MW01641094

The AMERICAN HERITAGE® *dic·tion·ar·y*

FOURTH EDITION

A Delta Book

Published by
Dell Publishing
a division of
Random House, Inc.
1540 Broadway
New York, New York 10036

Words included in this book that are known to have current trademark registrations are shown with an initial capital and are also identified as trademarks. No investigation has been made of common-law trademark rights in any word, because such investigation is impracticable. The inclusion of any word in this book is not, however, an expression of the Publisher's opinion as to whether or not it is subject to proprietary rights. Indeed, no definition in this book is to be regarded as affecting the validity of any trademark.

ISBN: 0-385-33576-8

Reprinted by arrangement with Houghton Mifflin Company

Manufactured in the United States of America

Published simultaneously in Canada

July 2001

10 9 8 7 6 5 4 3 2 1
QMB

Table of Contents

Tables and Charts

Editorial and Production Staff

Vice President, Director of Lexical Publishing, Production, and Manufacturing Services

Margery S. Berube

Executive Editor

Joseph P. Pickett

Editorial Project Director

David R. Pritchard

Managing Editor

Christopher Leonesio

Editors

Beth Anderson
Benjamin W. Fortson IV
Steven R. Kleinedler
Hanna Schonthal

Associate Editors

Jacquelyn Pope
Vali Tamm

Editorial Assistant

Uchenna C. Ikonné

Proofreading

Diane Fredrick
Ann-Marie Imbornoni
Julia Penelope

Production Supervisor

Judith Caldwell

Database Supervisor

Christopher Granniss

Senior Art and Production Coordinator

Margaret Anne Miles

Production and Manufacturing Coordinators

James W. Mitchell
Katherine P. Wilson

Text Design

Joyce Weston

GUIDE TO THE DICTIONARY

Main Entries. Entries are listed in alphabetical order without taking into account spaces or hyphens. Two or more entries with identical spellings but different origins are distinguished by superscript numbers. For example: **ground**[1], **ground**[2], **groundbreaking, ground floor, groundhog, groundless.** A pair of boldface guidewords at the top of each page shows the first and last main entries on that page. Thus **bandoleer** and **banquet** and all of the entries that fall alphabetically between them are entered and defined on page 68. Entry words of more than one syllable are divided by centered dots. Syllable dots are omitted for parts of compound words that are also main entries in the Dictionary; for example, see **Conestoga wagon** (p. 185).

Variant Forms. If a word has two or more different spellings, the definition appears at the spelling that is most frequently used. The variant spellings are shown in boldface type after the main entry. The word "or" separates two forms used with approximately equal frequency; "also" introduces a less frequent variant. Variant forms are listed separately when they fall more than ten entries away from the main entry.

Inflected Forms. Inflected forms regarded as being irregular or those offering possible spelling problems are entered in boldface type, often in shortened form. These regular inflections are also entered: degrees of adjectives and adverbs and regular plurals if irregular plurals are shown. Pronunciations are given only if they differ significantly from the base form of the word:

> **good** (go͝od) ▸ *adj.* **bet•ter** (bĕt′ər), **best 1.** Being…
> **com•pute** (kəm-pyo͞ot′) ▸ *v.* **-put•ed, -put•ing 1.** To…
> **ax•is** (ăk′sĭs) ▸ *n., pl.* **ax•es** (ăk′sēz′) **1.** A…

The inflected forms of verbs are given in the following order: past tense, past participle (if it differs from the past tense), and present participle.

Irregular inflected forms are listed separately when they fall more than ten entries away from the main entry.

Verbs. Verbal definitions indicate transitivity or intransitivity by their wording. In the following examples, **bloom** is defined intransitively and **shuck** transitively:

> **bloom** (blo͞om) ▸ *v.* **1.** To bear flowers.
> **shuck** (shŭk) ▸ *v.* **1.** To remove the husk or shell from.

Parentheses are used in certain transitive definitions to indicate a usual or typical direct object:

> **de•clas•si•fy** (dē-klăs′ə-fī′) ▸ *v.* To remove official security classification from (a document).

Parentheses are also used around a final preposition to indicate that a verb can be used either transitively or intransitively in that sense:

> **kink** (kĭngk) ▸ *n.* **1.** A tight curl… ▸ *v.* To form a kink (in).

Labels. The following labels, set in italics, indicate that an entry word or a definition is limited to a particular level or style of usage: *Nonstandard* is applied to forms and usages that educated speakers and writers consider unacceptable (e.g., **ain't**); *Informal* indicates a term whose acceptability is limited to conversation and informal writing (e.g., **enthuse**); *Slang* indicates a style of language that is distinguished by a striving for rhetorical effect through the use of extravagant, often facetious coinages or figures of speech (e.g., **boffo**); and *Offensive* is reserved for words and expressions considered insulting and derogatory. Other, usually abbreviated labels, such as *Geol.* and *Electron.*, identify the special area of knowledge to which an entry word or a definition applies, while such labels as *Scots* and *Chiefly Brit.* identify an entry as a form that is used chiefly in another part of the English-speaking world.

Undefined Forms. At the end of many entries additional boldface words appear without definitions. They are closely and clearly related in basic meaning to the entry word but may have different grammatical functions.

Etymologies. Etymologies appear in square brackets following the definitions. The symbol < is used to mean "from" and is often an indication that transitional stages have been omitted in order to give a concise history of the word. A word or word element printed in small capitals is an entry in the Dictionary and should be referred to for more etymological information. Linguistic forms that are not Modern English words appear in italics.

Abbreviations. Common abbreviations used in this Dictionary, such as *adj.*, *pl.*, *var.*, and *e.g.*, are main entries. Additional abbreviations and symbols are listed on page vii.

Additional Abbreviations in This Dictionary

At. no.	Atomic number
b.	born
c.	circa (about)
comp.	comparative
d.	died
dim.	diminutive
gen.	generally
imit.	imitative
imper.	imperative
indic.	indicative
orig.	origin, originally
p.	past
part.	participle
perh.	perhaps
pers.	person
poss.	possibly
pr.	present
prob.	probably
superl.	superlative
t.	tense
ult.	ultimately
var.	variant

Language Abbreviations Used in Etymologies

Afr.	Afrikaans
Am.Sp.	American Spanish
Ar.	Arabic
Aram.	Aramaic
Balt.	Baltic
Celt.	Celtic
Chin.	Chinese
Dan.	Danish
dial.	dialectal
Du.	Dutch
E.	English
Egypt.	Egyptian
Finn.	Finnish
Flem.	Flemish
Fr.	French
Gael.	Gaelic
Ger.	German
Gk.	Greek
Heb.	Hebrew
Hung.	Hungarian
Icel.	Icelandic
Ir.	Irish
Ital.	Italian
J.	Japanese
Lat.	Latin
LGer.	Low German
LGk.	Late Greek
LHeb.	Late Hebrew
LLat.	Late Latin
MDu.	Middle Dutch
ME	Middle English
Med.Gk.	Medieval Greek
Med.Lat.	Medieval Latin
MFlem.	Middle Flemish
MHGer.	Middle High German
MLGer.	Middle Low German
Mod.	Modern
MPers.	Middle Persian
NLat.	New Latin
Norw.	Norwegian
O	Old (in combination)
OE	Old English
OHGer.	Old High German
ONFr.	Old North French
Penn.Du.	Pennsylvania Dutch
Pers.	Persian
Pol.	Polish
Port.	Portuguese
Prov.	Provençal
Rom.	Romanian
Russ.	Russian
Sc.	Scots
Scand.	Scandinavian
Sc.Gael.	Scottish Gaelic
Skt.	Sanskrit
Slav.	Slavic
Sp.	Spanish
Swed.	Swedish
Turk.	Turkish
VLat.	Vulgar Latin

*	unattested
+	combined with
<	derived from
?	origin unknown

Pronunciation Key

Symbols	Examples
ă	pat
ā	pay
âr	care
ä	father
b	bib
ch	church
d	deed, milled
ĕ	pet
ē	bee
f	fife, phase, rough
g	gag
h	hat
hw	which
ĭ	pit
ī	pie, by
îr	pier
j	judge
k	kick, cat, pique
l	lid, needle (nēd′l)
m	mum
n	no, sudden (sŭd′n)
ng	thing
ŏ	pot
ō	toe
ô	caught, paw, for, horrid, hoarse*
oi	noise
o͝o	took

Symbols	Examples
o͞o	boot
ou	out
p	pop
r	roar
s	sauce
sh	ship, dish
t	tight, stopped
th	thin
th	this
ŭ	cut
ûr	urge, term, firm, word, heard
v	valve
w	with
y	yes
z	zebra, xylem
zh	vision, pleasure, garage
ə	about, item, edible, gallop, circus**
ər	butter

Foreign

œ	French feu German schön
ü	French tu German über
KH	German ich Scottish loch
N	French bon

Primary stress (′) **bi•ol′o•gy** (bī-ŏl′ə-jē)***
Secondary stress (′) **bi′o•log′i•cal** (bī′ə-lŏj′ĭ-kəl)***

*Regional pronunciations of *-or-* vary. In pairs such as **for, four; horse, hoarse;** and **morning, mourning,** the vowel varies between (ô) and (ō). In this Dictionary these vowels are represented as follows: **for** (fôr), **four** (fôr, fōr); **horse** (hôrs), **hoarse** (hôrs, hōrs); and **morning** (môr′nĭng), **mourning** (môr′nĭng, mōr′-). A similar variant occurs in words such as **coral**, **forest**, and **horrid**, where the pronunciation of *-or-* varies between (ôr) and (ŏr): **forest** (fôr′ĭst, fŏr′-).

**The symbol (ə) is called a *schwa*. It represents a vowel that receives the weakest level of stress within a word. The schwa sound varies, sometimes according to the vowel it is representing and often according to the sounds surrounding it.

***Stress, the relative degree of emphasis with which the syllables of a word (or phrase) are spoken, is indicated in three different ways. The strongest, or primary, stress is marked with a bold mark (′). An intermediate, or secondary, level of stress is marked with a similar but lighter mark (′). An unmarked syllable has the weakest stress in the word. Words of one syllable show no stress mark, since there is no other stress level to which the syllable is compared.

A

a[1] or **A** (ā) ▶*n., pl.* **a's** or **A's** also **as** or **As 1.** The 1st letter of the English alphabet. **2.** The 1st in a series. **3.** The best in quality or rank. **4.** *Mus.* The 6th tone in the scale of C major. **5. A** A type of blood in the ABO system.

a[2] (ə; ā *when stressed*) ▶*indef. art.* **1.** One: *a region; a person.* **2.** Any: *not a drop to drink.* [ME, var. of *an*, AN.]

a[3] (ə) ▶*prep.* Per: *once a day.* [< OE *an*, in.]

a[4] ▶*abbr.* **1.** acceleration **2.** are (measurement)

A ▶*abbr.* **1.** alto **2.** ampere **3.** or **Å** angstrom **4.** area

a. ▶*abbr.* **1.** acre **2.** adjective **3.** *Lat.* anno (in the year) **4.** *Lat.* annus (year) **5.** anode **6.** answer

a–[1] or **an–** ▶*pref.* Without; not: *amoral.* [Gk.]

a–[2] ▶*pref.* **1.** On; in: *abed.* **2.** In the direction of: *astern.* **3.** In a specified state: *aflutter.* [< OE < *an*, on.]

AA ▶*abbr.* **1.** Alcoholics Anonymous **2.** antiaircraft **3.** Associate in Arts

Aa•chen (ä′kən, ä′KHən) also **Aix-la-Cha•pelle** (āks′lä-shə-pĕl′, ĕks′-). A city of W Germany near the Belgian and Dutch borders. Pop. 246,671.

Aal•borg (ôl′bôrg′) See **Ålborg.**

A and R ▶*abbr.* artists and repertory

aard•vark (ärd′värk′) ▶*n.* A burrowing African mammal having large ears, a long tubular snout, and strong digging claws. [Obsolete Afr. : *aarde*, earth + *vark*, pig.]

Aar•hus (ôr′ho͞os′) See **Århus.**

Aar•on (âr′ən, ăr′-). In the Bible, the elder brother of Moses.

AAU ▶*abbr.* Amateur Athletic Union

AAVE ▶*abbr.* African American Vernacular English

AB[1] (ā′bē′) ▶*n.* A type of blood in the ABO system.

AB[2] ▶*abbr.* **1.** airman basic **2.** Alberta **3.** *Lat.* Artium Baccalaureus (Bachelor of Arts)

ab. ▶*abbr.* about

ab– ▶*pref.* Away from: *aboral.* [Lat.]

ABA ▶*abbr.* American Bar Association

a•back (ə-băk′) ▶*adv.* By surprise: *I was taken aback by her retort.*

ab•a•cus (ăb′ə-kəs, ə-băk′əs) ▶*n., pl.* **-cus•es** or **-ci** (ăb′ə-sī′, ə-băk′ī′). A manual computing device consisting of a frame holding parallel rods strung with movable counters. [< Gk. *abax*, counting board, perh. < Heb.]

abacus

Ab•a•dan (ä′bə-dän′, ăb′ə-dăn′) A city of SW Iran on **Abadan I.** at the head of the Persian Gulf. Pop. 296,081.

a•baft (ə-băft′) *Naut.* ▶*adv.* Toward the stern. ▶*prep.* Toward the stern from. [A–[2] + < OE *be-æftan*, behind.]

ab•a•lo•ne (ăb′ə-lō′nē) ▶*n.* A large, edible marine gastropod having an ear-shaped shell. [Am.Sp. *abulón.*]

a•ban•don (ə-băn′dən) ▶*v.* **1.** To forsake; desert. **2.** To give up completely: *abandoned the ship.* **3.** To quit: *abandoned the search.* ▶*n.* A complete surrender to feeling or impulse. [< OFr. *abandoner* < *a bandon*, in one's power.] **—a•ban′don•ment** *n.*

a•ban•doned (ə-băn′dənd) ▶*adj.* **1.** Deserted; forsaken. **2.** Recklessly unrestrained.

a•base (ə-bās′) ▶*v.* **a•based, a•bas•ing.** To humble or degrade. [< LLat. *bassus*, low.] **—a•base′ment** *n.*

a•bash (ə-băsh′) ▶*v.* To make ashamed; disconcert. See Syns at **embarrass.** [< OFr. *esbahir*, be abashed.] **—a•bash′ment** *n.*

a•bate (ə-bāt′) ▶*v.* **a•bat•ed, a•bat•ing 1.** To reduce in amount, degree, or intensity; lessen. **2.** *Law* To make void. [< OFr. *abattre*, beat down.] **—a•bate′ment** *n.*

ab•at•toir (ăb′ə-twär′) ▶*n.* A slaughterhouse. [< OFr. *abattre*, beat down.]

Abb. ▶*abbr.* **1.** abbess **2.** abbot

ab•ba•cy (ăb′ə-sē) ▶*n., pl.* **-cies.** The office, term, or jurisdiction of an abbot. [< LLat. *abbātia.*]

ab•bess (ăb′ĭs) ▶*n.* The superior of a convent.

ab•bey (ăb′ē) ▶*n., pl.* **-beys 1.** A monastery supervised by an abbot. **2.** A convent supervised by an abbess. **3.** A church that is or once was part of a monastery or convent. [< LLat. *abbātia.*]

ab•bot (ăb′ət) ▶*n.* The superior of a monastery. [< Aram. *'abbā*, my father.]

Ab•bott (ăb′ət), Sir **John Joseph Caldwell.** 1821–93. Canadian prime minister (1891–92).

abbr. or **abbrev.** ▶*abbr.* abbreviation

ab•bre•vi•ate (ə-brē′vē-āt′) ▶*v.* **-at•ed, -at•ing.** To make shorter. See Syns at **shorten.** [< LLat. *abbreviāre.*] **—ab•bre′vi•a′tor** *n.*

ab•bre•vi•a•tion (ə-brē′vē-ā′shən) ▶*n.* **1.** The act or product of shortening. **2.** A shortened form of a word or phrase, such as *Tex.* for *Texas.*

ABC (ā′bē-sē′) ▶*n.* often **ABCs 1.** The alphabet: *learned her ABCs.* **2.** The rudiments of reading and writing.

ab•di•cate (ăb′dĭ-kāt′) ▶*v.* **-cat•ed, -cat•ing.** To relinquish (power or responsibility) formally. [Lat. *abdicāre*, disclaim.] **—ab′di•ca′tion** *n.* **—ab′di•ca′tor** *n.*

ab•do•men (ăb′də-mən, ăb-dō′-) ▶*n.* **1.** The part of the body that lies between the thorax and the pelvis; belly. **2.** The posterior segment of the body in arthropods. [Lat. *abdōmen.*] **—ab•dom′i•nal** (ăb-dŏm′ə-nəl) *adj.* **—ab•dom′i•nal•ly** *adv.*

ab•duct (ăb-dŭkt′) ▶*v.* To carry off by force; kidnap. [Lat. *abdūcere*, lead away.] **—ab•duc′tion** *n.* **—ab•duc′tor** *n.*

a•beam (ə-bēm′) ▶*adv.* At right angles to the keel of a ship.

a•bed (ə-bĕd′) ▶*adv.* In bed.

A•bel (ā′bəl). In the Bible, the son of Adam and Eve; slain by Cain.

Ab•e•lard (ăb′ə-lärd′) also **A•bé•lard** (ä-bā-lär′), **Peter.** 1079–1142. French theologian and philosopher; secretly married Héloise.

Ab•e•na•ki (ä′bə-nä′kē, ăb′ə-năk′ē) or **Ab•na•ki** (äb-nä′kē, ăb-) ►*n.*, *pl.* **-ki** or **-kis 1.** A member of a group of Native American peoples of N New England and S Quebec. **2.** The Algonquian language of the Abenaki.

Ab•er•deen (ăb′ər-dēn′) A city of NE Scotland on the North Sea. Pop. 218,220.

Ab•er•nath•y (ăb′ər-năth′ē), **Ralph David.** 1926–90. Amer. civil rights leader.

Ralph Abernathy
photographed in 1968

ab•er•ra•tion (ăb′ə-rā′shən) ►*n.* **1.** A deviation from the normal, proper, or expected course. **2.** A defect of focus, such as blurring in an image. [< Lat. *aberrāre*, stray away.] —**ab•er′rant** (ăb′ər-ənt, ă-bĕr′-) *adj.*

a•bet (ə-bĕt′) ►*v.* **a•bet•ted, a•bet•ting.** To encourage or assist, esp. in wrongdoing. [< OFr. *abeter*, entice : *a-*, to + *beter*, to bait.] —**a•bet′ment** *n.* —**a•bet′tor, a•bet′ter** *n.*

a•bey•ance (ə-bā′əns) ►*n.* The condition of being temporarily set aside; suspension. [< OFr. *abeance*, desire < *abaer*, gape at.]

ab•hor (ăb-hôr′) ►*v.* **-horred, -hor•ring.** To regard with loathing; detest. [< Lat. *abhorrēre*, shrink from.] —**ab•hor′rer** *n.*

ab•hor•rence (ăb-hôr′əns, -hŏr′-) ►*n.* A feeling of repugnance or loathing. —**ab•hor′rent** *adj.* —**ab•hor′rent•ly** *adv.*

a•bide (ə-bīd′) ►*v.* **a•bode** (ə-bōd′) or **a•bid•ed, a•bid•ing 1.** To put up with; tolerate. **2.** To remain; endure. **3.** To dwell; reside. —***idiom:* abide by** To comply with: *abide by the rules.* [< OE *ābīdan.*] —**a•bid′er** *n.*

a•bid•ing (ə-bī′dĭng) ►*adj.* Lasting; enduring.

Ab•i•djan (ăb′ĭ-jän′) The de facto capital of Côte d'Ivoire, in the S part. Pop. 1,929,079.

a•bil•i•ty (ə-bĭl′ĭ-tē) ►*n.*, *pl.* **-ties 1.** The power to do something. **2.** A skill or talent. [< Lat. *habilis*, ABLE.]

ab•ject (ăb′jĕkt′) ►*adj.* **1.** Contemptible; despicable: *abject cowardice.* **2.** Miserable; wretched: *abject poverty.* [< Lat. *abicere*, *abiect-*, cast away.] —**ab′ject′ly** *adv.* —**ab•ject′ness, ab•jec′tion** *n.*

ab•jure (ăb-jo͝or′) ►*v.* **-jured, -jur•ing 1.** To renounce under oath. **2.** To recant solemnly; repudiate. **3.** To give up; abstain from. [< Lat. *abiūrāre.*] —**ab′ju•ra′tion** *n.*

Ab•kha•zia (ăb-kā′zhə, -zē-ə, -kä′-, äb- An autonomous republic of NW Georgia bordering on Russia and the Black Sea. —**Ab•kha′zi′an** *adj.* & *n.*

ab•la•tion (ă-blā′shən) ►*n.* **1.** Amputation of a body part. **2.** Reduction or dissipation, as by melting. [< Lat. *ablātus*, p.part. of *auferre*, carry off.]

ab•la•tive (ăb′lə-tĭv) ►*adj.* Of or being a grammatical case indicating separation, direction away from, and sometimes manner or agency. ►*n.* The ablative case. [< Lat. *ablātus*, carried off. See ABLATION.]

a•blaze (ə-blāz′) ►*adj.* **1.** Being on fire; blazing. **2.** Bright with color. —**a•blaze′** *adv.*

a•ble (ā′bəl) ►*adj.* **a•bler, a•blest 1.** Having sufficient ability or resources. **2.** Highly capable or talented. [< Lat. *habilis* < *habēre*, to handle.] —**a′bly** (ā′blē) *adv.*

-able or **-ible** ►*suff.* **1.** Susceptible, capable, or worthy of (an action): *debatable.* **2.** Inclined or given to: *changeable.* [< Lat. *-ābilis, -ibilis.*]

a•ble-bod•ied (ā′bəl-bŏd′ēd) ►*adj.* Physically strong and healthy.

able-bodied seaman ►*n.* A merchant seaman certified for all seaman's duties.

a•ble•ism (ā′bə-lĭz′əm) ►*n.* Discrimination or prejudice against people with disabilities, esp. physical disabilities. —**a′ble•ist** *adj.* & *n.*

a•bloom (ə-blo͞om′) ►*adj.* Being in bloom.

ab•lu•tion (ă-blo͞o′shən) ►*n.* A washing or cleansing of the body, esp. in a ritual manner. [< Lat. *abluere*, wash away.]

ABM (ā′bē-ĕm′) ►*n.* See **antiballistic missile.**

Ab•na•ki (äb-nä′kē, ăb-) ►*n.* Var. of **Abenaki.**

ab•ne•ga•tion (ăb′nĭ-gā′shən) ►*n.* Self-denial; renunciation. [< Lat. *abnegāre*, refuse.]

ab•nor•mal (ăb-nôr′məl) ►*adj.* Not typical or normal; deviant. —**ab′nor•mal′i•ty** (ăb′nôr-măl′ĭ-tē) *n.* —**ab•nor′mal•ly** *adv.*

abnormal psychology ►*n.* The study of mental and emotional disorders or of mental phenomena such as altered levels of consciousness.

a•board (ə-bôrd′, -bōrd′) ►*adv.* On or onto a passenger vehicle, such as a ship, train, or aircraft. ►*prep.* On board of; on; in.

a•bode (ə-bōd′) ►*v.* P.t. and p.part of **abide.** ►*n.* A dwelling place; home. [ME *abod* < *abiden*, ABIDE.]

a•bol•ish (ə-bŏl′ĭsh) ►*v.* To do away with; annul. [< Lat. *abolēre.*] —**a•bol′ish•er** *n.* —**a•bol′ish•ment** *n.*

ab•o•li•tion (ăb′ə-lĭsh′ən) ►*n.* **1.** The act of abolishing. **2.** Abolishment of slavery.

ab•o•li•tion•ism (ăb′ə-lĭsh′ə-nĭz′əm) ►*n.* Advocacy of the abolition of slavery. —**ab′o•li′tion•ist** *n.*

A-bomb (ā′bŏm′) ►*n.* See **atom bomb** 1.

a•bom•i•na•ble (ə-bŏm′ə-nə-bəl) ►*adj.* Utterly detestable; loathsome. —**a•bom′i•na•bly** *adv.*

abominable snowman ►*n.* A hairy humanlike animal supposedly inhabiting the snows of the high Himalaya Mountains.

a•bom•i•nate (ə-bŏm′ə-nāt′) ►*v.* **-nat•ed, -nat•ing.** To detest thoroughly; abhor. [Lat. *abōminārī*, deprecate as a bad omen.] —**a•bom′i•na′tion** *n.* —**a•bom′i•na′tor** *n.*

ab•o•rig•i•nal (ăb′ə-rĭj′ə-nəl) ►*adj.* **1.** Existing from the beginning. **2.** Of or relating to aborigines. See Usage Note at **native. 3.** often **Aboriginal** Relating to any of the indigenous peoples of Australia. ►*n.* An aborigine. —**ab′o•rig′i•nal•ly** *adv.*

ab•o•rig•i•ne (ăb′ə-rĭj′ə-nē) ►*n.* **1.** A member

of the earliest known population of a region. See Usage Note at **native. 2.** often **Aborigine** A member of any of the indigenous peoples of Australia. [< Lat. *aborīginēs*, original inhabitants.]

a•born•ing (ə-bôr′nĭng) ▸*adv.* While coming into being or getting under way.

a•bort (ə-bôrt′) ▸*v.* **1a.** To cause the abortion of (a fetus or embryo). **b.** To terminate (a pregnancy) by inducing abortion. **2.** To miscarry. **3.** To terminate before completion: *abort a takeoff.* ▸*n.* The act of terminating before completion. [< Lat. *aborīrī, abort-*, miscarry.] —**a•bor′tive** *adj.*

a•bor•ti•fa•cient (ə-bôr′tə-fā′shənt) ▸*adj.* Causing abortion. —**a•bor′ti•fa′cient** *n.*

a•bor•tion (ə-bôr′shən) ▸*n.* **1.** Induced termination of pregnancy and expulsion of an embryo or fetus before it is viable. **2.** A miscarriage. —**a•bor′tion•ist** *n.*

ABO system (ā′bē′ō′) ▸*n.* A system of classifying blood into four major groups, A, B, AB, and O, used in determining blood compatibility in transfusions.

a•bound (ə-bound′) ▸*v.* **1.** To be great in number or amount. **2.** To be fully supplied; teem. See Syns at **teem.** [< Lat. *abundāre*, overflow : AB– + *unda*, wave.]

a•bout (ə-bout′) ▸*adv.* **1.** Approximately. **2.** Almost. **3.** To a reversed position: *Turned about.* **4.** All around. **5.** In the vicinity. ▸*prep.* **1.** On all sides of. **2.** In the vicinity of. **3.** Relating to; concerning. **4.** On the point of: *about to go.* [< OE *onbūtan.*]

a•bout-face (ə-bout′fās′) ▸*n.* A sudden change to the opposite direction, attitude, or viewpoint. —**a•bout′-face′** *v.*

a•bove (ə-bŭv′) ▸*adv.* **1.** On high; overhead. **2.** In or to a higher place. **3.** In an earlier part of a text. ▸*prep.* **1.** Over or higher than. **2.** Superior to: *put principles above expediency.* ▸*n.* An earlier part of a given text. ▸*adj.* Appearing earlier in the same text. [< OE *abufan.*]

above all ▸*adv.* Exceeding all other factors in importance.

a•bove•board (ə-bŭv′bôrd′, -bōrd′) ▸*adv. & adj.* Without deceit or trickery. [Orig. a gambling term.]

Abp. ▸*abbr.* archbishop

ab•ra•ca•dab•ra (ăb′rə-kə-dăb′rə) ▸*n.* **1.** A magical charm believed to ward off disease or disaster. **2.** Gibberish. [LLat.]

a•brade (ə-brād′) ▸*v.* **a•brad•ed, a•brad•ing 1.** To wear away by friction; erode. See Syns at **chafe. 2.** To be abrasive; irritate. [Lat. *abrādere*, scrape off.] —**a•bra′sion** (ə-brā′zhən) *n.*

A•bra•ham (ā′brə-hăm′). In the Bible, the first patriarch and progenitor of the Hebrew people.

a•bra•sive (ə-brā′sĭv, -zĭv) ▸*adj.* **1.** Causing abrasion. **2.** Harsh or irritating in manner. ▸*n.* A substance that abrades. —**a•bra′sive•ly** *adv.* —**a•bra′sive•ness** *n.*

a•breast (ə-brĕst′) ▸*adv.* **1.** Side by side. **2.** Up to date with: *abreast of developments.*

a•bridge (ə-brĭj′) ▸*v.* **a•bridged, a•bridg•ing 1.** To reduce the length of (a text); condense. **2.** To cut short; curtail. See Syns at **shorten.** [< LLat. *abbreviāre*, abbreviate.] —**a•bridg′ment, a•bridge′ment** *n.*

a•broad (ə-brôd′) ▸*adv. & adj.* **1.** In or to a foreign country, esp. overseas. **2.** Away from home. **3.** In wide circulation; at large.

ab•ro•gate (ăb′rə-gāt′) ▸*v.* **-gat•ed, -gat•ing.** To abolish or annul, esp. by authority. [Lat. *abrogāre.*] —**ab′ro•ga′tion** *n.*

a•brupt (ə-brŭpt′) ▸*adj.* **1.** Unexpectedly sudden. **2.** Curt; brusque: *an abrupt retort.* **3.** Jerky; disconnected. **4.** Steeply inclined. See Syns at **steep**[1]. [< Lat. *abrumpere, abrupt-*, break off.] —**a•brupt′ly** *adv.* —**a•brupt′ness** *n.*

A•bruz•zi (ä-bro͞ot′sē, ə-bro͞ot′-) A region of central Italy on the Adriatic.

ab•scess (ăb′sĕs′) ▸*n.* A collection of pus surrounded by an inflamed area. ▸*v.* To form an abscess. [< Lat. *abscēdere, abscess-*, go away.]

ab•scis•sa (ăb-sĭs′ə) ▸*n., pl.* **-scis•sas** or **-scis•sae** (-sĭs′ē) *Symbol* **x** The coordinate representing the position of a point along a line perpendicular to the *y*-axis in a plane Cartesian coordinate system. [NLat. *(linea) abscissa*, cutoff (line).]

ab•scis•sion (ăb-sĭzh′ən) ▸*n.* The shedding of leaves, flowers, or fruits.

ab•scond (ăb-skŏnd′) ▸*v.* To leave secretly and hide, often to avoid the law. [Lat. *abscondere*, hide away.] —**ab•scond′er** *n.*

ab•sence (ăb′səns) ▸*n.* **1.** The state or a period of being away. **2.** Lack; nonexistence: *an absence of leadership.*

ab•sent (ăb′sənt) ▸*adj.* **1.** Not present. **2.** Not existent; lacking. **3.** Absent-minded; inattentive: *an absent nod.* ▸*v.* (ăb-sĕnt′). To keep (oneself) away. ▸*prep.* Without. [< Lat. *absēns*, pr.part. of *abesse*, be away.] —**ab′sent•ly** *adv.*

ab•sen•tee (ăb′sən-tē′) ▸*n.* One that is absent. ▸*adj.* Not in residence: *absentee landlords.*

absentee ballot ▸*n.* A ballot mailed in advance by a voter unable to go to the polls.

ab•sen•tee•ism (ăb′sən-tē′ĭz′əm) ▸*n.* Habitual absence, esp. from work or duty.

ab•sent-mind•ed (ăb′sənt-mīn′dĭd) ▸*adj.* **1.** Lost in thought; preoccupied. **2.** Inattentive; forgetful. —**ab′sent-mind′ed•ly** *adv.* —**ab′sent-mind′ed•ness** *n.*

ab•sinthe also **ab•sinth** (ăb′sĭnth) ▸*n.* A strong, bitter liqueur flavored with wormwood. [< Gk. *apsinthion*, wormwood.]

ab•so•lute (ăb′sə-lo͞ot′) ▸*adj.* **1.** Perfect in quality or nature; complete. **2.** Not mixed; pure. See Syns at **pure. 3a.** Not limited by restrictions or exceptions: *absolute trust; absolute power.* **b.** Total; utter: *absolute silence.* **4.** Certain; positive: *absolute proof.* **5.** *Phys.* **a.** Relating to measurements or units of measurement derived from fundamental units of length, mass, and time. **b.** Relating to a temperature scale whose zero is absolute zero. ▸*n.* Something that is absolute. [< Lat. *absolvere, absolūt-*, loosen.] —**ab′so•lute′ly** *adv.* —**ab′so•lute′ness** *n.*

absolute pitch ▸*n.* **1.** The precise pitch of an isolated tone as established by its rate of vibration. **2.** *Mus.* The ability to identify any pitch heard or sing any pitch named.

absolute value ▸*n.* The numerical value of a real number without regard to its sign.

absolute zero ▸*n.* The theoretical temperature at which substances possess no thermal energy, equal to –273.15°C, or –459.67°F.

ab•so•lu•tion (ăb′sə-lo͞o′shən) ▸*n.* **1.** The act of absolving. **2.** The formal remission of sin imparted by a priest, as in the sacrament of penance. [< Lat. *absolvere*, absolve.]

ab•so•lut•ism (ăb′sə-lo͞o′tĭz′əm) ►*n.* A form of government in which all power is vested in a single ruler or other authority. —**ab′so•lut′ist** *n.* —**ab′so•lu•tis′tic** *adj.*

ab•solve (əb-zŏlv′, -sŏlv′) ►*v.* **-solved, -solv•ing 1.** To pronounce clear of guilt or blame. **2.** To relieve of a requirement or obligation. **3.** To grant absolution to. [< Lat. *absolvere.*] —**ab•solv′a•ble** *adj.* —**ab•solv′er** *n.*

ab•sorb (əb-sôrb′, -zôrb′) ►*v.* **1.** To take (something) in through or as through pores or interstices. **2.** To occupy completely; engross. See Syns at **monopolize. 3.** *Phys.* To retain (e.g., sound) wholly, without reflection or transmission. **4.** To assimilate into a larger whole. **5.** To take on: *absorb a cost.* [< Lat. *absorbēre.*] —**ab•sorb′a•ble** *adj.* —**ab•sorb′er** *n.* —**ab•sorb′ing•ly** *adv.*

ab•sor•bent (əb-sôr′bənt, -zôr′-) ►*adj.* Capable of absorbing. —**ab•sor′ben•cy** *n.* —**ab•sor′bent** *n.*

ab•sorp•tion (əb-sôrp′shən, -zôrp′-) ►*n.* **1.** The act or process of absorbing. **2.** A state of mental concentration. —**ab•sorp′tive** (-tĭv) *adj.* —**ab′sorp•tiv′i•ty** *n.*

ab•stain (ăb-stān′) ►*v.* To refrain from something by one's own choice. See Syns at **refrain**[1]. [< Lat. *abstinēre*, hold back.] —**ab•stain′er** *n.*

ab•ste•mi•ous (ăb-stē′mē-əs) ►*adj.* Exercising self-restraint in appetites or behavior. [< Lat. *abstēmius.*] —**ab•ste′mi•ous•ly** *adv.* —**ab•ste′mi•ous•ness** *n.*

ab•sten•tion (ăb-stĕn′shən) ►*n.* The act or habit of abstaining. [< Lat. *abstinēre*, *abstent-*, hold back.]

ab•sti•nence (ăb′stə-nəns) ►*n.* **1.** Deliberate self-restraint. **2a.** Abstention from alcoholic beverages. **b.** Abstention from sexual activity; continence. —**ab′sti•nent** *adj.*

ab•stract (ăb-străkt′, ăb′străkt′) ►*adj.* **1.** Considered apart from concrete existence: *an abstract concept.* **2.** Not applied or practical. See Syns at **theoretical. 3.** Difficult to understand; abstruse. **4.** Considered without reference to a specific instance. **5.** Having an artistic content that depends on intrinsic form rather than on pictorial representation: *abstract painting.* ►*n.* (ăb′străkt′) **1.** A summary or condensation. **2.** Something abstract. ►*v.* (ăb-străkt′) **1.** To take away; remove. **2.** To steal; filch. **3.** (ăb′străkt′). To summarize. [< Lat. *abstrahere*, *abstract-*, draw away.] —**ab•stract′er** *n.* —**ab•stract′ly** *adv.* —**ab•stract′ness** *n.*

ab•stract•ed (ăb-străk′tĭd) ►*adj.* **1.** Removed; apart. **2.** Lost in thought; preoccupied. —**ab•stract′ed•ly** *adv.*

ab•strac•tion (ăb-străk′shən) ►*n.* **1a.** The act or process of abstracting. **b.** An abstract idea or term. **2.** Preoccupation; absent-mindedness. **3.** An abstract work of art.

ab•struse (ăb-stro͞os′) ►*adj.* Difficult to understand. [< Lat. *abstrūdere*, *abstrūs-*, hide away.] —**ab•struse′ly** *adv.* —**ab•struse′ness** *n.*

ab•surd (əb-sûrd′, -zûrd′) ►*adj.* **1.** Ridiculously incongruous or nonsensical. **2.** Devoid of meaning, value, or purpose. [Lat. *absurdus.*] —**ab•surd′i•ty, ab•surd′ness** *n.* —**ab•surd′ly** *adv.*

A•bu Dha•bi (ä′bo͞o dä′bē) A sheikdom and the capital of the United Arab Emirates, in E Arabia on the Persian Gulf. Pop. 242,975.

A•bu•ja (ä-bo͞o′jä) The official capital of Nigeria, in the center of the country. Pop. 379,000.

a•bu•li•a (ə-bo͞o′lē-ə, -byo͞o′-) ►*n.* Loss or impairment of the ability to make decisions. [< A–[1] + Gk. *boulē*, will.] —**a•bu′lic** *adj.*

a•bun•dant (ə-bŭn′dənt) ►*adj.* **1.** Richly supplied. See Syns at **plentiful. 2.** Abounding with. [< Lat. *abundāre*, ABOUND.] —**a•bun′dance** *n.* —**a•bun′dant•ly** *adv.*

a•buse (ə-byo͞oz′) ►*v.* **a•bused, a•bus•ing 1.** To use wrongly or improperly. **2.** To hurt or injure by maltreatment. **3.** To rape or molest. **4.** To insult; revile. ►*n.* (ə-byo͞os′) **1.** Misuse: *drug abuse.* **2.** Physical maltreatment. **3.** Insulting or coarse language. [< Lat. *abūtī*, *abūs-*.] —**a•bus′er** *n.* —**a•bu′sive** *adj.* —**a•bu′sive•ly** *adv.*

a•but (ə-bŭt′) ►*v.* **a•but•ted, a•but•ting 1.** To have a common boundary; lie adjacent. **2.** To border upon. [< OFr. *abouter.*] —**a•but′ter** *n.*

a•but•ment (ə-bŭt′mənt) ►*n.* **1.** The act of abutting. **2.** Something that abuts. **3.** A supporting structure, as at the end of a bridge.

a•bysm (ə-bĭz′əm) ►*n.* An abyss. [< LLat. *abyssus*, ABYSS.]

a•bys•mal (ə-bĭz′məl) ►*adj.* **1.** Very profound; limitless. **2.** Very bad: *an abysmal performance.* —**a•bys′mal•ly** *adv.*

a•byss (ə-bĭs′) ►*n.* **1.** An immeasurably deep chasm, depth, or void. **2a.** The primeval chaos. **b.** Hell. [< Gk. *abussos*, bottomless.]

Ab•ys•sin•i•a (ăb′ĭ-sĭn′ē-ə) See **Ethiopia.** —**Ab′ys•sin′i•an** *adj. & n.*

Ac ► The symbol for the element **actinium.**

AC ►*abbr.* **1.** alternating current **2.** area code

a/c ►*abbr.* **1.** account **2.** account current **3.** or **AC** air conditioning

a•ca•cia (ə-kā′shə) ►*n.* **1.** Any of various often spiny trees or shrubs having feathery leaves and heads or spikes of small flowers. **2.** See **gum arabic.** [< Gk. *akakia.*]

ac•a•deme (ăk′ə-dēm′) ►*n.* **1.** Academia. **2.** A scholar, esp. a pedant.

ac•a•de•mi•a (ăk′ə-dē′mē-ə) ►*n.* The academic life or environment.

ac•a•dem•ic (ăk′ə-dĕm′ĭk) ►*adj.* **1.** Of or relating to a school or college. **2a.** Liberal or classical rather than technical or vocational. **b.** Relating to scholarly performance: *a student's academic average.* **3.** Scholarly to the point of triviality. See Syns at **pedantic. 4.** Excessively abstract. See Syns at **theoretical.** ►*n.* A member of a college or university faculty. —**ac′a•dem′i•cal•ly** *adv.*

ac•a•de•mi•cian (ăk′ə-də-mĭsh′ən, ə-kăd′ə-) ►*n.* **1.** An academic. **2.** A member of an academy or learned society.

ac•a•dem•i•cism (ăk′ə-dĕm′ĭ-sĭz′əm) also **a•cad•e•mism** (ə-kăd′ə-mĭz′əm) ►*n.* Traditional formalism, esp. when reflected in art.

ac•a•dem•ics (ăk′ə-dĕm′ĭks) ►*n. (takes pl. v.)* College or university studies.

a•cad•e•my (ə-kăd′ə-mē) ►*n., pl.* **-mies 1.** A school for special instruction. **2.** A secondary or college-preparatory school, esp. a private one. **3a.** Academia. **b.** A society of scholars, scientists, or artists. [< Gk. *Akadēmia*, school where Plato taught.]

A•ca•di•a (ə-kā′dē-ə) A region and former French colony of E Canada and E ME. —**A•ca′di•an** *adj.* & *n.*

a•can•thus (ə-kăn′thəs) ►*n.*, *pl.* **-thus•es** or **-thi** (-thī′) **1.** Any of various Mediterranean shrubs with large, segmented, thistlelike leaves. **2.** *Archit.* A design patterned after acanthus leaves. [< Gk. *akantha*, thorn.]

acanthus

a cap•pel•la (ä′ kə-pĕl′ə) ►*adv. Mus.* Without instrumental accompaniment. [Ital., chapel style.]

Ac•a•pul•co (ăk′ə-po͝ol′kō, ä′kä-po͞ol′-) A city of S Mexico on the Pacific. Pop. 301,902.

ac•cede (ăk-sēd′) ►*v.* **-ced•ed, -ced•ing 1.** To give one's consent; agree. **2.** To come into an office or dignity: *accede to the throne.* [< Lat. *accēdere*, go near.] —**ac•ced′ence** *n.*

ac•cel•er•an•do (ä-chĕl′ə-rän′dō) ►*adv.* & *adj. Mus.* Gradually accelerating in tempo. [Ital.]

ac•cel•er•ate (ăk-sĕl′ə-rāt′) ►*v.* **-at•ed, -at•ing 1.** To make or become faster. **2.** To cause to occur sooner than expected. [Lat. *accelerāre.*] —**ac•cel′er•a′tion** *n.* —**ac•cel′er•a′tive** *adj.*

ac•cel•er•a•tor (ăk-sĕl′ə-rā′tər) ►*n.* **1.** A device, esp. the gas pedal of a motor vehicle, for increasing speed. **2.** *Phys.* A device, such as a cyclotron, that accelerates charged subatomic particles or nuclei to high energies.

ac•cel•er•om•e•ter (ăk-sĕl′ə-rŏm′ĭ-tər) ►*n.* An instrument used to measure acceleration.

ac•cent (ăk′sĕnt′) ►*n.* **1.** Vocal emphasis given to a particular syllable, word, or phrase. **2.** A characteristic manner of speech or pronunciation: *a British accent.* **3.** A mark placed over a letter to indicate vocal stress or phonetic quality: *an acute accent.* **4.** Rhythmical stress in a line of verse. **5.** A distinctive quality, as of decorative style. **6.** Particular importance or interest. See Syns at **emphasis.** ►*v.* To stress or emphasize. [< Lat. *accentus*, accentuation.]

ac•cen•tu•ate (ăk-sĕn′cho͞o-āt′) ►*v.* **-at•ed, -at•ing.** To stress; accent.

ac•cept ►*v.* **1.** To receive willingly. **2.** To admit to a group or place. **3.** To regard as proper or true: *accept a new theory.* **4.** To answer affirmatively: *accept an invitation.* **5.** To consent to pay, as by a signed agreement. [< Lat. *accipere*, take on, receive.]

ac•cept•a•ble (ăk-sĕp′tə-bəl) ►*adj.* Adequate; satisfactory. —**ac•cept′a•bil′i•ty** *n.* —**ac•cept′a•bly** *adv.*

ac•cep•tance (ăk-sĕp′təns) ►*n.* **1.** The act or process of accepting. **2.** The state of being accepted or acceptable. **3.** A formal agreement to pay a draft or bill of exchange.

ac•cep•ta•tion (ăk′sĕp-tā′shən) ►*n.* The usual meaning, as of a word or expression. See Syns at **meaning.**

ac•cept•ed (ăk-sĕp′tĭd) ►*adj.* Widely encountered, used, or recognized.

ac•cep•tor (ăk-sĕp′tər) ►*n. Chem.* The atom that contributes no electrons to a covalent bond.

ac•cess (ăk′sĕs) ►*n.* **1.** A means of approaching or entering; passage. **2.** The right to enter or make use of: *has access to classified material.* **3.** An outburst: *an access of rage.* ►*v.* To obtain access to. [< Lat. *accēdere, access-*, come toward.]

ac•ces•si•ble (ăk-sĕs′ə-bəl) ►*adj.* Easily approached, entered, or obtained. —**ac•ces′si•bil′i•ty, ac•ces′si•ble•ness** *n.* —**ac•ces′si•bly** *adv.*

ac•ces•sion (ăk-sĕsh′ən) ►*n.* **1.** The attainment of a dignity or rank. **2a.** Something acquired or added. **b.** An increase by means of something added. —**ac•ces′sion•al** *adj.*

ac•ces•so•ry (ăk-sĕs′ə-rē) ►*n.*, *pl.* **-ries 1a.** A supplementary item; adjunct. **b.** Something nonessential but desirable. **2.** *Law* One who though absent aids or assists in the commission of a crime. ►*adj.* Supplementary; adjunct.

ac•ci•dent (ăk′sĭ-dənt) ►*n.* **1a.** An unexpected, undesirable event. **b.** An unforeseen incident. **2.** Chance; fortuity: *discovered the secret by accident.* **3.** *Logic* An attribute that is not essential to the nature of something. [< Lat. *accidere*, happen.]

ac•ci•den•tal (ăk′sĭ-dĕn′tl) ►*adj.* **1.** Occurring unexpectedly, unintentionally, or by chance. **2.** Incidental. ►*n. Mus.* A sharp, flat, or natural not indicated in the key signature. —**ac′ci•den′tal•ly** *adv.*

ac•cip•i•ter (ăk-sĭp′ĭ-tər) ►*n.* Any of several hawks with short wings and a long tail. [Lat., hawk.]

ac•claim (ə-klām′) ►*v.* To praise openly and enthusiastically; applaud. ►*n.* Enthusiastic applause; acclamation. [< Lat. *acclāmāre*, shout at.] —**ac•claim′er** *n.*

ac•cla•ma•tion (ăk′lə-mā′shən) ►*n.* **1.** A show of enthusiastic approval. **2.** An oral vote, esp. a vote of approval taken without formal ballot. —**ac•clam′a•to′ry** (ə-klăm′ə-tôr′ē, -tōr′ē) *adj.*

ac•cli•mate (ə-klī′mĭt, ăk′lə-māt′) ►*v.* **-mat•ed, -mat•ing.** To make or become accustomed to a new environment or situation; adapt. See Syns at **harden.** [Fr. *acclimater.*] —**ac′cli•ma′tion** *n.*

ac•cli•ma•tize (ə-klī′mə-tīz′) ►*v.* **-tized, -tiz•ing.** To acclimate. See Syns at **harden.** —**ac•cli′ma•ti•za′tion** *n.*

ac•cliv•i•ty (ə-klĭv′ĭ-tē) ►*n.*, *pl.* **-ties.** An upward slope. [< Lat. *acclīvis*, uphill : *ad-*, ad- + *clīvus*, slope.]

ac•co•lade (ăk′ə-lād′, -läd′) ►*n.* **1.** High praise. **2.** A special acknowledgment or award. [< OFr. *acoler*, to embrace.]

ac•com•mo•date (ə-kŏm′ə-dāt′) ►*v.* **-dat•ed, -dat•ing 1.** To do a favor for. See Syns at **oblige. 2.** To provide or allow for: *accommodate the needs of both groups.* **3.** To hold or contain comfortably. **4.** To make suitable; adjust. See Syns at **adapt. 5.** To settle; reconcile. [Lat. *accommodāre*, make fit.]

ac•com•mo•dat•ing (ə-kŏm′ə-dā′tĭng) ►*adj.* Willing to do a favor; helpful or obliging.

—**ac•com′mo•dat′ing•ly** *adv.*
ac•com•mo•da•tion (ə-kŏm′ə-dā′shən) ▸*n.* **1.** The act of accommodating or the state of being accommodated. **2.** Something that meets a need. **3. accommodations** Room and board; lodgings.
ac•com•pa•ni•ment (ə-kŭm′pə-nē-mənt, ə-kŭmp′nē-) ▸*n.* **1.** *Mus.* A part that supports another, often solo, part. **2.** Something that accompanies or complements.
ac•com•pa•nist (ə-kŭm′pə-nĭst, ə-kŭmp′nĭst) ▸*n. Mus.* One who plays or sings an accompaniment.
ac•com•pa•ny (ə-kŭm′pə-nē, ə-kŭmp′nē) ▸*v.* **-nied, -ny•ing 1.** To go with as a companion. **2.** To add to; supplement. **3.** To occur with. **4.** *Mus.* To perform an accompaniment to. [< OFr. *acompagnier.*]
ac•com•plice (ə-kŏm′plĭs) ▸*n.* One who aids or abets a lawbreaker in a criminal act. [< Lat. *complex*, closely connected.]
ac•com•plish (ə-kŏm′plĭsh) ▸*v.* **1.** To succeed in doing; achieve. **2.** To finish; complete. [< OFr. *acomplir* < Lat. *complēre*, COMPLETE.] —**ac•com′plish•er** *n.*
ac•com•plished (ə-kŏm′plĭsht) ▸*adj.* **1.** Skilled; expert: *an accomplished pianist.* **2.** Definite: *an accomplished fact.*
ac•com•plish•ment (ə-kŏm′plĭsh-mənt) ▸*n.* **1.** The act of accomplishing or state of being accomplished. **2.** Something completed successfully; achievement. **3.** An acquired skill. **4.** Social poise and grace.
ac•cord (ə-kôrd′) ▸*v.* **1.** To cause to conform or agree. **2.** To grant or bestow. **3.** To be in agreement or harmony. ▸*n.* **1.** Agreement; harmony. **2.** A settlement or understanding, esp. between nations. **3.** Free or spontaneous choice: *signed up on my own accord.* [< Lat. *cor, cord-*, heart.]
ac•cor•dance (ə-kôr′dns) ▸*n.* Agreement: *in accordance with your instructions.*
ac•cord•ing•ly (ə-kôr′dĭng-lē) ▸*adv.* **1.** In accordance; correspondingly. **2.** So; consequently.
ac•cord•ing to (ə-kôr′dĭng) ▸*prep.* **1.** As stated or indicated by: *according to law.* **2.** In keeping with: *according to custom.*
ac•cor•di•on (ə-kôr′dē-ən) ▸*n.* A portable musical instrument with a small keyboard and free metal reeds that sound when air is forced past them by pleated bellows. [Ger. *Akkordion* < OFr. *acorder*, ACCORD.] —**ac•cor′di•on•ist** *n.*
ac•cost (ə-kôst′, -kŏst′) ▸*v.* To approach and speak to in an aggressive or hostile manner. [< Med.Lat. *accostāre*, adjoin.]
ac•count (ə-kount′) ▸*n.* **1a.** A narrative or record of events. **b.** A set of reasons; explanation. **2a.** A business arrangement, as with a bank or store, in which money is kept, exchanged, or owed. **b.** A detailed record, esp. of financial transactions. **3.** Worth or importance. **4.** Profit; advantage: *turned her skills to good account.* ▸*v.* To consider as being; regard. —***phrasal verb:* account for** To provide or constitute a reason for; explain. —***idioms:* on account of** Because of. **take into account** To take into consideration. [< OFr. *aconter*, reckon < Lat. *computāre*, COUNT[1].]
ac•count•a•ble (ə-koun′tə-bəl) ▸*adj.* Responsible; answerable. —**ac•count′a•bil′i•ty, ac•count′a•ble•ness** *n.* —**ac•count′a•bly** *adv.*
ac•coun•tant (ə-koun′tənt) ▸*n.* One trained in accounting. —**ac•coun′tan•cy** *n.*
ac•count•ing (ə-koun′tĭng) ▸*n.* The bookkeeping methods involved in recording business transactions and preparing the financial statements of a business.
ac•cou•ter or **ac•cou•tre** (ə-ko͞o′tər) ▸*v.* **-tered, -ter•ing** or **-tred, -tre•ing.** To outfit and equip, as for military duty. [< OFr. *acoustrer.*] —**ac•cou′ter•ments** *n.*
Ac•cra (ăk′rə, ə-krä′) The capital of Ghana, in the SE part on the Gulf of Guinea. Pop. 867,500.
ac•cred•it (ə-krĕd′ĭt) ▸*v.* **1.** To attribute to; credit. **2.** To supply with credentials. See Syns at **authorize. 3.** To certify as meeting a prescribed standard. [Fr. *accréditer.*] —**ac•cred′i•ta′tion** *n.*
ac•cre•tion (ə-krē′shən) ▸*n.* **1.** Growth or increase in size by gradual addition. **2.** The result of such growth or increase. [< Lat. *accrēscere, accrēt-*, grow.] —**ac•cre′tion•ar′y, ac•cre′tive** *adj.*
ac•crue (ə-kro͞o′) ▸*v.* **-crued, -cru•ing 1.** To come to one as a gain: *benefits that accrue from scientific research.* **2.** To increase or accumulate over time: *interest accruing in a bank account.* [< Lat. *accrēscere*, grow.] —**ac•cru′al** *n.*
ac•cul•tur•a•tion (ə-kŭl′chə-rā′shən) ▸*n.* The modification of the culture of a group or individual by contact with a different culture. —**ac•cul′tur•ate′** *v.*
ac•cu•mu•late (ə-kyo͞om′yə-lāt′) ▸*v.* **-lat•ed, -lat•ing.** To gather or pile up; amass. [Lat. *accumulāre* < *cumulus*, heap.] —**ac•cu′mu•la′tion** *n.* —**ac•cu′mu•la′tor** *n.*
ac•cu•ra•cy (ăk′yər-ə-sē) ▸*n.* **1.** Conformity to fact. **2.** Precision; exactness.
ac•cu•rate (ăk′yər-ĭt) ▸*adj.* **1.** Conforming exactly to fact; errorless. **2.** Capable of providing a correct reading or measurement: *an accurate scale.* [< Lat. *accūrāre*, attend to carefully.] —**ac′cu•rate•ly** *adv.* —**ac′cu•rate•ness** *n.*
ac•curs•ed (ə-kûr′sĭd, ə-kûrst′) also **ac•curst** (ə-kûrst′) ▸*adj.* **1.** Abominable; odious: *this accursed mud.* **2.** Being under a curse; doomed. —**ac•curs′ed•ly** *adv.*
ac•cu•sa•tive (ə-kyo͞o′zə-tĭv) ▸*adj.* Of or relating to the case of a noun, pronoun, adjective, or participle that is the direct object of a verb or the object of certain prepositions. ▸*n.* The accusative case.
ac•cuse (ə-kyo͞oz′) ▸*v.* **-cused, -cus•ing 1.** To charge with an error or offense. **2.** To bring charges against. [< Lat. *accūsāre.*] —**ac′cu•sa′tion** (ăk′yo͞o-zā′shən) *n.* —**ac•cus′er** *n.* —**ac•cus′ing•ly** *adv.*
ac•cused (ə-kyo͞ozd′) ▸*n.* The defendant or defendants in a criminal case.
ac•cus•tom (ə-kŭs′təm) ▸*v.* **-tomed, -tom•ing 1.** To familiarize, as by habit or frequent use: *accustom oneself to working late.* **2.** To adjust; adapt. [< OFr. *acostumer.*]
ac•cus•tomed (ə-kŭs′təmd) ▸*adj.* **1.** Usual; customary. **2.** Being in the habit of: *I am accustomed to sleeping late.*
ace (ās) ▸*n.* **1.** A playing card, die, or domino having one spot or pip. **2.** In racket games, a

serve that one's opponent fails to return. **3.** A fighter pilot who has destroyed five or more enemy aircraft. **4.** An expert in a given field. ▶*adj.* Top-notch; first-rate. ▶*v.* **aced, ac•ing 1.** To serve an ace against. **2.** *Slang* To triumph over; defeat. —***idioms:*** **ace in the hole** A hidden advantage. **within an ace of** Very near to. [< Lat. *as*, unit.]

a•cer•bic (ə-sûr′bĭk) also **a•cerb** (ə-sûrb′) ▶*adj.* Acid or biting, as in taste, manner, or tone. See Syns at **bitter.** [< Lat. *acerbus.*] —**a•cer′bi•cal•ly** *adv.*

a•cer•bi•ty (ə-sûr′bĭ-tē) ▶*n., pl.* **-ties.** Bitterness, acidness.

a•cet•a•min•o•phen (ə-sē′tə-mĭn′ə-fən) ▶*n.* A crystalline compound, $C_8H_9NO_2$, used in medicine to relieve pain and fever.

ac•e•tate (ăs′ĭ-tāt′) ▶*n.* **1.** A salt or ester of acetic acid. **2.** Cellulose acetate or a product, esp. fibers, derived from it.

a•ce•tic (ə-sē′tĭk) ▶*adj.* Of, relating to, or containing acetic acid or vinegar. [< Lat. *acētum*, vinegar.]

acetic acid ▶*n.* A clear, colorless organic acid, CH_3COOH, with a distinctive pungent odor, that is the chief acid of vinegar.

ac•e•tone (ăs′ĭ-tōn′) ▶*n.* A colorless, volatile, highly flammable liquid, CH_3COCH_3, used as an organic solvent.

a•ce•tyl•cho•line (ə-sēt′l-kō′lēn′) ▶*n.* A white crystalline compound, $C_7H_{17}NO_3$, that mediates transmission of nerve impulses across synapses.

a•cet•y•lene (ə-sĕt′l-ēn′, -ən) ▶*n.* A colorless, highly flammable or explosive gas, C_2H_2, used for metal welding and cutting.

a•ce•tyl•sal•i•cyl•ic acid (ə-sēt′l-săl′ĭ-sĭl′ĭk) ▶*n.* See **aspirin** 1.

ache (āk) ▶*v.* **ached, ach•ing 1.** To suffer a dull, sustained pain. **2.** To yearn painfully. ▶*n.* **1.** A dull, steady pain. See Syns at **pain. 2.** A longing or yearning. [< OE *acan.*] —**ach′y** *adj.*

a•chene (ā-kēn′) ▶*n.* A small, dry, one-seeded fruit with a thin wall. [NLat. *achenium* : A-[1] + Gk. *khainein*, yawn.]

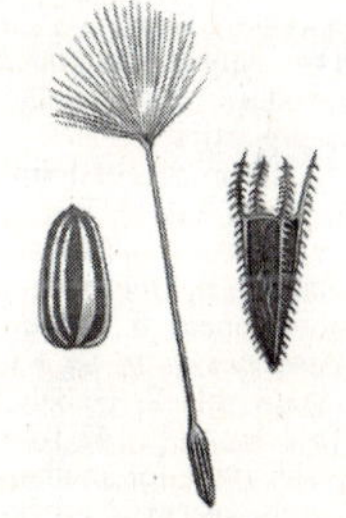

achene
left to right: sunflower, dandelion, and swamp beggar-ticks

a•chieve (ə-chēv′) ▶*v.* **a•chieved, a•chiev•ing 1.** To perform successfully; accomplish: *achieve a task.* **2.** To attain with effort: *achieve fame.* [< OFr. *achever* < *(venir) a chief*, (come) to a head.] —**a•chiev′a•ble** *adj.* —**a•chiev′er** *n.*

a•chieve•ment (ə-chēv′mənt) ▶*n.* **1.** The act of achieving. **2.** Something accomplished successfully. See Syns at **feat.**

A•chil•les (ə-kĭl′ēz) ▶*n.* *Gk. Myth.* The hero of Homer's *Iliad,* who slew Hector.

Achilles' heel ▶*n.* A seemingly small but fatal weakness. [From Achilles's being vulnerable only in one heel.]

Achilles tendon ▶*n.* The large tendon connecting the heel bone to the calf muscle.

ach•ro•mat•ic (ăk′rə-măt′ĭk) ▶*adj.* **1.** Designating a color, such as black or white, that has no hue. **2.** Refracting light without spectral color separation. —**ach′ro•mat′i•cal•ly** *adv.* —**a•chro′ma•tism** (ā-krō′mə-tĭz′əm) *n.*

ac•id (ăs′ĭd) ▶*n.* **1.** *Chem.* Any of a large class of sour-tasting substances whose aqueous solutions turn blue litmus red and react with bases, alkalis, or certain metals to form salts. **2.** A sour-tasting substance. **3.** *Slang* See **LSD.** ▶*adj.* **1.** *Chem.* **a.** Of an acid. **b.** Having a high concentration of acid. **2.** Having a sour taste. See Syns at **sour. 3.** Biting; sarcastic: *an acid wit.* [< Lat. *acidus*, sour < *acēre*, be sharp.] —**a•cid′ic** (ə-sĭd′ĭk) *adj.* —**a•cid′i•ty** *n.* —**ac′id•ly** *adv.* —**ac′id•ness** *n.*

a•cid•i•fy (ə-sĭd′ə-fī′) ▶*v.* **-fied, -fy•ing.** To make or become acid. —**a•cid′i•fi•ca′tion** *n.* —**a•cid′i•fi′er** *n.*

ac•i•doph•i•lus milk (ăs′ĭ-dŏf′ə-ləs) ▶*n.* Milk fermented by bacterial cultures, used to treat certain digestive disorders. [< NLat. *acidophilus*, bacteria species.]

ac•i•do•sis (ăs′ĭ-dō′sĭs) ▶*n.* An abnormal increase in the acidity of the body's fluids. —**ac′i•dot′ic** (-dŏt′ĭk) *adj.*

acid rain ▶*n.* Rain having an abnormally high acidity as a result of interactions with atmospheric pollutants.

acid re•flux (rē′flŭks′) ▶*n.* See **heartburn.**

acid rock ▶*n.* Rock music having a heavy repetitive beat and lyrics that suggest psychedelic experiences.

acid test ▶*n.* A decisive or critical test.

a•cid•u•late (ə-sĭj′ə-lāt′) ▶*v.* **-lat•ed, -lat•ing.** To make or become slightly acid.

a•cid•u•lous (ə-sĭj′ə-ləs) ▶*adj.* Slightly sour in taste or in manner. [< Lat. *acidulus* < *acidus*, ACID.]

a•ci•du•ri•a• (ăs′ĭ-dŏŏr′ē-ə,-dyŏŏr′-) ▶*n.* A condition marked by the presence of acid in the urine.

ac•knowl•edge (ăk-nŏl′ĭj) ▶*v.* **-edged, -edg•ing 1a.** To admit the existence, reality, or truth of. **b.** To recognize as being valid. **2a.** To express recognition of: *acknowledge a friend's smile.* **b.** To express thanks or gratitude for. **3.** To report the receipt of. [Prob. blend of ME *knowlechen*, acknowledge, and *aknouen*, recognize.] —**ac•knowl′edge•a•ble** *adj.* —**ac•knowl′edg•ment, ac•knowl′edge•ment** *n.*

ACLU ▶*abbr.* American Civil Liberties Union

ACM ▶*abbr.* asbestos-containing material

ac•me (ăk′mē) ▶*n.* The highest point, as of perfection. [Gk. *akmē.*]

ac•ne (ăk′nē) ▶*n.* An inflammatory disease of the oil glands and hair follicles of the skin, marked by pimples, esp. on the face. [Poss. < Gk. *akmē*, point. See ACME.] —**ac′ned** *adj.*

ac•o•lyte (ăk′ə-līt′) ▶*n.* **1.** One who attends or assists the celebrant in the performance of liturgical rites. **2.** A devoted follower or attendant.

[< Gk. *akolouthos*, attendant.]

A•con•ca•gua (ăk′ən-kä′gwə, ä′kən-) A mountain, about 7,025.4 m (23,034 ft), in the Andes of W Argentina; highest peak of the Western Hemisphere.

ac•o•nite (ăk′ə-nīt′) ►*n.* **1.** Any of various usu. poisonous plants with hooded flowers. **2.** The dried roots of these plants, used as a source of drugs. [< Gk. *akoniton*.]

a•corn (ā′kôrn′, -kərn) ►*n.* The fruit of an oak, consisting of a nut set in a woody, cuplike base. [< OE *æcern*.]

acorn squash ►*n.* A type of squash shaped somewhat like an acorn with a ridged rind and yellow to orange flesh.

a•cous•tic (ə-ko͞o′stĭk) also **a•cous•ti•cal** (-stĭ-kəl) ►*adj.* **1.** Of or relating to sound, the sense of hearing, or the science of sound. **2.** Designed to aid in hearing. **3.** *Mus.* Not electronically produced or modified: *an acoustic guitar.* [Gk. *akoustikos* < *akouein*, hear.] —**a•cous′ti•cal•ly** *adv.*

a•cous•tics (ə-ko͞o′stĭks) ►*n.* **1.** *(takes sing. v.)* The scientific study of sound. **2.** *(takes pl. v.)* The total effect of sound, esp. as produced in an enclosed space.

acpt. ►*abbr.* acceptance

ac•quaint (ə-kwānt′) ►*v.* To make familiar: *acquainted myself with the controls.* [< Med. Lat. *adcognitāre*, make known to.]

ac•quain•tance (ə-kwān′təns) ►*n.* **1.** Knowledge of a person less intimate than friendship. **2.** A person whom one knows. **3.** Personal knowledge or information. —**ac•quain′tance•ship′** *n.*

ac•qui•esce (ăk′wē-ĕs′) ►*v.* **-esced, -esc•ing.** To consent or comply without protest. [Lat. *acquiēscere*.] —**ac′qui•es′cense** *n.* —**ac′qui•es′cent** *adj.* —**ac′qui•es′cent•ly** *adv.*

Usage: *Acquiesce* usually takes the preposition *in* (*acquiesced in the ruling*) but sometimes takes *to* (*acquiesced to her parents' wishes*).

ac•quire (ə-kwīr′) ►*v.* **-quired, -quir•ing 1.** To gain possession of. **2.** To get by one's own efforts: *acquire proficiency in math.* [< Lat. *acquīrere*, *acquīsit-*, add to.] —**ac•quir′a•ble** *adj.* —**ac•quire′ment** *n.*

ac•quired (ə-kwīrd′) ►*adj.* **1.** Developing after birth; not congenital. **2.** Caused by exposure to something. **3.** Gained by one's own efforts.

acquired immune deficiency syndrome ►*n.* AIDS.

ac•qui•si•tion (ăk′wĭ-zĭsh′ən) ►*n.* **1.** The act of acquiring. **2.** Something acquired.

ac•quis•i•tive (ə-kwĭz′ĭ-tĭv) ►*adj.* Eager to gain and possess; grasping. —**ac•quis′i•tive•ly** *adv.* —**ac•quis′i•tive•ness** *n.*

ac•quit (ə-kwĭt′) ►*v.* **-quit•ted, -quit•ting 1.** *Law* To free from a charge or accusation. **2.** To discharge from a duty. **3.** To conduct (oneself) in a specified manner. [< OFr. *aquiter*.] —**ac•quit′tal** *n.*

ac•quit•tance (ə-kwĭt′ns) ►*n.* A written release from an obligation.

a•cre (ā′kər) ►*n.* See table at **measurement.** [< OE *æcer*, field.]

a•cre•age (ā′kər-ĭj) ►*n.* Land area in acres.

ac•rid (ăk′rĭd) ►*adj.* **1.** Unpleasantly sharp or bitter to the taste or smell. See Syns at **bitter.** **2.** Caustic in language or tone. [< Lat. *ācer*, bitter.] —**a•crid′i•ty** (ə-krĭd′ĭ-tē), **ac′rid•ness** *n.* —**ac′rid•ly** *adv.*

ac•ri•mo•ny (ăk′rə-mō′nē) ►*n.* Bitter, ill-natured animosity, esp. in speech or behavior. [< Lat. *ācer*, sharp.] —**ac′ri•mo′ni•ous** *adj.* —**ac′ri•mo′ni•ous•ly** *adv.*

acro– or **acr–** ►*pref.* **1.** Height; summit: *acrophobia.* **2.** Beginning: *acronym.* [< Gk. *akros*, extreme.]

ac•ro•bat (ăk′rə-băt′) ►*n.* One skilled in feats of agility in gymnastics. [< Gk. *akrobatē* : ACRO– + *bainein*, *bat-*, walk.] —**ac′ro•bat′ic** *adj.* —**ac′ro•bat′i•cal•ly** *adv.*

ac•ro•bat•ics (ăk′rə-băt′ĭks) ►*n.* *(takes sing. or pl. v.)* **1.** The gymnastic moves of an acrobat. **2.** A display of spectacular agility: *vocal acrobatics.*

ac•ro•nym (ăk′rə-nĭm′) ►*n.* A word formed from the initial letters of a name, such as *AIDS* for *a*cquired *i*mmune *d*eficiency *s*yndrome. —**ac′ro•nym′ic, a•cron′y•mous** (ə-krŏn′ə-məs) *adj.*

ac•ro•pho•bi•a (ăk′rə-fō′bē-ə) ►*n.* An abnormal fear of high places.

a•crop•o•lis (ə-krŏp′ə-lĭs) ►*n.* The fortified height or citadel of an ancient Greek city. [Gk. *akropolis* : ACRO– + *polis*, city.]

a•cross (ə-krôs′, -krŏs′) ►*prep.* On, at, to, or from the other side of. ►*adv.* **1.** From one side to the other: *The footbridge swayed when I ran across.* **2.** Crosswise; crossed. [< AN *an croiz*, crosswise.]

a•cross-the-board (ə-krôs′*th*ə-bôrd′, -bōrd′, ə-krŏs′-) ►*adj.* **1.** Including all categories or members. **2.** *Sports & Games* Combining win, place, or show in one bet.

a•cros•tic (ə-krô′stĭk, -krŏs′tĭk) ►*n.* A poem or series of lines in which certain letters, usu. the first in each line, form a name, motto, or message when read in sequence. [< Gk. *akrostikhis* : ACRO– + *stikhos*, line.] —**a•cros′tic** *adj.*

a•cryl•ic (ə-krĭl′ĭk) ►*n.* **1.** An acrylic resin. **2.** A paint containing acrylic resin. **3.** An acrylic fiber. [*acrolein*, an aldehyde + –YL + –IC.] —**a•cryl′ic** *adj.*

acrylic fiber ►*n.* Any of numerous synthetic fibers used in sweaters, knits, and carpets.

acrylic resin ►*n.* Any of numerous thermoplastics used to produce paints, synthetic rubbers, and lightweight plastics.

act (ăkt) ►*n.* **1.** The process of doing something. **2.** Something done; a deed. **3.** *Law* A statute, decree, or enactment. **4.** A formal written record of transactions. **5.** One of the major divisions of a play or opera. **6.** A manifestation of insincerity; pose: *put on an act.* ►*v.* **1.** To perform in a dramatic role. **2.** To behave; conduct oneself. **3.** To seem to be. **4.** To carry out an action. **5.** To substitute for another. **6.** To produce an effect. —***phrasal verbs:*** **act out 1.**To perform in or as if in a play. **2.** To express (e.g., unconscious impulses) without awareness or understanding. **act up 1.** To misbehave. **2.** To malfunction. —***idiom:*** **get (one's) act together** *Slang* To get organized. [< Lat. *agere*, *āct-*, do.]

ACTH (ā′sē′tē-āch′) ►*n.* A hormone produced by the pituitary gland that stimulates the secretion of cortisone and other hormones by the adrenal cortex. [*a(dreno)c(ortico)t(ropic) h(ormone)*.]

ac•tin (ăk′tĭn) ►*n.* A muscle protein that acts with myosin to produce muscle contraction. [Lat. *agere, āct-*, ACT + –IN.]

act•ing (ăk′tĭng) ►*adj.* Temporarily assuming the duties or authority of another. See Syns at **temporary.** ►*n.* The occupation of or performance as an actor or actress.

ac•ti•nide (ăk′tə-nīd′) ►*n.* Any of a series of chemically similar radioactive elements with atomic numbers ranging from 89 (actinium) through 103 (lawrencium).

ac•ti•nism (ăk′tə-nĭz′əm) ►*n.* The intrinsic property in radiation that produces photochemical activity. —**ac•tin′ic** (-tĭn′ĭk) *adj.*

ac•tin•i•um (ăk-tĭn′ē-əm) ►*n. Symbol* **Ac** A radioactive metallic element found in uranium ores and used as a source of alpha rays. At. no. 89. See table at **element.** [< Gk. *aktis*, ray.]

ac•ti•no•my•cin (ăk′tə-nō-mī′sĭn) ►*n.* Any of various red, often toxic antibiotics obtained from soil bacteria.

ac•tion (ăk′shən) ►*n.* **1.** The state or process of acting or doing. **2.** Something done; a deed or act. **3.** A movement or a series of movements. **4.** Manner of movement: *a gearshift with smooth action.* **5.** Habitual or vigorous activity; energy. **6.** often **actions** Behavior or conduct. **7.** The operating parts of a mechanism. **8.** The plot of a story or play. **9.** A lawsuit. **10.** Combat. **11.** Important or exciting work or activity.

ac•tion•a•ble (ăk′shə-nə-bəl) ►*adj.* Giving cause for legal action: *an actionable statement.* —**ac′tion•a•bly** *adv.*

Ac•ti•um (ăk′shē-əm, -tē-) A promontory and ancient town of W Greece.

ac•ti•vate (ăk′tə-vāt′) ►*v.* **-vat•ed, -vat•ing 1.** To make active. **2.** To organize or create (e.g., a military unit). **3.** To treat (sewage) with aeration and bacteria. **4.** *Phys.* To make radioactive. —**ac′ti•va′tion** *n.* —**ac′ti•va′tor** *n.*

ac•ti•vat•ed charcoal (ăk′tə-vā′tĭd) ►*n.* Highly absorbent carbon obtained by heating granulated charcoal to exhaust contained gases.

ac•tive (ăk′tĭv) ►*adj.* **1.** Being in motion. **2.** Capable of functioning; working. **3.** Disposed to make changes. **4.** Engaged in activity; participating. **5.** Being in action; not passive: *an active volcano.* **6a.** Energetic; lively. **b.** Requiring physical exertion: *active sports.* **7.** *Gram.* Of or being a verb form or voice used to indicate that the subject of the sentence is performing or causing the action. —**ac′tive•ly** *adv.* —**ac′tive•ness** *n.*

active immunity ►*n.* Immunity resulting from the production of antibodies in response to an antigen.

ac•tiv•ism (ăk′tə-vĭz′əm) ►*n.* A theory or practice based on often militant action to oppose or support a social or political end. —**ac′tiv•ist** *adj. & n.* —**ac•tiv•ist′ic** *adj.*

ac•tiv•i•ty (ăk-tĭv′ĭ-tē) ►*n., pl.* **-ties 1.** The state of being active. **2.** Energetic action; liveliness. **3a.** A pursuit or pastime. **b.** An educational procedure to stimulate learning through actual experience.

act of God ►*n.* An unforeseeable manifestation of the forces of nature beyond human intervention, such as a tornado or flood.

ac•tor (ăk′tər) ►*n.* **1.** A theatrical performer. **2.** A participant. **3.** *Law* One, such as an administrator, who acts for another.

ac•tress (ăk′trĭs) ►*n.* A woman who is an actor. See Usage Note at **–ess.**

Acts of the Apostles (ăkts) ►*pl.n. (takes sing. v.)* See table at **Bible.**

ac•tu•al (ăk′cho͞o-əl) ►*adj.* **1.** Existing in fact; real. **2.** Existing or acting at the present moment; current. [< Lat. *agere, āct-*, ACT.] —**ac′tu•al•ly** *adv.*

ac•tu•al•i•ty (ăk′cho͞o-ăl′ĭ-tē) ►*n., pl.* **-ties.** The state or fact of being actual; reality. See Syns at **existence.**

ac•tu•al•ize (ăk′cho͞o-ə-līz′) ►*v.* **-ized, -iz•ing.** To realize in action. —**ac′tu•al•i•za′tion** *n.*

ac•tu•ar•y (ăk′cho͞o-ĕr′ē) ►*n., pl.* **-ies.** A statistician who computes insurance risks and premiums. [< Lat. *ācta*, records < *agere*, ACT.] —**ac′tu•ar′i•al** (-âr′ē-əl) *adj.*

ac•tu•ate (ăk′cho͞o-āt′) ►*v.* **-at•ed, -at•ing.** To put into motion or action. [Med.Lat. *āctuāre, āctuāt-* < Lat. *agere*, ACT.] —**ac′tu•a′tion** *n.* —**ac′tu•a′tor** *n.*

a•cu•i•ty (ə-kyo͞o′ĭ-tē) ►*n.* Acuteness of vision or perception; keenness. [< Lat. *acūtus*, ACUTE.]

ac•u•men (ăk′yə-mən, ə-kyo͞o′-) ►*n.* Accuracy and keenness of judgment or insight. [Lat. *acūmen* < *acus*, needle.]

ac•u•pres•sure (ăk′yə-prĕsh′ər) ►*n.* See **shiatsu.** [ACU(PUNCTURE) + PRESSURE.]

ac•u•punc•ture (ăk′yo͞o-pŭngk′chər) ►*n.* A Chinese medical procedure in which specific body areas are pierced with fine needles for pain relief or other therapeutic purposes. [Lat. *acus*, needle + PUNCTURE.] —**ac′u•punc′ture** *v.* —**ac′u•punc′tur•ist** *n.*

a•cute (ə-kyo͞ot′) ►*adj.* **1.** Having a sharp point. **2.** Keenly perceptive or discerning. **3.** Sensitive. **4.** Crucial: *an acute lack of research funds.* **5.** Extremely sharp or severe: *acute pain.* **6.** *Medic.* Having a rapid onset and following a short but severe course: *acute disease.* **7.** *Geometry* Designating angles less than 90°. [< Lat. *acuere, acūt-*, sharpen < *acus*, needle.] —**a•cute′ly** *adv.* —**a•cute′ness** *n.*

acute accent ►*n.* A mark (´) indicating: **a.** Stress of a syllable. **b.** Metrical stress in poetry. **c.** Sound quality or quantity.

acute care ►*n.* Short-term medical treatment, usu. in a hospital, for acute illness or injury.

ACV ►*abbr.* actual cash value

a•cy•clo•vir (ā-sī′klō-vîr) ►*n.* A drug used topically to treat herpes simplex infections. [A–[1] + CYCLO– + VIR(US).]

ad (ăd) ►*n.* An advertisement.

A.D. ►*abbr.* often **A.D.** anno Domini

ad– ►*pref.* Toward; to; near: *adrenal.* [< Lat. *ad*, to.]

ad•age (ăd′ĭj) ►*n.* A short proverb; saying. [< Lat. *adagium.*]

a•da•gio (ə-dä′jō, -jē-ō′) ►*adv. & adj. Mus.* In a slow tempo. [Ital.]

Ad•am (ăd′əm). In the Bible, the first man and the husband of Eve.

ad•a•mant (ăd′ə-mənt) ►*adj.* Impervious to pleas or reason; unyielding. ►*n.* A legendary stone of impenetrable hardness. [< Gk. *adamas*, hard steel.]

Ad•ams (ăd′əmz), **Abigail Smith.** 1744–1818. First Lady of the US (1797–1801) and noted correspondent.

Adams, John. 1735–1826. The first Vice President (1789–97) and second President (1797–1801) of the US.

John Adams
1793 portrait

John Quincy Adams
1815 portrait

Adams, John Quincy. 1767–1848. The sixth US President (1825–29).

Adams, Samuel. 1722–1803. Amer. Revolutionary leader.

Adam's apple ►*n.* The slight projection at the front of the throat formed by the largest cartilage of the larynx.

a•dapt (ə-dăpt′) ►*v.* To make or become suitable for a specific use. [< Lat. *adaptāre*, fit to.] —**a•dapt′a•bil′i•ty** *n.* —**a•dapt′a•ble** *adj.* ***Syns:*** *adapt, accommodate, adjust, conform, fit, reconcile* **v.**

ad•ap•ta•tion (ăd′ăp-tā′shən) ►*n.* **1a.** The act or process of adapting. **b.** The state of being adapted. **2.** A composition recast into a new form: *The play is an adaptation of a short novel.* **3.** *Biol.* An alteration or adjustment by which a species or individual improves its condition in relationship to its environment. —**ad′ap•ta′tion•al** *adj.*

a•dapt•er also **a•dap•tor** (ə-dăp′tər) ►*n.* One that adapts, such as a device used to effect compatibility between different parts of a system.

a•dap•tive (ə-dăp′tĭv) ►*adj.* Capable of adapting or of being adapted: *an adaptive nature.* —**a•dap′tive•ness** *n.*

A•dar (ä-där′) ►*n.* A month of the Jewish calendar. See table at **calendar.** [Heb. *'ădār.*]

Adar She•ni (shā-nē′) ►*n.* An intercalary month in the Jewish calendar. See table at **calendar.** [Heb. *'ădār šēnî*, second Adar.]

ADC ►*abbr.* **1.** aide-de-camp **2.** Aid to Dependent Children

add (ăd) ►*v.* **1.** To combine (e.g., a column of figures) to form a sum. **2.** To join so as to increase in size, quantity, quality, or scope: *added 12 inches to the deck.* **3.** To say or write further. —***phrasal verb:*** **add up** To be reasonable or plausible: *an excuse that didn't add up.* —***idiom:*** **add up to** To constitute; mean. [< Lat. *addere* : AD– + *dare*, give.] —**add′a•ble, add′i•ble** *adj.*

ADD ►*abbr.* attention deficit disorder

Ad•dams (ăd′əmz), **Jane.** 1860–1935. Amer. social reformer and pacifist; shared 1931 Nobel Peace Prize.

ad•dend (ăd′ĕnd′) ►*n.* Any of a set of numbers to be added. [Short for ADDENDUM.]

ad•den•dum (ə-dĕn′dəm) ►*n.*, *pl.* **-da** (-də). Something added or to be added, esp. a supplement to a book. [Lat. < *addere*, ADD.]

add•er[1] (ăd′ər) ►*n.* One that adds, esp. a device that performs arithmetic addition.

ad•der[2] (ăd′ər) ►*n.* **1.** See **viper** 1. **2.** Any of several nonvenomous snakes, such as the milk snake of North America, popularly believed to be harmful. [< OE *nǣdre.*]

ad•dict (ə-dĭkt′) ►*v.* **1.** To give (oneself) habitually or compulsively: *We were addicted to gambling.* **2.** To cause to become compulsively and physiologically dependent on a habit-forming substance. ►*n.* (ăd′ĭkt). One who is addicted, as to narcotics. [Lat. *addīcere, addict-*, bind over to.] —**ad•dic′tion** *n.* —**ad•dic′tive** *adj.*

add-in (ăd′ĭn′) ►*n.* **1.** Something designed for use in conjunction with another. **2.** *Comp. Sci.* A software program that extends the capabilities of an existing application.

Ad•dis Ab•a•ba (ăd′ĭs ăb′ə-bə, ä′dĭs ä′bə-bä′) The capital of Ethiopia, in the central part. Pop. 2,316,400.

Ad•di•son (ăd′ĭ-sən), **Joseph.** 1672–1719. English essayist. —**Ad′di•so′ni•an** (-sō′nē-ən) *adj.*

ad•di•tion (ə-dĭsh′ən) ►*n.* **1.** The act or process of adding. **2.** Something added, such as a room to a building. —***idiom:*** **in addition** Also. See Usage Note at **together.** —**ad•di′tion•al** *adj.* —**ad•di′tion•al•ly** *adv.*

ad•di•tive (ăd′ĭ-tĭv) ►*n.* A substance added in small amounts to something else to improve or strengthen it. ►*adj.* Relating to addition.

ad•dle (ăd′l) ►*v.* **-dled, -dling 1.** To make or become confused. See Syns at **confuse. 2.** To become rotten; spoil. [< OE *adel*, filth.]

add-on (ăd′ŏn′, -ôn′) ►*n.* **1.** One thing added as a supplement to another. **2.** *Comp. Sci.* **a.** See **add-in** 2. **b.** A hardware device added to a computer to increase its capabilities.

ad•dress (ə-drĕs′) ►*v.* **1.** To speak to. **2.** To direct to the attention of. **3.** To mark with a destination. **4.** To direct one's efforts or attention to. ►*n.* **1.** A formal spoken or written communication. **2.** (*also* ăd′rĕs′). The directions on a deliverable item indicating destination. **3.** (*also* ăd′rĕs′). The location at which an organization or person may be found. **4.** (*also* ăd′rĕs′) *Comp. Sci.* **a.** A number assigned to a specific memory location. **b.** A name or character sequence that designates an e-mail account or website. [< OFr. *adresser*, direct to.]

ad•dress•ee (ăd′rĕ-sē′, ə-drĕs′ē′) ►*n.* The one to whom something is addressed.

ad•duce (ə-do͞os′, -dyo͞os′) ►*v.* **-duced, -duc•ing.** To cite as an example or means of proof in an argument. [Lat. *addūcere*, bring to.] —**ad•duce′a•ble, ad•duc′i•ble** *adj.*

-ade ►*suff.* A sweetened beverage of: *lemonade.* [< OFr. < Lat. *-ātus*, -ate.]

Ad•e•laide (ăd′l-ād′) A city of S Australia NW of Melbourne. Met. area pop. 1,071,100.

A•den (äd′n, ād′n) **1.** A former British colony and protectorate of S Arabia, part of Southern Yemen (now Yemen) since 1967. **2.** A city of S Yemen on the **Gulf of Aden,** an arm of the Arabian Sea between Yemen and Somalia. Pop. 400,783.

Ad•en•au•er (ăd′n-ou′ər, äd′-), **Konrad.** 1876–1967. German politician; first chancellor of West Germany (1949–63).

ad•e•nine (ăd′n-ēn′, -ĭn) ►*n.* A purine base, $C_5H_5N_5$, that is a constituent of DNA and RNA. [Gk. *adēn*, gland + –INE[2].]

ad•e•noid (ăd′n-oid′) ►*n.* A lymphoid tissue growth in the nose above the throat. Often used in the plural. [Gk. *adēn*, gland + –OID.]

ad•e•noi•dal (ăd′n-oid′l) ►*adj.* **1.** Of the adenoids. **2.** Nasal; stuffy: *an adenoidal voice.*

a•dept (ə-dĕpt′) ►*adj.* Very skilled; expert. [< Lat. *adipīscī*, *adept-*, attain to.] —**ad′ept′** (ăd′ĕpt′) *n.* —**a•dept′ly** *adv.*

ad•e•quate (ăd′ĭ-kwĭt) ►*adj.* **1.** Sufficient to satisfy a requirement. See Syns at **sufficient. 2.** Barely satisfactory. [< Lat. *adaequāre*, make equal to.] —**ad′e•qua•cy** (-kwə-sē) *n.* —**ad′e•quate•ly** *adv.*

ADHD ►*abbr.* attention deficit hyperactivity disorder

ad•here (ăd-hîr′) ►*v.* **-hered, -her•ing 1.** To stick fast, as by suction or glue. **2.** To be a devoted follower. **3.** To carry something out without deviation: *We will adhere to our plan.* [< Lat. *adhaerēre*, stick to.] —**ad•her′ence** *n.* —**ad•her′ent** *adj. & n.*

ad•he•sion (ăd-hē′zhən) ►*n.* **1.** The act or state of adhering. **2.** Attachment or devotion; loyalty. **3.** *Medic.* A condition in which normally separate bodily tissues grow together.

ad•he•sive (ăd-hē′sĭv, -zĭv) ►*adj.* **1.** Tending to adhere; sticky. **2.** Gummed so as to adhere. —**ad•he′sive** *n.* —**ad•he′sive•ly** *adv.* —**ad•he′sive•ness** *n.*

ad hoc (ăd hŏk′, hōk′) ►*adv.* For only the specific case or situation at hand. ►*adj.* Improvised; impromptu. [Lat., for this.]

ad hom•i•nem (hŏm′ə-nĕm′) ►*adj.* Attacking an opponent's character to avoid discussing the issues. [Lat., to the man.]

ad•i•a•bat•ic (ăd′ē-ə-băt′ĭk, ā′dī-) ►*adj.* Relating to a reversible process occurring without gain or loss of heat. [< Gk. *adiabatos*, impassable : A–[1] + *diabatos*, passable (*dia-*, across + *bainein*, *bat-*, go).]

a•dieu (ə-dyo͞o′, -do͞o′) ►*interj.* Used to express farewell. ►*n., pl.* **a•dieus** or **a•dieux** (ə-dyo͞oz′, -do͞oz′). A farewell. [< OFr.]

ad in•fi•ni•tum (ăd ĭn′fə-nī′təm) ►*adv. & adj.* To infinity; having no end. [Lat. *ad īnfīnītum.*]

ad•i•os (ăd′ē-ōs′, ä′dē-) ►*interj.* Used to express farewell. [Sp. *adiós.*]

ad•i•pose (ăd′ə-pōs′) ►*adj.* Relating to animal fat; fatty. [< Lat. *adeps*, *adip-*, fat.]

Ad•i•ron•dack Mountains (ăd′ə-rŏn′dăk′) A group of mountains in NE NY rising to about 1,630 m (5,344 ft).

adj. ►*abbr.* **1.** adjective **2.** adjunct **3. Adj.** adjutant

ad•ja•cent (ə-jā′sənt) ►*adj.* **1.** Close to; lying near: *adjacent cities.* **2.** Next to; adjoining: *adjacent garden plots.* [< Lat. *adiacēre*, lie near to.] —**ad•ja′cen•cy** *n.*

ad•jec•tive (ăj′ĭk-tĭv) ►*n.* The part of speech that modifies a noun or other substantive by limiting, qualifying, or specifying. [< Lat. *adicere*, *adiect-*, add to.] —**ad′jec•ti′val** (-tī′vəl) *adj.* —**ad′jec•ti′val•ly** *adv.*

ad•join (ə-join′) ►*v.* **1.** To be next to. **2.** To attach. [< Lat. *adiungere*, join to : AD– + *iungere*, join.]

ad•journ (ə-jûrn′) ►*v.* **1.** To suspend until a later time. **2.** To move from one place to another: *After the meal we adjourned to the living room.* [< OFr. *ajourner* < LLat. *diurnum*, day.] —**ad•journ′ment** *n.*

ad•judge (ə-jŭj′) ►*v.* **-judged, -judg•ing 1.** To determine or award by law. **2.** To regard; deem: *was adjudged incompetent.* [< Lat. *adiūdicāre.*]

ad•ju•di•cate (ə-jo͞o′dĭ-kāt′) ►*v.* **-cat•ed, -cat•ing.** To hear and settle (a case) by judicial procedure. [Lat. *adiūdicāre.*] —**ad•ju′di•ca′tion** *n.* —**ad•ju′di•ca′tive** *adj.* —**ad•ju′di•ca′tor** *n.*

ad•junct (ăj′ŭngkt′) ►*n.* One attached to another in a dependent or subordinate position. [< Lat. *adiungere*, *adiūnct-*, ADJOIN.] —**ad•junc′tive** *adj.*

ad•jure (ə-jo͝or′) ►*v.* **-jured, -jur•ing 1.** To command or enjoin solemnly, as under oath. **2.** To appeal to or entreat earnestly. [< Lat. *adiūrāre*, swear to.] —**ad′ju•ra′tion** (ăj′ə-rā′shən) *n.*

ad•just (ə-jŭst′) ►*v.* **1.** To change so as to match or fit. **2.** To bring into proper relationship. **3.** To adapt or conform, as to new conditions. See Syns at **adapt. 4.** To settle (an insurance claim). [< VLat. **adiūxtāre* : AD– + Lat. *iūxtā*, near.] —**ad•just′a•ble** *adj.* —**ad•just′er, ad•jus′tor** *n.* —**ad•just′ment** *n.*

ad•ju•tant (ăj′ə-tənt) ►*n.* **1.** A staff officer who helps a commanding officer with administration. **2.** An assistant. [< Lat. *adiūtāre*, give help to.] —**ad′ju•tan•cy** *n.*

Ad•ler (ăd′lər, ăd′-), **Alfred.** 1870–1937. Austrian psychiatrist. —**Ad•le′ri•an** (ăd-lîr′ē-ən) *adj.*

ad lib (ăd lĭb′) ►*adv.* In an unrestrained manner; spontaneously. [< Lat. *ad libitum*, at pleasure.]

ad-lib (ăd-lĭb′) ►*v.* **-libbed, -lib•bing.** To improvise and deliver extemporaneously. ►*n.* (ăd′lĭb′). Words, music, or actions uttered or performed extemporaneously. —**ad′-lib′** *adj.* —**ad-lib′ber** *n.*

ad loc. ►*abbr. Lat.* ad locum (to, or at, the place)

ad•min•is•ter (ăd-mĭn′ĭ-stər) ►*v.* **1.** To direct; manage. **2a.** To give or apply in a formal way: *administer the last rites.* **b.** To apply as a remedy: *administer a sedative.* **3.** To mete out; dispense: *administer justice.* **4.** To tender (an oath). [< Lat. *administrāre.*] —**ad•min′is•trant** *adj. & n.*

ad•min•is•tra•tion (ăd-mĭn′ĭ-strā′shən) ►*n.* **1.** The act of administering. **2.** Management, esp. of business affairs. **3.** The activity of a sovereign state in the exercise of its powers or duties. **4.** often **Administration** The executive branch of a government. **5.** Those who manage an institution, esp. a school or college. —**ad•min′is•tra′tive** (-strā′tĭv, -strə-) *adj.* —**ad•min′is•tra′tive•ly** *adv.*

ad•min•is•tra•tor (ăd-mĭn′ĭ-strā′tər) ►*n.* **1.** One who administers. **2.** One appointed to manage an estate.

ad•mi•ra•ble (ăd′mər-ə-bəl) ►*adj.* Deserving admiration. —**ad′mi•ra•bly** *adv.*

ad•mi•ral (ăd′mər-əl) ►*n.* **1.** The commander in chief of a fleet. **2.** A rank, as in the US Navy, above vice admiral and below fleet admiral. [< Ar. *'amīr al-* . . ., high commander of the . . ..]

ad•mi•ral•ty (ăd′mər-əl-tē) ►*n., pl.* **-ties 1a.** A court exercising jurisdiction over all maritime cases. **b.** Maritime law. **2. Admiralty** The department of the British government that once had control over all naval affairs.

ad•mire (ăd-mīr′) ►*v.* **-mired, -mir•ing 1.** To regard with pleasure, wonder, and approval. **2.** To esteem or respect. **3.** *Archaic* To marvel at. [< Lat. *admīrārī*, to wonder at.] —**ad′mi•ra′tion** (ăd′mə-rā′shən) *n.* —**ad•mir′er** *n.*

ad•mis•si•ble (ăd-mĭs′ə-bəl) ►*adj.* **1.** That can be accepted; allowable: *admissible evidence.* **2.** Worthy of admission. —**ad•mis′si•bil′i•ty, ad•mis′si•ble•ness** *n.*

ad•mis•sion (ăd-mĭsh′ən) ►*n.* **1.** The act of admitting. **2.** Right to enter; access. **3.** The price required for entering; entrance fee. **4.** A confession, as of having committed a crime. —**ad•mis′sive** (-mĭs′ĭv) *adj.*

ad•mit (ăd-mĭt′) ►*v.* **-mit•ted, -mit•ting 1.** To permit to enter. **2.** To serve as a means of entrance. **3.** To have room for; accommodate. **4.** To allow; permit. **5.** To acknowledge; confess. **6.** To grant as true or valid; concede. [< Lat. *admittere.*]

ad•mit•tance (ăd-mĭt′ns) ►*n.* **1.** The act of admitting. **2a.** Permission to enter. **b.** Right of entry.

ad•mit•ted•ly (ăd-mĭt′ĭd-lē) ►*adv.* By general admission; confessedly.

ad•mix•ture (ăd-mĭks′chər) ►*n.* **1.** The act of mixing. **2.** A mixture. **3.** Something added in mixing. —**ad•mix′** *v.*

ad•mon•ish (ăd-mŏn′ĭsh) ►*v.* **1.** To reprove gently but earnestly. **2.** To warn; caution. **3.** To remind of an obligation. [< Lat. *admonēre* : AD– + *monēre*, warn.] —**ad•mon′ish•ment, ad′mo•ni′tion** (ăd′mə-nĭsh′ən) *n.*

ad•mon•i•to•ry (ăd-mŏn′ĭ-tôr′ē, -tōr′ē) ►*adj.* Expressing admonition.

ad nau•se•am (ăd nô′zē-əm) ►*adv.* To a disgusting or absurd degree. [Lat., to nausea.]

a•do (ə-do͞o′) ►*n.* Bustle; fuss; bother. [< ME *at do*, to do.]

a•do•be (ə-dō′bē) ►*n.* **1.** A sun-dried, unburned brick of clay and straw. **2.** A structure built of adobe brick. [< Ar. *aṭ-ṭūba*, the brick.]

adobe
San Miguel Mission Church, Santa Fe, New Mexico

ad•o•les•cence (ăd′l-ĕs′əns) ►*n.* The period of physical and psychological development from the onset of puberty to maturity. [< Lat. *adolēscere*, grow up.] —**ad′o•les′cent** *adj.* & *n.*

A•don•is (ə-dŏn′ĭs, -dō′nĭs) ►*n.* **1.** *Gk. Myth.* A beautiful young man loved by Aphrodite. **2.** often **adonis** A handsome young man.

a•dopt (ə-dŏpt′) ►*v.* **1.** To take (a child) into one's family through legal means and raise as one's own. **2.** To take and follow (a course of action) by choice or assent. **3.** To take up and make one's own. [< Lat. *adoptāre*, opt for.] —**a•dopt′a•ble** *adj.* —**a•dopt′er** *n.* —**a•dop′tion** *n.*

Usage: One refers to an *adopted* child but to *adoptive* parents.

a•dop•tee (ə-dŏp′tē) ►*n.* One, such as a child, that is or has been adopted.

a•dop•tive (ə-dŏp′tĭv) ►*adj.* **1.** Of or relating to adoption. **2.** Related by adoption. See Usage Note at **adopt.** —**a•dop′tive•ly** *adv.*

a•dor•a•ble (ə-dôr′ə-bəl, -dōr′-) ►*adj.* **1.** Delightful, lovable, and charming. **2.** Worthy of adoration. —**a•dor′a•bly** *adv.*

a•dore (ə-dôr′, -dōr′) ►*v.* **a•dored, a•dor•ing 1.** To worship as divine. **2.** To regard with deep, often rapturous love. **3.** To like very much. [< Lat. *adōrāre*, pray to.] —**ad•o•ra′tion** (ăd′ə-rā′shən) *n.* —**a•dor′er** *n.*

a•dorn (ə-dôrn′) ►*v.* **1.** To lend beauty to; enhance. **2.** To decorate; embellish. [< Lat. *adōrnāre.*] —**a•dorn′ment** *n.*

ad•re•nal (ə-drē′nəl) ►*adj.* **1.** At, near, or on the kidneys. **2.** Of or relating to the adrenal glands or their secretions.

adrenal gland ►*n.* Either of two small endocrine glands, one located above each kidney.

a•dren•a•line (ə-drĕn′ə-lĭn) ►*n.* See **epinephrine** 1.

A•dri•at•ic Sea (ā′drē-ăt′ĭk) An arm of the Mediterranean between Italy and the Balkan Peninsula.

a•drift (ə-drĭft′) ►*adv.* & *adj.* **1.** Drifting or floating freely; not anchored. **2.** Without direction or purpose.

a•droit (ə-droit′) ►*adj.* **1.** Dexterous; deft. **2.** Proficient under pressing conditions. [Fr.] —**a•droit′ly** *adv.* —**a•droit′ness** *n.*

ad•sorb (ăd-sôrb′, -zôrb′) ►*v.* To take up and hold (liquid or gas) on the surface of a solid. [AD– + Lat. *sorbēre*, suck.] —**ad•sorb′a•ble** *adj.* —**ad•sorp′tion** (-sôrp′shən, -zôrp′-) *n.* —**ad•sorp′tive** *adj.*

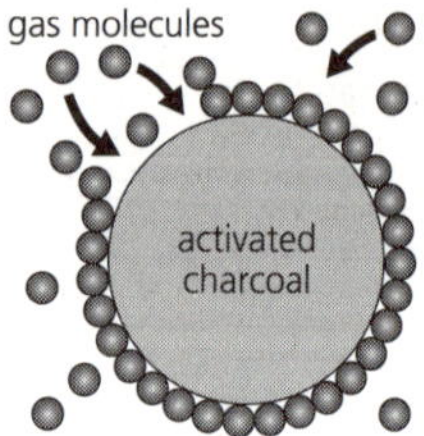

adsorb
Activated charcoal in a gas mask attracts toxic gas molecules, allowing the person wearing the mask to breathe fresh air.

ad•u•late (ăj′ə-lāt′) ►*v.* **-lat•ed, -lat•ing.** To praise or admire excessively; fawn on. [< Lat. *adūlārī*, to flatter.] —**ad′u•la′tion** *n.* —**ad′u•la•to′ry** (-lə-tôr′ē, -tōr′ē) *adj.*

a•dult (ə-dŭlt′, ăd′ŭlt) ►*n.* One that has attained maturity or legal age. ►*adj.* **1.** Fully developed; mature. **2.** For or befitting adults: *adult education.* [< Lat. *adolēscere, adult-*, grow up.] —**a•dult′hood′** *n.*

a•dul•ter•ate (ə-dŭl′tə-rāt′) ►*v.* **-at•ed, -at•ing.** To make impure by adding improper or inferior ingredients. [Lat. *adulterāre*, pollute.] —**a•dul′ter•ant** *adj.* & *n.* —**a•dul′ter•a′-**

tion *n.* —**a•dul′ter•a′tor** *n.*

Syns: *adulterate, debase, doctor* **v.**

a•dul•ter•y (ə-dŭl′tə-rē, -trē) ►*n., pl.* **-ies.** Voluntary sexual intercourse between a married person and a partner other than the lawful spouse. [< Lat. *adulter*, adulterer.] —**a•dul′ter•er** *n.* —**a•dul′ter•ess** (-trĭs, -tər-ĭs) *n.* —**a•dul′ter•ous** *adj.*

ad•um•brate (ăd′əm-brāt′, ə-dŭm′-) ►*v.* **-brat•ed, -brat•ing 1.** To give a sketchy outline of. **2.** To foreshadow. **3.** To disclose partially. [Lat. *adumbrāre*, shade in.] —**ad′um•bra′tion** *n.*

adv. ►*abbr.* **1.** adverb **2.** *Lat.* adversus (against)

ad•vance (ăd-văns′) ►*v.* **-vanced, -vanc•ing 1.** To move or bring forward. **2.** To put forward; suggest. **3a.** To aid the progress of. **b.** To make progress; proceed. **4.** To raise or rise in rank, amount, or value. **5.** To cause to occur sooner. **6.** To pay (money or interest) before due. **7.** To lend, esp. on credit. ►*n.* **1.** The act or process of moving or going forward. **2.** Improvement; progress. **3.** An increase of price or value. **4. advances** Opening approaches made to secure acquaintance, favor, or an agreement. **5.** Payment of money before due. ►*adj.* **1.** Made or given ahead of time: *an advance payment.* **2.** Going before or in front. —***idioms:* in advance** Ahead of time; beforehand. **in advance of** Ahead of. [< Lat. *ab ante*, from before.] —**ad•vanc′er** *n.*

Syns: *advance, forward, foster, further, promote* ***Ant:*** *retard* **v.**

ad•vanced (ăd-vănst′) ►*adj.* **1.** Highly developed or complex. **2.** At a higher level than others: *an advanced text in physics.* **3.** Progressive: *advanced teaching methods.* **4.** Far along in course or time: *an advanced stage of illness.*

ad•vance•ment (ăd-văns′mənt) ►*n.* **1.** The act of advancing. **2.** Progress: *the advancement of knowledge.* **3.** A promotion.

ad•van•tage (ăd-văn′tĭj) ►*n.* **1.** A beneficial factor or combination of factors. **2.** Benefit or profit; gain. **3.** A relatively favorable position. **4.** The first point scored in tennis after deuce. ►*v.* **-taged, -tag•ing.** To afford profit or gain to; benefit. —***idiom:* take advantage of 1.** To put to good use. **2.** To exploit. [< OFr. *avantage* < Lat. *ab ante*, from before.] —**ad•van•ta′geous** (-văn-tā′jəs) *adj.* —**ad′van•ta′geous•ly** *adv.*

ad•vec•tion (ăd-vĕk′shən) ►*n.* **1.** The transfer of an atmospheric property (e.g., temperature) by the motion of the air. **2.** The horizontal movement of water, as in a current. [< Lat. *advehere, advect-*, carry toward.]

ad•vent (ăd′vĕnt′) ►*n.* **1.** The coming or arrival, esp. of something important: *the advent of the computer.* **2.** also **Advent a.** The period of preparation for Christmas, beginning on the fourth Sunday before Christmas. **b.** *Christianity* The coming or birth of Jesus. [< Lat. *advenīre, advent-*, come to.]

ad•ven•ti•tious (ăd′vĕn-tĭsh′əs) ►*adj.* Not inherent but added extrinsically. [< Lat. *adventus*, ADVENT.] —**ad′ven•ti′tious•ly** *adv.*

ad•ven•ture (ăd-vĕn′chər) ►*n.* **1a.** An enterprise of a hazardous nature. **b.** An undertaking of a questionable nature, esp. intervention in another state's affairs. **2.** An unusual or exciting experience. **3.** A business venture. ►*v.* **-tured, -tur•ing 1.** To hazard or risk. **2.** To take risks. [< Lat. *advenīre, advent-*, come to. See ADVENT.]

ad•ven•tur•er (ăd-vĕn′chər-ər) ►*n.* **1.** One that seeks adventure. **2.** A soldier of fortune. **3.** A financial speculator. **4.** One who attempts to gain wealth and social position by unscrupulous means.

ad•ven•ture•some (ăd-vĕn′chər-səm) ►*adj.* Daring. See Syns at **adventurous.**

ad•ven•tur•ess (ăd-vĕn′chər-ĭs) ►*n.* A woman who seeks social and financial advancement by unscrupulous means. See Usage Note at **-ess.**

ad•ven•tur•ous (ăd-vĕn′chər-əs) ►*adj.* **1.** Inclined to undertake new and daring enterprises. **2.** Hazardous; risky. —**ad•ven′tur•ous•ly** *adv.* —**ad•ven′tur•ous•ness** *n.*

Syns: *adventurous, adventuresome, audacious, daredevil, daring, venturesome* **adj.**

ad•verb (ăd′vûrb) ►*n.* The part of speech that modifies a verb, an adjective, or another adverb. [< Lat. *adverbium.*] —**ad•ver′bi•al** *adj.* —**ad•ver′bi•al•ly** *adv.*

ad•ver•sar•i•al (ăd′vər-sâr′ē-əl) ►*adj.* Characteristic of an adversary; antagonistic.

ad•ver•sar•y (ăd′vər-sĕr′ē) ►*n., pl.* **-ies.** An opponent; enemy.

ad•verse (ăd-vûrs′, ăd′vûrs′) ►*adj.* **1.** Acting or serving to oppose; antagonistic: *adverse criticism.* **2.** Harmful or unfavorable: *adverse circumstances.* [< Lat. *advertere, advers-*, turn toward.] —**ad•verse′ly** *adv.*

ad•ver•si•ty (ăd-vûr′sĭ-tē) ►*n., pl.* **-ties 1.** Great hardship or affliction; misfortune. **2.** A calamitous event.

ad•vert (ăd-vûrt′) ►*v.* To call attention; refer: *advert to a problem.* See Syns at **refer.** [< Lat. *advertere*, turn toward.]

ad•ver•tise (ăd′vər-tīz′) ►*v.* **-tised, -tis•ing 1.** To make public announcement of, esp. to promote sales: *advertise a new product.* See Syns at **announce. 2.** To make known. **3.** To warn or notify. —**ad′ver•tis′er** *n.*

ad•ver•tise•ment (ăd′vər-tīz′mənt, ăd-vûr′tĭs-, -tĭz-) ►*n.* **1.** The act of advertising. **2.** A notice designed to attract public attention or patronage.

ad•ver•tis•ing (ăd′vər-tī′zĭng) ►*n.* **1.** The business of designing, preparing, and disseminating advertisements. **2.** Advertisements collectively.

ad•vice (ăd-vīs′) ►*n.* Opinion about a course of action; counsel. [< OFr. *avis* : *a*, to + Lat. *vidēre, vīs-*, see.]

Syns: *advice, counsel, recommendation* **n.**

ad•vis•a•ble (ăd-vī′zə-bəl) ►*adj.* Worthy of being recommended or suggested; prudent. —**ad•vis′a•bil′i•ty** *n.* —**ad•vis′a•bly** *adv.*

ad•vise (ăd-vīz′) ►*v.* **-vis•ed, -vis•ing 1.** To offer advice to; counsel. **2.** To recommend; suggest: *advised patience.* **3.** To inform; notify. [< OFr. *aviser* < *avis*, ADVICE.] —**ad•vis′er, ad•vi′sor** *n.*

Syns: *advise, counsel, recommend* **v.**

ad•vis•ed•ly (ăd-vī′zĭd-lē) ►*adv.* With careful consideration; deliberately.

ad•vise•ment (ăd-vīz′mənt) ►*n.* Careful consideration.

ad•vi•so•ry (ăd-vī′zə-rē) ►*adj.* **1.** Empowered to advise: *an advisory committee.* **2.** Containing advice, esp. a warning. ►*n., pl.* **-ries.** A report giving information, esp. a warning.

ad•vo•ca•cy (ăd′və-kə-sē) ▸*n.* The act of pleading or arguing in favor of something, such as a cause, idea, or policy; active support.

ad•vo•cate (ăd′və-kāt′) ▸*v.* **-cat•ed, -cat•ing.** To speak, plead, or argue in favor of. ▸*n.* (-kĭt, -kāt′) **1.** One that argues for a cause. **2.** One that pleads in another's behalf. **3.** A lawyer. [< Lat. *advocāre*, call to.] —**ad′vo•ca′tor** *n.*

adz or **adze** (ădz) ▸*n.* An axlike tool with a curved blade at right angles to the handle, used for dressing wood. [< OE *adesa.*]

Ae•ge•an Sea (ĭ-jē′ən) An arm of the Mediterranean off SE Europe between Greece and Turkey.

ae•gis also **e•gis** (ē′jĭs) ▸*n.* **1.** Protection. **2.** Sponsorship; patronage. **3.** *Gk. Myth.* The shield of Zeus, later an attribute of Athena. [< Gk. *aigis.*]

Ae•ne•as (ĭ-nē′əs) ▸*n. Gk. & Rom. Myth.* Trojan hero and ancestor of the Romans.

Ae•o•lis (ē′ə-lĭs) or **Ae•o•li•a** (ē-ō′lē-ə). An ancient region of W Asia Minor in present-day Turkey. —**Ae•o′li•an** *adj.*

ae•on (ē′ŏn′, ē′ən) ▸*n.* Var. of **eon.**

aer•ate (âr′āt) ▸*v.* **-at•ed, -at•ing 1.** To charge (liquid) with a gas, esp. with carbon dioxide. **2.** To expose to fresh air for purification. **3.** To oxygenate (blood) by respiration. —**aer•a′tion** *n.* —**aer′a′tor** *n.*

aer•i•al (âr′ē-əl) ▸*adj.* **1.** Of, in, or caused by the air. **2.** Lofty. **3.** Airy. **4.** Of, for, or by means of aircraft: *aerial photography.* **5.** *Bot.* Growing above the ground or water: *aerial roots.* ▸*n.* A radio antenna, esp. one extending into the air.

aer•i•al•ist (âr′ē-ə-lĭst) ▸*n.* An acrobat who performs in the air, as on a trapeze.

aer•ie or **aer•y** also **ey•rie** (âr′ē, îr′ē) ▸*n., pl.* **-ies.** A nest, as of an eagle, built on a high place. [< Lat. *ārea*, open space.]

aero– or **aer–** ▸*pref.* **1.** Air; atmosphere: *aerosol.* **2.** Aviation: *aeronaut.* [< Gk. *aēr*, air.]

aer•o•bat•ics (âr′ə-băt′ĭks) ▸*n. (takes sing. or pl. v.)* The performance of stunts by an airplane. [AERO– + (ACRO)BATICS.]

aer•obe (âr′ōb′) ▸*n.* An organism, such as a bacterium, requiring oxygen to live. [< AERO– + Gk. *bios*, life.]

aer•o•bic (â-rō′bĭk) ▸*adj.* **1.** Occurring or living only in the presence of oxygen. **2.** Relating to aerobics. —**aer•o′bi•cal•ly** *adv.*

aer•o•bics (â-rō′bĭks) ▸*n. (takes sing. or pl. v.)* An exercise regimen designed to strengthen the cardiovascular system.

aer•o•dy•nam•ic (âr′ō-dī-năm′ĭk) also **aer•o•dy•nam•i•cal** (-ĭ-kəl) ▸*adj.* **1.** Of or relating to aerodynamics. **2.** Styled with rounded edges to reduce wind drag. —**aer′o•dy•nam′i•cal•ly** *adv.*

aer•o•dy•nam•ics (âr′ō-dī-năm′ĭks) ▸*n. (takes sing. v.)* The dynamics of bodies moving relative to gases, esp. the interaction of moving objects with the atmosphere.

aer•om•e•ter (â-rŏm′ĭ-tər) ▸*n.* An instrument for determining the weight and density of a gas.

aer•o•naut (âr′ə-nôt′) ▸*n.* A pilot or navigator of a lighter-than-air craft, such as a balloon. [AERO– + Gk. *nautēs*, sailor.]

aer•o•nau•tics (âr′ə-nô′tĭks) ▸*n. (takes sing. v.)* **1.** The design and construction of aircraft. **2.** The theory and practice of aircraft navigation. —**aer′o•nau′tic, aer′o•nau′ti•cal** *adj.*

aer•o•pause (âr′ō-pôz′) ▸*n.* The region of the atmosphere above which aircraft cannot fly.

aer•o•plane (âr′ə-plān′) ▸*n. Chiefly Brit.* Var. of **airplane.**

aer•o•pon•ics (âr′ə-pŏn′ĭks) ▸*n. (takes sing. v.)* A technique for growing plants without soil by misting the roots with nutrient-laden water. [AERO– + (HYDRO)PONICS.]

aer•o•sol (âr′ə-sôl′, -sŏl′) ▸*n.* **1.** A gaseous suspension of fine solid or liquid particles. **2a.** A substance packaged under pressure for release as a spray of fine particles. **b.** An aerosol bomb. [AERO– + SOL(UTION).]

aerosol bomb ▸*n.* A usu. hand-held container from which an aerosol is released.

aer•o•space (âr′ō-spās′) ▸*adj.* **1.** Relating to Earth's atmosphere and the space beyond. **2.** Relating to the science or technology of flight. —**aer′o•space′** *n.*

aer•y (âr′ē, îr′ē) ▸*n.* Var. of **aerie.**

Aes•chy•lus (ĕs′kə-ləs, ē′skə-). 525–456 B.C. Greek tragic dramatist. —**Aes′chy•le′an** (-lē′ən) *adj.*

Ae•sop (ē′səp, -sŏp′). 6th cent. B.C. Greek storyteller. —**Ae•so′pi•an** (ē-sō′pē-ən), **Ae•sop′ic** (-sŏp′ĭk) *adj.*

aes•the•sia (ĕs-thē′zhə) ▸*n.* Var. of **esthesia.**

aes•thete or **es•thete** (ĕs′thēt) ▸*n.* One who cultivates a superior sensitivity to beauty, esp. in art. [< AESTHETIC.]

aes•thet•ic or **es•thet•ic** (ĕs-thĕt′ĭk) ▸*adj.* **1.** Relating to aesthetics. **2.** Of or concerning the appreciation of beauty. **3.** Artistic: *The play was an aesthetic success.* ▸*n.* A guiding principle in matters of artistic beauty. [< Gk. *aisthētikos*, of sense perception.] —**aes•thet′i•cal•ly** *adv.*

aes•thet•i•cism or **es•thet•i•cism** (ĕs-thĕt′ĭ-sĭz′əm) ▸*n.* **1.** Devotion to the beautiful. **2.** The doctrine that beauty is the basic principle from which all others are derived.

aes•thet•ics or **es•thet•ics** (ĕs-thĕt′ĭks) ▸*n. (takes sing. v.)* The branch of philosophy that deals with the nature and expression of beauty, as in the fine arts.

aes•ti•vate (ĕs′tə-vāt′) ▸*v.* Var. of **estivate.**

a•far (ə-fär′) ▸*adv.* From, at, or to a great distance: *traveled afar.*

AFB ▸*abbr.* air force base

AFDC ▸*abbr.* Aid to Families with Dependent Children

af•fa•ble (ăf′ə-bəl) ▸*adj.* Easy and pleasant to speak to; amiable. [< Lat. *affārī*, speak to.] —**af′fa•bil′i•ty** *n.* —**af′fa•bly** *adv.*

af•fair (ə-fâr′) ▸*n.* **1.** Something done or to be done. **2. affairs** Matters of personal or professional business. **3a.** An occurrence; event. **b.** A social function. **4.** A matter of personal concern. **5.** A sexual relationship between two people who are not married to each other. [< OFr. *a faire*, to do.]

Syns: *affair, business, concern* **n.**

af•fect[1] (ə-fĕkt′) ▸*v.* **1.** To influence or change. **2.** To touch the emotions of. ▸*n.* (ăf′ĕkt′). Feeling or emotion, esp. as expressed physically. [Lat. *afficere, affect-*, do to.]

Usage: *Affect*[1] and *effect* have no senses in common. As a verb *affect*[1] is most commonly used in the sense of "to influence" (*how smoking affects health*). *Effect* means "to bring about or execute" (*layoffs designed to effect savings*).

af•fect[2] (ə-fĕkt′) ►*v.* **1.** To put on a false or pretentious show of: *affected a British accent.* **2.** To fancy; like: *affects dramatic clothes.* [< Lat. *affectāre*, strive for < *afficere*, AFFECT[1].]

af•fec•ta•tion (ăf′ĕk-tā′shən) ►*n.* **1.** A show; pretense. **2.** Behavior that is assumed rather than natural.

af•fect•ed (ə-fĕk′tĭd) ►*adj.* **1.** Assumed or simulated to impress others. **2.** Mannered; artificial. [< AFFECT[2].] —**af•fect′ed•ly** *adv.*

af•fect•ing (ə-fĕk′tĭng) ►*adj.* Inspiring strong emotion; moving. —**af•fect′ing•ly** *adv.*

af•fec•tion (ə-fĕk′shən) ►*n.* A tender feeling toward another; fondness. —**af•fec′tion•ate** (-shə-nĭt) *adj.* —**af•fec′tion•ate•ly** *adv.*

af•fec•tive (ə-fĕk′tĭv) ►*adj. Psychol.* Influenced by or resulting from the emotions: *affective disorders.*

af•fer•ent (ăf′ər-ənt) ►*adj.* Carrying inward to a central organ or section. [< Lat. *afferre*, bring to : AD– + *ferre*, bring.]

af•fi•ance (ə-fī′əns) ►*v.* **-anced, -anc•ing.** To pledge to marry; betroth. [< Med.Lat. *affīdāre*, trust to : AD– + Lat. *fīdus*, faithful.]

af•fi•da•vit (ăf′ĭ-dā′vĭt) ►*n.* A written declaration made under oath before an authorized officer. [< Med.Lat. *affīdāre*, to pledge. See AFFIANCE.]

af•fil•i•ate (ə-fĭl′ē-āt′) ►*v.* **-at•ed, -at•ing.** To accept as a member, associate, or branch. ►*n.* (-ē-ĭt, -āt′). An associate or subordinate member: *network affiliates.* [< Lat. *fīlius*, son.] —**af•fil′i•a′tion** *n.*

af•fin•i•ty (ə-fĭn′ĭ-tē) ►*n., pl.* **-ties 1.** A natural attraction or feeling of kinship. **2.** Relationship by marriage. **3.** An inherent similarity. [< Lat. *affīnis*, related by marriage : AD– + *fīnis*, boundary.]

af•firm (ə-fûrm′) ►*v.* **1.** To declare firmly; maintain to be true. **2.** To uphold; confirm. [< Lat. *affirmāre*, strengthen.] —**af•firm′a•ble** *adj.* —**af•fir′mant** *adj. & n.* —**af′fir•ma′tion** (ăf′ər-mā′shən) *n.*

af•fir•ma•tive (ə-fûr′mə-tĭv) ►*adj.* **1.** Giving assent; confirming. **2.** Positive; optimistic: *an affirmative outlook.* ►*n.* **1.** A word or statement of assent. **2.** The side in a debate that upholds the proposition. —**af•fir′ma•tive•ly** *adv.*

affirmative action ►*n.* A policy that seeks to redress past discrimination by ensuring equal opportunity, as in education and employment.

af•fix (ə-fĭks′) ►*v.* **1.** To secure; attach. **2.** To add or append. ►*n.* (ăf′ĭks′) **1.** Something affixed. **2.** A word element, such as a prefix or suffix, that is attached to a base, stem, or root. [< Lat. *affīgere, affīx-*, fasten to.]

af•fla•tus (ə-flā′təs) ►*n.* **1.** A strong creative impulse. **2.** Divine inspiration. [< Lat. *afflāre*, breathe on.]

af•flict (ə-flĭkt′) ►*v.* To inflict grievous suffering on. [< Lat. *afflīgere, afflīct-*, strike down.] —**af•flic′tive** *adj.*

Syns: *afflict, agonize, rack, torment, torture* ***v.***

af•flic•tion (ə-flĭk′shən) ►*n.* **1.** A condition of distress. See Syns at **trial. 2.** A cause of distress. See Syns at **burden**[1]**.**

af•flu•ence (ăf′lo͞o-əns) ►*n.* **1.** Wealth; prosperity. **2.** A great quantity; abundance.

af•flu•ent (ăf′lo͞o-ənt) ►*adj.* **1.** Wealthy. See Syns at **rich. 2.** Plentiful; abundant. ►*n.* A stream; tributary. [< Lat. *affluere*, overflow with.] —**af′flu•ent•ly** *adv.*

af•ford (ə-fôrd′, -fōrd′) ►*v.* **1.** To have the financial means for. **2.** To be able to spare or give up. **3.** To provide: *a tree that affords ample shade.* [< OE *geforthian*, carry through.] —**af•ford′a•bil′i•ty** *n.* —**af•ford′a•ble** *adj.* —**af•ford′a•bly** *adv.*

af•for•est (ə-fôr′ĭst, -fŏr′-) ►*v.* To convert (open land) into a forest by planting trees. —**af•for′es•ta′tion** *n.*

af•fray (ə-frā′) ►*n.* A noisy quarrel or brawl. [< OFr. *esfraier*, frighten.]

af•front (ə-frŭnt′) ►*v.* **1.** To insult intentionally. **2.** To confront. ►*n.* An insult. [< OFr. *front*, face. See FRONT.]

Af•ghan (ăf′găn′) ►*n.* **1.** A native or inhabitant of Afghanistan. **2.** See **Pashto. 3. afghan** A coverlet knitted or crocheted in geometric designs. **4.** An Afghan hound. [Pers. *afghān*, an Afghan.] —**Af′ghan** *adj.*

Afghan hound ►*n.* A large slender hunting dog having long hair and drooping ears.

af•ghan•i (ăf-găn′ē, -gä′nē) ►*n.* See table at **currency.** [Pashto *afghānī.*]

Af•ghan•i•stan (ăf-găn′ĭ-stăn′) A landlocked country of SW-central Asia E of Iran. Cap. Kabul. Pop. 18,879,000.

a•fi•cio•na•do (ə-fĭsh′ē-ə-nä′dō) ►*n., pl.* **-dos.** A fan; devotee. [Sp., ult. < Lat. *affectiō*, liking.]

a•field (ə-fēld′) ►*adv.* **1.** Off the usual or desired track. See Syns at **amiss. 2.** Away from one's home or usual environment. **3.** To or on a field.

a•fire (ə-fīr′) ►*adv. & adj.* On fire.

AFL ►*abbr.* **1.** American Federation of Labor **2.** American Football League

a•flame (ə-flām′) ►*adv. & adj.* On fire.

af•la•tox•in (ăf′lə-tŏk′sĭn) ►*n.* A toxic compound that is produced by certain molds and contaminates stored food. [NLat. *A(spergillus) flā(vus)*, mold species + TOXIN.]

AFL-CIO ►*abbr.* American Federation of Labor and Congress of Industrial Organizations

a•float (ə-flōt′) ►*adv. & adj.* **1.** Floating. **2.** At sea. **3.** Awash; flooded. **4.** Financially sound.

a•flut•ter (ə-flŭt′ər) ►*adj.* **1.** Fluttering: *with flags aflutter.* **2.** Nervous and excited.

a•foot (ə-fo͝ot′) ►*adv. & adj.* **1.** On foot. **2.** In progress: *plans afoot to resign.*

a•fore•men•tioned (ə-fôr′mĕn′shənd, -fōr′-) ►*adj.* Mentioned previously. [< OE *onforan*, before.]

a•fore•said (ə-fôr′sĕd′, -fōr′-) ►*adj.* Spoken of earlier. [< OE *onforan*, before.]

a•fore•thought (ə-fôr′thôt′, -fōr′-) ►*adj.* Premeditated: *malice aforethought.*

a for•ti•o•ri (ä fôr′tē-ôr′ē, ā) ►*adv.* For a stronger reason. Used of a conclusion logically more certain than another. [Lat.]

a•foul of (ə-foul′) ►*prep.* In or into collision, entanglement, or conflict with.

Afr. ►*abbr.* **1.** Africa **2.** African

a•fraid (ə-frād′) ►*adj.* **1.** Filled with fear. **2.** Averse; opposed: *not afraid of hard work.* **3.** Regretful: *I'm afraid you're wrong.* [< OFr. *esfraier*, frighten.]

Syns: *afraid, apprehensive, fearful* ***adj.***

A-frame (ā′frām′) ►*n.* A structure with steeply angled sides in the shape of the letter A.

a•fresh (ə-frĕsh′) ►*adv.* Once more; anew; again: *start afresh.*

Af•ri•ca (ăf′rĭ-kə) The second-largest continent, S of Europe between the Atlantic and Indian oceans.

Af•ri•can (ăf′rĭ-kən) ►*adj.* Of or relating to Africa or its peoples, languages, or cultures. ►*n.* **1.** A native or inhabitant of Africa. **2.** A person of African descent.

Af•ri•ca•na (ăf′rĭ-kä′nə, -kăn′ə, -kā′nə) ►*n.* *(takes pl. v.)* Materials relating to the history or culture of African peoples.

African American ►*n.* A Black American of African ancestry. —**Af′ri•can-A•mer′i•can** *adj.*

Af•ri•can•ized bee (ăf′rĭ-kə-nīzd′) ►*n.* A hybrid strain of honeybee distinguished by aggressive traits, such as the tendency to sting with great frequency.

African violet ►*n.* Any of various East African plants having showy violet, pink, or white flowers and grown as house plants.

Af•ri•kaans (ăf′rĭ-käns′, -känz′) ►*n.* A language that developed from 17th-cent. Dutch and is an official language of South Africa.

Af•ri•ka•ner (ăf′rĭ-kä′nər) ►*n.* A South African descended from Dutch settlers, esp. one who speaks Afrikaans.

Af•ro (ăf′rō) ►*n., pl.* **-ros.** A rounded, thick, tightly curled hair style. ►*adj.* African in style or origin.

Afro– ►*pref.* African: *Afro-Asiatic.*

Af•ro-A•mer•i•can (ăf′rō-ə-mĕr′ĭ-kən) ►*n.* An African American. —**Af′ro-A•mer′i•can** *adj.*

Af•ro-A•si•at•ic (ăf′rō-ā′zhē-ăt′ĭk, -zē-) ►*n.* A family of languages spoken in N Africa and SW Asia. —**Af′ro-A′si•at′ic** *adj.*

Af•ro•cen•tric (ăf′rō-sĕn′trĭk) ►*adj.* Centered or focused on Africa or African peoples. —**Af′ro•cen′trism** *n.* —**Af′ro•cen′trist** *adj. & n.*

aft (ăft) ►*adv. & adj.* At, in, or toward a ship's stern or the rear of an aircraft. [< OE *æftan*, behind.]

AFT ►*abbr.* American Federation of Teachers

af•ter (ăf′tər) ►*prep.* **1.** Behind in place or order. **2.** In pursuit of. **3.** Concerning: *asked after you.* **4.** At a later time than. **5.** In the style of: *satires after Horace.* **6.** With the same name as. ►*adv.* **1.** Behind. **2.** Afterward: *forever after.* ►*adj.* **1.** Later: *in after years.* **2.** *Naut.* Nearer the stern. ►*conj.* Following the time that. [< OE *æfter.*]

after all (ăf′tər-ôl′) ►*adv.* **1.** In spite of everything. **2.** Ultimately.

af•ter•birth (ăf′tər-bûrth′) ►*n.* The placenta and fetal membranes expelled from the uterus following childbirth.

af•ter•burn•er (ăf′tər-bûr′nər) ►*n.* A device for augmenting jet engine thrust by burning additional fuel with the hot exhaust gases.

af•ter•ef•fect (ăf′tər-ĭ-fĕkt′) ►*n.* A delayed or prolonged response to a stimulus.

af•ter•glow (ăf′tər-glō′) ►*n.* **1.** The light emitted after removal of a source of energy. **2.** A lingering pleasantness.

af•ter-hours (ăf′tər-ourz′) ►*adj.* Occurring or operating after the usual closing time.

af•ter•im•age (ăf′tər-ĭm′ĭj) ►*n.* A visual image persisting for some time after the visual stimulus causing it has ceased to act.

af•ter•life (ăf′tər-līf′) ►*n.* A life or existence after death.

af•ter•math (ăf′tər-măth′) ►*n.* **1.** A consequence, esp. of a disaster or misfortune. **2.** A second crop in the same season. [AFTER + OE *mǣth*, mowing.]

af•ter•noon (ăf′tər-no͞on′) ►*n.* The part of day from noon until sunset.

af•ter•school (ăf′tər-sko͞ol′) ►*adj.* Of or being a program providing care for children following school classes. —**af′ter•school′** *n.*

af•ter-shave (ăf′tər-shāv′) ►*n.* A usu. fragrant lotion for use after shaving.

af•ter•shock (ăf′tər-shŏk′) ►*n.* **1.** A quake of lesser magnitude following a large earthquake. **2.** A subsequent shock or trauma.

af•ter•taste (ăf′tər-tāst′) ►*n.* **1.** A taste remaining after the original stimulus is gone. **2.** A lingering emotion or feeling.

af•ter•thought (ăf′tər-thôt′) ►*n.* An idea that occurs to one after an event or decision.

af•ter•ward (ăf′tər-wərd) also **af•ter•wards** (-wərdz) ►*adv.* At a later time; subsequently.

af•ter•word (ăf′tər-wûrd′) ►*n.* See **epilogue** 2.

af•ter•world (ăf′tər-wûrld′) ►*n.* A world believed to exist for those in the afterlife.

Ag ► The symbol for the element **silver** 1. [< Lat. *argentum*, silver.]

AG ►*abbr.* **1.** adjutant general **2.** attorney general

a•gain (ə-gĕn′) ►*adv.* **1.** Once more; anew. **2.** To a previous place, position, or state: *never went back again.* **3.** Furthermore. **4.** On the other hand. [< OE *ongeagn*, against.]

a•gainst (ə-gĕnst′) ►*prep.* **1.** In a direction opposite to. **2.** So as to hit or touch: *waves dashing against the shore.* **3.** Resting or pressing on: *leaned against the tree.* **4.** In opposition to. **5.** Contrary to: *against all advice.* **6.** As a safeguard from: *protection against the cold.* [< OE *ongeagn.*]

Ag•a•mem•non (ăg′ə-mĕm′nŏn′) ►*n.* *Gk. Myth.* King of Mycenae and leader of the Greeks in the Trojan War.

A•ga•na (ä-gä′nyä) The capital of Guam, on the W coast of the island. Pop. 1,139.

a•gape[1] (ə-gāp′, ə-găp′) ►*adv. & adj.* **1.** With the mouth wide open, as in wonder. **2.** Wide open.

a•ga•pe[2] (ä-gä′pā, ä′gə-pā′) ►*n.* Love as revealed in Jesus, seen as spiritual and selfless. [Gk. *agapē.*]

a•gar (ā′gär′, ä′gär′) also **a•gar-a•gar** (ā′gär-ā′gär′, ä′gär-ä′-) ►*n.* A gelatinous material prepared from certain saltwater algae and used in bacterial culture media and for thickening foods. [Malay *agar-agar.*]

Ag•as•siz (ăg′ə-sē), **(Jean) Louis (Rodolphe).** 1807–73. Swiss-born Amer. naturalist.

ag•ate (ăg′ĭt) ►*n.* **1.** A variety of chalcedony with colored bands. **2.** A marble made of agate or a glass imitation. [< Gk. *akhatēs.*]

a•ga•ve (ə-gä′vē, ə-gā′-) ►*n.* Any of various tropical American plants with tough sword-shaped leaves. [< Gk. *agauos*, noble.]

age (āj) ►*n.* **1.** The length of time that one has existed. **2.** The time of life when a person can assume certain civil and personal rights and responsibilities: *under age; of age.* **3.** A stage of life. **4.** Old age: *hair white with age.* **5.** often **Age a.** A distinctive period in human history. **b.** A period in the history of the earth: *the Ice Age.* **6. ages** *Informal* A long time: *left ages ago.* ►*v.* **aged, ag•ing 1.** To grow older or more mature. **2.** To bring or come to a desired ripeness. See Syns at **mature.** [< OFr. *aage* < Lat. *aetās.*]

-age ►*suff.* **1.** Collection; mass: *sewerage.* **2.** Relationship; connection: *parentage.* **3.** Condition; state: *vagabondage.* **4a.** An action: *blockage.* **b.** Result of an action: *breakage.* **5.** Residence or place of: *vicarage.* **6.** Charge or fee: *dockage.* [< Lat. *-āticum.*]

ag•ed (ā′jĭd) ►*adj.* **1.** Advanced in years; old. **2.** (ājd). Of the age of: *aged three.* **3.** (ājd). Of a desired ripeness or maturity: *aged cheese.* ►*n.* Elderly people. Used with *the.*

A•gee (ā′jē), **James.** 1909–55. Amer. writer and critic.

age•ism also **ag•ism** (ā′jĭz′əm) ►*n.* Discrimination based on age, esp. against the elderly. —**age′ist** *adj. & n.*

age•less (āj′lĭs) ►*adj.* **1.** Seeming never to grow old. **2.** Existing forever; eternal. —**age′less•ly** *adv.* —**age′less•ness** *n.*
Syns: *ageless, eternal, timeless* **adj.**

a•gen•cy (ā′jən-sē) ►*n., pl.* **-cies 1.** Action; operation. **2.** A mode of acting; means. **3.** A business or service acting for others: *an employment agency.* **4.** An administrative division of a government.

a•gen•da (ə-jĕn′də) ►*n., pl.* **-das.** A list or program of things to be done or considered. See Usage Note at **criterion.** [< Lat. *agere,* do.]

a•gent (ā′jənt) ►*n.* **1.** One that acts or has the power to act. **2.** One that acts for or represents another: *an insurance agent.* **3.** A means of doing something; instrument. **4.** Something that causes a change: *a chemical agent.* **5.** A member of a government agency. **6.** A spy. [< Lat. *agere,* do.]

Agent Orange ►*n.* A herbicide used in the Vietnam War to defoliate areas of forest.

a•gent pro•vo•ca•teur (ă-zhäɴ′ prô-vô′kä-tœr′) ►*n., pl.* **a•gents pro•vo•ca•teurs** (ă-zhäɴ′ prô-vô′kä-tœr′). One who infiltrates an organization in order to incite its members to commit illegal acts. [Fr.]

age-old (āj′ōld′) ►*adj.* Very old.

ag•er•a•tum (ăj′ə-rā′təm) ►*n.* Any of a genus of tropical New World plants having showy colorful flower heads. [< Gk. *agēratos,* ageless.]

age spot ►*n.* See **liver spot.**

ag•gie (ăg′ē) ►*n.* *Games* A playing marble. [AG(ATE) + -IE.]

ag•glom•er•ate (ə-glŏm′ə-rāt′) ►*v.* **-at•ed, -at•ing.** To gather into a rounded mass. ►*n.* (-ər-ĭt). A jumbled mass; heap. [Lat. *agglomerāre.*] —**ag•glom′er•a′tion** *n.*

ag•glu•ti•nate (ə-glo͞ot′n-āt′) ►*v.* **-nat•ed, -nat•ing 1.** To join; adhere. **2.** To cause (red blood cells or bacteria) to clump together. [Lat. *agglūtināre,* glue to.] —**ag•glu′ti•na′tion** *n.* —**ag•glu′ti•na′tive** *adj.*

ag•gran•dize (ə-grăn′dīz′, ăg′rən-) ►*v.* **-dized, -diz•ing.** To make greater; increase. [< OFr. *agrandir.*] —**ag•gran′dize•ment** (ə-grăn′dĭz-mənt, -dīz′-) *n.*

ag•gra•vate (ăg′rə-vāt′) ►*v.* **-vat•ed, -vat•ing 1.** To make worse or more troublesome. **2.** To exasperate; provoke. [Lat. *aggravāre.*] —**ag′gra•vat′ing•ly** *adv.* —**ag′gra•va′tion** *n.* —**ag′gra•va′tor** *n.*

ag•gre•gate (ăg′rĭ-gĭt) ►*adj.* Amounting to a whole; total. ►*n.* A whole considered with respect to its constituent parts. ►*v.* (-gāt′) **-gat•ed, -gat•ing.** To gather into a mass or whole. [< Lat. *aggregāre,* add to.] —**ag′gre•ga′tion** *n.* —**ag′gre•ga′tive** *adj.*

ag•gres•sion (ə-grĕsh′ən) ►*n.* **1.** The initiation of unprovoked hostilities. **2.** The launching of attacks. **3.** Hostile behavior. [< Lat. *aggredī, aggress-,* to attack.]

ag•gres•sive (ə-grĕs′ĭv) ►*adj.* **1.** Inclined to hostile behavior. **2.** Bold and enterprising: *an aggressive young executive.* **3.** Intense or harsh, as in color. —**ag•gres′sive•ly** *adv.* —**ag•gres′sive•ness** *n.* —**ag•gres′sor** *n.*

ag•grieve (ə-grēv′) ►*v.* **-grieved, -griev•ing 1.** To distress; afflict. **2.** To injure; wrong. [< Lat. *aggravāre,* make worse.]

ag•grieved (ə-grēvd′) ►*adj.* **1.** Distressed; afflicted. **2.** Treated wrongly or unjustly.

a•ghast (ə-găst′) ►*adj.* Struck by terror or amazement. [< OE *gǣstan,* frighten.]

ag•ile (ăj′əl, -īl′) ►*adj.* **1.** Quick, light, and easy in movement; nimble. **2.** Mentally alert. [< Lat. *agilis* < *agere,* do.] —**ag′ile•ly** *adv.* —**a•gil′i•ty** (ə-jĭl′ĭ-tē), **ag′ile•ness** *n.*

A•gin•court (ăj′ĭn-kôrt′, -kōrt′) A village of N France; site of English victory over a larger French army (1415).

ag•ing (ā′jĭng) ►*n.* The process of growing old or maturing.

ag•ism (ā′jĭz′əm) ►*n.* Var. of **ageism.**

ag•i•tate (ăj′ĭ-tāt′) ►*v.* **-tat•ed, -tat•ing 1.** To move with violence or sudden force. **2.** To upset; disturb. **3.** To stir up public interest in a cause. [Lat. *agitāre* < *agere,* do.] —**ag′i•tat′ed•ly** *adv.* —**ag′i•ta′tion** *n.*
Syns: *agitate, churn, convulse, rock, shake* **v.**

ag•i•ta•tor (ăj′ĭ-tā′tər) ►*n.* **1.** One who agitates, esp. in political struggles. **2.** An apparatus that shakes or stirs, as in a washing machine.

a•gleam (ə-glēm′) ►*adv. & adj.* Brightly shining.

a•glit•ter (ə-glĭt′ər) ►*adv. & adj.* Glittering; sparkling.

a•glow (ə-glō′) ►*adv. & adj.* Glowing.

Ag•new (ăg′no͞o′, -nyo͞o′), **Spiro Theodore.** 1918–96. Vice President of the US (1969–73); resigned.

ag•nos•tic (ăg-nŏs′tĭk) ►*n.* **1.** One who believes that there can be no proof of the existence of God but does not deny the possibility. **2.** One who is doubtful or noncommital about something. [< A-[1] + Gk. *gnōsis,* knowledge.] —**ag•nos′tic** *adj.* —**ag•nos′ti•cism** (-tĭ-sĭz′əm) *n.*

Ag•nus De•i (ăg′nəs dē′ī, än′yo͞os dā′ē) ►*n.* **1.** Lamb of God; an emblem of Jesus; Jesus. **2a.** A liturgical prayer. **b.** A musical setting for this prayer. [LLat. *Agnus Deī.*]

a•go (ə-gō′) ►*adv. & adj.* **1.** Gone by; past: *two years ago.* **2.** In the past: *It happened ages ago.* [< OE *āgān,* go away.]

a•gog (ə-gŏg′) ►*adv. & adj.* Full of eager excitement. [< OFr. *en gogue,* in merriment.]

ag•o•nist (ăg′ə-nĭst) ►*n.* A contracting muscle that is counteracted by the antagonist. [< Gk.

agōn, contest. See AGONY.]

ag•o•nize (ăg′ə-nīz′) ▸*v.* **-nized, -niz•ing 1.** To suffer or cause to suffer great anguish. See Syns at **afflict. 2.** To make a great effort; struggle. —**ag′o•niz′ing•ly** *adv.*

ag•o•ny (ăg′ə-nē) ▸*n., pl.* **-nies 1.** Intense physical or mental pain. **2.** The struggle that precedes death. **3.** An intense emotion: *an agony of doubt.* [< Gk. *agōn*, struggle < *agein*, drive.]

ag•o•ra (ăg′ər-ə) ▸*n., pl.* **-o•rae** (ə-rē′) or **-o•ras.** A place of congregation, esp. an ancient Greek marketplace. [Gk.]

ag•o•ra•pho•bi•a (ăg′ər-ə-fō′bē-ə) ▸*n.* An abnormal fear of open or public places. [< Gk. *agora*, market place.] —**ag′o•ra•pho′bic** (-fō′bĭk, -fŏb′ĭk) *adj. & n.*

A•gra (ä′grə) A city of N-central India on the Jumna R.; site of the Taj Mahal. Pop. 891,790.

a•grar•i•an (ə-grâr′ē-ən) ▸*adj.* **1.** Relating to land and its ownership. **2.** Relating to agriculture. ▸*n.* One who favors equitable distribution of land. [< Lat. *ager*, *agr-*, field.]

a•grar•i•an•ism (ə-grâr′ē-ə-nĭz′əm) ▸*n.* A movement for equitable distribution of land and for agrarian reform.

a•gree (ə-grē′) ▸*v.* **1.** To grant consent; accede. **2.** To come into or be in accord. **3.** To be of one opinion; concur. **4.** To come to an understanding or to terms. **5.** To be in correspondence: *The copy agrees with the original.* **6.** To be pleasing or healthful: *Spicy food does not agree with me.* **7.** *Gram.* To correspond in gender, number, case, or person. [< OFr. *agreer.*]

a•gree•a•ble (ə-grē′ə-bəl) ▸*adj.* **1.** To one's liking; pleasing. **2.** Suitable; conformable. **3.** Ready to consent or submit. —**a•gree′a•ble•ness** *n.* —**a•gree′a•bly** *adv.*

a•gree•ment (ə-grē′mənt) ▸*n.* **1.** Harmony of opinion; accord. **2.** An arrangement between parties regarding a method of action; a covenant. **3.** *Law* **4.** A properly executed and legally binding compact. **5.** *Gram.* Correspondence in gender, number, case, or person between words.

ag•ri•busi•ness (ăg′rə-bĭz′nĭs) ▸*n.* Farming as a large-scale business operation.

A•gric•o•la (ə-grĭk′ə-lə), **Gnaeus Julius.** A.D. 37–93. Roman soldier and politician.

ag•ri•cul•ture (ăg′rĭ-kŭl′chər) ▸*n.* The cultivation of the soil and raising of livestock; farming. [< Lat. *agrīcultūra.*] —**ag′ri•cul′tur•al** *adj.* —**ag′ri•cul′tur•al•ly** *adv.* —**ag′ri•cul′tur•ist, ag′ri•cul′tur•al•ist** *n.*

A•grip•pa (ə-grĭp′ə), **Marcus Vipsanius.** 63–12 B.C. Roman general.

Ag•rip•pi•na[1] (ăg′rə-pī′nə, -pē′-). "the Elder." 13 B.C.?–A.D. 33. Roman matron and mother of Caligula.

Ag•rip•pi•na[2] (ăg′rə-pī′nə, -pē′-). "the Younger." A.D. 15?–59. Roman empress; murdered by her son Nero.

a•gron•o•my (ə-grŏn′ə-mē) ▸*n.* Application of soil and plant sciences to farming. [Gk. *agros*, field + –NOMY.] —**ag′ro•nom′ic** (ăg′rə-nŏm′ĭk), **ag′ro•nom′i•cal** *adj.* —**a•gron′o•mist** *n.*

a•ground (ə-ground′) ▸*adv. & adj.* Stranded on a shore, reef, or in shallow water.

a•gue (ā′gyo͞o) ▸*n.* A fever with alternating chills and sweating, esp. associated with malaria. [< OFr. *(fievre) ague*, sharp (fever) < Lat. *acūtus*, ACUTE.] —**a′gu•ish** *adj.*

A•gui•nal•do (ä′gē-näl′dō), **Emilio.** 1869–1964. Philippine revolutionary leader.

A•gul•has (ə-gŭl′əs), **Cape.** A headland of South Africa at the S point of Africa.

ah (ä) ▸*interj.* Used to express various emotions, such as satisfaction, surprise, delight, dislike, or pain.

A.h. ▸*abbr.* ampere-hour

a•ha (ä-hä′) ▸*interj.* Used to express surprise, pleasure, or triumph.

A•hab (ā′hăb′). 9th cent. B.C. Pagan king of Israel and husband of Jezebel.

a•head (ə-hĕd′) ▸*adv.* **1.** At or to the front. **2a.** In advance; before: *Pay ahead.* **b.** In or into the future: *planned ahead.* **3.** Forward: *The train moved ahead slowly.* —***idioms:*** **be ahead** To be winning or in a superior position. **get ahead** To attain success.

a•hem (ə-hĕm′) ▸*interj.* Used to attract attention or to express doubt or warning.

Ah•ma•da•bad (ä′mə-də-bäd′) A city of NW India N of Mumbai. Pop. 2,876,710.

-aholic ▸*suff.* One that is compulsively in need of: *workaholic.* [< (ALC)OHOLIC.]

a•hoy (ə-hoi′) ▸*interj. Naut.* Used to hail a ship or person or to attract attention.

AI ▸*abbr.* artificial intelligence

aid (ād) ▸*v.* To help; support. ▸*n.* **1.** Assistance. **2a.** An assistant. **b.** A device that assists: *visual aids such as slides.* [< Lat. *adiuvāre*, give help to.] —**aid′er** *n.*

aide (ād) ▸*n.* **1.** An aide-de-camp. **2.** A helper. See Syns at **assistant.** [Fr. < *aider*, AID.]

aide-de-camp (ād′dĭ-kămp′) ▸*n., pl.* **aides-de-camp.** A military or naval officer acting as an assistant to a superior officer. [Fr.]

AIDS (ādz) ▸*n.* A severe immunological disorder caused by the retrovirus HIV, resulting in an increased susceptibility to opportunistic infections and to certain rare cancers, esp. Kaposi's sarcoma. [A(CQUIRED) I(MMUNE) D(EFICIENCY) S(YNDROME).]

ai•grette or **ai•gret** (ā-grĕt′, ā′grĕt′) ▸*n.* An ornamental tuft of plumes, esp. the tail feathers of an egret. [< OFr., EGRET.]

Ai•ken (ā′kən), **Conrad Potter.** 1889–1973. Amer. writer.

ai•ki•do (ī′kē-dō′, ī-kē′dō) ▸*n.* A Japanese art of self-defense that employs holds, locks, and principles of nonresistance. [Jap. *aikidō.*]

ail (āl) ▸*v.* **1.** To feel ill or have pain. **2.** To make ill or cause pain. [< OE *eglian.*]

ai•lan•thus (ā-lăn′thəs) ▸*n.* Any of several Asian trees, esp. the tree-of-heaven. [< Ambonese (Austronesian) *ai lanto.*]

ai•le•ron (ā′lə-rŏn′) ▸*n.* A movable flap on the wings of an airplane that controls rolling and banking. [< Lat. *āla*, wing.]

ail•ment (āl′mənt) ▸*n.* A mild illness.

aim (ām) ▸*v.* **1.** To direct (e.g., a weapon or remark) toward an intended target. **2.** To determine a course: *aim for a better life.* **3.** To propose to do something; intend. ▸*n.* **1a.** The act of aiming. **b.** Skill at hitting a target: *a good aim.* **2.** The line of fire of an aimed weapon. **3.** A purpose or intention. [< Lat. *aestimāre*, to estimate.]

Syns: *aim, direct, level, point, train* **v.**

aim•less (ām′lĭs) ▸*adj.* Without direction or purpose. —**aim′less•ly** *adv.* —**aim′less•ness** *n.*

ain't (ānt) ▸ *Nonstandard* **1.** Am not. **2.** Used also as a contraction for *are not, is not, has not,* and *have not.*
Usage: Although the use of *ain't* is often regarded as a sign of ignorance, *ain't* continues to enjoy extensive use in speech. Even educated speakers see no substitute in folksy expressions such as *Say it ain't so.*

Ai•nu (ī′no͞o) ▸ *n., pl.* **Ainu** or **-nus 1.** A member of an indigenous people inhabiting the northernmost islands of Japan. **2.** The language of the Ainu.

air (âr) ▸ *n.* **1a.** A colorless, odorless, tasteless, gaseous mixture, mainly nitrogen (78%) and oxygen (21%). **b.** The earth's atmosphere. **c.** The atmosphere in an enclosure. **2.** The sky; firmament. **3.** A breeze or wind. **4.** Aircraft: *send troops by air.* **5.** Airwaves. **6.** A characteristic impression; aura: *an air of mystery.* **7.** Personal bearing or manner. **8. airs** An affected pose. **9.** *Mus.* A melody or tune. ▸ *v.* **1.** To expose to air; ventilate. **2.** To give public utterance to. **3.** To broadcast on television or radio. —***idioms:* in the air** Abroad; prevalent: *Excitement was in the air.* **on** (or **off) the air** Being (or not being) broadcast on radio or television. **up in the air** Not yet decided; uncertain. [< Gk. *aēr.*]

air bag ▸ *n.* An automotive passive restraint that inflates upon collision and prevents passengers from pitching forward.

air•borne (âr′bôrn′, -bōrn′) ▸ *adj.* **1.** Carried by or through the air. **2.** In flight; flying.

air brake ▸ *n.* A brake, esp. on a motor vehicle, that is operated by compressed air.

air•brush (âr′brŭsh′) ▸ *n.* An atomizer using compressed air to spray a liquid, such as paint, on a surface. —**air′brush** *v.*

air•bus or **air bus** (âr′bŭs′) ▸ *n.* A commercial passenger jet used for short trips.

air conditioner ▸ *n.* An apparatus for lowering the temperature of an enclosed space. —**air′-con•di′tion** *v.* —**air conditioning** *n.*

air•craft (âr′krăft′) ▸ *n., pl.* **aircraft.** A machine, such as an airplane or helicopter, capable of atmospheric flight.

aircraft carrier ▸ *n.* A large naval vessel designed as a mobile air base.

air-cush•ion vehicle (âr′ko͝osh′ən) ▸ *n.* A usu. propeller-driven vehicle for traveling over land or water on a cushion of air.

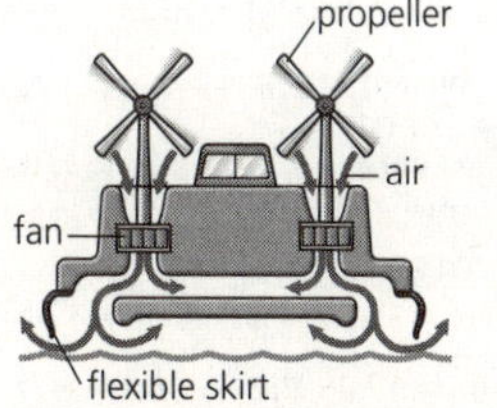

air-cushion vehicle
front cutaway view of a flexible skirt model hovercraft

air•drome (âr′drōm′) ▸ *n.* An airport.

air•drop (âr′drŏp′) ▸ *n.* A delivery, as of supplies, by parachute from aircraft. —**air′drop′** *v.*

Aire•dale (âr′dāl′) ▸ *n.* A large terrier with a wiry tan coat marked with black. [After *Airedale,* a valley of north-central England.]

air•fare (âr′fâr′) ▸ *n.* Fare for travel by aircraft.

air•field (âr′fēld′) ▸ *n.* **1.** A runway or landing strip. **2.** An airport.

air•foil (âr′foil′) ▸ *n.* An aircraft part or surface, such as a wing, that controls stability, direction, lift, thrust, or propulsion.

air force ▸ *n.* The aviation branch of a country's armed forces.

air gun ▸ *n.* A gun discharged by compressed air.

air•head¹ (âr′hĕd′) ▸ *n.* *Slang* A silly, stupid person.

air•head² (âr′hĕd′) ▸ *n.* An area of hostile or enemy-controlled territory secured by paratroops. [AIR + (BEACH)HEAD.]

air lane ▸ *n.* A regular route of travel for aircraft.

air•lift (âr′lĭft′) ▸ *n.* A system of transportation by aircraft when surface routes are blocked. —**air′lift′** *v.*

air•line (âr′līn′) ▸ *n.* **1.** A system for scheduled air transport. **2.** A business providing such a system.

air•lin•er (âr′lī′nər) ▸ *n.* A large passenger airplane.

air lock ▸ *n.* An airtight chamber, usu. located between two regions of unequal pressure, in which air pressure can be regulated.

air•mail (âr′māl′) ▸ *v.* To send (e.g., a letter) by air. ▸ *n.* **air mail** also **airmail 1.** The system of conveying mail by aircraft. **2.** Mail conveyed by aircraft. —**air′mail′** *adj.*

air•man (âr′mən) ▸ *n.* **1.** Any of the three lowest ranks in the US Air Force. **2.** An aviator.

air mass ▸ *n.* A large body of air with only small horizontal variations of temperature, pressure, and moisture.

air mile ▸ *n.* A nautical mile.

air•plane (âr′plān′) ▸ *n.* A self-propelled winged vehicle heavier than air and capable of flight.

air•play (âr′plā′) ▸ *n.* The broadcasting of a recording by a radio station.

air•port (âr′pôrt′, -pōrt′) ▸ *n.* A facility where aircraft can take off and land, with accommodations for passengers and cargo.

air•pow•er or **air power** (âr′pou′ər) ▸ *n.* The strategic strength of a country's air force.

air raid ▸ *n.* An attack by military aircraft.

air rifle ▸ *n.* A low-powered rifle, such as a BB gun, that uses manually compressed air to fire small pellets.

air sac ▸ *n.* See **alveolus** 2.

air•ship (âr′shĭp′) ▸ *n.* A self-propelled lighter-than-air craft with directional control surfaces; dirigible.

air•sick (âr′sĭk′) ▸ *adj.* Suffering nausea from the motion of air flight. —**air′sick′ness** *n.*

air•space or **air space** (âr′spās′) ▸ *n.* The portion of the atmosphere above a particular land area, esp. above a nation.

air speed ▸ *n.* The speed of an aircraft relative to the air.

air•strip (âr′strĭp′) ▸ *n.* See **landing strip.**

air•tight (âr′tīt′) ▸ *adj.* **1.** Impermeable by air. **2.** Solid; sound: *an airtight excuse.*

air•time (âr′tīm′) ▸ *n.* **1.** The time that a radio or television station is broadcasting. **2.** The scheduled time of a broadcast.

air-to-air (âr′tə-âr′) ►*adj.* Operating or fired between aircraft in flight: *air-to-air missiles.*

air-to-sur•face (âr′tə-sûr′fĭs) ►*adj.* Operating or fired from aircraft to ground targets or installations: *air-to-surface communications.*

air•wave (âr′wāv′) ►*n.* The medium for transmitting radio and television signals. Often used in the plural.

air•way (âr′wā′) ►*n.* **1.** A passageway or shaft in which air circulates. **2a.** See **air lane. b.** See **airline** 2.

air•wor•thy (âr′wûr′*thē*) ►*adj.* **-thi•er, -thi•est.** Fit to fly. —**air′wor′thi•ness** *n.*

air•y (âr′ē) ►*adj.* **-i•er, -i•est 1.** Of or like air. **2.** High in the air; lofty. **3.** Open to the air. **4.** Immaterial; unreal. **5.** Speculative and impractical. **6.** Displaying lofty nonchalance. **7.** Light-hearted; gay. —**air′i•ly** *adv.* —**air′i•ness** *n.*

Syns: *airy, diaphanous, ethereal, vaporous* ***adj.***

aisle (īl) ►*n.* **1.** A passageway between rows of seats, as in a theater or airplane. **2.** A part of a church separated from the nave by a row of pillars or columns. [< Lat. *āla*, wing.]

Aisne (ān) A river rising in N France and flowing about 266 km (165 mi) to the Oise R.

Aix-en-Pro•vence (āk′säɴ-prō-väɴs′, ĕk′-) A city of SE France N of Marseilles. Pop. 123,778.

Aix-la-Cha•pelle (āks′lä-shä-pĕl′, ĕks′-) See **Aachen.**

A•jac•cio (ä-yä′chō) A city of W Corsica, France, on the **Gulf of Ajaccio,** an inlet of the Mediterranean. Pop. 54,089.

a•jar (ə-jär′) ►*adv. & adj.* Partially opened: *left the door ajar.* [ME *on char*, in turning.]

AK ►*abbr.* Alaska

AKA ►*abbr.* also known as

Ak•bar (ăk′bär). "the Great." 1542–1605. Mogul emperor of India (1556–1605).

AKC ►*abbr.* American Kennel Club

A•khe•na•ton (ä′kə-nät′n, äk-nät′n). Orig. Amenhotep IV d. c. 1358 B.C. King of Egypt (1375?–1358?).

Akh•ma•to•va (ək-mä′tə-və), **Anna.** Anna Andreevna Gorenko. 1889–1966. Russian poet.

A•ki•hi•to (ä′kē-hē′tō). b. 1933. Emperor of Japan (since 1989).

a•kim•bo (ə-kĭm′bō) ►*adv. & adj.* With hands on hips and elbows bowed outward. [ME *in kenebowe*, in a sharp curve.]

a•kin (ə-kĭn′) ►*adj.* **1.** Of the same kin; related by blood. **2.** Similar in quality or character; analogous. **3.** *Ling.* Cognate.

Ak•kad (ăk′ăd′, ä′käd′) **1.** An ancient region of Mesopotamia in N Babylonia. **2.** An ancient city of Mesopotamia and capital of the Akkadian empire.

Ak•ka•di•an (ə-kā′dē-ən) ►*n.* **1.** A native of ancient Akkad. **2.** The Semitic language of Mesopotamia. —**Ak•ka′di•an** *adj.*

Ak•ron (ăk′rən) A city of NE OH SSE of Cleveland. Pop. 223,019.

Al ► The symbol for the element **aluminum.**

AL ►*abbr.* **1.** Alabama **2.** American League

-al[1] ►*suff.* Of, relating to, or characterized by: *parental.* [< Lat. *-ālis.*]

-al[2] ►*suff.* Action; process: *retrieval.* [< Lat. *-ālia.*]

a•la (ā′lə) ►*n., pl.* **a•lae** (ā′lē). A winglike structure or part. [Lat. *āla*, wing.]

Ala. ►*abbr.* Alabama

à la also **a la** (ä′ lä, ä′ lə) ►*prep.* In the style or manner of: *a poem à la Ogden Nash.* [< Fr. *à la mode de.*]

Al•a•bam•a (ăl′ə-băm′ə) A state of the SE US. Cap. Montgomery. Pop. 4,062,608. —**Al′a•ba′mi•an** (-bā′mē-ən), **Al′a•bam′an** *adj. & n.*

al•a•bas•ter (ăl′ə-băs′tər) ►*n.* **1.** A translucent white or tinted gypsum used esp. for carving. **2.** A translucent, often banded variety of calcite. [< Gk. *alabastros.*]

à la carte also **a la carte** (ä′lə kärt′) ►*adv. & adj.* With a separate price for each item on the menu. [Fr., by the menu.]

a•lac•ri•ty (ə-lăk′rĭ-tē) ►*n.* **1.** Cheerful willingness; eagerness. **2.** Speed or quickness. [< Lat. *alacer*, lively.] —**a•lac′ri•tous** *adj.*

A•lai (ä′lī′) A mountain range of SW Kirghiz.

Al•a•mo (ăl′ə-mō′) A mission in San Antonio, TX; besieged and taken by Mexico (1836) during the Texas Revolution.

à la mode (ä′lə mōd′) ►*adj.* **1.** In the prevailing fashion. **2.** Served with ice cream: *apple pie à la mode.* [Fr.]

Al•a•mo•gor•do (ăl′ə-mə-gôr′dō) A city of S-central NM; site of first atomic bomb explosion (1945). Pop. 27,596.

Al•ar•ic (ăl′ər-ĭk). A.D. 370?–410. King of the Visigoths (395–410).

a•larm (ə-lärm′) ►*n.* **1.** A sudden feeling of fear. **2.** A warning of danger. **3.** A device that signals a warning. **4.** The sounding mechanism of an alarm clock. **5.** A call to arms. ►*v.* **1.** To frighten. **2.** To warn. [< OItal. *all' arme*, to arms.] —**a•larm′ing•ly** *adv.*

a•larm•ist (ə-lär′mĭst) ►*n.* One who needlessly alarms others. —**a•larm′ism** *n.*

a•las (ə-lăs′) ►*interj.* Used to express sorrow, regret, or grief. [< OFr. *helas.*]

A•las•ka (ə-lăs′kə) A state of the US in extreme NW North America. Cap. Juneau. Pop. 551,947. —**A•las′kan** *adj. & n.*

Alaska Native ►*n.* A member of any of the aboriginal people of Alaska, including Native American and Eskimo peoples.

Alaska Peninsula. A peninsula of S-central to SW AK between the Bering Sea and the Pacific.

Alaska Range. A mountain range of S-central AK rising to about 6,198 m (20,320 ft).

alb (ălb) ►*n.* A long white linen robe worn by a priest at Mass. [< Lat. *albus*, white.]

Al•ba (ăl′bə), Duke of. See Duke of **Alva.**

al•ba•core (ăl′bə-kôr′, -kōr′) ►*n., pl.* **al•ba•core** or **-cores.** A large marine fish that is a major source of canned tuna. [< Ar. *al-bakūra.*]

Al•ba•ni•a (ăl-bā′nē-ə, -bān′yə) A country of SE Europe on the Adriatic Sea. Cap. Tiranë. Pop. 3,414,000.

Al•ba•ni•an (ăl-bā′nē-ən, -bān′yən) ►*n.* **1.** A native or inhabitant of Albania. **2.** The Indo-European language of the Albanians. —**Al•ba′ni•an** *adj.*

Al•ba•ny (ôl′bə-nē) The capital of NY, in the E part on the Hudson R. Pop. 101,082.

al•ba•tross (ăl′bə-trôs′, -trŏs′) ►*n., pl.* **-tross** or **-tross•es 1.** Any of several large web-footed sea birds. **2.** A constant, worrisome burden. [< Ar. *al-ġaṭṭās*, sea eagle.]

al•be•do (ăl-bē′dō) ►*n., pl.* **-dos 1.** The reflecting power of a surface, as of a planet. **2.** The white tissue inside a citrus fruit rind. [LLat. *albēdō*, whiteness.]

Al•bee (ôl′bē, ŏl′-), **Edward Franklin.** b. 1928. Amer. playwright.

al•be•it (ôl-bē′ĭt, ăl-) ►*conj.* Even though; although. [ME, although it be.]

Al•be•marle Sound (ăl′bə-märl′) A large body of water in NE NC.

Al•bert (ăl′bərt), Prince. 1819–61. German-born consort (1840–61) of Queen Victoria.

Albert, Lake. A lake of E-central Africa on the Zaire-Uganda border.

Al•ber•ta (ăl-bûr′tə) A province of W Canada between British Columbia and Saskatchewan. Cap. Edmonton. Pop. 2,237,724. —**Al•ber′tan** *adj. & n.*

Al•ber•tus Mag•nus (ăl-bûr′təs măg′nəs), Saint. 1206?–80. German theologian.

al•bi•no (ăl-bī′nō) ►*n., pl.* **-nos.** A person or animal lacking normal pigmentation, esp. one having abnormally white skin and hair and pink eyes. [Port. < Lat. *albus*, white.] —**al′bi•nism** (ăl′bə-nĭz′əm) *n.*

Ål•borg also **Aal•borg** (ôl′bôrg′). A city of N Denmark NNE of Århus. Pop. 157,270.

al•bum (ăl′bəm) ►*n.* **1.** A book or binder with blank pages for stamps, photographs, or autographs. **2a.** A set of phonograph records in one binding. **b.** A recording of different musical pieces, esp. a long-playing phonograph record. [Lat., blank tablet < *albus*, white.]

al•bu•men (ăl-byo͞o′mən) ►*n.* **1.** The white of an egg, mainly albumin dissolved in water. **2.** See **albumin.** [Lat. *albūmen* < *albus*, white.]

al•bu•min (ăl-byo͞o′mĭn) ►*n.* A class of proteins found in egg white, blood serum, milk, and many other animal and plant tissues. —**al•bu′mi•nous** *adj.*

Al•bu•quer•que (ăl′bə-kûr′kē) A city of central NM SW of Santa Fe. Pop. 384,736.

Al•ca•traz (ăl′kə-trăz′) A rocky island of W CA in San Francisco Bay; site of a prison until 1963.

al•caz•ar (ăl-kăz′ər, ăl′kə-zär′) ►*n.* A Spanish palace or fortress. [< Ar. *al-qaṣr*, castle.]

al•che•my (ăl′kə-mē) ►*n.* **1.** A medieval chemical philosophy concerned primarily with the transmutation of base metals into gold. **2.** A seemingly magical power. [< Ar. *al-kīmiyā'*, chemistry.] —**al•chem′i•cal** (ăl-kĕm′-ĭ-kəl), **al•chem′ic** *adj.* —**al•chem′i•cal•ly** *adv.* —**al′chem•ist** *n.*

Al•ci•bi•a•des (ăl′sə-bī′ə-dēz′). 450?–404 B.C. Athenian politician and general.

al•co•hol (ăl′kə-hôl′, -hŏl′) ►*n.* **1.** A colorless flammable liquid, C_2H_5OH, obtained by fermentation of sugars and starches and used as a solvent, in drugs, and in intoxicating beverages; ethanol. **2.** Intoxicating liquor containing alcohol. **3.** Any of a series of organic compounds with the general formula $C_nH_{2n+1}OH$. [< Ar. *al-kuḥl*, antimony powder.]

al•co•hol•ic (ăl′kə-hô′lĭk, -hŏl′ĭk) ►*adj.* **1.** Of, containing, or resulting from alcohol. **2.** Suffering from alcoholism. ►*n.* A person who suffers from alcoholism.

al•co•hol•ism (ăl′kə-hô-lĭz′əm, -hŏ-) ►*n.* **1.** The compulsive consumption of alcoholic beverages. **2.** A chronic pathological condition caused by this.

Al•cott (ôl′kət, -kŏt), **Louisa May.** 1832–88. Amer. writer and reformer.

al•cove (ăl′kōv′) ►*n.* A small recessed or partly enclosed extension of a room. [< Ar. *al-qubba*, vault.]

Al•dan (äl-dän′) A river of SE Russia flowing about 2,253 km (1,400 mi) around the **Aldan Plateau** to the Lena R.

al•de•hyde (ăl′də-hīd′) ►*n.* Any of a class of highly reactive organic chemical compounds obtained by oxidation of alcohols. [< NLat., *al(cohol) dehyd(rogenatum)*, dehydrogenized alcohol.]

Al•den (ôl′dən), **John.** 1599?–1687. Amer. Pilgrim colonist.

al•der (ôl′dər) ►*n.* A deciduous shrub or tree having toothed leaves and tiny fruits in woody, conelike catkins. [< OE *alor.*]

al•der•man (ôl′dər-mən) ►*n.* A member of a municipal legislative body. [< OE *ealdorman*, nobleman < *eald*, old.]

ale (āl) ►*n.* A fermented, bitter alcoholic beverage similar to beer. [< OE *ealu.*]

a•le•a•to•ry (ā′lē-ə-tôr′ē, -tōr′ē) ►*adj.* **1.** Dependent on chance. **2.** Relating to gambling. [< Lat. *ālea*, dice.]

a•lee (ə-lē′) ►*adv. Naut.* Away from the wind.

A•lem•bert (ăl′əm-bâr′, ä-läɴ-bĕr′), **Jean Le Rond d′.** 1717–83. French mathematician and philosopher.

a•lem•bic (ə-lĕm′bĭk) ►*n.* An apparatus formerly used for distilling. [< Ar. *al-'anbīq.*]

A•lep•po (ə-lĕp′ō) A city of NW Syria. Pop. 1,542,000.

a•lert (ə-lûrt′) ►*adj.* **1.** Vigilantly attentive; watchful. **2.** Mentally perceptive; quick. **3.** Brisk or lively. ►*n.* **1.** A signal that warns of attack or danger. **2.** A period of watchfulness or preparation for action. ►*v.* To notify of approaching danger; warn. —***idiom:* on the alert** Watchful for danger or opportunity. [< Ital. *all'erta*, on the watch.] —**a•lert′ness** *n.*

A•leut (ə-lo͞ot′, ăl′ē-o͞ot′) ►*n., pl.* **Aleut** or **A•leuts 1.** A member of a Native American people inhabiting the Aleutian Islands and coastal areas of SW Alaska. **2.** The language of the Aleut, related to Eskimo. See Usage Note at **Native American.** —**A•leu′tian** (ə-lo͞o′shən) *adj. & n.*

Aleutian Islands. A chain of volcanic islands of SW AK curving about 1,931 km (1,200 mi) W from the Alaska Peninsula and separating the Bering Sea from the Pacific.

Al•ex•an•der I[1] (ăl′ĭg-zăn′dər). 1777–1825. Czar of Russia (1801–25).

Alexander I[2]. 1876–1903. King of Serbia (1889–1903); assassinated.

Alexander I[3]. 1888–1934. King of Yugoslavia (1921–34).

Alexander II. 1818–81. Czar of Russia (1855–81); emancipated the serfs (1861).

Alexander III[1]. "Alexander the Great." 356–323 B.C. King of Macedonia (336–323) and conqueror of Asia Minor, Syria, Egypt, Babylonia, and Persia.

Alexander III[2]. d. 1181. Pope (1159–81); established papal supremacy.

Alexander Archipelago. A group of more than 1,000 islands off SE AK.

Al•ex•an•dri•a (ăl′ĭg-zăn′drē-ə) **1.** A city of N Egypt on the Mediterranean Sea at the W tip of the Nile Delta. Pop. 3,380,000. **2.** An independent city of N VA on the Potomac R. opposite Washington DC. Pop. 111,183.

Al•ex•an•dri•an (ăl′ĭg-zăn′drē-ən) ▸*adj.* **1.** Relating to Alexander the Great. **2.** Relating to Alexandria, Egypt. **3.** Relating to a learned school of Hellenistic literature, science, and philosophy at Alexandria in the last three centuries B.C.

al•ex•an•drine (ăl′ĭg-zăn′drĭn) ▸*n.* **1.** A line of English verse composed in iambic hexameter. **2.** A line of French verse consisting of 12 syllables. [< OFr. < *Alexandre,* a romance about Alexander the Great.]

a•lex•i•a (ə-lĕk′sē-ə) ▸*n.* Loss of the ability to read, usu. caused by brain lesions. [< A–[1] + Gk. *lexis,* speech.]

al•fal•fa (ăl-făl′fə) ▸*n.* A cloverlike perennial herb widely cultivated for forage. [< Ar. *al-faṣfaṣa.*]

Al•fon•so XIII (ăl-fŏn′sō). 1886–1941. King of Spain (1886–1931).

Al•fred (ăl′frĭd). "the Great." 849–899. King of the West Saxons (871–899).

al•fres•co (ăl-frĕs′kō) ▸*adv. & adj.* In the fresh air; outdoors. [Ital. *al fresco.*]

al•ga (ăl′gə) ▸*n., pl.* **-gae** (-jē). Any of various chiefly aquatic photosynthetic organisms, ranging from single-celled forms to the giant kelp. [Lat., seaweed.] —**al′gal** *adj.*

al•ge•bra (ăl′jə-brə) ▸*n.* A branch of mathematics in which symbols represent numbers or members of a specified set and express general relations that hold for all members in the set. [< Ar. *al-jabr.*] —**al′ge•bra′ic** (-brā′ĭk) *adj.*

Al•ge•ri•a (ăl-jîr′ē-ə) A country of NW Africa on the Mediterranean Sea E of Morocco and W of Tunisia and Libya. Cap. Algiers. Pop. 27,325,000. —**Al•ge′ri•an** *adj. & n.*

-algia ▸*suff.* Pain: *neuralgia.* [Gk. < *algos,* pain.]

Al•giers (ăl-jîrz′) The capital of Algeria, in the N on the **Bay of Algiers,** an arm of the Mediterranean Sea. Pop. 1,523,000.

Al•gon•qui•an (ăl-gŏng′kwē-ən, -kē-ən) also **Al•gon•ki•an** (-kē-ən) ▸*n., pl.* **-an** or **-ans 1.** A family of North American Indian languages spoken or formerly spoken in an area from Labrador to the Carolinas between the Atlantic coast and the Rocky Mountains. **2.** A member of a people speaking an Algonquian language. —**Al•gon′qui•an** *adj.*

Al•gon•quin (ăl-gŏng′kwĭn, -kĭn) also **Al•gon•kin** (-kĭn) ▸*n., pl.* **-quin** or **-quins** also **-kin** or **-kins 1.** A member of any of various Native American peoples inhabiting the Ottawa R. valley of Quebec and Ontario. **2.** Any of the varieties of Ojibwa spoken by these peoples.

al•go•rithm (ăl′gə-rĭth′əm) ▸*n.* A step-by-step problem-solving procedure. [Ult. after Muhammad ibn-Musa al-*Khwarizmi.*] —**al′go•rith′mic** *adj.*

A•li (ä-lē′), **Muhammad.** Orig. Cassius Marcellus Clay. b. 1942. Amer. prizefighter.

a•li•as (ā′lē-əs) ▸*n.* An assumed name. ▸*adv.* Also known as; otherwise. [Lat. *aliās,* otherwise.]

al•i•bi (ăl′ə-bī′) ▸*n., pl.* **-bis 1.** *Law* A form of defense whereby a defendant attempts to prove that he or she was elsewhere when the crime was committed. **2.** *Informal* An excuse. [Lat., elsewhere.]

Muhammad Ali
photographed in 1974

a•li•en (ā′lē-ən, āl′yən) ▸*adj.* **1.** Owing political allegiance to another country; foreign. **2.** Belonging to a very different place or society. See Syns at **foreign. 3.** Dissimilar or opposed: *ideas alien to her nature.* ▸*n.* **1.** An unnaturalized foreign resident of a country. **2.** A person from a very different group or place. **3.** An outsider. **4.** A creature from outer space. [< Lat. *aliēnus.*]

al•ien•a•ble (ăl′yə-nə-bəl, ā′lē-ə-) ▸*adj. Law* Transferrable to the ownership of another. —**al′ien•a•bil′i•ty** *n.*

al•ien•ate (āl′yə-nāt′, ā′lē-ə-) ▸*v.* **-at•ed, -at•ing 1.** To make unfriendly or hostile; estrange. **2.** *Law* To transfer (property) to the ownership of another. —**al′ien•a′tor** *n.*

al•ien•a•tion (āl′yə-nā′shən, ā′lē-ə-) ▸*n.* **1.** The act of alienating or the condition of being alienated. **2.** *Psychol.* A state of estrangement esp. between the self and the objective world.

al•ien•ist (āl′yə-nĭst, ā′lē-ə-) ▸*n. Law* A psychiatrist accepted by a court of law as an expert. [Fr. *aliéniste* < *aliéné,* insane.]

a•light[1] (ə-līt′) ▸*v.* **a•light•ed** or **a•lit** (ə-lĭt′), **a•light•ing 1.** To come down and settle, as after flight. **2.** To dismount. [< OE *ālīhtan.*]

a•light[2] (ə-līt′) ▸*adj.* **1.** Burning; lighted. **2.** Illuminated. —**a•light′** *adv.*

a•lign also **a•line** (ə-līn′) ▸*v.* **a•ligned, a•lign•ing** also **a•lined, a•lin•ing 1.** To arrange or be arranged in a straight line. **2.** To adjust (e.g., parts of a mechanism) to produce a proper orientation. **3.** To ally (oneself) with one side of an argument or cause. [< OFr. *ligne,* LINE[1].] —**a•lign′ment** *n.*

a•like (ə-līk′) ▸*adj.* Having close resemblance; similar. ▸*adv.* In the same manner or to the same degree. [< OE *gelīc.*] —**a•like′ness** *n.*

al•i•ment (ăl′ə-mənt) ▸*n.* **1.** Nourishment. **2.** Support. [< Lat. *alere,* nourish.]

al•i•men•ta•ry (ăl′ə-mĕn′tə-rē, -trē) ▸*adj.* **1.** Relating to food, nutrition, or digestion. **2.** Providing nourishment.

alimentary canal ▸*n.* The mucous membrane-lined tube of the digestive system that extends from the mouth to the anus and includes the pharynx, esophagus, stomach, and intestines.

al•i•mo•ny (ăl′ə-mō′nē) ▸*n., pl.* **-nies.** *Law* An allowance for support usu. made under court order to a divorced person by the former spouse. [Lat. *alimōnia,* sustenance.]

al•i•phat•ic (ăl′ə-făt′ĭk) ▸*adj.* Relating to a group of organic chemical compounds in which the carbon atoms are linked in open chains. [< Gk. *aleiphar, aleiphat-,* oil.]

al•i•quot (ăl′ĭ-kwŏt′) *Math.* ▶*adj.* Relating to an exact divisor or factor, esp. of an integer. ▶*n.* An aliquot part. [Lat. *aliquot*, a number of.]

a•lit (ə-lĭt′) ▶*v.* P.t. and p.part of **alight**[1].

a•live (ə-līv′) ▶*adj.* **1.** Having life; living. **2.** In existence or operation. **3.** Full of living things. **4.** Animated; lively. —***idiom:* alive to** Aware of; alert to. —**a•live′ness** *n.*

a•liz•a•rin (ə-lĭz′ər-ĭn) ▶*n.* An orange-red crystalline compound, $C_{14}H_6O_2(OH)_2$, used in dyes. [Prob. < Ar. *al-'uṣāra*, juice.]

al•ka•li (ăl′kə-lī′) ▶*n., pl.* **-lis** or **-lies 1.** A carbonate or hydroxide of an alkali metal, the aqueous solution of which is basic in reactions. **2.** Any of various soluble mineral salts found in natural water and arid soils. [< Ar. *al-qily*, ashes, lye.]

alkali metal ▶*n.* Any of a group of highly reactive metallic elements, including lithium, sodium, potassium, rubidium, cesium, and francium.

al•ka•line (ăl′kə-lĭn, -līn′) ▶*adj.* **1.** Relating to or containing an alkali. **2.** Having a pH greater than 7. —**al′ka•lin′i•ty** (-lĭn′ĭ-tē) *n.*

al•ka•line-earth metal (ăl′kə-lĭn-ûrth′, -līn′-) ▶*n.* Any of a group of metallic elements, esp. calcium, strontium, magnesium, and barium, but usu. including beryllium and radium.

al•ka•lize (ăl′kə-līz′) also **al•ka•lin•ize** (-lə-nīz′) ▶*v.* **-lized, -liz•ing** also **-ized, -iz•ing.** To make alkaline or become an alkali. —**al′ka•li•za′tion** *n.*

al•ka•loid (ăl′kə-loid′) ▶*n.* Any of various organic compounds containing nitrogen, occurring in many vascular plants, and including nicotine, quinine, cocaine, and caffeine. —**al′ka•loi′dal** *adj.*

al•ka•lo•sis (ăl′kə-lō′sĭs) ▶*n.* Abnormally high alkalinity of the blood and body fluids.

al•kyd (ăl′kĭd) ▶*n.* A widely used durable synthetic resin. [Ult. < ALCOHOL + (ACI)D.]

all (ôl) ▶*adj.* **1.** Being the total number, amount, or quantity. See Syns at **whole. 2.** Constituting or being the total. **3.** The utmost possible. **4.** Every: *all kinds of trouble.* **5.** Any whatsoever. ▶*n.* Everything one has: *They gave their all.* ▶*pron.* **1.** The total number; totality: *All the kittens are black.* **2.** Everyone; everything: *justice for all.* ▶*adv.* **1.** Wholly; completely: *directions that were all wrong.* **2.** Each; apiece: *a score of five all.* **3.** So much: *I am all the better for that experience.* —***idioms:* all along** From the beginning. **all but** Nearly; almost: *all but crying with relief.* **all in** Tired; exhausted. **all in all** Everything considered. **be all** *Informal* To say: *He's all, "Why did you do that?"* See Usage Note at **go**[1]. [< OE *eall.*]

Al•lah (ăl′ə, ä′lə) ▶*n.* God, esp. in Islam. [Ar. *Allāh* : al-, the + *'ilāh*, god.]

all-A•mer•i•can (ôl′ə-mĕr′ĭ-kən) ▶*adj.* **1.** Representative of the people of the US; typically American. **2.** *Sports* Chosen as the best amateur in the US at a particular position or event. **3.** Composed entirely of Americans or American materials. —**All′-A•mer′i•can** *n.*

all-a•round (ôl′ə-round′) also **all-round** (ôl′round′) ▶*adj.* **1.** Comprehensive: *a good all-around education.* **2.** Versatile: *an all-around athlete.* See Syns at **versatile.**

al•lay (ə-lā′) ▶*v.* **1.** To lessen or relieve. **2.** To calm or pacify. [< OE *ālecgan*, to lay aside.]

all clear ▶*n.* A signal, usu. by siren, that an air raid is over or a danger has passed.

al•lege (ə-lĕj′) ▶*v.* **-leged, -leg•ing 1.** To assert to be true, usu. without offering proof. **2.** To cite as a plea or excuse. [< LLat. **exlītigāre*, to clear : EX– + Lat. *lītigāre*, LITIGATE.] —**al′le•ga′tion** (ăl′ĭ-gā′shən) *n.* —**al•lege′a•ble** *adj.* —**al•leg′er** *n.*

al•leged (ə-lĕjd′, ə-lĕj′ĭd) ▶*adj.* Not proved; supposed. —**al•leg′ed•ly** (ə-lĕj′ĭd-lē) *adv.*

Usage: Newspapers and law enforcement officials sometimes misuse *alleged.* A person arrested for murder may be only an *alleged* murderer, for example, but he or she is a real, not an *alleged,* suspect.

Al•le•ghe•ny Mountains (ăl′ĭ-gā′nē) also **Al•le•ghe•nies** (-nēz). A range forming the W part of the Appalachian Mts. and extending from N PA to SW VA.

Allegheny River. A river rising in N-central PA and flowing about 523 km (325 mi) to Pittsburgh, where it forms the Ohio R.

al•le•giance (ə-lē′jəns) ▶*n.* Loyalty or the obligation of loyalty, as to a nation, sovereign, or cause. [< OFr. *lige*, LIEGE.]

al•le•go•ry (ăl′ĭ-gôr′ē, -gōr′ē) ▶*n., pl.* **-ries 1.** The use of characters or events to represent ideas or principles in a story, play, or picture. **2.** A story, play, or picture in which such representation occurs. [< Gk. *allēgorein*, interpret.] —**al′le•gor′ic, al′le•gor′i•cal** *adj.* —**al′le•gor′i•cal•ly** *adv.* —**al′le•go′rist** *n.*

al•le•gret•to (ăl′ĭ-grĕt′ō) ▶*adv. & adj. Mus.* In a moderately quick tempo. [Ital.]

al•le•gro (ə-lĕg′rō, ə-lā′grō) ▶*adv. & adj. Mus.* In a quick, lively tempo. [< Lat. *alacer*, lively.]

al•lele (ə-lēl′) ▶*n.* One member of a pair or series of genes that occupy a specific position on a specific chromosome. [Ger. *Allel.*] —**al•le′lic** (-lē′lĭk, -lĕl′ĭk) *adj.*

al•le•lop•a•thy (ə-lē-lŏp′ə-thē, ăl′ə-) ▶*n.* The inhibition of growth in one plant by chemicals produced by another plant. [Gk. *allēlōn*, reciprocally + –PATHY.] —**al•le′lo•path′ic** (-lē′lə-păth′ĭk, -lĕl′ə-) *adj.*

al•le•lu•ia (ăl′ə-lo͞o′yə) ▶*interj.* Hallelujah.

Al•len (ăl′ən), **Ethan.** 1738–89. Amer. Revolutionary soldier.

Al•len•de Gos•sens (ä-yĕn′dā gō′sĕns), **Salvador.** 1908–73. Chilean president (1970–73); assassinated.

Al•len•town (ăl′ən-toun′) A city of E PA NNW of Philadelphia. Pop. 105,090.

Allen wrench ▶*n.* A wrench used to secure screws threaded in hexagonally shaped nuts. [Orig. a trademark.]

al•ler•gen (ăl′ər-jən) ▶*n.* A substance that causes an allergy. —**al′ler•gen′ic** (-jĕn′ĭk) *adj.*

al•ler•gist (ăl′ər-jĭst) ▶*n.* A physician specializing in treating allergies.

al•ler•gy (ăl′ər-jē) ▶*n., pl.* **-gies.** An abnormally high sensitivity to certain substances, such as pollens, foods, or microorganisms. [< ALLO– + Gk. *ergon*, action.] —**al•ler′gic** (ə-lûr′jĭk) *adj.*

al•le•vi•ate (ə-lē′vē-āt′) ▶*v.* **-at•ed, -at•ing.** To make more bearable. [LLat. *alleviāre*, lighten.] —**al•le′vi•a′tion** *n.*

al•ley (ăl′ē) ▶*n., pl.* **-leys 1.** A narrow street or passageway between or behind buildings. **2.** A straight, narrow course or track. —***idiom:* up**

(one's) alley Compatible with one's interests or qualifications. [< OFr. *aller*, to walk < Lat. *ambulāre*.]
alley cat ▸*n.* A homeless or stray cat.
al•ley•way (ăl′ē-wā′) ▸*n.* A narrow passage between buildings.
al•li•ance (ə-lī′əns) ▸*n.* **1a.** A close, formal association of nations or other groups. **b.** A formal agreement establishing such an association. **2.** A connection based on kinship, marriage, or common interest. **3.** Close similarity in nature or type.
al•lied (ə-līd′, ăl′īd′) ▸*adj.* **1.** Joined in an alliance. **2.** Of a similar nature; related: *city planning and allied studies.*
al•li•ga•tor (ăl′ĭ-gā′tər) ▸*n.* **1.** A large amphibious reptile having sharp teeth, powerful jaws, and a broader, shorter snout than the related crocodile. **2.** Leather made from the hide of one of these reptiles. [< Sp. *el lagarto*, the lizard.]
alligator pear ▸*n.* See **avocado.**
all-im•por•tant (ôl′ĭm-pôr′tnt) ▸*adj.* Of the greatest importance; crucial.
al•lit•er•a•tion (ə-lĭt′ə-rā′shən) ▸*n.* The repetition of the same consonant sounds or of different vowel sounds at the beginning of words or in stressed syllables, as in *"When to the sessions of sweet silent thought"* (Shakespeare). [< AD– + Lat. *littera*, letter.] —**al•lit′er•ate** *v.* —**al•lit′er•a′tive** *adj.* —**al•lit′er•a•tive•ly** *adv.*
allo– ▸*pref.* Other; different: *allophone.* [Gk. < *allos*, other.]
al•lo•cate (ăl′ə-kāt′) ▸*v.* **-cat•ed, -cat•ing 1.** To set apart; designate. **2.** To distribute; allot. [Med.Lat. *allocāre*.] —**al′lo•ca•ble** (-kə-bəl) *adj.* —**al′lo•ca′tion** *n.*
Syns: *allocate, appropriate, designate, earmark* ***v.***
al•lo•morph (ăl′ə-môrf′) ▸*n.* Any of the variant forms of a morpheme. —**al′lo•mor′phic** *adj.* —**al′lo•mor′phism** *n.*
al•lo•phone (ăl′ə-fōn′) ▸*n.* A predictable phonetic variant of a phoneme. —**al′lo•phon′ic** (-fŏn′ĭk) *adj.*
al•lot (ə-lŏt′) ▸*v.* **-lot•ted, -lot•ting 1.** To parcel out; distribute by lot. **2.** To assign as a portion; allocate. [< OFr. *aloter*.] —**al•lot′ment** *n.* —**al•lot′ter** *n.*
al•lot•ro•py (ə-lŏt′rə-pē) ▸*n.* The existence, esp. in the solid state, of two or more crystalline or molecular structural forms of an element. —**al′lo•trope** (ăl′ə-trōp′) *n.* —**al′lo•trop′ic** (-trŏp′ĭk, -trō′pĭk), **al′lo•trop′i•cal** *adj.*
all-out (ôl′out′) ▸*adj.* Wholehearted: *an all-out sprint.*
all over ▸*adv.* **1.** Over the whole area. **2.** Everywhere. **3.** In all respects. —**all′-o′ver** *adj.*
al•low (ə-lou′) ▸*v.* **1.** To let do or happen; permit. **2.** To permit to have. **3.** To make provision for. **4.** To grant as a discount. **5.** *Regional* To admit; grant: *I allowed as how he was right.* —***phrasal verbs:*** **allow for** To make a provision for: *allow for bad weather.* **allow of** To admit: *a poem allowing of several interpretations.* [< OFr. *allouer*.] —**al•low′a•ble** *adj.* —**al•low′a•bly** *adv.*
al•low•ance (ə-lou′əns) ▸*n.* **1.** The act of allowing or an amount allowed. **2.** Something, such as money, given at regular intervals or for a specific purpose. **3.** A price reduction. **4.** A consideration for circumstances: *an allowance for breakage.*
al•low•ed•ly (ə-lou′ĭd-lē) ▸*adv.* By general admission; admittedly.
al•loy (ăl′oi′, ə-loi′) ▸*n.* **1.** A homogeneous mixture of two or more metals. **2.** Something added that lowers value or purity. [< Lat. *alligāre*, bind to.] —**al•loy′** *v.*
all-pur•pose (ôl′pûr′pəs) ▸*adj.* Having many uses.
all right ▸*adj.* **1.** In satisfactory order. **2.** Correct. **3.** Average; mediocre. ▸*adv.* **1.** In a satisfactory way; adequately. **2.** Very well; yes. **3.** Without a doubt.
all-round (ôl′round′) ▸*adj.* Var. of **all-around.**
All Saints' Day ▸*n.* Nov. 1, a Christian feast honoring all the saints.
All Souls' Day ▸*n.* *Rom. Cath. Ch.* Nov. 2, the day on which prayers are offered for the souls in purgatory.
all•spice (ôl′spīs′) ▸*n.* The dried, nearly ripe berries of a tropical American evergreen tree, used as a spice.
all-star (ôl′stär′) ▸*adj.* Made up wholly of star performers.
all-time (ôl′tīm′) ▸*adj.* Unsurpassed by any others: *an all-time broad jump record.*
all told ▸*adv.* With everything considered; in all: *All told, we won 100 games.*
al•lude (ə-lo͞od′) ▸*v.* **-lud•ed, -lud•ing.** To make an indirect reference. [Lat. *allūdere*, play with.] —**al•lu′sion** (-lo͞o′zhən) *n.* —**al•lu′sive** (-sĭv) *adj.* —**al•lu′sive•ly** *adv.*
al•lure (ə-lo͝or′) ▸*v.* **-lured, -lur•ing.** To attract with something desirable; entice. ▸*n.* The power to attract; enticement. [< OFr. *alurer*.] —**al•lure′ment** *n.* —**al•lur′ing•ly** *adv.*
al•lu•vi•on (ə-lo͞o′vē-ən) ▸*n.* **1.** See **alluvium. 2.** The flow of water against a shore or bank. [Lat. *alluviō*, *alluviōn-* < *alluere*, to wash against. See ALLUVIUM.]
al•lu•vi•um (ə-lo͞o′vē-əm) ▸*n.*, *pl.* **-vi•ums** or **-vi•a** (-vē-ə). Sediment deposited by flowing water, as in a river bed. [< Lat. *alluere*, wash against : AD– + *luere*, wash.] —**al•lu′vi•al** *adj.*
al•ly (ə-lī′, ăl′ī) ▸*v.* **-lied, -ly•ing 1.** To unite in a formal relationship, as by treaty or contract. **2.** To join with another or others out of mutual interest. ▸*n.*, *pl.* **-lies.** One allied with another, esp. by treaty or contract. [< Lat. *alligāre*, bind to.]
al•ma ma•ter or **Al•ma Ma•ter** (ăl′mə mä′tər, äl′mə) ▸*n.* **1.** The school that one has attended. **2.** The anthem of a school or college. [Lat. *alma māter*, nourishing mother.]
al•ma•nac (ôl′mə-năk′, ăl′-) ▸*n.* An annual publication in calendar form with weather forecasts, astronomical information, tide tables, and other information. [< Med.Lat.]
Al•ma•ty (äl′mə-tē′) The capital of Kazakhstan, in the SE near the Chinese border. Pop. 1,068,000.
al•might•y (ôl-mī′tē) ▸*adj.* Omnipotent; all-powerful. [< OE *ealmihtig* : *eall*, all + *miht*, MIGHT[1].] —**al•might′i•ly** *adv.*
al•mond (ä′mənd, äl′-, ôl′-, ăm′ənd) ▸*n.* **1.** A deciduous tree having pink flowers and leathery fruits. **2.** The kernel of this tree, eaten or used for flavoring. [< LLat. *amandula*.]
al•most (ôl′mōst′, ôl-mōst′) ▸*adv.* Slightly

short of; not quite. [< OE *ealmǣst.*]

alms (ämz) ►*pl.n.* Money or goods given as charity to the poor. [< Gk. *eleēmosunē* < *eleos*, pity.]

alms•house (ämz′hous′) ►*n.* A poorhouse.

al•oe (ăl′ō) ►*n.* **1.** Any of various chiefly African plants having rosettes of succulent, often spiny-margined leaves. **2. aloes** *(takes sing. v.)* A laxative obtained from the juice of a certain aloe. [< Gk. *aloē.*]

aloe ver•a (vĕr′ə, vîr′ə) ►*n.* **1.** An aloe native to the Mediterranean region. **2.** The gel obtained from its leaves, widely used in cosmetics. [Lat. *aloē*, ALOE + *vērus*, true.]

a•loft (ə-lôft′, -lŏft′) ►*adv.* **1.** In or into a high place. **2.** *Naut.* At or toward the upper rigging. [< ON *ā lopt*, in the air.]

a•lo•ha (ə-lō′ə, ä-lō′hä′) ►*interj.* Used as a greeting or farewell. See Regional Note at **ukulele.** [Hawaiian.]

a•lone (ə-lōn′) ►*adj.* **1.** Apart from others; solitary. **2.** Without anyone or anything else; only. **3.** Separate from all others of the same class. **4.** Without equal; unique. [ME.] —**a•lone′** *adv.* —**a•lone′ness** *n.*

a•long (ə-lông′, -lŏng′) ►*prep.* **1.** Over the length of. **2.** On a course parallel and close to. **3.** In accordance with: *The committee split along party lines.* ►*adv.* **1.** Forward; onward: *moving along.* **2.** As a companion: *Bring your friend along.* **3.** In accompaniment; together. See Usage Note at **together. 4.** With one; at hand: *had my camera along.* **5.** *Informal* Advanced to some degree: *getting along in years.* [< OE *andlang.*]

a•long•shore (ə-lông′shôr′, -shōr′, -lŏng′-) ►*adv.* Along, near, or by the shore.

a•long•side (ə-lông′sīd′, -lŏng′-) ►*adv.* Along, near, at, or to the side. ►*prep.* By the side of; side by side with.

a•loof (ə-lo͞of′) ►*adj.* Distant or reserved in manner or social relations. ►*adv.* Apart. [A–[2] + *luff*, windward side of a ship.] —**a•loof′ly** *adv.* —**a•loof′ness** *n.*

al•o•pe•cia (ăl′ə-pē′shə, -shē-ə) ►*n.* Loss of hair, esp. as a result of disease. [Lat. *alōpecia*, fox-mange, ult. < Gk. *alōpēx*, fox.]

a•loud (ə-loud′) ►*adv.* **1.** Using the voice; orally: *Read this passage aloud.* **2.** In a loud tone; loudly: *crying aloud for help.*

alp (ălp) ►*n.* A high mountain. [< the ALPS.]

al•pac•a (ăl-păk′ə) ►*n.*, *pl.* **-a** or **-as 1.** A domesticated South American mammal related to the llama and having fine long wool. **2a.** The silky wool of this mammal. **b.** Cloth made from alpaca. [Am.Sp.]

al•pen•horn (ăl′pən-hôrn′) ►*n.* A long curved wooden horn used by herders in the Alps to call cows to pasture. [Ger.]

al•pha (ăl′fə) ►*n.* The 1st letter of the Greek alphabet. [Gk., of Phoenician orig.]

al•pha•bet (ăl′fə-bĕt′) ►*n.* **1.** The letters of a language, arranged in a customary order. **2.** The basic principles; rudiments. [< Gk. *alpha*, ALPHA + *bēta*, BETA.]

al•pha•bet•i•cal (ăl′fə-bĕt′ĭ-kəl) also **al•pha•bet•ic** (-bĕt′ĭk) ►*adj.* **1.** Arranged in the customary order of the letters of a language. **2.** Relating to or expressed by an alphabet. —**al′pha•bet′i•cal•ly** *adv.*

al•pha•bet•ize (ăl′fə-bĭ-tīz′) ►*v.* **-ized, -iz•ing.** To arrange in alphabetical order. —**al′pha•bet′i•za′tion** *n.* —**al′pha•bet•iz′er** *n.*

alpha helix ►*n.* A protein structure characterized by a single, spiral chain of amino acids stabilized by hydrogen bonds.

al•pha•nu•mer•ic (ăl′fə-no͞o-mĕr′ĭk, -nyo͞o-) also **al•pha•mer•ic** (-fə-mĕr′ĭk) ►*adj.* Consisting of both letters and numbers.

alpha particle ►*n.* A positively charged particle, indistinguishable from a helium atom nucleus, consisting of two protons and two neutrons.

alpha ray ►*n.* A stream of alpha particles.

alpha wave also **alpha rhythm** ►*n.* A pattern of regular electrical oscillations in the brain that occur at a frequency of 8 to 13 hertz when a person is awake and relaxed.

al•pine (ăl′pīn′) ►*adj.* **1. Alpine** Relating to the Alps or their inhabitants. **2.** Of or relating to high mountains.

Alps (ălps) A mountain system of S-central Europe.

al•read•y (ôl-rĕd′ē) ►*adv.* **1.** By this or a specified time; before: *It was already dark at 5:00.* **2.** So soon: *Are you going already?* [ME *alredi* : *all*, ALL + *redi*, READY.]

al•right (ôl-rīt′) ►*adv.* *Nonstandard* All right.

Al•sace (ăl-săs′, -sās′) A region and former province of E France between the Rhine R. and the Vosges Mts.

Al•sa•tian (ăl-sā′shən) ►*adj.* Of or relating to Alsace. ►*n.* **1.** A native or inhabitant of Alsace. **2.** *Chiefly Brit.* A German shepherd.

al•so (ôl′sō) ►*adv.* **1.** In addition; besides. **2.** Likewise; too. ►*conj.* And in addition. [< OE *ealswā.*]

al•so-ran (ôl′sō-răn′) ►*n.* **1.** A horse that does not win, place, or show in a race. **2.** A loser in a competition.

alt. ►*abbr.* **1.** alternate **2.** altitude

Alta. ►*abbr.* Alberta

Al•ta California (äl′tə). Also **Upper California.** The Spanish possessions along the Pacific coast N of the peninsula of Baja California.

Al•ta•ic (ăl-tā′ĭk) ►*n.* A language family of Europe and Asia that includes the Turkic, Tungusic, and Mongolian subfamilies. ►*adj.* **1.** Of or relating to the Altai Mountains. **2.** Of or relating to Altaic.

Al•tai Mountains (ăl′tī′) A mountain system of central Asia.

al•tar (ôl′tər) ►*n.* An elevated place or structure before or upon which religious ceremonies may be performed. [< Lat. *altāre.*]

al•tar•piece (ôl′tər-pēs′) ►*n.* A piece of artwork, such as a painting or carving, that is placed above and behind an altar.

al•ter (ôl′tər) ►*v.* **1.** To change; modify. **2.** To adjust (a garment) for a better fit. **3.** To castrate or spay (an animal). [< Med.Lat. *alterāre*, make other.] —**al′ter•a•ble** *adj.* —**al′ter•a′tion** *n.*

al•ter•cate (ôl′tər-kāt′) ►*v.* **-cat•ed, -cat•ing.** To argue or dispute vehemently. [Lat. *altercārī* < *alter*, another.] —**al′ter•ca′tion** *n.*

alter ego ►*n.* **1.** Another side of oneself. **2.** An intimate friend. [Lat., other I.]

al•ter•nate (ôl′tər-nāt′, ăl′-) ►*v.* **-nat•ed, -nat•ing 1.** To perform or occur in successive turns. **2.** To pass back and forth from one state, action, or place to another. ►*adj.* (-nĭt) **1.** Happening or following in turns. **2.** Designating or relating to every other one of a series. **3.** Substitute: *an alternate plan.* ▸*n.* (-nĭt) **1.** A substitute. **2.** An alternative. [< Lat. *alternus*, by turns.] —**al′ter•nate•ly** *adv.* —**al′ter•na′tion** *n.*

al•ter•nat•ing current (ôl′tər-nā′tĭng, ăl′-) ▸*n.* An electric current that reverses direction at regular intervals.

al•ter•na•tive (ôl-tûr′nə-tĭv, ăl-) ▸*n.* **1.** The choice between two or more exclusive possibilities. **2.** One of these possibilities. ▸*adj.* **1.** Allowing or necessitating a choice between two or more things. **2.** Existing outside convention: *an alternative lifestyle.* —**al•ter′na•tive•ly** *adv.*

alternative medicine ▸*n.* Any of various health care practices that do not follow generally accepted medical methods.

alternative school ▸*n.* A school that is nontraditional, esp. in ideals or curriculum.

al•ter•na•tor (ôl′tər-nā′tər, ăl′-) ▸*n.* An electric generator that produces alternating current.

al•though also **al•tho** (ôl-*thō*′) ▸*conj.* Regardless of the fact that; even though. [ME.]

Usage: *Although* is usually placed at the beginning of its clause, whereas *though* may occur there or elsewhere and is more commonly used to link words or phrases, as in *wiser though poorer.*

al•tim•e•ter (ăl-tĭm′ĭ-tər) ▸*n.* An instrument for determining elevation. [Lat. *altus*, high + –METER.] —**al•tim′e•try** *n.*

al•ti•pla•no (äl′tĭ-plä′nō) ▸*n.*, *pl.* **-nos.** A high mountain plateau, as in Bolivia and Peru. [< Lat. *altus*, high + *plānum*, plain.]

al•ti•tude (ăl′tĭ-to͞od′, -tyo͞od′) ▸*n.* **1.** The height of a thing above a reference level, esp. above sea level. See Syns at **elevation. 2.** A high region. **3.** The angular height of a celestial object above the horizon. **4.** The perpendicular distance from the base of a geometric figure to the opposite vertex, parallel side, or parallel surface. [< Lat. *altus*, high.] —**al′ti•tu′di•nal** *adj.*

alt key (ôlt) ▸*n.* A key on a computer keyboard pressed in combination with another key to execute an alternate operation.

al•to (ăl′tō) ▸*n.*, *pl.* **-tos** *Mus.* **1.** A low female singing voice; contralto. **2.** The range between soprano and tenor. **3.** A singer, voice, or instrument having this range. [< Lat. *altus*, high.]

al•to•geth•er (ôl′tə-gĕ*th*′ər) ▸*adv.* **1.** Entirely. **2.** With all included or counted: *Altogether the bill came to $30.* **3.** On the whole. [ME *al togeder.*]

al•tru•ism (ăl′tro͞o-ĭz′əm) ▸*n.* Unselfish concern for the welfare of others; selflessness. [Fr. *altruisme*, ult. < Lat. *alter*, other.] —**al′tru•ist** *n.* —**al′tru•is′tic** *adj.* —**al′tru•is′ti•cal•ly** *adv.*

al•um (ăl′əm) ▸*n.* Any of various double sulfates of a trivalent metal and a univalent metal, esp. aluminum potassium sulfate, used as hardeners and purifiers. [< Lat. *alūmen.*]

a•lu•mi•na (ə-lo͞o′mə-nə) ▸*n.* Any of several forms of aluminum oxide, Al_2O_3, occurring naturally as corundum, in bauxite, and with various impurities as ruby, sapphire, and emery. [< Lat. *alūmen*, alum.]

al•u•min•i•um (ăl′yə-mĭn′ē-əm) ▸*n. Chiefly Brit.* Var. of **aluminum.**

a•lu•mi•nize (ə-lo͞o′mə-nīz′) ▸*v.* **-nized, -niz•ing.** To coat or cover with aluminum.

a•lu•mi•nous (ə-lo͞o′mə-nəs) ▸*adj.* Relating to or containing aluminum or alum.

a•lu•mi•num (ə-lo͞o′mə-nəm) ▸*n. Symbol* **Al** A silvery-white, ductile metallic element used to form many hard, light, corrosion-resistant alloys. At. no. 13. See table at **element.** [< ALUMINA.]

a•lum•na (ə-lŭm′nə) ▸*n.*, *pl.* **-nae** (-nē′). A female graduate of a school, college, or university. [Lat., female pupil.]

a•lum•nus (ə-lŭm′nəs) ▸*n.*, *pl.* **-ni** (-nī′). A male graduate of a school, college, or university. [Lat., male pupil.]

Al•va (ăl′və, äl′vä) also **Al•ba** (ăl′bə), Duke of. 1508–82. Spanish general and colonial administrator.

al•ve•o•lus (ăl-vē′ə-ləs) ▸*n.*, *pl.* **-li** (-lī′) **1.** A tooth socket in the jawbone. **2.** A tiny, capillary-rich sac in the lungs where the exchange of oxygen and carbon dioxide takes place. [Lat., small cavity.]

al•ways (ôl′wāz, -wĭz) ▸*adv.* **1.** At all times; invariably. **2.** For all time; forever. **3.** At any time; in any event. [< OE *ealne weg.*]

a•lys•sum (ə-lĭs′əm) ▸*n.* **1.** See **sweet alyssum. 2.** A Mediterranean weed or ornamental having white or yellow flowers. [< Gk. *alusson*, plant believed to cure rabies.]

Alz•hei•mer's disease (älts′hī-mərz, ălts′-) ▸*n.* A disease marked by progressive loss of mental capacity. [After Alois *Alzheimer* (1864–1915), German neurologist.]

am (ăm) ▸*v.* 1st pers. sing. pr. indic. of **be.** [< OE *eom.*]

Am ▸ The symbol for the element **americium.**

AM ▸*abbr.* **1.** airmail **2.** amplitude modulation **3.** *Lat.* artium magister (Master of Arts)

A.M. also **a.m.** ▸*abbr.* ante meridiem See Usage Note at **ante meridiem.**

AMA ▸*abbr.* American Medical Association

a•mal•gam (ə-măl′gəm) ▸*n.* **1.** An alloy of mercury with other metals, as with tin or silver. **2.** A combination of diverse elements. [< Med. Lat. *amalgama.*]

a•mal•ga•mate (ə-măl′gə-māt′) ▸*v.* **-mat•ed, -mat•ing.** To form into an integrated whole; unite. —**a•mal′ga•ma′tion** *n.*

a•man•u•en•sis (ə-măn′yo͞o-ĕn′sĭs) ▸*n.*, *pl.* **-ses** (-sēz). A secretary. [Lat. *āmanuēnsis.*]

am•a•ranth (ăm′ə-rănth′) ▸*n.* **1.** Any of various annuals having dense clusters of tiny flowers. **2.** An imaginary flower that never fades. [< Gk. *amarantos*, unfading.] —**am′a•ran′thine** *adj.*

Am•a•ril•lo (ăm′ə-rĭl′ō) A city of N TX in the Panhandle N of Lubbock. Pop. 157,615.

am•a•ryl•lis (ăm′ə-rĭl′ĭs) ▸*n.* A tropical American bulbous plant grown as an ornamental for its large lilylike flowers. [< Gk. *Amarullis*, name of a shepherdess.]

a•mass (ə-măs′) ▸*v.* To accumulate. [< OFr. *amasser.*] —**a•mass′ment** *n.*

am•a•teur (ăm′ə-tûr′, -cho͝or′, -tyo͝or′) ▸*n.* **1.** One who engages in an activity or study as a pastime and not as a profession. **2.** One lacking expertise. [< Lat. *amātor*, lover.] —**am′a•teur′ish** *adj.* —**am′a•teur′ish•ly** *adv.* —**am′a•teur•ism** *n.*

Syns: *amateur, dabbler, dilettante* ***Ant:*** *professional* ***n.***

A•ma•ti (ä-mä′tē), **Nicolò.** 1596–1684. Italian violin maker.

amaryllis

am•a•to•ry (ăm′ə-tôr′ē, -tōr′ē) ►*adj.* Relating to love, esp. sexual love. [< Lat. *amāre*, to love.]

a•maze (ə-māz′) ►*v.* **a•mazed, a•maz•ing.** To affect with great wonder; astonish. [< OE *āmasian*, bewilder.] —**a•maz′ed•ly** (-mā′zĭd-lē) *adv.* —**a•maze′ment** *n.* —**a•maz′ing•ly** *adv.*

Am•a•zon (ăm′ə-zŏn′) ►*n.* **1.** *Gk. Myth.* A member of a nation of women warriors. **2.** often **amazon** A tall, aggressive, strong-willed woman.

Am•a•zo•ni•a (ăm′ə-zō′nē-ə) The vast basin of the Amazon R. in N South America.

Am•a•zo•ni•an (ăm′ə-zō′nē-ən) ►*adj.* **1.** Relating to the Amazon R. or to Amazonia. **2.** Relating to an Amazon.

Amazon River. The world's second-longest river, flowing about 6,275 km (3,900 mi) from N Peru across N Brazil to a wide delta on the Atlantic.

am•bas•sa•dor (ăm-băs′ə-dər) ►*n.* A diplomat of the highest rank accredited as representative in residence by one government to another. [< Lat. *ambactus*, servant.] —**am•bas′sa•do′ri•al** (-dôr′ē-əl, -dōr′-) *adj.* —**am•bas′sa•dor•ship′** *n.*

am•bas•sa•dress (ăm-băs′ə-drĭs) ►*n.* A woman ambassador. See Usage Note at **-ess.**

am•ber (ăm′bər) ►*n.* **1.** A hard, translucent, brownish-yellow fossil resin, used esp. for making jewelry. **2.** A brownish yellow. [< Ar. *'anbar*, ambergris.] —**am′ber** *adj.*

am•ber•gris (ăm′bər-grĭs′, -grēs′) ►*n.* A waxy, grayish substance formed in the intestines of sperm whales and used in perfumes. [< OFr. *ambre gris.*]

ambi– ►*pref.* Both: *ambivalence.* [Lat., around.]

am•bi•ance also **am•bi•ence** (ăm′bē-əns) ►*n.* The special atmosphere of a particular environment. [< Lat. *ambiēns*, AMBIENT.]

am•bi•dex•trous (ăm′bĭ-dĕk′strəs) ►*adj.* **1.** Able to use both hands with equal facility. **2.** Unusually skillful; adroit. [< Med.Lat. *ambidexter* : AMBI– + Lat. *dexter*, right.] —**am′bi•dex•ter′i•ty** (-stĕr′ĭ-tē) *n.* —**am′bi•dex′trous•ly** *adv.*

am•bi•ent (ăm′bē-ənt) ►*adj.* Surrounding; encircling. [< Lat. *ambīre*, go around.]

am•big•u•ous (ăm-bĭg′yo͞o-əs) ►*adj.* **1.** Open to more than one interpretation. **2.** Doubtful or uncertain. [< Lat. *ambiguus* : AMBI– + *agere*, drive.] —**am′bi•gu′i•ty** (-bĭ-gyo͞o′ĭ-tē) *n.* —**am′big′u•ous•ly** *adv.*

am•bit (ăm′bĭt) ►*n.* **1.** An external boundary; circuit. **2.** Sphere or scope. See Syns at **range.** [Lat. *ambitus* < *ambīre*, go around.]

am•bi•tion (ăm-bĭsh′ən) ►*n.* **1.** A strong desire to achieve something. **2.** The object or goal desired. [< Lat. *ambīre*, solicit.]

am•bi•tious (ăm-bĭsh′əs) ►*adj.* **1.** Full of or motivated by ambition. **2.** Challenging: *an ambitious schedule.* —**am•bi′tious•ly** *adv.* —**am•bi′tious•ness** *n.*

am•biv•a•lence (ăm-bĭv′ə-ləns) ►*n.* The coexistence of opposing feelings toward a person, object, or idea. —**am•biv′a•lent** *adj.* —**am•biv′a•lent•ly** *adv.*

am•ble (ăm′bəl) ►*v.* **-bled, -bling.** To walk slowly or leisurely; stroll. [< Lat. *ambulāre*, walk.] —**am′ble** *n.* —**am′bler** *n.*

am•bro•sia (ăm-brō′zhə) ►*n.* **1.** *Gk. & Rom. Myth.* The food of the gods. **2.** Something with a delicious flavor or fragrance. [< Gk. *ambrotos*, immortal.] —**am•bro′sial** *adj.*

am•bu•lance (ăm′byə-ləns) ►*n.* A specially equipped vehicle used to transport the sick or injured. [< Fr. *ambulant*, AMBULANT.]

am•bu•lant (ăm′byə-lənt) ►*adj.* Moving or walking about. [< Lat. *ambulāre*, walk.]

am•bu•la•to•ry (ăm′byə-lə-tôr′ē, -tōr′ē) ►*adj.* **1.** Relating to or adapted for walking. **2.** Capable of walking; not bedridden: *an ambulatory patient.* **3.** Moving about. ►*n., pl.* **-ries.** A covered place for walking, as in a cloister. [< Lat. *ambulāre*, walk.]

am•bus•cade (ăm′bə-skād′) ►*n.* An ambush. ►*v.* **-cad•ed, -cad•ing.** To attack suddenly from a concealed place. See Syns at **ambush.** [< OItal. *imboscare*, to ambush.]

am•bush (ăm′bo͝osh) ►*n.* **1.** The act of lying in wait to attack by surprise. **2.** A sudden attack made from a concealed position. ►*v.* To attack from a concealed position. [< OFr. *embuschier*, to ambush.] —**am′bush′er** *n.*

Syns: *ambush, ambuscade, bushwhack, waylay* **n.**

a•me•ba (ə-mē′bə) ►*n.* Var. of **amoeba.**

a•me•lio•rate (ə-mēl′yə-rāt′) ►*v.* **-rat•ed, -rat•ing.** To make or become better; improve. [Alteration of MELIORATE.] —**a•me′lio•ra′tion** *n.*

a•men (ā-mĕn′, ä-) ►*interj.* Used at the end of a prayer or to express approval. [< Heb. *'āmēn*, verily.]

a•me•na•ble (ə-mē′nə-bəl, -mĕn′ə-) ►*adj.* **1.** Obedient; compliant. **2.** Responsible; accountable. [< OFr. *mener*, to lead.] —**a•me′na•bly** *adv.*

a•mend (ə-mĕnd′) ►*v.* **1.** To improve. **2.** To remove the errors in; correct. **3.** To alter (e.g., a law) formally by adding, deleting, or rephrasing. [< Lat. *ēmendāre.*]

a•mend•ment (ə-mĕnd′mənt) ►*n.* **1.** Improvement. **2.** Correction. **3a.** Formal revision, as of a bill or constitution. **b.** A statement of such a revision: *The 19th Amendment gave women the right to vote.*

a•mends (ə-mĕndz′) ►*pl.n. (takes sing. or pl. v.)* Recompense for grievance or injury.

A•men•ho•tep III (ä′mən-hō′tĕp). King of Egypt (1411?–1375 B.C.).

Amenhotep IV. See **Akhenaton.**

a•men•i•ty (ə-mĕn′ĭ-tē, -mē′nĭ-) ▸*n., pl.* **-ties** **1.** Pleasantness; agreeableness. **2.** Something that contributes to comfort. **3.** A feature that increases attractiveness or value. **4. amenities** Social courtesies; pleasantries. [< Lat. *amoenus*, pleasant.]

Syns: *amenity, comfort, convenience, facility* ***n.***

a•men•or•rhe•a or **a•men•or•rhoe•a** (ā-mĕn′ə-rē′ə) ▸*n.* Abnormal suppression or absence of menstruation. [A–[1] + Gk. *mēn*, month + –RRHEA.] —**a•men′or•rhe′ic** *adj.*

Amer. ▸*abbr.* **1.** America **2.** American

Am•er•a•sian (ăm′ə-rā′zhən, -shən) ▸*n.* A person of American and Asian descent. —**Am′er•a′sian** *adj.*

a•merce (ə-mûrs′) ▸*v.* **a•merced, a•merc•ing.** To punish, esp. by a fine imposed arbitrarily by the court. [< AN *amercier.*]

A•mer•i•ca (ə-mĕr′ĭ-kə) **1.** The United States. **2.** Also **the Americas.** The landmasses and islands of North America, Central America, and South America.

A•mer•i•can (ə-mĕr′ĭ-kən) ▸*adj.* **1.** Of or relating to the US. **2.** Of or relating to America or the Americas. ▸*n.* **1.** A citizen of the US. **2.** A native or inhabitant of America or the Americas.

A•mer•i•ca•na (ə-mĕr′ə-kä′nə, -kăn′ə, -kā′nə) ▸*n. (takes sing. or pl. v.)* Materials relating to American history, folklore, or geography.

American English ▸*n.* The English language as used in the US.

American Indian ▸*n.* See **Native American.** See Usage Note at **Native American.**

A•mer•i•can•ism (ə-mĕr′ĭ-kə-nĭz′əm) ▸*n.* **1.** A custom or trait originating in the US. **2.** A word, phrase, or idiom characteristic of American English.

A•mer•i•can•ize (ə-mĕr′ĭ-kə-nīz′) ▸*v.* **-ized, -iz•ing 1.** To make or become American, as in culture or method. **2.** To bring under American control. —**A•mer′i•can•i•za′tion** *n.*

American plan ▸*n.* A system of hotel management in which a guest pays a fixed daily rate for room and meals.

American Samoa. An unincorp. territory of the US in the S Pacific NE of Fiji. Cap. Pago Pago. Pop. 32,279.

American Sign Language ▸*n.* An American system of communication for the hearing-impaired that uses manual signs.

American Spanish ▸*n.* The Spanish language as used in the Western Hemisphere.

am•er•i•ci•um (ăm′ə-rĭsh′ē-əm) ▸*n. Symbol* **Am** A white metallic radioactive element used as a radiation source in research. At. no. 95. See table at **element.** [< AMERICA.]

Am•er•in•di•an (ăm′ə-rĭn′dē-ən) also **Am•er•ind** (ăm′ə-rĭnd′) ▸*n.* See **Native American.** —**Am′er•in′di•an, Am′er•ind′** *adj.*

am•e•thyst (ăm′ə-thĭst) ▸*n.* **1.** A purple or violet variety of transparent quartz or corundum used as a gemstone. **2.** A moderate to grayish purple. [< Gk. *amethustos.*] —**am′e•thys′tine** (-thĭs′tĭn, -tīn′) *adj.*

Amex ▸*abbr.* American Stock Exchange

Am•har•ic (ăm-hăr′ĭk, äm-hä′rĭk) ▸*n.* A Semitic language, the official language of Ethiopia.

a•mi•a•ble (ā′mē-ə-bəl) ▸*adj.* Friendly; good-natured. [< LLat. *amīcābilis*, AMICABLE.] —**a′mi•a•bil′i•ty, a′mi•a•ble•ness** *n.* —**a′mi•a•bly** *adv.*

am•i•ca•ble (ăm′ĭ-kə-bəl) ▸*adj.* Friendly; peaceable. [< Lat. *amīcus*, friend.] —**am′i•ca•bil′i•ty** *n.* —**am′i•ca•bly** *adv.*

a•mid (ə-mĭd′) also **a•midst** (ə-mĭdst′) ▸*prep.* Surrounded by; in the middle of.

a•mid•ships (ə-mĭd′shĭps′) also **a•mid•ship** (-shĭp′) ▸*adv. Naut.* Midway between the bow and the stern.

Am•i•ens (ăm′ē-ənz, ä-myăN′) A city of N France N of Paris. Pop. 131,880.

a•mi•go (ə-mē′gō) ▸*n., pl.* **-gos.** A friend. [Sp. < Lat. *amīcus.*]

A•min Da•da (ä-mēn′ dä-dä′), **Idi.** b. c. 1925. Ugandan dictator (1971–79).

a•mine (ə-mēn′, ăm′ēn) ▸*n.* Any of a group of organic compounds derived from ammonia by replacing one or more hydrogen atoms by a hydrocarbon radical. [AM(MONIUM) + –INE[2].]

a•mi•no acid (ə-mē′nō, ăm′ə-nō′) ▸*n.* Any of a class of organic compounds, esp. any of the 20 compounds that form proteins.

A•mish (ä′mĭsh, ăm′ĭsh) ▸*n.* A member of an Anabaptist sect that settled primarily in SE Pennsylvania in the late 17th cent. [After Jacob *Amman*, 17th-century Mennonite bishop.] —**A′mish** *adj.*

a•miss (ə-mĭs′) ▸*adj.* **1.** Out of proper order. **2.** Not in perfect shape; faulty. ▸*adv.* In a defective, unfortunate, or mistaken way. [Prob. < ON *ā mis.*]

Syns: *amiss, afield, astray, awry, wrong*
Ant: *aright* ***adj.***

am•i•ty (ăm′ĭ-tē) ▸*n., pl.* **-ties.** Peaceful relations, as between nations. [< OFr. *amitie* < Lat. *amīcus*, friend.]

Am•man (ä-män′) The capital of Jordan, in the N-central part. Pop. 965,000.

am•me•ter (ăm′mē′tər) ▸*n.* An instrument that measures electric current. [AM(PERE) + –METER.]

am•mo (ăm′ō) ▸*n. Informal* Ammunition.

am•mo•nia (ə-mōn′yə) ▸*n.* **1.** A colorless, pungent gas, NH_3, used to manufacture fertilizers and a wide variety of nitrogen-containing chemicals. **2.** See **ammonium hydroxide.** [< Lat. *(sal) ammōniacus*, (salt) of Amen, an Egyptian god.]

am•mon•ite (ăm′ə-nīt′) ▸*n.* The coiled, flat, chambered fossil shell of an extinct cephalopod mollusk. [< Lat. *(cornū) Ammōnis*, (horn) of Amen (Egypt. god), ammonite.]

am•mo•ni•um (ə-mō′nē-əm) ▸*n.* The chemical ion NH_4+. [AMMON(IA) + –IUM.]

ammonium chloride ▸*n.* A white crystalline compound, NH_4Cl, used in dry cells and as an expectorant.

ammonium hydroxide ▸*n.* A basic, aqueous solution of ammonia, NH_4OH, used as a household cleanser and in other products.

am•mu•ni•tion (ăm′yə-nĭsh′ən) ▸*n.* **1.** Projectiles that can be fired from guns or otherwise propelled. **2.** Explosive or destructive materials used in war. **3.** A means of offense or defense. [< OFr. *(la) munition*, MUNITIONS.]

am•ne•sia (ăm-nē′zhə) ▸*n.* Loss of memory. [Gk. *amnēsia* : A–[1] + *mimnēskein*, remember.] —**am•ne′si•ac′** (-zē-ăk′, -zhē-ăk′), **am•ne′sic** (-zĭk, -sĭk) *n. & adj.*

am•nes•ty (ăm′nĭ-stē) ▸*n., pl.* **-ties.** A general pardon, esp. for political offenses. [< Gk.

amnēstia : A–[1] + *mimnēskein*, remember.] —**am′nes•ty** *v.*

am•ni•o•cen•te•sis (ăm′nē-ō-sĕn-tē′sĭs) ►*n.*, *pl.* **-ses** (-sēz). A procedure in which a small sample of fluid is drawn out of the uterus, then analyzed to determine genetic abnormalities in, or the sex of, a fetus. [AMNION + Gk. *kentēsis*, pricking.]

am•ni•on (ăm′nē-ən) ►*n.*, *pl.* **-ni•ons** or **-ni•a** (-nē-ə). A membranous sac filled with a serous fluid that encloses the embryo or fetus of a mammal, bird, or reptile. [Gk. *amniōn*.] —**am′ni•ot′ic** (-ŏt′ĭk), **am′ni•on′ic** (-ŏn′ĭk) *adj.*

a•moe•ba also **a•me•ba** (ə-mē′bə) ►*n.*, *pl.* **-bas** or **-bae** (-bē). A protozoan occurring in water, soil, or as a parasite and consisting essentially of an indefinitely shaped mass of protoplasm. [< Gk. *amoibē*, change.] —**a•moe′bic** *adj.*

ammonite

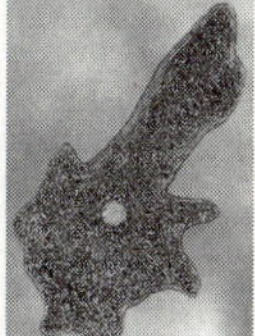

amoeba

a•mok (ə-mŭk′, ə-mŏk′) ►*adv.* Var. of **amuck.**

a•mong (ə-mŭng′) also **a•mongst** (ə-mŭngst′) ►*prep.* **1.** In the midst of; surrounded by. **2.** In the group or class of. **3.** With portions to each of: *Distribute this among you.* **4.** Each with the other. See Usage Note at **between.** [< OE *āmang*.]

a•mon•til•la•do (ə-mŏn′tl-ä′dō) ►*n.*, *pl.* **-dos.** A pale dry sherry. [Sp. *(vino) amontillado*, (wine) made in Montilla, Spain.]

a•mor•al (ā-môr′əl, -mŏr′-) ►*adj.* **1.** Neither moral nor immoral. **2.** Lacking moral sensibility; not caring about right and wrong. —**a•mor′al•ism** *n.* —**a′mo•ral′i•ty** (ā′mô-răl′ĭ-tē, -mə-) *n.* —**a•mor′al•ly** *adv.*

am•o•rous (ăm′ər-əs) ►*adj.* **1.** Strongly disposed to love, esp. sexual love. **2.** Showing or expressing love. [< Lat. *amor*, love.] —**am′or•ous•ly** *adv.* —**am′or•ous•ness** *n.*

a•mor•phous (ə-môr′fəs) ►*adj.* **1.** Lacking definite organization or form. See Syns at **shapeless. 2.** Of no particular type; anomalous. **3.** *Chem.* Lacking distinct crystalline structure. [< Gk. *amorphos*.]

am•or•tize (ăm′ər-tīz′, ə-môr′-) ►*v.* **-tized, -tiz•ing.** To liquidate (a debt) by installment payments. [< OFr. *amortir*.] —**am′or•tiz′a•ble** *adj.* —**am′or•ti•za′tion** *n.*

A•mos (ā′məs) ►*n. Bible* **1.** A Hebrew prophet of the 8th cent. B.C. **2.** See table at **Bible.**

a•mount (ə-mount′) ►*n.* **1.** The total quantity or number. **2.** A principal plus its interest, as in a loan. ►*v.* **1.** To add up in number. **2.** To add up in effect. **3.** To be equivalent. [< OFr. *amont*, upward.]

a•mour (ə-mo͝or′) ►*n.* A love affair, esp. an illicit one. [< OFr. < Lat. *amor*, love.]

a•mour-pro•pre (ä-mo͝or-prôp′rə) ►*n.* Self-respect. [Fr.]

a•mox•i•cil•lin (ə-mŏk′sĭ-sĭl′ĭn) ►*n.* A type of penicillin having antibacterial properties similar to ampicillin. [AM(INE) + OX(Y)– + (PEN)ICILLIN.]

A•moy (ä-moi′) See **Xiamen.**

amp (ămp) ►*n.* **1.** An ampere. **2.** An amplifier, esp. one used to amplify music.

am•per•age (ăm′pər-ĭj, ăm′pîr′-) ►*n.* The strength of an electric current expressed in amperes.

am•pere (ăm′pîr′) ►*n.* A unit of electric current strength, equal to a flow of one coulomb per second. [After André Marie AMPÈRE.]

Am•père (ăm′pîr, äɴ-pĕr′), **André Marie.** 1775–1836. French physicist.

am•per•sand (ăm′pər-sănd′) ►*n.* The character (&) representing the word *and.* [Contraction of *and per se and*, & (the sign) by itself (equals) and.]

am•phet•a•mine (ăm-fĕt′ə-mēn′, -mĭn) ►*n.* A colorless, volatile liquid, $C_9H_{13}N$, or one of its derivatives, used primarily as a central nervous system stimulant. [*a(lpha) m(ethyl) ph(enyl) et(hyl) amine.*]

am•phib•i•an (ăm-fĭb′ē-ən) ►*n.* **1.** A vertebrate that hatches as an aquatic larva with gills, then transforms into an adult having air-breathing lungs. **2.** An aircraft that can take off and land on land or water. **3.** A vehicle that can operate on land and in water. [< Gk. *amphibios*, AMPHIBIOUS.]

am•phib•i•ous (ăm-fĭb′ē-əs) ►*adj.* **1.** Able to live on land and in water. **2.** Able to operate on land and in water. [< Gk. *amphibios* : *amphi-*, both + *bios*, life.]

am•phi•bole (ăm′fə-bōl′) ►*n.* Any of a group of silicate minerals containing various combinations of sodium, calcium, magnesium, iron, and aluminum. [< Gk. *amphibolos*, doubtful.] —**am′phi•bol′ic** (-bŏl′ĭk) *adj.*

am•phi•the•a•ter (ăm′fə-thē′ə-tər) ►*n.* A round structure having tiers of seats rising gradually outward from a central arena. [< Gk. *amphitheatron*.]

am•pho•ra (ăm′fər-ə) ►*n.*, *pl.* **-pho•rae** (-fə-rē′) or **-pho•ras.** A two-handled jar with a narrow neck used by the ancient Greeks and Romans. [< Gk. *amphoreus* : *amphi-*, both + *pherein*, carry.]

am•pi•cil•lin (ăm′pĭ-sĭl′ĭn) ►*n.* A type of penicillin having a broad antibacterial spectrum and used to treat a variety of infections. [Blend of AMINE and PENICILLIN.]

am•ple (ăm′pəl) ►*adj.* **-pler, -plest 1.** Large in size or extent. See Syns at **spacious. 2.** Large in degree or quantity. **3.** Sufficient for a purpose. See Syns at **plentiful.** [< Lat. *amplus*.] —**am′ple•ness** *n.* —**am′ply** *adv.*

am•pli•fi•er (ăm′plə-fī′ər) ►*n.* **1.** One that amplifies. **2.** A device that produces amplification of an electrical signal.

am•pli•fy (ăm′plə-fī′) ►*v.* **-fied, -fy•ing 1.** To make greater; increase. **2.** To add to; make complete. **3.** To exaggerate. **4.** To increase the magnitude of a variable quantity, esp. of voltage, power, or current. [< Lat. *amplificāre*.] —**am′pli•fi•ca′tion** *n.*

am•pli•tude (ăm′plĭ-to͞od′, -tyo͞od′) ►*n.* **1.** Largeness; magnitude. **2.** Fullness; copiousness. **3.** *Phys.* The maximum absolute value of a periodically varying quantity. [< Lat. *amplus*, large.]

amplitude modulation ▸*n.* The encoding of a carrier wave by variation of its amplitude in accordance with an input signal.

am•poule also **am•pule** (ăm′po͝ol, -pyo͞ol) ▸*n.* A small sealed vial used as a container for a hypodermic injection solution. [< Lat. *ampulla*, dim. of *amphora*, AMPHORA.]

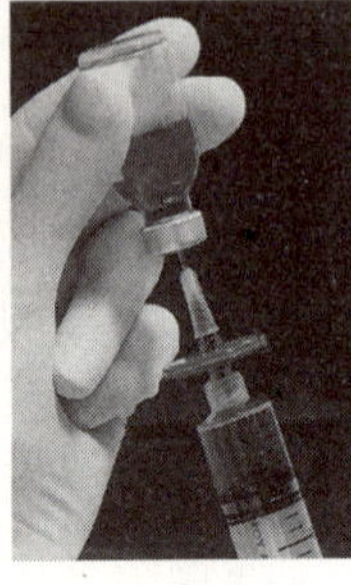

ampoule

am•pu•tate (ăm′pyo͞o-tāt′) ▸*v.* **-tat•ed, -tat•ing.** To cut off (a part of the body), esp. by surgery. [Lat. *amputāre*, cut around.] —**am′pu•ta′tion** *n.* —**am′pu•ta′tor** *n.*

am•pu•tee (ăm′pyo͞o-tē′) ▸*n.* A person who has had one or more limbs amputated.

Am•ster•dam (ăm′stər-dăm′) The constitutional capital of the Netherlands, in the W part. Pop. 721,976.

amu ▸*abbr.* atomic mass unit

a•muck (ə-mŭk′) also **a•mok** (ə-mŭk′, ə-mŏk′) ▸*adv.* **1.** In a frenzy to do violence or kill: *rioters running amuck.* **2.** In a jumbled or confused state: *The plans went amuck.* [Malay *amok.*]

A•mu Dar•ya (ä′mo͞o där′yə, ə-mo͞o′ dŭr-yä′) A river of central Asia flowing about 2,574 km (1,600 mi) from the Pamir Mts. to the S Aral Sea.

am•u•let (ăm′yə-lĭt) ▸*n.* An object worn, esp. around the neck, as a charm against evil or injury. [Lat. *amulētum.*]

A•mund•sen (ä′mənd-sən, ä′mo͞on-), **Roald.** 1872–1928. Norwegian explorer; first person to reach the South Pole (1911).

A•mur River (ä-mo͝or′) also **Hei•long Jiang** (hā′lông′ jyäng′). A river of NE Asia flowing about 2,896 km (1,800 mi) mainly along the border between China and Russia.

a•muse (ə-myo͞oz′) ▸*v.* **a•mused, a•mus•ing 1.** To occupy in an entertaining fashion. **2.** To cause to laugh. [< OFr. *amuser*, stupefy.] —**a•mus′a•ble** *adj.* —**a•muse′ment** *n.*

am•y•lase (ăm′ə-lās′) ▸*n.* Any of a group of enzymes that convert starch to sugar. [Lat. *amyl(um)*, starch + –ASE.]

an (ən; ăn *when stressed*) ▸*indef. art.* The form of *a* used before words beginning with a vowel or with an unpronounced *h: an elephant; an hour.* [< OE *ān*, one.]

an. ▸*abbr. Lat.* **1.** anno (in the year) **2.** ante (before)

an– ▸*pref.* Var. of **a–**[1].

–an ▸*suff.* **1.** Of or resembling: *Korean.* **2.** One relating to or characterized by: *librarian.* [< Lat. *-ānus*, adj. and n. suff.]

ana– ▸*pref.* Upward; up: *anabolism.* [< Gk. *ana*, up.]

–ana or **–iana** ▸*suff.* A collection of items relating to a specified person or place: *Americana.* [< Lat. *-āna*, neuter pl. adj. and n. suff.]

An•a•bap•tist (ăn′ə-băp′tĭst) ▸*n.* A member of a radical Protestant movement of the 16th-cent. Reformation. [< LGk. *anabaptizein*, baptize again.] —**An′a•bap′tism** *n.*

a•nab•o•lism (ə-năb′ə-lĭz′əm) ▸*n.* Metabolic activity in which complex substances are synthesized from simpler substances. [ANA– + (META)BOLISM.] —**an′a•bol′ic** (ăn′ə-bŏl′ĭk) *adj.*

a•nach•ro•nism (ə-năk′rə-nĭz′əm) ▸*n.* **1.** Representation of something as existing or happening outside its historical order. **2.** One that is out of its proper or chronological order. [< Gk. *ana-*, back + *khronos*, time.] —**a•nach′ro•nis′tic, a•nach′ro•nous** (-nəs) *adj.* —**a•nach′ro•nis′ti•cal•ly, a•nach′ro•nous•ly** *adv.*

an•a•con•da (ăn′ə-kŏn′də) ▸*n.* A large nonvenomous snake of tropical South America that suffocates its prey in its coils. [Perh. < Sinhalese *henakandayā*, whip snake.]

A•nac•re•on (ə-năk′rē-ən). 563?–478? B.C. Greek poet.

an•aer•obe (ăn′ə-rōb′, ăn-âr′ōb′) ▸*n.* An organism, such as a bacterium, that can live in the absence of atmospheric oxygen. —**an′aer•o′bic** *adj.* —**an′aer•o′bi•cal•ly** *adv.*

an•aes•the•sia (ăn′ĭs-thē′zhə) ▸*n.* Var. of **anesthesia.**

an•a•gram (ăn′ə-grăm′) ▸*n.* A word formed by reordering the letters of another word, such as *satin* to *stain.* [< Gk. *anagrammatizein*, rearrange letters : ANA– + *gramma*, letter.]

An•a•heim (ăn′ə-hīm′) A city of S CA SE of Los Angeles. Pop. 266,406.

a•nal (ā′nəl) ▸*adj.* **1.** Of or near the anus. **2.** Relating to the second stage of psychosexual development in psychoanalytic theory. —**a′nal•ly** *adv.*

an•al•ge•si•a (ăn′əl-jē′zē-ə, -zhə) ▸*n.* A deadening of the sense of pain without loss of consciousness. [Gk. *analgēsia.*]

an•al•ge•sic (ăn′əl-jē′zĭk, -sĭk) ▸*n.* A medication that reduces or eliminates pain. —**an′al•ge′sic** *adj.*

a•nal•o•gous (ə-năl′ə-gəs) ▸*adj.* **1.** Similar or alike in such a way as to permit the drawing of an analogy. **2.** *Biol.* Similar in function but not in structure and evolutionary origin. —**a•nal′o•gous•ly** *adv.*

an•a•logue also **an•a•log** (ăn′ə-lôg′, -lŏg′) ▸*n.* Something that is analogous. ▸*adj.* often **analog** Of or relating to the representation of data by measurable physical variables: *an analog computer.*

a•nal•o•gy (ə-năl′ə-jē) ▸*n., pl.* **-gies 1a.** Similarity in some respects between things otherwise dissimilar. **b.** A comparison based on such similarity. **2.** *Biol.* Correspondence in function between organs of dissimilar evolution. **3.** An inference that if two things are alike in some respects they must be alike in others. [< Gk. *analogos*, proportionate.]

a•nal•y•sis (ə-năl′ĭ-sĭs) ▸*n., pl.* **-ses** (-sēz′) **1.** The separation of a whole into its parts for study. **2.** A statement of the results of such a separation or study. **3.** Psychoanalysis. **4.** Systems analysis. [< Gk. *analusis*, a dissolving.] —**an′a•lyst** (ăn′ə-lĭst) *n.*

an•a•lyt•ic (ăn′ə-lĭt′ĭk) or **an•a•lyt•i•cal** (-ĭ-kəl) ►*adj.* **1.** Relating to analysis. **2.** Reasoning or acting from a perception of the parts and interrelations of a subject. **3.** Expert in or using analysis, esp. in thinking. See Syns at **logical.** [< Gk. *analutikos.*] —**an′a•lyt′i•cal•ly** *adv.*

an•a•lyze (ăn′ə-līz′) ►*v.* **-lyzed, -lyz•ing 1.** To make an analysis of. **2.** To psychoanalyze. [< Gk. *analusis*, analysis.]

Syns: *analyze, anatomize, dissect* ***v.***

an•a•pest (ăn′ə-pĕst′) ►*n.* A metrical foot composed of two short syllables followed by one long one. [< Gk. *anapaistos.*] —**an′a•pes′tic** *adj.*

an•ar•chism (ăn′ər-kĭz′əm) ►*n.* **1.** The theory that all forms of government are oppressive and should be abolished. **2.** Terrorism against the state. —**an′ar•chist** *n.* —**an′ar•chis′tic** *adj.*

an•ar•chy (ăn′ər-kē) ►*n., pl.* **-chies 1.** Absence of governmental authority or law. **2.** Disorder and confusion. [< Gk. *anarkhos*, without a ruler.] —**an•ar′chic** (ăn-är′kĭk), **an•ar′chi•cal** *adj.* —**an•ar′chi•cal•ly** *adv.*

A•na•sa•zi (ä′nə-sä′zē) ►*n., pl.* **-zi** or **-zis.** A member of a former Native American people of the SW US whose descendants are considered to include the present-day Pueblo peoples.

a•nath•e•ma (ə-năth′ə-mə) ►*n., pl.* **-mas 1.** A formal ecclesiastical ban or excommunication. **2.** One that is greatly reviled or shunned. [< Gk. *anathēma*, an accursed thing.]

An•a•to•li•a (ăn′ə-tō′lē-ə, -tōl′yə) The Asian part of Turkey; usu. considered synonymous with Asia Minor.

An•a•to•li•an (ăn′ə-tō′lē-ən) ►*n.* **1.** A native or inhabitant of Anatolia. **2.** An extinct group of Indo-European languages of ancient Anatolia, including Hittite. —**An′a•to′li•an** *adj.*

a•nat•o•mize (ə-năt′ə-mīz′) ►*v.* **-mized, -miz•ing 1.** To dissect (an organism) for study. **2.** To analyze. See Syns at **analyze.**

a•nat•o•my (ə-năt′ə-mē) ►*n., pl.* **-mies 1.** The structure of an organism or organ. **2.** The science of the structure of organisms and their parts. **3.** A detailed analysis. [< Gk. *anatomē*, a cutting up.] —**an′a•tom′ic** (ăn′ə-tŏm′ĭk), **an′a•tom′i•cal** *adj.* —**an′a•tom′i•cal•ly** *adv.* —**a•nat′o•mist** *n.*

An•ax•ag•o•ras (ăn′ăk-săg′ər-əs). 500?–428 B.C. Greek philosopher.

-ance ►*suff.* **1.** State or condition: *repentance.* **2.** Action: *utterance.* [ME < Lat. *-antia*, n. suff.]

an•ces•tor (ăn′sĕs′tər) ►*n.* **1.** A person from whom one is remotely descended; forebear. **2.** A forerunner or predecessor. **3.** *Biol.* The organism from which later kinds evolved. [< Lat. *antecessor*, predecessor.] —**an•ces′tral** *adj.* —**an•ces′tral•ly** *adv.*

Syns: *ancestor, forebear, forefather, progenitor* ***Ant:*** *descendant* ***n.***

an•ces•try (ăn′sĕs′trē) ►*n., pl.* **-tries 1.** Descent or lineage. **2.** Ancestors collectively.

an•chor (ăng′kər) ►*n.* **1.** A heavy object attached to a vessel and cast overboard to keep the vessel in place. **2.** A source of security or stability. **3.** *Sports* An athlete who runs the last stage of a relay race. **4.** An anchorperson. ►*v.* **1.** To hold fast by or as if by an anchor. See Syns at **fasten. 2.** *Sports* To serve as an anchor for (a team). **3.** To narrate or coordinate (a newscast). [< Gk. *ankura.*]

an•chor•age (ăng′kər-ĭj) ►*n.* A place for anchoring ships.

Anchorage. A city of S AK SSW of Fairbanks. Pop. 226,338.

an•cho•rite (ăng′kə-rīt′) ►*n.* A religious hermit. [< LGk. *anakhōrētēs*, one who withdraws.] —**an′cho•rit′ic** (-rĭt′ĭk) *adj.*

an•chor•man (ăng′kər-măn′) ►*n.* **1.** A man who anchors a newscast. **2.** See **anchor** 3.

an•chor•per•son (ăng′kər-pûr′sən) ►*n.* An anchorman or anchorwoman.

an•chor•wom•an (ăng′kər-wo͝om′ən) ►*n.* A woman who anchors a newscast.

an•cho•vy (ăn′chō′vē) ►*n., pl.* **-vy** or **-vies.** A small, edible, herringlike marine fish. [Sp. *anchova.*]

an•cien ré•gime (äN-syăN′ rā-zhēm′) ►*n.* **1.** The political and social system that existed in France before the Revolution of 1789. **2.** A former or outmoded sociopolitical system. [Fr., old regime.]

an•cient (ān′shənt) ►*adj.* **1.** Of great age; very old. **2.** Relating to times long past, esp. before the fall of Rome (A.D. 476). ►*n.* **1.** A very old person. **2. ancients** The peoples of classical antiquity. [< Lat. *ante*, before.] —**an′cient•ly** *adv.*

an•cil•lar•y (ăn′sə-lĕr′ē) ►*adj.* **1.** Subordinate. **2.** Auxiliary; helping. [< Lat. *ancilla*, maidservant.]

-ancy ►*suff.* Condition or quality: *buoyancy.* [Lat. *-antia.*]

and (ənd, ən; ănd *when stressed*) ►*conj.* **1.** Together with or along with; as well as. **2.** Added to; plus. [< OE.]

Usage: The use of *and* or *but* to begin a sentence has a long and respectable history in English, occurring in writers from Shakespeare to Virginia Woolf.

An•da•lu•sia (ăn′də-lo͞o′zhə, -zhē-ə) A region of S Spain on the Mediterranean. —**An′da•lu′sian** *adj. & n.*

An•da•man Islands (ăn′də-mən) A group of Indian islands in the E part of the Bay of Bengal S of Myanmar (Burma); separated from the Malay Peninsula by the **Andaman Sea.**

an•dan•te (än-dän′tā) ►*adv. & adj. Mus.* In a moderately slow tempo. [Ital. < *andare*, walk.]

an•dan•ti•no (än′dän-tē′nō) ►*adv. & adj. Mus.* In a tempo slightly faster or slower than andante. [Ital.]

An•der•sen (ăn′dər-sən), **Hans Christian.** 1805–75. Danish writer.

An•der•son (ăn′dər-sən), **Marian.** 1902–93. Amer. contralto.

Anderson, Maxwell. 1888–1959. Amer. playwright.

Anderson, Sherwood. 1876–1941. Amer. writer.

An•des (ăn′dēz) A mountain system of W South America extending from Venezuela to Tierra del Fuego. —**An′de•an** *adj. & n.*

and•i•ron (ănd′ī′ərn) ►*n.* One of a pair of metal supports for logs in a fireplace. [< OFr. *andier.*]

Regional Note: Once limited to the North, *andiron* (contrasting with Southern *dog iron* and *fire dog*), *faucet* (contrasting with Southern *spigot*), and *frying pan* (contrasting with Midland and Upper Southern *skillet*), are now used across the United States. Formerly Southern words now used nationwide include *feisty* and *gutters*.

andiron

and/or (ăn′dôr′) ► *conj.* Used to indicate that either or both of the items connected by it are involved.

An•dor•ra (ăn-dôr′ə, -dŏr′ə) A tiny country of SW Europe between France and Spain in the E Pyrenees. Cap. Andorra la Vella. Pop. 65,000. —**An•dor′ran** *adj.* & *n.*

An•dre•a del Sar•to (än-drā′ə dĕl sär′tō). 1486–1531. Italian painter.

An•drew (ăn′dro͞o), Saint. One of the 12 Apostles.

andro– or **andr–** ► *pref.* Male; masculine: *androgen.* [< Gk. *anēr, andr-*.]

an•dro•gen (ăn′drə-jən) ► *n.* A hormone that controls and maintains masculine characteristics. —**an′dro•gen′ic** (-jĕn′ĭk) *adj.*

an•drog•y•nous (ăn-drŏj′ə-nəs) ► *adj.* **1.** *Biol.* Having both female and male characteristics; hermaphroditic. **2.** Being neither distinguishably masculine nor feminine. [ANDRO– + Gk. *gunē*, woman.] —**an•drog′y•nous•ly** *adv.* —**an•drog′y•ny** *n.*

an•droid (ăn′droid′) ► *n.* An automaton created from biological materials and resembling a human. —**an′droid** *adj.*

–andry ► *suff.* Kind or number of husbands: *polyandry.* [< Gk. *anēr, andr-*, man.]

–ane ► *suff.* A saturated hydrocarbon: *propane.* [Alteration of –ENE.]

an•ec•dote (ăn′ĭk-dōt′) ► *n.* A short account of an interesting or humorous incident. [< Gk. *anekdotos*, unpublished : A–[1] + *ek-*, out + *didonai*, give.] —**an′ec•dot′al** *adj.*

an•e•cho•ic (ăn′ĕ-kō′ĭk) ► *adj.* Neither having nor producing echoes.

a•ne•mi•a (ə-nē′mē-ə) ► *n.* A pathological deficiency in the oxygen-carrying component of the blood. —**a•ne′mic** *adj.*

an•e•mom•e•ter (ăn′ə-mŏm′ĭ-tər) ► *n.* An instrument for measuring wind force and velocity. [< Gk. *anemos*, wind.]

a•nem•o•ne (ə-nĕm′ə-nē) ► *n.* **1.** A perennial plant having lobed leaves and large flowers with showy sepals. **2.** The sea anemone. [< Gk. *anemōnē*.]

a•nent (ə-nĕnt′) ► *prep.* Regarding; concerning. [< OE *onefn*, near.]

an•er•oid barometer (ăn′ə-roid′) ► *n.* A barometer in which variations of atmospheric pressure are indicated by the relative bulges of a thin elastic metal disk covering a partially evacuated chamber. [A–[1] + Gk. *nēron*, water.]

an•es•the•sia also **an•aes•the•sia** (ăn′ĭs-thē′zhə) ► *n.* Total or partial loss of physical sensation caused by disease or an anesthetic. [< Gk. *anaisthēsia*, lack of sensation.]

an•es•the•si•ol•o•gy also **an•aes•the•si•ol•o•gy** (ăn′ĭs-thē′zē-ŏl′ə-jē) ► *n.* The medical study and application of anesthetics. —**an′es•the′si•ol′o•gist** *n.*

an•es•thet•ic also **an•aes•thet•ic** (ăn′ĭs-thĕt′ĭk) ► *adj.* Causing anesthesia. ► *n.* An agent or substance that induces anesthesia. —**an′es•thet′i•cal•ly** *adv.*

a•nes•the•tize also **a•naes•the•tize** (ə-nĕs′thĭ-tīz′) ► *v.* **-tized, -tiz•ing.** To induce anesthesia in. —**an•es′the•tist** *n.* —**an•es′the•ti•za′tion** *n.*

an•eu•rysm also **an•eu•rism** (ăn′yə-rĭz′əm) ► *n.* A pathological, blood-filled dilatation of a blood vessel. [< Gk. *aneurusma*.]

a•new (ə-no͞o′, -nyo͞o′) ► *adv.* **1.** Once more; again. **2.** In a new and different way.

an•gel (ān′jəl) ► *n.* **1a.** A usu. benevolent celestial being that acts as an intermediary between heaven and earth. **b.** *Christianity* An angel of the lowest order. **2.** A good, kind person. **3.** *Informal* A financial backer of an enterprise, esp. a dramatic production. [< Gk. *angelos*, messenger.] —**an•gel′ic** (ăn-jĕl′ĭk), **an•gel′i•cal** *adj.*

Angel Fall or **Falls.** A waterfall, about 980 m (3,212 ft), in SE Venezuela.

an•gel•fish (ān′jəl-fĭsh′) ► *n.*, *pl.* **-fish** or **-fish•es.** A brightly colored tropical fish having a laterally compressed body.

an•gel•i•ca (ăn-jĕl′ĭ-kə) ► *n.* An herb in the parsley family, whose roots and fruits are used in flavoring. [Med.Lat. *(herba) angelica*, angelic (herb).]

An•gel•i•co (ăn-jĕl′ĭ-kō′), Fra. 1400?–55. Italian Dominican friar and painter.

an•ger (ăng′gər) ► *n.* A strong feeling of displeasure, resentment, or hostility. ► *v.* To make or become angry. [< ON *angr*, grief.]

An•gers (ăn′jərz, äɴ-zhā′) A city of W France ENE of Nantes. Pop. 141,354.

an•gi•na (ăn-jī′nə) ► *n.* **1.** Angina pectoris. **2.** A condition in which spasmodic attacks of suffocating pain occur. [< Gk. *ankhonē*, a strangling.]

angina pec•to•ris (pĕk′tər-ĭs) ► *n.* Severe paroxysmal pain in the chest associated with an insufficient supply of blood to the heart. [NLat., angina of the chest.]

an•gi•o•gen•e•sis (ăn′jē-ō-jĕn′ĭ-sĭs) ► *n.* The formation of new blood vessels. [Gk. *angeion*, vessel + –GENESIS.] —**an′gi•o•gen′ic** (-jĕn′ĭk) *adj.*

an•gi•o•gram (ăn′jē-ə-grăm′) ► *n.* An x-ray of the blood vessels, used in diagnosis of the cardiovascular system. [Gk. *angeion*, vessel + –GRAM.]

an•gi•o•plas•ty (ăn′jē-ə-plăs′tē) ► *n.*, *pl.* **-ties.** A surgical procedure that uses a catheter fitted with an inflatable tip to clear blocked arteries. [Gk. *angeion*, vessel + E. *-plasty*, surgical repair.]

an•gi•o•sperm (ăn′jē-ə-spûrm′) ► *n.* A seed-bearing plant whose ovules are enclosed in an ovary; a flowering plant. [Gk. *angeion*, vessel + SPERM.]

Ang•kor (ăng′kôr, -kōr) An archaeological site in NW Cambodia and capital of the Khmer empire (9th–15th cent.).

an•gle[1] (ăng′gəl) ► *v.* **-gled, -gling 1.** To fish

with a hook and line. **2.** To try to get something by using schemes or tricks. [< OE *angul*, fishhook.] —**an′gler** *n.*

an•gle² (ăng′gəl) ►*n.* **1.** *Math.* **a.** The figure formed by two lines diverging from a common point. **b.** The figure formed by two planes diverging from a common line. **c.** The space between such lines or surfaces. **2.** A corner, as of a building. **3a.** The place or direction from which an object is seen. **b.** A point of view. **4.** *Slang* A devious method; scheme. ►*v.* **-gled, -gling 1.** To move or turn at an angle. **2.** *Informal* To impart a biased point of view to. [< Lat. *angulus.*]

An•gle (ăng′gəl) ►*n.* A member of a Germanic people that migrated to England from S Jutland in the 5th cent. A.D. and formed part of the Anglo-Saxon peoples.

an•gle•worm (ăng′gəl-wûrm′) ►*n.* An earthworm used as bait in fishing.

An•gli•can (ăng′glĭ-kən) ►*adj.* Relating to the Church of England or to the churches in communion with it. —**An′gli•can** *n.* —**An′gli•can•ism** *n.*

An•gli•cism (ăng′glĭ-sĭz′əm) ►*n.* A word, phrase, or idiom peculiar to the English language, esp. as spoken in England.

An•gli•cize (ăng′glĭ-sīz′) ►*v.* **-cized, -ciz•ing.** To make or become English. —**An′gli•ci•za′tion** *n.*

An•glo (ăng′glō) ►*n., pl.* **-glos.** An English-speaking person, esp. a white North American. —**An′glo** *adj.*

Usage: In contemporary American usage, *Anglo* is used primarily in direct contrast to *Hispanic* or *Latino.* In this context it is not limited to persons of English or even British descent, but can be generally applied to any English-speaking, non-Hispanic white person.

Anglo– ►*pref.* England; English: *Anglophile.* [< LLat. *Anglī*, the Angles.]

An•glo-A•mer•i•can (ăng′glō-ə-mĕr′ĭ-kən) ►*n.* An American of English ancestry. ►*adj.* Relating to England and the US.

An•glo•cen•tric (ăng′glō-sĕn′trĭk) ►*adj.* Centered or focused on England or the English. —**An′glo•cen′trism** *n.* —**An′glo•cen′trist** *adj. & n.*

An•glo-Nor•man (ăng′glō-nôr′mən) ►*n.* **1.** A Norman settler in England after 1066. **2.** The dialect of Old French used by the Anglo-Normans. —**An′glo-Nor′man** *adj.*

An•glo•phile (ăng′glə-fīl′) also **An•glo•phil** (-fĭl) ►*n.* One who admires England and its culture. —**An′glo•phil′i•a** (-fĭl′ē-ə) *n.*

An•glo•phobe (ăng′glə-fōb′) ►*n.* One who dislikes England or its culture. —**An′glo•pho′bi•a** *n.* —**An′glo•pho′bic** *adj.*

An•glo•phone (ăn′glə-fōn′) ►*n.* An English-speaking person, esp. in a region of linguistic diversity.

An•glo-Sax•on (ăng′glō-săk′sən) ►*n.* **1.** A member of one of the Germanic peoples who migrated to Britain in the 5th and 6th cent. **2.** See **Old English. 3.** A person of English ancestry. —**An′glo-Sax′on** *adj.*

An•go•la (ăng-gō′lə, ăn-) A country of SW Africa bordering on the Atlantic Ocean. Cap. Luanda. Pop. 8,140,000. —**An•go′lan** *adj. & n.*

An•go•ra (ăng-gôr′ə, -gōr′ə) ►*n.* **1.** A cat, goat, or rabbit with long silky hair. **2.** often **angora** A yarn or fabric made from the hair of the Angora goat or rabbit. [After *Angora* (Ankara), Turkey.]

an•gry (ăng′grē) ►*adj.* **-gri•er, -gri•est 1.** Feeling or showing anger. **2.** Resulting from anger: *an angry silence.* **3.** Having a menacing aspect; threatening: *angry clouds.* **4.** Inflamed and painful.

Syns: *angry, furious, indignant, irate, ireful, mad, wrathful* **adj.**

angst (ängkst) ►*n.* A feeling of anxiety. [Ger.]

ang•strom or **ång•strom** (ăng′strəm) ►*n.* A unit of length equal to one hundred-millionth (10^{-8}) of a centimeter. [After Anders Jonas Ångström (1814–1874).]

An•guil•la (ăng-gwĭl′ə, ăn-) An island of the British West Indies in the N Leeward Is.

an•guish (ăng′gwĭsh) ►*n.* Agonizing physical or mental pain; torment. ►*v.* To cause or suffer anguish. [< Lat. *angustiae*, distress.]

an•gu•lar (ăng′gyə-lər) ►*adj.* **1.** Having an angle or angles. **2.** Measured by an angle. **3.** Bony and lean; gaunt. —**an′gu•lar′i•ty** (-lăr′ĭ-tē) *n.* —**an′gu•lar•ly** *adv.*

an•hy•dride (ăn-hī′drīd′) ►*n.* A chemical compound formed from another by the removal of water. [ANHYDR(OUS) + –IDE.]

an•hy•drous (ăn-hī′drəs) ►*adj.* Without water. [< Gk. *anudros* : AN– + *hudōr*, water.]

an•i•line also **an•i•lin** (ăn′ə-lĭn) ►*n.* A colorless, oily, poisonous benzene derivative, $C_6H_5NH_2$, used in rubber, dyes, resins, pharmaceuticals, and varnishes. [< *anil*, indigo.] —**an′i•line** *adj.*

an•i•mad•vert (ăn′ə-măd-vûrt′) ►*v.* To comment critically, usu. with disapproval. [< Lat. *animadvertere*, direct the mind to.] —**an′i•mad•ver′sion** *n.*

an•i•mal (ăn′ə-məl) ►*n.* **1.** An organism of the kingdom Animalia, differing from plants in certain typical characteristics such as capacity for locomotion. **2.** An animal organism other than a human. **3.** A brutish person. ►*adj.* **1.** Of or relating to animals. **2.** Relating to the physical as distinct from the spiritual nature of people: *animal instincts.* [Lat. < *anima*, spirit.]

an•i•mal•cule (ăn′ə-măl′kyo͞ol) ►*n.* A microscopic animal organism. [NLat. *animalculum.*]

animal husbandry ►*n.* The care and breeding of domestic animals.

animal rights ►*pl.n.* The rights to humane treatment claimed on behalf of animals.

an•i•mate (ăn′ə-māt′) ►*v.* **-mat•ed, -mat•ing 1.** To give life to. **2.** To impart interest to. **3.** To fill with spirit. See Syns at **encourage. 4.** To produce (e.g., a cartoon) with the illusion of motion. ►*adj.* (ăn′ə-mĭt) **1.** Possessing life; living. **2.** Relating to animal life. [Lat. *animāre* < *anima*, spirit.]

an•i•mat•ed (ăn′ə-mā′tĭd) ►*adj.* **1.** Spirited; lively. **2.** Designed so as to appear alive and moving. —**an′i•mat′ed•ly** *adv.*

animated cartoon ►*n.* A motion picture or television film consisting of a series of drawings, objects, or computer graphics photographed sequentially to simulate motion.

a•ni•ma•to (ä′nē-mä′tō) ►*adv. & adj. Mus.* In an animated or lively manner. [Ital. < Lat. *animāre*, ANIMATE.]

an•i•ma•tor (ăn′ə-mā′tər) ►*n.* One that animates, esp. an artist or technician who produces animated cartoons.

an•i•me (ăn′ə-mā′) ►*n.* A style of animation

marked by colorful art, futuristic settings, and violence. [Jap. < ANI MATION.]

an•i•mism (ăn′ə-mĭz′əm) ►*n.* The belief that natural phenomena or inanimate objects possess spirits. [< Lat. *anima*, spirit.] —**an′i•mist** *n.* —**an′i•mis′tic** *adj.*

an•i•mos•i•ty (ăn′ə-mŏs′ĭ-tē) ►*n.*, *pl.* **-ties.** Bitter hostility or open enmity. [< Lat. *animōsus*, bold.]

an•i•mus (ăn′ə-məs) ►*n.* **1.** An attitude; disposition. **2.** Animosity. [Lat., spirit.]

an•i•on (ăn′ī′ən) ►*n.* A negatively charged ion, esp. one that migrates to an anode. [< Gk. *anienai*, go up.] —**an′i•on′ic** (-ŏn′ĭk) *adj.* —**an′i•on′i•cal•ly** *adv.*

an•ise (ăn′ĭs) ►*n.* **1.** An annual aromatic Mediterranean herb in the parsley family used as flavoring. **2.** Anise seed. [< Gk. *anison.*]

anise seed or **an•i•seed** (ăn′ĭ-sēd′) ►*n.* The seedlike fruit of the anise.

an•i•sette (ăn′ĭ-sĕt′, -zĕt′) ►*n.* A liqueur flavored with anise. [Fr.]

An•jou[1] (ăn′jo͞o′, äN-zho͞o′) A historical region and former province of NW France in the Loire R. valley.

An•jou[2] (ăn′zho͞o, -jo͞o) ►*n.* A variety of pear.

An•ka•ra (ăng′kər-ə, äng′-) The capital of Turkey, in the W-central part. Pop. 2,782,200.

ankh (ăngk) ►*n.* A cross shaped like a T with a loop at the top. [Egypt. *ʻnḫ*, life.]

ankh

an•kle (ăng′kəl) ►*n.* **1.** The joint between the foot and the leg. **2.** The slender section of the leg above the foot. [ME *ancle.*]

an•kle•bone (ăng′kəl-bōn′) ►*n.* See **talus.**

an•klet (ăng′klĭt) ►*n.* **1.** An ornament worn around the ankle. **2.** A sock that reaches just above the ankle.

Ann (ăn), **Cape.** A peninsula of NE MA projecting into the Atlantic.

an•nals (ăn′əlz) ►*pl.n.* **1.** A chronological record of the events of successive years. **2.** A descriptive account or record; history. **3.** A periodical journal in which the records and reports of a learned field are compiled. [< Lat. *annus*, year.] —**an′nal•ist** *n.* —**an′nal•is′tic** *adj.*

An•nam (ə-năm′, ăn′ăm′) A region and former kingdom of E-central Vietnam on the South China Sea. —**An′na•mese′** (ăn′ə-mēz′, -mēs′) *adj. & n.*

An•nap•o•lis (ə-năp′ə-lĭs) The capital of MD, in the central part on an inlet of Chesapeake Bay SSE of Baltimore. Pop. 33,187.

An•na•pur•na (ăn′ə-po͝or′nə, -pûr′-) A massif of the Himalaya Mountains in N-central Nepal. It rises to approximately 8,084 m (26,504 ft) at **Annapurna I** in the W and approximately 7,943 m (26,041 ft) at **Annapurna II** in the E.

Ann Arbor. A city of SE MI W of Detroit. Pop. 109,592.

Anne (ăn). 1665–1714. Queen of Great Britain and Ireland (1702–14).

an•neal (ə-nēl′) ►*v.* **1.** To heat (glass or metal) and slowly cool it to toughen and reduce brittleness. **2.** To temper. [< OE *onǣlan.*]

an•ne•lid (ăn′ə-lĭd) ►*n.* Any of various worms with cylindrical segmented bodies, including the earthworm and leech. [< Lat. *ānellus*, small ring.]

an•nex (ə-nĕks′) ►*v.* **1.** To add, esp. to a larger thing. **2.** To incorporate (territory) into a larger existing political unit. ►*n.* (ăn′ĕks′). A building near or added on to a larger one. [< Lat. *annectere, annex-*, connect to.] —**an′nex•a′tion** *n.* —**an′nex•a′tion•ist** *n.*

an•ni•hi•late (ə-nī′ə-lāt′) ►*v.* **-lat•ed, -lat•ing.** To destroy completely. [LLat. *annihilāre.*] —**an•ni′hi•la′tion** *n.*

an•ni•ver•sa•ry (ăn′ə-vûr′sə-rē) ►*n.*, *pl.* **-ries.** The annually recurring date of a past event. [< Lat. *anniversārius*, returning yearly.]

an•no Dom•i•ni (ăn′ō dŏm′ə-nī′, -nē) ►*adv.* In a specified year of the Christian era. [Med. Lat., in the year of the Lord.]

an•no•tate (ăn′ō-tāt′) ►*v.* **-tat•ed, -tat•ing.** To furnish (a literary work) with critical commentary or explanatory notes. [Lat. *annotāre*, note down.] —**an′no•ta′tion** *n.* —**an′no•ta′tive** *adj.* —**an′no•ta′tor** *n.*

an•nounce (ə-nouns′) ►*v.* **-nounced, -nounc•ing 1.** To make known publicly. **2.** To proclaim the arrival of. **3.** To serve as an announcer (for). [< Lat. *annūntiāre*, report to.] —**an•nounce′ment** *n.*

Syns: *announce, advertise, broadcast, declare, proclaim, promulgate, publish* ***v.***

an•nounc•er (ə-noun′sər) ►*n.* One who announces, esp. a radio or television employee who provides program continuity and delivers announcements or commentaries.

an•noy (ə-noi′) ►*v.* To bother or irritate. [< VLat. **inodiāre*, make odious.] —**an•noy′ing•ly** *adv.*

an•noy•ance (ə-noi′əns) ►*n.* **1.** The act of annoying or the state of being annoyed. **2.** A cause of vexation; nuisance.

an•nu•al (ăn′yo͞o-əl) ►*adj.* **1.** Recurring or done every year; yearly. **2.** Determined by a year: *an annual income.* **3.** *Bot.* Living or growing for only one year or season. ►*n.* **1.** A periodical published yearly; yearbook. **2.** *Bot.* An annual plant. [< Lat. *annus*, year.] —**an′nu•al•ly** *adv.*

annual ring ►*n.* The layer of wood, esp. in a tree, formed during a single year.

an•nu•i•tant (ə-no͞o′ĭ-tənt, -nyo͞o′-) ►*n.* One that receives an annuity.

an•nu•i•ty (ə-no͞o′ĭ-tē, -nyo͞o′-) ►*n.*, *pl.* **-ties 1.** The annual payment of an allowance or income. **2.** An investment on which one receives fixed payments for a lifetime or for a specified period. [< Lat. *annuus*, yearly.]

an•nul (ə-nŭl′) ►*v.* **-nulled, -nul•ling.** To declare invalid, as a marriage or a law; nullify. [< LLat. *annullāre.*] —**an•nul′ment** *n.*

an•nu•lar (ăn′yə-lər) ►*adj.* Ring-shaped.

an•nu•lus (ăn′yə-ləs) ►*n.*, *pl.* **-lus•es** or **-li** (-lī′). A ringlike figure, part, structure, or marking. [Lat. *ānulus*, ring.]

an•nun•ci•ate (ə-nŭn′sē-āt′) ►*v.* **-at•ed, -at•ing.** To announce; proclaim. [Lat. *annūntiāre*, report to.]

an•nun•ci•a•tion (ə-nŭn′sē-ā′shən) ►*n.* **1.** The act of announcing. **2.** An announcement; proclamation. **3. Annunciation** *Christianity* The angel Gabriel's announcement to the Virgin Mary of the Incarnation.

an•ode (ăn′ōd′) ►*n.* A positively charged electrode. [Gk. *anodos*, a way up.]

an•o•dize (ăn′ə-dīz′) ►*v.* **-dized, -diz•ing.** To coat (a metal) electrolytically with an oxide.

an•o•dyne (ăn′ə-dīn′) ►*n.* **1.** A medicine that relieves pain. **2.** A source of comfort. [< Gk. *anōdunos*, free from pain : AN– + *odunē*, pain.] —**an′o•dyne** *adj.*

a•noint (ə-noint′) ►*v.* **1.** To apply oil or ointment to, esp. in a religious ceremony. **2.** To choose by or as if by divine intervention. [< Lat. *inunguere*.] —**a•noint′ment** *n.*

a•no•le (ə-nō′lē) ►*n.* Any of a genus of tropical American lizards having the ability to change color. [Of Cariban orig.]

a•nom•a•ly (ə-nŏm′ə-lē) ►*n.*, *pl.* **-lies 1.** Deviation from the normal order, form, or rule. **2.** One that is peculiar, abnormal, or difficult to classify. [< Gk. *anōmalos*, uneven.] —**a•nom′a•lis′tic** (-lĭs′tĭk) *adj.* —**a•nom′a•lous** *adj.*

a•non (ə-nŏn′) ►*adv. Archaic* At once; forthwith. [< OE *on ān*.]

anon. ►*abbr.* anonymous

a•non•y•mous (ə-nŏn′ə-məs) ►*adj.* Having an unknown or unacknowledged name, authorship, or agency. [< Gk. *anōnumos*, nameless.] —**an′o•nym′i•ty** (ăn′ə-nĭm′ĭ-tē) *n.* —**a•non′y•mous•ly** *adv.*

a•noph•e•les (ə-nŏf′ə-lēz′) ►*n.* A mosquito that transmits malaria to humans. [< Gk. *anōphelēs*, useless.]

an•o•rak (ăn′ə-răk′) ►*n.* A parka. [Inuit *annoraaq*.]

anorak

an•o•rec•tic (ăn′ə-rĕk′tĭk) ►*adj.* **1.** Marked by or causing loss of appetite. **2.** Of or afflicted with anorexia nervosa. [< Gk. *anorektos*.] —**an′o•rec′tic** *n.*

an•o•rex•i•a (ăn′ə-rĕk′sē-ə) ►*n.* **1.** Loss of appetite, esp. as a result of disease. **2.** Anorexia nervosa. [Gk.]

anorexia ner•vo•sa (nûr-vō′sə) ►*n.* A psychophysiological disorder usu. occurring in teenage women, marked by an abnormal fear of becoming obese. [NLat., nervous anorexia.]

an•o•rex•ic (ăn′ə-rĕk′sĭk) ►*adj.* **1.** Afflicted with anorexia nervosa. **2.** Anorectic. —**an′o•rex′ic** *n.*

an•oth•er (ə-nŭth′ər) ►*adj.* **1.** One more; an additional: *another cup of coffee.* **2.** Different: *tried another method.* **3.** Some other: *costumes from another era.* ►*pron.* **1.** An additional or different one. **2.** One of an undetermined number.

A•nou•ilh (ä-no͞o′ē), **Jean.** 1910–87. French playwright.

An•shan (än′shän′) A city of NE China SSW of Shenyang. Pop. 2,478,650.

ANSI ►*abbr.* American National Standards Institute

an•swer (ăn′sər) ►*n.* **1.** A spoken or written reply, as to a question. **2.** A solution, as to a problem. **3.** An act in response. ►*v.* **1.** To reply (to). **2.** To be liable or accountable. **3.** To suffice. See Syns at **satisfy. 4.** To correspond (to); match. [< OE *andswaru*.] —**an′swer•a•ble** *adj.* —**an′swer•a•bly** *adv.*

an•swer•ing machine (ăn′sər-ĭng) ►*n.* An electronic device for answering one's telephone and recording callers' messages.

ant (ănt) ►*n.* Any of various social insects usu. having wings only in the males and fertile females and living in complexly organized colonies. [< OE *ǣmete*.]

ant. ►*abbr.* antonym

Ant. ►*abbr.* Antarctica

ant– ►*pref.* Var. of **anti–.**

–ant ►*suff.* **1a.** Performing or promoting an action: *conversant.* **b.** In a state or condition: *expectant.* **2.** One that performs or promotes an action: *stimulant.* [< Lat. *-āns*, *-ant-*, present participle suff.]

ant•ac•id (ănt-ăs′ĭd) ►*adj.* Counteracting acidity, esp. of the stomach. ►*n.* A substance, such as sodium bicarbonate, that neutralizes acid.

an•tag•o•nism (ăn-tăg′ə-nĭz′əm) ►*n.* **1.** Hostility; enmity. **2.** The condition of being an opposing force.

an•tag•o•nist (ăn-tăg′ə-nĭst) ►*n.* **1.** One who opposes; adversary. **2.** The principal character in opposition to the protagonist or hero of a narrative or drama. **3.** *Physiol.* A muscle that counteracts the action of another muscle, the agonist. —**an•tag′o•nis′tic** *adj.* —**an•tag′o•nis′ti•cal•ly** *adv.*

an•tag•o•nize (ăn-tăg′ə-nīz′) ►*v.* **-nized, -niz•ing.** To incur the dislike of. [Gk. *antagōnizesthai*, struggle against : ANTI– + *agōn*, contest; see AGONY.]

An•ta•na•na•ri•vo (ăn′tə-năn′ə-rē′vō, än′tə-nä′nə-). Formerly **Ta•na•na•rive** (tə-năn′ə-rēv′, tä-nä-nä-rēv′). The capital of Madagascar, in the E-central part. Pop. 700,000.

Ant•arc•ti•ca (ănt-ärk′tĭ-kə, -är′tĭ-) An ice-covered continent asymmetrically centered on the South Pole. —**Ant•arc′tic** *adj.*

Antarctic Circle. The parallel of latitude (approx. 66°33′ S) that separates the South Temperate and South Frigid zones.

Antarctic Ocean. The waters surrounding Antarctica, actually the S extensions of the Atlantic, Pacific, and Indian oceans.

An•tar•es (ăn-târ′ēz, -tăr′-) ►*n.* The brightest star in the constellation Scorpio.

an•te (ăn′tē) ►*n.* **1.** The stake each poker player puts into the pool before receiving a hand or before receiving new cards. See Syns at **bet. 2.** A price to be paid, esp. as one's share. ►*v.* **-ted**

or **-teed, -te•ing 1.** To put up (one's stake) in poker. **2.** To pay (one's share). [< Lat., before.]

ante– ►*pref.* **1.** Earlier: *antedate.* **2.** In front of: *anteroom.* [Lat.]

ant•eat•er (ănt′ē′tər) ►*n.* Any of several tropical American mammals that lack teeth and feed on ants and termites.

an•te•bel•lum (ăn′tē-bĕl′əm) ►*adj.* Of the period before the American Civil War. [Lat. *ante bellum*, before the war.]

an•te•ce•dent (ăn′tĭ-sēd′nt) ►*adj.* Going before; preceding. ►*n.* **1.** One that precedes. **2.** A preceding occurrence or cause. **3. antecedents** One's ancestors. **4.** *Gram.* The word, phrase, or clause to which a pronoun refers. [< Lat. *antecēdere*, go before.] —**an′te•cede′** *v.* —**an′te•ce′dence** *n.*

an•te•cham•ber (ăn′tē-chām′bər) ►*n.* An anteroom.

an•te•date (ăn′tĭ-dāt′) ►*v.* **-dat•ed, -dat•ing 1.** To precede in time. **2.** To give a date earlier than the actual one.

an•te•di•lu•vi•an (ăn′tĭ-də-lo͞o′vē-ən) ►*adj.* **1.** Extremely old and antiquated. **2.** *Bible* Occurring before the Flood. [< ANTE– + Lat. *dīluvium*, flood (< *dīluere*, wash away; see DILUTE).] —**an′te•di•lu′vi•an** *n.*

an•te•lope (ăn′tl-ōp′) ►*n., pl.* **-lope** or **-lopes 1.** Any of various swift-running ruminant mammals of Africa and Asia, having long horns and a slender build. **2.** The pronghorn. [< LGk. *antholops*.]

an•te me•rid•i•em (ăn′tē mə-rĭd′ē-əm) ►*adv. & adj.* Before noon. [Lat.]

Usage: Strictly speaking, *12 A.M.* denotes midnight, and *12 P.M.* denotes noon, but there is sufficient confusion over these uses to make it advisable to use *12 noon* and *12 midnight* where clarity is required.

an•ten•na (ăn-tĕn′ə) ►*n., pl.* **-ten•nae** (-tĕn′ē) **1.** One of the paired, flexible sensory organs on the head of an insect, myriapod, or crustacean. **2.** *pl.* **-nas** An apparatus for sending or receiving electromagnetic waves. [< Lat., sail yard.]

an•te•pe•nult (ăn′tē-pē′nŭlt′) ►*n.* The third syllable from the end in a word, such as *te* in *antepenult.* [< LLat. *antepaenultimus*, next to last.]

an•te•ri•or (ăn-tîr′ē-ər) ►*adj.* **1.** Placed before or in front. **2.** Prior in time. [Lat.]

an•te•room (ăn′tē-ro͞om′, -ro͝om′) ►*n.* An outer room that opens into another room, often used as a waiting room.

an•them (ăn′thəm) ►*n.* **1.** A hymn of praise or loyalty. **2.** A sacred choral composition. [< LGk. *antiphōnos*, sounding in answer.]

an•ther (ăn′thər) ►*n.* The pollen-bearing part of the stamen. [Ult. < Gk. *anthos*, flower.]

ant•hill (ănt′hĭl′) ►*n.* A mound of earth formed by ants or termites in digging a nest.

an•thol•o•gy (ăn-thŏl′ə-jē) ►*n., pl.* **-gies.** A collection of selected writings. [< Gk. *anthologia*, gathering of flowers.] —**an•thol′o•gist** *n.* —**an•thol′o•gize′** *v.*

An•tho•ny (ăn′thə-nē), Saint. A.D. 250?–350? Egyptian ascetic monk considered the founder of Christian monasticism.

Anthony, Susan Brownell. 1820–1906. Amer. feminist leader and suffragist.

Susan B. Anthony

an•thra•cite (ăn′thrə-sīt′) ►*n.* A dense shiny coal that has a high carbon content. [Prob. < Gk. *anthrakitis*, a kind of coal.] —**an′thra•cit′ic** (-sĭt′ĭk) *adj.*

an•thrax (ăn′thrăks′) ►*n.* An infectious, usu. fatal bacterial disease esp. of cattle and sheep, marked by skin ulcers and transmissible to humans. [< Gk., carbuncle.]

anthropo– ►*pref.* Human: *anthropoid.* [< Gk. *anthrōpos*, human being.]

an•thro•po•cen•tric (ăn′thrə-pə-sĕn′trĭk) ►*adj.* Interpreting reality in terms of human values and experience. —**an′thro•po•cen′trism** *n.*

an•thro•po•gen•ic (ăn′thrə-pə-jĕn′ĭk) ►*adj.* **1.** Relating to the origin and development of humans. **2.** Caused by humans. —**an′thro•po•gen′i•cal•ly** *adv.*

an•thro•poid (ăn′thrə-poid′) ►*adj.* Resembling a human, as the great apes. ►*n.* A great ape, such as a gorilla.

an•thro•pol•o•gy (ăn′thrə-pŏl′ə-jē) ►*n.* The scientific study of the origin, culture, and development of humans. —**an′thro•po•log′i•cal** (-pə-lŏj′ĭ-kəl), **an′thro•po•log′ic** (-ĭk) *adj.* —**an′thro•pol′o•gist** *n.*

an•thro•po•mor•phism (ăn′thrə-pə-môr′fĭz′əm) ►*n.* Attribution of human characteristics to animals, inanimate objects, or natural phenomena. —**an′thro•po•mor′phic** *adj.* —**an′thro•po•mor′phize** *v.*

an•ti (ăn′tī, -tē) ►*n., pl.* **-tis.** One who is opposed. [< ANTI–.] —**an′ti** *adj. & prep.*

anti– or **ant–** ►*pref.* **1a.** Opposite: *antiparticle.* **b.** Opposed to: *antinuclear.* **c.** Counteracting: *antibody.* **2.** Inverse: *antilogarithm.* [< Gk. *anti*, opposite.]

an•ti•a•bor•tion (ăn′tē-ə-bôr′shən, ăn′tī-) ►*adj.* Opposed to abortion. —**an′ti•a•bor′tion•ist** *n.*

an•ti•bal•lis•tic missile (ăn′tĭ-bə-lĭs′tĭk, ăn′tī-) ►*n.* A defensive missile designed to intercept and destroy a ballistic missile in flight.

an•ti•bi•ot•ic (ăn′tĭ-bī-ŏt′ĭk, ăn′tī-) ►*n.* A substance, such as penicillin or streptomycin, that destroys or inhibits the growth of microorganisms and is widely used to treat infectious diseases. —**an′ti•bi•ot′ic** *adj.*

an•ti•bod•y (ăn′tĭ-bŏd′ē) ►*n.* A protein produced in the blood as an immune response to a specific antigen.

an•tic (ăn′tĭk) ►*n.* A ludicrous act or gesture. [Ital. *antico*, ancient.] —**an′tic** *adj.*

an•ti-choice (ăn′tē-chois′, ăn′tī-) ►*adj.* Opposed to the right of women to choose or reject abortion.

an•ti•christ (ăn′tĭ-krīst′, ăn′tī-) ►*n.* **1.** An enemy of Christ. **2. Antichrist** *Bible* The antagonist expected to oppose Christ in the last days. **3.** A false Christ.

an•tic•i•pate (ăn-tĭs′ə-pāt′) ►*v.* **-pat•ed, -pat•ing 1.** To foresee. **2.** To look forward to; expect. **3.** To act in advance to prevent; forestall. [Lat. *anticipāre*, take before.] —**an•tic′i•pa′tion** *n.* —**an•tic′i•pa′tor** *n.* —**an•tic′i•pa•to′ry** (-pə-tôr′ē, -tōr′ē) *adj.*

an•ti•cler•i•cal (ăn′tē-klĕr′ĭ-kəl, ăn′tī-) ►*adj.* Opposed to the influence of the church in politics. —**an′ti•cler′i•cal•ism** *n.*

an•ti•cli•max (ăn′tē-klī′măks′, ăn′tī-) ►*n.* **1.** A decline viewed in disappointing contrast to previous events. **2.** Something commonplace that concludes a series of significant events. —**an′ti•cli•mac′tic** *adj.*

an•ti•cy•clone (ăn′tē-sī′klōn′, ăn′tī-) ►*n.* A system of winds spiraling outward from a high-pressure center. —**an′ti•cy•clon′ic** (-klŏn′ĭk) *adj.*

an•ti•de•pres•sant (ăn′tē-dĭ-prĕs′ənt, ăn′tī-) ►*n.* A drug used to treat mental depression. —**an′ti•de•pres′sive** *adj.*

an•ti•dote (ăn′tĭ-dōt′) ►*n.* **1.** An agent that counteracts a poison. **2.** Something that relieves or counteracts. [< Gk. *antidoton* : ANTI–, anti- + *didonai*, *do-*, give.] —**an′ti•dot′al** *adj.*

Usage: *Antidote* may be followed by *to, for,* or *against: an antidote to boredom; an antidote for snakebite; an antidote against inflation.*

An•tie•tam (ăn-tē′təm) A creek of N-central MD emptying into the Potomac R.; site of a Civil War Battle (1862).

an•ti•freeze (ăn′tĭ-frēz′) ►*n.* A substance, such as ethylene glycol, mixed with another liquid to lower its freezing point.

an•ti•gen (ăn′tĭ-jən) ►*n.* A substance, such as a toxin, bacterium, or foreign cell, that when introduced into the body stimulates the production of an antibody. —**an′ti•gen′ic** (-jĕn′ĭk) *adj.* —**an′ti•ge•nic′i•ty** (-jə-nĭs′ĭ-tē) *n.*

An•ti•gua and Barbuda (ăn-tē′gə) A country in the N Leeward Is. of the Caribbean Sea, comprising the islands of **Antigua,** Barbuda, and Redonda. Cap. St. John's. Pop. 72,000. —**An•ti′guan** *adj. & n.*

an•ti•he•ro also **an•ti-he•ro** (ăn′tē-hîr′ō, ăn′tī-) ►*n., pl.* **-roes.** A fictional or dramatic character lacking traditional heroic qualities. —**an′ti•her•o′ic** (-hĭ-rō′ĭk) *adj.*

an•ti•her•o•ine or **an•ti-her•o•ine** (ăn′tē-hĕr′ō-ĭn, ăn′tī-) ►*n.* A woman protagonist who lacks traditional heroic qualities or who acts counter to traditional expectations of women.

an•ti•his•ta•mine (ăn′tē-hĭs′tə-mēn′, -mĭn) ►*n.* A drug used to counteract the physiological effects of histamine production in allergic reactions and colds. —**an′ti•his′ta•min′ic** (-mĭn′ĭk) *adj.*

an•ti•knock (ăn′tĭ-nŏk′) ►*n.* A substance added to gasoline to reduce engine knock.

An•til•les (ăn-tĭl′ēz) The islands of the West Indies except for the Bahamas, separating the Caribbean Sea from the Atlantic and divided into the **Greater Antilles** to the N and the **Lesser Antilles** to the E.

an•ti•lock (ăn′tē-lŏk′, ăn′tī-) ►*adj.* Of or being a motor vehicle braking system in which wheel speeds are electronically adjusted to prevent locking.

an•ti•log (ăn′tē-lôg′, -lŏg′, ăn′tī-) ►*n.* An antilogarithm.

an•ti•log•a•rithm (ăn′tē-lô′gə-rĭ*th*′əm, -lŏg′ə-, ăn′tī-) ►*n.* The number for which a given logarithm stands; e.g., where log *x* equals *y*, then *x* is the antilogarithm of *y*.

an•ti•ma•cas•sar (ăn′tē-mə-kăs′ər) ►*n.* A protective covering for the backs of chairs and sofas. [ANTI– + *Macassar*, a brand of hair oil.]

an•ti•mat•ter (ăn′tĭ-măt′ər, ăn′tī-) ►*n.* A hypothetical form of matter identical to physical matter except that it is composed of antiparticles.

an•ti•mo•ny (ăn′tə-mō′nē) ►*n. Symbol* **Sb** A metallic element used in a wide variety of alloys, esp. with lead in battery plates, and in paints, semiconductors, and ceramics. At. no. 51. See table at **element.** [< Med.Lat. *antimonium.*]

an•ti•neu•tron (ăn′tē-no͞o′trŏn′, -nyo͞o′-, ăn′tī-) ►*n.* The antiparticle of the neutron.

an′ti•air′craft′ *adj. & n.*
an′ti•al•ler′gic *adj.*
an′ti-A•mer′i•can *adj.*
an′ti•anx•i′e•ty *adj.*
an′ti•bac•te′ri•al *adj. & n.*
an′ti•can′cer *adj.*
an′ti•cap′i•tal•ist *n. & adj.*
an′ti-Cath′o•lic *adj. & n.*
an′ti•co•ag′u•lant *n. & adj.*
an′ti•co•lo′ni•al *adj. & n.*
an′ti•co•lo′ni•al•ism *n.*
an′ti•com′mu•nism *n.*
an′ti•com′mu•nist *n. & adj.*
an′ti•cor•ro′sive *adj. & n.*
an′ti•crime′ *adj.*
an′ti•dem′o•crat′ic *adj.*
an′ti•di′ar•rhe′al *n. & adj.*
an′ti•es•tab′lish•ment *n.*
an′ti•fas′cism *n.*
an′ti•fas′cist *n. & adj.*
an′ti•fem′i•nism *n.*
an′ti•fem′i•nist *adj. & n.*
an′ti•fun′gal *adj. & n.*
an′ti-im•pe′ri•al•ism *n.*
an′ti-im•pe′ri•al•ist *adj. & n.*
an′ti-in•fec′tive *adj. & n.*
an′ti-in•flam′ma•to′ry *adj. & n.*
an′ti-in′tel•lec′tu•al *adj. & n.*
an′ti-in′tel•lec′tu•al•ism *n.*
an′ti-i′so•la′tion•ist *n.*
an′ti•la′bor *adj.*
an′ti•lib′er•al *adj. & n.*
an′ti•ma•lar′i•al *adj.*
an′ti•mi•cro′bi•al *adj.*
an′ti•mil′i•ta•rism *n.*
an′ti•mi•tot′ic *adj. & n.*
an′ti•mon′ar•chist *n.*
an′ti•mo•nop′o•lis′tic *adj.*
an′ti•nar•cot′ic *n. & adj.*
an′ti•na′tion•al•ist *n.*
an′ti•ox′i•dant *n.*
an′ti•pac′i•fist *n.*
an′ti•par′a•sit′ic *adj. & n.*
an′ti•pole′ *n.*
an′ti•pol•lu′tion *adj.*
an′ti•pov′er•ty *adj.*
an′ti•Prot′es•tant *n. & adj.*
an′ti•rad′i•cal *adj. & n.*
an′ti•ra′tion•al *adj.*
an′ti•re•lig′ious *adj.*
an′ti•rev′o•lu′tion•ar′y *adj. & n.*
an′ti•slav′er•y *adj. & n.*
an′ti•spas•mod′ic *adj. & n.*
an′ti•stat′ic *adj. & n.*
an′ti•sub′ma•rine′ *adj.*
an′ti•take′o′ver *adj.*
an′ti•tank′ *adj.*
an′ti•ter′ror•ism *n.*
an′ti•ter′ror•ist *adj.*
an′ti•tu′mor *adj.*
an′ti•vi′ral *adj. & n.*
an′ti•viv′i•sec′tion *adj.*
an′ti•viv′i•sec′tion•ist *n.*
an′ti•war′ *adj.*
an′ti-Zi′on•ist *adj. & n.*

an•ti•nov•el (ăn′tē-nŏv′əl, ăn′tī-) ►*n.* A fictional work that lacks traditional elements of the novel, such as coherent plot structure or realistic character development.

an•ti•nu•cle•ar (ăn′tē-no͞o′klē-ər, -nyo͞o′-, ăn′tī-) ►*adj.* Opposing the production or use of nuclear power or nuclear weaponry.

An•ti•och (ăn′tē-ŏk′) An ancient town of Phrygia in SW Turkey.

an•ti•ox•i•dant (ăn′tē-ŏk′sĭ-dənt, ăn′tī-) ►*n.* **1.** A substance that inhibits oxidation. **2.** A substance, such as vitamin E, thought to protect body cells from the damaging effects of oxidation.

an•ti•par•ti•cle (ăn′tē-pär′tĭ-kəl, ăn′tī-) ►*n.* A subatomic particle, such as a positron or antiproton, having the same mass, lifetime, and spin as the particle to which it corresponds but having the opposite electric charge and magnetic properties.

an•ti•pas•to (än′tē-päs′tō) ►*n., pl.* **-tos** or **-ti** (-tē). An appetizer usu. of assorted meats, cheeses, and vegetables. [Ital.]

an•tip•a•thy (ăn-tĭp′ə-thē) ►*n., pl.* **-thies 1.** A strong aversion or repugnance. **2.** An object of aversion. [< Gk. *antipathēs*, of opposite feelings.] —**an•tip′a•thet′ic** (-thĕt′ĭk), **an•tip′a•thet′i•cal** *adj.*

an•ti•per•son•nel (ăn′tē-pûr′sə-nĕl′, ăn′tī-) ►*adj.* Designed to cause death or injury rather than material damage.

an•ti•per•spi•rant (ăn′tē-pûr′spər-ənt, ăn′tī-) ►*n.* A preparation applied to the skin to decrease perspiration.

an•ti•phon (ăn′tə-fŏn′) ►*n.* A devotional composition sung responsively as part of a liturgy. [LLat. *antiphona*, ANTHEM.] —**an•tiph′o•nal** (-tĭf′ə-nəl) *adj.*

an•tiph•o•ny (ăn-tĭf′ə-nē) ►*n., pl.* **-nies 1.** Responsive or antiphonal singing. **2.** An exchange, as of ideas or opinions.

an•ti•pode (ăn′tĭ-pōd′) ►*n.* A direct opposite. —**an•tip′o•dal** (-tĭp′ə-dəl) *adj.*

an•tip•o•des (ăn-tĭp′ə-dēz′) ►*pl.n.* **1.** Two places on diametrically opposite sides of the earth. **2.** *(takes sing. or pl. v.)* One that is the exact opposite of another. [< Gk. : ANTI– + *pous, pod-*, foot.]

Antipodes. A group of rocky islands of the S Pacific SE of New Zealand and diametrically opposite Greenwich, England.

an•ti•pope (ăn′tĭ-pōp′) ►*n.* One claiming to be pope in opposition to the one chosen by church law.

an•ti•pro•ton (ăn′tē-prō′tŏn′, ăn′tī-) ►*n.* The antiparticle of the proton.

an•ti•psy•chot•ic (ăn′tē-sī-kŏt′ĭk, ăn′tī-) ►*adj.* Counteracting the symptoms of psychotic disorders.

an•ti•py•ret•ic (ăn′tē-pī-rĕt′ĭk, ăn′tī-) ►*adj.* Reducing fever. ►*n.* A medication that reduces fever. —**an′ti•py•re′sis** (-rē′sĭs) *n.*

an•ti•quar•i•an (ăn′tĭ-kwâr′ē-ən) ►*adj.* **1.** Relating to the study or collecting of antiquities. **2.** Dealing in old or rare books. —**an′ti•quar′i•an** *adj. & n.*

an•ti•quar•y (ăn′tĭ-kwĕr′ē) ►*n., pl.* **-ies.** One who collects or deals in antiquities.

an•ti•quate (ăn′tĭ-kwāt′) ►*v.* **-quat•ed, -quat•ing.** To make obsolete. —**an′ti•qua′tion** *n.*

an•tique (ăn-tēk′) ►*adj.* **1.** Belonging to or made in an earlier period. **2.** Belonging to ancient times, esp. ancient Greece or Rome. ►*n.* An object considered valuable because of its age and artistry. ►*v.* **-tiqued, -tiqu•ing.** To give the appearance of an antique to. [< Lat. *antīquus*.] —**an•tique′ly** *adv.* —**an•tique′ness** *n.*

an•tiq•ui•ty (ăn-tĭk′wĭ-tē) ►*n., pl.* **-ties 1.** Ancient times, esp. those before the Middle Ages. **2.** The quality of being old or ancient: *a carving of great antiquity.* **3.** often **antiquities** Something dating from ancient times.

an•ti•re•jec•tion (ăn′tē-rĭ-jĕk′shən, ăn′tī-) ►*adj.* Preventing rejection of a transplanted tissue or organ.

an•ti•sat•el•lite (ăn′tē-săt′l-īt, ăn′tī-) ►*adj.* Directed against enemy satellites.

an•ti-Sem•ite (ăn′tē-sĕm′īt′, ăn′tī-) ►*n.* One who is prejudiced against Jews. —**an′ti-Se•mit′ic** (-sə-mĭt′ĭk) *adj.* —**an′ti-Sem′i•tism** (-sĕm′ĭ-tĭz′əm) *n.*

an•ti•sep•sis (ăn′tĭ-sĕp′sĭs) ►*n.* Destruction of disease-causing microorganisms to prevent infection.

an•ti•sep•tic (ăn′tĭ-sĕp′tĭk) ►*adj.* **1.** Relating to or producing antisepsis. **2.** Thoroughly clean; aseptic. See Syns at **clean.** —**an′ti•sep′tic** *n.* —**an′ti•sep′ti•cal•ly** *adv.*

an•ti•se•rum (ăn′tĭ-sîr′əm) ►*n., pl.* **-se•rums** or **-se•ra** (-sîr′ə). Serum containing antibodies that are specific for one or more antigens.

an•ti•smok•ing (ăn′tē-smō′kĭng, ăn′tī-) ►*adj.* Opposed to or prohibiting the smoking of tobacco, esp. in public.

an•ti•so•cial (ăn′tē-sō′shəl, ăn′tī-) ►*adj.* **1.** Shunning others; not sociable. **2.** Hostile to the established social order. —**an′ti•so′cial•ly** *adv.*

an•ti•theft (ăn′tē-thĕft′, ăn′tī-) ►*adj.* Designed to prevent theft.

an•tith•e•sis (ăn-tĭth′ĭ-sĭs) ►*n., pl.* **-ses** (-sēz′) **1.** Direct contrast; opposition. **2.** The direct opposite. **3.** The juxtaposition of contrasting ideas in parallel grammatical structures. [< Gk.] —**an′ti•thet′i•cal** (ăn′tĭ-thĕt′ĭ-kəl), **an′ti•thet′ic** *adj.*

an•ti•tox•in (ăn′tē-tŏk′sĭn) ►*n.* An antibody formed in response to and capable of neutralizing a specific biological toxin.

an•ti•trust (ăn′tē-trŭst′, ăn′tī-) ►*adj.* Opposing or regulating business monopolies, such as trusts or cartels.

an•ti•tus•sive (ăn′tē-tŭs′ĭv, ăn′tī-) ►*adj.* Relieving or suppressing coughing. [< ANTI– + Lat. *tussis*, cough.] —**an′ti•tus′sive** *n.*

an•ti•vi•ral (ăn′tē-vī′rəl, ăn′tī-) ►*adj.* **1.** Destroying or inhibiting viral growth and reproduction. **2.** *Comp. Sci.* Designed to inactivate a virus.

an•ti•vi•rus (ăn′tē-vī′rəs, ăn′tī-) ►*n.* An antiviral software program.

ant•ler (ănt′lər) ►*n.* One of a pair of branched bony growths on the head of a deer. [< OFr. *antoillier*.] —**ant′lered** *adj.*

ant lion ►*n.* **1.** An insect which at maturity resembles a dragonfly. **2.** The large-jawed larva of the ant lion, which digs holes to trap ants for food.

An•to•ni•nus Pi•us (ăn′tə-nī′nəs pī′əs). A.D. 86–161. Emperor of Rome (138–161).

an•to•nym (ăn′tə-nĭm′) ►*n.* A word meaning the opposite of another word. —**an′to•**

nym′ic *adj.* —**an•ton′y•mous** (ăn-tŏn′ə-məs) *adj.* —**an•ton′y•my** *n.*

ant•sy (ănt′sē) ►*adj.* **-si•er, -si•est** *Slang.* Restless or fidgety.

Ant•werp (ăn′twərp) A city of N Belgium N of Brussels. Pop. 470,349.

a•nus (ā′nəs) ►*n., pl.* **a•nus•es.** The excretory opening at the lower end of the alimentary canal. [< Lat. *ānus.*]

an•vil (ăn′vĭl) ►*n.* **1.** A heavy block of iron or steel with a smooth flat top on which metals are shaped by hammering. **2.** *Anat.* See **incus.** [< OE *anfilt.*]

anx•i•e•ty (ăng-zī′ĭ-tē) ►*n., pl.* **-ties 1.** A state or cause of uneasiness and apprehension; worry. **2.** *Psychiat.* Intense fear resulting from the anticipation of a threatening event. **3.** Eager, often agitated desire: *my anxiety to make a good impression.* [< Lat. *ānxius,* ANXIOUS.]

anx•ious (ăngk′shəs, ăng′-) ►*adj.* **1.** Uneasy and apprehensive; worried. **2.** *Informal* Eager; desirous: *was anxious to see the new show.* [< Lat. *ānxius* < *angere,* to torment.] —**anx′ious•ly** *adv.* —**anx′ious•ness** *n.*

an•y (ĕn′ē) ►*adj.* One, some, every, or all without specification: *Take any book you want. Are there any messages for me? Any child would love that.* See Usage Note at **every.** ►*pron. (takes sing. or pl. v.)* Any one or more persons, things, or quantities. ►*adv.* To any degree; at all: *didn't feel any better.* [< OE *ǣnig.*]

an•y•bod•y (ĕn′ē-bŏd′ē, -bŭd′ē) ►*pron.* Anyone. ►*n.* An important person: *Everybody who is anybody was there.*

an•y•how (ĕn′ē-hou′) ►*adv.* **1.** In whatever way or manner. **2.** Haphazardly. **3a.** In any case; at least. **b.** Nevertheless.

an•y•more (ĕn′ē-môr′, -mōr′) ►*adv.* **1a.** Any longer; still: *Do they make this model anymore?* **b.** From now on: *promised not to quarrel anymore.* **2.** *Regional* Nowadays.

Regional Note: The word *anymore* is widely used to mean "nowadays," especially in the South Midland and Midwestern states and the Western states that received settlers from those areas.

an•y•one (ĕn′ē-wŭn′, -wən) ►*pron.* Any person.

an•y•place (ĕn′ē-plās′) ►*adv.* To, in, or at any place; anywhere.

an•y•thing (ĕn′ē-thĭng′) ►*pron.* Any object or matter at all. —***idioms:*** **anything but** By no means: *anything but happy to do it.* **anything goes** Anything is permissible. **like anything** To an exceeding degree: *We worked like anything to meet the deadline.*

an•y•time (ĕn′ē-tīm′) ►*adv.* At any time: *Call me anytime.*

an•y•way (ĕn′ē-wā′) ►*adv.* **1.** In any manner whatever. **2.** Nevertheless: *It was raining but they played the game anyway.*

an•y•where (ĕn′ē-hwâr′, -wâr′) ►*adv.* **1.** To, in, or at any place. **2.** To any extent at all.

a/o ►*abbr.* account of

ao dai (ou′ dī, ô′) ►*n., pl.* **ao dais.** A traditional long tunic slit on the sides and worn over loose trousers by Vietnamese women. [Vietnamese *áo dài.*]

A-one also **A-1** (ā′wŭn′) ►*adj. Informal* First-class; excellent.

a•or•ta (ā-ôr′tə) ►*n., pl.* **-tas** or **-tae** (-tē). The main trunk of the systemic arteries, carrying blood to all bodily organs except the lungs. [< Gk. *aortē.*] —**a•or′tal, a•or′tic** *adj.*

ao dai

a•ou•dad (ä′o͞o-dăd′, ou′dăd′) ►*n.* A wild sheep of N Africa. [< Berber *audad.*]

aoudad

AP ►*abbr.* **1.** American plan **2.** antipersonnel **3.** Associated Press

a•pace (ə-pās′) ►*adv.* At a rapid pace; swiftly. [< OFr. *a pas.*]

A•pach•e (ə-păch′ē) ►*n., pl.* **-e** or **-es 1.** A member of a Native American people of the SW US and N Mexico, now mainly in Arizona, New Mexico, and Oklahoma. **2.** Any of the Athabaskan languages of the Apache.

a•part (ə-pärt′) ►*adv.* **1.** Separately or at a distance in place, position, or time. **2.** In or into pieces: *split apart.* **3.** One from another: *I can't tell the twins apart.* [< OFr. *a part.*] —**a•part′ness** *n.*

a•part•heid (ə-pärt′hīt′, -hāt′) ►*n.* A formerly official policy of racial segregation practiced in the Republic of South Africa. [Afr.]

a•part•ment (ə-pärt′mənt) ►*n.* **1.** A room or suite designed as a residence. **2.** An apartment building. [< Ital. *appartamento.*]

apartment building ►*n.* A building divided into apartments.

ap•a•thy (ăp′ə-thē) ►*n.* **1.** Lack of interest or concern, esp. in important matters. **2.** Lack of emotion; impassiveness. [< Gk. *apathēs,* without feeling.] —**ap′a•thet′ic** (-thĕt′ĭk) *adj.* —**ap′a•thet′i•cal•ly** *adv.*

a•pat•o•saur (ə-păt′ə-sôr′) or **a•pat•o•sau•rus** (ə-păt′ə-sôr′əs) ►*n.* A large herbivorous dinosaur of the Jurassic Period. [Gk. *apatē,* untruth, lie + *sauros,* lizard.]

APB ▸*abbr.* all points bulletin

ape (āp) ▸*n.* **1a.** A large tailless Old World primate such as the chimpanzee, gorilla, gibbon, and orangutan. **b.** A monkey. **2.** A mimic. **3.** *Informal* A clumsy person. ▸*v.* **aped, ap•ing.** To mimic. [< OE *apa.*]

Ap•en•nines (ăp′ə-nīnz′) A mountain system extending from NW Italy S to the Strait of Messina.

a•pé•ri•tif (ä-pĕr′ĭ-tēf′) ▸*n.* An alcoholic drink taken as an appetizer. [< Lat. *aperīre, apert-,* to open.]

ap•er•ture (ăp′ər-chər) ▸*n.* **1.** An opening, such as a hole or slit. **2.** A usu. adjustable opening in an optical instrument, such as a camera, that limits the amount of light passing through a lens. [< Lat. *aperīre, apert-,* to open.] —**ap′er•tur′al** *adj.*

a•pex (ā′pĕks) ▸*n., pl.* **-es** or **a•pi•ces** (ā′pĭ-sēz′, ăp′ĭ-). The highest point; peak. [Lat.]

Ap•gar score (ăp′gär) ▸*n.* A system of assessing the physical condition of a newborn infant. [After Virginia *Apgar* (1909–1974).]

a•pha•sia (ə-fā′zhə) ▸*n.* Partial or total loss of the ability to speak or comprehend spoken or written language, resulting from brain damage. [Gk.] —**a•pha′si•ac′** (-zē-ăk′) *n.* —**a•pha′sic** (-zĭk, -sĭk) *adj. & n.*

a•phe•li•on (ə-fē′lē-ən, ə-fēl′yən) ▸*n., pl.* **-li•a** (-lē-ə). The point on the orbit of a celestial body that is farthest from the sun. [Gk. *apo-,* away from + Gk. *hēlios,* sun.]

a•phid (ā′fĭd, ăf′ĭd) ▸*n.* Any of various small, soft-bodied insects that feed by sucking sap from plants. [NLat. *Aphis, Aphid-,* type genus.]

aph•o•rism (ăf′ə-rĭz′əm) ▸*n.* **1.** A maxim; adage. **2.** A brief statement of a principle. [< Gk. *aphorismos.*] —**aph′o•rist** *n.* —**aph′o•ris′tic** *adj.*

aph•ro•di•si•ac (ăf′rə-dē′zē-ăk′, -dĭz′ē-) ▸*adj.* Arousing or intensifying sexual desire. ▸*n.* An aphrodisiac food or drug. [< Gk. *Aphroditē,* Aphrodite.]

Aph•ro•di•te (ăf′rə-dī′tē) ▸*n. Gk. Myth.* The goddess of love and beauty.

API ▸*abbr.* Asian and Pacific Islander

A•pi•a (ə-pē′ə, ä′pē-ä′) The capital of Samoa, on the N coast of Upolo I. in the S Pacific. Pop. 32,099.

a•pi•ar•y (ā′pē-ĕr′ē) ▸*n., pl.* **-ies.** A place where bees are raised for their honey. [< Lat. *apis,* bee.] —**a′pi•a•rist** (-ə-rĭst) *n.*

a•pi•ces (ā′pĭ-sēz′, ăp′ĭ-) ▸*n.* Pl. of **apex.**

a•pi•cul•ture (ā′pĭ-kŭl′chər) ▸*n.* The raising of bees. [< Lat. *apis,* bee.] —**a′pi•cul′tur•al** *adj.* —**a′pi•cul′tur•ist** *n.*

a•piece (ə-pēs′) ▸*adv.* To or for each one.

a•plomb (ə-plŏm′, ə-plŭm′) ▸*n.* Self-confidence; poise. [< OFr. *a plomb,* perpendicular.]

ap•ne•a (ăp′nē-ə, ăp-nē′ə) ▸*n.* Temporary absence or cessation of breathing. [< Gk. *apnoia,* without breathing.]

APO ▸*abbr.* Army Post Office

a•poc•a•lypse (ə-pŏk′ə-lĭps′) ▸*n.* **1. Apocalypse** *Bible* The Book of Revelation. **2.** Great devastation; doom. [< Gk. *apokalupsis,* revelation.] —**a•poc′a•lyp′tic, a•poc′a•lyp′ti•cal** *adj.* —**a•poc′a•lyp′ti•cal•ly** *adv.*

A•poc•ry•pha (ə-pŏk′rə-fə) ▸*n. (takes sing. or pl. v.)* **1.** *Bible* The 14 books of the Septuagint included in the Vulgate but considered uncanonical by some. See table at **Bible. 2. apocrypha** Writings of questionable authenticity. [< Gk. *apokruphos,* hidden away.]

a•poc•ry•phal (ə-pŏk′rə-fəl) ▸*adj.* **1.** Of questionable authorship or authenticity. **2.** Erroneous; fictitious. **3. Apocryphal** *Bible* Of the Apocrypha. —**a•poc′ry•phal•ly** *adv.*

ap•o•gee (ăp′ə-jē) ▸*n.* **1.** The point in the orbit of the moon or of an artificial satellite most distant from the center of the earth. **2.** The farthest or highest point; apex. [< Gk. *apogaios,* far from earth.]

a•po•lit•i•cal (ā′pə-lĭt′ĭ-kəl) ▸*adj.* **1.** Having no interest in politics. **2.** Politically unimportant. —**a′po•lit′i•cal•ly** *adv.*

A•pol•lo (ə-pŏl′ō) ▸*n.* **1.** *Gk. Myth.* The god of prophecy, music, medicine, and poetry. **2. apollo,** *pl.* **-los** A beautiful young man.

a•pol•o•get•ic (ə-pŏl′ə-jĕt′ĭk) also **a•pol•o•get•i•cal** (-ĭ-kəl) ▸*adj.* Making an apology. ▸*n.* A formal defense or apology. —**a•pol′o•get′i•cal•ly** *adv.*

ap•o•lo•gi•a (ăp′ə-lō′jē-ə, -jə) ▸*n.* A formal defense or justification. [< Gk.] —**a•pol′o•gist** (ə-pŏl′ə-jĭst) *n.*

a•pol•o•gize (ə-pŏl′ə-jīz′) ▸*v.* **-gized, -giz•ing 1.** To make an apology. **2.** To make a formal defense or justification.

a•pol•o•gy (ə-pŏl′ə-jē) ▸*n., pl.* **-gies 1.** A statement expressing regret or asking pardon for a fault or offense. **2.** A formal justification or defense. **3.** An inferior substitute. [< Gk. *apologia.*]

ap•o•plex•y (ăp′ə-plĕk′sē) ▸*n.* **1.** Sudden impairment of neurological function, esp. resulting from a cerebral hemorrhage; stroke. **2.** A fit of extreme anger. [< Gk. *apoplēxia.*] —**ap′o•plec′tic** *adj.* —**ap′o•plec′ti•cal•ly** *adv.*

a•pos•ta•sy (ə-pŏs′tə-sē) ▸*n., pl.* **-sies.** Abandonment of one's religious faith, political party, or cause. [< Gk. *apostasis,* revolt : *apo-,* away + *histanai,* place.] —**a•pos′tate** (-tāt′) *n. & adj.* —**a•pos′ta•tize** (-tə-tīz′) *v.*

a pos•te•ri•o•ri (ä′ pŏ-stîr′ē-ôr′ē, -ōr′ē, ā′) ▸*adj.* Reasoning from particular facts to general principles; empirical. [Med.Lat., from the subsequent.]

a•pos•tle (ə-pŏs′əl) ▸*n.* **1. Apostle** One of the 12 disciples chosen by Jesus to preach the gospel. **2.** One who pioneers a cause. [< Gk. *apostolos,* messenger.]

ap•os•tol•ic (ăp′ə-stŏl′ĭk) ▸*adj.* **1.** Relating to an apostle. **2.** Relating to the teaching of the 12 Apostles. **3.** Papal.

a•pos•tro•phe[1] (ə-pŏs′trə-fē) ▸*n.* The sign (') used to indicate omission of a letter or letters from a word, the possessive case, and the plurals of numbers, letters, and abbreviations. [< Gk. *apostrophos.*]

a•pos•tro•phe[2] (ə-pŏs′trə-fē) ▸*n.* A rhetorical device in which a speaker or writer addresses an absent person, an abstraction, or an inanimate object. [< Gk. *apostrophē.*] —**ap′os•troph′ic** (ăp′ə-strŏf′ĭk) *adj.* —**a•pos′tro•phize** *v.*

a•poth•e•car•ies' measure (ə-pŏth′ĭ-kĕr′ēz) ▸*n.* A system of liquid volume measure used in pharmacy.

apothecaries' weight ▸*n.* A system of weights used in pharmacy and based on an ounce equal to 480 grains and a pound equal to 12 ounces.

a•poth•e•car•y (ə-pŏth′ĭ-kĕr′ē) ▸*n., pl.* **-ies**

1. A druggist; pharmacist. **2.** See **pharmacy** 2. [< Gk. *apothēkē*, storehouse.]

ap•o•thegm (ăp′ə-thĕm′) ►*n.* A proverb; maxim. [Gk. *apophthegma* < *apophthengesthai*, speak plainly.] —**ap′o•theg•mat′ic** (-thĕg-măt′ĭk) *adj.*

ap•o•them (ăp′ə-thĕm′) ►*n.* The perpendicular distance from the center of a regular polygon to any of its sides. [*apo-*, off + Gk. *thema*, something set down.]

a•poth•e•o•sis (ə-pŏth′ē-ō′sĭs, ăp′ə-thē′ə-sĭs) ►*n.*, *pl.* **-ses** (-sēz′) **1.** Exaltation to divine rank or stature; deification. **2.** An exalted or glorified example. [< Gk. *apotheoun*, deify.] —**a•poth′e•o•size′** *v.*

app (ăp) ►*n. Informal* A computer application.

Ap•pa•la•chi•a (ăp′ə-lā′chē-ə, -chə, -lăch′ē-ə, -lăch′ə) A region of the E US including the Appalachian Mts.

Ap•pa•la•chi•an Mountains (ăp′ə-lā′chē-ən, -chən, -lăch′ē-ən, -lăch′ən) A mountain system of E North America extending SW from E Canada to central AL.

ap•pall (ə-pôl′) ►*v.* To fill with horror or dismay. [< OFr. *apalir*, grow pallid, faint.] —**ap•pall′ing•ly** *adv.*

ap•pa•loo•sa (ăp′ə-lo͞o′sə) ►*n.* A horse having a spotted rump. [?]

ap•pa•rat•us (ăp′ə-răt′əs, -rā′təs) ►*n.*, *pl.* **-us** or **-us•es 1a.** The means by which a function or task is performed. **b.** A political organization or movement. **2a.** A machine or machinery. **b.** A group of materials or devices used for a particular purpose: *dental apparatus.* See Syns at **equipment. 3.** A system. [< Lat. *apparāre*, prepare.]

ap•par•el (ə-păr′əl) ►*n.* Clothing, esp. outer garments. ►*v.* **-eled, -el•ing** or **-elled, -el•ling.** To clothe or dress. [< OFr. *apareillier*, prepare.]

ap•par•ent (ə-păr′ənt, -pâr′-) ►*adj.* **1.** Readily seen; visible. **2.** Readily understood; obvious. **3.** Appearing as such but not necessarily so. [< Lat. *appārēre*, appear.] —**ap•par′ent•ly** *adv.*

Syns: *apparent, clear, clear-cut, distinct, evident, manifest, obvious, patent, plain* **adj.**

ap•pa•ri•tion (ăp′ə-rĭsh′ən) ►*n.* **1.** A ghost. **2.** A sudden or unusual sight. [< Lat. *appārēre*, appear.] —**ap′pa•ri′tion•al** *adj.*

ap•peal (ə-pēl′) ►*n.* **1.** An earnest request. **2.** An application to a higher authority: *an appeal to reason.* **3.** *Law* **a.** The transfer of a case from a lower to a higher court for a new hearing. **b.** A request for a new hearing. **4.** The power of attracting interest: *a city with appeal for tourists.* ►*v.* **1.** To make an earnest request, as for help. **2.** To have recourse. **3.** *Law* To make or apply for an appeal. **4.** To be attractive. [< Lat. *appellāre*, entreat.] —**ap•peal′a•ble** *adj.* —**ap•peal′er** *n.* —**ap•peal′ling•ly** *adv.*

ap•pear (ə-pîr′) ►*v.* **1.** To become visible. **2.** To come into existence. **3.** To seem. See Syns at **seem. 4.** To seem likely. **5.** To come before the public. **6.** *Law* To present oneself before a court. [< Lat. *appārēre*.]

ap•pear•ance (ə-pîr′əns) ►*n.* **1.** The act of appearing. **2.** Outward aspect: *an untidy appearance.* **3.** A pretense.

ap•pease (ə-pēz′) ►*v.* **-peased, -peas•ing 1.** To satisfy or relieve: *appease one's thirst.* **2.** To pacify (an enemy) by granting concessions. [< OFr. *apesier*.] —**ap•peas′a•ble** *adj.* —**ap•peas′ment** *n.* —**ap•peas′er** *n.*

ap•pel•lant (ə-pĕl′ənt) ►*adj.* Appellate. ►*n.* One who appeals a court decision.

ap•pel•late (ə-pĕl′ĭt) ►*adj.* Empowered to hear judicial appeals and review court decisions. [< Lat. *appellāre*, entreat.]

ap•pel•la•tion (ăp′ə-lā′shən) ►*n.* A name or title. [< Lat. *appellāre*, entreat.]

ap•pend (ə-pĕnd′) ►*v.* **1.** To add as a supplement. **2.** To attach. [Lat. *appendere*, hang upon.]

ap•pend•age (ə-pĕn′dĭj) ►*n.* **1.** Something attached to a larger entity. **2.** *Biol.* A subordinate external body part or organ, as an arm or tail.

ap•pen•dec•to•my (ăp′ən-dĕk′tə-mē) ►*n.*, *pl.* **-mies.** Surgical removal of the vermiform appendix.

ap•pen•di•ci•tis (ə-pĕn′dĭ-sī′tĭs) ►*n.* Inflammation of the vermiform appendix.

ap•pen•dix (ə-pĕn′dĭks) ►*n.*, *pl.* **-dix•es** or **-di•ces** (-dĭ-sēz′) **1.** Supplementary material at the end of a book. **2.** *Anat.* The vermiform appendix. [Lat. < *appendere*, hang upon.]

ap•per•tain (ăp′ər-tān′) ►*v.* To belong as a part. [< LLat. *appertinēre*, pertain.]

ap•pe•tite (ăp′ĭ-tīt′) ►*n.* **1.** A desire for food or drink. **2.** A strong wish or urge. [< Lat. *appetere*, strive after.] —**ap′pe•ti′tive** *adj.*

ap•pe•tiz•er (ăp′ĭ-tī′zər) ►*n.* A food or drink served before a meal.

ap•pe•tiz•ing (ăp′ĭ-tī′zĭng) ►*adj.* Stimulating the appetite. —**ap′pe•tiz′ing•ly** *adv.*

ap•plaud (ə-plôd′) ►*v.* To express approval (of), esp. by clapping hands. —**ap•plaud′a•ble** *adj.* —**ap•plaud′er** *n.*

Syns: *applaud, cheer, root* **v.**

ap•plause (ə-plôz′) ►*n.* Approval expressed esp. by the clapping of hands. [< Lat. *applaudere, applaus-*, applaud.]

ap•ple (ăp′əl) ►*n.* **1.** A deciduous tree having alternate white or pink flowers. **2.** Its firm, edible, usu. rounded fruit. —***idiom:* apple of (one's) eye** One that is treasured: *Her son is the apple of her eye.* [< OE *æppel*.]

ap•ple•jack (ăp′əl-jăk′) ►*n.* Brandy distilled from hard cider.

ap•ple•sauce (ăp′əl-sôs′) ►*n.* **1.** Apples stewed to a pulp. **2.** *Slang* Nonsense.

ap•plet (ăp′lĭt) ►*n.* A computer application with limited features and memory requirements. [APPL(ICATION) + -ET.]

ap•pli•ance (ə-plī′əns) ►*n.* A device, esp. one operated by gas or electricity, designed for household use. [< APPLY.]

ap•pli•ca•ble (ăp′lĭ-kə-bəl, ə-plĭk′ə-) ►*adj.* That can be applied; appropriate. —**ap′pli•ca•bil′i•ty** *n.* —**ap′pli•ca•bly** *adv.*

ap•pli•cant (ăp′lĭ-kənt) ►*n.* One who applies.

ap•pli•ca•tion (ăp′lĭ-kā′shən) ►*n.* **1.** The act of applying. **2.** Something applied. **3.** The act of putting something to a special use. **4.** The capacity of being usable; relevance. **5.** Close attention; diligence: *shows application to her work.* **6a.** A request, as for employment. **b.** The form on which such a request is made. **7.** *Comp. Sci.* A computer program with a user interface. ►*adj.* also **applications** *Comp. Sci.* Of or being a program designed for a specific task.

ap•pli•ca•tor (ăp′lĭ-kā′tər) ►*n.* An instrument for applying something, such as glue.

ap•plied (ə-plīd′) ►*adj.* Put into practice or a particular use: *applied physics.*

ap•pli•qué (ăp′lĭ-kā′) ►*n.* A decoration, as in needlework, cut from one material and applied to the surface of another. [< Fr. *appliquer*, APPLY.] —**ap′pli•qué′** *v.*

ap•ply (ə-plī′) ►*v.* **-plied, -ply•ing 1.** To bring into contact with something. **2.** To adapt for a special use. **3.** To put into action: *applied the brakes.* **4.** To devote (oneself or one's efforts) to something. **5.** To be relevant. **6.** To request or seek assistance, employment or admission. [< Lat. *applicāre*, affix to.]

ap•point (ə-point′) ►*v.* **1.** To select for an office or position. **2.** To fix or set by authority. **3.** To furnish; equip. [< OFr. *apointier*, arrange.]
Syns: *appoint, designate, name, nominate, tap* **v.**

ap•point•ee (ə-poin′tē′, ăp′oin-) ►*n.* One who is appointed to an office or position.

ap•poin•tive (ə-poin′tĭv) ►*adj.* Relating to or filled by appointment: *an appointive office.*

ap•point•ment (ə-point′mənt) ►*n.* **1.** The act of appointing. **2.** The office or position to which one has been appointed. **3.** An arrangement for a meeting. **4. appointments** Furnishings; equipment.

Ap•po•mat•tox (ăp′ə-măt′əks) A town of S-central VA E of Lynchburg; site of Confederate surrender that ended the Civil War (1865). Pop. 12,298.

Appomattox
lithograph depicting Lee's surrender

ap•por•tion (ə-pôr′shən, -pōr′-) ►*v.* To divide and assign by a plan; allot. [< OFr. *apportioner.*] —**ap•por′tion•ment** *n.*

ap•po•site (ăp′ə-zĭt) ►*adj.* Appropriate; relevant. [< Lat. *appōnere*, *apposit-*, place near to.] —**ap′po•site•ly** *adv.*

ap•po•si•tion (ăp′ə-zĭsh′ən) ►*n.* **1.** *Gram.* A construction in which a noun or noun phrase is placed with another as an explanatory equivalent, e.g., *Copley* and *the painter* in *The painter Copley was born in Boston.* **2.** Placement side by side. —**ap′po•si′tion•al** *adj.*

ap•pos•i•tive (ə-pŏz′ĭ-tĭv) ►*adj.* Being in apposition. —**ap•pos′i•tive** *n.*

ap•praise (ə-prāz′) ►*v.* **-praised, -prais•ing.** To evaluate, esp. in an official capacity. [< LLat. *appretiāre.*] —**ap•prais′a•ble** *adj.* —**ap•prais′al** *n.* —**ap•praise′ment** *n.* —**ap•prais′er** *n.*

ap•pre•cia•ble (ə-prē′shə-bəl) ►*adj.* Possible to estimate, measure, or perceive. —**ap•pre′cia•bly** *adv.*

ap•pre•ci•ate (ə-prē′shē-āt′) ►*v.* **-at•ed, -at•ing 1.** To recognize the quality, significance, or magnitude of. **2.** To be fully aware of; realize. **3.** To be thankful for. **4.** To increase in value. [LLat. *appretiāre*, appraise.] —**ap•pre′ci•a′tion** *n.* —**ap•pre′ci•a′tor** *n.*

ap•pre•cia•tive (ə-prē′shə-tĭv, -shē-ā′tĭv) ►*adj.* Capable of or showing appreciation. —**ap•pre′cia•tive•ly** *adv.*

ap•pre•hend (ăp′rĭ-hĕnd′) ►*v.* **1.** To arrest. **2.** To understand. **3.** To perceive. **4.** To anticipate with anxiety; dread. [< Lat. *apprehendere*, to grasp.] —**ap′pre•hen′sion** *n.*

ap•pre•hen•sive (ăp′rĭ-hĕn′sĭv) ►*adj.* Fearful about the future. See Syns at **afraid.** —**ap′pre•hen′sive•ly** *adv.*

ap•pren•tice (ə-prĕn′tĭs) ►*n.* **1.** One learning a trade under a skilled master. **2.** A beginner. ►*v.* **-ticed, -tic•ing.** To place or take on as an apprentice. [< Lat. *apprehendere*, seize.] —**ap•pren′tice•ship′** *n.*

ap•prise (ə-prīz′) ►*v.* **-prised, -pris•ing.** To give notice to; inform. [< OFr. *aprendre*, apprehend.]

ap•proach (ə-prōch′) ►*v.* **1.** To come near or nearer (to). **2.** To come close to, as in appearance; approximate. **3.** To make a proposal or overtures to. **4.** To begin to deal with: *approached the task with dread.* ►*n.* **1.** The act of approaching. **2.** A fairly close resemblance. **3.** A means of reaching something; access. [< LLat. *appropiāre.*] —**ap•proach′a•ble** *adj.*

ap•pro•ba•tion (ăp′rə-bā′shən) ►*n.* Approval; praise. [< Lat. *approbāre*, approve.]

ap•pro•pri•ate (ə-prō′prē-ĭt) ►*adj.* Suited to a particular condition or use; fitting. ►*v.* (-āt′) **-at•ed, -at•ing 1.** To set apart for a specific use. See Syns at **allocate. 2.** To take possession of, often without permission. [< LLat. *appropriāre*, make one's own.] —**ap•pro′pri•ate•ly** *adv.* —**ap•pro′pri•ate•ness** *n.* —**ap•pro′pri•a′tor** *n.*
Syns: *appropriate, arrogate, commandeer, confiscate, preempt, usurp* **v.**

ap•pro•pri•a•tion (ə-prō′prē-ā′shən) ►*n.* **1.** The act of appropriating. **2.** Something appropriated, esp. public funds set aside for a specific purpose.

ap•prov•al (ə-pro͞o′vəl) ►*n.* **1.** The act of approving. **2.** Approbation; sanction. **3.** Favorable regard. —***idiom:*** **on approval** For inspection by a customer with no obligation to buy.

ap•prove (ə-pro͞ov′) ►*v.* **-proved, -prov•ing 1a.** To consider right or good. **b.** To express approval. **2.** To consent to formally; authorize. [< Lat. *approbāre.*]

ap•prox•i•mate (ə-prŏk′sə-mĭt) ►*adj.* **1.** Almost exact or correct. **2.** Very similar. ►*v.* (-māt′) **-mat•ed, -mat•ing.** To come close to; be nearly the same as. [< LLat. *approximāre*, go near to.] —**ap•prox′i•mate•ly** *adv.* —**ap•prox′i•ma′tion** *n.*

ap•pur•te•nance (ə-pûr′tn-əns) ►*n.* **1.** Something added to a more important thing; appendage. **2. appurtenances** Equipment used for a specific task. [< LLat. *appertinēre*, PERTAIN.] —**ap•pur′te•nant** *adj.*

Apr. ►*abbr.* April

a•pri•cot (ăp′rĭ-kŏt′, ā′prĭ-) ►*n.* **a.** A deciduous tree having clusters of white flowers. **b.** Its edible, yellow-orange, peachlike fruit. [Ult. < Lat. *praecoquus*, ripe early.]

A•pril (āʹprəl) ▸*n.* The 4th month of the Gregorian calendar. See table at **calendar.** [< Lat. *aprīlis.*]

April Fools' Day ▸*n.* Apr. 1, marked by the playing of practical jokes.

a pri•o•ri (äʹ prē-ôrʹē, -ōrʹē) ▸*adj.* **1.** From a known or assumed cause to a necessarily related effect; deductive. **2.** Based on theory rather than on experiment. [Med.Lat., from the former.] —**aʹ pri•oʹri** *adv.*

a•pron (āʹprən) ▸*n.* **1.** A garment worn over the front of the body to protect clothing. **2.** The paved strip around airport hangars and terminal buildings. **3.** The part of a theater stage in front of the curtain. [< OFr. *naperon,* small tablecloth.]

ap•ro•pos (ăpʹrə-pōʹ) ▸*adj.* Appropriate; pertinent. ▸*adv.* **1.** Appropriately; opportunely. **2.** Incidentally. ▸*prep.* With regard to. [Fr. *à propos,* to the purpose.]

apropos of ▸*prep.* Speaking of.

apse (ăps) ▸*n.* A semicircular or polygonal, usu. domed projection of a church. [Var. of APSIS.] —**apʹsi•dal** (ăpʹsĭ-dəl) *adj.*

ap•sis (ăpʹsĭs) ▸*n., pl.* **-si•des** (-sĭ-dēzʹ). The nearest or farthest orbital point of a celestial body from a center of attraction. [< Gk. *hapsis,* arch.]

apt (ăpt) ▸*adj.* **1.** Exactly suitable; appropriate. **2.** Liable; likely: *The river is apt to flood in spring.* **3.** Quick to learn or understand: *an apt student.* [< Lat. *aptus* < *apere,* fasten.] —**aptʹly** *adv.* —**aptʹness** *n.*

apt. ▸*abbr.* apartment

ap•ti•tude (ăpʹtĭ-to͞odʹ, -tyo͞odʹ) ▸*n.* **1.** A natural ability; talent. **2.** Quickness in learning. **3.** Suitability. [< Lat. *aptus,* APT.]

Ap•u•lei•us (ăpʹyə-lēʹəs), **Lucius.** fl. 2nd cent. A.D. Roman philosopher and satirist.

A•qa•ba (äʹkə-bə), **Gulf of.** An arm of the Red Sea between the Sinai Peninsula and NW Saudi Arabia.

aq•ua (ăkʹwə, äʹkwə) ▸*n., pl.* **aq•uae** (ăkʹwē, äʹkwīʹ) or **aq•uas 1.** Water. **2.** An aqueous solution. **3.** A light blue-green to green-blue. [< Lat.] —**aqʹua** *adj.*

aq•ua•cul•ture (ăkʹwə-kŭlʹchər, äʹkwə-) ▸*n.* The cultivation of fish or shellfish for food. —**aqʹua•culʹtur•ist** *n.*

aq•ua•ma•rine (ăkʹwə-mə-rēnʹ, äʹkwə-) ▸*n.* **1.** A transparent blue-green beryl, used as a gemstone. **2.** A pale to light greenish blue. [Lat. *aqua marīna,* sea water.]

aq•ua•naut (ăkʹwə-nôtʹ, äʹkwə-) ▸*n.* One who works in scientific research conducted in underwater installations. [Lat. *aqua,* water + Gk. *nautēs,* sailor.]

aq•ua•plane (ăkʹwə-plānʹ, äʹkwə-) ▸*n.* A board pulled over the water by a motorboat and ridden by a person standing up. —**aqʹua•planeʹ** *v.*

aqua re•gi•a (rēʹjē-ə) ▸*n.* A corrosive, fuming mixture of hydrochloric and nitric acids, used for testing metals and dissolving platinum and gold. [NLat., royal water.]

a•quar•i•um (ə-kwârʹē-əm) ▸*n., pl.* **-i•ums** or **-i•a** (-ē-ə) **1.** A water-filled enclosure in which living aquatic animals and plants are kept. **2.** A place for the public exhibition of live aquatic animals and plants. [Ult. < Lat. *aqua,* water.]

A•quar•i•us (ə-kwârʹē-əs) ▸*n.* **1.** A constellation in the equatorial region of the Southern Hemisphere. **2.** The 11th sign of the zodiac. —**A•quarʹi•an** *adj. & n.*

a•quat•ic (ə-kwătʹĭk, ə-kwŏtʹ-) ▸*adj.* **1.** Living or growing in, on, or near the water. **2.** Taking place in or on the water: *an aquatic sport.* —**a•quatʹi•cal•ly** *adv.*

aq•ua•tint (ăkʹwə-tĭntʹ, äʹkwə-) ▸*n.* **1.** A process of etching capable of producing tonal variations in the resulting print. **2.** An etching so made. [< Ital. *acquatinta* : Lat. *aqua,* water; see AQUA + *tinta,* dyed.]

a•qua•vit (äʹkwə-vētʹ) ▸*n.* A strong clear liquor flavored with caraway seed. [Swed., Dan. and Norw. *akvavit,* AQUA VITAE.]

aqua vi•tae (vīʹtē) ▸*n.* A strong liquor such as brandy. [< Med.Lat. *aqua vītae* : Lat. *aqua,* water + Lat. *vīta,* life.]

aq•ue•duct (ăkʹwĭ-dŭktʹ) ▸*n.* **1.** A conduit for transporting water from a remote source. **2.** A bridgelike structure supporting a conduit or canal passing over a river or low ground. [Lat. *aquaeductus* : *aqua,* water + *ductus,* DUCT.]

a•que•ous (āʹkwē-əs, ăkʹwē-) ▸*adj.* Relating to, containing, or dissolved in water; watery. [< Lat. *aqua,* water.]

aqueous humor ▸*n. Anat.* The clear, watery fluid in the chamber of the eye between the cornea and the lens.

aq•ui•fer (ăkʹwə-fər, äʹkwə-) ▸*n.* An underground layer of earth, gravel, or porous stone that yields water.

aq•ui•line (ăkʹwə-līnʹ, -lĭn) ▸*adj.* **1.** Of or like an eagle. **2.** Curved like an eagle's beak: *an aquiline nose.* [< Lat. *aquila,* eagle.]

A•qui•nas (ə-kwīʹnəs), Saint **Thomas.** 1225–74. Italian Dominican theologian.

A•qui•no (ä-kēʹnō), **Corazón Cojuangco.** b. 1933. Philippine president (1986–92).

Aq•ui•taine (ăkʹwĭ-tānʹ) A historical region of SW France between the Pyrenees and the Garonne R.

Ar ▸ The symbol for the element **argon.**

AR ▸*abbr.* **1.** also **A/R** accounts receivable **2.** Arkansas

Ar. ▸*abbr.* **1.** Arabia **2.** Arabic

-ar ▸*suff.* Of, relating to, or resembling: *polar.* [< Lat. *-āris,* alteration of *-ālis,* -al.]

Ar•ab (ărʹəb) ▸*n.* **1.** A member of a Semitic people of Arabia whose language and Islamic religion spread widely throughout the Middle East and N Africa from the 7th cent. **2.** A member of an Arabic-speaking people. —**Arʹab** *adj.*

Arab. ▸*abbr.* Arabic

ar•a•besque (ărʹə-bĕskʹ) ▸*n.* **1.** A complex design of interwined floral, foliate, and geometric figures. **2.** A short, whimsical composition esp. for the piano. [< Ital. *arabesco,* in Arabian fashion.]

A•ra•bi•a (ə-rāʹbē-ə) also **A•ra•bi•an Peninsula** (-bē-ən). A peninsula of SW Asia between the Red Sea and the Persian Gulf. —**A•raʹbi•an** *adj. & n.*

Arabian Desert. A desert of E Egypt between the Nile Valley and the Red Sea.

Arabian Sea. The NW part of the Indian Ocean between Arabia and western India.

Ar•a•bic (ărʹə-bĭk) ▸*adj.* Of or relating to Arabia, the Arabs, their language, or their culture. ▸*n.* The Semitic language of the Arabs, spoken in numerous dialects throughout much of the

Middle East and parts of North Africa.

Arabic numeral ►*n.* One of the numerical symbols 1, 2, 3, 4, 5, 6, 7, 8, 9, or 0.

ar•a•ble (ăr′ə-bəl) ►*adj.* Fit for cultivation. [< Lat. *arāre*, to plow.] —**ar′a•bil′i•ty** *n.*

a•rach•nid (ə-răk′nĭd) ►*n.* Any of various eight-legged arthropods such as spiders, scorpions, mites, and ticks. [< Gk. *arakhnē*, spider.] —**a•rach′ni•dan** *adj. & n.*

Ar•a•fat (ăr′ə-făt′, är′ə-fät′), **Yasir.** b. 1929. Leader of the Palestine Liberation Organization; president of the Palestinian Authority (since 1996).

Yasir Arafat

Ar•a•gon (ăr′ə-gŏn′) A region and former kingdom of NE Spain. —**Ar′a•go•nese′** (-gə-nēz′, -nēs′) *adj. & n.*

A•ra•guaí•a or **A•ra•gua•ya** (är′ə-gwī′ə). A river rising in central Brazil and flowing about 2,092 km (1,300 mi) generally N.

Ar•al Sea (ăr′əl) An inland sea between S Kazakhstan and NW Uzbekistan.

Ar•a•ma•ic (ăr′ə-mā′ĭk) ►*n.* A Semitic language widely used throughout SW Asia from the 7th cent. B.C. to the 7th cent. A.D. —**Ar′a•ma′ic** *adj.*

Ar•an Islands (ăr′ən) Three small islands of W Ireland at the entrance to Galway Bay.

A•rap•a•ho (ə-răp′ə-hō′) ►*n., pl.* **-ho** or **-hos** **1.** A member of a Native American people formerly of E Colorado and SE Wyoming, now in Oklahoma and Wyoming. **2.** Their Algonquian language.

Ar•a•rat (ăr′ə-răt′), **Mount.** A massif of extreme E Turkey; traditional resting place of Noah's ark.

Ar•a•wak (ăr′ə-wäk′) ►*n., pl.* **-wak** or **-waks** **1.** A member of an American Indian people formerly inhabiting parts of the West Indies, now chiefly in NE South America. **2.** The Arawakan language of the Arawak.

Ar•a•wa•kan (ăr′ə-wä′kən) ►*n., pl.* **-kan** or **-kans** **1.** A family of South American Indian languages spoken in the Amazon Basin, NE South America, and formerly the Greater Antilles. **2.** A member of an Arawakan-speaking people. —**Ar′a•wa′kan** *adj.*

Ar•bil (îr′bĭl, är′-) or **Ir•bil** (îr′-). A city of N Iraq N of Baghdad. Pop. 485,968.

ar•bi•ter (är′bĭ-tər) ►*n.* One having the power to judge or decide. [< Lat.]

ar•bi•trage (är′bĭ-träzh′) ►*n.* The purchase of securities on one market for immediate resale on another in order to profit from a price discrepancy. [< OFr. *arbitration.*] —**ar′bi•trage′** *v.* —**ar′bi•tra•geur′** also **ar′bi•tra′ger** *n.*

ar•bit•ra•ment (är-bĭt′rə-mənt) ►*n.* **1.** The act of arbitrating. **2.** The judgment of an arbiter. [< OFr. *arbitrer*, ARBITRATE.]

ar•bi•trar•y (är′bĭ-trĕr′ē) ►*adj.* **1.** Determined by chance, whim, or impulse. **2.** Not limited by law; despotic. [< Lat. *arbiter*, judge.] —**ar′bi•trar′i•ly** (-trâr′ə-lē) *adv.* —**ar′bi•trar′i•ness** *n.*

Syns: *arbitrary, capricious, whimsical* ***adj.***

ar•bi•trate (är′bĭ-trāt′) ►*v.* **-trat•ed, -trat•ing** **1.** To judge or decide as an arbitrator. **2.** To submit (a dispute) to settlement by arbitration. **3.** To serve as an arbitrator. [Lat. *arbitrārī* < *arbiter*, judge.] —**ar′bi•tra′tion** *n.*

ar•bi•tra•tor (är′bĭ-trā′tər) ►*n.* A person chosen to settle a dispute.

ar•bor (är′bər) ►*n.* A shady resting place in a garden or park. [< OFr. *erbier*, garden.]

ar•bo•re•al (är-bôr′ē-əl, -bōr′-) ►*adj.* **1.** Of or like a tree. **2.** Living in trees. [< Lat. *arbor*, tree.]

ar•bo•re•tum (är′bə-rē′təm) ►*n., pl.* **-tums** or **-ta** (-tə). A place for the study and exhibition of trees. [< Lat. *arbor*, tree.]

ar•bor•vi•tae also **ar•bor vi•tae** (är′bər-vī′tē) ►*n.* Any of several evergreen trees having scalelike leaves and small cones. [Lat. *arbor*, tree + *vīta*, life.]

ar•bo•vi•rus (är′bə-vī′rəs) ►*n.* Any of a large group of viruses that cause encephalitis and yellow fever. [*ar(thropod-)bo(rne) virus.*]

ar•bu•tus (är-byōō′təs) ►*n.* The trailing arbutus. [Lat.]

arc (ärk) ►*n.* **1.** Something shaped like a curve or an arch. **2.** *Math.* A segment of a circle. **3.** A luminous electric discharge, as when a current jumps a gap between two electrodes. ►*v.* **arced** (ärkt), **arc•ing** (är′kĭng). To move in or form an arc. [< Lat. *arcus.*]

ARC[1] (ärk) ►*n.* A combination of symptoms first considered to be a precursor to AIDS, but now thought of as a milder form of the disease. [*A(IDS-)r(elated) c(omplex).*]

ARC[2] ►*abbr.* American Red Cross

ar•cade (är-kād′) ►*n.* **1.** A series of arches supported by columns. **2.** A roofed passageway, esp. one with shops on one or both sides. **3.** A commercial establishment featuring rows of coin-operated games. [< Ital. *arcata* < Lat. *arcus*, arch.]

Ar•ca•di•a (är-kā′dē-ə) also **Ar•ca•dy** (är′kə-dē). A region of ancient Greece proverbial for its simple pastoral life. —**Ar•ca′di•an** *adj. & n.*

ar•ca•na (är-kā′nə) ►*pl.n.* Specialized knowledge or detail that is mysterious to the average person.

ar•cane (är-kān′) ►*adj.* Known to only a few; esoteric. [Lat. *arcānus* < *arca*, chest.]

arch[1] (ärch) ►*n.* **1.** A structure forming the curved, pointed, or flat upper edge of an open space and supporting the weight above it. **2.** A structure, such as a monument, shaped like an inverted U. **3.** Something curved like an arch. ►*v.* **1.** To provide with an arch. **2.** To form or cause to form an arch. [< Lat. *arcus.*] —**arched** *adj.*

arch[2] (ärch) ►*adj.* **1.** Chief; principal: *their arch foe.* **2.** Mischievous: *an arch glance.* [<

ARCH–.] —**arch′ly** *adv.* —**arch′ness** *n.*

arch. ►*abbr.* **1a.** archaic **b.** archaism **2.** archipelago **3a.** architect **b.** architecture

arch– ►*pref.* **1.** Chief; highest: *archbishop.* **2.** Extreme: *archconservative.* [< Gk. *arkhi-*.]

–arch ►*suff.* Ruler; leader: *matriarch.* [< Gk. *arkhos*, ruler.]

ar•chae•ol•o•gy or **ar•che•ol•o•gy** (är′kē-ŏl′ə-jē) ►*n.* The systematic study of past human life and culture by the examination of remaining material evidence. [< Gk. *arkhaiologia*, antiquarian lore.] —**ar′chae•o•log′i•cal** (-ə-lŏj′ĭ-kəl), **ar′chae•o•log′ic** *adj.* —**ar′chae•ol′o•gist** *n.*

ar•cha•ic (är-kā′ĭk) ►*adj.* **1.** Belonging to an earlier time. **2.** No longer current; antiquated. **3.** Relating to words and language once in regular use but now rare and suggestive of an earlier style or period. [Gk. *arkhaikos* < *arkhē*, beginning.] —**ar•cha′i•cal•ly** *adv.*

ar•cha•ism (är′kē-ĭz′əm, -kā-) ►*n.* An archaic word, phrase, or style. —**ar′cha•ist** *n.*

arch•an•gel (ärk′ān′jəl) ►*n.* An angel of the next to the lowest order.

Archangel. See **Arkhangelsk.**

arch•bish•op (ärch-bĭsh′əp) ►*n.* A bishop of the highest rank. —**arch•bish′op•ric** *n.*

arch•dea•con (ärch-dē′kən) ►*n.* A church official, as in the Anglican Church, in charge of temporal and other affairs in a diocese. —**arch•dea′con•ate** (-kə-nĭt) *n.*

arch•di•o•cese (ärch-dī′ə-sĭs, -sēs′, -sēz′) ►*n.* The district under an archbishop's jurisdiction. —**arch′di•oc′e•san** (-ŏs′ĭ-sən) *adj.*

arch•duch•ess (ärch-dŭch′ĭs) ►*n.* A royal princess, esp. of imperial Austria.

arch•duke (ärch-do͞ok′, -dyo͞ok′) ►*n.* A royal prince, esp. of imperial Austria.

arch•en•e•my (ärch-ĕn′ə-mē) ►*n.* A principal enemy.

ar•che•ol•o•gy (är′kē-ŏl′ə-jē) ►*n.* Var. of **archaeology.**

arch•er (är′chər) ►*n.* One who shoots with a bow and arrow. [< LLat. *arcārius* < Lat. *arcus*, bow.] —**arch′er•y** *n.*

archer

arch•er•fish (är′chər-fĭsh′) ►*n.* Any of various freshwater fish that spit water at flying insects and prey on those that fall.

ar•che•type (är′kĭ-tīp′) ►*n.* **1.** An original model or type after which other similar things are patterned; prototype. **2.** An ideal example of a type. [< Gk. *arkhetupos*, original.] —**ar′che•typ′al** (-tī′pəl), **ar′che•typ′ic** (-tĭp′ĭk), **ar′che•typ′i•cal** *adj.*

arch•fiend (ärch-fēnd′) ►*n.* **1.** A principal fiend. **2. Archfiend** Satan.

ar•chi•e•pis•co•pal (är′kē-ĭ-pĭs′kə-pəl) ►*adj.* Relating to an archbishop.

ar•chi•man•drite (är′kə-măn′drīt′) ►*n. Eastern Orthodox Ch.* A cleric ranking below a bishop. [< LGk. *arkhimandritēs*.]

Ar•chi•me•des (är′kə-mē′dēz). 287?–212 B.C. Greek mathematician, engineer, and physicist. —**Ar′chi•me′de•an** *adj.*

ar•chi•pel•a•go (är′kə-pĕl′ə-gō′) ►*n., pl.* **-goes** or **-gos 1.** A large group of islands. **2.** A sea containing a large group of islands. [Ital. *Arcipelago*, the Aegean Sea.] —**ar′chi•pe•lag′ic** (-pə-lăj′ĭk) *adj.*

ar•chi•tect (är′kĭ-tĕkt′) ►*n.* **1.** One who designs and supervises the construction of buildings. **2.** One that plans or devises. [< Gk. *arkhitektōn*, master builder : *arkhi-*, chief + *tektōn*, builder.]

ar•chi•tec•ton•ics (är′kĭ-tĕk-tŏn′ĭks) ►*n.* *(takes sing. v.)* **1.** The science of architecture. **2.** Structural design, as in a musical work. —**ar′chi•tec•ton′ic** *adj.*

ar•chi•tec•ture (är′kĭ-tĕk′chər) ►*n.* **1.** The art and science of designing and erecting buildings. **2.** A style and method of design and construction: *Byzantine architecture.* —**ar′chi•tec′tur•al** *adj.*

ar•chi•trave (är′kĭ-trāv′) ►*n.* **1.** In classical architecture, the lowest part of an entablature, resting on top of a column. **2.** The molding around a door or window. [< OItal.]

ar•chive (är′kīv′) ►*n.* **1.** often **archives** Public records of historical interest. **2.** A place for storing archives. **3.** *Comp. Sci.* **a.** A storage area, usu. on magnetic tape, for files not in active use. **b.** A file containing data compressed for ease of storage or transfer. [< Gk. *arkheion*, town hall.] —**ar•chi′val** *adj.* —**ar′chive** *v.*

ar•chi•vist (är′kə-vĭst, -kī′-) ►*n.* One who is in charge of archives.

arch•ri•val (ärch′rī′vəl) ►*n.* A principal rival.

arch•way (ärch′wā′) ►*n.* **1.** A passageway under an arch. **2.** An arch over a passageway.

–archy ►*suff.* Rule; government: *oligarchy.*

arc lamp ►*n.* An electric light in which a current traverses a gas between two incandescent electrodes.

arc•tic (ärk′tĭk, är′tĭk) ►*adj.* Extremely cold; frigid. See Syns at **cold.** [< Gk. *arktikos* < *arktos*, bear, Ursa Major.]

Arctic. A region between the North Pole and the N timberlines of North America and Eurasia. —**Arctic** *adj.*

Arctic Archipelago. A group of islands of Northwest Terrs., Canada, in the Arctic between North America and Greenland.

Arctic Circle. The parallel of latitude (approx. 66°33′ N) that separates the North Temperate and North Frigid zones.

Arctic Ocean. The waters around the North Pole between North America and Eurasia.

–ard or **–art** ►*suff.* One who habitually or excessively is in a certain state or performs a certain action: *drunkard.* [< OFr.]

Ar•dennes (är-dĕn′) A plateau region of N France, SE Belgium, and N Luxembourg.

ar•dent (är′dnt) ►*adj.* **1.** Characterized by warmth of feeling; passionate. **2a.** Burning; fiery. **b.** Glowing; shining. [< Lat. *ārdēre*, burn.] —**ar′den•cy** *n.* —**ar′dent•ly** *adv.*

ar•dor (är′dər) ►*n.* **1.** Fiery intensity of feeling. **2.** Intense heat. [< Lat. *ārdor*.]

ar•du•ous (är′jo͞o-əs) ▶*adj.* **1.** Strenuous; difficult. **2.** Full of hardships. [< Lat. *arduus,* steep.] —**ar′du•ous•ly** *adv.*

are¹ (är) ▶*v.* 2nd pers. sing. and pl. and 1st and 3rd pers. pl. pr. indic. of **be.**

are² (âr, är) ▶*n.* A unit of area equal to 100 square meters. [< Lat. *ārea,* open space.]

ar•e•a (âr′ē-ə) ▶*n.* **1.** A portion of the space on a surface; region. **2.** A distinct part or section: *a storage area.* **3.** A division of experience or knowledge; field. **4.** *Math.* The extent of a planar region or of the surface of a solid. [Lat. *ārea,* open space.]

area code ▶*n.* A number used to distinguish broad geographic areas of telephone service, esp. a 3-digit number used in the US, Canada, and the Caribbean.

ar•e•a•way (âr′ē-ə-wā′) ▶*n.* A small sunken area allowing access or light and air to basement doors or windows.

a•re•na (ə-rē′nə) ▶*n.* **1.** A building for the presentation of sports events and spectacles. **2.** A sphere of activity: *the political arena.* [Lat. *arēna,* sand, sandy place.]

arena theater ▶*n.* A theater in which the stage is at the center of the auditorium.

aren't (ärnt, är′ənt) ▶ Are not.

Ar•es (âr′ēz) ▶*n. Gk. Myth.* The god of war.

ar•gent (är′jənt) ▶*n. Archaic* Silver. [< Lat. *argentum.*]

Ar•gen•ti•na (är′jən-tē′nə) A country of SE South America E of Chile extending to S Tierra del Fuego, an island it shares with Chile. Cap. Buenos Aires. Pop. 34,180,000. —**Ar′gen•tine′** (-tēn′, -tīn′), **Ar′gen•tin′e•an** (-tĭn′ē-ən) *adj. & n.*

Ar•go•lis (är′gə-lĭs) An ancient region of S Greece in the NE Peloponnesus.

ar•gon (är′gŏn′) ▶*n. Symbol* **Ar** A colorless, odorless, inert gaseous element constituting approx. one percent of Earth's atmosphere and used in electric light bulbs, fluorescent tubes, and welding. At. no. 18. See table at **element.** [< Gk. *argos,* inert : A–¹ + *ergon,* work.]

Ar•gonne (är-gŏn′, är′gŏn) A wooded hilly region of NE France between the Meuse and Aisne rivers.

ar•go•sy (är′gə-sē) ▶*n., pl.* **-sies 1.** A large merchant ship. **2.** A fleet of ships. [< Ital. *ragusea,* vessel of Ragusa, Croatia.]

ar•got (är′gō, -gət) ▶*n.* The specialized vocabulary of a group: *thieves' argot.* [Fr.]

ar•gu•a•ble (är′gyo͞o-ə-bəl) ▶*adj.* **1.** Open to argument. **2.** Defensible in argument; plausible. —**ar′gu•a•bly** *adv.*

ar•gue (är′gyo͞o) ▶*v.* **-gued, -gu•ing 1.** To put forth reasons for or against; debate. **2.** To maintain by reasoning; contend. **3.** To give evidence of. See Syns at **indicate. 4.** To quarrel; dispute. [< Lat. *arguere,* make clear.] —**ar′gu•er** *n.*

ar•gu•ment (är′gyə-mənt) ▶*n.* **1.** A discussion of differing points of view; debate. **2.** A quarrel; dispute. **3a.** A course of reasoning aimed at demonstrating truth or falsehood. **b.** A persuasive reason: *The low rates are an argument for buying now.*

ar•gu•men•ta•tion (är′gyə-mĕn-tā′shən) ▶*n.* The presentation and elaboration of an argument.

ar•gu•men•ta•tive (är′gyə-mĕn′tə-tĭv) ▶*adj.* **1.** Given to arguing; disputatious. **2.** Of or marked by argument. —**ar′gu•men′ta•tive•ness** *n.*

Syns: *argumentative, combative, contentious, disputatious, quarrelsome, scrappy* **adj.**

ar•gyle also **ar•gyll** (är′gīl′) ▶*n.* **1.** A knitting pattern of varicolored, diamond-shaped areas on a solid background. **2.** A sock knit in this pattern. [After Clan Campbell of County *Argyll,* Scotland.]

År•hus also **Aar•hus** (ôr′ho͞os′). A city of central Denmark on **Århus Bay,** an arm of the Kattegat. Pop. 250,404.

a•ri•a (ä′rē-ə) ▶*n.* A solo vocal piece with instrumental accompaniment, as in an opera. [Ital. < Gk. *aēr,* air.]

-arian ▶*suff.* Believer in; advocate of: *utilitarian.* [< Lat. *-ārius.*]

ar•id (ăr′ĭd) ▶*adj.* **1.** Lacking in rainfall; dry. **2.** Lifeless; dull. [Lat. *āridus.*] —**a•rid′i•ty** (ə-rĭd′ĭ-tē), **ar′id•ness** *n.*

Ar•ies (âr′ēz, âr′ē-ēz′) ▶*n.* **1.** A constellation in the Northern Hemisphere. **2.** The 1st sign of the zodiac. [< Lat. *ariēs,* ram.]

a•right (ə-rīt′) ▶*adv.* Properly; correctly.

ar•il (ăr′əl) ▶*n.* A fleshy, usu. brightly colored cover of a seed. [Med.Lat. *arillus,* grape seed.]

a•rise (ə-rīz′) ▶*v.* **a•rose** (ə-rōz′), **a•ris•en** (ə-rĭz′ən), **a•ris•ing 1.** To get up; rise. **2.** To move upward; ascend. **3.** To originate. **4.** To result or proceed. See Syns at **stem¹.** [< OE *ārīsan.*]

Ar•is•ti•des (ăr′ĭ-stī′dēz). "the Just." 530?–468? B.C. Athenian general and political leader.

ar•is•toc•ra•cy (ăr′ĭ-stŏk′rə-sē) ▶*n., pl.* **-cies 1.** A hereditary ruling class. **2.** Government by the nobility or by a privileged upper class. **3.** A group or class considered superior to others. [< Gk. *aristos,* best.] —**a•ris′to•crat′** (ə-rĭs′tə-krăt′, ăr′ĭs-) *n.* —**a•ris′to•crat′ic** *adj.*

Ar•is•toph•a•nes (ăr′ĭ-stŏf′ə-nēz). 448?–388? B.C. Athenian playwright.

Ar•is•tot•le (ăr′ĭ-stŏt′l). 384–322 B.C. Greek philosopher.

a•rith•me•tic (ə-rĭth′mĭ-tĭk) ▶*n.* The mathematics of integers, rational numbers, real numbers, or complex numbers under addition, subtraction, multiplication, and division. [< Gk. *arithmētikē (tekhnē),* (the art) of counting.] —**ar′ith•met′ic** (ăr′ĭth-mĕt′ĭk), **ar′ith•met′i•cal** (-ĭ-kəl) *adj.* —**ar′ith•met′i•cal•ly** *adv.*

arithmetic mean ▶*n.* The value obtained by dividing the sum of a set of quantities by the number of quantities in the set.

-arium ▶*suff.* A place or device containing or associated with: *planetarium.* [Lat., neuter of *-ārius,* -ary.]

A•ri•us (ə-rī′əs, ăr′ē-, âr′-). A.D. 256?–336. Greek Christian theologian.

Ariz. ▶*abbr.* Arizona

Ar•i•zo•na (ăr′ĭ-zō′nə) A state of the SW US on the Mexican border. Cap. Phoenix. Pop. 3,677,985. —**Ar′i•zo′nan** *adj. & n.*

ark (ärk) ▶*n.* **1.** often **Ark** *Bible* The chest containing the Ten Commandments, carried by the Hebrews during their desert wanderings. **2.** often **Ark** *Judaism* The Holy Ark. **3.** *Bible* The boat built by Noah for the Flood. [< Lat. *arca,* chest.]

Ark. ▶*abbr.* Arkansas

Ar•kan•sas (är′kən-sô′) A state of the S-central US Cap. Little Rock. Pop. 2,362,239. —**Ar•kan′san** (-kăn′zən) *adj. & n.*

Ar•kan•sas River (är′kən-sô′, är-kăn′zəs) A river of the S-central US rising in the Rocky Mts. in central CO and flowing about 2,333 km (1,450 mi) to the Mississippi R. in SE AR.

Ark•han•gelsk (är-kăn′gĕlsk, -KHän′-) or **Arch•an•gel** (ärk′ān′jəl). A city of NW Russia. Pop. 409,886.

Ark•wright (ärk′rīt′), Sir **Richard.** 1732–92. British inventor and manufacturer.

Ar•ling•ton (är′lĭng-tən) **1.** A city of N TX between Dallas and Fort Worth. Pop. 261,271. **2.** A county and unincorp. city of N VA across the Potomac R. from Washington DC. Pop. 152,700.

arm[1] (ärm) ►*n.* **1.** An upper limb of the human body. **2.** A part similar to a human arm. **3.** A narrow extension: *an arm of the sea.* See Syns at **branch. 4.** An administrative or functional branch. —***idiom:*** **with open arms** In a warm, friendly manner. [< OE *earm.*] —**armed** *adj.*

arm[2] (ärm) ►*n.* **1.** A weapon. **2.** A branch of a military force. **3. arms a.** Warfare: *a call to arms.* **b.** Military service. **4. arms** Heraldic bearings or insignia. ►*v.* **1.** To equip with weapons. **2.** To prepare for or as if for war. **3.** To prepare (a weapon) for use. —***idiom:*** **up in arms** Angry; indignant. [< Lat. *arma,* weapons.] —**armed** *adj.*

ar•ma•da (är-mä′də, -mā′-) ►*n.* A fleet of warships. [Sp. < Lat. *armāre,* to arm.]

ar•ma•dil•lo (är′mə-dĭl′ō) ►*n., pl.* **-los.** A burrowing mammal of South America and S North America having bony, armorlike plates. [Sp., dim. of *armado,* armored.]

Ar•ma•ged•don (är′mə-gĕd′n) ►*n.* **1.** *Bible* The scene of a final battle between the forces of good and evil. **2.** A catastrophic confrontation.

ar•ma•ment (är′mə-mənt) ►*n.* **1.** The weapons and supplies of a military unit. **2.** often **armaments** All the military forces and equipment of a country. [< Lat. *arma.*]

ar•ma•ture (är′mə-chŏŏr′, -chər) ►*n.* **1.** *Elect.* **a.** The rotating part of a dynamo, consisting of copper wire wound around an iron core. **b.** The moving part of an electromagnetic device such as a relay, buzzer, or loudspeaker. **c.** A piece of soft iron connecting the poles of a magnet. **2.** *Biol.* A protective covering or part. **3.** A supporting framework. [< Lat. *armāre,* to arm.]

arm•chair (ärm′chār′) ►*n.* A chair with sides to support the arms or elbows.

armed forces ►*pl.n.* The military forces of a country.

Ar•me•ni•a (är-mē′nē-ə, -mēn′yə) A region and republic of Asia Minor S of Georgia. Cap. Yerevan. Pop. 3,548,000.

Ar•me•ni•an (är-mē′nē-ən, -mēn′yən) ►*n.* **1a.** A native or inhabitant of Armenia. **b.** A person of Armenian ancestry. **2.** The Indo-European language of the Armenians. —**Ar•me′ni•an** *adj.*

arm•ful (ärm′fŏŏl′) ►*n.* The amount that an arm or arms can hold.

arm•hole (ärm′hōl′) ►*n.* An opening in a garment for an arm.

ar•mi•stice (är′mĭ-stĭs) ►*n.* A temporary cessation of fighting by mutual consent; truce. [< NLat. *armistitium* : Lat. *arma,* arms + Lat. *-stitium,* a stopping.]

arm•let (ärm′lĭt) ►*n.* A band worn esp. on the upper arm for ornament or identification.

ar•moire (ärm-wär′) ►*n.* A large, often ornate cabinet or wardrobe. [Fr. < Lat. *armārium,* chest.]

ar•mor (är′mər) ►*n.* **1.** A protective or defensive covering for the body. **2a.** Metal plates covering a military vehicle or ship. **b.** The armored vehicles of an army. ►*v.* To cover with armor. [< Lat. *armātūra,* ARMATURE.] —**ar′mored** *adj.*

ar•mo•ri•al (är-môr′ē-əl, -mōr′-) ►*adj.* Of or relating to heraldry or heraldic arms.

ar•mor•y (är′mə-rē) ►*n., pl.* **-ies 1.** A storehouse for arms and military equipment. **2.** An arms factory.

arm•pit (ärm′pĭt′) ►*n.* The hollow under the upper part of the arm at the shoulder.

arm•rest (ärm′rĕst′) ►*n.* A support for the arm.

Arm•strong (ärm′strông′), **Louis.** "Satchmo." 1900–71. Amer. jazz musician.

Armstrong, Neil Alden. b. 1930. Amer. astronaut; first to walk on the moon (1969).

Neil Armstrong
photographed in 1969

arm-twist (ärm′twĭst′) ►*v.* *Informal* To use pressure to persuade or to gain support.

ar•my (är′mē) ►*n., pl.* **-mies 1a.** A large body of people organized for warfare. **b.** often **Army** The entire military land forces of a country. **2.** A large group of people organized for a cause. **3.** A multitude. [< Lat. *armāta* < *armāre,* to arm.]

army ant ►*n.* Any of various rapacious tropical ants that move in swarms and subsist on other insects.

ar•ni•ca (är′nĭ-kə) ►*n.* **1.** A perennial herb having yellow flowers. **2.** A tincture of dried arnica flower heads used for bruises and sprains. [NLat. *Arnica,* genus name.]

Ar•no (är′nō) A river of central Italy rising in the N Apennines and flowing about 241 km (150 mi) to the Ligurian Sea.

Ar•nold (är′nəld), **Benedict.** 1741–1801. Amer. Revolutionary general and traitor.

Arnold, Matthew. 1822–88. British poet and critic.

a•ro•ma (ə-rō′mə) ►*n.* **1.** A quality that can be perceived by the olfactory sense. See Syns at **smell. 2.** A usu. pleasant characteristic odor, as of a plant, spice, or food. See Syns at **fragrance.** [< Gk. *arōma,* aromatic herb.] —**ar′o•mat′ic** (ăr′ə-măt′ĭk) *adj.*

a•rose (ə-rōz′) ►*v.* P.t. of **arise.**

a•round (ə-round′) ►*adv.* **1a.** On or to all

sides: *toys lying around.* **b.** In all directions. **2.** In a circle. **3.** In circumference. **4.** In succession. **5.** In the opposite direction: *wheeled around.* **6.** From one place to another: *wander around.* **7.** Nearby. **8.** Approximately: *weighed around 30 pounds.* ▶*prep.* **1.** On all sides of. **2a.** About the circumference of. **b.** So as to encircle or surround. **3a.** Here and there within: *walked around the city.* **b.** Near. **4.** On or to the farther side of: *around the corner.* **5.** So as to bypass or avoid. **6.** Approximately at: *left around seven.*

a•rouse (ə-rouz′) ▶*v.* **a•roused, a•rous•ing** **1.** To awaken from or as if from sleep. **2.** To stir up; excite: *aroused her curiosity.* [< ROUSE.] —**a•rous′al** *n.*

ar•peg•gi•o (är-pĕj′ē-ō′, -pĕj′ō) ▶*n., pl.* **-os** **1.** The playing of the tones of a chord in rapid succession rather than simultaneously. **2.** A chord played or sung in this manner. [Ital. < *arpa*, harp.]

arr. ▶*abbr.* **1.** arranged **2.** arrival

ar•raign (ə-rān′) ▶*v.* **1.** To call (an accused person) before a court to answer a charge. **2.** To denounce. [< VLat. **adrationāre*, call to account.] —**ar•raign′ment** *n.*

ar•range (ə-rānj′) ▶*v.* **-ranged, -rang•ing** **1.** To put into a specific order or relation. **2.** To plan: *arrange a picnic.* **3.** To agree about; settle. **4.** To reset (music) for other instruments or voices. [< OFr. *arengier.*] —**ar•range′ment** *n.* —**ar•rang′er** *n.*

Syns: *arrange, marshal, order, organize, sort, systematize* ***Ant:*** *disarrange* **v.**

ar•rant (ăr′ənt) ▶*adj.* Utter; thoroughgoing: *an arrant fool.* [Var. of ERRANT.]

ar•ras (ăr′əs) ▶*n.* **1.** A tapestry. **2.** A curtain or wall hanging. [ME, after *Arras*, France.]

ar•ray (ə-rā′) ▶*v.* **1.** To place in an orderly arrangement. **2.** To dress in finery; adorn. ▶*n.* **1.** An orderly arrangement. **2.** An impressively large number. See Syns at **display. 3.** Splendid attire; finery. **4.** *Math.* An arrangement of quantities in rows and columns. **5.** *Comp. Sci.* An arrangement of memory elements in one or more planes. [< VLat. **arrēdāre.*]

ar•rears (ə-rîrz′) ▶*pl.n.* **1.** An overdue debt. **2.** The state of being behind in fulfilling obligations: *an account in arrears.* [< OFr. *arere*, behind.] —**ar•rear′age** *n.*

ar•rest (ə-rĕst′) ▶*v.* **1.** To stop; check. **2.** To seize and hold by legal authority. **3.** To capture; engage: *arrested my attention.* ▶*n.* **1.** The act of stopping or the condition of being stopped. **2a.** The act of detaining in legal custody. **b.** The state of being so detained: *under arrest.* [< OFr. *arester* : AD– + RE– + Lat. *stāre*, stand.] —**ar•rest′er, ar•res′tor** *n.*

ar•rest•ing (ə-rĕs′tĭng) ▶*adj.* Attracting and holding the attention; striking.

ar•rhyth•mi•a (ə-rĭ*th*′mē-ə) ▶*n.* An irregularity in the force or rhythm of the heartbeat.

ar•ri•val (ə-rī′vəl) ▶*n.* **1.** The act of arriving. **2.** One that arrives or has arrived.

ar•rive (ə-rīv′) ▶*v.* **-rived, -riv•ing** **1.** To reach a destination. **2.** To come eventually: *The day of reckoning has arrived.* **3.** To achieve success or recognition. [< OFr. *ariver.*]

ar•ro•gant (ăr′ə-gənt) ▶*adj.* Unpleasantly or disdainfully self-important; haughty. [< Lat. *arrogāre*, arrogate.] —**ar′ro•gance** *n.* —**ar′ro•gant•ly** *adv.*

ar•ro•gate (ăr′ə-gāt′) ▶*v.* **-gat•ed, -gat•ing.** To take or claim for oneself without right. See Syns at **appropriate.** [Lat. *arrogāre.*] —**ar′ro•ga′tion** *n.* —**ar′ro•ga′tive** *adj.*

ar•row (ăr′ō) ▶*n.* **1.** A straight thin shaft with a pointed head and often stabilizing feathers, meant to be shot from a bow. **2.** Something, such as a directional symbol, shaped like an arrow. [< OE *arwe.*]

ar•row•head (ăr′ō-hĕd′) ▶*n.* The pointed, removable striking tip of an arrow.

ar•row•root (ăr′ō-ro͞ot′, -ro͝ot′) ▶*n.* **1.** An edible starch obtained from the rhizomes of a tropical American plant. **2.** This plant or its rhizome. [< Arawak *aru-aru*, meal of meals.]

ar•roy•o (ə-roi′ō) ▶*n., pl.* **-os.** A deep gully cut by an intermittent stream. [Sp.]

ar•se•nal (är′sə-nəl) ▶*n.* **1.** A place for the storage, manufacture, or repair of arms and ammunition. **2.** A stock or supply, esp. of weapons. [< Ar. *dār-aṣ-ṣināʽa*, place of manufacture.]

ar•se•nic (är′sə-nĭk) ▶*n. Symbol* **As** A highly poisonous metallic element used in insecticides, weed killers, solid-state doping agents, and various alloys. At. no. 33. See table at **element.** [< Gk. *arsenikon*, a yellow substance, of Iranian orig.]

ar•son (är′sən) ▶*n.* The crime of willfully setting fire to buildings or other property. [< LLat. *ārsiō* < Lat. *ārdēre*, to burn.] —**ar′son•ist** *n.*

art[1] (ärt) ▶*n.* **1a.** Creative or imaginative activity, esp. the expressive arrangement of elements within a medium. **b.** Works, such as paintings or poetry, resulting from such activity. **2.** A branch of artistic activity, such as musical composition, using a special medium and technique. **3.** The aesthetic values of an artist. **4.** Any of various disciplines, such as the humanities, that do not rely on the scientific method. **5.** A craft or trade and its methods. **6.** Contrivance; cunning. **7.** A practical skill; knack. [< Lat. *ars*, *art-*.]

Syns: *art, craft, expertise, knack, know-how, technique* **n.**

art[2] (ərt; ärt *when stressed*) ▶*v. Archaic* 2nd pers. sing. pr. indic. of **be.**

art. ▶*abbr.* article

-art ▶*suff.* Var. of **-ard.**

art dec•o (dĕk′ō) ▶*n.* A decorative style of the period 1925–40, marked by geometric designs and bold colors. [< *Exposition Internationale des Arts Décoratifs et Industriels Modernes*, held in 1925 in Paris.]

ar•te•fact (är′tə-făkt′) ▶*n.* Var. of **artifact.**

Ar•te•mis (är′tə-mĭs) ▶*n. Gk. Myth.* The virgin goddess of the hunt and the moon and twin sister of Apollo. [Gk.]

ar•te•ri•o•scle•ro•sis (är-tîr′ē-ō-sklə-rō′sĭs) ▶*n.* A chronic disease in which thickening and hardening of the arterial walls impair blood circulation. —**ar•te′ri•o•scle•rot′ic** (-rŏt′ĭk) *adj.*

ar•ter•y (är′tə-rē) ▶*n., pl.* **-ies** **1.** Any of a branching system of muscular tubes that carry blood away from the heart. **2.** A major transportation route into which local routes flow. [< Gk. *artēria.*] —**ar•te′ri•al** (-tîr′ē-əl) *adj.*

ar•te•sian well (är-tē′zhən) ▶*n.* A deep well in which water rises to the surface by internal hydrostatic pressure. [Fr. *(puit) artēsien*, (well) of Artois, France.]

art•ful (ärt′fəl) ►*adj.* **1.** Exhibiting art or skill. **2.** Deceitful; cunning; crafty: *an artful reply.* —**art′ful•ly** *adv.* —**art′ful•ness** *n.*

ar•thri•tis (är-thrī′tĭs) ►*n.* Inflammation of a joint or joints. —**ar•thrit′ic** (-thrĭt′ĭk) *adj.*

arthro– or **arthr–** ►*pref.* Joint: *arthropod.* [< Gk. *arthron*, joint.]

ar•thro•pod (är′thrə-pŏd′) ►*n.* Any of numerous invertebrates, including the insects, crustaceans, and arachnids, characterized by an exoskeleton, a segmented body, and paired, jointed limbs.

ar•thros•co•py (är-thrŏs′kə-pē) ►*n.*, *pl.* **-pies.** Endoscopic examination of a joint, such as the knee. —**ar′thro•scop′ic** (-skŏp′ĭk) *adj.*

Ar•thur (är′thər) ►*n.* A legendary British hero, said to have been king of the Britons in the 6th cent. A.D., who held court at Camelot. —**Ar•thu′ri•an** (-thoor′ē-ən) *adj.*

Arthur, Chester Alan. 1829–86. The 21st US President (1881–85).

Chester A. Arthur

ar•ti•choke (är′tĭ-chōk′) ►*n.* **1.** A thistlelike plant having large heads of bluish flowers. **2.** The edible, unopened flower head of this plant. [Ult. < Ar. *al-ḫaršūf.*]

ar•ti•cle (är′tĭ-kəl) ►*n.* **1.** An individual element of a class; item. **2.** A section in a written document. **3.** A nonfictional composition or essay in a publication. **4.** *Gram.* Any of a class of words, such as *a* or *the,* used to signal nouns and to specify their application. [< Lat. *articulus*, dim. of *artus*, joint.]

ar•tic•u•lar (är-tĭk′yə-lər) ►*adj.* Of a joint or joints. [< Lat. *articulus*, small joint.]

ar•tic•u•late (är-tĭk′yə-lĭt) ►*adj.* **1.** Endowed with speech. **2.** Composed of meaningful syllables or words. **3.** Using or characterized by clear, expressive language. **4.** *Anat.* Jointed. ►*v.* (är-tĭk′yə-lāt′) **-lat•ed, -lat•ing 1.** To pronounce distinctly; enunciate. **2.** To utter (a speech sound). **3.** To express in words. **4.** To fit together; unify. **5.** *Anat.* To unite by or form a joint. [< Lat. *articulāre*, divide into joints.] —**ar•tic′u•late•ly** *adv.* —**ar•tic′u•la′tion** *n.* —**ar•tic′u•la′tor** *n.*

ar•ti•fact also **ar•te•fact** (är′tə-făkt′) ►*n.* An object, such as a tool, made by human craft. [Lat. *ars*, art + *factum*, something made.]

ar•ti•fice (är′tə-fĭs) ►*n.* **1.** A crafty expedient; stratagem. **2.** Deception; trickery. **3.** Cleverness; ingenuity. [< Lat. *artificium.*]

ar•ti•fi•cial (är′tə-fĭsh′əl) ►*adj.* **1.** Made by humans rather than occurring in nature. **2.** Made in imitation of something natural. **3.** Not genuine: *an artificial smile.* [< Lat. *artificium*, artifice.] —**ar′ti•fi′ci•al′i•ty** (-ē-ăl′ĭ-tē) *n.* —**ar′ti•fi′cial•ly** *adv.*

artificial insemination ►*n.* Introduction of semen into the vagina or uterus without sexual contact.

artificial intelligence ►*n.* The ability of a computer to perform activities normally thought to require intelligence.

artificial life ►*n.* The simulation of biological phenomena through computer models, robotics, or biochemistry.

artificial respiration ►*n.* A procedure to restore respiration in a person who has stopped breathing by forcing air into and out of the lungs in a rhythmic fashion.

ar•til•ler•y (är-tĭl′ə-rē) ►*n.* **1.** Large-caliber weapons, such as cannon, operated by crews. **2.** Troops armed with artillery. [< OFr. *artillier*, equip.]

ar•ti•san (är′tĭ-zən, -sən) ►*n.* A skilled manual worker. [< Ital. *artigiano* < Lat. *ars*, art.] —**ar′ti•san•ship′** *n.*

art•ist (är′tĭst) ►*n.* **1.** One who practices any of the fine or performing arts, as painting or music. **2.** One whose work shows skill. —**ar•tis′tic** *adj.* —**ar•tis′ti•cal•ly** *adv.*

ar•tiste (är-tēst′) ►*n.* A public performer, esp. a singer or dancer. [Fr., artist.]

art•ist•ry (är′tĭ-strē) ►*n.* Artistic ability, quality, or craft.

art•less (ärt′lĭs) ►*adj.* **1.** Without cunning; guileless. **2.** Simple; natural. **3.** Lacking art; crude. —**art′less•ly** *adv.* —**art′less•ness** *n.*

artsy ►*adj.* **-sier, -siest.** Var. of **arty.**

art•y (är′tē) or **art•sy** (ärt′sē) ►*adj.* **-i•er, -i•est** or **-si•er, -si•est** *Informal.* Affectedly artistic. —**art′i•ly** *adv.* —**art′i•ness** *n.*

A•ru•ba (ə-roo′bə) An island of the Netherlands in the Netherlands Antilles N of the Venezuela coast.

a•ru•gu•la (ə-roo′gə-lə) ►*n.* See **rocket²**. [Ital. dial. < Lat. *ērūca.*]

ar•um (ăr′əm, âr′-) ►*n.* Any of several Old World plants having arrowhead-shaped leaves. [< Gk. *aron.*]

–ary ►*suff.* Of or relating to: *reactionary.* [< Lat. *-ārius*, adj. and n. suff.]

Ar•y•an (âr′ē-ən, ăr′-) ►*n.* **1.** See **Indo-Iranian. 2.** A member of the people who spoke Proto-Indo-European. **3.** A member of a people speaking an Indo-European language. **4.** In Nazism, a non-Jewish Caucasian, esp. one of Nordic type. [< Skt. *ārya-*, compatriot, Aryan.] —**Ar′y•an** *adj.*

as (ăz; əz *when unstressed*) ►*adv.* **1.** To the same extent or degree; equally. **2.** For instance: *large carnivores, as the bear or lion.* ►*conj.* **1.** To the same degree or quantity that: *as sweet as sugar.* See Usage Note at **like²**. **2.** In the same way that: *Think as I think.* **3.** At the same time that; while. **4.** Since; because. **5.** Though: *Trite as it sounds, it's true.* **6.** *Informal* That: *I don't know as I can.* ►*pron.* That; which; who: *I received the same grade as you did.* ►*prep.* **1.** In the role, capacity, or function of: *acting as a mediator.* **2.** In a manner similar to; the same as. —***idioms:*** **as is** *Informal* Just the way it is. **as it were** In a manner of speaking. [< OE *ealswā.*]

Usage: Use a comma before *as* to express a causal relation, as in *She won't be coming, as* *we didn't invite her.* To express a time relation, do not use a comma before *as: She was finishing the painting as I walked into the room.* In using a clause that starts with *as* at the beginning of a sentence, make clear whether *as* is used to mean "because" or "at the same time that." E.g., *As they were leaving, John walked to the door* may mean that John walked to the door either because they were leaving or at the same time they were leaving.

As ▸ The symbol for the element **arsenic.**

As. ▸ *abbr.* Asia

as•a•fet•i•da (ăs′ə-fĕt′ĭ-də) ▸ *n.* A brownish, bitter, foul-smelling resin. [< Med.Lat. *asa foetida.*]

A•sa•ma (ə-sä′mə), **Mount.** A volcano, about 2,544 m (8,340 ft), of central Honshu, Japan.

ASAP ▸ *abbr.* as soon as possible

ASAT ▸ *abbr.* antisatellite

as•bes•tos (ăs-bĕs′təs, ăz-) ▸ *n.* An incombustible, chemical-resistant, fibrous mineral used for fireproofing and electrical insulation. [< Gk. *asbestos*, unquenchable.]

as•bes•to•sis (ăs′bĕs-tō′sĭs, ăz′-) ▸ *n.* A progressive lung disease caused by prolonged inhalation of asbestos particles.

ASCAP ▸ *abbr.* American Society of Composers, Authors, and Publishers

as•cend (ə-sĕnd′) ▸ *v.* **1a.** To go or move upward; rise. **b.** To climb: *ascend the stairs.* **2.** To succeed to; occupy: *ascended the throne.* [< Lat. *ascendere.*]

as•cen•dan•cy also **as•cen•den•cy** (ə-sĕn′dən-sē) ▸ *n.* Decisive advantage; domination.

as•cen•dant also **as•cen•dent** (ə-sĕn′dənt) ▸ *adj.* **1.** Inclining or moving upward. **2.** Dominant; superior. ▸ *n.* The position or state of being dominant.

as•cen•sion (ə-sĕn′shən) ▸ *n.* **1.** The act or process of ascending. **2. Ascension** *Christianity* The bodily rising of Jesus into heaven on the 40th day after his Resurrection.

as•cent (ə-sĕnt′) ▸ *n.* **1.** The act of rising upward. **2.** An upward slope.

as•cer•tain (ăs′ər-tān′) ▸ *v.* To discover through investigation. See Syns at **discover.** [< OFr. *acertener* < *certain*, CERTAIN.] —**as′cer•tain′a•ble** *adj.*

as•cet•ic (ə-sĕt′ĭk) ▸ *n.* One who leads a life of austerity, esp. for religious reasons. [< Gk. *askētēs*, hermit.] —**as•cet′ic** *adj.* —**as•cet′i•cism** (-ĭ-sĭz′əm) *n.*

ASCII (ăs′kē) ▸ *n. Comp. Sci.* A standard for assigning numerical values to the set of letters in the Roman alphabet and typographic characters. [*A(merican) S(tandard) C(ode for) I(nformation) I(nterchange).*]

a•scor•bic acid (ə-skôr′bĭk) ▸ *n.* A vitamin, $C_6H_8O_6$, found in citrus fruits and leafy green vegetables and used to prevent scurvy; vitamin C. [A–[1] + SCORB(UT)IC.]

as•cot (ăs′kət) ▸ *n.* A broad scarf knotted so that its ends are laid flat upon each other. [From *Ascot*, England.]

as•cribe (ə-skrīb′) ▸ *v.* **-cribed, -crib•ing.** To attribute to a specified cause, source, or origin. [< Lat. *ascrībere.*] —**as•crib′a•ble** *adj.* —**as•crip′tion** (-skrĭp′shən) *n.*

ASE ▸ *abbr.* American Stock Exchange

-ase ▸ *suff.* Enzyme: *amylase.* [< *diastase*, an amylase found in germinating grains.]

a•sep•tic (ə-sĕp′tĭk, ā-) ▸ *adj.* Free of pathogenic microorganisms. —**a•sep′sis** *n.*

a•sex•u•al (ā-sĕk′shōō-əl) ▸ *adj.* **1.** Having no sex or sex organs; sexless. **2.** Not involving sex organs or the union of sex cells. **3.** Lacking interest in sex. —**a•sex′u•al•ly** *adv.*

as for ▸ *prep.* With regard to.

ash[1] (ăsh) ▸ *n.* **1.** The grayish-white to black powdery residue of combustion. **2.** *Geol.* Pulverized particulate matter ejected by volcanic eruption. **3. ashes** Ruins. **4. ashes** Human remains, esp. after cremation. [< OE *æsce.*]

ash[2] (ăsh) ▸ *n.* **1.** A deciduous ornamental or timber tree. **2.** The strong elastic wood of this tree. [< OE *æsc.*]

a•shamed (ə-shāmd′) ▸ *adj.* **1.** Feeling shame. **2.** Feeling inferior or embarrassed. **3.** Reluctant through fear of shame: *ashamed to tell.* [< OE *āsceamian*, feel shame.] —**a•sham′ed•ly** (-shā′mĭd-lē) *adv.*

A•shan•ti[1] (ə-shăn′tē, ə-shän′-) ▸ *n., pl.* **-ti** or **-tis 1.** A member of a people of central Ghana. **2.** The Twi language of the Ashanti.

A•shan•ti[2] (ə-shăn′tē, -shän′-) A region and former kingdom of W Africa in present-day central Ghana.

Ashe (ăsh), **Arthur Robert, Jr.** 1943–93. Amer. tennis player.

ash•en (ăsh′ən) ▸ *adj.* **1.** Consisting of ashes. **2.** Resembling ashes, esp. in color; pale.

Ash•ga•bat (äsh′gä-bät′) The capital of Turkmenistan, in the S-central part. Pop. 407,000.

Ash•ke•naz•i (äsh′kə-nä′zē) ▸ *n., pl.* **-naz•im** (-năz′ĭm, -nä′zĭm). A usu. Yiddish-speaking Jew of E and central Europe.

ash•lar (ăsh′lər) ▸ *n.* **1.** A squared block of building stone. **2.** Masonry of such stones. [< OFr. *aisselier*, board.]

a•shore (ə-shôr′, -shōr′) ▸ *adv.* To or on the shore.

ash•ram (äsh′rəm) ▸ *n.* A residence of a Hindu religious community and its guru. [Skt. *āśramaḥ.*]

ash•tray (ăsh′trā′) ▸ *n.* A receptacle for tobacco ashes and cigarette butts.

Ash Wednesday ▸ *n.* The 7th Wednesday before Easter and the 1st day of Lent.

ash•y (ăsh′ē) ▸ *adj.* **-i•er, -i•est 1.** Of or covered with ashes. **2.** Ashen; pale.

A•sia (ā′zhə, -shə) The largest continent, occupying the E part of the Eurasian landmass and its adjacent islands and separated from Europe by the Ural Mts.

Asia Minor. A peninsula of W Asia between the Black and Mediterranean seas.

A•sian (ā′zhən, -shən) ▸ *adj.* Of or relating to Asia or its peoples, languages, or cultures. ▸ *n.* **1.** A native or inhabitant of Asia. **2.** A person of Asian descent.

Usage: The term *Asian* is now preferred for persons of South and East Asian ancestry (Indians, Southeast Asians, Chinese, Koreans, Japanese, Indonesians, Filipinos, and others) in place of the term *Oriental*, an older usage for some of these groups.

Asian American ▸ *n.* A US citizen or resident of Asian descent. —**A′sian-A•mer′i•can** *adj.*

A•si•at•ic (ā′zhē-ăt′ĭk, -shē-, -zē-) ▸ *adj.* Asian. ▸ *n. Often Offensive* An Asian.

a•side (ə-sīd′) ▸ *adv.* **1.** To one side. **2.** Out of one's thoughts or mind. **3.** Apart. **4.** In reserve;

away. ▸*n.* Dialogue supposedly not heard by the other actors in a play.

aside from ▸*prep.* Excluding; except for.

as•i•nine (ăs′ə-nīn′) ▸*adj.* Stupid; silly. [Lat. *asinīnus* < *asinus*, ass.]

ask (ăsk) ▸*v.* **1.** To put a question to. **2.** To seek an answer to. **3.** To inquire. **4.** To request. **5.** To expect or demand. **6.** To invite. [< OE *āscian.*]

a•skance (ə-skăns′) ▸*adv.* **1.** With disapproval or distrust. **2.** With a sideways glance. [?]

a•skew (ə-skyo͞o′) ▸*adv. & adj.* To one side; awry.

ASL ▸*abbr.* American Sign Language

a•slant (ə-slănt′) ▸*adv. & adj.* Obliquely.

a•sleep (ə-slēp′) ▸*adj.* **1.** Sleeping. **2.** Inactive; dormant. **3.** Numb. —**a•sleep′** *adv.*

As•ma•ra (ăz-mä′rə) A city of N Ethiopia near the Red Sea. Pop. 358,100.

a•so•cial (ā-sō′shəl) ▸*adj.* **1.** Averse to the society of others. **2.** Unwilling to conform to normal social behavior; antisocial.

as of ▸*prep.* On; at: *payable as of May 1.*

asp (ăsp) ▸*n.* Any of several venomous African or Eurasian snakes. [< Gk. *aspis.*]

as•par•a•gus (ə-spăr′ə-gəs) ▸*n.* A plant having leaflike stems, scalelike leaves, and edible young shoots. [< Gk. *asparagos.*]

ASPCA ▸*abbr.* American Society for the Prevention of Cruelty to Animals

as•pect (ăs′pĕkt) ▸*n.* **1.** An appearance; air. **2.** An element; facet. **3.** A position facing a given direction. **4.** *Gram.* A category of the verb designating the duration or type of action. [< Lat. *aspicere*, look at : AD– + *specere*, look.]

as•pen (ăs′pən) ▸*n.* A poplar tree having leaves that flutter readily in even a light breeze. [< OE *æspe.*]

as•per•i•ty (ă-spĕr′ĭ-tē) ▸*n.* **1.** Roughness; harshness. **2.** Ill temper. [< Lat. *asper*, rough.]

as•per•sion (ə-spûr′zhən, -shən) ▸*n.* A slanderous remark. [< Lat. *aspergere*, scatter.]

as•phalt (ăs′fôlt′) ▸*n.* A brownish-black solid or semisolid mixture of bitumens used in paving, roofing, and waterproofing. [< Gk. *asphaltos*, pitch.] —**as•phal′tic** *adj.*

as•pho•del (ăs′fə-dĕl′) ▸*n.* A Mediterranean plant having clusters of white, pink, or yellow flowers. [< Gk. *asphodelos.*]

as•phyx•i•a (ăs-fĭk′sē-ə) ▸*n.* Lack of oxygen accompanied by an increase of carbon dioxide in the blood, leading to unconsciousness or death. [< Gk. *asphuxia*, stopping of the pulse.]

as•phyx•i•ate (ăs-fĭk′sē-āt′) ▸*v.* **-at•ed, -at•ing.** To suffocate; smother. —**as•phyx′i•a′tion** *n.* —**as•phyx′i•a′tor** *n.*

as•pic (ăs′pĭk) ▸*n.* A clear jelly made of meat, fish, or vegetable stock and gelatin. [Fr., asp (from its color).]

as•pi•dis•tra (ăs′pĭ-dĭs′trə) ▸*n.* A popular houseplant having large evergreen leaves. [< Gk. *aspis*, *aspid-*, shield.]

as•pi•rant (ăs′pər-ənt, ə-spīr′-) ▸*n.* One who aspires, as to advancement.

as•pi•rate (ăs′pə-rāt′) ▸*v.* **-rat•ed, -rat•ing 1.** *Ling.* To pronounce (e.g., a vowel) with the release of breath associated with English *h,* as in *he.* **2.** To inhale. **3.** *Medic.* To remove with a suction device. [Lat. *aspīrāre*, breathe on.] —**as′pi•rate** (-pər-ĭt) *n.*

as•pi•ra•tion (ăs′pə-rā′shən) ▸*n.* **1a.** A strong desire for achievement. **b.** An object of such desire; an ambition. **2.** The removal of fluids or gases from the body by suction. **3.** The pronunciation of an aspirated speech sound.

as•pi•ra•tor (ăs′pə-rā′tər) ▸*n.* A device for removing substances, such as mucus or serum, from a body cavity by suction.

as•pire (ə-spīr′) ▸*v.* **-pired, -pir•ing.** To have a great ambition; desire. [< Lat. *aspīrāre*, desire.] —**as•pir′er** *n.* —**as•pir′ing•ly** *adv.*

as•pi•rin (ăs′pər-ĭn, -prĭn) ▸*n.* **1.** A white crystalline compound derived from salicylic acid and used to relieve pain and reduce fever and inflammation. **2.** A tablet of aspirin. [Orig. a trademark.]

As•quith (ăs′kwĭth), **Herbert Henry.** 1852–1928. British prime minister (1908–16).

ass (ăs) ▸*n.* **1.** Any of several hoofed, long-eared mammals resembling and closely related to the horse. **2.** A vain, silly, or stupid person. [< OE *assa*, ult. < Lat. *asinus.*]

as•sail (ə-sāl′) ▸*v.* To attack violently. [< Lat. *assilīre*, jump on.] —**as•sail′a•ble** *adj.* —**as•sail′ant** *n.* —**as•sail′er** *n.*

as•sas•sin (ə-săs′ĭn) ▸*n.* A murderer, esp. of a prominent person. [< Ar. *ḥaššāšīn*, pl. of *ḥaššāš*, hashish user.]

as•sas•si•nate (ə-săs′ə-nāt′) ▸*v.* **-nat•ed, -nat•ing 1.** To murder by surprise attack, as for political reasons. **2.** To destroy (a rival's character). —**as•sas′si•na′tion** *n.*

as•sault (ə-sôlt′) ▸*n.* **1.** A violent physical or verbal attack. **2.** An unlawful threat or attempt to do bodily injury to another. **3.** The crime of rape. [< Lat. *assilīre*, *assult-*, jump on.] —**as•sault′** *v.* —**as•sault′er** *n.* —**as•saul′tive** *adj.*

assault and battery ▸*n.* *Law* A physical assault involving bodily injury to another.

assault weapon ▸*n.* An infantry weapon designed for individual use.

as•say (ăs′ā′, ă-sā′) ▸*n.* Qualitative or quantitative analysis of a substance, esp. of an ore or drug. ▸*v.* (ă-sā′, ăs′ā′) **1.** To subject to or undergo an assay. **2.** To evaluate; assess. **3.** To attempt. [< OFr. *assai*, ESSAY.] —**as•say′a•ble** *adj.* —**as•say′er** *n.*

as•sem•blage (ə-sĕm′blĭj) ▸*n.* **1.** The act of assembling or the state of being assembled. **2.** A collection of persons or things. **3.** A fitting together of parts, as in a machine. **4.** An art work consisting of an arrangement of miscellaneous objects, such as pieces of metal, cloth, and string.

as•sem•ble (ə-sĕm′bəl) ▸*v.* **-bled, -bling 1.** To bring or gather together. **2.** To fit together the parts of. [< OFr. *assembler.*]

as•sem•bler (ə-sĕm′blər) ▸*n.* **1.** One that assembles. **2.** A program that produces executable machine code from symbolic assembly language.

as•sem•bly (ə-sĕm′blē) ▸*n.*, *pl.* **-blies 1.** The act of assembling or the state of being assembled. **2.** A group of persons gathered together for a common purpose. **3. Assembly** The lower house of a legislature. **4a.** The putting together of parts to make a product. **b.** A set of parts so assembled. **5.** *Comp. Sci.* The automatic translation of symbolic code into machine code.

assembly language ▸*n.* A programming language that closely resembles machine code.

assembly line ▸*n.* An arrangement of workers

and tools in which the product passes from operation to operation until completed.

as•sent (ə-sĕnt′) ►*v.* To agree; concur. [< Lat. *assentārī.*] —**as•sent′** *n.* —**as•sent′er, as•sen′tor** *n.*

as•sert (ə-sûrt′) ►*v.* **1.** To state positively; affirm. **2.** To defend or maintain. **3.** To put (oneself) forward boldly or forcefully. [Lat. *asserere.*] —**as•ser′tive** *adj.* —**as•ser′tive•ly** *adv.* —**as•ser′tive•ness** *n.*

as•ser•tion (ə-sûr′shən) ►*n.* A positive, often unsupported declaration.

as•sess (ə-sĕs′) ►*v.* **1.** To evaluate, esp. for taxation. **2.** To set the amount of (a tax or fine). **3.** To charge with a tax or fine. **4.** To make a judgment about. [< Lat. *assidēre, assess-*, assist as judge : AD– + *sedēre*, sit.] —**as•sess′a•ble** *adj.* —**as•sess′ment** *n.* —**as•ses′sor** *n.*

as•set (ăs′ĕt′) ►*n.* **1.** A useful or valuable quality, person, or thing. **2. assets** All properties, such as cash or stock, that may cover the liabilities of a person or business. [< AN *asez*, enough.]

as•sev•er•ate (ə-sĕv′ə-rāt′) ►*v.* **-at•ed, -at•ing.** To declare positively; assert. [Lat. *assevērāre.*] —**as•sev′er•a′tion** *n.*

as•sid•u•ous (ə-sĭj′o͞o-əs) ►*adj.* Constant in application or attention; diligent. [< Lat. *assidēre*, attend to. See ASSESS.] —**as′si•du′i•ty** (ăs′ĭ-do͞o′ĭ-tē, dyo͞o′-) *n.* —**as•sid′u•ous•ly** *adv.* —**as•sid′u•ous•ness** *n.*

as•sign (ə-sīn′) ►*v.* **1.** To specify; designate. **2.** To select for a duty; appoint. **3.** To give out as a task; allot. **4.** To ascribe; attribute. **5.** *Law* To transfer (e.g., property) from one to another. [< Lat. *assignāre.*] —**as•sign′a•bil′i•ty** *n.* —**as•sign′a•ble** *adj.* —**as•sign′er** *n.*

as•sig•na•tion (ăs′ĭg-nā′shən) ►*n.* An appointment for a meeting between lovers.

as•sign•ment (ə-sīn′mənt) ►*n.* **1.** The act of assigning. **2.** Something assigned.

as•sim•i•late (ə-sĭm′ə-lāt′) ►*v.* **-lat•ed, -lat•ing 1.** To take in, digest, and transform (food) into living tissue. **2.** To take in and understand. **3.** To make or become similar. [< Lat. *assimilāre*, make similar to.] —**as•sim′i•la•ble** (-lə-bəl) *adj.* —**as•sim′i•la′•tion** *n.*

As•sin•i•boin (ə-sĭn′ə-boin′) ►*n., pl.* **-boin** or **-boins 1.** A member of a Native American people of N Montana and adjacent regions of Canada. **2.** Their Siouan language.

as•sist (ə-sĭst′) ►*v.* To help; support. ►*n.* An act of giving aid; help. [< Lat. *assistere* : AD– + *sistere*, stand.] —**as•sis′tance** *n.*

as•sis•tant (ə-sĭs′tənt) ►*n.* One that assists; helper. —**as•sis′tant** *adj.*

Syns: *assistant, aide, coadjutor, helper, lieutenant, second* **n.**

as•sist•ed living (ə-sĭs′tĭd) ►*n.* A living arrangement in which people with special needs reside in a facility that provides help with everyday tasks.

assisted suicide ►*n.* Suicide accomplished with the aid of another person, esp. a physician.

as•size (ə-sīz′) ►*n.* **1.** A session or a decree of a court. **2. assizes** One of the periodic court sessions formerly held in the counties of England and Wales. [< Lat. *assidēre*, sit beside : AD– + *sedēre*, sit.]

assn. ►*abbr.* association

assoc. ►*abbr.* **1.** associate **2.** association

as•so•ci•ate (ə-sō′shē-āt′, -sē-) ►*v.* **-at•ed, -at•ing 1.** To join or connect in a relationship. **2.** To connect in the mind or imagination. ►*n.* (-ĭt, -āt′) **1.** A partner; colleague. **2.** A companion; comrade. ►*adj.* (-ĭt, -āt′). Joined in equal or nearly equal status. [< Lat. *associāre*, join to.]

as•so•ci•a•tion (ə-sō′sē-ā′shən, -shē-) ►*n.* **1.** The act of associating or the state of being associated. **2.** An organized body of people; society. —**as•so′ci•a′tion•al** *adj.*

association football ►*n.* *Chiefly Brit.* Soccer.

as•so•ci•a•tive (ə-sō′shē-ā′tĭv, -sē-, -shə-tĭv) ►*adj.* **1.** Of or causing association. **2.** *Math.* Independent of the grouping of elements. —**as•so′ci•a′tive•ly** *adv.*

as•so•nance (ăs′ə-nəns) ►*n.* Resemblance esp. of the vowel sounds in words. [< Lat. *assonāre*, respond to.] —**as′so•nant** *adj.* & *n.* —**as′so•nan′tal** (-năn′tl) *adj.*

as•sort (ə-sôrt′) ►*v.* To separate into groups according to kind; classify. [< OFr. *assorter.*] —**as•sor′ta•tive** *adj.* —**as•sort′er** *n.*

as•sort•ed (ə-sôr′tĭd) ►*adj.* Of different kinds; various: *assorted sizes.*

as•sort•ment (ə-sôrt′mənt) ►*n.* **1.** The act of assorting. **2.** A collection of various kinds; variety.

ASSR ►*abbr.* Autonomous Soviet Socialist Republic

asst. ►*abbr.* assistant

as•suage (ə-swāj′) ►*v.* **-suaged, -suag•ing 1.** To make less severe; ease. **2.** To satisfy or appease. [< OFr. *assuagier* < Lat. *suavis*, sweet.]

as•sume (ə-so͞om′) ►*v.* **-sumed, -sum•ing 1.** To take upon oneself. **2.** To take on; adopt. **3.** To pretend; feign. **4.** To take for granted; suppose. [< Lat. *assūmere*, take to.] —**as•sum′a•ble** *adj.* —**as•sum′a•bly** *adv.*

as•sumed (ə-so͞omd′) ►*adj.* **1.** Feigned; pretended. **2.** Taken for granted; supposed. —**as•sum′ed•ly** (-so͞o′mĭd-lē) *adv.*

as•sum•ing (ə-so͞o′mĭng) ►*adj.* Presumptuous; arrogant. ►*conj.* Supposing.

as•sump•tion (ə-sŭmp′shən) ►*n.* **1.** The act of assuming. **2.** A statement accepted as true without proof; supposition. **3. Assumption** *Christianity* The bodily taking up of the Virgin Mary into heaven after her death.

as•sur•ance (ə-sho͝or′əns) ►*n.* **1.** The act of assuring. **2.** Freedom from doubt; certainty. **3.** Self-confidence. **4.** *Chiefly Brit.* Insurance, esp. life insurance.

as•sure (ə-sho͝or′) ►*v.* **-sured, -sur•ing 1.** To inform positively. **2.** To cause to feel sure. **3.** To make certain; ensure. **4.** *Chiefly Brit.* To insure, as against loss. [< VLat. **assēcūrāre*, make sure.] —**as•sur′er** *n.*

Usage: *Assure, ensure,* and *insure* all mean "to make secure or certain." Only *assure* is used for a person in the sense of "to set the mind at rest" and only *insure* is now used in American English in the sense of "to guarantee persons or property against risk."

as•sured (ə-sho͝ord′) ►*adj.* **1.** Certain; guaranteed. **2.** Confident; sure. —**as•sur′ed•ly** (-ĭd-lē) *adv.* —**as•sur′ed•ness** *n.*

As•syr•i•a (ə-sîr′ē-ə) An ancient empire and civilization of W Asia in the upper valley of the Tigris R.

As•syr•i•an (ə-sîr′ē-ən) ►*adj.* Of or relating to Assyria or its culture. ►*n.* **1.** A native or inhabitant of Assyria. **2.** See **Akkadian** 2.

A•staire (ə-stâr′), **Fred.** 1899–1987. Amer. dancer and actor.

as•ta•tine (ăs′tə-tēn′, -tĭn) ►*n. Symbol* **At** A highly unstable radioactive element used in medicine as a radioactive tracer. See table at **element.** [< Gk. *astatos*, unstable.]

as•ter (ăs′tər) ►*n.* Any of various plants having daisylike flower heads with white, pink, or violet rays and a usu. yellow disk. [< Gk. *astēr*, star.]

as•ter•isk (ăs′tə-rĭsk′) ►*n.* A star-shaped figure (*) used in printing to indicate an omission or a reference to a footnote. [< Gk. *asteriskos*, dim. of *astēr*, star.]

a•stern (ə-stûrn′) ►*adv. & adj.* **1.** Behind a vessel. **2.** At or to the stern of a vessel.

as•ter•oid (ăs′tə-roid′) ►*n.* Any of numerous small celestial bodies that revolve around the sun chiefly between Mars and Jupiter. [< Gk. *astēr*, star.]

asth•ma (ăz′mə, ăs′-) ►*n.* A respiratory disease, often arising from allergies, marked by labored breathing, chest constriction, and coughing. [< Gk.] —**asth•mat′ic** (-măt′ĭk) *adj. & n.*

a•stig•ma•tism (ə-stĭg′mə-tĭz′əm) ►*n.* A refractive defect of a lens, esp. of the eye, that prevents focusing of sharp, distinct images. [A–[1] + Gk. *stigma*, mark.] —**as′tig•mat′ic** (ăs′tĭg-măt′ĭk) *adj. & n.*

a•stir (ə-stûr′) ►*adj.* Moving about.

a•ston•ish (ə-stŏn′ĭsh) ►*v.* To fill with sudden wonder or amazement. [< OFr. *estoner*.] —**a•ston′ish•ing•ly** *adv.* —**a•ston′ish•ment** *n.*

As•tor (ăs′tər), **John Jacob.** 1763–1848. German-born Amer. fur trader and capitalist.

Astor, Nancy Witcher Langhorne. 1879–1964. Amer.-born British politician; first woman to serve in the House of Commons (1919–45).

a•stound (ə-stound′) ►*v.* To astonish and bewilder. [< ME *astoned*, astonished.] —**a•stound′ing** *adj.* —**a•stound′ing•ly** *adv.*

a•strad•dle (ə-străd′l) ►*adv. & prep.* Astride.

as•tra•khan (ăs′trə-kăn′, -kən) ►*n.* A curly, wavy fur made from the skins of young lambs from Astrakhan.

As•tra•khan (ăs′trə-kăn′, ä-strä-KHän′) A city of SW Russia on the Volga R. delta. Pop. 507,710.

as•tral (ăs′trəl) ►*adj.* Of or resembling the stars. [< Gk. *astron*, star.]

a•stray (ə-strā′) ►*adv.* **1.** Away from the correct direction or route. See Syns at **amiss. 2.** Into wrong or evil ways. [< OFr. *estraier*, STRAY.] —**a•stray′** *adj.*

a•stride (ə-strīd′) ►*adv. & prep.* With a leg on each side (of).

as•trin•gent (ə-strĭn′jənt) ►*adj.* **1.** *Medic.* Tending to draw together or constrict living tissues; styptic. **2.** Sharp; harsh: *astringent remarks.* ►*n.* An astringent agent or drug. [< Lat. *astringere*, bind together.] —**as•trin′gen•cy** *n.* —**as•trin′gent•ly** *adv.*

astro– or **astr–** ►*pref.* **1.** Star: *astrophysics.* **2.** Outer space: *astronaut.* [< Gk., *astron*, star.]

as•tro•labe (ăs′trə-lāb′) ►*n.* A medieval instrument used to determine the altitude of a celestial body. [< Gk. *(organon) astrolabon*, (instrument) for taking the stars.]

as•trol•o•gy (ə-strŏl′ə-jē) ►*n.* The study of the positions and aspects of celestial bodies with a view to predicting their influence on human affairs. —**as•trol′o•ger** *n.* —**as′tro•log′i•cal** (ăs′trə-lŏj′ĭ-kəl), **as′tro•log′ic** *adj.*

as•tro•naut (ăs′trə-nôt′) ►*n.* A person trained to pilot or otherwise participate in the flight of a spacecraft. [ASTRO– + Gk. *nautēs*, sailor.]

as•tro•nau•tics (ăs′trə-nô′tĭks) ►*n. (takes sing. or pl. v.)* The science and technology of space flight. —**as′tro•nau′tic, as′tro•nau′ti•cal** *adj.* —**as′tro•nau′ti•cal•ly** *adv.*

as•tro•nom•i•cal (ăs′trə-nŏm′ĭ-kəl) also **as•tro•nom•ic** (-nŏm′ĭk) ►*adj.* **1.** Of or relating to astronomy. **2.** Colossal; immense. —**as′tro•nom′i•cal•ly** *adv.*

astronomical unit ►*n.* A unit of length equal to the mean distance from Earth to the sun, approx. 150 million km (93 million mi).

as•tron•o•my (ə-strŏn′ə-mē) ►*n.* The scientific study of the positions, distribution, motion, and composition of celestial bodies. —**as•tron′o•mer** *n.*

as•tro•phys•ics (ăs′trō-fĭz′ĭks) ►*n. (takes sing. v.)* The branch of astronomy that deals with the physics of stellar phenomena. —**as′tro•phys′i•cal** *adj.* —**as′tro•phys′i•cist** (-fĭz′ĭ-sĭst) *n.*

As•tro•Turf (ăs′trō-tûrf′) ► A trademark for an artificial grasslike ground covering.

as•tute (ə-sto͞ot′, ə-styo͞ot′) ►*adj.* Having or showing keen judgment; shrewd. [Lat. *astūtus* < *astus*, craft.] —**as•tute′ly** *adv.* —**as•tute′ness** *n.*

A•sun•ción (ä-so͞on′syōn′) The capital of Paraguay, in the S part. Pop. 546,637.

a•sun•der (ə-sŭn′dər) ►*adv.* **1.** Into separate parts, pieces, or groups. **2.** Apart in position or direction. [< OE *on sundran*.]

a•sy•lum (ə-sī′ləm) ►*n.* **1.** An institution for the care of ill or needy people, esp. those with mental impairments. **2.** A place of safety; refuge. **3.** Protection granted by a government to a political refugee from another country. [< Gk. *asulos*, inviolable.]

a•sym•met•ri•cal (ā′sĭ-mĕt′rĭkəl) also **a•sym•met•ric** (-rĭk) ►*adj.* Not symmetrical. —**a′sym•met′ri•cal•ly** *adv.* —**a•sym′me•try** *n.*

a•symp•to•mat•ic (ā′sĭmp-tə-măt′ĭk) ►*adj.* Neither causing nor exhibiting symptoms of disease. —**a′symp•to•mat′i•cal•ly** *adv.*

as•ymp•tote (ăs′ĭm-tōt′, -ĭmp-) ►*n.* A line whose distance to a given curve tends to zero.

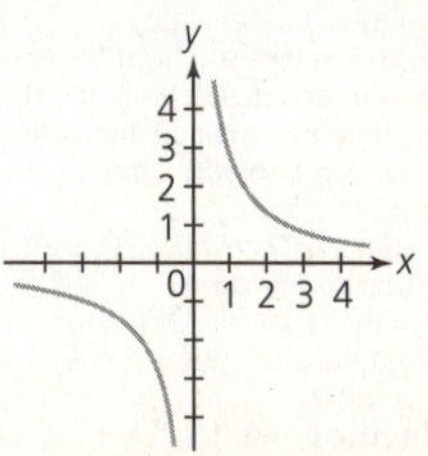

asymptote
the *x* and *y* axes are asymptotes of the hyperbola $xy = 1$

[< Gk. *asumptōtos,* not intersecting.] —**as′ymp•tot′ic** (-tŏt•ĭk), **as′ymp•tot′i•cal** *adj.*

at (ăt; ət *when unstressed*) ▶*prep.* **1.** In or near the position or area occupied by: *at the market; at the top of the page.* **2.** To or toward the direction or goal of: *looked at them; worked at the task.* **3.** In the state or condition of: *at peace.* **4.** In the activity or field of: *good at math; at work.* **5.** On, near, or by the time or age of: *at three o'clock.* **6.** Because of: *rejoice at a victory.* [< OE *æt.*]

At ▶ The symbol for the element **astatine.**

at•a•vism (ăt′ə-vĭz′əm) ▶*n.* The reappearance of a characteristic in an organism after several generations of absence. [< Lat. *atavus,* ancestor.] —**at′a•vis′tic** *adj.* —**at′a•vis′ti•cal•ly** *adv.*

ate (āt) ▶*v.* P.t. of **eat.**

-ate[1] ▶*suff.* **1a.** Having: *nervate.* **b.** Characterized by: *affectionate.* **c.** Resembling: *palmate.* **2.** Rank; office: *pastorate.* **3.** To act upon in a specified manner: *acidulate.* **4.** Product of an action or process: *distillate.* [< Lat. *-ātus,* p.part. suff.]

-ate[2] ▶*suff.* **1.** A derivative of a specified chemical compound or element: *silicate.* **2.** A salt or ester of a specified acid: *acetate.* [NLat. *-ātum* < Lat. *-ātus,* p.part. suff.]

at•el•ier (ăt′l-yā′) ▶*n.* A workshop or studio, esp. for an artist. [< OFr. *astelier.*]

Ath•a•bas•ca (ăth′ə-băs′kə) A river rising in the Rocky Mts. of SW Alberta, Canada, and flowing about 1,231 km (765 mi) to **Lake Athabasca** on the Saskatchewan border.

Ath•a•bas•kan or **Ath•a•bas•can** (ăth′ə-băs′kən) also **Ath•a•pas•can** (-păs′-) ▶*n.* **1.** A group of related Native American languages including Navajo, Apache, and languages of NW Canada. **2.** A member of an Athabaskan-speaking people.

a•the•ism (ā′thē-ĭz′əm) ▶*n.* **1a.** Disbelief in or denial of the existence of God. **b.** The doctrine that there is no God. **2.** Godlessness; immorality. [< Gk. *atheos,* without a god.] —**a′the•ist** *n.* —**a′the•is′tic** *adj.*

A•the•na (ə-thē′nə) also **A•the•ne** (-nē) ▶*n.* *Gk. Myth.* The goddess of wisdom, the practical arts, and warfare.

ath•e•nae•um also **ath•e•ne•um** (ăth′ə-nē′əm) ▶*n.* **1.** An institution for the promotion of learning. **2.** A library. [< Gk. *Athēnaion,* temple of Athena.]

Ath•ens (ăth′ənz) The capital of Greece, in the E part near the Saronic Gulf; reached the height of its power and cultural achievements in the 5th cent. B.C. Pop. 885,737. —**A•the′ni•an** (ə-thē′nē-ən) *adj. & n.*

ath•er•o•scle•ro•sis (ăth′ə-rō-sklə-rō′sĭs) ▶*n.* A form of arteriosclerosis in which plaque containing cholesterol and lipids is deposited on the inner walls of the arteries. [< Lat. *athērōma,* kind of tumor.]

a•thirst (ə-thûrst′) ▶*adj.* Strongly desirous; eager: *athirst for freedom.*

ath•lete (ăth′lēt′) ▶*n.* One who participates esp. in competitive sports. [< Gk. *athlētēs* < *athlein,* compete.]

ath•lete's foot (ăth′lēts) ▶*n.* A contagious fungal skin infection usu. affecting the feet, esp. the skin between the toes, marked by itching, blisters, cracking, and scaling.

ath•let•ic (ăth-lĕt′ĭk) ▶*adj.* **1.** Of or for athletics or athletes. **2.** Physically strong. See Syns at **muscular.** —**ath•let′i•cal•ly** *adv.* —**ath•let′i•cism** (-lĕt′ĭ-sĭz′əm) *n.*

ath•let•ics (ăth-lĕt′ĭks) ▶*n. (takes sing. or pl. v.)* **1.** Athletic activities. **2.** A system of training and practice for such activities.

athletic supporter ▶*n.* An elastic support for the male genitals, worn esp. during sports.

a•thwart (ə-thwôrt′) ▶*adv.* From side to side; crosswise. ▶*prep.* **1.** From one side to the other of; across. **2.** Contrary to.

a•tilt (ə-tĭlt′) ▶*adv. & adj.* In a tilted position.

-ation ▶*suff.* **1a.** Action or process: *strangulation.* **b.** The result of an action or process: *acculturation.* **2.** State, condition, or quality of: *moderation.* [< Lat. *-ātiō,* n. suff.]

-ative ▶*suff.* Relating to or characterized by: *talkative.* [< Lat. *-ātīvus* < *-ātus,* -ATE[1].]

At•lan•ta (ăt-lăn′tə) The capital of GA, in the NW part. Pop. 394,017. —**At•lan′tan** *n.*

Atlantic Ocean. The second-largest ocean, divided into the **North Atlantic** and the **South Atlantic** and extending from the Arctic in the N to the Antarctic in the S between the Americas and Europe and Africa.

At•lan•tis (ăt-lăn′tĭs) ▶*n.* A legendary sunken island in the Atlantic Ocean W of Gibraltar.

at•las (ăt′ləs) ▶*n.* A book or bound collection of maps. [After ATLAS, often depicted holding the world on his shoulders on the frontispiece of early atlases.]

Atlas ▶*n.* *Gk. Myth.* A Titan condemned by Zeus to hold up the heavens.

Atlas Mountains. A system of ranges and plateaus of NW Africa.

at•la•tl (ät-lät′l) ▶*n.* A device , usu. a stick fitted with a thong or socket, used for added leverage in throwing a spear. [Nahuatl.]

ATM ▶*abbr.* automated teller machine

at•mos•phere (ăt′mə-sfîr′) ▶*n.* **1.** The gaseous mass or envelope surrounding a celestial body, esp. Earth. **2.** *Phys.* A unit of pressure equal to the air pressure at sea level. **3.** Surroundings; environment. **4.** A dominant tone or attitude: *an atmosphere of distrust.* [Gk. *atmos,* vapor + Lat. *sphaera,* sphere.] —**at′mos•pher′ic** (-sfĕr′ĭk) *adj.* —**at′mos•pher′i•cal•ly** *adv.*

at•mos•pher•ics (ăt′mə-sfĕr′ĭks) ▶*n.* **1.** *(takes sing. v.)* Radio interference produced by electromagnetic radiation from natural phenomena. **2.** Features intended to create a particular mood or attitude.

at. no. ▶*abbr.* atomic number

a•toll (ăt′ôl′, -ŏl′, ā′tôl′, ā′tŏl′) ▶*n.* A ringlike coral island that encloses a lagoon. [Perh. < Tamil *aṭar,* be close together.]

at•om (ăt′əm) ▶*n.* **1.** An extremely small part, quantity, or amount. **2.** A unit of matter, the smallest unit of an element, having all the characteristics of that element and consisting of a dense, positively charged nucleus surrounded by a system of electrons. [< Gk. *atomos,* indivisible.]

atom bomb ▶*n.* **1.** An explosive weapon of great destructive power derived from the rapid release of energy in the fission of heavy atomic nuclei. **2.** A nuclear weapon.

a•tom•ic (ə-tŏm′ĭk) ▶*adj.* **1.** Of or relating to an atom. **2.** Of or employing nuclear energy: *an atomic submarine.* **3.** Very small; infinitesimal. —**a•tom′i•cal•ly** *adv.*

atomic bomb ▸*n.* See **atom bomb** 1.

atomic energy ▸*n.* See **nuclear energy.**

atomic number ▸*n.* The number of protons in an atomic nucleus.

atomic weight ▸*n.* The average mass of an atom of an element, usu. given relative to carbon 12, which is assigned a mass of 12.

at•om•ize (ăt′ə-mīz′) ▸*v.* **-ized, -iz•ing 1.** To reduce to fine or minute particles, as in a spray. **2.** To fragment; disintegrate. —**at′om•i•za′tion** *n.*

at•om•iz•er (ăt′ə-mī′zər) ▸*n.* A device for producing a fine spray of a liquid.

atom smasher ▸*n.* See **accelerator** 2.

a•ton•al (ā-tōn′əl) ▸*adj. Mus.* Lacking a traditional key or tonality. —**a′to•nal′i•ty** (-tō-năl′ĭ-tē) *n.* —**a•ton′al•ly** *adv.*

a•tone (ə-tōn′) ▸*v.* **a•toned, a•ton•ing.** To make amends (for). [< ME *at one*, of one mind.] —**a•ton′er** *n.*

a•tone•ment (ə-tōn′mənt) ▸*n.* Reparation made for an injury, wrong, or sin.

a•top (ə-tŏp′) ▸*adv.* To, on, or at the top. ▸*prep.* On top of. —**a•top′** *adj.*

-ator ▸*suff.* One that acts in a specified manner: *radiator.* [Lat. *-ātor.*]

-atory ▸*suff.* **1a.** Of or relating to: *reconciliatory.* **b.** Tending to: *derogatory.* **2.** One that is connected with: *observatory.* [< Lat. *-ātōrius.*]

ATP (ā′tē′pē′) ▸*n.* A nucleotide that supplies energy to cells. [*a(denosine) t(ri)p(hosphate)* (blend of ADENINE and RIBOSE).]

a•tri•um (ā′trē-əm) ▸*n., pl.* **a•tri•a** (ā′trē-ə) or **-ums 1a.** A usu. skylighted central area in a building, esp. a public building. **b.** An open central court in an ancient Roman house. **2.** A body cavity or chamber, esp. either of the upper chambers of the heart; auricle. [Lat. *ātrium.*]

a•tro•cious (ə-trō′shəs) ▸*adj.* **1.** Extremely evil, savage, or cruel: *an atrocious crime.* **2.** Exceptionally bad; abominable: *atrocious decor.* [< Lat. *atrōx*, cruel.] —**a•tro′cious•ly** *adv.* —**a•tro′cious•ness** *n.*

a•troc•i•ty (ə-trŏs′ĭ-tē) ▸*n., pl.* **-ties 1.** Atrocious state, quality, or behavior. **2.** An appalling act or object. **3.** An act of vicious cruelty, esp. the killing of unarmed people.

at•ro•phy (ăt′rə-fē) ▸*n., pl.* **-phies.** A wasting or shrinking of a bodily organ, tissue, or part. ▸*v.* **-phied, -phy•ing.** To waste or cause to waste away. [< Gk. *atrophos*, without food.] —**a•troph′ic** (ā-trŏf′ĭk) *adj.*

at•ro•pine (ăt′rə-pēn′, -pĭn) also **at•ro•pin** (-pĭn) ▸*n.* A poisonous, bitter, crystalline alkaloid, $C_{17}H_{23}NO_3$, obtained from belladonna and used to dilate the pupil of the eye. [< NLat. *Atropa*, belladonna.]

at•tach (ə-tăch′) ▸*v.* **1.** To fasten or become fastened; connect. **2.** To bind by ties of affection or loyalty. **3.** To affix or append: *attached her signature to the contract.* **4.** To seize by legal writ. [< OFr. *attachier.*] —**at•tach′a•ble** *adj.*

at•ta•ché (ăt′ə-shā′, ă-tă-) ▸*n.* One who is assigned to a diplomatic mission to serve in a particular capacity: *a cultural attaché.* [Fr., one attached.]

attaché case ▸*n.* A slim briefcase with flat sides and hinges.

at•tach•ment (ə-tăch′mənt) ▸*n.* **1.** The act of attaching or the condition of being attached. **2.** Something, such as a tie or band, that attaches one thing to another. **3.** A bond of affection or loyalty. **4.** A supplementary part, as of an appliance; accessory. **5.** *Law* **a.** Legal seizure of property or a person. **b.** The writ ordering this.

at•tack (ə-tăk′) ▸*v.* **1.** To set upon with violent force. **2.** To criticize strongly. **3.** To start work on with vigor. **4.** To affect harmfully: *a disease that attacked the nervous system.* ▸*n.* **1.** The act of attacking; assault. **2.** An expression of strong or hostile criticism. **3.** The onset of a disease, esp. a chronic disease. [< OFr. *attaquer.*] —**at•tack′er** *n.*

at•tain (ə-tān′) ▸*v.* **1.** To accomplish; achieve. **2.** To arrive at. [< Lat. *attingere*, reach to, touch.] —**at•tain′a•bil′i•ty** *n.* —**at•tain′a•ble** *adj.* —**at•tain′ment** *n.*

at•tain•der (ə-tān′dər) ▸*n.* Formerly, the loss of all civil rights by a person sentenced for a capital offense. [< OFr. *ataindre*, to convict.]

at•taint (ə-tānt′) ▸*v.* To pass a sentence of attainder against. [< OFr. *ataindre*, to convict. See ATTAIN.]

at•tar (ăt′ər) ▸*n.* A fragrant oil obtained from flowers. [< Ar. *'aṭir*, aromatic.]

at•tempt (ə-tĕmpt′) ▸*v.* To make an effort to do, perform, or achieve; try. ▸*n.* **1.** An effort; try. **2.** An attack; assault: *an attempt on someone's life.* [< Lat. *attemptāre*, try to.] —**at•tempt′a•ble** *adj.*

at•tend (ə-tĕnd′) ▸*v.* **1.** To be present (at). **2.** To accompany. **3.** To take care (of). See Syns at **tend**[2]. **4.** To take charge of; manage. **5.** To pay attention (to); heed. [< Lat. *attendere*, stretch toward, heed.]

at•ten•dance (ə-tĕn′dəns) ▸*n.* **1.** The act of attending. **2.** The number of persons present.

at•ten•dant (ə-tĕn′dənt) ▸*n.* **1.** A person who attends or waits on another. **2.** One who is present. **3.** An accompanying circumstance; consequence. ▸*adj.* Accompanying; consequent: *attendant conditions.*

at•ten•tion (ə-tĕn′shən) ▸*n.* **1.** Concentration of the mental powers upon an object. **2.** Observant consideration; notice. **3.** Courtesy or consideration: *attention to a guest's comfort.* **4. attentions** Acts of courtesy and consideration, esp. by a suitor. **5.** An erect military posture assumed on command. —**at•ten′tive** *adj.* —**at•ten′tive•ly** *adv.* —**at•ten′tive•ness** *n.*

attention deficit disorder ▸*n.* A syndrome, usu. diagnosed in childhood, marked by persistent impulsiveness and inattention, with or without hyperactivity.

attention deficit hyperactivity disorder ▸*n.* Attention deficit disorder with hyperactivity.

at•ten•u•ate (ə-tĕn′yo͞o-āt′) ▸*v.* **-at•ed, -at•ing 1.** To make or become thin or small. **2.** To weaken. **3.** To rarefy or dilute. [Lat. *attenuāre*, make thin.] —**at•ten′u•a′tion** *n.*

at•test (ə-tĕst′) ▸*v.* **1.** To affirm to be correct, true, or genuine, esp. by affixing one's signature as witness. **2.** To supply evidence of: *actions that attested their bravery.* See Syns at **indicate. 3.** To bear witness: *attested to their good faith.* [Lat. *attestārī*, be witness to.] —**at′tes•ta′tion** (ăt′ĕs-tā′shən) *n.* —**at•test′er, at•tes′tor** *n.*

at•tic (ăt′ĭk) ▸*n.* A story or room directly below the roof of a building, esp. a house. [Ult. < ATTIC.]

Attic ►*adj.* **1.** Of ancient Attica or Athens. **2.** Pure and simple: *Attic prose.* ►*n.* A dialect of ancient Greek.

At•ti•ca (ăt′ĭ-kə) An ancient region of E-central Greece around Athens.

At•ti•la (ăt′l-ə, ə-tĭl′ə). A.D. 406?–453. King of the Huns (433?–453).

at•tire (ə-tīr′) ►*v.* **-tired, -tir•ing.** To dress or clothe. ►*n.* Clothing or array; apparel. [< OFr. *atirier*, arrange in ranks.]

at•ti•tude (ăt′ĭ-to͞od′, -tyo͞od′) ►*n.* **1.** A position of the body or manner of carrying oneself: *stood in a belligerent attitude.* See Syns at **posture. 2.** A state of mind or a feeling; disposition: *an attitude of friendliness.* **3.** The orientation of an aircraft's axes esp. with respect to the horizon. **4.** The orientation of a spacecraft relative to its direction of motion. **5.** A position in which a ballet dancer stands on one leg with the other raised and bent at the knee. [< LLat. *aptitūdō*, fitness.] —**at′ti•tu′di•nal** *adj.*

attitude

Att•lee (ăt′lē), **Clement Richard.** 1883–1967. British prime minister (1945–51).

attn. ►*abbr.* attention

at•tor•ney (ə-tûr′nē) ►*n., pl.* **-neys.** A person, esp. a lawyer, legally appointed or empowered to act as another's agent. [< OFr. *atorner*, assign to.] —**at•tor′ney•ship′** *n.*

attorney at law ►*n., pl.* **attorneys at law.** An attorney.

attorney general ►*n., pl.* **attorneys general** or **attorney generals.** The chief law officer and counsel of a state or nation's government.

at•tract (ə-trăkt′) ►*v.* **1.** To cause to draw near or adhere. **2.** To arouse the interest, admiration, or attention of. [< Lat. *attrahere, attract-*, draw toward.] —**at•tract′a•ble** *adj.* —**at•trac′tive** *adj.* —**at•trac′tive•ness** *n.*

at•trac•tant (ə-trăk′tənt) ►*n.* A substance, such as a pheromone, that attracts insects or other animals.

at•trac•tion (ə-trăk′shən) ►*n.* **1.** The act or power of attracting. **2.** Allure; charm. **3.** A feature or characteristic that attracts. **4.** A public spectacle or entertainment.

at•trib•ute (ə-trĭb′yo͞ot) ►*v.* **-ut•ed, -ut•ing.** To regard as a particular cause, source, or agent; ascribe: *attributed their success to hard work.* ►*n.* **at•tri•bute** (ăt′rə-byo͞ot′) **1.** A distinctive feature of or object associated with someone or something. **2.** *Gram.* An attributive. [Lat. *attribuere*, allot to.] —**at•trib′ut•a•ble** *adj.* —**at•trib′ut•er, at•trib′u•tor** *n.* —**at′tri•bu′tion** (ăt′rə-byo͞o′shən) *n.*

at•trib•u•tive (ə-trĭb′yə-tĭv) ►*n.* A word or word group, such as an adjective, that is adjacent to the noun it modifies without a linking verb; e.g., *pale* in *the pale moon.* ►*adj.* **1.** Of or being an attributive. **2.** Of or like an attribute. —**at•trib′u•tive•ly** *adv.*

at•trit (ə-trĭt′) ►*v.* **-trit•ted, -trit•ting 1.** To lose (e.g., personnel) by attrition. **2.** To destroy or kill (e.g., troops). [< ATTRITION.]

at•tri•tion (ə-trĭsh′ən) ►*n.* **1.** A rubbing away or wearing down by friction. **2.** A gradual diminution in number or strength because of constant stress: *a war of attrition.* **3.** A gradual, natural reduction in membership or personnel, as through resignation or death. [< Lat. *atterere, attrit-*, rub against.]

At•tu (ăt′to͞o′) An island of SW AK, the westernmost of the Aleutians.

At•tucks (ăt′əks), **Crispus.** 1723?–70. Amer. patriot; killed in the Boston Massacre.

at•tune (ə-to͞on′, -tyo͞on′) ►*v.* **-tuned, -tun•ing 1.** To bring into harmony. **2.** To tune.

Atty. ►*abbr.* attorney

Atty. Gen. ►*abbr.* Attorney General

at. wt. ►*abbr.* atomic weight

a•typ•i•cal (ā-tĭp′ĭ-kəl) ►*adj.* Not typical; unusual or irregular. —**a•typ′i•cal•ly** *adv.*

Au ► The symbol for the element **gold** 1. [< Lat. *aurum*, gold.]

au•burn (ô′bərn) ►*n.* A reddish brown. [< Med.Lat. *alburnus*, whitish.] —**au′burn** *adj.*

Auck•land (ôk′lənd) A city of New Zealand, on NW North I. Pop. 316,900.

au cou•rant (ō′ ko͞o-räN′) ►*adj.* **1.** Up-to-date. **2.** Knowledgeable. [Fr.]

auc•tion (ôk′shən) ►*n.* A public sale in which property or items of merchandise are sold to the highest bidder. ►*v.* To sell at or by an auction. [< Lat. *augēre*, increase.] —**auc′tion•eer′** (-shə-nîr′) *n. & v.*

au•da•cious (ô-dā′shəs) ►*adj.* **1.** Fearlessly daring. See Syns at **adventurous. 2.** Arrogantly insolent; impudent. [< Lat. *audēre*, dare.] —**au•da′cious•ly** *adv.* —**au•da′cious•ness** *n.* —**au•dac′i•ty** (-dăs′ĭ-tē) *n.*

Au•den (ôd′n), **W(ystan) H(ugh).** 1907–73. British-born Amer. writer and critic.

au•di•al (ô′dē-əl) ►*adj.* Of or relating to the sense of hearing; aural. [AUDI(O)– + –AL[1].]

au•di•ble (ô′də-bəl) ►*adj.* That is or can be heard. [< Lat. *audīre*, hear.] —**au′di•bil′i•ty** *n.* —**au′di•bly** *adv.*

au•di•ence (ô′dē-əns) ►*n.* **1.** A gathering of spectators or listeners. **2.** All those reached by printed matter or a radio or television broadcast. **3.** A formal hearing or conference: *a papal audience.* **4.** An opportunity to be heard. [< Lat. *audīre*, hear.]

au•di•o (ô′dē-ō′) ►*adj.* **1.** Of or relating to audible sound. **2.** Of the broadcasting or reception of sound. **3.** Of the high-fidelity reproduction of sound. ►*n., pl.* **-di•os 1.** The audio part of television or motion-picture equipment. **2.** The broadcasting, reception, or reproduction of sound. **3.** Audible sound. [< AUDIO–.]

audio– ►*pref.* **1.** Hearing: *audiology.* **2.** Sound: *audiophile.* [< Lat. *audīre*, hear.]

audio book ►*n.* A taped reading of a book that is reproduced in cassette form.

au•di•o•cas•sette (ô′dē-ō-kə-sĕt′) ►*n.* A cassette containing audiotape.

audio frequency ▸*n.* A range of frequencies, usu. from 15 hertz to 20,000 hertz, characteristic of signals audible to the normal human ear.
au•di•ol•o•gy (ô′dē-ŏl′ə-jē) ▸*n.* The study of hearing, esp. hearing defects and their treatment. —**au′di•o•log′i•cal** (-ə-lŏj′ĭ-kəl) *adj.* —**au′di•ol′o•gist** *n.*
au•di•o•phile (ô′dē-ə-fīl′) ▸*n.* One who has an ardent interest in high-fidelity sound reproduction.
au•di•o•tape (ô′dē-ō-tāp′) ▸*n.* A magnetic tape recording of sound made for later playback. ▸*v.* **-taped, -tap•ing.** To record (sound) on magnetic tape.
au•di•o-vis•u•al (ô′dē-ō-vĭzh′o͞o-əl) ▸*adj.* Both audible and visible. ▸*n.* Educational material (e.g., a language film) in audible and visible form.
au•dit (ô′dĭt) ▸*n.* A formal examination or verification of financial accounts. ▸*v.* **1.** To formally examine or correct the financial accounts of: *audit a tax return.* **2.** To attend (a college course) without receiving academic credit. [< Lat. *audīre*, *audīt-*, hear.]
au•di•tion (ô-dĭsh′ən) ▸*n.* A hearing, esp. a trial performance of an actor, dancer, or musician, to obtain a particular role or position. ▸*v.* **1.** To take part in an audition. **2.** To evaluate (a performer) in an audition. [< Lat. *audīre*, *audīt-*, hear.]
au•di•tor (ô′dĭ-tər) ▸*n.* **1.** One who audits accounts. **2.** One who audits a college course. **3.** One who hears; listener.
au•di•to•ri•um (ô′dĭ-tôr′ē-əm, -tōr′-) ▸*n.* **1.** A large room to accommodate an audience. **2.** A building for public gatherings or entertainments.
au•di•to•ry (ô′dĭ-tôr′ē, -tōr′ē) ▸*adj.* Of or relating to the sense, the organs, or the experience of hearing.
Au•du•bon (ô′də-bŏn′, -bən), **John James.** 1785–1851. Haitian-born Amer. ornithologist and artist.
auf Wie•der•seh•en (ouf vē′dər-zā′ən) ▸*interj.* Farewell. [Ger.]
Aug. ▸*abbr.* August
au•ger (ô′gər) ▸*n.* A tool for boring holes in wood, ice, or the earth. [< OE *nafogār.*]

auger

aught¹ also **ought** (ôt) ▸*pron.* Anything whatever. [< OE *āuht.*]
aught² also **ought** (ôt) ▸*n.* **1.** A cipher; zero. **2.** *Archaic* Nothing. [< *a naught.*]
aug•ment (ôg-mĕnt′) ▸*v.* To make or become greater in size, extent, or quantity; increase. [< Lat. *augēre*, to increase.] —**aug′men•ta′tion** *n.*
au gra•tin (ō grät′n, grăt′n) ▸*adj.* Baked with a topping of bread crumbs and sometimes butter and grated cheese. [Fr.]
Augs•burg (ôgz′bûrg′, ouks′bo͝ork′) A city of S Germany WNW of Munich. Pop. 264,764.
au•gur (ô′gər) ▸*n.* A seer; soothsayer. ▸*v.* **1.** To predict, esp. from signs or omens. See Syns at **foretell. 2.** To serve as a sign or omen (of). [< Lat.]
au•gu•ry (ô′gyə-rē) ▸*n.*, *pl.* **-ries 1.** The art or practice of auguring. **2.** An omen.
au•gust (ô-gŭst′) ▸*adj.* **1.** Inspiring awe, reverence, or admiration; majestic. **2.** Venerable. [Lat. *augustus.*] —**au•gust′ly** *adv.*
August ▸*n.* The 8th month of the Gregorian calendar. See table at **calendar.** [After Augustus.]
Au•gus•ta (ô-gŭs′tə, ə) The capital of ME, in the SW part NNE of Portland. Pop. 21,325.
Au•gus•tine (ô′gə-stēn′, ô-gŭs′tĭn), Saint. A.D. 354–430. Early Christian church father and philosopher.
Au•gus•tus (ô-gŭs′təs). Orig. **Oc•ta•vi•an** (ŏk-tā′vē-ən). 63 B.C.–A.D. 14. 1st emperor of Rome (27 B.C.–A.D. 14); defeated Mark Antony and Cleopatra in 31 B.C.
au jus (ō zho͞os′, zhü′) ▸*adj.* Served with the natural juices or gravy. [Fr.]
auk (ôk) ▸*n.* A diving sea bird of northern regions, having a chunky body, short wings, and webbed feet. [< ON *ālka.*]
auld lang syne (ôld′ lăng zīn′, sīn′) ▸*n.* The good old days long past. [Sc., old long since.]
aunt (ănt, änt) ▸*n.* **1.** The sister of one's father or mother. **2.** The wife of one's uncle. [< Lat. *amita*, paternal aunt.]
au pair (ô pâr′) ▸*n.* A young foreigner who works for a family for room and board and in order to learn the language. [Fr.]
au•ra (ôr′ə) ▸*n.*, *pl.* **-ras** or **-rae** (ôr′ē) **1.** An invisible breath or emanation. **2.** A distinctive quality that seems to surround a person or thing; atmosphere. [< Gk., breath.]
au•ral¹ (ôr′əl) ▸*adj.* Of or perceived by the ear. [< Lat. *auris*, ear.] —**au′ral•ly** *adv.*
au•ral² (ôr′əl) ▸*adj.* Of or relating to an aura.
Au•re•lian (ô-rēl′yən, ô-rē′lē-ən). A.D. 212?–275. Roman emperor (A.D. 270–275).
au•re•ole (ôr′ē-ōl′) also **au•re•o•la** (ô-rē′ə-lə) ▸*n.* **1.** A halo. **2.** See **corona** 1. [< Lat. *aureolus*, golden.]
au re•voir (ō′ rə-vwär′) ▸*interj.* Farewell. [Fr.]
au•ri•cle (ôr′ĭ-kəl) ▸*n.* **1.** *Anat.* **a.** The outer projecting portion of the ear. **b.** See **atrium** 2. **2.** *Biol.* An earlobe-shaped part or appendage. [< Lat. *auricula*, dim. of *auris*, ear.] —**au′ri•cled** (-kəld) *adj.*
au•ric•u•lar (ô-rĭk′yə-lər) ▸*adj.* **1.** Aural. **2.** Received by or spoken into the ear. **3.** Shaped like an ear or earlobe. **4.** Of or relating to an auricle of the heart.
au•ro•ra (ə-rôr′ə, ə-rōr′ə) ▸*n.* **1.** Aurora borealis. **2.** Aurora australis. **3.** The dawn. [< Lat. *aurōra*, dawn.] —**au•ro′ral** *adj.*
Aurora¹ ▸*n.* *Rom. Myth.* The goddess of the dawn.
Aurora². A city of N-central CO, a suburb of Denver. Pop. 222,103.
aurora aus•tra•lis (ô-strā′lĭs) ▸*n.* A luminous

phenomenon of southern regions that corresponds to the aurora borealis; southern lights. [NLat., southern dawn.]

aurora bo•re•al•is (bôr′ē-ăl′ĭs, bōr′-) ►*n.* Luminous bands or streamers in the night skies of northern regions, likely caused by charged particles entering the earth's magnetic field; northern lights. [NLat., northern dawn.]

aus•cul•ta•tion (ô′skəl-tā′shən) ►*n.* Diagnostic monitoring of the sounds made by internal bodily organs. [< Lat. *auscultāre*, listen to.]

aus•pice (ô′spĭs) ►*n., pl.* **aus•pi•ces** (ô′spĭ-sĭz, -sēz′) **1.** also **auspices** Protection or support; patronage. **2.** A sign, portent, or omen. [Lat. *auspicium* < *auspex*, bird augur.]

aus•pi•cious (ô-spĭsh′əs) ►*adj.* **1.** Favorable; propitious. **2.** Successful; prosperous. —**aus•pi′cious•ly** *adv.*

Aust. ►*abbr.* Australia

Aus•ten (ô′stən), **Jane.** 1775–1817. British writer.

aus•tere (ô-stîr′) ►*adj.* **-ter•er, -ter•est 1.** Severe or stern; somber: *an austere Puritan minister.* **2.** Strict or severe in discipline; ascetic: *a nomad's austere life.* **3.** Without adornment; bare: *austere living quarters.* [< Gk. *austēros*, harsh.] —**aus•tere′ly** *adv.* —**aus•ter′i•ty** (-stĕr′ĭ-tē)

Aus•ter•litz (ô′stər-lĭts′, ous′tər-) A town of SE Czech Republic.

Aus•tin (ô′stən, ŏs′tən) The capital of TX, in the S-central part. Pop. 465,622.

Austin, Stephen Fuller. 1793–1836. Amer. colonizer and political leader in TX.

Austl. ►*abbr.* Australia

aus•tral (ô′strəl) ►*adj.* Southern. [< Lat. *auster*, south.]

Aus•tral•a•sia (ô′strə-lā′zhə, -shə) **1.** The islands of the S Pacific, including Australia, New Zealand, and New Guinea. **2.** Oceania. —**Aus′tral•a′sian** *adj. & n.*

Aus•tra•lia (ô-strāl′yə) **1.** The world's smallest continent, SE of Asia between the Pacific and Indian Oceans. **2.** A commonwealth comprising the continent of Australia, the island state of Tasmania, two external territories, and several dependencies. Cap. Canberra. Pop. 17,843,000.

Aus•tra•lian (ô-strāl′yən) ►*adj.* Of or relating to Australia. ►*n.* **1.** A native or inhabitant of Australia. **2a.** A member of an aboriginal people of Australia. **b.** Any of the aboriginal languages of Australia.

Australian Alps. A chain of mountain ranges of SE Australia.

Aus•tra•loid (ô′strə-loid′) ►*adj. Anthro.* Of or being a purported human racial classification distinguished by dark skin and dark curly hair and including peoples indigenous to Australia and parts of SE Asia. Not in scientific use. —**Aus′tra•loid′** *n.*

Aus•tri•a (ô′strē-ə) A landlocked country of central Europe W of Czech Republic and Hungary. Cap. Vienna. Pop. 8,031,000. —**Aus′tri•an** *adj. & n.*

Aus•tri•a-Hun•ga•ry (ô′strē-ə-hŭng′gə-rē) A former dual monarchy (1867–1918) of central Europe. —**Aus′tro-Hun•gar′i•an** (ô′strō-hŭng-gâr′ē-ən) *adj. & n.*

Aus•tro-A•si•at•ic (ô′strō-ā′zhē-ăt′ĭk, -shē-, -zē-) ►*n.* A family of languages of SE Asia once dominant in NE India and Indochina. —**Aus′tro-A′si•at′ic** *adj.*

Aus•tro•ne•sia (ô′strō-nē′zhə, -shə) The islands of the Pacific, including Indonesia, Melanesia, Micronesia, and Polynesia.

Aus•tro•ne•sian (ô′strō-nē′zhən, -shən) ►*adj.* Of or relating to Austronesia or its peoples, languages, or cultures. ►*n.* A family of languages that includes the Indonesian, Malay, Melanesian, Micronesian, and Polynesian subfamilies.

aut– ►*pref.* Var. of **auto–.**

au•tar•chy (ô′tär′kē) ►*n., pl.* **-chies.** Autocracy. [< Gk. *autarkhos*, self-governing.] —**au′tarch** *n.* —**au•tar′chic** *adj.*

au•then•tic (ô-thĕn′tĭk) ►*adj.* **1.** Conforming to fact and therefore worthy of trust, reliance, or belief. **2.** Having a claimed and verifiable origin or authorship. [< Gk. *authentēs*, author.] —**au•then′ti•cal•ly** *adv.* —**au′then•tic′i•ty** (-tĭs′ĭ-tē) *n.*

Syns: *authentic, bona fide, genuine, real, true* **Ant:** *counterfeit* **adj.**

au•then•ti•cate (ô-thĕn′tĭ-kāt′) ►*v.* **-cat•ed, -cat•ing.** To prove or establish as being genuine. —**au•then′ti•ca′tion** *n.*

au•thor (ô′thər) ►*n.* **1a.** The writer of a literary work. **b.** One who writes as a profession. **2.** One who originates or creates something. [< Lat. *auctor* < *augēre*, create.] —**au′thor** *v.* —**au•thor′i•al** (ô-thôr′ē-əl, -thŏr′-) *adj.* —**au′thor•ship′** *n.*

au•thor•i•tar•i•an (ə-thôr′ĭ-târ′ē-ən, -thŏr′-, ô-) ►*adj.* Marked by or favoring absolute obedience to authority. —**au•thor′i•tar′i•an** *n.* —**au•thor′i•tar′i•an•ism** *n.*

au•thor•i•ta•tive (ə-thôr′ĭ-tā′tĭv, -thŏr′-, ô-) ►*adj.* **1.** Having or arising from proper authority; official. **2.** Having or showing expert knowledge. —**au•thor′i•ta′tive•ly** *adv.* —**au•thor′i•ta′tive•ness** *n.*

au•thor•i•ty (ə-thôr′ĭ-tē, -thŏr′-, ô-) ►*n., pl.* **-ties 1a.** The right and power to enforce laws, exact obedience, command, determine, or judge. **b.** One that is invested with this right and power, esp. a government or government official. **2.** Authorization. **3a.** One that is an accepted source of expert information. **b.** A citation from such a source. **4.** Firm self-assurance; confidence.

au•thor•i•za•tion (ô′thər-ĭ-zā′shən) ►*n.* **1.** The act of authorizing. **2.** Something that authorizes. See Syns at **permission.**

au•thor•ize (ô′thə-rīz′) ►*v.* **-ized, -iz•ing 1.** To grant authority or power to. **2.** To give permission for; sanction. **3.** To justify.

Syns: *authorize, accredit, commission, empower, license* **v.**

au•tism (ô′tĭz′əm) ►*n.* A psychiatric disorder of childhood marked by withdrawal, preoccupation with fantasy, and language impairment. —**au•tis′tic** (-tĭs′-tĭk) *adj. & n.*

au•to (ô′tō) ►*n., pl.* **-tos.** An automobile.

auto– or **aut–** ►*pref.* **1.** Self; same: *autobiography.* **2.** Automatic: *autopilot.* [< Gk. *autos*, self.]

au•to•bahn (ô′tə-bän′, ou′tō-) ►*n.* An expressway in Germany. [Ger. : *Auto*, automobile + MHGer. *ban*, road.]

au•to•bi•og•ra•phy (ô′tō-bī-ŏg′rə-fē) ►*n., pl.* **-phies.** The biography of a person that is written by that same person. —**au′to•bi•og′ra•pher** *n.* —**au′to•bi′o•graph′ic** (-bī′ə-grăf′ĭk), **au′to•bi′o•graph′i•cal** *adj.*

au•toch•tho•nous (ô-tŏk′thə-nəs) ►*adj.* Originating where found; indigenous; native. [< Gk. *autokhthōn* : AUTO– + *khthōn*, earth.]

au•toc•ra•cy (ô-tŏk′rə-sē) ►*n., pl.* **-cies.** Government by a single person having unlimited power. —**au′to•crat′** *n.* —**au′to•crat′ic, au′to•crat′i•cal** *adj.*

au•to•di•dact (ô′tō-dī′dăkt′) ►*n.* One who is self-taught. [< Gk. *autodidaktos*, self-taught.] —**au′to•di•dac′tic** *adj.*

au•to•graph (ô′tə-grăf′) ►*n.* **1.** A person's own signature or handwriting. **2.** A manuscript in the author's handwriting. ►*v.* To write one's signature on; sign.

au•to•im•mune (ô′tō-ĭ-myo͞on′) ►*adj.* Of or relating to an immune response by the body against one of its own tissues or types of cells. —**au′to•im•mu′ni•ty** *n.*

au•to•mate (ô′tə-māt′) ►*v.* **-mat•ed, -mat•ing 1.** To convert to automatic operation. **2.** To operate by automation.

au•to•mat•ed teller machine (ô′tə-mā′tĭd) ►*n.* An electronic machine in a public place, connected to a bank's data system and activated by a customer to obtain specified banking services, esp. deposits and cash withdrawals.

au•to•mat•ic (ô′tə-măt′ĭk) ►*adj.* **1.** Acting or operating with little or no external influence or control. **2.** Involuntary; reflex. **3.** Responding or behaving in a mechanical way. **4.** Capable of firing continuously until ammunition is exhausted. ►*n.* A machine or device, esp. a firearm, that is automatic. [< Gk. *automatikos* : AUTO– + *-matos*, willing.] —**au′to•mat′i•cal•ly** *adv.*

automatic pilot ►*n.* A navigational mechanism, as on an aircraft, that automatically maintains a preset course; autopilot.

automatic teller machine ►*n.* See **automated teller machine.**

au•to•ma•tion (ô′tə-mā′shən) ►*n.* **1.** The automatic operation or control of equipment, a process, or a system. **2.** The techniques and equipment used to achieve automatic operation or control. **3.** The condition of being automatically controlled or operated.

au•tom•a•tism (ô-tŏm′ə-tĭz′əm) ►*n.* The state, quality, or action of being automatic.

au•tom•a•tize (ô-tŏm′ə-tīz′) ►*v.* **-tized, -tiz•ing.** To make automatic. —**au•tom′a•ti•za′tion** *n.*

au•tom•a•ton (ô-tŏm′ə-tən, -tŏn′) ►*n., pl.* **-tons** or **-ta** (-tə) **1.** An automatic machine or mechanism, esp. a robot. **2.** One that behaves or responds in an automatic or mechanical way. [< Gk. *automatos*, AUTOMATIC.]

au•to•mo•bile (ô′tə-mō-bēl′, -mō′bēl′) ►*n.* A self-propelled land vehicle, esp. a four-wheeled passenger car powered by an internal-combustion engine.

au•to•mo•tive (ô′tə-mō′tĭv) ►*adj.* **1.** Moving by itself; self-propelled. **2.** Of or relating to self-propelled vehicles, esp. automobiles.

au•to•nom•ic nervous system (ô′tə-nŏm′ĭk) ►*n.* The part of the vertebrate nervous system that regulates involuntary action, as of the intestines, heart, and glands.

au•ton•o•mous (ô-tŏn′ə-məs) ►*adj.* **1.** Not controlled by others; independent. **2.** Self-governing. [< Gk. *autonomos*, self-ruling.] —**au•ton′o•my** *n.*

au•to•pi•lot (ô′tō-pī′lət) ►*n.* Automatic pilot.

au•top•sy (ô′tŏp′sē, ô′təp-) ►*n., pl.* **-sies.** Examination of a dead body to find the cause of death; postmortem. [Gk. *autopsia*, seeing for oneself.] —**au′top′sist** *n.*

au•to•some (ô′tə-sōm′) ►*n.* A chromosome that is not a sex chromosome.

au•to•sug•ges•tion (ô′tō-səg-jĕs′chən) ►*n.* *Psychol.* The process by which a person induces self-acceptance of an opinion, belief, or plan of action.

au•to•troph (ô′tə-trŏf′, -trōf′) ►*n.* An organism capable of synthesizing its own food from inorganic substances. [AUTO– + Gk. *trophē*, food.] —**au′to•troph′ic** *adj.*

au•tumn (ô′təm) ►*n.* **1.** The season between summer and winter; fall. **2.** A period of maturity verging on decline. [< Lat. *autumnus.*] —**au•tum′nal** (-tŭm′nəl) *adj.*

Au•vergne (ō-vûrn′, -vĕrn′) A historical region and former province of central France.

aux. ►*abbr.* **1.** auxiliary **2.** auxiliary verb

aux•il•ia•ry (ôg-zĭl′yə-rē, -zĭl′ə-rē) ►*adj.* **1.** Giving assistance or support; helping. **2.** Subsidiary; supplementary. **3.** Held in or used as a reserve. ►*n., pl.* **-ries 1.** One that acts in a supporting capacity. **2.** An auxiliary verb. [< Lat. *auxilium*, help.]

auxiliary verb ►*n.* A verb, such as *have, can,* or *will,* that comes first in a verb phrase and helps form the mood, voice, aspect, and tense of the main verb.

aux•in (ôk′sĭn) ►*n.* Any of several plant growth hormones. [< Gk. *auxein*, grow.]

Av (äv, ôv) ►*n.* A month of the Jewish calendar. See table at **calendar.** [Heb. *'āb.*]

AV ►*abbr.* **1.** audio-visual **2.** Authorized Version

av. ►*abbr.* **1. Av.** avenue **2.** average **3.** avoirdupois

a.v. or **a/v** ►*abbr.* *Lat.* ad valorem (in proportion to the value)

a•vail (ə-vāl′) ►*v.* To be of use or advantage (to); help. ►*n.* Use, benefit, or advantage: *labored to no avail.* [< Lat. *valēre*, be strong, be worth.]

a•vail•a•ble (ə-vā′lə-bəl) ►*adj.* **1.** At hand; accessible. **2.** Capable of being used or gotten; obtainable. —**a•vail′a•bil′i•ty** *n.*

av•a•lanche (ăv′ə-lănch′) ►*n.* **1.** A slide of a large mass, as of snow or rock, down a mountainside. **2.** A massive amount: *an avalanche of mail.* [Fr.]

a•vant-garde (ä′vänt-gärd′, ăv′änt-) ►*n.* A group active in the invention and application of new techniques in a given field, esp. in the arts. [Fr., vanguard.] —**a′vant-garde′** *adj.*

av•a•rice (ăv′ə-rĭs) ►*n.* Extreme desire for wealth; greed. [< Lat. *avārus*, greedy.] —**av′a•ri′cious** (-ə-rĭsh′əs) *adj.*

a•vast (ə-văst′) ►*interj.* *Naut.* Used as a command to stop or desist. [< MDu. *hou vast*, hold fast.]

av•a•tar (ăv′ə-tär′) ►*n.* **1.** *Hinduism* One that is regarded as an incarnation, esp. of Vishnu. **2.** An embodiment or exemplar; archetype. [Skt. *avatāraḥ.*]

a•vaunt (ə-vônt′, ə-vänt′) ►*adv.* Hence; away. [< Lat. *ab ante*, forward.]

avdp. ►*abbr.* avoirdupois

Ave. ►*abbr.* avenue

a•venge (ə-vĕnj′) ►*v.* **a•venged, a•veng•**

ing 1. To take revenge for: *avenge a murder.* **2.** To take vengeance on behalf of: *avenged his father.* [< Lat. *vindicāre*, to claim.] —**a•veng′er** *n.*

av•e•nue (ăv′ə-no͞o′, -nyo͞o′) ►*n.* **1.** A wide street or thoroughfare. **2.** A means of access, approach, or achievement. [< Lat. *advenīre*, come to. See ADVENT.]

a•ver (ə-vûr′) ►*v.* **a•verred, a•ver•ring.** To assert positively; declare. [< VLat. **adverāre*, state as true.] —**a•ver′ment** *n.*

av•er•age (ăv′ər-ĭj, ăv′rĭj) ►*n.* **1a.** A number that typifies a set of numbers of which it is a function. **b.** See **arithmetic mean. 2.** A relative level, proportion, or degree that indicates position or achievement. ►*adj.* **1.** Of or constituting a mathematical average. **2.** Intermediate between extremes, as on a scale. **3.** Usual; ordinary: *a poll of average people.* ►*v.* **-aged, -ag•ing 1.** To calculate the average of. **2.** To do or have an average of: *averaged ten pages an hour.* **3.** To distribute proportionately. [< ME *averay*, charge above the cost of freight, ult. < Ar. *'awārīya*, damaged goods.]

a•verse (ə-vûrs′) ►*adj.* Strongly disinclined; reluctant. [< Lat. *āvertere, āvers-*, turn away.] —**a•verse′ly** *adv.*

a•ver•sion (ə-vûr′zhən, -shən) ►*n.* **1.** A fixed, intense dislike; repugnance. **2.** One that is intensely disliked and avoided.

a•vert (ə-vûrt′) ►*v.* **1.** To turn away: *avert one's eyes.* **2.** To ward off; prevent. [< Lat. *āvertere*.] —**a•vert′i•ble, a•vert′a•ble** *adj.*

avg. ►*abbr.* average

a•vi•an (ā′vē-ən) ►*adj.* Of or characteristic of birds. [< Lat. *avis*, bird.]

a•vi•ar•y (ā′vē-ĕr′ē) ►*n., pl.* **-ies.** A large enclosure for holding birds, as in a zoo. [< Lat. *avis*, bird.]

a•vi•a•tion (ā′vē-ā′shən, ăv′ē-) ►*n.* **1.** The operation of aircraft. **2.** The design, development, and production of aircraft. [< Lat. *avis*, bird.]

a•vi•a•tor (ā′vē-ā′tər, ăv′ē-) ►*n.* One who operates an aircraft; pilot.

a•vi•a•trix (ā′vē-ā′trĭks, ăv′ē-) ►*n.* A woman who operates an aircraft.

av•id (ăv′ĭd) ►*adj.* **1.** Having an ardent desire or craving; eager: *avid for adventure.* **2.** Passionate; enthusiastic: *an avid sports fan.* [Lat. *avidus.*] —**a•vid′i•ty** (ə-vĭd′ĭ-tē) —**av′id•ly** *adv.*

A•vi•gnon (ä-vē-nyôɴ′) A city of SE France on the Rhone R. Pop. 89,132.

a•vi•on•ics (ā′vē-ŏn′ĭks, ăv′ē-) ►*n.* *(takes sing. v.)* The science and technology of electronics as applied to aeronautics and astronautics. —**a′vi•on′ic** *adj.*

av•o•ca•do (ăv′ə-kä′dō, ä′və-) ►*n., pl.* **-dos 1.** A tropical American tree having pear-shaped fruit with leathery skin and yellowish-green flesh. **2.** The edible fruit of this tree. [< Nahuatl *ahuacatl.*]

av•o•ca•tion (ăv′ō-kā′shən) ►*n.* An activity taken up in addition to one's regular work, usu. for enjoyment; hobby. [< Lat. *āvocāre*, call away.] —**av′o•ca′tion•al** *adj.*

av•o•cet (ăv′ə-sĕt′) ►*n.* A long-legged shore bird with a long slender beak. [< Ital. *avocetta.*]

avocet
American avocet

A•vo•ga•dro's number (ä′vō-gä′drōz) ►*n.* The number of atoms or molecules in a mole of a substance, approximately 6.02×10^{23}. [After Amedeo *Avogadro* (1776–1856).]

a•void (ə-void′) ►*v.* **1.** To stay clear of; evade; shun. **2.** To keep from happening; prevent. **3.** To refrain from. [< AN *avoider*, empty out.] —**a•void′a•ble** *adj.* —**a•void′a•bly** *adv.* —**a•void′ance** *n.* —**a•void′er** *n.*

av•oir•du•pois weight (ăv′ər-də-poiz′) ►*n.* A system of weights and measures based on one pound containing 16 ounces or 7,000 grains and equal to 453.59 grams. [< OFr. *aver de peis*, goods of weight.]

A•von (ā′vŏn) A river of S-central England flowing 154.5 km (96 mi) to the Severn.

a•vouch (ə-vouch′) ►*v.* **1.** To affirm. **2.** To vouch for. [< Lat. *advocāre*, summon.]

a•vow (ə-vou′) ►*v.* **1.** To acknowledge openly; confess: *avow guilt.* **2.** To assert: *avowed the words to be true.* [< Lat. *advocāre*, summon.] —**a•vow′al** *n.* —**a•vowed′** *adj.* —**a•vow′ed•ly** (-ĭd-lē) *adv.*

a•vun•cu•lar (ə-vŭng′kyə-lər) ►*adj.* Of or like an uncle. [< Lat. *avunculus*, maternal uncle.]

AWACS (ā′wăks) ►*n., pl.* **AWACS.** An airborne military surveillance system capable of tracking distant aircraft. [*A(irborne) W(arning) A(nd) C(ontrol) S(ystem).*]

a•wait (ə-wāt′) ►*v.* **1.** To wait (for). **2.** To be in store (for): *Success awaits him. A busy day awaits.* [< ONFr. *awaitier.*]

a•wake (ə-wāk′) ►*v.* **a•woke** (ə-wōk′) or **a•waked, a•waked** or **a•wok•en** (ə-wō′kən), **a•wak•ing 1.** To rouse or become roused from sleep. **2.** To excite. **3.** To stir up (e.g., desire). **4.** To become aware: *awoke to reality.* ►*adj.* **1.** Not asleep. **2.** Vigilant; alert. [< OE *āwacan.*]

a•wak•en (ə-wā′kən) ►*v.* To awake. [< OE *āwæcnian.*] —**a•wak′en•ing** *adj. & n.*

a•ward (ə-wôrd′) ►*v.* **1.** To grant or declare as merited or due: *awarded damages to the plaintiff.* **2.** To bestow for performance or quality: *award a prize to the victor.* ►*n.* **1.** Something awarded; prize. **2.** A decision, as by a judge or arbitrator. [< AN *awarder*, decide (a legal case).]

a•ware (ə-wâr′) ►*adj.* Having knowledge or cognizance; mindful. [< OE *gewær.*] —**a•ware′ness** *n.*

a•wash (ə-wŏsh′, -wôsh′) ►*adj. & adv.* **1.** Level with or washed by waves. **2.** Flooded. **3.** Afloat.

a•way (ə-wā′) ►*adv.* **1.** From a particular thing or place: *ran away from the lion.* **2.** At or to a distance in space or time: *away off on the horizon.* **3.** In or to a different place or direction: *glanced away.* **4.** Out of existence: *music fading away.* **5.** From one's presence or possession: *gave the tickets away.* **6.** Continuously; steadily: *worked away.* **7.** At will; freely: *Fire away!* ▶*adj.* **1.** Absent: *The neighbors are away.* **2.** Distant, as in space or time: *miles away.* **3.** Played on an opponent's home grounds: *an away game.* [< OE *aweg.*]

awe (ô) ▶*n.* **1.** A mixed emotion of reverence, dread, and wonder. **2.** Respect tinged with fear. ▶*v.* **awed, aw•ing.** To inspire or fill with awe. [< ON *agi.*]

a•weigh (ə-wā′) ▶*adj.* Hanging clear of the bottom. Used of an anchor.

awe•some (ô′səm) ▶*adj.* **1.** Inspiring awe. **2.** *Slang* Superb; outstanding. —**awe′some•ly** *adv.* —**awe′some•ness** *n.*

awe•struck (ô′strŭk′) also **awe•strick•en** (-strĭk′ən) ▶*adj.* Full of awe.

aw•ful (ô′fəl) ▶*adj.* **1.** Very bad or unpleasant; terrible. **2.** Commanding, inspiring, or filled with awe. **3.** Great: *an awful burden.* —**aw′ful•ly** *adv.* —**aw′ful•ness** *n.*

a•while (ə-hwīl′, ə-wīl′) ▶*adv.* For a short time.

awk•ward (ôk′wərd) ▶*adj.* **1.** Lacking grace or dexterity; clumsy or ungainly. **2.** Hard to handle or manage; unwieldy: *an awkward bundle.* **3.** Uncomfortable; inconvenient: *an awkward pose; an awkward time.* **4.** Causing embarrassment: *an awkward remark.* [ME *awkeward*, in the wrong direction.] —**awk′ward•ly** *adv.* —**awk′ward•ness** *n.*

awl (ôl) ▶*n.* A pointed tool for making holes, as in wood or leather. [< OE *æl.*]

awn (ôn) ▶*n.* A slender bristle on the spikelets of many grasses. [< ON *ögn* and OE *agen*, ear of grain.] —**awned** *adj.*

awn•ing (ô′nĭng) ▶*n.* A canvas rooflike structure, as over a window or storefront, used to provide shade or shelter. [?]

a•woke (ə-wōk′) ▶*v.* P.t. of **awake.**

a•wok•en (ə-wō′kən) ▶*v.* P.part. of **awake.**

AWOL (ā′wôl′) ▶*adj. & adv.* Absent without leave. ▶*n.* One who is absent without leave, esp. from military service.

a•wry (ə-rī′) ▶*adv.* **1.** Askew. **2.** Wrong; amiss. See Syns at **amiss.** —**a•wry′** *adj.*

ax or **axe** (ăks) ▶*n., pl.* **ax•es** (ăk′sĭz) **1.** A chopping tool with a bladed head mounted on a handle. **2.** *Informal* A sudden termination, as of employment. ▶*v.* **axed, ax•ing 1.** To use an ax on in order to chop or fell. **2.** To remove ruthlessly or suddenly. —***idiom:* ax to grind** A selfish or subjective aim: *claimed disinterest but had an ax to grind.* [< OE *æx.*]

ax. ▶*abbr.* **1.** axiom **2.** axis

ax•i•al (ăk′sē-əl) ▶*adj.* **1.** Of, relating to, or forming an axis. **2.** Located on, around, or along an axis. —**ax′i•al•ly** *adv.*

ax•il•la (ăk-sĭl′ə) ▶*n., pl.* **-il•lae** (-sĭl′ē) **1.** The armpit. **2.** An analogous structure, as under a bird's wing. [Lat.]

ax•i•om (ăk′sē-əm) ▶*n.* **1.** A self-evident or universally recognized truth; maxim. **2.** A principle that is accepted as true without proof; postulate. [< Gk. *axiōma* < *axios*, worthy.] —**ax′i•o•mat′ic** *adj.*

ax•is (ăk′sĭs) ▶*n., pl.* **ax•es** (ăk′sēz′) **1.** A straight line about which an object rotates or can be conceived to rotate. **2.** *Math.* **a.** A line, ray, or line segment with respect to which a figure or object is symmetric. **b.** A reference line from which distances or angles are measured in a coordinate system. **3.** A center line to which parts of a structure or body may be referred. **4.** *Bot.* The main stem or central part about which plant parts, as branches, are arranged. **5.** An alliance of powers, such as nations, to promote mutual interests. [< Lat.]

ax•le (ăk′səl) ▶*n.* A supporting shaft on which a wheel or a set of wheels revolves. [< ON *öxull.*]

ax•le•tree (ăk′səl-trē′) ▶*n.* A crossbar, as on a cart, with terminal spindles on which the wheels revolve.

ax•on (ăk′sŏn′) ▶*n.* The usu. long process of a nerve cell that conducts impulses away from the cell body. [Gk. *axōn*, axis.]

a•ya•tol•lah (ī′ə-tō′lə) ▶*n. Islam* A high-ranking Shiite leader having religious and administrative authority. [< Ar. *'āyatu llāh*, sign of god.]

aye[1] also **ay** (ī) ▶*n.* An affirmative vote or voter. ▶*adv.* Yes; yea. [Perh. < AYE[2] + YEA.]

aye[2] also **ay** (ā) ▶*adv.* Always; ever: *for aye.* [< ON *ei.*]

AYH ▶*abbr.* American Youth Hostels

Ay•ma•ra (ī′mä-rä′, ī′mə-) ▶*n., pl.* **-ra** or **-ras** **1.** A member of a South American Indian people inhabiting parts of highland Bolivia and Peru. **2.** Their Aymaran language.

Ay•ma•ran (ī′mä-rän′) ▶*n.* A group of South American Indian languages, the most important being Aymara. —**Ay′ma•ran′** *adj.*

AZ ▶*abbr.* Arizona

a•zal•ea (ə-zāl′yə) ▶*n.* Any of a genus of shrubs cultivated for their showy, variously colored flowers. [< Gk. *azaleos*, dry.]

A•zer•bai•jan (ăz′ər-bī-jän′, ä′zər-) A region and republic of Transcaucasia N of Iran, formerly a kingdom that extended into NW Iran. Cap. Baku. Pop. 7,472,000. —**A′zer•bai•ja′ni** *adj. & n.*

az•i•muth (ăz′ə-məth) ▶*n.* The horizontal angular distance from a reference direction, usu. measured clockwise from due north, to the point where a vertical circle through a celestial body intersects the horizon. [< Ar. *as-sumūt*, pl. of *as-samt*, the way, bearing.]

A•zores (ā′zôrz, ə-zôrz′) A group of Portuguese volcanic islands in the N Atlantic about 1,448 km (900 mi) W of mainland Portugal. —**A•zor′e•an, A•zor′i•an** *adj. & n.*

A•zov (ăz′ôf, ā′zôf, ə-zôf′), **Sea of.** The N arm of the Black Sea between Russia and Ukraine.

AZT (ā′zē-tē′) ▶*n.* An antiviral drug that inhibits replication of the AIDS virus. [*az(ido)t(hymidine).*]

Az•tec (ăz′tĕk′) ▶*n.* **1.** A member of an American Indian people of central Mexico whose empire was at its height at the time of the Spanish conquest in the early 16th cent. **2.** The Nahuatl language of the Aztecs. —**Az′tec′, Az′tec′an** *adj.*

az•ure (ăzh′ər) ▶*n.* **1.** A light purplish blue. **2.** The blue sky. [< Ar. *al-lāzaward*, lapis lazuli.] —**az′ure** *adj.*

B

b or **B** (bē) ►*n., pl.* **b's** or **B's** also **bs** or **Bs 1.** The 2nd letter of the English alphabet. **2.** The 2nd in a series. **3.** The second best in quality or rank. **4.** *Mus.* The 7th tone in the scale of C major. **5. B** A type of blood in the ABO system.

B¹ ► The symbol for the element **boron.**

B² ►*abbr.* **1.** baryon number **2.** base **3.** *Mus.* bass **4.** bishop (chess)

b. ►*abbr.* born

B. ►*abbr.* bay

Ba ► The symbol for the element **barium.**

BA ►*abbr.* Bachelor of Arts

baa (bă, bä) ►*v.* **baaed, baa•ing.** To make a bleating sound, as a sheep or goat. [Imit.] —**baa** *n.*

Ba•al (bā′əl) ►*n., pl.* **-als** or **-al•im** (-ə-lĭm). Any of various fertility and nature gods of the ancient Semitic peoples.

ba•ba gan•ouj or **ba•ba ga•noosh** (bä′bə gə-no͞osh′, -no͞ozh′) ►*n.* A purée of roasted eggplant, tahini, garlic, and lemon juice. [Egypt. Ar. *bābā ġannūj.*]

Bab•bitt (băb′ĭt) ►*n.* A smug, provincial member of the American middle class. [After the main character in the novel *Babbitt* by Sinclair Lewis.] —**Bab′bitt•ry** *n.*

bab•ble (băb′əl) ►*v.* **-bled, -bling 1.** To utter meaningless words or sounds. **2.** To talk foolishly; chatter. **3.** To make a continuous low, murmuring sound. [ME *babelen.*] —**bab′ble** *n.* —**bab′bler** *n.*

babe (bāb) ►*n.* **1.** A baby. **2.** An innocent or naive person. **3.** *Slang* A woman. [ME.]

ba•bel (băb′əl, bā′bəl) ►*n.* A confusion of sounds or voices. [After BABEL.]

Ba•bel (bā′bəl, băb′əl) In the Bible, a city (now thought to be Babylon) in Shinar.

ba•boon (bă-bo͞on′) ►*n.* **1.** Any of several large African and Asian monkeys having an elongated, doglike muzzle. **2.** *Slang* A lout; oaf. [< OFr. *babuin.*]

ba•bush•ka (bə-bo͝osh′kə) ►*n.* A woman's head scarf, folded triangularly and tied under the chin. [Russ., grandmother.]

ba•by (bā′bē) ►*n., pl.* **-bies 1a.** A very young child; infant. **b.** The youngest member of a family or group. **c.** A very young animal. **2.** One who behaves in an infantile way. **3.** *Slang* A girl or young woman. **4.** *Slang* An object of personal concern: *The project is your baby.* ►*v.* **-bied, -by•ing.** To treat overindulgently; pamper. [ME.] —**ba′by•hood′** *n.* —**ba′by•ish** *adj.*

baby boom ►*n.* A sudden, large increase in the birthrate, esp. the one in the US after World War II. —**ba′by-boom′** *adj.* —**ba′by-boom′er** *n.*

baby carriage ►*n.* A four-wheeled, often hooded carriage for pushing an infant.

Bab•y•lon (băb′ə-lən, -lŏn′) The capital of ancient Babylonia, on the Euphrates R.

Bab•y•lo•ni•a (băb′ə-lō′nē-ə) An ancient empire of Mesopotamia in the Euphrates R. valley.

Bab•y•lo•ni•an (băb′ə-lō′nē-ən) ►*adj.* Of Babylonia or Babylon. ►*n.* **1.** A native or inhabitant of Babylon or Babylonia. **2.** The form of Akkadian used in Babylonia.

ba•by's breath (bā′bēz) ►*n.* A plant having panicles of numerous small white flowers.

ba•by-sit (bā′bē-sĭt′) ►*v.* To take care of a child or children, as when the parents are away. —**baby sitter** *n.*

bac•ca•lau•re•ate (băk′ə-lôr′ē-ĭt) ►*n.* **1.** See **bachelor's degree. 2.** A farewell address delivered to a graduating class. [Med.Lat. *baccalaureātus.*]

bac•ca•rat (bä′kə-rä′, băk′ə-) ►*n.* A card game in which the objective is to hold cards totaling closest to nine. [Fr. *baccara.*]

bac•cha•nal (băk′ə-năl′, -näl′) ►*n.* **1.** A drunken or riotous celebration. **2.** A reveler. [< Lat. *bacchānālis*, of Bacchus.]

Bac•cha•na•lia (băk′ə-nāl′yə, -nā′lē-ə) ►*n.* **1.** The ancient Roman festival in honor of Bacchus. **2. bacchanalia** A drunken festivity. [Lat. *bacchānālia.*] —**Bac′cha•na′lian** *adj. & n.*

Bac•chus (băk′əs) ►*n. Gk. & Rom. Myth.* See **Dionysus.** —**Bac′chic** *adj.*

Bach (bäKH, bäk), **Johann Sebastian.** 1685–1750. German composer and organist.

bach•e•lor (băch′ə-lər, băch′lər) ►*n.* **1.** An unmarried man. **2.** A person who holds a bachelor's degree. [Ult. < Med.Lat. *baccalārius*, tenant farmer.] —**bach′e•lor•hood′, bach′e•lor•dom** *n.*

bach•e•lor's button (băch′ə-lərz, băch′lərz) ►*n.* See **cornflower.**

bachelor's degree ►*n.* A college or university degree signifying completion of the undergraduate curriculum.

ba•cil•lus (bə-sĭl′əs) ►*n., pl.* **-cil•li** (-sĭl′ī′). Any of various rod-shaped aerobic bacteria. [LLat., little rod.] —**bac′il•lar′y** (băs′ə-lĕr′ē), **ba•cil′lar** *adj.*

bac•i•tra•cin (băs′ĭ-trā′sĭn) ►*n.* An antibiotic obtained from bacteria and used in the topical treatment of certain bacterial infections. [< BACI(LLUS) + Margaret *Tracy*, in whose blood it was first isolated.]

back (băk) ►*n.* **1a.** The part of the vertebrate body nearest or along the spine. **b.** The upper or dorsal region in invertebrates. **2a.** The backbone or spine. **b.** A part that supports or fits the human back: *the back of a chair.* **3.** The part farthest from or behind the front; the rear. **4.** The reverse side. **5.** *Sports* A player who takes a position behind the frontline. ►*v.* **1.** To move or cause to move backward. **2.** To support or sustain: *back a political cause.* **3.** To bet on. **4.** To form the back or backing of. —***phrasal verbs:*** **back down** To withdraw, as from a confrontation. **back off** To retreat, as from a position or commitment. **back out** To withdraw from something before completion. **back up 1.** To accumulate in a clogged state. **2.** To assist, support, or corroborate. **3.** *Comp. Sci.* To make a backup of. ►*adj.* **1.** At the rear. **2.** Distant; remote. **3.** Of a past date; not current: *a back issue of a periodical.* **4.** In arrears: *back pay.* **5.** Operating or directed backward. ►*adv.* **1.** To or toward the rear; backward. **2.** To or toward a former place, state, or time. **3.** In reserve or concealment. **4.** In check: *Barriers held the crowd back.* **5.** In reply or return. [< OE *bæc.*] —**back′less** *adj.*

back•ache (băk′āk′) ►*n.* Discomfort or a pain in the region of the back or spine.

back•beat (băk′bēt′) ►*n.* A loud, steady beat characteristic of rock music.

back•bench (băk′bĕnch′) ►*n. Chiefly Brit.* The rear benches in the House of Commons where junior members of Parliament sit. —**back•bench′er** *n.*

back•bite (băk′bīt′) ►*v.* To speak spitefully or slanderously about a person who is not present. —**back′bit′er** *n.*

back•board (băk′bôrd′, -bōrd′) ►*n.* **1.** A board placed under or behind something to provide support. **2.** *Basketball* The elevated board from which the basket projects.

back•bone (băk′bōn′) ►*n.* **1.** The vertebrate spine. **2.** A main support: *the backbone of a policy.* **3.** Strength of character.

back•break•ing (băk′brā′kĭng) ►*adj.* Demanding great exertion; arduous.

back•court (băk′kôrt′, -kōrt′) ►*n. Sports* The part of a court farthest from the net, goal, or front wall.

back•date (băk′dāt′) ►*v.* To supply (e.g., a check) with a date earlier than the actual date.

back•door (băk′dôr′, -dōr′) ►*adj.* Secret or surreptitious; clandestine.

back•drop (băk′drŏp′) ►*n.* **1.** A painted curtain hung at the back of a stage set. **2.** A setting; background.

back•er (băk′ər) ►*n.* One that backs a person, group, or enterprise: *a financial backer.*

back•field (băk′fēld′) ►*n.* **1.** *Football* The players stationed behind the line of scrimmage. **2.** The primarily defensive players in soccer, field hockey, and Rugby.

back•fire (băk′fīr′) ►*n.* **1.** An explosion of prematurely ignited fuel or of unburned exhaust in an engine. **2.** A fire started to extinguish or control a larger fire. ►*v.* **1.** To explode in a backfire. **2.** To produce an unexpected, undesired result.

back-for•ma•tion (băk′fôr-mā′shən) ►*n.* **1.** A new word created by removing an actual or supposed affix from an already existing word, as *laze* from *lazy.* **2.** This process.

back•gam•mon (băk′găm′ən) ►*n.* A board game for two persons, with moves determined by throws of dice.

back•ground (băk′ground′) ►*n.* **1.** The area or surface against which something is seen or depicted. **2.** A setting or context. **3.** A state of relative obscurity. **4.** The circumstances leading up to an event. **5.** One's total experience, training, and education. **6.** Sound or radiation present at a relatively constant low level.

back•hand (băk′hănd′) ►*n.* **1.** *Sports* A stroke, as of a racket, made with the back of the hand facing outward and the arm moving forward. **2.** Handwriting having letters that slant to the left. ►*adj.* Backhanded. —**back′hand′** *v. & adv.*

back•hand•ed (băk′hăn′dĭd) ►*adj.* **1.** *Sports* Backhand. **2.** Oblique or roundabout: *a backhanded compliment.* —**back′hand′ed•ly** *adv.* —**back′hand′ed•ness** *n.*

back•hoe (băk′hō′) ►*n.* An excavator with a boom that is drawn backward to the machine.

back•ing (băk′ĭng) ►*n.* **1.** Something forming a back: *the backing of a carpet.* **2a.** Support or aid. **b.** Approval or endorsement.

back•lash (băk′lăsh′) ►*n.* **1.** A sudden or violent backward whipping motion. **2.** A hostile reaction, esp. to a social or political movement. —**back′lash′** *v.*

back•light (băk′līt′) ►*v.* To light (a subject or scene) from behind. —**back′light′** *n.*

back•log (băk′lŏg′, -lôg′) ►*n.* **1.** A reserve supply or source. **2.** An accumulation, esp. of unfinished work or unfilled orders.

back•pack (băk′păk′) ►*n.* **1.** A knapsack, often on a lightweight frame, that is worn on the back. **2.** An apparatus designed to be used while carried on the back. ►*v.* To hike with a backpack. —**back′pack′er** *n.*

back•ped•al (băk′pĕd′l) ►*v.* **1.** To pedal backward, as in braking. **2.** To back off.

back•rest (băk′rĕst′) ►*n.* A rest or support for the back.

back seat ►*n.* **1.** A seat in the back, esp. of a vehicle. **2.** A subordinate position.

back-seat driver (băk′sēt′) ►*n.* One who gives unsolicited direction or advice.

back•side (băk′sīd′) ►*n. Informal* The buttocks.

back•slash (băk′slăsh′) ►*n.* A backward virgule (\ ).

back•slide (băk′slīd′) ►*v.* To revert esp. to sin or bad habits. —**back′slid′er** *n.*

back•space (băk′spās′) ►*v.* To move the cursor on a computer screen or the carriage of a typewriter back one or more spaces. ►*n.* The key used for backspacing.

back•spin (băk′spĭn′) ►*n.* A spin that tends to slow, stop, or reverse the linear motion of an object, esp. of a ball.

back•stage (băk′stāj′) ►*adv.* **1.** In or toward the area behind the performing space in a theater. **2.** In secret; privately.

back•stairs (băk′stârz′) ►*adj.* Furtively carried on; clandestine: *backstairs gossip.*

back•stop (băk′stŏp′) ►*n.* **1.** A screen or fence used to stop a ball from going beyond the playing area. **2.** *Baseball* A catcher.

back•stretch (băk′strĕch′) ►*n.* The part of an oval racecourse farthest from the spectators and opposite the homestretch.

back•stroke (băk′strōk′) ►*n.* **1.** A swimming stroke executed with the swimmer lying face up in the water. **2.** A backhanded stroke. —**back′stroke′** *v.*

back•swept (băk′swĕpt′) ►*adj.* Brushed or angled backward: *a backswept hairstyle.*

back talk ►*n.* Insolent or impudent retorts.

back•track (băk′trăk′) ►*v.* **1.** To retrace one's route. **2.** To reverse one's position.

back•up (băk′ŭp′) ►*n.* **1a.** A reserve or substitute. **b.** *Comp. Sci.* A copy of a program or file stored separately from the original. **2a.** Support or backing. **b.** *Mus.* A background accompaniment. **3.** An overflow or accumulation caused by clogging. ►*adj.* Auxiliary; standby.

back•ward (băk′wərd) ►*adj.* **1.** Directed or facing toward the back. **2.** Reversed. **3.** Unwilling; reluctant. **4.** Behind in progress or development. ►*adv.* or **back•wards** (-wərdz) **1.** To or toward the back. **2.** With the back leading. **3.** In a reverse manner. **4.** Toward a worse or less advanced condition. —***idiom:*** **bend** (or

lean) over backward To do one's utmost. —**back′ward•ly** *adv.* —**back′ward•ness** *n.*

Usage: The adverb forms *backward* and *backwards* are interchangeable: *stepped backward; a mirror facing backwards.* Only *backward* is an adjective: *a backward view.*

back•wash (băk′wŏsh′, -wôsh′) ▸*n.* **1.** A backward flow. **2.** An aftermath.

back•wa•ter (băk′wô′tər, -wŏt′ər) ▸*n.* **1.** Water that stagnates or flows backward, as at the edge of a current. **2.** A backward or isolated place.

back•woods (băk′wo͝odz′) ▸*pl.n. (takes sing. or pl. v.)* **1.** Heavily wooded, thinly settled areas. **2.** An isolated and uncultured place. —**back′woods′man** *n.*

ba•con (bā′kən) ▸*n.* The salted and smoked meat from the back and sides of a pig. [< OFr.]

Bacon[1], Francis. 1561–1626. English philosopher, essayist, and politician.

Bacon[2], Francis. 1909–92. Irish-born British painter.

Bacon, Roger. 1214?–92. English friar, scientist, and philosopher.

bac•te•ri•a (băk-tîr′ē-ə) ▸*n.* Pl. of **bacterium.**

bac•te•ri•cide (băk-tîr′ĭ-sīd′) ▸*n.* An agent that kills bacteria. —**bac•te′ri•cid′al** *adj.*

bac•te•ri•ol•o•gy (băk-tîr′ē-ŏl′ə-jē) ▸*n.* The scientific study of bacteria. —**bac•te′ri•o•log′ic** (-ə-lŏj′ĭk), **bac•te′ri•o•log′i•cal** *adj.* —**bac•te′ri•ol′o•gist** *n.*

bac•te•ri•o•phage (băk-tîr′ē-ə-fāj′) ▸*n.* A virus that destroys certain bacteria.

bac•te•ri•um (băk-tîr′ē-əm) ▸*n., pl.* **-te•ri•a** (-tîr′ē-ə). Any of numerous unicellular microorganisms existing in several typical shapes and variously associated with processes of putrefaction, fermentation, and causation of infectious disease in plants or animals. [< Gk. *baktērion*, little rod.] —**bac•te′ri•al** *adj.* —**bac•te′ri•al•ly** *adv.*

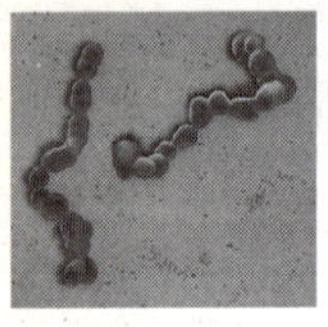
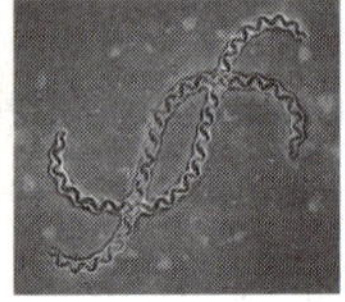

bacterium
left to right: chain-shaped and spiral-shaped bacteria

Bac•tri•a (băk′trē-ə) An ancient country of SW Asia. —**Bac′tri•an** *adj. & n.*

bad (băd) ▸*adj.* **worse** (wûrs), **worst** (wûrst) **1.** Of inferior quality; poor. **2.** Evil; sinful. **3.** Ill-behaved. **4.** Unpleasant or disturbing: *bad news.* **5.** Unfavorable: *a bad review.* **6.** Not fresh; spoiled. **7.** Detrimental: *bad habits.* **8.** Defective. **9.** Severe; intense: *a bad cold.* **10.** Being in poor health or condition. **11.** Sorry; regretful. ▸*n.* Something bad: *Take the good with the bad.* ▸*adv. Informal* Badly. [ME *badde.*] —**bad′ly** *adv.* —**bad′ness** *n.*

Usage: The use of *bad* as an adverb, while common in informal speech, is widely regarded as unacceptable in formal writing. Formal usage requires *His tooth ached badly* (not *bad*).

bad blood ▸*n.* Enmity or bitterness between persons or groups.

bade (băd, bād) ▸*v.* P.t. of **bid.**

Ba•den (bäd′n) A region of SW Germany.

Ba•den-Pow•ell (bād′n-pō′əl), Sir **Robert Stephenson Smyth.** 1857–1941. British founder of the Boy Scouts (1908) and with his sister **Agnes** (1858–1945) the Girl Guides (1910).

badge (băj) ▸*n.* A device or emblem worn as an insignia of rank, office, or honor. [< Norman Fr. *bage.*]

badg•er (băj′ər) ▸*n.* A carnivorous burrowing mammal with long front claws and a heavy grizzled coat. ▸*v.* To harry or pester persistently. [Perh. < BADGE.]

bad•i•nage (băd′n-äzh′) ▸*n.* Light, playful banter. [Fr. < *badin*, joker.]

Bad•lands also **Bad Lands** (băd′lăndz′). A heavily eroded arid region of SW SD and NW NE.

bad•min•ton (băd′mĭn′tən) ▸*n.* A sport played by volleying a shuttlecock over a net with long-handled rackets. [After *Badminton*, the Duke of Beaufort's country seat in western England.]

bad•mouth (băd′mouth′, -mouth′) ▸*v. Slang* To criticize or disparage, often spitefully.

Bae•de•ker (bā′dĭ-kər), **Karl.** 1801–59. German guidebook publisher.

Baf•fin (băf′ĭn), **William.** 1584?–1622. English explorer.

Baffin Bay. An ice-clogged body of water between NE Canada and Greenland.

Baffin Island. An island of E Nunavut, Canada, W of Greenland.

baf•fle (băf′əl) ▸*v.* **-fled, -fling 1.** To frustrate; stymie. **2.** To impede. ▸*n.* A barrier designed to check or regulate the flow of a liquid, gas, sound, or light. [Perh. < Fr. *bafouer*, to ridicule.] —**baf′fle•ment** *n.*

bag (băg) ▸*n.* **1a.** A nonrigid container, as of paper, plastic, or leather. **b.** A handbag; purse. **c.** A suitcase. **2.** An object that resembles a pouch. **3.** An amount of game taken at one time. **4.** *Baseball* A base. **5.** *Slang* An area of interest or skill: *Cooking is not my bag.* **6.** *Slang* A frumpy or homely woman. ▸*v.* **bagged, bag•ging 1.** To put into a bag. **2a.** To hang loosely. **b.** To bulge out. **3.** To capture or kill as game. —***idiom:* in the bag** Assured of a successful outcome. [< ON *baggi.*] —**bag′ful** *n.*

bag•a•telle (băg′ə-tĕl′) ▸*n.* **1.** A trifle. **2.** A short piece of music. [Fr. < Ital. dial. *bagata*, little property.]

ba•gel (bā′gəl) ▸*n.* A ring-shaped roll with a tough chewy texture. [Yiddish *beygl.*]

bag•gage (băg′ĭj) ▸*n.* **1.** The bags and belongings of a traveler. **2.** The movable supplies of an army. [< OFr. *bague*, bundle.]

bag•gy (băg′ē) ▸*adj.* **-gi•er, -gi•est.** Bulging or hanging loosely: *baggy trousers.* —**bag′gi•ly** *adv.* —**bag′gi•ness** *n.*

Bagh•dad or **Bag•dad** (băg′dăd′). The capital of Iraq, in the center on the Tigris R. Pop. 3,841,268.

bag•pipe (băg′pīp′) ▸*n.* often **bagpipes.** A wind instrument having an inflatable bag, a double-reed melody pipe, and one or more drone pipes. —**bag′pipe′** *v.* —**bag′pip′er** *n.*

ba•guette (bă-gĕt′) ►*n.* **1.** A gem cut in a narrow rectangle. **2.** A narrow loaf of French bread. [Fr., small rod.]

Ba•gui•o (bä′gē-ō′) The summer capital of the Philippines, on NW Luzon. Pop. 169,565.

Ba•ha•mas (bə-hä′məz, -hā′-) also **Ba•ha•ma Islands** (-mə). An island country in the Atlantic E of FL and Cuba. Cap. Nassau. Pop. 218,000. —**Ba•ha′mi•an** (-hā′mē-ən, -hä′-), **Ba•ha′man** *adj. & n.*

Bah•rain or **Bah•rein** (bä-rān′). An island country in the Persian Gulf between Qatar and Saudi Arabia. Cap. Manama. Pop. 549,000. —**Bah•rain′i** *adj. & n.*

baht (bät) ►*n., pl.* **bahts** or **baht.** See table at **currency.** [Thai *bāt.*]

Bai•kal or **Bay•kal** (bī-kôl′, -kŏl′), **Lake.** A deep lake of S-central Russia.

bail¹ (bāl) ►*n.* **1.** Security, usu. money, supplied as a guarantee that an arrested person will appear for trial. **2.** Release from imprisonment obtained by bail. ►*v.* To secure the release of by paying bail. —***phrasal verb:* bail out** *Informal* To extricate from trouble. [< Lat. *bāiulus,* carrier.] —**bail′er** *n.*

bail² (bāl) ►*v.* **1.** To remove (water) from a boat by dipping with a container. **2.** To empty (a boat) by bailing. —***phrasal verb:* bail out 1.** To parachute from an aircraft. **2.** To abandon a project or enterprise. [< OFr. *baille,* bucket.] —**bail′er** *n.*

bail³ (bāl) ►*n.* The arched, hooplike handle of a container, such as a pail. [ME *beil.*]

bail•ee (bā-lē′) ►*n.* A person to whom property is bailed.

bail•iff (bā′lĭf) ►*n.* **1.** A court attendant with duties such as the maintenance of order during a trial. **2.** An official who assists a British sheriff by executing writs and arrests. **3.** *Chiefly Brit.* An overseer of an estate. [< OFr. *baillis,* steward.]

bail•i•wick (bā′lə-wĭk′) ►*n.* **1.** One's specific area of interest, skill, or authority. See Syns at **field. 2.** The office or district of a bailiff. [ME *bailliwik,* bailiff's village.]

bail•or (bā′lər, bā-lôr′) ►*n.* One who bails property to another.

bails•man (bālz′mən) ►*n.* One who provides bail or security for another.

Bai•ri•ki (bī-rē′kē) The administrative center of Kiribati, in the N Gilbert Is. of the W-central Pacific. Pop. 1,956.

bairn (bârn) ►*n. Scots* A child. [< OE *bearn.*]

bait (bāt) ►*n.* **1.** Food or other lure used to catch fish or trap animals. **2.** An enticement; lure. ►*v.* **1.** To place bait in (a trap) or on (a fishhook). **2.** To entice; lure. **3.** To set dogs upon (a chained animal) for sport. **4.** To torment, esp. with criticism or ridicule. **5.** To tease. [< ON *beita,* food, to hunt with dogs.] —**bait′er** *n.*

bait and switch ►*n.* A sales tactic in which a bargain-priced item is used to attract customers who are then encouraged to purchase a more expensive similar item.

baize (bāz) ►*n.* A thick feltlike cloth used chiefly to cover gaming tables. [< Lat. *badius,* bay-colored.]

Ba•ja California (bä′hä). Also **Lower California.** A peninsula of W Mexico extending SSE between the Pacific and the Gulf of California.

bake (bāk) ►*v.* **baked, bak•ing 1.** To cook (food) with dry heat, esp. in an oven. **2.** To harden or dry in or as if in an oven: *bake bricks.* ►*n.* **1.** The act or process of baking. **2.** A social gathering at which food is baked and served. [< OE *bacan.*] —**bak′er** *n.*

Ba•ke•lite (bā′kə-līt′, bāk′līt′) ► A trademark for any of a group of synthetic resins and plastics found in a variety of manufactured articles.

Ba•ker (bā′kər), **Mount.** A peak, 3,287.3 m (10,778 ft), of NW WA in the Cascade Range.

bak•er's dozen (bā′kərz) ►*n.* A group of 13. [From adding an extra roll to avoid the possibility of 12 weighing light.]

Ba•kers•field (bā′kərz-fēld′) A city of S-central CA NNW of Los Angeles. Pop. 105,611.

bak•er•y (bā′kə-rē) ►*n., pl.* **-ies.** A place where products such as bread, cake, and pastries are baked or sold.

bak•ing powder (bā′kĭng) ►*n.* A mixture of baking soda, starch, and an acidic compound such as cream of tartar, used as a leavening agent in baking.

baking soda ►*n.* A white crystalline compound, $NaHCO_3$, used esp. in baking powder, effervescent beverages, pharmaceuticals, and fire extinguishers.

ba•kla•va (bä′klə-vä′) ►*n.* A dessert made of paper-thin layers of pastry, chopped nuts, and honey. [Turk.]

bak•sheesh (băk′shēsh′, băk-shēsh′) ►*n., pl.* **-sheesh.** A gratuity or tip in certain Near Eastern countries. [Pers. *bakhshish.*]

Ba•ku (bä-ko͞o′) The capital of Azerbaijan, in the E part on the Caspian Sea. Pop. 1,104,000.

Ba•ku•nin (bə-ko͞o′nĭn, -nyĭn), **Mikhail Aleksandrovich.** 1814–76. Russian anarchist and political theorist.

bal•a•lai•ka (băl′ə-lī′kə) ►*n.* A musical instrument with a triangular body, fretted neck, and three strings. [Russ. *balalaĭka.*]

bal•ance (băl′əns) ►*n.* **1.** A weighing device, esp. one consisting of a rigid beam suspended at its center and brought into equilibrium by adding known weights at one end while the unknown weight hangs from the other. **2a.** A state of equilibrium. **b.** An influence or force that tends to produce equilibrium. **3.** Emotional stability. **4.** A harmonious arrangement or proportion of parts. **5.** *Accounting* **a.** Equality of totals in the debit and credit sides of an account. **b.** A difference between such totals. **6.** Something left over; remainder. **7.** *Math.* Equality of symbolic quantities on each side of an equation. ►*v.* **-anced, -anc•ing 1.** To weigh in or as if in a balance. **2.** To bring into or be in a state of equilibrium. **3.** To counterbalance. **4.** *Accounting* To compute the difference between the debits and credits of (an account). —***idioms:* in the balance** With the result or outcome still uncertain. **on balance** Taking everything into consideration. [< Lat. *bilānx,* having two scales.]

balance beam ►*n.* A horizontal raised beam used in gymnastics for balancing exercises.

balance of power ►*n.* Distribution of power in which no single nation is able to dominate.

balance sheet ►*n.* A statement of the assets and liabilities of a business or institution.

balance wheel ▶*n.* A wheel that regulates rate of mechanical movement, as in a watch.

Bal•an•chine (băl′ən-chēn′), **George.** 1904–83. Russian-born Amer. ballet director and choreographer.

bal•bo•a (băl-bō′ə) ▶*n.* See table at **currency.** [After Vasco Núñez de BALBOA.]

Balboa, Vasco Núñez de. 1475–1517. Spanish explorer.

bal•co•ny (băl′kə-nē) ▶*n., pl.* **-nies 1.** A platform that projects from the wall of a building and is surrounded by a railing. **2.** A gallery that projects over the main floor in a theater or auditorium. [Ital. *balcone.*]

bald (bôld) ▶*adj.* **-er, -est 1.** Lacking hair on the head. **2.** Lacking a natural or usual covering; bare. **3.** *Zool.* Having white feathers or markings on the head. **4.** Plain; blunt: *the bald truth.* [ME *balled.*] —**bald′ly** *adv.* —**bald′ness** *n.*

bal•da•chin (bôl′də-kĭn, băl′-) also **bal•da•chi•no** (băl′də-kē′nō) ▶*n., pl.* **-chins** also **-chi•nos.** A canopy over an altar, throne, or dais. [< OItal. *Baldacco,* Baghdad.]

bald eagle ▶*n.* A North American eagle with a dark body and white head and tail.

bal•der•dash (bôl′dər-dăsh′) ▶*n.* Nonsense. [?]

bald-faced (bôld′fāst′) ▶*adj.* Blatant; brazen: *a bald-faced lie.*

bal•dric (bôl′drĭk) ▶*n.* A belt worn across the chest to support a sword or bugle. [< OFr. *baudre* and MHGer. *balderich.*]

Bald•win (bôld′wĭn), **James Arthur.** 1924–87. Amer. writer and essayist.

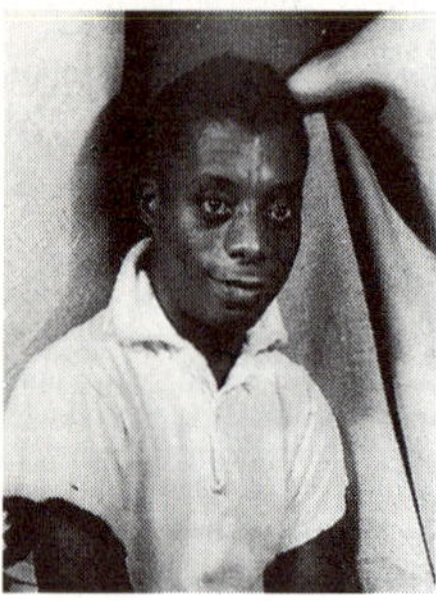

James Baldwin
photographed in 1955

Baldwin, Stanley. 1867–1947. British prime minister (1923–29 and 1935–37).

bale (bāl) ▶*n.* A large, tightly bound package of raw or finished material. ▶*v.* **baled, bal•ing.** To bind in bales. [ME.] —**bal′er** *n.*

Bal•e•ar•ic Islands (băl′ē-ăr′ĭk) An archipelago in the W Mediterranean Sea off the E coast of Spain.

ba•leen (bə-lēn′) ▶*n.* See **whalebone** 1. [< Lat. *balaena,* whale.]

bale•ful (bāl′fəl) ▶*adj.* **1.** Portending evil; ominous. **2.** Malignant in intent or effect. [*bale,* evil + -FUL.] —**bale′ful•ly** *adv.* —**bale′ful•ness** *n.*

Bal•four (băl′fo͝or′, -fôr′, -fōr′), **Arthur James.** 1848–1930. British prime minister (1902–05).

Ba•li (bä′lē) An island of S Indonesia in the Lesser Sundas E of Java.

Ba•li•nese (bä′lə-nēz′, -nēs′) ▶*n., pl.* **-nese 1.** A native or inhabitant of Bali. **2.** The Indonesian language of Bali. —**Ba′li•nese′** *adj.*

balk (bôk) ▶*v.* **1.** To stop short and refuse to go on. **2.** To refuse to proceed, as out of doubt or moral principle. **3.** *Baseball* To make an illegal motion before pitching, entitling any base runner to advance. ▶*n.* **1.** A hindrance, check, or defeat. **2.** *Baseball* An act of balking. [< OE *balca,* ridge.] —**balk′er** *n.* —**balk′y** *adj.*

Bal•kan Mountains (bôl′kən) also **Bal•kans** (-kənz). A mountain system of SE Europe extending about 563 km (350 mi) from E Serbia through central Bulgaria to the Black Sea.

Balkan Peninsula also **Balkans.** A peninsula of SE Europe bounded by the Black Sea, the Sea of Marmara, and the Aegean, Mediterranean, Ionian, and Adriatic seas. —**Bal′kan** *adj.*

Bal•khash (bäl-käsh′, -KHäsh′), **Lake.** A shallow lake of SE Kazakhstan.

ball[1] (bôl) ▶*n.* **1.** A spherical or almost spherical object or body. **2a.** Any of various round or rounded objects used in sports and games. **b.** A game played with such an object. **c.** A pitched baseball that does not pass through the strike zone and is not swung at by the batter. **3.** A usu. round projectile. **4.** A rounded part or protuberance: *the ball of the foot.* ▶*v.* To form or become formed into a ball. —***phrasal verb:* ball up** To confuse; bungle. —***idiom:* on the ball** *Informal* Alert or efficient. [ME.]

ball[2] (bôl) ▶*n.* **1.** A formal gathering for social dancing. **2.** *Slang* An extremely enjoyable time or experience: *had a ball on our vacation.* [< Gk. *ballizein,* to dance.]

bal•lad (băl′əd) ▶*n.* **1a.** A narrative poem, often of folk origin and intended to be sung, consisting of simple stanzas and usu. having a refrain. **b.** The music for such a poem. **2.** A slow, usu. romantic song. [< OProv. *balada,* dancing song.] —**bal′lad•eer′** *n.* —**bal′lad•ry** *n.*

bal•last (băl′əst) ▶*n.* **1.** Heavy material placed in the hold of a ship or the gondola of a balloon to enhance stability. **2.** Coarse gravel or crushed rock laid to form a roadbed. ▶*v.* To provide with ballast. [Of Scand. orig.]

ball bearing ▶*n.* **1.** A friction-reducing bearing, as for a rotating shaft, in which the moving and stationary parts are separated by hard metal balls revolving freely in a lubricated track. **2.** A hard ball used in such a bearing.

bal•le•ri•na (băl′ə-rē′nə) ▶*n.* A principal woman dancer in a ballet company. [Ital. < *ballare,* to dance.]

bal•let (bă-lā′, băl′ā′) ▶*n.* **1.** A classical dance form characterized by elaborate formal technique. **2.** A choreographed theatrical presentation danced to a musical accompaniment. **3.** A company that performs ballet. [< Ital. *ballare,* to dance.]

bal•let•o•mane (bă-lĕt′ə-măn′) ▶*n.* An admirer of ballet. [Fr. < *ballet,* BALLET.]

ball game ▶*n.* **1.** A game or sport played with a ball. **2.** *Slang* **a.** A highly competitive situation. **b.** A particular set of circumstances.

ballistic missile ▶*n.* A projectile that assumes a free-falling trajectory after an internally guided, self-powered ascent.

bal•lis•tics (bə-lĭs′tĭks) ►*n.* *(takes sing. v.)* **1.** The study of the dynamics or flight characteristics of projectiles. **2a.** The study of the functioning of firearms. **b.** The study of the firing, flight, and effects of ammunition. [< Gk. *ballein*, to throw.] —**bal•lis′tic** *adj.* —**bal•lis′ti•cal•ly** *adv.*

bal•loon (bə-lo͞on′) ►*n.* **1a.** A flexible bag inflated with a gas, such as helium, that causes it to rise in the atmosphere. **b.** Such a bag capable of lifting and transporting a gondola or other load. **2.** An inflatable toy rubber bag. **3.** An outline containing the words or thoughts of a cartoon character. ►*v.* **1.** To ride in a balloon. **2.** To expand or cause to expand like a balloon. See Syns at **bulge. 3.** To increase rapidly. [< Ital. dial. *ballone*, big ball.] —**bal•loon′ist** *n.*

bal•lot (băl′ət) ►*n.* **1.** A paper or card used to cast or register a vote. **2.** The act or method of voting. **3.** A list of candidates for office. **4.** The total of all votes cast in an election. **5.** The right to vote; franchise. ►*v.* To cast a ballot. [< Ital. *balla*, ball.]

ball•park (bôl′pärk′) ►*n.* **1.** A park or stadium in which ball games are played. **2.** *Slang* The approximately proper range, as of an estimate. —**ball′park′** *adj.*

ball•point pen (bôl′point′) ►*n.* A pen having a small, freely revolving ball as its writing point.

ball•room (bôl′ro͞om′, -ro͝om′) ►*n.* A large room for dancing.

bal•ly•hoo (băl′ē-ho͞o′) ►*n., pl.* **-hoos 1.** Sensational promotion or publicity. **2.** Clamor; uproar. ►*v.* To promote by sensational methods. [?]

balm (bäm) ►*n.* **1.** Any of several aromatic plants, esp. one used as a seasoning or for tea. **2.** An aromatic salve or oil. **3.** Something that soothes, heals, or comforts. [< Lat. *balsamum*, balsam.]

balm•y (bä′mē) ►*adj.* **-i•er, -i•est 1.** Having the quality or fragrance of balm. **2.** Mild and pleasant: *a balmy breeze.* **3.** *Slang* Eccentric or crazy. —**balm′i•ly** *adv.* —**balm′i•ness** *n.*

ba•lo•ney[1] (bə-lō′nē) ►*n.* Var. of **bologna.**

ba•lo•ney[2] (bə-lō′nē) ►*n.* *Slang* Nonsense. [Prob. var. of BOLOGNA.]

bal•sa (bôl′sə) ►*n.* **1.** A tropical American tree having very light, soft, buoyant wood. **2.** The wood of this tree. [Sp.]

bal•sam (bôl′səm) ►*n.* **1.** An aromatic resin obtained from various trees or plants. **2.** A tree, esp. the balsam fir, yielding balsam. **3.** See **jewelweed.** [< Gk. *balsamon.*]

balsam fir ►*n.* A North American evergreen tree that yields pulpwood and is widely used as a Christmas tree.

bal•sam•ic vinegar (bôl-săm′ĭk) ►*n.* Any of various aromatic vinegars, esp. a dark sweet aged Italian variety. [< *balsamic*, restorative (translation of Ital. *aceto balsamico*).]

Balt (bôlt) ►*n.* A member of a Baltic-speaking people.

Bal•tic (bôl′tĭk) ►*adj.* **1.** Of the Baltic Sea, the Baltic States, or a Baltic-speaking people. **2.** Of the branch of Indo-European that includes Latvian and Lithuanian. ►*n.* The Baltic language branch.

Baltic Sea. An arm of the Atlantic in N Europe.

Baltic States. Estonia, Latvia, and Lithuania, on the E coast of the Baltic Sea.

Bal•ti•more (bôl′tə-môr′, -mōr′) A city of N MD on an arm of Chesapeake Bay NE of Washington DC. Pop. 736,014.

Baltimore, Lord. See **Calvert.**

Baltimore oriole ►*n.* A subspecies of the northern oriole in its eastern range.

bal•us•ter (băl′ə-stər) ►*n.* One of the upright supports of a handrail. [< Ital. *balaustro.*]

bal•us•trade (băl′ə-strād′) ►*n.* A handrail and the row of balusters or posts that support it. [< Ital. *balaustrata.*]

Bal•zac (bôl′zăk′, bäl-zäk′), **Honoré de.** 1799–1850. French writer.

Ba•ma•ko (bä′mə-kō′) The capital of Mali, in the SW on the Niger R. Pop. 658,275.

bam•boo (băm-bo͞o′) ►*n., pl.* **-boos 1.** Any of various tall, usu. woody, temperate or tropical grasses. **2.** The hard hollow stems of any of these grasses, used in construction and crafts. [Malay *bambu.*]

bam•boo•zle (băm-bo͞o′zəl) ►*v.* **-zled, -zling** *Informal.* To trick or deceive; hoodwink. [?] —**bam•boo′zle•ment** *n.*

ban (băn) ►*v.* **banned, ban•ning.** To prohibit, esp. by official decree. See Syns at **forbid.** ►*n.* **1.** A condemnation by church officials. **2.** A prohibition imposed by law or official decree. **3.** A curse. [< OE *bannan*, summon, and ON *banna*, prohibit.]

ba•nal (bə-năl′, bā′nəl, bə-näl′) ►*adj.* Completely ordinary and commonplace; trite. [< OFr., held in common.] —**ba•nal′i•ty** (-năl′ĭ-tē) *n.* —**ba•nal′ly** *adv.*

ba•nan•a (bə-năn′ə) ►*n.* **1.** Any of several treelike tropical or subtropical plants having large leaves and hanging clusters of edible fruit. **2.** The elongated fruit of these plants, having yellowish to reddish skin and white pulpy flesh. [Of African orig.]

band[1] (bănd) ►*n.* **1.** A thin strip of flexible material used to encircle and bind together. **2.** A strip or stripe of a contrasting color or material. **3.** A simple ring, esp. a wedding ring. **4.** *Phys.* A range or interval, esp. of radio wavelengths or frequencies. ►*v.* **1.** To bind with or as if with a band. **2.** To tag (e.g., birds) with a band. [< OFr. *bande.*]

band[2] (bănd) ►*n.* **1.** A group of people or animals. **2.** A group of musicians who perform together. ►*v.* To assemble or unite in a group: *band together for safety.* [< OFr.]

Syns: *band, company, corps, party, troop, troupe* **n.**

band•age (băn′dĭj) ►*n.* A strip of material used to protect or support a wound or other injury. ►*v.* **-aged, -ag•ing.** To apply a bandage to. [< OFr. *bande*, strip.]

Band-Aid (bănd′ād′) ► A trademark for an adhesive bandage with a gauze pad in the center, used to protect minor wounds.

ban•dan•na or **ban•dan•a** (băn-dăn′ə) ►*n.* A large handkerchief, usu. patterned and brightly colored. [< Hindi *bāndhnā*, to tie.]

Ban•dar Se•ri Be•ga•wan (bŭn′dər sĕr′ē bə-gä′wən) The capital of Brunei, on the N coast of Borneo. Pop. 49,902.

band•box (bănd′bŏks′) ►*n.* A rounded box used to hold small articles of apparel.

ban•di•coot (băn′dĭ-ko͞ot′) ►*n.* **1.** A large rat of SE Asia. **2.** A ratlike Australian marsupial. [Telugu *bantikoku* : *banti*, ball + *kokku*, long beak.]

ban•dit (băn′dĭt) ►*n.* A robber, esp. one who is

armed. [Ital. *bandito*.] —**ban′dit•ry** *n.*

ban•do•leer or **ban•do•lier** (băn′də-lîr′) ▶*n.* A military belt for carrying cartridges that is worn across the chest. [< Sp. *bandolera*.]

band saw ▶*n.* A power saw having a toothed metal band driven around pulleys.

band•stand (bănd′stănd′) ▶*n.* A platform for a band or orchestra, often roofed when outdoors.

Ban•dung (bän′do͝ong′) A city of Indonesia in W Java SE of Jakarta. Pop. 1,462,637.

band•wag•on (bănd′wăg′ən) ▶*n.* **1.** A decorated wagon used to transport musicians in a parade. **2.** *Informal* A cause or party that attracts increasing numbers of adherents.

band•width (bănd′wĭdth′, -wĭth′) ▶*n.* *Comp. Sci.* The amount of data that can be passed along a communications channel in a given period of time.

ban•dy (băn′dē) ▶*v.* **-died, -dy•ing 1.** To toss back and forth. **2.** To discuss in a casual or frivolous manner. ▶*adj.* Bowed in an outward curve: *bandy legs.* [?]

bane (bān) ▶*n.* **1.** Fatal injury or ruin. **2.** A cause of death or ruin. **3.** A deadly poison. [< OE *bana*.] —**bane′ful** *adj.*

bang[1] (băng) ▶*n.* **1.** A sudden loud noise, blow, or thump. **2.** *Slang* A sense of excitement; thrill. ▶*v.* **1.** To hit noisily; bump. **2.** To handle noisily or violently. **3.** To make a loud, explosive noise. ▶*adv.* Exactly; precisely: *hit bang on the target.* [Prob. < ON *bang*, a hammering.]

bang[2] (băng) ▶*n.* often **bangs.** Hair cut straight across the forehead. [< BANG[1], suddenly, abruptly.]

Ban•ga•lore (băng′gə-lôr′, -lōr′) A city of S-central India W of Chennai. Pop. 2,660,088.

Bang•kok (băng′kŏk′) The capital of Thailand, in the SW. Pop. 5,876,000.

Bang•la•desh (bäng′glə-dĕsh′, băng′-) A country of S Asia between India and Myanmar (Burma) on the Bay of Bengal. Cap. Dhaka. Pop. 117,787,00. —**Bang′la•desh′i** *adj. & n.*

ban•gle (băng′gəl) ▶*n.* **1.** A hooplike bracelet or anklet. **2.** A hanging ornament. [Hindi *baṅgrī*, glass bracelet.]

Ban•gor (băng′gôr, -gər) A city of S-central ME. Pop. 33,181.

Ban•gui (bäng-gē′, bäɴ-) The capital of Central African Republic, in the S part on the Ubangi R. Pop. 473,817.

bang-up (băng′ŭp′) ▶*adj.* *Informal* Very good; excellent.

ban•ian (băn′yən) ▶*n.* Var. of **banyan.**

ban•ish (băn′ĭsh) ▶*v.* **1.** To force to leave a country or place by official decree; exile. **2.** To drive away; expel. [< OFr. *banir*.] —**ban′ish•ment** *n.*

ban•is•ter also **ban•nis•ter** (băn′ĭ-stər) ▶*n.* **1.** A handrail, esp. on a staircase. **2.** A baluster. [Var. of BALUSTER.]

ban•jo (băn′jō) ▶*n.*, *pl.* **-jos** or **-joes** *Mus.* A usu. fretted stringed instrument having a hollow circular body with a stretched diaphragm of vellum. [Prob. of African orig.] —**ban′jo•ist** *n.*

Ban•jul (bän′jo͞ol′) The capital of Gambia, at the mouth of the Gambia R. Pop. 49,181.

bank[1] (băngk) ▶*n.* **1.** A piled-up mass, as of snow or clouds. See Syns at **heap. 2.** A steep natural incline. **3.** An artificial embankment. **4.** often **banks** The slope of land adjoining a body of water, esp. a river, lake, or channel. **5.** often **banks** A large elevated area of a sea floor. **6.** Lateral tilting, as of an aircraft or vehicle in turning. ▶*v.* **1.** To border or protect with a bank. **2.** To pile up; amass. **3.** To cover (a fire) with ashes or fuel for continued low burning. **4.** To construct with a slope rising to the outside edge. **5.** To tilt (e.g., an aircraft) in turning. [Of Scand. orig.]

bank[2] (băngk) ▶*n.* **1a.** A business establishment authorized to perform financial transactions, such as receiving or lending money. **b.** The offices in which a bank is located. **2.** The funds held by a dealer or banker in some gambling games. **3.** A supply for future or emergency use: *a blood bank.* **4.** A place of storage: *a computer's memory bank.* ▶*v.* **1.** To deposit in a bank. **2.** To transact business with a bank. **3.** To operate a bank. —***phrasal verb:*** **bank on** To count on; rely on. [< OItal. *banca*, moneychanger's table.] —**bank′a•ble** *adj.* —**bank′er** *n.* —**bank′ing** *n.*

bank[3] (băngk) ▶*n.* **1.** A set of similar things arranged in a row: *a bank of elevators.* **2.** *Naut.* A bench for rowers or a row of oars in a galley. ▶*v.* To arrange in a row. [< LLat. *bancus*, bench.]

bank•book (băngk′bo͝ok′) ▶*n.* A booklet held by a depositor in which deposits and withdrawals are entered by the bank; passbook.

bank•card (băngk′kärd′) ▶*n.* A card issued by a bank, used for receiving credit or for operating an automated teller machine.

bank holiday ▶*n.* A day on which banks are legally closed.

bank note ▶*n.* A note issued by an authorized bank payable to the bearer on demand and acceptable as money.

bank•roll (băngk′rōl′) ▶*n.* **1.** A roll of paper money. **2.** *Informal* One's ready cash. ▶*v.* *Informal* To underwrite the expense of.

bank•rupt (băngk′rŭpt′, -rəpt) ▶*n.* A debtor that is judged legally insolvent and whose remaining property is then administered for the creditors or is distributed among them. ▶*adj.* **1a.** Having been legally declared insolvent. **b.** Financially ruined; impoverished. **2.** Lacking in quality or resources; depleted. ▶*v.* To cause to become financially bankrupt. [< Ital. *bancarotta*.] —**bank′rupt•cy** *n.*

ban•ner (băn′ər) ▶*n.* **1.** A piece of cloth attached to a staff and used as a standard by a monarch, military commander, or knight. **2.** A flag. **3.** A headline spanning the width of a newspaper page. ▶*adj.* Outstanding: *a banner crop.* [< OFr. *baniere*.]

ban•nis•ter (băn′ĭ-stər) ▶*n.* Var. of **banister.**

Bannister, Roger. b. 1929. British runner; first person to run the mile in under four minutes (1954).

ban•nock (băn′ək) ▶*n.* A flat, usu. unleavened bread made of oatmeal or barley flour. [< OE *bannuc*, of Celt. orig.]

banns (bănz) ▶*pl.n.* An announcement, esp. in a church, of an intended marriage. [< OE *gebann*, proclamation.]

ban•quet (băng′kwĭt) ▶*n.* **1.** An elaborate, sumptuous feast. **2.** A ceremonial dinner honoring a particular guest or occasion. ▶*v.* To honor at or partake of a banquet. [< OFr. *banc*, bench.] —**ban′quet•er** *n.*

ban•quette (băng-kĕt′) ►*n.* **1.** A platform lining a trench or parapet for soldiers when firing. **2.** A long upholstered bench along a wall. [< Prov. *banqueta.*]

ban•shee (băn′shē) ►*n.* A female spirit in Gaelic folklore believed to presage a death in a family by wailing. [Ir.Gael. *bean sídhe.*]

ban•tam (băn′təm) ►*n.* **1.** Any of various breeds of small domestic fowl. **2.** A small but aggressive person. ►*adj.* **1.** Diminutive; small. **2.** Aggressive and spirited. [After *Bantam,* Indonesia.]

ban•tam•weight (băn′təm-wāt′) ►*n.* A boxer weighing from 113 to 118 lbs., between a flyweight and a featherweight.

ban•ter (băn′tər) ►*n.* Good-humored, playful conversation. ►*v.* To exchange playful or teasing remarks. [?]

Syns: *banter, chaff, josh, kid, rag, razz, rib* ***v.***

Ban•tu (băn′to͞o) ►*n., pl.* **-tu** or **-tus 1.** A large group of related languages spoken in central, E-central, and S Africa, including Swahili, Zulu, and Xhosa. **2.** A member of a Bantu-speaking people. —**Ban′tu** *adj.*

ban•yan also **ban•ian** (băn′yən) ►*n.* A tropical fig tree having many aerial roots that descend from the branches and develop new trunks. [Short for *banyan tree,* merchant's tree < Skt. *vāṇijaḥ,* merchant.]

ban•zai (bän-zī′) ►*n.* A Japanese battle cry or patriotic cheer. [J., ten thousand years.]

ba•o•bab (bā′ō-băb′, bä′-) ►*n.* A tropical African tree with large, hard-shelled hanging fruits and a short swollen trunk that stores water. [Prob. < Ar. dial. *būḥibab,* fruit of many seeds : Ar. *'ab,* father, source + *ḥibāb,* pl. of *ḥabb,* seed.]

Bao•tou (bou′tō′) A city of N China on the Huang He (Yellow R.) west of Hohhot. Pop. 1,075,920.

bap•tism (băp′tĭz′əm) ►*n.* **1.** A Christian sacrament of spiritual rebirth marked by the symbolic use of water. **2.** A ceremony or an experience by which one is purified, given a name, or initiated. [< Gk. *baptismos.*] —**bap•tis′mal** *adj.*

Bap•tist (băp′tĭst) ►*n.* **1.** A member of an evangelical Protestant church that practices voluntary adult baptism. **2. baptist** One that baptizes. —**Bap′tist** *adj.*

bap•tis•ter•y also **bap•tis•try** (băp′tĭ-strē) ►*n., pl.* **-ies** also **-tries 1.** A part of a church or a separate building used for baptizing. **2.** A font used for baptism.

bap•tize (băp-tīz′, băp′tīz′) ►*v.* **-tized, -tiz•ing 1.** To administer baptism (to). **2a.** To cleanse or purify. **b.** To initiate. **3.** To give a first or Christian name to; christen. [< Gk. *baptein,* to dip.] —**bap•tiz′er** *n.*

bar (bär) ►*n.* **1.** A relatively long, straight, rigid piece of solid material. **2.** A solid oblong block of a substance, such as soap, candy, or gold. **3.** An obstacle. **4.** A narrow marking, as a stripe or band. **5.** *Law* The nullification or prevention of a claim or action. **6.** The railing in a courtroom in front of which the judges, lawyers, and defendants sit. **7.** *Law* **a.** Attorneys considered as a group. **b.** The legal profession. **8.** *Mus.* A vertical line drawn through a staff to mark off a measure. **9a.** A counter at which food and esp. drinks are served: *an oyster bar.* **b.** A place having such a counter. **10.**Var. of **barre.** ►*v.* **barred, bar•ring 1.** To fasten securely with a bar. **2.** To shut in or out with or as if with bars. **3.** To obstruct. **4a.** To forbid; prohibit. **b.** To exclude. **5.** To mark with stripes or bands. ►*prep.* Except for; excluding: *my best performance, bar none.* [< OFr. *barre.*]

Ba•rab•bas (bə-răb′əs). In the Bible, the prisoner whose release, instead of that of Jesus, was demanded by the multitude.

barb (bärb) ►*n.* **1.** A sharp backward-pointing projection, as on an arrow or fishhook. **2.** A cutting remark. **3.** A parallel filament projecting from the main shaft of a feather. **4.** *Bot.* A hooked bristle or hairlike projection. **5.** See **barbel.** ►*v.* To provide with a barb. [< Lat. *barba,* beard.] —**barbed** *adj.*

Bar•ba•dos (bär-bā′dōs′, -dōz′) An island country of the E West Indies. Cap. Bridgetown. Pop. 261,000. —**Bar•ba′di•an** *adj. & n.*

bar•bar•i•an (bär-bâr′ē-ən) ►*n.* **1.** A member of a people considered by others to have a primitive civilization. **2.** A savage, brutal, or cruel person. **3.** An insensitive, uncultured person. See Syns at **boor.** [< Lat. *barbarus,* BARBAROUS.] —**bar•bar′i•an** *adj.* —**bar•bar′i•an•ism** *n.*

bar•bar•ic (bär-băr′ĭk) ►*adj.* **1.** Of or typical of barbarians. **2.** Marked by crudeness in taste, style, or manner.

bar•ba•rism (bär′bə-rĭz′əm) ►*n.* **1.** An act or custom marked by brutality or crudity. **2.** The use of words or expressions considered incorrect or unacceptable.

bar•ba•rous (bär′bər-əs) ►*adj.* **1.** Primitive in culture and customs. **2.** Lacking refinement; coarse. **3.** Marked by savagery; brutal; cruel. **4.** Marked by the use of barbarisms in language. [< Gk. *barbaros,* foreign.] —**bar′ba•rize′** *v.* —**bar′ba•rous•ly** *adv.* —**bar′ba•rous•ness, bar•bar′i•ty** (-băr′ĭ-tē) *n.*

Bar•ba•ry (bär′bə-rē, -brē) A region of N Africa on the Mediterranean coast between Egypt and the Atlantic.

Barbary Coast. The Mediterranean coastal area of Barbary.

bar•be•cue (bär′bĭ-kyo͞o′) ►*n.* **1.** A grill, pit, or outdoor fireplace for roasting meat. **2.** Meat roasted over an open fire. **3.** A social gathering, usu. held outdoors, at which food is cooked over an open fire. ►*v.* **-cued, -cu•ing.** To roast (meat or seafood) over an open fire. [Of Taino orig.]

barbed wire ►*n.* Twisted strands of fence wire with barbs at regular intervals.

bar•bel (bär′bəl) ►*n.* One of the whiskerlike feelers of certain fishes, such as catfishes. [< Med.Lat. *barbula,* little beard.]

bar•bell (bär′bĕl′) ►*n.* A bar with weights at each end, lifted for sport or exercise.

bar•ber (bär′bər) ►*n.* One whose business is to cut hair and to shave or trim beards. ►*v.* To cut the hair or beard (of). [< Lat. *barba,* beard.]

bar•ber•ry (bär′bĕr′ē) ►*n.* Any of various often spiny shrubs having small reddish or blackish berries. [< Med.Lat. *berberis.*]

bar•ber•shop (bär′bər-shŏp′) ►*n.* The place of business of a barber. ►*adj.* Relating to sentimental songs sung in four-part harmony.

bar•bi•tal (bär′bĭ-tôl′, -tăl′) ►*n.* A barbiturate, $C_8H_{12}N_2O_3$, used as a sedative. [< BARBITURIC ACID.]

bar•bi•tu•rate (bär-bĭch′ər-ĭt, -ə-rāt′, -ə-wĭt) ►*n.* Any of a group of barbituric acid derivatives used as sedatives or hypnotics. [BARBITUR(IC ACID) + –ATE[2].]
bar•bi•tu•ric acid (bär′bĭ-to͝or′ĭk, -tyo͝or′-) ►*n.* An organic acid, $C_4H_4O_3N_2$, used in the manufacture of barbiturates.
Bar•bu•da (bär-bo͞o′də) An island of Antigua and Barbuda in the West Indies N of Antigua. —**Bar•bu′dan** *adj. & n.*
barb•wire (bärb′wīr′) ►*n.* Barbed wire.
Bar•ce•lo•na (bär′sə-lō′nə) A city of NE Spain on the Mediterranean. Pop. 1,770,296.
bar code ►*n.* A series of vertical bars of varying widths printed on consumer product packages and used esp. for inventory control.
bard (bärd) ►*n.* **1.** One of an ancient Celtic order of singing narrative poets. **2.** A poet, esp. an exalted national poet. [< Ir.Gael. *bárd* and < Welsh *bardd.*] —**bard′ic** *adj.*
bare (bâr) ►*adj.* **bar•er, bar•est 1.** Lacking the usual or appropriate covering or clothing; naked. **2.** Exposed to view. **3.** Lacking the usual furnishings, equipment, or decoration. **4.** Having no addition or qualification: *the bare facts.* **5.** Just sufficient: *the bare necessities.* ►*v.* **bared, bar•ing.** To make bare; reveal. [< OE *bær.*] —**bare′ness** *n.*
bare•back (bâr′băk′) ►*adj.* Using no saddle: *a bareback rider.* —**bare′back′** *adv.*
bare•faced (bâr′fāst′) ►*adj.* **1.** Having no covering or beard on the face. **2.** Shameless; brazen: *a barefaced lie.* —**bare′fac′ed•ly** (-fā′sĭd-lē, -fāst′lē) *adv.*
bare•foot (bâr′fo͝ot′) also **bare•foot•ed** (-fo͝ot′ĭd) ►*adj.* Wearing nothing on the feet. —**bare′foot** *adv.*
bare•hand•ed (bâr′hăn′dĭd) ►*adj.* Having no covering on the hands. —**bare′hand′ed** *adv.*
bare•head•ed (bâr′hĕd′ĭd) ►*adj.* Having no covering on the head. —**bare′head′ed** *adv.*
bare•leg•ged (bâr′lĕg′ĭd, -lĕgd′) ►*adj.* Having the legs uncovered. —**bare′leg′ged** *adv.*
bare•ly (bâr′lē) ►*adv.* **1.** By a very little; hardly. **2.** Sparsely; sparely: *a barely furnished room.*
Ba•rents Sea (băr′ənts, bä′rənts) A shallow section of the Arctic Ocean N of Norway and NW Russia.
barf (bärf) ►*v. Slang* To vomit. [Prob. imit.] —**barf** *n.*
bar•fly (bär′flī′) ►*n. Slang* One who frequents drinking establishments.
bar•gain (bär′gĭn) ►*n.* **1.** An agreement between parties fixing obligations that each promises to carry out. **2a.** An agreement establishing the terms of a sale or exchange of goods or services. **b.** The property acquired or services rendered as a result of such an agreement. **3.** Something offered or acquired at a price advantageous to the buyer. ►*v.* **1.** To negotiate the terms of a sale, exchange, or other agreement. **2.** To arrive at an agreement. **3.** To exchange; trade. —***phrasal verb:*** **bargain for** To count on; expect. —***idiom:*** **into** (or **in**) **the bargain** More than what is expected. [< OFr. *bargaignier*, haggle.] —**bar′gain•er** *n.*
Syns: *bargain, compact, contract, covenant, deal* ***n.***
barge (bärj) ►*n.* **1.** A long, large, usu. flat-bottomed boat for transporting freight. **2.** A large open pleasure boat used for parties. **3.** A powerboat reserved for the use of an admiral. ►*v.* **barged, barg•ing 1.** To carry by barge. **2.** To move about clumsily. **3.** To intrude. [< Lat. *barca*, boat.]
bar graph ►*n.* A graph consisting of parallel, usu. vertical bars or rectangles with lengths proportional to specified quantities.

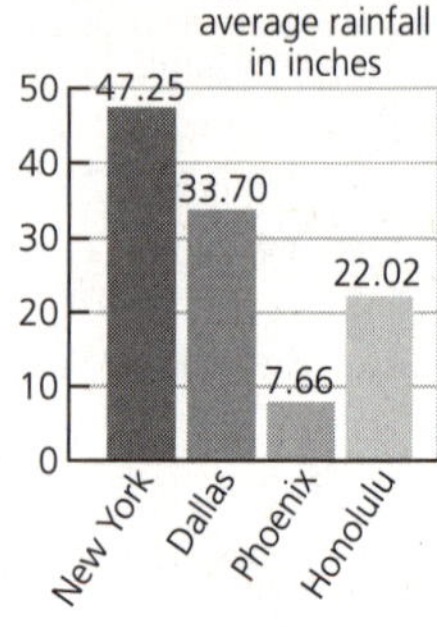

bar graph
average annual rainfall of several US cities

bar•ite (bâr′īt, băr′-) ►*n.* A crystalline mineral that is the chief source of barium compounds. [Gk. *barus*, heavy + –ITE[1].]
bar•i•tone (băr′ĭ-tōn′) ►*n.* **1.** A male singer or voice with a range higher than a bass and lower than a tenor. **2.** A wind instrument with a similar range. [< Gk. *barutonos*, deep-sounding.]
bar•i•um (bâr′ē-əm, băr′-) ►*n. Symbol* **Ba** A soft, silvery-white metal used to deoxidize copper and in various alloys. At. no. 56. See table at **element.** [< Gk. *barus*, heavy.]
bark[1] (bärk) ►*n.* The harsh, abrupt sound uttered by a dog. ►*v.* **1.** To utter a bark. **2.** To speak sharply; snap. —***idiom:*** **bark up the wrong tree** To misdirect one's efforts. [< OE *beorcan*, to bark.]
bark[2] (bärk) ►*n.* The tough outer covering of the stems and roots of trees and other woody plants. ►*v.* **1.** To remove bark from. **2.** To scrape; skin: *barked my shin.* [< ON *börkr.*]
bark[3] also **barque** (bärk) ►*n.* **1.** A sailing ship with from three to five masts. **2.** A boat, esp. a small sailing vessel. [< Lat. *barca*, boat.]
bar•keep•er (bär′kē′pər) also **bar•keep** (-kēp′) ►*n.* **1.** One who owns or runs a bar. **2.** See **bartender.**
bark•er (bär′kər) ►*n.* **1.** One that barks. **2.** One who stands at the entrance to a show, as at a carnival, and solicits customers with a loud colorful sales spiel.
bar•ley (bär′lē) ►*n.* A cereal grass that bears grain used as food, livestock feed, and for malt production. [< OE *bærlic.*]
bar•maid (bär′mād′) ►*n.* A woman who serves drinks in a bar.
bar•man (bär′mən) ►*n.* A man who serves drinks in a bar.
bar mitz•vah or **bar miz•vah** (bär mĭts′və) ►*n.* **1.** A 13-year-old Jewish boy, considered an adult and responsible for his moral and religious duties. **2.** The ceremony that confirms a boy as a bar mitzvah. [Heb. *bar miṣwâ.*]

barn (bärn) ►*n.* A large farm building used for storing farm products and sheltering livestock. [< OE *berærn.*]

bar•na•cle (bär′nə-kəl) ►*n.* A small, hard-shelled crustacean that attaches itself to submerged surfaces. [< Med.Lat. *bernaca.*]

Bar•nard (bär′nərd, bär-närd′), **Christiaan Neethling.** b. 1923. South African surgeon.

Bar•na•ul (bär′nə-o͞ol′) A city of S-central Russia S of Novosibirsk. Pop. 595,298.

barn owl ►*n.* An owl with a white, heart-shaped face, often nesting in barns.

barn•storm (bärn′stôrm′) ►*v.* **1.** To travel about making political speeches, giving lectures, or presenting plays. **2.** To tour as a stunt flyer. —**barn′storm′er** *n.*

Bar•num (bär′nəm), **P(hineas) T(aylor).** 1810–91. Amer. circus impresario.

barn•yard (bärn′yärd′) ►*n.* The area surrounding a barn, often enclosed by a fence.

bar•o•graph (băr′ə-grăf′) ►*n.* A recording barometer. [< Gk. *baros*, weight.] —**bar′o•graph′ic** *adj.*

ba•rom•e•ter (bə-rŏm′ĭ-tər) ►*n.* **1.** An instrument for measuring atmospheric pressure, used esp. in weather forecasting. **2.** An indicator of change. [< Gk. *baros*, weight.] —**bar′o•met′ric** (băr′ə-mĕt′rĭk), **bar′o•met′ri•cal** *adj.* —**ba•rom′e•try** *n.*

bar•on (băr′ən) ►*n.* **1a.** A British or Japanese nobleman of the lowest rank. **b.** A nobleman of continental Europe, ranked variously in different countries. **2.** One having great power in a specified field. [< OFr.] —**bar′on•age** *n.* —**ba•ro′ni•al** (bə-rō′nē-əl) *adj.* —**bar′o•ny** *n.*

bar•on•ess (băr′ə-nĭs) ►*n.* **1.** The wife or widow of a baron. **2.** A woman holding a baronial title.

bar•on•et (băr′ə-nĭt, băr′ə-nĕt′) ►*n.* A man holding a British hereditary title reserved for commoners. —**bar′on•et•cy** *n.*

bar•on•et•ess (băr′ə-nĭ-tĭs, băr′ə-nĕt′ĭs) ►*n.* A woman holding a British hereditary title reserved for commoners.

ba•roque (bə-rōk′) ►*adj.* **1.** also **Baroque a.** Of an artistic style current in Europe from the early 17th to mid-18th cent., typified by bold, curving forms and elaborate ornamentation. **b.** Of a musical style current in Europe from about 1600 to 1750, marked by strict forms and elaborate ornamentation. **2a.** Highly intricate or ornate. **b.** Grotesque; bizarre. [< Ital. *barocco.*] —**ba•roque′ly** *adv.* —**ba•roque′** *n.*

barque (bärk) ►*n.* Var. of **bark**[3].

Bar•qui•si•me•to (bär′kē-sē-mĕ′tō) A city of NW Venezuela WSW of Caracas. Pop. 692,599.

bar•rack (băr′ək) ►*v.* To house (e.g., soldiers) in quarters. ►*n.* often **bar•racks** (băr′əks) A building or group of buildings used to house military personnel. [< Sp. *barracas*, soldiers' tents.]

bar•ra•cu•da (băr′ə-ko͞o′də) ►*n.*, *pl.* **-da** or **-das.** A narrow-bodied, chiefly tropical marine fish with very sharp fanglike teeth. [< Sp. *barraco*, bucktooth.]

bar•rage (bə-räzh′) ►*n.* **1.** A heavy curtain of artillery or missile fire. **2.** An overwhelming outpouring: *a barrage of criticism.* ►*v.* **-raged, -rag•ing.** To direct a barrage at. [Fr. *(tir de) barrage*, barrier (fire).]

Syns: *barrage, bombard, pepper, shower* ***v.***

baroque
Bernini's *The Ecstasy of St. Theresa*

Bar•ran•quil•la (bä′rän-kē′yä) A city of N Colombia on the Magdalena R. near the Caribbean Sea. Pop. 917,486.

bar•ra•try (băr′ə-trē) ►*n.*, *pl.* **-tries 1.** *Law* The offense of instigating quarrels or groundless lawsuits. **2.** An unlawful breach of duty on the part of a ship's master or crew resulting in injury to the ship's owner. **3.** Sale or purchase of positions in church or state. [< OFr. *barater*, to cheat.]

barre also **bar** (bär) ►*n.* **1.** In ballet, a horizontal rail used as a support in exercises. **2.** *Mus.* A technique in which a finger is laid across a fingerboard to stop several strings at once. [Fr.]

bar•rel (băr′əl) ►*n.* **1.** A large cask usu. made of curved wooden staves bound with hoops and having a flat top and bottom. **2.** See table at **measurement. 3a.** The long tube of a firearm. **b.** A cylindrical machine part. **4.** *Informal* A great deal: *a barrel of fun.* ►*v.* **-reled, -rel•ing** or **-relled, -rel•ling 1.** To put or pack in a barrel. **2.** To move at a high speed. —***idiom:*** **over a barrel** In a difficult or frustrating position. [< OFr. *baril.*]

barrel organ ►*n.* A mechanical instrument on which a tune is played by a revolving cylinder turned by a hand crank.

barrel roll ►*n.* A flight maneuver in which an aircraft makes a complete rotation on its longitudinal axis.

bar•ren (băr′ən) ►*adj.* **1a.** Not producing offspring. **b.** Incapable of producing offspring; sterile. **2.** Lacking vegetation. **3.** Unproductive of results. See Syns at **futile. 4.** Devoid; lacking: *writing barren of insight.* ►*n.* often **barrens.** A tract of unproductive land. [< OFr. *brahaigne.*] —**bar′ren•ness** *n.*

bar•rette (bə-rĕt′) ►*n.* A hair clasp. [Fr.]

bar•ri•cade (băr′ĭ-kād′, băr′ĭ-kād′) ►*n.* A makeshift barrier or fortification set up across a route of access. ►*v.* **-cad•ed, -cad•ing.** To block or confine with a barricade. [< OProv. *barrica*, barrel.]

bar•ri•er (băr′ē-ər) ►*n.* **1.** A structure, such as a fence, built to bar passage. **2.** Something immaterial that impedes. **3.** A boundary or limit. [< VLat. *barra, bar.]

barrier island ►*n.* A long narrow island running parallel to the mainland.

barrier reef ►*n.* A long narrow ridge of coral parallel to a coastline and separated from it by a lagoon too deep for coral growth.

bar•ring (bär′ĭng) ►*prep.* Apart from the occurrence of; excepting.

bar•ri•o (bä′rē-ō′) ►*n., pl.* **-os.** A chiefly Spanish-speaking neighborhood in a US city. [< Ar. *barr*, open area.]

bar•ris•ter (băr′ĭ-stər) ►*n. Chiefly Brit.* A lawyer who argues cases in the superior courts. [Prob. < BAR.]

bar•room (bär′ro͞om′, -ro͝om′) ►*n.* A place where alcoholic beverages are sold at a bar.

bar•row[1] (băr′ō) ►*n.* **1.** A flat rectangular tray or cart with handles at each end. **2.** A wheelbarrow. [< OE *bearwe.*]

bar•row[2] (băr′ō) ►*n.* A large mound of earth or stones placed over a burial site. [< OE *beorg.*]

Barrow, Point. The northernmost point of AK, on the Arctic Ocean.

Bar•ry•more (băr′ĭ-môr′, -mōr′). Family of American actors, including **Lionel** (1878–1954), **Ethel** (1879–1959), and **John** (1882–1942).

bar•tend•er (bär′tĕn′dər) ►*n.* One who serves alcoholic drinks at a bar; barkeeper.

bar•ter (bär′tər) ►*v.* To trade (goods or services) without using money. [Prob. < OFr. *barater.*] —**bar′ter** *n.* —**bar′ter•er** *n.*

Bar•thol•di (bär-thŏl′dē, -tôl-dē′), **Frédéric Auguste.** 1834–1904. French sculptor of the Statue of Liberty.

Bar•thol•o•mew (bär-thŏl′ə-myo͞o′), Saint. One of the 12 Apostles.

Bart•lett (bärt′lĭt), **John.** 1820–1905. Amer. publisher and editor.

Bar•tók (bär′tŏk′, -tôk′), **Béla.** 1881–1945. Hungarian pianist and composer.

Bar•ton (bär′tn), **Clara.** 1821–1912. Amer. founder of the American Red Cross (1881).

Bar•uch (bâr′ək, bə-ro͞ok′) ►*n.* See table at **Bible.**

Ba•ruch (bə-ro͞ok′), **Bernard Mannes.** 1870–1965. Amer. stock broker and presidential adviser.

bar•y•on (băr′ē-ŏn′) ►*n.* Any of a family of subatomic particles, including protons and neutrons, that are composed of three quarks. [Gk. *barus*, heavy + -ON[1].]

bas•al (bā′səl, -zəl) ►*adj.* **1.** Of, located at, or forming a base. **2.** Of primary importance; basic. —**bas′al•ly** *adv.*

basal metabolism ►*n.* The minimum amount of energy required to maintain vital functions in an organism at complete rest.

ba•salt (bə-sôlt′, bā′sôlt′) ►*n.* A hard, dense, dark volcanic rock. [< Gk. *basanitēs*, touchstone.] —**ba•sal′tic** *adj.*

base[1] (bās) ►*n.* **1.** The lowest or bottom part. **2.** A foundation. **3.** The fundamental principle of a system or theory; basis. **4.** A chief constituent: *a paint with an oil base.* **5.** The fact, observation, or premise from which a reasoning process is begun. **6a.** *Games* A starting point, safety area, or goal. **b.** *Baseball* Any one of the four corners of an infield marked by a bag or plate. **7.** A center of organization, supply, or activity; headquarters. **8a.** A fortified center of operations. **b.** A supply center for a large force of military personnel. **9.** *Ling.* A morpheme regarded as a form to which affixes or other bases may be added. **10.** *Math.* The number that is raised to various powers to generate the principal counting units of a number system. **11.** A line used as a reference for measurement or computations. **12.** *Chem.* **a.** Any of a large class of compounds, including the hydroxides and oxides of metals, having a bitter taste, a slippery solution, the ability to turn litmus blue, and the ability to react with acids to form salts. **b.** A molecular or ionic substance capable of combining with a proton to form a new substance. ►*adj.* Forming or serving as a base. ►*v.* **based, bas•ing 1.** To form or assign a base for. **2.** To find a basis for; establish. —***idiom:*** **off base** Badly mistaken. [< Gk. *basis.*]

base[2] (bās) ►*adj.* **bas•er, bas•est 1.** Morally bad; contemptible. **2.** Lowly; menial. **3.** Inferior in value or quality. **4.** Containing inferior substances: *a base metal.* [< Med.Lat. *bassus*, low.] —**base′ly** *adv.* —**base′ness** *n.*

base•ball (bās′bôl′) ►*n.* **1.** A game played with a bat and ball by two teams of nine players, each team playing alternately in the field and at bat, the players at bat having to run a course of four bases laid out in a diamond pattern in order to score. **2.** The hard ball used in this game.

base•board (bās′bôrd′, -bōrd′) ►*n.* A molding that conceals the joint between an interior wall and the floor.

base•born (bās′bôrn′) ►*adj.* **1.** Ignoble; contemptible. **2a.** Born of unwed parents; illegitimate. **b.** Of humble birth.

base hit ►*n. Baseball* A hit by which the batter reaches base safely.

Ba•sel (bä′zəl) A city of N Switzerland on the Rhine R. Pop. 175,781.

base•less (bās′lĭs) ►*adj.* Having no basis or foundation in fact; unfounded.

Syns: *baseless, groundless, idle, unfounded, unwarranted* ***adj.***

base line ►*n.* **1.** A line serving as a basis, as for measurement or comparison. **2.** *Baseball* An area within which a base runner must stay when running between bases. **3.** *Sports* The boundary line at either end of a court, as in badminton or tennis.

base•man (bās′mən) ►*n. Baseball* A player assigned to first, second, or third base.

base•ment (bās′mənt) ►*n.* **1.** The substructure or foundation of a building. **2.** The lowest story of a building, usu. below ground.

ba•sen•ji (bə-sĕn′jē) ►*n.* A dog having a short smooth coat and lacking a bark. [Of Bantu orig.]

base on balls ►*n. Baseball* The advance of a batter to first base after four pitches that are balls.

ba•ses (bā′sēz′) ►*n.* Pl. of **basis.**

bash (băsh) ►*v.* **1.** To strike with a heavy crushing blow. **2.** *Informal* To criticize (another) harshly. ►*n.* **1.** *Informal* A heavy crushing blow. **2.** *Slang* A party. [?] —**bash′er** *n.*

bash•ful (băsh′fəl) ►*adj.* Shy and self-conscious. [< ME *basshen*, be discomfited.] —**bash′ful•ly** *adv.* —**bash′ful•ness** *n.*

ba•sic (bā′sĭk) ►*adj.* **1.** Of or forming a base; fundamental. **2.** First and necessary beyond all else. **3.** *Chem.* **a.** Of, producing, or resulting from a base. **b.** Containing a base, esp. in excess of acid. **c.** Containing oxide or hydroxide anions. Used of a salt. ►*n.* A fundamental element or entity: *the basics of math.* —**ba′si•cal•ly** *adv.* —**ba•sic′i•ty** (-sĭs′ĭ-tē) *n.*

BA•SIC or **Ba•sic** (bā′sĭk) ►*n.* A simple programming language. [*B(eginner's) A(ll-purpose) S(ymbolic) I(nstruction) C(ode).*]

bas•il (băz′əl, bā′zəl) ►*n.* An Old World aromatic herb with leaves used as seasoning. [< Gk. *basilikos*, royal.]

ba•sil•i•ca (bə-sĭl′ĭ-kə) ►*n.* **1a.** A public building of ancient Rome, used as a courtroom or assembly hall. **b.** A Christian church building having a nave with a semicircular apse. **2.** *Rom. Cath. Ch.* A church accorded certain privileges by the pope. [< Gk. *basilikē (stoa)*, royal (portico).]

bas•i•lisk (băs′ə-lĭsk′, băz′-) ►*n.* **1.** A legendary serpent with lethal breath and glance. **2.** Any of various crested tropical American lizards that can run on the hind legs. [< Gk. *basiliskos.*]

ba•sin (bā′sĭn) ►*n.* **1.** An open, shallow, usu. round container used esp. for holding liquids. **2.** A washbowl; sink. **3a.** An artificially enclosed area of a river or harbor. **b.** A small enclosed or partly enclosed body of water. **4.** A region drained by a single river system. **5.** A bowl-shaped depression in the surface of the land or ocean floor. [< OFr. *bacin.*] —**ba′sin•al** *adj.*

ba•sis (bā′sĭs) ►*n., pl.* **-ses** (-sēz′) **1.** A foundation upon which something rests. **2.** The chief constituent. **3.** A fundamental principle. [< Gk.]

bask (băsk) ►*v.* **1.** To expose oneself to pleasant warmth. **2.** To take great satisfaction: *basked in the teacher's praise.* [ME *basken.*]

bas•ket (băs′kĭt) ►*n.* **1.** A container made of interwoven material. **2.** A usu. open gondola on a hot-air balloon. **3.** *Basketball* A metal hoop from which an open-bottomed circular net is suspended, serving as a goal. [< VLat. **baskauta.*]

bas•ket•ball (băs′kĭt-bôl′) ►*n.* **1.** A game played between two teams of five players each, the object being to throw an inflated ball through an elevated basket on the opponent's side of the rectangular court. **2.** The ball for this game.

basket case ►*n. Informal* One that is in a completely hopeless or useless condition.

bas•ket•ry (băs′kĭ-trē) ►*n.* **1.** The craft of making baskets. **2.** Baskets collectively.

bas mitz•vah (bäs mĭts′və) ►*n.* Var. of **bat mitzvah.**

Basque (băsk) ►*n.* **1.** A member of a people of unknown origin inhabiting the W Pyrenees and the Bay of Biscay in France and Spain. **2.** The language of the Basques, of no known linguistic affiliation. —**Basque** *adj.*

Basque Provinces. A region comprising three provinces of N Spain on the Bay of Biscay.

Bas•ra (bäs′rə, bŭs′-) A city of SE Iraq on the Shatt al Arab. Pop. 406,296.

bas-re•lief (bä′rĭ-lēf′) ►*n.* See **low relief.** [< Ital. *bassorilievo.*]

bass[1] (băs) ►*n., pl.* **bass** or **-es.** Any of several freshwater or marine food and game fishes. [< OE *bærs.*]

bass[2] (bās) ►*n.* **1.** A low-pitched tone. **2.** The tones in the lowest register of an instrument. **3a.** The lowest singing voice of a man. **b.** The tonal range characteristic of a bass. **c.** A singer or voice having this range. **d.** An instrument, esp. a double bass or bass guitar, having this range. [ME *bas*, lowest musical part < Med.-Lat. *bassus*, low.] —**bass** *adj.*

bass clef (bās) ►*n. Mus.* A symbol centered on the fourth line from the bottom of a staff to indicate F below middle C.

Basse•terre (băs-târ′, bäs-) The capital of St. Kitts–Nevis, in the Leeward Is. of the West Indies. Pop. 29,522.

Basse-Terre (băs-târ′, bäs-) The capital of the French overseas department of Guadeloupe, on **Basse-Terre Island** in the Leeward Is. of the West Indies. Pop. 29,522.

basset hound (băs′ĭt) ►*n.* A short-haired dog with a long body, short legs, and drooping ears. [Fr. *basset*, very short.]

bas•si•net (băs′ə-nĕt′) ►*n.* An oblong basket-like bed for an infant. [Fr., small basin.]

bass•ist (bā′sĭst) ►*n.* One who plays a bass instrument, esp. a double bass or bass guitar.

bas•so (băs′ō, bä′sō) ►*n., pl.* **-sos** or **-si** (-sē). A bass singer, esp. an operatic bass. [Ital. < Med.Lat. *bassus*, low.]

bas•soon (bə-so͞on′, bă-) ►*n.* A low-pitched double-reed woodwind instrument having a long wooden body. [< Ital. *basso*, bass.] —**bas•soon′ist** *n.*

Bass Strait (băs) A channel between Tasmania and SE Australia connecting the Indian Ocean with the Tasman Sea.

bass viol (bās) ►*n.* See **double bass.**

bass•wood (băs′wo͝od′) ►*n.* **1.** See **linden. 2.** The soft wood of a linden. [< BAST.]

bast (băst) ►*n.* Fibrous plant material used to make cordage and textiles. [< OE *bæst.*]

bas•tard (băs′tərd) ►*n.* **1.** An illegitimate child. **2.** *Slang* A mean person. ►*adj.* **1.** Illegitimate. **2.** Not genuine; spurious. [< OFr.] —**bas′tard•ly** *adj.* —**bas′tard•y** *n.*

bas•tard•ize (băs′tər-dīz′) ►*v.* **-ized, -iz•ing.** To lower in quality or character; debase. —**bas′tard•i•za′tion** *n.*

baste[1] (bāst) ►*v.* **bast•ed, bast•ing.** To sew temporarily with large running stitches. [< OFr. *bastir.*]

baste[2] (bāst) ►*v.* **bast•ed, bast•ing.** To moisten (e.g., meat) periodically with a liquid while cooking. [ME *basten.*] —**bast′er** *n.*

baste[3] (bāst) ►*v.* **bast•ed, bast•ing 1.** To beat vigorously; thrash. See Syns at **beat. 2.** To lambaste. [Prob. of Scand. orig.]

Bas•tille Day (bă-stēl′) ►*n.* Jul. 14, observed in France to commemorate the storming of the Bastille prison in 1789.

bas•tion (băs′chən, -tē-ən) ►*n.* **1.** A projecting part of a fortification. **2.** A bulwark; stronghold. [< OFr. *bastille*, fortress.]

bat[1] (băt) ►*n.* **1.** A stout wooden stick; cudgel. **2.** A blow, as with a stick. **3.** *Sports* **a.** A rounded, tapered, usu. wooden club used to hit the ball in baseball. **b.** A flat-sided club used in cricket. **c.** A racket, as in table tennis. ►*v.* **bat•ted, bat•ting 1.** To hit with or as if with a bat. **2.** *Sports* **a.** To be the batter or batsman in baseball or cricket. **b.** To have (a certain batting average). **3.** *Informal* To discuss: *bat an idea around.* —***idioms:*** **at bat** Taking one's turn at hitting a pitched or bowled ball in baseball or cricket. **go to bat for** To support or defend. **off the bat** Immediately. [ME.]

bat² (băt) ►*n.* Any of various nocturnal flying mammals having membranous wings. [Of Scand. orig.]

bat³ (băt) ►*v.* **bat•ted, bat•ting.** To flutter (e.g., one's eyes). [Prob. < *bate*, flap one's wings.]

bat⁴ (băt) ►*n. Slang* A binge; spree. [Prob. < *batter*, spree.]

Ba•taan (bə-tăn′, -tän′) A peninsula of W Luzon, Philippines, between Manila Bay and the South China Sea.

batch (băch) ►*n.* **1.** An amount prepared or produced at one time. **2.** A group of persons or things. **3.** *Comp. Sci.* A set of data to be processed in a single program run. [< OE *bacan*, bake.] —**batch** *v.*

bate (bāt) ►*v.* **bat•ed, bat•ing.** To lessen the force of; moderate. [< ME *abaten*, abate.]

ba•teau (bă-tō′) ►*n.*, *pl.* **-teaux** (-tōz′). A light, flat-bottomed boat. [< OFr. *batel*, boat < OE *bāt*.]

BATF ►*abbr.* Bureau of Alcohol, Tobacco, and Firearms

bath (băth) ►*n.*, *pl.* **baths** (bă*th*z, băths) **1a.** The act of soaking or cleansing the body, as in water or steam. **b.** The water used for bathing. **2a.** A bathtub. **b.** A bathroom. **3.** A building equipped for bathing. **4.** often **baths** A spa. **5.** A liquid in which something is dipped or soaked in processing. [< OE *bæth*.]

Bath (băth, bäth) A city of SW England SE of Bristol. Pop. 84,100.

bathe (bā*th*) ►*v.* **bathed, bath•ing 1a.** To take a bath. **b.** To give a bath to. **2.** To go swimming. **3.** To wash or wet. **4.** To treat by applying a liquid. **5.** To suffuse, as with light. [< OE *bathian*.] —**bath′er** *n.*

bath•house (băth′hous′) ►*n.* **1.** A building with facilities for bathing. **2.** A building with dressing rooms for swimmers.

bath•ing suit (bā′*th*ĭng) ►*n.* A swimsuit.

ba•thos (bā′thŏs′, -thôs′) ►*n.* **1.** A ludicrously abrupt transition in style from the exalted to the commonplace. **2.** Grossly sentimental pathos. [Gk., depth.] —**ba•thet′ic** (bə-thĕt′ĭk) *adj.*

bath•robe (băth′rōb′) ►*n.* A loose-fitting robe worn before and after bathing and for lounging.

bath•room (băth′ro͞om′, -ro͝om′) ►*n.* A room equipped with a bathtub or shower and usu. a sink and toilet.

bath salts ►*pl.n.* Perfumed crystals for softening the water in a bathtub.

Bath•she•ba (băth-shē′bə, băth′shə-). In the Bible, the second wife of David and mother of Solomon.

bath•tub (băth′tŭb′) ►*n.* A tub or fixture for bathing.

bath•y•scaph (băth′ĭ-skăf′) also **bath•y•scaphe** (-skăf′, -skāf′) ►*n.* A free-diving deep-sea research vessel with a crewed observation capsule. [< Gk. *bathus*, deep + *skaphos*, hull.]

bath•y•sphere (băth′ĭ-sfîr′) ►*n.* A crewed spherical deep-diving chamber lowered by cable. [Gk. *bathus*, deep + SPHERE.]

ba•tik (bə-tēk′, băt′ĭk) ►*n.* **1.** A method of dyeing fabric by applying a design in removable wax. **2.** Fabric so dyed. [Malay *batek*.]

ba•tiste (bə-tēst′, bă-) ►*n.* A fine, plain-woven fabric. [< OFr.]

bat mitz•vah (bät mĭts′və) or **bas mitz•vah** (bäs) ►*n.* **1.** In Conservative and Reform Judaism, a Jewish girl of 12 to 14 years of age, considered an adult and responsible for her moral and religious duties. **2.** The ceremony that confirms a girl as a bat mitzvah. [Heb. *bat miṣwâ*.]

ba•ton (bə-tŏn′, băt′n) ►*n.* **1.** *Mus.* A slender rod used by a conductor to direct an orchestra. **2.** A hollow metal rod with heavy rubber tips twirled by a drum major or majorette. **3.** The hollow cylinder passed to each member of a relay team. [< VLat. **bastō*, stick.]

Bat•on Rouge (băt′n ro͞ozh′) The capital of LA, in the SE-central part. Pop. 219,531.

bats (băts) ►*adj. Slang* Crazy; insane.

bats•man (băts′mən) ►*n.* The player at bat in cricket and baseball.

bat•tal•ion (bə-tăl′yən) ►*n.* **1.** An army unit typically consisting of a headquarters and two or more companies or batteries. **2.** A large body of organized troops. [< VLat. **battalia*, battle.]

bat•ten (băt′n) ►*n.* A flexible wooden strip used esp. in flattening a sail or securing a hatch. ►*v.* To furnish or secure with battens: *batten down the hatches.* [< OFr. *bataunt*, clapper.]

bat•ter¹ (băt′ər) ►*v.* **1.** To hit repeatedly with heavy blows. See Syns at **beat. 2.** To damage. **3.** To inflict continuing physical injuries on, esp. within a family or marital relationship. [< Lat. *battuere*.]

Syns: *batter, maim, mangle, maul, mutilate* ***v.***

bat•ter² (băt′ər) ►*n.* The player at bat in baseball and cricket.

bat•ter³ (băt′ər) ►*n.* A beaten mixture, as of flour, milk, and eggs, used in cooking. [ME *bater*.]

bat•ter•ing ram (băt′ər-ĭng) ►*n.* A heavy beam used in ancient warfare to batter down walls and gates.

battering ram

bat•ter•y (băt′ə-rē) ►*n.*, *pl.* **-ies 1a.** The act of battering. **b.** The unlawful beating of a person. **2a.** An emplacement for artillery. **b.** A set of heavy guns, as on a warship. **3a.** An array: *a battery of tests.* **b.** An impressive body or group. **4.** The percussion section of an orchestra. **5.** *Elect.* A cell or group of connected cells that produces direct current, usu. by converting chemical to electrical energy. [< OFr. *batre*, to batter.]

bat•ting (băt′ĭng) ►*n.* Fiber wadded into rolls or sheets, as for lining quilts.

batting average ►*n. Baseball* The ratio of a batter's hits to the number of times at bat.

bat•tle (băt′l) ►*n.* **1a.** An encounter between opposing forces. **b.** Armed fighting; combat. **2a.** A protracted struggle. **b.** An intense competition. ►*v.* **-tled, -tling 1.** To engage in or as if in battle. **2.** To fight against. [< LLat. *battuālia*, fighting and fencing exercises.] —**bat′tler** *n.*

bat•tle-ax or **bat•tle-axe** (băt′l-ăks′) ►*n.* A broad heavy ax formerly used as a weapon.

battle cry ►*n.* **1.** A rallying cry uttered in combat. **2.** A militant slogan.

bat•tle•field (băt′l-fēld′) ►*n.* **1.** An area where a battle is fought. **2.** A sphere of conflict.

bat•tle•front (băt′l-frŭnt′) ►*n.* The area where opponents meet in battle.

bat•tle•ground (băt′l-ground′) ►*n.* A battlefield.

bat•tle•ment (băt′l-mənt) ►*n.* A parapet built on top of a wall, with notched indentations for decoration or defense. [< OFr. *batillement*, turret.]

battle royal ►*n., pl.* **battles royal 1.** An all-out fight. **2.** A battle with many combatants.

bat•tle•ship (băt′l-shĭp′) ►*n.* Any of the largest, most heavily armed and armored class of warships.

bat•ty (băt′ē) ►*adj.* **-ti•er, -ti•est** *Slang* Crazy.

bau•ble (bô′bəl) ►*n.* A trinket. [< OFr. *babel*, plaything.]

baud (bôd) ►*n. Comp. Sci.* A unit of speed in data transmission equal to one bit per second. [After Jean Maurice Emile *Baudot* (1845–1903).]

Baude•laire (bōd-lâr′), **Charles Pierre.** 1821–67. French writer, translator, and critic.

Bau•douin I (bō-dwăɴ′). 1930–93. King of Belgium (1951–93).

baux•ite (bôk′sīt′) ►*n.* The principal ore of aluminum, composed mainly of hydrous aluminum oxides and aluminum hydroxides. [After Les *Baux*, French commune.]

Ba•var•i•a (bə-vâr′ē-ə) A region of S Germany. —**Ba•var′i•an** *adj. & n.*

bawd (bôd) ►*n.* **1.** A woman who keeps a brothel. **2.** A prostitute. [ME.]

bawd•y (bô′dē) ►*adj.* **-i•er, -i•est 1.** Humorously indecent; risqué. **2.** Vulgar; lewd. —**bawd′i•ly** *adv.* —**bawd′i•ness** *n.*

bawl (bôl) ►*v.* **1.** To sob loudly; wail. **2.** To cry out loudly; bellow. See Syns at **shout.** —***phrasal verb:*** **bawl out** *Informal* To scold loudly or harshly. [Of Scand. orig.]

bay[1] (bā) ►*n.* A body of water partially enclosed by land but with a wide outlet to the sea. [< OFr. *baie*.]

bay[2] (bā) ►*n.* **1.** A part of a building marked off by vertical elements, such as columns. **2a.** A bay window. **b.** An opening or recess in a wall. **3.** A section or compartment set off for a specific purpose: *a cargo bay.* [< OFr. *baee*, an opening.]

bay[3] (bā) ►*adj.* Reddish-brown. ►*n.* **1.** A reddish brown. **2.** A reddish-brown animal, esp. a horse. [< Lat. *badius*.]

bay[4] (bā) ►*n.* A deep prolonged bark, as of a hound. —***idioms:*** **at bay** Held at a safe distance: *kept trouble at bay.* **to bay** Cornered by and facing pursuers: *bring quarry to bay.* [< OFr. *abaiier*, to bark.] —**bay** *v.*

bay[5] (bā) ►*n.* **1.** See **laurel** 1. **2.** A tree or shrub with aromatic foliage similar to the laurel. [< Lat. *bāca*, berry.]

Ba•ya•món (bä′yä-mōn′) A town of NE Puerto Rico, a suburb of San Juan. Pop. 222,102.

bay•ber•ry (bā′bĕr′ē) ►*n.* **1.** An aromatic shrub bearing waxy, fragrant, berrylike fruit. **2.** The fruit of this shrub.

Bay•kal (bī-kôl′, -kŏl′), **Lake.** See Lake **Baikal.**

bay leaf ►*n.* The dried aromatic leaf of the laurel, used as a seasoning.

bay•o•net (bā′ə-nĭt, -nĕt′, bā′ə-nĕt′) ►*n.* A blade adapted to fit the muzzle of a rifle, used in close combat. ►*v.* **-net•ed, -net•ing** or **-net•ted, -net•ting.** To stab with a bayonet. [After *Bayonne*, France.]

bay•ou (bī′o͞o, bī′ō) ►*n.* A marshy creek or small river tributary to a larger body of water. [Poss. < Choctaw *bayuk*.]

Bay•reuth (bī-roit′, bī′roit) A city of E-central Germany. Pop. 71,811.

bay window ►*n.* A large window or series of windows projecting from a building and forming an alcove within.

ba•zaar also **ba•zar** (bə-zär′) ►*n.* **1.** A market consisting of a street lined with shops and stalls, esp. in the Middle East. **2.** A fair or sale esp. for charity. [< Pers. *bāzār*.]

ba•zoo•ka (bə-zo͞o′kə) ►*n.* A shoulder-held, tube-shaped weapon for firing armor-piercing rockets at short range. [< *bazooka*, a crude wind instrument.]

BB[1] (bē′bē) ►*n.* A small size of lead pellet used in air rifles.

BB[2] ►*abbr.* base on balls

bbl. ►*abbr.* barrel

BBS ►*abbr. Comp. Sci.* bulletin board system

B.C. ►*abbr.* **1.** also **B.C.** before Christ **2.** or **BC** British Columbia

B.C.E. or **B.C.E.** ►*abbr.* before the Common Era

B cell ►*n.* A lymphocyte in the immune system responsible for the production of antibodies. [*b(ursa-dependent) cell.*]

bd. ft. ►*abbr.* board foot

bdrm. ►*abbr.* bedroom

be (bē) ►*v. 1st and 3rd pers. sing. p. indic.* **was** (wŭz, wŏz; wəz *when unstressed*), *2nd pers. sing. and pl. and 1st and 3rd pers. pl. p. indic.* **were** (wûr), *p. subjunctive* **were,** *p.part.* **been** (bĭn), *pr.part.* **be•ing** (bē′ĭng), *1st pers. sing. pr. indic.* **am** (ăm), *2nd pers. sing. and pl. and 1st and 3rd pers. pl. pr. indic.* **are** (är), *3rd pers. sing. pr. indic.* **is** (ĭz), *pr. subjunctive* **be 1.** To exist: *I think, therefore I am.* **2a.** To occupy a specified position: *The food is on the table.* **b.** To remain undisturbed or untouched: *Let the dog be.* **3.** To take place; occur. **4.** To go or come: *Have you ever been to Japan?* **5.** Used as a copula linking a subject and a predicate nominative, adjective, or pronoun, as: **a.** To equal in identity: *All athletes are hard workers.* **b.** To signify; symbolize: *A is excellent, C is passing.* **c.** To belong to a specified class or group: *The human being is a primate.* **d.** To have or show a specified quality or characteristic: *She is smart.* **6.** To belong; befall:

Woe is me. **7.** *Informal* Used in combination with *all* or *like* to introduce quotations. See Usage Note at **go**[1]. —*aux.* **1.** Used with the past participle of a transitive verb to form the passive voice: *The election is held annually.* **2.** Used with the present participle of a verb to express a continuing action: *We are trying to improve our services.* **3.** Used with the infinitive of a verb to express intention, obligation, or future action: *She was to call before she left.* **4.** *Archaic* Used with the past participle of certain intransitive verbs to form the perfect tense: *He is gone to a better place.* [< OE *bēon.*]

Be ► The symbol for the element **beryllium.**

be– ►*pref.* **1.** To make; cause to become: *benumb.* **2a.** To cover with: *befog.* **b.** On; over: *bedaub.* **3.** Used as an intensive: *belabor.* **4.** About: *bewail.* **5.** To remove: *behead.* [< OE.]

beach (bēch) ►*n.* The shore of a body of water, esp. when sandy or pebbly. ►*v.* To haul or run ashore. [Perh. < OE *bece*, stream.]

beach buggy ►*n.* See **dune buggy.**

beach•comb•er (bēch′kō′mər) ►*n.* One who scavenges along beaches.

beach•head (bēch′hĕd′) ►*n.* **1.** A position on an enemy shoreline captured by troops in advance of an invading force. **2.** A first achievement that opens the way; foothold.

bea•con (bē′kən) ►*n.* **1.** A lighthouse. **2.** A radio transmitter that emits a guidance signal for aircraft. **3.** A source of guidance. **4.** A signal fire. [< OE *bēacen.*]

bead (bēd) ►*n.* **1a.** A small piece of material pierced for stringing. **b. beads** A necklace made of beads. **c. beads** A rosary. **2.** A small round object, as: **a.** A drop of moisture. **b.** A knoblike forward sight on a firearm. ►*v.* To decorate with or collect into beads. —***idiom:*** **draw (**or **get) a bead on** To take careful aim at. [< OE *gebed*, prayer.]

bea•dle (bēd′l) ►*n.* A former minor parish official in an English church. [< OE *bydel.*]

bead•y (bē′dē) ►*adj.* **-i•er, -i•est.** Small, round, and shiny: *beady eyes.*

bea•gle (bē′gəl) ►*n.* A small hound with drooping ears and a smooth white, black, and tan coat. [ME *begle.*]

beak (bēk) ►*n.* **1.** The horny projecting mandibles of a bird; bill. **2.** A similar part or structure. [< Lat. *beccus*, of Celt. orig.]

beak•er (bē′kər) ►*n.* **1.** A wide glass cylinder with a pouring lip, used as a laboratory container. **2.** A wide-mouthed drinking cup. [< Med.Lat. *bicārius.*]

beam (bēm) ►*n.* **1.** A large timber or squared-off log used as a horizontal support in construction. **2a.** The maximum breadth of a ship. **b.** The side of a ship. **3.** A horizontal bar. **4a.** A ray of light. **b.** A concentrated stream of particles, waves, or signals. ►*v.* **1.** To radiate; shine. **2.** To emit or transmit (e.g., a signal). **3.** To smile expansively. —***idiom:*** **on the beam 1.** Following a radio beam, as an aircraft. **2.** On the right track. [< OE *bēam.*]

bean (bēn) ►*n.* **1a.** Any of various twining plants with edible pods and seeds. **b.** A seed or pod of a bean plant. **2.** Any of various plants related to or suggestive of beans. **3.** *Slang* The head. ►*v. Slang* To hit on the head. —***idioms:*** **full of beans 1.** Energetic; frisky. **2.** Badly mistaken. **spill the beans** To disclose a secret. [< OE *bēan.*]

bean•bag (bēn′băg′) ►*n.* A small bag filled with dried beans and thrown in games.

bean ball ►*n. Baseball* A pitch aimed at the batter's head.

bean curd ►*n.* Tofu.

bean•ie (bē′nē) ►*n.* A small brimless cap.

bean•o (bē′nō) ►*n., pl.* **-os.** A form of bingo.

bean sprouts ►*pl.n.* The tender, edible seedlings of certain beans, esp. the mung bean.

bear[1] (bâr) ►*v.* **bore** (bôr, bōr), **borne** (bôrn, bōrn) or **born** (bôrn), **bear•ing 1.** To hold up; support. **2.** To carry on one's person. **3.** To harbor: *bear a grudge.* **4.** To transmit; relate: *bearing glad tidings.* **5.** To have or exhibit. **6.** To conduct: *bore herself with dignity.* **7.** To be accountable for; assume: *bearing heavy responsibilities.* **8.** To endure: *couldn't bear the pain.* **9a.** To warrant: *This case bears investigation.* **b.** To have relevance; apply. **10.** *p.part.* **born** To give birth to. **11.** To yield: *bear flowers.* See Syns at **produce. 12.** To exert pressure or influence. **13.** To offer; render: *bear witness.* **14.** To proceed in a specified direction: *bear left.* —***phrasal verbs:*** **bear down 1.** To weigh on; overwhelm. **2.** To exert oneself. **bear out** To prove right; confirm. **bear up** To endure. **bear with** To be tolerant of or toward. —***idiom:*** **bear in mind** To remember. [< OE *beran.*] —**bear′a•ble** *adj.* —**bear′a•bly** *adv.*

bear[2] (bâr) ►*n.* **1.** Any of various large, usu. omnivorous mammals having a shaggy coat and short tail. **2.** A clumsy or grouchy person. **3.** One that sells securities or commodities in expectation of falling prices. [< OE *bera.*] —**bear′ish** *adj.*

beard (bîrd) ►*n.* **1.** The hair on a man's chin, cheeks, and throat. **2.** A hairy or hairlike growth, as on certain animals and plants. ►*v.* To confront boldly. [< OE.] —**beard′ed** *adj.*

bear•er (bâr′ər) ►*n.* **1.** One that bears. **2.** One that holds a check or note for payment.

bear hug ►*n.* A rough, tight hug.

bear•ing (bâr′ĭng) ►*n.* **1.** Deportment; demeanor. **2.** A device that supports, guides, and reduces the friction of motion between fixed and moving machine parts. **3.** Something that supports weight. **4.** Direction, esp. angular direction measured using geographical or celestial reference lines. **5.** often **bearings** Awareness of one's position relative to one's surroundings. **6.** Relevant relationship: *That has no bearing on our work.* **7.** A heraldic emblem.

béar•naise sauce (bâr-nāz′, bā′är-, -ər-) ►*n.* A sauce of egg yolk, butter, shallots, tarragon, and chervil. [Fr. *béarnaise*, of Béarn, former region of France.]

Bear River. A river, about 563 km (350 mi), of NE UT, SW WY, and SE ID.

bear•skin (bâr′skĭn′) ►*n.* **1.** A bear pelt. **2.** A tall military hat made of black fur.

beast (bēst) ►*n.* **1.** An animal, esp. a large four-footed mammal. **2.** Animal nature. **3.** A brutal person. [< Lat. *bēstia.*]

beast•ly (bēst′lē) ►*adj.* **-li•er, -li•est 1.** Of or like a beast; bestial. **2.** Very disagreeable; nasty: *beastly behavior.* —**beast′li•ness** *n.*

beat (bēt) ►*v.* **beat, beat•en** (bēt′n) or **beat, beat•ing 1a.** To strike repeatedly; pound. **b.** To punish by hitting. **2.** To flap, esp. wings. **3.** To sound by striking: *beat a drum.* **4a.** To shape by blows; forge. **b.** To make by trampling: *beat a path.* **5.** To mix rapidly: *beat eggs.* **6.** To pulsate; throb. **7.** To defeat. **8.** *Informal* To be better than: *Riding beats walking.* **9.** *Slang* To baffle: *It beats me.* **10.** *Informal* **a.** To circumvent: *beat the traffic.* **b.** To arrive or finish before (another). —***phrasal verb:*** **beat off** To drive away. ►*n.* **1.** A stroke or blow. **2.** A pulsation; throb. **3.** A rhythmic stress or stress pattern, as in meter or verse. **4.** An area regularly covered, as by a reporter or police officer. ►*adj.* **1.** *Informal* Worn-out; fatigued. **2.** Of or being a beatnik. —***idioms:*** **beat around (**or **about) the bush** To fail to confront a subject directly. **beat it** *Slang* To leave hurriedly. **beat the bushes** To make an exhaustive search. [< OE *bēaten.*] —**beat′er** *n.*

Syns: *beat, baste, batter, belabor, buffet, hammer, lambaste, pound, pummel, thrash* ***v.***

be•a•tif•ic (bē′ə-tĭf′ĭk) ►*adj.* Showing exalted joy or bliss: *a beatific smile.* [< Lat. *beātus,* blessed.] —**be′a•tif′i•cal•ly** *adv.*

be•at•i•fy (bē-ăt′ə-fī′) ►*v.* **-fied, -fy•ing 1.** To make blessedly happy. **2.** *Rom. Cath. Ch.* To proclaim (a deceased person) to be one of the blessed. —**be•at′i•fi•ca′tion** *n.*

be•at•i•tude (bē-ăt′ĭ-to͞od′, -tyo͞od′) ►*n.* Supreme blessedness.

beat•nik (bēt′nĭk) ►*n.* A member of a group or movement esp. of the 1950s stressing nonconformity to social and cultural mores. [*beat (generation),* unconventional group of the 1950s + -NIK.]

Be•a•trix (bā′ə-trĭks′, bē′-). b. 1938. Queen of the Netherlands (since 1980).

beat-up (bēt′ŭp′) ►*adj. Slang* Damaged or worn through neglect or heavy use.

beau (bō) ►*n., pl.* **beaus** or **beaux** (bōz) **1.** A suitor. **2.** A dandy; fop. [Fr., handsome.]

Beau•fort Sea (bō′fərt) A part of the Arctic Ocean N of NE AK and NW Canada.

beau geste (bō zhĕst′) ►*n., pl.* **beaux gestes** or **beau gestes** (bō zhĕst′) **1.** A gracious gesture. **2.** A gesture noble in form but meaningless in substance. [Fr.]

Beau•har•nais (bō-är-nā′), **Josephine de.** 1763–1814. Empress of the French (1804–09) as the wife of Napoleon I.

beau i•de•al (bō′ ī-dē′əl) ►*n., pl.* **beau ideals.** An ideal type or model. [Fr. *beau idéal.*]

Beau•mar•chais (bō-mär-shā′), **Pierre Augustin Caron de.** 1732–99. French writer.

beau monde (bō mŏnd′, môɴd′) ►*n., pl.* **beaux mondes** (bō môɴd′) or **beau mondes** (bō mŏndz′). Fashionable society. [Fr.]

Beau•mont (bō′mŏnt′) A city of SE TX NNE of Houston. Pop. 114,323.

Beau•mont (bō′mŏnt′, -mənt), **Francis.** 1584–1616. English poet and playwright who collaborated with John Fletcher.

beau•te•ous (byo͞o′tē-əs) ►*adj.* Beautiful. —**beau′te•ous•ly** *adv.*

beau•ti•cian (byo͞o-tĭsh′ən) ►*n.* One skilled in giving cosmetic treatments.

beau•ti•ful (byo͞o′tə-fəl) ►*adj.* Having beauty. —**beau′ti•ful•ly** *adv.*

beau•ti•fy (byo͞o′tə-fī′) ►*v.* **-fied, -fy•ing.** To make or become beautiful. —**beau′ti•fi•ca′tion** *n.* —**beau′ti•fi′er** *n.*

beau•ty (byo͞o′tē) ►*n., pl.* **-ties 1.** A quality that pleases or delights the senses or mind. **2.** One that is beautiful. **3.** An outstanding example. [< Lat. *bellus,* pretty.]

beauty mark ►*n.* A mole or birthmark.

beauty parlor ►*n.* An establishment providing women with such services as hair treatment, manicures, and facials.

Beau•voir (bō-vwär′), **Simone de.** 1908–86. French writer, existentialist, and feminist.

beaux (bōz) ►*n.* Pl. of **beau.**

beaux-arts (bō-zär′, -zärt′) ►*pl.n.* The fine arts. [Fr.]

bea•ver (bē′vər) ►*n.* **1.** A large aquatic rodent having thick brown fur, webbed hind feet, a broad flat tail, and sharp incisors adapted for felling trees to build dams. **2.** The fur of a beaver. [< OE *beofor.*]

bea•ver•board (bē′vər-bôrd′, -bōrd′) ►*n.* A wallboard of compressed wood pulp.

be•bop (bē′bŏp′) ►*n. Mus.* Bop. [Imitation of a two-beat phrase in this music.]

be•calm (bĭ-käm′) ►*v.* To render (e.g., a ship) motionless for lack of wind.

be•cause (bĭ-kôz′, -kŭz′) ►*conj.* For the reason that; since. [ME *bi cause.*]

beck (bĕk) ►*n.* A summons. —***idiom:*** **at (one's) beck and call** Ready to comply with any wish or command. [ME *bek* < *bekenen,* BECKON.]

Beck•et (bĕk′ĭt), Saint **Thomas à.** 1118?–70. English Roman Catholic martyr.

Beck•ett (bĕk′ĭt), **Samuel.** 1906–89. Irish-born writer; 1969 Nobel.

beck•on (bĕk′ən) ►*v.* **1.** To summon by nodding or waving. **2.** To be inviting or enticing (to); attract. [< OE *bēcnan.*]

be•cloud (bĭ-kloud′) ►*v.* To obscure.

be•come (bĭ-kŭm′) ►*v.* **be•came** (-kām′), **-come, -com•ing 1.** To grow or come to be. **2.** To be suitable to. —***phrasal verb:*** **become of** To be the fate of: *What will become of us?* [< OE *becuman.*]

be•com•ing (bĭ-kŭm′ĭng) ►*adj.* **1.** Appropriate or suitable. **2.** Pleasing or attractive. —**be•com′ing•ly** *adv.*

bed (bĕd) ►*n.* **1.** A place for sleeping, esp. a piece of furniture that frames or supports a mattress. **2.** A small plot of cultivated land: *a flower bed.* **3.** The bottom of a body of water, such as a stream. **4.** A supporting or underlying part; foundation. **5.** *Geol.* **a.** A large layer of rock or earth extending horizontally; stratum. **b.** A deposit, as of ore. ►*v.* **bed•ded, bed•ding 1.** To furnish with a bed or sleeping quarters. **2.** To put, send, or go to bed. **3.** To plant in a prepared plot of soil. **4.** To lay flat or arrange in layers. **5.** To embed. [< OE.]

be•daub (bĭ-dôb′) ►*v.* To smear; soil.

be•daz•zle (bĭ-dăz′əl) ►*v.* **-zled, -zling 1.** To dazzle so completely as to confuse or blind. **2.** To enchant. —**be•daz′zle•ment** *n.*

bed•bug (bĕd′bŭg′) ►*n.* A wingless, bloodsucking insect that infests dwellings and bedding.

bed•clothes (bĕd′klōz′, -klō*th*z′) ►*pl.n.* Coverings ordinarily used on a bed.

bed•ding (bĕd′ĭng) ►*n.* **1.** Bedclothes. **2.** Material, esp. straw, on which animals sleep. **3.** A foundation.

Bede (bēd). 673?–735. Anglo-Saxon theologian and historian.

be•deck (bĭ-dĕk′) ►*v.* To adorn or ornament.

be•dev•il (bĭ-dĕv′əl) ►*v.* **-iled, -il•ing** or **-illed, -il•ling 1.** To torment; harass. **2.** To worry, annoy, or frustrate. —**be•dev′il•ment** *n.*
be•dew (bĭ-do͞o′, -dyo͞o′) ►*v.* To wet with or as if with dew.
bed•fel•low (bĕd′fĕl′ō) ►*n.* **1.** One with whom a bed is shared. **2.** An often temporary associate, as for convenience.
bed•lam (bĕd′ləm) ►*n.* **1.** A place of noisy uproar and confusion. **2.** An insane asylum. [ME *Bedlem*, Hospital of Saint Mary of *Bethlehem*, London.]
Bed•ou•in also **Bed•u•in** (bĕd′o͞o-ĭn, bĕd′wĭn) ►*n., pl.* **-in** or **-ins.** An Arab of any of the nomadic tribes of the Arabian, Syrian, Nubian, or Sahara deserts. [< Ar. *badawī.*]
bed•pan (bĕd′păn′) ►*n.* A receptacle used as a toilet by a bedridden person.
bed•post (bĕd′pōst′) ►*n.* A vertical post at the corner of a bed.
be•drag•gled (bĭ-drăg′əld) ►*adj.* Wet, limp, or soiled, as by being dragged through mud.
bed•rid•den (bĕd′rĭd′n) ►*adj.* Confined to bed, esp. because of illness or infirmity. [< OE *bedrida*, bedridden person.]
bed•rock (bĕd′rŏk′) ►*n.* **1.** The solid rock that underlies the loose surface material of the earth. **2a.** Fundamental principles; foundation. **b.** The lowest point; bottom.
bed•roll (bĕd′rōl′) ►*n.* A portable roll of bedding used esp. for sleeping outdoors.
bed•room (bĕd′ro͞om′, -ro͝om′) ►*n.* A room in which to sleep.
bed•side (bĕd′sīd′) ►*n.* The space alongside a bed, esp. of a sick person. —**bed′side′** *adj.*
bed•sore (bĕd′sôr′, -sōr′) ►*n.* A pressure-induced ulceration of the skin occurring during long confinement to bed.
bed•spread (bĕd′sprĕd′) ►*n.* A usu. decorative covering for a bed.
bed•stead (bĕd′stĕd′) ►*n.* The frame supporting a bed.
bed•time (bĕd′tīm′) ►*n.* The time at which one goes to bed.
Bed•u•in (bĕd′o͞o-ĭn, bĕd′wĭn) ►*n.* Var. of **Bedouin.**
bee (bē) ►*n.* **1.** Any of several winged, hairy-bodied, usu. stinging insects that gather nectar and pollen from which some species produce honey. **2.** A social gathering where people work together or compete. —***idiom:* a bee in (one's) bonnet** A persistent notion, esp. an idea that keeps one angry or upset. [< OE *bēo.*]
beech (bēch) ►*n.* A deciduous tree having smooth gray bark, edible nuts, and strong heavy wood. [< OE *bēce.*]
Bee•cher (bē′chər), **Lyman.** 1775–1863. Amer. cleric; father of **Henry Ward Beecher** (1813–87), an abolitionist, and Harriet Beecher Stowe.
beech•nut (bēch′nŭt′) ►*n.* The small, three-angled nut of a beech tree.
beef (bēf) ►*n., pl.* **beeves** (bēvz) or **beef 1a.** A full-grown steer, bull, ox, or cow, esp. one intended for use as meat. **b.** The flesh of a slaughtered steer, bull, ox, or cow. **2.** *Informal* Human muscle; brawn. **3.** *pl.* **beefs** *Slang* A complaint. ►*v.* To complain. —***phrasal verb:* beef up** To build up; reinforce. [< Lat. *bōs.*]
beef•a•lo (bē′fə-lō′) ►*n., pl.* **-lo** or **-los** or **-loes.** A hybrid that results from a cross between the American buffalo, or bison, and beef cattle. [BEEF + (BUFF)ALO.]
beef•eat•er (bēf′ē′tər) ►*n.* A yeoman of the British monarch's royal guard.
beef•y (bē′fē) ►*adj.* **-i•er, -i•est.** Muscular in build; brawny. —**beef′i•ness** *n.*
bee•hive (bē′hīv′) ►*n.* **1.** A hive for bees. **2.** A place teeming with activity.
bee•keep•er (bē′kē′pər) ►*n.* One who raises or tends bees. —**bee′keep•ing** *n.*
bee•line (bē′līn′) ►*n.* A fast straight course.
Be•el•ze•bub (bē-ĕl′zə-bŭb′) ►*n.* The Devil. [Prob. < Heb. *ba'al zəbûl*, lord prince.]
been (bĭn) ►*v.* P.part. of **be.**
beep (bēp) ►*n.* A sound or signal, as from a horn or electronic device. —**beep** *v.*
beep•er (bē′pər) ►*n.* **1.** One that beeps. **2.** A portable electronic paging device that emits a beeping signal.
beer (bîr) ►*n.* **1.** An alcoholic beverage brewed from malt and hops. **2.** Any of various carbonated beverages made from roots and plants. [< OE *bēor.*] —**beer′y** *adj.*
bees•wax (bēz′wăks′) ►*n.* The wax secreted by honeybees for making honeycombs and used in candles, crayons, and polishes.
beet (bēt) ►*n.* **1.** A cultivated plant with a fleshy, usu. dark-red edible root. **2.** The sugar beet. [< Lat. *bēta.*]
Bee•tho•ven (bā′tō′vən), **Ludwig van.** 1770–1827. German composer.

Ludwig van Beethoven
1819 portrait

bee•tle¹ (bēt′l) ►*n.* Any of numerous insects with horny forewings that protect the membranous hind wings when at rest. [< OE *bitela* < *bītan*, bite.]
bee•tle² (bēt′l) ►*adj.* Jutting; overhanging: *beetle brows.* ►*v.* **-tled, -tling.** To jut. [< ME *bitel-brouwed*, grim-browed.]
beeves (bēvz) ►*n.* Pl. of **beef.**
be•fall (bĭ-fôl′) ►*v.* **-fell** (-fĕl′), **-fall•en** (-fô′lən), **-fall•ing 1.** To come to pass; happen. **2.** To happen to. See Syns at **happen.** [< OE *befallen*, fall.]
be•fit (bĭ-fĭt′) ►*v.* **-fit•ted, -fit•ting.** To be suitable to or appropriate for.
be•fog (bĭ-fôg′, -fŏg′) ►*v.* **-fogged, -fog•ging 1.** To fog. **2.** To confuse; muddle.
be•fore (bĭ-fôr′, -fōr′) ►*adv.* **1.** Earlier in time; previously. **2.** In front; ahead. ►*prep.* **1.** Prior to. **2.** In front of. **3.** In store for; awaiting. **4.** Into or in the presence of. **5.** Under the consideration of: *the case before the court.* **6.** In a position superior to: *She comes before him in*

rank. ▶*conj.* **1.** In advance of the time when: *See me before you leave.* **2.** Rather than; sooner than: *I will die before I will betray you.* [< OE *beforan.*]

before Christ ▶*adv.* In a specified year of the pre-Christian area.

be•fore•hand (bĭ-fôr′hănd′, -fōr′-) ▶*adv.* & *adj.* In advance; early.

be•foul (bĭ-foul′) ▶*v.* To make dirty; soil.

be•friend (bĭ-frĕnd′) ▶*v.* To act as a friend to.

be•fud•dle (bĭ-fŭd′l) ▶*v.* **-dled, -dling 1.** To confuse or muddle; perplex. See Syns at **confuse. 2.** To stupefy.

beg (bĕg) ▶*v.* **begged, beg•ging 1.** To ask for (alms or charity). See Syns at **cadge. 2.** To entreat. **3.** To evade; dodge: *begged the question.* —***phrasal verb:*** **beg off** To ask to be excused from something. [ME *beggen.*]

be•get (bĭ-gĕt′) ▶*v.* **-got** (-gŏt′), **-got•ten** (-gŏt′n) or **-got, -get•ting 1.** To father; sire. **2.** To cause; produce. [< OE *begetan.*]

beg•gar (bĕg′ər) ▶*n.* **1.** One who solicits alms for a living. **2.** A pauper. ▶*v.* **1.** To impoverish. **2.** To exceed the limits of: *beauty that beggars description.* [< OFr. *begart.*] —**beg′gar•ly** *adj.* —**beg′gar•y** *n.*

be•gin (bĭ-gĭn′) ▶*v.* **-gan** (-găn′), **-gun** (-gŭn′), **-gin•ning 1.** To commence or start. **2.** To come into being. [< OE *beginnan.*] —**be•gin′ner** *n.*

Be•gin (bā′gĭn), **Menachem.** 1913–92. Russian-born Israeli politician; shared the 1978 Nobel Peace Prize with Anwar el-Sadat of Egypt.

be•gin•ning (bĭ-gĭn′ĭng) ▶*n.* **1.** The act or process of bringing or being brought into being; start. **2.** The time when something begins or is begun. **3.** The place where something begins or is begun. **4.** A source; origin. **5.** The first part. **6.** often **beginnings** An early or rudimentary phase.

Syns: *beginning, birth, dawn, genesis, rise*
Ant: *end* ***n.***

be•gone (bĭ-gôn′, -gŏn′) ▶*interj.* Used chiefly to express dismissal.

be•go•nia (bĭ-gōn′yə) ▶*n.* Any of various plants cultivated for their brightly colored leaves and flowers. [After Michel *Bégon* (1638–1710).]

be•grime (bĭ-grīm′) ▶*v.* **-grimed, -grim•ing.** To smear or grime with or as if with dirt.

be•grudge (bĭ-grŭj′) ▶*v.* **-grudged, -grudg•ing 1.** To envy. **2.** To give with reluctance. —**be•grudg′ing•ly** *adv.*

be•guile (bĭ-gīl′) ▶*v.* **-guiled, -guil•ing 1.** To deceive by guile. **2.** To distract; divert. **3.** To pass (time) pleasantly. **4.** To amuse or delight. See Syns at **charm.** —**be•guile′ment** *n.* —**be•guil′ing•ly** *adv.*

be•gum (bā′gəm, bē′-) ▶*n.* A Muslim woman of rank. [Urdu *begam.*]

be•half (bĭ-hăf′, -häf′) ▶*n.* Interest, support, or benefit. —***idioms:*** **in behalf of** For the benefit of. **on behalf of** As the agent of. [< OE *be healfe*, on (his) side.]

be•have (bĭ-hāv′) ▶*v.* **-haved, -hav•ing 1a.** To conduct oneself in a specified way. **b.** To conduct oneself in a proper way. **2.** To act, react, function, or perform in a particular way. [ME *behaven* < *haven*, have.]

be•hav•ior (bĭ-hāv′yər) ▶*n.* **1.** The manner in which one behaves; deportment. **2.** The actions or reactions of persons or things under given circumstances. —**be•hav′ior•al** *adj.*

behavioral science ▶*n.* A scientific discipline, such as sociology, anthropology, or psychology, that deals with the study of human behavior.

be•hav•ior•ism (bĭ-hāv′yə-rĭz′əm) ▶*n.* A school of psychology that studies observable and quantifiable aspects of behavior but excludes subjective phenomena. —**be•hav′ior•ist** *n.* —**be•hav′ior•is′tic** *adj.*

be•head (bĭ-hĕd′) ▶*v.* To decapitate.

be•he•moth (bĭ-hē′məth, bē′ə-məth) ▶*n.* **1.** Something enormous in size or power. **2.** A huge animal described in the Bible. [< Heb. *bəhēmâ*, beast.]

be•hest (bĭ-hĕst′) ▶*n.* **1.** An authoritative command. **2.** An urgent request. [< OE *behǣs*, vow.]

be•hind (bĭ-hīnd′) ▶*adv.* **1.** In, to, or toward the rear. **2.** In a place or condition that has been passed or left: *I left my gloves behind.* **3.** In arrears; late. **4.** In or into an inferior position: *fell behind in class.* **5.** Slow: *My watch is running behind.* ▶*prep.* **1.** At the back or in the rear of. **2.** On the farther or other side of. **3.** In a former place, time, or situation. **4.** Later than: *behind schedule.* **5.** Below, as in rank or ability: *behind us in technology.* **6a.** Concealed by: *hatred behind a smile.* **b.** Underlying: *Behind your action is greed.* **7.** In support of. ▶*n. Informal* The buttocks. [< OE *behindan.*]

be•hind•hand (bĭ-hīnd′hănd′) ▶*adj.* **1.** Being in arrears. **2.** Being behind time; slow. —**be•hind′hand′** *adv.*

be•hold (bĭ-hōld′) ▶*v.* **-held** (-hĕld′), **-hold•ing 1.** To look upon; gaze at. **2.** Used in the imperative to direct attention. [< OE *behaldan.*] —**be•hold′er** *n.*

be•hold•en (bĭ-hōl′dən) ▶*adj.* Obliged or indebted, as from gratitude. [ME *biholden.*]

be•hoove (bĭ-ho͞ov′) ▶*v.* **-hooved, -hoov•ing.** To be necessary or proper for: *It behooves you at least to try.* [< OE *behōfian.*]

beige (bāzh) ▶*n.* A light grayish or yellowish brown. [< OFr. *bege*, undyed woolen fabric.] —**beige** *adj.*

Bei•jing (bā′jĭng′) also **Pe•king** (pē′kĭng′, pā′-). The capital of China, in the NE. Pop. 7,362,426.

be•ing (bē′ĭng) ▶*n.* **1.** The state or quality of existing. See Syns at **existence. 2a.** A person. **b.** One that exists or has a life. **3.** One's essential nature.

Bei•rut (bā-ro͞ot′) The capital of Lebanon, in the W part on the Mediterranean. Pop. 474,870.

be•jew•eled or **be•jew•elled** (bĭ-jo͞o′əld) ▶ *adj.* Decorated with or as if with jewels.

be•la•bor (bĭ-lā′bər) ▶*v.* **1.** To attack with blows. See Syns at **beat. 2.** To harp on.

Bel•a•rus (bĕl′ə-ro͞os′, byĕl′-) A country of E Europe E of Poland. Cap. Minsk. Pop. 10,355,000.

be•lat•ed (bĭ-lā′tĭd) ▶*adj.* Done or sent too late; delayed; tardy. —**be•lat′ed•ly** *adv.* —**be•lat′ed•ness** *n.*

be•lay (bĭ-lā′) ▶*v.* **1.** *Naut.* To secure or make fast (e.g., a rope). **2.** To secure (a mountain climber) at the end of a rope. **3.** To stop: *Belay there!* [< OE *belecgan*, surround.]

be•lay•ing pin (bĭ-lā′ĭng) ▶*n.* A pin fitted in the rail of a boat for securing running gear.

belch (bĕlch) ►*v.* **1.** To expel gas noisily from the stomach through the mouth. **2.** To gush forth violently. [ME *belchen.*] —**belch** *n.*

bel•dam or **bel•dame** (bĕl′dəm, -dăm) ►*n.* An old woman. [ME, grandmother.]

be•lea•guer (bĭ-lē′gər) ►*v.* **1.** To harass; beset. **2.** To surround with troops. [Prob. Du. *belegeren.*]

Be•lém (bə-lĕm′, -lāɴ′) A city of N Brazil on the Pará R. Pop. 1,244,688.

Bel•fast (bĕl′făst′, bĕl-făst′) The capital of Northern Ireland, in the E part on an inlet of the Irish Sea. Pop. 296,700.

bel•fry (bĕl′frē) ►*n., pl.* **-fries 1.** A bell tower, esp. one attached to a building. **2.** The part of a tower or steeple in which bells are hung. [< OFr. *berfrei*, siege tower.]

Bel•gium (bĕl′jəm) A country of NW Europe on the North Sea. Cap. Brussels. Pop. 10,080,000. —**Bel′gian** *adj. & n.*

Bel•grade (bĕl′grād′, -gräd′) The capital of Yugoslavia, in N-central Serbia at the confluence of the Danube and Sava rivers. Pop. 1,136,786.

be•lie (bĭ-lī′) ►*v.* **-lied, -ly•ing 1.** To misrepresent or disguise. **2.** To show to be false. **3.** To be counter to; contradict.

be•lief (bĭ-lēf′) ►*n.* **1.** Trust or confidence. **2.** A conviction or opinion. **3.** Something believed or accepted as true, esp. a tenet or body of tenets. [< OE *gelēafa.*]

Syns: *belief, credence, credit, faith* ***Ant:*** *disbelief* **n.**

be•liev•a•ble (bĭ-lē′və-bəl) ►*adj.* Capable of eliciting belief or trust. See Syns at **plausible.** —**be•liev′a•bil′i•ty** *n.*

be•lieve (bĭ-lēv′) ►*v.* **-lieved, -liev•ing 1.** To accept as true or real. **2.** To credit with veracity: *I believe you.* **3.** To have confidence (in); trust: *I believe in you. I believe the ruby to be genuine.* **4.** To suppose; think. **5.** To have firm faith. [< OE *belēfan.*] —**be•liev′er** *n.*

be•lit•tle (bĭ-lĭt′l) ►*v.* **-tled, -tling.** To speak of as small or unimportant; disparage. —**be•lit′tle•ment** *n.* —**be•lit′tler** *n.*

Be•lize (bə-lēz′) **1.** A country of Central America on the Caribbean Sea. Cap. Belmopan. Pop. 211,000. **2.** Also **Belize City.** The former capital of Belize, in the E part on the Caribbean Sea at the mouth of the **Belize River.** Pop. 39,771.

bell (bĕl) ►*n.* **1.** A hollow metal instrument, usu. cup-shaped with a flared opening, that emits a metallic tone when struck. **2.** Something shaped like bell. **3.** *Naut.* **a.** A stroke on a bell to mark the hour. **b.** The time thus marked. ►*v.* To put a bell on. [< OE *belle.*]

Bell, Alexander Graham. 1847–1922. Scottish-born Amer. inventor of the telephone.

bel•la•don•na (bĕl′ə-dŏn′ə) ►*n.* **1.** A poisonous plant with purplish-brown flowers and glossy black berries. **2.** A medicinal drug derived from this plant. [Ital.]

bell-bot•tom (bĕl′bŏt′əm) ►*adj.* Having legs that flare at the bottom: *bell-bottom pants.*

bell•boy (bĕl′boi′) ►*n.* A bellhop.

bell curve ►*n.* A curve symmetrical about the mean, used to show statistical probability in the distribution of measurements.

belle (bĕl) ►*n.* An attractive and admired girl or woman. [< Lat. *bella*, beautiful.]

belles-let•tres (bĕl-lĕt′rə) ►*pl.n. (takes sing. v.)* Literature regarded for its artistic value rather than for its content. [Fr.]

Alexander Graham Bell

bell•flow•er (bĕl′flou′ər) ►*n.* Any of various plants with bell-shaped bluish flowers.

bell•hop (bĕl′hŏp′) ►*n.* A hotel porter.

bel•li•cose (bĕl′ĭ-kōs′) ►*adj.* Warlike in manner; pugnacious; belligerent. [< Lat. *bellicus*, of war.] —**bel′li•cos′i•ty** (-kŏs′ĭ-tē) *n.*

bel•lig•er•ent (bə-lĭj′ər-ənt) ►*adj.* **1.** Eager to fight; aggressively hostile. **2.** Engaged in warfare. ►*n.* One that is engaged in war. [< Lat. *belligerāre*, wage war.] —**bel•lig′er•ence, bel•lig′er•en•cy** *n.* —**bel•lig′er•ent•ly** *adv.*

Bel•li•ni (bə-lē′nē). Family of Venetian painters, including **Jacopo** (1400?–70?) and his two sons, **Gentile** (1429?–1507) and **Giovanni** (1430?–1516).

Bellini, Vincenzo. 1801–35. Italian operatic composer.

bell jar ►*n.* A bell-shaped glass vessel used esp. to establish a controlled atmosphere in scientific experiments.

bel•low (bĕl′ō) ►*v.* **1.** To roar in the manner of a bull. **2.** To utter or cry out in a deep loud voice. See Syns at **shout.** [ME *belwen.*] —**bel′low** *n.*

Bellow, Saul. b. 1915. Canadian-born Amer. writer; 1976 Nobel.

bel•lows (bĕl′ōz, -əz) ►*pl.n. (takes sing. or pl. v.)* An apparatus for directing a strong current of air, as for increasing the draft to a fire. [< OE *belg*, bag.]

bell pepper ►*n.* A pepper plant cultivated for its edible, bell-shaped fruit.

bell•weth•er (bĕl′wĕ*th*′ər) ►*n.* One that is a leader or a leading indicator of future trends. [ME *bellewether*, belled wether, leader of a flock.]

bel•ly (bĕl′ē) ►*n., pl.* **-lies 1.** See **abdomen** 1. **2.** The underside of the body of an animal. **3.** *Informal* The stomach. **4.** A part that protrudes. ►*v.* **-lied, -ly•ing.** To protrude. See Syns at **bulge.** [< OE *belg*, bag.]

bel•ly•ache (bĕl′ē-āk′) ►*n.* **1.** Pain in the abdomen. **2.** *Slang* A whining complaint. ►*v.* *Slang* To complain in a whining manner.

bel•ly•but•ton (bĕl′ē-bŭt′n) ►*n.* *Informal* The navel; umbilicus.

belly dance ►*n.* A dance in which the performer makes sinuous movements of the belly. —**bel′ly-dance′** *v.* —**belly dancer** *n.*

belly flop ►*n.* *Informal* A dive in which the

front of the body hits flat against the surface of the water.

bel•ly•ful (bĕl′ē-fo͝ol′) ►*n. Informal* An undesirable or unendurable amount.

belly laugh ►*n.* A deep laugh.

bel•ly-up (bĕl′ē-ŭp′) ►*adj. Informal* Bankrupt.

Bel•mo•pan (bĕl′mō-păn′) The capital of Belize, in the N-central part. Pop. 44,087.

Be•lo Ho•ri•zon•te (bĕl′ō hôr′ĭ-zôn′tē) A city of E Brazil N of Rio de Janeiro. Pop. 2,017,127.

be•long (bĭ-lông′, -lŏng′) ►*v.* **1.** To have a proper or suitable place. **2.** To be a member of a group. **3.** To be owned by someone. **4.** To be a part of or in natural association with something. [ME *bilongen.*]

be•long•ing (bĭ-lông′ĭng, -lŏng′-) ►*n.* **1.** often **belongings** Personal possessions. **2.** Close, secure relationship: *a sense of belonging.*

Be•lo•rus•sia (bĕl′ō-rŭsh′ə, byĕl′-) See **Belarus.** —**Bel′o•rus′sian** *adj. & n.*

be•lov•ed (bĭ-lŭv′ĭd, -lŭvd′) ►*adj.* Dearly loved. —**be•lov′ed** *n.*

be•low (bĭ-lō′) ►*adv.* **1.** In or to a lower place or level; beneath. **2.** Later in a text: *See below.* **3.** On earth. ►*prep.* **1.** Lower than; under. **2.** Inferior to. [ME *biloghe.*]

Bel•shaz•zar (bĕl-shăz′ər). In the Bible, the last king of Babylon.

belt (bĕlt) ►*n.* **1.** A flexible, ornamental, or supportive band, as of leather or cloth, worn around the waist. **2.** A safety belt. **3.** A continuous moving band used in mechanics to transfer motion or to convey materials. **4.** A band of tough reinforcing material beneath the tread of a tire. **5.** A geographic region that is distinctive in a specific way. **6.** *Slang* A powerful blow; wallop. **7.** *Slang* A drink of hard liquor. ►*v.* **1.** To encircle; gird. **2.** To attach with a belt. **3.** *Slang* To strike forcefully; punch. **4.** *Slang* To sing loudly. **5.** *Slang* To swig (liquor). —***idioms:*** **below the belt** Against the rules; unfairly. **tighten (one's) belt** To exercise frugality. **under (one's) belt** In one's possession or experience. [< Lat. *balteus.*]

belt-tight•en•ing (bĕlt′-tīt′n-ĭng) ►*n.* A reduction in spending; frugality.

belt•way (bĕlt′wā′) ►*n.* **1.** A highway that skirts an urban area. **2. Beltway** The political establishment of Washington DC.

be•lu•ga (bə-lo͞o′gə) ►*n.* **1.** See **white whale. 2.** A large white sturgeon whose roe is used for caviar. [< Russ. *belyĭ*, white.]

bel•ve•dere (bĕl′vĭ-dîr′) ►*n.* A structure, such as an open, roofed gallery, situated so as to command a view. [Ital., beautiful view.]

be•moan (bĭ-mōn′) ►*v.* **1.** To mourn over; lament. **2.** To express pity or grief for.

be•muse (bĭ-myo͞oz′) ►*v.* **-mused, -mus•ing 1.** To cause to be bewildered. See Syns at **daze. 2.** To absorb; preoccupy. —**be•muse′ment** *n.*

bench (bĕnch) ►*n.* **1.** A long seat, often without a back, for two or more persons. **2.** *Law* **a.** The judge's seat in a court. **b.** The office or position of a judge. **c.** often **Bench** The court or judges composing a court. **3.** A worktable. **4.** *Sports* **a.** The place where team players sit when not playing. **b.** The reserve players on a team. ►*v.* **1.** To seat on a bench. **2.** *Sports* To remove (a player) from a game. [< OE *benc.*]

bench•mark (bĕnch′märk′) ►*n.* **1.** A standard by which something can be judged. See Syns at **standard. 2.** often **bench mark** A surveyor's mark made on a stationary object and used as a reference point.

bench•warm•er (bĕnch′wôr′mər) ►*n. Sports* A substitute player.

bench warrant ►*n.* A warrant issued by a judge or court ordering the apprehension of an offender.

bend (bĕnd) ►*v.* **bent** (bĕnt), **bend•ing 1.** To tighten: *bend a bow.* **2.** To curve or cause to curve. **3.** To stoop. **4.** To turn or deflect. **5a.** To render submissive; subdue. **b.** To yield; submit. **6.** To concentrate. **7.** *Naut.* To fasten. ►*n.* **1.** The act of bending or the state of being bent. **2.** Something bent; a curve or crook. **3. bends** *(takes sing. or pl. v.)* A manifestation of decompression sickness. [< OE *bendan.*]

bend•er (bĕn′dər) ►*n.* **1.** One that bends. **2.** *Slang* A drinking spree.

be•neath (bĭ-nēth′) ►*adv.* **1.** In a lower place; below. **2.** Underneath. ►*prep.* **1.** Lower than; under. **2.** Unworthy of. [< OE *beneothan.*]

Ben•e•dict XIV (bĕn′ĭ-dĭkt′). 1675–1758. Pope (1740–58).

Benedict XV. 1854–1922. Pope (1914–22).

ben•e•dic•tion (bĕn′ĭ-dĭk′shən) ►*n.* **1.** A blessing. **2.** An invocation of divine blessing, usu. at the end of a church service. [< Lat. *benedīcere*, bless.]

Benedict of Nur•si•a (nûr′shē-ə, -shə), Saint. A.D. 480?–547? Italian founder of the Benedictine order (c. 529). —**Ben′e•dic′tine** *adj. & n.*

ben•e•fac•tion (bĕn′ə-făk′shən, bĕn′ə-făk′-) ►*n.* **1.** The act of conferring a benefit. **2.** A charitable gift or deed. [< Lat. *benefacere*, do a service.]

ben•e•fac•tor (bĕn′ə-făk′tər) ►*n.* One that gives aid, esp. financial aid.

ben•e•fac•tress (bĕn′ə-făk′trĭs) ►*n.* A woman who gives aid, esp. financial aid.

ben•e•fice (bĕn′ə-fĭs) ►*n.* A church office endowed with fixed assets that provide a living. [< Lat. *beneficium*, benefit.]

be•nef•i•cence (bə-nĕf′ĭ-səns) ►*n.* **1.** The quality of being kind or charitable. **2.** A charitable act or gift. [< Lat. *beneficus*, charitable.] —**be•nef′i•cent** *adj.*

ben•e•fi•cial (bĕn′ə-fĭsh′əl) ►*adj.* Producing a favorable result; advantageous. —**ben′e•fi′cial•ly** *adv.*

ben•e•fi•ci•ar•y (bĕn′ə-fĭsh′ē-ĕr′ē, -fĭsh′ə-rē) ►*n., pl.* **-ies.** One that receives a benefit, as funds or property from an insurance policy or will. —**ben′e•fi′ci•ar′y** *adj.*

ben•e•fit (bĕn′ə-fĭt) ►*n.* **1a.** An advantage. **b.** A help; aid. **2.** A payment made or an entitlement available in accordance with a wage agreement, insurance policy, or public assistance program. **3.** A fund-raising public entertainment. ►*v.* **1.** To be helpful or advantageous to. **2.** To derive benefit; profit. [< Lat. *benefactum*, good deed.]

Syns: *benefit, capitalize, profit* **v.**

Be•nét (bĭ-nā′), **Stephen Vincent.** 1898–1943. American poet.

be•nev•o•lence (bə-nĕv′ə-ləns) ►*n.* **1.** An inclination to perform kind or charitable acts. **2.** A kindly or charitable act.

be•nev•o•lent (bə-nĕv′ə-lənt) ►*adj.* **1.** Having or showing benevolence. **2.** Organized to benefit charity. [< Lat. *benevolēns*, well-wishing.] —**be•nev′o•lent•ly** *adv.*

Syns: *benevolent, charitable, eleemosynary, philanthropic* **adj.**

Ben•gal (bĕn-gôl′, bĕng-) A region of E India and Bangladesh on the **Bay of Bengal,** an arm of the Indian Ocean between India and Burma. —**Ben′ga•lese′** (bĕn′gə-lēz′, -lēs′, bĕng′-) *adj. & n.*

Ben•ga•li (bĕn-gô′lē, bĕng-) ▸*n.* **1.** A native or inhabitant of Bengal. **2.** The modern Indic language of W Bengal and Bangladesh. —**Ben•ga′li** *adj.*

Ben•gha•zi (bĕn-gä′zē, bĕng-) A city of NE Libya on the Gulf of Sidra. Pop. 367,600.

Ben Gur•i•on (bĕn go͝or′ē-ən), **David.** 1886–1973. Polish-born Israeli prime minister (1948–53 and 1955–63).

be•night•ed (bĭ-nī′tĭd) ▸*adj.* Ignorant; unenlightened. —**be•night′ed•ness** *n.*

be•nign (bĭ-nīn′) ▸*adj.* **1.** Showing kindness, gentleness, and mildness. **2.** Favorable. **3.** *Pathol.* Not malignant. [< Lat. *benignus.*] —**be•nign′ly** *adv.*

be•nig•nant (bĭ-nĭg′nənt) ▸*adj.* Kind and gracious. —**be•nig′nant•ly** *adv.*

Be•nin (bə-nĭn′, bĕ-nēn′) **1.** A former kingdom of W Africa, now part of Nigeria. **2.** A country of W Africa. Cap. Porto-Novo. Pop. 5,387,000.

Benin, Bight of. A wide indentation of the Gulf of Guinea in W Africa.

Ben•nett (bĕn′ĭt), **Richard Bedford.** 1870–1947. Canadian prime minister (1930–35).

Ben Ne•vis (nē′vĭs, nĕv′ĭs) A peak, 1,343.8 m (4,406 ft), of W Scotland; highest mountain of Great Britain.

bent (bĕnt) ▸*v.* P.t. and p.part. of **bend.** ▸*adj.* **1.** Not being straight or even; crooked. **2.** Determined to take a course of action. **3.** *Chiefly Brit.* Corrupt; dishonest. ▸*n.* A tendency, disposition, or inclination.

Ben•tham (bĕn′thəm), **Jeremy.** 1748–1832. British writer, reformer, and philosopher.

Ben•ton (bĕn′tən), **Thomas Hart.** 1889–1975. Amer. artist.

be•numb (bĭ-nŭm′) ▸*v.* **1.** To numb, esp. by cold. **2.** To stupefy. See Syns at **daze.**

Ben•xi (bŭn′shē′) A city of NE China SSE of Shenyang. Pop. 937,805.

Ben•ze•drine (bĕn′zĭ-drēn′) ▸ A trademark formerly used for a brand of amphetamine.

ben•zene (bĕn′zēn′, bĕn-zēn′) ▸*n.* A clear flammable liquid, C_6H_6, derived from petroleum and used in products such as insecticides and motor fuels.

ben•zine (bĕn′zēn′, bĕn-zēn′) ▸*n.* A flammable liquid mixture of petroleum fractions, used in cleaning and as a motor fuel.

benzo– or **benz–** ▸*pref.* Benzene; benzoic acid: *benzoate.* [< BENZOIN.]

ben•zo•ate (bĕn′zō-āt′) ▸*n.* A salt or ester of benzoic acid.

ben•zo•ic acid (bĕn-zō′ĭk) ▸*n.* A crystalline acid, C_6H_5COOH, used to season tobacco and in perfumes and germicides.

ben•zo•in (bĕn′zō-ĭn, -zoin′) ▸*n.* A balsamic resin obtained from certain tropical Asian trees and used in perfumery and medicine. [< Ar. *lubān jāwī*, frankincense of Java.]

ben•zol (bĕn′zôl′, -zōl′, -zŏl′) ▸*n.* See **benzene.**

be•queath (bĭ-kwēth′, -kwēth′) ▸*v.* **1.** *Law* To leave or give (property) by will. **2.** To hand down. [< OE *becwethan.*] —**be•queath′al, be•queath′ment** *n.*

be•quest (bĭ-kwĕst′) ▸*n.* **1.** The act of bequeathing. **2.** Something bequeathed; legacy. [ME *biquest.*]

be•rate (bĭ-rāt′) ▸*v.* **-rat•ed, -rat•ing.** To scold angrily and at length. [BE– + RATE².]

Ber•ber (bûr′bər) ▸*n.* **1.** A member of a North African people living in settled or nomadic tribes from Morocco to Egypt. **2.** Any of their Afro-Asiatic languages.

ber•ceuse (bĕr-sœz′) ▸*n., pl.* **-ceuses** (-sœz′) *Mus.* **1.** A lullaby. **2.** A soothing composition similar to a lullaby. [Fr.]

be•reave (bĭ-rēv′) ▸*v.* **-reaved** or **-reft** (-rĕft′), **-reav•ing.** To leave desolate or alone, esp. by death. [< OE *berēafian.*] —**be•reave′ment** *n.*

be•reaved (bĭ-rēvd′) ▸*adj.* Suffering the loss of a loved one. ▸*n.* One who is or those who are bereaved.

be•reft (bĭ-rĕft′) ▸*v.* P.t. and p.part. of **bereave.** ▸*adj.* **1.** Lacking or deprived of something: *bereft of dignity.* **2.** Bereaved.

be•ret (bə-rā′) ▸*n.* A round, brimless cloth cap often worn to one side. [< LLat. *birrus*, hooded cloak.]

Ber•gen (bûr′gən, bĕr′-) A city of SW Norway. Pop. 218,144.

Berg•man (bûrg′mən), **Ingrid.** 1915–82. Swedish actress.

Berg•son (bĕrg′sən, bĕrg-sôN′), **Henri Louis.** 1859–1941. French philosopher and writer; 1927 Nobel.

ber•i•ber•i (bĕr′ē-bĕr′ē) ▸*n.* A thiamine-deficiency disease characterized by neurological symptoms, cardiovascular abnormalities, and edema. [Sinhalese.]

Ber•ing (bîr′ĭng, bâr′-), **Vitus.** 1681–1741. Danish navigator and explorer.

Bering Sea. A northward extension of the Pacific between Siberia and AK, connected with the Arctic Ocean by the **Bering Strait.**

Berke•ley (bûrk′lē) A city of W CA on San Francisco Bay N of Oakland. Pop. 103,328.

ber•ke•li•um (bər-kē′lē-əm, bûrk′lē-əm) ▸*n.* *Symbol* **Bk** A synthetic radioactive element. At. no. 97. See table at **element.** [After BERKELEY, California.]

Berk•shire Hills (bûrk′shîr′, -shər) also **Berk•shires** (-shîrz′, -shərz). A region of wooded hills in W MA.

Ber•lin (bər-lĭn′) The capital of Germany, in the NE part; formerly divided into **East Berlin** and **West Berlin** (1945–90). Pop. 3,475,392.

Berlin, Irving. 1888–1989. Russian-born Amer. songwriter.

Ber•lin•er (bûr′lə-nər), **Emile.** 1851–1929. German-born Amer. inventor.

Ber•li•oz (bĕr′lē-ōz′, -ōs′), **(Louis) Hector.** 1803–69. French composer.

berm (bûrm) ▸*n.* **1.** A raised bank or path, as along a roadway or canal. **2.** A protective mound or bank of earth. [< MDu. *bærm.*]

Ber•mu•da (bər-myo͞o′də) A self-governing British colony comprising about 300 islands in the Atlantic SE of Cape Hatteras. Cap. Hamilton, on **Bermuda Island.** Pop. 63,000. —**Ber•mu′di•an, Ber•mu′dan** *adj. & n.*

Bermuda onion ▸*n.* A large mild onion.

Bermuda shorts ▸*pl.n.* Short pants that end

berm

slightly above the knee.

Bern or **Berne** (bûrn, bĕrn). The capital of Switzerland, in the W-central part on the Aare R. Pop. 129,692.

Ber•nese Alps (bûr-nēz′, -nēs′) A range of the Alps in S-central Switzerland.

Bern•hardt (bûrn′härt′, bĕr-när′), **Sarah.** 1844–1923. French actress.

Sarah Bernhardt

Ber•ni•ni (bər-nē′nē, bĕr-), **Giovanni Lorenzo.** 1598–1680. Italian sculptor, painter, and architect.

Ber•noul•li effect (bər-no͞o′lē) ►*n.* The phenomenon of internal pressure reduction with increased stream velocity in a fluid. [After Daniel *Bernoulli* (1700–82).]

ber•ry (bĕr′ē) ►*n., pl.* **-ries 1.** *Bot.* A fruit derived from a single ovary and having the whole wall fleshy, such as the grape or tomato. **2.** A small, juicy, many-seeded fruit, such as a blackberry. ►*v.* **-ried, -ry•ing.** To hunt for or gather berries. [< OE *berie.*]

ber•serk (bər-sûrk′, -zûrk′) ►*adj.* **1.** Destructively violent. **2.** Crazed; deranged. [< ON *berserkr*, warrior.] —**ber•serk′** *adv.*

berth (bûrth) ►*n.* **1.** Sufficient space for a ship to maneuver. **2.** A space for a ship to dock or anchor. **3.** Employment, esp. on a ship. **4a.** A built-in bed, as on a ship or train. **b.** A place to sleep or stay; accommodations. **5.** A space where a vehicle can be parked. ►*v.* To bring (a ship) to a berth. —***idiom:*** **a wide berth** Ample space or distance to avoid any trouble. [ME *birth.*]

ber•yl (bĕr′əl) ►*n.* A hard glassy mineral, essentially $Be_3Al_2Si_6O_{18}$, the chief source of beryllium and used as a gem. [Of Indic orig.] —**ber′yl•line** (-ə-lĭn, -līn′) *adj.*

be•ryl•li•um (bə-rĭl′ē-əm) ►*n. Symbol* **Be** A high-melting, lightweight, corrosion-resistant, rigid, steel-gray metallic element used as a moderator in nuclear reactors and in sturdy light alloys. At. no. 4. See table at **element.** [< BERYL.]

be•seech (bĭ-sēch′) ►*v.* **-sought** (-sôt′) or **-seeched, -seech•ing.** To request urgently; implore. [< OE *sēcan*, seek.]

be•seem (bĭ-sēm′) ►*v. Archaic* To befit.

be•set (bĭ-sĕt′) ►*v.* **-set, -set•ting 1.** To attack from all sides. **2.** To trouble persistently; harass. [< OE *besettan.*]

be•side (bĭ-sīd′) ►*prep.* **1.** Next to. **2.** In comparison with. **3.** In addition to. **4.** Except for. **5.** Not relevant to: *beside the point.* —***idiom:*** **beside (oneself)** Extremely agitated or excited. [< OE *be sīdan.*]

be•sides (bĭ-sīdz′) ►*adv.* **1.** In addition; also. **2.** Moreover; furthermore. **3.** Otherwise; else. ►*prep.* **1.** In addition to. See Usage Note at **together. 2.** Except for.

be•siege (bĭ-sēj′) ►*v.* **-sieged, -sieg•ing 1.** To surround with hostile forces. **2.** To crowd around; hem in. **3.** To harass or importune, as with requests. —**be•sieg′er** *n.*

Bes•kids (bĕs′kĭdz′, bĕs-kēdz′) A mountain range of the W Carpathians extending along the Polish-Slovakian border.

be•smear (bĭ-smîr′) ►*v.* To smear.

be•smirch (bĭ-smûrch′) ►*v.* **1.** To stain; sully. **2.** To make dirty; soil. —**be•smirch′er** *n.*

be•sot (bĭ-sŏt′) ►*v.* **-sot•ted, -sot•ting.** To addle, as with liquor or infatuation.

be•spat•ter (bĭ-spăt′ər) ►*v.* To spatter with or as if with mud.

be•speak (bĭ-spēk′) ►*v.* **-spoke** (-spōk′), **-spo•ken** (-spō′kən) or **-spoke, -speak•ing 1.** To be or give a sign of; indicate. See Syns at **indicate. 2.** To engage, hire, or order in advance. **3.** To foretell.

be•sprin•kle (bĭ-sprĭng′kəl) ►*v.* **-kled, -kling.** To sprinkle.

Bes•sa•ra•bi•a (bĕs′ə-rā′bē-ə) A region of Moldova and W Ukraine. —**Bes′sa•ra′bi•an** *adj. & n.*

Bes•se•mer process (bĕs′ə-mər) ►*n.* A method for making steel by blasting compressed air through molten iron to burn out excess carbon and impurities. [After Sir Henry *Bessemer* (1813–98).]

best (bĕst) ►*adj.* Superl. of **good. 1.** Surpassing all others in quality. **2.** Most satisfactory or desirable: *the best solution.* **3.** Greatest; most: *the best part of an hour.* ►*adv.* Superl. of **well²**. **1.** Most creditably or advantageously. **2.** To the greatest degree or extent; most. ►*n.* **1.** One that surpasses all others. **2.** The best part, moment, or value: *Let's get the best out of life.* **3.** The optimum condition or quality: *look your best.* **4.** One's best clothing. **5.** The best effort one can make. **6.** One's regards: *Give them my best.* ►*v.* To surpass; beat. —***idioms:*** **at best 1.** Interpreted most favorably: *no more than 40 people at best.* **2.** Under the most favorable conditions: *runs 20 miles per hour at best.* **for the best** For the ultimate good. **get the best of** To outdo or outwit. [< OE *betst.*]

bes•tial (bĕs′chəl, bēs′-) ►*adj.* **1.** Beastlike. **2.** Marked by brutality or depravity. [< Lat. *bēstia*, beast.] —**bes′ti•al′i•ty** (-chē-ăl′ĭ-tē) *n.* —**bes′tial•ly** *adv.*

bes•ti•ar•y (bĕs′chē-ĕr′ē, bĕs′-) ►*n.*, *pl.* **-ies.** A medieval collection of stories providing descriptions of real and fabulous animals along with moral interpretation of their behavior. [< Lat. *bēstia*, beast.]

be•stir (bĭ-stûr′) ►*v.* **-stirred, -stir•ring.** To cause to become active; rouse.

best man ►*n.* A bridegroom's chief attendant.

be•stow (bĭ-stō′) ►*v.* To present as a gift or honor; confer. —**be•stow′al** *n.*

be•strew (bĭ-stro͞o′) ►*v.* **-strewed, -strewed** or **-strewn** (-stro͞on′), **-strew•ing.** To strew.

be•stride (bĭ-strīd′) ►*v.* **-strode** (-strōd′), **-strid•den** (-strĭd′n), **-strid•ing.** To sit or stand astride; straddle.

best•sell•er (bĕst′sĕl′ər) ►*n.* A product, such as a book, that is among those sold in the largest numbers.

bet (bĕt) ►*n.* **1.** A wager. **2.** The amount or object risked in a wager; stake. **3.** One on which a stake is or can be placed. ►*v.* **bet** or **bet•ted, bet•ting 1.** To stake (e.g., an amount) in a bet. **2.** To make a bet (with). —***idiom:* you bet** *Informal* Of course. [?]

Syns: *bet, ante, pot, stake, wager* **n.**

be•ta (bā′tə, bē′-) ►*n.* The 2nd letter of the Greek alphabet. [Gk. *bēta* < Phoenician **bēt*, house.]

be•ta-block•er (bā′tə-blŏk′ər, bē′-) ►*n.* A drug that blocks or reduces the heart's response to certain stimuli, used to treat angina, hypertension, and arrhythmia.

beta carotene ►*n.* An isomer of carotene efficiently converted to vitamin A by the body.

be•take (bĭ-tāk′) ►*v.* **-took** (-to͝ok′), **-tak•en** (-tā′kən), **-tak•ing.** To cause (oneself) to go.

beta particle ►*n.* A high-speed electron or positron, esp. from radioactive decay.

beta ray ►*n.* A stream of beta particles, esp. of electrons.

beta rhythm also **beta wave** ►*n.* A pattern of electrical oscillations occurring in the brain at a frequency of 13 to 30 hertz when a person is awake and alert.

beta test ►*n.* The final testing of software before its commercial release, done by testers other than its developers. —**be′ta-test′** (bā′tə-tĕst′, bē′-) *v.*

be•ta•tron (bā′tə-trŏn′, bē′-) ►*n.* A fixed-radius magnetic induction electron accelerator.

beta version ►*n.* The version of software used in a beta test.

be•tel (bēt′l) ►*n.* A climbing or trailing Asian shrub having usu. ovate leaves used to wrap betel nuts. [< Tamil *verrilai.*]

Be•tel•geuse (bēt′l-jo͞oz′, bĕt′l-jœz′) ►*n.* A bright-red variable star in the constellation Orion. [Prob. < Ar. *yad al-jawzā′*, hand of Orion.]

betel nut ►*n.* The seed of the betel palm, chewed with betel leaves, lime, and flavorings as a mild stimulant.

betel palm ►*n.* A tropical Asian feather-leaved palm cultivated for its seeds.

bête noire (bĕt nwär′) ►*n.* One that is an object of intense dislike or aversion. [Fr.]

be•think (bĭ-thĭngk′) ►*v.* **-thought** (-thôt′), **-think•ing.** To remind (oneself).

Beth•le•hem (bĕth′lĭ-hĕm′, -lē-əm) A town in the West Bank S of Jerusalem; traditional birthplace of Jesus. Pop. 25,000.

Be•thune (bə-tho͞on′, -thyo͞on′), **Mary McLeod.** 1875–1955. Amer. educator.

be•tide (bĭ-tīd′) ►*v.* **-tid•ed, -tid•ing.** To happen (to); befall. See Syns at **happen.** [< *tīdan*, happen.]

be•times (bĭ-tīmz′) ►*adv.* In good time; early.

be•to•ken (bĭ-tō′kən) ►*v.* To give a sign or portent of. See Syns at **indicate.**

be•took (bĭ-to͝ok′) ►*v.* P.t. of **betake.**

be•tray (bĭ-trā′) ►*v.* **1.** To commit treason against; be a traitor to. **2.** To be false or disloyal to. **3.** To make known unintentionally. **4.** To show; reveal. **5.** To lead astray; deceive. [< Lat. *trādere*, hand over.] —**be•tray′al** *n.* —**be•tray′er** *n.*

be•troth (bĭ-trōth′, -trôth′) ►*v.* To promise or engage to marry. —**be•troth′al** *n.*

be•trothed (bĭ-trōthd′, -trôtht′) ►*n.* The person to whom one is engaged to be married.

bet•ter (bĕt′ər) ►*adj.* Comp. of **good. 1.** Greater in excellence or higher in quality. **2.** More appropriate, useful, or desirable. **3.** Greater or larger: *the better part of an hour.* **4.** Healthier than before. ►*adv.* Comp. of **well**[2]. **1.** In a more excellent way. **2.** To a greater extent or degree. **3.** To greater use or advantage. **4.** More: *better than a year.* ►*n.* **1.** One that is better in excellence or quality. **2.** A superior, as in standing. ►*v.* **1.** To make or become better; improve. **2.** To surpass or exceed. —***idioms:* better off** In a wealthier or better condition. **for the better** Resulting in improvement. **had better** Ought to. **think better of** To change one's mind about. [< OE *betera.*]

bet•ter•ment (bĕt′ər-mənt) ►*n.* An improvement, often financially or educationally.

bet•tor also **bet•ter** (bĕt′ər) ►*n.* One that bets.

be•tween (bĭ-twēn′) ►*prep.* **1.** In or through the position or interval separating: *between the trees; between 11 and 12 o'clock.* **2.** Associating in a reciprocal relationship: *an agreement between workers and management.* **3a.** By the combined effort or effect of: *Between them they succeeded.* **b.** In the combined ownership of: *They had only a few dollars between them.* **4.** From one or another of: *choose between us.* ►*adv.* In an intermediate space, position, or time. —***idiom:* between you and me** In the strictest confidence. [< OE *betwēonum.*]

Usage: With exactly two entities, the only choice possible is *between: the choice between good and evil.* With more than two or an unspecified number of entities, use *between* if the entities are distinct and *among* if they are a mass or collection. In *The bomb landed between the houses,* the houses are points defining the impact area's boundary (*i.e.*, no house was hit). In *The bomb landed among the houses,* the impact area is the general location of the houses (*i.e.*, it is uncertain whether any house was hit).

be•twixt (bĭ-twĭkst′) ►*adv.* & *prep.* Between. —***idiom:* betwixt and between** In an intermediate position. [< OE *betwix.*]

BeV ►*abbr.* billion electron volts

bev•el (bĕv′əl) ►*n.* **1.** The angle or inclination of a line or surface that meets another at any angle but 90°. **2.** A rule with an adjustable arm used to measure or draw angles or to fix a surface at an angle. ►*v.* **-eled, -el•ing** or **-elled, -el•ling 1.** To cut at a bevel. **2.** To be inclined; slant. [Poss. < OFr.]

bev•er•age (bĕv′ər-ij, bĕv′rĭj) ▸*n.* Any one of various liquids for drinking, usu. excluding water. [< Lat. *bibere*, to drink.]

bev•y (bĕv′ē) ▸*n., pl.* **-ies 1.** A group of animals or birds, esp. quail. **2.** A group or assemblage. [< AN *bevee.*]

be•wail (bĭ-wāl′) ▸*v.* To express sorrow (about); lament.

be•ware (bĭ-wâr′) ▸*v.* **-wared, -war•ing.** To be on guard (against); be cautious (of). [ME *ben war.*]

be•wil•der (bĭ-wĭl′dər) ▸*v.* To confuse or befuddle, esp. with numerous conflicting situations, objects, or statements. [< obsolete *wilder*, disorient.] —**be•wil′der•ment** *n.*

be•witch (bĭ-wĭch′) ▸*v.* **1.** To place under one's power by or as if by magic; cast a spell over. **2.** To captivate completely; entrance. See Syns at **charm.** —**be•witch′ing•ly** *adv.* —**be•witch′ment** *n.*

bey (bā) ▸*n.* **1.** A provincial governor in the Ottoman Empire. **2.** A ruler of the former kingdom of Tunis. [Turk.]

be•yond (bē-ŏnd′, bĭ-yŏnd′) ▸*prep.* **1.** On the far side of; past. **2.** Later than; after. **3.** Past the understanding, reach, or scope of. **4.** To a degree or amount greater than. **5.** In addition to. [< OE *begeondan.*]

bez•el (bĕz′əl) ▸*n.* **1.** A slanting edge on a cutting tool. **2.** The faceted portion of a cut gem. [Perh. < Lat. *bis*, twice.]

bf ▸*abbr.* bold face

BF ▸*abbr.* **1.** board foot **2.** also **B/F** *Accounting* brought forward

Bh ▸ The symbol for the element **bohrium.**

B/H ▸*abbr.* bill of health

bhang (băng, bäng) ▸*n.* Marijuana. [< Skt. *bhaṅgā.*]

Bho•pal (bō-päl′) A city of central India NNW of Nagpur; site of a disastrous toxic gas leak (1984). Pop. 1,062,771.

BHT (bē′āch-tē′) ▸*n.* A crystalline phenolic antioxidant, $C_{15}H_{24}O$, that is used to preserve fats and oils, especially in foods. [*b(utylated) h(ydroxy)t(oluene), tolu*, a resin.]

Bhu•tan (bo͞o-tăn′, -tän′) A country of central Asia in the E Himalayas. Cap. Thimbu. Pop. 1,614,000. —**Bhu′tan•ese′** *adj. & n.*

Bi ▸ The symbol for the element **bismuth.**

bi– or **bin–** ▸*pref.* **1.** Two; twice: *bipolar.* **2.** Occurring twice during: *biweekly.* [Lat. *bis, bi-*, twice, and *bīnī*, two by two.]

Usage: *Bimonthly* and *biweekly* mean "once every two months" and "once every two weeks." For "twice a month" and "twice a week," *semimonthly* and *semiweekly* should be used. A writer is well advised to substitute phrases like *every two months* or *twice a month* where possible.

BIA ▸*abbr.* Bureau of Indian Affairs

Bi•a•fra (bē-ăf′rə, -ä′frə) A region of E Nigeria on the **Bight of Biafra,** an arm of the Gulf of Guinea stretching from the Niger R. delta to N Gabon. —**Bi•a′fran** *adj. & n.*

Bia•ly•stok (bē-ä′lĭ-stôk′) A city of NE Poland near the border of Belarus. Pop. 272,137.

bi•an•nu•al (bī-ăn′yo͞o-əl) ▸*adj.* Semiannual. —**bi•an′nu•al•ly** *adv.*

Biar•ritz (bē′ə-rĭts′) A city of SW France near the Spanish border. Pop. 26,598.

bi•as (bī′əs) ▸*n.* **1.** A line going diagonally across the grain of fabric. **2.** A preference or inclination that inhibits impartiality; prejudice. See Syns at **predilection.** ▸*adj.* Slanting or diagonal; oblique. ▸*v.* **-ased, -as•ing** or **-assed, -as•sing.** To cause to have a bias; prejudice. [Fr. *biais*, slant.]

Syns: *bias, color, jaundice, prejudice, warp* ***v.***

bi•ath•lon (bī-ăth′lən, -lŏn′) ▸*n.* An athletic competition that combines events in cross-country skiing and rifle shooting. [BI– + Gk. *athlon*, contest.]

bib (bĭb) ▸*n.* A cloth or plastic napkin secured under the chin and worn esp. by children to protect clothing while eating. [Prob. < ME *bibben*, drink heartily.]

Bib. ▸*abbr.* Bible

bi•be•lot (bē′bə-lō′, bē-blō′) ▸*n.* A small decorative object. [< OFr. *beubelet.*]

Bi•ble (bī′bəl) ▸*n.* **1a.** The sacred book of Christianity, which includes the Old Testament and the New Testament. **b.** The sacred book of Judaism, consisting of the Torah, the Prophets, and the Writings. See table p. 86. **2.** often **bible** A book considered authoritative in its field: *the bible of Chinese cooking.* [< Gk. *biblion*, book.] —**Bib′li•cal** (bĭb′lĭ-kəl) *adj.* —**Bib′li•cal•ly** *adv.*

biblio– ▸*pref.* Book: *bibliophile.* [< Gk. *biblion*, book.]

bib•li•og•ra•phy (bĭb′lē-ŏg′rə-fē) ▸*n., pl.* **-phies 1.** A list of the works of a specific author or publisher. **2.** A list of writings relating to a given subject. **3.** The description and identification of the editions, dates of issue, authorship, and typography of books or other written material. —**bib′li•og′ra•pher** *n.* —**bib′li•o•graph′i•cal** (-ə-grăf′ĭ-kəl), **bib′li•o•graph′ic** *adj.*

bib•li•o•phile (bĭb′lē-ə-fīl′) ▸*n.* A lover or connoisseur of books.

bib•u•lous (bĭb′yə-ləs) ▸*adj.* Given to convivial, often excessive alcoholic drinking. [< Lat. *bibere*, to drink.] —**bib′u•lous•ly** *adv.*

bi•cam•er•al (bī-kăm′ər-əl) ▸*adj.* Composed of two legislative branches. [BI– + Lat. *camera*, chamber.] —**bi•cam′er•al•ism** *n.*

bi•car•bon•ate (bī-kär′bə-nāt′, -nĭt) ▸*n.* The radical group HCO_3 or a compound, such as sodium bicarbonate, containing it.

bicarbonate of soda ▸*n.* See **baking soda.**

bi•cen•ten•a•ry (bī′sĕn-tĕn′ə-rē, bī-sĕn′tə-nĕr′ē) ▸*n., pl.* **-ries.** A bicentennial. —**bi′cen•ten′a•ry** *adj.*

bi•cen•ten•ni•al (bī′sĕn-tĕn′ē-əl) ▸*n.* A 200th anniversary or its celebration; bicentenary. —**bi′cen•ten′ni•al** *adj.*

bi•ceps (bī′sĕps′) ▸*n., pl.* **-ceps** or **-ceps•es** (-sĕp′sĭz). A muscle with two points of origin, esp. the large muscle at the front of the upper arm. [< Lat., two-headed.]

bick•er (bĭk′ər) ▸*v.* To engage in a petty quarrel; squabble. ▸*n.* A petty quarrel; squabble. [ME *bikeren*, to attack.]

bi•con•cave (bī′kŏn-kāv′, bī-kŏn′kāv′) ▸*adj.* Concave on both sides or surfaces. —**bi′con•cav′i•ty** (-kăv′ĭ-tē) *n.*

bi•con•vex (bī′kŏn-vĕks′, bī-kŏn′vĕks′) ▸*adj.* Convex on both sides or surfaces. —**bi′con•vex′i•ty** (-vĕk′sĭ-tē) *n.*

bi•cus•pid (bī-kŭs′pĭd) ▸*adj.* Having two points or cusps. ▸*n.* A bicuspid tooth, esp. a premolar. [BI– + Lat. *cuspis*, point.]

BOOKS OF THE BIBLE

Books of the Hebrew Scriptures appear as listed in the translation by the Jewish Publication Society of America. Books of the Christian Bible appear as listed in the Jerusalem Bible, a 1966 translation of the 1956 French Roman Catholic version. The Old Testament books shown in italic are considered apocryphal in many Christian churches, but they are accepted as canonical in the Roman Catholic Church, the Eastern Orthodox Church, and the Armenian and the Ethiopian Oriental Orthodox Church. The Christian Old Testament parallels the Hebrew Scriptures with the exception of these books.

Hebrew Scriptures

The Torah

Genesis
Exodus
Leviticus
Numbers
Deuteronomy

The Prophets

Joshua
Judges
I Samuel
II Samuel
I Kings
II Kings
Isaiah
Jeremiah
Ezekiel
Hosea
Joel
Amos
Obadiah
Jonah
Micah
Nahum
Habakkuk
Zephaniah
Haggai
Zechariah
Malachi

The Writings

Psalms
Proverbs
Job
Song of Songs
Ruth
Lamentations
Ecclesiastes
Esther
Daniel
Ezra
Nehemiah
I Chronicles
II Chronicles

Christian Bible

Old Testament

Genesis
Exodus
Leviticus
Numbers
Deuteronomy
Joshua
Judges
Ruth
I Samuel
II Samuel
I Kings
II Kings
I Chronicles
II Chronicles
Ezra
Nehemiah
Tobit
Judith
Esther
I Maccabees
II Maccabees
Job
Psalms
Proverbs
Ecclesiastes
Song of Songs (Song of Solomon)
Wisdom of Solomon
Ecclesiasticus
Isaiah
Jeremiah
Lamentations
Baruch
Ezekiel
Daniel
Hosea
Joel
Amos
Obadiah
Jonah
Micah
Nahum
Habakkuk
Zephaniah
Haggai
Zechariah
Malachi

New Testament

Matthew
Mark
Luke
John
Acts of the Apostles
Romans
I Corinthians
II Corinthians
Galatians
Ephesians
Philippians
Colossians
I Thessalonians
II Thessalonians
I Timothy
II Timothy
Titus
Philemon
Hebrews
James
I Peter
II Peter
I John
II John
III John
Jude
Revelation

bi•cy•cle (bī′sĭk′əl, -sĭ-kəl) ► *n.* A vehicle consisting of a metal frame mounted on two wire-spoked wheels and having a seat, handlebars for steering, brakes, and pedals. ► *v.* **-cled, -cling.** To ride or travel on a bicycle. [Fr.] —**bi′cy•cler, bi′cy•clist** *n.*

bid (bĭd) ► *v.* **bade** (băd, bād) or **bid, bid•den** (bĭd′n) or **bid, bid•ding 1.** To command; direct. **2.** To utter (a greeting or salutation). **3.** To invite to attend; summon. **4.** *p.t. and p.part.* **bid a.** To offer to pay or accept a specified price. **b.** To offer as a price. **c.** To state one's intention to take (tricks of a certain number or suit) in card games. ► *n.* **1a.** An offer of a price.

b. The amount offered. **2.** An invitation. **3a.** The act of bidding in card games. **b.** The number of tricks declared. **c.** A player's turn to bid. **4.** An earnest effort to gain something. [< OE *biddan*, to command, and *bēodan*, to offer.] —**bid′der** *n.*

bid•da•ble (bĭd′ə-bəl) ▸*adj.* **1.** Capable of being bid. **2.** Obedient; docile.

bid•dy (bĭd′ē) ▸*n.*, *pl.* **-dies.** A hen. [?]

bide (bīd) ▸*v.* **bid•ed** or **bode** (bōd), **bid•ed, bid•ing 1.** To remain; stay. **2.** To wait; tarry. **3.** *p.t.* **bided** To await. [< OE *bīdan*.]

bi•det (bē-dā′) ▸*n.* A fixture similar in design to a toilet, used for bathing the genitals and posterior parts of the body. [Fr.]

Bie•le•feld (bē′lə-fĕlt′) A city of NW Germany E of Münster. Pop. 324,674.

bi•en•ni•al (bī-ĕn′ē-əl) ▸*adj.* **1.** Lasting or living for two years. **2.** Happening every second year. **3.** *Bot.* Having a life cycle that normally takes two growing seasons. [< Lat. *biennium*, two-year period.] —**bi•en′ni•al** *n.* —**bi•en′ni•al•ly** *adv.*

bier (bîr) ▸*n.* A stand on which a corpse or a coffin is placed before burial. [< OE *bēr*.]

Bierce (bîrs), **Ambrose Gwinett.** 1842–1914? Amer. writer.

bi•fo•cal (bī-fō′kəl, bī′fō′-) ▸*adj.* **1.** Having two different focal lengths. **2.** Having one section that corrects for distant vision and another that corrects for near vision, as an eyeglass lens. ▸*pl.n.* **bi•fo•cals.** Eyeglasses with bifocal lenses.

bi•fur•cate (bī′fər-kāt′, bī-fûr′-) ▸*v.* **-cat•ed, -cat•ing.** To divide or separate into two parts or branches. [< Lat. *furca*, fork.] —**bi′fur•ca′tion** *n.*

big (bĭg) ▸*adj.* **big•ger, big•gest 1.** Of considerable size, number, quantity, or extent. See Syns at **large. 2.** Grown-up; adult. **3.** Pregnant: *big with child.* **4.** Of great significance: *a big decision.* **5.** *Informal* Self-important; cocky. ▸*adv.* **1.** In a self-important or boastful way. **2.** *Informal* With great success. —***idiom:*** **big on** Enthusiastic about; partial to. [ME, perh. of Scand. orig.] —**big′gish** *adj.* —**big′ness** *n.*

big•a•my (bĭg′ə-mē) ▸*n.*, *pl.* **-mies** *Law* The criminal offense of marrying one person while still legally married to another. [< LLat. *bigamus*, bigamous.] —**big′a•mist** *n.* —**big′a•mous** *adj.*

big bang theory ▸*n.* A cosmological theory holding that the universe originated approx. 20 billion years ago from the violent explosion of a small point source of extremely high density and temperature.

big brother also **Big Brother** ▸*n.* An omnipresent, seemingly benevolent figure representing the oppressive control over individuals exerted by an authoritarian government.

Big Dipper ▸*n.* A cluster of seven stars in the constellation Ursa Major forming a dipper-shaped configuration.

Big•foot (bĭg′fo͝ot′) ▸*n.* A very large, hairy, humanlike creature purported to inhabit the Pacific Northwest and Canada; Sasquatch.

big game ▸*n.* Large animals or fish hunted or caught for sport. —**big′-game′** *adj.*

big-heart•ed (bĭg′här′tĭd) ▸*adj.* Generous; kind. —**big′-heart′ed•ly** *adv.*

big•horn (bĭg′hôrn′) ▸*n.*, *pl.* **-horn** or **-horns.** A wild sheep of the mountains of W North America, the male of which has massive, curved horns.

bighorn
bighorn ram

Bighorn Mountains. A section of the Rocky Mts. of N WY and S MT.

bight (bīt) ▸*n.* **1.** A loop in a rope. **2a.** A bend or curve, esp. in a shoreline. **b.** A wide bay formed by a bight. [< OE *byht*, bend.]

big•mouth (bĭg′mouth′) ▸*n.* *Slang* A loud-mouthed or gossipy person.

big-name (bĭg′nām′) ▸*adj.* *Informal* Widely acclaimed; famous. —**big name** *n.*

big•ot (bĭg′ət) ▸*n.* One who is intolerant esp. in matters of religion, race, or politics. [OFr.] —**big′ot•ed** *adj.* —**big′ot•ry** *n.*

big shot ▸*n.* *Slang* An important or influential person. —**big′shot′, big′-shot′** *adj.*

Big Sur (sûr) A coastal resort region of central CA.

big-tick•et (bĭg′tĭk′ĭt) ▸*adj.* *Informal* Having a high price or cost: *big-ticket items.*

big time ▸*n.* *Informal* The highest level of attainment in a competitive field or profession. —**big′-time′** *adj.*

big top ▸*n.* **1.** The main tent of a circus. **2.** The circus.

big•wig (bĭg′wĭg′) ▸*n.* *Slang* A big shot.

bike (bīk) ▸*n.* **1.** A bicycle. **2.** A motorcycle. **3.** A motorbike. —**bike** *v.*

bik•er (bī′kər) ▸*n.* **1.** One who rides a bicycle or motorbike. **2.** A motorcyclist, esp. a member of a motorcycle gang.

bi•ki•ni (bĭ-kē′nē) ▸*n.* **1.** A woman's brief, close-fitting two-piece bathing suit. **2.** A man's brief bathing trunks. [After BIKINI.]

Bikini. An atoll of the Marshall Is. in the W-central Pacific.

bi•lat•er•al (bī-lăt′ər-əl) ▸*adj.* **1.** Having or formed of two sides; two-sided. **2.** Affecting or undertaken by two sides equally. —**bi•lat′er•al•ly** *adv.*

Bil•ba•o (bĭl-bä′ō, -bou′) A city of N Spain near the Bay of Biscay. Pop. 365,269.

bile (bīl) ▸*n.* **1.** A bitter greenish-yellow fluid that is secreted by the liver and aids in the digestion and absorption of fats. **2.** Ill temper; irascibility. [< Lat. *bīlis*.] —**bil′i•ar′y** (bĭl′ē-ĕr′ē) *adj.*

bilge (bĭlj) ▸*n.* **1.** The lowest inner part of a ship's hull. **2.** Bilge water. **3.** *Slang* Nonsense. [Prob. < BULGE.]

bilge water ▸*n.* **1.** Water that collects and stagnates in a ship's bilge. **2.** *Slang* Nonsense.

bi•lin•gual (bī-lĭng′gwəl) ▸*adj.* Expressed in

or able to speak two languages. [< BI– + Lat. *lingua*, tongue.] —**bi•lin′gual•ism** *n.* —**bi•lin′gual•ly** *adv.*

bil•ious (bĭl′yəs) ▸*adj.* **1.** Of or containing bile. **2.** Characterized by or experiencing gastric distress caused by a disorder of the liver or gallbladder. **3.** Irascible. —**bil′ious•ly** *adv.* —**bil′ious•ness** *n.*

bilk (bĭlk) ▸*v.* To defraud, cheat, or swindle. [Perh. < BALK.] —**bilk′er** *n.*

bill[1] (bĭl) ▸*n.* **1.** A statement of charges for goods or services. **2.** A list of particulars, such as a theater program or menu. **3.** The entertainment offered by a theater. **4.** A public notice, such as an advertising poster. **5.** A piece of legal paper money. **6.** A bill of exchange. **7a.** A draft of a law presented for approval to a legislative body. **b.** The law enacted from such a draft. **8.** *Law* A document containing a formal statement of a case, complaint, or petition. ▸*v.* **1.** To present a statement of costs or charges to. **2.** To enter on a bill. **3.** To advertise by public notice. [< Med.Lat. *bulla*, seal on a document.] —**bill′a•ble** *adj.*

bill[2] (bĭl) ▸*n.* **1.** The horny part of the jaws of a bird; beak. **2.** A beaklike mouth part, as of a turtle. **3.** The visor of a cap. ▸*v.* To touch beaks together. [< OE *bile*.]

bill•board (bĭl′bôrd′, -bōrd′) ▸*n.* A structure for the public display of advertisements.

bil•let (bĭl′ĭt) ▸*n.* **1a.** Lodging for troops. **b.** A written order directing that such lodging be provided. **2.** A position of employment; job. ▸*v.* To assign quarters to by billet. [< OFr. *billette*, official register.]

bil•let-doux (bĭl′ā-do͞o′) ▸*n.*, *pl.* **bil•lets-doux** (bĭl′ā-do͞oz′). A love letter. [Fr.]

bill•fold (bĭl′fōld′) ▸*n.* A wallet.

bil•liards (bĭl′yərdz) ▸*pl.n.* *(takes sing. v.)* A game played on a rectangular cloth-covered table, in which a cue is used to hit three small, hard balls against one another or the raised cushioned sides of the table. [< Fr. *billard*, cue.]

bill•ing (bĭl′ĭng) ▸*n.* The relative importance of performers as indicated by their listing on programs or advertisements: *top billing.*

Bil•lings (bĭl′ĭngz) A city of S MT on the Yellowstone R. ESE of Helena. Pop. 81,151.

bil•lings•gate (bĭl′ĭngz-gāt′, -gĭt) ▸*n.* Foul, abusive language. [After *Billingsgate*, a former fish market in London.]

bil•lion (bĭl′yən) ▸*n.* **1.** The cardinal number equal to 10^9. **2.** *Chiefly Brit.* The cardinal number equal to 10^{12}. [Fr., a million million.] —**bil′lion** *adj. & pron.*

bil•lion•aire (bĭl′yə-nâr′) ▸*n.* One whose wealth equals at least a billion dollars, pounds, or the equivalent in other currency. [BILLION + (MILLION)AIRE.]

bil•lionth (bĭl′yənth) ▸*n.* **1.** The ordinal number matching the number billion in a series. **2.** One of a billion equal parts. —**bil′lionth** *adj. & adv.*

bill of exchange ▸*n.* A written order directing that a specified sum of money be paid to a specified person.

bill of fare ▸*n.* A menu.

bill of goods ▸*n.* **1.** A consignment of items for sale. **2.** *Informal* A plan, promise, or offer, esp. one that is dishonest or misleading.

bill of lading ▸*n.* A document listing and acknowledging receipt of goods for transport.

bill of rights ▸*n.* **1.** A formal summary of the rights of a group of people: *a consumer bill of rights.* **2. Bill of Rights** The first ten amendments to the US Constitution.

bill of sale ▸*n.* A document that attests a transfer of personal property.

bil•low (bĭl′ō) ▸*n.* **1.** A large wave of water. **2.** A great swell or surge, as of smoke or windblown fabric. ▸*v.* **1.** To surge or roll in billows. **2.** To swell or cause to swell in billows. [< ON *bylgja*.] —**bil′low•y** *adj.*

bil•ly (bĭl′ē) ▸*n.*, *pl.* **-lies.** A billy club. [Perh. < BULLY.]

billy club ▸*n.* A short wooden club, esp. a police officer's.

billy goat ▸*n.* *Informal* A male goat.

bi•me•tal•lic (bī′mə-tăl′ĭk) ▸*adj.* **1.** Consisting of two metals. **2.** Of, based on, or using the principles of bimetallism.

bi•met•al•lism (bī-mĕt′l-ĭz′əm) ▸*n.* The use of both gold and silver in a fixed ratio of value as a monetary standard.

Bim•i•nis (bĭm′ə-nēz) A group of small islands of the W Bahamas in the Straits of Florida.

bi•mod•al (bī-mōd′l) ▸*adj.* Having two distinct modes or forms. —**bi′mo•dal′i•ty** *n.*

bi•month•ly (bī-mŭnth′lē) ▸*adj.* **1.** Happening every two months. **2.** Happening twice a month; semimonthly. ▸*n.*, *pl.* **-lies.** A bimonthly publication. See Usage Note at **bi–**. —**bi•month′ly** *adv.*

bin (bĭn) ▸*n.* A container or enclosed space for storage. [< OE *binne*.]

bin– ▸*pref.* Var. of **bi–**.

bi•na•ry (bī′nə-rē) ▸*adj.* **1.** Having two distinct parts or components. **2.** Of a number system having 2 as its base. [< Lat. *bīnī*, two by two.] —**bi′na•ry** *n.*

binary digit ▸*n.* Either of the digits 0 or 1, used in the binary number system.

binary number system ▸*n.* A method of representing numbers, using the digits 0 and 1, in which successive units are powers of 2.

binary star ▸*n.* A system consisting of two stars orbiting about a common center of mass and often appearing as a single object.

bin•au•ral (bī-nôr′əl, bĭn-ôr′-) ▸*adj.* **1.** Of or hearing with two ears. **2.** Relating to sound transmission from two sources, which may vary acoustically to give a stereophonic effect. —**bin•au′ral•ly** *adv.*

bind (bīnd) ▸*v.* **bound** (bound), **bind•ing 1.** To tie or encircle with or as with a rope or cord. **2.** To bandage. **3.** To hold or restrain. **4.** To compel or obligate. **5.** To place under legal obligation by contract or oath. **6.** To cohere or cause to cohere in a mass. **7.** To enclose and fasten (e.g., a book) between covers. **8.** To reinforce or ornament with an edge or border. **9.** To constipate. **10.** To be tight and uncomfortable. **11.** To be compelling or unifying: *the ties that bind.* ▸*n.* **1.** Something that binds. **2.** *Informal* A difficult or restrictive situation. [< OE *bindan*.] —**bind′er** *n.*

bind•er•y (bīn′də-rē) ▸*n.*, *pl.* **-ies.** A place where books are bound.

bind•ing (bīn′dĭng) ▸*n.* Something that binds, as: **a.** The cover that holds together the pages of a book. **b.** A strip sewn along an edge. **c.** Fastenings on a ski for securing the boot. ▸*adj.* **1.** Serving to bind. **2.** Commanding adherence to an obligation or commitment: *binding arbitration.*

binge (bĭnj) ►*n.* **1.** A drunken spree. **2.** A period of uncontrolled self-indulgence. ►*v.* **binged, bing•ing** or **binge•ing.** To be or go on a binge. [< dial. *binge*, to soak.]

Syns: *binge, fling, jag, orgy, spree* ***n.***

Bing•ham (bĭng′əm), **George Caleb.** 1811–79. Amer. painter.

bin•go (bĭng′gō) ►*n.* A game of chance in which players place markers on a pattern of numbered squares according to numbers drawn by a caller. ►*interj.* Used to express occurrence or completion. [?]

bin•na•cle (bĭn′ə-kəl) ►*n. Naut.* A case near the helm that supports a ship's compass. [< Lat. *habitāculum*, little house.]

bin•oc•u•lar (bə-nŏk′yə-lər, bī-) ►*adj.* Of or involving both eyes at the same time: *binocular vision.* ►*n.* often **binoculars.** A binocular optical device, such as field glasses.

bi•no•mi•al (bī-nō′mē-əl) ►*adj.* Consisting of or relating to two names or terms. ►*n.* **1.** *Math.* A polynomial with two terms. **2.** A taxonomic plant or animal name consisting of two terms. [< BI– + Lat. *nōmen*, name.] —**bi•no′mi•al•ly** *adv.*

bi•o (bī′ō) ►*n., pl.* **-os** *Informal* A biography.

bio– ►*pref.* Life; living organism: *biochemistry.* [< Gk. *bios*, life.]

bi•o•chem•is•try (bī′ō-kĕm′ĭ-strē) ►*n.* The study of the chemical substances and vital processes occurring in living organisms. —**bi′o•chem′i•cal** (-ĭ-kəl) *adj. & n.* —**bi′o•chem′i•cal•ly** *adv.* —**bi′o•chem′ist** *n.*

bi•o•con•ver•sion (bī′ō-kən-vûr′zhən, -shən) ►*n.* The conversion of organic materials into usable products or energy by biological means.

bi•o•de•grad•a•ble (bī′ō-dĭ-grā′də-bəl) ►*adj.* Capable of being decomposed by natural biological processes. —**bi′o•de•grad′a•bil′i•ty** *n.* —**bi′o•deg′ra•da′tion** (-dĕg′rə-dā′shən) *n.* —**bi′o•de•grade′** *v.*

bi•o•di•ver•si•ty (bī′ō-dĭ-vûr′sĭ-tē) ►*n.* The number and variety of organisms found in a specified geographic region or environment.

bi•o•feed•back (bī′ō-fēd′băk′) ►*n.* The technique of using monitoring devices to learn about an involuntary bodily function, such as blood pressure, in order to gain some voluntary control over that function.

bi•o•gas (bī′ō-găs′) ►*n.* A mixture of methane and carbon dioxide produced by bacterial degradation of organic matter and used as a fuel.

bi•o•gen•ic (bī′ō-jĕn′ĭk) ►*adj.* **1.** Produced by living organisms or biological processes. **2.** Necessary for the maintenance of life.

bi•o•ge•og•ra•phy (bī′ō-jē-ŏg′rə-fē) ►*n.* The biological study of the geographic distribution of plants and animals.

bi•og•ra•phy (bī-ŏg′rə-fē) ►*n., pl.* **-phies 1.** An account of a person's life written or produced by someone else. **2.** Biographies collectively, esp. when regarded as a literary form. —**bi•og′ra•pher** *n.* —**bi′o•graph′i•cal** (bī′ə-grăf′ĭ-kəl), **bi′o•graph′ic** *adj.*

bi•o•log•i•cal (bī′ə-lŏj′ĭ-kəl) also **bi•o•log•ic** ►*adj.* **1.** Of or relating to biology. **2.** Related by blood: *the child's biological parents.* —**bi′o•log′i•cal•ly** *adv.*

biological clock ►*n.* **1.** A mechanism in organisms that controls the periodic occurrence of functions or activities, such as metabolic change or photosynthesis. **2.** The span of a woman's fertility, from puberty to menopause.

biological warfare ►*n.* Warfare in which disease-producing microorganisms and bacteria are used to cause death or injury to humans, animals, or plants.

bi•ol•o•gy (bī-ŏl′ə-jē) ►*n.* **1.** The science of life and of living organisms. **2.** The life processes of a particular group or category of living organisms. —**bi•ol′o•gist** *n.*

bi•o•mass (bī′ō-măs′) ►*n.* **1.** The total mass of living matter within a given unit of environmental area. **2.** Plant material, vegetation, or agricultural waste used as a fuel.

bi•ome (bī′ōm′) ►*n.* A major regional biotic community, such as a grassland or desert.

bi•o•me•chan•ics (bī′ō-mĭ-kăn′ĭks) ►*n.* *(takes sing. v.)* The study of the mechanics of a living body, esp. of the forces exerted on the skeletal structure. —**bi′o•me•chan′i•cal** *adj.*

bi•o•med•i•cine (bī′ō-mĕd′ĭ-sĭn) ►*n.* The study of medicine as it relates to all biological systems. —**bi′o•med′i•cal** (-ĭ-kəl) *adj.*

bi•on•ic (bī-ŏn′ĭk) ►*adj.* **1.** Having anatomical structures that are replaced or enhanced esp. by electronic components. **2.** Superhuman. [BI(O)– + (ELECTR)ONIC.]

bi•o•phys•ics (bī′ō-fĭz′ĭks) ►*n.* *(takes sing. v.)* The physics of biological processes. —**bi′o•phys′i•cal** *adj.* —**bi′o•phys′i•cist** *n.*

bi•op•sy (bī′ŏp′sē) ►*n., pl.* **-sies.** The removal and examination of a sample of tissue from a living body for medical diagnosis.

bi•o•re•me•di•a•tion (bī′ō-rĭ-mē′dē-ā′shən) ►*n.* The use of biological agents, such as bacteria or plants, to decontaminate polluted soil or water.

bi•o•re•serve (bī′ō-rĭ-zûrv′) ►*n.* An area containing a wildlife preserve bordered by a zone of less restricted public access.

bi•o•rhythm (bī′ō-rĭ*th*′əm) ►*n.* An innate, cyclical biological process or function.

–biosis ►*suff.* A way of living: *symbiosis.* [< Gk. *biōsis* < *bios*, life.]

bi•o•sphere (bī′ə-sfîr′) ►*n.* The part of the earth and its atmosphere in which living organisms exist.

bi•o•ta (bī-ō′tə) ►*n.* The combined flora and fauna of a region. [< Gk. *biotē*, way of life < *bios*, life.]

bi•o•tech (bī′ō-tĕk′) ►*n. Informal* Biotechnology.

bi•o•tech•nol•o•gy (bī′ō-tĕk-nŏl′ə-jē) ►*n.* **1.** The use of microorganisms or biological substances to perform industrial or manufacturing processes. **2.** See **ergonomics.** —**bi′o•tech′no•log′i•cal** (-nə-lŏj′ĭ-kəl) *adj.*

bi•ot•ic (bī-ŏt′ĭk) ►*adj.* **1.** Of life or living organisms. **2.** Produced by living organisms. [Gk. *biōtikos* < *bios*, life.]

bi•o•tin (bī′ə-tĭn) ►*n.* A crystalline vitamin of the vitamin B complex, found esp. in liver, egg yolk, milk, and yeast. [< Gk. *biōtos*, life < *bios*.]

bi•par•ti•san (bī-pär′tĭ-zən, -sən) ►*adj.* Of, consisting of, or supported by members of two parties, esp. two major political parties. —**bi•par′ti•san•ship′** *n.*

bi•par•tite (bī-pär′tīt′) ►*adj.* **1.** Having or consisting of two parts. **2a.** Having two corresponding parts, one for each party: *a bipartite contract.* **b.** Having two participants: *a bipartite agreement.*

bi•ped (bī′pĕd′) ►*n.* An animal with two feet. ►*adj.* also **bi•ped•al** (bī-pĕd′l). Having two feet; two-footed.

bi•plane (bī′plān′) ►*n.* An airplane having two pairs of wings fixed at different levels, esp. one above and one below the fuselage.

bi•po•lar (bī-pō′lər) ►*adj.* **1.** Of or having two poles. **2.** Having two opposing sides or systems. **3.** *Psychiat.* Of or having a disorder marked by alternating episodes of mania and depression. —**bi′po•lar′i•ty** (-lăr′ĭ-tē) *n.*

bi•ra•cial (bī-rā′shəl) ►*adj.* **1.** Of or consisting of members of two races. **2.** Having parents of two different races. —**bi•ra′cial•ism** *n.*

birch (bûrch) ►*n.* **1a.** Any of various deciduous trees with bark that separates from the wood in sheets. **b.** The hard wood of a birch. **2.** A birch rod used for whipping. ►*v.* To whip with a birch. [< OE *birce.*]

bird (bûrd) ►*n.* **1.** A warm-blooded, egg-laying, feathered vertebrate with forelimbs modified to form wings. **2.** *Slang* A person: *a sly old bird.* —***idiom:*** **for the birds** Objectionable or worthless. [< OE *brid.*]

bird•bath (bûrd′băth′, -bäth′) ►*n.* A water basin for birds to drink from and bathe in.

bird•er (bûr′dər) ►*n.* **1.** A bird watcher. **2a.** A breeder of birds. **b.** A hunter of birds.

bird•house (bûrd′hous′) ►*n.* **1.** A box made as a nesting place for birds. **2.** An aviary.

bird•ie (bûr′dē) ►*n.* **1.** One stroke under par for a hole in golf. **2.** See **shuttlecock.** —**bird′ie** *v.*

bird•lime (bûrd′līm′) ►*n.* A sticky substance that is smeared on branches or twigs to capture small birds.

bird of paradise ►*n., pl.* **birds of paradise** **1.** Any of various New Guinean birds usu. having brilliant plumage and long tail feathers in the male. **2.** A plant having showy orange and blue flowers.

bird's-eye (bûrdz′ī′) ►*adj.* Marked with a spot or spots resembling a bird's eye.

bird•shot (bûrd′shŏt′) ►*n.* A small lead shot for shotgun shells.

bird watcher ►*n.* One who observes and identifies birds in their natural surroundings. —**bird watching** *n.*

bi•ret•ta (bə-rĕt′ə) ►*n.* A stiff square cap worn esp. by the Roman Catholic clergy. [< LLat. *birrus*, hooded cloak.]

Bir•ken•head (bûr′kən-hĕd′) A borough of NW England at the mouth of the Mersey R. near Liverpool. Pop. 341,000.

Bir•ming•ham (bûr′mĭng-hăm′) **1.** (*also* -əm) A city of central England NW of London. Pop. 1,012,351. **2.** A city of N-central AL NNE of Montgomery. Pop. 265,968.

birr (bîr) ►*n., pl.* **birr** or **birrs.** See table at **currency.** [Amharic *bərr*, be white.]

birth (bûrth) ►*n.* **1a.** The fact of being born. **b.** The act of bearing young. **2.** Origin or ancestry: *of Iraqi birth.* **3.** A beginning or commencement. See Syns at **beginning.** ►*v.* **1.** *Regional* To deliver (a baby). **2.** To bear (a child). [ME.]

birth canal ►*n.* The passage from the uterus through the cervix, vagina, and vulva.

birth control ►*n.* Voluntary limitation or control of the number of children conceived, esp. by use of contraceptive techniques.

birth•day (bûrth′dā′) ►*n.* The day or anniversary of one's birth.

birth defect ►*n.* A physiological abnormality present at the time of birth, esp. as a result of faulty development, heredity, or injury.

birth family ►*n.* A family consisting of one's biological, as opposed to adoptive, parents and their offspring.

birth•mark (bûrth′märk′) ►*n.* A mole or blemish present on the skin from birth.

birth parent ►*n.* A biological parent.

birth•place (bûrth′plās′) ►*n.* The place where someone is born or something originates.

birth•rate (bûrth′rāt′) ►*n.* The ratio of live births to total population in a specified community or area over a specified period.

birth•right (bûrth′rīt′) ►*n.* A right, possession, or privilege that is one's due by birth.

birth•stone (bûrth′stōn′) ►*n.* A gemstone associated with the specific month of a person's birth.

Bis•cay (bĭs′kā), **Bay of.** An arm of the Atlantic indenting the W coast of Europe from NW France to NW Spain.

Bis•cayne Bay (bĭs-kān′, bĭs′kān′) An inlet of the Atlantic in SW FL.

bis•cuit (bĭs′kĭt) ►*n.* **1.** A small cake of bread leavened with baking powder or soda. **2.** *Chiefly Brit.* **a.** A thin crisp cracker. **b.** A cookie. **3.** A pale brown. [< Med.Lat. *bis coctus*, twice cooked.]

bi•sect (bī′sĕkt′, bī-sĕkt′) ►*v.* **1.** To cut or divide into two parts, esp. two equal parts. **2.** To split; fork. —**bi•sec′tion** *n.* —**bi′sec′tor** *n.*

bi•sex•u•al (bī-sĕk′shōō-əl) ►*adj.* **1.** Of or relating to both sexes. **2.** Having both male and female organs. **3.** Of or having a sexual orientation to persons of either sex. —**bi•sex′u•al** *n.* —**bi′sex•u•al′i•ty** (-ăl′ĭ-tē) *n.* —**bi•sex′u•al•ly** *adv.*

Bish•kek (bĭsh′kĕk, bēsh′-). Formerly **Frunze.** The capital of Kyrgyzstan, in the N-central part. Pop. 627,800.

bish•op (bĭsh′əp) ►*n.* **1.** A high-ranking Christian cleric, usu. in charge of a diocese. **2.** *Games* A chess piece that can move diagonally across any number of free spaces. [< Gk. *episkopos*, overseer < *skopos*, watcher.]

bish•op•ric (bĭsh′ə-prĭk) ►*n.* The office, rank, or diocese of a bishop. [< OE *bisceoprīce*, diocese of a bishop.]

Bis•marck (bĭz′märk′) The capital of ND, in the S-central part. Pop. 49,256.

Bismarck, Prince **Otto Eduard Leopold von.** "the Iron Chancellor." 1815–98. Creator and first chancellor of the German Empire (1871–90). —**Bis•marck′i•an** *adj.*

Bismarck Archipelago. A group of volcanic islands and islets of Papua New Guinea in the SW Pacific.

bis•muth (bĭz′məth) ►*n.* *Symbol* **Bi** A white, crystalline, brittle metallic element used in low-melting alloys. At. no. 83. See table at **element.** [< obsolete Ger. *Wismuth.*]

bi•son (bī′sən, -zən) ►*n.* A bovine mammal of W North America, having a shaggy mane and massive head with short curved horns; buffalo. [Lat. *bisōn.*]

bisque (bĭsk) ►*n.* **1.** A cream soup made esp. from meat or seafood. **2.** Ice cream mixed with crushed macaroons or nuts. [Fr.]

Bis•sau (bĭ-sou′) The capital of Guinea-Bissau, on an estuary of the Atlantic. Pop. 109,486.

bis•tro (bē′strō, bĭs′trō) ►*n., pl.* **-tros 1.** A small bar, tavern, or nightclub. **2.** A small informal restaurant. [Fr.]

bit[1] (bĭt) ►*n.* **1.** A small portion, degree, or amount. **2.** A moment. **3.** An entertainment routine; act. **4.** A particular kind of action or behavior: *got tired of the macho bit.* **5.** *Informal* An amount equal to ⅛ of a dollar. —***idioms:* a bit** Somewhat: *a bit warm.* **bit by bit** Gradually. [< OE *bita.*]

bit[2] (bĭt) ►*n.* **1.** The sharp part of a tool, such as the cutting edge of an ax. **2.** A pointed and threaded tool for drilling and boring that is secured in a brace, bitstock, or drill press. **3.** The metal mouthpiece of a horse's bridle. [< OE, a biting.]

bit[3] (bĭt) ►*n. Comp. Sci.* A fundamental unit of information having just two possible values, as either of the binary digits 0 or 1. [B(INARY) + (DIG)IT.]

bitch (bĭch) ►*n.* **1.** A female canine animal, esp. a dog. **2.** *Offensive Slang* A spiteful or overbearing woman. **3.** *Slang* A complaint. **4.** *Slang* Something very unpleasant or difficult. ►*v. Slang* To complain. [< OE *bicce.*] —**bitch′y** *adj.*

bite (bīt) ►*v.* **bit** (bĭt), **bit•ten** (bĭt′n) or **bit, bit•ing 1.** To cut, grip, or tear with or as if with the teeth. **2.** To pierce the skin of with or as if with fangs. **3.** To cut into with or as if with a sharp instrument. **4.** To corrode. **5.** To pierce the skin of with or as with fangs. **6.** To take or swallow bait. ►*n.* **1.** The act of biting. **2.** A skin wound or puncture produced by biting. **3a.** A stinging or smarting sensation. **b.** An incisive, penetrating quality. **4a.** A mouthful. **b.** *Informal* A light meal or snack. **5.** The act of taking bait. **6.** The angle at which the upper and lower teeth meet; occlusion. —***idioms:* bite the bullet** *Slang* To face a painful situation bravely and stoically. **bite the dust** *Slang* To fall dead, esp. in combat. [< OE *bītan.*] —**bit′er** *n.*

bite•wing (bīt′wĭng′) ►*n.* A dental x-ray film with a central projection on which the teeth can close.

bit•ing (bī′tĭng) ►*adj.* **1.** Causing a stinging sensation. **2.** Incisive; penetrating.

bit map ►*n. Comp. Sci.* A set of bits representing a graphic image, with each bit or group of bits corresponding to a pixel in the image. —**bit′-mapped′** *adj.*

bit•ter (bĭt′ər) ►*adj.* **-er, -est 1.** Having or being a taste that is sharp and unpleasant. **2.** Causing sharp pain to the body or great discomfort to the mind: *a bitter wind; bitter sorrow.* **3.** Proceeding from or exhibiting strong animosity. **4.** Having or marked by resentment or disappointment: *bitter feelings.* ►*adv.* In an intense or harsh way; bitterly: *a bitter cold night.* ►*n.* **bitters** A bitter, usu. alcoholic liquid made with herbs or roots and used in cocktails or as a tonic. [< OE.] —**bit′ter•ly** *adv.* —**bit′ter•ness** *n.*

Syns: *bitter, acerbic, acrid* **adj.**

bit•tern (bĭt′ərn) ►*n.* A wading bird having mottled brownish plumage and a deep booming cry. [< OFr. *butor.*]

bit•ter•sweet (bĭt′ər-swēt′) ►*n.* **1.** A woody vine having small, round, yellow-orange fruits that split open to expose red seeds. **2.** See **bittersweet nightshade.** ►*adj.* **1.** Bitter and sweet at the same time. **2.** Producing or expressing a mixture of pain and pleasure.

bittersweet nightshade ►*n.* A poisonous climbing or trailing plant having violet flowers and red berries.

bit•ty (bĭt′ē) ►*adj.* **-ti•er, -ti•est.** *Informal* Tiny. —**bit•ti•ness** *n.*

bi•tu•men (bĭ-to͞o′mən, -tyo͞o′-, bī-) ►*n.* Any of various flammable mixtures of hydrocarbons and other substances that are constituents of asphalt and tar. [< Lat.]

bi•tu•mi•nous (bĭ-to͞o′mə-nəs, -tyo͞o′-, bī-) ►*adj.* Like or containing bitumen.

bituminous coal ►*n.* A mineral coal with a high percentage of volatile matter that burns with a smoky yellow flame; soft coal.

bi•va•lent (bī-vā′lənt) ►*adj. Chem.* Divalent.

bi•valve (bī′vălv′) ►*n.* A mollusk, such as an oyster or clam, that has a shell consisting of two hinged valves. —**bi′valve′** *adj.*

biv•ou•ac (bĭv′o͞o-ăk′, bĭv′wăk′) ►*n.* A temporary encampment, esp. one made by soldiers. ►*v.* **-acked, -ack•ing.** To camp in a bivouac. [Fr.]

bi•week•ly (bī-wēk′lē) ►*adj.* **1.** Happening every two weeks. **2.** Happening twice a week; semiweekly. ►*n., pl.* **-lies.** A publication issued every two weeks. See Usage Note at **bi–.** —**bi•week′ly** *adv.*

bi•year•ly (bī-yîr′lē) ►*adj.* **1.** Happening every two years. **2.** Happening twice a year; semiyearly. —**bi•year′ly** *adv.*

bi•zarre (bĭ-zär′) ►*adj.* Strikingly unconventional in style or appearance; odd. [< Sp. *bizarro,* brave.] —**bi•zarre′ly** *adv.*

Bi•zet (bē-zā′), **Alexandre César Léopold.** "Georges." 1838–75. French composer.

Bk ► The symbol for the element **berkelium.**

bl. ►*abbr.* barrel

B/L ►*abbr.* bill of lading

blab (blăb) ►*v.* **blabbed, blab•bing 1.** To reveal (secret matters) esp. through careless talk. **2.** To chatter indiscreetly. [ME *blabben.*] —**blab** *n.*

blab•ber (blăb′ər) ►*v.* To chatter; blab. [ME *blaberen.*] —**blab′ber** *n.*

blab•ber•mouth (blăb′ər-mouth′) ►*n. Informal* A gossip or chatterbox.

black (blăk) ►*adj.* **-er, -est 1.** Being of the color black. **2.** Without light: *a black, moonless night.* **3.** often **Black a.** Of or belonging to a racial group having brown to black skin, esp. one of African origin. **b.** African-American. **4.** Soiled, as from soot; dirty. **5.** Evil; wicked: *black deeds.* **6.** Depressing; gloomy. **7.** Angry; sullen. **8.** Marked by morbid or grimly satiric humor: *a black comedy.* ►*n.* **1.** The achromatic color of maximum darkness; the color of objects that absorb nearly all light of all visible wavelengths. **2.** Absence of light; darkness. **3.** Something colored black, esp. clothing worn for mourning. **4.** often **Black a.** A member of a racial group having brown to black skin. **b.** An African American. ►*v.* To make or become black. —***phrasal verb:* black out 1.** To lose consciousness or memory temporarily. **2.** To produce or cause a blackout. —***idiom:* in the black** On the credit side of a ledger. [< OE *blæc.*] —**black′ish** *adj.* —**black′ly** *adv.* —**black′ness** *n.*

Usage: *Black* is often capitalized in its use to denote persons, though the lowercased form *black* is still widely used by authors of all races. Use of the capitalized form has the advantage of acknowledging the parallel with other ethnic groups and nationalities, such as *Italian* and *Sioux.*

black-and-blue (blăk′ən-bloo′) ▶*adj.* Discolored from bruising.

black and white ▶*n.* **1.** Writing or print. **2.** A visual medium, such as photography, using black and white, and sometimes values of gray. —**black′-and-white′** *adj.*

black•ball (blăk′bôl′) ▶*n.* **1.** A negative vote, esp. one that blocks the admission of an applicant to an organization. **2.** A small black ball used as a negative ballot. ▶*v.* **1.** To vote against (e.g., an applicant). **2.** To ostracize.

Syns: *blackball, blacklist, boycott, ostracize* ***Ant:*** *admit* ***v.***

black bear ▶*n.* The common North American bear, having a black or dark brown coat.

black belt ▶*n.* **1.** The rank of expert in a martial art such as judo or karate. **2.** The black sash that symbolizes this rank.

black•ber•ry (blăk′bĕr′ē) ▶*n.* **1.** Any of various shrubs having usu. prickly, canelike stems and black or purplish edible fruit. **2.** The fruit of these plants.

black•bird (blăk′bûrd′) ▶*n.* Any of various birds, such as the grackle or cowbird, having predominantly black plumage.

black•board (blăk′bôrd′, -bōrd′) ▶*n.* A smooth panel for writing on with chalk.

black•bod•y (blăk′bŏd′ē) ▶*n.* A theoretically perfect absorber of all incident radiation.

black box ▶*n.* **1.** A usu. electronic device with known performance characteristics but unknown constituents and means of operation. **2.** See **flight recorder.**

Black Death ▶*n.* A form of bubonic plague pandemic in Europe and Asia in the 14th cent. [From the dark splotches it causes.]

Black Death
costume worn by a physician to ward off the disease

black•en (blăk′ən) ▶*v.* **1.** To make or become black. **2.** To defame. —**black′en•er** *n.*

black eye ▶*n.* **1.** Bruised discoloration of the skin around the eye. **2.** A dishonored reputation.

black-eyed Su•san (blăk′īd′ soo′zən) ▶*n.* A plant having daisylike flowers with orange-yellow rays and dark brown centers.

black•face (blăk′fās′) ▶*n.* Makeup for a conventionalized comic travesty of Black people, esp. in a minstrel show.

black•fish (blăk′fĭsh′) ▶*n.* See **pilot whale.**

Black•foot (blăk′fo͝ot′) ▶*n., pl.* **-foot** or **-feet** **1.** A member of a Native American confederacy of three tribes inhabiting the N Great Plains from central Alberta to NW Montana. **2.** Their Algonquian language.

Black Forest. A mountainous region of SW Germany between the Rhine and Neckar rivers.

black•guard (blăg′ərd, -ärd′) ▶*n.* A thoroughly unprincipled person; scoundrel.

Black Hawk. 1767–1838. Sauk leader in the Black Hawk War (1832).

black•head (blăk′hĕd′) ▶*n.* A plug of dried fatty matter that clogs a pore in the skin and is blackened at the surface.

Black Hills. A group of mountains of SW SD and NE WY.

black hole ▶*n.* An area of space-time with a gravitational field so intense that nothing can escape, not even light.

black•jack (blăk′jăk′) ▶*n.* **1.** A small leather-covered bludgeon with a short flexible shaft. **2.** A card game in which the object is to accumulate cards with a higher count than that of the dealer but not exceeding 21.

black light ▶*n.* Invisible ultraviolet or infrared radiation.

black•list (blăk′lĭst′) ▶*n.* A list of disapproved persons or organizations. ▶*v.* To place on a blacklist. See Syns at **blackball.**

black lung ▶*n.* A lung disease caused by the long-term inhalation of coal dust.

black magic ▶*n.* Magic practiced for evil purposes or in league with evil spirits.

black•mail (blăk′māl′) ▶*n.* **1.** Extortion by the threat of exposing something criminal or discreditable. **2.** Something extorted by blackmail. [BLACK + Sc. *mail*, rent.] —**black′mail′** *v.* —**black′mail′er** *n.*

black market ▶*n.* The illegal buying or selling of goods or currency. —**black′-mar′ket•er, black′-mar′ket•eer′** *n.*

Black Muslim ▶*n.* A member of the Nation of Islam, a religious group espousing Islamic principles and favoring social and economic independence for African Americans.

black•out (blăk′out′) ▶*n.* **1.** The concealment or extinguishment of lights that might be visible to enemy aircraft during an air raid. **2.** Lack of illumination caused by an electrical power failure. **3.** A temporary loss of memory or consciousness. **4a.** A suppression, as of news, by censorhip. **b.** Restriction of local telecasting of a sports event.

black pepper ▶*n.* **1.** A peppercorn. **2.** A pungent spice made from ground peppercorns.

Black Power ▶*n.* A movement among Black Americans to achieve equality esp. through Black political and cultural institutions.

Black Sea. An inland sea between Europe and Asia, connected with the Aegean by the Bosporus, the Sea of Marmara, and the Dardanelles.

black sheep ▶*n.* A member of a family or group who is considered disgraceful.

black•smith (blăk′smĭth′) ▶*n.* One who forges and shapes iron with an anvil and hammer.

black•snake (blăk′snāk′) ▶*n.* Any of various dark-colored, chiefly nonvenomous snakes.

Black•stone (blăk′stōn′, -stən), Sir **William.** 1723–80. British jurist and educator.

black•thorn (blăk′thôrn′) ►*n.* A thorny Eurasian shrub with white flowers and bluish-black, plumlike fruits used as a flavoring.

black tie ►*n.* **1.** A black bow tie worn with a dinner jacket. **2.** Semiformal evening wear, esp. for men.

black•top (blăk′tŏp′) ►*n.* A bituminous material, such as asphalt, used to pave roads.

Black•well (blăk′wĕl, -wəl), **Elizabeth.** 1821–1910. British-born Amer. physician.

black widow ►*n.* A black spider, the female of which has red markings and produces extremely toxic venom.

blad•der (blăd′ər) ►*n. Anat.* Any of various distensible membranous sacs, such as the urinary bladder or the swim bladder, found in most animals and that serve as receptacles for fluid or gas. [< OE *blǣdre.*]

blade (blād) ►*n.* **1.** The flat-edged cutting part of a sharpened weapon or tool. **2.** A dashing youth. **3.** A flat thin part or structure similar to a blade: *the blade of an oar; a blade of grass.* ►*v.* **blad•ed, blad•ing.** To skate on in-line skates. [< OE *blæd.*] —**blad′ed** *adj.*

blain (blān) ►*n.* A skin swelling or sore. [< OE *blegen.*]

Blair (blâr), **Anthony Charles Lynton.** "Tony." b. 1953. British prime minister (since 1997).

Tony Blair

Blake (blāk), **William.** 1757–1827. British poet and artist.

blam•a•ble also **blame•a•ble** (blā′mə-bəl) ►*adj.* Deserving blame; culpable. See Syns at **blameworthy.** —**blam′a•bly** *adv.*

blame (blām) ►*v.* **blamed, blam•ing 1.** To hold responsible. **2.** To find fault with; censure. ►*n.* **1.** Responsibility for a fault or error; culpability. **2.** Censure, as for a fault; condemnation. [< LLat. *blasphēmāre*, reproach. See BLASPHEME.] —**blame′less** *adj.*

blame•wor•thy (blām′wûr′*thē*) ►*adj.* Deserving blame. —**blame′wor′thi•ness** *n.*

Syns: *blameworthy, blamable, culpable, reprehensible* ***Ant:*** *blameless* ***adj.***

Blanc (blăngk, bläɴ), **Mont.** The highest peak of the Alps, rising to 4.810.2 m (15,771 ft) in SE France on the Italian border.

blanch (blănch) ►*v.* **1.** To bleach. **2.** To make or become pale or white. **3.** To scald (food) briefly, as before freezing. [< OFr. *blanchir.*]

blanc•mange (blə-mänj′, -mäɴzh′) ►*n.* A flavored, sweet milk pudding. [< OFr. *blanc mangier*, white food.]

bland (blănd) ►*adj.* **-er, -est 1.** Characterized by a moderate, unperturbed, or tranquil quality. **2.** Not irritating; soothing: *a bland diet.* **3.** Lacking a distinctive character; dull and insipid. [Lat. *blandus*, flattering.] —**bland′ly** *adv.* —**bland′ness** *n.*

blan•dish (blăn′dĭsh) ►*v.* To coax by flattery or wheedling; cajole. [< Lat. *blandus*, flattering.] —**blan′dish•ment** *n.*

blank (blăngk) ►*adj.* **-er, -est 1a.** Devoid of writing, images, or marks. **b.** Containing no information: *a blank diskette.* **2.** Not completed or filled in. **3.** Not having received final processing: *a blank key.* **4.** Lacking thought, impression, or expression; vacant: *a blank mind.* **5.** Appearing dazed or confused; bewildered: *a blank stare.* **6.** Absolute; complete: *a blank refusal.* ►*n.* **1.** An empty space or place; void. **2a.** A space to be filled in on a document. **b.** A document with such spaces. **3.** An unfinished manufactured article ready for final processing: *a key blank.* **4.** A gun cartridge with a powder charge but no bullet. ►*v.* **1.** To remove, as from view; obliterate. **2.** *Sports* To prevent (an opponent) from scoring. **3.** To become abstracted: *My mind blanked out for a few seconds.* [< OFr. *blanc*, white.] —**blank′ly** *adv.* —**blank′ness** *n.*

blank check ►*n.* **1.** A signed check without the amount filled in. **2.** Total freedom of action.

blan•ket (blăng′kĭt) ►*n.* **1.** A piece of woven material used as a covering. **2.** A layer that covers or encloses. ►*adj.* Applying to all conditions, instances, or members: *a blanket insurance policy.* ►*v.* To cover with or as if with a blanket. [< OFr., unbleached soft cloth < *blanc*, white.]

blank verse ►*n.* Unrhymed verse, esp. in iambic pentameter.

Blan•tyre (blăn-tīr′) A city of S Malawi. Pop. 331,588.

blare (blâr) ►*v.* **blared, blar•ing.** To sound or cause to sound loudly and stridently. [ME *bleren.*] —**blare** *n.*

blar•ney (blär′nē) ►*n.* Smooth, flattering talk. [After the *Blarney* Stone in Ireland.]

bla•sé (blä-zā′) ►*adj.* **1.** Uninterested or bored. **2.** Very sophisticated. [Fr.]

blas•pheme (blăs-fēm′, blăs′fēm′) ►*v.* **-phemed, -phem•ing.** To speak of (God or a sacred entity) in an irreverent, impious manner. [< Gk. *blasphēmein.*] —**blas•phem′er** *n.* —**blas′phe•mous** *adj.* —**blas′phe•mous•ly** *adv.* —**blas′phe•my** *n.*

blast (blăst) ►*n.* **1.** A strong gust of wind. **2.** A forcible stream of air, gas, or steam from an opening. **3.** A sudden loud sound, as of a whistle or trumpet. **4.** An explosion, as of dynamite or a bomb. **5.** Any of various plant diseases; blight. **6.** A powerful hit, blow, or shot. **7.** A violent verbal assault. **8.** *Slang* A highly exciting or pleasurable experience. ►*v.* **1.** To explode. **2.** To sound loudly; blare. **3.** To hit with great force. **4.** To have a harmful or destructive effect (on). **5.** To criticize vigorously. **6.** To shoot. —***phrasal verb:*** **blast off** To take off, as a rocket or space vehicle. —***idiom:*** **full blast** At full speed, volume, or capacity. [< OE *blǣst.*] —**blast′er** *n.*

Syns: *blast, blight, dash, nip, wreck* ***v.***

blast furnace ►*n.* A furnace in which combustion is intensified by a blast of air.

blast•off (blăst′ôf′, -ŏf′) ►*n.* The launch, esp. of a rocket or space vehicle.

bla•tant (blāt′nt) ►*adj.* **1.** Unpleasantly loud and noisy. **2.** Offensively conspicuous or undisguised: *a blatant lie.* [< Lat. *blatīre*, blab.] —**bla′tan•cy** *n.* —**bla′tant•ly** *adv.*

blath•er (blăth′ər) ►*v.* To talk foolishly or nonsensically. [ON *bladhra.*] —**blath′er** *n.* —**blath′er•er** *n.*

blaze¹ (blāz) ►*n.* **1a.** A brilliant burst of fire; flame. **b.** A destructive fire. **2.** A bright, direct, or steady light: *the blaze of the desert sun.* **3.** A brilliant, striking display: *a blaze of color.* **4.** A sudden outburst, as of activity or emotion. **5. blazes** Used as an intensive: *Where in blazes are my keys?* ►*v.* **blazed, blaz•ing 1.** To burn or shine brightly. **2.** To show strong emotion. **3.** To shoot rapidly and continuously. [< OE *blæse.*]

blaze² (blāz) ►*n.* **1.** A white or light-colored spot on the face of an animal. **2.** A mark cut or painted on a tree to indicate a trail. ►*v.* **blazed, blaz•ing.** To indicate (a trail) by marking trees with blazes. [Of Gmc. orig.]

blaze²

blaz•er (blā′zər) ►*n.* An informal sports jacket.

bla•zon (blā′zən) ►*v.* **1.** To adorn or embellish with or as if with a coat of arms. **2.** To display ostentatiously. ►*n.* A coat of arms. [< OFr. *blason*, shield.] —**bla′zon•ry** *n.*

bldg. ►*abbr.* building

bleach (blēch) ►*v.* To make or become white or colorless. ►*n.* A chemical agent used for bleaching. [< OE *blǣcan.*]

bleach•ers (blē′chərz) ►*pl.n.* An outdoor grandstand for seating spectators.

bleak (blēk) ►*adj.* **-er, -est 1.** Dreary and somber; depressing: *a bleak prognosis.* **2.** Cold; raw: *bleak winds.* **3.** Exposed to the elements; barren. [< ON *bleikr*, pale.] —**bleak′ly** *adv.* —**bleak′ness** *n.*

blear (blîr) ►*v.* **1.** To blur or redden (the eyes) with or as if with tears. **2.** To dim or obscure; blur. ►*adj.* Indistinct. [ME *bleren.*] —**blear′i•ly** *adv.* —**blear′i•ness** *n.* —**blear′y** *adj.*

bleat (blēt) ►*n.* **1.** The characteristic cry of a goat, sheep, or calf. **2.** A sound similar to this cry. [< OE *blǣtan.*] —**bleat** *v.*

bleed (blēd) ►*v.* **bled** (blĕd), **bleed•ing 1a.** To emit or lose blood. **b.** To extract blood from. **2.** To feel sympathetic grief or anguish: *My heart bleeds for you.* **3.** To exude or extract a fluid such as sap (from). **4.** To extort money from. **5.** To run together, as dyes on wet cloth or paper. **6.** To draw or drain liquid or gaseous contents from: *bleed the pipes.* [< OE *blēdan.*]

bleed•er (blē′dər) ►*n.* One that bleeds freely, esp. a hemophiliac.

bleed•ing heart (blē′dĭng) ►*n.* **1.** A garden plant having arching pink heart-shaped flowers. **2.** One who is excessively sympathetic toward others.

bleep (blēp) ►*n.* A brief high-pitched electronic sound. ►*v.* **1.** To emit a bleep or bleeps. **2.** To edit out (spoken material) from a broadcast or recording, esp. by replacing with bleeps. [Imit.]

blem•ish (blĕm′ĭsh) ►*v.* To mar, spoil, or impair by a flaw. ►*n.* A flaw or defect. [< OFr. *blemir*, make pale.]

blench (blĕnch) ►*v.* To draw back, as from fear; flinch. [< OE *blencan*, deceive.]

blend (blĕnd) ►*v.* **blend•ed** or **blent** (blĕnt), **blend•ing 1.** To make or form a uniform mixture. **2.** To combine (varieties or grades) to obtain a new mixture: *blend whiskeys.* **3.** To become merged into one; unite. **4.** To create a harmonious effect or result: *colors that blend well.* ►*n.* **1.** Something blended: *a blend of coffee and chicory.* **2.** *Ling.* A word produced by combining parts of other words, as *smog* from *smoke* and *fog.* [Prob. < ON *blanda.*]

blend•er (blĕn′dər) ►*n.* One that blends, esp. an appliance for chopping, mixing, or liquefying foods.

bless (blĕs) ►*v.* **blessed** or **blest** (blĕst), **bless•ing 1.** To make holy by religious rite; sanctify. **2.** To make the sign of the cross over. **3.** To invoke divine favor upon. **4.** To honor as holy; glorify: *Bless the Lord.* **5.** To confer well-being or prosperity upon. **6.** To endow, as with talent. [< OE *blētsian*, consecrate.]

bless•ed (blĕs′ĭd) ►*adj.* **1.** Worthy of worship; holy. **2.** Enjoying happiness; fortunate. **3.** Bringing happiness or pleasure. **4.** Used as an intensive: *I don't have a blessed dime.* —**bless′ed•ly** *adv.* —**bless′ed•ness** *n.*

bless•ing (blĕs′ĭng) ►*n.* **1.** The act or ceremony of one who blesses. **2.** A short prayer said at a meal; grace. **3.** Something promoting or contributing to happiness, well-being, or prosperity; boon. **4.** Approbation; approval: *This plan has my blessing.*

blew¹ (blo͞o) ►*v.* P.t. of **blow¹**.

blew² (blo͞o) ►*v.* P.t. of **blow³**.

Bligh (blī), **William.** 1754–1817. British naval officer.

blight (blīt) ►*n.* **1.** A plant disease caused esp. by a bacterium, fungus, or virus. **2.** An adverse environmental condition, such as air pollution. **3.** Something that impairs growth or withers hopes. ►*v.* **1.** To affect with blight. **2.** To ruin. See Syns at **blast. 3.** To frustrate. [?]

blimp (blĭmp) ►*n.* A nonrigid, buoyant airship. [?]

blind (blīnd) ►*adj.* **-er, -est 1a.** Sightless. **b.** Greatly impaired in vision. **2.** Of or for sightless persons. **3.** Performed by instruments and without the use of sight: *blind navigation.* **4.** Unable or unwilling to perceive or understand: *blind to a child's faults.* **5.** Not based on reason or evidence: *blind faith.* **6.** Hidden or screened from sight: *a blind seam; a blind intersection.* **7.** Closed at one end: *a blind passage.* **8.** Having no opening: *a blind wall.* ►*n.* **1.** Something, such as a window shade, that shuts out light. **2.** A shelter for concealing hunters. **3.** A subterfuge. ►*adv.* **1.** Without seeing; blindly. **2.** Used as an intensive: *Thieves robbed us blind.* ►*v.* **1.** To deprive of sight. **2.** To dazzle. **3.** To deprive of perception, insight, or reason: *Prejudice blinded them.* [< OE.] —**blind′ly** *adv.* —**blind′ness** *n.*

blind alley ►*n.* **1.** An alley or passageway that is closed at one end. **2.** A mistaken, unproductive undertaking.

blind date ►*n.* **1.** A social engagement between two persons who have not previously met. **2.** Either of the persons participating in such a date.

blind•ers (blīn′dərz) ►*pl.n.* A pair of leather flaps attached to a horse's bridle to curtail side vision.

blind•fold (blīnd′fōld′) ►*v.* **1.** To cover the eyes of with or as if with a bandage to prevent seeing. **2.** To mislead or delude. [< OE *geblindfellian*, strike blind.] —**blind′fold′** *n.* —**blind′fold′ed** *adj.*

blind side ►*n.* **1.** The side on which one's peripheral vision is obstructed. **2.** The side away from which one is directing one's attention.

blind-side (blīnd′sīd′) ►*v.* **1.** To hit or attack on the blind side. **2.** To take unawares, esp. with harmful results.

blind spot ►*n.* **1.** The small, optically insensitive region of the eye where the optic nerve enters the retina. **2.** A subject about which one is ignorant or prejudiced.

blink (blĭngk) ►*v.* **1.** To close and open (one or both eyes) rapidly. **2.** To flash on and off. **3.** To look with feigned ignorance: *blink at corruption.* ►*n.* **1.** A brief closing of the eyes. **2.** A flash of light; twinkle. —***idiom:* on the blink** Out of working order. [ME *blinken*, move suddenly.]

blink•er (blĭng′kər) ►*n.* **1.** One that blinks, esp. a light that conveys a signal. **2. blinkers.** See **blinders.**

blintz (blĭnts) ►*n.* A thin rolled pancake usu. filled with cottage cheese and often served with sour cream. [Yiddish *blintse.*]

blip (blĭp) ►*n.* **1.** A spot of light on a radar or sonar screen. **2.** A high-pitched electronic sound; bleep. ►*v.* **blipped, blip•ping.** To bleep. [Imit.]

bliss (blĭs) ►*n.* **1.** Extreme happiness; ecstasy. **2.** Religious ecstasy; spiritual joy. [< OE.] —**bliss′ful** *adj.* —**bliss′ful•ly** *adv.*

blis•ter (blĭs′tər) ►*n.* **1.** A local swelling of the skin that contains watery fluid and is caused by burning or irritation. **2.** Something resembling a blister, such as a raised plastic bubble. [Prob. < OFr. *blestre.*] —**blis′ter** *v.* —**blis′ter•y** *adj.*

blis•ter•ing (blĭs′tər-ĭng) ►*adj.* **1.** Intensely hot. **2.** Harsh; severe: *blistering criticism.* **3.** Very rapid: *a blistering pace.*

blister pack ►*n.* A form of packaging in which the merchandise is sealed into a transparent plastic blister.

BLit or **BLitt** ►*abbr.* *Lat.* Baccalaureus Litterarum (Bachelor of Literature)

blithe (blīth, blīth) ►*adj.* **blith•er, blith•est.** Carefree and lighthearted. [< OE *blīthe.*] —**blithe′ly** *adv.* —**blithe′ness** *n.*

blith•er (blĭth′ər) ►*v.* To blather. [Alteration of BLATHER.]

blithe•some (blīth′səm, blīth′-) ►*adj.* Cheerful; merry. —**blithe′some•ly** *adv.* —**blith′some•ness** *n.*

blitz (blĭts) ►*n.* **1a.** A blitzkrieg. **b.** A heavy aerial bombardment. **2.** An intense campaign: *a media blitz.* **3.** *Football* A rushing of the quarterback by the defensive team, esp. in a passing situation. [< BLITZKRIEG.] —**blitz** *v.*

blitz•krieg (blĭts′krēg′) ►*n.* A swift, sudden military offensive, usu. by combined air and land forces. [Ger., lightning war.]

bliz•zard (blĭz′ərd) ►*n.* A very heavy snowstorm with high winds. [?]

blk. ►*abbr.* **1.** block **2.** bulk

bloat (blōt) ►*v.* To make or become swollen or inflated, as with liquid or gas. [< ON *blautr*, soft.]

blob (blŏb) ►*n.* **1.** A soft formless mass: *a blob of wax.* **2.** A splotch of color. ►*v.* **blobbed, blob•bing.** To splotch. [< ME *blober*, bubble.]

bloc (blŏk) ►*n.* A group of nations, parties, or persons united by common interests. [< OFr. BLOCK.]

block (blŏk) ►*n.* **1.** A solid piece of a hard substance, such as wood or stone, having one or more flat sides. **2.** A stand from which articles are displayed at an auction. **3.** A pulley or a system of pulleys set in a casing. **4.** A set of like items, such as tickets or shares of stock, sold or handled as a unit. **5a.** A section of a city or town bounded on each side by consecutive streets. **b.** A segment of a street bounded by consecutive cross streets. **6.** The act of obstructing. **7.** Something that obstructs; obstacle; hindrance. **8.** *Sports* An act of bodily obstruction. **9.** *Medic.* Interruption, esp. obstruction, of a neural, digestive, or other physiological function. **10.** *Psychol.* Sudden cessation of speech or a thought process without an immediate observable cause. **11.** *Slang* The human head. ►*v.* **1.** To support, strengthen, or retain in place by means of a block. **2.** To shape or form with or on a block: *block a hat.* **3a.** To stop or impede the passage of: *block traffic.* **b.** To shut out from view: *a curtain blocking the stage.* **4.** To indicate broadly; sketch: *block out a plan of action.* **5.** *Sports* To obstruct by physical interference. **6.** *Medic.* To interrupt the proper functioning of (a physiological process). **7.** *Psychol.* To fail to remember. —***idiom:* on the block** Up for sale. [< MDu. *blok.*] —**block′age** *n.* —**block′er** *n.*

Syns: *block, hide, obscure, obstruct, screen, shroud* **v.**

block•ade (blŏ-kād′) ►*n.* **1.** The hostile isolation of a nation, city, or harbor so as to prevent traffic and commerce. **2.** The forces used in a blockade. ►*v.* **-ad•ed, -ad•ing.** To set up a blockade against.

block and tackle ►*n.* An apparatus of pulley blocks and ropes or cables used for hauling and hoisting.

block•bust•er (blŏk′bŭs′tər) ►*n.* **1.** Something, such as a film, that achieves enormous success. **2.** A high-explosive bomb used for demolition purposes.

block•bust•ing (blŏk′bŭs′tĭng) ►*n.* *Informal* The practice of persuading homeowners to sell quickly, usu. at a loss, by appealing to the fear that encroaching minority groups will cause property values to decline.

block grant ►*n.* An unrestricted federal grant, as to a state.

block•head (blŏk′hĕd′) ►*n.* A stupid person.

block•house (blŏk′hous′) ►*n.* **1.** A wooden or concrete fortification. **2.** A heavily reinforced building from which the launching of missiles or space vehicles is observed.

blockhouse
Ft. Abraham Lincoln State Park, Mandan, North Dakota

Bloem•fon•tein (blo͞om′fŏn-tān′) A city of central South Africa ESE of Kimberley. Pop. 104,381.

bloke (blōk) ►*n. Chiefly Brit.* A man. [?]

blond also **blonde** (blŏnd) ►*adj.* **blond•er, blond•est 1.** Having light or fair hair and skin. **2.** Of a flaxen or golden color: *blond hair.* ►*n.* **1.** A blond person. **2.** A light yellowish brown. [< OFr.] —**blond′ness** *n.*

blood (blŭd) ►*n.* **1a.** The fluid consisting of plasma, blood cells, and platelets that is circulated by the heart in vertebrates, carrying oxygen and nutrients to and waste materials away from all body tissues. **b.** A functionally similar fluid in an invertebrate. **2.** A vital force; lifeblood. **3.** Bloodshed; murder. **4.** Temperament or disposition: *hot blood; sporting blood.* **5.** Kinship: *related by blood.* **6.** National or racial ancestry. **7.** Membership; personnel: *new blood in the organization.* **8.** A dandy. —***idiom:* in cold blood** Deliberately and dispassionately. [< OE *blōd.*] —**blood′less** *adj.*

blood bank ►*n.* A place where whole blood or plasma is stored for use in transfusion.

blood•bath (blŭd′băth′, -bäth′) ►*n.* A massacre.

blood count ►*n.* A test in which the cells in a blood sample are classified and counted.

blood•cur•dling (blŭd′kûrd′lĭng) ►*adj.* Causing great horror; terrifying.

blood•ed (blŭd′ĭd) ►*adj.* **1.** Having blood or a temperament of a specified kind: *cold-blooded.* **2.** Thoroughbred: *blooded horses.*

blood group ►*n.* Any of several genetically determined classes of human blood that are based on the presence or absence of certain antigens.

blood•hound (blŭd′hound′) ►*n.* A hound with drooping ears, sagging jowls, and a keen sense of smell, used in tracking.

blood•let•ting (blŭd′lĕt′ĭng) ►*n.* **1.** Bloodshed. **2.** Phlebotomy.

blood•line (blŭd′līn′) ►*n.* Direct line of descent; pedigree.

blood poisoning ►*n.* **1.** See **septicemia. 2.** See **toxemia.**

blood pressure ►*n.* The pressure exerted by the blood against the walls of the blood vessels, esp. the arteries.

blood sausage also **blood pudding** ►*n.* A link sausage made of pig's blood and pork fat.

blood•shed (blŭd′shĕd′) ►*n.* The injury or killing of humans.

blood•shot (blŭd′shŏt′) ►*adj.* Red and inflamed from congested blood vessels: *bloodshot eyes.*

blood•stain (blŭd′stān′) ►*n.* A discoloration caused by blood. —**blood′stained′** *adj.*

blood•stream (blŭd′strēm′) ►*n.* The blood flowing through a circulatory system.

blood•suck•er (blŭd′sŭk′ər) ►*n.* **1.** An animal, such as a leech, that sucks blood. **2.** An extortionist. —**blood′suck′ing** *adj.*

blood•thirst•y (blŭd′thûr′stē) ►*adj.* Eager for bloodshed. —**blood′thirst′i•ly** *adv.* —**blood′thirst′i•ness** *n.*

blood vessel ►*n.* An elastic tubular channel, such as an artery, vein, or capillary, through which blood circulates.

blood•y (blŭd′ē) ►*adj.* **-i•er, -i•est 1.** Of, emitting, or stained with blood. **2.** Causing or marked by bloodshed: *a bloody fight.* **3.** Used as an intensive: *a bloody fool.* ►*adv.* Used as an intensive: *bloody well right.* ►*v.* **-ied, -y•ing.** To stain with or as if with blood. —**blood′i•ly** *adv.* —**blood′i•ness** *n.*

bloody mary also **Bloody Mary** ►*n.* A drink made with vodka and tomato juice.

bloom (blo͞om) ►*n.* **1.** The flower of a plant. **2a.** The condition or time of flowering: *a rose in bloom.* **b.** A time of vigor, freshness, and beauty; prime. **3.** A fresh, rosy complexion. **4.** A powdery coating on some fruits or leaves. **5.** A dense growth of plankton. ►*v.* **1.** To bear flowers. **2.** To shine with health and vigor; glow. **3.** To grow or flourish. [< ON *blōm.*]

Syns: *bloom, blossom, efflorescence, florescence, flower, flush, prime* **n.**

Bloom•er (blo͞o′mər), **Amelia Jenks.** 1818–94. Amer. social reformer.

bloom•ers (blo͞o′mərz) ►*pl.n.* Women's wide loose pants or underpants gathered at the knee. [< Amelia Jenks BLOOMER.]

bloop•er (blo͞o′pər) ►*n.* **1.** *Informal* An embarrassing mistake; faux pas. **2.** *Baseball* A short, weakly hit fly ball.

blos•som (blŏs′əm) ►*n.* **1.** A flower or cluster of flowers. **2.** The condition or time of flowering: *peach trees in blossom.* **3.** A period or condition of maximum development. See Syns at **bloom.** ►*v.* **1.** To flower; bloom. **2.** To develop; flourish. [< OE *blōstm.*]

blot (blŏt) ►*n.* **1.** A spot or stain: *a blot of ink.* **2.** A moral blemish; disgrace. See Syns at **stain.** ►*v.* **blot•ted, blot•ting 1.** To spot or stain. **2.** To bring moral disgrace to. **3.** To obliterate; cancel. **4.** To make obscure; hide. **5.** To soak up or dry with absorbent material. **6.** To make a blot. **7.** To become blotted. [ME.]

blotch (blŏch) ►*n.* **1.** A spot or blot; splotch. **2.** A discoloration on the skin; blemish. [Prob. blend of BLOT and BOTCH.] —**blotch** *v.* —**blotch′i•ness** *n.* —**blotch′y** *adj.*

blot•ter (blŏt′ər) ►*n.* **1.** A piece of blotting paper. **2.** A book containing daily records of occurrences: *a police blotter.*

blot•ting paper (blŏt′ĭng) ►*n.* Absorbent paper used to dry a surface or soak up excess ink.

blouse (blous, blouz) ►*n.* **1.** A loosely fitting shirtlike garment. **2.** The jacket of certain US armed forces uniforms. ►*v.* **bloused, blous•ing.** To hang loosely. [Fr.]

blow[1] (blō) ►*v.* **blew** (blo͞o), **blown** (blōn), **blow•ing 1.** To be in a state of motion, as air or wind. **2a.** To be carried by the wind: *Her hat blew away.* **b.** To cause to move by means of a current of air. **3.** To drive a current of air upon, in, or through. **4a.** To expel a current of air, as from a bellows. **b.** To expel (air), as from the mouth. **c.** To clear by forcing air through: *blow one's nose.* **5.** To sound by expelling a current of air: *blow a trumpet.* **6.** To pant. **7a.** To burst suddenly: *The tire blew.* **b.** To cause to explode. **8.** To melt (a fuse). **9.** To spout. Used of a whale. **10.** To shape (e.g., glass) by forcing air through at the end of a pipe. **11.** *Slang* To spend (money) freely. **12.** To handle ineptly. See Syns at **botch. 13.** To depart. —***phrasal verbs:* blow out 1.** To extinguish or be extinguished by blowing. **2.** To fail, as an electrical apparatus. **blow over 1.** To subside; wane. **2.** To be forgotten. **blow up 1.** To come into being: *A storm blew up.* **2.** To fill with air; inflate. **3.** To enlarge (a photographic image or print). **4.** To explode. **5.** To lose one's temper. ►*n.* **1.** The act of blowing. **2a.** A blast of air or wind. **b.** A storm. —***idioms:* blow off steam** To give release to one's anger or other pent-up emotion. **blow (one's) mind** *Slang* To amaze or shock. **blow (one's) top** *Informal* To lose one's temper. [< OE *blāwan.*] —**blow′er** *n.*

blow² (blō) ►*n.* **1.** A sudden hard stroke or hit, as with the fist. **2.** An unexpected shock or calamity. **3.** A sudden attack. [ME *blaw.*]

blow³ (blō) ►*n.* A mass of blossoms: *peach blow.* ►*v.* **blew** (blo͞o), **blown** (blōn), **blow•ing.** To bloom or cause to bloom. [< OE *blōwan,* to bloom.]

blow-by-blow (blō′-bī-blō′) ►*adj.* Describing in great detail.

blow-dry (blō′drī′) ►*v.* To dry or style (hair) with a hand-held dryer. —**blow dryer** *n.*

blow•fly (blō′flī′) ►*n.* A fly that deposits its eggs in carrion or open sores.

blow•gun (blō′gŭn′) ►*n.* A long narrow pipe through which darts may be blown.

blow•hard (blō′härd′) ►*n. Informal* A boaster or braggart.

blow•hole (blō′hōl′) ►*n.* An opening on the head of a cetacean for breathing.

blow•out (blō′out′) ►*n.* **1.** A sudden bursting, as of an automobile tire. **2.** A sudden escape of a confined gas or liquid, as from a well. **3.** *Slang* A large boisterous party.

blow•torch (blō′tôrch′) ►*n.* A portable burner that mixes gas and oxygen to produce a flame hot enough to melt soft metals.

blow•up (blō′ŭp′) ►*n.* **1.** An explosion. **2.** A violent outburst of temper. **3.** A photographic enlargement.

blow•zy also **blow•sy** (blou′zē) ►*adj.* **-zi•er, -zi•est** also **-si•er, -si•est.** Disheveled and frowzy. [< obsolete *blowze,* beggar girl.]

blub•ber¹ (blŭb′ər) ►*v.* To weep and sob noisily. ►*n.* A loud sobbing. [< ME *bluber,* bubbles, foam.]

blub•ber² (blŭb′ər) ►*n.* **1.** The fat of whales, seals, and other marine mammals, from which an oil is obtained. **2.** Excessive body fat. [ME *bluber,* foam.] —**blub′ber•y** *adj.*

bludg•eon (blŭj′ən) ►*n.* A short heavy club, usu. of wood, that is thicker or loaded at one end. ►*v.* **1.** To hit with or as if with a bludgeon. **2.** To threaten or intimidate. [?]

blue (blo͞o) ►*n.* **1a.** Any of a group of colors whose hue is that of a clear daytime sky. **b.** The hue of the visible spectrum lying between green and indigo. **2a.** The sky. **b.** The sea. ►*adj.* **blu•er, blu•est 1.** Of the color blue. **2.** Having a gray or purplish color, as from cold or bruising. **3.** Downhearted or low; gloomy. See Syns at **depressed. 4.** Puritanical; strict. **5.** Indecent; risqué: *a blue joke.* ►*v.* **blued, blu•ing.** To make or become blue. —***idiom:* out of the blue 1.** From an unforeseen source. **2.** At a completely unexpected time. [< OFr. *bleu,* of Gmc. orig.] —**blue′ness** *n.* —**blu′ish, blue′ish** *adj.*

blue baby ►*n.* An infant born with bluish skin from inadequate oxygenation of its blood.

blue•bell (blo͞o′bĕl′) ►*n.* Any of several plants having blue bell-shaped flowers.

blue•ber•ry (blo͞o′bĕr′ē) ►*n.* **1.** Any of numerous plants having edible blue-black berries. **2.** The fruit of a blueberry.

blue•bird (blo͞o′bûrd′) ►*n.* A North American songbird having blue plumage and usu. a rust-colored breast in the male.

blue blood ►*n.* **1.** Noble or aristocratic descent. **2.** A member of the aristocracy. [Prob. < the visible veins of fair-skinned aristocrats.] —**blue′-blood′ed** *adj.*

blue•bon•net (blo͞o′bŏn′ĭt) ►*n.* A plant with compound leaves and light blue flowers.

blue•bot•tle (blo͞o′bŏt′l) ►*n.* Any of several flies that have a bright metallic-blue body.

blue cheese ►*n.* A semisoft tangy cheese streaked with a greenish-blue mold.

blue chip ►*n.* **1.** A stock highly valued for its long record of steady earnings. **2.** A valuable property. —**blue′-chip′** *adj.*

blue-col•lar (blo͞o′kŏl′ər) ►*adj.* Of or relating to wage earners whose jobs involve skilled or semiskilled manual labor.

blue•fish (blo͞o′fĭsh′) ►*n.* A food and game fish of temperate and tropical waters.

blue•gill (blo͞o′gĭl′) ►*n.* A common edible sunfish of North American lakes and streams.

blue•grass (blo͞o′grăs′) ►*n.* **1.** A usu. bluish lawn and pasture grass. **2.** A type of lively folk music originating in the S US, typically played on banjos, guitars, and fiddles.

blue heron ►*n.* Any of several herons with blue or blue-gray plumage.

blue•ing (blo͞o′ĭng) ►*n.* Var. of **bluing.**

blue jay ►*n.* A North American jay having a crested head, predominantly blue plumage, and a harsh noisy cry.

blue jeans ►*pl.n.* Clothes, esp. pants, made of blue denim.

blue law ►*n.* A law designed to regulate Sunday activities.

blue moon ►*n. Informal* A relatively long period of time: *once in a blue moon.*

Blue Nile. A river of NE Africa flowing about 1,609 km (1,000 mi) from NW Ethiopia to Sudan. At Khartoum it merges with the White Nile to form the Nile R. proper.

blue•nose (blo͞o′nōz′) ►*n.* A puritanical person.

blue-pen•cil (blo͞o′pĕn′səl) ►*v.* To edit with or as if with a blue pencil.

blue•print (blo͞o′prĭnt′) ►*n.* **1.** A photographic reproduction, as of an architectural plan or technical drawing, rendered as white lines on a blue background. **2.** A detailed plan of action. See Syns at **plan.** —**blue′print′** *v.*

blue ribbon ►*n.* The first prize in a competition. —**blue′-rib′bon** *adj.*

Blue Ridge also **Blue Ridge Mountains.** A range of the Appalachian Mts. extending from S PA to N GA.

blues (blo͞oz) ►*pl.n. (takes sing. or pl. v.)* **1.** A state of depression or melancholy. **2.** A style of music evolved from southern African-American secular songs and usu. marked by a syncopated 4/4 rhythm, flatted thirds and sevenths, and a 12-bar structure. [< *blue devils*, depression.] —**blues′man** *n.*—**blues′y** *adj.*

blue•stock•ing (blo͞o′stŏk′ĭng) ►*n.* A woman with strong scholarly or literary interests. [After the *Blue Stocking* Society, a literary club of 18th-century London.]

blu•ets (blo͞o′ĭts) ►*pl.n. (takes sing. or pl. v.)* A low-growing plant having blue flowers with yellow centers. [< ME *bleu*, BLUE.]

blue whale ►*n.* A very large baleen whale having a bluish-gray back, yellow underparts, and several ventral throat grooves.

bluff[1] (blŭf) ►*v.* To mislead or intimidate, esp. by a false display of confidence. ►*n.* **1.** The act or practice of bluffing. **2.** One that bluffs. [< LGer. *bluffen.*] —**bluff′er** *n.*

bluff[2] (blŭf) ►*n.* A steep headland, riverbank, or cliff. ►*adj.* **-er, -est.** Rough and blunt but not unkind in manner. [Poss. < obsolete Du. *blaf.*] —**bluff′ly** *adv.* —**bluff′ness** *n.*

blu•ing also **blue•ing** (blo͞o′ĭng) ►*n.* **1.** A coloring agent used to counteract the yellowing of laundered fabrics. **2.** A rinsing agent used with gray hair.

blun•der (blŭn′dər) ►*n.* A usu. serious mistake caused by ignorance, confusion, or foolishness. ►*v.* **1.** To move clumsily or blindly. **2.** To make a stupid, usu. serious error. [Poss. of Scand. orig.] —**blun′der•er** *n.* —**blun′der•ing•ly** *adv.*

Syns: *blunder, bumble, flounder, lumber, lurch, stumble* **v.**

blun•der•buss (blŭn′dər-bŭs′) ►*n.* A short musket with a wide muzzle for scattering shot at close range. [< Du. *donderbus.*]

blunt (blŭnt) ►*adj.* **-er, -est 1.** Having a dull edge or end. **2.** Abrupt and frank in speech and manner; brusque. ►*v.* **1.** To make or become blunt. **2.** To make less effective; weaken. [ME.] —**blunt′ly** *adv.* —**blunt′ness** *n.*

blur (blûr) ►*v.* **blurred, blur•ring 1.** To make or become indistinct. **2.** To smear or stain. **3.** To lessen the perception of; dim. ►*n.* **1.** A smear or smudge. **2.** Something indistinct to sight or mind. [Prob. akin to ME *bleren*, blear.] —**blur′ry** *adj.*

blurb (blûrb) ►*n.* A brief favorable publicity notice, as on a book jacket. [Coined by Gelett Burgess (1866–1951).]

blurt (blûrt) ►*v.* To say suddenly and impulsively: *blurt a confession.* [Prob. imit.]

blush (blŭsh) ►*v.* **1.** To become red in the face, esp. from modesty, embarrassment, or shame; flush. **2.** To become red or rosy. **3.** To feel embarrassed or ashamed about something. [< OE *blyscan.*] —**blush** *n.*

blush•er (blŭsh′ər) or **blush** (blŭsh) ►*n.* Facial makeup used esp. on the cheeks to give a red or rosy tint.

blus•ter (blŭs′tər) ►*v.* **1.** To blow in loud violent gusts, as wind in a storm. **2.** To speak in a noisy, arrogant, or bullying manner. [< MLGer. *blüsteren.*] —**blus′ter** *n.* —**blus′ter•er** *n.* —**blus′ter•y** *adj.*

Blvd. ►*abbr.* boulevard

BM ►*abbr.* **1.** basal metabolism **2.** board measure **3.** bowel movement

bo•a (bō′ə) ►*n.* **1.** Any of various large, nonvenomous tropical snakes, including the python, anaconda, and boa constrictor, that coil around and suffocate their prey. **2.** A long scarf made of soft fluffy material, such as fur or feathers. [< Lat. *boa*, a snake.]

boa constrictor ►*n.* A large boa of tropical America having brown markings.

Bo•ad•i•ce•a (bō′ăd-ĭ-sē′ə). See **Boudicca.**

boar (bôr, bōr) ►*n.* **1.** An uncastrated male pig. **2.** A wild pig. [< OE *bār.*]

board (bôrd, bōrd) ►*n.* **1.** A flat length of sawed lumber; plank. **2.** A flat piece of wood or similar material adapted for a special use. **3.** A flat surface on which a game is played. **4. boards** A theater stage. **5a.** A table, esp. one set for serving food. **b.** Food or meals considered as a whole: *board and lodging.* **6.** A table at which official meetings are held. **7.** An organized body of administrators. **8.** A circuit board. **9.** The side of a ship. ►*v.* **1.** To cover or close with boards: *board up a broken window.* **2.** To provide with or receive food and lodging for a charge. **3.** To enter or go aboard (a ship, train, or plane). **4.** To come alongside (a ship). —***idiom:* On board 1.** Aboard. **2.** On the job. [< OE *bord.*] —**board′er** *n.*

board foot ►*n., pl.* **board feet.** A unit of cubic measure for lumber, equal to one foot square by one inch thick.

board•ing house also **board•ing•house** (bôr′dĭng-hous′, bōr′-) ►*n.* A house where paying guests are given meals and lodging.

boarding school ►*n.* A school where pupils are provided with meals and lodging.

board•walk (bôrd′wôk′, bōrd′-) ►*n.* A promenade, esp. of planks, along a beach.

boast (bōst) ►*v.* **1.** To talk in a self-admiring way. **2.** To talk about or speak with excessive pride. **3.** To possess or own (a desirable feature). ►*n.* **1.** An instance of bragging. **2.** A source of pride. [< ME *bost*, a brag.] —**boast′er** *n.* —**boast′ful** *adj.* —**boast′ful•ly** *adv.* —**boast′ful•ness** *n.*

boat (bōt) ►*n.* **1a.** A relatively small, usu. open water craft. **b.** A ship or submarine. **2.** A dish shaped like a boat: *a sauce boat.* ►*v.* To travel or transport by boat. —***idiom:* in the same boat** In the same situation. [< OE *bāt.*] —**boat′ing** *n.* —**boat′man** *n.*

boat•er (bō′tər) ►*n.* **1.** One who boats. **2.** A stiff straw hat with a flat crown.

boat•swain also **bo's'n** or **bos'n** or **bo•sun** (bō′sən) ►*n.* A warrant officer or petty officer in charge of a ship's rigging, anchors, cables, and deck crew.

bob[1] (bŏb) ►*v.* **bobbed, bob•bing.** To move or cause to move up and down. ►*n.* A quick jerky movement. [ME *bobben.*]

bob[2] (bŏb) ►*n.* **1.** A small, knoblike pendent object. **2.** A fishing float. **3.** A woman's or child's short haircut. **4.** The docked tail of a horse. ►*v.* **bobbed, bob•bing.** To cut short or reshape: *bobbed her hair.* [ME *bobbe.*]

bob[3] (bŏb) ►*n., pl.* **bob** *Chiefly Brit.* A shilling. [?]

bob•bin (bŏb′ĭn) ►*n.* A spool for thread, as on

a sewing machine. [Fr. *bobine*.]

bob•ble (bŏb′əl) ►*v.* **-bled, -bling 1.** To bob up and down. **2.** To fumble (e.g., a ball) momentarily. [< BOB[1].] —**bob′ble** *n.*

bob•by (bŏb′ē) ►*n., pl.* **-bies** *Chiefly Brit.* A police officer. [After Sir *Robert* PEEL.]

bobby pin ►*n.* A small metal hair clip with the ends pressed tightly together. [< BOB[2].]

bobby socks also **bobby sox** ►*pl.n. Informal* Ankle socks. [Poss. < BOB[2].]

bob•cat (bŏb′kăt′) ►*n.* A wild cat of North America, having spotted reddish-brown fur, tufted ears, and a short tail.

bob•o•link (bŏb′ə-lĭngk′) ►*n.* An American migratory songbird. [Imit. of its song.]

bob•sled (bŏb′slĕd′) ►*n.* **1.** A long racing sled with a steering mechanism controlling the front runners. **2.** A long sled made of two sleds joined in tandem. —**bob′sled′** *v.*

bob•tail (bŏb′tāl′) ►*n.* **1.** A short tail or one that has been cut short. **2.** An animal, esp. a horse, having a bobtail. —**bob′tailed′** *adj.*

bob•white (bŏb-hwīt′, -wīt′) ►*n.* A small North American quail. [Imit. of its call.]

Boc•cac•cio (bō-kä′chē-ō′, -chō′), **Giovanni.** 1313–75. French-born Italian writer.

Bo•chum (bō′kəm, -KHŏŏm) A city of W-central Germany E of Essen. Pop. 401,058.

bock beer (bŏk) ►*n.* A dark, usu. springtime beer. [< Ger. *Einbeckisch Bier*, beer from Einbeck, Germany.]

bod (bŏd) ►*n. Slang* The human body.

bode[1] (bōd) ►*v.* **bod•ed, bod•ing.** To be an omen of. [< OE *bodian*, announce.]

bode[2] (bōd) ►*v.* P.t. of **bide.**

bo•de•ga (bō-dā′gə) ►*n.* A small grocery store specializing in products from Latin America. [< Lat. *apothēca*, storehouse.]

bod•ice (bŏd′ĭs) ►*n.* The fitted upper part of a dress. [< *bodies*, pl. of BODY.]

bod•i•less (bŏd′ē-lĭs) ►*adj.* Having no body, form, or substance: *bodiless fears.*

bod•i•ly (bŏd′l-ē) ►*adj.* **1.** Of or belonging to the body. **2.** Physical: *bodily welfare.* ►*adv.* **1.** In person. **2.** As a complete physical entity: *lifted bodily from his chair.*

Syns: *bodily, corporal, corporeal, fleshly, physical, somatic* ***adj.***

bod•kin (bŏd′kĭn) ►*n.* **1.** An awl for piercing fabric or leather. **2.** A blunt needle for pulling ribbon through loops or a hem. **3.** A dagger. [ME *boidekin*.]

bod•y (bŏd′ē) ►*n., pl.* **-ies 1a.** The entire material or physical structure of an organism, esp. of a human or animal. **b.** A corpse or carcass. **2.** The trunk or torso. **3a.** A person. **b.** A group of individuals regarded as an entity: *a governing body.* **4.** A collection of related things: *a body of information.* **5.** The main or central part, as of a vehicle, document, or musical instrument. **6.** A well-defined object, mass, or collection of material: *a body of water.* **7.** Consistency of substance, as in paint, textiles, or wine. [< OE *bodig*.] —**bod′ied** *adj.*

body bag ►*n.* A zippered bag, usu. of rubber, for transporting a human corpse.

bod•y•board (bŏd′ē-bôrd′, -bōrd′) ►*n.* A short surfboard with one straight end, usu. ridden on one's chest. —**bod′y•board′** *v.* —**bod′y•board′er** *n.*

bod•y•build•ing (bŏd′ē-bĭl′dĭng) ►*n.* The process of developing the musculature of the body through diet and exercise, esp. for competitive exhibition. —**bod′y•build′er** *n.*

body count ►*n.* A count of individual bodies, as those killed in combat operations.

body English ►*n.* The tendency of a person to try to influence the movement of a propelled object, such as a ball, by twisting his or her body toward the desired goal.

bod•y•guard (bŏd′ē-gärd′) ►*n.* A person or group of persons, usu. armed, responsible for protecting another or others.

body language ►*n.* The gestures, postures, and facial expressions by which a person communicates nonverbally with others.

body politic ►*n.* The aggregate people of a politically organized nation or state.

body shop ►*n.* A garage where the bodies of automotive vehicles are repaired.

body stocking ►*n.* A tight-fitting, usu. one-piece garment that covers the torso and sometimes the arms and legs.

body suit ►*n.* A tight-fitting one-piece garment for the torso.

bod•y•surf (bŏd′ē-sûrf′) ►*v.* To ride waves to shore without a surfboard.

bod•y•work (bŏd′ē-wûrk′) ►*n.* **1.** The body of a motor vehicle. **2.** The manufacturing or repairing of motor vehicle bodies.

Boe•o•tia (bē-ō′shə, -shē-ə) An ancient region of Greece N of Attica and the Gulf of Corinth. —**Boe•o′tian** *adj. & n.*

Boer (bōr, bôr, bŏŏr) ►*n.* A Dutch colonist or descendant of a Dutch colonist in South Africa. [Afr. < MDu. *gheboer*, peasant.]

bof•fo (bŏf′ō) ►*adj. Slang* Extremely successful; great. [Prob. < B(OX) OFF(ICE).]

bog (bôg, bŏg) ►*n.* An area of soft, naturally waterlogged ground. ►*v.* **bogged, bog•ging.** To hinder or be hindered: *bogged down in the mud; bogged me down with details.* [< Ir.Gael. *bog*, soft.] —**bog′gy** *adj.*

Bo•gart (bō′gärt), **Humphrey DeForest.** 1899–1957. Amer. actor.

bo•gey (bō′gē) ►*n.* also **bo•gy** or **bo•gie,** *pl.* **-geys** also **-gies 1.** (*also* bŏŏg′ē, bŏŏ′gē). An evil or mischievous spirit; hobgoblin. **2.** One golf stroke over par on a hole. **3.** *Slang* An unidentified flying aircraft. ►*v.* **-geyed, -gey•ing.** To shoot (a hole in golf) one stroke over par. [Poss. < Sc. *bogill*.]

bo•gey•man or **bo•gy•man** also **boog•ey•man** (bŏŏg′ē-măn′, bō′gē-, bŏŏ′gē-) ►*n.* A terrifying specter; hobgoblin.

bog•gle (bŏg′əl) ►*v.* **-gled, -gling 1.** To hesitate or shy away as if in fear or doubt. **2.** To overwhelm with astonishment: *boggles the mind.* [Poss. < Sc. *bogill*, goblin.]

Bo•go•tá (bō′gə-tä′) The capital of Colombia, in the central part on a high plain in the E Andes. Pop. 5,025,989.

bo•gus (bō′gəs) ►*adj.* Counterfeit or fake. [< *bogus*, counterfeit money device.]

Bo Hai also **Po Hai** (bō′ hī′). An inlet of the Yellow Sea on the NE coast of China.

Bo•he•mi•a (bō-hē′mē-ə) A historical region and former kingdom of W Czech Republic. —**Bo•he′mi•an** *adj. & n.*

bo•he•mi•an (bō-hē′mē-ən) ►*n.* A person with artistic interests who disregards conventional standards of behavior. —**bo•he′mi•an** *adj.* —**bo•he′mi•an•ism** *n.*

Bohr (bôr, bōr), **Niels Henrik David.** 1885–

1962. Danish physicist; 1922 Nobel.

bohr•i•um (bôr′ē-əm, bōr′-) ►*n. Symbol* **Bh** A synthetic radioactive element. At. no. 107. See table at **element.** [After Niels Henrik David BOHR.]

boil[1] (boil) ►*v.* **1a.** To vaporize (a liquid) by applying heat. **b.** To bring to or reach the boiling point. **2.** To cook or clean by boiling. **3.** To be in a state of agitation; seethe: *a river boiling over the rocks.* **4.** To be greatly excited, as by rage. —***phrasal verbs:* boil down 1.** To reduce in bulk or size by boiling. **2.** To summarize. **boil over** To lose one's temper. ►*n.* The condition or act of boiling. [< Lat. *bullīre.*]

boil[2] (boil) ►*n.* A painful, pus-filled inflammation of the skin usu. caused by bacterial infection. [< OE *bȳle.*]

boil•er (boi′lər) ►*n.* **1.** An enclosed vessel in which water is heated and circulated, as either hot water or steam, for heating or power. **2.** A container for boiling liquids.

boil•er-room (boi′lər-ro͞om′, -ro͝om′) ►*adj. Informal* Of or involving often illegal, high-pressure telephone sales tactics.

boil•ing point (boi′lĭng) ►*n.* **1.** The temperature at which a liquid boils at a fixed pressure, esp. under standard atmospheric conditions. **2.** *Informal* The point at which one loses one's temper.

Boi•se (boi′sē, -zē) The capital of ID, in the SW part on the **Boise River,** about 257 km (160 mi). Pop. 102,160.

bois•ter•ous (boi′stər-əs, -strəs) ►*adj.* **1.** Rough and stormy. **2.** Loud, noisy, and unrestrained. [< ME *boistous,* rude.] —**bois′ter•ous•ly** *adv.* —**bois′ter•ous•ness** *n.*

bok choy (bŏk′ choi′) ►*n.* A cabbagelike Chinese vegetable. [Cantonese *paāk ts'oì.*]

bok choy

bongo[1]

bo•la (bō′lə) also **bo•las** (-ləs) ►*n.* A rope with round weights attached, used esp. in South America to catch cattle or game by entangling their legs. [< Sp. *bola,* ball.]

bold (bōld) ►*adj.* **-er, -est 1.** Fearless and daring; courageous. **2.** Requiring or exhibiting courage and bravery. **3.** Unduly forward and brazen. **4.** Clear and distinct to the eye. **5.** *Print.* Boldface. [< OE *bald.*] —**bold′ly** *adv.* —**bold′ness** *n.*

bold•face (bōld′fās′) ►*n. Print.* Type with thick, heavy lines. —**bold′face′, bold′-faced′** *adj.*

bole (bōl) ►*n.* A tree trunk. [< ON *bolr.*]

bo•le•ro (bō-lâr′ō, bə-) ►*n., pl.* **-ros 1.** A very short jacket worn open in the front. **2a.** A Spanish dance in triple meter. **b.** The music for this dance. [Sp. < *bola,* ball.]

Bol•eyn (bo͝ol′ĭn, bo͞o-lĭn′), **Anne.** 1507–36. Queen of England (1533–36) as second wife of Henry VIII; beheaded.

bo•li•var (bō-lē′vär, bŏl′ə-vər) ►*n., pl.* **-vars** or **-va•res** (bō-lē′vä-rĕs′). See table at **currency.** [After Simón BOLÍVAR.]

Bo•lí•var (bō-lē′vär), **Simón.** 1783–1830. South American revolutionary leader.

Bo•liv•i•a (bə-lĭv′ē-ə, bō-) A landlocked country of W-central South America. Caps. Sucre and La Paz. Pop. 7,230,000. —**Bo•liv′i•an** *adj. & n.*

bo•li•vi•a•no (bə-lĭv′ē-ä′nō, bō-) ►*n., pl.* **-nos.** See table at **currency.** [Sp., Bolivian.]

boll (bōl) ►*n.* The seedpod esp. of cotton and flax. [< MDu., round object.]

boll weevil ►*n.* A small, grayish, long-snouted beetle that lays its eggs in cotton buds and bolls, causing great damage.

bo•lo•gna (bə-lō′nē, -nə, -nyə) also **ba•lo•ney** or **bo•lo•ney** (-nē) ►*n.* A large smoked sausage made of mixed meats, such as beef, pork, and veal. [After BOLOGNA.]

Bo•lo•gna (bə-lōn′yə) A city of N-central Italy NNE of Florence. Pop. 404,322. —**Bo•lo′gnan, Bo′lo•gnese′** (bō′lə-nēz′, -lən-yēz′) *adj. & n.*

Bol•she•vik (bōl′shə-vĭk′, bŏl′-) ►*n., pl.* **-viks** or **-vi•ki** (-vē′kē) **1.** A member of the radical Marxist party that seized power in Russia (1917–22). **2.** A Communist. [< Russ. *bol'shoĭ,* large.] —**Bol′she•vik′** *adj.* —**Bol′she•vism** *n.* —**Bol′she•vist** *adj. & n.*

bol•ster (bōl′stər) ►*n.* A long narrow pillow or cushion. ►*v.* **1.** To support with or as if with a bolster. **2.** To buoy up; reinforce: *bolstered their morale.* [< OE.]

bolt[1] (bōlt) ►*n.* **1.** A sliding bar used to fasten a door or gate. **2.** A metal bar in a lock that is extended or withdrawn by turning the key. **3.** A threaded pin or rod with a head at one end, used with a mated nut to hold things together. **4.** A flash of lightning; thunderbolt. **5.** A sudden movement toward or away; dash. **6.** A large roll of cloth. ►*v.* **1.** To secure or lock with or as if with a bolt. **2.** To eat hurriedly; gulp. **3.** To desert (a political party). **4.** To move or spring suddenly. **5.** To run away. [< OE, heavy arrow.]

bolt[2] (bōlt) ►*v.* To sift (e.g., flour) through a sieve. [< MHGer. *biutel,* bag, purse.]

bo•lus (bō′ləs) ►*n., pl.* **-lus•es 1.** A small round mass. **2.** A large, round, usu. soft pill or tablet. [< Gk. *bōlos,* lump of earth.]

bomb (bŏm) ►*n.* **1a.** An explosive weapon detonated esp. by impact or a timing mechanism. **b.** A nuclear weapon. Used with *the.* **2.** A weapon detonated to release smoke or gas. **3.** A container that ejects a spray, foam, or gas under pressure. **4.** *Slang* A dismal failure. ►*v.* **1.** To attack or damage with bombs. **2.** *Slang* To fail miserably. [< Ital. *bomba.*]

bom•bard (bŏm-bärd′) ►*v.* **1.** To attack with bombs, explosive shells, or missiles. **2.** To assail persistently, as with requests. See Syns at **barrage. 3.** To irradiate (an atom). [Prob. < Lat. *bombus,* a booming.] —**bom•bard′ment** *n.*

bom•bar•dier (bŏm′bər-dîr′) ►*n.* The member of a combat aircraft crew who operates the bombing equipment. [< OFr. *bombarde,* BOMBARD.]

bom•bast (bŏm′băst′) ►*n.* Grandiloquent, pompous speech or writing. [< OFr. *bombace,* cotton padding.] —**bom•bas′tic** *adj.*

Bom•bay (bŏm-bā′) See **Mumbai.**

bom•ba•zine (bŏm′bə-zēn′) ►*n.* A fine twilled fabric often dyed black. [< Gk. *bombux*, silkworm.]

bombed (bŏmd) ►*adj. Slang* Drunk.

bomb•er (bŏm′ər) ►*n.* **1.** A combat aircraft designed to carry and drop bombs. **2.** One who bombs.

bomb•shell (bŏm′shĕl′) ►*n.* **1.** An explosive bomb. **2.** A shocking surprise.

bomb•sight (bŏm′sīt′) ►*n.* A device in a combat aircraft for aiming a bomb.

bo•na fide (bō′nə fīd′, fī′dē, bŏn′ə) ►*adj.* **1.** Made or carried out in good faith; sincere: *a bona fide offer.* **2.** Authentic; genuine: *a bona fide Rembrandt.* See Syns at **authentic.** [Lat. *bonā fidē*, in good faith.]

bo•nan•za (bə-năn′zə) ►*n.* **1.** A rich mine or vein of ore. **2.** A source of great wealth or prosperity. [Sp.]

Bo•na•parte (bō′nə-pärt′). Corsican family, all brothers of Napoleon I, including **Joseph** (1768–1844), king of Naples (1806–08) and Spain (1808–13); **Lucien** (1775–1840); **Louis** (1778–1846), king of Holland (1806–10); and **Jérôme** (1784–1860), king of Westphalia (1807–13).

bon•bon (bŏn′bŏn′) ►*n.* A coated candy with a creamy center. [Fr. < Lat. *bonus*, good.]

bond (bŏnd) ►*n.* **1.** Something that binds, ties, or fastens things together. **2.** often **bonds** Confinement in prison; captivity. **3.** A uniting force or tie; link: *the familial bond.* **4.** A binding agreement; covenant. **5.** A promise or obligation by which one is bound. **6.** A union or cohesion between two or more parts. **7.** A chemical bond. **8.** *Law* **a.** A sum of money paid as bail or surety. **b.** A bail bondsman. **9.** A certificate of debt issued by a government or corporation guaranteeing payment of the original investment plus interest by a specified future date. **10.** The condition of storing goods in a warehouse until the taxes or duties owed on them are paid. **11.** An insurance contract that guarantees payment to an employer for financial loss or theft by an employee. **12.** Bond paper. ►*v.* **1.** To mortgage or place a guaranteed bond on. **2.** To furnish bond or surety for. **3.** To place (e.g., an employee) under bond or guarantee. **4.** To join securely, as with glue. **5.** To form a close nurturing relationship. [< ON *band.*]

bond•age (bŏn′dĭj) ►*n.* The condition of a slave or serf; servitude. [Ult. < ON *būa*, live.]

bond•man (bŏnd′mən) ►*n.* A male bondservant.

bond paper ►*n.* A superior grade of white paper made wholly or in part from rag pulp.

bond•ser•vant (bŏnd′sûr′vənt) ►*n.* **1.** A person obligated to service without wages. **2.** A slave or serf. [< ME *bonde*, serf.]

bonds•man (bŏndz′mən) ►*n.* **1.** One who provides bond or surety for another. **2.** A male bondservant.

bond•wom•an (bŏnd′wo͝om′ən) ►*n.* A woman bondservant.

bone (bōn) ►*n.* **1a.** The dense, semirigid, porous, calcified tissue forming the skeleton of most vertebrates. **b.** A skeletal structure made of this material. **2.** An animal material, such as whalebone, resembling bone. **3.** Something made of bone or similar material. ►*v.* **boned, bon•ing 1.** To remove the bones from. **2.** *Informal* To study intensely, usu. at the last minute: *boned up on the chemical elements.* —***idioms:*** **bone of contention** The subject of dispute. **bone to pick** Grounds for a complaint or dispute. [< OE *bān.*] —**bone′less** *adj.* —**bon′i•ness** *n.* —**bon′y, bon′ey** *adj.*

bone•black also **bone black** (bōn′blăk′) ►*n.* A black material made by roasting animal bones and used esp. as a pigment.

bone-dry (bōn′drī′) ►*adj.* Completely dry.

bone meal ►*n.* Crushed and coarsely ground bones used as fertilizer and animal feed.

bon•er (bō′nər) ►*n. Informal* A blunder.

bon•fire (bŏn′fīr′) ►*n.* A large outdoor fire. [ME *bonnefire*, "bone fire".]

bong (bŏng, bông) ►*n.* A deep ringing sound, as of a bell. [Imit.] —**bong** *v.*

bon•go[1] (bŏng′gō, bông′-) ►*n., pl.* **-gos.** A large reddish-brown antelope of central Africa, having white stripes and spirally twisted horns. [Prob. of Bantu orig.]

bon•go[2] (bŏng′gō, bông′-) ►*n., pl.* **-gos** or **-goes.** One of a pair of connected tuned drums played by beating with the hands. [Am.Sp. *bongó.*]

bon•ho•mie (bŏn′ə-mē′) ►*n.* A pleasant and affable disposition; geniality. [Fr.]

Bo•nin Islands (bō′nĭn) An archipelago of volcanic islands in the W Pacific S of Japan.

bo•ni•to (bə-nē′tō) ►*n., pl.* **-to** or **-tos.** Any of several marine food and game fishes related to and resembling the tuna. [Sp.]

bon mot (bôɴ mō′) ►*n., pl.* **bons mots** (bôɴ mō′, mōz′). A witticism. [Fr.]

Bonn (bŏn, bôn) The former capital of West Germany, in the W-central part on the Rhine R. Pop. 296,859.

bon•net (bŏn′ĭt) ►*n.* **1.** A hat held in place by ribbons tied under the chin, esp. one worn by women and children. **2.** *Chiefly Brit.* The hood of an automobile. [< OFr. *bonet.*]

bon•ny also **bon•nie** (bŏn′ē) ►*adj.* **-ni•er, -ni•est** *Scots* **1.** Physically attractive or appealing; pretty. **2.** Excellent. [Prob. ult. < Fr. *bon*, good.]

bo•no•bo (bə-nō′bō) ►*n., pl.* **-bos.** A small anthropoid ape of W-central Africa having more arboreal habits than the closely related chimpanzee. [Of Central African orig.]

bon•sai (bŏn-sī′, bŏn′sī′, -zī′) ►*n., pl.* **-sai.** A dwarfed, ornamentally shaped tree grown in a shallow pot. [J., potted plant.]

bo•nus (bō′nəs) ►*n., pl.* **-es.** Something given or paid in addition to what is usual or expected. [< Lat., good.]

bon vi•vant (bôɴ′ vē-väɴ′) ►*n., pl.* **bons vi•vants** (bôɴ′ vē-väɴ′). One who enjoys good living. [Fr.]

bon voy•age (bôɴ′ vwä-yäzh′) ►*interj.* Used to express farewell and good wishes to a departing traveler. [Fr.]

boo (bo͞o) ►*n., pl.* **boos.** A sound uttered to show contempt, scorn, or disapproval or to frighten or startle. —**boo** *v.*

boob (bo͞ob) ►*n. Slang* A stupid or foolish person; dolt. [Short for BOOBY.]

boo•by (bo͞o′bē) ►*n., pl.* **-bies 1.** A stupid or foolish person. **2.** Any of several tropical sea birds resembling or related to the gannets. [Prob. < Lat. *balbus*, stammering.]

booby prize ►*n.* An award for the lowest score in a game or contest.

booby trap ►*n.* **1.** A concealed, often explosive device triggered when a harmless-looking object is touched. **2.** A situation that catches one off guard; pitfall. —**boo′by-trap′** *v.*

boo•dle (bo͝od′l) ►*n. Slang* **1a.** Money, esp. counterfeit money. **b.** Money accepted as a bribe. **2.** Stolen goods; swag. [< MDu. *bōdel*, estate.]

boog•ey•man (bo͝og′ē-măn′, bä′gē-, bo͞o′gē-) ►*n. Slang* Var. of **bogeyman.**

boog•ie (bo͝og′ē, bo͞o′gē) ►*v.* **-ied, -y•ing** *Slang* To dance to rock music. [< BOOGIE-WOOGIE.]

boog•ie-woog•ie (bo͝og′ē-wo͝og′ē, bo͞o′gē-wo͞o′gē) ►*n.* A style of blues piano playing marked by an up-tempo rhythm and a repeated melodic pattern in the bass. [Poss. < Black W African E. *bogi(-bogi)*, to dance.]

book (bo͝ok) ►*n.* **1.** A set of written, printed, or blank pages fastened along one side and encased between protective covers. **2a.** A printed or written literary work. **b.** A main division of a larger printed or written work. **3.** A volume in which financial transactions are recorded. **4.** **Book** The Bible. **5.** A packet of similar items bound together: *a book of matches.* **6.** A record of bets placed on a race. ►*v.* **1.** To reserve or schedule, as by listing in a book. **2.** To record charges against on a police blotter. —***idiom:*** **like a book** Thoroughly; completely. [< OE *bōc.*]

book•case (bo͝ok′kās′) ►*n.* A piece of furniture with shelves for holding books.

book•end (bo͝ok′ĕnd′) ►*n.* A prop used to keep a row of books upright.

book•ie (bo͝ok′ē) ►*n.* See **bookmaker** 2.

book•ing (bo͝ok′ĭng) ►*n.* A scheduled engagement, as for a performance.

book•ish (bo͝ok′ĭsh) ►*adj.* **1.** Fond of books; studious. **2.** Dull. See Syns at **pedantic.**

book•keep•ing (bo͝ok′kē′pĭng) ►*n.* The recording of the accounts and transactions of a business. —**book′keep′er** *n.*

book•let (bo͝ok′lĭt) ►*n.* A small bound book or pamphlet.

book•mak•er (bo͝ok′mā′kər) ►*n.* **1.** One who prints or publishes books. **2.** One who accepts and pays off bets, as on a horserace; bookie. —**book′mak′ing** *n.*

book•mark (bo͝ok′märk′) ►*n.* An object placed between book pages to mark one's place.

book•plate (bo͝ok′plāt′) ►*n.* A label bearing the owner's name pasted inside a book.

book value ►*n.* The worth of a business as shown in the account books as distinguished from the market value.

book•worm (bo͝ok′wûrm′) ►*n.* **1.** One who spends much time reading or studying. **2.** Any of various insects, esp. silverfish, that infest books and feed on the bindings.

Bool•e•an (bo͞o′lē-ən) ►*adj.* Of or relating to an algebraic system used in symbolic logic and in logic circuits in computer science. [After George *Boole* (1815–1864).]

boom[1] (bo͞om) ►*v.* **1.** To make a deep resonant sound. **2.** To flourish rapidly or vigorously. ►*n.* **1.** A booming sound. **2.** A sudden increase, as in growth, wealth, or popularity. [ME *bomben.*]

boom[2] (bo͞om) ►*n.* **1.** A long spar extending from a mast to hold or extend the bottom of a sail. **2.** A long pole extending upward at an angle from the mast of a derrick to support or guide objects being lifted. **3a.** A chain of floating logs enclosing other free-floating logs. **b.** A floating barrier used to contain an oil spill. **4.** A long movable arm used to maneuver a microphone. [< MDu., tree, pole.]

boom box ►*n. Slang* A portable audio system capable of high volume.

boo•mer•ang (bo͞o′mə-răng′) ►*n.* **1.** A flat, curved, usu. wooden missile configured so that when hurled it returns to the thrower. **2.** A statement or course of action that backfires. ►*v.* To have an opposite effect; backfire. [Dharuk (Australian) *bumarinʸ.*]

boon[1] (bo͞on) ►*n.* Something beneficial; blessing. [< ON *bōn*, prayer.]

boon[2] (bo͞on) ►*adj.* Convivial; jolly: *a boon companion to all.* [< Lat. *bonus*, good.]

boon•docks (bo͞on′dŏks′) ►*pl.n. Slang* **1.** A jungle. **2.** Rural country; hinterland. [< Tagalog *bundok*, mountain.]

boon•dog•gle (bo͞on′dô′gəl, -dŏg′əl) ►*n. Informal* Unnecessary, wasteful, and often counterproductive work. [< *boondoggle*, plaited leather cord.] —**boon′dog′gle** *v.*

Boone (bo͞on), **Daniel.** 1734–1820. Amer. frontier settler and folk hero.

boor (bo͝or) ►*n.* A crude person with rude, clumsy manners. [< MDu. *gheboer*, peasant.] —**boor′ish** *adj.* —**boor′ish•ly** *adv.* —**boor′ish•ness** *n.*

Syns: *boor, barbarian, churl, lout, vulgarian, yahoo* **n.**

boost (bo͞ost) ►*v.* **1.** To lift by or as if by pushing up from behind or below. **2.** To increase; raise. **3.** To promote vigorously; aid. ►*n.* **1.** A push upward or ahead. **2.** An increase. [Poss. < dial. *boostering*, active.]

boost•er (bo͞o′stər) ►*n.* **1.** A device for increasing power or effectiveness. **2.** A promoter. **3.** A rocket that provides the main thrust for the launch of a missile or space vehicle. **4.** A booster shot.

boost•er•ism (bo͞o′stə-rĭz′əm) ►*n.* The supportive activities of boosters.

booster shot ►*n.* A supplementary dose of a vaccine to sustain the immune response.

boot[1] (bo͞ot) ►*n.* **1.** Footgear covering the foot and part of the leg. **2.** A protective covering or sheath. **3.** *Chiefly Brit.* An automobile trunk. **4a.** A kick. **b.** *Slang* A dismissal, esp. from a job. **5.** A marine or navy recruit. **6.** The starting or restarting of a computer. ►*v.* **1.** To put boots on. **2.** To kick. **3.** *Slang* To discharge; dismiss. **4.** *Comp. Sci.* To start (a computer) by loading an operating system from a disk. [< OFr. *bote.*]

boot[2] (bo͞ot) ►*v.* To be of help; avail. ►*n. Regional* See **lagniappe.** —***idiom:*** **to boot** In addition. [< OE *bōt*, help.]

boot•black (bo͞ot′blăk′) ►*n.* One who polishes shoes for a living.

boot camp ►*n.* A training camp for military recruits.

boo•tee also **boo•tie** (bo͞o′tē) ►*n.* A soft, usu. knitted shoe for a baby.

booth (bo͞oth) ►*n., pl.* **booths** (bo͞o*thz*, bo͞oths) **1.** A small enclosed compartment; box: *a ticket booth.* **2.** A dining area in a restaurant having seats whose high backs serve as partitions. **3.** A small stall for the sale of goods. [ME *bothe.*]

Booth. Family of reformers, including **William** (1829–1912) and his wife, **Catherine Mumford Booth** (1829–90), who were the founders of the Salvation Army (1878).

Booth, John Wilkes. 1838–65. Amer. assassin of Abraham Lincoln.

Boo•thi•a Peninsula (bo͞o′thē-ə) The northernmost tip of the North American mainland, in NE Northwest Terrs., Canada.

boot•leg (bo͝ot′lĕg′) ▶ *v.* **-legged, -leg•ging.** To make, sell, or transport illegally, as liquor or record albums. —**boot′leg′** *n. & adj.* —**boot′leg′ger** *n.*

boot•less (bo͞ot′lĭs) ▶ *adj.* Useless. See Syns at **futile.** —**boot′less•ness** *n.*

boot•lick (bo͞ot′lĭk′) ▶ *v.* To behave in a servile manner. See Syns at **fawn[1].** —**boot′lick′er** *n.*

boot•strap (bo͞ot′străp′) ▶ *n.* A loop sewn at the top rear of a boot to help in pulling it on. —***idiom:* by one's (own) bootstraps** By one's own effort.

boo•ty (bo͞o′tē) ▶ *n., pl.* **-ties 1.** Plunder taken from an enemy in war. **2.** Seized or stolen goods. [Prob. < MLGer. *būte*, exchange.]

booze (bo͞oz) *Slang* ▶ *n.* Hard liquor. ▶ *v.* **boozed, booz•ing.** To drink alcoholic beverages excessively. [< MDu. *būsen*, drink to excess.] —**booz′er** *n.* —**booz′y** *adj.*

bop[1] (bŏp) *Informal* ▶ *v.* **bopped, bop•ping.** To hit or strike. ▶ *n.* A blow; punch. [Imit.]

bop[2] (bŏp) ▶ *n.* A style of jazz marked by rhythmic and harmonic complexity and improvised solo performances. ▶ *v.* **bopped, bop•ping 1.** To dance to bop. **2.** *Slang* To go: *bopped off to the movies.* [Short for BEBOP.] —**bop′per** *n.*

Bor. ▶ *abbr.* borough

bo•rate (bôr′āt′, bōr′-) ▶ *n.* A salt of boric acid.

bo•rax (bôr′ăks′, -əks, bōr′-) ▶ *n.* A sodium borate used in detergents and in making glass and ceramics. [< MPers. *būrak*.]

Bor•deaux[1] (bôr-dō′) A city of SW France on the Garonne R. Pop. 210,467.

Bor•deaux[2] (bôr-dō′) ▶ *n., pl.* **Bor•deaux** (bôr-dō′, -dōz′). A red or white wine from the region around Bordeaux.

bor•del•lo (bôr-dĕl′ō) ▶ *n., pl.* **-los.** A house of prostitution. [< OFr. *borde*, wooden hut.]

bor•der (bôr′dər) ▶ *n.* **1.** A part that forms the outer edge of something. **2.** A political or geographic boundary. ▶ *v.* **1.** To put a border on. **2.** To share a border with; be next to. **3.** To be almost like; approach: *an act that borders on heroism.* [< OFr. *border*, to border.]

bor•der•land (bôr′dər-lănd′) ▶ *n.* **1.** Land on or near a border. **2.** An indeterminate area.

bor•der•line (bôr′dər-līn′) ▶ *n.* **1.** A boundary. **2.** An indefinite area between two qualities or conditions. ▶ *adj.* **1.** Verging on a given condition: *borderline poverty.* **2.** Uncertain; dubious: *borderline qualifications.*

Border States. The slave states of DE, MD, VA, KY, and MO that were adjacent to the free states during the Civil War.

bore[1] (bôr, bōr) ▶ *v.* **bored, bor•ing 1.** To make a hole in or through with or as if with a drill. **2.** To form (e.g., a tunnel) by drilling, digging, or burrowing. ▶ *n.* **1.** A hole or passage made by or as if by drilling. **2.** The interior diameter of a hole, tube, or cylinder. **3.** The caliber of a firearm. **4.** A drilling tool. [< OE *borian*.] —**bor′er** *n.*

bore[2] (bôr, bōr) ▶ *v.* **bored, bor•ing.** To make weary by being dull, repetitive, or tedious: *The movie bored us.* ▶ *n.* One that is boring. [?]

bore[3] (bôr, bōr) ▶ *v.* P.t. of **bear[1].**

bo•re•al (bôr′ē-əl, bōr′-) ▶ *adj.* Northern. [< Lat. *Boreās*, the north wind.]

bore•dom (bôr′dəm, bōr′-) ▶ *n.* The condition of being bored; ennui.

Bor•gia (bôr′jə, -zhə). Italian family, including **Cesare** (1475?–1507), a religious and political leader, and **Lucrezia** (1489–1519), a patron of the arts.

bo•ric acid (bôr′ĭk, bōr′-) ▶ *n.* A white or colorless crystalline compound, H_3BO_3, used esp. as an antiseptic and preservative.

born (bôrn) ▶ *v.* P.part. of **bear[1].** ▶ *adj.* **1.** Brought into life by birth. **2.** Having a natural talent: *a born artist.* **3.** Resulting or coming from: *wisdom born of experience.*

borne (bôrn, bōrn) ▶ *v.* P.part. of **bear[1].**

Bor•ne•o (bôr′nē-ō′) An island of the W Pacific in the Malay Archipelago between the Sulu and Java seas. —**Bor′ne•an** *adj.*

Bo•ro•din (bôr′ə-dēn′), **Aleksandr Porfirevich.** 1833–87. Russian composer and chemist.

bo•ron (bôr′ŏn′, bōr′-) ▶ *n. Symbol* **B** A soft, brown, amorphous or crystalline nonmetallic element used in flares, nuclear reactor control elements, abrasives, and hard metallic alloys. At. no. 5. See table at **element.** [BOR(AX) + (CARB)ON.]

bor•ough (bûr′ō, bŭr′-ō) ▶ *n.* **1.** A self-governing incorporated town in some US states. **2.** One of the five administrative units of New York City. **3.** A civil division of Alaska equivalent to a county. **4.** *Chiefly Brit.* **a.** A town having a municipal corporation. **b.** A town that sends a representative to Parliament. [< OE *burg*, fortified town.]

bor•row (bŏr′ō, bôr′ō) ▶ *v.* **1.** To obtain or receive (something) on loan with the intent to return it. **2.** To adopt or use as one's own. [< OE *borgian*.] —**bor′row•er** *n.*

bor•row•ing (bŏr′ō-ĭng, bôr′-) ▶ *n.* Something borrowed, especially a word borrowed from one language for use in another.

borscht also **borsht** (bôrsht) ▶ *n.* A beet soup served hot or cold, usu. with sour cream. [< Russ. *borshch*.]

bor•zoi (bôr′zoi′) ▶ *n.* A tall slender dog having a narrow pointed head and silky coat. [< Russ. *borzoĭ*, swift.]

Bosch (bŏsh, bôsh), **Hieronymous.** 1450?–1516. Dutch painter.

bosh (bŏsh) ▶ *n. Informal* Nonsense. [< Turk. *boş*, empty.] —**bosh** *interj.*

bo's'n or **bos'n** (bō′sən) ▶ *n.* Vars. of **boatswain.**

Bos•ni•a (bŏz′nē-ə) The N part of Bosnia and Herzegovina. —**Bos′ni•an** *adj. & n.*

Bosnia and Herzegovina or **Bos•ni•a-Her•ze•go•vi•na** (bŏz′nē-ə-hĕrt′sə-gō′vē-nə, -gō-vē′-, hûrt′-). A region and republic of the NW Balkan Peninsula W of Serbia. Cap. Sarajevo. Pop. 3,527,000.

bos•om (bo͝oz′əm, bo͞o′zəm) ▶ *n.* **1a.** The human chest. **b.** A woman's breast or breasts. **2.** The heart or center: *the bosom of our family.* ▶ *adj.* Intimate: *a bosom friend.* [< OE *bōsm*.]

Bos•po•rus (bŏs′pər-əs) A narrow strait separating European and Asian Turkey and joining the Black Sea with the Sea of Marmara.

boss[1] (bôs, bŏs) ▶ *n.* **1.** An employer or supervisor. **2.** A politician who controls a political party or machine. ▶*v.* **1.** To supervise or control. See Syns at **supervise. 2.** To give orders to, esp. in a domineering manner. [Du. *baas,* master.] —**boss′y** *adj.*

boss² (bôs, bŏs) ▶*n.* A knoblike ornament. ▶*v.* To emboss. [< OFr. *boce.*]

Bos•ton (bô′stən, bŏs′tən) The capital of MA, in the E part on **Boston Bay,** an arm of Massachusetts Bay. Pop. 574,283. —**Bos•to′ni•an** (bô-stō′nē-ən, bŏs-) *adj. & n.*

bo•sun (bō′sən) ▶*n.* Var. of **boatswain.**

Bos•well (bŏz′wĕl′, -wəl), **James.** 1740–95. Scottish lawyer, diarist, and writer.

bot (bŏt) ▶*n.* A software program that imitates human behavior, as by querying search engines.

bot•a•ny (bŏt′n-ē) ▶*n.* The science or study of plants. [< Gk. *botanē,* plants.] —**bo•tan′i•cal** (bə-tăn′ĭ-kəl), **bo•tan′ic** *adj.* —**bot′a•nist** *n.*

botch (bŏch) ▶*v.* **1.** To ruin through clumsiness. **2.** To repair clumsily. [ME *bocchen,* mend.] —**botch** *n.* —**botch′er** *n.* —**botch′i•ly** *adv.* —**botch′y** *adj.*

Syns: *botch, blow, bungle, fumble, muff* **v.**

both (bōth) ▶*adj.* One and the other; of or being two in conjunction: *Both guests are here.* ▶*pron.* The one and the other: *Both were tall.* ▶*conj.* Used with *and* to indicate that each of two things in a coordinated phrase or clause is included: *Both on and off.* [< OE *bā thā,* both those.]

both•er (bŏ*th*′ər) ▶*v.* **1.** To disturb, annoy, or anger, esp. by minor irritations. **2.** To trouble or concern oneself. ▶*n.* A cause or state of disturbance. ▶*interj.* Used to express annoyance. [Poss. of Celt. orig.] —**both′er•some** (-səm) *adj.*

Both•ni•a (bŏth′nē-ə), **Gulf of.** An arm of the Baltic Sea between Sweden and Finland.

Bot•swa•na (bŏt-swä′nə) A landlocked country of S-central Africa. Cap. Gaborone. Pop. 1,443,000.

Bot•ti•cel•li (bŏt′ĭ-chĕl′ē), **Sandro.** 1444?–1510. Italian painter.

bot•tle (bŏt′l) ▶*n.* **1.** A receptacle having a narrow neck, usu. no handles, and a mouth that can be plugged, corked, or capped. **2.** *Informal* Intoxicating liquor. ▶*v.* **-tled, -tling 1.** To place in a bottle. **2.** To restrain: *bottled up my emotions.* [< LLat. *buttis,* cask.] —**bot′tle•ful′** *n.* —**bot′tler** *n.*

bot•tle•neck (bŏt′l-nĕk′) ▶*n.* **1.** A narrow or obstructed section, as of a highway or pipeline, where movement is slowed down. **2.** A hindrance to progress or production.

bot•tom (bŏt′əm) ▶*n.* **1.** The deepest or lowest part: *the bottom of a well; the bottom of the page.* **2.** The underside. **3.** The supporting part; base. **4.** The basic underlying quality; essence. **5.** The solid surface under a body of water. **6.** often **bottoms** Low-lying land adjacent to a river. **7.** *Informal* The buttocks. —***idiom:* at bottom** Basically. [< OE *botm.*] —**bot′tom•less** *adj.*

bot•tom•land (bŏt′əm-lănd′) ▶*n.* See **bottom** 6.

bottom line ▶*n.* **1.** The lowest line in a financial statement that shows net income or loss. **2.** The final result or statement; upshot. **3.** The main or essential point.

bot•u•lism (bŏch′ə-lĭz′əm) ▶*n.* A severe, sometimes fatal food poisoning caused by bacteria that grow in improperly canned foods. [< Lat. *botulus,* sausage.]

Bou•dic•ca (bo͞o-dĭk′ə) also **Bo•ad•i•ce•a** (bō′ăd-ĭ-sē′ə). 1st cent. A.D. Queen of ancient Britain.

bou•doir (bo͞o′dwär′, -dwôr′) ▶*n.* A woman's private room. [< OFr. *bouder,* sulk.]

bouf•fant (bo͞o-fänt′) ▶*adj.* Puffed-out; full: *a bouffant hair style.* [< OFr. *bouffer,* puff up.]

bou•gain•vil•le•a (bo͞o′gən-vĭl′ē-ə, -vĭl′yə) ▶*n.* A woody tropical shrub or vine with variously colored petallike bracts attached to the flowers. [After Louis Antoine de *Bougainville* (1729–1811).]

bough (bou) ▶*n.* A tree branch, esp. a large or main branch. [< OE *bōh.*]

bought (bôt) ▶*v.* P.t. and p.part. of **buy.**

bouil•la•baisse (bo͞o′yə-bās′, bo͞ol′yə-bās′) ▶*n.* A stew made of several kinds of fish and shellfish. [< Prov. *bouiabaisso.*]

bouil•lon (bo͞ol′yŏn′, -yən) ▶*n.* A clear thin meat broth. [< OFr. *boulir,* BOIL[1].]

Boul. ▶*abbr.* boulevard

boul•der (bōl′dər) ▶*n.* A large rounded mass of rock. [ME *bulder.*]

Boulder. A city of N-central CO NW of Denver. Pop. 83,312.

boul•e•vard (bo͞ol′ə-värd′, bo͞o′lə-) ▶*n.* **1.** A broad city street, often tree-lined and landscaped. **2.** *Regional* See **median strip.** See Regional Note at **neutral ground.** [< MDu. *bolwer,* BULWARK.]

bounce (bouns) ▶*v.* **bounced, bounc•ing 1.** To rebound or cause to rebound after having struck an object or surface. **2.** To move jerkily; bump: *The car bounced over the potholes.* **3.** To recover quickly: *bounced back to good health.* **4.** To bound; spring. **5.** *Informal* To be sent back by a bank as valueless: *a check that bounced.* ▶*n.* **1.** A bound or rebound. **2.** A spring or leap. **3.** The capacity to rebound: *The ball had lost its bounce.* **4.** Spirit; liveliness. [Prob. < ME *bounsen,* beat.] —**bounc′i•ly** *adv.* —**bounc′y** *adj.*

bounc•er (boun′sər) ▶*n. Slang* A person employed to expel disorderly persons from a public place, esp. a bar.

bounc•ing (boun′sĭng) ▶*adj.* Vigorous; healthy: *a bouncing baby.*

bound¹ (bound) ▶*v.* **1.** To leap or spring. **2.** To move by leaping. **3.** To bounce or rebound. ▶*n.* **1.** A leap; jump. **2.** A rebound; bounce. [< OFr. *bondir,* resound.]

bound² (bound) ▶*n.* **1.** often **bounds** A boundary; limit. **2. bounds** The territory on or within a boundary. ▶*v.* **1.** To limit or confine. **2.** To constitute the limit of. **3.** To demarcate. [< Med.Lat. *bodina.*]

bound³ (bound) ▶*v.* P.t. and p.part. of **bind.** ▶*adj.* **1.** Confined by or as if by bonds. **2.** Being under legal or moral obligation. **3.** Equipped with a cover or binding. **4.** Certain: *We're bound to be late.*

bound⁴ (bound) ▶*adj.* On the way: *bound for home.* [< ON *būinn,* p.part. of *būa,* get ready.]

bound•a•ry (boun′də-rē, -drē) ▶*n., pl.* **-ries.** Something that indicates a border or limit.

Boundary Peak. A mountain, 4,008.6 m (13,143 ft), of SW NV near the CA border.

bound•en (boun′dən) ▶*adj.* Obligatory: *their*

bounden duty. [ME, p.part. of *binden*, BIND.]

bound•er (boun′dər) ►*n. Chiefly Brit.* A cad.

bound•less (bound′lĭs) ►*adj.* Being without limits. See Syns at **infinite.** —**bound′less•ly** *adv.* —**bound′less•ness** *n.*

boun•te•ous (boun′tē-əs) ►*adj.* **1.** Giving generously. See Syns at **liberal. 2.** Copiously given; plentiful. —**boun′te•ous•ly** *adv.*

boun•ti•ful (boun′tə-fəl) ►*adj.* **1.** Giving generously. See Syns at **liberal. 2.** Marked by abundance; plentiful. —**boun′ti•ful•ly** *adv.*

boun•ty (boun′tē) ►*n., pl.* **-ties 1.** Liberality in giving: *a patron's bounty.* **2.** Something given liberally. **3.** A reward or inducement, esp. one given by a government for performing a service, such as killing predatory animals. [< Lat. *bonitās*, goodness.]

bou•quet (bō-kā′, bo͞o-) ►*n.* **1.** A cluster of flowers. **2.** A pleasant fragrance, esp. of a wine. See Syns at **fragrance.** [< OFr. *bosquet*, thicket.]

bour•bon (bûr′bən) ►*n.* A whiskey distilled from a fermented mash of corn, malt, and rye. [After *Bourbon* County, Kentucky.]

Bour•bon (bo͝or′bən, bo͝or-bôN′). French royal family descended from Louis I, Duke of Bourbon (1270?–1342), whose members have ruled in France, Spain, and Italy.

bour•geois (bo͝or-zhwä′, bo͝or′zhwä′) ►*n., pl.* **-geois 1.** One belonging to the middle class. **2.** In Marxist theory, a capitalist. ►*adj.* **1.** Of or typical of the middle class. **2.** Preoccupied with respectability and material values. [< OFr. *burgeis*, citizen of a town.]

bour•geoi•sie (bo͝or′zhwä-zē′) ►*n.* **1.** The middle class. **2.** In Marxist theory, the social group opposed to the proletariat. [Fr.]

Bourke-White (bûrk′hwīt′, -wīt′), **Margaret.** 1906–71. Amer. photographer and editor.

Margaret Bourke-White
photographed in 1940

Bourne•mouth (bôrn′məth, bōrn′-, bo͝orn′-) A borough of S England on an inlet of the English Channel SW of Southampton.

bout (bout) ►*n.* **1.** A contest; match: *a wrestling bout.* **2.** A period of time spent in a particular way; spell: *a bout of the flu.* [< ME *bought*, a turn < *bowen*, BOW².]

bou•tique (bo͞o-tēk′) ►*n.* A small retail shop that specializes in gifts, fashionable items, or food. [< Lat. *apothēca*, storehouse.]

bou•ton•niere (bo͞o′tə-nîr′, -tən-yâr′) ►*n.* A flower worn in a buttonhole. [< OFr., buttonhole < *bouton*, BUTTON.]

bo•vine (bō′vīn′, -vēn′) ►*adj.* **1.** Of or resembling an ox or cow. **2.** Sluggish, dull, and stolid. [< Lat. *bōs*, cow.] —**bo′vine′** *n.*

bow¹ (bou) ►*n.* The front section of a ship or boat. [Poss. of LGer. orig.]

bow² (bou) ►*v.* **1.** To bend the body, head, or knee in order to express greeting, consent, courtesy, or veneration. **2.** To acquiesce; submit. —***phrasal verb:* bow out** To remove oneself; withdraw. ►*n.* An act of bowing, as in respect. [< OE *būgan.*]

bow³ (bō) ►*n.* **1.** A curve or arch. **2.** A weapon consisting of a curved, flexible strip of wood, strung taut from end to end and used to launch arrows. **3.** *Mus.* A rod strung with horsehair, used in playing the violin and related instruments. **4.** A knot usu. having two loops and two ends, as a bowknot. **5.** A rainbow. ►*v.* **1.** To bend into a bow. **2.** *Mus.* To play (a stringed instrument) with a bow. [< OE *boga.*]

bowd•ler•ize (bōd′lə-rīz′, boud′-) ►*v.* **-ized, -iz•ing.** To expurgate (e.g., a book) for prudish reasons. [After Thomas *Bowdler* (1754–1825).] —**bowd′ler•i•za′tion** *n.*

bow•el (bou′əl, boul) ►*n.* **1a.** often **bowels** The intestine. **b.** A division of the intestine: *the large bowel.* **2. bowels** The interior of something: *in the bowels of the ship.* [< Lat. *botulus*, sausage.]

bow•er (bou′ər) ►*n.* A shaded, leafy recess. [< OE *būr*, dwelling.]

bow•ie knife (bō′ē, bo͞o′ē) ►*n.* A long, single-edged steel hunting knife. [After James *Bowie* (1796–1836).]

bow•knot (bō′nŏt′) ►*n.* **1.** A knot with large, decorative loops. **2.** A bowtie.

bowl¹ (bōl) ►*n.* **1a.** A rounded hollow vessel for food or fluids. **b.** The contents of such a vessel. **2.** A curved hollow part, as of a spoon or pipe. **3.** A bowl-shaped structure or edifice, such as a stadium. [< OE *bolla.*]

bowl² (bōl) ►*n.* **1.** A large solid ball rolled in certain games. **2.** A roll of the ball in bowling. ►*v.* **1.** To play the game of bowling. **2.** To roll a ball in bowling. —***phrasal verb:* bowl over 1.** To astound. **2.** To knock over. [< Lat. *bulla*, round object.]

bow•leg•ged (bō′lĕg′ĭd, -lĕgd′) ►*adj.* Having legs that curve outward at the knees.

bowl•er¹ (bō′lər) ►*n.* One who bowls.

bowl•er² (bō′lər) ►*n.* A derby hat. [Poss. < BOWL².]

bow•line (bō′lĭn, -līn′) ►*n.* A knot forming a loop that does not slip. [< MLGer. *bōlīne.*]

bowline

bowl•ing (bō′lĭng) ►*n.* **1a.** A game played by rolling a heavy ball down a wooden alley in order to knock down a triangular group of ten pins; tenpins. **b.** Any of various similar games, such as duckpins or candlepins. **2.** A game played on a bowling green by rolling a wooden ball as close as possible to a target ball.

bowling alley ►*n.* **1.** A level wooden lane used in bowling. **2.** A building or room containing such lanes.

bowling green ►*n.* A level grassy area for bowling.
bow•man (bō′mən) ►*n.* An archer.
bow•sprit (bou′sprĭt′, bō′-) ►*n.* A spar extending forward from the bow of a sailing ship. [< MLGer. *bōchsprēt.*]
bow•string (bō′strĭng′) ►*n.* The cord attached to both ends of an archer's bow.
bow tie (bō) ►*n.* A short necktie tied in a bowknot close to the collar.
box[1] (bŏks) ►*n.* **1a.** A container, usu. rectangular and often with a lid. **b.** The amount or quantity a box can hold. **2.** A square or rectangle. **3.** A separated seating compartment, as in a theater. **4.** A booth: *a sentry box.* **5.** A perplexing situation. ►*v.* **1.** To place in or as if in a box. **2.** To restrict to a narrow scope or position: *boxed in by new rules.* [< OE, ult. < Gk. *puxis.*] —**box′ful′** *n.* —**box′y** *adj.*
box[2] (bŏks) ►*n.* A slap or blow with the hand or fist. ►*v.* **1.** To hit with the hand or fist. **2.** To take part in a boxing match. [ME.]
box[3] (bŏks) ►*n., pl.* **box** or **box•es.** An evergreen shrub or tree having hard yellowish wood, widely grown as a hedge. [< OE, ult. < Gk. *puxos.*]
box•car (bŏks′kär′) ►*n.* A fully enclosed railroad car used to transport freight.
box•er[1] (bŏk′sər) ►*n.* *Sports* One who boxes, esp. professionally.
box•er[2] (bŏk′sər) ►*n.* A medium-sized, short-haired dog having a short, square-jawed muzzle. [Ger. < E. BOXER[1].]
box•ing (bŏk′sĭng) ►*n.* The sport of fighting with the fists.
box office ►*n.* A booth, as in a theater, where tickets are sold. —**box′-of′fice** *adj.*
box•wood (bŏks′wo͝od′) ►*n.* **1.** The box shrub or tree. **2.** The hard wood of the box.
boy (boi) ►*n.* A male child or youth. ►*interj.* Used to express mild elation or disgust. [ME *boi.*] —**boy′hood′** *n.* —**boy′ish** *adj.* —**boy′ish•ly** *adv.* —**boy′ish•ness** *n.*
boy•cott (boi′kŏt′) ►*v.* To abstain from buying or dealing with as a protest. See Syns at **blackball.** [After Charles C. *Boycott* (1832–1897).] —**boy′cott′** *n.*
boy•friend (boi′frĕnd′) ►*n.* **1.** A favored male companion or sweetheart. **2.** A male friend.
Boyle (boil), **Robert.** 1627–91. Irish-born British physicist and chemist.
Boy Scout ►*n.* A member of a worldwide organization of young men and boys, founded for character development, citizenship training, and outdoor skills.
boy•sen•ber•ry (boi′zən-bĕr′ē) ►*n.* **1.** A prickly bramble derived from a W North American blackberry. **2.** The edible wine-red fruit of this plant. [After Rudolph *Boysen* (d. 1950).]
BPOE ►*abbr.* Benevolent and Protective Order of Elks
Br ► The symbol for the element **bromine.**
Br. ►*abbr.* **1.** Britain **2.** British
bra (brä) ►*n.* A brassiere.
brace (brās) ►*n.* **1.** A clamp. **2.** A device, such as a beam in a building, that steadies or supports a weight. **3. braces** *Chiefly Brit.* Suspenders. **4.** An orthopedic appliance used to support a bodily part. **5.** often **braces** A dental appliance of bands and wires that is fixed to the teeth to correct irregular alignment. **6.** A cranklike handle for securing and turning a bit. **7.** A symbol, { or }, used to enclose written or printed lines that are considered a unit. ►*v.* **braced, brac•ing 1.** To support, strengthen, or hold steady. **2.** To prepare for a struggle, impact, or danger. **3.** To fill with energy; stimulate. [< Gk. *brakhiōn,* upper arm.]
brace•let (brās′lĭt) ►*n.* An ornamental band or chain worn around the wrist or arm. [< Gk. *brakhiōn,* upper arm.]
bra•chi•o•saur (brā′kē-ə-sôr′, brăk′ē-) or **bra•chi•o•sau•rus** (brā′kē-ə-sôr′əs, brăk′ē-) ►*n.* A massive, herbaceous dinosaur of the Jurassic and Cretaceous periods, having forelegs longer than the hind legs. [Gk. *brakhiōn,* upper arm + *sauros,* lizard.]
brack•en (brăk′ən) ►*n.* A weedy fern having large triangular fronds, tough stems, and often forming dense thickets. [ME *braken.*]
brack•et (brăk′ĭt) ►*n.* **1.** An L-shaped fixture, one arm of which is fastened to a vertical surface, the other projecting to support a shelf or other weight. **2.** A shelf supported by brackets. **3.** One of a pair of marks, [ ], used to enclose written or printed material. **4.** A classification or grouping, esp. by income, within a sequence of numbers or grades. [Poss. < Fr. *braguette,* codpiece.] —**brack′et** *v.*
brack•ish (brăk′ĭsh) ►*adj.* Containing a mixture of seawater and fresh water. [< Du. *brak.*] —**brack′ish•ness** *n.*
bract (brăkt) ►*n.* A leaflike plant part located just below a flower, flower stalk, or flower cluster. [< Lat. *bractea,* gold leaf.]
brad (brăd) ►*n.* A thin wire nail with a small head. [< ON *broddr,* spike.] —**brad** *v.*
Brad•bur•y (brăd′bĕr′ē, -bə-rē), **Ray Douglas.** b. 1920. Amer. writer.
Brad•dock (brăd′ək), **Edward.** 1695–1755. British general in America.
Brad•ford (brăd′fərd) A borough of N-central England.
Bradford[1], **William.** 1590–1657. English Puritan colonist in America.
Bradford[2], **William.** 1663–1752. English-born Amer. colonial printer.
Brad•ley (brăd′lē), **Omar Nelson.** 1893–1981. Amer. general.
Brad•street (brăd′strēt′), **Anne Dudley.** 1612–72. English-born Amer. colonial poet.
Bra•dy (brā′dē), **Mathew B.** 1823–96. Amer. pioneer photographer.

Mathew Brady

brag (brăg) ►*v.* **bragged, brag•ging.** To talk or assert boastfully. [ME *braggen.*] —**brag** *n.* —**brag′ger** *n.*
brag•ga•do•ci•o (brăg′ə-dō′sē-ō′, -shē-ō′)

►*n.*, *pl.* **-os 1.** A braggart. **2a.** Empty or pretentious bragging. **b.** A swaggering, cocky manner. [After *Braggadocchio* in *The Faerie Queene* by Spenser.]

brag•gart (brăg′ərt) ►*n.* One given to empty boasting; bragger. [< Fr. *braguer*, to brag, poss. < ME *braggen.*]

Brahe (brä, brä′hē), **Tycho.** 1546–1601. Danish astronomer.

Brah•ma (brä′mə) ►*n.* **1.** *Hinduism* The creator god, conceived chiefly as a member of the triad including also Vishnu and Shiva. **2.**Var. of **Brahman** 2.

Brah•man (brä′mən) also **Brah•min** (-mĭn) ►*n.* **1.** A member of the highest of the four major castes of traditional Indian society, responsible for officiating at religious rites and studying and teaching the Vedas. **2.** also **Brah•ma** (-mə) One of a breed of domestic cattle bred from stock originating in India, having a hump between the shoulders. [Skt. *brahma, brahmaṇ-*.]

Brah•man•ism (brä′mə-nĭz′əm) also **Brah•min•ism** (-mĭ-) ►*n.* *Hinduism* **1.** The religion of ancient India as reflected in the Vedas. **2.** The social and religious system of Hindus, esp. of Brahmins, based on a caste structure. —**Brah′man•ist** *n.*

Brah•ma•pu•tra (brä′mə-po͞o′trə) A river of S Asia rising in SW Xizang (Tibet) and flowing about 2,896 km (1,800 mi) to the Ganges R.

Brah•min (brä′mĭn) ►*n.* **1.**Var. of **Brahman. 2.** A member of a cultural and social elite: *a Boston Brahmin.* [< Skt. *brāhmaṇa-*, of Brahmins.] —**Brah•min′ic** (-mĭn′ĭk) *adj.*

Brahms (brämz), **Johannes.** 1833–97. German composer. —**Brahms′i•an** *adj.*

braid (brād) ►*v.* **1.** To interweave strands or lengths of. **2.** To make by weaving strands together. **3.** To decorate or edge with an interwoven trim. ►*n.* **1.** A braided segment or length, as of hair, fabric, or fiber. **2.** Ornamental cord or ribbon, used esp. for decorating or edging fabrics. [< OE *bregdan*, weave.] —**braid′er** *n.*

Bră•i•la (brə-ē′lə) A city of SE Romania on the Danube R. near the Moldavian and Ukranian borders. Pop. 236,344.

Braille or **braille** (brāl) ►*n.* A system of writing and printing for visually impaired people, in which raised dots represent letters and numerals. [After Louis BRAILLE.]

Braille, Louis. 1809–52. French inventor of a writing system for the blind (1829).

brain (brān) ►*n.* **1a.** The portion of the vertebrate central nervous system, enclosed within the cranium and composed of gray matter and white matter, that is the primary center for the regulation and control of bodily activities, the receiving and interpreting of sensory impulses, and the exercising of thought and emotion. **b.** A functionally similar portion of the invertebrate nervous system. **2.** often **brains** Intellectual power; intelligence. **3.** A highly intelligent person. ►*v.* *Slang* **1.** To smash in the skull of. **2.** To hit on the head. —***idioms:*** **beat (one's) brains (out)** *Informal* To try energetically. **on the brain** Obsessively in mind. **pick (someone's) brain** To explore another's ideas through questioning. [< OE *brægen.*] —**brain′i•ness** *n.* —**brain′less** *adj.* —**brain′less•ness** *n.* —**brain′y** *adj.*

Braille
alphabet and numerals

brain•child (brān′chīld′) ►*n.* An original idea, plan, or creation.

brain death ►*n.* Irreversible brain damage and loss of brain function, as evidenced by cessation of activity of the central nervous system. —**brain′-dead′** (brān′dĕd′) *adj.*

brain•pow•er (brān′pou′ər) ►*n.* Intellectual capacity.

brain•storm (brān′stôrm′) ►*n.* A sudden clever plan or idea. ►*v.* To attempt to solve a problem by a method in which the members of a group spontaneously propose ideas and solutions. —**brain′storm′ing** *n.*

brain•wash•ing (brān′wŏsh′ĭng, -wô′shĭng) ►*n.* Intensive, forcible indoctrination aimed at replacing a person's basic convictions with an alternative set of fixed beliefs. —**brain′-wash′** *v.*

brain wave ►*n.* A rhythmic fluctuation of electric potential between parts of the brain, as seen on an electroencephalogram.

braise (brāz) ►*v.* **braised, brais•ing.** To brown in fat and then simmer in a small quantity of liquid in a covered container. [< OFr. *brese*, hot coals.]

brake[1] (brāk) ►*n.* A device for slowing or stopping motion, as of a vehicle, esp. by contact friction. ►*v.* **braked, brak•ing 1.** To reduce the speed of with or as if with a brake. **2.** To operate or apply a brake. [Prob. < MLGer., curb.]

brake[2] (brāk) ►*n.* Any of several ferns, esp. bracken. [< ME.]

brake[3] (brāk) ►*n.* A densely overgrown area; thicket. [< MLGer.]

brake•man (brāk′mən) ►*n.* A railroad employee who assists the conductor and checks on the operation of a train's brakes.

bram•ble (brăm′bəl) ►*n.* A prickly plant or shrub, esp. the blackberry or raspberry. [< OE *bræmbel.*] —**bram′bly** *adj.*

Bramp•ton (brămp′tən) A city of S Ontario,

Canada, a suburb of Toronto. Pop. 149,030.

bran (brăn) ► *n.* The outer husks of cereal grain removed during the process of milling and used for dietary fiber. [< OFr.]

branch (brănch) ► *n.* **1a.** A secondary woody stem growing from the trunk, main stem, or limb of a tree or shrub. **b.** A similar structure or part. **2.** Something that resembles a branch of a tree, as the tine of a deer's antlers. **3.** A limited part of a larger or more complex unit or system. **4.** A division of a family or tribe. **5.** A tributary of a river. See Regional Note at **run.** ► *v.* **1.** To divide or spread out in branches. **2.** To enlarge one's scope: *branch out into new fields.* [< LLat. *branca*, paw.] —**branched** *adj.*

Syns: *branch, arm, fork, offshoot* **n.**

brand (brănd) ► *n.* **1a.** A trademark or distinctive name identifying a product or manufacturer. **b.** A product line so identified. **c.** A distinctive kind. **2.** A mark indicating ownership, burned on the hide of an animal. **3.** A mark formerly burned into the flesh of criminals. **4.** A mark of disgrace. See Syns at **stain. 5.** A branding iron. **6.** A piece of burning wood. ► *v.* **1.** To mark with or as if with a brand. See Syns at **mark[1]. 2.** To stigmatize. [< OE, torch.]

Bran•deis (brăn′dīs′, -dīz′), **Louis Dembitz.** 1856–1941. Amer. jurist; associate justice of the US Supreme Court (1916–39).

Bran•den•burg (brăn′dən-bûrg′) **1.** A region and former duchy of N-central Germany around which the kingdom of Prussia developed. **2.** A city of NE Germany WSW of Berlin. Pop. 95,133.

brand•ing iron (brăn′dĭng) ► *n.* An iron that is heated and used for branding.

bran•dish (brăn′dĭsh) ► *v.* **1.** To wave or flourish (e.g., a weapon) menacingly. **2.** To display ostentatiously. See Syns at **flourish.** [< OFr. *brandir* < *brand*, sword.]

brand name ► *n.* See **trade name** 1. —**brand′-name′** *adj.*

brand-new (brănd′no͞o′, -nyo͞o′) ► *adj.* Being fresh and unused; completely new.

Bran•do (brăn′dō), **Marlon.** b. 1924. Amer. actor.

Brandt (brănt, bränt), **Willy.** 1913–92. German political leader; 1971 Nobel Peace Prize.

bran•dy (brăn′dē) ► *n., pl.* **-dies.** An alcoholic liquor distilled from wine or fermented fruit juice. [< Du. *brandewijn.*] —**bran′dy** *v.*

brant (brănt) ► *n., pl.* **brant** or **brants.** A small wild goose having a black neck and head. [Poss. < ME *brende*, brindled.]

Brant, Joseph. 1742–1807. Mohawk leader.

Braque (bräk, brăk), **Georges.** 1882–1963. French cubist painter.

brash (brăsh) ► *adj.* **-er, -est 1.** Hasty and unthinking; rash. **2.** Bold; impudent. [Poss. imit.] —**brash′ly** *adv.* —**brash′ness** *n.*

Bra•sí•lia (brə-zĭl′yə) The capital of Brazil, in the central plateau NW of Rio de Janeiro. Pop. 1,598,415.

Bra•şov (brä-shôv′) A city of central Romania NNW of Bucharest. Pop. 324,104.

brass (brăs) ► *n.* **1a.** A yellowish alloy of copper and zinc. **b.** Objects made of brass. **2.** often **brasses** *Mus.* The brass instruments of an orchestra or band. **3.** *Informal* Bold self-assurance; effrontery. **4.** *Slang* High-ranking military officers. [< OE *bræs.*] —**brass′y** *adj.*

bras•se•rie (brăs′ə-rē′) ► *n.* A bar serving food as well as alcoholic beverages. [< OFr. *bracier*, to brew.]

Joseph Brant
c. 1807 portrait

brass hat ► *n. Slang* One of high rank or position, esp. a high-ranking military officer.

bras•siere (brə-zîr′) ► *n.* A woman's undergarment that supports the breasts. [OFr. *bras*, arm; see BRACE.]

brass tacks ► *pl.n. Informal* Essential facts; basics: *getting down to brass tacks.*

brat (brăt) ► *n.* A spoiled or ill-mannered child. [Poss. < OE *bratt*, coarse garment.] —**brat′ty** *adj.*

Bra•ti•sla•va (brăt′ĭ-slä′və, brä′tĭ-) The capital of Slovakia, in the SE part on the Danube R. Pop. 445,089.

Braun (brôn, broun), **Wernher Magnus Maximilian von.** 1912–77. German-born Amer. rocket engineer.

bra•va•do (brə-vä′dō) ► *n., pl.* **-dos** or **-does 1.** Defiant or swaggering behavior. **2.** A false show of bravery. [< Sp. *bravada.*]

brave (brāv) ► *adj.* **brav•er, brav•est 1.** Possessing or displaying courage; valiant. **2.** Making a fine display; splendid. **3.** Excellent; great. ► *n.* A Native American warrior. ► *v.* **braved, brav•ing 1.** To undergo or face courageously. **2.** To challenge; dare. See Syns at **defy.** [< OFr. *bravo.*] —**brave′ly** *adv.* —**brave′ness** *n.*

brav•er•y (brā′və-rē, brāv′rē) ► *n.* Courage.

bra•vo (brä′vō, brä-vō′) ► *interj.* Used to express approval, esp. of a performance. ► *n., pl.* **-vos.** A cry of "bravo." [Ital.]

bra•vu•ra (brə-vo͝or′ə, -vyo͝or′ə) ► *n.* **1.** *Mus.* Brilliant technique or style in performance. **2.** A showy manner or display. [Ital.]

brawl (brôl) ► *n.* A noisy quarrel or fight. [< ME *braullen*, to quarrel.] —**brawl** *v.* —**brawl′er** *n.*

Syns: *brawl, donnybrook, fracas, fray, free-for-all, melee, row* **n.**

brawn (brôn) ► *n.* **1.** Solid and well-developed muscles. **2.** Muscular strength. [< OFr. *braon*, meat, of Gmc. orig.]

brawn•y (brô′nē) ► *adj.* **-i•er, -i•est.** Well-muscled; strong. See Syns at **muscular.**

bray (brā) ► *v.* To utter the loud harsh cry of a donkey. [< OFr. *braire.*] —**bray** *n.*

braze (brāz) ► *v.* **brazed, braz•ing.** To solder together using a solder with a high melting point. [Prob. < OFr. *braser*, to burn.] —**braz′er** *n.*

bra•zen (brā′zən) ►*adj.* **1.** Rudely bold; insolent. **2.** Having a loud harsh sound. **3.** Made of or resembling brass. ►*v.* To face with bold self-assurance: *brazened out the crisis.* [< OE *bræsen*, made of brass.] —**bra′zen•ly** *adv.* —**bra′zen•ness** *n.*

bra•zier[1] (brā′zhər) ►*n.* One who works in brass. [ME *brasier* < *bras*, BRASS.]

bra•zier[2] (brā′zhər) ►*n.* A metal pan for holding burning coals or charcoal. [< OFr. *brese*, embers.]

Bra•zil (brə-zĭl′) A country of central and E South America. Cap. Brasília. Pop. 153,725,000. —**Bra•zil′i•an** *adj. & n.*

Brazil nut ►*n.* The hard-shelled edible seed of a South American tree.

Braz•os (brăz′əs) A river rising in E NM and flowing about 1,400 km (870 mi) across TX to the Gulf of Mexico.

Braz•za•ville (brăz′ə-vĭl′) The capital of the Republic of the Congo, in the S part on the Congo R. Pop. 596,200.

breach (brēch) ►*n.* **1.** An opening, tear, or rupture, esp. in a solid structure. **2.** A violation or infraction, as of a law or obligation. **3.** A disruption of friendly relations. **4.** A leap of a whale from the water. [< OE *brēc.*] —**breach** *v.*

bread (brĕd) ►*n.* **1.** A staple food made chiefly from moistened, usu. leavened flour or meal kneaded and baked. **2.** Food in general, regarded as necessary to sustain life. **3a.** Livelihood: *earn one's bread.* **b.** *Slang* Money. ►*v.* To coat with bread crumbs before cooking. [< OE *brēad.*]

bread•bas•ket (brĕd′băs′kĭt) ►*n.* An abundant grain-producing region.

bread•board (brĕd′bôrd′, -bōrd′) ►*n.* **1.** A slicing board. **2.** An experimental model, esp. of an electronic circuit.

bread•fruit (brĕd′fro͞ot′) ►*n.* **1.** A Malaysian timber tree having large round yellowish fruits. **2.** The edible fruit of this tree, having a breadlike texture when cooked.

bread•stuff (brĕd′stŭf′) ►*n.* **1.** Bread in any form. **2.** Flour or grain used in making bread.

breadth (brĕdth) ►*n.* **1.** The measure or dimension from side to side; width. **2a.** Wide range or scope. **b.** Tolerance; broadmindedness: *a jurist of great breadth and wisdom.* [< ME *brede*, broad.]

bread•win•ner (brĕd′wĭn′ər) ►*n.* One whose earnings are the primary source of support for one's dependents.

break (brāk) ►*v.* **broke** (brōk), **bro•ken** (brō′kən), **break•ing 1a.** To separate into or reduce to pieces by sudden force. **b.** To crack without separating into pieces. **2.** To make or become unusable or inoperative. **3.** To give way; collapse. **4.** To force or make a way into, through, or out of. **5.** To pierce the surface of. **6.** To disrupt the uniformity or continuity of: *break ranks.* **7.** To make or become known or noticed, esp. suddenly: *break a story.* **8.** To begin or emerge suddenly: *break into bloom.* **9.** To change suddenly: *broke to the left.* **10.** To surpass, outdo, or overcome: *broke the record.* **11.** To ruin or destroy, as in spirit or health. **12.** To reduce in rank. See Syns at **demote. 13.** To lessen in force or effect: *break a fall.* **14.** To fail to conform (to); violate: *break a law.* —***phrasal verbs:*** **break down** To undergo a breakdown. **break in 1.** To train. **2.** To enter forcibly or illegally. **3.** To interrupt. **break off 1.** To separate or become separated. **2.** To stop suddenly. **break out 1.** To develop suddenly. **2.** To erupt. **3.** To escape, as from prison. ►*n.* **1.** The act or an occurrence of breaking. **2.** The result of breaking, as a crack or separation. **3.** An emergence. **4.** A disruption in continuity. **5.** A sudden or marked change. **6.** A violation: *a security break.* **7.** A stroke of luck. —***idioms:*** **break bread** To eat together. **break even** To have neither losses or gains. **break new ground** To advance beyond previous achievements. [< OE *brecan.*] —**break′a•ble** *adj. & n.*

break•age (brā′kĭj) ►*n.* **1.** The act of breaking. **2.** A quantity broken. **3a.** Loss as a result of breaking. **b.** A commercial allowance for loss or damage.

break•down (brāk′doun′) ►*n.* **1a.** The act or process of failing to function. **b.** The condition resulting from this. **2.** A collapse in physical or mental health. **3.** An analysis, outline, or summary consisting of itemized data or essentials. **4.** Disintegration or decomposition into parts or elements.

break•er (brā′kər) ►*n.* **1.** One that breaks. **2.** *Elect.* A circuit breaker. **3.** A wave that breaks into foam, esp. against a shoreline.

break•fast (brĕk′fəst) ►*n.* The first meal of the day. [ME *brekfast.*] —**break′fast** *v.*

break•front (brāk′frŭnt′) ►*n.* A cabinet or bookcase having a central section projecting farther forward than the end sections.

break•neck (brāk′nĕk′) ►*adj.* **1.** Dangerously fast. **2.** Hazardous: *a breakneck curve.*

break•out (brāk′out′) ►*n.* A forceful emergence from a restrictive condition.

break•through (brāk′thro͞o′) ►*n.* **1.** An act of overcoming or penetrating an obstacle or restriction. **2.** A major success that permits further progress, as in technology.

break•up (brāk′ŭp′) ►*n.* **1.** A division, dispersal, or disintegration. **2.** The discontinuance of a relationship.

break•wa•ter (brāk′wô′tər, -wŏt′ər) ►*n.* A barrier that protects a harbor or shore from the full impact of waves.

bream (brēm, brĭm) ►*n., pl.* **bream** or **breams.** A freshwater fish having a flattened body and silvery scales. [< OFr. *breme.*]

breast (brĕst) ►*n.* **1.** The mammary gland, esp. of the human female. **2.** The upper front of the human body from the neck to the abdomen. **3.** The seat of affection and emotion. ►*v.* To meet or confront boldly. [< OE *brēost.*]

breast•bone (brĕst′bōn′) ►*n.* See **sternum.**

breast-feed (brĕst′fēd′) ►*v.* To suckle.

breast•plate (brĕst′plāt′) ►*n.* A piece of armor that covers the breast.

breast•stroke (brĕst′strōk′) ►*n.* A swimming stroke performed face down with the arms sweeping back to the sides while kicking.

breast•work (brĕst′wûrk′) ►*n.* A temporary, quickly constructed fortification, usu. breast-high.

breath (brĕth) ►*n.* **1.** The air inhaled and exhaled in respiration. **2.** The act or process of breathing; respiration. **3.** The ability to breathe. **4.** A slight breeze. **5.** A trace or suggestion. **6.** A whisper. —***idiom:*** **out of breath** Breathing with difficulty; gasping. [< OE *brǣth.*]

—**breath′less** *adj.* —**breath′less•ly** *adj.* —**breath′y** *adj.*

breathe (brēth) ► *v.* **breathed, breath•ing 1.** To inhale and exhale air. **2.** To be alive; live. **3.** To pause to rest. **4.** To utter quietly; whisper. —***idiom:* breathe down (someone's) neck** To threaten or annoy by proximity. [ME *brethen.*] —**breath′a•ble** *adj.*

breath•er (brē′*th*ər) ► *n.* **1.** One that breathes. **2.** *Informal* A short rest period.

breath•tak•ing (brĕth′tā′kĭng) ► *adj.* Inspiring awe. —**breath′tak′ing•ly** *adv.*

Brecht (brĕkt, brĕKHt), **Bertolt.** 1898–1956. German poet and playwright. —**Brecht′i•an** *adj.*

breech (brēch) ► *n.* **1.** The buttocks. **2. breech•es** (brĭch′ĭz) **a.** Knee-length trousers. **b.** *Informal* Trousers. **3.** The part of a firearm behind the barrel. [< OE *brēc*, trousers.]

breech•cloth (brēch′klôth′, -klŏth′) ► *n.* A loincloth.

breed (brēd) ► *v.* **bred** (brĕd), **breed•ing 1a.** To produce (offspring). **b.** To reproduce. **2.** To bring about; engender. **3.** To raise or mate animals. **4.** To rear or train; bring up. ► *n.* **1.** A genetic strain, esp. one developed and maintained by controlled propagation. **2.** A kind; sort. [< OE *brēdan.*]

breed•er (brē′dər) ► *n.* **1.** One who breeds animals or plants. **2.** A source or cause.

breeder reactor ► *n.* A nuclear reactor that produces as well as consumes fissionable material.

breed•ing (brē′dĭng) ► *n.* **1.** One's line of descent; ancestry. **2.** Training in the proper forms of social and personal conduct.

breeze (brēz) ► *n.* **1.** A light gentle wind. **2.** *Informal* Something, such as a task, that is easy to do. ► *v.* **breezed, breez•ing.** *Informal* To progress swiftly and effortlessly. [Perh. < OSpan. *briza*, northeast wind.] —**breez′i•ly** *adv.* —**breez′i•ness** *n.* —**breez′y** *adj.*

Syns: *breeze, cinch, pushover, snap* **n.**

breeze•way (brēz′wā′) ► *n.* A roofed, open-sided passageway connecting two structures, such as a house and garage.

Bre•men (brĕm′ən) A city of NW Germany SW of Hamburg. Pop. 551,604.

Bren•ner Pass (brĕn′ər) An Alpine pass, 1,371 m (4,495 ft), connecting Innsbruck, Austria, with Bolzano, Italy.

Bre•scia (brĕsh′ə) A city of N Italy E of Milan. Pop. 200,722.

Brest (brĕst) A city of SW Belarus on the Bug R. Pop. 287,200.

breth•ren (brĕ*th*′rən) ► *n.* Pl. of **brother** 2.

Bret•on (brĕt′n) ► *n.* **1.** A native or inhabitant of Brittany. **2.** The Celtic language of Brittany. —**Bret′on** *adj.*

Breu•ghel (broi′gəl). See **Brueghel.**

breve (brĕv, brēv) ► *n.* **1.** A symbol (˘) placed over a vowel to show that it has a short sound. **2.** *Mus.* A note equivalent to two whole notes. [< Lat. *brevis*, short.]

bre•vi•ar•y (brē′vē-ĕr′ē, brĕv′ē-) ► *n., pl.* **-ies.** A book containing the hymns, offices, and prayers for the canonical hours. [< Lat. *breviārium*, summary < *brevis*, short.]

brev•i•ty (brĕv′ĭ-tē) ► *n.* **1.** Briefness of duration. **2.** Concise expression; terseness. [< Lat. *brevis*, short.]

brew (bro͞o) ► *v.* **1.** To make (ale or beer) from malt and hops by infusion, boiling, and fermentation. **2.** To make (a beverage) by boiling or steeping. **3.** To be imminent: *Trouble's brewing.* [< OE *brēowan.*] —**brew** *n.* —**brew′er** *n.* —**brew′er•y** *n.*

Brezh•nev (brĕzh′nĕf), **Leonid Ilyich.** 1906–82. Soviet political leader.

Bri•an Bo•ru (brī′ən bə-ro͞o′). 926–1014. Irish king (1002–14).

bri•ar[1] also **bri•er** (brī′ər) ► *n.* **1.** A Mediterranean shrub whose woody roots are used to make tobacco pipes. **2.** A pipe made from this root. [< OFr. *bruyere*, heath.]

bri•ar[2] (brī′ər) ► *n.* Var. of **brier[1].**

bribe (brīb) ► *n.* Something, such as money or a favor, offered or given to induce or influence a person to act dishonestly. ► *v.* **bribed, brib•ing 1.** To give, offer, or promise a bribe (to). **2.** To gain influence over or corrupt by a bribe. [< OFr., alms.] —**brib′a•ble** *adj.* —**brib′er•y** *n.*

bric-a-brac (brĭk′ə-brăk′) ► *n.* Small objects usu. displayed as ornaments. [Fr. *bric-à-brac.*]

brick (brĭk) ► *n., pl.* **bricks** or **brick 1.** A molded rectangular block of clay baked until hard and used as a building and paving material. **2.** An object shaped like a brick: *a brick of cheese.* ► *v.* To construct, line, or pave with bricks. [< MDu. *bricke.*]

brick-and-mor•tar (brĭk′ənd-môr′tər) ► *adj.* Serving consumers in a physical facility rather than providing remote, esp. online, services.

brick•bat (brĭk′băt′) ► *n.* **1.** A piece of brick, esp. when thrown. **2.** A critical remark.

brick•lay•er (brĭk′lā′ər) ► *n.* A person skilled in building with bricks. —**brick′lay′ing** *n.*

bri•dal (brīd′l) ► *n.* A wedding. [< OE *brȳdealo.*] —**bri′dal** *adj.*

bride (brīd) ► *n.* A woman recently married or about to be married. [< OE *brȳd.*]

bride•groom (brīd′gro͞om′, -gro͝om′) ► *n.* A man who is about to be married or has recently been married. [< OE *brȳdguma* : *brȳd*, bride; see BRIDE + *guma*, man.]

brides•maid (brīdz′mād′) ► *n.* A woman who attends the bride at a wedding.

bridge[1] (brĭj) ► *n.* **1.** A structure spanning and providing passage over an obstacle. **2.** The upper bony ridge of the human nose. **3.** A fixed or removable replacement for missing natural teeth. **4.** *Mus.* A thin, upright piece of wood in some stringed instruments that supports the strings above the sounding board. **5.** A crosswise platform or enclosed area above the main deck of a ship from which the ship is con-

bridge[1]
on a viola da gamba

trolled. ▸*v.* **bridged, bridg•ing 1.** To build a bridge over. **2.** To cross by or as if by a bridge. [< OE *brycg*.] —**bridge′a•ble** *adj.*

bridge[2] (brĭj) ▸*n.* Any of several card games usu. for four people, derived from whist. [Poss. < Russ. *birich*, a call.]

bridge•head (brĭj′hĕd′) ▸*n.* A forward position seized by advancing troops in enemy territory as a foothold for further advance.

Bridge•port (brĭj′pôrt′, -pōrt′) A city of SW CT on Long Island Sound SW of New Haven. Pop. 141,686.

Bridge•town (brĭj′toun′) The capital of Barbados, in the West Indies. Pop. 7,466.

bridge•work (brĭj′wûrk′) ▸*n.* A dental bridge or bridges used to replace missing teeth.

bri•dle (brīd′l) ▸*n.* **1.** The harness fitted about a horse's head, used to restrain or guide. **2.** A curb or check. ▸*v.* **-dled, -dling 1.** To put a bridle on. **2.** To control or restrain with or as if with a bridle. **3.** To show anger: *bridled at the remark.* [< OE *brīdel*.]

brief (brēf) ▸*adj.* **-er, -est 1.** Short in duration or extent. **2.** Succinct; concise. ▸*n.* **1.** A short or condensed statement, esp. of a legal case or argument. **2. briefs** Short, tight-fitting underpants. ▸*v.* To give a briefing to. [< Lat. *brevis*, short.] —**brief′ly** *adv.* —**brief′ness** *n.*

brief•case (brēf′kās′) ▸*n.* A portable, often flat case, used esp. for carrying papers.

brief•ing (brē′fĭng) ▸*n.* **1.** The act of giving or receiving concise preparatory instructions or information. **2.** The information itself.

bri•er[1] also **bri•ar** (brī′ər) ▸*n.* Any of several prickly plants, such as certain rosebushes. [< OE *brēr*.] —**bri′er•y** *adj.*

bri•er[2] (brī′ər) ▸*n.* Var. of **briar**[1].

brig (brĭg) ▸*n.* **1.** A two-masted square-rigged sailing ship. **2.** A prison on board a US Navy or Coast Guard vessel.

bri•gade (brĭ-gād′) ▸*n.* **1.** A military unit consisting of a variable number of combat battalions, with supporting units and services. **2.** A group organized for a specific task: *a fire brigade.* [< OItal. *briga*, strife.]

brig•a•dier general (brĭg′ə-dîr′) ▸*n.*, *pl.* **brigadier generals.** A rank, as in the US Army, above colonel and below major general.

brig•and (brĭg′ənd) ▸*n.* A bandit, esp. one of an outlaw band. [< OItal. *brigare*, to fight.] —**brig′and•age** (-ən-dĭj) *n.*

brig•an•tine (brĭg′ən-tēn′) ▸*n.* A two-masted square-rigged sailing ship having a fore-and-aft mainsail. [< OItal. *brigante*, skirmisher.]

Brig Gen ▸*abbr.* brigadier general

bright (brīt) ▸*adj.* **-er, -est 1.** Emitting or reflecting light; shining. **2.** Brilliant in color; vivid. **3.** Glorious; splendid. **4.** Happy; cheerful. **5.** Clever; intelligent. [< OE *beorht*.] —**bright′ly** *adv.* —**bright′ness** *n.*

bright•en (brīt′n) ▸*v.* To make or become bright or brighter. —**bright′en•er** *n.*

Brigh•ton (brīt′n) A borough of SE England on the English Channel S of London. Pop. 154,370.

bril•liant (brĭl′yənt) ▸*adj.* **1.** Full of light; shining brightly. **2.** Bright and vivid in color. **3.** Glorious; magnificent. **4.** Highly intelligent: *a brilliant mind.* ▸*n.* A precious gem, esp. a diamond, cut with numerous facets. [< Fr. *briller*, shine.] —**bril′liance, bril′lian•cy** *n.* —**bril′liant•ly** *adv.*

bril•lian•tine (brĭl′yən-tēn′) ▸*n.* An oily, perfumed hairdressing. [Fr. *brillantine*.]

brim (brĭm) ▸*n.* **1.** The rim or uppermost edge of a cup or other vessel. **2.** A projecting rim, as on a hat. ▸*v.* **brimmed, brim•ming 1.** To be full to the brim. **2.** To overflow. [ME *brimme*.] —**brim′ful′** *adj.*

brim•stone (brĭm′stōn′) ▸*n.* Sulfur. [< OE *brynstān*.]

brin•dled (brĭn′dld) ▸*adj.* Tawny or grayish with streaks or spots of a darker color. [< ME *brended*, burned.]

brine (brīn) ▸*n.* **1.** Water saturated with salt. **2.** The ocean. [< OE *brīne*.] —**brin′i•ness** *n.* —**brin′y** *adj.*

bring (brĭng) ▸*v.* **brought** (brôt), **bring•ing 1.** To take with oneself to a place. **2.** To lead or force into a specified state or condition: *bring water to a boil; brought the meeting to a close.* **3.** To persuade; induce. **4.** To cause; produce. **5.** To sell for. —***phrasal verbs:*** **bring about** To cause to happen. **bring down** To cause to fall or collapse. **bring forth** To produce. **bring off** To accomplish successfully. **bring on** To result in; cause. **bring out 1.** To reveal or expose. **2.** To produce or publish. **bring to** To cause to recover consciousness. **bring up 1.** To rear as a parent. **2.** To mention. [< OE *bringan*.] —**bring′er** *n.*

Usage: *Bring* is used to denote motion toward the place of speaking or the place from which the action is regarded: *Bring it over here. Take* is used to denote motion away from such a place: *Take it over there.* When the relevant point of focus is not the place of speaking itself, the difference obviously depends on the context.

brink (brĭngk) ▸*n.* **1.** The upper edge of a steep place. **2.** The verge of something. [ME.]

brink•man•ship (brĭngk′mən-shĭp′) also **brinks•man•ship** (brĭngks′-) ▸*n.* A policy aimed at pushing a dangerous situation to the limit so that an opponent will concede.

bri•o (brē′ō) ▸*n.* Vigor; vivacity. [Ital.]

bri•oche (brē-ôsh′, -ōsh′) ▸*n.* A soft roll made from a dough of yeast, butter, and eggs. [< OFr. *brier*, knead.]

brioche

bri•quette also **bri•quet** (brĭ-kĕt′) ▸*n.* A block of compressed coal dust, charcoal, or sawdust, used for fuel and kindling. [Fr., small brick < MDu. *bricke*.]

bris (brĭs) ▸*n.*, *pl.* **bris•es** *Judaism* The rite of male circumcision. [Ashkenazi Heb. *brīs*, covenant (of circumcision).]

Bris•bane (brĭz′bən, -bān′) A city of E Australia on the **Brisbane River** on Moreton Bay, an inlet of the Pacific. Pop. 1,421,600.

brisk (brĭsk) ▸*adj.* **-er, -est 1.** Marked by speed, liveliness, and vigor; energetic. **2.** Stimulating and invigorating. [Prob. of Scand. orig.] —**brisk′ly** *adv.* —**brisk′ness** *n.*

bris•ket (brĭs′kĭt) ▶*n.* **1.** The chest of an animal. **2.** The ribs and meat taken from the brisket. [ME *brusket.*]

bris•ling (brĭz′lĭng, brĭs′-) ▶*n.* See **sprat** 1. [Norw. < LGer. *bretling.*]

bris•tle (brĭs′əl) ▶*n.* A stiff coarse hair. ▶*v.* **-tled, -tling 1.** To stand or erect stiffly on end like bristles. **2.** To raise the bristles stiffly. **3.** To react in an angry or offended manner. **4.** To abound with: *The path bristled with thorns.* [< OE *byrst.*] —**bris′tly** *adj.*

Bris•tol (brĭs′təl) A city of SW England W of London. Pop. 397,585.

Bristol Channel. An inlet of the Atlantic stretching W from the Severn R. and separating Wales from SW England.

Brit (brĭt) ▶*n. Informal* A British person.

Brit. ▶*abbr.* **1.** Britain **2.** British

Brit•ain[1] (brĭt′n) The island of Great Britain.

Brit•ain[2] (brĭt′n) See **United Kingdom.**

Bri•tan•nic (brĭ-tăn′ĭk) ▶*adj.* British.

britch•es (brĭch′ĭz) ▶*pl.n.* Breeches.

Brit•i•cism (brĭt′ĭ-sĭz′əm) ▶*n.* A word, phrase, or idiom peculiar to British English.

Brit•ish (brĭt′ĭsh) ▶*adj.* **1.** Of or relating to Great Britain. **2.** Of or relating to the ancient Britons. ▶*n.* **1.** The people of Great Britain. **2.** British English. **3.** The Celtic language of the ancient Britons.

British Columbia. A province of W Canada bordering on the Pacific Ocean. Cap. Victoria. Pop. 2,744,467.

British Commonwealth. See **Commonwealth of Nations.**

British English ▶*n.* The English language as used in England.

British Isles. A group of islands off the NW coast of Europe comprising Great Britain, Ireland, and adjacent smaller islands.

British thermal unit ▶*n.* Formerly, the quantity of heat required to raise the temperature of one pound of water by 1°F; now defined as 1,055.06 joules.

British Virgin Islands. A British colony in the E Caribbean E of Puerto Rico and the US Virgin Is. Cap. Road Town. Pop. 12,034.

British West Indies. The islands of the West Indies formerly under British control, including Jamaica, Barbados, Trinidad and Tobago, and the Bahamas.

Brit•on (brĭt′n) ▶*n.* **1.** A native or inhabitant of Great Britain. **2.** One of a Celtic people inhabiting ancient Britain at the time of the Roman invasion.

Brit•ta•ny (brĭt′n-ē) A historical region and former province of NW France on a peninsula between the English Channel and the Bay of Biscay.

Brit•ten (brĭt′n), **(Edward) Benjamin.** 1913–76. British composer.

brit•tle (brĭt′l) ▶*adj.* **-tler, -tlest.** Likely to break, snap, or crack; fragile. [ME *britel.*] —**brit′tle•ness** *n.*

Br•no (bûr′nō) A city of SE Czech Republic SE of Prague. Pop. 389,762.

Bro. ▶*abbr. Eccles.* brother

broach (brōch) ▶*v.* **1.** To bring up (a subject) for discussion or debate. **2.** To pierce in order to draw off liquid. ▶*n.* **1.** A tapered, serrated tool used to shape or enlarge a hole. **2.** A gimlet for tapping casks. [Prob. < OFr. *broche,* a spit.] —**broach′er** *n.*

Syns: *broach, introduce, moot, raise* **v.**

broad (brôd) ▶*adj.* **-er, -est 1.** Wide in extent from side to side. **2.** Large in expanse; spacious. **3.** Full; open: *broad daylight.* **4.** Covering a wide scope; general. **5.** Liberal; tolerant. See Syns at **broad-minded. 6.** Main; essential. **7.** Plain and clear; obvious: *gave us a broad hint to leave.* [< OE *brād.*] —**broad′ly** *adv.* —**broad′ness** *n.*

broad•band (brôd′bănd′) ▶*adj.* Of or having a wide band of electromagnetic frequencies.

broad bean ▶*n.* **1.** An annual Old World plant in the pea family. **2.** The edible seed or thick green pod of this plant.

broad•cast (brôd′kăst′) ▶*v.* **-cast** or **-cast•ed, -cast•ing 1a.** To transmit by radio or television. **b.** To be on the air. **2.** To make known over a wide area. See Syns at **announce. 3.** To sow (seed) widely, esp. by hand. ▶*n.* **1.** Transmission of a radio or television program or signal. **2.** A radio or television program. —**broad′cast′er** *n.*

broad•cloth (brôd′klôth′, -klŏth′) ▶*n.* **1.** A fine textured woolen cloth with a glossy texture. **2.** A closely woven silk, cotton, or synthetic fabric.

broad•en (brôd′n) ▶*v.* To make or become broad or broader. —**broad′en•er** *n.*

broad jump ▶*n. Sports* See **long jump.**

broad•loom (brôd′lo͞om′) ▶*adj.* Woven on a wide loom: *a broadloom carpet.*

broad-mind•ed (brôd′mīn′dĭd) ▶*adj.* Having or marked by tolerant or liberal views. —**broad′-mind′ed•ness** *n.*

Syns: *broad-minded, broad, liberal, open-minded, tolerant* ***Ant:*** *narrow-minded* **adj.**

broad•side (brôd′sīd′) ▶*n.* **1.** The side of a ship above the water line. **2.** The simultaneous discharge of all the guns on one side of a warship. **3.** A forceful verbal attack. ▶*adv.* With the side turned to a given object. ▶*v.* **-sid•ed, -sid•ing.** To collide with full on the side.

broad-spec•trum (brôd′spĕk′trəm) ▶*adj.* Widely applicable or effective: *a broad-spectrum antibiotic.*

broad•sword (brôd′sôrd′, -sōrd′) ▶*n.* A sword with a wide, usu. two-edged blade.

broad•tail (brôd′tāl′) ▶*n.* **1.** See **karakul. 2.** The flat, glossy, wavy pelt of a prematurely born karakul sheep.

Broad•way (brôd′wā′) The principal theater and amusement district of New York City, on the West Side of midtown Manhattan.

bro•cade (brō-kād′) ▶*n.* A heavy fabric interwoven with a rich, raised design. [< Ital. *brocco,* twisted thread.] —**bro•cade′** *v.*

broc•co•li (brŏk′ə-lē) ▶*n.* A plant with densely clustered green flower buds and stalks, eaten as a vegetable. [< Ital. *brocco,* sprout.]

bro•chette (brō-shĕt′) ▶*n.* A skewer. [< OFr., small spit.]

bro•chure (brō-sho͝or′) ▶*n.* A pamphlet, often containing promotional material. [< Fr. *brocher,* to stitch < OFr. *broche,* needle.]

Brod•sky (brôd′skē), **Joseph.** 1940–96. Russian writer; 1987 Nobel.

bro•gan (brō′gən) ▶*n.* A heavy ankle-high shoe. [Ir.Gael. *brōgan,* small brogue.]

brogue[1] (brōg) ▶*n.* A strong oxford shoe. [< OIr. *brōc,* shoe.]

brogue[2] (brōg) ►*n.* A strong dialectal accent, esp. an Irish accent. [Prob. < the brogues worn by peasants.]

broil (broil) ►*v.* **1.** To cook by direct radiant heat. **2.** To expose or be exposed to great heat. [< OFr. *bruler.*] —**broil** *n.*

broil•er (broi′lər) ►*n.* **1.** One that broils, esp. a small oven or the part of a stove used for broiling food. **2.** A tender young chicken suitable for broiling.

broke (brōk) ►*v.* P.t. of **break.** ►*adj. Informal* Lacking funds.

bro•ken (brō′kən) ►*v.* P.part. of **break.** ►*adj.* **1.** Shattered; fractured. **2.** Having been violated: *a broken promise.* **3.** Not continuous. **4.** Spoken imperfectly: *broken English.* **5.** Subdued totally; tamed or humbled. **6.** Not functioning; out of order. —**bro′ken•ly** *adv.*

bro•ken-down (brō′kən-doun′) ►*adj.* **1.** Out of working order. **2.** In poor condition.

bro•ken•heart•ed (brō′kən-här′tĭd) ►*adj.* Grievously sad or despairing.

bro•ker (brō′kər) ►*n.* One that acts as an agent and negotiates contracts, purchases, or sales in return for a fee or commission. ►*v.* To arrange or manage: *broker an agreement.* [< AN *brocour.*]

bro•ker•age (brō′kər-ĭj) ►*n.* **1.** The business of a broker. **2.** A fee or commission paid to a broker.

bro•me•li•ad (brō-mē′lē-ăd′) ►*n.* Any of various mostly epiphytic tropical American plants usu. having long, stiff leaves and colorful flowers. [After Olaf *Bromelius* (1639–1705).]

bro•mide (brō′mīd′) ►*n.* **1a.** A chemical compound of bromine with another element, such as silver. **b.** Potassium bromide. **2.** A platitude. See Syns at **cliché.** —**bro•mid′ic** (-mĭd′ĭk) *adj.*

bro•mine (brō′mēn) ►*n. Symbol* **Br** A heavy, volatile, corrosive, reddish-brown, nonmetallic liquid element used in gasoline antiknock mixtures, fumigants, dyes, and photographic chemicals. At. no. 35. See table at **element.** [< Gk. *brōmos,* stench.]

bron•chi•al (brŏng′kē-əl) ►*adj.* Of or relating to either bronchus or their extensions.

bron•chi•tis (brŏn-kī′tĭs, brŏng-) ►*n.* Inflammation of the mucous membrane of the bronchial tubes. —**bron•chit′ic** (-kĭt′ĭk) *adj.*

bron•cho•pul•mo•nar•y (brŏng′kō-po͝ol′mə-nĕr′ē, -pŭl′-) ►*adj.* Relating to the bronchi and the lungs.

bron•chus (brŏng′kəs) ►*n., pl.* **-chi** (-kī′, -kē′). Either of two main branches of the trachea, leading directly to the lungs. [< Gk. *bronkhos,* windpipe.]

bron•co (brŏng′kō) ►*n., pl.* **-cos.** A wild horse of W North America. [< Sp., wild.]

bron•co•bust•er (brŏng′kō-bŭs′tər) ►*n.* One who breaks wild horses to the saddle.

Bron•të (brŏn′tē). Family of British novelists and poets, including **Charlotte** (1816–55), **Emily,** (1818–48), and **Anne** (1820–49).

bron•to•saur (brŏn′tə-sôr′) or **bron•to•sau•rus** (brŏn′tə-sôr′əs) ►*n.* An apatosaur. [Gk. *brontē,* thunder + *sauros,* lizard.]

Bronx (brŏngks) A borough of New York City in SE NY on the mainland north of Manhattan. Pop. 1,203,789.

bronze (brŏnz) ►*n.* **1.** Any of various alloys consisting chiefly of copper and tin. **2.** A work of art made of bronze. **3.** A yellowish to olive brown. ►*v.* **bronzed, bronz•ing.** To give the color or appearance of bronze to. [< Ital. *bronzo.*] —**bronze** *adj.*

Bronze Age ►*n.* A period of human culture between the Stone Age and the Iron Age, characterized by weapons and implements made of bronze.

brooch (brōch, bro͞och) ►*n.* A decorative pin or clasp. [ME *broche.* See BROACH.]

brood (bro͞od) ►*n.* The young of certain animals, esp. a group of young birds or fowl hatched at one time. ►*v.* **1.** To sit on in order to hatch. **2.** To think deeply or worry anxiously. [< OE *brōd.*] —**brood′er** *n.* —**brood′ing•ly** *adv.*

Syns: *brood, dwell, fret, mope, stew, worry* ***v.***

brood•mare (bro͞od′mâr′) ►*n.* A mare used for breeding.

brook[1] (bro͝ok) ►*n.* A small stream; creek. See Regional Note at **run.** [< OE *brōc.*]

brook[2] (bro͝ok) ►*v.* To put up with; tolerate. [< OE *brūcan,* to use.]

Brooke (bro͝ok), **Rupert.** 1887–1915. British poet.

Brook•lyn (bro͝ok′lĭn) A borough of New York City in SE NY on W Long I. Pop. 2,300,664.

Brooks (bro͝oks), **Gwendolyn Elizabeth.** 1917–2000. Amer. poet.

brook trout ►*n.* A freshwater game fish of E North America.

broom (bro͞om, bro͝om) ►*n.* **1.** A bunch of twigs, straw, or bristles bound together, attached to a stick or handle, and used for sweeping. **2.** Any of various Mediterranean shrubs having compound leaves and usu. bright yellow flowers. [< OE *brōm.*]

bros. ►*abbr.* brothers

broth (brôth, brŏth) ►*n., pl.* **broths** (brôths, brŏths, brô*thz,* brŏ*thz*) **1.** The water in which meat, fish, or vegetables have been boiled; stock. **2.** A thin clear soup made with stock. [< OE.]

broth•el (brŏth′əl, brô′thəl) ►*n.* A house of prostitution. [< ME, prostitute.]

broth•er (brŭ*th*′ər) ►*n.* **1.** A male having one or both parents in common with another person. **2.** *pl.* **-ers** or **breth•ren** (brĕ*th*′rən) One sharing a common ancestry or allegiance with another, esp.: **a.** A kinsman. **b.** A close male friend. **c.** A fellow African-American male. **3.** A member of a Christian men's religious order who is not a priest. [< OE *brōthor.*] —**broth′er•li•ness** *n.* —**broth′er•ly** *adj.*

broth•er•hood (brŭ*th*′ər-ho͝od′) ►*n.* **1.** The state or relationship of being brothers. **2.** Fellowship. **3.** An association of men united for common purposes. **4.** All the members of a profession or trade.

broth•er-in-law (brŭ*th*′ər-ĭn-lô′) ►*n., pl.* **broth•ers-in-law** (-ərz-) **1.** The brother of one's husband or wife. **2.** The husband of one's sister. **3.** The husband of the sister of one's husband or wife.

brougham (bro͞om, bro͞o′əm, brōm) ►*n.* **1.** A closed four-wheeled carriage with an open driver's seat in front. **2.** An automobile with an open driver's seat. [After Henry P. *Brougham* (1778–1868).]

brought (brôt) ►*v.* P.t. and p.part. of **bring.**

brou•ha•ha (bro͞o′hä-hä′) ►*n.* An uproar. [Fr.]

brow (brou) ►*n.* **1a.** The ridge over the eyes. **b.** The eyebrow. **c.** The forehead. **2.** The projecting upper edge of a steep place. [< OE *brū*.]

brow•beat (brou′bēt′) ►*v.* To intimidate with an overbearing manner; bully.

brown (broun) ►*n.* Any of a group of colors between red and yellow in hue. ►*v.* **1.** To make or become brown. **2.** To cook until brown. [< OE *brūn*.] —**brown** *adj.* —**brown′ish** *adj.* —**brown′ness** *n.*

Brown, John. 1800–59. Amer. abolitionist.

John Brown

brown bear ►*n.* Any of several large bears of W North America and N Eurasia, such as the grizzly and Kodiak bears.

brown dwarf ►*n.* A starlike celestial body that does not emit light because it is too small to ignite internal nuclear fusion.

Browne (broun), Sir **Thomas.** 1605–82. English physician and writer.

brown•field (broun′fēld′) ►*n.* An abandoned, usu. contaminated commercial property that has potential for redevelopment.

brown•ie (brou′nē) ►*n.* **1. Brownie** A junior member of the Girl Scouts. **2.** A bar of moist, usu. chocolate cake often with nuts. **3.** A small helpful elf in folklore.

Brown•ing (brou′nĭng), **Elizabeth Barrett.** 1806–61. British poet.

Browning, Robert. 1812–89. British poet.

brown•out (broun′out′) ►*n.* A reduction or cutback in electric power.

brown rice ►*n.* Unpolished rice that retains the germ and outer layers.

brown sauce ►*n.* A sauce made from butter and flour browned together and stock.

brown•stone (broun′stōn′) ►*n.* **1.** A brownish-red sandstone. **2.** A house built or faced with brownstone.

brown sugar ►*n.* Unrefined or incompletely refined sugar that still retains some molasses.

browse (brouz) ►*v.* **browsed, brows•ing 1.** To inspect leisurely or casually. **2.** To look for information on the World Wide Web. **3.** To feed on leaves, young shoots, and other vegetation; graze. [< OFr. *brost*, twig.] —**browse** *n.*

brows•er (brou′zər) ►*n.* **1.** One that browses. **2.** A computer program that accesses and displays data from the Internet or other networks.

Bruck•ner (bro͝ok′nər), **Anton.** 1824–96. Austrian organist and composer.

Brue•ghel or **Brue•gel** also **Breu•ghel** (broi′gəl), **Pieter.** "the Elder." 1525?–69. Flemish painter.

Bruges (bro͞ozh) A city of NW Belgium connected by canal with the North Sea. Pop. 117,100.

bru•in (bro͞o′ĭn) ►*n.* A bear. [< MDu., brown.]

bruise (bro͞oz) ►*v.* **bruised, bruis•ing 1a.** To injure (body tissue) without breaking the skin. **b.** To suffer such injury. **2.** To damage (plant tissue), as by abrasion. **3.** To pound; crush. **4.** To hurt or offend. ►*n.* **1.** A bruised area, often marked by discoloration. **2.** A hurt, as to one's feelings. [< OE *brȳsan* and ONFr. *bruisier*, crush.]

bruis•er (bro͞o′zər) ►*n. Informal* A large, powerfully built person.

bruit (bro͞ot) ►*v.* To spread news of; repeat. [< OFr., noise.]

brunch (brŭnch) ►*n.* A meal eaten late in the morning combining breakfast and lunch.

Bru•nei (bro͞o-nī′) A sultanate of NW Borneo on the South China Sea. Cap. Bandar Seri Begawan. Pop. 280,000.

Bru•nel•le•schi (bro͞o′nə-lĕs′kē), **Filippo.** 1377–1446. Italian architect.

bru•net (bro͞o-nĕt′) ►*adj.* **1.** Of a dark complexion or coloring. **2.** Having dark or brown hair or eyes. ►*n.* A person with dark or brown hair. [< OFr. *brun*, brown.]

bru•nette (bro͞o-nĕt′) ►*n.* A girl or woman with dark or brown hair. [Fr. < *brunet*, BRUNET.] —**bru•nette′** *adj.*

Bru•no (bro͞o′nō), **Giordano.** 1548?–1600. Italian philosopher.

Bruns•wick (brŭnz′wĭk) A city of N-central Germany ESE of Hanover. Pop. 256,267.

brunt (brŭnt) ►*n.* The main impact or force, as of an attack or blow. [ME.]

brush[1] (brŭsh) ►*n.* **1.** A device consisting of bristles fastened into a handle, used in scrubbing, polishing, grooming the hair, or painting. **2.** A light touch in passing; graze. **3.** A bushy tail, as of a fox. **4.** A sliding connection completing a circuit between a fixed and a moving conductor. **5.** A brushoff. ►*v.* **1.** To use a brush (on). **2.** To apply or remove with or as if with motions of a brush. **3.** To dismiss abruptly: *brushed the matter aside.* **4.** To touch lightly in passing; graze. —***phrasal verb:*** **brush up 1.** To refresh one's memory. **2.** To renew a skill. [< OFr. *brosse*, brushwood.]

Syns: *brush, flick, glance, graze, shave, skim* **v.**

brush[2] (brŭsh) ►*n.* **1.** A dense growth of bushes or shrubs. **2.** Cut or broken branches. [< OFr. *brosse*.] —**brush′y** *adj.*

brush[3] (brŭsh) ►*n.* A brief, often alarming encounter. [< ME *brushen*, hasten.]

brush•off (brŭsh′ôf′, -ŏf′) ►*n.* An abrupt dismissal or snub.

brusque (brŭsk) ►*adj.* Abrupt and curt in manner or speech. [< Ital. *brusco*, coarse.] —**brusque′ly** *adv.* —**brusque′ness** *n.*

Brus•sels (brŭs′əlz) The capital of Belgium, in the central part. Pop.136,424.

Brussels sprouts ►*pl.n. (takes sing. or pl. v.)* The edible buds of a variety of cabbage, eaten as a vegetable.

bru•tal (bro͞ot′l) ►*adj.* **1.** Extremely ruthless or cruel. **2.** Crude or unfeeling. **3.** Harsh; unrelenting: *a brutal winter.* —**bru•tal′i•ty** (-tal′ĭtē) *n.* —**bru′tal•ly** *adv.*

bru•tal•ize (bro͞ot′l-īz′) ►*v.* **-ized, -iz•ing 1.** To make brutal. **2.** To treat in a brutal manner. —**bru′tal•i•za′tion** *n.*

brute (bro͞ot) ►*n.* **1.** An animal; beast. **2.** A brutal person. ►*adj.* **1.** Of or relating to beasts. **2a.** Entirely physical: *brute force.* **b.** Lacking reason or intelligence: *a brute impulse.* [< Lat. *brūtus*, stupid.] —**brut′ish** *adj.* —**brut′ish•ly** *adv.* —**brut′ish•ness** *n.*

Bru•tus (bro͞o′təs), **Marcus Junius.** 85?–42 B.C. Roman politician and general.

Bryan (brī′ən), **William Jennings.** 1860–1925. Amer. lawyer and politician.

Bry•ansk (brē-änsk′) A city of W Russia SW of Moscow. Pop. 456,202.

Bry•ant (brī′ənt), **William Cullen.** 1794–1878. Amer. poet, critic, and editor.

BS ▸*abbr.* Bachelor of Science

BSA ▸*abbr.* Boy Scouts of America

BTU or **Btu** ▸*abbr.* British thermal unit

bu. ▸*abbr.* **1.** bureau **2.** bushel

bub•ba (bŭb′ə) ▸*n. Slang* **1.** *Regional* Brother. **2.** A white working-class man of the S US, often seen as uneducated.

bub•ble (bŭb′əl) ▸*n.* **1.** A thin, usu. spherical or hemispherical film of liquid filled with air or gas. **2.** A globular body of air or gas formed within a liquid. **3a.** An illusion. **b.** A speculative scheme that comes to nothing. **4.** A usu. transparent glass or plastic dome. ▸*v.* **-bled, -bling.** To form or give off bubbles. [< ME *bubelen*, to bubble.] —**bub′bly** *adj.*

bub•ble•gum also **bubble gum** (bŭb′əl-gŭm′) ▸*n.* Chewing gum that can be blown into bubbles.

bubble top ▸*n.* A transparent glass or plastic dome, as over a swimming pool or open car.

Bu•ber (bo͞o′bər), **Martin.** 1878–1965. Austrian-born Judaic scholar and philosopher.

bu•bo (bo͞o′bō, byo͞o′-) ▸*n., pl.* **-boes.** An inflamed swelling of a lymph node, esp. near the armpit or groin. [< Gk. *boubōn*.]

bu•bon•ic plague (bo͞o-bŏn′ĭk, byo͞o-) ▸*n.* A contagious, often fatal epidemic disease caused by bacteria transmitted by fleas from an infected host, esp. a rat, and characterized by chills, fever, vomiting, diarrhea, and buboes.

Bu•ca•ra•man•ga (bo͞o′kə-rə-mäng′gə) A city of N-central Colombia. Pop. 351,687.

buc•ca•neer (bŭk′ə-nîr′) ▸*n.* A pirate. [< Fr. *boucaner*, cure meat.]

Bu•chan•an (byo͞o-kăn′ən, bə-), **James.** 1791–1868. The 15th US President (1857–61).

James Buchanan

Bu•cha•rest (bo͞o′kə-rĕst′, byo͞o′-) The capital of Romania, in the SE part on a tributary of the Danube R. Pop. 2,343,824.

buck¹ (bŭk) ▸*n.* **1.** The adult male of some animals, such as the deer or rabbit. **2.** A robust or high-spirited young man. ▸*v.* **1a.** To leap upward arching the back, as a horse or mule. **b.** To throw (a rider or burden) by bucking. **2.** To butt (against). **3.** To make sudden jerky movements; jolt. **4.** To resist stubbornly. **5.** *Informal* To strive with determination: *bucking for a promotion.* —***phrasal verb:* buck up** To raise (one's) spirits; hearten. ▸*adj.* Of the lowest rank: *a buck private.* [< OE *buc*, male deer, and *bucca*, male goat.] —**buck′er** *n.*

buck² (bŭk) ▸*n. Informal* A dollar. [< BUCKSKIN.]

Buck, Pearl Sydenstricker. 1892–1973. Amer. writer; 1938 Nobel.

buck•board (bŭk′bôrd′, -bōrd′) ▸*n.* A four-wheeled open carriage with the seat attached to a flexible board. [Obsolete *buck*, body of a wagon + BOARD.]

buck•et (bŭk′ĭt) ▸*n.* **1a.** A cylindrical vessel used for holding or carrying liquids or solids; pail. **b.** The amount that a bucket can hold. **2.** A receptacle, such as the scoop of a power shovel, used to gather and convey material. [< OFr. *buket*.]

bucket seat ▸*n.* A single, usu. low seat with a contoured back, as in some cars.

buck•eye (bŭk′ī′) ▸*n.* Any of various North American trees or shrubs having erect flower clusters and large, shiny brown seeds.

buck•le (bŭk′əl) ▸*n.* **1.** A clasp, esp. a frame with a movable tongue, for fastening two ends, as of straps or a belt. **2.** An ornament that resembles a buckle. **3.** A bend or bulge. ▸*v.* **-led, -ling 1.** To fasten or become fastened with a buckle. **2.** To bend, warp, or crumple under pressure or heat. **3.** To give way; collapse. **4.** To give in; succumb. —***phrasal verbs:* buckle down** To begin working hard. **buckle up** To use a safety belt, esp. in an automobile. [< Lat. *buccula*, cheek strap.]

buck•ler (bŭk′lər) ▸*n.* A small round shield. [< OFr. *boucle*, boss on a shield.]

buck•ram (bŭk′rəm) ▸*n.* A coarse cotton fabric heavily stiffened with glue, used for lining garments and in bookbinding. [Ult. < *Bukhara*, Central Asia.]

buck•saw (bŭk′sô′) ▸*n.* A woodcutting saw, usu. in an H-shaped frame. [< *buck*, sawhorse.]

buck•shot (bŭk′shŏt′) ▸*n.* A large lead shot for shotgun shells, used esp. in hunting big game.

buck•skin (bŭk′skĭn′) ▸*n.* **1.** A soft, grayish-yellow leather made from deerskin or sheepskin. **2. buckskins** Clothing made from buckskin.

buck•tooth (bŭk′to͞oth′) ▸*n.* A prominent, projecting upper front tooth. —**buck′-toothed′** (-to͞otht′) *adj.*

buck•wheat (bŭk′hwēt′, -wēt′) ▸*n.* **1.** A plant having small, seedlike, triangular fruits. **2.** The edible fruits of this plant, often ground into flour. [Prob. < MDu. *boecweite* : *boek*, beech + *weite*, wheat.]

bu•col•ic (byo͞o-kŏl′ĭk) ▸*adj.* Rustic; pastoral. [< Gk. *boukolos*, cowherd < *bous*, cow.] —**bu•col′i•cal•ly** *adv.*

bud (bŭd) ▸*n.* **1.** A small, protuberant plant structure containing an undeveloped shoot, leaf, or flower. **2.** An asexual reproductive structure, as in yeast or a hydra, that resembles a bud. **3.** One that is not yet fully developed. ▸*v.* **bud•ded, bud•ding 1.** To put forth or cause to put forth buds. **2.** To develop from or as if from a bud. [ME.]

Bu•da•pest (bo͞o′də-pĕst′, -pĕsht′) The capital of Hungary, in the N-central part on the Danube R. Pop. 2,002,121.
Bud•dha (bo͞o′də, bo͝od′ə). 563?–483? B.C. Indian mystic and founder of Buddhism.
Bud•dhism (bo͞o′dĭz′əm, bo͝od′ĭz′-) ►*n.* A religion founded on the teachings of Buddha, esp. that enlightenment obtained through right conduct and meditation releases one from suffering. —**Bud′dhist** *adj. & n.*
bud•ding (bŭd′ĭng) ►*n.* Asexual reproduction in which an outgrowth forms on the parent organism and detaches to produce a new individual.
bud•dy (bŭd′ē) ►*n., pl.* **-dies** *Informal* A good friend. [Prob. < BROTHER.]
buddy system ►*n.* An arrangement in which persons are paired, as for mutual safety or assistance.
budge (bŭj) ►*v.* **budged, budg•ing 1.** To move or cause to move slightly. **2.** To alter a position or attitude. [OFr. *bouger.*]
budg•er•i•gar (bŭj′ə-rē-gär′, bŭj′ə-rē′-) ►*n.* A small parakeet bred in green, yellow, or blue plumage. [Kamilaroi (Australian) *gijirrigaa.*]
budg•et (bŭj′ĭt) ►*n.* **1.** An itemized summary of probable expenditures and income for a given period. **2.** The sum of money allocated for a particular purpose or period of time. ►*v.* **1.** To make a budget. **2.** To plan in advance the expenditure of. **3.** To enter or account for in a budget. [< OFr. *bougette*, small leather bag.] —**budg′et•ar′y** (-ĭ-tĕr′ē) *adj.*
budg•ie (bŭj′ē) ►*n. Informal* A budgerigar.
Bue•nos Ai•res (bwā′nəs âr′ēz, bwĕ′nōs ī′rĕs) The capital of Argentina, in the E part on the Río de la Plata. Pop. 2,960,976.
buff[1] (bŭf) ►*n.* **1.** A soft, thick, undyed leather made chiefly from the skins of buffalo, elk, or oxen. **2.** A yellowish tan. **3.** A piece of soft material used for polishing. ►*adj.* Of the color buff. ►*v.* To polish or shine with a buff. [< LLat. *būfalus*, buffalo.]
buff[2] (bŭf) ►*n. Informal* One who is enthusiastic and knowledgeable about a particular subject.
buf•fa•lo (bŭf′ə-lō′) ►*n., pl.* **-lo** or **-loes** or **-los 1.** Any of several oxlike Old World mammals, such as the water buffalo. **2.** The North American bison. ►*v.* To intimidate or bewilder. [< Gk. *boubalos.*]
Buffalo. A city of W NY at the E end of Lake Erie. Pop. 328,123.
Buffalo Bill. See William Frederick **Cody.**
buff•er[1] (bŭf′ər) ►*n.* One that shines or polishes, esp. a soft cloth or a machine with a moving head.
buff•er[2] (bŭf′ər) ►*n.* **1.** Something that lessens, absorbs, or protects against the shock of an impact. **2.** Something that separates potentially antagonistic entities. **3.** *Chem.* A substance that minimizes change in the acidity of a solution when an acid or base is added to the solution. **4.** *Comp. Sci.* A device or area used to store data temporarily. [Perh. < *buff*, blow, buffet.] —**buf′fer** *v.*
buffer zone ►*n.* A neutral area between hostile forces that serves to prevent conflict.
buf•fet[1] (bə-fā′, bo͞o-) ►*n.* **1.** A large sideboard with drawers and cupboards. **2.** A counter or table, as in a restaurant, for serving refreshments. **3.** A meal at which guests serve themselves from dishes displayed on a table. [Fr.]
buf•fet[2] (bŭf′ĭt) ►*n.* A blow or cuff with or as if with the hand. ►*v.* To hit or strike against, esp. repeatedly. See Syns at **beat.** [< OFr. *bufet*, light blow.] —**buf′fet•er** *n.*
Buf•fon (bo͞o-fôɴ′), Comte **Georges Louis Leclerc de.** 1707–88. French naturalist.
buf•foon (bə-fo͞on′) ►*n.* A clown; jester. [< OItal. *buffa*, jest.] —**buf•foon′er•y** *n.*
bug (bŭg) ►*n.* **1.** Any of various often harmful insects such as the bedbug, louse, and chinch bug. **2.** Any insect or similar organism. **3.** A disease-producing microorganism; germ. **4.** A mechanical, electrical, or other defect, as in a system, design, or computer code. **5.** An enthusiast; buff. **6.** An electronic listening device, such as a wiretap, used in surveillance. ►*v.* **bugged, bug•ging 1.** To annoy; pester. **2.** To equip (e.g., a room) with a bug. **3.** To bulge out. Used of the eyes. [?] —**bug′ger** *n.*
bug•a•boo (bŭg′ə-bo͞o′) ►*n., pl.* **-boos.** An object of obsessive, usu. exaggerated fear or anxiety. [Perh. of Celt. orig.]
bug•bear (bŭg′bâr′) ►*n.* A bugaboo. [ME *bugge*, hobgoblin + BEAR[2].]
bug-eyed (bŭg′īd′) ►*adj.* Agog.
bug•gy[1] (bŭg′ē) ►*n., pl.* **-gies.** A small, light, usu. four-wheeled carriage. [?]
bug•gy[2] (bŭg′ē) ►*adj.* **-gi•er, -gi•est 1.** Infested with bugs. **2.** *Slang* Crazy.
bu•gle (byo͞o′gəl) ►*n.* A trumpetlike musical instrument lacking keys or valves. [< Lat. *būculus*, steer < *bōs*, ox.] —**bu′gle** *v.* —**bu′gler** *n.*
build (bĭld) ►*v.* **built** (bĭlt), **build•ing 1.** To make by combining parts; construct. **2.** To fashion; create. **3.** To add gradually to: *build support; build up strength.* **4.** To establish a basis for. —***phrasal verb:* build up** To develop or increase in stages or by degrees. ►*n.* Physical makeup; physique. [< OE *byldan.*] —**build′er** *n.*
build•ing (bĭl′dĭng) ►*n.* **1.** A structure; edifice. **2.** The act or art of constructing.
build•up (bĭld′ŭp′) ►*n.* **1.** The act of amassing or increasing. **2.** Widely favorable publicity, esp. by a systematic campaign.
built-in (bĭlt′ĭn′) ►*adj.* **1.** Constructed as part of a larger unit; not detachable. **2.** Forming a permanent element or quality; inherent.
Bu•jum•bu•ra (bo͞o′jəm-bo͝or′ə) The capital of Burundi, in the W part on Lake Tanganyika. Pop. 235,440.
Bu•kha•rin (bo͞o-kär′ĭn, -KHär′-), **Nikolai Ivanovich.** 1888–1938. Bolshevik revolutionary and Soviet politician; executed.
Bu•la•wa•yo (bo͞o′lə-wā′yō, -wä′-) A city of SW Zimbabwe. Pop. 621,742.
bulb (bŭlb) ►*n.* **1.** *Bot.* A short, modified underground stem, such as that of the onion or tulip, that contains stored food for the shoot within. **2.** A rounded projection or part. **3.** A light bulb. [< Gk. *bolbos*, bulbous plant.] —**bul′bous** *adj.*
Bul•finch (bo͝ol′fĭnch′), **Charles.** 1763–1844. Amer. architect.
Bulfinch, Thomas. 1796–1867. Amer. writer.
Bul•ga•nin (bo͝ol-găn′ĭn, -gä′nyĭn), **Nikolai Aleksandrovich.** 1895–1975. Soviet military and political leader.
Bul•gar (bŭl′gär′, bo͝ol′-) ►*n.* See **Bulgarian** 1. [< Turkic *bulghar*, of mixed origin.]

Bul•gar•i•a (bŭl-gâr′ē-ə, bo͝ol-) A country of SE Europe on the Black Sea. Cap. Sofia. Pop. 8,443,000.

Bul•gar•i•an (bŭl-gâr′ē-ən, bo͝ol-) ►*n.* **1.** A native or inhabitant of Bulgaria; Bulgar. **2.** The Slavic language of the Bulgarians. —**Bul•gar′i•an** *adj.*

bulge (bŭlj) ►*n.* A protruding part; swelling. ►*v.* **bulged, bulg•ing.** To swell or cause to swell outward. [< Lat. *bulga*, bag, of Celt. orig.] —**bulg′i•ness** *n.* —**bulg′y** *adj.*
Syns: *bulge, balloon, belly, jut, overhang, project, protrude* **v.**

bul•gur also **bul•ghur** (bo͝ol-go͝or′, bŭl′gər) ►*n.* Cracked wheat grains, often used in Middle Eastern dishes. [Ottoman Turk. *bulghūr*.]

bu•li•mi•a (bo͞o-lē′mē-ə, -lĭm′ē-, byo͞o-) ►*n.* An eating disorder esp. of young women that is marked by episodic binge eating and subsequent feelings of guilt and by measures to prevent weight gain, such as self-induced vomiting. [Gk. *boulimia*, ravenous hunger : *bous*, ox + *limos*, hunger.] —**bu•li′mic** *adj. & n.*

bulk (bŭlk) ►*n.* **1.** Size, mass, or volume, esp. when very large. **2.** The major portion of something. **3.** See **fiber** 6. ►*v.* To be or appear massive in size or importance; loom. —***idiom:*** **in bulk** Unpacked; loose. [ME < ON *bulki*, cargo.] —**bulk′i•ly** *adj.* —**bulk′i•ness** *n.* —**bulk′y** *adj.*

bulk•head (bŭlk′hĕd′) ►*n.* **1a.** One of the upright partitions dividing a ship into compartments. **b.** A partition in an aircraft or spacecraft. **2.** A retaining wall in a mine or along a waterfront. [Perh. < *bulk*, stall, partition.]

bull[1] (bo͝ol) ►*n.* **1a.** An adult male bovine mammal. **b.** The uncastrated adult male of domestic cattle. **c.** The male of certain other animals, such as the alligator, elephant, or moose. **2.** One who buys commodities or securities in anticipation of a rise in prices. **3.** *Slang* A police officer. **4.** *Slang* Empty talk; nonsense. ►*adj.* **1.** Male. **2.** Large and strong. **3.** Characterized by rising prices: *a bull market.* [< OE *bula.*] —**bull′ish** *adj.* —**bull′ish•ly** *adv.* —**bull′ish•ness** *n.*

bull[2] (bo͝ol) ►*n.* An official document issued by the pope. [< Lat. *bulla*, seal.]

bull•dog (bo͝ol′dôg′, -dŏg′) ►*n.* A short-haired dog having a large head, strong square jaws, and a stocky body. ►*adj.* Stubborn. ►*v.* **-dogged, -dog•ging.** To throw (a calf or steer) by seizing its horns and twisting its neck.

bull•doze (bo͝ol′dōz′) ►*v.* **-dozed, -doz•ing 1.** To clear, dig up, or move with a bulldozer. **2.** To bully. [Poss. < obsolete *bulldose*, severe beating.]

bull•doz•er (bo͝ol′dō′zər) ►*n.* A heavy, driver-operated machine for clearing and grading land, usu. having continuous treads and a broad hydraulic blade in front.

bul•let (bo͝ol′ĭt) ►*n.* **1.** A usu. metal projectile that is expelled from a firearm. **2.** *Print.* A heavy dot (•) used for highlighting. [< Lat. *bulla*, ball.] —**bul′let•proof** *adj.*

bul•le•tin (bo͝ol′ĭ-tn, -tĭn) ►*n.* **1.** A printed or broadcast statement on a matter of public interest. **2.** A periodical, esp. one published by an organization or society. [Prob. < Ital. *bolletta*, bill.]

bulletin board ►*n.* **1.** A board, usu. mounted on a wall, on which notices are posted. **2.** *Comp. Sci.* A system for sending or reading electronic messages of general interest.

bull•fight (bo͝ol′fīt′) ►*n.* A public spectacle, esp. in Spain, Portugal, and parts of Latin America, in which a matador engages and usu. kills a fighting bull. —**bull′fight′er** *n.*

bull•finch (bo͝ol′fĭnch′) ►*n.* A European bird having a short thick bill and a red breast.

bull•frog (bo͝ol′frôg′, -frŏg′) ►*n.* A large frog having a deep resonant croak.

bullfrog

bull•head (bo͝ol′hĕd′) ►*n.* A North American freshwater catfish.

bull•head•ed (bo͝ol′hĕd′ĭd) ►*adj.* Very stubborn; headstrong. —**bull′head′ed•ly** *adv.* —**bull′head′ed•ness** *n.*

bull•horn (bo͝ol′hôrn′) ►*n.* An electric megaphone used esp. to amplify the voice.

bul•lion (bo͝ol′yən) ►*n.* Gold or silver bars, ingots, or plates. [< OFr. *billon*, ingot, and *bouillon*, bubble.]

bul•lock (bo͝ol′ək) ►*n.* A steer or young bull. [OE *bulloc*, dim. of *bula*, bull.]

bull•pen (bo͝ol′pĕn′) ►*n.* *Baseball* An area where relief pitchers warm up.

Bull Run. A small stream of NE VA SW of Washington DC; site of two Civil War battles (Jul. 21, 1861, and Aug. 29–30, 1862).

bull session ►*n.* *Informal* An informal group discussion.

bull's-eye (bo͝olz′ī′) ►*n.* **1.** The small central circle on a target. **2.** A shot that hits this circle. **3.** A direct hit.

bull•whip (bo͝ol′hwĭp′, -wĭp′) ►*n.* A long plaited rawhide whip with a knotted end.

bul•ly (bo͝ol′ē) ►*n., pl.* **-lies.** One who is habitually cruel to smaller or weaker people. ►*v.* **-lied, -ly•ing.** To behave like a bully (toward). ►*adj.* Excellent; splendid. ►*interj.* Used to express approval. [Poss. < MDu. *broeder*, brother.]

bul•rush (bo͝ol′rŭsh′) ►*n.* Any of various grasslike marsh plants. [ME *bulrish.*]

bul•wark (bo͝ol′wərk, -wôrk′, bŭl′-) ►*n.* **1.** A wall or embankment raised as a defensive fortification. **2.** Something serving as a defense or safeguard. [< MHGer. *bolwerc* : *bole*, plank + OHGer. *werc*, work.]

bum (bŭm) ►*n.* **1.** A tramp; vagrant. **2.** One who seeks to live off others. ►*v.* **bummed, bum•ming 1.** To live or acquire by begging and scavenging. See Syns at **cadge. 2.** To loaf. ►*adj.* **1.** Inferior; worthless. **2.** Disabled; malfunctioning. **3.** Unfavorable or unfair. [Poss. < Ger. *Bummler*, loafer.]

bum•ble (bŭm′bəl) ►*v.* **-bled, -bling.** To speak, behave, or proceed in a faltering or clumsy manner. See Syns at **blunder.** [Poss. blend of BUNGLE and STUMBLE.] —**bum′bler** *n.*

bum•ble•bee (bŭm′bəl-bē′) ► *n.* Any of various large, hairy, social bees that nest underground. [< ME *bomblen*, to buzz.]

bump (bŭmp) ► *v.* **1.** To strike or collide (with). **2.** To knock: *bumped my knee on the table.* **3.** To jolt; jerk. **4.** To displace; oust. —***phrasal verbs:* bump into** To meet by chance. **bump off** *Slang* To murder. ► *n.* **1.** A blow, collision, or jolt. **2.** A slight swelling or lump. [Imit.] —**bump′i•ness** *n.* —**bump′y** *adj.*

bump•er[1] (bŭm′pər) ► *n.* A horizontal bar attached to either end of a motor vehicle to absorb the impact in a collision.

bump•er[2] (bŭm′pər) ► *n.* A drinking vessel filled to the brim. ► *adj.* Unusually abundant or full: *a bumper crop.* [Perh. < BUMP.]

bump•kin (bŭmp′kĭn, bŭm′-) ► *n.* An awkward, unsophisticated person. [Perh. < MDu. *bomme*, barrel.]

bump•tious (bŭmp′shəs) ► *adj.* Crudely or loudly assertive; pushy. [Poss. alteration of BUMP.] —**bump′tious•ly** *adv.*

bun (bŭn) ► *n.* **1.** A small bread roll, often sweetened. **2.** A roll of hair worn at the back of the head. [ME *bunne*.]

bunch (bŭnch) ► *n.* A group, cluster, or clump. [ME *bonche*.] —**bunch** *v.* —**bunch′y** *adj.*

Bunche (bŭnch), **Ralph Johnson.** 1904–71. Amer. diplomat; 1950 Nobel Peace Prize.

bun•co (bŭng′kō) ► *n., pl.* **-cos** *Informal* A confidence game; swindle. [Poss. < Sp. *banca*, a card game.] —**bun′co** *v.*

bun•dle (bŭn′dl) ► *n.* **1.** A group of objects held together, as by tying or wrapping; package. **2.** *Informal* A large sum of money. ► *v.* **-dled, -dling 1.** To tie, wrap, fold, or otherwise gather together. **2.** To dress warmly. [Prob. < MDu. *bondel*.]

bundt cake (bŭnt, bo͝ont) ► *n.* A ring-shaped cake with fluted sides, baked in a mold. [Orig. a trademark.]

bundt cake

bung (bŭng) ► *n.* A stopper for a bunghole. [< LLat. *puncta*, hole.] —**bung** *v.*

bun•ga•low (bŭng′gə-lō′) ► *n.* A small house or cottage usu. of one story. [< Hindi *baṅglā*, Bengali.]

bun•gee cord (bŭn′jē′) ► *n.* An elasticized rubber cord used to fasten, bear weight, or absorb shock. [< *bunjie*, rubber.]

bungee jumping ► *n.* The sport of jumping from a great height while attached to a bungee cord.

bung•hole (bŭng′hōl′) ► *n.* The hole in a cask, keg, or barrel through which liquid is poured in or drained out.

bun•gle (bŭng′gəl) ► *v.* **-gled, -gling.** To work, manage, or act ineptly or inefficiently. See Syns at **botch.** [Perh. of Scand. orig.] —**bun′gle** *n.* —**bun′gler** *n.*

bun•ion (bŭn′yən) ► *n.* A painful, inflamed swelling of the bursa at the first joint of the big toe. [Perh. < OFr. *bugne*, a swelling.]

bunk[1] (bŭngk) ► *n.* **1.** A narrow built-in bed. **2.** A bunk bed. **3.** A place for sleeping. [Perh. < BUNKER.] —**bunk** *v.*

bunk[2] (bŭngk) ► *n.* Empty talk; nonsense. [After *Buncombe* County, North Carolina.]

bunk bed ► *n.* A double-decker bed.

bun•ker (bŭng′kər) ► *n.* **1.** A bin or tank esp. for fuel storage, as on a ship. **2a.** An underground fortification. **b.** A reinforced chamber or observation post. **3.** A sand trap on a golf course. [Sc. *bonker*, chest.]

Bunker Hill. A hill of Charlestown, MA, near the site of the first major Revolutionary War battle (Jun. 17, 1775).

bunk•house (bŭngk′hous′) ► *n.* Sleeping quarters on a ranch or in a camp.

bun•ny (bŭn′ē) ► *n., pl.* **-nies.** A rabbit, esp. a young one. [dial. *bun*, rabbit's tail.]

Bun•sen burner (bŭn′sən) ► *n.* A small, adjustable gas-burning laboratory burner. [After R.W. *Bunsen* (1811–1899).]

bunt (bŭnt) ► *v.* **1.** *Baseball* To bat (a pitched ball) by tapping it lightly so that the ball rolls slowly in front of the infielders. **2.** To butt with the head. [dial., to push.] —**bunt** *n.* —**bunt′er** *n.*

bunt•ing[1] (bŭn′tĭng) ► *n.* **1.** A light cloth used for making flags. **2.** Flags collectively. **3.** Long colored strips of cloth or material used esp. for festive decoration. [Perh. < Ger. *bunt*, colored.]

bunt•ing[2] (bŭn′tĭng) ► *n.* Any of various birds having short, cone-shaped bills. [ME.]

Bun•yan (bŭn′yən), **John.** 1628–88. English preacher and writer.

buoy (bo͞o′ē, boi) ► *n.* **1.** A float, often having a bell or light, moored in water as a warning of danger or as a marker for a channel. **2.** A life buoy. ► *v.* **1.** To keep afloat or aloft. **2.** To hearten or inspire. [< OFr. *boue*.]

buoy•an•cy (boi′ən-sē, bo͞o′yən-) ► *n.* **1a.** The tendency to float in a liquid or to rise in a gas. **b.** The upward force a fluid exerts on an object less dense than itself. **2.** Ability to recover quickly from setbacks. **3.** Cheerfulness. —**buoy′ant** *adj.*

bur[1] also **burr** (bûr) ► *n.* **1.** A rough, prickly husk surrounding the seeds or fruits of certain plants. **2.** A rotary cutting tool designed to be attached to a drill. [ME.]

bur[2] (bûr) ► *n. & v.* Var. of **burr**[2].

bur. ► *abbr.* bureau

Bur•bank (bûr′băngk′), **Luther.** 1849–1926. Amer. horticulturist.

bur•den[1] (bûr′dn) ► *n.* **1.** Something that is carried. **2.** Something that is emotionally difficult to bear. **3.** A responsibility or duty. ► *v.* **1.** To weigh down; oppress. **2.** To load or overload. [< OE *byrthen*.] —**bur′den•some** *adj.*

Syns: *burden, affliction, cross, trial, tribulation* ***n.***

bur•den[2] (bûr′dn) ► *n.* **1.** A principal or recurring idea; theme. See Syns at **substance. 2.** *Mus.* A chorus or refrain. [< OFr. *bourdon*, drone.]

bur•dock (bûr′dŏk′) ► *n.* A weedy plant having purplish flowers surrounded by prickly bracts and forming a bur in fruit. [BUR[1] + DOCK[4].]

bu•reau (byo͝or′ō) ►*n., pl.* **-reaus** or **-reaux** (-ōz) **1.** A chest of drawers. **2a.** A government department or a subdivision of a department. **b.** An office or business that performs a specific duty: *a travel bureau.* [< OFr. *burel*, woolen cloth.]

bu•reauc•ra•cy (byo͝o-rŏk′rə-sē) ►*n., pl.* **-cies 1a.** Administration of a government chiefly through bureaus and departments staffed with nonelected officials. **b.** The departments and their officials as a group. **2.** An unwieldy administrative system. —**bu′reau•crat′** (byo͝or′ə -kăt′) *n.* —**bu′reau•crat′ic** *adj.* —**bu′reau•crat′i•cal•ly** *adv.*

bu•reauc•ra•tize (byo͝o-rŏk′rə-tīz′) ►*v.* **-tized, -tiz•ing.** To make into a bureaucracy. —**bu•reauc′ra•ti•za′tion** *n.*

bu•rette also **bu•ret** (byo͝o-rĕt′) ►*n.* A glass tube with fine gradations and a stopcock at the bottom, used esp. for accurate fluid dispensing. [< OFr. *buire*, vase.]

burg (bûrg) ►*n. Informal* A city or town. [< OE.]

bur•geon (bûr′jən) ►*v.* **1a.** To put forth new buds, leaves, or greenery; sprout. **b.** To begin to grow or blossom. **2.** To grow and flourish. [< OFr. *burjon*, bud.]

burg•er (bûr′gər) ►*n.* **1.** A hamburger. **2.** A sandwich with a nonbeef patty as a filling: *a crab burger.* [< HAMBURGER.]

bur•gess (bûr′jĭs) ►*n.* A freeman, citizen, or representative of an English borough. [< LLat. *burgēnsis*, of a town.]

burgh (bûrg) ►*n.* A chartered town or borough in Scotland. [Sc.]

burgh•er (bûr′gər) ►*n.* A solid citizen; bourgeois. [< OHGer. *burgārī.*]

bur•glar (bûr′glər) ►*n.* One who commits burglary; housebreaker. [< AN *burgler* and Med.Lat. *burgulator.*] —**bur′glar•ize** *v.* —**bur′glar•proof′** *adj.* —**bur′gla•ry** *n.*

bur•gle (bûr′gəl) ►*v.* **-gled, -gling.** To commit burglary (on). [< BURGLAR.]

bur•go•mas•ter (bûr′gə-măs′tər) ►*n.* The principal magistrate of some European cities. [Du. *burgemeester.*]

Bur•goyne (bûr-goin′, bûr′goin′), **John.** 1722–92. British general and playwright.

Bur•gun•dy[1] (bûr′gən-dē) also **Bour•gogne** (bo͞or-gôn′yə). A historical region and former province of E France. —**Bur•gun′di•an** (bər-gŭn′dē-ən) *adj. & n.*

Bur•gun•dy[2] (bûr′gən-dē) ►*n., pl.* **-dies 1.** Any of various red or white wines produced in Burgundy, France. **2. burgundy** A dark purplish red.

bur•i•al (bĕr′ē-əl) ►*n.* The act or process of burying. [< OE *byrgels.*]

Burke (bûrk), **Edmund.** 1729–97. Irish-born British politician and writer.

Bur•ki•na Fa•so (bər-kē′nə fä′sō). Formerly **Upper Volta.** A landlocked country of W Africa; gained independence from France in 1960. Cap. Ouagadougou. Pop. 9,889,000.

burl (bûrl) ►*n.* A large rounded outgrowth on a tree. [< OFr. *bourle*, tuft of wool.]

bur•lap (bûr′lăp′) ►*n.* A coarse cloth that is made of jute, flax, or hemp. [?]

bur•lesque (bər-lĕsk′) ►*n.* **1.** A ludicrous or mocking imitation. **2.** Vaudeville entertainment characterized by ribald comedy and display of nudity. ►*v.* **-lesqued, -lesqu•ing.** To imitate mockingly. [< Ital. *burla*, joke.]

Bur•ling•ton (bûr′lĭng-tən) A city of NW VT WNW of Montpelier. Pop. 39,127.

bur•ly (bûr′lē) ►*adj.* **-li•er, -li•est.** Heavy and strong. See Syns at **muscular.** [< OE **borlic*, excellent.] —**bur′li•ness** *n.*

Bur•ma (bûr′mə) See **Myanmar.**

Bur•mese (bər-mēz′, -mēs′) ►*n., pl.* **Bur•mese 1.** also **Bur•man** (bûr′mən) A native or inhabitant of Myanmar (Burma). **2.** The Sino-Tibetan language of Myanmar. —**Bur•mese′, Bur′man** *adj.*

burn (bûrn) ►*v.* **burned** or **burnt** (bûrnt), **burn•ing 1a.** To undergo or cause to undergo combustion. **b.** To destroy or be destroyed with fire. **2.** To consume or use as a fuel: *a furnace that burns coal.* **3.** To damage or be damaged by fire, heat, radiation, electricity, or a caustic agent. **4.** To execute, esp. by electrocution. **5.** To make or produce by fire or heat: *burn a hole in the rug.* **6.** To impart a sensation of intense heat to: *The chili burned my mouth.* **7.** To make or become very angry. **8.** To emit heat or light by or as if by fire. **9.** To feel or look hot. —***phrasal verbs:* burn out 1.** To stop burning from lack of fuel. **2.** To wear out or fail, esp. because of heat. **3.** To become exhausted from long-term stress. **burn up** To make or become very angry. ►*n.* **1.** An injury produced by fire, heat, radiation, electricity, or a caustic agent. **2.** A sunburn or windburn. **3.** *Aerospace* A firing of a rocket. —***idioms:* burn (one's) bridges** To eliminate the possibility of return or retreat. **to burn** In great amounts: *They had money to burn.* [< OE *beornan* and *bærnan.*]

Bur•na•by (bûr′nə-bē) A city of SW British Columbia, Canada, a suburb of Vancouver. Pop. 136,494.

burned-out (bûrnd′out′) or **burnt-out** (bûrnt′-) ►*adj.* Worn out or exhausted, esp. as a result of long-term stress.

burn•er (bûr′nər) ►*n.* **1.** One that burns, esp.: **a.** A device, as in a furnace, that is lighted to produce a flame. **b.** A device on a stovetop that produces heat. **2.** A unit, such as a furnace, in which fuel is burned.

bur•nish (bûr′nĭsh) ►*v.* To polish by or as if by rubbing. ►*n.* A glossy finish; luster. [< OFr. *burnir.*]

bur•noose (bər-no͞os′) ►*n.* A hooded cloak worn esp. by Arabs. [< Ar. *burnus.*]

burn•out (bûrn′out′) ►*n.* **1.** A failure in a device caused by excessive heat or friction. **2.** Termination of rocket or jet-engine operation due to fuel exhaustion or shutoff. **3a.** Exhaustion, esp. from long-term stress. **b.** One who is burned out.

Burns (bûrnz), **Robert.** 1759–96. Scottish poet. —**Burns′i•an** *adj.*

Burn•side (bûrn′sīd′), **Ambrose Everett.** 1824–81. Amer. general and politician.

burnt (bûrnt) ►*v.* P.t. and p.part. of **burn.**

burp (bûrp) ►*n.* A belch. ►*v.* **1.** To belch. **2.** To cause (a baby) to belch. [Imit.]

burr[1] (bûr) ►*n.* **1.** A rough edge remaining esp. on metal after it has been cast, cut, or drilled. **2.** Var. of **bur**[1]. ►*v.* **1.** To form a burr on. **2.** To remove burrs from. [Var. of BUR[1].]

burr[2] also **bur** (bûr) ►*n.* **1.** A trilling of the letter *r*, as in Scottish speech. **2.** A buzzing or whirring sound. [Imit.] —**burr** *v.*

Burr, Aaron. 1756–1836. Amer. politician; US Vice President (1801–05).

bur•ri•to (bo͝o-rē′tō, bə-) ▶*n., pl.* **-tos.** A flour tortilla wrapped around a filling, as of beef, beans, or cheese. [Am.Sp.]

bur•ro (bûr′ō, bo͝or′ō, bŭr′ō) ▶*n., pl.* **-ros.** A small donkey, esp. one used as a pack animal. [< LLat. *burrīcus*, small horse.]

bur•row (bûr′ō, bŭr′ō) ▶*n.* A hole or tunnel dug in the ground by an animal for habitation or refuge. ▶*v.* **1.** To dig a burrow. **2.** To move or progress by or as if by tunneling. [ME *borow.*] —**bur′row•er** *n.*

bur•sa (bûr′sə) ▶*n., pl.* **-sae** (-sē) or **-sas.** A saclike body cavity, esp. one located between moving structures. [< Gk., wineskin.]

Bur•sa (bûr′sə, bo͝or-sä′) A city of NW Turkey W of Ankara. Pop. 996,600.

bur•sar (bûr′sər, -sär′) ▶*n.* A treasurer, as at a college. [< LLat. *bursa*, PURSE.] —**bur′sa•ry** *n.*

bur•si•tis (bər-sī′tĭs) ▶*n.* Inflammation of a bursa, esp. in the shoulder, elbow, or knee.

burst (bûrst) ▶*v.* **burst, burst•ing 1a.** To come open or fly apart suddenly, esp. from internal pressure. **b.** To break, shatter, or explode. **2.** To be full to the breaking point. **3.** To emerge or arrive suddenly: *burst out of the door.* **4.** To give sudden utterance or expression: *burst out laughing.* ▶*n.* **1.** A sudden outbreak or explosion. **2.** The result of bursting. **3.** An abrupt increase: *a burst of speed.* [< OE *berstan.*]

Bur•ton (bûr′tn), Sir **Richard Francis.** 1821–90. British explorer.

Burton, Robert. 1577–1640. English cleric and writer.

Bu•run•di (bo͝o-ro͝on′dē, -ro͝on′-) A country of E-central Africa with a coastline on Lake Tanganyika. Cap. Bujumbura. Pop. 6,134,000. —**Bu•run′di•an** *adj. & n.*

bur•y (bĕr′ē) ▶*v.* **-ied, -y•ing 1.** To place in the ground: *bury a bone.* **2.** To place (a corpse) in a grave or tomb. **3.** To embed deeply; sink. **4.** To conceal; hide. **5.** To absorb: *I'm buried in work.* **6.** To abandon: *buried their quarrel.* —***idiom:*** **bury the hatchet** To stop fighting. [< OE *byrgan.*]

bus (bŭs) ▶*n., pl.* **bus•es** or **bus•ses 1.** A long motor vehicle for carrying passengers. **2.** A circuit that connects a computer's major components. ▶*v.* **bused, bus•ing** or **bussed, bus•sing 1.** To transport or travel in a bus. **2.** To clear (dishes) in a restaurant. [< OMNIBUS.]

bus•boy (bŭs′boi′) ▶*n.* A restaurant employee who clears dishes and sets tables.

bus•by (bŭz′bē) ▶*n., pl.* **-bies.** A tall, full-dress fur hat worn in certain regiments of the British army. [Poss. < *Busby.*]

bush (bo͝osh) ▶*n.* **1.** A low shrub with many branches. **2a.** Land covered with dense vegetation or undergrowth. **b.** Land remote from settlement. **3.** A shaggy mass, as of hair. ▶*v.* To grow or branch out like a bush. ▶*adj. Slang* Bush-league. [< OE *busc* and OFr. *bois*, wood.] —**bush′i•ness** *n.* —**bush′y** *adj.*

Bush, George Herbert Walker. b. 1924. The 41st US President (1989–93).

Bush, George Walker. b. 1946. The 43rd US President (since 2001).

bushed (bo͝osht) ▶*adj. Informal* Exhausted.

George H. W. Bush George W. Bush

bush•el (bo͝osh′əl) ▶*n.* **1.** See table at **measurement. 2.** A container with the capacity of a bushel. **3.** *Informal* A large amount. [< OFr. *boissiel*, of Celt. orig.]

bush•ing (bo͝osh′ĭng) ▶*n.* A cylindrical metal lining used to constrain, guide, or reduce friction. [Poss. < Du. *bus*, box.]

bush-league (bo͝osh′lēg′) ▶*adj. Slang* Second-rate.

Bush•man (bo͝osh′mən) ▶*n.* See **San.**

bush•mas•ter (bo͝osh′măs′tər) ▶*n.* A large venomous snake of tropical America.

bush•whack (bo͝osh′hwăk′, -wăk′) ▶*v.* **1.** To travel through dense growth by cutting away bushes and branches. **2.** To ambush. See Syns at **ambush.** —**bush′whack′er** *n.*

busi•ness (bĭz′nĭs) ▶*n.* **1.** The occupation in which a person is engaged. **2.** Commercial, industrial, or professional dealings. **3.** A commercial establishment. **4.** Volume of commercial trade: *Business had fallen off.* **5.** Patronage: *took my business elsewhere.* **6.** One's concern or interest. **7.** Serious work: *got down to business.* **8.** An affair or matter. See Syns at **affair. 9.** An incidental action performed by an actor on the stage, as to fill a pause. **10.** *Informal* Verbal abuse; scolding: *gave me the business for being late.* —**busi′ness•per′son** *n.*

business card ▶*n.* A small card printed with a person's name and business affiliation.

busi•ness•like (bĭz′nĭs-līk′) ▶*adj.* **1.** Methodical and systematic. **2.** Unemotional.

busi•ness•man (bĭz′nĭs-măn′) ▶*n.* A man engaged in business. See Usage Note at **man.**

busi•ness•wom•an (bĭz′nĭs-wo͝om′ən) ▶*n.* A woman engaged in business. See Usage Note at **man.**

bus•ing or **bus•sing** (bŭs′ĭng) ▶*n.* The transportation of children by bus to schools outside their neighborhoods, esp. to achieve racial integration.

busk (bŭsk) ▶*v.* To play music or perform entertainment in public, esp. while soliciting money. [Perh. ult. < Italian *buscare*, to prowl.] —**busk′er** *n.*

bus•kin (bŭs′kĭn) ▶*n.* **1.** A laced half boot worn by actors of Greek and Roman tragedies. **2.** Tragedy. [Poss. < obsolete Fr. *broisequin.*]

bus•man's holiday (bŭs′mənz) ▶*n. Informal* A vacation during which one engages in activity similar to one's usual work.

buss (bŭs) ▶*v.* To kiss. ▶*n.* A kiss. [Poss. < obsolete *bass.*]

bus•ses (bŭs′ĭz) ▶*n.* Pl. of **bus.**

bust¹ (bŭst) ▶*n.* **1.** A sculpture representing a person's head, shoulders, and upper chest. **2.** A woman's bosom. [< Ital. *busto.*]

bust² (bŭst) ▶*v.* **1.** *Slang* **a.** To burst or break.

b. To render or become inoperable. **2.** To break up: *bust the gang.* **3.** To break (a horse). **4.** To bankrupt. **5.** *Slang* To reduce in rank. See Syns at **demote. 6.** To hit; punch. **7.** *Slang* **a.** To arrest. **b.** To make a raid on. ►*n.* **1.** A failure; flop. **2.** A widespread financial depression. **3.** A punch. **4.** A spree. **5.** *Slang* A raid or arrest. [< BURST.]

bust•ed (bŭs′tĭd) ►*adj.* **1.** *Slang* **a.** Broken. **b.** Inoperable: *a busted car.* **2.** Bankrupt or out of funds. **3.** *Slang* Arrested: *a busted robber.*

bus•tle[1] (bŭs′əl) ►*v.* **-tled, -tling.** To move energetically and busily. ►*n.* A commotion; stir. [Poss. < *busk*, prepare oneself.]

bus•tle[2] (bŭs′əl) ►*n.* A frame or pad formerly worn under the back of a woman's skirt to add fullness. [?]

bus•y (bĭz′ē) ►*adj.* **-i•er, -i•est 1.** Engaged in work or activity. **2.** Full of activity: *a busy morning.* **3.** Meddlesome; prying. **4.** Being in use, as a telephone line. **5.** Cluttered with detail: *a busy design.* ►*v.* **-ied, -y•ing.** To make busy. [< OE *bisig.*] —**bus′i•ly** *adv.* —**bus′y•ness** *n.*

bus•y•bod•y (bĭz′ē-bŏd′ē) ►*n.* A meddlesome person.

bus•y•work (bĭz′ē-wûrk′) ►*n.* Activity that takes up time but does not necessarily yield productive results.

but (bŭt; bət *when unstressed*) ►*conj.* **1.** On the contrary. See Usage Notes at **and, not. 2.** Contrary to expectation; yet. **3.** Except; save. **4.** Except that: *would have come but I had to work.* **5.** *Informal* Without the result that: *It never rains but it pours.* **6.** *Informal* That. Often used after a negative: *no doubt but we'll win.* **7.** That . . . not. Used after a negative or question: *There never is a tax law but someone opposes it.* **8.** *Informal* Than: *no sooner arrived but they had to go.* ►*prep.* Except: *No one but us.* ►*adv.* Merely; only: *lasted but a moment.* [< OE *būtan.*]

bu•ta•di•ene (byo͞o′tə-dī′ēn′, -dī-ēn′) ►*n.* A gaseous hydrocarbon, C_4H_6, obtained from butane and used in making synthetic rubber. [BUTA(NE) + DI– + –ENE.]

bu•tane (byo͞o′tān′) ►*n.* Either of two isomers of a gaseous hydrocarbon, C_4H_{10}, cracked from petroleum and used as a household fuel. [BUT(YL) + –ANE.]

butch•er (bo͝och′ər) ►*n.* **1a.** One who slaughters and dresses animals for food. **b.** One who sells meats. **2.** A cruel or wanton killer. ►*v.* **1.** To slaughter or prepare (animals). **2.** To kill brutally or indiscriminately. **3.** To botch; bungle: *butchered the language.* [< OFr. *bouchier* < *bouc*, he-goat.] —**butch′er•er** *n.* —**butch′er•y** *n.*

bu•te•o (byo͞o′tē-ō′) ►*n.*, *pl.* **-os.** Any of various broad-winged, soaring hawks. [Lat. *būteō.*]

but•ler (bŭt′lər) ►*n.* The head servant in a household, usu. in charge of food service. [< OFr. *bouteillier*, bottle bearer.]

Butler, Samuel. 1835–1902. British writer.

butt[1] (bŭt) ►*v.* To hit with the head or horns. —***phrasal verb:* butt in** To interfere or meddle in other people's affairs. ►*n.* A push or blow with the head or horns. [< OFr. *bouter*, strike, of Gmc. orig.]

butt[2] (bŭt) ►*v.* To join or be joined end to end; abut. [< AN *butter.*] —**butt** *n.*

butt[3] (bŭt) ►*n.* An object of ridicule: *the butt of their jokes.* [< OFr. *but*, target.]

butt[4] (bŭt) ►*n.* **1.** The larger or thicker end: *the butt of a rifle.* **2a.** An unburned end, as of a cigarette. **b.** *Informal* A cigarette. **3.** A short or broken remnant; stub. **4.** *Informal* The buttocks. [< OFr. *but*, end.]

butt[5] (bŭt) ►*n.* A large cask. [< LLat. *buttis.*]

butte (byo͞ot) ►*n.* A flat-topped hill that rises abruptly from the surrounding area. [< OFr. *butt*, mound behind targets.]

but•ter (bŭt′ər) ►*n.* **1.** A soft yellowish fatty food churned from milk or cream. **2.** Any of various substances similar to butter. ►*v.* To put butter on or in. —***phrasal verb:* butter up** To flatter. [< Gk. *bouturon* : *bous*, cow + *turos*, cheese.] —**but′ter•y** *adj.*

butter bean ►*n.* *Regional* See **lima bean.**

but•ter•cup (bŭt′ər-kŭp′) ►*n.* Any of numerous plants with usu. glossy yellow flowers.

but•ter•fat (bŭt′ər-făt′) ►*n.* The natural fat of milk from which butter is made.

but•ter•fin•gers (bŭt′ər-fĭng′gərz) ►*pl.n.* *(takes sing. v.)* A person who tends to drop things. —**but′ter•fin′gered** *adj.*

but•ter•fish (bŭt′ər-fĭsh′) ►*n.* An Atlantic marine food fish having a flattened body.

but•ter•fly (bŭt′ər-flī′) ►*n.* **1.** Any of an order of insects having slender bodies and four broad, usu. colorful wings. **2.** The butterfly stroke. **3. butterflies** A feeling of unease caused esp. by fearful anticipation. [< OE *butorflēoge.*]

butterfly stroke ►*n.* A swimming stroke in which both arms are drawn upward and forward with a simultaneous kick.

but•ter•milk (bŭt′ər-mĭlk′) ►*n.* The sour liquid remaining after butterfat is removed from whole milk or cream by churning.

but•ter•nut (bŭt′ər-nŭt′) ►*n.* **1.** An E North American walnut having light brown wood and a nut enclosed in an egg-shaped husk. **2.** The edible, oily nut of this tree. **3.** A brownish dye obtained from the husks of the butternut. [From the nut's oiliness.]

butternut squash ►*n.* A winter squash with a smooth tan rind and edible orange flesh.

but•ter•scotch (bŭt′ər-skŏch′) ►*n.* A syrup, candy, or flavoring made by melting butter and brown sugar.

but•tock (bŭt′ək) ►*n.* **1.** Either of the two rounded prominences posterior to the hips. **2. buttocks** The rear pelvic area of the body. [< OE *buttuc*, strip of land.]

but•ton (bŭt′n) ►*n.* **1.** An often disk-shaped fastener on a garment, designed to fit through a buttonhole or loop. **2.** An object resembling a button, such as a push-button switch or a round flat pin. **3.** *Comp. Sci.* A defined area within an interface that one clicks to select a command. ►*v.* To fasten or be fastened with buttons. —***idiom:* on the button** Exactly. [< OFr. *bouter*, thrust.]

but•ton-down (bŭt′n-doun′) ►*adj.* **1.** Having the ends of the collar fastened down by buttons. **2.** Conservative; conventional.

but•ton•hole (bŭt′n-hōl′) ►*n.* A small slit in a garment or cloth for fastening a button. ►*v.* **-holed, -hol•ing.** To hold or detain (a person) in conversation.

but•tress (bŭt′rĭs) ►*n.* **1.** A structure, usu. brick or stone, built against a wall for support.

2. Something that serves to support or reinforce. ►*v.* To support with or as if with a buttress: *buttress a wall; buttress an argument.* [< OFr. *bouter*, strike against.]

bu•tyl (byo͞ot′l) ►*n.* A hydrocarbon radical, C_4H_9. [< Lat. *butyrum*, BUTTER + -YL.]

bux•om (bŭk′səm) ►*adj.* **1.** Healthily plump. **2.** Full-bosomed. [ME, obedient.]

buy (bī) ►*v.* **bought** (bôt), **buy•ing 1.** To acquire in exchange for money; purchase. **2.** To be capable of purchasing: *the best that money can buy.* **3.** To acquire by sacrifice, exchange, or trade: *buy love with favors.* **4.** To bribe. **5.** *Slang* To accept; believe: *didn't buy my lame excuse.* —***phrasal verbs:* buy off** To bribe. **buy out** To purchase the entire stock, business rights, or interests of. **buy up** To purchase all that is available of. ►*n.* **1.** Something bought. **2.** *Informal* A bargain. [< OE *bycgan.*] —**buy′er** *n.*

buy•back (bī′băk′) ►*n.* The repurchase of stock by the issuing company.

buy•out (bī′out′) ►*n.* **1.** The purchase of the entire holdings of an owner. **2.** The purchase of a company or business.

buzz (bŭz) ►*v.* **1.** To make a low droning or vibrating sound like that of a bee. **2.** To talk excitedly in low tones. **3.** To hum; bustle. **4.** To signal with a buzzer. **5.** *Informal* To fly low over: *buzzed the control tower.* **6.** To telephone: *Buzz me later.* —***phrasal verb:* buzz off** *Informal* To go away. ►*n.* **1.** A vibrating, humming, or droning sound. **2.** A low murmur. **3.** A telephone call. **4.** *Slang* Pleasant intoxication. [ME *bussen.*]

buz•zard (bŭz′ərd) ►*n.* **1.** Any of various North American vultures. **2.** *Chiefly Brit.* A broad-winged hawk. [< Lat. *būteō.*]

buzz•er (bŭz′ər) ►*n.* An electric signaling device that makes a buzzing sound.

buzz saw ►*n.* See **circular saw.**

buzz•word (bŭz′wûrd′) ►*n.* A word or phrase connected with a specialized field that is used esp. to impress laypersons.

BW ►*abbr.* **1.** biological warfare **2.** also **b/w** black and white

BWI ►*abbr.* British West Indies

by (bī) ►*prep.* **1.** Next to. **2.** With the use of; through. **3.** Up to and beyond; past. **4.** During: *sleeping by day.* **5.** Not later than: *by 5:30* P.M. **6a.** In the amount of: *letters by the thousands.* **b.** To the extent of: *shorter by two inches.* **7a.** According to: *played by the rules.* **b.** With respect to: *siblings by blood.* **8.** In the name of: *swore by the Bible.* **9.** Through the agency or action of: *killed by a bullet.* **10.** In succession to; after: *one by one.* **11a.** Used in multiplication and division: *4 by 6 is 24.* **b.** Used with measurements: *a room 12 by 18 feet.* **c.** Used with compass directions: *south by southeast.* ►*adv.* **1.** On hand; nearby: *Stand by.* **2.** Aside; away: *Put it by for later.* **3.** Up to, alongside, and past: *raced by.* **4.** Into the past: *as years go by.* —***idiom:* by and by** In a while. [< OE *bī.*]

by– ►*pref.* **1.** By: *bygone.* **2.** Secondary: *byway.* [ME.]

by-and-by (bī′ən-bī′) ►*n.* Some future time or occasion.

by and large ►*adv.* For the most part.

by-catch (bī′kăch′, -kĕch′) ►*n.* The unwanted portion of a fishing catch.

Byd•goszcz (bĭd′gôsh) A city of N-central Poland NE of Poznań. Population, 382,004.

bye[1] also **by** (bī) ►*n.* **1.** A side issue. **2.** *Sports* The position of one who draws no opponent for a round in a tournament and so advances to the next round. —***idiom:* by the bye** By the way; incidentally. [< BY.]

bye[2] (bī) ►*interj.* Used to express farewell. [< GOODBYE.]

bye-bye (bī′bī′, bī-bī′) ►*interj.* Used to express farewell. [Alteration of GOODBYE.]

by•gone (bī′gôn′, -gŏn′) ►*adj.* Gone by; past: *bygone days.* ►*n.* One, esp. a grievance, that is past: *Let bygones be bygones.*

by•law (bī′lô′) ►*n.* **1.** A law or rule governing the internal affairs of an organization. **2.** A secondary law. [ME *bilawe*, local regulations : ON *bȳr*, settlement + ON **lagu*, law.]

by•line also **by-line** (bī′līn′) ►*n.* A line at the head of a newspaper or magazine article carrying the writer's name. —**by′lin′er** *n.*

by•pass also **by-pass** (bī′păs′) ►*n.* **1.** A highway that passes around an obstructed or congested area. **2.** A means of circumvention. **3.** *Elect.* See **shunt** 3. **4.** *Medic.* **a.** An alternative passage created surgically to divert the flow of blood or other bodily fluid. **b.** A surgical procedure to create a bypass. ►*v.* **1.** To avoid (an obstacle) by using a bypass. **2.** To ignore: *bypass the rules.*

by-path (bī′păth′, -päth′) ►*n.* An indirect or rarely used path.

by-play (bī′plā′) ►*n.* Theatrical action or speech taking place on stage while the main action proceeds.

by•prod•uct or **by-prod•uct** (bī′prŏd′əkt) ►*n.* **1.** Something produced in the making of something else. **2.** A side effect.

Byrd (bûrd), **Richard Evelyn.** 1888–1957. Amer. polar explorer.

By•ron (bī′rən), **George Gordon.** Sixth Baron Byron of Rochdale. 1788–1824. British poet. —**By•ron′ic** (bī-rŏn′ĭk) *adj.*

by•stand•er (bī′stăn′dər) ►*n.* One who is present at an event without participating.

byte (bīt) ►*n.* A sequence of adjacent bits, usu. eight, operated on as a unit by a computer. [< BIT[3] and BITE.]

by•way (bī′wā′) ►*n.* **1.** A side road. **2.** A secondary or arcane field of study.

by•word also **by-word** (bī′wûrd′) ►*n.* **1a.** A proverb. **b.** An often-used word or phrase. **2.** One that represents a type, class, or quality: *Einstein is a byword for genius.*

Byz•an•tine (bĭz′ən-tēn′, -tīn′, bĭ-zăn′tĭn) ►*adj.* **1.** Relating to Byzantium or the Byzantine Empire. **2.** Of the richly decorative artistic or architectural style developed in the Byzantine Empire. **3.** Of the Eastern Orthodox Church or the rites performed in it. **4.** often **byzantine a.** Marked by intrigue; devious. **b.** Highly complex; intricate: *a byzantine tax law.* ►*n.* A native or inhabitant of Byzantium.

Byzantine Empire. The E part of the later Roman Empire, dating from A.D. 330.

By•zan•ti•um (bĭ-zăn′shē-əm, -tē-əm) **1.** The Byzantine Empire. **2.** An ancient city of Thrace on the site of present-day Istanbul, Turkey.

C

c¹ or **C** (sē) ▸ *n., pl.* **c's** or **C's** also **cs** or **Cs** **1.** The 3rd letter of the English alphabet. **2.** The 3rd in a series. **3.** The third best in quality or rank. **4.** *Mus.* The 1st tone in the scale of C major.

c² ▸ *abbr.* **1.** *Phys.* candle **2.** carat **3.** also **C** constant **4.** cubic

C¹ ▸ **1.** The symbol for the element **carbon** 1. **2.** also **c** The symbol for the Roman numeral 100. **3.** The symbol for **capacitance** 1, 2.

C² ▸ *abbr.* **1.** Celsius **2.** centigrade **3.** consonant **4.** coulomb

c. ▸ *abbr.* **1.** cent **2.** centavo **3.** centime **4.** circa **5.** copyright **6.** cup

C. ▸ *abbr.* **1.** cape **2.** or **c.** century **3.** chancellor

ca ▸ *abbr.* **1.** centare **2.** circa

Ca ▸ The symbol for the element **calcium.**

CA ▸ *abbr.* **1.** California **2.** Central America

c/a ▸ *abbr.* current account

CAA ▸ *abbr.* Civil Aeronautics Administration

cab (kăb) ▸ *n.* **1.** A taxicab. **2.** The enclosed compartment for the operator or driver of a heavy vehicle or machine. [< CABRIOLET.]

CAB ▸ *abbr.* Civil Aeronautics Board

ca•bal (kə-băl′, -bäl′) ▸ *n.* **1.** A conspiratorial group. **2.** A secret plot. [< Med.Lat. *cabala*, KABBALAH.]

cab•a•la (kăb′ə-lə, kə-bä′-) ▸ *n.* Var. of **kabbalah.**

ca•ban•a also **ca•ba•ña** (kə-băn′ə, -băn′yə) ▸ *n.* A shelter esp. on a beach, used as a bathhouse. [< LLat. *capanna*, hut.]

cab•a•ret (kăb′ə-rā′) ▸ *n.* **1.** A restaurant or nightclub providing live entertainment. **2.** The floor show in a cabaret. [< ONFr. *camberette*, taproom.]

cab•bage (kăb′ĭj) ▸ *n.* A vegetable of the mustard family, having a large round head of tightly overlapping green to purplish leaves. [< ONFr. *caboche*, head.] —**cab′bag•y** *adj.*

cab•by or **cab•bie** (kăb′ē) ▸ *n., pl.* **-bies.** A cab driver.

cab•in (kăb′ĭn) ▸ *n.* **1.** A small, roughly built house. **2.** A room in a ship used as living quarters. **3.** The enclosed space in an aircraft or spacecraft for the crew, passengers, or cargo. [< LLat. *capanna*, hut.]

cabin class ▸ *n.* A class of accommodations on some passenger ships, lower than first class and higher than tourist class.

cabin cruiser ▸ *n.* A powerboat with a cabin.

cab•i•net (kăb′ə-nĭt) ▸ *n.* **1.** An upright case or cupboard with shelves, drawers, or compartments for the safekeeping or display of objects. **2.** The box that houses a computer's main components. **3.** often **Cabinet** A body of persons appointed by a head of state or a prime minister to head the executive departments of the government and to act as official advisers. **4.** *Regional* See **milk shake.** See Regional Note at **milk shake.** [< ONFr. *cabine*, gambling-room.]

cab•i•net•mak•er (kăb′ə-nĭt-mā′kər) ▸ *n.* An artisan who makes fine articles of wooden furniture. —**cab′i•net•mak′ing** *n.*

cab•i•net•work (kăb′ə-nĭt-wûrk′) ▸ *n.* Finished furniture made by a cabinetmaker.

cabin fever ▸ *n.* Uneasiness resulting from confinement to a limited space or routine.

ca•ble (kā′bəl) ▸ *n.* **1.** A strong, large-diameter steel or fiber rope. **2.** *Elect.* A bound or sheathed group of mutually insulated conductors. **3.** A cablegram. **4.** Cable television. ▸ *v.* **-bled, -bling.** To send a cablegram (to). [< LLat. *capulum*, lasso.]

cable car ▸ *n.* A vehicle that is moved along a route by an endless cable.

ca•ble•cast (kā′bəl-kăst′) ▸ *n.* A telecast by cable television. —**ca′ble•cast′** *v.*

ca•ble•gram (kā′bəl-grăm′) ▸ *n.* A telegram sent by submarine cable.

cable television ▸ *n.* A television distribution system in which station signals received by a central antenna are delivered by cable to the receivers of subscribers.

ca•ble•vi•sion (kā′bəl-vĭzh′ən) ▸ *n.* See **cable television.**

cab•o•chon (kăb′ə-shŏn′) ▸ *n.* A highly polished, convex-cut, unfaceted gem. [< ONFr.]

ca•boo•dle (kə-bo͝od′l) ▸ *n. Informal* The lot, group, or bunch: *donated the whole caboodle.* [Alteration of BOODLE.]

ca•boose (kə-bo͞os′) ▸ *n.* The last car on a freight train, having kitchen and sleeping facilities for the train crew. [Poss. < obsolete Du. *cabūse*, ship's galley.]

Cab•ot (kăb′ət), **John.** 1450?–98? Italian-born explorer.

Cabot, Sebastian. 1476?–1557. Italian-born explorer and cartographer.

Ca•bri•ni (kə-brē′nē), Saint **Frances Xavier.** 1850–1917. Italian-born Amer. religious leader.

Mother Cabrini

cab•ri•o•let (kăb′rē-ə-lā′) ▸ *n.* **1.** A two-wheeled, one-horse carriage with a folding top. **2.** A convertible coupe. [Fr.]

ca•ca•o (kə-kä′ō, -kā′ō) ▸ *n., pl.* **-os** **1.** An evergreen tropical American tree having ribbed, reddish-brown fruits. **2.** The seed of this plant, used in making chocolate, cocoa, and cocoa butter. [< Nahuatl *cacahuatl*, cacao bean.]

cach•a•lot (kăsh′ə-lŏt′, -lō′) ▸ *n.* See **sperm whale.** [< Sp. or Port. *cachalote*, big head.]

cache (kăsh) ▸ *n.* **1.** A hiding place for storing provisions. **2.** A place for concealing valuables. **3.** The goods or valuables hidden in a cache. ▸ *v.* **cached, cach•ing.** To hide or

store in a cache. [< O.Fr. *cacher*, hide, ult. < Lat. *cōgere*, to force. See COGENT.]
ca•chet (kă-shā′) ►*n.* **1.** A mark or quality of distinction, individuality, or authenticity. **2.** A seal on a document. [< O.Fr. *cacher*, press. See CACHE.]
cack•le (kăk′əl) ►*v.* **-led, -ling 1.** To make the shrill cry characteristic of a hen after laying an egg. **2.** To laugh or talk in a shrill manner. ►*n.* **1.** The act or sound of cackling. **2.** Shrill laughter. [Prob. < MLGer. *kākeln.*] —**cack′ler** *n.*
ca•coph•o•ny (kə-kŏf′ə-nē) ►*n.*, *pl.* **-nies.** Jarring, discordant sound; dissonance. [< Gk. *kakophōnos*, dissonant.] —**ca•coph′o•nous** *adj.*
cac•tus (kăk′təs) ►*n.*, *pl.* **-ti** (-tī′) or **-tus•es.** Any of various fleshy-stemmed, spiny, usu. leafless plants native to arid regions of the New World. [< Gk. *kaktos*, thistle.]
cad (kăd) ►*n.* A man of unprincipled behavior, esp. toward women. [< CADDIE.] —**cad′dish** *adj.* —**cad′dish•ly** *adv.* —**cad′dish•ness** *n.*
CAD ►*abbr.* computer-aided design
ca•dav•er (kə-dăv′ər) ►*n.* A dead body, esp. one intended for dissection. [< Lat. *cadere*, to fall, die.]
ca•dav•er•ous (kə-dăv′ər-əs) ►*adj.* **1.** Suggestive of death; corpselike. **2.** Pale and gaunt. —**ca•dav′er•ous•ness** *n.*
cad•die also **cad•dy** (kăd′ē) ►*n.*, *pl.* **-dies.** One hired to attend a golfer, esp. by carrying the clubs. ►*v.* **-died, -dy•ing.** To serve as a caddie. [< Fr. *cadet*, CADET.]
Cad•do•an (kăd′ō-ən) ►*n.* A family of Native American languages of the E Great Plains from the Dakotas to Oklahoma, Texas, and Louisiana.
cad•dy (kăd′ē) ►*n.*, *pl.* **-dies 1.** A small container, esp. for tea. **2.** A case for loading a CD-ROM into a disk drive. [< Malay *kati*, a unit of weight.]
ca•dence (kād′ns) ►*n.* **1.** Balanced, rhythmic flow, as of poetry. **2.** The beat of movement, as in marching. **3.** Vocal inflection or modulation. **4.** *Mus.* A progression of chords moving to a harmonic close or sense of resolution. [< Lat. *cadere*, to fall.]
ca•den•cy (kād′n-sē) ►*n.*, *pl.* **-cies.** Cadence.
ca•den•za (kə-dĕn′zə) ►*n.* *Mus.* **1.** An ornamental melodic flourish, as in an aria. **2.** An extended virtuosic section for the soloist usu. near the end of a concerto movement. [< OItal., CADENCE.]
ca•det (kə-dĕt′) ►*n.* **1.** A student at a military school who is training to be an officer. **2.** A younger son or brother. [< LLat. *capitellum*, dim. of Lat. *caput*, head.]
cadge (kăj) ►*v.* **cadged, cadg•ing.** To beg or get by begging. [< ME *cadgear*, peddler.] —**cadg′er** *n.*
Syns: *cadge, beg, bum, mooch, panhandle* **v.**
Cad•il•lac (kăd′l-ăk′), Sieur **Antoine de la Mothe.** 1658–1730. French explorer and colonial administrator.
Cá•diz (kə-dĭz′, kä′dĭz) A city of SW Spain NW of Gibraltar on the **Gulf of Cádiz,** an inlet of the Atlantic. Pop. 152,187.
cad•mi•um (kăd′mē-əm) ►*n.* *Symbol* **Cd** A soft, bluish-white metallic element used in low-friction alloys, solders, dental amalgams, and nickel-cadmium storage batteries. At. no. 48. See table at **element.** [After *Cadmus*, founder of Thebes < Gk. *Kadmos.*] —**cad′mic** (-mĭk) *adj.*
cad•re (kä′drā, -drə, kăd′rē) ►*n.* **1.** A nucleus of trained personnel around which a larger organization can be built. **2a.** A tightly knit group, esp. of political activists. **b.** A member of such a group. [< Lat. *quadrum*, a square.]
ca•du•ce•us (kə-do͞o′sē-əs, -shəs, -dyo͞o′-) ►*n.*, *pl.* **-ce•i** (-sē-ī′) **1.** *Gk. Myth.* A winged staff with two serpents twined around it, carried by Hermes. **2.** This staff used as the symbol of the medical profession. [< Gk. *karukeion.*]
cae•cum (sē′kəm) ►*n.* Var. of **cecum.**
Caed•mon (kăd′mən). d. c. 680. The earliest English poet.
Caen (käɴ) A city of N France SW of Le Havre. Pop. 112,872.
cae•sar also **Cae•sar** (sē′zər) ►*n.* **1.** Used as a title for Roman emperors. **2.** A dictator or autocrat.
Caesar, Julius. Gaius Julius Caesar. 100–44 B.C. Roman political and military leader and historian. —**Cae•sar′e•an, Cae•sar′i•an** (sĭ-zâr′ē-ən) *adj.*
Cae•sa•re•a (sē′zə-rē′ə, sĕs′ə-, sĕz′ə-) An ancient seaport of Palestine S of present-day Haifa, Israel.
cae•sar•e•an or **cae•sar•i•an** (sĭ-zâr′ē-ən) ►*adj.* & *n.* Vars. of **cesarean.**
cae•si•um (sē′zē-əm) ►*n.* Var. of **cesium.**
cae•su•ra also **ce•su•ra** (sĭ-zho͝or′ə, -zo͝or′ə) ►*n.*, *pl.* **-su•ras** or **-su•rae** (-zho͝or′ē, -zo͝or′ē). A pause in a line of verse dictated by sense or speech rhythm rather than by metrics. [Lat. *caesūra*, a cutting.]
CAF ►*abbr.* cost and freight
ca•fé also **ca•fe** (kă-fā′, kə-) ►*n.* A coffee house, restaurant, or bar. [Fr. < Ital. *caffè*, COFFEE.]
ca•fé au lait (kă-fā′ ō lā′) ►*n.* **1.** Coffee with hot milk. **2.** A light yellowish brown. [Fr.]
caf•e•te•ri•a (kăf′ĭ-tîr′ē-ə) ►*n.* **1.** A restaurant in which customers are served at a counter and carry their meals on trays to tables. **2.** A dining area, as at a school, where meals may be purchased or brought from home. [Sp. *cafetería*, coffee shop < *café*, COFFEE.]
caf•feine also **caf•fein** (kă-fēn′, kăf′ēn′, kăf′ē-ĭn) ►*n.* A bitter white alkaloid, $C_8H_{10}N_4O_2$, often derived from tea or coffee and used chiefly as a mild stimulant. [Ger. *Kaffein* < Fr. *café*, COFFEE.] —**caf′fein•at′ed** (kăf′ə-nā′tĭd) *adj.*
caf•fe lat•te (kăf′ā lä′tā) ►*n.* Espresso coffee with steamed milk. [Ital. *caffé (e) latte*, coffee (with) milk.]
caf•tan or **kaf•tan** (kăf′tăn′, -tən, kăf-tăn′) ►*n.* A full-length sleeved garment worn chiefly in the Near East. [< Turk. *qaftān.*]
cage (kāj) ►*n.* **1.** A barred or grated enclosure for confining birds or animals. **2.** A similar enclosure or structure. **3.** An elevator car. **4a.** *Baseball* A wire backstop used in batting practice. **b.** A hockey or soccer goal. **c.** *Basketball* The basket. ►*v.* **caged, cag•ing.** To put in or as if in a cage. See Syns at **enclose.** [< Lat. *cavea.*]
ca•gey also **ca•gy** (kā′jē) ►*adj.* **-gi•er, -gi•est 1.** Wary; careful. **2.** Crafty; shrewd. [?] —**ca′gi•ly** *adv.* —**ca′gi•ness** *n.*

Ca•glia•ri (käl′yə-rē′) A city of Sardinia, Italy, on the S coast on the **Gulf of Cagliari,** an inlet of the Mediterranean. Pop. 203,254.

ca•hoots (kə-ho͞ots′) ▸*pl.n. Informal* Secret partnership: *in cahoots with organized crime.* [Perh. < OFr. *cahute*, cabin.]

CAI ▸*abbr.* computer-aided instruction

cai•man also **cay•man** (kā′mən) ▸*n., pl.* **-mans.** Any of various tropical American reptiles resembling and closely related to the alligators. [< Carib *acayuman.*]

Cain (kān). In the Bible, the eldest son of Adam and Eve; murdered Abel.

cairn (kârn) ▸*n.* A mound of stones erected as a memorial or marker. [< Sc.Gael. *carn.*]

Cai•ro (kī′rō) The capital of Egypt, in the NE part on the Nile R. Pop. 6,663,000.

cais•son (kā′sŏn′, -sən) ▸*n.* **1.** A watertight structure within which construction work is carried on under water. **2.** See **camel** 2. **3a.** A horse-drawn vehicle formerly used to carry artillery ammunition. **b.** A large ammunition box. [< OFr., large box.]

caisson disease ▸*n.* See **decompression sickness.**

cai•tiff (kā′tĭf) ▸*n.* A despicable coward. [< Lat. *captīvus.* See CAPTURE.] —**cai′tiff** *adj.*

ca•jole (kə-jōl′) ▸*v.* **-joled, -jol•ing.** To wheedle. [Fr. *cajoler.*] —**ca•jol′er** *n.* —**ca•jol′er•y** *n.* —**ca•jol′ing•ly** *adv.*

Ca•jun (kā′jən) ▸*n.* A member of a group of people in S Louisiana descended from French colonists exiled from Acadia in the 18th cent. [Alteration of ACADIAN.] —**Ca′jun** *adj.*

cake (kāk) ▸*n.* **1.** A sweet baked food typically made of flour, liquid, and eggs. **2.** A flat mass of baked or fried batter. **3.** A flat mass of chopped food; patty. **4.** A shaped mass, as of soap or ice. **5.** A coat or crust. ▸*v.* **caked, cak•ing.** To coat; encrust: *hands caked with mud.* [< ON *kaka.*]

cal ▸*abbr.* calorie (small calorie)

Cal ▸*abbr.* calorie (large calorie)

cal. ▸*abbr.* **1.** calendar **2.** caliber

Cal. or **Calif.** ▸*abbr.* California

cal•a•bash (kăl′ə-băsh′) ▸*n.* **1.** An annual vine having large hard-shelled gourds. **2.** A tropical American tree bearing hard-shelled, gourdlike fruits. **3.** The fruit of a calabash, often dried and hollowed for use as a utensil. [< Catalan *carabaça*, gourd.]

cal•a•boose (kăl′ə-bo͞os′) ▸*n. Slang* A jail. [< Sp. *calabozo*, dungeon.]

Ca•la•bri•a (kə-lā′brē-ə, -lä′-) A region of S Italy.

Ca•lais (kă-lā′, kăl′ā) A city of N France on the Strait of Dover opposite Dover, England. Pop. 76,527.

cal•a•mine (kăl′ə-mīn′, -mĭn) ▸*n.* A pink powder of zinc oxide with a small amount of ferric oxide, used in skin lotions. [< Med.Lat. *calamīna.*]

ca•lam•i•ty (kə-lăm′ĭ-tē) ▸*n., pl.* **-ties 1.** A disaster. **2.** Dire distress. [< Lat. *calamitās.*] —**ca•lam′i•tous** *adj.*

cal•car•e•ous (kăl-kâr′ē-əs) ▸*adj.* Composed of or containing calcium carbonate, calcium, or limestone. [< Lat. *calx, calc-*, lime.]

cal•ces (kăl′sēz′) ▸*n.* Pl. of **calx.**

calci– or **calc–** ▸*pref.* Calcium: *calciferous.* [< Lat. *calx, calc-*, lime.]

cal•cif•er•ous (kăl-sĭf′ər-əs) ▸*adj.* Of or containing calcium or calcium carbonate.

cal•ci•fy (kăl′sə-fī′) ▸*v.* **-fied, -fy•ing.** To make or become calcareous. —**cal′ci•fi•ca′tion** *n.*

cal•ci•mine (kăl′sə-mīn′) ▸*n.* A white or tinted liquid containing zinc oxide, water, and glue, used as a wash for walls and ceilings. [Orig. a trademark.] —**cal′ci•mine′** *v.*

cal•cine (kăl-sīn′, kăl′sīn′) ▸*v.* **-cined, -cin•ing.** To heat (a substance) to a high temperature but below the melting or fusing point, causing loss of moisture, reduction, or oxidation. [< LLat. *calcīna*, CALX.] —**cal′ci•na′tion** (-sə-nā′shən) *n.*

cal•cite (kăl′sīt′) ▸*n.* A common crystalline form of natural calcium carbonate. —**cal•cit′ic** (-sĭt′ĭk) *adj.*

cal•ci•um (kăl′sē-əm) ▸*n. Symbol* **Ca** A silvery metallic element that occurs in bone, shells, limestone, and gypsum and forms compounds used to make plaster, quicklime, cement, and metallurgic and electronic materials. At. no. 20. See table at **element.**

calcium carbonate ▸*n.* A colorless or white crystalline compound, $CaCO_3$, occurring naturally as chalk, limestone, and marble, and used in commercial chalk, medicines, and dentifrices.

calcium chloride ▸*n.* A white deliquescent compound, $CaCl_2$, used chiefly as a drying agent, refrigerant, and preservative and for controlling dust and ice on roads.

calcium hydroxide ▸*n.* A soft white powder, $Ca(OH)_2$, used in making mortar, cements, calcium salts, paints, and petrochemicals.

calcium oxide ▸*n.* A white, caustic, lumpy powder, CaO, used as a refractory, as a flux, in making steel, paper, and glass, and in waste treatment and insecticides.

cal•cu•late (kăl′kyə-lāt′) ▸*v.* **-lat•ed, -lat•ing 1.** To compute mathematically. **2.** To estimate; reckon. **3.** To intend: *a choice calculated to please.* **4.** *Regional* **a.** To suppose; guess. **b.** To depend; rely. [< Lat. *calculus*, small stone for counting.] —**cal′cu•la•ble** *adj.* —**cal′cu•la′tive** *adj.*

cal•cu•lat•ed (kăl′kyə-lā′tĭd) ▸*adj.* Undertaken after careful forethought: *a calculated risk.* —**cal′cu•lat′ed•ly** *adv.*

cal•cu•lat•ing (kăl′kyə-lā′tĭng) ▸*adj.* **1.** Shrewd; crafty. **2.** Coldly scheming.

cal•cu•la•tion (kăl′kyə-lā′shən) ▸*n.* **1a.** The act, process, or result of calculating. **b.** A probable estimate. **2.** Careful, often cunning forethought.

cal•cu•la•tor (kăl′kyə-lā′tər) ▸*n.* **1.** One who calculates. **2.** An electronic or mechanical device for the performance of mathematical computations.

cal•cu•lus (kăl′kyə-ləs) ▸*n., pl.* **-li** (-lī′) or **-lus•es 1.** *Pathol.* An abnormal mineral concretion in the body, as in the gallbladder or kidney; stone. **2.** *Dentistry* Tartar. **3.** *Math.* The mathematics of limits, instantaneous rates of change, and finding areas and volumes. [Lat., pebble.]

Cal•cut•ta (kăl-kŭt′ə) A city of E India on the Hooghly R. in the Ganges delta. Pop. 4,399,819.

Cal•der (kôl′dər, kŏl′-), **Alexander.** 1898–1976. Amer. sculptor.

cal•de•ra (kăl-dâr′ə, -dîr′ə, kôl-) ▸*n.* A large

THREE PRINCIPAL CALENDARS

In use throughout most of the modern world, the **Gregorian calendar** was first introduced in 1582 by Pope Gregory XIII. The **Jewish calendar** is used to mark the dates of annual religious events and is the official calendar of the Jewish religious community. The **Islamic calendar** is used throughout the Islamic world to mark religious festivals and is the official calendar in many Muslim countries. It is reckoned from the year of the Hegira in A.D. 622.

Gregorian

The solar year of the Gregorian calendar consists of 365 days. Every fourth year is a leap year of 366 days except for centennial years not evenly divisible by 400.

Months	Number of Days
January	31
February	28
in leap year	*29*
March	31
April	30
May	31
June	30
July	31
August	31
September	30
October	31
November	30
December	31

Jewish

The Jewish calendar is based on both the solar and lunar cycles. The average lunar year of 354 days is adjusted to the solar year with an intercalary month (Adar Sheni) in leap years. This ensures that the major religious festivals fall in their proper season.

Months		Number of Days
Tishri	(Sep.—Oct.)	30
Heshvan	(Oct.—Nov.)	29 or 30
Kislev	(Nov.—Dec.)	29 or 30
Tevet	(Dec.—Jan.)	30
Shevat	(Jan.—Feb.)	30
Adar	(Feb.—Mar.)	29 or 30
Adar Sheni *in leap year only*		29
Nisan	(Mar.—Apr.)	30
Iyar	(Apr.—May)	29
Sivan	(May—Jun.)	30
Tammuz	(Jun.—Jul.)	29
Av	(Jul.—Aug.)	30
Elul	(Aug.—Sept.)	29

Islamic

The Islamic calendar is based on the lunar year and consists of 354 or 355 days. The number of days in each month is adjusted throughout the year in accordance with each lunar cycle.

Months	Number of Days
Muharram	29 or 30
Safar	29 or 30
Rabi I	29 or 30
Rabi II	29 or 30
Jumada I	29 or 30
Jumada II	29 or 30
Rajab	29 or 30
Sha'ban	29 or 30
Ramadan	29 or 30
Shawwal	29 or 30
Dhu'l-Qa'dah	29 or 30
Dhu'l-Hijjah	29 or 30

crater formed by volcanic processes. [Sp. < LLat. *caldāria*, cauldron.]

cal•dron (kôl′drən) ►*n.* Var. of **cauldron.**

cal•en•dar (kăl′ən-dər) ►*n.* **1.** Any of various systems of reckoning the length and divisions of a year. **2.** A table showing the months, weeks, and days of a year. **3.** A chronological list. ►*v.* To enter in a calendar. [< Lat. *kalendārium*, moneylender's account book.] —**ca•len′dri•cal** (kə-lĕn′drĭ-kəl), **ca•len′dric** *adj.*

cal•en•der (kăl′ən-dər) ►*n.* A machine in which paper or cloth is made smooth and glossy by being pressed through rollers. [< Gk. *kulindros*, roller.] —**cal′en•der** *v.*

cal•ends (kăl′əndz, kā′ləndz) ►*n.*, *pl.* **-ends.** The first day of the month in the ancient Roman calendar. [< Lat. *kalendae*.]

calf[1] (kăf) ►*n.*, *pl.* **calves** (kăvz) **1a.** A young cow or bull. **b.** The young of certain other mammals, such as the elephant or whale. **2.** Calfskin. [< OE *cealf*.]

calf[2] (kăf) ►*n.*, *pl.* **calves** (kăvz). The fleshy muscular back of the human leg between the knee and ankle. [< ON *kālfi*.]

calf•skin (kăf′skĭn′) ►*n.* Fine leather made from the hide of a calf.

Cal•ga•ry (kăl′gə-rē) A city of S Alberta, Canada, S of Edmonton. Pop. 710,677.

Cal•houn (kăl-ho͞on′), **John Caldwell.** 1782–1850. Vice President of the US (1825–32).

Ca•li (kä′lē) A city of W Colombia on the **Cali River** SW of Bogotá. Pop. 1,369,331.

cal•i•ber (kăl′ə-bər) ►*n.* **1a.** The diameter of the inside of a round cylinder, esp. the bore of a firearm. **b.** The diameter of a bullet or projectile. **2.** Degree of worth; quality: *a school of high caliber.* [Fr. *calibre*.]

cal•i•brate (kăl′ə-brāt′) ►*v.* **-brat•ed, -brat•ing 1.** To check or adjust the graduations of (a quantitative measuring instrument). **2.** To determine the caliber of. **3.** To make fine corrections in. —**cal′i•bra′tion** *n.*

cal•i•bre (kăl′ə-bər) ►*n. Chiefly Brit.* Var. of **caliber.**

cal•i•co (kăl′ĭ-kō′) ►*n.*, *pl.* **-coes** or **-cos 1.** A coarse, brightly printed cloth. **2.** A cat having a white coat mottled with red and black. [< *Calicut*, India.] —**cal′i•co** *adj.*

Cal•i•for•nia (kăl′ĭ-fôr′nyə, -fôr′nē-ə) A state of the W US on the Pacific. Cap. Sacramento. Pop. 29,839,250. —**Cal′i•for′nian** *adj. & n.*

California, Gulf of. An arm of the Pacific in NW Mexico separating Baja California from the mainland.

California condor ►*n.* A very large, nearly extinct vulture of S California.

California poppy ►*n.* A plant of W North America having showy, often orange or yellow flowers.

cal•i•for•ni•um (kăl′ə-fôr′nē-əm) ►*n. Symbol* **Cf** A radioactive element produced synthetically from curium. At. no. 98. See table at **element.** [< CALIFORNIA.]

Ca•lig•u•la (kə-lĭg′yə-lə). A.D. 12–41. Emperor of Rome (A.D. 37–41).

cal•i•per also **cal•li•per** (kăl′ə-pər) ►*n.* **1.** often **calipers** An instrument consisting of two curved hinged legs, used to measure thickness and distances. **2.** A vernier caliper. [Alteration of CALIBER.]

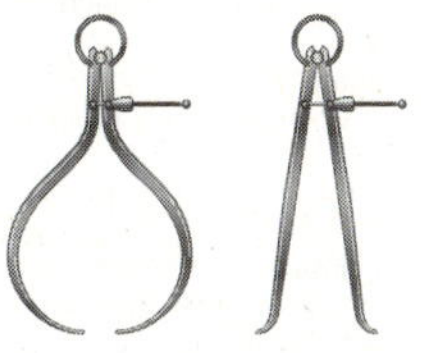

caliper
left to right: spring and inside calipers

ca•liph also **ca•lif** (kā′lĭf, kăl′ĭf) ►*n.* A leader of an Islamic polity, regarded as a successor of Muhammad. [< Ar. *ḫalīfa.*] —**ca′liph•ate′** (-fāt′, -fĭt) *n.*

cal•is•then•ics (kăl′ĭs-thĕn′ĭks) ►*n. (takes pl. v.)* Gymnastic exercises designed to develop muscular tone and promote physical well-being. [Gk. *kallos*, beauty + *sthenos*, strength.] —**cal′is•then′ic** *adj.*

calk (kôk) ►*v.* Var. of **caulk.**

call (kôl) ►*v.* **called, call•ing 1.** To cry or utter loudly or clearly. **2.** To summon. **3.** To telephone. **4.** To name; designate: *Don't call me a liar.* **5.** To consider; estimate: *Would you call him an expert?* **6.** To pay a brief visit. **7.** To demand payment of (a loan or bond issue). **8.** *Sports* **a.** To stop or postpone (a game), as for bad weather. **b.** To declare as an umpire or referee: *call a runner out.* **9.** To indicate accurately in advance: *call the outcome of the next election.* —***phrasal verbs:* call down** To reprimand. **call for 1.** To stop for: *I'll call for you on my way home.* **2.** To warrant. **call forth** To evoke. **call in 1.** To take out of circulation: *calling in silver dollars.* **2.** To summon for assistance or consultation. **call off 1.** To cancel or postpone. **2.** To restrain: *Call off your dogs!* **call out** To cause to assemble; summon. **call up 1.** To summon to military service. **2.** To bring to mind: *call up old times.* **call upon 1.** To order; require: *I call upon you to tell the truth.* **2.** To make a demand or appeal on. ►*n.* **1.** A loud cry; shout. **2.** The characteristic cry of an animal. **3.** A telephone communication. **4.** Demand; occasion: *There's no call for haste.* **5.** A short visit. **6.** A summons or invitation. **7.** A strong urge or prompting. **8.** *Sports* A decision made by an umpire or referee. **9.** A demand for payment, as of a debt. —***idioms:* call it a day** *Informal* To stop one's work for the day; quit. **call it quits** *Informal* To leave off; quit. **call the shots** *Informal* To be in charge. **call to mind** To remind of. **on call 1.** Available when summoned. **2.** Payable on demand. **within call** Accessible. [< ON *kalla.*] —**call′er** *n.*

Syns: *call, convene, convoke, muster, summon* **v.**

cal•la lily (kăl′ə) ►*n.* Any of several ornamental plants cultivated for their showy, usu. white or yellow spathes. [Perh. < Gk. *kallos*, beauty.]

Cal•la•o (kə-yä′ō, kä-you′) A city of W-central Peru on the Pacific near Lima. Pop. 515,200.

caller ID ►*n.* A telephone service that displays an incoming caller's name and telephone number.

cal•lig•ra•phy (kə-lĭg′rə-fē) ►*n.* The art of fine handwriting. [< Gk. *kallos*, beautiful + -GRAPHY.] —**cal•lig′ra•pher, cal•lig′ra•phist** *n.* —**cal′li•graph′ic** (kăl′ĭ-grăf′ĭk) *adj.*

call-in (kôl′ĭn′) ►*adj.* Inviting listeners or viewers to participate in a program by means of broadcasted telephone calls.

call•ing (kô′lĭng) ►*n.* **1.** An inner urge; strong impulse. **2.** An occupation; vocation.

calling card ►*n.* **1.** An engraved card bearing one's full name. **2.** A phone card.

cal•li•o•pe (kə-lī′ə-pē′, kăl′ē-ōp′) ►*n.* A musical instrument fitted with steam whistles, played from a keyboard. [< *Calliope*, muse of epic poetry.]

cal•li•per (kăl′ə-pər) ►*n.* Var. of **caliper.**

call letters ►*pl.n.* The identifying code letters or numbers of a radio or television station.

call loan ►*n.* A loan repayable on demand at any time.

call number ►*n.* A number used in libraries to classify a book and indicate its location on the shelves.

cal•los•i•ty (kə-lŏs′ĭ-tē) ►*n.*, *pl.* **-ties 1.** The condition of being calloused. **2.** Hardheartedness; insensitivity. **3.** See **callus.**

cal•lous (kăl′əs) ►*adj.* **1.** Having calluses; toughened. **2.** Insensitive: *a callous indifference to suffering.* ►*v.* To make or become callous. [< Lat. *callum*, callus.] —**cal′lous•ly** *adv.* —**cal′lous•ness** *n.*

cal•low (kăl′ō) ►*adj.* Lacking experience; immature: *a callow youth.* [< OE *calu*, bald.] —**cal′low•ness** *n.*

call-up (kôl′ŭp′) ►*n.* The summoning of reserve military personnel to active service.

cal•lus (kăl′əs) ►*n.*, *pl.* **-lus•es.** A localized thickening and enlargement of the horny layer of the skin. [Lat.] —**cal′lus** *v.*

call waiting ►*n.* A telephone service that alerts someone using the phone to an incoming call and allows switching between calls.

calm (käm) ►*adj.* **-er, -est 1.** Nearly or completely motionless; undisturbed: *calm seas.* **2.** Not excited or agitated; composed. ►*n.* **1.** An absence of motion; stillness. **2.** Serenity; peace. ►*v.* To make or become calm. [< LLat. *cauma*, heat of the day.] —**calm′ly** *adv.* —**calm′ness** *n.*

calm•a•tive (kä′mə-tĭv, kăl′mə-) ►*adj.* Having sedative properties. ►*n.* A sedative.

cal•o•mel (kăl′ə-mĕl′, -məl) ►*n.* A usu. white tasteless compound, Hg_2Cl_2, used as a purgative and insecticide. [NLat. *kalomelas.*]

ca•lor•ic (kə-lôr′ĭk, -lŏr′-) ►*adj.* **1.** Of or relating to heat. **2.** Of or relating to calories.

cal•o•rie (kăl′ə-rē) ►*n.* **1.** A unit of heat equal to the amount of heat required to raise the temperature of 1 gram of water by 1°C at 1 atmosphere pressure; small calorie. **2a.** A unit of heat equal to the amount of heat required to raise the temperature of 1 kilogram of water by 1°C at 1 atmosphere pressure; large calorie. **b.** A unit of energy-producing potential equal to this amount of heat that is contained in food. [< Lat. *calor*, heat.]

cal•o•rif•ic (kăl′ə-rĭf′ĭk) ►*adj.* Of or generating heat or calories.

cal•o•rim•e•ter (kăl′ə-rĭm′ĭ-tər) ►*n.* An apparatus for measuring the heat generated by a chemical reaction or change of state.

cal•u•met (kăl′yə-mĕt′, kăl′yə-mĕt′) ►*n.* A long-stemmed ceremonial tobacco pipe used by certain Native American peoples. [< Fr. dial., straw.]

ca•lum•ni•ate (kə-lŭm′nē-āt′) ►*v.* **-at•ed, -at•ing.** To slander or malign. —**ca•lum′ni•a′tion** *n.* —**ca•lum′ni•a′tor** *n.*

cal•um•ny (kăl′əm-nē) ►*n., pl.* **-nies 1.** A false statement maliciously made to injure another's reputation. **2.** The utterance of maliciously false statements; slander. [< Lat. *calumnia.*] —**ca•lum′ni•ous** (kə-lŭm′nē-əs) *adj.* —**ca•lum′ni•ous•ly** *adv.*

Cal•va•ry (kăl′və-rē) also **Gol•go•tha** (gŏl′gə-thə, gŏl-gŏth′ə). A hill outside ancient Jerusalem where Jesus was crucified.

calve (kăv) ►*v.* **calved, calv•ing 1.** To give birth to a calf. **2.** To break at an edge. Used of a glacier.

Cal•vert (kăl′vərt). Family of English colonists in America, including **George** (1580?–1632), 1st Baron Baltimore; **Cecilius** (1605–75), 2nd Baron Baltimore; **Leonard** (1606–47); and **Charles** (1637–1715), 3rd Baron Baltimore.

calves¹ (kăvz) ►*n.* Pl. of **calf¹.**

calves² (kăvz) ►*n.* Pl. of **calf².**

Cal•vin (kăl′vĭn), **John.** 1509–64. French-born Swiss theologian. —**Cal′vin•ism′** *n.* —**Cal′vin•ist** *adj. & n.*

calx (kălks) ►*n., pl.* **-es** or **cal•ces** (kăl′sēz′). The residue left after a mineral or metal has been calcined. [< Gk. *khalix*, pebble.]

Ca•lyp•so or **ca•lyp•so** (kə-lĭp′sō) ►*n., pl.* **-sos** also **-soes.** A type of West Indian music with improvised lyrics on topical or broadly humorous subjects. [?] —**Ca•lyp•so′ni•an** (kə-lĭp-sō′nē-ən, kăl′ĭp-) *n.*

ca•lyx (kā′lĭks, kăl′ĭks) ►*n., pl.* **-es** or **ca•ly•ces** (kā′lĭ-sēz′, kăl′ĭ-). The sepals of a flower that together form a cuplike base. [< Gk. *kalux.*]

cal•zo•ne (kăl-zō′nē, -zōn′) ►*n.* A baked turnover filled with vegetables, meat, or cheese. [Ital., pant leg, calzone.]

cam (kăm) ►*n.* A multiply curved wheel mounted on a rotating shaft, used to produce reciprocating motion. [Du. *kam*, cog, comb.]

CAM ►*abbr.* computer-aided manufacturing

Ca•ma•güey (kăm′ə-gwā′, kä′mä-) A city of E-central Cuba. Pop. 291,426.

ca•ma•ra•der•ie (kä′mə-rä′də-rē, kăm′ə-răd′ə-) ►*n.* Spirited goodwill among friends. [Fr.]

cam•ber (kăm′bər) ►*n.* **1.** A slightly arched surface, as of a road. **2.** A setting of automobile wheels in which they are closer together at the bottom than at the top. [< Lat. *camur*, curved.] —**cam′ber** *v.*

cam•bi•um (kăm′bē-əm) ►*n.* A layer of soft growing tissue in a plant body that develops into new bark and new wood and produces the annual rings. [< Med.Lat., exchange.]

Cam•bo•di•a (kăm-bō′dē-ə) A country of SE Asia on the Gulf of Siam. Cap. Phnom Penh. Pop. 9,568,000. —**Cam•bo′di•an** *adj. & n.*

Cam•bri•an (kăm′brē-ən) *Geol.* ►*adj.* Of or being the 1st and oldest period of the Paleozoic Era, marked by an abundance of marine invertebrates. ►*n.* The Cambrian Period.

cam•bric (kām′brĭk) ►*n.* A fine white linen or cotton fabric. [< *Cambrai*, France.]

Cam•bridge (kām′brĭj) **1.** A municipal borough of E-central England NNE of London. Pop. 100,200. **2.** A city of E MA on the Charles R. opposite Boston. Pop. 95,802.

cam•cord•er (kăm′kôr′dər) ►*n.* A lightweight, hand-held video camera that incorporates a videocassette recorder.

Cam•den (kăm′dən) A city of W NJ on the Delaware R. opposite Philadelphia. Pop. 87,492.

came (kām) ►*v.* P.t. of **come.**

cam•el (kăm′əl) ►*n.* **1.** A humped, long-necked ruminant mammal domesticated in Old World desert regions as a beast of burden. **2.** A hollow, watertight device used to raise sunken objects. [< Gk. *kamēlos.*]

cam•el•hair (kăm′əl-hâr′) also **cam•el's hair** (kăm′əlz) ►*n.* **1.** The soft fine hair of the camel or a substitute for it. **2.** A soft, heavy, usu. light tan cloth, made chiefly of camelhair.

ca•mel•lia (kə-mēl′yə) ►*n.* Any of a genus of evergreen Asian shrubs having showy, usu. red, white, or pink roselike flowers. [After Georg Josef *Kamel* (1661–1706).]

Cam•e•lot (kăm′ə-lŏt′) ►*n.* **1.** The legendary site of King Arthur's court. **2.** A place or time of idealized beauty, peacefulness, and enlightenment.

cam•e•o (kăm′ē-ō′) ►*n., pl.* **-os 1.** A gem or medallion with a design cut in raised relief, usu. of a contrasting color. **2.** A brief appearance of a prominent actor, as in a single scene. [Ital.]

cam•er•a (kăm′ər-ə, kăm′rə) ►*n.* **1.** An apparatus for taking photographs, consisting of a lightproof enclosure having an aperture with a shuttered lens through which an image is focused and recorded on a photosensitive film or plate. **2.** The part of a video transmitting apparatus that receives the primary image and transforms it into electrical impulses. [LLat., room.]

cam•er•a•man (kăm′ər-ə-măn′, kăm′rə-) ►*n.* A man who operates a movie or television camera. See Usage Note at **man.**

Cam•e•roon (kăm′ə-ro͞on′) also **Came•roun** (kăm-ro͞on′). A country of W-central Africa on the Bight of Biafra. Cap. Yaoundé. Pop. 12,871,000.

cam•i•sole (kăm′ĭ-sōl′) ►*n.* **1.** A woman's sleeveless undergarment. **2.** A short negligee. [< LLat. *camīsa*, shirt.]

Ca•mões (kə-moiNsh′) also **Ca•mo•ëns** (kăm′ō-ənz, kə-mō′-), **Luiz Vaz de.** 1524?–80. Portuguese writer.

cam•o•mile (kăm′ə-mīl′, -mēl′) ►*n.* Var. of **chamomile.**

cam•ou•flage (kăm′ə-fläzh′, -fläj′) ►*n.* A means of concealment or a disguise that creates the effect of being part of the natural surroundings. ►*v.* **-flaged, -flag•ing 1.** To conceal by camouflage. **2.** To mask. See Syns at **disguise.** [< Ital. *camuffare*, to disguise.] —**cam′ou•flag′er** *n.*

camp¹ (kămp) ►*n.* **1a.** A place of temporary residence or shelter, as for soldiers or travelers. **b.** The shelters, such as tents or cabins, at such a place. **2.** A usu. rural place offering organized recreation or instruction: *a girls' summer camp.* **3.** A group sharing a common cause or opinion. ►*v.* To set up or live in a camp. [< Lat. *campus*, field.]

camp² (kămp) ►*n.* An affectation, esp. for humor's sake, of manners commonly thought to be vulgar or banal. ►*adj.* Deliberately artificial, vulgar, or banal. ►*v.* To act in a camp manner. [?] —**camp′y** *adj.*

Cam•pa•gna di Ro•ma (kăm-pän′yə dē rō′mə, -mä, käm-) A low-lying region surrounding Rome, Italy.

cam•paign (kăm-pān′) ►*n.* **1.** A series of military operations undertaken to achieve a large-scale objective during a war. **2.** An organized operation to accomplish a purpose: *an ad campaign; a political campaign.* ►*v.* To engage in a campaign. [< LLat. *campānia,* battlefield.] —**cam•paign′er** *n.*

Syns: *campaign, drive, push* **n.**

Cam•pa•ni•a (kăm-pā′nē-ə, käm-pä′nyä) A region of S Italy on the Tyrrhenian Sea.

cam•pa•ni•le (kăm′pə-nē′lē) ►*n.* An often freestanding bell tower. [< LLat. *campāna,* bell.]

camp•er (kăm′pər) ►*n.* **1.** One who camps or attends a camp. **2.** A motor vehicle equipped, as with a rear compartment or attached trailer, for sleeping and housekeeping, used for recreational travel.

camp•fire (kămp′fīr′) ►*n.* **1.** An outdoor fire in a camp, used for cooking or warmth. **2.** A meeting held around such a fire.

camp•ground (kămp′ground′) ►*n.* An area for camping, esp. one containing individual campsites.

cam•phor (kăm′fər) ►*n.* A natural aromatic compound used in the manufacture of film and plastics and as an external medicinal preparation. [< Ar. *kāfūr.*] —**cam′phor•at′ed** (-fə-rā′tĭd) *adj.*

Cam•pi•nas (kăm-pē′nəs, kän-) A city of SE Brazil N of São Paulo. Pop. 846,434.

Cam•pi•on (kăm′pē-ən), **Thomas.** 1567–1620. English poet and composer.

camp meeting ►*n.* An evangelistic gathering held in a tent or outdoors.

Cam•pos (kän′po͝os) A city of SE Brazil NE of Rio de Janeiro. Pop. 178,457.

camp•site (kămp′sīt′) ►*n.* An area used or suitable for setting up a camp.

cam•pus (kăm′pəs) ►*n., pl.* **-pus•es.** The grounds of a school, college, university, or hospital. [Lat., field.]

cam•shaft (kăm′shăft′) ►*n.* An engine shaft fitted with a cam or cams.

Ca•mus (kä-mo͞o′, -mü′), **Albert.** 1913–60. French writer and philosopher; 1957 Nobel.

can¹ (kăn; kən *when unstressed*) ►*aux.v. P.t.* **could** (ko͝od) **1.** Used to indicate: **a.** Physical or mental ability: *I can carry both suitcases.* **b.** Possession of a power, right, or privilege: *The President can veto bills.* **c.** Possession of a capability or skill: *I can tune a piano.* **2.** Used to indicate: **a.** Possibility or probability: *I wonder if I could be sick.* **b.** That which is permitted, as by conscience or feelings: *I can hardly blame you for laughing.* **3.** Used to request or grant permission. [< OE *cunnan,* know how.]

Usage: Technically, *may* is used to express permission and *can* to express the capacity to do something. Although *can* has a long history of use by educated speakers to express permission, observance of the distinction is often advisable in the interests of clarity.

can² (kăn) ►*n.* **1.** A metal container: *a garbage can.* **2a.** An airtight storage container, usu. made of tin-coated iron and used esp. for foods. **b.** The contents of a can. **3.** *Slang* A jail. **4.** *Slang* A toilet. ►*v.* **canned, can•ning 1.** To seal in a can or jar; preserve. **2.** *Slang* To dismiss; fire. **3.** *Slang* To put a stop to: *Can the chatter.* [< OE *canne,* water container.] —**can′ner** *n.*

Can. ►*abbr.* **1.** Canada **2.** Canadian

Ca•naan (kā′nən) An ancient region made up of Palestine or the part of it between the Jordan R. and the Mediterranean. —**Ca′naan•ite′** *adj. & n.*

Can•a•da (kăn′ə-də) A country of N North America. Cap. Ottawa. Pop. 23,343,181. —**Ca•na′di•an** (kə-nā′dē-ən) *adj. & n.*

Canada Day ►*n.* July 1, observed in Canada in commemoration of the formation of the Dominion in 1867.

Canada goose or **Canadian goose** ►*n.* A common wild goose of North America, having grayish plumage, a black neck and head, and a white throat patch.

Canadian French ►*n.* The French language as used in Canada.

Canadian River. A river rising in NE NM and flowing about 1,458 km (906 mi) to the Arkansas R. in E OK.

ca•naille (kə-nī′, -nāl′) ►*n.* The common people. [< Ital. *canaglia* < Lat. *canis,* dog.]

ca•nal (kə-năl′) ►*n.* **1.** An artificial waterway used for travel, shipping, or irrigation. **2.** *Anat.* A tube or duct. [< Lat. *canālis,* channel.] —**can′al•i•za′tion** (kăn′ə-lĭ-zā′shən) *n.* —**can′al•ize′** *v.*

Canal Zone also **Panama Canal Zone.** A strip of land across the Isthmus of Panama, formerly administered by the US for the operation of the Panama Canal.

can•a•pé (kăn′ə-pā′, -pē) ►*n.* A cracker or small piece of bread topped with a spread. [Fr., couch, canapé.]

ca•nard (kə-närd′) ►*n.* An unfounded or false, deliberately misleading story. [Fr.]

ca•nar•y (kə-nâr′ē) ►*n., pl.* **-ies 1.** A small, greenish to yellow finch long bred as a cage bird. **2.** A sweet white wine. **3.** A light to vivid yellow. [After the CANARY ISLANDS.]

Canary Islands. A group of Spanish islands in the Atlantic off the NW coast of Africa.

ca•nas•ta (kə-năs′tə) ►*n.* A card game related to rummy and requiring two decks of cards. [Sp. < *canasto,* basket.]

Ca•nav•er•al (kə-năv′ər-əl, -năv′rəl), **Cape.** A sandy promontory extending into the Atlantic on the E-central coast of FL.

Can•ber•ra (kăn′bər-ə, -bĕr′ə) The capital of Australia, in the SE part. Pop. 298,200.

can•can (kăn′kăn′) ►*n.* An exuberant exhibition dance marked by high kicking. [Fr.]

can•cel (kăn′səl) ►*v.* **-celed, -cel•ing** also **-celled, -cel•ling 1.** To cross out with lines or other markings. **2.** To annul or invalidate. **3.** To mark or perforate (e.g., a postage stamp or check) to insure against further use. **4.** To counteract; offset. **5.** *Math.* **a.** To remove (a common factor) from the numerator and denominator of a fractional expression. **b.** To remove (a common factor or term) from both sides of an equation or inequality. [< Lat. *cancellus,* lattice.] —**can′cel•a•ble** *adj.* —**can′cel•er** *n.* —**can′cel•la′tion** *n.*

can•cer (kăn′sər) ►*n.* **1a.** A malignant tumor that tends to invade surrounding tissue and spread to new body sites. **b.** The pathological condition characterized by such growths. **2.** A pernicious, spreading evil. [< Lat.] —**can′cer•ous** (-sər-əs) *adj.*

Can•cer (kăn′sər) ►*n.* **1.** A constellation in the Northern Hemisphere. **2.** The 4th sign of the zodiac. [< Lat.]

can•del•a (kăn-dĕl′ə) ►*n.* A unit of luminous intensity equal to 1/60 of the luminous intensity per square cm of a blackbody radiating at the temperature of 2,046°K. [Lat. *candēla*, candle.]

can•de•la•bra (kăn′dl-ä′brə, -ăb′rə, -ā′brə) ►*n.* A candelabrum. [Lat. *candēlābra*, pl. of *candēlābrum*.]

can•de•la•brum (kăn′dl-ä′brəm, -ăb′rəm, -ā′brəm) ►*n.*, *pl.* **-bra** (-brə) or **-brums.** A large decorative candlestick having several arms or branches. [Lat. *candēlābrum*.]

candelabrum

can•des•cence (kăn-dĕs′əns) ►*n.* The state of being white hot; incandescence. [< Lat. *candēre*, shine.] —**can•des′cent** *adj.*

can•did (kăn′dĭd) ►*adj.* **1.** Free from prejudice; impartial. **2.** Direct and frank; straightforward: *my candid opinion.* **3.** Not posed or rehearsed: *a candid snapshot.* [Lat. *candidus*, white, pure < *candēre*, shine.] —**can′did•ly** *adv.* —**can′did•ness** *n.*

can•di•date (kăn′dĭ-dāt′, -dĭt) ►*n.* A person who seeks or is nominated for an office, prize, or honor. [Lat. *candidātus*, clothed in white.] —**can′di•da•cy** (-də-sē), **can′di•da•ture′** (-də-cho͝or′, -chər) *n.*

can•dle (kăn′dl) ►*n.* **1.** A solid, usu. cylindrical mass of tallow, wax, or other fatty substance with an embedded wick that is burned to provide light. **2.** See **candela.** ►*v.* **-dled, -dling.** To examine (an egg) in front of a bright light. [< Lat. *candēla* < *candēre*, shine.] —**can′dler** *n.*

can•dle•light (kăn′dl-līt′) ►*n.* **1.** Illumination from a candle or candles. **2.** Dusk; twilight.

can•dle•pin (kăn′dl-pĭn′) ►*n.* A slender bowling pin used with a smaller ball in a variation of the game of tenpins.

can•dle•pow•er (kăn′dl-pou′ər) ►*n.* Luminous intensity expressed in candelas.

can•dle•stick (kăn′dl-stĭk′) ►*n.* A holder with a cup or spike for a candle.

can•dor (kăn′dər) ►*n.* Frankness or sincerity of expression. [< Lat. < *candēre*, shine.]

C & W ►*abbr.* country and western

can•dy (kăn′dē) ►*n.*, *pl.* **-dies.** A sweet confection made with sugar and often with fruits or nuts. ►*v.* **-died, -dying.** To cook, preserve, saturate, or coat with sugar or syrup. [Ult. < Ar. *qand*, cane sugar.]

candy striper ►*n.* A usu. young volunteer worker in a hospital.

can•dy•tuft (kăn′dē-tŭft′) ►*n.* Any of several plants with white, pink, red, or purple flowers. [Obsolete *Candy*, Crete + TUFT.]

cane (kān) ►*n.* **1a.** A slender, strong but often flexible stem, as of certain bamboos or reeds. **b.** A plant with such a stem. **c.** Interwoven strips of such stems, esp. rattan. **2.** Sugar cane. **3.** A walking stick or similar rod. ►*v.* **caned, can•ing 1.** To make or repair with cane. **2.** To hit or beat with a rod. [< Gk. *kanna*, reed.] —**can′er** *n.*

cane•brake (kān′brāk′) ►*n.* A dense thicket of cane.

cane sugar ►*n.* Sucrose obtained from sugar cane.

ca•nine (kā′nīn) ►*adj.* **1.** Of or belonging to the family of carnivorous mammals that includes dogs, jackals, foxes, and wolves. **2.** Of or being one of the pointed conical teeth between the incisors and bicuspids. ►*n.* **1.** A canine animal, esp. a dog. **2.** A canine tooth; cuspid. [< Lat. *canis*, dog.]

Ca•nis Major (kā′nĭs, kăn′ĭs) ►*n.* A constellation in the Southern Hemisphere containing the star Sirius.

Canis Minor ►*n.* A constellation in the Southern Hemisphere.

can•is•ter (kăn′ĭ-stər) ►*n.* **1.** A usu. metal box or can used for holding dry foodstuffs. **2.** A metal cylinder packed with shot that are scattered when the cylinder is fired. [< Gk. *kanastron*, reed basket.]

can•ker (kăng′kər) ►*n.* Ulceration of the mouth and lips. [< Lat. *cancer*.] —**can′ker•ous** *adj.*

canker sore ►*n.* A small painful ulcer or sore, usu. of the mouth.

can•na (kăn′ə) ►*n.* Any of various tropical plants having large, showy red or yellow flowers. [Lat. *canna*, CANE.]

can•na•bis (kăn′ə-bĭs) ►*n.* **1.** A tall Asian plant having alternate leaves and tough bast fibers. **2.** The dried flowers and leaves of the cannabis, from which mildly euphoriant and intoxicating drugs, such as marijuana, are prepared. [< Gk. *kannabis*.]

canned (kănd) ►*adj.* **1.** Preserved and sealed in an airtight can or jar. **2.** *Informal* Recorded or taped: *canned laughter.*

can•ner•y (kăn′ə-rē) ►*n.*, *pl.* **-ies.** A factory where meat, fish, vegetables, fruit, or other foods are canned.

Cannes (kăn) A city of SE France on the Mediterranean near Nice. Pop. 72,259.

can•ni•bal (kăn′ə-bəl) ►*n.* **1.** A person who eats the flesh of other humans. **2.** An animal that feeds on others of its own kind. [< Carib *kar-ibna*, Carib (allegedly cannibalistic)] —**can′ni•bal•ism** *n.* —**can′ni•bal•is′tic** *adj.*

can•ni•bal•ize (kăn′ə-bə-līz′) ►*v.* **-ized, -iz•ing.** To remove serviceable parts from (e.g., damaged vehicles) for use in the repair of other equipment of the same kind. —**can′ni•bal•i•za′tion** *n.*

Can•ning (kăn′ĭng), **George.** 1770–1827. British prime minister (1827).

can•no•li (kə-nō′lē, kă-) ►*n.* A fried pastry roll with a sweet creamy filling. [Ital.]

can•non (kăn′ən) ▶*n., pl.* **-non** or **-nons.** A large mounted weapon, such as a gun or howitzer, that fires heavy projectiles. [< OItal. *cannone.*] —**can′non•eer′** *n.*

can•non•ade (kăn′ə-nād′) ▶*n.* An extended discharge of artillery. —**can′non•ade′** *v.*

can•non•ball (kăn′ən-bôl′) ▶*n.* **1.** A round projectile fired from a cannon. **2.** Something, such as a fast train, moving with great speed. —**can′non•ball′** *v.*

can•not (kăn′ŏt, kə-nŏt′, kă-) ▶*aux.v.* The negative form of **can**[1].

can•nu•la (kăn′yə-lə) ▶*n., pl.* **-las** or **-lae** (-lē′). A flexible tube inserted into a body cavity or vessel to drain fluid or administer a medication. [Lat., small tube < *canna*, reed.]

can•ny (kăn′ē) ▶*adj.* **-ni•er, -ni•est 1.** Careful and shrewd. **2.** Thrifty; frugal. [< CAN[1].] —**can′ni•ly** *adv.* —**can′ni•ness** *n.*

ca•noe (kə-no͞o′) ▶*n.* A light slender boat that has pointed ends and is propelled by paddles. ▶*v.* **-noed, -noe•ing.** To carry or travel by canoe. [< Sp. *canoa*, of Cariban orig.] —**ca•noe′ist** *n.*

ca•no•la (kə-nō′lə) ▶*n.* An oil made from rape seeds, high in monounsaturated fatty acids. [*Can(ada) o(il,) l(ow) a(cid).*]

can•on[1] (kăn′ən) ▶*n.* **1.** A code of laws established by a church council. **2.** An accepted standard. **3.** The books of the Bible officially accepted by a Christian church. **4.** *Mus.* A round. [< Gk. *kanōn*, rule.]

can•on[2] (kăn′ən) ▶*n.* A member of the clergy serving in a cathedral or collegiate church. [< LLat. *canōnicus* < *canōn*, CANON[1].]

ca•ñon (kăn′yən) ▶*n.* Var. of **canyon.**

ca•non•i•cal (kə-nŏn′ĭ-kəl) also **ca•non•ic** (-ĭk) ▶*adj.* **1.** Of or according to canon law. **2.** Conforming to standard or orthodox rules. —**ca•non′i•cal•ly** *adv.* —**can′on•ic′i•ty** (kăn′ə-nĭs′ĭ-tē) *n.*

canonical hours ▶*pl.n.* **1.** The times of day at which canon law prescribes certain prayers to be recited. **2.** The prayers recited.

can•on•ize (kăn′ə-nīz′) ▶*v.* **-ized, -iz•ing 1.** To declare (a deceased person) a saint. **2.** To exalt; glorify. —**can′on•i•za′tion** *n.*

canon law ▶*n.* The body of officially established rules governing a Christian church.

can•o•py (kăn′ə-pē) ▶*n., pl.* **-pies 1.** A usu. cloth covering suspended over a throne or bed or held aloft on poles, as over a monarch. **2.** *Archit.* An ornamental rooflike structure. **3.** An awning over a walkway or door. **4.** *Ecol.* The uppermost layer in a forest, formed by the crowns of the trees. **5.** A transparent enclosure over an aircraft cockpit. [< Gk. *kōnōpeion*, bed with mosquito netting.] —**can′o•py** *v.*

canst (kănst) ▶*aux.v. Archaic* 2nd pers. sing. pr.t. of **can**[1].

cant[1] (kănt) ▶*n.* **1.** Angular deviation from a vertical or horizontal plane or surface. **2.** A slanted or oblique surface. **3.** A thrust or motion that tilts something. ▶*v.* To slant or tilt. [< Lat. *canthus*, rim of a wheel.]

cant[2] (kănt) ▶*n.* **1.** Insincere speech full of platitudes or pious expressions. **2.** The special vocabulary peculiar to the members of a group. **3.** Whining or singsong speech, such as that of beggars. ▶*v.* **1.** To speak sententiously. **2.** To whine or plead. [< Lat. *cantāre*, sing.] —**cant′ing•ly** *adv.*

can't (kănt) ▶ Cannot.

can•ta•bi•le (kän-tä′bĭ-lā′) ▶*adv. Mus.* In a smooth, lyrical, flowing style. [< Lat. *cantāre*, sing.] —**can•ta′bi•le′** *adj. & n.*

can•ta•loupe also **can•ta•loup** (kăn′tl-ōp′) ▶*n.* A melon with a ribbed, rough rind and orange flesh. [Fr. *cantaloup.*]

can•tan•ker•ous (kăn-tăng′kər-əs) ▶*adj.* Ill-tempered and quarrelsome. [Perh. < ME *contek*, dissension.] —**can•tan′ker•ous•ly** *adv.* —**can•tan′ker•ous•ness** *n.*

can•ta•ta (kən-tä′tə) ▶*n. Mus.* An often sacred composition comprising recitatives, arias, and choruses. [Ital.]

can•teen (kăn-tēn′) ▶*n.* **1a.** A snack bar or small cafeteria. **b.** A store for on-base military personnel. **2.** An institutional recreation hall or social club. **3.** A temporary or mobile eating place, esp. one set up in an emergency. **4.** A flask for carrying drinking water. **5.** A soldier's mess kit. [< Ital. *cantina*, wine cellar.]

can•ter (kăn′tər) ▶*n.* A smooth gait, esp. of a horse, slower than a gallop but faster than a trot. [< *Canterbury gallop.*] —**can′ter** *v.*

Can•ter•bur•y (kăn′tər-bĕr′ē, -brē, -tə-) A borough of SE England ESE of London; site of Canterbury Cathedral. Pop. 36,000.

can•thus (kăn′thəs) ▶*n., pl.* **-thi** (-thī′). The angle formed by the meeting of the upper and lower eyelids at either side of the eye. [< Gk. *kanthos.*]

can•ti•cle (kăn′tĭ-kəl) ▶*n.* A liturgical chant. [< Lat. *canticulum*, dim. of *cantus*, song.]

can•ti•le•ver (kăn′tl-ē′vər, -ĕv′ər) ▶*n.* A projecting structure, such as a beam, that is supported at one end and carries a load at the other. [Poss. CANT[1] + LEVER.] —**can′ti•le′ver** *v.*

can•ti•na (kăn-tē′nə) ▶*n. Regional* A bar that serves liquor. [< Ital., wine cellar.]

can•tle (kăn′tl) ▶*n.* The raised rear part of a saddle. [< Med.Lat. *cantellus.*]

can•to (kăn′tō) ▶*n., pl.* **-tos.** One of the principal divisions of a long poem. [< Lat. *cantus*, song.]

can•ton (kăn′tən, -tŏn′) ▶*n.* A small territorial division of a country, esp. one of the states of Switzerland. [< OItal. *cantone*, corner.] —**can′ton•al** *adj.*

Can•ton (kăn′tŏn, kăn′tŏn′) See **Guangzhou.**

can•ton•ment (kăn-tōn′mənt, -tŏn′-) ▶*n.* **1.** Temporary quarters for troops. **2.** Assignment of troops to temporary quarters.

can•tor (kăn′tər) ▶*n.* **1.** The Jewish religious official who leads the musical part of a service. **2.** A precentor. [Lat., singer < *canere*, sing.] —**can•to′ri•al** (kăn-tôr′ē-əl, -tŏr′-) *adj.*

Ca•nute (kə-no͞ot′, -nyo͞ot′). 994?–1035. King of England (1016–35), Denmark (1018–35), and Norway (1028–35).

can•vas (kăn′vəs) ▶*n.* **1.** A heavy, closely woven fabric of cotton, hemp, or flax, used for tents and sails. **2.** A piece of such fabric on which a painting is executed. **3.** Sails. **4.** The floor of a boxing or wrestling ring. [< Lat. *cannabis*, hemp.]

can•vas•back (kăn′vəs-băk′) ▶*n.* A North American duck having a reddish-brown head and neck and a whitish back.

can•vass (kăn′vəs) ▶*v.* **1.** To scrutinize. **2a.** To go through (a region) in order to solicit votes or orders. **b.** To conduct a survey. ▶*n.* **1.**

An examination or discussion. **2.** A solicitation of votes, sales, orders, or opinions. [< obsolete *canvas*, to toss in a canvas sheet as punishment.] —**can′vass•er** *n.*

can•yon also **ca•ñon** (kăn′yən) ►*n.* A narrow chasm with steep cliff walls. [Sp. *cañon.*]

cap (kăp) ►*n.* **1.** A usu. soft and close-fitting head covering, with or without a visor. **2.** A protective cover or seal, esp. one that closes off an end or tip: *a bottle cap.* **3.** An upper limit; ceiling. **4a.** A percussion cap. **b.** A small explosive charge enclosed in paper for use in a toy gun. ►*v.* **capped, cap•ping 1.** To cover or seal with a cap. **2.** To lie on top of: *hills capped with snow.* **3.** To set an upper limit on. —***idiom:* cap in hand** Respectfully or humbly; unpretentiously. [< LLat. *cappa.*]

cap. ►*abbr.* **1.** capacity **2.** capital

ca•pa•ble (kā′pə-bəl) ►*adj.* **1.** Having ability; competent. **2.** Having the potential: *capable of violence.* [LLat. *capābilis.*] —**ca′pa•bil′i•ty** *n.* —**ca′pa•bly** *adv.*

ca•pa•cious (kə-pā′shəs) ►*adj.* Able to hold a large amount; roomy. See Syns at **spacious.** [< Lat. *capāx, capāc-.*] —**ca•pa′cious•ly** *adv.* —**ca•pa′cious•ness** *n.*

ca•pac•i•tance (kə-păs′ĭ-təns) ►*n. Symbol* **C 1.** The ratio of charge to potential on an isolated conductor. **2.** The ratio of the electric charge on one of a pair of conductors to the potential difference between them. **3.** The property of a circuit element that permits it to store charge. —**ca•pac′i•tive** *adj.*

ca•pac•i•tate (kə-păs′ĭ-tāt′) ►*v.* **-tat•ed, -tat•ing.** To render fit; enable.

ca•pac•i•tor (kə-păs′ĭ-tər) ►*n.* An electric circuit element used to store charge temporarily, consisting in general of two metallic plates separated by a dielectric.

ca•pac•i•ty (kə-păs′ĭ-tē) ►*n., pl.* **-ties 1.** The ability to receive, hold, or absorb. **2.** The maximum amount that can be contained. **3.** The maximum or optimum amount that can be produced. **4.** The ability to learn or retain knowledge. **5.** The quality of being suitable for or receptive to specified treatment: *the capacity of elastic to be stretched.* **6.** Position; role: *in your capacity as sales manager.* **7.** *Elect.* Capacitance. ►*adj.* As large or numerous as possible: *a capacity crowd.* [< Lat. *capāx, capāc-*, spacious.]

ca•par•i•son (kə-păr′ĭ-sən) ►*n.* An ornamental covering for a horse. [< Sp. *caparazón.*] —**ca•par′i•son** *v.*

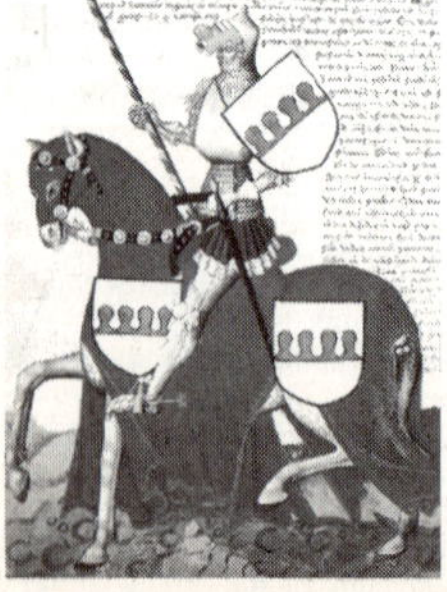

caparison

cape[1] (kāp) ►*n.* A sleeveless garment often tied at the throat and worn hanging over the shoulders. [< LLat. *cappa.*]

cape[2] (kāp) ►*n.* A headland projecting into a body of water. [< Lat. *caput*, head.]

Cape Bret•on Island (brĕt′n, brĭt′n) An island forming the NE part of Nova Scotia, Canada.

Cape buffalo ►*n.* A large African buffalo having massive downward-curving horns.

ca•per[1] (kā′pər) ►*n.* **1.** A playful leap or hop. **2.** A wild escapade. **3.** *Slang* An illegal enterprise, esp. one involving theft. ►*v.* To leap or frisk about. [Alteration of CAPRIOLE.]

ca•per[2] (kā′pər) ►*n.* The pickled flower bud of a Mediterranean shrub, used as a pungent condiment. [< Gk. *kapparis.*]

Ca•pet (kā′pĭt, kăp′ĭt, kă-pā′). A dynasty of French kings (987–1328), including **Hugh Capet** (940?–996).

Cape Town or **Cape•town** (kāp′toun′). The legislative capital of South Africa, in the extreme SW. Pop. 854,616.

Cape Verde (vûrd) An island country of the Atlantic W of Senegal. Cap. Praia. Pop. 381,000.

cap•il•lar•i•ty (kăp′ə-lăr′ĭ-tē) ►*n., pl.* **-ties.** The interaction between contacting surfaces of a liquid and a solid that distorts the liquid surface from a planar shape.

cap•il•lar•y (kăp′ə-lĕr′ē) ►*adj.* **1.** Of or resembling a hair; fine and slender. **2.** Having a very small internal diameter: *a capillary tube.* **3.** *Anat.* Of the capillaries. **4.** Of capillarity. ►*n., pl.* **-ies 1.** One of the minute blood vessels that connect the arteries and veins. **2.** A tube with a very small internal diameter. [< LLat. *capillus*, hair.]

capillary attraction ►*n.* The force that causes a liquid to be raised against a vertical surface, as water is in a clean glass tube.

cap•i•tal[1] (kăp′ĭ-tl) ►*n.* **1.** A town or city that is the official seat of government in a political entity. **2.** Wealth in the form of money or property. **3.** The net worth of a business. **4.** Capital stock. **5.** Capitalists considered as a group or class. **6.** An asset or advantage. **7.** A capital letter. ►*adj.* **1.** First and foremost; principal. **2.** First-rate; excellent: *a capital idea.* **3.** Of or being a political capital. **4.** Extremely serious: *a capital blunder.* **5.** Involving or punishable by death: *a capital offense.* **6.** Of or relating to financial assets, esp. those that add to the net worth of a business. **7.** Of or being a capital letter. [< Lat. *caput, capit-*, head.]

Usage: The term for a town or city that serves as a seat of government is *capital.* The term for the building in which a legislative assembly meets is *capitol.*

cap•i•tal[2] (kăp′ĭ-tl) ►*n. Archit.* The top part of a pillar or column. [< LLat. *capitellum.*]

capital gain ►*n.* The amount by which the sale of a capital asset exceeds the original cost.

cap•i•tal•ism (kăp′ĭ-tl-ĭz′əm) ►*n.* An economic system in which the means of production and distribution are privately or corporately owned and development is proportionate to the accumulation and reinvestment of profits gained in a free market.

cap•i•tal•ist (kăp′ĭ-tl-ĭst) ►*n.* **1.** A supporter of capitalism. **2.** An investor of capital in business. **3.** A person of great wealth. —**cap′i•tal•is′tic** *adj.*

cap•i•tal•ize (kăp′ĭ-tl-īz′) ►*v.* **-ized, -iz•ing 1.** To convert into capital. **2.** To supply with capital. **3a.** To print in capital letters. **b.** To begin (a word) with a capital letter. **4.** To turn something to one's advantage: *capitalize on another's error.* See Syns at **benefit.** —**cap′i•tal•i•za′tion** *n.*

capital letter ►*n.* A letter written or printed in a size larger than and often in a form differing from its corresponding lowercase letter; uppercase letter.

cap•i•tal•ly (kăp′ĭ-tl-ē) ►*adv.* Excellently.

capital punishment ►*n.* The death penalty.

capital stock ►*n.* **1.** The total amount of stock authorized for issue by a corporation. **2.** The total value of the permanently invested capital of a corporation.

cap•i•ta•tion (kăp′ĭ-tā′shən) ►*n.* A poll tax. [< Lat. *caput*, *capit-*, head.]

cap•i•tol (kăp′ĭ-tl) ►*n.* **1.** The building in which a legislature meets. See Usage Note at **capital**[1]. **2. Capitol** The building in Washington DC where the US Congress meets. [< Lat. *Capitōlium*, Jupiter's temple in Rome.]

ca•pit•u•late (kə-pĭch′ə-lāt′) ►*v.* **-lat•ed, -lat•ing 1.** To surrender under specified conditions. **2.** To give up all resistance; acquiesce. [Med.Lat. *capitulāre*, draw up in chapters.] —**ca•pit′u•la′tion** *n.*

cap•let (kăp′lĭt) ►*n.* A coated capsule-shaped medicine tablet intended to be tamper-resistant. [CAP(SULE) + (TAB)LET.]

ca•po[1] (kā′pō) ►*n.*, *pl.* **-pos.** A small movable bar placed across the fingerboard of a guitar to raise the pitch of all the strings uniformly. [< Ital. *capo*, head.]

ca•po[2] (kä′pō, kăp′ō) ►*n.*, *pl.* **-pos.** The head of a branch of an organized crime syndicate. [Ital.]

ca•pon (kā′pŏn′, -pən) ►*n.* A castrated rooster raised for food. [< Lat. *cāpō.*]

Cap•pa•do•cia (kăp′ə-dō′shə, -shē-ə) An ancient region of Asia Minor in present-day E-central Turkey. —**Cap′pa•do′cian** *adj.*

cap•puc•ci•no (kăp′ə-chē′nō, kä′pə-) ►*n.*, *pl.* **-nos.** Espresso coffee with steamed milk or cream. [Ital., Capuchin.]

Ca•pri (kə-prē′, kä′prē) An island of S Italy on the S edge of the Bay of Naples.

ca•pric•cio (kə-prē′chō, -chē-ō′) ►*n.*, *pl.* **-cios** *Mus.* An instrumental work with an improvisatory style and a free form. [Ital., CAPRICE.]

ca•price (kə-prēs′) ►*n.* **1a.** An impulsive change of mind. **b.** An inclination to change one's mind impulsively. **2.** *Mus.* A capriccio. [< Ital. *caporiccio*, a start.]

ca•pri•cious (kə-prĭsh′əs, -prē′shəs) ►*adj.* Impulsive and unpredictable. See Syns at **arbitrary.** —**ca•pri′cious•ly** *adv.* —**ca•pri′cious•ness** *n.*

Cap•ri•corn (kăp′rĭ-kôrn′) ►*n.* **1.** A constellation in the Southern Hemisphere. **2.** The 10th sign of the zodiac.

cap•ri•ole (kăp′rē-ōl′) ►*n.* An upward leap made by a trained horse without going forward. [< Lat. *capreolus*, small goat.]

cap•si•cum (kăp′sĭ-kəm) ►*n.* Any of a genus of tropical American pepper plants having pungent fruit used as a condiment. [Poss. < Lat. *capsa*, box.]

cap•sid (kăp′sĭd) ►*n.* The protein shell of a virus particle. [< Lat. *capsa*, box.]

cap•size (kăp′sīz′, kăp-sīz′) ►*v.* **-sized, -siz•ing.** To overturn or cause to overturn. Used of a boat. [?]

cap•stan (kăp′stən, -stăn′) ►*n.* **1.** *Naut.* A vertical spool-shaped revolving cylinder for hoisting weights by winding in a cable. **2.** A small cylindrical shaft used to drive magnetic tape at a constant speed in a tape recorder. [< Lat. *capistrum*, halter.]

cap•stone (kăp′stōn′) ►*n.* **1.** The top stone of a structure or wall. **2.** The crowning achievement; acme.

cap•su•late (kăp′sə-lāt′, -lĭt, -syo͞o-) also **cap•su•lat•ed** (-lā′tĭd) ►*adj.* Enclosed in or formed into a capsule. —**cap′su•la′tion** *n.*

cap•sule (kăp′səl, -so͞ol) ►*n.* **1.** A small soluble container, usu. of gelatin, that encloses a dose of oral medicine or vitamins. **2.** A fibrous, membranous, or fatty sheath that encloses a bodily organ or part. **3.** A seed case that dries and splits open. **4.** A pressurized compartment of an aircraft or spacecraft. ►*adj.* **1.** Condensed; brief. **2.** Very small; compact. [< Lat. *capsula*, dim. of *capsa*, box.] —**cap′su•lar** *adj.*

cap•sul•ize (kăp′sə-līz′, -syo͞o-) ►*v.* **-ized, -iz•ing.** To condense or summarize.

Capt. also **Capt** or **CAPT** ►*abbr.* captain

cap•tain (kăp′tən) ►*n.* **1.** One who commands, leads, or guides. **2.** The officer in command of a ship, aircraft, or spacecraft. **3a.** A rank, as in the US Army, above first lieutenant and below major. **b.** A rank, as in the US Navy, above commander and below commodore. **4.** A leading figure: *a captain of industry.* ►*v.* To command or direct. [< LLat. *capitāneus*, chief < Lat. *caput*, head.] —**cap′tain•cy** *n.* —**cap′tain•ship′** *n.*

cap•tion (kăp′shən) ►*n.* **1.** A short legend or description accompanying an illustration. **2.** A series of words superimposed on the bottom of television or motion picture frames. **3.** A title, as of a document or article. ►*v.* To furnish a caption for. [< Lat. *captiō*, arrest.]

cap•tious (kăp′shəs) ►*adj.* **1.** Inclined to find fault; critical. **2.** Intended to entrap or confuse. [< Lat. *capere*, seize.] —**cap′tious•ly** *adv.* —**cap′tious•ness** *n.*

cap•ti•vate (kăp′tə-vāt′) ►*v.* **-vat•ed, -vat•ing.** To attract and hold by charm, beauty, or excellence. See Syns at **charm.** —**cap′ti•va′tion** *n.* —**cap′ti•va′tor** *n.*

cap•tive (kăp′tĭv) ►*n.* **1.** A prisoner. **2.** One held in the grip of a strong emotion. ►*adj.* **1.** Held as prisoner. **2.** Kept under restraint or control: *captive birds; a captive nation.* **3.** Restrained by circumstances that prevent free choice: *a captive audience.* **4.** Enraptured. —**cap•tiv′i•ty** *n.*

cap•tor (kăp′tər, -tôr′) ►*n.* One who captures.

cap•ture (kăp′chər) ►*v.* **-tured, -tur•ing 1.** To take captive; seize. **2.** To gain possession or control of. **3.** To attract and hold: *capture the imagination.* **4.** To preserve in lasting form. ►*n.* **1.** The act of capturing; seizure. **2.** One that is seized, caught, or won. [< Lat. *capere*, seize.]

cap•u•chin (kăp′yə-chĭn, -shĭn, kə-pyo͞o′-) ►*n.* **1. Capuchin** A monk belonging to an independent order of Franciscans. **2.** Any of several long-tailed tropical American monkeys. [< Ital. *cappuccino*, pointed cowl, Capuchin.]

car (kär) ►*n.* **1.** An automobile. **2.** A conveyance with wheels that runs along tracks: *a railroad car.* **3.** A boxlike enclosure for passengers on a conveyance: *an elevator car.* [< Lat. *carrus*, cart.]

car. ►*abbr.* carat

car•a•bi•ner (kăr′ə-bē′nər) ►*n.* An oblong metal ring with a spring clip, used in mountaineering to secure ropes. [< Ger. *Karabiner(haken)*, (hook) for a carbine.]

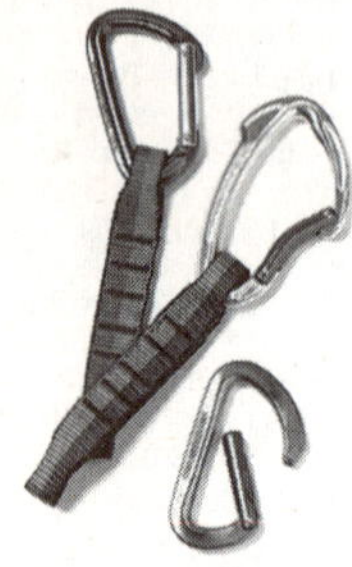

carabiner

Car•a•cal•la (kăr′ə-kăl′ə). A.D. 188–217. Emperor of Rome (211–217).

Ca•ra•cas (kə-rä′kəs) The capital of Venezuela, in the N part near the Caribbean coast. Pop. 1,964,846.

ca•rafe (kə-răf′) ►*n.* A glass or metal bottle, often with a flared lip, used for serving water or wine. [< Sp. *garrafa.*]

car•a•mel (kăr′ə-məl, -mĕl′, kär′məl) ►*n.* **1.** A smooth chewy candy made with sugar, butter, cream or milk, and flavoring. **2.** Burnt sugar, used for coloring and sweetening foods. [< Gk. *kalamos*, cane.]

car•a•pace (kăr′ə-pās′) ►*n. Zool.* A hard outer covering, such as the upper shell of a turtle. [< Sp. *carapacho.*]

car•at (kăr′ət) ►*n.* **1.** A unit of weight for precious stones, equal to 200 mg. **2.** Var. of **karat.** [< Gk. *keration*, small weight.]

Ca•ra•vag•gio (kăr′ə-vä′jō), **Michelangelo Merisi da.** 1573–1610. Italian painter.

car•a•van (kăr′ə-văn′) ►*n.* **1.** A company of travelers journeying together, esp. across a desert. **2.** A single file of vehicles or pack animals. **3.** A van. [< Pers. *kārvān.*]

car•a•van•sa•ry (kăr′ə-văn′sə-rē) also **car•a•van•se•rai** (-rī′) ►*n., pl.* **-ries** also **-rais.** An inn built around a large court for accommodating caravans in central or western Asia. [Pers. *kārvān*, caravan + *sarāy*, camp.]

car•a•vel or **car•a•velle** (kăr′ə-vĕl′) ►*n.* A small, light sailing ship used by the Spanish and Portuguese in the 15th and 16th cent. [< OPort. *caravela.*]

car•a•way (kăr′ə-wā′) ►*n.* A plant with pungent, aromatic, seedlike fruit used in cooking and flavoring. [< OFr. *carvi, caroi.*]

car•bide (kär′bīd′) ►*n.* A binary compound of carbon and a more electropositive element.

car•bine (kär′bēn′, -bīn′) ►*n.* A lightweight rifle with a short barrel. [Fr. *carabine.*]

carbo– or **carb–** ►*pref.* Carbon: *carbohydrate.* [Fr. < *carbone*, CARBON.]

car•bo•hy•drate (kär′bō-hī′drāt′) ►*n.* Any of a group of photosynthetically produced organic compounds that includes sugars, starches, celluloses, and gums and serves as a major energy source in the diet.

car•bol•ic acid (kär-bŏl′ĭk) ►*n.* See **phenol.** [CARB(O)– + Lat. *oleum*, oil + –IC.]

car•bon (kär′bən) ►*n.* **1.** *Symbol* **C** A naturally abundant nonmetallic element that occurs in many inorganic and in all organic compounds, exists freely as graphite and diamond, and is capable of chemical self-bonding to form an enormous number of chemically, biologically, and commercially important molecules. At. no. 6. See table at **element. 2a.** A sheet of carbon paper. **b.** A carbon copy. [< Lat. *carbō*, charcoal.] —**car′bon•ize** *v.* —**car′bon•ous** *adj.*

carbon 14 ►*n.* A naturally radioactive carbon isotope with atomic mass 14 and half-life 5,730 years, used in carbon dating.

car•bo•na•ceous (kär′bə-nā′shəs) ►*adj.* Of, consisting of, or yielding carbon.

car•bon•ate (kär′bə-nāt′) ►*v.* **-at•ed, -at•ing.** To charge (e.g., a beverage) with carbon dioxide gas. ►*n.* (-nāt′, -nĭt). A salt or ester of carbonic acid. —**car′bon•a′tion** *n.*

carbon black ►*n.* A finely divided form of carbon derived from the incomplete combustion of hydrocarbons and used principally in rubber, inks, paints, and polishes.

carbon copy ►*n.* **1.** A duplicate, as of a letter, made by using carbon paper. **2.** One that closely resembles another.

carbon dating ►*n.* See **radiocarbon dating.**

carbon dioxide ►*n.* A colorless, odorless, incombustible gas, CO_2, formed during respiration, combustion, and organic decomposition.

car•bon•ic acid (kär-bŏn′ĭk) ►*n.* A weak, unstable acid, H_2CO_3, present in solutions of carbon dioxide in water.

Car•bon•if•er•ous (kär′bə-nĭf′ər-əs) ►*adj.* **1.** *Geol.* Of or being a division of the Paleozoic Era comprising the Mississipian and Pennsylvanian periods and marked by the deposition of plant remains that later hardened into coal. **2. carboniferous** Producing or containing carbon or coal. ►*n.* The Carboniferous Period.

carbon monoxide ►*n.* A colorless, odorless, highly poisonous gas, CO, formed by the incomplete combustion of carbon.

carbon paper ►*n.* Thin paper coated with a dark waxy pigment, placed between blank sheets so that writing on the top sheet is copied onto the bottom sheet.

carbon tet•ra•chlo•ride (tĕt′rə-klôr′īd′, -klōr′-) ►*n.* A poisonous, nonflammable, colorless liquid, CCl_4, used as a solvent.

Car•bo•run•dum (kär′bə-rŭn′dəm) ► A trademark for a silicon carbide abrasive.

car•boy (kär′boi′) ►*n.* A large bottle, usu. encased in a protective covering and used to hold corrosive liquids. [Pers. *qarābah.*]

car•bun•cle (kär′bŭng′kəl) ►*n.* **1.** A painful, localized, pus-producing bacterial infection of the skin. **2.** A deep-red garnet. [< Lat. *carbunculus*, dim. of *carbō*, coal.] —**car•bun′cu•lar** (-kyə-lər) *adj.*

car•bu•ret (kär′bə-rāt′, -rĕt′, -byə-) ►*v.* **-ret•ed, -ret•ing** or **-ret•ted, -ret•ting.** To mix (air or a gas) with volatile hydrocarbons so as to increase available fuel energy. [< Fr. *carbure*, carbide.] —**car•bu•re′tion** *n.*

car•bu•re•tor (kär′bə-rā′tər, -byə-) ▸*n.* A device used in internal-combustion engines to produce an explosive mixture of vaporized fuel and air. [< CARBURET.]

car•bu•rize (kär′bə-rīz′, -byə-) ▸*v.* **-rized, -riz•ing 1.** To treat, combine, or impregnate with carbon. **2.** To carburet. [CARBUR(ET) + -IZE.] —**car′bu•ri•za′tion** *n.*

car•cass (kär′kəs) ▸*n.* A dead body, esp. of an animal. [< AN *carcais.*]

car•cin•o•gen (kär-sĭn′ə-jən, kär′sə-nə-jĕn′) ▸*n.* A cancer-causing substance or agent. [Gk. *karkinos,* cancer + -GEN.] —**car′ci•no•gen′e•sis** *n.* —**car′cin•o•gen′ic** *adj.*

car•ci•no•ma (kär′sə-nō′mə) ▸*n., pl.* **-mas** or **-ma•ta** (-mə-tə). A malignant tumor derived from epithelial tissue. [< Gk. *karkinos,* cancer.] —**car′ci•nom′a•tous** (-nŏm′ə-təs, -nō′mə-) *adj.*

car coat ▸*n.* A three-quarter-length overcoat.

card[1] (kärd) ▸*n.* **1.** A flat, usu. rectangular piece of stiff paper, cardboard, or plastic, esp.: **a.** One of a set of playing cards. **b.** A greeting card. **c.** A post card. **d.** A business card. **e.** A credit card. **2. cards** *(takes sing. or pl. v.)* A game using playing cards. **3.** A circuit board. **4.** A program, esp. for a sports event. **5.** *Informal* An eccentrically amusing person. ▸*v.* **1.** To furnish with or attach to a card. **2.** To list (something) on a card; catalog. **3.** To check the identification of, esp. in order to verify legal age. —***idioms:*** **card up (one's) sleeve** A secret resource or plan held in reserve. **in the cards** Likely or certain to happen. **put (**or **lay) (one's) cards on the table** To reveal frankly and clearly, as one's motives. [< Gk. *khartēs,* leaf of papyrus.]

card[2] (kärd) ▸*n.* A wire-toothed brush used to disentangle textile fibers. [< Lat. *carduus,* thistle.] —**card** *v.* —**card′er** *n.*

car•da•mom (kär′də-məm) or **car•da•mon** (-mən) ▸*n.* **1.** A tropical Asian plant having capsular fruits whose aromatic seeds are used as a spice or condiment. **2.** The seed of this plant. [< Gk. *kardamōmon.*]

card•board (kärd′bôrd′, -bōrd′) ▸*n.* A thick stiff material made of pressed paper pulp or pasted sheets of paper. ▸*adj.* **1.** Made of cardboard. **2.** Flimsy; insubstantial.

card-car•ry•ing (kärd′kăr′ē-ĭng) ▸*adj.* **1.** Being an enrolled member of an organization, esp. the Communist Party. **2.** Avidly devoted to a group or cause.

card catalog ▸*n.* An alphabetical listing, esp. of books in a library, made with a separate card for each item.

car•di•ac (kär′dē-ăk′) ▸*adj.* Of or near the heart. [< Gk. *kardia,* heart.]

cardiac arrest ▸*n.* Sudden cessation of heartbeat and cardiac function, resulting in the loss of effective circulation.

cardiac massage ▸*n.* A resuscitative procedure employing rhythmic compression of the chest and heart, as after cardiac arrest.

Car•diff (kär′dĭf) The capital of Wales, in the SE part on Bristol Channel. Pop. 298,697.

car•di•gan (kär′dĭ-gən) ▸*n.* A sweater or knitted jacket that opens down the front. [After the 7th Earl of *Cardigan* (1797–1868).]

car•di•nal (kär′dn-əl, kärd′nəl) ▸*adj.* **1.** Of foremost importance; paramount. **2.** Dark to deep or vivid red. ▸*n.* **1.** *Rom. Cath. Ch.* A high church official, ranking just below the pope. **2.** A North American finch having a crested head, a short thick bill, and bright red plumage in the male. [< Lat. *cardō, cardin-,* hinge.]

car•di•nal•ate (kär′dn-ə-lĭt, -lāt′, kärd′nə-) ▸*n. Rom. Cath. Ch.* The position, rank, dignity, or term of a cardinal.

cardinal number ▸*n.* A number, such as 3 or 11 or 412, used in counting to indicate quantity but not order.

cardinal point ▸*n.* One of the four principal directions on a compass: north, south, east, or west.

cardio– or **cardi–** ▸*pref.* Heart: *cardiovascular.* [< Gk. *kardia,* heart.]

car•di•o•gram (kär′dē-ə-grăm′) ▸*n.* **1.** The curve traced by a cardiograph, used in the diagnosis of heart disorders. **2.** See **electrocardiogram.**

car•di•o•graph (kär′dē-ə-grăf′) ▸*n.* **1.** An instrument used to record graphically the mechanical movements of the heart. **2.** See **electrocardiograph.** —**car′di•og′ra•phy** (-ŏg′rə-fē) *n.*

car•di•ol•o•gy (kär′dē-ŏl′ə-jē) ▸*n.* The study of the structure, functioning, and disorders of the heart. —**car′di•ol′o•gist** *n.*

car•di•o•pul•mo•nar•y (kär′dē-ō-po͝ol′mə-nĕr′ē, -pŭl′-) ▸*adj.* Of or involving the heart and lungs.

cardiopulmonary resuscitation ▸*n.* A procedure used after cardiac arrest in which cardiac massage, artificial respiration, and drugs are used to restore circulation.

car•di•o•vas•cu•lar (kär′dē-ō-văs′kyə-lər) ▸*adj.* Of or involving the heart and the blood vessels.

card•sharp (kärd′shärp′) ▸*n.* An expert in cheating at cards. —**card′sharp′ing** *n.*

care (kâr) ▸*n.* **1.** A burdened state of mind; worry. **2.** Mental suffering; grief. **3.** An object or source of attention or solicitude. **4.** Caution: *handle with care.* **5.** Charge or supervision: *in the care of a nurse.* **6.** Assistance or treatment: *emergency care.* ▸*v.* **1. cared, car•ing** To be concerned or interested. **2.** To provide assistance or supervision. **3.** To object or mind. [< OE *cearu.*]

Syns: *care, charge, custody, supervision, trust* ***n.***

CARE ▸*abbr.* Cooperative for American Relief Everywhere

ca•reen (kə-rēn′) ▸*v.* **1.** To rush headlong or carelessly; career. **2.** To cause (a ship) to lean to one side; tilt. [< Fr. *(en) carène,* (on the) keel < Lat. *carīna.*] —**ca•reen′er** *n.*

ca•reer (kə-rîr′) ▸*n.* **1.** A chosen pursuit; profession or occupation. **2.** The general progress in one's working or professional life. ▸*v.* To move or run at full speed; rush. [< OFr. *carriere,* racecourse.]

care•free (kâr′frē′) ▸*adj.* Free of worries and responsibilities.

care•ful (kâr′fəl) ▸*adj.* **1.** Attentive to potential danger, error, or harm; cautious. **2.** Thorough and painstaking; conscientious. —**care′ful•ly** *adv.* —**care′ful•ness** *n.*

Syns: *careful, heedful, mindful, observant, watchful* ***Ant:*** *careless* ***adj.***

care•giv•er (kâr′gĭv′ər) ▸*n.* **1.** One, such as a nurse or social worker, who assists in the treatment of an illness or disability. **2.** One who attends to the needs of a child or dependent adult. —**care′giv′ing** *adj. & n.*

care•less (kâr′lĭs) ▸*adj.* **1.** Inattentive; negligent. **2.** Marked by or resulting from lack of thought. **3.** Inconsiderate: *a careless remark.* **4.** Free from cares; cheerful. —**care′less•ly** *adv.* —**care′less•ness** *n.*

ca•ress (kə-rĕs′) ▸*n.* A gentle touch or gesture of fondness. ▸*v.* To touch or stroke fondly. [< Ital. *carezza.*] —**ca•ress′er** *n.*

Syns: *caress, cuddle, fondle, pet* ***v.***

car•et (kăr′ĭt) ▸*n.* A proofreading symbol (^) used to indicate where something is to be inserted in a line of printed or written matter. [Lat., there is lacking.]

care•tak•er (kâr′tā′kər) ▸*n.* One employed to look after or take charge of goods, property, or a person; custodian.

care•worn (kâr′wôrn′, -wōrn′) ▸*adj.* Showing the effects of worry or care.

car•fare (kär′fâr′) ▸*n.* The fare charged a passenger, as on a streetcar or bus.

car•go (kär′gō) ▸*n., pl.* **-goes** or **-gos.** The freight carried by a ship, aircraft, or other vehicle. [Sp. < *cargar,* to load.]

car•hop (kär′hŏp′) ▸*n.* One who waits on customers at a drive-in restaurant.

Car•ib (kăr′ĭb) ▸*n., pl.* **-ib** or **-ibs 1.** A member of a group of American Indian peoples of N South America, the Lesser Antilles, and the E coast of Central America. **2.** Any of the languages of the Carib.

Car•i•ban (kăr′ə-bən, kə-rē′bən) ▸*n.* A language family comprising the Carib languages.

Car•ib•be•an Sea (kăr′ə-bē′ən, kə-rĭb′ē-ən) An arm of the W Atlantic bounded by the coasts of Central and South America and the West Indies. —**Car′ib•be′an** *adj.*

car•i•bou (kăr′ə-bo͞o′) ▸*n., pl.* **-bou** or **-bous.** Any of several large reindeer native to N North America. [Micmac *ğalipu.*]

car•i•ca•ture (kăr′ĭ-kə-cho͝or′, -chər) ▸*n.* **1.** A representation, esp. pictorial, in which the subject's distinctive features or peculiarities are exaggerated for comic or grotesque effect. **2.** A mockery; farce. ▸*v.* **-tured, -tur•ing.** To represent or imitate in a caricature. [< Ital. *caricare,* exaggerate.] —**car′i•ca•tur′ist** *n.*

caricature
Dwight Eisenhower by Charles Dunn

car•ies (kâr′ēz) ▸*n., pl.* **-ies.** Decay of a bone or tooth. [Lat. *cariēs.*]

car•il•lon (kăr′ə-lŏn′, -lən) ▸*n.* A stationary set of bells hung in a tower and usu. played from a keyboard. [Fr. < LLat. *quaterniō,* set of four.] —**car′il•lon′** *v.*

car•ing (kâr′ĭng) ▸*adj.* Feeling and exhibiting concern and empathy for others.

car•jack or **car-jack** (kâr′jăk′) ▸*v.* To commit forcible theft of (a vehicle) from its users. [CAR + (HI)JACK.] —**car′jack′er** *n.*

Carl XVI Gus•tav (kärl gŭs′täv, -täf, go͞os′-). b. 1946. King of Sweden (since 1973).

car•load (kär′lōd′) ▸*n.* The quantity that a car, esp. a railroad car, can hold.

Car•lyle (kär-līl′, kär′līl), **Thomas.** 1795–1881. British historian and essayist.

Car•mel (kär′məl), **Mount.** A ridge of NW Israel extending about 24 km (15 mi) from the Plain of Esdraelon to the Mediterranean.

car•min•a•tive (kär-mĭn′ə-tĭv, kär′mə-nā′-) ▸*adj.* Inducing expulsion of intestinal gas. ▸*n.* A carminative drug or agent. [< Lat. *carmināre,* to card wool.]

car•mine (kär′mĭn, -mīn′) ▸*n.* A strong to vivid red. [< Med.Lat. *carminium.*] —**car′mine** *adj.*

car•nage (kär′nĭj) ▸*n.* Massive slaughter or bloodshed. [< Lat. *carō, carn-,* flesh.]

car•nal (kär′nəl) ▸*adj.* **1.** Relating to the physical and esp. sexual appetites. **2.** Not spiritual; worldly or earthly: *the carnal world.* [< Lat. *carō, carn-,* flesh.] —**car•nal′i•ty** (-năl′ĭ-tē) *n.* —**car′nal•ly** *adv.*

car•na•tion (kär-nā′shən) ▸*n.* A plant cultivated for its fragrant flowers with fringed petals. [Prob. < OFr., flesh-colored.]

car•nau•ba (kär-nô′bə, -nou′-, -no͞o′-) ▸*n.* **1.** A Brazilian palm tree. **2.** A hard wax obtained from its leaves, used esp. in polishes and floor waxes. [< Tupi *carnaúba.*]

Car•ne•gie (kär′nə-gē, kär-nā′gē, -nĕg′ē), **Andrew.** 1835–1919. Scottish-born Amer. industrialist and philanthropist.

Car•ne•gie (kär′nə-gē), **Dale.** 1888–1955. Amer. educator.

car•nel•ian (kär-nēl′yən) ▸*n.* A reddish variety of clear chalcedony. [< OFr. *corneline.*]

car•ni•val (kär′nə-vəl) ▸*n.* **1.** A festival marked by merrymaking and feasting just before Lent. **2.** A traveling amusement show. **3.** A festival or revel: *the winter carnival.* [Ital. *carnevale.*]

car•ni•vore (kär′nə-vôr′, -vōr′) ▸*n.* A flesh-eating animal, esp. one of a group including dogs, cats, and bears.

car•niv•o•rous (kär-nĭv′ər-əs) ▸*adj.* **1.** Of or relating to carnivores. **2.** Predatory. [< Lat. *carnivorus.*] —**car•niv′o•rous•ly** *adv.* —**car•niv′o•rous•ness** *n.*

car•ny also **car•ney** (kär′nē) ▸*n., pl.* **-nies** also **-neys** *Informal* **1.** A carnival. **2.** One who works with a carnival.

car•ob (kăr′əb) ▸*n.* **1.** A Mediterranean evergreen tree having large leathery pods. **2.** A chocolatelike powder made from the seeds and pods of the carob. [< Ar. *ḫarrūba,* carob pod.]

car•ol (kăr′əl) ▸*n.* A song of praise or joy, esp. for Christmas. [< OFr.] —**car′ol** *v.* —**car′ol•er** *n.*

Car•o•li•nas (kăr′ə-lī′nəz) The colonies (after 1729) or states of NC and SC.

Car•o•line Islands (kăr′ə-līn′, -lĭn) An archipelago of the W Pacific E of the Philippines.

car•om (kăr′əm) ▸*n.* **1.** A collision followed by a rebound. **2.** A shot in billiards in which the cue ball successively strikes two other balls. ▸*v.* **1.** To collide with and rebound. **2.** To make a carom in billiards. [< Sp. *carambola*, billiards shot.]

car•o•tene (kăr′ə-tēn′) ►*n.* An orange-yellow pigment found in plants such as carrots and squash and converted to vitamin A in the liver. [< Lat. *carōta*, CARROT.]

ca•rot•id (kə-rŏt′ĭd) ►*n.* Either of the two major arteries, one on each side of the neck, that carry blood to the head. [< Gk. *karōtides*, carotid arteries.]

ca•rouse (kə-rouz′) ►*n.* Boisterous, drunken merrymaking. ►*v.* **-roused, -rous•ing 1.** To engage in drunken revelry. **2.** To drink excessively. [Ger. *garaus*, all out, drink up.] —**ca•rous′al** *n.* —**ca•rous′er** *n.*

car•ou•sel or **car•rou•sel** (kăr′ə-sĕl′, -zĕl′) ►*n.* **1.** A merry-go-round. **2.** A circular conveyor on which objects are displayed or rotated. [Fr. *carrousel.*]

carp[1] (kärp) ►*v.* To find fault and complain fretfully. See Syns at **quibble.** [< ON *karpa*, boast.] —**carp′er** *n.*

carp[2] (kärp) ►*n., pl.* **carp** or **carps.** An edible freshwater fish, often bred commercially. [< Med.Lat. *carpa*, of Gmc. orig.]

-carp ►*suff.* Fruit; fruitlike structure: *mesocarp.* [< Gk. *karpos*, fruit.]

car•pal (kär′pəl) ►*adj.* Of or near the carpus. ►*n.* A bone of the carpus.

carpal tunnel syndrome ►*n.* A condition marked by pain and numbing in the hand, caused by compression of a nerve in the wrist.

Car•pa•thi•an Mountains (kär-pā′thē-ən) A mountain system of central Europe in Slovakia, S Poland, W Ukraine, and NE Romania.

car•pel (kär′pəl) ►*n.* One of the structural units of a pistil, representing a modified ovule-bearing leaf. [< Gk. *karpos*, fruit.]

car•pen•ter (kär′pən-tər) ►*n.* A skilled worker who makes, finishes, and repairs wooden objects and structures. [< Lat. *carpentārius (artifex)*, (maker) of a carriage.] —**car′pen•ter** *v.* —**car′pen•try** *n.*

car•pet (kär′pĭt) ►*n.* A heavy, usu. woven or piled covering for a floor. ►*v.* To cover with or as if with a carpet. —***idiom:* on the carpet** In a position of being reprimanded by one in authority. [< OItal. *carpita* < Lat. *carpere*, pluck.]

car•pet•bag (kär′pĭt-băg′) ►*n.* A traveling bag made of carpet fabric.

car•pet•bag•ger (kär′pĭt-băg′ər) ►*n.* A Northerner who went to the South after the Civil War for political or financial advantage. —**car′pet•bag′ger•y** *n.*

carpet beetle ►*n.* Any of various small beetles having larvae that are injurious to fabrics.

car•pet-bomb (kär′pĭt-bŏm′) ►*v.* To bomb in a close pattern over a large target area.

car pool ►*n.* **1.** An arrangement whereby several commuters travel together in one vehicle and share the costs. **2.** A group participating in a car pool. —**car′-pool′** *v.*

car•port (kär′pôrt′, -pōrt′) ►*n.* An open-sided shelter for an automobile formed by a roof projecting from a building.

car•pus (kär′pəs) ►*n., pl.* **-pi** (-pī′). The wrist or its bones. [Gk. *karpos.*]

car•ra•geen also **car•ra•gheen** (kăr′ə-gēn′) ►*n.* See **Irish moss.** [After *Carragheen*, Ireland.]

car•ra•geen•an also **car•ra•geen•in** (kăr′ə-gē′nən) ►*n.* A colloid derived esp. from Irish moss and used as a thickener, stabilizer, and emulsifier.

car•rel also **car•rell** (kăr′əl) ►*n.* A partially partitioned nook near the stacks in a library, used for private study. [ME *carole*, ring, round dance ring. See CAROL.]

car•riage (kăr′ĭj) ►*n.* **1.** A wheeled vehicle, esp. a four-wheeled horse-drawn passenger vehicle. **2.** A baby carriage. **3.** A wheeled support or frame. **4.** A machine part for holding or shifting another part. **5a.** The act of transporting or carrying. **b.** (kăr′ē-ĭj). The charge for transporting. **6.** Posture; bearing. See Syns at **posture.** [< ONFr. *carier*, CARRY.]

carriage trade ►*n.* Wealthy patrons or customers, as of a store.

car•ri•er (kăr′ē-ər) ►*n.* **1.** One that carries or conveys. **2.** One that transports passengers or goods. **3.** *Medic.* An immune organism that transmits a pathogen to others. **4.** *Genet.* An individual that carries one gene for a particular recessive trait. **5.** An aircraft carrier.

carrier pigeon ►*n.* A homing pigeon, esp. one trained to carry messages.

carrier wave ►*n.* An electromagnetic wave that can be modulated to transmit sound or images.

car•ri•on (kăr′ē-ən) ►*n.* Dead and decaying flesh. [< Lat. *carō*, flesh.]

Car•roll (kăr′əl), **Lewis.** See Charles Lutwidge **Dodgson.**

car•rot (kăr′ət) ►*n.* **1.** A plant widely cultivated for its edible taproot. **2.** Its fleshy orange root, eaten as a vegetable. **3.** A reward or inducement. [< Gk. *karōton.*]

car•rot-and-stick (kăr′ət-ən-stĭk′) ►*adj.* Combining a promised reward with a threatened penalty.

car•rou•sel (kăr′ə-sĕl′, -zĕl′) ►*n.* Var. of **carousel.**

car•ry (kăr′ē) ►*v.* **-ried, -ry•ing 1.** To hold while moving; bear. **2.** To convey or transport. **3.** To have on one's person: *carry cash.* **4.** To support the weight of. **5.** To hold (e.g., the head or body) in a certain way. **6.** To conduct (oneself) in a certain way. **7.** To have as a consequence: *The job carries a heavy workload.* **8.** To support (one that is weaker). **9.** To keep in one's accounts as a debtor. **10.** To offer for sale or keep in stock. **11.** To seize or capture. **12.** To win most of the votes in. **13.** To secure the adoption of (e.g., a bill or amendment). **14.** To print or broadcast. —***phrasal verbs:* carry away** To move or excite greatly. **carry forward** *Accounting* To transfer (an entry) to the next column or book. **carry off 1.** To cause the death of. **2.** To handle (e.g., a situation) successfully. **carry on 1.** To conduct; maintain. **2.** To engage in: *carry on a love affair.* **3.** To continue without halting: *carry on in the face of disaster.* **carry out 1.** To put into practice. **2.** To follow or obey. **carry over 1.** *Accounting* To transfer (an account) to the next column or book. **2.** To continue at or retain for a later time. **carry through 1.** To accomplish; complete. **2.** To enable to endure; sustain. ►*n., pl.* **-ries 1.** An act of carrying. **2.** The range of a gun or projectile. [< ONFr. *carre*, cart. See CAR.]

car•ry•all (kăr′ē-ôl′) ►*n.* A large receptacle, such as a bag, basket, or pocketbook.

car•ry•on (kăr′ē-ŏn′) ► *adj.* Small enough to be carried aboard an airplane by a passenger: *carryon luggage.* —**car′ry•on′** *n.*
car•ry•out (kăr′ē-out′) ► *adj.* Takeout.
car•sick (kär′sĭk′) ► *adj.* Nauseated by vehicular travel. —**car′sick′ness** *n.*
Car•son (kär′sən), **Christopher.** "Kit." 1809–68. Amer. frontier settler.
Carson, Rachel Louise. 1907–64. Amer. environmentalist and writer.

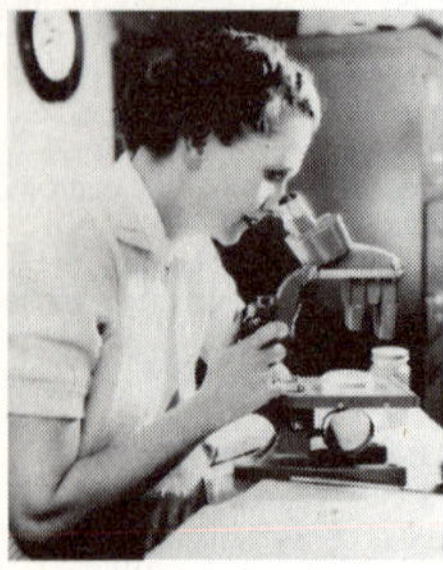

Rachel Carson

Carson City. The capital of NV, in the W part near the CA border. Pop. 40,443.
cart (kärt) ► *n.* **1.** A small wheeled vehicle typically pushed by hand: *a shopping cart.* **2.** A two-wheeled vehicle drawn by an animal. **3.** A light motorized vehicle: *a golf cart.* ► *v.* **1.** To convey in a cart or truck: *cart away garbage.* **2.** To convey laboriously or remove unceremoniously. [< OE *cræt* and ON *kartr*, wagon.] —**cart′er** *n.*
cart•age (kär′tĭj) ► *n.* **1.** Transportation by cart or truck. **2.** The cost of cartage.
Car•ta•ge•na (kär′tä-hĕ′nä) **1.** A city of NW Colombia on the Caribbean. Pop. 513,986. **2.** A city of SE Spain on the Mediterranean SSE of Murcia. Pop. 168,023.
carte blanche (kärt blänsh′, blänch′, blănch′) ► *n.* Unrestricted authority. [Fr.]
car•tel (kär-tĕl′) ► *n.* A monopolistic combination of independent business organizations. [< Ital. *cartello*, placard.]
Car•ter (kär′tər), **James Earl, Jr.** "Jimmy." b. 1924. The 39th US President (1977–81).

Jimmy Carter

Car•te•sian coordinate (kär-tē′zhən) ► *n.* A member of the set of numbers that locates a point in a Cartesian coordinate system.
Cartesian coordinate system ► *n.* A coordinate system in which the coordinates of a point are its distances from a set of perpendicular lines that intersect at an origin, such as two lines in a plane or three in space. [After René DESCARTES.]
Car•thage (kär′thĭj) An ancient city and state of N Africa on the Bay of Tunis NE of modern Tunis. —**Car′tha•gin′i•an** (-thə-jĭn′ē-ən) *adj. & n.*
Car•tier (kär-tyā′, kär′tē-ā′), **Jacques.** 1491–1557. French explorer.
car•ti•lage (kär′tl-ĭj) ► *n.* A tough white fibrous connective tissue found in various parts of the body, such as the joints, outer ear, and larynx. [< Lat. *cartilāgō.*] —**car′ti•lag′i•nous** (-ăj′ə-nəs) *adj.*
car•tog•ra•phy (kär-tŏg′rə-fē) ► *n.* The making of maps or charts. [Fr. *cartographie* < *carte*, CHART.] —**car•tog′ra•pher** *n.* —**car′to•graph′ic** (-tə-grăf′ĭk) *adj.*
car•ton (kär′tn) ► *n.* **1.** A container made from cardboard or coated paper. **2.** The contents of a carton. [< Ital. *cartone*, pasteboard.]
car•toon (kär-to͞on′) ► *n.* **1.** A humorous or satirical drawing, often with a caption. **2.** A preliminary full-scale sketch, as for a fresco. **3.** An animated cartoon. **4.** A comic strip. [< Ital. *cartone*, pasteboard.] —**car•toon′** *v.* —**car•toon′ist** *n.*
car•tridge (kär′trĭj) ► *n.* **1a.** A cylindrical, usu. metal casing containing the primer and powder of small arms ammunition. **b.** Such a casing fitted with a bullet. **2.** A small modular unit designed to be inserted into a larger piece of equipment: *an ink cartridge; a cartridge of film.* **3.** A magnetic tape cassette. [< Ital. *cartoccio*, small paper horn.]
cart•wheel (kärt′hwēl′, -wēl′) ► *n.* A handspring in which the body turns over sideways with the arms and legs extended.
Cart•wright (kärt′rīt′), **Edmund.** 1743–1823. British inventor.
Ca•ru•so (kə-ro͞o′sō, -zō), **Enrico.** 1873–1921. Italian operatic tenor.
carve (kärv) ► *v.* **carved, carv•ing 1.** To divide into pieces by cutting; slice. **2.** To disjoint, slice, and serve (meat or poultry). **3.** To make or form by or as if by cutting. [< OE *ceorfan.*] —**carv′er** *n.*
Car•ver (kär′vər), **George Washington.** 1864?–1943. Amer. botanist and educator.
carv•ing (kär′vĭng) ► *n.* **1.** The cutting of material such as stone or wood to form a figure or design. **2.** A figure or design so formed.
car•y•at•id (kăr′ē-ăt′ĭd) ► *n., pl.* **-ids** or **-i•des** (-ĭ-dēz′) *Archit.* A supporting column sculptured in the form of a woman. [< Gk. *Karuatides*, maidens of Caryae, Greece.]
ca•sa•ba (kə-sä′bə) ► *n.* A melon having a yellow rind and sweet whitish flesh. [After *Kasaba* (Turgutlu), Turkey.]
Cas•a•blan•ca (kăs′ə-blăng′kə, kä′sə-bläng′kə) A city of NW Morocco on the Atlantic SSW of Tangier. Pop. 2,943,000.
Ca•sals (kə-sälz′, -sälz′), **Pablo.** 1876–1973. Spanish cellist.
Cas•a•no•va de Sein•galt (kăs′ə-nō′və də săn-gält′), **Giovanni Jacopo.** 1725–98. Italian adventurer and writer.
cas•cade (kăs-kād′) ► *n.* **1.** A waterfall or series of small waterfalls. **2.** A fall of material, such as lace. **3.** A succession of stages, opera-

tions, or units. ►*v.* **-cad•ed, -cad•ing.** To fall in a cascade. [< Ital. *cascare*, fall.]

Cascade Range. A mountain chain extending from British Columbia, Canada, to N CA.

cas•car•a (kă-skăr′ə) ►*n.* A tree of NW North America, the dried bark of which is used as a laxative. [Sp. *cáscara*, bark.]

case[1] (kās) ►*n.* **1.** An instance of something; example. **2a.** An occurrence of a disease, disorder, or injury. **b.** A person or group being treated, assisted, or studied, as by a physician, attorney, or social worker. **3.** A set of circumstances or state of affairs; situation. **4.** A question or problem; matter. **5.** *Law* An action or suit or just grounds for an action. **6.** A persuasive argument, demonstration, or justification. **7.** *Ling.* An inflectional pattern or form of nouns, pronouns, and adjectives to express syntactic functions in a sentence. ►*v.* **cased, cas•ing** *Informal.* To examine (e.g., a place) carefully, as in planning a crime. —***idioms:*** **in any case** Regardless of what has occurred or will occur. **in case** If it happens that; if. **in case of** If there should happen to be. [< Lat. *cāsus* < *cadere*, fall.]

case[2] (kās) ►*n.* **1.** A container or receptacle. **2.** A decorative or protective covering. **3.** A set or pair: *a case of pistols.* **4.** The frame of a window, door, or stairway. **5.** A shallow tray with compartments for storing printing type. ►*v.* **cased, cas•ing.** To put into or cover with a case. [< Lat. *capsa*.]

case history ►*n.* A record of the facts affecting the development or condition of a person or group under treatment or study.

ca•sein (kā′sēn′, -sē-ĭn) ►*n.* A white, tasteless, odorless milk protein, used to make plastics, adhesives, paints, and foods. [< Lat. *cāseus*, cheese.]

case•load (kās′lōd′) ►*n.* The number of cases handled in a given period, as by an attorney or social services agency.

case•ment (kās′mənt) ►*n.* **1.** A window sash that opens outward by means of hinges. **2.** A window with casements. [ME, hollow molding.]

case study ►*n.* A detailed analysis of a person or group, esp. as a model of medical, psychiatric, or social phenomena.

case•work (kās′wûrk′) ►*n.* Social work dealing with the needs of a particular case. —**case′work′er** *n.*

cash (kăsh) ►*n.* **1.** Money in the form of bills or coins; currency. **2.** Immediate payment for goods or services in currency. ►*v.* To exchange for or convert into ready money. [Poss. obsolete Fr. *casse*, money box.]

cash•ew (kăsh′o͞o, kə-sho͞o′) ►*n.* **1.** A tropical American tree bearing edible nutlike seeds. **2.** The kidney-shaped nut or seed of the cashew. [< Tupi *acajú*.]

cash•ier[1] (kă-shîr′) ►*n.* **1.** The officer of a bank or business concern in charge of paying and receiving money. **2.** A store employee who handles cash transactions with customers. [< Fr. *caisse*, money box.]

ca•shier[2] (kă-shîr′) ►*v.* To dismiss in disgrace from a position of responsibility. See Syns at **dismiss.** [< LLat. *cassāre*, quash.]

ca•shier's check (kă-shîrz′) ►*n.* A check drawn by a bank on its own funds and signed by the bank's cashier.

cash machine ►*n.* See **automated teller machine.**

cash•mere (kăzh′mîr′, kăsh′-) ►*n.* **1.** Fine wool from an Asian goat. **2.** A soft fabric made from cashmere. [< KASHMIR.]

Cash•mere (kăsh′mîr′, kăsh-mîr′) See **Kashmir.**

cash register ►*n.* A machine that tabulates the amount of sales transactions and makes a permanent and cumulative record of them.

cas•ing (kā′sĭng) ►*n.* An outer cover; case.

ca•si•no (kə-sē′nō) ►*n.*, *pl.* **-nos.** A public room or building for gambling and other entertainment. [Ital. < Lat. *cāsa*, house.]

cask (kăsk) ►*n.* **1.** A barrel of any size. **2.** The amount a cask holds. [ME *caske*.]

cas•ket (kăs′kĭt) ►*n.* **1.** A small case or chest, as for jewels. **2.** A coffin. [ME.]

Cas•per (kăs′pər) A city of E-central WY NW of Cheyenne. Pop. 46,742.

Cas•pi•an Sea (kăs′pē-ən) A saline lake between SE Europe and W Asia.

casque (kăsk) ►*n.* A helmet. [< Sp. *casco*.]

Cas•san•dra (kə-săn′drə) ►*n.* **1.** *Gk. Myth.* A Trojan prophetess fated by Apollo never to be believed. **2.** One that utters unheeded prophecies. [< Gk. *Kassandra*.]

Cas•satt (kə-săt′), **Mary Stevenson.** 1844?–1926. Amer. painter.

Mary Cassatt
c. 1880 self-portrait

cas•sa•va (kə-sä′və) ►*n.* A tropical American plant grown for its tuberous starchy root, a staple food and the source of tapioca. [Ult. < Taino *casavi*, cassava flour.]

cas•se•role (kăs′ə-rōl′) ►*n.* **1.** A dish, usu. of earthenware, glass, or cast iron, in which food is baked and served. **2.** Food baked and served in a casserole. [Fr., saucepan.]

cas•sette (kə-sĕt′, kă-) ►*n.* A cartridge for holding and winding magnetic tape, photographic film, or typewriter ribbon. [< OFr., small box.]

cassette deck ►*n.* A tape deck designed for recording or playing audiocassettes.

cas•sia (kăsh′ə) ►*n.* **1.** Any of a genus of chiefly tropical trees or shrubs having usu. yellow flowers and long pods. **2.** A tropical Asian evergreen tree having cinnamonlike bark. [< Gk. *kassia*, of Semitic orig.]

Cas•si•o•pe•ia (kăs′ē-ə-pē′ə) ►*n.* A W-shaped constellation in the Northern Hemisphere.

cas•sit•er•ite (kə-sĭt′ə-rīt′) ►*n.* A yellow, brown, or black mineral, SnO_2, that is an important tin ore. [< Gk. *kassiteros*, tin.]

cas•sock (kăs′ək) ►*n.* An ankle-length garment worn by the clergy. [< Pers. *kazhāgand*, padded garment.]

cas•so•war•y (kăs′ə-wĕr′ē) ►*n.*, *pl.* **-ies.** A large flightless bird of Australia and New Guinea with brightly colored wattles. [Malay *kesuari.*]

cast (kăst) ►*v.* **cast, cast•ing 1.** To throw or fling. **2.** To shed or discard; molt. **3.** To deposit or indicate (a ballot or vote). **4.** To turn or direct: *cast a glance at me.* **5a.** To choose actors for. **b.** To assign a role to. **6.** To form (e.g., liquid metal) by molding. **7.** To add up (a column of figures); compute. ►*n.* **1.** A throw. **2.** A throw of dice. **3.** Something, such as molted skin, that is shed or thrown off. **4.** A mold. **5.** A rigid dressing, usu. made of gauze and plaster of Paris, used to immobilize an injured body part. **6.** Outward appearance; look. **7.** The actors in a theatrical presentation. **8.** A slight trace of color; tinge. [< ON *kasta.*]

cas•ta•nets (kăs′tə-nĕts′) ►*pl.n.* A percussion instrument consisting of a pair of ivory or hardwood shells held in the hand and clapped together with the fingers. [< Lat. *castanea*, CHESTNUT.]

cast•a•way (kăst′ə-wā′) ►*adj.* **1.** Cast adrift or ashore; shipwrecked. **2.** Thrown away; discarded. —**cast′a•way′** *n.*

caste (kăst) ►*n.* **1.** Any of the hereditary social classes of traditional Hindu society, stratified according to Hindu ritual purity. **2a.** A social class separated from others by distinctions of hereditary rank, profession, or wealth. **b.** Social position or status. [< Lat. *castus*, race.]

cast•er (kăs′tər) ►*n.* **1.** One that casts. **2.** also **castor** A small wheel on a swivel, attached to the underside of a heavy object to make it easier to move. **3.** also **castor** A small bottle or cruet for condiments.

cas•ti•gate (kăs′tĭ-gāt′) ►*v.* **-gat•ed, -gat•ing.** To chastise or criticize severely. [Lat. *castīgāre.*] —**cas′ti•ga′tion** *n.*

Cas•tile (kăs-tēl′) A region and former kingdom of central and N Spain.

Cas•til•ian (kă-stĭl′yən) ►*n.* **1.** A native or inhabitant of Castille. **2.** The Spanish dialect of Castille. —**Cas•til′ian** *adj.*

cast•ing (kăs′tĭng) ►*n.* **1.** Something cast in a mold. **2.** Something cast off or out.

cast iron ►*n.* A hard, brittle nonmalleable iron-carbon alloy containing 2 to 4.5% carbon, 0.5 to 3% silicon. —**cast′-i′ron** *adj.*

cast-i•ron plant (kăst′ī′ərn) ►*n.* See **aspidistra.**

cas•tle (kăs′əl) ►*n.* **1.** A large fortified building or group of buildings. **2.** A large imposing building. **3.** *Games* See **rook**[2]. [< Lat. *castellum.*]

Cas•tle•reagh (kăs′əl-rā′), Viscount. Robert Stewart. 1769–1822. British politician.

cast•off (kăst′ôf′, -ŏf′) ►*n.* One that has been discarded. —**cast′off** *adj.*

cas•tor (kăs′tər) ►*n.* Var. of **caster** 2, 3.

Castor ►*n.* A double star in Gemini.

castor oil ►*n.* An oil extracted from the seeds of a tropical plant and used as a laxative and industrially as a lubricant. [Prob. < *castor*, an oily secretion of beavers.]

cas•trate (kăs′trāt′) ►*v.* **-trat•ed, -trat•ing.** To remove the testicles of (a male) or ovaries of (a female). [Lat. *castrāre.*] —**cas′trat•er, cas′tra•tor** *n.* —**cas•tra′tion** *n.*

Cas•tries (kăs′trēz′, -trēs′) The capital of St. Lucia, in the Windward Is. of the British West Indies. Pop. 51,994.

Cas•tro (kăs′trō), **Fidel.** b. 1927. Cuban revolutionary leader.

ca•su•al (kăzh′o͞o-əl) ►*adj.* **1.** Occurring by chance. **2a.** Irregular; occasional. **b.** Unpremeditated; offhand: *a casual remark.* **3a.** Informal or relaxed. **b.** Suited for informal wear or use. **4.** Not thorough; superficial. **5.** Nonchalant. [< Lat. *cāsus*, CASE[1].] —**ca′su•al•ly** *adv.* —**ca′su•al•ness** *n.*

ca•su•al•ty (kăzh′o͞o-əl-tē) ►*n.*, *pl.* **-ties 1.** A disastrous accident. **2.** One injured or killed in an accident. **3.** One injured, killed, captured, or missing in military action.

ca•su•ist•ry (kăzh′o͞o-ĭ-strē) ►*n.* Specious or overly subtle reasoning intended to rationalize or mislead. [< Lat. *cāsus*, CASE[1].] —**ca′su•ist** *n.* —**ca′su•is′tic** *adj.*

cat (kăt) ►*n.* **1a.** A small carnivorous mammal domesticated as a catcher of rats and mice and as a pet. **b.** An animal related to the cat, including the lion, tiger, and leopard. **2.** *Slang* A person, esp. a man. [< OE *catt.*]

CAT ►*abbr.* **1.** clear-air turbulence **2.** computerized axial tomography

ca•tab•o•lism (kə-tăb′ə-lĭz′əm) ►*n.* Metabolic activity in which complex substances are broken down into simpler substances. [Gk. *kata-*, down + (META)BOLISM.] —**cat′a•bol′ic** (kăt′ə-bŏl′ĭk) *adj.*

cat•a•clysm (kăt′ə-klĭz′əm) ►*n.* A violent and sudden, usu. destructive upheaval. [< Gk. *katakluzein*, inundate.] —**cat′a•clys′mic, cat′a•clys′mal** *adj.*

cat•a•comb (kăt′ə-kōm′) ►*n.* often **catacombs** An underground chamber with recesses for graves. [< LLat. *catacumba.*]

cat•a•falque (kăt′ə-fălk′, -fôlk′) ►*n.* A decorated platform on which a coffin rests in state during a funeral. [< Ital. *catafalco.*]

Cat•a•lan (kăt′l-ăn′) ►*n.* **1.** A native or inhabitant of Catalonia. **2.** The Romance language of Catalonia. —**Cat′a•lan′** *adj.*

cat•a•lep•sy (kăt′l-ĕp′sē) ►*n.*, *pl.* **-sies** *Pathol.* Muscular rigidity, lack of awareness of environment, and lack of response to external stimuli. [< Gk. *katalambanein*, seize upon.] —**cat′a•lep′tic** *adj.*

cat•a•log or **cat•a•logue** (kăt′l-ôg′, -ŏg′) ►*n.* **1.** An itemized, often descriptive list. **2.** A publication containing a catalog. **3.** A card catalog. ►*v.* **-loged, -log•ing** or **-logued, -logu•ing.** To list in or make a catalog. [< Gk. *katalegein*, count off.] —**cat′a•log′er, cat′a•logu′er** *n.*

Cat•a•lo•nia (kăt′l-ōn′yə) A region of NE Spain bordering on France and the Mediterranean. —**Cat′a•lo′nian** *adj. & n.*

ca•tal•pa (kə-tăl′pə, -tôl′-) ►*n.* A North American tree having large heart-shaped leaves, showy white flower clusters, and long slender pods. [Creek *katałpa.*]

ca•tal•y•sis (kə-tăl′ĭ-sĭs) ►*n.*, *pl.* **-ses** (-sēz′). The action of a catalyst, esp. an increase in the rate of a chemical reaction. [< Gk. *kataluein*, dissolve.] —**cat′a•lyt′ic** (kăt′l-ĭt′ĭk) *adj.* —**cat′a•lyt′i•cal•ly** *adv.*

cat•a•lyst (kăt′l-ĭst) ►*n.* **1.** *Chem.* A substance that modifies and esp. increases the rate of a re-

action without being consumed in the process. **2.** An agent of change.
catalytic converter ▸ *n.* A device for reducing carbon monoxide and hydrocarbon pollutants in automobile exhaust.
cat•a•lyze (kăt′l-īz′) ▸ *v.* **-lyzed, -lyz•ing.** To modify the rate of (a chemical reaction) by catalysis. —**cat′a•lyz′er** *n.*
cat•a•ma•ran (kăt′ə-mə-răn′) ▸ *n.* A boat, esp. a light sailboat, with two parallel hulls or floats. [Tamil *kaṭṭumaram.*]
cat•a•mount (kăt′ə-mount′) ▸ *n.* See **mountain lion.** [< *cat of the mountain.*]
Ca•ta•nia (kə-tān′yə) A city of E Sicily, Italy on the **Gulf of Catania,** an inlet of the Ionian Sea. Pop. 330,037.
cat•a•pult (kăt′ə-pŭlt′, -po͝olt′) ▸ *n.* **1.** An ancient military machine for hurling large missiles. **2.** A mechanism for launching aircraft from the deck of a carrier. [< Gk. *katapaltēs.*] —**cat′a•pult′** *v.*
cat•a•ract (kăt′ə-răkt′) ▸ *n.* **1.** A large waterfall. **2.** A downpour. **3.** Opacity of the lens or capsule of the eye, causing partial or total blindness. [< Gk. *katarraktēs.*]
ca•tarrh (kə-tär′) ▸ *n.* Inflammation of mucous membranes, esp. of the nose and throat. [< Gk. *katarrous* : *kata-*, down + *rhein*, flow.] —**ca•tarrh′al** *adj.*
ca•tas•tro•phe (kə-tăs′trə-fē) ▸ *n.* A great, often sudden calamity; disaster. [< Gk. *katastrephein*, overturn.] —**cat′a•stroph′ic** (kăt′ə-strŏf′ĭk) *adj.* —**cat′a•stroph′i•cal•ly** *adv.*
cat•a•to•ni•a (kăt′ə-tō′nē-ə) ▸ *n.* An abnormal condition most often associated with schizophrenia and variously marked by stupor, mania, and either rigidity or extreme flexibility of the limbs. [< Gk. *katatonos*, stretching tight.] —**cat′a•ton′ic** (-tŏn′ĭk) *adj. & n.* —**cat′a•ton′i•cal•ly** *adv.*
Ca•taw•ba (kə-tô′bə) ▸ *n., pl.* **-ba** or **-bas 1.** A member of a Native American people now located in W South Carolina. **2.** The Siouan language of the Catawba.
cat•bird (kăt′bûrd′) ▸ *n.* A dark gray North American songbird with a mewing call.
cat•call (kăt′kôl′) ▸ *n.* A shrill call or cry of derision or disapproval. —**cat′call′** *v.*
catch (kăch, kĕch) ▸ *v.* **caught** (kôt), **catch•ing 1.** To capture, esp. after a chase. **2.** To snare or trap. **3.** To discover or come upon unexpectedly or accidentally. **4.** To take hold of or apprehend suddenly; grasp. **5.** To snatch; grab. **6a.** To intercept or overtake. **b.** To get to in time: *catch a plane.* **7.** To become or cause to become held, entangled, or fastened. **8.** To hold up; delay. **9.** To become subject to or contract, as by contagion. **10.** To apprehend or grasp mentally. **11.** *Informal* To go to see: *caught the late show.* —***phrasal verbs:*** **catch on 1.** To understand or perceive. **2.** To become popular. **catch up 1.** To come up from behind; overtake. **2.** To bring up to date: *caught up on my reading.* ▸ *n.* **1.** The act of catching. **2.** Something that catches, esp. a device for fastening or for checking motion. **3a.** Something caught. **b.** *Informal* One worth catching. **4.** A game of throwing and catching a ball. **5.** *Informal* An unsuspected drawback. —***idioms:*** **catch fire 1.** To ignite. **2.** To gain sudden popularity. **catch (one's) breath** To pause or rest briefly. [< Lat. *captāre*, chase.]
Syns: *catch, enmesh, ensnare, entangle, entrap, snare, tangle, trap* **v.**
Catch-22 (kăch′twĕn-tē-to͞o′, kĕch′-) ▸ *n.* A situation in which a desired outcome is impossible to attain because of a set of inherently contradictory rules or conditions. [After the novel *Catch-22* by Joseph Heller.]
catch•all (kăch′ôl′, kĕch′-) ▸ *n.* A receptacle or storage area for odds and ends.
catch•er (kăch′ər, kĕch′-) ▸ *n.* One that catches, esp. the baseball player positioned behind home plate.
catch•ing (kăch′ĭng, kĕch′-) ▸ *adj.* **1.** Infectious or contagious. **2.** Attractive; alluring.
catch•up (kăch′əp, kĕch′-) ▸ *n.* Var. of **ketchup.**
catch•word (kăch′wûrd′, kĕch′-) ▸ *n.* A well-known word or phrase, esp. one that exemplifies a notion, class, or quality.
catch•y (kăch′ē, kĕch′ē) ▸ *adj.* **-i•er, -i•est 1.** Easily remembered: *a catchy tune.* **2.** Tricky; deceptive. —**catch′i•ness** *n.*
cat•e•chism (kăt′ĭ-kĭz′əm) ▸ *n.* A book giving a brief summary of the basic principles of Christianity in question-and-answer form. [< LGk. *katēkhismos.*] —**cat′e•chist** *n.* —**cat′e•chize′** *v.*
cat•e•chu•men (kăt′ĭ-kyo͞o′mən) ▸ *n.* One who is being taught the principles of Christianity. [< Gk. *katēkhein*, instruct.]
cat•e•gor•i•cal (kăt′ĭ-gôr′ĭ-kəl, -gŏr′-) also **cat•e•gor•ic** (-ĭk) ▸ *adj.* **1.** Being without exception or qualification; absolute. See Syns at **explicit. 2.** Of or included in a category. —**cat′e•gor′i•cal•ly** *adv.*
cat•e•go•rize (kăt′ĭ-gə-rīz′) ▸ *v.* **-rized, -riz•ing.** To put into categories. —**cat′e•go•riz′a•ble** *adj.* —**cat′e•go•ri•za′tion** *n.*
cat•e•go•ry (kăt′ĭ-gôr′ē, -gōr′ē) ▸ *n., pl.* **-ries.** A specifically defined division in a system of classification; class. [< Gk. *katēgoria*, accusation.]
ca•ter (kā′tər) ▸ *v.* **1.** To provide food and service (for). **2.** To be attentive or solicitous: *catered to our every need.* [< Norman Fr. *acatour*, buyer.] —**ca′ter•er** *n.*
cat•er-cor•nered (kăt′ər-kôr′nərd, kăt′ē-) also **cat•ty-cor•nered** (kăt′ē-kôr′nərd) or **cat•ty-cor•ner** (-nər) ▸ *adj.* Diagonal. ▸ *adv.* Diagonally. [< *cater*, four at dice < Lat. *quattuor.*]
cat•er•pil•lar (kăt′ər-pĭl′ər, kăt′ə-) ▸ *n.* The wormlike, often hairy larva of a butterfly or moth. [Prob. < ONFr. **catepelose.*]
cat•er•waul (kăt′ər-wôl′) ▸ *v.* To make a discordant sound or shriek. [ME **caterwawlen.*] —**cat′er•waul′** *n.*
cat•fish (kăt′fĭsh′) ▸ *n.* Any of numerous scaleless fishes with whiskerlike feelers near the mouth.
cat•gut (kăt′gŭt′) ▸ *n.* A tough cord made from the dried intestines of certain animals.
ca•thar•sis (kə-thär′sĭs) ▸ *n., pl.* **-ses** (-sēz) **1.** *Medic.* Purgation, esp. for the digestive system. **2.** A purging of the emotions as a result of experiencing esp. a dramatic work of art. [< Gk. *kathairein*, purge.]
ca•thar•tic (kə-thär′tĭk) ▸ *adj.* Inducing catharsis; purgative. ▸ *n.* A purgative.
ca•the•dral (kə-thē′drəl) ▸ *n.* The principal church of a bishop's diocese. [< Gk. *kathedra*,

seat : *kat-*, down + *hedra*, seat.]
Cath•er (kăth′ər), **Willa Sibert.** 1873–1947. Amer. writer.
Cath•e•rine I (kăth′ər-ĭn, kăth′rĭn). 1684?–1727. Empress of Russia (1725–27).
Catherine II. "Catherine the Great." 1729–96. Empress of Russia (1762–96).
Catherine de Mé•di•cis (də mĕd′ĭ-chē′, də mā-dē-sēs′). 1519–89. Queen of France as wife of Henry II and regent during the minority (1560–63) of her son Charles IX.
Catherine of Aragon. 1485–1536. The first wife of Henry VIII.
cath•e•ter (kăth′ĭ-tər) ►*n.* A hollow flexible tube for insertion into a bodily channel to allow the passage of fluids or to distend a passageway. [< Gk. *kathienai*, send down.]
cath•ode (kăth′ōd′) ►*n.* **1.** A negatively charged electrode. **2.** The positively charged terminal of a primary cell or storage battery. [Gk. *kathodos*, a way down.] —**ca•thod′ic** (kă-thŏd′ĭk) *adj.*
cath•ode-ray tube (kăth′ōd-rā′) ►*n.* A vacuum tube in which a hot cathode emits electrons that are accelerated and focused on a phosphorescent screen.
cath•o•lic (kăth′ə-lĭk, kăth′lĭk) ►*adj.* **1.** Universal; general. **2. Catholic** Of or involving the Roman Catholic Church or Catholics. ►*n.* **Catholic.** A member of the Roman Catholic Church. [< Gk. *katholikos*, universal.] —**ca•thol′i•cal•ly** (kə-thŏl′ĭk-lē) *adv.* —**cath′o•lic′i•ty** (-ə-lĭs′ĭ-tē) *n.*
Ca•thol•i•cism (kə-thŏl′ĭ-sĭz′əm) ►*n.* The faith, doctrine, system, and practice of the Roman Catholic Church.
Cat•i•line (kăt′l-īn′). 108?–62 B.C. Roman politician and conspirator.
cat•i•on (kăt′ī′ən) ►*n.* An ion or group of ions having a positive charge and characteristically moving toward a negative electrode in electrolysis. [Gk. *kation*, (thing) going down.] —**cat′i•on′ic** (-ŏn′ĭk) *adj.*
cat•kin (kăt′kĭn) ►*n.* A dense, often drooping cluster of scalelike flowers found in willows, birches, and oaks. [< obsolete Du. *katteken*, kitten.]
cat•nap (kăt′năp′) ►*n.* A short nap; light sleep. —**cat′nap′** *v.*
cat•nip (kăt′nĭp′) ►*n.* An aromatic plant to which cats are strongly attracted.
Ca•to[1] (kā′tō), **Marcus Porcius.** "the Elder." 234–149 B.C. Roman politician and general.
Cato[2], **Marcus Porcius.** "the Younger." 95–46 B.C. Roman politician and great-grandson of Cato the Elder.
cat-o′-nine-tails (kăt′ə-nīn′tālz′) ►*n.*, *pl.* **cat-o′-nine-tails.** A flogging whip consisting of nine knotted cords fastened to a handle.
CAT scanner (kăt) ►*n.* A device that produces cross-sectional views of an internal body structure using computerized axial tomography. —**CAT scan** *n.*
cat's cradle (kăts) ►*n.* A game in which an intricately looped string is transferred from the hands of one player to another.
cat's-eye (kăts′ī′) ►*n.* A semiprecious gem displaying a band of reflected light that shifts position as the gem is turned.
Cats•kill Mountains (kăt′skĭl′) A range of the Appalachian Mts. in SE NY.
cat's-paw also **cats•paw** (kăts′pô′) ►*n.* A person used by another as a dupe or tool.
cat•sup (kăt′səp, kăch′əp, kĕch′-) ►*n.* Var. of **ketchup.**
Catt (kăt), **Carrie (Lane) Chapman.** 1859–1947. Amer. suffragist.
cat•tail (kăt′tāl′) ►*n.* A tall-stemmed marsh plant having long straplike leaves and a dense brown cylindrical head.
cat•tle (kăt′l) ►*pl.n.* Bovine mammals such as cows, steers, bulls, and oxen, often raised for meat and dairy products. [< Med.Lat. *capitāle*, property.] —**cat′tle•man** *n.*
cat•ty (kăt′ē) ►*adj.* **-ti•er, -ti•est.** Slyly malicious. —**cat′ti•ly** *adv.* —**cat′ti•ness** *n.*
cat•ty-cor•nered (kăt′ē-kôr′nərd) or **cat•ty-cor•ner** (-nər) ►*adj. & adv.* Vars. of **cater-cornered.**
Ca•tul•lus (kə-tŭl′əs), **Gaius Valerius.** 84?–54? B.C. Roman lyric poet.
CATV ►*abbr.* community antenna television
cat•walk (kăt′wôk′) ►*n.* A narrow, often elevated walkway, as on the sides of a bridge.
Cau•ca•sian (kô-kā′zhən) ►*adj.* **1.** Of or being a purported human racial classification traditionally distinguished by light to brown skin color and including peoples indigenous to Europe, N Africa, W Asia, and India. Not in scientific use. **2.** Of the Caucasus. ►*n.* **1.** *Anthro.* A member of the Caucasian racial classification. **2.** A native or inhabitant of the Caucasus.
Cau•ca•soid (kô′kə-soid′) ►*adj.* Of or relating to the Caucasian racial classification. Not in scientific use. —**Cau′ca•soid′** *n.*
Cau•ca•sus (kô′kə-səs) also **Cau•ca•sia** (kô-kā′zhə, -shə). A region between the Black and Caspian seas that includes Russia, Georgia, Azerbaijan, and Armenia.
Caucasus Mountains. A range extending from the N to the SE in the Caucasus.
cau•cus (kô′kəs) ►*n.*, *pl.* **-cus•es** or **-cus•ses** **1.** A meeting of the local members of a political party esp. to select delegates to a convention. **2.** A group within a legislative body seeking to represent a specific interest or policy. [After the *Caucus* Club of Boston.] —**cau′cus** *v.*
cau•dal (kôd′l) ►*adj.* Of, at, or near the tail or hind parts; posterior. [< Lat. *cauda*, tail.]
cau•dil•lo (kô-dēl′yō, -dē′yō) ►*n.*, *pl.* **-los.** A leader or chief, esp. a military dictator. [Sp. < LLat. *capitellum*, small head.]
caught (kôt) ►*v.* P.t. and p.part. of **catch.**
caul (kôl) ►*n.* A portion of the amnion, esp. when it covers the head of a fetus at birth. [< OE *cawl*, basket.]
caul•dron also **cal•dron** (kôl′drən) ►*n.* **1.** A large kettle or vat. **2.** A situation of seething unrest. [< LLat. *caldāria*, cooking pot.]
cau•li•flow•er (kô′lĭ-flou′ər, kŏl′ĭ-) ►*n.* A plant related to the cabbage and broccoli and having a whitish undeveloped flower with a large edible head. [Prob. < Lat. *caulis*, stem + *flōs*, flower.]
cauliflower ear ►*n.* An ear swollen and deformed by repeated blows.
caulk also **calk** (kôk) ►*v.* **1.** To make (e.g., pipes) watertight or airtight by sealing. **2.** To make (a boat) watertight by packing seams with oakum or tar. ►*n.* Caulking. [< ONFr. *cauquer*, to press.] —**caulk′er** *n.*
caulk•ing (kô′kĭng) ►*n.* A usu. impermeable substance used to caulk or seal.
caus•al (kô′zəl) ►*adj.* Of, constituting, or ex-

pressing a cause : *a causal relationship.* —**cau•sal′i•ty** (-zăl′ĭ-tē) *n.* —**caus′al•ly** *adv.*

cau•sa•tion (kô-zā′shən) ►*n.* **1.** The act or process of causing. **2.** A causal agency.

cause (kôz) ►*n.* **1.** The one, such as a person, event, or condition, responsible for an action or result. **2.** A reason; motive. **3.** A goal or principle. **4a.** A ground for legal action. **b.** A lawsuit. ►*v.* **caused, caus•ing.** To be the cause of; bring about. [< Lat. *causa*, reason.] —**cause′less** *adj.*

cause cé•lè•bre (kōz′ sā-lĕb′rə) ►*n., pl.* **causes cé•lè•bres** (kōz′ sā-lĕb′rə) **1.** An issue arousing widespread controversy or heated debate. **2.** A celebrated legal case. [Fr.]

cause•way (kôz′wā′) ►*n.* A raised roadway across water or marshland. [ME *caucewei.*]

caus•tic (kô′stĭk) ►*adj.* **1.** Capable of burning, corroding, or dissolving by chemical action. **2.** Sarcastic; biting. ►*n.* A caustic substance. [< Gk. *kaustikos.*]

cau•ter•ize (kô′tə-rīz′) ►*v.* **-ized, -iz•ing.** To burn or sear so as to stop bleeding and prevent infection. [< Gk. *kautērion*, branding iron.] —**cau′ter•i•za′tion** *n.*

cau•tion (kô′shən) ►*n.* **1.** Careful forethought to avoid danger or harm. **2.** A warning or admonition. ►*v.* To warn. [< Lat. *cavēre, caut-*, take care.] —**cau′tion•ar′y** *adj.*

cau•tious (kô′shəs) ►*adj.* Showing or practicing caution; careful. —**cau′tious•ly** *adv.* —**cau′tious•ness** *n.*

cav•al•cade (kăv′əl-kād′, kăv′əl-kād′) ►*n.* **1.** A procession of riders or horse-drawn carriages. **2.** A ceremonial procession. [< Med. Lat. *caballicāre*, ride on horseback.]

cav•a•lier (kăv′ə-lîr′) ►*n.* **1.** A gallant gentleman. **2.** A mounted soldier; knight. **3. Cavalier** A supporter of Charles I of England. ►*adj.* **1.** Haughty; disdainful. **2.** Carefree and nonchalant; jaunty. [< Med.Lat. *caballārius*, horseman.] —**cav′a•lier′ly** *adv.*

cav•al•ry (kăv′əl-rē) ►*n., pl.* **-ries.** Troops trained to fight on horseback or in light armored vehicles. [< Ital. *cavalleria* < *cavaliere*, CAVALIER.] —**cav′al•ry•man** *n.*

cavalry
Captain Dodge's Colored Troopers to the Rescue by Frederic Remington

cave (kāv) ►*n.* A hollow or natural passage under or into the earth with an opening to the surface. ►*v.* **caved, cav•ing 1.** To fall in; collapse. **2.** To capitulate; yield: *caved in to their demands.* **3.** To explore and study caves. [< Lat. *cava.*] —**cav′er** *n.*

ca•ve•at (kăv′ē-ăt′, kä′vē-ät′) ►*n.* A warning or caution. [< Lat., let him beware.]

cave-in (kāv′ĭn′) ►*n.* A collapse, as of a tunnel or structure.

cave•man (kāv′măn′) ►*n.* **1.** A prehistoric human who lived in caves. **2.** *Informal* A man who is crude or brutal, esp. toward women.

cav•ern (kăv′ərn) ►*n.* A large cave. [< Lat. *caverna.*] —**cav′ern•ous** *adj.*

cav•i•ar also **cav•i•are** (kăv′ē-är′, kä′vē-) ►*n.* The roe of a large fish, esp. a sturgeon, salted and eaten as a delicacy. [< Turk. *havyar* < Pers. *khāvyār*; akin to MPers. *khāyak*, egg.]

cav•il (kăv′əl) ►*v.* **-iled, -il•ing** also **-illed, -il•ling.** To find fault unnecessarily. See Syns at **quibble.** [< Lat. *cavillārī*, jeer.] —**cav′il** *n.* —**cav′il•er** *n.*

cav•i•ty (kăv′ĭ-tē) ►*n., pl.* **-ties 1.** A hollow or hole. **2.** A pitted area in a tooth caused by decay. [< Lat. *cavus*, hollow.]

ca•vort (kə-vôrt′) ►*v.* To leap about; caper. [Poss. alteration of *curvet*, a leap.]

Ca•vour (kə-vo͝or′, kä-vo͝or′), Conte **Camillo Benso di.** 1810–61. Italian political leader.

caw (kô) ►*n.* The hoarse raucous sound of a crow or similar bird. [Imit.] —**caw** *v.*

Cax•ton (kăk′stən), **William.** 1422?–91. English printer.

cay (kē, kā) ►*n.* A small low island of coral or sand; key. [< Sp. *cayo.*]

Cay•enne (kī-ĕn′, kā-) The capital of French Guiana, on **Cayenne Island** at the mouth of the **Cayenne River.** Pop. 41,164.

cayenne pepper ►*n.* A condiment made from the fruit of a pungent variety of capsicum pepper. [< Tupi *quiínia.*]

cay•man (kā′mən) ►*n.* Var. of **caiman.**

Cay•man Islands (kā-măn′, kā′mən) A British-administered group of three islands in the Caribbean Sea NW of Jamaica. Cap. Georgetown. Pop. 30,000.

Ca•yu•ga (kā-yo͞o′gə, kī-) ►*n., pl.* **-ga** or **-gas 1.** A member of a Native American people formerly of W-central New York, now living in W New York, Wisconsin, and Oklahoma. **2.** Their Iroquoian language.

cay•use (kī-yo͞os′, kī′yo͞os′) ►*n.* A horse, esp. an Indian pony of the Pacific Northwest.

Cayuse ►*n., pl.* **-use** or **-us•es 1.** A member of a Native American people of NE Oregon and SE Washington. **2.** Their language.

CB (sē-bē′) ►*abbr.* citizens band

CBD ►*abbr.* **1.** cash before delivery **2.** central business district

CBW ►*abbr.* chemical and biological warfare

cc ►*abbr.* **1.** carbon copy **2.** cubic centimeter

CCC ►*abbr.* **1.** Civilian Conservation Corps **2.** Commodity Credit Corporation

cckw. or **ccw.** ►*abbr.* counterclockwise

CCTV ►*abbr.* closed-circuit television

CCU ►*abbr.* coronary care unit

cd ►*abbr.* candela

Cd ► The symbol for the element **cadmium.**

CD ►*abbr.* **1.** also **C/D** certificate of deposit **2.** civil defense **3.** compact disk

cd. ►*abbr.* cord

CDC ►*abbr.* Centers for Disease Control and Prevention

CDR ►*abbr.* commander

CD-ROM (sē′dē′rŏm′) ►*n.* A compact disk that functions as read-only memory.

CD-RW ►*abbr.* compact disk–rewritable

CDT ►*abbr.* Central Daylight Time

Ce ► The symbol for the element **cerium.**

CE ►*abbr.* **1.** chemical engineer **2.** civil engineer

C.E. or C.E. ▸*abbr.* Common Era

cease (sēs) ▸*v.* **ceased, ceas•ing.** To bring or come to an end. See Syns at **stop.** [< Lat. *cessāre.*]

cease-fire (sēs′fīr′) ▸*n.* **1.** An order to stop firing. **2.** Suspension of hostilities; truce.

cease•less (sēs′lĭs) ▸*adj.* Never ending. —**cease′less•ly** *adv.* —**cease′less•ness** *n.*

Ce•bu (sĕ-bo͞o′) An island of the central Philippines in the Visayan Is. The city of **Cebu** (pop. 688,196) is on the E coast.

Cec•il (sĕs′əl), **Robert.** 1st Viscount Cranborne and 1st Earl of Salisbury. 1563?–1612. English political leader.

Cecil, Robert Arthur Talbot Gascoyne. 3rd Marquis of Salisbury. 1830–1903. British prime minister (1885–92 and 1895–1902).

Ce•cil•ia (sĭ-sēl′yə), Saint. 3rd cent. A.D. Christian martyr.

ce•cum also **cae•cum** (sē′kəm) ▸*n., pl.* **-ca** (-kə). The large blind pouch forming the beginning of the large intestine. [< Lat. *(intestīnum) caecum,* blind (intestine).] —**ce′cal** *adj.* —**ce′cal•ly** *adv.*

ce•dar (sē′dər) ▸*n.* Any of a genus of evergreen trees having large erect cones and aromatic, usu. reddish wood. [< Gk. *kedros.*]

Cedar Rapids. A city of E-central IA WNW of Davenport. Pop. 108,751.

cede (sēd) ▸*v.* **ced•ed, ced•ing 1.** To surrender possession of, esp. by treaty. **2.** To yield or grant. [< Lat. *cēdere.*]

ce•di (sā′dē) ▸*n., pl.* **-dis.** See table at **currency.** [Poss. < Akan (African) *sedį,* cowry.]

ce•dil•la (sĭ-dĭl′ə) ▸*n.* A mark (̧) placed beneath the letter *c,* as in *façade,* to indicate that the letter is to be pronounced (s). [Obsolete Sp., dim. of *ceda,* the letter *z.*]

cei•ba (sā′bə) ▸*n.* The silk-cotton tree. [Sp.]

ceil•ing (sē′lĭng) ▸*n.* **1.** The upper interior surface of a room. **2.** An upper limit: *wage and price ceilings.* **3.** The highest altitude under particular weather conditions from which the ground is visible. [ME *celing.*]

Cel•e•bes (sĕl′ə-bēz′, sə-lē′bēz′) See **Sulawesi.**

Celebes Sea. A section of the W Pacific between Sulawesi and the S Philippines.

cel•e•brate (sĕl′ə-brāt′) ▸*v.* **-brat•ed, -brat•ing 1.** To observe (a day or event) with ceremonies of respect, festivity, or rejoicing. **2.** To perform (a religious ceremony). **3.** To extol or praise. [< Lat. *celeber,* famous.] —**cel′e•brant** *n.* —**cel′e•bra′tion** *n.* —**cel′e•bra′tor** *n.* —**cel′e•bra•to′ry** (sĕl′ə-brə-tôr′ē, -tōr′ē, sə-lĕb′rə-) *adj.*

cel•e•brat•ed (sĕl′ə-brā′tĭd) ▸*adj.* Known and praised widely. See Syns at **noted.**

ce•leb•ri•ty (sə-lĕb′rĭ-tē) ▸*n., pl.* **-ties 1.** A famous person. **2.** Renown; fame. [< Lat. *celeber,* famous.] —**ce•leb′ri•ty•hood′** *n.*

Syns: *celebrity, luminary, name, notable, personage* **n.**

ce•ler•i•ty (sə-lĕr′ĭ-tē) ▸*n.* Swiftness; speed. See Syns at **haste.** [< Lat. *celer,* swift.]

cel•er•y (sĕl′ə-rē) ▸*n.* A plant having edible roots, leafstalks, leaves, and seedlike fruits. [< Gk. *selinon.*]

ce•les•ta (sə-lĕs′tə) also **ce•leste** (-lĕst′) ▸*n.* A keyboard instrument with metal plates struck by hammers. [< Fr. *céleste,* CELESTIAL.]

ce•les•tial (sə-lĕs′chəl) ▸*adj.* **1.** Of or relating to the sky or the heavens. **2.** Of or suggestive of heaven; heavenly. [< Lat. *caelestis.*]

celestial equator ▸*n.* A great circle on the celestial sphere in the same plane as the earth's equator.

celestial navigation ▸*n.* Navigation based on the positions of celestial bodies.

celestial sphere ▸*n.* An imaginary sphere of infinite extent with the earth at its center.

cel•i•bate (sĕl′ə-bĭt) ▸*adj.* **1.** Abstaining from sexual intercourse, esp. by reason of religious vows. **2.** Unmarried. [< Lat. *caelebs.*] —**cel′i•ba•cy** (-bə-sē) *n.* —**cel′i•bate** *n.*

cell (sĕl) ▸*n.* **1.** A narrow confining room, as in a prison or convent. **2.** A small enclosed space, as in a honeycomb. **3.** A rectangular box on a spreadsheet where a column and a row intersect. **4.** *Biol.* The smallest structural unit of an organism that is capable of independent functioning, consisting of one or more nuclei, cytoplasm, and various organelles, all surrounded by a semipermeable membrane. **5.** The smallest organizational unit esp. of a revolutionary political party. **6.** *Elect.* **a.** A single unit for electrolysis or conversion of chemical into electric energy, usu. consisting of a container with electrodes and an electrolyte. **b.** A unit that converts radiant energy into electric energy. [< Lat. *cella,* chamber.]

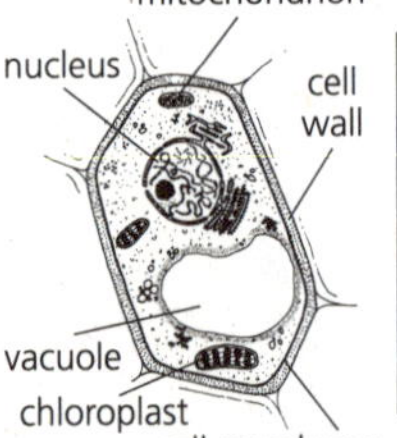

cell
plant (*left*) and animal cells

cel•lar (sĕl′ər) ▸*n.* **1.** An underground room usu. beneath a building. **2.** A stock of wines. [< LLat. *cellārium,* pantry.]

cell•block (sĕl′blŏk′) ▸*n.* A group of cells that make up a unit of a prison.

Cel•li•ni (chə-lē′nē, chĕ-), **Benvenuto.** 1500–71. Italian writer and sculptor.

cell•mate (sĕl′māt′) ▸*n.* One with whom a cell is shared, esp. in a prison.

cel•lo (chĕl′ō) ▸*n., pl.* **-los** *Mus.* An instrument of the violin family, pitched lower than the viola but higher than the double bass. [< VIOLONCELLO.] —**cel′list** *n.*

cel•lo•phane (sĕl′ə-fān′) ▸*n.* A thin, flexible, transparent cellulose material used as a moistureproof wrapping. [Orig. a trademark.]

cell phone ▸*n.* A cellular telephone.

cel•lu•lar (sĕl′yə-lər) ▸*adj.* **1.** Of or resembling a cell. **2.** Consisting of cells.

cellular telephone ▸*n.* A mobile radiotelephone that uses a network of transmitters to connect to regular telephone lines.

cel•lu•lite (sĕl′yə-līt′, -lēt′) ▸*n.* A fatty deposit causing dimpled skin as around the thighs. [Fr. : *cellule,* cell + NLat. *-ītis,* -itis.]

cel•lu•loid (sĕl′yə-loid′) ►*n.* A colorless flammable material made from nitrocellulose and camphor, used to make photographic film. [Orig. a trademark.]

cel•lu•lose (sĕl′yə-lōs′, -lōz′) ►*n.* A complex carbohydrate, $(C_6H_{10}O_5)_n$, the main constituent of the cell wall in most plants, used in the manufacture of paper, textiles, and explosives. [Fr.]

cellulose acetate ►*n.* A cellulose resin used in lacquers and photographic film.

Cel•si•us (sĕl′sē-əs, -shəs) ►*adj.* Of or according to a temperature scale that registers the freezing point of water as 0° and the boiling point as 100° under normal atmospheric pressure. See table at **measurement.** [After Anders *Celsius* (1701–1744).]

Celt (kĕlt, sĕlt) ►*n.* **1.** One of an ancient people of central and W Europe, esp. a Briton or Gaul. **2.** A speaker of a Celtic language.

Celt•ic (kĕl′tĭk, sĕl′-) ►*n.* A subfamily of the Indo-European language family that includes Welsh, Irish Gaelic, Scottish Gaelic, Breton, and Gaulish. ►*adj.* Of or relating to the Celts or the Celtic languages.

cem•ba•lo (chĕm′bə-lō′) ►*n., pl.* **-los** *Mus.* A harpsichord. [Ital.] —**cem′ba•list** *n.*

ce•ment (sĭ-mĕnt′) ►*n.* **1.** A building material made by grinding calcined limestone and clay to a fine powder, which can be mixed with water and poured to set as a solid mass or used as an ingredient in making mortar or concrete. **2.** A substance that hardens to act as an adhesive; glue. **3.**Var. of **cementum.** ►*v.* **1.** To bind with or as if with cement. **2.** To cover or coat with cement. [< Lat. *caementum*, rough-cut stone.]

cement mixer ►*n.* A machine, often mounted on a truck, having a revolving drum in which cement, sand, gravel, and water are combined into concrete.

ce•men•tum (sĭ-mĕn′təm) also **ce•ment** (-mĕnt′) ►*n.* A bonelike substance covering the root of a tooth. [< Lat. *caementum*, rough stone.]

cem•e•ter•y (sĕm′ĭ-tĕr′ē) ►*n., pl.* **-ies.** A place for burying the dead; graveyard. [< Gk. *koimētērion.*]

-cene ►*suff.* Recent: *Oligocene, Pleistocene.* [< Gk. *kainos*, new.]

cen•o•taph (sĕn′ə-tăf′) ►*n.* A monument to commemorate a dead person whose remains lie elsewhere. [< Gk. *kenotaphion.*]

Ce•no•zo•ic (sē′nə-zō′ĭk, sĕn′ə-) ►*adj.* Of or being the 4th and most recent geologic era, including the Tertiary and Quaternary periods and marked by the formation of modern continents and the diversification of mammals, birds, and plants. ►*n.* The Cenozoic Era. [Gk. *kainos*, new + -ZOIC.]

cen•ser (sĕn′sər) ►*n.* A vessel in which incense is burned, esp. during religious services. [< OFr. *encens*, INCENSE[2].]

cen•sor (sĕn′sər) ►*n.* **1.** One authorized to examine books, films, or other material and remove or suppress what is considered objectionable. **2.** A Roman official who was responsible for supervising the census. ►*v.* To examine and expurgate. [< Lat. *cēnsēre*, assess.] —**cen•so′ri•al** (sĕn-sôr′ē-əl, -sōr′-) *adj.*

cen•so•ri•ous (sĕn-sôr′ē-əs, -sōr′-) ►*adj.* Tending to censure; critical. —**cen•so′ri•ous•ly** *adv.*

cen•sor•ship (sĕn′sər-shĭp′) ►*n.* **1.** The act or process of censoring. **2.** The office of a Roman censor.

cen•sure (sĕn′shər) ►*n.* **1.** An expression of disapproval, blame, or criticism. **2.** An official rebuke. ►*v.* **-sured, -sur•ing.** To criticize severely; blame. —**cen′sur•a•ble** *adj.*

cen•sus (sĕn′səs) ►*n.* A periodic official population count. [< Lat. *cēnsēre*, assess.]

cent (sĕnt) ►*n.* **1.** A monetary unit equal to $\frac{1}{100}$ of the US dollar. **2.** A monetary unit equal to $\frac{1}{100}$ of various standard monetary units. [< Lat. *centum*, hundred.]

cent. ►*abbr.* **1.** centigrade **2.** *Lat.* centum (hundred) **3.** century

cen•taur (sĕn′tôr′) ►*n. Gk. Myth.* One of a race of monsters having the head, arms, and trunk of a man and the body and legs of a horse. [< Gk. *Kentauros.*]

cen•ta•vo (sĕn-tä′vō) ►*n., pl.* **-vos 1.** A monetary unit equal to $\frac{1}{100}$ of the Portuguese escudo. **2.** A similar unit used in various Central and South American countries. [Sp., hundredth.]

cen•te•nar•i•an (sĕn′tə-nâr′ē-ən) ►*n.* One that is 100 years or older. —**cen′te•nar′i•an** *adj.*

cen•ten•a•ry (sĕn-tĕn′ə-rē, sĕn′tə-nĕr′ē) ►*n., pl.* **-ries.** A centennial. [< Lat. *centēnārius*, of a hundred.] —**cen•ten′a•ry** *adj.*

cen•ten•ni•al (sĕn-tĕn′ē-əl) ►*n.* A 100th anniversary. [Lat. *centum*, hundred + (BI)ENNIAL.] —**cen•ten′ni•al** *adj.*

cen•ter (sĕn′tər) ►*n.* **1.** A point equidistant from the sides or outer boundaries of something; middle. **2a.** A point equidistant from the vertices of a regular polygon. **b.** A point equidistant from all points on the circumference of a circle or on the surface of a sphere. **3.** A point around which something revolves; axis. **4.** A place of concentrated activity, service, or influence: *a medical center.* **5.** One occupying a middle position. **6.** A political group with views midway between the right and the left. **7.** *Sports* A player who holds a middle position. ►*v.* **1.** To place in, on, or at the center. **2.** To have a center; focus. [< Gk. *kentron.*]

Syns: *center, focus, headquarters, heart, hub, seat* **n.**

cen•ter•board (sĕn′tər-bôrd′, -bōrd′) ►*n.* A movable keel in a sailboat that can be pivoted upward, as in shallow water.

center field ►*n. Baseball* The middle third of the outfield, behind second base. —**center fielder** *n.*

cen•ter•fold (sĕn′tər-fōld′) ►*n.* A magazine center spread, esp. an oversize feature that folds out.

center of mass ►*n., pl.* **centers of mass.** The point in a system at which its mass may be considered to be concentrated.

cen•ter•piece (sĕn′tər-pēs′) ►*n.* **1.** A decorative arrangement placed at the center of a table. **2.** The most important feature.

cen•tes•i•mal (sĕn-tĕs′ə-məl) ►*adj.* Relating to or divided into hundredths. [< Lat. *centēsimus.*] —**cen•tes′i•mal•ly** *adv.*

centi- ►*pref.* **1.** One hundredth part (10^{-2}): *centiliter.* **2.** One hundred: *centipede.* [< Lat. *centum*, hundred.]

cen•ti•grade (sĕn′tĭ-grād′) ►*adj.* Celsius.

cen•ti•gram (sĕn′tĭ-grăm′) ►*n.* See table at **measurement.**

cen•ti•li•ter (sĕn′tə-lē′tər) ►*n.* See table at **measurement.**

cen•time (sän′tēm′, säN-tēm′) ►*n.* A monetary unit equal to 1/100 of the standard unit in France and various other countries. [Fr.]

cen•ti•me•ter (sĕn′tə-mē′tər) ►*n.* See table at **measurement.**

cen•ti•pede (sĕn′tə-pēd′) ►*n.* A wormlike arthropod having many legs and body segments. [Lat. *centipeda* : CENTI– + *pēs, pedīs* foot; see –PED.]

cen•tral (sĕn′trəl) ►*adj.* **1.** At, in, near, or being the center. **2.** Key; essential. ►*n.* **1.** A telephone exchange. **2.** A coordinating office at the center of a group of related activities. —**cen•tral′i•ty** (-trăl′ĭ-tē) *n.* —**cen′tral•ly** *adv.*

Central African Republic. A country of central Africa. Cap. Bangui. Pop. 2,395,000.

Central America. A region of S North America extending from the S border of Mexico to the N border of Colombia. —**Central American** *adj. & n.*

cen•tral•ize (sĕn′trə-līz′) ►*v.* **-ized, -iz•ing.** To bring or come to a center or under a central authority. —**cen′tral•i•za′tion** *n.* —**cen′tral•iz′er** *n.*

central nervous system ►*n.* The portion of the vertebrate nervous system consisting of the brain and spinal cord.

central processing unit ►*n.* The part of a computer that interprets and executes instructions.

cen•tre (sĕn′tər) ►*n. & v. Chiefly Brit.* Var. of **center.**

cen•trif•u•gal (sĕn-trĭf′yə-gəl, -trĭf′ə-) ►*adj.* **1.** Moving or directed away from a center or axis. **2.** Operated by means of centrifugal force. [< Lat. *centrum*, center + *fugere*, flee.] —**cen•trif′u•gal•ly** *adv.*

centrifugal force ►*n.* The apparent force, equal and opposite to the centripetal force, drawing a rotating body away from the center of rotation, caused by the inertia of the body.

cen•tri•fuge (sĕn′trə-fyo͞oj′) ►*n.* A compartment spun about a central axis to separate contained materials of different densities or to simulate gravity with centrifugal force. [< Fr. CENTRIFUGAL.]

cen•trip•e•tal (sĕn-trĭp′ĭ-tl) ►*adj.* **1.** Moving or directed toward a center or axis. **2.** Operated by means of centripetal force. [< Lat. *centrum*, center + *petere*, seek.] —**cen•trip′e•tal•ly** *adv.*

centripetal force ►*n.* The component of force acting on a body in curvilinear motion that is directed toward the center of curvature or axis of rotation.

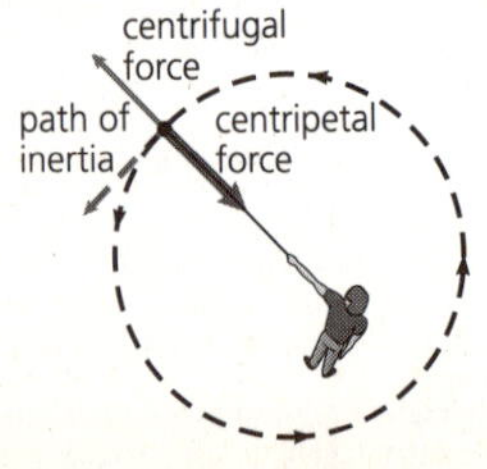

centripetal force

cen•trism (sĕn′trĭz′əm) ►*n.* The political philosophy of avoiding the extremes of right and left by taking a moderate position. —**cen′trist** *adj. & n.*

centro– or **centr–** or **centri–** ►*pref.* Center: *centrism.* [< Lat. *centrum*, CENTER.]

cen•tu•ri•on (sĕn-to͝or′ē-ən, -tyo͝or′-) ►*n.* The commander of a century in the ancient Roman army. [< Lat. *centuriō*.]

cen•tu•ry (sĕn′chə-rē) ►*n., pl.* **-ries 1.** A period of 100 years. **2.** A unit of the ancient Roman army orig. consisting of 100 men. [Lat. *centuria*, a group of a hundred.]

CEO ►*abbr.* chief executive officer

ce•phal•ic (sə-făl′ĭk) ►*adj.* Of or relating to the head. [< Gk. *kephalē*, head.]

ceph•a•lo•pod (sĕf′ə-lə-pŏd′) ►*n.* Any of various marine mollusks, such as the octopus or squid, having a large head, tentacles, and usu. an ink sac for protection or defense. [Gk. *kephalē*, head + –POD.]

ce•ram•ic (sə-răm′ĭk) ►*n.* **1.** Any of various hard, brittle, heat-resistant and corrosion-resistant materials made by firing clay or other nonmetallic minerals. **2a.** An object made of ceramic. **b. ceramics** *(takes sing. v.)* The art of making objects of ceramic, esp. from fired clay. [< Gk. *keramos*, clay.] —**ce•ram′ic** *adj.* —**ce•ram′ist** *n.*

ce•re•al (sîr′ē-əl) ►*n.* **1.** A grass such as wheat, oats, or corn, whose starchy grains are used as food. **2.** A food prepared from such grains. [< Lat. *Cerēs*, Ceres.]

cer•e•bel•lum (sĕr′ə-bĕl′əm) ►*n., pl.* **-lums** or **-bel•la** (-bĕl′ə). The structure of the brain responsible for control of voluntary muscular movement. [< Lat., dim. of *cerebrum*, brain.] —**cer′e•bel′lar** *adj.*

cer•e•bral (sĕr′ə-brəl, sə-rē′-) ►*adj.* **1.** Of the brain or cerebrum. **2.** Intellectual rather than emotional. —**cer•e′bral•ly** *adv.*

cerebral cortex ►*n.* The outer layer of gray matter that covers the two parts of the cerebrum, largely responsible for higher nervous functions.

cerebral palsy ►*n.* A disorder usu. caused by brain damage at or before birth and marked by muscular impairment and often poor coordination.

cer•e•brum (sĕr′ə-brəm, sə-rē′-) ►*n., pl.* **-brums** or **-bra** (-brə). The large rounded structure of the brain occupying most of the cranial cavity and divided into two cerebral hemispheres. [Lat., brain.]

cere•cloth (sîr′klôth′, -klŏth′) ►*n.* Cloth coated with wax, formerly used for wrapping the dead. [< Lat. *cēra*, wax.]

cer•e•ment (sĕr′ə-mənt, sîr′mənt) ►*n.* **1.** Cerecloth. **2.** often **cerements** A burial garment. [Fr. *cirement* < OFr. *cirer*, cover with wax.]

cer•e•mo•ni•al (sĕr′ə-mō′nē-əl) ►*adj.* **1.** Of or characterized by ceremony. **2.** Used in ceremonies: *ceremonial garb.* ►*n.* **1.** A set of ceremonies for a specific occasion; ritual. **2.** A ceremony. —**cer′e•mo′ni•al•ly** *adv.*

cer•e•mo•ni•ous (sĕr′ə-mō′nē-əs) ►*adj.* **1.** Strictly observant of ceremony or etiquette; punctilious. **2.** Characterized by ceremony; formal. —**cer′e•mo′ni•ous•ly** *adv.*

cer•e•mo•ny (sĕr′ə-mō′nē) ►*n., pl.* **-nies 1.** A formal act performed as prescribed by ritual, custom, or etiquette. **2.** A conventional social gesture or courtesy: *the ceremony of shaking hands.* **3.** Strict observance of formalities or etiquette. [< Lat. *caerimōnia*, religious rite.]

Ce•res (sîr′ēz) ►*n. Rom. Myth.* The goddess of agriculture.

ce•re•us (sîr′ē-əs) ►*n.* Any of a genus of cactus that includes the saguaro and several night-blooming species. [< Lat. *cēreus*, candle.]

ce•rise (sə-rēs′, -rēz′) ►*n.* A purplish red. [< OFr., CHERRY.]

ce•ri•um (sîr′ē-əm) ►*n. Symbol* **Ce** A lustrous, iron-gray, malleable metallic element, used in various metallurgical and nuclear applications. At. no. 58. See table at **element.** [< the asteroid *Ceres.*]

Cer•ro de Pun•ta (sĕr′ō də pōōn′tə, -tä) A mountain, 1,338.6 m (4,389 ft), of central Puerto Rico in the Cordillera Central.

cer•tain (sûr′tn) ►*adj.* **1.** Definite; fixed. **2.** Sure to come or happen. **3.** Established beyond doubt. **4.** Having no doubt; confident. **5.** Not identified but assumed to be known: *a certain teacher.* **6.** Limited: *to a certain degree.* ►*pron.* An indefinite number; some. [< Lat. *cernere, cert-*, determine.] —**cer′tain•ly** *adv.*

Syns: *certain, inescapable, inevitable, sure, unavoidable* **adj.**

cer•tain•ty (sûr′tn-tē) ►*n., pl.* **-ties 1.** The fact, quality, or state of being certain. **2.** Something that is clearly established.

cer•tif•i•cate (sər-tĭf′ĭ-kĭt) ►*n.* **1.** A document testifying to the truth of something. **2.** A document certifying completion of requirements, as of a course of study. **3.** A document certifying ownership. [< LLat. *certificāre*, CERTIFY.]

cer•ti•fi•ca•tion (sûr′tə-fĭ-kā′shən) ►*n.* **1a.** The act of certifying. **b.** The state of being certified. **2.** A certified statement.

cer•ti•fied check (sûr′tə-fīd′) ►*n.* A check guaranteed by a bank to be covered by sufficient funds on deposit.

certified public accountant ►*n.* An accountant certified by a state examining board as having met the state's legal requirements.

cer•ti•fy (sûr′tə-fī′) ►*v.* **1. -fied, -fy•ing** To confirm formally as true, accurate, or genuine. **2.** To acknowledge on (a check) that the maker has sufficient funds on deposit for payment. **3.** To issue a certificate to. **4.** To declare legally insane. [< Lat. *certus*, CERTAIN.] —**cer′ti•fi′a•ble** *adj.* —**cer′ti•fi′a•bly** *adv.* —**cer′ti•fi′er** *n.*

cer•ti•tude (sûr′tĭ-tōōd′, -tyōōd′) ►*n.* The state of being certain. [< Lat. *certus*, CERTAIN.]

ce•ru•le•an (sə-rōō′lē-ən) ►*adj.* Azure; sky-blue. [< Lat. *caeruleus*, dark blue.]

ce•ru•men (sə-rōō′mən) ►*n.* See **earwax.** [< Lat. *cēra*, wax.] —**ce•ru′mi•nous** *adj.*

Cer•van•tes Sa•a•ve•dra (sər-văn′tēz sä′ə-vā′drə), **Miguel de.** 1547–1616. Spanish writer.

cer•vi•cal (sûr′vĭ-kəl) ►*adj.* Of or relating to a neck or cervix.

cer•vix (sûr′vĭks) ►*n., pl.* **-vix•es** or **-vi•ces** (-vĭ-sēz′, sər-vī′sēz) **1.** The neck. **2.** A neck-shaped anatomical structure, such as the outer end of the uterus. [Lat. *cervīx.*]

ce•sar•e•an also **cae•sar•e•an** or **cae•sar•i•an** or **ce•sar•i•an** (sĭ-zâr′ē-ən) ►*n.* A cesarean section. —**ce•sar′e•an** *adj.*

cesarean section ►*n.* A surgical incision through the abdominal wall and uterus to deliver a fetus. [< the tradition that Julius CAESAR was so delivered.]

ce•si•um also **cae•si•um** (sē′zē-əm) ►*n. Symbol* **Cs** A soft, silvery-white, highly electropositive metallic element, used in photoelectric cells. At. no. 55. See table at **element.** [< Lat. *caesius*, bluish gray.]

ces•sa•tion (sĕ-sā′shən) ►*n.* A ceasing; halt. [< Lat. *cessāre*, cease.]

ces•sion (sĕsh′ən) ►*n.* A ceding or surrendering, as of territory to another country by treaty. [< Lat. *cēdere, cess-*, yield.]

cess•pool (sĕs′pōōl′) ►*n.* A covered hole or pit for receiving drainage, waste, or sewage. [< ME *suspiral*, vent.]

ce•su•ra (sĭ-zhŏŏr′ə, -zŏŏr′ə) ►*n.* Var. of **caesura.**

ce•ta•cean (sĭ-tā′shən) ►*n.* Any of a group of aquatic, chiefly marine mammals that includes the whales, dolphins, and porpoises. [< Lat. *cētus*, whale.] —**ce•ta′cean, ce•ta′ceous** *adj.*

Ceu•ta (syōō′tə, sĕ′ōō-tä) A Spanish city of NW Africa, an enclave in Morocco on the Strait of Gibraltar. Pop. 68,882.

Cey•lon (sĭ-lŏn′, sā-) See **Sri Lanka.** —**Cey′lo•nese′** (-nēz′, -nēs′) *adj. & n.*

Cé•zanne (sā-zăn′, -zän′), **Paul.** 1839–1906. French postimpressionist artist.

Cf ► The symbol for the element **californium.**

CF ►*abbr.* **1.** cost and frieght **2.** cystic fibrosis

cf. ►*abbr. Lat.* confer (compare)

C/F ►*abbr. Accounting* carried forward

CFC ►*abbr.* chlorofluorocarbon

CFI ►*abbr.* cost, freight, and insurance

CFIDS (sē′fĭdz′) ►*abbr.* chronic fatigue immune dysfunction syndrome

CFS ►*abbr.* chronic fatigue syndrome

cg ►*abbr.* centigram

CG ►*abbr.* coast guard

ch ►*abbr.* chain (measurement)

ch. ►*abbr.* **1.** chapter **2.** check (bank order)

Ch. ►*abbr.* **1.** chaplain **2.** church

Cha•blis (shă-blē′, shä-, shăb′lē) ►*n.* A very dry white Burgundy wine. [After *Chablis*, France.]

cha-cha (chä′chä) ►*n.* A rhythmic ballroom dance that originated in Latin America. [Am.Sp. *chachachá.*] —**cha′-cha** *v.*

Chad (chăd) A country of N-central Africa. Cap. N'Djamena. Pop. 4,405,000. —**Chad′i•an** *adj. & n.*

Chad, Lake. A lake of N-central Africa in Chad, Cameroon, Niger, and Nigeria.

Chad•ic (chăd′ĭk) ►*n.* A branch of the Afro-Asiatic language family.

cha•dor (chä-dôr′) ►*n.* A loose, usu. black robe worn by Muslim women that covers the body and most of the face. [< Skt. *chattram*, screen.]

chafe (chāf) ►*v.* **chafed, chaf•ing 1.** To make or become worn or sore by rubbing. **2.** To annoy; vex. **3.** To heat or warm by rubbing. [< Lat. *calefacere*, make warm.]

Syns: *chafe, abrade, excoriate, fret, gall* **v.**

chaff[1] (chăf) ►*n.* **1.** Grain husks, as of wheat, removed during threshing. **2.** Trivial or worthless matter. [< OE *ceaf.*]

chaff[2] (chăf) ►*v.* To tease good-naturedly. See Syns at **banter.** [Poss. < CHAFE.] —**chaff** *n.*

chaf•finch (chăf′ĭnch) ►*n.* A small European songbird. [< OE *ceaffinc.*]

chaf•ing dish (chā′fĭng) ►*n.* A pan mounted above a heating device, used to cook food at the table.

Cha•gall (shə-gäl′), **Marc.** 1887–1985. Russian-born artist.

cha•grin (shə-grĭn′) ►*n.* A feeling of embarrassment, humiliation, or annoyance. ►*v.* To cause to feel chagrin. See Syns at **embarrass.** [Fr.]

chain (chān) ►*n.* **1.** A connected, flexible series of links. **2. chains a.** Bonds, fetters, or shackles. **b.** Bondage. **3.** A series of related things. **4.** A number of commercial establishments under common ownership. **5.** A range of mountains. **6a.** An instrument used in surveying, consisting of 100 linked pieces of iron or steel. **b.** A unit of length equal to 100 links, or 66 ft (20.1 m). ►*v.* **1.** To bind or make fast with a chain. **2.** To fetter. [< Lat. *catēna.*]

chain gang ►*n.* A group of convicts chained together, esp. for outdoor labor.

chain mail ►*n.* Flexible armor made of joined metal links or scales.

chain reaction ►*n.* **1.** A series of events in which each induces or influences the next. **2.** *Phys.* A multistage nuclear reaction, esp. a self-sustaining series of fissions in which the release of neutrons from the splitting of one atom leads to the splitting of others. **3.** *Chem.* A series of reactions in which one product of a reacting set is a reactant in the following set. —**chain′-re•act′** *v.*

chain saw ►*n.* A portable power saw with teeth linked in an endless chain.

chain-smoke (chān′smōk′) ►*v.* To smoke (e.g., cigarettes) in close succession. —**chain smoker** *n.*

chain store ►*n.* One of a number of retail stores under the same ownership and dealing in the same merchandise.

chair (châr) ►*n.* **1.** A seat with a back, designed to accommodate one person. **2a.** A seat of office, authority, or dignity, such as that of a bishop, chairperson, or professor. **b.** One who holds such a chair. **3.** *Slang* The electric chair. **4.** A sedan chair. ►*v.* To preside over as chairperson. [< Gk. *kathedra.* See CATHEDRAL.]

chair lift ►*n.* A mechanized, cable-suspended chair assembly used to transport people up or down a mountain slope.

chair•man (châr′mən) ►*n.* The presiding officer of a meeting, committee, or board. See Usage Note at **man.** —**chair′man•ship′** *n.*

chair•per•son (châr′pûr′sən) ►*n.* A chairman or chairwoman. See Usage Note at **man.**

chair•wom•an (châr′wo͝om′ən) ►*n.* A woman presiding officer of a meeting, committee, or board. See Usage Note at **man.**

chaise (shāz) ►*n.* **1.** A two-wheeled, horse-drawn carriage with a collapsible hood. **2.** A post chaise. [< OFr. *chaiere,* CHAIR.]

chaise longue (lông′) ►*n., pl.* **chaise longues** (lông′). A reclining chair with a lengthened seat to support the outstretched legs. [Fr.]

chal•ced•o•ny (kăl-sĕd′n-ē) ►*n., pl.* **-nies.** A translucent milky or grayish quartz. [< Gk. *khalkēdōn,* a mystical stone.]

Chal•de•a or **Chal•dae•a** (kăl-dē′ə). An ancient region of S Mesopotamia. —**Chal•de′an** *adj. & n.*

cha•let (shă-lā′, shăl′ā) ►*n.* **1.** A wooden dwelling with a sloping roof and overhanging eaves, common in Alpine regions. **2.** The hut of an Alpine herder. [Fr.]

chal•ice (chăl′ĭs) ►*n.* **1.** A cup or goblet. **2.** A cup for the consecrated wine of the Eucharist. [< Lat. *calix.*]

chalk (chôk) ►*n.* **1.** A soft compact calcite, $CaCO_3$, derived chiefly from fossil seashells. **2.** A piece of chalk used for marking on a surface such as a blackboard. ►*v.* To mark, draw, or write with chalk. —***phrasal verb:* chalk up** **1.** To earn or score. **2.** To credit or ascribe: *Chalk that up to experience.* [< Lat. *calx,* limestone.] —**chalk′y** *adj.*

chalk•board (chôk′bôrd′, -bōrd′) ►*n.* A blackboard.

chal•lenge (chăl′ənj) ►*n.* **1.** A call to engage in a contest, fight, or competition. **2.** A demand for an explanation. **3.** A sentry's call for identification. **4.** A formal objection, esp. to the qualifications of a juror or voter. ►*v.* **-lenged, -leng•ing 1a.** To call to engage in a contest. **b.** To invite with defiance; dare. See Syns at **defy. 2.** To call into question; dispute. **3.** To order to halt and be identified. **4.** To take formal objection to (a juror or voter). **5.** To summon to action or effort; stimulate. [< Lat. *calumnia,* accusation.] —**chal′leng•er** *n.*

chal•lenged (chăl′ənjd) ►*adj.* **1.** Having a disability or impairment. **2.** Deficient or lacking: *ethically challenged.*

Usage: People who object to the terms *disabled* and *handicapped* as too negative sometimes propose the substitution of *challenged.* While popular, especially in the phrase *physically challenged,* the use of the word can be taken as condescending.

chal•leng•ing (chăl′ən-jĭng) ►*adj.* Calling for full use of one's abilities or resources.

chal•lis (shăl′ē) ►*n.* A lightweight, usu. printed fabric of wool, cotton, or rayon. [Poss. < the surname *Challis.*]

cham•ber (chām′bər) ►*n.* **1.** A room, esp. a bedroom. **2. chambers** A judge's office. **3.** A hall, esp. for the meetings of a legislative or other assembly. **4.** A legislative, judicial, or deliberative body. **5.** An enclosed space; a compartment or cavity. **6.** A compartment in a firearm that holds the cartridge. [< LLat. *camera.*] —**cham′bered** *adj.*

cham•ber•lain (chām′bər-lĭn) ►*n.* **1a.** A chief steward. **b.** A high-ranking official in a royal court. **2.** A treasurer. [< OFr. *chamberlenc.*]

Chamberlain, (Arthur) Neville. 1869–1940. British prime minister (1937–40).

Chamberlain, Wilton Norman. "Wilt." 1936–99. Amer. basketball player.

cham•ber•maid (chām′bər-mād′) ►*n.* A maid who cleans bedrooms, as in a hotel.

chamber music ►*n.* Music, as for a trio or quartet, appropriate for performance in a small concert hall.

chamber of commerce ►*n.* An association of businesses for the promotion of commercial interests in the community.

cham•bray (shăm′brā′) ►*n.* A fine, lightweight fabric woven with white threads across a colored warp. [After *Cambrai,* France.]

cha•me•leon (kə-mēl′yən, -mē′lē-ən) ►*n.* **1.** Any of various tropical Old World lizards capable of changing color. **2.** See **anole. 3.** A changeable person. [< Gk. *khamaileōn* : *kha-*

mai, on the ground + *leōn*, lion.]

chameleon
Meller's chameleon

cham•fer (chăm′fər) ►*v.* **1.** To cut off the edge or corner of; bevel. **2.** To cut a groove in; flute. [Poss. < OFr. *chanfreindre*, to bevel.] —**cham′fer** *n.*

cham•ois (shăm′ē) ►*n., pl.* **cham•ois** (shăm′ēz) **1.** A goat antelope of mountainous regions of Europe. **2.** also **cham•my** or **sham•my** (shăm′ē), *pl.* **-mies a.** A soft leather made from the hide of a chamois. **b.** A piece of such leather used esp. as a polishing cloth. [< LLat. *camōx.*]

cham•o•mile or **cam•o•mile** (kăm′ə-mīl′, -mēl′) ►*n.* An aromatic plant having daisylike white flower heads that are used for herbal tea and in flavorings. [< Gk. *khamaimēlon* : *khamai*, on the ground + *mēlon*, apple.]

champ[1] (chămp) ►*v.* To chew upon noisily. —***idiom:* champ at the bit** To show impatience at being delayed. [Prob. imit.]

champ[2] (chămp) ►*n. Informal* A champion.

cham•pagne (shăm-pān′) ►*n.* A sparkling white wine orig. produced in Champagne.

Cham•pagne (shăm-pān′, shäN-pän′yə) A region and former province of NE France.

cham•pi•on (chăm′pē-ən) ►*n.* **1.** One that holds first place or wins first prize in a contest. **2.** An ardent defender or supporter of a cause or another person. ►*v.* To fight for, defend, or support as a champion. [< Med.Lat. *campiō* < Lat. *campus*, field.]

cham•pi•on•ship (chăm′pē-ən-shĭp′) ►*n.* **1.** The position or title of a champion. **2.** Defense or support. **3.** A competition held to determine a champion.

Cham•plain (shăm-plān′), **Lake.** A lake of NE NY, NW VT, and S Quebec, Canada.

Cham•plain (shăm-plān′, shäN-plăN′), **Samuel de.** 1567?–1635. French explorer.

chance (chăns) ►*n.* **1a.** The unknown and unpredictable element in happenings that seems to have no assignable cause. **b.** This element viewed as a cause of events; luck. **2.** often **chances** The likelihood of something happening; probability. **3.** An accidental or unpredictable event. **4.** An opportunity. **5.** A risk or hazard. **6.** A raffle or lottery ticket. ►*v.* **chanced, chanc•ing 1.** To come about by chance. See Syns at **happen. 2.** To risk; hazard. —***phrasal verb:* chance on** To find accidentally; happen upon. [< OFr. < Lat. *cadere*, befall.]

chan•cel (chăn′səl) ►*n.* The space around the altar of a church for the clergy and often the choir. [< OFr. < LLat. *cancellus*, latticework.]

chan•cel•ler•y or **chan•cel•lor•y** (chăn′sə-lə-rē, -slə-rē) ►*n., pl.* **-ies 1.** The rank or position of a chancellor. **2.** The official place of business of an embassy or consulate.

chan•cel•lor (chăn′sə-lər, -slər) ►*n.* **1.** The chief minister of state in some countries. **2.** The head of a university. **3.** *Law* The presiding judge of a court of equity. [< LLat. *cancellārius*, doorkeeper.] —**chan′cel•lor•ship′** *n.*

chan•cer•y (chăn′sə-rē) ►*n., pl.* **-ies 1.** *Law* **a.** A court with jurisdiction in equity. **b.** An office of archives. **2.** The office of a chancellor. [< ME *chancelrie*, chancellery.]

chan•cre (shăng′kər) ►*n.* A dull red, hard, insensitive lesion that is the first sign of syphilis. [< Lat. *cancer*, crab, tumor.] —**chan′crous** (-krəs) *adj.*

chanc•y (chăn′sē) ►*adj.* **-i•er, -i•est.** Uncertain as to outcome; risky.

chan•de•lier (shăn′də-lîr′) ►*n.* A branched lighting fixture holding bulbs or candles, usu. suspended from a ceiling. [< Lat. *candēlābrum*, candelabrum.]

chan•dler (chănd′lər) ►*n.* **1.** One that makes or sells candles. **2.** A dealer in specified goods: *a ship chandler.* [< Lat. *candēla*, CANDLE.] —**chan′dler•y** (chănd′lə-rē) *n.*

change (chānj) ►*v.* **changed, chang•ing 1.** To be or cause to be different; alter. **2.** To interchange. **3.** To exchange for or replace with another. **4.** To transfer from (one conveyance) to another: *change planes.* **5.** To give or receive an equivalent sum of money in lower denominations or in foreign currency. **6.** To put fresh clothes or coverings on. ►*n.* **1.** The act or result of changing. **2.** A fresh set of clothing. **3a.** Money of smaller denomination changed for money of higher denomination. **b.** The balance of money returned when an amount given is more than what is due. **c.** Coins. [< Lat. *cambiāre*, exchange.] —**change′a•bil′i•ty, change′a•ble•ness** *n.* —**change′a•ble** *adj.* —**change′less** *adj.* —**chang′er** *n.*

change•ling (chānj′lĭng) ►*n.* A child secretly exchanged for another.

change of life ►*n.* Menopause.

change•o•ver (chānj′ō′vər) ►*n.* A conversion, as from one system to another.

Chang Jiang (chäng′ jyäng′) or **Yang•tze River** (yăng′sē′, -tsē′). The longest river of China and of Asia, flowing about 5,551 km (3,450 mi) from Xizang (Tibet) to the East China Sea.

Chang•sha (chäng′shä′) A city of S China on the Xiang Jiang WSW of Shanghai. Pop. 1,328,950.

chan•nel (chăn′əl) ►*n.* **1.** The bed of a stream or river. **2.** The deeper part of a river or harbor, esp. a navigable passage. **3.** A strait. **4.** A trench, furrow, or groove. **5.** A tubular passage. **6.** A means of passage. **7.** often **channels** Official routes of communication. **8.** A specified frequency band for the transmission and reception of electromagnetic signals. **9.** A site on a network where online conversations are held in real time. ►*v.* **-neled, -nel•ing** also **-nelled, -nel•ling 1.** To make or form channels in. **2.** To direct along a channel or path. [< Lat. *canālis.*] —**chan′nel•i•za′tion** *n.* —**chan′nel•ize′** *v.*

Channel Islands. A group of British islands in the English Channel off the coast of Normandy, France.

chan•nel-surf (chăn′əl-sûrf′) ►*v.* To watch a number of different television channels in rapid succession. —**channel surfer** *n.*

chan•son (shäN-sôN′) ►*n.* A song, esp. a French one. [< OFr. < Lat. *cantāre*, sing.]

chant (chănt) ►*n.* **1a.** A series of syllables sung on the same note or a limited range of notes. **b.** A canticle sung thus. **2.** A monotonous rhythmic call or shout. ►*v.* **1.** To sing (a chant). **2.** To celebrate in song. **3.** To utter (e.g., a slogan) in the manner of a chant. [< Lat. *cantus*, song.] —**chant′er** *n.*

chan•teuse (shäN-tœz′) ►*n.* A woman singer, esp. in a nightclub. [Fr. < *chanter*, sing.]

chan•tey (shăn′tē, chăn′-) ►*n.*, *pl.* **-teys.** A song sailors sing to the rhythm of their work. [Prob. < OFr. *chanter*, sing.]

chan•ti•cleer (chăn′tĭ-klîr′, shăn′-) ►*n.* A rooster. [< OFr. *chantecler.*]

Cha•nu•kah (KHä′nə-kə, hä′-) ►*n.* Var. of **Hanukkah.**

cha•os (kā′ŏs′) ►*n.* **1.** Great disorder or confusion. **2. Chaos** The disordered state held to have existed before the ordered universe. [< Gk. *khaos*, unformed matter.] —**cha•ot′ic** *adj.* —**cha•ot′i•cal•ly** *adv.*

chap[1] (chăp) ►*v.* **chapped, chap•ping.** To split or roughen (the skin), esp. from cold or exposure. [ME *chappen.*]

chap[2] (chăp) ►*n. Informal* A man or boy; fellow. [< CHAPMAN.]

chap•ar•ral (shăp′ə-răl′) ►*n.* A dense thicket of shrubs. [Sp.]

cha•pa•ti (chə-pä′tē) ►*n.*, *pl.* **-ti.** A flat, unleavened, disk-shaped bread of N India. [Hindi *capātī.*]

chap•el (chăp′əl) ►*n.* **1.** A place of worship that is smaller than and subordinate to a church, esp. in a prison, college, or hospital. **2.** A place of worship for those not belonging to an established church. **3.** The services held at a chapel. [< OFr. *chapele.*]

chap•er•on or **chap•er•one** (shăp′ə-rōn′) ►*n.* **1.** A person, esp. an older or married woman, who accompanies and supervises young unmarried people. **2.** An older person who attends and supervises a social gathering for young people. ►*v.* **-oned, -on•ing.** To act as chaperon to or for. [< OFr., hood.]

chap•lain (chăp′lĭn) ►*n.* A member of the clergy attached to a chapel, legislative assembly, or military unit. [< Med.Lat. *capellānus* < *capella*, chapel.] —**chap′lain•cy, chap′lain•ship′** *n.*

chap•let (chăp′lĭt) ►*n.* **1.** A wreath for the head. **2.** *Rom. Cath. Ch.* A rosary having beads for five decades. **3.** A string of beads. [< OFr. *chapelet*, small hat.]

Chap•lin (chăp′lĭn), Sir **Charles Spencer.** "Charlie." 1889–1977. British-born actor, director, and producer.

chap•man (chăp′mən) ►*n. Chiefly Brit.* A peddler. [< OE *cēapman.*]

chaps (chăps, shăps) ►*pl.n.* Heavy leather trousers without a seat, worn by horseback riders to protect their legs. [< Am.Sp. *chaparreras.*]

chap•ter (chăp′tər) ►*n.* **1.** A main division of a book. **2.** A local branch of a club or fraternity. **3.** An assembly of members, as of a religious order. [< Lat. *capitulum.*]

char[1] (chär) ►*v.* **charred, char•ring 1.** To scorch or become scorched. **2.** To reduce or be reduced to carbon or charcoal by incomplete combustion. [< CHARCOAL.]

char[2] (chär) ►*n.*, *pl.* **char** or **chars.** Any of several fishes related to the trout. [?]

char[3] (chär) *Chiefly Brit.* ►*n.* A charwoman. ►*v.* **charred, char•ring.** To work as a charwoman. [< OE *cierr*, a turn, job.]

char•ac•ter (kăr′ək-tər) ►*n.* **1.** The qualities that distinguish one person from another. **2.** A distinguishing feature or attribute. **3.** *Genet.* A structure, function, or attribute determined by a gene or group of genes. **4.** Moral or ethical strength. **5.** Reputation. **6.** An eccentric person. **7.** A person portrayed in a drama or novel. **8.** A symbol in a writing system. **9.** *Comp. Sci.* **a.** A symbol, such as a letter or number, that expresses information. **b.** The code that represents such a symbol. [< Gk. *kharaktēr.*]

char•ac•ter•is•tic (kăr′ək-tə-rĭs′tĭk) ►*adj.* Distinctive; typical. ►*n.* A distinguishing attribute. —**char′ac•ter•is′ti•cal•ly** *adv.*

char•ac•ter•ize (kăr′ək-tə-rīz′) ►*v.* **-ized, -iz•ing 1.** To describe the qualities of. **2.** To be a distinctive trait or mark of. —**char′ac•ter•iz′er** *n.* —**char′ac•ter•i•za′tion** *n.*

cha•rade (shə-rād′) ►*n.* **1. charades** *(takes sing. or pl. v.)* A game in which words or phrases are represented in pantomime until guessed by the other players. **2.** A pretense; sham. [Fr.]

char•broil (chär′broil′) ►*v.* To broil over charcoal: *charbroil a steak.*

char•coal (chär′kōl′) ►*n.* **1.** A black, porous, carbonaceous material produced by the destructive distillation of wood and used as a fuel, filter, and absorbent. **2.** A drawing pencil made from charcoal. **3.** A dark gray. [ME *charcol.*]

chard (chärd) ►*n.* Swiss chard. [< Fr. *carde.*]

charge (chärj) ►*v.* **charged, charg•ing 1.** To impose a duty or responsibility on. **2.** To set as a price. **3.** To demand payment from. **4.** To purchase on credit. **5a.** To load or fill. **b.** To saturate: *an atmosphere charged with tension.* **6.** To instruct or command authoritatively. **7.** To accuse or blame. **8.** To attack violently. **9.** *Elect.* **a.** To cause formation of a net electric charge on or in (a conductor). **b.** To energize (a storage battery). ►*n.* **1.** Price; cost. **2a.** A burden; load. **b.** The quantity that a container or apparatus can hold. **3.** A quantity of explosive to be set off at one time. **4.** A duty or responsibility. **5.** One entrusted to another's care. **6a.** Supervision; management. **b.** Care; custody: *a child put in my charge.* See Syns at **care. 7.** A command or injunction. **8.** An accusation or indictment. **9.** A rushing, forceful attack. **10.** A debt in an account. **11.** *Symbol* **q** *Phys.* **a.** The intrinsic property of matter responsible for all electric phenomena, occurring in two forms arbitrarily designated *negative* and *positive.* **b.** A measure of this property. **12.** *Informal* A feeling of pleasant excitement; thrill. [< LLat. *carricāre*, to load.]

Syns: *charge, imbue, impregnate, permeate, pervade, saturate, suffuse* **v.**

charge account ►*n.* A credit arrangement in which a customer receives purchased goods or services before paying for them.

charge card ►*n.* See **credit card.**

char•gé d'af•faires (shär-zhā′ də-fâr′, dä-) ►*n.*, *pl.* **char•gés d'affaires** (-zhā′, -zhāz′). A diplomat who temporarily substitutes for an absent ambassador or minister. [Fr.]

charg•er (chär′jər) ►*n.* **1.** One that charges,

such as a device that charges storage batteries. **2.** A horse trained for battle.

char•i•ot (chăr′ē-ət) ►*n.* An ancient horse-drawn two-wheeled vehicle used in war, races, and processions. [< Lat. *carrus*, vehicle.] —**char′i•o•teer′** *n.*

cha•ris•ma (kə-rĭz′mə) ►*n.* A personal quality attributed to those who arouse fervent popular devotion and enthusiasm. [Gk. *kharisma*, divine favor.]

char•is•mat•ic (kăr′ĭz-măt′ĭk) ►*adj.* **1.** Of or relating to charisma. **2.** Of or being a type of Christianity that emphasizes personal religious experience and divinely inspired powers. ►*n.* A member of a Christian charismatic group.

char•i•ta•ble (chăr′ĭ-tə-bəl) ►*adj.* **1.** Generous to the needy. **2.** Tolerant in judging others. **3.** Of or for charity. See Syns at **benevolent.** —**char′i•ta•bly** *adv.*

char•i•ty (chăr′ĭ-tē) ►*n., pl.* **-ties 1.** Help or relief given to the poor. **2.** An organization or fund that helps the needy. **3.** Benevolence toward others. **4.** Forbearance in judging others. **5.** often **Charity** *Christianity* Love directed first toward God but also toward oneself and one's neighbors. [< Lat. *cāritās*, affection.]

char•la•tan (shär′lə-tən) ►*n.* A person who makes elaborate and fraudulent claims to skill or knowledge. [< Ital. *ciarlatano.*] —**char′la•tan•ism, char′la•tan•ry** *n.*

Char•le•magne (shär′lə-mān′). Also called Charles I or "Charles the Great." 742?–814. King of the Franks (768–814); emperor of the West (800–814).

Charles (chärlz). Prince of Wales. b. 1948. Prince of Wales (since 1969).

Charles I. 1600–49. King of England, Scotland, and Ireland (1625–49).

Charles II. 1630–85. King of England, Scotland, and Ireland (1660–85).

Charles V. 1500–58. Holy Roman emperor (1519–58) and king of Spain as Charles I (1516–56).

Charles VII. 1403–61. King of France (1422–61).

Charles IX. 1550–74. King of France (1560–74).

Charles X. 1757–1836. King of France (1824–30).

Charles Mar•tel (mär-tĕl′). 688?–741. Frankish ruler (715–741).

Charles•ton[1] (chärl′stən) **1.** A city of SE SC NE of Savannah. Pop. 80,414. **2.** The capital of WV, in the W-central part. Pop. 57,287.

Charles•ton[2] (chärl′stən) ►*n.* A fast ballroom dance popular in the 1920s. [After CHARLESTON [1], South Carolina.]

char•ley horse (chär′lē) ►*n. Informal* A muscle cramp. [?]

Char•lotte (shär′lət) A city of S NC SSW of Winston-Salem. Pop. 395,934.

Charlotte A•ma•lie (ə-mäl′yə) The capital of the US Virgin Islands, on St. Thomas I. in the West Indies E of Puerto Rico. Pop. 11,842.

Char•lotte•town (shär′lət-toun′) The capital of Prince Edward I., Canada, on the S coast. Pop. 15,282.

charm (chärm) ►*n.* **1.** The quality of pleasing or delighting. **2.** A small ornament worn on a bracelet. **3.** An item worn for its supposed magical benefit; amulet. **4.** An action or formula thought to have magical power. ►*v.* **1.** To attract or delight greatly. **2.** To cast or seem to cast a spell on; bewitch. [< Lat. *carmen*, incantation.] —**charm′er** *n.* —**charm′ing•ly** *adj.* —**charm′less** *adj.*

Syns: *charm, beguile, bewitch, captivate, enchant, entrance, fascinate* **v.**

char•nel house (chär′nəl) ►*n.* **1.** A repository for the bones or bodies of the dead. **2.** A scene of great carnage or loss of life. [< Lat. *carnālis*, of flesh.]

Char•on (kâr′ən) ►*n. Gk. Myth.* The ferryman of Hades.

chart (chärt) ►*n.* **1.** A map. **2.** A sheet presenting information in the form of graphs or tables. ►*v.* **1.** To make a chart of. **2.** To plan. [< Lat. *charta*, papyrus paper. See CARD[1].]

char•ter (chär′tər) ►*n.* **1.** A document issued by a government authority, creating a corporation and defining its privileges and purposes. **2.** A document outlining the organization of a corporate body. **3.** An authorization from an organization to establish a local chapter. **4a.** A contract to lease a vessel. **b.** The hiring of an aircraft, vessel, or other vehicle. ►*v.* **1.** To grant a charter to. **2.** To hire or lease by charter. [< Lat. *chartula*, piece of papyrus.]

charter member ►*n.* An original member of an organization.

charter school ►*n.* An independent public school, often with a distinct curriculum and educational philosophy.

Char•tres (shärt, shär′trə) A city of N France SW of Paris. Pop. 37,119.

char•treuse (shär-tro͞oz′) ►*n.* A strong greenish yellow to yellow green. [< *Chartreuse*, trademark for a type of liqueur.]

char•wom•an (chär′wo͝om′ən) ►*n.* A cleaning woman.

char•y (châr′ē) ►*adj.* **-i•er, -i•est 1.** Very cautious. **2.** Not giving freely; sparing. [< OE *cearig*, sorrowful.] —**char′i•ly** *adv.* —**char′i•ness** *n.*

chase[1] (chās) ►*v.* **chased, chas•ing 1.** To follow rapidly in order to catch; pursue. **2.** To hunt. **3.** To put to flight: *chased the dog away.* ►*n.* **1.** The act of chasing. **2.** The hunting of game. [< Lat. *captāre.*]

chase[2] (chās) ►*n.* **1.** A groove cut in an object; slot. **2.** A trench or channel for drainpipes or wiring. ►*v.* **chased, chas•ing.** To decorate (metal) by engraving or embossing. [Prob. < Lat. *capsa*, box.]

chas•er (chā′sər) ►*n.* **1.** One that chases. **2.** *Informal* A drink of beer or water taken after hard liquor.

chasm (kăz′əm) ►*n.* **1.** A deep opening in the earth; gorge. **2.** A great disparity, as of opinion or interests. [< Gk. *khasma.*]

Chas•sid (KHä′sĭd, KHô′-, hä′-) ►*n.* Var. of **Hasid.** —**Chas•si′dic** *adj.* —**Chas•si′dism** *n.*

chas•sis (shăs′ē, chăs′ē) ►*n., pl.* **chas•sis** (-ēz) **1.** The rectangular steel frame that holds the body and motor of an automotive vehicle. **2.** The landing gear of an aircraft. **3.** The framework to which the components of a radio, television, or other electronic equipment are attached. [< OFr., frame < Lat. *capsa*, box.]

chaste (chāst) ►*adj.* **chast•er, chast•est 1.** Morally pure; modest. **2.** Abstaining from illicit sexual acts or thoughts. **3.** Simple in design or style; austere. [< Lat. *castus.*]

—**chaste′ly** *adv.* —**chaste′ness** *n.* —**chas′ti•ty** (chăs′tĭ-tē) *n.*

chas•ten (chā′sən) ►*v.* **1.** To correct by punishment or reproof. **2.** To restrain; subdue. [< Lat. *castigāre.*] —**chas′ten•er** *n.*

chas•tise (chăs-tīz′, chăs′tīz′) ►*v.* **-tised, -tis•ing 1.** To punish, as by beating. **2.** To criticize severely. [< ME *chastien,* CHASTEN.] —**chas•tise′ment** *n.* —**chas•tis′er** *n.*

chas•u•ble (chăz′ə-bəl, chăzh′-, chăs′-) ►*n.* A long sleeveless vestment worn over the alb by a priest at Mass. [< LLat. *casubla,* hooded garment, dim. of *casa,* house.]

chat (chăt) ►*v.* **chat•ted, chat•ting 1.** To converse in an easy manner. **2.** To converse in real time over a computer network. ►*n.* **1.** An informal conversation. **2.** Any of several birds with a chattering call. [< ME *chattern,* chatter.] —**chat′ti•ness** *n.* —**chat′ty** *adj.*

cha•teau also **châ•teau** (shă-tō′) ►*n., pl.* **-teaus** or **-teaux** (-tōz′) **1.** A French castle. **2.** A large country house. [< OFr. *chastel,* CASTLE.]

Châ•teau•bri•and (shä-tō′brē-äN′, shă-), Vicomte **François René de.** 1768–1848. French diplomat and writer.

chat•room (chăt′ro͞om′, -ro͝om′) ►*n.* A site on a computer network where online conversations are held in real time.

Chat•ta•noo•ga (chăt′ə-no͞o′gə) A city of SE TN SE of Nashville. Pop. 152,466.

chat•tel (chăt′l) ►*n.* **1.** *Law* An article of personal, movable property. **2.** A slave. [< Med. Lat. *capitāle,* property.]

chat•ter (chăt′ər) ►*v.* **1.** To talk rapidly and incessantly on trivial subjects. **2.** To utter inarticulate speechlike sounds. **3.** To click quickly and repeatedly, as the teeth from cold. [ME *chateren.*] —**chat′ter** *n.*

chat•ter•box (chăt′ər-bŏks′) ►*n.* An extremely talkative person.

Chat•ter•ton (chăt′ər-tən), **Thomas.** 1752–70. British poet.

Chau•cer (chô′sər), **Geoffrey.** 1340?–1400. English poet. —**Chau•cer′i•an** (-sîr′ē-ən) *adj. & n.*

Chaucer
from a page of *The Canterbury Tales*

chauf•feur (shō′fər, shō-fûr′) ►*n.* One employed to drive an automobile. [Fr., stoker.] —**chauf′feur** *v.*

chau•vin•ism (shō′və-nĭz′əm) ►*n.* **1.** Fanatical patriotism. **2.** Prejudiced belief in the superiority of one's own group. [Fr. *chauvinisme,* after Nicolas *Chauvin,* legendary French soldier.] —**chau′vin•ist** *n.* —**chau′vin•is′tic** *adj.* —**chau′vin•is′ti•cal•ly** *adv.*

cheap (chēp) ►*adj.* **-er, -est 1.** Inexpensive. **2.** Charging low prices. **3.** Achieved with little effort. **4.** Of little value. **5.** Of poor quality; inferior. **6.** Vulgar or contemptible. **7.** Stingy. ►*adv.* **-er, -est.** Inexpensively: *got the new car cheap.* [< OE *cēap,* trade < Lat. *caupō,* shopkeeper.] —**cheap′ly** *adv.* —**cheap′ness** *n.*

cheap•en (chē′pən) ►*v.* **1.** To make or become cheap. **2.** To debase or degrade.

cheap shot ►*n.* An unfair verbal attack on a vulnerable target.

cheap•skate (chēp′skāt′) ►*n. Slang* A miser.

cheat (chēt) ►*v.* **1.** To deceive by trickery; swindle. **2.** To act dishonestly. **3.** To elude; escape: *cheat death.* **4.** To be sexually unfaithful. ►*n.* **1.** A fraud or swindle. **2.** One that cheats; swindler. [ME *cheten,* confiscate.] —**cheat′er** *n.* —**cheat′ing•ly** *adv.*

Che•bok•sa•ry (chĭ-bŏk-sär′ē) A city of W-central Russia. Pop. 445,707.

Chech•en (chĕch′ən) ►*n.* **1.** A native or inhabitant of Chechnya. **2.** The Caucasian language of the Chechens.

Chech•nya (chĕch′nē-ə, chĕch-nyä′) A region of SW Russia in the N Caucasus bordering on Georgia.

check (chĕk) ►*n.* **1.** A curb or restraint. **2.** An abrupt stop or halt. **3.** An instance of inspecting or testing. **4.** A standard for inspecting or evaluating. **5.** A mark to show verification. **6.** A slip for identification: *a baggage check.* **7.** A bill at a restaurant or bar. **8.** A written order to a bank to pay an amount from funds on deposit. **9a.** A pattern of small squares. **b.** A fabric patterned with squares. **10.** *Games* A move in chess that directly attacks an opponent's king. **11.** *Sports* The act of checking in ice hockey. ►*v.* **1.** To arrest the motion of abruptly. **2.** To curb; restrain. **3.** To inspect, as to determine accuracy or quality: *check the brakes.* **4.** To verify: *check a spelling in the dictionary.* **5.** To put a check mark on. **6.** To deposit for temporary safekeeping: *check one's coat.* **7.** *Sports* To block or impede (an opposing player with the puck) in ice hockey by using one's body or one's stick. —***phrasal verbs:*** **check in** To register, as at a hotel. **check out 1.** To settle one's bill and leave, as from a hotel. **2.** To withdraw (an item) after recording the withdrawal: *check out books.* **3.** To pay for purchases, as at a supermarket. [< Ar. *šāh,* check in chess < Pers., king.] —**check′a•ble** *adj.*

check•book (chĕk′bo͝ok′) ►*n.* A book containing blank checks issued by a bank.

check•er (chĕk′ər) ►*n.* **1a.** One that checks. **b.** One who receives items for temporary safekeeping: *a baggage checker.* **2.** *Games* **a. checkers** *(takes sing. v.)* A game played on a checkerboard by two players, each using 12 pieces. **b.** One of the round flat pieces used in this game. ►*v.* To mark with a checked or squared pattern. [< OFr. *eschequier,* chessboard.]

check•er•board (chĕk′ər-bôrd′, -bōrd′) ►*n.* A board on which chess and checkers are played, divided into 64 squares of two alternating colors.

check•ered (chĕk′ərd) ►*adj.* **1.** Divided into squares. **2.** Having light and dark patches. **3.**

Marked by great changes in fortune: *a professional boxer with a checkered career.*

check•ing account (chĕk′ĭng) ►*n.* A bank account against which checks may be written drawing from amounts on deposit.

check•mate (chĕk′māt′) ►*v.* **-mat•ed, -mat•ing 1.** To attack (a chess opponent's king) in such a manner that no escape or defense is possible, thus ending the game. **2.** To defeat completely. [< Ar. *šāh māt*, the king is dead < Pers.] —**check′mate′** *n.*

check•out (chĕk′out′) ►*n.* **1.** The act, time, or place of checking out, as at a hotel, library, or supermarket. **2.** A test, as of a machine, for proper functioning. **3.** An investigation or inspection.

check•point (chĕk′point′) ►*n.* A place where surface traffic is stopped for inspection.

check•rein (chĕk′rān′) ►*n.* A short rein that extends from a horse's bit to the saddle to keep the horse from lowering its head.

check•room (chĕk′ro͝om′, -ro͞om′) ►*n.* A place where items, such as hats or packages, can be stored temporarily.

check•up (chĕk′ŭp′) ►*n.* **1.** An examination or inspection. **2.** A physical examination.

Ched•dar also **ched•dar** (chĕd′ər) ►*n.* Any of several types of smooth hard cheese varying in flavor from mild to extra sharp. [After *Cheddar*, England.]

cheek (chēk) ►*n.* **1.** The fleshy part of either side of the face below the eye and between the nose and ear. **2.** Either of the buttocks. **3.** Impertinence. —***idiom:* cheek by jowl** Close together. [< OE *cēace.*]

cheek•bone (chēk′bōn′) ►*n.* A small bone forming the prominence of the cheek.

cheek•y (chē′kē) ►*adj.* **-i•er, -i•est.** Impertinent. —**cheek′i•ly** *adv.* —**cheek′i•ness** *n.*

cheep (chēp) ►*n.* A faint shrill sound like that of a young bird. ►*v.* To chirp. [Imit.]

cheer (chîr) ►*n.* **1.** Gaiety or joy. **2.** A source of happiness or comfort. **3.** A shout of encouragement or congratulation. ►*v.* **1.** To make or become happier. **2.** To encourage with cheers. See Syns at **encourage. 3.** To salute or acclaim with cheers. See Syns at **applaud. 4.** To shout cheers. [< OFr. *chiere*, face.] —**cheer′y** *adj.* —**cheer′less** *adj.* —**cheer′i•ly** *adv.* —**cheer′i•ness** *n.*

cheer•ful (chîr′fəl) ►*adj.* **1.** In good spirits. **2.** Promoting cheer. —**cheer′ful•ly** *adv.* —**cheer′ful•ness** *n.*

cheer•lead•er (chîr′lē′dər) ►*n.* One who leads spectators in cheering, as at a sports contest.

cheers (chîrz) ►*interj.* Used as a toast.

cheese (chēz) ►*n.* A solid food prepared from the pressed curd of milk. [< Lat. *cāseus.*]

cheese•burg•er (chēz′bûr′gər) ►*n.* A hamburger topped with melted cheese.

cheese•cake (chēz′kāk′) ►*n.* **1.** A cake made of cottage or cream cheese, eggs, milk, and sugar. **2.** *Informal* Photographs of minimally attired women.

cheese•cloth (chēz′klôth′, -klŏth′) ►*n.* A coarse, loosely woven cotton gauze.

chees•y (chē′zē) ►*adj.* **-i•er, -i•est 1.** Containing or resembling cheese. **2.** *Informal* Of poor quality; shoddy. —**chees′i•ness** *n.*

chee•tah (chē′tə) ►*n.* A long-legged, swift-running spotted wild cat of Africa and SW Asia. [< Skt. *citrakāyaḥ*, leopard.]

Chee•ver (chē′vər), **John.** 1912–82. Amer. writer.

chef (shĕf) ►*n.* A cook, esp. a chief cook. [Fr. CHIEF.]

chef-d'oeu•vre (shā-dœ′vrə, -dûrv′) ►*n.*, *pl.* **chefs-d'oeuvre** (shā-). A masterpiece. [Fr.]

chef's salad (shĕfs) ►*n.* A tossed green salad usu. with raw vegetables, hard-boiled eggs, and julienne strips of cheese and meat.

Che•khov (chĕk′ôf, -ŏf), **Anton Pavlovich.** 1860–1904. Russian writer. —**Che•kho′vi•an** (chĕ-kō′vē-ən) *adj.*

Che•lya•binsk (chĕl-yä′bĭnsk) A city of SW Russia S of Sverdlovsk. Pop. 1,129,661.

chem•i•cal (kĕm′ĭ-kəl) ►*adj.* **1.** Of or relating to chemistry. **2.** Involving or produced by chemicals. ►*n.* A substance produced by or used in a chemical process. [< Med.Lat. *alchimicus.*] —**chem′i•cal•ly** *adv.*

chemical abuse ►*n.* See **substance abuse.**

chemical bond ►*n.* Any of several forces or mechanisms, esp. the ionic bond, covalent bond, and metallic bond, by which atoms or ions are bound in a molecule or crystal.

chemical dependency ►*n.* A physical and psychological habituation to a mood- or mind-altering drug, such as alcohol or cocaine.

chemical engineering ►*n.* The technology of large-scale chemical production. —**chemical engineer** *n.*

chemical warfare ►*n.* Warfare involving poisons, contaminants, and irritants.

chem•i•lu•mi•nes•cence (kĕm′ə-lo͞o′mə-nĕs′əns) ►*n.* Emission of light as a result of a chemical reaction at environmental temperatures. —**chem′i•lu′mi•nes′cent** *adj.*

che•mise (shə-mēz′) ►*n.* **1.** A woman's loose, shirtlike undergarment. **2.** A dress that hangs straight from the shoulders. [< LLat. *camisia*, shirt.]

chem•ist (kĕm′ĭst) ►*n.* **1.** A scientist specializing in chemistry. **2.** *Chiefly Brit.* A pharmacist.

chem•is•try (kĕm′ĭ-strē) ►*n.*, *pl.* **-tries 1.** The science of the composition, structure, properties, and reactions of matter, esp. of atomic and molecular systems. **2.** The composition, structure, properties, and reactions of a substance. **3.** The interrelation of elements in a complex entity. **4.** Mutual attraction; rapport: *The chemistry was good between the partners.*

Chem•nitz (kĕm′nĭts) A city of E-central Germany SE of Leipzig. Pop. 279,520.

che•mo (kē′mō, kĕm′ō) ►*n.* *Informal* Chemotherapy.

chemo– or **chemi–** or **chem–** ►*pref.* Chemicals; chemical: *chemurgy.* [< CHEMICAL.]

che•mo•re•cep•tion (kē′mō-rĭ-sĕp′shən, kĕm′ō-) ►*n.* The response of a sense organ to a chemical stimulus. —**che′mo•re•cep′tive** *adj.* —**che′mo•re′cep•tiv′i•ty** *n.* —**che′mo•re•cep′tor** *n.*

che•mo•syn•the•sis (kē′mō-sĭn′thĭ-sĭs, kĕm′ō-) ►*n.* Synthesis of carbohydrate from carbon dioxide and water using energy from a chemical reaction rather than from light. —**che′mo•syn•thet′ic** *adj.*

che•mo•ther•a•py (kē′mō-thĕr′ə-pē, kĕm′ō-) ►*n.* The treatment of cancer and other diseases using specific chemical agents or drugs. —**che′mo•ther′a•peu′tic** *adj.* —**che′mo•ther′a•pist** *n.*

chem•ur•gy (kĕm′ər-jē, kĭ-mûr′-) ►*n.* The development of new industrial chemical products from organic raw materials, esp. from those of agricultural origin. —**che•mur′gic, che•mur′gi•cal** *adj.*

Cheng•chow (jŭng′jō′) See **Zhengzhou.**

Cheng•du also **Cheng•tu** (chŭng′dōō′). A city of S-central China WNW of Chongqing. Pop. 3,483,834.

che•nille (shə-nēl′) ► *n.* **1.** A soft tufted cord of silk, cotton, or worsted. **2.** Fabric made of this cord. [< Lat. *canīcula*, caterpillar.]

Chen•nai (chə-nī′). Formerly **Ma•dras** (mə-drăs′, -dräs′). A city of SE India on the Bay of Bengal. Pop. 3,841,396.

Che•ops (kē′ŏps). 2590–2567 B.C. Second king of the IV Dynasty of Egypt.

cheque (chĕk) ► *n. Chiefly Brit.* Var. of **check.**

cheq•uer (chĕk′ər) ► *n. Chiefly Brit.* Var. of **checker.**

cher•ish (chĕr′ĭsh) ► *v.* To treat with affection; hold dear. [< Lat. *cārus*, dear.]

Cher•no•byl (chər-nō′bəl) A city of N-central Ukraine NNW of Kiev; site of a nuclear power plant accident (Apr. 16, 1986).

Cher•o•kee (chĕr′ə-kē′, chĕr′ə-kē′) ► *n., pl.* **-kee** or **-kees 1.** A member of a Native American people formerly of the S Appalachians, now living in NE Oklahoma and W North Carolina. **2.** Their Iroquoian language.

che•root (shə-rōōt′) ► *n.* A cigar with square-cut ends. [< Tamil *curruṭṭu*.]

cher•ry (chĕr′ē) ► *n., pl.* **-ries 1.** Any of several trees or shrubs having pink or white flowers and small juicy drupes. **2.** The yellow, red, or blackish fruit of any of these plants. **3.** The wood of a cherry tree. **4.** A strong red to purplish red. [< Gk. *kerasia, kerasos*, cherry tree.]

cherry tomato ► *n.* A variety of tomato having red to yellow, cherry-sized fruits.

chert (chûrt) ► *n.* A variety of silica containing microcrystalline quartz. [?]

cher•ub (chĕr′əb) ► *n.* **1.** *pl.* **cher•u•bim** (chĕr′ə-bĭm′, -yə-bĭm′) One of the 2nd order of angels. **2.** *pl.* **cher•ubs** A small angel, portrayed as a winged child with a chubby, rosy face. [< Heb. *kərûb*.] —**che•ru′bic** (chə-rōō′bĭk) *adj.*

cher•vil (chûr′vəl) ► *n.* A Eurasian herb with parsleylike leaves used as a seasoning or garnish. [< Gk. *khairephullon*.]

Ches•a•peake (chĕs′ə-pēk′) A city of SE VA S of Norfolk. Pop. 151,976.

Chesapeake Bay. An inlet of the Atlantic separating the Delmarva Peninsula from mainland MD and VA.

chess (chĕs) ► *n.* A board game for two players, each beginning with 16 pieces, with the objective of checkmating the opposing king. [< OFr. *eschec*, CHECK.]

chess•board (chĕs′bôrd′, -bōrd′) ► *n.* A board with 64 squares, used in playing chess.

chess•man (chĕs′măn′, -mən) ► *n.* One of the pieces used in chess.

chest (chĕst) ► *n.* **1.** The part of the body between the neck and the abdomen. **2a.** A sturdy box with a lid, used for storage. **b.** A small closet or cabinet: *a medicine chest.* **3.** A bureau; dresser. [< Gk. *kistē*, box.]

ches•ter•field (chĕs′tər-fēld′) ► *n.* An overcoat with a velvet collar. [After a 19th-century earl of *Chesterfield*.]

Chesterfield, 4th Earl of. Philip Dormer Stanhope. 1694–1773. English politician and writer.

Ches•ter•ton (chĕs′tər-tən), **Gilbert Keith.** 1874–1936. British writer and critic.

chest•nut (chĕs′nŭt′, -nət) ► *n.* **1.** Any of several deciduous trees having nuts enclosed in a prickly husk. **2.** The often edible nut of these trees. **3.** The wood of a chestnut tree. **4.** A deep reddish brown. **5.** A stale joke or story. [< Gk. *kastanea*.]

chev•a•lier (shĕv′ə-lîr′) ► *n.* **1.** A member of certain orders of knighthood or merit. **2.** A French nobleman of the lowest rank. [< LLat. *caballārius*, horseman.]

Chev•i•ot (shĕv′ē-ət, chĕv′-) ► *n.* **1.** A hornless sheep with short thick wool. **2.** also **cheviot** A woolen fabric with a coarse twill weave. [From the *Cheviot* Hills, England.]

chev•ron (shĕv′rən) ► *n.* A badge or insignia consisting of stripes meeting at an angle, worn on the sleeve of a military or police uniform to indicate rank, merit, or length of service. [< OFr. *chevron*, rafter.]

chew (chōō) ► *v.* **1.** To grind and crush with the teeth. **2.** To ponder: *chew a problem over.* —***phrasal verb:* chew out** *Slang* To scold. ► *n.* **1.** The act of chewing. **2.** Something chewed. —***idiom:* chew the fat** *Slang* To talk in a leisurely way. [< OE *cēowan*.] —**chew′a•ble** *adj.* —**chew′er** *n.*

chew•ing gum (chōō′ĭng) ► *n.* A sweetened, flavored preparation for chewing, usu. made of chicle.

chew•y (chōō′ē) ► *adj.* **-i•er, -i•est.** Needing much chewing. —**chew′i•ness** *n.*

Chey•enne[1] (shī-ĕn′, -ăn′) ► *n., pl.* **-enne** or **-ennes 1.** A member of a Native American people of the W Great Plains, now living in Montana and Oklahoma. **2.** The Algonquian language of the Cheyenne.

Chey•enne[2] (shī-ăn′, -ĕn′) The capital of WY, in the SE part. Pop. 50,008.

chi[1] (kī) ► *n.* The 22nd letter of the Greek alphabet. [Gk. *khi*.]

chi[2] (chē) ► *n.* The vital force believed in Taoism and other Chinese thought to be inherent in all things. [Mandarin *qì*.]

Chiang Kai-shek (chăng′ kī′shĕk′, jyäng′). 1887–1975. Chinese military and political leader.

chi•a•ro•scu•ro (kē-är′ə-skōōr′ō, -skyōōr′ō) ► *n.* The technique of using light and shade in pictorial representation. [Ital., light and dark.] —**chi•a′ro•scu′rist** *n.*

Chi•ba (chē′bä′) A city of E-central Honshu, Japan. Pop. 850,631.

chic (shēk) ► *adj.* **chic•er, chic•est.** Stylish. See Syns at **fashionable.** [Fr.] —**chic** *n.* —**chic′ly** *adv.* —**chic′ness** *n.*

Chi•ca•go (shĭ-kä′gō, -kô′-) A city of NE IL on Lake Michigan. Pop. 2,783,726. —**Chi•ca′go•an** *n.*

Chi•ca•na (chĭ-kä′nə, shĭ-) ► *n.* A Mexican-American woman or girl. See Usage Note at **Chicano.** [< Am.Sp. *Mexicana*.]

chi•can•er•y (shĭ-kā′nə-rē, chĭ-) ► *n., pl.* **-ies 1.** Deception by trickery. **2.** A trick; subterfuge. [< OFr. *chicaner*, to quibble.]

Chi•ca•no (chĭ-kä′nō, shĭ-) ► *n., pl.* **-nos.** A Mexican American. [< Am.Sp. *Mexicano*.] —**Chi•ca′no** *adj.*

Usage: *Chicano* is used only of Mexican

Americans, not of Mexicans living in Mexico. While *Chicano* is a term of pride for many, it is not necessarily espoused by all Mexican Americans, and outsiders may be better off using the term *Mexican American* instead. See Usage Note at **Hispanic.**

chi•chi (shē′shē) ▸*adj.* **-chi•er, -chi•est.** Ostentatiously stylish. [Fr.]

chick (chĭk) ▸*n.* **1.** A young chicken. **2.** Any young bird. **3.** *Slang* A young woman.

chick•a•dee (chĭk′ə-dē′) ▸*n.* A small, gray, dark-crowned North American bird. [Imit. of its call.]

Chick•a•saw (chĭk′ə-sô′) ▸*n., pl.* **-saw** or **-saws 1.** A member of a Native American people formerly of NE Mississippi and NW Alabama, now living in Oklahoma. **2.** The Muskogean language of the Chickasaw.

chick•en (chĭk′ən) ▸*n.* **1.** The common domestic fowl or its young. **2.** The flesh of this fowl. **3.** *Slang* A coward. ▸*adj. Slang* Afraid; cowardly. ▸*v. Slang* To act in a cowardly manner: *chickened out at the last moment.* [< OE *cīcen.*]

chicken feed ▸*n. Slang* A trifling amount of money.

chick•en-fried (chĭk′ən-frīd′) ▸*adj.* Coated with batter and seasoned flour and fried.

chick•en-heart•ed (chĭk′ən-här′tĭd) ▸*adj.* Cowardly. —**chick′en•heart′ed•ness** *n.*

chick•en-liv•ered (chĭk′ən-lĭv′ərd) ▸*adj.* Cowardly; timid.

chick•en•pox or **chicken pox** (chĭk′ən-pŏks′) ▸*n.* A contagious viral disease, primarily of children, characterized by skin eruptions and slight fever.

chicken wire ▸*n.* A light-gauge galvanized wire fencing usu. of hexagonal mesh.

chick•pea (chĭk′pē′) ▸*n.* **1.** An Old World plant cultivated for its edible pealike seeds. **2.** A seed of this plant. [< Lat. *cicer.*]

chick•weed (chĭk′wēd′) ▸*n.* A low weedy plant with small white flowers.

chic•le (chĭk′əl, chē′klĕ) ▸*n.* The coagulated milky juice of a tropical American tree, used as the principal ingredient of chewing gum. [< Nahuatl *chictli.*]

chic•o•ry (chĭk′ə-rē) ▸*n., pl.* **-ries 1.** A plant having blue daisylike flowers and leaves used as salad. **2.** The roasted ground roots of this plant, used as a coffee admixture or substitute. [< Gk. *kikhora.*]

chide (chīd) ▸*v.* **chid•ed** or **chid** (chĭd), **chid•ed** or **chid** or **chid•den** (chĭd′n), **chid•ing.** To scold mildly; reprimand. [< OE *cīdan.*] —**chid′er** *n.* —**chid′ing•ly** *adv.*

chief (chēf) ▸*n.* **1.** One who is highest in rank or authority. **2.** often **Chief a.** A chief petty officer. **b.** The chief engineer of a ship. ▸*adj.* **1.** Highest in rank or authority. **2.** Most important. [< OFr. *chef* < Lat. *caput*, head.] —**chief′ly** *adj. & adv.*

chief justice also **Chief Justice** ▸*n.* The presiding judge of a high court having several judges, esp. the US Supreme Court.

chief master sergeant ▸*n.* The highest noncommissioned rank in the US Air Force.

chief of staff ▸*n., pl.* **chiefs of staff 1.** often **Chief of Staff** The ranking officer of the US Army, Navy, or Air Force, responsible to the secretary of his or her branch as well as to the President. **2.** The senior military staff officer at the division level or higher.

chief of state ▸*n., pl.* **chiefs of state.** The formal head of a nation, distinct from the head of the government.

chief petty officer ▸*n.* A rank, as in the US Navy, below senior chief petty officer.

chief•tain (chēf′tən) ▸*n.* The leader esp. of a clan or tribe. [< LLat. *capitāneus.*]

chif•fon (shĭ-fŏn′, shĭf′ŏn′) ▸*n.* A fabric of sheer silk or rayon. [< Fr. *chiffe*, old rag.]

chif•fo•nier (shĭf′ə-nîr′) ▸*n.* A narrow, high chest of drawers. [< Fr. *chiffon*, rag. See CHIFFON.]

chig•ger (chĭg′ər) ▸*n.* **1.** A parasitic mite larva that lodges on the skin and whose bite causes severe itching. **2.** See **chigoe** 1. [Alteration of CHIGOE.]

chi•gnon (shēn-yŏn′, shēn′yŏn′) ▸*n.* A roll of hair worn esp. at the nape of the neck. [< OFr. *chaignon*, CHAIN.]

chig•oe (chĭg′ō, chē′gō) ▸*n.* **1.** A small tropical flea, the fertilized female of which burrows under the skin and causes intense irritation and sores. **2.** See **chigger** 1. [Poss. < Galibi (Carib) *chico*, or of African orig.]

Chi•hua•hua[1] (chə-wä′wä, chē-) A city of N Mexico S of Ciudad Juárez. Pop. 385,603.

Chi•hua•hua[2] (chĭ-wä′wä, -wə) ▸*n.* A very small dog having pointed ears and a short smooth coat. [< CHIHUAHUA[1].]

chil•blain (chĭl′blān′) ▸*n.* An inflammation of the hands, feet, or ears, due to exposure to moist cold. [CHIL(L) + *blain*, a pain.]

child (chīld) ▸*n., pl.* **chil•dren** (chĭl′drən) **1.** A person between birth and puberty. **2.** An immature person. **3.** A son or daughter; offspring. [< OE *cild.*] —**child′hood′** *n.* —**child′less** *adj.* —**child′like′** *adj.*

child•bear•ing (chīld′bâr′ĭng) ▸*n.* Pregnancy and childbirth. —**child′bear′ing** *adj.*

child•birth (chīld′bûrth′) ▸*n.* Parturition.

child-care or **child•care** (chīld′kâr′) ▸*adj.* Of or providing care for children, esp. preschoolers. —**child′care′** *n.*

child•ish (chīl′dĭsh) ▸*adj.* **1.** Of or suitable for a child. **2.** Immature in behavior. —**child′ish•ly** *adv.* —**child′ish•ness** *n.*

child•proof (chīld′pro͞of′) ▸*adj.* Designed to resist tampering by young children.

chil•dren (chĭl′drən) ▸*n.* Pl. of **child.**

child's play (chīldz) ▸*n.* **1.** Something very easy to do. **2.** A trivial matter.

Chil•e (chĭl′ē) A country of SW South America with a long Pacific coastline. Cap. Santiago. Pop. 13,994,000. —**Chil′e•an** *adj. & n.*

chil•i (chĭl′ē) also **chil•e** or **chil•li** ▸*n., pl.* **-ies** also **-es** or **-lis 1.** The pungent pod of several varieties of capsicum pepper, used esp. as a flavoring in cooking. **2.** Chili con carne. [< Nahuatl *chilli.*]

chil•i•bur•ger (chĭl′ē-bûr′gər) ▸*n.* A hamburger covered with chili con carne.

chili con car•ne (kŏn kär′nē) ▸*n.* A highly spiced dish made of chili peppers, meat, and often beans. [Sp.]

chil•i•dog (chĭl′ē-dôg′, -dŏg′) ▸*n.* A hot dog covered with chili con carne.

chili sauce ▸*n.* A spiced sauce made with chilies and tomatoes.

chill (chĭl) ▸*n.* **1.** A moderate but penetrating cold. **2.** A cold or clammy sensation, as from fever or fear, often accompanied by shivering and pallor. **3.** A dampening of enthusiasm or spirit. ►*adj.* Chilly. ►*v.* **1.** To make or become cold. **2.** To dispirit. **3.** *Slang* To calm down or relax. Often used with *out.* [< OE *cele.*] —**chill′ness** *n.*

chill•y (chĭl′ē) ►*adj.* **-i•er, -i•est 1.** Cold enough to cause shivering. See Syns at **cold. 2.** Seized with cold; shivering. **3.** Cool; unfriendly. —**chill′i•ness** *n.*

Chi-lung (jē′lo͝ong′, chē′-) or **Kee•lung** (kē′-). A city of N Taiwan on the East China Sea. Pop. 349,686.

chime (chīm) ►*n.* **1.** often **chimes** A set of tuned bells used as a musical instrument. **2.** The sound produced by or as if by a bell or bells. ►*v.* **chimed, chim•ing 1.** To sound with a harmonious ring when struck. **2.** To agree; harmonize. **3.** To signal by chiming: *The clock chimed noon.* —***phrasal verb:* chime in** To interrupt, as in a conversation. [< Lat. *cymbalum,* CYMBAL.] —**chim′er** *n.*

Chi•me•ra (kī-mîr′ə, kĭ-) ►*n.* **1.** *Gk. Myth.* A fire-breathing she-monster usu. represented as a composite of a lion, goat, and serpent. **2. chimera** An impossible or foolish fantasy. [< Gk. *khimaira.*]

Chimera **Chinese lantern**

chi•mer•i•cal (kī-mĕr′ĭ-kəl, -mîr′-, kĭ-) ►*adj.* **1.** Imaginary; unreal. **2.** Given to unrealistic fantasies. —**chi•mer′i•cal•ly** *adv.*

chim•ney (chĭm′nē) ►*n., pl.* **-neys 1.** A usu. vertical passage through which smoke and gases escape from a fire or furnace. **2.** A glass tube for enclosing the flame of a lamp. [< LLat. *camīnāta,* fireplace.]

chim•ney•piece (chĭm′nē-pēs′) ►*n.* **1.** The mantel of a fireplace. **2.** A decoration over a fireplace.

chimney pot ►*n.* A short pipe placed on the top of a chimney to improve the draft.

chimney sweep ►*n.* A worker employed to clean soot from chimneys.

chimney swift ►*n.* A small swallowlike New World bird that often nests in chimneys.

chimp (chĭmp) ►*n. Informal* A chimpanzee.

chim•pan•zee (chĭm′păn-zē′, chĭm-păn′zē) ►*n.* A gregarious anthropoid ape of tropical Africa, having long dark hair. [< Vili (African) *ci-mpenzi.*]

chin (chĭn) ►*n.* The central forward portion of the lower jaw. ►*v.* **chinned, chin•ning.** To pull (oneself) up with the arms while grasping an overhead horizontal bar until the chin is level with the bar. [< OE *cin.*]

Chin. ►*abbr.* Chinese

chi•na (chī′nə) ►*n.* **1.** High-quality porcelain or ceramic ware. **2.** Porcelain or earthenware used for the table. [< *China ware.*]

China. A country of E Asia. Cap. Beijing. Pop. 1,237,000,000.

China, Republic of. See **Taiwan.**

China Sea. The W part of the Pacific extending from S Japan to the Malay Peninsula.

chinch (chĭnch) ►*n. Regional* See **bedbug.** [< Lat. *cīmex,* bug.]

chinch bug ►*n.* A small black and white insect that is destructive to grains and grasses.

chin•chil•la (chĭn-chĭl′ə) ►*n.* **1a.** A squirrellike South American rodent having soft, pale-gray fur. **b.** The fur of this animal. **2.** A thick wool cloth used for overcoats. [Sp.]

chine (chīn) ►*n.* **1a.** The backbone or spine, esp. of an animal. **b.** A cut of meat containing part of the backbone. **2.** A ridge or crest. [< OFr. *eschine,* of Gmc. orig.]

Chi•nese (chī-nēz′, -nēs′) ►*adj.* Of or relating to China or its peoples, languages, or cultures. ►*n., pl.* **-nese 1a.** A native or inhabitant of China. **b.** A person of Chinese ancestry. **c.** See **Han. 2a.** A branch of the Sino-Tibetan language family that consists of the various dialects spoken by the Chinese people. **b.** Any of these dialects.

Chinese cabbage ►*n.* A plant related to the common cabbage, having an elongated head of overlapping, crinkled edible leaves.

Chinese checkers ►*pl.n. (takes sing. or pl. v.)* A game played with marbles on a board shaped like a six-pointed star.

Chinese lantern ►*n.* A decorative collapsible lantern of thin, brightly colored paper.

Chinese puzzle ►*n.* **1.** A very intricate puzzle. **2.** Something very difficult or complex.

chink[1] (chĭngk) ►*n.* A narrow opening, such as a crack or fissure. ►*v.* To fill cracks or chinks in. [Prob. < OE *cine,* crack.]

chink[2] (chĭngk) ►*n.* A slight clinking sound. ►*v.* To make a chink. [Imit.]

chi•no (chē′nō, shē′-) ►*n., pl.* **-nos 1.** A coarse twilled cotton fabric. **2.** often **chinos** Trousers made of chino. [Am.Sp., yellowish.]

chi•nook (shĭ-no͝ok′, chĭ-) ►*n.* **1.** A moist warm marine wind in the Pacific NW. **2.** A warm dry wind of the E Rocky Mountains. [< *Chinook wind.*]

Chinook ►*n., pl.* **-nook** or **-nooks 1.** A member of any of various Chinookan-speaking peoples of the Columbia River valley in Washington and Oregon. **2.** Any of their Chinookan languages.

Chi•nook•an (shĭ-no͝ok′ən, chĭ-) ►*n.* A Native American language family of Washington and Oregon. —**Chi•nook′an** *adj.*

Chinook Jargon ►*n.* A pidgin language combining words from Native American languages, French, and English, formerly used as a lingua franca in the Pacific Northwest.

Chinook salmon ►*n.* A very large, commercially valuable salmon of N Pacific waters.

chin•qua•pin (chĭng′kə-pĭn′) ►*n.* **1.** Any of several deciduous shrubs or small trees related to the chestnut. **2.** A large evergreen tree of the Pacific Northwest. **3.** The nut of a chinquapin. [Of Algonquian orig.]

chintz (chĭnts) ►*n.* A printed and glazed cotton fabric, usu. of bright colors. [< Hindi *cīṃṭ,* calico cloth.]

chintz•y (chĭnt′sē) ►*adj.* **-i•er, -i•est 1.** Gaudy or cheap; trashy. **2.** Stingy; miserly.

chin-up (chĭn′ŭp′) ►*n.* The act of chinning oneself, practiced esp. as a fitness exercise.

chip (chĭp) ►*n.* **1.** A small broken or cut off

piece, as of wood, stone, or glass. **2.** A crack or flaw caused by the removal of such a piece. **3a.** A coinlike disk used as a counter, as in poker. **b. chips** *Slang* Money. **4a.** *Electron.* A minute slice of a semiconducting material, such as silicon, processed to have specified electrical characteristics, esp. before it is developed into an electronic component or integrated circuit; microchip. **b.** An integrated circuit. **5a.** often **chips** A thin, usu. fried slice of food: *a potato chip.* **b. chips** *Chiefly Brit.* French fries. **6.** *Sports* A chip shot. ►*v.* **chipped, chip•ping.** To break, chop, or cut a small piece from. —***phrasal verb:*** **chip in** To contribute. —***idioms:*** **chip off the old block** A child who closely resembles his or her parent. **chip on (one's) shoulder** A habitually hostile attitude. [< Lat. *cippus*, beam.] —**chip′per** *n.*

Chip•e•wy•an (chĭp′ə-wī′ən) ►*n., pl.* **-an** or **-ans 1.** A member of a Native American people of N-central Canada. **2.** The Athabaskan language of the Chipewyan.

chip•munk (chĭp′mŭngk′) ►*n.* Any of several small terrestrial squirrels having a striped back. [Perh. < Ojibwa *ajidamoon?*, red squirrel.]

chipped beef (chĭpt) ►*n.* Dried beef smoked and sliced very thin.

chip•per (chĭp′ər) ►*adj.* In lively spirits; cheerful. [Perh. < dial. *kipper*, lively.]

Chip•pe•wa (chĭp′ə-wô′, -wä′, -wā′) ►*n., pl.* **-wa** or **-was.** See **Ojibwa.**

chip shot ►*n.* A short lofted golf stroke, used in approaching the green.

chiro– ►*pref.* Hand: *chiropractic.* [< Gk. *kheir.*]

chi•ro•man•cy (kī′rə-măn′sē) ►*n.* Palmistry. [CHIRO– + Gk. *manteia*, divination.] —**chi′ro•man′cer** *n.*

chi•rop•o•dy (kĭ-rŏp′ə-dē, shĭ-) ►*n.* See **podiatry.** —**chi•rop′o•dist** *n.*

chi•ro•prac•tic (kī′rə-prăk′tĭk) ►*n.* A system of therapy typically involving manipulation of the spinal column and other bodily structures. [CHIRO– + Gk. *praktikos*, effective.] —**chi′ro•prac′tor** *n.*

chirp (chûrp) ►*n.* A short, high-pitched sound, such as that made by a small bird or insect. [Imit.] —**chirp** *v.*

chis•el (chĭz′əl) ►*n.* A metal tool with a sharp beveled edge, used to cut and shape stone, wood, or metal. ►*v.* **-eled, -el•ing** or **-elled, -el•ling 1.** To shape or cut with a chisel. **2.** *Informal* To swindle or obtain by swindling; cheat. [< OFr. *cisiel.*] —**chis′el•er** *n.*

Chi•şi•nău (kĭsh′ə-nou′) or **Ki•shi•nev** (-nĕf′, -nôf′). The capital of Moldova, in the S part near the Romanian border NW of Odessa. Pop. 667,100.

chit[1] (chĭt) ►*n.* A voucher for an amount owed for food and drink. [< Hindi *ciṭṭhī*, note.]

chit[2] (chĭt) ►*n.* **1.** A child. **2.** A saucy girl or young woman. [ME, young animal.]

chit•chat (chĭt′chăt′) ►*n.* Casual conversation. [Reduplication of CHAT.] —**chit′chat′** *v.*

chi•tin (kīt′n) ►*n.* A tough protective substance that is the principal component of crustacean shells and insect exoskeletons. [< Gk. *khitōn*, chiton.] —**chi′tin•ous** *adj.*

chi•ton (kīt′n, kī′tŏn′) ►*n.* **1.** Any of a class of marine mollusks that live on rocks and have shells with eight overlapping calcareous plates. **2.** A tunic worn by men and women in ancient Greece. [Gk. *khitōn*, tunic.]

Chit•ta•gong (chĭt′ə-gông′, -gŏng′) A city of SE Bangladesh. Pop. 1,363,998.

chit•ter•lings also **chit•lins** or **chit•lings** (chĭt′lĭnz) ►*pl.n.* The small intestines of pigs, cooked as food. [< ME *chiterling.*]

chiv•al•ry (shĭv′əl-rē) ►*n., pl.* **-ries 1.** The medieval system of knighthood. **2a.** Qualities, such as bravery, honor, and gallantry toward women, idealized by knighthood. **b.** A gallant or courteous act. [< OFr. *chevalier*, knight. See CHEVALIER.] —**chiv′al•rous, chi•val′ric** *adj.*

chive (chīv) ►*n.* often **chives.** A plant with grasslike onion-flavored leaves used as seasoning. [< Lat. *cēpa*, onion.]

chla•myd•i•a (klə-mĭd′ē-ə) ►*n., pl.* **-i•ae** (-ē-ē′) **1.** Any of various spherical microorganisms pathogenic to humans and other animals. **2.** Any of several often asymptomatic sexually transmitted diseases caused by one of these microorganisms. [NLat., genus name < Gk. *khlamus*, hood.]

chlo•ral (klôr′əl, klōr′-) ►*n.* A colorless oily liquid used to manufacture DDT and chloral hydrate. [CHLOR(O)– + AL(COHOL).]

chloral hydrate ►*n.* A colorless crystalline compound, $CCl_3CH(OH)_2$, used medicinally as a sedative and hypnotic.

chlo•rate (klôr′āt′, klōr′-) ►*n.* The inorganic group ClO_3 or a compound containing it.

chlor•dane (klôr′dān′, klōr′-) also **chlor•dan** (-dăn′) ►*n.* A colorless, odorless, viscous liquid, $C_{10}H_6Cl_8$, used as an insecticide. [CHLOR(O)– + *(in)d(ene)* + –ANE.]

chlo•rel•la (klə-rĕl′ə) ►*n.* Any of a genus of unicellular green algae often used in studies of photosynthesis. [< Gk. *khlōros*, green.]

chlo•ric acid (klôr′ĭk, klōr′-) ►*n.* A strongly oxidizing unstable acid, $HClO_3 \cdot 7H_2O$.

chlo•ride (klôr′īd′, klōr′-) ►*n.* A binary compound of chlorine. —**chlo•rid′ic** (klə-rĭd′ĭk) *adj.*

chlo•ri•nate (klôr′ə-nāt′, klōr′-) ►*v.* **-nat•ed, -nat•ing.** To treat or combine with chlorine or a chlorine compound. —**chlo′ri•na′tion** *n.* —**chlo′ri•na′tor** *n.*

chlo•rine (klôr′ēn′, -ĭn, klōr′-) ►*n. Symbol* **Cl** A highly reactive, poisonous greenish-yellow gaseous element used to purify water, as a disinfectant and bleaching agent, and in the manufacture of many compounds. At. no. 17. See table at **element.**

chloro– or **chlor–** ►*pref.* **1.** Green: *chlorophyll.* **2.** Chlorine: *chloroform.* [< Gk. *khlōros*, green.]

chlo•ro•fluor•o•car•bon (klôr′ō-flŏŏr′ō-kär′bən, -flôr′-, -flōr′-, klōr′-) ►*n.* Any of various gaseous compounds of carbon, hydrogen, chlorine, and fluorine, once used widely as aerosol propellants and refrigerants, now believed to cause depletion of the atmospheric ozone layer.

chlo•ro•form (klôr′ə-fôrm′, klōr′-) ►*n.* A clear colorless liquid, $CHCl_3$, used in refrigerants, propellants, and resins, as a solvent, and sometimes as an anesthetic. ►*v.* To anesthetize or kill with chloroform. [CHLORO– + *formyl.*]

chlo•ro•phyll (klôr′ə-fĭl, klōr′-) ►*n.* Any of a group of green pigments essential in photosynthesis. [CHLORO– + Gk. *phullon*, leaf.]

chlo•ro•plast (klôr′ə-plăst′, klōr′-) ►*n.* A

chlorophyll-containing plastid found in algal and green plant cells. [CHLORO– + Gk. *plastos*, molded.]

chlor•tet•ra•cy•cline (klôr′tĕt-rə-sī′klēn′, -klĭn, klōr′-) ►*n.* An antibiotic obtained from a soil bacterium.

chock (chŏk) ►*n.* A block or wedge placed under something else, such as a wheel, to keep it from moving. ►*v.* To secure by a chock. [Poss. < ONFr. *choque*, log.]

chock-a-block or **chock•a•block** (chŏk′ə-blŏk′) ►*adj.* Squeezed together; jammed.

chock-full or **chock•full** (chŏk′fo͝ol′) ►*adj.* As full as possible.

choc•o•late (chô′kə-lĭt, chôk′lĭt, chŏk′-) ►*n.* **1.** Fermented, roasted, and ground cacao seeds, often sweetened. **2.** A candy or beverage made from chocolate. [< Nahuatl *xocolatl.*] —**choc′o•late** *adj.*

Choc•taw (chŏk′tô) ►*n., pl.* **-taw** or **-taws 1.** A member of a Native American people formerly of S Mississippi and SW Alabama, now living in Mississippi and Oklahoma. **2.** The Muskogean language of the Choctaw.

choice (chois) ►*n.* **1.** The act of choosing; selection. **2.** The power, right, or liberty to choose. **3.** One that is chosen. **4.** A number or variety from which to choose. **5.** The best part. ►*adj.* **choic•er, choic•est 1.** Of very fine quality. See Syns at **delicate. 2.** Selected with care. [< OFr. *choisir*, choose.] —**choice′ness** *n.*

choir (kwīr) ►*n.* **1.** An organized company of singers, esp. one singing in a church. **2.** The part of a church used by a choir. **3.** A group of similar orchestral instruments. [< Lat. *chorus*, choral dance. See CHORUS.]

choke (chōk) ►*v.* **choked, chok•ing 1a.** To have difficulty in breathing, swallowing, or speaking. **b.** To cause to choke, as by constricting or obstructing the windpipe. **2.** To check or repress forcibly. **3.** To block up or obstruct; clog. **4.** To reduce the air intake of (a carburetor), thereby enriching the fuel mixture. **5.** To fail to perform effectively because of nervous tension. —***phrasal verb:* choke up** To be unable to speak because of strong emotion. ►*n.* **1.** The act or sound of choking. **2.** A device used in choking a carburetor. [< OE *āceōcian.*]

choke collar ►*n.* A chain collar that tightens like a noose when the leash is pulled, used in canine obedience training.

chok•er (chō′kər) ►*n.* **1.** One that chokes. **2.** A tight-fitting necklace.

chol•er (kŏl′ər, kō′lər) ►*n.* Anger; irritability. [< Gk. *kholera*, jaundice < *kholē*, bile.]

chol•er•a (kŏl′ər-ə) ►*n.* An infectious, often fatal epidemic disease characterized by profuse watery diarrhea, vomiting, muscle cramps, and severe dehydration. [< Lat. See CHOLER.] —**chol′e•ra′ic** (-ə-rā′ĭk) *adj.*

chol•er•ic (kŏl′ə-rĭk, kə-lĕr′ĭk) ►*adj.* Easily angered; bad-tempered; irritable.

cho•les•ter•ol (kə-lĕs′tə-rôl′, -rōl′) ►*n.* A white crystalline substance, $C_{27}H_{45}OH$, found in animal tissues and various foods, that is normally synthesized by the liver and is thought to be a factor in atherosclerosis. [Gk. *kholē*, bile + *stereos*, solid + -OL.]

chol•la (choi′ə) ►*n.* Any of a genus of spiny, shrubby, or treelike cacti having cylindrical, often detachable stem segments. [Am.Sp.]

chomp (chŏmp) ►*v.* To chew or bite on noisily or repeatedly. [Var. of CHAMP[1].]

Chong•qing (chông′chĭng′, cho͞ong′-) also **Chung•king** (cho͞ong′kĭng′, jo͞ong′gĭng′). A city of S-central China on the Chang Jiang (Yangtze R.) Pop. 3,122,704.

choose (cho͞oz) ►*v.* **chose** (chōz), **cho•sen** (chō′zən), **choos•ing 1.** To decide on and pick out; select. **2.** To prefer above others. [< OE *cēosan.*] —**choos′er** *n.*

choos•y also **choos•ey** (cho͞o′zē) ►*adj.* **-i•er, -i•est.** Highly selective. —**choos′i•ness** *n.*

chop[1] (chŏp) ►*v.* **chopped, chop•ping 1a.** To cut by striking with a heavy sharp tool. **b.** To mince. **2.** *Sports* To hit with a short, swift downward stroke. ►*n.* **1a.** A swift, short, cutting blow or stroke. **b.** *Sports* A short downward stroke. **2.** A cut of meat, usu. taken from the rib, shoulder, or loin and containing a bone. **3.** A short irregular motion of waves. [ME *choppen.*]

chop[2] (chŏp) ►*n.* **1.** An official stamp or permit in the Far East. **2.** Quality; class. [Hindi *chāp*, seal.]

chop•house (chŏp′hous′) ►*n.* A restaurant that specializes in steaks and chops.

Cho•pin (shō′păn′, shō-păN′), **Frédéric François.** 1810–49. Polish-born French composer and pianist.

chop•per (chŏp′ər) ►*n.* *Informal* **1.** A helicopter. **2. choppers** Teeth or dentures. **3.** A usu. customized motorcycle.

chop•ping block (chŏp′ĭng) ►*n.* A wooden block on which food or wood is chopped.

chop•py (chŏp′ē) ►*adj.* **-pi•er, -pi•est 1.** Having many small waves. **2.** Marked by abrupt starts and stops. —**chop′pi•ly** *adv.*

chops (chŏps) ►*pl.n.* The jaws, cheeks, or jowls. [< CHOP[1].]

chop shop ►*n.* *Slang* A place where stolen cars are disassembled for parts that are then sold.

chop•stick (chŏp′stĭk′) ►*n.* One of a pair of slender sticks used as an eating utensil chiefly in Asian countries. [< Pidgin E. *chop*, quick.]

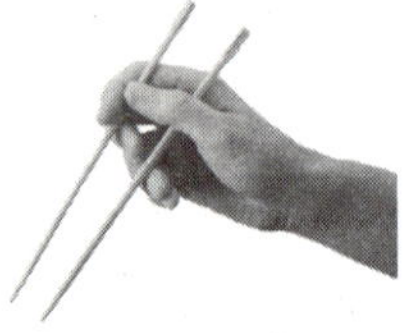

chopsticks

chop su•ey (so͞o′ē) ►*n.* A Chinese-American dish consisting of small pieces of meat or chicken cooked with bean sprouts and other vegetables and served with rice. [Cantonese *tsaāpsuì*, mixed pieces.]

cho•ral (kôr′əl, kōr′-) ►*adj.* *Mus.* Of or for a chorus or choir. —**cho′ral•ly** *adv.*

cho•rale also **cho•ral** (kə-răl′, -räl′) ►*n.* **1.** A harmonized hymn. **2.** A chorus or choir. [Ger. *Choral(gesang)*, choral (song).]

chord[1] (kôrd, kōrd) *Mus.* ►*n.* A combination of three or more pitches sounded simultaneously. ►*v.* To play chords on: *chord a guitar.* [< OFr. *acorde*, agreement. See ACCORD.]

chord[2] (kôrd, kōrd) ►*n.* **1.** A line segment that

joins two points on a curve. **2.** *Anat.* Var. of **cord** 3. **3.** An emotional feeling or response: *a sympathetic chord.* [Alteration of CORD.]

chore (chôr, chōr) ►*n.* **1. chores** Daily or routine domestic tasks. **2.** An unpleasant task. [Var. of CHAR[3].]

cho•re•a (kô-rē′ə, kō-, kə-) ►*n.* A nervous disorder, esp. of children, marked by uncontrollable movements, esp. of the arms, legs, and face. [< Gk. *khoreia,* choral dance.]

cho•re•og•ra•phy (kôr′ē-ŏg′rə-fē, kōr′-) ►*n.* The art of creating and arranging dances or ballets. [Gk. *khoreia,* choral dance + –GRAPHY.] —**cho′re•o•graph′** (kôr′ē-ə-grăf′, kōr′-) *v.* —**cho′re•og′ra•pher** *n.* —**cho′re•o•graph′ic** *adj.*

cho•ris•ter (kôr′ĭ-stər, kōr′-, kŏr′-) ►*n.* A singer in a choir. [< Med.Lat. *chorista.*]

cho•ri•zo (chə-rē′zō, -sō) ►*n.* A spicy pork sausage seasoned esp. with garlic. [Sp.]

cho•roid (kôr′oid′, kōr′-) or **cho•ri•oid** (kôr′ē-oid′, kōr′-) ►*n.* The vascular coat of the eye between the sclera and retina. [< Gk. *khoroeidēs,* like an afterbirth.]

chor•tle (chôr′tl) ►*n.* A snorting, joyful laugh or chuckle. [Blend of CHUCKLE and SNORT.] —**chor′tle** *v.* —**chor′tler** *n.*

cho•rus (kôr′əs, kōr′-) ►*n., pl.* **-rus•es 1.** *Mus.* **a.** A composition written for a large number of singers. **b.** A body of singers who perform choral compositions. **c.** A line or group of lines repeated at intervals in a song. **2.** A body of vocalists and dancers who support the leading performers in operas, musical comedies, and revues. **3.** A group of persons who speak or recite together, esp. in a play. **4.** A simultaneous utterance by many voices. [Lat., choral dance < Gk. *khoros.*] —**cho′rus** *v.*

chose (chōz) ►*v.* P.t. of **choose.**

cho•sen (chō′zən) ►*v.* P.part. of **choose.** ►*adj.* Selected from or preferred above others.

Chou En-lai (jō′ ĕn-lī′). See **Zhou Enlai.**

chow[1] (chou) ►*n.* A heavy-set dog having a usu. reddish-brown coat and a blue-black tongue. [Poss. < Cantonese *gŏu,* dog.]

chow[2] (chou) *Slang* ►*n.* Food. ►*v.* To eat: *chowed down on pizza.* [Poss. < Cantonese *tsaāp,* mixture, food.]

chow•der (chou′dər) ►*n.* **1.** A thick seafood soup often with a milk base. **2.** A similar soup: *corn chowder.* [< LLat. *caldāria,* stew pot.]

chow mein (chou′ mān′) ►*n.* A Chinese-American dish consisting of various stewed vegetables and meat served over fried noodles. [Mandarin *chăo miàn.*]

Chré•tien (krā-tyăN′), **Jean.** b. 1934. Canadian prime minister (since 1993).

chrism (krĭz′əm) ►*n.* Consecrated oil and balsam, used for anointing, esp. in baptism and confirmation. [< Gk. *khrisma,* an anointing.] —**chris′mal** *adj.*

Christ (krīst) ►*n.* **1.** The Messiah, as foretold by the prophets of the Heb. Scriptures. **2.** Jesus. [< Gk. *khristos,* anointed.] —**Christ′like′** *adj.* —**Christ′ly** *adj.*

Christ•church (krīst′chûrch′) A city of E South I. Pop. 293,700.

chris•ten (krĭs′ən) ►*v.* **1a.** To baptize into a Christian church. **b.** To give a name to at baptism. **2.** To name and dedicate ceremonially: *christen a ship.* [< OE *cristnian.*] —**chris′ten•ing** *n.*

Chris•ten•dom (krĭs′ən-dəm) ►*n.* **1.** Christians collectively. **2.** The Christian world.

Chris•tian (krĭs′chən) ►*adj.* **1.** Professing belief in Christianity. **2.** Of or derived from Jesus's teachings. **3.** Of Christianity or its adherents. ►*n.* An adherent of Christianity. —**Chris′tian•ize′** *v.*

Christian era ►*n.* The period beginning with the birth of Jesus.

chris•ti•an•i•a (krĭs′tē-ăn′ē-ə, -ä′nē-ə, krĭs′-chē-) ►*n.* A christie. [After *Christiania* (Oslo), Norway.]

Chris•ti•an•i•ty (krĭs′chē-ăn′ĭ-tē, krĭs′tē-) ►*n.* **1.** The Christian religion, founded on the life and teachings of Jesus. **2.** Christendom. **3.** The state or fact of being a Christian.

Christian name ►*n.* A name given at birth or baptism.

Christian Science ►*n.* The church and the religious system founded by Mary Baker Eddy, emphasizing healing through spiritual means. —**Christian Scientist** *n.*

chris•tie or **chris•ty** (krĭs′tē) ►*n., pl.* **-ties.** A ski turn in which the skis are kept parallel. [Short for CHRISTIANIA.]

Chris•tie (krĭs′tē), Dame **Agatha Mary Clarissa.** 1890–1976. British writer.

Chris•ti•na (krĭ-stē′nə). 1626–89. Queen of Sweden (1632–54).

Christ•mas (krĭs′məs) ►*n.* A Christian feast commemorating the birth of Jesus, celebrated on Dec. 25. [< OE *Crīstes mæsse,* Christ's festival.]

Christ•mas•tide (krĭs′məs-tīd′) ►*n.* The season of Christmas.

Christmas tree ►*n.* An evergreen or artificial tree decorated during the Christmas season.

Chris•to•pher (krĭs′tə-fər), Saint. fl. 3rd cent. A.D. Legendary Christian martyr.

chro•mat•ic (krō-măt′ĭk) ►*adj.* **1.** Relating to colors or color. **2.** *Mus.* Proceeding by half tones: *a chromatic scale.* [< Gk. *khrōma,* color.] —**chro•mat′i•cal•ly** *adv.* —**chro•mat′i•cism** *n.*

chrome (krōm) ►*n.* **1.** Chromium or a chromium alloy. **2.** Something plated with a chrome. [< Gk. *khrōma,* color.]

chro•mi•um (krō′mē-əm) ►*n.* *Symbol* **Cr** A lustrous, hard, steel-gray metallic element used to harden steel alloys, to produce stainless steels, and in corrosion-resistant platings. At. no. 24. See table at **element.** [< Fr. *chrome,* CHROME.]

chromo– or **chrom–** ►*pref.* Color: *chromosome.* [< Gk. *khrōma,* color.]

chro•mo•some (krō′mə-sōm′) ►*n.* A linear strand of DNA and associated proteins in the nucleus of animal and plant cells that carries the genes determining heredity. —**chro′mo•so′mal** *adj.*

chron•ic (krŏn′ĭk) ►*adj.* **1.** Of long duration; continuing or lingering: *chronic money problems; chronic colitis.* **2.** Firmly established by habit: *a chronic liar.* [< Gk. *khronos,* time.] —**chron′i•cal•ly** *adv.*

Syns: *chronic, confirmed, habitual, inveterate* **adj.**

chronic fatigue syndrome ►*n.* A syndrome marked by debilitating fatigue and flulike symptoms.

chron•i•cle (krŏn′ĭ-kəl) ►*n.* **1.** A chronological account of historical events. **2. Chronicles**

(takes sing. v.) See table at **Bible.** ►*v.* **-cled, -cling.** To record in or in the form of a chronicle. [< Gk. *khronika*, annals.]

chrono– or **chron–** ►*pref.* Time: *chronometer.* [< Gk. *khronos*, time.]

chron•o•log•i•cal (krŏn′ə-lŏj′ĭ-kəl, krō′nə-) also **chron•o•log•ic** (-lŏj′ĭk) ►*adj.* **1.** Arranged in order of time of occurrence. **2.** Relating to or in accordance with chronology. —**chron′o•log′i•cal•ly** *adv.*

chro•nol•o•gy (krə-nŏl′ə-jē) ►*n., pl.* **-gies 1.** The determination of dates and sequence of events. **2.** The arrangement of events in time. **3.** A chronological list or table. —**chro•nol′o•gist** *n.*

chro•nom•e•ter (krə-nŏm′ĭ-tər) ►*n.* An exceptionally precise timepiece.

chrys•a•lis (krĭs′ə-lĭs) ►*n.* A pupa, esp. of a moth or butterfly, enclosed in a firm case or cocoon. [< Gk. *khrusallis.*]

chry•san•the•mum (krĭ-săn′thə-məm, -zăn′-) ►*n.* Any of a genus of plants cultivated for their showy flower heads. [< Gk. *khrusanthemon*, gold flower.]

chub (chŭb) ►*n., pl.* **chub** or **chubs 1.** Any of a family of freshwater fishes related to the carps and minnows. **2.** Any of several North American food fishes. [ME *chubbe.*]

chub•by (chŭb′ē) ►*adj.* **-bi•er, -bi•est.** Rounded and plump. [Prob. < CHUB.] —**chub′bi•ly** *adv.* —**chub′bi•ness** *n.*

chuck[1] (chŭk) ►*v.* **1.** To pat or squeeze playfully, esp. under the chin. **2a.** To throw or toss. **b.** *Informal* To throw out; discard. [Perh. < OFr. *choc*, SHOCK[1].] —**chuck** *n.*

chuck[2] (chŭk) ►*n.* **1.** A cut of beef extending from the neck to the ribs. **2.** A clamp that holds a tool or the material being worked, as in a drill or lathe. [dial. *chuck*, lump.]

chuck•hole (chŭk′hōl′) ►*n.* See **pothole.** [Prob. < CHUCK[1].]

chuck•le (chŭk′əl) ►*v.* **-led, -ling.** To laugh quietly. ►*n.* A quiet laugh of mild amusement. [Poss. < ME *chukken*, to cluck.]

chuck wagon ►*n.* A wagon equipped with food and cooking utensils, as on a ranch.

chug[1] (chŭg) ►*n.* A brief dull explosive sound made by or as if by a laboring engine. ►*v.* **chugged, chug•ging 1.** To make chugs. **2.** To move at a steady speed. [Imit.]

chug[2] (chŭg) ►*v. Slang* To chugalug.

chug•a•lug (chŭg′ə-lŭg′) ►*v.* **-lugged, -lug•ging** *Slang* To swallow (a liquid) without pausing. [Imit.]

chuk•ka (chŭk′ə) ►*n.* An ankle-length, usu. suede leather boot. [< CHUKKER.]

chuk•ker also **chuk•kar** (chŭk′ər) ►*n.* A period of play, lasting 7½ minutes, in a polo match. [< Skt. *cakram*, circle.]

Chu•la Vis•ta (cho͞o′lə vĭs′tə) A city of S CA S of San Diego. Pop. 135,163.

chum[1] (chŭm) ►*n.* An intimate friend. ►*v.* **chummed, chum•ming.** To spend time with a friend. [Perh. < *chamber fellow*, roommate.]

chum[2] (chŭm) ►*n.* Bait, esp. oily fish, ground up and scattered on the water. [?]

Chu•mash (cho͞o′măsh) ►*n., pl.* **-mash** or **-mash•es.** A member of a Hokan-speaking Native American people of S California.

chum•my (chŭm′ē) ►*adj.* **-mi•er, -mi•est.** Intimate; friendly: *chummy work relations.* —**chum′mi•ly** *adv.* —**chum′mi•ness** *n.*

chump (chŭmp) ►*n.* A dupe. [Poss. blend of CHUNK and LUMP[1] or STUMP.]

Chung•king (cho͝ong′kĭng′, jo͝ong′gĭng′) See **Chongqing.**

chunk (chŭngk) ►*n.* **1.** A thick mass or piece. **2.** *Informal* A substantial amount. [Poss. < CHUCK[2].]

chunk•y (chŭng′kē) ►*adj.* **-i•er, -i•est.** Short and thick; stocky. —**chunk′i•ness** *n.*

church (chûrch) ►*n.* **1.** A building for public, esp. Christian worship. **2.** often **Church** All Christians regarded as a spiritual body. **3.** A congregation. **4.** A religious service. **5.** The clergy. **6.** Ecclesiastical power: *the separation of church and state.* [< Gk. *kuriakos*, of the lord.]

church•go•er (chûrch′gō′ər) ►*n.* One who attends church. —**church′go′ing** *adj. & n.*

Chur•chill (chûr′chĭl′, chûrch′hĭl′), Sir **Winston Leonard Spenser.** 1874–1965. British prime minister (1940–45 and 1951–55) and writer; 1953 Nobel Prize for literature. —**Chur•chill′i•an** (chûr-chĭl′ē-ən) *adj.*

Winston Churchill

church key ►*n.* A can or bottle opener having a usu. triangular head.

church•man (chûrch′mən) ►*n.* **1.** A clergyman. **2.** A man who is a member of a church. See Usage Note at **man.**

Church of Christ, Scientist ►*n.* See **Christian Science.**

Church of England ►*n.* The Anglican church as established in England and headed by the Archbishop of Canterbury.

Church of Jesus Christ of Latter-day Saints ►*n.* See **Mormon Church.**

church•war•den (chûrch′wôr′dn) ►*n.* A lay officer who handles the secular affairs of an Anglican or Episcopal church.

church•wom•an (chûrch′wo͝om′ən) ►*n.* **1.** A clergywoman. **2.** A woman who is a member of a church. See Usage Note at **man.**

church•yard (chûrch′yärd′) ►*n.* A yard adjacent to a church, esp. a cemetery.

churl (chûrl) ►*n.* A rude, surly person. See Syns at **boor.** [< OE *ceorl*, peasant.] —**churl′ish** *adj.* —**churl′ish•ness** *n.*

churn (chûrn) ►*n.* A vessel or device in which cream or milk is agitated to make butter. ►*v.* **1a.** To agitate or stir (milk or cream) in a churn. **b.** To make (butter) by churning. **2.** To shake or stir vigorously. See Syns at **agitate.** —***phrasal verb:* churn out** To produce in an abundant and automatic manner: *churns out four novels a year.* [< OE *cyrn.*]

chute (sho͞ot) ►*n.* **1.** An inclined trough or passage through or down which things may pass. **2.** A parachute. [< Fr. *cheoir*, to fall.]

chut•ney (chŭt′nē) ►*n.* A pungent relish made of fruits, spices, and herbs. [Hindi *caṭni.*]

chutz•pah (KHo͝ot′spə, ho͝ot′-) ►*n.* Utter nerve; gall. [< Mishnaic Heb. *ḥuṣpâ.*]

Chuuk Islands (cho͝ok) or **Truk Islands** (trŭk, tro͝ok). An island group of the W Pacific in the central Caroline Is.

Ci ►*abbr.* curie

CIA ►*abbr.* Central Intelligence Agency

ciao (chou) ►*interj.* Used to express greeting or farewell. [Ital.]

ci•bo•ri•um (sĭ-bôr′ē-əm, -bōr′-) ►*n., pl.* **-bo•ri•a** (-bôr′ē-ə, -bōr′-) **1.** A vaulted canopy over an altar. **2.** A covered receptacle for the consecrated wafers of the Eucharist. [< Gk. *kibōrion*, drinking cup.]

ci•ca•da (sĭ-kā′də, -kä′-) ►*n., pl.* **-das** or **-dae** (-dē′). A large insect with membranous wings and in the male a pair of organs that produce a shrill drone. [< Lat. *cicāda.*]

cic•a•trix (sĭk′ə-trĭks′, sĭ-kā′trĭks) ►*n., pl.* **-tri•ces** (-trī′sēz, -trĭ-sēz′). A scar. [< Lat. *cicātrīx.*] —**cic′a•tri′cial** (-trĭsh′əl) *adj.*

Cic•e•ro (sĭs′ə-rō′), **Marcus Tullius.** 106–43 B.C. Roman political leader and orator. —**Cic′e•ro′ni•an** *adj.*

Cid (sĭd), **the.** Rodrigo Díaz de Vivar. 1043?–99. Spanish soldier and hero.

-cide ►*suff.* **1.** Killer: *pesticide.* **2.** Act of killing: *genocide.* [< Lat. *caedere*, kill.]

ci•der (sī′dər) ►*n.* The juice pressed esp. from apples, used as a beverage or to make vinegar. [< Semitic; akin to Heb. *šēkār*, intoxicating drink.]

CIF ►*abbr.* cost, insurance, and freight

ci•gar (sĭ-gär′) ►*n.* A compact roll of tobacco leaves prepared for smoking. [Sp. *cigarro.*]

cig•a•rette also **cig•a•ret** (sĭg′ə-rĕt′, sĭg′ə-rĕt′) ►*n.* A small roll of finely cut tobacco for smoking, usu. enclosed in a wrapper of thin paper. [Fr., dim. of *cigare*, CIGAR.]

ci•lan•tro (sĭ-lăn′trō) ►*n.* See **coriander** 2. [Sp. < Lat. *coriandrum*, CORIANDER.]

cil•i•a (sĭl′ē-ə) ►*n.* Pl. of **cilium.**

cil•i•ar•y (sĭl′ē-ĕr′ē) ►*adj.* Of or resembling cilia.

cil•i•ate (sĭl′ē-ĭt, -āt′) ►*adj.* Ciliated. ►*n.* Any of a class of protozoans characterized by numerous cilia.

cil•i•at•ed (sĭl′ē-ā′tĭd) ►*adj.* Having cilia.

cil•i•um (sĭl′ē-əm) ►*n., pl.* **-i•a** (-ē-ə) **1.** A microscopic hairlike process extending from a cell or unicellular organism and capable of rhythmical motion. **2.** An eyelash. [Lat., eyelid.]

cinch (sĭnch) ►*n.* **1.** A girth for holding a pack or saddle in place. **2.** A firm grip. **3.** Something easy to accomplish. See Syns at **breeze. 4.** A sure thing; certainty. [< Lat. *cingere*, gird.] —**cinch** *v.*

cin•cho•na (sĭng-kō′nə, sĭn-chō′-) ►*n.* **1.** Any of a genus of South American trees whose bark yields quinine and other medicinal alkaloids. **2.** The dried bark of a cinchona. [Supposedly after Francisca H. de Ribera (1576–1639), Countess of *Chinchón.*]

Cin•cin•na•ti (sĭn′sə-năt′ē, -năt′ə) A city of SW OH on the Ohio R. Pop. 364,040.

Cin•cin•na•tus (sĭn′sə-năt′əs, -nā′təs), **Lucius Quinctius.** 519?–438 B.C. Roman statesman.

cinc•ture (sĭngk′chər) ►*n.* A belt or sash; girdle. [< Lat. *cingere*, gird.] —**cinc′ture** *v.*

cin•der (sĭn′dər) ►*n.* **1a.** A burned substance that is not reduced to ashes but cannot be burned further. **b.** A glowing coal. **2. cinders** Ashes. **3. cinders** *Geol.* See **scoria** 1. **4.** *Metall.* See **scoria** 2. [< OE *sinder*, dross.] —**cin′der•y** *adj.*

cinder block ►*n.* A usu. hollow building block made with concrete and coal cinders.

cin•e•ma (sĭn′ə-mə) ►*n.* **1a.** A film or movie. **b.** A movie theater. **2a.** Films or movies collectively. **b.** The film or movie industry. **3.** The art of making films; filmmaking. [Fr. *cinéma* < *cinématographe*, motion-picture projector.] —**cin′e•mat′ic** (-măt′ĭk) *adj.* —**cin′e•mat′i•cal•ly** *adv.*

cin•e•ma•tize (sĭn′ə-mə-tīz′) ►*v.* **-tized, -tiz•ing.** To adapt (e.g., a novel or play) for film or movies. —**cin′e•mat′i•za′tion** *n.*

cin•e•ma•tog•ra•phy (sĭn′ə-mə-tŏg′rə-fē) ►*n.* The art or technique of movie photography. —**cin′e•ma•tog′ra•pher** *n.* —**cin′e•mat′o•graph′ic** (-măt′ə-grăf′ĭk) *adj.*

ci•né•ma vé•ri•té (sē′nā-mä′ vā′rē-tā′) ►*n.* Documentary filmmaking that stresses unbiased realism. [Fr.]

cin•e•rar•i•a (sĭn′ə-râr′ē-ə) ►*n.* Any of several tropical plants cultivated as house plants for their showy, daisylike flowers. [< Lat. *cinerārius*, of ashes.]

cin•e•rar•i•um (sĭn′ə-râr′ē-əm) ►*n., pl.* **-i•a** (-ē-ə). A place for keeping the ashes of a cremated body. [< Lat. *cinis, ciner-*, ashes.] —**cin′er•ar′y** (sĭn′ə-rĕr′ē) *adj.*

cin•na•bar (sĭn′ə-bär′) ►*n.* **1.** A heavy reddish compound, HgS, that is the principal ore of mercury. **2.** See **vermilion** 2. [< Gk. *kinnabari.*]

cin•na•mon (sĭn′ə-mən) ►*n.* **1.** The aromatic reddish or yellowish-brown bark of certain tropical Asian trees, dried and often ground for use as a spice. **2.** A light reddish brown. [< Gk. *kinnamōmon.*] —**cin′na•mon** *adj.*

CIO ►*abbr.* **1.** chief information officer **2.** Congress of Industrial Organizations

ciop•pi•no (chə-pē′nō) ►*n., pl.* **-nos.** A stew of fish and shellfish, tomatoes, and white wine. [Ital.]

ci•pher (sī′fər) ►*n.* **1.** The mathematical symbol (0) denoting absence of quantity; zero. **2.** An Arabic numeral or figure. **3.** A nonentity. **4a.** A system of secret writing in which units of plain text are substituted according to a predetermined key. **b.** The key to a cipher. **c.** A message in cipher. ►*v.* To compute arithmetically. [< Ar. *ṣifr.*]

cir•ca (sûr′kə) ►*prep.* About: *born circa 1900.* [Lat. *circā.*]

cir•ca•di•an (sər-kā′dē-ən, -kăd′ē-, sûr′kə-dī′ən, -dē′-) ►*adj. Biol.* Of or exhibiting approx. 24-hour periodicity. [< Lat. *circā*, around + *diēs*, day.]

cir•cle (sûr′kəl) ►*n.* **1.** A plane curve everywhere equidistant from a given fixed point, the center. **2.** A planar region bounded by a circle. **3.** Something shaped like a circle. **4.** A group of people sharing an interest or activity. **5.** A sphere of influence or interest. ►*v.* **-cled, -cling 1.** To make a circle around. See Syns at **surround. 2.** To move in a circle (around). [< Gk. *kirkos.*]

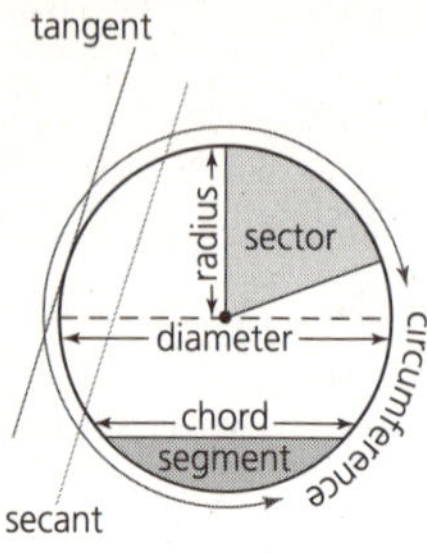

circle

cir•clet (sûr′klĭt) ►*n.* A small circle.

cir•cuit (sûr′kĭt) ►*n.* **1a.** A closed, usu. circular line around an area. See Syns at **circumference. b.** The region enclosed by such a line. **2.** A closed path or route. **3a.** A closed path followed by an electric current. **b.** A configuration of electrically or electromagnetically connected components or devices. **4a.** A regular or accustomed course from place to place, as that of a salesperson. **b.** The area or district thus covered, esp. a territory served by a circuit court. ►*v.* To make a circuit (of). [< Lat. *circumīre*, go around.]

circuit board ►*n. Comp. Sci.* An insulated board on which interconnected circuits and components such as microchips are mounted or etched.

circuit breaker ►*n.* An automatic switch that interrupts an overloaded electric circuit.

circuit court ►*n.* A state court that holds sessions periodically at several different places within a judicial district.

cir•cu•i•tous (sər-kyo͞o′ĭ-təs) ►*adj.* Being or taking a roundabout course. —**cir•cu′i•tous•ly** *adv.* —**cir•cu′i•ty, cir•cu′i•tous•ness** *n.*

cir•cuit•ry (sûr′kĭ-trē) ►*n., pl.* **-ries 1.** The design of or a detailed plan for an electric circuit. **2.** Electric circuits collectively.

cir•cu•lar (sûr′kyə-lər) ►*adj.* **1.** Of or relating to a circle. **2a.** Shaped like a circle; round. **b.** Moving in or forming a circle. **3.** Circuitous. **4.** Self-referential: *circular reasoning.* ►*n.* A printed advertisement or notice for mass distribution. —**cir′cu•lar′i•ty** (-lăr′ĭ-tē) *n.* —**cir′cu•lar•ly** *adv.*

circular saw ►*n.* A power saw consisting of a toothed disk rotated at high speed.

cir•cu•late ►*v.* **-lat•ed, -lat•ing 1.** To move in or flow through a circle or circuit. **2.** To move around, as from person to person or place to place. **3.** To move or cause to move, as air. **4.** To disseminate. —**cir′cu•la′tive** *adj.* —**cir′cu•la′tor** *n.* —**cir′cu•la•to′ry** (-lə-tôr′ē, -tōr′ē) *adj.*

cir•cu•la•tion (sûr′kyə-lā′shən) ►*n.* **1.** Movement in a circle or circuit. **2.** The movement of blood through bodily vessels as a result of the heart's pumping action. **3.** The passing of something, such as money, from place to place or person to person. **4a.** The distribution of printed material, esp. newspapers or magazines. **b.** The number of copies sold or distributed.

circulatory system ►*n.* The heart, blood vessels, and lymphatic system of the body.

circum– ►*pref.* Around; about: *circumlunar.* [Lat. < *circum*, around.]

cir•cum•cise (sûr′kəm-sīz′) ►*v.* **-cised, -cis•ing 1.** To remove the prepuce of (a male). **2.** To remove a part of the clitoris of (a female). [< Lat. *circumcīdere, circumcīs-*, cut around.] —**cir′cum•ci′sion** (-sĭzh′ən) *n.*

cir•cum•fer•ence (sər-kŭm′fər-əns) ►*n.* **1.** The boundary line of a circle. **2a.** The boundary line of a figure, area, or object. **b.** The length of such a boundary. [< Lat. *circumferre*, carry around : CIRCUM– + *ferre*, carry.] —**cir•cum′fer•en′tial** (-fə-rĕn′shəl) *adj.*

Syns: *circumference, circuit, compass, perimeter, periphery* **n.**

cir•cum•flex (sûr′kəm-flĕks′) ►*n.* Any of several marks, especially (ˆ), used over a vowel to indicate quality of pronunciation. [< Lat. *circumflectere*, bend around.]

cir•cum•lo•cu•tion (sûr′kəm-lō-kyo͞o′shən) ►*n.* **1.** The use of wordy and indirect language. **2.** A roundabout expression.

cir•cum•lu•nar (sûr′kəm-lo͞o′nər) ►*adj.* Revolving about or surrounding the moon.

cir•cum•nav•i•gate (sûr′kəm-năv′ĭ-gāt′) ►*v.* **-gat•ed, -gat•ing.** To go or proceed completely around: *circumnavigating the earth.* —**cir′cum•nav′i•ga′tion** *n.*

cir•cum•po•lar (sûr′kəm-pō′lər) ►*adj.* Located or found in one of the polar regions.

cir•cum•scribe (sûr′kəm-skrīb′) ►*v.* **-scribed, -scrib•ing 1.** To draw a line around. **2.** To confine within bounds; restrict. **3.** To enclose (a polygon or polyhedron) within a configuration of lines, curves, or surfaces so that every vertex of the enclosed object touches the enclosing configuration. [< Lat. *circumscrībere*, write around.] —**cir′cum•scrip′tion** (-skrip′shən) *n.*

cir•cum•so•lar (sûr′kəm-sō′lər) ►*adj.* Revolving around or surrounding the sun.

cir•cum•spect (sûr′kəm-spĕkt′) ►*adj.* Heedful of potential consequences; prudent. [< Lat. *circumspicere*, take heed : CIRCUM– + *specere*, look.] —**cir′cum•spec′tion** *n.* —**cir′cum•spect′ly** *adv.*

cir•cum•stance (sûr′kəm-stăns′) ►*n.* **1.** A condition or fact attending an event and having some bearing on it. **2.** often **circumstances** The sum of determining factors beyond willful control. **3. circumstances** Financial status or means. **4.** Formal display; ceremony: *pomp and circumstance.* —***idioms:*** **under no circumstances** Never. **under** (or **in**) **the circumstances** Given these conditions. [< Lat. *circumstāre*, stand around : CIRCUM– + *stāre*, stand.]

cir•cum•stan•tial (sûr′kəm-stăn′shəl) ►*adj.* **1.** Of or dependent on circumstances. **2.** Of minor import; incidental. **3.** Complete and particular. —**cir′cum•stan′tial•ly** *adv.*

circumstantial evidence ►*n.* Evidence not bearing directly on the fact in dispute but on various attendant circumstances from which the judge or jury might infer the occurrence of the fact in dispute.

cir•cum•stan•ti•ate (sûr′kəm-stăn′shē-āt′)

►*v.* **-at•ed, -at•ing.** To give detailed proof or description of. —**cir′cum•stan′ti•a′tion** *n.*

cir•cum•ter•res•tri•al (sûr′kəm-tə-rĕs′trē-əl) ►*adj.* Revolving around or surrounding the earth.

cir•cum•vent (sûr′kəm-vĕnt′) ►*v.* **1.** To entrap or overcome by ingenuity. **2.** To avoid or get around: *circumvent a regulation.* [< Lat. *circumvenīre* : CIRCUM– + *venīre*, go.] —**cir′cum•ven′tion** *n.* —**cir′cum•ven′tive** *adj.*

cir•cus (sûr′kəs) ►*n.* **1a.** A public entertainment consisting typically of a variety of performances by acrobats, clowns, and trained animals. **b.** A traveling company that performs such entertainments, often under a tent. **2.** *Informal* A humorous or rowdy time or event. [< Lat., CIRCLE.] —**cir′cus•y** *adj.*

cirque (sûrk) ►*n.* A steep hollow, often containing a small lake, at the upper end of a mountain valley. [< Lat. *circus*, CIRCLE.]

cir•rho•sis (sĭ-rō′sĭs) ►*n.* A chronic, sometimes fatal liver disease caused esp. by alcohol abuse or hepatitis. [< Gk. *kirros*, tawny.] —**cir•rhot′ic** (-rŏt′ĭk) *adj.*

cir•ro•cu•mu•lus (sĭr′ō-kyo͞om′yə-ləs) ►*n.* A high-altitude cloud composed of a series of small, regularly arranged cloudlets in the form of ripples or grains.

cir•ro•stra•tus (sĭr′ō-strā′təs, -străt′əs) ►*n.* A high-altitude, thin hazy cloud or cloud cover, often producing a halo effect.

cir•rus (sĭr′əs) ►*n.*, *pl.* **cir•ri** (sĭr′ī′). A high-altitude cloud composed of thin, usu. white fleecy bands or patches. [Lat., curl of hair.]

cis•tern (sĭs′tərn) ►*n.* A receptacle for holding water, esp. a tank for catching and storing rainwater. [< Lat. *cisterna.*]

cit. ►*abbr.* **1.** citation **2.** cited

cit•a•del (sĭt′ə-dəl, -dĕl′) ►*n.* **1.** A fortress in a commanding position in or near a city. **2.** A stronghold. [< Ital. *cittadella*, small city.]

cite (sīt) ►*v.* **cit•ed, cit•ing 1.** To quote as an authority or example. See Usage Note at **quote. 2.** To mention as support, illustration, or proof. **3.** To commend officially for meritorious action, esp. in military service. **4.** To summon before a court of law. [< Lat. *citāre.*] —**ci•ta′tion** *n.*

cit•i•fy (sĭt′ĭ-fī′) ►*v.* **-fied, -fy•ing 1.** To make urban. **2.** To impart the styles and manners of a city to. —**cit′i•fi•ca′tion** *n.* —**cit′i•fied′** *adj.*

cit•i•zen (sĭt′ĭ-zən) ►*n.* **1.** A person owing loyalty to and entitled by birth or naturalization to the protection of a state or nation. **2.** A resident of a city or town. [< AN *citesein.*] —**cit′i•zen•ly** *adj.*

Syns: *citizen, national, subject* **n.**

cit•i•zen•ry (sĭt′ĭ-zən-rē) ►*n.*, *pl.* **-ries.** Citizens collectively.

cit•i•zens band (sĭt′ĭ-zənz) ►*n.* A radio-frequency band officially allocated for private use by individuals.

cit•i•zen•ship (sĭt′ĭ-zən-shĭp′) ►*n.* The status of a citizen with its duties, rights, and privileges.

cit•rate (sĭt′rāt′) ►*n.* A salt or ester of citric acid.

cit•ric acid (sĭt′rĭk) ►*n.* A colorless acid derived from citrus and pineapple juices and used in flavorings and metal polishes.

ci•trine (sĭ-trēn′, sĭt′rēn′) ►*n.* **1.** A pale yellow quartz resembling topaz. **2.** A light yellow. [< Lat. *citrus*, citron.] —**ci•trine′** *adj.*

cit•ron (sĭt′rən) ►*n.* **1.** A thorny evergreen shrub with large, lemonlike fruits. **2.** Its fruit, whose rind is often candied and used in confections. [< Lat. *citreum*, citrus.]

cit•ro•nel•la (sĭt′rə-nĕl′ə) ►*n.* A pale yellow aromatic oil obtained from a tropical Asian grass and used in perfumery, insect repellents, and flavorings. [< Fr. *citronnelle.*]

cit•rus (sĭt′rəs) ►*n.*, *pl.* **-rus** or **-rus•es.** Any of various evergreen shrubs or trees such as the grapefruit, lemon, or orange, bearing juicy edible fruits with an aromatic rind. [Lat., citron tree.]

cit•y (sĭt′ē) ►*n.*, *pl.* **-ies 1.** A town of significant size and importance. **2.** An incorporated US municipality with definite boundaries and legal powers set forth in a state charter. **3.** The inhabitants of a city as a group. [< Lat. *cīvitās.*]

city council ►*n.* The governing body of a city.

city desk ►*n.* The newspaper department that handles local news.

city hall ►*n.* **1.** The building housing the administrative offices of a municipal government. **2.** A municipal government.

city manager ►*n.* An administrator appointed by a city council to manage municipal affairs.

cit•y-state (sĭt′ē-stāt′) ►*n.* A sovereign state consisting of an independent city and its surrounding territory.

Ci•u•dad Juá•rez (sē′o͞o-däd′ wär′ĕz) A city of N Mexico on the Rio Grande opposite El Paso, TX. Pop. 544,496.

civ•et (sĭv′ĭt) ►*n.* **1.** A catlike mammal of Africa and Asia that secretes a musky fluid. **2.** This fluid, used in perfumery. [< Ar. *zabād*, civet perfume.]

civ•ic (sĭv′ĭk) ►*adj.* Of a city, a citizen, or citizenship. [< Lat. *cīvis*, citizen.]

civ•ics (sĭv′ĭks) ►*n.* *(takes sing. v.)* The study of civic affairs and the rights and duties of citizens.

civ•ies (sĭv′ēz) ►*pl.n.* *Slang* Var. of **civvies.**

civ•il (sĭv′əl) ►*adj.* **1.** Of or relating to a citizen or citizens. **2.** Of ordinary community life as distinguished from the military or the ecclesiastical. **3.** Civilized. **4.** Not rude; polite. [< Lat. *cīvis*, citizen.] —**civ′il•ly** *adv.*

civil defense ►*n.* Emergency measures to be taken by organized civilian volunteers for protection of life and property in the event of natural disaster or enemy attack.

civil disobedience ►*n.* Refusal to obey civil laws in an effort to induce change in governmental policy or legislation, characterized by nonviolent means.

civil engineer ►*n.* An engineer trained in the design and construction of public works, as bridges or dams. —**civil engineering** *n.*

ci•vil•ian (sĭ-vĭl′yən) ►*n.* A person following the pursuits of civil or nonmilitary life. —**ci•vil′ian** *adj.*

ci•vil•i•ty (sĭ-vĭl′ĭ-tē) ►*n.*, *pl.* **-ties 1.** Politeness; courtesy. **2.** A courteous act.

civ•i•li•za•tion (sĭv′ə-lĭ-zā′shən) ►*n.* **1.** An advanced state of cultural and material development in human society, marked by political and social complexity and progress in the arts and sciences. **2.** The culture developed by a particular society or epoch. **3.** Cultural refinement. **4.** Modern society with its conveniences.

civ•i•lize (sĭv′ə-līz′) ►*v.* **-lized, -liz•ing 1.** To raise (a society) to an advanced stage of development. **2.** To educate in manners; sophisticate. —**civ′i•liz′er** *n.*

civil law ►*n.* The body of laws dealing with the rights of private citizens.

civil liberties ►*pl.n.* Fundamental individual rights, such as freedom of speech and religion, protected by legal guarantee.

civil rights ►*pl.n.* The rights belonging to an individual by virtue of citizenship, esp. the rights to due process, equal protection of the laws, and freedom from discrimination. —**civil rights, civ′il-rights′** *adj.*

civil service ►*n.* Those branches of public service that are not legislative, judicial, or military. —**civil servant** *n.*

civil war ►*n.* **1.** A war between factions or regions of the same country. **2. Civil War** The war between the Union and the Confederacy from 1861 to 1865.

civ•vies also **civ•ies** (sĭv′ēz) ►*pl.n. Slang* Civilian clothes.

CJ ►*abbr.* Chief Justice

cl ►*abbr.* centiliter

Cl ► The symbol for the element **chlorine.**

clab•ber (klăb′ər) ►*n.* Sour curdled milk. ►*v.* To curdle. [< Ir.Gael. *bainne clabair.*]

clack (klăk) ►*v.* **1.** To make or cause to make a sharp sound, as by the collision of hard surfaces. **2.** To chatter. ►*n.* A clacking sound. [< ON *klaka.*] —**clack′er** *n.*

clad[1] (klăd) ►*v.* **clad, clad•ding.** To cover (a metal) with a bonded metal coating. [Poss. < CLAD[2].]

clad[2] (klăd) ►*v.* P.t. and p.part of **clothe.**

clad•dagh (klä′də) ►*n.* A ring formed of two hands clasping a crowned heart. [After *Claddagh*, suburb of Galway.]

claim (klām) ►*v.* **1.** To ask for as one's due: *claim a reward.* See Syns at **demand. 2.** To state to be true; assert. **3.** To call for: *problems that claim her attention.* ►*n.* **1.** A demand for something as one's due. **2.** A title or right. **3.** Something claimed formally or legally. **4.** A statement of something as a fact. —***idiom:* lay claim to** To assert one's right to. [< Lat. *clāmāre*, to call.] —**claim′a•ble** *adj.*

claim•ant (klā′mənt) ►*n.* One making a claim.

clair•voy•ance (klâr-voi′əns) ►*n.* The supposed power to see objects or events that cannot be perceived by the senses. [Fr. : *clair*, CLEAR + Lat. *vidēre*, see.] —**clair•voy′ant** *adj. & n.*

clam (klăm) ►*n.* **1.** Any of a class of bivalve mollusks, many of which are edible. **2.** *Slang* A dollar. ►*v.* **clammed, clam•ming.** To hunt for clams. —***phrasal verb:* clam up** *Informal* To refuse to talk. [< *clam*, clamp.] —**clam′mer** *n.*

clam•bake (klăm′bāk′) ►*n.* A picnic where clams, corn, and other foods are baked in layers on hot stones covered with seaweed.

clam•ber (klăm′bər, klăm′ər) ►*v.* To climb with difficulty, esp. on all fours; scramble. [ME *clambren.*] —**clam′ber•er** *n.*

clam•my (klăm′ē) ►*adj.* **-mi•er, -mi•est.** Disagreeably moist, sticky, and usu. cold. [ME, sticky.] —**clam′mi•ness** *n.*

clam•or (klăm′ər) ►*n.* **1.** A loud outcry; hubbub. **2.** A vehement expression of discontent. [< Lat. *clāmor*, shout.] —**clam′or** *v.* —**clam′or•ous** *adj.* —**clam′or•ous•ly** *adv.*

clamp (klămp) ►*n.* Any of various devices used to join, grip, support, or compress mechanical or structural parts. ►*v.* To fasten or grip with or as if with a clamp. —***phrasal verb:* clamp down** To become more repressive. [< MDu. *klampe.*]

clamp•down (klămp′doun′) ►*n.* An imposing of restrictions or controls.

clan (klăn) ►*n.* **1.** A traditional social unit in the Scottish Highlands, consisting of a number of families claiming a common ancestor. **2.** A division of a tribe tracing descent from a common ancestor. **3.** A large group of relatives or associates. [< OIr. *cland*, offspring.] —**clan′nish** *adj.* —**clan′nish•ness** *n.* —**clans′man** *n.* —**clans′wom′an** *n.*

clan•des•tine (klăn-dĕs′tĭn) ►*adj.* Kept or done in secret. [Lat. *clandestīnus.*]

clang (klăng) ►*n.* A loud, resonant, metallic sound. [Prob. < Lat. *clangere*, to ring.] —**clang** *v.*

clan•gor (klăng′ər, klăng′gər) ►*n.* **1.** A repeated clanging. **2.** A din. [Lat. < *clangere*, to clang.] —**clan′gor** *v.*

clank (klăngk) ►*n.* A sharp, hard metallic sound. [Prob. imit.] —**clank** *v.*

clap (klăp) ►*v.* **clapped, clap•ping 1.** To strike the palms of the hands together with a sudden explosive sound, as in applauding. **2.** To come together suddenly with a sharp sound. **3.** To strike lightly with the open hand, as in greeting. **4.** To put or send promptly or suddenly: *clapped the thief in jail.* ►*n.* **1.** The act or sound of clapping the hands. **2.** A loud or explosive sound: *a clap of thunder.* **3.** A slap. [< OE *clæppan*, throb, and ON *klappa*, clap.]

clap•board (klăb′ərd, klăp′bôrd′, -bōrd′) ►*n.* A long narrow board with one edge thicker than the other, overlapped horizontally to cover the outer walls of frame structures. [< Du. *klaphout*, split board.]

clap•per (klăp′ər) ►*n.* One that claps, esp. the hammerlike tongue of a bell.

clap•trap (klăp′trăp′) ►*n.* Pretentious, insincere, or empty language.

claque (klăk) ►*n.* A group of persons hired to applaud at a performance. [Fr.]

clar•et (klăr′ĭt) ►*n.* A dry red table wine. [< OFr. *(vin) claret*, (light-colored) wine.]

clar•i•fy (klăr′ə-fī′) ►*v.* **-fied, -fy•ing.** To make or become clear. [< LLat. *clārificāre.*] —**clar′i•fi•ca′tion** *n.*

clar•i•net (klăr′ə-nĕt′) ►*n.* A woodwind instrument having a straight cylindrical tube with a flaring bell and a single-reed mouthpiece. [< Lat. *clārus*, clear.] —**clar′i•net′ist, clar′i•net′tist** *n.*

clar•i•on (klăr′ē-ən) ►*adj.* Loud and clear. [< Lat. *clārus*, clear.]

clar•i•ty (klăr′ĭ-tē) ►*n.* The quality or condition of being clear. [< Lat. *clārus*, clear.]

Clark (klärk), **Charles Joseph.** "Joe." b. 1939. Canadian prime minister (1979–80).

Clark, George Rogers. 1752–1818. Amer. military leader and pioneer.

Clark, William. 1770–1838. Amer. explorer.

clash (klăsh) ►*v.* **1.** To collide or strike together with a loud harsh noise. **2.** To conflict; disagree. ►*n.* **1.** A loud metallic noise. **2.** A usu. hostile conflict. [Imit.]

clasp (klăsp) ►*n.* **1.** A fastening, such as a hook,

used to hold two objects or parts together. **2a.** An embrace. **b.** A grip of the hand. ►*v.* **1.** To fasten with or as if with a clasp. **2.** To hold in a tight embrace. **3.** To grip firmly in or with the hand. [ME *claspe.*]

class (klăs) ►*n.* **1.** A group whose members have certain attributes in common; category. **2.** A division based on quality or grade. **3.** A social or economic stratum whose members share similar characteristics. **4.** *Informal* Elegance of style or manner. **5a.** A group of students or alumni who have the same year of graduation. **b.** A group of students who meet to study the same subject. **6.** *Biol.* A taxonomic category ranking below a phylum and above an order. ►*v.* To classify. [< Lat. *classis*, class of citizens.]

class action ►*n.* A lawsuit brought by one or more plaintiffs on behalf of a large group of others who have a common interest.

clas•sic (klăs′ĭk) ►*adj.* **1a.** Of highest rank or class. **b.** Serving as the established model or standard: *a classic example.* **2.** Adhering to established standards and principles. **3.** Relating to ancient Greek and Roman literature and art; classical. **4.** Having lasting historical or literary associations. ►*n.* **1.** An artist, author, or work gen. considered to be of the highest rank. **2.** **classics** The languages and literature of ancient Greece and Rome. **3.** A typical example. **4.** *Informal* An outstanding example of its kind: *His excuse was a classic.* **5.** A traditional event, as in sports.

clas•si•cal (klăs′ĭ-kəl) ►*adj.* **1a.** Of or relating to the ancient Greeks and Romans, esp. their art, literature, or culture. **b.** Conforming to the artistic models of ancient Greece and Rome. **2.** *Mus.* **a.** Of European music during the later 18th and early 19th cent. **b.** Of concert music, such as symphony and opera, as opposed to popular or folk music. **3.** Standard and authoritative rather than new or experimental. —**clas′si•cal•ly** *adv.*

clas•si•cism (klăs′ĭ-sĭz′əm) ►*n.* **1.** Aesthetic attitudes and principles manifested in the art, architecture, and literature of ancient Greece and Rome and characterized by emphasis on form, simplicity, proportion, and restraint. **2.** Adherence to such attitudes and principles. **3.** Classical scholarship.

clas•si•cist (klăs′ĭ-sĭst) ►*n.* **1.** A classical scholar. **2.** An adherent of classicism.

clas•si•fied (klăs′ə-fīd′) ►*adj.* **1.** Arranged in classes or categories. **2.** Available to authorized persons only; secret.

classified advertisement ►*n.* An advertisement, usu. brief and in small type, in a newspaper or magazine with others of the same kind.

clas•si•fy (klăs′ə-fī′) ►*v.* **-fied, -fy•ing 1.** To arrange or organize according to class or category. **2.** To designate (e.g., a document) as confidential, secret, or top secret. —**clas′si•fi•ca′tion** *n.* —**clas′si•fi′er** *n.*

class•less (klăs′lĭs) ►*adj.* Lacking social or economic distinctions of class.

class•mate (klăs′māt′) ►*n.* A member of the same class at school.

class•room (klăs′ro͞om′, -ro͝om′) ►*n.* A room in which academic classes meet.

class•y (klăs′ē) ►*adj.* **-i•er, -i•est** *Informal.* Highly stylish; elegant. —**class′i•ness** *n.*

clat•ter (klăt′ər) ►*v.* To make or cause to make a rattling sound. ►*n.* **1.** A rattling sound. **2.** A din; racket. [ME *clateren.*]

Clau•di•us I (klô′dē-əs). 10 B.C.–A.D. 54. Emperor of Rome (A.D. 41–54).

clause (klôz) ►*n.* **1.** *Gram.* A group of words containing a subject and a predicate and forming part of a compound or complex sentence. **2.** A distinct article, stipulation, or provision in a document. [< Lat. *claudere, claus-*, to close.] —**claus′al** *adj.*

claus•tro•pho•bi•a (klô′strə-fō′bē-ə) ►*n.* An abnormal fear of being in narrow or enclosed spaces. [< Lat. *claustrum*, enclosed place.] —**claus′tro•phobe′** *n.* —**claus′tro•pho′bic** *adj.*

clav•i•chord (klăv′ĭ-kôrd′) ►*n. Mus.* An early keyboard instrument. [< Lat. *clāvis*, key + *chorda*, string.] —**clav′i•chord′ist** *n.*

clav•i•cle (klăv′ĭ-kəl) ►*n.* Either of two slender bones that connect the sternum and the scapula; collarbone. [< Lat. *clāvīcula*, dim. of *clāvis*, key.]

cla•vier (klə-vîr′, klā′vē-ər, klăv′ē-) ►*n. Mus.* **1.** A keyboard. **2.** A stringed keyboard instrument. [Ult. < Lat. *clāvis*, key.]

claw (klô) ►*n.* **1.** A sharp curved nail on the toe of a mammal, reptile, or bird. **2.** A pincerlike part, as of a lobster. **3.** Something resembling a claw. ►*v.* To scratch or dig with or as if with claws. [< OE *clawu.*]

clay (klā) ►*n.* **1.** A fine-grained, firm earth that is pliable when wet and hardens when heated, used in making bricks, tiles, and pottery. **2.** Moist sticky earth. **3.** The mortal human body. [< OE *clæg.*] —**clay′ey** (klā′ē), **clay′ish** *adj.*

Clay[1], Cassius Marcellus. 1810–1903. Amer. abolitionist.

Clay[2], Cassius Marcellus. See Muhammad **Ali**.

Clay, Henry. 1777–1852. Amer. politician.

Clay•ma•tion (klā-mā′shən) ► A service mark for an animation process in which clay figures are manipulated and filmed to produce an image of lifelike motion.

clay•more mine (klā′môr′, -mōr′) ►*n.* A ground-emplaced antipersonnel mine. [< *claymore*, a Scottish sword.]

clay pigeon ►*n.* A clay disk thrown as a flying target for skeet and trapshooting.

clean (klēn) ►*adj.* **-er, -est 1.** Free from dirt or impurities. **2.** Free from foreign matter, pollution, or infection. **3.** Even; regular: *a clean, straight line.* **4.** Thorough; complete: *a clean getaway.* **5.** Morally pure; virtuous. **6.** Obeying the rules; honest or fair. ►*adv.* **-er, -est 1.** In a clean manner. **2.** *Informal* Entirely; wholly: *clean forgot.* ►*v.* To make or become clean. —***phrasal verbs:* clean out** *Informal* **1.** To deprive completely, as of money. **2.** To drive or force out. **clean up** *Slang* To make a large profit. —***idiom:* clean house** *Slang* To eliminate or discard what is undesirable. [< OE *clǣne.*] —**clean′a•ble** *adj.* —**clean′er** *n.* —**clean′ness** *n.*

Syns: *clean, antiseptic, cleanly, immaculate, spotless* ***Ant:*** *dirty* **adj.**

clean-cut (klēn′kŭt′) ►*adj.* **1.** Clearly defined. **2.** Neat and trim in appearance.

clean•ly (klĕn′lē) ►*adj.* **-li•er, -li•est.** Habitually neat and clean. See Syns at **clean.** ►*adv.* (klēn′lē). In a clean manner. —**clean′li•ness** (klĕn′lē-nĭs) *n.*

clean room ►*n.* A room kept virtually free of contaminants, used for laboratory work and in the production of precision parts.

clean room

cleanse (klĕnz) ►*v.* **cleansed, cleans•ing.** To free from dirt, defilement, or guilt. [< OE *clǣnsian.*] —**cleans′er** *n.*

clean•up (klēn′ŭp′) ►*n.* **1.** A thorough cleaning or ordering. **2.** *Slang* A very large profit. **3.** *Baseball* The 4th position in the batting order.

clear (klîr) ►*adj.* **-er, -est 1.** Free from anything that dims, obscures, or darkens. **2.** Free from impediment; open. **3.** Easily seen through; transparent. **4.** Evident. See Syns at **apparent. 5.** Easily perceptible; distinct. **6.** Discerning or perceiving easily: *a clear mind.* **7.** Free from doubt or confusion. **8.** Free from qualification or limitation. **9.** Free from burden, obligation, or guilt. **10.** Freed from contact or connection: *clear of the danger; clear of the reef.* ►*adv.* **1.** Distinctly; clearly. **2.** Out of the way. **3.** *Informal* Completely; entirely. ►*v.* **1.** To make or become light, clear, or bright. **2.** To rid of impurities or blemishes. **3.** To make plain or intelligible. **4.** To rid of obstructions. **5.** To remove the occupants of: *clear the theater.* **6.** To free from a charge of guilt. **7.** To pass by, under, or over without contact. **8.** To gain as net profit. **9.** To pass through a clearinghouse, as a check. **10.** To authorize. **11.** To free (the throat) of phlegm. —***phrasal verb:*** **clear out** *Informal* To leave a place, usu. quickly. [< Lat. *clārus.*] —**clear′ly** *adv.* —**clear′ness** *n.*
Syns: *clear, limpid, lucid, pellucid, transparent* ***Ant:*** *opaque* **adj.**

clear•ance (klîr′əns) ►*n.* **1.** The act or process of clearing. **2.** The amount by which a moving object clears something. **3.** Permission to proceed.

clear-cut (klîr′kŭt′) ►*adj.* **1.** Distinctly defined or outlined. **2.** Not ambiguous; obvious. See Syns at **apparent.** ►*v.* To log (an area) by removing all the trees at one time.

clear•ing (klîr′ĭng) ►*n.* An open space, esp. a tract of woodland clear of trees.

clear•ing-house (klîr′ĭng-hous′) ►*n.* An office where banks exchange checks and drafts and settle accounts.

cleat (klēt) ►*n.* A wooden, metallic, or hard rubber projection used to grip, provide support, or prevent slipping. [ME *clete.*]

cleav•age (klē′vĭj) ►*n.* **1.** The act of splitting or cleaving. **2.** A fissure or division.

cleave[1] (klēv) ►*v.* **cleft** (klĕft) or **cleaved** or **clove** (klōv), **cleft** or **cleaved** or **clo•ven** (klō′vən), **cleav•ing 1.** To split; divide. **2.** To pierce. [< OE *clēofan.*]

cleave[2] (klēv) ►*v.* **cleaved, cleav•ing.** To adhere, cling, or stick fast. [< OE *cleofian.*]

cleav•er (klē′vər) ►*n.* A heavy, broad-bladed knife or hatchet used esp. by butchers.

clef (klĕf) ►*n.* *Mus.* A symbol indicating the pitch represented by one line of a staff, from which the others can be determined. [Fr., key < Lat. *clāvis.*]

cleft (klĕft) ►*v.* P.t. and p.part of **cleave**[1]. ►*adj.* Divided; split. ►*n.* A crevice.

cleft lip ►*n.* A congenital cleft or pair of clefts in the upper lip.

cleft palate ►*n.* Cleft lip involving fissuring of the palate.

clem•a•tis (klĕm′ə-tĭs, klĭ-măt′ĭs) ►*n.* Any of a genus of vines having showy, variously colored flowers. [< Gk. *klēma*, twig.]

Cle•men•ceau (klĕm′ən-sō′), **Georges.** 1841–1929. French premier (1906–09 and 1917–20).

clem•en•cy (klĕm′ən-sē) ►*n., pl.* **-cies 1.** Leniency; mercy. **2.** Mildness, as of weather.

Clem•ens (klĕm′ənz), **Samuel Langhorne.** Pen name Mark Twain. 1835–1910. Amer. author.

clem•ent (klĕm′ənt) ►*adj.* **1.** Lenient or merciful. **2.** Mild; pleasant: *clement weather.* [< Lat. *clēmēns.*] —**clem′ent•ly** *adv.*

clench (klĕnch) ►*v.* **1.** To close tightly: *clench one's teeth; clenched my fists in anger.* **2.** To grasp or grip tightly. **3.** To clinch (e.g., a bolt). ►*n.* **1.** A tight grip or grasp. **2.** A device that clenches. [< OE *beclencan.*]

Cle•o•pat•ra (klē′ə-păt′rə). 69–30 B.C. Egyptian queen (51–49 and 48–30).

clere•sto•ry (klîr′stôr′ē, -stōr′ē) ►*n., pl.* **-ries.** A windowed wall above the roofed section of a building. [ME *clerestorie.*]

cler•gy (klûr′jē) ►*n., pl.* **-gies.** The body of people ordained for religious service. See Usage Note at **collective noun.** [< LLat. *clēricus*, CLERK.]

cler•gy•man (klûr′jē-mən) ►*n.* A man who is a member of the clergy.

cler•gy•wom•an (klûr′jē-wo͝om′ən) ►*n.* A woman who is a member of the clergy.

cler•ic (klĕr′ĭk) ►*n.* A member of the clergy. [< LLat. *clēricus*, CLERK.]

cler•i•cal (klĕr′ĭ-kəl) ►*adj.* **1.** Of or relating to clerks or office workers or their work. **2.** Of the clergy.

cler•i•cal•ism (klĕr′ĭ-kə-lĭz′əm) ►*n.* A policy of supporting the power and influence of the clergy in political or secular matters.

clerk (klûrk; *British* klärk) ►*n.* **1.** One who works in an office performing such tasks as keeping records and filing. **2.** One who performs the business of a court or legislative body. **3.** A salesclerk. ►*v.* To work or serve as a clerk. [< Gk. *klērikos*, of the clergy.] —**clerk′ship′** *n.*

Cleve•land (klēv′lənd) A city of NE OH on Lake Erie. Pop. 505,616.

Cleveland, (Stephen) Grover. 1837–1908. The 22nd and 24th US President.

clev•er (klĕv′ər) ►*adj.* **-er, -est 1.** Mentally quick and original; bright. **2.** Dexterous; nimble. **3.** Ingenious; shrewd. [ME *cliver*, of LGer.

Grover Cleveland

Bill Clinton

orig.] —**clev′er•ly** *adv.* —**clev′er•ness** *n.*

Regional Note: In the 17th and 18th centuries, *clever* acquired certain positive senses in regional British speech, such as "neat and convenient to use" and "of an agreeable disposition." American regional speech has preserved some of these senses, as in the South, where *clever* can mean "good-natured, amiable."

clev•is (klĕv′ĭs) ►*n.* A U-shaped metal fastener. [Poss. of Scand. orig.]

clew (klo͞o) ►*n.* **1.** A ball of yarn or thread. **2.** *Naut.* A metal loop attached to the lower corner of a sail. [< OE *cliwen.*]

cli•ché (klē-shā′) ►*n.* A trite expression or idea. [< Fr. *clicher*, to stereotype.]

Syns: *cliché, bromide, commonplace, platitude, truism* **n.**

cli•chéd (klē-shād′) ►*adj.* Trite; hackneyed.

click (klĭk) ►*n.* **1.** A brief sharp sound. **2.** An act of clicking. ►*v.* **1.** To make or cause to make a click. **2.** *Comp. Sci.* To press down and release a button on a pointing device, as to select an icon. **3.** *Slang* **a.** To be a great success. **b.** To function well together. [Imit.]

click•er (klĭk′ər) ►*n.* One that clicks, as: **a.** A remote control. **b.** A computer mouse.

cli•ent (klī′ənt) ►*n.* **1.** One for whom professional services are rendered. **2.** A customer. **3.** A computer or program that can download files, run applications, or request services from a file server. [< Lat. *cliēns*, dependent.]

cli•en•tele (klī′ən-tĕl′, klē′än-) ►*n.* Clients or customers collectively. [< Lat. *clientēla*, clientship < *cliēns*, CLIENT.]

cliff (klĭf) ►*n.* A high, steep, or overhanging face of rock. [< OE *clif.*] —**cliff′y** *adj.*

cliff dweller ►*n.* A member of an Anasazi people of the SW US who built dwellings in the sides of cliffs. —**cliff dwelling** *n.*

cliff•hang•er (klĭf′hăng′ər) ►*n.* **1.** A melodramatic serial in which each episode ends in suspense. **2.** A close, suspenseful contest.

cli•mac•ter•ic (klī-măk′tər-ĭk, klī′măk-tĕr′ĭk) ►*n.* **1.** A period of life marked in women by the end of reproductive capacity and terminating with the completion of menopause. **2.** A critical period. [< Gk. *klimaktēr*, crisis < *klimax*. See CLIMAX.]

cli•mac•tic (klī-măk′tĭk) ►*adj.* Of or constituting a climax. —**cli•mac′ti•cal•ly** *adv.*

cli•mate (klī′mĭt) ►*n.* **1.** The prevailing weather conditions in a particular region. **2.** A region having certain weather conditions: *lives in a cold climate.* **3.** A general atmosphere or attitude: *a climate of unrest.* [< Gk. *klima*, region.] —**cli•mat′ic** (-măt′ĭk) *adj.* —**cli•mat′i•cal•ly** *adv.*

cli•ma•tol•o•gy (klī′mə-tŏl′ə-jē) ►*n.* The meteorological study of climate. —**cli′ma•to•log′ic** (-mə-tl-ŏj′ĭk), **cli′ma•to•log′i•cal** *adj.* —**cli′ma•tol′o•gist** *n.*

cli•max (klī′măks′) ►*n.* **1.** The point of greatest intensity, force, or effect in an ascending series. **2.** See **orgasm. 3.** *Ecol.* A stage in which a community of organisms, esp. plants, reaches a stable, self-perpetuating balance. ►*v.* To bring to or reach a climax. [< Gk. *klimax*, ladder.]

climb (klīm) ►*v.* **1a.** To move up or ascend, esp. by using the hands and feet. **b.** To move in a specified direction: *climbed down the ladder.* **2.** To grow upward. **3.** To rise: *prices climbed in June.* ►*n.* **1.** An act of climbing. **2.** A place to be climbed. [< OE *climban.*] —**climb′er** *n.*

clime (klīm) ►*n.* Climate.

clinch (klĭnch) ►*v.* **1.** To fasten securely, as with a nail or bolt. **2.** To settle conclusively. **3.** *Sports* To embrace so as to immobilize an opponent's arms. ►*n.* An act or instance of clinching. [Var. of CLENCH.]

clinch•er (klĭn′chər) ►*n.* One that clinches, esp. a decisive point, fact, or remark.

cling (klĭng) ►*v.* **clung** (klŭng), **cling•ing 1.** To hold fast or adhere to something or someone. **2.** To remain emotionally attached. [< OE *clingan.*] —**cling′y** *adj.*

cling•stone (klĭng′stōn′) ►*n.* A fruit, esp. a peach, having flesh that adheres closely to the stone. —**cling′stone′** *adj.*

clin•ic (klĭn′ĭk) ►*n.* **1.** A facility, often associated with a hospital, that deals mainly with outpatients. **2.** A medical establishment run by several specialists working in cooperation. **3.** A center that offers special counseling or instruction. **4.** A training session in which medical students observe the examination and treatment of patients, as at the bedside. [< Gk. *klinikos*, clinical < *klinē*, couch, bed.]

clin•i•cal (klĭn′ĭ-kəl) ►*adj.* **1.** Of or connected with a clinic. **2.** Of or based on direct observation of patients. **3.** Objective; analytical. —**clin′i•cal•ly** *adv.*

cli•ni•cian (klĭ-nĭsh′ən) ►*n.* A physician, psychologist, or psychiatrist specializing in clinical studies or practice.

clink¹ (klĭngk) ►*v.* To make or cause to make a light sharp ringing sound. [< MDu. *klinken.*] —**clink** *n.*

clink² (klĭngk) ►*n.* *Slang* A prison or jail. [After *Clink*, a London prison.]

clink•er (klĭng′kər) ►*n.* **1.** A fused lump of incombustible residue that remains after coal has burned. **2.** A mistake; blunder. [Obsolete Du. *klinckaerd.*]

Clinton (klĭn′tən), **William Jefferson.** "Bill." b. 1946. The 42nd US President (since 1993).

cli•o•met•rics (klī′ə-mĕt′rĭks) ►*n.* *(takes sing. v.)* The study of history using advanced mathematical methods of data processing and analysis. [< *Clio*, the muse of history.] —**cli′o•met′ric** *adj.*

clip¹ (klĭp) ►*v.* **clipped, clip•ping 1.** To cut off or out with or as if with shears. **2.** To shorten; trim. **3.** *Informal* To hit with a sharp blow. **4.** *Slang* To cheat; swindle. ►*n.* **1.** Something clipped off, esp. a short extract from a film or videotape. **2.** *Informal* A sharp blow. **3.** *Informal* A brisk pace. **4. clips** A pair of clippers. [< ON *klippa.*]

clip² (klĭp) ►*n.* **1.** A clasp or fastener. **2.** A container for holding cartridges. ►*v.* **clipped,**

clip•ping 1. To hold tightly; fasten. **2.** *Football* To block (an opponent) illegally. [< OE *clyppan*, to embrace.]

clip art ▸*n.* Ready-made computerized graphic art used in decorating documents.

clip•board (klĭp′bôrd′, -bōrd′) ▸*n.* A small writing board with a spring clip at the top for holding papers or a pad.

clip•per (klĭp′ər) ▸*n.* **1.** often **clippers** A tool for cutting, clipping, or shearing. **2.** A sailing vessel built for great speed.

clip•ping (klĭp′ĭng) ▸*n.* Something cut out, esp. an item from a newspaper.

clique (klēk, klĭk) ▸*n.* A small, exclusive group of people. [Fr.] —**cliqu′ey, cliqu′y** *adj.*

clit•o•ris (klĭt′ər-ĭs, klĭ-tôr′-, klī′tər-) ▸*n.* A small erectile organ at the upper part of the vulva, homologous with the penis. [< Gk. *kleitoris.*] —**clit′o•ral** *adj.*

Clive (klīv), **Robert.** 1725–74. British colonial administrator in India.

clo•a•ca (klō-ā′kə) ▸*n., pl.* **-cae** (-sē′) **1.** The cavity into which the intestinal, genital, and urinary tracts open in reptiles, birds, amphibians, and most fishes. **2.** A similar cavity in certain invertebrates. [Lat. *cloāca*, sewer.]

cloak (klōk) ▸*n.* **1.** A loose outer garment, such as a cape. **2.** Something that covers or conceals: *a cloak of secrecy.* ▸*v.* **1.** To cover with a cloak. **2.** To conceal. See Syns at **disguise.** [< Med.Lat. *clocca*, bell.]

cloak-and-dag•ger (klōk′ən-dăg′ər) ▸*adj.* Marked by melodramatic intrigue and spying.

clob•ber (klŏb′ər) ▸*v. Slang* **1.** To hit or pound with great force. **2.** To defeat decisively. [?]

cloche (klōsh) ▸*n.* A close-fitting woman's hat with a bell-like shape. [< OFr., bell.]

clock (klŏk) ▸*n.* An instrument for measuring or indicating time. ▸*v.* **1.** To time, as with a stopwatch. **2.** To measure the speed of. [< Med.Lat. *clocca*, bell.] —**clock′er** *n.*

clock•wise (klŏk′wīz′) ▸*adv.* & *adj.* In the same direction as the rotating hands of a clock.

clock•work (klŏk′wûrk′) ▸*n.* A mechanism of geared wheels driven by a wound spring, as in a mechanical clock. —***idiom:* like clockwork** With machinelike precision.

clod (klŏd) ▸*n.* **1.** A lump or chunk, esp. of earth or clay. **2.** A dull, stupid person; dolt. [ME < OE *clot.*] —**clod′dish** *adj.* —**clod′dish•ly** *adv.* —**clod′dish•ness** *n.*

clod•hop•per (klŏd′hŏp′ər) ▸*n.* **1.** A rube or bumpkin. **2.** A big heavy shoe.

clog (klôg, klŏg) ▸*n.* **1.** An obstruction or hindrance. **2.** A heavy, usu. wooden-soled shoe. ▸*v.* **clogged, clog•ging 1.** To make or become obstructed. **2.** To hamper or impede. [ME *clogge*, block attached to an animal's leg.]

cloi•son•né (kloi′zə-nā′, klə-wä′zə-) ▸*n.* Enamelware in which the surface decoration is formed by different colors of enamel separated by thin strips of metal. [< OFr. *cloison*, partition.] —**cloi•son•né′** *adj.*

clois•ter (kloi′stər) ▸*n.* **1.** A covered walk with an open colonnade on one side, running along the walls of buildings that face a quadrangle. **2.** A monastery or convent. ▸*v.* To seclude in or as if in a cloister. [< Lat. *claustrum*, enclosed place.] —**clois′tral** *adj.*

clone (klōn) ▸*n.* **1.** One or more organisms descended asexually from and genetically identical to a single common ancestor. **2.** A replica of a DNA sequence, such as a gene, produced by genetic engineering. **3.** One that closely resembles another, as in appearance or function. ▸*v.* **cloned, clon•ing 1.** To make multiple identical copies of (a DNA sequence). **2.** To reproduce asexually. **3.** To propagate (an organism) as a clone. [Gk. *klōn*, twig.] —**clon′al** *adj.*

clop (klŏp) ▸*n.* A sharp hollow sound, as of a horse's hoof striking pavement. [Imit.] —**clop** *v.*

close (klōs) ▸*adj.* **clos•er, clos•est 1.** Being near in space, time, or relation. **2.** Bound by mutual interests or affections; intimate. **3.** Compact: *a close weave.* **4.** Being near a surface, as of the skin: *a close haircut.* **5.** Decided by a narrow margin; almost even: *a close election.* **6.** Faithful to the original: *a close copy.* **7.** Rigorous; thorough: *close attention.* **8.** Shut or shut in. **9.** Confined in space; crowded. **10.** Fitting tightly. **11.** Lacking fresh air; stuffy. **12.** Confined to specific persons; restricted. **13.** Hidden; secluded. **14.** Taciturn in manner; reticent. **15.** Stingy; miserly. ▸*v.* (klōz) **closed, clos•ing 1a.** To shut or become shut. **b.** To shut in; enclose. **2.** To fill or stop up. **3.** To bring or come to an end; finish. **4.** To join or unite; bring into contact. **5.** To reach an agreement. **6.** To cease operation: *The shop closes at six.* —***phrasal verb:* close out** To dispose of (a line of merchandise) at reduced prices. ▸*n.* (klōz). A conclusion; finish. ▸*adv.* (klōs) **clos•er, clos•est.** In a close manner. [< Lat. *claudere, claus-*, to close.] —**close′ly** *adv.* —**close′ness** *n.*

Syns: *close, immediate, near, nearby* ***Ant:*** *far* **adj.**

closed-cap•tioned (klōzd′kăp′shənd) ▸*adj.* Broadcast with captions that can be seen only on a specially equipped receiver.

closed circuit (klōzd) ▸*n.* **1.** An electric circuit providing an uninterrupted, endless path for the flow of current. **2.** Television that is transmitted to a limited number of receivers. —**closed′-cir′cuit** *adj.*

closed shop ▸*n.* See **union shop.**

close-fist•ed (klōs′fĭs′tĭd) ▸*adj.* Stingy.

close-mind•ed (klōs′mīn′dĭd, klōz′-) or **closed-mind•ed** (klōzd′-) ▸*adj.* Intolerant of the beliefs and opinions of others. —**close′-mind′ed•ness** *n.*

close-mouthed (klōs′mou*th*d′, -moutht′) ▸*adj.* Giving little information; tightlipped.

close•out (klōz′out′) ▸*n.* A sale in which all remaining stock is disposed of, usu. at greatly reduced prices.

clos•et (klŏz′ĭt, klô′zĭt) ▸*n.* **1.** A small room for storing supplies or clothing. **2.** A small private room. **3.** A state of secrecy or cautious privacy. ▸*v.* To enclose in a private room, as for discussion. ▸*adj.* Private; secret: *a closet liberal.* [< OFr. < Lat. *clausum*, enclosure.]

clos•et•ed (klŏz′ĭ-tĭd, klô′zĭ-) ▸*adj.* Being in a state of secrecy or cautious privacy.

close-up (klōs′ŭp′) ▸*n.* **1.** A photograph or film shot in which the subject is tightly framed and shown at a relatively large scale. **2.** An intimate view or description. —**close′-up′** *adj.*

clos•ing (klō′zĭng) ▸*n.* **1.** A concluding part. **2.** A meeting for concluding esp. a real estate transaction.

clo•sure (klō′zhər) ▸*n.* **1.** The act of closing or

the state of being closed. **2.** Something that closes or shuts. **3.** See **cloture.**

clot (klŏt) ►*n.* A thick or solid mass or lump formed from liquid. ►*v.* **clot•ted, clot•ting.** To form or cause to form into a clot. [< OE *clott.*]

cloth (klôth, klŏth) ►*n., pl.* **cloths** (klôths, klô*th*z, klŏths, klŏ*th*z) **1.** Fabric formed by weaving, knitting, or pressing natural or synthetic fibers. **2.** A piece of fabric used for a specific purpose, as a tablecloth. **3.** The characteristic attire of a profession, esp. that of the clergy. [< OE *clāth.*]

clothe (klō*th*) ►*v.* **clothed** or **clad** (klăd), **cloth•ing 1.** To put clothes on; dress. **2.** To cover as if with clothing. [< OE *clāthian.*]

clothes (klōz, klō*th*z) ►*pl.n.* Articles of dress; wearing apparel; garments.

clothes•horse (klōz′hôrs′, klō*th*z′-) ►*n.* **1.** A frame on which clothes are hung to dry. **2.** One excessively concerned with dress.

clothes•pin (klōz′pĭn′, klō*th*z′-) ►*n.* A clip for fastening clothes to a line.

cloth•ier (klō*th*′yər, klō′*th*ē-ər) ►*n.* One that makes or sells clothing or cloth.

cloth•ing (klō′*th*ĭng) ►*n.* Clothes collectively.

clo•ture (klō′chər) ►*n.* A parliamentary procedure by which debate is ended and an immediate vote is taken. [< OFr. *closture*, closure.]

cloud (kloud) ►*n.* **1a.** A visible body of fine water droplets or ice particles suspended in the earth's atmosphere. **b.** A similar mass, as of dust, suspended in the atmosphere or in outer space. **2.** A swarm. **3.** Something that darkens or fills with gloom. ►*v.* **1.** To cover with or as if with clouds. **2.** To become overcast. **3.** To make or become gloomy or troubled. **4.** To cast aspersions on. [< OE *clūd*, hill.] —**cloud′less** *adj.*

cloud•burst (kloud′bûrst′) ►*n.* A sudden heavy rainstorm; downpour.

cloud chamber ►*n.* A device in which the path of charged subatomic particles can be detected by the formation of chains of droplets on ions generated by their passage.

cloud nine ►*n. Informal* A state of elation or great happiness.

cloud•y (klou′dē) ►*adj.* **-i•er, -i•est 1.** Full of or covered with clouds. **2.** Of or like clouds. **3.** Not transparent. **4.** Obscure or vague. —**cloud′i•ly** *adv.* —**cloud′i•ness** *n.*

clout (klout) ►*n.* **1.** A blow, esp. with the fist. **2.** *Informal* **a.** Influence; pull. **b.** Power; muscle. ►*v.* To hit, esp. with the fist. [Prob. < OE *clūt*, cloth patch.]

clove[1] (klōv) ►*n.* An evergreen tree whose aromatic dried flower buds are used as a spice. [< OFr. *clou (de girofle)*, nail (of the clove tree) < Lat. *clāvus.*]

clove[2] (klōv) ►*n.* A small section of a separable bulb, as that of garlic. [< OE *clufu.*]

clove[3] (klōv) ►*v.* P.t. of **cleave**[1]**.**

clo•ven (klō′vən) ►*v.* P.part. of **cleave**[1]. ►*adj.* Split; divided: *a cloven hoof.*

clo•ver (klō′vər) ►*n.* Any of various plants having compound leaves with three leaflets and small flowers. [< OE *clāfre.*]

clo•ver•leaf (klō′vər-lēf′) ►*n.* A highway interchange whose curving entrance and exit ramps resemble a four-leaf clover.

Clo•vis I (klō′vĭs). A.D. 466?–511. King of the Franks (481–511).

clown (kloun) ►*n.* **1.** A buffoon who entertains by jokes, antics, and tricks, as in a circus. **2.** A coarse, rude person. ►*v.* To behave like a clown. [Of Scand. or LGer. orig.] —**clown′ish** *adj.* —**clown′ish•ly** *adv.*

cloy (kloi) ►*v.* To surfeit, esp. with something too rich or sweet. [< ME *acloien.*] —**cloy′ing•ly** *adv.* —**cloy′ing•ness** *n.*

CLU ►*abbr.* chartered life underwriter

club (klŭb) ►*n.* **1.** A heavy stick, usu. thicker at one end, suitable for use as a weapon. **2.** *Sports* A stick used in some games to drive a ball. **3.** *Games* Any of a suit of playing cards marked with a black figure shaped like a clover leaf. **4.** A group of people organized for a common purpose. **5.** The facilities used for the meetings of a club. **6.** A nightclub. ►*v.* **clubbed, club•bing 1.** To strike or beat with or as if with a club. **2.** To contribute or combine for common purpose. [< ON *klubba.*]

club car ►*n.* A railroad passenger car equipped with a buffet or bar and other comforts.

club•foot (klŭb′fo͝ot′) ►*n.* **1.** A congenital deformity of the foot, usu. marked by a curled shape of the ankle, heel, and toes. **2.** A foot so deformed. —**club′foot′ed** *adj.*

club•house (klŭb′hous′) ►*n.* **1.** A building occupied by a club. **2.** The locker room of an athletic team.

club sandwich ►*n.* A sandwich, usu. of three slices of bread with a filling of various meats, tomato, lettuce, and dressing.

club soda ►*n.* See **soda water** 1.

club steak ►*n.* See **Delmonico steak.**

cluck (klŭk) ►*n.* **1.** The low, short, throaty sound made by a hen when brooding or calling its chicks. **2.** *Informal* A stupid or foolish person. [< OE *cloccian.*] —**cluck** *v.*

clue (klo͞o) ►*n.* Something that guides or directs in the solution of a problem or mystery. ►*v.* **clued, clue•ing** or **clu•ing.** To give guiding information to. [< CLEW.]

clue•less (klo͞o′lĭs) ►*adj.* Lacking understanding or knowledge.

clump (klŭmp) ►*n.* **1.** A clustered mass or thick grouping; lump. **2.** A heavy dull sound. ►*v.* **1.** To form clumps (of). **2.** To walk with a heavy dull sound. [Prob. < MLGer. *klumpe.*]

clum•sy (klŭm′zē) ►*adj.* **-si•er, -si•est 1.** Lacking physical coordination, skill, or grace; awkward. **2.** Gauche; inept: *a clumsy excuse.* [< ME *clomsen*, be numb with cold.] —**clum′si•ly** *adv.* —**clum′si•ness** *n.*

clung (klŭng) ►*v.* P.t. and p.part. of **cling.**

clunk (klŭngk) ►*n.* A dull heavy sound. [Imit.] —**clunk** *v.*

clunk•y (klŭng′kē) ►*adj.* **-i•er, -i•est.** Clumsy in form or manner; awkward.

clus•ter (klŭs′tər) ►*n.* A group of things gathered or occurring closely together; bunch. ►*v.* To gather, grow, or form into clusters. [< OE *clyster.*]

clutch[1] (klŭch) ►*v.* **1.** To grasp or attempt to grasp and hold tightly. **2.** To work a motor vehicle's clutch. ►*n.* **1.** A hand, claw, talon, or paw in the act of grasping. **2.** A tight grasp. **3.** often **clutches** Control or power. **4.** A device for engaging and disengaging two working parts of a shaft or of a shaft and a driving mechanism. **5.** A tense, critical situation. [< OE *clyccan.*]

clutch[2] (klŭch) ►*n.* **1.** A set of eggs produced at one time. **2.** A brood of chickens. **3.** A cluster. [< dial. *cletch*, hatch < ON *klekja*.]

clut•ter (klŭt′ər) ►*n.* A confused or disordered state or collection. [< ME *cloteren*, to clot.] —**clut′ter** *v.*

Clyde (klīd) A river of SW Scotland flowing about 171 km (106 mi) NW to the **Firth of Clyde,** an estuary of the North Channel.

Clydes•dale (klīdz′dāl′) ►*n.* A large powerful draft horse having white feathered hair on the fetlocks. [After the CLYDE Valley.]

cm ►*abbr.* centimeter

Cm ► The symbol for the element **curium.**

CMA ►*abbr.* certified medical assistant

Cmdr. ►*abbr.* commander

cni•dar•i•an (nī-dâr′ē-ən) ►*n.* Any of a phylum of chiefly marine invertebrates having a radially symmetrical body and saclike internal cavity and including the jellyfishes and corals. [< Gk. *knidē*, sea nettle.]

Co ► The symbol for the element **cobalt.**

CO ►*abbr.* **1.** *Accounting* carried over **2.** cash order **3.** Colorado **4.** commanding officer **5.** conscientious objector

co. ►*abbr.* **1.** company **2.** county

c/o ►*abbr.* care of

co– ►*pref.* **1.** Together; joint; jointly: *coeducation.* **2a.** Partner or associate in an activity: *coauthor.* **b.** Subordinate or assistant: *copilot.* **3.** To the same extent or degree: *coextensive.* **4.** Complement of an angle: *cotangent.* [< Lat.]

coach (kōch) ►*n.* **1a.** A bus. **b.** A railroad passenger car. **2.** A large, closed, four-wheeled carriage with an elevated exterior seat for the driver. **3.** An economical passenger class on an airplane or train. **4.** One who trains or directs athletes or athletic teams. **5.** One who gives private instruction. ►*v.* To train or instruct; teach. [< Hung. *kocsi*.]

coach•man (kōch′mən) ►*n.* A man who drives a coach.

co•ad•ju•tor (kō′ə-jo͞o′tər, kō-ăj′ə-tər) ►*n.* **1.** An assistant or coworker. See Syns at **assistant. 2.** An assistant to a bishop. [< Lat. *coadiūtor*.]

co•ag•u•lant (kō-ăg′yə-lənt) ►*n.* An agent that causes coagulation. —**co•ag′u•lant** *adj.*

co•ag•u•late (kō-ăg′yə-lāt′) ►*v.* **-lat•ed, -lat•ing.** To form a soft semisolid or solid mass. [< Lat. *coāgulum*, rennet : CO– + *agere*, drive.] —**co•ag′u•la′tion** *n.*

coal (kōl) ►*n.* **1.** A natural dark brown to black carbon-containing material formed from fossilized plants and used as a fuel. **2.** An ember. [< OE *col*.]

co•a•lesce (kō′ə-lĕs′) ►*v.* **-lesced, -lesc•ing.** To grow or come together so as to form one whole; fuse; unite. [Lat. *coalēscere*.] —**co′a•les′cence** *n.* —**co′a•les′cent** *adj.*

coal gas ►*n.* A gaseous mixture distilled from bituminous coal and used as a fuel.

co•a•li•tion (kō′ə-lĭsh′ən) ►*n.* An alliance or union, esp. a temporary one. [< Lat. *coalēscere*, grow together.]

coal oil ►*n.* See **kerosene.**

coal tar ►*n.* A viscous black liquid distilled from bituminous coal, used for waterproofing and insulating and in many dyes, drugs, and paints.

coarse (kôrs, kōrs) ►*adj.* **coars•er, coars•est 1.** Of common or inferior quality. **2a.** Lacking refinement. **b.** Vulgar or indecent. **3.** Consisting of large particles: *coarse sand.* **4.** Rough, esp. to the touch: *a coarse tweed.* [ME *cors*.] —**coarse′ly** *adv.* —**coarse′ness** *n.*

coars•en (kôr′sən, kōr′-) ►*v.* To make or become coarse.

coast (kōst) ►*n.* **1.** Land next to the sea. **2.** A hill or slope. **3.** The act of coasting. ►*v.* **1.** To slide down an incline through the effect of gravity. **2.** To move without accelerating. **3.** To act or move aimlessly. **4.** To sail along the coast (of). [< Lat. *costa*, side.] —**coast′al** (kō′stəl) *adj.*

coast•er (kō′stər) ►*n.* **1.** One that coasts. **2.** A disk or small mat used to protect a table top or other surface beneath.

coast guard also **Coast Guard** ►*n.* The branch of a nation's armed forces that is responsible for coastal defense, protection of life and property at sea, and enforcement of customs, immigration, and navigation laws.

coast•line (kōst′līn′) ►*n.* The shape or outline of a coast.

Coast Mountains. A range of W British Columbia, Canada, and SE AK.

Coast Ranges. A series of mountain ranges of W North America from SE AK to Baja California along the Pacific coast.

coat (kōt) ►*n.* **1.** A sleeved outer garment extending from the shoulders to the waist or below. **2.** A natural or outer covering, such as the fur of an animal. **3.** A layer of material covering something else. ►*v.* To provide or cover with a coat or layer. [< OFr. *cote*.] —**coat′ed** *adj.* —**coat′ing** *n.*

co•a•ti (kō-ä′tē) ►*n.* An omnivorous mammal of tropical America related to and resembling the raccoon. [< Tupi *coati*.]

co•a•ti•mun•di (kō-ä′tē-mŭn′dē) ►*n.* A coati. [Poss. Tupi *coati* + *mundé*, animal trap.]

coat of arms ►*n.*, *pl.* **coats of arms.** A shield blazoned with heraldic bearings indicating ancestry and distinction.

coat of arms
of Christopher Columbus

coat of mail ►*n.*, *pl.* **coats of mail.** An armored coat made of chain mail.

coat•tail (kōt′tāl′) ►*n.* The lower back part of a coat. —***idiom:*** **on (someone's) coattails** With the help or on the success of another.

co•au•thor or **co-au•thor** (kō-ô′thər) ►*n.* A joint author. —**co•au′thor** *v.*

coax (kōks) ►*v.* **1.** To persuade by pleading or flattery. **2.** To obtain by persistent persuasion. [Obsolete *cokes*, to fool.]

co•ax•i•al (kō-ăk′sē-əl) ►*adj.* Having or mounted on a common axis.

coaxial cable ►*n.* A cable consisting of a conducting outer metal tube insulated from a central conducting core, used for transmission of electronic signals.

cob (kŏb) ►*n.* **1.** A corncob. **2.** A male swan. **3.** A thickset, short-legged horse. [Prob. < obsolete *cob*, round object.]

co•balt (kō′bôlt′) ►*n. Symbol* **Co** A hard, brittle metallic element used for magnetic alloys, high-temperature alloys, and for blue glass and ceramic pigments. At. no. 27. See table at **element.** [< MHGer. *kobolt*, goblin.]

cobalt blue ►*n.* A vivid blue to greenish blue.

cob•ble (kŏb′əl) ►*v.* **-bled, -bling 1.** To make or mend (boots or shoes). **2.** To put together clumsily. [Prob. < COBBLER[1].]

cob•bler[1] (kŏb′lər) ►*n.* One who mends or makes boots and shoes. [ME *cobeler.*]

cob•bler[2] (kŏb′lər) ►*n.* A deep-dish fruit pie with a thick top crust. [?]

cob•ble•stone (kŏb′əl-stōn′) ►*n.* A naturally rounded paving stone. [ME *cobelston.*]

CO•BOL or **Co•bol** (kō′bôl′) ►*n.* A programming language, used esp. for business applications, that is closer to English than many other high-level languages. [*Co(mmon) B(usiness-)O(riented) L(anguage).*]

co•bra (kō′brə) ►*n.* A venomous snake of Asia and Africa capable of expanding the skin of the neck to form a flattened hood. [< Lat. *colubra*, snake.]

cob•web (kŏb′wĕb′) ►*n.* **1a.** The web spun by a spider to catch its prey. **b.** A single thread of such a web. **2.** Something resembling a cobweb. [ME *coppeweb.*]

co•ca (kō′kə) ►*n.* **1.** An Andean evergreen shrub whose leaves contain cocaine. **2.** Dried coca leaves chewed for a stimulating effect and used for extraction of cocaine. [< Quechua *kúka.*]

co•caine (kō-kān′, kō′kān′) ►*n.* A narcotic alkaloid extracted from coca leaves, sometimes used as a local anesthetic and widely as an illegal drug. [Fr. *cocaïne* < Sp. *coca*, cocaine plant.]

coc•cus (kŏk′əs) ►*n., pl.* **coc•ci** (kŏk′sī, kŏk′ī). A bacterium having a spherical or spheroidal shape. [< Gk. *kokkos*, grain.]

-coccus ►*suff.* A microorganism of spheroidal shape: *streptococcus.* [< COCCUS.]

coc•cyx (kŏk′sĭks) ►*n., pl.* **coc•cy•ges** (kŏk-sī′jēz, kŏk′sĭ-jēz′). A small bone at the base of the spinal column. [< Gk. *kokkux*, cuckoo.]

Co•cha•bam•ba (kō′chə-bäm′bə) A city of W-central Bolivia NNW of Sucre. Pop. 448,756.

coch•i•neal (kŏch′ə-nēl′, kŏch′ə-nēl′, kō′chə-, kō′chə-) ►*n.* A brilliant red dye made of the dried bodies of a tropical American insect. [< Lat. *coccinus*, scarlet < Gk. *kokkos*, a kind of berry.]

Co•chise (kō-chēs′, -chēz′). 1812?–74. Apache leader.

coch•le•a (kŏk′lē-ə, kō′klē-ə) ►*n., pl.* **-le•ae** (-lē-ē′, -lē-ī′) also **-le•as.** A spiral tube of the inner ear that contains nerve endings essential for hearing. [< Gk. *kokhlias*, snail.] —**coch′le•ar** *adj.*

cock[1] (kŏk) ►*n.* **1a.** An adult male chicken; rooster. **b.** An adult male of various other birds. **2.** A faucet or valve. **3a.** The hammer of a firearm. **b.** Its position when ready for firing. ►*v.* **1.** To set the hammer of (a firearm) in position for firing. **2.** To tilt: *cock an eyebrow.* **3.** To raise or draw back in preparation to throw or hit. [< OE *cocc.*]

cock[2] (kŏk) ►*n.* A cone-shaped pile of straw or hay. [ME *cok.*]

cock•ade (kŏ-kād′) ►*n.* An ornament, such as a rosette, usu. worn on the hat as a badge. [< OFr. *coquarde*, cocky.]

cock•a•tiel also **cock•a•teel** (kŏk′ə-tēl′) ►*n.* A small crested Australian parrot having gray and yellow plumage. [Du. *kaketielje*, ult. < Malay *kakatua*, cockatoo.]

cock•a•too (kŏk′ə-to͞o′) ►*n., pl.* **-toos.** A large parrot of Australia and adjacent areas, having a long erectile crest. [< Malay *kakatua.*]

cock•a•trice (kŏk′ə-trĭs, -trīs′) ►*n. Myth.* A serpent having the power to kill by its glance. [< Med.Lat. *cocātrīx.*]

cocked hat (kŏkt) ►*n.* A three-cornered hat.

cock•er•el (kŏk′ər-əl) ►*n.* A young rooster. [ME *cokerel*, dim. of *cok*, COCK[1].]

cock•er spaniel (kŏk′ər) ►*n.* A dog having long drooping ears and a variously colored silky coat. [Used in hunting woodcock.]

cock•eyed (kŏk′īd′) ►*adj. Informal* **1.** Foolish; ridiculous: *a cockeyed idea.* **2.** Askew; crooked. **3.** Intoxicated; drunk.

cock•fight (kŏk′fīt′) ►*n.* A fight between gamecocks, often fitted with metal spurs, held as a spectacle. —**cock′fight′ing** *n.*

cock•le[1] (kŏk′əl) ►*n.* **1.** Any of various bivalve mollusks having rounded or heart-shaped ribbed shells. **2.** *Naut.* A cockleshell. [< Gk. *konkhulion*, small mussel.]

cock•le[2] (kŏk′əl) ►*n.* Any of several weedy plants growing esp. in grain fields. [< OE *coccel.*]

cock•le•shell (kŏk′əl-shĕl′) ►*n.* **1.** The shell of a cockle. **2.** A small light boat.

cock•ney (kŏk′nē) ►*n., pl.* **-neys 1.** often **Cockney** A native of the East End of London. **2.** The dialect or accent of cockneys. [ME *cokenei*, pampered child : *cok*, COCK[1] + *ei*, egg (< OE *ǣg*).]

cock•pit (kŏk′pĭt′) ►*n.* **1.** The space set apart in the fuselage of an aircraft for the pilot and crew. **2.** A pit or enclosed area for cockfights. **3.** An area in a small vessel toward the stern, from which it is steered.

cock•roach (kŏk′rōch′) ►*n.* Any of various oval, flat-bodied insects common as household pests. [< Sp. *cucaracha.*]

cocks•comb (kŏks′kōm′) ►*n.* **1.** The comb of a rooster. **2.** The cap of a jester, decorated to resemble a rooster's comb. **3.** An annual plant having fan-shaped or plumelike clusters of red or yellow flowers.

cock•sure (kŏk′sho͝or′) ►*adj.* **1.** Completely sure; certain. **2.** Too sure; overconfident.

cock•tail (kŏk′tāl′) ►*n.* **1.** A mixed alcoholic drink. **2.** An appetizer, usu. seafood or fruit. **3.** A combination of drugs used as part of a treatment regimen. [?]

cock•y (kŏk′ē) ►*adj.* **-i•er, -i•est.** Overly self-assertive or self-confident. —**cock′i•ly** *adv.* —**cock′i•ness** *n.*

Co•co (kō′kō) A river rising in N Nicaragua and flowing about 483 km (300 mi) along the Honduras border to the Caribbean Sea.

co•coa (kō′kō) ►*n.* **1.** A powder made from processed cacao seeds. **2.** A beverage made by mixing this powder with sugar in hot water or milk. [Alteration of CACAO.]

co•co•nut also **co•coa•nut** (kō′kə-nŭt′, -nət) ►*n.* **1.** The fruit of the coconut palm, consisting of a fibrous husk surrounding a large seed. **2.** The hard-shelled seed of the coconut, having edible white flesh and a hollow center filled with milky fluid. [Port. *côco*, skull, coconut + NUT.]

coconut palm ►*n.* A tropical feather-leaved palm cultivated for food, beverages, oil, thatching, and fiber.

co•coon (kə-ko͞on′) ►*n.* **1.** A protective case of silk or fibrous material spun by the larvae of moths and other insects. **2.** A private, comfortable retreat; refuge. [< Prov. *coucoun*, little shell.] —**co•coon′** *v.*

cod (kŏd) ►*n., pl.* **cod** or **cods.** An important food fish of N Atlantic waters. [ME.]

Cod, Cape. A hook-shaped peninsula of SE MA.

COD ►*abbr.* **1.** cash on delivery **2.** collect on delivery

co•da (kō′də) ►*n. Mus.* The final passage of a movement or work. [< Lat. *cauda*, tail.]

cod•dle (kŏd′l) ►*v.* **-dled, -dling 1.** To cook in water just below the boiling point. **2.** To treat indulgently; baby. [< *caudle*, a medicinal drink.] —**cod′dler** *n.*

code (kōd) ►*n.* **1.** A systematic, comprehensive collection of laws or rules. **2a.** A system of signals for transmitting messages. **b.** A system of symbols or words given arbitrary meanings, used for transmitting brief or secret messages. **3.** A system of symbols and rules used to represent instructions to a computer. **4.** The genetic code. ►*v.* **cod•ed, cod•ing 1.** To arrange or convert into a code. **2.** To write or revise a computer program. [< Lat. *cōdex*, book.]

co•deine (kō′dēn′, -dē-ĭn) ►*n.* An alkaloid narcotic derived from opium or morphine and used esp. for relieving pain. [< Gk. *kōdeia*, poppy head.]

co-de•pen•dent (kō′dĭ-pĕn′dənt) ►*adj.* **1.** Mutually dependent. **2.** Of a relationship in which one person is psychologically dependent on someone addicted to self-destructive behavior. —**co′-de•pen′dence, co′-de•pen′den•cy** *n.* —**co′-de•pen′dent** *n.*

co•dex (kō′dĕks′) ►*n., pl.* **co•di•ces** (kō′dĭ-sēz′, kŏd′ĭ-). A manuscript volume, esp. of an ancient text. [Lat. *cōdex*.]

cod•fish (kŏd′fĭsh′) ►*n.* See **cod.**

codg•er (kŏj′ər) ►*n. Informal* A somewhat eccentric man, esp. an old one. [Poss. < obsolete *cadger*, peddler.]

cod•i•cil (kŏd′ə-sĭl) ►*n.* A supplement or appendix to a will. [< Lat. *cōdex*, volume.]

cod•i•fy (kŏd′ĭ-fī′, kō′də-) ►*v.* **-fied, -fy•ing.** To arrange or systematize. —**cod′i•fi•ca′tion** *n.*

cod-liv•er oil (kŏd′lĭv′ər) ►*n.* Oil obtained from the liver esp. of a cod and used as a source of vitamins A and D.

Co•dy (kō′dē), **William Frederick.** "Buffalo Bill." 1846–1917. Amer. frontier scout and performer.

co•ed (kō′ĕd′) *Informal* ►*n.* A woman who attends a coeducational college or university. ►*adj.* Coeducational.

co•ed•u•ca•tion (kō-ĕj′ə-kā′shən) ►*n.* The education of both men and women at the same institution. —**co•ed′u•ca′tion•al** *adj.*

co•ef•fi•cient (kō′ə-fĭsh′ənt) ►*n.* **1.** A number or symbol multiplied with a variable in an algebraic term, as 4 in the term $4x$. **2.** A numerical measure of a physical or chemical property that is constant for a specified system.

coe•len•ter•ate (sĭ-lĕn′tə-rāt′, -tər-ĭt) ►*n.* Any of a phylum of aquatic invertebrates such as the jellyfishes and hydras, having a radially symmetrical, saclike body. [Gk. *koilos*, hollow + *enteron*, intestine.]

coe•lom (sē′ləm) ►*n.* The body cavity of all animals higher than the coelenterates. [Ger. *Koelom* < Gk. *koilōma*, cavity < *koilos*, hollow.]

co•e•qual (kō-ē′kwəl) ►*adj.* Equal with one another, as in rank or size. ►*n.* An equal. —**co′e•qual′i•ty** (-kwŏl′ĭ-tē) *n.*

co•erce (kō-ûrs′) ►*v.* **-erced, -erc•ing 1.** To force to act or think in a certain way; compel. **2.** To dominate, restrain, or control forcibly. **3.** To bring about by force. [Lat. *coercēre*, confine.] —**co•erc′er** *n.* —**co•erc′i•ble** *adj.* —**co•er′cion** (kō-ûr′zhən, -shən) *n.* —**co•er′cive** *adj.*

Coeur d'A•lene (kôr′ də-lān′, kôrd′l-ān′, kûrd′-) A city of N ID on **Coeur D'Alene Lake** in the Panhandle E of Spokane, WA. Pop. 24,563.

co•e•val (kō-ē′vəl) ►*adj.* Of, originating, or existing during the same period or time. [< LLat. *coaevus* < *aevum*, age.] —**co•e′val** *n.* —**co•e′val•ly** *adv.*

co•ev•o•lu•tion (kō′ĕv-ə-lo͞o′shən, -ē-və-) ►*n.* The evolution of two or more interdependent species, each adapting to changes in the other. —**co′ev•o•lu′tion•ar•y** *adj.* —**co′e•volve′** (-ĭ-vŏlv′) *v.*

co•ex•ist (kō′ĭg-zĭst′) ►*v.* **1.** To exist together, at the same time, or in the same place. **2.** To live in peace with another or others despite differences. —**co′ex•is′tence** *n.*

co•ex•ten•sive (kō′ĭk-stĕn′sĭv) ►*adj.* Having the same limits, boundaries, or scope.

C. of C. ►*abbr.* chamber of commerce

C. of E. ►*abbr.* Church of England

cof•fee (kô′fē, kŏf′ē) ►*n.* **1a.** A stimulating, aromatic beverage prepared from the roasted ground beanlike seeds of a tropical tree. **b.** The whole or ground seeds themselves. **2.** A dark brown. [< Ar. *qahwa*.]

cof•fee•cake (kô′fē-kāk′, kŏf′ē-) ►*n.* A cake or sweetened bread, often containing nuts or raisins.

cof•fee•house also **coffee house** (kô′fē-hous′, kŏf′ē-) ►*n.* A restaurant serving coffee and refreshments and often having musical entertainment.

coffee klatch or **coffee klatsch** (klăch, kläch) ►*n.* A casual social gathering for coffee and conversation. [Ger. *Kaffeeklatsch* < *Klatsch*, gossip.]

cof•fee•mak•er (kô′fē-mā′kər, kŏf′ē-) ►*n.* An apparatus used to brew coffee.

cof•fee•pot (kô′fē-pŏt′, kŏf′ē-) ►*n.* A pot for brewing or serving coffee.

coffee shop ►*n.* A small restaurant in which coffee and light meals are served.

coffee table ►*n.* A long low table, often placed before a sofa.

cof•fer (kô′fər, kŏf′ər) ►*n.* **1.** A strongbox. **2.** often **coffers** Financial resources; funds. [<

Lat. *cophinus*, basket. See COFFIN.]
cof•fer•dam (kô′fər-dăm′, kŏf′ər-) ►*n.* A temporary watertight enclosure that is pumped dry to expose the bottom of a body of water so that construction, as of piers, may be undertaken.
cof•fin (kô′fĭn, kŏf′ĭn) ►*n.* A box in which a corpse is buried. [< Gk. *kophinos*, basket.]
cog (kŏg, kôg) ►*n.* **1.** One of the teeth on the rim of a wheel or gear. **2.** A subordinate member of an organization. [ME *cogge.*]
co•gen•er•a•tion (kō-jĕn′ə-rā′shən) ►*n.* A process in which a factory uses its waste energy to produce heat or electricity.
co•gent (kō′jənt) ►*adj.* Forcefully convincing: *a cogent argument.* [< Lat. *cōgere*, to force : CO– + *agere*, drive.] —**co′gen•cy** (-jən-sē) *n.* —**co′gent•ly** *adv.*
cog•i•tate (kŏj′ĭ-tāt′) ►*v.* **-tat•ed, -tat•ing.** To think carefully (about); ponder. [Lat. *cōgitāre* : CO– + *agitāre*, consider; see AGITATE.] —**cog′i•ta′tion** *n.*
co•gnac (kōn′yăk′, kŏn′-, kôn′-) ►*n.* A fine French brandy. [After *Cognac*, France.]
cog•nate (kŏg′nāt′) ►*adj.* **1.** Having a common ancestor or origin, esp. culturally or linguistically akin. **2.** Analogous in nature. [Lat. *cognātus.*] —**cog′nate′** *n.*
cog•ni•tion (kŏg-nĭsh′ən) ►*n.* **1.** The mental process or faculty of knowing. **2.** That which comes to be known. [< Lat. *cognōscere*, learn.] —**cog′ni•tive** *adj.*
cog•ni•zance (kŏg′nĭ-zəns) ►*n.* **1.** Conscious knowledge or recognition; awareness. **2.** Observance; notice. [< Lat. *cognōscere*, know.] —**cog′ni•zant** *adj.*
cog•no•men (kŏg-nō′mən) ►*n.*, *pl.* **-no•mens** or **-nom•i•na** (-nŏm′ə-nə) **1.** A surname. **2.** A nickname. [Lat. *cognōmen.*]
co•gno•scen•te (kŏn′yə-shĕn′tē, kŏg′nə-) ►*n.*, *pl.* **-ti** (-tē). A connoisseur. [Obsolete Italian < Lat. *cognōscere*, know.]
cog•wheel (kŏg′hwēl′, -wēl′, kôg′-) ►*n.* A toothed gear wheel within a mechanism.
co•hab•it (kō-hăb′ĭt) ►*v.* To live together as spouses, esp. when not legally married. [LLat. *cohabitāre*, live together.] —**co•hab′i•ta′tion** *n.*
Co•han (kō′hăn′), **George Michael.** 1878–1942. Amer. songwriter and playwright.
co•here (kō-hîr′) ►*v.* **-hered, -her•ing 1.** To stick or hold together. **2.** To be logically connected. [Lat. *cohaerēre*, *cohaes-*.] —**co•her′ence, co•her′en•cy** *n.* —**co•her′ent** *adj.*
co•he•sion (kō-hē′zhən) ►*n.* **1.** The process or condition of cohering. **2.** *Phys.* The attraction by which the elements of a body are held together. —**co•he′sive** (-sĭv, -zĭv) *adj.* —**co•he′sive•ly** *adv.* —**co•he′sive•ness** *n.*
co•hort (kō′hôrt′) ►*n.* **1.** A group or band of people. **2.** A companion or associate. [< Lat. *cohors*, an army division.]
co•host or **co-host** (kō′hōst′) ►*n.* A joint host, as of a social event. —**co′host′** *v.*
coif (koif) ►*n.* **1.** (*also* kwäf). A coiffure. **2.** A tight-fitting cap. ►*v.* (*also* kwäf). To style or dress (the hair). [< LLat. *cofea*, helmet.]
coif•fure (kwä-fyo͝or′) ►*n.* A hairstyle. [Fr. < *coiffer*, arrange hair.]
coil (koil) ►*n.* **1.** A series of connected spirals or concentric rings formed by gathering or winding: *a coil of rope.* **2.** A spiral or ring. **3.** *Elect.* A wound spiral of insulated wire. [< Lat. *colligere*, gather together.] —**coil** *v.*
coin (koin) ►*n.* **1.** A piece of metal authorized by a government for use as money. **2.** Metal money collectively. ►*v.* **1.** To make coins from metal. **2.** To invent (a new word or phrase). [< Lat. *cuneus*, wedge, stamp.] —**coin′er** *n.*
coin•age (koi′nĭj) ►*n.* **1.** The process of making coins. **2.** Metal currency.
co•in•cide (kō′ĭn-sīd′) ►*v.* **-cid•ed, -cid•ing 1.** To occupy the same position in space. **2.** To happen at the same time. **3.** To correspond exactly. [Med.Lat. *coincidere*, occur together.]
co•in•ci•dence (kō-ĭn′sĭ-dəns, -dĕns′) ►*n.* **1.** The act or state of coinciding. **2.** A sequence of events that although accidental seems to have been planned or arranged. —**co•in′ci•den′tal, co•in′ci•dent** *adj.* —**co•in′ci•den′tal•ly** *adv.*
co•i•tus (kō′ĭ-təs, kō-ē′-) ►*n.* Sexual intercourse. [Lat.] —**co′i•tal** *adj.*
coke[1] (kōk) ►*n.* The solid residue of coal after removal of volatile material, used as fuel. [Poss. < ME *colk*, core.]
coke[2] (kōk) ►*n.* *Slang* Cocaine.
Coke (ko͝ok, kōk), Sir **Edward.** 1552–1634. English jurist.
Col. ►*abbr.* **1.** also **Col** or **COL** colonel **2.** Colorado
col–[1] ►*pref.* Var. of **com–.**
col–[2] ►*pref.* Var. of **colo–.**
co•la[1] (kō′lə) ►*n.* A carbonated soft drink containing an extract of the cola nut.
co•la[2] (kō′lə) ►*n.* Pl. of **colon**[2]**.**
co•la[3] also **ko•la** (kō′lə) ►*n.* Either of two African evergreens having nutlike seeds used in carbonated beverages and pharmaceuticals. [Of West African orig.]
COLA ►*abbr.* cost-of-living adjustment
col•an•der (kŭl′ən-dər, kŏl′-) ►*n.* A perforated, bowl-shaped kitchen utensil for draining off liquids. [< OProv. *colador*, strainer < Lat. *cōlāre*, strain.]
Col•bert (kôl-bĕr′, kōl-), **Jean Baptiste.** 1619–83. French adviser to Louis XIV.
cold (kōld) ►*adj.* **-er, -est 1.** Having a low temperature. **2.** Having a subnormal body temperature. **3.** Feeling uncomfortably chilled. **4.** Lacking emotion; objective. **5.** Not friendly; aloof. **6.** No longer fresh: *a cold scent.* **7.** Unconscious: *knocked cold.* ►*adv.* Totally; thoroughly. ►*n.* **1.** Relative lack of warmth. **2.** The sensation of lacking warmth. **3.** A viral infection of the mucous membranes of the upper respiratory passages. —***idiom:*** **out in the cold** Neglected; ignored. [< OE *ceald.*] —**cold′ly** *adv.* —**cold′ness** *n.*
Syns: *cold, arctic, chilly, cool, frigid, frosty, gelid, glacial, icy* **Ant:** *hot* **adj.**
cold-blood•ed (kōld′blŭd′ĭd) ►*adj.* **1.** Lacking feeling or emotion: *a cold-blooded killer.* **2.** Ectothermic. —**cold′-blood′ed•ly** *adv.* —**cold′-blood′ed•ness** *n.*
cold cream ►*n.* An emulsion for softening and cleansing the skin.
cold cuts ►*pl.n.* Slices of cold cooked meat.
cold drink ►*n.* *Regional* See **soft drink.** See Regional Note at **tonic.**
cold duck ►*n.* A beverage made of sparkling Burgundy and champagne. [Translation of Ger. *Kalte Ente.*]
cold feet ►*pl.n.* *Slang* Failure of nerve.
cold frame ►*n.* An unheated outdoor structure

consisting of a usu. wooden frame and glass top, used for protecting young plants.

cold-heart•ed (kōld′här′tĭd) ►*adj.* Lacking sympathy or feeling. —**cold′-heart′ed•ly** *adv.* —**cold′-heart′ed•ness** *n.*

cold shoulder ►*n. Informal* Deliberate coldness or disregard. —**cold′shoul′der** *v.*

cold sore ►*n.* A small blister occurring on the lips, caused by a herpes virus.

cold turkey ►*n. Slang* Immediate, complete withdrawal esp. from an addictive drug.

cold war ►*n.* A state of political tension and military rivalry between nations that stops short of full-scale war. —**cold warrior** *n.*

Cole•ridge (kōl′rĭj, kō′lə-rĭj), **Samuel Taylor.** 1772–1834. British poet and critic.

cole•slaw also **cole slaw** (kōl′slô′) ►*n.* A salad of shredded raw cabbage. [Du. *koolsla.*]

Co•lette (kŏ-lĕt′, kô-), **(Sidonie Gabrielle Claudine).** 1873–1954. French novelist.

co•le•us (kō′lē-əs) ►*n.* A plant of the mint family, cultivated for its showy leaves. [< Gk. *koleos*, sheath.]

col•ic (kŏl′ĭk) ►*n.* Severe abdominal pain. [< Gk. *kōlikos*, having colic < *kolon*, colon.] —**col′ick•y** (kŏl′ĭ-kē) *adj.*

col•i•se•um (kŏl′ĭ-sē′əm) ►*n.* A large public amphitheater. [< Lat. *Colossēum*, an amphitheater in Rome < *colossus*, COLOSSUS.]

coliseum
the Colosseum, Rome

co•li•tis (kə-lī′tĭs) ►*n.* Inflammation of the colon.

col•lab•o•rate (kə-lăb′ə-rāt′) ►*v.* **-rat•ed, -rat•ing 1.** To work together, esp. in a joint intellectual effort. **2.** To cooperate treasonably. [LLat. *collabōrāre.*] —**col•lab′o•ra′tion** *n.* —**col•lab′o•ra′tive** *adj.* —**col•lab′o•ra′tor** *n.*

col•lage (kō-läzh′, kə-) ►*n.* An artistic composition of materials and objects pasted over a surface. [Fr. < *coller*, to glue.]

col•la•gen (kŏl′ə-jən) ►*n.* The fibrous protein constituent of bone, cartilage, and connective tissue. [Gk. *kolla*, glue + -GEN.]

col•lapse (kə-lăps′) ►*v.* **-lapsed, -laps•ing 1.** To fall down or inward suddenly; cave in. **2.** To break down suddenly in strength or health and thereby cease to function. **3.** To fold compactly: *collapse a folding bed for storage.* [Lat. *collābī, collāps-*, fall together.] —**col•lapse′** *n.* —**col•laps′i•ble** *adj.*

col•lar (kŏl′ər) ►*n.* **1.** The part of a garment that encircles the neck. **2.** A restraining or identifying band around the neck of an animal. **3.** *Biol.* An encircling structure or bandlike marking suggestive of a collar. **4.** A ringlike device used to limit, guide, or secure a part. **5.** *Slang* An arrest. ►*v. Slang* To seize or detain. [< Lat. *collum*, neck.] —**col′lared** *adj.*

col•lar•bone (kŏl′ər-bōn′) ►*n.* See **clavicle.**

col•lard (kŏl′ərd) ►*n.* **1.** See **kale. 2. collards** The leaves of kale, used as a vegetable. [Var. of *colewort*, a kind of cabbage.]

col•late (kə-lāt′, kŏl′āt′, kō′lāt′) ►*v.* **-lat•ed, -lat•ing 1.** To examine and compare (texts) carefully. **2.** To assemble pages in proper sequence. [< Lat. *collātus*, p.part. of *cōnferre*, bring together.]

col•lat•er•al (kə-lăt′ər-əl) ►*adj.* **1.** Situated or running side by side. **2.** Serving to corroborate. **3.** Of a secondary nature; subordinate. **4.** Of or guaranteed by a security pledged against the performance of an obligation. **5.** Having an ancestor in common but descended from a different line. ►*n.* Property acceptable as security for a loan. [< Med.Lat. *collāterālis.*]

col•la•tion (kə-lā′shən, kŏ-, kō-) ►*n.* **1.** The act or process of collating. **2.** A light meal.

col•league (kŏl′ēg′) ►*n.* A fellow member of a profession; associate. [< Lat. *collēga.*]

col•lect ►*v.* **1.** To bring or come together in a group; gather. **2.** To accumulate: *collect signatures.* **3.** To obtain payment of: *collect taxes.* **4.** To recover control of: *collect one's emotions.* ►*adv. & adj.* With payment to be made by the receiver: *called collect.* [< Lat. *colligere, collēct-.*] —**col•lect′i•ble, col•lect′a•ble** *adj. & n.* —**col•lec′tion** *n.* —**col•lec′tor** *n.*

col•lect•ed (kə-lĕk′tĭd) ►*adj.* Self-possessed; composed.

col•lec•tive (kə-lĕk′tĭv) ►*adj.* **1.** Assembled into a whole. **2.** Of or made by a number of people acting as a group: *a collective decision.* ►*n.* An undertaking or business controlled by the workers involved. —**col•lec′tive•ly** *adv.* —**col′lec•tiv′i•ty** *n.* —**col•lec′tiv•ize′** *v.* —**col•lec′tiv•i•za′tion** *n.*

collective bargaining ►*n.* Negotiation between the representatives of organized workers and an employer.

collective noun ►*n.* A noun denoting a group of persons or things regarded as a unit.

Usage: A collective noun takes a singular verb when it refers to the collection considered as a whole, as in *The family was united on this question.* It takes a plural verb when it refers to the members of the group as individuals, as in *My family are always fighting among themselves.* Among the common collective nouns are *committee, clergy, company, enemy, group, family, flock, public,* and *team.*

col•lec•tiv•ism (kə-lĕk′tə-vĭz′əm) ►*n.* The principles or system of ownership and control of the means of production and distribution by the people collectively. —**col•lec′tiv•ist** *n.*

col•leen (kŏ-lēn′, kŏl′ēn′) ►*n.* An Irish girl. [Ir. Gael. *cailín.*]

col•lege (kŏl′ĭj) ►*n.* **1.** An institution of higher learning that grants the bachelor's degree. **2.** An undergraduate division or school of a university. **3.** A technical or professional school. **4.** The building or buildings occupied by any such school. **5.** A body of persons having a common purpose or shared duties. [< Lat. *collēgium*, association < *collēga*, colleague.] —**col•le′giate** (kə-lē′jĭt, -jē-ĭt) *adj.*

col•le•gi•al (kə-lē′jē-əl, -jəl) ►*adj.* Having power and authority vested equally among colleagues.

col•le•gian (kə-lē′jən, -jē-ən) ►*n.* A college

student or recent college graduate.

col•le•gi•um (kə-lē′jē-əm, -lĕg′ē-) ►*n., pl.* **-le•gi•a** (-lē′jē-ə, -lĕg′ē-ə) or **-le•gi•ums.** A governing council in which all members have equal authority. [< Lat. *collēgium*, association. See COLLEGE.]

col•lide (kə-līd′) ►*v.* **-lid•ed, -lid•ing 1.** To come together with violent, direct impact. **2.** To clash; conflict. [Lat. *collīdere*, strike together.] —**col•li′sion** (-lĭzh′ən) *n.*

col•lie (kŏl′ē) ►*n.* A large, long-haired dog orig. used to herd sheep. [Sc.]

col•lier (kŏl′yər) ►*n.* **1.** A coal miner. **2.** A coal ship. [< OE *col*, coal.]

col•lier•y (kŏl′yə-rē) ►*n., pl.* **-ies.** A coal mine and its outbuildings.

col•lin•e•ar (kə-lĭn′ē-ər, kŏ-) ►*adj.* **1.** Lying on the same line. **2.** Containing a common line; coaxial.

col•lo•cate (kŏl′ə-kāt′) ►*v.* **-cat•ed, -cat•ing.** To place together, esp. side by side. [Lat. *collocāre*.] —**col′lo•ca′tion** *n.*

col•lo•di•on (kə-lō′dē-ən) ►*n.* A highly flammable, syrupy solution used in topical medications and photographic plates. [< Gk. *kollōdēs*, gluelike.]

col•loid (kŏl′oid′) ►*n.* A suspension of finely divided particles in a continuous medium from which the particles do not settle out rapidly and cannot be readily filtered. [< Gk. *kolla*, glue.] —**col•loi′dal** (kə-loid′l, kŏ-) *adj.*

col•lo•qui•al (kə-lō′kwē-əl) ►*adj.* Characteristic of or appropriate to informal speech or writing. [< COLLOQUY.] —**col•lo′qui•al•ism** *n.* —**col•lo′qui•al•ly** *adv.*

col•lo•qui•um (kə-lō′kwē-əm) ►*n., pl.* **-qui•ums** or **-qui•a** (-kwē-ə) **1.** An informal conference. **2.** An academic seminar. [< Lat. *colloquī*, talk together.]

col•lo•quy (kŏl′ə-kwē) ►*n., pl.* **-quies.** A conversation, esp. a formal one. [Lat. *colloquium*, COLLOQUIUM.]

col•lude (kə-lo͞od′) ►*v.* **-lud•ed, -lud•ing.** To act together secretly to achieve a fraudulent, illegal, or deceitful purpose; conspire. [Lat. *collūdere*.] —**col•lu′sion** *n.* —**col•lu′sive** *adj.*

Colo. ►*abbr.* Colorado

colo– or **col–** ►*pref.* Colon: *colostomy.* [< COLON².]

co•logne (kə-lōn′) ►*n.* A scented liquid made of alcohol and fragrant oils. [< Fr. *(eau de) Cologne*, (water of) Cologne.]

Cologne. A city of W Germany on the Rhine R. N of Bonn. Pop. 962,517.

Co•lom•bi•a (kə-lŭm′bē-ə) A country of NW South America with coastlines on the Pacific Ocean and the Caribbean Sea. Cap. Bogotá. Pop. 26,525,670. —**Co•lom′bi•an** *adj. & n.*

Co•lom•bo (kə-lŭm′bō) The capital of Sri Lanka, on the W coast on the Indian Ocean. Pop. 615,000.

co•lon¹ (kō′lən) ►*n., pl.* **-lons.** A punctuation mark (:) used to introduce a quotation, explanation, example, or series. [< Gk. *kōlon*, metrical unit.]

co•lon² (kō′lən) ►*n., pl.* **-lons** or **-la** (-lə). The section of the large intestine extending from the cecum to the rectum. [< Gk. *kolon*.] —**co•lon′ic** (kə-lŏn′ĭk) *adj.*

co•lon³ (kō-lōn′) ►*n., pl.* **-lons** or **-lo•nes** (-lō′nās′). See table at **currency.** [Sp. *colón*, after Cristóbal *Colón*, Christopher Columbus.]

colo•nel (kûr′nəl) ►*n.* A rank, as in the US Army, above lieutenant colonel and below brigadier general. [< OItal. *colonello* < dim. of *colonna*, COLUMN.] —**colo′nel•cy** *n.*

co•lo•ni•al (kə-lō′nē-əl) ►*adj.* **1.** Of or possessing a colony or colonies. **2.** often **Colonial** Of or relating to the 13 original colonies that became the United States of America. ►*n.* A native or inhabitant of a colony. —**co•lo′ni•al•ly** *adv.*

co•lo•ni•al•ism (kə-lō′nē-ə-lĭz′əm) ►*n.* A policy by which a nation maintains or extends its control over foreign dependencies. —**co•lo′ni•al•ist** *n.*

col•o•nist (kŏl′ə-nĭst) ►*n.* An inhabitant or original settler of a colony.

col•o•nize (kŏl′ə-nīz′) ►*v.* **-nized, -niz•ing.** To establish a colony (in). —**col′o•ni•za′tion** *n.* —**col′o•niz′er** *n.*

col•on•nade (kŏl′ə-nād′) ►*n. Archit.* A series of regularly spaced columns. [< Ital. *colonna*, COLUMN.] —**col′on•nad′ed** *adj.*

col•o•ny (kŏl′ə-nē) ►*n., pl.* **-nies 1.** A group of emigrants who settle in a distant territory but remain subject to their parent country. **2.** A region controlled by a distant country. **3.** A group of people with the same interests concentrated in a particular area. **4.** A group of the same kind of organisms living together. [< Lat. *colōnus*, settler.]

col•o•phon (kŏl′ə-fŏn′, -fən) ►*n.* An inscription placed usu. at the end of a book, giving facts about its publication. [< Gk. *kolophōn*, finishing touch.]

col•or (kŭl′ər) ►*n.* **1.** The visible aspect of things caused by differing qualities of the light reflected or emitted by them. **2.** A dye, pigment, or paint that imparts a hue. **3.** Skin tone. **4. colors** A flag or banner, as of a country or military unit. **5.** Outward appearance, often deceptive. **6.** Vivid, picturesque detail. ►*v.* **1.** To impart color to. **2.** To give a distinctive character to; influence. See Syns at **bias. 3.** To misrepresent. **4.** To blush. [< Lat.] —**col′or•er** *n.*

Usage: Though the use of *colored* to refer to persons of non-European origin is now generally considered offensive, the terms *person of color* and *people of color* are increasingly popular in American English and are generally regarded as not only acceptable but respectful. See Usage Note at **black.**

Col•o•ra•do (kŏl′ə-răd′ō, -rä′dō) A state of the W-central US. Cap. Denver. Pop. 3,307,912. —**Col′o•ra′dan** *adj. & n.*

Colorado Desert. An arid region of SE CA W of the Colorado R.

Colorado River 1. A river of the SW US rising in the Rocky Mts. and flowing about 2,333 km (1,450 mi) to the Gulf of California in NW Mexico. **2.** A river rising in NW TX and flowing about 1,438 km (894 mi) to an inlet of the Gulf of Mexico.

Colorado Springs. A city of central CO at the foot of Pikes Peak S of Denver. Pop. 281,140.

col•or•ant (kŭl′ər-ənt) ►*n.* Something, esp. a dye, that colors something else.

col•or•a•tion (kŭl′ə-rā′shən) ►*n.* Arrangement of colors.

col•or•a•tu•ra (kŭl′ər-ə-to͝or′ə, -tyo͝or′ə) ►*n.* Ornamental trills and runs in vocal music. [< LLat. *colōrātūra*, coloring.]

color bar ►*n.* See **color line.**

col•or•blind or **col•or-blind** (kŭl′ər-blīnd′) ►*adj.* **1.** Partially or totally unable to distinguish certain colors. **2.** Not subject to racial prejudices. —**col′or•blind′ness** *n.*

col•or-code (kŭl′ər-kōd′) ►*v.* To color, as wires or papers, according to a code for easy identification.

col•ored (kŭl′ərd) ►*adj.* **1.** Having color. **2.** *Often Offensive* Of or belonging to a racial group not categorized as white. **3.** Distorted or biased, as by incorrect information.

col•or•ful (kŭl′ər-fəl) ►*adj.* **1.** Full of color. **2.** Vividly distinctive. —**col′or•ful•ly** *adv.*

color guard ►*n.* A ceremonial escort for the flag, esp. of a country.

col•or•ing (kŭl′ər-ĭng) ►*n.* **1.** A substance used to color something. **2.** Appearance with regard to color. **3.** False or misleading appearance.

col•or•less (kŭl′ər-lĭs) ►*adj.* **1.** Lacking color. **2.** Drab; lifeless. See Syns at **dull.** —**col′or•less•ly** *adv.* —**col′or•less•ness** *n.*

color line ►*n.* A barrier, created by custom, law, or economic differences, separating nonwhite persons from whites.

co•los•sal (kə-lŏs′əl) ►*adj.* Immense in size, extent, or degree. —**co•los′sal•ly** *adv.*

Co•los•sians (kə-lŏsh′ənz) ►*pl.n. (takes sing. v.)* See table at **Bible.**

co•los•sus (kə-lŏs′əs) ►*n., pl.* **-los•si** (-lŏs′ī′) or **-sus•es 1.** A huge statue. **2.** Something of enormous size or importance. [< Gk. *kolossos.*]

colossus
the Colossus of Rhodes

co•los•to•my (kə-lŏs′tə-mē) ►*n., pl.* **-mies.** Surgical construction of an artificial excretory opening from the colon. [COLO– + Gk. *stoma,* opening.]

co•los•trum (kə-lŏs′trəm) ►*n.* The thin yellowish fluid secreted by the mammary glands at the time of parturition. [Lat.]

col•our (kŭl′ər) ►*n. & v. Chiefly Brit.* Var. of **color.**

colt (kōlt) ►*n.* A young male horse. [< OE.] —**colt′ish** *adj.* —**colt′ish•ness** *n.*

Co•lum•bi•a (kə-lŭm′bē-ə) The capital of SC, in the central part. Pop. 98,052.

Columbia River. A river rising in SE British Columbia, Canada, and flowing about 1,947 km (1,210 mi) along the WA-OR border to the Pacific.

col•um•bine (kŏl′əm-bīn′) ►*n.* Any of various plants with variously colored flowers that have five spurred petals. [< Lat. *columba,* dove.]

Co•lum•bus (kə-lŭm′bəs) **1.** A city of W GA SSW of Atlanta. Pop. 179,278. **2.** The capital of OH, in the central part. Pop. 632,910.

Columbus, Christopher. 1451–1506. Italian explorer in the service of Spain and discoverer (1492) of the New World.

Christopher Columbus

Columbus Day ►*n.* Oct. 12, observed in the US on the 2nd Monday in Oct. in honor of Christopher Columbus.

col•umn (kŏl′əm) ►*n.* **1.** A supporting pillar used in building construction. **2.** Something resembling a pillar in form or function. **3.** *Print.* One of two or more vertical sections of a page. **4.** A feature article that appears regularly in a publication. **5.** A formation in rows or ranks, as of troops. [< Lat. *columna.*] —**co•lum′nar** (kə-lŭm′nər) *adj.* —**col′umned** *adj.*

col•um•nist (kŏl′əm-nĭst, -ə-mĭst) ►*n.* A writer of a column in a publication.

Com. ►*abbr.* **1.** commander **2.** commodore

com– or **col–** or **con–** ►*pref.* Together; jointly: *commingle.* [< Lat.]

co•ma (kō′mə) ►*n.* A deep prolonged unconsciousness, usu. the result of injury, disease, or poison. [Gk. *kōma,* deep sleep.]

Co•man•che (kə-măn′chē) ►*n., pl.* **-che** or **-ches 1.** A member of a Native American people formerly of the S Great Plains, now living in Oklahoma. **2.** The Uto-Aztecan language of the Comanche.

co•ma•tose (kō′mə-tōs′, kŏm′ə-) ►*adj.* **1.** Of or affected with coma; unconscious. **2.** Lethargic; torpid.

comb (kōm) ►*n.* **1.** A thin toothed strip, as of plastic, used to arrange the hair. **2.** Something resembling a comb in shape or use. **3.** The fleshy crest on the crown of the head of domestic fowl and other birds. **4.** A honeycomb. ►*v.* **1.** To arrange with or as if with a comb. **2.** To card (wool or other fiber). **3.** To search thoroughly. [< OE.]

comb. ►*abbr.* **1.** combination **2.** combustion

com•bat (kəm-băt′, kŏm′băt′) ►*v.* **-bat•ed, -bat•ing** or **-bat•ted, -bat•ting 1.** To fight against. **2.** To oppose vigorously. ►*n.* (kŏm′băt′). Fighting, esp. armed battle. [< LLat. *combattere,* beat together.] —**com•bat′ant** *n.*

combat fatigue ►*n.* A nervous disorder characterized by anxiety, depression, and irritability, caused by the stress of combat.

com•bat•ive (kəm-băt′ĭv) ►*adj.* Eager or disposed to fight; belligerent. See Syns at **argumentative.** —**com•bat′ive•ly** *adv.* —**com•bat′ive•ness** *n.*

comb•er (kō′mər) ►*n.* **1.** One that combs

something, as wool. **2.** A long cresting wave.

com•bi•na•tion (kŏm′bə-nā′shən) ►*n.* **1.** The act of combining or the state of being combined. **2.** A sequence of numbers or letters used to open certain locks.

com•bine (kəm-bīn′) ►*v.* **-bined, -bin•ing 1.** To make or become united. **2.** To join (two or more substances) to make a single substance. ►*n.* (kŏm′bīn′) **1.** A harvesting machine that cuts, threshes, and cleans grain. **2.** An association of people united for political or commercial interests. [< LLat. *combīnāre.*]

com•bo (kŏm′bō) ►*n., pl.* **-bos.** A small jazz band. [< COMBINATION.]

com•bust (kəm-bŭst′) ►*v.* **1a.** To catch fire. **b.** To burn. **2.** To become suddenly angry. [Back-formation from COMBUSTION.]

com•bus•ti•ble (kəm-bŭs′tə-bəl) ►*adj.* Capable of igniting and burning. ►*n.* A substance that ignites and burns easily. —**com•bus′ti•bil′i•ty** *n.* —**com•bus′ti•bly** *adv.*

com•bus•tion (kəm-bŭs′chən) ►*n.* **1.** The process of burning. **2.** A chemical change, esp. oxidation, accompanied by heat and light. [< Lat. *combūrere, combust-*, burn up.] —**com•bus′tive** (-tĭv) *adj.*

Comdr. ►*abbr.* commander

Comdt. ►*abbr.* commandant

come (kŭm) ►*v.* **came** (kām), **come, com•ing 1.** To advance; approach. **2.** To make progress. **3.** To arrive. **4.** To move into view. **5.** To occur: *Happiness came to her late in life.* **6.** To arrive at a particular result or condition. **7.** To issue forth; originate. **8.** To become: *The knot came loose.* **9.** To be obtainable. —***phrasal verbs:*** **come about** To happen. **come across 1.** To meet by chance. **2.** *Slang* To give an impression: *come across as honest.* **come around 1.** To recover. **2.** To change one's opinion. **come by** To acquire. **come into** To inherit. **come off 1.** To happen. **2.** To be successful. **come out 1.** To become known. **2.** To be issued. **come through** To do what is required. **come to** To recover consciousness. —***idioms:*** **come clean** To confess all. **come to grips with** To confront squarely and resolutely. **come to light** To be clearly revealed or disclosed. **come up with** To produce or discover. [< OE *cuman.*]

come•back (kŭm′băk′) ►*n.* **1.** A return to former status or prosperity. **2.** A retort.

co•me•di•an (kə-mē′dē-ən) ►*n.* **1.** A professional entertainer who tells jokes or performs various other comic acts. **2.** A writer of comedy.

co•me•di•enne (kə-mē′dē-ĕn′) ►*n.* A female professional entertainer who tells jokes or performs various other comic acts. [Fr. *comédienne.*]

come•down (kŭm′doun′) ►*n.* **1.** A decline in status or level. **2.** A cause or feeling of disappointment or depression.

com•e•dy (kŏm′ĭ-dē) ►*n., pl.* **-dies 1.** A dramatic work that is humorous and usu. has a happy ending. **2.** The genre made up of such works. **3.** A literary work having humorous themes or characters. **4.** Popular entertainment composed of jokes and satire. [< Gk. *kōmōidia.*]

come•ly (kŭm′lē) ►*adj.* **-li•er, -li•est.** Pleasing in appearance; attractive. [< OE *cȳmlic.*] —**come′li•ness** *n.*

come-on (kŭm′ŏn′, -ôn′) ►*n.* Something offered to allure or attract; inducement.

com•er (kŭm′ər) ►*n.* **1.** One that comes. **2.** One showing promise of attaining success.

co•mes•ti•ble (kə-mĕs′tə-bəl) ►*adj.* Edible. [< Lat. *comedere, comēs-*, eat up : COM– + *edere*, eat.] —**co•mes′ti•ble** *n.*

com•et (kŏm′ĭt) ►*n.* A celestial body consisting of a dense nucleus of frozen gases and dust, which develops a luminous halo and tail when its orbit approaches the sun. [< Gk. *(astēr) komētēs*, long-haired (star).]

come•up•pance (kŭm′ŭp′əns) ►*n.* A punishment that one deserves.

com•fit (kŭm′fĭt, kŏm′-) ►*n.* A confection; candy. [< Lat. *cōnficere*, prepare.]

com•fort (kŭm′fərt) ►*v.* To soothe in time of affliction or distress. ►*n.* **1.** A condition of pleasurable ease or well-being. **2.** Solace. **3.** One that brings or provides comfort. See Syns at **amenity. 4.** The capacity to give physical ease. [< LLat. *cōnfortāre*, strengthen.] —**com′fort•ing** *adj.*

Syns: *comfort, console, solace* **v.**

com•fort•a•ble (kŭm′fər-tə-bəl, kŭmf′tə-bəl, kŭmf′tər-) ►*adj.* **1.** Providing comfort. **2.** At ease. **3.** Sufficient; adequate: *comfortable earnings.* —**com′fort•a•ble•ness** *n.* —**com′fort•a•bly** *adv.*

com•fort•er (kŭm′fər-tər) ►*n.* **1.** One that comforts. **2.** A quilted bedcover.

com•frey (kŭm′frē) ►*n.* Any of a genus of Eurasian herbs used in herbal medicine. [< Lat. *cōnfervēre*, boil together.]

com•fy (kŭm′fē) ►*adj.* **-fi•er, -fi•est** *Informal.* Comfortable.

com•ic (kŏm′ĭk) ►*adj.* **1.** Of or relating to comedy. **2.** Amusing; humorous. ►*n.* **1.** A comedian. **2. comics** Comic strips. [< Gk. *kōmos*, revel.]

com•i•cal (kŏm′ĭ-kəl) ►*adj.* Causing amusement; funny. —**com′i•cal′i•ty** (-kăl′ĭ-tē), **com′i•cal•ness** *n.* —**com′i•cal•ly** *adv.*

comic book ►*n.* A book of comic strips.

comic relief ►*n.* A humorous incident introduced into a serious literary work to relieve tension or heighten emotional impact.

comic strip ►*n.* A narrative series of cartoons.

com•ing (kŭm′ĭng) ►*adj.* **1.** Approaching; next. **2.** Showing promise of success. ►*n.* Arrival; advent.

com•i•ty (kŏm′ĭ-tē) ►*n., pl.* **-ties.** Civility; courtesy. [< Lat. *cōmis*, friendly.]

com•ma (kŏm′ə) ►*n.* A punctuation mark (,) used to indicate a separation of ideas or elements within the structure of a sentence. [< Gk. *komma*, short clause.]

com•mand (kə-mănd′) ►*v.* **1.** To give orders to. **2.** To have authority (over). **3.** To receive as due; exact: *command respect.* **4.** To dominate by position; overlook. ►*n.* **1.** The act of commanding. **2.** An order given with authority. **3.** *Comp. Sci.* A signal that initiates an operation defined by an instruction. **4.** Ability to control. **5.** A military unit or region under the control of one officer. [< LLat. *commandāre*, entrust to.]

com•man•dant (kŏm′ən-dănt′, -dänt′) ►*n.* The commanding officer of a military organization.

com•man•deer (kŏm′ən-dîr′) ►*v.* To seize for military use; confiscate. 2. To take or seize arbitrarily. See Syns at **appropriate.** [Afr. *kom-*

mandeer < Fr. *commander,* command.]

com•mand•er (kə-măn′dər) ►*n.* **1.** One who commands. **2.** A rank, as in the US Navy, above lieutenant commander and below captain.

commander in chief ►*n., pl.* **commanders in chief.** The supreme commander of all the armed forces of a nation.

com•mand•ing (kə-măn′dĭng) ►*adj.* **1.** Having command; controlling. **2.** Dominating: *a commanding view; a commanding lead.*

com•mand•ment (kə-mănd′mənt) ►*n.* **1.** A command. **2.** One of the Ten Commandments.

command module ►*n.* The portion of a spacecraft in which the astronauts live and operate controls during a flight.

com•man•do (kə-măn′dō) ►*n., pl.* **-dos** or **-does.** A member of a small military unit specially trained to make quick raids. [Afr. *kommando,* ult. < LLat. *commandāre,* to command.]

com•mem•o•rate (kə-mĕm′ə-rāt′) ►*v.* **-rat•ed, -rat•ing 1.** To honor the memory of. **2.** To serve as a memorial to. [Lat. *commemorāre,* remind.] **—com•mem′o•ra′tion** *n.* **—com•mem′o•ra•tive** (-ər-ə-tĭv, -ə-rā′-) *adj. & n.*

com•mence (kə-mĕns′) ►*v.* **-menced, -menc•ing.** To make or have a beginning; start. [< VLat. **cominitiāre.*]

com•mence•ment (kə-mĕns′mənt) ►*n.* **1.** A beginning; start. **2.** A graduation ceremony.

com•mend (kə-mĕnd′) ►*v.* **1.** To represent as worthy or qualified; recommend. **2.** To praise. **3.** To put in the care of another; entrust. [< Lat. *commendāre.*] **—com•mend′a•ble** *adj.* **—com•mend′a•bly** *adv.*

com•men•da•tion (kŏm′ən-dā′shən) ►*n.* **1.** The act of commending. **2.** An official award or citation.

com•men•da•to•ry (kə-mĕn′də-tôr′ē, -tōr′ē) ►*adj.* Serving to commend.

com•men•sal•ism (kə-mĕn′sə-lĭz′əm) ►*n.* *Biol.* A symbiotic relationship between two organisms of different species in which one derives some benefit while the other is unaffected.

com•men•su•ra•ble (kə-mĕn′sər-ə-bəl, -shər-) ►*adj.* Measurable by a common standard. [LLat. *commēnsūrābilis.*] **—com•men′su•ra•bly** *adv.*

com•men•su•rate (kə-mĕn′sər-ĭt, -shər-) ►*adj.* **1.** Of the same size, extent, or duration. **2.** Corresponding in scale; proportionate. [LLat. *commēnsūrātus.*] **—com•men′su•rate•ly** *adv.* **—com•men′su•ra′tion** *n.*

com•ment (kŏm′ĕnt) ►*n.* **1.** An explanation, illustration, or criticism. **2.** A statement of opinion. [< LLat. *commentum,* interpretation < Lat. *comminīscī,* devise.] **—com′ment** *v.*

Syns: *comment, observation, remark* ***n.***

com•men•tar•y (kŏm′ən-tĕr′ē) ►*n., pl.* **-ies.** A series of explanations or interpretations.

com•men•tate (kŏm′ən-tāt′) ►*v.* **-tat•ed, -tat•ing.** To serve as commentator.

com•men•ta•tor (kŏm′ən-tā′tər) ►*n.* A broadcaster or writer who reports and analyzes events in the news.

com•merce (kŏm′ərs) ►*n.* The buying and selling of goods, esp. on a large scale. [< Lat. *commercium* : COM– + *merx,* merchandise.]

com•mer•cial (kə-mûr′shəl) ►*adj.* **1.** Of or engaged in commerce. **2.** Having profit as a chief aim. **3.** Supported by advertising. ►*n.* An advertisement on television or radio. **—com•mer′cial•ism** *n.* **—com•mer′cial•ist** *n.* **—com•mer′cial•is′tic** *adj.* **—com•mer′cial•ly** *adv.*

commercial bank ►*n.* A bank whose principal functions are to receive demand deposits and to make short-term loans.

com•mer•cial•ize (kə-mûr′shə-līz′) ►*v.* **-ized, -iz•ing.** To apply methods of business to for profit. **—com•mer′cial•i•za′tion** *n.*

com•min•gle (kə-mĭng′gəl) ►*v.* **-gled, -gling.** To blend together; mix.

com•mis•er•ate (kə-mĭz′ə-rāt′) ►*v.* **-at•ed, -at•ing.** To feel or express sympathy (for). [Lat. *commiserārī.*] **—com•mis′er•a′•tion** *n.* **—com•mis′er•a′tive** *adj.* **—com•mis′er•a′tor** *n.*

com•mis•sar (kŏm′ĭ-sär′) ►*n.* A Communist Party official in charge of indoctrination and enforcement of party loyalty. [Russ. *komissar.*]

com•mis•sar•i•at (kŏm′ĭ-sâr′ē-ĭt) ►*n.* An army department in charge of providing food and supplies. [< Med.Lat. *commissārius,* agent. See COMMISSARY.]

com•mis•sar•y (kŏm′ĭ-sĕr′ē) ►*n., pl.* **-ies 1.** A store where food and equipment are sold, esp. on a military post. **2.** A cafeteria, esp. in a film studio. [< Med.Lat. *commissārius,* agent < Lat. *committere,* entrust.]

com•mis•sion (kə-mĭsh′ən) ►*n.* **1a.** Authorization to carry out a task. **b.** The authority so granted. **c.** The task so authorized. **d.** A document conferring such authorization. **2.** A group authorized to perform certain duties or functions. **3.** A committing; perpetrating: *the commission of a crime.* **4.** An allowance to a sales representative or agent for services rendered. **5.** A document conferring the rank of a military officer. ►*v.* **1.** To grant a commission to. See Syns at **authorize. 2.** To place an order for. **—*idioms:* in commission** In use or in usable condition. **out of commission** Not in use or in working condition. [< Lat. *committere,* entrust.]

com•mis•sioned officer (kə-mĭsh′ənd) ►*n.* A military officer who holds a commission and ranks above an enlisted person, a noncommissioned officer, or a warrant officer.

com•mis•sion•er (kə-mĭsh′ə-nər) ►*n.* **1.** A member of a commission. **2.** A government official in charge of a department. **3.** An administrative head of a professional sport.

com•mit (kə-mĭt′) ►*v.* **-mit•ted, -mit•ting 1.** To do, perform, or perpetrate: *commit murder.* **2.** To consign; entrust. **3.** To place in confinement or custody. **4.** To pledge or obligate (oneself). [< Lat. *committere,* entrust.] **—com•mit′ment** *n.* **—com•mit′ta•ble** *adj.* **—com•mit′tal** *n.*

com•mit•tee (kə-mĭt′ē) ►*n.* A group of people officially delegated to perform a function, such as investigating, considering, reporting, or acting on a matter. See Usage Note at **collective noun.** [< AN *comité,* trustee < *cometre,* COMMIT.] **—com•mit′tee•man** *n.* **—com•mit′tee•wom′an** *n.*

com•mode (kə-mōd′) ►*n.* **1.** A low cabinet or chest of drawers. **2.** A movable stand containing a washbowl. **3.** A toilet. [Fr., convenient. See COMMODIOUS.]

com•mo•di•ous (kə-mō′dē-əs) ▸*adj.* Spacious; roomy. See Syns at **spacious.** [< Lat. *commodus,* convenient.] —**com•mo′di•ous•ly** *adv.* —**com•mo′di•ous•ness** *n.*

com•mod•i•ty (kə-mŏd′ĭ-tē) ▸*n., pl.* **-ties 1.** Something useful that can be turned to commercial advantage. **2.** A transportable article of trade or commerce, esp. an agricultural or mining product that can be processed and resold. [< Lat. *commodus,* convenient.]

com•mo•dore (kŏm′ə-dôr′, -dōr′) ▸*n.* **1.** A rank, as in the US Navy, above captain and below rear admiral. **2.** The senior captain of a naval squadron or merchant fleet. [Prob. < Du. *komandeur,* commander < Fr. *commandeur.*]

Com•mo•dus (kŏm′ə-dəs), **Lucius Aelius Aurelius.** A.D. 161–192. Emperor of Rome (180–192).

com•mon (kŏm′ən) ▸*adj.* **-er, -est 1.** Belonging equally to all; joint. See Syns at **general. 2.** Of or relating to the whole community; public: *the common good.* **3.** Widespread; prevalent. **4.** Frequent or habitual; usual. **5.** Most widely known; ordinary. **6.** Without noteworthy characteristics; average. **7.** Unrefined; coarse. ▸*n.* **1.** often **Commons.** See **House of Commons. 2.** A tract of land belonging to a whole community. —***idiom:*** **in common** Equally with or by all. [< Lat. *commūnis.*] —**com′mon•ly** *adv.* —**com′mon•ness** *n.*

com•mon•al•ty (kŏm′ə-nəl-tē) ▸*n., pl.* **-ties.** The common people, as distinct from the upper classes. [< LLat. *commūnālis,* of the community.]

common denominator ▸*n.* **1.** A quantity into which all the denominators of a set of fractions may be divided without a remainder. **2.** A commonly shared trait.

com•mon•er (kŏm′ə-nər) ▸*n.* A person without noble rank.

Common Era ▸*n.* The period coinciding with the Christian era.

common fraction ▸*n.* A fraction whose numerator and denominator are both integers.

common ground ▸*n.* A foundation for mutual understanding.

common law ▸*n.* An unwritten system of law based on court decisions, customs, and usages. —**com′mon-law′** *adj.*

common logarithm ▸*n.* A logarithm to the base 10.

common market ▸*n.* An economic association of nations.

Common Market. See **European Economic Community.**

common multiple ▸*n.* A quantity into which each of two or more quantities may be divided with zero remainder.

com•mon•place (kŏm′ən-plās′) ▸*adj.* Unremarkable; ordinary. ▸*n.* Something ordinary or common, esp. a trite or obvious remark. See Syns at **cliché.**

common sense ▸*n.* Native good judgment.

common stock ▸*n.* Ordinary capital shares of a corporation, usu. giving the owners a vote.

common time ▸*n. Mus.* A meter with four quarter notes to the measure.

com•mon•weal (kŏm′ən-wēl′) ▸*n.* **1.** The public good. **2.** *Archaic* A commonwealth.

com•mon•wealth (kŏm′ən-wĕlth′) ▸*n.* **1.** The people of a nation or state. **2.** A nation or state governed by the people; republic. **3.** A union of self-governing states.

Commonwealth of Independent States. A federation of self-governing states in E Europe, Asia Minor, and central Asia; formerly republics of the Soviet Union.

Commonwealth of Nations also **British Commonwealth.** An association comprising the United Kingdom, its dependencies, and many former British colonies.

com•mo•tion (kə-mō′shən) ▸*n.* Violent or turbulent motion; agitation; tumult. [< Lat. *commovēre, commōt-,* disturb.]

com•mu•nal (kə-myōō′nəl, kŏm′yə-) ▸*adj.* **1.** Of or relating to a commune or community. **2.** Public. —**com•mu′nal•ly** *adv.*

com•mune[1] (kə-myōōn′) ▸*v.* **-muned, -mun•ing 1.** To experience heightened receptivity: *hikers communing with nature.* **2.** To receive the Eucharist. [< OFr. *communier.*]

com•mune[2] (kŏm′yōōn′, kə-myōōn′) ▸*n.* **1a.** A small, often rural community whose members share work and income and often own property collectively. **b.** The members of a commune. **2.** The smallest local political division of various European countries. [< Lat. *commūnis,* common.]

com•mu•ni•ca•ble (kə-myōō′nĭ-kə-bəl) ▸*adj.* **1.** Capable of being transmitted or communicated. **2.** Talkative. —**com•mu′ni•ca•bil′i•ty** *n.* —**com•mu′ni•ca•bly** *adv.*

com•mu•ni•cant (kə-myōō′nĭ-kənt) ▸*n.* **1.** A person who receives Communion. **2.** One who communicates.

com•mu•ni•cate (kə-myōō′nĭ-kāt′) ▸*v.* **-cat•ed, -cat•ing 1.** To make known; impart. **2.** To spread, as a disease. **3.** To receive Communion. [Lat. *commūnicāre.*] —**com•mu′ni•ca′tive** (-kā′tĭv, -kə-tĭv) *adj.* —**com•mu′ni•ca′tive•ly** *adv.* —**com•mu′ni•ca′tive•ness** *n.* —**com•mu′ni•ca′tor** *n.*

com•mu•ni•ca•tion (kə-myōō′nĭ-kā′shən) ▸*n.* **1.** The act of communicating. **2.** The exchange of thoughts, messages, or information. **3.** Something communicated; message. **4. communications a.** A system for communicating. **b.** The art and technology of communicating. —**com•mu′ni•ca′tion•al** *adj.*

com•mun•ion (kə-myōōn′yən) ▸*n.* **1.** A sharing of thoughts or feelings. **2.** Religious or spiritual fellowship. **3.** A Christian denomination. **4. Communion a.** The Eucharist. **b.** The consecrated elements of the Eucharist. [< Lat. *commūniō,* mutual participation.]

com•mu•ni•qué (kə-myōō′nĭ-kā′, -myōō′nĭ-kā′) ▸*n.* An official announcement. [Fr. < p.part. of *communiquer,* announce.]

com•mu•nism (kŏm′yə-nĭz′əm) ▸*n.* **1.** An economic system characterized by collective ownership of property and by the organization of labor for common advantage. **2. Communism a.** A system of government in which the state plans and controls the economy and a single, often authoritarian party holds power. **b.** The Marxist-Leninist version of Communist doctrine. [< Fr. *commun,* COMMON.] —**com′mu•nist** *n.* —**com′mu•nis′tic** *adj.* —**com′mu•nis′ti•cal•ly** *adv.*

Communism Peak. A mountain, 7,500 m (24,590 ft), of NE Tajikistan in the Pamirs near the Chinese border.

com•mu•ni•ty (kə-myōō′nĭ-tē) ▸*n., pl.* **-ties 1a.** A group of people living in the same locality and under the same government. **b.** The locality in which such a group lives. **2.** A group of people having common interests. **3.** Similarity: *a community of interests.* **4.** Society as a whole. **5.** *Ecol.* A group of plants and animals living with one another in a specific region. [< Lat. *commūnitās.*]

community college ▸*n.* A junior college without residential facilities that is often funded by the government.

community property ▸*n. Law* Property owned jointly by spouses.

com•mu•nize (kŏm′yə-nīz′) ▸*v.* **-nized, -niz•ing 1.** To subject to public ownership or control. **2.** To convert to Communist principles or control. —**com′mu•ni•za′tion** *n.*

com•mu•ta•tion (kŏm′yə-tā′shən) ▸*n.* **1.** A substitution or exchange. **2.** The travel of a commuter. **3.** *Law* Reduction of a penalty to a less severe one.

com•mu•ta•tive (kŏm′yə-tā′tĭv, kə-myōō′tə-tĭv) ▸*adj.* **1.** Of or involving substitution, interchange, or exchange. **2.** Logically or mathematically independent of order. —**com•mu′ta•tiv′i•ty** (kə-myōō′tə-tĭv′ĭ-tē) *n.*

com•mu•ta•tor (kŏm′yə-tā′tər) ▸*n.* A device in a direct current motor or generator that reverses current direction.

com•mute (kə-myōōt′) ▸*v.* **-mut•ed, -mut•ing 1.** To travel as a commuter. **2.** To substitute; interchange. **3.** To change (a penalty or payment) to a less severe one. ▸*n.* A trip made by a commuter. [< Lat. *commūtāre*, transform.]

com•mut•er (kə-myōō′tər) ▸*n.* One who travels regularly from one place to another, esp. between home and work.

Co•mo (kō′mō) A resort city of N Italy near the Swiss border at the SW end of **Lake Como.** Pop. 95,183.

Com•o•ros (kŏm′ə-rōz′) An island country in the **Comoro Islands** of the Indian Ocean between Mozambique and Madagascar. Cap. Moroni. Pop. 630,000.

com•pact[1] (kəm-păkt′, kŏm-, kŏm′păkt′) ▸*adj.* **1.** Closely and firmly packed together. **2.** Occupying little space. **3.** Concise. ▸*v.* (kəm-păkt′). To press or join together. ▸*n.* (kŏm′păkt′) **1.** A small cosmetic case. **2.** A small automobile. [< Lat. *compingere, compāct-*, join together.] —**com•pact′ly** *adv.* —**com•pact′ness** *n.*

com•pact[2] (kŏm′păkt′) ▸*n.* An agreement or a covenant. See Syns at **bargain.** [< Lat. *compacīscī, compact-*, make an agreement.]

com•pact disk (kŏm′păkt′) or **compact disc** ▸*n.* A small optical disk on which data such as music, text, or graphic images is digitally encoded.

Usage: The computer industry generally uses the spelling *disk* in compounds like *hard disk* and *compact disk.* The music and entertainment industry generally prefers *disc,* as in *disc jockey* and *compact disc.*

com•pac•tor or **com•pact•er** (kəm-păk′tər, kŏm′păk′-) ▸*n.* An apparatus that compresses refuse for disposal.

com•pa•dre (kəm-pä′drā) ▸*n. Regional* A close friend; companion. [Sp., godfather, friend.]

com•pan•ion (kəm-păn′yən) ▸*n.* **1.** An associate; comrade. **2.** A person employed to live or travel with another. **3.** One of a pair or set of things. [< VLat. **compāniō.*] —**com•pan′ion•ship′** *n.*

com•pan•ion•a•ble (kəm-păn′yə-nə-bəl) ▸*adj.* Sociable; friendly. See Syns at **social.** —**com•pan′ion•a•bly** *adv.*

com•pan•ion•way (kəm-păn′yən-wā′) ▸*n.* A staircase leading below deck on a ship. [Prob. < OFr. *compagne*, storeroom.]

com•pa•ny (kŭm′pə-nē) ▸*n., pl.* **-nies 1.** A group of persons. See Syns at **band**[2]. **2.** One's companions or associates. **3.** A guest or guests. **4.** Companionship; fellowship. **5.** A business enterprise; firm. **6.** A troupe of dramatic or musical performers. **7.** *Military* A subdivision of a regiment or battalion. **8.** A ship's crew and officers. See Usage Note at **collective noun.** [< OFr. *compaignie* < VLat. **compāniō*, companion.]

com•pa•ra•ble (kŏm′pər-ə-bəl) ▸*adj.* **1.** Admitting of comparison. **2.** Similar or equivalent. —**com′pa•ra•bil′i•ty** *n.* —**com′pa•ra•bly** *adv.*

com•par•a•tive (kəm-păr′ə-tĭv) ▸*adj.* **1.** Of, based on, or involving comparison. **2.** Relative: *a comparative newcomer.* **3.** *Gram.* Of or being the intermediate degree of comparison of adjectives or adverbs. ▸*n. Gram.* **1.** The comparative degree. **2.** An adjective, such as *bigger,* or adverb, such as *more distinctly,* expressing the comparative degree. —**com•par′a•tive•ly** *adv.*

com•pare (kəm-pâr′) ▸*v.* **-pared, -par•ing 1.** To describe as similar, equal, or analogous. **2.** To examine in order to note the similarities or differences of. **3.** *Gram.* To form the positive, comparative, or superlative degree of (an adjective or adverb). ▸*n.* Comparison: *rich beyond compare.* —***idiom:*** **compare notes** To exchange ideas or opinions. [< Lat. *comparāre*, match up.]

com•par•i•son (kəm-păr′ĭ-sən) ▸*n.* **1.** The act of comparing. **2.** Similarity. **3.** *Gram.* The modification or inflection of an adjective or adverb to denote the positive, comparative, or superlative degree. [< Lat. *comparātiō.*]

com•part•ment (kəm-pärt′mənt) ▸*n.* One of the parts or spaces into which an area is subdivided. [< LLat. *compartīrī*, share with.] —**com′part•ment′al** (kŏm′pärt-mĕn′tl) *adj.*

com•part•men•tal•ize (kŏm′pärt-mĕn′tl-īz′, kəm-pärt′-) ▸*v.* **-ized, -iz•ing.** To separate into distinct areas or categories. —**com′part•men′tal•i•za′tion** (-ĭ-zā′shən) *n.*

com•pass (kŭm′pəs, kŏm′-) ▸*n.* **1.** A device used to determine geographic direction, usu. consisting of a magnetic needle that is free to pivot until aligned with the magnetic field of Earth. **2.** A hinged V-shaped device for drawing circles or circular arcs. **3.** An enclosing line or boundary; circumference. See Syns at **circumference. 4.** A restricted space or area. **5.** Range or scope. See Syns at **range.** ▸*v.* **1.** To make a circuit of; circle. **2.** To surround; encircle. See Syns at **surround. 3.** To accomplish. **4.** To scheme; plot. [< VLat. **compassāre*, pace off.]

com•pas•sion (kəm-păsh′ən) ▸*n.* Deep awareness of the suffering of another. [< LLat. *compatī, compass-*, suffer with.]

com•pas•sion•ate (kəm-păsh′ə-nĭt) ▸*adj.* Feeling or showing compassion. See Syns at

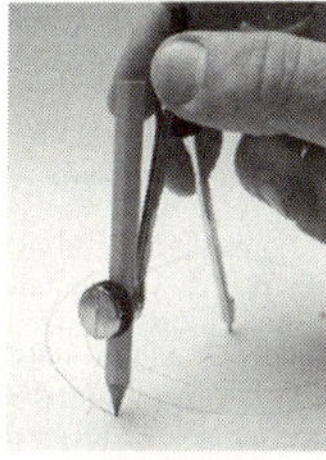

compass
top to bottom: directional and drawing models

humane. —com•pas′sion•ate•ly *adv.*

com•pat•i•ble (kəm-păt′ə-bəl) ►*adj.* **1.** Capable of existing or functioning well with another or others. **2.** *Medic.* Capable of being grafted or transplanted from one individual to another without rejection. [< LLat. *compatī*, sympathize with.] **—com•pat′i•bil′i•ty** *n.* **—com•pat′i•bly** *adv.*

com•pa•tri•ot (kəm-pā′trē-ət, -ŏt′) ►*n.* A person from one's own country.

com•peer (kŏm′pîr′, kəm-pîr′) ►*n.* A person of equal status; peer.

com•pel (kəm-pĕl′) ►*v.* **-pelled, -pel•ling.** To force; constrain. [< Lat. *compellere*, force together.]

com•pel•ling (kəm-pĕl′ĭng) ►*adj.* **1.** Urgently requiring attention. **2.** Drivingly forceful.

com•pen•di•um (kəm-pĕn′dē-əm) ►*n., pl.* **-di•ums** or **-di•a** (-dē-ə) **1.** A short detailed summary. **2.** A list or collection of items. [Lat., a shortening < *compendere*, weigh together.]

com•pen•sate (kŏm′pən-sāt′) ►*v.* **-sat•ed, -sat•ing 1.** To make up for; offset; counterbalance. **2.** To make payment to; reimburse. [Lat. *compēnsāre*, weigh together.] **—com′pen•sa′tion** *n.* **—com•pen′sa•to′ry** (kəm-pĕn′sə-tôr′ē, -tōr′ē) *adj.*

com•pete (kəm-pēt′) ►*v.* **-pet•ed, -pet•ing.** To strive with another or others. [LLat. *competere*, to strive together.]

com•pe•tence (kŏm′pĭ-təns) also **com•pe•ten•cy** (-tən-sē) ►*n.* **1.** The state or quality of being competent. **2.** A specific range of skill, knowledge, or ability.

com•pe•tent (kŏm′pĭ-tənt) ►*adj.* **1.** Properly or well qualified. **2.** Adequate for the purpose. **3.** Legally qualified to perform an act. [< Lat. *competere*, be suitable.] **—com′pe•tent•ly** *adv.*

com•pe•ti•tion (kŏm′pĭ-tĭsh′ən) ►*n.* **1.** The act of competing. **2.** A contest. **3.** A competitor: *The competition has cornered the market.* **—com•pet′i•tive** (kəm-pĕt′ĭ-tĭv) *adj.* **—com•pet′i•tive•ly** *adv.* **—com•pet′i•tive•ness** *n.*

com•pet•i•tor (kəm-pĕt′ĭ-tər) ►*n.* One who competes, as in sports or business; rival.

com•pile (kəm-pīl′) ►*v.* **-piled, -pil•ing 1.** To gather into a single book. **2.** To compose from materials gathered from several sources. **3.** *Comp. Sci.* To translate (a program) into machine language. [< OFr. *compiler.*] **—com′pi•la′tion** (kŏm′pə-lā′shən) *n.* **—com•pil′er** *n.*

com•pla•cence (kəm-plā′səns) also **com•pla•cen•cy** (-sən-sē) ►*n.* **1.** Contented self-satisfaction. **2.** Lack of concern. [< Lat. *complacēre*, to please.] **—com•pla′cent** *adj.* **—com•pla′cent•ly** *adv.*

com•plain (kəm-plān′) ►*v.* **1.** To express feelings of pain, dissatisfaction, or resentment. **2.** To make a formal accusation or bring a formal charge. [< VLat. **complangere*, to lament.] **—com•plain′er** *n.*

com•plain•ant (kəm-plā′nənt) ►*n.* A party that files a formal charge, as in a court of law; plaintiff.

com•plaint (kəm-plānt′) ►*n.* **1.** An expression of pain, dissatisfaction, or resentment. **2.** A cause or reason for complaining; grievance. **3.** A bodily disorder or disease. **4.** A formal charge or accusation. [< OFr. *complainte.*]

com•plai•sance (kəm-plā′səns, -zəns) ►*n.* Willing compliance; amiability. [< OFr. *complaire*, to please.] **—com•plai′sant** *adj.* **—com•plai′sant•ly** *adv.*

com•ple•ment (kŏm′plə-mənt) ►*n.* **1.** Something that completes or makes up a whole. **2.** The quantity or number needed to make up a whole. **3.** An angle related to another so that the sum of their measures is 90°. **4.** *Gram.* A word or group of words that completes a predicate construction. **5.** *Immunol.* Any of several blood proteins that combine with antibodies to destroy antigens. ►*v.* (-mĕnt′). To serve as a complement to. [< Lat. *complēmentum* < *complēre*, fill out.]

Usage: *Complement* means "something that completes or brings to perfection": *The antique silver was a complement to the beautifully set table. Compliment* means "an expression of courtesy or praise": *They gave us a compliment on our beautiful table.*

com•ple•men•ta•ry (kŏm′plə-mĕn′tə-rē, -trē) ►*adj.* **1.** Forming or serving as a complement. **2.** Supplying mutual needs or offsetting mutual lacks. **—com′ple•men′ta•ri•ly** *adv.*

com•plete (kəm-plēt′) ►*adj.* **-plet•er, -plet•est 1.** Having all necessary or normal parts. **2.** Ended; concluded. **3.** Thorough; total: *a complete coward.* ►*v.* **-plet•ed, -plet•ing 1.** To end. **2.** To make whole. [< Lat. *complēre*, *complēt-*, fill out.] **—com•plete′ly** *adv.* **—com•plete′ness** *n.* **—com•ple′tion** *n.*

com•plex (kəm-plĕks′, kŏm′plĕks′) ►*adj.* **1.** Consisting of two or more interconnected parts. **2.** Intricate; complicated. **3.** *Gram.* **a.** Containing at least one bound morpheme. Used of a word. **b.** Consisting of an independent clause and at least one other clause. Used of a sentence. ►*n.* (kŏm′plĕks′) **1.** A whole composed of interconnected parts. **2.** *Psychol.* A group of repressed ideas and impulses that compel patterns of feelings and behavior. No longer in scientific use. [< Lat. *complectī*, *complex-*, entwine.] **—com•plex′i•ty** *n.* **—com•plex′ly** *adv.* **—com•plex′ness** *n.*

complex fraction ►*n.* A fraction in which the

numerator or the denominator or both contain fractions.

com•plex•ion (kəm-plĕk′shən) ►*n.* **1.** The natural color, texture, and appearance of the skin. **2.** General character or appearance. [< LLat. *complexiō*, balance of the humors.]

complex number ►*n.* A number of the form $a + bi$, where a and b are real numbers and $i^2 = -1$.

com•pli•ance (kəm-plī′əns) also **com•pli•an•cy** (-ən-sē) ►*n.* **1.** The act of complying with a wish, request, or demand. **2.** A disposition or tendency to yield to others. —**com•pli′ant** *adj.* —**com•pli′ant•ly** *adv.*

com•pli•cate (kŏm′plĭ-kāt′) ►*v.* **-cat•ed, -cat•ing.** To make or become complex, intricate, or perplexing. [Lat. *complicāre*, fold together.] —**com′pli•ca′tion** *n.*

com•pli•cat•ed (kŏm′plĭ-kā′tĭd) ►*adj.* **1.** Containing intricately combined parts. **2.** Convoluted. See Syns at **elaborate.**

com•plic•i•ty (kəm-plĭs′ĭ-tē) ►*n.*, *pl.* **-ties.** Involvement as an accomplice in a questionable act or a crime. [< LLat. *complex*, *complic-*, accomplice.]

com•pli•ment (kŏm′plə-mənt) ►*n.* **1.** An expression of praise or admiration. See Usage Note at **complement. 2. compliments** Good wishes; regards. ►*v.* To pay a compliment to. [< Lat. *complēre*, fill up.]

com•pli•men•ta•ry (kŏm′plə-mĕn′tə-rē, -trē) ►*adj.* **1.** Expressing a compliment. **2.** Given free as a favor or courtesy. —**com′pli•men′ta•ri•ly** *adv.*

com•ply (kəm-plī′) ►*v.* **-plied, -ply•ing.** To act in accordance with another's command or wish. [< Lat. *complēre*, fill up.]

com•po•nent (kəm-pō′nənt) ►*n.* An element of a system. See Syns at **element.** ►*adj.* Being or functioning as a constituent. [< Lat. *compōnere*, put together.] —**com′po•nen′tial** (kŏm′pə-nĕn′shəl) *adj.*

com•port (kəm-pôrt′, -pōrt′) ►*v.* **1.** To conduct (oneself) in a particular manner. **2.** To agree; harmonize: *a policy that comports with democratic principles.* [< Lat. *comportāre*, bring together.] —**com•port′ment** *n.*

com•pose (kəm-pōz′) ►*v.* **-posed, -pos•ing 1.** To make up; constitute: *the many ethnic groups that compose our nation.* See Usage Note at **comprise. 2.** To make by putting together parts or elements. **3.** To create (a literary or musical piece). **4.** To make calm or tranquil. **5.** To settle; adjust. **6.** *Print.* To arrange or set (type). [< Lat. *compōnere*, put together.] —**com•pos′er** *n.*

com•posed (kəm-pōzd′) ►*adj.* Serenely self-possessed; calm. —**com•pos′ed•ly** (-pō′zĭd-lē) *adv.*

com•pos•ite (kəm-pŏz′ĭt) ►*adj.* **1.** Made up of distinct components or elements. **2.** *Math.* Having factors. **3.** Of or belonging to a family of flowering plants, such as the daisy, having flower heads consisting of many small flowers. ►*n.* **1.** A composite structure or entity. **2.** A composite plant. [< Lat. *compōnere*, *composit-*, put together.] —**com•pos′ite•ly** *adv.*

com•po•si•tion (kŏm′pə-zĭsh′ən) ►*n.* **1.** The act of composing. **2.** General makeup: *the changing composition of the electorate.* **3.** The arrangement of artistic parts so as to form a unified whole. **4a.** A work of music, literature, or art. **b.** A short essay. **5.** Typesetting. —**com′po•si′tion•al** *adj.*

com•pos•i•tor (kəm-pŏz′ĭ-tər) ►*n.* A typesetter.

com•post (kŏm′pōst′) ►*n.* A mixture of decaying organic matter used as fertilizer. ►*v.* **1.** To fertilize with compost. **2.** To convert (organic matter) to compost. [< Lat. *compositum*, mixture.]

com•po•sure (kəm-pō′zhər) ►*n.* Calmness and self-possession; equanimity.

com•pote (kŏm′pōt) ►*n.* **1.** Fruit stewed or cooked in syrup. **2.** A long-stemmed dish used for holding fruit, nuts, or candy. [< OFr. *composte*, mixture.]

com•pound[1] (kŏm-pound′, kŏm′pound′) ►*v.* **1.** To combine; mix. **2.** To produce by combining. **3.** To compute (interest) on the principal and accrued interest. **4.** To add to; increase. ►*adj.* (kŏm′pound′, kŏm-pound′). Consisting of two or more parts. ►*n.* (kŏm′pound′) **1.** A combination of two or more elements or parts. **2.** A word, such as *loudspeaker* or *baby-sit*, that consists of two or more elements that are independent words. **3.** A substance consisting of atoms or ions of two or more different elements in definite proportions, usu. having properties unlike those of its constituent elements. [< Lat. *compōnere*, put together.] —**com•pound′a•ble** *adj.* —**com•pound′er** *n.*

com•pound[2] (kŏm′pound′) ►*n.* A building or buildings set off and enclosed by a barrier. [Alteration of Malay *kampong*, village.]

compound eye ►*n.* The eye of most insects and some crustaceans, composed of many visual units that each form a portion of an image.

compound fraction ►*n.* See **complex fraction.**

compound interest ►*n.* Interest computed on accumulated unpaid interest as well as on the original principal.

compound number ►*n.* A quantity expressed in two or more different units, such as 3 feet 4 inches.

compound sentence ►*n.* A sentence of two or more independent clauses.

com•pre•hend (kŏm′prĭ-hĕnd′) ►*v.* **1.** To understand the meaning or importance of. **2.** To take in; include. [< Lat. *comprehendere.*] —**com′pre•hen′si•ble** *adj.* —**com′pre•hen′si•bly** *adv.* —**com′pre•hen′sion** *n.*

com•pre•hen•sive (kŏm′prĭ-hĕn′sĭv) ►*adj.* Large in scope; including much. —**com′pre•hen′sive•ly** *adv.* —**com′pre•hen′sive•ness** *n.*

com•press (kəm-prĕs′) ►*v.* **1.** To press together; compact. **2.** To make smaller or shorter; condense. ►*n.* (kŏm′prĕs′). A soft pad applied to a part of the body to control bleeding or reduce pain. [< LLat. *compressāre.*] —**com•press′i•bil′i•ty** *n.* —**com•press′i•ble** *adj.* —**com•pres′sion** *n.*

com•pres•sor (kəm-prĕs′ər) ►*n.* One that compresses, esp. a machine used to compress gases.

com•prise (kəm-prīz′) ►*v.* **-prised, -pris•ing 1.** To consist of. **2.** To include. [< Lat. *comprehendere.*] —**com•pris′a•ble** *adj.*

Usage: The traditional rule states that the whole *comprises* the parts and the parts *compose* the whole. In strict usage: *The Union com-*

prises 50 states. Fifty states compose (or *constitute* or *make up*) *the Union.* Even though careful writers often maintain this distinction, *comprise* is increasingly used in place of *compose,* especially in the passive, as in *The Union is comprised of 50 states.*

com•pro•mise (kŏm′prə-mīz′) ►*n.* **1.** A settlement of differences in which each side makes concessions. **2.** Something that combines qualities of different things. ►*v.* **-mised, -mis•ing 1a.** To settle by concessions. **b.** To make a compromise. **2.** To expose to danger, suspicion, or disrepute. [< Lat. *comprōmissum,* mutual promise.] —**com′pro•mis′er** *n.*

comp time (kŏmp) ►*n. Informal* Time off given to an employee in place of overtime pay. [< *compensatory time.*]

comp•trol•ler (kən-trō′lər, kŏmp-trō′-) ►*n.* Var. of **controller** 2.

com•pul•sion (kəm-pŭl′shən) ►*n.* **1.** The act of compelling. **2.** The state of being compelled. **3.** An irresistible impulse to act. [< Lat. *compellere, compuls-,* compel.] —**com•pul′sive** *adj.* —**com•pul′sive•ly** *adv.* —**com•pul′sive•ness** *n.*

com•pul•so•ry (kəm-pŭl′sə-rē) ►*adj.* **1.** Obligatory; required. **2.** Coercive. —**com•pul′so•ri•ly** *adv.*

com•punc•tion (kəm-pŭngk′shən) ►*n.* A strong uneasiness caused by guilt. See Syns at **penitence.** [< LLat. *compungere, compūnct-,* to sting.]

com•pute (kəm-pyo͞ot′) ►*v.* **-put•ed, -put•ing 1.** To determine by mathematics, esp. by numerical methods. **2.** To determine by use of a computer. [Lat. *computāre.*] —**com•put′a•ble** *adj.* —**com′pu•ta′tion** (kŏm′pyo͞o-tā′shən) *n.* —**com′pu•ta′tion•al** *adj.*

com•put•er (kəm-pyo͞o′tər) ►*n.* **1.** A device that computes, esp. a programmable electronic machine that performs high-speed mathematical or logical operations or that assembles, stores, correlates, or processes information. **2.** One who computes.

com•put•er•ize (kəm-pyo͞o′tə-rīz′) ►*v.* **-ized, -iz•ing 1.** To furnish with a computer or computer system. **2.** To enter, process, or store (information) in a computer or computer system. —**com•put′er•i•za′tion** *n.*

com•rade (kŏm′răd′, -rəd) ►*n.* A friend, associate, or companion. [< OFr. *camarade,* roommate.] —**com′rade•ship′** *n.*

con¹ (kŏn) ►*adv.* Against. ►*n.* An argument or opinion against something. [< CONTRA–.]

con² (kŏn) ►*v.* **conned, con•ning 1.** To study, peruse, or examine carefully. **2.** To memorize. [< OE *cunnan,* know.]

con³ (kŏn) *Slang* ►*v.* **conned, con•ning.** To swindle or dupe. ►*n.* A swindle. ►*adj.* Of or involving a swindle. [< CONFIDENCE.]

con⁴ (kŏn) ►*n. Slang* A convict.

con– ►*pref.* Var. of **com–.**

Con•a•kry (kŏn′ə-krē) The capital of Guinea, in the SW part on the Atlantic. Pop. 600,000.

con•cat•e•nate (kŏn-kăt′n-āt′, kən-) ►*v.* **-nat•ed, -nat•ing.** To connect or link in a series. [LLat. *concatēnāre* < Lat. *catēna,* chain.] —**con•cat′e•nate** (-nĭt, -nāt′) *adj.* —**con•cat′e•na′tion** *n.*

con•cave (kŏn-kāv′, kŏn′kāv′) ►*adj.* Curved like the inner surface of a sphere. [< Lat. *concavus,* vaulted.] —**con•cave′ly** *adv.* —**con•cav′i•ty** (-kăv′ĭ-tē), **con•cave′ness** *n.*

con•ceal (kən-sēl′) ►*v.* To keep from being seen, found, or discovered; hide. [< Lat. *concēlāre.*] —**con•ceal′a•ble** *adj.* —**con•ceal′er** *n.* —**con•ceal′ment** *n.*

con•cede (kən-sēd′) ►*v.* **-ced•ed, -ced•ing 1.** To acknowledge, often reluctantly, as being true. **2.** To grant (e.g., a privilege). **3.** To make a concession; yield. [< Lat. *concēdere.*] —**con•ced′er** *n.*

con•ceit (kən-sēt′) ►*n.* **1.** An unduly high opinion of oneself. **2.** An elaborate metaphor. [< LLat. *conceptus,* CONCEPT.]

Syns: *conceit, egoism, egotism, narcissism, vanity* **Ant:** *humility* **n.**

con•ceit•ed (kən-sē′tĭd) ►*adj.* Vain. —**con•ceit′ed•ly** *adv.* —**con•ceit′ed•ness** *n.*

con•ceive (kən-sēv′) ►*v.* **-ceived, -ceiv•ing 1.** To become pregnant (with). **2.** To form in the mind; devise. **3.** To think; imagine. [< Lat. *concipere.*] —**con•ceiv′a•ble** *adj.* —**con•ceiv′a•bly** *adv.* —**con•ceiv′er** *n.*

con•cen•trate (kŏn′sən-trāt′) ►*v.* **-trat•ed, -trat•ing 1.** To direct or draw toward a common center; focus. **2.** To direct one's thoughts or attention. **3.** To make (a solution) less dilute. ►*n.* A product of concentration: *orange juice concentrate.* [< Lat. *com-,* com- + *centrum,* center.] —**con′cen•tra′tive** *adj.* —**con′cen•tra′tor** *n.*

con•cen•tra•tion (kŏn′sən-trā′shən) ►*n.* **1.** The act of concentrating or state of being concentrated. **2.** Something concentrated. **3.** *Chem.* The amount of one substance in a unit amount of another substance.

concentration camp ►*n.* A camp where prisoners of war, enemy aliens, and political prisoners are confined.

con•cen•tric (kən-sĕn′trĭk) also **con•cen•tri•cal** (-trĭ-kəl) ►*adj.* Having a common center. [< Lat. *com-,* com- + *centrum,* center.] —**con•cen′tri•cal•ly** *adv.* —**con′cen•tric′i•ty** (kŏn′sĕn-trĭs′ĭ-tē) *n.*

Con•cep•ción (kōn′sĕp-syōn′) A city of W-central Chile near the Pacific coast SSW of Santiago. Pop. 306,464.

con•cept (kŏn′sĕpt′) ►*n.* **1.** A general idea derived from specific instances. **2.** A thought or notion. **3.** A plan. [< Lat. *concipere, concept-,* conceive.] —**con•cep′tu•al** (kən-sĕp′cho͞o-əl) *adj.* —**con•cep′tu•al•ly** *adv.*

con•cep•tion (kən-sĕp′shən) ►*n.* **1.** Formation of a viable zygote by the union of the male sperm and the female ovum; fertilization. **2.** The ability to form or understand mental concepts. **3.** A concept, plan, design, or thought. [< Lat. *concipere, concept-,* conceive.] —**con•cep′tion•al** *adj.*

con•cep•tu•al•ize (kən-sĕp′cho͞o-ə-līz′) ►*v.* **-ized, -iz•ing.** To form concepts (of). —**con•cep′tu•al•i•za′tion** *n.*

con•cern (kən-sûrn′) ►*v.* **1.** To have to do with; relate to. **2.** To engage the attention of; involve. **3.** To cause anxiety or uneasiness in. ►*n.* **1.** A matter that relates to or affects one. See Syns at **affair. 2.** Serious interest in. **3.** A troubled state of mind. **4.** A business establishment. [< LLat. *concernere,* mingle together.]

con•cerned (kən-sûrnd′) ►*adj.* **1.** Interested. **2.** Anxious; troubled.

con•cern•ing (kən-sûr′nĭng) ►*prep.* In reference to.

con•cert (kŏn′sûrt′, -sərt) ►*n.* **1.** A public musical performance. **2.** Agreement in purpose, feeling, or action. ►*v.* (kən-sûrt′). To plan by mutual agreement. —***idiom:*** **in concert** All together; in agreement. [< Ital. *concerto.*]

con•cert•ed (kən-sûr′tĭd) ►*adj.* Planned or accomplished together: *a concerted effort to solve the problem.* —**con•cert′ed•ly** *adv.*

con•cer•ti•na (kŏn′sər-tē′nə) ►*n.* A small hexagonal accordion with buttons for keys.

con•cert•mas•ter (kŏn′sərt-măs′tər) ►*n.* The first violinist in a symphony orchestra.

con•cer•to (kən-chĕr′tō) ►*n., pl.* **-tos** or **-ti** (-tē). A composition for an orchestra and one or more solo instruments. [Ital.]

con•ces•sion (kən-sĕsh′ən) ►*n.* **1.** The act of conceding. **2.** Something conceded. **3.** Land granted by a government to be used for a specific purpose. **4a.** The privilege of maintaining a subsidiary business in a certain place. **b.** The business itself. [< Lat. *concēdere, concess-,* concede.]

con•ces•sion•aire (kən-sĕsh′ə-nâr′) ►*n.* The holder or operator of a concession. [Fr.]

conch (kŏngk, kŏnch) ►*n., pl.* **conchs** (kŏngks) or **conch•es** (kŏn′chĭz). A tropical marine mollusk having a large spiral shell and edible flesh. [< Gk. *konkhē,* mussel.]

con•cierge (kôn-syârzh′) ►*n.* A staff member of a hotel or apartment complex, esp. in France, who assists guests or residents. [< Lat. *cōnservus,* fellow slave.]

con•cil•i•ate (kən-sĭl′ē-āt′) ►*v.* **-at•ed, -at•ing 1.** To overcome the distrust of; appease. **2.** To make compatible; reconcile. [Lat. *conciliāre* < *concilium,* meeting.] —**con•cil′i•a′tion** *n.* —**con•cil′i•a′tor** *n.* —**con•cil′i•a•to′ry** (-ə-tôr′ē, -tōr′ē) *adj.*

con•cise (kən-sīs′) ►*adj.* Expressing much in few words; clear and succinct. [Lat. *concīsus,* p.part. of *concīdere,* cut up.] —**con•cise′ly** *adv.* —**con•cise′ness** *n.* —**con•ci′sion** (-sĭzh′ən) *n.*

con•clave (kŏn′klāv′, kŏng′-) ►*n.* A secret meeting, esp. one in which the cardinals of the Catholic Church meet to elect a pope. [< Lat. *conclāve,* lockable room.]

con•clude (kən-klo͞od′) ►*v.* **-clud•ed, -clud•ing 1.** To bring or come to an end; close. **2.** To come to an agreement or settlement of. **3.** To reach a decision about. **4.** To arrive at (a logical conclusion) by reasoning. [< Lat. *conclūdere.*]

con•clu•sion (kən-klo͞o′zhən) ►*n.* **1.** The close or finish. **2.** A result; outcome. **3.** A determination. See Syns at **decision. 4.** A final arrangement.

con•clu•sive (kən-klo͞o′sĭv) ►*adj.* Serving to put an end to doubt. See Syns at **decisive.** —**con•clu′sive•ly** *adv.*

con•coct (kən-kŏkt′) ►*v.* **1.** To prepare by mixing ingredients. **2.** To devise. [Lat. *concoquere, concoct-,* cook up.] —**con•coct′er, con•coc′tor** *n.* —**con•coc′tion** *n.*

con•com•i•tant (kən-kŏm′ĭ-tənt) ►*adj.* Occurring or existing concurrently. ►*n.* One that is concomitant with another. [< Lat. *concomitārī,* accompany.] —**con•com′i•tant•ly** *adv.* —**con•com′i•tance** *n.*

con•cord (kŏn′kôrd′, kŏng′-) ►*n.* Agreement of interests or feelings; accord. [< Lat. *concors, concord-,* agreeing : COM– + *cor,* heart.]

Con•cord (kŏng′kərd) **1.** A city of W-central CA NE of Oakland. Pop. 111,348. **2.** A town of E MA WNW of Boston; site of an early battle of the Revolutionary War. Pop. 17,076. **3.** The capital of NH, in the S-central part. Pop. 36,006.

con•cor•dance (kən-kôr′dns) ►*n.* **1.** Agreement; concord. **2.** An index of the words in a text or texts, showing every context in which they occur.

con•cor•dant (kən-kôr′dnt) ►*adj.* Harmonious; agreeing. —**con•cor′dant•ly** *adv.*

con•cor•dat (kən-kôr′dăt′) ►*n.* A formal agreement. [< Med.Lat. *concordātum.*]

con•course (kŏn′kôrs′, -kōrs′, kŏng′-) ►*n.* **1.** A large open space for the gathering or passage of crowds. **2.** A broad thoroughfare. **3.** A crowd; throng. [< Lat. *concursus.*]

con•cres•cence (kən-krĕs′əns) ►*n. Biol.* The growing together of related parts. [< Lat. *concrēscere,* grow together.] —**con•cres′cent** *adj.*

con•crete (kŏn-krēt′, kŏng-, kŏn′krēt′, kŏng′-) ►*adj.* **1.** Relating to an actual, specific thing or instance; particular. **2.** Existing in reality or in real experience. **3.** Formed by the coalescence of separate particles or parts into one mass; solid. **4.** Made of concrete. ►*n.* (kŏn′krēt′, kŏng′-, kŏn-krēt′, kŏng-) **1.** A construction material consisting of sand, conglomerate gravel, broken stone, or slag in a mortar or cement matrix. **2.** A mass formed by the coalescence of particles. ►*v.* (kŏn′krēt′, kŏng′-, kŏn-krēt′, kŏng-) **-cret•ed, -cret•ing 1.** To build, treat, or cover with concrete. **2.** To form into a mass by coalescence or cohesion of particles. [< Lat. *concrētus,* p.part. of *concrēscere,* grow together.] —**con•crete′ly** *adv.* —**con•crete′ness** *n.*

con•cre•tion (kən-krē′shən) ►*n.* **1.** The act or process of concreting into a mass; coalescence. **2.** A solid, hard mass.

con•cu•bine (kŏng′kyə-bīn′, kŏn′-) ►*n. Law* A woman who cohabits with a man without being legally married to him. [< Lat. *concubīna.*]

con•cu•pis•cence (kŏn-kyo͞o′pĭ-səns) ►*n.* Sexual desire; lust. [< Lat. *concupere,* desire strongly.] —**con•cu′pis•cent** *adj.*

con•cur (kən-kûr′) ►*v.* **-curred, -cur•ring 1.** To agree. **2.** To act together. **3.** To occur at the same time. [< Lat. *concurrere,* coincide.] —**con•cur′rence** *n.* —**con•cur′rent** *adj.* —**con•cur′rent•ly** *adv.*

con•cus•sion (kən-kŭsh′ən) ►*n.* **1.** A violent jarring. **2.** An injury to an organ, esp. the brain, produced by a violent blow. [< Lat. *concutere, concuss-,* strike together.] —**con•cus′sive** (-kŭs′ĭv) *adj.*

con•demn (kən-dĕm′) ►*v.* **1.** To express disapproval of. **2.** To pronounce judgment against; sentence. **3.** To declare unfit for use. **4.** *Law* To appropriate (property) for public use. [< Lat. *condemnāre.*] —**con•dem′na•ble** (-dĕm′nə-bəl) *adj.* —**con′dem•na′tion** (kŏn′dĕm-nā′shən) *n.* —**con•dem′na•to′ry** (-nə-tôr′ē, -tōr′ē) *adj.*

Syns: *condemn, damn, doom, sentence* **v.**

con•dense (kən-dĕns′) ►*v.* **-densed, -dens•ing 1.** To make or become more compact. **2.** To abridge. **3.** To cause (a gas or vapor) to change to a liquid. [< Lat. *condēnsāre,* thicken.] —**con•dens′a•bil′i•ty** *n.* —**con•**

dens'a•ble, con•dens'i•ble *adj.* —**con'-den•sa'tion** (kŏn'dĕn-sā'shən) *n.*

con•dens•er (kən-dĕn'sər) ►*n.* **1.** One that condenses, esp. an apparatus that condenses vapor. **2.** See **capacitor.**

con•de•scend (kŏn'dĭ-sĕnd') ►*v.* **1.** To descend to the level of one considered inferior. See Syns at **stoop**[1]. **2.** To deal with people in a patronizing manner. [< LLat. *condēscendere.*] —**con'de•scend'ing** *adj.* —**con'de•scend'ing•ly** *adv.* —**con'de•scen'sion** *n.*

con•dign (kən-dīn') ►*adj.* Deserved; adequate: *condign censure.* [< Lat. *condignus.*]

con•di•ment (kŏn'də-mənt) ►*n.* A substance, such as a relish, vinegar, or spice, used to complement food. [< Lat. *condīmentum.*]

con•di•tion (kən-dĭsh'ən) ►*n.* **1.** A mode or state of being. **2.** A state of health. **3.** A disease or ailment. **4.** A prerequisite. **5.** A qualification. **6. conditions** The existing circumstances. **7.** *Gram.* The dependent clause of a conditional sentence. ►*v.* **1.** To make conditional. **2.** To render fit for work or use. **3.** To adapt: *condition oneself to physical labor.* **4.** *Psychol.* To cause to respond in a specific manner to a specific stimulus. [< Lat. *condiciō,* stipulation.]

con•di•tion•al (kən-dĭsh'ə-nəl) ►*adj.* **1.** Imposing, depending on, or containing a condition. See Syns at **dependent. 2.** *Gram.* Stating or implying a condition. ►*n. Gram.* A mood, tense, clause, or word expressing a condition. —**con•di'tion•al•ly** *adv.*

con•di•tioned (kən-dĭsh'ənd) ►*adj.* **1.** Subject to conditions. **2.** Physically fit. **3.** Prepared for a specific action. **4.** *Psychol.* Exhibiting or trained to exhibit a specific response.

con•do (kŏn'dō') ►*n., pl.* **-dos** *Informal.* A condominium.

con•dole (kən-dōl') ►*v.* **-doled, -dol•ing.** To express sympathy or sorrow. [LLat. *condolēre,* grieve with.] —**con•do'lence** *n.*

con•dom (kŏn'dəm, kŭn'-) ►*n.* A usu. latex sheath used to cover the penis during sex to prevent conception or disease. [?]

con•do•min•i•um (kŏn'də-mĭn'ē-əm) ►*n., pl.* **-min•i•ums** also **-min•i•a** (-mĭn'ē-ə) **1a.** An apartment complex in which individuals own their apartments and share joint ownership in common elements with other unit owners. **b.** A unit in such a complex. **2.** Joint sovereignty, esp. joint rule over a territory. [COM– + Lat. *dominium,* property.]

con•done (kən-dōn') ►*v.* To overlook, forgive, or disregard (an offense) without protest or censure. [Lat. *condōnāre,* give, permit.] —**con•don'a•ble** *adj.*

con•dor (kŏn'dôr', -dər) ►*n.* Either of two large vultures of the Andes or mountains of California. [< Quechua *cuntur.*]

Con•dor•cet (kôn-dôr-sĕ'). Marie Jean Antoine Nicolas Caritat. 1743–94. French mathematician and philosopher.

con•duce (kən-do͞os', -dyo͞os') ►*v.* **-duced, -duc•ing.** To lead to a specific result. [Lat. *condūcere.*] —**con•du'cive** *adj.* —**con•du'cive•ness** *n.*

con•duct (kən-dŭkt') ►*v.* **1.** To direct the course of; control. **2.** To lead or guide. **3.** To serve as a medium for conveying; transmit. **4.** To behave (oneself) in a specified way. ►*n.* (kŏn'dŭkt') **1.** The way one acts; behavior. **2.** Management. [< Lat. *condūcere.*] —**con•duct'i•ble** *adj.*

con•duc•tance (kən-dŭk'təns) ►*n.* A measure of a material's ability to conduct electric charge.

con•duc•tion (kən-dŭk'shən) ►*n.* Transmission through a medium or passage, esp. the transmission of electric charge or heat. —**con•duc'tive** *adj.* —**con'duc•tiv'i•ty** (kŏn'dŭk-tĭv'ĭ-tē) *n.*

con•duc•tor (kən-dŭk'tər) ►*n.* **1.** One who conducts. **2.** One in charge of a train, bus, or streetcar. **3.** One who directs a musical group. **4.** A substance that conducts heat, light, sound, or esp. an electric charge.

con•duit (kŏn'do͞o-ĭt, -dĭt) ►*n.* **1.** A pipe or channel for conveying fluids. **2.** A tube or duct for enclosing electric wires or cable. **3.** A means of passing or transmitting. [< OFr. < Lat. *condūcere, conduct-,* lead to.]

cone (kōn) ►*n.* **1.** *Math.* **a.** The surface generated by a straight line passing through a fixed point or vertex and moving along a fixed curve. **b.** The figure formed by such a surface, bound by its vertex and an intersecting plane. **2.** *Bot.* A scaly, rounded or cylindrical seed-bearing structure, as of a pine. **3.** *Physiol.* A photoreceptor in the retina. [< Gk. *kōnos.*]

cone•flow•er (kōn'flou'ər) ►*n.* Any of various North American plants having disk flowers on a cone-shaped central receptacle surrounded by colorful rays.

Con•es•to•ga wagon (kŏn'ĭ-stō'gə) ►*n.* A heavy covered wagon with broad wheels, used by American pioneers. [After *Conestoga,* Pennsylvania.]

co•ney also **co•ny** (kō'nē, kŭn'ē) ►*n., pl.* **-neys** also **-nies 1.** A rabbit, esp. of an Old World species. **2.** The fur of a rabbit. **3.** See **pika. 4.** See **hyrax.** [< Lat. *cunīculus.*]

Co•ney Island (kō'nē) A resort district of Brooklyn, NY, on the Atlantic Ocean.

con•fab•u•late (kən-făb'yə-lāt') ►*v.* **-lat•ed, -lat•ing.** To talk casually; chat. [Lat. *cōnfābulārī.*] —**con•fab'u•la'tion** *n.*

con•fec•tion (kən-fĕk'shən) ►*n.* A sweet preparation, such as candy. [< Lat. *cōnficere, cōnfect-,* put together.] —**con•fec'tion•er** *n.*

con•fec•tion•er•y (kən-fĕk'shə-nĕr'ē) ►*n., pl.* **-ies 1.** Candies and other confections collectively. **2.** A confectioner's shop.

con•fed•er•a•cy (kən-fĕd'ər-ə-sē) ►*n., pl.* **-cies 1.** A political union of persons, parties, or states; league. **2. Confederacy** The 11 Southern states that seceded from the US in 1860 and 1861.

con•fed•er•ate (kən-fĕd'ər-ĭt) ►*n.* **1.** An associate; ally. **2.** An accomplice. **3. Confederate** A supporter of the American Confederacy. ►*v.* (-ə-rāt') **-at•ed, -at•ing.** To form into or become part of a confederacy. [< LLat. *cōnfoederāre,* unite.] —**con•fed'er•ate** (-ĭt) *adj.*

con•fed•er•a•tion (kən-fĕd'ə-rā'shən) ►*n.* **1a.** The act of confederating. **b.** The state of being confederated. **2.** A confederacy.

con•fer (kən-fûr') ►*v.* **-ferred, -fer•ring 1.** To bestow (e.g., an honor). **2.** To hold a meeting. [Lat. *cōnferre* : *com-,* com- + *ferre,* bring.] —**con'fer•ee'** (kŏn'fə-rē') *n.* —**con•fer'ral** *n.* —**con•fer'rer** *n.*

con•fer•ence (kŏn'fər-əns, -frəns) ►*n.* **1.** A meeting for consultation or discussion. **2.**

Sports An association of teams.

conference call ▸*n.* A telephone call that connects three or more persons at once.

con•fess (kən-fĕs′) ▸*v.* **1.** To disclose (something damaging about oneself); admit. **2.** To tell one's sins to a priest for absolution. **3.** To recognize the reality or truth of. [< Lat. *cōnfitērī, cōnfess-*, admit to.] —**con•fess′ed•ly** (-ĭd-lē) *adv.*

con•fes•sion (kən-fĕsh′ən) ▸*n.* **1.** The act of confessing. **2.** Something confessed, esp. disclosure of one's sins to a priest for absolution. **3.** A formal statement acknowledging one's guilt. **4.** A church or group of worshipers adhering to a specific creed.

con•fes•sion•al (kən-fĕsh′ə-nəl) ▸*n.* A small booth in which a priest hears confessions.

con•fes•sor (kən-fĕs′ər) ▸*n.* **1.** One who confesses. **2.** A priest who hears confessions.

con•fet•ti (kən-fĕt′ē) ▸*pl.n. (takes sing. v.)* Small pieces of colored paper scattered during festive occasions. [Ital., candies.]

con•fi•dant (kŏn′fĭ-dănt′, -dänt′, kŏn′fĭ-dănt′, -dänt′) ▸*n.* One to whom secrets or private matters are disclosed.

con•fide (kən-fīd′) ▸*v.* **-fid•ed, -fid•ing 1.** To tell (something) in confidence. **2.** To put into another's keeping. [< Lat. *cōnfīdere*.]

con•fi•dence (kŏn′fĭ-dəns) ▸*n.* **1.** Trust or faith in a person or thing. **2.** A trusting relationship. **3a.** Something confided. **b.** A feeling of assurance that a confidant will keep a secret. **4.** Self-assurance. —**con′fi•dent** *adj.* —**con′fi•dent•ly** *adv.*

confidence game ▸*n.* A swindle in which the victim is defrauded after his or her confidence has been won.

confidence man ▸*n.* A man who swindles his victims by using a confidence game.

con•fi•den•tial (kŏn′fĭ-dĕn′shəl) ▸*adj.* **1.** Told in confidence; secret. **2.** Entrusted with the confidence of another. —**con′fi•den′ti•al′i•ty** (-shē-ăl′ĭ-tē) *n.* —**con′fi•den′tial•ly** *adv.*

con•fig•u•ra•tion (kən-fĭg′yə-rā′shən) ▸*n.* Arrangement of parts or elements. —**con•fig′u•ra′tive, con•fig′u•ra′tion•al** *adj.*

con•fig•ure (kən-fĭg′yər) ▸*v.* **-ured, -ur•ing.** To design, arrange, or shape for specific applications or uses. [< Lat. *cōnfigūrāre*, give form to.]

con•fine (kən-fīn′) ▸*v.* **-fined, -fin•ing 1.** To keep within bounds; restrict. **2.** To imprison. [< Lat. *cōnfīnis*, adjoining.] —**con•fin′a•ble, con•fine′a•ble** *adj.* —**con•fine′ment** *n.* —**con•fin′er** *n.*

con•fines (kŏn′fīnz′) ▸*pl.n.* **1.** The limits of a space or area. **2.** Restraining elements: *escape the confines of bureaucracy.*

con•firm (kən-fûrm′) ▸*v.* **1.** To establish the validity of; verify. **2.** To make firmer; strengthen. **3.** To ratify. **4.** To administer the religious rite of confirmation to. [< Lat. *cōnfirmāre*.] —**con•firm′a•ble** *adj.* —**con•firm′a•to′ry** (-fûr′mə-tôr′ē, -tōr′ē) *adj.*

con•fir•ma•tion (kŏn′fər-mā′shən) ▸*n.* **1.** The act of confirming. **2.** A verification. **3a.** A Christian rite admitting a baptized person to full membership in a church. **b.** A ceremony in Judaism that marks the end of a young person's religious training.

con•firmed (kən-fûrmd′) ▸*adj.* **1.** Firmly settled in habit. See Syns at **chronic. 2.** Ratified; verified. **3.** Having received confirmation. —**con•firm′ed•ly** (-fûr′mĭd-lē) *adv.*

con•fis•cate (kŏn′fĭ-skāt′) ▸*v.* **-cat•ed, -cat•ing 1.** To seize (private property) for the public treasury. **2.** To seize by or as if by authority. See Syns at **appropriate.** [Lat. *cōnfiscāre* < *fiscus*, treasury.] —**con′fis•ca′tion** *n.* —**con′fis•ca′tor** *n.* —**con•fis′ca•to′ry** (kən-fĭs′kə-tôr′ē, -tōr′ē) *adj.*

con•fla•gra•tion (kŏn′flə-grā′shən) ▸*n.* A large destructive fire. [< Lat. *cōnflagrāre*, burn up.]

con•flict (kŏn′flĭkt′) ▸*n.* **1.** Prolonged fighting. **2.** Disharmony between incompatible or antithetical persons, ideas, or interests. **3.** *Psychol.* A struggle, often unconscious, between mutually exclusive impulses or desires. ▸*v.* (kən-flĭkt′). To be in opposition; differ. [< Lat. *cōnflīgere, cōnflīct-*, strike together.] —**con•flic′tive** *adj.*

con•flu•ence (kŏn′flo͞o-əns) ▸*n.* **1a.** A flowing together of two or more streams. **b.** The point where such streams meet. **2.** A gathering together. [< Lat. *cōnfluere*, flow together.] —**con′flu•ent** *adj.*

con•flux (kŏn′flŭks′) ▸*n.* A confluence.

con•form (kən-fôrm′) ▸*v.* **1.** To correspond; be similar. **2.** To act or be in agreement; comply. **3.** To act in accordance with current customs or modes. See Syns at **adapt.** [< Lat. *cōnfōrmāre*, shape after.] —**con•form′a•bil′i•ty** *n.* —**con•form′a•ble** *adj.* —**con•form′a•bly** *adv.* —**con•form′er** *n.*

con•for•mance (kən-fôr′məns) ▸*n.* Conformity.

con•for•ma•tion (kŏn′fər-mā′shən) ▸*n.* **1.** The structure or shape of an item or entity. **2.** A symmetrical arrangement of parts.

con•form•ist (kən-fôr′mĭst) ▸*n.* A person who uncritically conforms to the customs or styles of a group. —**con•form′ist** *adj.*

con•form•i•ty (kən-fôr′mĭ-tē) ▸*n., pl.* **-ties 1.** Similarity; agreement. **2.** Behavior conforming to current customs or styles.

con•found (kən-found′, kŏn-) ▸*v.* **1.** To confuse or perplex. **2.** To mix up. [< Lat. *cōnfundere*, confuse.] —**con•found′er** *n.*

con•found•ed (kən-foun′dĭd, kŏn-) ▸*adj.* **1.** Confused; befuddled. **2.** Used as an intensive: *a confounded fool.* —**con•found′ed•ly** *adv.* —**con•found′ed•ness** *n.*

con•fra•ter•ni•ty (kŏn′frə-tûr′nĭ-tē) ▸*n., pl.* **-ties.** An association of persons united in a common purpose or profession.

con•frere (kŏn′frâr′) ▸*n.* A colleague. [< Med. Lat. *cōnfrāter* : COM– + Lat. *frāter*, brother.]

con•front (kən-frŭnt′) ▸*v.* **1.** To bring or come face to face with, esp. with hostility. **2.** To meet; encounter. [< Med.Lat. *cōnfrontāre*.] —**con′fron•ta′tion** (kŏn′frŭn-tā′shən) *n.* —**con′fron•ta′tion•al** *adj.*

Con•fu•cius (kən-fyo͞o′shəs). c. 551–479 B.C. Chinese philosopher. —**Con•fu′cian** *adj. & n.* —**Con•fu′cian•ism** *n.* —**Con•fu′cian•ist** *n.*

con•fuse (kən-fyo͞oz′) ▸*v.* **-fused, -fus•ing 1.** To cause to be unclear in mind or purpose. **2.** To mistake (one thing for another). **3.** To make unclear; blur. [< Lat. *cōnfundere, cōnfūs-*, mix together.] —**con•fu′sion** *n.* —**con•fus′ed•ly** (-fyo͞o′zĭd-lē) *adv.*

Confucius

Syns: *confuse, addle, befuddle, fuddle, muddle, throw* **v.**

con•fused (kən-fyo͞ozd′) ►*adj.* **1.** Unclear in mind; addled. **2a.** Lacking logical order or sense: *a confused set of instructions.* **b.** Chaotic; jumbled. —**con•fus′ed•ly** (-fyo͞o′zĭd-lē) *adv.* —**con•fus′ed•ness** *n.*

con•fute (kən-fyo͞ot′) ►*v.* **-fut•ed, -fut•ing.** To prove to be wrong or false; refute decisively. [Lat. *cōnfūtāre.*] —**con•fut′a•ble** *adj.* —**con′fu•ta′tion** (kŏn′fyo͞o-tā′shən) *n.*

con game ►*n. Slang* A confidence game.

con•geal (kən-jēl′) ►*v.* **1.** To solidify by or as if by freezing. **2.** To coagulate; jell. [< Lat. *congelāre* : COM– + *gelāre*, freeze.] —**con•geal′a•ble** *adj.* —**con•geal′ment** *n.*

con•gen•ial (kən-jēn′yəl) ►*adj.* **1.** Having the same tastes or temperament. **2.** Friendly. **3.** Suited to one's needs or nature; agreeable. [Prob. < CON– + Lat. *genius*, spirit.] —**con•ge′ni•al′i•ty** (-jē′nē-ăl′ĭ-tē), **con•gen′ial•ness** *n.* —**con•gen′ial•ly** *adv.*

con•gen•i•tal (kən-jĕn′ĭ-tl) ►*adj.* **1.** Existing at or before birth. **2.** Constitutional; inherent. [< Lat. *congenitus*, born with.] —**con•gen′i•tal•ly** *adv.*

con•ger (kŏng′gər) ►*n.* A large scaleless marine eel. [< Gk. *gongros.*]

con•ge•ries (kən-jîr′ēz′, kŏn′jə-rēz′) ►*n.* *(takes sing. v.)* A collection; aggregation. [Lat. *congeriēs* < *congerere*, heap together.]

con•gest (kən-jĕst′) ►*v.* **1.** To overfill; clog. **2.** To cause the accumulation of excessive blood or fluid in (a vessel or organ). [Lat. *congerere, congest-*, heap together.] —**con•ges′tion** *n.* —**con•ges′tive** *adj.*

con•glom•er•ate (kən-glŏm′ə-rāt′) ►*v.* **-at•ed, -at•ing.** To form or cause to form into an adhering or rounded mass. ►*n.* (-ər-ĭt) **1.** A corporation that is made up of several different companies in diversified fields. **2.** A collected heterogeneous mass; cluster. **3.** *Geol.* A rock consisting of pebbles and gravel embedded in cement. [Lat. *conglomerāre* < *glomus*, ball.] —**con•glom′er•ate** (-ĭt) *adj.* —**con•glom′er•a′tion** *n.*

Con•go (kŏng′gō) **1.** Officially **Democratic Republic of the Congo.** Formerly (1971–97) **Za•ire** (zī′îr, zä-îr′). A country of central Africa astride the equator. Cap. Kinshasa. Pop. 42,552,000. **2.** Officially **Republic of the Congo.** A country of W-central Africa with a short coastline on the Atlantic Ocean. Cap. Brazzaville. Pop. 2,516,000. —**Con′go•lese′** (-lēz′, -lēs′) *adj. & n.*

Congo River also **Zaire River.** A river of central Africa flowing about 4,666 km (2,900 mi) through Congo (formerly Zaire) to the Atlantic.

con•grat•u•late (kən-grăch′ə-lāt′, -grăj′-, kəng-) ►*v.* **-lat•ed, -lat•ing.** To extend congratulations to. [Lat. *congrātulārī.*] —**con•grat′u•la′tor** *n.* —**con•grat′u•la•to′ry** (-lə-tôr′ē, -tōr′ē) *adj.*

con•grat•u•la•tion (kən-grăch′ə-lā′shən, -grăj′-, kəng-) ►*n.* **1.** The act of expressing joy or acknowledgment, as for the achievement or good fortune of another. **2.** often **congratulations** An expression of such joy or acknowledgment.

con•gre•gate (kŏng′grĭ-gāt′) ►*v.* **-gat•ed, -gat•ing.** To bring or come together in a group; assemble. [< Lat. *congregāre.*] —**con′gre•ga′tor** *n.*

con•gre•ga•tion (kŏng′grĭ-gā′shən) ►*n.* **1.** The act of assembling. **2.** An assemblage; gathering. **3.** The members of a specific religious group who regularly worship at a church or synagogue.

con•gre•ga•tion•al (kŏng′grĭ-gā′shə-nəl) ►*adj.* **1.** Of or relating to a congregation. **2. Congregational** Of or relating to a Protestant denomination in which each member church is self-governing. —**con′gre•ga′tion•al•ism** *n.* —**con′gre•ga′tion•al•ist** *n.*

con•gress (kŏng′grĭs) ►*n.* **1.** A formal assembly to discuss problems. **2.** The national legislative body of a nation, esp. a republic. **3. Congress** The US legislature, consisting of the Senate and the House of Representatives. [< Lat. *congredī, congress-*, convene.] —**con•gres′sion•al** (kən-grĕsh′ə-nəl, kəng-) *adj.* —**con•gres′sion•al•ly** *adv.* —**con′gress•man** *n.* —**con′gress•per′son** *n.* —**con′gress•wom′an** *n.*

Con•greve (kŏn′grēv′, kŏng′-), **William.** 1670–1729. English playwright.

con•gru•ent (kŏng′gro͞o-ənt, kən-gro͞o′-) ►*adj.* **1.** Corresponding; congruous. **2.** *Math.* Coinciding exactly when superimposed. [< Lat. *congruere*, agree.] —**con′gru•ence, con′gru•en•cy** *n.* —**con′gru•ent•ly** *adv.*

con•gru•ous (kŏng′gro͞o-əs) ►*adj.* **1.** Corresponding in character or kind; harmonious. **2.** *Math.* Congruent. [< Lat. *congruere*, agree.] —**con•gru′i•ty** (kən-gro͞o′ĭ-tē, kŏn-) *n.* —**con′gru•ous•ly** *adv.* —**con′gru•ous•ness** *n.*

con•ic (kŏn′ĭk) or **con•i•cal** (-ĭ-kəl) ►*adj.* Of or shaped like a cone.

conic section ►*n.* The intersection of a cone and a plane, which generates a group of curves, including the circle, ellipse, hyperbola, and parabola.

con•i•fer (kŏn′ə-fər, kō′nə-) ►*n.* A cone-bearing tree such as a pine or fir. [< Lat. *cōnifer*, cone-bearing : *cōnus*, CONE + –FER.] —**co•nif′er•ous** (kō-nĭf′ər-əs, kə-) *adj.*

conj. ►*abbr.* **1.** conjugation **2.** conjunction

con•jec•tur•al (kən-jĕk′chər-əl) ►*adj.* Based on or involving conjecture. See Syns at **supposed.** —**con•jec′tur•al•ly** *adv.*

con•jec•ture (kən-jĕk′chər) ►*n.* Inference based on incomplete evidence; guesswork. ►*v.* **-tured, -tur•ing.** To guess. [< Lat. *conicere*,

coniect-, infer.] —**con•jec′tur•a•ble** *adj.*
con•join (kən-join′) ►*v.* To join together; unite. [< Lat. *coniungere* : COM– + *iungere*, join.] —**con•join′er** *n.* —**con•joint′** *adj.* —**con•joint′ly** *adv.*
con•ju•gal (kŏn′jə-gəl, kən-jo͞o′-) ►*adj.* Of or relating to marriage or the marital relationship. [< Lat. *coniūnx*, *coniug-*, spouse < *coniungere*, CONJOIN.] —**con′ju•gal′i•ty** *n.* —**con′ju•gal•ly** *adv.*
con•ju•gate (kŏn′jə-gāt′) ►*v.* **-gat•ed, -gat•ing.** To inflect (a verb). ►*adj.* (-gĭt, -gāt′). Joined together, esp. in pairs. [Lat. *coniugāre*, join together : COM– + *iugum*, yoke.] —**con′ju•gate′ly** *adv.* —**con′ju•ga′tive** *adj.*
con•ju•ga•tion (kŏn′jə-gā′shən) ►*n.* **1a.** The inflection of a verb. **b.** A presentation of the inflected forms of a verb. **2.** *Biol.* A process in which two one-celled organisms unite to transfer nuclear material. —**con′ju•ga′tion•al** *adj.* —**con′ju•ga′tion•al•ly** *adv.*
con•junct (kən-jŭngkt′, kŏn′jŭngkt′) ►*adj.* Joined together; united. [< Lat. *coniungere*, *coniūnct-*, CONJOIN.] —**con•junct′ly** *adv.*
con•junc•tion (kən-jŭngk′shən) ►*n.* **1.** The act of joining or state of being joined. **2.** A joint or simultaneous occurrence. **3.** A word such as *and, but,* and *because* that connects other words, phrases, clauses, or sentences. —**con•junc′tion•al** *adj.* —**con•junc′tion•al•ly** *adv.*
con•junc•ti•va (kŏn′jŭngk-tī′və) ►*n., pl.* **-vas** or **-vae** (-vē). The mucous membrane that lines the inner surface of the eyelid and the exposed surface of the eyeball. [< Med.Lat. *(membrāna) coniūnctīva*, connective (membrane).] —**con′junc•ti′val** *adj.*
con•junc•tive (kən-jŭngk′tĭv) ►*adj.* **1.** Connective. **2.** Joined together; combined. **3.** *Gram.* Used as a conjunction. ►*n.* A conjunction. —**con•junc′tive•ly** *adv.*
con•junc•ti•vi•tis (kən-jŭngk′tə-vī′tĭs) ►*n.* Inflammation of the conjunctiva.
con•junc•ture (kən-jŭngk′chər) ►*n.* A critical set of circumstances; crisis.
con•jure (kŏn′jər, kən-jo͝or′) ►*v.* **-jured, -jur•ing 1.** To summon (a spirit) by magical power. **2.** To evoke: *a song that conjured up old memories.* **3.** To perform magic tricks. [< Lat. *coniūrāre*, swear together.] —**con′ju•ra′tion** *n.* —**con′jur•er, con′jur•or** *n.*
conk (kŏngk) ►*v. Slang* To hit, esp. on the head. —***phrasal verb:* conk out 1.** To stop functioning; fail. **2.** To fall asleep, esp. suddenly or heavily. [?]
con man ►*n. Slang* A confidence man.
Conn. ►*abbr.* Connecticut
con•nect ►*v.* **1.** To join or become joined together. **2.** To associate or consider as related. **3.** To join to or by means of a communications circuit. **4.** To make a connection. [< Lat. *cōnectere*, tie together.] —**con•nec′tor, con•nect′er** *n.*
Con•nect•i•cut (kə-nĕt′ĭ-kət) A state of the NE US. Cap. Hartford. Pop. 3,295,669.
Connecticut River. A river of the NE US flowing about 655 km (407 mi) from N NH to Long Island Sound.
con•nec•tion (kə-nĕk′shən) ►*n.* **1.** Union; junction. **2.** A link. **3.** An association or relation. **4.** The logical ordering of words or ideas; coherence. **5.** Reference to something else; context. **6.** A person, esp. one of influence, with whom one is associated. **7.** A scheduled run providing service between means of transportation. **8.** A line of communication between two points in a telephone system.
con•nec•tive (kə-nĕk′tĭv) ►*adj.* Serving or tending to connect. ►*n.* A connecting word, such as a conjunction. —**con•nec′tive•ly** *adv.* —**con′nec•tiv′i•ty** *n.*
connective tissue ►*n.* Tissue, such as cartilage and bone, that forms the supporting and connecting structures of the body.
con•nip•tion (kə-nĭp′shən) ►*n. Informal* A fit of violent emotion. [?]
con•nive (kə-nīv′) ►*v.* **-nived, -niv•ing 1.** To cooperate secretly in an illegal action. **2.** To scheme; plot. **3.** To feign ignorance of a wrong, thus implying consent. [Lat. *cōnīvēre*, close one's eyes.] —**con•niv′ance** *n.* —**con•niv′er** *n.* —**con•niv′er•y** *n.*
con•nois•seur (kŏn′ə-sûr′, -so͝or′) ►*n.* A person of discriminating taste. [Obsolete Fr., ult. < Lat. *cognōscere*, learn.]
con•note (kə-nōt′) ►*v.* **-not•ed, -not•ing 1.** To suggest or imply in addition to literal meaning: *Spring connotes flowers and new life.* See Usage Note at **denote. 2.** To have as a related condition: *For a political leader, hesitation is apt to connote weakness.* [Med.Lat. *connotāre*, to mark along with.] —**con′no•ta′tion** (kŏn′ə-tā′shən) *n.* —**con′no•ta′tive** *adj.*
con•nu•bi•al (kə-no͞o′bē-əl, -nyo͞o′-) ►*adj.* Relating to marriage or the married state; conjugal. [< Lat. *cōnūbium*, marriage.] —**con•nu′bi•al•ly** *adv.*
con•quer ►*v.* **1.** To defeat or subdue by or as if by force of arms. **2.** To overcome; surmount: *conquered my fear of heights.* [< Lat. *conquīrere*, procure.] —**con′quer•a•ble** *adj.* —**con′quer•or, con′quer•er** *n.*
con•quest (kŏn′kwĕst′, kŏng′-) ►*n.* **1.** The act or process of conquering. **2.** Something acquired by conquering. [< VLat. **conquaesīta* < **conquaerere*, CONQUER.]
con•quis•ta•dor (kŏn-kwĭs′tə-dôr′, kŏng-kē′stə-) ►*n., pl.* **-dors** or **-dor•es** (-dôr′ās, -ēz). One of the 16th-cent. Spanish conquerors of Mexico, Central America, or Peru. [Sp. < *conquistar*, CONQUER.]
Con•rad (kŏn′răd′), **Joseph.** 1857–1924. Polish-born British novelist.
con•san•guin•e•ous (kŏn′săn-gwĭn′ē-əs, -săng-) also **con•san•guine** (kŏn-săng′gwĭn, kən-) ►*adj.* Having a common ancestor. [< Lat. *cōnsanguineus* : COM– + *sanguis*, blood.] —**con′san•guin′e•ous•ly** *adv.* —**con′san•guin′i•ty** *n.*
con•science (kŏn′shəns) ►*n.* **1.** The awareness of a moral or ethical aspect to one's conduct. **2.** Conformity to one's own sense of right conduct. [< Lat. *cōnscīre*, be conscious of.]
con•sci•en•tious (kŏn′shē-ĕn′shəs) ►*adj.* **1.** Guided by one's conscience; principled. **2.** Thorough and careful: *a conscientious worker.* —**con′sci•en′tious•ly** *adv.* —**con′sci•en′tious•ness** *n.*
conscientious objector ►*n.* One who refuses to participate in military service on the basis of moral or religious beliefs.
con•scious (kŏn′shəs) ►*adj.* **1a.** Having an awareness of one's environment and one's own existence. **b.** Not asleep; awake. **2.** Capable of

thought, will, or perception. **3.** Subjectively known: *conscious remorse.* **4.** Deliberate: *a conscious insult.* **5.** Sensible; mindful: *conscious of being stared at.* [< Lat. *cōnscius.*] —**con′scious•ly** *adv.*

con•scious•ness (kŏn′shəs-nĭs) ►*n.* **1.** A sense of one's personal or collective identity. **2.** Special awareness of or sensitivity to a particular issue or situation.

con•script (kŏn′skrĭpt′) ►*n.* One compulsorily enrolled for service, esp. in the armed forces. [< Lat. *cōnscrībere, cōnscrīpt-*, enroll.] —**con•script′** (kən-skrĭpt′) *v.* —**con•scrip′tion** *n.*

con•se•crate (kŏn′sĭ-krāt′) ►*v.* **-crat•ed, -crat•ing 1.** To declare or set apart as sacred. **2.** *Christianity* To change (bread and wine) into the body and blood of Jesus. **3.** To initiate (a priest) into the order of bishops. **4.** To dedicate to a service or goal. [< Lat. *cōnsecrāre.*] —**con′se•cra′tion** *n.* —**con′se•cra′tive** *adj.* —**con′se•cra′tor** *n.*

con•sec•u•tive (kən-sĕk′yə-tĭv) ►*adj.* Following one after another without interruption. [< Lat. *cōnsequī, cōnsecūt-*, follow closely.] —**con•sec′u•tive•ly** *adv.* —**con•sec′u•tive•ness** *n.*

con•sen•su•al (kən-sĕn′sho͞o-əl) ►*adj.* **1.** *Law* Entered into by mutual consent. **2.** Involving the willing participation of both or all parties. —**con•sen′su•al•ly** *adv.*

con•sen•sus (kən-sĕn′səs) ►*n.* **1.** An opinion or position reached by a group as a whole or by majority will. **2.** General agreement. See Usage Note at **redundancy.** [Lat. *cōnsēnsus* < *cōnsentīre*, agree.]

con•sent (kən-sĕnt′) ►*v.* To give assent; agree. ►*n.* Acceptance; agreement. See Syns at **permission.** [< Lat. *cōnsentīre.*]

con•se•quence (kŏn′sĭ-kwĕns′, -kwəns) ►*n.* **1.** Something that follows from an action or condition. **2.** Significance; importance: *an issue of consequence.*

con•se•quent (kŏn′sĭ-kwĕnt′, -kwənt) ►*adj.* Following as an effect, result, or conclusion. [< Lat. *cōnsequī*, follow closely.] —**con′se•quent′ly** *adv.*

con•se•quen•tial (kŏn′sĭ-kwĕn′shəl) ►*adj.* **1.** Having important consequences. **2.** Important; influential. —**con′se•quen′ti•al′i•ty** *n.* —**con′se•quen′tial•ly** *adv.*

con•ser•va•tion (kŏn′sûr-vā′shən) ►*n.* **1.** The act or process of conserving. **2.** The controlled use and systematic protection of natural resources. —**con′ser•va′tion•al** *adj.* —**con′ser•va′tion•ist** *n.*

con•ser•va•tism (kən-sûr′və-tĭz′əm) ►*n.* **1.** The inclination, esp. in politics, to maintain the existing or traditional order. **2.** Caution or moderation, as in behavior or outlook.

con•ser•va•tive (kən-sûr′və-tĭv) ►*adj.* **1.** Favoring traditional views and values; tending to oppose change. **2.** Traditional in style. **3.** Moderate; cautious: *a conservative estimate.* **4.** Of a branch of Judaism that allows certain authorized modifications in the law. ►*n.* A conservative person. —**con•ser′va•tive•ly** *adv.* —**con•ser′va•tive•ness** *n.*

con•ser•va•tor (kən-sûr′və-tər, kŏn′sər-vā′tər) ►*n.* **1.** A person in charge of maintaining or restoring valuable items. **2.** *Law* A guardian.

con•ser•va•to•ry (kən-sûr′və-tôr′ē, -tōr′ē) ►*n., pl.* **-ries 1.** A greenhouse, esp. one in which plants are arranged for display. **2.** A school of music or drama.

con•serve (kən-sûrv′) ►*v.* **-served, -serv•ing 1a.** To protect from loss or depletion; preserve. **b.** To use carefully or sparingly: *conserve energy.* **2.** To preserve (fruits). ►*n.* (kŏn′sûrv′). A jam made of stewed fruits. [< Lat. *cōnservāre.*] —**con•serv′a•ble** *adj.*

con•sid•er (kən-sĭd′ər) ►*v.* **1.** To think carefully about. **2.** To regard as. **3.** To take into account. [< Lat. *cōnsīderāre* < *sīdus, sīder-*, star.]

con•sid•er•a•ble (kən-sĭd′ər-ə-bəl) ►*adj.* **1.** Large in amount, extent, or degree. **2.** Worthy of consideration; significant. —**con•sid′er•a•bly** *adv.*

con•sid•er•ate (kən-sĭd′ər-ĭt) ►*adj.* Having regard for the needs or feelings of others; thoughtful. —**con•sid′er•ate•ly** *adv.* —**con•sid′er•ate•ness** *n.*

con•sid•er•a•tion (kən-sĭd′ə-rā′shən) ►*n.* **1.** Careful thought. **2.** A factor to be considered in making a decision. **3.** Thoughtful concern for others. **4.** Recompense.

con•sid•ered (kən-sĭd′ərd) ►*adj.* Reached after careful thought; deliberate.

con•sid•er•ing (kən-sĭd′ər-ĭng) ►*prep.* In view of; taking into consideration. ►*adv. Informal* All things considered: *We had a good trip, considering.*

con•sign (kən-sīn′) ►*v.* **1.** To give over to the care of another; entrust. **2.** To deliver (merchandise) for sale. **3.** To set apart, as for a special use or purpose. [< Lat. *cōnsignāre*, certify.] —**con•sign′a•ble** *adj.* —**con•sig′nor, con•sign′er** *n.*

con•sign•ment (kən-sīn′mənt) ►*n.* **1.** The act of consigning. **2.** Something consigned. —***idiom:* on consignment** With the provision that payment is expected only on completed sales.

con•sist (kən-sĭst′) ►*v.* **1.** To be made up or composed. **2.** To reside: *Its beauty consists in its simplicity.* [Lat. *cōnsistere* : COM– + *sistere*, cause to stand.]

con•sis•ten•cy (kən-sĭs′tən-sē) ►*n., pl.* **-cies 1.** Agreement or coherence among things or parts. **2.** Uniformity of successive results or events. **3.** Degree or texture of firmness. —**con•sis′tent** *adj.* —**con•sis′tent•ly** *adv.*

con•sis•to•ry (kən-sĭs′tə-rē) ►*n., pl.* **-ries 1.** *Rom. Cath. Ch.* An assembly of cardinals presided over by the pope. **2.** A council.

con•so•la•tion (kŏn′sə-lā′shən) ►*n.* **1a.** The act or an instance of consoling. **b.** The state of being consoled. **2.** One that consoles; a comfort: *Your kindness was a consolation to me in my grief.*

consolation prize ►*n.* A prize given to a competitor who loses.

con•sole[1] (kən-sōl′) ►*v.* **-soled, -sol•ing.** To allay the sorrow or grief of. See Syns at **comfort.** [< Lat. *cōnsōlārī.*] —**con•sol′a•ble** *adj.* —**con′so•la′tion** *n.* —**con•so′la•to′ry** (-sō′lə-tôr′ē, -tōr′ē, -sŏl′ə-) *adj.* —**con•sol′er** *n.* —**con•sol′ing•ly** *adv.*

con•sole[2] (kŏn′sōl′) ►*n.* **1.** A freestanding cabinet for a radio, television set, or phonograph. **2.** *Mus.* The part of an organ containing the keyboard, stops, and pedals. **3.** A central control panel for a mechanical or electronic system. **4.** *Archit.* A usu. scroll-shaped bracket. [Fr.]

con•sol•i•date (kən-sŏl′ĭ-dāt′) ►*v.* **-dat•ed, -dat•ing 1.** To unite into one system or whole; combine. **2.** To make strong or secure; strengthen. [Lat. *cōnsolidāre* < *solidus*, solid.] —**con•sol′i•da′tion** *n.* —**con•sol′i•da′tor** *n.*

con•som•mé (kŏn′sə-mā′, kŏn′sə-mā′) ►*n.* A clear soup made of meat or vegetable stock. [Fr., p.part of *consommer*, use up.]

con•so•nance (kŏn′sə-nəns) ►*n.* **1.** Agreement; harmony. **2.** The repetition of consonants esp. at the ends of words, as in *blank* and *think*.

con•so•nant (kŏn′sə-nənt) ►*adj.* **1.** In agreement or accord. **2.** Harmonious in sound. ►*n.* **1.** A speech sound produced by partial or complete obstruction of the air stream. **2.** A letter or character representing a consonant. [< Lat. *cōnsonāre*, agree.] —**con′so•nan′tal** *adj.* —**con′so•nan′tal•ly** *adv.* —**con′so•nant•ly** *adv.*

con•sort (kŏn′sôrt′) ►*n.* A husband or wife, esp. of a monarch. ►*v.* (kən-sôrt′) **1.** To keep company; associate. **2.** To be in agreement. [< Lat. *cōnsors*, partner.]

con•sor•ti•um (kən-sôr′tē-əm, -shē-əm) ►*n.*, *pl.* **-ti•a** (-tē-ə, -shē-ə) **1.** An association of businesses, financial institutions, or investors engaging in a joint venture. **2.** A cooperative arrangement among institutions. [Lat. *cōnsortium*, partnership.]

con•spic•u•ous (kən-spĭk′yo͞o-əs) ►*adj.* **1.** Obvious. **2.** Attracting attention; noticeable. [< Lat. *cōnspicere*, observe : COM– + *specere*, look.] —**con•spic′u•ous•ly** *adv.* —**con•spic′u•ous•ness** *n.*

con•spir•a•cy (kən-spîr′ə-sē) ►*n.*, *pl.* **-cies.** A plot, esp. an illegal one. [< Lat. *cōnspīrātiō*.]

con•spire (kən-spīr′) ►*v.* **-spired, -spir•ing 1.** To plan together secretly to commit an illegal act. **2.** To join or act together; combine. [< Lat. *cōnspīrāre*.] —**con•spir′a•tor** (-spîr′ə-tər) *n.* —**con•spir′a•tor′i•al** *adj.* —**con•spir′a•tor′i•al•ly** *adv.*

con•sta•ble (kŏn′stə-bəl, kŭn′-) ►*n.* **1.** A peace officer with less authority than a sheriff. **2.** *Chiefly Brit.* A police officer. [< LLat. *comes stabulī*, officer of the stable : *comes*, officer + Lat. *stabulum*, stable.]

Con•sta•ble (kŭn′stə-bəl, kŏn′-), **John.** 1776–1837. British landscape painter.

con•stab•u•lar•y (kən-stăb′yə-lĕr′ē) ►*n.*, *pl.* **-ies 1.** The body of constables of a district or city. **2.** An armed police force organized like a military unit.

con•stant (kŏn′stənt) ►*adj.* **1.** Continually occurring; persistent. **2.** Unchanging; invariable. **3.** Steadfast; faithful. ►*n.* **1.** Something unchanging. **2.** A condition, factor, or quantity that is invariant in specified circumstances. [< Lat. *cōnstāre*, stand firm : COM– + *stāre*, stand.] —**con′stan•cy** *n.* —**con′stant•ly** *adv.*

Con•stan•ţa (kən-stän′sə, kôn-stän′tsä) A city of SE Romania on the Black Sea E of Bucharest. Pop. 348,985.

Con•stan•tine (kŏn′stən-tēn′) A city of NE Algeria E of Algiers. Pop. 344,454.

Con•stan•tine I (kŏn′stən-tēn′, -tīn′). "Constantine the Great." A.D. 285?–337. Emperor of Rome (306–337).

Con•stan•ti•no•ple (kŏn′stăn-tə-nō′pəl) See **Istanbul.**

con•stel•la•tion (kŏn′stə-lā′shən) ►*n.* **1.** A formation of stars perceived as a figure or design. **2.** The configuration of planets at one's birth, regarded by astrologers as determining one's character or fate. **3.** A gathering or assemblage. [< LLat. *cōnstellātiō* : COM– + *stēlla*, star.]

con•ster•na•tion (kŏn′stər-nā′shən) ►*n.* Great agitation or dismay. [< Lat. *cōnsternāre*, to dismay.]

con•sti•pa•tion (kŏn′stə-pā′shən) ►*n.* Difficult, incomplete, or infrequent evacuation of the bowels. [< Lat. *cōnstīpāre*, crowd together.] —**con′sti•pate′** *v.*

con•stit•u•en•cy (kən-stĭch′o͞o-ən-sē) ►*n.*, *pl.* **-cies 1a.** The voters represented by an elected legislator or official. **b.** The district so represented. **2.** A group of supporters.

con•stit•u•ent (kən-stĭch′o͞o-ənt) ►*adj.* **1.** Serving as part of a whole; component. **2.** Authorized to make or amend a constitution: *a constituent assembly.* ►*n.* **1.** A component. See Syns at **element. 2.** A resident of a district represented by an elected official. [< Lat. *cōnstituere*, set up. See CONSTITUTE.] —**con•stit′u•ent•ly** *adv.*

con•sti•tute (kŏn′stĭ-to͞ot′, -tyo͞ot′) ►*v.* **-tut•ed, -tut•ing 1.** To be the parts of; compose. **2.** To set up; establish. **3.** To appoint to an office; designate. [Lat. *cōnstituere*, set up : COM– + *statuere*, set up.]

con•sti•tu•tion (kŏn′stĭ-to͞o′shən, -tyo͞o′-) ►*n.* **1.** The act or process of composing or establishing. **2a.** The composition of something. **b.** The physical makeup of a person. **3a.** The system of laws and principles that prescribes the functions and limits of a government. **b.** The written document describing such a system.

con•sti•tu•tion•al (kŏn′stĭ-to͞o′shə-nəl, -tyo͞o′-) ►*adj.* **1.** Of or relating to a constitution. **2.** Consistent with, sanctioned by, or operating under a constitution. **3.** Basic; inherent: *a constitutional inability to lie.* ►*n.* A walk taken regularly for one's health. —**con′sti•tu′tion•al′i•ty** *n.* —**con′sti•tu′tion•al•ly** *adv.*

con•sti•tu•tive (kŏn′stĭ-to͞o′tĭv, -tyo͞o′-) ►*adj.* Inherent; essential.

con•strain (kən-strān′) ►*v.* **1.** To compel by physical, moral, or circumstantial force; oblige. **2.** To confine. **3.** To restrain. [< Lat. *cōnstringere*, compress.] —**con•strain′a•ble** *adj.* —**con•strain′er** *n.*

con•straint (kən-strānt′) ►*n.* **1.** Force used to compel another; coercion. **2.** Restraint; confinement. **3.** Something that restricts; check. **4.** Reticence; awkwardness.

con•strict (kən-strĭkt′) ►*v.* **1.** To make smaller or narrower; compress. **2.** To restrict; cramp: *lives constricted by poverty.* [Lat. *cōnstringere*, *cōnstrict-*.] —**con•stric′tion** *n.* —**con•stric′tive** *adj.*

con•stric•tor (kən-strĭk′tər) ►*n.* **1.** One that constricts, as a muscle that contracts a part of the body. **2.** A snake, such as the boa, that coils around and asphyxiates its prey.

con•struct (kən-strŭkt′) ►*v.* To form by assembling or combining parts; build. ►*n.* (kŏn′strŭkt′) **1.** Something formed from parts. **2.** A schematic idea. [Lat. *cōnstruere*, *cōnstrūct-*.] —**con•struct′i•ble** *adj.* —**con•**

struc′tor, con•struct′er *n.*

con•struc•tion (kən-strŭk′shən) ►*n.* **1.** The act, process, or business of building. **2.** A structure. **3.** An interpretation: *put a favorable construction on his reply.* **4.** *Gram.* An arrangement of words that forms a phrase, clause, or sentence.

construction paper ►*n.* A heavy paper in a variety of colors, used in artwork.

con•struc•tive (kən-strŭk′tĭv) ►*adj.* **1.** Serving to improve; helpful. **2.** Structural. —**con•struc′tive•ly** *adv.* —**con•struc′tive•ness** *n.*

con•strue (kən-stro͞o′) ►*v.* **-strued, -stru•ing 1.** To interpret. **2.** To translate. [< Lat. *cōnstruere*, build.]

con•sul (kŏn′səl) ►*n.* **1.** An official appointed by a government to reside in a foreign country and represent its interests there. **2.** Either of the two chief magistrates of the Roman Republic. [< Lat. *cōnsul.*] —**con′su•lar** *adj.* —**con′sul•ship′** *n.*

con•su•late (kŏn′sə-lĭt) ►*n.* The residence or official premises of a consul.

con•sult (kən-sŭlt′) ►*v.* **1.** To seek advice or information of. **2.** To exchange views. **3.** To work or serve in an advisory capacity. [< Lat. *cōnsulere*, *cōnsult-*, take counsel.] —**con•sul′tant** *n.* —**con′sul•ta′tion** *n.* —**con′sul•ta′tive** *adj.*

con•sul•tan•cy (kən-sŭl′tn-sē) ►*n.*, *pl.* **-cies.** A business offering expert advice in a field.

con•sume (kən-so͞om′) ►*v.* **-sumed, -sum•ing 1.** To eat or drink up. See Syns at **eat. 2.** To expend; use up. **3.** To purchase (goods or services) for use or ownership. **4.** To squander. See Syns at **waste. 5.** To destroy totally; ravage. **6.** To absorb; engross. See Syns at **monopolize.** [< Lat. *cōnsūmere.*] —**con•sum′a•ble** *adj. & n.*

con•sum•er (kən-so͞o′mər) ►*n.* One that consumes, esp. a buyer of goods or services.

consumer goods ►*pl.n.* Goods, such as food and clothing, that satisfy human wants through their direct consumption or use.

con•sum•er•ism (kən-so͞o′mə-rĭz′əm) ►*n.* **1.** A movement seeking to protect and inform consumers by requiring honest packaging and advertising, product guarantees, and improved standards. **2.** Materialism. —**con•sum′er•ist** *n.*

consumer price index ►*n.* An index of prices used to measure the change in the cost of basic goods and services in comparison with a fixed base period.

con•sum•mate (kŏn′sə-māt′) ►*v.* **-mat•ed, -mat•ing 1.** To bring to completion; conclude. **2.** To complete (a marriage) with the first act of sexual intercourse. ►*adj.* (kən-sŭm′ĭt, kŏn′sə-mət) **1.** Complete; lacking nothing. See Syns at **perfect. 2.** Supremely accomplished. [< Lat. *cōnsummāre* : COM– + *summa*, SUM[1].] —**con•sum′mate•ly** *adv.* —**con′sum•ma′tion** *n.* —**con′sum•ma′tor** *n.*

con•sump•tion (kən-sŭmp′shən) ►*n.* **1a.** The act or process of consuming. **b.** An amount consumed. **2.** The using up of goods and services esp. by consumer purchasing. **3.** *Pathol.* **a.** A wasting away of body tissue. **b.** Pulmonary tuberculosis. [< Lat. *cōnsūmere*, *cōnsūmpt-*, consume.]

con•sump•tive (kən-sŭmp′tĭv) ►*adj.* **1.** Wasteful. **2.** *Pathol.* Of or afflicted with consumption. ►*n.* A person afflicted with consumption. —**con•sump′tive•ly** *adv.*

cont. ►*abbr.* **1.** contents **2.** continent **3.** continued **4.** contraction

con•tact (kŏn′tăkt′) ►*n.* **1.** A coming together or touching, as of objects or surfaces. **2.** Interaction; communication. **3.** An association; relationship. **4.** A useful person; connection. **5.** A connection between two electric conductors. **6.** A contact lens. ►*v.* (kŏn′tăkt′, kən-tăkt′) **1.** To bring or put in contact. **2.** To get in touch with. [< Lat. *contingere*, *contāct-*, to touch.]

contact lens ►*n.* A thin corrective lens fitted directly over the cornea.

con•ta•gion (kən-tā′jən) ►*n.* **1a.** Disease transmission by direct or indirect contact. **b.** A disease so transmitted. **2.** The tendency to spread, as of a doctrine, influence, or emotional state. [< Lat. *contāgiō.*]

con•ta•gious (kən-tā′jəs) ►*adj.* **1.** Transmissible by direct or indirect contact; communicable. **2.** Carrying or capable of transmitting disease. **3.** Tending to spread: *a contagious smile.* —**con•ta′gious•ly** *adv.* —**con•ta′gious•ness** *n.*

con•tain (kən-tān′) ►*v.* **1.** To have within; hold. **2.** To include; comprise. **3.** To hold back; restrain. [< Lat. *continēre.*] —**con•tain′a•ble** *adj.*

con•tain•er (kən-tā′nər) ►*n.* A receptacle.

con•tain•er•ize ►*v.* **-ized, -iz•ing.** To package (cargo) in large standardized containers for efficient shipping and handling. —**con•tain′er•i•za′tion** *n.*

con•tain•ment (kən-tān′mənt) ►*n.* **1.** A policy of checking the expansion of a hostile power or ideology. **2.** A system designed to prevent the accidental release of radioactive materials from a reactor.

con•tam•i•nate (kən-tăm′ə-nāt′) ►*v.* **-nated, -nat•ing 1.** To make impure or unclean by contact or mixture. **2.** To permeate with radioactivity. [< Lat. *contāmināre.*] —**con•tam′i•nant** *n.* —**con•tam′i•na′tion** *n.* —**con•tam′i•na′tive** *adj.* —**con•tam′i•na′tor** *n.*

Syns: *contaminate, foul, poison, pollute, taint* **v.**

contd. ►*abbr.* continued

con•temn (kən-tĕm′) ►*v.* To view with contempt. See Syns at **despise.** [< Lat. *contemnere.*]

con•tem•plate (kŏn′təm-plāt′) ►*v.* **-plat•ed, -plat•ing 1.** To consider or ponder thoughtfully. **2.** To intend or anticipate. [Lat. *contemplārī.*] —**con′tem•pla′tion** *n.* —**con•tem′pla•tive** (kən-tĕm′plə-tĭv) *adj.* —**con•tem′pla•tive•ly** *adv.* —**con′tem•pla′tor** *n.*

con•tem•po•ra•ne•ous (kən-tĕm′pə-rā′nē-əs) ►*adj.* Existing or happening during the same period of time. [< Lat. *contemporāneus* : COM– + *tempus*, *tempor-*, time.] —**con•tem′po•ra•ne′i•ty** (-pər-ə-nē′ĭ-tē, -nā′-), **con•tem′po•ra′ne•ous•ness** *n.* —**con•tem′po•ra•ne′ous•ly** *adv.*

con•tem•po•rar•y (kən-tĕm′pə-rĕr′ē) ►*adj.* **1.** Contemporaneous. **2.** Current; modern. ►*n.*, *pl.* **-ies 1.** One of the same time or age. **2.** A person of the present age. —**con•tem′po•rar′i•ly** (-râr′ə-lē) *adv.*

con•tempt (kən-tĕmpt′) ►*n.* **1.** Disparaging or haughty disdain; scorn. **2.** The state of being despised; disgrace. **3.** Open disrespect or willful disobedience of the authority of a court of law. [< Lat. *contemptus*, p.part. of *contemnere*, despise.]

con•tempt•i•ble (kən-tĕmp′tə-bəl) ►*adj.* Deserving of contempt; despicable. —**con•tempt′i•bil′i•ty** *n.* —**con•tempt′i•bly** *adv.*

con•temp•tu•ous (kən-tĕmp′cho͞o-əs) ►*adj.* Manifesting or feeling contempt; scornful. —**con•temp′tu•ous•ly** *adv.* —**con•temp′tu•ous•ness** *n.*

con•tend (kən-tĕnd′) ►*v.* **1.** To strive in opposition; struggle. **2.** To compete. **3.** To maintain or assert. [< Lat. *contendere.*] —**con•tend′er** *n.*

con•tent[1] (kŏn′tĕnt′) ►*n.* **1.** often **contents** Something contained in a receptacle. **2.** often **contents** The subject matter of a written work. **3.** The meaning or significance of a literary or artistic work. **4.** The proportion of a specified substance. [< Lat. *continēre*, *content-*, contain.]

con•tent[2] (kən-tĕnt′) ►*adj.* Satisfied; happy. ►*v.* To make satisfied. ►*n.* Contentment; satisfaction. [< Lat. *contentus*, p.part. of *continēre*, to contain.]

con•tent•ed (kən-tĕn′tĭd) ►*adj.* Satisfied; happy. —**con•tent′ed•ly** *adv.*

con•ten•tion (kən-tĕn′shən) ►*n.* **1.** Controversy; dispute. **2.** Rivalry: *in contention for first place.* [< Lat. *contendere*, *content-*, contend.]

con•ten•tious (kən-tĕn′shəs) ►*adj.* Quarrelsome. See Syns at **argumentative.** —**con•ten′tious•ly** *adv.* —**con•ten′tious•ness** *n.*

con•tent•ment (kən-tĕnt′mənt) ►*n.* The state of being contented.

con•ter•mi•nous (kən-tûr′mə-nəs) also **co•ter•mi•nous** (kō-) ►*adj.* Having a boundary in common; contiguous. [< Lat. *conterminus.*] —**con•ter′mi•nous•ly** *adv.*

con•test (kŏn′tĕst′) ►*n.* **1.** A struggle between rivals. **2.** A competition. ►*v.* (kən-tĕst′, kŏn′tĕst′) **1.** To compete for. **2.** To dispute: *contest a will.* [< Lat. *contestārī*, call to witness.] —**con•test′a•ble** *adj.* —**con′tes•ta′tion** *n.* —**con•test′er** *n.*

con•tes•tant (kən-tĕs′tənt, kŏn′tĕs′tənt) ►*n.* A competitor, as in a contest or game.

con•text (kŏn′tĕkst′) ►*n.* **1.** The part of a text or statement that surrounds a particular word or passage and determines its meaning. **2.** The circumstances in which an event occurs. [< Lat. *contexere*, join together : COM– + *texere*, weave.] —**con•tex′tu•al** (kən-tĕks′cho͞o-əl) *adj.* —**con•tex′tu•al•ly** *adv.*

con•tig•u•ous (kən-tĭg′yo͞o-əs) ►*adj.* **1.** Touching. **2.** Neighboring; adjacent. [< Lat. *contingere*, *contig-*, touch.] —**con′ti•gu′i•ty** (kŏn′tĭ-gyo͞o′ĭ-tē) —**con•tig′u•ous•ly** *adv.* —**con•tig′u•ous•ness** *n.*

con•ti•nence (kŏn′tə-nəns) ►*n.* **1.** Self-restraint; moderation. **2.** Voluntary control over bladder and bowel functions. **3.** Sexual abstinence. [< Lat. *continēre*, contain.] —**con′ti•nent** *adj.*

con•ti•nent (kŏn′tə-nənt) ►*n.* **1.** One of the principal land masses of the earth. **2. the Continent** The mainland of Europe. [Lat. *(terra) continēns*, continuous (land).]

con•ti•nen•tal (kŏn′tə-nĕn′tl) ►*adj.* **1.** Of or relating to a continent. **2.** often **Continental** European. **3. Continental** Of the American colonies during the Revolutionary War. ►*n.* **1.** often **Continental** A European. **2. Continental** An American Revolutionary War soldier. —**con′ti•nen′tal•ly** *adv.*

continental divide ►*n.* A watershed that separates continental river systems flowing in opposite directions.

Continental Divide. A series of mountain ridges extending from AK to Mexico that forms the watershed of North America.

continental shelf ►*n.* A submerged, relatively shallow border of a continent.

con•tin•gen•cy (kən-tĭn′jən-sē) ►*n., pl.* **-cies.** An event that may occur; possibility. —**con•tin′gen•cy** *adj.*

con•tin•gent (kən-tĭn′jənt) ►*adj.* **1.** Liable to occur but not certain; possible. **2.** Conditional. See Syns at **dependent.** ►*n.* **1.** A share or quota, as of troops. **2.** A representative group. [< Lat. *contingere*, touch.] —**con•tin′gent•ly** *adv.*

contingent worker ►*n.* A temporary or part-time worker.

con•tin•u•al (kən-tĭn′yo͞o-əl) ►*adj.* **1.** Recurring frequently. **2.** Not interrupted; constant. —**con•tin′u•al•ly** *adv.*

con•tin•u•ance (kən-tĭn′yo͞o-əns) ►*n.* **1.** The act or fact of continuing. **2.** Duration. **3.** A continuation or sequel. **4.** *Law* Postponement or adjournment to a future date.

con•tin•u•a•tion (kən-tĭn′yo͞o-ā′shən) ►*n.* **1.** The act of continuing. **2.** An extension. **3.** A resumption after an interruption.

con•tin•ue (kən-tĭn′yo͞o) ►*v.* **-ued, -u•ing 1.** To persist. **2.** To endure; last. **3.** To remain in a state, capacity, or place. **4.** To go on after an interruption; resume. **5.** To extend. **6.** To retain. **7.** To postpone or adjourn. [< Lat. *continuāre.*] —**con•tin′u•er** *n.*

con•ti•nu•i•ty (kŏn′tə-no͞o′ĭ-tē, -nyo͞o′-) ►*n., pl.* **-ties 1.** The state of being continuous. **2.** An uninterrupted succession.

con•tin•u•ous (kən-tĭn′yo͞o-əs) ►*adj.* Uninterrupted in time, sequence, substance, or extent. —**con•tin′u•ous•ly** *adv.* —**con•tin′u•ous•ness** *n.*

con•tin•u•um (kən-tĭn′yo͞o-əm) ►*n., pl.* **-tin•u•a** (-tĭn′yo͞o-ə) or **-tin•u•ums.** A continuous extent or whole, no part of which can be distinguished from neighboring parts except by arbitrary division. [< Lat. *continuus*, continuous.]

con•tort (kən-tôrt′) ►*v.* To twist or wrench out of shape. [Lat. *contorquēre*, *contort-*, twist together.] —**con•tor′tion** *n.* —**con•tor′tive** *adj.*

con•tor•tion•ist (kən-tôr′shə-nĭst) ►*n.* One who contorts, esp. an acrobat capable of twisting into extraordinary positions. —**con•tor′tion•is′tic** *adj.*

con•tour (kŏn′to͝or′) ►*n.* **1.** The outline of a figure or body. See Syns at **outline. 2.** often **contours** A surface, esp. of a curving form. ►*v.* To make or shape the outline of. ►*adj.* Following the contour of something. [< Ital. *contornare*, draw in outline.]

contour map ►*n.* A map showing elevations and surface configuration by means of spaced lines.

contra– ►*pref.* Against; opposite; contrasting: *contraindicate.* [< Lat. *contrā*, against.]

con•tra•band (kŏn′trə-bănd′) ►*n.* Goods prohibited in trade. [Ital. *contrabbando* : CONTRA– + *bando*, proclamation.] —**con′tra•band′ist** *n.*

con•tra•bass (kŏn′trə-bās′) ►*n.* See **double bass.** [Obsolete Ital. *contrabasso* : *contra-*, against (< Lat. *contrā-*, CONTRA–) + *basso*, bass (< LLat. *bassus*, low).]

con•tra•cep•tion (kŏn′trə-sĕp′shən) ►*n.* Prevention of conception, as by use of a device, drug, or chemical agent. —**con′tra•cep′tive** *adj. & n.*

con•tract (kŏn′trăkt′) ►*n.* An enforceable agreement between parties. See Syns at **bargain.** ►*v.* (kən-trăkt′, kŏn′trăkt′) **1.** To enter into or establish by contract. **2.** To catch (a disease). **3.** To shrink by drawing together. **4.** To shorten (a word or words) by omitting some of the letters or sounds. [< Lat. *contrahere, contract-*, draw together.] —**con•tract′i•bil′i•ty** *n.* —**con•tract′i•ble** *adj.* —**con•trac′tion** *n.*

con•trac•tile (kən-trăk′təl, -tīl′) ►*adj.* Capable of contracting, as muscle tissue.

con•trac•tor (kŏn′trăk′tər) ►*n.* One that agrees to perform services at a specified price, esp. for construction work.

con•trac•tu•al (kən-trăk′cho͞o-əl) ►*adj.* Of or like a contract. —**con•trac′tu•al•ly** *adv.*

con•tra•dict (kŏn′trə-dĭkt′) ►*v.* **1.** To assert the opposite of. **2.** To deny the statement of. See Syns at **deny. 3.** To be contrary to or inconsistent with. [Lat. *contrādīcere*, speak against.] —**con′tra•dict′a•ble** *adj.* —**con′tra•dict′er, con′tra•dic′tor** *n.* —**con′tra•dic′tion** *n.* —**con′tra•dic′to•ry** *adj.*

con•tra•dis•tinc•tion (kŏn′trə-dĭ-stĭngk′shən) ►*n.* Distinction by contrasting qualities. —**con′tra•dis•tinc′tive** *adj.* —**con′tra•dis•tinc′tive•ly** *adv.*

con•trail (kŏn′trāl′) ►*n.* A visible trail of condensed water vapor or ice crystals formed in the wake of an aircraft at high altitudes. [*con(densation) trail.*]

contrail

con•tra•in•di•cate (kŏn′trə-ĭn′dĭ-kāt′) ►*v.* To indicate the inadvisability of. —**con′tra•in′di•ca′tion** *n.* —**con′tra•in•dic′a•tive** (-ĭn-dĭk′ə-tĭv) *adj.*

con•tral•to (kən-trăl′tō) ►*n., pl.* **-tos 1.** The lowest female voice or voice part. **2.** A woman having a contralto voice. [Ital.]

con•trap•tion (kən-trăp′shən) ►*n.* A mechanical device; gadget. [Perh. blend of CONTRIVE and TRAP.]

con•tra•pun•tal (kŏn′trə-pŭn′tl) ►*adj. Mus.* Of, relating to, or incorporating counterpoint. [< Obsolete Ital. *contrapunto*, counterpoint.] —**con′tra•pun′tal•ly** *adv.*

con•trar•i•an (kən-trâr′ē-ən) ►*n.* An investor who makes decisions that contradict prevailing wisdom.

con•trar•i•wise (kŏn′trĕr′ē-wīz′, kən-trâr′-) ►*adv.* **1.** From a contrasting point of view. **2.** In the opposite way.

con•trar•y (kŏn′trĕr′ē) ►*adj.* **1.** Opposed; counter: *contrary opinions.* **2.** Opposite, as in character or direction. **3.** Adverse; unfavorable. **4.** (*also* kən-trâr′ē). Willful or perverse. ►*n., pl.* **-ies.** Something that is opposite or contrary. ►*adv.* Contrariwise; counter. [< Lat. *contrārius* < *contrā*, against.] —**con′trar′i•ly** (kŏn′trĕr′ə-lē, kən-trâr′-) *adv.* —**con′tra•ri′e•ty** (-trə-rī′ĭ-tē) *n.* —**con′trar′i•ness** *n.*

con•trast (kən-trăst′, kŏn′trăst′) ►*v.* **1.** To set in opposition in order to show differences. **2.** To show differences when compared. ►*n.* (kŏn′trăst′) **1.** The act of contrasting or the state of being contrasted. **2.** A difference between things compared. **3.** One thing that is strikingly different from another. [< Med.Lat. *contrāstāre* : CONTRA– + Lat. *stāre*, stand.] —**con•trast′a•ble** *adj.* —**con•trast′ing•ly** *adv.*

con•tra•vene (kŏn′trə-vēn′) ►*v.* **-vened, -ven•ing 1.** To act or be counter to; violate. **2.** To contradict. See Syns at **deny.** [< LLat. *contrāvenīre*, oppose : CONTRA– + Lat. *venīre*, come.] —**con′tra•ven′tion** (-vĕn′shən) *n.*

con•tre•temps (kŏn′trə-täN′, kôN′trə-täN′) ►*n., pl.* **-temps** (-täNz′, -täNz′). An inopportune or embarrassing occurrence. [Fr.]

con•trib•ute (kən-trĭb′yo͞ot) ►*v.* **-ut•ed, -ut•ing 1.** To give or supply a share (to); participate (in). **2.** To help bring about a result. [Lat. *contribuere*, bring together.] —**con′tri•bu′tion** (kŏn′trĭ-byo͞o′shən) *n.* —**con•trib′u•tive** *adj.* —**con•trib′u•tor** *n.* —**con•trib′u•to′ry** (-tôr′ē, -tōr′ē) *adj.*

con•trite (kən-trīt′, kŏn′trīt′) ►*adj.* Repentant; penitent. [< Lat. *contrītus*, p.part. of *conterere*, grind up.] —**con•trite′ly** *adv.*

con•tri•tion (kən-trĭsh′ən) ►*n.* Remorse for wrongdoing. See Syns at **penitence.**

con•triv•ance (kən-trī′vəns) ►*n.* **1.** A mechanical device. **2.** A clever plan; scheme.

con•trive (kən-trīv′) ►*v.* **-trived, -triv•ing 1.** To plan with ingenuity; devise. **2.** To invent or fabricate, esp. by improvisation. **3.** To bring about or manage. [< Med.Lat. *contropāre*, compare.] —**con•triv′er** *n.*

con•trived (kən-trīvd′) ►*adj.* Not spontaneous; labored: *a contrived plot.* —**con•triv′ed•ly** (-trī′vĭd-lē, -trīvd′lē) *adv.*

con•trol (kən-trōl′) ►*v.* **-trolled, -trol•ling 1.** To exercise authority or influence over; direct. **2.** To hold in restraint; check. **3.** To verify or regulate by systematic comparison. ►*n.* **1.** Power to manage, direct, or dominate. **2.** often **controls** A set of instruments used to operate a machine. **3.** A restraint; curb. **4.** A standard of comparison for verifying experimental results. [< Med.Lat. *contrārotulāre*, to check by duplicate register < Lat. *rotulus*, roll.] —**con•trol′la•bil′i•ty** *n.* —**con•trol′la•ble** *adj.*

control key ►*n.* A key on a computer keyboard pressed in combination with other keys to activate a command.

con•trolled substance (kən-trōld′) ►*n.* A drug or chemical substance whose possession and use are regulated by law.

con•trol•ler (kən-trō′lər) ►*n.* **1.** One that controls, esp. a regulating mechanism in a vehicle or machine. **2.** also **comp•trol•ler** (kən-trō′-lər, kŏmp-trō′-) An executive or official who supervises financial affairs.

control stick ►*n.* A lever used to control the motion of an aircraft by changing the angle of the elevators and ailerons.

control tower ►*n.* An observation tower at an airfield from which air traffic is controlled by radio.

con•tro•ver•sy (kŏn′trə-vûr′sē) ►*n., pl.* **-sies.** A dispute, esp. a public one, between sides holding opposing views. [< Lat. *contrōversus*, disputed.] —**con′tro•ver′sial** (-shəl, -sē-əl) *adj.* —**con′tro•ver′sial•ly** *adv.*

con•tro•vert (kŏn′trə-vûrt′, kŏn′trə-vûrt′) ►*v.* To argue against; contradict. —**con′tro•vert′i•ble** *adj.*

con•tu•ma•cious (kŏn′tə-mā′shəs, -tyə-) ►*adj.* Obstinately disobedient or rebellious; insubordinate. [< Lat. *contumāx*, insolent.] —**con′tu•ma′cious•ly** *adv.*

con•tu•me•ly (kŏn′to͞o-mə-lē, -tyo͞o-, -təm-lē) ►*n., pl.* **-lies.** Insulting treatment; insolence. [< Lat. *contumēlia.*]

con•tuse (kən-to͞oz′, -tyo͞oz′) ►*v.* **-tused, -tus•ing.** To injure without breaking the skin; bruise. [< Lat. *contundere, contūs-*, beat up.] —**con•tu′sion** *n.*

co•nun•drum (kə-nŭn′drəm) ►*n.* **1.** A riddle. **2.** A dilemma. [?]

con•ur•ba•tion (kŏn′ər-bā′shən) ►*n.* A predominantly urban region including adjacent towns. [CON– + Lat. *urbs*, city + –ATION.]

con•va•lesce (kŏn′və-lĕs′) ►*v.* **-lesced, -lesc•ing.** To recuperate from an illness or injury. [Lat. *convalēscere* < *valēre*, be strong.] —**con′va•les′cence** *n.* —**con′va•les′cent** *adj. & n.*

con•vect (kən-vĕkt′) ►*v.* To transfer by or undergo convection. [< CONVECTION.]

con•vec•tion (kən-vĕk′shən) ►*n.* Heat transfer in a gas or liquid by the circulation of currents from one region to another. [< LLat. *convehere, convect-*, carry together.] —**con•vec′tion•al** *adj.* —**con•vec′tive** *adj.*

convection
Air heated by a space heater rises, is replaced by cool air, and creates a convection current that circulates hot air throughout a room.

con•vene (kən-vēn′) ►*v.* **-vened, -ven•ing** **1.** To meet or assemble formally. **2.** To convoke. See Syns at **call.** [< Lat. *convenīre* : COM– + *venīre*, come.] —**con•ven′a•ble** *adj.* —**con•ven′er** *n.*

con•ven•ience (kən-vēn′yəns) ►*n.* **1.** Suitability to one's purposes or needs; handiness. **2.** Personal comfort or advantage. **3.** Something that increases comfort or saves work. See Syns at **amenity.**

con•ven•ient (kən-vēn′yənt) ►*adj.* **1.** Suited to one's comfort or needs. **2.** Easy to reach; accessible. [< Lat. *convenīre*, be suitable.] —**con•ven′ient•ly** *adv.*

con•vent (kŏn′vənt, -vĕnt′) ►*n.* A monastic community or house, esp. of nuns. [< Lat. *convenīre*, assemble. See CONVENE.] —**con•ven′tu•al** (kən-vĕn′cho͞o-əl) *adj.*

con•ven•ti•cle (kən-vĕn′tĭ-kəl) ►*n.* A religious meeting, esp. a secret one. [< Lat. *conventiculum*, dim. of *conventus*, assembly.]

con•ven•tion (kən-vĕn′shən) ►*n.* **1a.** A formal meeting or assembly, as of a political party. **b.** The delegates attending such an assembly. **2.** An international agreement or compact. **3.** General usage or custom. **4.** An accepted or prescribed practice. [< Lat. *convenīre, convent-*, CONVENE.]

con•ven•tion•al (kən-vĕn′shə-nəl) ►*adj.* **1.** Following accepted practice; customary. **2.** Unimaginative or commonplace; ordinary. **3.** Using means other than nuclear weapons or energy. —**con•ven′tion•al′i•ty** *n.* —**con•ven′tion•al•ly** *adv.*

con•ven•tion•al•ize (kən-vĕn′shə-nə-līz′) ►*v.* **-ized, -iz•ing.** To make conventional. —**con•ven′tion•al•i•za′tion** *n.*

con•verge (kən-vûrj′) ►*v.* **-verged, -verg•ing.** To tend or move toward a common point or result. [LLat. *convergere*, incline together.] —**con•ver′gence** *n.* —**con•ver′gent** *adj.*

con•ver•sant (kən-vûr′sənt, kŏn′vər-) ►*adj.* Familiar, as by study or experience. —**con•ver′sant•ly** *adv.*

con•ver•sa•tion (kŏn′vər-sā′shən) ►*n.* An informal exchange of speech. —**con′ver•sa′tion•al** *adj.* —**con′ver•sa′tion•al•ly** *adv.*

con•ver•sa•tion•al•ist (kŏn′vər-sā′shə-nə-lĭst) ►*n.* One given to conversation.

conversation piece ►*n.* An unusual object that arouses comment or interest.

con•verse[1] (kən-vûrs′) ►*v.* **-versed, -vers•ing.** To engage in conversation. ►*n.* (kŏn′vûrs′). Conversation. [< Lat. *conversārī*, associate with.]

con•verse[2] (kən-vûrs′, kŏn′vûrs′) ►*adj.* Reversed in position, order, or action. ►*n.* (kŏn′vûrs′). The reverse or opposite of something. [Lat. *conversus*, p.part. of *convertere*, turn around.] —**con•verse′ly** *adv.*

con•ver•sion (kən-vûr′zhən, -shən) ►*n.* **1.** The act of converting or the state of being converted. **2.** A change in which one adopts a new religion or belief. **3.** The unlawful appropriation of another's property. **4.** *Football* A score made on a try for a point or points after a touchdown.

con•vert (kən-vûrt′) ►*v.* **1.** To change into another form, substance, or state. **2.** To adapt to a new or different purpose. **3.** To persuade or be persuaded to adopt a particular religion or belief. **4.** To exchange for something of equal value. **5.** To express in alternative units: *convert feet into meters.* **6.** To misappropriate. **7.** *Football* To make a conversion. ►*n.* (kŏn′vûrt′). One who has been converted, esp. from one belief to another. [< Lat. *convertere*, turn around.] —**con•vert′er, con•ver′tor** *n.*

Syns: *convert, metamorphose, transfigure, transform, transmogrify, transmute* ***v.***

con•vert•i•ble (kən-vûr′tə-bəl) ►*adj.* That can be converted. ►*n.* **1.** Something that can be converted. **2.** An automobile with a top that can be folded back or removed.

con•vex (kŏn′vĕks′, kən-vĕks′) ►*adj.* Curved outward, as the exterior of a sphere. [Lat. *convexus.*] —**con•vex′i•ty** *n.* —**con′vex′ly** *adv.*

con•vey (kən-vā′) ►*v.* **1.** To carry; transport. **2.** To transmit. **3.** To communicate; impart. **4.** *Law* To transfer ownership of or title to. [< Med.Lat. *conviāre*, to escort.] —**con•vey′a•ble** *adj.* —**con•vey′or, con•vey′er** *n.*

con•vey•ance (kən-vā′əns) ►*n.* **1.** The act of conveying. **2.** A vehicle. **3.** A document effecting the transfer of title to property.

conveyor belt ►*n.* A continuous moving belt that transports materials from one place to another.

con•vict (kən-vĭkt′) ►*v.* To find or prove guilty of an offense or crime. ►*n.* (kŏn′vĭkt′). A person found guilty of a crime, esp. one serving a prison sentence. [< Lat. *convincere, convict-*, prove wrong.]

con•vic•tion (kən-vĭk′shən) ►*n.* **1.** The act of convicting or the state of being convicted. **2.** A strong opinion or belief.

con•vince (kən-vĭns′) ►*v.* **-vinced, -vinc•ing.** To bring to belief by argument or evidence; persuade. [Lat. *convincere*, prove wrong.] —**con•vinc′ing** *adj.* —**con•vinc′ing•ly** *adv.*

con•viv•i•al (kən-vĭv′ē-əl) ►*adj.* **1.** Fond of social pleasures. See Syns at **social. 2.** Merry; festive. [< Lat. *convīvium*, banquet : COM– + *vīvere*, live.] —**con•viv′i•al′i•ty** (-ăl′ĭ-tē) *n.* —**con•viv′i•al•ly** *adv.*

con•vo•ca•tion (kŏn′və-kā′shən) ►*n.* **1.** The act of convoking. **2.** A formal assembly.

con•voke (kən-vōk′) ►*v.* **-voked, -vok•ing.** To cause to assemble; convene. See Syns at **call.** [< Lat. *convocāre*, call together.]

con•vo•lut•ed (kŏn′və-lo͞o′tĭd) ►*adj.* **1.** Having numerous overlapping coils or folds. **2.** Intricate; complex. [< Lat. *convolūtus*, p.part. of *convolvere*, roll together.]

con•vo•lu•tion (kŏn′və-lo͞o′shən) ►*n.* **1.** A form or part that is folded, coiled, or twisted. **2.** One of the convex folds of the surface of the brain.

con•voy (kŏn′voi′) ►*n.* **1.** An accompanying and protecting force, as of ships. **2.** A group traveling together for safety. ►*v.* (kŏn′voi′, kən-voi′). To accompany, esp. for protection. [< OFr. *convoier*, CONVEY.]

con•vulse (kən-vŭls′) ►*v.* **-vulsed, -vuls•ing 1.** To disturb violently. See Syns at **agitate. 2.** To throw into convulsions. [Lat. *convellere, convuls-*, pull violently.] —**con•vul′sive** *adj.* —**con•vul′sive•ly** *adv.*

con•vul•sion (kən-vŭl′shən) ►*n.* **1.** An intense, paroxysmal, involuntary muscular contraction. **2.** An uncontrolled fit, as of laughter; paroxysm. **3.** Violent turmoil.

co•ny (kō′nē, kŭn′ē) ►*n.* Var. of **coney.**

coo (ko͞o) ►*v.* **1.** To utter the murmuring sound of a dove or pigeon. **2.** To talk in fond or amorous murmurs. [Imit.] —**coo** *n.*

cook (ko͝ok) ►*v.* **1.** To prepare (food) for eating by applying heat. **2.** To prepare or treat by heating. **3.** *Slang* To alter or falsify; doctor. —***phrasal verb:* cook up** *Informal* To concoct: *cook up an excuse.* ►*n.* One who prepares food for eating. [< Lat. *coquere.*]

Cook, James. "Captain Cook." 1728–79. British navigator and explorer.

Cook, Mount. The highest mountain, 3,766.4 m (12,349 ft), of New Zealand, on South I. in the Southern Alps.

cook•book (ko͝ok′bo͝ok′) ►*n.* A book with recipes and advice about food preparation.

cook•er•y (ko͝ok′ə-rē) ►*n., pl.* **-ies.** The art or practice of preparing food.

cook•ie also **cook•y** (ko͝ok′ē) ►*n., pl.* **-ies 1.** A small cake, usu. flat and crisp, made from sweetened dough. **2.** Information stored on a Web user's computer, used by websites to identify previous visitors to that site. [Du. *koekje*, dim. of *koek*, cake.]

Cook Inlet. An inlet of the Gulf of Alaska in S AK W of the Kenai Peninsula.

Cook Islands. An island group of the S Pacific SE of Samoa.

cook•out (ko͝ok′out′) ►*n.* A meal cooked and served outdoors.

Cook Strait. A narrow channel separating North I. and South I. in New Zealand.

cook•top (ko͝ok′tŏp′) ►*n.* A flat cooking surface, as on a stove, usu. consisting of glass-covered electric heating elements.

cool (ko͞ol) ►*adj.* **-er, -est 1.** Moderately cold. See Syns at **cold. 2.** Giving or suggesting relief from heat. **3.** Marked by calm self-control. **4.** Marked by indifference, disdain, or dislike. **5.** *Slang* Excellent; first-rate. ►*v.* **1.** To make or become less warm. **2.** To make or become less intense or ardent. ►*n.* **1.** A cool place, part, or time. **2.** *Slang* Composure; poise. —***idiom:* cool it** *Slang* To calm down; relax. [< OE *cōl.*] —**cool′ly** *adv.* —**cool′ness** *n.*

cool•ant (ko͞o′lənt) ►*n.* Something that cools, esp. a fluid that draws off heat by circulating through or over an engine or part.

cool•er (ko͞o′lər) ►*n.* **1.** A device or container that cools or keeps something cool. **2.** A tall cold drink. **3.** *Slang* A jail.

Coo•lidge (ko͞o′lĭj), **(John) Calvin.** 1872–1933. The 30th US President (1923–29).

Calvin Coolidge

coo•lie (ko͞o′lē) ► *n. Offensive* An unskilled Asian laborer. [Hindi *qulī*.]

coon (ko͞on) ► *n. Informal* A raccoon. [Short for RACCOON.]

coon•skin (ko͞on′skĭn′) ► *n.* **1.** The pelt of a raccoon. **2.** An article made of coonskin.

coop (ko͞op) ► *n.* A cage, esp. one for poultry. ► *v.* To confine in or as if in a coop. See Syns at **enclose.** [ME *coupe*.]

co-op (kō′ŏp′, kō-ŏp′) ► *n.* A cooperative.

coop•er (ko͞o′pər) ► *n.* One who makes wooden barrels and tubs. [< MDu. *kūper* < *kūpe*, basket, tub.] —**coop′er•age** *n.*

Cooper, James Fenimore. 1789–1851. Amer. novelist.

co•op•er•ate (kō-ŏp′ə-rāt′) ► *v.* **-at•ed, -at•ing.** To work together for a common end. [LLat. *cooperārī*, work together.] —**co•op′er•a′tion** *n.* —**co•op′er•a′tor** *n.*

co•op•er•a•tive (kō-ŏp′ər-ə-tĭv, -ə-rā′tĭv, -ŏp′rə-) ► *adj.* **1.** Willing to cooperate. **2.** Engaged in joint economic activity. ► *n.* An enterprise owned and operated by those who use its services. —**co•op′er•a•tive•ly** *adv.* —**co•op′er•a•tive•ness** *n.*

co-opt (kō-ŏpt′, kō′ŏpt′) ► *v.* **1.** To elect or appoint as a fellow member or colleague. **2.** To appropriate. **3.** To take over through assimilation into an established group or culture. [Lat. *cooptāre*.] —**co′-op•ta′tion** *n.*

co•or•di•nate (kō-ôr′dn-āt′, -ĭt) ► *n.* **1.** One that is equal in rank or degree. **2.** *Math.* Any of a set of numbers that determines the position of a point in a space of a given dimension. ► *adj.* (-ĭt, -āt′) **1.** Of equal rank or degree. **2.** Of or involving coordination. **3.** Of or based on coordinates. ► *v.* (-āt′) **-nat•ed, -nat•ing 1.** To place in the same order, class, or rank. **2.** To harmonize in a common action or effort. **3.** To be coordinate. [CO– + ORDINATE.] —**co•or′di•nate•ly** (-ĭt-lē) *adv.* —**co•or′di•na′tive** *adj.* —**co•or′di•na′tor** *n.*

co•or•di•na•tion (kō-ôr′dn-ā′shən) ► *n.* **1.** The act of coordinating or the state of being coordinated. **2.** Harmonious functioning of muscles in the execution of movements. [< CO– + Lat. *ōrdinātus*, put in order.]

coot (ko͞ot) ► *n.* **1.** A gray water bird with a black head and white bill. **2.** *Informal* An eccentric person. [ME *coote*.]

coo•tie (ko͞o′tē) ► *n. Slang* A body louse. [Poss. < Malay *kutu*.]

cop[1] (kŏp) ► *n. Slang* A police officer. [Short for COPPER[2].]

cop[2] (kŏp) ► *v.* **copped, cop•ping** *Slang* **1.** To steal. **2.** To seize; catch. —***phrasal verb:*** **cop out** To avoid fulfilling a commitment or responsibility. —***idiom:*** **cop a plea** To plead guilty to a lesser charge to avoid a more serious charge. [< *copper*, prob. < Lat. *capere*, catch.]

co•pa•cet•ic or **co•pa•set•ic** (kō′pə-sĕt′ĭk) ► *adj.* Excellent; first-rate. [?]

co•part•ner (kō-pärt′nər, kō′pärt′-) ► *n.* A joint partner. —**co•part′ner•ship′** *n.*

co•pay•ment (kō′pā′mənt) ► *n.* A fixed fee paid by members of a medical plan to a provider of medical services.

cope[1] (kōp) ► *v.* **coped, cop•ing.** To contend with difficulties, esp. successfully. [< OFr. *couper*, strike < LLat. *colpus*, a blow < Gk. *kolaphos*.]

cope[2] (kōp) ► *n.* **1.** A long ecclesiastical cape-like vestment. **2.** A coping. [< LLat. *cappa*, cloak.]

Co•pen•ha•gen (kō′pən-hā′gən, -hä′-) The capital of Denmark, in the E part. Pop. 619,288.

Co•per•ni•cus (kō-pûr′nə-kəs, kə-), **Nicolaus.** 1473–1543. Polish astronomer.

cop•i•er (kŏp′ē-ər) ► *n.* One that copies, esp. an office machine that makes copies.

co•pi•lot (kō′pī′lət) ► *n.* The second or relief pilot of an aircraft.

cop•ing (kō′pĭng) ► *n.* The top layer of a wall, usu. slanted to shed water. [< COPE[2].]

co•pi•ous (kō′pē-əs) ► *adj.* Ample; abundant. See Syns at **plentiful.** [< Lat. *cōpia*, abundance.] —**co′pi•ous•ly** *adv.* —**co′pi•ous•ness** *n.*

Cop•land (kōp′lənd), **Aaron.** 1900–90. Amer. composer.

Cop•ley (kŏp′lē), **John Singleton.** 1738–1815. Amer. painter.

cop-out (kŏp′out′) ► *n. Slang* A failure to fulfill a commitment or responsibility.

cop•per[1] (kŏp′ər) ► *n.* **1.** *Symbol* **Cu** A ductile, malleable, reddish-brown metallic element that is an excellent conductor of heat and electricity and is used for electrical wiring, water piping, and corrosion-resistant parts. At. no. 29. See table at **element. 2.** A copper object or coin. **3.** A reddish brown. [< Lat. *Cyprium (aes)*, (metal) of Cyprus.] —**cop′per•y** *adj.*

cop•per[2] (kŏp′ər) ► *n. Slang* A police officer. [< COP[2].]

cop•per•head (kŏp′ər-hĕd′) ► *n.* A venomous reddish-brown snake of the E US.

co•pra (kō′prə, kŏp′rə) ► *n.* Dried coconut meat from which coconut oil is extracted. [< Malayalam *koppara*.]

co•proc•es•sor (kō′prŏs′ĕs-ər) ► *n.* A microprocessor that performs specialized functions not performed by the central processing unit.

copse (kŏps) ► *n.* A thicket of small trees. [< OFr. *copeiz* < *couper*, cut. See COPE[1].]

Copt (kŏpt) ► *n.* **1.** A member of the people of pre-Islamic Egypt. **2.** A member of the Christian church of Egypt. —**Cop′tic** *adj.*

cop•ter (kŏp′tər) ► *n. Informal* A helicopter.

cop•u•la (kŏp′yə-lə) ► *n.* A verb, such as a form of *be* or *seem*, that identifies the predicate of a sentence with the subject. [Lat. *cōpula*, link.] —**cop′u•lar** *adj.* —**cop′u•la′tive** *adj.* & *n.* —**cop′u•la′tive•ly** *adv.*

cop•u•late (kŏp′yə-lāt′) ► *v.* **-lat•ed, -lat•ing.** To engage in coitus or sexual intercourse. [< Lat. *cōpula*, link.] —**cop′u•la′tion** *n.* —**cop′u•la•to′ry** (-lə-tôr′ē, -tōr′ē) *adj.*

cop•y (kŏp′ē) ► *n., pl.* **-ies 1.** An imitation or reproduction of an original; duplicate. **2.** One specimen of a printed text or picture. **3.** Material, such as a manuscript, that is to be set in type. **4.** Suitable source material for journalism. ► *v.* **-ied, -y•ing 1.** To make a copy or copies (of). **2.** To follow as a model or pattern; imitate. [< Lat. *cōpia*, profusion.]

cop•y•book (kŏp′ē-bo͝ok′) ► *n.* A book of models of penmanship for imitation.

cop•y•cat (kŏp′ē-kăt′) ► *n. Informal* An imitator. —**cop′y•cat′** *adj.*

copy desk ► *n.* The desk in a news office where copy is edited and prepared for typesetting.

cop•y•ed•it or **cop•y-ed•it** (kŏp′ē-ĕd′ĭt) ► *v.* To correct and prepare (a manuscript) for typesetting. —**cop′y•ed′i•tor** *n.*

copy protection ►*n.* Prevention of unauthorized copying of a software product, esp. by means of a routine incorporated into a program. —**cop′y-pro•tect′ed** *adj.*

cop•y•right (kŏp′ē-rīt′) ►*n.* The legal right to exclusive publication, production, sale, or distribution of a literary or artistic work. ►*adj.* also **cop•y•right•ed** (-rī′tĭd) Protected by copyright. ►*v.* To secure a copyright for.

cop•y•writ•er (kŏp′ē-rī′tər) ►*n.* One who writes copy, esp. for advertising.

co•quette (kō-kĕt′) ►*n.* A flirtatious woman. [Fr. < OFr. *coc*, cock.] —**co•quet′tish** *adj.* —**co•quet′tish•ness** *n.*

cor•a•cle (kôr′ə-kəl, kŏr′-) ►*n.* A boat made of waterproof material stretched over a wicker or wooden frame. [Welsh *corwgl.*]

cor•al (kôr′əl, kŏr′-) ►*n.* **1a.** Any of a class of marine polyps that secrete a rocklike skeleton. **b.** Such skeletons collectively, often forming reefs or islands in warm seas. **c.** The secretions of certain corals used in jewelry. **2.** A strong pink to red or reddish orange. [< Gk. *korallion.*] —**cor′al** *adj.*

Coral Sea. An arm of the SW Pacific bounded by Vanuatu, NE Australia, and SE New Guinea.

coral snake ►*n.* A venomous snake having red, yellow, and black banded markings.

cor•bel (kôr′bəl, -bĕl′) ►*n.* A usu. stone bracket projecting from the face of a wall and used to support a cornice or arch. [< OFr., dim. of *corp*, raven < Lat. *corvus.*] —**cor′bel** *v.*

cord (kôrd) ►*n.* **1.** A string of twisted strands or fibers. **2.** An insulated, flexible electric wire fitted with a plug. **3.** also **chord** *Anat.* A long ropelike structure: *a spinal cord.* **4a.** A raised rib on the surface of cloth. **b.** A fabric with such ribs. **5.** A unit of quantity for cut fuel wood, equal to a stack measuring 4 × 4 × 8 ft or 128 cu ft (3.62 cu m). ►*v.* **1.** To fasten or bind with a cord. **2.** To pile (wood) in cords. [< Gk. *khordē.*] —**cord′er** *n.*

cord•age (kôr′dĭj) ►*n.* Cords or ropes, esp. the ropes in the rigging of a ship.

Cor•day (kôr-dā′, kôr′dā), **Charlotte.** 1768–98. French Revolutionary heroine.

cor•dial (kôr′jəl) ►*adj.* Warm and sincere; friendly. See Syns at **gracious.** ►*n.* **1.** A stimulant; tonic. **2.** A liqueur. [< Lat. *cor, cord-*, heart.] —**cor•dial′i•ty** (-jăl′ĭ-tē, -jē-ăl′-) *n.* —**cor′dial•ly** *adv.*

cor•dil•le•ra (kôr′dl-yâr′ə, kôr-dĭl′ər-ə) ►*n.* A mountain chain. [Sp. < *cuerda*, CORD.] —**cor′dil•le′ran** (-yâr′ən) *adj.*

Cor•dil•le•ras (kôr′dĭl-yĕr′əz, -dē-yĕ′räs) The entire complex of mountain ranges in W North America, Mexico, Central America, and South America, extending from AK to Cape Horn.

cord•ite (kôr′dīt′) ►*n.* A smokeless explosive powder consisting of nitrocellulose, nitroglycerin, and petrolatum.

cord•less (kôrd′lĭs) ►*adj.* Having no cord; battery operated: *a cordless telephone.*

cor•do•ba (kôr′də-bə, -və) ►*n.* See table at **currency.** [After Francisco Fernández de *Córdoba* (1475?–1526).]

Cór•do•ba (kôr′də-bə, *-thō*-vä) A city of S Spain ENE of Seville. Pop. 305,894. —**Cor′do•van** (-vən) *adj. & n.*

cor•don (kôr′dn) ►*n.* **1.** A line of people, military posts, or ships stationed around an area to enclose or guard it. **2.** A ribbon worn as an ornament, badge of honor, or decoration. ►*v.* To form a cordon around. [< OFr. < *corde*, CORD.]

cor•do•van (kôr′də-vən) ►*n.* A soft fine-grained leather. [After *Córdova* (Córdoba), Spain.]

cor•du•roy (kôr′də-roi′) ►*n.* **1.** A durable ribbed fabric, usu. made of cotton. **2. corduroys** Corduroy trousers. [Prob. CORD + obsolete *duroy*, coarse woolen fabric.]

core (kôr, kōr) ►*n.* **1.** The hard or fibrous central part of certain fruits, such as the apple, containing the seeds. **2.** The central or innermost part. **3.** The most important part. See Syns at **substance. 4.** An internal computer memory. **5.** The part of a nuclear reactor where fission occurs. ►*v.* **cored, cor•ing.** To remove the core of. [ME.]

CORE ►*abbr.* Congress of Racial Equality

co•re•lig•ion•ist (kō′rĭ-lĭj′ə-nĭst) ►*n.* One having the same religion as another.

co•re•spon•dent (kō′rĭ-spŏn′dənt) ►*n.* A person charged as an adulterer with the defendant in a divorce suit.

co•ri•an•der (kôr′ē-ăn′dər, kōr′-) ►*n.* **1.** An aromatic Eurasian herb having seedlike fruit used as a seasoning. **2.** The leafy plantlets of this herb, used in salads and as a flavoring; cilantro. [< Gk. *koriandron.*]

Cor•inth (kôr′ĭnth, kŏr′-) A city of ancient Greece in the NE Peloponnesus on the Gulf of Corinth.

Corinth, Gulf of. An inlet of the Ionian Sea between the Peloponnesus and central Greece.

Corinth, Isthmus of. A narrow isthmus connecting central Greece with the Peloponnesus.

Co•rin•thi•an (kə-rĭn′thē-ən) ►*adj.* Of or relating to ancient Corinth. ►*n.* **1.** A native or inhabitant of Corinth. **2. Corinthians** *(takes sing. v.)* See table at **Bible.**

Corinthian order ►*n. Archit.* A classical order marked by slender fluted columns with ornate capitals.

co•ri•um (kôr′ē-əm, kōr′-) ►*n., pl.* **-ri•a** (-ē-ə) *Anat.* See **dermis.** [Lat., skin.]

cork (kôrk) ►*n.* **1.** The lightweight, porous, elastic outer bark of a Mediterranean tree, used for stoppers, insulation, and floats. **2.** Something made of cork, esp. a bottle stopper. **3.** *Bot.* The outermost layer of the bark in woody plants. [< Sp. *alcorque*, cork-soled shoe.] —**cork** *v.* —**cork′y** *adj.*

Cork. A city of S Ireland near the head of **Cork Harbor,** an inlet of the Atlantic. Pop. 127,253.

cork•er (kôr′kər) ►*n. Slang* One that is remarkable or astounding.

cork•screw (kôrk′skrōō′) ►*n.* A device for drawing corks from bottles. ►*adj.* Spiral in shape: *a corkscrew turn.*

corm (kôrm) ►*n.* A rounded food-storing underground stem similar to a bulb. [< Gk. *kormos*, a trimmed tree trunk.]

cor•mo•rant (kôr′mər-ənt, -mə-rănt′) ►*n.* A diving bird having dark plumage, webbed feet, and a hooked bill. [< OFr. : *corp*, raven; see CORBEL + *marenc*, MARINE.]

corn[1] (kôrn) ►*n.* **1a.** A tall, widely cultivated cereal plant bearing grains or kernels on large ears. **b.** The edible grains or kernels of this plant. **2.** A single grain of various cereal plants. **3.** *Slang* Something trite or overly sentimental. ►*v.* To preserve in brine. [< OE, grain.]

corn² (kôrn) ▶*n.* A horny thickening of the skin, usu. on or near a toe, resulting from pressure or friction. [< Lat. *cornū*, horn.]

corn•ball (kôrn′bôl′) ▶*adj. Slang* Mawkish; corny: *cornball humor.*

corn bread or **corn•bread** (kôrn′brĕd′) ▶*n.* Bread made from cornmeal.

corn•cob (kôrn′kŏb′) ▶*n.* The woody core of an ear of corn.

corn•crib (kôrn′krĭb′) ▶*n.* A ventilated structure for storing and drying ears of corn.

corn dog ▶*n.* A baked or fried frankfurter encased in corn bread.

cor•ne•a (kôr′nē-ə) ▶*n.* The tough transparent membrane of the eyeball, covering the iris and the pupil. [Med.Lat. *cornea (tēla)*, horny (tissue).] —**cor′ne•al** *adj.*

Cor•neille (kôr-nā′), **Pierre.** 1606–84. French playwright.

cor•ner (kôr′nər) ▶*n.* **1a.** The position at which two lines, surfaces, or edges meet and form an angle. **b.** The area enclosed or bounded by such an angle. **2.** The place where two roads or streets meet. **3.** A position from which escape is difficult. **4.** A remote or secret place. **5.** A speculative monopoly of a stock or commodity created by controlling the available supply so as to raise its price. ▶*v.* **1.** To place or drive into a corner. **2.** To form a corner in (a stock or commodity). **3.** To turn, as at a corner. [< AN < Lat. *cornū*, horn.]

corner kick ▶*n.* In soccer, a direct free kick given to the offense when the defense has driven the ball out of bounds beyond the goal line.

cor•ner•stone (kôr′nər-stōn′) ▶*n.* **1.** A stone at the corner of a building uniting two intersecting walls, esp. one laid with a special ceremony. **2.** A fundamental basis: *The cornerstone of the government's policy.*

cor•net (kôr-nĕt′) ▶*n.* A three-valved brass wind instrument resembling a trumpet. [< OFr. < Lat. *cornū*, horn.] —**cor•net′ist** *n.*

corn•flow•er (kôrn′flou′ər) ▶*n.* An annual plant having showy blue, purple, pink, or white flowers; bachelor's button.

cor•nice (kôr′nĭs) ▶*n.* **1.** A horizontal molded projection that crowns or completes a building or wall. **2.** The top part of an entablature. [< Ital.]

Cor•nish (kôr′nĭsh) ▶*adj.* Of or relating to Cornwall or the Cornish language. ▶*n.* The extinct Celtic language of Cornwall.

corn•meal (kôrn′mēl′) ▶*n.* Coarse meal made from corn.

corn•pone or **corn pone** (kôrn′pōn′) ▶*n. Regional* See **johnnycake.** See Regional Note at **pone.** [CORN¹ + Virginia Algonquian *poan*, cornbread.]

corn•row (kôrn′rō′) ▶*n.* A portion of hair braided close to the scalp to form a row with others. —**corn′row′** *v.*

corn•stalk (kôrn′stôk′) ▶*n.* The stalk or stem of a corn plant.

corn•starch (kôrn′stärch′) ▶*n.* Starch prepared from corn grains, used industrially and as a thickener in cooking.

corn syrup ▶*n.* A syrup prepared from cornstarch, used esp. as a sweetener.

cor•nu•co•pi•a (kôr′nə-kō′pē-ə, -nyə-) ▶*n.* **1.** A cone-shaped container overflowing with fruit, flowers, and grain; horn of plenty. **2.** An abundance. [< Lat. *cornū cōpiae*, horn of plenty.]

Corn•wall (kôrn′wôl′) A region of extreme SW England on a peninsula bounded by the Atlantic Ocean and English Channel. —**Cor′nish•man** *n.* —**Cor′nish•wom′an** *n.*

Corn•wal•lis (kôrn-wŏl′ĭs, -wô′lĭs), **Charles.** 1st Marquis and 2nd Earl Cornwallis. 1738–1805. British military and political leader.

corn•y (kôr′nē) ▶*adj.* **-i•er, -i•est.** Trite, dated, or mawkish. —**corn′i•ness** *n.*

co•rol•la (kə-rŏl′ə, -rō′lə) ▶*n.* The petals of a flower considered as a unit. [Lat. *corōlla*, dim. of *corōna*, CROWN.]

cor•ol•lar•y (kôr′ə-lĕr′-ē, kŏr′-) ▶*n., pl.* **-ies** **1.** A proposition that follows with little or no proof required from one already proven. **2.** A natural consequence or effect; result. [< Lat. *corōllārium*, gratuity < *corōlla*, garland. See COROLLA.]

Cor•o•man•del Coast (kôr′ə-măn′dl) A region of SE India bounded by the Bay of Bengal and the Eastern Ghats.

co•ro•na (kə-rō′nə) ▶*n., pl.* **-nas** or **-nae** (-nē) **1.** A ring of diffracted light visible esp. around the sun or moon during hazy conditions. **2.** The luminous outer atmosphere of the sun. [Lat. *corōna*, CROWN.]

Co•ro•na•do (kôr′ə-nä′dō, kŏr′-), **Francisco Vásquez de.** 1510–54. Spanish explorer.

cor•o•nar•y (kôr′ə-nĕr′ē, kŏr′-) ▶*adj.* **1.** Of or relating to either of two arteries that originate in the aorta and supply blood directly to the heart tissues. **2.** Relating to the heart. ▶*n., pl.* **-ies.** A coronary thrombosis. [< Lat. *corōna*, CROWN.]

coronary thrombosis ▶*n.* Obstruction of a coronary artery by a blood clot, often leading to destruction of heart muscle.

cor•o•na•tion (kôr′ə-nā′shən, kŏr′-) ▶*n.* The act or ceremony of crowning a sovereign. [< Lat. *corōna*, CROWN.]

cor•o•ner (kôr′ə-nər, kŏr′-) ▶*n.* A public officer who investigates any death thought to be of other than natural causes. [< AN *corouner*, officer of the crown.]

cor•o•net (kôr′ə-nĕt′, kŏr′-) ▶*n.* **1.** A small crown worn by nobles below the rank of sovereign. **2.** A jeweled headband. [< OFr. *coronette*, dim. of *corone*, CROWN.]

Co•rot (kô-rō′, kə-), **Jean Baptiste Camille.** 1796–1875. French painter.

corp. ▶*abbr.* corporation

cor•po•ra (kôr′pər-ə) ▶*n.* Pl. of **corpus.**

cor•po•ral¹ (kôr′pər-əl, kôr′prəl) ▶*adj.* Of the body; bodily. See Syns at **bodily.** [< Lat. *corpus*, *corpor-*, body.] —**cor′po•ral′i•ty** (-pə-răl′ĭ-tē) *n.* —**cor′po•ral•ly** *adv.*

cor•po•ral² (kôr′pər-əl, kôr′prəl) ▶*n.* The lowest noncommissioned rank, as in the US Army or Marine Corps. [< OItal. *caporale* < *capo*, head.]

cor•po•rate (kôr′pər-ĭt, kôr′prĭt) ▶*adj.* **1.** Formed into a corporation; incorporated. **2.** Of a corporation. **3.** United or combined into one body; collective. [< Lat. *corpus*, *corpor-*, body.] —**cor′po•rate•ly** *adv.*

cor•po•ra•tion (kôr′pə-rā′shən) ▶*n.* **1.** A body of persons acting under a legal charter as a separate entity having its own rights, privileges, and liabilities. **2.** Such a body created for purposes of government.

cor•po•re•al (kôr-pôr′ē-əl, -pōr′-) ▸*adj.* **1.** Of the body. See Syns at **bodily. 2.** Of a material nature; tangible. [< Lat. *corporeus* < *corpus*, body.] —**cor•po′re•al′i•ty** (-ăl′ĭ-tē) *n.* —**cor•po′re•al•ly** *adv.*

corps (kôr, kōr) ▸*n., pl.* **corps** (kôrz, kōrz) **1.** A specialized branch or department of the armed forces. **2.** A body of persons under common direction. See Syns at **band²**. [< OFr. < Lat. *corpus*, body.]

corpse (kôrps) ▸*n.* A dead body, esp. of a human. [< Lat. *corpus*, body.]

corps•man (kôr′mən, kōr′-, kôrz′mən, kōrz′-) ▸*n.* An enlisted person in the armed forces trained in first aid.

cor•pu•lence (kôr′pyə-ləns) ▸*n.* Excessive fatness; obesity. [< Lat. *corpulentia* < *corpus*, body.] —**cor′pu•lent** *adj.*

cor•pus (kôr′pəs) ▸*n., pl.* **-po•ra** (-pər-ə) **1.** A large collection of specialized writings. **2.** *Anat.* The main part of a bodily structure or organ. [< Lat., body.]

Corpus Chris•ti (krĭs′tē) A city of S TX on **Corpus Christi Bay,** an arm of the Gulf of Mexico. Pop. 257,453.

cor•pus•cle (kôr′pə-səl, -pŭs′əl) ▸*n.* **1.** An unattached or free-moving body cell, such as a blood or lymph cell. **2.** A minute globular particle. [Lat. *corpusculum*, dim. of *corpus*, body.] —**cor•pus′cu•lar** (kôr-pŭs′kyə-lər) *adj.*

corpus de•lic•ti (dĭ-lĭk′tī′) ▸*n.* **1.** *Law* The material evidence showing that a crime has been committed. **2.** A corpse, esp. of a murder victim. [NLat., body of crime.]

cor•ral (kə-răl′) ▸*n.* An enclosure for confining livestock. ▸*v.* **-ralled, -ral•ling 1.** To drive into and hold in a corral. **2.** To seize or procure. [Sp. < Lat. *currere*, run.]

cor•rect (kə-rĕkt′) ▸*v.* **1a.** To remove errors from. **b.** To mark the errors in. **2.** To punish for the purpose of improving. **3.** To remedy or counteract: *correct a malfunction.* ▸*adj.* **1.** True; accurate. **2.** Conforming to standards; proper. [< Lat. *corrigere, corrēct-*, make right.] —**cor•rect′a•ble, cor•rect′i•ble** *adj.* —**cor•rec′tive** *adj. & n.* —**cor•rect′ly** *adv.* —**cor•rect′ness** *n.*

cor•rec•tion (kə-rĕk′shən) ▸*n.* **1.** The act or process of correcting. **2.** Something offered or substituted for a mistake or fault. **3.** Punishment intended to improve. **4.** A quantity added or subtracted in order to correct. —**cor•rec′tion•al** *adj.*

Cor•reg•gio (kə-rĕj′ō, -ē-ō′), **Antonio Allegri da.** 1494–1534. Italian High Renaissance painter.

Cor•reg•i•dor (kə-rĕg′ĭ-dôr′, -dōr′) An island of the N Philippines at the entrance to Manila Bay.

cor•re•la•tion (kôr′ə-lā′shən, kŏr′-) ▸*n.* A complementary, parallel, or reciprocal relationship: *a correlation between drug abuse and crime.* [Med.Lat. *correlātiō*.] —**cor′re•late′** *v. & adj.* —**cor′re•la′tion•al** *adj.*

cor•rel•a•tive (kə-rĕl′ə-tĭv) ▸*adj.* **1.** Related; corresponding. **2.** *Gram.* Reciprocally related, as the conjunctions *neither* and *nor.* ▸*n.* **1.** Either of two correlative entities. **2.** *Gram.* A correlative word or expression. —**cor•rel′a•tive•ly** *adv.*

cor•re•spond (kôr′ĭ-spŏnd′, kŏr′-) ▸*v.* **1.** To be in agreement, harmony, or conformity. **2.** To be similar, parallel, or equivalent, as in nature or function. **3.** To communicate by letter. [< Med.Lat. *correspondēre.*] —**cor′re•spond′ing•ly** *adv.*

cor•re•spon•dence (kôr′ĭ-spŏn′dəns, kŏr′-) ▸*n.* **1.** The act, fact, or state of agreeing or conforming. **2.** Similarity or analogy. **3a.** Communication by the exchange of letters. **b.** The letters written or received.

cor•re•spon•dent (kôr′ĭ-spŏn′dənt, kŏr′-) ▸*n.* **1.** One who communicates by letter. **2.** One employed by the media to supply news, esp. from a distant place. **3.** Something that corresponds; correlative. ▸*adj.* Corresponding.

cor•ri•dor (kôr′ĭ-dər, -dôr′, kŏr′-) ▸*n.* **1.** A narrow hallway or passageway, often with rooms opening onto it. **2.** A narrow tract of land, esp. through another country. **3.** A thickly populated strip of land connecting urban areas. [Fr. < Lat. *currere*, run.]

cor•ri•gen•dum (kôr′ə-jĕn′dəm, kŏr′-) ▸*n., pl.* **-da** (-də) **1.** An error to be corrected. **2. corrigenda** A list of errors in a book along with their corrections. [Lat. < *corrigere*, to correct.]

cor•rob•o•rate (kə-rŏb′ə-rāt′) ▸*v.* **-rat•ed, -rat•ing.** To strengthen or support (other evidence). [Lat. *corrōborāre* : COM– + *rōborāre*, strengthen (< *rōbur*, strength).] —**cor•rob′o•ra′tion** *n.* —**cor•rob′o•ra′tive** (-ə-rā′tĭv, -ər-ə-tĭv) *adj.* —**cor•rob′o•ra′tor** *n.*

cor•rode (kə-rōd′) ▸*v.* **-rod•ed, -rod•ing.** To wear away gradually, esp. by chemical action. [< Lat. *corrōdere*, gnaw away.] —**cor•rod′i•ble, cor•ro′si•ble** (-rō′sə-bəl) *adj.* —**cor•ro′sion** *n.* —**cor•ro′sive** *adj. & n.* —**cor•ro′sive•ness** *n.*

cor•ru•gate (kôr′ə-gāt′, kŏr′-) ▸*v.* **-gat•ed, -gat•ing.** To make folds or parallel and alternating ridges and grooves (in). [Lat. *corrūgāre*, wrinkle up.] —**cor′ru•ga′tion** *n.*

cor•rupt (kə-rŭpt′) ▸*adj.* **1.** Marked by immorality; depraved. **2.** Open to bribery; dishonest: *a corrupt mayor.* **3.** *Archaic* Tainted; putrid. ▸*v.* **1.** To make or become corrupt. **2.** To damage (data) in a file or on a disk. [< Lat. *corrumpere, corrupt-*, destroy.] —**cor•rupt′er, cor•rup′tor** *n.* —**cor•rupt′i•ble** *adj.* —**cor•rup′tion** *n.* —**cor•rupt′ly** *adv.* —**cor•rupt′ness** *n.*

Syns: *corrupt, debase, debauch, deprave, pervert, vitiate* **v.**

cor•sage (kôr-säzh′, -säj′) ▸*n.* A small bouquet worn usu. at the shoulder. [< OFr., torso.]

cor•sair (kôr′sâr′) ▸*n.* **1.** A pirate. **2.** A swift pirate ship. [< Med.Lat. *cursārius.*]

cor•set (kôr′sĭt) ▸*n.* A close-fitting undergarment, often reinforced by stays, worn esp. to shape the waist and hips. [< OFr.]

Cor•si•ca (kôr′sĭ-kə) An island of France in the Mediterranean Sea north of Sardinia. —**Cor′si•can** *adj. & n.*

cor•tege (kôr-tĕzh′) ▸*n.* **1.** A train of attendants. **2.** A ceremonial procession, esp. for a funeral. [< OItal. *corte*, COURT.]

Cor•tés (kôr-tĕz′, -tĕs′), **Hernando.** 1485–1547. Spanish explorer and conquistador.

cor•tex (kôr′tĕks′) ▸*n., pl.* **-ti•ces** (-tĭ-sēz′) or **-tex•es 1a.** The outer layer of a bodily organ. **b.** The layer of gray matter covering most of the brain. **2.** The region of tissue in a root or stem surrounding the vascular tissue. [Lat., bark.] —**cor′ti•cal** *adj.*

cor•ti•co•ste•roid (kôr′tĭ-kō-stîr′oid′, -stĕr′-) ►*n.* Any of the steroid hormones produced by the adrenal cortex or their synthetic equivalents.

cor•ti•sone (kôr′tĭ-sōn′, -zōn′) ►*n.* A corticosteroid active in carbohydrate metabolism and used esp. to treat rheumatoid arthritis. [Alteration of *corticosterone*, a type of hormone.]

co•run•dum (kə-rŭn′dəm) ►*n.* An extremely hard mineral, aluminum oxide, occurring in gem varieties and in a common form used chiefly in abrasives. [Tamil *kuruntam.*]

cor•us•cate (kôr′ə-skāt′, kŏr′-) ►*v.* **-cat•ed, -cat•ing.** To sparkle and glitter. [Lat. *coruscāre.*] —**cor′us•ca′tion** *n.*

cor•vette (kôr-vĕt′) ►*n.* **1.** A fast, lightly armed warship, smaller than a destroyer. **2.** An obsolete sailing warship, smaller than a frigate. [Fr., a kind of warship.]

cor•ymb (kôr′ĭmb, -ĭm, kŏr′-) ►*n.* A usu. flat-topped flower cluster. [< Gk. *korumbos*, head.]

co•ry•za (kə-rī′zə) ►*n.* See **cold** 3. [< Gk. *koruza*, catarrh.]

cos ►*abbr.* cosine

Cos (kŏs, kôs) See **Kos.**

co•se•cant (kō-sē′kănt′, -kənt) ►*n.* The reciprocal of the sine of an angle.

co•sign (kō-sīn′) ►*v.* **1.** To sign (a document) jointly. **2.** To endorse (another's signature), as for a loan. —**co•sign′er** *n.*

co•sig•na•to•ry (kō-sĭg′nə-tôr′ē) ►*adj.* Signed jointly. ►*n., pl.* **-ries.** A cosigner.

co•sine (kō′sīn′) ►*n.* In a right triangle, the ratio of the length of the side adjacent to an acute angle to the length of the hypotenuse.

cos•met•ic (kŏz-mĕt′ĭk) ►*adj.* **1.** Serving to beautify the body. **2.** Serving to improve the appearance of a physical feature. **3.** Lacking significance; superficial. ►*n.* A cosmetic preparation. [< Gk. *kosmētikos*, skilled in arranging.] —**cos•met′i•cal•ly** *adv.*

cos•me•tol•o•gy (kŏz′mĭ-tŏl′ə-jē) ►*n.* The study or art of cosmetics and their use. [Fr. *cosmétologie.*] —**cos′me•tol′o•gist** *n.*

cos•mic (kŏz′mĭk) ►*adj.* **1.** Relating to the universe, esp. as distinct from Earth. **2.** Limitless; vast. —**cos′mi•cal•ly** *adv.*

cosmic ray ►*n.* A stream of ionizing radiation, consisting chiefly of protons, alpha particles, and other atomic nuclei but including some high-energy electrons, that enters the atmosphere from outer space.

cosmo– or **cosm–** ►*pref.* Universe; world: *cosmology.* [< Gk. *kosmos*, universe.]

cos•mo•chem•is•try (kŏz′mō-kĕm′ĭ-strē) ►*n.* The science of the chemical composition of the universe. —**cos′mo•chem′i•cal** *adj.*

cos•mog•o•ny (kŏz-mŏg′ə-nē) ►*n.* The study of the origin and evolution of the universe. [Gk. *kosmogonia*, creation of the world.] —**cos•mog′o•nist** *n.*

cos•mog•ra•phy (kŏz-mŏg′rə-fē) ►*n., pl.* **-phies 1.** The study of the visible universe. **2.** A description of the world or universe. —**cos•mog′ra•pher** *n.*

cos•mol•o•gy (kŏz-mŏl′ə-jē) ►*n., pl.* **-gies 1.** The study of the physical universe as a totality of phenomena in time and space. **2.** The astrophysical study of the history, structure, and constituent dynamics of the universe. —**cos′mo•log′ic** (-mə-lŏj′ĭk), **cos′mo•log′i•cal** *adj.* —**cos•mol′o•gist** *n.*

cos•mo•naut (kŏz′mə-nôt′) ►*n.* A Soviet astronaut. [Russ. *kosmonavt.*]

cos•mo•pol•i•tan (kŏz′mə-pŏl′ĭ-tn) ►*adj.* **1.** Common to the whole world. **2.** Of the entire world or from many different parts of the world. **3.** At home in all parts of the world or in many spheres of interest. ►*n.* A cosmopolitan person.

cos•mop•o•lite (kŏz-mŏp′ə-līt′) ►*n.* A cosmopolitan person. [Gk. *kosmopolitēs*, citizen of the world.]

cos•mos (kŏz′məs, -mŏs′, -mōs′) ►*n.* **1.** The universe regarded as an orderly harmonious whole. **2.** Any system regarded as ordered, harmonious, and whole. **3.** A garden annual with daisylike flowers. [Gk. *kosmos.*]

co•spon•sor (kō-spŏn′sər) ►*n.* A joint sponsor, as of legislation. —**co•spon′sor** *v.* —**co•spon′sor•ship′** *n.*

Cos•sack (kŏs′ăk) ►*n.* A member of a people of S European Russia, noted as cavalrymen esp. during czarist times. [< Turk. *kazak*, adventurer.] —**Cos′sack′** *adj.*

cost (kôst) ►*n.* **1.** An amount paid or required in payment for a purchase. **2.** A loss, sacrifice, or penalty. **3. costs** *Law* The charges fixed for litigation. ►*v.* **cost, cost•ing.** To require a specified payment, expenditure, effort, or loss. [< Lat. *cōnstāre*, be fixed. See CONSTANT.]

co•star also **co-star** (kō′stär′) ►*n.* A starring actor or actress given equal status with another or others in a play or film. —**co′star′** *v.*

Cos•ta Ri•ca (kŏs′tə rē′kə, kôs′stə, kō′-) A country of Central America between Panama and Nicaragua. Cap. San José. Pop. 3,071,000. —**Cos′ta Ri′can** (-kən) *adj. & n.*

cost•ly (kôst′lē) ►*adj.* **-li•er, -li•est 1.** Of high price or value; expensive. **2.** Entailing great loss or sacrifice. —**cost′li•ness** *n.*

cost of living ►*n.* **1.** The average cost of the necessities of life, such as food, shelter, and clothing. **2.** The cost of necessities as defined by an accepted standard.

cost-of-liv•ing adjustment (kôst′əv-lĭv′ĭng) ►*n.* An adjustment made in wages that corresponds with a change in the cost of living.

cost-of-living index ►*n.* See **consumer price index.**

cost-plus (kôst′plŭs′) ►*n.* The cost of production plus a fixed rate of profit.

cos•tume (kŏs′to͞om′, -tyo͞om′) ►*n.* **1.** A style of dress characteristic of a particular country or period. **2.** A set of clothes for a particular occasion or season. **3.** An outfit worn by one playing a part. [< Ital., style.] —**cos′tum•er** *n.*

costume jewelry ►*n.* Jewelry made from inexpensive metals and imitation or semiprecious stones.

co•sy (kō′zē) ►*adj., v., & n.* Var. of **cozy.**

cot[1] (kŏt) ►*n.* A narrow bed, esp. a collapsible one. [< Skt. *khaṭvā.*]

cot[2] ►*abbr.* cotangent

co•tan•gent (kō-tăn′jənt) ►*n.* The reciprocal of the tangent of an angle.

cote (kōt) ►*n.* A small shed or shelter for sheep or birds. [< OE.]

Côte d'A•zur (kōt′ də-zo͞or′, dä-zür′) The Mediterranean coast of SE France.

Côte d'I•voire (dē-vwär′) also **Ivory Coast.** A country of W Africa on the Gulf of Guinea.

Caps. Abidjan and Yamoussoukro. Pop. 13,695,000. —**I•vo′ri•an** (ī-vôr′ē-ən, ī-vōr′-) *adj. & n.*

co•ter•ie (kō′tə-rē, kō′tə-rē′) ►*n.* A close circle of friends or associates. [Fr.]

co•ter•mi•nous (kō-tûr′mə-nəs) ►*adj.* Var. of **conterminous.**

co•til•lion (kō-tĭl′yən, kə-) ►*n.* **1.** A formal debutante ball. **2.** A lively group dance. [< OFr. *cotillon*, petticoat.]

Co•to•nou (kōt′n-ōō′) A city of S Benin on the Gulf of Guinea. Pop. 536,827.

cot•tage (kŏt′ĭj) ►*n.* **1.** A small house, esp. in the country. **2.** A small vacation house. [< AN *cotage*, of Gmc. orig.] —**cot′tag•er** *n.*

cottage cheese ►*n.* A soft mild white cheese made of strained curds of skim milk.

cot•ter (kŏt′ər) ►*n.* A bolt or pin inserted through a slot to hold parts together. [?]

cotter pin ►*n.* A split cotter inserted through holes in two or more pieces and bent at the ends to fasten the pieces together.

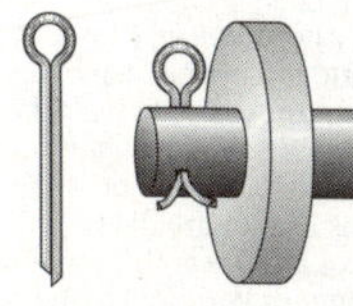

cotter pin

cot•ton (kŏt′n) ►*n.* **1a.** Any of various shrubby plants grown for the soft, white, downy fibers surrounding oil-rich seeds. **b.** The fiber of any of these plants, used esp. in making textiles. **2.** Thread or cloth made from cotton fiber. ►*v. Informal* To take a liking; become friendly. [< Ar. *quṭn*.]

cotton candy ►*n.* A candy of threaded sugar, often tinted and twirled onto a stick.

cotton gin ►*n.* A machine that separates the seeds and seed hulls from cotton fibers.

cot•ton•mouth (kŏt′n-mouth′) ►*n.* See **water moccasin.**

cot•ton•seed (kŏt′n-sēd′) ►*n.* The seed of the cotton plant, used as a source of oil and meal.

cot•ton•tail (kŏt′n-tāl′) ►*n.* A New World rabbit having a tail with a white underside.

cot•ton•wood (kŏt′n-wŏŏd′) ►*n.* A North American poplar having triangular leaves and seeds with a tuft of cottony hairs.

cot•y•le•don (kŏt′l-ēd′n) ►*n.* An embryonic plant leaf, the first to appear from a sprouting seed. [< Gk. *kotulēdōn*, a kind of plant.] —**cot′y•le′do•nous** *adj.*

couch (kouch) ►*n.* A sofa. ►*v.* To word in a certain manner; phrase. [< OFr. *couchier*, lie down.]

cou•gar (kōō′gər) ►*n.* See **mountain lion.** [Ult. < Tupi *suasuarana*.]

cough (kôf, kŏf) ►*v.* **1.** To expel air from the lungs suddenly and noisily. **2.** To expel by coughing. [ME *coughen*.] —**cough** *n.*

could (kŏŏd) ►*aux.v.* P.t. of **can**[1]. **1.** Used to indicate ability, possibility, or permission in the past. **2.** Used to indicate condition or politeness: *If we could help, we would.*

cou•lee (kōō′lē) ►*n.* A deep ravine, esp. in the W US. [< Fr. *couler*, flow.]

cou•lomb (kōō′lŏm′, -lōm′) ►*n.* A unit of electric charge equal to the quantity of charge in approx. 6×10^{18} electrons. [After Charles A. de *Coulomb* (1736–1806).]

coun•cil (koun′səl) ►*n.* **1.** An assembly of persons called together for deliberation or discussion. **2.** An administrative, legislative, or advisory body. [< Lat. *concilium*.] —**coun′cil•man** *n.* —**coun′cil•wom′an** *n.*

Usage: *Council* and *councilor* refer principally to a deliberative assembly, its work, and its membership. *Counsel* and *counselor* pertain chiefly to advice and guidance in general and to a person who provides it.

coun•cil•or also **coun•cil•lor** (koun′sə-lər, -slər) ►*n.* A member of a council. See Usage Note at **council.**

coun•sel (koun′səl) ►*n.* **1.** The act of exchanging opinions and ideas; consultation. **2.** Advice or guidance. See Syns at **advice. 3.** A plan of action. **4.** Private thoughts or opinions: *keep one's own counsel.* **5.** A lawyer or group of lawyers. ►*v.* **-seled, -sel•ing** or **-selled, -sel•ling 1.** To give counsel (to). See Syns at **advise. 2.** To recommend: *counseled caution in negotiating the contract.* See Usage Note at **council.** [< Lat. *cōnsilium*.]

coun•sel•or also **coun•sel•lor** (koun′sə-lər, -slər) ►*n.* **1.** An adviser. **2.** An attorney, esp. a trial lawyer. **3.** One who supervises at a summer camp. See Usage Note at **council.** —**coun′se•lor•ship′** *n.*

count[1] (kount) ►*v.* **1.** To name or list one by one in order to determine a total. **2.** To recite numerals in ascending order. **3.** To include in a reckoning: *ten dogs, counting the puppies.* **4.** To believe or consider to be. **5.** To merit consideration. **6.** To have a specified importance or value: *count for little; counts for two points.* —***phrasal verb:*** **count on** To rely on; depend on. ►*n.* **1.** The act of counting. **2.** A number reached by counting. **3.** *Law* Any of the charges in an indictment. [< Lat. *computāre*, calculate.] —**count′a•ble** *adj.*

Syns: *count, import, matter, signify, weigh* **v.**

count[2] (kount) ►*n.* A nobleman in some European countries. [< LLat. *comes*, occupant of a state office.]

count•down (kount′doun′) ►*n.* The counting backward to indicate the time remaining before an event or operation, such as the launching of a missile or space vehicle.

coun•te•nance (koun′tə-nəns) ►*n.* **1.** Appearance, esp. the expression of the face. **2.** The face. **3.** Support or approval. ►*v.* **-nanced, -nanc•ing.** To approve or sanction. [< OFr. *contenance*.] —**coun′te•nanc•er** *n.*

coun•ter[1] (koun′tər) ►*adj.* Contrary; opposing. ►*n.* One that is counter; opposite. ►*v.* To move or act in opposition (to). ►*adv.* In a contrary manner or direction. [< COUNTER–.]

count•er[2] (koun′tər) ►*n.* **1.** A flat surface on which money is counted, business is transacted, or food is prepared or served. **2.** A piece, as of wood or ivory, used for keeping a count or a place in games. [< Med.Lat. *computātōrium*, countinghouse.]

count•er[3] (koun′tər) ►*n.* One that counts, esp. an electronic or mechanical device that automatically counts occurrences or repetitions of phenomena or events.

counter– ►*pref.* **1.** Contrary; opposing: *coun-*

teract. **2.** Reciprocation: *countersign.* [< Lat. *contrā*, against.]

coun•ter•act (koun′tər-ăkt′) ►*v.* To oppose and lessen the effects of by contrary action; check. —**coun′ter•ac′tion** *n.*

coun•ter•at•tack (koun′tər-ə-tăk′) ►*n.* A return attack. —**coun′ter•at•tack′** *v.*

coun•ter•bal•ance (koun′tər-băl′əns) ►*n.* **1.** A force or influence equally counteracting another. **2.** A weight that acts to balance another. —**coun′ter•bal′ance** *v.*

coun•ter•charge (koun′tər-chärj′) ►*n.* A charge in opposition to another charge. —**coun′ter•charge′** *v.*

coun•ter•claim (koun′tər-klām′) ►*n.* A claim filed in opposition to another claim. —**coun′ter•claim′** *v.* —**coun′ter•claim′ant** *n.*

coun•ter•clock•wise (koun′tər-klŏk′wīz′) ►*adv. & adj.* In a direction opposite to the rotating hands of a clock.

coun•ter•cul•ture (koun′tər-kŭl′chər) ►*n.* A culture, esp. of young people, with antiestablishment values or lifestyles.

coun•ter•es•pi•o•nage (koun′tər-ĕs′pē-ə-näzh′, -nĭj) ►*n.* Espionage undertaken to detect and counteract enemy espionage.

coun•ter•feit (koun′tər-fĭt′) ►*v.* **1.** To make a copy of, usu. with intent to defraud; forge. **2.** To pretend; feign. ►*adj.* **1.** Made in imitation of what is genuine, usu. with intent to defraud. **2.** Simulated; feigned. ►*n.* A fraudulent imitation. [< OFr. *contrefait*, made in imitation.] —**coun′ter•feit′er** *n.*

coun•ter•in•sur•gen•cy (koun′tər-ĭn-sûr′jən-sē) ►*n.* Political and military action undertaken to suppress insurgency. —**coun′ter•in•sur′gent** *n.*

coun•ter•in•tel•li•gence (koun′tər-ĭn-tĕl′ə-jəns) ►*n.* The branch of an intelligence service charged with keeping sensitive information from an enemy and preventing subversion and sabotage.

coun•ter•in•tu•i•tive (koun′tər-ĭn-to͞o′ĭ-tĭv, -tyo͞o′-) ►*adj.* Contrary to what intuition and common sense would indicate. —**coun′ter•in•tu′i•tive•ly** *adv.*

coun•ter•mand (koun′tər-mănd′) ►*v.* **1.** To reverse (an order). **2.** To recall by a contrary order. [< OFr. *contremander*.]

coun•ter•meas•ure (koun′tər-mĕzh′ər) ►*n.* A measure or action taken to counter or offset another one.

coun•ter•of•fen•sive (koun′tər-ə-fĕn′sĭv) ►*n.* A large-scale counterattack by an armed force, intended to stop an enemy offensive.

coun•ter•pane (koun′tər-pān′) ►*n.* A cover for a bed; bedspread. [< OFr. *coultepointe* < Med.Lat. *culcita pūncta*, stitched quilt.]

coun•ter•part (koun′tər-pärt′) ►*n.* One that closely resembles another, as in function, characteristics, or relation.

coun•ter•plot (koun′tər-plŏt′) ►*n.* **1.** A plot or scheme intended to subvert another plot. **2.** See **subplot.** ►*v.* To plot against; thwart with a counterplot.

coun•ter•point (koun′tər-point′) ►*n.* **1.** *Mus.* The technique of combining two or more melodic lines so that they establish a harmonic relationship while retaining their linear individuality. **2.** A contrasting but parallel element or theme.

coun•ter•poise (koun′tər-poiz′) ►*n.* **1.** A counterbalancing weight. **2.** A force or influence that balances or counteracts another. **3.** The state of being balanced or in equilibrium. —**coun′ter•poise′** *v.*

coun•ter•pro•duc•tive (koun′tər-prə-dŭk′tĭv) ►*adj.* Tending to hinder rather than serve one's purpose.

coun•ter•rev•o•lu•tion (koun′tər-rĕv′ə-lo͞o′shən) ►*n.* A movement arising in opposition to a previous revolution. —**coun′ter•rev′o•lu′tion•ar′y** *adj. & n.*

coun•ter•sign (koun′tər-sīn′) ►*v.* To sign (a previously signed document), as for authentication. ►*n.* **1.** A second or confirming signature. **2.** A password.

coun•ter•sig•na•ture (koun′tər-sĭg′nə-chər) ►*n.* See **countersign** 1.

coun•ter•sink (koun′tər-sĭngk′) ►*n.* **1.** A hole with the top part enlarged so that the head of a screw or bolt will lie flush with or below the surface. **2.** A tool for making such a hole. ►*v.* **1.** To make a countersink on or in. **2.** To set into a countersink.

coun•ter•spy (koun′tər-spī′) ►*n.* A spy working in opposition to enemy espionage.

coun•ter•ten•or (koun′tər-tĕn′ər) ►*n.* A male singer with a range above a tenor's.

coun•ter•weight (koun′tər-wāt′) ►*n.* A weight used as a counterbalance.

count•ess (koun′tĭs) ►*n.* **1.** A woman holding the title of count or earl. **2.** The wife or widow of a count or earl.

count•ing•house also **count•ing house** (koun′tĭng-hous′) ►*n.* An office in which a business firm carries on operations such as accounting and correspondence.

count•less (kount′lĭs) ►*adj.* Innumerable. See Syns at **incalculable.**

coun•tri•fied also **coun•try•fied** (kŭn′trĭ-fīd′) ►*adj.* **1.** Characteristic of country life; rural. **2.** Lacking sophistication.

coun•try (kŭn′trē) ►*n., pl.* **-tries 1a.** A nation or state. **b.** The territory or people of a nation or state. **2.** The land of a person's birth or citizenship. **3.** A large tract of land distinguishable by features of topography, biology, or culture: *hill country; cattle country.* **4.** A rural area. **5.** *Informal* Country music. [< VLat. **(terra) contrāta*, (land) opposite.]

country and western ►*n.* See **country music.**

country club ►*n.* A suburban club for social and sports activities.

coun•try-dance (kŭn′trē-dăns′) ►*n.* A folk dance of English origin in which two lines of dancers face each other.

coun•try•man (kŭn′trē-mən) ►*n.* **1.** A person from one's own country; compatriot. **2.** A rustic.

country mile ►*n. Informal* A great distance.

country music ►*n.* Popular music based on folk styles of the rural American South and West.

coun•try•side (kŭn′trē-sīd′) ►*n.* **1.** A rural region. **2.** The inhabitants of a rural region.

coun•try•wom•an (kŭn′trē-wo͝om′ən) ►*n.* **1.** A woman from one's own country; compatriot. **2.** A rustic woman.

coun•ty (koun′tē) ►*n., pl.* **-ties.** An administrative subdivision of a state or territory. [< Med.Lat. *comitātus*, territory of a count.]

coup (ko͞o) ►*n., pl.* **coups** (ko͞oz) **1.** A brilliantly executed stratagem. **2.** A coup d'état. [Fr., a stroke. See COPE[1].]

coup de grâce (ko͞o' də gräs') ►*n., pl.* **coups de grâce 1.** A deathblow delivered to end the misery of a mortally wounded victim. **2.** A finishing or decisive stroke. [Fr.]

coup d'é•tat (dā-tä') ►*n., pl.* **coups d'état.** The sudden overthrow of a government by a usu. small group of persons in or previously in authority. [Fr.]

coupe (ko͞op) ►*n.* A closed two-door automobile. [Fr. *coupé.*]

Cou•pe•rin (ko͞o-pə-răɴ', ko͞op-răɴ'), **François.** 1668–1733. French composer.

cou•ple (kŭp'əl) ►*n.* **1.** Two items of the same kind; pair. **2.** Something that joins two things; link. **3.** *(takes sing. or pl. v.)* **a.** Two people united, as by marriage. **b.** Two people together. **4.** *Informal* A few; several: *a couple of days.* ►*v.* **-pled, -pling 1.** To link together. **2.** To form pairs. [< Lat. *cōpula*, bond, pair.] —**cou'pler** *n.*

Usage: When used to refer to two people who function socially as a unit, as in *a married couple,* the word *couple* may take either a singular or a plural verb, depending on whether the members are considered individually or collectively.

cou•plet (kŭp'lĭt) ►*n.* Two successive lines of verse, usu. rhyming and having the same meter. [< OFr., dim. of *couple*, COUPLE.]

cou•pling (kŭp'lĭng) ►*n.* **1.** The act of forming couples. **2.** A device that links or connects.

cou•pon (ko͞o'pŏn', kyo͞o'-) ►*n.* **1.** A negotiable certificate attached to a bond that represents a sum of interest due. **2a.** A redeemable certificate: *a food coupon.* **b.** A certificate that entitles the bearer to certain benefits, such as a cash refund. **3.** A printed form, as in an advertisement, to be used as an order blank. [Fr.]

cour•age (kûr'ĭj, kŭr'-) ►*n.* The quality of mind that enables one to face danger with self-possession, confidence, and resolution; bravery. [< OFr. *corage* < Lat. *cor*, heart.] —**cou•ra'geous** (kə-rā'jəs) *adj.* —**cou•ra'geous•ly** *adv.*

Cour•bet (ko͞or-bā', -bĕ'), **Gustave.** 1819–77. French painter.

cou•ri•er (ko͝or'ē-ər, kûr'-, kŭr'-) ►*n.* A messenger, esp. one on urgent or official business. [< OItal. *corriere*, runner.]

course (kôrs, kōrs) ►*n.* **1.** Onward movement in a particular direction. **2.** The route or path taken by something, such as a stream, that moves. **3.** Duration: *in the course of a year.* **4.** A mode of action or behavior. **5.** Regular development. **6a.** A body of prescribed studies constituting a curriculum. **b.** A unit of such a curriculum. **7.** A part of a meal served as a unit at one time. ►*v.* **coursed, cours•ing 1.** To move swiftly (through or over); traverse. **2.** To hunt (game) with hounds. —***idioms:*** **in due course** At the proper or right time. **of course** Without any doubt; certainly. [< Lat. *cursus* < p.part. of *currere*, run.]

cours•er (kôr'sər, kōr'-) ►*n.* A swift horse.

court (kôrt, kōrt) ►*n.* **1.** A courtyard. **2.** A short street. **3a.** A royal mansion or palace. **b.** The retinue of a sovereign. **c.** A sovereign's governing body, including ministers and advisers. **4a.** A person or persons whose task is to hear and submit a decision on legal cases. **b.** The place where such cases are heard. **c.** The regular session of a judicial assembly. **5.** An open, level area marked with appropriate lines, upon which a game, such as tennis or basketball, is played. ►*v.* **1.** To attempt to gain; seek. **2.** To behave so as to invite: *court disaster.* **3.** To woo. **4.** To attempt to gain the favor of by attention or flattery. —***idiom:*** **pay court to 1.** To flatter in an attempt to obtain something. **2.** To woo. [< Lat. *cohors.*]

cour•te•ous (kûr'tē-əs) ►*adj.* Graciously considerate of others. —**cour'te•ous•ly** *adv.* —**cour'te•ous•ness** *n.*

cour•te•san (kôr'tĭ-zən, kōr'-) ►*n.* A woman prostitute, esp. one whose clients are men of rank or wealth. [< OItal. *cortigiana* < *corte*, COURT.]

cour•te•sy (kûr'tĭ-sē) ►*n., pl.* **-sies 1a.** Polite behavior. **b.** A polite gesture or remark. **2.** Generosity, esp. as a sponsor. [< OFr. *courtesie.*]

court•house (kôrt'hous', kōrt'-) ►*n.* A building housing judicial courts.

court•i•er (kôr'tē-ər, -tyər, kōr'-) ►*n.* An attendant at a sovereign's court.

court•ly (kôrt'lē, kōrt'-) ►*adj.* **-li•er, -li•est.** Elegant in manners. —**court'li•ness** *n.*

court-mar•tial (kôrt'mär'shəl, kōrt'-) ►*n., pl.* **courts-mar•tial** (kôrts'-, kōrts'-) **1.** A military or naval court of officers appointed by a commander to try persons for offenses under military law. **2.** A trial by court-martial. —**court'-mar'tial** *v.*

court order ►*n.* An order issued by a court that requires a person to do or refrain from doing something.

court•room (kôrt'ro͞om', -ro͝om', kōrt'-) ►*n.* A room for court proceedings.

court•ship (kôrt'shĭp', kōrt'-) ►*n.* The act or period of courting or wooing.

court•yard (kôrt'yärd', kōrt'-) ►*n.* An open space surrounded by walls or buildings.

cous•cous (ko͞os'ko͞os') ►*n.* A pasta of North African origin made of crushed and steamed semolina. [< Ar. *kuskus.*]

cous•in (kŭz'ĭn) ►*n.* **1.** A child of one's aunt or uncle. **2.** A relative descended from a common ancestor. **3.** A member of a kindred group. [< Lat. *cōnsōbrīnus* : COM– + *sōbrīnus*, maternal cousin.]

cou•ture (ko͞o-to͝or') ►*n.* The business of designing, making, and selling highly fashionable clothing for women. [Fr., sewing < Lat. *cōnsuere*, sew together : COM– + *suere*, sew.]

cou•tu•rier (ko͞o-to͝or'ē-ər, -ē-ā') ►*n.* One who designs for or owns an establishment engaged in couture. [Fr.]

co•va•lent bond (kō-vā'lənt) ►*n.* A chemical bond formed by the sharing of one or more electrons between atoms.

cove (kōv) ►*n.* A small sheltered bay of a sea, river, or lake. [< OE *cofa*, cave.]

cov•en (kŭv'ən, kō'vən) ►*n.* An assembly of 13 witches. [Perh. < ME *covent*, CONVENT.]

cov•e•nant (kŭv'ə-nənt) ►*n.* A formal binding agreement; compact; contract. See Syns at **bargain.** ►*v.* To enter into a covenant (with). [< OFr. *convenir*, agree.] —**cov'e•nant•er** *n.*

Cov•en•try (kŭv'ĭn-trē) A city of central England ESE of Birmingham. Pop. 304,097.

cov•er (kŭv'ər) ►*v.* **1.** To place something upon, over, or in front of so as to protect, shut in, or conceal. **2.** To clothe. **3a.** To spread over the surface of: *Dust covered the table.* **b.** To extend over: *a farm covering 100 acres.* **4.** To hide or conceal: *covered up their mistakes.* **5.** To protect by insurance. **6.** To defray or meet the cost of. **7.** To deal with; treat of. **8.** To travel or pass over. **9.** To report the details of (an event or situation). **10.** To hold within the range and aim of a weapon, such as a firearm. **11.** To act as a substitute during someone's absence. ►*n.* **1.** Something that covers. **2.** Something that provides shelter. **3.** Something that screens, conceals, or disguises. **4.** A table setting for one person. **5.** An envelope or wrapper for mail. [< Lat. *cooperīre*, cover completely.]

cov•er•age (kŭv′ər-ĭj) ►*n.* **1.** The extent or degree to which something is observed, analyzed, and reported. **2.** The protection given by an insurance policy.

cov•er•alls (kŭv′ər-ôlz′) ►*pl.n.* A loose-fitting one-piece garment worn to protect clothes.

cover charge ►*n.* A fixed amount added to the bill at a nightclub, esp. for entertainment.

cover crop ►*n.* A crop, such as clover, planted to prevent soil erosion and provide humus or nitrogen when plowed under.

covered wagon (kŭv′ərd) ►*n.* A large wagon with an arched canvas top, used esp. by American pioneers for prairie travel.

cov•er•ing (kŭv′ər-ĭng) ►*n.* Something that covers, so as to protect or conceal.

cov•er•let (kŭv′ər-lĭt) ►*n.* A bedspread.

cov•ert (kŭv′ərt, kō′vərt, kō-vûrt′) ►*adj.* **1.** Concealed, hidden, or secret. **2.** Sheltered. ►*n.* **1.** A covered shelter or hiding place. **2.** Thick underbrush affording cover for game. [< OFr., covered.] —**cov′ert•ly** *adv.*

cov•er-up or **cov•er•up** (kŭv′ər-ŭp′) ►*n.* An effort or strategy designed to conceal something, such as a crime or scandal.

cov•et (kŭv′ĭt) ►*v.* **1.** To desire (that which is rightfully another's). **2.** To wish for longingly. See Syns at **desire.** [< OFr. *coveitier.*]

cov•et•ous (kŭv′ĭ-təs) ►*adj.* Excessively desirous of another's possessions. See Syns at **jealous.** —**cov′et•ous•ness** *n.*

cov•ey (kŭv′ē) ►*n.*, *pl.* **-eys.** A small flock or group, esp. of birds. [< OFr. *covee*, brood.]

cow[1] (kou) ►*n.* **1.** The mature female of cattle. **2.** The mature female of other large animals, such as whales or elephants. **3.** A domesticated bovine. [< OE *cū.*]

cow[2] (kou) ►*v.* To frighten with threats; intimidate. [Prob. of Scand. orig.]

cow•ard (kou′ərd) ►*n.* One who lacks courage in the face of danger, pain, or hardship. [< OFr. *coue*, tail.] —**cow′ard•ly** *adv.*

Coward, Sir **Noel Pierce.** 1899–1973. British actor, playwright, and composer.

cow•ard•ice (kou′ər-dĭs) ►*n.* Lack of courage or resoluteness.

cow•bird (kou′bûrd′) ►*n.* A blackbird that lays its eggs in other birds' nests.

cow•boy (kou′boi′) ►*n.* A hired man, esp. in the American West, who tends cattle, typically on horseback.

cow•catch•er (kou′kăch′ər, -kĕch′-) ►*n.* The metal frame projecting from the front of a locomotive and serving to clear the track of obstructions.

cow•er (kou′ər) ►*v.* To cringe in fear. [ME *couren*, of Scand. orig.]

cowcatcher

cow•girl (kou′gûrl′) ►*n.* A hired woman, esp. in the American West, who tends cattle, typically on horseback.

cow•hand (kou′hănd′) ►*n.* A cowboy or cowgirl.

cow•herd (kou′hûrd′) ►*n.* One who herds or tends cattle.

cow•hide (kou′hīd′) ►*n.* **1.** The hide of a cow. **2.** The leather made from this hide.

cowl (koul) ►*n.* **1.** The hood or hooded robe worn esp. by a monk. **2.** A draped neckline on a woman's garment. [< Lat. *cucullus*, hood.]

Cow•ley (kou′lē), **Abraham.** 1618–67. English metaphysical poet.

cow•lick (kou′lĭk′) ►*n.* A projecting tuft of hair on the head that will not lie flat.

cowl•ing (kou′lĭng) ►*n.* A removable metal covering esp. for an aircraft engine.

co•work•er (kō′wûr′kər) ►*n.* A colleague.

Cow•per (ko͞o′pər, kou′-, ko͝op′ər), **William.** 1731–1800. British poet.

cow•poke (kou′pōk′) ►*n.* A cowhand.

cow•pox (kou′pŏks′) ►*n.* A skin disease of cattle caused by a virus that is isolated and used to vaccinate humans against smallpox.

cow•punch•er (kou′pŭn′chər) ►*n.* A cowhand.

cow•rie or **cow•ry** (kou′rē) ►*n.*, *pl.* **-ries.** Any of various tropical marine gastropods having glossy, often brightly marked shells. [< Skt. *kapardikā*, small shell.]

cow•slip (kou′slĭp′) ►*n.* **1.** A Eurasian primrose having fragrant yellow flowers. **2.** See **marsh marigold.** [< OE *cūslyppe* : *cū*, cow + *slypa*, slime.]

cox•comb (kŏks′kōm′) ►*n.* A conceited dandy; fop. [ME *cokkes comb*, cock's comb.]

cox•swain (kŏk′sən, -swān′) ►*n.* **1.** One who steers a ship's boat. **2.** One who directs the crew of a racing shell. [ME *cokswaynne.*]

coy (koi) ►*adj.* **-er, -est 1.** Shy, esp. flirtatiously so. **2.** Annoyingly unforthcoming. [< Lat. *quiētus*, quiet.] —**coy′ly** *adv.* —**coy′ness** *n.*

coy•o•te (kī-ō′tē, kī′ōt′) ►*n.* A small wolflike predator native to W North America, now widely dispersed. [< Nahuatl *cóyotl.*]

coz•en (kŭz′ən) ►*v.* To deceive; cheat. [Perh. < ME *cosin*, trickery.]

co•zy also **co•sy** (kō′zē) ►*adj.* **-zi•er, -zi•est** also **-si•er, -si•est.** Snug, comfortable, and warm. ►*v.* **-zied, -zy•ing** also **-sied, -sy•ing** *Informal.* To ingratiate oneself: *cozy up to the* *boss.* ▸ *n., pl.* **-zies** also **-sies.** A padded insulating cover for a teapot. [Prob. of Scand. orig.] —**co′zi•ly** *adv.* —**co′zi•ness** *n.*

cp ▸ *abbr.* candlepower

CP ▸ *abbr.* **1.** command post **2.** Communist Party

cp. ▸ *abbr.* compare

CPA ▸ *abbr.* certified public accountant

cpd. ▸ *abbr.* compound

CPI ▸ *abbr.* consumer price index

CPO ▸ *abbr.* chief petty officer

CPR ▸ *abbr.* cardiopulmonary resuscitation

cps ▸ *abbr.* **1.** characters per second **2.** cycles per second

CPT ▸ *abbr.* captain

CPU ▸ *abbr.* central processing unit

Cr ▸ The symbol for the element **chromium.**

crab[1] (krăb) ▸ *n.* **1.** Any of various chiefly marine crustaceans having a broad flattened body with a shell-like covering. **2.** A horseshoe crab. **3.** A crab louse. [< OE *crabba.*]

crab[2] (krăb) ▸ *n.* A quarrelsome, ill-tempered person. [ME *crabbe.*] —**crab** *v.*

crab apple ▸ *n.* **1.** A tree with white, pink, or reddish flowers. **2.** The small tart applelike fruit of such a tree.

crab•bed (krăb′ĭd) ▸ *adj.* **1.** Irritable; ill-tempered. **2.** Difficult to read, as handwriting. [ME < *crabbe*, CRAB[1].] —**crab′bed•ly** *adv.* —**crab′bed•ness** *n.*

crab•by (krăb′ē) ▸ *adj.* **-bi•er, -bi•est.** Grouchy; ill-tempered. —**crab′bi•ly** *adv.* —**crab′bi•ness** *n.*

crab•grass (krăb′grăs′) ▸ *n.* A coarse spreading grass usu. considered a weed in lawns.

crab louse ▸ *n.* A body louse that infests the pubic region and causes severe itching.

crack (krăk) ▸ *v.* **1.** To break with a sharp snapping sound. **2.** To break without complete separation of parts. **3.** To change sharply in pitch or timbre, as the voice from emotion. **4.** To strike. **5.** To break open or into. **6.** To discover the solution to, esp. after great effort. **7.** *Informal* To tell (a joke). **8.** To reduce (petroleum) to simpler compounds. —***phrasal verbs:*** **crack down** *Informal* To become more severe or strict. **crack up** *Informal* **1.** To crash; collide. **2.** To have a mental or physical breakdown. **3.** To laugh or cause to laugh boisterously. ▸ *n.* **1.** A sharp snapping sound. **2a.** A partial split or break; fissure. **b.** A narrow space: *The window was open a crack.* **3.** A sharp resounding blow. **4.** A cracking of the voice. **5.** A try; chance: *gave him a crack at it.* **6.** A witty or sarcastic remark. **7.** *Slang* Chemically purified crystallized cocaine prepared for smoking. ▸ *adj.* Superior; first rate. [< OE *cracian.*]

crack•down (krăk′doun′) ▸ *n.* An act or instance of cracking down.

cracked (krăkt) ▸ *adj.* **1.** Broken without dividing into parts: *a cracked mirror.* **2.** *Informal* Crazy.

crack•er (krăk′ər) ▸ *n.* **1.** A thin crisp wafer or biscuit. **2.** A firecracker.

crack•er•jack (krăk′ər-jăk′) ▸ *adj. Slang* Of excellent quality. —**crack′er•jack′** *n.*

crack•le (krăk′əl) ▸ *v.* **-led, -ling 1.** To make or cause to make a succession of slight sharp snapping noises. **2.** To develop a network of fine cracks. [< CRACK.] —**crack′le** *n.* —**crack′ly** *adj.*

crack•pot (krăk′pŏt′) ▸ *n.* An eccentric or harebrained person.

crack•up (krăk′ŭp′) ▸ *n. Informal* **1.** A crash or collision, as of an automobile. **2.** A mental or physical breakdown.

Crac•ow (krăk′ou, krä′kou, -ko͞of) See **Kraków.**

–cracy ▸ *suff.* Government; rule: *technocracy.* [< Gk. *-kratia* < *kratos*, power.]

cra•dle (krād′l) ▸ *n.* **1.** A low bed for an infant, often with rockers. **2.** A place of origin. **3.** The part of a telephone on which the handset is supported. **4.** A supporting framework. ▸ *v.* **-dled, -dling.** To place gently in or as if in a cradle. [< OE *cradel.*]

cra•dle•board (krād′l-bôrd′, -bōrd′) ▸ *n.* A board or frame used by certain Native Americans as a portable cradle or to carry an infant on the back.

cradleboard

craft (krăft) ▸ *n.* **1.** Skill in doing or making something, as in the arts. See Syns at **art**[1]. **2.** Skill in evasion or deception; guile. **3a.** A trade, esp. one requiring skilled artistry. **b.** The membership of such a trade; guild. **4.** *pl.* **craft** A boat, ship, or aircraft. ▸ *v.* To make or devise, esp. with great care. [< OE *cræft.*] —**crafts′man** *n.* —**crafts′man•ship′** *n.* —**crafts′per′son** *n.* —**crafts′wom′an** *n.*

craft•y (krăf′tē) ▸ *adj.* **-i•er, -i•est.** Marked by underhandedness, deviousness, or deception. —**craft′i•ly** *adv.* —**craft′i•ness** *n.*

crag (krăg) ▸ *n.* A steeply projecting mass of rock. [ME, of Celt. orig.] —**crag′gy** *adj.*

crag
Black Crag, Lake District, England

cram (krăm) ►*v.* **crammed, cram•ming 1.** To squeeze into an insufficient space; stuff. **2.** To fill too tightly. **3.** To gorge with food. **4.** *Informal* To study intensively just before an examination. [< OE *crammian.*]

cramp[1] (krămp) ►*n.* **1.** A sudden painful involuntary muscular contraction. **2.** A temporary partial paralysis of habitually or excessively used muscles. **3. cramps** Sharp persistent abdominal pains. ►*v.* To be affected with or as if with a cramp. [< OFr. *crampe*, of Gmc. orig.]

cramp[2] (krămp) ►*n.* Something that confines or restricts. ►*v.* **1.** To restrict; hamper. **2.** To jam (a wheel) by a short turn. [Prob. MDu. *crampe*, hook.]

cram•pon (krăm′pŏn′, -pən) ►*n.* An iron spike attached to the shoe to prevent slipping on ice. [< OFr., of Gmc. orig.]

cran•ber•ry (krăn′bĕr′ē) ►*n.* A mat-forming, evergreen shrub of E North America, bearing tart red edible berries and used in jellies and relishes. [< LGer. *Kraanbere.*]

crane (krān) ►*n.* **1.** A large wading bird having a long neck, long legs, and a long bill. **2.** A machine for hoisting heavy objects. ►*v.* **craned, cran•ing.** To stretch (one's neck) for a better view. [< OE *cran.*]

Crane, (Harold) Hart. 1899–1932. Amer. poet.

Crane, Stephen. 1871–1900. Amer. writer.

cra•ni•um (krā′nē-əm) ►*n., pl.* **-ni•ums** or **-ni•a** (-nē-ə) **1.** The skull of a vertebrate. **2.** The portion of the skull enclosing the brain. [< Gk. *kranion.*] —**cra′ni•al** *adj.*

crank (krăngk) ►*n.* **1.** A device for transmitting rotary motion, consisting of a handle attached at right angles to a shaft. **2.** *Informal* **a.** A grouchy person. **b.** An eccentric person. ►*v.* To start or operate by turning a crank. —***phrasal verb:* crank out** To produce rapidly and mechanically. [< OE **cranc.*]

crank•case (krăngk′kās′) ►*n.* The metal case enclosing a crankshaft.

crank•shaft (krăngk′shăft′) ►*n.* A shaft that turns or is turned by a crank.

crank•y (krăng′kē) ►*adj.* **-i•er, -i•est 1.** Ill-tempered; peevish. **2.** Eccentric; odd. **3.** Working or operating unpredictably.

Cran•mer (krăn′mər), **Thomas.** 1489–1556. English archbishop of Canterbury (1533–53).

cran•ny (krăn′ē) ►*n., pl.* **-nies.** A small opening, as in a wall; crevice. [Perh. < OFr. *cran*, notch.]

crap (krăp) ►*n. Slang* **1.** Nonsense; bunk. **2.** Worthless or shoddy material or work. **3.** Junk; clutter. **4.** Insolent talk or behavior. [< ME *crappe*, chaff.]

crape (krāp) ►*n.* **1.** See **crepe** 1. **2.** A black band worn as a sign of mourning. [Alteration of Fr. *crêpe.* See CREPE.]

crap•pie (krŏp′ē) ►*n., pl.* **-pies.** Either of two edible North American sunfishes. [Canadian Fr. *crapet.*]

craps (krăps) ►*pl.n. (takes sing. or pl. v.)* A gambling game played with two dice. [Louisiana Fr.]

crap•shoot (krăp′sho͞ot′) ►*n. Slang* A risky enterprise.

crap•shoot•er (krăp′sho͞o′tər) ►*n.* One who plays craps.

crash (krăsh) ►*v.* **1.** To fall or collide violently or noisily. **2.** To make a sudden loud noise. **3.** To fail suddenly, as a market or computer. **4.** To cause to collide or fail. **5.** *Informal* To join or enter uninvited: *crash a party.* ►*n.* **1.** A sudden loud noise. **2.** A wreck or collision. **3.** A sudden economic or business failure. **4.** *Comp. Sci.* A sudden failure of a hard drive, program, or operating system. ►*adj. Informal* All-out: *a crash diet.* [ME *crasshen.*]

crash-land (krăsh′lănd′) ►*v.* To land and usu. damage an aircraft or spacecraft under emergency conditions. —**crash landing** *n.*

crass (krăs) ►*adj.* **-er, -est.** Crude and undiscriminating; coarse. [Lat. *crassus*, dense.] —**crass′ly** *adv.* —**crass′ness** *n.*

-crat ►*suff.* A participant in or supporter of a specified form of government: *technocrat.* [< Gk. *-kratēs*, ruler < *kratos*, power.]

crate (krāt) ►*n.* An often slatted wooden shipping box. ►*v.* **crat•ed, crat•ing.** To pack into a crate. [Lat. *crātis*, wickerwork.]

cra•ter (krā′tər) ►*n.* **1.** A bowl-shaped depression at the mouth of a volcano. **2.** A depression or pit made by an explosion or impact. [< Gk. *kratēr*, mixing vessel.] —**cra′ter** *v.*

Crater Lake. A lake of SW OR in a volcanic crater of the Cascade Range.

cra•ton (krā′tŏn′) ►*n.* A large portion of a continental plate that has been relatively undisturbed since the Precambrian Era.

cra•vat (krə-văt′) ►*n.* A necktie. [Fr. *cravate.*]

crave (krāv) ►*v.* **craved, crav•ing 1.** To want intensely. See Syns at **desire. 2.** To beg earnestly for; implore. [< OE *crafian*, beg.]

cra•ven (krā′vən) ►*adj.* Cowardly. [ME *cravant.*] —**cra′ven•ly** *adv.* —**cra′ven•ness** *n.*

crav•ing (krā′vĭng) ►*n.* A consuming desire.

craw (krô) ►*n.* The crop of a bird or stomach of an animal. [ME *crawe.*]

craw•dad (krô′dăd′) ►*n. Regional* See **crayfish.** [Prob. alteration of *crawfish*, crayfish.]

crawl (krôl) ►*v.* **1.** To move slowly by dragging the body along the ground. **2.** To advance slowly or feebly. **3.** To be or feel as if covered with moving things. See Syns at **teem.** ►*n.* **1.** A very slow pace. **2.** A rapid swimming style with alternating overarm strokes. [< ON *krafla.*] —**crawl′er** *n.* —**crawl′y** *adj.*

cray•fish (krā′fĭsh′) also **craw•fish** (krô′-) ►*n., pl.* **-fish** or **-fish•es.** A small freshwater lobsterlike crustacean. [< OFr. *crevice*, of Gmc. orig.]

cray•on (krā′ŏn′, -ən) ►*n.* A stick of colored wax, charcoal, or chalk, used for drawing. [Fr. < Lat. *crēta*, chalk.] —**cray′on′** *v.*

craze (krāz) ►*v.* **crazed, craz•ing.** To drive insane. ►*n.* A fad. [ME *crasen*, shatter.]

cra•zy (krā′zē) ►*adj.* **-zi•er, -zi•est 1.** Mentally unbalanced; insane. **2.** *Informal* Departing from proportion or moderation. —**cra′zi•ly** *adv.* —**cra′zi•ness** *n.*

Crazy Horse. 1849?–77. Sioux leader.

crazy quilt ►*n.* A patchwork quilt with irregular pieces of cloth arranged haphazardly.

creak (krēk) ►*v.* To make or move with a squeaking sound. ►*n.* A grating or squeaking sound. [ME *creken.*] —**creak′i•ly** *adv.* —**creak′i•ness** *n.* —**creak′y** *adj.*

cream (krēm) ►*n.* **1.** The yellowish fatty part of milk. **2.** A yellowish white. **3.** The choicest part. ►*v.* **1.** To beat into a creamy consistency. **2.** To prepare in a cream sauce. **3.** *Slang* To defeat overwhelmingly. [< OFr. *craime.*]

—**cream′i•ness** *n.* —**cream′y** *adj.*

cream cheese ►*n.* A soft white cheese made of cream and milk.

cream•er (krē′mər) ►*n.* **1.** A small pitcher for cream. **2.** A substitute for cream.

cream•er•y (krē′mə-rē) ►*n., pl.* **-ies.** An establishment where dairy products are prepared or sold.

cream puff ►*n.* **1.** A light pastry filled with whipped cream or custard. **2.** *Slang* A weakling.

cream sauce ►*n.* A white sauce made by mixing flour and butter with milk or cream.

crease (krēs) ►*n.* A line made by pressing, folding, or wrinkling. [Perh. < ME *creste,* ridge. See CREST.] —**crease** *v.* —**crease′less** *adj.* —**crease′proof′** *adj.*

cre•ate (krē-āt′) ►*v.* **-at•ed, -at•ing 1.** To cause to exist. See Syns at **found**[1]. **2.** To cause; produce. [< Lat. *creāre.*]

cre•a•tion (krē-ā′shən) ►*n.* **1.** The act of creating. **2.** A product of invention or imagination. **3.** The world and all things in it. **4. Creation** In various religions, the divine act by which the world was created.

cre•a•tion•ism (krē-ā′shə-nĭz′əm) ►*n.* Belief in the literal interpretation of the account of the Creation in the Bible. —**cre•a′tion•ist** *n.*

cre•a•tive (krē-ā′tĭv) ►*adj.* Characterized by originality; imaginative. —**cre•a′tive•ly** *adv.* —**cre′a•tiv′i•ty, cre•a′tive•ness** *n.*

cre•a•tor (krē-ā′tər) ►*n.* One that creates.

crea•ture (krē′chər) ►*n.* **1.** A living being, esp. an animal. **2.** A human.

crèche (krĕsh) ►*n.* A representation of the Nativity. [< OFr. *cresche,* crib, of Gmc. orig.]

cre•dence (krēd′ns) ►*n.* Acceptance as true; belief. See Syns at **belief.** [< Lat. *crēdere,* believe.]

cre•den•tial (krĭ-dĕn′shəl) ►*n.* **1.** Something that entitles one to confidence or authority. **2. credentials** Evidence concerning one's authority. [< Med.Lat. *crēdentia,* trust, authority. See CREDENCE.]

cre•den•za (krĭ-dĕn′zə) ►*n.* A buffet or sideboard, esp. one without legs. [Ital. < Med.Lat. *crēdentia,* trust. See CREDENCE.]

cred•i•ble (krĕd′ə-bəl) ►*adj.* **1.** Believable. See Syns at **plausible. 2.** Trustworthy; reliable. [< Lat. *crēdere,* believe.] —**cred′i•bil′i•ty** *n.* —**cred′i•bly** *adv.*

cred•it (krĕd′ĭt) ►*n.* **1.** Confidence in the truth of something. See Syns at **belief. 2.** The quality of being trustworthy. **3.** A source of honor: *a credit to her family.* **4.** Approval; praise. **5.** often **credits** An acknowledgment of work done, as in a motion picture. **6.** Certification of completion of a course of study. **7.** Reputation for solvency and integrity. **8.** An arrangement for deferred payment of a loan or purchase. **9.** *Accounting* Deduction of a payment made by a debtor from an amount due. **10.** The amount remaining in a person's account. ►*v.* **1.** To believe in; trust. **2.** To ascribe to; attribute. **3.** To give credit to. [< Lat. *crēditum,* a loan < *crēdere,* believe.]

cred•it•a•ble (krĕd′ĭ-tə-bəl) ►*adj.* Deserving of commendation. —**cred′it•a•bly** *adv.*

credit card ►*n.* A card authorizing the holder to buy goods or services on credit.

cred•i•tor (krĕd′ĭ-tər) ►*n.* One to whom money is owed.

credit union ►*n.* A cooperative organization that makes low-interest loans to its members.

cre•do (krē′dō, krā′-) ►*n., pl.* **-dos.** A creed. [< Lat. *crēdō,* I believe < *crēdere,* believe.]

cred•u•lous (krĕj′ə-ləs) ►*adj.* Disposed to believe too readily; gullible. [< Lat. *crēdulus* < *crēdere,* believe.] —**cre•du′li•ty** (krĭ-dōō′lĭ-tē, -dyōō′-) *n.* —**cred′u•lous•ly** *adv.* —**cred′u•lous•ness** *n.*

Cree (krē) ►*n., pl.* **Cree** or **Crees 1.** A member of a Native American people formerly of central Canada, now living from E Canada to Alberta. **2.** Their Algonquian language.

creed (krēd) ►*n.* A formal statement of religious belief. [< OE *crēda* < Lat. *crēdō,* I believe. See CREDO.]

creek (krēk, krĭk) ►*n.* A small stream, often a tributary to a river. See Regional Note at **run.** —***idiom:* up the creek** *Informal* In a difficult position. [Prob. < ON *kriki,* bend.]

Creek (krēk) ►*n., pl.* **Creek** or **Creeks 1a.** A member of a Native American people formerly of Alabama, Georgia, and NW Florida, now chiefly in Oklahoma. **b.** The Muskogean language of the Creek. **2.** A member of a confederacy of the Creek and various smaller tribes.

creel (krēl) ►*n.* A wicker basket used to carry fish. [< Lat. *crātīcula,* fine wattle.]

creep (krēp) ►*v.* **crept** (krĕpt), **creep•ing 1.** To move with the body close to the ground. **2.** To move stealthily or slowly. **3.** *Bot.* To grow along a surface, as a vine. **4.** To have a tingling sensation. ►*n.* **1.** The act of creeping. **2.** *Slang* An annoying or repulsive person. **3. creeps** *Informal* A sensation of fear or repugnance. [< OE *crēopan.*]

creep•er (krē′pər) ►*n.* A plant that spreads by means of stems that creep.

creep•y (krē′pē) ►*adj.* **-i•er, -i•est** *Informal* **1.** Inducing a sensation of uneasiness or fear, as of things crawling on one's skin. **2.** Annoyingly unpleasant. —**creep′i•ness** *n.*

cre•mate (krē′māt′, krĭ-māt′) ►*v.* **-mat•ed, -mat•ing.** To incinerate (a corpse). [Lat. *cremāre.*] —**cre•ma′tion** *n.*

cre•ma•to•ri•um (krē′mə-tôr′ē-əm, -tōr′-) ►*n., pl.* **-to•ri•ums** or **-to•ri•a** (-tôr′ē-ə, -tōr′-). A furnace or establishment for the incineration of corpses.

cre•ma•to•ry (krē′mə-tôr′ē, -tōr′ē, krĕm′ə-) ►*n., pl.* **-ries.** A crematorium.

crème car•a•mel (krĕm′ kăr′ə-mĕl′) ►*n.* A custard baked in a caramel-lined mold. [Fr.]

cren•e•lat•ed also **cren•el•lat•ed** (krĕn′ə-lā′tĭd) ►*adj.* Having battlements. [< OFr. *crenel,* notch.] —**cren′e•la′tion** *n.*

cren•shaw (krĕn′shô′) ►*n.* A winter melon with a greenish rind and pink flesh. [?]

Cre•ole (krē′ōl′) ►*n.* **1.** A person of European descent born in the West Indies or Spanish America. **2a.** A person descended from the original French settlers of Louisiana. **b.** The French dialect of these people. **3.** often **creole** A person of mixed Black and European, esp. French or Spanish descent. **4. creole** A pidgin that has developed and become the native language of its users. ►*adj.* **creole** Cooked with a spicy sauce containing tomatoes, onions, and peppers. [< Port. *crioulo,* of the household.]

cre•o•sote (krē′ə-sōt′) ►*n.* An oily liquid obtained from coal tar and used as a wood preservative and disinfectant. [Ger. *Kreosot.*]

crepe also **crêpe** (krāp) ►*n.* **1.** A thin crinkled fabric of silk, cotton, wool, or other fiber. **2.** See **crape** 2. **3.** Crepe paper. **4.** (*also* krĕp). A thin small pancake. [< OFr. *crespe*, curly < Lat. *crīspus*.]

crepe paper ►*n.* Crinkled tissue paper, used for decorations.

crept (krĕpt) ►*v.* P.t. and p.part. of **creep.**

cre•pus•cu•lar (krĭ-pŭs′kyə-lər) ►*adj.* **1.** Of or like twilight. **2.** *Zool.* Active at twilight. [< Lat. *crepusculum*, twilight.]

cres•cen•do (krə-shĕn′dō) ►*n.*, *pl.* **-dos 1.** *Mus.* A gradual increase in the volume of sound. **2.** A steady increase in intensity or force. [Ital. < Lat. *crēscere*, increase.] —**cres•cen′do** *adj. & adv.*

cres•cent (krĕs′ənt) ►*n.* **1.** The figure of the moon in its first or last quarter, with concave and convex edges terminating in points. **2.** Something shaped like a crescent. ►*adj.* Crescent-shaped. [< AN *cressaunt* < Lat. *crēscere*, increase.]

cress (krĕs) ►*n.* Any of several related plants with pungent leaves, often used in salads. [< OE *cœrse, cresse*.]

crest (krĕst) ►*n.* **1.** A tuft or similar projection on the head of a bird or other animal. **2.** *Her.* A device placed above the shield on a coat of arms. **3.** The top, as of a hill or wave. ►*v.* **1.** To form into a crest. **2.** To reach the crest (of). [< Lat. *crista*.]

crest•fall•en (krĕst′fô′lən) ►*adj.* Dispirited; dejected.

Cre•ta•ceous (krĭ-tā′shəs) *Geol.* ►*adj.* Of or being the 3rd and last period of the Mesozoic Era, marked by the development of flowering plants and the disappearance of dinosaurs. ►*n.* The Cretaceous Period. [< Lat. *crēta*, chalk.]

Crete (krēt) An island of SE Greece in the E Mediterranean Sea. —**Cre′tan** *adj. & n.*

cre•tin (krēt′n) ►*n.* A person afflicted with cretinism. [< VLat. **christiānus*, Christian.] —**cre′tin•oid′** *adj.*

cre•tin•ism (krēt′n-ĭz′əm) ►*n.* A thyroid deficiency resulting in dwarfed stature and mental retardation.

cre•tonne (krĭ-tŏn′, krē′tŏn′) ►*n.* A heavy unglazed cotton or linen fabric used for draperies and slipcovers. [From *Creton*, France.]

cre•vasse (krĭ-văs′) ►*n.* **1.** A deep fissure, as in a glacier. **2.** A crack in a levee. [< OFr. *crevace*, CREVICE.]

crevasse

crev•ice (krĕv′ĭs) ►*n.* A narrow crack. [< OFr. *crevace* < Lat. *crepāre*, to crack.]

crew¹ (kro͞o) ►*n.* **1.** A group of people working together. **2.** All personnel operating a boat, ship, or aircraft. **3.** A team of rowers. [ME *creue*, military reinforcement.]

crew² (kro͞o) ►*v. Chiefly Brit.* P.t. of **crow².**

crew•cut or **crew cut** (kro͞o′kŭt′) ►*n.* A closely cropped haircut.

crewed (kro͞od) ►*adj.* Operated by an onboard crew: *a crewed space flight.*

crew•el (kro͞o′əl) ►*n.* Loosely twisted worsted yarn used for embroidery. [ME *crule*.]

crew•mate (kro͞o′māt′) ►*n.* A fellow member of a crew.

crew neck ►*n.* A round, close-fitting neckline.

crib (krĭb) ►*n.* **1.** A child's bed with high sides. **2.** A small building for storing corn. **3.** A rack or trough for fodder. **4a.** A petty theft. **b.** Plagiarism. **c.** See **pony** 2. ►*v.* **cribbed, crib•bing 1.** To confine in or as if in a crib. **2.** To plagiarize. **3.** To steal. [< OE *cribb*, manger.] —**crib′ber** *n.*

crib•bage (krĭb′ĭj) ►*n.* A card game scored by inserting pegs into holes on a board. [< CRIB.]

crib death ►*n.* See **sudden infant death syndrome.**

crick¹ (krĭk) ►*n.* A painful cramp, as in the neck. [ME *crike*.]

crick² (krĭk) ►*n. Regional* A creek. See Regional Note at **run.**

crick•et¹ (krĭk′ĭt) ►*n.* A leaping insect, the male of which produces a shrill chirping sound. [< OFr. *criquet* < *criquer*, to click.]

crick•et² (krĭk′ĭt) ►*n.* A game played with bats, a ball, and wickets by two teams of 11 players each. [Poss. < OFr. *criquet*, target stick in a bowling game.] —**crick′et•er, crick′et•eer′** (-ĭ-tîr′) *n.*

cri•er (krī′ər) ►*n.* One who shouts out public announcements.

crime (krīm) ►*n.* **1.** An act committed or omitted in violation of a law. **2.** An unjust or senseless act. [< Lat. *crīmen*.]

Cri•me•a (krī-mē′ə, krĭ-) A region and peninsula of S Ukraine on the Black Sea and Sea of Azov. —**Cri•me′an** *adj.*

crim•i•nal (krĭm′ə-nəl) ►*adj.* **1.** Of or involving crime. **2.** Guilty of crime. ►*n.* One who has committed a crime. —**crim′i•nal′i•ty** (-năl′ĭ-tē) *n.* —**crim′i•nal•ly** *adv.*

crim•i•nal•ist (krĭm′ə-nə-lĭst) ►*n.* A specialist in the collection and examination of the physical evidence of crime.

crim•i•nal•ize (krĭm′ə-nə-līz′) ►*v.* **-ized, -iz•ing.** To make criminal; outlaw. —**crim′i•nal•i•za′tion** *n.*

crim•i•nol•o•gy (krĭm′ə-nŏl′ə-jē) ►*n.* The scientific study of crime and criminals. —**crim′i•no•log′i•cal** (-nə-lŏj′ĭ-kəl) *adj.* —**crim′i•no•log′i•cal•ly** *adv.* —**crim′i•nol′o•gist** *n.*

crimp (krĭmp) ►*v.* **1.** To press or pinch into small folds or ridges. **2.** To curl (hair). **3.** To have a hampering or obstructive effect on. ►*n.* **1.** The act of crimping. **2.** An obstructing agent or force. [Du. or LGer. *krimpen*.] —**crimp′er** *n.*

crim•son (krĭm′zən) ►*n.* A vivid purplish red. [< Ar. *qirmizī*.] —**crim′son** *adj. & v.*

cringe (krĭnj) ►*v.* **cringed, cring•ing 1.** To shrink back, as in fear; cower. **2.** To fawn. [ME *crengen*.] —**cringe** *n.*

crin•kle (krĭng′kəl) ►*v.* **-kled, -kling.** To form

wrinkles or ripples. [< ME *crinkled*, wrinkled.] —**crin′kle** *n.* —**crin′kly** *adj.*

crin•o•line (krĭn′ə-lĭn) ►*n.* **1.** A stiff fabric used to line garments. **2.** A petticoat made of this fabric. [Fr. < Ital. *crinolino*.]

crip•ple (krĭp′əl) ►*n.* One that is partially disabled or lame. ►*v.* **-pled, -pling.** To disable or damage. [< OE *crypel*.]

cri•sis (krī′sĭs) ►*n., pl.* **-ses** (-sēz) **1.** A crucial point or situation; turning point. **2.** A sudden change in a disease or fever toward improvement or deterioration. [< Gk. *krisis* < *krinein*, to separate.]

Syns: *crisis, crossroad, exigency, head, juncture, pass* **n.**

crisp (krĭsp) ►*adj.* **-er, -est 1.** Firm but easily broken; brittle. **2.** Firm and fresh: *crisp celery.* **3.** Bracing; invigorating. **4.** Clear and concise: *a crisp reply.* [< OE *curly* < Lat. *crīspus*.] —**crisp** *v.* —**crisp′ly** *adv.* —**crisp′ness** *n.* —**crisp′•y** *adj.*

criss•cross (krĭs′krôs′, -krŏs′) ►*v.* **1.** To mark with crossing lines. **2.** To move back and forth through or over. ►*n.* A pattern of crossing lines. [< ME *Crist crosse*, mark of a cross.] —**criss′cross′** *adj. & adv.*

cri•te•ri•on (krī-tîr′ē-ən) ►*n., pl.* **-te•ri•a** (-tîr′ē-ə) or **-te•ri•ons.** A standard or test on which a judgment can be based. See Syns at **standard.** [Gk. *kritērion*.]

Usage: Like the analogous etymological plurals *agenda* and *data, criteria* is widely used as a singular form. Unlike them, however, it is not yet acceptable in that use.

crit•ic (krĭt′ĭk) ►*n.* **1.** One who analyzes, interprets, or evaluates artistic works. **2.** A faultfinder. [< Gk. *kritikos*, able to discern < *krinein*, to separate.]

crit•i•cal (krĭt′ĭ-kəl) ►*adj.* **1.** Inclined to judge severely. **2.** Marked by careful evaluation. **3.** Of or relating to critics or criticism. **4.** Of or forming a crisis: *a critical food shortage.* **5.** Crucial; decisive. —**crit′i•cal•ly** *adv.*

crit•i•cism (krĭt′ĭ-sĭz′əm) ►*n.* **1.** The act of criticizing, esp. adversely. **2.** A critical comment or judgment. **3.** The practice of analyzing, interpreting, or evaluating artistic works. **4.** A critical essay; critique.

crit•i•cize (krĭt′ĭ-sīz′) ►*v.* **-cized, -ciz•ing 1.** To find fault with. **2.** To judge the merits and faults of; evaluate. —**crit′i•ciz′er** *n.*

cri•tique (krĭ-tēk′) ►*n.* A critical review or commentary. [Fr.] —**cri•tique′** *v.*

crit•ter (krĭt′ər) ►*n.* *Regional* A creature, esp. a domestic animal. [< CREATURE.]

croak (krōk) ►*n.* A low hoarse sound, as that of a frog. ►*v.* **1.** To utter a croak. **2.** *Slang* To die. [< ME *croken*, to croak.]

Cro•at (krō′ăt′, -ät′, krōt) ►*n.* **1.** A native or inhabitant of Croatia. **2.** Serbo-Croatian as used by the Croats.

Cro•a•tia (krō-ā′shə, -shē-ə) A country of SE Europe along the NE Adriatic coast; declared independence in Jun. 1991. Cap. Zagreb. Pop. 4,396,397.

Cro•a•tian (krō-ā′shən) ►*n.* See **Croat.** ►*adj.* Of or relating to Croatia or the Croats.

Cro•ce (krō′chĕ), **Benedetto.** 1866–1952. Italian philosopher, historian, and critic.

cro•chet (krō-shā′) ►*v.* **-cheted** (-shād′), **-chet•ing** (-shā′ĭng). To make (a piece of needlework) by looping thread with a hooked needle. ►*n.* Needlework made by crocheting. [< OFr., hook.]

crock (krŏk) ►*n.* An earthenware vessel. [< OE *crocc*.]

crocked (krŏkt) ►*adj.* *Slang* Drunk. [Perh. < *crock*, worn-out old nag.]

crock•er•y (krŏk′ə-rē) ►*n.* Earthenware.

Crock•ett (krŏk′ĭt), **David.** "Davy." 1786–1836. Amer. pioneer and politician.

croc•o•dile (krŏk′ə-dīl′) ► *n.* **1.** A large tropical aquatic reptile with armorlike skin and long tapering jaws. **2.** A similar or related reptile, such as a caiman. —**croc′o•dil′i•an** (krŏk′ə-dĭl′ē-ən, -dĭl′yən) *adj. & n.*

crocodile tears ►*pl.n.* An insincere display of grief.

cro•cus (krō′kəs) ►*n., pl.* **-cus•es** or **-ci** (-sī, -kī). A garden plant with showy, variously colored flowers. [< Gk. *krokos*.]

Croe•sus (krē′səs). d. c. 546 B.C. Last king of Lydia (560–546).

Crohn's disease (krōnz) ►*n.* A form of ileitis marked by abdominal pain, ulceration, and fibrous tissue buildup. [After Burrill Bernard *Crohn* (1884–1983).]

crois•sant (krwä-säɴ′, krə-sänt′) ►*n.* A rich, crescent-shaped roll. [< OFr. *creissant*, CRESCENT.]

Cro-Mag•non (krō-măg′nən, -măn′yən) ►*n.* An early form of modern human of Europe in the late Paleolithic Era. [After *Cro-Magnon* cave, France.] —**Cro-Mag′non** *adj.*

Crom•well (krŏm′wĕl′, -wəl, krŭm′-), **Oliver.** 1599–1658. English military, political, and religious leader. —**Crom•well′i•an** *adj.*

crone (krōn) ►*n.* **1.** An old woman. **2.** A hag. [< VLat. **carōnia*, CARRION.]

cro•ny (krō′nē) ►*n., pl.* **-nies.** A close friend or companion. [Perh. < Gk. *khronios*, long-lasting < *khronos*, time.]

cro•ny•ism (krō′nē-ĭz′əm) ►*n.* Favoritism shown to old friends without regard for their qualifications.

crook (kro͝ok) ►*n.* **1.** A bent or curved implement, such as a staff. **2.** A curve or bend. **3.** *Informal* A thief; swindler. ►*v.* To curve or bend. [< ON *krōkr*.]

crook•ed (kro͝ok′ĭd) ►*adj.* **1.** Having bends or curves. **2.** *Informal* Dishonest; fraudulent. —**crook′ed•ly** *adv.* —**crook′ed•ness** *n.*

croon (kro͞on) ►*v.* To hum or sing softly. [< MDu. *krōnen*, to lament.] —**croon** *n.* —**croon′er** *n.*

crop (krŏp) ►*n.* **1a.** Agricultural produce. **b.** The total yield of such produce. **2.** A group. **3.** A short haircut. **4a.** A short riding whip. **b.** The stock of a whip. **5.** *Zool.* A pouchlike enlargement of a bird's gullet in which food is digested or stored. ►*v.* **cropped, crop•ping 1.** To cut or bite off the tops of. **2.** To cut very short. **3.** To trim. —***phrasal verb:*** **crop up** To appear unexpectedly. [< OE *cropp*, ear of grain.]

crop-dust•ing (krŏp′dŭs′tĭng) ►*n.* The process of spraying crops with insecticides from an airplane. —**crop′-dust′** *v.*

crop•per (krŏp′ər) ►*n.* A sharecropper.

cro•quet (krō-kā′) ►*n.* An outdoor game in which players drive wooden balls through wickets using mallets. [< ONFr., crook.]

cro•quette (krō-kĕt′) ►*n.* A small cake of minced food usu. fried in deep fat. [Fr.]

cro•sier or **cro•zier** (krō′zhər) ►*n.* A crooked

staff, esp. of a bishop. [< OFr. *crosse*.]

crosier

cross (krôs, krŏs) ►*n.* **1.** An upright post with a transverse piece near the top. **2a.** often **Cross** A symbolic representation of the structure on which Jesus was crucified. **b.** Any of various modifications of the cross design. **3.** A trial or affliction. See Syns at **burden¹**. **4.** A pattern formed by the intersection of two lines. **5.** *Biol.* **a.** A hybrid plant or animal. **b.** A hybridization. ►*v.* **1.** To go or extend across. **2.** To intersect. **3.** To draw a line across. **4.** To place crosswise. **5.** To encounter in passing. **6.** To thwart or obstruct. **7.** *Biol.* To breed by hybridizing. ►*adj.* **1.** Lying crosswise. **2.** Contrary or opposing. **3.** Showing ill humor; annoyed. **4.** Hybrid. [< Lat. *crux*.] —**cross′ly** *adv.* —**cross′ness** *n.*

cross
left to right: Maltese, Calvary, and St. Andrew's crosses

cross•bar (krôs′bär′, krŏs′-) ►*n.* A horizontal bar or line.

cross•bones (krôs′bōnz′, krŏs′-) ►*pl.n.* Two bones placed crosswise, usu. under a skull.

cross•bow (krôs′bō′, krŏs′-) ►*n.* A weapon consisting of a bow fixed crosswise on a wooden stock.

cross•breed (krôs′brēd′, krŏs′-) ►*v.* To hybridize. ►*n.* A hybrid.

cross-coun•try (krôs′kŭn′trē, krŏs′-) ►*adj.* **1.** Moving across open country rather than roads. **2.** From one side of a country to the opposite side. —**cross′-coun′try** *adv.*

cross-country skiing ►*n.* The sport of skiing over the countryside rather than downhill.

cross-cul•tur•al (krôs′kŭl′chər-əl, krŏs′-) ►*adj.* Comparing or dealing with different cultures. —**cross′-cul′tur•al•ly** *adv.*

cross•cur•rent (krôs′kûr′ənt, -kŭr′-, krŏs′-) ►*n.* **1.** A current flowing across another. **2.** A conflicting tendency.

cross•cut (krôs′kŭt′, krŏs′-) ►*v.* To cut or run crosswise. ►*adj.* **1.** Used for cutting crosswise. **2.** Cut across the grain.

cross-dress (krôs′drĕs′, krŏs′-) ►*v.* To dress in the clothing characteristic of the opposite sex. —**cross′-dress′er** *n.*

cross-ex•am•ine (krôs′ĭg-zăm′ĭn, krŏs′-) ►*v.* To question (a person) closely, esp. with regard to answers or information given previously. —**cross′-ex•am′i•na′tion** *n.*

cross-eye (krôs′ī′, krŏs′ī′) ►*n.* A form of strabismus in which one or both eyes deviate toward the nose. —**cross′-eyed′** *adj.*

cross•fire (krôs′fīr′, krŏs′-) ►*n.* **1.** Lines of gunfire crossing each other. **2.** Rapid, heated discussion.

cross•hatch (krôs′hăch′, krŏs′-) ►*v.* To shade (e.g., a drawing) with sets of intersecting parallel lines. —**cross′hatch•ing** *n.*

cross•ing (krô′sĭng, krŏs′ĭng) ►*n.* **1.** An intersection, as of roads. **2.** A place at which something, as a river, may be crossed.

cross•piece (krôs′pēs′, krŏs′-) ►*n.* A transverse or horizontal piece, as of a structure.

cross-pol•li•nate (krôs′pŏl′ə-nāt′, krŏs′-) ►*v.* To fertilize (a flower) with pollen from another. —**cross′pol′li•na′tion** *n.*

cross-pur•pose (krôs′pûr′pəs, krŏs′-) ►*n.* A conflicting or contrary purpose. —***idiom:* at cross-purposes** Acting under a misunderstanding of each other's purposes.

cross-ques•tion (krôs′kwĕs′chən, krŏs′-) ►*v.* To cross-examine. —**cross′ques′tion** *n.*

cross-ref•er•ence (krôs′rĕf′ər-əns, -rĕf′rəns, krŏs′-) ►*n.* A reference from one part of a book or file to another part containing related information. —**cross′re•fer′** *v.*

cross•road (krôs′rōd′, krŏs′-) ►*n.* **1.** A road that intersects another. **2.** **crossroads** *(takes sing. v.)* A place where two or more roads meet. **3.** A crucial point. See Syns at **crisis.**

cross section ►*n.* **1a.** A section formed by a plane cutting through an object, usu. at right angles to an axis. **b.** A piece so cut or a graphic representation of it. **2.** A sample meant to be representative of the whole.

cross-train (krôs′trān′, krŏs′-) ►*v.* **1.** To train in different tasks or skills. **2.** To train in different sports, esp. by alternating regimens.

cross•walk (krôs′wôk′, krŏs′-) ►*n.* A street crossing marked for pedestrians.

cross•wise (krôs′wīz′, krŏs′-) also **cross•ways** (-wāz′) ►*adv.* So as to be in a cross direction; across. —**cross′wise′** *adj.*

cross•word (krôs′wûrd′, krŏs′-) ►*n.* A puzzle consisting of numbered squares to be filled with words in answer to clues.

crotch (krŏch) ►*n.* The angle formed by the junction of two parts, as branches or legs. [Poss. < CRUTCH and OFr. *croche*, crook.]

crotch•et (krŏch′ĭt) ►*n.* An odd or whimsical notion. [ME *crochet* < OFr. See CROCHET.] —**crotch′et•y** *adj.*

crouch (krouch) ►*v.* **1.** To stoop, esp. with the knees bent. **2.** To cower or cringe. [Prob. < ONFr. **crouchir*, be bent.] —**crouch** *n.*

croup (kro͞op) ►*n.* Inflammation of the larynx, esp. in children, marked by labored breathing and a hoarse cough. [< dial. *croup*, croak.] —**croup′ous, croup′y** *adj.*

crou•pi•er (kro͞o′pē-ər, -pē-ā′) ►*n.* An attendant at a gaming table. [Fr.]

crou•ton (kro͞o′tŏn′, kro͞o-tŏn′) ►*n.* A small piece of toasted bread. [Fr. *croûton*, dim. of *croûte*, crust.]

crow¹ (krō) ►*n.* A large, glossy black bird with a raucous call. —***idiom:* as the crow flies** In a straight line. [< OE *crāwe*.]

crow² (krō) ►*v.* **1.** To utter the shrill cry of a rooster. **2.** To exult loudly; boast. **3.** To make an inarticulate sound of pleasure or delight. [< OE *crāwan*.] —**crow** *n.*

Crow ►*n., pl.* **Crow** or **Crows 1.** A member of a Native American people of the N Great Plains. **2.** The Siouan language of the Crow.

crow•bar (krō′bär′) ►*n.* A metal bar with the working end shaped like a forked chisel, used as a lever.

crowd (kroud) ►*n.* **1.** A large number of persons gathered together. **2.** A particular group: *the over-30 crowd.* ►*v.* **1.** To gather closely together; throng. **2.** To advance by pressing or shoving. **3.** To press or force tightly together. [< OE *crūdan*, hasten.]

Syns: *crowd, crush, flock, horde, mob, press, throng* **n.**

crown (kroun) ►*n.* **1.** An ornamental circlet worn as a symbol of sovereignty. **2.** often **Crown** The power of a monarch. **3.** A distinction for achievement, esp. a title signifying championship in a sport. **4.** Something resembling a crown in shape. **5.** A former British coin. **6.** The top part of something, as the head. **7.** The part of a tooth above the gum line. ►*v.* **1.** To put a crown on. **2.** To invest with regal power. **3.** To confer honor upon. **4.** To be the highest part of. [< Gk. *korōnē*, wreath.]

crown prince ►*n.* The male heir apparent to a throne.

crown princess ►*n.* **1.** The female heir apparent to a throne. **2.** The wife of a crown prince.

crow's-feet (krōz′fēt′) ►*pl.n.* Wrinkles at the outer corner of the eye.

crow's-nest (krōz′nĕst′) ►*n.* A small lookout platform near the top of a ship's mast.

cro•zier (krō′zhər) ►*n.* Var. of **crosier.**

CRT ►*abbr.* cathode-ray tube

cru•ces (kro͞o′sēz) ►*n.* Pl. of **crux.**

cru•cial (kro͞o′shəl) ►*adj.* **1.** Extremely significant or important. **2.** Vital to the resolution of a crisis. See Syns at **decisive.** [< Lat. *crux*, *cruc-*, cross.] —**cru′cial•ly** *adv.*

cru•ci•ble (kro͞o′sə-bəl) ►*n.* **1.** A vessel used for melting materials at high temperatures. **2.** A severe test. See Syns at **trial.** [< Med.Lat. *crūcibulum*.]

cru•ci•fix (kro͞o′sə-fĭks′) ►*n.* An image of Jesus on the cross. [< Lat. *crucifīgere*, *crucifīx-*, crucify.]

cru•ci•fix•ion (kro͞o′sə-fĭk′shən) ►*n.* **1.** Execution on a cross. **2. Crucifixion** The crucifying of Jesus. **3.** A crucifix.

cru•ci•form (kro͞o′sə-fôrm′) ►*adj.* Shaped like a cross. [< Lat. *crux*, *cruc-*, cross.]

cru•ci•fy (kro͞o′sə-fī′) ►*v.* **-fied, -fy•ing 1.** To put to death by nailing or binding to a cross. **2.** To torture; torment. [< Lat. *crucifīgere*.]

crude (kro͞od) ►*adj.* **crud•er, crud•est 1.** In an unrefined or natural state; raw. **2.** Lacking tact, refinement, or taste. **3.** Roughly made. See Syns at **rude.** ►*n.* Unrefined petroleum. [< Lat. *crūdus*.] —**crude′ly** *adv.* —**cru′di•ty, crude′ness** *n.*

cru•el (kro͞o′əl) ►*adj.* **-el•er, -el•est** or **-el•ler, -el•lest.** Causing suffering; painful. [< Lat. *crūdēlis*.] —**cru′el•ly** *adv.* —**cru′el•ty** *n.*

cru•et (kro͞o′ĭt) ►*n.* A small glass bottle for vinegar or oil. [< OFr. *crue*, flask.]

cruet

Cruik•shank (kro͝ok′shăngk′), **George.** 1792–1878. British illustrator.

cruise (kro͞oz) ►*v.* **cruised, cruis•ing 1.** To sail or travel about, as for pleasure. **2.** To travel at a steady or efficient speed. [Du. *kruisen*, to cross.] —**cruise** *n.*

cruise missile ►*n.* An unpiloted aircraft that serves as a self-contained bomb.

cruis•er (kro͞o′zər) ►*n.* **1.** One of a class of fast warships of medium tonnage. **2.** A cabin cruiser. **3.** See **squad car.**

crul•ler (krŭl′ər) ►*n.* A small cake of deep-fried sweet dough. [< MDu. *crulle*, curly.]

crumb (krŭm) ►*n.* **1.** A very small piece broken from bread or pastry. **2.** A fragment or scrap. ►*v.* **1.** To break into crumbs. **2.** To cover with crumbs. [< OE *cruma*.]

crum•ble (krŭm′bəl) ►*v.* **-bled, -bling 1.** To break into small pieces. **2.** To disintegrate. [< OE **crymelen*, break into crumbs.] —**crum′bly** *adj.*

crum•my also **crumb•y** (krŭm′ē) ►*adj.* **-mi•er, -mi•est** also **-i•er, -i•est** *Slang* **1.** Miserable. **2.** Shabby; cheap. [< CRUMB.]

crum•pet (krŭm′pĭt) ►*n.* A small flat round of bread, baked on a griddle. [Poss. < ME *crompid (cake)*, curled (cake).]

crum•ple (krŭm′pəl) ►*v.* **-pled, -pling 1.** To crush together into wrinkles; rumple. **2.** To fall apart; collapse. [ME *crumplen*, prob. < *crumpen*, curl up.] —**crum′ply** *adj.*

crunch (krŭnch) ►*v.* **1.** To chew with a crackling noise. **2.** To crush or grind noisily. [Prob. imit.] —**crunch** *n.* —**crunch′y** *adj.*

cru•sade (kro͞o-sād′) ►*n.* **1.** often **Crusade** Any of the Christian military expeditions undertaken in the 11th, 12th, and 13th cent. to seize the Holy Land from the Muslims. **2.** A vigorous concerted movement for a cause or against an abuse. ►*v.* **-sad•ed, -sad•ing.** To engage in a crusade. [< Lat. *crux*, cross.] —**cru•sad′er** *n.*

crush (krŭsh) ►*v.* **1.** To press or squeeze so as to break or injure. **2.** To break, pound, or grind into small fragments or powder. **3.** To put down; subdue. **4.** To shove or crowd. **5.** To extract by pressing or squeezing. ►*n.* **1.** The act of crushing. **2.** A throng. See Syns at **crowd. 3.** *Informal* A temporary infatuation. [< OFr. *croissir*.] —**crush′er** *n.*

Syns: *crush, mash, pulp, smash, squash* **v.**

crust (krŭst) ►*n.* **1.** The usu. hard outer surface of bread. **2.** A hard and dry or stale piece of bread. **3.** A pastry shell, as of a pie. **4.** A hard covering or surface. **5.** *Geol.* The exterior layer of the earth. ►*v.* To cover with or harden into a crust. [< Lat. *crūsta*, shell.] —**crust′y** *adj.*

crus•ta•cean (krŭ-stā′shən) ►*n.* Any of a class

of chiefly aquatic arthropods, including lobsters, crabs, and shrimps, having a segmented body with a hard outer shell. [< Lat. *crūsta*, shell.]

crutch (krŭch) ▸*n.* **1.** A staff or support used as an aid in walking, usu. designed to fit under the armpit. **2.** Something depended upon for support. [< OE *crycc*.]

crux (krŭks, kro͝oks) ▸*n., pl.* **crux•es** or **cru•ces** (kro͞o′sēz) **1.** A central or critical point. **2.** A puzzling problem. [< Lat., cross.]

cru•zei•ro (kro͞o-zâr′ō, -zā′ro͞o) ▸*n., pl.* **-ros.** See table at **currency.** [Port. < *cruz*, CROSS.]

cry (krī) ▸*v.* **cried** (krīd), **cry•ing 1.** To sob or shed tears, as out of grief or pain. **2.** To call loudly; shout. **3.** To proclaim or announce in public. **4.** To utter a characteristic sound or call, as does an animal. **5.** To demand or require remedy: *grievances crying out for redress.* ▸*n., pl.* **cries** (krīz) **1.** A loud shout, exclamation, or utterance. **2.** A fit of weeping. **3.** An urgent appeal. **4.** The characteristic call of an animal. —***idioms:* cry over spilled milk** To regret in vain what cannot be undone. **cry wolf** To raise a false alarm. [< Lat. *quirītāre*, cry out.]

cry•ba•by (krī′bā′bē) ▸*n.* One who cries or complains frequently with little cause.

cryo– ▸*pref.* Cold; freezing: *cryogenics.* [< Gk. *kruos*, icy cold.]

cry•o•gen (krī′ə-jən) ▸*n.* A refrigerant that produces very low temperatures. —**cry′o•gen′ic** *adj.*

cry•o•gen•ics (krī′ə-jĕn′ĭks) ▸*n. (takes sing. or pl. v.)* The study of low-temperature phenomena.

cry•o•sur•ger•y (krī′ō-sûr′jə-rē) ▸*n.* Destruction of abnormal tissue by exposure to extreme cold.

crypt (krĭpt) ▸*n.* An underground vault, esp. one used as a burial place. [< Gk. *kruptē*.]

cryp•tic (krĭp′tĭk) ▸*adj.* Having an ambiguous or hidden meaning. [< Gk. *kruptikos*.] —**cryp′ti•cal•ly** *adv.*

crypto– or **crypt–** ▸*pref.* Hidden; secret: *cryptogram.* [< Gk. *kruptos*, hidden.]

cryp•to•gram (krĭp′tə-grăm′) ▸*n.* A piece of writing in code or cipher.

cryp•tog•ra•phy (krĭp-tŏg′rə-fē) ▸*n.* The process or skill of using or deciphering secret writings. —**cryp•tog′ra•pher** *n.*

crys•tal (krĭs′təl) ▸*n.* **1.** A homogenous solid formed by a repeating, three-dimensional pattern of atoms, ions, or molecules and having fixed distances between constituent parts. **2.** A mineral, esp. a transparent form of quartz, having a crystalline structure. **3.** A high-quality clear glass. **4.** A clear protective cover for a watch or clock face. [< Gk. *krustallos*.] —**crys′tal•line** *adj.*

crys•tal•lize (krĭs′tə-līz′) ▸*v.* **-lized, -liz•ing 1.** To form or cause to form a crystalline structure. **2.** To assume or cause to assume a definite and permanent form. —**crys′tal•li•za′tion** (-lĭ-zā′shən) *n.*

crys•tal•log•ra•phy (krĭs′tə-lŏg′rə-fē) ▸*n.* The science of crystal structure and phenomena. —**crys′tal•log′ra•pher** *n.*

Cs ▸ The symbol for the element **cesium.**

csc ▸*abbr.* cosecant

C-sec•tion (sē′sĕk′shən) ▸*n.* A cesarean section.

CST ▸*abbr.* Central Standard Time

CT ▸*abbr.* **1.** computerized tomography **2.** Connecticut

ct. ▸*abbr.* **1.** cent **2.** certificate

Ct. ▸*abbr.* **1.** Connecticut **2.** count (title) **3.** court

Cu ▸ The symbol for the element **copper** 1. [Lat. *cuprum*.]

cu. ▸*abbr.* cubic

cub (kŭb) ▸*n.* **1.** The young of certain carnivorous animals, such as the bear. **2.** A youth or novice. [?]

Cu•ba (kyo͞o′bə) An island country in the Caribbean Sea S of FL. Cap. Havana. Pop. 10,960,000. —**Cu′ban** *adj. & n.*

Cuban sandwich ▸*n. Regional* See **submarine** 2. See Regional Note at **submarine.**

cub•by•hole (kŭb′ē-hōl′) ▸*n.* A small or cramped space. [< *cub*, pen, hutch.]

cube (kyo͞ob) ▸*n.* **1.** *Math.* A solid having six congruent square faces. **2a.** Something shaped like a cube. **b.** A cubicle, used for work or study. **3.** *Math.* The third power of a number or quantity. ▸*v.* **cubed, cub•ing 1.** *Math.* To raise (a quantity or number) to the third power. **2.** To form or cut into cubes; dice. [< Gk. *kubos*.]

cu•bic (kyo͞o′bĭk) ▸*adj.* **1.** Having the shape of a cube. **2a.** Having three dimensions. **b.** Having a volume equal to a cube whose edge is of a stated length: *a cubic foot.* **3.** *Math.* Of the third power, order, or degree.

cu•bi•cal (kyo͞o′bĭ-kəl) ▸*adj.* **1.** Cubic. **2.** Of or relating to volume. —**cu′bi•cal•ly** *adv.*

cu•bi•cle (kyo͞o′bĭ-kəl) ▸*n.* A small compartment, as for work or sleeping. [< Lat. *cubiculum* < *cubāre*, lie down.]

cub•ism (kyo͞o′bĭz′əm) ▸*n.* A 20th-cent. school of painting and sculpture characterized by abstract, often geometric structures. —**cub′ist** *n.* —**cu•bis′tic** *adj.*

cu•bit (kyo͞o′bĭt) ▸*n.* An ancient unit of linear measure, approx. 17 to 22 in. (43 to 56 cm). [< Lat. *cubitum*.]

cuck•old (kŭk′əld, ko͝ok′-) ▸*n.* A man married to an adulterous wife. ▸*v.* To make a cuckold of. [< AN **cucuald* < *cucu*, cuckoo.]

cuck•oo (ko͞o′ko͞o, ko͝ok′o͞o) ▸*n., pl.* **-oos 1.** A grayish European bird that lays its eggs in the nests of other birds. **2.** Its two-note call. ▸*adj. Slang* Foolish or crazy. [ME *cuccu*, of imit. orig.]

cu•cum•ber (kyo͞o′kŭm′bər) ▸*n.* **1.** A vine bearing an edible cylindrical fruit with a green rind and crisp white flesh. **2.** The fruit itself. [< Lat. *cucumis*, *cucumer-*.]

Cú•cu•ta (ko͞o′kə-tə, -ko͞o-tä′) A city of NE Colombia. Pop. 383,584.

cud (kŭd) ▸*n.* Food regurgitated from the first stomach to the mouth of a ruminant and chewed again. [< OE *cudu*.]

cud•dle (kŭd′l) ▸*v.* **-dled, -dling 1.** To hug tenderly. See Syns at **caress. 2.** To nestle; snuggle. [?] —**cud′dly** *adj.*

cudg•el (kŭj′əl) ▸*n.* A short heavy club. [< OE *cycgel*.] —**cudg′el** *v.*

cue[1] (kyo͞o) ▸*n.* A long tapered rod used to strike the cue ball in billiards and pool. [Var. of QUEUE.] —**cue** *v.*

cue[2] (kyo͞o) ▸*n.* **1.** A word or signal, as in a play, used esp. to prompt another actor's speech or entrance. **2.** A reminder or hint. ▸*v.*

cued, cu•ing. To give a cue to. [Perh. < *q* < Lat. *quandō*, when.]

cue ball ►*n.* The white ball propelled with the cue in billiards and pool.

Cuen•ca (kwĕng′kə, -kä) A city of S-central Ecuador SE of Guayaquil. Pop. 194,981.

cuff[1] (kŭf) ►*n.* **1.** A fold or band at the bottom of a sleeve. **2.** The turned-up fold at the bottom of a trouser leg. —***idiom:* off the cuff** Extemporaneously. [ME *cuffe*, mitten.]

cuff[2] (kŭf) ►*v.* To strike with the open hand; slap. [?] —**cuff** *n.*

cuff link ►*n.* A paired or jointed fastening for a shirt cuff.

cui•sine (kwĭ-zēn′) ►*n.* **1.** A manner or style of preparing food: *Cuban cuisine.* **2.** Food; fare. [< Lat. *coquīna*, cookery.]

cul-de-sac (kŭl′dĭ-săk′, ko͝ol′-) ►*n., pl.* **culs-de-sac** (kŭlz′-, ko͝olz′-) or **cul-de-sacs 1.** A dead-end street. **2.** An impasse. [Fr.]

Cu•lia•cán (ko͞ol′yə-kän′) A city of W Mexico WNW of Durango. Pop. 304,826.

cu•li•nar•y (kyo͞o′lə-nĕr′ē, kŭl′ə-) ►*adj.* Of or relating to cooking or cookery. [< Lat. *culīna*, kitchen.]

cull (kŭl) ►*v.* **1.** To pick out from others; select. **2.** To gather; collect. [< Lat. *colligere*, collect.] —**cull′er** *n.*

Cul•len (kŭl′ən), **Countée.** 1903–46. Amer. poet.

cul•mi•nate (kŭl′mə-nāt′) ►*v.* **-nat•ed, -nat•ing 1.** To reach the highest point or degree. **2.** To end. [< Lat. *culmen*, peak.] —**cul′mi•na′tion** *n.*

cu•lottes (ko͞o-lŏts′, kyo͞o-, ko͞o′lŏts′, kyo͞o′-) ►*pl.n.* A woman's full trousers cut to resemble a skirt. [Fr., dim. of *cul*, rump.]

cul•pa•ble (kŭl′pə-bəl) ►*adj.* Deserving of blame. See Syns at **blameworthy.** [< Lat. *culpa*, fault.] —**cul′pa•bil′i•ty** *n.* —**cul′pa•bly** *adv.*

cul•prit (kŭl′prĭt) ►*n.* One charged with or guilty of a crime. [< *cul. prit* : abbr. of AN *culpable*, guilty + **prit*, ready.]

cult (kŭlt) ►*n.* **1.** A system of religious worship and ritual. **2.** A religion or sect considered extremist or false. **3a.** Obsessive devotion to a person or principle. **b.** The object of such devotion. [Lat. *cultus*, worship.] —**cult′ish** *adj.* —**cult′ism** *n.* —**cult′ist** *n.*

cul•ti•var (kŭl′tə-vär′, -vâr′) ►*n.* A plant variety produced by selective breeding.

cul•ti•vate (kŭl′tə-vāt′) ►*v.* **-vat•ed, -vat•ing 1.** To improve and prepare (land) for raising crops. **2.** To grow or tend (a plant or crop). **3.** To foster. See Syns at **nurture. 4.** To form and refine, as by education. **5.** To seek the acquaintance or good will of. [Med.Lat. *cultivāre* < Lat. *colere*, *cult-*, till.] —**cul′ti•va′tion** *n.* —**cul′ti•va′tor** *n.*

cul•ture (kŭl′chər) ►*n.* **1.** The behavior patterns, arts, beliefs, institutions, and all other products of human work and thought, esp. as expressed in a particular community or period. **2.** Intellectual and artistic activity and the works produced. **3.** Development of the intellect through training or education. **4.** The breeding of animals or growing of plants, esp. to improve stock. **5.** *Biol.* The growing esp. of microorganisms in a specially prepared nutrient medium. ►*v.* **-tured, -tur•ing.** To grow (microorganisms) in a nutrient medium. [< Lat. *cultūra* < *colere*, cultivate.] —**cul′tur•al** *adj.* —**cul′tur•al•ly** *adv.* —**cul′tured** *adj.*

cul•vert (kŭl′vərt) ►*n.* A drain crossing under a road or embankment. [?]

cum•ber (kŭm′bər) ►*v.* To weigh down. [< OFr. *combrer*, annoy < *combre*, hindrance.] —**cum′brous** *adj.*

Cum•ber•land Gap (kŭm′bər-lənd) A natural passage through the Cumberland Plateau near the junction of KY, VA, and TN.

Cumberland Plateau or **Cumberland Mountains.** The SW section of the Appalachian Mts., from S WV to N AL.

cum•ber•some (kŭm′bər-səm) ►*adj.* Unwieldy and burdensome.

cum•in (kŭm′ĭn, ko͞o′mĭn, kyo͞o′-) ►*n.* A plant having aromatic seedlike fruit used for seasoning. [< Gk. *kuminon*.]

cum•mer•bund (kŭm′ər-bŭnd′) ►*n.* A broad pleated sash worn with a tuxedo. [Hindi *kamarband*.]

Cum•mings (kŭm′ĭngz), **Edward Estlin.** e. e. cummings. 1894–1962. Amer. poet.

cu•mu•la•tive (kyo͞om′yə-lā′tĭv, -yə-lə-tĭv) ►*adj.* Increasing or enlarging by successive addition. [< Lat. *cumulāre*, heap up.]

cu•mu•lo•nim•bus (kyo͞om′yə-lō-nĭm′bəs) ►*n., pl.* **-bus•es** or **-bi** (-bī). An extremely dense cumulus extending to great heights, usu. producing heavy rains or thunderstorms. [CUMUL(US) + NIMBUS.]

cu•mu•lus (kyo͞om′yə-ləs) ►*n., pl.* **-li** (-lī′). A dense, white, fluffy flat-based cloud with a multiple rounded top and a well-defined outline. [Lat., heap.]

cu•ne•i•form (kyo͞o′nē-ə-fôrm′, kyo͞o-nē′-) ►*adj.* Wedge-shaped, as the characters used in ancient Mesopotamian writing. ►*n.* Cuneiform writing. [< Lat. *cuneus*, wedge.]

cun•ning (kŭn′ĭng) ►*adj.* **1.** Shrewdly deceptive. **2.** Exhibiting ingenuity. **3.** Delicately pleasing; cute. ►*n.* **1.** Skill in deception; guile. **2.** Dexterity. [< OE *cunnan*, know.] —**cun′ning•ly** *adv.*

cup (kŭp) ►*n.* **1a.** A small open container used for drinking. **b.** Such a container and its contents. **2.** See table at **measurement. 3.** A cuplike object. ►*v.* **cupped, cup•ping.** To shape like a cup: *cup one's hand.* [< LLat. *cuppa*, drinking vessel.]

cup•board (kŭb′ərd) ►*n.* A storage closet or cabinet.

cup•cake (kŭp′kāk′) ►*n.* A small, cup-shaped cake.

Cu•pid (kyo͞o′pĭd) ►*n.* **1.** *Rom. Myth.* The god of love. **2. cupid** A representation of Cupid as a boy having wings and a bow and arrow. [< Lat. *cupere*, to desire.]

cu•pid•i•ty (kyo͞o-pĭd′ĭ-tē) ►*n.* Excessive desire, esp. for wealth. [< Lat. *cupere*, to desire.]

cu•po•la (kyo͞o′pə-lə) ►*n.* A small, usu. domed structure surmounting a roof. [Ital.]

cur (kûr) ►*n.* **1.** A mongrel dog. **2.** A base person. [ME *curre*.]

Cu•ra•çao (ko͝or′ə-sou′, -sō′, ko͝or′ə-sou′, kyo͝or′-) An island of the Netherlands Antilles in the S Caribbean Sea off the NW coast of Venezuela.

cu•ra•re also **cu•ra•ri** (ko͞o-rä′rē, kyo͞o-) ►*n.* A South American plant extract used as an arrow poison and medicinally as a muscle relaxant. [Of Cariban and Tupian orig.]

cu•rate (kyo͝or′ĭt) ►*n.* **1.** A cleric who has charge of a parish. **2.** A cleric who assists a rector or vicar. [< Med.Lat. *cūrātus* < Lat. *cūra*, care.]

cu•ra•tive (kyo͝or′ə-tĭv) ►*adj.* Serving or tending to cure. —**cur′a•tive** *n.*

cu•ra•tor (kyo͝o-rā′tər, kyo͝or′ə-tər) ►*n.* One in charge of a collection, as at a museum or library. [< Lat. *cūrātor*, overseer < *cūra*, care.] —**cu′ra•to′ri•al** (kyo͝or′ə-tôr′ē-əl, -tōr′-) *adj.* —**cu•ra′tor•ship′** *n.*

curb (kûrb) ►*n.* **1.** A concrete or stone edging along a street. **2.** Something that checks or restrains. **3.** A chain or strap used with a bit to restrain a horse. ►*v.* To check, restrain, or control. [< Lat. *curvus*, curved.]

curb•stone (kûrb′stōn′) ►*n.* A stone or row of stones that constitutes a curb.

curd (kûrd) ►*n.* The coagulated part of sour milk, used to make cheese. [ME, var. of *crud*.]

cur•dle (kûr′dl) ►*v.* **-dled, -dling.** To change into curd.

cure (kyo͝or) ►*n.* **1.** Restoration of health. **2.** A method or course of medical treatment. **3.** An agent, such as a drug, that restores health. ►*v.* **cured, cur•ing 1.** To restore to health. **2.** To effect a recovery from. **3.** To preserve (e.g., meat), as by salting, smoking, or aging. [< Lat. *cūra*, care.] —**cur′a•ble** *adj.* —**cur′er** *n.* —**cure′less** *adj.*

Syns: *cure, heal, remedy* **v.**

cure-all (kyo͝or′ôl′) ►*n.* Something that cures all diseases or evils; panacea.

cu•ret•tage (kyo͝or′ĭ-täzh′) ►*n.* Surgical scraping of a body cavity. [Fr. < *curette*, surgical scoop < Lat. *cūra*, care.]

cur•few (kûr′fyo͞o) ►*n.* **1.** A regulation requiring certain or all people to leave the streets at a prescribed hour. **2.** The signal, as a bell, announcing the hour of a curfew. [< OFr. *cuevrefeu* : *covrir*, COVER + *feu*, fire.]

cu•ri•a or **Cu•ri•a** (ko͝or′ē-ə, kyo͝or′-) ►*n.*, *pl.* **-ri•ae** (-ē-ē′). The central administration governing the Catholic Church. [Lat. *cūria*, council.] —**cu′ri•al** *adj.*

cu•rie (kyo͝or′ē, kyo͝o-rē′) ►*n.* A unit of radioactivity, equal to the amount of a radioactive isotope that decays at the rate of 3.7×10^{10} disintegrations per second. [After Marie CURIE.]

Cu•rie (kyo͝or′ē, kyo͝o-rē′) also **Cu•rie-Jo•liot** (-zhō-lyō′), **Irène.** See Irène **Joliot-Curie.**

Curie, Marie. 1867–1934. Polish-born French chemist; shared a 1903 Nobel with her husband, **Pierre Curie** (1859–1906), and won a second Nobel in 1911.

cu•ri•o (kyo͝or′ē-ō′) ►*n.*, *pl.* **-os.** A curious or unusual object. [Short for CURIOSITY.]

cu•ri•ous (kyo͝or′ē-əs) ►*adj.* **1.** Eager to learn. **2.** Unduly inquisitive; prying. **3.** Unusual or extraordinary; singular. [< Lat. *cūriōsus* < *cūra*, care.] —**cu′ri•ous•ly** *adv.* —**cu′ri•os′i•ty** (-ŏs′ĭ-tē) *n.*

Cu•ri•ti•ba (ko͝or′ĭ-tē′bə) A city of SE Brazil SW of São Paulo. Pop. 1,313,094.

cu•ri•um (kyo͝or′ē-əm) ►*n. Symbol* **Cm** A silvery metallic synthetic radioactive element. At. no. 96. See table at **element.** [After Marie CURIE and Pierre CURIE.]

curl (kûrl) ►*v.* **1.** To form or twist into ringlets or coils. **2.** To assume or form into a coiled or spiral shape. ►*n.* **1.** A ringlet of hair. **2.** Something with a spiral or coiled shape. [< ME *crulle*, curly.] —**curl′y** *adj.* —**curl′i•ness** *n.* —**curl′er** *n.*

Marie Curie

cur•lew (kûrl′yo͞o, kûr′lo͞o) ►*n.* A brownish, long-legged shore bird with a slender, downward-curving bill. [< OFr. *courlieu*.]

curl•i•cue (kûr′lĭ-kyo͞o′) ►*n.* A fancy twist or curl. [CURLY + *cue*, tail.]

curl•ing (kûr′lĭng) ►*n.* A game in which two four-person teams slide stones toward the center of a circle at either end of a length of ice.

cur•mudg•eon (kər-mŭj′ən) ►*n.* A cantankerous person. [?]

cur•rant (kûr′ənt, kŭr′-) ►*n.* **1.** Any of a genus of shrubs having edible, variously colored berries. **2.** The fruits of any of these plants. **3.** A small seedless raisin. [< ME *(raysons of) coraunte*, (raisins of) Corinth.]

cur•ren•cy (kûr′ən-sē, kŭr′-) ►*n.*, *pl.* **-cies 1.** Money in any form when in actual use as a medium of exchange. **2.** General acceptance or use: *the currency of a slang term.*

cur•rent (kûr′ənt, kŭr′-) ►*adj.* **1.** Belonging to the present time. **2.** Prevalent, esp. at the present time. ►*n.* **1.** A steady onward movement. See Syns at **flow. 2.** The part of a body of liquid or gas that is in flow. **3.** *Symbol* **I a.** A flow of electric charge. **b.** The amount of charge flowing past a specified circuit point per unit time. [< Lat. *currere*, run.] —**cur′rent•ly** *adv.*

cur•ric•u•lum (kə-rĭk′yə-ləm) ►*n.*, *pl.* **-la** (-lə) or **-lums.** The courses of study offered by an educational institution. [Lat., course.] —**cur•ric′u•lar** *adj.*

curriculum vi•tae (vī′tē, vē′tī) ►*n.*, *pl.* **curricula vitae.** A summary of one's education, professional history, and job qualifications. [Lat. *curriculum vītae*, the race of life.]

cur•ry[1] (kûr′ē kŭr′ē) ►*v.* **-ried, -ry•ing 1.** To groom (a horse) with a currycomb. **2.** To prepare (tanned hides) for use. —***idiom:* curry favor** To seek favor by flattery. [< VLat. **conrēdāre* : COM– + **-rēdāre*, make ready.]

cur•ry[2] (kûr′ē, kŭr′ē) ►*n.*, *pl.* **-ries 1.** A pungent seasoning made from ground spices, including cumin and coriander. **2.** A sauce or dish seasoned with curry. ►*v.* **-ried, -ry•ing.** To season (food) with curry. [Tamil *kaṟi*.]

cur•ry•comb (kûr′ē-kōm′, kŭr′-) ►*n.* A comb with metal teeth, used for grooming horses.

curse (kûrs) ►*n.* **1a.** An appeal for evil or misfortune to befall a person or thing. **b.** Evil or misfortune resulting from or as if from a curse.

CURRENCY TABLE: LISTED BY BASIC UNIT

Unit	Country
afghani	Afghanistan
baht	Thailand
balboa	Panama
birr	Ethiopia
bolivar	Venezuela
boliviano	Bolivia
cedi	Ghana
colon	Costa Rica
	El Salvador
cordoba	Nicaragua
dalasi	Gambia
denar	Macedonia
deutsche mark	Germany
dinar	Algeria
	Bahrain
	Iraq
	Jordan
	Kuwait
	Libya
	Sudan
	Tunisia
	Yugoslavia
dirham	Morocco
	United Arab Emirates
dobra	São Tomé and Principé
dollar	Antigua and Barbuda
	Australia
	Bahamas
	Barbados
	Belize
	Brunei
	Canada
	Dominica
	Fiji
	Grenada
	Guyana
	Hong Kong
	Jamaica
	Kiribati
	Liberia
	Marshall Islands
	Micronesia
	Namibia
	Nauru
	New Zealand
	Palau
	Saint Kitts and Nevis
	Saint Lucia
	Saint Vincent and the Grenadines
	Singapore
	Solomon Islands
	Trinidad and Tobago
	Tuvalu
	United States
	Zimbabwe
dong	Vietnam
drachma	Greece
dram	Armenia
escudo	Cape Verde
	Portugal
forint	Hungary
franc	Belgium
	Benin
	Burkina Faso
	Burundi
	Cameroon
	Central African Republic
	Chad
	Comoros
	Congo (Rep. of)
	Congo (Dem. Rep. of)
	Côte d'Ivoire
	Djibouti
	Equatorial Guinea
	France
	Gabon
	Guinea
	Guinea-Bissau
	Liechtenstein
	Luxembourg
	Madagascar
	Mali
	Monaco
	Niger
	Rwanda
	Senegal
	Switzerland
	Togo
gourde	Haiti
guarani	Paraguay
guilder	Netherlands
	Suriname
hryvnia	Ukraine
kina	Papua New Guinea
kip	Laos
koruna	Czech Republic
	Slovakia
krona	Iceland
	Sweden
krone	Denmark
	Norway
kroon	Estonia
kuna	Croatia
kwacha	Malawi
	Zambia
kwanza	Angola
kyat	Myanmar
lari	Georgia
lats	Latvia
lek	Albania
lempira	Honduras
leone	Sierra Leone
leu	Moldova
	Romania
lev	Bulgaria
lilangeni	Swaziland
lira	Italy
	Malta
	San Marino
	Turkey
	Vatican City
litas	Lithuania
livre	Lebanon
loti	Lesotho
manat	Azerbaijan
	Turkmenistan
marka	Bosnia and Herzegovina
markka	Finland
metical	Mozambique
naira	Nigeria
nakfa	Eritrea
ngultrum	Bhutan
ouguiya	Mauritania
pa'anga	Tonga
pataca	Macao
peseta	Andorra
	Spain
peso	Argentina
	Chile
	Colombia
	Cuba
	Dominican Republic
	Mexico
	Philippines
	Uruguay
pound	Cyprus
	Egypt
	Ireland
	Lebanon
	Syria
	United Kingdom
pula	Botswana
quetzal	Guatemala
rand	South Africa
real	Brazil
rial	Iran
	Oman
	Yemen
riel	Cambodia
ringgit	Malaysia
riyal	Qatar
	Saudi Arabia
rubel	Belarus
ruble	Russia
	Tajikistan
rufiyaa	Maldives
rupee	India
	Mauritius
	Nepal
	Pakistan
	Seychelles
	Sri Lanka
rupiah	Indonesia
schilling	Austria
sheqel	Israel
shilling	Kenya
	Somalia
	Tanzania
	Uganda
sol	Peru
som	Kyrgyzstan
sucre	Ecuador
sum	Uzbekistan
taka	Bangladesh
tala	Samoa
tenge	Kazakhstan
tolar	Slovenia
tugrik	Mongolia
vatu	Vanuatu
won	North Korea
	South Korea
yen	Japan
yuan	China
zloty	Poland

2. A source or cause of evil. **3.** A profane word or phrase. ▶*v.* **cursed** or **curst** (kûrst), **curs•ing 1.** To invoke evil upon. **2.** To swear (at). **3.** To bring a curse upon. [< OE *curs.*]

curs•ed (kûr′sĭd, kûrst) also **curst** (kûrst) ▶*adj.* Detestable; damned.

cur•sive (kûr′sĭv) ▶*adj.* Having the successive letters joined: *cursive writing.* [< Med.Lat. *(scrīpta) cursīva*, running (script).]

cur•sor (kûr′sər) ▶*n. Comp. Sci.* A bright, usu. blinking, movable indicator on a display, marking the position at which a character can be entered or deleted. [< Lat., runner.]

cur•so•ry (kûr′sə-rē) ▶*adj.* Performed with haste and scant attention to detail. [< Lat. *currere, curs-*, run.] —**cur′so•ri•ly** *adv.*

curt (kûrt) ▶*adj.* **-er, -est 1.** Rudely brief or abrupt. **2.** Concise. [< Lat. *curtus*, cut short.] —**curt′ly** *adv.* —**curt′ness** *n.*

cur•tail (kər-tāl′) ▶*v.* To cut short; abbreviate. See Syns at **shorten.** [< OFr. *courtauld*, docked + *tailler*, cut; see TAILOR.] —**cur•tail′ment** *n.*

cur•tain (kûr′tn) ▶*n.* **1.** Material that hangs in a window or other opening as a decoration, shade, or screen. **2.** Something resembling a screen: *a curtain of fire.* **3.** The drape in a theater that separates the stage from the auditorium. [< LLat. *cōrtīna* < Lat. *cōrs, cōrt-*, COURT.] —**cur′tain** *v.*

curt•sy or **curt•sey** (kûrt′sē) ▶*n., pl.* **-sies** or **-seys.** A gesture of respect or reverence made chiefly by women by bending the knees with one foot forward. [Var. of COURTESY.] —**curt′sy** *v.*

cur•va•ceous (kûr-vā′shəs) ▶*adj.* Having a full or voluptuous figure.

cur•va•ture (kûr′və-chŏŏr′, -chər) ▶*n.* The act of curving or the state of being curved.

curve (kûrv) ▶*n.* **1a.** A line that deviates from straightness in a smooth, continuous fashion. **b.** A surface that deviates from planarity in such a fashion. **2.** Something that has the shape of a curve. ▶*v.* **curved, curv•ing.** To move in, form, or cause to form a curve. [< Lat. *curvus.*] —**curv′y** *adj.*

cush•ion (kŏŏsh′ən) ▶*n.* **1.** A soft pad or pillow for resting, reclining, or kneeling. **2.** Something that absorbs or softens an impact. **3.** The rim bordering a billiard table. ▶*v.* **1.** To absorb the shock of. **2.** To protect from impacts or disturbing effects. [< Lat. *coxa*, hip.]

Cush•it•ic (kŏŏ-shĭt′ĭk) ▶*n.* A branch of the Afro-Asiatic language family spoken in Somalia, Ethiopia, and N Kenya.

cush•y (kŏŏsh′ē) ▶*adj.* **-i•er, -i•est** *Informal.* Making few demands; comfortable. [?]

cusp (kŭsp) ▶*n.* A point or pointed end, as of a tooth or crescent. [Lat. *cuspis.*]

cus•pid (kŭs′pĭd) ▶*n.* See **canine** 2. [< Lat. *cuspis, cuspid-*, point.]

cus•pi•dor (kŭs′pĭ-dôr′, -dōr′) ▶*n.* A spittoon. [Port. < *cuspir*, to spit.]

cuss (kŭs) *Informal* ▶*v.* To curse (at). ▶*n.* **1.** A curse. **2.** A stubborn individual. [Alteration of CURSE.]

cus•tard (kŭs′tərd) ▶*n.* A dish of milk, eggs, flavoring, and sugar, cooked until set. [< Lat. *crūsta*, crust.]

Cus•ter (kŭs′tər), **George Armstrong.** 1839–76. Amer. soldier.

cus•to•di•al (kŭ-stō′dē-əl) ▶*adj.* Of or relating to custody or a custodian.

cus•to•di•an (kŭ-stō′dē-ən) ▶*n.* **1.** One that has charge of something; caretaker. **2.** A janitor. —**cus•to′di•an•ship′** *n.*

cus•to•dy (kŭs′tə-dē) ▶*n., pl.* **-dies 1.** The act or right of guarding, esp. such a right granted by a court. **2.** Charge; supervision. See Syns at **care. 3.** The state of being held under guard. [< Lat. *custōs, custōd-*, guard.]

cus•tom (kŭs′təm) ▶*n.* **1.** A practice followed by people of a particular group or region. **2.** A person's habitual practice. **3. customs a.** Duties or taxes on imported goods. **b.** *(takes sing. v.)* The governmental agency authorized to collect these duties. ▶*adj.* **1.** Made to order. **2.** Specializing in made-to-order goods. [< Lat. *cōnsuētūdo.*]

cus•tom•ar•y (kŭs′tə-mĕr′ē) ▶*adj.* **1.** Commonly practiced or used; usual. **2.** Established by custom. —**cus′tom•ar′i•ly** (-mâr′ə-lē) *adv.*

cus•tom•er (kŭs′tə-mər) ▶*n.* One that buys goods or services.

cus•tom•house (kŭs′təm-hous′) ▶*n.* A building or office where customs are collected.

cus•tom•ize (kŭs′tə-mīz′) ▶*v.* **-ized, -iz•ing.** To make or alter to individual specifications. —**cus′tom•i•za′tion** *n.*

cus•tom-made (kŭs′təm-mād′) ▶*adj.* Made according to the specifications of the buyer.

customs union ▶*n.* An international organization organized to eliminate customs restrictions between member nations and to set a tariff policy toward nonmembers.

cut (kŭt) ▶*v.* **cut, cut•ting 1.** To penetrate with or as if with a sharp edge. **2.** To separate into parts with a sharp-edged instrument; slice. **3.** To trim; shorten. **4.** To mow; harvest. **5.** To have (a new tooth) grow through the gums. **6.** To form or shape by incising. **7.** To sever or detach. **8.** *Comp. Sci.* To remove (e.g., text) from a file for storage in a buffer. **9.** To reduce the size, amount, or duration of. **10.** To dilute. **11.** To hurt keenly. **12.** To fail to attend purposely: *cut a class.* **13.** *Informal* To stop: *cut the noise.* **14.** To stop filming (a movie scene). **15.** To make a recording of. —***phrasal verbs:* cut back** To prune. **cut down 1.** To kill. **2.** To reduce consumption or use. **cut in 1.** To enter a line out of turn. **2.** To interrupt. **cut off 1.** To isolate. **2.** To discontinue. **cut out 1.** To be suited: *not cut out to be a hero.* **2.** To stop. **cut up** *Informal* To behave in a playful way. ▶*n.* **1.** The act or result of cutting. **2.** A piece cut from an animal: *a cut of beef.* **3.** A passage made by digging or eroding. **4.** A reduction. **5.** The style in which a garment is cut. **6.** *Informal* A share. **7.** An insult. **8a.** An engraved block or plate. **b.** A print made from such a block. —***idiom:* cut corners** To do something in the easiest or cheapest way. [ME *cutten.*]

cut-and-dried (kŭt′n-drīd′) ▶*adj.* In accordance with a standard formula; routine.

cu•ta•ne•ous (kyŏŏ-tā′nē-əs) ▶*adj.* Of or affecting the skin. [< Lat. *cutis*, skin.]

cut•back (kŭt′băk′) ▶*n.* A decrease; curtailment: *cutbacks in federal funding.*

cute (kyŏŏt) ▶*adj.* **cut•er, cut•est 1.** Delightfully pretty or dainty. **2.** Clever. [Short for ACUTE.] —**cute′ly** *adv.* —**cute′ness** *n.*

cute•sy (kyŏŏt′sē) ▶*adj.* **-si•er, -si•est** *Informal.* Deliberately or affectedly cute.

cu•ti•cle (kyōō′tĭ-kəl) ►*n.* **1.** The epidermis. **2.** The strip of hardened skin at the base of a fingernail or toenail. [< *cutis*, skin.]

cut•lass (kŭt′ləs) ►*n.* A short heavy sword with a curved blade. [< Lat. *cultellus*, dim. of *culter*, knife.]

cut•ler•y (kŭt′lə-rē) ►*n.* Cutting instruments and tools, esp. tableware. [< OFr. *coutel*, knife. See CUTLASS.]

cut•let (kŭt′lĭt) ►*n.* A thin slice of meat, usu. veal or lamb, cut from the leg or ribs. [Fr. *côtelette* < OFr. *costelette* < Lat. *costa*.]

cut•off (kŭt′ôf′, -ŏf′) ►*n.* **1.** A designated limit or end. **2.** A shortcut or bypass. **3.** A device that cuts off a flow of fluid.

cut•out (kŭt′out′) ►*n.* Something cut out or intended to be cut out from something else.

cut-rate (kŭt′rāt′) ►*adj.* Reduced in price.

cut•ter (kŭt′ər) ►*n.* **1.** A person or device that cuts. **2.** A ship's boat used for transporting stores or passengers. **3.** A small, lightly armed Coast Guard boat.

cut•throat (kŭt′thrōt′) ►*n.* **1.** A murderer. **2.** A ruthless person. ►*adj.* **1.** Cruel; murderous. **2.** Merciless: *cutthroat competition.*

cut•ting (kŭt′ĭng) ►*n.* A part cut off from a main body, esp. a shoot removed from a plant for rooting or grafting.

cut•tle•bone (kŭt′l-bōn′) ►*n.* The chalky internal shell of a cuttlefish, used as a dietary supplement for cage birds.

cut•tle•fish (kŭt′l-fĭsh′) ►*n.* A ten-armed, squidlike marine mollusk that has a chalky internal shell. [< OE *cudele*.]

cut•up (kŭt′ŭp′) ►*n. Informal* A prankster.

Cu•vier (kyōō′vē-ā′, kü-vyā′), Baron **Georges Léopold Chrétien Frédéric Dagobert.** 1769–1832. French naturalist.

cwt ►*abbr.* hundredweight

-cy ►*suff.* **1.** Condition; quality: *bankruptcy.* **2.** Rank; office: *baronetcy.* **3.** Action; practice: *conspiracy.* [< Lat. *-cia, -tia* and Gk. *-kia, -tia*.]

cy•an (sī′ăn′, -ən) ►*n.* A greenish blue, considered a primary color in printing and photography. [Gk. *kuanos*, dark blue.]

cy•a•nide (sī′ə-nīd′) ►*n.* Any of various compounds containing a CN group, esp. the poisonous compounds potassium cyanide and sodium cyanide.

cyano– or **cyan–** ►*pref.* **1.** Blue: *cyanosis.* **2.** Cyanide: *cyanogen.* [< Gk. *kuanos*, dark blue.]

cy•an•o•gen (sī-ăn′ə-jən) ►*n.* A colorless, flammable, highly poisonous gas, C_2N_2, used as a rocket propellant.

cy•a•no•sis (sī′ə-nō′sĭs) ►*n.* A bluish discoloration of the skin and mucous membranes resulting from inadequate oxygenation of the blood. —**cy′a•not′ic** (-nŏt′ĭk) *adj.*

cyber– ►*pref.* **1.** Computer: *cyberpunk.* **2.** Computer network: *cyberspace.* See Usage Note at **virtual.**

cy•ber•net•ics (sī′bər-nĕt′ĭks) ►*n. (takes sing. v.)* The theoretical study of control processes in biological, mechanical, and electronic systems. [< Gk. *kubernētēs*, governor.] —**cy′ber•net′ic** *adj.*

cy•ber•punk (sī′bər-pŭnk′) ►*n.* Fast-paced science fiction involving futuristic computer-based societies. —**cy′ber•punk′** *adj.*

cy•ber•space (sī′bər-spās′) ►*n.* The electronic medium of computer networks, in which online communication or browsing takes place.

Cyc•la•des (sĭk′lə-dēz′) A group of islands of SE Greece in the S Aegean.

cy•cla•mate (sī′klə-māt′, sĭk′lə-) ►*n.* A salt of cyclamic acid formerly used as an artificial sweetener.

cy•cla•men (sī′klə-mən, sĭk′lə-) ►*n.* A plant with showy, variously colored flowers. [< Gk. *kuklaminos*.]

cyc•la•mic acid (sĭk′lə-mĭk′, sī′klə-) ►*n.* A crystalline acid used to produce cyclamates. [Short for *cycl(ohexylsulf)amic acid*.]

cy•cle (sī′kəl) ►*n.* **1.** An interval of time during which a regularly repeated event occurs. **2a.** A single occurrence of a periodically repeated phenomenon. **b.** A periodically repeated sequence of events. **3.** The orbit of a celestial body. **4.** A group of literary or musical works about a central theme or hero. **5.** A bicycle or motorcycle. ►*v.* **-cled, -cling 1.** To occur in or pass through a cycle. **2.** To ride a bicycle or motorcycle. [< Gk. *kuklos*, circle.] —**cy′cler** *n.* —**cy′clic** (sī′klĭk, sĭk′lĭk), **cy′cli•cal** *adj.*

cy•clist (sī′klĭst) ►*n.* One who rides a vehicle such as a bicycle or motorcycle.

cyclo– or **cycl–** ►*pref.* Circle: *cyclometer.* [< Gk. *kuklos*.]

cy•clom•e•ter (sī-klŏm′ĭ-tər) ►*n.* **1.** An instrument that records the revolutions of a wheel to indicate distance traveled. **2.** An instrument that measures circular arcs.

cy•clone (sī′klōn′) ►*n.* **1.** An atmospheric system characterized by the rapid inward circulation of air masses about a low-pressure center. **2.** A violent rotating windstorm. [< Gk. *kuklōn* < *kuklos*, circle.] —**cy•clon′ic** (-klŏn′ĭk) *adj.*

Cy•clops (sī′klŏps) ►*n., pl.* **Cy•clo•pes** (sī-klō′pēz′) *Gk. Myth.* **1.** Any of three one-eyed Titans. **2.** Any of a race of one-eyed giants reputedly descended from these Titans.

cy•clo•tron (sī′klə-trŏn′) ►*n.* A device that accelerates charged subatomic particles in a spiral path by an alternating electric field in a constant magnetic field.

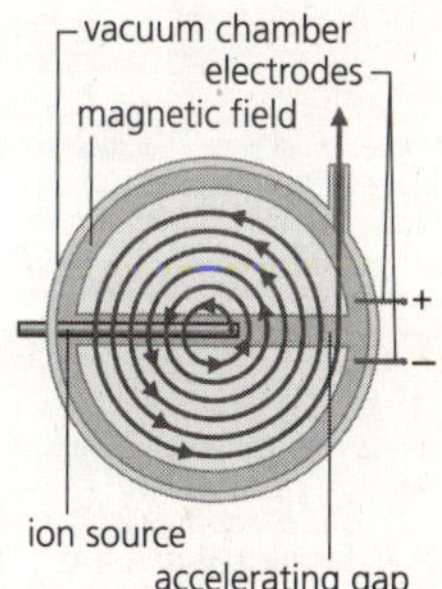

cyclotron

cyg•net (sĭg′nĭt) ►*n.* A young swan. [< Gk. *kuknos*, swan.]

Cyg•nus (sĭg′nəs) ►*n.* A constellation in the Northern Hemisphere. [Lat. < Gk. *kuknos*, swan.]

cyl•in•der (sĭl′ən-dər) ►*n.* **1.** *Math.* **a.** The surface generated by a straight line intersecting and moving along a closed plane curve while remaining parallel to a fixed straight line that is not on or parallel to the plane of the closed curve. **b.** A solid bounded by two parallel planes and such a surface having a closed curve, esp. a circle. **2.** A cylindrical object. **3.** The chamber in which a piston moves. **4.** The rotating chamber of a revolver that holds the cartridges. [< Gk. *kulindros.*] —**cy•lin′dri•cal** *adj.* —**cy•lin′dri•cal•ly** *adv.*

cym•bal (sĭm′bəl) ►*n. Mus.* A concave brass plate that makes a loud clashing tone when hit with a drumstick or when used in pairs. [< Gk. *kumbalon.*]

cyn•ic (sĭn′ĭk) ►*n.* A person who believes all people are motivated by selfishness. [< Gk. *kunikos*, like a dog < *kuōn*, dog.] —**cyn′i•cal** *adj.* —**cyn′i•cal•ly** *adv.* —**cyn′i•cism** *n.*

cy•no•sure (sī′nə-shŏŏr′, sĭn′ə-) ►*n.* A focal point of attention and admiration. [< Gk. *kunosoura*, Ursa Minor.]

cy•press (sī′prĭs) ►*n.* Any of a genus of evergreen trees or shrubs having scalelike leaves and woody cones. [< Gk. *kuparissos.*]

Cy•prus (sī′prəs) An island country in the E Mediterranean S of Turkey. Cap. Nicosia. Pop. 734,000. —**Cyp′ri•an** (sĭp′re-ən), **Cyp′ri•ot** (-ət, -ŏt′) *adj. & n.*

Cy•ra•no de Ber•ge•rac (sîr′ə-nō də bûr′zhə-răk′, bĕr′-), **Savinien de.** 1619–55. French satirist and duelist.

Cyr•il (sîr′əl), Saint. 827–869. Christian missionary and theologian.

Cy•ril•lic (sə-rĭl′ĭk) ►*adj.* Of or being an alphabet based esp. on that of Byzantine Greek and used for some Slavic languages, such as Russian and Serbian.

Cyrus II (sī′rəs). "Cyrus the Great." 600?–529 B.C. King of Persia (550–529) and founder of the Persian Empire.

cyst (sĭst) ►*n. Pathol.* An abnormal membranous sac containing a gaseous, liquid, or semisolid substance. [< Gk. *kustis*, bladder.]

cys•tic fibrosis (sĭs′tĭk) ►*n.* A hereditary disease of the exocrine glands, usu. resulting in chronic respiratory infections and impaired pancreatic function.

cys•to•scope (sĭs′tə-skōp′) ►*n.* A tubular instrument used to examine the urinary bladder. [Gk. *kustis*, bladder + –SCOPE.]

–cyte ►*suff.* Cell: *leukocyte.* [< Gk. *kutos*, hollow vessel.]

cyto– or **cyt–** ►*pref.* Cell: *cytoplasm.* [< Gk. *kutos*, hollow vessel.]

cy•tol•o•gy (sī-tŏl′ə-jē) ►*n.* The branch of biology that deals with the formation, structure, and function of cells. —**cy′to•log′ic** (-tə-lŏj′ĭk), **cy′to•log′i•cal** *adj.* —**cy•tol′o•gist** *n.*

cy•to•plasm (sī′tə-plăz′əm) ►*n.* The protoplasm outside the cell nucleus. —**cy′to•plas′mic** *adj.*

cy•to•sine (sī′tə-sēn′) ►*n.* A pyrimidine base that is an essential constituent of RNA and DNA. [CYT(O)– + (RIB)OS(E) + –INE[2].]

czar (zär, tsär) ►*n.* **1.** also **tsar** or **tzar** (zär, tsär) A king or emperor, esp. one of the former emperors of Russia. **2.** An autocrat. **3.** *Informal* An official having special authority: *an energy czar.* [Russ. *tsar′* < Lat. *Caesar*, emperor.]

cza•ri•na (zä-rē′nə, tsä-) ►*n.* The wife of a czar. [Alteration of Russ. *tsaritsa*, feminine of *tsar′*, czar.]

czar•ism (zär′ĭz′əm, tsär′-) ►*n.* The system of government in Russia under the czars. —**czar′ist** *adj. & n.*

Czech (chĕk) ►*n.* **1.** A native or inhabitant of the Czech Republic. **2.** The Slavic language of the Czech Republic. —**Czech** *adj.*

Czech•o•slo•va•ki•a (chĕk′ə-slə-vä′kē-ə, -ō-slō-) A former country of central Europe; divided in Jan. 1993 into Czech Republic and Slovakia. —**Czech′o•slo′vak, Czech′o•slo•va′ki•an** *adj. & n.*

Czech Republic. A country of central Europe; part of Czechoslovakia until Jan. 1993. Cap. Prague. Pop. 10,333,000.

D

d or **D** (dē) ►*n., pl.* **d's** or **D's** also **ds** or **Ds 1.** The 4th letter of the English alphabet. **2.** The 4th in a series. **3.** *Mus.* The 2nd tone of the C major scale. **4. D** The lowest passing grade given to a student.

D[1] also **d** ► The symbol for the Roman numeral 500.

D[2] ►*abbr.* **1.** day **2.** Democrat

d. ►*abbr.* **1.** date **2.** daughter **3.** died **4.** *Chiefly British* penny ($\frac{1}{12}$ of a shilling)

DA ►*abbr.* **1.** district attorney **2.** Doctor of Arts

dab (dăb) ►*v.* **dabbed, dab•bing 1.** To apply with short poking strokes. **2.** To pat lightly. ►*n.* **1.** A small amount. **2.** A quick light pat. [ME *dabben.*]

dab•ble (dăb′əl) ►*v.* **-bled, -bling 1.** To splash or spatter with or as if with a liquid. **2.** To undertake something superficially or without serious intent. [Poss. < Du. *dabbelen.*]

dab•bler (dăb′lər) ►*n.* One who dabbles in a subject or activity. See Syns at **amateur.**

da ca•po (dä kä′pō) ►*adv. Mus.* From the beginning. Used as a direction. [Ital.]

Dac•ca (dăk′ə, dä′kə) See **Dhaka.**

dace (dās) ►*n., pl.* **dace** or **dac•es.** A small freshwater fish related to the carps and minnows. [< LLat. *darsus.*]

da•cha (dä′chə) ►*n.* A Russian country house. [Russ.]

dachs•hund (däks′hŏŏnt′, dăk′sənt, -sənd) ►*n.* A small dog having a long body, drooping ears, and very short legs. [Ger. : OHGer. *dahs*, badger + OHGer. *hunt*, dog.]

Da•ci•a (dā′shē-ə, -shə) An ancient region and Roman province corresponding to modern Romania. —**Da′ci•an** *adj. & n.*

Da•cron (dā′krŏn′, dăk′rŏn′) ► A trademark for a synthetic polyester fabric or fiber.

dac•tyl (dăk′təl) ►*n.* A metrical foot consisting of one accented syllable followed by two unaccented ones. [< Gk. *daktulos*, finger, dactyl.] —**dac•tyl′ic** (-tĭl′ĭk) *adj. & n.*

dad (dăd) ►*n. Informal* A father. [Of baby-talk orig.]

Da•da (dä′dä) ▸*n.* A European artistic and literary movement (1916–23) that flouted conventional values in works marked by nonsense and incongruity. [Fr.] —**Da′da•ism** *n.* —**Da′da•ist** *adj. & n.*

dad•dy (dăd′ē) ▸*n., pl.* **-dies** *Informal.* A father.

daddy long•legs (lông′lĕgz′, lŏng′-) ▸*n., pl.* **daddy longlegs.** A spiderlike arachnid with a small rounded body and long slender legs.

da•do (dā′dō) ▸*n., pl.* **-does 1.** The section of a pedestal between the base and cornice or cap. **2.** The lower portion of an interior wall, decorated differently from the upper section. [Ital. < Lat. *dare, dat-*, give.]

daf•fo•dil (dăf′ə-dĭl) ▸*n.* A bulbous plant having showy, usu. yellow flowers with a trumpet-shaped central crown. [Alteration of ME *affodil*, ASPHODEL.]

daf•fy (dăf′ē) ▸*adj.* **-fi•er, -fi•est** *Informal* **1.** Silly; zany. **2.** Crazy. [< ME *daffe*, fool.] —**daf′fi•ly** *adv.* —**daf′fi•ness** *n.*

daft (dăft) ▸*adj.* **-er, -est 1.** Mad; crazy. **2.** Foolish; stupid. [< OE *gedæfte*, meek.] —**daft′ly** *adv.* —**daft′ness** *n.*

dag•ger (dăg′ər) ▸*n.* **1.** A short pointed weapon with sharp edges. **2.** *Print.* See **obelisk** 2. —***idiom:* look daggers at** To glare at angrily. [ME *daggere.*]

da•guerre•o•type (də-gâr′ə-tīp′) ▸*n.* A photograph made by an early process with the image developed on a light-sensitive silver-coated metallic plate. [After Louis J.M. *Daguerre* (1789–1851).]

dahl (däl) ▸*n.* A spicy East Indian stew made with lentils or other legumes. [< Skt. *dalaḥ*, piece split off.]

dahl•ia (dăl′yə, däl′-, dāl′-) ▸*n.* A New World plant cultivated for its showy, variously colored flowers. [After Anders *Dahl* (1751–87).]

dai•kon (dī′kŏn′, -kən) ▸*n.* A large white radish of Japan. [J.]

dai•ly (dā′lē) ▸*adj.* Happening or done every day. ▸*adv.* **1.** Every day. **2.** Once a day. ▸*n., pl.* **-lies.** A newspaper published every day. [< OE *dæglīc.*]

daily double ▸*n.* A bet won by choosing both winners of two specified races on one day, as in horse racing.

dain•ty (dān′tē) ▸*adj.* **-ti•er, -ti•est 1.** Delicately beautiful; exquisite. **2.** Delicious or choice. See Syns at **delicate. 3.** Of refined taste. **4.** Fastidious; squeamish. ▸*n., pl.* **-ties.** A delicacy. [< Lat. *dignitās*, excellence.] —**dain′ti•ly** *adv.* —**dain′ti•ness** *n.*

daiq•ui•ri (dăk′ə-rē, dī′kə-) ▸*n., pl.* **-ris.** An iced cocktail of rum, lime or lemon juice, and sugar. [After *Daiquirí*, Cuba.]

dair•y (dâr′ē) ▸*n., pl.* **-ies 1.** An establishment for processing or selling milk and milk products. **2.** A dairy farm. [< ME *daie*, dairymaid + AN *-erie*, place.] —**dair′y** *adj.* —**dair′y•maid′** *n.* —**dair′y•man** *n.* —**dair′y•wom′an** *n.*

dair•y•ing (dâr′ē-ĭng) ▸*n.* The business of operating a dairy or a dairy farm.

da•is (dā′ĭs, dī′) ▸*n.* A raised platform, as in a lecture hall, for honored guests. [< LLat. *discus*, table. See DISK.]

dai•sy (dā′zē) ▸*n., pl.* **-sies.** Any of several plants of the composite family, esp. a widely naturalized species having flower heads with a yellow center and white rays. [< OE *dæges ēage*, day's eye.]

daisy wheel ▸*n.* A printing device consisting of type characters fixed at the ends of spokes on a wheel.

Da•kar (də-kär′, dăk′är′) The capital of Senegal, in the W part. Pop. 1,641,358.

Da•ko•ta (də-kō′tə) ▸*n., pl.* **-ta** or **-tas 1.** A Sioux, esp. a member of the Santee branch. **2.** The Siouan language of the Dakota. —**Da•ko′tan** *adj. & n.*

Da•lai Lama (dä′lī) ▸*n.* The traditional ruler and highest priest of Buddhism in Tibet and Mongolia, held to be compassion incarnate. [Tibetan, ocean monk.]

Dalai Lama

Salvador Dali

da•la•si (dä-lä′sē) ▸*n., pl.* **-si.** See table at **currency.** [Mandingo.]

dale (dāl) ▸*n.* A valley. [< OE *dæl.*]

Da•li (dä′lē), **Salvador.** 1904–89. Spanish surrealist artist. —**Da′li•esque′** *adj.*

Dal•las (dăl′əs) A city of NE TX E of Fort Worth. Pop. 1,006,877.

dal•ly (dăl′ē) ▸*v.* **-lied, -ly•ing 1.** To play amorously. See Syns at **flirt. 2.** To waste time; dawdle. [< OFr. *dalier.*] —**dal′li•ance** *n.* —**dal′li•er** *n.*

Dal•ma•ti•a (dăl-mā′shə) A historical region of SE Europe on the Adriatic Sea.

Dal•ma•tian (dăl-mā′shən) ▸*n.* **1.** A native or inhabitant of Dalmatia. **2.** also **dalmatian** A dog with a short white coat covered with black spots. ▸*adj.* Relating to Dalmatia.

dam¹ (dăm) ▸*n.* A barrier built across a waterway to control the flow of water. ▸*v.* **dammed, dam•ming 1.** To build a dam across. **2.** To hold back; check. [ME.]

dam² (dăm) ▸*n.* A female parent of a four-legged animal. [ME *dame*, lady. See DAME.]

dam•age (dăm′ĭj) ▸*n.* **1.** Impairment of the usefulness or value of person or property; harm. **2. damages** *Law* Money ordered to be paid as compensation for injury or loss. ▸*v.* **-aged, -ag•ing.** To cause damage to. [< Lat. *damnum*, loss.] —**dam′age•a•ble** *adj.*

Da•mas•cus (də-măs′kəs) The capital of Syria, in the SW part. Pop. 1,549,000. —**Dam′a•scene′** (dăm′ə-sēn′) *adj. & n.*

dam•ask (dăm′əsk) ▸*n.* **1.** A rich patterned fabric esp. of silk or wool. **2.** A fine twilled table linen. [ME, Damascus.]

damask rose ▸*n.* A rose with fragrant red or pink flowers used as a source of attar.

dame (dām) ▸*n.* **1.** A married woman. **2.** *Slang* A woman. **3.** *Chiefly Brit.* **a.** A woman holding a nonhereditary title. **b.** The wife of a knight. [< Lat. *domina*, lady.]

damn (dăm) ▸*v.* **1.** To criticize adversely. See

Syns at **condemn.** **2.** To bring to ruin. **3.** To condemn to everlasting punishment; doom. **4.** To swear at. ►*interj.* Used to express anger, contempt, or disappointment. ►*n. Informal* The least bit; jot: *not worth a damn.* ►*adv.* & *adj.* Damned. [< Lat. *damnum*, damage.] —**dam•na′tion** (-nā′shən) *n.*

dam•na•ble (dăm′nə-bəl) ►*adj.* Deserving condemnation; odious. —**dam′na•bly** *adv.*

damned (dămd) ►*adj.* **-er, -est 1.** Condemned; doomed. **2.** *Informal* Dreadful; awful. **3.** Used as an intensive: *a damned fool.* ►*adv.* **-er, -est.** Used as an intensive: *a damned poor excuse.* ►*n.* Souls doomed to eternal punishment.

Dam•o•cles (dăm′ə-klēz′). fl. 4th cent. B.C. Greek courtier who according to legend was forced to sit under a sword suspended by a single hair.

damp (dămp) ►*adj.* **-er, -est.** Slightly wet; moist. ►*n.* **1.** Moisture in the air; humidity. **2.** Foul or poisonous gas in coal mines. ►*v.* **1.** To moisten. **2.** To restrain or check. **3.** *Phys.* To decrease the amplitude of (a wave). [ME, poison gas.] —**damp′ish** *adj.* —**damp′ly** *adv.* —**damp′ness** *n.*

damp•en (dăm′pən) ►*v.* **1.** To make or become damp. **2.** To deaden or depress: *dampen one's spirits.* **3.** To soundproof. —**damp′en•er** *n.*

damp•er (dăm′pər) ►*n.* **1.** One that deadens or depresses: *Rain put a damper on our plans.* **2.** An adjustable plate in a flue for controlling the draft.

dam•sel (dăm′zəl) ►*n.* A young woman or girl; maiden. [< VLat. **dominicella* < Lat. *domina*, lady.]

dam•sel•fly (dăm′zəl-flī′) ►*n.* A predatory insect related to the dragonfly but having wings that fold together at rest.

dam•son (dăm′zən, -sən) ►*n.* A Eurasian plum tree bearing oval, bluish-black fruit. [< Lat. *Damascēnum*, of Damascus.]

Dan (dăn). In the Bible, a son of Jacob and the forebear of one of the tribes of Israel.

Da•na (dā′nə), **Richard Henry.** 1815–82. Amer. lawyer and writer.

Da Nang or **Da•nang** (də-năng′, dä′näng′). A city of central Vietnam on the South China Sea. Pop. 382,674.

dance (dăns) ►*v.* **danced, danc•ing 1.** To move rhythmically usu. to music. **2.** To leap or skip about. **3.** To bob up and down. ►*n.* **1.** A series of motions and steps, usu. performed to music. **2.** The art of dancing. **3.** A party at which people dance. **4.** One round or turn of dancing: *May I have this dance?* [< OFr. *danser.*] —**dance′a•ble** *adj.* —**danc′er** *n.*

D and C ►*n.* Dilation and curettage.

dan•de•li•on (dăn′dl-ī′ən) ►*n.* A weedy plant having many-rayed yellow flower heads. [< OFr. *dent de lion* : Lat. *dēns, dent-*, tooth + Lat. *leō*, lion.]

dan•der[1] (dăn′dər) ►*n. Informal* Temper: *got my dander up.* [?]

dan•der[2] (dăn′dər) ►*n.* Scurf from the coat or feathers of various animals, often of an allergenic nature. [Alteration of DANDRUFF.]

dan•dle (dăn′dl) ►*v.* **-dled, -dling.** To move (a small child) up and down on one's knees in a playful way. [?]

dan•druff (dăn′drəf) ►*n.* Small flakes of dead skin formed on and shed from the scalp. [*dand-*, of unknown orig. + dial. *hurf*, scurf.]

dan•dy (dăn′dē) ►*n., pl.* **-dies 1.** A man who affects extreme elegance in clothes; fop. **2.** *Informal* Something very good of its kind. ►*adj.* **-di•er, -di•est 1.** Foppish. **2.** *Informal* Fine; good. [Perh. < *jack-a-dandy*, fop.] —**dan′di•fy′** *v.* —**dan′dy•ism** *n.*

Dane (dān) ►*n.* A native or inhabitant of Denmark.

dan•ger (dān′jər) ►*n.* **1.** Exposure or vulnerability to harm or risk. **2.** A source of risk or peril. [< VLat. **dominiārium*, power < Lat. *dominus*, lord.]

dan•ger•ous (dān′jər-əs) ►*adj.* **1.** Full of danger. **2.** Able or likely to do harm. —**dan′ger•ous•ly** *adv.* —**dan′ger•ous•ness** *n.*

dan•gle (dăng′gəl) ►*v.* **-gled, -gling.** To hang or cause to hang loosely and swing to and fro. [Poss. of Scand. orig.] —**dan′gler** *n.*

dan•gling (dăng′glĭng) ►*n.* Of or being a modifier, especially a participle or participial phrase, that grammatically modifies the subject of its sentence but semantically modifies another element or an unstated referent, as *approaching Dallas* in the sentence *Approaching Dallas, the skyline came into view.*

Dan•iel (dăn′yəl) ►*n. Bible* **1.** A Hebrew prophet of the 6th cent. B.C. **2.** See table at **Bible.**

da•ni•o (dā′nē-ō′) ►*n., pl.* **-os.** A small, brightly colored freshwater fish popular as an aquarium fish. [NLat., genus name.]

Dan•ish (dā′nĭsh) ►*adj.* Of Denmark, the Danes, or the Danish language. ►*n.* **1.** The Germanic language of the Danes. **2.** *pl.* **-ish** or **-ish•es** A Danish pastry.

Danish pastry ►*n.* A sweet buttery pastry made with raised dough.

dank (dăngk) ►*adj.* **-er, -est.** Disagreeably damp or humid. [ME.] —**dank′ly** *adv.* —**dank′ness** *n.*

Dan•te A•li•ghie•ri (dän′tā ä′lē-gyĕ′rē, dăn′tē). 1265–1321. Italian poet. —**Dan′te•an** *adj.* & *n.* —**Dan•tesque′** (dăn-tĕsk′, dăn-) *adj.*

Dan•ton (däN-tôN′), **Georges Jacques.** 1759–94. French Revolutionary leader.

Dan•ube (dăn′yo͞ob) A river of S-central Europe rising in SW Germany and flowing about 2,848 km (1,770 mi) to the Black Sea. —**Dan•u′bi•an** *adj.*

Dan•zig (dăn′sĭg, dän′tsĭk) See **Gdańsk.**

dap•per (dăp′ər) ►*adj.* **1a.** Neatly dressed; trim. **b.** Stylish. **2.** Spry. [ME *daper*, elegant.] —**dap′per•ly** *adv.* —**dap′per•ness** *n.*

dap•ple (dăp′əl) ►*v.* **-pled, -pling.** To mark or mottle with spots. ►*adj.* Dappled. [< DAPPLED.]

dap•pled (dăp′əld) ►*adj.* Spotted; mottled. [Prob. < ON *depill*, small pool, splash.]

DAR ►*abbr.* Daughters of the American Revolution

Dar•da•nelles (där′dn-ĕlz′). Formerly **Hellespont.** A strait connecting the Aegean Sea with the Sea of Marmara.

dare (dâr) ►*v.* **dared, dar•ing 1.** To have the courage required for. **2.** To challenge (someone) to do something requiring boldness. **3.** To confront boldly. See Syns at **defy.** ►*n.* A challenge. [< OE *durran.*] —**dar′er** *n.*

Dare, Virginia. 1587–87? The first child of English parents born in America.

dare•dev•il (dâr′dĕv′əl) ►*n.* One who is recklessly bold. ►*adj.* Recklessly bold. See Syns at **adventurous.**

dare•say (dâr′sā′) ►*v.* To think very likely. Used in the 1st person sing. present tense: *I daresay you're wrong.*

Dar es Sa•laam (där′ ĕs sə-läm′) The de facto capital of Tanzania, in the E part. Pop. 1,096,000.

dar•ing (dâr′ĭng) ►*adj.* Bold and venturesome. See Syns at **adventurous.** ►*n.* Audacious bravery. —**dar′ing•ly** *adv.* —**dar′ing•ness** *n.*

Da•ri•us I (də-rī′əs). "Darius the Great." 550?–486 B.C. King of Persia (521–486).

dark (därk) ►*adj.* **-er, -est 1.** Lacking light or brightness. **2.** Of a shade of color tending toward black. **3.** Gloomy; dismal. **4.** Sullen or threatening: *a dark scowl.* **5.** Obscure; mysterious. **6.** Lacking enlightenment: *a dark era.* **7.** Evil; sinister. ►*n.* **1.** Absence of light. **2.** Night; nightfall. —***idiom:*** **in the dark 1.** In secret. **2.** In ignorance; uninformed. [< OE *deorc.*] —**dark′ish** *adj.* —**dark′ly** *adv.* —**dark′ness** *n.*

Dark Ages ►*pl.n.* The early part of the Middle Ages from about A.D. 476 to A.D. 1000.

dark•en (där′kən) ►*v.* **1.** To make or become dark or darker. **2.** To make somber or gloomy. **3.** To tarnish: *darkened their good name.* —**dark′en•er** *n.*

dark horse ►*n.* A little-known, unexpectedly successful entrant in a race or contest.

dark matter ►*n.* Non-luminous physical objects, such as very dim stars, believed to be part of the universe's missing mass.

dark•room (därk′ro͞om′, -ro͝om′) ►*n.* A room in which photographic materials are processed in complete darkness or with a safelight.

dar•ling (där′lĭng) ►*n.* **1.** A dearly beloved person. **2.** A favorite. ►*adj.* **1.** Much loved. **2.** *Informal* Charming or adorable: *a darling hat.* [< OE *dēorling.*]

Darling River. A river rising in SE Australia and flowing about 2,739 km (1,702 mi) to the Murray R.

darn[1] (därn) ►*v.* To mend by weaving thread across a hole. ►*n.* A hole repaired by darning. [Fr. dial. *darner.*] —**darn′er** *n.*

darn[2] (därn) ►*v., interj., n., adv., & adj.* Damn. [Alteration of DAMN.]

darned (därnd) ►*adj. & adv.* Damned.

darn•ing needle (där′nĭng) ►*n.* **1.** A long, large-eyed needle used in darning. **2.** A dragonfly. See Regional Note at **dragonfly.**

Dar•row (dăr′ō), **Clarence Seward.** 1857–1938. Amer. lawyer.

dart (därt) ►*n.* **1.** A slender pointed missile thrown by hand or shot from a blowgun. **2. darts** *(takes sing. or pl. v.)* A game in which darts are thrown at a target. **3.** A sudden rapid movement. **4.** A tapered tuck sewn in a garment. ►*v.* To move suddenly and rapidly. [< OFr., of Gmc. orig.]

dart•er (där′tər) ►*n.* Any of various small, often brilliantly colored freshwater fishes.

Dar•win (där′wĭn), **Charles Robert.** 1809–82. British naturalist. —**Dar•win′i•an** *adj. & n.*

Dar•win•ism (där′wĭ-nĭz′əm) ►*n.* A theory of biological evolution developed by Charles Darwin and others, stating that species of organisms arise and develop through the natural selection of inherited variations that increase the individual's ability to survive and reproduce. —**Dar′win•ist** *n.* —**Dar′win•is′tic** *adj.*

dash (dăsh) ►*v.* **1.** To break or smash to pieces. **2.** To hurl or thrust violently. **3.** To splash; spatter. **4.** To move with haste; rush: *dashed inside.* **5.** To perform or complete hastily: *dash off a letter.* **6.** To ruin. See Syns at **blast.** ►*n.* **1.** A swift blow or stroke. **2a.** A splash. **b.** A small amount of an added ingredient. **3.** A sudden movement; rush. **4.** *Sports* A relatively short footrace run at top speed. **5.** Verve. See Syns at **vigor. 6.** A punctuation mark (—) used to indicate a break or omission. **7.** A long sound or symbol used esp. in Morse code. **8.** A dashboard. [ME *dashen.*] —**dash′er** *n.*

dash•board (dăsh′bôrd′, -bōrd′) ►*n.* A panel under the windshield of a vehicle, containing indicator dials and controls.

da•shi•ki (də-shē′kē) ►*n., pl.* **-kis.** A loose, brightly colored African tunic. [Yoruba *dàńṣíkí.*]

dash•ing (dăsh′ĭng) ►*adj.* **1.** Bold and gallant; spirited. **2.** Stylish; splendid. See Syns at **fashionable.** —**dash′ing•ly** *adv.*

das•tard (dăs′tərd) ►*n.* A sneaking, malicious coward. [ME.] —**das′tard•li•ness** *n.* —**das′tard•ly** *adj.*

DAT ►*abbr.* digital audiotape

dat. ►*abbr.* dative

da•ta (dā′tə, dăt′ə, dä′tə) ►*pl.n. (takes sing. or pl. v.)* **1.** Factual information, esp. information organized for analysis or used to make decisions. **2.** Numerical information suitable for processing by computer. **3.** Pl. of **datum** 1. [Lat., pl. of *datum*, something given < p.part. of *dare*, give.]

Usage: Although *data* came from a Latin plural form and is sometimes used with a plural verb in English, scientists and researchers usually think of data as a singular mass entity like information and use it with a singular verb. Most people do the same in general usage. See Usage Note at **criterion.**

da•ta•base (dā′tə-bās′, dăt′ə-) ►*n. Comp. Sci.* A collection of data arranged for ease of search and retrieval.

data processing ►*n.* **1.** Conversion of data into a form that can be processed by computer. **2.** The storing or processing of such data. —**data processor** *n.*

date[1] (dāt) ►*n.* **1a.** Time stated in terms of the day, month, and year. **b.** A statement of calendar time, as on a document. **2.** A specified day of a month. **3.** A particular time at which something happened or is expected to happen. **4.** The period to which something belongs. **5a.** An appointment, esp. to go out socially. **b.** A person's companion on such an outing. **6.** An engagement for a performance. ►*v.* **dat•ed, dat•ing 1.** To mark or supply with a date: *date a letter.* **2.** To determine the date of. **3.** To betray the age of. **4.** To have origin in a particular time in the past: *This statue dates from 500 B.C.* **5.** To go on a date or dates (with). —***idiom:*** **to date** Up to the present time. [< Lat. *data (Romae)*, issued (at Rome) (on a certain day) < *dare*, give.] —**dat′a•ble, date′a•ble** *adj.*

date[2] (dāt) ►*n.* The sweet edible oblong fruit of the date palm. [< Gk. *daktulos*, date.]

dat•ed (dā′tĭd) ►*adj.* **1.** Marked with a date. **2.**

Old-fashioned. —**dat′ed•ness** *n.*
date•line (dāt′līn′) ►*n.* A phrase in a news story that gives its date and place of origin.
date palm ►*n.* A palm tree native to W Asia and N Africa, having featherlike leaves and clusters of dates.
date rape ►*n.* Rape perpetrated by the victim's social escort.
da•tive (dā′tĭv) ►*adj.* Of or being the grammatical case that marks the indirect object. ►*n.* The dative case. [< Lat. *(cāsus) datīvus*, (case) of giving < *dare*, give.]
da•tum (dā′təm, dăt′əm, dä′təm) ►*n.* **1.** *pl.* **-ta** (-tə) A fact or proposition used to draw a conclusion or make a decision. See Usage Note at **data. 2.** *pl.* **-tums** A point, line, or surface used as a reference, as in surveying. [Lat., something given, neuter p.part. of *dare*, give.]
daub (dôb) ►*v.* **1.** To cover or smear with a soft sticky substance. **2.** To paint quickly or crudely. [< Lat. *dēalbāre*, to whitewash.] —**daub** *n.* —**daub′er** *n.*
daugh•ter (dô′tər) ►*n.* **1.** One's female child. **2.** A female descendant. **3.** A woman considered as if in a relationship of child to parent: *a daughter of the nation.* [< OE *dohtor.*] —**daugh′ter•ly** *adj.*
daugh•ter-in-law (dô′tər-ĭn-lô′) ►*n., pl.* **daugh•ters-in-law** (-tərz-). The wife of one's son.
Dau•mier (dō-myā′), **Honoré.** 1808–79. French artist.
daunt (dônt, dänt) ►*v.* To intimidate or discourage. [< Lat. *domitāre*, to tame.]
daunt•less (dônt′lĭs, dänt′-) ►*adj.* Fearless. —**daunt′less•ly** *adv.*
dau•phin (dô′fĭn) ►*n.* The eldest son of the king of France from 1349 to 1830. [< OFr. < *dalfin*, dolphin.]
dau•phine (dô-fēn′) ►*n.* The wife of a dauphin. [Fr.]
dav•en•port (dăv′ən-pôrt′, -pōrt′) ►*n.* A large sofa. [< *davenport*, a small writing desk.]
Davenport. A city of E IA on the Mississippi R. Pop. 95,333.
Da•vid (dā′vĭd). d. c. 962 B.C. The 2nd king of Judah and Israel.
Da•vid (dä-vēd′), **Jacques Louis.** 1748–1825. French painter.
Da•vis (dā′vĭs), **Bette.** 1908–89. Amer. actress.
Davis, Jefferson. 1808–89. Amer. soldier and president of the Confederacy (1861–65).

Jefferson Davis
detail of an 1849 portrait

dav•it (dăv′ĭt, dā′vĭt) ►*n.* A small crane that projects over the side of a ship, used to hoist boats, anchors, and cargo. [< Norman Fr. *daviot*, dim. of *Davi*, David.]
Da•vy (dā′vē), Sir **Humphry.** 1778–1829. British chemist.
daw•dle (dôd′l) ►*v.* **-dled, -dling 1.** To take more time than necessary. **2.** To waste time; idle. [Perh. alteration of dial. *daddle.*] —**daw′dler** *n.*
Dawes (dôz), **Charles Gates.** 1865–1951. Vice President of the US (1925–29); shared the 1925 Nobel Peace Prize.
dawn (dôn) ►*n.* **1.** The time each morning at which daylight begins. **2.** A first appearance. See Syns at **beginning.** ►*v.* **1.** To begin to become light in the morning. **2.** To begin to exist. **3.** To become apparent: *The truth dawned on us.* [< OE *dagung.*]
day (dā) ►*n.* **1.** The period of light between dawn and nightfall. **2a.** The 24-hour period during which the earth completes one rotation on its axis. **b.** The analogous period of a celestial body. **3.** One of the numbered 24-hour periods into which a week, month, or year is divided. **4.** The portion of a day that is devoted to work or school: *an eight-hour day.* **5.** A period of activity or prominence: *a writer who has had her day.* **6.** often **days** A period of time: *in the days of the Roman Empire.* —***idiom:*** **day in, day out** All the time; continuously. [< OE *dæg.*]
Da•yan (dä-yän′), **Moshe.** 1915–81. Israeli military leader.
day bed ►*n.* A couch convertible into a bed.
day•book (dā′bo͝ok′) ►*n.* **1.** A book in which daily entries are recorded. **2.** A diary.
day•break (dā′brāk′) ►*n.* Dawn.
day•care or **day care** (dā′kâr′) ►*n.* Provision of daytime supervision, training, and recreation, esp. for preschool children.
day•dream (dā′drēm′) ►*n.* A dreamlike musing or fantasy while awake. ►*v.* To have daydreams. —**day′dream′er** *n.*
Day-Glo (dā′glō′) ► A trademark for fluorescent coloring agents and materials.
day labor ►*n.* Labor hired and paid by the day. —**day laborer** *n.*
day•light (dā′līt′) ►*n.* **1.** The light of day. **2a.** Dawn. **b.** Daytime. **3.** Exposure to public notice. **4.** An approaching end, as of a complicated task. **5. daylights** *Slang* One's wits: *scared the daylights out of me.*
day•light-sav•ing time (dā′līt-sā′vĭng) ►*n.* Time during which clocks are set one hour or more ahead of standard time to provide more daylight at the end of the working day.
day lily ►*n.* A perennial garden plant with yellow, orange, or purplish lilylike flowers.
Day of Atonement ►*n.* See **Yom Kippur.**
day school ►*n.* A private school for pupils living at home.
day student ►*n.* A nonresident student at a residential school or college.
day•time (dā′tīm′) ►*n.* The time between sunrise and sunset. —**day′time′** *adj.*
day-to-day (dā′tə-dā′) ►*adj.* **1.** Occurring on a daily basis. **2.** Subsisting one day at a time.
Day•ton (dāt′n) A city of SW OH NNE of Cincinnati. Pop. 182,044.
day trade ►*n.* A trade of a security that is bought and sold on the same day. —**day trader** *n.* —**day trading** *n.*
day-trip•per (dā′trĭp′ər) ►*n.* One who takes a

one-day trip without staying overnight.

daze (dāz) ▸ *v.* **dazed, daz•ing 1.** To stun, as with a blow or shock. **2.** To dazzle. ▸ *n.* A stunned or bewildered condition. [ME *dasen*, of Scand. orig.]

Syns: *daze, bemuse, benumb, stun, stupefy* ***v.***

daz•zle (dăz′əl) ▸ *v.* **-zled, -zling 1.** To dim the vision of, esp. to blind with intense light. **2.** To amaze or bewilder with spectacular display. [Frequentative of DAZE.] **—daz′zle** *n.* **—daz′zler** *n.* **—daz′zling•ly** *adv.*

dB ▸ *abbr.* decibel

Db ▸ The symbol for the element **dubnium.**

DC ▸ *abbr.* **1.** da capo **2.** direct current **3.** District of Columbia **4.** Doctor of Chiropractic

DCM ▸ *abbr.* Distinguished Conduct Medal

DD ▸ *abbr.* **1.** dishonorable discharge **2.** *Lat.* Divinitatis Doctor (Doctor of Divinity)

D-day (dē′dā′) ▸ *n.* The unnamed day on which an operation or offensive is to be launched. [*D* (abbr. of DAY) + DAY.]

DDS ▸ *abbr.* **1.** Doctor of Dental Science **2.** Doctor of Dental Surgery

DDT (dē′dē-tē′) ▸ *n.* An insecticide banned since 1972 from US agricultural use for its persistent toxicity in the environment. [*d(ichloro)d(iphenyl)t(richloroethane).*]

DE ▸ *abbr.* Delaware

de– ▸ *pref.* **1.** Reverse: *deactivate.* **2.** Remove: *defog.* **3.** Out of: *deplane.* **4.** Reduce: *degrade.* [ME *de-* < Lat. *dē*, from.]

dea•con (dē′kən) ▸ *n.* **1.** A cleric ranking just below a priest in the Anglican, Eastern Orthodox, and Roman Catholic churches. **2.** A lay assistant to a Protestant minister. [< Gk. *diakonos*, attendant.] **—dea′con•ry** *n.*

dea•con•ess (dē′kə-nĭs) ▸ *n.* A laywoman serving as assistant to a Protestant minister.

de•ac•ti•vate (dē-ăk′tə-vāt′) ▸ *v.* **1.** To render inactive or ineffective. **2.** To remove from active military status. **—de•ac′ti•va′tion** *n.*

dead (dĕd) ▸ *adj.* **-er, -est 1.** No longer alive. **2.** Lacking feeling; unresponsive. **3.** Weary and worn-out. **4a.** Inanimate. **b.** Lifeless; barren: *dead soil.* **5a.** No longer in existence or use. **b.** No longer relevant. **c.** Dormant: *a dead volcano.* **6.** Not circulating; stagnant: *dead air.* **7.** Dull; quiet: *a dead town; a dead party.* **8.** Having grown cold: *dead coals.* **9.** Lacking elasticity or bounce. **10.** Not running or working: *The motor is dead.* **11a.** Sudden; abrupt: *a dead stop.* **b.** Complete: *dead silence.* **c.** Exact: *dead center.* **12a.** Lacking connection to a source of electric current. **b.** Discharged: *a dead battery.* ▸ *n.* **1.** One who has died. **2.** A period of greatest intensity: *the dead of winter.* ▸ *adv.* **1.** Absolutely; altogether: *dead sure.* **2.** Directly; exactly: *dead ahead.* **3.** Suddenly: *stop dead.* [< OE *dēad.*] **—dead′ness** *n.*

dead•beat (dĕd′bēt′) ▸ *n.* *Slang* **1.** One who does not pay one's debts. **2.** A lazy person; loafer.

dead bolt ▸ *n.* A bolt on a lock that is moved by turning the key or knob without activation of a spring.

dead•en (dĕd′n) ▸ *v.* **1.** To make less intense, sensitive, or strong: *deaden the pain; deaden curiosity.* **2.** To make soundproof. **3.** To make dull.

dead end ▸ *n.* **1.** An end of a passage that affords no exit. **2.** An impasse.

dead-end (dĕd′ĕnd′) ▸ *adj.* **1.** Having no exit. **2.** Permitting no opportunity for advancement: *a dead-end job.* **—dead′-end′** *v.*

dead•eye (dĕd′ī′) ▸ *n.* *Slang* An expert shooter.

dead hand ▸ *n.* **1.** The oppressive influence of past events. **2.** Mortmain. [ME *dede hond.*]

dead heat ▸ *n.* A race in which two or more contestants finish at the same time.

dead letter ▸ *n.* An unclaimed or undelivered letter.

dead•line (dĕd′līn′) ▸ *n.* A time limit, as for completion of a task.

dead•lock (dĕd′lŏk′) ▸ *n.* A standstill resulting from the opposition of two unrelenting forces. ▸ *v.* To bring or come to a deadlock.

dead•ly (dĕd′lē) ▸ *adj.* **-li•er, -li•est 1.** Causing or capable of causing death. **2.** Suggestive of death. **3.** Mortal; implacable: *deadly enemies.* **4.** Destructive in effect. **5.** Absolute; utter. **6.** Dull: *a deadly lecture.* ▸ *adv.* To an extreme: *deadly serious.* **—dead′li•ness** *n.*

deadly nightshade ▸ *n.* See **belladonna** 1.

deadly sin ▸ *n.* One of the seven sins—anger, covetousness, envy, gluttony, lust, pride, and sloth—supposed to be fatal to one's spiritual development.

dead•pan (dĕd′păn′) ▸ *adj.* & *adv.* With a blank expressionless face. **—dead′pan′** *v.*

dead reckoning ▸ *n.* Navigation without astronomical observations, as by applying to a previously determined position the course and distance traveled since. [Poss. < *ded.*, abbr. of *deduced.*]

Dead Sea. A salt lake between Israel and Jordan.

dead weight ▸ *n.* **1.** The unrelieved weight of a heavy motionless mass. **2.** An oppressive burden or difficulty.

dead•wood (dĕd′wo͝od′) ▸ *n.* One that is burdensome or superfluous.

deaf (dĕf) ▸ *adj.* **-er, -est 1.** Partially or completely unable to hear. **2.** Unwilling to listen: *was deaf to our pleas.* ▸ *n. (takes pl. v.)* **1.** Deaf people collectively. **2. Deaf** The community of deaf people who use American Sign Language as a primary means of communication. [< OE *dēaf.*] **—deaf′en** *v.* **—deaf′ly** *adv.* **—deaf′ness** *n.*

Usage: When spelled with a capital letter, *Deaf* refers to deaf persons belonging to *Deaf culture*—the community of those who use American Sign Language as the primary means of communication. Only persons who are self-identified as belonging to Deaf culture are appropriately referred to as *Deaf.*

deaf-mute also **deaf mute** (dĕf′myo͞ot′) ▸ *n.* *Often Offensive* A person who can neither hear nor speak. See Usage Note at **mute. —deaf-mute′** *adj.*

deal[1] (dēl) ▸ *v.* **dealt** (dĕlt), **deal•ing 1.** To distribute or apportion. **2.** To sell. **3.** To administer; deliver: *deal a blow.* **4.** To distribute (playing cards) among players. **5.** To have to do; treat: *a book that deals with ecology.* **6.** To behave in a specified way toward another or others. **7.** To take action: *deal with a complaint.* See Syns at **treat. 8.** To do business; trade: *deal in furs.* ▸ *n.* **1.** The act of dealing. **2a.** The cards dealt in a card game; hand. **b.** The right or turn of a player to deal. **3.** An indefinite quantity or degree: *a great deal of luck.*

4. An often secret arrangement or pact. **5a.** A business transaction. **b.** An agreement. See Syns at **bargain. 6.** *Informal* A good buy. **7.** *Informal* Treatment received: *a fair deal.* [< OE *dǣlan.*]

deal² (dēl) ►*n.* Fir or pine wood, esp. cut to standard size. [< MLGer. *dele*, plank.]

deal•er (dē′lər) ►*n.* **1.** One who buys and sells. **2.** *Games* The one who deals the cards.

deal•er•ship (dē′lər-shĭp′) ►*n.* A franchise to sell specified items in a certain area.

deal•ing (dē′lĭng) ►*n.* **1. dealings** Transactions or relations with others, usu. in business. **2.** Conduct in relation to others.

dean (dēn) ►*n.* **1.** An administrative officer in a high school, college, or university. **2.** The senior member of a body or group. [< LLat. *decānus*, chief of ten.]

dear (dîr) ►*adj.* **-er, -est 1.** Loved and cherished. **2.** Highly esteemed or regarded. **3.** High-priced. ►*n.* A greatly loved person; darling. ►*interj.* Used as a polite exclamation. [< OE *dēore.*] —**dear′ly** *adv.* —**dear′ness** *n.*

dearth (dûrth) ►*n.* A scarce supply; lack. [< OE **dēorthu*, costliness < *dēore*, costly.]

death (dĕth) ►*n.* **1.** The act of dying or state of being dead; termination of life. **2.** The cause or manner of dying. **3.** Termination; extinction. —***idiom:* to death** To an extreme degree: *worried to death.* [< OE *dēath.*]

death•bed (dĕth′bĕd′) ►*n.* **1.** The bed on which a person dies. **2.** The last hours before death.

death•blow (dĕth′blō′) ►*n.* A fatal blow or event.

death•less (dĕth′lĭs) ►*adj.* Undying; immortal. —**death′less•ness** *n.*

death•ly (dĕth′lē) ►*adj.* Of, resembling, or characteristic of death. ►*adv.* Extremely; very: *deathly pale.*

death rate ►*n.* The ratio of deaths to total population in a specified community over a specified period of time.

death rattle ►*n.* A gurgling or rattling sound sometimes made in the throat of a dying person.

death row (rō) ►*n.* The part of a prison for housing inmates who have received the death penalty.

death's-head (dĕths′hĕd′) ►*n.* The human skull as a symbol of mortality or death.

death squad ►*n.* A clandestine, usu. military, group employed for political assassinations.

death•trap (dĕth′trăp′) ►*n.* An unsafe building or other structure.

Death Valley. An arid desert basin of E CA and W NV.

death•watch (dĕth′wŏch′) ►*n.* A vigil kept beside a dying or dead person.

deb (dĕb) ►*n.* *Informal* A debutante.

de•ba•cle (dĭ-bä′kəl, -băk′əl, dĕb′ə-kəl) ►*n.* A sudden disastrous collapse, downfall, or defeat. [< OFr. *desbacler*, unbar.]

de•bar (dē-bär′) ►*v.* **-barred, -bar•ring 1.** To exclude or shut out; bar. **2.** To forbid or prevent. [< OFr. *desbarer*, unbar.] —**de•bar′ment** *n.*

de•bark (dĭ-bärk′) ►*v.* To unload; disembark. [Fr. *débarquer* : DE– + *barque*, ship.] —**de′bar•ka′tion** (dē′bär-kā′shən) *n.*

de•base (dĭ-bās′) ►*v.* **-based, -bas•ing.** To lower in character, quality, or value; degrade. See Syns at **adulterate, corrupt.** —**de•base′ment** *n.* —**de•bas′er** *n.*

de•bate (dĭ-bāt′) ►*v.* **-bat•ed, -bat•ing 1.** To consider; deliberate. **2.** To discuss opposing points. **3.** To discuss or argue formally. ►*n.* **1.** An argument. **2.** Deliberation; consideration. **3.** A formal contest of argumentation in which two opposing teams defend and attack a given proposition. [< OFr. *debatre.*] —**de•bat′a•ble** *adj.* —**de•bat′er** *n.*

de•bauch (dĭ-bôch′) ►*v.* **1.** To corrupt morally. **2.** To reduce the value or quality of; debase. See Syns at **corrupt.** [< OFr. *desbauchier*, roughhew timber, lead astray.] —**de•bauch′er** *n.* —**de•bauch′er•y** *n.*

de•ben•ture (dĭ-bĕn′chər) ►*n.* **1.** A voucher acknowledging a debt. **2.** An unsecured bond issued by a civil or governmental agency. [< Lat. *dēbentur*, they are due.]

de•bil•i•tate (dĭ-bĭl′ĭ-tāt′) ►*v.* **-tat•ed, -tat•ing.** To sap the strength of; enervate. [< Lat. *dēbilis*, weak.] —**de•bil′i•ta′tion** *n.* —**de•bil′i•ta′tive** *adj.*

de•bil•i•ty (dĭ-bĭl′ĭ-tē) ►*n.*, *pl.* **-ties.** The state of being weak; feebleness.

deb•it (dĕb′ĭt) ►*n.* **1.** An item of debt as recorded in an account. **2.** The sum of such entries. ►*v.* **1.** To enter a debit in an account. **2.** To charge with a debit. [< Lat. *dēbitum*, DEBT.]

debit card ►*n.* A bankcard used in charging electronic transactions against funds on deposit.

deb•o•nair also **deb•o•naire** (dĕb′ə-nâr′) ►*adj.* **1.** Suave; urbane. **2.** Carefree; jaunty. [< OFr. *de bon aire*, of good disposition.] —**deb′o•nair′ly** *adv.*

De•bre•cen (dĕb′rĭt-sĕn′, -rĕ-tsĕn′) A city of E Hungary E of Budapest. Pop. 217,497.

de•brief (dē-brēf′) ►*v.* To question to obtain knowledge gathered, esp. on a military mission. —**de•brief′ing** *n.*

de•bris also **dé•bris** (də-brē′, dā-, dā′brē′) ►*n.* The scattered remains of something broken or destroyed; rubble or wreckage. [< OFr. *debrisier*, break to pieces.]

Debs (dĕbz), **Eugene Victor.** 1855–1926. Amer. labor organizer and socialist leader.

debt (dĕt) ►*n.* **1.** Something owed, as money, goods, or services. **2.** The condition of owing; indebtedness. [< Lat. *dēbitum* < p.part. of *dēbēre*, owe.] —**debt′or** *n.*

de•bug (dē-bŭg′) ►*v.* **-bugged, -bug•ging 1.** To remove a hidden electronic surveillance device from. **2.** To search for and eliminate malfunctioning elements or errors in (e.g., computer software). —**de•bug′ger** *n.*

de•bunk (dē-bŭngk′) ►*v.* To expose or ridicule the falseness or exaggerated claims of. —**de•bunk′er** *n.*

De•bus•sy (dĕb′yo͞o-sē′), **Claude Achille.** 1862–1918. French composer.

de•but also **dé•but** (dā-byo͞o′, dā′byo͞o′) ►*n.* **1.** A first public appearance. **2.** The formal presentation of a young woman to society. **3.** The beginning of something. ►*v.* **-buted** (-byo͞od′), **-but•ing** (-byo͞o′ĭng). To make a debut. [Fr. *début* < *débuter*, begin.]

deb•u•tante (dĕb′yo͞o-tänt′, dā′byo͞o-) ►*n.* A young woman making a formal debut into society. [Fr. *débutante* < *débuter*, begin.]

Dec. ►*abbr.* December

deca– or **dec–** also **deka–** or **dek–** ►*pref.*

Ten: *decagram.* [< Gk. *deka*, ten.]
dec•ade (dĕk′ād′, dĕ-kād′) ▶*n.* A period of ten years. [< Gk. *dekas*, group of ten.]
dec•a•dence (dĕk′ə-dəns, dĭ-kād′ns) ▶*n.* A process, condition, or period of deterioration; decay. [< VLat. **dēcadere*, DECAY.] —**dec′a•dent** *adj. & n.* —**dec′a•dent•ly** *adv.*
de•caf (dē′kăf′) ▶*n. Informal* Decaffeinated coffee. —**de′caf′** *adj.*
de•caf•fein•at•ed (dē-kăf′ə-nā′tĭd, -kăf′ē-ə-) ▶*adj.* Having the caffeine removed. —**de•caf′fein•ate′** *v.* —**de•caf′fein•a′tion** *n.*
dec•a•gon (dĕk′ə-gŏn′) ▶*n.* A polygon with ten sides. —**de•cag′o•nal** (dĭ-kăg′ə-nəl) *adj.* —**de•cag′o•nal•ly** *adv.*
dec•a•gram or **dek•a•gram** (dĕk′ə-grăm′) ▶*n.* See table at **measurement.**
dec•a•he•dron (dĕk′ə-hē′drən) ▶*n., pl.* **-drons** or **-dra** (-drə). A polyhedron with ten faces. —**dec′a•he′dral** *adj.*
de•cal (dē′kăl′, dĭ-kăl′) ▶*n.* **1.** A design transferred by decalcomania. **2.** A decorative sticker.
de•cal•ci•fy (dē-kăl′sə-fī′) ▶*v.* **-fied, -fy•ing.** To remove calcium or calcium compounds from. —**de•cal′ci•fi•ca′tion** *n.* —**de•cal′ci•fi′er** *n.*
de•cal•co•ma•ni•a (dē-kăl′kə-mā′nē-ə,-mān′yə) ▶*n.* The process of transferring designs printed on specially prepared paper to materials such as glass or metal. [< Fr. *décalquer*, transfer by tracing.]
dec•a•li•ter or **dek•a•li•ter** (dĕk′ə-lē′tər) ▶*n.* See table at **measurement.**
Dec•a•logue or **Dec•a•log** (dĕk′ə-lôg′, -lŏg′) ▶*n. Bible* The Ten Commandments. [< Gk. *dekalogos*.]
dec•a•me•ter or **dek•a•me•ter** (dĕk′ə-mē′tər) ▶*n.* See table at **measurement.**
de•camp (dĭ-kămp′) ▶*v.* **1.** To depart secretly or suddenly. **2.** To break camp. [< OFr. *descamper*.] —**de•camp′ment** *n.*
de•cant (dĭ-kănt′) ▶*v.* **1.** To pour off (e.g., wine) without disturbing the sediment. **2.** To pour (a liquid) from one container into another. [< Med.Lat. *dēcanthāre* : DE– + Lat. *canthus*, rim.] —**de′can•ta′tion** (dē′kăn-tā′shən) *n.*
de•cant•er (dĭ-kăn′tər) ▶*n.* A vessel used for decanting, esp. a bottle for serving wine.
de•cap•i•tate (dĭ-kăp′ĭ-tāt′) ▶*v.* **-tat•ed, -tat•ing.** To cut off the head of. [LLat. *dēcapitāre* < Lat. *caput*, *capit-*, head.] —**de•cap′i•ta′tion** *n.* —**de•cap′i•ta′tor** *n.*
dec•a•syl•la•ble (dĕk′ə-sĭl′ə-bəl) ▶*n.* A line of verse having ten syllables. —**dec′a•syl•lab′ic** (-sə-lăb′ĭk) *adj.*
de•cath•lon (dĭ-kăth′lən, -lŏn′) ▶*n.* An athletic contest in which each contestant participates in ten track and field events. [DECA– + Gk. *athlon*, contest.] —**de•cath′lete** *n.*
De•ca•tur (dĭ-kā′tər), **Stephen.** 1779–1820. Amer. naval officer.
de•cay (dĭ-kā′) ▶*v.* **1.** To decompose; rot. **2.** *Phys.* To diminish by radioactive decay. **3.** To decline or decrease in quality or quantity. ▶*n.* **1.** Decomposition. **2.** *Phys.* Radioactive decay. **3.** A gradual deterioration. **4.** A falling into ruin. [< VLat. **dēcadere*, fall away.]
de•cease (dĭ-sēs′) ▶*v.* **-ceased, -ceas•ing.** To die. ▶*n.* Death. [< Lat. *dēcēdere*, go away, die.]
de•ceased (dĭ-sēst′) ▶*adj.* No longer living; dead. ▶*n., pl.* **deceased.** A dead person.
de•ce•dent (dĭ-sēd′nt) ▶*n. Law* A dead person. [< Lat. *dēcēdere*, go away, die.]
de•ceit (dĭ-sēt′) ▶*n.* **1.** Misrepresentation; deception. **2.** A stratagem; trick. [< OFr. *deceite* < p.part. of *deceveir*, DECEIVE.] —**de•ceit′ful** *adj.* —**de•ceit′ful•ly** *adv.* —**de•ceit′ful•ness** *n.*
de•ceive (dĭ-sēv′) ▶*v.* **-ceived, -ceiv•ing.** To cause to believe what is not true; mislead. [< Lat. *dēcipere*.] —**de•ceiv′er** *n.* —**de•ceiv′ing•ly** *adv.*
de•cel•er•ate (dē-sĕl′ə-rāt′) ▶*v.* **-at•ed, -at•ing.** To decrease in speed. [DE– + (AC)CELERATE.] —**de•cel′er•a′tion** *n.*
De•cem•ber (dĭ-sĕm′bər) ▶*n.* The 12th month of the Gregorian calendar. See table at **calendar.** [< Lat., the tenth month.]
de•cen•ni•al (dĭ-sĕn′ē-əl) ▶*adj.* **1.** Of or lasting for ten years. **2.** Occurring every ten years. ▶*n.* A tenth anniversary. [< Lat. *decennium*, decade.] —**de•cen′ni•al•ly** *adv.*
de•cent (dē′sənt) ▶*adj.* **1.** Conforming to standards of propriety. **2.** Free from indelicacy; modest. **3.** Meeting accepted standards; adequate. **4.** Kind or obliging. **5.** *Informal* Properly or modestly dressed. [< Lat. *decēre*, be fitting.] —**de′cen•cy** *n.* —**de′cent•ly** *adv.* —**de′cent•ness** *n.*
de•cen•tral•ize (dē-sĕn′trə-līz′) ▶*v.* **-ized, -iz•ing 1.** To distribute the functions of (a central authority) among local authorities. **2.** To cause to withdraw from an area of concentration. —**de•cen′tral•i•za′tion** *n.*
de•cep•tion (dĭ-sĕp′shən) ▶*n.* **1.** The use of deceit. **2.** The fact or state of being deceived. [< Lat. *dēcipere*, *dēcept-*, deceive.]
de•cep•tive (dĭ-sĕp′tĭv) ▶*adj.* Intended or tending to deceive. —**de•cep′tive•ly** *adv.* —**de•cep′tive•ness** *n.*
deci– ▶*pref.* One tenth (10^{-1}): *decigram.* [< Lat. *decimus*, tenth.]
de•ci•bel (dĕs′ə-bəl, -bĕl′) ▶*n.* A unit used to express relative difference in power, usu. between acoustic or electric signals, equal to ten times the common logarithm of the ratio of the two levels. [DECI– + *bel*, after Alexander Graham BELL.]
de•cide (dĭ-sīd′) ▶*v.* **-cid•ed, -cid•ing 1.** To settle conclusively all uncertainty about. **2.** To influence or determine the outcome of. **3.** To make up one's mind. [< Lat. *dēcīdere*, cut off.] —**de•cid′a•ble** *adj.* —**de•cid′er** *n.*
de•cid•ed (dĭ-sī′dĭd) ▶*adj.* **1.** Without doubt or question; definite. **2.** Resolute. —**de•cid′ed•ly** *adv.* —**de•cid′ed•ness** *n.*
de•cid•u•ous (dĭ-sĭj′o͞o-əs) ▶*adj.* **1.** Falling off at a specific season or stage of growth. **2.** Shedding foliage at the end of the growing season: *deciduous trees.* [< Lat. *dēciduus* < *dēcidere*, fall off.] —**de•cid′u•ous•ly** *adv.* —**de•cid′u•ous•ness** *n.*
dec•i•gram (dĕs′ĭ-grăm′) ▶*n.* See table at **measurement.**
de•cil•lion (dĭ-sĭl′yən) ▶*n.* **1.** The cardinal number equal to 10^{33}. **2.** *Chiefly Brit.* The cardinal number equal to 10^{60}. [Lat. *decem*, ten + (M)ILLION.] —**de•cil′lion** *adj.* —**de•cil′lionth** *adj. & n.*
dec•i•mal (dĕs′ə-məl) ▶*n.* **1.** A linear array of integers that represents a fraction, every decimal place indicating a multiple of a negative

power of 10. For example, the decimal 0.1 = $\frac{1}{10}$, 0.12 = $\frac{12}{100}$, 0.003 = $\frac{3}{1000}$. **2.** A number written using the base 10. ► *adj.* **1.** Expressed or expressible as a decimal. **2a.** Based on 10. **b.** Numbered or ordered by groups of 10. [< Lat. *decima*, tenth part.] —**dec′i•mal•ly** *adv.*

decimal place ► *n.* The position of a digit to the right of a decimal point, usu. identified by successive ascending ordinal numbers with the digit immediately to the right of the decimal point being first.

decimal point ► *n.* A dot written in a decimal number to indicate where the place values change from positive to negative powers of 10.

dec•i•mate (dĕs′ə-māt′) ► *v.* **-mat•ed, -mat•ing 1.** To destroy or kill a large part of. **2.** *Informal* **a.** To inflict great damage on: *Deer decimated the new garden.* **b.** To reduce markedly in amount: *hospital bills that decimated our savings.* [Lat. *decimāre* < *decimus*, tenth.] —**dec′i•ma′tion** *n.*

Usage: *Decimate* originally referred to killing every tenth person, but commonly can be extended to include killing any large proportion of a group. Use of *decimate* to refer to large-scale destruction other than killing is less acceptable.

dec•i•me•ter (dĕs′ə-mē′tər) ► *n.* See table at **measurement.**

de•ci•pher (dĭ-sī′fər) ► *v.* **1.** To read or interpret (obscure or illegible matter). See Syns at **solve. 2.** To decode. —**de•ci′pher•a•ble** *adj.* —**de•ci′pher•ment** *n.*

de•ci•sion (dĭ-sĭzh′ən) ► *n.* **1.** The passing of judgment on an issue. **2.** A conclusion or judgment; verdict. **3.** Firmness of character or action; determination. **4.** *Sports* A victory in boxing won on points when no knockout has occurred. [< Lat. *dēcīdere, dēcīs-*, decide.]

Syns: *decision, conclusion, determination* **n.**

de•ci•sive (dĭ-sī′sĭv) ► *adj.* **1.** Conclusive. **2.** Determined; resolute. **3.** Beyond doubt; unmistakable. —**de•ci′sive•ly** *adv.* —**de•ci′sive•ness** *n.*

Syns: *decisive, conclusive, crucial, definitive, determinative* ***Ant:*** *indecisive* **adj.**

deck[1] (dĕk) ► *n.* **1.** A platform extending horizontally from one side of a ship to the other. **2.** A similar platform or surface, esp. a roofless floored area adjoining a house. **3.** A pack of playing cards. [MDu. *dec*, covering.]

deck[2] (dĕk) ► *v.* **1.** To clothe with finery; adorn. **2.** To decorate. [< MDu. *decken*, to cover.]

deck chair ► *n.* A folding chair, usu. with arms and a leg rest.

de•claim (dĭ-klām′) ► *v.* To speak loudly and with rhetorical effect. [< Lat. *dēclāmāre*, cry out.] —**de•claim′er** *n.* —**dec′la•ma′tion** (dĕk′lə-mā′shən) *n.* —**de•clam′a•to′ry** (dĭ-klăm′ə-tôr′ē, -tōr′ē) *adj.*

de•clare (dĭ-klâr′) ► *v.* **-clared, -clar•ing 1.** To make known formally, officially, or authoritatively. See Syns at **announce. 2.** To reveal or show. **3.** To make a full statement of (e.g., dutiable goods). **4.** To proclaim one's support or opinion. [< Lat. *dēclārāre.*] —**dec′la•ra′tion** (dĕk′lə-rā′shən) *n.* —**de•clar′a•tive** *adj.* —**de•clar′er** *n.*

de•clas•si•fy (dē-klăs′ə-fī′) ► *v.* To remove official security classification from (a document). —**de•clas′si•fi•ca′tion** *n.*

de•clen•sion (dĭ-klĕn′shən) ► *n.* **1.** *Ling.* **a.** The inflection of nouns, pronouns, and adjectives for case, number, and gender. **b.** A class of words with the same inflections. **2.** A descent. **3.** A decline or deterioration. [< Lat. *dēclīnātiō* < *dēclīnāre*, decline.] —**de•clen′sion•al** *adj.*

de•cline (dĭ-klīn′) ► *v.* **-clined, -clin•ing 1.** To express polite refusal. **2.** To slope downward. **3.** To deteriorate gradually; fail. **4.** *Gram.* To inflect (a noun, pronoun, or adjective). ► *n.* **1.** The process or result of declining. **2.** A downward slope. **3.** A disease that gradually weakens the body. [< Lat. *dēclīnāre*, turn aside : DE– + *-clīnāre*, lean.] —**de•clin′a•ble** *adj.* —**dec′li•na′tion** (dĕk′lə-nā′shən) *n.* —**dec′li•na′tion•al** *adj.* —**de•clin′er** *n.*

de•cliv•i•ty (dĭ-klĭv′ĭ-tē) ► *n., pl.* **-ties.** A downward slope. [< Lat. *dēclīvis*, sloping down : DE– + *clīvus*, slope.]

de•code (dē-kōd′) ► *v.* To convert from code into plain text. —**de•cod′er** *n.*

dé•colle•tage (dā′kôl-täzh′) ► *n.* A low neckline, esp. on a dress. [Fr. < *décolleter*, lower a neckline.]

décolletage

dé•colle•té (dā′kôl-tā′) ► *adj.* Cut low at the neckline. [Fr.]

de•col•o•nize (dē-kŏl′ə-nīz′) ► *v.* To free (a colony) from dependent status. —**de•col′o•ni•za′tion** *n.*

de•com•mis•sion (dē′kə-mĭsh′ən) ► *v.* To withdraw (e.g., a ship) from active service.

de•com•pose (dē′kəm-pōz′) ► *v.* **1.** To separate into components or basic elements. **2.** To rot or cause to rot. —**de′com•pos′a•ble** *adj.* —**de′com•pos′er** *n.* —**de•com′po•si′tion** (dē-kŏm′pə-zĭsh′ən) *n.*

de•com•press (dē′kəm-prĕs′) ► *v.* To relieve of pressure. —**de′com•pres′sion** *n.*

decompression sickness ► *n.* A disorder, seen esp. in deep-sea divers, caused by nitrogen bubbles in the blood and characterized by severe pain and paralysis.

de•con•gest (dē′kən-jĕst′) ► *v.* To relieve the congestion of (e.g., sinuses). —**de′con•ges′tion** *n.* —**de′con•ges′tive** *adj.*

de•con•ges•tant (dē′kən-jĕs′tənt) ► *n.* A medication that breaks up congestion, esp. in the sinuses.

de•con•tam•i•nate (dē′kən-tăm′ə-nāt′) ► *v.* **1.** To eliminate contamination in. **2.** To make safe by eliminating poisonous or harmful substances, such as radioactive material. —**de′con•tam′i•nant** *n.* —**de′con•tam′i•na′tion** *n.*

de•con•trol (dē'kən-trōl') ▶ *v.* To stop control of, esp. by the government: *decontrol prices.*

dé•cor or **de•cor** (dā'kôr', dā-kôr') ▶ *n.* **1.** Decoration. **2.** A decorative style or scheme, as of a room. [Fr.]

dec•o•rate (dĕk'ə-rāt') ▶ *v.* **-rat•ed, -rat•ing 1.** To provide or adorn with something ornamental. **2.** To confer a medal or other honor on. [< Lat. *decorāre* < *decus*, ornament.] **—dec'o•ra'tion** *n.* **—dec'o•ra•tive** *adj.* **—dec'o•ra•tive•ly** *adv.*

dec•o•ra•tor (dĕk'ə-rā'tər) ▶ *n.* One that decorates, esp. an interior decorator.

dec•o•rous (dĕk'ər-əs, dĭ-kôr'əs, -kōr'-) ▶ *adj.* Marked by decorum; proper. [< Lat. *decor*, seemliness.] **—dec'o•rous•ly** *adv.* **—dec'o•rous•ness** *n.*

de•co•rum (dĭ-kôr'əm, -kōr'-) ▶ *n.* **1.** Appropriateness of behavior or conduct; propriety. **2.** Artistic or literary appropriateness. [Lat. *decōrum.*]

de•cou•page also **dé•cou•page** (dā'ko͞o-päzh') ▶ *n.* The technique of decorating a surface with cutouts, as of paper. [Fr. *découpage* < *découper*, cut up.]

de•coy (dē'koi', dĭ-koi') ▶ *n.* **1.** A living or artificial animal used to entice game. **2.** A means used to mislead or lead into danger. ▶ *v.* (dĭ-koi'). To lure or entrap by or as if by a decoy. [Poss. < Du. *de kooi*, the cage.] **—de•coy'er** *n.*

de•crease (dĭ-krēs') ▶ *v.* **-creased, -creas•ing.** To diminish gradually; reduce. ▶ *n.* (dē'krēs'). The act or process of decreasing. [< Lat. *dēcrēscere* : DE– + *crēscere*, grow.]

de•cree (dĭ-krē') ▶ *n.* **1.** An authoritative order; edict. **2.** *Law* The judgment of a court of equity, admiralty, probate, or divorce. ▶ *v.* **-creed, -cree•ing.** To ordain, establish, or decide by decree. See Syns at **dictate.** [< Lat. *dēcrētum* < p.part. of *dēcernere*, decide.]

dec•re•ment (dĕk'rə-mənt) ▶ *n.* **1.** A gradual decrease. **2.** The amount lost by gradual diminution or waste. [Lat. *dēcrēmentum* < *dēcrēscere*, DECREASE.] **—dec're•ment'al** *adj.*

de•crep•it (dĭ-krĕp'ĭt) ▶ *adj.* Weakened, worn out, or broken down by old age, illness, or hard use. [< Lat. *dēcrepitus.*] **—de•crep'it•ly** *adv.* **—de•crep'i•tude'** *n.*

de•cre•scen•do (dā'krə-shĕn'dō, dē'-) ▶ *n.*, *pl.* **-dos** *Mus.* A gradual decrease in force or loudness. [Ital.] **—de'cre•scen'do** *adv.* & *adj.*

de•crim•i•nal•ize (dē-krĭm'ə-nə-līz') ▶ *v.* **-ized, -iz•ing.** To reduce or abolish criminal penalties for. **—de•crim'i•nal•i•za'tion** *n.*

de•cry (dĭ-krī') ▶ *v.* **-cried, -cry•ing.** To condemn openly. [< OFr. *descrier.*] **—de•cri'er** *n.*

ded•i•cate (dĕd'ĭ-kāt') ▶ *v.* **-cat•ed, -cat•ing 1.** To set apart for a special use. **2.** To commit (oneself) to a course of action. **3.** To inscribe (e.g., a book) to another. **4.** To open to public use: *dedicate a new library.* [< Lat. *dēdicāre.*] **—ded'i•ca'tion** *n.* **—ded'i•ca'tive, ded'i•ca•to'ry** (-kə-tôr'ē, -tōr'ē) *adj.*

de•duce (dĭ-do͞os', -dyo͞os') ▶ *v.* **-duced, -duc•ing.** To infer from a general principle; reason deductively. [< Lat. *dēdūcere*, lead away.] **—de•duc'i•ble** *adj.*

de•duct (dĭ-dŭkt') ▶ *v.* To take away or subtract. [< Lat. *dēdūcere*, *dēduct-*.]

de•duct•i•ble (dĭ-dŭk'tə-bəl) ▶ *adj.* That can be deducted, esp. for income taxes. ▶ *n.* **1.** Something, such as an expense, that can be deducted. **2.** A clause in an insurance policy exempting the insurer from paying an initial specified amount after an accident. **—de•duct'i•bil'i•ty** *n.*

de•duc•tion (dĭ-dŭk'shən) ▶ *n.* **1.** The act of deducting; subtraction. **2.** An amount that is or may be deducted. **3.** *Logic* **a.** The process of reasoning in which a conclusion follows necessarily from the stated premises. **b.** A conclusion reached by this process. **—de•duc'tive** *adj.* **—de•duc'tive•ly** *adv.*

deed (dēd) ▶ *n.* **1.** An act; feat; exploit. **2.** Action or performance in general: *Deeds, not words, matter most.* **3.** *Law* A document sealed as an instrument of bond, contract, or conveyance, esp. relating to property. ▶ *v.* To transfer by means of a deed. [< OE *dǣd.*]

deem (dēm) ▶ *v.* To judge; consider; think. [< OE *dēman.*]

deep (dēp) ▶ *adj.* **-er, -est 1.** Extending far downward, inward, backward, or from side to side; far down or in. **2.** Difficult to understand. **3.** Of a grave or extreme nature. **4.** Very absorbed or involved. **5.** Profound in quality or feeling. **6.** Of an intense shade of color. **7.** Low in pitch; resonant. ▶ *adv.* To a great depth; deeply. ▶ *n.* **1.** A deep place in land or in a body of water. **2.** The most intense or extreme part. **3.** The ocean. **—*idiom:* in deep water** In difficulty. [< OE *dēop.*] **—deep'ly** *adv.* **—deep'ness** *n.*

deep•en (dē'pən) ▶ *v.* To make or become deep or deeper.

deep-fry (dēp'frī') ▶ *v.* To fry by immersing in a deep pan of fat or oil. **—deep'-fried'** *adj.*

deep-root•ed (dēp'ro͞o'tĭd, -ro͝ot'ĭd) ▶ *adj.* Firmly implanted; well-established.

deep-sea (dēp'sē') ▶ *adj.* Of or occurring in deep parts of the sea.

deep-seat•ed (dēp'sē'tĭd) ▶ *adj.* Deeply rooted; ingrained.

deep-set (dēp'sĕt') ▶ *adj.* Deeply set or placed: *deep-set eyes.*

deep-six (dēp'sĭks') ▶ *v.* *Slang* **1.** To toss overboard. **2.** To get rid of.

deep space ▶ *n.* The regions beyond the gravitational influence of Earth, encompassing interplanetary, interstellar, and intergalactic space.

deer (dîr) ▶ *n.*, *pl.* **deer.** Any of various hoofed mammals, including the elk, moose, and caribou, having seasonally shed antlers borne chiefly by the males. [< OE *dēor*, beast.]

deer fly ▶ *n.* Any of various blood-sucking flies smaller than the related horsefly.

deer•skin (dîr'skĭn') ▶ *n.* Leather made from the hide of a deer.

de-es•ca•late (dē-ĕs'kə-lāt') ▶ *v.* To decrease the scope or intensity of. **—de-es'ca•la'tion** *n.*

de•face (dĭ-fās') ▶ *v.* **-faced, -fac•ing.** To mar or spoil the appearance or surface of. **—de•face'ment** *n.* **—de•fac'er** *n.*

de fac•to (dĭ făk'tō, dā) ▶ *adv.* In reality or fact; actually. ▶ *adj.* **1.** Actual: *de facto segregation.* **2.** Actually exercising power. [Lat. *dē factō*, according to the fact.]

de•fal•cate (dĭ-făl'kāt', -fôl'-, dĕf'əl-) ▶ *v.* **-cat•ed, -cat•ing.** To embezzle. [Med.Lat. *dēfalcāre*, mow < Lat. *falx*, sickle.] **—de'fal•**

ca′tion *n.* —**de•fal′ca′tor** *n.*
de•fame (dĭ-fām′) ▶*v.* **-famed, -fam•ing.** To damage the reputation or good name of by slander or libel. [< Lat. *diffāmāre.*] —**def′a•ma′tion** (dĕf′ə-mā′shən) *n.* —**de•fam′a•to′ry** (dĭ-făm′ə-tôr′ē, -tōr′ē) *adj.*
de•fault (dĭ-fôlt′) ▶*n.* **1.** Failure to perform a task or fulfill an obligation. **2.** Failure to participate in a contest. **3.** *Comp. Sci.* A particular value for a variable assigned automatically by an operating system. ▶*v.* **1a.** To fail to do what is required. **b.** To fail to pay money when it is due. **2.** To lose by not appearing, completing, or participating. [< OFr. *defaute* < *defaillir*, fail.] —**de•fault′er** *n.*
de•feat (dĭ-fēt′) ▶*v.* **1.** To win victory over; beat. **2.** To prevent the success of; thwart: *defeat one's own purposes.* ▶*n.* The act of defeating or state of being defeated. [< OFr. *desfait*, p.part. of *desfaire*, destroy.]
de•feat•ism (dĭ-fē′tĭz′əm) ▶*n.* Acceptance of or resignation to the prospect of defeat. —**de•feat′ist** *adj. & n.*
def•e•cate (dĕf′ĭ-kāt′) ▶*v.* **-cat•ed, -cat•ing.** To void feces from the bowels. [< *faex, faec-*, dregs.] —**def′e•ca′tion** *n.*
de•fect (dē′fĕkt′, dĭ-fĕkt′) ▶*n.* **1.** The lack of something necessary or desirable. **2.** An imperfection; shortcoming. ▶*v.* (dĭ-fĕkt′). To disown allegiance to a country, position, or group and adopt or join another. [< Lat. *dēfectus* < p.part. of *dēficere*, be wanting.] —**de•fec′tion** *n.* —**de•fec′tor** *n.*
de•fec•tive (dĭ-fĕk′tĭv) ▶*adj.* Having a defect. —**de•fec′tive•ly** *adv.*
de•fence (dĭ-fĕns′) ▶*n. & v. Chiefly Brit.* Var. of **defense.**
de•fend (dĭ-fĕnd′) ▶*v.* **1.** To protect from danger or harm. **2.** To support or maintain; justify. **3.** *Law* **a.** To represent (a defendant) in a civil or criminal action. **b.** To contest (an action or claim). [< Lat. *dēfendere*, ward off.] —**de•fend′a•ble** *adj.* —**de•fend′er** *n.*
de•fen•dant (dĭ-fĕn′dənt) ▶*n. Law* The party against which an action is brought.
de•fense (dĭ-fĕns′) ▶*n.* **1.** The act of defending. **2.** A means or method of defending or protecting. **3.** An argument in support or justification. **4.** *Law* **a.** The action of the defendant in opposition to complaints against him or her. **b.** The defendant and his or her legal counsel. **5.** (*often* dē′fĕns′) *Sports* The players on a team attempting to stop the opposition from scoring. [< Lat. *dēfēnsa* < *dēfendere*, ward off.] —**de•fense′less** *adj.* —**de•fense′less•ly** *adv.* —**de•fense′less•ness** *n.*
defense mechanism ▶*n.* A physical or psychological reaction of an organism used in self-protection.
de•fen•si•ble (dĭ-fĕn′sə-bəl) ▶*adj.* Capable of being defended or justified. —**de•fen′si•bil′i•ty** *n.* —**de•fen′si•bly** *adv.*
de•fen•sive (dĭ-fĕn′sĭv) ▶*adj.* **1.** Of, intended for, or relating to defense. **2.** *Psychol.* Constantly protecting oneself from perceived threats to the ego. ▶*n.* An attitude or position of defense. —***idiom:* on the defensive** Prepared to withstand attack. —**de•fen′sive•ly** *adv.* —**de•fen′sive•ness** *n.*
de•fer[1] (dĭ-fûr′) ▶*v.* **-ferred, -fer•ring.** To put off; postpone. [ME *differren.* See DIFFER.] —**de•fer′ra•ble** *adj.*
Syns: *defer, postpone, shelve, stay, suspend* **v.**
de•fer[2] (dĭ-fûr′) ▶*v.* **-ferred, -fer•ring.** To submit to the opinion, wishes, or decision of another. [< Lat. *dēferre*, refer to : DE– + *ferre*, carry.] —**de•fer′rer** *n.*
def•er•ence (dĕf′ər-əns, dĕf′rəns) ▶*n.* **1.** Submission or courteous yielding to the opinion, wishes, or judgment of another. **2.** Courteous respect. —**def′er•en′tial** *adj.* —**def′er•en′tial•ly** *adv.*
de•fer•ment (dĭ-fûr′mənt) ▶*n.* **1.** The act or an instance of delaying. **2.** Official postponement of compulsory military service.
de•fer•ral (dĭ-fûr′əl) ▶*n.* Deferment.
de•fi•ant (dĭ-fī′ənt) ▶*adj.* **1.** Marked by bold resistance to authority or an opposing force. **2.** Deliberately provocative. —**de•fi′ance** *n.* —**de•fi′ant•ly** *adv.*
deficiency disease ▶*n.* A disease, such as scurvy, caused by a dietary deficiency of specific nutrients.
de•fi•cient (dĭ-fĭsh′ənt) ▶*adj.* **1.** Lacking an essential quality or element. **2.** Inadequate; insufficient. [< Lat. *dēficere*, be wanting.] —**de•fi′cien•cy** *n.* —**de•fi′cient•ly** *adv.*
def•i•cit (dĕf′ĭ-sĭt) ▶*n.* **1.** Inadequacy or insufficiency. **2.** The amount by which a sum of money falls short of the required amount. [< Lat. *dēficit*, it is lacking.]
deficit spending ▶*n.* The spending of public funds obtained by borrowing rather than taxation.
de•fi•er (dĭ-fī′ər) ▶*n.* One that defies: *a defier of tradition.*
de•file[1] (dĭ-fīl′) ▶*v.* **-filed, -fil•ing 1.** To make filthy or dirty. **2.** To corrupt. **3.** To profane or sully (e.g., a good name). **4.** To desecrate. **5.** To violate the chastity of. [< OE *fȳlan*, befoul, and OFr. *defouler*, trample.] —**de•file′ment** *n.* —**de•fil′er** *n.*
de•file[2] (dĭ-fīl′) ▶*v.* **-filed, -fil•ing.** To march in single file or in columns. ▶*n.* **1.** A narrow gorge or pass. **2.** A march in a line. [Fr. *défiler* < OFr. *filer*, spin thread.]
de•fine (dĭ-fīn′) ▶*v.* **-fined, -fin•ing 1.** To state the precise meaning of (e.g., a word). **2.** To describe the nature or basic qualities of. **3.** To delineate. **4.** To specify distinctly; distinguish. [< Lat. *dēfīnīre* < *fīnis*, boundary.] —**de•fin′a•ble** *adj.* —**de•fin′a•bly** *adv.* —**de•fin′er** *n.*
def•i•nite (dĕf′ə-nĭt) ▶*adj.* **1.** Having distinct limits. **2.** Indisputable; certain. **3.** Clearly defined; precise. See Syns at **explicit.** [< Lat. *dēfīnīre*, DEFINE.] —**def′i•nite•ly** *adv.* —**def′i•nite•ness** *n.*
definite article ▶*n.* A determiner that particularizes a noun. In English, *the* is the definite article.
def•i•ni•tion (dĕf′ə-nĭsh′ən) ▶*n.* **1a.** A statement conveying fundamental character. **b.** A statement of the meaning of a word, phrase, or term, as in a dictionary entry. **2.** The act of making clear and distinct. **3.** A determination of outline, extent, or limits.
de•fin•i•tive (dĭ-fĭn′ĭ-tĭv) ▶*adj.* **1.** Precisely defined or explicit. **2.** Being a final settlement; conclusive. See Syns at **decisive. 3.** Authoritative and complete. —**de•fin′i•tive•ly** *adv.* —**de•fin′i•tive•ness** *n.*
de•flate (dĭ-flāt′) ▶*v.* **-flat•ed, -flat•ing 1a.**

To release contained air or gas from. **b.** To collapse by such a release. **2.** To reduce or lessen the size or importance of. **3.** *Econ.* To reduce the amount or availability of (currency or credit), effecting a decline in prices. [DE– + (IN)FLATE.] —**de•fla′tion** *n.* —**de•fla′tion•ar•y** *adj.* —**de•fla′tor** *n.*

de•flect (dĭ-flĕkt′) ► *v.* To turn aside or cause to turn aside. [Lat. *dēflectere.*] —**de•flect′a•ble** *adj.* —**de•flec′tion** *n.* —**de•flec′tive** *adj.* —**de•flec′tor** *n.*

De•foe (dĭ-fō′), **Daniel.** 1660–1731. British writer.

de•fog (dē-fôg′, -fŏg′) ► *v.* To remove fog from. —**de•fog′ger** *n.*

de•fo•li•ant (dē-fō′lē-ənt) ► *n.* A chemical sprayed or dusted on plants to cause the leaves to fall off.

de•fo•li•ate (dē-fō′lē-āt′) ► *v.* **-at•ed, -at•ing.** To deprive of leaves, esp. by the use of chemicals. —**de•fo′li•ate** (-ĭt) *adj.* —**de•fo′li•a′tion** *n.* —**de•fo′li•a′tor** *n.*

de•for•est (dē-fôr′ĭst, -fŏr′-) ► *v.* To clear away trees from. —**de•for′es•ta′tion** *n.*

de•form (dĭ-fôrm′) ► *v.* **1.** To spoil the beauty or appearance of; disfigure. **2.** To become disfigured. —**de•form′a•ble** *adj.* —**de′for•ma′tion** (dē′fôr-mā′shən, dĕf′ər-) *n.*

de•for•mi•ty (dĭ-fôr′mĭ-tē) ► *n.*, *pl.* **-ties 1.** The state of being deformed. **2.** A bodily malformation or disfigurement. **3.** A deformed person or thing.

de•fraud (dĭ-frôd′) ► *v.* To swindle. —**de′fraud•a′tion** *n.* —**de•fraud′er** *n.*

de•fray (dĭ-frā′) ► *v.* To undertake the payment of; pay. [< OFr. *desfrayer.*] —**de•fray′a•ble** *adj.* —**de•fray′al** *n.*

de•frock (dē-frŏk′) ► *v.* To strip of priestly or other privileges and functions.

de•frost (dē-frôst′, -frŏst′) ► *v.* **1.** To remove ice or frost from. **2.** To cause to thaw. **3.** To become thawed. —**de•frost′er** *n.*

deft (dĕft) ► *adj.* **-er, -est.** Skillful; adroit: *a deft maneuver.* [< ME *dafte*, DAFT.] —**deft′ly** *adv.* —**deft′ness** *n.*

de•funct (dĭ-fŭngkt′) ► *adj.* No longer in existence, operation, or use. [Lat. *dēfūnctus*, p.part. of *dēfungī*, finish.]

de•fuse (dē-fyo͞oz′) ► *v.* **-fused, -fus•ing 1.** To remove the fuse from (an explosive). **2.** To make less dangerous or hostile.

de•fy (dĭ-fī′) ► *v.* **-fied, -fy•ing 1.** To oppose or resist with boldness. **2.** To resist or withstand. **3.** To dare (someone) to do something. [< VLat. **disfīdāre.*]

Syns: *defy, brave, challenge, dare, face* **v.**

deg. ► *abbr.* degree

De•gas (də-gä′), **(Hilaire Germain) Edgar.** 1834–1917. French artist.

de Gaulle (də gōl′, gôl′), **Charles André Joseph Marie.** 1890–1970. French general and politician.

de•gauss (dē-gous′) ► *v.* **1.** To neutralize the magnetic field of. **2.** To erase information from (e.g., a magnetic disk). [DE– + *gauss*, unit of electromagnetism.]

de•gen•er•ate (dĭ-jĕn′ər-ĭt) ► *adj.* Having declined, as in function, from a former state. ► *n.* A depraved or corrupt person. ► *v.* (-ə-rāt′) **-at•ed, -at•ing 1.** To fall below a normal or desirable state. **2.** To decline in quality. [< Lat. *dēgenerāre*, deteriorate.] —**de•gen′er•ate•ly** *adv.* —**de•gen′er•ate•ness, de•gen′er•a•cy** *n.* —**de•gen′er•a′tion** *n.* —**de•gen′er•a•tive** *adj.*

de•grad•a•ble (dĭ-grā′də-bəl) ► *adj.* That can be chemically degraded: *degradable plastic.* —**de•grad′a•bil′i•ty** *n.*

de•grade (dĭ-grād′) ► *v.* **-grad•ed, -grad•ing 1.** To reduce in rank or status. See Syns at **demote. 2.** To dishonor or disgrace. **3.** To reduce in worth or value. [< LLat. *dēgradāre.*] —**deg′ra•da′tion** (dĕg′rə-dā′shən) *n.*

de•gree (dĭ-grē′) ► *n.* **1.** One of a series of steps in a process or course; stage. **2.** Relative social or official rank or position. **3.** Relative intensity. **4.** The extent or measure of a state of being or action. **5.** A unit division of a temperature scale. **6.** *Math.* A unit of angular measure equal in magnitude to $\frac{1}{360}$ of a complete revolution. **7.** A unit of latitude or longitude, equal to $\frac{1}{360}$ of a great circle. **8.** *Math.* The greatest sum of the exponents of the variables in a term of a polynomial or polynomial equation. **9.** An academic title given to someone who has completed a course of study or as an honorary distinction. **10.** *Law* A classification of a crime or injury according to its seriousness. **11.** *Gram.* One of the forms used in the comparison of adjectives and adverbs. **12.** *Mus.* One of the seven notes of a diatonic scale. —***idiom:* to a degree** In a limited way. [< VLat. **dēgradus* : DE– + Lat. *gradus*, step.]

de•gree-day (dĭ-grē′dā′) ► *n.* A unit of measurement equal to a difference of one degree between the mean outdoor temperature on a certain day and a reference temperature, used in estimating the energy needs for heating or cooling a building.

de•hisce (dĭ-hĭs′) ► *v.* **-hisced, -hisc•ing 1.** *Bot.* To open at definite places, discharging seeds or other contents, as the ripe capsules or pods of some plants. **2.** *Medic.* To rupture or break open. [< Lat. *hīscere*, split.] —**de•hisc′ent** *adj.* —**de•hisc′ence** *n.*

de•hu•man•ize (dē-hyo͞o′mə-nīz′) ► *v.* **1.** To deprive of human qualities such as individuality or compassion. **2.** To render mechanical and routine. —**de•hu′man•i•za′tion** *n.*

de•hu•mid•i•fy (dē′hyo͞o-mĭd′ə-fī′) ► *v.* To remove atmospheric moisture from. —**de′hu•mid′i•fi•ca′tion** *n.* —**de′hu•mid′i•fi′er** *n.*

de•hy•drate (dē-hī′drāt′) ► *v.* **1.** To lose water or bodily fluids. **2.** To deplete the bodily fluids of. See Syns at **dry.** —**de′hy•dra′tion** *n.* —**de•hy′dra′tor** *n.*

de•hy•dro•gen•ate (dē′hī-drŏj′ə-nāt′, dē-hī′drə-jə-) ► *v.* To remove hydrogen from. —**de•hy′dro•gen•a′tion** *n.*

de•ice (dē-īs′) ► *v.* To make or keep free of ice. —**de•ic′er** *n.*

de•i•fy (dē′ə-fī′, dā′-) ► *v.* **-fied, -fy•ing 1.** To make a god of. **2.** To worship; exalt. [< LLat. *deificāre.*] —**de′i•fi•ca′tion** *n.*

deign (dān) ► *v.* To consider appropriate to one's dignity; condescend. See Syns at **stoop[1].** [< Lat. *dignārī*, regard as worthy.]

de•in•sti•tu•tion•al•ize (dē-ĭn′stĭ-to͞o′shə-nə-līz′, -tyo͞o′-) ► *v.* **1.** To remove the status of an institution from. **2.** To release (e.g., a mental health patient) from an institution for placement and care in the community. —**de•in′sti•tu′tion•al•i•za′tion** *n.*

de•ism (dē′ĭz′əm) ► *n.* An 18th-cent. system of

natural religion affirming the existence of God while denying the validity of revelation. [< Lat. *deus*, god.] —**de′ist** *n.* —**de•is′tic** *adj.* —**de•is′ti•cal•ly** *adv.*

de•i•ty (dē′ĭ-tē, dā′-) ►*n.*, *pl.* **-ties 1.** A god or goddess. **2.** Divinity. **3. Deity** God. [< Lat. *deus*.]

dé•jà vu (dā′zhä vü′) ►*n.* An impression of having seen or experienced something before. [Fr., already seen.]

de•ject (dĭ-jĕkt′) ►*v.* To lower the spirits of; dishearten. [< Lat. *dēicere*, *dēiect-*, cast down.] —**de•jec′tion** *n.*

de•ject•ed (dĭ-jĕk′tĭd) ►*adj.* Being in low spirits; depressed. See Syns at **depressed.** —**de•ject′ed•ly** *adv.* —**de•ject′ed•ness** *n.*

de ju•re (dē jo͝or′ē, dā yo͝or′ā) ►*adv. & adj.* According to law; by right. [Lat. *dē iūre*.]

dek– or **deka–** ►*pref.* Vars. of **deca–.**

Del. ►*abbr.* Delaware

De•la•croix (də-lä-krwä′), **(Ferdinand Victor) Eugène.** 1798–1863. French romantic painter.

de la Mare (də lə mâr′, dĕl′ə-mâr′), **Walter John.** 1873–1956. British writer.

Del•a•ware¹ (dĕl′ə-wâr′) ►*n.*, *pl.* **-ware** or **-wares 1.** A member of a group of Native American peoples formerly of the Delaware and lower Hudson river valleys, now chiefly in Oklahoma. **2.** The Algonquian language of the Delaware.

Del•a•ware² (dĕl′ə-wâr′) A state of the E US on the Atlantic Ocean. Cap. Dover. Pop. 688,696.

Delaware River. A river rising in SE NY and flowing about 451 km (280 mi) to the **Delaware Bay** in N DE.

De La Warr (dĕl′ə wâr′, wər), Baron. Thomas West. 1577–1618. English-born Amer. colonial administrator.

de•lay (dĭ-lā′) ►*v.* **1.** To postpone; defer. **2.** To cause to be later than expected. **3.** To procrastinate. ►*n.* **1.** The act of delaying or condition of being delayed; postponement. **2.** The period of time one is delayed. [< OFr. *deslaier*.] —**de•lay′er** *n.*

de•lec•ta•ble (dĭ-lĕk′tə-bəl) ►*adj.* **1.** Delightful. **2.** Pleasing to the taste. See Syns at **delicious.** [< Lat. *dēlectāre*, to please.] —**de•lec′ta•bil′i•ty** *n.* —**de•lec′ta•bly** *adv.*

de•lec•ta•tion (dē′lĕk-tā′shən) ►*n.* Delight; pleasure. [< Lat. *dēlectāre*, to please.]

del•e•gate (dĕl′ĭ-gāt′, -gĭt) ►*n.* **1.** A person authorized to act as representative for another. **2.** A representative to a convention. ►*v.* (-gāt′) **-gat•ed, -gat•ing 1.** To authorize and send (another person) as one's representative. **2.** To commit or entrust to another. [< Lat. *dēlēgāre*, to dispatch.]

del•e•ga•tion (dĕl′ĭ-gā′shən) ►*n.* **1.** The act of delegating. **2.** A body of delegates.

de•lete (dĭ-lēt′) ►*v.* **-let•ed, -let•ing.** To remove by striking out or canceling. [Lat. *dēlēre*.] —**de•le′tion** *n.*

del•e•te•ri•ous (dĕl′ĭ-tîr′ē-əs) ►*adj.* Harmful; injurious. [< Gk. *dēlētēr*, destroyer.] —**del′e•te′ri•ous•ly** *adv.* —**del′e•te′ri•ous•ness** *n.*

delft (dĕlft) ►*n.* A style of glazed earthenware, usu. blue and white. [< *Delft*, a city of the Netherlands.]

Del•hi (dĕl′ē) A city of N-central India on the Yamuna R. Pop. 7,206,704.

del•i (dĕl′ē) ►*n.*, *pl.* **-is** *Informal.* A delicatessen.

de•lib•er•ate (dĭ-lĭb′ər-ĭt) ►*adj.* **1.** Done with full consciousness of the effects; intentional. **2.** Marked by careful consideration. **3.** Unhurried in action or manner. ►*v.* (-ə-rāt′) **-at•ed, -at•ing.** To consider or discuss a matter carefully. [< Lat. *dēlīberāre*, consider.] —**de•lib′er•ate•ly** *adv.* —**de•lib′er•ate•ness** *n.*

de•lib•er•a•tion (dĭ-lĭb′ə-rā′shən) ►*n.* **1.** The act or process of deliberating. **2. deliberations** Careful discussion and consideration. —**de•lib′er•a′tive** *adj.* —**de•lib′er•a′tive•ly** *adv.*

del•i•ca•cy (dĕl′ĭ-kə-sē) ►*n.*, *pl.* **-cies 1.** The quality of being delicate. **2.** A choice food. **3.** Elegance; refinement; sensitivity; tact.

del•i•cate (dĕl′ĭ-kĭt) ►*adj.* **1.** Pleasing to the senses, esp. in a subtle way. **2.** Exquisitely fine or dainty; easily damaged. **3.** Frail in constitution. **4.** Sensitive; considerate. **5.** Concerned with propriety; fastidious; precise. **6.** Tactful; skillful; subtle. [< Lat. *dēlicātus*, pleasing.] —**del′i•cate•ly** *adv.* —**del′i•cate•ness** *n.*

Syns: *delicate, choice, dainty, elegant, exquisite, fine* **adj.**

del•i•ca•tes•sen (dĕl′ĭ-kə-tĕs′ən) ►*n.* A shop that sells prepared foods ready for serving. [Ger. *Delikatessen*, delicacies.]

de•li•cious (dĭ-lĭsh′əs) ►*adj.* **1.** Highly pleasing to the taste. **2.** Gratifying; sweet: *a delicious revenge.* [< Lat. *dēlicia*, pleasure.] —**de•li′cious•ly** *adv.* —**de•li′cious•ness** *n.*

Syns: *delicious, delectable, luscious* **adj.**

de•light (dĭ-līt′) ►*n.* **1.** Great pleasure; joy. **2.** Something that gives great pleasure or enjoyment. ►*v.* **1.** To take great pleasure or joy. **2.** To please greatly. See Syns at **please.** [< Lat. *dēlectāre*, to please.] —**de•light′ed•ly** *adv.* —**de•light′ed•ness** *n.*

de•light•ful (dĭ-līt′fəl) ►*adj.* Greatly pleasing. —**de•light′ful•ly** *adv.*

De•li•lah (də-lī′lə). In the Bible, Samson's lover who betrayed him by having his hair shorn, thus depriving him of his strength.

de•lim•it (dĭ-lĭm′ĭt) ►*v.* To establish the limits of. [< Lat. *līmes*, boundary line.] —**de•lim′i•ta′tion** *n.* —**de•lim′it•er** *n.*

de•lin•e•ate (dĭ-lĭn′ē-āt′) ►*v.* **-at•ed, -at•ing 1.** To draw or trace the outline of. **2.** To depict; describe. See Syns at **represent.** [Lat. *dēlīneāre*.] —**de•lin′e•a′tion** *n.* —**de•lin′e•a′tive** *adj.* —**de•lin′e•a′tor** *n.*

de•lin•quent (dĭ-lĭng′kwənt, -lĭn′-) ►*adj.* **1.** Failing to do what is required. **2.** Overdue in payment: *a delinquent account.* ►*n.* **1.** A juvenile delinquent. **2.** A person who fails to do what is required. [< Lat. *dēlinquere*, offend.] —**de•lin′quen•cy** *n.* —**de•lin′quent•ly** *adv.*

del•i•quesce (dĕl′ĭ-kwĕs′) ►*v.* **-quesced, -quesc•ing.** To dissolve and become liquid by absorbing moisture from the air. [Lat. *dēliquēscere* < *liquēre*, be liquid.] —**del′i•ques′cence** *n.* —**del′i•ques′cent** *adj.*

de•lir•i•um (dĭ-lîr′ē-əm) ►*n.*, *pl.* **-i•ums** or **-i•a** (-ē-ə) **1.** A temporary state of mental confusion resulting from high fever, intoxication, or shock, marked by anxiety, disorientation, hallucinations, delusions, trembling, and incoherence. **2.** Uncontrolled excitement or emotion.

[Lat. *dēlīrium* : *dē-*, out of + *līra*, furrow.] —**de•lir′i•ous** *adj.* —**de•lir′i•ous•ly** *adv.* —**de•lir′i•ous•ness** *n.*

delirium tre•mens (trē′mənz) ►*n.* An acute delirium caused by withdrawal from alcohol. [NLat., trembling delirium.]

De•lius (dē′lē-əs, dēl′yəs), **Frederick.** 1862–1934. British composer.

de•liv•er (dĭ-lĭv′ər) ►*v.* **1.** To take to the proper place or recipient. **2.** To throw or hurl. **3.** To utter. **4a.** To give birth to. **b.** To assist (a woman) in giving birth. **5.** To give forth or produce. **6.** To set free. **7.** To produce what is expected; make good. [< LLat. *dēlīberāre*, set free.] —**de•liv′er•a•bil′i•ty** *n.* —**de•liv′er•a•ble** *adj.* —**de•liv′er•ance** *n.* —**de•liv′er•er** *n.*

de•liv•er•y (dĭ-lĭv′ə-rē, -lĭv′rē) ►*n., pl.* **-ies 1.** The act of delivering. **2.** Something delivered. **3.** The act or manner of throwing or discharging. **4.** Childbirth. **5.** The act or manner of speaking or singing.

delivery system ►*n.* **1.** A procedure for providing a product or service. **2.** The technology for conveying nuclear weapons to their targets.

dell (dĕl) ►*n.* A small wooded valley. [< OE.]

Del•mon•i•co steak (dĕl-mŏn′ĭ-kō′) ►*n.* A small, often boned steak from the front section of the short loin of beef; club steak. [After Lorenzo *Delmonico* (1813–81).]

De•los (dē′lŏs′, dĕl′ōs) An island of SE Greece in the S Aegean.

Del•phi (dĕl′fī′) An ancient town of central Greece near Mount Parnassus.

del•phin•i•um (dĕl-fĭn′ē-əm) ►*n.* A tall cultivated plant having showy, variously colored spurred flowers. [< Gk. *delphinion*, larkspur, dim. of *delphis*, dolphin.]

del•ta (dĕl′tə) ►*n.* **1.** The 4th letter of the Greek alphabet. **2.** A usu. triangular deposit at the mouth of a river. [Gk. < Phoenician **dalt*, door.]

delta wing ►*n.* An aircraft with wings that together form an isosceles triangle.

delta wing

del•toid (dĕl′toid′) ►*n.* A thick triangular muscle covering the shoulder joint, used to raise the arm from the side. [< Gk. *deltoeidēs*, triangular : *delta*, DELTA + –OID.]

de•lude (dĭ-lo͞od′) ►*v.* **-lud•ed, -lud•ing.** To deceive the mind or judgment of. [< Lat. *dēlūdere.*] —**de•lud′er** *n.*

del•uge (dĕl′yo͞oj) ►*n.* **1.** A great flood; downpour. **2.** Something that overwhelms. **3. Deluge** The Flood. ►*v.* **-uged, -ug•ing.** To overrun with or as if with water; inundate. [< Lat. *dīluvium* < *dīluere*, wash away : DIS– + *-luere*, wash.]

de•lu•sion (dĭ-lo͞o′zhən) ►*n.* **1.** The act of deluding or state of being deluded. **2.** A false belief or opinion. —**de•lu′sion•al, de•lu′sive** *adj.* —**de•lu′sive•ly** *adv.*

de•luxe also **de luxe** (dĭ-lŭks′, -lo͝oks′) ►*adj.* Particularly elegant and luxurious. ►*adv.* In an elegant manner. [Fr., of luxury.]

delve (dĕlv) ►*v.* **delved, delv•ing.** To search deeply and laboriously. [< OE *delfan*, dig.]

dem. ►*abbr.* demonstrative

Dem. ►*abbr.* **1.** Democrat **2.** Democratic

de•mag•net•ize (dē-măg′nĭ-tīz′) ►*v.* To remove magnetic properties from. —**de•mag′net•i•za′tion** *n.*

dem•a•gogue or **dem•a•gog** (dĕm′ə-gôg′, -gŏg′) ►*n.* A leader who obtains power by appealing to the emotions and prejudices of the populace. [Gk. *dēmagōgos*, popular leader : *dēmos*, people + *agein*, to lead.] —**dem′a•gog′ic** (-gŏj′ĭk, -gŏg′-), **dem′a•gog′i•cal** *adj.* —**dem′a•gogu′er•y** *n.* —**dem′a•gog′y** (-gŏj′ē, -gô′jē, -gŏg′ē) *n.*

de•mand (dĭ-mănd′) ►*v.* **1.** To ask for insistently. **2.** To claim as just or due. **3.** To require; call for. ►*n.* **1.** The act of demanding. **2.** Something demanded. **3.** An urgent requirement or need. **4.** The state of being sought after. **5.** *Econ.* **a.** The desire to possess something combined with the ability to purchase it. **b.** The amount of something that people are ready to buy for a given price. [< Lat. *dēmandāre*, entrust.] —**de•mand′a•ble** *adj.* —**de•mand′er** *n.*

Syns: *demand, claim, exact, require* **v.**

de•mand•ing (dĭ-măn′dĭng) ►*adj.* Requiring much effort or attention. —**de•mand′ing•ly** *adv.*

de•mar•cate (dĭ-mär′kāt′, dē′mär-kāt′) ►*v.* **-cat•ed, -cat•ing.** To set the boundaries of; delimit. —**de•mar′ca′tor** *n.*

de•mar•ca•tion (dē′mär-kā′shən) ►*n.* **1.** The setting or marking of boundaries or limits. **2.** A separation. [Sp. *demarcación.*]

de•mean[1] (dĭ-mēn′) ►*v.* To behave (oneself) in a particular manner. [< OFr. *mener*, to conduct.]

de•mean[2] (dĭ-mēn′) ►*v.* To debase in dignity or social standing.

de•mean•or (dĭ-mē′nər) ►*n.* The way a person behaves. [< OFr. *demener*, govern.]

de•ment•ed (dĭ-mĕn′tĭd) ►*adj.* Mentally ill; insane. [< Lat. *dēmēns*, *dēment-*, senseless : DE– + *mēns*, mind.]

de•men•tia (dĭ-mĕn′shə) ►*n.* Deterioration of intellectual faculties resulting from an organic disease of the brain. [Lat. *dēmentia.*]

de•mer•it (dĭ-mĕr′ĭt) ►*n.* A mark made against one's record for a fault or misconduct. [< Lat. *dēmeritum*, neuter p.part. of *dēmerēre*, deserve.]

Dem•er•ol (dĕm′ə-rôl′, -rŏl′, -rōl′) ► A trademark for an analgesic similar to morphine.

de•mesne (dĭ-mān′, -mēn′) ►*n.* **1.** The grounds of an estate. **2.** An extensive piece of landed property. **3.** A district; territory. [< OFr. *demaine*, DOMAIN.]

De•me•ter (dĭ-mē′tər) ►*n.* *Gk. Myth.* The goddess of the harvest.

dem•i•god (dĕm′ē-gŏd′) ►*n.* **1.** *Myth.* **a.** A male being, the offspring of a deity and a mortal. **b.** A minor god. **2.** A person who is highly revered. [*demi-*, partly + GOD.]

dem•i•john (dĕm′ē-jŏn′) ►*n.* A large bottle usu. encased in wickerwork. [Prob. < Fr. *dame-Jeanne*, lady Jane.]

demijohn

de•mil•i•ta•rize (dē-mĭl′ĭ-tə-rīz′) ►*v.* To prohibit or eliminate military forces or installations. —**de•mil′i•ta•ri•za′tion** *n.*

De Mille (də mĭl′), **Agnes George.** 1905–93. Amer. choreographer.

De Mille, Cecil Blount. 1881–1959. Amer. filmmaker.

dem•i•mon•daine (dĕm′ē-mŏn-dān′, -mŏn′dān′) ►*n.* A woman belonging to the demimonde. [Fr.]

dem•i•monde (dĕm′ē-mŏnd′) ►*n.* **1a.** A class of women kept by wealthy lovers or protectors. **b.** Women prostitutes collectively. **2.** A group whose respectability is dubious. [Fr.]

de•min•er•al•ize (dē-mĭn′ər-ə-līz′) ►*v.* To remove minerals or mineral salts from (a liquid). —**de•min′er•al•i′zer** *n.*

de•mise (dĭ-mīz′) ►*n.* **1.** Death. **2.** The end; termination. [< OFr. *dimis*, transfer of property < *demettre*, release.]

dem•i•tasse (dĕm′ē-tăs′, -täs′) ►*n.* A small cup of strong coffee. [Fr.]

dem•o (dĕm′ō) ►*n.*, *pl.* **-os** *Informal* **1.** A demonstration, as of a product. **2.** A recording used to illustrate the qualities of a musician. —**dem′o** *v.*

de•mo•bil•ize (dē-mō′bə-līz′) ►*v.* To discharge from military service or use. —**de•mo′bil•i•za′tion** *n.*

de•moc•ra•cy (dĭ-mŏk′rə-sē) ►*n.*, *pl.* **-cies 1.** Government by the people, exercised either directly or through elected representatives. **2.** A political unit that has such a government. **3.** Majority rule. **4.** The principles of social equality and respect for the individual within a community. [< Gk. *dēmokratia*.]

dem•o•crat (dĕm′ə-krăt′) ►*n.* **1.** An advocate of democracy. **2. Democrat** A member of the Democratic Party.

dem•o•crat•ic (dĕm′ə-krăt′ĭk) ►*adj.* **1.** Characterized by or advocating democracy. **2.** Of or for the people in general. **3.** Believing in or practicing social equality. **4. Democratic** Of or relating to the Democratic Party. —**dem′o•crat′i•cal•ly** *adv.*

Democratic Party ►*n.* One of the two major US political parties.

de•moc•ra•tize (dĭ-mŏk′rə-tīz′) ►*v.* **-tized, -tiz•ing.** To make democratic. —**de•moc′ra•ti•za′tion** *n.*

De•moc•ri•tus (dĭ-mŏk′rĭ-təs). 460?–370? B.C. Greek philosopher.

de•mod•u•late (dē-mŏj′ə-lāt′, -mŏd′yə-) ►*v.* **-lat•ed, -lat•ing.** To extract (information) from a modulated carrier wave. —**de•mod′u•la′tion** *n.* —**de•mod′u•la′tor** *n.*

dem•o•graph•ics (dĕm′ə-grăf′ĭks, dē′mə-) ►*n.* *(takes pl. v.)* The characteristics of human population segments, esp. for identifying consumer markets.

de•mog•ra•phy (dĭ-mŏg′rə-fē) ►*n.* The statistical study of human populations. [Gk. *dēmos*, people + -GRAPHY.] —**de•mog′ra•pher** *n.* —**dem′o•graph′ic** (dĕm′ə-grăf′ĭk, dē′mə-) *adj.* —**dem′o•graph′i•cal•ly** *adv.*

de•mol•ish (dĭ-mŏl′ĭsh) ►*v.* To tear down completely; raze. [< Lat. *dēmōlīrī*.]

dem•o•li•tion (dĕm′ə-lĭsh′ən, dē′mə-) ►*n.* The act or process of destroying, esp. by explosives. —**dem′o•li′tion•ist** *n.*

de•mon (dē′mən) ►*n.* **1.** An evil supernatural being; devil. **2.** A persistently tormenting person, force, or passion. **3.** One who is extremely zealous or diligent. [< Gk. *daimōn*, divine power.] —**de•mon′ic** (dĭ-mŏn′ĭk) *adj.* —**de•mon′i•cal•ly** *adv.*

de•mon•e•tize (dē-mŏn′ĭ-tīz′, -mŭn′-) ►*v.* To divest (currency) of monetary value. —**de•mon′e•ti•za′tion** *n.*

de•mo•ni•ac (dĭ-mō′nē-ăk′) also **de•mo•ni•a•cal** (dē′mə-nī′ə-kəl) ►*adj.* **1.** Possessed by or as if by a demon. **2.** Devilish; fiendish. —**de′mo•ni′a•cal•ly** *adv.*

de•mon•ize (dē′mə-nīz′) ►*v.* **-ized, -iz•ing 1.** To turn into or as if into a demon. **2.** To represent as evil. —**de′mon•i•za′tion** *n.*

de•mon•ol•o•gy (dē′mə-nŏl′ə-jē) ►*n.* The study of demons. —**de′mon•ol′o•gist** *n.*

de•mon•stra•ble (dĭ-mŏn′strə-bəl) ►*adj.* Capable of being shown or proved. —**de•mon′stra•bil′i•ty** *n.* —**de•mon′stra•bly** *adv.*

dem•on•strate (dĕm′ən-strāt′) ►*v.* **-strat•ed, -strat•ing 1.** To show clearly and deliberately. **2.** To show to be true by reasoning or evidence. **3.** To explain and illustrate. **4.** To show the use of (a product) to a prospective buyer. **5.** To participate in a public display of opinion. [Lat. *dēmōnstrāre* : *dē-*, completely + *mōnstrum*, portent (< *monēre*, warn).] —**dem′on•stra′tion** *n.* —**dem′on•stra′tor** *n.*

de•mon•stra•tive (dĭ-mŏn′strə-tĭv) ►*adj.* **1.** Serving to manifest or prove. **2.** Given to the open expression of emotion. **3.** *Gram.* Specifying the person or thing referred to: *the demonstrative pronouns* these *and* that. ►*n.* *Gram.* A demonstrative pronoun or adjective. —**de•mon′stra•tive•ly** *adv.*

de•mor•al•ize (dĭ-môr′ə-līz′, -mŏr′-) ►*v.* **-ized, -iz•ing 1.** To undermine the confidence or morale of; dishearten. **2.** To corrupt. —**de•mor′al•i•za′tion** *n.* —**de•mor′al•iz′er** *n.*

De•mos•the•nes (dĭ-mŏs′thə-nēz′). 384–322 B.C. Greek orator.

de•mote (dĭ-mōt′) ►*v.* **-mot•ed, -mot•ing.** To reduce in grade or rank. [DE- + (PRO)MOTE.] —**de•mo′tion** *n.*

Syns: *demote, break, bust, degrade, downgrade, reduce* **Ant:** *promote* **v.**

de•mot•ic (dĭ-mŏt′ĭk) ►*adj.* **1.** Of or relating to the common people; popular. **2.** Of or written in a simplified ancient Egyptian hieratic script. **3. Demotic** Relating to a form of modern Greek based on colloquial use. [< Gk. *dēmotēs*, commoner.]

de•mul•cent (dĭ-mŭl′sənt) ►*adj.* Soothing. ►*n.* A soothing, usu. jellylike or oily substance, used to relieve pain. [< Lat. *dēmulcēre*, soften.]

de•mur (dĭ-mûr′) ►*v.* **-murred, -mur•ring.** To voice opposition; object. [< Lat. *dēmorārī*, to delay.]

de•mure (dĭ-myo͝or′) ►*adj.* **-mur•er, -mur•est 1.** Modest in manner; reserved. **2.** Affectedly modest or reserved. [ME.] —**de•mure′ly** *adv.* —**de•mure′ness** *n.*

de•mys•ti•fy (dē-mĭs′tə-fī′) ►*v.* To make less mysterious; clarify.

de•my•thol•o•gize (dē′mĭ-thŏl′ə-jīz′) ►*v.* To rid of mythological elements. —**de′my•thol′o•gi•za′tion** *n.*

den (dĕn) ►*n.* **1.** The shelter or retreat of a wild animal; lair. **2.** A hidden or squalid dwelling place. **3.** A secluded room for study or relaxation. **4.** A unit of about eight to ten Cub Scouts. [< OE *denn.*]

De•na•li (də-nä′lē) See Mount **McKinley.**

den•ar (dĕn′är) ►*n., pl.* **-a•ri** (-är-ē). See table at **currency.** [Macedonian.]

de•na•ture (dē-nā′chər) ►*v.* **-tured, -tur•ing.** To render unfit to eat or drink, esp. to add methanol to. —**de•na′tur•ant** *n.*

den•drite (dĕn′drīt′) ►*n.* A branched protoplasmic extension of a nerve cell that conducts impulses toward the cell body.

dendro– or **dendri–** or **dendr–** ►*pref.* Tree; treelike: *dendrite.* [< Gk. *dendron*, tree.]

den•gue (dĕng′gē, -gā) ►*n.* An acute infectious tropical disease transmitted by mosquitoes. [< Swahili *ki-dinga.*]

Deng Xiao•ping (dŭng′ shou′pĭng′). 1904–97. Chinese Communist leader.

de•ni•a•ble (dĭ-nī′ə-bəl) ►*adj.* **1.** Possible to declare untrue: *deniable charges.* **2.** Being such that plausible disavowal is possible. —**de•ni′a•bil′i•ty** *n.* —**de•ni′a•bly** *adv.*

de•ni•al (dĭ-nī′əl) ►*n.* **1.** A refusal to comply with a request. **2.** A refusal to grant the truth of a statement. **3.** A disavowal; repudiation. **4.** Self-denial.

den•ier (dən-yā′, dĕn′yər) ►*n.* A unit of fineness for rayon, nylon, and silk fibers. [< OFr. *dener*, a coin < Lat. *dēnārius.*]

den•i•grate (dĕn′ĭ-grāt′) ►*v.* **-grat•ed, -grat•ing.** To attack the reputation of; defame. [Lat. *dēnigrāre* < *niger*, black.] —**den′i•gra′tion** *n.* —**den′i•gra′tor** *n.*

den•im (dĕn′ĭm) ►*n.* **1.** A coarse cotton cloth used for jeans, overalls, and work uniforms. **2. denims** Garments made of this cloth. [Fr. *(serge) de Nîmes*, (serge) of Nîmes.]

den•i•zen (dĕn′ĭ-zən) ►*n.* An inhabitant; resident. [< LLat. *dēintus*, from within.]

Den•mark (dĕn′märk′) A country of N Europe on Jutland and adjacent islands. Cap. Copenhagen. Pop. 5,205,000.

de•nom•i•nate (dĭ-nŏm′a-nāt") *v.* **-nat•ed, -nat•ing 1.** To issue or express in terms of a given monetary unit. **2.** To give a name to; designate.

de•nom•i•na•tion (dĭ-nŏm′ə-nā′shən) ►*n.* **1.** An organized group of religious congregations. **2.** A unit of specified value in a system of currency or weights. **3.** A name or designation, esp. for a class or group. [< Lat. *dēnōmināre*, designate < *nōmen*, name.] —**de•nom′i•na′tion•al** *adj.*

de•nom•i•na•tor (dĭ-nŏm′ə-nā′tər) ►*n.* **1.** *Math.* The expression written below the line in a fraction that indicates the number of parts into which one whole is divided. **2.** A common trait or characteristic.

de•note (dĭ-nōt′) ►*v.* **-not•ed, -not•ing 1.** To mark; indicate. **2.** To signify directly; refer to specifically. [< Lat. *dēnotāre.*] —**de′no•ta′tion** *n.* —**de•no′ta•tive** *adj.* —**de•no′ta•tive•ly** *adv.*

Usage: In speaking of words, *denote* is used to indicate the thing it conventionally names, whereas *connote* indicates the images or associations it evokes.

de•noue•ment also **dé•noue•ment** (dā′no͞o-mäɴ′) ►*n.* **1.** The resolution of a dramatic or narrative plot. **2.** The outcome of a sequence of events. [< OFr. *desnouement*, an untying.]

de•nounce (dĭ-nouns′) ►*v.* **-nounced, -nounc•ing 1.** To condemn openly as being evil or reprehensible. **2.** To accuse formally. [< Lat. *dēnūntiāre.*] —**de•nounce′ment** *n.* —**de•nounc′er** *n.*

dense (dĕns) ►*adj.* **dens•er, dens•est 1.** Having relatively high density. **2.** Crowded together. **3.** Thick. **4.** Stupid. [Lat. *dēnsus.*] —**dense′ly** *adv.* —**dense′ness** *n.*

den•si•ty (dĕn′sĭ-tē) ►*n., pl.* **-ties 1a.** The quantity of something per unit measure, esp. per unit length, area, or volume. **b.** The mass per unit volume of a substance under specified conditions of pressure and temperature. **2.** Thickness of consistency. **3.** Stupidity.

dent (dĕnt) ►*n.* **1.** A depression in a surface made by pressure or a blow. **2.** *Informal* Meaningful progress; headway. ►*v.* To make a dent in. [< OE *dynt*, a blow.]

den•tal (dĕn′tl) ►*adj.* **1.** Of or relating to the teeth. **2.** *Ling.* Articulated with the tip of the tongue near or against the upper front teeth. ►*n.* *Ling.* A dental consonant.

dental floss ►*n.* A thread used to clean between the teeth.

dental hygienist ►*n.* One who assists a dentist.

denti– or **dent–** ►*pref.* Tooth: *dentition.* [< Lat. *dēns, dent-*, tooth.]

den•ti•frice (dĕn′tə-frĭs′) ►*n.* A substance, such as a paste, for cleaning the teeth. [< Lat. *dentifricium* : DENTI– + *fricāre*, rub.]

den•tin (dĕn′tĭn) or **den•tine** (-tēn′) ►*n.* The calcified part of a tooth, beneath the enamel. —**den′tin•al** (dĕn′tə-nəl, dĕn-tē′-) *adj.*

den•tist (dĕn′tĭst) ►*n.* A person trained and licensed in the diagnosis, prevention, and treatment of diseases of the teeth and gums. [Fr. *dentiste* < Lat. *dēns, dent-*, tooth.] —**den′tist•ry** *n.*

den•ti•tion (dĕn-tĭsh′ən) ►*n.* The type, number, and arrangement of a set of teeth.

den•ture (dĕn′chər) ►*n.* A set of artificial teeth.

de•nude (dĭ-no͞od′, -nyo͞od′) ►*v.* **-nud•ed, -nud•ing.** To strip of covering; make bare. [Lat. *dēnūdāre.*] —**de′nu•da′tion** (dē′no͞o-dā′shən, -nyo͞o-, dĕn′yo͞o-) *n.*

de•nun•ci•a•tion (dĭ-nŭn′sē-ā′shən, -shē-) ►*n.* The act of denouncing, esp. a public condemnation. —**de•nun′ci•a′tive, de•nun′ci•a•to′ry** (-ə-tôr′ē, -tōr′ē) *adj.*

Den•ver (dĕn′vər) The capital of CO, in the N-central part. Pop. 467,610.

de•ny (dĭ-nī′) ►*v.* **-nied, -ny•ing 1.** To declare untrue. **2.** To refuse to believe; reject. **3.** To refuse to recognize. **4a.** To decline to grant: *deny a request.* **b.** To restrain (oneself) esp. from indulgence in pleasures. [< Lat. *dēnegāre.*]

Syns: *deny, contradict, contravene, gainsay, negate* ***Ant:*** *affirm* **v.**

de•o•dor•ant (dē-ō′dər-ənt) ►*n.* A substance used to counteract undesirable odors.

de•o•dor•ize (dē-ō′də-rīz′) ►*v.* **-ized, -iz•ing.** To mask or neutralize the odor of. **—de•o′dor•i•za′tion** *n.* **—de•o′dor•iz′er** *n.*

de•ox•y•ri•bo•nu•cle•ic acid (dē-ŏk′sē-rī′-bō-no͞o-klē′ĭk, -klā′-, -nyo͞o-) ►*n.* DNA.

de•part (dĭ-pärt′) ►*v.* **1.** To go away; leave. **2.** To die. **3.** To vary; deviate: *depart from custom.* See Syns at **swerve.** [< OFr. *departir,* divide, split.]

de•part•ment (dĭ-pärt′mənt) ►*n.* **1.** A distinct, usu. specialized division of an organization, business, government, or institution. **2.** *Informal* An area of particular knowledge or responsibilty. [Fr. *département.*] **—de′part•men′tal** (dē′pärt-mĕn′tl) *adj.* **—de′part•men′tal•ly** *adv.*

de•part•men•tal•ize (dē′pärt-mĕn′tl-īz′) ►*v.* **-ized, -iz•ing.** To organize into departments. **—de′part•men′tal•i•za′tion** *n.*

department store ►*n.* A large retail store offering a variety of merchandise.

de•par•ture (dĭ-pär′chər) ►*n.* **1.** The act of leaving. **2.** A starting out, as on a trip. **3.** A divergence, as from a set procedure.

de•pend (dĭ-pĕnd′) ►*v.* **1.** To rely, esp. for support: *depend on one's parents.* **2.** To place trust or confidence: *You can depend on her.* **3.** To be determined, conditioned, or contingent. **4.** To have a dependence. [< Lat. *dēpendēre,* hang from.]

Usage: *Depend,* indicating condition or contingency, is always followed by *on* or *upon,* as in *It depends on who is in charge.*

de•pend•a•ble (dĭ-pĕn′də-bəl) ►*adj.* Trustworthy. See Syns at **reliable. —de•pend′a•bil′i•ty** *n.* **—de•pend′a•bly** *adv.*

de•pen•dence also **de•pen•dance** (dĭ-pĕn′dəns) ►*n.* **1.** The state of being dependent, as for support. **2.** Condition; contingency. **3.** Trust; reliance. **4.** A compulsive or chronic need; addiction.

de•pen•den•cy also **de•pen•dan•cy** (dĭ-pĕn′dən-sē) ►*n., pl.* **-cies 1.** Dependence. **2.** A territory under the jurisdiction of another country of which it is not an integral part.

de•pen•dent (dĭ-pĕn′dənt) ►*adj.* **1.** Contingent on another. **2.** Subordinate. **3.** Relying on the aid of another for support: *dependent children.* ►*n.* also **de•pen•dant.** One who relies on another for financial support. **—de•pen′dent•ly** *adv.*

Syns: *dependent, conditional, contingent, relative, subject* ***Ant:*** *independent* **adj.**

de•pict (dĭ-pĭkt′) ►*v.* **1.** To represent in a picture. **2.** To describe in words. See Syns at **represent.** [< Lat. *dēpingere, dēpict-.*] **—de•pic′tion** *n.*

de•pil•a•to•ry (dĭ-pĭl′ə-tôr′ē, -tōr′ē) ►*n., pl.* **-ries.** A substance used to remove hair. [< Lat. *dēpilāre,* remove hair.] **—de•pil′a•to′ry** *adj.*

de•plane (dē-plān′) ►*v.* **-planed, -plan•ing.** To disembark from an airplane.

de•plete (dĭ-plēt′) ►*v.* **-plet•ed, -plet•ing.** To use up or empty out. [Lat. *dēplēre,* to empty : DE– + *plēre,* fill.] **—de•ple′tion** *n.*

de•plore (dĭ-plôr′, -plōr′) ►*v.* **-plored, -plor•ing 1.** To feel or express strong disapproval of. **2.** To regret; bemoan. [< Lat. *dēplōrāre.*] **—de•plor′a•ble** *adj.* **—de•plor′a•bly** *adv.*

de•ploy (dĭ-ploi′) ►*v.* **1.** To distribute (persons or forces) systematically or strategically. **2.** To put into use or action. [< Lat. *displicāre,* scatter.] **—de•ploy′a•bil′i•ty** *n.* **—de•ploy′a•ble** *adj.* **—de•ploy′ment** *n.*

de•po•nent (dĭ-pō′nənt) ►*n.* One who testifies under oath, esp. in writing. [< Lat. *dēpōnere,* put down.]

de•pop•u•late (dē-pŏp′yə-lāt′) ►*v.* To reduce sharply the population of. **—de•pop′u•la′tion** *n.*

de•port (dĭ-pôrt′, -pōrt′) ►*v.* **1.** To expel from a country. **2.** To conduct (oneself) in a given manner. [< Lat. *dēportāre,* carry away.] **—de′por•ta′tion** (dē′pôr-tā′shən, -pōr-) *n.* **—de′por•tee′** *n.*

de•port•ment (dĭ-pôrt′mənt, -pōrt′-) ►*n.* Personal conduct; behavior.

de•pose (dĭ-pōz′) ►*v.* **-posed, -pos•ing 1.** To remove from office or power. **2.** *Law* **a.** To give a deposition; testify. **b.** To take a deposition from. [< OFr. *deposer.*]

de•pos•it (dĭ-pŏz′ĭt) ►*v.* **1.** To put or set down. **2.** To lay down by a natural process. **3.** To place for safekeeping, as money in a bank. **4.** To give as partial payment or security. ►*n.* **1.** Something entrusted for safekeeping, as money in a bank. **2.** The condition of being deposited: *funds on deposit with a broker.* **3.** A partial or initial payment of a cost or debt. **4.** Something deposited, esp. by a natural process: *rich deposits of natural gas.* [Lat. *dēpōnere, dēposit-,* put aside.] **—de•pos′i•tor** *n.*

dep•o•si•tion (dĕp′ə-zĭsh′ən) ►*n.* **1.** The act of deposing, as from high office. **2.** The act of depositing. **3.** A deposit. **4.** *Law* Testimony under oath, esp. a written statement admissible in court. **—dep′o•si′tion•al** *adj.*

de•pos•i•to•ry (dĭ-pŏz′ĭ-tôr′ē, -tōr′ē) ►*n., pl.* **-ries.** A place where something is deposited, as for safekeeping.

de•pot (dē′pō, dĕp′ō) ►*n.* **1.** A railroad or bus station. **2.** A warehouse or storehouse. **3.** A storage installation for military equipment and supplies. [< Lat. *dēpositum,* something deposited.]

de•prave (dĭ-prāv′) ►*v.* **-praved, -prav•ing.** To debase, esp. morally. See Syns at **corrupt.** [< Lat. *dēprāvāre.*] **—de•praved′** *adj.* **—de•prav′i•ty** (-prăv′ĭ-tē) *n.*

dep•re•cate (dĕp′rĭ-kāt′) ►*v.* **-cat•ed, -cat•ing 1.** To express disapproval of. **2.** To belittle; depreciate. [Lat. *dēprecārī,* ward off by prayer.] **—dep′re•ca′tion** *n.* **—dep′re•ca′tor** *n.* **—dep′re•ca•to′ry** (-kə-tôr′ē, -tōr′ē) *adj.*

de•pre•ci•ate (dĭ-prē′shē-āt′) ►*v.* **-at•ed, -at•ing 1.** To diminish in price or value. **2.** To belittle. [< Lat. *dēpretiāre* < *pretium,* price.] **—de•pre′ci•a′tion** *n.* **—de•pre′ci•a′tor** *n.* **—de•pre′cia•to′ry** (-shə-tôr′ē, -tōr′ē), **de•pre′cia•tive** *adj.*

dep•re•da•tion (dĕp′rĭ-dā′shən) ►*n.* **1.** An act of plunder or ravage. **2.** Damage or destruction. [< LLat. *dēpraedārī,* to plunder.]

de•press (dĭ-prĕs′) ►*v.* **1.** To lower in spirits; deject. **2.** To push or press down; lower. **3.** To lessen the activity or force of; weaken. [< Lat. *dēprimere, dēpress-.*] —**de•pres′sive** *adj.* —**de•pres′sive•ly** *adv.* —**de•pres′sor** *n.*

de•pres•sant (dĭ-prĕs′ənt) ►*adj.* Tending to slow vital physiological activities. ►*n.* A depressant drug.

de•pressed (dĭ-prĕst′) ►*adj.* **1.** Low in spirits; dejected. **2.** Suffering from psychological depression. **3.** Lower in amount, degree, or position. **4.** Suffering from socioeconomic hardship.

Syns: *depressed, blue, dejected, dispirited, downcast, downhearted* **adj.**

de•pres•sion (dĭ-prĕsh′ən) ►*n.* **1.** The act of depressing or condition of being depressed. **2.** A sunken area; hollow. **3.** The condition of feeling sad or despondent. **4.** *Psychol.* A condition marked by an inability to concentrate, insomnia, and feelings of dejection and hopelessness. **5.** A period of drastic decline in an economy. **6.** A region of low barometric pressure.

de•prive (dĭ-prīv′) ►*v.* **-prived, -priv•ing 1.** To take something away from. **2.** To keep from possessing or enjoying. [< Med.Lat. *dēprīvāre.*] —**dep′ri•va′tion** (dĕp′rə-vā′shən) *n.*

de•pro•gram (dē-prō′grăm′, -grəm) ►*v.* To counteract the effect of an indoctrination, esp. a cult indoctrination. —**de•pro′gram′mer** *n.*

dept. ►*abbr.* **1.** department **2.** deputy

depth (dĕpth) ►*n.* **1.** The quality of being deep. **2.** The extent or dimension downward, backward, or inward. **3.** often **depths** A deep part or place. **4.** The most profound or intense part or stage. **5.** The severest or worst part. **6.** Intellectual complexity; profundity. **7.** The range of one's competence: *out of my depth.* **8.** Thoroughness. [ME *depthe* < *dep*, DEEP.]

depth charge ►*n.* A charge designed for detonation under water, used esp. against submarines.

dep•u•ta•tion (dĕp′yə-tā′shən) ►*n.* **1.** A person or group appointed to represent others. **2.** The act of deputing.

de•pute (dĭ-pyo͞ot′) ►*v.* **-put•ed, -put•ing.** To appoint or authorize as a representative. [< LLat. *dēputāre*, allot.]

dep•u•tize (dĕp′yə-tīz′) ►*v.* **-tized, -tiz•ing.** To appoint as a deputy.

dep•u•ty (dĕp′yə-tē) ►*n., pl.* **-ties 1.** A person empowered to act for another. **2.** An assistant exercising full authority in the absence of a superior. **3.** A legislative representative in certain countries. [< OFr. *depute* < *deputer*, DEPUTE.]

De Quin•cey (dĭ kwĭn′sē, -zē), **Thomas.** 1785–1859. British writer.

de•rac•i•nate (də-răs′ə-nāt′) ►*v.* **-nat•ed, -nat•ing 1.** To uproot. **2.** To displace from one's native or accustomed environment. —**de•rac′i•na′tion** *n.*

de•rail (dē-rāl′) ►*v.* **1.** To run or cause to run off the rails. **2.** To come or bring to a sudden halt: *a campaign derailed by lack of funds.* —**de•rail′ment** *n.*

de•rail•leur (dĭ-rā′lər) ►*n.* A device for shifting gears on a bicycle by moving the chain between sprocket wheels of different sizes. [< Fr. *dérailler*, derail.]

de•range (dĭ-rānj′) ►*v.* **-ranged, -rang•ing 1.** To disarrange. **2.** To make insane. [< OFr. *desrengier.*] —**de•range′ment** *n.*

der•by (dûr′bē; *British* där′bē) ►*n., pl.* **-bies 1.** An annual horse race, esp. for three-year-olds. **2.** A race open to all contestants. **3.** A stiff felt hat with a round crown and narrow brim. [After the 12th Earl of *Derby* (1752–1834).]

Der•by (där′bē) A city of central England W of Nottingham. Pop. 228,648.

der•e•lict (dĕr′ə-lĭkt′) ►*adj.* **1.** Deserted by an owner; abandoned. **2.** Neglectful of duty. See Syns at **negligent.** ►*n.* **1.** Abandoned property, esp. a ship abandoned at sea. **2.** A homeless or vagrant person. [< Lat. *dērelinquere, dērelict-*, abandon.]

der•e•lic•tion (dĕr′ə-lĭk′shən) ►*n.* **1.** Willful neglect, as of duty. **2.** Abandonment.

de•ride (dĭ-rīd′) ►*v.* **-rid•ed, -rid•ing.** To speak of or treat with contemptuous mirth. [Lat. *dērīdēre.*] —**de•ri′sion** (-rĭzh′ən) *n.* —**de•ri′sive** (-rī′sĭv) *adj.* —**de•ri′sive•ly** *adv.*

de ri•gueur (də rē-gœr′) ►*adj.* Socially obligatory. [Fr., of rigor, strictness.]

der•i•va•tion (dĕr′ə-vā′shən) ►*n.* **1.** The act or process of deriving. **2.** The origin or source of something. **3.** The historical origin and development of a word; etymology. —**der′i•va′tion•al** *adj.*

de•riv•a•tive (dĭ-rĭv′ə-tĭv) ►*adj.* **1.** Resulting from derivation. **2.** Unoriginal: *a derivative prose style.* ►*n.* **1.** Something derived. **2.** A word formed from another by derivation. —**de•riv′a•tive•ly** *adv.*

de•rive (dĭ-rīv′) ►*v.* **-rived, -riv•ing 1a.** To obtain from a source. **b.** To originate. See Syns at **stem**[1]. **2.** To deduce or infer. **3.** To trace the origin or development of (a word). **4.** To produce or obtain (a compound) from another substance by chemical reaction. [< Lat. *dērīvāre.*] —**de•riv′a•ble** *adj.*

der•ma (dûr′mə) ►*n.* See **dermis.** [Gk. *derma, dermat-*, skin.]

der•ma•ti•tis (dûr′mə-tī′tĭs) ►*n.* Inflammation of the skin.

der•ma•tol•o•gy (dûr′mə-tŏl′ə-jē) ►*n.* The medical study of the skin and its diseases. —**der′ma•tol′o•gist** *n.*

der•mis (dûr′mĭs) ►*n.* The layer of the skin below the epidermis, containing nerve endings, sweat glands, and blood and lymph vessels. [NLat. < EPIDERMIS.] —**der′mal** *adj.*

der•o•gate (dĕr′ə-gāt′) ►*v.* **-gat•ed, -gat•ing 1.** To take away; detract. **2.** To disparage; belittle. [< Lat. *dērogāre.*] —**der′o•ga′tion** *n.*

de•rog•a•to•ry (dĭ-rŏg′ə-tôr′ē, -tōr′ē) ►*adj.* Disparaging; belittling: *a derogatory comment.* —**de•rog′a•to′ri•ly** *adv.*

der•rick (dĕr′ĭk) ►*n.* **1.** A machine for hoisting and moving heavy objects. **2.** A tall framework over a drilled hole, esp. an oil well, used to support equipment. [Obsolete *derick*, hangman, gallows.]

der•ri•ère also **der•ri•ere** (dĕr′ē-âr′) ►*n.* The buttocks. [< OFr. *deriere*, in back of.]

der•ring-do (dĕr′ĭng-do͞o′) ►*n.* Daring or reckless action. [< ME *durring don*, daring to do.]

der•rin•ger (dĕr′ĭn-jər) ►*n.* A small, short-barreled pistol. [After Henry *Deringer* (1786–1868).]

der•vish (dûr′vĭsh) ►*n.* A member of any of various Muslim ascetic orders, some of which perform whirling dances in ecstatic devotion. [< Pers. *darvēsh*, mendicant.]

dervish

de•sal•i•nate (dē-săl′ə-nāt′) ►*v.* **-nat•ed, -nat•ing.** To desalinize. —**de•sal′i•na′tion** *n.* —**de•sal′i•na′tor** *n.*

de•sal•i•nize (dē-săl′ə-nīz′) ►*v.* **-nized, -niz•ing.** To remove salts and other chemicals from (e.g., sea water). —**de•sal′i•ni•za′tion** *n.*

des•cant (dĕs′kănt′) ►*n.* **1.** *Mus.* An ornamental melody sung or played above a theme. **2.** A discourse on a theme. [< Med.Lat. *discantus*, refrain.] —**des′cant′** *v.*

Des•cartes (dā-kärt′), **René.** 1596–1650. French mathematician and philosopher.

de•scend (dĭ-sĕnd′) ►*v.* **1.** To move from a higher to a lower place; come or go down. **2.** To slope, extend, or incline downward. **3.** To come from an ancestor. **4.** To pass by inheritance. **5.** To lower oneself; stoop. **6.** To arrive or attack in an overwhelming manner: *tourists descending on the village.* [< Lat. *dēscendere.*]

de•scen•dant (dĭ-sĕn′dənt) ►*n.* One descended from specified ancestors. ►*adj.* Var. of **descendent.**

de•scen•dent also **de•scen•dant** (dĭ-sĕn′dənt) ►*adj.* **1.** Moving downward. **2.** Proceeding from an ancestor.

de•scent (dĭ-sĕnt′) ►*n.* **1.** The act or an instance of descending. **2.** A downward incline. **3.** Hereditary derivation; lineage. **4.** A decline, as in status. **5.** A sudden attack. [< OFr.]

de•scribe (dĭ-skrīb′) ►*v.* **-scribed, -scrib•ing 1.** To give a verbal account of. **2.** To depict. **3.** To trace the outline of. [< Lat. *dēscrībere*, write down.] —**de•scrib′a•ble** *adj.*

Syns: *describe, narrate, recite, recount, relate, report* ***v.***

de•scrip•tion (dĭ-skrĭp′shən) ►*n.* **1.** The act of describing. **2.** An account describing something. **3.** A kind or sort: *cars of every description.* —**de•scrip′tive** *adj.* —**de•scrip′tive•ly** *adv.* —**de•scrip′tive•ness** *n.*

de•scry (dĭ-skrī′) ►*v.* **-scried, -scry•ing 1.** To catch sight of. **2.** To discover by careful observation. [< OFr. *descrier*, call, cry out.]

des•e•crate (dĕs′ĭ-krāt′) ►*v.* **-crat•ed, -crat•ing.** To violate the sacredness of; profane. [DE– + (CON)SECRATE.] —**des′e•crat′er, des′e•cra′tor** *n.* —**des′e•cra′tion** *n.*

de•seg•re•gate (dē-sĕg′rĭ-gāt′) ►*v.* To abolish segregation in. —**de•seg′re•ga′tion** *n.* —**de•seg′re•ga′tion•ist** *n.*

de•sen•si•tize (dē-sĕn′sĭ-tīz′) ►*v.* To make less sensitive. —**de•sen′si•ti•za′tion** *n.*

des•ert[1] (dĕz′ərt) ►*n.* A dry, often sandy region of little rainfall and sparse vegetation. [< LLat. *dēsertum.*]

de•sert[2] (dĭ-zûrt′) ►*n.* often **deserts** Something deserved, esp. a punishment. [< OFr. *deserte* < p.part. of *deservir*, DESERVE.]

de•sert[3] (dĭ-zûrt′) ►*v.* **1.** To forsake or leave alone; abandon. **2.** To forsake one's duty or post, esp. in the armed forces. [< Lat. *dēserere, dēsert-*, abandon.] —**de•sert′er** *n.* —**de•ser′tion** *n.*

de•sert•i•fi•ca•tion (dĭ-zûr′tə-fĭ-kā′shən) ►*n.* The transformation of arable or habitable land to desert.

de•serve (dĭ-zûrv′) ►*v.* **-served, -serv•ing.** To be worthy of; merit. See Syns at **earn.** [< Lat. *dēservīre*, serve zealously.]

de•served (dĭ-zûrvd′) ►*adj.* Merited or earned. —**de•serv′ed•ly** (-zûr′vĭd-lē) *adv.*

de•serv•ing (dĭ-zûr′vĭng) ►*adj.* Worthy, as of reward or praise. —**de•serv′ing•ly** *adv.*

des•ic•cant (dĕs′ĭ-kənt) ►*n.* A substance used as a drying agent.

des•ic•cate (dĕs′ĭ-kāt′) ►*v.* **-cat•ed, -cat•ing 1.** To dry out thoroughly. **2.** To preserve (foods) by removing the moisture. See Syns at **dry.** [Lat. *dēsiccāre* < *siccus*, dry.] —**des′ic•ca′tion** *n.* —**des′ic•ca′tive** *adj.*

de•sid•er•a•tum (dĭ-sĭd′ə-rā′təm, -rä′-) ►*n.*, *pl.* **-ta** (-tə). Something necessary or desirable. [< Lat. *dēsīderāre*, to desire.]

de•sign (dĭ-zīn′) ►*v.* **1.** To conceive; invent. **2.** To formulate a plan for; devise. **3.** To have as a goal or purpose; intend. ►*n.* **1.** A drawing or sketch, esp. a detailed plan for construction or manufacture. **2.** The purposeful arrangement of parts or details. **3.** The art or practice of making designs. **4.** An ornamental pattern. See Syns at **figure. 5.** A plan or project. See Syns at **plan. 6.** A reasoned purpose; intent. **7.** often **designs** A secretive plot or scheme. [< Lat. *dēsignāre*, designate.] —**de•sign′er** *n.*

des•ig•nate (dĕz′ĭg-nāt′) ►*v.* **-nat•ed, -nat•ing 1.** To indicate or specify. **2.** To give a name to. **3.** To select and set aside for a duty, office, or purpose. See Syns at **allocate, appoint.** ►*adj.* (-nĭt). Appointed but not yet installed in office. [Lat. *dēsignāre.*] —**des′ig•na′tion** *n.* —**des′ig•na′tive** *adj.*

des•ig•nat•ed driver (dĕz′ĭg-nā′tĭd) ►*n.* One who agrees to remain sober, as at a party, in order to drive others home safely.

designated hitter ►*n.* *Baseball* A player designated to bat instead of the pitcher.

de•sign•ing (dĭ-zī′nĭng) ►*adj.* Conniving.

de•sir•a•ble (dĭ-zīr′ə-bəl) ►*adj.* **1.** Worth having or seeking. **2.** Worth doing. **3.** Arousing desire. —**de•sir′a•bil′i•ty, de•sir′a•ble•ness** *n.* —**de•sir′a•bly** *adv.*

de•sire (dĭ-zīr′) ►*v.* **-sired, -sir•ing 1.** To wish or long for; want. **2.** To express a wish for. ►*n.* **1.** A wish or longing. **2.** A request. **3.** The object of longing. **4.** Sexual appetite. [< Lat. *dēsīderāre.*] —**de•sir′er** *n.*

Syns: *desire, covet, crave, want, wish* ***v.***

de•sir•ous (dĭ-zīr′əs) ►*adj.* Wanting; desiring.

de•sist (dĭ-sĭst′, -zĭst′) ►*v.* To cease doing something. See Syns at **stop.** [< Lat. *dēsistere* < *sistere*, stop.]

desk (dĕsk) ►*n.* **1.** A piece of furniture typically having a flat top for writing. **2.** A counter or booth at which specified services are performed. **3.** A specialized department of a large organization: *a newspaper city desk.* [< OItal. *desco*, table.]

desk•top (dĕsk′tŏp′) ▶*adj.* **1.** Designed for use on a desk. **2.** Small enough to fit conveniently in an individual workspace.

desktop publishing ▶*n.* The design and production of publications using personal computers with graphics capability.

Des Moines (dĭ moin′) The capital of IA, in the S-central part. Pop. 193,187.

des•o•late (dĕs′ə-lĭt, dĕz′-) ▶*adj.* **1.** Devoid of inhabitants; deserted. **2.** Rendered unfit for habitation or use. **3.** Dreary; dismal. **4.** Lonely; forlorn. ▶*v.* (-lāt′) **-lat•ed, -lat•ing.** To make desolate. [< Lat. *dēsōlātus*, p.part. of *dēsōlāre*, abandon.] —**des′o•late•ly** *adv.* —**des′o•la′tion** *n.*

de So•to (dĭ sō′tō, dĕ), **Hernando** or **Fernando.** 1496?–1542. Spanish explorer.

de•spair (dĭ-spâr′) ▶*v.* To lose all hope. ▶*n.* **1.** Complete loss of hope. **2.** One that causes despair. [< Lat. *dēspērāre*, lose hope.]

des•per•a•do (dĕs′pə-rä′dō, -rā′-) ▶*n.*, *pl.* **-does** or **-dos.** A bold or desperate outlaw. [Sp. < p.part. of *desesperar*, DESPAIR.]

des•per•ate (dĕs′pər-ĭt) ▶*adj.* **1.** Having lost all hope; despairing. **2.** Reckless or violent because of despair. **3.** Undertaken as a last resort. **4.** Nearly hopeless; critical. **5.** Extreme; great: *a desperate urge.* [< Lat. *dēspērātus*, p.part. of *dēspērāre*, lose hope.] —**des′per•ate•ly** *adv.* —**des′per•a′tion** (dĕs′pə-rā′shən) *n.*

de•spic•a•ble (dĭ-spĭk′ə-bəl, dĕs′pĭ-kə-) ▶*adj.* Deserving of contempt or scorn; vile. [< Lat. *dēspicārī*, despise.] —**de•spic′a•ble•ness** *n.* —**de•spic′a•bly** *adv.*

de•spise (dĭ-spīz′) ▶*v.* **-spised, -spis•ing 1.** To regard with scorn. **2.** To dislike intensely. [< Lat. *dēspicere* : *dē-*, down + *specere*, look.] —**de•spis′er** *n.*

Syns: *despise, contemn, disdain, scorn* ***Ant:*** *esteem* ***v.***

de•spite (dĭ-spīt′) ▶*prep.* In spite of. [< OFr. *despit*, spite < Lat. *dēspicere*, DESPISE.]

de•spoil (dĭ-spoil′) ▶*v.* To sack; plunder. [< Lat. *dēspoliāre.*] —**de•spoil′ment** *n.* —**de•spo′li•a′tion** (-spō′lē-ā′shən) *n.*

de•spond (dĭ-spŏnd′) ▶*v.* To become discouraged. ▶*n.* Despondency. [Lat. *dēspondēre*, give up.] —**de•spond′ing•ly** *adv.*

de•spon•den•cy (dĭ-spŏn′dən-sē) ▶*n.* Loss of hope; dejection. —**de•spon′dent** *adj.* —**de•spon′dent•ly** *adv.*

des•pot (dĕs′pət) ▶*n.* A ruler with absolute power; tyrant. [< Gk. *despotēs.*] —**des•pot′ic** (dĭ-spŏt′ĭk) *adj.* —**des•pot′i•cal•ly** *adv.* —**des′pot•ism′** *n.*

des•sert (dĭ-zûrt′) ▶*n.* A usu. sweet dish served at the end of a meal. [Fr. < OFr. *desservir*, clear the table.]

de•sta•bi•lize (dē-stā′bə-līz′) ▶*v.* **-lized, -liz•ing 1.** To upset the stability of. **2.** To undermine the power of (a government). —**de•sta′bi•li•za′tion** *n.*

des•ti•na•tion (dĕs′tə-nā′shən) ▶*n.* **1.** The place to which one is going or directed. **2.** An ultimate purpose or goal.

des•tine (dĕs′tĭn) ▶*v.* **-tined, -tin•ing 1.** To determine beforehand. **2.** To assign for a specific end, use, or purpose. **3.** To direct toward a given destination: *a flight destined for Tokyo.* [< Lat. *dēstināre*, determine.]

des•ti•ny (dĕs′tə-nē) ▶*n.*, *pl.* **-nies 1.** One's inevitable fate. **2.** A predetermined course of events. **3.** The power or agency thought to predetermine events. [< OFr. *destiner*, DESTINE.]

des•ti•tute (dĕs′tĭ-to͞ot′, -tyo͞ot′) ▶*adj.* **1.** Utterly lacking; devoid: *destitute of any experience.* **2.** Lacking means of subsistence; impoverished. [< Lat. *dēstitūtus*, p.part. of *dēstituere*, abandon : DE– + *statuere*, to set.] —**des′ti•tu′tion** *n.*

de•stroy (dĭ-stroi′) ▶*v.* **1.** To ruin completely. **2.** To tear down; demolish. **3.** To kill. [< Lat. *dēstruere.*]

de•stroy•er (dĭ-stroi′ər) ▶*n.* **1.** One that destroys. **2.** A small fast warship.

de•struct (dĭ-strŭkt′, dē′strŭkt′) ▶*n.* The intentional, usu. remote-controlled destruction of a space vehicle, rocket, or missile after launching. —**de•struct′** *v.*

de•struc•ti•ble (dĭ-strŭk′tə-bəl) ▶*adj.* Easily destroyed. —**de•struc′ti•bil′i•ty** *n.*

de•struc•tion (dĭ-strŭk′shən) ▶*n.* **1.** The act of destroying or condition of having been destroyed. **2.** The cause or means of destroying. [< Lat. *dēstrūctiō* < *dēstruere*, destroy.] —**de•struc′tive** *adj.* —**de•struc′tive•ly** *adv.* —**de•struc′tive•ness** *n.*

des•ue•tude (dĕs′wĭ-to͞od′, -tyo͞od′) ▶*n.* A state of disuse. [< Lat. *dēsuētūdō.*]

des•ul•to•ry (dĕs′əl-tôr′ē, -tōr′ē, dĕz′-) ▶*adj.* **1.** Without purpose or intent; aimless. **2.** Occurring haphazardly; random. [< Lat. *dēsultor*, a leaper.] —**des′ul•to′ri•ly** *adv.*

de•tach (dĭ-tăch′) ▶*v.* To separate; disconnect. [< OFr. *destachier.*] —**de•tach′a•bil′i•ty** *n.* —**de•tach′a•ble** *adj.*

de•tached (dĭ-tăcht′) ▶*adj.* **1.** Separated; disconnected. **2.** Free from emotional involvement; cool; aloof.

de•tach•ment (dĭ-tăch′mənt) ▶*n.* **1.** The act or process of disconnecting; separation. **2.** Indifference to the concerns of others; aloofness. **3.** Impartiality; disinterest. **4a.** The dispatch of troops or ships from a larger body for special duty. **b.** A small permanent unit organized for special duties.

de•tail (dĭ-tāl′, dē′tāl′) ▶*n.* **1.** An individual part. See Syns at **item. 2.** Itemized or minute treatment of particulars: *attention to detail.* **3.** An inconsequential item or aspect. **4a.** A group of military personnel selected to do a specified task. **b.** The task assigned. ▶*v.* (dĭ-tāl′) **1.** To report or relate minutely. **2.** To name or state explicitly. **3.** To provide with decorative detail. [< OFr., piece cut off.]

de•tain (dĭ-tān′) ▶*v.* **1.** To keep from proceeding; delay. **2.** To keep in custody or confinement. [< Lat. *dētinēre*, hold back.] —**de•tain′ment** *n.* —**de′tain•ee′** (dē′tā-nē′, dĭ-tā′-) *n.*

de•tect (dĭ-tĕkt′) ▶*v.* To discover or ascertain the existence, presence, or fact of. [< Lat. *dētegere, dētēct-*, uncover.] —**de•tect′a•ble, de•tect′i•ble** *adj.* —**de•tec′tion** *n.* —**de•tect′er** *n.*

de•tec•tive (dĭ-tĕk′tĭv) ▶*n.* A person, usu. a member of a police force, who investigates crimes and obtains evidence.

de•tec•tor (dĭ-tĕk′tər) ▶*n.* One that detects, esp. a mechanical or electrical device that identifies and records a stimulus.

dé•tente (dā-tänt′, -täNt′) ►*n.* A relaxing of tension between nations. [Fr., a releasing.]

de•ten•tion (dĭ-tĕn′shən) ►*n.* **1.** The act of detaining or condition of being detained. **2.** A forced or punitive confinement. [< Lat. *dētinēre*, detain.]

de•ter (dĭ-tûr′) ►*v.* **-terred, -ter•ring.** To prevent or discourage from acting, as by means of fear or doubt. See Syns at **dissuade.** [Lat. *dēterrēre*, frighten away.] —**de•ter′ment** *n.*

de•ter•gent (dĭ-tûr′jənt) ►*n.* A cleansing substance made from chemical compounds rather than fats and lye. ►*adj.* Having cleansing power. [< Lat. *dētergēre*, wipe off.]

de•te•ri•o•rate (dĭ-tîr′ē-ə-rāt′) ►*v.* **-rat•ed, -rat•ing 1.** To diminish in quality or value. **2.** To weaken or disintegrate. [< Lat. *dēterior*, worse.] —**de•te′ri•o•ra′tion** *n.*

de•ter•mi•nant (dĭ-tûr′mə-nənt) ►*adj.* Determinative. ►*n.* A determining factor.

de•ter•mi•nate (dĭ-tûr′mə-nĭt) ►*adj.* **1.** Precisely limited or defined; definite. **2.** Conclusively settled; final.

de•ter•mi•na•tion (dĭ-tûr′mə-nā′shən) ►*n.* **1a.** The act of arriving at a decision. See Syns at **decision. b.** The decision reached. **2.** Firmness of purpose; resolve. **3.** The ascertaining or fixing of the quantity, quality, position, or character of something.

de•ter•mi•na•tive (dĭ-tûr′mə-nā′tĭv, -nə-) ►*adj.* Tending, able, or serving to determine. See Syns at **decisive.** ►*n.* A determining factor. —**de•ter′mi•na′tive•ly** *adv.*

de•ter•mine (dĭ-tûr′mĭn) ►*v.* **-mined, -min•ing 1.** To decide, establish, or ascertain definitely. See Syns at **discover. 2.** To cause to come to a conclusion or resolution; influence. **3.** To limit; regulate. **4.** To give direction to. [< Lat. *dētermindruare*, to limit < *terminus*, boundary.] —**de•ter′min•a•ble** *adj.* —**de•ter′min•a•bly** *adv.*

de•ter•mined (dĭ-tûr′mĭnd) ►*adj.* Showing determination. —**de•ter′mined•ly** *adv.*

de•ter•min•er (dĭ-tûr′mə-nər) ►*n.* A word belonging to a group of noun modifiers that includes articles, demonstratives, and possessive adjectives, and, in English, occupying the first position in a noun phrase.

de•ter•min•ism (dĭ-tûr′mə-nĭz′əm) ►*n.* The philosophical doctrine that every state of affairs, including every human event, act, and decision, is the inevitable consequence of antecedent states of affairs. —**de•ter′min•ist** *n.* —**de•ter′min•is′tic** *adj.*

de•ter•rent (dĭ-tûr′ənt, -tŭr′-) ►*adj.* Tending to deter. ►*n.* Something that deters. —**de•ter′rence** *n.*

de•test (dĭ-tĕst′) ►*v.* To dislike intensely; abhor. [< Lat. *dētestārī*, to curse.] —**de•test′a•ble** *adj.* —**de•test′a•bly** *adv.* —**de′tes•ta′tion** (dē′tĕ-stā′shən) *n.*

de•throne (dē-thrōn′) ►*v.* **-throned, -thron•ing.** To remove from the throne; depose. —**de•throne′ment** *n.*

det•o•nate (dĕt′n-āt′) ►*v.* **-nat•ed, -nat•ing.** To explode or cause to explode. [Lat. *dētonāre*, thunder down.] —**det′o•na′tion** *n.* —**det′o•na′tor** *n.*

de•tour (dē′to͝or′, dĭ-to͝or′) ►*n.* A roundabout way, esp. a road used temporarily instead of a main route. ►*v.* To go or cause to go by a detour. [< OFr. *destorner*, turn away.]

de•tox (dē-tŏks′) *Informal* ►*v.* To detoxify. ►*n.* (dē′tŏks′). A place where patients are detoxified.

de•tox•i•fy (dē-tŏk′sə-fī′) ►*v.* **-fied, -fy•ing 1.** To remove poison or the effects of poison from. **2.** To treat (an individual) for alcohol or drug dependence, usu. under medical supervision. —**de•tox′i•fi•ca′tion** *n.*

de•tract (dĭ-trăkt′) ►*v.* To take away (from); diminish. [< Lat. *dētrahere*, *dētract-*.] —**de•trac′tion** *n.* —**de•trac′tor** *n.*

de•train (dē-trān′) ►*v.* To leave or cause to leave a railroad train.

det•ri•ment (dĕt′rə-mənt) ►*n.* **1.** Damage, harm, or loss. See Syns at **disadvantage. 2.** Something that causes damage, harm, or loss. [< Lat. *dētrīmentum*.] —**det′ri•men′tal** *adj.* —**det′ri•men′tal•ly** *adv.*

de•tri•tus (dĭ-trī′təs) ►*n., pl.* **-tus 1.** Loose fragments or grains worn away from rock. **2.** Debris: *the detritus of past civilizations.* [< Lat. *dētrītus*.]

De•troit (dĭ-troit′) A city of SE MI opposite Windsor, Ontario. Pop. 1,027,974.

deuce[1] (do͞os, dyo͞os) ►*n.* **1.** A playing card or side of a die having two spots. **2.** A tied score in tennis in which each player or side has 40 points. [< Lat. *duōs*, two.]

deuce[2] (do͞os, dyo͞os) ►*n.* *Informal* The devil. Used as a mild oath. [Prob. < LGer. *duus*, a throw of two in dice games.]

deu•te•ri•um (do͞o-tîr′ē-əm, dyo͞o-) ►*n.* A hydrogen isotope with an atomic weight of 2.014. [< Gk. *deuteros*, second.]

Deu•ter•on•o•my (do͞o′tə-rŏn′ə-mē, dyo͞o′-) ►*n.* See table at **Bible.** [< Gk. *deuteronomion*, a second law.]

deut•sche mark also **deut•sche•mark** (doi′chə-märk′) ►*n.* See table at **currency.** [Ger., German mark.]

De Va•le•ra (dĕv′ə-lĕr′ə, -lîr′ə), **Eamon.** 1882–1975. Amer.-born Irish political leader; first president of the Republic of Ireland (1959–73).

de•val•ue (dē-văl′yo͞o) also **de•val•u•ate** (-văl′yo͞o-āt′) ►*v.* **-ued, -u•ing** also **-at•ed, -at•ing 1.** To lessen the value of. **2.** To lower the exchange value of (a currency). —**de•val′u•a′tion** *n.*

dev•as•tate (dĕv′ə-stāt′) ►*v.* **-tat•ed, -tat•ing 1.** To lay waste; destroy. **2.** To overwhelm; confound. [< Lat. *vāstus*.] —**dev′as•ta′tion** *n.* —**dev′as•ta′tor** *n.*

de•vel•op (dĭ-vĕl′əp) ►*v.* **1.** To bring, grow, or evolve from latency to or toward fulfillment. See Syns at **mature. 2.** To expand or enlarge; elaborate. **3.** To appear, disclose, or acquire. **4.** To make available and usable. **5.** To process (a photosensitive material), esp. with chemicals, to render a recorded image visible. [< OFr. *desveloper*.] —**de•vel′op•er** *n.* —**de•vel′op•ment** *n.* —**de•vel′op•ment′al** *adj.* —**de•vel′op•men′tal•ly** *adv.*

de•vi•ant (dē′vē-ənt) ►*adj.* Differing or deviating from accepted social or moral standards. —**de′vi•ance** *n.* —**de′vi•ant** *n.*

de•vi•ate (dē′vē-āt′) ►*v.* **-at•ed, -at•ing.** To differ or move away from an established course, way, or prescribed mode of behavior. See Syns at **swerve.** ►*n.* (-ĭt). A deviant. [LLat. *dēviāre*.] —**de′vi•a′tion** *n.*

de•vice (dĭ-vīs′) ►*n.* **1.** Something designed for a particular purpose, esp. a machine. **2.** A plan or scheme; trick. **3.** A literary contrivance, such as parallelism or personification, used to achieve a particular effect. **4.** A decorative design, figure, or pattern, as one used in embroidery. See Syns at **figure. 5.** A graphic symbol or motto, esp. in heraldry. [< OFr. *deviser*, devise.]

dev•il (dĕv′əl) ►*n.* **1.** often **Devil** In some religions, the major spirit of evil and foe of God. Used with *the.* **2.** A subordinate evil spirit; demon. **3.** A wicked or malevolent person. **4.** A person: *a handsome devil; the poor devil.* **5.** A mischievous or daring person. **6.** A printer's apprentice. ►*v.* **-iled, -il•ing** or **-illed, -il•ling 1.** To season (food) heavily. **2.** To annoy, torment, or harass. [< Gk. *diabolos*, slanderer.]

dev•il•ish (dĕv′ə-lĭsh) ►*adj.* **1.** Of or like a devil; fiendish. **2.** Mischievous. **3.** Excessive; extreme: *devilish heat.* ►*adv.* Extremely; very. —**dev′il•ish•ly** *adv.*

Dev•il's Island (dĕv′ĭlz) An island in the Caribbean Sea off French Guiana.

dev•il•try (dĕv′əl-trē) or **dev•il•ry** (-əl-rē) ►*n., pl.* **-tries** or **-ries 1.** Reckless mischief. **2.** Wickedness. **3.** Evil magic. [Alteration of *devilry.*]

de•vi•ous (dē′vē-əs) ►*adj.* **1.** Not straightforward; deceitful. **2.** Deviating from the straight or direct course: *a devious route.* [< Lat. *dēvius*, out-of-the-way.] —**de′vi•ous•ly** *adv.* —**de′vi•ous•ness** *n.*

de•vise (dĭ-vīz′) ►*v.* **-vised, -vis•ing 1.** To plan or arrange in the mind; invent. **2.** *Law* To transmit (real property) by will. ►*n. Law* **1.** The act of transmitting real property by will. **2.** A will or clause in a will devising real property. [< Lat. *dīvidere, dīvīs-*, divide.] —**de•vis′a•ble** *adj.* —**de•vis′er** *n.*

de•vi•tal•ize (dē-vīt′l-īz′) ►*v.* To diminish or destroy the strength or vitality of.

de•void (dĭ-void′) ►*adj.* Completely lacking; destitute: *a novel devoid of wit.* [< OFr. *desvoidier*, remove.]

de•volve (dĭ-vŏlv′) ►*v.* **-volved, -volv•ing.** To pass on or be passed on to a substitute or successor. [< Lat. *dēvolvere*, roll down.] —**dev′o•lu′tion** (dĕv′ə-lo͞o′shən) *n.*

De•vo•ni•an (dĭ-vō′nē-ən) *Geol.* ►*adj.* Of or being the 4th period of the Paleozoic Era, marked by the appearance of forests and amphibians. ►*n.* The Devonian Period. [After *Devon*, England.]

de•vote (dĭ-vōt′) ►*v.* **-vot•ed, -vot•ing 1.** To give or apply (one's time, attention, or self) entirely. **2.** To set apart for a specific purpose. **3.** To dedicate or consecrate. [Lat. *dēvovēre, dēvōt-*, to vow.]

de•vot•ed (dĭ-vō′tĭd) ►*adj.* Feeling or displaying strong affection or attachment; ardent. —**de•vot′ed•ly** *adv.*

dev•o•tee (dĕv′ə-tē′, -tā′) ►*n.* An enthusiast.

de•vo•tion (dĭ-vō′shən) ►*n.* **1.** Ardent attachment or affection. **2.** Religious ardor. **3.** often **devotions** Prayers, esp. when private. —**de•vo′tion•al** *adj.*

de•vour (dĭ-vour′) ►*v.* **1.** To eat up greedily. See Syns at **eat. 2.** To destroy, consume, or waste. **3.** To take in eagerly. **4.** To prey upon voraciously; engulf: *devoured by jealousy.* [< Lat. *dēvorāre*, swallow up.]

de•vout (dĭ-vout′) ►*adj.* **-er, -est 1.** Deeply religious; pious. **2.** Sincere; earnest. [< Lat. *dēvōtus*, devoted.] —**de•vout′ly** *adv.* —**de•vout′ness** *n.*

De Vries (də vrēs′), **Hugo.** 1848–1935. Dutch botanist.

dew (do͞o, dyo͞o) ►*n.* **1.** Water droplets condensed from the air, usu. at night, onto cool surfaces. **2.** Something moist, fresh, pure, or renewing. [< OE *dēaw.*] —**dew′i•ly** *adv.* —**dew′i•ness** *n.* —**dew′y** *adj.*

DEW ►*abbr.* distant early warning

dew•ber•ry (do͞o′bĕr′ē, dyo͞o′-) ►*n.* **1.** Any of several trailing plants. **2.** The edible fruit of the dewberry.

dew•claw (do͞o′klô′, dyo͞o′-) ►*n.* A vestigial digit on the feet of certain mammals. [?]

dew•drop (do͞o′drŏp′, dyo͞o′-) ►*n.* A drop of dew.

Dew•ey (do͞o′ē, dyo͞o′ē), **George.** 1837–1917. Amer. naval officer.

Dewey, John. 1859–1952. Amer. philosopher and educator.

dew•lap (do͞o′lăp′, dyo͞o′-) ►*n.* A fold of loose skin hanging from the neck of certain animals. [ME *dewlappe.*]

dew point ►*n.* The temperature at which air becomes saturated and produces dew.

dex•ter•i•ty (dĕk-stĕr′ĭ-tē) ►*n.* **1.** Skill in the use of the hands or body; adroitness. **2.** Mental skill or cleverness.

dex•ter•ous (dĕk′stər-əs, -strəs) also **dex•trous** (-strəs) ►*adj.* **1.** Skillful in the use of the hands or mind. **2.** Done with dexterity. [< Lat. *dexter*, skillful.] —**dex′ter•ous•ly** *adv.*

dex•trin (dĕk′strĭn) ►*n.* A pale powder obtained from starch, used mainly as an adhesive. [< Lat. *dexter*, right.]

dex•trose (dĕk′strōs′) ►*n.* A colorless sugar, $C_6H_{12}O_6 \cdot H_2O$, found in animal and plant tissue and also made synthetically from starch. [*dexter*, right + -OSE[2].]

DFC ►*abbr.* Distinguished Flying Cross

dg ►*abbr.* decigram

DH ►*abbr.* **1.** designated hitter **2.** Doctor of Humanities

Dha•ka or **Dac•ca** (dăk′ə, dä′kə). The capital of Bangladesh, in the E-central part. Pop. 3,397,187.

dhar•ma (där′mə, dûr′-) ►*n. Hinduism & Buddhism* **1.** The principle or law that orders the universe. **2.** Individual conduct in conformity with this principle. [Skt.]

Dhau•la•gi•ri (dou′lə-gîr′ē) A peak, 8,177.1 m (26,810 ft), in the Himalayas of W-central Nepal.

Dhu'l-Hij•jah (do͞ol-hĭj′ä) ►*n.* The 12th month of the Muslim calendar. See table at **calendar.** [Ar. *ḏū-l-ḥijja.*]

Dhu'l-Qa•'dah (do͞ol-kä′dä) ►*n.* The 11th month of the Muslim calendar. See table at **calendar.** [Ar. *ḏū-l-qa'da.*]

di– ►*pref.* **1.** Two; twice; double: *digraph.* **2.** Containing two atoms, radicals, or groups: *dioxide.* [Gk.]

dia. ►*abbr.* Diameter.

di•a•be•tes (dī′ə-bē′tĭs, -tēz) ►*n.* Any of several metabolic disorders marked by excessive discharge of urine and persistent thirst, esp. diabetes mellitus. [< Gk. *diabētēs*, siphon, diabetes : *dia-*, through + *bainein*, go.] —**di′a•bet′ic** (-bĕt′ĭk) *adj. & n.*

diabetes mel•li•tus (mə-lī′təs, mĕl′ĭ-) ►*n.* A chronic disease of pancreatic origin marked by insulin deficiency that results in excess sugar in the blood and urine. [NLat., honey-sweet diabetes.]

di•a•bol•i•cal (dī′ə-bŏl′ĭ-kəl) also **di•a•bol•ic** (-ĭk) ►*adj.* Fiendish; wicked. [< Lat. *diabolus*, DEVIL.] —**di′a•bol′i•cal•ly** *adv.*

di•a•crit•ic (dī′ə-krĭt′ĭk) ►*adj.* **1.** Diacritical. **2.** *Medic.* Diagnostic or distinctive. ►*n.* A mark added to a letter to indicate a special phonetic value. [Gk. *diakritikos*, distinguishing.]

di•a•crit•i•cal (dī′ə-krĭt′ĭ-kəl) ►*adj.* **1.** Marking a distinction; distinguishing. **2.** Able to distinguish. **3.** Serving as a diacritic. —**di′a•crit′i•cal•ly** *adv.*

Dí•a de la Ra•za (dē′ä dĕ lä rä′sä) ►*n.* Oct. 12, celebrated in many Spanish-speaking areas in commemoration of Christopher Columbus.

di•a•dem (dī′ə-dĕm′, -dəm) ►*n.* **1.** A crown or headband. **2.** Royal power or dignity. [< Gk. *diadēma*.]

di•aer•e•sis (dī-ĕr′ĭ-sĭs) ►*n.* Var. of **dieresis.**

di•ag•no•sis (dī′əg-nō′sĭs) ►*n.*, *pl.* **-ses** (-sēz). Identification, esp. of a disease, by examination and analysis. [Gk. *diagnōsis*, discernment.] —**di′ag•nose′** *v.* —**di′ag•nos′tic** (-nŏs′tĭk) *adj.* —**di′ag•nos′ti•cal•ly** *adv.* —**di′ag•nos•ti′cian** (-stĭsh′ən) *n.*

di•ag•o•nal (dī-ăg′ə-nəl) ►*adj.* **1.** *Math.* Joining two nonadjacent vertices. **2.** Having a slanted or oblique direction. ►*n.* *Math.* A diagonal line or plane. [< Gk. *diagōnios*, from angle to angle.] —**di•ag′o•nal•ly** *adv.*

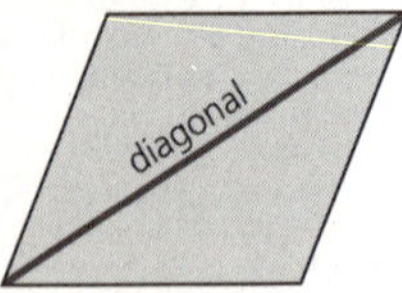

diagonal

di•a•gram (dī′ə-grăm′) ►*n.* A schematic plan or drawing designed to explain how something works or to clarify the relationship between the parts of a whole. ►*v.* **-grammed**, **-gram•ming** or **-gramed,** or **-gram•ing.** To represent by a diagram. [< Gk. *diagramma* : *dia-*, across + *graphein*, write.] —**di′a•gram•mat′ic** (-grə-măt′ĭk), **di′a•gram•mat′i•cal** *adj.*

di•al (dī′əl) ►*n.* **1.** A graduated surface or face on which a measurement, as of time, speed, or temperature, is indicated by a moving pointer. **2.** A sundial. **3.** A rotatable disk, as of a telephone, radio, or television, for making connections or changing frequency channels. ►*v.* **-aled, -al•ing** or **-alled, -al•ling 1.** To indicate or select by means of a dial. **2.** To call on a telephone. [< Med.Lat. *diālis*, daily.]

di•a•lect (dī′ə-lĕkt′) ►*n.* **1.** A regional variety of a language. **2.** A language considered as part of a larger family of languages or a linguistic branch. [< Gk. *dialektos*, speech.] —**di′a•lec′tal** *adj.*

di•a•lec•tic (dī′ə-lĕk′tĭk) ►*n.* **1.** The art or practice of arriving at the truth by the exchange of logical arguments. **2. dialectics** *(takes sing. v.)* A method of argument that weighs contradictory facts or ideas with a view to resolving real or apparent contradictions. [< Gk. *dialektikē (tekhnē)*, (art) of debate.] —**di′a•lec′ti•cal, di′a•lec′tic** *adj.*

dialog box ►*n.* A window that appears on a computer screen, presenting information or requesting input.

di•a•logue or **di•a•log** (dī′ə-lôg′, -lŏg′) ►*n.* **1.** A conversation between two or more people. **2.** Conversation between characters in a drama or narrative. **3.** An exchange of ideas or opinions. [< Gk. *dialogos*.]

dial-up (dī′əl-ŭp′, dīl′-) ►*adj.* Relating to a network connection, usu. to the Internet, made by dialing a phone number.

di•al•y•sis (dī-ăl′ĭ-sĭs) ►*n.*, *pl.* **-ses** (-sēz′). The separation of smaller molecules from larger molecules or of dissolved substances from colloidal particles in a solution by selective diffusion through a semipermeable membrane. [Gk. *dialusis*, separating.]

di•a•mag•net•ic (dī′ə-măg-nĕt′ĭk) ►*adj.* Of or relating to a substance that is repelled by a magnet. [Gk. *dia*, through + MAGNETIC.] —**di′a•mag′ne•tism** *n.*

di•am•e•ter (dī-ăm′ĭ-tər) ►*n.* **1a.** A straight line segment passing through the center of a figure, esp. of a circle or sphere. **b.** The length of such a segment. **2.** Thickness or width. [< Gk. *diametros*.]

di•a•met•ri•cal (dī′ə-mĕt′rĭ-kəl) also **di•a•met•ric** (-rĭk) ►*adj.* **1.** Of or along a diameter. **2.** Exactly opposite; contrary. —**di′a•met′ri•cal•ly** *adv.*

di•a•mond (dī′ə-mənd, dī′mənd) ►*n.* **1.** An extremely hard, highly refractive crystalline form of carbon, usu. colorless, used as a gemstone when pure and chiefly in abrasives and cutting tools otherwise. **2.** A rhombus or lozenge. **3.** Any of a suit of playing cards marked with a red, diamond-shaped symbol. **4.** *Baseball* **a.** An infield. **b.** The whole playing field. [< Lat. *adamās*, ADAMANT.]

di•a•mond•back rattlesnake (dī′ə-mənd-băk′, dī′mənd-) ►*n.* A large venomous rattlesnake of SW North America.

Diamond Head. A promontory, 232.1 m (761 ft), on the SE coast of Oahu, HI.

Di•an•a (dī-ăn′ə) ►*n.* *Rom. Myth.* The goddess of chastity, hunting, and the moon.

di•a•pa•son (dī′ə-pā′zən, -sən) ►*n.* *Mus.* **1.** The entire range of an instrument or voice. **2.** Either of the two principal stops on a pipe organ that form the tonal basis for the entire scale of the instrument. [< Gk. *(dia) pasōn (khordōn)*, (through) all (the notes).]

di•a•per (dī′ə-pər, dī′pər) ►*n.* A piece of absorbent material, such as paper or cloth, that is placed between a baby's legs and fastened at the waist to serve as underpants. ►*v.* To put a diaper on. [< OFr. *diaspre*, a patterned fabric.]

di•aph•a•nous (dī-ăf′ə-nəs) ►*adj.* **1.** Of such fine texture as to be transparent or translucent. See Syns at **airy. 2.** Vague or insubstantial. [< Gk. *diaphainein*, be transparent.] —**di•aph′a•nous•ly** *adv.*

di•a•pho•re•sis (dī′ə-fə-rē′sĭs, dī-ăf′ə-) ►*n.* Copious perspiration, esp. when medically induced. [< Gk. *diaphorēsis* : *dia-*, through + *pherein*, carry.]

di•a•phragm (dī′ə-frăm′) ►*n.* **1.** A muscular membranous partition separating the abdominal and thoracic cavities and functioning in respiration. **2.** A similar membranous part that divides or separates. **3.** A thin disk, esp. in a microphone or telephone receiver, that vibrates in response to sound waves to produce electric signals, or vice versa. **4.** A contraceptive device consisting of a flexible disk that covers the uterine cervix. **5.** A disk used to restrict the amount of light that passes through a lens or optical system. [< Gk. *diaphragma*, partition.] —**di′a•phrag•mat′ic** (-frăg-măt′ĭk) *adj.*

di•ar•rhe•a also **di•ar•rhoe•a** (dī′ə-rē′ə) ►*n.* Excessively frequent bowel movements, usu. indicating gastrointestinal disorder. [< Gk. *diarrhoia* : *dia-*, through + *rhein*, flow.]

di•a•ry (dī′ə-rē) ►*n., pl.* **-ries 1.** A daily record, esp. of personal experiences and observations; journal. **2.** A book for keeping such a record. [Lat. *diārium.*] —**di′a•rist** *n.*

Di•as (dē′əs, -əsh), **Bartolomeu.** 1450?–1500. Portuguese navigator.

di•as•to•le (dī-ăs′tə-lē) ►*n.* The normal rhythmically occurring relaxation and dilatation of the heart chambers, esp. the ventricles, during which they fill with blood. [Gk. *diastolē*, dilation.] —**di′as•tol′ic** (dī′ə-stŏl′ĭk) *adj.*

di•a•ther•my (dī′ə-thûr′mē) ►*n.* The therapeutic generation of local heat in body tissues by high-frequency electromagnetic currents. [Gk. *dia*, through + *thermē*, heat.] —**di′a•ther′mic** *adj.*

di•a•tom (dī′ə-tŏm′) ►*n.* Any of a class of microscopic one-celled algae having cell walls of silica consisting of two interlocking valves. [< Gk. *diatomos*, cut in half.]

di•a•to•ma•ceous (dī′ə-tə-mā′shəs, dī-ăt′ə-) ►*adj.* Consisting of diatoms or their skeletons.

di•a•tom•ic (dī′ə-tŏm′ĭk) ►*adj.* Made up of two atoms: *a diatomic molecule.*

di•a•ton•ic (dī′ə-tŏn′ĭk) ►*adj. Mus.* Of or using the seven tones of a standard scale. [< Gk. *diatonikos.*] —**di′a•ton′i•cal•ly** *adv.* —**di′a•ton′i•cism** (-ĭ-sĭz′əm) *n.*

di•a•tribe (dī′ə-trīb′) ►*n.* A bitter, abusive denunciation. [< Gk. *diatribē*, lecture.]

di•az•e•pam (dī-ăz′ə-păm′) ►*n.* An antianxiety drug. [*diaz(o)* + *ep(oxide)* + AM(MONIA).]

dib•ble (dĭb′əl) ►*n.* A pointed implement used to make holes in soil, esp. for planting bulbs. [ME *dibbel.*] —**dib′ble** *v.*

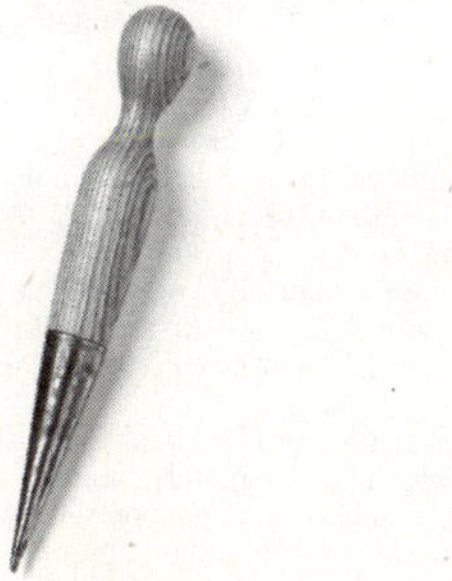

dibble

dibs (dĭbz) ►*pl.n. Slang* A claim; rights. [< *dibstones*, counters used in a game.]

dice (dīs) ►*n.* **1.** *Games* Pl. of **die²** 2. **2.** *pl.* **dice** also **dic•es** A small cube, as of food. ►*v.* **diced, dic•ing 1.** *Games* To play or gamble with dice. **2.** To cut into small cubes. [Pl. of DIE².]

dic•er (dī′sər) ►*n.* A device used for dicing food.

dic•ey (dī′sē) ►*adj.* **-i•er, -i•est.** Involving or full of danger or risk. [< DICE.]

di•chot•o•my (dī-kŏt′ə-mē) ►*n., pl.* **-mies.** Division into two usu. contradictory parts, categories, or opinions. [< Gk. *dikhotomos*, cut in two.] —**di•chot′o•mous** *adj.*

dick (dĭk) ►*n. Slang* A detective.

dick•ens (dĭk′ənz) ►*n. Informal* **1.** A severe reprimand. Used with *the.* **2.** Used as an intensive: *What in the dickens is that?* [Perh. < the name *Dickens.*]

Dickens, Charles John Huffam. 1812–70. British writer. —**Dick•en′si•an** (dĭ-kĕn′zē-ən) *adj.*

dick•er (dĭk′ər) ►*v.* To bargain; barter. [Poss. < ME *diker*, quantity of ten.]

dick•ey also **dick•ie** or **dick•y** (dĭk′ē) ►*n., pl.* **-eys** also **-ies 1a.** A woman's blouse front worn under a jacket or low-necked garment. **b.** A man's detachable shirt front. **2.** A small bird. [< *Dick*, nickname for *Richard.*]

Dick•in•son (dĭk′ĭn-sən), **Emily Elizabeth.** 1830–86. Amer. poet.

di•cot•y•le•don (dī′kŏt′l-ēd′n) also **di•cot** (dī′kŏt′) ►*n.* A plant with two embryonic seed leaves that usu. appear at germination. —**di′cot′y•le′don•ous** *adj.*

dic•tate (dĭk′tāt′, dĭk-tāt′) ►*v.* **-tat•ed, -tat•ing 1.** To say or read aloud for transcription. **2.** To prescribe or command with authority. ►*n.* (dĭk′tāt′) **1.** A directive; command. **2.** A guiding principle: *the dictates of conscience.* [Lat. *dictāre* < *dīcere*, say.] —**dic•ta′tion** *n.*

Syns: *dictate, decree, impose, ordain, prescribe* **v.**

dic•ta•tor (dĭk′tā′tər, dĭk-tā′-) ►*n.* **1.** A ruler having absolute power, esp. a tyrant. **2.** One who dictates. —**dic•ta′tor•ship** *n.*

dic•ta•to•ri•al (dĭk′tə-tôr′ē-əl, -tōr′-) ►*adj.* **1.** Domineering. **2.** Relating to or characteristic of a dictator or dictatorship; autocratic. —**dic′ta•to′ri•al•ly** *adv.*

dic•tion (dĭk′shən) ►*n.* **1.** Choice and use of words in speech or writing. **2.** Clarity and distinctness of pronunciation. [< Lat. *dictiō-*, rhetorical delivery < *dīcere*, say.]

dic•tion•ar•y (dĭk′shə-nĕr′ē) ►*n., pl.* **-ies.** A reference book containing an alphabetical list of words, with information given for each word, usu. including meaning, pronunciation, and etymology, or equivalent translations into another language.

dic•tum (dĭk′təm) ►*n., pl.* **-ta** (-tə) or **-tums 1.** An authoritative, often formal pronouncement. **2.** *Law* See **obiter dictum** 1. [Lat. < p.part. of *dīcere*, say.]

did (dĭd) ►*v.* P.t. of **do¹**.

di•dac•tic (dī-dăk′tĭk) also **di•dac•ti•cal** (-tĭ-kəl) ►*adj.* **1.** Intended to instruct. **2.** Morally instructive. [< Gk. *didaskein*, *didak-*, teach.] —**di•dac′ti•cal•ly** *adv.*

did•dle¹ (dĭd′l) ►*v.* **-dled, -dling.** *Slang* To cheat or swindle. [?] —**did′dler** *n.*

did•dle² (dĭd′l) ►*v.* **1.** To toy or fiddle: *diddling with the controls.* **2.** To waste time: *diddled around all day.* [Prob. ult. < Low Ger.]

Di•de•rot (dē′də-rō′, dē-drō′), **Denis.** 1713–84. French philosopher and writer.

did•n't (dĭd′nt) ► Did not.

Did•rik•son (dĭd′rĭk-sən), **Mildred Ella.** See Mildred Ella Didrikson **Zaharias.**

didst (dĭdst) ► *v. Archaic* 2nd pers. sing. p.t. of **do**[1].

die[1] (dī) ► *v.* **died, dy•ing** (dī′ĭng) **1.** To cease living; become dead; expire. **2.** To cease existing, esp. by degrees. **3.** *Informal* To desire greatly. **4.** To lose force or vitality; cease operation. —***phrasal verb:*** **die out** To become extinct: *customs that died out centuries ago.* [Prob. < ON *deyja.*]

die[2] (dī) ► *n.* **1.** *pl.* **dies** A device used for cutting out, forming, punching, or stamping materials. **2.** *pl.* **dice** (dīs) A small cube marked on each side with from one to six dots, usu. used in pairs in gambling and in various other games. —***idiom:*** **no dice** No. Used as a refusal to a request. [< OFr. *de*, gaming die < Lat. *dare*, give.]

Die•fen•ba•ker (dē′fən-bā′kər), **John George.** 1895–1979. Canadian prime minister (1957–63).

die-hard also **die•hard** (dī′härd′) ► *adj.* Stubbornly resisting change or clinging to a cause. —**die′-hard′** *n.*

di•e•lec•tric (dī′ĭ-lĕk′trĭk) ► *n.* A nonconductor of electricity. [Gk. *dia*, through + ELECTRIC.] —**di′e•lec′tric** *adj.*

di•er•e•sis or **di•aer•e•sis** (dī-ĕr′ĭ-sĭs) ► *n., pl.* **-ses** (-sēz′). A mark (¨) placed over the second of two adjacent vowels to indicate that they are to be pronounced as separate sounds rather than a dipthong. [< Gk. *diairesis*, separation.]

die•sel (dē′zəl, -səl) ► *n.* A vehicle powered by a diesel engine.

diesel engine ► *n.* An internal-combustion engine that uses the heat of highly compressed air to ignite a spray of fuel introduced after the start of the compression stroke. [After Rudolf *Diesel* (858–1913).]

di•et[1] (dī′ĭt) ► *n.* **1.** One's usual food and drink. **2.** A regulated selection of foods, esp. as for medical reasons or cosmetic weight loss. ► *v.* To eat and drink according to a regulated or prescribed system. [< Gk. *diaita*, way of living.] —**di′e•tar′y** *adj.* —**di′et•er** *n.*

di•et[2] (dī′ĭt) ► *n.* A legislative assembly. [< Med.Lat. *diēta*, ult. < Gk. *diaita*. See DIET[1].]

di•e•tet•ic (dī′ĭ-tĕt′ĭk) ► *adj.* Specially prepared or processed for restrictive diets.

di•e•tet•ics (dī′ĭ-tĕt′ĭks) ► *n. (takes sing. v.)* The study of diet and nutrition.

di•e•ti•tian or **di•e•ti•cian** (dī′ĭ-tĭsh′ən) ► *n.* A person specializing in dietetics.

dif•fer (dĭf′ər) ► *v.* **1.** To be unlike. **2.** To disagree with something or have a different opinion. [< Lat. *differre* : *dis-*, apart + *ferre*, carry.]

Syns: *differ, disagree, vary* ***Ant:*** *agree* ***v.***

dif•fer•ence (dĭf′ər-əns, dĭf′rəns) ► *n.* **1.** The fact, condition, or degree of being unlike. **2a.** A disagreement, controversy, or quarrel. **b.** A cause of disagreement. **3.** *Math.* **a.** The amount by which one quantity is greater or less than another. **b.** A remainder.

dif•fer•ent (dĭf′ər-ənt, dĭf′rənt) ► *adj.* **1.** Unlike or dissimilar. **2.** Distinct or separate. **3.** Unusual or distinctive. —**dif′fer•ent•ly** *adv.* —**dif′fer•ent•ness** *n.*

dif•fer•en•tial (dĭf′ə-rĕn′shəl) ► *adj.* Of, showing, or constituting a difference. ► *n.* **1.** An amount or degree of difference between similar kinds or individuals: *a wage differential.* **2.** A differential gear.

differential gear ► *n.* An arrangement of gears that permits one turning shaft to drive two others at different speeds.

dif•fer•en•ti•ate (dĭf′ə-rĕn′shē-āt′) ► *v.* **-at•ed, -at•ing 1.** To constitute or perceive a distinction. **2.** To make or become different, distinct, or specialized. —**dif′fer•en′ti•a′tion** *n.*

dif•fi•cult (dĭf′ĭ-kŭlt′, -kəlt) ► *adj.* **1.** Hard to do, accomplish, or comprehend; arduous. **2.** Hard to please, satisfy, or manage. [< DIFFICULTY.] —**dif′fi•cult′ly** *adv.*

dif•fi•cul•ty (dĭf′ĭ-kŭl′tē, -kəl-) ► *n., pl.* **-ties 1.** The condition or quality of being difficult. **2.** often **difficulties a.** A troublesome or embarrassing state of affairs: *in financial difficulty.* **b.** Problems or conflicts: *emotional difficulties.* **3.** Great effort; trouble. [< Lat. *difficultās.*]

Syns: *difficulty, hardship, rigor, vicissitude* ***n.***

dif•fi•dent (dĭf′ĭ-dənt, -dĕnt′) ► *adj.* Lacking self-confidence; timid. [< Lat. *diffīdere*, to mistrust.] —**dif′fi•dence** *n.*

dif•frac•tion (dĭ-frăk′shən) ► *n.* Change in the directions and intensities of light or other radiation after passing by an obstacle or through an aperture. [< Lat. *diffringere, diffrāct-*, shatter.]

dif•fuse (dĭ-fyo͞oz′) ► *v.* **-fused, -fus•ing.** To pour or spread out and disperse. ► *adj.* (dĭ-fyo͞os′) **1.** Widely spread or scattered. **2.** Verbose. See Syns at **wordy.** [< Lat. *diffundere, diffūs-*, spread.] —**dif•fuse′ly** (-fyo͞os′lē) *adv.* —**dif•fu′sion** *n.*

dig (dĭg) ► *v.* **dug** (dŭg), **dig•ging 1.** To break up, turn over, or remove (e.g., earth or sand) with a tool or the hands. **2.** To make (an excavation) by or as if by digging. **3.** To learn or discover: *dug up the evidence.* **4.** To thrust against; poke or prod: *dug me in the ribs.* **5.** *Slang* To understand, take notice of, or enjoy. —***phrasal verb:*** **dig in 1.** To begin to work intensively. **2.** To begin to eat heartily. ► *n.* **1.** A poke or thrust. **2.** A sarcastic remark; gibe. **3.** An archaeological excavation. [ME *diggen.*] —**dig′ger** *n.*

dig•er•a•ti (dĭj′ə-rä′tē) ► *pl.n.* People knowledgeable about digital technologies. [DIG(ITAL) + (LIT)ERATI.]

di•gest (dī-jĕst′, dĭ-) ► *v.* **1.** To convert (food) into a form that can easily be absorbed and assimilated by the body. **2.** To absorb mentally; comprehend. **3.** To organize into a systematic arrangement. ► *n.* (dī′jĕst′). A collection of written material in condensed form. [< Lat. *dīgerere, dīgest-*, to separate.] —**di•gest′i•ble** *adj.* —**di•ges′tion** *n.* —**di•ges′tive** *adj.*

digestive system ► *n.* The alimentary canal along with the glands, such as the liver, salivary glands, and pancreas, that produce substances needed in digestion.

dig•it (dĭj′ĭt) ► *n.* **1.** A finger or toe. **2.** One of the ten Arabic number symbols, 0 through 9. [< Lat. *digitus*, finger, toe.]

dig•i•tal (dĭj′ĭ-tl) ► *adj.* **1.** Of a digit. **2.** Expressed as or giving a readout in digits: *a digital clock.* **3.** *Comp. Sci.* **a.** Relating to a device that can read, write, or store data in numerical form. **b.** Capable of being read by a computer. See Usage Note at **virtual.** —**dig′i•tal•ly** *adv.*

digital computer ►*n.* A computer that performs calculations and logical operations with quantities represented as digits, usu. in the binary number system.

dig•i•tal•is (dĭj′ĭ-tăl′ĭs) ►*n.* A drug prepared from the seeds and dried leaves of the foxglove, used in medicine as a cardiac stimulant. [Lat. *digitālis*, finger-shaped.]

dig•ni•fy (dĭg′nə-fī′) ►*v.* **-fied, -fy•ing.** To give dignity or honor to. [< LLat. *dignificāre.*]

dig•ni•tar•y (dĭg′nĭ-tĕr′ē) ►*n., pl.* **-ies.** A person of high rank or position.

dig•ni•ty (dĭg′nĭ-tē) ►*n., pl.* **-ties 1.** The quality or state of being worthy of esteem or respect. **2.** Nobility of character, manner, or language. **3.** A high office or rank. [< Lat. *dignitās* < *dignus*, worthy.]

di•graph (dī′grăf′) ►*n.* A pair of letters representing a single speech sound.

di•gress (dī-grĕs′, dĭ-) ►*v.* To stray, esp. from the main subject in writing or speaking. See Syns at **swerve.** [Lat. *dīgredī, dīgress-.*] —**di•gres′sion** *n.* —**di•gres′sive** *adj.* —**di•gres′sive•ly** *adv.*

Di•jon (dē-zhôN′) A city of E France N of Lyon. Pop. 146,723.

dike (dīk) ►*n.* **1.** A wall or embankment of earth and rock built to hold back water and prevent floods. **2.** A ditch or channel. [< OE *dīc*, trench, and ON *dīki*, ditch.]

di•lap•i•dat•ed (dĭ-lăp′ĭ-dā′tĭd) ►*adj.* In a state of disrepair, deterioration, or ruin. [< Lat. *dīlapidāre*, demolish.] —**di•lap′i•da′tion** *n.*

dil•a•ta•tion (dĭl′ə-tā′shən, dī′lə-) ►*n.* **1.** The process of expanding; dilation. **2.** The condition of being expanded.

di•late (dī-lāt′, dī′lāt′) ►*v.* **-lat•ed, -lat•ing.** To make or become wider or larger; expand. [< Lat. *dīlātāre*, expand.] —**di•lat′a•ble** *adj.* —**di•la′tion** *n.* —**di•la′tor** *n.*

dilation and curettage also **dilatation and curettage** ►*n.* A surgical procedure performed for the diagnosis and treatment of various uterine conditions.

dil•a•to•ry (dĭl′ə-tôr′ē, -tōr′ē) ►*adj.* Tending to delay. [< Lat. *dīlātus*, p.part. of *differre*, to delay.] —**dil′a•to′ri•ly** *adv.*

di•lem•ma (dĭ-lĕm′ə) ►*n.* A situation that requires a choice between options, usu. equally unfavorable or mutually exclusive. [< Gk. *dilēmma*, ambiguous proposition.]

dil•et•tante (dĭl′ĭ-tänt′, dĭl′ĭ-tănt′, -tän′tē) ►*n., pl.* **-tantes** also **-tan•ti** (-tän′tē, -tăn′-). A dabbler in an art or a field of knowledge. See Syns at **amateur.** [< Lat. *dēlectāre*, delight.] —**dil′et•tan′tism** *n.*

dil•i•gent (dĭl′ə-jənt) ►*adj.* Marked by or done with persevering, painstaking effort and care. [< Lat. *dīligere*, to love.] —**dil′i•gence** *n.* —**dil′i•gent•ly** *adv.*

dill (dĭl) ►*n.* An herb having aromatic leaves and seeds used as seasoning. [< OE *dile.*]

dil•ly (dĭl′ē) ►*n., pl.* **-lies** *Slang.* One that is remarkable, as in size. [< DELIGHTFUL.]

dil•ly-dal•ly (dĭl′ē-dăl′ē) ►*v.* **-lied, -lying.** To waste time, esp. in indecision; dawdle or vacillate. [< DALLY.]

dil•u•ent (dĭl′yo͞o-ənt) ►*n. Chem.* An inert substance used to dilute. [< Lat. *dīluere*, DILUTE.] —**dil′u•ent** *adj.*

di•lute (dī-lo͞ot′, dĭ-) ►*v.* **-lut•ed, -lut•ing.** To make thinner or weaker, as by adding a liquid such as water. ►*adj.* Weakened; diluted. [Lat. *dīluere* : *dis-*, away + *-luere*, wash.] —**di•lu′tion** *n.*

dim (dĭm) ►*adj.* **dim•mer, dim•mest 1.** Faintly lighted. **2.** Lacking luster; dull. **3.** Obscure or indistinct; faint. **4.** Lacking sharpness or clarity in sight or understanding. **5.** Negative, unfavorable, or disapproving. ►*v.* **dimmed, dim•ming 1.** To make or become dim. **2.** To put on low beam: *dimmed the headlights.* ►*n.* Low beam. [< OE.] —**dim′ly** *adv.* —**dim′ness** *n.*

dim. ►*abbr.* **1.** dimension **2.** diminished **3.** diminutive

dime (dīm) ►*n.* A US or Canadian coin worth ten cents. [< Lat. *decima (pars)*, tenth (part).]

di•men•sion (dĭ-mĕn′shən, dī-) ►*n.* **1.** A measure of spatial extent, esp. width, height, or length. **2.** often **dimensions** Extent or magnitude; scope. **3.** *Math.* One of the least number of independent coordinates required to specify uniquely a point in space. **4.** *Phys.* A physical property, such as mass, length, or time, regarded as a fundamental measure. [< Lat. *dīmēnsiō.*] —**di•men′sion•al** *adj.* —**di•men′sion•al′i•ty** (-shə-năl′ĭ-tē) *n.* —**di•men′sion•al•ly** *adv.*

dime store ►*n.* See **five-and-ten.**

di•min•ish (dĭ-mĭn′ĭsh) ►*v.* **1.** To make or become smaller or less important. **2.** To taper. [ME *diminishen.*] —**di•min′ish•a•ble** *adj.* —**di•min′ish•ment** *n.*

di•min•u•en•do (dĭ-mĭn′yo͞o-ĕn′dō) ►*n., adv., & adj. Mus.* Decrescendo. [Ital.]

dim•i•nu•tion (dĭm′ə-no͞o′shən, -nyo͞o′-) ►*n.* The act, process, or result of diminishing. [Lat. *dīminūtiō* < *dīminuere*, diminish.]

di•min•u•tive (dĭ-mĭn′yə-tĭv) ►*adj.* **1.** Extremely small in size; tiny. See Syns at **small. 2.** Of or being a suffix that indicates smallness or affection, as *-let* in *booklet.* ►*n.* A diminutive suffix, word, or name.

dim•i•ty (dĭm′ĭ-tē) ►*n., pl.* **-ties.** A sheer crisp cotton fabric with raised woven stripes or checks. [< Gk. *dimitos*, double-threaded.]

dim•mer (dĭm′ər) ►*n.* A device used to vary the brightness of an electric light.

dim•ple (dĭm′pəl) ►*n.* **1.** A small natural indentation in the flesh on a part of the human body, esp. in the cheek or chin. **2.** A slight depression in a surface. ►*v.* **-pled, -pling.** To form dimples, as by smiling. [ME *dimpel.*]

dim sum (dĭm′ so͝om′) ►*n.* Small portions of a variety of traditional Chinese foods, including steamed or fried dumplings, served in succession. [< Cantonese *tímsam*, light refreshments.]

dim•wit (dĭm′wĭt′) ►*n. Slang* A stupid person. —**dim′wit′ted** *adj.*

din (dĭn) ►*n.* A jumble of loud, usu. discordant sounds. ►*v.* **dinned, din•ning 1.** To instill by wearying repetition. **2.** To stun with or make a din. [< OE *dyne.*]

di•nar (dĭ-när′, dē′när′) ►*n.* See table at **currency.** [Ar. *dīnār.*]

Di•nar•ic Alps (dĭ-năr′ĭk) A range of the Balkan Peninsula extending about 644 km (400 mi) along the E coast of the Adriatic Sea.

dine (dīn) ▸ *v.* **dined, din•ing 1.** To have dinner. **2.** To give dinner to. [< OFr. *diner.*]

din•er (dī′nər) ▸ *n.* **1.** One that dines. **2.** A railroad dining car. **3.** A restaurant shaped like a dining car.

di•nette (dī-nĕt′) ▸ *n.* A nook or alcove used for informal meals.

ding[1] (dĭng) ▸ *v.* To ring or cause to ring; clang. ▸ *n.* A ringing sound. [Imit.]

ding[2] (dĭng) ▸ *n. Informal* A small dent or nick, as in the body of a car. [< *ding,* to strike.] —**ding** *v.*

din•ghy (dĭng′ē) ▸ *n., pl.* **-ghies.** A small open boat, esp. a rowboat. [Hindi *ḍīṅgī.*]

din•go (dĭng′gō) ▸ *n., pl.* **-goes.** A wild dog of Australia, having a reddish-brown or yellow coat. [Dharuk (Australian) *diŋgu.*]

din•gus (dĭng′əs) ▸ *n. Slang* An article whose name is unknown or forgotten. [Du. *dinges.*]

din•gy (dĭn′jē) ▸ *adj.* **-gi•er, -gi•est 1.** Dirty, soiled, or grimy. **2.** Shabby, drab, or squalid. [Poss. < ME *dinge,* dung.] —**din′gi•ly** *adv.* —**din′gi•ness** *n.*

din•ky (dĭng′kē) ▸ *adj.* **-ki•er, -ki•est** *Informal.* Of small size or consequence; insignificant. [Prob. < Sc. *dink,* neat.]

din•ner (dĭn′ər) ▸ *n.* **1.** The main meal of the day. **2.** A formal banquet. [< OFr. *disner,* dine, morning meal.]

dinner jacket ▸ *n.* See **tuxedo.**

di•no•saur (dī′nə-sôr′) ▸ *n.* Any of various extinct, often gigantic, carnivorous or herbivorous reptiles of the Mesozoic Era. [Gk. *deinos,* monstrous + *sauros,* lizard.]

dint (dĭnt) ▸ *n.* **1.** Force or effort: *succeeded by dint of hard work.* **2.** A dent. [ME DENT.]

di•o•cese (dī′ə-sĭs, -sēs′, -sēz′) ▸ *n.* The district or churches under the jurisdiction of a bishop; bishopric. [< Gk. *dioikēsis,* administration.] —**di•oc′e•san** (dī-ŏs′ə-sən) *adj.*

Di•o•cle•tian (dī′ə-klē′shən). A.D. 245?–313? Emperor of Rome (284–305).

di•ode (dī′ōd′) ▸ *n.* A two-terminal semiconductor device, esp. one that restricts current flow chiefly to one direction.

Di•og•e•nes (dī-ŏj′ə-nēz′). d. c. 320 B.C. Greek philosopher.

Di•o•nys•i•an (dī′ə-nĭsh′ən, -nĭzh′ən, -nĭs′ē-ən) ▸ *adj.* **1.** *Gk. Myth.* Of or relating to Dionysus. **2.** often **dionysian** Of an orgiastic or irrational nature.

Di•o•ny•sus (dī′ə-nī′səs, -nē′-) ▸ *n. Gk. & Rom. Myth.* The god of wine, drama, and of an orgiastic religion celebrating the power and fertility of nature. [< Gk. *Dionusos.*]

di•o•ram•a (dī′ə-răm′ə, -rä′mə) ▸ *n.* A three-dimensional scene with modeled figures against a painted background. [Gk. *dia,* through + (PAN)ORAMA.]

di•ox•ide (dī-ŏk′sīd) ▸ *n.* A compound with two oxygen atoms per molecule.

di•ox•in (dī-ŏk′sĭn) ▸ *n.* Any of several carcinogenic or teratogenic hydrocarbons that occur as impurities in petroleum-derived herbicides. [DI– + *ox(o)-,* oxygen + –IN.]

dip (dĭp) ▸ *v.* **dipped, dip•ping 1.** To plunge briefly into a liquid. **2.** To immerse (an animal) in a disinfectant solution. **3.** To scoop up (liquid). **4.** To lower and raise (a flag) in salute. **5.** To drop or sink suddenly. **6.** To slope downward; decline. **7.** To dabble: *dip into medieval history.* ▸ *n.* **1.** A brief plunge or immersion, esp. a quick swim. **2.** A liquid into which something is dipped. **3.** A savory creamy mixture into which crackers or other foods may be dipped. **4.** An amount taken up by dipping. **5.** A downward slope. **6.** A decline: *a dip in prices.* **7.** A hollow or depression. **8.** *Slang* A foolish or stupid person. [< OE *dyppan.*]

Syns: *dip, douse, duck, dunk* **v.**

diph•the•ri•a (dĭf-thîr′ē-ə, dĭp-) ▸ *n.* An acute infectious bacterial disease marked by high fever, weakness, and the formation of a false membrane in the throat and other respiratory passages, causing difficulty in breathing. [< Gk. *diphthera,* piece of leather.] —**diph′the•rit′ic** (-thə-rĭt′ĭk), **diph•ther′ic** (-thĕr′ĭk), **diph•the′ri•al** *adj.*

diph•thong (dĭf′thông′, -thŏng′, dĭp′-) ▸ *n.* A complex speech sound that begins with one vowel and gradually changes to another vowel within the same syllable, as (oi) in *boil.* [< Gk. *diphthongos.*]

dip•loid (dĭp′loid′) ▸ *adj.* Having two sets of chromosomes. [< Gk. *diploos,* double.] —**dip′loid′** *n.*

di•plo•ma (dĭ-plō′mə) ▸ *n.* **1.** A document issued by an educational institution, such as a university, testifying that the recipient has earned a degree or successfully completed a course of study. **2.** A certificate conferring a privilege or honor. [< Gk. *diplōma,* folded document < *diploos,* double.]

di•plo•ma•cy (dĭ-plō′mə-sē) ▸ *n.* **1.** The art or practice of conducting international relations. **2.** Tact and skill in dealing with people. [Ult. < Gk. *diplōma,* document.]

dip•lo•mat (dĭp′lə-măt′) ▸ *n.* One skilled or working in diplomacy.

dip•lo•mat•ic (dĭp′lə-măt′ĭk) ▸ *adj.* **1.** Of or involving diplomacy or diplomats. **2.** Tactful. —**dip′lo•mat′i•cal•ly** *adv.*

di•pole (dī′pōl′) ▸ *n.* **1.** *Phys.* A pair of electric charges or magnetic poles, of equal magnitude but of opposite sign or polarity, separated by a small distance. **2.** *Electron.* An antenna, usu. fed from the center, consisting of two equal rods extending outward in a straight line. —**di•po′lar** *adj.*

dip•per (dĭp′ər) ▸ *n.* **1.** One that dips, esp. a long-handled cup for taking up water. **2.** A small bird that dives into swift streams and feeds along the bottom.

dip•so•ma•ni•a (dĭp′sə-mā′nē-ə, -mān′yə) ▸ *n.* An insatiable, often periodic craving for alcoholic beverages. [Gk. *dipsa,* thirst + -MANIA.] —**dip′so•ma′ni•ac′** *adj. & n.*

dip•stick (dĭp′stĭk′) ▸ *n.* A graduated rod for measuring the depth of liquid.

dire (dīr) ▸ *adj.* **dir•er, dir•est 1.** Warning of disaster. **2.** Urgent; desperate: *in dire poverty.* [Lat. *dīrus,* terrible.] —**dire′ful** *adj.* —**dire′ful•ly** *adv.* —**dire′ly** *adv.*

di•rect (dĭ-rĕkt′, dī-) ▸ *v.* **1.** To conduct the affairs of; manage. **2.** To have or take charge of; control. **3.** To aim, guide, or address (something or someone). See Syns at **aim. 4.** To give interpretive dramatic guidance and instruction to the actors in a play or film. **5.** To conduct (musicians) in a performance or rehearsal. ▸ *adj.* **1.** Proceeding in a straight course or line. **2.** Straightforward. **3.** Having no intervening persons, conditions, or agencies; immediate. **4.** By action of voters, rather than through elected delegates. **5.** Being of unbroken descent; lineal. **6.** Consisting of the exact words of the writer or speaker: *a direct quotation.* **7.** Absolute; total: *direct opposites.* **8.** *Math.* Varying in the same manner as another quantity, esp. increasing if another quantity increases or decreasing if it decreases. ▸*adv.* Straight; directly. [< Lat. *dīrigere, dīrēct-*.] —**di•rect′ness** *n.*

direct current ▸*n.* An electric current flowing in one direction only.

direct deposit ▸*n.* The electronic transfer of a payment from the payer's account to that of the payee.

di•rec•tion (dĭ-rĕk′shən, dī-) ▸*n.* **1.** The act or function of directing. **2.** often **directions** An instruction or series of instructions for doing or finding something. **3.** An order or command. **4a.** The distance-independent relationship between two points in space that specifies the angular position of either with respect to the other. **b.** A position to which motion or another position is referred. **c.** The line or course along which a person or thing moves. **5.** Tendency toward a particular end or goal. —**di•rec′tion•al** *adj.* —**di•rec′tion•al′i•ty** *n.*

di•rec•tive (dĭ-rĕk′tĭv, dī-) ▸*n.* An order or instruction, esp. from a central authority.

di•rect•ly (dĭ-rĕkt′lē, dī-) ▸*adv.* **1.** In a direct line or manner. **2.** Without anyone or anything intervening. **3.** Exactly. **4.** Instantly.

direct mail ▸*n.* Advertising circulars or other printed matter sent directly through the mail to prospective customers or contributors. —**di•rect′-mail′** *adj.*

direct object ▸*n.* The word or phrase in a sentence referring to the receiver of the action of a transitive verb. For example, in *call him, him* is the direct object.

di•rec•tor (dĭ-rĕk′tər, dī-) ▸*n.* **1.** A manager. **2.** One of a group chosen to govern the affairs of an institution or corporation. **3.** One who supervises or guides the performers in a play, film, or musical performance. —**di•rec′to′ri•al** (-tôr′ē-əl, -tōr′-) *adj.* —**di•rec′tor•ship′** *n.*

di•rec•tor•ate (dĭ-rĕk′tər-ĭt, dī-) ▸*n.* **1.** The office or position of a director. **2.** A board of directors.

di•rec•to•ry (dĭ-rĕk′tə-rē, dī-) ▸*n., pl.* **-ries 1.** An alphabetical or classified listing of names, addresses, and usu. telephone numbers. **2.** *Comp. Sci.* A listing of the files contained in a storage device.

dirge (dûrj) ▸*n.* **1.** A funeral song. **2.** A slow mournful piece of music. [< Med.Lat. *dīrige Domine*, direct, O Lord.]

dir•ham (də-răm′) ▸*n.* See table at **currency.** [Ar. < Gk. *drakhmē*, drachma.]

dir•i•gi•ble (dĭr′ə-jə-bəl, də-rĭj′ə-bəl) ▸*n.* See **airship.** [< Lat. *dīrigere*, to direct.]

dirk (dûrk) ▸*n.* A dagger. [Sc. *durk*.]

dirn•dl (dûrn′dl) ▸*n.* A full skirt with a gathered waistband. [< Ger. *Dirndlkleid*.]

dirt (dûrt) ▸*n.* **1.** Earth or soil. **2.** A filthy or soiling substance, such as mud. **3.** One that is contemptible or vile. **4a.** Obscene language. **b.** Malicious or scandalous gossip. [< ON *drit*, filth.]

dirt bike ▸*n.* A motorbike or bicycle designed for use on rough surfaces.

dirt-cheap (dûrt′chēp′) ▸*adv. & adj.* Very cheap.

dirt•y (dûr′tē) ▸*adj.* **-i•er, -i•est 1.** Soiled or grimy; unclean. **2.** Obscene or indecent. **3.** Dishonorable or unfair: *a dirty fighter.* **4.** Expressing hostility: *a dirty look.* **5.** Dull in color. **6.** Stormy: *dirty weather.* ▸*v.* **-ied, -y•ing.** To make or become soiled. —**dirt′i•ly** *adv.* —**dirt′i•ness** *n.*

dis (dĭs) ▸*v.* **dissed, dis•sing** *Informal* To show disrespect to. [*dis(respect)*.]

dis– ▸*pref.* **1.** Not: *dissimilar.* **2a.** Absence of: *disinterest.* **b.** Opposite of: *disfavor.* **3.** Undo: *disarrange.* **4a.** Deprive of: *disfranchise.* **b.** Remove: *disbar.* [< Lat. *dis*, apart.]

dis•a•bil•i•ty (dĭs′ə-bĭl′ĭ-tē) ▸*n.* **1.** The condition of being disabled; incapacity. **2.** A disadvantage or deficiency, esp. a physical or mental impairment that prevents or restricts normal achievement. See Usage Note at **handicapped.**

dis•a•ble (dĭs-ā′bəl) ▸*v.* **-bled, -bling.** To deprive of capability or effectiveness, esp. to impair the physical abilities of.

dis•a•bled (dĭs-ā′bəld) ▸*adj.* **1.** Inoperative: *a disabled vehicle.* **2.** Impaired, as in physical functioning: *a disabled veteran.* ▸*n.* Physically impaired people as a group: *the disabled.* See Usage Note at **handicapped.**

dis•a•buse (dĭs′ə-byo͞oz′) ▸*v.* **-bused, -bus•ing.** To free from a falsehood or misconception. [Fr. *désabuser*.]

di•sac•cha•ride (dī-săk′ə-rīd′) ▸*n.* Any of a class of carbohydrates, including lactose and sucrose, that yield two monosaccharides upon hydrolysis.

dis•ad•van•tage (dĭs′əd-văn′tĭj) ▸*n.* **1.** An unfavorable condition or circumstance. **2.** Damage, harm, or loss. —**dis•ad′van•ta′geous** (dĭs-ăd′vən-tā′jəs) *adj.*

Syns: *disadvantage, detriment, drawback, handicap* ***Ant:*** *advantage* **n.**

dis•ad•van•taged (dĭs′əd-văn′tĭjd) ▸*adj.* **1.** Socially or economically deprived. **2.** Being at a disadvantage. ▸*n. (takes pl. v.)* Deprived people collectively: *the disadvantaged.*

dis•af•fect (dĭs′ə-fĕkt′) ▸*v.* To cause to lose affection or loyalty. —**dis′af•fect′ed** *adj.* —**dis′af•fec′tion** *n.*

dis•a•gree (dĭs′ə-grē′) ▸*v.* **1.** To fail to correspond. See Syns at **differ. 2.** To have a differing opinion. **3.** To dispute; quarrel. **4.** To have bad effects. —**dis′a•gree′ment** *n.*

dis•a•gree•a•ble (dĭs′ə-grē′ə-bəl) ▸*adj.* **1.** Unpleasant, distasteful, or offensive. **2.** Bad-tempered; quarrelsome. —**dis′a•gree′a•ble•ness** *n.* —**dis′a•gree′a•bly** *adv.*

dis•al•low (dĭs′ə-lou′) ▸*v.* To refuse to allow; reject. —**dis′al•low′ance** *n.*

dis•ap•pear (dĭs′ə-pîr′) ▸*v.* **1.** To pass out of sight. **2.** To cease to exist. —**dis′ap•pear′ance** *n.*

Syns: *disappear, evanesce, evaporate, fade, vanish* ***Ant:*** *appear* **v.**

dis•ap•point (dĭs′ə-point′) ▸*v.* To fail to satisfy the hope, desire, or expectation of. [< OFr. *desapointier*, remove from office.] —**dis′ap•point′ing•ly** *adv.* —**dis′ap•point′ment** *n.*

dis•ap•pro•ba•tion (dĭs-ăp′rə-bā′shən) ▸*n.* Moral disapproval; condemnation.

dis•ap•prov•al (dĭs′ə-pro͞o′vəl) ▸*n.* The act of disapproving; condemnation or censure.

dis•ap•prove (dĭs′ə-pro͞ov′) ▸*v.* **1.** To have an unfavorable opinion (of). **2.** To refuse to approve. —**dis′ap•prov′ing•ly** *adv.*

dis•arm (dĭs-ärm′) ► *v.* **1a.** To divest or deprive of weapons. **b.** To render helpless or harmless. **2.** To overcome the hostility of. **3.** To reduce one's arms or armed forces.

dis•ar•ma•ment (dĭs-är′mə-mənt) ► *n.* A reduction of armed forces and armaments.

dis•ar•range (dĭs′ə-rānj′) ► *v.* To upset the arrangement of. —**dis′ar•range′ment** *n.*

dis•ar•ray (dĭs′ə-rā′) ► *n.* **1.** A state of disorder; confusion. **2.** Disordered dress. ► *v.* To throw into confusion; upset.

dis•as•sem•ble (dĭs′ə-sĕm′bəl) ► *v.* To take or come apart.

dis•as•so•ci•ate (dĭs′ə-sō′shē-āt′, -sē-) ► *v.* To dissociate. —**dis′as•so′ci•a′tion** *n.*

dis•as•ter (dĭ-zăs′tər, -săs′-) ► *n.* Great destruction, distress, or misfortune. [< Ital. *disastro* : DIS– + *astro*, star (< Gk. *astron*).] —**dis•as′trous** *adj.* —**dis•as′trous•ly** *adv.*

dis•a•vow (dĭs′ə-vou′) ► *v.* To disclaim knowledge of, responsibility for, or association with. —**dis′a•vow′al** *n.*

dis•band (dĭs-bănd′) ► *v.* To dissolve or become dissolved. —**dis•band′ment** *n.*

dis•bar (dĭs-bär′) ► *v.* **-barred, -bar•ring.** To expel (an attorney) from the legal profession. —**dis•bar′ment** *n.*

dis•be•lieve (dĭs′bĭ-lēv′) ► *v.* To refuse to believe (in). —**dis′be•lief′** *n.*

dis•burse (dĭs-bûrs′) ► *v.* **-bursed, -burs•ing.** To pay out, as from a fund; expend. [< OFr. *desborser* < LLat. *bursa*, PURSE.] —**dis•burse′ment, dis•bur′sal** *n.*

disc (dĭsk) ► *n.* Var. of **disk.**

dis•card (dĭ-skärd′) ► *v.* **1.** To throw away; reject. **2.** *Games* To throw out (a playing card) from one's hand. ► *n.* (dĭs′kärd′) **1.** The act of discarding. **2.** One that is discarded or rejected.

dis•cern (dĭ-sûrn′, -zûrn′) ► *v.* **1.** To detect or perceive with the eyes or intellect. **2.** To perceive the distinctions of; discriminate. [< Lat. *discernere.*] —**dis•cern′i•ble** *adj.* —**dis•cern′i•bly** *adv.* —**dis•cern′ment** *n.*

dis•cern•ing (dĭ-sûr′nĭng, -zûr′-) ► *adj.* Insightful or perceptive.

dis•charge (dĭs-chärj′) ► *v.* **-charged, -charg•ing 1.** To relieve or be relieved of a burden or of contents. **2.** To unload or empty (contents). **3.** To release or dismiss: *discharge a patient; discharge an employee.* See Syns at **dismiss. 4.** To send or pour forth; emit. **5.** To shoot (a projectile or weapon). **6.** To perform the obligations or demands of (a duty). **7.** To comply with the terms of (e.g., a debt or promise). **8.** To cause or undergo electrical discharge. ► *n.* (dĭs′chärj′, dĭs-chärj′) **1.** The act of removing a load or burden. **2.** The act of shooting a projectile or weapon. **3a.** A pouring forth; emission: *a discharge of pus.* **b.** The amount or rate of emission or ejection. **c.** Something that is discharged: *a watery discharge.* **4.** A relieving from an obligation. **5a.** Dismissal or release from employment, service, care, or confinement. **b.** An official document certifying such release, esp. from military service. **6.** *Elect.* **a.** Release of stored energy in a capacitor by the flow of current between its terminals. **b.** Conversion of chemical energy to electric energy in a storage battery. **c.** A flow of electricity in a dielectric, esp. in a rarefied gas. [< LLat. *discarricāre*, unload.]

dis•ci•ple (dĭ-sī′pəl) ► *n.* **1.** One who embraces and assists in spreading the teachings of another. **2.** often **Disciple** One of the 12 original followers of Jesus. [< Lat. *discipulus*, pupil < *discere*, learn.]

dis•ci•pli•nar•i•an (dĭs′ə-plə-nâr′ē-ən) ► *n.* One that enforces or believes in strict discipline.

dis•ci•pli•nar•y (dĭs′ə-plə-nĕr′ē) ► *adj.* Of or used for discipline.

dis•ci•pline (dĭs′ə-plĭn) ► *n.* **1.** Training expected to produce a specific character or pattern of behavior. **2.** Controlled behavior resulting from such training. **3.** A state of order based on submission to rules and authority. **4.** Punishment intended to correct or train. **5.** A set of rules or methods. **6.** A branch of knowledge or teaching. ► *v.* **-plined, -plin•ing 1.** To train by instruction and practice. **2.** To punish. [< Lat. *disciplīna* < *discipulus*, DISCIPLE.]

dis•ci•plined (dĭs′ə-plĭnd) ► *adj.* Possessing or indicative of discipline: *a disciplined mind.*

disc jockey also **disk jockey** ► *n.* An announcer who presents popular recorded music, esp. on the radio.

dis•claim (dĭs-klām′) ► *v.* **1.** To deny or renounce any claim to or connection with. **2.** To renounce a legal right or claim (to).

dis•claim•er (dĭs-klā′mər) ► *n.* A repudiation or denial of responsibility, connection, or claim.

dis•close (dĭ-sklōz′) ► *v.* **1.** To expose to view. **2.** To make known (something secret). —**dis•clo′sure** (-sklō′zhər) *n.*

dis•co (dĭs′kō) ► *n.*, *pl.* **-cos 1.** A discotheque. **2.** Popular dance music, esp. of the late 1970s, marked by strong repetitive bass rhythms. —**dis′co** *adj.*

dis•col•or (dĭs-kŭl′ər) ► *v.* To make or become a different color, as by staining or fading. —**dis•col′or•a′tion** *n.*

dis•com•bob•u•late (dĭs′kəm-bŏb′yə-lāt′) ► *v.* **-lat•ed, -lat•ing.** To throw into a state of confusion; upset. [Perh. < DISCOMPOSE.]

dis•com•fit (dĭs-kŭm′fĭt) ► *v.* **1.** To make uneasy or perplexed; disconcert. See Syns at **embarrass. 2.** To thwart the plans of; frustrate. [< OFr. *desconfit*, p.part of *desconfire*, to defeat.] —**dis•com′fi•ture** *n.*

dis•com•fort (dĭs-kŭm′fərt) ► *n.* **1.** Mental or bodily distress. **2.** Something that disturbs comfort. ► *v.* To make uncomfortable.

dis•com•mode (dĭs′kə-mōd′) ► *v.* **-mod•ed, -mod•ing.** To inconvenience; disturb. [< DIS– + Lat. *commodus*, convenient.]

dis•com•pose (dĭs′kəm-pōz′) ► *v.* **1.** To disturb the composure of; perturb. **2.** To put into disorder. —**dis′com•po′sure** *n.*

dis•con•cert (dĭs′kən-sûrt′) ► *v.* **1.** To upset; perturb. See Syns at **embarrass. 2.** To throw into confusion or disarray. —**dis′con•cert′ing•ly** *adv.*

dis•con•nect (dĭs′kə-nĕkt′) ► *v.* **1.** To sever the connection of or between. **2.** To shut off the current to. —**dis′con•nec′tion** *n.*

dis•con•nect•ed (dĭs′kə-nĕk′tĭd) ► *adj.* **1.** Not connected. **2.** Marked by unrelated parts; incoherent. —**dis′con•nect′ed•ly** *adv.*

dis•con•so•late (dĭs-kŏn′sə-lĭt) ► *adj.* **1.** Hopelessly sad; extremely dejected. **2.** Gloomy; dismal. [< Med.Lat. *discōnsōlātus.*] —**dis•con′so•late•ly** *adv.* —**dis•con′so•late•ness** *n.*

dis•con•tent (dĭs′kən-tĕnt′) ►*n.* Absence of contentment; dissatisfaction. ►*adj.* Discontented. ►*v.* To make discontented. —**dis′con•tent′ment** *n.*

dis•con•tent•ed (dĭs′kən-tĕn′tĭd) ►*adj.* Restlessly unhappy; not satisfied; malcontent. —**dis′con•tent′ed•ly** *adv.* —**dis′con•tent′ed•ness** *n.*

dis•con•tin•ue (dĭs′kən-tĭn′yo͞o) ►*v.* **1.** To put a stop to. **2.** To give up; abandon. **3.** To come to an end. See Syns at **stop.** —**dis′con•tin′u•ance, dis′con•tin′u•a′tion** *n.*

dis•con•tin•u•ous (dĭs′kən-tĭn′yo͞o-əs) ►*adj.* Marked by breaks or interruptions. —**dis•con′ti•nu′i•ty** (dĭs-kŏn′tə-no͞o′ĭ-tē, -nyo͞o′-) *n.* —**dis′con•tin′u•ous•ly** *adv.*

dis•cord (dĭs′kôrd′) ►*n.* **1.** Lack of agreement; dissension. **2.** A harsh mingling of sounds. **3.** *Mus.* An inharmonious combination of simultaneously sounded tones; dissonance. [< Lat. *discordia* : DIS– + *cor*, heart.] —**dis•cor′dant** *adj.* —**dis•cor′dant•ly** *adv.*

dis•co•theque (dĭs′kə-tĕk′, dĭs′kə-tĕk′) ►*n.* A nightclub, usu. with showy lighting, featuring dancing to recorded or live music. [Fr. *discothèque.*]

dis•count (dĭs′kount′, dĭs-kount′) ►*v.* **1.** To deduct or subtract from a cost or price. **2a.** To purchase or sell (a promissory note) after deducting the interest. **b.** To lend money after deducting the interest. **3.** To offer for sale at a reduced price. **4.** To disregard as being untrustworthy or exaggerated. **5.** To anticipate and make allowance for. ►*n.* (dĭs′kount′) **1.** A reduction from the full amount of a price or debt. **2a.** The interest deducted prior to purchasing or selling a promissory note. **b.** The rate of interest so deducted. **3.** The act or an instance of discounting. [< OFr. *desconter.*]

dis•coun•te•nance (dĭs-koun′tə-nəns) ►*v.* **1.** To view with disfavor. **2.** To disconcert.

discount store ►*n.* A store that sells merchandise below the suggested retail price.

dis•cour•age (dĭ-skûr′ĭj, -skŭr′-) ►*v.* **-aged, -ag•ing 1.** To deprive of confidence, hope, or spirit. **2.** To hamper. **3.** To try to deter, as by raising objections. See Syns at **dissuade.** —**dis•cour′age•ment** *n.* —**dis•cour′ag•ing•ly** *adv.*

Syns: *discourage, dishearten, dispirit* ***Ant:*** *encourage* ***v.***

dis•course (dĭs′kôrs′, -kōrs′) ►*n.* **1.** Verbal exchange; conversation. **2.** A formal discussion of a subject, either written or spoken. ►*v.* (dĭ-skôrs′, -skōrs′) **-coursed, -cours•ing.** To speak or write formally and at length. [< Med. Lat. *discursus.*]

dis•cour•te•ous (dĭs-kûr′tē-əs) ►*adj.* Lacking courtesy; not polite. —**dis•cour′te•ous•ly** *adv.* —**dis•cour′te•sy** *n.*

dis•cov•er (dĭ-skŭv′ər) ►*v.* **1.** To obtain knowledge of through observation or study. **2.** To be the first to find, learn of, or observe. [< LLat. *discooperīre*, uncover.] —**dis•cov′er•a•ble** *adj.* —**dis•cov′er•er** *n.*

Syns: *discover, ascertain, determine, learn* ***v.***

dis•cov•er•y (dĭ-skŭv′ə-rē) ►*n., pl.* **-ies 1.** The act or an instance of discovering. **2.** Something discovered.

dis•cred•it (dĭs-krĕd′ĭt) ►*v.* **1.** To disgrace; dishonor. **2.** To cast doubt on. **3.** To refuse to believe. ►*n.* **1.** Damage to one's reputation. **2.** Lack or loss of trust or belief. —**dis•cred′it•a•ble** *adj.* —**dis•cred′i•ta•bly** *adv.*

dis•creet (dĭ-skrēt′) ►*adj.* Having or showing prudence and self-restraint in speech and behavior. [< Med.Lat. *discrētus* < Lat. *discernere*, discern.] —**dis•creet′ly** *adv.* —**dis•creet′ness** *n.*

dis•crep•an•cy (dĭ-skrĕp′ən-sē) ►*n., pl.* **-cies.** Lack of agreement, as between facts or claims; difference.

dis•crep•ant (dĭ-skrĕp′ənt) ►*adj.* Marked by discrepancy. [< Lat. *discrepāre*, disagree.]

dis•crete (dĭ-skrēt′) ►*adj.* **1.** Individually distinct; separate. **2.** Consisting of unconnected distinct parts. See Syns at **distinct.** [< Lat. *discrētus*, p.part. of *discernere*, to separate.]

dis•cre•tion (dĭ-skrĕsh′ən) ►*n.* **1.** The quality of being discreet. **2.** Freedom of action or judgment: *The choice was left to our discretion.* —**dis•cre′tion•ar′y** *adj.*

dis•crim•i•nate (dĭ-skrĭm′ə-nāt′) ►*v.* **-nat•ed, -nat•ing 1.** To make a clear distinction; differentiate. **2.** To make distinctions on the basis of preference or prejudice: *accused of discriminating against women.* [Lat. *discrīmināre.*] —**dis•crim′i•na′tion** *n.* —**dis•crim′i•na′tive, dis•crim′i•na•to′ry** *adj.*

dis•crim•i•nat•ing (dĭ-skrĭm′ə-nā′tĭng) ►*adj.* **1.** Able to recognize or draw fine distinctions; discerning. **2.** Showing careful judgment or fine taste.

dis•cur•sive (dĭ-skûr′sĭv) ►*adj.* Covering a wide field of subjects; digressive. [< Lat. *discursus*, running about.] —**dis•cur′sive•ly** *adv.* —**dis•cur′sive•ness** *n.*

dis•cus (dĭs′kəs) ►*n.* A disk, typically wooden or plastic, that is thrown for distance in athletic competitions. [Lat. DISK.]

dis•cuss (dĭ-skŭs′) ►*v.* **1.** To speak with others about; talk over. **2.** To examine (a subject) in speech or writing. [< Lat. *discutere*, break up.] —**dis•cus′sion** *n.*

dis•cus•sant (dĭ-skŭs′ənt) ►*n.* A participant in a formal discussion.

dis•dain (dĭs-dān′) ►*v.* **1.** To regard or treat with contempt. See Syns at **despise. 2.** To reject aloofly. ►*n.* Haughty contempt. [< Lat. *dēdignārī.*] —**dis•dain′ful** *adj.* —**dis•dain′ful•ly** *adv.*

dis•ease (dĭ-zēz′) ►*n.* A condition of an organism that impairs physiological functioning, resulting from causes such as infection, genetic defect, or environmental stress. [< OFr. *disese*, misery.] —**dis•eased′** *adj.*

dis•em•bark (dĭs′ĕm-bärk′) ►*v.* **1.** To put, go, or cause to go ashore from a ship. **2.** To leave an aircraft or vehicle. —**dis•em′bar•ka′tion** *n.*

dis•em•bod•y (dĭs′ĕm-bŏd′ē) ►*v.* **1.** To free (the spirit) from the body. **2.** To divest of material form or existence. —**dis′em•bod′i•ment** *n.*

dis•em•bow•el (dĭs′ĕm-bou′əl) ►*v.* **-eled, -el•ing** or **-elled, -el•ling.** To remove the entrails from. —**dis′em•bow′el•ment** *n.*

dis•en•chant (dĭs′ĕn-chănt′) ►*v.* To free from enchantment or false belief; disillusion. —**dis′en•chant′ment** *n.*

dis•en•cum•ber (dĭs′ĕn-kŭm′bər) ►*v.* To relieve of burdens or hardships.

dis•en•fran•chise (dĭs′ĕn-frăn′chīz′) ►*v.* To

disfranchise. —**dis′en•fran′chise′ment** (-chīz′mənt, -chĭz-) *n.*

dis•en•gage (dĭs′ĕn-gāj′) ►*v.* To release from something that holds fast, connects, or obliges. See Syns at **extricate.** —**dis′en•gage′ment** *n.*

dis•en•tan•gle (dĭs′ĕn-tăng′gəl) ►*v.* To free from entanglement. See Syns at **extricate.** —**dis′en•tan′gle•ment** *n.*

dis•es•tab•lish (dĭs′ĭ-stăb′lĭsh) ►*v.* To alter the established status of, esp. of a nationally established church. —**dis′es•tab′lish•ment** *n.*

dis•fa•vor (dĭs-fā′vər) ►*n.* **1.** Disapproval. **2.** The condition of being regarded with disapproval. —**dis•fa′vor** *v.*

dis•fig•ure (dĭs-fĭg′yər) ►*v.* **-ured, -ur•ing.** To spoil the appearance or shape of; mar. —**dis•fig′ure•ment** *n.*

dis•fran•chise (dĭs-frăn′chīz′) ►*v.* To deprive of a privilege, an immunity, or a right of citizenship, esp. the right to vote. —**dis•fran′chise′ment** *n.*

dis•gorge (dĭs-gôrj′) ►*v.* **-gorged, -gorg•ing 1.** To vomit. **2.** To discharge violently; spew. [< OFr. *desgorger.*] —**dis•gorge′ment** *n.*

dis•grace (dĭs-grās′) ►*n.* **1.** Loss of honor, respect, or reputation; shame. **2.** The condition of being strongly disapproved. **3.** One that brings disgrace. ►*v.* **-graced, -grac•ing.** To bring shame or dishonor on. [< Ital. *disgrazia.*] —**dis•grace′ful** *adj.* —**dis•grace′ful•ly** *adv.*

dis•grun•tle (dĭs-grŭn′tl) ►*v.* **-tled, -tling.** To make discontented or ill-humored. [DIS– + *gruntle*, grumble.] —**dis•grun′tle•ment** *n.*

dis•guise (dĭs-gīz′) ►*v.* **-guised, -guis•ing 1.** To modify the manner or appearance of in order to prevent recognition. **2.** To conceal or obscure by false show; misrepresent. ►*n.* **1.** Clothes or accessories worn to conceal one's true identity. **2.** A pretense or misrepresentation. [< OFr. *desguiser.*]

Syns: *disguise, camouflage, cloak, dissemble, dissimulate, mask* ***v.***

dis•gust (dĭs-gŭst′) ►*v.* To make (someone) feel sick, repelled, averse, or offended. ►*n.* A feeling of profound aversion, repugnance, or offensiveness. [< OFr. *desgouster*, lose one's appetite.] —**dis•gust′ed** *adj.* —**dis•gust′ed•ly** *adv.*

Syns: *disgust, nauseate, repel, revolt, sicken* ***v.***

dis•gust•ing (dĭs-gŭs′tĭng) ►*adj.* Arousing disgust; repugnant. See Syns at **offensive.** —**dis•gust′ing•ly** *adv.*

dish (dĭsh) ►*n.* **1.** A flat or shallow container for holding, cooking, or serving food. **2.** A particular variety or preparation of food. **3.** Something shaped like a dish. **4.** *Electron.* A dish antenna. ►*v.* To serve in or as if in a dish. —***phrasal verb:* dish out** To dispense freely. [< OE *disc* < Lat. *discus*, DISK.]

dis•ha•bille (dĭs′ə-bēl′, -bē′) ►*n.* The state of being partially, casually, or sloppily dressed. [Fr. *déshabillé* < p.part. of *déshabiller*, to undress.]

dish antenna ►*n.* A transmitter or receiver of electromagnetic energy, esp. microwaves or radiowaves, consisting of a concave parabolic reflector.

dish antenna

dis•har•mo•ny (dĭs-här′mə-nē) ►*n.* Lack of harmony; discord. —**dis′har•mo′ni•ous** (-mō′nē-əs) *adj.* —**dis′har•mo′ni•ous•ly** *adv.*

dish•cloth (dĭsh′klôth′, -klŏth′) ►*n.* A cloth for washing dishes; dishrag.

dis•heart•en (dĭs-här′tn) ►*v.* To shake or destroy the courage, spirit, or resolution of. See Syns at **discourage.** —**dis•heart′en•ing•ly** *adv.*

di•shev•el (dĭ-shĕv′əl) ►*v.* **-eled, -el•ing** or **-elled, -el•ling.** To put into disarray or disorder, esp. hair or clothing. [< OFr. *descheveler*, disarrange one's hair.] —**di•shev′el•ment** *n.*

dis•hon•est (dĭs-ŏn′ĭst) ►*adj.* **1.** Disposed to lie, cheat, defraud, or deceive; untrustworthy. **2.** Resulting from or marked by fraud. —**dis•hon′est•ly** *adv.* —**dis•hon′es•ty** *n.*

dis•hon•or (dĭs-ŏn′ər) ►*n.* **1.** Loss of honor, respect, or reputation; disgrace. **2.** A cause of loss of honor. **3.** Failure to pay a note, bill, or other commercial obligation. ►*v.* **1.** To bring shame or disgrace upon. **2.** To fail or refuse to pay. —**dis•hon′or•a•ble** *adj.* —**dis•hon′or•a•bly** *adv.*

dishonorable discharge ►*n.* Discharge from the armed forces for a grave offense, such as cowardice, murder, or sabotage.

dish•rag (dĭsh′răg′) ►*n.* See **dishcloth.**

dish•wash•er (dĭsh′wŏsh′ər, -wô′shər) ►*n.* One, esp. a machine, that washes dishes.

dis•il•lu•sion (dĭs′ĭ-lo͞o′zhən) ►*v.* To free or deprive of illusion; disenchant. —**dis′il•lu′sion•ment** *n.*

dis•in•cline (dĭs′ĭn-klīn′) ►*v.* To make or be reluctant. —**dis•in′cli•na′tion** (-klə-nā′shən) *n.*

dis•in•fect (dĭs′ĭn-fĕkt′) ►*v.* To rid of disease-carrying microorganisms. —**dis′in•fec′tant** *adj. & n.* —**dis′in•fec′tion** *n.*

dis•in•gen•u•ous (dĭs′ĭn-jĕn′yo͞o-əs) ►*adj.* Not straightforward or candid; crafty. —**dis′in•gen′u•ous•ly** *adv.* —**dis′in•gen′u•ous•ness** *n.*

dis•in•her•it (dĭs′ĭn-hĕr′ĭt) ►*v.* To exclude from inheriting or the right to inherit.

dis•in•te•grate (dĭs-ĭn′tĭ-grāt′) ►*v.* **1.** To separate into pieces; fragment. **2.** To decay or undergo a transformation, as an atomic nucleus. —**dis•in′te•gra′tion** *n.* —**dis•in′te•gra′tive** *adj.* —**dis•in′te•gra′tor** *n.*

dis•in•ter (dĭs′ĭn-tûr′) ►*v.* To remove from a grave or tomb. —**dis′in•ter′ment** *n.*

dis•in•ter•est•ed (dĭs-ĭn′trĭ-stĭd, -ĭn′tə-rĕs′tĭd) ►*adj.* **1.** Free of bias and self-interest;

impartial. **2.** *Informal* Not interested; indifferent. —**dis•in'ter•est** *n.* —**dis•in'ter•est•ed•ly** *adv.* —**dis•in'ter•est•ed•ness** *n.*

Usage: Many maintain that *disinterested* can legitimately be used only in its sense of "unbiased or impartial."

dis•join (dĭs-join') ►*v.* To separate.

dis•joint (dĭs-joint') ►*v.* **1.** To take or come apart at the joints. **2.** To separate or disconnect; disjoin.

dis•joint•ed (dĭs-join'tĭd) ►*adj.* **1.** Separated at the joints. **2.** Lacking order or coherence. —**dis•joint'ed•ly** *adv.* —**dis•joint'ed•ness** *n.*

disk also **disc** (dĭsk) ►*n.* **1.** A thin, flat, circular object or plate. **2.** The central part of a composite flower, such as the daisy. **3.** *Anat.* A broad cartilaginous plate lying between adjacent vertebrae. **4.** *Comp. Sci.* **a.** An optical disk, esp. a compact disk. **b.** A magnetic disk, esp. a floppy or hard disk. **5.** often **disc** A phonograph record. See Usage Note at **compact disk.** [< Gk. *diskos*, quoit.]

disk drive ►*n. Comp. Sci.* A device that reads data stored on a disk and writes data onto it for storage.

disk•ette (dĭ-skĕt') ►*n.* See **floppy disk.**

disk operating system ►*n.* DOS.

dis•like (dĭs-līk') ►*v.* To regard with distaste or aversion. ►*n.* An attitude or feeling of distaste or aversion.

dis•lo•cate (dĭs'lō-kāt', dĭs-lō'kāt) ►*v.* **1.** To move out of the normal position, esp. to displace (a bone) from a socket or joint. **2.** To disrupt. —**dis'lo•ca'tion** *n.*

dis•lodge (dĭs-lŏj') ►*v.* To force out of a position previously occupied. —**dis•lodge'ment, dis•lodg'ment** *n.*

dis•loy•al (dĭs-loi'əl) ►*adj.* Lacking loyalty. —**dis•loy'al•ly** *adv.* —**dis•loy'al•ty** *n.*

dis•mal (dĭz'məl) ►*adj.* Causing or showing gloom or depression; dreary. [< Med.Lat. *diēs malī*, evil days.] —**dis'mal•ly** *adv.*

dis•man•tle (dĭs-măn'tl) ►*v.* **-tled, -tling 1.** To take apart; tear down; disassemble. **2.** To strip of furnishings or equipment. [< OFr. *desmanteler*, demolish fortifications.] —**dis•man'tle•ment** *n.*

dis•may (dĭs-mā') ►*v.* To fill with dread or apprehension; daunt. ►*n.* Consternation or apprehension. [< AN **desmaiier* : DE– + VLat. **exmagāre*, deprive of power (EX– + Gmc. **magan*, be able).]

dis•mem•ber (dĭs-mĕm'bər) ►*v.* **1.** To cut, tear, or pull off the limbs of. **2.** To divide into pieces. —**dis•mem'ber•ment** *n.*

dis•miss (dĭs-mĭs') ►*v.* **1.** To discharge, as from employment or service. **2.** To direct or allow to leave: *dismiss students.* **3a.** To rid one's mind of; dispel. **b.** To reject or repudiate. **4.** *Law* To put (a claim or action) out of court without further hearing. [< Lat. *dīmittere, dīmiss-*, send away.] —**dis•miss'i•ble** *adj.* —**dis•miss'al** *n.*

Syns: *dismiss, cashier, discharge, drop, fire, sack* **v.**

dis•mis•sive (dĭs-mĭs'ĭv) ►*adj.* **1.** Serving to dismiss. **2.** Showing indifference or disregard.

dis•mount (dĭs-mount') ►*v.* **1.** To get off or down, as from a horse or vehicle. **2.** To remove (a rider) from a horse. **3.** To remove from a support, setting, or mounting. **4.** To disassemble (e.g., a mechanism). —**dis'mount'** *n.* —**dis•mount'a•ble** *adj.*

Dis•ney (dĭz'nē), **Walter Elias.** "Walt" 1901–66. Amer. animator and film producer.

dis•o•be•di•ence (dĭs'ə-bē'dē-əns) ►*n.* Refusal or failure to obey. —**dis'o•be'di•ent** *adj.* —**dis'o•be'di•ent•ly** *adv.*

dis•o•bey (dĭs'ə-bā') ►*v.* To fail to obey.

dis•o•blige (dĭs'ə-blīj') ►*v.* **1.** To refuse or fail to comply with the wishes of. **2.** To inconvenience. **3.** To offend.

dis•or•der (dĭs-ôr'dər) ►*n.* **1.** A lack of order; confusion. **2.** A public disturbance. **3.** An ailment. ►*v.* To throw into disorder.

dis•or•der•ly (dĭs-ôr'dər-lē) ►*adj.* **1.** Not neat or tidy. **2.** Undisciplined; unruly. **3.** *Law* Disturbing the public peace. —**dis•or'der•li•ness** *n.*

dis•or•gan•ize (dĭs-ôr'gə-nīz') ►*v.* To destroy the systematic arrangement of. —**dis•or'gan•i•za'tion** *n.*

dis•o•ri•ent (dĭs-ôr'ē-ĕnt', -ōr'-) ►*v.* To cause to lose orientation. —**disori•en•ta'tion** *n.*

dis•own (dĭs-ōn') ►*v.* To refuse to acknowledge or accept as one's own; repudiate.

dis•par•age (dĭ-spăr'ĭj) ►*v.* **-aged, -ag•ing.** To speak of in a slighting way; belittle. [< OFr. *desparager*, degrade.] —**dis•par'age•ment** *n.* —**dis•par'ag•ing•ly** *adv.*

dis•pa•rate (dĭs'pər-ĭt, dĭ-spăr'ĭt) ►*adj.* Entirely distinct or different. [Lat. *disparātus*, p.part. of *disparāre*, to separate.] —**dis'pa•rate•ly** *adv.* —**dis•par'i•ty** (dĭ-spăr'ĭ-tē) *n.*

dis•pas•sion•ate (dĭs-păsh'ə-nĭt) ►*adj.* Not influenced by emotion or bias. —**dis•pas'sion** *n.* —**dis•pas'sion•ate•ly** *adv.*

dis•patch (dĭ-spăch') ►*v.* **1.** To send to a specific destination. See Syns at **send. 2.** To perform or transact promptly. **3.** To kill. ►*n.* **1.** The act of dispatching. **2.** Speed in performance or movement. See Syns at **haste. 3.** An important message. **4.** (*also* dĭs'păch'). A news item sent to a news organization, as by a correspondent. [Sp. *despachar* or Ital. *dispacciare.*] —**dis•patch'er** *n.*

dis•pel (dĭ-spĕl') ►*v.* **-pelled, -pel•ling.** To rid of by or as if by scattering: *dispel doubts.* [< Lat. *dispellere*, drive away.]

dis•pens•a•ble (dĭ-spĕn'sə-bəl) ►*adj.* Capable of being dispensed with.

dis•pen•sa•ry (dĭ-spĕn'sə-rē) ►*n., pl.* **-ries.** A place where medical supplies, preparations, and treatments are dispensed.

dis•pen•sa•tion (dĭs'pən-sā'shən, -pĕn-) ►*n.* **1a.** The act of dispensing. **b.** Something dispensed. **2.** A system for ordering or administering affairs. **3.** An official exemption or release from an obligation or rule. **4.** A religious system or code of commands considered to have been divinely appointed.

dis•pense (dĭ-spĕns') ►*v.* **-pensed, -pens•ing 1.** To deal out in portions; distribute. **2.** To prepare and give out (medicines). **3.** To carry out or administer (e.g., laws). —***phrasal verb:*** **dispense with 1.** To manage without; forgo. **2.** To get rid of. [< Lat. *dispēnsāre* < *dispendere*, weigh out.] —**dis•pens'er** *n.*

dis•perse (dĭ-spûrs') ►*v.* **-persed, -pers•ing 1.** To break up and scatter. **2.** To disseminate or distribute. [< Lat. *dispergere.*] —**dis•pers'i•ble** *adj.* —**dis•per'sion** (-spûr'zhən, -shən), **dis•per'sal** *n.*

dis•pir•it (dĭ-spĭr′ĭt) ►*v.* To lower the spirits of; dishearten. See Syns at **discourage.** [DI(S)– + SPIRIT.]
dis•pir•it•ed (dĭ-spĭr′ĭ-tĭd) ►*adj.* Affected or marked by low spirits; dejected. See Syns at **depressed.** —**dis•pir′it•ed•ly** *adv.*
dis•place (dĭs-plās′) ►*v.* **1.** To move from the usual place or position. **2.** To take the place of; supplant. **3.** To cause a displacement of.
dis•place•ment (dĭs-plās′mənt) ►*n.* **1.** The act of displacing. **2a.** The weight or volume of a fluid displaced by a floating body. **b.** The distance from an initial position to a subsequent position assumed by a body.
displacement ton ►*n.* A unit for measuring the displacement of a ship afloat, equivalent to one long ton.
dis•play (dĭ-splā′) ►*v.* **1.** To present or hold up to view. **2.** *Comp. Sci.* To provide (information or graphics) on a computer screen. ►*n.* **1a.** The act of displaying. **b.** Something displayed, esp. an elaborate public exhibition. **2.** *Comp. Sci.* A device that accepts video signals from a computer and gives information in a visual form, as on a screen. [< Lat. *displicāre*, scatter.]
Syns: *display, array, panoply, parade, pomp* ***n.***
dis•please (dĭs-plēz′) ►*v.* To cause annoyance or vexation (to). —**dis•pleas′ing•ly** *adv.* —**dis•pleas′ure** (-plĕzh′ər) *n.*
dis•port (dĭ-spôrt′, -spōrt′) ►*v.* To play; frolic. [< OFr. *desporter*, divert.]
dis•pos•a•ble (dĭ-spō′zə-bəl) ►*adj.* **1.** Designed to be disposed of after use: *disposable razors.* **2a.** Remaining after taxes have been deducted: *disposable income.* **b.** Free for use; available: *all disposable means.* ►*n.* An article that can be disposed of after one use. —**dis•pos′a•bil′i•ty** *n.*
dis•pos•al (dĭ-spō′zəl) ►*n.* **1.** A particular order, distribution, or placement. **2.** A method of attending to or settling matters. **3.** Transference by gift or sale. **4.** The act of throwing out or away. **5.** A device installed below a sink that grinds and flushes garbage away. **6.** The power to use something.
dis•pose (dĭ-spōz′) ►*v.* **-posed, -pos•ing 1.** To place in a particular order; arrange. **2.** To put into a certain frame of mind. See Syns at **incline. 3.** To settle a matter. —***phrasal verb:*** **dispose of** To get rid of, as by attending to, selling, or throwing out. [< Lat. *dispōnere.*] —**dis•pos′er** *n.*
dis•po•si•tion (dĭs′pə-zĭsh′ən) ►*n.* **1.** Temperament. **2.** A tendency or inclination. **3.** Arrangement, positioning, or distribution. **4.** A final settlement. **5.** An act of disposing of something.
dis•pos•sess (dĭs′pə-zĕs′) ►*v.* To deprive of possession of (e.g., land or property). —**dis′pos•ses′sion** *n.*
dis•praise (dĭs-prāz′) ►*v.* To disparage. ►*n.* Disapproval; reproach.
dis•pro•por•tion (dĭs′prə-pôr′shən, -pōr′-) ►*n.* Absence of proper proportion or harmony. —**dis′pro•por′tion•al, dis′pro•por′tion•ate** (-nĭt) *adj.* —**dis′pro•por′tion•al•ly, dis′pro•por′tion•ate•ly** *adv.*
dis•prove (dĭs-pro͞ov′) ►*v.* To prove to be false. —**dis•prov′al** *n.*
dis•pu•ta•tion (dĭs′pyə-tā′shən) ►*n.* **1.** An argument or debate. **2.** An oral defense of a thesis done as an academic exercise.
dis•pu•ta•tious (dĭs′pyə-tā′shəs) ►*adj.* Inclined to dispute. See Syns at **argumentative.** —**dis′pu•ta′tious•ly** *adv.* —**dis′pu•ta′tious•ness** *n.*
dis•pute (dĭ-spyo͞ot′) ►*v.* **-put•ed, -put•ing 1.** To argue (about); debate. **2.** To question the truth or validity of; doubt. **3.** To strive against; oppose. ►*n.* **1.** An argument; debate. **2.** A quarrel. [< Lat. *disputāre*, examine.] —**dis•put′a•ble** *adj.* —**dis•put′a•bly** *adv.* —**dis•pu′tant, dis•put′er** *n.*
dis•qual•i•fy (dĭs-kwŏl′ə-fī′) ►*v.* To declare or render unqualified or ineligible. —**dis•qual′i•fi•ca′tion** *n.*
dis•qui•et (dĭs-kwī′ĭt) ►*v.* To trouble; bother. ►*n.* Disquietude.
dis•qui•e•tude (dĭs-kwī′ĭ-to͞od′, -tyo͞od′) ►*n.* A condition of worried unease; anxiety.
dis•qui•si•tion (dĭs′kwĭ-zĭsh′ən) ►*n.* A formal discourse or treatise. [< Lat. *disquīrere, disquīsit-*, investigate.]
Dis•rae•li (dĭz-rā′lē), **Benjamin.** First Earl of Beaconsfield. 1804–81. British prime minister (1868 and 1874–80) and novelist.
dis•re•gard (dĭs′rĭ-gärd′) ►*v.* To pay no attention to; ignore. ►*n.* Lack of thoughtful attention or due regard.
dis•re•pair (dĭs′rĭ-pâr′) ►*n.* The condition of being in need of repair.
dis•rep•u•ta•ble (dĭs-rĕp′yə-tə-bəl) ►*adj.* Lacking respectability, as in character or behavior. —**dis•rep′u•ta•bly** *adv.*
dis•re•pute (dĭs′rĭ-pyo͞ot′) ►*n.* Damage to or loss of reputation; disgrace.
dis•re•spect (dĭs′rĭ-spĕkt′) ►*n.* Lack of respect; rudeness. —**dis′re•spect′** *v.* —**dis′re•spect′ful** *adj.* —**dis′re•spect′ful•ly** *adv.*
dis•robe (dĭs-rōb′) ►*v.* To undress.
dis•rupt (dĭs-rŭpt′) ►*v.* **1.** To throw into confusion. **2.** To break apart. [Lat. *disrumpere, disrupt-*, break apart.] —**dis•rupt′er, dis•rup′tor** *n.* —**dis•rup′tion** *n.* —**dis•rup′tive** *adj.*
dis•sat•is•fac•tion (dĭs-săt′ĭs-făk′shən) ►*n.* **1.** Discontent. **2.** A cause of discontent. —**dis•sat′is•fac′to•ry** (-tə-rē) *adj.*
dis•sat•is•fy (dĭs-săt′ĭs-fī′) ►*v.* To fail to satisfy; disappoint.
dis•sect (dĭ-sĕkt′, dī-, dī′sĕkt′) ►*v.* **1.** To cut apart or separate (tissue), esp. for anatomical study. **2.** To analyze or criticize in minute detail. See Syns at **analyze.** [Lat. *dissecāre, dissect-*, cut apart.] —**dis•sec′tion** *n.*
dis•sem•ble (dĭ-sĕm′bəl) ►*v.* **-bled, -bling 1.** To conceal the real nature or motives of. See Syns at **disguise. 2.** To simulate; feign. [< OFr. *dessembler*, be different.] —**dis•sem′bler** *n.*
dis•sem•i•nate (dĭ-sĕm′ə-nāt′) ►*v.* **-nat•ed, -nat•ing.** To spread or become spread; diffuse. [Lat. *dissēmināre.*] —**dis•sem′i•na′tion** *n.* —**dis•sem′i•na′tor** *n.*
dis•sen•sion (dĭ-sĕn′shən) ►*n.* A difference of opinion, esp. one causing strife within a group. [< Lat. *dissentīre*, to dissent.]
dis•sent (dĭ-sĕnt′) ►*v.* **1.** To disagree; differ. **2.** To withhold assent. ►*n.* **1.** Difference of opinion. **2.** The refusal to conform to the authority or doctrine of an established church. [< Lat. *dissentīre.*] —**dis•sent′er** *n.* —**dis•sent′ing** *adj.*

dis•ser•ta•tion (dĭs′ər-tā′shən) ►*n.* A treatise, esp. one written as a doctoral thesis. [< Lat. *dissertāre*, to deal with.]

dis•ser•vice (dĭs-sûr′vĭs) ►*n.* A harmful action.

dis•si•dent (dĭs′ĭ-dənt) ►*adj.* Disagreeing, as in opinion or belief. ►*n.* One who disagrees; dissenter. [< *dissidēre*, disagree : *dis-*, apart + *sedēre*, sit.] —**dis′si•dence** *n.*

dis•sim•i•lar (dĭ-sĭm′ə-lər) ►*adj.* Different or distinct; unlike. —**dis•sim′i•lar′i•ty** (-lăr′ĭ-tē) *n.* —**dis•sim′i•lar•ly** *adv.*

dis•si•mil•i•tude (dĭs′ə-mĭl′ĭ-to͞od′, -tyo͞od′) ►*n.* Lack of resemblance.

dis•sim•u•late (dĭ-sĭm′yə-lāt′) ►*v.* **-lat•ed, -lat•ing.** To disguise under a feigned appearance; dissemble. See Syns at **disguise.** [< Lat. *dissimulāre.*] —**dis•sim′u•la′tion** *n.* —**dis•sim′u•la′tor** *n.*

dis•si•pate (dĭs′ə-pāt′) ►*v.* **-pat•ed, -pat•ing 1.** To break up and drive away. **2.** To vanish or disappear. **3.** To spend wastefully; squander. See Syns at **waste. 4.** To indulge in the intemperate pursuit of pleasure. [< Lat. *dissipāre.*] —**dis′si•pat′ed** *adj.* —**dis′si•pa′tion** *n.*

dis•so•ci•ate (dĭ-sō′shē-āt′, -sē-) ►*v.* **-at•ed, -at•ing.** To separate or cause to separate. [Lat. *dissociāre.*] —**dis•so′ci•a′tion** *n.* —**dis•so′ci•a′tive** *adj.*

dis•so•lute (dĭs′ə-lo͞ot′) ►*adj.* Lacking in moral. restraint; wanton. [< Lat. *dissolūtus*, p.part. of *dissolvere*, dissolve.] —**dis′so•lute′ly** *adv.* —**dis′so•lute′ness** *n.*

dis•so•lu•tion (dĭs′ə-lo͞o′shən) ►*n.* **1.** Decomposition into fragments; disintegration. **2.** Sensual indulgence; debauchery. **3.** Termination or extinction by dispersion. **4.** Death. **5.** Termination of a legal bond or contract. **6.** Formal dismissal of an assembly. **7.** Reduction to a liquid form.

dis•solve (dĭ-zŏlv′) ►*v.* **-solved, -solv•ing 1.** To enter or cause to pass into solution. **2.** To make or become liquid; melt. **3.** To vanish or cause to vanish. **4.** To break or become broken into component parts. **5.** To terminate or dismiss. **6.** To collapse emotionally. [< Lat. *dissolvere.*] —**dis•solv′a•ble** *adj.* —**dis•solv′er** *n.*

dis•so•nance (dĭs′ə-nəns) ►*n.* **1.** A harsh, disagreeable combination of sounds; discord. **2.** *Mus.* A combination of harsh tones considered to suggest unrelieved tension. [< Lat. *dissonāre*, be dissonant.] —**dis′so•nant** *adj.* —**dis′so•nant•ly** *adv.*

dis•suade (dĭ-swād′) ►*v.* **-suad•ed, -suad•ing.** To deter from a course of action or purpose. [Lat. *dissuādēre* : DIS– + *suādēre*, advise.] —**dis•sua′sion** *n.* —**dis•sua′sive** *adj.*

Syns: *dissuade, deter, discourage* ***Ant:*** *persuade* **v.**

dist. ►*abbr.* **1.** distance **2.** district

dis•taff (dĭs′tăf′) ►*n.* **1.** A staff that holds on its cleft end the flax, wool, or tow in spinning. **2.** Women collectively. [< OE *distæf.*]

distaff side ►*n.* The maternal family line.

dis•tal (dĭs′təl) ►*adj.* **1.** Anatomically located far from the point of attachment, as a bone. **2.** Situated farthest from the middle front of the jaw, as a tooth. [< DISTANT.]

dis•tance (dĭs′təns) ►*n.* **1.** Separation in space or time. **2.** The interval separating any two specified instants in time. **3.** *Math.* The length of a line segment joining two points. **4a.** The degree of deviation or difference that separates two things in a relationship. **b.** The degree of progress between two points in a trend or course. **5.** A point or area that is far away. **6.** The whole way: *went the distance.* **7.** Chillness of manner; aloofness. ►*v.* **-tanced, -tanc•ing 1.** To place at or as if at a distance. **2.** To outrun or outstrip.

dis•tant (dĭs′tənt) ►*adj.* **1a.** Separate or apart in space or time. **b.** Far removed; remote. **2.** Coming from, located at, or going to a distance. **3.** Far apart in relationship: *a distant cousin.* **4.** Aloof or chilly. [< Lat. *dīstāre*, be remote : *dī-*, *dis-*, apart + *stāre*, stand.] —**dis′tant•ly** *adv.*

dis•taste (dĭs-tāst′) ►*n.* Dislike. —**dis•taste′ful** *adj.* —**dis•taste′ful•ly** *adv.*

Dist. Atty. ►*abbr.* district attorney

dis•tem•per (dĭs-tĕm′pər) ►*n.* An infectious, often fatal viral disease occurring in dogs, cats, and certain other mammals.

dis•tend (dĭ-stĕnd′) ►*v.* To swell or cause to swell. [< Lat. *distendere.*] —**dis•ten′si•ble** *adj.* —**dis•ten′tion, dis•ten′sion** *n.*

dis•till also **dis•til** (dĭ-stĭl′) ►*v.* **-tilled, -till•ing 1.** To subject to or derive from distillation. **2.** To separate from. **3.** To exude in drops. [< Lat. *dēstillāre*, drip down.] —**dis•till′er** *n.* —**dis•till′er•y** *n.*

dis•til•late (dĭs′tə-lāt′, -lĭt, dĭ-stĭl′ĭt) ►*n.* A liquid condensed from vapor in distillation.

dis•til•la•tion (dĭs′tə-lā′shən) ►*n.* The evaporation of a liquid and subsequent condensation and collection of the vapors as a means of purification or of extraction of volatile components.

dis•tinct (dĭ-stĭngkt′) ►*adj.* **1.** Distinguishable from all others. **2.** Easily perceived; clear. See Syns at **apparent. 3.** Clearly defined; unquestionable: *at a distinct disadvantage.* [< Lat. *dīstīnctus*, p.part. of *dīstinguere*, distinguish.] —**dis•tinct′ly** *adv.* —**dis•tinct′ness** *n.*

Syns: *distinct, discrete, separate, several* **adj.**

dis•tinc•tion (dĭ-stĭngk′shən) ►*n.* **1.** The act of distinguishing; differentiation. **2.** A difference. **3.** A distinguishing factor or characteristic. **4.** Excellence or eminence. **5.** Honor: *graduated with distinction.*

dis•tinc•tive (dĭ-stĭngk′tĭv) ►*adj.* Serving to distinguish or set apart from others. —**dis•tinc′tive•ly** *adv.* —**dis•tinc′tive•ness** *n.*

dis•tin•guish (dĭ-stĭng′gwĭsh) ►*v.* **1.** To recognize as being distinct. **2.** To perceive distinctly; discern. **3.** To discriminate. **4.** To set apart. **5.** To make eminent. [< Lat. *dīstinguere.*] —**dis•tin′guish•a•ble** *adj.* —**dis•tin′guish•a•bly** *adv.*

dis•tin•guished (dĭ-stĭng′gwĭsht) ►*adj.* **1.** Characterized by excellence or distinction; eminent. **2.** Dignified in conduct or appearance.

dis•tort (dĭ-stôrt′) ►*v.* **1.** To twist out of a proper or natural shape or position. **2.** To give a false or misleading account of; misrepresent. [Lat. *distorquēre, distort-.*] —**dis•tor′tion** *n.*

dis•tract (dĭ-străkt′) ►*v.* **1.** To sidetrack; divert. **2.** To upset emotionally; unsettle. [ME *distracten* < Lat. *distrahere, distract-*, pull away.] —**dis•tract′ing•ly** *adv.* —**dis•trac′tion** *n.*

dis•traught (dĭ-strôt′) ►*adj.* **1.** Deeply agitated or anxious. **2.** Mad; crazed. [< ME *distract*, p.part. of *distracten*, DISTRACT.]
dis•tress (dĭ-strĕs′) ►*v.* **1.** To cause anxiety or suffering to. See Syns at **trouble. 2.** To mar or treat (e.g., an object or fabric) to give the appearance of an antique. ►*n.* **1.** Pain or suffering of mind or body. **2.** Severe psychological strain. **3.** The condition of being in need of immediate assistance. [< Lat. *dīstrictus*, p.part. of *dīstringere*, draw tight.] —**dis•tress′ful** *adj.* —**dis•tress′ing•ly** *adv.*
dis•trib•ute (dĭ-strĭb′yo͞ot) ►*v.* **-ut•ed, -ut•ing 1.** To divide and give out in portions. **2.** To market, esp. as a wholesaler. **3.** To deliver or hand out. **4.** To spread or diffuse over an area. **5.** To classify. [< Lat. *distribuere*.] —**dis′tri•bu′tion** *n.* —**dis•trib′u•tive** *adj.*
dis•trib•u•tor (dĭ-strĭb′yə-tər) ►*n.* **1.** One that distributes, esp. a device that applies electric current to the spark plugs of an engine. **2.** One that markets goods, esp. a wholesaler.
dis•trict (dĭs′trĭkt) ►*n.* **1.** A division of an area, as for administrative purposes. **2.** A region having a distinguishing feature. ►*v.* To divide into districts. [< Med.Lat. *dīstrictus* < Lat. *dīstringere*, hinder.]
district attorney ►*n.* The prosecuting officer of a judicial district.
District of Columbia. A federal district of the E US on the Potomac R. between VA and MD; coextensive with the city of Washington.
dis•trust (dĭs-trŭst′) ►*n.* Lack of trust or confidence; suspicion. ►*v.* To have no confidence in. —**dis•trust′ful** *adj.* —**dis•trust′ful•ly** *adv.* —**dis•trust′ful•ness** *n.*
dis•turb (dĭ-stûrb′) ►*v.* **1.** To destroy the tranquillity or settled state of. **2.** To trouble emotionally or mentally. **3.** To intrude on or interfere with; interrupt. **4.** To disarrange. [< Lat. *disturbāre*.] —**dis•tur′bance** *n.* —**dis•turb′er** *n.* —**dis•turb′ing•ly** *adv.*
dis•u•nite (dĭs′yo͞o-nīt′) ►*v.* **-nit•ed, -nit•ing.** To separate; divide.
dis•u•ni•ty (dĭs-yo͞o′nĭ-tē) ►*n., pl.* **-ties.** Lack of unity; dissension.
dis•use (dĭs-yo͞os′) ►*n.* The state of not being used or no longer being in use.
ditch (dĭch) ►*n.* A trench dug in the ground. ►*v.* **1.** To dig or make a ditch. **2.** To drive (a vehicle) into a ditch. **3.** *Slang* To discard. **4.** To crash-land on water. [< OE *dīc*.]
dith•er (dĭ*th*′ər) ►*n.* Indecisive agitation. [< ME *didderen*, tremble.] —**dith′er** *v.*
dit•to (dĭt′ō) ►*n., pl.* **-tos 1.** The same as stated above or before. **2.** A duplicate or copy. **3.** A pair of small marks (") used as a symbol for the word *ditto*. [Ital. dial., said.]
dit•ty (dĭt′ē) ►*n., pl.* **-ties.** A simple song. [< Lat. *dictātum* < p.part. of *dictāre*, DICTATE.]
di•u•ret•ic (dī′ə-rĕt′ĭk) ►*adj.* Tending to increase the discharge of urine. [< Gk. *diourētikos* < *diourein*, pass urine.] —**di′u•ret′ic** *n.*
di•ur•nal (dī-ûr′nəl) ►*adj.* **1.** Of or occurring in a 24-hour period; daily. **2.** Occurring or active during the daytime. [< Lat. *diurnus*.] —**di•ur′nal•ly** *adv.*
div. ►*abbr.* **1.** dividend **2.** divorced
di•va (dē′və) ►*n., pl.* **-vas** or **-ve** (-vā) **1.** An operatic prima donna. **2.** A very successful female singer of nonoperatic music. [< Lat. *dīva*, goddess.]
di•va•gate (dī′və-gāt′, dĭv′ə-) ►*v.* **-gat•ed, -gat•ing 1.** To wander or drift about. **2.** To ramble; digress. [LLat. *dīvagārī* < Lat. *vagus*, wandering.] —**di′va•ga′tion** *n.*
di•va•lent (dī-vā′lənt) ►*adj.* Having a valence of 2.
di•van (dĭ-văn′, dī′văn′) ►*n.* A long backless sofa; couch. [< Pers. *dīvān*, place of assembly.]
dive (dīv) ►*v.* **dived** or **dove** (dōv), **dived, div•ing 1.** To plunge, esp. headfirst, into water. **2.** To submerge: *dive for pearls.* **3.** To fall or drop sharply and rapidly; plummet. **4.** To lunge, leap, or dash. See Regional Note at **wake**[1]. ►*n.* **1.** The act or an instance of diving. **2.** A quick pronounced drop. **3.** *Slang* A disreputable or run-down bar or nightclub. [< OE *dȳfan*, dip, and *dūfan*, sink.] —**div′er** *n.*
dive-bomb (dīv′bŏm′) ►*v.* To bomb from an airplane at the end of a steep dive toward the target. —**dive′-bomb′er** *n.*
di•verge (dĭ-vûrj′, dī-) ►*v.* **-verged, -verg•ing 1.** To extend in different directions from a common point. **2.** To differ, as in opinion. **3.** To deviate from a norm. See Syns at **swerve.** [Lat. *dīvergere*, bend apart.] —**di•ver′gent** *adj.* —**di•ver′gent•ly** *adv.*
di•ver•gence (dĭ-vûr′jəns, dī-) ►*n.* **1.** An act or instance of diverging. **2.** Departure from a norm; deviation. **3.** Difference, as of opinion.
di•vers (dī′vərz) ►*adj.* Various; sundry. [ME DIVERSE.]
di•verse (dĭ-vûrs′, dī-, dī′vûrs′) ►*adj.* **1.** Distinct in kind; unlike. **2.** Having variety in form; diversified. [< Lat. *dīversus*, p.part. of *dīvertere*, divert.] —**di•verse′ly** *adv.* —**di•verse′ness** *n.*
di•ver•si•fy (dĭ-vûr′sə-fī′, dī-) ►*v.* **-fied, -fy•ing 1.** To make diverse; vary. **2.** To spread out activities or investments, esp. in business. —**di•ver′si•fi•ca′tion** *n.*
di•ver•sion (dĭ-vûr′zhən, -shən, dī-) ►*n.* **1.** The act or an instance of diverting. **2.** That which diverts. —**di•ver′sion•ar′y** *adj.*
di•ver•si•ty (dĭ-vûr′sĭ-tē, dī-) ►*n., pl.* **-ties 1.** The fact or quality of being diverse; difference. **2.** Variety or multiformity.
di•vert (dĭ-vûrt′, dī-) ►*v.* **1.** To turn aside from a course or direction. **2.** To distract. **3.** To amuse or entertain. [< Lat. *dīvertere*.]
di•ver•ti•men•to (dĭ-vĕr′tə-mĕn′tō) ►*n., pl.* **-tos** also **-ti** (-tē). A chiefly 18th-cent. form of instrumental chamber music having several short movements. [Ital.]
di•vest (dĭ-vĕst′, dī-) ►*v.* **1.** To strip, as of clothes. **2.** To deprive, as of rights; dispossess. [< OFr. *desvestir*.] —**di•vest′ment** *n.*
di•ves•ti•ture (dĭ-vĕs′tĭ-chər, -cho͝or′, dī-) ►*n.* **1.** An act of divesting. **2.** The sale, liquidation, or spinoff of a corporate division or subsidiary.
di•vide (dĭ-vīd′) ►*v.* **-vid•ed, -vid•ing 1.** To separate or become separated into parts, sections, or groups. **2.** To classify. **3.** To set at odds; disunite. **4.** To separate from something else; cut off. **5.** To distribute among a number; apportion. **6.** *Math.* **a.** To subject to the process of division. **b.** To be an exact divisor of. **7.** To branch out, as a river. ►*n.* A watershed. [< Lat. *dīvidere*.]
div•i•dend (dĭv′ĭ-dĕnd′) ►*n.* **1.** *Math.* A quantity to be divided. **2.** A share of profits received by a stockholder. **3.** A bonus. [< Lat. *dīvidere*, divide.]

di•vid•er (dĭ-vīʹdər) ►*n.* **1.** One that divides, esp. a partition. **2.** A compasslike device used for dividing lines and transferring measurements.

div•i•na•tion (dĭvʹə-nāʹshən) ►*n.* **1.** The art or act of foretelling future events or revealing occult knowledge by means of augury or alleged supernatural agency. **2.** An inspired guess or presentiment.

di•vine (dĭ-vīnʹ) ►*adj.* **-vin•er, -vin•est 1a.** Being a deity. **b.** Of or relating to a deity. **2.** Superhuman; godlike. **3.** Supremely good; magnificent. ►*n.* **1.** A cleric. **2.** A theologian. ►*v.* **-vined, -vin•ing 1.** To prophesy through or practice divination. See Syns at **foretell. 2.** To guess, infer, or conjecture. [< Lat. *dīvīnus*, foreseeing, divine.] —**di•vineʹly** *adv.* —**di•vinʹer** *n.*

diving board ►*n.* A flexible board from which a dive may be executed.

di•vin•ing rod (dĭ-vīʹnĭng) ►*n.* A forked rod believed to indicate underground water or minerals by bending downward when held over a source.

di•vin•i•ty (dĭ-vĭnʹĭ-tē) ►*n.*, *pl.* **-ties 1.** The state or quality of being divine. **2. the Divinity** God. **3.** Theology.

di•vis•i•ble (dĭ-vĭzʹə-bəl) ►*adj.* Capable of being divided. —**di•visʹi•bilʹi•ty** *n.*

di•vi•sion (dĭ-vĭzhʹən) ►*n.* **1.** The act or process of dividing or the state of being divided. **2.** Something that serves to divide or separate. **3.** One of the parts, sections, or groups into which something is divided. **4.** A self-contained military unit smaller than a corps. **5.** Disagreement; disunion. **6.** *Math.* The operation of determining how many times one quantity is contained in another. [< Lat. *dīvidere*, *dīvīs-*, divide.] —**di•viʹsion•al** *adj.*

di•vi•sive (dĭ-vīʹsĭv) ►*adj.* Creating dissension or discord. —**di•viʹsive•ly** *adv.* —**di•viʹsive•ness** *n.*

di•vi•sor (dĭ-vīʹzər) ►*n.* The quantity by which another, the dividend, is divided.

di•vorce (dĭ-vôrsʹ, -vōrsʹ) ►*n.* **1.** The legal dissolution of a marriage. **2.** A complete severance. ►*v.* **-vorced, -vorc•ing 1.** To dissolve the marriage bond between. **2.** To separate or disunite. [< Lat. *dīvortium* < *dīvertere*, divert.]

di•vor•cé (dĭ-vôr-sāʹ, -sēʹ, -vōr-) ►*n.* A divorced man. [Fr.]

di•vor•cée (dĭ-vôr-sāʹ, -sēʹ, -vōr-) ►*n.* A divorced woman. [Fr.]

div•ot (dĭvʹət) ►*n.* A piece of turf torn up by a golf club in striking a ball. [Sc., a turf.]

di•vulge (dĭ-vŭljʹ) ►*v.* **-vulged, -vulg•ing.** To make known (something secret). [< Lat. *dīvulgāre*, publish.] —**di•vulʹgence** *n.*

div•vy (dĭvʹē) ►*v.* **-vied, -vy•ing** *Slang* To divide: *divvied up the loot.* [< DIVIDEND.]

Dix (dĭks), **Dorothea Lynde.** 1802–87. Amer. reformer and educator.

Dorothea Dix
c. 1849 daguerreotype

Dix•ie (dĭkʹsē) A region of the S and E US, usu. comprising the states that joined the Confederacy during the Civil War.

Dix•ie•land (dĭkʹsē-lăndʹ) ►*n.* An instrumental jazz style associated with New Orleans and marked by a two-beat rhythm and improvisation.

DIY ►*abbr.* do-it-yourself

di•zy•got•ic (dīʹzī-gŏtʹĭk) ►*adj.* Derived from two separately fertilized eggs. Used esp. of fraternal twins.

diz•zy (dĭzʹē) ►*adj.* **-zi•er, -zi•est 1.** Having a whirling sensation. See Syns at **giddy. 2.** Bewildered or confused. **3.** *Slang* Scatterbrained or silly. [< OE *dysig*, foolish.] —**dizʹzi•ly** *adv.* —**dizʹzi•ness** *n.* —**dizʹzy** *v.*

DJ ►*abbr.* **1.** disc jockey **2.** district judge **3.** *Lat.* Doctor Juris (Doctor of Law)

Dja•kar•ta (jə-kärʹtə) See **Jakarta.**

Dji•bou•ti (jĭ-bo͞oʹtē) **1.** A country of E Africa on the Gulf of Aden. Pop. 566,000. **2.** The capital of Djibouti, in the SE part on an inlet of the Gulf of Aden. Pop. 300,000.

dkg ►*abbr.* decagram

dkl ►*abbr.* decaliter

dkm ►*abbr.* decameter

DLit or **DLitt** ►*abbr.* *Lat.* Doctor Litterarum (Doctor of Letters; Doctor of Literature)

DM ►*abbr.* deutsche mark

DMD ►*abbr.* *Lat.* Dentariae Medicinae Doctor (Doctor of Dental Medicine)

DMZ ►*abbr.* demilitarized zone

DNA (dēʹĕn-āʹ) ►*n.* A nucleic acid that carries the genetic information which determines individual hereditary characteristics, consists of two long chains of nucleotides twisted into a double helix, and is capable of self-replication and RNA synthesis. [D(EOXYRIBO)N(UCLEIC) A(CID).]

Dnie•per (nēʹpər) A river rising in W-central Russia and flowing about 2,285 km (1,420 mi) through Belarus and Ukraine to the Black Sea.

Dnies•ter (nēʹstər) A river rising in W Ukraine and flowing about 1,368 km (850 mi) to the Black Sea near Odessa.

Dni•pro•pe•trovs'k (nēʹprō-pə-trôfskʹ) A city of E-central Ukraine on the Dnieper R. SSW of Kharkiv. Pop. 1,189,900.

DNR ►*abbr.* **1.** Department of Natural Resources **2.** do not resuscitate

do[1] (do͞o) ►*v.* **did** (dĭd), **done** (dŭn), **do•ing, does** (dŭz) **1.** To perform or execute. **2.** To fulfill; complete. **3.** To produce: *do a play on Broadway.* **4.** To bring about; effect: *Crying won't do any good now.* **5.** To render: *do equal justice to both sides.* **6.** To put forth; exert: *Do the best you can.* **7.** To prepare, as by cleaning or washing: *did the dishes.* **8.** To work at: *What do you do?* **9.** To work out: *do homework.* **10.** *Informal* To travel (a specified distance). **11a.** To meet the needs of sufficiently; suit. **b.** To be adequate. **12.** To set or style (the hair). **13.** *Informal* To serve (a prison term). **14.** *Slang* To cheat; swindle: *did her out of an inheritance.*

15. To behave; act: *Do as I say.* **16.** To get along; fare: *doing well.* **17.** Used as a substitute for an antecedent verb: *worked as hard as everyone else did.* —*aux.* **1.** Used in questions, negative statements, and inverted phrases: *Do you understand? I did not sleep well. Little did we know.* **2.** Used for emphasis: *I do want to be sure.* —***phrasal verbs:* do away with 1.** Make an end of; eliminate. **2.** To destroy; kill. **do in** *Slang* **1.** To tire completely; exhaust. **2.** To kill. **do up** To adorn or dress lavishly. ►*n., pl.* **do's** or **dos.** A statement of what should be done: *a list of the do's and don'ts.* [< OE *dōn.*]

do² (dō) ►*n. Mus.* The 1st tone of the diatonic scale. [Ital.]

DOA ►*abbr.* dead on arrival

do•a•ble (do͞o′ə-bəl) ►*adj.* Possible to do.

DOB ►*abbr.* date of birth

Do•ber•man pin•scher (dō′bər-mən pĭn′shər) ►*n.* A fairly large dog of a breed originating in Germany, with a smooth short-haired coat. [Ger. *Dobermann* (after Ludwig *Dobermann*) + *Pinscher*, terrier.]

do•bra (dō′brə) ►*n.* See table at **currency.** [Port.]

doc•ile (dŏs′əl, -īl′) ►*adj.* Easily managed or taught; tractable. [Lat. *docilis* < *docēre*, teach.] —**do•cil′i•ty** (dŏ-sĭl′ĭ-tē, dō-) *n.*

dock¹ (dŏk) ►*n.* **1.** The area of water between two piers or alongside a pier that receives a ship. **2.** A pier or wharf. **3.** often **docks** A group of piers on a commercial waterfront. **4.** A loading platform for trucks or trains. ►*v.* **1.** To maneuver into or next to a dock. **2.** To couple (two or more spacecraft) in space. [< MDu. *doc.*]

dock² (dŏk) ►*v.* **1.** To clip short or cut off (e.g., an animal's tail). **2.** To withhold or deduct a part from (one's salary or wages). [ME *dokken.*]

dock³ (dŏk) ►*n.* An enclosed place where the defendant stands or sits in a court of law. [Obsolete Flem. *docke*, cage.]

dock⁴ (dŏk) ►*n.* See **sorrel¹.** [< OE *docce.*]

dock•age (dŏk′ĭj) ►*n.* **1.** A charge for docking privileges. **2.** Facilities for docking vessels.

dock•et (dŏk′ĭt) ►*n.* **1a.** A calendar of the cases awaiting action in a court. **b.** A brief entry of the court proceedings in a legal case. **c.** The book containing such entries. **2.** A list of things to be done; agenda. **3.** A label affixed to a package listing contents or directions. ►*v.* To enter in a court calendar. [ME *doggett*, summary, digest.]

dock•hand (dŏk′hănd′) ►*n.* A dockworker.

dock•work•er (dŏk′wûr′kər) ►*n.* A worker who loads and unloads ships; stevedore.

dock•yard (dŏk′yärd′) ►*n.* A shipyard.

doc•tor (dŏk′tər) ►*n.* **1.** A person, esp. a physician, dentist, or veterinarian, trained in the healing arts and licensed to practice. **2.** One holding the highest academic degree awarded by a college or university. ►*v.* **1.** *Informal* To give medical treatment to. **2.** To repair, esp. in a makeshift manner. **3.** To falsify or change: *doctored the evidence.* **4.** To add ingredients to: *doctor the soup with a dash of sherry.* See Syns at **adulterate.** [< Lat., teacher < *docēre*, teach.] —**doc′tor•al** *adj.*

doc•tor•ate (dŏk′tər-ĭt) ►*n.* The degree or status of an academic doctor.

doc•tri•naire (dŏk′trə-nâr′) ►*adj.* Marked by inflexible attachment to a practice or theory without regard to its practicality. [Fr.] —**doc′tri•nair′ism** *n.*

doc•trine (dŏk′trĭn) ►*n.* **1.** A body of principles presented for acceptance or belief, as by a religious, political, or philosophic group. **2.** A statement of official government policy, esp. in foreign affairs. [< Lat. *doctrīna*, teaching.] —**doc′tri•nal** (dŏk′trə-nəl, dŏk-trī′-) *adj.*

***Syns:** doctrine, dogma, tenet* **n.**

doc•u•dra•ma (dŏk′yə-drä′mə, -drăm′ə) ►*n.* A television or movie dramatization based on fact. [DOCU(MENTARY) + DRAMA.]

doc•u•ment (dŏk′yə-mənt) ►*n.* **1.** A paper that provides evidence or information. **2.** Something, such as a photograph or computer file, that contains information. ►*v.* (-mĕnt′). To support (a claim) with evidence. [< Lat. *documentum*, example < *docēre*, teach.] —**doc′u•men•ta′tion** *n.*

doc•u•men•ta•ry (dŏk′yə-mĕn′tə-rē) ►*adj.* **1.** Of or based on documents. **2.** Of or being a documentary. ►*n., pl.* **-ries.** A work, such as a film or television program, presenting factual information without editorial comment or fictional elements.

dod•der (dŏd′ər) ►*v.* To shake or tremble, as from old age. [ME *daderen.*]

do•dec•a•gon (dō-dĕk′ə-gŏn′) ►*n.* A polygon with 12 sides. [Gk. *dōdeka*, twelve + -GON.]

do•dec•a•he•dron (dō′dĕk-ə-hē′drən) ►*n., pl.* **-drons** or **-dra** (-drə). A polyhedron with 12 faces. [Gk. *dōdeka*, twelve + -HEDRON.]

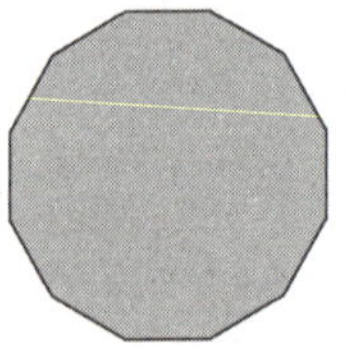

dodecagon

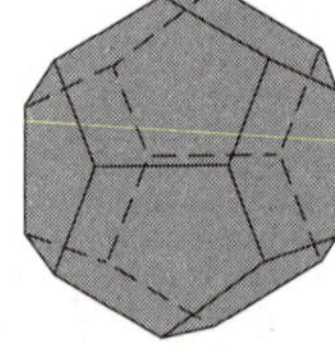

dodecahedron

Do•dec•a•nese (dō-dĕk′ə-nēz′, -nēs′) An island group of SE Greece in the Aegean between Turkey and Crete.

dodge (dŏj) ►*v.* **dodged, dodg•ing 1.** To avoid by moving quickly aside. **2.** To evade by cunning or deceit. **3.** To move aside by twisting suddenly. ►*n.* **1.** The act of dodging. **2.** An ingenious expedient intended to evade or trick. [?] —**dodg′er** *n.*

Dodg•son (dŏj′sən), **Charles Lutwidge.** Lewis Carroll. 1832–98. British mathematician and writer.

do•do (dō′dō) ►*n., pl.* **-does** or **-dos 1.** A large flightless bird extinct since the 17th cent. **2.** *Informal* **a.** One who is hopelessly passé. **b.** A stupid person. [Port. *dodó.*]

Do•do•ma (dō′də-mä, -dō-) The official capital of Tanzania, in the central part. Pop. 203,833.

doe (dō) ►*n., pl.* **doe** or **does.** The female of a deer or certain other animals, such as the hare or kangaroo. [< OE *dā.*]

do•er (do͞o′ər) ►*n.* One who does something, esp. an active, energetic person.

does (dŭz) ►*v.* 3rd pers. sing. pr.t. of **do¹.**

doe•skin (dō′skĭn′) ▸*n.* **1.** Soft leather made from the skin of a doe. **2.** A fine, soft, smooth woolen fabric.

does•n't (dŭz′ənt) ▸ Does not.

doff (dôf, dŏf) ▸*v.* **1.** To take off: *doff one's clothes.* **2.** To tip or lift (one's hat) in salutation. [< ME *don off*, do off.]

dog (dôg, dŏg) ▸*n.* **1.** A domesticated canine mammal related to the foxes and wolves. **2.** Any of various other canines, such as the dingo. **3.** A male canine animal. **4.** *Informal* A person: *a lucky dog.* **5.** A contemptible person. **6.** An inferior product or creation. **7. dogs** *Slang* The feet. **8.** *Slang* A hot dog. ▸*v.* **dogged, dog•ging.** To track or trail persistently. —***idiom:*** **go to the dogs** To go to ruin. [< OE *docga.*]

dog•cart (dôg′kärt′, dŏg′-) ▸*n.* A one-horse vehicle for two persons seated back to back.

dog•catch•er (dôg′kăch′ər, dŏg′-) ▸*n.* An official charged with impounding stray dogs.

doge (dōj) ▸*n.* The elected chief magistrate of the former republics of Venice and Genoa. [Ital. dial. < Lat. *dux*, leader.]

dog-ear (dôg′îr′, dŏg′-) ▸*n.* A turned-down corner of a page in a book. —**dog′-ear′** *v.* —**dog′-eared′** *adj.*

dog-eat-dog (dôg′ēt-dôg′, dŏg′ēt-dŏg′) ▸*adj.* Ruthlessly acquisitive or competitive.

dog•fight (dôg′fīt′, dŏg′-) ▸*n.* An aerial battle between fighter planes.

dog•fish (dôg′fĭsh′, dŏg′-) ▸*n.* Any of various small sharks.

dog•ged (dô′gĭd, dŏg′ĭd) ▸*adj.* Stubbornly persevering; tenacious. —**dog′ged•ly** *adv.* —**dog′ged•ness** *n.*

dog•ger•el (dô′gər-əl, dŏg′ər-) ▸*n.* Clumsy verse, often irregular in form and humorous in effect. [< ME, worthless.]

dog•gy or **dog•gie** (dô′gē, dŏg′ē) ▸*n.*, *pl.* **-gies.** A dog, esp. a small one.

dog•house (dôg′hous′, dŏg′-) ▸*n.* A shelter for a dog. —***idiom:*** **in the doghouse** *Slang* In trouble.

do•gie also **do•gy** (dō′gē) ▸*n.*, *pl.* **-gies** *Regional.* A stray or motherless calf. [?]

dog iron ▸*n.* See **andiron.** See Regional Note at **andiron.** [(FIRE)DOG + (AND)IRON.]

dog•leg (dôg′lĕg′, dŏg′-) ▸*n.* A sharp bend or turn. —**dog′leg′** *v.*

dog•ma (dôg′mə, dŏg′-) ▸*n.*, *pl.* **-mas** or **-ma•ta** (-mə-tə) **1.** A corpus of doctrines set forth by a religion. **2.** An authoritative principle or belief, esp. one considered to be absolutely true. See Syns at **doctrine.** [< Gk., opinion < *dokein*, seem.]

dog•mat•ic (dôg-măt′ĭk, dŏg-) ▸*adj.* Marked by an authoritative, arrogant assertion of unproved principles. —**dog•mat′i•cal•ly** *adv.* —**dog′ma•tism′** *n.* —**dog′ma•tist** *n.*

do-good•er (do͞o′go͝od′ər) ▸*n.* A naive idealist who supports philanthropic or humanitarian causes.

dog paddle ▸*n.* A prone swimming stroke in which the limbs remain submerged.

dog tag ▸*n.* **1.** An identification disk attached to a dog's collar. **2.** A metal identification tag worn around the neck by members of the armed forces.

dog•trot (dôg′trŏt′, dŏg′-) ▸*n.* A steady trot like that of a dog. —**dog′trot′** *v.*

dog•wood (dôg′wo͝od′, dŏg′-) ▸*n.* A tree with small greenish flowers surrounded by large, showy white or pink petallike bracts.

Do•ha (dō′hə, -hä) The capital of Qatar, on the Persian Gulf. Pop. 217,294.

doi•ly (doi′lē) ▸*n.*, *pl.* **-lies.** A small ornamental mat, usu. of lace or linen. [After *Doily* or *Doyly*, 18th-century London draper.]

doily

do•ings (do͞o′ĭngz) ▸*pl.n.* Activities, esp. social activities.

do-it-your•self (do͞o′ĭt-yər-sĕlf′) ▸*adj.* Of or designed to be done by an amateur or as a hobby. —**do′-it-your•self′er** *n.*

dol•drums (dōl′drəmz′, dôl′-, dŏl′-) ▸*pl.n.* *(takes sing. or pl. v.)* **1a.** A period of stagnation or slump. **b.** A period of depression or unhappy listlessness. **2.** An ocean region near the equator, marked by calms. [< obsolete *doldrum*, dullard.]

dole (dōl) ▸*n.* **1.** Charitable dispensation of goods, esp. money, food, or clothing. **2.** A share of such goods. **3.** *Chiefly Brit.* Government welfare or relief. ▸*v.* **doled, dol•ing 1.** To dispense as charity. **2.** To distribute, esp. sparingly: *doled out the food rations.* [< OE *dāl*, portion.]

dole•ful (dōl′fəl) ▸*adj.* Filled with grief; mournful. [< Lat. *dolus*, grief.] —**dole′ful•ly** *adv.* —**dole′ful•ness** *n.*

doll (dŏl) ▸*n.* **1.** A child's toy having the likeness of a human. **2.** *Slang* **a.** An attractive person. **b.** A woman. **c.** A sweetheart. ▸*v.* To dress smartly: *dolled themselves up for the party.* [< *Doll*, nickname for *Dorothy.*]

dol•lar (dŏl′ər) ▸*n.* See table at **currency.** [< LGer. *Daler*, a silver coin.]

dol•lop (dŏl′əp) ▸*n.* A lump or portion, as of ice cream. [Perh. of Scand. orig.]

dol•ly (dŏl′ē) ▸*n.*, *pl.* **-lies 1.** *Informal* A doll. **2.** A low wheeled platform used for transporting heavy loads. **3.** A wheeled apparatus used to transport a movie or television camera about a set.

dol•men (dōl′mən, dŏl′-) ▸*n.* See **portal tomb.** [Fr. < Breton.]

dol•o•mite (dō′lə-mīt′, dŏl′ə-) ▸*n.* A magnesia-rich sedimentary rock resembling limestone. [After Déodat de *Dolomieu* (1750–1801).] —**dol′o•mit′ic** (-mĭt′ĭk) *adj.*

Dolomite Alps. A range of the E Alps in NE Italy.

do•lor (dō′lər) ▸*n.* Sorrow; grief. [< Lat., pain.] —**do′lor•ous** *adj.* —**do′lor•ous•ly** *adv.* —**do′lor•ous•ness** *n.*

dol•phin (dŏl′fĭn, dôl′-) ▸*n.* **1.** Any of a family of marine mammals related to the whales but generally smaller and having a beaklike snout. **2.** Either of two marine game fishes having iridescent coloring. [< Gk. *delphis*.]

dolt (dōlt) ▸*n.* A stupid person. [ME *dulte* < *dul*, dull.] —**dolt'ish** *adj.*

-dom ▸*suff.* **1.** State; condition: *stardom.* **2a.** Domain; position; rank: *dukedom.* **b.** A group having a specified position, office, or character: *officialdom.* [< OE *-dōm*.]

do•main (dō-mān') ▸*n.* **1.** A territory over which control is exercised. **2.** A sphere of activity, concern, or function. See Syns at **field. 3.** *Comp. Sci.* A group of networked computers having a common communications address. [< Lat. *dominium*, property < *dominus*, lord.]

dome (dōm) ▸*n.* **1.** A vaulted roof of gen. hemispherical shape. **2.** A geodesic dome. **3.** Something resembling a dome. [< Lat. *domus* and Gk. *dōma*, house.] —**domed** *adj.*

do•mes•tic (də-mĕs'tĭk) ▸*adj.* **1.** Of or relating to the family or household. **2.** Fond of home life and household affairs. **3.** Tame or domesticated. **4.** Of or relating to a country's internal affairs. **5.** Produced in or indigenous to a particular country. ▸*n.* A household servant. [< Lat. *domesticus* < *domus*, house.] —**do•mes'ti•cal•ly** *adv.* —**do'mes•tic'i•ty** (dō'mĕ-stĭs'ĭ-tē) *n.*

do•mes•ti•cate (də-mĕs'tĭ-kāt') ▸*v.* **-cat•ed, -cat•ing.** To adapt or make fit for domestic use or life; tame. —**do•mes'ti•ca'tion** *n.*

domestic partner ▸*n.* A person, other than a spouse, with whom one cohabits.

dom•i•cile (dŏm'ĭ-sīl', -səl, dō'mĭ-) ▸*n.* A legal residence; home. [< Lat. *domicilium* < *domus*, house.] —**dom'i•cile'** *v.*

dom•i•nant (dŏm'ə-nənt) ▸*adj.* **1.** Exercising the most influence or control. **2.** Most prominent, as in position. **3.** *Genet.* Producing the same phenotypic effect whether inherited with an identical or dissimilar gene. —**dom'i•nance** *n.* —**dom'i•nant•ly** *adv.*

dom•i•nate (dŏm'ə-nāt') ▸*v.* **-nat•ed, -nat•ing 1.** To control, govern, or rule. **2.** To enjoy a commanding position in or over. **3.** To overlook from a height. **4.** To occupy a position more elevated or superior to others. [Lat. *dominārī* < *dominus*, lord.] —**dom'i•na'tion** *n.* —**dom'i•na'tor** *n.*

dom•i•neer (dŏm'ə-nîr') ▸*v.* To rule over arrogantly; tyrannize. [Du. *domineren*, ult. < Lat. *dominārī*, DOMINATE.]

Dom•i•nic (dŏm'ə-nĭk), Saint. 1170?–1221. Spanish-born priest who founded the Dominican order of friars (1216). —**Do•min'i•can** *adj. & n.*

Dom•i•ni•ca (dŏm'ə-nē'kə, də-mĭn'ĭ-kə) An island country of the E Caribbean between Guadeloupe and Martinique. Cap. Roseau. Pop. 71,000. —**Dom'i•ni'can** *adj. & n.*

Do•min•i•can Republic (də-mĭn'ĭ-kən) A country of the West Indies on the E part of the island of Hispaniola. Cap. Santo Domingo. Pop. 7,760,000. —**Do•min'i•can** *adj. & n.*

do•min•ion (də-mĭn'yən) ▸*n.* **1.** Control or exercise of control; sovereignty. **2.** A sphere of influence or control; realm. **3.** often **Dominion** A self-governing nation within the British Commonwealth. [< Lat. *dominium*, property. See DOMAIN.]

Dominion Day ▸*n.* See **Canada Day.**

dom•i•no¹ (dŏm'ə-nō') ▸*n., pl.* **-noes** or **-nos 1.** A small rectangular block marked by one to six dots. **2. dominoes** or **dominos** *(takes sing. or pl. v.)* A game played with dominoes. [Fr., prob. < *domino*, mask. See DOMINO².]

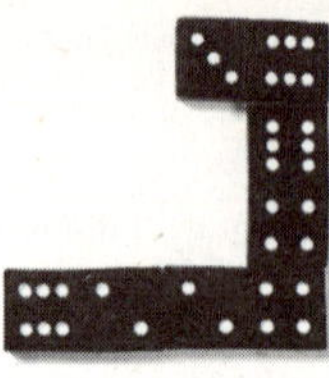

domino¹

dom•i•no² (dŏm'ə-nō') ▸*n., pl.* **-noes** or **-nos 1a.** A hooded robe worn with an eye mask at a masquerade. **b.** The mask so worn. **2.** One wearing this costume. [Fr., prob. < Lat. *(benedīcāmus) dominō*, (let us praise) the Lord. See DOMAIN.]

domino effect ▸*n.* An effect produced when one event sets off a chain of similar events.

Do•mi•tian (də-mĭsh'ən). A.D. 51–96. Emperor of Rome (81–96) who completed the conquest of Britain.

don¹ (dŏn) ▸*n.* **1. Don** A Spanish courtesy title for a man. **2.** *Chiefly Brit.* A teacher at a college of Oxford or Cambridge. **3.** The leader of an organized-crime family. [< Lat. *dominus*, lord.]

don² (dŏn) ▸*v.* **donned, don•ning.** To put on (clothing). [< ME *do on*, put on.]

Do•ña (dō'nyä) ▸*n.* A Spanish courtesy title for a woman. [< Lat. *domina*, feminine of *dominus*, lord.]

do•nate (dō'nāt', dō-nāt') ▸*v.* **-nat•ed, -nat•ing.** To give to a fund or cause; contribute. [< Lat. *dōnāre* < *dōnum*, gift.] —**do•na'tion** *n.* —**do'na•tor** *n.*

Don•a•tel•lo (dŏn'ə-tĕl'ō, dō'nä-tĕl'lō). 1386?–1466. Italian sculptor.

done (dŭn) ▸*v.* P.part. of **do¹.** ▸*adj.* **1.** Completely accomplished or finished. **2.** Cooked adequately. **3.** Socially acceptable.

Do•nets Basin (də-nĕts') also **Don•bas** (dŏn'bäs). An industrial region of E Ukraine and SW Russia.

Do•nets'k (də-nĕtsk') A city of E Ukraine ESE of Kiev. Pop. 1,121,400.

dong (dông, dŏng) ▸*n.* See table at **currency.** [Vietnamese < Chin. *tóng*, copper coin.]

Don•i•zet•ti (dŏn'ĭ-zĕt'ē), **Gaetano.** 1797–1848. Italian composer.

don•key (dŏng'kē, dŭng'-, dông'-) ▸*n., pl.* **-keys 1.** The domesticated ass. **2.** *Slang* An obstinate or stupid person. [?]

Donne (dŭn), **John.** 1572–1631. English metaphysical poet.

don•ny•brook (dŏn'ē-brŏŏk') ▸*n.* A free-for-all. See Syns at **brawl.** [After *Donnybrook* fair, Ireland.]

do•nor (dō'nər) ▸*n.* One that contributes, gives, or donates. [< Lat. *dōnātor* < *dōnāre*, give.]

Don River. A river of W Russia flowing about 1,963 km (1,220 mi) into the NE Sea of Azov.

don't (dōnt) ▸ Do not.

do•nut (dō'nŭt', -nət) ▸*n.* Var. of **doughnut.**

doo•dad (dōō'dăd') ▸*n.* *Informal* An unnamed or nameless gadget or trinket. [?]

doo•dle (dōōd'l) ▸*v.* **-dled, -dling.** To scribble aimlessly, esp. when preoccupied. [E. dial.,

fritter away time.] —**doo′dle** *n.*
doo•dle•bug (do͞od′l-bŭg′) ►*n.* See **ant lion** 2. [Perh. < LGer. *dudel*, fool, simpleton.]
doom (do͞om) ►*n.* **1.** Condemnation to a severe penalty. **2.** Fate, esp. a tragic or ruinous one. **3.** Inevitable destruction or ruin. ►*v.* To condemn to ruination or death. See Syns at **condemn.** [< OE *dōm*, judgment.]
doom•say•er (do͞om′sā′ər) ►*n.* One who predicts calamity at every opportunity.
dooms•day (do͞omz′dā′) ►*n.* Judgment Day. [< OE *dōmes dæg*.]
door (dôr, dōr) ►*n.* **1.** A movable panel used to close off an entrance. **2.** An entrance to a room, building, or passage. **3.** A means of approach or access. [< OE *duru.*]
do-or-die (do͞o′ər-dī′) ►*adj.* Requiring supreme effort to avoid dire consequences: *a do-or-die situation.*
door•jamb (dôr′jăm′, dōr′-) ►*n.* Either of the two vertical pieces framing a doorway.
door•keep•er (dôr′kē′pər, dōr′-) ►*n.* One employed to guard an entrance or gateway.
door•knob (dôr′nŏb′, dōr′-) ►*n.* A knob-shaped handle for opening and closing a door.
door•man (dôr′măn′, -mən, dōr′-) ►*n.* An attendant at the entrance of a building.
door•mat (dôr′măt′, dōr′-) ►*n.* **1.** A mat placed before a doorway for wiping the shoes. **2.** *Slang* One who submits meekly to mistreatment by others.
door prize ►*n.* A prize awarded by lottery to a ticketholder at a function.
door•step (dôr′stĕp′, dōr′-) ►*n.* A step leading to a door.
door•yard (dôr′yärd′, dōr′-) ►*n.* The yard in front of the door of a house.
doo•zy or **doo•zie** (do͞o′zē) ►*n., pl.* **-zies** *Slang.* Something extraordinary or bizarre. [Poss. blend of DAISY and *Duesenberg*, a luxury car.]
do•pa (dō′pə) ►*n.* An amino acid formed in the liver and converted to dopamine in the brain. [*d(ihydr)o(xy)p(henyl)a(lanine).*]
do•pa•mine (dō′pə-mēn′) ►*n.* A monoamine neurotransmitter formed in the brain, essential to the normal functioning of the central nervous system. [DOP(A) + *amine*, a nitrogen compound.]
dope (dōp) ►*n.* **1.** *Informal* **a.** A narcotic. **b.** An illicit drug, esp. marijuana. **2.** A narcotic preparation used to stimulate a racehorse. **3.** *Informal* A stupid person. **4.** *Informal* Factual information. ►*v.* **doped, dop•ing** *Informal* **1.** To add or administer a narcotic to. **2.** To figure out (e.g., a puzzle). [Du. *doop*, sauce.] —**dop′er** *n.*
dope•ster (dōp′stər) ►*n.* One who forecasts future events, as in sports or politics.
dop•ey also **dop•y** (dō′pē) ►*adj.* **-i•er, -i•est** *Slang* **1.** Dazed or lethargic, as if drugged. **2.** Stupid; foolish.
Dop•pler effect (dŏp′lər) ►*n. Phys.* An apparent change in the frequency of waves when the source and observer are either approaching or moving apart. [After Christian Johann *Doppler* (1803–53).]
Do•ré (dô-rā′), **(Paul) Gustave.** 1832–83. French artist.
Dor•ic (dôr′ĭk, dŏr′-) ►*n.* A dialect of ancient Greek. —**Dor′ic** *adj.*
Doric order ►*n. Archit.* A classical order marked by heavy fluted columns with plain, saucer-shaped capitals and no base.
dork (dôrk) ►*n. Slang* A stupid, inept, or foolish person. [?] —**dork′y** *adj.*
dorm (dôrm) ►*n. Informal* A dormitory.
dor•mant (dôr′mənt) ►*adj.* **1.** In a state resembling sleep. **2.** Latent. **3.** Temporarily inactive: *a dormant volcano.* **4.** *Biol.* In a condition of suspended growth or development. [< Lat. *dormīre*, to sleep.] —**dor′man•cy** *n.*
dor•mer (dôr′mər) ►*n.* A window set vertically in a gable projecting from a sloping roof. [Obsolete Fr. *dormeor*, sleeping room < *dormir*, to sleep. See DORMANT.]

dormer

dor•mi•to•ry (dôr′mĭ-tôr′ē, -tōr′ē) ►*n., pl.* **-ries 1.** A room providing sleeping quarters for several people. **2.** A residence hall, as at a school. [< Lat. *dormīre*, to sleep.]
dor•mouse (dôr′mous′) ►*n.* A small squirrellike Old World rodent. [ME.]
dor•sal (dôr′səl) ►*adj.* Of, toward, on, or near the back. [< Lat. *dorsum*, back.] —**dor′sal•ly** *adv.*
Dort•mund (dôrt′mənd, -mo͝ont′) A city of W-central Germany NNE of Cologne. Pop. 601,966.
do•ry (dôr′ē, dōr′ē) ►*n., pl.* **-ries.** A small flat-bottomed boat with high sides. [?]
DOS (dŏs, dôs) ►*n. Comp. Sci.* An operating system that resides on a disk.
dose (dōs) ►*n.* A specified quantity of a therapeutic agent to be taken at one time or at stated intervals. ►*v.* **dosed, dos•ing.** To give a dose to. [< Gk. *dosis* < *didonai*, give.] —**dos′age** *n.*
do•sim•e•ter (dō-sĭm′ĭ-tər) ►*n.* An instrument that measures amounts of x-rays or radiation.
Dos Pas•sos (dōs păs′ōs), **John Roderigo.** 1896–1970. Amer. writer.
dos•si•er (dŏs′ē-ā′, dô′sē-ā′) ►*n.* A collection of papers giving detailed information about a particular person or subject. [< OFr., bundle of papers labeled on the back < *dos*, back.]
Dos•to•yev•sky or **Dos•to•ev•ski** (dŏs′tə-yĕf′skē, -toi-, dŭs-), **Feodor Mikhailovich.** 1821–81. Russian writer. —**Dos′to•yev′ski•an** *adj.*
dot (dŏt) ►*n.* **1.** A tiny round mark made by or as if by a pointed instrument; spot. **2.** The short sound or signal used in combination with the dash to represent letters or numbers in a code. **3.** *Mus.* A mark after a note indicating an increase in time value by half. **4.** A decimal point. **5.** *Comp. Sci.* A period that separates

strings of characters, as in e-mail addresses or URLs. ▶*v.* **dot•ted, dot•ting 1.** To mark with a dot. **2.** To cover with or as if with dots. ***idiom:* on (or at) the dot** Exactly at the appointed time. [< OE *dott*, head of a boil.]

dot•age (dō′tĭj) ▶*n.* A deterioration of the mind; senility.

dot•ard (dō′tərd) ▶*n.* A senile person. [< ME *doten*, dote.]

dot-com (dŏt′kŏm′) ▶*adj.* Of or relating to business conducted on the Internet: *dot-com advertising.* ▶*n.* A dot-com company. [Pronunciation of *.com*, used in company Internet addresses.]

dote (dōt) ▶*v.* **dot•ed, dot•ing.** To show excessive love or fondness. [ME *doten.*]

doth (dŭth) ▶*v. Archaic* 3rd pers. sing. pr.t. of **do**[1].

dot matrix ▶*n.* A dense grid of dots used to form characters or designs, as by some computer printers.

dot•ty (dŏt′ē) ▶*adj.* **-ti•er, -ti•est.** Eccentric; daft; absurd. [< ME *doten*, dote.]

Dou•a•la also **Du•a•la** (do͞o-ä′lä). A city of SW Cameroon on the Bight of Biafra. Pop. 1,029,731.

dou•ble (dŭb′əl) ▶*adj.* **1.** Twice as much in size, strength, number, or amount. **2.** Composed of two parts. **3.** Twofold; dual. **4.** Designed for two. **5.** Duplicitous. ▶*n.* **1.** Something increased twofold. **2.** A duplicate; counterpart. **3.** An actor's understudy or stand-in. **4.** A sharp turn; reversal. **5. doubles** *Sports* A game, such as tennis or handball, having two players on each side. **6.** *Baseball* A hit enabling the batter to reach second base. **7.** *Games* A bid doubling one's opponent's bid in bridge. ▶*v.* **-bled, -bling 1.** To make or become twice as great. **2.** To be twice as much as. **3.** To fold in two. **4.** *Baseball* To make a double. **5.** *Games* To challenge with a double in bridge. **6.** To reverse one's direction. **7.** To serve in an additional capacity. ▶*adv.* **1.** To twice the amount or extent; doubly. **2.** Two together; in pairs. **3.** In two: *bent double.* —***phrasal verb:* double up 1.** To bend suddenly, as in pain or laughter. **2.** To share accommodations meant for one person. [< Lat. *duplus.*] —**dou′bly** *adv.*

double agent ▶*n.* A spy working simultaneously for two opposed governments.

double bass (bās) ▶*n.* The largest and lowest-pitched member of the violin family.

double blind ▶*n.* A testing procedure, designed to eliminate biased results, in which the identity of those receiving a test treatment is concealed from both administrators and subjects until after the study is completed. —**dou′ble-blind′** *adj.*

dou•ble-breast•ed (dŭb′əl-brĕs′tĭd) ▶*adj.* Fastened by lapping one edge of the front over the other: *a double-breasted jacket.*

dou•ble-click (dŭb′əl-klĭk′) ▶*v.* To press a button, esp. on a pointing device, twice in rapid succession to activate a command.

dou•ble-cross (dŭb′əl-krôs′, -krŏs′) ▶*v.* To betray by acting in contradiction to a prior agreement. —**dou′ble-cross′** *n.* —**dou′ble-cross′er** *n.*

dou•ble-deal•ing (dŭb′əl-dē′lĭng) ▶*n.* Duplicity; treachery. —**dou′ble-deal′er** *n.* —**dou′ble-deal′ing** *adj.*

dou•ble-deck•er (dŭb′əl-dĕk′ər) ▶*n.* Something, as a vehicle or sandwich, that has two decks or layers. —**dou′ble-deck′er** *adj.*

dou•ble-dig•it (dŭb′əl-dĭj′ĭt) ▶*adj.* Being between 10 and 99 percent: *double-digit inflation.*

dou•ble-en•ten•dre (dŭb′əl-än-tän′drə, do͞o-bläɴ-täɴ′drə) ▶*n.* A word or phrase having a double meaning, esp. when one meaning is risqué. [Obsolete Fr.]

dou•ble-head•er (dŭb′əl-hĕd′ər) ▶*n.* Two games or events held in succession on the same program, esp. in baseball.

double helix ▶*n.* The coiled structure of double-stranded DNA in which strands form a spiral configuration.

double jeopardy ▶*n.* The act of putting a person through a second trial for an offense for which he or she has already been prosecuted or convicted.

dou•ble-joint•ed (dŭb′əl-join′tĭd) ▶*adj.* Having unusually flexible joints, esp. of the limbs or fingers.

double negative ▶*n. Gram.* A construction that employs two negatives, esp. to express a single negation.

Usage: A double negative is considered unacceptable when it is used to convey or reinforce a negative meaning, as in *He didn't say nothing.*

double play ▶*n. Baseball* A play in which two players are put out.

dou•ble•speak (dŭb′əl-spēk′) ▶*n.* See **double talk** 2.

double star ▶*n.* See **binary star.**

dou•blet (dŭb′lĭt) ▶*n.* **1.** A close-fitting jacket formerly worn by European men. **2.** One of a pair of similar things. [< OFr.]

double take ▶*n.* A delayed reaction to an unusual remark or circumstance.

double talk ▶*n.* **1.** Meaningless speech that consists of nonsense syllables mixed with intelligible words; gibberish. **2.** Deliberately ambiguous or evasive language.

dou•bloon (dŭ-blo͞on′) ▶*n.* An obsolete Spanish gold coin. [Sp. *doblón.*]

doubt (dout) ▶*v.* **1.** To be uncertain or skeptical about. **2.** To distrust. ▶*n.* **1.** A lack of certainty or conviction. **2.** A lack of trust. [< Lat. *dubitāre*, waver.] —**doubt′er** *n.*

doubt•ful (dout′fəl) ▶*adj.* **1.** Subject to or causing doubt. **2.** Experiencing or showing doubt. **3.** Of uncertain outcome. **4.** Questionable in character; suspicious. —**doubt′ful•ly** *adv.* —**doubt′ful•ness** *n.*

doubt•less (dout′lĭs) ▶*adv.* **1.** Certainly. **2.** Presumably; probably. ▶*adj.* Certain; assured. —**doubt′less•ly** *adv.*

douche (do͞osh) ▶*n.* **1.** A stream of water or air applied to a body part or cavity. **2.** An instrument for applying a douche. [Fr., shower.] —**douche** *v.*

dough (dō) ▶*n.* **1.** A soft thick mixture of flour and other ingredients that is kneaded, shaped, and baked, esp. as bread or pastry. **2.** *Slang* Money. [< OE *dāg.*] —**dough′y** *adj.*

dough•boy (dō′boi′) ▶*n.* An American infantryman in World War I.

dough•nut also **do•nut** (dō′nŭt′, -nət) ▶*n.* A small ring-shaped cake made of rich light dough and fried in deep fat.

dough•ty (dou′tē) ▶*adj.* **-ti•er, -ti•est.** Stouthearted; brave. [< OE *dohtig.*]

Doug•las (dŭg′ləs), **Stephen Arnold.** 1813–1861. Amer. politician.

Douglas fir ►*n.* A tall evergreen timber tree of NW North America. [After David *Douglas* (1798–1834).]

Doug•lass (dŭg′ləs), **Frederick.** 1817–95. Amer. abolitionist.

Frederick Douglass

dour (do͝or, dour) ►*adj.* **-er, -est 1.** Stern; forbidding. **2.** Silently ill-humored; gloomy. [Prob. < Lat. *dūrus*, hard.] —**dour′ness** *n.*

Dou•ro (dôr′o͞o, dō′ro͞o) A river rising in N-central Spain and flowing about 772 km (480 mi) along the Spanish-Portuguese border to the Atlantic.

douse¹ (dous) ►*v.* **doused, dous•ing 1.** To plunge into liquid; immerse. See Syns at **dip. 2.** To wet thoroughly; drench. **3.** To put out; extinguish. [< obsolete *douse*, strike.] —**dous′er** *n.*

douse² (douz) ►*v.* Var. of **dowse.**

dove¹ (dŭv) ►*n.* **1.** A pigeon or related bird, esp. an undomesticated species. **2.** A person who advocates peace and negotiation instead of war. [< OE **dūfe.*] —**dov′ish** *adj.* —**dov′ish•ness** *n.*

dove² (dōv) ►*v.* P.t. of **dive.** See Regional Note at **wake¹.**

Do•ver (dō′vər) **1.** A municipal borough of SE England on the Strait of Dover opposite Calais, France. Pop. 33,700. **2.** The capital of DE, in the central part. Pop. 27,630.

Dover, Strait of. A narrow channel at the E end of the English Channel between SE England and N France.

dove•tail (dŭv′tāl′) ►*n.* A fan-shaped tenon that forms a tight interlocking joint when fitted into a corresponding mortise. ►*v.* **1.** To join by means of dovetails. **2.** To combine or interlock into a unified whole.

dow•a•ger (dou′ə-jər) ►*n.* **1.** A widow with a title derived from her husband. **2.** An elderly woman of high social station. [< OFr. *douage*, dowry, ult. < Lat. *dōs*, dowry.]

dow•dy (dou′dē) ►*adj.* **-di•er, -di•est.** Lacking stylishness; shabby. [< ME *doude*, unattractive woman.] —**dow′di•ness** *n.*

dow•el (dou′əl) ►*n.* A usu. round pin that fits into a corresponding hole to fasten or align two adjacent pieces. [ME *doule*, part of a wheel.]

dow•er (dou′ər) ►*n.* **1.** The part of a deceased man's real estate allotted by law to his widow for her lifetime. **2.** See **dowry.** ►*v.* To give a dower to; endow. [< Med.Lat. *dōtārium.* See DOWRY.]

down¹ (doun) ►*adv.* **1.** From a higher to a lower place. **2.** In or to a lower position, point, or condition. **3.** Southward: *flew down to Florida.* **4.** To a source: *tracking a rumor down.* **5.** From earlier times or people: *tradition handed down.* **6.** To a concentrated form: *pared the lecture down.* **7.** In writing; on paper: *wrote it all down.* **8.** In partial payment at the time of purchase: *put ten dollars down.* ►*adj.* **1a.** Moving or directed downward: *a down elevator.* **b.** Low or lower: *Stock prices are down.* **2.** Sick: *down with a cold.* **3.** Malfunctioning or not operating, esp. temporarily: *The computer is down.* **4.** Low in spirits; depressed: *feeling down today.* **5.** *Sports & Games* Trailing an opponent: *down 20 points.* **6.** Learned or known perfectly: *had algebra down.* ►*prep.* In a descending direction along, upon, into, or through. ►*n.* **1.** A downward movement; descent. **2.** *Football* Any of a series of four plays during which a team must advance at least ten yards to retain possession of the ball. ►*v.* **1.** To bring, put, strike, or throw down. **2.** To swallow hastily. —***idiom:* down on** Hostile toward. [< OE *dūne*, downwards < *dūn*, hill.]

down² (doun) ►*n.* **1.** Fine, soft, fluffy feathers. **2.** Something similar to down. [< ON *dūnn.*] —**down′y** *adj.*

down³ (doun) ►*n.* often **downs** A rolling, grassy, upland expanse. [< OE *dūn.*]

down-and-out (doun′ənd-out′, -ən-) ►*adj.* **1.** Lacking funds, resources, or prospects; destitute. **2.** Incapacitated; prostrate.

down•beat (doun′bēt′) ►*n.* **1.** The downward stroke of a conductor to indicate the first beat of a measure of music. **2.** The first beat of a measure. ►*adj.* Cheerless; pessimistic.

down•cast (doun′kăst′) ►*adj.* **1.** Directed downward: *a downcast glance.* **2.** Low in spirits; depressed. See Syns at **depressed.**

Down East also **down East.** New England, esp. Maine. —**Down East′er** *n.*

down•er (dou′nər) ►*n.* *Slang* **1.** A depressant or sedative drug, such as a barbiturate or tranquilizer. **2.** A depressing experience.

down•fall (doun′fôl′) ►*n.* **1.** A sudden loss of wealth or reputation; ruin. **2.** A downpour. —**down′fall′en** *adj.*

down•grade (doun′grād′) ►*n.* A descending slope, as in a road. ►*v.* **1.** To lower the status or salary of. **2.** To minimize the importance or value of. See Syns at **demote.**

down•heart•ed (doun′här′tĭd) ►*adj.* Low in spirit; depressed. See Syns at **depressed.**

down•hill (doun′hĭl′) ►*adv.* **1.** Down the slope of a hill. **2.** Toward a worse condition. —**down′hill′** *adj.*

down-home (doun′hōm′) ►*adj.* Of or reminiscent of a simple life, esp. that associated with the rural S US.

Down•ing Street (dou′nĭng) ►*n.* The British government.

down•load (doun′lōd′) ►*v.* **1.** To unload. **2.** To transfer (data or programs) from a server or host computer to one's own computer.

down payment ►*n.* A partial payment made at the time of purchase.

down•play (doun′plā′) ►*v.* To minimize the significance of.

down•pour (doun′pôr′, -pōr′) ▶ *n.* A heavy fall of rain.

down•range (doun′rānj′) ▶ *adv. & adj.* In a direction away from the launch site and along the flight line of a missile test range.

down•right (doun′rīt′) ▶ *adj.* **1.** Thoroughgoing; unequivocal: *a downright lie.* **2.** Forthright; candid. ▶ *adv.* Thoroughly.

down•size (doun′sīz′) ▶ *v.* To reduce in size, as a corporation.

down•stage (doun′stāj′) ▶ *adv.* Toward or at the front of a stage. —**down′stage′** *adj.*

down•stairs (doun′stârz′) ▶ *adv.* **1.** Down the stairs. **2.** To or on a lower floor. —**down′stairs′** *adj.* —**down′stairs′** *n.*

down•stream (doun′strēm′) ▶ *adj.* In the direction of a stream's current. —**down′stream′** *adv.*

down•swing (doun′swĭng′) ▶ *n.* **1.** A swing downward, as of a golf club. **2.** A decline, as of a business.

Down syndrome (doun) or **Down's syndrome** (dounz) ▶ *n.* A congenital disorder marked by mild to moderate mental retardation and short stature. [After John L.H. *Down* (1828–96).]

down•time (doun′tīm′) ▶ *n.* The period of time when something is not in operation.

down-to-earth (doun′to͝o-ûrth′, -tə-) ▶ *adj.* Realistic; sensible.

down•town (doun′toun′) ▶ *n.* The business center of a city or town. ▶ *adv.* (doun′toun′). To, toward, or in the business center of a city or town. —**down′town′** *adj.*

down•trod•den (doun′trŏd′n) ▶ *adj.* Oppressed; tyrannized.

down•turn (doun′tûrn′) ▶ *n.* A tendency downward, esp. in economic activity.

down•ward (doun′wərd) ▶ *adv. & adj.* **1.** From a higher to a lower place, point, or level. **2.** From a prior source or earlier time. —**down′ward•ly** *adv.* —**down′wards** *adv.*

down•wind (doun′wĭnd′) ▶ *adv.* In the direction in which the wind blows. —**down′wind′** *adj.*

dow•ry (dou′rē) ▶ *n., pl.* **-ries.** Money or property brought by a bride to her husband at marriage. [< Med.Lat. *dōtārium*, dower < Lat. *dōs*, dowry.]

dowse also **douse** (douz) ▶ *v.* **dowsed, dows•ing** also **doused, dous•ing.** To use a divining rod to search for underground water or minerals. [?]

dows•er (dou′zər) ▶ *n.* **1.** A person who dowses. **2.** A divining rod.

dox•ol•o•gy (dŏk-sŏl′ə-jē) ▶ *n., pl.* **-gies.** An expression of praise to God, esp. a short hymn sung as part of a Christian liturgy. [< Gk. *doxologia*, praise.] —**dox′o•log′i•cal** (dŏk′sə-lŏj′ĭ-kəl) *adj.*

Doyle (doil), Sir **Arthur Conan.** 1859–1930. British writer.

doz. ▶ *abbr.* dozen

doze (dōz) ▶ *v.* **dozed, doz•ing.** To sleep lightly; nap. [Prob. of Scand. orig.] —**doze** *n.*

doz•en (dŭz′ən) ▶ *n.* **1.** *pl.* **dozen** A set of twelve. **2. dozens** An indefinite, large number: *had dozens of errands to run before dinner.* ▶ *adj.* Twelve. [< Lat. *duodecim*, twelve.] —**doz′enth** *adj.*

DP ▶ *abbr.* **1.** data processing **2.** double play

DPhil ▶ *abbr.* Doctor of Philosophy

DPT ▶ *abbr.* diphtheria, pertussis, tetanus (vaccine)

dr ▶ *abbr.* dram

DR ▶ *abbr.* dining room

Dr. ▶ *abbr.* **1.** doctor **2.** drive

drab[1] (drăb) ▶ *adj.* **drab•ber, drab•best 1.** Of a dull light brown or khaki color. **2.** Dull or commonplace; dreary. See Syns at **dull.** [< OFr. *drap*, cloth < LLat. *drappus.*] —**drab** *n.* —**drab′ly** *adv.* —**drab′ness** *n.*

drab[2] (drăb) ▶ *n.* A negligible amount. [Prob. alteration of *drib.*]

drach•ma (drăk′mə) ▶ *n., pl.* **-mas** or **-mae** (-mē) **1.** See table at **currency. 2.** An ancient Greek silver coin. [< Gk. *drakhmē.*]

Dra•co (drā′kō). 7th cent. B.C. Athenian lawgiver and politician.

dra•co•ni•an (drā-kō′nē-ən, drə-) ▶ *adj.* Exceedingly harsh; very severe: *draconian budget cuts.* [After DRACO.]

draft (drăft) ▶ *n.* **1.** A current of air. **2.** A device that controls air circulation. **3a.** The act of pulling loads; traction. **b.** The load pulled or drawn. **4.** *Naut.* The depth of a vessel's keel below the water line. **5.** A document for transferring money. **6a.** A gulp, swallow, or inhalation. **b.** The amount taken in by such an act. **7.** The drawing, or the amount drawn, of a liquid, as from a keg. **8a.** The selection of individuals from a group, as for military duty. **b.** Compulsory enrollment in the armed forces; conscription. **9.** *Sports* A system in which new players are distributed among professional teams. **10.** A preliminary outline of a plan, document, or picture. ▶ *v.* **1.** To take, as for compulsory military service. **2.** To draw up a preliminary version of. ▶ *adj.* **1.** Suited for drawing heavy loads. **2.** Drawn from a cask or tap. [ME *draught*, a drawing.]

draft•ee (drăf-tē′) ▶ *n.* One who is drafted, esp. for military service.

draft•ing (drăf′tĭng) ▶ *n.* The drawing of mechanical and architectural structures to scale.

drafts•man (drăfts′mən) ▶ *n.* One who draws plans or designs, as of structures to be built. —**drafts′man•ship′** *n.*

draft•y (drăf′tē) ▶ *adj.* **-i•er, -i•est.** Having or exposed to drafts of air. —**draft′i•ness** *n.*

drag (drăg) ▶ *v.* **dragged, drag•ging 1.** To pull along with effort, esp. by force; haul. See Syns at **pull. 2.** To pull along the ground. **3.** To search or sweep the bottom of (a body of water), as with a grappling hook. **4.** *Comp. Sci.* **a.** To move (e.g., a mouse) while pressing one of its buttons. **b.** To move (e.g. an icon) on a screen using a pointing device. **5.** To prolong tediously. **6.** To proceed slowly or laboriously. **7.** To draw on a cigarette, pipe, or cigar. ▶ *n.* **1.** The act of dragging. **2.** Something, as a harrow, dragged along the ground. **3.** Something that retards motion or progress. **4.** The degree of resistance involved in dragging or hauling. **5.** *Slang* Something obnoxiously tiresome. **6.** A puff on a cigarette, pipe, or cigar. **7.** *Slang* A street or road: *the main drag.* **8.** The clothing characteristic of one sex when worn by a member of the opposite sex. [Prob. < ON *draga.*] —**drag′ger** *n.*

drag•net (drăg′nĕt′) ▶ *n.* **1.** A system of procedures for apprehending criminal suspects. **2.** A net for trawling.

drag•o•man (drăg′ə-mən) ►*n., pl.* **-mans** or **-men.** An interpreter of Arabic, Turkish, or Persian. [< Ar. *tarjumān.*]

drag•on (drăg′ən) ►*n.* A mythical monster usu. represented as a gigantic winged reptile with lion's claws. [< Gk. *drakōn*, large serpent.]

drag•on•fly (drăg′ən-flī′) ►*n.* Any of an order of large slender insects with two pairs of net-veined wings.

Regional Note: Regional terms for the dragonfly distinguish dialect boundaries in the United States. The South gives us *snake doctor* and the Midland *snake feeder* (both from folk belief). In the Lower South we find *mosquito hawk* and in the South Atlantic states *skeeter hawk.* The insect's shape provides *darning needle* or *devil's darning needle* (Upper Northern); *spindle* (coastal New Jersey); and *ear sewer* (Northern California).

dra•goon (drə-gōōn′, dră-) ►*n.* Formerly, a heavily armed trooper. ►*v.* To subjugate or compel by violent measures; coerce. [< OFr. *dragon*, DRAGON.]

drag race ►*n.* An acceleration race between two cars. —**drag racer** *n.* —**drag racing** *n.*

drag•ster (drăg′stər) ►*n.* **1.** An automobile built or modified for drag racing. **2.** A person who races such an automobile.

drain (drān) ►*v.* **1.** To draw or flow off by a gradual process. **2.** To make or become empty or dry. **3.** To deplete gradually, esp. to the point of exhaustion. ►*n.* **1.** A pipe or channel by which liquid is drawn off. **2.** The act or process of draining. **3a.** A gradual loss; consumption or depletion. **b.** Something that causes a gradual loss. [< OE *drēahnian.*] —**drain′er** *n.*

drain•age (drā′nĭj) ►*n.* **1.** The action or a method of draining. **2.** A system of drains. **3.** Something drained off.

drain•pipe (drān′pīp′) ►*n.* A pipe for carrying off water or sewage.

drake (drāk) ►*n.* A male duck. [ME.]

Drake, Sir **Francis.** 1540?–96. English naval hero and explorer.

dram[1] (drăm) ►*n.* See table at **measurement.** [< Lat. *drachma*, DRACHMA.]

dram[2] (dräm) ►*n.* See table at **currency.** [Armenian.]

dra•ma (drä′mə, drăm′ə) ►*n.* **1.** A prose or verse composition, esp. one for performance by actors; a play. **2.** Plays of a given type or period. **3.** The art of writing or producing dramatic works. **4.** A situation that involves conflicts or suspense and builds to a climax. [< Gk.] —**dra•mat′ic** *adj.* —**dra•mat′i•cal•ly** *adv.*

dra•mat•ics (drə-măt′ĭks) ►*n.* *(takes sing. or pl. v.)* **1.** The art or practice of acting and stagecraft. **2.** Dramatic or stagy behavior.

dram•a•tist (drăm′ə-tĭst, drä′mə-) ►*n.* One who writes plays; playwright.

dram•a•tize (drăm′ə-tīz′, drä′mə-) ►*v.* **-tized, -tiz•ing 1.** To adapt (a literary work) for dramatic presentation, as in a theater. **2.** To present or view in a dramatic or melodramatic way. —**dram′a•ti•za′tion** *n.*

drank (drăngk) ►*v.* P.t. of **drink.**

dr. ap. ►*abbr.* apothecaries' dram

drape (drāp) ►*v.* **draped, drap•ing 1.** To cover, dress, or hang with or as if with cloth in loose folds. **2.** To arrange in loose folds. **3.** To hang or rest limply: *draped my legs over the chair.* ►*n.* **1.** A drapery; curtain. **2.** A cloth arranged over a patient's body during a medical procedure. **3.** The way that a cloth falls or hangs. [< LLat. *drappus*, cloth.]

drap•er•y (drā′pə-rē) ►*n., pl.* **-ies 1.** Cloth gracefully arranged in loose folds. **2.** Heavy fabric hanging straight in loose folds, used as a curtain. **3.** Cloth; fabric.

dras•tic (drăs′tĭk) ►*adj.* Severe or radical in nature; extreme. [Gk. *drastikos*, active < *dran*, do.] —**dras′ti•cal•ly** *adv.*

draught (drăft) ►*n., v., & adj. Chiefly Brit.* Var. of **draft.**

draughts (drăfts, dräfts) ►*n.* *(takes sing. or pl. v.) Chiefly Brit.* The game of checkers. [< ME *draught*, a move at chess.]

dr. avdp. ►*abbr.* avoirdupois dram

Dra•vid•i•an (drə-vĭd′ē-ən) ►*n.* **1.** A large family of languages spoken esp. in S India and N Sri Lanka that includes Tamil, Telugu, and Malayalam. **2.** A speaker of a Dravidian language. —**Dra•vid′i•an** *adj.*

draw (drô) ►*v.* **drew** (drōō), **drawn** (drôn), **draw•ing 1a.** To cause to move in a given direction by applying continuous force; drag. See Syns at **pull. b.** To cause to move in a given direction or to a given position, as by leading: *drew us into the room.* **2.** To cause to flow forth: *a blow that drew blood.* **3.** To suck or take in (e.g., air); inhale. **4.** To take or pull out; extract. **5.** To eviscerate; disembowel. **6.** To attract; entice. **7.** To select or take in. **8.** To bring on oneself as a result; provoke. **9.** To elicit: *drew jeers from the audience.* **10.** To earn; gain: *draw interest.* **11.** To withdraw (money). **12.** To receive on a regular basis: *draw a pension.* **13.** To take or receive by chance: *draw lots.* **14.** *Games* To take (cards) from a dealer or stack. **15.** To end or leave (a contest) tied. **16.** To pull back the string of (a bow). **17a.** To inscribe (a line or lines) with a marking implement. **b.** To make a likeness of on a surface; depict with lines. **18.** To formulate or devise from evidence at hand: *draw a comparison.* **19.** To compose in legal format: *draw a deed.* —***phrasal verbs:*** **draw out** To prolong; protract. **draw up** To compose or write in a set form. ►*n.* **1.** An act or result of drawing. **2:** Something drawn, esp. a lot or card. **3.** An inhalation, as on a pipe or cigar. **4.** Something that attracts interest, customers, or spectators. **5.** A contest ending with neither side winning. —***idioms:*** **draw a blank** To fail to find or remember something. **draw straws** To decide by a lottery with straws of unequal lengths. [< OE *dragan.*]

draw•back (drô′băk′) ►*n.* A disadvantage or inconvenience. See Syns at **disadvantage.**

draw•bridge (drô′brĭj′) ►*n.* A bridge that can be raised or drawn aside to permit passage beneath it.

draw•er (drô′ər) ►*n.* **1.** One that draws, esp. one that draws an order for the payment of money. **2.** (*also* drôr). A sliding boxlike compartment in furniture. **3. drawers** (drôrz) Underpants.

draw•ing (drô′ĭng) ►*n.* **1.** The art of representing objects or forms on a surface by means of lines. **2.** A work so produced.

drawing card ►*n.* An attraction drawing large audiences.

drawing room ►*n.* **1.** A large room in which

guests are entertained. **2.** A large private room on a railroad sleeping car. [< *withdrawing room.*]

drawl (drôl) ►*v.* To speak with lengthened or drawn-out vowels. [Poss. < LGer. *drauelen,* loiter.] —**drawl** *n.*

drawn (drôn) ►*v.* P.part. of **draw.** ►*adj.* Haggard, as from fatigue or ill health.

draw•string (drô′strĭng′) ►*n.* A cord or ribbon run through a hem or casing and pulled to tighten or close an opening.

dray (drā) ►*n.* A low heavy cart without sides. [ME *draie,* cart < OE *dragan,* draw.]

dread (drĕd) ►*v.* **1.** To be in terror of. **2.** To anticipate with alarm, distaste, or reluctance. ►*n.* **1.** Profound fear; terror. **2.** Fearful or distasteful anticipation. ►*adj.* **1.** Causing terror or fear. **2.** Inspiring awe. [< OE *adrǣdan.*]

dread•ful (drĕd′fəl) ►*adj.* **1.** Inspiring dread; terrible. **2.** Extremely unpleasant; distasteful or shocking. —**dread′ful•ly** *adv.* —**dread′ful•ness** *n.*

dread•locks (drĕd′lŏks′) ►*pl.n.* **1.** A natural hairstyle in which the hair is twisted into long matted or ropelike locks. **2.** A similar hairstyle consisting of long thin braids.

dread•nought (drĕd′nôt′) ►*n.* A heavily armed battleship.

dreads (drĕdz) *pl.n. Informal* Dreadlocks.

dream (drēm) ►*n.* **1.** A series of images, ideas, emotions, and sensations occurring during sleep. **2.** A daydream; reverie. **3.** A wild fancy or hope. **4.** An ambition; aspiration. **5.** One that is exceptionally gratifying, excellent, or beautiful. ►*v.* **dreamed** or **dreamt** (drĕmt), **dream•ing 1.** To experience a dream in sleep. **2.** To daydream. **3.** To aspire. **4.** To conceive of; imagine. **5.** To pass (time) idly or in reverie. —***phrasal verb:* dream up** To invent; concoct. [< OE *drēam,* joy.] —**dream′er** *n.* —**dream′i•ly** *adv.* —**dream′i•ness** *n.* —**dream′y** *adj.*

dream•land (drēm′lănd′) ►*n.* **1.** An ideal or imaginary land. **2.** A state of sleep.

drear (drîr) ►*adj.* Dreary.

drea•ry (drîr′ē) ►*adj.* **-ri•er, -ri•est 1.** Dismal; bleak. **2.** Boring; dull. [< OE *drēor,* blood, gore.] —**drea′ri•ly** *adv.* —**drea′ri•ness** *n.*

dredge[1] (drĕj) ►*n.* **1.** A machine used to deepen harbors and waterways. **2.** *Naut.* A boat or barge equipped with a dredge. **3.** A net fixed to a frame, used for gathering shellfish. ►*v.* **dredged, dredg•ing.** To deepen or bring up with or as if with a dredge. [ME *dreg-* < OE *dragan,* draw.] —**dredg′er** *n.*

dredge[2] (drĕj) ►*v.* **dredged, dredg•ing.** To coat (food) by sprinkling, as with flour. [< Gk. *tragēmata,* sweetmeats.]

dregs (drĕgz) ►*pl.n.* **1.** The sediment in a liquid; lees. **2.** The least desirable portion. [< ON *dregg.*]

drei•del also **drei•dl** (drād′l) ►*n.* A small spinning top used in games played at Hanukkah. [Yiddish *dreydl* < *dreyen,* to turn.]

Drei•ser (drī′sər, -zər), **Theodore Herman Albert.** 1871–1945. Amer. writer and editor.

drench (drĕnch) ►*v.* To wet thoroughly; soak. [< OE *drencan,* give to drink.]

Dres•den (drĕz′dən) A city of E-central Germany on the Elbe R. ESE of Leipzig. Pop. 479,273.

dress (drĕs) ►*v.* **1.** To put clothes on; clothe. **2.** To decorate or adorn. **3.** To arrange a display in. **4.** To apply medication or bandages. **5.** To arrange (the hair). **6.** To clean (fish or fowl) for cooking or sale. **7.** To wear formal clothes. —***phrasal verbs:* dress down** To scold; reprimand. **dress up** To wear formal or fancy clothes. ►*n.* **1.** Clothing; apparel. **2.** A style of clothing. **3.** A one-piece outer garment for women or girls. ►*adj.* **1.** Suitable for formal occasions. **2.** Requiring formal clothes. [< OFr. *drecier,* arrange < Lat. *dīrigere,* DIRECT.]

dreidel

dres•sage (drə-säzh′, drĕ-) ►*n.* The guiding of a horse through a series of complex maneuvers by slight movements of the hands, legs, and weight.

dress•er[1] (drĕs′ər) ►*n.* One that dresses or assists in dressing.

dress•er[2] (drĕs′ər) ►*n.* A chest of drawers used for holding clothes and personal items. [< OFr. *dreceur,* table for preparing food < *drecier,* arrange. See DRESS.]

dress•ing (drĕs′ĭng) ►*n.* **1.** Therapeutic material applied to a wound. **2.** A sauce, as for salads. **3.** A stuffing, as for poultry.

dressing gown ►*n.* A robe worn for lounging.

dressing table ►*n.* A low table with a mirror at which one sits while applying makeup.

dress•mak•er (drĕs′mā′kər) ►*n.* A tailor of women's clothing. —**dress′mak′ing** *n.*

dress•y (drĕs′ē) ►*adj.* **-i•er, -i•est 1.** Showy or elegant in dress. **2.** Smart; stylish. —**dress′i•ness** *n.*

drew (dro͞o) ►*v.* P.t. of **draw.**

Drey•fus (drī′fəs, drā-), **Alfred.** 1859–1935. French army officer.

drib•ble (drĭb′əl) ►*v.* **-bled, -bling 1.** To flow or fall in drops or an unsteady stream; trickle. **2.** To let saliva drip from the mouth; drool. **3.** *Sports* To move (a ball) by repeated light bounces or kicks, as in basketball or soccer. [Frequentative of obsolete *drib,* alteration of DRIP.] —**drib′ble** *n.* —**drib′bler** *n.*

drib•let (drĭb′lĭt) ►*n.* **1.** A falling drop of liquid. **2.** A small amount or portion. [< alteration of DRIP.]

dried (drīd) ►*v.* P.t. and p.part. of **dry.**

dri•er[1] also **dry•er** (drī′ər) ►*n.* A substance added to paint, varnish, or ink to speed drying.

dri•er[2] (drī′ər) ►*adj.* Comp. of **dry.**

dries (drīz) ►*v.* 3rd pers. sing. pr.t. of **dry.**

dri•est (drī′ĭst) ►*adj.* Superl. of **dry.**

drift (drĭft) ►*v.* **1.** To be carried along by currents of air or water. **2.** To move unhurriedly and smoothly. **3.** To move from place to place, esp. without purpose or regular employment. **4.** To wander; stray. **5.** To be piled up in banks or heaps by the force of a current. ►*n.* **1.** The act or condition of drifting. **2.** Something that drifts. **3.** A bank or pile, as of sand or snow, heaped up by currents of air or water. **4.** A general trend, as of opinion. **5.** The main idea; gist. [< ME, act of driving.] —**drift′y** *adj.*

drift•er (drĭf′tər) ► *n.* A person who moves aimlessly from place to place or job to job.

drift net ► *n.* A large fishing net buoyed up by floats that is carried along with the current or tide.

drift•wood (drĭft′wo͝od′) ► *n.* Wood floating in or washed up by the water.

drill[1] (drĭl) ► *n.* **1.** An implement for boring holes in hard materials. **2.** Disciplined, repetitious exercise as a means of teaching a skill or procedure. **3.** A task or exercise for teaching a skill or procedure. ► *v.* **1.** To make a hole with a drill. **2.** To instruct thoroughly by repetition. [< MDu. *drillen*, to bore.] —**drill′er** *n.*

drill[2] (drĭl) ► *n.* **1.** A shallow trench or furrow in which seeds are planted. **2.** A row of planted seeds. **3.** An implement for planting seeds. [?] —**drill** *v.*

drill[3] (drĭl) ► *n.* Durable cotton or linen twill. [< Lat. *trilīx*, triple-twilled.]

drill instructor ► *n.* A noncommissioned officer who instructs recruits in military drill and discipline.

drill•mas•ter (drĭl′măs′tər) ► *n.* A military drill instructor.

drill press ► *n.* A powered vertical drilling machine in which the drill is pressed to the work automatically or by a hand lever.

drink (drĭngk) ► *v.* **drank** (drăngk), **drunk** (drŭngk), **drink•ing 1.** To swallow (a liquid). **2.** To soak up; absorb. **3.** To take in eagerly through the senses or intellect: *drank in every word.* **4a.** To propose (a toast). **b.** To toast (e.g., a person). **5.** To imbibe alcoholic liquors, esp. to excess. ► *n.* **1.** A liquid for drinking; beverage. **2.** An amount of liquid swallowed. **3.** An alcoholic beverage. **4.** Excessive indulgence in alcohol. [< OE *drincan.*] —**drink′a•bil′i•ty** *n.* —**drink′a•ble** *adj.* —**drink′er** *n.*

drip (drĭp) ► *v.* **dripped, drip•ping 1.** To fall or let fall in drops. **2.** To shed drops. ► *n.* **1.** The process of forming and falling in drops. **2.** Liquid that falls in drops. **3.** The sound made by dripping liquid. **4.** *Slang* A tiresome person. [ME *drippen.*]

drip•pings (drĭp′ĭngz) ► *pl.n.* The fat and juices exuded from roasting meat.

drive (drīv) ► *v.* **drove** (drōv), **driv•en** (drĭv′ən), **driv•ing 1.** To push, propel, or urge onward forcibly. **2.** To repulse forcefully; put to flight. **3a.** To guide, control, or direct (a vehicle). **b.** To operate or be transported in a vehicle. **4.** To motivate; cause to function: *Steam drives the engine.* **5.** To compel or force to work, often excessively. **6.** To force into a particular act or state: *drives me crazy.* **7.** To force to go through or penetrate: *drive a nail.* **8.** To carry through vigorously to a conclusion. **9.** To throw or strike (e.g., a ball), hard or rapidly. **10.** To rush or advance violently: *The wind drove into my face.* —***phrasal verb:* drive at** To mean to do or say. ► *n.* **1.** A trip or journey in a vehicle. **2.** A road, esp. a driveway, for vehicles. **3.** The apparatus for transmitting motion or power to or in a machine. **4.** *Comp. Sci.* A device that reads data from and writes data onto a storage medium, such as a floppy disk. **5.** A strong organized effort to accomplish a purpose. See Syns at **campaign. 6.** Energy; initiative. **7.** *Psychol.* A strong motivating tendency or instinct. **8.** A massive sustained military offensive. **9.** The act of propelling a ball forcefully. **10.** The act of driving cattle. [< OE *drīfan.*] —**driv′a•bil′i•ty** *n.* —**driv′a•ble** *adj.*

drive-by (drīv′bī′) ► *adj.* Performed from a moving vehicle: *a drive-by shooting.* —**drive′-by′** *n.*

drive-in (drīv′ĭn′) ► *n.* An establishment, esp. an outdoor movie theater, that permits customers to remain in their motor vehicles while being accommodated. —**drive′-in′** *adj.*

driv•el (drĭv′əl) ► *v.* **-eled, -el•ing** or **-elled, -el•ling 1.** To slobber; drool. **2.** To talk stupidly or childishly. [< OE *dreflian.*] —**driv′el** *n.* —**driv′el•er** *n.*

drive•line (drīv′līn′) ► *n.* The components of an automotive vehicle that connect the transmission with the driving axles and include the universal joint and drive shaft.

driv•er (drī′vər) ► *n.* **1.** One that drives. **2.** A tool, such as a screwdriver, used to impart forceful pressure on another object. **3.** A golf club used for long shots from the tee.

drive shaft ► *n.* A rotating shaft that transmits mechanical power from an engine to a point of application.

drive train ► *n.* See **driveline.**

drive•way (drīv′wā′) ► *n.* A short private road, as to a house or garage.

driz•zle (drĭz′əl) ► *v.* **-zled, -zling.** To rain gently in fine mistlike drops. [< ME *drisning*, fall of dew.] —**driz′zle** *n.* —**driz′zly** *adj.*

drogue (drōg) ► *n.* A parachute used to slow a fast-moving object, such as a spacecraft during reentry. [Poss. < DRAG.]

droll (drōl) ► *adj.* **-er, -est.** Amusingly odd or whimsically comical. [Fr. *drôle.*] —**droll′er•y, droll′ness** *n.* —**drol′ly** *adv.*

-drome ► *suff.* **1.** Racecourse: *hippodrome.* **2.** Field; arena: *airdrome.* [< Gk. *dromos*, racecourse.]

drom•e•dar•y (drŏm′ĭ-dĕr′ē, drŭm′-) ► *n., pl.* **-ies.** The one-humped domesticated camel of N Africa and W Asia. [< LLat. *dromedārius* < Gk. *dromas*, running.]

drone[1] (drōn) ► *n.* **1.** A male bee, esp. a honeybee. **2.** An idle person who lives off others. **3.** A pilotless, remote-controlled aircraft. [< OE *drān.*]

drone[2] (drōn) ► *v.* **droned, dron•ing 1.** To make a continuous low dull humming sound. **2.** To speak in a monotonous tone. [Prob. < DRONE[1].] —**drone** *n.*

drool (dro͞ol) ► *v.* **1.** To let saliva run from the mouth; drivel. **2.** *Informal* To make an extravagant show of desire. [Perh. alteration of DRIVEL.] —**drool** *n.*

droop (dro͞op) ► *v.* **1.** To bend or hang downward. **2.** To sag in dejection or exhaustion. [< ON *drūpa.*] —**droop** *n.* —**droop′i•ly, droop′ing•ly** *adv.* —**droop′y** *adj.*

drop (drŏp) ► *n.* **1.** A quantity of liquid heavy enough to fall in a spherical mass. **2.** Something resembling a drop. **3.** The act of falling. **4.** A swift decline or decrease, as in quality. **5.** The vertical distance from a higher to a lower level. **6.** A sheer incline, such as a cliff. **7.** Personnel and equipment landed by parachute. **8.** A place where something, such as mail, is brought and distributed. ► *v.* **dropped, drop•ping 1.** To fall or let fall in drops. **2.** To fall or let fall from a higher to a lower place. **3.** To become less, as in amount or intensity. **4.** To descend. **5.** To sink into a state of exhaustion. **6.** To pass into a specified condition: *dropped into a doze.* **7.** To say or offer casually: *drop a hint.* **8.** To write at leisure: *drop me a note.* **9.** To cease consideration or treatment of: *drop the subject.* **10.** To stop participating in; quit: *drop a course.* **11.** To fire. See Syns at **dismiss. 12.** To leave out (e.g., a letter) in speaking or writing. —***phrasal verbs:* drop by** To visit briefly. **drop off** To fall asleep. **drop out 1.** To leave school without graduating. **2.** To withdraw from society. [< OE *dropa.*]

drop•let (drŏp′lĭt) ►*n.* A tiny drop.

drop-off (drŏp′ôf′, -ŏf′) ►*n.* **1.** An abrupt downward slope. **2.** A noticeable decrease.

drop•out (drŏp′out′) ►*n.* One who drops out, as from school.

drop•per (drŏp′ər) ►*n.* A small tube with a suction bulb at one end for drawing in a liquid and releasing it in drops.

drop•sy (drŏp′sē) ►*n.* Edema. No longer in scientific use. [< Gk. *hudrōps* < *hudōr*, water.] —**drop′si•cal** (-sĭ-kəl) *adj.*

dro•soph•i•la (drō-sŏf′ə-lə, drə-) ►*n.* A fruit fly used extensively in genetic research. [< Gk. *drosos*, dew + NLat. *-philus*, -phile.]

dross (drŏs, drôs) ►*n.* **1.** A waste product formed on the surface of molten metal. **2.** Worthless or trivial matter. [< OE *drōs*, dregs.]

drought (drout) also **drouth** (drouth) ►*n.* **1.** A long period of low rainfall. **2.** A prolonged dearth or shortage. [< OE *drūgoth.*]

drove[1] (drōv) ►*v.* P.t. of **drive.**

drove[2] (drōv) ►*n.* A flock, herd, or large group being driven or moving in a body. [< OE *drāf* < *drīfan*, drive.]

drov•er (drō′vər) ►*n.* One who drives cattle or sheep.

drown (droun) ►*v.* **1.** To die or kill by suffocating in water or another liquid. **2.** To cover with or as if with a liquid. **3.** To mask (a sound) by a louder sound. [ME *drounen.*]

drowse (drouz) ►*v.* **drowsed, drows•ing.** To be half-asleep; doze. [Perh. < OE *drūsian*, be sluggish.] —**drowse** *n.*

drows•y (drou′zē) ►*adj.* **-i•er, -i•est 1.** Sleepy. **2.** Causing sleepiness; soporific. —**drows′i•ly** *adv.* —**drows′i•ness** *n.*

dr. t. ►*abbr.* troy dram

drub (drŭb) ►*v.* **drubbed, drub•bing 1.** To thrash with a stick. **2.** To instill forcefully. **3.** To defeat thoroughly. [Perh. Ar. *ḍaraba*, to beat.] —**drub′ber** *n.*

drudge (drŭj) ►*n.* A person who does tedious, menial, or unpleasant work. ►*v.* **drudged, drudg•ing.** To do the work of a drudge. [< ME *druggen*, to labor.] —**drudg′er•y** *n.*

drug (drŭg) ►*n.* **1.** A medicine used in treating a disease. **2.** A narcotic or hallucinogen. ►*v.* **drugged, drug•ging 1.** To administer a drug to. **2.** To mix a drug into (food or drink). **3.** To stupefy or dull with or as if with a drug. [< OFr. *drogue.*]

drug•gist (drŭg′ĭst) ►*n.* A pharmacist.

drug•store also **drug store** (drŭg′stôr′, -stōr′) ►*n.* A store where prescriptions are filled and drugs and other articles are sold.

dru•id also **Dru•id** (dro͞o′ĭd) ►*n.* A member of an order of priests in ancient Gaul and Britain who appear in legend as prophets and sorcerers. [< Lat. *druidēs*, druids, of Celt. orig.] —**dru•id′ic, dru•id′i•cal** *adj.* —**dru′id•ism** *n.*

drum (drŭm) ►*n.* **1.** A percussion instrument consisting of a hollow cylinder with a membrane stretched tightly over one or both ends, played by beating with the hands or sticks. **2.** Something like a drum in shape or structure. ►*v.* **drummed, drum•ming 1.** To play or perform on a drum. **2.** To thump or tap rhythmically or continually. **3.** To summon by or as if by beating a drum. **4.** To instill by constant repetition: *drummed the answers into my head.* **5.** To expel or dismiss in disgrace: *was drummed out of the army.* —***phrasal verb:* drum up** To bring about by continuous effort: *drum up new business.* [ME *drom* < MDu. *tromme.*] —**drum′mer** *n.*

drum•beat (drŭm′bēt′) ►*n.* The sound produced by beating a drum.

drum•lin (drŭm′lĭn) ►*n.* An elongated hill or ridge of glacial drift. [< Ir.Gael. *druim*, ridge.]

drum major ►*n.* A man who leads a marching band, often twirling a baton.

drum ma•jor•ette (mā′jə-rĕt′) ►*n.* A woman who leads a marching band, often twirling a baton.

drum•stick (drŭm′stĭk′) ►*n.* **1.** A stick for beating a drum. **2.** The lower part of the leg of a cooked fowl.

drunk (drŭngk) ►*v.* P.part. of **drink.** ►*adj.* **1.** Intoxicated with alcohol; inebriated. **2.** Overcome by emotion: *drunk with power.* ►*n.* **1.** A drunkard. **2.** A bout of drinking.

drunk•ard (drŭng′kərd) ►*n.* One who is habitually drunk.

drunk•en (drŭng′kən) ►*adj.* **1.** Intoxicated: *a drunken guest.* **2.** Habitually drunk. **3.** Of or occurring during intoxication: *a drunken brawl.* —**drunk′en•ly** *adv.* —**drunk′en•ness** *n.*

drupe (dro͞op) ►*n.* A fleshy fruit, as a peach or plum, with a single hard stone that encloses a seed. [< Gk. *drupa*, olive.]

drupe•let (dro͞op′lĭt) ►*n.* A small drupe, such as one of the many subdivisions of a raspberry or blackberry.

dry (drī) ►*adj.* **dri•er, dri•est** or **dry•er, dry•est 1.** Free or freed from liquid or moisture. **2.** Marked by little or no rain. **3.** Not under water. **4.** No longer yielding milk: *a dry cow.* **5.** Lacking a mucous or watery discharge: *a dry cough.* **6.** Thirsty. **7.** Of solid rather than liquid commodities: *dry weight.* **8.** Not sweet: *a dry wine.* **9.** Matter-of-fact; impersonal. **10.** Wearisome; dull: *a dry lecture.* **11.** Humorous in a subtle way: *dry wit.* **12.** Prohibiting the sale of alcoholic beverages. ►*v.* **dried, dry•ing 1.** To make or become dry. **2.** To preserve food by extracting the moisture. [< OE *drȳge.*] —**dry′ly, dri′ly** *adv.* —**dry′ness** *n.*

Syns: *dry, dehydrate, desiccate, parch* ***Ant:*** *moisten* **v.**

dry•ad (drī′əd, -ăd′) ►*n. Gk. Myth.* A wood nymph. [< Gk. *Druas*, *Druad-*.]

dry cell ►*n.* An electric cell having an electrolyte in the form of moist paste.

dry-clean (drī′klēn′) ►*v.* To clean (fabrics) with chemical solvents that have little or no water. —**dry cleaner** *n.* —**dry cleaning** *n.*

Dry•den (drīd′n), **John.** 1631–1700. English writer.

dry dock ►*n.* A large basinlike dock from

which the water can be emptied, used for building or repairing ships.

dry•er (drī′ər) ►*n.* **1.** An appliance that removes moisture. **2.**Var. of **drier**[1].

dry farming ►*n.* Farming practiced in arid areas without irrigation. —**dry′-farm′** *v.*

dry goods ►*pl.n.* Textiles, clothing, and related articles of trade.

dry ice ►*n.* Solid carbon dioxide used primarily as a coolant.

dry measure ►*n.* A system of units for measuring dry commodities such as grains.

dry rot ►*n.* A fungous disease of plants in which the tissue remains relatively dry.

dry run ►*n.* A trial exercise or rehearsal, as a military exercise without live ammunition.

dry wall or **dry•wall** (drī′wôl′) ►*n.* Plasterboard.

DSC ►*abbr.* Distinguished Service Cross

DSM ►*abbr.* Distinguished Service Medal

DSO ►*abbr.* Distinguished Service Order

d.s.p. ►*abbr. Lat.* decessit sine prole (died without issue)

DST ►*abbr.* daylight-saving time

DTP ►*abbr.* diphtheria, tetanus, pertussis (vaccine)

DTs or **DT's** (dē′tēz′) ►*n. (takes sing. or pl. v.)* Delirium tremens.

du•al (do͞o′əl, dyo͞o′-) ►*adj.* **1.** Composed of two parts; double. **2.** Having a double character or purpose. [Lat. *duālis* < *duo*, two.] —**du•al′i•ty** (-ăl′ĭ-tē) *n.* —**du′al•ly** *adv.*

Du•a•la (do͞o-ä′lä) See **Douala.**

du•al•ism (do͞o′ə-lĭz′əm, dyo͞o′-) ►*n.* **1.** The condition of being dual. **2.** *Philos.* The view that the world consists of two fundamental entities, such as mind and matter. —**du′al•is′tic** *adj.*

dub[1] (dŭb) ►*v.* **dubbed, dub•bing 1.** To confer knighthood on. **2.** To give a nickname. [< OE *dubbian.*]

dub[2] (dŭb) ►*v.* **dubbed, dub•bing 1a.** To transfer (recorded material) onto a new recording medium. **b.** To copy (a record or tape). **2.** To insert a new sound track into (a film). **3.** To add (sound) into a film or tape. [< DOUBLE.] —**dub** *n.* —**dub′ber** *n.*

Du Bar•ry (do͞o băr′ē, dyo͞o-, dü bä-rē′), Comtesse. Marie Jeanne Bécu. 1743–93. French courtier and lover of Louis XV.

Du•bayy or **Du•bai** (do͞o-bī′). A city and sheikdom of E United Arab Emirates on the Persian Gulf. Pop. 265,702.

du•bi•e•ty (do͞o-bī′ĭ-tē, dyo͞o-) ►*n., pl.* **-ties 1.** A feeling of uncertainty. **2.** A matter of doubt. [LLat. *dubietās* < Lat. *dubius*, doubtful.]

du•bi•ous (do͞o′bē-əs, dyo͞o′-) ►*adj.* **1.** Fraught with uncertainty; undecided. **2.** Arousing doubt; questionable. [< Lat. *dubius.*] —**du′bi•ous•ly** *adv.* —**du′bi•ous•ness** *n.*

Dub•lin (dŭb′lĭn) The capital of Ireland, in the E-central part on the Irish Sea. Pop. 533,929. —**Dub′lin•er** *n.*

dub•ni•um (do͞ob′nē-əm) ►*n. Symbol* **Db** A short-lived, synthetic radioactive element. At. no. 105. See table at **element.**

Du Bois (do͞o bois′), **W(illiam) E(dward) B(urghardt).** 1868–1963. Amer. writer and civil rights leader.

du•cal (do͞o′kəl, dyo͞o′-) ►*adj.* Of or relating to a duke or dukedom.

duc•at (dŭk′ət) ►*n.* Any of various gold coins formerly used in Europe. [< Med.Lat. *ducātus*, DUCHY.]

duch•ess (dŭch′ĭs) ►*n.* **1.** A woman holding title to a duchy. **2.** The wife or widow of a duke. [< Med.Lat. *ducissa* < Lat. *dux*, leader.]

duch•y (dŭch′ē) ►*n., pl.* **-ies.** The territory ruled by a duke or duchess; dukedom. [< Med. Lat. *ducātus* < Lat. *dux*, leader.]

duck[1] (dŭk) ►*n.* **1.** Any of various water birds having a broad flat bill, short legs, and webbed feet. **2.** A female duck. [< OE *dūce.*]

duck[2] (dŭk) ►*v.* **1.** To lower quickly, esp. to avoid something. **2.** To evade; dodge. **3.** To push suddenly under water. See Syns at **dip.** [ME *douken*, dive.] —**duck** *n.*

duck[3] (dŭk) ►*n.* **1.** A durable, closely woven cotton fabric. **2. ducks** Clothing made of duck, esp. white trousers. [< MDu. *doec*, cloth.]

duck•bill (dŭk′bĭl′) ►*n.* See **platypus.**

duck•board (dŭk′bôrd′, -bōrd′) ►*n.* A board or boardwalk laid across wet or muddy ground or flooring.

duck•ling (dŭk′lĭng) ►*n.* A young duck.

duck•pin (dŭk′pĭn′) ►*n.* **1.** A bowling pin shorter and squatter than a tenpin. **2. duckpins** *(takes sing. v.)* A bowling game played with such pins.

duck•weed (dŭk′wēd′) ►*n.* Any of various small, free-floating, stemless aquatic flowering plants.

duck•y (dŭk′ē) ►*adj.* **-i•er, -i•est** *Slang.* Excellent; fine.

duct (dŭkt) ►*n.* **1.** A channel for conveying a substance, esp. a liquid or gas. **2.** *Anat.* A tubular bodily passage, esp. one for carrying glandular secretions. **3.** A tube or pipe for enclosing electrical cables or wires. [Lat. *ductus*, act of leading < *dūcere*, to lead.] —**duct′ed** *adj.* —**duct′less** *adj.*

duc•tile (dŭk′təl, -tīl′) ►*adj.* **1.** Easily drawn into wire or hammered thin. **2.** Capable of being readily influenced; tractable. [< Lat. *ductilis* < *dūcere*, to lead.] —**duc•til′i•ty** (-tĭl′ĭ-tē), **duc′ti•li•bil′i•ty** *n.*

duct•less gland (dŭkt′lĭs) ►*n.* See **endocrine gland.**

dud (dŭd) ►*n.* **1.** A bomb, shell, or explosive that fails to detonate. **2.** *Informal* One that is disappointingly ineffective or unsuccessful. **3. duds** *Informal* Clothing or personal belongings. [ME *dudde*, cloak.]

dude (do͞od, dyo͞od) ►*n.* **1.** *Informal* An Easterner or city person vacationing on a ranch in the West. **2.** *Informal* A dandy. **3.** *Slang* A fellow; chap. ►*v.* **dud•ed, dud•ing.** *Slang* To dress elaborately. [?]

dude ranch ►*n.* A resort patterned after a Western ranch, featuring outdoor activities.

dudg•eon (dŭj′ən) ►*n.* A sullen, angry, or indignant humor. [?]

Dud•ley (dŭd′lē), **Robert.** 1st Earl of Leicester. 1532?–88. English courtier.

due (do͞o, dyo͞o) ►*adj.* **1.** Payable immediately or on demand. **2.** Owed as a debt or right; owing. **3.** Meeting special requirements; sufficient. **4.** Expected or scheduled. **5.** Anticipated; looked for. **6.** Capable of being attributed. See Usage Note at **due to.** ►*n.* **1.** Something owed or deserved. **2. dues** A membership fee. ►*adv.* Straight; directly: *due west.* [< OFr. *deu* < Lat. *dēbēre*, owe.]

du•el (do͞o′əl, dyo͞o′-) ►*n.* **1.** A prearranged formal combat between two persons, usu. fought to settle a point of honor. **2.** A struggle for domination between two persons or groups. ▸*v.* **-eled, -el•ing** or **-elled,** or **-el•ling.** To fight in a duel. [< Lat. *duellum*, war.] —**du′el•er, du′el•ist** *n.*

due process ▸*n.* An established course for judicial proceedings designed to safeguard the legal rights of the individual.

du•et (do͞o-ĕt′, dyo͞o-) ▸*n.* **1.** *Mus.* A composition for two voices or instruments. **2.** The two performers of such a composition. [Ital. *duetto*, dim. of *duo* < Lat. *duō*, two.]

due to ▸*prep.* Because of.

Usage: According to some critics, it is incorrect to say *The concert was canceled due to the rain,* where *due to* is a compound preposition, as opposed to the acceptable *The cancellation of the concert was due to the rain,* where *due* functions as an adjective modifying *cancellation.*

duff•er (dŭf′ər) ▸*n. Informal* An incompetent or dull-witted person. [?]

duf•fle bag (dŭf′əl) or **duf•fel bag** ▸*n.* A large cylindrical cloth bag for carrying personal belongings.

duffle bag

dug¹ (dŭg) ▸*n.* A breast or teat. [?]

dug² (dŭg) ▸*v.* P.t. and p.part. of **dig.**

dug•out (dŭg′out′) ▸*n.* **1.** A boat or canoe made of a hollowed-out log. **2.** A pit dug into the ground or on a hillside and used as a shelter. **3.** *Baseball* A sunken shelter at the side of a field where players stay while not on the field.

duh (dŭ) ▸*interj.* Used to express disdain, esp. for something deemed obvious. [Imit. of utterance attributed to stupid people.]

DUI ▸*abbr.* driving under the influence (of drugs or alcohol)

Duis•burg (do͞os′bûrg′, do͞oz′-) A city of W-central Germany at the confluence of the Rhine and Ruhr rivers. Pop. 536,797.

du jour (də zho͝or, do͞o) ▸*adj.* **1.** Offered on a given day: *the soup du jour.* **2.** Current: *the trend du jour.* [Fr., of the day.]

duke (do͞ok, dyo͞ok) ▸*n.* **1.** A nobleman with the highest hereditary rank, esp. in Great Britain. **2.** A sovereign prince who rules an independent duchy. **3.** often **dukes** *Slang* A fist: *Put up your dukes!* ▸*v.* **duked, duk•ing.** To fight, esp. with fists: *duking it out.* [< Lat. *dux*, leader.] —**duke′dom** *n.*

dul•cet (dŭl′sĭt) ▸*adj.* **1.** Pleasing to the ear; melodious. **2.** Soothing; agreeable. [< OFr. *doucet* < Lat. *dulcis.*]

dul•ci•mer (dŭl′sə-mər) ▸*n. Mus.* **1.** A zitherlike instrument played by striking with padded hammers. **2.** A long, narrow, usu. four-stringed fretted instrument played by plucking or strumming. [< OFr. *doulcemer.*]

dull (dŭl) ▸*adj.* **-er, -est 1.** Intellectually obtuse; stupid. **2.** Lacking alertness; insensitive. **3.** Dispirited; depressed. **4.** Not brisk or rapid; sluggish. **5.** Not having a sharp edge; blunt. **6.** Not keenly felt. **7.** Uninteresting; boring. **8.** Not bright or vivid. **9.** Muffled; indistinct. ▸*v.* To make or become dull. [ME *dul.*] —**dull′ish** *adj.* —**dull′ness, dul′ness** *n.* —**dul′ly** *adv.*

Syns: *dull, colorless, drab, humdrum, lackluster, pedestrian, stodgy, uninspired* ***Ant:*** *lively* ***adj.***

dull•ard (dŭl′ərd) ▸*n.* A mentally dull person; dolt.

Du•luth (də-lo͞oth′) A city of NE MN on Lake Superior opposite Superior, WI. Pop. 85,493.

du•ly (do͞o′lē, dyo͞o′-) ▸*adv.* **1.** In a proper manner. **2.** At the expected time.

Du•mas (do͞o-mä′, dyo͞o-, dü-), **Alexandre.** "Dumas *père.*" 1802–70. French writer.

dumb (dŭm) ▸*adj.* **-er, -est 1.** Stupid; silly. **2.** Unintentional: *dumb luck.* **3.** Lacking the power or faculty of speech: *a dumb animal.* **4.** Temporarily speechless, as with shock or fear. [< OE.] —**dumb′ly** *adv.* —**dumb′ness** *n.*

dumb•bell (dŭm′bĕl′) ▸*n.* **1.** A weight consisting of a short bar with a metal ball or disk at each end lifted for muscular exercise. **2.** *Slang* A stupid person.

dumb•found also **dum•found** (dŭm′found′) ▸*v.* To fill with astonishment and perplexity; confound. [DUMB + (CON)FOUND.]

dum-dum (dŭm′dŭm′) ▸*n.* **1.** A soft-nosed bullet designed to expand on impact. **2.** *Slang* A stupid person. [After *Dum Dum*, India. Sense 2 < DUMB.]

dum•my (dŭm′ē) ▸*n., pl.* **-mies 1.** An imitation of a real object used as a substitute. **2a.** A mannequin used in displaying clothes. **b.** A figure of a person or animal manipulated by a ventriloquist. **3.** A stupid person. **4.** A person secretly in the service of another. **5.** *Print.* A model page with text and illustrations to direct the printer. **6.** *Games* **a.** The partner in bridge who exposes his or her hand to be played by the declarer. **b.** The hand thus exposed. **7.** *Comp. Sci.* A piece of information entered into a computer only to meet prescribed conditions, such as word length. ▸*adj.* **1.** Simulating or replacing something but lacking its function. **2.** Serving as a front for another: *a dummy corporation.* **3.** *Comp. Sci.* Entered or provided only to meet prescribed conditions: *a dummy variable.* [< DUMB.]

dump (dŭmp) ▸*v.* **1.** To release in a large mass. **2.** To empty (material) out of a container or vehicle. **3.** To get rid of; discard. **4.** To place (e.g., goods or stock) on the market in large quantities at a low price. **5.** *Comp. Sci.* To transfer (data) from one place to another, as from a memory to a printout, without processing. ▸*n.* **1.** A place where refuse is dumped. **2.** A storage place; depot. **3.** *Comp. Sci.* An instance or the result of dumping stored data. **4.** *Slang* A poorly maintained or disreputable place. [ME *dumpen.*] —**dump′er** *n.*

dump•ling (dŭmp′lĭng) ▸*n.* **1.** A piece of dough, sometimes filled, cooked in liquid such as soup. **2.** Sweetened dough wrapped around fruit and served as a dessert. [Perh. < *dump*, lump.]

dumps (dŭmps) ▸*pl.n.* A gloomy, melancholy state of mind; depression. [Prob. < Du. *domp*, haze.]

dump truck ▸*n.* A truck having a bed that tilts

backward to dump loose material.
dump•y[1] (dŭm′pē) ▸*adj.* **-i•er, -i•est.** Short and stout; squat. [Prob. < *dump*, lump.] —**dump′i•ly** *adv.*—**dump′i•ness** *n.*
dum•py[2] (dŭm′pē) ▸*adj.* **-i•er, -i•est.** Resembling a dump; shabby; disreputable.
dun[1] (dŭn) ▸*v.* **dunned, dun•ning.** To importune (a debtor) for payment. [?] —**dun** *n.*
dun[2] (dŭn) ▸*n.* A neutral brownish gray. [< OE *dunn.*]
Dun•bar (dŭn′bär), **Paul Laurence.** 1872–1906. Amer. writer.
Dun•can (dŭng′kən), **Isadora.** 1878–1927. Amer. dancer.
dunce (dŭns) ▸*n.* A stupid person. [After John *Duns* Scotus (1265?–1308).]
Dun•dee (dŭn-dē′) A burgh of E-central Scotland. Pop. 170,120.
dun•der•head (dŭn′dər-hĕd′) ▸*n.* A dunce. [Perh. Du. *donder*, thunder + HEAD.]
dune (do͞on, dyo͞on) ▸*n.* A hill or ridge of windblown sand. [< MDu. *dūne.*]
dune buggy ▸*n.* A recreational vehicle having oversize tires designed for use on sand.
dung (dŭng) ▸*n.* Animal excrement; manure. [< OE.]
dun•ga•ree (dŭng′gə-rē′) ▸*n.* **1.** A sturdy, often blue denim fabric. **2. dungarees** Trousers or overalls made of denim. [Hindi *duṁgrī.*]
dun•geon (dŭn′jən) ▸*n.* A dark, often underground prison cell. [Poss. < Med.Lat. *domniō*, lord's tower < Lat. *dominus*, lord.]
dung•hill (dŭng′hĭl′) ▸*n.* A heap of dung.
dunk (dŭngk) ▸*v.* **1.** To plunge into liquid; immerse. See Syns at **dip. 2.** To dip (food) into a liquid food, such as sauce, before eating it. **3.** *Basketball* To slam (a ball) through the basket. **4.** To submerge oneself briefly in water. [Penn. Du. *dunke.*] —**dunk** *n.*
Dun•kirk (dŭn′kûrk′) A city of N France on the North Sea. Pop. 73,120.
du•o (do͞o′ō, dyo͞o′ō) ▸*n., pl.* **-os 1.** *Mus.* A duet. **2.** A pair. [Ital. < Lat. *duō*, two.]
du•o•dec•i•mal (do͞o′ə-dĕs′ə-məl, dyo͞o′-) ▸*adj.* Of or based on the number 12. [< Lat. *duodecim*, twelve.]
du•o•de•num (do͞o′ə-dē′nəm, dyo͞o′-, do͞o-ŏd′n-əm, dyo͞o-) ▸*n., pl.* **du•o•de•na** (-nə) or **du•o•de•nums.** The beginning portion of the small intestine. [< Med.Lat. *intestīnum duodēnum digitōrum*, (intestine) of twelve (fingers' length).] —**du′o•de′nal** *adj.*
dupe (do͞op, dyo͞op) ▸*n.* **1.** An easily deceived person. **2.** A person who functions as the tool of another. ▸*v.* **duped, dup•ing.** To deceive. [< OFr.] —**dup′a•bil′i•ty** *n.* —**dup′a•ble** *adj.* —**dup′er** *n.*
du•ple (do͞o′pəl, dyo͞o′-) ▸*adj.* **1.** Double. **2.** *Mus.* Consisting of two or a multiple of two beats to the measure. [Lat. *duplus.*]
du•plex (do͞o′plĕks′, dyo͞o′-) ▸*adj.* Twofold; double. ▸*n.* A house divided into two living units, usu. with separate entrances. [Lat.]
du•pli•cate (do͞o′plĭ-kĭt, dyo͞o′-) ▸*adj.* **1.** Identically copied from an original. **2.** Existing in two corresponding parts; double. ▸*n.* An identical copy; facsimile. ▸*v.* (-kāt′) **-cat•ed, -cat•ing 1.** To make an exact copy of. **2.** To make or perform again; repeat. [< Lat. *duplicāre*, to double.] —**du′pli•ca′tion** *n.*
du•pli•ca•tor (do͞o′plĭ-kā′tər, dyo͞o′-) ▸*n.* A machine that reproduces printed or written material.
du•plic•i•ty (do͞o-plĭs′ĭ-tē, dyo͞o-) ▸*n., pl.* **-ties.** Deliberate deceptiveness in behavior or speech. [< Lat. *duplex*, *duplic-*, twofold.] —**du•plic′i•tous** *adj.* —**du•plic′i•tous•ness** *n.*
du•ra•ble (do͝or′ə-bəl, dyo͝or′-) ▸*adj.* **1.** Capable of withstanding wear and tear. **2.** *Econ.* Not depleted or consumed by use. [< Lat. *dūrāre*, to last.] —**du′ra•bil′i•ty, du′ra•ble•ness** *n.* —**du′ra•bly** *adv.*
du•ra ma•ter (do͝or′ə mā′tər, mä′-, dyo͝or′ə) ▸*n.* The tough fibrous membrane covering the brain and spinal cord. [< Med.Lat. *dūra mater*, hard mother.]
du•rance (do͝or′əns, dyo͝or′-) ▸*n.* Imprisonment. [< Lat. *dūrāre*, to last.]
Du•ran•go (do͞o-răng′gō) A city of N-central Mexico NNW of Guadalajara. Pop. 257,915.
du•ra•tion (do͞o-rā′shən, dyo͞o-) ▸*n.* **1.** Continuance in time. **2.** A period of existence or persistence. [< Lat. *dūrāre*, to last.]
Dur•ban (dûr′bən) A city of E South Africa on **Durban Bay,** an inlet of the Indian Ocean. Pop. 715,669.
Dü•rer (do͝or′ər, dyo͝or′-, dü′rər), **Albrecht.** 1471–1528. German painter and engraver.
du•ress (do͞o-rĕs′, dyo͞o-) ▸*n.* **1.** Constraint by threat; coercion. **2.** *Law* Illegal coercion or confinement. [< Lat. *dūritia*, hardness.]
Dur•ham (dûr′əm) A city of N-central NC E of Greensboro. Pop. 136,611.
dur•ing (do͝or′ĭng, dyo͝or′-) ▸*prep.* **1.** Throughout the course of. **2.** At some time in. [ME < *duren*, to last < Lat. *dūrāre.*]
du•rum (do͝or′əm, dyo͝or′-, dûr′-, dŭr′-) ▸*n.* A hardy wheat used chiefly in making pasta. [< Lat. *dūrus*, hard.]
Du•se (do͞o′zĕ), **Eleonora.** 1859?–1924. Italian actress.
Du•shan•be (do͞o-shäm′bə) The capital of Tajikistan, in the W part. Pop. 602,000.
dusk (dŭsk) ▸*n.* The darker stage of twilight. [< OE *dox.*]
dusk•y (dŭs′kē) ▸*adj.* **-i•er, -i•est 1.** Marked by inadequate light; shadowy. **2.** Rather dark in color. —**dusk′i•ness** *n.*
Düs•sel•dorf (do͝os′əl-dôrf′, düs′-) A city of W-central Germany on the Rhine R. NNW of Cologne. Pop. 514,936.
dust (dŭst) ▸*n.* **1.** Fine dry particles of matter. **2.** The earthy remains of a dead body. **3.** The surface of the ground. **4.** Something of no worth. ▸*v.* **1.** To remove dust from by wiping or brushing. **2.** To sprinkle with a powdery substance. —***idiom:* in the dust** Far behind, as in a race. [< OE *dūst.*] —**dust′y** *adj.*
dust bowl ▸*n.* A region reduced to aridity by drought and dust storms.
dust devil ▸*n.* A small whirlwind that swirls dust and debris.
dust•er (dŭs′tər) ▸*n.* **1.** One that dusts. **2.** A cloth or brush used to remove dust. **3.** A smock worn to protect clothing from dust. **4.** A woman's loose housecoat.
dust•ing (dŭs′tĭng) ▸*n.* **1.** A light sprinkling. **2.** *Slang* A beating or defeat.
dust•pan (dŭst′păn′) ▸*n.* A short-handled pan into which dust is swept.
dust storm ▸*n.* A severe windstorm that sweeps clouds of dust across an arid region.

Dutch (dŭch) ▶*adj.* **1.** Of or relating to the Netherlands or its people or language. **2.** *Archaic* German. ▶*n.* **1.** The people of the Netherlands. **2.** The Germanic language of the Netherlands. **3.** *Slang* Anger or temper. —***idioms:* go Dutch** To pay one's own expenses on a date. **in Dutch** In trouble. —**Dutch′man** *n.* —**Dutch′wom′an** *n.*

Dutch door ▶*n.* A door divided horizontally so that either part can be left open or closed.

Dutch door

Dutch elm disease ▶*n.* A disease of elm trees caused by a fungus and resulting in death.

Dutch oven ▶*n.* A large heavy pot, usu. of cast iron, used for slow cooking.

Dutch treat ▶*n.* An outing, as for dinner or a movie, in which all persons pay their own expenses.

du•te•ous (do͞o′tē-əs, dyo͞o′-) ▶*adj.* Obedient; dutiful. —**du′te•ous•ly** *adv.*

du•ti•a•ble (do͞o′tē-ə-bəl, dyo͞o′-) ▶*adj.* Subject to import tax.

du•ti•ful (do͞o′tĭ-fəl, dyo͞o′-) ▶*adj.* **1.** Careful to fulfill obligations. **2.** Expressing or filled with a sense of duty. —**du′ti•ful•ly** *adv.* —**du′ti•ful•ness** *n.*

du•ty (do͞o′tē, dyo͞o′-) ▶*n., pl.* **-ties 1.** An act or course of action required of one. **2.** Moral obligation. **3.** A task assigned to one, esp. in the armed forces. **4.** Function or work; service: *jury duty.* See Syns at **function. 5.** A tax charged by a government, esp. on imports. [< AN *duete* < *due*, var. of OFr. *deu*, DUE.]

DVD (dē′vē-dē′) ▶*n.* A high-density compact disk esp. for high-resolution audio-visual data. [*d(igital) v(ideo)d(isk)* and *d(igital) v(ersatile) d(isk).*]

DVM ▶*abbr.* Doctor of Veterinary Medicine

Dvoř•ák (dvôr′zhäk, -zhăk), **Anton.** 1841–1904. Czech composer.

dwarf (dwôrf) ▶*n., pl.* **dwarfs** or **dwarves** (dwôrvz) **1.** An abnormally small, often atypically proportioned person, animal, or plant. **2.** A small creature appearing in fairy tales. ▶*v.* **1.** To check the growth of; stunt. **2.** To cause to appear small by comparison. [< OE *dweorh.*] —**dwarf′ish** *adj.* —**dwarf′ish•ness** *n.*

dwell (dwĕl) ▶*v.* **dwelt** (dwĕlt) or **dwelled, dwell•ing 1.** To live as a resident; reside. **2.** To exist in a given place or state. **3a.** To fasten one's attention. See Syns at **brood. b.** To speak or write at length. [< OE *dwellan*, mislead, delay.] —**dwell′er** *n.*

dwell•ing (dwĕl′ĭng) ▶*n.* A place to live in; abode.

DWI ▶*abbr.* driving while intoxicated

dwin•dle (dwĭn′dl) ▶*v.* **-dled, -dling.** To make or become gradually less until little remains. [< OE *dwīnan*, shrink.]

Dy ▶ The symbol for the element **dysprosium.**

dyb•buk (dĭb′o͝ok, dē-bo͝ok′) ▶*n., pl.* **-buks** or **dyb•buk•im** (dĭ-bo͝ok′ĭm, dē′bo͞o-kēm′). In Jewish folklore, the soul of a dead person that enters and takes control of the body of a living person. [< Heb. *dibbūq.*]

dye (dī) ▶*n.* **1.** A substance used to color materials. **2.** A color imparted by dyeing. ▶*v.* **dyed, dye•ing 1.** To color (a material) with a dye. **2.** To take on or impart color. [< OE *dēag, dēah.*] —**dy′er** *n.*

Dy•er (dī′ər), **Mary.** d. 1660. English-born Amer. Quaker martyr.

dye•stuff (dī′stŭf′) ▶*n.* See **dye** 1.

dy•ing (dī′ĭng) ▶*adj.* **1.** About to die. **2.** Drawing to an end; declining. **3.** Done or uttered just before death.

dy•nam•ic (dī-năm′ĭk) ▶*adj.* also **dy•nam•i•cal** (-ĭ-kəl) **1.** Of or relating to energy or to objects in motion. **2.** Marked by continuous change or activity. **3.** Marked by intensity and vigor; forceful. ▶*n.* **1.** An interactive system, esp. one involving conflicting forces. **2.** A force, esp. political, social, or psychological. [< Gk. *dunamis*, power.] —**dy•nam′i•cal•ly** *adv.*

dy•nam•ics (dī-năm′ĭks) ▶*n.* **1.** *(takes sing. v.)* The branch of mechanics concerned with the effects of forces on the motion of a body or system, esp. of forces not originating in the system. **2.** *(takes pl. v.)* The social, intellectual, or moral forces that produce activity and change in a given sphere.

dy•na•mite (dī′nə-mīt′) ▶*n.* **1.** A powerful explosive composed of nitroglycerin or ammonium nitrate dispersed in an absorbent medium. **2.** *Slang* Something exceptionally exciting or dangerous. ▶*v.* **-mit•ed, -mit•ing.** To blow up or destroy with or as if with dynamite. ▶*adj.* *Slang* Outstanding; superb. [Swed. *dynamit.*]

dy•na•mo (dī′nə-mō′) ▶*n., pl.* **-mos 1.** A generator, esp. one for producing direct current. **2.** An energetic and forceful person. [< *dynamo electric machine.*]

dy•na•mom•e•ter (dī′nə-mŏm′ĭ-tər) ▶*n.* An instrument used to measure mechanical power. [Fr. *dynamomètre.*] —**dy′na•mom′e•try** *n.*

dy•nas•ty (dī′nə-stē) ▶*n., pl.* **-ties 1.** A succession of rulers from the same family or line. **2.** A group that maintains power for several generations. [< Gk. *dunasteia*, lordship.] —**dy•nas′tic** (dī-năs′tĭk) *adj.*

dys– ▶*pref.* Abnormal; impaired; difficult; bad: *dysplasia.* [< Gk. *dus-.*]

dys•en•ter•y (dĭs′ən-tĕr′ē) ▶*n.* An inflammatory disorder of the lower intestinal tract, resulting in severe diarrhea often with blood and mucus. [< Gk. *dusenteria.*] —**dys′en•ter′ic** *adj.*

dys•func•tion (dĭs-fŭngk′shən) ▶*n.* Abnormal or impaired functioning, esp. of a bodily system or organ. —**dys•func′tion•al** *adj.*

dys•lex•i•a (dĭs-lĕk′sē-ə) ▶*n.* A learning disorder marked by impairment of the ability to read. [DYS– + Gk. *lexis*, speech.] —**dys•lex′ic** *adj. & n.*

dys•pep•sia (dĭs-pĕp′shə, -sē-ə) ▶*n.* Indigestion. [< Gk. *duspepsia.*] —**dys•pep′tic** *adj.* & *n.*

dys•pla•sia (dĭs-plā′zhə, -zhē-ə) ►*n.* Abnormal development of tissues, organs, or cells. —**dys•plas′tic** (-plăs′tĭk) *adj.*

dys•pro•si•um (dĭs-prō′zē-əm, -zhē-əm) ►*n.* *Symbol* **Dy** A soft, silvery rare-earth element used in nuclear research. At. no. 66. See table at **element.** [< Gk. *dusprositos*, difficult to approach (from its rarity in nature).]

dys•tro•phy (dĭs′trə-fē) ►*n.* **1.** A degenerative disorder caused by inadequate nutrition. **2.** Any of several disorders, esp. muscular dystrophy, in which the muscles weaken and atrophy. —**dys•troph′ic** *adj.*

dz. ►*abbr.* dozen

E

e[1] or **E** (ē) ►*n.*, *pl.* **e's** or **E's** also **es** or **Es 1.** The 5th letter of the English alphabet. **2.** The 5th in a series. **3.** *Mus.* The 3rd tone of the C major scale. **4. E** A failing grade.

e[2] ►*abbr.* electron

E ►*abbr.* **1.** east **2.** *Baseball* error

e– ►*pref.* Computer or computer network: *e-commerce.* See Usage Note at **virtual.** [< ELECTRONIC.]

ea. ►*abbr.* each

each (ēch) ►*adj.* Being one of two or more considered individually; every. See Usage Note at **every.** ►*pron.* Every one of a group considered individually; each one. ►*adv.* For or to each one; apiece. [< OE *ǣlc.*]

each other ►*pron.* Each the other. Used to indicate a reciprocal relationship or action: *The children like each other.*

ea•ger (ē′gər) ►*adj.* **-er, -est.** Having or showing keen interest or impatient expectancy. [< Lat. *ācer*, sharp.] —**ea′ger•ly** *adv.* —**ea′ger•ness** *n.*

ea•gle (ē′gəl) ►*n.* **1.** A large bird of prey with a powerful hooked bill and strong soaring flight. **2.** A former US gold coin having a face value of ten dollars. **3.** A golf score of two under par on a hole. [< Lat. *aquila.*]

ea•glet (ē′glĭt) ►*n.* A young eagle.

Ea•kins (ā′kĭnz), **Thomas.** 1844–1916. Amer. painter.

ear[1] (îr) ►*n.* **1.** *Anat.* **a.** The vertebrate organ of hearing, responsible for maintaining equilibrium and sensing sound. **b.** The visible outer part of this organ. **2.** The sense of hearing. **3.** Aural sensitivity, esp. to differences in musical pitch **4.** Sympathetic attention. **5.** Something resembling the vertebrate ear. **6. ears** *Informal* Headphones. —***idioms:* all ears** *Informal* Acutely attentive. **play it by ear** *Informal* To improvise. **up to (one's) ears** *Informal* Deeply involved. [< OE *ēare.*] —**eared** *adj.* —**ear′less** *adj.*

ear[2] (îr) ►*n.* The seed-bearing spike of a cereal plant, such as corn. [< OE *ēar.*]

ear•ache (îr′āk′) ►*n.* Pain in the ear.

ear•drum (îr′drŭm′) ►*n.* The thin membrane that separates the middle ear from the external ear.

ear•flap (îr′flăp′) ►*n.* A flap attached to a cap used to cover the ears.

ear•ful (îr′fo͝ol′) ►*n.* **1.** An excessive amount of something heard. **2.** Scandalous gossip. **3.** A reprimand.

Ear•hart (âr′härt′), **Amelia.** 1897?–1937. Amer. aviator.

earl (ûrl) ►*n.* A British nobleman next in rank above a viscount and below a marquis. [< OE *eorl*, nobleman.] —**earl′dom** *n.*

Amelia Earhart

ear•lobe (îr′lōb′) ►*n.* The soft pendulous lower part of the external ear.

ear•ly (ûr′lē) ►*adj.* **-li•er, -li•est 1.** Of or occurring near the beginning of a series, period of time, or course of events. **2.** Belonging to a previous or remote period of time: *early mammals.* **3.** Occurring or developing before the expected time. **4.** Occurring in the near future: *predicted an early end to the negotiations.* ►*adv.* **-lier, -liest 1.** Near the beginning of a given series, period of time, or course of events. **2.** At or during a remote or initial period. **3.** Before the expected or usual time: *arrived early.* [< OE *ǣrlīce.*] —**ear′li•ness** *n.*

ear•mark (îr′märk′) ►*n.* **1.** An identifying feature or characteristic. **2.** A brand on the ear of a domestic animal. ►*v.* **1.** To set aside for a particular purpose. See Syns at **allocate. 2.** To brand with an earmark.

ear•muff (îr′mŭf′) ►*n.* Either of a pair of ear coverings worn to protect against the cold.

earn (ûrn) ►*v.* **1.** To gain esp. for the performance of service or labor. **2.** To acquire or deserve as a result of effort or action. **3.** To yield as return or profit. [< OE *earnian.*] —**earn′er** *n.*

Syns: *earn, deserve, merit, rate, win* **v.**

earned run (ûrnd) ►*n.* *Baseball* A run scored without the aid of an error.

ear•nest[1] (ûr′nĭst) ►*adj.* **1.** Showing deep sincerity or seriousness. **2.** Of an important nature; grave. —***idiom:* in earnest** With a purposeful or sincere intent. [< OE *eornoste.*] —**ear′nest•ly** *adv.* —**ear′nest•ness** *n.*

ear•nest[2] (ûr′nĭst) ►*n.* Money paid in advance as part payment to bind a contract or bargain. [Ult. < Canaanite* *'irrabōn.*]

earn•ings (ûr′nĭngz) ►*pl.n.* **1.** Salary or wages. **2.** Profits from business or investments.

ear•phone (îr′fōn′) ►*n.* A device that converts

electric signals to audible sound and fits over or in the ear.

ear•piece (îr′pēs′) ► *n.* **1.** A part, as of a telephone receiver, that fits in or is held next to the ear. **2.** See **earphone. 3.** Either of the two parts of an eyeglasses frame that extend over the ear.

ear•plug (îr′plŭg′) ► *n.* **1.** A soft plug fitted into the ear canal to keep out water or sound. **2.** An earphone that fits into the ear.

ear•ring (îr′rĭng, îr′ĭng) ► *n.* An ornament worn on the ear, esp. the earlobe.

ear•shot (îr′shŏt′) ► *n.* The range within which sound can be heard.

ear•split•ting (îr′splĭt′ĭng) ► *adj.* Loud and shrill enough to hurt the ears. See Syns at **loud.**

earth (ûrth) ► *n.* **1a.** The land surface of the world. **b.** Soil, esp. productive soil. **2.** often **Earth** The 3rd planet from the sun, at a mean distance of approx. 149 million km (92.96 million mi) and with an average radius of 6,374 km (3,959 mi). **3.** The realm of mortal existence. —***idioms:* down to earth** Sensible; realistic. **on earth** Among all the possiblities: *Why on earth did you go?* [< OE *eorthe.*]

earth•en (ûr′thən, *-thən*) ► *adj.* Made of earth or clay.

earth•en•ware (ûr′thən-wâr′, *-thən-*) ► *n.* Pottery made from a porous clay fired at low temperatures.

earth•ling (ûrth′lĭng) ► *n.* One that inhabits the planet Earth.

earth•ly (ûrth′lē) ► *adj.* **1.** Of or characteristic of this earth; terrestrial. **2.** Not heavenly or divine; worldly. **3.** Conceivable; possible: *no earthly reason.* —**earth′li•ness** *n.*

earth•mov•er (ûrth′mo͞o′vər) ► *n.* A machine, such as a bulldozer, used for digging or pushing earth. —**earth′mov′ing** *adj.*

earth•quake (ûrth′kwāk′) ► *n.* A sudden movement of the earth's crust caused by stress accumulated along geologic faults or by volcanic activity.

earth science ► *n.* Any of several geologic sciences concerned with the origin, structure, and physical phenomena of the earth.

earth•shak•ing (ûrth′shā′kĭng) ► *adj.* Of great consequence or importance.

earth•ward (ûrth′wərd) ► *adv.* & *adj.* To or toward the earth. —**earth′wards** *adv.*

earth•work (ûrth′wûrk′) ► *n.* An earthen embankment, esp. one used as a fortification.

earth•worm (ûrth′wûrm′) ► *n.* Any of a class of annelid worms that burrow into and aerate soil.

earth•y (ûr′thē) ► *adj.* **-i•er, -i•est 1.** Of, consisting of, or resembling earth. **2.** Crude; indecent. **3.** Hearty or uninhibited. —**earth′i•ly** *adv.* —**earth′i•ness** *n.*

ear•wax (îr′wăks′) ► *n.* The waxlike secretion of glands lining the canal of the external ear.

ear•wig (îr′wĭg′) ► *n.* An elongate insect having a pair of pincerlike appendages protruding from the rear of the abdomen. [< OE *ēarwicga* : *ēar*, EAR[1] + *wicga*, insect.]

ease (ēz) ► *n.* **1.** Freedom from pain, worry, or agitation. **2.** Freedom from constraint or embarrassment; naturalness. **3.** Freedom from difficulty, hardship, or effort. **4.** Freedom from financial difficulty; affluence. **5.** Dexterity in performance; facility. ► *v.* **eased, eas•ing 1.** To free or become free from pain, worry, or agitation. **2.** To lessen the discomfort or pain of. **3.** To give respite from. **4.** To slacken; loosen. **5.** To reduce the difficulty of. **6.** To maneuver slowly and carefully. [< OFr. *aise*, perh. < Lat. *adiacēns*, ADJACENT.]

ea•sel (ē′zəl) ► *n.* An upright frame for supporting an artist's canvas. [< MDu. *esel*, ass.]

ease•ment (ēz′mənt) ► *n.* **1.** The act of easing or the condition of being eased. **2.** *Law* A right afforded a person to make limited use of another's real property.

east (ēst) ► *n.* **1a.** The direction of the earth's axial rotation; the direction of sunrise. **b.** The compass point 90° clockwise from north. **2.** often **East** The eastern part of a region or country. **3.** often **East** Asia. ► *adj.* **1.** To, toward, of, or in the east. **2.** Coming from the east: *an east wind.* ► *adv.* In, from, or toward the east. [< OE *ēast.*] —**east′ward, east′ward•ly** *adj.* & *adv.* —**east′wards** *adv.*

East An•gli•a (ăng′glē-ə) A region and Anglo-Saxon kingdom of E England.

East Asia. A region of Asia coextensive with the Far East. —**East Asian** *adj.* & *n.*

East China Sea. An arm of the W Pacific bounded by China, South Korea, Taiwan, and the Ryukyu and Kyushu islands.

Eas•ter (ē′stər) ► *n.* A Christian feast commemorating the Resurrection of Jesus, observed on a Sunday in March or April. [< OE *ēastre.*]

Easter Island. An island of Chile in the S Pacific about 3,701 km (2,300 mi) W of the mainland, famous for its colossal heads carved from volcanic rock.

Easter Island

east•er•ly (ē′stər-lē) ► *adj.* **1.** Situated toward the east. **2.** From the east: *easterly winds.* —**east′er•ly** *adv.*

east•ern (ē′stərn) ► *adj.* **1.** Of, in, or toward the east. **2.** From the east: *eastern breezes.* **3.** often **Eastern** Of or characteristic of eastern regions or the East. **4. Eastern a.** Of the Eastern Church. **b.** Of the Eastern Orthodox Church. [< OE *ēasterne.*]

Eastern Church ► *n.* Any of the Christian churches formerly within the Byzantine Empire, esp. the Eastern Orthodox Church.

east•ern•er also **East•ern•er** (ē′stər-nər) ► *n.* A native or inhabitant of the east, esp. the E US.

Eastern Europe. The countries of E Europe,

esp. those allied with the USSR in the Warsaw Pact (1955–91).

Eastern Hemisphere. The half of the earth comprising Europe, Africa, Asia, and Australia.

Eastern Orthodox Church ▶*n.* Any of the Christian churches in communion with the patriarch of Constantinople.

East Germany. A former country of N Europe on the Baltic Sea (1949–90). —**East German** *adj. & n.*

East Indies 1. The islands comprising Indonesia. **2.** A general term formerly used for India and SE Asia. —**East Indian** *adj.*

East•man (ēst′mən), **George.** 1854–1932. Amer. inventor.

eas•y (ē′zē) ▶*adj.* **-i•er, -i•est 1.** Capable of being accomplished without difficulty. **2.** Free from worry, anxiety, trouble, or pain. **3.** Causing little hardship or distress. **4.** Socially at ease. **5a.** Relaxed in attitude; easygoing. **b.** Not strict or severe; lenient. **6.** Readily exploited, imposed on, or tricked. **7.** Not hurried or forced; moderate. ▶*adv.* Without strain or difficulty; in a relaxed manner. [< OFr. *aaisier*, to put at ease < *aise*, EASE.] —**eas′i•ly** *adv.* —**eas′i•ness** *n.*

easy chair ▶*n.* A large comfortable chair.

eas•y•go•ing (ē′zē-gō′ĭng) ▶*adj.* Living without worry or concern; relaxed.

eat (ēt) ▶*v.* **ate** (āt), **eat•en** (ēt′n), **eat•ing 1.** To consume (food). **2.** To consume or ravage as if by eating. **3.** To erode or corrode. **4.** *Slang* To absorb the cost of. **5.** *Informal* To bother or annoy. —***idioms:*** **eat crow** To be forced to accept a humiliating defeat. **eat (one's) words** To retract an assertion. **eat out of (someone's) hand** To be manipulated by another. [< OE *etan.*] —**eat′a•ble** *adj. & n.* —**eat′er** *n.*

Syns: *eat, consume, devour, ingest* ***v.***

eat•er•y (ē′tə-rē) ▶*n., pl.* **-ies** *Informal.* A restaurant.

eat•ing disorder (ē′tĭng) ▶*n.* A psychological disorder, such as anorexia nervosa, that involves insufficient or excessive food intake.

eaves (ēvz) ▶*pl.n.* The projecting overhang at the lower edge of a roof. [< OE *efes.*]

eaves•drop (ēvz′drŏp′) ▶*v.* **-dropped, -drop•ping.** To listen secretly to private conversations. [< ME *evesdrop*, place where water falls from the eaves.]

E•ban (ē′bən), **Abba.** b. 1915. South African-born Israeli politician.

ebb (ĕb) ▶*n.* **1.** The period of a tide between high tide and a following low tide. **2.** A period of decline or diminution. ▶*v.* **1.** To recede, as the tide. **2.** To decline or diminish. See Syns at **recede.** [< OE *ebba.*]

EbN ▶*abbr.* east by north

eb•on•ite (ĕb′ə-nīt′) ▶*n.* A hard rubber used as an electrical insulating material.

eb•on•y (ĕb′ə-nē) ▶*n., pl.* **-ies 1.** The hard dark wood of a tropical Asian tree. **2.** The color black. ▶*adj.* Of or like ebony; black. [< Gk. *ebeninos*, of ebony, of Egypt. orig.]

Eb•ro (ē′brō, ĕ′vrō) A river rising in N Spain and flowing about 925 km (575 mi) to the Mediterranean Sea.

EbS ▶*abbr.* east by south

e•bul•lient (ĭ-bo͝ol′yənt, ĭ-bŭl′-) ▶*adj.* **1.** Zestfully enthusiastic. **2.** Boiling or seeming to boil; bubbling. [< Lat. *ēbullīre*, to bubble up.] —**e•bul′lience** *n.* —**e•bul′lient•ly** *adv.*

eb•ul•li•tion (ĕb′ə-lĭsh′ən) ▶*n.* **1.** The state or process of boiling. **2.** A sudden outpouring, as of emotion.

ec•cen•tric (ĭk-sĕn′trĭk, ĕk-) ▶*adj.* **1.** Departing from a conventional pattern. **2.** Deviating from a circular path, as in an elliptical orbit. **3.** Not situated at or in the geometric center. ▶*n.* **1.** One that deviates from conventional patterns. **2.** *Phys.* A disk or wheel having its axis of revolution displaced from its center so that it is capable of imparting reciprocating motion. [< Gk. *ekkentros*, not having the same center.] —**ec•cen′tri•cal•ly** *adv.* —**ec′cen•tric′i•ty** *n.*

Ec•cle•si•as•tes (ĭ-klē′zē-ăs′tēz′) ▶*n. (takes sing. v.)* See table at **Bible.**

ec•cle•si•as•tic (ĭ-klē′zē-ăs′tĭk) ▶*adj.* Ecclesiastical. ▶*n.* A minister or priest; cleric. [< Gk. *ekklēsiastēs*, member of the assembly.]

ec•cle•si•as•ti•cal (ĭ-klē′zē-ăs′tĭ-kəl) ▶*adj.* Of or relating to a church, esp. as an institution. —**ec•cle′si•as′ti•cal•ly** *adv.*

Ec•cle•si•as•ti•cus (ĭ-klē′zē-ăs′tĭ-kəs) ▶*n.* See table at **Bible.**

ec•dy•sis (ĕk′dĭ-sĭs) ▶*n., pl.* **-ses** (-sēz′). The shedding of an outer integument or layer of skin, as by insects, crustaceans, and snakes; molting. [Gk. *ekdusis*, a stripping off < *ekduein*, to take off.]

ECG ▶*abbr.* **1.** electrocardiogram **2.** electrocardiograph

ech•e•lon (ĕsh′ə-lŏn′) ▶*n.* **1.** A steplike formation, as of troops or aircraft. **2.** A subdivision of a military force. **3.** A level of authority in a hierarchy; rank. [< OFr. *eschelon*, rung of a ladder.]

ech•i•na•ce•a (ĕk′ə-nā′sē-ə, -nā′shə) ▶*n.* Any of several usu. pinkish-purple coneflower plants used in herbal medicine. [Ult. < Lat. *echīnus*, sea urchin (from its rough leaves).]

e•chi•no•derm (ĭ-kī′nə-dûrm′) ▶*n.* Any of various gen. spiny marine invertebrates having an internal calcareous skeleton, including starfishes and sea urchins. [< Gk. *ekhinos*, sea urchin.]

ech•o (ĕk′ō) ▶*n., pl.* **-oes 1a.** Repetition of a sound by reflection of sound waves from a surface. **b.** The sound produced in this manner. **2.** A remnant or vestige. **3.** One who imitates another. **4.** A consequence or repercussion. ▶*v.* **-oed, -o•ing 1.** To repeat or be repeated by or as if by an echo; imitate: *followers echoing the cries of their leader.* **2.** To resound; reverberate. [< Gk. *ēkhō.*] —**ech′o•er** *n.* —**e•cho′ic** *adj.*

Syns: *echo, reecho, reflect, resound, reverberate* ***v.***

Echo ▶*n. Gk. Myth.* A nymph whose unrequited love for Narcissus caused her to pine away until only her voice remained.

echo chamber ▶*n.* A room with acoustically reflective walls used in broadcasting and recording.

ech•o•gram (ĕk′ō-grăm′) ▶*n.* See **sonogram.**

ech•o•lo•ca•tion (ĕk′ō-lō-kā′shən) ▶*n.* **1.** *Zool.* A sensory system, as in bats or dolphins, in which usu. high-pitched sounds are emitted and their echoes interpreted to determine the direction and distance of objects. **2.** *Electron.*

Ranging by acoustical echo analysis. —**ech′o•lo•cate′** *v.*

é•clair (ā-klâr′, ā′klâr′) ►*n.* An elongated pastry filled with custard or whipped cream and usu. iced with chocolate. [< OFr. *esclair,* lightning.]

é•clat (ā-klä′, ā′klä′) ►*n.* **1.** Great brilliance, as of achievement. **2.** Great acclamation. [< OFr. *esclater,* burst out.]

e•clec•tic (ĭ-klĕk′tĭk) ►*adj.* Selecting or employing individual elements from a variety of sources, systems, or styles. [< Gk. *eklegein,* select.] —**e•clec′tic** *n.* —**e•clec′ti•cal•ly** *adv.* —**e•clec′ti•cism′** *n.*

e•clipse (ĭ-klĭps′) ►*n.* **1a.** The partial or complete obscuring of one celestial body by another. **b.** The period of time during which such an obscuration occurs. **2.** A fall into obscurity or disuse; decline. ►*v.* **e•clipsed, e•clips•ing 1.** To cause an eclipse of. **2.** To surpass; outshine. [< Gk. *ekleipsis* < *ekleipein,* fail to appear.]

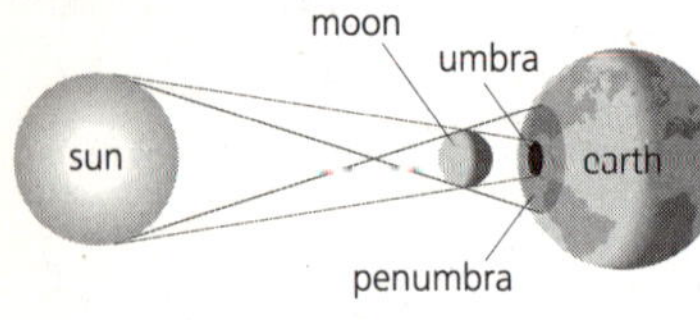

eclipse
solar eclipse

e•clip•tic (ĭ-klĭp′tĭk) ►*n.* The apparent path of the sun and the planets among the stars in one year. [< Med.Lat. *(līnea) eclīptica,* (line) of eclipses.]

ec•logue (ĕk′lôg′, -lŏg′) ►*n.* A pastoral poem. [< Gk. *eklogē,* selection.]

ECM ►*abbr.* European Common Market

e•col•o•gy (ĭ-kŏl′ə-jē) ►*n.* **1.** The science of the relationships between organisms and their environments. **2.** The study of the detrimental effects of human civilization on the environment. [Ger. *Ökologie* : Gk. *oikos,* house + -LOGY.] —**ec′o•log′i•cal** (ĕk′ə-lŏj′ĭ-kəl, ē′kə-), **ec′o•log′ic** *adj.* —**ec′o•log′i•cal•ly** *adv.* —**e•col′o•gist** *n.*

e-com•merce (ē′kŏm′ərs) ►*n.* Commerce transacted electronically, as over the Internet.

e•con•o•met•rics (ĭ-kŏn′ə-mĕt′rĭks) ►*n.* *(takes sing. v.)* Application of mathematical and statistical techniques to economics.

ec•o•nom•ic (ĕk′ə-nŏm′ĭk, ē′kə-) ►*adj.* **1.** Of or relating to the production, development, and management of material wealth, as of a country. **2.** Of or relating to the necessities of life. **3.** Efficient; economical.

ec•o•nom•i•cal (ĕk′ə-nŏm′ĭ-kəl, ē′kə-) ►*adj.* **1.** Prudent and thrifty; not wasteful. **2.** Intended to save money, as by efficient operation. —**ec′o•nom′i•cal•ly** *adv.*

ec•o•nom•ics (ĕk′ə-nŏm′ĭks, ē′kə-) ►*n.* **1.** *(takes sing. v.)* The science that deals with the production, distribution, and consumption of goods and services. **2.** *(takes sing. or pl. v.)* Economic matters. —**e•con′o•mist** (ĭ-kŏn′ə-mĭst) *n.*

e•con•o•mize (ĭ-kŏn′ə-mīz′) ►*v.* **-mized, -miz•ing.** To practice economy, as by avoiding waste. —**e•con′o•miz′er** *n.*

e•con•o•my (ĭ-kŏn′ə-mē) ►*n., pl.* **-mies 1a.** Careful, thrifty management of resources. **b.** An example of such management. **2.** The system of economic activity in a country or region. **3.** Efficient or sparing use. [< Gk. *oikonomia,* management of a household.]

e•co•sys•tem (ē′kō-sĭs′təm, ĕk′ō-) ►*n.* An ecological community together with its environment, functioning as a unit.

e•co•tour•ism (ē′kō-to͝or′ĭz′əm, ĕk′ō-) ►*n.* Travel to areas of ecological interest, usu. under guidance of a naturalist. [ECO(LOGY) + TOURISM.]

ec•ru (ĕk′ro͞o, ā′kro͞o) ►*n.* A light tan color. [< OFr. *escru,* raw, unbleached.]

ec•sta•sy (ĕk′stə-sē) ►*n., pl.* **-sies.** Intense joy or delight; rapture. [< Gk. *ekstasis,* astonishment : *ex-,* out of + *histanai,* to place.] —**ec•stat′ic** (ĕk-stăt′ĭk) *adj.* —**ec•stat′i•cal•ly** *adv.*

-ectomy ►*suff.* Surgical removal: *tonsillectomy.* [Gk. *ek-,* out + NLat. *-tomia,* a cutting.]

ec•top•ic pregnancy (ĕk-tŏp′ĭk) ►*n.* Implantation and subsequent development of a fertilized ovum outside the uterus, as in a fallopian tube. [< Gk. *ektopos,* out of place.]

ec•to•therm (ĕk′tə-thûrm′) ►*n.* An organism that regulates its body temperature largely by exchanging heat with its surroundings. [Gk. *ektos,* outside + *thermos,* heat.] —**ec′to•ther′mic, ec′to•ther′mal, ec′to•ther′mous** *adj.*

ECU ►*abbr.* European currency unit

Ec•ua•dor (ĕk′wə-dôr′) A country of NW South America on the Pacific Ocean. Cap. Quito. Pop. 11,221,000. —**Ec′ua•dor′i•an** *adj. & n.*

ec•u•men•i•cal (ĕk′yə-mĕn′ĭ-kəl) also **ec•u•men•ic** (-mĕn′ĭk) ►*adj.* **1.** Of worldwide scope or applicability; universal. **2.** Of or relating to ecumenism. [< Gk. *(hē) oikoumenē (gē),* (the) inhabited (world) < *oikein,* inhabit.] —**ec′u•men′i•cal•ly** *adv.*

ec•u•me•nism (ĕk′yə-mə-nĭz′əm, ĭ-kyo͞o′-) ►*n.* A movement promoting unity among Christian churches or denominations. —**ec′u•men′ist** *n.*

ec•ze•ma (ĕk′sə-mə, ĕg′zə-, ĭg-zē′-) ►*n.* A noncontagious skin inflammation marked by redness, itching, and lesions. [< Gk. *ekzema* < *ekzein,* boil over.]

ed. ►*abbr.* **1.** edition **2.** editor

-ed¹ ►*suff.* Used to form the past tense of regular verbs: *waited.* [< OE *-ade, -ede, -ode.*]

-ed² ►*suff.* Used to form the past participle of regular verbs: *linked.* [< OE *-ad, -ed, -od.*]

-ed³ ►*suff.* Having; characterized by; resembling: *pointed.* [< OE *-ed, -od.*]

E•dam (ē′dəm, ē′dăm′) ►*n.* A mild yellow Dutch cheese, usu. covered with red wax. [After *Edam,* the Netherlands.]

ed•dy (ĕd′ē) ►*n., pl.* **-dies.** A current, as of water or air, moving contrary to the direction of the main current, esp. in a circular motion. [ME *ydy.*] —**ed′dy** *v.*

Eddy, Mary (Morse) Baker. 1821–1910. Amer. religious leader who founded Christian Science (1879).

e•del•weiss (ā′dəl-vīs′, -wīs′) ►*n.* An alpine plant having downy leaves and small whitish flowers. [Ger.]

e•de•ma (ĭ-dē′mə) ►*n.* *Pathol.* An excessive

Mary Baker Eddy

Thomas Edison

accumulation of serous fluid in tissues. [< Gk. *oidēma*, a swelling.] —**e•dem′a•tous** (ĭ-dĕm′ə-təs) *adj.*

E•den (ēd′n) ►*n.* **1.** *Bible* The garden of God and first home of Adam and Eve. **2.** A state of innocence or bliss. [< Heb. *'ēden*, delight.] —**E•den′ic** (ē-dĕn′ĭk) *adj.*

Eden, Sir **(Robert) Anthony.** 1st Earl of Avon. 1897–1977. British prime minister (1955–57).

edge (ĕj) ►*n.* **1.** A thin sharpened side, as of the blade of a cutting instrument. **2.** Keenness; zest. **3.** The line of intersection of two surfaces. **4.** A rim or brink. **5.** A dividing line; border. **6.** An advantage. ►*v.* **edged, edg•ing 1.** To give an edge to. **2.** To advance or push gradually. —***idiom:*** **on edge** Highly tense or nervous; irritable. [< OE *ecg*.] —**edg′er** *n.*

edge•wise (ĕj′wīz′) also **edge•ways** (-wāz′) ►*adv.* With the edge foremost.

edg•ing (ĕj′ĭng) ►*n.* Something that forms an edge or border.

edg•y (ĕj′ē) ►*adj.* **-i•er, -i•est 1.** Nervous or irritable. **2.** Having a sharp or biting edge. —**edg′i•ly** *adv.* —**edg′i•ness** *n.*

ed•i•ble (ĕd′ə-bəl) ►*adj.* Fit to be eaten. [< Lat. *edere*, eat.] —**ed′i•bil′i•ty, ed′i•ble•ness** *n.* —**ed′i•ble** *n.*

e•dict (ē′dĭkt′) ►*n.* A proclamation issued by an authority. [Lat. *ēdictum* < p.part. of *ēdīcere*, declare.]

ed•i•fice (ĕd′ə-fĭs) ►*n.* A building, esp. one of imposing size. [< Lat. *aedificium*.]

ed•i•fy (ĕd′ə-fī′) ►*v.* **-fied, -fy•ing.** To instruct, esp. to encourage moral or spiritual improvement. [< Lat. *aedificāre*, build.] —**ed′i•fi•ca′tion** *n.* —**ed′i•fi′er** *n.*

Ed•in•burgh (ĕd′n-bûr′ə, -bŭr′ə, -brə) The capital of Scotland, in the E part on the Firth of Forth. Pop. 441,620.

Ed•i•son (ĕd′ĭ-sən), **Thomas Alva.** 1847–1931. Amer. inventor.

ed•it (ĕd′ĭt) ►*v.* **1.** To prepare (e.g., a manuscript) for publication, as by correcting or revising. **2.** To supervise the publication of. **3.** To assemble the components of (e.g., a film or soundtrack), as by cutting and splicing. [< Lat. *ēdere*, *ēdit-*, publish : EX– + *dare*, give.] —**ed′it** *n.* —**ed′i•tor** *n.* —**ed′i•tor•ship′** *n.*

e•di•tion (ĭ-dĭsh′ən) ►*n.* **1.** The form in which a book is published. **2.** The entire number of copies of a publication issued at one time. **3.** One that resembles an original; version.

ed•i•to•ri•al (ĕd′ĭ-tôr′ē-əl, -tōr′-) ►*n.* **1.** An article in a publication expressing the opinion of its editors or publishers. **2.** A commentary on television or radio expressing the opinion of the station or network. ►*adj.* **1.** Of or relating to editing. **2.** Of or like an editorial. —**ed′i•to′ri•al•ist** *n.* —**ed′i•to′ri•al•ly** *adv.*

ed•i•to•ri•al•ize (ĕd′ĭ-tôr′ē-ə-līz′, -tōr′-) ►*v.* **-ized, -iz•ing 1.** To express an opinion in or as if in an editorial. **2.** To present an opinion in the guise of an objective report.

Ed•mon•ton (ĕd′mən-tən) The capital of Alberta, Canada, in the central part of the province. Pop. 616,741.

E•dom (ē′dəm) An ancient country of Palestine between the Dead Sea and the Gulf of Aqaba. —**E′dom•ite′** *n.*

EDP ►*abbr.* electronic data processing

EDT ►*abbr.* Eastern Daylight Time

ed•u•ca•ble (ĕj′ə-kə-bəl) ►*adj.* Capable of being educated. —**ed′u•ca•bil′i•ty** *n.*

ed•u•cate (ĕj′ə-kāt′) ►*v.* **-cat•ed, -cat•ing 1.** To provide esp. with formal knowledge or training. **2.** To provide with information: *educate the public about the dangers of smoking.* **3.** To bring to an understanding. [< Lat. *ēducāre*.] —**ed′u•ca′tor** *n.*

ed•u•cat•ed (ĕj′ə-kā′tĭd) ►*adj.* **1.** Having an education, esp. one above the average. **2.** Showing evidence of schooling, training, or experience. **3.** Based on experience or knowledge: *an educated guess.*

ed•u•ca•tion (ĕj′ə-kā′shən) ►*n.* **1.** The act or process of educating or being educated. **2.** The knowledge or skill obtained. **3.** The field of study concerned with teaching and learning. —**ed′u•ca′tion•al** *adj.*

e•duce (ĭ-do͞os′, ĭ-dyo͞os′) ►*v.* **e•duced, e•duc•ing 1.** To draw out; elicit. **2.** To deduce. [< Lat. *ēdūcere*.]

ed•u•tain•ment (ĕj′o͞o-tān′mənt, ĕj′ə-) ►*n.* Educational entertainment, esp. through media such as television or computer software. [EDU(CATION) + (ENTER)TAINMENT.]

Ed•ward[1] (ĕd′wərd). "the Confessor." 1003?–66. King of the English (1042–66).

Edward[2]**.** Prince of Wales. "the Black Prince." 1330–76. English soldier during the Hundred Years' War.

Edward I. 1239–1307. King of England (1272–1307).

Edward II. 1284–1327. King of England (1307–27).

Edward III. 1312–77. King of England (1327–77).

Edward IV. 1442–83. King of England (1461–70 and 1471–83).

Edward V. 1470–83. King of England (1483); murdered.
Edward VI. 1537–53. King of England and Ireland (1547–53).
Edward VII. 1841–1910. King of Great Britain and Ireland (1901–10).
Edward VIII. Duke of Windsor. 1894–1972. King of Great Britain and Ireland (1936); abdicated.
Ed•wards (ĕd′wərdz), **Jonathan.** 1703–58. Amer. theologian and philosopher.
EE ▸*abbr.* **1.** electrical engineer **2.** electrical engineering
-ee¹ ▸*suff.* **1.** One that receives or benefits from a specified action: *addressee.* **2.** One that performs a specified action: *standee.* [< Lat. *-ātus*, –ATE¹.]
-ee² ▸*suff.* **1.** One resembling: *goatee.* **2.** A particular, esp. a diminutive kind of: *bootee.* [Var. of –Y¹.]
EEC ▸*abbr.* European Economic Community
EEG ▸*abbr.* **1.** electroencephalogram **2.** electroencephalograph
eel (ēl) ▸*n., pl.* **eel** or **eels.** Any of various long snakelike marine or freshwater fishes. [< OE *ǣl.*]
EEOC ▸*abbr.* Equal Employment Opportunity Commission
-eer ▸*suff.* One concerned with or engaged in: *auctioneer.* [< Lat. *-ārius*, –ARY.]
ee•rie or **ee•ry** (îr′ē) ▸*adj.* **-ri•er, -ri•est 1.** Inspiring inexplicable fear or uneasiness. **2.** Suggestive of the supernatural; mysterious. [< OE *earg*, timid.] —**ee′ri•ly** *adv.* —**ee′ri•ness** *n.*
ef•face (ĭ-fās′) ▸*v.* **-faced, -fac•ing 1.** To wipe out; erase. **2.** To make indistinct. **3.** To conduct (oneself) inconspicuously. [< OFr. *esfacier.*] —**ef•face′ment** *n.*
ef•fect (ĭ-fĕkt′) ▸*n.* **1.** Something brought about by a cause or agent; result. **2.** The power to achieve a result; influence. **3.** Advantage; avail. **4.** The condition of being in full force. **5.** Something that produces a specific impression. **6.** The basic or general meaning: *words to that effect.* **7. effects** Movable belongings. ▸*v.* **1.** To bring into existence. **2.** To produce as a result. See Usage Note at **affect¹**. —***idiom:* in effect** In essence; to all purposes. [< Lat. *effectus*, p.part. of *efficere*, accomplish.]
ef•fec•tive (ĭ-fĕk′tĭv) ▸*adj.* **1.** Having an intended or expected effect. **2.** Producing a strong impression or response; striking. **3.** Operative; in effect. —**ef•fec′tive•ly** *adv.*
ef•fec•tor (ĭ-fĕk′tər) ▸*n.* A muscle, gland, or organ capable of responding to a stimulus, esp. a nerve impulse.
ef•fec•tu•al (ĭ-fĕk′cho͞o-əl) ▸*adj.* Producing or sufficient to produce a desired effect; fully adequate. —**ef•fec′tu•al•ly** *adv.*
ef•fec•tu•ate (ĭ-fĕk′cho͞o-āt′) ▸*v.* **-at•ed, -at•ing.** To bring about; effect. [< Lat. *effectus*, EFFECT.] —**ef•fec′tu•a′tion** *n.*
ef•fem•i•nate (ĭ-fĕm′ə-nĭt) ▸*adj.* Having qualities or characteristics more often associated with women than men. [< Lat. *effēmināre*, make feminine.] —**ef•fem′i•na•cy** *n.* —**ef•fem′i•nate•ly** *adv.*
ef•fer•ent (ĕf′ər-ənt) ▸*adj.* **1.** Directed away from a central organ or section. **2.** Carrying impulses from the central nervous system to an effector. ▸*n.* An efferent organ. [< Lat. *efferre*, carry away : EX– + *ferre*, carry.]
ef•fer•vesce (ĕf′ər-vĕs′) ▸*v.* **-vesced, -vesc•ing 1.** To emit small bubbles of gas, as a carbonated liquid. **2.** To show high spirits or excitement. [Lat. *effervēscere*, boil over.] —**ef′fer•ves′cence** *n.* —**ef′fer•ves′cent** *adj.*
ef•fete (ĭ-fēt′) ▸*adj.* **1.** Depleted of vitality or effectiveness; exhausted. **2.** Marked by self-indulgence or triviality. [Lat. *effētus*, worn out, exhausted.] —**ef•fete′ly** *adv.* —**ef•fete′ness** *n.*
ef•fi•ca•cious (ĕf′ĭ-kā′shəs) ▸*adj.* Producing a desired effect; effective. [< Lat. *efficāx.*] —**ef′fi•ca′cious•ly** *adv.* —**ef′fi•ca′cious•ness** *n.* —**ef′fi•ca•cy** (ĕf′ĭ-kə-sē) *n.*
ef•fi•cient (ĭ-fĭsh′ənt) ▸*adj.* **1.** Acting to produce an effect with a minimum of waste or effort. **2.** Exhibiting a high ratio of output to input. [< Lat. *efficere*, bring about.] —**ef•fi′cien•cy** *n.* —**ef•fi′cient•ly** *adv.*
ef•fi•gy (ĕf′ə-jē) ▸*n., pl.* **-gies.** A likeness or image, esp. a crude figure or dummy representing a hated person or group. [< Lat. *effigiēs*, likeness.]
ef•flo•resce (ĕf′lə-rĕs′) ▸*v.* **-resced, -resc•ing.** To blossom; bloom. [Lat. *efflōrēscere* < *flōs, flōr-*, flower.]
ef•flo•res•cence (ĕf′lə-rĕs′əns) ▸*n.* **1.** *Bot.* A state or time of flowering. **2a.** A gradual process of unfolding or developing. **b.** The highest point; culmination. See Syns at **bloom.** —**ef′flo•res′cent** *adj.*
ef•flu•ent (ĕf′lo͞o-ənt) ▸*adj.* Flowing out or forth. ▸*n.* Something that flows out or forth, esp. outflow from a sewer or a discharge of liquid waste. [< Lat. *effluere*, flow out.] —**ef′flu•ence** *n.*
ef•flu•vi•um (ĭ-flo͞o′vē-əm) ▸*n., pl.* **-vi•a** (-vē-ə) or **-vi•ums.** A usu. invisible emanation, often foul or harmful. [Lat. < *effluere*, flow out.] —**ef•flu′vi•al** *adj.*
ef•fort (ĕf′ərt) ▸*n.* **1.** The use of physical or mental energy to do something; exertion. **2.** An earnest attempt. **3.** Something done through exertion; achievement. [< Med.Lat. *exfortiāre*, to force < Lat. *fortis*, strong.] —**ef′fort•less** *adj.*
ef•front•er•y (ĭ-frŭn′tə-rē) ▸*n., pl.* **-ies.** Brazen boldness; presumptuousness. [Poss. < LLat. *effrōns*, shameless.]
ef•ful•gent (ĭ-fo͝ol′jənt, ĭ-fŭl′-) ▸*adj.* Shining brilliantly; resplendent. [< Lat. *effulgēre*, shine out.] —**ef•ful′gence** *n.*
ef•fuse (ĭ-fyo͞os′) ▸*adj.* *Bot.* Spreading out loosely. ▸*v.* (ĭ-fyo͞oz′) **-fused, -fus•ing 1.** To pour out (a liquid). **2.** To radiate; diffuse. [< Lat. *effundere, effūs-*, pour out.]
ef•fu•sion (ĭ-fyo͞o′zhən) ▸*n.* **1.** Pouring forth; effusing. **2.** An unrestrained outpouring of feeling. —**ef•fu′sive** *adj.* —**ef•fu′sive•ly** *adv.* —**ef•fu′sive•ness** *n.*
eft (ĕft) ▸*n.* An immature newt. [< OE *efeta.*]
e.g. ▸*abbr.* *Lat.* exempli gratia (for example)
e•gal•i•tar•i•an (ĭ-găl′ĭ-târ′ē-ən-) ▸*adj.* Affirming political, economic, and social equality for all. [< Fr. *égalité*, equality.] —**e•gal′i•tar′i•an** *n.* —**e•gal′i•tar′i•an•ism** *n.*
egg¹ (ĕg) ▸*n.* **1a.** A female reproductive cell; ovum. **b.** The round or oval reproductive body of various animals, such as birds, reptiles, fishes, and insects, containing the embryo and covered with a shell or membrane. **2.** A hen's

egg used as food. [< ON, bird's egg.]

egg² (ĕg) ►*v.* To encourage or incite to action: *egged them on.* [< ON *eggja.*]

egg•beat•er (ĕg′bē′tər) ►*n.* A kitchen utensil with rotating blades for beating or mixing.

egg•head (ĕg′hĕd′) ►*n.* *Informal* An intellectual; highbrow.

egg•nog (ĕg′nŏg′) ►*n.* A drink consisting of milk, sugar, and eggs, often mixed with an alcoholic liquor. [EGG¹ + *nog*, ale.]

egg•plant (ĕg′plănt′) ►*n.* **1.** A plant cultivated for its large, ovoid, purple-skinned fruit. **2.** The fruit of this plant.

egg roll ►*n.* A deep-fried cylindrical casing of thin egg dough, filled with minced vegetables and often meat.

egg•shell (ĕg′shĕl′) ►*n.* **1.** The thin, brittle, exterior covering of an egg. **2.** A yellowish white. —**egg′shell′** *adj.*

e•gis (ē′jĭs) ►*n.* Var. of **aegis.**

eg•lan•tine (ĕg′lən-tīn′, -tēn′) ►*n.* See **sweetbrier.** [< VLat. **aculentum* < Lat. *acūleus*, spine < *acus*, needle.]

e•go (ē′gō, ĕg′ō) ►*n., pl.* **e•gos 1.** The self, esp. as distinct from all others. **2.** In psychoanalysis, the part of the psyche that is conscious, controls thought and behavior, and is most in touch with external reality. **3.** An exaggerated sense of self-importance; conceit. [Lat., I.]

e•go•cen•tric (ē′gō-sĕn′trĭk, ĕg′ō-) ►*adj.* Interested only in one's own needs or affairs. —**e′go•cen′tric** *n.* —**e′go•cen•tric′i•ty** (-trĭs′ĭ-tē) *n.* —**e′go•cen′trism** *n.*

e•go•ism (ē′gō-ĭz′əm, ĕg′ō-) ►*n.* **1.** The belief that self-interest is the just and proper motive for all human conduct. **2.** Egotism; conceit. See Syns at **conceit.** —**e′go•ist** *n.* —**e′go•is′tic, e′go•is′ti•cal** *adj.* —**e′go•is′ti•cal•ly** *adv.*

e•go•ma•ni•a (ē′gō-mā′nē-ə, -mān′yə, ĕg′ō-) ►*n.* Obsessive preoccupation with the self. —**e′go•ma′ni•ac′** *n.* —**e′•go•ma•ni′a•cal** (-mə-nī′ə-kəl) *adj.* —**e′go•ma•ni′a•cal•ly** *adv.*

e•go•tism (ē′gə-tĭz′əm, ĕg′ə-) ►*n.* **1.** The tendency to speak or write of oneself excessively and boastfully. **2.** An inflated sense of one's own importance; conceit. See Syns at **conceit.** —**e′go•tist** *n.* —**e′go•tis′tic, e′go•tis′ti•cal** *adj.* —**e′go•tis′ti•cal•ly** *adv.*

ego trip ►*n.* *Slang* An act, experience, or course of behavior that gratifies the ego.

e•gre•gious (ĭ-grē′jəs, -jē-əs) ►*adj.* Conspicuously bad or offensive. [< Lat. *ēgregius*, outstanding.] —**e•gre′gious•ly** *adv.* —**e•gre′gious•ness** *n.*

e•gress (ē′grĕs′) ►*n.* An act of or opening for going out. [Lat. *ēgressus* < *ēgredī*, go out.]

e•gret (ē′grĭt, ĕg′rĭt) ►*n.* Any of several usu. white herons having long, showy, drooping plumes. [OFr., ult.< OProv. *aigron*, heron.]

E•gypt (ē′jĭpt) A country of NE Africa on the Mediterranean Sea. Cap. Cairo. Pop. 48,503,000.

E•gyp•tian (ĭ-jĭp′shən) ►*n.* **1.** A native or inhabitant of Egypt. **2.** The extinct Afro-Asiatic language of the ancient Egyptians. —**E•gyp′tian** *adj.*

EHF ►*abbr.* extremely high frequency

ei•der (ī′dər) ►*n.* A large sea duck of northern regions, having soft, commercially valuable down. [< ON *æðhr.*]

ei•der•down also **eider down** (ī′dər-doun′) ►*n.* The down of the eider.

eight (āt) ►*n.* **1.** The cardinal number equal to 7 + 1. **2.** The 8th in a set or sequence. [< OE *eahta.*] —**eight** *adj. & pron.*

eight ball ►*n.* *Games* A black pool ball that bears the number 8. —***idiom:* behind the eight ball** *Slang* In an unfavorable position.

eight•een (ā-tēn′) ►*n.* **1.** The cardinal number equal to 17 + 1. **2.** The 18th in a set or sequence. —**eight•een′** *adj. & pron.*

eight•eenth (ā-tēnth′) ►*n.* **1.** The ordinal number matching the number 18 in a series. **2.** One of 18 equal parts. —**eight•eenth′** *adv. & adj.*

eighth (ātth, āth) ►*n.* **1.** The ordinal number matching the number 8 in a series. **2.** One of eight equal parts. —**eighth** *adv. & adj.*

eight•i•eth (ā′tē-ĭth) ►*n.* **1.** The ordinal number matching the number 80 in a series. **2.** One of 80 equal parts. —**eight′i•eth** *adv. & adj.*

eight•y (ā′tē) ►*n., pl.* **-ies.** The cardinal number equal to 8 × 10. —**eight′y** *adj. & pron.*

Eind•ho•ven (īnt′hō′vən) A city of S Netherlands SE of Rotterdam. Pop. 195,632.

Ein•stein (īn′stīn′), **Albert.** 1879–1955. German-born Amer. theoretical physicist; 1921 Nobel.

ein•stei•ni•um (īn-stī′nē-əm) ►*n.* *Symbol* **Es** A synthetic radioactive element first produced in a thermonuclear explosion. At. no. 99. See table at **element.** [After Albert EINSTEIN.]

Eir•e (âr′ə, ī′rə) See **Ireland².**

Ei•sen•how•er (ī′zən-hou′ər), **Dwight David.** 1890–1969. 34th US President (1953–61).

Dwight D. Eisenhower

ei•ther (ē′*th*ər, ī′*th*ər) ►*pron.* One or the other of two. ►*conj.* Used before the first of two or more coordinates or clauses linked by *or*: *Either we go now or we remain here forever.* ►*adj.* **1.** Any one of two; one or the other: *Wear either coat.* **2.** One and the other; each: *rings on either hand.* ►*adv.* Likewise; also: *If you don't order a dessert, I won't either.* [< OE *ǣghwæther.*]

e•jac•u•late (ĭ-jăk′yə-lāt′) ►*v.* **-lat•ed, -lat•ing 1.** To eject abruptly, esp. to discharge (semen) in orgasm. **2.** To utter suddenly and passionately; exclaim. ►*n.* (-lĭt). Semen ejaculated in orgasm. [Lat. *ēiaculārī.*] —**e•jac′u•la′tion** *n.* —**e•jac′u•la′tor** *n.* —**e•jac′u•la•to′ry** (-lə-tôr′y, -tōr′y) *adj.*

e•ject (ĭ-jĕkt′) ►*v.* To throw out forcefully; expel. [< Lat. *ēicere, ēiect-.*] —**e•jec′tion** *n.* —**e•jec′tor** *n.*

ejection seat ▸*n.* A seat designed to eject the occupant clear of an aircraft during an in-flight emergency.
eke (ēk) ▸*v.* **eked, ek•ing.** To make or supplement with effort: *eked out an income by working two jobs.* [< OE *ēcan*, increase.]
EKG ▸*abbr.* electrocardiogram
el. ▸*abbr.* elevation
e•lab•o•rate (ĭ-lăb′ər-ĭt) ▸*adj.* **1.** Planned or executed with attention to details. **2.** Intricate and rich in detail. ▸*v.* (-ə-rāt′) **-rat•ed, -rat•ing 1.** To work out carefully; develop thoroughly. **2.** To express at greater length or in greater detail. [Lat. *ēlabōrātus*, p.part. of *ēlabōrāre*, work out.] —**e•lab′o•rate•ly** *adv.* —**e•lab′o•rate•ness** *n.* —**e•lab′o•ra′tion** *n.* —**e•lab′o•ra′tor** *n.*
Syns: *elaborate, complicated, intricate* ***Ant:*** *simple* **adj.**
El Al•a•mein (ĕl ăl′ə-mān′, ä′lə-) A town of N Egypt on the Mediterranean Sea; site of a British victory over Germany (1942).
E•lam (ē′ləm) An ancient country of SW Asia in present-day SW Iran.
é•lan (ā-läɴ′, ā-län′) ▸*n.* **1.** Enthusiastic vigor and liveliness. **2.** Distinctive style or flair. [< OFr. *eslancer*, hurl.]
e•land (ē′lənd) ▸*n., pl.* **eland** also **e•lands.** Either of two large African antelopes having spirally twisted horns. [Ult. of Balt. orig.]
el•a•pid (ĕl′ə-pĭd) ▸*n.* Any of a family of venomous snakes that includes cobras, mambas, and coral snakes. [< Med.Gk. *elaps*, fish.]
e•lapse (ĭ-lăps′) ▸*v.* **e•lapsed, e•laps•ing.** To slip by, as time; pass. [Lat. *ēlābī, ēlāps-*.]
e•las•mo•branch (ĭ-lăz′mə-brăngk′) ▸*n.* Any of a class of cartilaginous fishes that includes sharks, rays, and skates. [Gk. *elasmos*, beaten metal + LLat. *branchia*, gill.]
e•las•tic (ĭ-lăs′tĭk) ▸*adj.* **1.** Easily resuming original shape after being stretched or expanded; flexible. **2.** Quick to recover, as from disappointment. **3.** Capable of adapting to change or a variety of circumstances. ▸*n.* **1.** A flexible, stretchable fabric. **2.** A rubber band. [< LGk. *elastos*, beaten, ductile.] —**e•las′ti•cal•ly** *adv.* —**e•las•tic′i•ty** (ĭ-lă-stĭs′ĭ-tē, ē′lă-) *n.*
e•late (ĭ-lāt′) ▸*v.* **e•lat•ed, e•lat•ing.** To make proud or joyful; fill with delight. [< Lat. *ēlātus*, p.part. of *efferre*, carry away.] —**e•la′tion** *n.*
El•ba (ĕl′bə) An island of Italy in the Tyrrhenian Sea between Corsica and the mainland.
El•be (ĕl′bə, ĕlb) A river of Czech Republic and Germany flowing about 1,167 km (725 mi) to the North Sea.
El•bert (ĕl′bərt), **Mount.** A peak, 4,402.1 m (14,433 ft), in the Sawatch Range of central CO.
el•bow (ĕl′bō′) ▸*n.* **1a.** The joint or bend of the arm between the forearm and the upper arm. **b.** The bony outer projection of this joint. **2.** Something, esp. a length of pipe, bent like an elbow. ▸*v.* **1.** To push or jostle with the elbow. **2.** To make one's way by elbowing. [< OE *elnboga*.]
elbow grease ▸*n. Informal* Strenuous effort.
el•bow•room (ĕl′bō-ro͞om′, -ro͝om′) ▸*n.* Room to move around or work freely. See Syns at **room.**
El•brus (ĕl-bro͞os′), **Mount.** A peak, 5,645.6 m (18,510 ft), in the Caucasus Mts. of SW Russia; highest mountain of Europe.
El•burz Mountains (ĕl-bo͝orz′) A range of N Iran rising to 5,774.9 m (18,934 ft).
eld•er[1] (ĕl′dər) ▸*adj.* **1.** Older. **2.** Superior to another, as in rank. ▸*n.* **1.** An older person. **2.** An older, influential member of a family, tribe, or community. **3.** A governing officer of a church. [< OE *eldra*.]
Usage: *Elder* and *eldest* generally apply to persons, unlike *older* and *oldest,* which also apply to things. *Elder* and *eldest* are used principally with reference to seniority: *elder sister; elder statesman; John the Elder.*
el•der[2] (ĕl′dər) ▸*n.* Any of various shrubs having small white flowers and red or black drupes. [< OE *ellærn*.]
el•der•ber•ry (ĕl′dər-bĕr′ē) ▸*n.* **1.** The small edible fruit of an elder. **2.** The elder.
eld•er•ly (ĕl′dər-lē) ▸*adj.* **1.** Approaching old age. **2.** Of or characteristic of older persons. ▸*n., pl.* **elderly** *(takes pl. v.)* Older people collectively. Used with *the.*
eld•est (ĕl′dĭst) ▸*adj.* Greatest in age or seniority. See Usage Note at **elder**[1]**.**
El Do•ra•do (də-rä′dō) ▸*n.* A place of fabulous wealth. [Sp., legendary South American land.]
El•ea•nor of Aquitaine (ĕl′ə-nər, -nôr′). 1122?–1204. Queen of France (1137–52) and England (1152–1204).
e•lect (ĭ-lĕkt′) ▸*v.* **1.** To select by vote for an office or for membership. **2.** To pick out; select: *elect an art course.* ▸*adj.* **1.** Chosen deliberately; singled out. **2.** Elected but not yet installed: *the governor-elect.* ▸*n.* **1.** One that is chosen or selected. **2.** *(takes pl. v.)* An exclusive group of people. [< Lat. *ēligere, ēlēct-*.] —**e•lec′tion** *n.*
e•lec•tion•eer (ĭ-lĕk′shə-nîr′) ▸*v.* To work actively for a candidate or political party.
e•lec•tive (ĭ-lĕk′tĭv) ▸*adj.* **1.** Filled or obtained by election. **2.** Having the power to elect. **3.** Optional. ▸*n.* An optional academic course or subject.
e•lec•tor (ĭ-lĕk′tər) ▸*n.* **1.** A qualified voter. **2.** A member of the Electoral College. —**e•lec′tor•al** *adj.*
Electoral College ▸*n.* A body of electors chosen to elect the President and Vice President of the US.
e•lec•tor•ate (ĭ-lĕk′tər-ĭt) ▸*n.* A body of qualified voters.
E•lec•tra (ĭ-lĕk′trə) ▸*n. Gk. Myth.* Daughter of Agamemnon who with her brother Orestes avenged their father's murder by killing their mother Clytemnestra.
e•lec•tric (ĭ-lĕk′trĭk) ▸*adj.* **1.** Of or operated by electricity. **2.** Amplified by an electronic device: *an electric guitar.* **3.** Emotionally exciting; thrilling. —**e•lec′tri•cal•ly** *adv.*
electric chair ▸*n.* A chair used in the electrocution of a prisoner sentenced to death.
electric eel ▸*n.* An eellike freshwater fish of South America that produces a powerful electric discharge.
electric eye ▸*n.* See **photoelectric cell.**
e•lec•tri•cian (ĭ-lĕk-trĭsh′ən, ē′lĕk-) ▸*n.* One whose occupation is the installation, maintenance, repair, or operation of electric equipment and circuitry.
e•lec•tric•i•ty (ĭ-lĕk-trĭs′ĭ-tē, ē′lĕk-) ▸*n.* **1.** The physical phenomena arising from the at-

traction of particles with opposite charges and the repulsion of particles with the same charge. **2.** Electric current used or regarded as a source of power. **3.** Intense emotional excitement.

e•lec•tri•fy (ĭ-lĕk′trə-fī′) ►*v.* **-fied, -fy•ing 1.** To produce electric charge on or in. **2.** To wire or equip for the use of electric power. **3.** To thrill, startle greatly, or shock. —**e•lec′tri•fi•ca′tion** *n.*

electro– or **electr–** ►*pref.* **1.** Electric; electricity: *electrochemistry.* **2.** Electron: *electrode.* [< Gk. *ēlektron*, amber.]

e•lec•tro•car•di•o•gram (ĭ-lĕk′trō-kär′dē-ə-grăm′) ►*n.* The curve traced by an electrocardiograph.

e•lec•tro•car•di•o•graph (ĭ-lĕk′trō-kär′dē-ə-grăf′) ►*n.* An instrument that measures electrical potentials associated with heart muscle activity. —**e•lec′tro•car′di•o•graph′ic** *adj.* —**e•lec′tro•car′di•og′ra•phy** (-kär′dē-ŏg′rə-fē) *n.*

e•lec•tro•chem•is•try (ĭ-lĕk′trō-kĕm′ĭ-strē) ►*n.* The science of the interaction of electric and chemical phenomena. —**e•lec′tro•chem′i•cal•ly** *adv.*

e•lec•tro•con•vul•sive therapy (ĭ-lĕk′trō-kən-vŭl′sĭv) ►*n.* Administration of electric current to the brain to induce unconsciousness and brief convulsions, used esp. to treat acute depression.

e•lec•tro•cute (ĭ-lĕk′trə-kyo͞ot′) ►*v.* **-cut•ed, -cut•ing 1.** To kill with electricity. **2.** To execute (a prisoner) by electricity. [ELECTRO– + (EXE)CUTE.] —**e•lec′tro•cu′tion** *n.*

e•lec•trode (ĭ-lĕk′trōd′) ►*n.* A solid electric conductor through which an electric current enters or leaves an electrolytic cell or other medium.

e•lec•tro•dy•nam•ics (ĭ-lĕk′trō-dī-năm′ĭks) ►*n.* *(takes sing. v.)* The physics of the relationship between electric current and magnetic or mechanical phenomena. —**e•lec′tro•dy•nam′ic** *adj.*

e•lec•tro•en•ceph•a•lo•gram (ĭ-lĕk′trō-ĕn-sĕf′ə-lə-grăm′) ►*n.* A graphic record of the electrical activity of the brain as recorded by an electroencephalograph.

e•lec•tro•en•ceph•a•lo•graph (ĭ-lĕk′trō-ĕn-sĕf′ə-lə-grăf′) ►*n.* An instrument that measures electrical potentials on the scalp and generates a record of the electrical activity of the brain. —**e•lec′tro•en•ceph′a•lo•graph′ic** *adj.* —**e•lec′tro•en•ceph′a•log′ra•phy** (-lŏg′rə-fē) *n.*

e•lec•trol•o•gist (ĭ-lĕk-trŏl′ə-jĭst, ē′lĕk-) ►*n.* One who removes body hair by means of an electric current.

e•lec•trol•y•sis (ĭ-lĕk-trŏl′ĭ-sĭs, ē′lĕk-) ►*n.* **1.** Chemical change, esp. decomposition, produced in an electrolyte by an electric current. **2.** Destruction of living tissue, esp. of hair roots, by an electric current.

e•lec•tro•lyte (ĭ-lĕk′trə-līt′) ►*n.* **1.** A chemical compound that ionizes when dissolved or molten to produce an electrically conductive medium. **2.** *Physiol.* Any of various ions required by cells to regulate the electric charge and flow of water molecules across the cell membrane.

e•lec•tro•lyt•ic (ĭ-lĕk′trə-lĭt′ĭk) ►*adj.* **1.** Of or relating to electrolysis. **2.** Of electrolytes. —**e•lec′tro•lyt′i•cal•ly** *adv.*

e•lec•tro•mag•net (ĭ-lĕk′trō-măg′nĭt) ►*n.* A magnet consisting essentially of a coil of insulated wire wrapped around a soft iron core that is magnetized only when current flows through the wire.

electromagnetic spectrum ►*n.* The entire range of radiation that includes, in order of decreasing frequency, cosmic-ray photons, gamma rays, x-rays, ultraviolet radiation, visible light, infrared radiation, microwaves, and radio waves.

e•lec•tro•mag•net•ism (ĭ-lĕk′trō-măg′nĭ-tĭz′əm) ►*n.* **1.** Magnetism produced by electric charge in motion. **2.** The physics of electricity and magnetism. —**e•lec′tro•mag•net′ic** *adj.*

e•lec•tro•mo•tive (ĭ-lĕk′trō-mō′tĭv) ►*adj.* Of or producing electric current.

electromotive force ►*n.* The energy per unit charge that is converted reversibly from chemical, mechanical, or other forms of energy into electrical energy in a battery or dynamo.

e•lec•tron (ĭ-lĕk′trŏn′) ►*n.* A stable elementary particle having a unit negative electric charge and a rest mass of approx. 9.1×10^{-28} gram.

e•lec•tron•ic (ĭ-lĕk-trŏn′ĭk, ē′lĕk-) ►*adj.* **1.** Of or involving electrons or electronics. **2.** Implemented on or controlled by a computer. —**e•lec′tron′i•cal•ly** *adv.*

e•lec•tron•ics (ĭ-lĕk′trŏn′ĭks, ē′lĕk-) ►*n.* **1.** *(takes sing. v.)* The science dealing with the controlled conduction of electrons, esp. in a vacuum, gas, or semiconductor. **2.** *(takes pl. v.)* Electronic devices and systems.

electron microscope ►*n.* A microscope that uses electrons rather than visible light to produce magnified images.

electron tube ►*n.* A sealed enclosure, either highly evacuated or containing a controlled quantity of gas, in which electrons can be made sufficiently mobile to act as the principal carriers of current between at least one pair of electrodes.

electron volt ►*n.* A unit of energy equal to the energy acquired by an electron falling through a potential difference of one volt.

e•lec•tro•pho•re•sis (ĭ-lĕk′trō-fə-rē′sĭs) ►*n.* The migration of charged colloidal particles or molecules through a solution under the influence of an applied electric field.

e•lec•tro•plate (ĭ-lĕk′trə-plāt′) ►*v.* **-plat•ed, -plat•ing.** To coat or cover electrolytically with a thin layer of metal.

e•lec•tro•shock (ĭ-lĕk′trō-shŏk′) ►*n.* See **electroconvulsive therapy.** ►*v.* To administer electroconvulsive therapy to.

e•lec•tro•stat•ic (ĭ-lĕk′trō-stăt′ĭk) ►*adj.* **1.** Of or relating to electric charges at rest. **2.** Of electrostatics. —**e•lec′tro•stat′i•cal•ly** *adv.*

e•lec•tro•stat•ics (ĭ-lĕk′trō-stăt′ĭks) ►*n.* *(takes sing. v.)* The physics of electrostatic phenomena.

e•lec•tro•type (ĭ-lĕk′trə-tīp′) ►*n.* A metal plate used in letterpress, made by electroplating a mold of the page to be printed. —**e•lec′tro•type′** *v.* —**e•lec′tro•typ′er** *n.* —**e•lec′tro•typ′ic** (-trō-tĭp′ĭk) *adj.*

el•ee•mos•y•nar•y (ĕl′ə-mŏs′ə-nĕr′ē, ĕl′ē-ə-) ►*adj.* Of or dependent on charity. See Syns at **benevolent.** [< LLat. *eleēmosyna*, ALMS.]

el•e•gance (ĕl′ĭ-gəns) ►*n.* **1.** Refinement and

PERIODIC TABLE OF THE ELEMENTS

The periodic table arranges the chemical elements in two ways. The first is by **atomic number**, starting with hydrogen (atomic number = 1) in the upper left-hand corner and continuing in ascending order from left to right. The second is by the number of electrons in the outermost **shell**. Elements having the same number of electrons in the outermost shell are grouped in the same column. Since the number of electrons in the outermost shell in large part determines the chemical nature of an element, elements in the same column have similar chemical properties.

This arrangement of the elements was devised by **Dmitri Mendeleev** in 1869, before many of

KEY

1 — atomic number
H — symbol
Hydrogen
1.00794 — atomic weight (or mass number of most stable isotope if in parentheses)

	1	2	3	4	5	6	7	8	9
1	1 **H** Hydrogen 1.00794								
2	3 **Li** Lithium 6.941	4 **Be** Beryllium 9.0122							
3	11 **Na** Sodium 22.9898	12 **Mg** Magne- sium 24.305							
4	19 **K** Potassium 39.098	20 **Ca** Calcium 40.08	21 **Sc** Scandium 44.956	22 **Ti** Titanium 47.87	23 **V** Vanadium 50.942	24 **Cr** Chro- mium 51.996	25 **Mn** Manga- nese 54.9380	26 **Fe** Iron 55.845	27 **Co** Cobalt 58.9332
5	37 **Rb** Rubidium 85.47	38 **Sr** Strontium 87.62	39 **Y** Yttrium 88.906	40 **Zr** Zirconium 91.22	41 **Nb** Niobium 92.906	42 **Mo** Molyb- denum 95.94	43 **Tc** Tech- netium (98)	44 **Ru** Ruthe- nium 101.07	45 **Rh** Rhodium 102.905
6	55 **Cs** Cesium 132.905	56 **Ba** Barium 137.33	57—71* Lantha- nides	72 **Hf** Hafnium 178.49	73 **Ta** Tantalum 108.948	74 **W** Tungsten 183.84	75 **Re** Rhenium 186.2	76 **Os** Osmium 190.2	77 **Ir** Iridium 192.2
7	87 **Fr** Francium (223)	88 **Ra** Radium (226)	89— 103** Actinides	104 **Rf** Ruther- fordium (261)	105 **Db** Dubnium (262)	106 **Sg** Seabor- gium (266)	107 **Bh** Bohrium (264)	108 **Hs** Hassium (265)	109 **Mt** Meit- nerium (268)
***LANTHANIDES**			57 **La** Lantha- num 138.91	58 **Ce** Cerium 140.12	59 **Pr** Praseo- dymium 140.908	60 **Nd** Neodym- ium 144.24	61 **Pm** Prome- thium (145)	62 **Sm** Samarium 150.36	63 **Eu** Europium 151.96
****ACTINIDES**			89 **Ac** Actinium (227)	90 **Th** Thorium 232.038	91 **Pa** Protac- tinium 231.036	92 **U** Uranium 238.03	93 **Np** Neptu- nium (237)	94 **Pu** Plutonium (244)	95 **Am** Ameri- cium (243)

grace in movement, appearance, or manners. **2.** Tasteful opulence in form, decoration, or presentation. **3a.** Restraint and grace of style. **b.** Scientific exactness and precision.

el•e•gant (ĕl′ĭ-gənt) ►*adj.* Marked by refined, tasteful beauty of manner, form, or style. See Syns at **delicate.** [< Lat. *ēligere*, select.] —**el′e•gant•ly** *adv.*

el•e•gi•ac (ĕl′ə-jī′ək, ĭ-lē′jē-ăk′) ►*adj.* **1.** Of or relating to an elegy. **2.** Expressing sorrow; mournful. —**el′•e•gi′ac** *n.* —**el′e•gi′a•cal** *adj.* —**el′e•gi′a•cal•ly** *adv.*

el•e•gy (ĕl′ə-jē) ►*n., pl.* **-gies.** A mournful poem or song, esp. one lamenting a dead person. [< Gk. *elegos*, song.] —**el′e•gist** *n.*

el•e•ment (ĕl′ə-mənt) ►*n.* **1.** A substance composed of atoms having an identical number of protons in each nucleus and not reducible to a simpler substance. **2.** A fundamental or essential part of a whole. **3.** *Math.* **a.** A member of a set. **b.** A point, line, or plane. **c.** A part of a geometric configuration, as an angle in a triangle. **4. elements** The forces that constitute the weather, esp. inclement weather. **5.** An en-

PERIODIC TABLE OF THE ELEMENTS, continued

the elements now known were discovered. To maintain the overall logic of the table, Mendeleev allowed space for undiscovered elements whose existence he predicted. This space has since been partly filled in, most recently by the addition of elements 104–112. Elements 110–112 have been isolated experimentally but not yet officially named.

The **lanthanide** series (elements 57–71) and the **actinide** series (elements 89–103) are composed of elements whose chemical properties are similar to those of elements in column 3. They are placed below the main body of the table to make it easier to read.

10	11	12	13	14	15	16	17	18
								2 **He** Helium 4.0026
			5 **B** Boron 10.811	6 **C** Carbon 12.011	7 **N** Nitrogen 14.0067	8 **O** Oxygen 15.9994	9 **F** Fluorine 18.9984	10 **Ne** Neon 20.183
			13 **Al** Alum-inum 26.9815	14 **Si** Silicon 28.086	15 **P** Phospho-rus 30.9738	16 **S** Sulfur 32.066	17 **Cl** Chlorine 35.453	18 **Ar** Argon 39.948
28 **Ni** Nickel 58.69	29 **Cu** Copper 63.546	30 **Zn** Zinc 65.39	31 **Ga** Gallium 69.72	32 **Ge** German-ium 72.61	33 **As** Arsenic 74.9216	34 **Se** Selenium 78.96	35 **Br** Bromine 79.904	36 **Kr** Krypton 83.80
46 **Pd** Palladium 106.4	47 **Ag** Silver 107.868	48 **Cd** Cadmium 112.41	49 **In** Indium 114.82	50 **Sn** Tin 118.71	51 **Sb** Antimony 121.76	52 **Te** Tellurium 127.60	53 **I** Iodine 126.9045	54 **Xe** Xenon 131.29
78 **Pt** Platinum 195.08	79 **Au** Gold 196.967	80 **Hg** Mercury 200.59	81 **Tl** Thallium 204.38	82 **Pb** Lead 207.2	83 **Bi** Bismuth 208.98	84 **Po** Polonium (210)	85 **At** Astatine (210)	86 **Rn** Radon (222)
110 (269)	111 (272)	112 (277)						

64 **Gd** Gadolin-ium 157.25	65 **Tb** Terbium 158.925	66 **Dy** Dyspro-sium 162.50	67 **Ho** Holmium 164.930	68 **Er** Erbium 167.26	69 **Tm** Thulium 168.934	70 **Yb** Ytterbium 173.04	71 **Lu** Lutetium 174.97
96 **Cm** Curium (247)	97 **Bk** Berkelium (247)	598 **Cf** Califor-nium (251)	99 **Es** Einstein-ium (252)	100 **Fm** Fermium (257)	101 **Md** Mende-levium (258)	102 **No** Nobelium (259)	103 **Lr** Lawren-cium (262)

vironment naturally suited to or associated with an individual. [< Lat. *elementum*, fundamental constituent.]

Syns: *element, component, constituent, factor, ingredient* **n.**

element 110 ►*n.* A short-lived, synthetic radioactive element. See table at **element.**

element 111 ►*n.* A short-lived, synthetic radioactive element. See table at **element.**

element 112 ►*n.* A short-lived, synthetic radioactive element. See table at **element.**

el•e•men•tal (ĕl′ə-mĕn′tl) ►*adj.* **1.** Of or being an element. **2.** Fundamental or essential. **3.** Of or resembling a force of nature in power or effect. —**el′e•men′tal** *n.* —**el′e•men′tal•ly** *adv.*

el•e•men•ta•ry (ĕl′ə-mĕn′tə-rē, -trē) ►*adj.* **1.** Of or constituting the essential or fundamental part. **2.** Of or involving the fundamental or simplest aspects of a subject. —**el′e•men•ta′ri•ly** (-tĕr′ə-lē) *adv.* —**el′e•men′ta•ri•ness** *n.*

elementary particle ►*n.* A subatomic particle, esp. one regarded as irreducible.

elementary school ►*n.* A school attended for

the first six to eight years of a child's formal education.

el•e•phant (ĕl′ə-fənt) ▸ *n.* A very large herbivorous mammal of Africa and Asia with a long flexible trunk and long tusks. [< Gk. *elephas*.]

el•e•phan•ti•a•sis (ĕl′ə-fən-tī′ə-sĭs) ▸ *n.* Enlargement and hardening of tissues, esp. of the lower body, resulting from lymphatic obstruction and usually caused by parasitic worms. [< Gk.]

el•e•phan•tine (ĕl′ə-făn′tēn′, -tīn′, ĕl′ə-fən-) ▸ *adj.* **1.** Of or relating to an elephant. **2a.** Enormous in size or strength. **b.** Ponderously clumsy.

elev. ▸ *abbr.* elevation

el•e•vate (ĕl′ə-vāt′) ▸ *v.* **-vat•ed, -vat•ing 1.** To raise to a higher position; lift. **2.** To promote to a higher rank. **3.** To raise to a higher moral, cultural, or intellectual level. **4.** To lift the spirits of; elate. [< Lat. *ēlevāre*.]

el•e•va•tion (ĕl′ə-vā′shən) ▸ *n.* **1.** The act of elevating or condition of being elevated. **2.** An elevated place or position. **3.** The height to which something is elevated above a point of reference such as the ground.

Syns: *elevation, altitude, height* ***n.***

el•e•va•tor (ĕl′ə-vā′tər) ▸ *n.* **1.** A platform or enclosure raised and lowered in a vertical shaft to transport people or freight. **2.** A movable control surface on an aircraft, used to move the aircraft up or down. **3.** A granary with devices for hoisting and discharging grain.

e•lev•en (ĭ-lĕv′ən) ▸ *n.* **1.** The cardinal number equal to 10 + 1. **2.** The 11th in a set or sequence. [< OE *endleofan*.] —**e•lev′en** *adj. & pron.*

e•lev•enth (ĭ-lĕv′ənth) ▸ *n.* **1.** The ordinal number matching the number 11 in a series. **2.** One of 11 equal parts. —**e•lev′enth** *adv. & adj.*

elf (ĕlf) ▸ *n., pl.* **elves** (ĕlvz). A small, often mischievous fairy. [< OE *ælf*.] —**elf′in** *adj.* —**elf′ish** *adj.*

ELF ▸ *abbr.* extremely low frequency

El•gar (ĕl′gär′, -gər), Sir **Edward.** 1857–1934. British composer.

El Grec•o (grĕk′ō). See El **Greco.**

e•lic•it (ĭ-lĭs′ĭt) ▸ *v.* **1.** To bring or draw out. **2.** To call forth; evoke. [Lat. *ēlicere*.] —**e•lic′i•ta′tion** *n.*

e•lide (ĭ-līd′) ▸ *v.* **e•lid•ed, e•lid•ing 1.** To omit or slur over (a syllable or word) in pronunciation. **2.** To eliminate or leave out of consideration. [Lat. *ēlīdere*, strike out.]

el•i•gi•ble (ĕl′ĭ-jə-bəl) ▸ *adj.* **1.** Qualified to be chosen. **2.** Worthy of choice, esp. for marriage. [< Lat. *ēligere*, select.] —**el′i•gi•bil′i•ty** *n.* —**el′i•gi•bly** *adv.*

E•li•jah (ĭ-lī′jə). 9th cent. B.C. Hebrew prophet.

e•lim•i•nate (ĭ-lĭm′ə-nāt′) ▸ *v.* **-nat•ed, -nat•ing 1.** To get rid of; remove. **2.** To leave out or omit; reject. **3.** *Physiol.* To excrete (bodily wastes). [Lat. *ēlīmināre*, banish.] —**e•lim′i•na′tion** *n.* —**e•lim′i•na′tive, e•lim′i•na•to′ry** (-nə-tôr′ē, -tōr′ē) *adj.* —**e•lim′i•na′tor** *n.*

Syns: *eliminate, eradicate, liquidate, purge* ***v.***

El•i•ot (ĕl′ē-ət), **George.** Pen name of Mary Ann Evans. 1819–80. British writer.

Eliot, T(homas) S(tearns). 1888–1965. Amer.-born British writer; 1948 Nobel.

E•li•sha (ĭ-lī′shə). 9th cent. B.C. Hebrew prophet.

e•lite or **é•lite** (ĭ-lēt′, ā-lēt′) ▸ *n., pl.* **elite** or **e•lites 1.** A group or class enjoying superior intellectual, social, or economic status. **2.** A size of type on a typewriter, equal to 12 characters per linear inch. [< OFr. *eslire*, ELECT.] —**e•lite′** *adj.*

e•lit•ism or **é•lit•ism** (ĭ-lē′tĭz′əm, ā-lē′-) ▸ *n.* **1.** The belief that certain persons or members of certain classes or groups deserve favored treatment. **2a.** The sense of entitlement enjoyed by such a group or class. **b.** Control, rule, or domination by such a group or class. —**e•lit′ist** *adj. & n.*

e•lix•ir (ĭ-lĭk′sər) ▸ *n.* **1.** A sweetened aromatic solution of alcohol and water containing medicine. **2.** A substance believed to cure all ills. [< Ar. *al-'iksīr*.]

E•liz•a•beth (ĭ-lĭz′ə-bəth) A city of NE NJ S of Newark. Pop. 110,002.

Elizabeth I. 1533–1603. Queen of England and Ireland (1558–1603).

Elizabeth II. b. 1926. Queen of Great Britain and Northern Ireland (since 1952).

Elizabeth II
photographed in 1995

E•liz•a•be•than (ĭ-lĭz′ə-bē′thən, -bĕth′ən) ▸ *adj.* Of or characteristic of Elizabeth I of England or her reign. —**E•liz′a•be′than** *n.*

elk (ĕlk) ▸ *n., pl.* **elk** or **elks 1.** See **wapiti. 2.** The moose. [Prob. < OE *eolh*.]

ell[1] (ĕl) ▸ *n.* A wing of a building at right angles to the main structure. [Poss. from L.]

ell[2] (ĕl) ▸ *n.* An English linear measure equal to 45 in. (114 cm). [< OE *eln*, the length from elbow to finger tips.]

El•ling•ton (ĕl′ĭng-tən), **Edward Kennedy.** "Duke." 1899–1974. Amer. jazz composer and musician.

el•lipse (ĭ-lĭps′) ▸ *n.* A plane curve that is the locus of points for which the sum of the distances from each point to two fixed points is equal. [< Gk. *elleipsis*.]

el•lip•sis (ĭ-lĭp′sĭs) ▸ *n., pl.* **-ses** (-sēz) **1.** The omission of a word or phrase that is not necessary for understanding. **2.** A mark or series of marks, often three periods (...), used to indicate an omission. [< Gk. *elleipsis*.]

el•lip•soid (ĭ-lĭp′soid′) ▸ *n.* A geometric surface whose plane sections are ellipses or circles. —**el•lip′soid′, el′lip•soi′dal** (-soid′l) *adj.*

el•lip•tic (ĭ-lĭp′tĭk) or **el•lip•ti•cal** (-tĭ-kəl) ▸ *adj.* **1.** Of or shaped like an ellipse. **2.** Containing an ellipsis. **3.** Obscure or incomplete. [< Gk. *elleiptikos* < *elleipsis*, ellipsis.]

El•lis (ĕl′ĭs), **(Henry) Havelock.** 1859–1939. British psychologist and writer.

Ellis Island. An island of Upper New York Bay SW of Manhattan; chief immigration station of the US (1892–1943).

El•li•son (ĕl′ĭ-sən), **Ralph Waldo.** 1914–94. Amer. novelist.

elm (ĕlm) ▸*n.* **1.** Any of various deciduous trees having arching or curving branches and serrate leaves. **2.** The wood of an elm. [< OE.]

El Mis•ti (mē′stē) A dormant volcano, 5,825.8 m (19,101 ft), in the Cordillera Occidental of S Peru.

El Ni•ño (nēn′yō) ▸*n.* A periodic warming of the ocean surface off the W coast of South America that affects Pacific and other weather patterns. [Sp., the (Christ) child (< its onset being around Christmas).]

el•o•cu•tion (ĕl′ə-kyo͞o′shən) ▸*n.* The art of public speaking, emphasizing gesture and vocal delivery. [< Lat. *ēloquī*, speak out.] —**el′o•cu′tion•ar′y** *adj.* —**el′o•cu′tion•ist** *n.*

e•lon•gate (ĭ-lông′gāt′, ĭ-lŏng′-) ▸*v.* **-gat•ed, -gat•ing.** To make or grow longer. [LLat. *ēlongāre.*] —**e•lon′ga′tion** *n.*

e•lope (ĭ-lōp′) ▸*v.* **e•loped, e•lop•ing.** To run away with a lover, esp. to get married. [Poss. AN *aloper*, to run away from one's husband with a lover.] —**e•lope′ment** *n.*

el•o•quent (ĕl′ə-kwənt) ▸*adj.* **1.** Marked by fluent, persuasive discourse. **2.** Vividly or movingly expressive. See Syns at **expressive.** [< Lat. *ēloquī*, speak out.] —**el′o•quence** *n.* —**el′o•quent•ly** *adv.*

El Pas•o (păs′ō) A city of extreme W TX on the Rio Grande. Pop. 515,342.

El Sal•va•dor (săl′və-dôr′) A country of Central America bordering on the Pacific Ocean. Cap. San Salvador. Pop. 4,949,000. —**El Sal′va•dor′i•an** *adj. & n.*

else (ĕls) ▸*adj.* **1.** Other; different: *Ask somebody else.* **2.** Additional; more: *Would you like anything else?* ▸*adv.* **1.** In a different time, place, or manner: *Where else would you like to go?* **2.** If not; otherwise: *Be careful, or else you may err.* [< OE *elles.*]

Usage: When a pronoun is followed by *else*, the possessive form is generally written thus: *someone else's* (not *someone's else*). Both *who else's* and *whose else* are in use, but not *whose else's.*

else•where (ĕls′hwâr′, -wâr′) ▸*adv.* In or to another place.

e•lu•ci•date (ĭ-lo͞o′sĭ-dāt′) ▸*v.* **-dat•ed, -dat•ing.** To make clear or plain; clarify. [LLat. *ēlūcidāre* < Lat. *lūcidus*, bright.] —**e•lu′ci•da′tion** *n.*

e•lude (ĭ-lo͞od′) ▸*v.* **e•lud•ed, e•lud•ing 1.** To evade or escape from, as by daring or skill. **2.** To escape the understanding or grasp of. [Lat. *ēlūdere.*]

E•lul (ĕl′o͝ol, ĕ-lo͞ol′) ▸*n.* A month of the Jewish calendar. See table at **calendar.** [Heb. *'Elûl* < Akkadian.]

e•lu•sive (ĭ-lo͞o′sĭv, -zĭv) ▸*adj.* **1.** Tending to elude. **2.** Evasive; slippery. —**e•lu′sive•ly** *adv.* —**e•lu′sive•ness** *n.*

e•lute (ĭ-lo͞ot′) ▸*v.* **e•lut•ed, e•lut•ing.** To extract (one material) from another. [< Lat. *ēluere, ēlūt-*, wash out : *ē-, ex-*, ex- + *-luere*, wash.] —**e•lu′tion** *n.*

el•ver (ĕl′vər) ▸*n.* A young or immature eel. [< *eelfare*, the migration of young eels.]

elves (ĕlvz) ▸*n.* Pl. of **elf.**

E•ly•si•um (ĭ-lĭz′ē-əm, ĭ-lĭzh′-) ▸*n.* A place or condition of ideal happiness. —**E•ly′sian** (-lĭzh′ən) *adj.*

em (ĕm) ▸*n. Print.* **1.** The width of a square piece of type, used as a unit of measure for matter set in that size of type. **2.** A pica.

em–[1], **em–**[2] ▸*pref.* Var. of **en–**[1], **en–**[2].

'em (əm) ▸*pron. Informal* Them. [< OE *heom.*]

e•ma•ci•ate (ĭ-mā′shē-āt′) ▸*v.* **-at•ed, -at•ing.** To make or become extremely thin, esp. from starvation. [Lat. *ēmaciāre*, make thin.] —**e•ma′ci•a′tion** *n.*

e-mail or **e•mail** (ē′māl′) ▸*n.* A message or messages sent and received electronically over a computer network. [*e(lectronic) mail.*] —**e′-mail′** *v.*

em•a•lan•ge•ni (ĕm′ə-läng-gĕn′ē) ▸*n.* Pl. of **lilangeni.**

em•a•nate (ĕm′ə-nāt′) ▸*v.* **-nat•ed, -nat•ing.** To come or send forth from a source; issue; stem. [Lat. *ēmānāre*, flow out.] —**em′a•na′tion** *n.*

e•man•ci•pate (ĭ-măn′sə-pāt′) ▸*v.* **-pat•ed, -pat•ing.** To free from bondage, oppression, or restraint; liberate. [Lat. *ēmancipāre.*] —**e•man′ci•pa′tion** *n.* —**e•man′ci•pa′tor** *n.*

e•mas•cu•late (ĭ-măs′kyə-lāt′) ▸*v.* **-lat•ed, -lat•ing 1.** To castrate. **2.** To make weak. [Lat. *ēmasculāre.*] —**e•mas′cu•la′tion** *n.* —**e•mas′cu•la′tive, e•mas′cu•la•to′ry** (-lə-tôr′ē, -tōr′ē) *adj.* —**e•mas′cu•la′tor** *n.*

em•balm (ĕm-bäm′) ▸*v.* To treat (a corpse) with preservatives in order to prevent decay. [< OFr. *embasmer* < *basme*, BALM.] —**em•balm′er** *n.* —**em•balm′ment** *n.*

em•bank (ĕm-băngk′) ▸*v.* To confine, support, or protect with a bank, as of earth or stone. —**em•bank′ment** *n.*

em•bar•ca•de•ro (ĕm-bär′kə-dâr′ō) ▸*n., pl.* **-ros** *Regional* A pier or wharf, esp. on a river. [Sp.]

em•bar•go (ĕm-bär′gō) ▸*n., pl.* **-goes 1.** A government order prohibiting the movement of merchant ships into or out of its ports. **2.** A prohibition by a government on certain or all trade with a foreign nation. ▸*v.* To impose an embargo on. [Sp. < *embargar*, impede.]

em•bark (ĕm-bärk′) ▸*v.* **1.** To board or cause to board a vessel or aircraft, esp. at the start of a journey. **2.** To set out; commence. [Fr. *embarquer.*] —**em′bar•ka′tion** *n.*

em•bar•rass (ĕm-băr′əs) ▸*v.* **1.** To cause to feel self-conscious or ill at ease; disconcert. **2.** To hamper with financial difficulties. [< Ital. *imbarazzo*, obstacle.] —**em•bar′rass•ing•ly** *adv.* —**em•bar′rass•ment** *n.*

Syns: *embarrass, abash, chagrin, discomfit, disconcert, faze, rattle* **v.**

em•bas•sy (ĕm′bə-sē) ▸*n., pl.* **-sies 1.** A building containing the offices of an ambassador and staff. **2.** The position or function of an ambassador. **3.** A mission headed by an ambassador. [< Med.Lat. *ambactiāta* < Lat. *ambactus*, servant.]

em•bat•tled (ĕm-băt′ld) ▸*adj.* Beset with attackers, criticism, or controversy.

em•bed (ĕm-bĕd′) also **im•bed** (ĭm-) ▸*v.* **-bed•ded, -bed•ding.** To fix or become fixed firmly in a surrounding mass.

em•bel•lish (ĕm-bĕl′ĭsh) ►*v.* **1.** To make beautiful, as by ornamentation; decorate. **2.** To add fictitious details to. [< OFr. *embellir* < *bel*, beautiful.] —**em•bel′lish•ment** *n.*

em•ber (ĕm′bər) ►*n.* **1.** A piece of live coal or wood from a fire. **2. embers** The smoldering remains of a fire. [< OE *ǣmerge.*]

em•bez•zle (ĕm-bĕz′əl) ►*v.* **-zled, -zling.** To take (e.g., money) for one's own use in violation of a trust. [< AN *enbesiler.*] —**em•bez′zle•ment** *n.* —**em•bez′zler** *n.*

em•bit•ter (ĕm-bĭt′ər) ►*v.* **1.** To make bitter. **2.** To arouse bitter feelings in. —**em•bit′ter•ment** *n.*

em•bla•zon (ĕm-blā′zən) ►*v.* **1.** To ornament richly, esp. with heraldic devices. **2.** To make resplendent with brilliant colors. **3.** To mark or inscribe boldly. —**em•bla′zon•er** *n.* —**em•bla′zon•ment** *n.*

em•blem (ĕm′bləm) ►*n.* **1.** An object or representation that functions as a symbol. **2.** A distinctive badge, design, or device. [< Gk. *emblēma*, embossed design.] —**em′blem•at′ic, em′blem•at′i•cal** *adj.* —**em′blem•at′i•cal•ly** *adv.*

em•bod•y (ĕm-bŏd′ē) ►*v.* **-bod•ied, -bod•y•ing 1.** To give a bodily form to. **2.** To personify. **3.** To make part of a system or whole; incorporate. —**em•bod′i•ment** *n.*

em•bold•en (ĕm-bōl′dən) ►*v.* To foster boldness or courage in. See Syns at **encourage.**

em•bo•lism (ĕm′bə-lĭz′əm) ►*n.* **1.** Obstruction or occlusion of a blood vessel by an embolus. **2.** An embolus. [< Gk. *embolismos*, insertion.]

em•bo•lus (ĕm′bə-ləs) ►*n., pl.* **-li** (-lī′). A mass in the bloodstream that lodges so as to block a blood vessel. [< Gk. *embolos*, stopper.]

em•boss (ĕm-bôs′, -bŏs′) ►*v.* **1.** To mold or carve in relief. **2.** To decorate with a raised design. [< OFr. *embocer* < *boce*, knob.]

em•bou•chure (äm′bo͞o-sho͝or′) ►*n.* **1.** The mouthpiece of a wind instrument. **2.** The manner in which the lips and tongue are applied to such a mouthpiece. [< OFr. *emboucher*, put in the mouth < *bouche*, mouth.]

em•bow•er (ĕm-bou′ər) ►*v.* To enclose in or as if in a bower.

em•brace (ĕm-brās′) ►*v.* **-braced, -brac•ing 1.** To clasp or hold close with the arms. **2.** To surround; enclose: *The warm water embraced us.* **3.** To include as part of something broader. **4.** To take up willingly or eagerly: *embrace a cause.* ►*n.* An act of embracing. [< OFr. *embracer* < *brace*, the two arms.] —**em•brace′a•ble** *adj.* —**em•brace′ment** *n.*

em•bra•sure (ĕm-brā′zhər) ►*n.* **1.** An opening in a thick wall for a door or window. **2.** A flared opening for a gun in a wall or parapet. [Fr.]

em•bro•cate (ĕm′brə-kāt′) ►*v.* **-cat•ed, -cat•ing.** To moisten and rub (a part of the body) with a liniment or lotion. [< Gk. *embrekhein.*] —**em′bro•ca′tion** *n.*

em•broi•der (ĕm-broi′dər) ►*v.* **1.** To ornament with needlework. **2.** To add embellishments or fanciful details to: *embroider the truth.* [ME *embrouderen.*] —**em•broi′der•er** *n.*

em•broi•der•y (ĕm-broi′də-rē) ►*n., pl.* **-ies 1.** The act or art of embroidering. **2.** Something that has been embroidered.

em•broil (ĕm-broil′) ►*v.* **1.** To involve in argument, contention, or hostile actions. **2.** To throw into confusion or disorder; entangle. [Fr. *embrouiller.*] —**em•broil′ment** *n.*

em•bry•o (ĕm′brē-ō′) ►*n., pl.* **-os 1.** An organism in its early stages of development, esp. before it has reached a distinctively recognizable form. **2.** A rudimentary or beginning stage. [< Gk. *embruon.*] —**em′bry•on′ic** (-ŏn′ĭk) *adj.* —**em′bry•on′i•cal•ly** *adv.*

em•bry•ol•o•gy (ĕm′brē-ŏl′ə-jē) ►*n.* The branch of biology that deals with the formation, early growth, and development of living organisms. —**em′bry•o•log′ic** (-ə-lŏj′ĭk), **em′bry•o•log′i•cal** *adj.* —**em′bry•ol′o•gist** *n.*

em•cee (ĕm′sē′) ►*n.* A master of ceremonies. ►*v.* **-ceed, -cee•ing.** To act as master of ceremonies (of). [Pronunciation of *M.C.*, abbr. of *master of ceremonies.*]

e•mend (ĭ-mĕnd′) ►*v.* To improve (a text) by critical editing. [< Lat. *ēmendāre.*] —**e•men′da′tion** *n.* —**e•mend′er** *n.*

em•er•ald (ĕm′ər-əld, ĕm′rəld) ►*n.* **1.** A brilliant transparent green beryl, used as a gemstone. **2.** A strong yellowish green. [< Gk. *smaragdos.*] —**em′er•ald** *adj.*

e•merge (ĭ-mûrj′) ►*v.* **e•merged, e•merg•ing 1.** To rise up or come forth; issue. **2.** To become evident. **3.** To come into existence. [Lat. *ēmergere.*] —**e•mer′gence** *n.* —**e•mer′gent** *adj.*

e•mer•gen•cy (ĭ-mûr′jən-sē) ►*n., pl.* **-cies.** A serious, unexpected situation or occurrence that demands immediate action.

e•mer•i•tus (ĭ-mĕr′ĭ-təs) ►*adj.* Retired but retaining an honorary title: *a professor emeritus.* [Lat. *ēmeritus*, p.part. of *ēmerēre*, earn by service.]

Em•er•son (ĕm′ər-sən), **Ralph Waldo.** 1803–82. Amer. writer and philosopher. —**Em′er•so′ni•an** (-sō′nē-ən) *adj.*

em•er•y (ĕm′ə-rē, ĕm′rē) ►*n.* A fine-grained impure corundum used for grinding and polishing. [< LLat. *smericulum* < Gk. *smiris.*]

e•met•ic (ĭ-mĕt′ĭk) ►*adj.* Causing vomiting. [< Gk. *emein*, to vomit.] —**e•met′ic** *n.*

EMF ►*abbr.* electromotive force

-emia or **-hemia** or also **-aemia** or **-haemia** ►*suff.* Blood: *leukemia.* [< Gk. *haima*, blood.]

em•i•grate (ĕm′ĭ-grāt′) ►*v.* **-grat•ed, -grat•ing.** To leave one country or region to settle in another. See Usage Note at **migrate.** [Lat. *ēmigrāre.*] —**em′i•grant** (-grənt) *n.* —**em′i•gra′tion** *n.*

é•mi•gré (ĕm′ĭ-grā′) ►*n.* One who has left a native country, esp. for political reasons. [Fr.]

em•i•nence (ĕm′ə-nəns) ►*n.* **1.** A position of great distinction or superiority. **2.** A rise of ground; hill. **3.** A person of high station or great achievements.

em•i•nent (ĕm′ə-nənt) ►*adj.* **1.** Rising above others; prominent. **2.** Of high rank or station. **3.** Outstanding; distinguished. See Syns at **noted.** [< Lat. *ēminēre*, stand out.] —**em′i•nent•ly** *adv.*

eminent domain ►*n.* The right of a government to appropriate private property for public use.

e•mir (ĭ-mîr′, ā-mîr′) ►*n.* A prince, chieftain, or governor, especially in the Middle East. [< Ar. *'amīr*, commander, prince.]

e•mir•ate (ĭ-mîr′ĭt, -āt′) ►*n.* **1.** The office of an emir. **2.** The nation or territory ruled by an emir.

em•is•sar•y (ĕm′ĭ-sĕr′ē) ►*n., pl.* **-ies.** An agent sent on a mission to represent another. [Lat. *ēmissārius.*]

e•mit (ĭ-mĭt′) ►*v.* **e•mit•ted, e•mit•ting 1.** To release or send out matter or energy. **2.** To utter; express. **3.** To put (currency) into circulation. [Lat. *ēmittere.*] —**e•mis′sion** (ĭ-mĭsh′ən) *n.* —**e•mit′ter** *n.*

e•mol•lient (ĭ-mŏl′yənt) ►*adj.* Softening and soothing, esp. to the skin. [< Lat. *ēmollīre,* soften.] —**e•mol′lient** *n.*

e•mol•u•ment (ĭ-mŏl′yə-mənt) ►*n.* Payment for an office or employment; compensation. [< Lat. *ēmolumentum.*]

e•mote (ĭ-mōt′) ►*v.* **e•mot•ed, e•mot•ing.** To express emotion, esp. in an excessive or theatrical manner. [< EMOTION.]

e•mo•ti•con (ĭ-mō′tĭ-kŏn′) ►*n.* A series of keyed characters used, as in e-mail, to indicate an emotion or attitude, as [:-)] to indicate intended humor. [EMOT(ION) + ICON.]

e•mo•tion (ĭ-mō′shən) ►*n.* **1.** A strong feeling, as of joy, sorrow, or hate. **2.** A state of mental agitation or disturbance. [< VLat. **exmovēre, exmōt-,* excite.]

e•mo•tion•al (ĭ-mō′shə-nəl) ►*adj.* **1.** Of or exhibiting emotion. **2.** Readily affected with emotion. **3.** Arousing the emotions: *an emotional appeal.* —**e•mo′tion•al•ism** *n.* —**e•mo′tion•a•lize′** *v.* —**e•mo′tion•al•ly** *adv.*

e•mo•tive (ĭ-mō′tĭv) ►*adj.* **1.** Of or relating to emotion. **2.** Expressing or exciting emotion: *an emotive trial lawyer.* —**e•mo′tive•ly** *adv.* —**e•mo′tive•ness** *n.*

em•pa•na•da (ĕm′pə-nä′də) ►*n.* A turnover with a flaky crust and a spicy or sweet filling. [Sp.< *pan,* bread.]

em•pan•el (ĕm-păn′əl) ►*v.* Var. of **impanel.**

em•pa•thy (ĕm′pə-thē) ►*n.* Identification with and understanding of another's situation, feelings, and motives. [EN–[2] + –PATHY.] —**em′pa•thet′ic, em•path′ic** (-păth′ĭk) *adj.* —**em′pa•thize′** *v.*

em•per•or (ĕm′pər-ər) ►*n.* The male ruler of an empire. [< Lat. *imperātor.*]

em•pha•sis (ĕm′fə-sĭs) ►*n., pl.* **-ses** (-sēz′) **1.** Special forcefulness of expression that gives importance to something singled out. **2.** Stress given to a syllable, word, or words. [Gk. < *emphainein,* to exhibit.] —**em′pha•size′** *v.* —**em•phat′ic** (-făt′ĭk) *adj.* —**em•phat′i•cal•ly** *adv.*

Syns: *emphasis, accent, stress* **n.**

em•phy•se•ma (ĕm′fĭ-sē′mə, -zē′-) ►*n.* A disease of the lungs marked by an abnormal increase in the size of the air spaces, resulting in labored breathing and an increased susceptibility to infection. [Gk. *emphusēma,* inflation.] —**em′phy•se′mic** *adj. & n.*

em•pire (ĕm′pīr′) ►*n.* **1.** A political unit having an extensive territory or comprising a number of territories or nations and ruled by a single supreme authority. **2.** An extensive enterprise under a central authority: *a publishing empire.* **3.** Imperial sovereignty, domination, or control. [< Lat. *imperium.*]

em•pir•i•cal (ĕm-pîr′ĭ-kəl) ►*adj.* **1.** Based on observation or experiment. **2.** Guided by practical experience and not theory. [< Gk. *empeirikos,* experienced.] —**em•pir′i•cal•ly** *adv.*

em•pir•i•cism (ĕm-pîr′ĭ-sĭz′əm) ►*n.* **1.** The view that experience, esp. of the senses, is the only source of knowledge. **2.** Employment of empirical methods, as in science. —**em•pir′i•cist** *n.*

em•place•ment (ĕm-plās′mənt) ►*n.* **1.** A prepared position for a military weapon. **2.** Position; location. [Fr.]

em•ploy (ĕm-ploi′) ►*v.* **1.** To engage the services of; put to work. **2.** To put to use or service. ►*n.* Employment. [< Lat. *implicāre,* involve.] —**em•ploy′a•bil′i•ty** *n.* —**em•ploy′a•ble** *adj.* —**em•ploy′er** *n.*

em•ploy•ee also **em•ploy•e** (ĕm-ploi′ē, ĭm-, ĕm′ploi-ē′) ►*n.* A person who works for another in return for compensation.

em•ploy•ment (ĕm-ploi′mənt) ►*n.* **1.** The act of employing. **2.** The state of being employed. **3.** The work in which one is engaged; occupation.

em•po•ri•um (ĕm-pôr′ē-əm, -pōr′-) ►*n., pl.* **-po•ri•ums** or **-po•ri•a** (-pôr′ē-ə, -pōr′-) **1.** A marketplace. **2.** A large retail store carrying a variety of goods. [< Gk. *emporion.*]

em•pow•er (ĕm-pou′ər) ►*v.* To invest esp. with legal power. See Syns at **authorize.** —**em•pow′er•ment** *n.*

em•press (ĕm′prĭs) ►*n.* **1.** The woman ruler of an empire. **2.** The wife or widow of an emperor. [< OFr. *emperesse.*]

emp•ty (ĕmp′tē) ►*adj.* **-ti•er, -ti•est 1.** Containing nothing. **2.** Having no occupants or inhabitants; vacant. **3.** Lacking purpose or substance; meaningless. See Syns at **vain.** ►*v.* **-tied, -ty•ing 1.** To make or become empty. **2.** To pour or discharge: *The river empties into a bay.* ►*n., pl.* **-ties** *Informal* An empty container. [< OE *ǣmetta,* leisure.] —**emp′ti•ly** *adv.* —**emp′ti•ness** *n.*

emp•ty-hand•ed (ĕmp′tē-hăn′dĭd) ►*adj.* **1.** Bearing nothing. **2.** Having received or gained nothing.

em•py•re•an (ĕm′pī-rē′ən, ĕm-pîr′ē-ən) ►*n.* **1.** The highest reaches of heaven. **2.** The sky. [< Gk. *empurios,* fiery < *pur,* fire.] —**em′py•re′an** *adj.*

EMT ►*abbr.* emergency medical technician

e•mu (ē′myo͞o) ►*n.* A large flightless Australian bird related to and resembling the ostrich. [Port. *ema,* flightless bird of South America.]

em•u•late (ĕm′yə-lāt′) ►*v.* **-lat•ed, -lat•ing.** To strive to equal or excel, esp. through imitation. [Lat. *aemulārī.*] —**em′u•la′tion** *n.* —**em′u•la′tive** *adj.* —**em′u•la′tor** *n.*

e•mul•si•fy (ĭ-mŭl′sə-fī′) ►*v.* **-fied, -fy•ing.** To make into an emulsion. —**e•mul′si•fi•ca′tion** *n.* —**e•mul′si•fi′er** *n.*

e•mul•sion (ĭ-mŭl′shən) ►*n.* **1.** A suspension of small globules of one liquid in a second liquid with which the first will not mix. **2.** A photosensitive coating, usu. of silver halide grains in a thin gelatin layer, on photographic film, paper, or glass. [< Lat. *ēmulgēre, ēmuls-,* milk out.] —**e•mul′sive** *adj.*

en (ĕn) ►*n. Print.* A space equal to half the width of an em.

en–[1] or **em–** or **in–** ►*pref.* **1a.** To put into or onto: *encapsulate.* **b.** To go into or onto: *entrain.* **2.** To cover or provide with: *enrobe.* **3.** To cause to be: *endear.* **4.** Thoroughly. Used often as an intensive: *entangle.* [< Lat. *in,* in.]

en–² or **em–** ►*pref.* In; into; within: *endemic.* [< Gk.]

–en¹ ►*suff.* **1a.** To cause to be: *cheapen.* **b.** To become: *redden.* **2a.** To cause to have: *hearten.* **b.** To come to have: *lengthen.* [< OE *-nian.*]

–en² ►*suff.* Made of; resembling: *earthen.* [< OE.]

en•a•ble (ĕ-nā′bəl) ►*v.* **-bled, -bling 1.** To supply with the means, knowledge, or opportunity; make able. **2.** To give legal power, capacity, or sanction to. **3.** To make (e.g., a device) operational. —**en•a′bler** *n.*

en•act (ĕn-ăkt′) ►*v.* **1.** To make (a bill) into law. **2.** To act out, as on a stage. —**en•act′ment** *n.* —**en•ac′tor** *n.*

e•nam•el (ĭ-năm′əl) ►*n.* **1.** A vitreous, usu. opaque protective coating on metal, glass, or ceramic ware. **2.** A paint that dries to a hard glossy finish. **3.** The hard substance covering the exposed portion of a tooth. ►*v.* **-eled, -el•ing** or **-elled, -el•ling.** To coat or decorate with enamel. [< AN *enamailler,* to put on enamel.] —**e•nam′el•ware′** *n.*

en•am•or (ĭ-năm′ər) ►*v.* To inspire with love; captivate. [< OFr. *enamourer* < *amour,* love. See AMOUR.]

en•am•our (ĭ-năm′ər) ►*v. Chiefly Brit.* Var. of **enamor.**

en bloc (äɴ blôk′, ĕn blŏk′) ►*adv.* As a unit; all together. [Fr.]

enc. ►*abbr.* **1.** enclosed **2.** enclosure

en•camp (ĕn-kămp′) ►*v.* To set up or live in a camp. —**en•camp′ment** *n.*

en•cap•su•late (ĕn-kă p′sə-lāt′) ►*v.* **-lat•ed, -lat•ing 1.** To encase in or as if in a capsule. **2.** To express in a brief summary. —**en•cap′su•la′tion** *n.*

en•case (ĕn-kās′) also **in•case** (ĭn-) ►*v.* **-cased, -cas•ing.** To enclose in or as if in a case. —**en•case′ment** *n.*

–ence ►*suff.* **1.** State or condition: *dependence.* **2.** Action: *emergence.* [< Lat. *-entia.*]

en•ceph•a•li•tis (ĕn-sĕf′ə-lī′tĭs) ►*n.* Inflammation of the brain. —**en•ceph′a•lit′ic** (-lĭt′ĭk) *adj.*

encephalo– or **encephal–** ►*pref.* Brain: *encephalitis.* [< Gk. *enkephalos,* in the head.]

en•ceph•a•lo•gram (ĕn-sĕf′ə-lə-grăm′, -ə-lō-) ►*n.* An x-ray picture of the brain. —**en•ceph′a•log′ra•phy** (ĕn-sĕf′ə-lŏg′rə-fē) *n.*

en•ceph•a•lon (ĕn-sĕf′ə-lŏn′) ►*n., pl.* **-la** (-lə). The brain of a vertebrate. [Gk. *enkephalon.*] —**en•ceph′a•lous** *adj.*

en•chain (ĕn-chān′) ►*v.* To bind with or as if with chains. —**en•chain′ment** *n.*

en•chant (ĕn-chănt′) ►*v.* **1.** To cast a spell over; bewitch. **2.** To attract and delight; entrance. See Syns at **charm.** [< Lat. *incantāre,* cast a spell.] —**en•chant′er** *n.* —**en•chant′ment** *n.* —**en•chant′ress** *n.*

en•chi•la•da (ĕn′chə-lä′də) ►*n.* A rolled tortilla with a meat or cheese filling, served with a sauce spiced with chili. [Am.Sp.]

en•ci•pher (ĕn-sī′fər) ►*v.* To put (a message) into cipher. —**en•ci′pher•ment** *n.*

en•cir•cle (ĕn-sûr′kəl) ►*v.* **-cled, -cling 1.** To form a circle around. See Syns at **surround. 2.** To move or go around; make a circuit of. —**en•cir′cle•ment** *n.*

encl. ►*abbr.* **1.** enclosed **2.** enclosure

en•clave (ĕn′klāv′, ŏn′-) ►*n.* A distinctly bounded area enclosed within a larger unit, esp. a country or part of a country lying wholly within the boundaries of another. [< VLat. **inclāvāre,* enclose.]

en•close (ĕn-klōz′) also **in•close** (ĭn-) ►*v.* **-closed, -clos•ing 1.** To surround on all sides; close in. **2.** To include in the same envelope or package: *enclose a check with the order.* [< Lat. *inclūdere, inclūs-.*] —**en•clo′sure** (-klō′zhər) *n.*

Syns: *enclose, cage, coop, fence, hem, pen, wall* **v.**

en•code (ĕn-kōd′) ►*v.* **-cod•ed, -cod•ing 1.** To put (e.g., a message) into code. **2.** *Comp. Sci.* To convert into machine language. —**en•cod′er** *n.*

en•co•mi•um (ĕn-kō′mē-əm) ►*n., pl.* **-mi•ums** or **-mi•a** (-mē-ə). Lofty praise; tribute. [< Gk. *enkōmios,* of the victory procession.]

en•com•pass (ĕn-kŭm′pəs) ►*v.* **1.** To enclose. See Syns at **surround. 2.** To constitute or include. —**en•com′pass•ment** *n.*

en•core (ŏn′kôr′, -kōr′) ►*n.* **1.** A demand by an audience for an additional performance. **2.** An additional performance in response to such a demand. ►*interj.* Used to demand an encore. [Fr., again.]

en•coun•ter (ĕn-koun′tər) ►*n.* **1.** A meeting, esp. one that is unexpected or brief. **2.** A hostile confrontation; clash. ►*v.* **1.** To meet, esp. unexpectedly. **2.** To confront in battle. [< LLat. *incontrāre,* meet with.]

en•cour•age (ĕn-kûr′ĭj, -kŭr′-) ►*v.* **-aged, -ag•ing 1.** To inspire with hope, courage, or confidence. **2.** To give support to; foster. [< OFr. *encoragier* < *corage,* COURAGE.] —**en•cour′age•ment** *n.* —**en•cour′ag•er** *n.* —**en•cour′ag•ing•ly** *adv.*

Syns: *encourage, animate, cheer, embolden, hearten, inspirit* ***Ant:*** *discourage* **v.**

en•croach (ĕn-krōch′) ►*v.* To take another's possessions or rights gradually or stealthily. [< OFr. *encrochier,* seize.] —**en•croach′er** *n.* —**en•croach′ment** *n.*

en•crust (ĕn-krŭst′) also **in•crust** (ĭn-) ►*v.* To cover with or as if with a crust. —**en′crust•a′tion** *n.*

en•crypt (ĕn-krĭpt′) ►*v.* **1.** To put into code or cipher. **2.** *Comp. Sci.* To alter (e.g., a file) using a secret code so as to be unintelligible to unauthorized parties. —**en•cryp′tion** *n.*

en•cum•ber (ĕn-kŭm′bər) ►*v.* **1.** To weigh down; burden. **2.** To hinder or impede. **3.** To burden with legal or financial obligations. [< OFr. *encombrer,* block up.] —**en•cum′brance** *n.*

–ency ►*suff.* Condition or quality: *complacency.* [ME, var. of *-ence,* -ence.]

en•cyc•li•cal (ĕn-sĭk′lĭ-kəl) ►*n. Rom. Cath. Ch.* A papal letter addressed to the bishops. [< Gk. *enkuklios,* circular.]

en•cy•clo•pe•di•a (ĕn-sī′klə-pē′dē-ə) ►*n.* A comprehensive reference work containing articles on a wide range of subjects or on numerous aspects of a particular field. [< Gk. *enkuklios paideia,* general education.] —**en•cy′clo•pe′dic** *adj.*

en•cyst (ĕn-sĭst′) ►*v.* To enclose or become enclosed in a cyst. —**en•cyst′ment, en′cys•ta′tion** *n.*

end (ĕnd) ►*n.* **1.** Either extremity of something that has length. **2.** The point in time when an action, event, or phenomenon ceases or is completed; conclusion. **3.** A result; outcome. **4.** Something toward which one strives; goal. **5.** Death. **6.** The ultimate extent; the very limit. **7.** A remainder; remnant. **8.** A share of a responsibility or obligation. **9.** *Football* Either of the players in the outermost position on the line of scrimmage. ▸*v.* **1.** To bring or come to a conclusion. **2.** To form the concluding part of. **3.** To destroy. —***idioms:* in the end** Eventually; ultimately. **no end** A great deal. [< OE *ende.*]

en•dan•ger (ĕn-dān′jər) ▸*v.* To expose to harm or danger; imperil. —**en•dan′ger•ment** *n.* —**en•dan′gered** *adj.*

Syns: *endanger, imperil, jeopardize, risk* **v.**

endangered species ▸*n.* A species present in such small numbers that it is at risk of extinction.

en•dear (ĕn-dîr′) ▸*v.* To make beloved.

en•dear•ment (ĕn-dîr′mənt) ▸*n.* An expression of affection.

en•deav•or (ĕn-dĕv′ər) ▸*n.* A concerted effort toward an end; earnest attempt. ▸*v.* To attempt through concerted effort: *endeavored to improve my grades.* [< ME *(putten) in dever,* (put oneself) under obligation.]

En•de•cott also **En•di•cott** (ĕn′dĭ-kət, -kŏt′), **John.** 1588?–1665. English-born Amer. colonial administrator.

en•dem•ic (ĕn-dĕm′ĭk) ▸*adj.* Prevalent in or peculiar to a particular locality, region, or people. [< Gk. *endēmos,* among the people.] —**en•dem′i•cal•ly** *adv.*

en•dive (ĕn′dīv′, ŏn′dēv′) ▸*n.* **1.** A plant with crisp succulent leaves used in salads. **2.** A variety of chicory with a narrow pointed cluster of whitish leaves used in salads. [< Gk. *entubon.*]

endive
left to right: Belgian and curly

end•less (ĕnd′lĭs) ▸*adj.* **1.** Being or seeming to be without an end or limit; boundless. **2.** Formed with the ends joined; continuous. —**end′less•ly** *adv.* —**end′less•ness** *n.*

end•most (ĕnd′mōst′) ▸*adj.* Being at or closest to the end; last.

endo– or **end–** ▸*pref.* Inside; within: *endogenous.* [< Gk. *endon,* within.]

en•do•crine (ĕn′də-krĭn, -krēn′, -krīn′) ▸*adj.* **1.** Secreting internally. **2.** Of or relating to endocrine glands or the hormones secreted by them. [Fr. : ENDO– + Gk. *krinein,* to separate.]

endocrine gland ▸*n.* A gland, such as the thyroid, adrenal, or pituitary, having hormonal secretions that pass directly into the bloodstream.

en•do•cri•nol•o•gy (ĕn′də-krə-nŏl′ə-jē) ▸*n.* The study of the glands and hormones of the body and their disorders. —**en′do•cri′no•log′ic** (-krĭn′ə-lŏj′ĭk), **en′do•crin′o•log′i•cal** *adj.* —**en′do•cri•nol′o•gist** *n.*

en•do•don•tics (ĕn′dō-dŏn′tĭks) ▸*n.* *(takes sing. v.)* The branch of dentistry that deals with diseases of the tooth root, dental pulp, and surrounding tissue. [ENDO– + (ORTHO)DONTICS.] —**en′do•don′tic** *adj.* —**en′do•don′tist** *n.*

en•dog•e•nous (ĕn-dŏj′ə-nəs) ▸*adj. Biol.* Originating within an organism or part. —**en•dog′e•nous•ly** *adv.*

en•do•me•tri•o•sis (ĕn′dō-mē′trē-ō′sĭs) ▸*n.* A usu. painful condition marked by the abnormal occurrence of endometrial tissue outside the uterus.

en•do•me•tri•um (ĕn′dō-mē′trē-əm) ▸*n., pl.* **-tri•a** (-trē-ə). The glandular mucous membrane that lines the uterus. [NLat. : ENDO– + Gk. *mētra,* uterus.] —**en′do•me′tri•al** *adj.*

en•do•plasm (ĕn′də-plăz′əm) ▸*n.* A central, less viscous portion of the cytoplasm distinguishable in certain cells. —**en′do•plas′mic** *adj.*

en•dor•phin (ĕn-dôr′fĭn) ▸*n.* Any of a group of peptide hormones that bind to opiate receptors and are found mainly in the brain. [ENDO(GENOUS) + (MO)RPHIN(E).]

en•dorse (ĕn-dôrs′) also **in•dorse** (ĭn-) ▸*v.* **-dorsed, -dors•ing 1.** To write one's signature on the back of (e.g., a check), esp. in return for the cash or credit indicated on its face. **2.** To give approval of or support to, esp. by public statement; sanction. [< Med.Lat. *indorsāre* < Lat. *dorsum,* back.] —**en•dorse′ment** *n.* —**en•dors′er, en•dor′sor** *n.*

en•do•scope (ĕn′də-skōp′) ▸*n.* An instrument for viewing the interior of a body canal or a hollow organ such as the colon or stomach. —**en′do•scop′ic** (-skŏp′ĭk) *adj.* —**en•dos′co•py** (ĕn-dŏs′kə-pē) *n.*

en•do•therm (ĕn′də-thûrm′) ▸*n.* An organism that generates heat to maintain its body temperature, typically above the temperature of its surroundings. [ENDO– + Gk. *thermos,* heat.]

en•dow (ĕn-dou′) ▸*v.* **1.** To provide with property, income, or a source of income. **2.** To equip or supply with a talent or quality. [< AN *endouer* : EN–[1] + Lat. *dōtāre,* provide a dowry (< *dōs,* dowry).] —**en•dow′ment** *n.*

en•due (ĕn-do͞o′, -dyo͞o′) ▸*v.* **-dued, -du•ing.** To provide with a quality or trait. [< Lat. *indūcere,* INDUCT, and *induere,* put on.]

en•dure (ĕn-do͝or′, -dyo͝or′) ▸*v.* **-dured, -dur•ing 1.** To carry on through, despite hardships; undergo. **2.** To continue in existence; last. **3.** To suffer patiently without yielding. [< Lat. *indūrāre,* make hard.] —**en•dur′a•ble** *adj.* —**en•dur′ance** *n.*

end•wise (ĕnd′wīz′) also **end•ways** (-wāz′) ▸*adv.* **1.** On end; upright. **2.** With the end foremost.

end zone ▸*n. Football* The area at either end of the playing field between the goal line and the end line.

ENE ▸*abbr.* east-northeast

-ene ▸*suff.* An unsaturated organic compound, esp. one containing a double bond between carbon atoms: *ethylene.* [< Gk. *-ēnē,* feminine adj. suff.]

en•e•ma (ĕn′ə-mə) ▸*n.* The injection of liquid into the rectum for cleansing or other therapeutic purposes. [< Gk. < *enienai,* send in.]

en•e•my (ĕn′ə-mē) ▸*n., pl.* **-mies 1.** One who feels hatred toward, intends injury to, or opposes the interests of another; foe. **2.** A hostile power or force, such as a nation. **3.** A group of foes or hostile forces. See Usage Note at **collective noun.** [< Lat. *inimīcus.*] —**en′e•my** *adj.*

Syns: *enemy, foe, opponent* ***n.***

en•er•get•ic (ĕn′ər-jĕt′ĭk) ►*adj.* **1.** Possessing, exerting, or displaying energy. **2.** Of or relating to energy. [Gk. *energētikos* < *energos,* active. See ENERGY.] —**en′er•get′i•cal•ly** *adv.*

en•er•gize (ĕn′ər-jīz′) ►*v.* **-gized, -giz•ing 1.** To give energy to; invigorate. **2.** To supply with an electric current. —**en′er•giz′er** *n.*

en•er•gy (ĕn′ər-jē) ►*n., pl.* **-gies 1.** The capacity for work or vigorous activity. **2.** Exertion of vigor or power. **3.** Usable heat or power. **4.** *Phys.* The capacity of a physical system to do work. [< Gk. *energos,* active : EN–[2] + *ergon,* work.]

en•er•vate (ĕn′ər-vāt′) ►*v.* **-vat•ed, -vat•ing.** To weaken or destroy the strength or vitality of. [Lat. *ēnervāre.*] —**en′er•va′tion** *n.* —**en′er•va′tive** *adj.*

En•e•we•tak or **En•i•we•tok** (ĕn′ə-wē′tŏk′, ə-nē′wĭ-). An atoll of the Marshall Is. in the W-central Pacific.

en•fee•ble (ĕn-fē′bəl) ►*v.* **-bled, -bling.** To make feeble. —**en•fee′ble•ment** *n.*

en•fi•lade (ĕn′fə-lād′, -läd′) ►*n.* Gunfire directed along the length of a target, as a column of troops. [< OFr. *enfiler,* to thread.]

en•fold (ĕn-fōld′) ►*v.* **1.** To cover with or as if with folds; envelop. **2.** To embrace.

en•force (ĕn-fôrs′, -fōrs′) ►*v.* **-forced, -forc•ing.** To compel observance of or obedience to. —**en•force′a•bil′i•ty** *n.* —**en•force′a•ble** *adj.* —**en•force′ment** *n.* —**en•forc′er** *n.*

en•fran•chise (ĕn-frăn′chīz′) ►*v.* **-chised, -chis•ing 1.** To bestow a franchise on. **2.** To endow with the rights of citizenship, esp. the right to vote. **3.** To free, as from bondage. —**en•fran′chise′ment** *n.*

Eng. ►*abbr.* **1.** England **2.** English

en•gage (ĕn-gāj′) ►*v.* **-gaged, -gag•ing 1.** To hire; employ. **2.** To reserve. **3.** To pledge, esp. to marry. **4.** To attract and hold: *a project that engaged her interest.* **5.** To participate: *engage in conversation.* **6.** To enter into conflict with: *engage the enemy.* **7.** To interlock or cause to interlock; mesh. **8.** To assume an obligation; agree. [< OFr. *engagier,* pledge something as security.]

en•gaged (ĕn-gājd′) ►*adj.* **1.** Employed, occupied, or busy. **2.** Pledged to marry; betrothed. **3.** Involved in conflict or battle. **4.** Being in gear; meshed.

en•gage•ment (ĕn-gāj′mənt) ►*n.* **1.** The act of engaging or the state of being engaged. **2.** Betrothal. **3.** A promise or agreement to be at a particular place at a particular time. **4.** Employment, esp. for a specified time. **5.** A hostile encounter; battle.

en•gag•ing (ĕn-gā′jĭng) ►*adj.* Charming; attractive. —**en•gag′ing•ly** *adv.*

en garde (äɴ gärd′) ►*interj.* Used to warn a fencer to assume the position preparatory to a match. [Fr.]

Eng•els (ĕng′əlz, -əls), **Friedrich.** 1820–95. German social theorist and writer.

en•gen•der (ĕn-jĕn′dər) ►*v.* **1.** To give rise to. **2.** To propagate. [< Lat. *ingenerāre.*]

en•gine (ĕn′jĭn) ►*n.* **1.** A machine that converts energy into mechanical force or motion. **2.** A mechanical appliance, instrument, or tool. **3.** A locomotive. **4.** *Comp. Sci.* A search engine. [< Lat. *ingenium,* skill.]

engine block ►*n.* The cast metal block containing the cylinders of an internal-combustion engine.

en•gi•neer (ĕn′jə-nîr′) ►*n.* **1.** One trained or professionally engaged in a branch of engineering. **2.** One who operates an engine. ►*v.* **1.** To plan, construct, or manage as an engineer. **2.** To alter or produce by methods of genetic engineering. **3.** To plan, manage, and put through by contrivance; maneuver. [< Med.Lat. *ingeniātor,* contriver.]

en•gi•neer•ing (ĕn′jə-nîr′ĭng) ►*n.* The application of scientific principles to practical ends, as the design, manufacture, and operation of structures and machines.

Eng•land (ĭng′glənd) A division of the United Kingdom, in S Great Britain. Cap. London. Pop. 46,220,955.

Eng•lish (ĭng′glĭsh) ►*adj.* **1.** Of or characteristic of England or its people or culture. **2.** Of the English language. ►*n.* **1.** The people of England. **2.** The Germanic language of England, the US, and other countries. **3.** A course in the study of English language, literature, or composition. **4.** often **english** *Sports & Games* The spin given to a ball by striking it on one side or releasing it with a sharp twist. —**Eng′lish•man** *n.* —**Eng′lish•wom′an** *n.*

English Channel. An arm of the Atlantic between W France and S England.

English horn ►*n.* A double-reed woodwind instrument similar to but larger than the oboe and pitched lower by a fifth.

English setter ►*n.* Any of a breed of medium-sized dog developed in England having a long silky white coat usu. with black or brownish markings.

en•gorge (ĕn-gôrj′) ►*v.* **-gorged, -gorg•ing 1.** To devour greedily. **2.** To fill to excess, as with fluid. [< OFr. *engorgier* < *gorge,* throat. See GORGE.] —**en•gorge′ment** *n.*

en•graft (ĕn-grăft′) ►*v.* To graft (a scion) onto or into another plant.

en•grave (ĕn-grāv′) ►*v.* **-graved, -grav•ing 1.** To carve, cut, or etch into a material. **2a.** To cut into a block or surface used for printing. **b.** To print from a block or plate made by such a process. **3.** To impress deeply as if by carving or etching. —**en•grav′er** *n.*

en•grav•ing (ĕn-grā′vĭng) ►*n.* **1.** The art or technique of one that engraves. **2.** An engraved surface for printing. **3.** A print made from an engraved plate or block.

en•gross (ĕn-grōs′) ►*v.* To occupy exclusively; absorb. See Syns at **monopolize.** [< OFr. *en gros,* in large quantity.]

en•gulf (ĕn-gŭlf′) ►*v.* To swallow up or overwhelm by or as if by overflowing and enclosing.

en•hance (ĕn-hăns′) ►*v.* **-hanced, -hanc•ing.** To make greater, as in value, reputation, or usefulness. [< LLat. *inaltāre,* heighten.] —**en•hance′ment** *n.* —**en•hanc′er** *n.*

e•nig•ma (ĭ-nĭg′mə) ►*n.* One that is puzzling, ambiguous, or inexplicable. [< Gk. *ainigma.*] —**en′ig•mat′ic** (ĕn′ĭg-măt′ĭk), **en′ig•mat′i•cal** *adj.*

En•i•we•tok (ĕn′ə-wē′tŏk′, ə-nē′wĭ-) See **Enewetak.**

en•join (ĕn-join′) ▸*v.* **1.** To direct or impose with authority and emphasis. **2.** To forbid. See Syns at **forbid.** [< Lat. *iniungere* < *iungere*, join.] —**en•join′ment** *n.*

en•joy (ĕn-joi′) ▸*v.* **1.** To receive pleasure or satisfaction from. **2.** To have the use or benefit of: *enjoys good health.* [< OFr. *enjoir.*] —**en•joy′a•ble** *adj.* —**en•joy′a•bly** *adv.* —**en•joy′ment** *n.*

en•large (ĕn-lärj′) ▸*v.* **-larged, -larg•ing 1.** To make or become larger. **2.** To give greater scope to; expand. **3.** To speak or write at greater length or in greater detail; elaborate. —**en•large′ment** *n.* —**en•larg′er** *n.*

en•light•en (ĕn-līt′n) ▸*v.* **1.** To give spiritual or intellectual insight to. **2.** To inform or instruct. —**en•light′en•ment** *n.*

en•list (ĕn-lĭst′) ▸*v.* **1.** To engage (a person) for service in the armed forces. **2.** To engage the support or cooperation of. **3.** To enter the armed forces. —**en•list′ment** *n.*

en•liv•en (ĕn-lī′vən) ▸*v.* To make lively or spirited; animate. —**en•liv′en•ment** *n.*

en masse (ŏn măs′) ▸*adv.* In one group or body; all together. [Fr.]

en•mesh (ĕn-mĕsh′) also **im•mesh** (ĭm-) ▸*v.* To entangle, involve, or catch in or as if in a mesh. See Syns at **catch.**

en•mi•ty (ĕn′mĭ-tē) ▸*n.*, *pl.* **-ties.** Deep-seated, often mutual hatred. [< Lat. *inimīcus*, enemy.]

en•no•ble (ĕn-nō′bəl) ▸*v.* **-bled, -bling 1.** To make noble. **2.** To confer nobility upon. —**en•no′ble•ment** *n.*

en•nui (ŏn-wē′, ŏn′wē) ▸*n.* Listlessness and dissatisfaction resulting from lack of interest; boredom. [< OFr. *enui* < *ennuier*, ANNOY.]

e•nol•o•gy also **oe•nol•o•gy** (ē-nŏl′ə-jē) ▸*n.* The study of wine and winemaking. [Gk. *oinos*, wine + -LOGY.] —**e•nol′o•gist** *n.*

e•nor•mi•ty (ĭ-nôr′mĭ-tē) ▸*n.*, *pl.* **-ties 1.** Excessive wickedness or outrageousness. **2.** A monstrous offense or evil; outrage. **3.** *Informal* Great size; immensity.

e•nor•mous (ĭ-nôr′məs) ▸*adj.* Very great in size, extent, number, or degree. [< Lat. *ēnormis.*] —**e•nor′mous•ly** *adv.* —**e•nor′mous•ness** *n.*

e•nough (ĭ-nŭf′) ▸*adj.* Sufficient to meet a need or satisfy a desire; adequate. See Syns at **sufficient.** ▸*pron.* An adequate quantity. ▸*adv.* **1.** To a satisfactory amount or degree. **2.** Very; quite: *glad enough to leave.* **3.** Tolerably; rather: *She sang well enough.* ▸*interj.* Used to express impatience or exasperation. [< OE *genōg.*]

en•quire (ĕn-kwīr′) ▸*v.* Var. of **inquire.** —**en•quir′er** *n.* —**en•quir′y** *n.*

en•rage (ĕn-rāj′) ▸*v.* **-raged, -rag•ing.** To put into a rage; infuriate.

en•rap•ture (ĕn-răp′chər) ▸*v.* **-tured, -tur•ing.** To fill with rapture or delight.

Syns: *enrapture, entrance, ravish, thrill, transport* **v.**

en•rich (ĕn-rĭch′) ▸*v.* **1.** To make rich or richer. **2.** To make fuller, more meaningful, or more rewarding. **3.** To add nutrients to. **4.** To add to the beauty or character of; adorn. —**en•rich′ment** *n.*

en•roll also **en•rol** (ĕn-rōl′) ▸*v.* **-rolled, -roll•ing.** To enter or register in a roll, list, or record. —**en•roll′ment, en•rol′ment** *n.*

en route (ŏn ro͞ot′, ĕn) ▸*adv. & adj.* On or along the way. [Fr.]

ENS or **Ens.** ▸*abbr.* ensign

en•sconce (ĕn-skŏns′) ▸*v.* **-sconced, -sconc•ing 1.** To settle securely or comfortably. **2.** To place or conceal in a secure place. [EN-[1] + *sconce*, small fort.]

en•sem•ble (ŏn-sŏm′bəl) ▸*n.* **1.** A unit or group of complementary parts that contribute to a single effect. **2.** A coordinated outfit or costume. **3.** A group of musicians, singers, dancers, or actors who perform together. **4.** *Mus.* A work for two or more vocalists or instrumentalists. [< LLat. *īnsimul*, at the same time.]

en•shrine (ĕn-shrīn′) ▸*v.* **-shrined, -shrin•ing 1.** To enclose in or as if in a shrine. **2.** To cherish as sacred. —**en•shrine′ment** *n.*

en•shroud (ĕn-shroud′) ▸*v.* To cover with or as if with a shroud.

en•sign (ĕn′sən, -sīn′) ▸*n.* **1.** A standard or banner, as of a military unit. **2.** (ĕn′sən). The lowest commissioned rank in the US Navy or Coast Guard. **3.** A badge of office or power; emblem. [< Lat. *īnsignia*, INSIGNIA.]

en•si•lage (ĕn′sə-lĭj) ▸*n.* The process of storing and fermenting green fodder in a silo. —**en′sil•age** *v.*

en•sile (ĕn-sīl′) ▸*v.* **-siled, -sil•ing.** To store (fodder) in a silo. [< Sp. *ensilar.*]

en•slave (ĕn-slāv′) ▸*v.* **-slaved, -slav•ing.** To make into or as if into a slave. —**en•slave′ment** *n.* —**en•slav′er** *n.*

en•snare (ĕn-snâr′) ▸*v.* **-snared, -snar•ing.** To catch in or as if in a snare. See Syns at **catch.** —**en•snare′ment** *n.* —**en•snar′er** *n.*

en•sue (ĕn-so͞o′) ▸*v.* **-sued, -su•ing 1.** To follow as a result. **2.** To take place subsequently. [< Lat. *īnsequī*, follow.]

en•sure (ĕn-sho͝or′) ▸*v.* **-sured, -sur•ing.** To make sure or certain; insure. See Usage Note at **assure.**

-ent ▸*suff.* **1a.** Performing, promoting, or causing a specified action: *absorbent.* **b.** Being in a specified state or condition: *different.* **2.** One that performs, promotes, or causes a specified action: *resident.* [< Lat. *-ēns, -ent-*, present participle suff.]

en•tab•la•ture (ĕn-tăb′lə-cho͝or′) ▸*n.* The horizontal upper section of a classical building, resting on the columns. [Obsolete Fr. < Ital. *intavolatura.*]

en•tail (ĕn-tāl′, ĭn-) ▸*v.* **1.** To have, impose, or require as a necessary accompaniment or consequence. **2.** To limit the inheritance of (property) to a specified succession of heirs. [ME *entaillen*, limit inheritance to specific heirs.] —**en•tail′ment** *n.*

en•tan•gle (ĕn-tăng′gəl) ▸*v.* **-gled, -gling 1.** To twist together into a confusing mass; snarl. **2.** To complicate; confuse. **3.** To involve in or as if in a tangle. See Syns at **catch.** —**en•tan′gle•ment** *n.*

en•tente (ŏn-tŏnt′) ▸*n.* **1.** An agreement between two or more governments or powers for cooperative action or policy. **2.** The parties to such an agreement. [Fr.]

en•ter (ĕn′tər) ▸*v.* **1.** To come or go into. **2.** To penetrate; pierce. **3.** To insert. **4.** To become or cause to become a participant, member, or part of; join or enroll. **5.** To embark on; begin. **6.** To write or put in. **7.** To place formally on record; submit. **8.** To go to or occupy in order to claim possession of (land). —***phrasal verbs:* enter into 1.** To participate in. **2.** To become party to (a contract). **enter on** (or **upon**) To set out on; begin. [< Lat. *intrāre*.]

en•ter•ic (ĕn-tĕr′ĭk) also **en•ter•al** (ĕn′tər-əl) ▶*adj.* Of or being within the intestine. [< Gk. *enteron*, intestine.]

en•ter•i•tis (ĕn′tə-rī′tĭs) ▶*n.* Inflammation of the intestine. [< Gk. *enteron*, intestine.]

en•ter•prise (ĕn′tər-prīz′) ▶*n.* **1.** An undertaking, esp. one of some scope, complication, and risk. **2.** A business organization. **3.** Industrious, systematic activity, esp. when directed toward profit. **4.** Willingness to undertake new ventures; initiative. [ME < OFr. *entreprise* < OFr. *entreprendre*, undertake.]

en•ter•pris•ing (ĕn′tər-prī′zĭng) ▶*adj.* Willing and eager to undertake new projects.

en•ter•tain (ĕn′tər-tān′) ▶*v.* **1.** To hold the attention of with something amusing or diverting. **2.** To extend hospitality to. **3.** To consider; contemplate. [< OFr. *entretenir*.] —**en′ter•tain′er** *n.* —**en′ter•tain′ment** *n.*

en•thrall (ĕn-thrôl′) ▶*v.* **1.** To hold spellbound. **2.** To enslave. —**en•thrall′ment** *n.*

en•throne (ĕn-thrōn′) ▶*v.* **-throned, -thron•ing 1.** To seat on a throne. **2.** To raise to a lofty position; exalt. —**en•throne′ment** *n.*

en•thuse (ĕn-thōōz′) ▶*v.* **-thused, -thus•ing** *Informal* To make or act enthusiastic.

en•thu•si•asm (ĕn-thōō′zē-ăz′əm) ▶*n.* **1.** Great excitement for or interest in a subject or cause. **2.** A source or cause of great excitement or interest. [< Gk. *enthousiasmos*.] —**en•thu′si•ast′** *n.* —**en•thu′si•as′tic** *adj.* —**en•thu′si•as′ti•cal•ly** *adv.*

en•tice (ĕn-tīs′) ▶*v.* **-ticed, -tic•ing.** To attract by arousing hope or desire; lure. [< OFr. *enticier*, instigate.] —**en•tice′ment** *n.* —**en•tic′er** *n.* —**en•tic′ing•ly** *adv.*

en•tire (ĕn-tīr′) ▶*adj.* **1.** Having no part excluded or left out. See Syns at **whole. 2.** Complete: *gave us his entire attention.* [< Lat. *integer*.] —**en•tire′ly** *adv.*

en•tire•ty (ĕn-tī′rĭ-tē, -tīr′tē) ▶*n., pl.* **-ties 1.** Wholeness. **2.** The entire amount or extent.

en•ti•tle (ĕn-tīt′l) ▶*v.* **-tled, -tling 1.** To give a name to. **2.** To furnish with a right or claim to something. [< Med.Lat. *intitulāre* < Lat. *titulus*, title.] —**en•ti′tle•ment** *n.*

entitlement program ▶*n.* A government program that guarantees benefits to all members of a particular group.

en•ti•ty (ĕn′tĭ-tē) ▶*n., pl.* **-ties 1.** Something that exists as a particular and discrete unit. **2.** The fact of existence; being. [< Lat. *ēns*, *ent-*, pr.part. of *esse*, be.]

en•tomb (ĕn-tōōm′) ▶*v.* **1.** To place in or as if in a tomb or grave. **2.** To serve as a tomb for. —**en•tomb′ment** *n.*

en•to•mol•o•gy (ĕn′tə-mŏl′ə-jē) ▶*n.* The scientific study of insects. [< Gk. *entomon*, insect.] —**en′to•mo•log′ic** (-mə-lŏj′ĭk), **en′to•mo•log′i•cal** *adj.* —**en′to•mol′o•gist** *n.*

en•tou•rage (ŏn′tōō-räzh′) ▶*n.* A group of attendants or associates; retinue. [< OFr. *entour*, surroundings.]

en•tr′acte (ŏn′trăkt′, äɴ-träkt′) ▶*n.* **1.** The interval between two acts of a theatrical performance. **2.** Another performance, as of music or dance, provided between two acts of a theatrical performance. [Fr.]

en•trails (ĕn′trālz′, -trəlz) ▶*pl.n.* The internal organs, esp. the intestines. [< Med.Lat. *intrālia* < Lat. *interāneus*, internal.]

en•train (ĕn-trān′) ▶*v.* To go or put aboard a train.

en•trance[1] (ĕn′trəns) ▶*n.* **1.** The act or an instance of entering. **2.** A means or point by which to enter. **3.** Permission or power to enter; admission: *gained entrance to law school.* [< OFr. *entraunce* < *entrer*, ENTER.]

en•trance[2] (ĕn-trăns′) ▶*v.* **-tranced, -tranc•ing 1.** To put into a trance. **2.** To fill with delight, wonder, or enchantment. See Syns at **charm, enrapture.** —**en•trance′ment** *n.* —**en•tranc′ing•ly** *adv.*

en•trant (ĕn′trənt) ▶*n.* One that enters a competition.

en•trap (ĕn-trăp′) ▶*v.* **-trapped, -trap•ping 1.** To catch in or as if in a trap. **2.** To lure into danger or a compromising situation. See Syns at **catch.** —**en•trap′ment** *n.*

en•treat (ĕn-trēt′) ▶*v.* To make an earnest request of; plead. [< AN *entreter*.] —**en•treat′ing•ly** *adv.* —**en•treat′ment** *n.*

en•treat•y (ĕn-trē′tē) ▶*n., pl.* **-ies.** An earnest request; plea.

en•trée or **en•tree** (ŏn′trā, ŏn-trā′) ▶*n.* **1.** The main dish of a meal. **2.** The power or liberty to enter. [< OFr., entry.]

en•trench (ĕn-trĕnch′) ▶*v.* **1.** To dig or provide with a trench. **2.** To fix (e.g., an idea or custom) firmly. **3.** To encroach or trespass. —**en•trench′ment** *n.*

en•tre•pre•neur (ŏn′trə-prə-nûr′, -nōōr′) ▶*n.* A person who organizes, operates, and assumes the risk for a business venture. [< OFr. *entreprendre*, undertake.] —**en′tre•pre•neur′i•al** *adj.* —**en′tre•pre•neur′ism** *n.* —**en′tre•pre•neur′ship′** *n.*

en•tro•py (ĕn′trə-pē) ▶*n., pl.* **-pies 1.** For a closed thermodynamic system, a measure of the amount of thermal energy not available to do work. **2.** A measure of the disorder or randomness of a system. [Ger. *Entropie*.] —**en•tro′pic** (ĕn-trō′pĭk, -trŏp′ĭk) *adj.*

en•trust (ĕn-trŭst′) also **in•trust** (ĭn-) ▶*v.* **1.** To give over (something) to another for care, protection, or performance. **2.** To give as a trust to (someone).

en•try (ĕn′trē) ▶*n., pl.* **-tries 1.** The act or an instance of entering. **2.** A means by which to enter. **3a.** The inclusion of an item, as in a record. **b.** An item entered in this way. **4.** An entry word, as in a dictionary; headword. **5.** One entered in a competition.

en•twine (ĕn-twīn′) ▶*v.* **-twined, -twin•ing.** To twine around or together.

e•nu•mer•ate (ĭ-nōō′mə-rāt′, ĭ-nyōō′-) ▶*v.* **-at•ed, -at•ing 1.** To name one by one; list. **2.** To determine the number of; count. [Lat. *ēnumerāre*, count out.] —**e•nu′mer•a′tion** *n.* —**e•nu′mer•a′tive** (-mə-rā′tĭv, -mər-ə-) *adj.* —**e•nu′mer•a′tor** *n.*

e•nun•ci•ate (ĭ-nŭn′sē-āt′) ▶*v.* **-at•ed, -at•ing 1.** To pronounce, esp. with clarity; articulate. **2.** To announce; proclaim. [Lat. *ēnūntiāre*.] —**e•nun′ci•a′tion** *n.* —**e•nun′ci•a′tor** *n.*

en•vel•op (ĕn-vĕl′əp) ▶*v.* **-oped, -op•ing.**

To enclose completely with or as if with a covering. [< OFr. *envoloper*, wrap up.] —**en•vel′op•er** *n.* —**en•vel′op•ment** *n.*
en•ve•lope (ĕn′və-lōp′, ŏn′-) ►*n.* **1.** A flat, folded paper container, esp. for a letter. **2.** Something that envelops or encloses. **3.** The bag containing the gas in a balloon or airship. [< OFr. *envoloper*, wrap up.]
en•ven•om (ĕn-vĕn′əm) ►*v.* **1.** To make poisonous or noxious. **2.** To embitter.
en•vi•a•ble (ĕn′vē-ə-bəl) ►*adj.* So desirable as to arouse envy. —**en′vi•a•bly** *adv.*
en•vi•ous (ĕn′vē-əs) ►*adj.* Feeling, expressing, or characterized by envy. See Syns at **jealous.** —**en′vi•ous•ly** *adv.* —**en′vi•ous•ness** *n.*
en•vi•ron•ment (ĕn-vī′rən-mənt, -vī′ərn-) ►*n.* **1.** The circumstances or conditions that surround one; surroundings. **2.** The totality of circumstances surrounding an organism or a group of organisms. —**en•vi′ron•men′tal** *adj.* —**en•vi′ron•men′tal•ly** *adv.*
en•vi•ron•men•tal•ism (ĕn-vī′rən-mĕn′tl-ĭz′əm, -vī′ərn-) ►*n.* Advocacy for or work toward protecting the natural environment from destruction or pollution. —**en•vi′ron•men′tal•ist** *n.*
en•vi•rons (ĕn-vī′rənz, -vī′ərnz) ►*pl.n.* A surrounding area, esp. of a city. [< OFr. *environ*, around.]
en•vis•age (ĕn-vĭz′ĭj) ►*v.* **-aged, -ag•ing.** To conceive an image or picture of, esp. as a future possibility. [Fr. *envisager*.]
en•vi•sion (ĕn-vĭzh′ən) ►*v.* To picture in the mind; imagine.
en•voy[1] (ĕn′voi′, ŏn′-) ►*n.* **1.** A representative of a government who is sent on a special diplomatic mission. **2.** A messenger; agent. [< OFr. *envoier*, send < LLat. *inviāre*, be on the way.]
en•voy[2] also **en•voi** (ĕn′voi′, ŏn′-) ►*n.* A short closing stanza in certain verse forms dedicating the poem to a patron or summarizing its main ideas. [< OFr. *envoier*, send. See ENVOY[1].]
en•vy (ĕn′vē) ►*n.*, *pl.* **-vies 1.** Discontent and resentment aroused by desire for the possessions or qualities of another. **2.** The object of such feeling. ►*v.* **-vied, -vy•ing.** To feel envy toward. [< Lat. *invidia* < *invidēre*, look at with envy : *in-*, in, on + *vidēre*, see.] —**en′vi•er** *n.*
en•zyme (ĕn′zīm) ►*n.* Any of numerous proteins that are produced by living organisms and function as biochemical catalysts. [< Med.Gk. *enzumos*, leavened.] —**en′zy•mat′ic** (-zə-măt′ĭk) *adj.*
eo– ►*pref.* Most primitive; earliest: *Eocene.* [< Gk. *ēōs*, dawn.]
E•o•cene (ē′ə-sēn′) *Geol.* ►*adj.* Of or being the 2nd epoch of the Tertiary Period, marked by the rise of mammals. ►*n.* The Eocene Epoch.
EOE ►*abbr.* equal opportunity employer
e•o•li•an (ē-ō′lē-ən, ē-ōl′yən) ►*adj.* Relating to, caused by, or carried by the wind. [< *Aeolus*, god of the winds in classical myth.]
EOM ►*abbr.* end of month
e•on also **ae•on** (ē′ŏn′, ē′ən) ►*n.* **1.** An indefinitely long period of time; age. **2.** The longest division of geologic time, containing two or more eras. [< Gk. *aiōn*.]
E•os (ē′ŏs′) ►*n.* *Gk. Myth.* The goddess of the dawn.
e•o•sin (ē′ə-sən) ►*n.* An acidic dye, used in biology to stain cells. [Gk. *ēōs*, dawn + –IN.]
–eous ►*suff.* Characterized by; resembling: *beauteous.* [< Lat. *-ōsus* and Lat. *-eus.*]
EP ►*abbr.* **1.** European plan **2.** extended play
EPA ►*abbr.* Environmental Protection Agency
ep•au•let also **ep•au•lette** (ĕp′ə-lĕt′, ĕp′ə-lĕt′) ►*n.* A shoulder ornament, esp. a fringed strap on a uniform. [< OFr. *espaule*, shoulder < LLat. *spatula*.]
é•pée also **e•pee** (ā-pā′, ĕp′ā) ►*n.* A fencing sword with a bowl-shaped guard and a long narrow blade that has no cutting edge. [Fr. < Lat. *spatha*, sword.]
e•phed•rine (ĭ-fĕd′rĭn, ĕf′ĭ-drēn′) ►*n.* A white odorless alkaloid, $C_{10}H_{15}NO$, used in the treatment of allergies and asthma. [< Lat. *ephedra*, horsetail : Gk. *epi*, upon + *hedra*, seat.]
e•phem•er•al (ĭ-fĕm′ər-əl) ►*adj.* Lasting for a brief time; fleeting; evanescent. [< Gk. *ephēmeros*.] —**e•phem′er•al′i•ty, e•phem′er•al•ness** *n.* —**e•phem′er•al•ly** *adv.*
E•phe•sian (ĭ-fē′zhən) ►*n.* **1.** A native or inhabitant of ancient Ephesus. **2. Ephesians** *(takes sing. v.)* See table at **Bible.** [< Gk. *Ephesioi*, inhabitants of Ephesus.] —**E•phe′sian** *adj.*
Eph•e•sus (ĕf′ĭ-səs) An ancient Greek city of Asia Minor in present-day W Turkey.
epi– or **ep–** ►*pref.* **1.** On; upon: *epiphyte.* **2.** Over; above: *epicenter.* **3.** Around; covering: *epithelium.* [< Gk. *epi*.]
ep•ic (ĕp′ĭk) ►*n.* **1.** A long narrative poem celebrating the feats of a traditional hero. **2.** A literary or dramatic composition that suggests the characteristics of epic poetry. ►*adj.* **1.** Of or resembling an epic; heroic; grand. **2.** Of great size or duration. [< Gk. *epos*, song.]
ep•i•cene (ĕp′ĭ-sēn′) ►*adj.* **1.** Having the characteristics of both the male and the female. **2.** Effeminate. **3.** Sexless. ►*n.* One that is epicene. [< Gk. *epikoinos*.]
ep•i•cen•ter (ĕp′ĭ-sĕn′tər) ►*n.* The point of the earth's surface directly above the focus of an earthquake.
Ep•ic•te•tus (ĕp′ĭk-tē′təs). A.D. 55?–135? Phrygian-born Stoic philosopher.
ep•i•cure (ĕp′ĭ-kyŏŏr′) ►*n.* A person with refined taste, esp. in food. [< EPICURUS.]
ep•i•cu•re•an (ĕp′ĭ-kyŏŏ-rē′ən, -kyŏŏr′ē-) ►*adj.* **1.** Devoted to the pursuit of pleasure. **2.** Suited to the tastes of an epicure. —**ep′i•cu•re′an** *n.*
Ep•i•cu•rus (ĕp′ĭ-kyŏŏr′əs). 341?–270 B.C. Greek philosopher.
ep•i•dem•ic (ĕp′ĭ-dĕm′ĭk) ►*adj.* Spreading rapidly among many individuals in an area. ►*n.* **1.** A contagious disease that spreads rapidly. **2.** A rapid spread or development. [< Gk. *epidēmos*, prevalent.]
ep•i•der•mis (ĕp′ĭ-dûr′mĭs) ►*n.* The outer, protective layer of the skin. —**ep′i•der′mal** *adj.*
ep•i•du•ral (ĕp′ĭ-dŏŏr′əl, -dyŏŏr′-) ►*adj.* Located on or over the dura mater. ►*n.* An injection, esp. of an anesthetic, into the epidural space of the spine.
ep•i•glot•tis (ĕp′ĭ-glŏt′ĭs) ►*n.* The elastic flap of cartilage located at the root of the tongue that prevents food from entering the windpipe during swallowing.
ep•i•gram (ĕp′ĭ-grăm′) ►*n.* A short witty poem or remark. [< Gk. *epigramma*, inscription

< *epigraphein*, write on. See EPIGRAPH.] —**ep′i•gram•mat′ic** *adj.*

ep•i•graph (ĕp′ĭ-grăf′) ►*n.* **1.** An inscription, as on a statue or building. **2.** A motto or quotation, as at the beginning of a book, setting forth a theme. [< Gk. *epigraphein*, write on : EPI– + *graphein*, write.] —**ep′i•graph′ic** *adj.*

e•pig•ra•phy (ĭ-pĭg′rə-fē) ►*n.* The study esp. of ancient inscriptions. —**e•pig′ra•pher** *n.*

ep•i•lep•sy (ĕp′ə-lĕp′sē) ►*n.* Any of various neurological disorders marked by loss of consciousness or convulsive seizures. [< Gk. *epilēpsis*, a taking hold.] —**ep′i•lep′tic** *adj.* & *n.*

ep•i•logue (ĕp′ə-lôg′, -lŏg′) ►*n.* **1.** A short poem or speech spoken directly to the audience at the end of a play. **2.** A short section at the end of a literary or dramatic work, often discussing the future of its characters; afterword. [< Gk. *epilogos*.]

ep•i•neph•rine also **ep•i•neph•rin** (ĕp′ə-nĕf′rĭn) ►*n.* **1.** An adrenal hormone that constricts blood vessels and raises blood pressure; adrenaline. **2.** A crystalline compound, $C_9H_{13}NO_3$, used as a heart stimulant, vasoconstrictor, and bronchial relaxant. [EPI– + NEPHR(O)– + –INE[2].]

e•piph•a•ny (ĭ-pĭf′ə-nē) ►*n.*, *pl.* **-nies 1. Epiphany** A Christian feast observed on Jan. 6 celebrating the visit of the Magi to Jesus. **2.** A revelatory manifestation esp. of a divine being. [< Gk. *epiphaneia*, manifestation.]

ep•i•phyte (ĕp′ə-fīt′) ►*n.* A plant, such as Spanish moss or a tropical orchid, that grows on another plant or object that provides support but not nutrients. —**ep′i•phyt′ic** (-fĭt′ĭk) *adj.*

e•pis•co•pa•cy (ĭ-pĭs′kə-pə-sē) ►*n.*, *pl.* **-cies 1.** See **episcopate** 3. **2.** A system of church government headed by bishops.

e•pis•co•pal (ĭ-pĭs′kə-pəl) ►*adj.* **1.** Of or relating to a bishop. **2.** Governed by bishops. **3. Episcopal** Of the Episcopal Church. [< Gk. *episkopos*, overseer : EPI– + *skopos*, watcher.]

Episcopal Church ►*n.* The church in the US that is in communion with the see of Canterbury.

E•pis•co•pa•lian (ĭ-pĭs′kə-pā′lē-ən, -pāl′yən) ►*adj.* Of or belonging to the Episcopal Church. —**E•pis′co•pa′lian** *n.*

e•pis•co•pate (ĭ-pĭs′kə-pĭt, -pāt′) ►*n.* **1.** The position, term, or office of a bishop. **2.** The jurisdiction of a bishop; diocese. **3.** Bishops collectively.

e•pis•i•ot•o•my (ĭ-pĭz′ē-ŏt′ə-mē, ĭ-pē′zē-) ►*n.*, *pl.* **-mies.** Surgical incision of the perineum during childbirth to ease delivery. [Gk. *epision*, pubic region + –TOMY.]

ep•i•sode (ĕp′ĭ-sōd′) ►*n.* **1.** An incident in the course of an experience. **2.** An incident that forms a unit in a narrative or dramatic work. [< Gk. *epeisodion*, parenthetic narrative.] —**ep′i•sod′ic** (-sŏd′ĭk) *adj.*

e•pis•te•mol•o•gy (ĭ-pĭs′tə-mŏl′ə-jē) ►*n.* The branch of philosophy that studies the nature and theory of knowledge. [< Gk. *epistēmē*, knowledge < *epistasthai*, understand : EPI– + *histanai*, *stē-*, place, determine.] —**e•pis′te•mo•log′i•cal** *adj.* —**e•pis′te•mol′o•gist** *n.*

e•pis•tle (ĭ-pĭs′əl) ►*n.* **1.** A letter, esp. a formal one. **2. Epistle** *Bible* A letter written by an Apostle and included in the New Testament. [< Gk. *epistolē*.] —**e•pis′to•lar′y** (-tə-lĕr′ē) *adj.*

ep•i•taph (ĕp′ĭ-tăf′) ►*n.* An inscription, as on a tombstone, in memory of a deceased person. [< Gk. *epitaphion*, funeral oration.]

ep•i•the•li•um (ĕp′ə-thē′lē-əm) ►*n.*, *pl.* **-li•ums** or **-li•a** (-lē-ə). A membranous tissue composed of one or more layers of cells that covers most internal and external surfaces of the body and its organs. [< EPI– + Gk. *thēlē*, nipple.] —**ep′i•the′li•al** *adj.*

ep•i•thet (ĕp′ə-thĕt′) ►*n.* A term, often abusive or contemptuous, used to characterize a person or thing. [< Gk. *epithetos*, added.]

e•pit•o•me (ĭ-pĭt′ə-mē) ►*n.* **1.** A typical or perfect example of its kind. **2.** A brief summary. [< Gk. *epitomē*, an abridgment.]

e•pit•o•mize (ĭ-pĭt′ə-mīz′) ►*v.* **-mized, -miz•ing 1.** To make an epitome of; sum up. **2.** To be a typical example of; embody.

ep•och (ĕp′ək, ē′pŏk′) ►*n.* **1.** A particular period of history, esp. one that is noteworthy; era. **2.** A unit of geologic time that is a division of a period. [< Gk. *epokhē*, point in time.] —**ep′och•al** *adj.*

ep•o•nym (ĕp′ə-nĭm′) ►*n.* A real or mythical person whose name is the source of the name of something, such as an era or city. [< Gk. *epōnumos*, named after.] —**e•pon′y•mous** (ĭ-pŏn′ə-məs) *adj.*

ep•ox•y (ĭ-pŏk′sē) ►*n.*, *pl.* **-ies.** Any of various usu. thermosetting resins used esp. in surface coatings and adhesives. [EP(I)– + OXY(GEN).] —**ep•ox′y** *v.*

ep•si•lon (ĕp′sə-lŏn′, -lən) ►*n.* The 5th letter of the Greek alphabet. [Gk. *e psilon*, simple e.]

Ep•som salts (ĕp′səm) ►*pl.n.* *(takes sing. v.)* Hydrated magnesium sulfate, used as a cathartic and to reduce inflammation. [After *Epsom*, England.]

EQ (ē′kyo͞o′) ►*n.* Intelligence regarding the emotions, esp. in monitoring the emotions of oneself or others.

eq. ►*abbr.* **1.** equal **2.** equation **3.** equivalent

eq•ua•ble (ĕk′wə-bəl, ē′kwə-) ►*adj.* **1.** Unvarying; steady. **2.** Even-tempered. [< Lat. *aequāre*, make even.] —**eq′ua•bil′i•ty** *n.* —**eq′ua•bly** *adv.*

e•qual (ē′kwəl) ►*adj.* **1.** Having the same capability, quantity, effect, measure, or value as another. **2.** *Math.* Being identical to in value. **3.** Having the same privileges, status, or rights. **4.** Having the requisite qualities for a task or situation. ►*n.* One that is equal to another. ►*v.* **e•qualed, e•qual•ing** or **e•qualled, e•qual•ling 1.** To be equal to, esp. in value. **2.** To do, make, or produce something equal to: *equaled the world record.* [< Lat. *aequus*.] —**e•qual′i•ty** (ĭ-kwŏl′ĭ-tē) *n.* —**e′qual•ly** *adv.*

e•qual•ize (ē′kwə-līz′) ►*v.* **-ized, -iz•ing.** To make equal, uniform, or balanced. —**e′qual•i•za′tion** *n.* —**e′qual•iz′er** *n.*

equal sign ►*n.* The symbol (=) used to indicate mathematical equality.

e•qua•nim•i•ty (ē′kwə-nĭm′ĭ-tē, ĕk′wə-) ►*n.* Calmness; composure. [< Lat. *aequanimis*, even-tempered.]

e•quate (ĭ-kwāt′) ►*v.* **e•quat•ed, e•quat•ing.** To make, treat, or regard as equal or equivalent. [< Lat. *aequāre* < *aequus*, even.]

e•qua•tion (ĭ-kwā′zhən, -shən) ►*n.* **1.** The act or process of equating or the condition of being equated. **2.** A statement, as in mathematics, asserting that two expressions are equal. **3.** A complex of variable elements or factors.

e•qua•tor (ĭ-kwā′tər) ►*n.* **1.** The imaginary great circle around the earth's surface, equidistant from the poles and perpendicular to the earth's axis of rotation, that divides the earth into the Northern Hemisphere and the Southern Hemisphere. **2.** A similar great circle on a celestial body. [< Med.Lat. *aequātor (diēī et noctis)*, equalizer (of day and night).] —**e′qua•to′ri•al** (ē′kwə-tôr′ē-əl, -tōr′-, ĕk′wə-) *adj.*

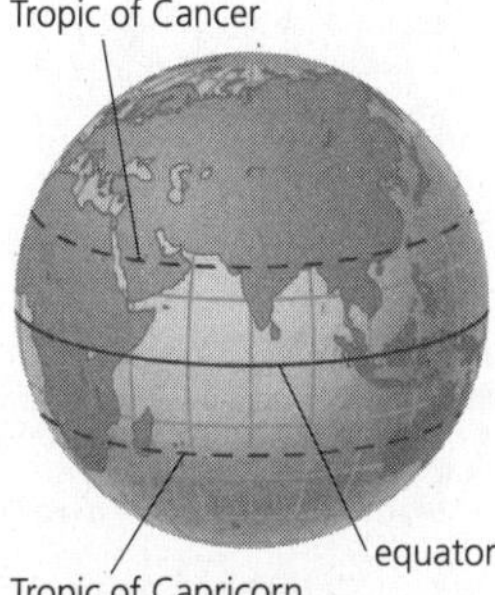

equator

Equatorial Guinea. A country of W-central Africa including islands in the Gulf of Guinea. Cap. Malabo. Pop. 389,000.

eq•uer•ry (ĕk′wə-rē) ►*n., pl.* **-ries 1.** An attendant to the British royal household. **2.** An officer in charge of the horses in a royal or noble household. [< OFr. *escuier*, SQUIRE.]

e•ques•tri•an (ĭ-kwĕs′trē-ən) ►*adj.* **1.** Of or relating to horseback riding. **2.** Depicted or represented on horseback. ►*n.* One who rides a horse or performs on horseback. [< Lat. *equester* < *eques*, horseman.] —**e•ques′tri•an•ism** *n.*

equi– ►*pref.* Equal; equally: *equiangular.* [< Lat. *aequus*, equal.]

e•qui•an•gu•lar (ē′kwē-ăng′gyə-lər, ĕk′wē-) ►*adj.* Having all angles equal.

e•qui•dis•tant (ē′kwĭ-dĭs′tənt, ĕk′wĭ-) ►*adj.* Equally distant. —**e′qui•dis′tance** *n.*

e•qui•lat•er•al (ē′kwə-lăt′ər-əl, ĕk′wə-) ►*adj.* Having all sides equal. —**e′qui•lat′er•al** *n.*

e•qui•lib•ri•um (ē′kwə-lĭb′rē-əm, ĕk′wə-) ►*n.* A condition of balance between opposed forces, influences, or actions. [Lat. *aequilībrium.*]

e•quine (ē′kwīn′, ĕk′wīn′) ►*adj.* **1.** Of or like a horse. **2.** Of the taxonomic family which includes the horses, asses, and zebras. [< Lat. *equus*, horse.] —**e′quine′** *n.*

e•qui•noc•tial (ē′kwə-nŏk′shəl, ĕk′wə-) ►*adj.* Relating to an equinox.

e•qui•nox (ē′kwə-nŏks′, ĕk′wə-) ►*n.* Either of the two times during a year when the sun crosses the celestial equator and when the length of day and night are approx. equal. [< Lat. *aequinoctium* : EQUI– + *nox*, night.]

e•quip (ĭ-kwĭp′) ►*v.* **e•quipped, e•quip•ping.** To supply with the necessary materials for an undertaking. [< OFr. *esquiper.*]

e•quip•ment (ĭ-kwĭp′mənt) ►*n.* **1.** The act of equipping or the state of being equipped. **2.** The things with which one is equipped.

Syns: *equipment, apparatus, gear, materiel, outfit, paraphernalia* **n.**

e•qui•poise (ē′kwə-poiz′, ĕk′wə-) ►*n.* **1.** Equality in distribution, as of weight. **2.** A counterbalance.

eq•ui•ta•ble (ĕk′wĭ-tə-bəl) ►*adj.* Just and fair; impartial. [< OFr. *equite*, EQUITY.] —**eq′ui•ta•ble•ness** *n.* —**eq′ui•ta•bly** *adv.*

eq•ui•ta•tion (ĕk′wĭ-tā′shən) ►*n.* The art and practice of riding a horse. [< Lat. *equitāre*, ride horseback.]

eq•ui•ty (ĕk′wĭ-tē) ►*n., pl.* **-ties 1.** The state or quality of being just, impartial, and fair. **2.** Something that is equitable. **3.** *Law* A system of rules and principles supplementing civil and common law. **4.** The residual value of a business or property beyond any mortgage or liability. **5.** Corporate stock. [< Lat. *aequitās.*]

e•quiv•a•lent (ĭ-kwĭv′ə-lənt) ►*adj.* **1.** Equal. **2.** Similar or identical in function or effect. [< LLat. *aequivalēre*, have equal force.] —**e•quiv′a•lence, e•quiv′a•len•cy** *n.* —**e•quiv′a•lent** *n.* —**e•quiv′a•lent•ly** *adv.*

e•quiv•o•cal (ĭ-kwĭv′ə-kəl) ►*adj.* **1.** Ambiguous. **2.** Questionable or inconclusive. [< LLat. *aequivocus.*] —**e•quiv′o•cal•ly** *adv.*

e•quiv•o•cate (ĭ-kwĭv′ə-kāt′) ►*v.* **-cat•ed, -cat•ing.** To use ambiguous language; hedge. [< Med.Lat. *aequivocāre.*] —**e•quiv′o•ca′tion** *n.* —**e•quiv′o•ca′tor** *n.*

Er ► The symbol for the element **erbium.**

ER ►*abbr.* emergency room

–er¹ ►*suff.* **1a.** One that performs a specified action: *swimmer.* **b.** One that undergoes a specified action: *broiler.* **c.** One that has: *ten-pounder.* **d.** One associated or involved with: *banker.* **2a.** Native or resident of: *New Yorker.* **b.** One that is: *foreigner.* [< OE *-ere* and < Lat. *-ārius*, -ary.]

–er² ►*suff.* Used to form the comparative degree of adjectives and adverbs: *darker; faster.* [< OE *-re, -ra.*]

e•ra (îr′ə, ĕr′ə) ►*n.* **1.** A period of time using a specific date in history as a basis. **2.** A period of time characterized by a particular circumstance, event, or person. **3.** The longest division of geologic time, made up of one or more periods. [< Lat. *aera*, counters.]

ERA ►*abbr.* **1.** earned run average **2.** Equal Rights Amendment

e•rad•i•cate (ĭ-răd′ĭ-kāt′) ►*v.* **-cat•ed, -cat•ing.** To get rid of or remove completely; uproot. See Syns at **eliminate.** [< Lat. *ērādīcāre* : EX– + *rādīx*, root.] —**e•rad′i•ca•ble** *adj.* —**e•rad′i•ca′tion** *n.* —**e•rad′i•ca′tor** *n.*

e•rase (ĭ-rās′) ►*v.* **e•rased, e•ras•ing 1.** To remove (e.g., something written) by or as if by rubbing. **2.** To remove (recorded material) from a magnetic tape or diskette. **3.** To remove all traces of. [Lat. *ērādere, ērās-*, scratch out.] —**e•ras•a•ble** *adj.* —**e•ras′er** *n.* —**e•ra′sure** *n.*

E•ras•mus (ĭ-răz′məs), **Desiderius.** 1466?–1536. Dutch scholar and theologian.

er•bi•um (ûr′bē-əm) ►*n.* *Symbol* **Er** A soft, malleable, silvery rare-earth element. At. no. 68. See table at **element.** [After *Ytterby*, Sweden.]

ere (âr) ►*prep.* Previous to; before. ►*conj.* Rather than; before. [< OE *ǣr.*]

Er•e•bus (ĕr′ə-bəs), **Mount.** A volcanic peak, 3,796.6 m (12,448 ft), on Ross I. in Antarctica.

e•rect (ĭ-rĕkt′) ►*adj.* **1.** Being in a vertical, upright position. **2.** *Physiol.* Stiff; rigid. ►*v.* **1.** To build or construct. **2.** To raise upright. **3.** To set up; establish. [< Lat. *ērēctus*, p.part. of *ērigere*, set up.] —**e•rect′ly** *adv.* —**e•rect′ness** *n.* —**e•rec′tor** *n.*

e•rec•tile (ĭ-rĕk′təl, -tīl′) ►*adj. Physiol.* Of or relating to vascular tissue that is capable of filling with blood and becoming rigid.

e•rec•tion (ĭ-rĕk′shən) ►*n.* **1.** The act of erecting or the state of being erected. **2.** *Physiol.* The condition of erectile tissue when filled with blood.

ere•long (âr-lông′, -lŏng′) ►*adv.* Before long; soon.

er•e•mite (âr′ə-mīt′) ►*n.* A hermit, esp. a religious recluse. [< Gk. *erēmitēs*, HERMIT.]

E•re•van (yĕ′rĭ-vän′) See **Yerevan.**

erg (ûrg) ►*n.* A unit of energy or work equal to 10^{-7} joule. [< Gk. *ergon*, work.]

er•go (ûr′gō, âr′-) ►*conj. & adv.* Consequently; therefore. [Lat. *ergō*.]

er•go•nom•ics (ûr′gə-nŏm′ĭks) ►*n. (takes sing. v.)* The applied science of equipment design intended to reduce operator fatigue and discomfort. [Gk. *ergon*, work + (ECO)NOMICS.] —**er′go•nom′ic, er′go•no•met′ric** *adj.*

er•got (ûr′gət, -gŏt′) ►*n.* **1.** A fungus that infects rye and other cereal plants. **2.** The disease caused by such a fungus. **3.** A drug or medicine made from dried ergot. [< OFr. *argot*, cock's spur.]

Er•ic•son (ĕr′ĭk-sən), **Leif.** fl. c. 1000. Norwegian navigator.

Er•ic the Red (ĕr′ĭk). fl. 10th cent.. Norwegian navigator.

E•rie[1] (îr′ē) ►*n., pl.* **E•rie** or **E•ries 1.** A member of a Native American people formerly inhabiting the S shore of Lake Erie. **2.** The Iroquoian language of the Erie.

E•rie[2] (îr′ē) A city of NW PA on Lake Erie SW of Buffalo, NY. Pop. 108,718.

Erie, Lake. One of the Great Lakes, bounded by S Ontario, W NY, NW PA, N OH, and SE MI.

Erie Canal. An artificial waterway extending about 579 km (360 mi) across central NY from Albany to Buffalo; now part of the New York State Barge Canal.

Er•in (ĕr′ĭn) A poetic name for Ireland.

ERISA ►*abbr.* Employee Retirement Income Security Act

Er•i•tre•a (ĕr′ĭ-trē′ə) A country of NE Africa bordering on the Red Sea; it was part of Ethiopia from 1952–93. Pop. 3,437,000 —**Er′i•tre′an** *adj. & n.*

er•mine (ûr′mĭn) ►*n.* **1.** A weasel having dark brown fur that in winter changes to white. **2.** The white fur of this animal. [< OFr.]

Ernst (ĕrnst), **Max.** 1891–1976. German-born artist.

e•rode (ĭ-rōd′) ►*v.* **e•rod•ed, e•rod•ing 1.** To wear away or destroy gradually by or as if by abrasion. **2.** To eat into or away; corrode. [Lat. *ērōdere*, eat away.] —**e•rod′i•ble** *adj.*

e•rog•e•nous (ĭ-rŏj′ə-nəs) ►*adj.* **1.** Responsive to sexual stimulation. **2.** Arousing sexual desire. [< Gk. *erōs*, sexual love.]

Er•os (ĕr′ŏs′, îr′-) ►*n. Gk. Myth.* The god of love, son of Aphrodite.

e•ro•sion (ĭ-rō′zhən) ►*n.* The process of eroding or the condition of being eroded. —**e•ro′sive** *adj.* —**e•ro′sive•ness** *n.*

erosion

e•rot•ic (ĭ-rŏt′ĭk) ►*adj.* **1.** Of, concerning, or tending to arouse sexual desire. **2.** Dominated by sexual desire. [< Gk. *erōs*, *erōt-*, sexual love.] —**e•rot′i•cal•ly** *adv.* —**e•rot′i•cism** *n.*

e•rot•i•ca (ĭ-rŏt′ĭ-kə) ►*pl.n. (takes sing. or pl. v.)* Literature or art intended to arouse sexual desire. [Gk. *erōtika* < *erōtikos*, EROTIC.]

err (ûr, ĕr) ►*v.* **1.** To make an error or mistake. **2.** To sin. [< Lat. *errāre*, wander.]

er•rand (ĕr′ənd) ►*n.* **1.** A short trip taken to perform a specified task. **2.** The purpose or object of an errand. [< OE *ǣrend*.]

er•rant (ĕr′ənt) ►*adj.* **1.** Roving, esp. in search of adventure. **2.** Straying from proper moral standards. **3.** Roving aimlessly. [< AN *erraunt*.] —**er′rant•ly** *adv.* —**er′rant•ry** *n.*

er•rat•ic (ĭ-răt′ĭk) ►*adj.* **1.** Lacking consistency or uniformity; irregular. **2.** Unconventional; eccentric. [< Lat. *errāticus*, wandering.] —**er•rat′i•cal•ly** *adv.*

er•ra•tum (ĭ-rä′təm, ĭ-rā′-) ►*n., pl.* **-ta** (-tə). An error in a printed text. [Lat. *errātum*.]

Er Rif (ĕr rĭf′) A hilly region along the coast of N Morocco.

er•ro•ne•ous (ĭ-rō′nē-əs) ►*adj.* Incorrect or mistaken. [< Lat. *errō*, *errōn-*, vagabond.] —**er•ro′ne•ous•ly** *adv.*

er•ror (ĕr′ər) ►*n.* **1.** An unintentional deviation from is what is correct, right, or true. **2.** The condition of being incorrect or wrong. **3.** *Baseball* A defensive misplay. [< Lat.] —**er′ror•less** *adj.*

er•satz (ĕr′zäts′, ĕr-zäts′) ►*adj.* Being a substitute; artificial. [Ger., replacement < OHGer. *irsezzan*, replace : *ir-*, out + *sezzan*, set.]

Erse (ûrs) ►*n.* **1.** See **Irish Gaelic. 2.** See **Scottish Gaelic.** [< OE *Iras*, the Irish.] —**Erse** *adj.*

erst•while (ûrst′hwīl′, -wīl′) ►*adv.* In the past. ►*adj.* Former. [< OE *ǣrest*.]

e•ruct (ĭ-rŭkt′) ►*v.* To belch. [Lat. *ērūctāre*.] —**e•ruc•ta′tion** *n.*

er•u•dite (ĕr′yə-dīt′, ĕr′ə-) ►*adj.* Marked by erudition; scholarly. See Syns at **learned.** [< Lat. *ērudītus*, p.part. of *ērudīre*, instruct, polish.] —**er′u•dite′ly** *adv.*

er•u•di•tion (ĕr′yə-dĭsh′ən, ĕr′ə-) ►*n.* Deep, extensive learning; scholarship.

e•rupt (ĭ-rŭpt′) ►*v.* **1.** To break out violently

from restraint or limits: *erupt in anger.* **2.** To become violently active, as a volcano. **3.** To appear on the skin. Used of a rash or blemish. [Lat. *ērumpere, ērupt-.*] —**e•rup′tion** *n.* —**e•rup′tive** *adj.*

–ery or **–ry** ►*suff.* **1.** A place for: *bakery.* **2.** A collection or class: *finery.* **3.** A state or condition: *slavery.* **4.** Act; practice: *bribery.* **5.** Characteristics or qualities of: *snobbery.* [< OFr. *-erie.*]

er•y•sip•e•las (ĕr′ĭ-sĭp′ə-ləs, îr′-) ►*n.* An acute disease of the skin caused by a streptococcus and marked by spreading inflammation and fever. [< Gk. *erusipelas* : *erusi-*, red + *-pelas*, skin.]

e•ryth•ro•cyte (ĭ-rĭth′rə-sīt′) ►*n.* See **red blood cell.** [Gk. *eruthros*, red + -CYTE.] —**e•ryth′ro•cyt′ic** (-sĭt′ĭk) *adj.*

e•ryth•ro•my•cin (ĭ-rĭth′rə-mī′sĭn) ►*n.* An antibiotic obtained from a strain of fungus and effective against many bacteria. [Gk. *eruthros*, red + -MYCIN.]

Erz•ge•bir•ge (ĕrts′gə-bîr′gə) A mountain range on the border of Germany and Czech Republic rising to 1,244.4 m (4,080 ft).

Es ► The symbol for the element **einsteinium.**

–es[1] ►*suff.* Var. of **–s**[1].

–es[2] ►*suff.* Var. of **–s**[2].

E•sau (ē′sô). In the Bible, the eldest son of Isaac and Rebecca.

es•ca•late (ĕs′kə-lāt′) ►*v.* **-lat•ed, -lat•ing.** To increase or intensify. [< ESCALATOR.] —**es′ca•la′tion** *n.*

es•ca•la•tor (ĕs′kə-lā′tər) ►*n.* A moving stairway consisting of steps attached to a continuously circulating belt. [Orig. trademark.]

es•ca•pade (ĕs′kə-pād′) ►*n.* A reckless adventure. [< VLat. **excappāre*, ESCAPE.]

es•cape (ĭ-skāp′) ►*v.* **-caped, -cap•ing 1.** To break out (of). **2.** To avoid capture, danger, or harm. **3.** To succeed in avoiding. **4.** To elude: *Her name escapes me.* **5.** To leak or issue (from). ►*n.* **1.** The act or a means of escaping. **2.** A leakage. **3.** A means of obtaining temporary freedom from worry or care. *Comp. Sci.* A key used esp. to interrupt a command or exit a program. [< VLat. **excappāre* < Med.Lat. *cappa*, cloak.] —**es•cap′er** *n.*

es•cap•ee (ĭ-skā′pē′, ĕs′kā-) ►*n.* One that has escaped, esp. an escaped prisoner.

escape velocity ►*n.* The minimum velocity that a body must attain to overcome the gravitational attraction of another body, such as the earth.

es•cap•ism (ĭ-skā′pĭz′əm) ►*n.* The avoidance of reality through daydreaming, fantasy, or entertainment. —**es•cap′ist** *adj. & n.*

es•ca•role (ĕs′kə-rōl′) ►*n.* A salad plant having leaves with frilled edges. [< LLat. *ēscāriola*, chicory < Lat. *ēsca*, food < *edere*, eat.]

es•carp•ment (ĭ-skärp′mənt) ►*n.* **1.** A steep slope or long cliff. **2.** A steep slope in front of a fortification. [< Ital. *scarpa*, slope.]

–escence ►*suff.* State; process: *luminescence.* [< Lat. *-ēscentia.*]

–escent ►*suff.* **1.** Beginning to be; becoming: *obsolescent.* **2.** Characterized by; resembling: *evanescent.* [< Lat. *-ēscēns.*]

es•chew (ĕs-cho͞o′) ►*v.* To avoid or shun. [< OFr. *eschivir*, of Gmc. orig.]

es•cort (ĕs′kôrt′) ►*n.* **1.** One that accompanies another to guide, protect, or show honor. **2.** A man who is the companion of a woman, esp. socially. ►*v.* (ĭ-skôrt′, ĕs′kôrt′). To accompany as an escort. [< Ital. *scorta* < *scorgere*, to guide.]

es•cri•toire (ĕs′krĭ-twär′) ►*n.* A writing table. [< Med.Lat. *scrīptōrium*, a study.]

es•crow (ĕs′krō′, ĕ-skrō′) ►*n.* Money, property, a deed, or a bond put into the custody of a third party until fulfillment of certain conditions. [< AN *escrowe*, SCROLL.]

es•cu•do (ĭ-sko͞o′dō) ►*n., pl.* **-dos.** See table at **currency.** [< Lat. *scūtum*, shield.]

es•cutch•eon (ĭ-skŭch′ən) ►*n.* A shield or shield-shaped emblem bearing a coat of arms. [< Lat. *scūtum*, shield.]

ESE ►*abbr.* east-southeast

–ese ►*suff.* **1.** Of, characteristic of, or originating in a specified place: *Vietnamese.* **2.** Native or inhabitant of: *Taiwanese.* **3a.** Language or dialect of: *Chinese.* **b.** Literary style or diction of: *journalese.* [< Lat. *-ēnsis*, originating in.]

Es•fa•han (ĕs′fə-hän′) or **Is•fa•han** (ĭs′-). A city of central Iran S of Tehran. Pop. 1,220,595.

Es•ki•mo (ĕs′kə-mō′) ►*n., pl.* **-mo** or **-mos 1.** A member of a group of peoples inhabiting the Arctic coast of North America and parts of Greenland and NE Siberia. **2.** Any of the languages of the Eskimo. —**Es′ki•mo′, Es′ki•mo′an** *adj.*

ESL ►*abbr.* English as a second language

e•soph•a•gus (ĭ-sŏf′ə-gəs) ►*n., pl.* **-gi** (-jī′, -gī′). A muscular tube for passing food from the pharynx to the stomach. [< Gk. *oisophagos.*] —**e•soph′a•ge′al** (-jē′əl) *adj.*

es•o•ter•ic (ĕs′ə-tĕr′ĭk) ►*adj.* **1.** Intended for or understood by only a few. **2.** Not publicly disclosed; confidential. [< Gk. *esōterō*, further in.] —**es′o•ter′i•cal•ly** *adv.*

ESP (ē′ĕs-pē′) ►*n.* Communication or perception by means other than the physical senses. [*e(xtra)s(ensory) p(erception).*]

esp. ►*abbr.* especially

es•pa•drille (ĕs′pə-drĭl′) ►*n.* A shoe usu. having a fabric upper and a rope or rubber sole. [< Prov. *espardilho.*]

espadrille

es•pal•ier (ĭ-spăl′yər, -yā′) ►*n.* A tree or shrub trained to grow in a flat plane against a wall or framework, often in a pattern. [< Ital. *spalliera*, shoulder support.] —**es•pal′ier** *v.*

es•pe•cial (ĭ-spĕsh′əl) ►*adj.* Of special importance or significance; particular; exceptional. [< Lat. *speciālis*, of a kind < *speciēs*, kind.] —**es•pe′cial•ly** *adv.*

Es•pe•ran•to (ĕs′pə-răn′tō, -rän′-) ►*n.* An artificial international language based on many European languages. [After Dr. *Esperanto*, pseudonym of L.L. Zamenhof (1859–1917).]

es•pi•o•nage (ĕs′pē-ə-näzh′, -nĭj) ►*n.* The act

or practice of spying. [< OItal. *spione*, of Gmc. orig.]

es•pla•nade (ĕs′plə-näd′, -nād′) ►*n.* A flat, open stretch of pavement or grass used as a promenade. [< Lat. *explānāre*, make plain.]

Es•poo (ĕs′pō, -pô) A town of S Finland, a suburb of Helsinki. Pop. 180,851.

es•pous•al (ĭ-spou′zəl, -səl) ►*n.* **1a.** A betrothal. **b.** A wedding ceremony. **2.** Adoption of or support for an idea or cause.

es•pouse (ĭ-spouz′) ►*v.* **-poused, -pous•ing 1.** To marry. **2.** To give one's loyalty or support to; adopt. [< Lat. *spondēre*, betroth.]

es•pres•so (ĭ-sprĕs′ō, ĕ-sprĕs′ō) ►*n., pl.* **-sos.** A strong coffee brewed by forcing steam through darkly roasted, powdered beans. [< Ital., p.part. of *esprimere*, press out.]

es•prit (ĕ-sprē′) ►*n.* **1.** Liveliness of mind and expression; spirit. **2.** Esprit de corps. See Syns at **morale.** [< Lat. *spīritus*, SPIRIT.]

esprit de corps (də kôr′) ►*n.* A common spirit of enthusiasm and devotion among members of a group. See Syns at **morale.** [Fr.]

es•py (ĭ-spī′) ►*v.* **-pied, -py•ing.** To catch sight of; glimpse. [< OFr. *espier*, to watch, of Gmc. orig.]

Esq. ►*abbr.* esquire (title)

-esque ►*suff.* In the manner of; resembling: *picturesque.* [< VLat. *-iscus*, of Gmc. orig.]

es•quire (ĕs′kwīr′, ĭ-skwīr′) ►*n.* **1.** A member of the English gentry ranking directly below a knight. **2. Esquire** Used as an honorific, usu. in its abbreviated form *Esq.*, esp. after the name of an attorney or a consular officer. **3.** A candidate for knighthood serving a knight as attendant. [< LLat. *scūtārius*, shield bearer.]

-ess ►*suff.* Female: *lioness.* [< Gk. *-issa.*]

Usage: Critics have argued that sexist connotations are implicit in the use of the feminine suffix *-ess,* as in words such as *sculptress, stewardess,* and *hostess,* in that the suffix implies a difference in the denoted roles when performed by women instead of men. For occupational titles, the use of *-ess* has been largely replaced by gender-neutral compounds such as *flight attendant* or by the *-er/-or* forms. See Usage Note at **man.**

es•say (ĕs′ā′) ►*n.* **1.** A short literary composition on a single subject, usu. presenting the personal view of the author. **2.** (*also* ĕ-sā′). An initial attempt or endeavor, esp. a tentative one. ►*v.* (ĕ-sā′, ĕs′ā′). To make an attempt at; try. [< LLat. *exagium*, a weighing : EX- + Lat. *agere*, drive.] **—es•say′er** *n.*

es•say•ist (ĕs′ā′ĭst) ►*n.* A writer of essays.

Es•sen (ĕs′ən) A city of W-central Germany near the confluence of the Ruhr and Rhine rivers N of Cologne. Pop. 622,380.

es•sence (ĕs′əns) ►*n.* **1.** The intrinsic or indispensable properties that identify something. **2.** A concentrated extract of a substance that retains its fundamental properties. **3.** A perfume or scent. [< Lat. *essentia* < *esse*, be.]

es•sen•tial (ĭ-sĕn′shəl) ►*adj.* **1.** Constituting or being part of the essence of something; inherent. **2.** Basic or indispensable; necessary. See Syns at **indispensable.** ►*n.* Something essential. **—es•sen′ti•al′i•ty, es•sen′tial•ness** *n.* **—es•sen′tial•ly** *adv.*

essential oil ►*n.* A volatile oil obtained from aromatic plants, used in perfumes and flavorings.

EST ►*abbr.* Eastern Standard Time

est. ►*abbr.* **1.** established **2.** estate **3.** estimate

-est¹ ►*suff.* Used to form the superlative degree of adjectives and adverbs: *greatest; earliest.* [< OE.]

-est² or **-st** ►*suff.* Used to form the archaic 2nd person sing. of English verbs: *comest.* [< OE.]

es•tab•lish (ĭ-stăb′lĭsh) ►*v.* **1.** To found or create; set up. See Syns at **found¹. 2.** To place or settle in a secure position or condition. **3.** To cause to be recognized and accepted. **4.** To prove the truth of. [< Lat. *stabilīre* < *stabilis*, firm.] **—es•tab′lish•er** *n.*

es•tab•lish•ment (ĭ-stăb′lĭsh-mənt) ►*n.* **1.** The act of establishing or the condition of being established. **2.** A place of residence or business with its members, staff, and possessions. **3.** often **the Establishment** An exclusive or powerful group who control or strongly influence a government, society, or field of activity.

es•tate (ĭ-stāt′) ►*n.* **1.** A landed property, usu. of considerable size. **2.** All of one's possessions, esp. those left at death. **3.** A stage, condition, or status of life. [< OFr. *estat*, STATE.]

es•teem (ĭ-stēm′) ►*v.* **1.** To regard with respect; prize. **2.** To regard as; consider. ►*n.* Favorable regard; respect. [< Lat. *aestimāre*, appraise.]

es•ter (ĕs′tər) ►*n.* Any of a class of organic compounds chemically corresponding to inorganic salts. [Ger. < *Essigäther* : *Essig*, vinegar (< Lat. *acētum*) + *Äther*, ETHER.]

Es•ther (ĕs′tər) ►*n.* **1.** In the Bible, the Jewish queen of Persia who saved her people from massacre. **2.** See table at **Bible.**

es•the•sia also **aes•the•sia** (ĕs-thē′zhə) ►*n.* The ability to receive sense impressions. [< ANESTHESIA.]

es•thete (ĕs′thēt) ►*n.* Var. of **aesthete. —es•thet′ic** (ĕs-thĕt′ĭk) *adj.* **—es•thet′i•cal•ly** *adv.* **—es•thet′i•cism** *n.* **—es•thet′ics** *n.*

es•ti•ma•ble (ĕs′tə-mə-bəl) ►*adj.* **1.** Possible to estimate. **2.** Deserving of esteem; admirable. **—es′ti•ma•bly** *adv.*

es•ti•mate (ĕs′tə-māt′) ►*v.* **-mat•ed, -mat•ing 1.** To calculate approximately the amount, extent, magnitude, position, or value of. **2.** To evaluate. ►*n.* (-mĭt) **1.** A rough calculation. **2.** A preliminary statement of the cost of work to be done. **3.** An opinion. [Lat. *aestimāre.*] **—es′ti•ma′tion** *n.* **—es′ti•ma′tor** *n.*

es•ti•vate also **aes•ti•vate** (ĕs′tə-vāt′) ►*v.* **-vat•ed, -vat•ing** *Zool.* To pass the summer in a dormant or torpid state. [< Lat. *aestās*, summer.] **—es′ti•va′tion** *n.*

Es•to•ni•a (ĕ-stō′nē-ə) A country of NE Europe. Cap. Tallinn. Pop. 1,499,000.

Es•to•ni•an (ĕ-stō′nē-ən) ►*n.* **1.** A native or inhabitant of Estonia. **2.** The Finno-Ugric language of Estonia. **—Es•to′ni•an** *adj.*

es•trange (ĭ-strānj′) ►*v.* **-tranged, -trang•ing.** To make hostile, unsympathetic, or indifferent; alienate. [< Lat. *extrāneāre*, treat as a stranger.] **—es•trange′ment** *n.*

es•tro•gen (ĕs′trə-jən) ►*n.* Any of several hormones produced chiefly by the ovaries that act to regulate certain female reproductive functions and maintain female secondary sex characteristics. [ESTR(US) + -GEN.]

es•trus (ĕs′trəs) ► *n.* The state of sexual excitement in most female mammals that immediately precedes ovulation; heat. [< Gk. *oistros*, gadfly, frenzy.] —**es′trous** *adj.*

es•tu•ar•y (ĕs′cho͞o-ĕr′ē) ► *n., pl.* **-ies 1.** The wide lower course of a river where its current is met by the tides. **2.** An inland arm of the sea that meets the mouth of a river. [< Lat. *aestus*, heat, tide, surge.]

ET ► *abbr.* **1.** Eastern Time **2.** elapsed time **3.** extraterrestrial

–et ► *suff.* **1.** Small: *eaglet.* **2.** Something worn on: *anklet.* [< VLat. **-ittum.*]

e•ta (ā′tə, ē′tə) ► *n.* The 7th letter of the Greek alphabet. [Gk. *ēta.*]

ETA ► *abbr.* estimated time of arrival

e-tail•er (ē′tā′lər) ► *n.* One that sells goods or commodities electronically, as over the Internet. [E– + (RE)TAILER.]

et al. ► *abbr. Lat.* et alii (and others)

etc. ► *abbr.* et cetera

et cet•er•a (ĕt sĕt′ər-ə, sĕt′rə) ► And other unspecified things of the same class; and so forth. [Lat. *et cētera*, and the rest.]

etch (ĕch) ► *v.* **1.** To make (a pattern) on a surface with acid. **2.** To impress, delineate, or imprint clearly. [< OHGer. *ezzen*, eat.] —**etch′er** *n.*

etch•ing (ĕch′ĭng) ► *n.* **1.** The art or technique of preparing etched plates, esp. metal plates. **2.** A design etched on a plate. **3.** An impression made from an etched plate.

ETD ► *abbr.* estimated time of departure

e•ter•nal (ĭ-tûr′nəl) ► *adj.* **1.** Being without beginning or end; existing outside time. See Syns at **infinite. 2.** Forever true or changeless: *eternal truths.* See Syns at **ageless. 3.** Seemingly endless; interminable. **4.** Of or relating to existence after death. [< Lat. *aeternus.*] —**e•ter′nal•ly** *adv.* —**e•ter′nal•ness** *n.*

e•ter•ni•ty (ĭ-tûr′nĭ-tē) ► *n., pl.* **-ties 1.** Continuance without beginning or end. **2.** The state or quality of being eternal. **3.** Immortality. **4.** A very long or seemingly endless time. [< Lat. *aeternus*, eternal.]

–eth[1] or **–th** ► *suff.* Used to form the archaic 3rd person sing. of English verbs: *leadeth.* [< OE.]

–eth[2] ► *suff.* Var. of **–th**[2].

eth•ane (ĕth′ān′) ► *n.* A colorless, odorless gas, C_2H_6, that occurs in natural gas and is used as a fuel and refrigerant. [ETH(YL) + –ANE.]

eth•a•nol (ĕth′ə-nôl′, -nōl′, -nŏl′) ► *n.* See **alcohol** 1. [ETHAN(E) + –OL.]

Eth•el•bert (ĕth′əl-bûrt′). 552?–616. Anglo-Saxon king who codified English law (604).

Eth•el•red II (ĕth′əl-rĕd′). "the Unready." 968?–1016. King of the English (978–1016).

e•ther (ē′thər) ► *n.* **1.** Any of a class of organic compounds in which two hydrocarbon groups are linked by an oxygen atom. **2.** A highly flammable liquid, $C_2H_5OC_2H_5$, widely used as a reagent, solvent, and anesthetic. **3.** The regions of space beyond the earth's atmosphere; the clear sky. **4.** An all-pervading, infinitely elastic, massless medium formerly postulated as the medium of propagation of electromagnetic waves. [< Gk. *aithēr*, the upper air.]

e•the•re•al (ĭ-thîr′ē-əl) ► *adj.* **1.** Highly refined; delicate. See Syns at **airy. 2.** Heavenly. [< Gk. *aitherios.*] —**e•the′re•al•ly** *adv.* —**e•the′re•al•ness** *n.*

eth•ic (ĕth′ĭk) ► *n.* **1.** A principle of right or good conduct or a body of such principles. **2.** A system of moral principles or values. **3. ethics** *(takes sing. v.)* The study of the general nature of morals and of specific moral choices; moral philosophy. **4. ethics** *(takes sing. or pl. v.)* The rules or standards governing the conduct of the members of a profession. [< Gk. *ēthos*, character.]

eth•i•cal (ĕth′ĭ-kəl) ► *adj.* **1.** Of or dealing with ethics. **2.** Being in accordance with the accepted principles that govern the conduct of a group, esp. of a profession. —**eth′i•cal•ly** *adv.*

E•thi•o•pi•a (ē′thē-ō′pē-ə). Formerly **Ab•ys•sin•i•a** (ăb′ĭ-sĭn′ē-ə). A country of NE Africa. Cap. Addis Ababa. Pop. 32,775,000. —**E′thi•o′pi•an** *adj. & n.*

eth•nic (ĕth′nĭk) ► *adj.* Of or relating to sizable groups of people sharing a common and distinctive racial, national, religious, linguistic, or cultural heritage. ► *n.* A member of an ethnic group. —**eth′ni•cal•ly** *adv.*

ethnic cleansing ► *n.* The systematic elimination of an ethnic group from a region or society, as by expulsion or genocide.

eth•nic•i•ty (ĕth-nĭs′ĭ-tē) ► *n.* Ethnic character, background, or affiliation.

ethno– ► *pref.* Race; people: *ethnology.* [< Gk. *ethnos.*]

eth•no•cen•trism (ĕth′nō-sĕn′trĭz′əm) ► *n.* Belief in the superiority of one's own ethnic group. —**eth′no•cen′tric** *adj.* —**eth′no•cen′tri•cal•ly** *adv.*

eth•nol•o•gy (ĕth-nŏl′ə-jē) ► *n.* **1.** The science that analyzes and compares human cultures, as in social structure, language, religion, and technology. **2.** The branch of anthropology that deals with the origin, distribution, and characteristics of ethnic groups and the relations among them. —**eth′no•log′ic** (ĕth′nə-lŏj′ĭk), **eth′no•log′i•cal** *adj.* —**eth′no•log′i•cal•ly** *adv.* —**eth•nol′o•gist** *n.*

e•thol•o•gy (ĭ-thŏl′ə-jē, ē-thŏl′-) ► *n.* **1.** The scientific study of animal behavior. **2.** The study of human ethos. [Gk. *ēthos*, character + –LOGY.] —**eth′o•log′i•cal** (ĕth′ə-lŏj′ĭ-kəl) *adj.* —**e•thol′o•gist** *n.*

e•thos (ē′thŏs′) ► *n.* The character or values peculiar to a specific person, people, culture, or movement. [Gk. *ēthos*, character.]

eth•yl (ĕth′əl) ► *n.* An organic radical, C_2H_5. [ETH(ER) + –YL.]

ethyl alcohol ► *n.* See **alcohol** 1.

eth•yl•ene (ĕth′ə-lēn′) ► *n.* A colorless flammable gas, C_2H_4, derived from natural gas and petroleum.

ethylene glycol ► *n.* A colorless syrupy alcohol used as an antifreeze.

e•ti•ol•o•gy (ē′tē-ŏl′ə-jē) ► *n., pl.* **-gies 1.** The study of causes, origins, or reasons. **2.** The cause or origin of a disease or disorder as determined by medical diagnosis. [< Gk. *aitiologia* < *aitia*, a cause.] —**e′ti•o•log′ic** (-ə-lŏj′ĭk), **e′ti•o•log′i•cal** *adj.* —**e′ti•o•log′i•cal•ly** *adv.* —**e′ti•ol′o•gist** *n.*

et•i•quette (ĕt′ĭ-kĕt′, -kĭt) ► *n.* The practices and forms prescribed by social convention or by authority. [< OFr. *estiquet*, label.]

Et•na (ĕt′nə), **Mount.** An active volcano, 3,325.1 m (10,902 ft), of E Sicily.

E•tru•ri•a (ĭ-tro͝or′ē-ə) An ancient country of

W-central Italy in modern Tuscany and parts of Umbria. —**E•tru′ri•an** *adj. & n.*

E•trus•can (ĭ-trŭs′kən) ▸*n.* **1.** A native or inhabitant of ancient Etruria. **2.** The extinct language of the Etruscans, of unknown affiliation. —**E•trus′can** *adj.*

-ette ▸*suff.* **1.** Small; diminutive: *kitchenette.* **2.** Female: *suffragette.* **3.** An imitation or inferior kind of cloth: *leatherette.* [< OFr., feminine of *-et*, –ET.]

e•tude (ā′to͞od′, -tyo͞od′) ▸*n. Mus.* A composition for developing a specific point of technique. [< OFr. *estudie*, a study.]

et•y•mol•o•gy (ĕt′ə-mŏl′ə-jē) ▸*n., pl.* **-gies** **1.** The origin and development of a word. **2.** An account of the history of a word. **3.** The branch of linguistics that deals with etymologies. [< Gk. *etumon*, true sense of a word.] —**et′y•mo•log′i•cal** (-mə-lŏj′ĭ-kəl) *adj.* —**et′y•mol′o•gist** *n.*

Eu ▸ The symbol for the element **europium.**

EU ▸*abbr.* European Union

eu– ▸*pref.* Good; well; true: *euphony.* [< Gk.]

eu•ca•lyp•tus (yo͞o′kə-lĭp′təs) ▸*n., pl.* **-tus•es** or **-ti** (-tī′). Any of numerous Australian trees yielding valuable timber and an aromatic medicinal oil. [EU– + Gk. *kaluptos*, covered.]

Eu•cha•rist (yo͞o′kər-ĭst) ▸*n.* The Christian sacrament instituted at the Last Supper, in which bread and wine are consecrated and consumed in remembrance of Jesus's death; Communion. [< Gk. *eukharistia*, gratitude.] —**Eu′cha•ris′tic** *adj.*

eu•chre (yo͞o′kər) ▸*n.* A card game played usu. with the highest 32 cards. ▸*v.* **-chred, -chring.** To deceive or cheat. [?]

Eu•clid (yo͞o′klĭd). 3rd cent. B.C. Greek mathematician.

Eu•clid•e•an (yo͞o-klĭd′ē-ən) ▸*adj.* Of or relating to Euclid's geometric principles.

Eu•gene (yo͞o-jēn′) A city of W OR on the Willamette R. S of Salem. Pop. 112,669.

eu•gen•ics (yo͞o-jĕn′ĭks) ▸*n. (takes sing. v.)* The study of hereditary improvement of the human race by controlled selective breeding. —**eu•gen′ic** *adj.*

Eu•gé•nie (yo͞o-jē′nē, œ-zhā-nē′). 1826–1920. Empress of France (1853–71) as the wife of Napoleon III.

eu•kar•y•ote (yo͞o-kăr′ē-ōt, -ē-ət) ▸*n.* An organism whose cells contain a distinct membrane-bound nucleus. [EU– + Gk. *karuon*, nut, kernel.] —**eu•kar′y•ot′ic** (-ŏt′ĭk) *adj.*

eu•lo•gize (yo͞o′lə-jīz′) ▸*v.* **-gized, -giz•ing.** To praise highly in speech or writing. —**eu′lo•giz′er** *n.*

eu•lo•gy (yo͞o′lə-jē) ▸*n., pl.* **-gies.** A spoken or written tribute, esp. one praising someone who has died. [< Gk. *eulogia*, praise.] —**eu′lo•gist** *n.* —**eu′lo•gis′tic** *adj.*

eu•nuch (yo͞o′nək) ▸*n.* A castrated man. [< Gk. *eunoukhos*.]

eu•phe•mism (yo͞o′fə-mĭz′əm) ▸*n.* The substitution of an inoffensive term for one considered blunt or offensive. [< Gk. *euphēmia*, use of auspicious words.] —**eu′phe•mist** *n.* —**eu′phe•mis′tic** *adj.* —**eu′phe•mis′ti•cal•ly** *adv.* —**eu′phe•mize′** *v.*

eu•pho•ny (yo͞o′fə-nē) ▸*n., pl.* **-nies.** Agreeable sound, esp. of words pleasing to the ear. —**eu•pho′ni•ous** (-fō′nē-əs) *adj.*

eu•pho•ri•a (yo͞o-fôr′ē-ə, -fōr′-) ▸*n.* A feeling of great happiness or well-being. [Gk. < *euphoros*, healthy : EU– + *pherein*, carry.] —**eu•phor′ic** (-fôr′ĭk, -fŏr′-) *adj.*

eu•pho•ri•ant (yo͞o-fôr′ē-ənt, -fōr′-) ▸*n.* A drug that induces euphoria. —**eu•pho′ri•ant** *adj.*

Eu•phra•tes (yo͞o-frā′tēz) A river of SW Asia flowing about 2,735 km (1,700 mi) from central Turkey to Iraq, where it joins the Tigris R. to form the Shatt al Arab.

Eur•a•sia (yo͞o-rā′zhə) The land mass comprising the continents of Europe and Asia.

Eur•a•sian (yo͞o-rā′zhən) ▸*adj.* **1.** Of or relating to Eurasia. **2.** Of mixed European and Asian descent. ▸*n.* A person of mixed European and Asian descent.

eu•re•ka (yo͞o-rē′kə) ▸*interj.* Used to express triumph upon finding or discovering something. [Gk. *heurēka*, I have found (it).]

Eu•rip•i•des (yo͞o-rĭp′ĭ-dēz′). 480?–406 B.C. Greek dramatist. —**Eu•rip′i•de′an** *adj.*

eu•ro or **Eu•ro** (yo͝or′ō) ▸*n., pl.* **-ros.** The basic unit of currency in participating European Union countries, introduced for noncash transactions in 1999.

Eu•ro-A•mer•i•can (yo͝or′ō-ə-mĕr′ĭ-kən) ▸*n.* A US citizen or resident of European descent. ▸*adj.* **1.** Relating to Euro-Americans. **2.** Relating to Europe and America.

Eu•ro•bond (yo͝or′ō-bŏnd′) ▸*n.* A bond of a US corporation issued in Europe.

Eu•ro•cen•tric (yo͝or′ō-sĕn′trĭk) ▸*adj.* Centered or focused on Europe or European peoples. —**Eu′ro•cen′trism** *n.* —**Eu′ro•cen′trist** *adj. & n.*

Eu•ro•cur•ren•cy (yo͝or′ō-kûr′ən-sē, -kŭr′-) ▸*n., pl.* **-cies.** Currency held and traded in a bank outside the currency's country of origin.

Eu•ro•dol•lar (yo͝or′ō-dŏl′ər) ▸*n.* A US dollar on deposit in a foreign bank.

Eu•ro•pa (yo͞o-rō′pə) ▸*n. Gk. Myth.* A Phoenician princess abducted to Crete by Zeus, who had assumed the form of a white bull.

Eu•rope (yo͝or′əp) The sixth-largest continent, consisting of the section of Eurasia that extends W from the Dardanelles, Black Sea, and Ural Mountains.

Eu•ro•pe•an (yo͝or′ə-pē′ən) ▸*n.* **1.** A native or inhabitant of Europe. **2.** A person of European descent. ▸*adj.* Of Europe or its peoples, languages, or cultures.

European Community. An economic and political organization formed in 1967 by the members of the European Economic Community.

European Economic Community. Informally the **Common Market.** An economic union among the countries of W Europe.

European plan ▸*n.* A hotel plan in which the rates include only the charges for a room and not for meals.

European Union. An economic and political union established in 1993 by members of the European Community.

eu•ro•pi•um (yo͞o-rō′pē-əm) ▸*n. Symbol* **Eu** A silvery-white, soft rare-earth element used in lasers and nuclear research. At. no. 63. See table at **element.** [< EUROPE.]

Eu•ryd•i•ce (yo͞o-rĭd′ĭ-sē) ▸*n. Gk. Myth.* The wife of Orpheus.

eu•sta•chian tube or **Eu•sta•chian tube** (yo͞o-stā′shən, -shē-ən, -kē-ən) ▸*n.* A narrow tube that connects the middle ear with the pharynx and serves to equalize air pressure on either side of the eardrum. [After B. *Eustachio* (1520–74).]

eu•tha•na•sia (yo͞o′thə-nā′zhə, -zhē-ə) ▸*n.* The act of painlessly ending the life of a person for reasons of mercy. [Gk.] —**eu′than•ize′** *v.*

eu•then•ics (yo͞o-thĕn′ĭks) ▸*n. (takes sing. v.)* The study of the improvement of human functioning and well-being by improvement of living conditions. [< Gk. *euthenein*, to flourish.] —**eu•then′ist** *n.*

eV ▸*abbr.* electron volt

EVA ▸*abbr.* extravehicular activity

e•vac•u•ate (ĭ-văk′yo͞o-āt′) ▸*v.* **-at•ed, -at•ing 1a.** To remove the contents of. **b.** To create a vacuum in. **2.** To excrete waste matter from (the bowel). **3.** To withdraw, esp. from a threatened area. [< Lat. *ēvacuāre.*] —**e•vac′u•a′tion** *n.*

e•vac•u•ee (ĭ-văk′yo͞o-ē′) ▸*n.* A person evacuated from a dangerous or threatened area.

e•vade (ĭ-vād′) ▸*v.* **e•vad•ed, e•vad•ing.** To escape or avoid by cleverness or deceit. [< Lat. *ēvādere.*] —**e•vad′er** *n.*

e•val•u•ate (ĭ-văl′yo͞o-āt′) ▸*v.* **-at•ed, -at•ing.** To ascertain or fix the value of. [< OFr. *evaluer.*] —**e•val′u•a′tion** *n.* —**e•val′u•a•tor** *n.*

ev•a•nesce (ĕv′ə-nĕs′) ▸*v.* **-nesced, -nesc•ing.** To dissipate gradually; fade away like vapor. See Syns at **disappear.** [Lat. *ēvānēscere*, vanish < *vānus*, empty.] —**ev′a•nes′cence** *n.* —**ev′a•nes′cent** *adj.* —**ev′a•nes′cent•ly** *adv.*

e•van•gel•i•cal (ē′văn-jĕl′ĭ-kəl, ĕv′ən-) also **e•van•gel•ic** (-jĕl′ĭk) ▸*adj.* **1.** Of or in accordance with the Christian gospel or Gospels. **2. Evangelical** Of or being a Protestant church that stresses personal spiritual transformation and the inerrancy of the Bible. [< Gk. *evangelos*, bringing good news.] —**E′van•gel′i•cal** *n.* —**e′van•gel′i•cal•ism** *n.* —**e′van•gel′i•cal•ly** *adv.*

e•van•gel•ism (ĭ-văn′jə-lĭz′əm) ▸*n.* Zealous preaching of the gospel, as through missionary work. —**e•van′gel•is′tic** *adj.* —**e•van′gel•is′ti•cal•ly** *adv.*

e•van•gel•ist (ĭ-văn′jə-lĭst) ▸*n.* **1.** often **Evangelist** Any one of the authors of the New Testament Gospels. **2.** One who practices evangelism, esp. a Protestant preacher or missionary.

e•van•gel•ize (ĭ-văn′jə-līz′) ▸*v.* **-ized, -iz•ing 1.** To preach the gospel (to). **2.** To convert to Christianity.

Ev•ans•ville (ĕv′ənz-vĭl′) A city of extreme SW IN on the Ohio R. and the KY border. Pop. 126,272.

e•vap•o•rate (ĭ-văp′ə-rāt′) ▸*v.* **-rat•ed, -rat•ing 1.** To change into a vapor. **2.** To remove or be removed in or as if in a vapor. **3.** To vanish. See Syns at **disappear.** [< Lat. *ēvapōrāre.*] —**e•vap′o•ra′tion** *n.* —**e•vap′o•ra′tive** *adj.* —**e•vap′o•ra′tor** *n.*

e•va•sion (ĭ-vā′zhən) ▸*n.* **1.** The act of evading. **2.** A means of evading. [< LLat. *ēvāsiō.*]

e•va•sive (ĭ-vā′sĭv) ▸*adj.* **1.** Inclined or intended to evade: *took evasive action.* **2.** Intentionally vague or ambiguous. —**e•va′sive•ly** *adv.* —**e•va′sive•ness** *n.*

eve (ēv) ▸*n.* **1.** The evening or day preceding a holiday. **2.** The period immediately preceding a certain event: *the eve of war.* **3.** Evening. [ME, var. of EVEN[2].]

Eve. In the Bible, the first woman and the wife of Adam.

e•ven[1] (ē′vən) ▸*adj.* **1a.** Flat: *an even floor.* **b.** Smooth. **c.** Level; parallel: *The picture is even with the window.* **2a.** Uniform, steady, or regular: *an even rhythm of breathing.* **b.** Placid; calm: *an even temperament.* **3.** Equal in degree, extent, or amount; balanced. **4.** *Math.* **a.** Exactly divisible by 2. **b.** Characterized by a number exactly divisible by 2. **5a.** Having an even number in a series. **b.** Having an even number of members. **6.** Exact: *an even pound.* ▸*adv.* **1.** To a greater degree: *an even worse condition.* **2.** In fact: *unhappy, even weeping.* **3.** At that very time: *Even as we watched, the building collapsed.* **4.** In spite of: *Even with his head start, I beat him.* ▸*v.* To make or become even. [< OE *efen.*] —**e′ven•ly** *adv.* —**e′ven•ness** *n.*

e•ven[2] (ē′vən) ▸*n. Archaic* Evening. [< OE *ǣfen.*]

e•ven•hand•ed (ē′vən-hăn′dĭd) ▸*adj.* Showing no partiality; fair. —**e′ven•hand′ed•ly** *adv.* —**e′ven•hand′ed•ness** *n.*

eve•ning (ēv′nĭng) ▸*n.* Late afternoon and early night. [< OE *ǣfnung.*]

evening star ▸*n.* A planet, esp. Venus or Mercury, that is prominent in the west shortly after sunset.

e•vent (ĭ-vĕnt′) ▸*n.* **1.** An occurrence or incident, esp. one of significance. **2.** A social gathering or activity. **3.** A contest or an item in a sports program. [Lat. *ēventus* < p.part. of *ēvenīre*, happen : EX– + *venīre*, come.]

e•vent•ful (ĭ-vĕnt′fəl) ▸*adj.* **1.** Full of events. **2.** Important; momentous. —**e•vent′ful•ly** *adv.* —**e•vent′ful•ness** *n.*

e•ven•tide (ē′vən-tīd′) ▸*n.* Evening. [< OE *ǣfentīd.*]

e•ven•tu•al (ĭ-vĕn′cho͞o-əl) ▸*adj.* Occurring at an unspecified time in the future: *her eventual success.* [Fr. *éventuel.*] —**e•ven′tu•al•ly** *adv.*

e•ven•tu•al•i•ty (ĭ-vĕn′cho͞o-ăl′ĭ-tē) ▸*n., pl.* **-ties.** Something that may occur; possibility.

e•ven•tu•ate (ĭ-vĕn′cho͞o-āt′) ▸*v.* **-at•ed, -at•ing.** To result ultimately; culminate.

ev•er (ĕv′ər) ▸*adv.* **1.** At all times; always: *ever hoping to strike it rich.* **2.** At any time: *Have you ever been to India?* **3.** In any way; at all: *How did they ever manage?* **4.** To a great extent or degree: *He was ever so sorry. Was she ever mad!* [< OE *ǣfre.*]

Ev•er•est (ĕv′ər-ĭst, ĕv′rĭst), **Mount.** A mountain, 8,853.5 m (29,035 ft), of the central Himalayas on the border of Xizang (Tibet) and Nepal.

ev•er•glade (ĕv′ər-glād′) ▸*n.* A tract of marshland, usu. under water.

Ev•er•glades (ĕv′ər-glādz′) A subtropical swamp area of S FL including **Everglades National Park.**

ev•er•green (ĕv′ər-grēn′) ▸*adj.* Having foliage that persists and remains green throughout the year. ▸*n.* An evergreen tree, shrub, or plant.

ev•er•last•ing (ĕv′ər-lăs′tĭng) ▸*adj.* Lasting forever; eternal. —**ev′er•last′ing•ly** *adv.*

ev•er•more (ĕv′ər-môr′, -mōr′) ▸*adv.* **1.** Forever; always. **2.** In a future time.

eve•ry (ĕv′rē) ►*adj.* **1.** Each without exception: *every student in the class.* **2.** Being each of a specified series: *every third seat; every two hours.* **3.** Being of the highest degree or expression: *showed us every attention.* —***idioms:*** **every bit** *Informal* In all ways; equally. **every so often** Occasionally. [< OE *ǣfre ǣlc*, ever each.]

Usage: *Every* is representative of a large class of English words and expressions that are singular in form but felt to be plural in sense. The class includes, for example, noun phrases introduced by *every, any,* and certain uses of *some.* These expressions invariably take a singular verb: *Every car has been tested.*

eve•ry•bod•y (ĕv′rē-bŏd′ē, -bŭd′ē) ►*pron.* Every person; everyone.

eve•ry•day (ĕv′rē-dā′) ►*adj.* **1.** Appropriate for ordinary occasions. **2.** Commonplace; ordinary.

eve•ry•one (ĕv′rē-wŭn′) ►*pron.* Every person; everybody.

eve•ry•thing (ĕv′rē-thĭng′) ►*pron.* All things or all relevant matters.

eve•ry•where (ĕv′rē-hwâr′, -wâr′) ►*adv.* In every place; in all places.

e•vict (ĭ-vĭkt′) ►*v.* **1.** To expel (a tenant) by legal process. **2.** To eject. [< Lat. *ēvincere, ēvict-*, vanquish.] —**e•vic′tion** *n.* —**e•vic′tor** *n.*

ev•i•dence (ĕv′ĭ-dəns) ►*n.* **1.** The data on which a conclusion or judgment can be established. **2.** Something indicative; an outward sign: *the house showed evidence of neglect.* **3.** The statements and material objects admissible as testimony in a court of law. ►*v.* **-denced, -denc•ing.** To indicate clearly. —***idiom:*** **in evidence** Plainly visible; conspicuous.

ev•i•dent (ĕv′ĭ-dənt) ►*adj.* Easily seen or understood; obvious. See Syns at **apparent.** [< Lat. *ēvidēns* : *ē-, ex-*, ex- + *vidēre*, see.] —**ev′i•dent•ly** *adv.*

ev•i•den•tial (ĕv′ĭ-dĕn′shəl) ►*adj.* Of, providing, or constituting legal evidence.

e•vil (ē′vəl) ►*adj.* **-er, -est 1.** Morally bad or wrong; wicked. **2.** Harmful or injurious. ►*n.* **1.** The quality of being morally bad or wrong; wickedness. **2.** Something that causes harm, misfortune, suffering, or destruction. [< OE *yfel.*] —**e′vil•ly** *adv.* —**e′vil•ness** *n.*

e•vil•do•er (ē′vəl-dōō′ər) ►*n.* One that performs evil acts. —**e′vil•do′ing** *n.*

evil eye ►*n.* A look believed to have the power to cause injury to others, esp. by magic or supernatural means.

e•vince (ĭ-vĭns′) ►*v.* **e•vinced, e•vinc•ing.** To show or demonstrate clearly; manifest. [Lat. *ēvincere*, prove.] —**e•vinc′i•ble** *adj.*

e•vis•cer•ate (ĭ-vĭs′ə-rāt′) ►*v.* **-at•ed, -at•ing 1.** To remove the entrails of. **2.** To take away a vital or essential part of. [Lat. *ēviscerāre* < *viscera*, VISCERA.] —**e•vis′cer•a′tion** *n.*

ev•i•ta•ble (ĕv′ĭ-tə-bəl) ►*adj.* Avoidable. [< Lat. *ēvītāre*, shun.]

e•voke (ĭ-vōk′) ►*v.* **e•voked, e•vok•ing.** To summon or call forth; elicit: *evoke memories.* [Lat. *ēvocāre.*] —**ev′o•ca•ble** (ĕv′ə-kə-bəl, ĭ-vō′kə-) *adj.* —**ev′o•ca′tion** *n.* —**e•voc′a•tive** (ĭ-vŏk′ə-tĭv) *adj.* —**e•voc′a•tive•ly** *adv.*

ev•o•lu•tion (ĕv′ə-lōō′shən, ē′və-) ►*n.* **1.** A gradual process in which something changes into a different and usu. more complex form. **2.** *Biol.* **a.** The theory that groups of organisms change with the passage of time, mainly as a result of natural selection, so that descendants differ morphologically and physiologically from their ancestors. **b.** The historical development of a related group of organisms; phylogeny. **3.** *Math.* The extraction of a root of a quantity. [< Lat. *ēvolvere, ēvolūt-*, unroll.] —**ev′o•lu′tion•ar′y** *adj.* —**ev′o•lu′tion•ism** *n.* —**ev′o•lu′tion•ist** *n.*

e•volve (ĭ-vŏlv′) ►*v.* **e•volved, e•volv•ing 1.** To develop or work out; achieve gradually: *evolve a plan.* **2.** *Biol.* To develop by evolutionary processes. [Lat. *ēvolvere*, unroll.] —**e•volve′ment** *n.*

e•vul•sion (ĭ-vŭl′shən) ►*n.* A forcible extraction. [< Lat. *ēvellere, ēvuls-*, pull out.]

ewe (yōō) ►*n.* A female sheep. [< OE *eōwu.*]

ew•er (yōō′ər) ►*n.* A pitcher, esp. one with a flaring spout. [< VLat. **aquāria* < Lat. *aqua*, water.]

ewer

ex[1] (ĕks) ►*prep.* Not including; without: *a stock price ex dividend.* [Lat.]

ex[2] (ĕks) ►*n. Slang* A former spouse or partner. [< EX–.]

ex. ►*abbr.* **1.** examination **2.** example

ex– ►*pref.* **1.** Outside; out of; away from: *exurbia.* **2.** Former: *ex-president.* [< Lat. *ex*, out of.]

ex•ac•er•bate (ĭg-zăs′ər-bāt′) ►*v.* **-bat•ed, -bat•ing.** To increase the severity of; aggravate: *exacerbate tensions; exacerbate pain.* [Lat. *exacerbāre* < *acerbus*, harsh.] —**ex•ac′er•ba′tion** *n.*

ex•act (ĭg-zăkt′) ►*adj.* Strictly accurate; precise. ►*v.* To obtain by or as if by force or authority. See Syns at **demand.** [Lat. *exāctus*, p.part of *exigere*, demand : EX– + *agere*, weigh.] —**ex•act′ly** *adv.* —**ex•act′ness** *n.*

ex•act•ing (ĭg-zăk′tĭng) ►*adj.* **1.** Making rigorous demands. **2.** Requiring great care or effort. —**ex•act′ing•ly** *adv.*

ex•ac•ti•tude (ĭg-zăk′tĭ-tōōd, -tyōōd′) ►*n.* The state or quality of being exact.

ex•ag•ger•ate (ĭg-zăj′ə-rāt′) ►*v.* **-at•ed, -at•ing.** To enlarge, increase, or represent (something) beyond normal bounds. [Lat. *exaggerāre.*] —**ex•ag′ger•a′tion** *n.* —**ex•ag′ger•a′tive, ex•ag′ger•a•to′ry** (-ə-tôr′ē, -tōr′ē) *adj.* —**ex•ag′ger•a′tor** *n.*

Syns: *exaggerate, inflate, magnify, overstate* ***Ant:*** *minimize* **n.**

ex•alt (ĭg-zôlt′) ►*v.* **1.** To raise in rank or status; elevate. **2.** To glorify, praise, or honor. **3.** To inspire; heighten: *art that exalts the imagination.* [< Lat. *exaltāre* < *altus*, high.] —**ex′-**

al•ta′tion (ĕg′zôl-tā′shən) *n.*

ex•am (ĭg-zăm′) ►*n.* An examination; test.

ex•am•i•na•tion (ĭg-zăm′ə-nā′shən) ►*n.* **1.** The act of examining or the state of being examined. **2.** A set of questions or exercises testing knowledge or skill. —**ex•am′i•na′tion•al** *adj.*

ex•am•ine (ĭg-zăm′ĭn) ►*v.* **-ined, -in•ing 1.** To inspect or analyze (a person, thing, or situation) in detail. **2.** To determine the aptitude or skills of by questioning. **3.** To question formally to elicit facts; interrogate. [< Lat. *exāmināre* < *exigere*, weigh out. See EXACT.] —**ex•am′in•ee′** *n.* —**ex•am′in•er** *n.*

ex•am•ple (ĭg-zăm′pəl) ►*n.* **1.** One that is representative of a group as a whole. **2.** One serving as a pattern of a specific kind: *set a good example.* **3.** One that serves as a warning or deterrent. **4.** A problem used to illustrate a principle. [< Lat. *exemplum.*]

ex•as•per•ate (ĭg-zăs′pə-rāt′) ►*v.* **-at•ed, -at•ing.** To make very angry or impatient; provoke. [Lat. *exasperāre* < *asper*, rough.] —**ex•as′per•at′ing•ly** *adv.* —**ex•as′per•a′tion** *n.*

Exc. ►*abbr.* Excellency

ex•ca•vate (ĕk′skə-vāt′) ►*v.* **-vat•ed, -vat•ing 1.** To dig or hollow out. **2.** To remove (soil) by digging. **3.** To uncover by digging. [Lat. *excavāre.*] —**ex′ca•va′tion** *n.* —**ex′ca•va′tor** *n.*

ex•ceed (ĭk-sēd′) ►*v.* **1.** To be greater than; surpass. **2.** To go or be beyond the limits of: *exceeded their authority.* [< Lat. *excēdere.*]

ex•ceed•ing (ĭk-sē′dĭng) ►*adj.* Extreme; extraordinary. —**ex•ceed′ing•ly** *adv.*

ex•cel (ĭk-sĕl′) ►*v.* **-celled, -cel•ling.** To be superior to; surpass; outdo. [< Lat. *excellere.*]

ex•cel•lence (ĕk′sə-ləns) ►*n.* **1.** The quality or condition of excelling; superiority. **2.** Something in which one excels. **3. Excellence** Excellency.

Ex•cel•len•cy (ĕk′sə-lən-sē) ►*n., pl.* **-cies.** Used with *His, Her,* or *Your* as a title for certain high officials.

ex•cel•lent (ĕk′sə-lənt) ►*adj.* Of the highest or finest quality; exceptionally good; superb. —**ex′cel•lent•ly** *adv.*

ex•cel•si•or (ĭk-sĕl′sē-ər) ►*n.* Wood shavings used esp. for packing. [Orig. a trademark.]

ex•cept (ĭk-sĕpt′) ►*prep.* Other than; but. ►*conj.* If it were not for the fact that; only. ►*v.* To leave out; exclude. [< Lat. *exceptus*, p.part. of *excipere*, take out.]

Usage: *Except* in the sense of "other than" is generally construed as a preposition, not a conjunction. A personal pronoun that follows *except* is therefore in the objective case: *No one except me knew it.*

ex•cept•ing (ĭk-sĕp′tĭng) ►*prep.* With the exception of; except.

ex•cep•tion (ĭk-sĕp′shən) ►*n.* **1.** The act of excepting; exclusion. **2.** One that is excepted. **3.** An objection.

ex•cep•tion•a•ble (ĭk-sĕp′shə-nə-bəl) ►*adj.* Open to objection. —**ex•cep′tion•a•bly** *adv.*

ex•cep•tion•al (ĭk-sĕp′shə-nəl) ►*adj.* Uncommon; extraordinary. —**ex•cep′tion•al•ly** *adv.*

ex•cerpt (ĕk′sûrpt′) ►*n.* A passage or segment taken from a longer work, such as a speech, book, or film. [< Lat. *excerpere, excerpt-*, pick out.] —**ex•cerpt′** *v.*

ex•cess (ĭk-sĕs′, ĕk′sĕs′) ►*n.* **1.** An amount or quantity beyond what is required; surplus. **2.** Intemperance; overindulgence: *drank to excess.* ►*adj.* Being more than what is required. See Syns at **superfluous.** [< Lat. *excessus*, p.part. of *excēdere*, exceed.] —**ex•ces′sive** *adj.* —**ex•ces′sive•ly** *adv.* —**ex•ces′sive•ness** *n.*

ex•change (ĭks-chānj′) ►*v.* **-changed, -chang•ing 1.** To give and receive reciprocally; trade; interchange. **2.** To turn in for replacement. ►*n.* **1.** The act or an instance of exchanging. **2.** One that is exchanged. **3.** A place where things are exchanged, esp. a center where securities are traded. **4.** A central system that establishes connections between individual telephones. **5.** A bill of exchange. **6.** A rate of exchange. [< VLat. **excambiāre.*] —**ex•change′a•ble** *adj.*

ex•cheq•uer (ĕks′chĕk′ər, ĭks-chĕk′ər) ►*n.* A treasury, as of a nation or organization. [< OFr. *eschequier*, counting table.]

ex•cip•i•ent (ĭk-sĭp′ē-ənt) ►*n.* An inert substance used as a diluent or vehicle for a drug. [< Lat. *excipere*, take out.]

ex•cise[1] (ĕk′sīz′) ►*n.* A tax on the production, sale, or consumption of a commodity within a country. [MDu. *excijs.*]

ex•cise[2] (ĭk-sīz′) ►*v.* **-cised, -cis•ing.** To remove by or as if by cutting. [Lat. *excīdere, excīs-*, cut out.] —**ex•ci′sion** (-sĭzh′ən) *n.*

ex•cit•a•ble (ĭk-sī′tə-bəl) ►*adj.* Capable of being easily excited. —**ex•cit′a•bil′i•ty, ex•cit′a•ble•ness** *n.* —**ex•cit′a•bly** *adv.*

ex•ci•tant (ĭk-sīt′nt) ►*n.* An agent or stimulus that excites; stimulant. —**ex•ci′tant** *adj.*

ex•cite (ĭk-sīt′) ►*v.* **-cit•ed, -cit•ing 1.** To stir to activity; stimulate. **2.** To call forth; elicit: *excited my curiosity.* **3.** To arouse strong feeling in; provoke. **4.** *Phys.* To raise (e.g., an atom) to a higher energy level. [< Lat. *excitāre.*] —**ex′ci•ta′tion** (ĕk′sī-tā′shən) *n.* —**ex•cit′ed•ly** *adv.* —**ex•cite′ment** *n.* —**ex•cit′ing•ly** *adv.*

ex•claim (ĭk-sklām′) ►*v.* To cry out or speak suddenly or vehemently. [< Lat. *exclāmāre.*]

ex•cla•ma•tion (ĕk′sklə-mā′shən) ►*n.* **1.** A sudden forceful utterance. **2.** *Gram.* An interjection. —**ex•clam′a•to′ry** (ĭk-sklăm′ə-tôr′ē, -tōr′ē) *adj.*

exclamation point ►*n.* A punctuation mark (!) used after an exclamation.

ex•clude (ĭk-sklo͞od′) ►*v.* **-clud•ed, -clud•ing 1.** To prevent from entering; keep out; bar. **2.** To reject: *excluded the improperly obtained evidence.* **3.** To put out; expel. [< Lat. *exclūdere*, shut out.] —**ex•clu′sion** *n.*

ex•clu•sive (ĭk-sklo͞o′sĭv) ►*adj.* **1.** Not divided or shared with others: *exclusive rights.* **2.** Admitting only certain people, as for membership or participation. **3.** Fancy; expensive: *exclusive shops.* ►*n.* **1.** A news item initially released to only one publication or broadcaster. **2.** An exclusive right. —**ex•clu′sive•ly** *adv.* —**ex•clu′sive•ness, ex′clu•siv′i•ty** (ĕk′sklo͞o-sĭv′ĭ-tē) *n.*

ex•com•mu•ni•cate (ĕks′kə-myo͞o′nĭ-kāt′) ►*v.* **-cat•ed, -cat•ing.** To deprive of the right of church membership by ecclesiastical authority. ►*n.* (-kĭt). A person who has been excommunicated. [< LLat. *excommūnicāre.*] **—ex′com•mu′ni•ca′tion** *n.* **—ex′com•mu′ni•ca′tor** *n.*

ex•co•ri•ate (ĭk-skôr′ē-āt′, -skōr′-) ►*v.* **-at•ed, -at•ing 1.** To tear or wear off the skin of. See Syns at **chafe. 2.** To censure strongly; denounce. [< Lat. *excoriāre* < *corium*, skin.] **—ex•co′ri•a′tion** *n.*

ex•cre•ment (ĕk′skrə-mənt) ►*n.* Bodily waste, esp. fecal matter. [Lat. *excrēmentum* < *excernere*, excrete.] **—ex′cre•men′tal** *adj.*

ex•cres•cence (ĭk-skrĕs′əns) ►*n.* An outgrowth or enlargement, esp. an abnormal one. [< Lat. *excrēscere*, grow out.] **—ex•cres′cent** *adj.*

ex•cre•ta (ĭk-skrē′tə) ►*pl.n.* Waste matter, such as sweat, urine, or feces, discharged from the body. [Lat. *excrēta.*]

ex•crete (ĭk-skrēt′) ►*v.* **-cret•ed, -cret•ing.** To separate and discharge (waste matter) from the blood, tissues, or organs. [Lat. *excernere, excrēt-.*] **—ex•cre′tion** *n.* **—ex′cre•to′ry** (-skrĭ-tôr′ē, -tōr′ē) *adj.*

ex•cru•ci•at•ing (ĭk-skrōō′shē-ā′tĭng) ►*adj.* Intensely painful or distressing. [< Lat. *excruciāre*, crucify, torture.] **—ex•cru′ci•at′ing•ly** *adv.*

ex•cul•pate (ĕk′skəl-pāt′, ĭk-skŭl′-) ►*v.* **-pat•ed, -pat•ing.** To clear of guilt or blame. [Med.Lat. *exculpāre.*] **—ex′cul•pa′tion** *n.* **—ex•cul′pa•to′ry** (ĭk-skŭl′pə-tôr′ē, -tōr′ē) *adj.*

ex•cur•sion (ĭk-skûr′zhən) ►*n.* **1.** A usu. short journey; outing. **2.** A short pleasure trip. **3.** A digression from a main topic. [Lat. *excursiō.*] **—ex•cur′sion•ist** *n.*

ex•cur•sive (ĭk-skûr′sĭv) ►*adj.* Marked by digression; rambling. **—ex•cur′sive•ly** *adv.* **—ex•cur′sive•ness** *n.*

ex•cuse (ĭk-skyōōz′) ►*v.* **-cused, -cus•ing 1.** To offer an apology or explanation for (a fault or offense). **2a.** To pardon; forgive. **b.** To make allowance for; overlook. **3.** To justify: *Brilliance does not excuse bad manners.* **4.** To free, as from an obligation. ►*n.* (ĭk-skyōōs′) **1.** An explanation offered to obtain forgiveness. **2.** A reason for being excused. **3.** *Informal* An inferior example: *a poor excuse for a car.* [< Lat. *excūsāre.*] **—ex•cus′a•ble** *adj.* **—ex•cus′er** *n.*

ex•e•cra•ble (ĕk′sĭ-krə-bəl) ►*adj.* **1.** Detestable or hateful. **2.** Extremely inferior. **—ex′e•cra•bly** *adv.*

ex•e•crate (ĕk′sĭ-krāt′) ►*v.* **-crat•ed, -crat•ing 1.** To protest vehemently against; denounce. **2.** To loathe; abhor. [Lat. *execrārī.*] **—ex′e•cra′tion** *n.* **—ex′e•cra′tor** *n.*

ex•e•cute (ĕk′sĭ-kyōōt′) ►*v.* **-cut•ed, -cut•ing 1.** To carry out; perform. **2.** To make valid or legal, as by signing. **3.** To carry out what is required by: *execute a will.* **4.** To put to death, esp. by a lawful sentence. **5.** *Comp. Sci.* To run (a program or instruction). [< Med.Lat. *execūtāre.*] **—ex′e•cut′a•ble** *adj.* **—ex′e•cut′er** *n.* **—ex′e•cu′tion** *n.*

ex•e•cu•tion•er (ĕk′sĭ-kyōō′shə-nər) ►*n.* One who administers capital punishment.

ex•ec•u•tive (ĭg-zĕk′yə-tĭv) ►*n.* **1.** A person or group having administrative or managerial authority in an organization. **2.** The branch of government charged with putting a country's laws into effect. ►*adj.* **1.** Relating to or capable of carrying out or executing: *executive powers.* **2.** Of or relating to the executive branch of government.

ex•ec•u•tor (ĭg-zĕk′yə-tər, ĕk′sĭ-kyōō′tər) ►*n.* *Law* A person designated to execute the terms of a will.

ex•e•ge•sis (ĕk′sə-jē′sĭs) ►*n., pl.* **-ses** (-sēz). Critical interpretation or explanation of a text. [Gk. *exēgēsis*, interpretation.] **—ex′e•get′ic** (-jĕt′ĭk), **ex′e•get′i•cal** *adj.*

ex•em•plar (ĭg-zĕm′plär′, -plər) ►*n.* **1.** One that is worthy of imitation; model. **2.** One that is typical; example. [< LLat. *exemplārium* < Lat. *exemplum*, example.] **—ex•em′pla•ry** *adj.*

ex•em•pli•fy (ĭg-zĕm′plə-fī′) ►*v.* **-fied, -fy•ing 1.** To illustrate by example. **2.** To serve as an example of. [< Lat. *exemplum*, example.] **—ex•em′pli•fi•ca′tion** *n.*

ex•empt (ĭg-zĕmpt′) ►*v.* To free from an obligation, duty, or liability to which others are subject. [< Lat. *eximere, exēmpt-*, take out.] **—ex•empt′** *adj.* **—ex•empt′i•ble** *adj.* **—ex•emp′tion** *n.*

ex•er•cise (ĕk′sər-sīz′) ►*n.* **1.** An act of using or putting into effect. **2.** The discharge of a duty, function, or office. **3.** Physical activity, esp. to develop or maintain fitness. **4.** A task, problem, or other effort designed to develop understanding or skill. **5. exercises** A public program that includes speeches, awards, and other ceremonial activities. ►*v.* **-cised, -cis•ing 1.** To take exercise. **2.** To put into operation; employ. **3.** To put through exercises. See Syns at **practice. 4.** To worry, upset, or make anxious. [< Lat. *exercēre, exercit-*, to exercise.] **—ex′er•cis′er** *n.*

ex•ert (ĭg-zûrt′) ►*v.* **1.** To bring to bear: *exert influence.* **2.** To put (oneself) to strenuous effort. [Lat. *exserere, exsert-*, put forth.] **—ex•er′tion** *n.*

ex•hale (ĕks-hāl′, ĕk-sāl′) ►*v.* **-haled, -hal•ing 1.** To breathe out. **2.** To emit (e.g., smoke). [< Lat. *exhālāre.*] **—ex′ha•la′tion** (ĕks′hə-lā′shən, ĕk′sə-) *n.*

ex•haust (ĭg-zôst′) ►*v.* **1.** To wear out completely; tire. **2.** To use up completely; consume. **3.** To treat or cover thoroughly: *exhaust all possibilities.* **4.** To let out or draw off (a liquid or gas). ►*n.* **1a.** The escape or release of waste gases or vapors, as from an engine. **b.** Vapors or gases so released. **2.** A device or system that pumps gases out or allows them to escape. [Lat. *exhaurīre, exhaust-.*] **—ex•haust′i•bil′i•ty** *n.* **—ex•haust′i•ble** *adj.* **—ex•haus′tion** *n.*

ex•haus•tive (ĭg-zô′stĭv) ►*adj.* Comprehensive; thorough: *an exhaustive study.* **—ex•haus′tive•ly** *adv.* **—ex•haus′tive•ness** *n.*

ex•hib•it (ĭg-zĭb′ĭt) ►*v.* To show or display, esp. to public view. ►*n.* **1.** The act of exhibiting. **2.** Something exhibited. **3.** *Law* Something introduced as evidence in court. [< Lat. *exhibēre, exhibit-.*] **—ex•hib′i•tor** *n.* **—ex′hi•bi′tion** (ĕk′sə-bĭsh′ən) *n.*

ex•hi•bi•tion•ism (ĕk′sə-bĭsh′ə-nĭz′əm) ►*n.* The practice of behaving so as to attract attention. **—ex′hi•bi′tion•ist** *n.* **—ex′hi•bi′tion•is′tic** *adj.*

ex•hil•a•rate (ĭg-zĭl′ə-rāt′) ►*v.* **-rat•ed, -rat•ing 1.** To make joyous and energetic; elate. **2.** To invigorate or stimulate. [Lat. *exhilarāre* <

hilaris, cheerful.] —**ex•hil′a•ra′tion** *n.* —**ex•hil′a•ra′tive** *adj.*
ex•hort (ĭg-zôrt′) ▶*v.* To urge by strong argument, admonition, advice, or appeal. [< Lat. *exhortārī*.] —**ex′hor•ta′tion** *n.* —**ex•hor′ta•tive** *adj.* —**ex•hort′er** *n.*
ex•hume (ĭg-zo͞om′, -zyo͞om′, ĕks-hyo͞om′) ▶*v.* **-humed, -hum•ing 1.** To remove from a grave. **2.** To bring to light, esp. after a period of obscurity. [< Med.Lat. *exhumāre* : EX– + Lat. *humus*, ground.] —**ex′hu•ma′tion** *n.*
ex•i•gence (ĕk′sə-jəns) ▶*n.* Exigency.
ex•i•gen•cy (ĕk′sə-jən-sē, ĭg-zĭj′ən-) ▶*n.*, *pl.* **-cies 1.** A pressing or urgent situation. See Syns at **crisis. 2.** often **exigencies** Urgent requirements. [< Lat. *exigere*, to demand. See EXACT.] —**ex′i•gent** *adj.*
ex•ig•u•ous (ĭg-zĭg′yo͞o-əs, ĭk-sĭg′-) ▶*adj.* Scanty; meager. [< Lat. *exigere*, measure. See EXACT.] —**ex′i•gu′i•ty** (ĕk′sĭ-gyo͞o′ĭ-tē) *n.* —**ex•ig′u•ous•ly** *adv.*
ex•ile (ĕg′zīl′, ĕk′sīl′) ▶*n.* **1.** Enforced removal or self-imposed absence from one's native country. **2.** One who chooses or is sent into exile. ▶*v.* **-iled, -il•ing.** To send into exile; banish. [< Lat. *exilium*.]
ex•ist (ĭg-zĭst′) ▶*v.* **1.** To have actual being; be real. **2.** To have life; live. **3.** To occur. [Lat. *exsistere*, be manifest : *ex*-, ex- + *sistere*, stand.]
ex•is•tence (ĭg-zĭs′təns) ▶*n.* **1.** The fact or state of existing. **2.** Presence; occurrence. —**ex•is′tent** *adj.*
Syns: *existence, actuality, being* ***Ant:*** *nonexistence* ***n.***
ex•is•ten•tial (ĕg′zĭ-stĕn′shəl, ĕk′sĭ-) ▶*adj.* **1.** Of or relating to existence. **2.** Based on experience; empirical. **3.** Of or relating to existentialism. —**ex′is•ten′tial•ly** *adv.*
ex•is•ten•tial•ism (ĕg′zĭ-stĕn′shə-lĭz′əm, ĕk′sĭ-) ▶*n.* A philosophy that emphasizes the uniqueness and isolation of the individual in a hostile or indifferent universe and stresses freedom of choice and responsibility for the consequences of one's acts. —**ex′is•ten′tial•ist** *adj. & n.*
ex•it (ĕg′zĭt, ĕk′sĭt) ▶*n.* **1.** The act of going out. **2.** A passage or way out. **3.** The departure of a performer from the stage. [< Lat. *exīre*, go out.] —**ex′it** *v.*
exo– ▶*pref.* Outside; external: *exoskeleton.* [< Gk. *exō*, outside of.]
ex•o•bi•ol•o•gy (ĕk′sō-bī-ŏl′ə-jē) ▶*n.* The scientific search for extraterrestrial life. —**ex′o•bi•ol′o•gist** *n.*
ex•o•crine (ĕk′sə-krĭn, -krēn, -krīn′) ▶*adj.* Having or secreting through a duct: *an exocrine gland.* [EXO– + Gk. *krinein*, to separate.]
ex•o•dus (ĕk′sə-dəs) ▶*n.* **1.** A departure or emigration of a large number of people. **2. Exodus.** See table at **Bible.** [< Gk. *exodos*.]
ex of•fi•ci•o (ĕks′ ə-fĭsh′ē-ō′) ▶*adv. & adj.* By virtue of office or position. [Lat. *ex officiō*.]
ex•og•e•nous (ĕk-sŏj′ə-nəs) ▶*adj.* Originating outside an organism or part: *an exogenous disease.* —**ex•og′e•nous•ly** *adv.*
ex•on•er•ate (ĭg-zŏn′ə-rāt′) ▶*v.* **-at•ed, -at•ing.** To free from blame or responsibility. [< Lat. *exonerāre*, to free from a burden.] —**ex•on′er•a′tion** *n.* —**ex•on′er•a′tive** *adj.* —**ex•on′er•a′tor** *n.*
ex•or•bi•tant (ĭg-zôr′bĭ-tənt) ▶*adj.* Exceeding reasonable bounds or limits; excessive. [< LLat. *exorbitāre*, deviate.] —**ex•or′bi•tance** *n.* —**ex•or′bi•tant•ly** *adv.*
ex•or•cise (ĕk′sôr-sīz′, -sər-) ▶*v.* **-cised, -cis•ing 1.** To expel (an evil spirit) by or as if by incantation or prayer. **2.** To free from evil spirits. [< Gk. *exorkizein* < *horkos*, oath.] —**ex′or•cism** *n.* —**ex′or•cist** *n.*
ex•o•skel•e•ton (ĕk′sō-skĕl′ĭ-tn) ▶*n.* A hard outer structure, such as the shell of an insect or crustacean, that provides protection or support for an organism. —**ex′o•skel′e•tal** (-ĭ-tl) *adj.*
ex•o•sphere (ĕk′sō-sfîr′) ▶*n.* The outermost layer of the earth's atmosphere.
ex•o•ther•mic (ĕk′sō-thûr′mĭk) also **ex•o•ther•mal** (-məl) ▶*adj.* Releasing heat: *an exothermic reaction.* —**ex′o•ther′mi•cal•ly** *adv.*
ex•ot•ic (ĭg-zŏt′ĭk) ▶*adj.* **1.** From another part of the world. See Syns at **foreign. 2.** Intriguingly unusual, different, or beautiful. [< Gk. *exōtikos* < *exō*, outside.] —**ex•ot′ic** *n.* —**ex•ot′i•cal•ly** *adv.*
exp ▶*abbr.* **1.** exponent **2.** exponential
exp. ▶*abbr.* **1.** expenses **2.** experiment **3.** expiration **4.** export **5.** express
ex•pand (ĭk-spănd′) ▶*v.* **1.** To increase or become increased in size, quantity, or scope. **2.** To express in detail; enlarge on: *expanded his remarks.* **3.** To spread out; unfold. [< Lat. *expandere*.] —**ex•pand′a•ble** *adj.*
ex•panse (ĭk-spăns′) ▶*n.* A wide, open extent, as of land, sea, or sky. [Lat. *expānsum* < p.part. of *expandere*, spread out.]
ex•pan•sion (ĭk-spăn′shən) ▶*n.* **1.** The act or process of expanding or the state of being expanded. **2.** A product of expanding.
ex•pan•sion•ism (ĭk-spăn′shə-nĭz′əm) ▶*n.* A nation's practice or policy of territorial or economic expansion. —**ex•pan′sion•ar′y** *adj.* —**ex•pan′sion•ist** *adj. & n.*
ex•pan•sive (ĭk-spăn′sĭv) ▶*adj.* **1.** Capable of expanding or tending to expand. **2.** Broad; comprehensive. **3.** Kind and generous; outgoing. —**ex•pan′sive•ly** *adv.* —**ex•pan′sive•ness** *n.*
ex par•te (ĕks pär′tē) ▶*adv. & adj. Law* From or on one side only. [Lat.]
ex•pa•ti•ate (ĭk-spā′shē-āt′) ▶*v.* **-at•ed, -at•ing.** To speak or write at length; elaborate. [Lat. *expatiārī* < *spatium*, space.] —**ex•pa′ti•a′tion** *n.*
ex•pa•tri•ate (ĕk-spā′trē-āt′) ▶*v.* **-at•ed, -at•ing 1.** To exile; banish. **2.** To leave one's country to reside in another. [Med.Lat. *expatriāre* : EX– + Lat. *patria*, native land (< *pater*, father).] —**ex•pa′tri•ate** (-ĭt, -āt′) *adj. & n.* —**ex•pa′tri•a′tion** *n.*
ex•pect (ĭk-spĕkt′) ▶*v.* **1.** To look forward to the occurrence or appearance of. **2.** To consider reasonable or due. **3.** *Informal* To presume or suppose. **4.** To be pregnant. Used in progressive tenses: *My wife is expecting.* [Lat. *exspectāre* : EX– + *spectāre*, look at (< *specere*, see).]
ex•pec•tan•cy (ĭk-spĕk′tən-sē) ▶*n.*, *pl.* **-cies 1.** Expectation. **2.** Something expected, esp. an amount calculated on statistical probability: *life expectancy.*
ex•pec•tant (ĭk-spĕk′tənt) ▶*adj.* **1.** Expecting. **2.** Pregnant. —**ex•pec′tant•ly** *adv.*
ex•pec•ta•tion (ĕk′spĕk-tā′shən) ▶*n.* **1.** The

act or condition of expecting. **2.** Eager anticipation. **3. expectations** Prospects or hopes, esp. of success or gain.

ex•pec•to•rant (ĭk-spĕk′tər-ənt) ►*adj.* Promoting secretion or expulsion of mucus or other matter from the respiratory system. —**ex•pec′to•rant** *n.*

ex•pec•to•rate (ĭk-spĕk′tə-rāt′) ►*v.* **-rat•ed, -rat•ing.** To eject from the mouth; spit. [Lat. *expectorāre*, drive from the chest.] —**ex•pec′to•ra′tion** *n.*

ex•pe•di•ence (ĭk-spē′dē-əns) ►*n.* Expediency.

ex•pe•di•en•cy (ĭk-spē′dē-ən-sē) ►*n., pl.* **-cies 1.** Appropriateness to a purpose. **2.** Adherence to self-serving means.

ex•pe•di•ent (ĭk-spē′dē-ənt) ►*adj.* **1.** Appropriate to a particular purpose. **2.** Serving narrow or selfish interests. ►*n.* Something expedient. See Syns at **makeshift.** [< Lat. *expedīre*, make ready. See EXPEDITE.] —**ex•pe′di•ent•ly** *adv.*

ex•pe•dite (ĕk′spĭ-dīt′) ►*v.* **-dit•ed, -dit•ing 1.** To speed the progress of; facilitate. **2.** To perform quickly. [Lat. *expedīre*, make ready : EX– + *pēs*, *ped-*, foot.] —**ex′pe•dit′er, ex′pe•di′tor** *n.*

ex•pe•di•tion (ĕk′spĭ-dĭsh′ən) ►*n.* **1a.** A journey undertaken with a definite objective. **b.** The group making such a journey. **2.** Speed in performance. See Syns at **haste.**

ex•pe•di•tion•ar•y (ĕk′spĭ-dĭsh′ə-nĕr′ē) ►*adj.* Of or being an expedition, esp. a military one.

ex•pe•di•tious (ĕk′spĭ-dĭsh′əs) ►*adj.* Acting or done with speed and efficiency. —**ex′pe•di′tious•ly** *adv.*

ex•pel (ĭk-spĕl′) ►*v.* **-pelled, -pel•ling 1.** To force or drive out; eject forcefully. **2.** To dismiss officially. [< Lat. *expellere*.] —**ex•pel′la•ble** *adj.* —**ex•pel′ler** *n.*

ex•pend (ĭk-spĕnd′) ►*v.* **1.** To spend. **2.** To use up; waste. [< Lat. *expendere*, pay out.]

ex•pend•a•ble (ĭk-spĕn′də-bəl) ►*adj.* **1.** Subject to use or consumption. **2.** Nonessential; dispensable.

ex•pen•di•ture (ĭk-spĕn′də-chər) ►*n.* **1.** The act or process of expending. **2.** Something expended, esp. money.

ex•pense (ĭk-spĕns′) ►*n.* **1a.** Something spent to accomplish a purpose. **b.** Something given up for something gained; sacrifice. **2. expenses a.** Charges incurred by an employee in the performance of work. **b.** *Informal* Money allotted for payment of such charges. **3.** Something requiring the expenditure of money. [< Lat. *expēnsus*, paid out.]

ex•pen•sive (ĭk-spĕn′sĭv) ►*adj.* Having a high price; costly. —**ex•pen′sive•ly** *adv.* —**ex•pen′sive•ness** *n.*

ex•pe•ri•ence (ĭk-spîr′ē-əns) ►*n.* **1.** The apprehension of an object, thought, or emotion through the senses or mind. **2a.** Activity or practice through which knowledge or skill is gained. **b.** Knowledge or skill so derived. **3a.** An event or a series of events undergone or lived through. **b.** The totality or effect of such events. ►*v.* **-enced, -enc•ing.** To have as an experience; undergo. [< Lat. *experīrī*, try.]

ex•pe•ri•enced (ĭk-spîr′ē-ənst) ►*adj.* Skilled or knowledgeable through experience.

ex•pe•ri•en•tial (ĭk-spîr′ē-ĕn′shəl) ►*adj.* Relating to or derived from experience. —**ex•pe′ri•en′tial•ly** *adv.*

ex•per•i•ment (ĭk-spĕr′ə-mənt) ►*n.* A test made to demonstrate a known truth, examine the validity of a hypothesis, or determine the nature of something. ►*v.* (-mĕnt′) **1.** To conduct an experiment. **2.** To try something new: *experiment with new methods of teaching.* [< Lat. *experīmentum.*] —**ex•per′i•men′tal** *adj.* —**ex•per′i•men′tal•ly** *adv.* —**ex•per′i•men•ta′tion** *n.*

ex•pert (ĕk′spûrt′) ►*n.* A person with a high degree of skill in or knowledge of a certain subject or field. ►*adj.* (ĕk′spûrt, ĭk-spûrt′). Highly skilled or knowledgeable. [< Lat. *expertus*, p.part. of *experīrī*, try.] —**ex′pert′ly** *adv.* —**ex′pert′ness** *n.*

ex•per•tise (ĕk′spûr-tēz′) ►*n.* Expert skill or knowledge. See Syns at **art**[1]. [Fr. < *expert*, experienced.]

ex•pi•ate (ĕk′spē-āt′) ►*v.* **-at•ed, -at•ing.** To atone or make amends (for). [Lat. *expiāre.*] —**ex′pi•a′tion** *n.* —**ex′pi•a′tor** *n.* —**ex′pi•a•to′ry** (-ə-tôr′ē, -tōr′ē) *adj.*

ex•pire (ĭk-spīr′) ►*v.* **-pired, -pir•ing 1.** To come to an end; terminate. **2.** To die. **3.** To exhale. [< Lat. *exspīrāre*, breathe out.] —**ex′pi•ra′tion** (ĕk′spə-rā′shən) *n.*

ex•pi•ry (ĭk-spīr′ē) ►*n., pl.* **-ries 1.** An expiration, esp. of a contract. **2.** Death.

ex•plain (ĭk-splān′) ►*v.* **1.** To make plain or comprehensible. **2.** To define; expound. **3.** To offer reasons for; justify. [< Lat. *explānāre*, make plain.] —**ex•plain′a•ble** *adj.* —**ex′pla•na′tion** (ĕk′splə-nā′shən) *n.* —**ex•plan′a•to′ri•ly** *adv.* —**ex•plan′a•to′ry** (-splăn′ə-tôr′ē, -tōr′ē) *adj.*

ex•ple•tive (ĕk′splĭ-tĭv) ►*n.* An exclamation or oath. [< Lat. *explēre*, *explēt-*, fill out.]

ex•plic•a•ble (ĭk-splĭk′ə-bəl, ĕk′splĭ-kə-) ►*adj.* Possible to explain. —**ex′plic•a•bly** *adv.*

ex•pli•cate (ĕk′splĭ-kāt′) ►*v.* **-cat•ed, -cat•ing.** To explain, esp. in detail. [Lat. *explicāre*, unfold.] —**ex′pli•ca′tion** *n.* —**ex′pli•ca′tive** *adj.* —**ex′pli•ca′tor** *n.*

ex•plic•it (ĭk-splĭs′ĭt) ►*adj.* Fully and clearly expressed, defined, or formulated. [Lat. *explicitus*, p.part of *explicāre*, unfold.] —**ex•plic′it•ly** *adv.* —**ex•plic′it•ness** *n.*

Syns: *explicit, categorical, definite, express, specific* ***Ant:*** *ambiguous* **adj.**

ex•plode (ĭk-splōd′) ►*v.* **-plod•ed, -plod•ing 1.** To cause or undergo an explosion. **2.** To burst or cause to burst by explosion. **3.** To burst forth or break out suddenly. **4.** To increase suddenly, sharply, and without control. **5.** To show to be false; refute. [Lat. *explōdere*, drive out by clapping.] —**ex•plod′a•ble** *adj.*

ex•ploit (ĕk′sploit′, ĭk-sploit′) ►*n.* An act or deed, esp. a heroic one. See Syns at **feat.** ►*v.* (ĭk-sploit′, ĕk′sploit′) **1.** To utilize fully or advantageously. **2.** To make use of selfishly or unethically. See Syns at **manipulate.** [< Lat. *explicitum.*] —**ex•ploit′a•ble** *adj.* —**ex′ploi•ta′tion** *n.* —**ex•ploit′a•tive** *adj.* —**ex•ploit′er** *n.*

ex•plore (ĭk-splôr′, -splōr′) ►*v.* **-plored, -plor•ing 1.** To investigate systematically. **2.** To search or travel into for the purpose of discovery. **3.** *Medic.* To examine for diagnostic purposes. [Lat. *explōrāre.*] —**ex′plo•ra′tion**

(ĕk′splə-rā′shən) *n.* —**ex•plor′a•to′ry** (-tôr′ē, -tōr′ē) *adj.* —**ex•plor′er** *n.*

ex•plo•sion (ĭk-splō′zhən) ►*n.* **1a.** A sudden violent release of mechanical, chemical, or nuclear energy. **b.** The loud sound accompanying such a release. **2.** A sudden, often vehement outburst, esp. of emotion. **3.** A sudden sharp increase: *a population explosion.* [Lat. *explōsiō.*]

ex•plo•sive (ĭk-splō′sĭv) ►*adj.* **1.** Of or causing an explosion. **2.** Tending to explode. **3.** Highly unstable; volatile. ►*n.* A substance, esp. a prepared chemical, that explodes or causes explosion. —**ex•plo′sive•ly** *adv.* —**ex•plo′sive•ness** *n.*

ex•po•nent (ĭk-spō′nənt, ĕk′spō′nənt) ►*n.* **1.** One that expounds, interprets, or advocates. **2.** A number or symbol, as 3 in $(x + y)^3$, placed to the right of and above another number, symbol, or expression, denoting the power to which it is to be raised. [< Lat. *expōnere,* set forth.] —**ex′po•nen′tial** (ĕk′spə-nĕn′shəl) *adj.* —**ex′po•nen′tial•ly** *adv.*

ex•port (ĭk-spôrt′, -spōrt′, ĕk′spôrt′, -spōrt′) ►*v.* **1.** To send or transport abroad, esp. for trade or sale. **2.** *Comp. Sci.* To send (data) from one program to another. ►*n.* (ĕk′spôrt′, -spōrt′). Exportation. [< Lat. *exportāre,* carry out.] —**ex•port′a•ble** *adj.* —**ex•port′er** *n.*

ex•por•ta•tion (ĕk′spôr-tā′shən, -spōr-) ►*n.* **1.** The act of exporting. **2.** Something exported; export.

ex•pose (ĭk-spōz′) ►*v.* **-posed, -pos•ing 1a.** To subject or allow to be subjected to an action or influence. **b.** To subject (a photographic film or plate) to the action of light. **2.** To make visible or known; reveal. **3.** To lay bare; uncover. [< Lat. *expōnere,* to set out.] —**ex•pos′er** *n.*

ex•po•sé (ĕk′spō-zā′) ►*n.* A public revelation of something discreditable. [Fr.]

ex•po•si•tion (ĕk′spə-zĭsh′ən) ►*n.* **1.** The systematic explanation of a subject. **2.** A discourse that conveys information about or explains a subject. **3.** A public exhibition of broad scope. —**ex•pos′i•tor** (ĭk-spŏz′ĭ-tər) *n.* —**ex•pos′i•to′ry** (-tôr′ē, -tōr′ē) *adj.*

ex post fac•to (ĕks′ pōst făk′tō) ►*adj.* Formulated, enacted, or operating retroactively. [Lat. *ex postfactō,* from what is done afterwards.]

ex•pos•tu•late (ĭk-spŏs′chə-lāt′) ►*v.* **-lat•ed, -lat•ing.** To reason earnestly with someone, esp. to dissuade or correct. [Lat. *expostulāre,* demand strongly.] —**ex•pos′tu•la′tion** *n.* —**ex•pos′tu•la′tor** *n.* —**ex•pos′tu•la•to′ry** (-lə-tôr′ē, -tōr′ē) *adj.*

ex•po•sure (ĭk-spō′zhər) ►*n.* **1.** The act or an instance of exposing or the condition of being exposed. **2.** A position in relation to direction of weather conditions. **3a.** The act or time of exposing a photographic film or plate. **b.** A film or plate so exposed.

ex•pound (ĭk-spound′) ►*v.* To give a detailed statement (of); explain. [< Lat. *expōnere,* set forth.] —**ex•pound′er** *n.*

ex•press (ĭk-sprĕs′) ►*v.* **1.** To make known or indicate, as by words, facial aspect, or symbols. **2.** To press out, as juice from an orange. **3.** To send by rapid transport. ►*adj.* **1.** Definitely and clearly stated. See Syns at **explicit. 2a.** Sent by rapid direct transportation. **b.** Direct, rapid, and usu. nonstop: *an express bus.* ►*adv.* By express transportation. ►*n.* **1.** A rapid, efficient system for the delivery of goods and mail. **2.** A means of transport, such as a train, that travels rapidly, usu. nonstop. [< Med.Lat. *expressāre.*] —**ex•press′i•ble** *adj.* —**ex•press′ly** *adv.*

ex•pres•sion (ĭk-sprĕsh′ən) ►*n.* **1.** Communication, as of an idea or emotion, esp. by words, art, music, or movement. **2.** A symbol, sign, or indication. **3.** *Math.* A symbol or combination of symbols representing a quantity or a relationship between quantities. **4.** A manner of expressing, esp. in speaking, depicting, or performing. **5.** A word or phrase. **6.** A facial aspect or tone of voice conveying feeling. —**ex•pres′sion•less** *adj.*

ex•pres•sion•ism (ĭk-sprĕsh′ə-nĭz′əm) ►*n.* A movement in the fine arts that emphasized subjective expression of the artist's inner experiences. —**ex•pres′sion•ist** *n.* —**ex•pres′sion•is′tic** *adj.*

ex•pres•sive (ĭk-sprĕs′ĭv) ►*adj.* **1.** Expressing or serving to express or indicate. **2.** Full of expression or meaning. —**ex•pres′sive•ly** *adv.* —**ex•pres′sive•ness** *n.*

Syns: *expressive, eloquent, meaningful, significant* **adj.**

ex•press•way (ĭk-sprĕs′wā′) ►*n.* A major divided highway designed for high-speed travel.

ex•pro•pri•ate (ĕk-sprō′prē-āt′) ►*v.* **-at•ed, -at•ing.** To acquire or take (land or other property) from another, esp. for public use. [< Med.Lat. *expropriāre* < Lat. *proprius,* one's own.] —**ex•pro′pri•a′tion** *n.* —**ex•pro′pri•a′tor** *n.*

ex•pul•sion (ĭk-spŭl′shən) ►*n.* The act of expelling or the state of being expelled.

ex•punge (ĭk-spŭnj′) ►*v.* **-punged, -pung•ing.** To erase or strike out. [Lat. *expungere.*]

ex•pur•gate (ĕk′spər-gāt′) ►*v.* **-gat•ed, -gat•ing.** To remove obscene or objectionable material from. [Lat. *expūrgāre,* purify.] —**ex′pur•ga′tion** *n.* —**ex′pur•ga′tor** *n.*

ex•qui•site (ĕk′skwĭ-zĭt, ĭk-skwĭz′ĭt) ►*adj.* **1.** Beautifully made or designed. **2.** Of or having great delicacy or beauty. See Syns at **delicate. 3.** Acutely refined or discriminating. **4.** Intense; keen. [< Lat. *exquīsītus,* p.part. of *exquīrere,* search out.] —**ex′qui•site•ly** *adv.* —**ex′qui•site•ness** *n.*

ex•tant (ĕk′stənt, ĕk-stănt′) ►*adj.* Still in existence; not destroyed, lost, or extinct. [< Lat. *exstāre,* stand out : EX– + *stāre,* stand.]

ex•tem•po•ra•ne•ous (ĭk-stĕm′pə-rā′nē-əs) ►*adj.* Carried out or performed with little or no preparation; impromptu. [< Lat. *ex tempore,* extempore.] —**ex•tem′po•ra′ne•ous•ly** *adv.* —**ex•tem′po•ra′ne•ous•ness** *n.*

ex•tem•po•rar•y (ĭk-stĕm′pə-rĕr′ē) ►*adj.* Extemporaneous. [< EXTEMPORE.]

ex•tem•po•re (ĭk-stĕm′pə-rē) ►*adj.* Extemporaneous. ►*adv.* Extemporaneously. [Lat. *ex tempore,* out of the time.]

ex•tem•po•rize (ĭk-stĕm′pə-rīz′) ►*v.* **-rized, -riz•ing.** To do or perform (something) extemporaneously; improvise. —**ex•tem′po•ri•za′tion** *n.*

ex•tend (ĭk-stĕnd′) ►*v.* **1.** To stretch, spread, or enlarge to greater length, area, or scope; expand. **2.** To exert vigorously or to full capacity: *extended herself to learn the new job.* **3.** To offer; tender: *extend credit.* [< Lat. *extendere.*] —**ex•tend′i•bil′i•ty, ex•ten′si•bil′i•ty** *n.* —**ex•tend′i•ble, ex•ten′si•ble** *adj.*

ex•ten•sion (ĭk-stĕn′shən) ►*n.* **1.** The act of

extending or condition of being extended. **2.** An extended or added part. [< Lat. *extēnsiō*.]

ex•ten•sive (ĭk-stĕn′sĭv) ▶*adj.* Large in extent, range, or amount. —**ex•ten′sive•ly** *adv.* —**ex•ten′sive•ness** *n.*

ex•ten•sor (ĭk-stĕn′sər) ▶*n.* A muscle that extends or straightens a limb or body part. [NLat. < Lat. *extendere*, stretch out.]

ex•tent (ĭk-stĕnt′) ▶*n.* **1.** The area or distance over which a thing extends; size. **2.** The range or degree to which a thing extends; scope. [< Lat. *extendere*, extend.]

ex•ten•u•ate (ĭk-stĕn′yo͞o-āt′) ▶*v.* **-at•ed, -at•ing.** To lessen the seriousness of, esp. by providing partial excuses. See Syns at **palliate.** [Lat. *extenuāre*, make thin.] —**ex•ten′u•a′tion** *n.* —**ex•ten′u•a′tor** *n.*

ex•te•ri•or (ĭk-stîr′ē-ər) ▶*adj.* Outer; external. ▶*n.* An outer or outward part, surface, or aspect. [Lat., comp. of *exter*, outward.]

ex•ter•mi•nate (ĭk-stûr′mə-nāt′) ▶*v.* **-nat•ed, -nat•ing.** To destroy completely; wipe out. [Lat. *extermināre*, drive out.] —**ex•ter′mi•na′tion** *n.* —**ex•ter′mi•na′tor** *n.*

ex•ter•nal (ĭk-stûr′nəl) ▶*adj.* **1.** Of, on, or for the outside or outer part. **2.** Acting or coming from the outside. **3.** For outward show; superficial. **4.** Relating to foreign countries. ▶*n.* **externals** Outward appearances. [< Lat. *externus*.] —**ex•ter′nal•ly** *adv.*

external ear ▶*n.* The outer portion of the ear including the auricle and the passage leading to the eardrum.

ex•tinct (ĭk-stĭngkt′) ▶*adj.* **1.** No longer existing or living. **2.** No longer burning or active. [< Lat. *exstīnctus*, p.part. of *exstinguere*, EXTINGUISH.] —**ex•tinc′tion** *n.*

ex•tin•guish (ĭk-stĭng′gwĭsh) ▶*v.* **1.** To put out (e.g., a fire); quench. **2.** To put an end to; destroy. [Lat. *exstinguere*.] —**ex•tin′guish•a•ble** *adj.* —**ex•tin′guish•er** *n.*

ex•tir•pate (ĕk′stər-pāt′) ▶*v.* **-pat•ed, -pat•ing 1.** To uproot or cut out. **2.** To destroy totally; exterminate. [Lat. *exstirpāre*, root out.] —**ex′tir•pa′tion** *n.* —**ex′tir•pa′tive** *adj.* —**ex′tir•pa′tor** *n.*

ex•tol also **ex•toll** (ĭk-stōl′) ▶*v.* **-tolled, -tol•ling.** To praise highly. [< Lat. *extollere*, lift up.] —**ex•tol′ler** *n.* —**ex•tol′ment** *n.*

ex•tort (ĭk-stôrt′) ▶*v.* To obtain from by coercion or intimidation. [Lat. *extorquēre*, *extort-*, wring out.] —**ex•tor′tion** *n.* —**ex•tor′tion•ate** (-ĭt) *adj.* —**ex•tor′tion•ist** *n.* —**ex•tor′tive** *adj.*

ex•tra (ĕk′strə) ▶*adj.* More than what is usual, expected, or necessary. See Syns at **superfluous.** ▶*n.* **1.** Something that is extra. **2.** A special edition of a newspaper. **3.** A performer hired to play a minor part, as in a crowd scene in a film. ▶*adv.* Especially; unusually. [Prob. < EXTRAORDINARY.]

extra– ▶*pref.* Outside; beyond: *extraterrestrial.* [< Lat. *extrā*, outside.]

ex•tract (ĭk-străkt′) ▶*v.* **1.** To draw or pull out forcibly. **2.** To obtain despite resistance, as by threatening. **3.** To obtain in a concentrated form by chemical or mechanical action. **4.** To remove for separate consideration or publication; excerpt. **5.** *Math.* To determine or calculate (a root). ▶*n.* (ĕk′străkt′) **1.** A literary excerpt. **2.** A substance prepared by extracting; essence; concentrate. [< Lat. *extrahere*, *extract-*, draw out.] —**ex•tract′a•ble, ex•tract′i•ble** *adj.* —**ex•trac′tor** *n.*

ex•trac•tion (ĭk-străk′shən) ▶*n.* **1.** The act of extracting or the condition of being extracted. **2.** Something obtained by extracting; extract. **3.** Origin; lineage.

ex•tra•cur•ric•u•lar (ĕk′strə-kə-rĭk′yə-lər) ▶*adj.* Being outside a regular course of study.

ex•tra•dite (ĕk′strə-dīt′) ▶*v.* **-dit•ed, -dit•ing.** To give up or deliver (e.g., a fugitive) to the legal jurisdiction of another government or authority. [< Fr. *extradition*, extradition : EX– + Lat. *trāditiō*, handing over; see TRADITION.] —**ex′tra•dit′a•ble** *adj.* —**ex′tra•di′tion** (ĕk′strə-dĭsh′ən) *n.*

ex•tra•ga•lac•tic (ĕk′strə-gə-lăk′tĭk) ▶*adj.* Located or originating beyond the Milky Way.

ex•tra•le•gal (ĕk′strə-lē′gəl) ▶*adj.* Not permitted or governed by law. —**ex′tra•le′gal•ly** *adv.*

ex•tra•mar•i•tal (ĕk′strə-măr′ĭ-tl) ▶*adj.* Violating marriage vows; adulterous.

ex•tra•mu•ral (ĕk′strə-myo͝or′əl) ▶*adj.* Occurring or situated outside of the walls or boundaries, as of a community or school. [< EXTRA– + Lat. *mūrus*, wall.]

ex•tra•ne•ous (ĭk-strā′nē-əs) ▶*adj.* **1.** Not essential. See Syns at **irrelevant. 2.** Coming from the outside. [< Lat. *extrāneus* < *extrā*, outside.] —**ex•tra′ne•ous•ly** *adv.* —**ex•tra′ne•ous•ness** *n.*

ex•traor•di•nar•y (ĭk-strôr′dn-ĕr′ē, ĕk′strə-ôr′-) ▶*adj.* Beyond what is ordinary or usual; exceptional; remarkable. —**ex•traor′di•nar′i•ly** *adv.*

ex•trap•o•late (ĭk-străp′ə-lāt′) ▶*v.* **-lat•ed, -lat•ing.** To infer (unknown information) from known information. [EXTRA– + (INTER)POLATE.] —**ex•trap′o•la′tion** *n.*

ex•tra•sen•so•ry (ĕk′strə-sĕn′sə-rē) ▶*adj.* Being outside the normal range of sense perception.

ex•tra•ter•res•tri•al (ĕk′strə-tə-rĕs′trē-əl) ▶*adj.* From or occurring outside Earth or its atmosphere. —**ex′tra•ter•res′tri•al** *n.*

ex•tra•ter•ri•to•ri•al (ĕk′strə-tĕr′ĭ-tôr′ē-əl, -tōr′-) ▶*adj.* Located outside the territorial boundaries of a nation or state.

ex•tra•ter•ri•to•ri•al•i•ty (ĕk′strə-tĕr′ĭ-tôr′ē-ăl′ĭ-tē, -tōr′-) ▶*n.* Exemption from local legal jurisdiction, such as that granted to foreign diplomats.

ex•trav•a•gance (ĭk-străv′ə-gəns) ▶*n.* **1.** The quality of being extravagant. **2.** Immoderate expense or display. **3.** Something extravagant. See Syns at **luxury.**

ex•trav•a•gant (ĭk-străv′ə-gənt) ▶*adj.* **1.** Lavish or imprudent in spending money. **2.** Exceeding reasonable bounds; excessive. [< Med. Lat. *extrāvagārī*, wander.] —**ex•trav′a•gant•ly** *adv.*

ex•trav•a•gan•za (ĭk-străv′ə-găn′zə) ▶*n.* An elaborate, spectacular entertainment or display. [Ital. *estravaganza*.]

ex•tra•ve•hic•u•lar activity (ĕk′strə-vē-hĭk′yə-lər) ▶*n.* Maneuvers performed by an astronaut outside a spacecraft in space.

ex•treme (ĭk-strēm′) ▶*adj.* **1.** Most remote; outermost or farthest. **2.** Very great; intense. **3.** Extending far beyond the norm. **4.** Drastic; severe. ▶*n.* **1.** The greatest or utmost degree. **2.** Either of the two things at opposite ends of a scale, series, or range. **3.** An extreme condition. **4.** A drastic expedient. [< Lat. *extrēmus.*] —**ex•treme′ly** *adv.* —**ex•treme′ness** *n.*

extravehicular activity

ex•trem•ist (ĭk-strē′mĭst) ►*n.* One with extreme views, esp. in politics. —**ex•trem′ism** *n.*
ex•trem•i•ty (ĭk-strĕm′ĭ-tē) ►*n., pl.* **-ties 1.** The outermost or farthest point or part. **2.** The utmost degree. **3.** Grave danger, necessity, or distress. **4.** An extreme or severe measure. **5a.** A bodily limb or appendage. **b.** A hand or foot.
ex•tri•cate (ĕk′strĭ-kāt′) ►*v.* **-cat•ed, -cat•ing.** To release from an entanglement or difficulty. [Lat. *extricāre.*] —**ex′tri•ca•ble** (-kə-bəl) *adj.* —**ex′tri•ca′tion** *n.*
Syns: *extricate, disengage, disentangle, untangle* **v.**
ex•trin•sic (ĭk-strĭn′sĭk, -zĭk) ►*adj.* **1.** Not essential or inherent. **2.** Originating from the outside; external. [Lat. *extrīnsecus*, from outside.] —**ex•trin′si•cal•ly** *adv.*
ex•tro•vert also **ex•tra•vert** (ĕk′strə-vûrt′) ►*n.* One who is socially outgoing and communicative. [< EXTRA– + Lat. *vertere*, turn.] —**ex′tro•ver′sion** *n.*
ex•trude (ĭk-strōōd′) ►*v.* **-trud•ed, -trud•ing 1.** To thrust out. **2.** To shape (e.g., a plastic) by forcing through a die. [Lat. *extrūdere.*] —**ex•tru′sion** *n.* —**ex•tru′sive** *adj.*
ex•u•ber•ant (ĭg-zōō′bər-ənt) ►*adj.* **1.** High-spirited; lively. **2.** Lavish; effusive. **3.** Growing abundantly. See Syns at **profuse.** [< Lat. *exūberāre*, be exuberant.] —**ex•u′ber•ance** *n.* —**ex•u′ber•ant•ly** *adv.*
ex•ude (ĭg-zōōd′, ĭk-sōōd′) ►*v.* **-ud•ed, -ud•ing 1.** To ooze or pour forth gradually. **2.** To give off; radiate: *exude trust and confidence.* [Lat. *exsūdāre.*] —**ex′u•date′** (ĕks′yōō-dāt′) *n.* —**ex′u•da′tion** *n.*
ex•ult (ĭg-zŭlt′) ►*v.* To rejoice greatly, as in triumph. [Lat. *exsultāre*, leap up.] —**ex•ul′tant** *adj.* —**ex•ul′tant•ly** *adv.* —**ex′ul•ta′tion** (ĕk′səl-tā′shən, ĕg′zəl-) *n.*
ex•urb (ĕk′sûrb′) ►*n.* A mostly rural, often wealthy residential region lying beyond the suburbs of a city. [EX– + (SUB)URB.] —**ex•ur′ban** *adj.* —**ex•ur′ban•ite′** *n.*
ex•ur•bi•a (ĕk-sûr′bē-ə, ĕg-zûr′-) ►*n.* A typically exurban area.
-ey ►*suff.* Var. of **-y¹**.
Eyck (īk), **Jan van.** 1390?–1441. And his brother **Hubert** (d. 1426). Flemish painters.
eye (ī) ►*n.* **1.** An organ of vision or of light sensitivity. **2.** The faculty of seeing; vision. **3.** The ability to perceive or discern. **4.** A point of view; opinion. **5.** Attention. **6.** Something suggestive of an eye: *the eye of a needle; the eye of a potato.* ►*v.* **eyed, eye•ing** or **ey•ing.** To look at. —***idiom:* eye to eye** In agreement. [< OE *ēage.*]
eye•ball (ī′bôl′) ►*n.* The ball-shaped part of the eye enclosed by the socket and eyelids.
eye•brow (ī′brou′) ►*n.* The hairs covering the bony ridge over the eye.
eye•drop•per (ī′drŏp′ər) ►*n.* A dropper for applying liquid medicines, esp. to the eye.
eye•ful (ī′fōōl′) ►*n.* **1.** A good or thorough look. **2.** A pleasing sight.
eye•glass (ī′glăs′) ►*n.* **1a. eyeglasses** Glasses for the eyes. **b.** A monocle. **2.** See **eyepiece.**
eye•lash (ī′lăsh′) ►*n.* Any of the short hairs fringing the edge of the eyelid.
eye•let (ī′lĭt) ►*n.* **1.** A small hole for a lace, cord, or hook to fit through. **2.** A metal ring designed to reinforce such a hole. [< OFr. *oillet*, dim. of *oil*, eye < Lat. *oculus.*]
eye•lid (ī′lĭd′) ►*n.* Either of two folds of skin and muscle that can be closed over an eye.
eye opener ►*n.* *Informal* A startling or shocking revelation.
eye•piece (ī′pēs′) ►*n.* The lens or lens group closest to the eye in an optical instrument.
eye shadow ►*n.* A cosmetic applied esp. to the eyelids to enhance the eyes.
eye•sight (ī′sīt′) ►*n.* The faculty or range of sight; vision.
eye•sore (ī′sôr′, ī′sōr′) ►*n.* An ugly sight.
eye•strain (ī′strān′) ►*n.* Pain and fatigue in one or more of the eye muscles.
eye•tooth (ī′tōōth′) ►*n.* A canine tooth of the upper jaw.
eye•wash (ī′wŏsh′, ī′wôsh′) ►*n.* **1.** A solution applied as a cleanser for the eyes. **2.** *Informal* Nonsense; hogwash.
eye•wit•ness (ī′wĭt′nĭs) ►*n.* One who has personally seen someone or something and can bear witness to the fact.
ey•rie (âr′ē, îr′ē) ►*n.* Var. of **aerie.**
E•ze•ki•el (ĭ-zē′kē-əl) ►*n.* **1.** 6th cent. B.C. Hebrew prophet. **2.** See table at **Bible.**
e-zine (ē′zēn′) ►*n.* A magazine that is published electronically, esp. on the Internet.
Ez•ra (ĕz′rə) ►*n.* **1.** 5th cent. B.C. Hebrew high priest. **2.** See table at **Bible.**

F

f¹ or **F** (ĕf) ►*n., pl.* **f's** or **F's** also **fs** or **Fs 1.** The 6th letter of the English alphabet. **2. F** A failing grade. **3.** *Mus.* The 4th tone of the C major scale.
f² ►*abbr.* **1.** feminine **2.** focal length **3.** function
F¹ ► The symbol for the element **fluorine.**
F² ►*abbr.* **1.** Fahrenheit **2.** farad **3.** female **4.** franc **5.** Friday

F. ▸*abbr.* **1.** also **f.** folio **2.** French
f/ ▸*abbr.* f-stop
fa (fä) ▸*n. Mus.* The 4th tone of the diatonic scale.
FAA ▸*abbr.* Federal Aviation Administration
fa•ble (fā′bəl) ▸*n.* **1.** A fictitious story making a moral point and often using animals as characters. **2.** A story about legendary persons and exploits. **3.** A falsehood; lie. ▸*v.* **-bled, -bling.** To recount as if true. [< Lat. *fābula.*] —**fab′u•list** (făb′yə-lĭst) *n.*
fa•bled (fā′bəld) ▸*adj.* **1.** Legendary. **2.** Fictitious.
fab•ric (făb′rĭk) ▸*n.* **1.** A cloth produced esp. by knitting or weaving fibers. **2.** A complex underlying structure; framework: *the fabric of society.* [< Lat. *fabrica*, workshop.]
fab•ri•cate (făb′rĭ-kāt′) ▸*v.* **-cat•ed, -cat•ing 1.** To make; create. **2.** To construct or build. **3.** To make up in order to deceive: *fabricated an excuse.* —**fab′ri•ca′tion** *n.*
fab•u•lous (făb′yə-ləs) ▸*adj.* **1.** Barely credible; astonishing. **2.** Extremely pleasing or successful: *a fabulous vacation.* **3a.** Of the nature of a fable; legendary. **b.** Told of or celebrated in fables. [< Lat. *fābula*, fable.] —**fab′u•lous•ly** *adv.* —**fab′u•lous•ness** *n.*
fa•çade also **fa•cade** (fə-säd′) ▸*n.* **1.** The face of a building, esp. the principal face. **2.** An artificial or deceptive appearance: *put on a façade of sincerity.* [< Ital. *facciata.*]
face (fās) ▸*n.* **1.** The surface of the front of the head. **2.** A facial expression; countenance. **3.** A grimace. **4.** Outward appearance; aspect. **5.** Value or standing; prestige: *lose face.* **6.** Effrontery; impudence. **7.** The front or most significant surface of an object: *the face of a clock.* **8.** *Geom.* A planar surface of a geometric solid. ▸*v.* **faced, fac•ing 1.** To turn or be turned in the direction of. **2.** To front on: *a window that faces the south.* **3a.** To confront. See Syns at **defy. b.** To encounter: *face problems later on.* **4.** To furnish with a surface or cover of a different material. **5.** To trim the edge of (cloth), esp. with contrasting material. —***phrasal verbs:*** **face down** To overcome by a stare or a resolute manner. **face off** *Sports* To start play with a face-off. **face up to** To confront with resolution. —***idioms:*** **face the music** To accept unpleasant consequences. **face to face 1.** In each other's presence. **2.** Directly confronting: *face to face with death.* **in the face of 1.** Despite the opposition of. **2.** In view of. **on the face of it** From appearances alone. **to (one's) face** In one's presence. [< Lat. *faciēs.*] —**face′less** *adj.*
face card ▸*n. Games* A king, queen, or jack of a deck of playing cards.
face•less (fās′lĭs) ▸*adj.* **1.** Having no face. **2.** Without character; anonymous.
face-lift also **face•lift** (fās′lĭft′) ▸*n.* **1.** Plastic surgery to tighten facial tissues. **2.** A renovation, as of a building. —**face′-lift′** *v.*
face-off (fās′ôf′, -ŏf′) ▸*n.* **1.** A method of starting play, as in ice hockey or lacrosse, by releasing the puck or ball between two opposing players. **2.** A confrontation.
fac•et (făs′ĭt) ▸*n.* **1.** One of the flat surfaces cut on a gemstone. **2.** *Anat.* A small, smooth, flat surface, as on a bone or tooth. **3.** An aspect; phase. [< OFr. *facette*, dim. of *face*, FACE.] —**fac′et•ed** *adj.*
fa•ce•tious (fə-sē′shəs) ▸*adj.* Playfully jocular; humorous. [< Lat. *facētus*, witty.] —**fa•ce′tious•ly** *adv.* —**fa•ce′tious•ness** *n.*
face value ▸*n.* **1.** The value printed on the face, as of a bill or bond. **2.** Apparent significance or value.
fa•cial (fā′shəl) ▸*adj.* Of the face. ▸*n.* A cosmetic treatment for the face.
fac•ile (făs′əl) ▸*adj.* **1.** Simple; easy. **2.** Possessing effortless skill or fluency. **3.** Excessively simple; superficial: *a facile solution to a complex problem.* [< Lat. *facilis.*] —**fac′ile•ly** *adv.* —**fac′ile•ness** *n.*
fa•cil•i•tate (fə-sĭl′ĭ-tāt′) ▸*v.* **-tat•ed, -tat•ing.** To make easy or easier; assist. [< Ital. *facilitare.*] —**fa•cil′i•ta′tion** *n.* —**fa•cil′i•ta′tor** *n.*
fa•cil•i•ty (fə-sĭl′ĭ-tē) ▸*n., pl.* **-ties 1.** Ease in doing resulting from skill or aptitude. **2.** often **facilities** Something that facilitates an action or process. See Syns at **amenity. 3. facilities** *Informal* A restroom.
fac•ing (fā′sĭng) ▸*n.* **1.** A piece of material sewn to the edge of a garment as lining or decoration. **2.** A coating applied to a surface for protection or decoration.
fac•sim•i•le (făk-sĭm′ə-lē) ▸*n.* **1.** An exact copy or reproduction. **2.** See **fax.** [< Lat. *fac simile*, make similar.]
fact (făkt) ▸*n.* **1.** Information presented as true and accurate. **2.** Something having real, demonstrable existence. **3.** Something done, esp. a crime: *an accessory before the fact.* [Lat. *factum*, deed < p.part. of *facere*, do.]
fact-find•ing (făkt′fīn′dĭng) ▸*n.* Discovery or determination of facts. —**fact′-find′ing** *adj.*
fac•tion[1] (făk′shən) ▸*n.* **1.** A cohesive, usu. contentious minority within a larger group. **2.** Internal dissension or discord. [< Lat. *factiō* < p.part. of *facere*, do.] —**fac′tion•al** *adj.* —**fac′tion•al•ism** *n.*
fac•tion[2] (făk′shən) ▸*n.* A genre or work of literature or film that mixes fact and fiction. [Blend of FACT and FICTION.]
-faction ▸*suff.* Production; making: *petrifaction.* [< Lat. *-factiō.*]
fac•tious (făk′shəs) ▸*adj.* **1.** Produced or marked by faction. **2.** Tending to cause conflict or dissension; divisive. —**fac′tious•ly** *adv.*
fac•ti•tious (făk-tĭsh′əs) ▸*adj.* **1.** Produced artificially. **2.** False; sham. [< Lat. *factīcius* < *factus* < *facere*, make.]
fact of life ▸*n.* **1.** Something unavoidable that must be dealt with. **2. facts of life** The basic physiological functions involved in sex and reproduction.
fac•toid (făk′toid) ▸*n.* **1.** A piece of unverified or inaccurate information accepted as true because of frequent repetition. **2.** A brief, somewhat interesting fact.
fac•tor (făk′tər) ▸*n.* **1.** One that actively contributes to a result or process. See Syns at **element. 2.** One who acts for someone else; agent. **3.** *Math.* One of two or more quantities that divides a given quantity without a remainder: *2 and 3 are factors of 6.* ▸*v. Math.* **1.** To determine the factors of. **2.** To figure: *factor in inflation.* [< Lat., maker.]
fac•to•ry (făk′tə-rē) ▸*n., pl.* **-ries.** A building or group of buildings in which goods are manufactured; plant.
fac•to•tum (făk-tō′təm) ▸*n.* An employee or

assistant with a wide range of duties. [< Lat. *fac tōtum*, do everything.]

fac•tu•al (făk′cho͞o-əl) ▶ *adj.* Based on or containing facts. —**fac′tu•al′i•ty** (-ăl′ĭ-tē) *n.* —**fac′tu•al•ly** *adv.*

fac•ul•ty (făk′əl-tē) ▶ *n., pl.* **-ties 1.** An inherent power or ability. **2.** An aptitude or power of the human mind. **3a.** A division of learning at a college or university. **b.** The teachers in a college, university, or school. [< Lat. *facultās* < *facilis*, easy.]

fad (făd) ▶ *n.* A briefly popular fashion; craze. [?] —**fad′dist** *n.* —**fad′dish** *adj.*

fade (fād) ▶ *v.* **fad•ed, fad•ing 1.** To lose or cause to lose brightness or loudness; dim. **2.** To lose strength or freshness; wither. **3.** To disappear gradually; vanish. See Syns at **disappear.** [< OFr. *fader.*]

fade-in (fād′ĭn′) ▶ *n.* A gradual increase in the visibility of an image or the audibility of a sound, as in cinema, television, or radio.

fade-out (fād′out′) or **fade•out** ▶ *n.* A gradual disappearance of an image or sound, as in cinema, television, or radio.

fa•er•ie (fā′ə-rē, fâr′ē) ▶ *n.* **1.** A fairy. **2.** Fairyland. [ME *faierie*, FAIRY.]

Faer•oe Islands or **Far•oe Islands** (fâr′ō). A group of volcanic islands in the N Atlantic between Iceland and the Shetland Is. —**Faer′o•ese′** *adj. & n.*

fag¹ (făg) ▶ *n.* A drudge. ▶ *v.* **fagged, fag•ging.** To exhaust or work to exhaustion; fatigue. [< *fag*, droop.]

fag² (făg) ▶ *n. Slang* A cigarette. [< FAG END.]

fag end ▶ *n.* **1.** The frayed end of a length of cloth or rope. **2.** The last and least useful part. [ME *fag.*]

fag•ot also **fag•got** (făg′ət) ▶ *n.* A bundle of twigs or sticks. [< OProv.] —**fag′ot** *v.*

Fahd (fäd). Fahd ibn Abdel Aziz al-Saud. b. 1922. King of Saudi Arabia (since 1982).

Fahr. ▶ *abbr.* Fahrenheit

Fahr•en•heit (făr′ən-hīt′, fä′rən-) ▶ *adj.* Of or according to a temperature scale that registers the freezing point of water as 32°F and the boiling point as 212°F at one atmosphere of pressure. See table at **measurement.** [After Gabriel Daniel *Fahrenheit* (1686–1736).]

fa•ience also **fa•ïence** (fī-äns′, -äɴs′, fā-) ▶ *n.* Earthenware decorated with colorful opaque glazes. [After *Faenza*, Italy.]

faience
c. 1750 Austrian jar

fail (fāl) ▶ *v.* **1.** To be deficient or unsuccessful. **2.** To give or receive an unacceptable academic grade. **3.** To decline, weaken, or cease to function. **4.** To disappoint or forsake. **5.** To omit or neglect: *failed to appear.* **6.** To become bankrupt. ▶ *n.* Failure. —***idiom:* without fail** Absolutely. [ME *failen* < VLat. **fallīre*, deceive.]

fail•ing (fā′lĭng) ▶ *n.* A minor fault; shortcoming. ▶ *prep.* In the absence of.

faille (fīl, fāl) ▶ *n.* A ribbed woven fabric of silk, cotton, or rayon. [Fr.]

fail-safe (fāl′sāf′) ▶ *adj.* **1.** Compensating automatically for a failure, as of a mechanical system. **2.** Containing built-in safeguards, as against military attack.

fail•ure (fāl′yər) ▶ *n.* **1.** The act, condition, or fact of failing. **2.** One that fails. **3.** The act or fact of becoming bankrupt.

fain (fān) ▶ *adv.* Happily; gladly. ▶ *adj. Archaic* **1.** Willing; glad. **2.** Obliged or required. [< OE *fægen*, glad.]

faint (fānt) ▶ *adj.* **-er, -est 1.** Lacking strength or vigor; feeble. **2a.** Lacking brightness; dim. **b.** Indistinct. **3.** Suddenly dizzy and weak. ▶ *n.* An abrupt, usu. brief loss of consciousness; blackout. ▶ *v.* To fall into a faint. [< OFr., p.part. of *feindre*, feign.] —**faint′ly** *adv.* —**faint′ness** *n.*

faint-hearted (fānt′här′tĭd) ▶ *adj.* Lacking conviction or courage; timid. —**faint′-heart′ed•ly** *adv.* —**faint′-heart′ed•ness** *n.*

fair¹ (fâr) ▶ *adj.* **-er, -est 1.** Beautiful; lovely. **2.** Light in color: *fair hair.* **3.** Clear and sunny. **4.** Unblemished; clean. **5.** Promising; favorable. **6.** Just; equitable. **7.** Consistent with rules; permissible. **8.** Moderately good; average. ▶ *adv.* **1.** In a fair manner; properly. **2.** Directly; straight. —***idiom:* fair and square** Just and honest. [ME < OE *fæger.*] —**fair′ness** *n.*

fair² (fâr) ▶ *n.* **1.** A gathering for buying and selling goods; market. **2.** An exhibition, as of farm products or handicrafts, usu. judged competitively. **3.** A fund-raising event, as for a charity. [< Lat. *fēriae*, holidays.]

Fair•banks (fâr′băngks′) A city of central AK NNE of Anchorage. Pop. 30,843.

fair•ground (fâr′ground′) ▶ *n.* Open land where fairs are held.

fair•ly (fâr′lē) ▶ *adv.* **1.** In a fair or just manner; equitably. **2.** Actually; fully. **3.** Moderately; rather.

fair-mind•ed (fâr′mīn′dĭd) ▶ *adj.* Just and impartial. —**fair′-mind′ed•ness** *n.*

fair shake ▶ *n. Informal* A fair chance, as at achieving success.

fair-trade (fâr′trād′) ▶ *adj.* Of or being an agreement under which retailers sell a given item at no less than a minimum price set by the manufacturer.

fair•way (fâr′wā′) ▶ *n.* The mowed part of a golf course from the tee to the green.

fair-weath•er (fâr′wĕth′ər) ▶ *adj.* Dependable only in good times: *fair-weather friends.*

fair•y (fâr′ē) ▶ *n., pl.* **-ies.** A tiny imaginary being depicted as possessing magical powers. [< OFr. *faerie* < VLat. *Fāta*, goddess of fate.]

fair•y•land (fâr′ē-lănd′) ▶ *n.* **1.** The imaginary land of the fairies. **2.** A charming place.

fairy tale ▶ *n.* **1.** A fanciful tale of legendary deeds and creatures, usu. intended for children. **2.** A fanciful story or explanation. —**fair′y-tale′** *adj.*

Fai•sal (fī′səl). Faisal ibn Abdel Aziz al-Saud. 1906?–75. King of Saudi Arabia (1964–75); assassinated.

Fai•sa•la•bad (fī′sä-lə-bäd′). Formerly **Lyall-**

pur. A city of NE Pakistan W of Lahore. Pop. 1,104,209.

fait ac•com•pli (fā′tä-kôN-plē′, fĕt′ä-) ▸*n., pl.* **faits ac•com•plis** (fā′tä-kôN-plē′, -plēz′, fĕt′ä-). An accomplished deed or fact. [Fr.]

faith (fāth) ▸*n.* **1.** Confident belief or trust in a person, idea, or thing. See Syns at **belief. 2.** Loyalty; allegiance. **3.** often **Faith** *Christianity* Secure belief in God and acceptance of God's will. **4.** A religion. [< Lat. *fidēs.*] —**faith′less** *adj.* —**faith′less•ness** *n.*

faith•ful (fāth′fəl) ▸*adj.* **1.** Adhering firmly and devotedly; loyal. **2.** Worthy of trust; reliable. **3.** Accurate; true. ▸*n., pl.* **-ful** or **-fuls 1.** The practicing members of a religious faith. **2.** An adherent of a cause: *the party faithful.* —**faith′ful•ly** *adv.* —**faith′ful•ness** *n.*

fa•ji•ta (fə-hē′tə) ▸*n.* often **fajitas** A dish of grilled strips of marinated meat served in a tortilla, usu. with spicy condiments. [Am.Sp.]

fake (fāk) ▸*adj.* Not genuine; fraudulent. ▸*n.* One that is not authentic or genuine; a counterfeit, impostor, or sham. ▸*v.* **faked, fak•ing 1.** To contrive and present as genuine; counterfeit. **2.** To pretend; feign. [?] —**fak′er** *n.* —**fak′er•y** *n.*

fa•kir (fə-kîr′, fä-, fă-) ▸*n.* A Muslim or Hindu religious mendicant, esp. one who performs feats of magic or endurance. [Ar. *faqīr.*]

fa•la•fel or **fe•la•fel** (fə-lä′fəl) ▸*n.* Ground spiced chickpeas shaped into balls and fried. [Ar. *falāfil*, pl. of *filfil*, pepper.]

fal•con (făl′kən, fôl′-, fô′kən) ▸*n.* Any of various swift hawklike birds of prey with long pointed wings. [< LLat. *falcō.*]

fal•con•ry (făl′kən-rē, fôl′-, fô′kən-) ▸*n.* **1.** Hunting of small game with falcons. **2.** The art of training falcons for hunting. —**fal′con•er** *n.*

Falk•land Islands (fôk′lənd, fôlk′-) A group of islands in the S Atlantic E of the Strait of Magellan.

fall (fôl) ▸*v.* **fell** (fĕl), **fall•en** (fô′lən), **fall•ing 1.** To drop freely under the influence of gravity. **2.** To move oneself to a lower position. **3.** To be killed or severely wounded. **4.** To hang down: *Her hair fell in ringlets.* **5.** To assume an expression of disappointment: *His face fell.* **6.** To be conquered or overthrown. **7.** To slope downward. **8.** To lessen in amount or degree. **9.** To pass into a particular state or condition: *We fell silent.* **10.** To decline in rank, status, or importance. **11.** To err or sin. **12.** To come as if by descending: *A hush fell on the crowd.* **13.** To occur at a specified time or place. **14.** To be allotted: *The task fell to me.* **15.** To be within the range of something. **16.** To come to rest by chance: *My gaze fell on the letter.* —***phrasal verbs:*** **fall back** To retreat. **fall behind** To fail to keep up with. **fall for 1.** To become infatuated with. **2.** To be deceived or swindled by. **fall in** To take one's place in a military formation. **fall on** To attack suddenly. **fall out** To quarrel. **fall through** To fail or miscarry. **fall to** To begin energetically. **fall back on** To rely on. ▸*n.* **1.** The act or an instance of falling. **2.** Something that has fallen: *a fall of hail.* **3a.** An amount that has fallen: *a light fall of rain.* **b.** The distance that something falls. **4.** Autumn. **5. falls** *(takes sing. or pl. v.)* A waterfall. **6.** A hanging article of dress, as a veil or hairpiece. **7.** An overthrow or collapse: *the fall of a government.* **8.** A decline or reduction. **9.** A moral lapse. —***idioms:*** **fall back on** To rely on. **fall flat** To fail miserably. **fall in with 1.** To agree with. **2.** To associate with. **fall short** To fail to reach or attain. [< OE *feallan.*]

fal•la•cious (fə-lā′shəs) ▸*adj.* **1.** Containing or based on a fallacy. **2.** Tending to mislead; deceptive. —**fal•la′cious•ly** *adv.*

fal•la•cy (făl′ə-sē) ▸*n., pl.* **-cies 1.** A false idea or notion. **2.** Incorrectness of reasoning or belief. [< Lat. *fallācia*, deceit.]

fall•back (fôl′băk′) ▸*n.* A last resort or retreat.

fall guy ▸*n. Slang* **1.** A scapegoat. **2.** A dupe.

fal•li•ble (făl′ə-bəl) ▸*adj.* Capable of making an error. [< Lat. *fallere*, deceive.] —**fal′li•bil′i•ty** *n.* —**fal′li•bly** *adv.*

fall•ing-out (fô′lĭng-out′) ▸*n., pl.* **fall•ings-out** or **fall•ing-outs.** A quarrel.

fall•ing star (fô′lĭng) ▸*n.* See **meteor.**

fal•lo•pi•an tube also **Fal•lo•pi•an tube** (fə-lō′pē-ən) ▸*n.* Either of a pair of slender ducts through which ova pass from the ovaries to the uterus in the female reproductive system of humans and higher mammals. [After Gabriele *Fallopio* (1523–62).]

fall•out (fôl′out′) ▸*n.* **1a.** The slow descent of minute particles of radioactive debris in the atmosphere after a nuclear explosion. **b.** These particles. **2.** An incidental result or side effect: *political fallout.*

fal•low (făl′ō) ▸*adj.* **1.** Plowed but left unseeded during a growing season. **2.** Inactive. [< OE *fealh*, fallow land.]

fallow deer ▸*n.* A small Eurasian deer having broad flat antlers in the male. [< OE *fealu*, reddish yellow.]

false (fôls) ▸*adj.* **fals•er, fals•est 1.** Contrary to fact or truth. **2.** Unfaithful or disloyal. **3.** Not real; artificial. **4.** *Mus.* Of incorrect pitch. [< Lat. *falsus*, p.part. of *fallere*, deceive.] —**false′ly** *adv.* —**false′ness** *n.*

false alarm ▸*n.* **1.** An emergency alarm set off unnecessarily. **2.** A groundless warning.

false arrest ▸*n.* Unlawful arrest.

false-heart•ed (fôls′här′tĭd) ▸*adj.* Deceitful.

false•hood (fôls′ho͝od′) ▸*n.* **1.** A lie. **2.** The practice of lying. **3.** Lack of conformity to truth or fact; inaccuracy.

fal•set•to (fôl-sĕt′ō) ▸*n., pl.* **-tos.** A male voice in an upper register beyond its normal range. [Ital.] —**fal•set′to** *adv.*

fal•si•fy (fôl′sə-fī′) ▸*v.* **-fied, -fy•ing 1.** To state untruthfully. **2.** To alter (e.g., a document) so as to deceive. **3.** To counterfeit; forge. [< LLat. *falsificāre.*] —**fal′si•fi•ca′tion** *n.* —**fal′si•fi′er** *n.*

fal•si•ty (fôl′sĭ-tē) ▸*n., pl.* **-ties 1.** The quality or condition of being false. **2.** A lie.

fal•ter (fôl′tər) ▸*v.* **1.** To weaken or be unsteady in purpose or action; waver. **2.** To stammer. **3.** To stumble. ▸*n.* **1.** Unsteadiness in speech or action. **2.** A faltering sound. [ME *falteren*, stagger.] —**fal′ter•er** *n.* —**fal′ter•ing•ly** *adv.*

fame (fām) ▸*n.* Great reputation and recognition; renown. [< Lat. *fāma.*] —**famed** *adj.*

fa•mil•iar (fə-mĭl′yər) ▸*adj.* **1.** Often encountered; common. **2.** Having knowledge of something. **3.** Intimate. **4.** Unduly forward; bold. ▸*n.* A close friend or associate. [< Lat. *familiāris*, of the family.] —**fa•mil′iar•ly** *adv.*

fa•mil•iar•i•ty (fə-mĭl′yăr′ĭ-tē, -mĭl′ē-ăr′-)

►*n.*, *pl.* **-ties 1.** Considerable acquaintance with or knowledge of something. **2.** Close friendship; intimacy. **3.** An excessively familiar act; an impropriety.

fa•mil•iar•ize (fə-mĭl′yə-rīz′) ►*v.* **-ized, -iz•ing.** To make (oneself or another) acquainted with. —**fa•mil′iar•i•za′tion** *n.*

fam•i•ly (făm′ə-lē, făm′lē) ►*n.*, *pl.* **-lies 1.** Parents and their children. **2.** The members of one household. **3.** A group of persons related by blood or marriage. See Usage Note at **collective noun. 4.** A group of like things; class. **5.** *Biol.* The category ranking below an order and above a genus in the hierarchy of taxonomic classification. **6.** *Ling.* A group of languages descended from the same parent language. [< Lat. *familia*, household.] —**fa•mil′ial** (fə-mĭl′yəl) *adj.*

family leave ►*n.* A usu. unpaid absence from work granted for taking care of a family member, such as a baby or sick parent.

family name ►*n.* See **surname.**

family planning ►*n.* The regulation of the number and spacing of children in a family through birth-control techniques.

family tree ►*n.* A genealogical diagram of a family's ancestry.

fam•ine (făm′ĭn) ►*n.* **1.** A drastic, wide-reaching food shortage. **2.** A drastic lack; dearth. [< OFr. < Lat. *famēs*, hunger.]

fam•ish (făm′ĭsh) ►*v.* To starve. [< VLat. **affamāre*, be hungry.] —**fam′ished** *adj.*

fa•mous (fā′məs) ►*adj.* **1.** Well or widely known. See Syns at **noted. 2.** *Informal* First-rate; excellent. [< Lat. *fāmōsus* < *fāma*, fame.] —**fa′mous•ly** *adv.*

fan[1] (făn) ►*n.* **1.** A hand-held, usu. wedge-shaped device that is waved to create a cool breeze. **2.** An electrical device that rotates rigid vanes in order to move air, as for cooling. **3.** Something resembling an open hand-held fan. ►*v.* **fanned, fan•ning 1.** To direct a current of air upon, esp. in order to cool. **2.** To stir up: *fanned resentment.* **3.** *Baseball* To strike out. **4.** To spread: *fanned out on their search.* [< Lat. *vannus.*]

fan[2] (făn) ►*n.* *Informal* An ardent devotee; enthusiast. [Short for FANATIC.]

fa•nat•ic (fə-năt′ĭk) ►*n.* One who is fanatical. ►*adj.* Fanatical. [< Lat. *fānum*, temple.]

fa•nat•i•cal (fə-năt′ĭ-kəl) ►*adj.* Possessed with extreme zeal or enthusiasm. —**fa•nat′i•cal•ly** *adv.* —**fa•nat′i•cism** *n.*

fan•ci•er (făn′sē-ər) ►*n.* One who has a special enthusiasm or interest, as for raising a specific plant or animal.

fan•ci•ful (făn′sĭ-fəl) ►*adj.* **1.** Created in the fancy; imaginary: *a fanciful story.* **2.** Tending to indulge in fancy. **3.** Quaint or whimsical in design. —**fan′ci•ful•ly** *adv.*

fan•cy (făn′sē) ►*n.*, *pl.* **-cies 1.** Imagination, esp. of a whimsical or fantastic nature. **2.** A notion or whim. **3.** A capricious liking or inclination. ►*adj.* **-ci•er, -ci•est 1a.** Ingeniously or intricately designed. **b.** Stylish: *a fancy outfit.* **2.** Whimsical. **3.** Done with great technical skill: *fancy footwork.* **4.** Of superior grade: *fancy preserves.* ►*v.* **-cied, -cy•ing 1.** To imagine. **2.** To be fond of. **3.** To suppose; guess. [< ME *fantsy*, FANTASY.] —**fan′ci•ly** *adv.* —**fan′ci•ness** *n.*

fancy dress ►*n.* A masquerade costume.

fan•cy-free (făn′sē-frē′) ►*adj.* **1.** Having no restrictions; carefree. **2.** Not in love; unattached.

fan•cy•work (făn′sē-wûrk′) ►*n.* Decorative needlework, such as embroidery.

fan•dan•go (făn-dăng′gō) ►*n.*, *pl.* **-gos.** A lively Spanish or Latin dance. [Sp.]

fan•fare (făn′fâr′) ►*n.* **1.** A flourish of trumpets. **2.** A spectacular public display. [Fr.]

fang (făng) ►*n.* A long pointed tooth, especially: **a.** A hollow, poison-injecting tooth of a venomous snake. **b.** A canine tooth of a carnivorous animal. [< OE, what is taken.] —**fanged** *adj.*

fan•jet also **fan-jet** (făn′jĕt′) ►*n.* An aircraft powered by a jet engine with a ducted fan that draws in extra air.

fan•light (făn′līt′) ►*n.* A half-circle window, often with sash bars arranged like the ribs of a fan.

fan•ny (făn′ē) ►*n.*, *pl.* **-nies.** *Slang* The buttocks.

fan•tail (făn′tāl′) ►*n.* **1.** A fanlike tail or end. **2.** The stern overhang of a ship. —**fan′tailed′** *adj.*

fan•ta•sia (făn-tā′zhə, -zhē-ə, făn′tə-zē′ə) ►*n.* *Mus.* A freeform composition. [Ital.]

fan•ta•size (făn′tə-sīz′) ►*v.* **-sized, -siz•ing 1.** To indulge in fantasies. **2.** To imagine.

fan•tas•tic (făn-tăs′tĭk) also **fan•tas•ti•cal** (-tĭ-kəl) ►*adj.* **1.** Strange in conception or appearance. **2.** Bizarre, as in form or appearance; grotesque. **3.** Unreal or illusory. **4.** Superb. [< Gk. *phantastikos*, creating mental images.] —**fan•tas′ti•cal•ly** *adv.*

fan•ta•sy (făn′tə-sē, -zē) ►*n.*, *pl.* **-sies 1.** The creative imagination. **2.** A product of the fancy; illusion. **3.** A delusion. **4.** Fiction marked by highly fanciful elements. **5.** A daydream. **6.** *Mus.* See **fantasia.** [< Gk. *phantasia*, appearance.] —**fan′ta•sy** *v.*

fan•zine (făn′zēn) ►*n.* An amateur-produced fan magazine. [FAN[2] + (MAGA)ZINE.]

FAQ (făk) ►*n.* A list of frequently asked questions and their answers. [*f(requently) a(sked) q(uestions).*]

far (fär) ►*adv.* **far•ther** (fär′*th*ər), **far•thest** (fär′*th*ĭst) or **fur•ther** (fûr′*th*ər), **fur•thest** (fûr′*th*ĭst) **1.** To, from, or at considerable distance. **2.** To or at a specific distance, degree, or position. **3.** To a considerable degree; much: *felt far better.* ►*adj.* **farther, farthest** or **further, furthest 1.** Being at considerable distance: *a far country.* **2.** More distant or remote: *the far corner.* **3.** Extensive or lengthy: *a far trek.* —***idioms:*** **as far as** To the extent that. **by far** To the most extreme degree. **far and away** By a great margin. **far and wide** Everywhere. **far cry** A long way. **far from** Not at all: *far from satisfied.* **so far** Up to now. [< OE *feor*, distant.]

far•ad (făr′əd, -ăd′) ►*n.* The unit of capacitance equal to that of a capacitor that acquires a charge of 1 coulomb when a potential difference of 1 volt is applied. [After Michael *Faraday* (1791–1867).]

far•a•way (fär′ə-wā′) ►*adj.* **1.** Very distant; remote. **2.** Abstracted; dreamy.

farce (färs) ►*n.* **1.** A humorous play having a highly improbable plot and exaggerated characters. **2.** A ludicrous, empty show; mockery. [< Lat. *farcīre*, to stuff.] —**far′ci•cal** *adj.* —**far′ci•cal•ly** *adv.*

fare (fâr) ▸*v.* **fared, far•ing 1.** To get along. **2.** To travel; go. ▸*n.* **1.** A transportation charge. **2.** A passenger transported for a fee. **3.** Food and drink. [< OE *faran.*] —**far′er** *n.*

Far East. The countries and regions of E and SE Asia, esp. China, Japan, North Korea, South Korea, Taiwan, and Mongolia. —**Far Eastern** *adj.*

fare•well (fâr-wĕl′) ▸*interj.* Used to express an acknowledgment of parting. ▸*n.* **1.** A goodbye. **2.** A leave-taking.

far-fetched (fär′fĕcht′) ▸*adj.* Implausible.

far-flung (fär′flŭng′) ▸*adj.* **1.** Remote; distant. **2.** Widely distributed; wide-ranging.

Far•go (fär′gō) A city of E ND on the Red R. E of Bismarck. Pop. 74,111.

fa•ri•na (fə-rē′nə) ▸*n.* Fine meal, as of cereal grain, often used as a cooked cereal or in puddings. [< Lat. *farīna.*]

far•i•na•ceous (făr′ə-nā′shəs) ▸*adj.* **1.** Made from or containing starch. **2.** Mealy or powdery in texture.

farm (färm) ▸*n.* **1.** A tract of land on which crops or animals are raised. **2.** An area of water used for raising aquatic animals: *a trout farm.* ▸*v.* **1.** To raise crops or livestock. **2.** To use (land) for this purpose. —***phrasal verb:* farm out** To send out (work) to be done elsewhere. [< OFr. *ferme*, leased land.] —**farm′er** *n.* —**farm′ing** *n.*

farm hand ▸*n.* A hired farm laborer.

farm•house (färm′hous′) ▸*n.* A dwelling on a farm.

farm•land (färm′lănd′, -lənd) ▸*n.* An expanse of land suitable or used for farming.

farm•stead (färm′stĕd′) ▸*n.* A farm, including its land and buildings.

farm•yard (färm′yärd′) ▸*n.* An area surrounded by or adjacent to farm buildings.

far•o (fâr′ō) ▸*n.* A card game in which the players bet on the top card of the dealer's pack. [Alteration of PHARAOH.]

Far•oe Islands (fâr′ō) See **Faeroe Islands.**

far-off (fär′ôf′, -ŏf′) ▸*adj.* Remote in space or time; distant.

Fa•rouk I (fə-ro͞ok′). 1920–65. King of Egypt (1936–52).

far-out (fär′out′) ▸*adj. Slang* Extremely unconventional.

far•ra•go (fə-rä′gō, -rā′-) ▸*n., pl.* **-goes.** An assortment or medley; conglomeration. [Lat. *farrāgō.*]

Far•ra•gut (făr′ə-gət), **David Glasgow.** 1801–70. Amer. naval commander.

far-reach•ing (fär′rē′chĭng) ▸*adj.* Having a wide range, influence, or effect.

Far•rell (făr′əl), **James Thomas.** 1904–79. Amer. writer.

far•row (făr′ō) ▸*n.* A litter of pigs. ▸*v.* To give birth to a farrow. [< OE *fearh*, pig.]

far•see•ing (fär′sē′ĭng) ▸*adj.* Foresighted.

far•sight•ed or **far-sight•ed** (fär′sī′tĭd) ▸*adj.* **1.** Able to see distant objects better than objects at close range. **2.** Prudent; foresighted. —**far′sight′ed•ness** *n.*

far•ther (fär′*th*ər) ▸*adv.* Comp. of **far. 1.** To or at a more distant point. **2.** To or at a more advanced point or stage. **3.** To a greater extent or degree. ▸*adj.* Comp. of **far.** More distant; remoter. [ME, var. of *further*, FURTHER.]

far•ther•most (fär′*th*ər-mōst′) ▸*adj.* Most distant; farthest.

far•thest (fär′*th*ĭst) ▸*adj.* Superl. of **far.** Most remote or distant. ▸*adv.* Superl. of **far. 1.** To or at the most distant or remote point. **2.** To or at the most advanced point or stage. **3.** By the greatest extent or degree. [ME *ferthest.*]

far•thing (fär′*th*ĭng) ▸*n.* **1.** A coin formerly used in Great Britain worth one fourth of a penny. **2.** Something of little value. [< OE *fēorthung.*]

far•thin•gale (fär′*th*ĭn-gāl′, -*th*ĭng-) ▸*n.* A support, such as a hoop, worn beneath a skirt by European women in the 16th and 17th cent. [< OSpan. *verdugado.*]

fas•ci•cle (făs′ĭ-kəl) ▸*n.* **1.** A small bundle. **2.** One of the parts of a book published in separate sections. [Lat. *fasciculus.*] —**fas′ci•cled** *adj.*

fas•ci•nate (făs′ə-nāt′) ▸*v.* **-nat•ed, -nat•ing 1.** To hold an intense interest or attraction for. See Syns at **charm. 2.** To hold motionless; spellbind. [< Lat. *fascinum*, evil spell.] —**fas′ci•na′tion** *n.* —**fas′ci•na′tor** *n.*

fas•cism (făsh′ĭz′əm) ▸*n.* **1.** often **Fascism a.** Totalitarianism marked by right-wing dictatorship and bellicose nationalism. **b.** A political philosophy or movement based on or advocating such a system of government. **2.** Oppressive, dictatorial control. [< Ital. *fascio*, group.] —**fas′cist** *adj. & n.* —**fas•cis′tic** (fə-shĭs′tĭk) *adj.*

fash•ion (făsh′ən) ▸*n.* **1.** The prevailing style or custom, as in dress. **2.** Manner; way. **3.** Kind; sort. ▸*v.* **1.** To give shape or form to; make. **2.** To adapt, as to a purpose or an occasion. —***idiom:* after a fashion** To a limited extent. [< Lat. *factiō*, a making.] —**fash′ion•er** *n.*

fash•ion•a•ble (făsh′ə-nə-bəl) ▸*adj.* **1.** In the current style; stylish. **2.** Associated with persons of fashion. —**fash′ion•a•ble•ness** *n.* —**fash′ion•a•bly** *adv.*

Syns: *fashionable, chic, dashing, in, modish, posh, sharp, smart, stylish, swank, trendy* ***Ant:*** *unfashionable* **adj.**

fast[1] (făst) ▸*adj.* **-er, -est 1.** Acting or moving quickly; swift. **2.** Accomplished in little time. **3.** Indicating a time ahead of the actual time: *The clock is fast.* **4.** Adapted to or suitable for speed: *a fast running track.* **5.** Designed for a short exposure time: *fast film.* **6.** Flouting moral standards; wild. **7.** Resistant: *fast colors.* **8.** Firmly fixed or fastened. **9.** Secure. **10.** Firm in loyalty: *fast friends.* **11.** Deep; sound: *in a fast sleep.* ▸*adv.* **1.** Securely; tightly. **2.** Deeply: *fast asleep.* **3.** Rapidly; quickly. **4.** In quick succession: *New ideas followed fast.* **5.** In a dissipated, immoderate way: *living fast.* [< OE *fæst*, firm, fixed.]

fast[2] (făst) ▸*v.* To abstain from food, esp. as a religious discipline. ▸*n.* The act or a period of abstention from food. [< OE *fæstan.*]

fast•back (făst′băk′) ▸*n.* An automobile designed with a curving downward slope from roof to rear.

fas•ten (făs′ən) ▸*v.* **1.** To attach or become attached to something else; join; connect. **2.** To make fast or secure; close. **3.** To fix or direct steadily. [< OE *fæstnian.*] —**fas′ten•er** *n.* —**fas′ten•ing** *n.*

Syns: *fasten, anchor, fix, moor, secure* ***Ant:*** *unfasten* **v.**

fast food ▸*n.* Inexpensive food, such as hamburgers and fried chicken, prepared and served quickly. —**fast′-food′** *adj.*

fast-for•ward (făst-fôr′wərd) ►*n.* A function on a tape recorder or player that permits rapid advancement of the tape. —**fast-for′ward** *v.*

fas•tid•i•ous (fă-stĭd′ē-əs, fə-) ►*adj.* **1.** Attentive to detail. **2.** Difficult to please; exacting. **3.** Scrupulous, esp. in matters of taste or propriety. [< Lat. *fastīdium*, squeamishness.] —**fas•tid′i•ous•ness** *n.*

fast•ness (făst′nĭs) ►*n.* **1.** Rapidity; swiftness. **2.** A secure or fortified place.

fast-talk (făst′tôk′) ►*v. Informal* To persuade, mislead, or obtain with smooth talk. —**fast′-talk′er** *n.*

fast track ►*n. Informal* The quickest and most direct route to achievement of a goal. —**fast′-track′** *adj.* —**fast track′er** *n.*

fat (făt) ►*n.* **1a.** Any of various soft, solid, or semisolid organic compounds occurring widely in animal and plant tissue. **b.** Organic tissue containing such substances. **c.** A solidified animal or vegetable oil. **2.** Obesity; corpulence. **3.** The best or richest part: *living off the fat of the land.* **4.** Unnecessary excess. ►*adj.* **fat•ter, fat•test 1.** Having much flesh. **2.** Full of fat or oil; greasy. **3.** Abounding in desirable elements. **4.** Fertile or productive; rich. **5.** Having an abundance; well-stocked: *a fat larder.* **6a.** Lucrative or rewarding: *a fat promotion.* **b.** Prosperous; wealthy: *grew fat on profits.* **7.** Thick; large: *a fat book.* —***idiom:*** **fat chance** *Slang* Little or no chance. [< OE *fætt*, fatted.] —**fat′ly** *adv.* —**fat′ness** *n.* —**fat′ti•ness** *n.* —**fat′ty** *adj.*

fa•tal (fāt′l) ►*adj.* **1.** Causing or capable of causing death. **2.** Causing destruction. **3.** Of decisive importance; fateful. [< Lat. *fātālis* < *fātum*, FATE.] —**fa′tal•ly** *adv.*

fa•tal•ism (fāt′l-ĭz′əm) ►*n.* The doctrine that all events are determined by fate and are therefore unalterable. —**fa′tal•ist** *n.* —**fa′tal•is′tic** *adj.* —**fa′tal•is′ti•cal•ly** *adv.*

fa•tal•i•ty (fā-tăl′ĭ-tē, fə-) ►*n., pl.* **-ties.** A death resulting from an accident or disaster.

fat•back (făt′băk′) ►*n.* Salt-cured fat from the upper part of a side of pork.

fat cat ►*n. Slang* **1.** A wealthy and privileged person. **2.** A wealthy contributor to a political campaign.

fate (fāt) ►*n.* **1.** The supposed force or power that determines events. **2.** A final result; outcome. **3.** Unfavorable destiny; doom. **4. Fates** *Gk. & Rom. Myth.* The three goddesses, Clotho, Lachesis, and Atropos, who control human destiny. [< Lat. *fātum* < p.part. of *fārī*, speak.]

fat•ed (fā′tĭd) ►*adj.* **1.** Predetermined. **2.** Doomed.

fate•ful (fāt′fəl) ►*adj.* **1.** Being of great consequence; momentous. **2.** Controlled by or as if by fate. **3.** Bringing death or disaster; fatal. **4.** Ominously prophetic; portentous. —**fate′ful•ly** *adv.* —**fate′ful•ness** *n.*

fath or **fath.** ►*abbr.* fathom

fat•head (făt′hĕd′) ►*n. Slang* A stupid person. —**fat′head′ed** *adj.*

fa•ther (fä′*th*ər) ►*n.* **1.** A man who begets or raises a child. **2.** A male ancestor. **3. Father** God. **4.** A title used for a male priest in some Christian churches. ►*v.* To beget; sire. [< OE *fæder*.]—**fa′ther•hood′** *n.* —**fa′ther•li•ness** *n.* —**fa′ther•ly** *adj.*

father figure ►*n.* An older man who elicits the emotions usu. reserved for a father.

fa•ther-in-law (fä′*th*ər-ĭn-lô′) ►*n., pl.* **fa•thers-in-law** (-ərz-). The father of one's spouse.

fa•ther•land (fä′*th*ər-lănd′) ►*n.* One's native land.

fa•ther•less (fä′*th*ər-lĭs) ►*adj.* **1.** Having no living father. **2.** Having no known father. —**fa′ther•less•ness** *n.*

fath•om (făth′əm) ►*n., pl.* **-om** or **-oms.** A unit of length equal to 6 ft (1.83 m), used principally in the measurement of marine depths. ►*v.* **1.** To determine the depth of; sound. **2.** To comprehend. [< OE *fæthm*, outstretched arms.] —**fath′om•a•ble** *adj.*

fath•om•less (făth′əm-lĭs) ►*adj.* **1.** Too deep to be fathomed or measured. **2.** Too obscure or complicated to be understood.

fa•tigue (fə-tēg′) ►*n.* **1.** Physical or mental weariness resulting from exertion. **2. fatigues** Clothing worn by military personnel for labor or field duty. ►*v.* **-tigued, -tigu•ing.** To tire out; weary. [< Lat. *fatīgāre*, to fatigue.] —**fat′i•ga•ble** (făt′ĭ-gə-bəl) *adj.*

fat•ten (făt′n) ►*v.* To make or become plump or fat. —**fat′ten•er** *n.*

fatty acid ►*n.* Any of a large group of organic acids, esp. those found in animal and vegetable fats and oils, having the general formula $C_nH_{2n+1}COOH$.

fa•tu•i•ty (fə-to͞o′ĭ-tē, -tyo͞o′-) ►*n.* Smug stupidity; utter foolishness.

fat•u•ous (făch′o͞o-əs) ►*adj.* Smugly and unconsciously foolish. [< Lat. *fatuus*.] —**fat′u•ous•ly** *adv.* —**fat′u•ous•ness** *n.*

fat•wa (făt′wä′) ►*n.* A ruling issued by an Islamic scholar. [Ar. *fatwā*.]

fau•cet (fô′sĭt) ►*n.* A device for regulating the flow of a liquid, as from a pipe. See Regional Note at **andiron.** [< OFr. *fausser*, break in.]

Faulk•ner (fôk′nər), **William.** 1897–1962. Amer. writer; 1949 Nobel. —**Faulk•ner′i•an** (-nîr′ē-ən) *adj.*

fault (fôlt) ►*n.* **1.** A character weakness, esp. a minor one. **2.** A mistake; error. **3.** Responsibility for a mistake or offense. **4.** *Geol.* A fracture in the continuity of a rock formation caused by a shifting or dislodging of the earth's crust, in which adjacent surfaces are differentially displaced parallel to the plane of fracture. **5.** *Sports* A bad service, as in tennis. ►*v.* **1.** To find error or defect in; criticize or blame. **2.** *Geol.* To produce a fault in; fracture. **3.** To commit a mistake or an error. —***idioms:*** **at fault** Guilty. **find fault** To criticize. **to a**

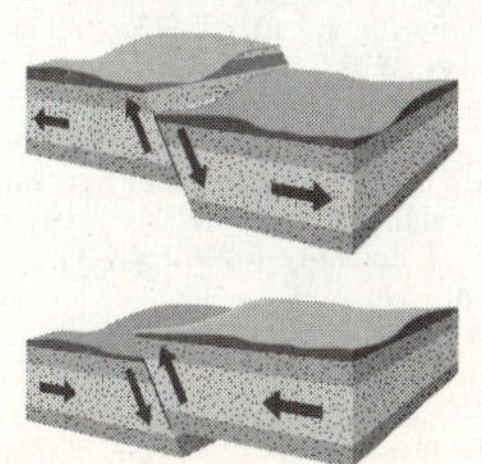

fault
top to bottom: normal and reverse faults

fault To an excessive degree. [< Lat. *fallere*, to deceive, fail.] —**fault'i•ly** *adv.* —**fault'i•ness** *n.* —**fault'y** *adj.*

fault•find•ing (fôlt'fīn'dĭng) ►*n.* Petty or nagging criticism; carping. ►*adj.* Disposed to find fault; critical. —**fault'find'er** *n.*

fault•less (fôlt'lĭs) ►*adj.* Being without fault. See Syns at **perfect.** —**fault'less•ly** *adv.* —**fault'less•ness** *n.*

faun (fôn) ►*n. Rom. Myth.* Any of a group of rural deities represented as part man and part goat. [< Lat. *Faunus*, Roman god of nature.]

fau•na (fô'nə) ►*n., pl.* **-nas** or **-nae** (-nē'). Animals, esp. of a region or period. [< Lat. *Fauna*, Roman goddess of nature.] —**fau'nal** *adj.* —**fau'nal•ly** *adv.*

Faust (foust) also **Faus•tus** (fou'stəs, fô'-) ►*n.* A magician and alchemist in German legend who sells his soul to the devil for power and knowledge. —**Faust'i•an** (fou'stē-ən) *adj.*

fau•vism (fō'vĭz'əm) ►*n.* An early 20th-cent. movement in painting marked by the use of bold, often distorted forms and vivid colors. [Fr. *fauvisme* < *fauve*, wild animal.] —**fau'vist** *adj.*

faux (fō) ►*adj.* Artificial; fake. *faux pearls.* [Fr.]

faux pas (fō pä') ►*n., pl.* **faux pas** (fō päz'). A social blunder. [Fr.]

fa•va bean (fä'və) ►*n.* See **broad bean.** [Ital. *fava* < Lat. *faba*, broad bean.]

fa•vor (fā'vər) ►*n.* **1.** A gracious, friendly, or obliging act that is freely granted. **2a.** Friendly regard; approval or support. **b.** A state of being held in such regard. **3.** Unfair partiality; favoritism. **4a.** A privilege or concession. **b. favors** Sexual privileges, esp. as granted by a woman. **5.** A small gift given to each guest at a party. **6.** Advantage; benefit. ►*v.* **1.** To oblige. See Syns at **oblige. 2.** To treat or regard with approval or support. **3.** To be partial to. **4.** To make easier; facilitate. **5.** To be gentle with. **6.** *Regional* To resemble: *She favors her father.* —***idiom:* in favor of 1.** In support of. **2.** To the advantage of. [< Lat.]

fa•vor•a•ble (fā'vər-ə-bəl, fāv'rə-) ►*adj.* **1.** Advantageous; helpful: *favorable winds.* **2.** Encouraging; propitious: *a favorable diagnosis.* **3.** Manifesting approval; commendatory: *a favorable report.* **4.** Winning approval; pleasing: *a favorable impression.* **5.** Granting what has been requested. —**fa'vor•a•ble•ness** *n.* —**fa'vor•a•bly** *adv.*

fa•vor•ite (fā'vər-ĭt, fāv'rĭt) ►*n.* **1a.** One enjoying special favor or regard. **b.** One trusted or preferred above others, esp. by a superior. **2.** A competitor regarded as most likely to win. [< OItal. *favorito*, p.part of *favorire*, to favor.] —**fa'vor•ite** *adj.*

favorite son ►*n.* A man favored for nomination as a presidential candidate by his own state delegates at a national political convention.

fa•vor•it•ism (fā'vər-ĭ-tĭz'əm, fāv'rĭ-) ►*n.* A display of partiality toward a favored person or group.

Fawkes (fôks), **Guy.** 1570–1606. English Gunpowder Plot conspirator; executed.

fawn[1] (fôn) ►*v.* **1.** To exhibit affection or attempt to please, as a dog. **2.** To seek favor or attention by obsequiousness. [< OE *fagnian*, rejoice < *fægen*, glad.] —**fawn'er** *n.* —**fawn'ing•ly** *adv.*

Syns: *fawn, bootlick, kowtow, slaver, toady, truckle* **v.**

fawn[2] (fôn) ►*n.* **1.** A young deer. **2.** A grayish yellow brown. [< OFr. *faon*; young animal < Lat. *fētus*, offspring.]

fax (făks) ►*n.* **1.** A fax machine. **2.** A printed page or image transmitted or received by a fax machine. ►*v.* To transmit (printed matter or an image) by electronic means. [Alteration of FACSIMILE.]

fax machine ►*n.* A device that sends and receives printed pages over telephone lines.

fay (fā) ►*n.* A fairy or elf. [< OFr. *fae.* See FAIRY.]

faze (fāz) ►*v.* **fazed, faz•ing.** To disconcert. See Syns at **embarrass.** [< OE *fēsian*, drive away.]

FBI ►*abbr.* Federal Bureau of Investigation

FCC ►*abbr.* Federal Communications Commission

F clef ►*n.* See **bass clef.**

FDA ►*abbr.* Food and Drug Administration

FDIC ►*abbr.* Federal Deposit Insurance Corporation

Fe ► The symbol for the element **iron** 1. [Lat. *ferrum*, iron.]

fe•al•ty (fē'əl-tē) ►*n., pl.* **-ties 1.** The fidelity owed by a vassal to his feudal lord. **2.** Faithfulness; allegiance. [< Lat. *fidēlitās*, faithfulness.]

fear (fîr) ►*n.* **1a.** A feeling of agitation and anxiety caused by the presence or imminence of danger. **b.** A state marked by this feeling. **2.** A feeling of disquiet or apprehension. **3.** Reverence or awe, as toward a deity. **4.** A reason for dread or apprehension. ►*v.* **1.** To be afraid of. **2.** To be apprehensive about. **3.** To be in awe of. **4.** To expect: *I fear you are wrong.* [< OE *fǣr*, danger.] —**fear'er** *n.* —**fear'less** *adj.* —**fear'less•ly** *adv.* —**fear'less•ness** *n.*

fear•ful (fîr'fəl) ►*adj.* **1.** Causing or capable of causing fear; frightening. **2.** Experiencing fear; frightened. See Syns at **afraid. 3.** Timid; nervous. **4.** Indicating anxiety or terror. **5.** Feeling dread or awe. **6.** Extreme, as in degree or extent. —**fear'ful•ly** *adv.* —**fear'ful•ness** *n.*

fear•some (fîr'səm) ►*adj.* **1.** Causing or capable of causing fear. **2.** Fearful; timid. —**fear'some•ly** *adv.* —**fear'some•ness** *n.*

fea•si•ble (fē'zə-bəl) ►*adj.* **1.** Capable of being accomplished or brought about; possible. **2.** Used successfully; suitable. [< OFr. *faire*, *fais-*, do.] —**fea'si•bil'i•ty, fea'si•ble•ness** *n.* —**fea'si•bly** *adv.*

feast (fēst) ►*n.* **1.** A large elaborate meal; banquet. **2.** A religious festival. ►*v.* **1.** To entertain or feed sumptuously. **2.** To eat heartily. **3.** To experience something with gratification or delight. —***idiom:* feast (one's) eyes on** To be delighted by the sight of. [< Lat. *fēstum.*] —**feast'er** *n.*

feat (fēt) ►*n.* A notable act or deed, esp. of courage. [< Lat. *factum.*]

Syns: *feat, achievement, exploit, masterstroke* **n.**

feath•er (fĕ*th*'ər) ►*n.* **1.** One of the light, flat, hollow-shafted growths forming the plumage of birds. **2. feathers** Plumage. **3.** Character, kind, or nature. ►*v.* **1.** To cover, dress, or decorate with or as if with feathers. **2.** To fit (an arrow) with a feather. **3.** To turn (an oar blade) almost horizontal as it is carried back after each stroke. **4.** To alter the pitch of (a propeller) so that the chords of the blades are parallel with the line of flight. —*idioms:* **feather in (one's cap)** An act or deed to one's credit. **feather (one's) nest** To grow wealthy esp. by abusing a position of trust. **in fine feather** In excellent form, health, or humor. [< OE *fether.*] —**feath′er•y** *adj.*

feath•er•bed (fĕ*th*′ər-bĕd′) ▶*v.* **-bed•ded, -bed•ding.** To employ more workers than are needed for a job.

feather bed ▶*n.* A mattress stuffed with feathers.

feath•er•brain (fĕ*th*′ər-brān′) ▶*n.* A flighty or empty-headed person. —**feath′er•brained′** *adj.*

feath•er•edge (fĕ*th*′ər-ĕj′) ▶*n.* A thin fragile edge.

feath•er•stitch (fĕ*th*′ər-stĭch′) ▶*n.* An embroidery stitch that produces a decorative zigzag line. —**feath′er•stitch′** *v.*

feath•er•weight (fĕ*th*′ər-wāt′) ▶*n.* **1.** *Sports* A boxer weighing from 119 to 126 lbs., between a bantamweight and a lightweight. **2.** An insignificant person.

fea•ture (fē′chər) ▶*n.* **1a.** Any of the distinct parts of the face, as the eyes or mouth. **b.** often **features** The overall appearance of the face. **2.** A prominent or distinctive quality or characteristic. **3a.** The main film presentation at a theater. **b.** A full-length film. **4.** A prominent article or story in a newspaper or periodical. **5.** An item offered as an inducement. ▶*v.* **-tured, -tur•ing 1.** To publicize or make prominent. **2.** To include as a prominent part or characteristic. **3.** To draw the features of. [< Lat. *factūra*, a making.]

Feb. ▶*abbr.* February

feb•ri•fuge (fĕb′rə-fyo͞oj′) ▶*n.* A medication that reduces a fever. [Lat. *febris*, fever + *fugāre*, drive away.]

feb•rile (fĕb′rəl, fē′brəl) ▶*adj.* Relating to or having a fever. [< Lat. *febris*, fever.]

Feb•ru•ar•y (fĕb′ro͞o-ĕr′ē, fĕb′yo͞o-) ▶*n.*, *pl.* **-ies.** The 2nd month of the Gregorian calendar. See table at **calendar.** [< Lat. *Februārius.*]

fe•ces (fē′sēz) ▶*pl.n.* Waste eliminated from the bowels; excrement. [< Lat. *faex*, *faec-*, dregs.] —**fe′cal** (fēkəl) *adj.*

feck•less (fĕk′lĭs) ▶*adj.* **1.** Lacking purpose or vitality; ineffective. **2.** Careless; irresponsible. [Sc. *feck*, effect + –LESS.] —**feck′less•ly** *adv.* —**feck′less•ness** *n.*

fe•cund (fē′kənd, fĕk′ənd) ▶*adj.* Capable of producing offspring or vegetation; fruitful. See Syns at **fertile.** [< Lat. *fēcundus.*] —**fe•cun′di•ty** (fĭ-kŭn′dĭ-tē) *n.*

fe•cun•date (fē′kən-dāt′, fĕk′ən-) ▶*v.* **-dat•ed, -dat•ing.** To impregnate; fertilize. —**fe′cun•da′tion** *n.*

fed (fĕd) ▶*v.* P.t. and p.part. of **feed.**

fed. ▶*abbr.* **1.** federal **2.** federation

fed•er•al (fĕd′ər-əl, fĕd′rəl) ▶*adj.* **1.** Relating to or being a form of government in which a union of states recognizes a central authority while retaining certain powers of government. **2. Federal** Of or loyal to the Union cause during the American Civil War. **3.** often **Federal** Of or being the central government of the US. ▶*n.* **1. Federal** A Union soldier or supporter during the American Civil War. **2.** often **Federal** A federal agent or official. [< Lat. *foedus*, *foeder-*, league.] —**fed′er•al•ly** *adv.*

fed•er•al•ism (fĕd′ər-ə-lĭz′əm, fĕd′rə-) ▶*n.* **1.** A system of federal government. **2.** Advocacy of such a system of government. **3. Federalism** The doctrine of the Federalist Party.

fed•er•al•ist (fĕd′ər-ə-lĭst, fĕd′rə-) ▶*n.* **1.** An advocate of federalism. **2. Federalist** A member of a US political party of the 1790s advocating a strong federal government. —**fed′er•al•ist** *adj.*

fed•er•al•ize (fĕd′ər-ə-līz′, fĕd′rə-) ▶*v.* **-ized, -iz•ing 1.** To unite in a federal union. **2.** To put under federal control. —**fed′er•al•i•za′tion** *n.*

fed•er•ate (fĕd′ə-rāt′) ▶*v.* **-at•ed, -at•ing.** To join or unite in a league, federal union, or similar association. [Lat. *foederāre.*] —**fed′er•a′tion** *n.* —**fed′er•a′tive** *adj.* —**fed′er•a′tive•ly** *adv.*

fe•do•ra (fĭ-dôr′ə, -dōr′ə) ▶*n.* A soft felt hat with a fairly low crown creased lengthwise and a flexible brim. [After *Fédora*, a play by Victorien Sardou (1831–1908).]

fed up ▶*adj.* Unable or unwilling to put up with something any longer.

fee (fē) ▶*n.* **1.** A fixed sum charged for a privilege. **2.** A charge for professional services. **3.** *Law* An inherited or heritable estate in land. **4.** In feudal law, an estate granted by a lord to a vassal on condition of homage and service. [< OFr. *fie, fief*, of Gmc. orig.]

fee•ble (fē′bəl) ▶*adj.* **-bler, -blest 1.** Lacking strength; weak. **2.** Lacking vigor, force, or effectiveness. [< Lat. *flēbilis*, lamentable.] —**fee′ble•ness** *n.* —**fee′bly** *adv.*

fee•ble-mind•ed (fē′bəl-mīn′dĭd) ▶*adj.* **1.** *Offensive* Deficient in intelligence. **2.** Exhibiting a marked lack of intelligent consideration: *feeble-minded excuses.* —**fee′ble-mind′ed•ly** *adv.* —**fee′ble-mind′ed•ness** *n.*

feed (fēd) ▶*v.* **fed** (fĕd), **feed•ing 1a.** To give food to; nourish. **b.** To eat. **2.** To supply with something essential for growth, maintenance, or operation. **3.** To distribute (a local broadcast) to a larger audience by network or satellite. **4.** To support or promote; encourage. ▶*n.* **1.** Food for animals or birds. **2.** *Informal* A meal, esp. a large one. **3a.** Material supplied, as to a machine. **b.** The act of supplying such material. **4.** Distribution of a locally broadcast program by network or satellite to a larger audience. [< OE *fēdan.*] —**feed′er** *n.*

feed•back (fēd′băk′) ▶*n.* **1a.** The return of a portion of the output of a process or system to the input. **b.** The portion of the output so returned. **2.** An evaluative response.

feed•lot (fēd′lŏt′) ▶*n.* A place where livestock are fattened for market.

feed•stuff (fēd′stŭf′) ▶*n.* Food for livestock; fodder.

feel (fēl) ▶*v.* **felt** (fĕlt), **feel•ing 1.** To perceive through the sense of touch. **2a.** To touch. **b.** To examine by touching. **3.** To test or explore with caution. **4a.** To undergo the experience of. **b.** To be aware of; sense. **5.** To believe; think. **6.** To have compassion or sympathy. ▶*n.* **1.** Perception by or as if by touch; sensation. **2.** The sense of touch. **3.** The quality of something perceived by or as if by touch. **4.** Overall effect; atmosphere. **5.** Intuitive awareness or natural ability. —*idiom:* **feel like** *Informal* To have an inclination for. [< OE *fēlan.*]

feel•er (fē′lər) ▶*n.* **1.** Something, such as a hint

or question, designed to elicit the attitudes or intentions of others. **2.** *Zool.* A sensory organ, such as an antenna.

feel•ing (fē′lĭng) ►*n.* **1a.** The sensation involving perception by touch. **b.** A sensation experienced through touch. **c.** A physical sensation. **2.** An awareness or impression. **3.** An emotional state or disposition; an emotion. **4. feelings** Susceptibility to emotional response; sensibilities. **5.** Opinion based on sentiment. **6.** A general impression. **7.** Intuitive awareness or aptitude. ►*adj.* **1.** Sensitive. **2.** Sympathetic. —**feel′ing•ly** *adv.*

feet (fēt) ►*n.* Pl. of **foot.**

feign (fān) ►*v.* **1.** To give a false appearance (of). **2.** To represent falsely; pretend to. [< Lat. *fingere*, to shape, form.]

feint (fānt) ►*n.* A feigned attack designed to draw defensive action away from an intended target. [< OFr. *feinte*.] —**feint** *v.*

feist•y (fī′stē) ►*adj.* **-i•er, -i•est 1.** Touchy; quarrelsome. **2.** Spirited; frisky. See Regional Note at **andiron.** [< dial. *feist*, a small dog.] —**feist′i•ness** *n.*

fe•la•fel (fə-lä′fəl) ►*n.* Var. of **falafel.**

feld•spar (fĕld′spär′, fĕl′-) ►*n.* Any of a group of abundant rock-forming minerals consisting of silicates of aluminum with potassium, sodium, calcium, and, rarely, barium. [< obsolete Ger. *Feldspath*.]

fe•lic•i•tate (fĭ-lĭs′ĭ-tāt′) ►*v.* **-tat•ed, -tat•ing.** To congratulate. —**fe•lic′i•ta′tion** *n.*

fe•lic•i•tous (fĭ-lĭs′ĭ-təs) ►*adj.* **1.** Admirably suited; apt. **2.** Exhibiting an agreeable manner or style. —**fe•lic′i•tous•ness** *n.*

fe•lic•i•ty (fĭ-lĭs′ĭ-tē) ►*n., pl.* **-ties 1.** Great happiness; bliss. **2.** A cause of happiness. **3.** An appropriate and pleasing manner or style. [< Lat. *fēlīx*, *fēlīc-*, fortunate.]

fe•line (fē′līn′) ►*adj.* **1.** Of or belonging to cats or related animals, as lions and tigers. **2.** Suggestive of a cat, as in suppleness or stealthiness. ►*n.* A feline animal. [< Lat. *fēlēs*, cat.] —**fe•lin′i•ty** (fĭ-lĭn′ĭ-tē) *n.*

fell[1] (fĕl) ►*v.* **1.** To cut or knock down. **2.** To kill. [< OE *fyllan*.] —**fell′a•ble** *adj.*

fell[2] (fĕl) ►*adj.* **1.** Cruel; fierce. **2.** Deadly; lethal. **3.** Dire; sinister. [< OFr. *fel*.]

fell[3] (fĕl) ►*n.* The hide of an animal; pelt. [< OE *fell*.]

fell[4] (fĕl) ►*v.* P.t. of **fall.**

fel•lah (fĕl′ə, fə-lä′) ►*n., pl.* **fel•la•hin** or **-heen** (fĕl′ə-hēn′, fə-lä-hēn′). A peasant or agricultural laborer in Arab countries. [< Ar. *fallāḥ*.]

fel•low (fĕl′ō) ►*n.* **1.** A man or boy. **2.** *Informal* A boyfriend. **3.** A comrade or associate. **4.** One of a pair; mate. **5.** A member of a learned society. **6.** A graduate student receiving financial aid for further study. ►*adj.* Being of the same kind, group, occupation, or locality: *fellow workers*. [< ON *fēlagi*, business partner : *fē*, property + *lag*, a laying down.]

fel•low•ship (fĕl′ō-shĭp′) ►*n.* **1.** The sharing of similar interests, ideals, or experiences, as by reason of profession, religion, or nationality. **2.** Friendship; comradeship. **3a.** The financial grant made to a fellow in a college or university. **b.** The status of having been awarded such a grant.

fellow traveler ►*n.* One who sympathizes with the tenets and program of an organized group, such as the Communist Party, without being a member.

fel•on (fĕl′ən) ►*n.* One who has committed a felony. [< Med.Lat. *fellō*, villain.]

fel•o•ny (fĕl′ə-nē) ►*n., pl.* **-nies** *Law* A serious crime, such as murder, rape, or burglary. —**fe•lo′ni•ous** (fə-lō′nē-əs) *adj.*

felt[1] (fĕlt) ►*n.* **1.** A fabric of matted, compressed fibers, as of wool. **2.** A material resembling this fabric. [< OE.] —**felt** *adj.*

felt[2] (fĕlt) ►*v.* P.t. and p.part. of **feel.**

fem. ►*abbr.* **1.** female **2.** feminine

FEMA ►*abbr.* Federal Emergency Management Agency

fe•male (fē′māl′) ►*adj.* **1a.** Relating to or being the sex that produces ova or bears young. **b.** Consisting of members of this sex. **2.** *Bot.* **a.** Of or being an organ, such as a pistil or ovary, that produces seeds after fertilization. **b.** Bearing pistils but not stamens. **3.** Having a recessed part, such as a slot or receptacle, designed to receive a complementary part, such as a plug. ►*n.* A member of the female sex. [< Lat. *fēmella*, dim. of *fēmina*, woman.] —**fe′male′ness** *n.*

fem•i•nine (fĕm′ə-nĭn) ►*adj.* **1.** Of or relating to women or girls. **2.** Marked by qualities gen. attributed to a woman. **3.** *Gram.* Of or being the gender of words referring to things classified as female. ►*n. Gram.* **1.** The feminine gender. **2.** A word belonging to this gender. [< Lat. *fēminīnus*.] —**fem′i•nine•ly** *adv.* —**fem′i•nine•ness** *n.* —**fem′i•nin′i•ty** *n.*

fem•i•nism (fĕm′ə-nĭz′əm) ►*n.* **1.** Belief in the social, political, and economic equality of the sexes. **2.** The movement organized around this belief. —**fem′i•nist** *n.*

femme fa•tale (fĕm′ fə-tăl′, -täl′) ►*n., pl.* **femmes fa•tales** (fĕm′ fə-tăl′, -tălz′, -täl′, -tälz′) **1.** A seductive woman. **2.** An alluring and mysterious woman. [Fr.]

fe•mur (fē′mər) ►*n., pl.* **fe•murs** or **fem•o•ra** (fĕm′ər-ə). A bone of the lower or hind limb in vertebrates, situated between the pelvis and knee in humans. [Lat., thigh.] —**fem′or•al** *adj.*

fen (fĕn) ►*n.* Low swampy land; bog. [< OE *fenn*.] —**fen′ny** *adj.*

fence (fĕns) ►*n.* **1.** An enclosure, barrier, or boundary, usu. made of posts or stakes joined together by boards, wire, or rails. **2a.** One who receives and sells stolen goods. **b.** A place where stolen goods are received and sold. ►*v.* **fenced, fenc•ing 1.** To enclose with or as if with a fence. See Syns at **enclose. 2a.** To act as a conduit for stolen goods. **b.** To sell (stolen goods) to a fence. **3.** To practice the art or sport of fencing. **4.** To avoid giving direct answers; hedge. —***idiom:* on the fence** *Informal* Undecided; neutral. [ME *fens* < *defens*, DEFENSE.] —**fenc′er** *n.*

fenc•ing (fĕn′sĭng) ►*n.* **1.** The art or sport of using a foil, épée, or saber. **2.** Skillful repartee, esp. as a defense against having to give direct answers. **3.** Material for fences.

fend (fĕnd) ►*v.* **1.** To ward off; repel. **2.** To manage; get by: *You'll have to fend for yourself.* [ME *fenden* < *defenden*, DEFEND.]

fend•er (fĕn′dər) ►*n.* **1.** A guard over a wheel of a vehicle. **2.** A screen or metal framework placed in front of a fireplace.

fen•es•tra•tion (fĕn′ĭ-strā′shən) ►*n.* The design and placement of windows in a building. [< Lat. *fenestra*, window.]

feng shui (fŭng′ shwā′) ▶*n.* The traditional Chinese practice of positioning objects, esp. buildings and graves, so as to harmonize with the flow of chi. [Mandarin *fēng shuǐ*, wind (and) water.]

Fe•ni•an (fē′nē-ən) ▶*n.* **1.** One of a legendary group of heroic Irish warriors of the 2nd and 3rd cent. A.D. **2.** A member of a secret revolutionary organization in the US and Ireland in the mid-19th cent. dedicated to the overthrow of British rule in Ireland. —**Fe′ni•an** *adj.* —**Fe′ni•an•ism** *n.*

fen•nel (fĕn′əl) ▶*n.* **1.** A plant having aromatic seeds used as flavoring. **2.** The seeds or edible stalks of this plant. [< Lat. *faeniculum.*]

–fer ▶*suff.* One that bears: *conifer.* [< Lat. *ferre*, carry.]

fe•ral (fîr′əl, fĕr′-) ▶*adj.* **1.** Existing in a wild or untamed state. **2.** Of or suggestive of a wild animal; savage. [< Lat. *ferus*, wild.]

Fer•ber (fûr′bər), **Edna.** 1887–1968. Amer. writer.

fer-de-lance (fĕr′dl-ăns′, -äns′) ▶*n.*, *pl.* **fer-de-lance.** A venomous tropical American pit viper having brown and grayish markings. [Fr., spearhead.]

Fer•di•nand I (fûr′dn-ănd′). 1503–64. King of Bohemia and Hungary (1526–64); Holy Roman emperor (1558–64).

Ferdinand V. 1452–1516. Spanish king of Aragon, Castile, Sicily, and Naples.

fer•ment (fûr′mĕnt′) ▶*n.* **1.** Something, such as yeast, that causes fermentation. **2.** A state of agitation or unrest. ▶*v.* (fər-mĕnt′) **1.** To produce by or as if by fermentation. **2.** To undergo or cause to undergo fermentation. **3.** To be turbulent; seethe. [< Lat. *fermentum.*] —**fer•ment′a•bil′i•ty** *n.* —**fer•ment′a•ble** *adj.*

fer•men•ta•tion (fûr′mən-tā′shən, -mĕn-) ▶*n.* **1.** A chemical reaction that splits complex organic compounds into relatively simple substances, esp. the conversion of sugar to carbon dioxide and alcohol by yeast. **2.** Unrest; agitation. —**fer•men′ta•tive** (fər-mĕn′tə-tĭv) *adj.*

Fer•mi (fĕr′mē), **Enrico.** 1901–54. Italian-born Amer. physicist; 1938 Nobel.

fer•mi•um (fûr′mē-əm, fĕr′-) ▶*n.* *Symbol* **Fm** A synthetic metallic element. At. no. 100. See table at **element.** [After Enrico FERMI.]

fern (fûrn) ▶*n.* Any of numerous flowerless plants having fronds and reproducing by spores. [< OE *fearn.*] —**fern′y** *adj.*

fe•ro•cious (fə-rō′shəs) ▶*adj.* **1.** Extremely savage; fierce. **2.** Intense; extreme: *ferocious heat.* [< Lat. *ferōx*, *ferōc-*, fierce.] —**fe•ro′cious•ly** *adv.* —**fe•ro′cious•ness, fe•roc′i•ty** (fə-rŏs′ĭ-tē) *n.*

–ferous ▶*suff.* Bearing; producing; containing: *carboniferous.* [–FER + –OUS.]

fer•ret (fĕr′ĭt) ▶*n.* **1.** An Old World, usu. albino weasel related to the polecat and often trained to hunt rats or rabbits. **2.** A North American weasel with black masklike markings. ▶*v.* **1.** To hunt with ferrets. **2.** To drive out, as from a hiding place; expel. **3.** To uncover and bring to light by searching: *ferret out the solution.* [< VLat. **fūrittus* < Lat. *fūr*, thief.]

fer•ric (fĕr′ĭk) ▶*adj.* Of or containing iron, esp. with a valence of 3.

ferric oxide ▶*n.* A dark red compound, Fe_2O_3, occurring naturally as rust.

Fer•ris wheel also **fer•ris wheel** (fĕr′ĭs) ▶*n.* A large upright, rotating wheel having suspended seats that remain in a horizontal position as the wheel revolves. [After George W.G. *Ferris* (1859–96).]

ferro– or **ferr–** ▶*pref.* Iron: *ferromagnetic.* [< Lat. *ferrum*, iron.]

fer•ro•mag•net•ic (fĕr′ō-măg-nĕt′ĭk) ▶*adj.* Of or characteristic of substances such as iron or nickel and various alloys that exhibit magnetic properties. —**fer′ro•mag′net** (-măg′nĭt) *n.* —**fer′ro•mag′net•ism** *n.*

fer•ro•man•ga•nese (fĕr′ō-măng′gə-nēz′, -nēs′) ▶*n.* An alloy of iron and manganese used in the production of steel.

fer•ro•type (fĕr′ə-tīp′) ▶*n.* A positive photograph made directly on an iron plate varnished with a thin sensitized film.

fer•rous (fĕr′əs) ▶*adj.* Of or containing iron, esp. with a valence of 2.

ferrous oxide ▶*n.* A black powder, FeO, used in the manufacture of steel and glass.

fer•rule (fĕr′əl) ▶*n.* A metal ring or cap placed around a pole or shaft for reinforcement. [< Lat. *viriola*, little bracelet.]

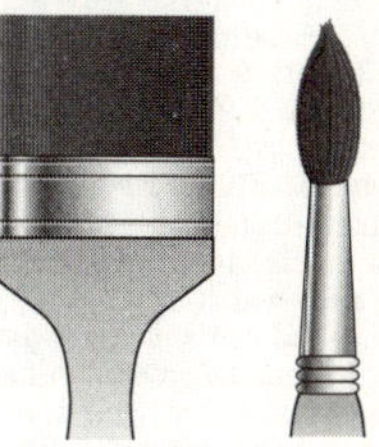

ferrule
left to right: household paintbrush and round paintbrush models

fer•ry (fĕr′ē) ▶*v.* **-ried, -ry•ing 1.** To transport by boat across a body of water. **2.** To cross by a ferry. **3.** To transport from one point to another. ▶*n.*, *pl.* **-ries 1.** A ferryboat. **2.** A place where a ferryboat embarks. **3.** A service for delivering an aircraft under its own power to its eventual user. [< OE *ferian.*]

fer•ry•boat (fĕr′ē-bōt′) ▶*n.* A boat used to ferry passengers, vehicles, or goods.

fer•tile (fûr′tl) ▶*adj.* **1.** *Biol.* Capable of initiating, sustaining, or supporting reproduction. **2.** Rich in material needed to sustain plant growth: *fertile soil.* **3.** Highly or continuously productive; prolific: *a fertile imagination.* [< Lat. *fertilis* < *ferre*, to bear.] —**fer′tile•ly** *adv.* —**fer•til′i•ty** (fər-tĭl′ĭ-tē), **fer′tile•ness** *n.*

Syns: *fertile, fecund, fruitful, productive, prolific* **Ant:** *infertile* **adj.**

Fertile Crescent. A region of the Middle East extending from the Nile Valley to the Tigris and Euphrates rivers.

fer•til•ize (fûr′tl-īz′) ▶*v.* **-ized, -iz•ing 1.** To initiate biological reproduction, esp. to provide with pollen or sperm. **2.** To make fertile, as by spreading fertilizer. —**fer′til•iz′a•ble** *adj.* —**fer′til•i•za′tion** *n.*

fer•til•iz•er (fûr′tl-ī′zər) ▶*n.* Any of a large number of natural and synthetic materials, including manure and chemical compounds, added to soil to increase its capacity to support plant growth.

fer•ule (fĕr′əl) ►*n.* A cane or flat stick used in punishing children. [< Lat. *ferula*, rod.]

fer•vent (fûr′vənt) ►*adj.* **1.** Greatly emotional or zealous; ardent. **2.** Extremely hot; glowing. [< Lat. *fervēre*, to boil.] —**fer′ven•cy** *n.* —**fer′vent•ly** *adv.*

fer•vid (fûr′vĭd) ►*adj.* **1.** Passionate; zealous. **2.** Extremely hot. [Lat. *fervidus*.] —**fer′vid•ly** *adv.* —**fer′vid•ness** *n.*

fer•vor (fûr′vər) ►*n.* **1.** Great warmth and intensity of emotion. **2.** Intense heat. [< Lat.]

fes•cue (fĕs′kyo͞o) ►*n.* Any of various grasses often cultivated as pasturage. [< Lat. *festūca*, straw.]

fes•tal (fĕs′təl) ►*adj.* Of a feast or festival; festive. [< Lat. *fēstum*, feast.]

fes•ter (fĕs′tər) ►*v.* **1.** To generate pus. **2.** To undergo decay; rot. **3.** To be or become a source of irritation; rankle. [< Lat. *fistula*, fistula.] —**fes′ter** *n.*

fes•ti•val (fĕs′tə-vəl) ►*n.* **1.** A feast or celebration, esp. a religious one. **2.** A programmed series of cultural performances, exhibitions, or competitions: *a film festival.* **3.** Revelry; conviviality.

fes•tive (fĕs′tĭv) ►*adj.* **1.** Relating to or appropriate for a feast or festival. **2.** Merry; joyous. [Lat. *fēstīvus*.] —**fes′tive•ly** *adv.* —**fes′tive•ness** *n.*

fes•tiv•i•ty (fĕ-stĭv′ĭ-tē) ►*n., pl.* **-ties 1.** A joyous feast or celebration. **2.** The gaiety of a festival or celebration. **3. festivities** The activities of a festival.

fes•toon (fĕ-sto͞on′) ►*n.* **1.** A garland, as of leaves or flowers, between two looped points. **2.** A representation of such a garland, as in painting. ►*v.* **1.** To decorate with or as if with festoons. **2.** To form festoons. [< Ital. *festone*.]

fet•a (fĕt′ə, fā′tə) ►*n.* A white semisoft cheese made usu. from goat's or ewe's milk. [Mod.Gk. *(turi) pheta*, (cheese) slice.]

fe•tal also **foe•tal** (fēt′l) ►*adj.* Of or relating to a fetus.

fetal alcohol syndrome ►*n.* A complex of birth defects in an infant born to an alcoholic mother.

fetal position ►*n.* A position of the body at rest in which the spine is curved, the head is bowed, and the limbs are drawn in toward the chest. [From its resemblance to the position of a fetus in the womb.]

fetch (fĕch) ►*v.* **1.** To go after and bring back; retrieve. **2.** To cause to come; bring forth. **3.** To bring as a price. [< OE *feccean*.] —**fetch′er** *n.*

fetch•ing (fĕch′ĭng) ►*adj.* Attractive; charming. —**fetch′ing•ly** *adv.*

fete also **fête** (fāt, fĕt) ►*n.* **1.** A festival or feast. **2.** An elaborate outdoor party. ►*v.* **fet•ed, fet•ing** also **fêt•ed, fêt•ing 1.** To celebrate or honor with a feast or elaborate entertainment. **2.** To pay honor to. [< OFr. *feste*, FEAST.]

fet•id (fĕt′ĭd, fē′tĭd) also **foe•tid** (fē′tĭd) ►*adj.* Having an offensive odor. [< Lat. *fētidus*.] —**fet′id•ly** *adv.* —**fet′id•ness** *n.*

fet•ish also **fet•ich** (fĕt′ĭsh, fē′tĭsh) ►*n.* **1.** An object believed to have spiritual powers. **2.** An object of excessive attention or reverence. **3.** An obsessive attachment; fixation. [< Lat. *factīcius*, artificial.] —**fet′ish•ism** *n.* —**fet′ish•ist** *n.* —**fet′ish•is′tic** *adj.*

fet•lock (fĕt′lŏk′) ►*n.* A projection on the lower part of the leg of a horse or related animal, above and behind the hoof. [ME *fitlok*.]

fet•ter (fĕt′ər) ►*n.* **1.** A chain or shackle for the ankles. **2.** Something that restricts or restrains. ►*v.* **1.** To shackle. **2.** To restrict the freedom of. See Syns at **hamper**[1]. [< OE *feter*.]

fet•tle (fĕt′l) ►*n.* Condition; emotional state: *in fine fettle.* [< ME *fetlen*, make ready.]

fet•tuc•ci•ne (fĕt′ə-chē′nē) ►*n.* Pasta in narrow flat strips. [Ital., pl. dim. of *fettucia*, ribbon.]

fe•tus also **foe•tus** (fē′təs) ►*n., pl.* **-tus•es.** The unborn young of a viviparous vertebrate; in humans the unborn young from the end of the eighth week after conception to birth, as distinguished from the earlier embryo. [< Lat. *fētus*, offspring.]

feud (fyo͞od) ►*n.* A bitter, often prolonged quarrel or state of enmity. [< OFr. *faide*, of Gmc. orig.] —**feud** *v.*

feu•dal (fyo͞od′l) ►*adj.* Of or characteristic of feudalism. [< Med.Lat. *feudum*, feudal estate.] —**feu′dal•ly** *adv.*

feu•dal•ism (fyo͞od′l-ĭz′əm) ►*n.* A political and economic system of medieval Europe by which a landowner granted land to a vassal in exchange for homage and military service. —**feu′dal•ist** *n.* —**feu′dal•is′tic** *adj.* —**feu′dal•i•za′tion** *n.* —**feu′dal•ize′** *v.*

feu•da•to•ry (fyo͞o′də-tôr′ē, -tōr′ē) ►*n., pl.* **-ries 1.** A vassal. **2.** A feudal fee. ►*adj.* Owing feudal allegiance.

fe•ver (fē′vər) ►*n.* **1.** Abnormally high body temperature. **2.** A disease marked by such temperature. **3.** Heightened activity or excitement. **4.** A usu. short-lived enthusiasm or craze. [< Lat. *febris*.] —**fe′ver•ish** *adj.* —**fe′ver•ish•ly** *adv.* —**fe′ver•ish•ness** *n.*

fever blister ►*n.* See **cold sore.**

few (fyo͞o) ►*adj.* **-er, -est.** Amounting to or consisting of a small number. ►*n. (takes pl. v.)* **1.** An indefinitely small number: *A few of the cars are new.* **2.** An exclusive or limited number: *the fortunate few.* ►*pron. (takes pl. v.)* A small number: *Few of them are left.* [< OE *fēawe*.] —**few′ness** *n.*

Usage: *Fewer* is used with expressions denoting things that can be counted (*fewer than four players*), while *less* is used with mass terms denoting things of measurable extent (*less paper*). However, *less* is idiomatic in *less than* used before a plural noun that denotes a measure of time, amount, or distance, as in *less than 50 miles,* and is sometimes used with plural nouns in the expressions *no less than* and *or less.*

fey (fā) ►*adj.* Otherworldly, magical, or fairylike. [< OE *fǣge*, fated to die.] —**fey′ness** *n.*

fez (fĕz) ►*n., pl.* **fez•zes.** A man's felt cap shaped like a flat-topped cone, usu. red with a black tassel hanging from the crown. [< FEZ.]

Fez. A city of N-central Morocco NE of Casablanca. Pop. 564,000.

FHA ►*abbr.* Federal Housing Administration

fi•an•cé (fē′än-sā′, fē-än′sā′) ►*n.* A man engaged to be married. [Fr. < p.part. of *fiancer*, betroth, ult. < Lat. *fīdere*, trust.]

fi•an•cée (fē′än-sā′, fē-än′sā′) ►*n.* A woman engaged to be married.

fi•as•co (fē-ăs′kō, -ä′skō) ►*n., pl.* **-coes** or **-cos.** A complete failure. [< Ital., bottle.]

fez

fi•at (fē′ət, -ăt′, -ät′) ►*n.* An arbitrary order or decree. [< Lat., let it be done < *fierī*, become, be done.]

fib (fĭb) ►*n.* An insignificant or childish lie. ►*v.* **fibbed, fib•bing.** To tell a fib. [Perh. < alteration of FABLE.] —**fib′ber** *n.*

fi•ber (fī′bər) ►*n.* **1.** A slender threadlike structure. **2.** *Bot.* An elongated, thick-walled cell strengthening and supporting plant tissue. **3.** *Anat.* Any of various elongated cells, esp. a muscle or nerve fiber. **4.** A filament, as of cotton or nylon, capable of being spun into yarn. **5a.** Something that provides substance or texture. **b.** Basic strength or toughness; fortitude. **6.** Indigestible plant matter, consisting esp. of cellulose, that stimulates intestinal peristalsis. [< Lat. *fibra*.] —**fi′brous** (fī′brəs) *adj.*

fi•ber•board (fī′bər-bôrd′, -bōrd′) ►*n.* A building material composed of wood chips or plant fibers bonded together and compressed into rigid sheets.

fi•ber•glass (fī′bər-glăs′) ►*n.* A material consisting of glass fibers in resin.

fiber optics ►*n.* *(takes sing. v.)* **1.** The technology of light transmission through very fine, flexible glass or plastic fibers. **2.** A bundle of such fibers. —**fi′ber-op′tic** *adj.*

fi•bril (fī′brəl, fĭb′rəl) ►*n.* A small slender fiber or filament. [NLat. *fibrilla* < Lat. *fibra*, fiber.]

fib•ril•la•tion (fĭb′rə-lā′shən, fī′brə-) ►*n.* Rapid uncoordinated twitching movements in the atria or ventricles of the heart. —**fib′ril•late′** *v.*

fi•brin (fī′brĭn) ►*n.* An elastic, insoluble, whitish protein that forms in blood clots.

fi•brin•o•gen (fī-brĭn′ə-jən) ►*n.* A protein in the blood plasma that is a precursor of fibrin.

fibro– or **fibr–** ►*pref.* Fiber, esp. fibrous tissue: *fibroma.* [< Lat. *fibra*, fiber.]

fi•broid (fī′broid′) ►*adj.* Composed of or resembling fibrous tissue. ►*n.* A fibroma occurring esp. in the uterine wall.

fi•bro•ma (fī-brō′mə) ►*n.*, *pl.* **-mas** or **-ma•ta** (-mə-tə). A benign, usu. enclosed neoplasm of primarily fibrous tissue.

fi•bro•sis (fī-brō′sĭs) ►*n.* The formation of excessive fibrous tissue. —**fi•brot′ic** (-brŏt′ĭk) *adj.*

fi•bro•vas•cu•lar (fī′brō-văs′kyə-lər) ►*adj.* Having both fibrous and vascular tissue.

fib•u•la (fĭb′yə-lə) ►*n.*, *pl.* **-lae** (-lē′) or **-las.** The outer and narrower of two bones of the human lower leg or of the hind leg of an animal. [Lat. *fībula*, clasp < *fīgere*, fasten.]

-fic ►*suff.* Causing; making: *honorific.* [Lat. *-ficus* < *facere*, make.]

FICA ►*abbr.* Federal Insurance Contributions Act

-fication ►*suff.* Production; making: *certification.* [< Lat. *-ficāre*, make < *facere*.]

fiche (fēsh) ►*n.* A microfiche.

Fich•te (fĭk′tə, fĭKH′-), **Johann Gottlieb.** 1762–1814. German philosopher.

fich•u (fĭsh′o͞o, fē-sho͞o′) ►*n.* A woman's triangular scarf, worn over the shoulders and crossed or tied in a loose knot at the breast. [Fr. < p.part. of *ficher*, FIX.]

fick•le (fĭk′əl) ►*adj.* Erratic or changeable, esp. in affections; capricious. [< OE *ficol*, deceitful.] —**fick′le•ness** *n.* —**fick′ly** *adv.*

fic•tion (fĭk′shən) ►*n.* **1.** An imaginative creation or pretense. **2.** A lie. **3a.** A literary work, such as a novel, whose content is produced by the imagination and is not necessarily based on fact. **b.** The category of literature comprising works of this kind. [< Lat. *fictiō* < *fingere*, to form.] —**fic′tion•al** *adj.* —**fic′tion•al•i•za′tion** *n.* —**fic′tion•al•ize′** *v.* —**fic′tion•al•ly** *adv.*

fic•ti•tious (fĭk-tĭsh′əs) ►*adj.* **1.** Nonexistent; imaginary. **2.** Purposely deceptive; false: *a fictitious name.* [< Lat. *fictīcius*.] —**fic•ti′tious•ly** *adv.* —**fic•ti′tious•ness** *n.*

fic•tive (fĭk′tĭv) ►*adj.* **1.** Relating to or being fiction; fictional. **2.** Not genuine; sham.

fid•dle (fĭd′l) ►*n.* A violin. ►*v.* **-dled, -dling 1.** To play a violin. **2.** To play idly; tinker: *fiddled with the knobs.* **3.** To meddle; tamper. —***phrasal verb:*** **fiddle away** To waste or squander. [< OE *fithele*.] —**fid′dler** *n.*

fiddler crab ►*n.* A burrowing crab with one of the front claws much larger in the male.

fid•dle•sticks (fĭd′l-stĭks′) ►*interj.* Used to express mild annoyance or impatience.

fi•del•i•ty (fĭ-dĕl′ĭ-tē, fī-) ►*n.*, *pl.* **-ties 1.** Faithfulness to obligations or duties. **2.** Exact correspondence with fact; accuracy. **3.** The degree to which an electronic system reproduces the sound or image of its input signal. [< Lat. *fidēlis*, faithful.]

fidg•et (fĭj′ĭt) ►*v.* To move nervously or restlessly. ►*n.* often **fidgets** Restlessness manifested by nervous movements. [< obsolete *fidge*, move about restlessly.] —**fidg′et•i•ness** *n.* —**fidg′et•y** *adj.*

fi•du•ci•ar•y (fĭ-do͞o′shē-ĕr′ē, -shə-rē, -dyo͞o′-) ►*adj.* **1.** Relating to a holding in trust for another. **2.** Held in trust. ►*n.*, *pl.* **-ies.** A trustee. [< Lat. *fīdūcia*, a trust.]

fie (fī) ►*interj.* Used to express distaste or disapproval.

fief (fēf) ►*n.* **1.** See **fee** 4. **2.** A fiefdom. [< OFr. FEE.]

fief•dom (fēf′dəm) ►*n.* **1.** The estate of a feudal lord. **2.** Something over which one person or group exercises control.

field (fēld) ►*n.* **1a.** A broad, level, open expanse of land. **b.** A meadow. **c.** A cultivated expanse of land. **d.** A portion of land or a geologic formation containing a specified natural resource. **2.** A battleground. **3.** A background area, as on a flag. **4.** *Sports* **a.** An area in which an athletic event takes place. **b.** All the contestants in an event. **5a.** An area of human activity. **b.** Profession, employment, or business. **c.** A setting of practical activity outside an office, school, or laboratory: *a product tested in the field.* **d.** An area where business activities are conducted. **6.** *Phys.* A region of space characterized by a physical property, such as gravitational force, having a determinable value at every point in the region. **7.** *Comp. Sci.* An interface element in a GUI that accepts the input of text. ►*v.* **1.** *Sports* **a.** To retrieve (a ball) and perform the required maneuver, esp. in baseball. **b.** To place in the field to play. **2.** To give an unrehearsed response to (a question). [< OE *feld.*] —**field′er** *n.*

Syns: *field, bailiwick, domain, province, realm, sphere, territory* **n.**

field day ►*n.* **1.** A day set aside for sports or athletic competition. **2.** *Informal* A time of great pleasure, activity, or opportunity.

field event ►*n.* A throwing or jumping event of a track-and-field meet.

field glass ►*n.* A portable binocular telescope.

field goal ►*n.* **1.** *Football* A score worth three points made on an ordinary down by kicking the ball over the crossbar and between the goal posts. **2.** *Basketball* A score made by throwing the ball through the basket in regulation play.

field hockey ►*n.* A game played on turf in which two opposing teams use curved sticks to drive a ball into a goal.

Field•ing (fēl′dĭng), **Henry.** 1707–54. British writer.

field magnet ►*n.* A magnet used to produce a magnetic field in an electrical device such as a generator or motor.

field marshal ►*n.* An officer in some European armies, usu. ranking just below the commander in chief.

field mouse ►*n.* Any of various small mice inhabiting meadows and fields.

field of force ►*n.* A region of space throughout which the force produced by a single agent, such as an electric current, is operative.

field-test (fēld′tĕst′) ►*v.* To test (e.g., a product) in actual operation or use.

field trial ►*n.* **1.** A test of young, untried hunting dogs for their competence in pointing and retrieving. **2.** A trial of a new product in actual use.

field trip ►*n.* A group excursion for firsthand observation, as to a museum.

field•work (fēld′wûrk′) ►*n.* Work done or observations made in the field as opposed to laboratory work. —**field′work′er** *n.*

fiend (fēnd) ►*n.* **1.** An evil spirit; devil. **2.** An evil or wicked person. **3.** *Informal* One obsessed with a job or pastime: *a puzzle fiend.* [< OE *fēond.*] —**fiend′ish** *adj.* —**fiend′ish•ly** *adv.* —**fiend′ish•ness** *n.*

fierce (fîrs) ►*adj.* **fierc•er, fierc•est 1.** Having a violent nature; ferocious: *a fierce beast.* **2.** Severe or violent: *a fierce storm.* **3.** Intense or ardent: *fierce loyalty.* See Syns at **intense.** [< Lat. *ferus.*] —**fierce′ly** *adv.* —**fierce′ness** *n.*

fier•y (fīr′ē, fī′ə-rē) ►*adj.* **-i•er, -i•est 1.** Consisting of, containing, or like fire. **2a.** Easily excited: *a fiery temper.* **b.** Charged with emotion: *a fiery speech.* [< ME *fier,* FIRE.] —**fier′i•ly** *adv.* —**fier′i•ness** *n.*

fi•es•ta (fē-ĕs′tə) ►*n.* **1.** A festival or religious holiday, esp. in Spanish-speaking regions. **2.** A party. [Sp. < VLat. **fēsta,* FEAST.]

fife (fīf) ►*n.* A small, high-pitched flute used to accompany drums in a military or marching band. [< VLat. **pīpa.*] —**fif′er** *n.*

FIFO (fī′fō) ►*n.* See **first-in, first-out.**

fif•teen (fĭf-tēn′) ►*n.* **1.** The cardinal number equal to 14 + 1. **2.** The 15th in a set or sequence. [< OE *fīftēne.*] —**fif•teen′** *adj. & pron.*

fif•teenth (fĭf-tēnth′) ►*n.* **1.** The ordinal number matching the number 15 in a series. **2.** One of 15 equal parts. —**fif•teenth′** *adv. & adj.*

fifth (fĭfth) ►*n.* **1.** The ordinal number matching the number 5 in a series. **2.** One of five equal parts. **3.** One fifth of a gallon or four fifths of a quart of liquor. **4.** *Mus.* A tone five degrees above or below a given tone in a diatonic scale. [< OE *fīfta.*] —**fifth** *adv. & adj.*

fifth column ►*n.* A secret organization working within a country to further an enemy's aims.

fifth wheel ►*n.* One that is unnecessary.

fif•ti•eth (fĭf′tē-ĭth) ►*n.* **1.** The ordinal number matching the number 50 in a series. **2.** One of 50 equal parts. —**fif′ti•eth** *adv. & adj.*

fif•ty (fĭf′tē) ►*n., pl.* **-ties.** The cardinal number equal to 5 × 10. [< OE *fīftig.*] —**fif′ty** *adj. & pron.*

fif•ty-fif•ty (fĭf′tē-fĭf′tē) ►*adj.* **1.** Divided in two equal portions. **2.** Being equally likely and unlikely. —**fif′ty-fif′ty** *adv.*

fig (fĭg) ►*n.* **1a.** Any of several Mediterranean trees or shrubs widely cultivated for their edible fruit. **b.** The sweet, pear-shaped fruit of this plant. **2.** A trivial amount: *not worth a fig.* [< Lat. *fīcus.*]

fight (fīt) ►*v.* **fought** (fôt), **fight•ing 1.** To harm or subdue an adversary by blows or with weapons. **2.** To quarrel; argue. **3.** To strive vigorously and resolutely: *fight for justice.* **4.** To contend with physically or in battle. **5.** To wage or carry on (a battle). **6.** To struggle against: *fight temptation.* **7.** To box or wrestle in a ring. —***phrasal verb:*** **fight off** To defend against or drive back. ►*n.* **1.** A confrontation in which each opponent attempts to harm or subdue the other. **2.** A quarrel or conflict. **3.** A physical conflict between two or more individuals. **4.** A struggle for an objective. **5.** The inclination to fight; pugnacity. [< OE *feohtan.*]

fight•er (fī′tər) ►*n.* **1.** One that fights. **2.** A fast, maneuverable combat aircraft. **3.** A pugnacious or determined person.

fig•ment (fĭg′mənt) ►*n.* Something invented or made up. [< Lat. *figmentum.*]

fig•u•ra•tive (fĭg′yər-ə-tĭv) ►*adj.* **1.** Based on figures of speech; metaphorical. **2.** Represented by a figure or resemblance; symbolic. —**fig′u•ra•tive•ly** *adv.*

fig•ure (fĭg′yər) ►*n.* **1.** A written or printed symbol, esp. a number. **2. figures** Mathematical calculations. **3.** An amount represented in numbers. **4.** The outline, form, or silhouette of a thing, esp. a human body. **5.** A person, esp. a well-known one. **6.** Impression or appearance made. **7.** A diagram, design, or pattern. **8.** A distinct group of steps or movements in a dance or in ice skating. ►*v.* **-ured, -ur•ing 1.** To calculate with numbers; compute. **2.** To make a likeness of; depict. **3.** To adorn with a design or figures. **4.** *Informal* To conclude, believe, or predict. **5.** To be pertinent or involved. **6.** *Informal* To seem reasonable or expected: *It figures.* —***phrasal verbs:*** **figure on** *Informal* **1.** To count on. **2.** To expect: *figured on an hour's delay.* **figure out** *Informal* To discover, decide, or solve. [< Lat. *figūra.*] —**fig′ur•er** *n.*

Syns: *figure, design, device, motif, pattern* ***n.***

fig•ure•head (fĭg′yər-hĕd′) ►*n.* **1.** A person with nominal leadership but no actual authority. **2.** A figure on the prow of a ship.

figure of speech ►*n.* An expression that uses words in a nonliteral way or that changes normal word order to heighten rhetorical effect.

figure skating ►*n.* Ice skating in which the skater traces prescribed, usu. elaborate figures. —**figure skater** *n.*

fig•u•rine (fĭg′yə-rēn′) ►*n.* A small sculptured figure; statuette. [< Ital. *figurina.*]

Fi•ji (fē′jē) A country of the SW Pacific comprising about 320 islands. Cap. Suva. Pop. 784,000.

fil•a•ment (fĭl′ə-mənt) ►*n.* **1.** A fine thin thread, fiber, or wire. **2.** A fine wire heated electrically to incandescence in an electric lamp. [< Lat. *fīlum,* thread.] —**fil′a•men′tous** (-mĕn′təs), **fil′a•men′ta•ry** (-mĕn′tə-rē, -mĕn′trē) *adj.*

fi•lar•i•a (fə-lâr′ē-ə) ►*n., pl.* **-i•ae** (-ē-ē′). Any of various slender parasitic nematode worms often transmitted as larvae by mosquitos. [NLat. < Lat. *fīlum,* thread.] —**fi•lar′i•al, fi•lar′i•an** *adj.*

fil•bert (fĭl′bərt) ►*n.* **1.** See **hazel** 1. **2.** See **hazelnut.** [< AN *philber,* after Saint *Philibert* (d. 684).]

filch (fĭlch) ►*v.* To steal; snitch. [ME *filchen.*] —**filch′er** *n.*

file[1] (fīl) ►*n.* **1.** A container, such as a cabinet or folder, for keeping papers in order. **2.** A collection of papers or published materials kept in convenient order. **3.** *Comp. Sci.* A collection of related data or program records stored as a unit. **4.** A line of persons, animals, or things positioned one behind the other. ►*v.* **filed, fil•ing 1.** To put or keep in useful order; catalog. **2.** To enter (a legal document) on record. **3.** To send (copy) to a newspaper. **4.** To carry out the first stage of: *filed charges against my associate.* **5.** To march or walk in a line. —***idiom:*** **on file** In or as if in a file for easy reference. [< Lat. *fīlum,* thread.]

file[2] (fīl) ►*n.* A tool with sharp, edged ridges for smoothing or grinding esp. metallic surfaces. ►*v.* **filed, fil•ing.** To smooth or grind with or as if with a file. [< OE *fīl.*]

file clerk ►*n.* One employed to maintain office files and records.

file server ►*n.* A computer that controls a central repository of data.

fi•let[1] (fĭ-lā′, fĭl′ā′) ►*n.* A lace with a simple pattern of squares. [< OFr.]

fi•let[2] (fĭ-lā′, fĭl′ā′) ►*n.* Var. of **fillet** 2. ►*v.* Var. of **fillet** 2.

fi•let mi•gnon (fĭ-lā′ mēn-yôN′, fĭl′ā) ►*n., pl.* **fi•lets mi•gnons** (fĭ-lā′ mēn-yôN′, fĭl′ā). A small, round, choice cut of beef from the loin. [Fr.]

fil•i•al (fĭl′ē-əl) ►*adj.* Of or befitting a son or daughter: *filial respect.* [< Lat. *fīlius,* son.] —**fil′i•al•ly** *adv.*

fil•i•bus•ter (fĭl′ə-bŭs′tər) ►*n.* **1.** The use of obstructionist tactics, esp. prolonged speechmaking, for the purpose of delaying legislative action. **2.** An adventurer engaged in private warfare abroad. [< Sp. *filibustero,* freebooter.] —**fil′i•bus′ter** *v.* —**fil′i•bus′ter•er** *n.*

fil•i•gree (fĭl′ĭ-grē′) ►*n.* Delicate and intricate ornamental work made from gold, silver, or other fine twisted wire. [< Ital. *filigrana* : Lat. *fīlum,* thread + Lat. *grānum,* grain.] —**fil′i•gree′** *v.*

fil•ing (fī′lĭng) ►*n.* A particle removed by a file.

Fil•i•pi•no (fĭl′ə-pē′nō) ►*n., pl.* **-nos 1.** A native or inhabitant of the Philippines. **2.** The official language of the Philippines, based on Tagalog. —**Fil′i•pi′no** *adj.*

fill (fĭl) ►*v.* **1.** To make or become full. **2.** To build up the level of (low-lying land) with material such as earth or gravel. **3.** To stop or plug up. **4.** To satisfy or meet; fulfill. See Syns at **satisfy. 5.** To complete (something) by insertion or addition: *fill in the blanks.* **6.** To supply as required: *fill a prescription.* **7.** To place a person in: *fill a job vacancy.* **8.** To occupy completely; pervade. —***phrasal verb:*** **fill in 1.** To provide with missing information. **2.** To take another's place. ►*n.* **1.** An amount needed to make full, complete, or satisfied: *eat one's fill.* **2.** Material for filling. —***idiom:*** **fill the bill** *Informal* To serve a particular purpose. [< OE *fyllan.*]

fill•er (fĭl′ər) ►*n.* **1.** Something added to augment weight or size or to fill space. **2.** A material used to fill in flaws in a surface. **3.** A short item to fill space in a publication or radio or television program.

fil•let (fĭl′ĭt) ►*n.* **1.** A narrow strip of ribbon or similar material. **2.** also **fi•let** (fĭ-lā′, fĭl′ā′) A boneless piece of meat or fish, esp. the beef tenderloin. ►*v.* **1.** To bind or decorate with or as if with a fillet. **2.** also **fi•let** (fĭ-lā′, fĭl′ā′) To make into fillets. [< OFr., dim. of *fil,* thread < Lat. *fīlum.*]

fill•ing (fĭl′ĭng) ►*n.* **1.** Something used to fill a space, cavity, or container: *a gold filling in a tooth.* **2.** An edible mixture used to fill pastries, sandwiches, or cakes: *pie filling.* **3.** The horizontal threads that cross the warp in weaving; weft.

filling station ►*n.* See **service station.**

fil•lip (fĭl′əp) ►*n.* **1.** A snap of the fingers. **2.** An incentive; stimulus. [Imit.] —**fil′lip** *v.*

Fill•more (fĭl′môr′, -mōr′), **Millard.** 1800–74. The 13th US President (1850–53).

Millard Fillmore

fil•ly (fĭl′ē) ►*n., pl.* **-lies.** A young female horse. [< ON *fylja.*]

film (fĭlm) ►*n.* **1.** A thin skin or membrane. **2.** A thin covering or coating. **3.** A thin transparent sheet, as of plastic, used in packaging. **4.** A thin sheet or strip of flexible material, such as a cellulose derivative, coated with a photosensitive emulsion and used to make photographic negatives or transparencies. **5a.** A movie. **b.** Movies collectively. ►*v.* **1.** To cover with or as if with a film. **2.** To make a movie (of). [< OE *filmen,* thin coating.] —**film′i•ly** *adv.* —**film′i•ness** *n.* —**film′y** *adj.*

film•mak•ing (fĭlm′mā′kĭng) ►*n.* The making of movies. —**film′mak′er** *n.*

film noir (nwär) ►*n.* A movie marked by low-key lighting, a bleak urban setting, and corrupt, cynical characters. [Fr., black film.]

film•strip (fĭlm′strĭp′) ►*n.* A length of film containing graphic matter prepared for still projection one frame at a time.

fil•ter (fĭl′tər) ►*n.* **1.** A porous material through which a liquid or gas is passed in order to separate the fluid from suspended particulate matter. **2.** Any of various devices used to reject signals, vibrations, or radiations of certain frequencies while passing others. **3.** *Comp. Sci.* A program that blocks access to data that meet a particular criterion. ►*v.* **1.** To pass through a filter. **2.** To remove by passing through a filter. [< Med.Lat. *filtrum,* of Gmc. orig.] —**fil′ter•a•bil′i•ty** *n.* —**fil′ter•a•ble, fil′tra•ble** *adj.*

filth (fĭlth) ►*n.* **1.** Foul or dirty matter. **2.** Corruption; vileness. **3.** Something considered obscene or immoral. [< OE *fӯlth.*] —**filth′i•ly** *adv.* —**filth′i•ness** *n.* —**filth′y** *adj.*

fil•trate (fĭl′trāt′) ►*v.* **-trat•ed, -trat•ing.** To put or go through a filter. ►*n.* Material that has passed through a filter. [< Med.Lat. *filtrum,* FILTER.] —**fil•tra′tion** *n.*

fin (fĭn) ►*n.* **1.** A membranous appendage extending from the body of a fish or other aquatic animal, used for propelling, steering, or balancing the body in the water. **2.** Something, such as an airfoil, that resembles a fin. **3.** See **flipper** 2. [< OE *finn.*] —**fin′ny** *adj.*

fi•na•gle (fə-nā′gəl) ►*v.* **-gled, -gling** *Informal.* To obtain or achieve by indirect, usu. deceitful methods. [Prob. < dial. *fainaigue,* cheat.] —**fi•na′gler** *n.*

fi•nal (fī′nəl) ►*adj.* **1.** Forming or occurring at the end; last. **2.** Of or constituting the end result of a succession or process; ultimate. **3.** Definitive; unalterable. ►*n.* **1.** The last of a series of contests. **2.** The last examination of an academic course. [< Lat. *fīnis,* end.] —**fi•nal′i•ty** (fī-năl′ĭ-tē, fə-) *n.* —**fi′nal•ly** *adv.*

fi•nal•e (fə-năl′ē, -nä′lē) ►*n.* The concluding part, esp. of a musical composition. [Ital.]

fi•nal•ist (fī′nə-lĭst) ►*n.* A contestant in the final session of a competition.

fi•nal•ize (fī′nə-līz′) ►*v.* **-ized, -iz•ing.** To put into final form. —**fi′nal•i•za′tion** *n.*

Usage: Although *finalize* has been criticized for its association with the language of bureaucracy, it is becoming more acceptable in general use. Rough synonyms can be found in *complete, conclude, make final,* and *put into final form.*

fi•nance (fə-năns′, fī-, fī′năns′) ►*n.* **1.** The management of money, banking, investments, and credit. **2. finances** Monetary resources; funds. ►*v.* **-nanced, -nanc•ing 1.** To provide or raise the funds or capital for. **2.** To furnish credit to. [< OFr. *finer,* pay ransom.] —**fi•nan′cial** *adj.* —**fi•nan′cial•ly** *adv.*

fin•an•cier (fĭn′ən-sîr′, fə-năn′-, fī′nən-) ►*n.* One dealing in large-scale financial affairs. [Fr.]

finch (fĭnch) ►*n.* Any of various small birds having a short stout bill. [< OE *finc.*]

find (fīnd) ►*v.* **found** (found), **find•ing 1.** To come upon, often by accident. **2.** To come upon after a search. **3.** To discover through observation, experience, or study. **4.** To perceive to be: *found the movie dull.* **5.** To recover; regain. **6.** To arrive at; attain: *found happiness at last.* **7.** To decide on and make a declaration about: *find a verdict of guilty.* —***phrasal verb:* find out 1.** To ascertain, as through examination or inquiry. **2.** To detect the true character of; expose. ►*n.* **1.** The act of finding. **2.** An unexpectedly valuable discovery. [< OE *findan.*] —**find′a•ble** *adj.* —**find′er** *n.*

fin-de-siè•cle (făN′də-sē-ĕk′lə) ►*adj.* Of or characteristic of the last part of the 19th cent., esp. its artistic climate of effete sophistication. [Fr.]

find•ing (fīn′dĭng) ►*n.* **1.** A conclusion reached after examination or investigation. **2.** A document containing an authoritative conclusion.

fine[1] (fīn) ►*adj.* **fin•er, fin•est 1.** Of superior quality, skill, or appearance. **2.** Very small in size, weight, or thickness. **3.** Very sharp: *a blade with a fine edge.* **4.** Exhibiting superior artistry: *fine china.* See Syns at **delicate. 5.** Consisting of very small particles: *fine dust.* **6.** Subtle or precise: *a fine difference.* **7.** Marked by refinement or elegance. **8.** First-rate; splendid. **9.** Being in good condition or health. **10.** Used as an intensive: *a fine mess.* ►*adv. Informal* Very well: *doing fine.* [< Lat. *fīnis,* end.] —**fine′ly** *adv.* —**fine′ness** *n.*

fine[2] (fīn) ►*n.* A sum of money imposed as a penalty for an offense. ►*v.* **fined, fin•ing.** To impose a fine on. —***idiom:* in fine 1.** In conclusion. **2.** In brief. [< Lat. *fīnis,* end.]

fi•ne[3] (fē′nā) ►*n. Mus.* The end. [Ital. < Lat. *fīnis,* end.]

fine art (fīn) ►*n.* **1.** Art intended primarily for beauty rather than utility. **2.** often **fine arts** Any of the art forms, such as sculpture, painting, and music, used to create this art.

fine print ►*n.* The portion of a document that contains qualifications or restrictions in small type or obscure language.

fin•er•y (fī′nə-rē) ►*n., pl.* **-ies.** Elaborate adornment, esp. fine clothing.

fi•nesse (fə-nĕs′) ►*n.* **1.** Refinement and delicacy of performance, execution, or artisanship. **2.** Subtlety; tact. ►*v.* **-nessed, -ness•ing.** To handle with subtle or evasive strategy: *finesse an embarrasing question.* [Fr. < *fin,* FINE[1].]

fine-tune (fīn′to͞on′, -tyo͞on′) ►*v.* To make small adjustments in for optimal performance or effectiveness.

fin•ger (fĭng′gər) ►*n.* **1.** One of the five digits of the hand, esp. one other than the thumb. **2.** The part of a glove that fits a finger. **3.** Something that resembles a finger. ►*v.* **1.** To touch with the fingers; handle. **2.** *Mus.* To play (an instrument) by using the fingers in a particular order or way. **3.** *Slang* **a.** To inform on. **b.** To designate, esp. as an intended victim. [< OE.]

fin•ger•board (fĭng′gər-bôrd′, -bōrd′) ►*n.* A strip of wood on the neck of a stringed instrument against which the strings are pressed in playing.

finger bowl ►*n.* A small bowl that holds water for rinsing the fingers at the table.

fin•ger•ing (fĭng′gər-ĭng) ►*n.* The indication

on a musical score of which fingers are to be used in playing.

Finger Lakes. A group of elongated glacial lakes in W-central NY.

fin•ger•ling (fĭng′gər-lĭng) ►*n.* A young or small fish.

fin•ger•nail (fĭng′gər-nāl′) ►*n.* The nail on a finger.

fin•ger•print (fĭng′gər-prĭnt′) ►*n.* **1.** An impression formed by the curves in the ridges on a fingertip, used esp. as a means of identification. **2.** A distinctive mark or characteristic. —**fin′ger•print′** *v.*

fin•ger•tip (fĭng′gər-tĭp′) ►*n.* The extreme end of a finger. —***idiom:*** **at (one's) fingertips** Readily available.

fin•i•al (fĭn′ē-əl) ►*n.* An ornamental projection or terminating part, as on an arch. [ME.]

fin•ick•y (fĭn′ĭ-kē) ►*adj.* **-i•er, -i•est.** Difficult to please; fussy. [Prob. ult. < FINE[1].] —**fin′ick•i•ness** *n.*

fin•is (fĭn′ĭs, fī′nĭs, fē-nē′) ►*n.* The end. [ME < Lat. *fīnis*.]

fin•ish (fĭn′ĭsh) ►*v.* **1.** To reach the end (of). **2.** To bring to an end; terminate. **3.** To consume all of; use up. **4.** To give (a surface) a desired texture. **5.** To destroy; kill. ►*n.* **1.** The final part; the conclusion. **2.** Surface texture. **3.** Completeness or refinement of execution; polish. [< Lat. *fīnīre*, to complete.] —**fin′ish•er** *n.*

fi•nite (fī′nīt′) ►*adj.* **1.** Having bounds; limited. **2.** *Math.* Being neither infinite nor infinitesimal. **3.** *Gram.* Limited by person, number, tense, and mood. Used of a verb. [< Lat. *fīnītus*.] —**fi′nite′ly** *adv.* —**fi′nite′ness** *n.*

fink (fĭngk) *Slang* ►*n.* **1.** A contemptible person. **2.** An informer. ►*v.* **1.** To inform against another person. **2.** To let another down. [?]

Fin•land (fĭn′lənd) A country of N Europe on the Gulf of Bothnia and the Gulf of Finland. Cap. Helsinki. Pop. 5,095,000.

Finland, Gulf of. An arm of the Baltic Sea bordered by Finland, Russia, and Estonia.

Finn (fĭn) ►*n.* A native or inhabitant of Finland.

fin•nan had•die (fĭn′ən hăd′ē) ►*n.* Smoked haddock. [< *Findon* or *Findhorn*, Scotland.]

Fin•nic (fĭn′ĭk) ►*n.* A branch of Finno-Ugric that includes Finnish, Estonian, and Lapp.

Finn•ish (fĭn′ĭsh) ►*adj.* Of or relating to Finland or its people or language. ►*n.* The Finno-Ugric language of the Finns.

Fin•no-U•gric (fĭn′ō-o͞o′grĭk, -yo͞o′-) also **Fin•no-U•gri•an** (-o͞o′grē-ən, -yo͞o′-) ►*n.* A subfamily of the Uralic language family that includes Finnish, Hungarian, and other languages of E and NE Europe. —**Finno-Ugric** *adj.*

fiord (fyôrd, fyōrd) ►*n.* Var. of **fjord.**

fir (fûr) ►*n.* **1.** Any of a genus of evergreen trees having flattened needles and erect cones. **2.** The wood of a fir. [ME *firre*.]

fire (fīr) ►*n.* **1.** A rapid, persistent chemical change that releases heat and light and is accompanied by flame, esp. the burning of a combustible substance. **2a.** Burning fuel or other material. **b.** A destructive burning: *insured against fire.* **3.** Enthusiasm; ardor. **4.** Brilliance; sparkle. **5.** The discharge of firearms. **6.** Intense, repeated attack or criticism. ►*v.* **fired, fir•ing 1.** To ignite. **2.** To maintain fire in. **3.** To bake in a kiln. **4.** To arouse the emotions of. **5.** To detonate or discharge (a weapon). **6.** To throw with force; hurl. **7.** To discharge from a position; dismiss. See Syns at **dismiss.** —***idiom:*** **on fire 1.** Ignited; ablaze. **2.** Ardent; impassioned. [< OE *fȳr*.] —**fir′er** *n.*

fire ant ►*n.* Any of a genus of ants of the S US and tropical America having a painful sting.

fire•arm (fīr′ärm′) ►*n.* A weapon, esp. a pistol or rifle, capable of firing a projectile.

fire•ball (fīr′bôl′) ►*n.* **1.** A brilliantly burning sphere. **2.** A highly luminous, intensely hot spherical cloud generated by a nuclear explosion. **3.** An energetic person.

fire•base (fīr′bās′) ►*n.* A military site from which fire is directed against the enemy.

fire•bomb (fīr′bŏm′) ►*n.* A bomb designed to start a fire. —**fire′bomb′** *v.*

fire•brand (fīr′brănd′) ►*n.* **1.** A piece of burning wood. **2.** One who stirs up trouble; agitator.

fire•break (fīr′brāk′) ►*n.* A strip of cleared or plowed land used to stop the spread of a fire.

fire•brick (fīr′brĭk′) ►*n.* A refractory brick, usu. of fire clay, used for lining furnaces, chimneys, or fireplaces.

fire•bug (fīr′bŭg′) ►*n.* *Informal* An arsonist; pyromaniac.

fire clay (fīr′klā′) ►*n.* A type of heat-resistant clay used esp. to make firebricks.

fire•crack•er (fīr′krăk′ər) ►*n.* A small explosive charge and a fuse in a heavy paper casing, exploded to entertain.

fire•damp (fīr′dămp′) ►*n.* A combustible gas, chiefly methane, that occurs in coal mines and forms an explosive mixture with air.

fire•dog (fīr′dôg′, -dŏg′) ►*n.* See **andiron.** See Regional Note at **andiron.**

fire engine ►*n.* A large truck that carries firefighters and equipment to a fire.

fire escape ►*n.* An outside stairway for emergency exit in the event of fire.

fire extinguisher ►*n.* A portable apparatus containing chemicals that can be discharged in a jet to extinguish a small fire.

fire•fight (fīr′fīt′) ►*n.* An exchange of gunfire, as between infantry units.

fire•fight•er (fīr′fī′tər) ►*n.* One who fights fires, esp. for a living. See Usage Note at **man.** —**fire′fight′ing** *adj. & n.*

fire•fly (fīr′flī′) ►*n.* Any of various nocturnal beetles having luminescent chemicals in the posterior tip of the abdomen that produce a flashing light. See Regional Note at **lightning bug.**

fire•house (fīr′hous′) ►*n.* See **fire station.**

fire hydrant ►*n.* An upright pipe with a nozzle or spout for drawing water from a water main.

fire irons ►*pl.n.* Implements, such as tongs and a poker, used to tend a fireplace.

fire•man (fīr′mən) ►*n.* **1.** A firefighter. See Usage Note at **man.** **2.** A man who tends fires; stoker.

fire•place (fīr′plās′) ►*n.* An open recess for holding a fire at the base of a chimney; hearth.

fire•plug (fīr′plŭg′) ►*n.* See **fire hydrant.**

fire•pow•er (fīr′pou′ər) ►*n.* The capacity, as of a military unit, for delivering fire.

fire•proof (fīr′pro͞of′) ►*adj.* Impervious to damage by fire. ►*v.* To make fireproof.

fire•side (fīr′sīd′) ►*n.* **1.** The area immediately surrounding a fireplace. **2.** A home.

fire station ►*n.* A building for fire equipment and firefighters.

fire tower ►*n.* A tower in which a lookout for fires is posted.

fire•trap (fīr′trăp′) ►*n.* A building that can catch fire easily or is difficult to escape from in the event of fire.

fire•wall (fīr′wôl) ►*n.* **1.** A fireproof wall used as a barrier to prevent the spread of fire. **2.** *Comp. Sci.* A security scheme that prevents unauthorized users from accessing a network.

fire•wa•ter (fīr′wô′tər, -wŏt′ər) ►*n. Slang* Strong liquor, esp. whiskey. [Translation of Ojibwa *ishkodewaaboo*, whiskey.]

fire•wood (fīr′wo͝od′) ►*n.* Wood used as fuel.

fire•works (fīr′wûrks′) ►*pl.n.* **1.** Explosives and combustibles set off to generate colored lights, smoke, and noise for amusement. **2a.** A spectacular display, as of musical virtuosity. **b.** A fiery verbal attack.

fir•ing line (fīr′ĭng) ►*n.* **1.** The line of positions from which fire is directed at a target. **2.** The forefront of an activity; vanguard.

firing pin ►*n.* The part of the bolt of a firearm that strikes the primer and detonates the charge of a projectile.

firm[1] (fûrm) ►*adj.* **-er, -est 1.** Resistant to externally applied pressure. **2.** Marked by the tone and resiliency of healthy tissue: *firm muscles.* **3.** Securely fixed in place. **4.** Indicating determination or resolution. **5.** Constant; steadfast. **6.** Fixed and definite: *a firm offer.* **7.** Strong and sure: *a firm grasp.* ►*v.* To make or become firm. ►*adv.* **-er, -est.** Resolutely: *stand firm.* [< Lat. *firmus*.] —**firm′ly** *adv.* —**firm′ness** *n.*

firm[2] (fûrm) ►*n.* A commercial partnership of two or more persons, esp. when unincorporated. [< Med.Lat. *firmāre*, ratify by signature, ult. < Lat. *firmus*, firm.]

fir•ma•ment (fûr′mə-mənt) ►*n.* The vault or expanse of the heavens; the sky. [< Lat. *firmāmentum*, support.]

firm•ware (fûrm′wâr′) ►*n. Comp. Sci.* Instructions that are stored in ROM.

first (fûrst) ►*n.* **1.** The ordinal number matching the number 1 in a series. **2.** The one coming, occurring, or ranking first. **3.** The beginning; outset: *from the first.* **4.** The lowest forward gear in a motor vehicle. **5.** The winning position in a contest. ►*adj.* **1.** Coming before all others in order or location. **2.** Prior to all others in time; earliest. **3.** Ranking above all others; foremost. ►*adv.* **1.** Before or above all others in time, order, rank, or importance. **2.** For the first time. **3.** Rather; preferably: *would die first.* **4.** To begin with: *First we need to make sure of our facts.* [< OE *fyrst*.]

first aid ►*n.* Emergency treatment administered to an injured or sick person before professional medical care is available. —**first′-aid′** *adj.*

first base ►*n. Baseball* The first base to be reached by a runner. —**first baseman** *n.*

first•born (fûrst′bôrn′) ►*adj.* First in order of birth. —**first′born′** *n.*

first class ►*n.* **1.** The first, highest, or best group in a system of classification. **2.** The most expensive class of accommodations. **3.** A class of mail sealed against inspection. —**first′-class′** *adj. & adv.*

first cousin ►*n.* See **cousin** 1.

first-de•gree burn (fûrst′dĭ-grē′) ►*n.* A mild burn that produces redness of the skin but no blistering.

first-gen•er•a•tion (fûrst′jĕn′ə-rā′shən) ►*adj.* **1.** Of or relating to an immigrant to another country. **2.** Of or relating to one whose parents are immigrants.

first•hand (fûrst′hănd′) ►*adj.* Received from the original source. —**first′hand′** *adv.*

first-in, first-out (fûrst′ĭn′ fûrst′out′) ►*n.* A method of inventory accounting in which the oldest remaining items are assumed to have been the first sold.

first lieutenant ►*n.* A rank, as in the US Army, above second lieutenant and below captain.

first•ly (fûrst′lē) ►*adv.* To begin with.

first mate ►*n.* An officer on a merchant ship ranking immediately below the captain.

first person ►*n.* The form of a verb or pronoun designating the speaker of the sentence in which it appears.

first-rate (fûrst′rāt′) ►*adj.* Foremost in quality, rank, or importance. ►*adv. Informal* Very well; excellently.

first sergeant ►*n.* **1.** A rank in the US Army and Marine Corps below sergeant major. **2.** Any of three senior noncommissioned ranks in the US Air Force.

first strike ►*n.* The initial use of strategic nuclear weapons against a nuclear-armed adversary. —**first′-strike′** *adj.*

first-string (fûrst′strĭng′) ►*adj.* Of or being a regular member of a team rather than a substitute. —**first′-string′er** *n.*

firth (fûrth) ►*n. Scots* A long narrow inlet of the sea. [< ON *fjördhr*.]

fis•cal (fĭs′kəl) ►*adj.* **1.** Of or relating to government expenditures, revenues, and debt. **2.** Of finance or finances. [< Lat. *fiscus*, treasury.] —**fis′cal•ly** *adv.*

fiscal year ►*n.* A 12-month period for which an organization plans the use of its funds.

fish (fĭsh) ►*n., pl.* **fish** or **fish•es 1.** Any of numerous cold-blooded aquatic vertebrates having fins, gills, and a streamlined body. **2.** The edible flesh of a fish. ►*v.* **1.** To catch or try to catch fish. **2.** To grope: *fished in both pockets for a coin.* **3.** To seek something indirectly: *fish for compliments.* [< OE *fisc*.] —**fish′er** *n.* —**fish′ing** *n.*

fish•bowl (fĭsh′bōl′) ►*n.* **1.** A transparent bowl in which live fish are kept. **2.** *Informal* A place or situation lacking in privacy.

fish•er•man (fĭsh′ər-mən) ►*n.* **1.** One who fishes as an occupation or for sport. **2.** A commercial fishing vessel.

fish•er•y (fĭsh′ə-rē) ►*n., pl.* **-ies 1.** The industry devoted to the catching, processing, or selling of fish. **2.** A fishing ground. **3.** A hatchery for fish.

fish•eye (fĭsh′ī′) ►*adj.* Of or being a camera lens that covers an angle of about 180°.

fish hawk ►*n.* See **osprey.**

fish•hook (fĭsh′ho͝ok′) ►*n.* A barbed metal hook for catching fish.

fishing rod ►*n.* A rod used with a line for catching fish.

fish ladder ►*n.* A steplike series of pools by which fish can pass around a dam.

fish•meal (fĭsh′mēl′) ►*n.* Ground dried fish used as animal feed and fertilizer.

fish•net (fĭsh′nĕt′) ►*n.* **1.** Netting used to catch fish. **2.** A large-mesh fabric.

fish story ►*n. Informal* A boastful and implausible or highly exaggerated story.

fish•wife (fĭsh′wīf′) ►*n.* **1.** A woman who sells fish. **2.** A woman regarded as coarse and abusive.

fish•y (fĭsh′ē) ►*adj.* **-i•er, -i•est 1.** Resembling or suggestive of fish. **2.** *Informal* Inspiring doubt or suspicion. —**fish′i•ly** *adv.* —**fish′i•ness** *n.*

fis•sile (fĭs′əl, -īl′) ►*adj.* **1.** Possible to split. **2.** *Phys.* Fissionable, esp. by neutrons of all energies. [< Lat. *findere, fiss-*, split.] —**fis•sil′i•ty** (fĭ-sĭl′ĭ-tē) *n.*

fis•sion (fĭsh′ən) ►*n.* **1.** The act or process of splitting into parts. **2.** A nuclear reaction in which an atomic nucleus splits into fragments, generating from 100 million to several hundred million electron volts of energy. **3.** *Biol.* An asexual reproductive process in which a unicellular organism divides into two or more independently maturing cells. [< Lat. *findere, fiss-*, split.] —**fis′sion•a•ble** *adj.*

fis•sure (fĭsh′ər) ►*n.* A long narrow opening; cleft. [< Lat. *fissūra* < *findere*, split.] —**fis′sure** *v.*

fist (fĭst) ►*n.* The hand closed tightly with the fingers bent against the palm. [< OE *fȳst.*]

fist•fight (fĭst′fīt′) ►*n.* A fight with the bare fists.

fist•ful (fĭst′fo͝ol′) ►*n., pl.* **-fuls.** A handful.

fist•i•cuffs (fĭs′tĭ-kŭfs′) ►*pl.n.* A fistfight.

fis•tu•la (fĭs′chə-lə) ►*n., pl.* **-las** or **-lae** (-lē′). An abnormal duct or passage that connects a hollow organ to the body surface or to another hollow organ. [< Lat.]

fit[1] (fĭt) ►*v.* **fit•ted** or **fit, fit•ted, fit•ting 1.** To be the proper size and shape (for). **2.** To be appropriate to; suit. **3.** To make suitable. See Syns at **adapt. 4.** To equip; outfit: *fit out a ship.* **5.** To provide a place or time for: *The doctor can fit you in today.* ►*adj.* **fit•ter, fit•test 1.** Suited, adapted, or acceptable for a given circumstance or purpose. **2.** Appropriate; proper. **3.** Physically sound; healthy. ►*n.* The manner in which something fits: *a jacket with a tight fit.* [ME *fitten*, be suitable.] —**fit′ly** *adv.* —**fit′ter** *n.*

fit[2] (fĭt) ►*n.* **1.** *Medic.* **a.** A seizure or convulsion, esp. one caused by epilepsy. **b.** The sudden appearance of a symptom such as coughing or sneezing. **2.** A sudden outburst: *a fit of jealousy.* **3.** A sudden period of vigorous activity. [ME, hardship.]

fit•ful (fĭt′fəl) ►*adj.* Intermittent; irregular. —**fit′ful•ly** *adv.* —**fit′ful•ness** *n.*

fit•ness (fĭt′nĭs) ►*n.* The state of being physically fit, esp. as the result of exercise and proper nutrition.

fit•ting (fĭt′ĭng) ►*adj.* Suitable; appropriate. ►*n.* **1.** The act of trying on clothes for fit. **2.** A small detachable part for a machine. —**fit′ting•ly** *adv.* —**fit′ting•ness** *n.*

Fitz•ger•ald (fĭts-jĕr′əld), **Ella.** 1917–96. Amer. singer.

Fitzgerald, F(rancis) Scott (Key). 1896–1940. Amer. writer.

FitzGerald, Edward. 1809–83. British poet and translator.

five (fīv) ►*n.* **1.** The cardinal number equal to 4 + 1. **2.** The 5th in a set or sequence. [< OE *fīf.*] —**five** *adj. & pron.*

five-and-ten (fīv′ən-tĕn′) ►*n.* A retail store selling a wide variety of inexpensive articles. [Short for *five-and-ten-cent store.*]

fisheye

Ella Fitzgerald photographed in 1954

fix (fĭks) ►*v.* **1a.** To place securely. See Syns at **fasten. b.** To secure to another; attach. **2a.** To put into a stable or unalterable form. **b.** To make (a chemical substance) nonvolatile or solid. **c.** To convert (nitrogen) into stable, biologically assimilable compounds. **d.** To prevent discoloration of (a photographic image) by coating with a chemical preservative. **3.** To direct steadily: *fixed her eyes on the road.* **4.** To establish definitely; specify: *fix a time to meet.* **5.** To assign; attribute: *fix blame.* **6.** To correct or set right; adjust. **7.** To restore to proper condition; repair. **8.** To make ready; prepare. **9.** To spay or castrate (an animal). **10.** *Informal* To get even with. **11.** To influence the outcome of by improper or unlawful means. ►*n.* **1.** The act of adjusting, correcting, or repairing. **2.** A solution: *a quick fix.* **3.** The position, as of a ship or aircraft, determined by observation or equipment. **4.** An instance of prearranging an improper or illegal outcome, esp. by means of bribery. **5.** A predicament. **6.** *Slang* A dose of a narcotic. [< Lat. *fīgere, fīx-*, fasten.] —**fix′a•ble** *adj.* —**fix′er** *n.*

fix•ate (fĭk′sāt′) ►*v.* **-at•ed, -at•ing 1.** To make fixed or stationary. **2.** To preoccupy obsessively. **3.** *Psychol.* To attach (oneself) to a person or thing in an immature or neurotic fashion. —**fix•a′tion** *n.*

fix•a•tive (fĭk′sə-tĭv) ►*n.* A substance that fixes or preserves. —**fix′a•tive** *adj.*

fixed (fĭkst) ►*adj.* **1.** Firmly in position; stationary. **2.** Determined; established: *a fixed price.* **3.** Invariable; constant: *a fixed income.* **4.** *Chem.* **a.** Nonvolatile. **b.** In a stable, combined form. **5.** Firmly, often dogmatically held: *fixed notions.* **6.** Illegally prearranged: *a fixed election.* —**fix′ed•ly** (fĭk′sĭd-lē) *adv.* —**fix′ed•ness** *n.*

fix•ings (fĭk′sĭngz) ►*pl.n.* *Informal* Accessories; trimmings: *turkey with all the fixings.*

fix•i•ty (fĭk′sĭ-tē) ►*n.* The quality or condition of being fixed; stability.

fix•ture (fĭks′chər) ►*n.* **1.** Something attached as a permanent apparatus or appliance: *plumbing fixtures.* **2.** One long associated with a place or setting. [< LLat. *fīxūra.*]

fizz (fĭz) ►*n.* **1.** A hissing or bubbling sound. **2.** Effervescence. [Imit.] —**fizz** *v.* —**fizz′y** *adj.*

fiz•zle (fĭz′əl) ►*v.* **-zled, -zling 1.** To make a hissing or sputtering sound. **2.** *Informal* To fail or end weakly, esp. after a hopeful beginning. ►*n.* *Informal* A failure. [Prob. < obsolete *fist*, break wind.]

fjord or **fiord** (fyôrd, fyōrd) ►*n.* A long, narrow, deep inlet of the sea between steep slopes. [< ON *fjördhr.*]

FL ▶*abbr.* **1.** also **Fla.** Florida **2.** focal length

fl. ▶*abbr.* **1.** *Lat.* floruit (flourished) **2.** fluid

flab (flăb) ▶*n.* Soft, fatty body tissue. [< FLABBY.]

flab•ber•gast (flăb′ər-găst′) ▶*v.* To overwhelm with astonishment; astound. [?]

flab•by (flăb′ē) ▶*adj.* **-bi•er, -bi•est 1.** Lacking firmness; slack. See Syns at **limp. 2.** Lacking force; feeble. [< *flappy*, tending to flap < FLAP.] —**flab′bi•ly** *adv.* —**flab′bi•ness** *n.*

flac•cid (flăs′ĭd, flăk′sĭd) ▶*adj.* Lacking firmness, resilience, or muscle tone. See Syns at **limp.** [< Lat. *flaccus.*] —**flac•cid′i•ty, flac′cid•ness** *n.* —**flac′cid•ly** *adv.*

flack (flăk) ▶*n.* Var. of **flak.**

flac•on (flăk′ən, -ŏn′) ▶*n.* A small stoppered bottle. [< OFr. FLAGON.]

flag¹ (flăg) ▶*n.* **1.** A piece of cloth of distinctive color and design, used as a symbol, signal, or emblem. **2.** A marker; tag. ▶*v.* **flagged, flag•ging 1.** To mark with a flag. **2.** To signal with or as if with a flag: *flagged the car to stop.* [?] —**flag′ger** *n.*

flag² (flăg) ▶*n.* A plant, as an iris, that has long bladelike leaves. [ME *flagge*, reed.]

flag³ (flăg) ▶*v.* **flagged, flag•ging 1.** To hang limply; droop. **2.** To decline in vigor or strength. [Poss. of Scand. orig.]

flag⁴ (flăg) ▶*n.* A flagstone. [< ON *flaga*, slab of stone.]

flag•el•late (flăj′ə-lāt′) ▶*v.* **-lat•ed, -lat•ing.** To whip or flog; scourge. [< Lat. *flagellum*, FLAIL.] —**flag′el•la′tion** *n.*

fla•gel•lum (flə-jĕl′əm) ▶*n., pl.* **-gel•la** (-jĕl′ə) **1.** *Biol.* A whiplike extension of certain cells or unicellular organisms that serves in locomotion. **2.** A whip. [Lat. FLAIL.]

flag•on (flăg′ən) ▶*n.* A large vessel with a handle and spout, used for holding wine or liquors. [< LLat. *flascō*, bottle. See FLASK.]

flag•pole (flăg′pōl′) ▶*n.* A pole on which a flag is raised.

fla•grant (flā′grənt) ▶*adj.* Conspicuously bad, offensive, or reprehensible. [< Lat. *flagrāre*, burn.] —**fla′gran•cy, fla′grance** *n.* —**fla′grant•ly** *adv.*

flag•ship (flăg′shĭp′) ▶*n.* **1.** A ship bearing the flag of a fleet or squadron commander. **2.** The chief one of a group: *the flagship of a newspaper chain.*

flag•staff (flăg′stăf′) ▶*n.* See **flagpole.**

flag•stone (flăg′stōn′) ▶*n.* A flat, evenly layered paving stone.

flag-wav•ing (flăg′wā′vĭng) ▶*n.* Excessive or fanatical patriotism. —**flag′-wav′er** *n.*

flail (flāl) ▶*n.* A manual threshing device with a long wooden handle and a short, free-swinging stick on the end. ▶*v.* **1.** To beat with or as if with a flail. **2.** To move wildly. [< LLat. *flagellum* < Lat. *flagrum*, whip.]

flair (flâr) ▶*n.* **1.** A talent or aptitude. **2.** Instinctive discernment; keenness. **3.** Distinctive elegance or style. [< OFr., fragrance < Lat. *frāgrāre*, emit an odor.]

flak also **flack** (flăk) ▶*n.* **1a.** Antiaircraft artillery. **b.** The bursting shells fired from such artillery. **2.** *Informal* **a.** Excessive criticism. **b.** Dissension; opposition. [Ger.]

flake (flāk) ▶*n.* **1.** A flat thin piece or layer; chip. **2.** A crystal of snow. **3.** *Slang* A somewhat eccentric person; oddball. ▶*v.* **flaked, flak•ing.** To break into or come off in flakes. [ME.] —**flak′er** *n.* —**flak′i•ly** *adv.* —**flak′i•ness** *n.* —**flak′y, flak′ey** *adj.*

flam•bé (fläm-bā′, fläɴ-) ▶*adj.* Served flaming in ignited liquor. [Fr., p.part. of *flamber*, to flame.] —**flam•bé′** *v.*

flam•boy•ant (flăm-boi′ənt) ▶*adj.* **1.** Highly elaborate; ornate. **2.** Richly colored; resplendent. **3.** Marked by striking audacity or verve. **4.** Ostentatious. See Syns at **showy.** [< OFr. *flamboyer*, to blaze.] —**flam•boy′ance, flam•boy′an•cy** *n.* —**flam•boy′ant•ly** *adv.*

flame (flām) ▶*n.* **1.** The zone of burning gases and fine suspended matter associated with rapid combustion. **2.** A violent or intense passion. **3.** *Informal* A sweetheart. **4.** An insulting or malicious remark, as on a computer network. ▶*v.* **flamed, flam•ing 1.** To burn brightly; blaze. **2.** To color or flash suddenly. **3.** To insult or criticize provokingly, as on a computer network. [< Lat. *flamma.*] —**flam′er** *n.*

fla•men•co (flə-mĕng′kō) ▶*n., pl.* **-cos 1.** A dance style of the Andalusian Gypsies, with forceful, often improvised rhythms. **2.** The guitar music that usu. accompanies such a dance. [Sp., Flemish < MDu. *Vlāming.*]

flamenco

flame•out (flām′out′) ▶*n.* Failure of a jet aircraft engine, esp. in flight.

flame•throw•er (flām′thrō′ər) ▶*n.* A weapon that projects a steady stream of ignited fuel.

fla•min•go (flə-mĭng′gō) ▶*n., pl.* **-gos** or **-goes.** A large tropical wading bird with pink plumage, long legs, and a long flexible neck. [Prob. < OProv. *flamenc.*]

flam•ma•ble (flăm′ə-bəl) ▶*adj.* Easily ignited and capable of burning rapidly. [< Lat. *flammāre*, set fire to.] —**flam′ma•bil′i•ty** *n.* —**flam′ma•ble** *n.*

Usage: Because some people mistakenly believe that *inflammable* means "not flammable," use *flammable* to avoid confusion.

flan (flăn, flän, fläɴ) ▶*n.* **1.** A tart with a filling of custard, fruit, or cheese. **2.** See **crème caramel.** [< LLat. *fladō*, flat cake, of Gmc. orig.]

Flan•ders (flăn′dərz) A historical region of NW Europe including parts of N France, W Belgium, and SW Netherlands.

flange (flănj) ▶*n.* A protruding rim or edge, as on a wheel, used to strengthen an object or hold it in place. [Perh. ult. < Fr. *flanc*, side.] —**flange** *v.*

flank (flăngk) ▶*n.* **1.** The fleshy section of the side between the last rib and the hip. **2.** A cut of meat from the flank of an animal. **3.** A lateral part or side. **4.** The right or left side of a military formation. ►*v.* **1.** To protect or guard the flank of. **2.** To menace or attack the flank of. **3.** To be placed or situated at the flank of. [< OFr. *flanc*.]

flan•nel (flăn′əl) ►*n.* **1.** A soft woven cloth of wool or a wool blend. **2. flannels** Trousers or undergarments made of wool. [ME.]

flan•nel•ette (flăn′ə-lĕt′) ►*n.* A soft napped cotton cloth.

flap (flăp) ►*n.* **1.** A flat, usu. thin piece attached at only one side, as on an envelope. **2.** The act or sound of flapping. **3.** A blow given with something flat. **4.** *Informal* A commotion or disturbance. ►*v.* **flapped, flap•ping 1.** To wave (e.g., wings) up and down. **2.** To wave loosely; flutter. **3.** To hit with something broad and flat. [ME *flappe*, a slap.]

flap•jack (flăp′jăk′) ►*n.* See **pancake.**

flap•per (flăp′ər) ►*n.* **1.** A broad, flexible part, such as a flipper. **2.** A young woman in the 1920s who showed disdain for conventional dress and behavior.

flare (flâr) ►*v.* **flared, flar•ing 1.** To flame up with a bright, wavering light. **2.** To burst into intense, sudden flame. **3.** To erupt or intensify suddenly. **4.** To expand or open outward in shape, as a skirt. ►*n.* **1.** A brief, wavering blaze of light. **2.** A device that produces a bright light for signaling or illumination. **3.** An outbreak, as of emotion. **4.** An expanding outward. [?]

flare-up (flâr′ŭp′) ►*n.* A sudden outburst, as of flame or anger.

flash (flăsh) ►*v.* **1.** To burst forth into or as if into flame. **2.** To give off light or be lighted in sudden or intermittent bursts. **3.** To appear or cause to appear suddenly. **4.** To move rapidly. **5.** To communicate (information) at great speed. **6.** To display ostentatiously; flaunt. ►*n.* **1.** A sudden, brief, intense display of light. **2.** A sudden perception. **3.** A split second; instant. **4.** A brief news dispatch or transmission. **5a.** Instantaneous illumination for photography. **b.** A device used to produce such illumination. [ME *flashen*, to splash.]

flash•back (flăsh′băk′) ►*n.* **1.** A literary or cinematic device in which an earlier event is inserted into the normal chronological order of a narrative. **2.** An unexpected recurrence of the effects of a hallucinogenic drug.

flash•bulb or **flash bulb** (flăsh′bŭlb′) ►*n.* A glass bulb filled with finely shredded metal foil that is ignited by electricity to produce a bright flash for taking photographs.

flash flood ►*n.* A sudden violent flood.

flash-for•ward (flăsh′fôr′wərd) ►*n.* A literary or cinematic device in which the chronological sequence of events is interrupted by the interjection of a future event.

flash•gun (flăsh′gŭn′) ►*n.* A dry-cell powered photographic apparatus that holds and electrically triggers a flashbulb.

flash•ing (flăsh′ĭng) ►*n.* Sheet metal used to reinforce and weatherproof the joints and angles of a roof.

flash lamp ►*n.* An electric lamp for producing a brief bright light for use in photography.

flash•light (flăsh′līt′) ►*n.* A small portable lamp usu. powered by batteries.

flash point ►*n.* The lowest temperature at which the vapor of a combustible liquid can be made to ignite.

flash•y (flăsh′ē) ►*adj.* **-i•er, -i•est 1.** Cheap and showy. See Syns at **gaudy. 2.** Giving a momentary or superficial brilliance. —**flash′i•ly** *adv.* —**flash′i•ness** *n.*

flask (flăsk) ►*n.* **1.** A flat, relatively thin container for liquor. **2.** A vial or round long-necked vessel for laboratory use. [< LLat. *flascō*, of Gmc. orig.]

flat[1] (flăt) ►*adj.* **flat•ter, flat•test 1.** Having a horizontal surface without a slope, tilt, or curvature. **2.** Stretched out or lying at full length along the ground; prone. **3.** Free of qualification; absolute: *a flat refusal.* **4.** Fixed; unvarying: *a flat rate.* **5.** Lacking interest or excitement; dull. **6a.** Lacking in flavor. **b.** Having lost effervescence. **7.** Deflated, as a tire. **8.** *Mus.* **a.** Being below the correct pitch. **b.** Being one half step lower than the corresponding natural key. ►*adv.* **1.** Level with the ground; horizontally. **2.** On or up against a flat surface; at full length. **3a.** Directly; completely: *flat broke.* **b.** Exactly; precisely: *arrived in six minutes flat.* **4.** *Mus.* Below the intended pitch. ►*n.* **1.** A flat surface or part. **2.** often **flats** A stretch of level ground. **3.** A shallow frame or box for seeds or seedlings. **4.** A deflated tire. **5.** A shoe with a flat heel. **6.** *Mus.* **a.** A sign (♭) used to indicate that a note is to be lowered by a half step. **b.** A note that is lowered a half step. ►*v.* **flat•ted, flat•ting 1.** To make flat; flatten. **2.** *Mus.* **a.** To lower (a note) a semitone. **b.** To sing or play below the proper pitch. [< ON *flatr*.] —**flat′ly** *adv.* —**flat′ness** *n.*

flat[2] (flăt) ►*n.* An apartment on one floor of a building. [< OE *flet*, floor, dwelling.]

flat•bed (flăt′bĕd′) ►*n.* An open truck bed or trailer with no sides.

flat•boat (flăt′bōt′) ►*n.* A boat with a flat bottom used for transporting freight.

flat•car (flăt′kär′) ►*n.* A railroad freight car without sides or roof.

flat•fish (flăt′fĭsh′) ►*n.* Any of numerous chiefly marine fishes, including flounders and soles, having a laterally compressed body with both eyes on the upper side.

flat•foot (flăt′fo͝ot′) ►*n.* **1.** *pl.* **-feet** (-fēt′) A condition in which the arch of the foot is flattened so that the entire sole makes contact with the ground. **2.** *pl.* **-foots** *Slang* A police officer. —**flat′-foot′ed** *adj.*

Flat•head (flăt′hĕd′) ►*n.*, *pl.* **-head** or **-heads 1.** A member of a Native American people of W Montana and N Idaho. **2.** The Salishan language of the Flathead.

flat•i•ron (flăt′ī′ərn) ►*n.* An iron for pressing clothes.

flat•ten (flăt′n) ►*v.* **1.** To make or become flat or flatter. **2.** To knock down. —**flat′ten•er** *n.*

flat•ter (flăt′ər) ►*v.* **1.** To compliment excessively and often insincerely, esp. to win favor. **2.** To please or gratify the vanity of. **3.** To portray favorably. [< OFr. *flater*, of Gmc. orig.] —**flat′ter•er** *n.* —**flat′ter•ing•ly** *adv.* —**flat′ter•y** *n.*

flat•top (flăt′tŏp′) ►*n.* *Informal* **1.** An aircraft carrier. **2.** A short level haircut.

flat•u•lent (flăch′ə-lənt) ►*adj.* **1.** Afflicted with or caused by excessive gas in the digestive tract. **2.** Pompous; bloated. [< Lat. *flātus*, a blowing, snorting.] —**flat′u•lence** *n.* —**flat′u•lent•ly** *adv.*

flat•ware (flăt′wâr′) ►*n.* **1.** Tableware that is

fairly flat and fashioned usu. of a single piece, as plates. **2.** Table utensils such as knives, forks, and spoons.

flat•worm (flăt′wûrm′) ►*n.* Any of various flat-bodied worms, as the tapeworm.

Flau•bert (flō-bâr′), **Gustave.** 1821–80. French writer.

flaunt (flônt) ►*v.* To exhibit ostentatiously or shamelessly; show off. [?] —**flaunt′er** *n.* —**flaunt′ing•ly** *adv.*

Usage: For some time now *flaunt* has been used in the sense "to flout or show contempt for," even by educated users of English. This usage is still widely seen as erroneous and is best avoided.

flau•tist (flô′tĭst, flou′-) ►*n.* A flutist. [Ital. *flautista* < *flauto*, flute.]

fla•vor (flā′vər) ►*n.* **1.** Distinctive taste; savor. See Syns at **taste. 2.** A distinctive quality. **3.** A flavoring. ►*v.* To give flavor to. [< VLat. *flātor, aroma.] —**fla′vor•ful** *adj.* —**fla′vor•less** *adj.*

fla•vor•ing (flā′vər-ĭng) ►*n.* A substance, as an extract or spice, that imparts flavor.

flaw (flô) ►*n.* An imperfection or blemish; defect. ►*v.* To make or become defective. [ME *flaue*, splinter.]

flaw•less (flô′lĭs) ►*adj.* Being entirely without flaw or imperfection. See Syns at **perfect.** —**flaw′less•ly** *adv.* —**flaw′less•ness** *n.*

flax (flăks) ►*n.* **1.** Any of several plants having blue flowers and slender fibrous stems. **2.** The fine yellowish textile fiber obtained from flax. [< OE *fleax.*]

flax•en (flăk′sən) ►*adj.* **1.** Made of or resembling flax. **2.** Having the pale yellowish color of flax fiber.

flay (flā) ►*v.* **1.** To strip off the skin of. **2.** To scold or criticize harshly. [< OE *flēan.*] —**flay′er** *n.*

fl. dr. ►*abbr.* fluid dram

flea (flē) ►*n.* Any of various small, wingless, bloodsucking insects that are parasitic on warm-blooded animals. [< OE *flēah.*]

flea collar ►*n.* A pet collar containing a substance that repels or kills fleas.

flea market ►*n.* A market, usu. held outdoors, where antiques, used household goods, and curios are sold.

fleck (flĕk) ►*n.* **1.** A tiny mark or spot. **2.** A small bit or flake. ►*v.* To spot or streak. [Prob. < ME *flekked*, spotted.]

fledg•ling also **fledge•ling** (flĕj′lĭng) ►*n.* **1.** A young bird that has recently acquired its flight feathers. **2.** A young or inexperienced person. [Prob. < OE *flycge, featherbed.] —**fledg′ling** *adj.*

flee (flē) ►*v.* **fled** (flĕd), **flee•ing 1.** To run away, as from trouble or danger. **2.** To pass swiftly away; vanish. [< OE *flēon.*] —**fle′er** *n.*

fleece (flēs) ►*n.* **1.** The coat of wool of a sheep or similar animal. **2.** A soft woolly covering or mass. **3.** Fabric with a soft deep pile. ►*v.* **fleeced, fleec•ing 1.** To defraud of money or property; swindle. **2.** To shear the fleece from. [< OE *flēos.*] —**fleec′er** *n.* —**fleec′i•ly** *adv.* —**fleec′i•ness** *n.* —**fleec′y** *adj.*

fleet[1] (flēt) ►*n.* **1.** A number of warships operating under one command. **2.** A group of vessels or vehicles, such as taxicabs, owned or operated as a unit. [< OE *flēot* < *flēotan*, float.]

fleet[2] (flēt) ►*adj.* **-er, -est 1.** Moving swiftly; rapid or nimble. **2.** Fleeting; evanescent. ►*v.* To move or pass swiftly. [Prob. < ON *fliōtr.*] —**fleet′ly** *adv.* —**fleet′ness** *n.*

Fleet Admiral ►*n.* The highest rank in the US Navy.

fleet•ing (flē′tĭng) ►*adj.* Passing quickly; ephemeral. —**fleet′ing•ly** *adv.*

Flem•ing (flĕm′ĭng) ►*n.* **1.** A native or inhabitant of Flanders. **2.** A Belgian who speaks Flemish.

Fleming, Sir **Alexander.** 1881–1955. British bacteriologist; 1945 Nobel.

Flem•ish (flĕm′ĭsh) ►*adj.* Of Flanders or the Flemings. ►*n.* **1.** The Germanic language of the Flemings. **2.** The Flemings.

flesh (flĕsh) ►*n.* **1.** The soft tissue of the body, consisting mainly of skeletal muscle and fat. **2.** The meat of animals as distinguished from the edible tissue of fish or fowl. **3.** *Bot.* The pulpy, usu. edible part of a fruit or vegetable. **4.** The body as opposed to the mind or soul. **5.** Humankind in general; humanity. ►*v.* To give substance or detail to; fill out. —***idiom:* in the flesh 1.** Alive. **2.** In person; present. [< OE *flǣsc.*]

flesh•ly (flĕsh′lē) ►*adj.* **-li•er, -li•est 1.** Of or relating to the body. See Syns at **bodily. 2.** Of or inclined to carnality; sensual. **3.** Not spiritual; worldly. —**flesh′li•ness** *n.*

flesh•y (flĕsh′ē) ►*adj.* **-i•er, -i•est 1.** Of or resembling flesh. **2.** Having abundant flesh; plump. **3.** Having a juicy or pulpy texture. **4.** Fleshly; carnal. —**flesh′i•ness** *n.*

Fletch•er (flĕch′ər), **John.** 1579–1625. English playwright.

fleur-de-lis (flûr′də-lē′, flŏŏr′-) ►*n.*, *pl.* **fleurs-de-lis** (flûr′də-lēz′, flŏŏr′-). A decorative motif consisting of a stylized three-petaled iris flower. [< OFr. *flor de lis*, flower of the lily.]

fleur-de-lis

flew (flōō) ►*v.* P.t. of **fly[1].**

flex (flĕks) ►*v.* **1.** To bend (something pliant or elastic). **2.** To contract (e.g., a muscle). **3.** To exhibit or show off the strength of. [Lat. *flectere, flex-*, bend.]

flex•i•ble (flĕk′sə-bəl) ►*adj.* **1.** Capable of being bent or flexed; pliable. **2.** Responsive to change; adaptable. —**flex′i•bil′i•ty, flex′i•ble•ness** *n.* —**flex′i•bly** *adv.*

flex•or (flĕk′sər) ►*n.* A muscle that when contracted acts to bend a joint or limb in the body. [< Lat. *flectere, flex-*, bend.]

flex•time (flĕks′tīm′) ►*n.* An arrangement by which employees may set their own work schedules. [FLEX(IBLE) + TIME.]

flex•ure (flĕk′shər) ►*n.* A curve, turn, or fold.

flick[1] (flĭk) ►*n.* **1.** A light quick blow or touch. **2.** A light splash, dash, or daub. ►*v.* **1.** To touch or hit with a light quick blow. See Syns at

brush[1]. **2.** To cause to move with a light blow: *flick a switch.* [Imit.]

flick[2] (flĭk) ►*n. Slang* A movie. [< FLICKER[1].]

flick•er[1] (flĭk′ər) ►*v.* **1.** To move waveringly; flutter. **2.** To burn unsteadily or fitfully. ►*n.* **1.** A brief movement; tremor. **2.** An inconstant or wavering light. **3.** A brief sensation. [< OE *flicerian*, flutter.]

flick•er[2] (flĭk′ər) ►*n.* A large woodpecker with a brown back, spotted breast, and white rump. [Perh. < FLICK[1].]

flied (flīd) ►*v.* P.t. and p.part. of **fly**[1] 6.

fli•er also **fly•er** (flī′ər) ►*n.* **1.** One that flies, esp. a pilot. **2.** A passenger in an aircraft. **3.** A circular for mass distribution.

flight[1] (flīt) ►*n.* **1.** The act or process of flying. **2.** A swift passage or movement. **3.** A scheduled airline trip. **4.** A group, esp. of birds or aircraft, flying together. **5.** An exuberant or transcendent effort or display: *a flight of the imagination.* **6.** A series of stairs rising from one landing to another. [< OE *flyht.*]

flight[2] (flīt) ►*n.* An act of running away. [< OE **flyht.*]

flight deck ►*n.* **1.** The upper deck of an aircraft carrier, used as a runway. **2.** An elevated compartment in certain aircraft, used by the pilot, copilot, and flight engineer.

flight engineer ►*n.* The crew member responsible for the mechanical performance of an aircraft in flight.

flight•less (flīt′lĭs) ►*adj.* Incapable of flying, as certain birds.

flight recorder ►*n.* A device, as on certain aircraft, that documents preflight checks, in-flight procedures, and the landing.

flight•y (flī′tē) ►*adj.* **-i•er, -i•est 1.** Capricious or impulsive. **2.** Irresponsible or silly. **3.** Easily excited. —**flight′i•ly** *adv.* —**flight′i•ness** *n.*

flim•flam (flĭm′flăm′) ►*n. Informal* **1.** Nonsense; humbug. **2.** A deception; swindle. [Prob. of Scand. orig.] —**flim′flam′** *v.* —**flim′flam′mer** *n.* —**flim′flam′mer•y** *n.*

flim•sy (flĭm′zē) ►*adj.* **-si•er, -si•est 1.** Light, thin, and insubstantial. **2.** Lacking solidity or strength. **3.** Lacking plausibility; unconvincing. [?] —**flim′si•ly** *adv.* —**flim′si•ness** *n.*

flinch (flĭnch) ►*v.* **1.** To start or wince involuntarily, as from pain. **2.** To recoil, as from something unpleasant. [Obsolete Fr. *flenchir*, of Gmc. orig.] —**flinch** *n.* —**flinch′er** *n.*

fling (flĭng) ►*v.* **flung** (flŭng), **fling•ing 1.** To throw or move quickly and forcefully. **2.** To throw (oneself) into an activity with abandon and energy. **3.** To cast aside; discard. ►*n.* **1.** The act of flinging. **2.** A brief period of indulging one's impulses. See Syns at **binge. 3.** *Informal* A usu. brief attempt or effort. [ME *flingen*, of Scand. orig.]

flint (flĭnt) ►*n.* **1.** A very hard, fine-grained quartz that sparks when struck with steel. **2.** A small solid cylinder of a spark-producing alloy, used in lighters to ignite the fuel. [< OE.] —**flint′y** *adj.*

Flint. A city of SE-central MI NNW of Detroit. Pop. 140,761.

flint•lock (flĭnt′lŏk′) ►*n.* **1.** An obsolete gunlock in which a flint ignites the charge. **2.** A firearm having a flintlock.

flip (flĭp) ►*v.* **flipped, flip•ping 1.** To throw or toss with a light brisk motion. **2.** To toss in the air, imparting a spin. **3a.** To turn over, esp. with a quick motion. **b.** To turn through; leaf. **4.** To flick. **5.** To move or operate (e.g., a lever or switch). **6.** To turn a somersault. **7a.** *Slang* To go crazy. **b.** To react strongly and esp. enthusiastically. ►*n.* The act of flipping, esp.: **a.** A flick. **b.** A short quick movement. **c.** A somersault. ►*adj.* **flip•per, flip•pest** *Informal.* Marked by casual disrespect; impertinent. [Perh. imit.]

flip-flop (flĭp′flŏp′) ►*n.* **1.** A backward somersault or handspring. **2.** *Informal* A reversal, as of a stand or position. **3.** A backless, often foam rubber sandal. —**flip′-flop′** *v.*

flip•pant (flĭp′ənt) ►*adj.* Casually disrespectful; pert. [Prob. < FLIP.] —**flip′pan•cy** *n.* —**flip′pant•ly** *adv.*

flip•per (flĭp′ər) ►*n.* **1.** A wide flat limb, as of a seal, adapted for swimming. **2.** A wide rubber covering for the foot, used in swimming.

flirt (flûrt) ►*v.* **1.** To make coyly romantic or sexual overtures. **2.** To deal triflingly with: *flirt with danger.* ►*n.* One given to flirting. [?] —**flir•ta′tion** *n.* —**flir•ta′tious** *adj.* —**flir•ta′tious•ly** *adv.* —**flir•ta′tious•ness** *n.*

Syns: *flirt, dally, play, toy, trifle* **v.**

flit (flĭt) ►*v.* **flit•ted, flit•ting.** To move quickly and nimbly. [< ON *flytja*, carry about.] —**flit′ter** *n.*

flit•ter (flĭt′ər) ►*v.* To flutter. [Frequentative of FLIT.]

float (flōt) ►*v.* **1a.** To remain or cause to remain suspended in or on a fluid without sinking. **b.** To be or cause to be suspended in space. **2.** To move from place to place at random. **3.** To move easily or lightly. **4.** To release (a security) for sale. **5.** To offer for consideration; suggest: *floated an idea.* ►*n.* **1.** Something that floats. **2.** A buoyant object that holds a net or fishing line afloat. **3.** A decorated exhibit on a mobile platform in a parade. **4.** A soft drink with ice cream floating in it. [< OE *flotian.*]

float•er (flō′tər) ►*n.* **1.** One that floats. **2.** One who wanders; drifter. **3.** An employee reassigned from job to job or shift to shift within an operation. **4.** An insurance policy that protects movable property in transit.

flock[1] (flŏk) ►*n.* **1.** A group of animals that live, travel, or feed together. **2.** A group of people, esp. under the leadership of one person. See Syns at **crowd. 3.** A large number; host. See Usage Note at **collective noun.** ►*v.* To congregate or travel in a flock or crowd. [< OE *floc.*]

flock[2] (flŏk) ►*n.* **1.** A tuft, as of fiber or hair. **2.** Pulverized fibers applied to paper or cloth to produce a texture or pattern. [< Lat. *floccus*, tuft of wool.] —**flock** *v.*

floe (flō) ►*n.* A large flat mass of floating ice. [Prob. < ON *flō*, layer.]

flog (flŏg, flôg) ►*v.* **flogged, flog•ging.** To beat severely with a whip or rod. [Perh. < Lat. *flagellāre*, FLAGELLATE.] —**flog′ger** *n.*

flood (flŭd) ►*n.* **1.** An overflowing of water onto normally dry land. **2.** An abundant flow or outpouring: *a flood of applications.* See Syns at **flow. 3.** A floodlight. **4. Flood** The universal deluge recorded in the Bible. ►*v.* **1.** To cover with or as if with a flood; inundate. **2.** To fill with an abundance or excess. [< OE *flōd.*]

flood•gate (flŭd′gāt′) ►*n.* **1.** A gate that controls the flow of a body of water. **2.** Something that restrains a flood or outpouring.

flood•light (flŭd′līt′) ►*n.* **1.** Artificial light in an intensely bright and broad beam. **2.** A unit that produces such a beam. ►*v.* To illuminate with a floodlight.

flood•plain (flŭd′plăn′) ►*n.* A plain bordering a river and subject to flooding.

floor (flôr, flōr) ►*n.* **1.** The surface of a room on which one stands. **2.** A story or level of a building. **3a.** The part of a legislative chamber where members are seated and from which they speak. **b.** The right to address an assembly. **c.** The body of assembly members. **4.** The part of a room or building where the principal business or work takes place. **5.** The ground or lowermost surface, as of a forest or ocean. **6.** A lower limit or base: *a pricing floor.* ►*v.* **1.** To provide with a floor. **2.** To knock down. **3.** To stun; overwhelm. [< OE *flōr.*]

floor leader ►*n.* The member of a legislature chosen by fellow party members to be in charge of the party's activities on the floor.

floor plan ►*n.* A scale diagram of a room or building.

floor•show (flôr′shō′, flōr′-) ►*n.* The entertainment presented in a nightclub.

floor•walk•er (flôr′wô′kər, flōr′-) ►*n.* An employee of a department store who supervises sales personnel and assists customers.

floo•zy also **floo•zie** (flo͞o′zē) ►*n., pl.* **-zies** *Slang.* A gaudy or tawdry woman. [?]

flop (flŏp) ►*v.* **flopped, flop•ping 1.** To fall or lie down heavily and noisily. **2.** To move about loosely or limply. **3.** *Informal* To fail utterly. ►*n.* **1.** The act or sound of flopping. **2.** *Informal* An utter failure. [Alteration of FLAP.]

flop•house (flŏp′hous′) ►*n.* A cheap hotel.

flop•py (flŏp′ē) ►*adj.* **-pi•er, -pi•est.** Tending to flop; loose and flexible. See Syns at **limp.** ►*n., pl.* **-pies** *Comp. Sci.* A floppy disk. —**flop′pi•ly** *adv.* —**flop′pi•ness** *n.*

floppy disk ►*n.* A flexible plastic disk coated with magnetic material, used to store computer data magnetically; diskette.

flo•ra (flôr′ə, flōr′ə) ►*n., pl.* **flo•ras** or **flo•rae** (flôr′ē′, flōr′ē′). Plants collectively, esp. the plants of a particular region or time. [< Lat. *flōs, flōr-*, flower.]

flo•ral (flôr′əl, flōr′-) ►*adj.* Of or relating to flowers. —**flo′ral•ly** *adv.*

Flor•ence (flôr′əns, flŏr′-) A city of central Italy E of Pisa. Pop. 402,316.

flo•res•cence (flô-rĕs′əns, flə-) ►*n.* A condition, time, or period of flowering. See Syns at **bloom.** [< Lat. *flōrēscere*, begin to bloom.] —**flo•res′cent** *adj.*

flor•id (flôr′ĭd, flŏr′-) ►*adj.* **1.** Flushed with rosy color; ruddy. **2.** Very ornate; flowery. [< Lat. *flōridus* < *flōs*, flower.] —**flo•rid′i•ty** (flə-rĭd′ĭ-tē, flô-), **flor′id•ness** *n.* —**flor′id•ly** *adv.*

Flor•i•da (flôr′ĭ-də, flŏr′-) A state of the SE US. Cap. Tallahassee. Pop. 13,003,362. —**Flo•rid′i•an** (flə-rĭd′ē-ən), **Flor′i•dan** (-ĭd-n) *adj. & n.*

Florida, Straits of. A sea passage between Cuba and the Florida Keys, linking the Gulf of Mexico with the Atlantic.

Florida Keys. A chain of small islands extending about 241 km (150 mi) from S of Miami to Key West.

flor•in (flôr′ĭn, flŏr′-) ►*n.* **1.** A guilder. **2.** A former British coin worth two shillings. [< OItal. *fiore*, flower.]

flo•rist (flôr′ĭst, flōr′-, flŏr′-) ►*n.* One who raises or sells flowers and plants. [< Lat. *flōs, flōr-*, flower.]

floss (flôs, flŏs) ►*n.* **1.** Dental floss. **2.** Short or waste silk fibers. **3.** A soft, loosely twisted thread. **4.** A silky fibrous substance. ►*v.* To clean between (teeth) with dental floss. [Perh. < Lat. *floccus*, tuft of wool.]

floss•y (flô′sē, flŏs′ē) ►*adj.* **-i•er, -i•est 1.** Superficially stylish; slick. **2.** Made of or resembling floss. —**floss′i•ness** *n.*

flo•ta•tion (flō-tā′shən) ►*n.* The act or condition of floating.

flo•til•la (flō-tĭl′ə) ►*n.* **1.** A small fleet. **2.** A fleet of small craft. [< ON *floti*, fleet.]

flot•sam (flŏt′səm) ►*n.* Wreckage or cargo that remains afloat after a ship has sunk. [< OFr. *floter*, float, of Gmc. orig.]

flounce[1] (flouns) ►*n.* A strip of usu. gathered material attached by one edge, as to a skirt or curtain. [< OFr. *fronce*, pleat.]

flounce[2] (flouns) ►*v.* **flounced, flounc•ing.** To move with exaggerated motions expressive esp. of displeasure or impatience. ►*n.* An act of flouncing. [Poss. of Scand. orig.]

floun•der[1] (floun′dər) ►*v.* **1.** To move or thrash about clumsily. **2.** To act or proceed in confusion. See Syns at **blunder.** See Usage Note at **founder.** [Poss. alteration of FOUNDER.]

floun•der[2] (floun′dər) ►*n., pl.* **-der** or **-ders.** Any of various marine flatfishes that are important food fishes. [< AN *floundre.*]

flour (flou′ər, flour) ►*n.* **1.** A fine powdery foodstuff obtained by grinding grain, esp. wheat. **2.** A soft fine powder. ►*v.* To cover or coat with flour. [ME.] —**flour′y** *adj.*

flour•ish (flûr′ĭsh, flŭr′-) ►*v.* **1.** To grow well or luxuriantly; thrive. **2.** To do or fare well; succeed. **3.** To wield or exhibit dramatically. ►*n.* **1.** A dramatic movement or gesture. **2.** An embellishment or ornamentation, esp. in handwriting. [< VLat. **flōrīre* < Lat. *flōs*, flower.]

Syns: *flourish, brandish, wave* ***v.***

flout (flout) ►*v.* To show contempt for; scorn. See Usage Note at **flaunt.** [Poss. < ME *flouten*, play the flute.] —**flout′er** *n.*

flow (flō) ►*v.* **1.** To move or run freely in or as if in a stream. **2.** To circulate, as the blood in the body. **3.** To proceed steadily and easily. **4.** To appear smooth, harmonious, or graceful. **5.** To hang loosely and gracefully. **6.** To rise. Used of the tide. **7.** To arise. See Syns at **stem**[1]. **8.** To abound or teem. ►*n.* **1.** The smooth motion characteristic of fluids. **2.** A stream or current. **3a.** A continuous output: *a flow of ideas.* **b.** A continuous movement or circulation: *the flow of traffic.* **4.** The amount that flows in a given period of time. **5.** The rising of the tide. [< OE *flōwan.*]

Syns: *flow, current, flood, flux, rush, stream, tide* ***n.***

flow chart ►*n.* A schematic representation of a sequence of operations.

flow•er (flou′ər) ►*n.* **1.** The reproductive structure of a seed-bearing plant, having specialized male and/or female organs and usu. colorful petals. **2.** A plant cultivated for its blossoms. **3.** The period of highest development; peak. See

Syns at **bloom. 4.** The highest example or best representative: *the flower of our generation.* ►*v.* **1.** To produce flowers; blossom. **2.** To develop fully; reach a peak. [< OFr. *flor* < Lat. *flōs.*]

flow•er•ing plant (flou′ər-ĭng) ►*n.* A plant that produces flowers and fruit.

flow•er•pot (flou′ər-pŏt′) ►*n.* A pot in which plants are grown.

flow•er•y (flou′ə-rē) ►*adj.* **-i•er, -i•est 1.** Full of or suggestive of flowers: *a flowery perfume.* **2.** Full of ornate or grandiloquent expressions. **—flow′er•i•ness** *n.*

flown (flōn) ►*v.* P.part. of **fly**[1].

fl. oz. ►*abbr.* fluid ounce

flu (flo͞o) ►*n. Informal* Influenza.

flub (flŭb) ►*v.* **flubbed, flub•bing** *Informal* To botch or bungle. [?] **—flub** *n.*

fluc•tu•ate (flŭk′cho͞o-āt′) ►*v.* **-at•ed, -at•ing 1.** To change or vary irregularly. **2.** To rise and fall in or as if in waves. [< Lat. *flūctus*, a flowing < *fluere*, flow.] **—fluc′tu•ant** (-ənt) *adj.* **—fluc′tu•a′tion** *n.*

flue (flo͞o) ►*n.* A pipe, tube, or channel for conveying hot air, gas, steam, or smoke, as in a chimney. [?]

flu•ent (flo͞o′ənt) ►*adj.* **1.** Having facility in the use of a language. **2.** Flowing smoothly and naturally; polished. **3.** Flowing or capable of flowing; fluid. [< Lat. *fluere*, to flow.] **—flu′en•cy** *n.* **—flu′ent•ly** *adv.*

fluff (flŭf) ►*n.* **1.** Light down or fuzz. **2.** Something having a light, soft, or frothy consistency or appearance. **3.** Something of little consequence. **4.** *Informal* An error or lapse of memory, esp. by an actor or announcer. ►*v.* **1.** To make light and puffy by shaking or patting into a soft loose mass: *fluff a pillow.* **2.** *Informal* To misread or forget: *fluff a line of dialogue.* [?] **—fluff′i•ness** *n.* **—fluff′y** *adj.*

flu•id (flo͞o′ĭd) ►*n.* A substance, such as air or water, whose molecules move freely past one another and that tends to assume the shape of its container. ►*adj.* **1.** Capable of flowing **2.** Smooth and graceful. **3.** Readily changing or tending to change; variable. **4.** Convertible into cash: *fluid assets.* [< Lat. *fluere*, flow.] **—flu•id′i•ty, flu′id•ness** *n.* **—flu′id•ly** *adv.*

fluid ounce ►*n.* See table at **measurement.**

fluke[1] (flo͞ok) ►*n.* **1.** Any of various flatfishes, esp. a flounder. **2.** See **trematode.** [< OE *flōc.*]

fluke[2] (flo͞ok) ►*n.* **1.** The triangular blade at the end of an arm of an anchor. **2.** A barb or barbed head, as on an arrow or harpoon. **3.** Either of the two flattened divisions of a whale's tail. [Poss. < FLUKE[1].]

fluke[3] (flo͞ok) ►*n.* An accidental stroke of good luck. [?] **—fluk′y** *adj.*

flume (flo͞om) ►*n.* **1.** A narrow gorge, usu. with a stream flowing through it. **2.** An open artificial channel or chute for carrying a stream of water. [< Lat. *flūmen*, river.]

flum•mox (flŭm′əks) ►*v. Informal* To confuse; perplex. [Prob. of dialectal orig.]

flung (flŭng) ►*v.* P.t. and p.part. of **fling.**

flunk (flŭngk) ►*v. Informal* To fail, esp. in a course or examination. [?]

flun•ky also **flun•key** (flŭng′kē) ►*n., pl.* **-kies** also **-keys 1.** A person of slavish or fawning obedience; lackey. **2.** One who does menial or trivial work; drudge. [Sc.]

fluo•resce (flo͞o-rĕs′, flô-, flō-) ►*v.* **-resced, -resc•ing.** To undergo, produce, or show fluorescence.

fluo•res•cence (flo͞o-rĕs′əns, flô-, flō-) ►*n.* **1.** The emission of electromagnetic radiation, esp. of visible light, stimulated in a substance by the absorption of incident radiation and persisting only as long as the stimulating radiation is continued. **2.** The radiation so emitted. **—fluo•res′cent** *adj.*

fluorescent lamp ►*n.* A lamp consisting of a glass tube whose inner wall is coated with a material that fluoresces when an electrical current causes a vapor within the tube to discharge electrons.

fluor•i•date (flo͝or′ĭ-dāt′, flôr′-, flōr′-) ►*v.* **-dat•ed, -dat•ing.** To add a fluorine compound to (e.g., a water supply) for the purpose of reducing tooth decay. **—fluor′i•da′tion** *n.*

fluor•ide (flo͝or′īd′, flôr′-, flōr′-) ►*n.* A binary compound of fluorine with another element.

fluor•ine (flo͝or′ēn′, -ĭn, flôr′-, flōr′-) ►*n. Symbol* **F** A pale-yellow, corrosive, poisonous gaseous element used in a wide variety of industrially important compounds. At. no. 9. See table at **element.** [NLat. *fluor*, mineral used as a flux + -INE[2].]

fluoro– or **fluor–** ►*pref.* **1.** Fluorine: *fluorocarbon.* **2.** Fluorescence: *fluoroscope.* [< FLUORINE.]

fluor•o•car•bon (flo͝or′ō-kär′bən, flôr′-, flōr′-) ►*n.* Any of various compounds in which fluorine replaces hydrogen, used as aerosol propellants, refrigerants, and solvents and in making plastics and resins.

fluor•o•scope (flo͝or′ə-skōp′, flôr′-, flōr′-) ►*n.* A mounted fluorescent screen on which the internal structures of an optically opaque object may be viewed as shadows formed by the transmission of x-rays through the object. **—fluor′o•scope′** *v.* **—fluor′o•scop′ic** (-skŏp′ĭk) *adj.* **—fluo•ros′co•py** (flo͞o-rŏs′kə-pē) *n.*

flur•ry (flûr′ē, flŭr′ē) ►*n., pl.* **-ries 1.** A brief light snowfall. **2.** A sudden gust of wind. **3.** A sudden burst of activity; stir: *a flurry of preparations.* [Poss. < *flurr*, scatter.] **—flur′ry** *v.*

flush[1] (flŭsh) ►*v.* **1.** To redden or cause to redden; blush. **2.** To glow, esp. with a reddish color. **3.** To flow suddenly and abundantly. **4.** To wash out or clean by a rapid brief flow of water. **5.** To excite or elate. ►*n.* **1.** A brief copious flow or rush, as of water. **2.** A reddish tinge; blush. **3.** A rush of strong feeling: *a flush of pride.* **4.** A state of freshness, vigor, or growth. See Syns at **bloom.** ►*adj.* **-er, -est 1.** Having a healthy reddish color; blushing. **2.** Prosperous; affluent. **3.** Abundant; plentiful: *flush times.* **4a.** Having surfaces in the same plane; even. **b.** Arranged with adjacent sides, surfaces, or edges close together. **5.** Direct or straightforward. ►*adv.* **1.** So as to be even, in one plane, or aligned with a margin. **2.** Squarely or solidly: *a hit flush on the face.* [Poss. < FLUSH[3].] **—flush′ness** *n.*

flush[2] (flŭsh) ►*n.* A hand in certain card games in which all the cards are of the same suit but not in numerical sequence. [< Lat. *flūxus*, FLUX.]

flush[3] (flŭsh) ►*v.* To drive or be driven from cover, as a game bird. [ME *flusshen.*]

flus•ter (flŭs′tər) ►*v.* To make or become nervous or upset. ► *n.* A state of agitation or excitement. [< ME *flostring*, agitation, prob. of Scand. orig.]

flute (flo͞ot) ► *n.* **1.** A high-pitched tubular woodwind instrument. **2a.** *Archit.* A long, usu. rounded groove incised on the shaft of a column. **b.** A groove in cloth, such as a pleat. [< OProv. *flauto*.] —**flut′ed** *adj.* —**flut′ing** *n.*

flut•ist (flo͞o′tĭst) ► *n.* One who plays the flute.

flut•ter (flŭt′ər) ► *v.* **1.** To wave or flap lightly, rapidly, and irregularly. **2.** To fly by a quick light flapping of the wings. **3.** To vibrate or beat rapidly or erratically. **4.** To move quickly in a nervous, restless, or excited fashion. ► *n.* **1.** The act of fluttering. **2.** A condition of nervous excitement or agitation. [< OE *floterian*.] —**flut′ter•y** *adj.*

flu•vi•al (flo͞o′vē-əl) ► *adj.* Of, inhabiting, or produced by a river or stream. [< Lat. *fluvius*, river.]

flux (flŭks) ► *n.* **1a.** A flow or flowing. **b.** A rush or flood. See Syns at **flow. 2.** Constant or frequent change; fluctuation. **3.** A substance applied to facilitate flowing, as of solder or plastics, or to prevent formation of oxides. ► *v.* **1.** To melt; fuse. **2.** To apply a flux to. [< Lat. *flūxus* < *fluere*, flow.]

fly[1] (flī) ► *v.* **flew** (flo͞o), **flown** (flōn), **fly•ing** **1.** To engage in flight, esp.: **a.** To move through the air by means of wings or winglike parts. **b.** To travel by air. **c.** To operate an aircraft or spacecraft. **2.** To rise, float, or cause to float in the air. **3a.** To hasten; rush. **b.** To try to escape; flee. **4.** To pass by swiftly. **5.** To disappear rapidly; vanish. **6.** *p.t. and p.part* **flied** (flīd) *Baseball* To hit a baseball in a high arc. ► *n., pl.* **flies 1.** An overlapping fold of cloth that covers a fastening of a garment. **2.** A flap that covers an entrance, as of a tent. **3.** A baseball batted in a high arc. **4. flies** The area directly over the stage and behind the proscenium of a theater. —***idioms:* fly high** To be elated. **fly off the handle** *Informal* To become suddenly enraged. **on the fly** On the run; in a hurry. [< OE *flēogan*.] —**fly′a•ble** *adj.*

fly[2] (flī) ► *n., pl.* **flies 1a.** Any of a large order of two-winged insects such as the housefly, horsefly, and fruit fly. **b.** Any of various other flying insects. **2.** A fishing lure simulating a fly. [< OE *flēoge*.]

fly•blown (flī′blōn′) ► *adj.* **1.** Contaminated with fly eggs. **2.** Dirty; squalid.

fly•by also **fly-by** (flī′bī′) ► *n., pl.* **-bys.** A flight, as of a spacecraft, passing close to a specified target or position.

fly-by-night (flī′bī-nīt′) ► *adj. Informal* **1.** Unreliable, esp. in business. **2.** Temporary.

fly•catch•er (flī′kăch′ər, -kĕch′-) ► *n.* Any of various birds that feed on insects, usu. catching them in flight.

fly•er (flī′ər) ► *n.* Var. of **flier.**

fly-fish (flī′fĭsh′) ► *v.* To angle using artificial flies for bait and usu. a fly rod for casting. —**fly′-fish′er** *n.*

fly•ing buttress (flī′ĭng) ► *n.* An arched masonry support serving to bear thrust away from a main structure to an outer pier or buttress.

flying fish ► *n.* A marine fish having enlarged winglike fins capable of sustaining it in brief gliding flights over the water.

flying saucer ► *n.* Any of various unidentified flying objects of presumed extraterrestrial origin, typically described as luminous moving disks.

flying squirrel ► *n.* Any of various nocturnal squirrels having membranes between the forelegs and hind legs that enable them to glide between trees.

fly•leaf (flī′lēf′) ► *n.* A blank page at the beginning or end of a book.

fly•pa•per (flī′pā′pər) ► *n.* Paper coated with a sticky substance used to catch flies.

fly•speck (flī′spĕk′) ► *n.* **1.** A stain made by the excrement of a fly. **2.** A minute spot.

fly•way (flī′wā′) ► *n.* A seasonal route followed by birds migrating to and from their breeding areas.

fly•weight (flī′wāt′) ► *n.* A boxer weighing 112 lbs. or less, lighter than a bantamweight.

fly•wheel (flī′hwēl′, -wēl′) ► *n.* A heavy-rimmed rotating wheel used to keep a shaft of a machine turning at a steady speed.

Fm ► The symbol for the element **fermium.**

FM ► *abbr.* frequency modulation

fm. ► *abbr.* fathom

fn. ► *abbr.* footnote

FNMA ► *abbr.* Federal National Mortgage Association

f-num•ber (ĕf′nŭm′bər) ► *n.* The ratio of the focal length of a lens or lens system to the effective diameter of its aperture. [F(OCAL LENGTH) + NUMBER.]

foal (fōl) ► *n.* The young offspring of an equine animal, esp. one under a year old. ► *v.* To give birth to a foal. [< OE *fola*.]

foam (fōm) ► *n.* **1a.** A mass of bubbles in a matrix of liquid film, esp. on the surface of a liquid. **b.** A thick chemical froth, such as shaving cream. **2.** Frothy saliva. **3.** Any of various light, porous, semirigid or spongy materials used for thermal insulation or shock absorption, as in packaging. ► *v.* To form or issue as foam. [< OE *fām*.] —**foam′i•ness** *n.* —**foam′y** *adj.*

foam rubber ► *n.* A light, firm, spongy rubber used in upholstery and for insulation.

fob[1] (fŏb) ► *n.* **1.** A short chain on a pocket watch. **2.** An ornament attached to a watch chain. [Prob. of Gmc. orig.]

fob[2] (fŏb) ► *v.* **fobbed, fob•bing** *Archaic* To cheat or deceive (another). —***phrasal verb:* fob off** To dispose of (something) by fraud or deception: *fobbed off the zircon as a diamond.* [ME *fobben*.]

FOB ► *abbr.* free on board

fo•cac•ci•a (fə-kä′chē-ə, -chə, fō-) ► *n.* A flat Italian bread flavored with olive oil. [Ital., hearth-cake < Lat. *focus*, hearth.]

focal length ► *n.* The distance of the focus from the surface of a lens or mirror.

focal point ► *n.* See **focus** 1.

Foch (fôsh, fŏsh), **Ferdinand.** 1851–1929. French World War I army commander.

fo′c′s′le (fōk′səl) ► *n.* Var. of **forecastle.**

fo•cus (fō′kəs) ► *n., pl.* **-cus•es** or **-ci** (-sī′, -kī′) **1a.** A point at which rays of light or other radiation converge or from which they appear to diverge, as after refraction or reflection in an optical system. **b.** See **focal length. 2a.** The distinctness or clarity of an image rendered by an optical system. **b.** Adjustment for distinctness or clarity. **3.** A center of interest or activity. See Syns at **center.** ► *v.* **-cused, -cus•ing** or **-cussed, -cus•sing 1.** To converge or cause to converge at a focus. **2a.** To produce a clear image (of). **b.** To adjust (e.g., a lens) to produce a clear image. **3.** To concentrate (on). [Lat., hearth.] —**fo′cal** *adj.* —**fo′cal•ly** *adv.*

fod•der (fŏd′ər) ►*n.* Feed for livestock, esp. coarsely chopped hay or straw. [< OE *fōdor.*]

foe (fō) ►*n.* **1.** A personal enemy. **2.** An enemy in war. **3.** An adversary; opponent. See Syns at **enemy.** [< OE *gefā* < *fāh*, hostile.]

foe•tid (fē′tĭd) ►*adj.* Var. of **fetid.**

foe•tus (fē′təs) ►*n.* Var. of **fetus.** —**foe′tal** *adj.*

fog (fôg, fŏg) ►*n.* **1.** Condensed water vapor in cloudlike masses close to the ground. **2.** A mist or film clouding a surface. **3.** Confusion or bewilderment. **4.** A dark blur on a developed photographic negative. ►*v.* **fogged, fog•ging.** To cover or be obscured with or as if with fog. [Perh. of Scand. orig.] —**fog′gi•ly** *adv.* —**fog′gi•ness** *n.* —**fog′gy** *adj.*

fog•horn (fôg′hôrn′, fŏg′-) ►*n.* A horn used to warn ships of danger in fog or darkness.

fo•gy also **fo•gey** (fō′gē) ►*n., pl.* **-gies** also **-geys.** A person of old-fashioned habits and attitudes. [Sc. *fogey.*] —**fo′gy•ish** *adj.*

foi•ble (foi′bəl) ►*n.* A minor weakness or failing of character. [< OFr. *feble*, weak. See FEEBLE.]

foil[1] (foil) ►*v.* To prevent from being successful; thwart. [ME *foilen*, trample.]

foil[2] (foil) ►*n.* **1.** A thin flexible leaf or sheet of metal. **2.** One that by contrast enhances the distinctive characteristics of another. **3a.** An airfoil. **b.** A hydrofoil. [< Lat. *folium*, leaf.]

foil[3] (foil) ►*n.* A light fencing sword having a usu. circular guard and a thin flexible blade with a blunt point. [?]

foist (foist) ►*v.* **1.** To pass off as genuine, valuable, or worthy. **2.** To impose upon another by coercion or trickery. [< MDu. *vuist*, fist.]

fold[1] (fōld) ►*v.* **1.** To bend over or double up so that one part lies on another part. **2.** To bring from an extended to a closed position. **3.** To place together and intertwine: *fold one's arms.* **4.** To envelop or clasp; enfold. **5.** To blend in (a cooking ingredient) by slowly and gently turning one part over another. **6.** *Informal* To close, esp. for lack of financial success; fail. ►*n.* **1.** The act or an instance of folding. **2.** A line, layer, pleat, or crease formed by folding. **3.** *Geol.* A bend in a stratum of rock. [< OE *fealdan.*]

fold[2] (fōld) ►*n.* **1.** A fenced enclosure for domestic animals, esp. sheep. **2.** A flock of sheep. **3.** A group of people or institutions bound together by common beliefs and aims. [< OE *fald.*]

-fold ►*suff.* **1.** Divided into a specified number of parts: *fourfold.* **2.** Multiplied by a specified number: *twofold.* [< OE *-feald.*]

fold•er (fōl′dər) ►*n.* **1.** One that folds. **2.** A booklet made of one or more folded sheets of paper. **3.** A folded sheet of heavy paper used as a holder for loose paper.

fol•de•rol (fŏl′də-rŏl′) ►*n.* **1.** Nonsense. **2.** A trinket. [From a refrain in some old songs.]

fold•out (fōld′out′) ►*n.* **1.** *Print.* A folded insert or section, as of a cover, whose full size exceeds that of the regular page. **2.** A piece or part that folds out. —**fold′out′** *adj.*

fo•li•age (fō′lē-ĭj, fō′lĭj) ►*n.* Plant leaves, esp. tree leaves, considered as a group. [< OFr. *foille*, leaf. See FOIL[2].]

fo•lic acid (fō′lĭk, fŏl′ĭk) ►*n.* A compound of the vitamin B complex, occurring esp. in dark leafy vegetables and citrus fruits. [< Lat. *folium*, leaf.]

fo•li•o (fō′lē-ō′) ►*n., pl.* **-os 1a.** A large sheet of paper folded once in the middle. **b.** A book of the largest common size, consisting of such folded sheets. **2.** A page number in a book. [< Lat. *folium*, leaf.]

folk (fōk) ►*n., pl.* **folk** or **folks 1.** The common people of a society or region. **2. folks** *Informal* People in general. **3.** often **folks** People of a specified group or kind: *rich folks.* **4. folks** *Informal* One's family or relatives. ►*adj.* Of or originating among the common people: *a folk hero.* [< OE *folc.*]

folk•lore (fōk′lôr′, -lōr′) ►*n.* The traditional beliefs, legends, and practices of a people, passed down orally. —**folk′lor′ist** *n.*

folk magic ►*n.* The practice of using charms, spells, or rituals to attempt to control natural or chance events.

folk music ►*n.* Music originating among the common people of a nation or region.

folk-rock (fōk′rŏk′) ►*n.* Music combining elements of rock 'n' roll and folk music.

folk•sing•er (fōk′sĭng′ər) ►*n.* A singer of folksongs.

folk•song (fōk′sông′, -sŏng′) ►*n.* A song belonging to the folk music of a people or area, often existing in several versions.

folk•sy (fōk′sē) ►*adj.* **-si•er, -si•est** *Informal.* Simple; unpretentious. —**folk′si•ness** *n.*

folk•way (fōk′wā′) ►*n.* A practice, custom, or belief shared by the members of a group as part of their common culture.

fol•li•cle (fŏl′ĭ-kəl) ►*n.* **1.** A small body cavity or sac, such as one in the skin from which hair grows. **2.** A cavity in an ovary containing a mature ovum. [Lat. *folliculus*, little bag.]

fol•low (fŏl′ō) ►*v.* **1.** To come or go after. **2.** To pursue. **3.** To move along the course of: *follow a path.* **4.** To adhere to. **5.** To comply with; obey. **6.** To engage in. **7.** To come after in order, time, or position: *Night follows day.* **8.** To result or ensue. **9.** To be attentive to. **10.** To grasp the meaning or logic of; understand. [< OE *folgian.*]

fol•low•er (fŏl′ō-ər) ►*n.* **1.** One that follows. **2.** One who subscribes to the teachings or methods of another; adherent. **3.** An attendant or servant; subordinate.

fol•low•ing (fŏl′ō-ĭng) ►*adj.* **1.** Coming next in time or order. **2.** Now to be mentioned or listed. ►*n.* A group or gathering of followers. ►*prep.* Subsequent to; after.

fol•low-up or **fol•low•up** (fŏl′ō-ŭp′) ►*n.* **1.** The act of repeating or adding to previous action. **2.** The means used to do this.

fol•ly (fŏl′ē) ►*n., pl.* **-lies 1.** A lack of good sense, understanding, or foresight. **2a.** An act or instance of foolishness. **b.** A costly undertaking having an absurd or ruinous outcome. **3. follies** *(takes sing. or pl. v.)* An elaborate theatrical revue consisting of music, dance, and skits. [< OFr. *folie* < LLat. *follis*, FOOL.]

fo•ment (fō-mĕnt′) ►*v.* **1.** To promote the growth of; incite. **2.** To treat (e.g., the skin) with heat and moisture. [< Lat. *fōmentum*, a poultice.] —**fo′men•ta′tion** *n.*

fond (fŏnd) ►*adj.* **-er, -est 1.** Having a strong liking, inclination, or affection: *fond of ballet.*

2. Affectionate; tender. 3. Foolishly affectionate; doting. 4. Deeply felt; dear: *my fondest hopes.* [Prob. < ME *fonne*, a fool.] —**fond′ly** *adv.* —**fond′ness** *n.*

Fon•da (fŏn′də), **Henry.** 1905–82. Amer. actor.

fon•dle (fŏn′dl) ►*v.* **-dled, -dling.** To handle or stroke lovingly. See Syns at **caress.** [< obsolete *fond*, show affection for.]

fon•due also **fon•du** (fŏn-do͞o′, -dyo͞o′) ►*n.* A hot dish usu. made of melted cheese and wine. [Fr. < *fondre*, melt.]

font[1] (fŏnt) ►*n.* **1.** A basin for holding baptismal or holy water. **2.** An abundant source. [< Lat. *fōns*, fountain.]

font[2] (fŏnt) ►*n. Print.* A complete set of type of one size and face. [< Lat. *fundere*, pour out.]

Fon•teyn (fŏn-tān′), Dame **Margot.** 1919–91. British ballerina.

Foo•chow (fo͞o′jō′, -chou′) See **Fuzhou.**

food (fo͞od) ►*n.* **1.** Material, usu. of plant or animal origin, that contains essential body nutrients, taken in and assimilated by an organism to maintain life and growth; nourishment. **2.** A specified kind of nourishment: *plant food.* **3.** Nourishment eaten in solid form. **4.** Something that stimulates or encourages: *food for thought.* [< OE *fōda.*]

food chain ►*n.* **1.** A succession of organisms, each kind serving as a source of nourishment as it consumes a lower member and in turn is preyed upon by a higher member. **2.** *Informal* A competitive hierarchy.

food poisoning ►*n.* An acute, often severe gastrointestinal disorder caused by eating food contaminated with bacteria or natural toxins.

food stamp ►*n.* A stamp or coupon issued by the government to persons with low incomes and redeemable for food at stores.

food•stuff (fo͞od′stŭf′) ►*n.* A substance that can be used or prepared for use as food.

food web ►*n.* A complex of interrelated food chains in an ecological community.

fool (fo͞ol) ►*n.* **1.** One who is deficient in judgment, sense, or understanding. **2.** One who can easily be tricked; dupe. **3.** A jester. ►*v.* **1.** To deceive or trick; dupe. **2.** To take unawares; surprise. **3.** *Informal* To speak or act in jest; joke. **4.** To toy, tinker, or meddle: *shouldn't fool with matches.* —***phrasal verb:* fool around** *Informal* **1.** To waste time; idle. **2.** To mess around; play. [< Lat. *follis*, bellows.]

fool•er•y (fo͞o′lə-rē) ►*n., pl.* **-ies 1.** Foolish behavior or speech. **2.** A jest.

fool•har•dy (fo͞ol′här′dē) ►*adj.* **-di•er, -di•est.** Unwisely bold, daring, or venturesome; rash. [< OFr. *fol hardi.*] —**fool′har′di•ly** *adv.* —**fool′har′di•ness** *n.*

fool•ish (fo͞o′lĭsh) ►*adj.* **1.** Lacking good sense or judgment; unwise. **2.** Absurd or ridiculous: *a foolish grin.* —**fool′ish•ly** *adv.* —**fool′ish•ness** *n.*

fool•proof (fo͞ol′pro͞of′) ►*adj.* **1.** Designed so as to be impervious to incompetence, error, or misuse. **2.** Effective; infallible: *a foolproof scheme.*

fools•cap (fo͞olz′kăp′) ►*n. Chiefly Brit.* A sheet of writing paper approx. 13 by 16 in. [From the watermark orig. used for this paper.]

fool's gold (fo͞olz) ►*n.* See **pyrite.**

foot (fo͝ot) ►*n., pl.* **feet** (fēt) **1.** The lower extremity of the leg that is in direct contact with the ground in standing or walking. **2.** An invertebrate structure used for locomotion. **3.** Something suggestive of a foot in position or function: *the foot of a mountain; the foot of a bed.* **4.** A unit of poetic meter consisting of stressed and unstressed syllables in various set combinations. **5.** See table at **measurement.** ►*v.* **1.** To walk: *had to foot it home.* **2.** To dance. **3.** To add up; total: *footed up the bill.* **4.** To pay: *footed the travel expenses.* —***idioms:* foot in the door** *Slang* An initial opportunity for entry. **on foot** Walking rather than riding. **on (one's) feet 1.** Standing up. **2.** Fully recovered, as after an illness. [< OE *fōt.*]

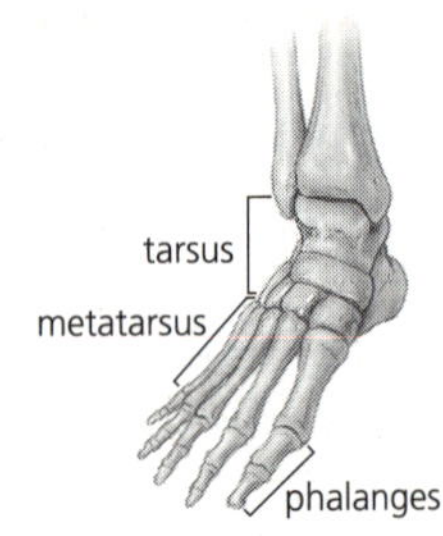

foot

foot•age (fo͝ot′ĭj) ►*n.* **1.** Length, extent, or amount based on measurement in feet. **2.** A portion of film or videotape: *news footage.*

foot•ball (fo͝ot′bôl′) ►*n.* **1a.** A game played by two teams of 11 players each on a 100-yard-long field with goal posts at either end. **b.** The inflated oval ball used in this game. **2.** *Chiefly Brit.* **a.** Rugby or soccer. **b.** The ball used in Rugby or soccer.

foot•board (fo͝ot′bôrd′, -bōrd′) ►*n.* **1.** An upright board across the foot of a bedstead. **2.** A board or small raised platform on which to support or rest the feet.

foot•bridge (fo͝ot′brĭj′) ►*n.* A bridge designed for pedestrians.

foot•ed (fo͝ot′ĭd) ►*adj.* Having feet or a specified kind or number of feet: *a footed sofa; web-footed; four-footed.*

foot•fall (fo͝ot′fôl′) ►*n.* See **footstep** 1.

foot•gear (fo͝ot′gîr) ►*n.* Sturdy footwear, such as shoes or boots.

foot•hill (fo͝ot′hĭl′) ►*n.* A low hill near the base of a mountain or mountain range.

foot•hold (fo͝ot′hōld′) ►*n.* **1.** A place providing support for the foot in climbing or standing. **2.** A firm or secure position that provides a base for further advancement.

foot•ing (fo͝ot′ĭng) ►*n.* **1.** Secure placement of the feet in standing or moving. **2.** A basis or foundation. **3a.** Position in relation to others. **b.** Terms of social interaction.

foot•lights (fo͝ot′līts′) ►*pl.n.* **1.** Lights placed in a row along the front of a stage floor. **2.** The theater as a profession.

foot•lock•er (fo͝ot′lŏk′ər) ►*n.* A small trunk for storing personal belongings.

foot•loose (fo͝ot′lo͞os′) ►*adj.* Having no attachments or ties.

foot•man (fo͝ot′mən) ►*n.* A man employed as a servant to wait at table, attend the door, and run various errands, as in a palace.

foot•note (fo͝ot′nōt′) ►*n.* A note of comment or reference at the bottom of a page of a book. —**foot′note′** *v.*

foot•path (fo͝ot′păth′, -päth′) ►*n.* A narrow path for persons on foot.

foot•print (fo͝ot′prĭnt′) ►*n.* An outline or indentation left by a foot on a surface.

foot•race (fo͝ot′rās′) ►*n.* A race run by contestants on foot.

foot•rest (fo͝ot′rĕst′) ►*n.* A support on which to rest the feet.

foot soldier ►*n.* A soldier in the infantry.

foot•sore (fo͝ot′sôr′, -sōr′) ►*adj.* Having sore or tired feet. —**foot′sore′ness** *n.*

foot•step (fo͝ot′stĕp′) ►*n.* **1a.** A step with the foot. **b.** The sound of a foot stepping; footfall. **2.** The distance covered by a step: *a footstep away.* **3.** A footprint.

foot•stool (fo͝ot′sto͞ol′) ►*n.* A low stool for supporting the feet.

foot•wear (fo͝ot′wâr′) ►*n.* Attire, such as shoes or slippers, for the feet.

foot•work (fo͝ot′wûrk′) ►*n.* The manner in which the feet are used or maneuvered, as in boxing, figure skating, or dancing.

fop (fŏp) ►*n.* A man preoccupied with clothes and manners; dandy. [ME, fool.] —**fop′per•y** *n.* —**fop′pish** *adj.* —**fop′pish•ly** *adv.* —**fop′pish•ness** *n.*

for (fôr; fər *when unstressed*) ►*prep.* **1a.** Used to indicate the object or purpose of an action or activity: *plans to run for senator.* **b.** Used to indicate a destination: *headed for town.* **2a.** On behalf of: *spoke for us all.* **b.** In favor of: *I'm for the proposal.* **3a.** As equivalent or equal to: *word for word.* **b.** As against: *two steps back for one step forward.* **4.** Used to indicate amount, extent, or duration: *walked for miles.* **5.** As being: *mistook me for the boss.* **6.** As a result of: *jumped for joy.* **7.** Used to indicate appropriateness or suitability: *not for us to decide.* **8.** Notwithstanding; despite: *For all the problems, it was worth it.* **9.** Considering the nature of: *was spry for his age.* **10.** In honor of: *named for her.* ►*conj.* Because; since. [< OE.]

fo•ra (fôr′ə, fōr′ə) ►*n.* Pl. of **forum.**

for•age (fôr′ĭj, fŏr′-) ►*n.* **1.** Food for domestic animals; fodder. **2.** A search for food or provisions. ►*v.* **-aged, -ag•ing.** To search, as for food. [< OFr. *fourrage* < *feurre,* fodder.] —**for′ag•er** *n.*

For•a•ker (fôr′ə-kər, fŏr′-), **Mount.** A peak, 5,307 m (17,400 ft), in the Alaska Range of S-central AK.

for•ay (fôr′ā′, fōr′ā′, fŏr′ā′) ►*n.* **1.** A sudden raid or military advance. **2.** A first venture or attempt. [< ME *forraien,* to plunder.] —**for′ay′** *v.*

forb (fôrb) ►*n.* A broad-leaved herb other than a grass. [< Gk. *phorbē,* fodder.]

for•bear[1] (fôr-bâr′) ►*v.* **-bore** (-bôr′, -bōr′), **-borne** (-bôrn′, -bōrn′), **-bear•ing 1.** To refrain or desist (from); resist. See Syns at **refrain**[1]. **2.** To be tolerant or patient. [< OE *forberan,* endure.] —**for•bear′ance** *n.*

for•bear[2] (fôr′bâr′, fōr′-) ►*n.* Var. of **forebear.**

for•bid (fər-bĭd′, fôr-) ►*v.* **-bade** (-băd′, -bād′) or **-bad** (-băd′), **-bid•den** (-bĭd′n) or **-bid, -bid•ding 1.** To command (someone) not to do something. **2.** To command against doing (something). **3.** To preclude. [< OE *forbēodan.*] —**for•bid′dance** *n.*

Syns: *forbid, ban, enjoin, interdict, prohibit, proscribe* ***Ant:*** *permit* ***v.***

for•bid•ding (fər-bĭd′ĭng, fôr-) ►*adj.* Tending to frighten or menace; threatening.

force (fôrs, fōrs) ►*n.* **1a.** Energy, strength, or active power. **b.** The exertion of such power. **2a.** Physical power or violence. **b.** Intellectual power or vigor. **c.** Moral strength. **3.** A body of persons organized for a certain purpose, esp. for the use of military power. **4.** *Phys.* A vector quantity that tends to produce an acceleration of a body in the direction of its application. ►*v.* **forced, forc•ing 1.** To compel to perform an action. **2a.** To gain by force or coercion. **b.** To move (something) against resistance. **c.** To inflict or impose. **3.** To produce with effort: *force a laugh.* **4.** To move, break down, open, or clear by force: *forced our way.* **5.** *Bot.* To cause to grow or mature artificially. —***idiom:* in force 1.** In full strength. **2.** In effect; operative: *a rule now in force.* [< Lat. *fortis,* strong.] —**force′ful** *adj.* —**force′ful•ly** *adv.* —**force′ful•ness** *n.*

force-feed (fôrs′fēd′, fōrs′-) ►*v.* To compel to ingest food, esp. by mechanical means.

force field ►*n.* See **field of force.**

for•ceps (fôr′səps, -sĕps) ►*n., pl.* **-ceps.** An instrument used for grasping, manipulating, or extracting, esp. in surgery. [Lat.]

forc•i•ble (fôr′sə-bəl, fōr′-) ►*adj.* **1.** Effected through force. **2.** Characterized by force; powerful. —**forc′i•bly** *adv.*

ford (fôrd, fōrd) ►*n.* A shallow place in a body of water where one can walk, ride, or drive across. [< OE.] —**ford** *v.* —**ford′a•ble** *adj.*

Ford, Gerald Rudolph. b. 1913. The 38th US President (1974–77).

Gerald Ford

Ford, Henry. 1863–1947. Amer. automobile manufacturer.

fore (fôr, fōr) ►*adj. & adv.* At, in, near, or toward the front; forward. ►*n.* The front part. ►*interj. Sports* Used by a golfer to warn those ahead that a ball is headed in their direction. [< OE, beforehand.]

fore– ►*pref.* **1.** Before; earlier: *forebode.* **2.** In front of; front: *foreground.* [< OE.]

fore-and-aft (fôr′ən-ăft′, fōr′-) ►*adj.* Parallel with the length of a structure, as a ship.

fore•arm[1] (fôr-ärm′, fōr-) ►*v.* To arm or prepare in advance of a conflict.

fore•arm[2] (fôr′ärm′, fōr′-) ►*n.* The part of the arm between the wrist and elbow.

fore•bear also **for•bear** (fôr′bâr′, fōr′-) ►*n.* A person from whom one is descended. See Syns at **ancestor.** [ME : FORE– + *been,* BE.]

fore•bode (fôr-bōd′, fōr-) ►*v.* **1.** To indicate the likelihood of; portend. **2.** To have a premonition of (a future misfortune). —**fore•bod′ing** *n.*

fore•cast (fôr′kăst′, fōr′-) ►*v.* **-cast** or **-cast•ed, -cast•ing 1.** To estimate, calculate, or indicate in advance: *forecast tomorrow's weather.* **2.** To foreshadow. ►*n.* A prediction. [ME *forecasten*, plan beforehand.] —**fore′cast′er** *n.*

fore•cas•tle (fōk′səl, fôr′kăs′əl, fōr′-) also **fo′c's′le** (fōk′səl) ►*n.* **1.** The section of the upper deck of a ship located forward of the foremast. **2.** The crew's quarters at the bow of a merchant ship. [ME *forecastel.*]

fore•close (fôr-klōz′, fōr-) ►*v.* **-closed, -clos•ing 1.** To deprive (a mortgagor) of mortgaged property, as for payment. **2.** To preclude; bar. [< OFr. *forclore*, exclude.] —**fore•clo′sure** *n.*

fore•court (fôr′kôrt′, fōr′kōrt′) ►*n.* **1.** A courtyard in front of a building. **2.** *Sports* The part of a court nearest the net or wall, as in tennis or handball.

fore•fa•ther (fôr′fä′*th*ər, fōr′-) ►*n.* **1.** An ancestor. See Syns at **ancestor. 2.** A founder or originator.

fore•fin•ger (fôr′fĭng′gər, fōr′-) ►*n.* See **index finger.**

fore•foot (fôr′fo͝ot′, fōr′-) ►*n.* Either of the front feet of an animal.

fore•front (fôr′frŭnt′, fōr′-) ►*n.* **1.** The foremost part or area. **2.** The most important position.

fore•go[1] (fôr-gō′, fōr-) ►*v.* To precede, as in time or place. —**fore•go′er** *n.*

fore•go[2] (fôr-gō′, fōr-) ►*v.* Var. of **forgo.**

fore•go•ing (fôr-gō′ĭng, fōr-, fôr′gō′ĭng, fōr′-) ►*adj.* Just before or past; previous.

fore•gone ►*adj.* (fôr′gôn′, -gŏn′, fōr′-). So certain as to be known in advance: *a foregone conclusion.* [< FOREGO[1].]

fore•ground (fôr′ground′, fōr′-) ►*n.* **1.** The part of a scene or picture nearest to the viewer. **2.** The forefront; vanguard.

fore•hand (fôr′hănd′, fōr′-) ►*adj.* Made or done with the hand moving palm forward: *a forehand tennis stroke.* ►*n.* A forehand stroke. —**fore′hand′** *adv.*

fore•head (fôr′hĕd′, -ĭd′, fōr′-) ►*n.* The part of the face between the eyebrows and the normal hairline. [< OE *forhēafod.*]

for•eign (fôr′ĭn, fōr′-) ►*adj.* **1.** Located away from one's native country. **2.** Characteristic of or from a place or country other than one's own: *a foreign custom.* **3.** Conducted or involved with other nations: *foreign trade.* **4.** Situated in an abnormal or improper place. **5.** Not natural; alien. **6.** Irrelevant. [< LLat. *forānus*, outsider < Lat. *forās*, outside.] —**for′eign•ness** *n.*

Syns: *foreign, alien, exotic, strange* **adj.**

for•eign•er (fôr′ə-nər, fōr′-) ►*n.* One who is from a foreign country or place.

foreign minister ►*n.* A cabinet minister in charge of a nation's foreign affairs.

foreign office ►*n.* The governmental department in charge of foreign affairs in certain countries.

fore•knowl•edge (fôr-nŏl′ĭj, fōr-) ►*n.* Knowledge of something before its occurrence.

fore•leg (fôr′lĕg′, fōr′-) ►*n.* Either of the front legs of an animal.

fore•limb (fôr′lĭm′, fōr′-) ►*n.* A front part, such as a leg, wing, or flipper.

fore•lock (fôr′lŏk′, fōr′-) ►*n.* A lock of hair that grows from or falls on the forehead.

forelock

fore•man (fôr′mən, fōr′-) ►*n.* **1.** A man in charge of a group of workers, as at a factory or ranch. **2.** A man who chairs and speaks for a jury.

fore•mast (fôr′məst, -măst′, fōr′-) ►*n.* The forward mast on a sailing vessel.

fore•most (fôr′mōst′, fōr′-) ►*adj. & adv.* First in position or rank. [< ME *formest* < OE *forma*, first.]

fore•noon (fôr′no͞on′, fōr′-) ►*n.* The period between sunrise and noon; morning.

fo•ren•sic (fə-rĕn′sĭk, -zĭk) ►*adj.* Of or used in legal proceedings or formal debate. [< Lat. *forēnsis*, of the forum.] —**fo•ren′si•cal•ly** *adv.*

fo•ren•sics (fə-rĕn′sĭks, -zĭks) ►*n.* *(takes sing. v.)* The art or study of formal debate.

fore•or•dain (fôr′ôr-dān′, fōr′-) ►*v.* To determine or appoint beforehand; predestine.

fore•part (fôr′pärt′, fōr′-) ►*n.* The first or foremost part.

fore•quar•ter (fôr′kwôr′tər, fōr′-) ►*n.* **1.** The front section of a side of meat. **2.** The foreleg and shoulder of an animal.

fore•run•ner (fôr′rŭn′ər, fōr′-) ►*n.* **1.** A predecessor. **2.** One that comes before and indicates the approach of another.

fore•sail (fôr′səl, -sāl′, fōr′-) ►*n.* The principal square sail hung to the foremast of a square-rigged sailing vessel.

fore•see (fôr-sē′, fōr-) ►*v.* To see or know beforehand. —**fore•see′a•ble** *adj.*

fore•shad•ow (fôr-shăd′ō, fōr-) ►*v.* To present an indication or hint of beforehand.

fore•shore (fôr′shôr′, fōr′shōr′) ►*n.* The part of a shore that is covered at high tide.

fore•short•en (fôr-shôr′tn, fōr-) ►*v.* To shorten the lines of (a figure or design) in a drawing or painting so as to produce an illusion of depth or distance.

fore•sight (fôr′sīt′, fōr′-) ►*n.* **1.** The ability to foresee. **2.** Care or prudence in providing for the future. **3.** The act of looking forward. —**fore′sight′ed** *adj.* —**fore′sight′ed•ly** *adv.* —**fore′sight′ed•ness** *n.*

fore•skin (fôr′skĭn′, fōr′-) ►*n.* The loose fold of skin that covers the glans of the penis.

for•est (fôr′ĭst, fōr′-) ►*n.* **1.** A dense growth of trees, plants, and underbrush covering a large area. **2.** Something resembling a forest. [< Med.Lat. *forestis (silva)*, outside (forest) < Lat. *forīs*, outside.] —**for′es•ta′tion** *n.*

fore•stall (fôr-stôl′, fōr-) ▸*v.* **1.** To delay, hinder, or prevent by taking measures beforehand. **2.** To anticipate. [< OE *foresteall*, an ambush.]

for•est•ry (fôr′ĭ-strē, fŏr′-) ▸*n.* The science and art of cultivating, maintaining, and developing forests.

fore•taste (fôr′tāst′, fōr′-) ▸*n.* An advance realization, token, or warning. —**fore•taste′** *v.*

fore•tell (fôr-tĕl′, fōr-) ▸*v.* To tell of or indicate beforehand; predict. —**fore•tell′er** *n.*

Syns: *foretell, augur, divine, prophesy*

fore•thought (fôr′thôt′, fōr′-) ▸*n.* Advance deliberation, consideration, or planning.

fore•to•ken (fôr-tō′kən, fōr-) ▸*v.* To foreshadow; presage. —**fore′to′ken** *n.*

for•ev•er (fôr-ĕv′ər, fər-) ▸*adv.* **1.** For all time; eternally. **2.** Always; incessantly.

for•ev•er•more (fôr-ĕv′ər-môr′, -mōr′, fər-) ▸*adv.* Forever.

fore•warn (fôr-wôrn′, fōr-) ▸*v.* To warn in advance.

fore•wing (fôr′wĭng′, fōr′-) ▸*n.* Either of a pair of front wings of a four-winged insect.

fore•wom•an (fôr′wo͝om′ən, fōr′-) ▸*n.* **1.** A woman who serves as the leader of a work crew, as in a factory. **2.** A woman who chairs and speaks for a jury.

fore•word (fôr′wərd, fōr′-) ▸*n.* A preface or introductory note, esp. in a book.

for•feit (fôr′fĭt) ▸*n.* **1.** Something surrendered as punishment for a crime, offense, or breach of contract. **2.** Something placed in escrow and then redeemed after payment of a fine. **3.** A forfeiture. ▸*v.* To surrender or be forced to surrender as a forfeit. [< OFr. *forfaire*, act outside the law.]

for•fei•ture (fôr′fĭ-cho͝or′, -chər) ▸*n.* **1.** The act of forfeiting. **2.** Something forfeited.

for•gath•er (fôr-găth′ər, fōr-) ▸*v.* To gather together; assemble.

forge[1] (fôrj, fōrj) ▸*n.* A furnace or hearth where metals are heated and wrought; smithy. ▸*v.* **forged, forg•ing 1.** To form (e.g., metal) by heating in a forge and beating or hammering into shape. **2.** To give form or shape to; devise: *forge a treaty.* **3.** To fashion or reproduce fraudulently; counterfeit: *forge a signature.* [< Lat. *fabrica.*] —**forg′er** *n.* —**for′ger•y** *n.*

forge[2] (fôrj, fōrj) ▸*v.* **forged, forg•ing 1.** To advance gradually but steadily. **2.** To surge forward. [Poss. < FORGE[1].]

for•get (fər-gĕt′, fôr-) ▸*v.* **-got** (-gŏt′), **-got•ten** (-gŏt′n) or **-got, -get•ting 1.** To be unable to remember or call to mind. **2.** To treat with inattention; neglect. **3.** To fail to become aware at the proper moment: *forget an appointment.* —***idiom:*** **forget oneself** To lose one's reserve, temper, or self-restraint. [< OE *forgietan.*] —**for•get′ful** *adj.* —**for•get′ful•ly** *adv.* —**for•get′ful•ness** *n.* —**for•get′ta•ble** *adj.*

for•get-me-not (fər-gĕt′mē-nŏt′, fôr-) ▸*n.* A low-growing plant with small blue flowers.

for•give (fər-gĭv′, fôr-) ▸*v.* **-gave** (-gāv′), **-giv•en** (-gĭv′ən), **-giv•ing 1.** To excuse for a fault or offense; pardon. **2.** To stop feeling anger or resentment against. **3.** To absolve from payment of. [< OE *forgiefan.*] —**for•giv′a•ble** *adj.* —**for•give′ness** *n.*

for•go also **fore•go** (fôr-gō′, fōr-) ▸*v.* **-went** (-wĕnt′), **-gone** (-gôn′, -gŏn′), **-go•ing.** To give up; relinquish. [< OE *forgān.*]

fo•rint (fôr′ĭnt′) ▸*n.* See table at **currency.** [Hung. < Ital. *fiorino*, FLORIN.]

fork (fôrk) ▸*n.* **1.** A utensil with two or more prongs, used for eating or serving food. **2.** A pronged implement or part, esp. a farm or garden tool used for digging. **3a.** A separation into two or more branches. **b.** The place of such a separation. **c.** One of the branches: *took the right fork.* See Syns at **branch.** ▸*v.* **1.** To raise, carry, or pierce with a fork. **2.** To shape as a fork. **3.** To divide into branches. **4.** *Informal* To pay: *forked over $50.* [< Lat. *furca.*] —**fork′ful′** *n.*

forked (fôrkt, fôr′kĭd) ▸*adj.* **1.** Having a fork: *a forked river.* **2.** Shaped like a fork: *forked lightning.*

fork•lift (fôrk′lĭft′) ▸*n.* An industrial vehicle with a power-operated pronged platform that can be raised and lowered for lifting and carrying loads.

for•lorn (fər-lôrn′, fôr-) ▸*adj.* **1.** Deserted or abandoned. **2.** Pitiful in appearance. **3.** Nearly hopeless; desperate. [< OE *forlēosan*, abandon.] —**for•lorn′ly** *adv.* —**for•lorn′ness** *n.*

form (fôrm) ▸*n.* **1a.** The shape and structure of an object. **b.** The body, esp. of a person; figure. **2a.** The essence of something. **b.** The mode in which a thing exists; kind: *a form of animal life.* **3a.** Procedure as determined by regulation or custom. **b.** A fixed order of words or procedures, as in a ceremony. **4.** A document with blanks for the insertion of requested information. **5.** Manners as governed by etiquette. **6.** Performance according to recognized criteria. **7.** Fitness with regard to health or training. **8a.** Style or manner in literary or musical composition. **b.** The structure of a work of art. **9.** A model for making a mold. **10.** A meaningful unit of language. **11.** A grade level esp. in a British school. ▸*v.* **1a.** To shape or become shaped. **b.** To develop in the mind: *form an opinion.* **2a.** To shape into a particular form. **b.** To draw up; arrange. **c.** To develop by instruction or precept: *form a child's mind.* **3.** To develop or acquire: *form a habit.* **4.** To constitute a part of. [< Lat. *fōrma*, perh. < Gk. *morphē.*]

-form ▸*suff.* Having the form of: *cruciform.*

for•mal (fôr′məl) ▸*adj.* **1a.** Of or involving outward form or structure. **b.** Being or relating to essential form or constitution: *a formal principle.* **2.** Following accepted forms or conventions: *a formal education.* **3.** Marked by strict observation of forms. **4.** Stiff or reserved: *a formal manner.* **5.** Done for the sake of procedure only: *a formal requirement.* ▸*n.* Something, such as a gown or social affair, that is formal in nature. —**for′mal•ly** *adv.*

for•mal•de•hyde (fôr-măl′də-hīd′) ▸*n.* A gaseous compound, HCHO, used in aqueous solution as a preservative and disinfectant. [*form(ic acid)*, HCOOH + ALDEHYDE.]

for•mal•ism (fôr′mə-lĭz′əm) ▸*n.* Rigorous or excessive adherence to recognized forms, as in religion or art. —**for′mal•ist** *adj.* & *n.* —**for′mal•is′tic** *adj.*

for•mal•i•ty (fôr-măl′ĭ-tē) ▸*n.*, *pl.* **-ties 1.** The quality or condition of being formal. **2.** Rigorous or ceremonious adherence to rules. **3.** An established rule or custom.

for•mal•ize (fôr′mə-līz′) ►*v.* **-ized, -iz•ing 1.** To make formal. **2.** To give formal endorsement to. —**for′mal•i•za′tion** *n.*

for•mat (fôr′măt′) ►*n.* **1.** A plan for the organization and arrangement of something. **2.** The layout of a publication. **3.** *Comp. Sci.* The arrangement of data for storage or display. ►*v.* **-mat•ted, -mat•ting 1.** To plan or arrange in a specified form. **2.** *Comp. Sci.* **a.** To determine the arrangement of (data) for storage or display. **b.** To divide (a disk) into sectors so that it may store data. [< Lat. *fōrma*, FORM.]

for•ma•tion (fôr-mā′shən) ►*n.* **1.** The act or process of forming. **2.** Something formed: *cloud formations.* **3.** The manner in which something is formed; structure. **4.** A specified arrangement, as of troops. —**for•ma′tion•al** *adj.*

for•ma•tive (fôr′mə-tĭv) ►*adj.* **1.** Forming or capable of forming. **2.** Of or relating to formation or growth: *his formative years.*

for•mer (fôr′mər) ►*adj.* **1.** Occurring earlier in time. **2.** Coming before in place or order. **3.** Being the first of two mentioned. **4.** Having been in the past: *a former ambassador.* [< OE *forma*, first.]

for•mer•ly (fôr′mər-lē) ►*adv.* At an earlier or former time; once.

form•fit•ting (fôrm′fĭt′ĭng) ►*adj.* Snugly fitting the body's contours: *formfitting jeans.*

For•mi•ca (fôr-mī′kə) ► A trademark for a variety of high-pressure laminated plastic sheets used esp. as heat- and chemical-resistant surfaces.

for•mi•da•ble (fôr′mĭ-də-bəl, fôr-mĭd′ə-) ►*adj.* **1.** Arousing fear, dread, or awe. **2.** Difficult to surmount. [< Lat. *formīdō*, fear.] —**for′mi•da•bil′i•ty** *n.* —**for′mi•da•bly** *adv.*

form•less (fôrm′lĭs) ►*adj.* Having no definite form. See Syns at **shapeless.** —**form′less•ly** *adv.* —**form′less•ness** *n.*

form letter ►*n.* A letter in a standardized format sent to many recipients.

For•mo•sa (fôr-mō′sə) See **Taiwan.**

for•mu•la (fôr′myə-lə) ►*n.*, *pl.* **-las** or **-lae** (-lē′) **1.** A set of words, symbols, or rules for use in a ceremony or procedure. **2.** *Chem.* A set of symbols that show the composition and structure of a compound. **3.** A recipe. **4.** A liquid food prescribed for an infant to substitute for or supplement human milk. **5.** *Math.* A statement, esp. an equation, of a fact, rule, principle, or other logical relation. [Lat. *fōrmula* < *fōrma*, FORM.] —**for′mu•la′ic** (-lā′ĭk) *adj.*

for•mu•late (fôr′myə-lāt′) ►*v.* **-lat•ed, -lat•ing 1.** To state as a formula. **2.** To express in systematic terms or concepts. **3.** To prepare according to a specified formula. —**for′mu•la′tion** *n.* —**for′mu•la′tor** *n.*

for•ni•ca•tion (fôr′nĭ-kā′shən) ►*n.* Sexual intercourse between partners who are not married. [< Lat. *fornix*, brothel.] —**for′ni•cate′** *v.* —**for′ni•ca′tor** *n.*

for•sake (fôr-sāk′, fər-) ►*v.* **-sook** (-so͝ok′), **-sak•en** (-sā′kən), **-sak•ing 1.** To give up; renounce. **2.** To leave altogether; abandon; desert. [< OE *forsacan.*]

for•sooth (fôr-so͞oth′, fər-) ►*adv.* In truth; indeed. [< OE *forsōth.*]

For•ster (fôr′stər), **E(dward) M(organ).** 1879–1970. British writer.

for•swear (fôr-swâr′, fōr-) ►*v.* **-swore** (fôr-swôr′, fōr-swōr′), **-sworn** (fôr-swôrn′, fōr-swōrn′), **-swear•ing 1.** To renounce seriously or under oath. **2.** To commit perjury. [< OE *forswerian.*]

for•syth•i•a (fôr-sĭth′ē-ə, -sī′thē-ə, fər-) ►*n.* A widely cultivated shrub with early-blooming yellow flowers. [After William *Forsyth* (1737–1804).]

fort (fôrt, fōrt) ►*n.* A fortified place, esp. an army post. [< Lat. *fortis*, strong.]

For•ta•le•za (fôr′tl-ā′zə, -tə-lĕ′-) A city of NE Brazil NW of Natal on the Atlantic. Pop. 1,765,794.

Fort-de-France (fôr-də-fräɴs′) The capital of Martinique, on the W coast. Pop. 99,844.

for•te¹ (fôr′tā′, fôrt, fōrt) ►*n.* Something in which one excels. [< OFr. *fort*, strong.]

Syns: *forte, métier, specialty, thing* **n.**

Usage: The word *forte* (from French *fort*) is traditionally pronounced with one syllable. Often, however, it is pronounced (fôr′tā′), probably influenced by the music term *forte,* which was borrowed from Italian.

for•te² (fôr′tā′) ►*adv. & adj. Mus.* In a loud, forceful manner. [Ital.] —**for′te′** *n.*

forth (fôrth, fōrth) ►*adv.* **1.** Forward or onward. **2.** Out into view. [< OE.]

Forth. A river of S-central Scotland flowing about 187 km (116 mi) to the **Firth of Forth,** an inlet of the North Sea.

forth•com•ing (fôrth-kŭm′ĭng, fōrth-) ►*adj.* **1.** About to appear or take place. **2.** Available when required or as promised. **3.** Willing to help; cooperative.

forth•right (fôrth′rīt′, fōrth′-) ►*adj.* Direct and without evasion; straightforward. —**forth′right′ly** *adv.* —**forth′right′ness** *n.*

forth•with (fôrth-wĭ*th*′, -wĭth′, fōrth-) ►*adv.* At once; immediately.

for•ti•eth (fôr′tē-ĭth) ►*n.* **1.** The ordinal number matching the number 40 in a series. **2.** One of 40 equal parts. —**for′ti•eth** *adv. & adj.*

for•ti•fy (fôr′tə-fī′) ►*v.* **-fied, -fy•ing 1.** To strengthen and secure (a position) militarily. **2.** To strengthen physically; invigorate. **3.** To give moral or mental strength to; encourage. **4.** To enrich (food), as by adding vitamins. **5.** To add alcohol to (wine). [< Lat. *fortis*, strong.] —**for′ti•fi•ca′tion** *n.*

for•tis•si•mo (fôr-tĭs′ə-mō′) ►*adv. & adj. Mus.* In a very loud manner. [Ital.] —**for•tis′si•mo′** *n.*

for•ti•tude (fôr′tĭ-to͞od′, -tyo͞od′) ►*n.* Strength of mind that allows one to endure pain or adversity with courage. [< Lat. *fortis*, strong.]

Fort Lau•der•dale (lô′dər-dāl′) A city of SE FL on the Atlantic coast N of Miami Beach. Pop. 149,377.

fort•night (fôrt′nīt′) ►*n.* A period of 14 days; two weeks. [ME *fourtenight* : OE *fēowertēne*, FOURTEEN + OE *niht*, NIGHT.]

fort•night•ly (fôrt′nīt′lē) ►*adj.* Happening or appearing once in or every two weeks. —**fort′night′ly** *adv.*

FOR•TRAN (fôr′trăn′) ►*n.* A programming language for problems that can be expressed algebraically. [*for(mula) tran(slation).*]

for•tress (fôr′trĭs) ►*n.* A fortified place, esp. one that includes a town. [< Med.Lat. *fortalitia* < Lat. *fortis*, strong.]

Fort Smith. A city of W AR WNW of Little Rock. Pop. 72,798.

for•tu•i•tous (fôr-to͞o′ĭ-təs, -tyo͞o′-) ▸*adj.* Happening by accident or chance; unplanned. [< Lat. *forte*, by chance.] —**for•tu′i•tous•ly** *adv.* —**for•tu′i•tous•ness** *n.*

for•tu•i•ty (fôr-to͞o′ĭ-tē, -tyo͞o′-) ▸*n., pl.* **-ties** **1.** A chance occurrence or event. **2.** The quality or condition of being fortuitous.

for•tu•nate (fôr′chə-nĭt) ▸*adj.* Occurring by or having good fortune. See Syns at **happy.** —**for′tu•nate•ly** *adv.*

for•tune (fôr′chən) ▸*n.* **1a.** Fate; destiny. **b.** Good or bad luck. **2. fortunes** The turns of luck in one's lifetime. **3a.** Wealth; riches. **b.** A large sum of money. [< Lat. *fortūna.*]

for•tune•tell•er (fôr′chən-tĕl′ər) ▸*n.* One who, usu. for a fee, professes to predict future events. —**for′tune•tell′ing** *adj. & n.*

Fort Wayne. A city of NE IN NE of Indianapolis. Pop. 173,072.

Fort Worth. A city of NE TX W of Dallas. Pop. 447,619.

for•ty (fôr′tē) ▸*n., pl.* **-ties.** The cardinal number equal to 4 × 10. [< OE *fēowertig.*] —**for′ty** *adj. & pron.*

for•ty-five (fôr′tē-fīv′) ▸*n.* **1.** A.45-caliber pistol. **2.** A phonograph record designed to be played at 45 revolutions per minute.

for•ty-nin•er (fôr′tē-nī′nər) ▸*n.* One who took part in the 1849 California gold rush.

forty winks ▸*pl.n. Informal* A short nap.

fo•rum (fôr′əm, fōr′-) ▸*n., pl.* **fo•rums** also **fo•ra** (fôr′ə, fōr′ə) **1.** The public square or marketplace of an ancient Roman city. **2.** A public place or medium for open discussion. **3.** A court of law; tribunal. [< Lat.]

for•ward (fôr′wərd) ▸*adj.* **1.** At, near, belonging to, or located in the front. **2.** Going, tending, or moving toward a position in front. **3.** Presumptuous or bold. **4.** Being ahead of current economic, political, or technological trends; progressive. **5.** Mentally, physically, or socially advanced; precocious. ▸*adv.* **1.** Toward or tending to the front; frontward: *step forward.* **2.** In or toward the future: *looking forward to seeing you.* **3.** Earlier or later: *moved the appointment forward.* ▸*n. Sports* A player in the front line, as in basketball or hockey. ▸*v.* **1.** To send on to a subsequent destination or address. See Syns at **send. 2.** To help advance; promote. See Syns at **advance.** [< OE *fōreweard.*] —**for′ward•ly** *adv.* —**for′ward•ness** *n.*

for•wards (fôr′wərdz, fōr′-) ▸*adv.* To or tending to the front; forward.

for•went (fôr-wĕnt′, fōr-) ▸*v.* P.t. of **forgo.**

fos•sil (fŏs′əl) ▸*n.* **1.** A remnant or trace of an organism of a past geologic age, such as a skeleton or leaf imprint, embedded in the earth's crust. **2.** One that is outdated. [< Lat. *fossilis*, dug up < *fodere*, dig.]

fossil fuel ▸*n.* A hydrocarbon deposit, such as natural gas, derived from living matter of a previous geologic time and used for fuel.

fos•sil•ize (fŏs′ə-līz′) ▸*v.* **-ized, -iz•ing 1.** To convert into or become a fossil. **2.** To make or become outmoded, rigid, or fixed; antiquate. —**fos′sil•i•za′tion** *n.*

fos•ter (fô′stər, fŏs′tər) ▸*v.* **1.** To bring up; rear. See Syns at **nurture. 2.** To promote the development of; cultivate. See Syns at **advance.** ▸*adj.* Giving or receiving parental care although not related legally or by blood: *foster parents.* [< OE *fōstor*, food.]

Fos•ter (fô′stər), **Stephen Collins.** 1826–64. Amer. composer of popular songs.

Fou•cault (fo͞o-kō′), **Jean Bernard Léon.** 1819–68. French physicist and inventor.

fought (fôt) ▸*v.* P.t. and p.part. of **fight.**

foul (foul) ▸*adj.* **-er, -est 1.** Offensive to the senses; revolting: *a foul flavor.* **2.** Having an offensive odor. **3.** Rotten or putrid. **4a.** Dirty; filthy. **b.** Full of impurities; polluted: *foul air.* **5.** Morally detestable; wicked. **6.** Vulgar; obscene. **7.** Bad or unfavorable; unpleasant: *foul weather.* **8.** Unfair; dishonorable: *win by foul means.* **9a.** *Sports* Contrary to the rules of a game or sport. **b.** Designating lines that limit the playing area. **10.** Entangled or twisted, as a rope. ▸*n.* **1a.** *Sports* An infraction of the rules. **b.** *Baseball* A foul ball, hit, or move. **2.** An entanglement or collision. ▸*adv.* In a foul manner. ▸*v.* **1.** To make or become foul; pollute. See Syns at **contaminate. 2.** To bring into dishonor. **3.** To clog or obstruct. **4.** To entangle or become entangled, as a rope. **5.** To commit a foul (against). —***phrasal verb:* foul up** To blunder or cause to blunder because of mistakes or poor judgment. [< OE *fūl.*] —**foul′ly** *adv.* —**foul′ness** *n.*

fou•lard (fo͞o-lärd′) ▸*n.* A lightweight twill or plain-woven fabric of silk, usu. having a printed design, esp. used for neckties. [Fr.]

foul•mouthed (foul′mouthd′, -moutht′) ▸*adj.* Using abusive or obscene language.

foul play ▸*n.* Unfair or treacherous action, esp. when involving violence.

foul shot ▸*n. Basketball* An unobstructed shot awarded to a fouled player and scored as one point if successful.

foul-up (foul′ŭp′) ▸*n.* **1.** A condition of confusion caused by mistakes or poor judgment. **2.** A mechanical failure.

found¹ (found) ▸*v.* **1.** To establish or set up (e.g., a college). **2.** To establish the foundation or basis of. [< Lat. *fundāre.*] —**found′er** *n.*

Syns: *found, create, establish, institute, organize* **v.**

found² (found) ▸*v.* **1.** To melt (metal) and pour into a mold. **2.** To make (objects) by founding. [< Lat. *fundere.*] —**found′er** *n.*

found³ (found) ▸*v.* P.t. and p.part. of **find.**

foun•da•tion (foun-dā′shən) ▸*n.* **1.** The act of founding, esp. the establishment of an institution. **2.** The basis on which a thing stands; underlying support; base. **3a.** An endowment. **b.** An endowed institution. **4.** A cosmetic used as a base for facial makeup. —**foun•da′tion•al** *adj.*

foun•der (foun′dər) ▸*v.* **1.** To sink or cause to sink below the water. **2.** To fail utterly; collapse. **3.** To go lame, as a horse. [< OFr. *fondrer*, sink to the ground.]

Usage: *Founder* means "to fail utterly, collapse." *Flounder* means "to proceed in confusion." If John is foundering in a course, he had better drop it. If he is floundering, he may yet pull through.

found•ling (found′lĭng) ▸*n.* An abandoned child of unknown parentage. [ME.]

foun•dry (foun′drē) ▸*n., pl.* **-dries.** A place where metal is melted and molded.

fount¹ (fount) ▸*n.* **1.** A fountain. **2.** A source. [< Lat. *fōns, font-.*]

fount² (fount) ▸*n. Chiefly Brit.* Var. of **font².**

foun•tain (foun′tən) ▸*n.* **1a.** An artificially created stream of water. **b.** A structure or device from which such a stream issues. **2.** A spring of water from the earth, esp. a stream's source. **3.** A soda fountain. **4.** A point of origin. [< LLat. *fontāna* < Lat. *fōns, font-*.]

foun•tain•head (foun′tən-hĕd′) ▸*n.* **1.** A spring that is the source of a stream. **2.** A chief and copious source or origin.

fountain pen ▸*n.* A pen filled from an external source and containing an ink reservoir that automatically feeds the writing point.

four (fôr, fōr) ▸*n.* **1.** The cardinal number equal to 3 + 1. **2.** The 4th in a set or sequence. [< OE *fēower*.] —**four** *adj. & pron.*

four-flush (fôr′flŭsh′, fōr′-) ▸*v.* **1.** *Games* To bluff in poker with a hand having only four out of five cards of the same suit. **2.** *Slang* To mislead; bluff. —**four′-flush′er** *n.*

4-H Club or **Four-H Club** (fôr′āch′, fōr′-) ▸*n.* A youth organization sponsored by the Department of Agriculture and teaching agriculture and home economics. [From its goals of improving head, heart, hands, and health.]

Fou•rier (fo͝or′ē-ā′, fo͞o-ryā′), **(François Marie) Charles.** 1772–1837. French socialist.

Fourier, Baron **Jean Baptiste Joseph.** 1768–1830. French mathematician and physicist.

four-in-hand (fôr′ĭn-hănd′, fōr′-) ▸*n.* **1.** A team of four horses controlled by one driver. **2.** A necktie tied in a slipknot with long ends left hanging one in front of the other.

four-leaf clover (fôr′lēf′, fōr′-) ▸*n.* A clover leaf having four leaflets instead of three, considered an omen of good luck.

four-o'clock (fôr′ə-klŏk′, fōr′-) ▸*n.* A plant cultivated for its tubular, variously colored flowers that open late in the afternoon.

401(k) (fôr′ō-wŭn-kā′, fōr′-) ▸*n.* A retirement plan for investing a portion of one's wages in a tax-deferred account.

four-post•er (fôr′pō′stər, fōr′-) ▸*n.* A bed having tall corner posts orig. intended to support curtains or a canopy.

four•score (fôr′skôr′, fōr′skōr′) ▸*adj.* Four times twenty; eighty.

four•some (fôr′səm, fōr′-) ▸*n.* **1.** A group of four persons or things, esp. two couples. **2.** Four players in a game, two on each side, esp. in golf or bridge.

four•square (fôr′skwâr′, fōr′-) ▸*adj.* **1.** Square. **2.** Marked by firm, unwavering conviction or expression; forthright. —**four′-square′** *adv.*

four•teen (fôr-tēn′, fōr-) ▸*n.* **1.** The cardinal number equal to 13 + 1. **2.** The 14th in a set or sequence. [< OE *fēowertēne*.] —**four•teen′** *adj. & pron.*

four•teenth (fôr-tēnth′, fōr-) ▸*n.* **1.** The ordinal number matching the number 14 in a series. **2.** One of 14 equal parts. —**four•teenth′** *adv. & adj.*

fourth (fôrth, fōrth) ▸*n.* **1.** The ordinal number matching the number 4 in a series. **2.** One of four equal parts. **3.** *Mus.* A tone four degrees above or below a given tone in a diatonic scale. [< OE *fēorth*.] —**fourth** *adv. & adj.*

fourth dimension ▸*n.* Time regarded as a coordinate dimension and required by relativity theory, along with three spatial dimensions, to specify fully the location of any event.

fourth estate ▸*n.* Journalists collectively.

Fourth of July ▸*n.* See **Independence Day.**

four-wheel drive (fôr′hwēl′, -wēl, fōr′) ▸*n.* An automotive drive system in which mechanical power is transmitted from the drive shaft to all four wheels.

fowl (foul) ▸*n., pl.* **fowl** or **fowls 1.** A bird used as food, esp. the common domesticated chicken. **2.** A bird used as food or hunted as game. ▸*v.* To hunt, trap, or shoot wildfowl. [< OE *fugol*.]

fox (fŏks) ▸*n., pl.* **-es** also **fox 1a.** A carnivorous mammal related to the dogs and wolves, having a pointed snout and a long bushy tail. **b.** The fur of a fox. **2.** A crafty or sly person. **3.** *Slang* A sexually attractive person. ▸*v.* To trick or fool by ingenuity or cunning; outwit. [< OE.] —**fox′i•ly** *adv.* —**fox′i•ness** *n.* —**fox′y** *adj.*

Fox ▸*n., pl.* **Fox** or **-es 1.** A member of a Native American people formerly of the upper Midwest, now in central Iowa and Oklahoma. **2.** Their Algonquian language.

Fox, Charles James. 1749–1806. British politician.

Fox, George. 1624–1691. English founder of the Quakers (1647–48).

fox•fire (fŏks′fīr′) ▸*n.* A phosphorescent glow, esp. that of fungi on rotting wood.

fox•glove (fŏks′glŭv′) ▸*n.* A plant having a long cluster of large, tubular, pinkish-purple flowers and leaves that are the source of the medicinal drug digitalis.

fox•hole (fŏks′hōl′) ▸*n.* A pit dug by a soldier for protection against enemy fire.

fox terrier ▸*n.* A small terrier having a white coat with dark markings.

fox trot ▸*n.* A ballroom dance in 4/4 time, encompassing a variety of slow and fast steps. —**fox′trot′** (fŏks′trŏt′) *v.*

foy•er (foi′ər, foi′ā′) ▸*n.* **1.** A lobby, as of a theater or hotel. **2.** An entrance hall; vestibule. [< VLat. **focārium*, fireplace < Lat. *focus*, hearth.]

fps ▸*abbr.* **1.** feet per second **2.** foot-pound-second **3.** frames per second

Fr ▸ The symbol for the element **francium.**

fr. ▸*abbr.* **1.** frame **2.** franc **3.** from

Fr. ▸*abbr.* **1.** *Eccles.* father (title) **2.** French **3.** Frau **4.** friar **5.** Friday

fra•cas (frā′kəs, frăk′əs) ▸*n.* A rowdy fight. See Syns at **brawl.** [< Ital. *fracasso*.]

frac•tal (frăk′təl) ▸*n.* A geometric pattern that is repeated at ever smaller scales to produce irregular shapes that cannot be represented by classical geometry. [< Lat. *frangere, frāct-*, break.]

frac•tion (frăk′shən) ▸*n.* **1.** *Math.* A quotient of two quantities shown as a numerator over a denominator. **2.** A disconnected piece; fragment. **3.** A small part; bit. [< Lat. *frangere, frāct-*, break.] —**frac′tion•al** *adj.* —**frac′tion•al•ly** *adv.*

frac•tious (frăk′shəs) ▸*adj.* **1.** Inclined to make trouble; unruly. **2.** Having a peevish nature; cranky. [< FRACTION, discord.] —**frac′tious•ly** *adv.* —**frac′tious•ness** *n.*

frac•ture (frăk′chər) ▸*n.* **1.** The act or process of breaking or the condition of being broken. **2.** A break, rupture, or crack, esp. in bone or cartilage. ▶ *v.* **-tured, -tur•ing.** To break or cause to break; crack. [< Lat. *frangere, frāct-,* break.]

frag•ile (frăj′əl, -īl′) ▶ *adj.* **1.** Easily broken or damaged; delicate. **2.** Tenuous or flimsy: *a fragile claim to fame.* [< Lat. *fragilis* < *frangere,* break.] —**frag′ile•ly** *adv.* —**fra•gil′i•ty** (frə-jĭl′ĭ-tē), **frag′ile•ness** *n.*

frag•ment (frăg′mənt) ▶ *n.* **1.** A small part broken off. **2.** Something incomplete. ▶ *v.* (-mĕnt′). To break into fragments. [< Lat. *fragmentum* < *frangere,* break.] —**frag′men•ta′tion** *n.*

frag•men•tar•y (frăg′mən-tĕr′ē) ▶ *adj.* Consisting of small, disconnected parts. —**frag′men•tar′i•ly** (-târ′ə-lē) *adv.*

fragmentation bomb ▶ *n.* An aerial antipersonnel bomb that scatters shrapnel over a wide area upon explosion.

Fra•go•nard (frăg′ə-när′, frä-gô-), **Jean Honoré.** 1732–1806. French artist.

fra•grance (frā′grəns) ▶ *n.* A sweet or pleasant odor. [< Lat. *frāgrāre,* emit an odor.] —**fra′grant** *adj.* —**fra′grant•ly** *adv.*

Syns: *fragrance, aroma, bouquet, perfume, redolence, scent* **n.**

frail (frāl) ▶ *adj.* **-er, -est 1.** Physically weak. **2.** Not substantial; slight. **3.** Easily broken. [< Lat. *fragilis,* FRAGILE.] —**frail′ly** *adv.*

frail•ty (frāl′tē) ▶ *n., pl.* **-ties 1.** The condition or quality of being frail. **2.** A fault, esp. one arising from human weakness.

frame (frām) ▶ *v.* **framed, fram•ing 1.** To build or construct. **2.** To conceive or design. **3.** To arrange or adjust for a purpose. **4.** To put into words; compose. **5.** To enclose in or as if in a frame. **6.** *Informal* To rig evidence or events so as to incriminate (a person) falsely. ▶ *n.* **1.** Something composed of parts fitted and joined together. **2.** A skeletal structure: *the frame of a house.* **3.** An open structure or rim: *a window frame.* **4.** The human body; physique. **5.** A general structure or system: *the frame of government.* **6.** A general state or condition: *frame of mind.* **7.** A round of play in some games, such as bowling. **8.** A single picture on a roll of movie film, videotape, or television images. **9.** *Comp. Sci.* A segment within a browser's window that can be scrolled independently of other such segments. [< OE *framian,* to further.] —**fram′er** *n.*

frame-up (frām′ŭp′) ▶ *n. Informal* A fraudulent scheme, esp. one that involves falsified charges or evidence to incriminate an innocent person.

frame•work (frām′wûrk′) ▶ *n.* **1.** A structure for supporting or enclosing something. **2.** A fundamental system or design. **3.** A set of assumptions constituting a way of viewing reality.

franc (frăngk) ▶ *n.* See table at **currency.** [< OFr.]

France (frăns) A country of W Europe on the Atlantic and the English Channel. Cap. Paris. Pop. 54,334,871.

France (frăns, fräNs), **Anatole.** 1844–1924. French critic and writer; 1921 Nobel.

fran•chise (frăn′chīz′) ▶ *n.* **1.** A privilege granted a person or a group; charter. **2.** A constitutional or statutory right, as the right to vote. **3.** Authorization granted to someone to sell a company's goods or services. **4.** The territory or limits within which a privilege or right may be exercised. ▶ *v.* **-chised, -chis•ing.** To grant a franchise to. [< OFr. *franchise,* freedom, exemption.] —**fran′chis•ee′** *n.* —**fran′chis′er, fran′chi′sor** *n.*

Fran•cis I (frăn′sĭs). 1494–1547. King of France (1515–47).

Francis II. 1768–1835. Last Holy Roman emperor (1792–1806); emperor of Austria (1804–35) as Francis I.

Francis Fer•di•nand (fûr′dn-ănd′). 1863–1914. Austrian archduke whose assassination precipitated World War I.

Francis Jo•seph I (jō′zəf, -səf, yō′zĕf) also **Franz Jo•sef I** (fränts yō′zĕf). 1830–1916. Emperor of Austria (1848–1916); king of Hungary (1867–1916).

Francis of As•si•si (ə-sē′zē, -sē, ə-sĭs′ē), Saint. 1182?–1226. Italian friar; founder of the Franciscan order (1209). —**Fran•cis′can** *adj. & n.*

fran•ci•um (frăn′sē-əm) ▶ *n. Symbol* **Fr** An extremely unstable synthetic radioactive element. At. no. 87. See table at **element.** [After FRANCE.]

Franck (frängk, fräNk), **César Auguste.** 1822–90. French organist and composer.

Fran•co (frăng′kō, fräng′-), **Francisco.** 1892–1975. Spanish soldier and dictator.

Franco- ▶ *pref.* French: *Francophone.* [< LLat. *Francus,* a Frank.]

Fran•co•phone (frăng′kə-fōn′) ▶ *n.* A French-speaking person, esp. in a region of linguistic diversity. ▶ *adj.* French-speaking.

fran•gi•ble (frăn′jə-bəl) ▶ *adj.* Easily broken; breakable. [< Lat. *frangere,* break.] —**fran′gi•bil′i•ty, fran′gi•ble•ness** *n.*

frank[1] (frăngk) ▶ *adj.* **-er, -est.** Open and sincere in expression; straightforward. ▶ *v.* **1.** To put an official mark on (a piece of mail) so that it can be sent free of charge. **2.** To send (mail) free of charge. ▶ *n.* **1.** A mark or signature on a piece of mail to indicate the right to send it free. **2.** The right to send mail free. [< OFr. *franc,* free.] —**frank′ly** *adv.* —**frank′ness** *n.*

frank[2] (frăngk) ▶ *n. Informal* A frankfurter.

Frank ▶ *n.* A member of a Germanic people who conquered Gaul about A.D. 500. —**Frank′ish** *adj.*

Frank (frăngk, frängk), **Anne.** 1929–45. German Jewish diarist.

Anne Frank

Frank•en•stein (frăng′kən-stīn′) ▶ *n.* **1.** A creation that destroys its creator. **2.** A monster having the appearance of a man. [After *Frankenstein,* the creator of the artificial monster in *Frankenstein* by Mary W. Shelley.]

Frank•fort (frăngk′fərt) The capital of KY, in the N-central part NW of Lexington. Pop. 25,968.

Frank•furt (frănk′fərt, frängk′fŏŏrt′) **1.** Also **Frankfurt an der O•der** (än dər ō′dər). A city of E Germany on the Polish border. Pop. 84,072. **2.** Also **Frankfurt am Main** (äm mīn′). A city of W-central Germany on the Main R. Pop. 659,803.

frank•furt•er (frănk′fər-tər) ►*n.* A smoked sausage of beef or beef and pork made in long reddish links. [After *Frankfurt* am Main, Germany.]

Frankfurter, Felix. 1882–1965. Austrian-born Amer. jurist and a founder of the American Civil Liberties Union.

frank•in•cense (frăng′kĭn-sĕns′) ►*n.* An aromatic gum resin used chiefly as incense. [< OFr. *franc encens*, pure incense.]

Frank•lin (frăngk′lĭn), **Benjamin.** 1706–90. Amer. public official, writer, scientist, and printer.

Franklin, Sir **John.** 1786–1847. British explorer.

fran•tic (frăn′tĭk) ►*adj.* Distraught, as from fear or worry. [< OFr. *frenetique*, FRENETIC.] —**fran′ti•cal•ly, fran′tic•ly** *adv.*

Franz Jo•sef I (fränts yō′zĕf). See **Francis Joseph I.**

Franz Josef Land (lănd, länt) An archipelago in the Arctic Ocean N of Novaya Zemlya.

frappe (frăp) ►*n.* *Regional* See **milk shake.** See Regional Note at **milk shake.** [Alteration of FRAPPÉ.]

frap•pé (fră-pā′, frăp) ►*n.* **1.** A frozen mixture similar to sherbet. **2.** A beverage poured over shaved ice. [< Fr., chilled.]

Fra•ser River (frā′zər) A river of British Columbia, Canada, flowing about 1,368 km (850 mi) from the Rocky Mts. to the Strait of Georgia at Vancouver.

fra•ter•nal (frə-tûr′nəl) ►*adj.* **1a.** Of brothers. **b.** Brotherly. **2.** Of or constituting a fraternity. **3.** *Biol.* Of or being a twin developed from separately fertilized ova. [< Lat. *frāter*, brother.] —**fra•ter′nal•ism** *n.* —**fra•ter′nal•ly** *adv.*

fra•ter•ni•ty (frə-tûr′nĭ-tē) ►*n., pl.* **-ties 1.** A group of people associated or joined by similar backgrounds, occupations, or interests. **2.** A chiefly social organization of male college students. **3.** Brotherhood.

frat•er•nize (frăt′ər-nīz′) ►*v.* **-nized, -niz•ing 1.** To associate with others in a brotherly or congenial way. **2.** To associate with an enemy or opposing group. —**frat′er•ni•za′tion** *n.* —**frat′er•niz′er** *n.*

frat•ri•cide (frăt′rĭ-sīd′) ►*n.* **1.** The killing of one's brother or sister. **2.** One who has killed a sibling. [Lat. *frāter*, brother + -CIDE.] —**frat′ri•cid′al** *adj.*

Frau (frou) ►*n., pl.* **Frau•en** (frou′ən). A German courtesy title for a woman. [Ger.]

fraud (frôd) ►*n.* **1.** A deliberate deception for unfair or unlawful gain; swindle. **2a.** One that defrauds; cheat. **b.** One who assumes a false pose; impostor. [< Lat. *fraus, fraud-*.]

fraud•u•lent (frô′jə-lənt) ►*adj.* Constituting or gained by fraud. [< Lat. *fraudulentus.*] —**fraud′u•lence** *n.* —**fraud′u•lent•ly** *adv.*

fraught (frôt) ►*adj.* **1.** Filled with a specified element; charged: *work fraught with danger.* **2.** Distressful; upsetting. [ME < *fraughten*, to load.]

Fräu•lein (froi′līn′, frou′-) ►*n., pl.* **-lein.** A German courtesy title for a girl or young woman. [Ger., dim. of *Frau*, Frau.]

fray[1] (frā) ►*n.* **1.** A fight or scuffle. See Syns at **brawl. 2.** A heated dispute. [< ME *affrai*, AFFRAY.]

fray[2] (frā) ►*v.* **1.** To strain; chafe: *fray the nerves.* **2.** To wear away, unravel, or tatter by rubbing. [< Lat. *fricāre*, rub.]

fraz•zle (frăz′əl) ►*v.* **-zled, -zling** *Informal* **1.** To fray. **2.** To exhaust physically or emotionally. [Perh. blend of FRAY[2] and dial. *fazzle*, unravel.] —**fraz′zle** *n.*

FRB ►*abbr.* Federal Reserve Board

freak (frēk) ►*n.* **1.** A person, thing, or event that is abnormal or markedly unusual. **2.** A whim; vagary. **3.** *Slang* **a.** A drug addict. **b.** A fan or enthusiast. ►*adj.* Highly unusual or irregular: *a freak storm.* ►*v.* *Slang* **1.** To experience or cause to experience hallucinations or feelings of paranoia, esp. as induced by a drug. Often used with *out.* **2.** To make or become agitated or excited: *a find that freaked me out.* [?] —**freak′i•ly** *adv.* —**freak′ish** *adj.* —**freak′ish•ly** *adv.* —**freak′ish•ness** *n.* —**freak′y** *adj.*

freak-out (frēk′out′) ►*n.* *Slang* An act or an instance of freaking out.

freck•le (frĕk′əl) ►*n.* A brownish spot on the skin, often darkening with exposure to the sun. ►*v.* **-led, -ling.** To dot or become dotted with freckles or spots. [< ME *fraknes*, freckles.] —**freck′ly** *adj.*

Fred•er•ick I (frĕd′rĭk, -ər-ĭk). "Frederick Barbarossa." 1123?–90. Holy Roman emperor (1152–90); king of Germany (1152–90) and Italy (1155–90).

Frederick II[1]. 1194–1250. Holy Roman emperor (1212–50); king of Sicily (1198–1250) as Frederick I.

Frederick II[2]. "Frederick the Great." 1712–86. King of Prussia (1740–86).

Fred•er•ic•ton (frĕd′rĭk-tən, -ər-ĭk-) The capital of New Brunswick, Canada, in the S-central part NW of St. John. Pop. 46,466.

free (frē) ►*adj.* **fre•er, fre•est 1.** Not bound or constrained; at liberty. **2.** Not under obligation or necessity. **3a.** Having political independence. **b.** Governed by consent and possessing civil liberties. **4a.** Not affected by a given condition or circumstance. **b.** Exempt: *free of all taxes.* **5.** Not literal or exact: *a free translation.* **6.** Costing nothing; gratuitous. **7.** Not occupied or used. **8.** Unobstructed. **9.** Guileless; frank. **10.** Taking undue liberties. **11.** Liberal or lavish. ►*adv.* **1.** In a free manner. **2.** Without charge. ►*v.* **freed, free•ing 1.** To set at liberty. **2.** To rid of; release. **3.** To disengage or untangle. [< OE *frēo.*] —**free′ly** *adv.*

free•base or **free-base** (frē′bās′) ►*v.* **-based, -bas•ing.** To prepare or use purified cocaine by burning it and inhaling the fumes.

free•bie also **free•bee** (frē′bē) ►*n.* *Slang* Something given or received free. [< FREE.]

free•board (frē′bôrd′, -bōrd′) ►*n.* The distance between the water line and the uppermost full deck of a ship.

free•boot•er (frē′bōō′tər) ►*n.* A pirate or plunderer. [< Du. *vrijbuit*, plunder.]

free•born (frē′bôrn′) ►*adj.* **1.** Born as a free person. **2.** Of or befitting a person born free.

freed•man (frēd′mən) ►*n.* A man who has been freed from slavery.

free•dom (frē′dəm) ►*n.* **1.** The condition of

being free. **2a.** Political independence. **b.** Possession of civil rights. **3.** Ease of movement. **4.** Frankness or boldness. **5.** Unrestricted use or access. [< OE *frēodōm.*]

freed•wom•an (frēd′wo͝om′ən) ►*n.* A woman who has been freed from slavery.

free enterprise ►*n.* The freedom of private businesses to operate competitively for profit with minimal government regulation.

free fall or **free-fall** (frē′fôl′) ►*n.* The fall of a body toward the earth without a drag-producing device such as a parachute.

free flight ►*n.* Flight, as of a spacecraft, after termination of powered flight.

free-for-all (frē′fər-ôl′) ►*n.* A fight or competition in which everyone present takes part. See Syns at **brawl.**

free•form (frē′fôrm′) ►*adj.* Having a usu. flowing asymmetrical shape or outline: *free-form sculpture.* —**free′form′** *adv.*

free•hand (frē′hănd′) ►*adj.* Drawn by hand without mechanical aids. —**free′hand′** *adv.*

free hand ►*n.* Freedom to do as one sees fit.

free•hand•ed (frē′hăn′dĭd) ►*adj.* Openhanded; generous. See Syns at **liberal.** —**free′hand′ed•ly** *adv.* —**free′hand′ed•ness** *n.*

free•hold (frē′hōld′) ►*n.* **1.** An estate held in fee or for life. **2.** The tenure by which such an estate is held. —**free′hold′er** *n.*

free kick ►*n.* An unobstructed kick of a stationary ball, as in soccer.

free•lance (frē′lăns′) ►*n.* A person, esp. a writer or artist, who sells his or her services to employers as those services are needed. —**free′lance′** *v. & adj.* —**free′lanc′er** *n.*

free•load (frē′lōd′) ►*v.* To take advantage of the generosity or hospitality of others. —**free′load′er** *n.*

free love ►*n.* The belief in or practice of living together without marriage.

free lunch ►*n. Slang* Something acquired without due effort or cost.

free•man (frē′mən) ►*n.* **1.** A person not in slavery. **2.** One who possesses the rights or privileges of a citizen.

Free•ma•son (frē′mā′sən) ►*n.* A member of the Free and Accepted Masons, an international fraternal charitable organization with secret rites and signs. —**Free′ma′son•ry** *n.*

free on board ►*adj. & adv.* Without charge to the buyer for delivery on board a carrier at a specified location.

free port ►*n.* A port where imported goods can be processed free of customs duties before reexport.

free radical ►*n.* An unstable, highly reactive atom or group of atoms that can damage cells in animal tissue.

free-range (frē′rānj′) ►*adj.* Of or produced by animals, esp. poultry, that range freely for food rather than being confined.

free speech ►*n.* The right to express any opinion in public without censorship or restraint.

free•stand•ing (frē′stăn′dĭng) ►*adj.* Standing without support or attachment.

free•stone (frē′stōn′) ►*n.* **1.** A stone, such as limestone, soft enough to be cut easily without shattering. **2.** A fruit, esp. a peach, that has a stone not adhering to the pulp.

free•style (frē′stīl′) ►*n.* **1.** A swimming event in which any stroke is permissible. **2.** A competition, as in skiing, in which any maneuver is allowed and competitors are judged on their artistic expression and technical skill. —**free′style′** *adv. & adj.*

free•think•er (frē′thĭng′kər) ►*n.* One who rejects authority and dogma, esp. in religious thinking. —**free′think′ing** *adj. & n.*

free throw ►*n.* See **foul shot.**

Free•town (frē′toun′) The capital of Sierra Leone, in the W part on the Atlantic. Pop. 469,776.

free trade ►*n.* Trade between nations without protective customs tariffs.

free verse ►*n.* Verse composed of lines having no fixed metrical pattern.

free•ware (frē′wâr′) ►*n.* Free software, usu. available over the Internet.

free•way (frē′wā′) ►*n.* **1.** See **expressway.** **2.** A highway without tolls.

free•wheel•ing (frē′hwē′lĭng, -wē′-) ►*adj.* **1.** Free of restraints or rules, as in organization or procedure. **2.** Heedless; carefree.

free•will (frē′wĭl′) ►*adj.* Voluntary.

free will ►*n.* **1.** The ability or discretion to choose. **2.** The power to make choices that are unconstrained, as by fate.

freeze (frēz) ►*v.* **froze** (frōz), **fro•zen** (frō′zən), **freez•ing 1a.** To pass or cause to pass from liquid to solid by loss of heat. **b.** To acquire a surface of ice. **2.** To be at that degree of temperature at which ice forms. **3.** To damage or be damaged by cold or frost. **4.** To be uncomfortably cold. **5.** To make or become inoperative by or as if by frost or ice. **6.** To become unable to act or react, as from fear or shyness. **7.** To become icily silent. **8.** To make or become rigid and inflexible. **9.** To preserve by subjecting to freezing temperatures. **10a.** To fix (prices or wages) at a current level. **b.** To prohibit further manufacture or use of. **c.** To prevent or restrict the exchange, liquidation, or granting of by law. **11.** To anesthetize by chilling. —***phrasal verb:* freeze out** To exclude. ►*n.* **1.** The act of freezing or the condition of being frozen. **2.** A cold spell; frost. [< OE *frēosan.*]

freeze-dry (frēz′drī′) ►*v.* To preserve by rapid freezing and drying in a high vacuum.

freez•er (frē′zər) ►*n.* An insulated compartment, cabinet, or room for the rapid freezing and storing of perishable food.

freez•ing point (frē′zĭng) ►*n.* The temperature at which a given liquid solidifies under a specified pressure, esp. a pressure equal to that of the atmosphere.

freight (frāt) ►*n.* **1.** Goods carried by a vessel or vehicle; cargo. **2.** A burden; load. **3a.** Commercial transportation of goods. **b.** The charge for transporting goods by cargo carrier. **4.** A railway train carrying goods only. ►*v.* **1.** To convey commercially as cargo. **2.** To load with cargo. **3.** To load, as with meaning. [< MDu. or MLGer. *vrecht.*]

freight•er (frā′tər) ►*n.* A vehicle, esp. a ship, used for carrying freight.

Fre•mont (frē′mŏnt′) A city of W CA SE of Oakland. Pop. 173,339.

Fré•mont (frē′mŏnt′), **John Charles.** 1813–1890. Amer. explorer and politician.

fre•na (frē′nə) ►*n.* Pl. of **frenum.**

French (frĕnch) ►*adj.* Of or relating to France or its people or language. ►*n.* **1.** The Romance language of France, Quebec, and various other areas. **2.** The people of France. —**French′man** *n.* —**French′wom′an** *n.*

French-Canadian also **French Canadian** ▸*n.* A Canadian of French descent. —**French′-Ca•na′di•an** *adj.*

French curve ▸*n.* A flat drafting tool with curved edges and scroll-shaped cutouts used to draw curves esp. in engineering.

French curve

French door ▸*n.* A door with glass panes extending for most of its length.

French door

French fry ▸*n.* A potato strip fried in deep fat.

French-fry (frĕnch′frī′) ▸*v.* To fry in deep fat.

French Guiana. A French overseas department of NE South America on the Atlantic. Cap. Cayenne. Pop. 72,012.

French horn ▸*n.* A valved brass wind instrument with a long narrow coiled tube that ends in a flaring bell.

French leave ▸*n.* An unauthorized departure.

French Polynesia. A French overseas territory in the S-central Pacific, including the Society, Marquesas, and Austral islands and the Tuamotu archipelago. Cap. Papeete, on Tahiti. Pop. 166,753.

French toast ▸*n.* Sliced bread soaked in a batter of milk and egg and lightly fried.

fre•net•ic or **phre•net•ic** (frə-nĕt′ĭk) also **fre•net•i•cal** or **phre•net•i•cal** (-ĭ-kəl) ▸*adj.* Wildly excited or active; frantic; frenzied. [< Gk. *phrenitis*, inflammation of the brain < *phrēn*, mind.] —**fre•net′i•cal•ly** *adv.*

fre•num (frē′nəm) ▸*n., pl.* **-nums** or **-na** (-nə) *Anat.* The band of tissue that connects the tongue to the floor of the mouth. [Lat. *frēnum*, bridle < *frendere*, to grind.]

fren•zy (frĕn′zē) ▸*n., pl.* **-zies 1.** Violent mental agitation or wild excitement. **2.** Temporary madness. **3.** A mania; craze. [< Lat. *phrenēsis* < *phrenēticus*, FRENETIC.] —**fren′zied** *adj.* —**fren′zied•ly** *adv.*

fre•quen•cy (frē′kwən-sē) ▸*n., pl.* **-cies 1.** The property of occurring at frequent intervals. **2.** *Math. & Phys.* The number of times a specified phenomenon occurs within a specified interval, as the number of complete cycles of a periodic process occurring per unit time. [< Lat. *frequentia*, multitude.]

frequency modulation ▸*n.* The encoding of a carrier wave by variation of its frequency in accordance with an input signal.

fre•quent (frē′kwənt) ▸*adj.* Occurring or appearing often or at close intervals. ▸*v.* (*also* frē-kwĕnt′). To visit (a place) often. [< Lat. *frequēns.*] —**fre•quent′er** *n.* —**fre′quent•ly** *adv.* —**fre′quent•ness** *n.*

fres•co (frĕs′kō) ▸*n., pl.* **-coes** or **-cos 1.** The art of painting on fresh plaster with pigments dissolved in water. **2.** A painting executed in this way. [Ital., fresh.]

fresh (frĕsh) ▸*adj.* **-er, -est 1.** New to one's experience; not encountered before. **2.** Novel; different. **3.** Recently made, produced, or harvested; not stale or spoiled. **4.** Not preserved, as by canning or freezing. **5.** Not salty: *fresh water.* **6.** Not yet used or soiled; clean: *a fresh sheet of paper.* **7.** Free from impurity or pollution: *fresh air.* **8.** Additional; new: *fresh evidence.* **9.** Not dull or faded: *a fresh memory.* **10.** Having the unspoiled appearance of youth: *a fresh complexion.* **11.** Untried; inexperienced: *fresh recruits.* **12.** Revived; refreshed. **13.** *Informal* Bold and saucy; impudent. ▸*adv.* Recently; newly: *fresh out of milk.* [< OFr. *freis*, of Gmc. orig.] —**fresh′ly** *adv.* —**fresh′ness** *n.*

fresh•en (frĕsh′ən) ▸*v.* **1.** To make or become fresh. **2.** To add to or strengthen (a drink). —**fresh′en•er** *n.*

fresh•et (frĕsh′ĭt) ▸*n.* A sudden overflow of a stream due to a heavy rain or a thaw.

fresh•man (frĕsh′mən) ▸*n.* **1.** A first-year student of a US high school or college. **2.** A beginner; novice. —**fresh′man** *adj.*

fresh•wa•ter (frĕsh′wô′tər, -wŏt′ər) ▸*adj.* Of, living in, or consisting of water that is not salty.

Fres•no (frĕz′nō) A city of central CA SSE of Sacramento. Pop. 354,202.

fret[1] (frĕt) ▸*v.* **fret•ted, fret•ting 1.** To rub or chafe. See Syns at **brood. 2a.** To gnaw or wear away. **b.** To produce a hole or worn spot in; corrode. See Syns at **chafe.** ▸*n.* Irritation of mind. [< OE *fretan*, devour.] —**fret′ful** *adj.* —**fret′ful•ly** *adv.*

fret[2] (frĕt) ▸*n. Mus.* One of several ridges set across the fingerboard of a stringed instrument. [?]

fret[3] (frĕt) ▸*n.* A design of repeated symmetrical figures within a band or border. [< OFr. *frete.*]

fret•work (frĕt′wûrk′) ▸*n.* **1.** Ornamental work consisting of three-dimensional frets. **2.** Fretwork represented two dimensionally.

Freud (froid), **Anna.** 1895–1982. Austrian-born British psychoanalyst.

Freud, Sigmund. 1856–1939. Austrian physician who was the founder of psychoanalysis. —**Freud′i•an** *adj.*

Frey (frā) also **Freyr** (frâr) ▸*n. Myth.* The Norse god of peace and prosperity.

Frey•a also **Frey•ja** (frā′ə) ▸*n. Myth.* The Norse goddess of love and beauty.

Fri. ▸*abbr.* Friday

fri•a•ble (frī′ə-bəl) ▸*adj.* Readily crumbled; brittle. [< Lat. *friāre*, crumble.]

fri•ar (frī′ər) ▸*n.* A man who is a member of a usu. mendicant Roman Catholic order. [< Lat. *frāter*, brother.]

fric•as•see (frĭk′ə-sē′, frĭk′ə-sē′) ►*n.* Poultry or meat cut up and stewed in gravy. [< OFr. *fricasser*, fry.] —**fric′as•see′** *v.*

fric•a•tive (frĭk′ə-tĭv) ►*n.* A consonant, such as *f* or *s* in English, produced by the forcing of breath through a constricted passage. [< Lat. *fricāre*, rub.] —**fric′a•tive** *adj.*

fric•tion (frĭk′shən) ►*n.* **1.** The rubbing of one object or surface against another. **2.** Conflict, as between persons having dissimilar ideas or interests; clash. **3.** *Phys.* A force that resists the relative motion or tendency to such motion of two bodies in contact. [< Lat. *fricāre*, *frict-*, rub.] —**fric′tion•al** *adj.* —**fric′tion•al•ly** *adv.*

friction tape ►*n.* A sturdy, moisture-resistant adhesive tape used chiefly to insulate electrical conductors.

Fri•day (frī′dē, -dā′) ►*n.* The 6th day of the week. [< OE *Frīgedæg*.]

fridge (frĭj) ►*n.* *Informal* A refrigerator.

friend (frĕnd) ►*n.* **1.** A person whom one knows, likes, and trusts. **2.** One who supports, sympathizes with, or patronizes a group, cause, or movement. **3. Friend** A member of the Society of Friends; Quaker. [< OE *frēond*.] —**friend′ship** *n.*

friend•ly (frĕnd′lē) ►*adj.* **-li•er, -li•est 1.** Of or befitting a friend. **2.** Favorably disposed; not antagonistic. **3.** Warm; comforting. **4.** Easy for one to use or understand: *a reader-friendly type design.* —**friend′li•ly** *adv.* —**friend′li•ness** *n.*

fri•er (frī′ər) ►*n.* Var. of **fryer.**

frieze (frēz) ►*n.* **1.** The part of an entablature between the architrave and cornice. **2.** A decorative horizontal band, as along the upper part of a wall in a room. [< Med.Lat. *frisium*, embroidery.]

frig•ate (frĭg′ĭt) ►*n.* **1.** A US warship larger than a destroyer and smaller than a cruiser. **2.** A high-speed, medium-sized sailing war vessel of the 17th, 18th, and 19th cent. [< Ital. *fregata*.]

fright (frīt) ►*n.* **1.** Sudden intense fear. **2.** *Informal* Something extremely unsightly or alarming. [< OE *fyrhto*.]

fright•en (frīt′n) ►*v.* **1.** To make or become suddenly afraid; alarm. **2.** To drive or force by arousing fear. —**fright′en•ing•ly** *adv.*

fright•ful (frīt′fəl) ►*adj.* **1.** Causing disgust or shock; horrifying. **2.** Causing fright; terrifying. **3.** *Informal* **a.** Excessive; extreme: *a frightful liar.* **b.** Disagreeable; distressing. —**fright′ful•ly** *adv.* —**fright′ful•ness** *n.*

frig•id (frĭj′ĭd) ►*adj.* **1.** Extremely cold. See Syns at **cold. 2.** Lacking warmth of feeling; cold in manner. [< Lat. *frīgus*, the cold.] —**fri•gid′i•ty** (frĭ-jĭd′ĭ-tē), **frig′id•ness** *n.* —**frig′id•ly** *adv.*

Frigid Zone. Either of the earth's two extreme latitude zones, the **North Frigid Zone** or the **South Frigid Zone,** between the polar circles and the poles.

frill (frĭl) ►*n.* **1.** A ruffled, gathered, or pleated border or projection. **2.** *Informal* Something desirable but not essential. See Syns at **luxury.** [?] —**frill** *v.* —**fril′li•ness** *n.* —**frill′y** *adj.*

Friml (frĭm′əl), **(Charles) Rudolf.** 1879–1972. Czech-born American pianist.

fringe (frĭnj) ►*n.* **1.** A decorative border or edging of hanging threads, cords, or strips. **2.** Something like a fringe. **3.** A marginal or secondary part. **4.** Those members of a group or political party holding extreme views. **5.** A fringe benefit. [< LLat. *fimbria*.] —**fringe** *v.* —**fring′y** *adj.*

fringe benefit ►*n.* An employment benefit given in addition to wages or salary.

frip•per•y (frĭp′ə-rē) ►*n.*, *pl.* **-ies 1.** Gaudy or showy ornaments or dress. **2.** Something trivial or nonessential. [< OFr. *frepe*, rag.]

Fri•sian Islands (frĭzh′ən, frē′zhən) A chain of islands in the North Sea off the coast of the Netherlands, Germany, and Denmark. —**Fri′sian** *adj.* & *n.*

frisk (frĭsk) ►*v.* **1.** To move about briskly and playfully. **2.** To search (a person) for something concealed, esp. a weapon, by passing the hands quickly over clothes or through pockets. [< OFr. *frisque*, lively, of Gmc. orig.] —**frisk** *n.* —**frisk′er** *n.*

frisk•y (frĭs′kē) ►*adj.* **-i•er, -i•est.** Energetic and playful. —**frisk′i•ness** *n.*

frit•ta•ta (frĭ-tä′tə) ►*n.* An open-faced omelet with other ingredients mixed into the eggs before cooking. [Ital. < *friggere*, to fry.]

frit•ter[1] (frĭt′ər) ►*v.* To reduce or squander little by little. See Syns at **waste.** [Prob. < *fritter*, fragment.]

frit•ter[2] (frĭt′ər) ►*n.* A small fried cake made of batter and often fruit, vegetables, or fish. [< LLat. *frīctūra* < Lat. *frīgere*, fry.]

friv•o•lous (frĭv′ə-ləs) ►*adj.* **1.** Unworthy of serious attention; trivial. **2.** Inappropriately silly. [Prob. < Lat. *frīvolus*.] —**friv′o•lous•ly** *adv.* —**friv′o•lous•ness, fri•vol′i•ty** (frĭ-vŏl′ĭ-tē) *n.*

frizz (frĭz) ►*v.* To form or be formed into small tight curls. ►*n.* A small tight curl. [< OFr. *friser*.] —**friz′zly, friz′zy** *adj.*

friz•zle[1] (frĭz′əl) ►*v.* **-zled, -zling 1.** To fry until crisp and curled. **2.** To fry or sear with a sizzling noise. [Poss. blend of FRY[1] and SIZZLE.]

friz•zle[2] (frĭz′əl) ►*v.* **-zled, -zling.** To form or cause to be formed into small tight curls. ►*n.* A small tight curl. [?]

fro (frō) ►*adv.* Away; back: *moving to and fro.* [ME, prob. < ON *frā*.]

Fro•bish•er (frō′bĭ-shər, frŏb′ĭ-), Sir **Martin.** 1535?–94. English explorer.

frock (frŏk) ►*n.* **1.** A woman's dress. **2.** A long loose outer garment; smock. **3.** A robe worn by monks and other clerics; habit. [< OFr. *froc*, habit, of Gmc. orig.]

frock coat ►*n.* A man's dress coat or suit coat with knee-length skirts.

frog (frôg, frŏg) ►*n.* **1.** Any of numerous tailless, chiefly aquatic amphibians characteristically having a smooth moist skin, webbed feet, and long hind legs adapted for leaping. **2.** An ornamental looped braid or cord with a button or knot for fastening the front of a garment. **3.** *Informal* Hoarseness or phlegm in the throat. [< OE *frogga*.]

frog•man (frôg′măn′, -mən, frŏg′-) ►*n.* A swimmer equipped to execute underwater maneuvers, esp. military maneuvers.

Frois•sart (froi′särt′, frwä-sär′), **Jean.** 1333?–1405? French historian.

frol•ic (frŏl′ĭk) ►*n.* **1.** Gaiety; merriment. **2.** A gay, carefree time. ►*v.* **-icked, -ick•ing 1.** To behave playfully; romp. **2.** To engage in merrymaking. [< MDu. *vrolijc*, merry.] —**frol′ick•er** *n.* —**frol′ic•some** *adj.*

from (frŭm, frŏm; frəm *when unstressed*) ►*prep.* **1.** Used to indicate: **a.** A place or time as a starting point: *from six o'clock on.* **b.** A specified point as the first of two limits: *from a to z.* **c.** A source, cause, agent, or instrument: *a note from me.* **d.** Separation, removal, or exclusion: *freed from bondage.* **e.** Differentiation: *know right from wrong.* **2.** Because of: *faint from hunger.* [< OE.]

frond (frŏnd) ►*n.* The leaf esp. of a fern or palm. [Lat. *frōns, frond-*, foliage.]

front (frŭnt) ►*n.* **1.** The forward part or surface. **2.** The area, location, or position directly ahead. **3.** A position of leadership or superiority. **4.** Demeanor or bearing, especially in the presence of danger or difficulty. **5.** A false appearance or manner: *a good front.* **6.** Land bordering a lake, river, or street. **7.** The most forward line of a combat force. **8.** *Meteorol.* The interface between air masses of different temperatures or densities. **9.** A field of activity: *the economic front.* **10a.** A united movement; coalition. **b.** A nominal leader lacking in real authority; figurehead. **c.** An apparently respectable person or business used as a cover for secret or illegal activities. ►*adj.* Of, aimed at, or located in the front. ►*v.* **1.** To look out on; face. **2.** To confront. **3.** To provide or serve as a front for. [< Lat. *frōns, front-*.]

front•age (frŭn′tĭj) ►*n.* **1a.** The front part of a piece of property. **b.** The land between a building and the street. **2.** Land adjacent to something, as a street or body of water.

fron•tal (frŭn′tl) ►*adj.* **1.** Of, directed toward, or situated at the front. **2.** *Anat.* Of or in the region of the forehead. **3.** Of a meteorological front. —**fron′tal•ly** *adv.*

Fron•te•nac (frŏn′tə-năk′, frôNt-näk′), Comte de. 1620?–98. French colonial administrator in Canada.

fron•tier (frŭn-tîr′, frŏn-) ►*n.* **1.** An international border or the area along it. **2.** A region just beyond or beside a settled area. **3.** An undeveloped area for discovery or research. [< OFr. < *front*, FRONT.] —**fron•tiers′man** *n.* —**fron•tiers′wom•an** *n.*

fron•tis•piece (frŭn′tĭ-spēs′) ►*n.* An illustration that faces or immediately precedes the title page of a book. [< LLat. *frontispicium*, façade : Lat. *frōns*, front + Lat. *specere*, look at.]

front•line also **front line** (frŭnt′līn′) ►*n.* **1.** A front or boundary, esp. between military or political positions. **2.** *Football* A team's linemen. ►*adj.* or **front-line 1.** Located or used at a military front. **2.** Being in the forefront; leading. **3.** *Sports* Of the frontline.

front money ►*n.* Money paid in advance.

front office ►*n.* The executive or policymaking officers of an organization.

front-run•ner (frŭnt′rŭn′ər) ►*n.* One in a leading position in a competition.

frost (frôst, frŏst) ►*n.* A deposit of minute ice crystals formed when water vapor condenses at a temperature below freezing. ►*v.* **1.** To cover or become covered with frost. **2.** To damage or kill by frost. **3.** To cover (glass or metal) with frosting. **4.** To decorate with icing. [< OE.]

Frost, Robert Lee. 1874–1963. Amer. poet.

frost•bite (frôst′bīt′, frŏst′-) ►*n.* Destruction of body tissue resulting from prolonged exposure to freezing or subfreezing temperatures. —**frost′bite′** *v.*

frost•ing (frô′stĭng, frŏs′tĭng) ►*n.* **1.** Icing, as on a cake. **2.** A roughened or speckled surface imparted to glass or metal.

frost line ►*n.* The depth to which frost penetrates the earth.

frost•y (frô′stē, frŏs′tē) ►*adj.* **-i•er, -i•est 1.** Producing or marked by frost; freezing. See Syns at **cold. 2.** Covered with or as if with frost. **3.** Cold in manner. —**frost′i•ly** *adv.* —**frost′i•ness** *n.*

froth (frôth, frŏth) ►*n.* **1.** A mass of bubbles in or on a liquid; foam. **2.** Salivary foam released as a result of disease or exhaustion. **3.** Something unsubstantial or trivial. ►*v.* (*also* frô*th*, frŏ*th*) **1.** To cover with foam. **2.** To exude or expel foam. [< ON *frodha*.] —**froth′i•ly** *adv.* —**froth′i•ness** *n.* —**froth′y** *adj.*

frou•frou also **frou-frou** (frōō′frōō) ►*n.* **1.** Fussy or showy dress or ornamentation. **2.** A rustling sound, as of silk. [Fr.]

fro•ward (frō′wərd, -ərd) ►*adj.* Stubbornly contrary and disobedient. [ME < *fro*, FRO.] —**fro′ward•ly** *adv.* —**fro′ward•ness** *n.*

Froward, Cape. The southernmost point of mainland South America, in S Chile on the Str. of Magellan.

frown (froun) ►*v.* **1.** To wrinkle the brow, as in thought or displeasure. **2.** To regard something with disapproval or distaste. ►*n.* A wrinkling of the brow; scowl. [< OFr. *frogne*, a grimace, of Celt. orig.]

Syns: *frown, glower, lower, scowl* **v.**

frow•zy also **frow•sy** (frou′zē) ►*adj.* **-zi•er, -zi•est** also **-si•er, -si•est.** Unkempt; slovenly. [?] —**frow′zi•ness** *n.*

froze (frōz) ►*v.* P.t. of **freeze.**

fro•zen (frō′zən) ►*v.* P.part. of **freeze.** ►*adj.* **1.** Made into, covered with, or surrounded by ice. **2.** Very cold. **3.** Preserved by freezing. **4.** Rendered immobile. **5.** Expressive of cold unfriendliness or disdain. **6a.** Kept at a fixed level: *frozen rents.* **b.** Impossible to withdraw, sell, or liquidate: *frozen assets.*

fruc•ti•fy (frŭk′tə-fī′, frōōk′-) ►*v.* **-fied, -fy•ing.** To be or make fruitful or productive. [< Lat. *frūctificāre* < *frūctus*, FRUIT.] —**fruc′ti•fi•ca′tion** *n.*

fruc•tose (frŭk′tōs′, frōōk′-) ►*n.* A sweet sugar, $C_6H_{12}O_6$, occurring in many fruits and honey. [Lat. *frūctus*, FRUIT + -OSE[2].]

fru•gal (frōō′gəl) ►*adj.* **1.** Practicing or marked by economy. **2.** Costing little; inexpensive. [< Lat. *frūx, frūg-*, produce, value.] —**fru•gal′i•ty** (frōō-găl′ĭ-tē), **fru′gal•ness** *n.* —**fru′gal•ly** *adv.*

fruit (frōōt) ►*n., pl.* **fruit** or **fruits 1.** The ripened, seed-bearing part of a plant, esp. when fleshy and edible. **2.** The fertile, often spore-bearing structure of a plant that does not bear seeds. **3.** A plant crop or product. **4.** Result; outcome. ►*v.* To produce fruit. [< Lat. *frūctus* < *fruī*, enjoy.]

fruit•cake (frōōt′kāk′) ►*n.* **1.** A heavy spiced cake containing nuts and candied or dried fruits. **2.** *Slang* An eccentric person.

fruit fly ►*n.* Any of various small flies that feed on ripening or fermenting fruits and vegetables.

fruit•ful (frōōt′fəl) ►*adj.* **1.** Producing fruit. **2.** Producing in abundance; prolific. **3.** Producing results; profitable. See Syns at **fertile.** —**fruit′ful•ly** *adv.* —**fruit′ful•ness** *n.*

fru•i•tion (fro͞o-ĭsh′ən) ►*n.* **1.** Realization of something desired or worked for. **2.** The condition of bearing fruit.

fruit•less (fro͞ot′lĭs) ►*adj.* **1.** Producing no fruit. **2.** Unproductive of success. See Syns at **futile.** —**fruit′less•ly** *adv.* —**fruit′less•ness** *n.*

fruit•y (fro͞o′tē) ►*adj.* **-i•er, -i•est 1.** Tasting or smelling of fruit. **2.** Excessively sentimental or sweet. **3.** *Slang* Eccentric. —**fruit′i•ness** *n.*

frump (frŭmp) ►*n.* A dull, plain, or unfashionable person. [Poss. < MDu. *verrompelen*, to wrinkle.] —**frump′i•ly** *adv.* —**frump′i•ness** *n.* —**frump′y** *adj.*

frump•ish (frŭm′pĭsh) ►*adj.* **1.** Dull or plain. **2.** Prim and sedate. —**frump′ish•ly** *adv.* —**frump′ish•ness** *n.*

Frun•ze (fro͞on′zə) See **Bishkek.**

frus•trate (frŭs′trāt′) ►*v.* **-trat•ed, -trat•ing 1.** To prevent from accomplishing a purpose or fulfilling a desire; thwart. **2.** To cause discouragement or bafflement in. **3.** To make ineffectual or invalid. [< Lat. *frūstrārī* < *frūstrā*, in vain.] —**frus•tra′tion** *n.*

fry[1] (frī) ►*v.* **fried** (frīd), **fry•ing.** To cook over direct heat in hot oil or fat. ►*n., pl.* **fries** (frīz) **1.** A French fry. **2.** A social gathering at which fried food is served. [< Lat. *frīgere.*]

fry[2] (frī) ►*pl.n.* **1.** Small fish, esp. hatchlings. **2.** Individuals, esp. young persons. [Prob. < AN *frie.*]

fry•er also **fri•er** (frī′ər) ►*n.* **1.** One that fries, as a deep utensil usu. equipped with a basket and used for frying foods. **2.** A young chicken suitable for frying.

fry•ing pan (frī′ĭng) ►*n.* A shallow, long-handled pan used for frying food. See Regional Note at **andiron.**

Regional Note: *Frying pan* and *skillet,* now virtually interchangeable, were formerly so regional as to be distinct dialect markers. *Frying pan* and *fry pan* were New England terms. *Skillet* seems to have been confined to the Midland including the Upper South.

FSLIC ►*abbr.* Federal Savings and Loan Insurance Corporation

f-stop (ĕf′stŏp′) ►*n.* A camera lens aperture setting that corresponds to an f-number. [F(OCAL LENGTH) + STOP.]

ft. ►*abbr.* **1.** or **ft** foot **2. Ft.** fort

FTC ►*abbr.* Federal Trade Commission

fth. ►*abbr.* fathom

FTP (ĕf′tē-pē′) ►*n.* A protocol governing file transfers over a computer network. ►*v.* **FTPed, FTPing.** To transfer (a file) using FTP. [*F(ile) T(ransfer) P(rotocol).*]

Fu•chou (fo͞o′jō′, -chou′) See **Fuzhou.**

fuch•sia (fyo͞o′shə) ►*n.* **1.** A widely cultivated plant with showy, drooping purplish, reddish, or white flowers. **2.** A vivid purplish red. [After Leonhard *Fuchs* (1501–66).] —**fuch′sia** *adj.*

fud•dle (fŭd′l) ►*v.* **-dled, -dling 1.** To put into a state of confusion; befuddle. See Syns at **confuse. 2.** To make drunk; intoxicate. [?] —**fud′dle** *n.*

fud•dy-dud•dy (fŭd′ē-dŭd′ē) ►*n., pl.* **-dies.** An old-fashioned, fussy person. [?]

fudge (fŭj) ►*n.* **1.** A soft rich candy made of sugar, milk, and butter. **2.** Nonsense; humbug. ►*v.* **fudged, fudg•ing 1.** To fake or falsify. **2.** To evade; dodge. [?]

fu•el (fyo͞o′əl) ►*n.* Something consumed to produce energy, esp.: **a.** A material such as wood or oil burned to produce heat or power. **b.** Fissionable material used in a nuclear reactor. **c.** Nutritive material metabolized by a living organism; food. ►*v.* **-eled, -el•ing** also **-elled, -el•ling.** To provide with or take in fuel. [< VLat. *_focālia_ < Lat. *focus*, hearth.] —**fu′el•er** *n.*

fuel cell ►*n.* A device in which a fuel and an oxidant react and the energy released is converted into electricity.

fuel oil ►*n.* A liquid petroleum product that is used to generate heat or power.

fuel rod ►*n.* A protective metal tube containing pellets of fuel for a nuclear reactor.

Fuen•tes (fo͞o-ĕn′tās′, fwĕn′tĕs), **Carlos.** b. 1928. Mexican writer.

Carlos Fuentes

fu•gi•tive (fyo͞o′jĭ-tĭv) ►*adj.* **1.** Running away or fleeing, as from the law. **2.** Lasting only a short time; fleeting: *fugitive hours.* ►*n.* One who flees. [< Lat. *fugere*, flee.]

fugue (fyo͞og) ►*n. Mus.* A polyphonic composition in which one or more themes stated successively are developed contrapuntally. [< Lat. *fuga*, flight.] —**fu′gal** (fyo͞o′gəl) *adj.* —**fu′gal•ly** *adv.*

füh•rer also **fueh•rer** (fyo͝or′ər) ►*n.* **1.** A leader, esp. a dictator. **2. Führer** Adolf Hitler's title as leader of Nazi Germany. [Ger.]

Fu•ji (fo͞o′jē), **Mount.** Also **Fu•ji•ya•ma** (fo͞o′jē-yä′mə, -mä). The highest peak, 3,778.6 m (12,389 ft), in Japan, in central Honshu WSW of Tokyo.

Fu•ku•o•ka (fo͞o′ko͞o-ō′kə, -kä) A city of NW Kyushu, Japan. Pop. 1,268,626.

-ful ►*suff.* **1.** Full of: *playful.* **a.** Marked by; resembling: *masterful.* **b.** Tending, given, or able to: *useful.* **2.** A quantity that fills: *armful.* [< OE.]

ful•crum (fo͝ol′krəm, fŭl′-) ►*n., pl.* **-crums** or **-cra** (-krə). The point or support on which a lever pivots. [Lat., bedpost.]

ful•fill also **ful•fil** (fo͝ol-fĭl′) ►*v.* **-filled, -fill•ing 1.** To bring into actuality; effect. **2.** To carry out. **3.** To measure up to; satisfy. See Syns at **satisfy. 4.** To bring to an end; complete. [< OE *fullfyllan.*] —**ful•fill′ment, ful•fil′ment** *n.*

full[1] (fo͝ol) ►*adj.* **-er, -est 1.** Containing all that is normal or possible. **2.** Complete in every particular. **3.** Of maximum or highest degree. **4.** Having a great deal or many: *full of errors.* **5.** Totally qualified or accepted: *a full member.* **6a.** Rounded in shape. **b.** Of generous dimensions; wide. **7.** Satiated, esp. with food or drink. **8.** Having depth and body. ►*adv.* **1.** To a complete extent; entirely: *knowing full well.* **2.** Exactly; directly: *full in the path of the truck.* ►*n.* The maximum or complete size or amount. [< OE.] —**full′ness, ful′ness** *n.*

full² (fo͝ol) ►*v.* To increase the weight and bulk of (cloth) by shrinking and beating or pressing. [< VLat. **fullāre.*]

full•back (fo͝ol′băk′) ►*n.* **1.** *Football* An offensive backfield player whose position is behind the quarterback and halfbacks. **2.** *Sports* A primarily defensive backfield player in field hockey, soccer, or Rugby.

full-blood•ed (fo͝ol′blŭd′ĭd) ►*adj.* **1.** Of unmixed ancestry; purebred. **2.** Vigorous; vital. —**full′-blood′ed•ness** *n.*

full-blown (fo͝ol′blōn′) ►*adj.* **1.** Having blossomed or opened completely. **2.** Fully developed or matured.

full-bod•ied (fo͝ol′bŏd′ēd) ►*adj.* Having richness of flavor or aroma.

full dress ►*n.* Attire appropriate for formal or ceremonial events.

Ful•ler (fo͝ol′ər), **R(ichard) Buckminster.** 1895–1983. Amer. architect and inventor.

Fuller, (Sarah) Margaret. 1810–50. Amer. writer and critic.

ful•ler•ene (fo͝ol′ə-rēn′) ►*n.* Any of various nearly spherical carbon molecules. [After R. Buckminster FULLER.]

Ful•ler•ton (fo͝ol′ər-tən) A city of S CA SE of Los Angeles. Pop. 114,144.

full-fledged (fo͝ol′flĕjd′) ►*adj.* **1.** Having reached full development; mature. **2.** Having full status or rank: *a full-fledged lawyer.*

full moon ►*n.* The moon when it is visible as a fully illuminated disk.

full-scale (fo͝ol′skāl′) ►*adj.* **1.** Of actual or full size. **2.** Employing all resources.

ful•ly (fo͝ol′ē) ►*adv.* **1.** Totally or completely. **2.** At least.

ful•mi•nate (fo͝ol′mə-nāt′, fŭl′-) ►*v.* **-nat•ed, -nat•ing 1.** To issue a severe denunciation. **2.** To explode. [< Lat. *fulmen, fulmin-*, lightning.] —**ful′mi•na′tion** *n.*

ful•some (fo͝ol′səm) ►*adj.* Offensively flattering or insincere. See Syns at **unctuous.** [ME *fulsom*, abundant, disgusting.] —**ful′some•ly** *adv.* —**ful′some•ness** *n.*

Ful•ton (fo͝ol′tən), **Robert.** 1765–1815. Amer. engineer and inventor.

fum•ble (fŭm′bəl) ►*v.* **-bled, -bling 1.** To touch or handle nervously or idly. **2.** To grope awkwardly to find something. **3.** To proceed awkwardly and uncertainly; blunder. **4.** *Sports* To mishandle or drop a ball that is in play. **5.** To bungle. See Syns at **botch.** ►*n.* **1.** The act or an instance of fumbling. **2.** *Sports* A ball that has been fumbled. [ME *fomelen*, grope.] —**fum′bler** *n.*

fume (fyo͞om) ►*n.* **1.** Vapor, gas, or smoke, esp. if irritating, harmful, or strong. **2.** A strong or acrid odor. ►*v.* **fumed, fum•ing 1.** To subject to or treat with fumes. **2.** To give off in or as if in fumes. **3.** To feel or show resentment or anger. [< Lat. *fūmus.*]

fu•mi•gate (fyo͞o′mĭ-gāt′) ►*v.* **-gat•ed, -gat•ing.** To treat with fumes in order to exterminate pests. [Lat. *fūmigāre*, to smoke : *fūmus*, smoke + *agere*, make.] —**fu′mi•ga′tion** *n.* —**fu′mi•ga′tor** *n.*

fun (fŭn) ►*n.* **1.** A source of enjoyment, amusement, or pleasure. **2.** Enjoyment; amusement. **3.** Playful, often noisy activity. —***idiom:* for fun** As a joke; playfully. [Poss. < ME *fonne*, a fool.]

func•tion (fŭngk′shən) ►*n.* **1.** The action for which one is particularly fitted or employed. **2.** The duty, occupation, or role of a person. **3.** An official ceremony or a formal social occasion. **4.** Something closely related to another thing and dependent on it for its existence or value. **5.** *Math.* A rule of correspondence between two sets such that there is a unique element in the second set assigned to each element in the first set. **6.** *Comp. Sci.* A procedure within an application. ►*v.* To have or perform a function; serve. [< Lat. *fungī, fūnct-*, perform.]

Syns: *function, duty, office, role* **n.**

func•tion•al (fŭngk′shə-nəl) ►*adj.* **1.** Of or relating to a function. **2.** Designed for or adapted to a particular purpose. **3.** Capable of performing; operative. **4.** *Pathol.* Involving functions rather than a physiological or structural cause. —**func′tion•al•ly** *adv.*

func•tion•al•i•ty (fŭngk′shə-năl′ĭ-tē) ►*n.* **1.** The quality of being functional. **2.** A useful function in a computer program. **3.** The capacity of a computer program to provide a useful function.

func•tion•ar•y (fŭngk′shə-nĕr′ē) ►*n., pl.* **-ies.** One who holds an office or performs a particular function; official.

function key ►*n.* A key on a computer keyboard used to activate functions.

function word ►*n.* A word, such as a preposition or article, that indicates a grammatical relationship.

fund (fŭnd) ►*n.* **1.** A source of supply; stock. **2.** A sum of money or other resources set aside for a specific purpose. **3. funds** Available money. ►*v.* **1.** To make provision for paying off (a debt). **2.** To furnish money for. [Lat. *fundus*, piece of land.]

fun•da•men•tal (fŭn′də-mĕn′tl) ►*adj.* **1.** Basic; elementary: *fundamental laws of nature.* **2.** Of central importance; essential. **3.** Involving all aspects; radical: *fundamental change.* [< Lat. *fundāmentum*, foundation < *fundus*, bottom.] —**fun′da•men′tal•ly** *adv.*

fun•da•men•tal•ism (fŭn′də-mĕn′tl-ĭz′əm) ►*n.* **1.** often **Fundamentalism** A Protestant movement holding the Bible to be the sole authority. **2.** A movement marked by rigid adherence to basic principles. —**fun′da•men′tal•ist** *adj. & n.*

fund•rais•er (fŭnd′rā′zər) ►*n.* **1.** One that raises funds. **2.** A social function held for raising funds.

Fun•dy (fŭn′dē), **Bay of.** An inlet of the Atlantic in SE Canada between New Brunswick and Nova Scotia.

fu•ner•al (fyo͞o′nər-əl) ►*n.* **1.** The ceremonies held in connection with the burial or cremation of the dead. **2.** The procession accompanying a body to the grave. [< Lat. *fūnus.*] —**fu′ner•ar′y** (-nə-rĕr′ē) *adj.*

funeral director ►*n.* One whose business is to arrange burials or cremations.

funeral home ▶*n.* An establishment in which the dead are prepared for burial or cremation.

fu•ne•re•al (fyo͞o-nîr′ē-əl) ▶*adj.* Appropriate for or suggestive of a funeral; mournful. [< Lat. *fūnus, fūner-*, funeral.] —**fu•ne′re•al•ly** *adv.*

fun•gi•cide (fŭn′jĭ-sīd′, fŭng′gĭ-) ▶*n.* A substance that destroys fungi. —**fun′gi•cid′al** *adj.*

fun•go (fŭng′gō) ▶*n., pl.* **-goes** *Baseball.* A fly ball hit for fielding practice with a long thin bat. [?]

fun•gus (fŭng′gəs) ▶*n., pl.* **fun•gi** (fŭn′jī, fŭng′gī) or **-gus•es.** Any of numerous plant organisms which lack chlorophyll, including the yeasts, molds, smuts, and mushrooms. [Lat.] —**fun′gal, fun′gous** *adj.*

fu•nic•u•lar (fyo͞o-nĭk′yə-lər, fə-) ▶*n.* A cable railway on a steep incline, esp. one with simultaneously ascending and descending cars counterbalancing one another. [< Lat. *funiculus*, thin rope.]

funk[1] (fŭngk) ▶*n.* **1.** A state of cowardly fright. **2.** A state of severe depression. [Poss. < obsolete Flem. *fonck*, agitation.]

funk[2] (fŭngk) ▶*n.* A type of popular music combining elements of jazz, blues, and soul. [Back-formation < FUNKY.]

funk•y (fŭng′kē) ▶*adj.* **-i•er, -i•est 1.** Having a strong offensive odor. **2.** *Slang* Of or relating to music that has an earthy quality reminiscent of the blues. **3.** *Slang* Eccentric in style or manner: *funky clothes.* [< *funk*, strong smell.] —**funk′i•ness** *n.*

fun•nel (fŭn′əl) ▶*n.* **1.** A conical utensil with a narrow tube at the bottom, used to channel the flow of a substance into a container. **2.** A flue or stack, esp. the smokestack of a ship. ▶*v.* **-neled, -nel•ing** or **-nelled, -nel•ling.** To move through or as if through a funnel. [< LLat. *fundibulum.*]

fun•ny (fŭn′ē) ▶*adj.* **-ni•er, -ni•est 1.** Causing laughter or amusement. **2.** Strangely or suspiciously odd. ▶*n., pl.* **-nies** *Informal* **1.** A joke. **2. funnies** Comic strips. —**fun′ni•ly** *adv.* —**fun′ni•ness** *n.*

funny bone ▶*n. Informal* **1.** A point on the elbow where pressure against the underlying nerve produces a sharp tingling sensation. **2.** A sense of humor.

fur (fûr) ▶*n.* **1.** The thick coat of soft hair covering the skin of various mammals. **2.** The dressed pelt of such a mammal, used esp. for clothing. **3.** A furlike coating. [Prob. < OFr. *fuerre*, lining.] —**furred** *adj.*

fur. ▶*abbr.* furlong

fur•be•low (fûr′bə-lō′) ▶*n.* **1.** A ruffle on a garment. **2.** A piece of showy ornamentation. [Prob. < Prov. *farbello*, fringe.]

fur•bish (fûr′bĭsh) ▶*v.* **1.** To brighten by cleaning or rubbing; polish. **2.** To renovate. [< OFr. *fourbir*, of Gmc. orig.]

fu•ri•ous (fyo͝or′ē-əs) ▶*adj.* **1.** Extremely angry; raging. See Syns at **angry. 2.** Violent or intense, as in speed or action. [< Lat. *furia*, fury.] —**fu′ri•ous•ly** *adv.*

furl (fûrl) ▶*v.* To roll up and secure (a flag or sail) to something else. [< OFr. *ferlier*, tie firmly.]

fur•long (fûr′lông′, -lŏng′) ▶*n.* See table at **measurement.** [< OE *furlang.*]

fur•lough (fûr′lō) ▶*n.* A leave of absence or vacation, esp. of a member of the armed forces. [< MDu. *verlof.*] —**fur′lough** *v.*

fur•nace (fûr′nĭs) ▶*n.* An enclosure in which heat is generated by the combustion of a suitable fuel. [< Lat. *fornāx.*]

fur•nish (fûr′nĭsh) ▶*v.* **1.** To equip, esp. with furniture. **2.** To supply; give. [< OFr. *fournir*, of Gmc. orig.] —**fur′nish•er** *n.*

fur•nish•ings (fûr′nĭ-shĭngz) ▶*pl.n.* **1.** The furniture and other movable articles in a home or building. **2.** Clothes and accessories.

fur•ni•ture (fûr′nĭ-chər) ▶*n.* The movable articles in a room or establishment that equip it for living or working. [OFr. *fourniture* < *fournir*, furnish.]

fu•ror (fyo͝or′ôr′, -ər) ▶*n.* **1.** A public uproar. **2.** Violent anger; frenzy. **3.** Intense excitement. [< Lat. < *furere*, to rage.]

fur•ri•er (fûr′ē-ər) ▶*n.* One who designs, sells, or repairs furs. [Alteration (influenced by CLOTHIER) < AN *furrere.*]

fur•ring (fûr′ĭng) ▶*n.* Strips of wood or metal attached to a wall or other surface to provide a level substratum, as for paneling.

fur•row (fûr′ō, fŭr′ō) ▶*n.* **1.** A long shallow trench made in the ground by a plow or other tool. **2.** A deep wrinkle in the skin. [< OE *furh.*] —**fur′row** *v.*

fur•ry (fûr′ē, fŭr′ē) ▶*adj.* **-ri•er, -ri•est 1.** Consisting of or similar to fur. **2.** Covered with fur or a furlike substance. —**fur′ri•ness** *n.*

fur seal ▶*n.* An eared seal having thick soft underfur that is valued commercially.

fur•ther (fûr′*th*ər) ▶*adj.* Comp. of **far. 1.** More distant in degree, time, or space. **2.** Additional. ▶*adv.* Comp. of **far. 1.** To a greater extent; more. **2.** In addition; furthermore. **3.** At or to a more distant or advanced point. ▶*v.* To help the progress of. See Syns at **advance.** [< OE *furthor.*] —**fur′ther•ance** *n.*

fur•ther•more (fûr′*th*ər-môr′, -mōr′) ▶*adv.* In addition; moreover.

fur•ther•most (fûr′*th*ər-mōst′) ▶*adj.* Most distant or remote.

fur•thest (fûr′*th*ĭst) ▶*adj.* Superl. of **far.** Most distant in degree, time, or space. ▶*adv.* Superl. of **far. 1.** To the greatest extent or degree. **2.** At or to the most distant point in space or time. [ME.]

fur•tive (fûr′tĭv) ▶*adj.* Marked by stealth; surreptitious. [< Lat. *furtum*, theft < *fūr*, thief.] —**fur′tive•ly** *adv.* —**fur′tive•ness** *n.*

fu•ry (fyo͝or′ē) ▶*n., pl.* **-ries 1.** Violent anger; rage. **2.** Violent, uncontrolled action. **3. Furies** *Gk. & Rom. Myth.* The three terrible, winged goddesses who pursue and punish doers of unavenged crimes. [< Lat. *furia* < *furere*, to rage.]

furze (fûrz) ▶*n.* See **gorse.** [< OE *fyrs.*]

fuse[1] also **fuze** (fyo͞oz) ▶*n.* **1.** A cord of readily combustible material that is lighted at one end to carry a flame along its length to detonate an explosive at the other end. **2.** often **fuze** A mechanical or electrical mechanism used to detonate an explosive device. [< Lat. *fūsus*, spindle.] —**fuse** *v.*

fuse[2] (fyo͞oz) ▶*v.* **fused, fus•ing 1.** To liquefy or reduce to a plastic state by heating; melt. **2.** To mix together by or as if by melting. ▶*n.* A safety device for an electric circuit that melts when current exceeds a specific amperage, thus opening the circuit. [< Lat. *fundere, fūs-*, melt.] —**fus′i•ble** *adj.*

fu•see also **fu•zee** (fyo͞o-zē′) ▶*n.* **1.** A large

friction match that can burn in a wind. **2.** A colored flare used as a warning signal for trucks and trains. [< Lat. *fūsus*, spindle.]

fu•se•lage (fyōō′sə-läzh′, -zə-) ▸*n.* The central body of an aircraft, to which the wings and tail assembly are attached. [Fr. < *fuselé*, spindle-shaped.]

Fu•shun (fōō′shōōn′) A city of NE China E of Shenyang. Pop. 1,388,011.

fu•sil•lade (fyōō′sə-läd′, -lād′, -zə-) ▸*n.* **1.** A simultaneous or rapid discharge from many firearms. **2.** A barrage: *a fusillade of insults.* [Fr. < *fusiller*, shoot.]

fu•sion (fyōō′zhən) ▸*n.* **1.** The act or procedure of liquefying or melting by heat. **2.** The liquid or melted state induced by heat. **3.** The merging of different elements into a union. **4.** *Phys.* A nuclear reaction in which nuclei release energy when combining to form more massive nuclei.

fuss (fŭs) ▸*n.* **1.** Useless or nervous activity; commotion. **2.** Needless concern or worry. **3.** An angry or fretful protest. **4.** A display of affectionate excitement and attention: *made a fuss over the baby.* ▸*v.* **1.** To worry over trifles. **2.** To be excessively careful or solicitous. **3.** To be in a state of nervous activity: *fussed with his collar.* **4.** To fret or complain. [?]

fuss•budg•et (fŭs′bŭj′ĭt) ▸*n.* A person who fusses over trifles.

fuss•y (fŭs′ē) ▸*adj.* **-i•er, -i•est 1.** Easily upset; given to bouts of ill temper. **2.** Frequently complaining or making demands. **3.** Meticulous; fastidious. **4.** Requiring attention to small details. —**fuss′i•ly** *adv.* —**fuss′i•ness** *n.*

fus•tian (fŭs′chən) ▸*n.* **1.** A coarse sturdy cloth. **2.** Pompous language. [< Med.Lat. *fustāneum.*] —**fus′tian** *adj.*

fus•ty (fŭs′tē) ▸*adj.* **-ti•er, -ti•est 1.** Smelling of mildew or decay; musty. **2.** Old-fashioned; antique. [< OFr. *fust*, wine cask.] —**fus′ti•ly** *adv.* —**fus′ti•ness** *n.*

fut. ▸*abbr.* future

fu•tile (fyōōt′l, fyōō′tīl′) ▸*adj.* Having no useful result. [Lat. *fūtilis.*] —**fu′tile•ly** *adv.* —**fu•til′i•ty** (fyōō-tĭl′ĭ-tē) *n.*

Syns: *futile, barren, bootless, fruitless, unavailing, useless, vain* ***Ant:*** *useful* ***adj.***

fu•ton (fōō′tŏn) ▸*n.* A pad usu. of tufted cotton batting used on a floor or on a raised frame as a bed. [J., bedding.]

fu•ture (fyōō′chər) ▸*n.* **1.** The indefinite time yet to come. **2.** Something that will happen in time to come. **3.** Chance of success or advancement: *a position with no future.* **4. futures** *Bus.* Commodities or stocks bought or sold upon agreement of delivery in time to come. **5.** *Gram.* The form of a verb used in speaking of action in the future. ▸*adj.* That is to be or to come. [< Lat. *futūrus*, about to be.]

fu•tur•is•tic (fyōō′chə-rĭs′tĭk) ▸*adj.* **1.** Of or relating to the future. **2.** Expressing a vision of life and society in the future. —**fu′tur•is′ti•cal•ly** *adj.*

fu•tu•ri•ty (fyōō-tōōr′ĭ-tē, -tyōōr′-, -chōōr′-) ▸*n.*, *pl.* **-ties 1.** The future. **2.** The quality or condition of being in or of the future. **3.** A future event or possibility.

fu•tur•ol•o•gy (fyōō′chə-rŏl′ə-jē) ▸*n.* The study or forecasting of potential developments, as in science, technology, and society, using current trends as a point of departure.

fuze (fyōōz) ▸*n.* & *v.* Var. of **fuse**[1].

fu•zee (fyōō-zē′) ▸*n.* Var. of **fusee.**

Fu•zhou (fōō′jō′) also **Foo•chow** or **Fu•chou** (fōō′jō′, -chou′). A city of SE China on the Min R. delta. Pop. 1,395,739.

fuzz[1] (fŭz) ▸*n.* A mass or coating of fine light fibers, hairs, or particles; down. ▸*v.* To make blurred or indistinct. [Perh. < FUZZY.]

fuzz[2] (fŭz) ▸*n.* *Slang* The police. [?]

fuzz•y (fŭz′ē) ▸*adj.* **-i•er, -i•est 1.** Covered with fuzz. **2.** Of or resembling fuzz. **3.** Not clear; indistinct. [Perh. < LGer. *fussig*, spongy.] —**fuzz′i•ly** *adv.* —**fuzz′i•ness** *n.*

fwd ▸*abbr.* forward

FY ▸*abbr.* fiscal year

-fy or **-ify** ▸*suff.* Cause to become; make: *calcify.* [< Lat. *-ficāre* < *-ficus*, –FIC.]

FYI ▸*abbr.* for your information

G

g[1] or **G** (jē) ▸*n.*, *pl.* **g's** or **G's** also **gs** or **Gs 1.** The 7th letter of the English alphabet. **2.** *Mus.* The 5th tone in the C major scale. **3.** A unit of acceleration equal to the acceleration caused by gravity at the earth's surface, about 9.8 m (32 ft.) per second per second.

g[2] ▸*abbr.* gram

G[1] (jē) ▸ A trademark for a movie rating granting admission to persons of all ages.

G[2] ▸*abbr.* gravitational constant

Ga ▸ The symbol for the element **gallium.**

GA ▸*abbr.* **1.** general agent **2.** General Assembly **3.** also **Ga.** Georgia (US)

gab (găb) ▸*v.* **gabbed, gab•bing** *Slang* To talk idly or incessantly; chatter. [< ON *gabba*, scoff.] —**gab** *n.* —**gab′ber** *n.*

gab•ar•dine (găb′ər-dēn′, găb′ər-dēn′) ▸*n.* A sturdy fabric of cotton, wool, or rayon twill. [< OFr. *galvardine*, a long cloak.]

gab•ble (găb′əl) ▸*v.* **-bled, -bling 1.** To speak rapidly or incoherently; jabber. **2.** To make low muttering or quacking sounds, as a goose or duck. [Poss. < GAB.] —**gab′ble** *n.*

gab•by (găb′ē) ▸*adj.* **-bi•er, -bi•est** *Slang.* Talkative; garrulous. —**gab′bi•ness** *n.*

ga•ble (gā′bəl) ▸*n.* A usu. triangular end section of wall between the two slopes of a pitched roof. [OFr.] —**ga′bled** *adj.*

Gable, (William) Clark. 1901–60. Amer. actor.

Ga•bon (gă-bōN′) A country of W-central Africa on the Atlantic Ocean. Cap. Libreville. Pop. 1,283,000.

Ga•bo•ro•ne (gä′bə-rō′nē) The capital of Botswana, in the SE part near the South African border. Pop. 133,468.

gad (găd) ▸*v.* **gad•ded, gad•ding.** To move about restlessly, as in search of social activity. [ME *gadden*, to hurry.] —**gad′der** *n.*

gad•a•bout (găd′ə-bout′) ▸*n.* One who roams about in search of amusement or social activity.

gad•fly (găd′flī′) ►*n.* **1.** A persistent, irritating critic. **2.** One that provokes or goads. **3.** Any of various flies that bite or annoy livestock. [*goad*, a gad + FLY[2].]

gadg•et (găj′ĭt) ►*n.* A small specialized mechanical or electronic device. [?] —**gadg′et•ry** *n.*

gad•o•lin•i•um (găd′l-ĭn′ē-əm) ►*n. Symbol* **Gd** A silvery-white, malleable rare-earth element used in improving the high-temperature characteristics of alloys. At. no. 64. See table at **element.** [After Johan *Gadolin* (1760–1852).]

Gae•a (jē′ə) also **Gai•a** (gā′ə) ►*n. Gk. Myth.* The goddess of the earth, who bore and married Uranus and became the mother of the Titans and the Cyclops.

Gael (gāl) ►*n.* A Gaelic-speaking Celt of Scotland, Ireland, or the Isle of Man.

Gael•ic (gā′lĭk) ►*n.* Any of the Celtic languages of Ireland, Scotland, or the Isle of Man. —**Gael′ic** *adj.*

gaff (găf) ►*n.* **1.** A large iron hook attached to a pole and used to land large fish. **2.** A spar used to extend the upper edge of a fore-and-aft sail. [< OProv. *gaf.*] —**gaff** *v.*

gaffe also **gaff** (găf) ►*n.* **1.** A clumsy social error. **2.** A blatant mistake. [Fr.]

gaf•fer (găf′ər) ►*n.* **1.** An electrician in charge of lighting on a movie or television set. **2.** *Chiefly Brit.* An old man. [Poss. < GODFATHER.]

gag (găg) ►*n.* **1.** Something forced into or put over the mouth to prevent speaking or crying out. **2.** An obstacle to free speech. **3.** A surgical device placed in the mouth to keep it open. **4a.** A practical joke. **b.** A comic remark. ►*v.* **gagged, gag•ging 1.** To prevent from speaking by using a gag. **2.** To restrain from exercising free speech. **3.** To choke or retch. **4.** To make jokes. [< ME *gaggen*, suffocate.]

ga•ga (gä′gä′) ►*adj. Informal* **1.** Silly; crazy. **2.** Completely absorbed or infatuated. [< Fr., old fool.]

Ga•ga•rin (gə-gär′ĭn), **Yuri Alekseyevich.** 1934–68. Soviet cosmonaut.

gage[1] (gāj) ►*n.* **1.** Something deposited or given as security; pledge. **2.** Something, such as a glove, that is offered or thrown down as a challenge to fight. [< OFr.]

gage[2] (gāj) ►*n.* & *v.* Var. of **gauge.**

Gage, Thomas. 1721–87. British general and colonial administrator.

gag•gle (găg′əl) ►*n.* **1.** A flock of geese. **2.** A group. [ME *gagel* < *gagelen*, cackle.]

gag order ►*n.* A court order forbidding public reporting or commentary on a case currently before the court.

gag rule ►*n.* A rule, as in a legislative body, limiting discussion or debate on an issue.

Gai•a (gā′ə) ►*n. Gk. Myth.* Var. of **Gaea.**

gai•e•ty (gā′ĭ-tē) ►*n.*, *pl.* **-ties 1.** Joyful exuberance or merriment; vivacity. **2.** Merry activity; festivity. [< OFr. *gai*, cheerful.]

gai•ly (gā′lē) ►*adv.* **1.** In a joyful, cheerful, or happy manner. **2.** Colorfully; showily.

gain (gān) ►*v.* **1.** To come into possession of; acquire. **2.** To win. **3.** To obtain through effort or merit. **4.** To earn. **5.** To increase by: *gained 15 pounds.* **6.** To reach. **7.** To increase; grow: *gained in wisdom.* **8.** To close a gap; get closer. ►*n.* Something gained or acquired; profit; advantage; increase. [< OFr. *gaaignier*, of Gmc. orig.]

gain•er (gā′nər) ►*n.* **1.** One that gains. **2.** *Sports* A dive in which the diver leaves the board facing forward, does a back somersault, and enters the water feet first.

gain•ful (gān′fəl) ►*adj.* Providing a gain or profit. —**gain′ful•ly** *adv.*

gain•say (gān-sā′, gān′sā′) ►*v.* **-said** (-săd′, -sĕd′), **-say•ing.** To declare false. See Syns at **deny.** [ME *gainsayen*, speak against.]

Gains•bor•ough (gānz′bûr′ō, -bər-ə), **Thomas.** 1727–88. British portrait and landscape painter.

gait (gāt) ►*n.* **1.** A way of moving on foot. **2.** Any of the ways a horse can move by lifting the feet in different order or rhythm. **3.** A rate or pace. [< ON *gata*, path.]

gai•ter (gā′tər) ►*n.* **1.** A cloth or leather covering for the legs extending from the instep to the ankle or knee. **2.** An ankle-high shoe with elastic sides. **3.** An overshoe with a cloth top. [Fr. *guêtre.*]

gal (găl) ►*n. Informal* A girl. [Alteration of GIRL.]

gal. ►*abbr.* gallon

ga•la (gā′lə, găl′ə, gä′lə) ►*n.* A festive occasion, esp. a lavish social event. [< OFr. *galer*, make merry.] —**ga′la** *adj.*

ga•lac•tose (gə-lăk′tōs′) ►*n.* A simple sugar commonly occurring in lactose. [Gk. *gala*, *galakt-*, milk + -OSE[2].]

Gal•a•had (găl′ə-hăd′) ►*n.* **1.** In Arthurian legend, the purest Knight of the Round Table. **2.** A model of nobleness and purity.

Ga•lá•pa•gos Islands (gə-lä′pə-gəs, -lăp′ə-) A group of volcanic islands in the Pacific W of Ecuador, to which they belong.

Ga•la•tia (gə-lā′shə, -shē-ə) An ancient country of central Asia Minor in the region surrounding modern Ankara, Turkey. —**Ga•la′tian** *adj.* & *n.*

Ga•la•tians (gə-lā′shənz) ►*pl.n. (takes sing. v.)* See table at **Bible.**

gal•ax•y (găl′ək-sē) ►*n.*, *pl.* **-ies 1a.** Any of numerous large-scale aggregates of stars, gas, and dust, containing an average of 100 billion solar masses and ranging in diameter from 1,500 to 300,000 light-years. **b.** often **Galaxy** The Milky Way. **2.** An assembly of brilliant, glamorous, or distinguished persons or things. [< Gk. *galaxias*, milky.] —**ga•lac′tic** (gə-lăk′tĭk) *adj.*

gale (gāl) ►*n.* **1.** A very strong wind. **2.** A forceful outburst, as of laughter. [?]

Ga•len (gā′lən). A.D. 130?–200? Greek anatomist, physician, and writer.

ga•le•na (gə-lē′nə) ►*n.* A gray mineral, essentially PbS, the principal ore of lead. [Lat. *galēna*, lead ore.]

Ga•li•cia (gə-lĭsh′ə, -ē-ə) **1.** A historical region of central Europe in SE Poland and W Ukraine. **2.** A region and ancient kingdom of NW Spain on the Atlantic S of the Bay of Biscay. —**Ga•li′cian** *adj.* & *n.*

Gal•i•lee (găl′ə-lē′) A region of N Israel. —**Gal′i•le′an** *adj.* & *n.*

Galilee, Sea of. Formerly **Lake Tiberias.** A freshwater lake of NE Israel.

Ga•li•le•o Ga•li•lei (găl′ə-lē′ō găl′ə-lā′, -lā′ō). 1564–1642. Italian astronomer and physicist. —**Gal′i•le′an** *adj.*

gall[1] (gôl) ►*n.* **1.** See **bile** 1. **2a.** Bitterness of feeling; rancor. **b.** Something bitter to endure. **3.** Outrageous insolence; effrontery. [< OE *gealla.*]

gall[2] (gôl) ►*n.* **1.** A skin sore caused by rubbing. **2.** Exasperation; vexation. ►*v.* **1.** To make or become sore by rubbing. See Syns at **chafe. 2.** To exasperate. [< OE *gealla.*]

gall[3] (gôl) ►*n.* An abnormal swelling of plant tissue caused by insects, microorganisms, or external injury. [< Lat. *galla.*]

gal•lant (găl′ənt) ►*adj.* **1.** Smartly stylish; dashing. **2.** Courageous; valiant. **3.** Nobly or selflessly resolute. **4.** (gə-lănt′, -länt′) **a.** Courteously attentive; chivalrous. **b.** Flirtatious. ►*n.* (gə-lănt′, -länt′, găl′ənt) **1.** A fashionable young man. **2a.** A man courteously attentive to women. **b.** A woman's lover; paramour. [< OFr. *galer*, make merry, of Gmc. orig.] —**gal′lant•ly** *adv.* —**gal′lant•ry** *n.*

gall•blad•der also **gall bladder** (gôl′blăd′ər) ►*n.* A small muscular sac under the right lobe of the liver, in which bile secreted by the liver is stored.

gal•le•on (găl′ē-ən, găl′yən) ►*n.* A large three-masted sailing ship used from the 15th to 17th cent. for trade or warfare. [Sp. *galeón* < OFr. *galie*, GALLEY.]

gal•ler•y (găl′ə-rē) ►*n., pl.* **-ies 1a.** A roofed promenade, esp. one along the wall of a building. **b.** A long interior or exterior balcony. **2a.** A long enclosed passage, esp. a corridor between two parts of a building. **b.** An underground tunnel. **3.** *Regional* See **veranda. 4a.** A rear or side balcony in a theater or auditorium. **b.** The seats in such a section. **c.** The cheapest seats in a theater. **d.** The audience occupying these seats. **5.** A group of spectators, as at a tennis match. **6.** The general public. **7a.** A building, institution, or room for the exhibition of artistic work. **b.** An establishment that displays and sells works of art. **8.** A collection; assortment. [Ult. < Lat. *Galilea*, Galilee.]

gal•ley (găl′ē) ►*n., pl.* **-leys 1a.** A large medieval ship propelled by sails and oars, used for trade or warfare in the Mediterranean. **b.** An ancient Mediterranean ship propelled by oars. **2.** The kitchen of an airliner or a ship. **3.** *Print.* **a.** A long tray for holding composed type. **b.** A printer's proof taken from such type. [< Med.Gk. *galea.*]

Gal•lic (găl′ĭk) ►*adj.* Of or relating to Gaul or France; French.

Gal•li•cism (găl′ĭ-sĭz′əm) ►*n.* A French phrase appearing in another language.

gal•li•um (găl′ē-əm) ►*n. Symbol* **Ga** A rare metallic element, liquid near room temperature, used in semiconductors. At. no. 31. See table at **element.** [< Lat. *gallus*, cock.]

gal•li•vant (găl′ə-vănt′) ►*v.* **1.** To roam about in search of pleasure or amusement. **2.** To flirt. [Perh. alteration of GALLANT.]

gal•lon (găl′ən) ►*n.* See table at **measurement.** [< ONFr. *galon*, a liquid measure.]

gal•lop (găl′əp) ►*n.* **1.** A natural three-beat gait of a horse, faster than a canter. **2.** A rapid pace. [< OFr. *galoper*, to gallop, of Gmc. orig.] —**gal′lop** *v.*

gal•lows (găl′ōz) ►*n., pl.* **gallows** or **-lows•es.** A framework from which a noose is suspended, used for execution by hanging. [< OE *galga.*]

gallows humor ►*n.* Humorous treatment of a grave or dire situation.

gall•stone (gôl′stōn′) ►*n.* A small hard mass formed in the gallbladder or in a bile duct.

ga•lore (gə-lôr′, -lōr′) ►*adj.* In great numbers; in abundance: *opportunities galore.* [Ir.Gael. *go leór*, enough.]

ga•losh (gə-lŏsh′) ►*n.* A waterproof overshoe. [< OFr. *galoche*, wooden-soled shoe.]

Gals•wor•thy (gălz′wûr′*th*ē), **John.** 1867–1933. British writer; 1932 Nobel.

Gal•va•ni (găl-vä′nē, gäl-), **Luigi.** 1737–98. Italian physiologist and physician.

gal•van•ic (găl-văn′ĭk) ►*adj.* **1.** Of or relating to direct-current electricity, esp. when produced chemically. **2.** Having the effect of an electric shock; jolting. [After Luigi GALVANI.] —**gal′van•ism** *n.*

gal•va•nize (găl′və-nīz′) ►*v.* **-nized, -niz•ing 1.** To stimulate or shock with an electric current. **2.** To arouse to awareness or action; spur. **3.** To coat (iron or steel) with rust-resistant zinc. —**gal′va•ni•za′tion** *n.*

gal•va•nom•e•ter (găl′və-nŏm′ĭ-tər) ►*n.* An instrument used to detect or measure small electric currents by means of mechanical effects produced by a coil in a magnetic field. [GALVAN(IC) + -METER.] —**gal′va•no•met′ric** (-nō-mĕt′rĭk), **gal′va•no•met′ri•cal** *adj.*

Gal•ves•ton (găl′vĭ-stən) A city of SE TX SSE of Houston on **Galveston Bay,** an arm of the Gulf of Mexico. Pop. 59,070.

Gal•way (gôl′wā′) **1.** A region of W-central Ireland. **2.** A city of W-central Ireland on **Galway Bay,** an inlet of the Atlantic. Pop. 37,835.

Ga•ma (găm′ə, gä′mə), **Vasco da.** 1460?–1524. Portuguese explorer and colonial administrator.

Gam•bi•a (găm′bē-ə) A country of W Africa on the Atlantic. Cap. Banjul. Pop. 1,081,000. —**Gam′bi•an** *adj. & n.*

Gambia River. A river of W Africa flowing about 1,126 km (700 mi) from N Guinea through SE Senegal and Gambia to the Atlantic.

gam•bit (găm′bĭt) ►*n.* **1.** A chess opening in which a minor piece, as a pawn, is offered in exchange for a favorable position. **2.** A maneuver or ploy. **3.** A remark intended to open a conversation. [< Ital. *gambetto*, a tripping up < *gamba*, leg.]

gam•ble (găm′bəl) ►*v.* **-bled, -bling 1a.** To bet on an uncertain outcome, as of a contest. **b.** To play a game of chance for stakes. **2.** To take a risk in the hope of gaining an advantage. **3.** To expose to hazard: *gamble one's life.* ►*n.* **1.** A wager. **2.** A risk. [Perh. < OE *gamenian*, to play.] —**gam′bler** *n.*

gam•bol (găm′bəl) ►*v.* **-boled, -bol•ing** or **-bolled, -bol•ling.** To leap about playfully; frolic. [< OItal. *gamba*, leg.] —**gam′bol** *n.*

gam•brel roof (găm′brəl) ►*n.* A ridged roof with two slopes on each side, the lower slope having the steeper pitch. [< ONFr. *gamberel*, hock of an animal < *gambe*, leg.]

game[1] (gām) ►*n.* **1.** An activity providing entertainment or amusement; pastime. **2a.** A competitive activity or sport. **b.** A single instance of such an activity. **3.** The total number of points required to win a game. **4.** A particular style or manner of playing a game. **5.** *Informal* A business or occupation: *the insurance* *game.* **6.** *Informal* A calculated strategy; scheme: *saw through their game.* **7.** Wild animals, birds, or fish hunted for food or sport. **8.** An object of attack or pursuit: *fair game.* ▸*v.* **gamed, gam•ing.** To gamble. ▸*adj.* **gam•er, gam•est 1.** Unyielding in spirit; resolute. **2.** Ready and willing. [< OE *gamen.*] —**game′ly** *adv.* —**game′ness** *n.*

game² (gām) ▸*adj.* **gam•er, gam•est.** Lame: *a game leg.* [?]

game•cock (gām′kŏk′) ▸*n.* A rooster trained for cockfighting.

game•keep•er (gām′kē′pər) ▸*n.* One employed to protect and maintain wildlife, esp. on an estate or preserve.

games•man•ship (gāmz′mən-shĭp′) ▸*n.* The practice of using dubious maneuvers to further one's aims or better one's position.

game•ster (gām′stər) ▸*n.* A habitual gambler.

gam•ete (găm′ēt′, gə-mēt′) ▸*n.* A reproductive cell, esp. a mature sperm or egg capable of participating in fertilization. [< Gk. *gametēs*, husband.] —**ga•met′ic** (-mĕt′ĭk) *adj.*

gam•in (găm′ĭn) ▸*n.* A boy who lives on or roams the streets. [Fr.]

ga•mine (gă-mēn′, găm′ēn) ▸*n.* **1.** A girl who lives on or roams the streets. **2.** A girl or woman of impish appeal.

gam•ma (găm′ə) ▸*n.* The 3rd letter of the Greek alphabet. [Gk.]

gamma globulin ▸*n.* A protein fraction of blood serum containing numerous antibodies, used in the prevention and treatment esp. of measles, polio, and hepatitis.

gamma ray ▸*n.* Electromagnetic radiation emitted by radioactive decay and having energies from ten thousand to ten million electron volts.

gam•mon (găm′ən) ▸*n.* A victory in backgammon reached before the loser has removed a single piece. [Prob. < ME *gamen*, game.]

-gamous ▸*suff.* Having a specified number of marriages: *monogamous.* [< Gk. *gamos*, marriage.]

gam•ut (găm′ət) ▸*n.* A complete range or extent. [< Med.Lat. *gamma ut*, low G.]

gam•y also **gam•ey** (gā′mē) ▸*adj.* **-i•er, -i•est 1.** Having the flavor or odor of game, esp. slightly spoiled game. **2.** Spirited; plucky. **3a.** Corrupt; tainted. **b.** Racy; risqué. —**gam′i•ness** *n.*

-gamy ▸*suff.* Marriage: *polygamy.* [< Gk. *gamos*, marriage.]

gan•der (găn′dər) ▸*n.* **1.** A male goose. **2.** *Informal* A look or glance. [< OE *gandra.*]

Gan•dhi (gän′dē, găn′-), **Indira Nehru.** 1917–84. Indian prime minister (1966–77 and 1980–84); assassinated.

Gandhi, Mohandas Karamchand. "Mahatma." 1869–1948. Indian nationalist and spiritual leader; assassinated.

gang (găng) ▸*n.* **1.** A group of criminals or hoodlums. **2.** A group of youths who band together for social and often criminal purposes. **3.** *Informal* A group of people who associate or work together. **4.** A work crew. **5.** A matched set, as of tools. ▸*v.* To band together as a group or gang. —***phrasal verb:* gang up** To join together esp. in opposition or attack. [< OE, journey, and ON *gangr*, group.]

Gan•ges (găn′jēz′) A river of N India and Bangladesh rising in the Himalayas and flowing about 2,510 km (1,560 mi) to the Bay of Bengal.

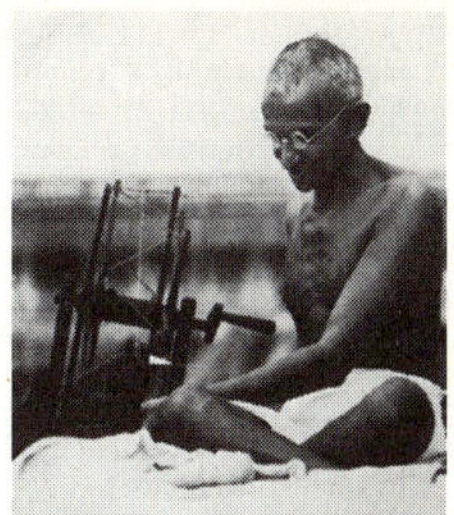

Mahatma Gandhi
photographed in 1925

gan•gling (găng′glĭng) ▸*adj.* Awkwardly tall or long-limbed. [Poss. < dial. *gang*, go.]

gan•gli•on (găng′glē-ən) ▸*n., pl.* **-gli•a** (-glē-ə) or **-gli•ons.** A group of nerve cells forming a nerve center, esp. one located outside the brain or spinal cord. [Gk., cystlike tumor.] —**gan′gli•on′ic** (-ŏn′ĭk) *adj.*

gan•gly (găng′glē) ▸*adj.* **-gli•er, -gli•est.** Gangling. [Alteration of GANGLING.]

gang•plank (găng′plăngk′) ▸*n.* A board or ramp used as a removable footway between a ship and a pier. [< GANG, a going.]

gan•grene (găng′grēn′, găng-grēn′) ▸*n.* Death and decay of body tissue caused by insufficient blood supply, usu. following injury or disease. [< Gk. *gangraina.*] —**gan′grene** *v.* —**gan′gre•nous** (găng′grə-nəs) *adj.*

gang•ster (găng′stər) ▸*n.* A member of an organized group of criminals; racketeer. —**gang′ster•dom** *n.* —**gang′ster•ism** *n.*

gang•way (găng′wā′) ▸*n.* **1.** A passage along a ship's upper deck. **2.** See **gangplank.** ▸*interj.* Used to clear a passage through a crowded area. [< GANG, a going.]

gan•ja (gän′jə) ▸*n.* Marijuana. [< Skt. *gañjaḥ*, hemp.]

gan•net (găn′ĭt) ▸*n.* A large sea bird of N Atlantic coastal regions, having white plumage with black wingtips. [< OE *ganot.*]

gant•let (gônt′lĭt, gänt′-) ▸*n.* **1.** Var. of **gauntlet¹**. **2.** Var. of **gauntlet²**.

gan•try (găn′trē) ▸*n., pl.* **-tries 1.** A bridgelike mount for a traveling crane. **2.** A massive vertical frame used in assembling or servicing a rocket. [< Lat. *canthērius*, wooden frame.]

GAO ▸*abbr.* General Accounting Office

gaol (jāl) ▸*n.* & *v.* *Chiefly Brit.* Var. of **jail.**

gap (găp) ▸*n.* **1.** An opening, as in a wall; breach. **2.** A pass through mountains. **3.** A space between objects or points. **4.** An interruption of continuity. **5.** A wide difference; disparity: *the gap between rich and poor.* [< ON, chasm.]

gape (gāp, găp) ▸*v.* **gaped, gap•ing 1.** To open the mouth wide; yawn. **2.** To stare wonderingly or stupidly, often with the mouth open. **3.** To open wide. ▸*n.* **1.** An act of gaping. **2.** A large opening. [< ON *gapa.*]

gar (gär) ▸*n.* Any of several fishes having long narrow jaws, an elongated body, and a long snout. [Short for *garfish* < OE *gār*, spear.]

GAR ▸*abbr.* Grand Army of the Republic

ga•rage (gə-räzh′, -räj′) ►*n.* **1.** A structure for housing a motor vehicle. **2.** A commercial establishment where cars are repaired, serviced, or parked. [Fr. < *garer*, to shelter.] —**ga•rage′** *v.*

garage sale ►*n.* A sale of used household items or clothing held at one's home.

garb (gärb) ►*n.* **1.** A distinctive style of clothing; dress. **2.** An outward appearance; guise. [< Ital. *garbo*, grace.] —**garb** *v.*

gar•bage (gär′bĭj) ►*n.* **1a.** Food wastes, as from a kitchen. **b.** Refuse; trash. **2.** Worthless matter. [ME, offal from fowls.]

gar•ban•zo (gär-bän′zō) ►*n.*, *pl.* **-zos.** See **chickpea.** [Sp. < OSpan. *arvanço*.]

gar•ble (gär′bəl) ►*v.* **-bled, -bling.** To mix up or distort (e.g., a message) to such an extent as to make misleading or unintelligible. [Ult. < Lat. *crībrum*, sieve.] —**gar′bler** *n.*

Gar•bo (gä′bəl), **Greta.** 1905–90. Swedish-born Amer. actress.

Gar•cí•a Lor•ca (gär-sē′ə lôr′kä, gär-thē′ä), **Federico.** 1898–1936. Spanish writer.

Gar•cí•a Már•quez (gär-sē′ə mär′kəs, -kĕs), **Gabriel.** b. 1928. Colombian-born writer; 1982 Nobel.

gar•den (gär′dn) ►*n.* **1.** A plot of land used for growing flowers, vegetables, herbs, or fruit. **2.** often **gardens** Grounds laid out with ornamental plants and trees and used for public recreation or display. **3.** A yard or lawn. **4.** A fertile, well-cultivated region. ►*v.* To plant or tend a garden. [< ONFr. *gardin*, of Gmc. orig.] —**gar′den•er** *n.*

Garden Grove. A city of S CA, a suburb of Los Angeles. Pop. 143,050.

gar•de•nia (gär-dēn′yə) ►*n.* **1.** A shrub having glossy evergreen leaves. **2.** The large fragrant white flower of this plant. [After Alexander *Garden* (1730?–91).]

gar•den-va•ri•e•ty (gär′dn-və-rī′ĭ-tē) ►*adj.* Common; unremarkable.

Gar•field (gär′fēld′), **James Abram.** 1831–81. The 20th President of the US (1881); assassinated.

James Garfield

gar•gan•tu•an (gär-găn′cho͞o-ən) ►*adj.* Of immense size; gigantic. [After the hero of *Gargantua and Pantagruel* by Rabelais.]

gar•gle (gär′gəl) ►*v.* **-gled, -gling 1.** To force exhaled air through a liquid held in the back of the mouth in order to cleanse or medicate the mouth or throat. **2.** To produce the sound of gargling when speaking or singing. ►*n.* **1.** A medicated solution for gargling. **2.** A gargling sound. [< OFr. *gargouiller*.]

gar•goyle (gär′goil′) ►*n.* A roof spout in the form of a grotesque or fantastic creature. [< OFr. *gargouille*, throat.]

Gar•i•bal•di (găr′ə-bôl′dē), **Giuseppe.** 1807–82. Italian general and nationalist.

gar•ish (gâr′ĭsh, găr′-) ►*adj.* Excessively or stridently decorated. See Syns at **gaudy.** [?] —**gar′ish•ly** *adv.* —**gar′ish•ness** *n.*

gar•land (gär′lənd) ►*n.* A wreath or festoon, esp. of plaited flowers or leaves. ►*v.* To ornament with a garland. [< OFr. *garlande*.]

Garland. A city of NE TX, a suburb of Dallas. Pop. 180,650.

Garland, Judy. Frances Gumm. 1922–69. Amer. actress and singer.

gar•lic (gär′lĭk) ►*n.* **1.** An onionlike plant having a bulb with a strong distinctive odor and flavor. **2.** The bulb of this plant, divisible into separate cloves and used as a seasoning. [< OE *gārlēac*.] —**gar′lick•y** *adj.*

gar•ment (gär′mənt) ►*n.* An article of clothing. [< OFr. *garnement* < *garnir*, equip.]

gar•ner (gär′nər) ►*v.* To amass; acquire. [< Lat. *grānārium*, GRANARY.]

gar•net (gär′nĭt) ►*n.* **1.** Any of several common, usu. crystallized silicate minerals, colored red, brown, black, green, yellow, or white and used as gemstones and abrasives. **2.** A dark to very dark red. [< OFr. *grenat*, pomegranate-colored.]

gar•nish (gär′nĭsh) ►*v.* **1.** To embellish; adorn. **2.** To decorate (food or drink) with small items such as parsley or lemon slices. **3.** *Law* To garnishee. [< OFr. *garnir*, equip.] —**gar′nish** *n.*

gar•nish•ee (gär′nĭ-shē′) ►*v.* **-eed, -ee•ing.** To attach by garnishment.

gar•nish•ment (gär′nĭsh-mənt) ►*n.* A proceeding whereby money or property belonging to a debtor but in the possession of another is turned over to the creditor.

Ga•ronne (gä-rôn′) A river of SW France flowing about 563 km (350 mi) from the Spanish Pyrenees to the Dordogne R.

gar•ret (găr′ĭt) ►*n.* An attic room or rooms, typically under a pitched roof. [< OFr. *garite*, watchtower < *garir*, defend.]

Gar•rick (găr′ĭk), **David.** 1717–79. British actor and theater manager.

gar•ri•son (găr′ĭ-sən) ►*n.* A permanent military post or the troops stationed there. ►*v.* To assign (troops) to a military post. [< OFr. *garison* < *garir*, defend.]

Garrison, William Lloyd. 1805–79. Amer. abolitionist leader.

gar•rote or **gar•rotte** (gə-rŏt′, -rōt′) ►*n.* **1a.** A method of execution by strangulation with an iron collar. **b.** The collar used for this. **2a.** Strangulation, esp. in order to rob. **b.** A cord or wire used for strangling. [Sp. *garrote*, instrument of torture.] —**gar•rote′** *v.* —**gar•rot′er** *n.*

gar•ru•lous (găr′ə-ləs, găr′yə-) ►*adj.* Tiresomely talkative; rambling. [< Lat. *garrulus*.] —**gar′ru•lous•ly** *adv.* —**gar′ru•lous•ness** *n.*

gar•ter (gär′tər) ►*n.* An elastic band or suspender worn to hold up hose. [< ONFr. *gartier* < *garet*, bend of the knee.] —**gar′ter** *v.*

garter snake ►*n.* A nonvenomous North American snake with longitudinal stripes.

Gar•vey (gär′vē), **Marcus (Moziah) Aurelius.** 1887–1940. Jamaican Black nationalist active in the US.

Gar•y (gâr′ē, găr′ē) A city of NW IN on Lake Michigan near the IL border. Pop. 116,646.

gas (găs) ►*n., pl.* **gas•es** or **gas•ses 1a.** The state of matter distinguished from the solid and liquid states by relatively low density and viscosity, the ability to diffuse readily, and the spontaneous tendency to become distributed uniformly throughout any container. **b.** A substance in this state. **2.** A gaseous fuel, such as natural gas. **3.** Gasoline. **4.** A gaseous asphyxiant, irritant, or poison. **5.** A gaseous anesthetic. **6.** Flatulence. **7.** *Slang* Idle or boastful talk. **8.** *Slang* One that provides great fun or entertainment. ►*v.* **gassed, gas•sing 1.** To treat chemically with gas. **2.** To overcome or kill with poisonous fumes. —***phrasal verb:* gas up** To supply a vehicle with gasoline. [Du. < Gk. *khaos*, chaos.] —**gas′e•ous** (găs′ē-əs, găsh′əs) *adj.*

gas chamber ►*n.* A sealed enclosure in which prisoners are executed by poison gas.

Gas•co•ny (găs′kə-nē) A historical region and former province of SW France. —**Gas′con** *adj. & n.*

gash (găsh) ►*v.* To make a long deep cut in. [< ONFr. *garser*, to slit.] —**gash** *n.*

gas•ket (găs′kĭt) ►*n.* Any of a variety of seals used between matched machine parts or around pipe joints to prevent the escape of a gas or fluid. [Perh. < Fr. *garcette*, small cord.]

gas•light (găs′līt′) ►*n.* **1.** Light produced by burning illuminating gas. **2.** A gas lamp.

gas mask ►*n.* A respirator that contains a chemical air filter and is worn over the face as protection against toxic gases.

gas•o•hol (găs′ə-hôl′) ►*n.* A blend of ethyl alcohol and unleaded gasoline used as a fuel. [GAS(OLINE) + (ALC)OHOL.]

gas•o•line (găs′ə-lēn′, găs′ə-lēn′) ►*n.* A volatile mixture of flammable liquid hydrocarbons derived chiefly from crude petroleum and used as a fuel for internal-combustion engines and as a solvent and thinner.

gasp (găsp) ►*v.* **1.** To draw in or catch the breath sharply, as from shock. **2.** To make violent or labored attempts at breathing. [< ON *geispa*, to yawn.] —**gasp** *n.*

Gas•pé Peninsula (găs-pā′) A peninsula of E Quebec, Canada, between Chaleur Bay and the mouth of the St. Lawrence R.

gas•sy (găs′ē) ►*adj.* **-si•er, -si•est.** Containing, full of, or resembling gas. —**gas′si•ness** *n.*

gas•tric (găs′trĭk) ►*adj.* Of or associated with the stomach.

gastric juice ►*n.* The watery, acidic digestive fluid secreted by glands in the stomach.

gas•tri•tis (gă-strī′tĭs) ►*n.* Chronic or acute inflammation of the stomach.

gastro– or **gastr–** ►*pref.* Stomach: *gastritis.* [Gk. < *gastēr*, belly.]

gas•tro•en•ter•i•tis (găs′trō-ĕn′tə-rī′tĭs) ►*n.* Inflammation of the mucous membrane of the stomach and intestines.

gas•tro•in•tes•ti•nal (găs′trō-ĭn-tĕs′tə-nəl) ►*adj.* Of the stomach and intestines.

gas•trol•o•gy (gă-strŏl′ə-jē) ►*n.* The medical study of the stomach and its diseases. —**gas′tro•log′i•cal** (găs′trə-lŏj′ĭ-kəl), **gas′tro•log′ic** *adj.* —**gas′tro•log′i•cal•ly** *adv.* —**gas•trol′o•gist** *n.*

gas•tron•o•my (gă-strŏn′ə-mē) ►*n., pl.* **-mies 1.** The art of good eating. **2.** Cooking, as of a particular region. [< Gk. *gastronomia.*] —**gas′tro•nome′** (găs′trə-nōm′) *n.* —**gas′tro•nom′ic** (găs′trə-nŏm′ĭk) *adj.*

gas•tro•pod (găs′trə-pŏd′) ►*n.* Any of a class of mollusks, such as the snail or slug, having a single, usu. coiled shell or no shell at all and a muscular foot for locomotion.

gas•works (găs′wûrks′) ►*pl.n. (takes sing. v.)* A factory where gas for heating and lighting is produced.

gate (gāt) ►*n.* **1a.** A structure that can be swung, drawn, or lowered to block an entrance or passageway. **b.** A gateway. **2.** A passageway, as in an airport terminal, through which passengers arrive or depart. **3.** The total paid attendance at a public event. **4.** A device for controlling the passage of water or gas through a dam or conduit. **5.** *Electron.* A circuit with one output that is energized only by certain combinations of two or more inputs. [< OE *geat.*]

gate•crash•er (gāt′krăsh′ər) ►*n. Slang* One who gains admittance, as to a party or concert, without being invited or without paying. —**gate′crash′** *v.*

gat•ed community (gā′tĭd) ►*n.* A private neighborhood with entry permitted only to residents and guests.

Gates (gāts), **Horatio.** 1728?–1806. Amer. Revolutionary general.

Gates•head (gāts′hĕd′) A borough of NE England on the Tyne R. Pop. 202,850.

gate•way (gāt′wā′) ►*n.* **1.** An opening, as in a wall or fence, that may be closed by a gate. **2.** A means of access.

gath•er (găth′ər) ►*v.* **1.** To bring or come together. **2.** To accumulate gradually. **3.** To harvest or pick. **4.** To grow or increase by degrees: *gather speed.* **5.** To draw (e.g., cloth) into small folds or puckers. **6.** To draw about or bring closer: *gathered the shawl about my shoulders.* **7.** To conclude; infer: *I gather you're ready.* **8.** To summon up: *gathered up my courage.* ►*n.* **1.** An act of gathering. **2.** A small fold or pucker in cloth. [< OE *gadrian.*] —**gath′er•er** *n.* —**gath′er•ing** *n.*

ga•tor or **ga•ter** (gā′tər) ►*n. Informal* An alligator.

gauche (gōsh) ►*adj.* Lacking social polish; tactless. [< OFr., awkward.] —**gauche′ly** *adv.* —**gauche′ness** *n.*

gau•cho (gou′chō) ►*n., pl.* **-chos.** A cowboy of the South American pampas. [Am.Sp.]

gaud•y (gô′dē) ►*adj.* **-i•er, -i•est.** Showy in a tasteless or vulgar way. [Ult. < Lat. *gaudēre*, make merry.] —**gaud′i•ly** *adv.* —**gaud′i•ness** *n.*

Syns: *gaudy, flashy, garish, loud, tawdry* ***adj.***

gauge also **gage** (gāj) ►*n.* **1a.** A standard or scale of measurement. **b.** A standard dimension, quantity, or capacity. See Syns at **standard. 2.** An instrument for measuring or testing. **3.** A means of estimating or evaluating. **4a.** The distance between the two rails of a railroad. **b.** The distance between two wheels on an axle. **5.** The diameter of a shotgun barrel. **6.** Thickness or diameter, as of sheet metal or wire. ►*v.* **gauged, gaug•ing** also **gaged, gag•ing 1.** To measure precisely. **2.** To determine the capacity, volume, or contents of. **3.** To evaluate. [< ONFr., measuring rod.]

Gau•guin (gō-găN′), **(Eugène Henri) Paul.** 1848–1903. French artist.

Gaul¹ (gôl) ► *n.* A Celt of ancient Gaul.
Gaul² (gôl) An ancient region of W Europe corresponding roughly to modern-day France and Belgium.
Gaul•ish (gô′lĭsh) ► *n.* The extinct Celtic language of Gaul.
gaunt (gônt) ► *adj.* **-er, -est 1.** Thin and bony. **2.** Emaciated. **3.** Bleak; desolate. [ME.] —**gaunt′ly** *adv.* —**gaunt′ness** *n.*
gaunt•let¹ also **gant•let** (gônt′lĭt, gänt′-) ► *n.* **1.** A protective glove. **2.** A challenge to fight or compete. [< OFr. *gant*, glove.]
gaunt•let² also **gant•let** (gônt′lĭt, gänt′-) ► *n.* **1.** A form of punishment in which two lines of persons facing each other and armed with sticks or clubs beat the person forced to run between them. **2.** A severe trial; ordeal: *run the gauntlet of public scrutiny.* [< Swed. *gatlopp.*]
Gau•tier (gō-tyā′), **Théophile.** 1811–72. French writer.
gauze (gôz) ► *n.* **1.** A thin, transparent fabric with a loose open weave. **2.** A thin, loosely woven surgical dressing. [Fr. *gaze.*] —**gauz′i•ly** *adv.* —**gauz′i•ness** *n.* —**gauz′y** *adj.*
gave (gāv) ► *v.* P.t. of **give.**
gav•el (găv′əl) ► *n.* A small mallet used by a presiding officer or an auctioneer to signal for attention or order or to conclude a transaction. [?] —**gav′el** *v.*
ga•votte (gə-vŏt′) ► *n.* A French peasant dance in duple meter. [< Prov. *gavoto.*]
gawk (gôk) ► *n.* An awkward, loutish person; oaf. ► *v.* To stare or gape stupidly. [Perh. < obsolete *gaw*, gape.] —**gawk′er** *n.* —**gawk′y** *adj.*
gay (gā) ► *adj.* **-er, -est 1.** Of or having a sexual orientation to persons of the same sex. **2.** Cheerful and lighthearted; merry. **3.** Bright or lively, esp. in color. ► *n.* A person whose sexual orientation is to persons of the same sex. [< OFr. *gai.*] —**gay′ness** *n.*
Usage: The word *gay* is distinguished from *homosexual* in emphasizing the cultural and social aspects of homosexuality as opposed to sexual practice. Many writers reserve *gay* for males, but since the word is also used to refer to both sexes, the phrase *gay and lesbian* is often useful to avoid ambiguity.
Gay, John. 1685–1732. English writer.
Ga•za (gä′zə, găz′ə, gā′zə) A city of SW Asia in the **Gaza Strip,** a narrow coastal area along the Mediterranean Sea adjoining Israel and Egypt. Pop. 118,272.
gaze (gāz) ► *v.* **gazed, gaz•ing.** To look steadily, intently, and with fixed attention. [ME *gasen.*] —**gaze** *n.* —**gaz′er** *n.*
ga•ze•bo (gə-zā′bō, -zē′-) ► *n., pl.* **-bos** or **-boes.** A small, usu. open-sided roofed structure in a garden or park. [?]
ga•zelle (gə-zĕl′) ► *n.* Any of various small swift antelopes of Africa and Asia. [< Ar. *ġazāl.*]
ga•zette (gə-zĕt′) ► *n.* **1.** A newspaper. **2.** An official journal. [< Ital. *gazzetta.*]
gaz•et•teer (găz′ĭ-tîr′) ► *n.* A geographic dictionary or index.
Ga•zi•an•tep (gä′zē-än-tĕp′) A city of S Turkey N of Aleppo, Syria. Pop. 716,000.
gaz•pa•cho (gə-spä′chō, gəz-pä′-) ► *n.* A chilled soup of chopped tomatoes, cucumbers, onions, peppers, and herbs. [Sp.]
GB ► *abbr.* **1.** gigabyte **2.** Great Britain
G clef ► *n.* See **treble clef.** [From its locating the note G above middle C.]
GCT ► *abbr.* Greenwich civil time
Gd ► The symbol for the element **gadolinium.**
Gdańsk (gə-dänsk′, -dănsk′, -dīnsk′) also **Dan•zig** (dăn′sĭg, dän′tsĭk). A city of N Poland on the Baltic Sea. Pop. 465,395.
GDP ► *abbr.* gross domestic product
Ge ► The symbol for the element **germanium.**
gear (gîr) ► *n.* **1a.** A toothed machine part, such as a wheel or cylinder, that meshes with another toothed part to transmit motion or to change speed or direction. **b.** A transmission configuration for a specific ratio of engine to axle torque in a motor vehicle. **2.** Equipment, such as tools or clothing, used for a particular activity. See Syns at **equipment. 3.** Personal belongings. ► *v.* **1a.** To equip with or connect by gears. **b.** To put into gear. **2.** To adjust or adapt. [< ON *gervi*, equipment.]
gear•box (gîr′bŏks′) ► *n.* **1.** See **transmission** 3. **2.** A casing for a system of gears.
gear•shift (gîr′shĭft′) ► *n.* A mechanism for changing from one gear to another in a transmission.
geck•o (gĕk′ō) ► *n., pl.* **-os** or **-oes.** Any of various usu. small tropical and subtropical lizards having toes with adhesive pads for climbing. [Javanese *ge'kok.*]
gee (jē) ► *interj.* Used as an exclamation, as of surprise. [Alteration of JESUS.]
geek (gēk) ► *n. Slang* **1a.** An inept or clumsy person. **b.** One accomplished in scientific or technical pursuits but regarded as socially inept. **2.** A carnival performer featuring bizarre acts. [Perh. < LGer. *gek*, fool.] —**geek′y** *adj.*
geese (gēs) ► *n.* Pl. of **goose.**
gee•zer (gē′zər) ► *n.* An eccentric old man. [Prob. < dial. *guiser*, masquerader.]
Gei•ger counter (gī′gər) ► *n.* An instrument that detects and measures the intensity of radiation, such as particles from radioactive material. [After H.W. *Geiger* (1882–1945).]
gei•sha (gā′shə, gē′-) ► *n., pl.* **-sha** or **-shas.** One of a class of professional women in Japan trained to entertain men. [J.]

geisha
Geisha Serving a Samurai
by Suzuki Harunobu

gel (jĕl) ► *n.* A jellylike mixture formed when the particles of a colloid become relatively large. [< GELATIN.] —**gel** *v.*

gel•a•tin also **gel•a•tine** (jĕl′ə-tn) ►*n.* **1.** A transparent brittle protein formed by boiling the specially prepared skin, bones, and connective tissue of animals and used in foods, drugs, and photographic film. **2.** A jelly made with gelatin. [< Ital. *gelata*, jelly < Lat. *gelāre*, freeze.] —**ge•lat′i•nous** (jə-lăt′n-əs) *adj.*

geld (gĕld) ►*v.* **geld•ed** or **gelt** (gĕlt), **geld•ing.** To castrate (e.g., a horse). [< ON *gelda*.] —**geld′ing** *n.*

gel•id (jĕl′ĭd) ►*adj.* Very cold. See Syns at **cold.** [Lat. *gelidus* < *gelū*, frost.] —**ge•lid′i•ty** (jə-lĭd′ĭ-tē), **gel′id•ness** *n.*

gel•ig•nite (jĕl′ĭg-nīt′) ►*n.* An explosive mixture composed of nitroglycerine, guncotton, wood pulp, and potassium nitrate. [GEL(ATIN) + Lat. *ignis*, fire + –ITE[1].]

Gel•sen•kir•chen (gĕl′zən-kîr′kən, -KHən) A city of W-central Germany in the Ruhr Valley NE of Essen. Pop. 295,037.

gem (jĕm) ►*n.* **1.** A pearl or mineral that has been cut and polished for use as an ornament. **2.** Something valued highly. [< Lat. *gemma*.] —**gem′my** *adj.*

Gem•i•ni (jĕm′ə-nī′, -nē′) ►*pl.n.* *(takes sing. v.)* **1.** A constellation in the Northern Hemisphere containing the stars Castor and Pollux. **2.** The 3rd sign of the zodiac. [< Lat. *Geminī*, twins.]

gem•ol•o•gy or **gem•mol•o•gy** (jĕ-mŏl′ə-jē) ►*n.* The study of precious or semiprecious stones. —**gem′o•log′i•cal** (jĕm′ə-lŏj′ĭ-kəl) *adj.* —**gem•ol′o•gist** *n.*

gem•stone (jĕm′stōn′) ►*n.* A precious or semiprecious stone that may be used as a jewel when cut and polished.

Gen. or **GEN** ►*abbr.* general

–gen or **–gene** ►*suff.* Producer: *androgen.* [< Gk. *-genēs*, born.]

gen•darme (zhän′därm′, zhäN′därm′) ►*n.* A member of the French national police. [< OFr. *gens d'armes*, men-at-arms.]

gen•der (jĕn′dər) ►*n.* **1.** *Gram.* A category used in the analysis of nouns, pronouns, adjectives, and, in some languages, verbs that determines agreement with modifiers, referents, or grammatical forms. **2.** Sexual category; males or females as a group. [< Lat. *genus*, *gener-*, kind.] —**gen′der•less** *adj.*

Usage: In recent years *gender* has become well established in its use to refer to sex-based categories, as in phrases such as *gender gap* and *the politics of gender.*

gene (jēn) ►*n.* A hereditary unit that occupies a specific location on a chromosome, determines a particular characteristic in an organism, and can undergo mutation. [< Gk. *genos*, race.]

ge•ne•al•o•gy (jē′nē-ŏl′ə-jē, -ăl′-, jĕn′ē-) ►*n.*, *pl.* **-gies 1.** A record of ancestral descent; family tree. **2.** Direct descent from an ancestor. **3.** The study of ancestry. [< Gk. *genea*, family.] —**ge′ne•a•log′i•cal** (-ə-lŏj′ĭ-kəl) *adj.* —**ge′ne•al′o•gist** *n.*

gene pool ►*n.* The collective genetic information contained within a population of sexually reproducing organisms.

gen•er•a (jĕn′ər-ə) ►*n.* Pl. of **genus.**

gen•er•al (jĕn′ər-əl) ►*adj.* **1.** Applicable to or affecting the whole or every member of a category. **2.** Widespread; prevalent. **3.** Of or affecting the entire body: *general malaise; general anesthetic.* **4.** Being usually the case. **5.** Not limited in scope or category: *a general rule; general merchandise.* **6.** Broad but not thorough: *a general grasp of the subject.* **7.** Highest or superior in rank: *the general manager.* ►*n.* A rank, as in the US Army, above lieutenant general. —***idiom:* in general** For the most part. [< Lat. *genus*, *gener-*, kind.] —**gen′er•al•ly** *adv.*

Syns: *general, common, universal* ***Ant:*** *particular* ***adj.***

general anesthetic ►*n.* An anesthetic that causes loss of sensation in the entire body and induces unconsciousness.

general assembly ►*n.* **1.** A legislative body. **2. General Assembly** The main deliberative body of the United Nations, in which each member nation has one vote.

gen•er•al•is•si•mo (jĕn′ər-ə-lĭs′ə-mō′) ►*n.*, *pl.* **-mos.** The commander in chief of all the armed forces in certain countries. [Ital.]

gen•er•al•i•ty (jĕn′ə-răl′ĭ-tē) ►*n.*, *pl.* **-ties 1.** The state of being general. **2.** An observation or principle having general application; generalization. **3.** A vague statement or idea.

gen•er•al•ize (jĕn′ər-ə-līz′) ►*v.* **-ized, -iz•ing 1.** To render general rather than specific. **2.** To draw inferences or a general conclusion (from). **3.** To deal in generalities; speak or write vaguely. —**gen′er•al•i•za′tion** *n.*

General of the Air Force ►*n.* The highest rank in the US Air Force.

General of the Army ►*n.* The highest rank in the US Army.

general practitioner ►*n.* A physician who does not specialize in a particular area but treats a variety of medical problems.

general relativity ►*n.* The geometric theory of gravitation developed by Albert Einstein, extending the theory of special relativity to accelerated frames of reference and introducing the principle that gravitational and inertial forces are equivalent.

gen•er•al•ship (jĕn′ər-əl-shĭp′) ►*n.* **1.** The rank, office, or tenure of a general. **2.** Skill in the conduct of war. **3.** Leadership.

gen•er•ate (jĕn′ə-rāt′) ►*v.* **-at•ed, -at•ing.** To bring into being; produce. [Lat. *generāre*.] —**gen′er•a•tive** (-ər-ə-tĭv, -ə-rā′-) *adj.*

gen•er•a•tion (jĕn′ə-rā′shən) ►*n.* **1.** All of the offspring that are at the same stage of descent from a common ancestor. **2.** The average interval of time between the birth of parents and the birth of their offspring. **3.** A group of contemporaneous individuals. **4.** A period of sequential technological development and innovation. **5.** The act of generating. —**gen•er•a′tion•al** *adj.*

Generation X ►*n.* The generation following the post–World War II baby boom, esp. in the US and Canada. [< title of a novel by Douglas Coupland (b. 1961).]

gen•er•a•tor (jĕn′ə-rā′tər) ►*n.* One that generates, esp. a machine that converts mechanical energy into electrical energy.

ge•ner•ic (jə-nĕr′ĭk) ►*adj.* **1.** Relating to or descriptive of an entire group. **2.** *Biol.* Of or relating to a genus. **3.** Not having a trademark or brand name. ►*n.* A product or substance sold under a generic name. [< Lat. *genus*, *gener-*, kind.] —**ge•ner′i•cal•ly** *adv.*

gen•er•ous (jĕn′ər-əs) ►*adj.* **1.** Liberal in giving or sharing. See Syns at **liberal. 2.** Not petty or mean; magnanimous. **3.** Abundant; ample. [< Lat. *generōsus*, of noble birth.] —**gen′er•os′i•ty** (-ə-rŏs′-ĭ-tē) *n.* —**gen′er•ous•ly** *adv.* —**gen′er•ous•ness** *n.*

gen•e•sis (jĕn′ĭ-sĭs) ▸*n.*, *pl.* **-ses** (-sēz′) **1.** The origin of something. See Syns at **beginning. 2. Genesis.** See table at **Bible.** [< Gk.]

–genesis ▸*suff.* Origin; production: *morphogenesis.* [< Gk.]

Ge•net (zhə-nā′), **Jean.** 1910–86. French writer.

gene therapy ▸*n.* Treatment of esp. genetic disorders by introducing engineered genes into a subject's cells.

ge•net•ic (jə-nĕt′ĭk) also **ge•net•i•cal** (-ĭ-kəl) ▸*adj.* **1a.** Of or relating to genetics. **b.** Affecting or affected by genes. **2.** Of, relating to, or influenced by the origin or development of something. [< Gk. *genetikos*, genitive < *genesis*, origin.] —**ge•net′i•cal•ly** *adv.*

genetic code ▸*n.* The nucleotide sequence in DNA or RNA that determines protein synthesis and constitutes the basis of heredity.

genetic engineering ▸*n.* Scientific alteration of the structure of genetic material in a living organism. —**genetic engineer** *n.*

ge•net•ics (jə-nĕt′ĭks) ▸*n.* *(takes sing. v.)* The branch of biology that deals with heredity, esp. the mechanisms of hereditary transmission and the variation of inherited characteristics. —**ge•net′i•cist** *n.*

Ge•ne•va (jə-nē′və) A city of SW Switzerland, bisected by the Rhone R. Pop. 170,861.

Geneva, Lake. A lake on the Swiss-French border between the Alps and the Jura Mts.

Gen•ghis Khan (jĕng′gĭs kän′, gĕng′-) also **Jen•ghis Khan** (jĕn′gĭs kän′, jĕng′-). 1162?–1227. Mongol conqueror.

gen•ial (jēn′yəl) ▸*adj.* Having a pleasant or friendly disposition or manner. See Syns at **gracious.** [< Lat. *genius*, spirit.] —**ge′ni•al′i•ty** (jē′nē-ăl′ĭ-tē), **gen′ial•ness** *n.* —**gen′ial•ly** *adv.*

–genic ▸*suff.* **1.** Producing; generating: *allergenic.* **2.** Produced or generated by: *psychogenic.* **3.** Suitable for production or reproduction by a specified medium: *photogenic.* [–GEN + –IC.]

ge•nie (jē′nē) ▸*n.* A supernatural creature who does one's bidding when summoned. [< Lat. *genius*, guardian spirit.]

gen•i•tal (jĕn′ĭ-tl) ▸*adj.* **1.** Of or relating to biological reproduction. **2.** Of the genitalia. **3.** Of the third and final stage of psychosexual development in psychoanalytic theory. ▸*n.* **genitals.** The genitalia. [< Lat. *genitālis*.] —**gen′i•tal•ly** *adv.*

gen•i•ta•li•a (jĕn′ĭ-tā′lē-ə, -tāl′yə) ▸*pl.n.* The reproductive organs, esp. the external sex organs. [< Lat. *genitālis*, GENITAL.]

gen•i•tive (jĕn′ĭ-tĭv) ▸*adj.* Of or designating a grammatical case that expresses possession, measurement, or source. ▸*n.* The genitive case. See Usage Note at **of.** [< Lat. *(cāsus) genetīvus*, (case) of origin.]

gen•i•to•u•ri•nar•y (jĕn′ĭ-tō-yo͝or′ə-nĕr′ē) ▸*adj.* Of or relating to the genital and urinary organs or their functions.

gen•ius (jēn′yəs) ▸*n.*, *pl.* **-ius•es 1a.** Extraordinary intellectual and creative power. **b.** A person of extraordinary intellect and talent. **2.** A strong natural talent or aptitude. **3.** The distinctive character of a place, person, or era. **4.** *pl.* **ge•ni•i** (jē′nē-ī′) *Rom. Myth.* The guardian spirit of a person or place. [Lat., guardian spirit.]

Gen•o•a (jĕn′ō-ə) A city of NW Italy on the Ligurian Sea. Pop. 675,659. —**Gen′o•ese′** (-ēz′, -ēs′), **Gen′o•vese′** (-vēz′, -vēs′) *adj.* & *n.*

gen•o•cide (jĕn′ə-sīd′) ▸*n.* The systematic, planned extermination of an entire national, racial, political, or ethnic group. [Gk. *genos*, race + –CIDE.] —**gen′o•cid′al** (-sīd′l) *adj.* —**gen′o•cid′al•ly** *adv.*

ge•nome (jē′nōm′) ▸*n.* **1.** The genetic material contained in a haploid set of chromosomes in eukaryotes, in a single chromosome in bacteria, or in the DNA or RNA of viruses. **2.** An organism's genetic material. [GEN(E) + Gk. *-ōma*, n. suff.] —**ge•nom′ic** (-nŏm′ĭk) *adj.*

ge•no•mics (jə-nō′mĭks) ▸*n.* *(takes sing. v.)* The study of the genome of a cell or organism.

gen•o•type (jĕn′ə-tīp′, jē′nə-) ▸*n.* **1.** The genetic constitution of an organism or group of organisms. **2.** A group or class of organisms having the same genetic constitution. [Gk. *genos*, race + TYPE.] —**gen′o•typ′ic** (-tĭp′ĭk), **gen′o•typ′i•cal** *adj.*

–genous ▸*suff.* **1.** Producing; generating: *erogenous.* **2.** Produced by or in a specified manner: *endogenous.* [–GEN + –OUS.]

gen•re (zhän′rə) ▸*n.* **1.** A type or class. **2.** An established class or category of artistic composition, as in literature or film. **3.** A realistic style of painting that depicts everyday life. [< OFr., a kind < Lat. *genus*, *gener-*.]

gent (jĕnt) ▸*n.* *Informal* A gentleman.

gen•teel (jĕn-tēl′) ▸*adj.* **1.** Refined in manner; well-bred and polite. **2.** Elegantly stylish. **3.** Striving to convey an appearance of refinement and respectability. [< OFr. *gentil*. See GENTLE.] —**gen•teel′ly** *adv.* —**gen•teel′ness** *n.*

gen•tian (jĕn′shən) ▸*n.* Any of numerous plants having showy, usu. blue flowers. [< Lat. *gentiāna*.]

gen•tile or **Gen•tile** (jĕn′tīl′) ▸*n.* **1.** One who is not a Jew. **2.** A Christian. **3.** *Archaic* A pagan or heathen. [< LLat. *gentīlis*, pagan. See GENTLE.]

gen•til•i•ty (jĕn-tĭl′ĭ-tē) ▸*n.* **1.** The quality of being well-mannered. **2.** The condition of being born to the gentry.

gen•tle (jĕn′tl) ▸*adj.* **-tler, -tlest 1.** Considerate or kindly. **2.** Not harsh or severe; soft; mild. **3.** Easily managed or handled; docile. **4.** Not steep or sudden; gradual. **5.** Of good family; wellborn. [< Lat. *gentīlis*, of the same clan < *gēns*, *gent-*, clan.] —**gen′tle** *v.* —**gen′tle•ness** *n.* —**gen′tly** *adv.*

gen•tle•man (jĕn′tl-mən) ▸*n.* **1.** A man of superior social position. **2.** A polite or well-mannered man. **3.** A man of independent means who does not need to work for a living. **4.** A man. —**gen′tle•man•ly** *adj.*

gen•tle•wom•an (jĕn′tl-wo͝om′ən) ▸*n.* **1.** A woman of superior social position. **2.** A polite or well-mannered woman.

gen•tri•fi•ca•tion (jĕn′trə-fĭ-kā′shən) ▸*n.* The restoration and upgrading of deteriorated urban property by the middle classes, often resulting in displacement of lower-income people. —**gen′tri•fy′** *v.*

gen•try (jĕn′trē) ▸*n.*, *pl.* **-tries 1.** People of

good family or high social position. **2.** The class of English landowners ranking just below the nobility. [< OFr. *genterise*, nobility < OFr. *gentil*, noble. See GENTLE.]

gen•u•flect (jĕn′yə-flĕkt′) ►*v.* To bend the knee or touch one knee to the floor or ground, as in worship. [LLat. *genūflectere*.] —**gen′u•flec′tion** *n.*

gen•u•ine (jĕn′yo͞o-ĭn) ►*adj.* **1.** Actually possessing the alleged or apparent attribute or character. **2.** Not spurious or counterfeit. See Syns at **authentic.** [Lat. *genuīnus*, natural.] —**gen′u•ine•ly** *adv.* —**gen′u•ine•ness** *n.*

ge•nus (jē′nəs) ►*n., pl.* **gen•er•a** (jĕn′ər-ə) **1.** *Biol.* The category ranking below a family and above a species in the hierarchy of taxonomic classification. **2.** A class, group, or kind with common attributes. [Lat., a kind.]

-geny ►*suff.* Production; origin: *ontogeny.* [< Gk. *-genēs*, born.]

geo– ►*pref.* **1.** Earth: *geocentric.* **2.** Geography: *geopolitics.* [< Gk. *gē*, earth.]

ge•o•cen•tric (jē′ō-sĕn′trĭk) ►*adj.* **1.** Of or measured from the center of the earth. **2.** Having the earth as a center. —**ge′o•cen′tri•cal•ly** *adv.*

ge•o•chro•nol•o•gy (jē′ō-krə-nŏl′ə-jē) ►*n.* The chronology of the earth's history as determined by geologic events. —**ge′o•chron′o•log′ic** (-krŏn′ə-lŏj′ĭk), **ge′o•chron′o•log′i•cal** *adj.* —**ge′o•chro•nol′o•gist** *n.*

ge•ode (jē′ōd′) ►*n.* A hollow, usu. spheroidal rock with crystals lining the inside wall. [< Gk. *geōdēs*, earthlike : GEO– + –OID.]

ge•o•des•ic (jē′ə-dĕs′ĭk, -dē′sĭk) ►*n.* The shortest line between two points on any mathematically defined surface, such as a sphere. ►*adj.* Of geodeosy or a geodesic.

geodesic dome ►*n.* A domed or vaulted structure of lightweight straight elements that form interlocking polygons.

geodesic dome

ge•od•e•sy (jē-ŏd′ĭ-sē) ►*n.* The geologic science of the size and shape of the earth. [< Gk. *geōdaisia*.] —**ge•od′e•sist** *n.*

Geof•frey of Mon•mouth (jĕf′rē; mŏn′məth). 1100?–54. English prelate and chronicler.

ge•og•ra•phy (jē-ŏg′rə-fē) ►*n., pl.* **-phies 1.** The science dealing with the earth's natural features, climate, resources, and population. **2.** The physical characteristics, esp. the surface features, of an area. **3.** A book on geography. —**ge•og′ra•pher** *n.* —**ge′o•graph′ic** (jē′ə-grăf′ĭk) *adj.* —**ge′o•graph′i•cal•ly** *adv.*

ge•ol•o•gy (jē-ŏl′ə-jē) ►*n., pl.* **-gies 1.** The science of the origin, history, and structure of the earth. **2.** The structure of a specific region of the earth's crust. —**ge′o•log′ic** (jē′ə-lŏj′ĭk), **ge′o•log′i•cal** *adj.* —**ge′o•log′i•cal•ly** *adv.* —**ge•ol′o•gist** *n.*

ge•o•mag•net•ism (jē′ō-măg′nĭ-tĭz′əm) ►*n.* The magnetism of the earth. —**ge′o•mag•net′ic** (-nĕt′ĭk) *adj.* —**ge′o•mag•net′i•cal•ly** *adv.*

geometric progression ►*n. Math.* A sequence, such as 1, 3, 9, 27, 81, in which each term is multiplied by the same factor to obtain the next term.

ge•om•e•try (jē-ŏm′ĭ-trē) ►*n., pl.* **-tries 1.** The mathematics of the properties, measurement, and relationships of points, lines, angles, surfaces, and solids. **2.** Configuration; arrangement. **3.** A surface shape. [< Gk. *geōmetrein*, measure land.] —**ge′o•met′ric** (jē′ə-mĕt′rĭk) *adj.* —**ge′o•met′ri•cal•ly** *adv.* —**ge•om′e•tri′cian** (jē-ŏm′ĭ-trĭsh′ən, jē′ə-mĭ-), **ge•om′e•ter** *n.*

ge•o•phys•ics (jē′ō-fĭz′ĭks) ►*n. (takes sing. v.)* The physics of geologic phenomena. —**ge′o•phys′i•cal** *adj.* —**ge′o•phys′i•cal•ly** *adv.* —**ge′o•phys′i•cist** (-ĭ-sĭst) *n.*

ge•o•pol•i•tics (jē′ō-pŏl′ĭ-tĭks) ►*n. (takes sing. v.)* The study of the relationship between politics and geography. —**ge′o•po•lit′i•cal** (-pə-lĭt′ĭ-kəl) *adj.* —**ge′o•po•lit′i•cal•ly** *adv.*

George (jŏrj), Saint. d. c. A.D. 303. Christian martyr and patron saint of England.

George I. 1660–1727. King of Great Britain and Ireland (1714–27).

George II. 1683–1760. King of Great Britain and Ireland (1727–60).

George III. 1738–1820. King of Great Britain and Ireland (1760–1820).

George IV. 1762–1830. King of Great Britain and Ireland (1820–30).

George V. 1865–1936. King of Great Britain and Northern Ireland (1910–36).

George VI. 1895–1952. King of Great Britain and Northern Ireland (1936–52).

Geor•ges Bank (jôr′jĭz) A submerged sandbank in the Atlantic E of Cape Cod, MA.

George•town (jôrj′toun′) **1.** The capital of the Cayman Is., on Grand Cayman in the West Indies W of Jamaica. Pop. 7,617. **2.** The capital of Guyana, in the N part on the Atlantic coast. Pop. 78,500.

George Town. A city of W Malaysia on Pinang I. in the Strait of Malacca. Pop. 250,578.

Geor•gia (jôr′jə) **1.** A region and republic of Asia Minor in the Caucasus on the Black Sea S of Russia. Cap. Tbilisi. Pop. 5,450,000. **2.** A state of the SE US. Cap. Atlanta. Pop. 6,508,419. —**Geor′gian** *adj. & n.*

Georgia, Strait of. A channel that separates Vancouver I. from mainland British Columbia and N WA State.

ge•o•sta•tion•ar•y (jē′ō-stā′shə-nĕr′ē) ►*adj.* Of or being a satellite that travels above the earth's equator at a speed matching that of the earth's rotation, thus remaining stationary in relation to the earth.

ge•o•syn•chro•nous (jē′ō-sĭng′krə-nəs, -sĭn′-) ►*adj.* Geostationary. —**ge′o•syn′chro•nous•ly** *adv.*

ge•o•ther•mal (jē′ō-thûr′məl) also **ge•o•ther•mic** (-mĭk) ►*adj.* Of or relating to the internal heat of the earth. —**ge′o•ther′mal•ly** *adv.*

Ger. ▸*abbr.* German

ge•ra•ni•um (jə-rā′nē-əm) ▸*n.* **1.** A plant having palmately divided leaves and pink or purplish flowers. **2.** A related plant widely cultivated for its rounded, often variegated leaves and showy clusters of red, pink, or white flowers. [< Gk. *geranos*, crane.]

ger•bil (jûr′bəl) ▸*n.* A small mouselike rodent of arid regions of Africa and Asia Minor. [< NLat. *Gerbillus*, dim. of *gerbō*, JERBOA.]

ger•i•at•rics (jĕr′ē-ăt′rĭks) ▸*n. (takes sing. v.)* The branch of medicine that deals with the diagnosis and treatment of diseases and problems specific to old age. [< Gk. *gēras*, old age.] —**ger′i•at′ric** *adj. & n.*

germ (jûrm) ▸*n.* **1.** *Biol.* A small mass of protoplasm or cells from which a new organism or one of its parts may develop. **2.** The earliest form of an organism; a seed, bud, or spore. **3.** A microorganism, esp. a pathogen. **4.** Something that may serve as the basis of further growth or development: *The germ of an idea.* [< Lat. *germen*, bud.]

Ger•man (jûr′mən) ▸*adj.* Of or relating to Germany or its people or language. ▸*n.* **1.** A native or inhabitant of Germany. **2.** The Germanic language of Germany, Austria, and part of Switzerland.

ger•mane (jər-mān′) ▸*adj.* Being both pertinent and fitting. [< Lat. *germānus*, having the same parents.] —**ger•mane′ly** *adv.* —**ger•mane′ness** *n.*

Ger•man•ic (jər-măn′ĭk) ▸*adj.* **1.** Of or relating to Germany. **2.** Teutonic. **3.** Of or relating to the Germanic languages. ▸*n.* A branch of the Indo-European language family that includes English.

ger•ma•ni•um (jər-mā′nē-əm) ▸*n. Symbol* **Ge** A brittle, crystalline, gray-white element, widely used as a semiconductor and as an alloying agent and catalyst. At. no. 32. See table at **element.** [< Lat. *Germānia*, Germany.]

German measles ▸*n. (takes sing. or pl. v.)* See **rubella.**

German shepherd ▸*n.* A large dog having a dense brownish or black coat and often trained to assist police or the blind.

Ger•ma•ny (jûr′mə-nē) A country of N-central Europe bordered on the N by the Baltic and North seas; formerly divided into **East Germany** and **West Germany** (1949–90). Cap. Berlin. Pop. 81,410,000.

germ cell ▸*n.* An ovum or a sperm cell or one of its developmental precursors.

ger•mi•cide (jûr′mĭ-sīd′) ▸*n.* An agent that kills germs; disinfectant. —**ger′mi•cid′al** (-sīd′l) *adj.*

ger•mi•nal (jûr′mə-nəl) ▸*adj.* **1.** Of or relating to a germ cell. **2.** Of or relating to the earliest stage of development. [< Lat. *germen*, *germin-*, seed.] —**ger′mi•nal•ly** *adv.*

ger•mi•nate (jûr′mə-nāt′) ▸*v.* **-nat•ed, -nat•ing.** To begin or cause to sprout or grow. [< Lat. *germen*, *germin-*, seed.] —**ger′mi•na′tion** *n.* —**ger′mi•na′tive** *adj.*

Ge•ron•i•mo (jə-rŏn′ə-mō′). 1829–1909. Apache leader.

ger•on•toc•ra•cy (jĕr′ən-tŏk′rə-sē) ▸*n., pl.* **-cies.** Government based on rule by elders. —**ge•ron′to•crat′** (jə-rŏn′tə-krăt′) *n.* —**ge•ron′to•crat′ic** *adj.*

ger•on•tol•o•gy (jĕr′ən-tŏl′ə-jē) ▸*n.* The study of the biological, psychological, and sociological phenomena associated with old age and aging. [< Gk. *gerōn*, *geront-*, old man.] —**ge•ron′to•log′i•cal** (jə-rŏn′tə-lŏj′ĭ-kəl), **ge•ron′to•log′ic** *adj.* —**ger′on•tol′o•gist** *n.*

Geronimo

Ger•ry (gĕr′ē), **Elbridge.** 1744–1814. Vice President of the US (1813–14).

ger•ry•man•der (jĕr′ē-măn′dər, gĕr′-) ▸*v.* To divide (a geographic area) into voting districts so as to give unfair advantage to one political party in elections. [After Elbridge GERRY + (SALA)MANDER.] —**ger′ry•man′der** *n.*

Gersh•win (gûrsh′wĭn), **George.** 1898–1937. Amer. composer.

ger•und (jĕr′ənd) ▸*n.* A verbal noun ending in *-ing*, as *singing* in *We admired the choir's singing.* [< Lat. *gerendum*, gerundive of *gerere*, carry on.] —**ge•run′di•al** (jə-rŭn′dē-əl) *adj.*

ge•run•dive (jə-rŭn′dĭv) ▸*n.* A Latin verbal adjective that expresses the notion of fitness or obligation or is used as a future passive participle. [< LLat. *gerundium*, GERUND.]

ge•stalt or **Ge•stalt** (gə-shtält′, -shtôlt′, -stält′, -stôlt′) ▸*n.* A configuration or pattern of elements so unified as a whole that its properties cannot be derived from a simple summation of its parts. [Ger., shape, form.]

Gestalt psychology ▸*n.* The school in psychology holding that psychological, physiological, and behavioral phenomena are irreducible experiential configurations.

Ge•sta•po (gə-stä′pō, -shtä′-) ▸*n.* The German internal security police during the Nazi regime. [Ger. *Ge(heime) Sta(ats)po(lizei)*, secret state police.]

ges•ta•tion (jĕ-stā′shən) ▸*n.* The period of development in the uterus from conception until birth; pregnancy. [< Lat. *gestāre*, bear.] —**ges′tate′** *v.* —**ges′ta•to′ry** (jĕs′tə-tôr′ē, -tōr′ē), **ges•ta′tion•al** *adj.*

ges•tic•u•late (jĕ-stĭk′yə-lāt′) ▸*v.* **-lat•ed, -lat•ing.** To make gestures, esp. while speaking. [< Lat. *gesticulus*, dim. of *gestus*, GESTURE.] —**ges•tic′u•la′tive** *adj.* —**ges•tic′u•la′tor** *n.*

ges•tic•u•la•tion (jĕ-stĭk′yə-lā′shən) ▸*n.* **1.** The act of gesticulating. **2.** An emphatic gesture.

ges•ture (jĕs′chər) ▸*n.* **1.** A motion of the limbs or body made to express thought or to emphasize speech. **2.** An act or remark made as a formality or as a sign of intention or attitude. [< Lat. *gestus* < p.part. of *gerere*, behave.] —**ges′ture** *v.* —**ges′tur•er** *n.*

ge•sund•heit (gə-zo͝ont′hīt′) ▸*interj.* Used to wish good health to a person who has just sneezed. [Ger., health.]

get (gĕt) ▸*v.* **got** (gŏt), **got•ten** (gŏt′n) or **got** or **get•ting 1.** To receive: *got a present from a friend.* **2a.** To go after and bring. **b.** To buy. **3a.** To obtain or acquire: *get knowledge from a book.* **b.** To earn. **4.** To capture. **5.** To reach or catch: *get the bus.* **6.** To contract; catch: *get the flu.* **7.** To understand: *They don't get your point.* **8.** To hear: *Did you get her name?* **9.** To cause to be in a specific condition: *got the shirt clean.* **10a.** To cause to move or go: *Get me out of here!* **b.** To go or come: *We'll get to the hotel at noon.* **11.** To prevail upon: *Get him to come early.* **12.** To take revenge on: *I'll get you for that.* **13.** *Informal* To hit or strike: *The bullet got him in the arm.* **14.** To puzzle or annoy: *His cold manner gets me.* **15.** To begin: *Let's get working on this.* **16.** To become or be: *Get well soon.* **17.** Used in the present perfect: **a.** To have or possess: *I've got lots of friends.* **b.** To have as an obligation: *You've got to see this.* —***phrasal verbs:*** **get across** To make or be understandable. **get along 1.** To be on friendly terms. **2.** To manage with reasonable success. **get around 1.** To evade or circumvent. **2.** To become known; circulate. **get away** To escape. **get by** To manage; survive. **get into** To be interested or involved in: *got into computers.* **get off 1.** To write and send. **2.** To escape from punishment. **get on 1.** To be on friendly terms. **2.** To make progress; continue. **get out 1.** To leave or escape. **2.** To become public: *The secret got out.* **get over** To recover from. **get through** To finish or complete. **get to 1.** To start to deal with: *finally got to the housework.* **2.** To annoy. **get up 1.** To arise, as from bed. **2.** To create or organize. **3.** To find within oneself: *got up the courage to speak.* ▸*n.* Progeny; offspring. —***idioms:*** **get around to** To find the time for. **get away with** To escape the consequences of. **get down to** To give one's attention to. **get even** To obtain revenge. **get somewhere** *Informal* To make progress. [< ON *geta.*]

get•a•way (gĕt′ə-wā′) ▸*n.* **1.** An act of escaping. **2.** The start, as of a race.

get-to•geth•er (gĕt′tə-gĕ*th*′ər) ▸*n.* *Informal* A casual social gathering.

Get•tys•burg (gĕt′ēz-bûrg′) A town of S PA ESE of Chambersburg; site of a Union victory in the Civil War (July 1–3, 1863). Pop. 7,025.

get•up (gĕt′ŭp′) ▸*n.* *Informal* An outfit or costume.

gew•gaw (gyo͞o′gô′, go͞o′-) ▸*n.* A trinket; bauble. [ME *giuegaue.*]

gey•ser (gī′zər) ▸*n.* A natural hot spring that intermittently ejects a column of water and steam into the air. [< ON *geysa*, gush.]

Gha•na (gä′nə, găn′ə) A country of W Africa on the N shore of the Gulf of Guinea. Pop. 16,944,000. —**Gha′na•ian** (gä′nə-yən, gə-nā′ən), **Gha′ni•an** (gä′nē-ən) *adj. & n.*

ghast•ly (găst′lē) ▸*adj.* **-li•er, -li•est 1.** Inspiring shock or revulsion; terrifying. **2.** Resembling ghosts. **3.** Extremely unpleasant. [< ME *gasten*, terrify. See AGHAST.] —**ghast′li•ness** *n.*

Ghats (gôts) Two mountain ranges of S India, the **Eastern Ghats** extending along the coast of the Bay of Bengal, and the **Western Ghats** along the coast of the Arabian Sea.

Ghent (gĕnt) A city of W Belgium WNW of Brussels. Pop. 230,446.

gher•kin (gûr′kĭn) ▸*n.* A small cucumber, esp. one used for pickling. [< Du. *agurk.*]

ghet•to (gĕt′ō) ▸*n., pl.* **-tos** or **-toes 1.** A section of a city occupied by a minority group who live there esp. because of social, economic, or legal pressure. **2.** An often walled quarter in a European city to which Jews were restricted beginning in the Middle Ages. [Ital.]

ghet•to•ize (gĕt′ō-īz′) ▸*v.* **-ized, -iz•ing.** To set apart in or as if in a ghetto. —**ghet′to•i•za′tion** *n.*

ghost (gōst) ▸*n.* **1.** The spirit of a dead person, esp. one believed to haunt living persons. **2.** A faint trace. **3.** A faint false image produced along with the correct television or photographic image. **4.** *Informal* A ghostwriter. ▸*v.* *Informal* To ghostwrite. [< OE *gāst*, spirit.] —**ghost′ly** *adj.*

ghost town ▸*n.* A once thriving town, esp. a boomtown of the American West, that has been completely abandoned.

ghost•writ•er (gōst′rī′tər) ▸*n.* One who writes for and gives credit of authorship to another. —**ghost′write′** *v.*

ghoul (go͞ol) ▸*n.* **1.** One who delights in the revolting, morbid, or loathsome. **2.** A grave robber. **3.** An evil spirit in Muslim folklore believed to plunder graves and feed on corpses. [Ar. *ġūl.*] —**ghoul′ish** *adj.* —**ghoul′ish•ly** *adv.* —**ghoul′ish•ness** *n.*

GHQ ▸*abbr.* general headquarters

gi or **gi.** ▸*abbr.* gill (liquid measure)

GI[1] (jē′ī′) ▸*n.* An enlisted person in or a veteran of the US armed forces. [Abbr. of *government issue.*] —**GI** *adj.*

GI[2] ▸*abbr.* **1.** gastrointestinal **2.** general issue **3.** Government Issue

Gia•co•met•ti (jä-kə-mĕt′ē), **Alberto.** 1901–66. Swiss sculptor and painter.

gi•ant (jī′ənt) ▸*n.* **1.** A person of great size, power, or importance. **2.** *Myth.* A humanlike being of enormous strength and stature. ▸*adj.* Of exceptionally great size, magnitude, or power. [< Gk. *gigas.*]

gi•ant•ess (jī′ən-tĭs) ▸*n.* A female giant.

gib•ber•ish (jĭb′ər-ĭsh) ▸*n.* **1.** Unintelligible or nonsensical talk or writing. **2.** Unnecessarily pretentious or vague language. [Prob. *gibber*, speak nonsense + -ISH.] —**gib′ber** *v.*

gib•bet (jĭb′ĭt) ▸*n.* A gallows. ▸*v.* **-bet•ed, -bet•ing** or **-bet•ted, -bet•ting 1.** To execute by hanging on a gibbet. **2.** To expose to public ridicule. [< OFr. *gibe*, staff.]

gib•bon (gĭb′ən) ▸*n.* Any of several small arboreal apes of SE Asia and the East Indies, having a slender body, long arms, and no tail. [Fr.]

Gibbon, Edward. 1737–94. British historian.

gib•bous (gĭb′əs) ▸*adj.* More than half but less than fully illuminated: *the gibbous moon.* [< Lat. *gibbus*, hump.] —**gib′bous•ly** *adv.*

gibe also **jibe** (jīb) ▸*v.* **gibed, gib•ing** also **jibed, jib•ing.** To make taunting, heckling, or jeering remarks. [Poss. < OFr. *giber*, handle roughly.] —**gibe** *n.* —**gib′er** *n.* —**gib′ing•ly** *adv.*

gib•lets (jĭb′lĭts) ▸*pl.n.* The heart, liver, and gizzard of a fowl. [< OFr. *gibelet*, game stew.]

Gi•bral•tar (jə-brôl′tər) A British colony at the NW end of the **Rock of Gibraltar**, a peninsula on the S-central coast of Spain in the **Strait of Gibraltar,** connecting the Mediterranean and the Atlantic between Spain and N Africa. Pop. 31,874

Gibraltar

Gib•son (gĭb′sən), **Althea.** b. 1927. Amer. tennis player.

Althea Gibson
at Wimbledon in 1957

gid•dy (gĭd′ē) ►*adj.* **-di•er, -di•est 1a.** Dizzy. **b.** Causing dizziness: *a giddy climb.* **2.** Frivolous; flighty. ►*v.* **-died, -dy•ing.** To become or make giddy. [< OE *gidig.*] —**gid′di•ly** *adv.* —**gid′di•ness** *n.*
Syns: *giddy, dizzy, vertiginous* **adj.**

Gide (zhēd), **André.** 1869–1951. French writer; 1947 Nobel.

gift (gĭft) ►*n.* **1.** Something bestowed voluntarily and without compensation. **2.** The act, right, or power of giving. **3.** A talent or aptitude. [< ON.]

gift•ed (gĭf′tĭd) ►*adj.* **1.** Endowed with great natural ability, intelligence, or talent. **2.** Revealing special talent. —**gift′ed•ness** *n.*

gig¹ (gĭg) ►*n.* **1.** A light, two-wheeled horse-drawn carriage. **2.** A long, light ship's boat. [< obsolete *gig*, spinning top.]

gig² (gĭg) ►*n.* A pronged spear for fishing. [< *fishgig*, spear for fishing.] —**gig** *v.*

gig³ (gĭg) ►*n. Slang* A demerit given in the military. [?] —**gig** *v.*

gig⁴ (gĭg) ►*n. Slang* A job, esp. a booking for musicians. [?]

giga– ►*pref.* One billion (10^9): *gigahertz.* [< Gk. *gigas*, giant.]

gig•a•byte (jĭg′ə-bīt′, gĭg′-) ►*n.* A unit of computer memory equal to 1,024 megabytes (2^{30} bytes).

gig•a•hertz (jĭg′ə-hûrtz′, gĭg′-) ►*n.* One billion cycles per second.

gi•gan•tic (jī-găn′tĭk) ►*adj.* Extremely large or extensive; huge. [< Gk. *gigas, gigant-*, giant.] —**gi•gan′ti•cal•ly** *adv.*

gig•gle (gĭg′əl) ►*v.* **-gled, -gling.** To laugh in a half-suppressed or nervous way. [Imit.] —**gig′gle** *n.* —**gig′gler** *n.* —**gig′gly** *adj.*

gig•o•lo (jĭg′ə-lō′, zhĭg′-) ►*n., pl.* **-los 1.** A man supported financially by a woman in return for sexual favors. **2.** A professional male escort. [Fr.]

Gi•jón (hē-hōn′) A city of NW Spain on the Bay of Biscay W of Santander. Pop. 259,067.

Gi•la monster (hē′lə) ►*n.* A venomous lizard of arid regions of the SW US and W Mexico. [After the GILA RIVER.]

Gila River. A river rising in the mountains of W NM and flowing about 1,014 km (630 mi) across S AZ to the Colorado R..

Gil•bert (gĭl′bərt), Sir **William Schwenck.** 1836–1911. British playwright and lyricist.

Gilbert Islands. A group of islands of W Kiribati in the central Pacific.

gild (gĭld) ►*v.* **gild•ed** or **gilt** (gĭlt), **gild•ing 1.** To cover with or as if with a thin layer of gold. **2.** To give an often deceptively attractive appearance to. [< OE *gyldan.*]

Gil•e•ad (gĭl′ē-əd) A mountainous region of ancient Palestine E of the Jordan R.

gill¹ (gĭl) ►*n.* The respiratory organ of most aquatic animals that breathe water to obtain oxygen. [ME *gile.*] —**gilled** *adj.*

gill² (jĭl) ►*n.* **1.** See table at **measurement. 2.** A unit of volume equal to ¼ of a British Imperial pint (142 ml). [< LLat. *gillō*, vessel.]

gil•ly•flow•er (jĭl′ē-flou′ər) ►*n.* A carnation or other plant with fragrant flowers. [< Gk. *karuophullon*, clove.]

gilt (gĭlt) ►*v.* P.t. and p.part. of **gild.** ►*adj.* Gilded. ►*n.* A thin layer of gold or goldlike material applied in gilding.

gilt-edged (gĭlt′ĕjd′) ►*adj.* **1.** Having gilded edges, as book pages. **2.** Of the highest quality or value: *gilt-edged securities.*

gim•bal (gĭm′bəl, jĭm′-) ►*n.* often **gimbals.** A device consisting of two rings mounted on axes at right angles to each other so that an object, such as a ship's compass, will remain suspended in a horizontal plane between them regardless of any motion of its support. [< Lat. *gemellus*, twin.]

gim•crack (jĭm′krăk′) ►*n.* A cheap showy object of little or no use. [Poss. < ME *gibecrake*, ornament.] —**gim′crack′er•y** *n.*

gim•let (gĭm′lĭt) ►*n.* **1.** A small hand tool used for boring holes. **2.** A cocktail made with vodka or gin and sweetened lime juice. [< AN *guimbelet.*]

gim•mick (gĭm′ĭk) ►*n.* **1.** A device employed to cheat, deceive, or trick. **2.** A stratagem used esp. to promote a project. **3.** A significant feature that is obscured or misrepresented; catch. [?] —**gim′mick•ry** *n.* —**gim′mick•y** *adj.*

gimp (gĭmp) ►*n. Slang* A limp or limping gait. [?] —**gimp** *v.* —**gimp′y** *adj.*

gin¹ (jĭn) ►*n.* A strong, colorless alcoholic liquor distilled from grain spirits and flavored usu. with juniper berries. [< VLat. **iiniperus*, JUNIPER.] —**gin′ny** *adj.*

gin² (jĭn) ►*n.* **1.** A snare or trap for game. **2.** A cotton gin. ►*v.* **ginned, gin•ning.** To remove the seeds from (cotton) with a cotton gin. [< OFr. < *engin*, skill. See ENGINE.]

gin³ (jĭn) ►*n.* Gin rummy.

gin•ger (jĭn′jər) ►*n.* **1.** A plant of SE Asia having a pungent aromatic rhizome. **2.** The rhizome of this plant, used as a spice. **3.** *Informal* Liveliness; vigor. [< Gk. *zingiberis.*] —**gin′ger•y** *adj.*

ginger ale ►*n.* A carbonated soft drink flavored with ginger.

gin•ger•bread (jĭn′jər-brĕd′) ►*n.* **1.** A dark molasses cake flavored with ginger. **2.** Elaborate ornamentation, esp. in architecture.

gin•ger•ly (jĭn′jər-lē) ►*adv.* With great care; cautiously. [Poss. < OFr. *gensor*, gentler.] —**gin′ger•li•ness** *n.* —**gin′ger•ly** *adj.*

gin•ger•snap (jĭn′jər-snăp′) ►*n.* A flat brittle cookie spiced with ginger and sweetened with molasses.

ging•ham (gĭng′əm) ►*n.* A yarn-dyed cotton fabric woven in stripes, checks, plaids, or solid colors. [< Malay *ginggang.*]

gin•gi•va (jĭn′jə-və, jĭn-jī′-) ►*n., pl.* **-vae** (-vē′). See **gum²**. [< Lat. *gingīva.*]

gin•gi•vi•tis (jĭn′jə-vī′tĭs) ►*n.* Inflammation of the gums.

gink•go also **ging•ko** (gĭng′kō) ►*n., pl.* **-goes** also **-koes.** A Chinese tree having fan-shaped leaves and fleshy yellowish seeds with a disagreeable odor. [J. *ginkyō*, silver apricot.]

gin rummy ►*n.* A variety of rummy in which a player may win by matching all his or her cards or may end the game by melding.

Gins•berg (gĭnz′bərg), **Allen.** 1926–97. Amer. poet.

gin•seng (jĭn′sĕng′) ►*n.* A plant of E Asia or North America, having forked roots believed to have medicinal properties. [Mandarin *rén shēn.*]

ginseng

Gior•gio•ne (jôr-jō′nē, -nĕ). 1478?–1510. Italian painter.

Giot•to (jŏt′ō, jō′tō). 1267?–1337. Florentine painter, architect, and sculptor.

gip (jĭp) ►*v. & n. Slang* Var. of **gyp.**

Gip•sy (jĭp′sē) ►*n.* Var. of **Gypsy.**

gi•raffe (jə-răf′) ►*n., pl.* **-raffes** or **-raffe.** An African ruminant with a long neck and legs, a tan coat with orange-brown blotches, and short horns. [< Ar. dial. *zirāfa.*]

Gi•rau•doux (zhē-rō-do͞o′), **(Hippolyte) Jean.** 1882–1944. French writer.

gird (gûrd) ►*v.* **gird•ed** or **girt** (gûrt), **gird•ing 1.** To encircle or fasten with a belt or band. **2.** To surround. See Syns at **surround. 3.** To prepare (oneself) for action. [< OE *gyrdan.*]

gird•er (gûr′dər) ►*n.* A strong horizontal beam used as a main support in building.

gir•dle (gûr′dl) ►*n.* **1.** A belt or sash worn around the waist. **2.** A woman's elasticized flexible undergarment worn over the waist and hips. ►*v.* **-dled, -dling.** To encircle with or as if with a belt. See Syns at **surround.** [< OE *gyrdel.*] —**gird′ler** *n.*

girl (gûrl) ►*n.* A female child or youth. [ME *girle.*] —**girl′hood′** *n.* —**girl′ish** *adj.* —**girl′ish•ly** *adv.* —**girl′ish•ness** *n.*

girl•friend (gûrl′frĕnd′) ►*n.* **1.** A favored female companion or sweetheart. **2.** A female friend.

Girl Scout ►*n.* A member of an organization of young women and girls founded for character development and citizenship training.

girth (gûrth) ►*n.* **1.** The distance around something; circumference. **2.** A strap encircling an animal's body in order to secure a load or saddle. [< ON *gjördh*, girdle.]

Gis•card d'Es•taing (zhĭ-skär′ dĕs-tăng′, -tăN′), **Valéry.** b. 1926. French president (1974–81).

gist (jĭst) ►*n.* The central idea; essence. See Syns at **substance.** [< AN, it lies.]

give (gĭv) ►*v.* **gave** (gāv), **giv•en** (gĭv′ən), **giv•ing 1.** To make a present of: *We gave her flowers.* **2.** To place in the hands of; pass: *Give me the scissors.* **3.** To deliver in exchange or recompense; pay: *give five dollars for the book.* **4.** To administer: *gave him some medicine.* **5a.** To convey: *Give her my best wishes.* **b.** To inflict, esp. as punishment: *She gave me a bloody nose.* **6.** To grant or bestow: *give permission.* **7.** To furnish or contribute: *gave time to help others.* **8.** To permit one to have or take: *Give me an hour to get ready.* **9.** To emit or utter: *gave a groan.* **10.** To submit for consideration or opinion: *give me your opinion.* **11.** To offer as entertainment: *give a party.* **12.** To cause to catch: *The draft gave me a cold.* **13.** To yield or produce: *Cows give milk.* —***phrasal verbs:*** **give away 1.** To make a gift of. **2.** To present (a bride) to the bridegroom at a wedding ceremony. **3.** To expose or betray. **give back** To return. **give in** To surrender; yield. **give off** To send forth; emit: *The radiator gave off heat.* **give out 1.** To distribute. **2.** To break down. **3.** To become used up. **give up 1.** To surrender. **2.** To stop: *gave up smoking.* **3.** To part with; relinquish. ►*n.* Resilience; springiness. —***idioms:*** **give it to** *Informal* To punish or reprimand. **give way 1.** To yield the right of way. **2.** To collapse. [< OE *giefan* and ON *gefa.*] —**giv′er** *n.*

give-and-take (gĭv′ən-tāk′) ►*n.* **1.** The practice of compromise. **2.** Lively exchange of ideas or conversation.

give•a•way (gĭv′ə-wā′) ►*n.* **1.** Something given away at no charge. **2.** Something that accidentally exposes or betrays.

giv•en (gĭv′ən) ►*v.* P.part. of **give.** ►*adj.* **1.** Specified; fixed: *meet at a given time.* **2.** Granted as a supposition; acknowledged or assumed. **3.** Having a tendency; inclined: *given to lavish spending.* —**giv′en** *n.*

given name ►*n.* A name given at birth or at baptism as distinguished from a surname.

Gi•za (gē′zə) A city of N Egypt on the Nile R.; site of the Great Pyramids and the Sphinx. Pop. 2,144,000.

giz•zard (gĭz′ərd) ►*n.* A digestive organ in

birds, often containing ingested grit. [< Lat. *gigēria*, cooked entrails of poultry.]

Gk. ▸ *abbr.* Greek

gla•cial (glā′shəl) ▸ *adj.* **1.** Of or derived from a glacier. **2.** Marked or dominated by the existence of glaciers: *a glacial epoch.* **3.** Extremely cold. See Syns at **cold.** [< Lat. *glaciālis*, icy < *glaciēs*, ice.] —**gla′cial•ly** *adv.*

gla•ci•ate (glā′shē-āt′, -sē-) ▸ *v.* **-at•ed, -at•ing 1.** To subject to glacial action. **2.** To freeze. [< Lat. *glaciēs*, ice.] —**gla′ci•a′tion** *n.*

gla•cier (glā′shər) ▸ *n.* A huge mass of ice slowly flowing over a land mass, formed from compacted snow. [< Lat. *glaciēs*, ice.]

Glacier Bay. A narrow inlet of the Pacific in SE AK NW of Juneau.

glad (glăd) ▸ *adj.* **glad•der, glad•dest 1.** Experiencing, showing, or giving joy and pleasure. **2.** Very willing: *glad to help.* [< OE *glæd.*] —**glad′ly** *adv.* —**glad′ness** *n.*

glad•den (glăd′n) ▸ *v.* To make glad. See Syns at **please.**

glade (glād) ▸ *n.* An open space in a forest. [ME, perh. < *glad*, shining. See GLAD.]

glad hand ▸ *n. Informal* A hearty but often insincere greeting. —**glad′-hand′** *v.* —**glad′-hand′er** *n.*

glad•i•a•tor (glăd′ē-ā′tər) ▸ *n.* A man trained to entertain the public by engaging in mortal combat in ancient Roman arenas. [< Lat. *gladius*, sword.] —**glad′i•a•to′ri•al** (-ə-tôr′ē-əl, -tōr′-) *adj.*

glad•i•o•lus (glăd′ē-ō′ləs) ▸ *n., pl.* **-li** (-lī, -lē) or **-lus•es.** Any of a genus of plants having sword-shaped leaves and showy, variously colored flowers. [< Lat., wild iris, dim. of *gladius*, sword.]

glad•some (glăd′səm) ▸ *adj.* Causing or showing gladness or joy. —**glad′some•ly** *adv.*

Glad•stone (glăd′stōn′, -stən), **William Ewart.** 1809–98. British prime minister (1868–74, 1880–85, 1886, and 1892–94).

glam•or•ize also **glam•our•ize** (glăm′ə-rīz′) ▸ *v.* **-ized, -iz•ing.** To make glamorous. —**glam′or•i•za′tion** *n.* —**glam′or•iz′er** *n.*

glam•our also **glam•or** (glăm′ər) ▸ *n.* An air of compelling charm, romance, and excitement. [Sc., magic spell, alteration of GRAMMAR.] —**glam′or•ous** *adj.* —**glam′or•ous•ly** *adv.* —**glam′or•ous•ness** *n.*

glance (glăns) ▸ *v.* **glanced, glanc•ing 1.** To direct the gaze briefly. **2.** To strike a surface and be deflected. See Syns at **brush**[1]**.** ▸ *n.* **1.** A brief or cursory look. **2.** A gleam. [ME *glauncen* < OFr. *glacer*, to slide.]

glanc•ing (glăn′sĭng) ▸ *adj.* **1.** Oblique in direction; deflected. **2.** Not straightforward; indirect. —**glanc′ing•ly** *adv.*

gland (glănd) ▸ *n.* An organ that produces a secretion for use elsewhere in the body. [< Lat. *glāns, gland-*, acorn.] —**glan′du•lar** (glăn′jə-lər) *adj.* —**glan′du•lar•ly** *adv.*

glans (glănz) ▸ *n., pl.* **glan•des** (glăn′dēz). The tip of the penis or clitoris. [Lat. *glāns*, acorn.]

glare[1] (glâr) ▸ *v.* **glared, glar•ing 1.** To stare fixedly and angrily. **2.** To shine intensely and blindingly. **3.** To stand out obtrusively. ▸ *n.* **1.** A fierce or angry stare. **2.** An intense, blinding light. [ME *glaren*, glitter.]

glare[2] (glâr) ▸ *n.* A sheet or surface of glassy and very slippery ice. [Prob. < GLARE[1].]

glar•ing (glâr′ĭng) ▸ *adj.* **1.** Shining intensely. **2.** Conspicuous; obvious. **3.** Staring with anger or hostility. —**glar′ing•ly** *adv.*

Glas•gow (glăs′kō, -gō, glăz′-) A city of SW Scotland on the Clyde R. Pop. 681,470.

glas•nost (gläs′nəst, -nôst) ▸ *n.* An official policy of the former Soviet government emphasizing candid discussion of social problems. [Russ. *glasnost'*, public information.]

glass (glăs) ▸ *n.* **1.** Any of a large class of materials that solidify from the molten state without crystallization, are gen. transparent or translucent, and are considered to be supercooled liquids rather than true solids. **2.** Something usu. made of glass, esp.: **a.** A drinking vessel. **b.** A mirror. **c.** A window or windowpane. **3. glasses** A pair of lenses mounted in a light frame, used to correct faulty vision or protect the eyes. **4.** The quantity contained by a drinking vessel; glassful. [< OE *glæs.*] —**glass′i•ly** *adv.* —**glass′i•ness** *n.* —**glass′y** *adj.*

glass ceiling ▸ *n.* An unofficial discriminatory barrier that keeps women and minorities from positions of power, as in a corporation.

glau•co•ma (glou-kō′mə, glô-) ▸ *n.* An eye disease characterized by abnormally high intraocular fluid pressure, hardening of the eyeball, and partial to complete loss of vision. [< Gk. *glaukōma*, cataract.]

glau•cous (glô′kəs) ▸ *adj.* Of a pale grayish green. [Lat. *glaucus* < Gk. *glaukos.*]

glaze (glāz) ▸ *n.* **1.** A thin, smooth, shiny coating, as on ceramics. **2.** A thin glassy coating of ice. **3.** A coating, as of syrup, applied to food. ▸ *v.* **glazed, glaz•ing 1.** To furnish with glass: *glaze a window.* **2.** To apply a glaze to. **3.** To become glassy. [ME *glasen* < *glas*, GLASS.] —**glaz′er** *n.*

gla•zier (glā′zhər) ▸ *n.* One that cuts and fits glass, as for windows. —**gla′zier•y** *n.*

gleam (glēm) ▸ *n.* **1.** A brief flash of light. **2.** A steady but subdued shining; glow. **3.** A brief or dim indication: *a gleam of intelligence.* ▸ *v.* **1.** To flash or glow. **2.** To be manifested briefly or faintly. [< OE *glǣm.*]

glean (glēn) ▸ *v.* **1.** To gather grain left behind by reapers. **2.** To collect bit by bit. [< LLat. *glennāre.*] —**glean′er** *n.* —**glean′ings** *pl.n.*

glee (glē) ▸ *n.* **1.** Jubilant delight; joy. **2.** An unaccompanied choral song. [< OE *glēo.*] —**glee′ful** *adj.* —**glee′ful•ly** *adv.*

glee club ▸ *n.* A group of singers who perform usu. short pieces of choral music.

glen (glĕn) ▸ *n.* A valley. [< OIr. *glenn.*]

Glen•dale (glĕn′dāl′) **1.** A city of S-central AZ, a suburb of Phoenix. Pop. 148,134. **2.** A city of S CA, a suburb of Los Angeles. Pop. 180,038.

Glenn (glĕn), **John Herschel, Jr.** b. 1921. Amer. astronaut and politician.

glib (glĭb) ▸ *adj.* **glib•ber, glib•best.** Marked by verbal ease and fluency that often suggests insincerity or superficiality. [Poss. of LGer. orig.] —**glib′ly** *adv.* —**glib′ness** *n.*

glide (glīd) ▸ *v.* **glid•ed, glid•ing 1.** To move smoothly and effortlessly. **2.** To fly without propulsion. [< OE *glīdan.*] —**glide** *n.*

glid•er (glī′dər) ▸ *n.* **1.** A light engineless aircraft designed to glide after being towed aloft. **2.** A swinging couch suspended from a vertical frame.

glim•mer (glĭm′ər) ►*n.* **1.** A dim or intermittent light. **2.** A faint suggestion or indication. ►*v.* **1.** To give off a glimmer. **2.** To appear faintly. [< ME *glimeren,* to glitter.]

glimpse (glĭmps) ►*n.* A brief, incomplete look. ►*v.* **glimpsed, glimps•ing.** To get a glimpse of. [< ME *glimsen,* to glance.]

glint (glĭnt) ►*n.* A brief flash of light; sparkle. [ME *glent.*] —**glint** *v.*

glis•san•do (glĭ-sän′dō) ►*n., pl.* **-di** (-dē) or **-dos.** A rapid slide through a series of consecutive musical tones. [< Fr. *glissade,* a sliding.]

glis•ten (glĭs′ən) ►*v.* To shine with reflected light. [< OE *glisnian.*] —**glis′ten** *n.*

glitch (glĭch) ►*n.* **1.** A minor malfunction. **2.** A false electronic signal caused by a brief power surge. [Yiddish *glitsh,* a slip.]

glit•ter (glĭt′ər) ►*n.* **1.** A sparkling or glistening light. **2.** Showy, often superficial attractiveness. **3.** Small pieces of reflective decorative material. ►*v.* To sparkle brilliantly; glisten. [< ON *glitra,* to sparkle.] —**glit′ter•ing•ly** *adv.* —**glit′ter•y** *adj.*

glitz (glĭts) ►*n. Informal* Ostentatious showiness; flashiness. [Prob. < Ger. *glitzern,* to glitter.] —**glitz′i•ness** *n.* —**glitz′y** *adj.*

gloam•ing (glō′mĭng) ►*n.* Twilight; dusk. [< OE *glōm.*]

gloat (glōt) ►*v.* To feel or express great, often malicious, pleasure or self-satisfaction. [Perh. of Scand. orig.] —**gloat′er** *n.*

glob (glŏb) ►*n.* **1.** A globule. **2.** A soft lump or mass. [< Lat. *globus,* globular mass.]

glob•al (glō′bəl) ►*adj.* **1.** Involving the entire earth; worldwide. **2.** Comprehensive; total. **3.** *Comp. Sci.* Of an entire program or document. —**glob′al•i•za′tion** *n.* —**glob′al•ize′** *v.* —**glob′al•ly** *adv.*

Global Positioning System ►*n.* A system for determining one's position on the earth by comparing radio signals received from different satellites.

global warming ►*n.* An increase in the average temperature of the earth's atmosphere, esp. one sufficient to cause climatic change.

globe (glōb) ►*n.* **1.** A spherical body, esp. a model of the earth as a hollow ball. **2.** The earth. **3.** A spherical or bowllike object. [< Lat. *globus.*]

globe artichoke ►*n.* See **artichoke.**

globe•trot (glōb′trŏt′) ►*v.* To travel widely, esp. for sightseeing. —**globe′trot′ter** *n.* —**globe′trot′ting** *n.*

glob•u•lar (glŏb′yə-lər) ►*adj.* **1.** Spherical. **2.** Consisting of globules. —**glob′u•lar•ly** *adv.* —**glob′u•lar•ness** *n.*

glob•ule (glŏb′yo͞ol) ►*n.* A small spherical mass, as of liquid. [< Lat. *globulus.*]

glob•u•lin (glŏb′yə-lĭn) ►*n.* Any of a class of proteins found extensively in blood plasma, milk, muscle, and plant seeds.

glock•en•spiel (glŏk′ən-spēl′, -shpēl′) ►*n.* A percussion instrument with a series of metal bars played with two light hammers. [Ger.]

gloom (glo͞om) ►*n.* **1.** Partial or total darkness. **2.** A state of melancholy or depression. [Prob. < ME *gloumen,* become dark.]

gloom•y (glo͞o′mē) ►*adj.* **-i•er, -i•est 1.** Partially or totally dark. **2.** Showing or filled with gloom. **3.** Causing gloom; depressing. —**gloom′i•ly** *adv.* —**gloom′i•ness** *n.*

glo•ri•fy (glôr′ə-fī′, glōr′-) ►*v.* **-fied, -fy•ing 1.** To give honor or high praise to; exalt. **2.** To exaggerate the glory or excellence of. **3.** To worship; extol. [< Lat. *glōrificāre.*] —**glo′ri•fi•ca′tion** *n.* —**glo′ri•fi′er** *n.*

glo•ri•ous (glôr′ē-əs, glōr′-) ►*adj.* **1.** Having or deserving glory; famous. **2.** Splendid; magnificent. **3.** Delightful. —**glo′ri•ous•ly** *adv.* —**glo′ri•ous•ness** *n.*

glo•ry (glôr′ē, glōr′ē) ►*n., pl.* **-ries 1.** Great honor or distinction; renown. **2.** A highly praiseworthy asset. **3.** Adoration and praise offered in worship. **4.** Majestic beauty. **5.** A height of achievement, enjoyment, or prosperity. ►*v.* **-ried, -ry•ing.** To rejoice triumphantly; exult. [< Lat. *glōria.*]

gloss[1] (glôs, glŏs) ►*n.* **1.** Surface shine; luster. **2.** A superficially attractive appearance. ►*v.* To make attractive or acceptable esp. by superficial treatment: *glossed over the candidate's faults.* See Syns at **palliate.** [Perh. of Scand. orig.]

gloss[2] (glôs, glŏs) ►*n.* **1.** A brief explanatory note or translation of a difficult or technical expression. **2.** A translation or commentary accompanying a text. ►*v.* To provide (e.g., a text) with a gloss. [< LLat. *glōssa,* foreign word < Gk., language.] —**gloss′er** *n.*

glos•sa•ry (glô′sə-rē, glŏs′ə-) ►*n., pl.* **-ries.** A list of difficult or specialized words with their definitions. [< Lat. *glōssārium.*]

gloss•y (glô′sē, glŏs′ē) ►*adj.* **-i•er, -i•est 1.** Having a smooth shiny surface. See Syns at **sleek. 2.** Superficially attractive; slick. ►*n., pl.* **-ies.** A photographic print on smooth shiny paper. —**gloss′i•ly** *adv.* —**gloss′i•ness** *n.*

glot•tal stop (glŏt′l) ►*n.* A speech sound produced by closure and release of the glottis.

glot•tis (glŏt′ĭs) ►*n., pl.* **-tis•es** or **glot•ti•des** (glŏt′ĭ-dēz′). The opening between the vocal cords at the upper part of the larynx. [Gk. *glōttis* < *glōtta,* tongue.]

glove (glŭv) ►*n.* **1.** A fitted covering for the hand with a separate sheath for each finger and the thumb. **2.** *Sports* An oversized padded leather covering for the hand, esp. one used in baseball or boxing. [< OE *glōf.*] —**glove** *v.*

glow (glō) ►*v.* **1.** To shine brightly and steadily, esp. without a flame. **2.** To have a bright ruddy color. **3.** To be exuberant or radiant: *glowing with pride.* ►*n.* **1.** A light produced by a heated body. **2.** Brilliance or warmth of color. **3.** A warm feeling. [< OE *glōwan.*] —**glow′ing** *adj.*

glow•er (glou′ər) ►*v.* To look or stare angrily or sullenly. See Syns at **frown.** [ME *gloren.*] —**glow′er** *n.* —**glow′er•ing•ly** *adv.*

glow•worm (glō′wûrm′) ►*n.* Any of various luminous female beetles or beetle larvae.

glox•in•i•a (glŏk-sĭn′ē-ə) ►*n.* A tropical South American plant grown as a houseplant for its showy, variously colored flowers. [After B.P. *Gloxin,* 18th-cent. botanist.]

gloze (glōz) ►*v.* **glozed, gloz•ing.** To minimize; gloss: *glozed over the errors.* See Syns at **palliate.** [< OFr. *gloser* < *glose,* GLOSS[2].]

glu•ca•gon (glo͞o′kə-gŏn′) ►*n.* A pancreatic hormone that raises blood sugar levels. [Prob. GLUC(OSE) + Gk. *agōn,* pr.part. of *agein,* lead, drive.]

glu•cose (glo͞o′kōs′) ►*n.* **1.** A monosaccharide sugar, $C_6H_{12}O_6$, that occurs widely in most plant and animal tissue and is the major energy source of the body. **2.** A syrupy mixture of dextrose, maltose, and dextrins with water, used in confectionery and alcoholic fermentation. [< Gk. *gleukos*, sweet wine.]

glue (glo͞o) ►*n.* **1.** A strong liquid adhesive, esp. one made from animal parts. **2.** An adhesive force or factor. ►*v.* **glued, glu•ing.** To stick or fasten with or as if with glue. [< Lat. *glūten*.] —**glu′ey** *adj.* —**glu′i•ness** *n.*

glum (glŭm) ►*adj.* **glum•mer, glum•mest.** Moody and melancholy; dejected. [Prob. akin to ME *gloumen*, darken.] —**glum′ly** *adv.* —**glum′ness** *n.*

glu•on (glo͞o′ŏn) ►*n. Phys.* A hypothetical particle believed to mediate the strong interaction that binds quarks. [GLU(E) + –ON[1].]

glut (glŭt) ►*v.* **glut•ted, glut•ting 1.** To fill beyond capacity, esp. with food; satiate. **2.** To flood (a market) so that supply exceeds demand. ►*n.* An oversupply. [< Lat. *gluttīre*, eat greedily.]

glu•ten (glo͞ot′n) ►*n.* A mixture of plant proteins occurring in cereal grains. [< Lat. *glūten*, glue.] —**glu′ten•ous** *adj.*

glu•te•us (glo͞o′tē-əs, glo͞o-tē′-) ►*n., pl.* **-te•i** (-tē-ī′, -tē′ī′). Any of three large muscles of the buttocks. [< Gk. *gloutos*, buttock.] —**glu′te•al** *adj.*

glu•ti•nous (glo͞ot′n-əs) ►*adj.* Gluey; sticky. [< Lat. *glūten*, glue.] —**glu′ti•nous•ness, glu′ti•nos′i•ty** (-ŏs′ĭ-tē) *n.*

glut•ton (glŭt′n) ►*n.* One who eats or consumes immoderate amounts. [< Lat. *gluttō*.] —**glut′ton•y** *n.*

glut•ton•ous (glŭt′n-əs) ►*adj.* **1.** Given to gluttony; greedy. **2.** Inordinately fond or eager. See Syns at **voracious.** —**glut′ton•ous•ly** *adv.*

glyc•er•in also **glyc•er•ine** (glĭs′ər-ĭn) ►*n.* Glycerol. [< Gk. *glukeros*, sweet.]

glyc•er•ol (glĭs′ə-rôl′, -rōl′, -rŏl′) ►*n.* A syrupy liquid obtained from fats and oils and used as a solvent, antifreeze, and sweetener and in making dynamite, soaps, and lubricants. [GLYCER(IN) + –OL.]

gly•co•gen (glī′kə-jən) ►*n.* A polysaccharide, $(C_6H_{10}O_5)_n$, that is the main form of carbohydrate storage in animals and occurs primarily in the liver. [Gk. *glukus*, sweet + –GEN.] —**gly′co•gen′ic** (-jĕn′ĭk) *adj.*

glyph (glĭf) ►*n.* **1.** *Archit.* A vertical groove. **2.** A symbol, such as an informative figure or arrow, on a sign. [Gk. *gluphē*, carving.]

glyph

gm. ►*abbr.* gram

GMT ►*abbr.* Greenwich mean time

GMW ►*abbr.* gram molecular weight

gnarl (närl) ►*n.* A protruding knot on a tree. [< ME *knarre*, knot in wood.] —**gnarled** *adj.*

gnash (năsh) ►*v.* To grind (the teeth) together. [< ME *gnasten*.]

gnat (năt) ►*n.* Any of various small biting flies. [< OE *gnæt*.]

gnaw (nô) ►*v.* **1.** To bite or chew on with the teeth. **2.** To erode or diminish gradually as if by gnawing. **3.** To cause persistent worry or pain. [< OE *gnagan*.] —**gnaw′er** *n.*

gneiss (nīs) ►*n.* A banded, granitelike metamorphic rock. [Ger. *Gneis*.]

GNMA ►*abbr.* Government National Mortgage Association

gnoc•chi (nyô′kē) ►*pl.n.* Dumplings made of flour or potatoes. [Ital.]

gnome (nōm) ►*n.* One of a fabled race of dwarflike creatures who live underground and guard treasure hoards. [< NLat. *gnomus*.] —**gnom′ish** *adj.*

Gnos•tic (nŏs′tĭk) ►*adj.* **1. gnostic** Of or relating to intellectual or spiritual knowledge. **2.** Of Gnosticism. [< Gk. *gnōsis*, knowledge.] —**Gnos′tic** *n.*

Gnos•ti•cism (nŏs′tĭ-sĭz′əm) ►*n.* The doctrines of certain pre-Christian pagan, Jewish, and early Christian sects.

GNP ►*abbr.* gross national product

gnu (no͞o, nyo͞o) ►*n.* A large bearded African antelope with curved horns. [< Xhosa *i-ngu*.]

go[1] (gō) ►*v.* **went** (wĕnt), **gone** (gôn, gŏn), **go•ing, goes** (gōz) **1.** To move or travel. **2.** To move away; depart. **3.** To extend in a certain direction: *The road goes west.* **4.** To function properly: *The car won't go.* **5.** Used to indicate future intent or expectation: *I am going to do it.* **6.** To become: *go mad.* **7.** To continue in a certain condition or continue an activity: *go barefoot all day.* **8.** To belong: *Where do the plates go?* **9.** To be allotted. **10.** To serve: *It goes to show how it is.* **11.** To elapse, as time. **12.** To be used up. **13.** To be discarded or abolished: *The foolish policy has to go.* **14.** To fail: *Her eyes are going.* **15.** To come apart or break up. **16.** To die. **17.** To get along; fare. **18.** To be suitable; harmonize: *The shirt and tie don't go.* **19.** To participate up to: *go halves on a dessert.* **20.** *Informal* To say. —***phrasal verbs:* go about** To undertake: *went about my chores.* **go along** To cooperate. **go down 1.** To fall or sink. **2.** To be accepted: *His proposal went down well.* **3.** To be remembered. **go for** *Informal* To have a liking for. **go off 1.** To be fired; explode. **2.** To make a noise: *The siren went off at noon.* **go on 1.** To happen. **2.** To continue: *Life goes on.* **3.** To proceed. **go out 1.** To be extinguished. **2.** To socialize outside the home. **go over 1.** To gain acceptance. **2.** To examine. **go through 1.** To examine carefully. **2.** To experience; undergo. **go under** To fail or be ruined. ►*n., pl.* **goes 1.** An attempt; try: *had a go at it.* **2.** A turn, as in a game. **3.** *Informal* Energy; vitality: *had lots of go.* —***idioms:* go back on** To fail to honor. **go in for** To have an interest in. **go places** *Informal* To be successful. **go steady** To date someone exclusively. **go to pieces** To lose one's self-control. **on the go** Constantly busy. **to go** To be taken out, as restaurant food. [< OE *gān*.]

Usage: Many speakers now use *go* in informal conversation to report speech, as in *Then he goes, "You think you're* real *smart, don't you?"* This usage is much like that of the quotation introducers *be all* and *be like,* although these constructions can also be used to express statements that sum up an attitude, as in *He's all, "No way!"* By contrast, *go* is largely restricted to relating dialogue in the present-tense narration.

go² (gō) ►*n.* A Japanese board game. [J.]

goad (gōd) ►*n.* **1.** A long pointed stick for prodding animals. **2.** A means of prodding; stimulus. [< OE *gād.*] —**goad** *v.*

go-a•head (gō′ə-hĕd′) ►*n. Informal* Permission to proceed.

goal (gōl) ►*n.* **1.** A desired purpose; objective. **2.** *Sports* **a.** The finish line of a race. **b.** A structure or zone into or over which players try to advance a ball or puck. **c.** The score awarded for this. [ME *gol,* boundary.]

goal•ie (gō′lē) ►*n.* See **goalkeeper.**

goal•keep•er (gōl′kē′pər) ►*n.* A player assigned to protect the goal in various sports.

goal kick ►*n.* A free kick in soccer awarded to a defensive team when the ball is driven out of bounds over the goal line by an opponent.

goal line ►*n.* **1.** *Sports* A line crossing either end of a playing area, on which a goal or goal post is positioned. **2.** *Football* A line crossing either end of the playing field over which the ball must be moved to score a touchdown.

goat (gōt) ►*n.* **1.** Any of a genus of horned, bearded mammals widely domesticated for wool, milk, and meat. **2.** A lecherous man. [< OE *gāt.*] —**goat′ish** *adj.*

goat antelope ►*n.* Any of various ruminants resembling both goats and antelopes.

goat•ee (gō-tē′) ►*n.* A pointed chin beard.

goat•skin (gōt′skĭn′) ►*n.* **1.** The skin of a goat, used for leather. **2.** A container, as for wine, made from goatskin.

gob¹ (gŏb) ►*n.* **1.** A small mass or lump. **2.** often **gobs** *Informal* A large quantity. [Prob. < OFr. *gobe,* mouthful.]

gob² (gŏb) ►*n. Slang* A sailor. [?]

gob•ble¹ (gŏb′əl) ►*v.* **-bled, -bling 1.** To devour greedily. **2.** To take greedily; grab: *gobble up scarce resources.* [< ME *gobben,* drink greedily. See GOB¹.]

gob•ble² (gŏb′əl) ►*n.* The guttural chortling sound of a male turkey. [Imit.] —**gob′ble** *v.* —**gob′bler** *n.*

gob•ble•dy•gook also **gob•ble•de•gook** (gŏb′əl-dē-go͝ok′) ►*n.* Unclear, wordy jargon. [Imit. of the gobbling of a turkey.]

go-be•tween (gō′bĭ-twēn′) ►*n.* An intermediary between two sides.

Go•bi (gō′bē) A desert of SE Mongolia and N China.

gob•let (gŏb′lĭt) ►*n.* A drinking glass with a stem and base. [< OFr. *gobelet,* small cup.]

gob•lin (gŏb′lĭn) ►*n.* A grotesque elfin creature thought to work mischief or evil. [< Norman Fr. **gobelin,* a famous ghost.]

god (gŏd) ►*n.* **1. God** A being conceived as the perfect, omnipotent, omniscient originator and ruler of the universe, the principal object of faith and worship in monotheistic religions. **2.** A being of supernatural powers, believed in and worshiped by a people. **3.** One that is worshiped or idealized. [< OE.] —**god′hood′** *n.* —**god′like′** *adj.*

god•child (gŏd′chīld′) ►*n.* A child for whom a person serves as sponsor at baptism.

God•dard (gŏd′ərd), **Robert Hutchings.** 1882–1945. Amer. rocketry pioneer.

god•daugh•ter (gŏd′dô′tər) ►*n.* A female godchild.

god•dess (gŏd′ĭs) ►*n.* **1.** A female deity. **2.** A woman of great beauty or grace.

god•fa•ther (gŏd′fä′*th*ər) ►*n.* **1.** A man who sponsors a child at baptism. **2.** *Slang* The leader of an organized crime family.

god•for•sak•en (gŏd′fər-sā′kən) ►*adj.* **1.** Located in a dismal or remote area. **2.** Desolate; forlorn.

god•head (gŏd′hĕd′) ►*n.* Divinity; godhood. [ME *godhede* < OE *godhād.*]

god•less (gŏd′lĭs) ►*adj.* **1.** Recognizing or worshiping no god. **2.** Wicked or impious. —**god′less•ly** *adv.* —**god′less•ness** *n.*

god•ly (gŏd′lē) ►*adj.* **-li•er, -li•est 1.** Pious. **2.** Divine. —**god′li•ness** *n.*

god•moth•er (gŏd′mŭ*th*′ər) ►*n.* A woman who sponsors a child at baptism.

god•par•ent (gŏd′pâr′ənt, -păr′-) ►*n.* A godfather or godmother.

god•send (gŏd′sĕnd′) ►*n.* Something wanted or needed that comes unexpectedly.

god•son (gŏd′sŭn′) ►*n.* A male godchild.

Godt•håb (gôt′hôp′) The capital of Greenland, on the SW coast. Pop. 12,483.

Go•du•nov (go͝od′n-ôf′, gŏd′-), **Boris Fyodorovich.** 1551?–1605. Czar of Russia (1598–1605).

God•win Aus•ten (gŏd′wĭn ô′stən), **Mount.** See **K2.**

goes (gōz) ►*v.* 3rd pers. sing. pr.t. of **go¹.**

Goe•thals (gō′thəlz), **George Washington.** 1858–1928. Amer. army engineer.

Goe•the (gœ′tə), **Johann Wolfgang von.** 1749–1832. German writer and scientist.

go-get•ter (gō′gĕt′ər, -gĕt′-) ►*n. Informal* An enterprising person.

gog•gle (gŏg′əl) ►*v.* **-gled, -gling.** To stare with wide and bulging eyes. ►*n.* **goggles.** Tight-fitting, often tinted eyeglasses worn to protect the eyes, as from dust, glare, or flying debris. [ME *gogelen,* squint.] —**gog′gly** *adj.*

goggle

go-go (gō′gō′) ►*adj. Informal* Of or relating to discotheques or to the energetic music and dancing performed at discotheques. [< Fr. *à gogo,* galore.]

Go•gol (gô′gəl, gō′gôl), **Nikolai Vasilievich.** 1809–52. Russian writer.

Goi•â•ni•a (goi-ä′nē-ə) A city of S Brazil SW of Brasília. Pop. 920,840.

go•ing (gō′ĭng) ►*n.* **1.** Departure. **2.** The condition underfoot as it affects walking or riding. **3.** *Informal* Progress toward a goal. ►*adj.* **1.** Working; running. **2.** Current; prevailing: *The going rates are high.*

goi•ter (goi′tər) ►*n.* A noncancerous enlargement of the thyroid gland, visible as a swelling at the front of the neck. [< Lat. *guttur*, throat.] —**goi′trous** (-trəs) *adj.*

Go•lan Heights (gō′län′) An upland region between NE Israel and SW Syria NE of the Sea of Galilee.

gold (gōld) ►*n.* **1a.** *Symbol* **Au** A soft, yellow, corrosion-resistant, highly malleable and ductile metallic element used as an international monetary standard, in jewelry, for decoration, and as a plated coating on a wide variety of electrical and mechanical components. At. no. 79. See table at **element. b.** Coinage made of gold. **2.** Money; riches. **3.** A moderate to vivid yellow. [< OE.] —**gold** *adj.*

gold•brick (gōld′brĭk′) ►*n. Slang* One who avoids assigned duties or work; shirker. —**gold′brick′** *v.*

Gold Coast. A section of coastal W Africa along the Gulf of Guinea roughly corresponding to present-day Ghana.

gold•en (gōl′dən) ►*adj.* **1.** Made of or containing gold. **2.** Having the color of gold. **3.** Suggestive of gold, as in richness or splendor: *a golden voice.* **4.** Precious: *golden memories.* **5.** Marked by prosperity: *a golden era.* **6.** Excellent: *a golden opportunity.*

golden eagle ►*n.* A large eagle with a brownish-yellow head and neck.

Golden Gate. A strait in W CA joining the Pacific and San Francisco Bay.

golden mean ►*n.* The course between extremes.

gold•en•rod (gōl′dən-rŏd′) ►*n.* Any of a genus of North American plants having feathery clusters of small yellow flowers.

gold•finch (gōld′fĭnch′) ►*n.* A small American finch having yellow plumage with a black forehead, wings, and tail.

gold•fish (gōld′fĭsh′) ►*n.* A typically reddish freshwater Asian fish bred in many ornamental forms as an aquarium fish.

gold leaf ►*n.* Gold beaten into extremely thin sheets, used for gilding.

Gold•man (gōld′mən), **Emma.** 1869–1940. Russian-born Amer. anarchist.

gold rush ►*n.* A rush of migrants to an area where gold has been discovered.

gold•smith (gōld′smĭth′) ►*n.* An artisan who makes or deals in articles of gold.

Goldsmith, Oliver. 1730?–74. British writer.

gold standard ►*n.* A monetary standard under which the basic unit of currency is equal in value to a specified amount of gold.

go•lem (gō′ləm) ►*n.* In Jewish folklore, an artificially created human supernaturally endowed with life. [Heb. *gōlem*, fool.]

golf (gŏlf, gôlf) ►*n.* A game played on a 9- or 18-hole course, the object being to hit a small ball with the use of various clubs into each hole with as few strokes as possible. [ME.] —**golf** *v.* —**golf′er** *n.*

Gol•go•tha (gŏl′gə-thə, gŏl-gŏth′ə) See **Calvary.**

Go•li•ath (gə-lī′əth). In the Bible, a giant warrior who was slain by David.

Go•mel (gō′məl) See **Homyel′.**

Go•mor•rah (gə-môr′ə, -mŏr′ə) An ancient city of Palestine near Sodom.

Gom•pers (gŏm′pərz), **Samuel.** 1850–1924. British-born Amer. labor leader.

-gon ►*suff.* A figure having a specified kind or number of angles: *polygon.* [< Gk. *gōnia*, angle.]

go•nad (gō′năd′) ►*n.* An organ in animals that produces gametes, esp. a testis or ovary. [< Gk. *gonos*, procreation.] —**go•nad′al, go•nad′ic** *adj.*

gon•do•la (gŏn′dl-ə, gŏn-dō′lə) ►*n.* **1.** A lightweight narrow barge used on the canals of Venice. **2.** An open shallow freight car with low sides. **3.** A compartment suspended from a balloon or dirigible. **4.** An enclosed passenger cabin that moves along an overhead cable. [Ital.]

gondola

gon•do•lier (gŏn′dl-îr′) ►*n.* The person who propels a Venetian gondola.

gone (gôn, gŏn) ►*v.* P.part. of **go**[1]. ►*adj.* **1.** Past; bygone. **2.** Dying or dead. **3.** Ruined; lost. **4.** Carried away; absorbed. **5.** Used up; exhausted. **6.** *Slang* Infatuated.

gon•er (gô′nər, gŏn′ər) ►*n. Slang* One that is ruined or doomed.

gong (gông, gŏng) ►*n.* A metal disk struck to produce a loud sonorous tone. [Malay *gōng.*]

gon•or•rhe•a (gŏn′ə-rē′ə) ►*n.* A sexually transmitted disease of the genital and urinary tracts, often marked by a purulent discharge and painful or difficult urination. [< Gk. *gonorrhoia.*]

goo (go͞o) ►*n. Informal* A sticky, wet, viscous substance. [Perh. < *burgoo*, thick oatmeal gruel.] —**goo′ey** *adj.*

goo•ber (go͞o′bər) ►*n.* A peanut. [Of Bantu orig.]

Regional Note: *Goober*, related to *n-guba*, "peanut," in a Bantu language of west-central Africa, is one of a small group of African language borrowings brought over by slaves. *Gumbo* is also of Bantu origin, and *okra* and *yam* of West African.

good (go͝od) ►*adj.* **bet•ter** (bĕt′ər), **best** (bĕst) **1.** Being positive or desirable in nature. **2a.** Having desirable qualities. **b.** Suitable; appropriate. **3a.** Not spoiled. **b.** In excellent condition; sound. **4.** Superior to the average: *a good student.* **5a.** Of high quality: *good books.* **b.** Discriminating: *good taste.* **6.** Beneficial; salutary: *a good night's rest.* **7.** Competent; skilled. **8.** Complete; thorough. **9a.** Reliable; sure. **b.** Valid or true. **c.** Genuine; real. **10.** In effect; operative. **11a.** Ample; substantial. **b.** Bountiful. **12.** Full: *a good mile away.* **13a.** Pleasant; enjoyable. **b.** Favorable. **14a.** Virtuous; upright. **b.** Benevolent; kind. **15a.** Well-behaved; obedient. **b.** Socially correct; proper. ►*n.* **1.** Something good. **2.** Welfare; benefit. **3.** Goodness; virtue. **4. goods a.** Commodities; wares. **b.** Portable personal property. —***idioms:*** **as good as** Nearly; almost. **for good**

Permanently. **good and** *Informal* Very; thoroughly. [< OE *gōd*.]

Usage: *Good* is properly used as an adjective with linking verbs such as *be, seem,* or *appear: The future looks good.* It should not be used as an adverb with other verbs: *The car runs well* (not *good*).

good•bye or **good-bye** also **good-by** (go͝od-bī′) ▸*interj.* Used to express farewell. [< *God be with you*.] —**good•bye′** *n.*

Good Friday ▸*n.* The Friday before Easter, observed by Christians in commemoration of the crucifixion of Jesus.

good•heart•ed (go͝od′här′tĭd) ▸*adj.* Kind and generous; benevolent. —**good′heart′ed•ly** *adv.* —**good′heart′ed•ness** *n.*

Good Hope, Cape of. A promontory on the SW coast of South Africa S of Cape Town.

good-hu•mored (go͝od′hyo͞o′mərd) ▸*adj.* Cheerful; amiable. —**good′-hu′mored•ly** *adv.* —**good′-hu′mored•ness** *n.*

good-look•ing (go͝od′lo͝ok′ĭng) ▸*adj.* Of a pleasing appearance; attractive.

good•ly (go͝od′lē) ▸*adj.* **-li•er, -li•est 1.** Of pleasing appearance; comely. **2.** Somewhat large; considerable. —**good′li•ness** *n.*

good-na•tured (go͝od′nā′chərd) ▸*adj.* Having an easygoing, cheerful disposition. —**good′-na′tured•ly** *adv.*

good•ness (go͝od′nĭs) ▸*n.* **1.** The state or quality of being good. **2.** The beneficial part. ▸*interj.* Used to express mild surprise.

Good Samaritan ▸*n.* A person who unselfishly helps others. [From the parable of the good Samaritan in the New Testament.]

good•will also **good will** (go͝od′wĭl′) ▸*n.* **1.** An attitude of kindness or friendliness; benevolence. **2.** Cheerful willingness. **3.** A good relationship, as between nations.

good•y (go͝od′ē) ▸*n., pl.* **-ies** *Informal* Something attractive or delectable, esp. something sweet to eat. —**good′y** *interj.*

good•y-good•y (go͝od′ē-go͝od′ē) ▸*adj.* Affectedly sweet, good, or virtuous. —**good′y-good′y** *n.*

goof (go͞of) *Slang* ▸*n.* **1.** An incompetent, foolish, or stupid person. **2.** A careless mistake; slip. ▸*v.* **1.** To blunder. **2.** To waste or kill time: *goofed off all day.* [Poss. < dial. *goff*, fool.] —**goof′i•ly** *adv.* —**goof′i•ness** *n.* —**goof′y** *adj.*

goof•ball (go͞of′bôl′) ▸*n. Slang* **1.** A foolish or goofy person. **2.** A barbiturate or tranquilizer in pill form. —**goof′ball** *adj.*

goo•gol (go͞o′gôl′) ▸*n.* The number 10 raised to the power 100 (10^{100}). [A coinage.]

gook (go͝ok, go͞ok) ▸*n.* Var. of **guck.**

goon (go͞on) ▸*n. Slang* **1.** A thug hired to intimidate or harm opponents. **2.** A stupid or oafish person. [Prob. < *gooney*, albatross.]

goose (go͞os) ▸*n., pl.* **geese** (gēs) **1.** Any of various water birds related to the ducks and swans. **2.** The female of such a bird. **3.** The flesh of such a bird used as food. **4.** *Informal* A silly person. [< OE *gōs*.]

goose•ber•ry (go͞os′bĕr′ē, -bə-rē, go͞oz′-) ▸*n.* **1.** A spiny shrub having edible greenish berries. **2.** The fruit of this plant. [< Fr. *groseille*.]

goose bumps ▸*pl.n.* Momentary roughness of the skin in response esp. to cold or fear.

goose flesh ▸*n.* See **goose bumps.**

goose•neck (go͞os′nĕk′) ▸*n.* A slender curved object or part, such as the flexible shaft of a type of desk lamp. —**goose′necked′** *adj.*

goose step ▸*n.* A military parade step executed by swinging the legs from the hips with the knees locked. —**goose′-step′** *v.*

GOP ▸*abbr.* Grand Old Party (Republican Party)

go•pher (gō′fər) ▸*n.* Any of various burrowing North American rodents having external cheek pouches. [?]

Gor•ba•chev (gôr′bə-chôf′, -chŏf′), **Mikhail Sergeyevich.** b. 1931. Soviet politician; 1990 Nobel Peace Prize.

Gor•di•mer (gôr′də-mər), **Nadine.** b. 1923. South African writer; 1991 Nobel.

gore[1] (gôr, gōr) ▸*v.* **gored, gor•ing.** To pierce with a horn or tusk. [< OE *gār*, spear.]

gore[2] (gôr, gōr) ▸*n.* A triangular or tapering piece of cloth, as in a skirt or sail. [< OE *gāra*, triangular land.] —**gore** *v.* —**gored** *adj.*

gore[3] (gôr, gōr) ▸*n.* Blood, esp. from a wound. [< OE *gor*, filth.]

Gore, Albert, Jr. "Al." b. 1948. US Vice President (since 1993).

gorge (gôrj) ▸*n.* **1.** A deep narrow passage with steep sides. **2.** The throat; gullet. **3.** Something swallowed. ▸*v.* **gorged, gorg•ing 1.** To stuff (oneself) with food; glut. **2.** To eat greedily. [< LLat. *gurga*, throat.]

gor•geous (gôr′jəs) ▸*adj.* **1.** Dazzlingly beautiful or magnificent: *a gorgeous gown.* **2.** *Informal* Wonderful; delightful. [< OFr. *gorgias*, elegant.] —**gor′geous•ly** *adv.* —**gor′geous•ness** *n.*

go•ril•la (gə-rĭl′ə) ▸*n.* An African ape, the largest of the great apes, having a stocky body and coarse dark hair. [< Gk. *Gorillai*, a tribe of hairy women.]

Gor•ky or **Gor•ki** (gôr′kē). See **Nizhniy Novgorod.**

Gorky also **Gorki, Maksim.** 1868–1936. Russian writer.

Gor•lov•ka (gôr-lôf′kə) See **Horlivka.**

gor•mand•ize (gôr′mən-dīz′) ▸*v.* **-ized, -iz•ing.** To eat gluttonously. [< OFr. *gormandise*, gluttony.] —**gor′mand•iz′er** *n.*

gorse (gôrs) ▸*n.* A spiny European shrub having fragrant yellow flowers. [< OE *gorst*, bramble.]

go•ry (gôr′ē, gōr′ē) ▸*adj.* **-ri•er, -ri•est 1.** Covered with gore; bloody. **2.** Full of bloodshed and violence. —**gor′i•ly** *adv.* —**gor′i•ness** *n.*

gosh (gŏsh) ▸*interj.* Used to express mild surprise. [Alteration of GOD.]

gos•hawk (gŏs′hôk′) ▸*n.* A large hawk having broad rounded wings and gray or brownish plumage. [< OE *gōshafoc*.]

gos•ling (gŏz′lĭng) ▸*n.* A young goose. [< ON *gæslingr*.]

gos•pel (gŏs′pəl) ▸*n.* **1.** often **Gospel** The proclamation of the redemption preached by Jesus and the Apostles. **2.** often **Gospel** *Bible* One of the first four books of the New Testament. **3.** Gospel music. **4.** Something accepted as unquestionably true. [< OE *gōdspel*, good news.]

gospel music ▸*n.* An American religious music associated with Christian evangelism and blending elements of folk music, spirituals, and jazz.

gos•sa•mer (gŏs′ə-mər) ▸*n.* **1.** A soft, sheer,

gauzy fabric. **2.** Something delicate or flimsy. **3.** A fine film of cobwebs often seen floating in the air or caught on bushes. [ME *gossomer.*] **—gos′sa•mer, gos′sa•mer•y** *adj.*

gos•sip (gŏs′əp) ▸*n.* **1.** Rumor or talk of a personal, sensational, or intimate nature. **2.** A person who habitually indulges in gossip. [< OE *godsibb*, godparent.] **—gos′sip** *v.* **—gos′sip•er** *n.* **—gos′sip•y** *adj.*

got (gŏt) ▸*v.* P.t. and p.part. of **get.**

Gö•te•borg (yœ′tə-bôr′ē) A city of SW Sweden on the Kattegat. Pop. 433,811.

Goth (gŏth) ▸*n.* A member of a Germanic people who invaded the Roman Empire in the early centuries of the Christian era.

Goth•ic (gŏth′ĭk) ▸*adj.* **1a.** Of the Goths or their language. **b.** Germanic. **2.** Medieval. **3.** Of an architectural style prevalent in W Europe from the 12th through the 15th cent., marked esp. by pointed arches and strong vertical elements. **4.** often **gothic** Of a style of fiction that emphasizes the grotesque and mysterious: *a gothic novel.* ▸*n.* The extinct Germanic language of the Goths.

Got•land (gŏt′lənd, gôt′lŭnd) A region of SE Sweden comprising several islands in the Baltic Sea, including **Gotland Island.**

got•ten (gŏt′n) ▸*v.* P.part. of **get.**

Gou•da (go͞o′də, gou′-) ▸*n.* A mild, close-textured, pale yellow cheese. [After *Gouda*, city in Netherlands.]

gouge (gouj) ▸*n.* **1.** A chisel with a rounded troughlike blade. **2.** A groove or hole scooped with or as if with such a chisel. ▸*v.* **gouged, goug•ing 1.** To cut or scoop out with or as if with a gouge. **2.** *Informal* To extort from. **3.** *Slang* To swindle. [< LLat. *gubia*, of Celt. orig.] **—goug′er** *n.*

gou•lash (go͞o′läsh′, -lăsh′) ▸*n.* A meat and vegetable stew seasoned esp. with paprika. [Hung. *gulyás (hús)*, herdsman's (meat).]

Gou•nod (go͞o′nō, go͞o-nō′), **Charles François.** 1818–93. French composer.

gourd (gôrd, gōrd, go͝ord) ▸*n.* **1.** A vine related to the pumpkin and cucumber and bearing fruits with a hard rind. **2.** The fruit of such a plant. **3.** The dried and hollowed-out shell of one of these fruits, often used as a drinking utensil. [< Lat. *cucurbita.*]

gourde (go͝ord) ▸*n.* See table at **currency.** [Haitian < Fr. *gourd*, dull.]

gour•mand (go͝or-mänd′, go͝or′mənd) ▸*n.* **1.** A lover of good food. **2.** A gluttonous eater. [< OFr. *gormant*, glutton.]

gour•met (go͝or-mā′, go͝or′mā′) ▸*n.* A connoisseur of fine food and drink. [< OFr. *groumet*, wine merchant's servant < ME *grom*, a groom.]

gout (gout) ▸*n.* **1.** A disease of uric-acid metabolism occurring esp. in males, marked by arthritis and painful inflammation of the joints. **2.** A large blob or clot. [< Lat. *gutta*, drop.] **—gout′i•ness** *n.* **—gout′y** *adj.*

Gov. ▸*abbr.* governor

gov•ern (gŭv′ərn) ▸*v.* **1.** To make and administer public policy and affairs. **2.** To regulate. **3.** To control; restrain. **4.** To decide or determine. [Ult. < Gk. *kubernan.*] **—gov′ern•a•ble** *adj.* **—gov′er•nance** *n.*

gov•er•ness (gŭv′ər-nĭs) ▸*n.* A woman employed to educate and train the children of a private household.

gov•ern•ment (gŭv′ərn-mənt) ▸*n.* **1.** The act or process of governing, esp. the administration of public policy. **2.** The means by which a governing agent or agency uses authority. **3.** A governing body or organization. **4.** Political science. **—gov′ern•men′tal** (-mĕn′tl) *adj.* **—gov′ern•men′tal•ly** *adv.*

Usage: In American usage, *government* always takes a singular verb. In British usage, in the sense of a governing group of officials *government* is usually construed as a plural collective and therefore takes a plural verb. See Usage Note at **collective noun.**

gov•er•nor (gŭv′ər-nər) ▸*n.* **1.** A person who governs, esp. the chief executive of a state in the US. **2.** The manager or administrative head of an organization or institution. **3.** A commandant. **4.** A device on an engine that regulates speed, pressure, or temperature. **—gov′er•nor•ship′** *n.*

govt. ▸*abbr.* government

gown (goun) ▸*n.* **1.** A long, loose, flowing garment, as a robe or nightgown. **2.** A woman's formal dress. **3.** A distinctive outer robe worn on ceremonial occasions, as by scholars or clerics. **4.** The faculty and student body of a university: *town and gown.* [< LLat. *gunna*, leather garment.]

Go•ya y Lu•ci•en•tes (goi′ə ē lo͞o-syĕn′tēs), **Francisco José de.** 1746–1828. Spanish painter and etcher.

Francisco Goya
1799 self-portrait

GP ▸*abbr.* general practitioner

GPA ▸*abbr.* grade point average

GPO ▸*abbr.* **1.** general post office **2.** Government Printing Office

GPS ▸*abbr.* Global Positioning System

GQ ▸*abbr.* general quarters

gr. ▸*abbr.* **1.** grain (measurement) **2.** gram **3.** gross

Gr. ▸*abbr.* Greek

grab (grăb) ▸*v.* **grabbed, grab•bing 1.** To take or grasp suddenly. **2.** To capture or restrain; arrest. **3.** To obtain or appropriate unscrupulously or illegally. **4.** To take hurriedly. [< MDu. or MLGer. *grabben.*] **—grab** *n.* **—grab′ber** *n.* **—grab′by** *adj.*

grab bag ▸*n.* **1.** A container filled with articles, such as party gifts, to be drawn unseen. **2.** *Slang* A miscellaneous collection.

Grac•chus (grăk′əs), **Tiberius Sempronius.** 163–133 B.C. Roman social reformer; known with his brother **Gaius Sempronius Gracchus** (153–121 B.C.) as "the Gracchi."

grace (grās) ▶*n.* **1.** Seemingly effortless beauty of movement, form, or proportion. **2.** A pleasing characteristic or quality. **3.** A sense of fitness or propriety. **4a.** Good will. **b.** Mercy; clemency. **5.** A temporary immunity or exemption; reprieve. **6. Graces** *Gk. & Rom. Myth.* Three sister goddesses who dispense charm and beauty. **7a.** Divine love and protection bestowed freely on people. **b.** The state of being protected by God. **8.** A short prayer said at mealtime. **9. Grace** Used with *His, Her,* or *Your* as a title for a duke, duchess, or archbishop. ▶*v.* **graced, grac•ing 1.** To honor or favor. **2.** To give beauty, elegance, or charm to. —***idiom:* in the good** (or **bad) graces of** In (or out of) favor with. [< Lat. *grātia.*] —**grace′ful** *adj.* —**grace′ful•ly** *adv.* —**grace′ful•ness** *n.* —**grace′less** *adj.* —**grace′less•ly** *adv.* —**grace′less•ness** *n.*

grace note ▶*n. Mus.* A note added as an embellishment and not counted in rhythm.

grace period ▶*n.* **1.** A period in which a debt may be paid without accruing further interest or penalty. **2.** A period in which an insurance policy is effective even though the premium is past due.

gra•cious (grā′shəs) ▶*adj.* **1.** Marked by kindness and warm courtesy. **2.** Tactful. **3.** Merciful or compassionate. **4.** Marked by elegance and good taste. [< Lat. *grātiōsus.*] —**gra′cious•ly** *adv.* —**gra′cious•ness** *n.*

Syns: *gracious, cordial, genial, sociable*
Ant: *ungracious* **adj.**

grack•le (grăk′əl) ▶*n.* Any of several American blackbirds with iridescent blackish plumage. [< Lat. *grāculus,* jackdaw.]

grad (grăd) ▶*n. Informal* A graduate.

gra•da•tion (grā-dā′shən) ▶*n.* **1.** A series of gradual, successive stages. **2.** A degree or stage in such a progression. See Syns at **nuance. 3.** The act of arranging in grades. [< Lat. *gradus,* step.] —**gra•da′tion•al** *adj.*

grade (grād) ▶*n.* **1.** A stage or degree in a process. **2.** A position in a scale. **3.** An accepted standard. **4.** A set of persons or things all falling in the same specified limits; class. **5.** A class at an elementary school or the pupils in it. **6.** A mark indicating a student's level of accomplishment. **7.** A military, naval, or civil service rank. **8.** The degree of inclination of a slope or other surface. **9.** A slope or gradual inclination, esp. of a road or railroad track. ▶*v.* **grad•ed, grad•ing 1.** To arrange in degrees; rank; sort. **2a.** To evaluate. **b.** To give a grade to. **3.** To level or smooth (a surface) to a desired gradient. [< Lat. *gradus,* step.] —**grad′er** *n.*

grade school ▶*n.* See **elementary school.** —**grade′-school′er** *n.*

gra•di•ent (grā′dē-ənt) ▶*n.* A rate of inclination; slope. [Perh. < GRADE.]

grad•u•al (grăj′ōō-əl) ▶*adj.* Occurring in small stages or advancing by regular or continuous degrees. [< Lat. *gradus,* step.] —**grad′u•al•ism** *n.* —**grad′u•al•ly** *adv.*

grad•u•ate (grăj′ōō-āt′) ▶*v.* **-at•ed, -at•ing 1.** To grant or be granted an academic degree or diploma. **2.** To arrange into categories, steps, or grades. **3.** To divide into marked intervals, esp. for use in measurement. ▶*n.* (-ĭt). One who has received an academic degree or diploma. ▶*adj.* (-ĭt) **1.** Possessing an academic degree or diploma. **2.** Of studies beyond a bachelor's degree. [< Med.Lat. *graduāri,* take a degree.]

grad•u•a•tion (grăj′ōō-ā′shən) ▶*n.* **1.** Conferral or receipt of an academic degree or diploma marking completion of studies. **2.** A commencement ceremony. **3.** An interval on a graduated scale.

graf•fi•to (grə-fē′tō) ▶*n., pl.* **-ti** (-tē). often **graffiti** A drawing or inscription made on a wall or other surface, usu. to be seen by the public. [Ital. < *graffiare,* scribble, ult. < Gk. *graphein,* write.]

graft[1] (grăft) ▶*v.* **1.** To unite (a shoot, bud, or plant) with a growing plant by insertion or placing in close contact. **2.** To transplant or implant (tissue) into a bodily part. ▶*n.* **1a.** A detached shoot or bud grafted onto a growing plant. **b.** The point of union of such plant parts. **2.** Material, esp. tissue or an organ, grafted onto a bodily part. [< OFr. *graffe,* stylus < Lat. *graphium* < Gk. *graphein,* write.] —**graft′er** *n.*

graft[2] (grăft) ▶*n.* **1.** Illegal use of one's position for profit or advantages. **2.** Money or advantage thus gained. [?] —**graft** *v.* —**graft′er** *n.*

Graham (grăm, grā′əm), **Martha.** 1894–1991. Amer. dancer and choreographer.

graham flour ▶*n.* Whole-wheat flour. [After Sylvester *Graham* (1794–1851).]

grail (grāl) ▶*n.* **1. Grail** A legendary cup or plate used by Jesus at the Last Supper, later the object of chivalrous quests. **2.** often **Grail** The object of a prolonged endeavor. [< Med.Lat. *gradālis,* flat dish.]

grain (grān) ▶*n.* **1a.** A small, one-seeded fruit of a cereal grass. **b.** The fruits of cereal grasses collectively, esp. after harvesting. **2.** Cereal grasses collectively. **3.** A small amount. **4.** See table at **measurement. 5.** The arrangement, direction, or pattern of the fibrous tissue in wood. **6.** Texture. **7.** Basic temperament; disposition. —***idiom:* with a grain of salt** With reservations; skeptically. [< Lat. *grānum.*] —**grain′i•ness** *n.* —**grain′y** *adj.*

grain alcohol ▶*n.* See **alcohol** 1.

grain elevator ▶*n.* A tall building used for storing grain.

gram (grăm) ▶*n.* See table at **measurement.** [< Gk. *gramma,* small weight.]

-gram ▶*suff.* Something written or drawn; a record: *cardiogram.* [< Gk. *gramma,* letter.]

gram•mar (grăm′ər) ▶*n.* **1a.** The study of how words and their component parts combine to form sentences. **b.** The study of structural relationships in language or in a language. **2.** The system of inflections, syntax, and word formation of a language. **3a.** A normative or prescriptive set of rules setting forth the current standard of usage. **b.** Writing or speech judged with regard to such rules. **4.** A book containing the inflectional, syntactic, and semantic rules for a specific language. [< Lat. *grammatica* < Gk. *gramma,* letter.] —**gram•mar′i•an** (grə-mâr′ē-ən) *n.* —**gram•mat′i•cal** (grə-măt′ĭ-kəl) *adj.* —**gram•mat′i•cal•ly** *adv.*

grammar school ▶*n.* See **elementary school.**

gram-mo•lec•u•lar weight (grăm′mə-lĕk′yə-lər) ▶*n.* The mass in grams of one mole of a substance.

gram molecule ▶*n.* See **mole**[4]**.**

gram-neg•a•tive or **Gram-neg•a•tive** (grăm′nĕg′ə-tĭv) ▶*adj.* Not retaining the violet

stain that is used in Gram's method.
gram•o•phone (grăm′ə-fōn′) ►*n.* A phonograph. [Orig. a trademark.]
Gram•pi•an Mountains (grăm′pē-ən) A mountain range of central Scotland forming a natural barrier between the Highlands and the Lowlands.
gram-pos•i•tive or **Gram-pos•i•tive** (grăm′pŏz′ĭ-tĭv) ►*adj.* Retaining the violet stain used in Gram's method.
gram•pus (grăm′pəs) ►*n.* A marine mammal related to and resembling the dolphins. [< Med. Lat. *craspiscis*, fat fish.]
Gram's method (grămz) ►*n.* A staining technique used to classify bacteria based on the ability or inability to retain a violet stain. [After H.C.J. *Gram* (1853–1938).]
Gra•na•da (grə-nä′də) A city of S Spain SE of Córdoba. Pop. 256,784.
gran•a•ry (grăn′ə-rē, grā′nə-) ►*n.*, *pl.* **-ries.** A building for storing threshed grain. [Lat. *grānārium* < *grānum*, grain.]
grand (grănd) ►*adj.* **-er, -est 1.** Large and impressive in size, scope, or extent. **2a.** Rich and sumptuous. **b.** Of a solemn or stately nature. **3.** Wonderful; very pleasing. **4.** Having higher rank than others of the same category: *a grand admiral.* **5.** Most important; principal: *the grand ballroom.* **6.** Including or covering all units or aspects: *the grand total.* ►*n.* **1.** A grand piano. **2.** *Slang* A thousand dollars. [< Lat. *grandis*.] —**grand′ly** *adv.* —**grand′ness** *n.*
gran•dam (grăn′dăm′, -dəm) also **gran•dame** (-dām′, -däm, -dəm) ►*n.* **1.** A grandmother. **2.** An old woman. [< OFr. *dame-grande*, great lady.]
Grand Banks. An area of shoals in the W Atlantic off SE Newfoundland, Canada.
Grand Canal 1. An inland waterway, about 1,609 km (1,000 mi), of E China extending from Tianjin in the N to Hangzhou in the S. **2.** The principal waterway of Venice, Italy.
Grand Canyon. A gorge of the Colorado R. in NW AZ, up to 1.6 km (1 mi) deep, 6.4–29 km (4–18 mi) wide, and more than 321.8 km (200 mi) long.
grand•child (grănd′chīld′, grăn′-) ►*n.* A child of one's son or daughter.
grand•daugh•ter (grăn′dô′tər) ►*n.* A daughter of one's son or daughter.
gran•deur (grăn′jər, -jŏŏr′) ►*n.* The quality of being grand; magnificence. [< OFr. < *grand*, GRAND.]
grand•fa•ther (grănd′fä′*th*ər, grăn′-) ►*n.* **1.** The father of one's mother or father. **2.** A forefather; ancestor. ►*v.* To exempt (one already existing) from new regulations.
gran•dil•o•quence (grăn-dĭl′ə-kwəns) ►*n.* Pompous or bombastic speech or expression. [< Lat. *grandiloquus*, speaking loftily.] —**gran•dil′o•quent** *adj.* —**gran•dil′o•quent•ly** *adv.*
gran•di•ose (grăn′dē-ōs′, grăn′dē-ōs′) ►*adj.* **1.** Great in scope or intent; grand. **2.** Affectedly grand; pompous. [< Ital. *grandioso* < Lat. *grandis*, great.] —**gran′di•os′i•ty** (-ŏs′ĭ-tē), **gran′di•ose′ness** *n.*
grand jury ►*n.* A jury convened in private to evaluate criminal accusations against persons and to determine whether the evidence warrants indictment.
grand•ma (grănd′mä′, grăn′-, grăm′mä′, grăm′ə) ►*n.* *Informal* A grandmother.
grand mal (grăn′ mäl′, măl′, grănd′) ►*n.* A severe form of epilepsy marked by severe seizures and loss of consciousness. [Fr.]
grand•moth•er (grănd′mŭ*th*′ər, grăn′-) ►*n.* **1.** The mother of one's father or mother. **2.** A female ancestor.
grand•pa (grănd′pä′, grăn′-, grăm′pä′, grăm′pə) ►*n.* *Informal* A grandfather.
grand•par•ent (grănd′pâr′ənt, -păr′-, grăn′-) ►*n.* A parent of one's mother or father.
grand piano ►*n.* A piano having the strings strung in a horizontal harp-shaped frame.
Grand Rapids. A city of W-central MI on the Grand R. WNW of Lansing. Pop. 189,126.
grand slam ►*n.* **1.** The winning of all the tricks during a hand in bridge. **2.** *Baseball* A home run hit with three runners on base.
grand•son (grănd′sŭn′, grăn′-) ►*n.* A son of one's son or daughter.
grand•stand (grănd′stănd′, grăn′-) ►*n.* A roofed stand for spectators at a stadium or racetrack. ►*v.* To act ostentatiously to impress an audience. —**grand′stand′er** *n.*
grand unified theory ►*n.* *Phys.* A theory in which the known interactions between elementary forces are viewed as low-energy manifestations of a single unified interaction.
grange (grānj) ►*n.* **1. Grange** A US farmers' association founded in 1867. **2.** *Chiefly Brit.* A farm with its outbuildings. [< VLat. **grānica*, granary < Lat. *grānum*, GRAIN.]
gran•ite (grăn′ĭt) ►*n.* A common, coarse-grained, hard igneous rock consisting chiefly of quartz and feldspar, used esp. in monuments and for building. [< Ital. *granito*, grainy < *grano*, GRAIN.] —**gra•nit′ic** (gră-nĭt′ĭk, grə-) *adj.*
gran•ny or **gran•nie** (grăn′ē) ►*n.*, *pl.* **-nies.** *Informal* A grandmother. [< GRANDMOTHER.]
gra•no•la (grə-nō′lə) ►*n.* Rolled oats often mixed with dried fruit, brown sugar, and nuts and used esp. as a breakfast cereal. [Orig. a trademark.]
grant (grănt) ►*v.* **1.** To consent to the fulfillment of. **2.** To accord as a favor. **3a.** To bestow; confer. **b.** To transfer (property) by a deed. **4.** To concede; acknowledge. ►*n.* **1.** The act of granting. **2a.** Something granted. **b.** A giving of funds for a specific purpose. **3a.** A transfer of property by deed. **b.** The property so transferred. **c.** The deed of transfer. [< VLat. **crēdentāre*, assure < Lat. *crēdere*, believe.] —**grant′er, gran′tor** *n.*
Grant, Cary. Archibald Alexander Leach. 1904–86. British-born Amer. actor.
Grant, Ulysses Simpson. 1822–1885. The 18th US President (1869–77) and a Civil War general.
gran•u•lar (grăn′yə-lər) ►*adj.* **1.** Composed of granules or grains. **2.** Having a grainy texture. —**gran′u•lar′i•ty** (-lăr′ĭ-tē) *n.*
gran•u•late (grăn′yə-lāt′) ►*v.* **-lat•ed, -lat•ing 1.** To form into grains or granules. **2.** To make rough and grainy. —**gran′u•la′tion** *n.* —**gran′u•la′tive** *adj.*
gran•ule (grăn′yōōl) ►*n.* A small grain or particle. [LLat. *grānulum* < Lat. *grānum*, GRAIN.]
grape (grāp) ►*n.* **1.** Any of a genus of woody vines bearing clusters of edible fruit. **2.** The fleshy, smooth-skinned, purple, red, or green fruit of a grape. **3.** Grapeshot. [< OFr., bunch of grapes.]

Ulysses S. Grant

grape•fruit (grāp′fro͞ot′) ►*n.* **1.** A large round citrus fruit having a yellow rind and juicy acid pulp. **2.** The semitropical tree bearing this fruit.

grape•shot (grāp′shŏt′) ►*n.* A cluster of small iron balls formerly used as a cannon charge.

grape sugar ►*n.* Dextrose from grapes.

grape•vine (grāp′vīn′) ►*n.* **1.** A vine on which grapes grow. **2.** The informal transmission of information, gossip, or rumor from person to person.

graph (grăf) ►*n.* **1.** A diagram that exhibits a relationship between two sets of numbers. **2.** Any drawing or diagram used to display quantitative relationships. ►*v.* **1.** To represent by a graph. **2.** To plot (a function) on a graph. [< *graphic formula.*]

-graph ►*suff.* **1.** Something written or drawn: *monograph.* **2.** An instrument for writing, drawing, or recording: *seismograph.* [< Gk. *graphein*, write.]

-grapher ►*suff.* One who writes about a specified subject or in a specified manner: *stenographer.*

graph•ic (grăf′ĭk) ►*adj.* also **graph•i•cal** (-ĭ-kəl) **1.** Relating to written or pictorial representation. **2.** Relating to a graph. **3.** Vividly described or set forth. **4.** Of the graphic arts. ►*n.* **1.** A work of graphic art. **2.** A graphic image or display, esp. one generated by a computer. [< Gk. *graphein*, to write.] —**graph′i•cal•ly** *adv.*

Syns: *graphic, lifelike, realistic, vivid* **adj.**

graphical user interface ►*n.* GUI.

graphic arts ►*pl.n.* The arts, such as painting, drawing, and engraving, that involve representing, writing, or printing on two-dimensional surfaces.

graph•ics (grăf′ĭks) ►*n.* **1.** *(takes sing. v.)* The making of drawings, as in engineering or architecture. **2.** *(takes sing. or pl. v.)* The pictorial representation and manipulation of data, as used in computer-aided design, typesetting, and the graphic arts.

graph•ite (grăf′īt′) ►*n.* A soft, steel-gray to black form of carbon used in lead pencils, lubricants, paints, and coatings. [Gk. *graphein*, write + –ITE[1].] —**gra•phit′ic** (gră-fĭt′ĭk) *adj.*

gra•phol•o•gy (gră-fŏl′ə-jē) ►*n.* The study of handwriting. —**graph′o•log′i•cal** (grăf′ə-lŏj′ĭ-kəl) *adj.* —**gra•phol′o•gist** *n.*

-graphy ►*suff.* **1.** A writing or representation produced in a specified manner or by a specified process: *photography.* **2.** A writing about a specified subject: *oceanography.* [< Gk. *graphein*, write.]

grap•nel (grăp′nəl) ►*n.* **1.** A small anchor with three or more flukes. **2.** See **grapple** 1. [Prob. < OFr. *grapin*, hook.]

grap•ple (grăp′əl) ►*n.* **1a.** An iron shaft with claws at one end, esp. one formerly used for drawing and holding an enemy ship alongside. **b.** See **grapnel** 1. **2.** The act of grappling. ►*v.* **-pled, -pling 1.** To seize and hold fast. **2.** To grip or grasp firmly, as in wrestling. **3.** To struggle: *grapple with one's conscience.* [< OFr. *grapil*, small hook.] —**grap′pler** *n.*

grappling iron ►*n.* See **grapple** 1.

grasp (grăsp) ►*v.* **1.** To seize or attempt to seize firmly; clutch. **2.** To comprehend. ►*n.* **1.** A firm hold or grip. **2.** The ability or power to seize; reach. **3.** Understanding; comprehension. [ME *graspen.*]

grasp•ing (grăs′pĭng) ►*adj.* Greedy; avaricious. —**grasp′ing•ly** *adv.*

grass (grăs) ►*n.* **1a.** Any of various plants with narrow leaves, jointed stems, and spikes or clusters of minute flowers. **b.** Such plants collectively. **2.** Ground, such as a lawn, covered with grass. **3.** *Slang* Marijuana. [< OE *græs.*] —**grass′y** *adj.*

Grass (gräs), **Günter Wilhelm.** b. 1927. German writer; 1999 Nobel.

grass•hop•per (grăs′hŏp′ər) ►*n.* Any of various related insects having long powerful hind legs adapted for jumping.

grass•land (grăs′lănd′) ►*n.* An area, such as a prairie, of grass or grasslike vegetation.

grass roots ►*pl.n. (takes sing. or pl. v.)* People or society at a local level rather than at the center of a political organization. —**grass′-roots′** *adj.*

grate[1] (grāt) ►*v.* **grat•ed, grat•ing 1.** To shred or pulverize by rubbing against a rough surface. **2.** To make or cause to make a harsh rasping sound. **3.** To irritate persistently. ►*n.* A harsh rasping sound. [< OFr. *grater*, scrape.] —**grat′er** *n.*

grate[2] (grāt) ►*n.* **1.** A framework of parallel or latticed bars over an opening. **2.** A framework of metal bars used to hold fuel or food in a stove, furnace, or fireplace. [< Lat. *crātis*, wickerwork.] —**grat′ed** *adj.*

grate•ful (grāt′fəl) ►*adj.* **1.** Appreciative; thankful. **2.** Expressing gratitude. **3.** Pleasing; agreeable. [< Lat. *grātus*, pleasing.] —**grate′ful•ly** *adv.* —**grate′ful•ness** *n.*

Gra•tian (grā′shən, -shē-ən). A.D. 359–383. Emperor of Rome (367–383) who ruled jointly (from 379) with Theodosius I.

grat•i•fy (grăt′ə-fī′) ►*v.* **-fied, -fy•ing 1.** To please or satisfy. See Syns at **please. 2.** To give what is desired to; indulge. [< Lat. *grātificārī*, to favor.] —**grat′i•fi•ca′tion** *n.* —**grat′i•fi′er** *n.* —**grat′i•fy′ing** *adj.*

grat•ing (grā′tĭng) ►*n.* A grill or network of bars; grate.

grat•is (grăt′ĭs, grä′tĭs, grā′-) ►*adv. & adj.* Without charge. [< Lat. *grātīs.*]

grat•i•tude (grăt′ĭ-to͞od′, -tyo͞od′) ►*n.* Thankfulness. [< Lat. *grātus*, pleasing.]

gra•tu•i•tous (grə-to͞o′ĭ-təs, -tyo͞o′-) ►*adj.* **1.** Given without return; unearned. **2.** Unnecessary or unwarranted: *gratuitous criticism.* [< Lat. *grātuītus.*] —**gra•tu′i•tous•ly** *adv.* —**gra•tu′i•tous•ness** *n.*

gra•tu•i•ty (grə-to͞o′ĭ-tē, -tyo͞o′-) ►*n., pl.* **-ties.** A tip for service. [< Med.Lat. *grātuītās.*]

grave[1] (grāv) ►*n.* **1.** An excavation for a burial.

2. A place of burial. [< OE *græf.*]

grave² (grāv) ►*adj.* **grav•er, grav•est 1.** Requiring serious thought; momentous. **2.** Fraught with danger or harm. **3.** Dignified in conduct or character. **4.** (*also* gräv). Written with the mark (`), as the è in *Sèvres.* ►*n.* (*also* gräv). The grave accent. [< Lat. *gravis*, heavy.] —**grave′ly** *adv.* —**grave′ness** *n.*

grave³ (grāv) ►*v.* **graved, grav•en** (grā′vən) or **graved, grav•ing.** To engrave. [< OE *grafan.*] —**grav′er** *n.*

grav•el (grăv′əl) ►*n.* A loose mixture of rock fragments or pebbles. [< OFr. *gravele*, dim. of *grave*, pebbly shore.] —**grav′el•ly** *adj.*

Graves (grāvz), **Robert Ranke.** 1895–1985. British writer and critic.

grave•stone (grāv′stōn′) ►*n.* A tombstone.

grave•yard (grāv′yärd′) ►*n.* A cemetery.

graveyard shift ►*n.* A work shift that runs during the early morning hours, as from midnight to 8 A.M.

grav•id (grăv′ĭd) ►*adj.* Pregnant. [Lat. *gravidus.*] —**gra•vid′i•ty** (grə-vĭd′ĭ-tē) *n.*

grav•i•met•ric (grăv′ə-mĕt′rĭk) also **grav•i•met•ri•cal** (-rĭ-kəl) ►*adj.* Of measurement by weight. [< Lat. *gravis*, heavy + -METER.] —**grav′i•met′ri•cal•ly** *adv.*

grav•i•tate (grăv′ĭ-tāt′) ►*v.* **-tat•ed, -tat•ing 1.** To move in response to the force of gravity. **2.** To be attracted. —**grav′i•tat′er** *n.*

grav•i•ta•tion (grăv′ĭ-tā′shən) ►*n.* **1a.** The natural phenomenon of attraction between massive bodies. **b.** The act of gravitating. **2.** A movement toward a source of attraction. —**grav′i•ta′tion•al** *adj.* —**grav′i•ta′tion•al•ly** *adv.* —**grav′i•ta′tive** *adj.*

grav•i•ton (grăv′ĭ-tŏn′) ►*n.* A massless particle hypothesized to be the quantum of gravitational interaction.

grav•i•ty (grăv′ĭ-tē) ►*n.* **1.** *Phys.* **a.** The force of attraction between any two massive bodies, which is directly proportional to the product of their masses and inversely proportional to the square of the distance between them, esp. the gravitational force exerted by a celestial body such as the earth. **b.** Gravitation. **2.** Grave consequence; seriousness. **3.** Solemnity or dignity of manner. [< Lat. *gravis*, heavy.]

gra•vure (grə-vyo͝or′) ►*n.* **1.** A method of printing with etched plates or cylinders. **2.** Photogravure. [< OFr. *graver*, engrave.]

gra•vy (grā′vē) ►*n., pl.* **-vies 1.** The juices that drip from cooking meat. **2.** A sauce made from these juices. **3.** *Slang* Money or profit gained easily. [< OFr. *grave.*]

gray also **grey** (grā) ►*n.* A neutral color between black and white. ►*adj.* **-er, -est 1.** Of the color gray. **2.** Dull or dark; gloomy. **3.** Having gray hair. **4.** Intermediate in character or position. [< OE *grǣg.*] —**gray′ish** *adj.* —**gray′ness** *n.*

Gray, Thomas. 1716–71. British poet.

gray•beard (grā′bîrd′) ►*n.* An old man.

gray matter ►*n.* **1.** The brownish-gray nerve tissue of the brain and spinal cord. **2.** *Informal* Brains; intellect.

gray whale ►*n.* A baleen whale of N Pacific waters having grayish-black coloring with white blotches.

gray wolf ►*n.* A large, tawny gray wolf of N North America and Eurasia.

Graz (gräts) A city of SE Austria on the Mur R. SSW of Vienna. Pop. 237,810.

graze¹ (grāz) ►*v.* **grazed, graz•ing 1.** To feed on growing grasses and herbage. **2.** *Informal* To eat frequent snacks. [< OE *grasian* < *græs*, grass.] —**graz′er** *n.*

graze² (grāz) ►*v.* **grazed, graz•ing.** To touch or scrape lightly in passing. See Syns at **brush¹**. [Perh. < GRAZE¹.] —**graze** *n.*

grease (grēs) ►*n.* **1.** Melted animal fat. **2.** A thick oil or viscous lubricant. ►*v.* (grēs, grēz) **greased, greas•ing 1.** To coat, smear, lubricate, or soil with grease. **2.** To facilitate the progress of, as with money or bribes. [< Lat. *crassus*, fat.] —**grease′less** *adj.*

grease•paint (grēs′pānt′) ►*n.* Theatrical makeup.

grease•wood (grēs′wo͝od′) ►*n.* A spiny shrub of W North America, having white stems and greenish flowers.

greas•y (grē′sē, -zē) ►*adj.* **-i•er, -i•est 1.** Coated or soiled with grease. **2.** Containing grease, esp. too much grease. —**greas′i•ly** *adv.* —**greas′i•ness** *n.*

great (grāt) ►*adj.* **-er, -est 1.** Very large in size, quantity, or number. See Syns at **large. 2.** Remarkable in magnitude or extent: *a great crisis.* **3.** Of outstanding importance: *a great work of art.* **4.** Powerful; influential. **5.** Eminent; distinguished: *a great leader.* **6.** *Informal* Very good: *great at algebra.* **7.** *Informal* First-rate: *had a great time.* **8.** Being one generation removed from the relative specified: *a great-granddaughter.* ►*n.* One that is great: *the greats of the opera world.* [< OE *grēat*, thick.] —**great′ly** *adv.* —**great′ness** *n.*

great ape ►*n.* Any of a family of anthropoid apes including chimpanzees, gorillas, and orangutans.

Great Barrier Reef. The world's largest coral reef, about 2,011 km (1,250 mi), off the NE coast of Australia.

Great Basin. A desert region of the W US comprising most of NV and parts of UT, CA, ID, WY, and OR.

Great Bear Lake. A lake of NW mainland Northwest Terrs., Canada.

Great Britain 1. An island off the W coast of Europe comprising England, Scotland, and Wales. **2.** See **United Kingdom.**

great circle ►*n.* A circle described by the intersection of the surface of a sphere with a plane passing through its center.

great•coat (grāt′kōt′) ►*n.* A heavy overcoat.

Great Dane ►*n.* A large powerful dog having a short smooth coat and narrow head.

Great Dane

great•er (grā′tər) ►*adj.* Of or being a city considered together with its suburbs.

Greater Antilles. An island group of the N

West Indies including Cuba, Jamaica, Hispaniola, and Puerto Rico.

Great Falls. A city of central MT on the Missouri R. NNE of Helena. Pop. 55,097.

great horned owl ▸*n.* A large North American owl having prominent ear tufts and brownish plumage with a white throat.

Great Lakes. A group of five freshwater lakes of central North America between the US and Canada, including Lakes Superior, Huron, Erie, Ontario, and Michigan.

Great Plains. A vast grassland region of central North America extending from the Canadian provinces of Alberta, Saskatchewan, and Manitoba S to TX.

Great Rift Valley. A geologic depression of SW Asia and E Africa extending from the Jordan R. valley to Mozambique.

Great Salt Lake. A saline lake of NW UT.

Great Slave Lake. A lake of S Northwest Terrs., Canada.

Great Smoky Mountains. A range of the Appalachian Mts. on the NC–TN border.

great white shark ▸*n.* A large shark of temperate and tropical waters that feeds on marine mammals.

grebe (grēb) ▸*n.* Any of various diving birds having a pointed bill and lobed fleshy membranes along each toe. [Fr. *grèbe.*]

Gre•cian (grē′shən) ▸*adj.* Greek. ▸*n.* A native or inhabitant of Greece.

Grec•o (grĕk′ō), **El.** 1541–1614. Greek-born Spanish painter of religious works.

Grec•o-Ro•man (grĕk′ō-rō′mən, grē′kō-) ▸*adj.* Relating to both Greece and Rome.

Greece (grēs) A country of SE Europe on the S Balkan Peninsula and including numerous islands in the Mediterranean, Aegean, and Ionian seas. Cap. Athens. Pop. 9,740,417.

greed (grēd) ▸*n.* An excessive desire for more than one needs or deserves. [< GREEDY.]

greed•y (grē′dē) ▸*adj.* **-i•er, -i•est.** Wishing to possess more than one needs or deserves. [< OE *grǣdig.*] —**greed′i•ly** *adv.* —**greed′i•ness** *n.*

Greek (grēk) ▸*n.* **1.** The Indo-European language of the Greeks. **2.** A native or inhabitant of Greece. **3.** *Informal* Something unintelligible: *Quantum mechanics is Greek to me.* —**Greek** *adj.*

Greek Orthodox Church ▸*n.* The state church of Greece, an autonomous part of the Eastern Orthodox Church.

Gree•ley (grēlē), **Horace.** 1811–72. Amer. journalist and politician.

green (grēn) ▸*n.* **1a.** Any of a group of colors whose hue is that of growing grass. **b.** The hue of the visible spectrum lying between yellow and blue. **2. greens** Leafy plants or plant parts used as food or for decoration. **3.** A grassy lawn or plot: *a putting green.* ▸*adj.* **-er, -est 1.** Of the color green. **2.** Covered with green growth or foliage. **3.** Made with leafy vegetables. **4.** Not mature or ripe. **5.** Inexperienced. ▸*v.* To make or become green. [< OE *grēne.*] —**green′ish** *adj.* —**green′ness** *n.*

green•back (grēn′băk′) ▸*n.* A note of US currency.

green bean ▸*n.* See **string bean.**

green card ▸*n.* An official document issued by the US government to aliens, allowing them to work legally in the US.

Greene (grēn), **(Henry) Graham.** 1904–91. British writer.

Greene, Nathanael. 1742–86. Amer. Revolutionary general.

green•er•y (grē′nə-rē) ▸*n.*, *pl.* **-ies.** Green foliage; verdure.

green-eyed (grēn′īd′) ▸*adj.* Jealous.

green•horn (grēn′hôrn′) ▸*n.* An inexperienced or immature person, esp. one who is easily deceived. [ME *greene horn,* horn of a freshly slaughtered animal.]

green•house (grēn′hous′) ▸*n.* A structure, usu. of glass, in which temperature and humidity can be controlled for the cultivation or protection of plants.

greenhouse effect ▸*n.* The phenomenon whereby the earth's atmosphere traps solar radiation, caused by gases such as carbon dioxide and methane that allow incoming sunlight to pass through but absorb heat radiated back from the earth's surface.

greenhouse gas ▸*n.* An atmospheric gas that contributes to the greenhouse effect.

Green•land (grēn′lənd, -lănd′) An island of Denmark in the N Atlantic off NE Canada. —**Green•land′ic** *adj.*

green light ▸*n.* **1.** The green-colored light that signals traffic to proceed. **2.** *Informal* Permission to proceed.

Green Mountains. A range of the Appalachian Mts. extending from Canada through VT to MA.

Greens•bor•o (grēnz′bûr′ə, -bûr′ō) A city of N-central NC. Pop. 183,521.

green•sward (grēn′swôrd′) ▸*n.* Ground that is green with grass; turf.

green tea ▸*n.* Tea made from leaves that are not fermented before being dried.

green thumb ▸*n.* An unusual ability to make plants grow well.

Green•wich (grĕn′ĭch) A borough of Greater London in SE England; on the prime meridian. Pop. 214,836

Greenwich time ▸*n.* See **universal time.**

greet (grēt) ▸*v.* **1.** To welcome or salute in a friendly and respectful way. **2.** To receive with a specified reaction. **3.** To be perceived by: *A terrible din greeted our ears.* [< OE *grētan.*] —**greet′er** *n.*

greet•ing (grē′tĭng) ▸*n.* A word or gesture of welcome or salutation.

greeting card ▸*n.* A folded card bearing a message, as of greeting or congratulation.

gre•gar•i•ous (grĭ-gâr′ē-əs) ▸*adj.* **1.** Seeking and enjoying the company of others; sociable. See Syns at **social. 2.** Tending to move in or form a group. [< Lat. *gregārius* < *grex, greg-,* flock.] —**gre•gar′i•ous•ly** *adv.* —**gre•gar′i•ous•ness** *n.*

Gre•go•ri•an calendar (grĭ-gôr′ē-ən, -gōr′-) ▸*n.* The calendar in use throughout most of the world, sponsored by Pope Gregory XIII in 1582. See table at **calendar.**

Gregorian chant ▸*n. Rom. Cath. Ch.* An unaccompanied, monophonic liturgical chant. [After Saint GREGORY I.]

Greg•o•ry I (grĕg′ə-rē), Saint. "Gregory the Great." 540?–604. Pope (590–604).

Gregory VII. 1020?–85. Pope (1073–85).

Gregory XIII. 1502–85. Pope (1572–85).

grem•lin (grĕm′lĭn) ▸*n.* An imaginary gnomelike creature to whom mechanical problems are attributed. [Perh. < Ir.Gael. *gruamín.*]

Gre•na•da (grə-nā′də) A country in the Windward Is. of the West Indies comprising the island of **Grenada** and the S Grenadines. Cap. St. George's. Pop. 92,000.

gre•nade (grə-nād′) ▸*n.* A small bomb detonated by a fuse and thrown by hand or fired from a launcher. [< OFr. *(pome) grenate,* POMEGRANATE.]

gren•a•dier (grĕn′ə-dîr′) ▸*n.* Formerly, a foot soldier equipped with grenades. [Fr. < *grenade,* GRENADE.]

gren•a•dine (grĕn′ə-dēn′, grĕn′ə-dēn′) ▸*n.* A thick sweet syrup made from pomegranates. [< OFr. *grenate,* POMEGRANATE.]

Gren•a•dines (grĕn′ə-dēnz′) An archipelago in the Windward Is. of the E Caribbean, divided between Grenada and the country of St. Vincent and the Grenadines.

Gre•no•ble (grə-nō′bəl, -nôbl′) A city of SE France. Pop. 150,815.

Gretz•ky (grĕt′skē), **Wayne.** b. 1961. Canadian hockey player.

grew (gro͞o) ▸*v.* P.t. of **grow.**

grey (grā) ▸*adj. & n.* Var. of **gray.**

Grey, Charles. 1764–1845. British prime minister (1830–34).

Grey, Lady **Jane.** 1537–54. Queen of England for nine days (1553); executed.

Grey, Zane. 1875–1939. Amer. writer.

grey•hound (grā′hound′) ▸*n.* A slender, swift-running dog having a narrow head and long legs. [< OE *grīghund.*]

grid (grĭd) ▸*n.* **1.** A framework of crisscrossed or parallel bars. **2.** A pattern of regularly spaced horizontal and vertical lines forming squares, as on a map, used as a reference for locating points. **3a.** An interconnected system for the distribution of electricity or electromagnetic signals over a wide area, esp. a network of high-tension cables and power stations. **b.** A conducting plate in a storage battery. **c.** A network or coil of fine wires located between the plate and the filament in an electron tube. [< GRIDIRON.]

grid•dle (grĭd′l) ▸*n.* A flat pan or metal surface used for frying. [< Lat. *crātīcula* < *crātis,* lattice work.]

grid•dle•cake (grĭd′l kāk′) ▸*n.* See **pancake.**

grid•i•ron (grĭd′ī′ərn) ▸*n.* **1.** A football field. **2.** A flat metal grid or grate used for broiling. [< ME *gridere,* alteration of *gridel,* GRIDDLE.]

grid•lock (grĭd′lŏk′) ▸*n.* A traffic jam in which no vehicular movement is possible. —**grid′lock′** *v.* —**grid′locked′** *adj.*

grief (grēf) ▸*n.* **1.** Deep mental anguish, as that arising from bereavement. **2.** A source of sorrow or anguish. **3.** Annoyance or frustration. [< OFr. < *grever,* GRIEVE.]

Grieg (grēg, grĭg), **Edvard Hagerup.** 1843–1907. Norwegian composer.

griev•ance (grē′vəns) ▸*n.* **1.** A circumstance regarded as just cause for protest. **2.** A complaint based on such a circumstance.

grieve (grēv) ▸*v.* **grieved, griev•ing 1.** To cause sorrow to; distress. **2.** To feel or express grief. [< Lat. *gravāre,* to burden.]

Syns: *grieve, lament, mourn, sorrow* ***Ant:*** *rejoice* ***v.***

griev•ous (grē′vəs) ▸*adj.* **1.** Causing grief, pain, or anguish. **2.** Serious; grave. —**griev′ous•ly** *adv.* —**griev′ous•ness** *n.*

grif•fin also **grif•fon** or **gryph•on** (grĭf′ən) ▸*n.* A fabulous beast with the head and wings of an eagle and the body of a lion. [< Lat. *grȳphus* < Gk. *grups.*]

Grif•fith (grĭf′ĭth), **D(avid Lewelyn) W(ark).** 1875–1948. Amer. filmmaker.

grill (grĭl) ▸*n.* **1.** A cooking surface of parallel metal bars. **2.** Food broiled on a grill. **3.** A restaurant where grilled foods are served. **4.** Var. of **grille.** ▸*v.* **1.** To broil on a grill. **2.** *Informal* To question relentlessly; cross-examine. [< Lat. *crātīcula,* GRIDDLE.]

grille also **grill** (grĭl) ▸*n.* A usu. metal grating used as a screen or barrier, as in a window or on the front of an automobile. [< OFr. *greille,* gridiron. See GRIDDLE.]

grim (grĭm) ▸*adj.* **grim•mer, grim•mest 1.** Unrelenting; stern. **2.** Terrible in aspect; forbidding. **3.** Ghastly; sinister. **4.** Dismal; gloomy. [< OE, fierce.] —**grim′ly** *adv.* —**grim′ness** *n.*

grim•ace (grĭm′ĭs, grĭ-mās′) ▸*n.* A contortion of the face expressive of pain, contempt, or disgust. [< OFr. *grimache.*] —**grim′ace** *v.*

grime (grīm) ▸*n.* Black dirt or soot clinging to or ingrained in a surface. [ME *grim.*] —**grim′i•ness** *n.* —**grim′y** *adj.*

Grim•ké (grĭm′kē), **Sarah Moore.** 1792–1873. Amer. feminist and abolitionist.

Grimm (grĭm). **Jakob Ludwig Karl** (1785–1863) and **Wilhelm Karl** (1786–1859). German philologists and folklorists.

grin (grĭn) ▸*v.* **grinned, grin•ning.** To smile broadly, showing the teeth. [< OE *grennian,* to grimace.] —**grin** *n.* —**grin′ner** *n.*

grind (grīnd) ▸*v.* **ground** (ground), **grind•ing 1a.** To crush or pulverize by friction. **b.** To shape, sharpen, or refine with friction: *grind a lens.* **2a.** To rub together harshly; gnash: *grind the teeth.* **b.** To move with noisy friction: *grind to a halt.* **3.** To bear down on harshly; crush. **4.** To oppress or weaken gradually. **5.** To operate or produce by turning a crank. **6.** To produce mechanically or without inspiration: *grinding out novels.* **7.** *Informal* To devote oneself to study or work. ▸*n.* **1.** The act of grinding. **2.** A specific degree of pulverization, as of coffee beans. **3.** *Informal* A laborious task, routine, or study. **4.** *Informal* A student thought to work or study excessively. [< OE *grindan.*] —**grind′ing•ly** *adv.*

grind•er (grīn′dər) ▸*n.* **1.** One that grinds, esp.: **a.** One who sharpens cutting edges. **b.** A mechanical device that grinds. **2.** See **submarine** 2. See Regional Note at **submarine.**

grind•stone (grīnd′stōn′) ▸*n.* **1.** A revolving stone disk used for grinding, polishing, or sharpening tools. **2.** A millstone. —***idiom:*** **put (one's) nose to the grindstone** *Informal* To work in earnest.

grip (grĭp) ▸*n.* **1.** A tight hold; firm grasp. **2.** A manner of grasping and holding. **3.** Mastery; command: *a good grip on the subject.* **4.** A part designed to be grasped; handle. **5.** A suitcase. **6.** A stagehand or member of a film crew who helps move scenery or adjust lighting and props. ▸*v.* **gripped, grip•ping 1.** To secure and maintain a tight hold on. **2.** To hold the interest or attention of. [< OE *gripe.*] —**grip′per** *n.* —**grip′ping•ly** *adv.*

gripe (grīp) ▸*v.* **griped, grip•ing 1.** *Informal*

To complain naggingly or petulantly; grumble. **2.** To cause or have sharp pains in the bowels. **3.** *Informal* To irritate; annoy: *Your meddling really gripes me.* ►*n.* **1.** *Informal* A complaint. **2. gripes** Sharp pains in the bowels. [< OE *grīpan.*] —**grip′er** *n.*

grippe also **grip** (grĭp) ►*n.* See **influenza.** [Fr. < OFr. *gripper*, seize.] —**grip′py** *adj.*

Gris (grēs), **Juan.** 1887–1927. Spanish painter.

gris•ly (grĭz′lē) ►*adj.* **-li•er, -li•est.** Horrifying; gruesome: *a grisly murder.* [< OE *grislīc.*] —**gris′li•ness** *n.*

grist (grĭst) ►*n.* Grain to be ground or already ground. —***idiom:* grist for (one's) mill** Something that can be used to advantage. [< OE *grīst.*]

gris•tle (grĭs′əl) ►*n.* Cartilage, esp. in meat. [< OE.] —**gris′tly** *adj.*

grit (grĭt) ►*n.* **1.** Tiny rough granules, as of sand or stone. **2.** *Informal* Indomitable spirit. ►*v.* **grit•ted, grit•ting.** To clamp (the teeth) together. [< OE *grēot.*] —**grit′ti•ly** *adv.* —**grit′ti•ness** *n.* —**grit′ty** *adj.*

grits (grĭts) ►*pl.n. (takes sing. or pl. v.)* **1.** A coarse meal made of ground hominy. **2.** A mush made from this meal. [< OE *grytta*, coarse meal.]

griz•zled (grĭz′əld) ►*adj.* Grizzly.

griz•zly (grĭz′lē) ►*adj.* **-zli•er, -zli•est.** Grayish or flecked with gray. ►*n., pl.* **-zlies.** A grizzly bear. [< OFr. *grisel*, gray < *gris.*]

grizzly bear ►*n.* The brown bear of NW North America.

groan (grōn) ►*v.* To voice a deep inarticulate sound, as of pain, grief, or displeasure. [< OE *grānian.*] —**groan** *n.*

groats (grōts) ►*pl.n. (takes sing. or pl. v.)* Hulled, usu. crushed grain, esp. oats. [< OE *grotan.*]

gro•cer (grō′sər) ►*n.* One that sells foodstuffs and household supplies. [< Med.Lat. *grossārius*, wholesale dealer.]

gro•cer•y (grō′sə-rē) ►*n., pl.* **-ies 1.** A store selling foodstuffs and household supplies. **2. groceries** Goods sold by a grocer.

grog (grŏg) ►*n.* An alcoholic liquor, esp. rum diluted with water. [After Old *Grog*, Admiral Edward Vernon (1684–1757).]

grog•gy (grŏg′ē) ►*adj.* **-gi•er, -gi•est.** Unsteady and dazed; shaky. —**grog′gi•ly** *adv.* —**grog′gi•ness** *n.*

groin (groin) ►*n.* **1.** The crease where the thigh meets the trunk, with the area nearby. **2.** *Archit.* The curved edge at the junction of two intersecting vaults. [< ME *grinde.*]

grom•met (grŏm′ĭt) ►*n.* A reinforced eyelet, as in cloth or leather, through which a fastener may be passed. [Prob. < OFr. *gormette*, chain joining the ends of a bit.]

Gro•my•ko (grə-mē′kō, grō-), **Andrei Andreyevich.** 1909–89. Soviet political leader.

groom (gro͞om, gro͝om) ►*n.* **1.** A man or boy employed to take care of horses. **2.** A bridegroom. ►*v.* **1.** To make neat and trim. **2.** To clean and brush (an animal). **3.** To prepare, as for a specific position. [ME *grom.*] —**groom′er** *n.*

groove (gro͞ov) ►*n.* **1.** A long narrow furrow or channel. **2.** *Slang* A settled routine. **3.** *Slang* A pleasurable experience. ►*v.* **grooved, groov•ing 1.** To cut a groove or grooves. **2.** *Slang* To enjoy oneself. [Prob. < MDu. *groeve*, ditch.]

groov•y (gro͞o′vē) ►*adj.* **-i•er, -i•est** *Slang.* Delightful; wonderful. —**groov′i•ness** *n.*

grope (grōp) ►*v.* **groped, grop•ing 1.** To reach about uncertainly; feel one's way. **2.** To search blindly or uncertainly: *grope for an answer.* ►*n.* The act of groping. [< OE *grāpian.*] —**grop′er** *n.* —**grop′ing•ly** *adv.*

Gro•pi•us (grō′pē-əs), **Walter Adolph.** 1883–1969. German-born Amer. architect.

gros•beak (grōs′bēk′) ►*n.* Any of various finches having a thick conical bill. [< Fr. *grosbec.*]

gro•schen (grō′shən) ►*n., pl.* **-schen.** See table at **currency.** [Ger. < LLat. *grossus*, thick.]

gross (grōs) ►*adj.* **-er, -est 1.** Exclusive of deductions; total: *gross profits.* **2.** Utter: *gross incompetence.* **3.** Glaringly obvious; flagrant: *gross injustice.* **4a.** Coarse; crude. **b.** Disgusting. **5.** Overweight; corpulent. **6.** Broad; general. ►*n.* **1.** *pl.* **gross•es** The entire body or amount, as of income. **2.** *pl.* **gross** A group of 144 items; 12 dozen. ►*v.* To earn as a total before deductions. —***phrasal verb:* gross out** *Slang* To fill with disgust. [< LLat. *grossus*, thick.] —**gross′ly** *adv.* —**gross′ness** *n.*

gross national product ►*n.* The total market value of all the goods and services produced by a nation during a specified period.

grosz (grôsh) ►*n., pl.* **gro•szy** (grô′shē). See table at **currency.** [Pol., ult. < LLat. *grossus*, thick.]

Grosz (grōs), **George.** 1893–1959. German-born Amer. artist.

gro•tesque (grō-tĕsk′) ►*adj.* **1.** Marked by ludicrous or incongruous distortion, as of appearance. **2.** Outlandish or bizarre. [< Ital. *grottesco*, of a grotto.] —**gro•tesque′** *n.* —**gro•tesque′ly** *adv.* —**gro•tesque′ness** *n.* —**gro•tes′que•ry** *n.*

Gro•ti•us (grō′shē-əs, -shəs), **Hugo.** 1583–1645. Dutch jurist and politician.

grot•to (grŏt′ō) ►*n., pl.* **-toes** or **-tos.** A cave or cavelike excavation. [< Ital. *grotta* < Lat. *crypta*, CRYPT.]

grouch (grouch) ►*n.* **1.** A habitually complaining or irritable person. **2.** A complaint. ►*v.* To grumble or sulk. [< ME *grucchen*, complain. See GRUDGE.] —**grouch′i•ly** *adv.* —**grouch′i•ness** *n.* —**grouch′y** *adj.*

ground[1] (ground) ►*n.* **1.** The solid surface of the earth. **2.** Soil; earth. **3.** often **grounds** An area of land designated for a particular purpose. **4. grounds** The land surrounding a building. **5.** A position contested in or as if in battle. **6.** A background. **7.** often **grounds** The foundation or basis for an argument or action. **8.** often **grounds** The underlying condition prompting an action; cause: *grounds for suspicion.* **9. grounds** The sediment at the bottom of a liquid. **10.** *Elect.* **a.** A large conducting body, such as the earth, used as an arbitrary zero of potential. **b.** A conducting object, such as a wire, connected to such a position of zero potential. ►*v.* **1.** To place on or cause to touch the ground. **2.** To provide a basis for: *ground a theory in facts.* **3.** To supply with basic information. **4a.** To prevent (an aircraft or pilot) from flying. **b.** *Informal* To restrict (someone) to a certain place as a punishment. **5.** *Elect.* To connect (an electric circuit) to a ground. **6.** To run

(a vessel) aground. **7.** *Baseball* To hit (a ball) on the ground. [< OE *grund.*]
ground² (ground) ▶ *v.* P.t. and p.part. of **grind.**
ground•break•ing (ground′brā′kĭng) ▶ *n.* The act or ceremony of breaking ground to begin a construction project. ▶ *adj.* Highly original; new: *a groundbreaking technology.*
ground floor ▶ *n.* **1.** The floor of a building at or nearest ground level. **2.** *Informal* The beginning of a venture.
ground•hog (ground′hôg′, -hŏg′) ▶ *n.* See **woodchuck.**
ground•less (ground′lĭs) ▶ *adj.* Having no ground or foundation; unsubstantiated. See Syns at **baseless.** —**ground′less•ly** *adv.*
ground rule ▶ *n.* **1.** *Sports* A rule governing the playing of a game on a particular field, course, or court. **2.** A basic rule.
ground squirrel ▶ *n.* Any of several burrowing or terrestrial squirrels resembling the chipmunk.
ground•swell (ground′swĕl′) ▶ *n.* **1.** A broad gathering of force, as of public opinion. **2.** A deep swell of the ocean.
ground water also **ground•wa•ter** (ground′wô′tər, -wŏt′ər) ▶ *n.* Subterranean water that supplies wells and springs.
ground•work (ground′wûrk′) ▶ *n.* A foundation; basis.
ground zero ▶ *n.* The point of detonation of a nuclear weapon.
group (gro͞op) ▶ *n.* A number of persons or objects gathered, located, or classified together. See Usage Note at **collective noun.** ▶ *v.* To place in or form a group. [< Ital. *gruppo*, prob. of Gmc. orig.]
grou•per (gro͞o′pər) ▶ *n., pl.* **-er** or **-pers.** Any of various large food and game fishes which inhabit warm seas. [Port. *garupa.*]
group•ie (gro͞o′pē) ▶ *n. Slang* A fan, esp. a young woman, who follows a rock group around on tours.
grouse¹ (grous) ▶ *n., pl.* **grouse** or **grous•es.** A plump chickenlike game bird having mottled brown or grayish plumage. [?]
grouse² (grous) ▶ *v.* **groused, grous•ing** *Informal* To complain. [Perh. < OFr. *grouchier*, grumble.] —**grouse** *n.* —**grous′er** *n.*
grout (grout) ▶ *n.* A thin mortar used to fill cracks and crevices in masonry. ▶ *v.* To fill or finish with grout. [< OE *grūt*, coarse meal.] —**grout′er** *n.*
grove (grōv) ▶ *n.* A small stand of trees that lacks undergrowth. [< OE *grāf.*]
grov•el (grŏv′əl, grŭv′-) ▶ *v.* **-eled, -el•ing** also **-elled, -el•ling.** To behave in a servile manner; cringe. [< ON *ā grūfu*, lying face down.] —**grov′el•er** *n.* —**grov′el•ing•ly** *adv.*
grow (grō) ▶ *v.* **grew** (gro͞o), **grown** (grōn), **grow•ing 1a.** To increase or cause to increase in size by a natural process. **b.** To cultivate; raise: *grow vegetables.* **2.** To expand or intensify. **3.** To develop and reach maturity. **4.** To originate; stem: *love that grew from friendship.* **5.** To become: *grow angry; grow closer.* —***phrasal verbs:* grow on** To become more pleasurable or acceptable to: *a way of singing that grows on you.* **grow up** To become an adult. [< OE *grōwan.*] —**grow′er** *n.*
growl (groul) ▶ *n.* A low, guttural, menacing sound, as of a dog. [Prob. < OFr. *grouler*, of Gmc. orig.] —**growl** *v.* —**growl′er** *n.* —**growl′y** *adj.*
grown (grōn) ▶ *v.* P.part. of **grow.** ▶ *adj.* Adult; mature.
grown•up also **grown-up** (grōn′ŭp′) ▶ *n.* An adult.
grown-up (grōn′ŭp′) ▶ *adj.* Of or intended for adults; mature.
growth (grōth) ▶ *n.* **1.** The process of growing or developing. **2.** Evolution. **3.** An increase, as in size or number. **4.** Something that has grown: *a new growth of grass.* **5.** *Pathol.* An abnormal mass of tissue in or on a living organism.
growth ring ▶ *n.* A growth layer in secondary xylem seen in a cross section.
Groz•ny (grôz′nē) The capital of Chechnya in SW Russia. Pop. 393,000.
grub (grŭb) ▶ *v.* **grubbed, grub•bing 1.** To dig up by or as if by the roots. **2.** To clear of roots and stumps. **3a.** To search laboriously; rummage. **b.** To toil arduously; drudge. **4.** *Slang* To obtain by begging: *grub a cigarette.* ▶ *n.* **1.** The thick wormlike larva of certain insects. **2.** *Slang* Food. [ME *grubben.*] —**grub′ber** *n.*
grub•by (grŭb′ē) ▶ *adj.* **-bi•er, -bi•est.** Dirty; grimy. —**grub′bi•ly** *adv.* —**grub′bi•ness** *n.*
grub•stake (grŭb′stāk′) ▶ *n.* Supplies or funds advanced to a mining prospector or a person starting a business in return for a share of the profits. —**grub′stake′** *v.*
grudge (grŭj) ▶ *v.* **grudged, grudg•ing.** To be reluctant to give or admit. ▶ *n.* A feeling of resentment. [< OFr. *grouchier*, grumble.] —**grudg′er** *n.* —**grudg′ing•ly** *adv.*
gru•el (gro͞o′əl) ▶ *n.* A thin watery porridge. [< OFr., of Gmc. orig.]
gru•el•ing also **gru•el•ling** (gro͞o′ə-lĭng, gro͞o′lĭng) ▶ *adj.* Physically or mentally demanding. —**gru′el•ing•ly** *adv.*
grue•some (gro͞o′səm) ▶ *adj.* Causing horror and repugnance; frightful and shocking. [Obsolete *grue*, to shudder + -SOME[1].] —**grue′some•ly** *adv.* —**grue′some•ness** *n.*
gruff (grŭf) ▶ *adj.* **-er, -est 1.** Brief and unfriendly: *a gruff reply.* **2.** Hoarse; harsh. [< MDu. *grof.*] —**gruff′ly** *adv.* —**gruff′ness** *n.*
grum•ble (grŭm′bəl) ▶ *v.* **-bled, -bling.** To mutter discontentedly. [< MDu. *grommelen.*] —**grum′ble** *n.* —**grum′bler** *n.* —**grum′bly** *adj.*
grump (grŭmp) ▶ *n.* **1.** A cranky, complaining person. **2.** often **grumps** A fit of ill temper. [?] —**grump** *v.* —**grump′i•ly** *adv.* —**grump′i•ness** *n.* —**grump′y** *adj.*
grunge (grŭnj) ▶ *n. Slang* **1.** Filth; dirt. **2.** Rock music incorporating punk rock and heavy metal styles, often having lyrics exhibiting nihilism, dissatisfaction, or apathy. [Back-formation from GRUNGY.]
grun•gy (grŭn′jē) ▶ *adj.* **-gi•er, -gi•est** *Slang.* In a dirty or run-down condition. [?]
grun•ion (grŭn′yən) ▶ *n.* A small fish of California coastal waters that spawns inshore at night. [Perh. < Sp. *gruñón*, grumbler.]
grunt (grŭnt) ▶ *v.* To utter (with) a deep guttural sound, as a hog does. ▶ *n.* **1.** A deep guttural sound. **2.** Any of various tropical fishes that produce grunting sounds. **3.** *Slang* An infantryman in the US military. **4.** *Slang* A menial;

drudge. [< OE *grunnettan.*] —**grunt′er** *n.*

gr. wt. ▸*abbr.* gross weight

gryph•on (grĭf′ən) ▸*n.* Var. of **griffin.**

GSA ▸*abbr.* **1.** General Services Administration **2.** Girl Scouts of America

Gt. Brit. ▸*abbr.* Great Britain

GU ▸*abbr.* **1.** genitourinary **2.** Guam

gua•ca•mo•le (gwä′kə-mō′lē) ▸*n.* A thick paste of mashed and seasoned avocado, served as a dip. [< Nahuatl *ahuacamolli.*]

Gua•da•la•ja•ra (gwŏd′l-ə-hä′rə) A city of W-central Mexico WNW of Mexico City. Pop. 1,626,152.

Gua•dal•ca•nal (gwŏd′l-kə-năl′) A volcanic island of the SE Solomon group in the W Pacific.

Gua•de•loupe (gwŏd′l-o͞op′, gwŏd′l-o͞op′) An overseas department of France in the Leeward Is. of the West Indies. Cap. Basse-Terre. Pop. 421,000.

Guam (gwäm) An unincorp. territory of the US, the largest of the Mariana Is. in the W Pacific. Cap. Agana. Pop. 156,974. —**Gua•ma′ni•an** (gwä-mā′nē-ən) *adj. & n.*

gua•na•ba•na (gwə-nä′bə-nə) ▸*n.* See **soursop.** [Am.Sp. *guanábana.*]

Gua•na•ba•ra Bay (gwä′nə-bär′ə) An inlet of the Atlantic on the SE coast of Brazil.

Guang•zhou (gwäng′jō′) also **Kwang•chow** (kwäng′chō′). Formerly **Canton.** A city of S China on a delta near the South China Sea. Pop. 3,918,010.

gua•nine (gwä′nēn′) ▸*n.* A purine base, $C_5H_5ON_5$, that is an essential constituent of both RNA and DNA. [< GUANO.]

gua•no (gwä′nō) ▸*n., pl.* **-nos.** The dung of sea birds or bats, used as fertilizer. [< Quechua *huanu*, dung.]

Guan•tá•na•mo (gwän-tä′nə-mō′) A city of SE Cuba N of **Guantánamo Bay,** an inlet of the Caribbean Sea. Pop. 206,311.

guar (gwär) ▸*n.* An annual plant cultivated in semiarid regions as a forage crop and for its seeds. [Hindi *guār.*]

gua•ra•ni (gwä′rə-nē′) ▸*n., pl.* **-ni** or **-nis.** See table at **currency.** [Sp. *guaraní*, Guarani.]

Guarani ▸*n., pl.* **-ni** or **-nis 1.** A member of a South American Indian people of Paraguay, N Argentina, and S Brazil. **2.** The language of the Guarani.

guar•an•tee (găr′ən-tē′) ▸*n.* **1.** Something assuring a particular outcome or condition. **2.** An assurance, esp. in writing, attesting to the quality or durability of a product or service. **3.** A guaranty. **4.** A guarantor. ▸*v.* **-teed, -tee•ing 1.** To assume responsibility for the debt or default of. **2.** To assume responsibility for the quality or performance of. **3.** To undertake to accomplish. **4.** To make certain. **5.** To furnish security for. **6.** To declare with conviction. [< OFr. *garant*, a warrant.]

guar•an•tor (găr′ən-tôr′, găr′ən-tər) ▸*n.* One that gives a promise, assurance, or pledge.

guar•an•ty (găr′ən-tē) ▸*n., pl.* **-ties 1.** An agreement by which one person assumes the responsibility of assuring payment of another's debts or obligations. **2a.** Something given as security for the execution or completion of something else. **b.** The act of providing such security. **3.** A guarantor. [< OFr. *garant*, a warrant.]

guard (gärd) ▸*v.* **1.** To protect from harm; watch over. **2.** To watch over to prevent escape. **3.** *Sports* To keep (an opposing player) from scoring. **4.** To keep watch at. ▸*n.* **1.** One who protects or keeps watch. **2.** One who supervises prisoners. **3.** A group of people serving as an escort on ceremonial occasions. **4.** *Football* One of the two offensive linemen on either side of the center. **5.** *Basketball* Either of the two players positioned in the backcourt. **6.** A device or attachment that prevents injury, damage, or loss. —***idiom:*** **on** (or **off**) **(one's) guard** Being (or not being) alert and watchful. [< OFr. *guarder.*] —**guard′er** *n.*

guard•ed (gär′dĭd) ▸*adj.* **1.** Protected; supervised. **2.** Cautious; restrained. —**guard′ed•ly** *adv.* —**guard′ed•ness** *n.*

guard•house (gärd′hous′) ▸*n.* **1.** A building that accommodates a military guard. **2.** A military jail.

guard•i•an (gär′dē-ən) ▸*n.* **1.** One that guards or protects. **2.** One legally responsible for the care and management of the person or property of an incompetent or minor. —**guard′i•an•ship′** *n.*

guards•man (gärdz′mən) ▸*n.* A member of the National Guard.

guar gum ▸*n.* A paste made from the seeds of the guar, used as an ingredient in foods and pharmaceuticals.

Guar•ne•ri (gwär-nĕr′ē, -nyĕr′ē). Family of Italian violin makers, including **Andrea** (1626?–98) and **Giuseppe** (1687?–1745).

Gua•te•ma•la (gwä′tə-mä′lə) **1.** A country of N Central America. Cap. Guatemala. Pop. 10,322,000. **2.** Also **Guatemala City.** The capital of Guatemala, in the S-central part. Pop. 1,675,589. —**Gua′te•ma′lan** *adj. & n.*

gua•va (gwä′və) ▸*n.* The yellow-skinned fruit of a tropical American tree, used for jellies and preserves. [Sp. *guayaba.*]

guava

Gua•ya•quil (gwī′ə-kēl′) A city of W Ecuador near the **Gulf of Guayaquil,** an inlet of the Pacific. Pop. 1,508,444.

gu•ber•na•to•ri•al (go͞o′bər-nə-tôr′ē-əl, -tōr′-, gyo͞o′-) ▸*adj.* Of or relating to a governor. [< Lat. *gubernātor*, governor.]

guck (gŭk, go͝ok) also **gook** (go͝ok, go͞ok) ▸*n.* *Slang* A thick messy substance, such as sludge. [Poss. G(OO) + (M)UCK.]

Guern•sey[1] (gûrn′zē) An island of S Great Britain, one of the Channel Is.

Guern•sey[2] (gûrn′zē) ▸*n., pl.* **-seys.** Any of a breed of brown and white dairy cattle orig. developed on the island of Guernsey.

guer•ril•la or **gue•ril•la** (gə-rĭl′ə) ▸*n.* A

member of an irregular military force operating in small bands in occupied territory to harass and undermine the enemy. [Sp., raiding party < *guerra*, war.]

guess (gĕs) ►*v.* **1.** To predict (a result or event) without sufficient information. **2.** To estimate correctly. **3.** To suppose; think: *I guess he was wrong.* ►*n.* **1.** An act of guessing. **2.** A conjecture arrived at by guessing. [ME *gessen.*] —**guess′er** *n.*

guess•work (gĕs′wûrk′) ►*n.* The process or result of making guesses.

guest (gĕst) ►*n.* **1.** One who receives hospitality at the home or table of another. **2.** One who pays for meals or accommodations at a restaurant or hotel. **3.** A visiting performer or contestant, as on a television program. [< ON *gestr.*]

guest worker ►*n.* A foreigner permitted to work in a country on a temporary basis.

Gue•va•ra (gə-vär′ə), **Ernesto.** "Che." 1928–67. Argentine-born Cuban revolutionary leader.

Che Guevara
photographed in 1961

guff (gŭf) ►*n. Slang* **1.** Nonsense; baloney. **2.** Back talk. [Perh. imit.]

guf•faw (gə-fô′) ►*n.* A boisterous burst of laughter. [Prob. imit.] —**guf•faw′** *v.*

GUI (gō͞o′ē) ►*n. Comp. Sci.* An interface in which a pointing device, such as a mouse, is used to manipulate graphical images on a monitor. [*g(raphical) u(ser) i(nterface).*]

Gui•an•a (gē-ăn′ə, -ä′nə, gī-) A region of NE South America including SE Venezuela, part of N Brazil, and French Guiana, Suriname, and Guyana.

guid•ance (gīd′ns) ►*n.* **1.** The act or process of guiding. **2.** Counseling; advice. **3.** Any of various processes for guiding the path of a vehicle, esp. a missile.

guide (gīd) ►*n.* **1.** One who shows the way by leading, directing, or advising, esp. a person employed to conduct others, as on a tour or expedition. **2.** Something, such as a pamphlet, that offers basic information or instruction. **3.** Something that serves to direct. **4.** A device, such as a ruler, that serves as an indicator or regulates motion. ►*v.* **guid•ed, guid•ing 1.** To serve as a guide for; conduct. **2.** To direct the course of; steer. **3.** To exert control or influence over. [< OProv. *guidar*, to guide, of Gmc. orig.] —**guid′er** *n.*

Syns: *guide, lead, pilot, shepherd, steer, usher* **v.**

guide•book (gīd′bo͝ok′) ►*n.* A handbook of information, esp. for travelers or tourists.

guid•ed missile (gī′dĭd) ►*n.* A self-propelled missile that can be guided while in flight.

guide dog ►*n.* A dog trained to guide a visually impaired or sightless person.

guide dog

guide•line (gīd′līn′) ►*n.* A statement or rule of policy or procedure.

guide•post (gīd′pōst′) ►*n.* A post with a sign giving directions for travelers.

Gui•do d'A•rez•zo (gwē′dō dä-rĕt′sō). 990?–1050. Benedictine monk and music theorist.

gui•don (gī′dŏn′, gīd′n) ►*n.* A small flag carried by a military unit. [< OItal. *guidone* < *guidare*, GUIDE.]

guild (gĭld) ►*n.* An association of persons of the same trade, formed to protect common interests and maintain standards. [< ON *gildi*, payment.]

guil•der (gĭl′dər) ►*n.* See table at **currency.** [< MDu. *gulden*, golden.]

guile (gīl) ►*n.* Treacherous cunning; skillful deceit. [< OFr.] —**guile′ful** *adj.* —**guile′ful•ly** *adv.* —**guile′less** *adj.* —**guile′less•ly** *adv.* —**guile′less•ness** *n.*

guil•lo•tine (gĭl′ə-tēn′, gē′ə-) ►*n.* A device consisting of a heavy blade held aloft between upright guides and dropped to behead the victim below. ►*v.* **-tined, -tin•ing.** To behead with a guillotine. [After J.I. *Guillotin* (1738–1814).]

guilt (gĭlt) ►*n.* **1.** The fact of being responsible for the commission of an offense. **2.** *Law* Culpability for a crime that carries a legal penalty. **3a.** Remorseful awareness of having done something wrong. **b.** Self-reproach, as for inadequacy. [< OE *gylt*, crime.] —**guilt′less** *adj.* —**guilt′less•ly** *adv.*

guilt•y (gĭl′tē) ►*adj.* **-i•er, -i•est 1.** Responsible for a crime or wrongdoing. **2.** *Law* Adjudged to have committed a crime. **3.** Suffering from or prompted by a sense of guilt. —**guilt′i•ly** *adv.* —**guilt′i•ness** *n.*

guin•ea (gĭn′ē) ►*n.* A former English gold coin worth one pound and one shilling. [After the *Guinea* coast of Africa.]

Guinea. A country of W Africa on the Atlantic. Cap. Conkary. Pop. 6,501,000. —**Guin′e•an** *adj. & n.*

Guinea, Gulf of. A broad inlet of the Atlantic formed by the great bend in the W-central coast of Africa.

Guin•ea-Bis•sau (gĭn′ē-bĭ-sou′) A country of

W Africa on the Atlantic. Cap. Bissau. Pop. 1,050,000.

guinea fowl ▸*n.* A domesticated pheasantlike African bird having blackish plumage flecked with small white spots. [After the *Guinea* coast of Africa.]

guinea pig ▸*n.* **1.** A small, short-eared rodent having variously colored hair and no visible tail, often kept as pets or used as experimental animals. **2.** *Informal* A person used for experimentation or research, often unknowingly. [Poss. alteration of GUIANA.]

Guin•e•vere (gwĭn′ə-vîr′) also **Guen•e•vere** (gwĕn′-) ▸*n.* The wife of King Arthur and lover of Lancelot in Arthurian legend.

guise (gīz) ▸*n.* **1.** Outward appearance; aspect. **2.** False appearance. **3.** Mode of dress. [< OFr., manner.]

gui•tar (gĭ-tär′) ▸*n.* A musical instrument having a large flat-backed sound box, a long fretted neck, and usu. six strings. [< Gk. *kithara*, lyre.] —**gui•tar′ist** *n.*

Gui•yang (gwē′yäng′) also **Kwei•yang** (kwā′-). A city of SW China. Pop. 1,664,709.

Gui•zot (gē-zō′), **François Pierre Guillaume.** 1787–1874. French historian and politician.

gu•lag also **Gu•lag** (go͞o′läg) ▸*n.* A network of forced labor camps in the former Soviet Union, esp. for political dissidents. [Russ.]

gulch (gŭlch) ▸*n.* A small ravine. [Perh. < ME *gulchen*, spew.]

gulf (gŭlf) ▸*n.* **1.** A large area of a sea or ocean partially enclosed by land. **2.** A deep, wide chasm; abyss. **3.** A wide gap, as in understanding. [< Gk. *kolpos.*]

Gulf States 1. The countries bordering the Persian Gulf in SW Asia. **2.** The states of the S US with coastlines on the Gulf of Mexico.

Gulf Stream. A generally N-flowing warm ocean current of the N Atlantic off E North America.

gulf•weed (gŭlf′wēd′) ▸*n.* A brownish, tropical Atlantic seaweed often forming dense floating masses.

gull[1] (gŭl) ▸*n.* Any of various chiefly coastal water birds having long wings, webbed feet, and usu. gray and white plumage. [ME *gulle*, poss. of Celt. orig.]

gull[2] (gŭl) ▸*n.* A person who is easily tricked; dupe. ▸*v.* To deceive or cheat. [Prob. < *gull*, to swallow.]

Gul•lah (gŭl′ə) ▸*n.* **1.** One of a group of people of African ancestry inhabiting coastal areas of South Carolina, Georgia, and N Florida. **2.** The English-based creole of the Gullahs.

gul•let (gŭl′ĭt) ▸*n.* **1.** The esophagus. **2.** The throat. [< OFr. *goulet* < Lat. *gula.*]

gul•li•ble (gŭl′ə-bəl) ▸*adj.* Easily deceived or duped. —**gul′li•bil′i•ty** *n.* —**gul′li•bly** *adv.*

gul•ly (gŭl′ē) ▸*n., pl.* **-lies.** A deep ditch cut in the earth by running water. [< GULLET.]

gulp (gŭlp) ▸*v.* **1.** To swallow greedily or rapidly in large amounts. **2.** To swallow air audibly, as in nervousness. ▸*n.* **1.** The act of gulping. **2.** A large mouthful. [ME *gulpen.*]

gum[1] (gŭm) ▸*n.* **1.** Any of various viscous plant substances that dry into water-soluble, noncrystalline, brittle solids. **2.** A sticky or adhesive substance. **3.** Any of various trees yielding gum. **4.** Chewing gum. ▸*v.* **gummed, gum•ming 1.** To cover, seal, or fix in place with gum. **2.** To become sticky or clogged. —***phrasal verb:* gum up** To ruin or bungle. [< Gk. *kommi.*] —**gum′mi•ness** *n.* —**gum′my** *adj.*

gum[2] (gŭm) ▸*n.* The firm connective tissue that surrounds the bases of the teeth. ▸*v.* **gummed, gum•ming.** To chew (food) with toothless gums. [< OE *gōma*, palate.]

gum arabic ▸*n.* A gum exuded by various African trees, used as a thickener and in pills, candies, and mucilage.

gum•bo (gŭm′bō) ▸*n., pl.* **-bos 1a.** See **okra** 1. **b.** *Regional* See **okra** 2. See Regional Note at **goober. 2.** A soup or stew thickened with okra pods. [Louisiana Fr. *gombo.*]

gum•drop (gŭm′drŏp′) ▸*n.* A small candy made of sweetened gum arabic or gelatin.

gump•tion (gŭmp′shən) ▸*n. Informal* Boldness of enterprise; initiative. [Sc.]

gum•shoe (gŭm′sho͞o′) ▸*n.* **1.** A rubber overshoe. **2.** *Slang* A detective.

gun (gŭn) ▸*n.* **1.** A weapon consisting of a metal tube from which a projectile is fired. **2.** A portable firearm. **3.** A device that discharges something under pressure or at great speed: *a grease gun.* ▸*v.* **gunned, gun•ning 1.** To shoot (a person): *gun down a robber.* **2.** To open the throttle of: *gunned the engine.* —***phrasal verb:* gun for** To seek to overcome, ruin, or obtain. —***idiom:* under the gun** Under great pressure or under threat. [< shortening of ME *Gunilda*, woman's name applied to a siege engine < ON *gunnr*, war.]

gun•boat (gŭn′bōt′) ▸*n.* A small armed vessel.

gun•cot•ton (gŭn′kŏt′n) ▸*n.* See **nitrocellulose.**

gun•fight (gŭn′fīt′) ▸*n.* A duel or battle with firearms. —**gun′fight′er** *n.*

gun•fire (gŭn′fīr′) ▸*n.* The firing of guns.

gung ho (gŭng′ hō′) ▸*adj. Slang* Extremely enthusiastic and dedicated. [< Mandarin *gōng hé*, work together.]

gun•lock (gŭn′lŏk′) ▸*n.* A device for igniting the charge of a firearm.

gun•man (gŭn′mən) ▸*n.* A man, esp. a criminal, armed with a gun.

gun•met•al (gŭn′mĕt′l) ▸*n.* **1.** An alloy of copper with tin. **2.** Metal used for guns. **3.** A dark gray.

gun•nel (gŭn′əl) ▸*n.* Var. of **gunwale.**

gun•ner (gŭn′ər) ▸*n.* A member of the armed forces who operates a gun.

gun•ner•y (gŭn′ə-rē) ▸*n.* The science of constructing and operating guns.

gunnery sergeant ▸*n.* A rank in the US Marine Corps above staff sergeant.

gun•ny (gŭn′ē) ▸*n.* A coarse heavy fabric made of jute or hemp. [< Skt. *goṇī*, sack.]

gun•ny•sack (gŭn′ē-săk′) ▸*n.* A sack made of burlap or gunny.

gun•play (gŭn′plā′) ▸*n.* An exchange of gunfire.

gun•pow•der (gŭn′pou′dər) ▸*n.* An explosive powder used to propel projectiles from guns.

gun•shot (gŭn′shŏt′) ▸*n.* **1.** The shooting of a gun. **2.** The range of a gun: *within gunshot.* **3.** Shot fired from a gun.

gun-shy (gŭn′shī′) ▸*adj.* **1.** Afraid of loud noise, esp. gunfire. **2.** Extremely wary.

gun•smith (gŭn′smĭth′) ▸*n.* One who makes or repairs firearms.

gun•wale also **gun•nel** (gŭn′əl) ►*n.* The upper edge of the side of a ship or boat.

gup•py (gŭp′ē) ►*n., pl.* **-pies.** A small, brightly colored freshwater fish popular in home aquariums. [After R.J. Lechmere *Guppy* (1836–1916).]

gur•gle (gûr′gəl) ►*v.* **-gled, -gling 1.** To flow in a broken, irregular current with a bubbling sound. **2.** To make a sound similar to this. [< Lat. *gurguliō*, gullet.] —**gur′gle** *n.* —**gur′gling•ly** *adv.*

gur•ney (gûr′nē) ►*n., pl.* **-neys.** A metal stretcher with wheeled legs, used for transporting patients. [Prob. after J. Theodore *Gurney*.]

gu•ru (go͝or′o͞o, go͞o-ro͞o′) ►*n., pl.* **-rus 1.** *Hinduism* A personal spiritual teacher. **2.** A revered teacher or mentor. **3.** A recognized leader: *the guru of high finance.* [< Skt. *guru-*, venerable.]

gush (gŭsh) ►*v.* **1.** To flow forth suddenly in great volume. **2.** To make an excessive display of sentiment or enthusiasm. ►*n.* A copious outflow. [ME *gushen.*] —**gush′i•ly** *adv.* —**gush′i•ness** *n.* —**gush′y** *adj.*

gush•er (gŭsh′ər) ►*n.* One that gushes, esp. a gas or oil well.

gus•set (gŭs′ĭt) ►*n.* A triangular insert for added strength or expansion in a garment. [< OFr. *gousset.*]

gus•sy (gŭs′ē) ►*v.* **-sied, -sy•ing** *Slang.* To dress or adorn elaborately. [Poss. < Australian slang *gussie*, effeminate man.]

gust (gŭst) ►*n.* **1.** A strong abrupt rush of wind. **2.** An outburst of emotion. ►*v.* To blow in gusts. [< ON *gustr.*] —**gust′i•ly** *adv.* —**gust′i•ness** *n.* —**gust′y** *adj.*

gus•ta•to•ry (gŭs′tə-tôr′ē, -tōr′ē) ►*adj.* Of or relating to the sense of taste. [< Lat. *gustāre*, to taste.] —**gus′ta•to′ri•ly** *adv.*

Gus•ta•vus I (gŭs-tā′vəs, -tä′-). 1496–1560. King of Sweden (1523–60).

Gustavus II. 1594–1632. King of Sweden (1611–32).

Gustavus IV. 1778–1837. King of Sweden (1792–1809).

Gustavus V. 1858–1950. King of Sweden (1907–50).

Gustavus VI. 1882–1973. King of Sweden (1950–73).

gus•to (gŭs′tō) ►*n.* Vigorous enjoyment. See Syns at **zest.** [Ital.]

gut (gŭt) ►*n.* **1.** The alimentary canal or a portion thereof, esp. the intestine or stomach. **2. guts** The bowels; entrails. **3.** *Slang* **a.** One's innermost being. **b. guts** The inner working parts. **4. guts** *Slang* **a.** Courage; fortitude. **b.** Nerve; audacity. **5.** A tough cord made from animal intestines. ►*v.* **gut•ted, gut•ting 1.** To disembowel. **2.** To remove the essence or substance of. **3.** To destroy the interior of: *Fire gutted the house.* ►*adj. Slang* Deeply felt: *a gut response.* [< OE *guttas*, entrails.]

Gu•ten•berg (go͞ot′n-bûrg′), **Johann.** 1400?–68? German printer; traditionally considered the inventor of movable type.

Guth•rie (gŭth′rē), **Woodrow Wilson.** "Woody." 1912–67. Amer. folk singer and composer.

gut•less (gŭt′lĭs) ►*adj. Slang* Lacking courage or drive. —**gut′less•ness** *n.*

guts•y (gŭt′sē) ►*adj.* **-i•er, -i•est** *Slang.* Marked by courage or daring; plucky. —**guts′i•ly** *adv.* —**guts′i•ness** *n.*

gut•ta-per•cha (gŭt′ə-pûr′chə) ►*n.* A rubbery substance obtained from certain tropical trees, used as an electrical insulator and in golf balls. [Malay *getah perca.*]

gut•ter (gŭt′ər) ►*n.* **1.** A channel for draining off water along the edge of a street or roof. See Regional Note at **andiron. 2.** A trough on either side of a bowling alley. **3.** A squalid state of human existence. ►*v.* **1.** To flow in channels. **2.** To melt away: *The candle guttered and died.* [< Lat. *gutta*, a drop.]

gut•ter•snipe (gŭt′ər-snīp′) ►*n.* A street urchin.

gut•tur•al (gŭt′ər-əl) ►*adj.* **1.** Of or produced in the throat. **2.** Harsh; throaty. **3.** *Ling.* Velar. [< Lat. *guttur*, throat.] —**gut′tur•al•ly** *adv.*

guy[1] (gī) ►*n.* A rope, cord, or cable used to steady, guide, or secure something. [< OFr. *guier*, to guide and < LGer. *gie*, a guide.] —**guy** *v.*

guy[2] (gī) ►*n. Informal* **1.** A man; fellow. **2. guys** Persons of either sex. [After *Guy* Fawkes.]

Guy•a•na (gī-ăn′ə, -ä′nə) A country of NE South America on the Atlantic. Cap. Georgetown. Pop. 825,000. —**Guy′a•nese′** (-nēz′, -nēs′) *adj. & n.*

guz•zle (gŭz′əl) ►*v.* **-zled, -zling.** To drink greedily. [?] —**guz′zler** *n.*

gym (jĭm) ►*n.* **1.** A gymnasium. **2.** A school course in physical education.

gym•na•si•um (jĭm-nā′zē-əm) ►*n., pl.* **-si•ums** or **-si•a** (-zē-ə) **1.** A room or building equipped for indoor sports. **2.** (gĭm-nä′zē-o͞om′). A college-preparatory school in some European countries. [< Gk. *gumnasion*, school < *gumnos*, nude.]

gym•nas•tics (jĭm-năs′tĭks) ►*n. (takes pl. v.)* Physical exercises that develop and display strength, balance, and agility, esp. those performed on or with specialized apparatus. [< Gk. *gumnastēs*, athletic trainer.] —**gym′nast′** *n.* —**gym•nas′tic** *adj.* —**gym•nas′ti•cal•ly** *adv.*

gym•no•sperm (jĭm′nə-spûrm′) ►*n.* A plant, such as a conifer, whose seeds are not enclosed within an ovary. [< Gk. *gumnospermos*, having naked seeds.] —**gym′no•sper′mous** *adj.* —**gym′no•sper′my** *n.*

gy•ne•col•o•gy (gī′nĭ-kŏl′ə-jē, jĭn′ĭ-, jī′nĭ-) ►*n.* The branch of medicine dealing with the health of women and esp. of the female reproductive system. [Gk. *gunē*, *gunaik-*, woman + -logy.] —**gy′ne•co•log′i•cal** (-kə-lŏj′ĭ-kəl), **gy′ne•co•log′ic** *adj.* —**gy′ne•col′o•gist** *n.*

gyp also **gip** (jĭp) *Slang* ►*v.* **gypped, gyp•ping** also **gipped, gip•ping.** To cheat or swindle. ►*n.* A fraud or swindle. [Prob. < Gypsy.] —**gyp′per** *n.*

gyp•sum (jĭp′səm) ►*n.* A white mineral, $CaSO_4 \cdot 2H_2O$, used in the manufacture of plaster of Paris, various plaster products, and fertilizers. [< Gk. *gupsos.*]

Gyp•sy also **Gip•sy** (jĭp′sē) ►*n., pl.* **-sies 1.** A member of a nomadic people orig. migrating from N India to Europe around the 14th cent., now also living in North America and Australia. **2.** See **Romany** 2. **3. gypsy** One inclined to a nomadic way of life.

gypsy moth ►*n.* A moth having hairy caterpillars that are destructive to trees.

gy•rate (jī′rāt′) ►*v.* **-rat•ed, -rat•ing 1.** To revolve around a fixed point or axis. **2.** To revolve in a circle or spiral. [< Lat. *gȳrus*, circle.] —**gy•ra′tion** *n.* —**gy′ra′tor** *n.*

gyr•fal•con (jûr′făl′kən, -fôl′-, -fô′-) ►*n.* A large Arctic falcon with color phases from black to gray to white. [< OFr. *girfaut*.]

gy•ro[1] (jī′rō) ►*n., pl.* **-ros.** A gyroscope.

gy•ro[2] (jī′rō, jē′-) ►*n., pl.* **-ros.** A sandwich made usu. of sliced roasted lamb, onion, and tomato on pita bread. [< Mod.Gk. *guros*, a turning (from the turning of the spit).]

gy•ro•com•pass (jī′rō-kŭm′pəs, -kŏm′-) ►*n.* A compass with a motorized gyroscope that maintains a true north-south orientation.

gy•ro•scope (jī′rə-skōp′) ►*n.* A device consisting of a spinning mass, usu. a disk or wheel, mounted on a base so that its axis can turn freely in one or more directions and thereby maintain its orientation regardless of any movement of the base. [Gk. *guros*, circle + -SCOPE.] —**gy′ro•scop′ic** (-skŏp′ĭk) *adj.* —**gy′ro•scop′i•cal•ly** *adv.*

H

h[1] or **H** (āch) ►*n., pl.* **h's** or **H's** also **hs** or **Hs.** The 8th letter of the English alphabet.

h[2] ►*abbr.* **1.** height **2.** hour

H[1] ► The symbol for the element **hydrogen.**

H[2] ►*abbr.* **1.** *Baseball* hit **2.** humidity

ha[1] also **hah** (hä) ►*interj.* Used to express surprise, laughter, or triumph.

ha[2] ►*abbr.* hectare

Haar•lem (här′ləm) A city of W Netherlands near the North Sea. Pop. 149,764.

Ha•bak•kuk (hăb′ə-kŭk′, -ko͝ok′, hə-băk′ək) ►*n.* **1.** A Hebrew prophet of the late 7th cent. B.C. **2.** See table at **Bible.**

ha•be•as corpus (hā′bē-əs) ►*n.* A writ issued to bring a party before a court or judge, used to protect the party from unlawful restraint. [< Med.Lat. *habeās corpus*, you must have the body.]

hab•er•dash•er (hăb′ər-dăsh′ər) ►*n.* A dealer in men's attire. [< AN *haberdassher*.]

hab•er•dash•er•y (hăb′ər-dăsh′ə-rē) ►*n., pl.* **-ies 1.** A haberdasher's shop. **2.** Men's furnishings.

ha•bil•i•ment (hə-bĭl′ə-mənt) ►*n.* **1.** often **habiliments** Clothing or dress, esp. that typical of an occasion or office. **2. habiliments** Characteristic furnishings or equipment; trappings. [< OFr. *habiller*, clothe.]

hab•it (hăb′ĭt) ►*n.* **1.** A pattern of behavior acquired through repetition. **2.** Customary practice. **3.** An addiction. **4.** Characteristic appearance or manner of growth, as of a plant. **5.** A distinctive costume. [< Lat. *habitus*, p.part. of *habēre*, have.]

hab•it•a•ble (hăb′ĭ-tə-bəl) ►*adj.* Suitable to live in. [< Lat. *habitāre*, inhabit.] —**hab′it•a•bil′i•ty** *n.* —**hab′it•a•bly** *adv.*

hab•i•tat (hăb′ĭ-tăt′) ►*n.* **1.** The area or environment in which an organism or ecological community normally lives or occurs. **2.** The place in which a person or thing is likely to be found. [< Lat., it dwells.]

hab•i•ta•tion (hăb′ĭ-tā′shən) ►*n.* **1.** The act of inhabiting or the state of being inhabited. **2a.** A natural environment or locality. **b.** A place of residence. [< Lat. *habitāre*, dwell.]

hab•it-form•ing (hăb′ĭt-fôr′mĭng) ►*adj.* Tending to become a habit, esp. as a result of physiological dependence.

ha•bit•u•al (hə-bĭch′o͞o-əl) ►*adj.* **1a.** Of the nature of a habit: *habitual lying.* **b.** Being such by force of habit: *a habitual liar.* See Syns at **chronic. 2.** Customary; usual. —**ha•bit′u•al•ly** *adv.* —**ha•bit′u•al•ness** *n.*

ha•bit•u•ate (hə-bĭch′o͞o-āt′) ►*v.* **-at•ed, -at•ing.** To accustom by repetition or long exposure. [< Lat. *habitus*, HABIT.] —**ha•bit′u•a′tion** *n.*

hab•i•tude (hăb′ĭ-to͞od′, -tyo͞od′) ►*n.* A customary behavior. [< Lat. *habitūdō*.]

ha•bit•u•é (hə-bĭch′o͞o-ā′, hə-bĭch′o͞o-ā′) ►*n.* One who frequents a particular place, as a café or bar. [Fr.]

Habs•burg (hăps′bûrg′). See **Hapsburg.**

ha•ci•en•da (hä′sē-ĕn′də) ►*n.* **1.** A large estate in Spanish-speaking countries. **2.** The main house of such an estate. [Sp.]

hack[1] (hăk) ►*v.* **1.** To cut or chop with heavy, irregular blows. **2.** To cough roughly or harshly. **3.** *Slang* To cope with successfully; manage. **4.** *Comp. Sci.* **a.** To alter (a program): *hacked her text editor to read HTML.* **b.** To access illegally: *hacked into a government network.* ►*n.* **1.** A cut made by hacking. **2.** A tool used for hacking. **3.** A rough, dry cough. [< OE *-haccian*.]

hack[2] (hăk) ►*n.* **1.** A hackney. **2.** A worn-out horse for hire. **3a.** A hireling. **b.** A writer hired to produce routine writing. **4.** *Informal* **a.** A taxicab. **b.** or **hackie.** A taxicab driver. ►*v.* To employ or work as a hack. ►*adj.* **1.** By or for a hack. **2.** Hackneyed. [< HACKNEY.]

hack•a•more (hăk′ə-môr′, -mōr′) ►*n.* A halter used in breaking horses to a bridle. [< Sp. *jáquima*, halter < Ar. *šakīma*, bit.]

hack•er (hăk′ər) ►*n.* **1a.** A computer buff. **b.** One who illegally gains access to another's electronic system. **2.** An enthusiastic amateur at a sport. [< *hacker*, inept golf player, or < *hack*, clever trick.]

hack•le (hăk′əl) ►*n.* **1.** Any of the long slender feathers on the neck of a bird. **2. hackles** The erectile hairs along the back of the neck of an animal, esp. a dog. **3.** A tuft of feathers trimming a fishing fly. —***idiom:* get (one's) hackles up** To be extremely insulted or irritated. [ME *hakell*.]

hack•ney (hăk′nē) ►*n., pl.* **-neys 1.** A horse suited for routine riding or driving. **2.** A coach or carriage for hire. ►*v.* To make banal and trite. [ME *hakenei*.]

hack•neyed (hăk′nēd) ►*adj.* Banal; trite.

hack•saw (hăk′sô′) ►*n.* A tough, fine-toothed saw stretched in a frame, used for cutting metal. [< ME *hagge-saw*.] —**hack′saw′** *v.*

had (hăd) ►*v.* P.t. and p.part. of **have.**

had•dock (hăd′ək) ►*n., pl.* **-dock** or **-docks.** A N Atlantic food fish related to the cod. [ME *haddok.*]

Ha•des (hā′dēz) ►*n.* **1.** *Gk. Myth.* The abode of the dead. **2.** also **hades** Hell. [Gk. *Haidēs.*]

had•n't (hăd′nt) ► Had not.

Ha•dri•an (hā′drē-ən). A.D. 76–138. Emperor of Rome (117–138).

had•ron (hăd′rŏn′) ►*n.* Any of a class of subatomic particles, including protons and neutrons, that take part in the strong interaction. [Gk. *hadros*, thick + -ON[1].]

had•ro•saur (hăd′rə-sôr′) ►*n.* Any of various amphibious dinosaurs that had webbed feet and a ducklike bill. [Gk. *hadros*, thick + *sauros*, lizard.]

hadst (hădst) ►*v. Archaic* 2nd pers. sing. p.t. of **have.**

-haemia ►*suff.* Var. of **-emia.**

haf•ni•um (hăf′nē-əm) ►*n. Symbol* **Hf** A brilliant silvery metallic element used in nuclear reactor control rods and in the manufacture of tungsten filaments. At. no. 72. See table at **element.** [After *Hafnia*, Medieval Latin name for Copenhagen, Denmark.]

haft (hăft) ►*n.* A handle or hilt, esp. of a tool or weapon. [< OE *hæft.*]

hag (hăg) ►*n.* **1.** An ugly old woman. **2.** A witch; sorceress. [Perh. < OE *hægtesse*, witch.] —**hag′gish** *adj.*

Hag•ga•i (hăg′ē-ī′, hăg′ī′) ►*n.* **1.** A Hebrew prophet of the 6th cent. B.C. **2.** See table at **Bible.**

hag•gard (hăg′ərd) ►*adj.* Appearing worn and gaunt. [< OFr. *hagard*, wild hawk.] —**hag′gard•ly** *adv.* —**hag′gard•ness** *n.*

hag•gle (hăg′əl) ►*v.* **-gled, -gling.** To argue in an attempt to bargain. [< ON *höggva*, cut.] —**hag′gle** *n.* —**hag′gler** *n.*

hag•i•og•ra•phy (hăg′ē-ŏg′rə-fē, hā′jē-) ►*n., pl.* **-phies 1.** Biography of saints. **2.** A worshipful or idealizing biography. [Gk. *hagios*, holy + -GRAPHY.] —**hag′i•og′raph•er** *n.* —**hag′i•o•graph′ic** (-ə-grăf′ĭk), **hag′i•o•graph′i•cal** *adj.*

Hague (hāg), **The.** The de facto capital of the Netherlands, in the W part near the North Sea. Pop. 444,392.

hah (hä) ►*interj.* Var. of **ha**[1].

Hai•da (hī′də) ►*n., pl.* **-da** or **-das 1.** A member of a Native American people inhabiting the Queen Charlotte Is. of W British Columbia, Canada, and Prince of Wales I. in S Alaska. **2.** The language of the Haida.

Hai•fa (hī′fə) A city of NW Israel on the **Bay of Haifa,** an inlet of the Mediterranean. Pop. 248,200.

hai•ku (hī′ko͞o) ►*n., pl.* **-ku** also **-kus.** An unrhymed Japanese poem having three lines of five, seven, and five syllables. [J.]

hail[1] (hāl) ►*n.* **1.** Precipitation in the form of ice pellets. **2.** Something with the force of a shower of hail: *a hail of criticism.* ►*v.* **1.** To precipitate hail. **2.** To pour down or forth. [< OE *hægel.*]

hail[2] (hāl) ►*v.* **1a.** To salute or greet. **b.** To greet or acclaim enthusiastically. **2.** To signal or call out to: *hail a cabdriver.* —***phrasal verb:*** **hail from** To come or originate from. ►*n.* **1.** The act of hailing. **2.** Hailing distance. ►*interj.* Used to express a greeting or tribute. [< ON *(ves) heill*, (be) healthy.] —**hail′er** *n.*

Hai•le Se•las•sie (hī′lē sə-lăs′ē, -lä′sē). Title of Ras Tafari Makonnen. 1892–1975. Emperor of Ethiopia (1930–74).

hail•stone (hāl′stōn′) ►*n.* A pellet of hail.

hail•storm (hāl′stôrm′) ►*n.* A storm with hail.

Hai•phong (hī′fŏng′) A city of NE Vietnam on the Red River delta near the Gulf of Tonkin. Pop. 783,133.

hair (hâr) ►*n.* **1a.** A fine threadlike outgrowth, esp. from the skin of a mammal. **b.** A covering of such outgrowths, as on the human head. **2a.** A minute distance or narrow margin: *won by a hair.* **b.** A precise degree: *calibrated to a hair.* [< OE *hǣr.*] —**hair′less** *adj.*

hair•breadth (hâr′brĕdth′) ►*adj.* Extremely close: *a hairbreadth escape.*

hair•brush (hâr′brŭsh′) ►*n.* A brush for the hair.

hair•cloth (hâr′klôth′, -klŏth′) ►*n.* A wiry fabric woven esp. from horsehair and used for upholstering.

hair•cut (hâr′kŭt′) ►*n.* **1.** The act or an instance of cutting the hair. **2.** A style in which hair is cut. —**hair′cut′ter** *n.* —**hair′cut′ting** *adj. & n.*

hair•do (hâr′do͞o′) ►*n., pl.* **-dos.** A hairstyle.

hair•dress•er (hâr′drĕs′ər) ►*n.* One who cuts or arranges hair. —**hair′dress•ing** *n.*

hair•line (hâr′līn′) ►*n.* **1.** The outline of the growth of hair on the head, esp. across the front. **2.** A very slender line.

hair•piece (hâr′pēs′) ►*n.* A covering or bunch of human or artificial hair used to conceal baldness or give shape to a hairstyle.

hair•pin (hâr′pĭn′) ►*n.* **1.** A thin U-shaped pin used to secure a hairdo or headdress. **2.** A sharp U-shaped turn in a road.

hair-rais•ing (hâr′rā′zĭng) ►*adj.* Causing excitement, terror, or thrills.

hair•split•ting (hâr′splĭt′ĭng) ►*n.* The making of unreasonably fine distinctions. —**hair′split′ter** *n.* —**hair′split′ting** *adj.*

hair spray ►*n.* A preparation sprayed on the hair to keep it in place.

hair•spring (hâr′sprĭng′) ►*n.* A fine coiled spring that regulates the movement of the balance wheel in a watch or clock.

hair•style (hâr′stīl′) ►*n.* A style in which hair is arranged. —**hair′styl′ing** *n.* —**hair′styl′ist** *n.*

hair trigger ►*n.* A gun trigger adjusted to respond to a very slight pressure.

hair-trig•ger (hâr′trĭg′ər) ►*adj.* Responding to the slightest provocation or stimulation: *a hair-trigger temper.*

hair•weav•ing (hâr′wē′vĭng) ►*n.* The process of interweaving a hairpiece of human hair with the wearer's own hair.

hair•y (hâr′ē) ►*adj.* **-i•er, -i•est 1.** Covered with hair. **2.** Of or like hair. **3.** *Slang* Fraught with difficulties; hazardous. —**hair′i•ness** *n.*

Hai•ti (hā′tē) **1.** A country of the West Indies comprising the W part of the island of Hispaniola and two offshore islands. Cap. Port-au-Prince. Pop. 7,041,000. **2.** See **Hispaniola.** —**Hai′tian** *adj. & n.*

haj (hăj) ►*n., pl.* **-es** *Islam* A pilgrimage to Mecca. [Ar. *ḥajj.*]

haj•i (hăj′ē) ►*n., pl.* **-is** *Islam* One who has made a pilgrimage to Mecca. [Pers. *ḥājī.*]

hake (hāk) ►*n., pl.* **hake** or **hakes.** A marine food fish related to the cod. [ME.]

Hak•luyt (hăk′lo͞ot′), **Richard.** 1552?–1616. English geographer.

ha•ku (hä′ko͞o) ►*n.* A crown made of fresh flowers. See Regional Note at **ukulele.** [Hawaiian.]

haku

hal– ►*pref.* Var. of **halo–.**

hal•berd (hăl′bərd, hôl′-) ►*n.* A weapon of the 15th and 16th cent. having an axlike blade and a steel spike mounted on the end of a long shaft. [< MHGer. *helmbarte.*]

hal•cy•on (hăl′sē-ən) ►*adj.* **1.** Calm and peaceful. **2.** Prosperous; golden: *halcyon years.* [< Gk. *alkuōn, halkuōn,* mythical bird.]

hale[1] (hāl) ►*adj.* **hal•er, hal•est.** Sound in health. [< OE *hāl.*] —**hale′ness** *n.*

hale[2] (hāl) ►*v.* **haled, hal•ing.** To compel to go. [< OFr. *haler,* HAUL.]

Hale, Edward Everett. 1822–1909. Amer. cleric and writer.

Hale, Nathan. 1755–76. Amer. Revolutionary soldier.

Ha•le•a•ka•la Crater (hä′lē-ä′kə-lä′) An enormous volcanic crater, 829.6 m (2,720 ft) deep, of E Maui, HI.

half (hăf) ►*n., pl.* **halves** (hăvz) **1a.** One of two equal parts that constitute a whole. **b.** One part approx. equal to the remaining part. **2.** *Sports* **a.** One of two playing periods into which a game is divided. **b.** A halfback. ►*adj.* **1a.** Being one of two equal parts. **b.** Being approx. a half. **2.** Partial or incomplete: *a half smile.* ►*adv.* **1.** To the extent of exactly or nearly a half: *The tank is half empty.* **2.** Not completely; partly: *only half right.* —***idioms:*** **by half 1.** By a considerable extent. **2.** By an excessive amount: *too clever by half.* **by halves** In a reluctant manner; unenthusiastically. **not half** Not at all: *not half bad.* [< OE *healf.*]

half•back (hăf′băk′) ►*n.* *Sports* **1.** One of the two football players near the flanks behind the line of scrimmage. **2.** One of several players stationed behind the forward line in various sports.

half-baked (hăf′bākt′) ►*adj.* **1.** Only partly baked. **2.** *Informal* Insufficiently thought out: *a half-baked scheme.* **3.** *Informal* Lacking common sense.

half boot ►*n.* A low boot extending just above the ankle.

half-breed (hăf′brēd′) ►*n.* *Offensive* A person of mixed racial descent.

half brother ►*n.* A brother related through one parent only.

half-caste (hăf′kăst′) ►*n.* *Offensive* A person of mixed racial descent. —**half′-caste′** *adj.*

half•cocked (hăf′kŏkt′) ►*adj.* *Informal* Inadequately or poorly prepared. ►*adv.* In a halfcocked manner: *go off halfcocked.*

half-dol•lar (hăf′dŏl′ər) ►*n.* A US silver coin worth 50 cents.

half•heart•ed (hăf′här′tĭd) ►*adj.* Exhibiting or feeling little interest or enthusiasm. —**half′heart′ed•ly** *adv.* —**half′heart′ed•ness** *n.*

half-life (hăf′līf′) ►*n.* **1.** *Phys.* The time required for half the nuclei in a sample of a specific isotopic species to undergo radioactive decay. **2.** *Biol.* The time required for half the quantity of a drug or other substance to be metabolized or eliminated.

half-mast (hăf′măst′) ►*n.* The position about halfway up a mast or pole at which a flag is flown as a symbol of mourning or as a signal of distress.

half-moon (hăf′mo͞on′) ►*n.* **1.** The moon when only half its disk is illuminated. **2.** Something shaped like a crescent.

half nelson ►*n.* A wrestling hold in which one arm is passed under the opponent's arm from behind to the back of the neck.

half note ►*n.* *Mus.* A note having half the value of a whole note.

half note
from *Fra Jacopino* by Girolamo Frescobaldi
A. half note
B. quarter note

half sister ►*n.* A sister related through one parent only.

half-slip (hăf′slĭp′) ►*n.* A woman's slip that hangs from the waist.

half sole ►*n.* A shoe sole that extends from the shank to the toe.

half-staff (hăf′stăf′) ►*n.* See **half-mast.**

half step ►*n.* See **semitone.**

half•time (hăf′tīm′) ►*n.* The intermission between halves in a game, such as basketball or football.

half-track (hăf′trăk′) ►*n.* A lightly armored military motor vehicle, with caterpillar treads in place of wheels.

half-truth (hăf′tro͞oth′) ►*n.* A statement, esp. one intended to deceive, that is only partially true.

half•way (hăf′wā′) ►*adj.* **1.** Midway between two points or conditions. **2.** Partial: *halfway measures.* —**half′way′** *adv.*

half-wit (hăf′wĭt′) ►*n.* A foolish or stupid person. —**half′-wit′ted** *adj.* —**half′-wit′ted•ly** *adv.* —**half′-wit′ted•ness** *n.*

hal•i•but (hăl′ə-bət, hŏl′-) ►*n., pl.* **-but** or **-buts.** Any of several large edible flatfishes of N Atlantic or Pacific waters. [ME.]

hal•ide (hăl′īd′, hā′līd′) ►*n.* A chemical compound of a halogen with a more electropositive element or group.

Hal•i•fax (hăl′ə-făks′) The capital of Nova Scotia, Canada, in the S-central part on the Atlantic. Pop. 328,699.

hal•ite (hăl′īt′, hā′līt′) ►*n.* Rock salt.

hal•i•to•sis (hăl′ĭ-tō′sĭs) ►*n.* Stale or foul-smelling breath. [< Lat. *hālitus,* breath.]

hall (hôl) ► *n.* **1.** A corridor or passageway in a building. **2.** A large entrance room; lobby. **3a.** A building with a large room for public gatherings or entertainments. **b.** The room itself. **4.** A building used by a social or religious organization. **5a.** A college or university building. **b.** A large room in such a building. **6.** The main house on a landed estate. **7.** The castle or house of a medieval monarch or noble. [< OE *heall.*]

Hal•le (hä′lə) A city of central Germany WNW of Leipzig. Pop. 295,372.

hal•le•lu•jah (hăl′ə-lo͞o′yə) ► *interj.* Used to express praise or joy. [Heb. *hallǝlû-yāh.*]

Hal•ley (hăl′ē), **Edmund** or **Edmond.** 1656–1742. English astronomer.

hall•mark (hôl′märk′) ► *n.* **1.** A mark indicating quality or excellence. **2.** A conspicuous feature or characteristic. [After Goldsmith's *Hall*, London.]

hall of fame ► *n.* **1.** A group of persons judged outstanding, as in a sport. **2.** A building housing memorials to illustrious persons.

hal•loo (hə-lo͞o′) ► *interj.* Used to catch someone's attention. ► *n.* A shout of "halloo." [< obsolete *holla*, stop!] —**hal•loo′** *n.*

hal•low (hăl′ō) ► *v.* **1.** To make or set apart as holy. **2.** To respect or honor greatly; revere. [< OE *hālgian.*]

Hal•low•een also **Hal•low•e'en** (hăl′ə-wēn′, hŏl′-) ► *n.* Oct. 31, celebrated by children wearing costumes and begging treats. [< *All Hallow Even.*]

hal•lu•ci•na•tion (hə-lo͞o′sə-nā′shən) ► *n.* **1a.** False or distorted perception of objects or events with a compelling sense of their reality. **b.** The objects or events so perceived. **2.** A false or mistaken idea; delusion. [< Lat. *ālūcinārī*, to dream.] —**hal•lu′ci•nate** *v.* —**hal•lu′ci•na′tion•al, hal•lu′ci•na′tive** *adj.* —**hal•lu′ci•na•to′ry** (hə-lo͞o′sə-nə-tôr′ē, -tōr′ē) *adj.*

hal•lu•ci•no•gen (hə-lo͞o′sə-nə-jən) ► *n.* A substance that induces hallucination. —**hal•lu′ci•no•gen′ic** (-jĕn′ĭk) *adj.*

hall•way (hôl′wā′) ► *n.* **1.** A corridor in a building. **2.** An entrance hall.

ha•lo (hā′lō) ► *n., pl.* **-los** or **-loes 1.** A circular band of colored light around a light source, as around the sun or moon. **2.** A luminous ring of light surrounding the heads or bodies of sacred figures in religious paintings. [< Gk. *halōs.*] —**ha′lo** *v.*

halo– or **hal–** ► *pref.* **1.** Salt: *halite.* **2.** Halogen: *halocarbon.* [< Gk. *hals.*]

hal•o•car•bon (hăl′ə-kär′bən) ► *n.* A compound consisting of carbon and a halogen.

hal•o•gen (hăl′ə-jən) ► *n.* Any of a group of five chemically related nonmetallic elements including fluorine, chlorine, bromine, iodine, and astatine. —**ha•log′e•nous** (hă-lŏj′ə-nəs) *adj.*

Hals (hälz, häls), **Frans.** 1580?–1666. Dutch painter.

Hal•sey (hôl′zē), **William Frederick.** "Bull." 1882–1959. Amer. naval officer.

halt[1] (hôlt) ► *n.* A suspension of movement or progress; stop. ► *v.* **1.** To cause to stop. **2.** To stop; pause. See Syns at **stop.** [< OHGer. *haltan*, hold back.]

halt[2] (hôlt) ► *v.* **1.** To proceed or act with uncertainty; waver. **2.** To limp or hobble. [< OE *healtian.*]

hal•ter (hôl′tər) ► *n.* **1.** A device made of rope or leather straps that fits around the head or neck of an animal, used to lead or secure it. **2.** A noose used for execution by hanging. **3.** A bodice for women that ties behind the neck and across the back. ► *v.* **1.** To put a halter on. **2.** To control with or as if with a halter. [< OE *hælftre.*]

halt•ing (hôl′tĭng) ► *adj.* **1.** Hesitant or wavering: *a halting voice.* **2.** Limping; lame. —**halt′ing•ly** *adv.*

hal•vah (häl-vä′, häl′vä) ► *n.* A confection of honey and crushed sesame seeds. [< Ar. *ḥalwā.*]

halve (hăv) ► *v.* **halved, halv•ing 1.** To divide into two equal parts. **2.** To lessen or reduce by half: *halved the recipe.* **3.** *Informal* To share equally: *The twins halve everything.* [ME *halven* < *half*, HALF.]

halves (hăvz) ► *n.* Pl. of **half.**

hal•yard (hăl′yərd) ► *n.* A rope used to raise or lower a sail, flag, or yard. [< ME *halier* < *halen*, pull. See HALE[2].]

ham (hăm) ► *n.* **1.** The thigh of the hind leg of an animal, esp. a hog. **2.** A cut of meat from the ham. **3.** The back of the knee or thigh. **4. hams** The buttocks. **5.** A performer who exaggerates or overacts. **6.** A licensed amateur radio operator. ► *v.* **hammed, ham•ming.** To exaggerate or overact. [< OE *hamm.*]

Ham. In the Bible, a son of Noah and the brother of Japheth and Shem.

Ha•ma or **Ha•mah** (hä′mä). A city of W Syria SSW of Aleppo. Pop. 273,000.

ham•a•dry•ad (hăm′ə-drī′əd) ► *n., pl.* **-ads** or **-a•des** (-ə-dēz′) *Gk. & Rom. Myth.* A wood nymph. [< Gk. *Hamadruas.*]

Ham•burg (hăm′bûrg′) A city of N Germany on the Elbe R. NE of Bremen. Pop. 1,702,887.

ham•burg•er (hăm′bûr′gər) also **ham•burg** (-bûrg′) ► *n.* **1a.** Ground meat, usu. beef. **b.** A cooked patty of such meat. **2.** A sandwich made with a patty of ground meat usu. in a roll or bun. [After HAMBURG.]

Ha•mil•car Bar•ca (hə-mĭl′kär′ bär′kə, hăm′əl-). 270?–228? B.C. Carthaginian general and father of Hannibal.

Ham•il•ton (hăm′əl-tən) **1.** The capital of Bermuda, on Bermuda I. Pop. 1,100. **2.** A city of SE Ontario, Canada, at the W end of Lake Ontario SW of Toronto. Pop. 318,499.

Hamilton, Alexander. 1755?–1804. Amer. politician; killed in a duel with Aaron Burr. —**Ham′il•to′ni•an** (-tō′nē-ən) *adj. & n.*

Hamilton, Edith. 1867–1963. German-born Amer. classicist.

Ham•ite (hăm′īt′) ► *n.* A member of a group of peoples of N and NE Africa, including the Berbers, the Tuaregs, and the ancient Egyptians. —**Ha•mit′ic** (hă-mĭt′ĭk) *adj.*

ham•let (hăm′lĭt) ► *n.* A small village. [< OFr. *ham*, village.]

Ham•mar•skjöld (hăm′ər-shōld′, hä′mär-shœld′), **Dag Hjalmar Agné Carl.** 1905–61. Swedish political leader and diplomat; 1961 Nobel Peace Prize.

ham•mer (hăm′ər) ► *n.* **1.** A hand tool used for striking, consisting of a handle with a perpendicularly attached head. **2.** A tool or device similar in function or action, as: **a.** The part of a gunlock that hits the primer or firing pin or explodes the percussion cap. **b.** *Mus.* One of the padded wooden pieces of a piano that strikes the strings. **c.** A part of an apparatus that strikes a gong or bell, as in a clock. **3.** See **malleus. 4.** *Sports* A metal ball having a long handle from which it is thrown for distance. ►*v.* **1.** To hit, esp. repeatedly. See Syns at **beat. 2.** To fashion or shape with or as if with repeated blows. **3.** *Informal* To keep at something continuously: *hammered away at the problem.* [< OE *hamor.*] —**ham′mer•er** *n.*

ham•mer•head (hăm′ər-hĕd′) ►*n.* **1.** The head of a hammer. **2.** A large predatory shark having eyes set in wide fleshy extensions at the sides of the head.

ham•mer•lock (hăm′ər-lŏk′) ►*n.* A wrestling hold in which the opponent's arm is pulled behind the back and twisted upward.

ham•mock (hăm′ək) ►*n.* A hanging bed of canvas or heavy netting suspended between two supports. [< Taino *hamaca.*]

Ham•mu•ra•bi (hăm′ə-rä′bē, hä′mo͝o-). d. 1750 B.C. Babylonian king (1792–1750).

ham•my (hăm′ē) ►*adj.* **-mi•er, -mi•est.** Marked by overacting; affectedly dramatic.

ham•per¹ (hăm′pər) ►*v.* To prevent the free movement, action, or progress of. [ME *hamperen.*]

Syns: *hamper, fetter, handcuff, hobble, hogtie, manacle, shackle, trammel* **v.**

ham•per² (hăm′pər) ►*n.* A large basket, usu. with a cover. [< OFr. *hanepier*, case for holding goblets.]

Hamp•ton (hămp′tən) An independent city of SE VA opposite Norfolk on **Hampton Roads,** the outlet of three rivers into Chesapeake Bay. Pop. 133,793.

ham•ster (hăm′stər) ►*n.* A small rodent with large cheek pouches and a short tail, often kept as a pet or used in laboratory research. [Poss. < OHGer. *hamustro*, of Slav. orig.]

ham•string (hăm′strĭng′) ►*n.* **1.** Any of the tendons at the rear hollow of the human knee. **2.** or **hamstrings** The muscles constituting the back of the upper leg. **3.** The large tendon in the back of the hock of a quadruped. ►*v.* **1.** To cripple by cutting the hamstring. **2.** To hinder the efficiency of.

Han (hän) ►*n., pl.* **Han** or **Hans.** A member of the principal ethnic group of China.

Han•cock (hăn′kŏk′), **John.** 1737–93. Amer. politician and Revolutionary leader.

hand (hănd) ►*n.* **1.** The terminal part of the human arm, consisting of the wrist, palm, four fingers, and thumb. **2.** A unit of length equal to 4 in. (10.2 cm), used esp. to specify the height of a horse. **3.** Something suggesting the shape or function of the human hand, esp.: **a.** A rotating pointer on the face of a clock. **b.** A pointer on a gauge or dial. **4.** See **index** 3. **5.** Lateral direction: *at my right hand.* **6.** Handwriting; penmanship. **7.** A round of applause. **8.** Assistance; help: *lend a hand.* **9a.** The cards held by or dealt to a player in a card game. **b.** A full round of play: *a hand of poker.* **10a.** A manual laborer: *a factory hand.* **b.** A member of a group or crew. **11.** A participant: *an old hand at diplomacy.* **12.** often **hands a.** Possession or keeping. **b.** Control; care: *His fate is in your hands.* **13a.** Involvement or participation. **b.** An influence or effect: *had a hand in all the decisions.* **c.** Craft or skill. **14.** A pledge to wed. ►*v.* **1.** To give or pass with or as if with the hands. **2.** To aid, direct, or conduct with the hands. —***phrasal verbs:*** **hand down 1.** To bequeath as an inheritance. **2.** To deliver (a verdict). **hand in** To turn in; submit. **hand out** To distribute; disseminate. **hand over** To relinquish to another. —***idioms:*** **at hand 1.** Close by; near. **2.** Soon; imminent. **by hand** Performed manually. **hand in glove** In close association. **hand it to** To give credit to. **hand over fist** At a tremendous rate. **hands down** Easily: *won hands down.* **in hand 1.** Under control. **2.** Accessible at the present time. **off (one's) hands** No longer in one's care or within one's responsibility. **on hand** Available. **on (one's) hands** In one's care or possession, often as an imposition. **out of hand** Out of control: *The fire got out of hand.* **show** (or **tip**) **(one's) hand** To reveal one's intentions. **to hand 1.** Nearby. **2.** In one's possession. [< OE.]

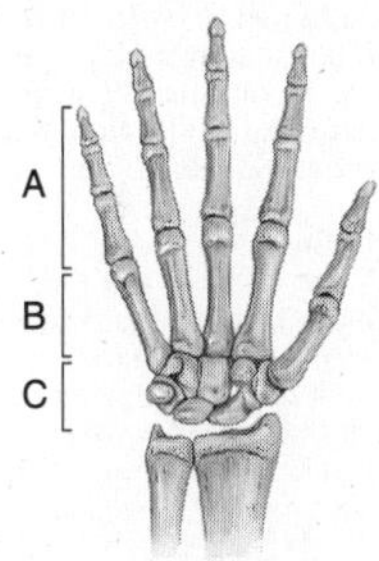

hand
A. phalanges
B. metacarpus
C. carpus

hand•bag (hănd′băg′) ►*n.* **1.** A woman's purse. **2.** A piece of small hand luggage.

hand•ball (hănd′bôl′) ►*n.* **1.** A game played by two or more players who hit a ball against a wall with their hands. **2.** The small rubber ball used in this game.

hand•bill (hănd′bĭl′) ►*n.* A printed sheet or pamphlet distributed by hand.

hand•book (hănd′bo͝ok′) ►*n.* A manual or reference book providing information or instruction about a subject or place.

hand•car (hănd′kär′) ►*n.* A small open railroad car propelled by a hand pump or a small motor.

hand•cart (hănd′kärt′) ►*n.* A small, usu. two-wheeled cart pulled or pushed by hand.

hand•clasp (hănd′klăsp′) ►*n.* A handshake.

hand•cuff (hănd′kŭf′) ►*n.* often **handcuffs.** A restraining device consisting of a pair of strong connected hoops that can be tightened and locked about the wrists. ►*v.* **1.** To restrain with or as if with handcuffs. **2.** To render ineffective. See Syns at **hamper¹.**

hand•ed (hăn′dĭd) ►*adj.* **1.** Of or relating to dexterity or preference with respect to a hand or hands: *one-handed; left-handed.* **2.** Relating to a specified number of people: *a four-handed card game.*

Han•del (hăn′dl), **George Frideric.** 1685–1759. German-born composer.

hand•ful (hănd′fo͝ol′) ►*n., pl.* **-fuls 1.** The amount that a hand can hold. **2.** A small, undefined number or quantity: *a handful of people.* **3.** *Informal* One that is difficult to control or manage: *Our toddler is a handful.*

hand•gun (hănd′gŭn′) ►*n.* A firearm that can be used with one hand.

hand•i•cap (hăn′dē-kăp′) ►*n.* **1a.** A race or contest in which advantages or compensations are given different contestants to equalize the chances of winning. **b.** Such an advantage or penalty. **2.** A physical or mental disability. See Syns at **disadvantage. 3.** A hindrance. ►*v.* **-capped, -cap•ping 1.** To assign a handicap to (a contestant). **2.** To hinder; impede. [< obsolete *hand in cap,* a game in which forfeits were held in a cap.]

hand•i•capped (hăn′dē-kăpt′) ►*adj.* Physically or mentally disabled. ►*n.* Physically or mentally disabled people as a group: *the handicapped.*

Usage: Although *handicapped* is widely used in both law and everyday speech to refer to people having physical or mental disabilities, those described by the word tend to prefer the expressions *disabled* or *people with disabilities.*

hand•i•craft (hăn′dē-krăft′) also **hand•craft** (hănd′krăft′) ►*n.* **1.** Skill and facility with the hands. **2.** An occupation requiring such skill. **3.** Work produced by skilled hands.

hand in hand ►*adv.* In cooperation; jointly.

hand•i•work (hăn′dē-wûrk′) ►*n.* **1.** Work performed by hand. **2.** The product of a person's efforts and actions.

hand•ker•chief (hăng′kər-chĭf, -chēf′) ►*n., pl.* **-chiefs** also **-chieves** (-chĭvz, -chēvz′). A small square of cloth used esp. for wiping the nose or mouth.

han•dle (hăn′dl) ►*v.* **-dled, -dling 1.** To touch, lift, or hold with the hands. **2.** To operate with the hands. **3.** To have responsibility for; manage: *handles legal matters.* See Syns at **treat. 4.** To cope with or dispose of. **5.** To act or function in a given way while in operation: *a car that handles well in the snow.* ►*n.* **1.** A part held or operated with the hand. **2.** An opportunity or means. **3.** *Slang* A person's name. —***idiom:*** **get a handle on** *Informal* To achieve an understanding of. [< OE *handlian.*]

han•dle•bar (hăn′dl-bär′) ►*n.* often **handlebars.** A curved metal steering bar, as on a bicycle.

han•dler (hănd′lər) ►*n.* **1.** One that handles or directs something or someone: *the candidate's campaign handlers.* **2.** One who trains or exhibits an animal, such as a dog.

hand•made (hănd′mād′) ►*adj.* Made or prepared by hand rather than by machine.

hand•maid (hănd′mād′) also **hand•maid•en** (-mād′n) ►*n.* A woman attendant or servant.

hand-me-down (hănd′mē-doun′) ►*adj.* **1.** Handed down to one person after being used and discarded by another. **2.** Of inferior quality; shabby. ►*n.* Something handed down from one person to another.

hand•off (hănd′ôf′, -ŏf′) ►*n. Football* A play in which one player hands the ball to another.

hand•out (hănd′out′) ►*n.* **1.** Food, clothing, or money given to the needy. **2.** A folder or leaflet circulated free of charge. **3.** A prepared news or publicity release.

hand•pick (hănd′pĭk′) ►*v.* **1.** To gather or pick by hand. **2.** To select personally: *handpicked the winning team.* —**hand′picked′** *adj.*

hand•rail (hănd′rāl′) ►*n.* A narrow railing to be grasped with the hand for support.

hand•set (hănd′sĕt′) ►*n.* The handle of a telephone, containing the receiver and transmitter and often a dial or push buttons.

hand•shake (hănd′shāk′) ►*n.* The grasping of hands by two people, as in greeting.

hands-off (hăndz′ôf′, -ŏf′) ►*adj.* Marked by nonintervention.

hand•some (hăn′səm) ►*adj.* **-som•er, -som•est 1.** Pleasing and dignified in form or appearance. **2.** Generous or copious: *a handsome reward.* See Syns at **liberal. 3.** Large: *a handsome price.* [ME *handsom,* handy.] —**hand′some•ly** *adv.* —**hand′some•ness** *n.*

hands-on (hăndz′ŏn′, -ôn′) ►*adj.* Involving active participation.

hand•spring (hănd′sprĭng′) ►*n.* A gymnastic feat in which the body is flipped completely forward or backward from an upright position, landing first on the hands and then on the feet.

hand•stand (hănd′stănd′) ►*n.* The act of balancing on the hands with one's feet in the air.

hand-to-hand (hănd′tə-hănd′) ►*adj.* Being at close quarters: *hand-to-hand combat.* —**hand to hand** *adv.*

hand-to-mouth (hănd′tə-mouth′) ►*adj.* Having or providing only the bare essentials.

hand•work (hănd′wûrk′) ►*n.* Work done by hand rather than by machine.

hand•writ•ing (hănd′rī′tĭng) ►*n.* **1.** Writing done with the hand. **2.** The writing characteristic of a particular person.

hand•y (hăn′dē) ►*adj.* **-i•er, -i•est 1.** Skillful in using one's hands. **2.** Readily accessible. **3.** Easy to use or handle. —**hand′i•ly** *adv.* —**hand′i•ness** *n.*

Handy, William Christopher. "W.C. Handy." 1873–1958. Amer. musician and composer.

hand•y•man (hăn′dē-măn′) ►*n.* A man who does odd jobs or various small tasks.

hang (hăng) ►*v.* **hung** (hŭng), **hang•ing 1.** To fasten from above with no support from below; suspend. **2.** To suspend or fasten so as to allow free movement at or about the point of suspension: *hang a door.* **3.** *p.t. and p.part* **hanged** (hăngd) To execute by suspending by the neck. **4.** To attach at an appropriate angle. **5.** To furnish by suspending objects about: *hang a room with curtains.* **6.** To hold or incline downward; droop: *hang one's head.* **7.** To attach to a wall, esp. to display: *hang wallpaper; hang a painting.* **8.** To deadlock (a jury) by failing to render a unanimous verdict. **9.** To attach oneself as a dependent; cling. **10.** To depend: *It all hangs on one vote.* —***phrasal verbs:*** **hang around** To loiter. **hang back** To hesitate; hold back. **hang on 1.** To cling to something. **2.** To persevere. **hang out** *Slang* **1.** To spend one's free time in a certain place. **2.** To pass time idly; loiter. **hang up 1.** To end a telephone conversation by replacing the receiver. **2.** To delay or impede; hinder. ►*n.* **1.** The way in which something hangs. **2.** Particular meaning or significance. **3.** *Informal* The proper method for doing or using something: *get the hang of a new tool.* —***idioms:*** **give** (or

care) a hang To be concerned. **let it all hang out** *Slang* **1.** To be relaxed. **2.** To be completely candid. [< OE *hangian* and *hōn.*]

Usage: *Hanged,* as a past tense and a past participle of *hang,* is used only in the sense of "to put to death by hanging."

han•gar (hăng′ər, hăng′gər) ►*n.* A shelter for housing or repairing aircraft. [< OFr. *hangard,* shelter.]

hang•dog (hăng′dôg′, -dŏg′) ►*adj.* **1.** Shamefaced or guilty. **2.** Downcast; intimidated.

hang•er (hăng′ər) ►*n.* **1.** One who hangs something. **2.** A contrivance to which something hangs or by which something is hung.

hang•er-on (hăng′ər-ŏn′, -ôn′) ►*n., pl.* **hang•ers-on** (hăng′ərz-). A sycophant; parasite.

hang glider ►*n.* **1.** A kitelike device from which a harnessed rider hangs while gliding from a height. **2.** The rider of such a device. —**hang′-glide′** *v.*

hang•ing (hăng′ĭng) ►*n.* **1.** Execution on a gallows. **2.** Something, such as a tapestry, that is hung.

hang•man (hăng′mən) ►*n.* One employed to execute condemned prisoners by hanging.

hang•nail (hăng′nāl′) ►*n.* A small, partly detached piece of dead skin at the side or the base of a fingernail. [< OE *angnægel.*]

hang•out (hăng′out′) ►*n. Slang* A frequently visited place.

hang•o•ver (hăng′ō′vər) ►*n.* **1.** Unpleasant physical effects following the heavy use of alcohol. **2.** A vestige; holdover.

hang-up (hăng′ŭp′) ►*n. Informal* **1.** A psychological or emotional difficulty or inhibition. **2.** An obstacle.

Hang•zhou (häng′jō′) also **Hang•chow** or **Hang•chou** (hăng′chou′, häng′jō′). A city of E China at the head of **Hangzhou Bay,** an inlet of the East China Sea. Pop. 2,589,504.

hank (hăngk) ►*n.* A coil or loop. [< ON *hönk.*]

han•ker (hăng′kər) ►*v.* To have a strong, often restless desire. [Perh. < Du. dial. *hankeren.*] —**hank′er•er** *n.* —**hank′er•ing** *n.*

han•kie also **han•ky** (hăng′kē) ►*n., pl.* **-kies** *Informal* A handkerchief.

han•ky-pan•ky (hăng′kē-păng′kē) ►*n. Slang* Devious or mischievous activity. [< alteration of HOCUS-POCUS.]

Han•na (hăn′ə), **Marcus Alonzo.** "Mark." 1837–1904. Amer. financier and politician.

Han•ni•bal (hăn′ə-bəl). 247–183? B.C. Carthaginian general.

Ha•noi (hă-noi′, hə-) The capital of Vietnam, in the N part on the Red R. Pop. 1,089,760.

Han•o•ver or **Han•no•ver** (hăn′ō′vər, hä-nō′-) **1.** A former kingdom and province of NW Germany. **2.** A city of NW Germany SE of Bremen. Pop. 524,823.

Han River. A river, about 1,126 km (700 mi), of E-central China flowing to the Chang Jiang (Yangtze R.).

Hans•ber•ry (hănz′bĕr-ē), **Lorraine.** 1930–65. Amer. playwright.

han•som (hăn′səm) ►*n.* A two-wheeled covered carriage with the driver's seat at the rear. [After J.A. *Hansom* (1803–82).]

Ha•nuk•kah or **Ha•nu•kah** also **Cha•nu•kah** (KHä′nə-kə, hä′-) ►*n. Judaism* An eight-day festival commemorating the victory of the Maccabees over Antiochus Epiphanes. [Heb. *ḥănukkâ,* dedication.]

hao•le (hou′lē, -lā) ►*n.* A person, esp. a white person, who is not native Hawaiian. See Regional Note at **ukulele.** [Hawaiian.]

hap (hăp) ►*n.* **1.** Fortune; chance. **2.** An occurrence. [< ON *happ.*]

hap•haz•ard (hăp-hăz′ərd) ►*adj.* Dependent upon or marked by mere chance. —**hap•haz′ard•ly** *adv.* —**hap•haz′ard•ness** *n.*

hap•less (hăp′lĭs) ►*adj.* Luckless. See Syns at **unfortunate.** —**hap′less•ly** *adv.*

hap•loid (hăp′loid′) ►*adj.* **1.** Having the same number of chromosomes as a gamete or half as many as a somatic cell. **2.** Having a single set of chromosomes. [Gk. *haplous,* single + -OID.]

hap•ly (hăp′lē) ►*adv.* By chance or accident.

hap•pen (hăp′ən) ►*v.* **1a.** To come to pass. **b.** To come into being. **2.** To take place by chance. **3.** To come upon something by chance. **4.** To appear by chance; turn up. [ME *happenen* < *hap,* HAP.]

Syns: *happen, befall, betide, chance, occur* **v.**

hap•pen•ing (hăp′ə-nĭng) ►*n.* **1.** An occurrence. **2.** An improvised, often spontaneous spectacle.

hap•pen•stance (hăp′ən-stăns′) ►*n.* A chance circumstance.

hap•py (hăp′ē) ►*adj.* **-pi•er, -pi•est 1.** Lucky; fortunate. **2.** Enjoying, showing, or marked by pleasure. **3.** Well adapted; felicitous: *a happy turn of phrase.* **4.** Cheerful; willing. [ME < *hap,* luck. See HAP.] —**hap′pi•ly** *adv.* —**hap′pi•ness** *n.*

Syns: *happy, fortunate, lucky* **adj.**

hap•py-go-luck•y (hăp′ē-gō-lŭk′ē) ►*adj.* Taking things easily; carefree.

happy hour ►*n.* A period of time during which a bar features drinks at reduced prices.

Haps•burg also **Habs•burg** (hăps′bûrg′). German royal family that supplied rulers to several European states from the late Middle Ages until the 20th cent.

ha•ra-ki•ri (hăr′ĭ-kîr′ē, hä′rē-) ►*n., pl.* **-ris.** See **seppuku.** [J.]

ha•rangue (hə-răng′) ►*n.* **1.** A long pompous speech. **2.** A tirade. [< OItal. *aringare,* speak in public.] —**ha•rangue** *v.* —**ha•rangu′er** *n.*

Ha•ra•re (hə-rär′ā). Formerly **Salisbury.** The capital of Zimbabwe, in the NE part. Pop. 1,189,103.

ha•rass (hə-răs′, hăr′əs,) ►*v.* **1.** To irritate or torment persistently. **2.** To wear out; exhaust. **3.** To exhaust (an enemy) by repeated attacks. [Poss. < OFr. *harer,* set a dog on.] —**ha•rass′er** *n.* —**ha•rass′ment** *n.*

Usage: Educated usage appears to be evenly divided on the pronunciation of *harass.* In a recent survey 50 percent of the Usage Panel preferred a pronunciation with stress on the first syllable, while 50 percent preferred stress on the second syllable.

Har•bin (här′bĭn′) A city of NE China N of Jilin. Pop. 3,597,404.

har•bin•ger (här′bĭn-jər) ►*n.* One that indicates or foreshadows what is to come; forerunner. [< OFr. *herbergeor,* one sent to arrange lodgings.]

har•bor (här′bər) ►*n.* **1.** A sheltered part of a body of water deep enough to provide anchorage for ships. **2.** A place of shelter; refuge. ►*v.* **1.** To give shelter to. **2.** To provide a place or habitat for. **3.** To hold or nourish: *harbor a* *grudge.* [ME *herberwe.*] —**har′bor•er** *n.*

hard (härd) ▸*adj.* **-er, -est 1.** Resistant to pressure; not readily penetrated. **2.** Physically or mentally tough. **3.** Difficult to do, understand, or endure. **4.** Intense in force or degree: *a hard blow.* **5a.** Stern or strict. **b.** Lacking compassion; callous. **6.** Oppressive or unjust. **7a.** Harsh or severe. **b.** Bitter; resentful. **8.** Bad; adverse: *hard luck.* **9.** Diligent; assiduous: *a hard worker.* **10a.** Real and unassailable: *hard evidence.* **b.** Definite; firm. **11.** Backed by bullion rather than by credit. Used of currency. **12a.** Having high alcoholic content. **b.** Fermented: *hard cider.* **13.** Containing salts that interfere with the lathering of soap. Used of water. **14.** *Ling.* Velar, as the *c* in *cape.* **15.** Physically addictive: *a hard drug.* —***idioms:*** **hard and fast** Fixed and invariable. **hard of hearing** Having a partial loss of hearing. **hard put** Undergoing great difficulty. **hard up** *Informal* In need; poor. [< OE *heard.*] —**hard** *adv.* —**hard′ness** *n.*

hard•back (härd′băk′) ▸*adj. & n.* Hardcover.

hard•ball (härd′bôl′) ▸*n.* **1.** Baseball. **2.** *Informal* The use of any means, however ruthless, to attain an objective.

hard-bit•ten (härd′bĭt′n) ▸*adj.* Toughened by experience.

hard-boiled (härd′boild′) ▸*adj.* **1.** Cooked to a solid consistency by boiling. Used of eggs. **2.** Callous or unfeeling; tough.

hard coal ▸*n.* See **anthracite.**

hard copy ▸*n.* A printed copy of the output of a computer.

hard-core (härd′kôr′, -kōr′) ▸*adj.* **1.** Intensely loyal; die-hard. **2.** Stubbornly resistant to change: *hard-core poverty.* **3.** Extremely explicit: *hard-core pornography.*

hard•cov•er (härd′kŭv′ər) ▸*adj.* Bound in cloth, cardboard, or leather rather than paper. Used of books. —**hard′cov′er** *n.*

hard disk ▸*n.* A rigid magnetic disk fixed permanently within a drive unit and used for storing computer data.

hard drive ▸*n.* A disk drive that reads data stored on hard disks.

hard•en (här′dn) ▸*v.* **1.** To make hard or harder. **2.** To enable to withstand hardship. **3.** To make unsympathetic or callous.

Syns: *harden, acclimate, acclimatize, season, toughen* ***Ant:*** *soften* ***v.***

hard•hat or **hard-hat** (härd′hăt′) ▸*n.* **1a.** A protective helmet worn esp. by construction workers. **b.** *Informal* A construction worker. **2.** *Slang* An aggressively patriotic and politically conservative person. —**hard′hat′** *adj.*

hard•head•ed (härd′hĕd′ĭd) ▸*adj.* **1.** Stubborn; willful. **2.** Pragmatic. —**hard′head′ed•ly** *adv.* —**hard′head′ed•ness** *n.*

hard•heart•ed (härd′här′tĭd) ▸*adj.* Lacking in feeling or compassion; cold. —**hard′heart′ed•ly** *adv.* —**hard′heart′ed•ness** *n.*

har•di•hood (här′dē-hŏŏd′) ▸*n.* **1.** Boldness and daring. **2.** Impudence or insolence.

Har•ding (här′dĭng), **Warren Gamaliel.** 1865–1923. The 29th US President (1921–23); died in office.

Warren G. Harding

hard line ▸*n.* An uncompromising position or stance. —**hard′-line′** *adj.* —**hard′-lin′er** *n.*

hard•ly (härd′lē) ▸*adv.* **1.** Barely; just. **2.** To almost no degree; almost not: *I could hardly hear the speaker.* **3.** Probably or almost surely not. [< OE *heardlīce*, boldly.]

Usage: The use of *hardly, rarely,* and *scarcely* with a negative, as in *I couldn't hardly see him,* is avoided in Standard English.

hard-nosed (härd′nōzd′) ▸*adj.* Hardheaded.

hard palate ▸*n.* The relatively hard, bony anterior portion of the palate.

hard•pan (härd′păn′) ▸*n.* A layer of hard subsoil or clay.

hard-pressed (härd′prĕst′) ▸*adj.* Experiencing great difficulty.

hard rock ▸*n.* A style of rock 'n' roll marked by harsh, amplified sound and loud, distorted electric guitars.

hard sauce ▸*n.* A creamy sauce of butter and sugar with liquor or vanilla flavoring.

hard sell ▸*n.* *Informal* Aggressive, high-pressure selling or promotion.

hard•ship (härd′shĭp′) ▸*n.* **1.** Extreme privation; suffering. **2.** A cause of privation or suffering. See Syns at **difficulty.**

hard•tack (härd′tăk′) ▸*n.* A hard biscuit or bread made with only flour and water. [HARD + *tack*, food.]

hard•top (härd′tŏp′) ▸*n.* An automobile designed to look like a convertible but having a rigidly fixed, hard top.

hard•ware (härd′wâr′) ▸*n.* **1.** Metal goods and utensils. **2a.** A computer and the associated physical equipment directly involved in data processing or communications. **b.** Machines and other physical equipment directly involved in performing an industrial, technological, or military function.

hard-wire (härd′wīr′) ▸*v.* *Comp. Sci.* To implement (a capability) through permanently connected logic circuitry not subject to change by programming.

hard•wood (härd′wŏŏd′) ▸*n.* **1.** The wood of a broad-leaved flowering tree as distinguished from that of a conifer. **2.** Such a tree.

har•dy (här′dē) ▸*adj.* **-di•er, -di•est 1.** Being in robust and sturdy good health. **2.** Courageous; intrepid. **3.** Brazenly daring; audacious. **4.** Capable of surviving unfavorable conditions, such as cold weather. [< OFr. *hardi*, hardened, of Gmc. orig.] —**har′di•ly** *adv.* —**har′di•ness** *n.*

Hardy, Thomas. 1840–1928. British writer.

hare (hâr) ▸*n.* A mammal similar to a rabbit but having longer ears and legs. [< OE *hara.*]

hare•brained (hâr′brānd′) ▸*adj.* Foolish; crazy.

hare•lip (hâr′lĭp′) ▸*n.* Cleft lip. No longer in scientific use. —**hare′lipped′** *adj.*

har•em (hâr′əm, hăr′-) ►*n.* **1.** A house or rooms reserved for the women of a Muslim household. **2.** The women occupying a harem. [< Ar. *ḥarīm*, forbidden place.]

hark (härk) ►*v.* To listen attentively. —***idiom:* hark back** To return to a previous point, as in a narrative. [ME *herken.*]

Har•lem (här′ləm) A section of New York City in N Manhattan. —**Har′lem•ite′** *n.*

har•le•quin (här′lĭ-kwĭn, -kĭn) ►*n.* **1. Harlequin** A conventional buffoon of comic theater, traditionally presented in a mask and parti-colored tights. **2.** A clown; buffoon. [< OFr. *Herlequin*, a demon.]

har•lot (här′lət) ►*n.* A prostitute. [< OFr. *arlot*, vagabond.] —**har′lot•ry** (-lə-trē) *n.*

harm (härm) ►*n.* **1.** Physical or psychological injury or damage. **2.** Wrong; evil. ►*v.* To do harm to. [< OE *hearm.*] —**harm′ful** *adj.* —**harm′ful•ly** *adv.* —**harm′ful•ness** *n.* —**harm′less** *adj.* —**harm′less•ly** *adv.* —**harm′less•ness** *n.*

har•mon•ic (här-mŏn′ĭk) ►*adj.* **1.** Of or relating to musical harmony or harmonics. **2.** Pleasing to the ear. ►*n.* **1.** A tone produced on a stringed instrument by lightly touching a vibrating string at a given fraction of its length so that both segments vibrate. **2. harmonics** *(takes sing. v.)* The theory or study of the physical properties of musical sound. —**har•mon′i•cal•ly** *adv.*

har•mon•i•ca (här-mŏn′ĭ-kə) ►*n.* A small rectangular musical instrument played by exhaling or inhaling through a row of reeds. [< Ital. *armonico*, harmonious.]

har•mo•ni•ous (här-mō′nē-əs) ►*adj.* **1.** Exhibiting accord in feeling or action. **2.** Having elements pleasingly combined. **3.** Marked by harmony of sound; melodious. —**har•mo′ni•ous•ly** *adv.* —**har•mo′ni•ous•ness** *n.*

har•mo•ni•um (här-mō′nē-əm) ►*n.* An organlike keyboard instrument with metal reeds. [Fr. < *harmonie*, HARMONY.]

har•mo•nize (här′mə-nīz′) ►*v.* **-nized, -niz•ing 1.** To bring or come into harmony. **2a.** To provide harmony for (a melody). **b.** To sing or play in harmony. —**har′mo•ni•za′tion** *n.* —**har′mo•niz′er** *n.*

har•mo•ny (här′mə-nē) ►*n.*, *pl.* **-nies 1.** Agreement in feeling or opinion; accord. **2.** A pleasing combination of elements in a whole. **3.** Combination and progression of chords in musical structure. [< Gk. *harmonia*, articulation < *harmos*, joint.]

har•ness (här′nĭs) ►*n.* **1.** The gear or tackle with which a draft animal pulls a vehicle or implement. **2.** Something resembling such gear. ►*v.* **1.** To put a harness on. **2.** To control and direct the force of. —***idiom:* in harness** On duty or at work. [< OFr. *harneis*, of Gmc. orig.] —**har′ness•er** *n.*

Har•old I (hăr′əld). d. 1040. King of England (1035–40).

Harold II. 1022?–66. King of England (1066) and the last of the Anglo-Saxon monarchs.

harp (härp) ►*n.* A musical instrument consisting of a large upright frame with strings of graded length played by plucking. ►*v.* To play a harp. —***phrasal verb:* harp on** To dwell on tediously. [< OE *hearpe.*] —**harp′ist** *n.*

Har•pers Ferry (här′pərz) A locality of NE WV; scene of John Brown's rebellion (1859).

har•poon (här-po͞on′) ►*n.* A spearlike weapon with a barbed head used in hunting whales and large fish. [< OFr. *harpon.*] —**har•poon′** *v.* —**har•poon′er** *n.*

harp•si•chord (härp′sĭ-kôrd′, -kōrd′) ►*n.* A keyboard instrument whose strings are plucked by means of quills or plectrums. [< Ital. *arpicordo.*] —**harp′si•chord′ist** *n.*

Har•py (här′pē) ►*n.*, *pl.* **-pies 1.** *Gk. Myth.* A monster with the head and trunk of a woman and the tail, wings, and talons of a bird. **2. harpy a.** A predatory person. **b.** A shrewish woman.

har•que•bus (här′kə-bəs, -kwə-) ►*n.* A heavy, portable matchlock gun invented during the 15th cent. [< MDu. *hakebus.*]

har•ri•dan (hăr′ĭ-dn) ►*n.* A shrewish woman. [Poss. < Fr. *haridelle*, old nag.]

har•ri•er[1] (hăr′ē-ər) ►*n.* **1.** One that harries. **2.** A slender, narrow-winged hawk.

har•ri•er[2] (hăr′ē-ər) ►*n.* **1.** Any of a breed of small hound orig. used in hunting hares and rabbits. **2.** A cross-country runner. [Poss. < OFr. *errier*, wanderer.]

Har•ris (hăr′ĭs), **Joel Chandler.** 1848–1908. Amer. writer and journalist.

Har•ris•burg (hăr′ĭs-bûrg′) The capital of PA, in the SE-central part. Pop. 52,376.

Har•ri•son[1] (hăr′ĭ-sən), **Benjamin.** 1726–91. Amer. Revolutionary leader.

Har•ri•son[2] (hăr′ĭ-sən), **Benjamin.** 1833–1901. The 23rd US President (1889–93).

Harrison, William Henry. 1773–1841. The 9th US President (1841).

Benjamin Harrison[2]

William Henry Harrison

har•row (hăr′ō) ►*n.* A farm implement consisting of a heavy frame with teeth or upright disks, used to break up and even off plowed ground. ►*v.* **1.** To break up and level (soil) with a harrow. **2.** To inflict great distress or torment on. [ME *harwe.*]

har•row•ing (hăr′ō-ĭng) ►*adj.* Extremely distressing; agonizing.

har•ry (hăr′ē) ►*v.* **-ried, -ry•ing 1.** To disturb or distress by or as if by repeated attacks. **2.** To raid; pillage. [< OE *hergian.*]

harsh (härsh) ►*adj.* **-er, -est 1.** Disagreeable to the senses, esp. to the sense of hearing. **2.** Extremely severe or exacting; stern. [ME *harsk.*] —**harsh′ly** *adv.* —**harsh′ness** *n.*

hart (härt) ►*n.*, *pl.* **harts** or **hart.** A male deer, esp. a male red deer. [< OE *heorot.*]

Harte (härt), **(Francis) Bret.** 1836–1902. Amer. writer.

Hart•ford (härt′fərd) The capital of CT, in the N-central part on the Connecticut R. Pop. 139,739.

har•um-scar•um (hâr′əm-skâr′əm, hăr′əm-skăr′əm) ► *adj.* Reckless. ► *adv.* With abandon; recklessly. [< *hare*, frighten + SCARE.]

har•vest (här′vĭst) ► *n.* **1.** The gathering in of a crop. **2a.** The crop that ripens or is gathered in a season. **b.** The time or season of such gathering. **3.** The result or consequence of an activity. [< OE *hærfest*.] —**har′vest** *v.* —**har′vest•er** *n.*

harvest moon ► *n.* The full moon that occurs nearest the autumnal equinox.

Har•vey (här′vē), **William.** 1578–1657. English physician and anatomist.

has (hăz) ► *v.* 3rd pers. sing. pr.t. of **have.**

has-been (hăz′bĭn′) ► *n. Informal* One that is no longer famous, successful, or useful.

hash[1] (hăsh) ► *n.* **1.** A dish of chopped meat and potatoes, usu. browned. **2.** A jumble; hodgepodge. ► *v.* **1.** To chop into pieces; mince. **2.** *Informal* To discuss carefully; review: *hash over future plans.* [< OFr. *hachier*, chop up < *hache*, ax.]

hash[2] (hăsh) ► *n. Slang* Hashish.

hash•ish (hăsh′ēsh′, hă-shēsh′) ► *n.* A purified resin prepared from marijuana. [Ar. *ḥašīš*, hemp.]

hash mark ► *n.* A service stripe on the sleeve of an enlisted person's uniform. [Alteration of HATCH[3].]

Ha•sid or **Has•sid** also **Chas•sid** (KHä′sĭd, hä′-) ► *n., pl.* **-si•dim** (KHä-sē′dĭm, KHô-, hä-). A member of a Jewish mystic movement founded in 18th-cent. E Europe that reacted against Talmudic learning. [< Heb. *ḥāsîd*, pious.] —**Ha•si′dic** *adj.* —**Ha•si′dism** *n.*

has•n't (hăz′ənt) ► Has not.

hasp (hăsp) ► *n.* A metal fastener that fits over a staple and is secured by a pin, bolt, or padlock. [< OE *hæpse*.] —**hasp** *v.*

has•si•um (hä′sē-əm) ► *n. Symbol* **Hs** A synthetic radioactive element. At. no. 108. See table at **element.** [< Med.Lat. *Hassia*, Hesse (German state where it was first synthesized).]

has•sle (hăs′əl) *Informal* ► *n.* **1.** An argument or fight. **2.** Trouble; bother. ► *v.* **-sled, -sling** **1.** To argue or fight. **2.** To bother or harass. [?]

has•sock (hăs′ək) ► *n.* A thick cushion used as a footstool or for kneeling. [< OE *hassuc*, clump of grass.]

hast (hăst) ► *v. Archaic* 2nd pers. sing. pr.t. of **have.**

haste (hāst) ► *n.* **1.** Rapidity of action or motion. **2.** Overeagerness to act. **3.** Rash or headlong action. —***idiom:* make haste** To move or act swiftly; hurry. [< OFr.]

Syns: *haste, celerity, dispatch, expedition, hurry, speed* **Ant:** *deliberation* ***n.***

has•ten (hā′sən) ► *v.* **1.** To move or cause to move swiftly. **2.** To speed up: *a drug to hasten clotting.*

Has•tings (hā′stĭngz) A borough of SE England on the English Channel at the entrance to the Strait of Dover. Pop. 75,900.

Hastings, Warren. 1732–1818. British colonial administrator in India.

hast•y (hā′stē) ► *adj.* **-i•er, -i•est** **1.** Marked by speed; rapid. **2.** Done or made too quickly to be accurate or wise; rash: *a hasty decision.* —**hast′i•ly** *adv.* —**hast′i•ness** *n.*

hat (hăt) ► *n.* A covering for the head, esp. one with a shaped crown and brim. —***idioms:* at the drop of a hat** At the slightest pretext or provocation. **hat in hand** Humbly. **pass the hat** To take up a collection of money. **take (one's) hat off to** To admire or congratulate. [< OE *hæt*.]

hatch[1] (hăch) ► *n.* **1.** An opening, as in the deck of a ship or in an aircraft. **2.** The cover for such an opening. **3.** A hatchway. [< OE *hæc*, small door.]

hatch[2] (hăch) ► *v.* **1.** To emerge from an egg. **2.** To produce (young) from an egg. **3.** To cause (an egg) to produce young. **4.** To devise or originate, esp. in secret: *hatch a plot.* [ME *hacchen*.] —**hatch′er** *n.*

hatch[3] (hăch) ► *v.* To shade by drawing fine parallel or crossed lines on. [< OFr. *hachier*, cut up. See HASH[1].] —**hatch** *n.*

hatch•back (hăch′băk′) ► *n.* An automobile having a sloping back with a hatch that opens upward.

hatch•er•y (hăch′ə-rē) ► *n., pl.* **-ies.** A place where eggs, esp. of fish or poultry, are hatched.

hatch•et (hăch′ĭt) ► *n.* **1.** A small, short-handled ax. **2.** A tomahawk. [< OFr. *hachete*, dim. of *hache*, ax.]

hatchet man ► *n. Slang* **1.** A man hired to commit murder. **2.** One who is assigned to carry out a disagreeable task.

hatch•ling (hăch′lĭng) ► *n.* A newly hatched bird, amphibian, fish, or reptile.

hatch•way (hăch′wā′) ► *n.* **1.** A hatch leading to a hold, compartment, or cellar. **2.** A ladder or stairway within a hatchway.

hate (hāt) ► *v.* **hat•ed, hat•ing** **1.** To feel hostility or animosity toward; detest. **2.** To feel dislike or distaste for. ► *n.* **1.** Hatred. **2.** An object of hatred. [< OE *hatian*.] —**hate′ful** *adj.* —**hate′ful•ly** *adv.* —**hate′ful•ness** *n.* —**hat′er** *n.*

hate crime ► *n.* A crime motivated by prejudice against a social group.

hath (hăth) ► *v. Archaic* 3rd pers. sing. pr.t. of **have.**

Hath•a•way (hăth′ə-wā′), **Anne.** 1556?–1623. The wife of William Shakespeare; married in 1582.

ha•tha yoga (hŭ′tə, hä′thə) ► *n.* A system of yoga exercises emphasizing specific postures and controlled breathing. [Skt. *haṭhayogaḥ*, force yoga.]

ha•tred (hā′trĭd) ► *n.* Intense animosity or hostility. [ME.]

Hat•shep•sut (hăt-shĕp′so͞ot′) also **Hat•shep•set** (-sĕt′). d. c. 1482 B.C. Queen of Egypt (1503–1482).

Hat•ter•as Island (hăt′ər-əs) A long barrier island off the E coast of NC between Pamlico Sound and the Atlantic, with **Cape Hatteras** projecting from the SE part.

hau•berk (hô′bərk) ► *n.* A tunic of chain mail. [< OFr. *hauberc*, of Gmc. orig.]

haugh•ty (hô′tē) ► *adj.* **-ti•er, -ti•est.** Scornfully and condescendingly proud. [< Lat. *altus*, high.] —**haugh′ti•ly** *adv.* —**haugh′ti•ness** *n.*

haul (hôl) ► *v.* **1.** To pull or drag forcibly. See Syns at **pull. 2.** To transport, as with a truck or cart. ► *n.* **1.** The act of hauling. **2.** A distance, esp. over which something is hauled. **3.** Something hauled. **4.** An amount collected or ac-

Hatshepsut
c. 15th century B.C. granite sculpture

quired: *a haul of fish.* [< OFr. *haler*, of Gmc. orig.] —**haul′er** *n.*

haul•age (hô′lĭj) ►*n.* **1.** The act or process of hauling. **2.** A charge made for hauling.

haunch (hônch, hŏnch) ►*n.* **1.** The hip, buttock, and upper thigh. **2.** The loin and leg of an animal, esp. as used for food. [< OFr. *hanche*, of Gmc. orig.]

haunt (hônt, hŏnt) ►*v.* **1.** To inhabit, visit, or appear to in the form of a ghost or spirit. **2.** To frequent. **3.** To come to the mind of continually. ►*n.* A place much frequented. [< OFr. *hanter*, to frequent.] —**haunt′ing•ly** *adv.*

Haupt•mann (houpt′män′, houp′-), **Gerhart.** 1862–1946. German writer; 1912 Nobel.

Hau•sa (hou′sə, -zə) ►*n.*, *pl.* **-sa** or **-sas 1.** A member of a people of N Nigeria and S Niger. **2.** Their Chadic language.

haute couture (ōt) ►*n.* **1.** The leading designers of exclusive fashions for women. **2a.** The creation of exclusive fashions for women. **b.** The fashions created. [Fr.]

haute cuisine ►*n.* Elaborate or skillfully prepared food. [Fr.]

hau•teur (hō-tûr′, ō-tœr′) ►*n.* Haughtiness; arrogance. [Fr. < OFr. *haut*, HAUGHTY.]

Ha•van•a (hə-văn′ə) The capital of Cuba, in the NW part on the Gulf of Mexico. Pop. 2,160,368. —**Ha•van′an** *adj. & n.*

Ha•var•ti (hə-vär′tē) ►*n.* A mild, pale yellow cheese of Danish origin. [After *Havarti*, experimental farm in Denmark.]

have (hăv) ►*v.* **had** (hăd), **hav•ing, has** (hăz) **1.** To possess; own. **2.** To possess as a characteristic or part: *He has a lot of energy. The car has bad brakes.* **3.** To stand in relation to. **4.** To hold in the mind; know or entertain. **5.** To exhibit: *have compassion.* **6.** To accept; take: *I'll have some peas.* **7a.** To suffer from: *has a bad cold.* **b.** To experience: *had a great summer.* **8.** To cause to: *had him run an errand.* **9.** To permit. **10.** To beget or give birth to. **11.** To partake of. **12.** To be obliged to: *I have to go.* —*aux.* Used with a past participle to form the present perfect, past perfect, and future perfect tenses: *I have written you. I had given up smoking for a year. I will have left when you get there.* —***phrasal verbs:*** **have at** To attack. **have on 1.** To wear. **2.** To be scheduled: *We have a dinner party on for tomorrow.* ►*n.* One who has wealth. —***idioms:*** **have done with** To stop; cease. **have had it 1.** To be exhausted or disgusted. **2.** To be beyond remedy or repair. **have it in for** To intend to harm. **have it out** To settle, esp. by an argument. **have to do with** To be concerned or associated with. [< OE *habban.*]

Ha•vel (hä′vəl), **Václav.** b. 1936. Czech writer and politician.

haven (hā′vən) ►*n.* **1.** A harbor; port. **2.** A place of refuge or rest. [< OE *hæfen.*]

have-not (hăv′nŏt′) ►*n.* One having little or no material wealth.

hav•er•sack (hăv′ər-săk′) ►*n.* A bag carried over one shoulder to transport supplies. [< obsolete Ger. *Habersack*, oat sack.]

hav•oc (hăv′ək) ►*n.* **1.** Widespread destruction; devastation. **2.** Disorder or chaos. [< OFr. *havot*, plundering.]

haw[1] (hô) ►*v.* To fumble in speaking. [Imit.]

haw[2] (hô) ►*n.* **1.** The fruit of a hawthorn. **2.** A hawthorn or similar tree. [< OE *haga.*]

Ha•wai•i (hə-wä′ē, -wī′ē) A state of the US in the central Pacific comprising the Hawaiian Islands. Cap. Honolulu. Pop. 1,115,274.

Ha•wai•ian (hə-wä′yən) ►*n.* **1.** A native or inhabitant of Hawaii or the Hawaiian Islands. **2a.** A member of the indigenous Polynesian people of the Hawaiian Islands. **b.** The Polynesian language of Hawaii. —**Ha•wai′ian** *adj.*

Hawaiian Islands. A group of islands in the central Pacific coextensive with HI.

hawk[1] (hôk) ►*n.* **1.** Any of various birds of prey characteristically having a short hooked bill and strong claws adapted for seizing. **2.** One who favors an aggressive or warlike foreign policy. [< OE *hafoc.*] —**hawk′ish** *adj.* —**hawk′ish•ly** *adv.* —**hawk′ish•ness** *n.*

hawk[2] (hôk) ►*v.* To peddle goods aggressively, esp. by calling out. [Prob. < MLGer. *höken*, peddle.] —**hawk′er** *n.*

hawk[3] (hôk) ►*v.* To clear the throat by or as if by coughing up phlegm. [Imit.] —**hawk** *n.*

hawk-eyed (hôk′īd′) ►*adj.* Having very keen eyesight.

haw•ser (hô′zər) ►*n.* A cable or rope used in mooring or towing a ship. [< OFr. *haucier*, to hoist < VLat. **altiāre.*]

haw•thorn (hô′thôrn′) ►*n.* A usu. thorny tree or shrub having white or pinkish flowers and reddish fruits. [< OE *hagathorn.*]

Haw•thorne (hô′thôrn′), **Nathaniel.** 1804–64. Amer. writer.

hay (hā) ►*n.* Grass or other plants cut and dried for fodder. ►*v.* To mow and cure grass and herbage for hay. [< OE *hīeg.*]

Haydn (hīd′n), **Franz Joseph.** 1732–1809. Austrian composer.

Hayes (hāz), **Rutherford Birchard.** 1822–93. The 19th US President (1877–81).

Rutherford B. Hayes

hay fever ►*n.* An allergic condition affecting the mucous membranes of the upper respiratory tract and the eyes, usu. caused by an abnormal sensitivity to airborne pollen.

hay•fork (hā′fôrk′) ►*n.* **1.** A pitchfork. **2.** A machine-operated fork for moving hay.

hay•loft (hā′lôft′, -lŏft′) ►*n.* A loft for storing hay.

hay•seed (hā′sēd′) ►*n.* **1.** Chaff that falls from hay. **2.** *Slang* A bumpkin; yokel.

hay•stack (hā′stăk′) ►*n.* A large stack of hay, esp. as left in a field to dry.

Hay•ward (hā′wərd) A city of W CA SE of Oakland. Pop. 111,498.

hay•wire (hā′wīr′) ►*adj. Informal* **1.** Crazy. **2.** Not functioning properly; broken.

haz•ard (hăz′ərd) ►*n.* **1.** A chance; accident. **2.** A possible source of danger: *a fire hazard.* **3.** An obstacle on a golf course. ►*v.* To venture: *hazard a guess.* [Poss. < Ar. *az-zahr*, gaming die.] —**haz′ard•ous** *adj.* —**haz′ard•ous•ly** *adv.*

hazardous waste ►*n.* A substance, such as nuclear waste, that is potentially harmful to the environment and living organisms.

haze[1] (hāz) ►*n.* **1.** Atmospheric moisture, dust, smoke, and vapor that diminishes visibility. **2.** A vague or confused state of mind. [Prob. < HAZY.]

haze[2] (hāz) ►*v.* **hazed, haz•ing.** To persecute or harass with meaningless, difficult, or humiliating tasks. [Perh. < OFr. *haser*, annoy.] —**haz′er** *n.*

ha•zel (hā′zəl) ►*n.* **1.** A shrub or small tree bearing edible nuts enclosed in a leafy husk. **2.** A light or yellowish brown. [< OE *hæsel.*] —**ha′zel** *adj.*

ha•zel•nut (hā′zəl-nŭt′) ►*n.* The nut of a hazel.

Haz•litt (hăz′lĭt, hāz′-), **William.** 1778–1830. British essayist.

haz•y (hā′zē) ►*adj.* **-i•er, -i•est 1.** Marked by the presence of haze. **2.** Not clearly defined; unclear or vague. [?] —**haz′i•ly** *adv.* —**haz′i•ness** *n.*

Hb ►*abbr.* hemoglobin

H-bomb (āch′bŏm′) ►*n.* A hydrogen bomb.

hcf ►*abbr.* highest common factor

HDL (āch′dē-ĕl′) ►*n.* A complex of lipids and proteins that transports cholesterol in the blood, high levels of which may decrease the risk of heart disease. [*h(igh-)d(ensity) l(ipoprotein).*]

hdqrs. ►*abbr.* headquarters

HDTV ►*abbr.* high-definition television

he (hē) ►*pron.* **1.** Used to refer to the male previously mentioned or implied. See Usage Note at **I**[1]. **2.** Used to refer to a person whose gender is unspecified or unknown. ►*n.* A male person or animal: *Is the cat a he?* [< OE *hē.*]

Usage: Use of *he* as a gender-neutral pronoun, as in *No one seems to take any pride in his work anymore,* is often considered sexist. The easiest way to avoid such constructions is to change to the plural, so that *they* is the pronoun, or to use forms such as *he/she* or *he or she,* although these can be cumbersome in sustained use.

He ► The symbol for the element **helium.**

head (hĕd) ►*n.* **1.** The uppermost or forwardmost part of the body, containing the brain and in vertebrates the eyes, ears, nose, mouth, and jaws. **2.** The intellect or mind; intelligence. **3a.** Mental ability or aptitude. **b.** Self-control: *Don't lose your head.* **4.** *Slang* A drug user. **5.** often **heads** *(takes sing. v.)* The side of a coin having the principal design. **6a.** An individual: *charged five dollars a head.* **b.** *pl.* **head** A single herd animal: *20 head of cattle.* **7.** A leader, chief, or director. **8.** The foremost or leading position. **9.** Pressure: *a head of steam.* **10.** A turning point: *bring matters to a head.* See Syns at **crisis. 11.** A projecting or striking part. **12.** A rounded compact mass, as of leaves or buds: *a head of cabbage.* **13.** The uppermost part; the top. **14.** The end considered the most important: *the head of the table.* **15.** A toilet, esp. on a ship. **16.** A headline or heading. ►*adj.* **1.** Foremost in rank or importance. **2.** Placed at the top or the front. ►*v.* **1.** To be in charge of; lead. **2.** To be in the first or foremost position of. **3.** To aim or proceed in a certain direction: *headed the horses up the hill; head for town.* **4.** To provide with a head. —***phrasal verb:*** **head off** To intercept. —***idioms:*** **head over heels 1.** Rolling, as in a somersault. **2.** Completely; hopelessly: *head over heels in love.* **off (**or **out of) (one's) head** Insane; crazy. [< OE *hēafod.*] —**head′less** *adj.*

head•ache (hĕd′āk′) ►*n.* **1.** A pain in the head. **2.** *Informal* An annoying problem. —**head′ach′y** *adj.*

head•band (hĕd′bănd′) ►*n.* A band worn around the head.

head•board (hĕd′bôrd′, -bōrd′) ►*n.* A board or panel that forms the head, as of a bed.

head•dress (hĕd′drĕs′) ►*n.* A covering or an ornament for the head.

head•first (hĕd′fûrst′) ►*adv.* **1.** With the head leading; headlong. **2.** Impetuously; brashly. —**head′first′** *adj.*

head•gear (hĕd′gîr′) ►*n.* A covering, such as a hat or helmet, for the head.

head•hunt•ing (hĕd′hŭn′tĭng) ►*n.* **1.** The custom of cutting off and preserving the heads of enemies as trophies. **2.** *Informal* The business of recruiting personnel, esp. executive personnel, as for a corporation. —**head′hunt′er** *n.*

head•ing (hĕd′ĭng) ►*n.* **1.** The title, subtitle, or topic that stands at the top or beginning, as of a text. **2.** The direction in which a ship or an aircraft is moving.

head•land (hĕd′lənd, -lănd′) ►*n.* A point of land extending out into a body of water.

head•light (hĕd′līt′) ►*n.* **1.** A light with a reflector mounted on the front of a vehicle. **2.** A lamp mounted on a miner's or spelunker's hard hat.

head•line (hĕd′līn′) ►*n.* The title or caption of a newspaper article, usu. set in large type. ►*v.* **-lined, -lin•ing 1.** To supply (a page or passage) with a headline. **2.** To receive prominent billing at: *headline a variety show.* —**head′lin′er** *n.*

head•lock (hĕd′lŏk′) ►*n.* A wrestling hold in which the head of one wrestler is encircled and locked by the arm and body of the other.

head•long (hĕd′lông′, -lŏng′) ►*adv.* **1.** Headfirst. **2.** In an impetuous manner; rashly. **3.** At breakneck speed. [ME *(bi) hedlong.*] —**head′long′** *adj.*

head•man (hĕd′mən, -măn′) ►*n.* The chief man esp. of a tribal or traditional village.

head•mas•ter (hĕd′măs′tər) ►*n.* A man who is a principal, usu. of a private school.

head•mis•tress (hĕd′mĭs′trĭs) ►*n.* A woman

who is a principal, usu. of a private school.

head-on (hĕd′ŏn′, -ôn′) ► *adj.* **1.** Facing forward; frontal. **2.** With the front end foremost: *a head-on collision.* —**head′-on′** *adv.*

head•phone (hĕd′fōn′) ► *n.* A receiver held to the ear by a headband.

head•piece (hĕd′pēs′) ► *n.* **1.** A protective covering for the head. **2.** A headset.

head•pin (hĕd′pĭn′) ► *n.* See **kingpin** 1.

head•quar•ters (hĕd′kwôr′tərz) ► *pl.n.* *(takes sing. or pl. v.)* **1.** The offices of a commander, as of a military unit. **2.** A center of operations or administration. See Syns at **center.**

Usage: The noun *headquarters* is more commonly used with a plural verb when reference is to physical location: *The headquarters are in Boston.* But the singular is sometimes preferred when reference is to authority: *Battalion headquarters has approved the retreat.*

head•rest (hĕd′rĕst′) ► *n.* A support for the head.

head•room (hĕd′ro͞om′, -ro͝om′) ► *n.* Space above one's head, as in a vehicle or tunnel; clearance.

head•set (hĕd′sĕt′) ► *n.* A pair of headphones, often with microphone attached.

head shop ► *n.* *Slang* A shop that sells paraphernalia for use with illegal drugs.

head•stall (hĕd′stôl′) ► *n.* The section of a bridle that fits over a horse's head.

head•stand (hĕd′stănd′) ► *n.* A position in which one supports oneself vertically on one's head with the hands braced for support on the floor.

head start ► *n.* **1.** A start before other contestants in a race. **2.** An early start that confers an advantage.

head•stone (hĕd′stōn′) ► *n.* **1.** A memorial stone set at the head of a grave. **2.** See **keystone** 1.

head•strong (hĕd′strông′, -strŏng′) ► *adj.* Determined to have one's own way; willful.

head•wait•er (hĕd′wā′tər) ► *n.* A waiter in charge of the other waiters and waitresses in a restaurant.

head•wa•ters (hĕd′wô′tərz, -wŏt′ərz) ► *pl.n.* The waters from which a river rises.

head•way (hĕd′wā′) ► *n.* **1.** Forward movement, esp. of a ship. **2.** Progress toward a goal. **3.** Overhead clearance; headroom.

head•wind (hĕd′wĭnd′) ► *n.* A wind blowing directly against the course of an aircraft or ship.

head•work (hĕd′wûrk′) ► *n.* Mental activity or work; thought. —**head′work′er** *n.*

head•y (hĕd′ē) ► *adj.* **-i•er, -i•est 1.** Intoxicating. **2.** Impetuous; rash. —**head′i•ly** *adv.* —**head′i•ness** *n.*

heal (hēl) ► *v.* **1.** To restore to or regain health or soundness. See Syns at **cure. 2.** To set right; repair: *healed the rift between us.* [< OE *hǣlan.*] —**heal′a•ble** *adj.* —**heal′er** *n.*

health (hĕlth) ► *n.* **1.** The overall condition of an organism at a given time. **2.** Soundness, esp. of body or mind. **3.** A condition of well-being. [< OE *hǣlth.*] —**health′ful** *adj.* —**health′ful•ly** *adv.* —**health′ful•ness** *n.*

health care ► *n.* The prevention and treatment of illness through the delivery of medical services. —**health-care** *adj.*

health food ► *n.* A food believed to be beneficial to one's health. —**health′-food′** *adj.*

health maintenance organization ► *n.* An HMO.

health•y (hĕl′thē) ► *adj.* **-i•er, -i•est 1.** Possessing good health. **2.** Conducive to good health; healthful. **3.** Indicative of sound thinking or mind: *a healthy attitude.* **4.** Sizable; considerable: *a healthy portion.* —**health′i•ly** *adv.* —**health′i•ness** *n.*

Hea•ney (hē′nē), **Seamus Justin.** b. 1939. Irish poet; 1995 Nobel.

heap (hēp) ► *n.* **1.** A group of things placed or thrown, one on top of the other. **2.** often **heaps** *Informal* A great deal; a lot. **3.** *Slang* An old or run-down car. ► *v.* **1.** To put or throw in a pile. **2.** To fill to capacity. **3.** To bestow in abundance: *heaped abuse on them.* [< OE *hēap.*]

Syns: *heap, bank, mound, pile, stack* **n.**

hear (hîr) ► *v.* **heard** (hûrd), **hear•ing 1.** To perceive by the ear. **2.** To learn by hearing. **3a.** To listen to attentively. **b.** To listen to in an official capacity. **c.** To attend: *hear Mass.* [< OE *hīeran.*] —**hear′er** *n.*

hear•ing (hîr′ĭng) ► *n.* **1.** The sense by which sound is perceived. **2.** Range of audibility; earshot. **3.** An opportunity to be heard. **4.** A preliminary examination of an accused person. **5.** A session at which testimony is taken from witnesses.

hearing aid ► *n.* A small electronic amplifying device that is worn to aid poor hearing.

hear•ing-im•paired (hîr′ĭng-ĭm-pârd′) ► *adj.* **1.** Hard of hearing. **2.** Completely incapable of hearing; deaf. —**hear′ing-im•paired′** *n.*

hear•ken (här′kən) ► *v.* To listen attentively; give heed. [< OE *hercnian.*]

hear•say (hîr′sā′) ► *n.* Information heard from another.

hearse (hûrs) ► *n.* A vehicle for conveying a coffin to a church or cemetery. [ME *herse,* frame for holding candles < Lat. *hirpex,* harrow.]

Hearst (hûrst), **William Randolph.** 1863–1951. Amer. newspaper and magazine publisher.

heart (härt) ► *n.* **1.** The chambered, muscular organ that pumps blood received from the veins into the arteries, maintaining the flow of blood through the circulatory system. **2.** The vital center and source of one's being, feelings, and emotions. **3a.** Sympathy or generosity; compassion. **b.** Love; affection. **4.** Resolution; fortitude: *lose heart.* **5.** The most important or essential part. See Syns at **center. 6.** Any of a suit of playing cards marked with a red, heart-shaped figure. —***idioms:* by heart** By memory. **heart and soul** Completely; entirely. **take to heart** To take seriously and be affected by. **with all (one's) heart 1.** With great willingness or pleasure. **2.** With deepest feeling. [< OE *heorte.*]

heart•ache (härt′āk′) ► *n.* Emotional anguish; sorrow.

heart attack ► *n.* Sudden interruption or insufficiency of blood supply to the heart, typically resulting from obstruction of a coronary artery.

heart•beat (härt′bēt′) ► *n.* A single complete pulsation of the heart.

heart•break (härt′brāk′) ► *n.* Overwhelming sorrow, grief, or disappointment, esp. in love. —**heart′break′er** *n.* —**heart′break′ing** *adj.* —**heart′break′ing•ly** *adv.*

heart•bro•ken (härt′brō′kən) ► *adj.* Suffering

from heartbreak. —**heart′bro′ken•ly** *adv.*

heart•burn (härt′bûrn′) ►*n.* A burning sensation, usu. in the middle of the chest, caused by acidic stomach fluids.

heart disease ►*n.* A structural or functional abnormality of the heart or of the blood vessels supplying the heart.

heart•en (här′tn) ►*v.* To give strength, courage, or hope to. See Syns at **encourage.**

heart•felt (härt′fĕlt′) ►*adj.* Deeply or sincerely felt; earnest.

hearth (härth) ►*n.* **1.** The floor of a fireplace, usu. extending into a room. **2.** Family life; the home. **3.** The lowest part of a blast furnace, from which the molten metal flows. [< OE *heorth.*]

hearth

hearth•stone (härth′stōn′) ►*n.* **1.** Stone used in the construction of a hearth. **2.** Family life; the home.

heart•land (härt′lănd′) ►*n.* A central region, esp. one that is vital to a nation.

heart•less (härt′lĭs) ►*adj.* Devoid of compassion or feeling; pitiless. —**heart′less•ly** *adv.* —**heart′less•ness** *n.*

heart-rend•ing (härt′rĕn′dĭng) ►*adj.* Causing anguish or arousing deep sympathy.

heart•sick (härt′sĭk′) ►*adj.* Profoundly disappointed; despondent. —**heart′sick′ness** *n.*

heart•strings (härt′strĭngz′) ►*pl.n.* The deepest feelings or affections.

heart•throb (härt′thrŏb′) ►*n.* **1.** A heartbeat. **2.** Sentimental emotion. **3.** A sweetheart.

heart-to-heart (härt′tə-härt′) ►*adj.* Candid; frank. ►*n.* An intimate conversation.

heart•wood (härt′wŏŏd′) ►*n.* The older inactive central wood of a tree or woody plant.

heart•y (här′tē) ►*adj.* **-i•er, -i•est 1.** Expressed warmly and exuberantly. **2.** Complete or thorough. **3.** Vigorous; robust. **4.** Nourishing; satisfying: *a hearty stew.* ►*n., pl.* **-ies.** A good fellow; comrade. —**heart′i•ly** *adv.* —**heart′i•ness** *n.*

heat (hēt) ►*n.* **1.** A form of energy associated with the motion of atoms or molecules and transferred from a body at a higher temperature to one at a lower temperature. **2.** The sensation or perception of such energy as warmth or hotness. **3.** A degree of warmth or hotness: *low heat.* **4.** The warming of a room or building, as by a furnace. **5.** Intensity, as of emotion. **6.** Estrus. **7.** *Sports* **a.** One round of several in a competition. **b.** A preliminary contest held to determine finalists. **8.** *Informal* Pressure; stress. **9.** *Slang* An intensification of police activity in pursuing criminals. **10.** *Slang* Adverse comments or criticism. ►*v.* **1.** To make or become warm or hot. **2.** To excite the feelings of; inflame. [< OE *hǣtu.*]

heat•ed (hē′tĭd) ►*adj.* Angry; vehement: *a heated argument.* —**heat′ed•ly** *adv.*

heat•er (hē′tər) ►*n.* **1.** An apparatus that heats or provides heat. **2.** *Slang* A pistol.

heat exhaustion ►*n.* A condition caused by exposure to heat, resulting in dehydration and causing weakness, dizziness, nausea, and often collapse.

heath (hēth) ►*n.* **1.** Any of various usu. low-growing shrubs having small evergreen leaves and small, colorful flowers. **2.** A tract of uncultivated open land covered with low shrubs; moor. [< OE *hǣth.*]

Heath, Edward Richard George. b. 1916. British prime minister (1970–74).

hea•then (hē′*th*ən) ►*n., pl.* **-thens** or **-then 1.** One who adheres to a religion other than Judaism, Christianity, or Islam. **2.** One regarded as irreligious, uncivilized, or unenlightened. [< OE *hǣthen.*] —**hea′then, hea′then•ish** *adj.* —**hea′then•dom, hea′then•ry** *n.*

heath•er (hĕ*th*′ər) ►*n.* **1.** A low shrub growing in dense masses and having small evergreen leaves and pinkish-purple flowers. **2.** See **heath** 1. [< ME *hather.*]

heat lightning ►*n.* Intermittent flashes of light near the horizon without thunder.

heat rash ►*n.* An inflammatory skin condition caused by obstruction of the sweat gland ducts and marked by itching or prickling.

heat stroke ►*n.* A condition caused by prolonged exposure to excessive heat and marked by cessation of sweating, headache, fever, hot dry skin, and sometimes collapse and coma.

heave (hēv) ►*v.* **heaved, heav•ing 1.** To raise or lift, esp. with great effort or force. **2.** To throw, esp. with great effort. **3.** To utter with effort or pain: *heaved a sigh.* **4.** To vomit. **5.** *p.t. and p.part* **hove a.** To raise or haul by means of a rope, line, or cable. **b.** To position or be positioned in a certain way: *the ship hove alongside.* **c.** To push at a capstan bar. **6.** To rise up or swell. ►*n.* **1.** The effort of heaving. **2.** A throw. **3.** An upward movement. **4.** An act of gagging or vomiting. **5. heaves** *(takes sing. or pl. v.)* A pulmonary disease of horses marked by coughing. [< OE *hebban.*]

heav•en (hĕv′ən) ►*n.* **1.** often **heavens** The sky or universe; firmament. **2.** often **Heaven** The abode of God, the angels, and the souls of those who are granted salvation. **3. Heaven** God. **4.** A state or place of great happiness. [< OE *heofon.*] —**heav′en•li•ness** *n.* —**heav′en•ly** *adj.*

heav•y (hĕv′ē) ►*adj.* **-i•er, -i•est 1.** Having relatively great weight. **2.** Having relatively high density. **3.** Large, as in number, quantity, or yield: *a heavy turnout.* **4.** Of great intensity: *heavy fighting.* **5a.** Having great power or force. **b.** Violent; rough: *heavy seas.* **6a.** Equipped with massive armaments and weapons: *heavy infantry.* **b.** Large enough to fire powerful shells: *heavy guns.* **7.** Indulging or participating to a great degree: *a heavy drinker.* **8.** Of great import or seriousness; grave. **9a.** Dense; thick: *a heavy fog; a heavy coat.* **b.** Too rich to digest easily: *a heavy dessert.* **10a.**

Weighed down; burdened. **b.** Marked by weariness: *heavy lids.* **c.** Sad or painful: *heavy news.* **11a.** Hard to do; arduous. **b.** Not easily borne; oppressive: *heavy taxes.* **12.** Lacking vitality. **13.** Sharply inclined; steep. **14.** Of or involving large-scale production: *heavy industry.* **15.** *Phys.* Of an isotope with an atomic mass greater than the average mass of that element. **16.** *Slang* Of great significance or profundity. ►*n., pl.* **-ies 1.** A serious or tragic role in a play. **2.** *Slang* A villain in a story or play. **3.** *Slang* One that is important or influential. [< OE *hefig.*] —**heav′i•ness** *n.* —**heav′y, heav′i•ly** *adv.*

heav•y-dut•y (hĕv′ē-do͞o′tē, -dyo͞o′-) ►*adj.* Made to withstand hard use or wear.

heav•y-hand•ed (hĕv′ē-hăn′dĭd) ►*adj.* **1.** Clumsy; awkward. **2.** Tactless; indiscreet. **3.** Oppressive; harsh. —**heav′y-hand′ed•ly** *adv.* —**heav′y-hand′ed•ness** *n.*

heav•y-heart•ed (hĕv′ē-här′tĭd) ►*adj.* Melancholy; depressed; sad. —**heav′y-heart′ed•ly** *adv.* —**heav′y-heart′ed•ness** *n.*

heavy metal ►*n.* **1.** A metal with a specific gravity greater than about 5.0. **2.** Very loud, brash rock music.

heav•y•set (hĕv′ē-sĕt′) ►*adj.* Having a stout or compact build.

heavy water ►*n.* An isotopic variety of water, esp. with deuterium replacing hydrogen.

heav•y•weight (hĕv′ē-wāt′) ►*n.* **1.** One of above average weight. **2.** A contestant in the heaviest weight class of a sport, esp. a boxer weighing more than 175 pounds. **3.** *Informal* A person of great importance.

He•bra•ic (hĭ-brā′ĭk) ►*adj.* Of or relating to the Hebrews or their language or culture.

He•bra•ism (hē′brā-ĭz′əm) ►*n.* **1.** A manner or custom of the Hebrews. **2.** Judaism.

He•bra•ist (hē′brā′ĭst) ►*n.* A Hebrew scholar. —**He′bra•is′tic, He′bra•is′ti•cal** *adj.*

He•brew (hē′bro͞o) ►*n.* **1.** A member of a Semitic people claiming descent from Abraham, Isaac, and Jacob; Israelite. **2a.** The Semitic language of the ancient Hebrews. **b.** Any of the various later forms of this language, esp. the language of the Israelis. **3. Hebrews** *(takes sing. v.)* See table at **Bible.** —**He′brew** *adj.*

Hebrew Scriptures ►*pl.n.* The Torah, the Prophets, and the Writings. See table at **Bible.**

Heb•ri•des (hĕb′rĭ-dēz′) An island group of W and NW Scotland in the Atlantic, divided into the **Inner Hebrides,** closer to the Scottish mainland, and the **Outer Hebrides,** to the NW. —**Heb′ri•de′an** *adj. & n.*

heck (hĕk) ►*interj.* Used as a mild oath. [Alteration of HELL.]

heck•le (hĕk′əl) ►*v.* **-led, -ling.** To try to embarrass and annoy, as with gibes. [ME *hekelen,* to comb flax.] —**heck′ler** *n.*

hec•tare (hĕk′târ′) ►*n.* See table at **measurement.**

hec•tic (hĕk′tĭk) ►*adj.* **1.** Marked by intense activity, confusion, or haste. **2.** Consumptive; feverish. **3.** Flushed. [< Gk. *hektikos,* habitual.] —**hec′ti•cal•ly** *adv.*

hecto– or **hect–** ►*pref.* One hundred (10^2): *hectare.* [< Gk. *hekaton,* hundred.]

hec•to•gram (hĕk′tə-grăm′) ►*n.* See table at **measurement.**

hec•to•li•ter (hĕk′tə-lē′tər) ►*n.* See table at **measurement.**

hec•to•me•ter (hĕk′tə-mē′tər, hĕk-tŏm′ĭ-tər) ►*n.* See table at **measurement.**

hec•tor (hĕk′tər) ►*v.* To intimidate in a blustering way. [< HECTOR.]

Hector ►*n. Gk. Myth.* A Trojan prince killed by Achilles in Homer's *Iliad.*

he'd (hēd) ► **1.** He had. **2.** He would.

hedge (hĕj) ►*n.* **1.** A row of closely planted shrubs or low-growing trees forming a boundary. **2.** Protection, esp. against financial loss: *a hedge against inflation.* **3.** An intentionally ambiguous statement. ►*v.* **hedged, hedg•ing 1.** To enclose or bound with or as if with hedges. **2.** To limit the financial risk of (e.g., a bet) by a counterbalancing transaction. **3.** To avoid making a clear, direct response. [< OE *hecg.*] —**hedg′er** *n.*

hedge•hog (hĕj′hôg′, -hŏg′) ►*n.* A small insectivorous Old World mammal having the back covered with dense, erectile spines.

he•don•ism (hēd′n-ĭz′əm) ►*n.* **1.** Pursuit of or devotion to pleasure. **2.** The ethical doctrine that only what is pleasant is intrinsically good. [< Gk. *hēdonē,* pleasure.] —**he′don•ist** *n.* —**he′don•is′tic** *adj.* —**he′don•is′ti•cal•ly** *adv.*

–hedral ►*suff.* Having a specified kind or number of surfaces: *tetrahedral.* [< –HEDRON.]

–hedron ►*suff.* A crystal or geometric figure having a specified kind or number of surfaces: *polyhedron.* [< Gk. *hedra,* face.]

hee•bie-jee•bies (hē′bē-jē′bēz) ►*pl.n. Slang* A feeling of uneasiness; jitters. [Coined by Billy *De Beck* (1890–1942).]

heed (hēd) ►*v.* To pay attention (to). ►*n.* Close attention; notice. [< OE *hēdan.*] —**heed′less** *adj.* —**heed′less•ly** *adv.* —**heed′less•ness** *n.*

heed•ful (hēd′fəl) ►*adj.* Attentive; mindful. See Syns at **careful.** —**heed′ful•ly** *adv.*

heel¹ (hēl) ►*n.* **1a.** The rounded posterior portion of the human foot under and behind the ankle. **b.** The corresponding part of the hind foot of other vertebrates. **2.** The part, as of a sock or shoe, that covers or supports the heel. **3.** One of the crusty ends of a loaf of bread. **4.** A lower, rearward surface. **5.** *Informal* A cad. ►*v.* **1.** To furnish with a heel. **2.** To follow at one's heels. —***idioms:* down at the heels** Shabby; poor. **on** (or **upon**) **the heels of 1.** Directly behind. **2.** Immediately following. **take to (one's) heels** To flee. [< OE *hēla.*]

heel² (hēl) ►*v.* To tilt or cause to tilt (e.g., a boat) to one side. [< OE *hieldan.*] —**heel** *n.*

heel²

heft (hĕft) ► *n.* Weight; heaviness. ► *v.* **1.** To judge the weight of by lifting. **2.** To hoist; heave. [ME < *heven*, HEAVE.]

heft•y (hĕf′tē) ► *adj.* **-i•er, -i•est 1.** Heavy. **2.** Rugged and powerful. **3.** *Informal* Large; substantial. —**heft′i•ness** *n.*

He•gel (hā′gəl), **Georg Wilhelm Friedrich.** 1770–1831. German philosopher.

he•gem•o•ny (hĭ-jĕm′ə-nē, hĕj′ə-mō′nē) ► *n., pl.* **-nies.** The dominance of one state over others. [< Gk. *hēgemōn*, leader.] —**heg′e•mon′ic** (hĕj′ə-mŏn′ĭk) *adj.* —**he•gem′o•nism** *n.* —**he•gem′o•nist** *adj. & n.*

he•gi•ra (hĭ-jī′rə, hĕj′ər-ə) ► *n.* **1.** A flight to escape danger. **2.** also **Hegira** The flight of Muhammad from Mecca to Medina in 622. [< Ar. *hijra*, emigration.]

Hei•deg•ger (hī′dĕg′ər, -dĭ-gər), **Martin.** 1889–1976. German philosopher.

Hei•del•berg (hīd′l-bûrg′) A city of SW Germany NNW of Stuttgart. Pop. 139,429.

heif•er (hĕf′ər) ► *n.* A young cow, esp. one that has not calved. [< OE *hēahfore.*]

Hei•fetz (hī′fĭts), **Jascha.** 1901–87. Russian-born Amer. violinist.

height (hīt) ► *n.* **1a.** The distance from the base of something to the top. **b.** Elevation above a given level; altitude. See Syns at **elevation. 2a.** The condition of being high or tall. **b.** Stature, esp. of the human body. **3.** The highest or uppermost point. **4a.** The most advanced degree; zenith. **b.** The point of highest intensity; climax. **5.** An eminence, such as a hill. [< OE *hēahthu.*]

height•en (hīt′n) ► *v.* **1.** To rise or increase in quantity or degree; intensify. **2.** To make or become high or higher.

Hei•long•jiang (hā′lông′jyäng′) also **Hei•lung•kiang** (hā′lo͝ong′kyäng′). A province of NE China bordering Russia. Pop. 35,214,873.

Hei•long Jiang (hā′lông′ jyäng′) See **Amur River.**

Heim•lich maneuver (hīm′lĭk′, -lĭKH′) ► *n.* A firm embrace with clasped hands just below the rib cage, applied from behind to force an object from the trachea of a choking person. [After Henry J. *Heimlich* (b. 1920).]

Hei•ne (hī′nə), **Heinrich.** 1797–1856. German writer.

hei•nous (hā′nəs) ► *adj.* Grossly wicked or abominable. [< OFr. *haine*, hatred.] —**hei′nous•ly** *adv.* —**hei′nous•ness** *n.*

heir (âr) ► *n.* A person who inherits or is entitled to inherit the estate, rank, title, or office of another. [< Lat. *hērēs.*]

heir apparent ► *n., pl.* **heirs apparent.** An heir whose right to inheritance is indisputable provided he or she survives an ancestor.

heir•ess (âr′ĭs) ► *n.* A woman who is an heir. See Usage Note at **-ess.**

heir•loom (âr′lo͞om′) ► *n.* **1.** A valued possession passed down in a family through succeeding generations. **2.** *Law* An article of personal property included in an inherited estate. [ME *heirlome.*]

heir presumptive ► *n., pl.* **heirs presumptive.** An heir whose claim can be defeated by the birth of a closer relative before the death of the ancestor.

Hei•sen•berg (hī′zən-bûrg′), **Werner Karl.** 1901–76. German physicist; 1932 Nobel.

heist (hīst) *Slang* ► *v.* To steal; rob. ► *n.* A robbery; burglary. [Alteration of HOIST.]

held (hĕld) ► *v.* P.t. and p.part. of **hold**[1].

Hel•en (hĕl′ən) ► *n. Gk. Myth.* The wife of Menelaus whose abduction by Paris caused the Trojan War.

Hel•e•na (hĕl′ə-nə) The capital of Montana, in the W-central part NNE of Butte. Pop. 24,569.

hel•i•cal (hĕl′ĭ-kəl, hē′lĭ-) ► *adj.* Shaped like a helix; spiral. —**hel′i•cal•ly** *adv.*

hel•i•cop•ter (hĕl′ĭ-kŏp′tər) ► *n.* An aircraft that derives its lift from blades that rotate about an approx. vertical central axis. [Fr. *hélicoptère.*] —**hel′i•cop′ter** *v.*

helio– or **heli–** ► *pref.* Sun: *heliocentric.* [< Gk. *hēlios*, sun.]

he•li•o•cen•tric (hē′lē-ō-sĕn′trĭk) also **he•li•o•cen•tri•cal** (-trĭ-kəl) ► *adj.* Having the sun as a center. —**he′li•o•cen•tric′i•ty** (-sĕn-trĭs′ĭ-tē) *n.*

He•li•op•o•lis (hē′lē-ŏp′ə-lĭs) An ancient city of N Egypt in the Nile River delta N of modern Cairo.

he•li•o•trope (hē′lē-ə-trōp′) ► *n.* **1.** Any of several plants having small, highly fragrant purplish flowers. **2.** Any of various plants that turn toward the sun. [< Gk. *hēliotropion.*]

hel•i•port (hĕl′ə-pôrt′, -pōrt′) ► *n.* A place for helicopters to land and take off.

he•li•um (hē′lē-əm) ► *n. Symbol* **He** A colorless, odorless inert gaseous element used in lasers and as a refrigerant and a lifting gas for balloons. At. no. 2. See table at **element.** [< Gk. *hēlios*, sun.]

he•lix (hē′lĭks) ► *n., pl.* **-lix•es** or **hel•i•ces** (hĕl′ĭ-sēz′, hē′lĭ-) **1.** A three-dimensional curve that lies on a cylinder or cone, so that its angle to a plane perpendicular to the axis is constant. **2.** A spiral form. [< Gk.]

hell (hĕl) ► *n.* **1.** often **Hell** The abode of condemned souls and devils. **2.** The abode of the dead; underworld. **3a.** A situation or place of evil, misery, or destruction. **b.** Torment; anguish. **4.** *Informal* One that causes trouble, agony, or annoyance. **5.** A sharp scolding: *gave me hell.* ► *interj.* Used to express anger, disgust, or impatience. —***idiom:* for the hell of it** For no particular reason. [< OE *helle.*]

he'll (hēl) ► **1.** He will. **2.** He shall.

hell-bent (hĕl′bĕnt′) ► *adj.* Recklessly determined to do something.

hel•le•bore (hĕl′ə-bôr′, -bōr′) ► *n.* Any of various chiefly poisonous plants, esp. a North American species yielding a toxic alkaloid used medicinally. [< Gk. *helleboros.*]

Hel•lene (hĕl′ēn′) ► *n.* A Greek.

Hel•len•ic (hĕ-lĕn′ĭk) ► *adj.* Of or relating to the ancient Hellenes or their language; Greek. ► *n.* The branch of Indo-European that consists only of Greek.

Hel•le•nism (hĕl′ə-nĭz′əm) ► *n.* **1.** A manner or custom of the Greeks. **2.** The civilization of ancient Greece. **3.** Admiration for Greek culture. —**Hel′le•ni•za′tion** *n.* —**Hel′le•nize′** *v.* —**Hel′le•niz′er** *n.*

Hel•le•nist (hĕl′ə-nĭst) ► *n.* **1.** A devotee or student of Greek literature, language, or civilization. **2.** In ancient times, a non-Greek who adopted Greek language and culture.

Hel•le•nis•tic (hĕl′ə-nĭs′tĭk) ► *adj.* **1.** Of or relating to the Hellenists. **2.** Relating to postclassical Greek history and civilization from the death of Alexander the Great (323 B.C.) to the battle of Actium (31 B.C.); Alexandrian.

Hel•les•pont (hĕl′ĭ-spŏnt′) See **Dardanelles.**

hell•gram•mite (hĕl′grə-mīt′) ►*n.* A large brownish aquatic insect larva, often used as fishing bait. [?]

hell•hole (hĕl′hōl′) ►*n.* A place of extreme wretchedness or squalor.

hel•lion (hĕl′yən) ►*n. Informal* A mischievous, troublesome person. [Prob. alteration of dial. *hallion*, worthless person.]

hell•ish (hĕl′ĭsh) ►*adj.* **1.** Of, resembling, or worthy of hell; fiendish. **2.** Highly unpleasant. —**hell′ish•ly** *adv.* —**hell′ish•ness** *n.*

Hell•man (hĕl′mən), **Lillian.** 1905–84. Amer. playwright.

hel•lo (hĕ-lō′, hə-) ►*interj.* Used to greet someone, answer the telephone, or express surprise. ►*n., pl.* **-los.** A calling or greeting of "hello." [< obsolete *holla*, stop!]

Hells Canyon (hĕlz) A gorge of the Snake R. on the ID-OR border.

helm (hĕlm) ►*n.* **1.** The steering gear of a ship, esp. the tiller or wheel. **2.** A position of leadership or control. [< OE *helma.*]

hel•met (hĕl′mĭt) ►*n.* A protective head covering, as of metal or plastic. [< OFr.]

hel•minth (hĕl′mĭnth′) ►*n.* A worm, esp. a parasitic roundworm or tapeworm. [< Gk. *helmins, helminth-.*]

helms•man (hĕlmz′mən) ►*n.* A person who steers a ship.

Hé•lo•ise (ĕl′ə-wēz′, ā-lô-ēz′). 1098?–1164. French philosopher and religious figure; secretly married Peter Abelard (c. 1118).

help (hĕlp) ►*v.* **1.** To give assistance (to); aid. **2.** To contribute; promote. **3.** To give relief to: *help the needy.* **4.** To ease; relieve: *medication to help your cold.* **5.** To change for the better; improve. **6.** To refrain from: *couldn't help laughing.* **7.** To wait on, as in a store. ►*n.* **1.** Aid or assistance. **2.** Relief; remedy. **3.** One that helps. **4a.** A person employed to help. **b.** Such employees in general. —***idiom:*** **help (oneself) to** To serve or provide oneself with. [< OE *helpan.*]

help•er (hĕl′pər) ►*n.* One that helps. See Syns at **assistant.**

help•ful (hĕlp′fəl) ►*adj.* Providing help; useful. —**help′ful•ly** *adv.* —**help′ful•ness** *n.*

help•ing (hĕl′pĭng) ►*n.* A single portion of food.

help•less (hĕlp′lĭs) ►*adj.* **1.** Unable to manage by oneself; incompetent. **2.** Lacking power or strength; impotent. **3.** Involuntary: *helpless laughter.* —**help′less•ly** *adv.* —**help′less•ness** *n.*

help•mate (hĕlp′māt′) ►*n.* A helper and companion, esp. a spouse. [Alteration of HELPMEET.]

help•meet (hĕlp′mēt′) ►*n.* A helpmate. [< misunderstanding of *an help meet,* a suitable helper.]

Hel•sin•ki (hĕl′sĭng′kē, hĕl-sĭng′-) The capital of Finland, in the S part on the Gulf of Finland. Pop. 505,051.

hel•ter-skel•ter (hĕl′tər-skĕl′tər) ►*adv.* **1.** In disorderly haste; confused. **2.** Haphazardly. ►*adj.* **1.** Hurried and confused. **2.** Haphazard. ►*n.* Turmoil; confusion. [?]

Hel•ve•tia (hĕl-vē′shə, -shē-ə) An ancient region of central Europe between the Alps and the Jura Mts. —**Hel•ve′tian** *adj. & n.*

hem[1] (hĕm) ►*n.* **1.** A smooth, even edge on a piece of cloth made by folding the selvage edge under and stitching it down. **2.** A hemline. ►*v.* **hemmed, hem•ming 1.** To fold back and stitch down the edge of. **2.** To surround and shut in. See Syns at **enclose.** [< OE.] —**hem′mer** *n.*

hem[2] (hĕm) ►*n.* A short cough or clearing of the throat, as to gain attention, warn another, or hide embarrassment. ►*v.* **hemmed, hem•ming.** To utter a hem. —***idiom:*** **hem and haw** To be hesitant and indecisive. [< ME *heminge*, coughing.]

he-man (hē′măn′) ►*n. Informal* A strong, virile man.

he•ma•tite (hē′mə-tīt′) ►*n.* A blackish-red to brick-red mineral, essentially Fe_2O_3, the chief ore of iron. [< Gk. *(lithos) haimatitēs*, bloodlike (stone).]

hemato– or **hemat–** ►*pref.* Blood: *hematology.* [< Gk. *haima, haimat-*, blood.]

he•ma•tol•o•gy (hē′mə-tŏl′ə-jē) ►*n.* The science encompassing the medical study of the blood and blood-producing organs. —**he′ma•to•log′ic** (-tə-lŏj′ĭk), **he′ma•to•log′i•cal** *adj.* —**he′ma•tol′o•gist** *n.*

he•ma•to•ma (hē′mə-tō′mə) ►*n.* A localized swelling filled with blood.

heme (hēm) ►*n.* The deep red, nonprotein, ferrous component of hemoglobin. [Ult. < Gk. *haima*, blood.]

–hemia ►*suff.* Var. of **–emia.**

Hem•ing•way (hĕm′ĭng-wā′), **Ernest Miller.** 1899–1961. Amer. writer; 1954 Nobel.

hem•i•sphere (hĕm′ĭ-sfîr′) ►*n.* **1a.** A half of a sphere bounded by a great circle. **b.** A half of a symmetrical, approx. spherical object as divided by a plane of symmetry. **2.** Either the northern or southern half of the earth as divided by the equator or the eastern or western half as divided by a meridian. **3.** *Anat.* Either of the lateral halves of the cerebrum. [< Gk. *hēmisphairion.*] —**hem′i•spher′ic** (-sfîr′ĭk, -sfĕr′-), **hem′i•spher′i•cal** *adj.*

hem•line (hĕm′līn′) ►*n.* **1.** The bottom edge of a skirt, dress, or coat. **2.** The height of a hemline from the floor.

hem•lock (hĕm′lŏk′) ►*n.* **1a.** Any of a genus of coniferous evergreen trees having small cones and short flat leaves. **b.** The wood of a hemlock. **2a.** The poison hemlock. **b.** A poison obtained from the poison hemlock. [< OE *hymlice*, poisonous hemlock.]

hemo– ►*pref.* Blood: *hemodialysis.* [< Gk. *haima*, blood.]

he•mo•di•al•y•sis (hē′mō-dī-ăl′ĭ-sĭs) ►*n., pl.* **-ses** (-sēz′). The removal esp. of metabolic waste products from the bloodstream by dialysis.

he•mo•glo•bin (hē′mə-glō′bĭn) ►*n.* The iron-containing respiratory pigment in red blood cells. [Short for *hematinoglobulin.*]

he•mo•phil•i•a (hē′mə-fĭl′ē-ə, -fēl′yə) ►*n.* Any of several hereditary blood-coagulation disorders occurring only in males, in which the blood fails to clot normally because of a defective clotting factor. —**he′mo•phil′i•ac′** *n.*

hem•or•rhage (hĕm′ər-ĭj) ►*n.* Copious or excessive bleeding. [< Gk. *haimorrhagia.*] —**hem′or•rhage** *v.* —**hem′or•rhag′ic** (hĕm′ə-răj′ĭk) *adj.*

hem•or•rhoid (hĕm′ə-roid′) ►*n.* **1.** An itching or painful mass of dilated veins in swollen anal tissue. **2. hemorroids** The pathological condition in which hemorrhoids occur. [< Gk. *haimorrhoïs* : HEMO– + *rhein*, to flow.] —**hem′or•rhoi′dal** *adj.*

he•mo•stat (hē′mə-stăt′) ►*n.* **1.** An agent used to stop bleeding. **2.** A surgical clamp used to constrict a blood vessel. —**he′mo•stat′ic** *adj.*

hemp (hĕmp) ►*n.* **1.** Cannabis. **2.** The tough coarse fiber of the cannabis plant, used to make cordage. [< OE *hænep.*]

hem•stitch (hĕm′stĭch′) ►*n.* A decorative stitch used esp. on hems. —**hem′stitch′** *v.*

hen (hĕn) ►*n.* A female bird, esp. the adult female of the domestic fowl. [< OE.]

hence (hĕns) ►*adv.* **1.** For this reason; therefore. **2.** From this time; from now. **3.** Away from here. [< OE *heonan*, from here.]

hence•forth (hĕns′fôrth′) ►*adv.* From this time forth; from now on.

hence•for•ward (hĕns-fôr′wərd) ►*adv.* Henceforth.

hench•man (hĕnch′mən) ►*n.* **1.** A loyal follower or subordinate. **2.** A person who supports a political figure for selfish interests. [ME *hengsman*, squire.]

hen•na (hĕn′ə) ►*n.* **1a.** A tree or shrub having fragrant white or reddish flowers. **b.** A reddish-orange cosmetic dye prepared from the dried and ground leaves of this plant. **2.** A reddish brown. ►*v.* To dye with henna. [Ar. *ḥinnā'*.] —**hen′na** *adj.*

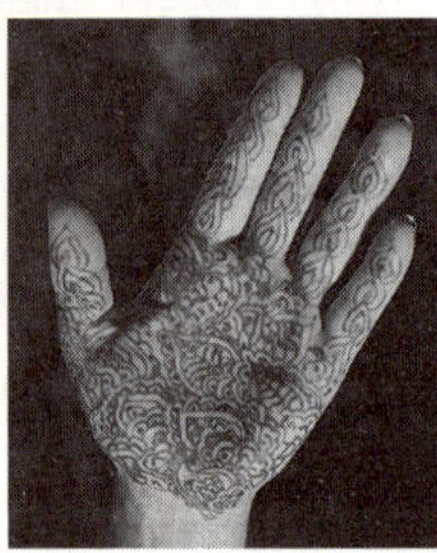

henna
tattoos made with henna dye

hen•peck (hĕn′pĕk′) ►*v. Informal* To dominate (one's husband) with nagging.

hen•ry (hĕn′rē) ►*n., pl.* **-ries** or **-rys.** The unit of inductance in which an induced electromotive force of one volt is produced when the current is varied at the rate of one ampere per second. [After Joseph *Henry* (1791–1878).]

Henry I. 1068–1135. King of England (1100–35).

Henry II. 1133–89. King of England (1154–89).

Henry III[1]**.** 1207–72. King of England (1216–72).

Henry III[2]**.** 1551–89. King of France (1574–89).

Henry IV[1]**.** 1050–1106. Holy Roman emperor and king of Germany (1056–1106).

Henry IV[2]**.** 1366?–1413. King of England (1399–1413).

Henry IV[3]**.** "Henry of Navarre." 1553–1610. King of France (1589–1610).

Henry V. 1387–1422. King of England (1413–22).

Henry VI. 1421–71. King of England (1422–61 and 1470–71); executed.

Henry VII. "Henry Tudor." 1457–1509. King of England (1485–1509).

Henry VIII. 1491–1547. King of England (1509–47).

Henry, Patrick. 1736–99. Amer. Revolutionary leader and orator.

hep (hĕp) ►*adj. Slang* Var. of **hip**[2]**.**

HEPA ►*abbr.* **1.** high-efficiency particulate air **2.** high-efficiency particulate arresting

hep•a•rin (hĕp′ər-ĭn) ►*n.* An organic acid, found esp. in lung and liver tissue, that slows blood clotting. [< Gk. *hēpar*, liver.]

he•pat•ic (hĭ-păt′ĭk) ►*adj.* **1.** Of or relating to the liver. **2.** Acting on or occurring in the liver. [< Gk. *hēpar, hēpat-*, liver.]

he•pat•i•ca (hĭ-păt′ĭ-kə) ►*n.* A woodland plant having three-lobed leaves and white or lavender flowers. [< Med.Lat. *hēpatica*, liverwort.]

hep•a•ti•tis (hĕp′ə-tī′tĭs) ►*n.* Inflammation of the liver, caused by infectious or toxic agents and characterized by jaundice, fever, liver enlargement, and abdominal pain. [Gk. *hēpar, hēpat-*, liver + –ITIS.]

Hep•burn (hĕp′bûrn′), **Audrey.** Edda von Heemstra Hepburn-Ruston. 1929–93. Belgian-born Amer. actress.

Hepburn, Katharine Houghton. b. 1909. Amer. actress.

He•phaes•tus (hĭ-fĕs′təs) ►*n. Gk. Myth.* The god of fire and metalworking.

hepta– or **hept–** ►*pref.* Seven: *heptagon.* [Gk. < *hepta*, seven.]

hep•ta•gon (hĕp′tə-gŏn′) ►*n.* A seven-sided polygon. —**hep•tag′o•nal** (-tăg′ə-nəl) *adj.*

her (hər, ər; hûr *when stressed*) ►*adj.* The possessive form of **she.** Used as a modifier before a noun: *her mother; her goals.* ►*pron.* The objective case of **she. 1.** Used as a direct or indirect object: *I know her; They gave her a ride.* **2.** Used as the object of a preposition: *The call is for her.* See Usage Note at **I**[1]**.** [< OE *hire.*]

He•ra (hîr′ə) ►*n. Gk. Myth.* The sister and wife of Zeus.

Her•a•cli•tus (hĕr′ə-klī′təs). fl. 500 B.C. Greek philosopher. —**Her′a•cli′te•an** (-tē-ən) *adj.*

her•ald (hĕr′əld) ►*n.* **1.** One who proclaims important news; messenger. **2.** One that gives a sign or indication of something to come. **3.** An official formerly charged with making royal proclamations. ►*v.* To proclaim; announce. [< AN, of Gmc. orig.]

he•ral•dic (hə-răl′dĭk) ►*adj.* Of heralds or heraldry. —**he•ral′di•cal•ly** *adv.*

her•ald•ry (hĕr′əl-drē) ►*n., pl.* **-ries 1.** The study or art of devising, granting, and blazoning arms, tracing genealogies, and ruling on questions of rank or protocol. **2.** Armorial ensigns or devices. **3.** Pomp and ceremony; pageantry. —**her′ald•ist** *n.*

He•rat (hĕ-rät′) A city of NW Afghanistan on the Hari Rud E of Kabul. Pop. 177,300.

herb (ûrb, hûrb) ►*n.* **1.** A plant that does not have a woody stem and usu. dies back at the end of each growing season. **2.** Any of various often aromatic plants used in medicine or as seasoning. [< Lat. *herba.*]

her•ba•ceous (hûr-bā′shəs, ûr-) ►*adj.* **1.** Relating to an herb as distinguished from a woody plant. **2.** Green and leaflike in appearance or texture.

herb•age (ûr′bĭj, hûr′-) ►*n.* **1.** Herbaceous plant growth, esp. as used for pasturage. **2.** The fleshy, often edible parts of plants.

herb•al (ûr′bəl, hûr′-) ►*adj.* Relating to or containing herbs. ►*n.* A book about plants and herbs, esp. those useful to humans.

herb•al•ism (ûr′bə-lĭz′əm, hûr′-) ►*n.* The study or use of medicinal herbs; herbal medicine. —**herb′al•ist** *n.*

herbal medicine ►*n.* **1.** The study or use of medicinal herbs to prevent or treat disease. **2.** A medicinal preparation made from plants.

her•bar•i•um (hûr-bâr′ē-əm, ûr-) ►*n., pl.* **-i•ums** or **-i•a** (-ē-ə) **1.** A collection of dried plants mounted and labeled for scientific study. **2.** A place where such a collection is kept. [LLat. *herbārium.*]

Her•bert (hûr′bərt), **George.** 1593–1633. English metaphysical poet.

Herbert, Victor. 1859–1924. Amer. composer and conductor.

her•bi•cide (hûr′bĭ-sīd′, ûr′-) ►*n.* A chemical substance used to destroy plants, esp. weeds. —**her′bi•cid′al** (-sīd′l) *adj.*

her•bi•vore (hûr′bə-vôr′, -vōr′, ûr′-) ►*n.* An animal that feeds chiefly on plants. [< NLat. *herbivorus*, plant-eating.]

her•biv•o•rous (hûr-bĭv′ər-əs, ûr-) ►*adj.* Feeding on plants; plant-eating. —**her•biv′o•rous•ly** *adv.*

Her•cu•la•ne•um (hûr′kyə-lā′nē-əm) An ancient city of S-central Italy on the Bay of Naples; destroyed by the eruption of Mount Vesuvius (A.D. 79).

Her•cu•les (hûr′kyə-lēz′) ►*n. Gk. & Rom. Myth.* A hero of extraordinary strength. —**Her′cu•le′an** (hûr′kyə-lē′ən, hûr-kyo͞o′lē-) *adj.*

herd (hûrd) ►*n.* **1.** A group of animals, as domestic cattle kept or living together. **2.** A large number of people; crowd. ►*v.* **1.** To come together in a herd. **2.** To gather, keep, or drive in or as if in a herd. [< OE *heord.*] —**herd′er** *n.* —**herds′man** *n.*

Her•der (hĕr′dər), **Johann Gottfried von.** 1744–1803. German philosopher.

here (hîr) ►*adv.* **1.** At or in this place: *Stop here for a rest.* **2.** At this time; now: *We'll adjourn the meeting here.* **3.** At or on this point or item: *Here I must disagree.* **4.** To this place: *Come here.* See Usage Note at **there.** ►*interj.* Used esp. to respond to a roll call, attract attention, command an animal, or concur. —***idiom:* neither here nor there** Irrelevant. [< OE *hēr.*]

here•a•bout (hîr′ə-bout′) also **here•a•bouts** (-bouts′) ►*adv.* In this vicinity.

here•af•ter (hîr-ăf′tər) ►*adv.* **1.** After this; from here or now on. **2.** In a future time or state. ►*n.* The afterlife.

here•by (hîr-bī′) ►*adv.* By this means.

he•red•i•tar•y (hə-rĕd′ĭ-tĕr′ē) ►*adj.* **1.** *Law* **a.** Passing down by inheritance. **b.** Having title or possession through inheritance. **2.** Genetically transmitted or transmissible. **3.** Derived from or fostered by one's ancestors. —**he•red′i•tar′i•ly** (-târ′ə-lē) *adv.*

he•red•i•ty (hə-rĕd′ĭ-tē) ►*n., pl.* **-ties 1.** The genetic transmission of characteristics from parent to offspring. **2.** The set of characteristics transmitted genetically to an individual organism. [< Lat. *hērēs, hērēd-*, heir.]

here•in (hîr-ĭn′) ►*adv.* In or into this.

here•of (hîr-ŭv′, -ŏv′) ►*adv.* Of this.

here•on (hîr-ŏn′, -ôn′) ►*adv.* On this.

her•e•sy (hĕr′ĭ-sē) ►*n., pl.* **-sies 1.** An opinion or doctrine at variance with religious orthodoxy. **2a.** A controversial or unorthodox opinion or doctrine, as in politics, philosophy, or science. **b.** Adherence to such opinion. [< Gk. *hairesis*, faction.]

her•e•tic (hĕr′ĭ-tĭk) ►*n.* A person who holds unorthodox opinions. [< Gk. *hairetikos*, factious.] —**he•ret′i•cal** (hə-rĕt′ĭ-kəl) *adj.*

here•to (hîr-to͞o′) ►*adv.* To this document or matter.

here•to•fore (hîr′tə-fôr′, -fōr′) ►*adv.* Before this; previously. [ME.]

here•un•to (hîr-ŭn′to͞o) ►*adv.* Hereto.

here•up•on (hîr′ə-pŏn′, -pôn′) ►*adv.* **1.** Immediately after this. **2.** At or on this.

here•with (hîr-wĭth′, -wĭ*th*′) ►*adv.* **1.** Along with this. **2.** By this means; hereby.

her•i•ta•ble (hĕr′ĭ-tə-bəl) ►*adj.* Capable of being inherited; hereditary. [< OFr.] —**her′i•ta•bil′i•ty** *n.* —**her′i•ta•bly** *adv.*

her•i•tage (hĕr′ĭ-tĭj) ►*n.* **1.** Property that is or can be inherited. **2.** Something passed down from preceding generations; tradition. [< OFr. < *heriter*, inherit.]

Syns: *heritage, inheritance, legacy, tradition* ***n.***

her•maph•ro•dite (hər-măf′rə-dīt′) ►*n.* One having the reproductive organs and many of the secondary sex characteristics of both sexes. [< Gk. *Hermaphroditos*, Hermaphroditus, son of Hermes and Aphrodite.] —**her•maph′ro•dit′ic** (-dĭt′ĭk) *adj.*

Her•mes (hûr′mēz) ►*n. Gk. Myth.* The god of commerce, invention, cunning, and theft.

her•met•ic (hər-mĕt′ĭk) also **her•met•i•cal** (-ĭ-kəl) ►*adj.* **1.** Completely sealed, esp. against the escape or entry of air. **2.** Impervious to outside interference or influence. [< Med. Lat. *Hermēs Trismegistus*, legendary alchemist.] —**her•met′i•cal•ly** *adv.*

her•mit (hûr′mĭt) ►*n.* One who lives a solitary existence; recluse. [< Gk. *erēmitēs* < *erēmos*, solitary.] —**her•mit′ic** *adj.*

her•mit•age (hûr′mĭ-tĭj) ►*n.* **1.** The habitation of a hermit. **2.** A hideaway or retreat.

hermit crab ►*n.* Any of various soft-bodied crabs that occupy and carry the empty shell of a snail or other mollusk.

Her•mo•sil•lo (ĕr′-mō-sē′ō) A city of NW Mexico near the Gulf of California W of Chihuahua. Pop. 297,175.

her•ni•a (hûr′nē-ə) ►*n., pl.* **-ni•as** or **-ni•ae** (-nē-ē′). The protrusion of an organ or other bodily structure through the wall that normally contains it; rupture. [< Lat.] —**her′ni•al** *adj.*

he•ro (hîr′ō) ►*n., pl.* **-roes 1.** In mythology and legend, a man celebrated for his bold exploits. **2.** A person noted for feats of courage or nobility of purpose. **3.** A person noted for special achievement in a particular field. **4.** The principal male character in a literary work. **5.** See **submarine** 2. See Regional Note at **submarine.** [< Gk. *hērōs.*]

Her•od (hĕr′əd). "the Great." 73?–4 B.C. King of Judea (40–4).

Herod An•ti•pas (ăn′tĭ-păs′, -pəs). Died c. A.D. 40. Ruler of Judea and tetrarch in Galilee (4 B.C. –A.D. 40).

He•rod•o•tus (hĭ-rŏd′ə-təs). 5th cent. B.C. Greek historian.

he•ro•ic (hĭ-rō′ĭk) also **he•ro•i•cal** (-ĭ-kəl) ►*adj.* **1.** Of or like the heroes of literature, legend, or myth. **2.** Nobly or selflessly brave. **3.** Impressive in size or scope; grand: *heroic undertakings.* ►*n.* **heroics 1.** Heroic acts; heroism. **2.** Melodramatic behavior or language. —**he•ro′i•cal•ly** *adv.*

heroic couplet ►*n.* A verse unit of two rhymed lines in iambic pentameter.

her•o•in (hĕr′ō-ĭn) ►*n.* A white, odorless, highly addictive narcotic derived from morphine. [Ger., orig. a trademark.]

her•o•ine (hĕr′ō-ĭn) ►*n.* **1.** A woman noted for courage and daring action. **2.** A woman noted for special achievement in a particular field. **3.** The principal female character in a literary work. [< Gk. *hērōinē.*]

her•o•ism (hĕr′ō-ĭz′əm) ►*n.* **1.** Heroic conduct or behavior. **2.** Selfless courage.

her•on (hĕr′ən) ►*n.* Any of various wading birds having a long neck, long legs, and a long pointed bill. [< OFr., of Gmc. orig.]

her•pes (hûr′pēz) ►*n.* Any of several viral diseases causing the eruption of small blisterlike vesicles on the skin or mucous membranes. [< Gk. *herpēs.*] —**her•pet′ic** (hər-pĕt′ĭk) *adj.*

herpes sim•plex (sĭm′plĕks′) ►*n.* Either of two recurrent viral diseases marked by the eruption of blisters on the mouth and face or on the genitals. [NLat., simple herpes.]

her•pe•tol•o•gy (hûr′pĭ-tŏl′ə-jē) ►*n.* The branch of zoology that deals with reptiles and amphibians. [< Gk. *herpeton*, reptile.] —**her′pe•to•log′ic** (-tə-lŏj′ĭk), **her′pe•to•log′i•cal** *adj.* —**her′pe•tol′o•gist** *n.*

Herr (hĕr) ►*n., pl.* **Her•ren** (hĕr′ən). A German courtesy title for a man. [Ger.]

Her•rick (hĕr′ĭk), **Robert.** 1591–1674. English lyric poet.

her•ring (hĕr′ĭng) ►*n., pl.* **-ring** or **-rings.** A commercially important food fish of Atlantic and Pacific waters. [< OE *hǣring.*]

her•ring•bone (hĕr′ĭng-bōn′) ►*n.* **1.** A pattern consisting of rows of short, slanted parallel lines with the direction of the slant alternating row by row. **2.** A twilled fabric woven in this pattern.

herring gull ►*n.* A common seagull having gray and white plumage with black wing tips.

hers (hûrz) ►*pron. (takes sing. or pl. v.)* Used to indicate the one or ones belonging to her: *I found my keys, but not hers.* [ME *hires.*]

Her•schel (hûr′shəl). Family of British astronomers, including Sir **William Herschel** (1738–1822), **Caroline Herschel** (1750–1848), and Sir **John Frederick William Herschel** (1792–1871).

her•self (hûr-sĕlf′) ►*pron.* **1.** That one identical with her: **a.** Used reflexively as the direct or indirect object of a verb or as the object of a preposition: *She hurt herself.* **b.** Used for emphasis: *She herself saw it.* **2.** Her normal or healthy condition: *She's feeling herself again.*

hertz (hûrts) ►*n., pl.* **hertz.** A unit of frequency equal to one cycle per second. [After Heinrich Rudolf *Hertz* (1857–94).]

Her•ze•go•vi•na (hĕrt′sə-gō′vē-nə, -gō-vē′-, hûrt′-) The S region of Bosnia and Herzegovina.

Her•zl (hĕrt′səl), **Theodor.** 1860–1904. Hungarian-born Austrian founder of Zionism.

he's (hēz) ► **1.** He is. **2.** He has.

Hesh•van also **Hesh•wan** (KHĕsh′vən, -vän) ►*n.* A month of the Jewish calendar. See table at **calendar.** [Heb. *ḥešwān.*]

He•si•od (hē′sē-əd, hĕs′ē-). fl. 8th cent. B.C. Greek poet.

hes•i•tant (hĕz′ĭ-tənt) ►*adj.* Inclined or tending to hesitate. —**hes′i•tan•cy** *n.* —**hes′i•tant•ly** *adv.*

hes•i•tate (hĕz′ĭ-tāt′) ►*v.* **-tat•ed, -tat•ing** **1.** To be slow to act, speak, or decide; waver. **2.** To be reluctant. **3.** To speak haltingly; falter. [Lat. *haesitāre.*] —**hes′i•tat′ing•ly** *adv.* —**hes′i•ta′tion** *n.*

Hes•se (hĕs′ə), **Hermann.** 1877–1962. German-born Swiss writer; 1946 Nobel.

Hes•ti•a (hĕs′tē-ə) ►*n. Gk. Myth.* The goddess of the hearth.

hetero– or **heter–** ►*pref.* Other; different: *heterosexual.* [Gk. < *heteros*, other.]

het•er•o•dox (hĕt′ər-ə-dŏks′) ►*adj.* **1.** Not in agreement with accepted beliefs, esp. in theology. **2.** Holding unorthodox opinions. [Gk. *heterodoxos.*] —**het′er•o•dox′y** *n.*

het•er•o•ge•ne•ous (hĕt′ər-ə-jē′nē-əs, -jēn′yəs) ►*adj.* **1.** also **het•er•og•e•nous** (hĕt′ə-rŏj′ə-nəs) Consisting of dissimilar elements or parts; not homogeneous. **2.** Completely different; incongruous. [< Gk. *heterogenēs.*] —**het′er•o′ge•ne′i•ty** *n.* —**het′er•o•ge′ne•ous•ly** *adv.* —**het′er•o•ge′ne•ous•ness** *n.*

het•er•o•sex•u•al (hĕt′ə-rō-sĕk′shōō-əl) ►*adj.* **1.** Sexually oriented to persons of the opposite sex. **2.** Of or relating to different sexes. ►*n.* A heterosexual person. —**het′er•o•sex′u•al′i•ty** *n.* —**het′er•o•sex′u•al•ly** *adv.*

het•er•o•troph (hĕt′ər-ə-trŏf′, -trōf′) ►*n.* An organism that cannot synthesize its own food and depends on complex organic substances for nutrition. [HETERO– + Gk. *trophos*, feeder; see –TROPHY.] —**het′er•o•troph′ic** (-trŏf′ĭk, -trō′fĭk) *adj.* —**het′er•o•troph′i•cal•ly** *adv.* —**het′er•ot′ro•phy** (-ə-rŏt′rə-fē) *n.*

heu•ris•tic (hyōō-rĭs′tĭk) ►*adj.* **1.** Of an educational method in which students learn through investigation and discovery. **2.** *Comp. Sci.* Of a problem-solving technique in which the best solution is selected at successive stages of a program. [< Gk. *heuriskein*, find.] —**heu•ris′tic** *n.* —**heu•ris′ti•cal•ly** *adv.* —**heu•ris′tics** *n.*

hew (hyōō) ►*v.* **hewed, hewn** (hyōōn) or **hewed, hew•ing 1.** To make or shape with or as if with an ax. **2.** To cut down with an ax. **3.** To adhere or conform strictly: *hew to the line.* [< OE *hēawan.*] —**hew′er** *n.*

hex[1] (hĕks) ►*n.* **1.** An evil spell; curse. **2.** One that brings bad luck. ►*v.* **1.** To put a hex on. **2.** To bring or wish bad luck to. [Penn.Du. < Ger. *Hexe*, witch.] —**hex′er** *n.*

hex[2] (hĕks) ►*adj.* Hexagonal. Used of hardware; *a hex wrench.*

hexa– or **hex–** ►*pref.* Six: *hexagon.* [Gk. < *hex*, six.]

hex•a•dec•i•mal (hĕk′sə-dĕs′ə-məl) ▸*adj.* Of or based on the number 16.

hex•a•gon (hĕk′sə-gŏn′) ▸*n.* A polygon having six sides. —**hex•ag′o•nal** (hĕk-săg′ə-nəl) *adj.* —**hex•ag′o•nal•ly** *adv.*

hex•am•e•ter (hĕk-săm′ĭ-tər) ▸*n.* A line of verse consisting of six metrical feet. —**hex′a•met′ric** (hĕk-sə-mĕt′rĭk), **hex′a•met′ri•cal** (-rĭ-kəl) *adj.*

hey (hā) ▸*interj.* Used to attract attention or to express surprise, appreciation, wonder, or pleasure.

hey•day (hā′dā′) ▸*n.* The period of greatest popularity, success, or power; prime. [Perh. < ME *hey*, hey.]

Hey•er•dahl (hā′ər-däl′, hī′-), **Thor.** b. 1914. Norwegian ethnologist and explorer.

Hf ▸ The symbol for the element **hafnium.**

HF ▸*abbr.* high frequency

Hg ▸ The symbol for the element **mercury** 1. [< Lat. *hydrargyrus*, mercury : HYDRO– + Gk. *arguros*, silver.]

hgt. ▸*abbr.* height

HH ▸*abbr.* **1.** His (or Her) Highness **2.** His Holiness

HHFA ▸*abbr.* Housing and Home Finance Agency

hi (hī) ▸*interj.* Used to express greeting.

HI ▸*abbr.* **1.** Hawaii **2.** high intensity **3.** humidity index

H.I. ▸*abbr.* Hawaiian Islands

Hi•a•le•ah (hī′ə-lē′ə) A city of SE FL NW of Miami. Pop. 188,004.

hi•a•tus (hī-ā′təs) ▸*n., pl.* **-tus•es** or **-tus.** A gap or an interruption in space, time, or continuity; break. [Lat. *hiātus* < *hiāre*, gape.] —**hi•a′tal** *adj.*

Hi•a•wa•tha (hī′ə-wŏth′ə, -wô′thə, hē′ə-). fl. 1570. Onondagan leader.

hi•ba•chi (hĭ-bä′chē) ▸*n., pl.* **-chis.** A portable charcoal-burning brazier. [J.]

hibachi

hi•ber•nate (hī′bər-nāt′) ▸*v.* **-nat•ed, -nat•ing.** To pass the winter in a dormant or torpid state. [< Lat. *hībernus*, of winter.] —**hi′ber•na′tion** *n.* —**hi′ber•na′tor** *n.*

Hi•ber•ni•a (hī-bûr′nē-ə) The Latin and poetic name for Ireland. —**Hi•ber′ni•an** *adj. & n.*

hi•bis•cus (hī-bĭs′kəs) ▸*n.* Any of a genus of chiefly tropical shrubs or trees having large, showy, variously colored flowers. [LLat. < Lat. *hibiscum*, marsh mallow.]

hic•cup also **hic•cough** (hĭk′əp) ▸*n.* **1.** A spasm of the diaphragm resulting in a rapid involuntary inhalation that is stopped by the sudden closure of the glottis. **2. hiccups** also **hiccoughs** An attack of these spasms. ▸*v.* **-cupped, -cup•ping** also **-coughed, -cough•ing.** To have the hiccups. [Imit.]

hick (hĭk) *Informal* ▸*n.* A gullible, provincial person; yokel. ▸*adj.* Provincial; unsophisticated. [< *Hick*, a nickname for *Richard*.]

Hick•ok (hĭk′ŏk′), **James Butler.** "Wild Bill." 1837–76. Amer. frontier scout and marshal.

hick•o•ry (hĭk′ə-rē) ▸*n., pl.* **-ries 1.** Any of a genus of North American trees having smooth or shaggy bark, compound leaves, and hard nuts with an edible kernel. **2.** The wood of a hickory. [Of Algonquian orig.]

hi•dal•go (hĭ-dăl′gō) ▸*n., pl.* **-gos.** A member of the minor nobility in Spain. [Sp.]

hide¹ (hīd) ▸*v.* **hid** (hĭd), **hid•den** (hĭd′n) or **hid, hid•ing 1.** To put or keep out of sight. **2.** To prevent the disclosure of. See Syns at **block. 3.** To cut off from sight; cover up. **4.** To seek refuge. [< OE *hȳdan*.]

hide² (hīd) ▸*n.* The skin of an animal, esp. of a large animal. [< OE *hȳd*.]

hide-and-seek (hīd′n-sēk′) ▸*n.* A children's game in which one player tries to find and catch others who are hiding.

hide•a•way (hīd′ə-wā′) ▸*n.* **1.** A place of concealment; hide-out. **2.** A secluded or isolated place.

hide•bound (hīd′bound′) ▸*adj.* Stubbornly narrow-minded or inflexible.

hid•e•ous (hĭd′ē-əs) ▸*adj.* Repulsive, esp. to the sight. See Syns at **ugly.** [< OFr. *hide*, fear.] —**hid′e•ous•ly** *adv.* —**hid′e•ous•ness** *n.*

hide•out (hīd′out′) ▸*n.* A place of shelter or concealment.

hie (hī) ▸*v.* **hied, hie•ing** or **hy•ing** (hī′ĭng). To go quickly; hasten. [< OE *hīgian*, exert oneself.]

hi•er•ar•chy (hī′ə-rär′kē, hī′rär′-) ▸*n., pl.* **-chies 1.** A body of persons having authority. **2.** An arrangement of persons or things in a graded series, as by rank or ability. [< Gk. *hierarkhia*, rule of a high priest.] —**hi′er•ar′chal, hi′er•ar′chic, hi′er•ar′chi•cal** *adj.* —**hi′er•ar′chi•cal•ly** *adv.*

hi•er•at•ic (hī′ə-răt′ĭk, hī-răt′-) ▸*adj.* **1.** Of or relating to sacred persons or offices; sacerdotal. **2.** Of or relating to a simplified style of Egyptian hieroglyphic script. [Lat. *hierāticus* < Gk. *hieratikos* < Gk. *hiereus*, priest.] —**hi′er•at′i•cal•ly** *adv.*

hi•er•o•glyph (hī′ər-ə-glĭf′, hī′rə-) ▸*n.* **1.** A symbol used in hieroglyphic writing. **2.** Something that suggests a hieroglyph.

hi•er•o•glyph•ic (hī′ər-ə-glĭf′ĭk, hī′rə-) ▸*adj.* Of or being a system of writing, such as that of ancient Egypt, in which pictorial symbols represent meaning or sound or both. ▸*n.* **1a.** A character in hieroglyphic writing. **b.** often **hieroglyphics** *(takes sing. or pl. v.)* Hieroglyphic writing, esp. that of the ancient Egyptians. **2.** Something illegible or undecipherable. [< Gk. *hieroglaphikos* : *hieros*, holy + *gluphein*, carve.] —**hi′er•o•glyph′i•cal•ly** *adv.*

hi-fi (hī′fī′) ▸*n., pl.* **-fis** *Informal* **1.** High fidelity. **2.** An electronic system, esp. a phonograph, for reproducing high-fidelity sound. —**hi′-fi′** *adj.*

hig•gle•dy-pig•gle•dy (hĭg′əl-dē-pĭg′əl-dē) ▸*adv.* In utter disorder or confusion. [?]

high (hī) ▸*adj.* **-er, -est 1a.** Relatively great in elevation. **b.** Extending a specified distance. **2a.** At or near a peak or culminating stage. **b.** Advanced in development or complexity. **3.** Piercing in tone or pitch. **4a.** Of great importance: *a high priority on housing.* **b.** Eminent in rank or status: *a high official.* **c.** Serious; grave: *high crimes.* **d.** Constituting a climax: *the high point of a film.* **5.** Lofty or exalted in quality. **6a.** Relatively great, as in quantity or degree. **b.** Favorable: *has a high opinion of him.* **7a.** Indicating excitement or euphoria. **b.** *Slang* Intoxicated by or as if by alcohol or a drug. ▸*adv.* **-er, -est.** At, in, or to a lofty position, level, or degree. ▸*n.* **1.** A high level, degree, or point. **2.** The gear configuration of a transmission that produces the highest range of output speeds. **3.** A center of high atmospheric pressure. **4.** *Slang* An intoxicated or euphoric condition. —***idioms:*** **high and dry** Helpless; stranded. **high and low** Everywhere: *searched high and low.* [< OE *hēah.*] —**high′ly** *adv.*

high•ball (hī′bôl′) ▸*n.* A mixed alcoholic beverage served in a tall glass.

high beam ▸*n.* The beam of a vehicle's headlight that provides long-range illumination.

high•born (hī′bôrn′) ▸*adj.* Of noble birth.

high•boy (hī′boi′) ▸*n.* A tall chest of drawers supported on four legs.

high•bred (hī′brĕd′) ▸*adj.* Of superior breed or stock.

high•brow (hī′brou′) ▸*adj.* Highly cultured or intellectual. ▸*n.* One who has or affects a high degree of culture or learning. —**high′brow′, high′browed′** (-broud′) *adj.*

high•chair (hī′châr′) ▸*n.* A very young child's feeding chair that has long legs.

high-class (hī′klăs′) ▸*adj.* Of superior quality; first-class.

high•er-up (hī′ər-ŭp′) ▸*n.* *Informal* One who has a superior rank, position, or status.

high•fa•lu•tin or **hi•fa•lu•tin** (hī′fə-lo͞ot′n) ▸*adj.* *Informal* Pompous; pretentious. [?]

Regional Note: Although *highfalutin* is characteristic of American folk speech, it is too widespread to be a true regionalism. The second element, *-falutin,* may come from the verb *flute*—hence *high-fluting,* a comical indictment of a conceited person.

high fashion ▸*n.* **1.** See **high style. 2.** See **haute couture.**

high fidelity ▸*n.* The electronic reproduction of sound with minimal distortion. —**high′-fi•del′i•ty** *adj.*

high•flown (hī′flōn′) ▸*adj.* Highly pretentious or inflated.

high frequency ▸*n.* A radio frequency in the range between 3 and 30 megahertz.

High German ▸*n.* **1.** German as used in central and S Germany. **2.** See **German** 2.

high•hand•ed (hī′hăn′dĭd) ▸*adj.* Arrogant; overbearing. —**high′hand′ed•ly** *adv.* —**high′hand′ed•ness** *n.*

high-hat (hī′hăt′) *Informal* ▸*v.* **-hat•ted, -hat•ting.** To treat condescendingly or superciliously. ▸*adj.* Snobbish; haughty.

high jinks or **hi•jinks** (hī′jĭnks′) ▸*pl.n.* Playful, often noisy and rowdy activity.

high jump ▸*n.* A jump for height made over a horizontal bar in a track-and-field contest. —**high jumper** *n.*

high•land (hī′lənd) ▸*n.* **1.** Elevated land. **2. highlands** A mountainous section of a country. —**high′land** *adj.* —**high′land•er** *n.*

High•lands (hī′ləndz) A mountainous region of central and N Scotland. —**High′land** *adj.* —**High′land•er** *n.*

high•light (hī′līt′) ▸*n.* An especially notable detail or event. ▸*v.* **1.** To make prominent; emphasize. **2.** To be a highlight of.

high-mind•ed (hī′mīn′dĭd) ▸*adj.* Elevated in ideals or conduct; noble. —**high′-mind′ed•ly** *adv.* —**high′-mind′ed•ness** *n.*

high•ness (hī′nĭs) ▸*n.* **1.** The quality or condition of being high. **2. Highness** Used with *His, Her,* or *Your* as a title for a prince or princess.

high-pres•sure (hī′prĕsh′ər) ▸*adj.* **1.** Relating to pressures higher than normal. **2.** *Informal* Aggressive and persistent. **3.** Full of or imposing great stress or tension.

high profile ▸*n.* An intentionally conspicuous, well-publicized presence or stance. —**high′-pro′file** *adj.*

high relief ▸*n.* Sculptural relief in which the modeled forms project from the background by at least half their depth.

high-rise also **high rise** (hī′rīz′) ▸*n.* A multistoried building equipped with elevators. —**high′-rise′** *adj.*

high•road or **high road** (hī′rōd′) ▸*n.* **1.** A direct or sure path. **2.** *Chiefly Brit.* A main road; highway.

high school ▸*n.* A secondary school that usu. includes grades 9 or 10 through 12. —**high′-school′** *adj.* —**high school′er** *n.*

high seas ▸*pl.n.* The open ocean waters beyond the territorial limits of a country.

high-sound•ing (hī′soun′dĭng) ▸*adj.* Pretentious; pompous.

high-spir•it•ed (hī′spĭr′ĭ-tĭd) ▸*adj.* **1.** Having a proud or unbroken spirit. **2.** Vivacious; lively. —**high′-spir′it•ed•ness** *n.*

high-strung (hī′strŭng′) ▸*adj.* Tending to be very nervous and easily excited.

high style ▸*n.* The latest in fashion, usu. for an exclusive clientele. —**high′-style′** *adj.*

high•tail (hī′tāl′) ▸*v.* *Slang* To go as fast as possible, esp. in retreat.

high-tech (hī′tĕk′) ▸*adj.* *Informal* Of or resembling high technology.

high technology ▸*n.* Technology involving highly advanced systems or devices. —**high′-tech•nol′o•gy** *adj.*

high-ten•sion (hī′tĕn′shən) ▸*adj.* Having a high voltage.

high-test (hī′tĕst′) ▸*adj.* **1.** Of or being highly volatile high-octane gasoline. **2.** Meeting exacting standards. —**high′test′** *n.*

high tide ▸*n.* **1a.** The tide at its highest level. **b.** The time at which this tide occurs. **2.** A point of culmination; climax.

high-toned (hī′tōnd′) ▸*adj.* **1.** Intellectually, morally, or socially superior. **2.** *Informal* Pretentiously elegant or fashionable.

high•way (hī′wā′) ▸*n.* A main public road.

high•way•man (hī′wā′mən) ▸*n.* A robber who holds up travelers on a road.

high wire ▸*n.* A tightrope for aerialists that is stretched high above the ground. —**high′-wire′** *adj.*

hi•jack also **high•jack** (hī′jăk′) ▸*v.* *Informal* **1.** To steal (goods) from a vehicle in transit. **2.** To seize control of (a moving vehicle) by force, esp. to reach an alternate destination. —**hi′jack′er** *n.*

hike (hīk) ▸*v.* **hiked, hik•ing 1.** To go on a long walk for pleasure or exercise. **2.** To increase in amount. **3.** To pull or raise abruptly:

hiked up her socks. **4.** *Football* To snap (the ball). ►*n.* **1.** A long walk. **2.** An often abrupt increase or rise: *a price hike.* **3.** *Football* See **snap** 9. [?] —**hik′er** *n.*

hi•lar•i•ous (hĭ-lâr′ē-əs, -lăr′-, hī-) ►*adj.* Boisterously funny. [< Gk. *hilaros*, cheerful.] —**hi•lar′i•ous•ly** *adv.* —**hi•lar′i•ty** *n.*

Hil•de•gard von Bing•en (hĭl′də-gärd′ vŏn bĭng′ən). 1098–1178. German nun, poet, and composer.

hill (hĭl) ►*n.* **1.** A well-defined natural elevation smaller than a mountain. **2.** A small heap, pile, or mound. **3. Hill** The US Congress. —***idiom:* over the hill** *Informal* Past one's prime. [< OE *hyll.*] —**hill′i•ness** *n.* —**hill′y** *adj.*

Hil•la•ry (hĭl′ə-rē), Sir **Edmund Percival.** b. 1919. New Zealand mountaineer.

hill•bil•ly (hĭl′bĭl′ē) ►*n., pl.* **-lies** *Informal.* A person from the backwoods or a remote mountain area.

hill•ock (hĭl′ək) ►*n.* A small hill. [ME *hillok.*]

hill•side (hĭl′sīd′) ►*n.* The slope of a hill.

hill•top (hĭl′tŏp′) ►*n.* The crest of a hill.

hilt (hĭlt) ►*n.* The handle of a weapon or tool. —***idiom:* to the hilt** To the limit; completely. [< OE.]

Hil•ton (hĭl′tən), **James.** 1900–54. British novelist.

him (hĭm) ►*pron.* The objective case of **he. 1.** Used as a direct or indirect object: *They chose him; I gave him a raise.* **2.** Used as the object of a preposition: *This call is for him.* See Usage Note at **I**[1]. [< OE.]

Him•a•la•ya Mountains (hĭm′ə-lā′ə, hĭ-mäl′yə) A mountain system of S-central Asia extending about 2,414 km (1,500 mi) through Kashmir, N India, S Xizang (Tibet), Nepal, Sikkim, and Bhutan. —**Him′a•la′yan** *adj.*

him•self (hĭm-sĕlf′) ►*pron.* **1.** That one identical with him: **a.** Used reflexively as the direct or indirect object of a verb or the object of a preposition: *He cut himself.* **b.** Used for emphasis: *He himself did it.* **2.** His normal or healthy condition: *He's feeling himself again.*

hind[1] (hīnd) ►*adj.* Located at or forming the back or rear; posterior: *hind legs.* [< OE *bihindan.*]

hind[2] (hīnd) ►*n.* A female red deer. [< OE.]

Hin•de•mith (hĭn′də-mĭth, -mĭt), **Paul.** 1895–1963. German violist and composer.

Hin•den•burg (hĭn′dən-bûrg′), **Paul von.** 1847–1934. German general and politician.

hin•der (hĭn′dər) ►*v.* **1.** To be or get in the way of. **2.** To obstruct or delay the progress of. [< OE *hindrian.*] —**hin′der•er** *n.*

Hin•di (hĭn′dē) ►*n.* **1.** A group of Indic dialects spoken in N India. **2.** The literary and official language based on these dialects. —**Hin′di** *adj.*

hind•most (hīnd′mōst′) also **hind•er•most** (hīn′dər-) ►*adj.* Farthest to the rear; last.

hind•quar•ter (hīnd′kwôr′tər) ►*n.* **1.** The back portion of a side of meat. **2. hindquarters** The rump of a four-footed animal.

hin•drance (hĭn′drəns) ►*n.* **1.** The act of hindering or condition of being hindered. **2.** One that hinders.

hind•sight (hīnd′sīt′) ►*n.* Understanding of events after their occurrence.

Hin•du (hĭn′do͞o) ►*adj.* Of Hinduism or the Hindus. ►*n.* **1.** An adherent of Hinduism. **2.** A native of India, esp. N India.

Hin•du•ism (hĭn′do͞o-ĭz′əm) ►*n.* A diverse body of religion, philosophy, and culture native to India.

Hindu Kush (ko͝osh, kŭsh) A mountain range of SW Asia extending W from N Pakistan to NE Afghanistan.

Hin•du•stan (hĭn′do͞o-stän′, -stăn′) **1.** A historical region of India considered at various times to include only the upper Ganges R. plateau or all of N India. **2.** The entire Indian subcontinent.

Hin•du•sta•ni (hĭn′do͞o-stä′nē, -stăn′ē) ►*n.* A group of Indic dialects that includes Urdu and Hindi. ►*adj.* Of or relating to Hindustan or the Hindustani language.

hinge (hĭnj) ►*n.* **1.** A jointed device that allows the turning of a part, such as a door, on a frame. **2.** A similar structure or part. ►*v.* **hinged, hing•ing 1.** To attach by or equip with or as if with a hinge. **2.** To be contingent on a single factor; depend: *The safety of the team hinges on the weather.* [ME.]

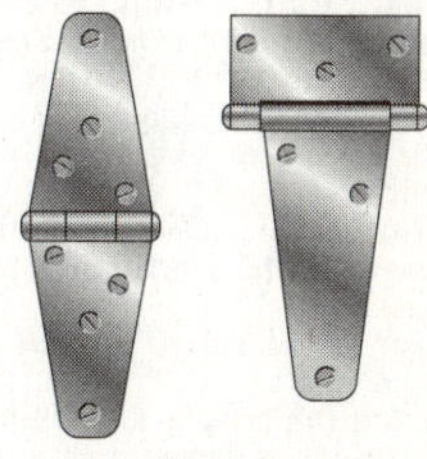

hinge
left to right: strap and T-hinge models

hint (hĭnt) ►*n.* **1.** A slight indication or intimation. **2.** A barely perceptible amount: *just a hint of color.* ►*v.* **1.** To make known in an indirect manner. **2.** To give a hint. [Poss. < OE *hentan*, to grasp.] —**hint′er** *n.*

hin•ter•land (hĭn′tər-lănd′) ►*n.* **1.** The land adjacent to and inland from a coast. **2.** A region remote from urban areas. [Ger.]

hip[1] (hĭp) ►*n.* **1.** The part of the human body that projects outward over the hipbone between the waist and the thigh. **2.** The hip joint. [< OE *hype.*]

hip[2] (hĭp) also **hep** (hĕp) ►*adj.* **hip•per, hip•pest** also **hep•per, hep•pest** *Slang* **1.** Keenly aware of the latest trends or developments. **2.** Cognizant; wise. **3.** Very fashionable or stylish. [Poss. of African orig.] —**hip′ness** *n.*

hip[3] (hĭp) ►*n.* The fleshy, usu. red fruit of the rose, used for tea. [< OE *hēope.*]

hip•bone (hĭp′bōn′) ►*n.* Either of two large flat bones each forming one of the halves of the pelvis.

hip-hop (hĭp′hŏp′) ►*n.* **1.** A popular urban youth culture, closely associated with rap music and the style of inner-city African Americans. **2.** Rap music. [Prob. HIP[2] + HOP[1].]

hip joint ►*n.* The ball-and-socket joint between the femur and the hipbone.

hip•pie also **hip•py** (hĭp′ē) ►*n., pl.* **-pies** *Slang.* A member of a social and political movement advocating such practices as pacifism, nonconformity in dress and behavior, and often the use of psychedelic drugs. [< HIP[2].] —**hip′pie•dom** *n.*

hip•po (hĭp′ō) ▸*n., pl.* **-pos.** A hippopotamus.

Hip•poc•ra•tes (hĭ-pŏk′rə-tēz′). 460?–377? B.C. Greek physician. —**Hip′po•crat′ic** (hĭp′ə-krăt′ĭk) *adj.*

Hippocratic oath ▸*n.* An oath of ethical professional behavior sworn by new physicians. [After HIPPOCRATES.]

hip•po•drome (hĭp′ə-drōm′) ▸*n.* An arena used esp. for horse shows. [< Gk. *hippodromos.*]

hip•po•pot•a•mus (hĭp′ə-pŏt′ə-məs) ▸*n., pl.* **-mus•es** or **-mi** (-mī′). A large African river mammal having thick, dark, almost hairless skin, short legs, and a broad, wide-mouthed muzzle. [< Gk. *hippopotamos.*]

hip roof or **hipped roof** (hĭpt) ▸*n.* A four-sided roof having sloping ends and sides.

hip•ster (hĭp′stər) ▸*n. Slang* One who is hip.

hi•ra•ga•na (hîr′ə-gä′nə) ▸*n.* A cursive kana used for polite, informal, or casual writing. [J. : *hira*, ordinary, plain + *kana*, kana.]

hire (hīr) ▸*v.* **hired, hir•ing.** To engage the services or use of for a fee: *hired a new clerk; hire a car for the day.* ▸*n.* **1.** The act of hiring or the condition of being hired. **2.** Payment for services or the use of something. [< OE *hȳrian.*] —**hir′er** *n.*

hire•ling (hīr′lĭng) ▸*n.* One who works solely for compensation, esp. at performing tasks considered offensive.

Hi•ro•hi•to (hîr′ō-hē′tō). 1901–89. Emperor of Japan (1926–89).

Hi•ro•shi•ma (hîr′ə-shē′mə, hĭ-rō′shə-mə) A city of SW Honshu, Japan; destroyed by US forces with the first atomic bomb used in warfare (August 6, 1945). Pop. 1,102,047.

hir•sute (hûr′so͞ot′, hîr′-, hər-so͞ot′) ▸*adj.* Hairy. [Lat. *hirsūtus.*] —**hir′sute′ness** *n.*

his (hĭz) ▸*adj.* The possessive form of **he.** Used as a modifier before a noun: *his brother; his ideas.* ▸*pron. (takes sing. or pl. v.)* Used to indicate the one or ones belonging to him: *If you can't find your hat, take his.* [< OE.]

His•pan•ic (hĭ-spăn′ĭk) ▸*adj.* **1.** Relating to Spain or Spanish-speaking Latin America. **2.** Relating to Hispanic Americans. ▸*n.* **1.** A Spanish-speaking person. **2.** A Hispanic American.

Usage: Though often used interchangeably, *Hispanic* and *Latino* are not identical terms. *Hispanic* is arguably the broader of the two, potentially encompassing all Spanish-speaking peoples in both hemispheres and emphasizing the common denominator of language between otherwise diverse communities. *Latino* refers more exclusively to persons of Latin American origin, and, with its Spanish sound and its ability to show the feminine form *Latina* when used of women, is favored by some as a term of ethnic pride. See Usage Note at **Chicano.**

Hispanic American ▸*n.* **1.** A US citizen or resident of Latin-American or Spanish descent. **2.** A Spanish American. —**His•pan′ic-A•mer′i•can** *adj.*

His•pan•io•la (hĭs′pən-yō′lə). Formerly **Haiti.** An island of the West Indies E of Cuba, divided between Haiti and the Dominican Republic.

hiss (hĭs) ▸*n.* **1.** A sharp sibilant sound similar to a sustained *s.* **2.** An expression of disapproval or contempt conveyed by a hiss. ▸*v.* **1.** To make a hiss. **2.** To express disapproval by hissing. [ME *hissen*, to hiss.]

his•ta•mine (hĭs′tə-mēn′, -mĭn) ▸*n.* A white crystalline compound, $C_5H_9N_3$, found in plant and animal tissue, that dilates blood vessels, stimulates gastric secretions, and is released by the body in allergic reactions. [*hist(idine)*, an amino acid + AMINE.] —**his′ta•min′ic** (-mĭn′ĭk) *adj.*

his•to•com•pat•i•bil•i•ty (hĭs′tō-kəm-păt′ə-bĭl′ĭ-tē) ▸*n., pl.* **-ties.** A state or condition in which the absence of immunological interference permits the grafting of tissue or the transfusion of blood without rejection. —**his′to•com•pat′i•ble** *adj.*

his•to•gram (hĭs′tə-grăm′) ▸*n.* A bar graph of a frequency distribution in which the areas of the bars are proportional to the classes into which the variable has been divided and their frequencies. [Gk. *histos*, bar + -GRAM.]

his•tol•o•gy (hĭ-stŏl′ə-jē) ▸*n., pl.* **-gies 1.** The anatomical study of the microscopic structure of animal and plant tissues. **2.** The microscopic structure of tissue. [< Gk. *histos*, tissue.] —**his′to•log′i•cal** (hĭs′tə-lŏj′ĭ-kəl), **his′to•log′ic** *adj.* —**his′to•log′i•cal•ly** *adv.* —**his•tol′o•gist** *n.*

his•to•ri•an (hĭ-stôr′ē-ən, -stōr′-, -stŏr′-) ▸*n.* A writer, student, or scholar of history.

his•tor•ic (hĭ-stôr′ĭk, -stŏr′-) ▸*adj.* Having importance in or influence on history.

Usage: *Historic* and *historical* are differentiated in usage, though their senses overlap. *Historic* refers to what is important in history. *Historical* refers to whatever existed in the past, whether regarded as important or not: *a historical character.*

his•tor•i•cal (hĭ-stôr′ĭ-kəl, -stŏr′-) ▸*adj.* **1.** Of or relating to history. **2.** Based on or concerned with events in history. **3.** Important or famous in history. See Usage Note at **historic.** —**his•tor′i•cal•ly** *adv.*

his•to•ri•og•ra•phy (hĭ-stôr′ē-ŏg′rə-fē, -stōr′-) ▸*n.* **1.** The principles or methodology of historical research. **2.** The writing of history. **3.** Historical literature. —**his•to′ri•og′ra•pher** *n.* —**his•to′ri•o•graph′ic** (-ē-ə-grăf′ĭk), **his•to′ri•o•graph′i•cal** *adj.*

his•to•ry (hĭs′tə-rē) ▸*n., pl.* **-ries 1.** A narrative of events; story. **2.** A chronological record of events. **3.** The branch of knowledge that records and analyzes past events. **4.** The events of the past. **5.** An interesting past: *a house with a history.* [< Gk. *historia* < *historein*, inquire < *histōr*, learned person.]

his•tri•on•ic (hĭs′trē-ŏn′ĭk) also **his•tri•on•i•cal** (-ĭ-kəl) ▸*adj.* **1.** Of or relating to actors or acting. **2.** Excessively dramatic or emotional; affected. [< Lat. *histriō*, actor.] —**his′tri•on′i•cal•ly** *adv.*

his•tri•on•ics (hĭs′trē-ŏn′ĭks) ▸*n. (takes sing. or pl. v.)* Exaggerated emotional behavior calculated for effect.

hit (hĭt) ▸*v.* **hit, hit•ting 1.** To come or cause to come into contact with forcefully; strike. **2.** To deal a blow to. **3.** To press or push (a key or button). **4.** To propel (e.g., a ball) with a blow. **5.** *Baseball* To execute (a base hit) successfully. **6.** To affect adversely. **7.** *Informal* To discover, esp. by chance. **8.** *Informal* To attain or reach: *Sales hit a new high.* ▸*n.* **1.** A collision or impact. **2.** A successfully executed shot, blow, or throw. **3.** A successful or popular venture. **4.** *Baseball* A base hit. **5.** *Comp. Sci.* **a.** A match of data in a search string against data that one is searching. **b.** A connection made to a website. **6.** *Slang* A dose of a narcotic drug. **7.** *Slang* A murder, esp. for hire. —***idioms:*** **hit it off** *Informal* To get along well together. **hit the hay** *Slang* To go to bed. **hit the road** *Slang* To set out; leave. **hit the roof** *Slang* To express vehement anger. **hit the spot** To satisfy a specific desire. [< ON *hitta.*] —**hit′ter** *n.*

hit-and-run (hĭt′n-rŭn′) ►*adj.* Of or being a vehicular accident in which the driver at fault leaves the scene.

hitch (hĭch) ►*v.* **1.** To fasten or catch temporarily with or as if with a loop, hook, or noose. **2.** To connect or attach: *hitch an ox to the plow.* **3.** To move or raise by pulling or jerking. **4.** *Informal* **a.** To obtain (a free ride). **b.** To hitchhike. **5.** To get married. ►*n.* **1.** A knot used as a temporary fastening. **2.** A short jerk or tug. **3.** A hobble or limp. **4.** An impediment or delay. **5.** A term of military service. [Prob. < ME *hytchen*, move, jerk.] —**hitch′er** *n.*

hitch•hike (hĭch′hīk′) ►*v.* **-hiked, -hik•ing.** To travel by soliciting free rides along a road. —**hitch′hik′er** *n.*

hith•er (hĭ*th*′ər) ►*adv.* To or toward this place: *Come hither.* ►*adj.* Located on the near side. [< OE *hider.*]

hith•er•to (hĭ*th*′ər-to͞o′, hĭ*th*′ər-to͞o′) ►*adv.* Until this time.

Hit•ler (hĭt′lər), **Adolf.** 1889–1945. Austrian-born German Nazi dictator. —**Hit•ler′i•an** (hĭt-lîr′ē-ən) *adj.*

hit man ►*n. Slang* A hired killer.

hit-or-miss (hĭt′ər-mĭs′) ►*adj.* Haphazard; random. —**hit or miss** *adv.*

hit squad ►*n. Slang* A squad or team of hired executioners.

Hit•tite (hĭt′īt′) ►*n.* **1.** A member of an ancient people living in Anatolia and N Syria about 2000–1200 B.C. **2.** The Indo-European language of the Hittites.

HIV (āch′ī-vē′) ►*n.* A retrovirus that causes AIDS. [*h(uman) i(mmunodeficiency) v(irus).*]

hive (hīv) ►*n.* **1.** A structure for housing bees, esp. honeybees. **2.** A colony of bees living in a hive. **3.** A place swarming with activity. [< OE *hȳf.*] —**hive** *v.*

hives (hīvz) ►*pl.n. (takes sing. or pl. v.)* A skin condition marked by itching welts and caused by an allergic reaction, as to a food, infection, or nervous state. [?]

HM ►*abbr.* Her (or His) Majesty

HMO (āch′ĕm-ō′) ►*n.* A corporation providing curative and preventive medicine within certain limits to enrolled members. [H(EALTH) M(AINTENANCE) O(RGANIZATION).]

Hmong (hmông) ►*n., pl.* **Hmong** or **Hmongs** **1.** A member of a people inhabiting parts of S China, Vietnam, Laos, and Thailand. **2.** The language of the Hmong.

HMS ►*abbr.* Her (or His) Majesty's Ship

Ho ► The symbol for the element **holmium.**

hoa•gie also **hoa•gy** (hō′gē) ►*n., pl.* **-gies** *Regional* See **submarine** 2. See Regional Note at **submarine.** [Alteration of *hoggy.*]

hoard (hôrd, hōrd) ►*n.* A supply hidden or stored for future use. ►*v.* To accumulate a hoard (of). [< OE *hord.*] —**hoard′er** *n.*

hoar•frost (hôr′frôst′, -frŏst′, hōr′-) ►*n.* Frozen dew that forms a white coating on a surface. [< OE *hār.*]

hoarse (hôrs, hōrs) ►*adj.* **hoars•er, hoars•est.** Rough or grating in sound. [< OE *hās.*] —**hoarse′ly** *adv.* —**hoarse′ness** *n.*

hoar•y (hôr′ē, hōr′ē) ►*adj.* **-i•er, -i•est** **1.** Gray or white with or as if with age. **2.** Very old; ancient. [< OE *hār.*] —**hoar′i•ness** *n.*

hoax (hōks) ►*n.* An act intended to deceive or trick. ►*v.* To deceive or cheat by using a hoax. [Perh. < HOCUS-POCUS.] —**hoax′er** *n.*

hob (hŏb) ►*n. Chiefly Brit.* A hobgoblin, sprite, or elf. [< ME *Hob*, nickname for Robert.]

Hobbes (hŏbz), **Thomas.** 1588–1679. English philosopher and political theorist. —**Hobbes′i•an** *adj.*

hob•ble (hŏb′əl) ►*v.* **-bled, -bling** **1.** To walk with difficulty; limp. **2.** To impede the movement or progress of. See Syns at **hamper**[1]**.** ►*n.* **1.** A hobbling walk or gait. **2.** A device used to join the legs esp. of a horse so as to hamper but not prevent its movement. [ME *hobblen*, of LGer. orig.] —**hob′bler** *n.*

hob•by (hŏb′ē) ►*n., pl.* **-bies.** An activity or interest pursued at one's leisure for enjoyment. [< ME *hobi*, small horse.] —**hob′by•ist** *n.*

hob•by•horse (hŏb′ē-hôrs′) ►*n.* **1.** A riding toy made of a long stick with an imitation horse's head on one end. **2.** See **rocking horse.** **3.** A favorite or obsessive topic.

hob•gob•lin (hŏb′gŏb′lĭn) ►*n.* **1.** An ugly, mischievous elf or goblin. **2.** An object or source of fear or dread; bugaboo.

hob•nail (hŏb′nāl′) ►*n.* A short nail with a thick head used to protect the soles of shoes or boots. [*hob*, peg + NAIL.] —**hob′nailed′** *adj.*

hob•nob (hŏb′nŏb′) ►*v.* **-nobbed, -nob•bing.** To associate familiarly: *hobnobs with the executives.* [< *(drink) hob or nob*, (toast) one another alternately.]

ho•bo (hō′bō) ►*n., pl.* **-boes** or **-bos.** A homeless person, esp. a vagrant. [?]

Ho Chi Minh (hō′ chē′ mĭn′). 1890–1969. Vietnamese leader and first president of North Vietnam (1954–69).

Ho Chi Minh City. Formerly **Saigon.** A city of S Vietnam near the South China Sea. Pop. 3,015,743.

hock[1] (hŏk) ►*n.* The joint of the hind leg of a quadruped, such as a horse, corresponding to the human ankle. [< OE *hōh*, heel.]

hock[2] (hŏk) *Slang* ►*v.* To pawn. ►*n.* **1.** The state of being in pawn. **2.** Debt: *in hock for 500 dollars.* [Prob. < Du. *hok*, prison.]

hock•ey (hŏk′ē) ►*n.* **1.** Ice hockey. **2.** Field hockey. [?]

hock•shop (hŏk′shŏp′) ►*n. Slang* A pawnshop.

ho•cus-po•cus (hō′kəs-pō′kəs) ►*n.* **1.** Nonsense words or phrases used when performing magic tricks. **2.** Deception; trickery. [Poss. alteration of Lat. *hoc est corpus (meum)*, this is (my) body (a phrase used in the Eucharist).]

hod (hŏd) ►*n.* **1.** A trough carried over the shoulder for transporting loads, as of bricks or mortar. **2.** A coal scuttle. [Perh. < OFr. *hotte*, pannier.]

hodge•podge (hŏj′pŏj′) ►*n.* A haphazard mixture; jumble. [< OFr. *hochepot*, stew.]

Hodg•kin (hŏj′kĭn), **Dorothy Mary Crow-**

foot. 1910–94. Egyptian-born British chemist; 1964 Nobel.

Hodg•kin's disease (hŏj′kĭnz) ►*n.* A malignant, progressive, sometimes fatal disease marked by enlargement of the lymph nodes, spleen, and liver. [After Thomas *Hodgkin* (1798–1866), British physician.]

hoe (hō) ►*n.* A tool with a flat blade attached to a long handle, used for weeding, cultivating, and gardening. [< OFr. *houe*, of Gmc. orig.] —**hoe** *v.* —**ho′er** *n.*

hoe•down (hō′doun′) ►*n.* A square dance.

hog (hôg, hŏg) ►*n.* **1a.** An animal of the pig family, such as the boar or wart hog. **b.** A domesticated pig, esp. one full-grown. **2.** A gluttonous person. ►*v.* **hogged, hog•ging** *Informal* To take more than one's share of. —***idiom:*** **high on the hog** In high or lavish style. [< OE *hogg.*]

ho•gan (hō′gän′, -gən) ►*n.* A usu. earth-covered Navajo dwelling, traditionally facing east. [Navajo *hooghan.*]

hogan

Ho•garth (hō′gärth′), **William.** 1697–1764. British artist. —**Ho•garth′i•an** *adj.*

hogs•head (hôgz′hĕd′, hŏgz′-) ►*n.* **1.** A large barrel or cask. **2.** A unit of capacity used in the US, equal to 63 gal. (238 l).

hog•tie also **hog-tie** (hôg′tī′, hŏg′-) ►*v.* **1.** To tie together the feet or legs of. **2.** *Informal* To impede in movement or action. See Syns at **hamper**[1].

hog•wash (hôg′wôsh′, -wŏsh′, hŏg′-) ►*n.* **1.** Worthless, false, or ridiculous language; nonsense. **2.** Garbage fed to hogs; swill.

hog-wild (hôg′wīld′, hŏg′-) ►*adj. Informal* So excited as to be devoid of good judgment. —**hog′-wild′** *adv.*

hoi pol•loi (hoi′ pə-loi′) ►*n.* The common people. [Gk., the many.]

hoist (hoist) ►*v.* To raise or haul up. ►*n.* **1.** An apparatus for lifting heavy or cumbersome objects. **2.** The act of hoisting; lift. [< dial. *hoise.*] —**hoist′er** *n.*

Ho•kan (hō′kən) ►*n.* A proposed grouping of a number of Native American language families of W North America.

Hok•kai•do (hŏ-kī′dō, hô′kī-dō′) An island of Japan N of Honshu.

hol– ►*pref.* Var. of **holo–.**

Hol•bein (hōl′bīn, hôl′-). **Hans** (1465?–1524), "the Elder," and **Hans** (1497?–1543), "the Younger." German artists.

hold[1] (hōld) ►*v.* **held** (hĕld), **hold•ing 1.** To have in one's grasp. **2.** To support; keep up. **3.** To retain the attention of. **4.** To contain. **5.** To have in one's possession. **6.** To maintain control over. **7.** To maintain occupation of by force. **8.** To maintain in a given condition or situation. **9.** To restrain; curb. **10.** To stop or delay. **11.** To keep from use: *Hold the tickets for us.* **12.** To obligate: *held me to my promise.* **13a.** To regard or consider. **b.** To assert; affirm. **14.** To cause to take place: *hold a yard sale.* **15.** To withstand pressure or stress. **16.** To continue in a direction or condition. **17.** To be valid or true. —***phrasal verbs:*** **hold forth** To talk at great length. **hold out 1.** To continue in supply; last. **2.** To continue to resist. **hold over 1.** To postpone. **2.** To keep in an earlier state. **hold up 1.** To obstruct or delay. **2.** To rob. **3.** To endure. ►*n.* **1.** The act or means of grasping. **2.** Something that may be grasped, as for support. **3.** Control or power. **4.** A prison cell. —***idioms:*** **hold the line** To maintain the current position or state. **hold water** To be valid or acceptable. **on hold** Into a state of delay. [< OE *healdan.*] —**hold′er** *n.*

hold[2] (hōld) ►*n.* The interior of a ship or airplane in which cargo is stored. [< OE *hulu*, hull.]

hold•ing (hōl′dĭng) ►*n.* **1.** Land rented or leased from another. **2.** often **holdings** Legally owned property, as land or stocks.

holding company ►*n.* A company with partial or complete control over other companies.

hold•out (hōld′out′) ►*n.* One that withholds agreement or consent.

hold•o•ver (hōld′ō′vər) ►*n.* One that remains from an earlier time.

hold•up (hōld′ŭp′) ►*n.* **1.** An interruption; delay. **2.** An armed robbery.

hole (hōl) ►*n.* **1.** A cavity in a solid. **2.** An opening or perforation; gap. **3.** An animal's burrow. **4.** An ugly, squalid, or depressing place. **5.** A bad situation; predicament. **6.** *Sports* **a.** The small pit lined with a cup into which a golf ball must be hit. **b.** One of the divisions of a golf course, from tee to cup. [< OE *hol.*]

Hol•guín (ōl-gēn′) A city of E Cuba NNW of Santiago de Cuba. Pop. 239,000.

hol•i•day (hŏl′ĭ-dā′) ►*n.* **1.** A day free from work, esp. one on which custom or the law dictates a halt to ordinary business to commemorate or celebrate a particular event. **2.** A holy day. **3.** *Chiefly Brit.* A vacation. [< OE *hālig dæg*, holy day.]

Holiday, Eleanora. "Billie." 1915–59. Amer. singer.

ho•li•ness (hō′lē-nĭs) ►*n.* **1.** The quality of being holy; sanctity. **2. Holiness** *Rom. Cath. Ch.* Used with *His* or *Your* as a title for the pope.

ho•lism (hō′lĭz′əm) ►*n.* A theory or belief emphasizing the importance of the whole and the interdependence of its parts. —**ho′list** *n.* —**ho•lis′tic** *adj.* —**ho•lis′ti•cal•ly** *adv.*

holistic medicine ►*n.* Medical care emphasizing treatment of a person's complete physical and mental state.

Hol•land (hŏl′ənd) See **Netherlands.**

hol•lan•daise sauce (hŏl′ən-dāz′) ►*n.* A sauce of butter, egg yolks, and lemon juice or vinegar. [< Fr. *Hollandais*, Dutch.]

hol•ler (hŏl′ər) ►*v.* To yell. See Syns at **shout.** [< obsolete *hollo*, stop!] —**hol′ler** *n.*

hol•low (hŏl′ō) ►*adj.* **-er, -est 1.** Having a cavity or space within. **2a.** Deeply concave. **b.** Sunken; indented: *hollow cheeks.* **3.** Without substance or character. See Syns at **vain.** **4.** Devoid of truth; specious. **5.** Having a deep reverberating sound. ►*n.* **1.** A cavity or interior space. **2.** An indented or concave surface or area. **3.** A void. **4.** also **hol•ler** (hŏl′ər) *Regional* A mountain valley. ►*v.* To make hollow. [< OE *holh*, hole.] —**hol′low•ly** *adv.* —**hol′low•ness** *n.*

hol•ly (hŏl′ē) ►*n., pl.* **-lies.** A tree or shrub usu. having bright red berries and glossy evergreen leaves with spiny margins. [< OE *holen.*]

hol•ly•hock (hŏl′ē-hŏk′) ►*n.* A tall garden plant with showy, variously colored flowers. [ME *holihocke*, marsh mallow.]

Hol•ly•wood (hŏl′ē-wŏŏd′) **1.** A district of Los Angeles, CA; a film and entertainment center. **2.** A city of SE FL on the Atlantic Coast N of Miami Beach. Pop. 121,697.

Holmes (hōmz, hōlmz), **Oliver Wendell.** 1809–94. Amer. physician and writer.

Holmes, Oliver Wendell, Jr. 1841–1935. Amer. jurist; associate justice of the US Supreme Court (1902–32).

hol•mi•um (hōl′mē-əm) ►*n. Symbol* **Ho** A relatively soft, malleable, rare-earth element. At. no. 67. See table at **element.** [After *Holmia* (Stockholm), Sweden.]

holo– or **hol–** ►*pref.* Whole; entire; entirely: *holograph.* [< Gk. *holos.*]

hol•o•caust (hŏl′ə-kôst′, hō′lə-) ►*n.* **1.** Great or total destruction, esp. by fire. **2. Holocaust** The genocide of European Jews and others by the Nazis during World War II. [< Gk. *holokaustos*, burnt whole.]

Hol•o•cene (hŏl′ə-sēn′, hō′lə-) *Geol.* ►*adj.* Of or being the more recent epoch of the Quaternary Period, extending to the present. ►*n.* The Holocene Epoch.

hol•o•gram (hŏl′ə-grăm′, hō′lə-) ►*n.* The pattern produced on a photosensitive medium that has been exposed by holography and then photographically developed.

hol•o•graph (hŏl′ə-grăf′, hō′lə-) ►*n.* **1.** A document written wholly in the handwriting of its signer. **2.** See **hologram.** —**hol′o•graph′ic, hol′o•graph′i•cal** *adj.* —**hol′o•graph′i•cal•ly** *adv.*

ho•log•raph•y (hō-lŏg′rə-fē) ►*n.* A method of producing a three-dimensional image of an object by recording the pattern of interference formed by a split laser beam and then illuminating the pattern.

Hol•stein[1] (hōl′stīn′, -stēn′) A region and former duchy of N Germany at the base of the Jutland Peninsula.

Hol•stein[2] (hōl′stīn′, -stēn′) ►*n.* Any of a breed of large black and white dairy cattle.

hol•ster (hōl′stər) ►*n.* **1.** A leather case shaped to hold a pistol. **2.** A belt designed to carry small tools. [Du.] —**hol′stered** *adj.*

ho•ly (hō′lē) ►*adj.* **-li•er, -li•est 1.** Of or associated with a divine power; sacred. **2.** Worthy of veneration or awe; revered. **3.** Spiritually pure; saintly. [< OE *hālig.*] —**ho′li•ly** *adv.* —**ho′li•ness** *n.*

Holy Ark ►*n. Judaism* The cabinet in a synagogue in which the Torah scrolls are kept.

Holy Communion ►*n.* The Eucharist.

holy day ►*n.* A day for religious observance.

Holy Ghost ►*n.* The Holy Spirit.

Holy Land. The biblical region of Palestine.

Holy Roman Empire. A loosely federated political entity of central and W Europe (962–1806).

Holy Spirit ►*n.* The third person of the Christian Trinity.

holy war ►*n.* A war declared for a religious or high moral purpose.

hom•age (hŏm′ĭj, ŏm′-) ►*n.* Special honor or respect shown or expressed publicly. [< OFr., prob. < Lat. *homō*, person.]

hom•bre (ŏm′brā′, -brē) ►*n. Slang* A man; fellow. [Sp. < Lat. *homō.*]

Hom•burg also **hom•burg** (hŏm′bûrg′) ►*n.* A man's felt hat having a high dented crown and a stiff, slightly rolled brim. [*Homburg*, Germany.]

home (hōm) ►*n.* **1.** A place where one lives; residence. **2.** A structure or unit for domestic living. **3.** A household. **4.** A place of origin. **5.** The native habitat, as of a plant or animal. **6a.** *Baseball* Home plate. **b.** *Games* Home base. **7.** An institution where people are cared for. ►*adv.* **1.** At or to the direction of home. **2.** On target: *The arrow struck home.* **3.** To the very center: *Your comment struck home.* ►*v.* **homed, hom•ing 1.** To go or return home. **2.** To be guided to a target automatically, as by radio waves. **3.** To move toward a goal: *home in on the truth.* —***idiom:* at home** Comfortable and relaxed. [< OE *hām.*]

home base ►*n.* **1a.** *Games* An objective toward which players progress. **b.** *Baseball* Home plate. **2.** A base of operations.

home•bod•y (hōm′bŏd′ē) ►*n., pl.* **-ies.** One whose interests center on the home.

home•boy (hōm′boi′) ►*n. Slang* **1.** A male friend from one's neighborhood or hometown. **2.** A fellow male gang member.

home•com•ing (hōm′kŭm′ĭng) ►*n.* **1.** A return home. **2.** An annual event at schools and colleges for visiting graduates.

home economics ►*n. (takes sing. or pl. v.)* The science and art of home management. —**home economist** *n.*

home front ►*n.* The civilian population or the civilian activities of a country at war.

home•girl (hōm′gûrl′) ►*n. Slang* **1.** A female friend from one's neighborhood or hometown. **2.** A fellow female gang member.

home•land (hōm′lănd′) ►*n.* **1.** One's native land. **2.** A state or region closely identified with a particular people.

home•less (hōm′lĭs) ►*adj.* Having no home or haven. ►*n. (takes pl. v.)* People without homes considered as a group.

home•ly (hōm′lē) ►*adj.* **-li•er, -li•est 1.** Not attractive or good-looking. **2.** Simple or unpretentious; plain: *homely truths.* **3.** Characteristic of the home. —**home′li•ness** *n.*

home•made (hōm′mād′) ►*adj.* **1.** Made or prepared in the home. **2.** Crudely or simply made.

home•mak•er (hōm′mā′kər) ►*n.* One who manages a household. —**home′mak′ing** *n.*

homeo– ►*pref.* Similar; constant: *homeostasis.* [< Gk. *homoios.*]

ho•me•op•a•thy (hō′mē-ŏp′ə-thē) ►*n., pl.* **-thies.** A system for treating disease based on the administration of minute doses of a drug that in massive amounts produces symptoms similar to those of the disease itself. —**ho′me•o•path′** (-ə-păth′), **ho′me•op′a•thist** *n.* —**ho′me•o•path′ic** *adj.*

ho•me•o•sta•sis (hō′mē-ō-stā′sĭs) ►*n.* The ability of an organism or cell to maintain internal equilibrium by adjusting its physiological processes. —**ho′me•o•stat′ic** (-stăt′ĭk) *adj.*

ho•me•o•therm (hō′mē-ə-thûrm′) ►*n.* An organism, such as a mammal or bird, having a constant body temperature independent of the temperature of its surroundings.

home•page or **home page** (hōm′pāj′) ►*n.* The main page of a website, usu. providing information about the site.

home plate ►*n.* *Baseball* The base at which a batter stands when hitting and which a runner must cross safely in order to score.

hom•er (hō′mər) ►*n.* *Baseball* A home run. ►*v.* To hit a home run.

Homer. fl. 850 B.C. Greek epic poet.

Homer, Winslow. 1836–1910. Amer. painter.

home rule ►*n.* Self-government in the internal affairs of a dependent country or region.

home run ►*n.* *Baseball* A hit that allows the batter to make a complete circuit of the diamond and score a run.

home•school (hōm′sko͞ol′) ►*v.* To educate at home rather than in an established school. —**home′school′er** *n.*

home•sick (hōm′sĭk′) ►*adj.* Longing for one's home. —**home′sick′ness** *n.*

home•spun (hōm′spŭn′) ►*adj.* **1.** Spun or woven in the home. **2.** Made of a homespun fabric. **3.** Simple; unpretentious. ►*n.* A plain, coarse cloth made of homespun yarn.

home•stead (hōm′stĕd′) ►*n.* A house, esp. a farmhouse, with adjoining buildings and land. ►*v.* To settle and farm land. —**home′stead′er** *n.*

home•stretch (hōm′strĕch′) ►*n.* **1.** The part of a racetrack from the last turn to the finish line. **2.** The final stage of a task.

home•ward (hōm′wərd) ►*adv.* & *adj.* Toward home. —**home′wards** (-wərdz) *adv.*

home•work (hōm′wûrk′) ►*n.* **1.** Work, such as schoolwork, done at home. **2.** Preparatory or preliminary work.

hom•ey also **hom•y** (hō′mē) ►*adj.* **-i•er, -i•est** *Informal* Having a feeling of home; comfortable. —**hom′ey•ness** *n.*

hom•i•cide (hŏm′ĭ-sīd′, hō′mĭ-) ►*n.* **1.** The killing of one person by another. **2.** A person who kills another. [< Lat. *homō*, person + -CIDE.] —**hom′i•cid′al** *adj.*

hom•i•let•ic (hŏm′ə-lĕt′ĭk) ►*adj.* **1.** Of or like a homily. **2.** Relating to preaching. [< Gk. *homilētos*, conversation.] —**hom′i•let′i•cal•ly** *adv.* —**hom′i•let′ics** *n.*

hom•i•ly (hŏm′ə-lē) ►*n.*, *pl.* **-lies 1.** A sermon. **2.** A tedious moralizing lecture. [< Gk. *homilia*, discourse < *homilos*, crowd.] —**hom′i•list** *n.*

hom•ing pigeon (hō′mĭng) ►*n.* A pigeon trained to return to its home roost.

hom•i•nid (hŏm′ə-nĭd) ►*n.* A primate of the family Hominidae, of which *Homo sapiens* is the only extant species. [< Lat. *homō, homin-*, person.] —**hom′i•nid** *adj.*

hom•i•ny (hŏm′ə-nē) ►*n.* Hulled and dried kernels of corn, prepared as food by boiling. See Regional Note at **pone.** [Of Algonquian orig.]

homo– or **hom–** ►*pref.* Same; like: *homophone; homograph.* [< Gk. *homos*.]

ho•mo•ge•ne•ous (hō′mə-jē′nē-əs, -jēn′yəs) ►*adj.* **1.** Of the same or similar nature or kind. **2.** Uniform in composition throughout. [< Gk. *homogenēs*.] —**ho′mo•ge•ne′i•ty** (-jə-nē′ĭ-tē, -nā′-) *n.* —**ho′mo•ge′ne•ous•ly** *adv.* —**ho′mo•ge′ne•ous•ness** *n.*

ho•mog•e•nize (hə-mŏj′ə-nīz′, hō-) ►*v.* **-nized, -niz•ing 1.** To make homogeneous. **2a.** To reduce to particles and disperse throughout a fluid. **b.** To make uniform in consistency, esp. to render (milk) uniform in consistency by emulsifying the fat content. [< HOMOGENEOUS.] —**ho•mog′e•ni•za′tion** *n.* —**ho•mog′e•niz′er** *n.*

ho•mog•e•ny (hə-mŏj′ə-nē, hō-) ►*n.* Similarity of structure between organs related by common descent. [Gk. *homogenia*, community of origin.] —**ho•mog′e•nous** *adj.*

hom•o•graph (hŏm′ə-grăf′, hō′mə-) ►*n.* One of two or more words that have the same spelling but differ in origin and meaning, as *light,* "not dark," and *light,* "not heavy." —**hom′o•graph′ic** *adj.*

ho•mol•o•gous (hə-mŏl′ə-gəs, hō-) ►*adj.* **1.** Corresponding or similar esp. in structure or function. **2.** *Biol.* Similar in structure and evolutionary origin but not necessarily in function. [< Gk. *homologos*, agreeing.] —**hom′o•logue′, hom′o•log′** (hŏm′ə-lôg′, -lŏg′, hō′mē-ə-) *n.* —**ho•mol′o•gy** (-ə-jē) *n.*

hom•o•nym (hŏm′ə-nĭm′, hō′mə-) ►*n.* One of two or more words that have the same sound and often the same spelling but differ in meaning, as *bear,* "carry"; *bear,* (the animal); and *bare,* "naked." [< Gk. *homōnumon*.] —**hom′o•nym′ic, ho•mon′y•mous** (hō-mŏn′ə-məs, hə-) *adj.*

ho•mo•pho•bi•a (hō′mə-fō′bē-ə) ►*n.* Fear of or contempt for lesbians and gay men. —**ho′mo•phobe′** *n.* —**ho′mo•pho′bic** *adj.*

hom•o•phone (hŏm′ə-fōn′, hō′mə-) ►*n.* One of two or more words, such as *night* and *knight,* that are pronounced the same but differ in meaning, origin, and sometimes spelling. —**ho•moph′o•nous** (hō-mŏf′ə-nəs) *adj.*

Ho•mo sa•pi•ens (hō′mō sā′pē-ənz, -ĕnz′) ►*n.* The modern species of humans. [NLat. *Homō sapiēns*, wise man.]

ho•mo•sex•u•al (hō′mə-sĕk′sho͞o-əl, -mō-) ►*adj.* Of or having a sexual orientation to persons of the same sex. ►*n.* A homosexual person; a gay man or lesbian. See Usage Note at **gay.** —**ho′mo•sex′u•al′i•ty** *n.*

Homs (hômz, hôms) A city of W-central Syria N of Damascus. Pop. 558,000.

hom•y (hō′mē) ►*adj.* Var. of **homey.**

Ho•myel′ (hō′myĕl) or **Go•mel** (gō′məl). A city of E Belarus SE of Minsk. Pop. 503,000.

Hon. ►*abbr.* **1.** honorable (title) **2. hon.** honorary

hon•cho (hŏn′chō) ►*n.*, *pl.* **-chos** *Slang* One who is in charge; leader. [J., squad leader.]

Hon•du•ras (hŏn-do͝or′əs, -dyo͝or′-) A country of N Central America. Cap. Tegucigalpa. Pop. 5,770,000. —**Hon•du′ran** *adj.* & *n.*

hone (hōn) ►*n.* A fine-grained whetstone for sharpening a tool. ►*v.* **honed, hon•ing.** To sharpen on or as if on a hone. [< OE *hān*.]

hon•est (ŏn′ĭst) ►*adj.* **1.** Marked by or displaying integrity; upright. **2.** Not deceptive or fraudulent; genuine. **3a.** True; not false: *honest reporting.* **b.** Sincere; frank: *an honest critique.*

4. Without affectation; plain: *honest folk.* [< Lat. *honestus* < *honōs*, honor.] —**hon′est•ly** *adv.* —**hon′es•ty** *n.*

hon•ey (hŭn′ē) ►*n., pl.* **-eys 1.** A sweet, thick fluid produced by bees from the nectar of flowers. **2.** Sweetness. **3.** Flattery. **4.** *Informal* Sweetheart. [< OE *hunig.*]

hon•ey•bee (hŭn′ē-bē′) ►*n.* Any of several social bees that produce honey.

hon•ey•comb (hŭn′ē-kōm′) ►*n.* **1.** A structure of hexagonal, thin-walled cells constructed from beeswax by honeybees to hold honey and larvae. **2.** Something resembling this structure. ►*v.* To fill with or as if with holes; riddle.

hon•ey•dew melon (hŭn′ē-do͞o′, -dyo͞o′) ►*n.* A melon having a smooth whitish rind and green flesh.

hon•eyed also **hon•ied** (hŭn′ēd) ►*adj.* Sweet; sugary: *honeyed words.*

hon•ey•moon (hŭn′ē-mo͞on′) ►*n.* **1.** A trip taken by a newly married couple. **2.** An early harmonious period in a relationship. —**hon′ey•moon′** *v.* —**hon′ey•moon′er** *n.*

hon•ey•suck•le (hŭn′ē-sŭk′əl) ►*n.* A shrub or vine having fragrant, usu. paired tubular flowers. [< OE *hunīsūce.*]

Hong Kong (hŏng′kŏng′, hông′kông′) An administrative region of SE China, on the coast SE of Guangzhou, including **Hong Kong Island** and adjacent areas. Cap. Victoria. Pop. 6,061,000.

Ho•ni•a•ra (hō′nē-är′ə) The capital of the Solomon Is., on the NW coast of Guadalcanal. Pop. 35,288.

honk (hôngk, hŏngk) ►*n.* **1.** The raucous, resonant sound of a goose. **2.** A similar sound, esp. the blaring sound of an automobile horn. [Imit.] —**honk** *v.* —**honk′er** *n.*

hon•ky-tonk (hông′kē-tôngk′, hŏng′kē-tŏngk′) ►*n. Slang* **1.** A cheap, noisy bar or dance hall. **2.** A type of ragtime music typically played on a tinny piano. [?] —**hon′ky-tonk′** *adj. & v.*

Hon•o•lu•lu (hŏn′ə-lo͞o′lo͞o) The capital of HI, on the SE coast of Oahu. Pop. 365,272.

hon•or (ŏn′ər) ►*n.* **1.** High respect; esteem. **2a.** Recognition; distinction. **b.** A token or gesture of respect or distinction: *the place of honor.* **3.** Great privilege. **4. Honor** Used with *His, Her,* or *Your* as a form of address for certain officials, such as judges and mayors. **5. honors a.** Special recognition for unusual academic achievement. **b.** A program of individual advanced study for exceptional students. ►*v.* **1a.** To esteem. **b.** To show respect for. **2.** To confer distinction on. **3.** To accept or pay as valid: *honor a check.* [< Lat.] —**hon′or•ee′** *n.*

hon•or•a•ble (ŏn′ər-ə-bəl) ►*adj.* **1.** Deserving or winning honor and respect. **2.** Bringing distinction or recognition. **3.** Possessing integrity. **4.** Illustrious. **5. Honorable** Used as a title of respect for certain high government officials. —**hon′or•a•bly** *adv.*

honorable discharge ►*n.* Discharge from the armed forces with a commendable record.

hon•o•rar•i•um (ŏn′ə-râr′ē-əm) ►*n., pl.* **-i•ums** or **-i•a** (-ē-ə). A payment given to a professional person for services for which fees are not legally or traditionally required. [Lat. *honōrārium.*]

hon•or•ar•y (ŏn′ə-rĕr′ē) ►*adj.* Held or given as a mark of honor, without fulfillment of the usual requirements: *an honorary degree.*

hon•or•if•ic (ŏn′ə-rĭf′ĭk) ►*adj.* Conferring or showing respect or honor. ►*n.* A title or grammatical form conveying respect. —**hon′or•if′i•cal•ly** *adv.*

hon•our (ŏn′ər) ►*n. & v. Chiefly Brit.* Var. of **honor.**

Hon•shu (hŏn′sho͞o) The largest island of Japan, in the central part between the Sea of Japan and the Pacific.

hood[1] (ho͝od) ►*n.* **1.** A loose pliable covering for the head and neck. **2.** Something resembling a hood. **3.** The hinged metal lid over the engine of a motor vehicle. ►*v.* To supply or cover with a hood. [< OE *hōd.*] —**hood′ed** *adj.*

hood[2] (ho͝od) ►*n. Slang* A hoodlum.

Hood, Mount. A volcanic peak, 3,426.7 m (11,235 ft), in the Cascade Range of NW OR.

-hood ►*suff.* **1a.** Condition; state; quality: *manhood.* **b.** An instance of a specified state or quality: *falsehood.* **2.** A group sharing a specified state or quality: *sisterhood.* [< OE *-hād.*]

hood•lum (ho͝od′ləm, ho͞od′-) ►*n.* **1.** A gangster; thug. **2.** A tough, often aggressive young man. [?] —**hood′lum•ism** *n.*

hoo•doo (ho͞o′do͞o) ►*n., pl.* **-doos 1.** Magic healing and control, esp. in African-based folk medicine. **2.** Voodoo. **3a.** Bad luck. **b.** One that brings bad luck. [Of West African orig.] —**hoo′doo** *v.*

hood•wink (ho͝od′wĭngk′) ►*v.* To deceive; cheat. —**hood′wink′er** *n.*

hoo•ey (ho͞o′ē) ►*n. Slang* Nonsense. [?]

hoof (ho͝of, ho͞of) ►*n., pl.* **hooves** (ho͝ovz, ho͞ovz) or **hoofs 1.** The horny sheath covering the foot of some mammals. **2.** A hoofed foot, esp. of a horse. ►*v. Slang* **1.** To walk. **2.** To dance. [< OE *hōf.*] —**hoofed** *adj.*

Hoogh•ly (ho͞o′glē) See **Hugli.**

hook (ho͝ok) ►*n.* **1.** A curved or sharply bent device, usu. of metal, used to catch, drag, suspend, or fasten something. **2.** Something shaped like a hook. **3.** *Slang* A means of attracting interest; enticement. **4.** *Sports* **a.** A short swinging blow in boxing delivered with a crooked arm. **b.** A thrown or struck ball that curves. ►*v.* **1.** To catch, suspend, fasten, or connect with or as if with a hook. **2.** *Slang* To steal; snatch. **3.** *Slang* To cause to become addicted. —***phrasal verb:* hook up 1.** To assemble or wire (a mechanism). **2.** *Slang* To connect. —***idioms:* by hook or (by) crook** By whatever means possible. **off the hook** Freed, as from blame or obligation. [< OE *hōc.*] —**hooked** *adj.*

hook•ah (ho͝ok′ə) ►*n.* A pipe in which the smoke is cooled by passing through a long tube submerged in an urn of water. [< Ar. *ḥuqqa*, the hookah's water urn.]

hook and eye ►*n.* A fastener consisting of a small hook that is inserted in a loop.

hook•er (ho͝ok′ər) ►*n. Slang* A prostitute.

Hooker, Thomas. 1586?–1647. English-born Amer. colonizer.

hook•up (ho͝ok′ŭp′) ►*n. Elect.* **1.** A system of circuits and equipment designed to operate together. **2.** A configuration of parts or devices providing a link between a supply source and a user.

hook•worm (ho͝ok′wûrm′) ►*n.* A parasitic nematode worm having hooked mouthparts that fasten to the intestinal walls of a host.

hook•y (ho͝ok′ē) ►*n. Informal* Truancy: *play hooky.* [Perh. < *hook it*, to make off.]

hoo•li•gan (ho͞o′lĭ-gən) ►*n. Informal* A rowdy or aggressive person; ruffian. [?] —**hoo′li•gan•ism** *n.*

hoop (ho͞op, ho͝op) ►*n.* **1.** A circular band put around a cask or barrel to bind the staves together. **2.** Something resembling a hoop. **3.** A circular support for a hoop skirt. **4.** A circular earring. **5.** *Basketball* The basket. [ME *hop.*] —**hoop** *v.*

hoop•la (ho͞op′lä′, ho͝op′-) ►*n. Slang* **1.** Great commotion or fuss. **2.** Extravagant publicity. [< Fr. *houp-là*, an interjection.]

hoop skirt ►*n.* A long full skirt belled out with a series of connected hoops.

hoo•ray (ho͞o-rā′, hə-) ►*interj., n., & v.* Var. of **hurrah.**

hoose•gow (ho͞os′gou′) ►*n. Slang* A jail. [Sp. *juzgado*, courtroom < *juzgar*, JUDGE.]

hoot (ho͞ot) ►*v.* **1.** To utter the characteristic cry of an owl. **2.** To make a loud, derisive cry. **3.** To drive off with jeering cries. [ME *houten.*] —**hoot** *n.* —**hoot′er** *n.*

hoot•en•an•ny (ho͞ot′n-ăn′ē) ►*n., pl.* **-nies.** An informal performance by folk singers. [?]

Hoo•ver (ho͞o′vər), **Herbert Clark.** 1874–1964. The 31st US President (1929–33).

Herbert Hoover

Hoover, J(ohn) Edgar. 1895–1972. Amer. director of the FBI (1924–72).

hooves (ho͝ovz, ho͞ovz) ►*n.* Pl. of **hoof.**

hop[1] (hŏp) ►*v.* **hopped, hop•ping 1.** To move with light bounding skips or leaps. **2.** To jump on one foot. **3.** To make a quick trip, esp. in an airplane. **4.** To jump aboard. ►*n.* **1.** A light springy jump or leap. **2a.** A short distance. **b.** A short trip, esp. by air. **3.** *Informal* A dance or dance party. —***idiom:* hop to it** To begin a task energetically. [< OE *hoppian.*]

hop[2] (hŏp) ►*n.* **1.** A twining vine having lobed leaves and spikes of green flowers. **2. hops** The dried flowers of this plant, used as a flavoring in brewing beer. ►*v.* **hopped, hop•ping.** To flavor with hops. —***phrasal verb:* hop up** *Slang* **1.** To increase the power of. **2.** To stimulate with or as if with a narcotic. [< MDu. *hoppe.*]

hope (hōp) ►*v.* **hoped, hop•ing.** To wish for something with expectation. ►*n.* **1.** A desire accompanied by confident expectation. **2.** Something hoped for. **3.** One that is a source of or reason for hope. [< OE *hopian.*] —**hope′ful** *adj.* —**hope′ful•ness** *n.*

hope•ful•ly (hōp′fə-lē) ►*adv.* **1.** In a hopeful manner. **2.** *Informal* It is to be hoped.

Usage: Writers who use *hopefully* as a sentence adverb, as in *Hopefully the measures will be adopted,* should be aware that the usage is unacceptable to a large majority of the Usage Panel.

hope•less (hōp′lĭs) ►*adj.* **1.** Having no hope. **2.** Dismal; bleak. —**hope′less•ly** *adv.*

Ho•pi (hō′pē) ►*n., pl.* **-pi** or **-pis 1.** A member of a Pueblo people of NE Arizona. **2.** The Uto-Aztecan language of the Hopi.

Hop•kins (hŏp′kĭnz), **Gerard Manley.** 1844–89. British poet.

hop•per (hŏp′ər) ►*n.* **1.** One that hops. **2.** A funnel-shaped container in which materials are held ready for dispensing.

hop•scotch (hŏp′skŏch′) ►*n.* A children's game in which players hop or jump through a pattern of numbered spaces to retrieve a thrown object.

ho•ra also **ho•rah** (hôr′ə, hōr′ə) ►*n.* A traditional dance of Romania and Israel usu. performed in a circle. [Mod.Heb. *hōrâ.*]

Hor•ace (hôr′əs, hŏr′-). 65–8 B.C. Roman lyric poet. —**Ho•ra′tian** (hə-rā′shən) *adj.*

horde (hôrd, hōrd) ►*n.* A throng or swarm. See Syns at **crowd.** [Ult. < O. Turkic *ordï*, residence.]

hore•hound (hôr′hound′, hōr′-) ►*n.* An aromatic plant having downy leaves that yield a bitter extract used in flavoring and as a cough remedy. [< OE *hārehūne.*]

ho•ri•zon (hə-rī′zən) ►*n.* **1.** The apparent intersection of the earth and sky as seen by an observer. **2.** The range of one's knowledge, experience, or interest. [< Gk. *horizein*, to limit.]

hor•i•zon•tal (hôr′ĭ-zŏn′tl, hŏr′-) ►*adj.* **1.** Of or near the horizon. **2.** At right angles to a vertical line. ►*n.* Something horizontal. [< Lat. *horizōn, horizont-*, HORIZON.] —**hor′i•zon′tal•ly** *adv.*

horizontal bar ►*n.* A gymnastic apparatus consisting of a single bar mounted approx. eight ft. above the ground and used for swinging maneuvers.

Hor•liv•ka (hôr′ləf-kə) or **Gor•lov•ka** (gôr′ləf-). A city of SE Ukraine in the Donets Basin N of Donetsk. Pop. 336,100.

hor•mone (hôr′mōn′) ►*n.* **1.** A substance produced by one tissue and conveyed by the bloodstream to another tissue to effect physiological activity, such as growth or metabolism. **2.** A compound that acts like a hormone in the body. [< Gk. *horman*, urge on.] —**hor•mon′al** (-mō′nəl) *adj.* —**hor•mon′al•ly** *adv.*

Hor•muz (hôr′mŭz′, hôr-mo͞oz′), **Strait of.** Also **Strait of Ormuz.** A waterway linking the Persian Gulf with the Gulf of Oman.

horn (hôrn) ►*n.* **1a.** One of the hard, usu. permanent structures projecting from the head of certain mammals, such as cattle or sheep. **b.** The hard, smooth material forming the outer covering of a horn. **2.** A growth or protuberance similar to a horn. **3.** A container made from a horn: *a powder horn.* **4.** *Mus.* **a.** A brass wind instrument, esp. a French horn. **b.** A trumpet. **c.** A saxophone. **5.** A signaling device that produces a loud, resonant sound: *an automobile horn.* [< OE.] —**horned** *adj.* —**horn′less** *adj.* —**horn′y** *adj.*

Horn, Cape. A headland of extreme S Chile in the Tierra del Fuego archipelago.

horn
left: white rhinoceros
right: American bighorn ram

Horne (hôrn), **Lena.** b. 1917. Amer. actress and singer.

Lena Horne

horned toad ▸*n.* A lizard having hornlike projections on the head and a spiny body.

hor•net (hôr′nĭt) ▸*n.* Any of various stinging wasps that typically build large papery nests. [< OE *hyrnet.*]

horn of plenty ▸*n., pl.* **horns of plenty.** See **cornucopia** 1.

horn•pipe (hôrn′pīp′) ▸*n.* A spirited British folk dance.

ho•rol•o•gy (hô-rŏl′ə-jē) ▸*n.* **1.** The science of measuring time. **2.** The art of making timepieces. [Gk. *hōra,* hour + -LOGY.] —**ho•rol′o•gist** *n.*

hor•o•scope (hôr′ə-skōp′, hŏr′-) ▸*n.* A diagram of the positions of the planets and stars at a given moment, such as the moment of a person's birth, used by astrologers. [< Gk. *hōroskopos* : *hōra,* hour + *skopos,* observer.]

Ho•ro•witz (hôr′ə-wĭts, hŏr′-), **Vladimir.** 1904–89. Russian-born Amer. pianist.

hor•ren•dous (hô-rĕn′dəs, hə-) ▸*adj.* Hideous. [< Lat. *horrendus,* gerundive of *horrēre,* tremble.] —**hor•ren′dous•ly** *adv.*

hor•ri•ble (hôr′ə-bəl, hŏr′-) ▸*adj.* **1.** Arousing horror; dreadful. **2.** Very unpleasant. [< Lat. *horribilis* < *horrēre,* tremble.] —**hor′ri•ble•ness** *n.* —**hor′ri•bly** *adv.*

hor•rid (hôr′ĭd, hŏr′-) ▸*adj.* **1.** Causing horror; dreadful. **2.** Extremely disagreeable; offensive. [< ME *horred,* bristling < Lat. *horrēre,* tremble.] —**hor′rid•ly** *adv.* —**hor′rid•ness** *n.*

hor•rif•ic (hô-rĭf′ĭk, hŏ-) ▸*adj.* Terrifying. [Lat. *horrificus* < *horrēre,* tremble.] —**hor•rif′i•cal•ly** *adv.*

hor•ri•fy (hôr′ə-fī′, hŏr′-) ▸*v.* **-fied, -fy•ing 1.** To cause to feel horror. **2.** To cause unpleasant surprise to; shock. [Lat. *horrificāre.*] —**hor′ri•fi•ca′tion** *n.* —**hor′ri•fy′ing•ly** *adv.*

hor•ror (hôr′ər, hŏr′-) ▸*n.* **1.** An intense feeling of repugnance and fear. **2.** Intense dislike; abhorrence. **3.** A cause of horror. [< Lat. *horror.*]

hors de com•bat (ôr′ də kôɴ-bä′) ▸*adv. & adj.* Out of action; disabled. [Fr.]

hors d'oeuvre (ôr dûrv′) ▸*n., pl.* **hors d'oeuvres** (ôr dûrvz′) or **hors d'oeuvre.** An appetizer served before a meal. [Fr.]

horse (hôrs) ▸*n.* **1.** A large hoofed mammal having a long mane and tail, domesticated for riding and for drawing or carrying loads. **2.** A supporting frame, usu. with four legs. **3.** *Sports* A vaulting horse. **4.** often **horses** Horsepower. ▸*v.* **horsed, hors•ing.** To provide with a horse. —***phrasal verb:*** **horse around** *Informal* To indulge in horseplay or frivolous activity. —***idioms:*** **hold (one's) horses** To check or restrain oneself. **the horse's mouth** The original source. [< OE *hors.*]

horse•back (hôrs′băk′) ▸*adv. & adj.* On the back of a horse.

horse chestnut ▸*n.* **1.** A tree having erect clusters of white flowers and shiny brown seeds. **2.** The seed of this tree.

horse•flesh (hôrs′flĕsh′) ▸*n.* **1.** The flesh of a horse. **2.** Horses collectively.

horse•fly (hôrs′flī′) ▸*n.* Any of numerous large flies, the females of which suck the blood of various mammals.

horse•hair (hôrs′hâr′) ▸*n.* **1.** The hair of a horse, esp. from the mane or tail. **2.** Cloth made of horsehair.

horse•hide (hôrs′hīd′) ▸*n.* **1.** The hide of a horse. **2.** Leather made from this hide.

horse•man (hôrs′mən) ▸*n.* A man who rides a horse or breeds and raises horses.

horse•man•ship (hôrs′mən-shĭp′) ▸*n.* The skill of riding horses.

horse•play (hôrs′plā′) ▸*n.* Rowdy play.

horse•pow•er (hôrs′pou′ər) ▸*n.* A unit of power equal to 745.7 watts or 33,000 foot-pounds per minute.

horse•rad•ish (hôrs′răd′ĭsh) ▸*n.* **1.** A coarse plant having a thick, whitish, pungent root. **2.** A condiment made of its grated roots.

horse sense ▸*n.* *Informal* Common sense.

horse•shoe (hôrs′sho͞o′, hôrsh′-) ▸*n.* **1.** A flat U-shaped metal plate fitted and nailed to a horse's hoof. **2. horseshoes** *(takes sing. v.)* A game in which players toss horseshoes at a stake to encircle it.

horseshoe crab ▸*n.* A marine arthropod having a rounded body and a stiff pointed tail.

horse•tail (hôrs′tāl′) ▸*n.* A nonflowering plant having a jointed hollow stem and narrow leaves.

horse•whip (hôrs′hwĭp′, -wĭp′) ▸*n.* A whip used to control a horse. —**horse′whip′** *v.*

horse•wom•an (hôrs′wo͝om′ən) ▸*n.* A woman who rides a horse or breeds and raises horses.

hors•y also **hors•ey** (hôr′sē) ▸*adj.* **-i•er, -i•est 1.** Of or resembling a horse. **2.** Devoted to horses or riding. **3.** Large and clumsy. —**hors′i•ly** *adv.* —**hors′i•ness** *n.*

hor•ta•to•ry (hôr′tə-tôr′ē, -tōr′ē) ▸*adj.* Marked by exhortation. [< Lat. *hortārī,* exhort.]

hor•ti•cul•ture (hôr′tĭ-kŭl′chər) ►*n.* The science or art of cultivating fruits, vegetables, flowers, or ornamental plants. [Lat. *hortus*, garden + (AGRI)CULTURE.] —**hor′ti•cul′tur•al** *adj.* —**hor′ti•cul′tur•al•ly** *adv.* —**hor′ti•cul′tur•ist** *n.*

ho•san•na also **ho•san•nah** (hō-zăn′ə) ►*interj.* Used to express praise or adoration to God. [< Heb. *hôšaʻnā'*, deliver us.]

hose (hōz) ►*n.* **1.** *pl.* **hose** Stockings; socks. **2.** *pl.* **hos•es** A flexible tube for conveying liquids or gases. ►*v.* **hosed, hos•ing.** To water or wash with a hose. [< OE *hosa.*]

Ho•se•a (hō-zē′ə, -zā′ə) ►*n.* **1.** 8th cent. B.C. Hebrew prophet. **2.** See table at **Bible.**

ho•sier•y (hō′zhə-rē) ►*n.* Socks and stockings. [< ME HOSE.]

hos•pice (hŏs′pĭs) ►*n.* **1.** A shelter or lodging for travelers or the needy. **2.** A program that provides medical and other care for terminally ill patients. [< Lat. *hospitium*, hospitality < *hospes*, host.]

hos•pi•ta•ble (hŏs′pĭ-tə-bəl, hŏ-spĭt′ə-bəl) ►*adj.* **1.** Cordial and generous to guests. **2.** Favorable to growth and development. [< Lat. *hospes*, *hospit-*, host.] —**hos′pi•ta•bly** *adv.*

hos•pi•tal (hŏs′pĭ-tl, -pĭt′l) ►*n.* An institution that provides medical, surgical, or psychiatric care and treatment for the sick or the injured. [< Lat. *hospitālis*, of a guest < *hospes*, guest.]

hos•pi•tal•i•ty (hŏs′pĭ-tăl′ĭ-tē) ►*n.*, *pl.* **-ties.** Cordial and generous reception of guests.

hos•pi•tal•ize (hŏs′pĭt-l-īz′) ►*v.* **-ized, -iz•ing.** To place in a hospital for treatment or observation. —**hos′pi•tal•i•za′tion** *n.*

host[1] (hōst) ►*n.* **1.** One who receives or entertains guests. **2.** One that furnishes facilities and resources for an event. **3.** The emcee or interviewer on a radio or television program. **4.** *Biol.* The organism on or in which a parasite lives. ►*v. Informal* To serve as host to or for. [< Lat. *hospes*, *hospit-*.]

host[2] (hōst) ►*n.* **1.** An army. **2.** A great number; multitude. [< Lat. *hostis*, enemy.]

host[3] also **Host** (hōst) ►*n. Eccles.* The consecrated bread or wafer of the Eucharist. [< Lat. *hostia*, sacrifice.]

hos•tage (hŏs′tĭj) ►*n.* A person held by force as security that specified terms will be met. [< OFr., prob. < *host*, guest. See HOST[1].]

hos•tel (hŏs′təl) ►*n.* **1.** A supervised inexpensive lodging for young travelers. **2.** An inn. [< Med.Lat. *hospitāle*, inn. See HOSPITAL.] —**hos′tel•er** *n.*

hos•tel•ry (hŏs′təl-rē) ►*n.*, *pl.* **-ries.** An inn.

host•ess (hō′stĭs) ►*n.* **1.** A woman who receives or entertains guests. **2.** A woman employed to greet and assist patrons, as in a restaurant. See Usage Note at **-ess.**

hos•tile (hŏs′təl, -tīl′) ►*adj.* **1.** Of or characteristic of an enemy. **2.** Feeling or showing enmity: *a hostile remark.* [< Lat. *hostis*, enemy.] —**hos′tile** *n.* —**hos′tile•ly** *adv.*

hos•til•i•ty (hŏ-stĭl′ĭ-tē) ►*n.*, *pl.* **-ties 1.** Antagonism or enmity. **2a.** A hostile act. **b. hostilities** Overt warfare.

hos•tler (hŏs′lər, ŏs′-) ►*n.* One who tends horses, esp. at an inn. [< AN *hostiler* < OFr. *hostel*, HOSTEL.]

hot (hŏt) ►*adj.* **hot•ter, hot•test 1a.** Having or giving off great heat. **b.** Being at a high temperature. **2.** Warmer than normal or desirable. **3a.** Causing a burning sensation. **b.** Spicy: *hot peppers.* **4a.** Charged or as if charged with electricity. **b.** Radioactive. **5.** Marked by intensity of emotion. **6.** *Informal* Arousing intense interest or controversy: *a hot topic.* **7.** *Slang* Recently stolen: *a hot car.* **8.** *Informal* **a.** Most recent; new: *a hot news item.* **b.** Currently popular: *the hottest young talents.* **9.** *Slang* **a.** Performing with great skill. **b.** Unusually lucky. —***idioms:*** **hot under the collar** *Informal* Angry. **hot water** Trouble; difficulty. [< OE *hāt.*] —**hot′ly** *adv.* —**hot′ness** *n.*

hot air ►*n. Slang* Empty, exaggerated talk.

hot•bed (hŏt′bĕd′) ►*n.* An environment conducive to growth or development, esp. of something undesirable: *a hotbed of intrigue.*

hot-blood•ed (hŏt′blŭd′ĭd) ►*adj.* Easily excited or aroused. —**hot′-blood′ed•ness** *n.*

hot•box (hŏt′bŏks′) ►*n.* An axle or journal box, as on a railway car, overheated by friction.

hot button ►*n. Slang* Something that elicits a strong emotional response. —**hot′-but′ton** *adj.*

hot•cake (hŏt′kāk′) ►*n.* See **pancake.** —***idiom:*** **go (**or **sell) like hotcakes** To be in great demand.

hot dog or **hot•dog** (hŏt′dôg′, -dŏg′) ►*n.* **1.** A frankfurter. **2.** *Slang* One who performs showy, often dangerous stunts. —**hot′-dog′** *v.* —**hot′-dog′ger** *n.*

ho•tel (hō-tĕl′) ►*n.* An establishment that provides lodging and often meals esp. for travelers. [< OFr. *hostel*, HOSTEL.]

hot flash ►*n.* A sudden brief sensation of heat sometimes experienced during menopause.

hot•foot (hŏt′fo͝ot′) ►*v. Informal* To go in haste: *hotfoot it out of town.*

hot•head•ed (hŏt′hĕd′ĭd) ►*adj.* **1.** Easily angered; quick-tempered. **2.** Impetuous; rash. —**hot′head′** *n.* —**hot′head′ed•ly** *adv.*

hot•house (hŏt′hous′) ►*n.* A heated greenhouse. ►*adj.* Delicate; sensitive.

hot line or **hot•line** (hŏt′līn′) ►*n.* A communications line for use in a crisis.

hot•link (hŏt′lĭngk′) ►*n. Comp. Sci.* See **link** 3.

hot plate ►*n.* An electrically heated plate for cooking food.

hot rod also **hot-rod** (hŏt′rŏd′) ►*n. Slang* An automobile modified for speed and acceleration. —**hot′-rod′** *v.* —**hot rodder, hot′-rod′der** *n.*

hot seat ►*n.* **1.** *Slang* The electric chair. **2.** *Informal* A position of stress or discomfort.

hot•shot (hŏt′shŏt′) ►*n. Slang* A person of impressive, often aggressive skill. —**hot′shot′** *adj.*

hot toddy ►*n.* A drink made of usu. whiskey mixed with hot water, sugar, and spices.

hot tub ►*n.* A large tub filled with hot water for bathing or soaking.

hot-wire (hŏt′wīr′) ►*v. Informal* To start the engine of (e.g., an automobile) without a key, as by short-circuiting the ignition system.

Hou•di•ni (ho͞o-dē′nē), **Harry.** Ehrich Weiss. 1874–1926. Amer. escape artist.

hound (hound) ►*n.* **1a.** Any of various hunting dogs usu. having drooping ears and a deep resonant voice. **b.** A dog. **2.** A scoundrel. **3.** An avid enthusiast. ►*v.* **1.** To pursue relentlessly. **2.** To nag. [< OE *hund.*]

hour (our) ►*n.* **1.** One of the 24 equal parts of a day. **2.** The time of day. **3a.** A customary time: *the dinner hour.* **b. hours** A specified time: *banking hours.* [< Gk. *hōra*, season, time.]

hour•glass (our′glăs′) ►*n.* An instrument that measures time by trickling sand from an upper to a lower glass chamber.

hou•ri (ho͝or′ē, ho͞o′rē) ►*n.*, *pl.* **-ris.** One of the beautiful virgins of the Koranic paradise. [Pers. *ḥūrī.*]

hour•ly (our′lē) ►*adj.* **1.** Occurring every hour. **2.** Frequent; continual. **3.** By the hour as a unit: *hourly pay.* ►*adv.* **1.** At or during every hour. **2.** Frequently; continually.

house (hous) ►*n.*, *pl.* **hous•es** (hou′zĭz, -sĭz) **1a.** A structure serving as a dwelling for one or more persons. **b.** A household. **2a.** A building used for a particular purpose: *a movie house.* **b.** The audience or patrons of such a place: *a full house.* **3a.** A commercial firm: *a brokerage house.* **b.** A publishing company. **4.** often **House** A legislative assembly. ►*v.* (houz) **housed, hous•ing 1.** To provide living quarters for; lodge. **2.** To shelter, keep, or store. **3.** To contain; harbor. —***idiom:* on the house** At the expense of the establishment; free. [< OE *hūs.*]

house•boat (hous′bōt′) ►*n.* A barge equipped for use as a dwelling.

house•break•ing (hous′brā′kĭng) ►*n.* The unlawful breaking into and entering another's house. —**house′break′er** *n.*

house•bro•ken (hous′brō′kən) ►*adj.* **1.** Trained to have excretory habits appropriate for indoor living. **2.** Compliant.

house•fly (hous′flī′) ►*n.* A common fly that frequents human dwellings and transmits a wide variety of diseases.

house•hold (hous′hōld′) ►*n.* A domestic unit consisting of the people who live together in a single dwelling. ►*adj.* Commonly known; familiar: *a household name.* [ME.] —**house′hold′er** *n.*

house•keep•er (hous′kē′pər) ►*n.* One hired to perform or direct the domestic tasks in a household.

house•keep•ing (hous′kē′pĭng) ►*n.* **1.** Performance or management of household tasks. **2.** Routine maintenance; upkeep.

house•moth•er (hous′mŭ*th*′ər) ►*n.* A woman employed as supervisor of a residence for young people.

House of Commons ►*n.* The lower house of Parliament in the United Kingdom and Canada.

House of Lords ►*n.* The upper house of Parliament in the United Kingdom.

house organ ►*n.* A periodical published by an organization for its employees or clients.

house•plant (hous′plănt′) ►*n.* A usu. decorative plant suitable for growing indoors.

house•wares (hous′wârz′) ►*pl.n.* Articles used in a home, esp. in the kitchen.

house•warm•ing (hous′wôr′mĭng) ►*n.* A celebration of the occupancy of a new home.

house•wife (hous′wīf′) ►*n.* A woman, esp. a married woman, who manages her household as her main occupation. —**house′wife′ly** *adj.* —**house′wif′er•y** *n.*

house•work (hous′wûrk′) ►*n.* The tasks, such as cleaning and cooking, performed in housekeeping.

hous•ing (hou′zĭng) ►*n.* **1a.** Buildings in which people live. **b.** A dwelling. **2.** Provision of lodging or shelter. **3.** Something that covers, protects, or supports, esp. something that protects a mechanical part.

Hous•man (hous′mən), **Alfred Edward.** 1859–1936. British poet and scholar.

Hous•ton (hyo͞o′stən) A city of SE TX NW of Galveston. Pop. 1,630,553. —**Hous•to′ni•an** (-stō′nē-ən) *n.*

Houston, Samuel. 1793–1863. Amer. general and politician.

Sam Houston

Julia Ward Howe photographed in 1908

HOV ►*abbr.* high-occupancy vehicle

hove (hōv) ►*v.* P.t. and p.part. of **heave** 5.

hov•el (hŭv′əl, hŏv′-) ►*n.* A small miserable dwelling. [ME, hut.]

hov•er (hŭv′ər, hŏv′-) ►*v.* **1.** To remain floating or suspended in the air. **2.** To linger in a place. **3.** To remain in an uncertain state; waver. [ME *hoveren.*]

hov•er•craft (hŭv′ər-krăft′, hŏv′-) ►*n.* See **air-cushion vehicle.**

HOV lane (āch′ō-vē′) ►*n.* An expressway lane restricted to vehicles with a set minimum of occupants, usu. two.

how (hou) ►*adv.* **1.** In what manner or way; by what means. **2.** In what state or condition. **3.** To what extent, amount, or degree. **4.** For what reason or purpose; why. **5.** With what meaning: *How should I take that remark?* ►*conj.* **1.** The manner or way in which: *forgot how it was done.* **2.** In whatever way or manner: *Cook it how you please.* —***idioms:* how about** What is your thought or feeling regarding: *How about a cup of tea?* **how come** *Informal* How is that; why. [< OE *hū.*]

How•ard (hou′ərd), **Catherine.** 1520?–42. Queen of England as the fifth wife of Henry VIII (1540–42); executed.

how•be•it (hou-bē′ĭt) ►*adv.* Nevertheless.

how•dah (hou′də) ►*n.* A covered seat on the back of an elephant or camel. [< Ar. *hawdaj.*]

Howe (hou), **Elias.** 1819–67. Amer. inventor.

Howe, Julia Ward. 1819–1910. Amer. writer and feminist.

How•ells (hou′əlz), **William Dean.** 1837–1920. Amer. writer and editor.

how•ev•er (hou-ĕv′ər) ►*adv.* **1.** In whatever manner or way. See Usage Note at **whatever.** **2.** To whatever degree or extent. **3.** In spite of that; nevertheless. **4.** On the other hand; by contrast. ►*conj.* In whatever manner or way.

how•it•zer (hou′ĭt-sər) ►*n.* A short cannon that delivers shells at a medium velocity and usu. high trajectory. [< Czech *haufnice.*]

howl (houl) ▸*v.* **1.** To utter a long mournful sound. **2.** To cry or wail loudly. See Syns at **shout. 3.** *Slang* To laugh heartily. [ME *houlen.*] —**howl** *n.*

howl•er (hou′lər) ▸*n.* **1.** One that howls. **2.** *Slang* A laughably stupid blunder.

How•rah (hou′rə, -rä) A city of E India opposite Calcutta. Pop. 950,435.

how•so•ev•er (hou′sō-ev′ər) ▸*adv.* **1.** To whatever extent. **2.** By whatever means.

hoy•den (hoid′n) ▸*n.* A high-spirited, boisterous, or saucy woman. [Prob. < MDu. *heiden,* heathen.] —**hoy′den•ish** *adj.*

hp ▸*abbr.* horsepower

HQ ▸*abbr.* headquarters

HR ▸*abbr.* **1.** House of Representatives **2.** home run

hr. ▸*abbr.* hour

HRH ▸*abbr.* Her (or His) Royal Highness

hryv•nia (hrĭv′nyä) ▸*n.* See table at **currency.** [Ukrainian.]

Hs ▸ The symbol for the element **hassium.**

HST ▸*abbr.* Hawaii-Aleutian Standard Time

ht ▸*abbr.* height

HTLV–I (āch′tē-ĕl′vē-wŭn′) ▸*n.* A retrovirus that causes diseases similar to multiple sclerosis. [*h(uman) T(-cell) l(ymphotropic) v(irus) I.*]

HTLV–III (āch′tē-ĕl′vē-thrē′) ▸*n.* HIV. [*h(uman) T(-cell) l(ymphotropic) v(irus) III.*]

HTML (āch′tē-ĕm-ĕl′) ▸*n.* A markup language used to structure and set up hypertext links between documents, esp. on the World Wide Web. [*h(yper)t(ext) m(arkup) l(anguage).*]

HTTP or **http** (āch′tē-tē-pē′) ▸*n.* A protocol used to request and transmit files, esp. over the Internet. [*h(yper)t(ext) t(ransfer) p(rotocol).*]

Hua Guo•feng (hwä′ gwô′fŭng′) also **Hua Kuo•feng** (kwô′fŭng′, gwô′-). b. 1920. Chinese prime minister (1976–80).

Huang He (hwäng′ hə′) also **Hwang Ho** (hwäng′ hō′) or **Yellow River.** A river of N China rising in the Kunlun Mts. and flowing about 4,827 km (3,000 mi) to the Gulf of Bo Hai.

hua•ra•che (wə-rä′chē, hə-) ▸*n.* A flat-heeled sandal with an upper of woven leather strips. [Am.Sp.]

huarache

Huas•ca•rán (wäs′kə-rän′, -kä-) An extinct volcano, 6,770.4 m (22,198 ft), in the Andes of W-central Peru.

hub (hŭb) ▸*n.* **1.** The center part of a wheel, fan, or propeller. **2.** A center of activity or interest. See Syns at **center.** [Prob. < *hob,* projection.]

hub•bub (hŭb′ŭb′) ▸*n.* **1.** Loud noise; din. **2.** Confusion; tumult. [Prob. of Ir. Gael. orig.]

hub•cap (hŭb′kăp′) ▸*n.* A round covering over the hub of an automobile wheel.

hu•bris (hyo͞o′brĭs) ▸*n.* Overbearing pride; arrogance. [Gk.]

huck•le•ber•ry (hŭk′əl-bĕr′ē) ▸*n.* **1.** A shrub related to the blueberry. **2.** The glossy blackish edible fruit of this plant. [Prob. alteration of *hurtleberry,* a kind of berry.]

huck•ster (hŭk′stər) ▸*n.* **1.** A peddler or hawker. **2.** An aggressive salesperson or promoter. [ME.] —**huck′ster•ism** *n.*

HUD ▸*abbr.* (Department of) Housing and Urban Development

hud•dle (hŭd′l) ▸*n.* **1.** A densely packed group. **2.** *Football* A brief gathering of a team's players behind the line of scrimmage to receive instructions for the next play. **3.** A small private conference. ▸*v.* **-dled, -dling 1.** To crowd together. **2.** To curl up or crouch. **3.** *Football* To gather in a huddle. **4.** *Informal* To gather together for consultation. [Poss. of LGer. orig.] —**hud′dler** *n.*

Hud•son (hŭd′sən), **Henry.** d. 1611. English navigator and explorer.

Hudson, William Henry. 1841–1922. British naturalist and writer.

Hudson Bay. An inland sea of E-central Canada connected to the Atlantic by **Hudson Strait.**

Hudson River. A river rising in NE NY and flowing about 507 km (315 mi) to Upper New York Bay at New York City.

hue (hyo͞o) ▸*n.* **1.** The property of colors by which they can be perceived as ranging from red through yellow, green, and blue. **2.** A particular gradation of color; shade or tint. **3.** Color. [< OE *hīw.*]

Hue (hyo͞o-ā′, hwā) A city of central Vietnam near the South China Sea NW of Da Nang. Pop. 219,149.

hue and cry ▸*n.* A public clamor, as of protest or demand. [< AN *hu e cri.*]

huff (hŭf) ▸*n.* A fit of anger or annoyance; pique. ▸*v.* **1.** To puff; blow. **2.** To bluster. [Imit.] —**huff′i•ly** *adv.* —**huff′i•ness** *adj.* —**huff′y** *adj.*

hug (hŭg) ▸*v.* **hugged, hug•ging 1.** To clasp or hold closely; embrace. **2.** To cherish. **3.** To stay close to. ▸*n.* A close embrace. [Prob. of Scand. orig.] —**hug′ger** *n.*

huge (hyo͞oj) ▸*adj.* **hug•er, hug•est.** Exceedingly large; tremendous. [< OFr. *ahuge.*] —**huge′ly** *adv.* —**huge′ness** *n.*

Hughes (hyo͞oz), **Charles Evans.** 1862–1948. Amer. jurist and politician.

Hughes, (James) Langston. 1902–67. Amer. writer.

Hu•gli or **Hoogh•ly** (ho͞o′glē). A channel, about 257 km (160 mi), of the Ganges R. in E India.

Hu•go (hyo͞o′gō, ü-gō′), **Victor Marie.** 1802–85. French writer.

Hu•gue•not (hyo͞o′gə-nŏt′) ▸*n.* A French Protestant of the 16th and 17th cent.

huh (hŭ) ▸*interj.* Used to express interrogation, surprise, contempt, or indifference.

hu•la (ho͞o′lə) ▸*n.* A Polynesian dance marked by undulating hips and rhythmic miming movements of the arms and hands. See Regional Note at **ukulele.** [Hawaiian.]

hulk (hŭlk) ▸*n.* **1.** An unwieldy or unseaworthy ship. **2.** A wrecked hull. **3.** One that is bulky, clumsy, or unwieldy. ▸*v.* To loom as a massive form. [< Med.Lat. *hulcus.*]

hula

hulk•ing (hŭl′kĭng) also **hulk•y** (hŭl′kē) ►*adj.* Unwieldy or bulky; massive.

hull (hŭl) ►*n.* **1.** The dry outer covering of a fruit, seed, or nut; husk. **2.** The frame or body of a ship. **3.** The outer casing of a rocket, guided missile, or spaceship. ►*v.* To remove the hulls of (fruit or seeds). [< OE *hulu.*]

Hull, Cordell. 1871–1955. Amer. public official.

hul•la•ba•loo also **hul•la•bal•loo** (hŭl′ə-bə-lo͞o′) ►*n., pl.* **-loos.** Great noise or excitement; uproar. [< alteration of *holla*, hello.]

hum (hŭm) ►*v.* **hummed, hum•ming 1.** To emit a continuous low droning sound. **2.** To be in a state of busy activity. **3.** To sing without opening the lips. [ME *hummen.*] —**hum** *n.* —**hum′ma•ble** *adj.* —**hum′mer** *n.*

hu•man (hyo͞o′mən) ►*n.* **1.** A member of the genus *Homo* and esp. of the species *H. sapiens.* **2.** A person: *remarkable humans who explored Antarctica.* ►*adj.* **1.** Of or characteristic of humans. **2.** Made up of humans: *formed a human bridge across the ice.* [< Lat. *hūmānus.*] —**hu′man•hood′** *n.* —**hu′man•ly** *adv.* —**hu′man•ness** *n.*

human being ►*n.* A human.

hu•mane (hyo͞o-mān′) ►*adj.* **1.** Kind or compassionate. **2.** Emphasizing humanistic values and concerns. [ME *humain*, HUMAN.] —**hu•mane′ly** *adv.* —**hu•mane′ness** *n.*

Syns: *humane, compassionate, humanitarian, merciful* **Ant:** *inhumane* **adj.**

hu•man•ism (hyo͞o′mə-nĭz′əm) ►*n.* **1.** A system of thought that centers on humans and their values, capacities, and worth. **2. Humanism** A Renaissance movement that emphasized secular concerns as a result of the rediscovery of classical literature, art, and civilization. —**hu′man•ist** *n.* —**hu′man•is′tic** *adj.*

hu•man•i•tar•i•an (hyo͞o-măn′ĭ-târ′ē-ən) ►*n.* One devoted to the promotion of human welfare. ►*adj.* Compassionate. See Syns at **humane.** —**hu•man′i•tar′i•an•ism** *n.*

hu•man•i•ty (hyo͞o-măn′ĭ-tē) ►*n., pl.* **-ties 1.** Humans considered as a group; the human race. **2.** The condition or quality of being human. **3.** The quality of being humane. **4. humanities** Those disciplines, such as philosophy and art, concerned with human thought and culture; the liberal arts.

hu•man•ize (hyo͞o′mə-nīz′) ►*v.* **-ized, -iz•ing 1.** To make human or humanlike. **2.** To make humane; civilize. —**hu′man•i•za′tion** *n.* —**hu′man•iz′er** *n.*

hu•man•kind (hyo͞o′mən-kīnd′) ►*n.* The human race.

hu•man•oid (hyo͞o′mə-noid′) ►*adj.* Having human characteristics or form. ►*n.* **1.** A being having human form. **2.** See **android.**

hum•ble (hŭm′bəl) ►*adj.* **-bler, -blest 1.** Meek or modest. **2.** Deferentially respectful. **3.** Low in rank or station. ►*v.* **-bled, -bling 1.** To humiliate. **2.** To cause to be meek. **3.** To make lower or lesser; abase. [< Lat. *humilis* < *humus*, ground.] —**hum′ble•ness** *n.* —**hum′bler** *n.* —**hum′bly** *adv.*

Hum•boldt (hŭm′bōlt′), Baron **(Friedrich Heinrich) Alexander von.** 1769–1859. German naturalist and writer.

Humboldt Bay. A sheltered inlet of the Pacific in NW California.

Humboldt Current ►*n.* A cold ocean current of the South Pacific, flowing N along the W coast of South America.

Humboldt River. A river, about 467 km (290 mi), of N NV.

hum•bug (hŭm′bŭg′) ►*n.* **1.** A hoax or fraud. **2.** An impostor. **3.** Nonsense; rubbish. ►*v.* **-bugged, -bug•ging.** To deceive or trick. [?] —**hum′bug′** *interj.* —**hum′bug′ger** *n.* —**hum′bug′ger•y** *n.*

hum•ding•er (hŭm′dĭng′ər) ►*n. Slang* One that is extraordinary. [?]

hum•drum (hŭm′drŭm′) ►*adj.* Monotonous; boring. See Syns at **dull.** [Poss. < HUM.]

Hume (hyo͞om), **David.** 1711–76. Scottish philosopher and historian.

hu•mer•us (hyo͞o′mər-əs) ►*n., pl.* **-mer•i** (-mə-rī′). The long bone of the arm, extending from the shoulder to the elbow. [Lat., upper arm.]

hu•mid (hyo͞o′mĭd) ►*adj.* Containing a high amount of water vapor. [Lat. *hūmidus* < *hūmēre*, be moist.] —**hu•mid′i•ty** *n.*

hu•mid•i•fy (hyo͞o-mĭd′ə-fī′) ►*v.* **-fied, -fy•ing.** To make humid. —**hu•mid′i•fi•ca′tion** *n.* —**hu•mid′i•fi′er** *n.*

hu•mi•dor (hyo͞o′mĭ-dôr′) ►*n.* A container designed for storing cigars at a constant humidity. [HUMID + -OR[1].]

hu•mil•i•ate (hyo͞o-mĭl′ē-āt′) ►*v.* **-at•ed, -at•ing.** To lower the pride, dignity, or self-respect of; degrade. [LLat. *humiliāre* < *humilis*, HUMBLE.] —**hu•mil′i•a′tion** *n.*

hu•mil•i•ty (hyo͞o-mĭl′ĭ-tē) ►*n.* The quality or condition of being humble. [< *humilis*, HUMBLE.]

hum•ming•bird (hŭm′ĭng-bûrd′) ►*n.* Any of a family of very small birds having brilliant iridescent plumage, a long slender bill, and hovering flight.

hum•mock (hŭm′ək) ►*n.* A low mound or ridge of earth. [?] —**hum′mock•y** *adj.*

hum•mus (ho͝om′əs, hŭm′-) ►*n.* A thick dip or spread made of mashed chickpeas, tahini, oil, lemon juice, and garlic. [Ar. *ḥummuṣ*, chickpea.]

hu•mor (hyo͞o′mər) ►*n.* **1.** The quality that makes something laughable or amusing. **2.** The ability to perceive, enjoy, or express what is amusing or comical. **3.** *Physiol.* A body fluid, such as blood, lymph, or bile. **4.** An often temporary state of mind; mood: *a bad humor.* **5.** A sudden whim. ►*v.* To comply with the wishes or ideas of; indulge. [< Lat. *ūmor*, fluid.] —**hu′mor•ist** *n.* —**hu′mor•less** *adj.* —**hu′mor•less•ly** *adv.* —**hu′mor•less•ness** *n.* —**hu′mor•ous** *adj.* —**hu′mor•**

ous•ly *adv.* —**hu′mor•ous•ness** *n.*

hump (hŭmp) ▸*n.* **1.** A rounded mass, as on the back of a camel. **2.** A low mound. ▸*v.* **1.** To bend into a hump; arch. **2.** *Slang* To exert (oneself). **3.** *Slang* To hurry. —***idiom:* over the hump** Past the worst stage. [Prob. of LGer. orig.]

hump•back (hŭmp′băk′) ▸*n.* **1.** See **hunchback** 1. **2.** A humped upper back. **3.** A humpback whale. —**hump′backed′** *adj.*

humpback whale ▸*n.* A large baleen whale noted for its communicative songs.

Hum•phrey (hŭm′frē, hŭmp′-), **Hubert Horatio.** 1911–78. Vice President of the US (1965–69).

hu•mus (hyōō′məs) ▸*n.* A brown or black organic substance consisting of decayed vegetable or animal matter. [Lat., soil.]

Hun (hŭn) ▸*n.* **1.** A member of a nomadic Mongolian people who invaded Europe in the 4th and 5th cent. A.D. **2.** often **hun** A barbarous person.

hunch (hŭnch) ▸*n.* An intuitive feeling. ▸*v.* **1.** To bend or draw up into a hump. **2.** To assume a crouched or cramped posture. [?]

hunch•back (hŭnch′băk′) ▸*n.* **1.** One whose back is hunched due to abnormal curvature of the upper spine. **2.** An abnormally humped back. —**hunch′backed′** *adj.*

hun•dred (hŭn′drĭd) ▸*n., pl.* **-dred** or **-dreds** **1.** The cardinal number equal to 10 × 10 or 10^2. **2. hundreds** The numbers between 100 and 999: *a crowd numbering in the hundreds.* [< OE.] —**hun′dred** *adj. & pron.*

hun•dredth (hŭn′drĭdth) ▸*n.* **1.** The ordinal number matching the number 100 in a series. **2.** One of 100 equal parts. —**hun′dredth** *adj.*

hun•dred•weight (hŭn′drĭd-wāt′) ▸*n., pl.* **-weight** or **-weights** **1.** A unit of weight equal to 100 lbs. (45.36 kg). **2.** *Chiefly Brit.* A unit equal to 112 lbs. (50.80 kg).

hung (hŭng) ▸*v.* P.t. and p.part of **hang.** See Usage Note at **hang.**

Hun•gar•i•an (hŭng-gâr′ē-ən) ▸*n.* **1.** A native or inhabitant of Hungary. **2.** The Finno-Ugric language of the Hungarians. —**Hun•gar′i•an** *adj.*

Hun•ga•ry (hŭng′gə-rē) A country of central Europe E of Austria. Cap. Budapest. Pop. 10,261,000.

hun•ger (hŭng′gər) ▸*n.* **1a.** A strong desire for food. **b.** The discomfort, weakness, or pain caused by a lack of food. **2.** A strong desire or craving. ▸*v.* **1.** To have a need or desire for food. **2.** To have a strong desire or craving; yearn. [< OE *hungor.*] —**hun′gri•ly** *adv.* —**hun′gri•ness** *n.* —**hun′gry** *adj.*

hung jury ▸*n.* A jury unable to agree on a verdict.

hunk (hŭngk) ▸*n.* **1.** *Informal* A large piece. **2.** *Slang* An attractive man. [Perh. < Flem. *hunke,* a piece of food.]

hun•ker (hŭng′kər) ▸*v.* **1.** To squat; crouch. **2.** To assume a defensive position: *hunkered down against the unfavorable criticism.* [Perh. of Scand. orig.]

hun•ky-do•ry (hŭng′kē-dôr′ē, -dōr′ē) ▸*adj.* *Slang* Perfectly satisfactory; fine. [Prob. < alteration of obsolete *hunk,* goal < Frisian.]

hunt (hŭnt) ▸*v.* **1.** To pursue (game) for food or sport. **2.** To search for prey: *hunted the backwoods.* **3.** To pursue so as to capture. **4.** To search (for). ▸*n.* **1.** The act or sport of hunting. **2.** A hunting expedition. **3.** A diligent search. [< OE *huntian.*] —**hunt′er** *n.* —**hunt′ress** *n.*

Hun•ting•ton (hŭn′tĭng-tən) A city of W WV W of Charleston. Pop. 54,844.

Huntington Beach. A city of S CA on the Pacific SE of Long Beach. Pop. 181,519.

hunts•man (hŭnts′mən) ▸*n.* A man who hunts, esp. one who manages a pack of hounds in the field.

Hunts•ville (hŭnts′vĭl′) A city of N AL ENE of Decatur. Pop. 159,789.

hur•dle (hûr′dl) ▸*n.* **1.** *Sports* **a.** A framelike barrier to be jumped over in certain races. **b. hurdles** A race in which such barriers must be jumped. **2.** An obstacle to be overcome. ▸*v.* **-dled, -dling** **1.** To leap over (a barrier). **2.** To overcome; surmount. [< OE *hyrdel.*] —**hur′dler** *n.*

hur•dy-gur•dy (hûr′dē-gûr′dē, hûr′dē-gûr′dē) ▸*n., pl.* **-dies.** A musical instrument, such as a barrel organ, played by turning a crank. [Prob. imit.]

hurl (hûrl) ▸*v.* **1.** To throw forcefully; fling. **2.** To utter vehemently: *hurl insults.* **3.** To pitch a baseball. [ME *hurlen.*] —**hurl** *n.*

hur•ly-bur•ly (hûr′lē-bûr′lē) ▸*n., pl.* **-lies.** Noisy confusion; tumult. [< HURL.]

Hu•ron (hyŏŏr′ən, -ŏn′) ▸*n., pl.* **-ron** or **-rons** **1.** A member of a Native American confederacy formerly of SE Ontario, now in Quebec and Oklahoma. **2.** The Iroquoian language of the Huron.

Huron, Lake. The second largest of the Great Lakes, between SE Ontario, Canada, and E MI.

hur•rah (hŏŏ-rä′, -rô′, hə-) also **hoo•ray** or **hur•ray** (-rā′) ▸*interj.* Used as an exclamation of pleasure, approval, elation, or victory. —**hur•rah′** *n. & v.*

hur•ri•cane (hûr′ĭ-kān′, hŭr′-) ▸*n.* A tropical cyclone usu. involving heavy rains and winds exceeding 74 mph (119 kph). [< Carib *huracan.*]

hur•ry (hûr′ē, hŭr′-) ▸*v.* **-ried, -ry•ing** **1.** To move or cause to move with speed or haste. **2.** To act or cause to act with undue haste; rush. **3.** To speed the completion of; expedite. ▸*n., pl.* **-ries** **1.** The act of hurrying. **2.** Haste. See Syns at **haste.** [Poss. ME *horien.*] —**hur′ried** *adj.* —**hur′ried•ly** *adv.*

Hur•ston (hûr′stən), **Zora Neale.** 1901?–60. Amer. writer.

Zora Neale Hurston
photographed in 1938

hurt (hûrt) ▸*v.* **hurt, hurt•ing** **1.** To feel or cause to feel pain. **2.** To aggrieve; distress. **3.**

To damage or impair. ▸*n.* **1.** Something that hurts. **2.** Mental suffering; anguish. **3.** A wrong; harm. [Poss. < OFr. *hurter*, bang into.] —**hurt′ful** *adj.* —**hurt′ful•ly** *adv.*

hur•tle (hûr′tl) ▸*v.* **-tled, -tling 1.** To move with or as if with great speed. **2.** To throw forcefully; hurl. [ME *hurtlen*, collide.]

Hus or **Huss** (hŭs, ho͝os), **Jan** or **John.** 1372?–1415. Bohemian religious reformer.

hus•band (hŭz′bənd) ▸*n.* A male spouse. ▸*v.* To use economically: *husband one's energy.* [< ON *hūsbōndi* : *hūs*, house + *būandi*, householder (< *būa*, dwell).]

hus•band•man (hŭz′bənd-mən) ▸*n.* A farmer.

hus•band•ry (hŭz′bən-drē) ▸*n.* **1.** Farming; agriculture. **2.** Careful management of resources; economy.

hush (hŭsh) ▸*v.* **1.** To make or become silent. **2.** To calm; soothe. **3.** To suppress mention of: *hush up the evidence.* ▸*n.* A silence or stillness. [Prob. < ME *husht*, silent.]

hush-hush (hŭsh′hŭsh′) ▸*adj. Informal* Secret; confidential.

hush puppy ▸*n.* A small round cornmeal fritter fried in deep fat. [?]

husk (hŭsk) ▸*n.* **1.** The outer covering of some fruits or seeds, as that of an ear of corn. **2.** A shell or outer covering, esp. when considered worthless. ▸*v.* To remove the husk from. [ME.] —**husk′er** *n.*

husk•y[1] (hŭs′kē) ▸*adj.* **-i•er, -i•est.** Hoarse or throaty. [< HUSK.] —**husk′i•ly** *adv.*

husk•y[2] (hŭs′kē) ▸*adj.* **-i•er, -i•est.** Strongly built; burly. [Perh. < HUSK.]

hus•ky[3] (hŭs′kē) ▸*n., pl.* **-kies.** An Arctic sled dog having a dense, variously colored coat. [Prob. < alteration of ESKIMO.]

Huss (hŭs, ho͝os), **John.** See Jan **Hus.**

hus•sar (hə-zär′, -sär′) ▸*n.* A member of any of various European units of light cavalry. [< OItal. *corsaro*, CORSAIR.]

Hus•sein (ho͞o-sān′). 1935–99. King of Jordan (1953–99).

Hussein, Saddam. b. 1937. Iraqi military and political leader.

Hus•serl (ho͝os′ərl, -ĕrl), **Edmund.** 1859–1938. Austrian-born German philosopher and mathematician.

hus•sy (hŭz′ē, hŭs′ē) ▸*n., pl.* **-sies 1.** A brazen or immoral woman. **2.** A saucy or impudent girl. [< ME *houswif*, housewife.]

hust•ings (hŭs′tĭngz) ▸*pl.n. (takes sing. or pl. v.)* A political campaign or its activities. [< ON *hūsthing*, assembly, court.]

hus•tle (hŭs′əl) ▸*v.* **-tled, -tling 1.** To jostle or shove roughly. **2.** To hurry along. **3.** To work busily. **4.** *Slang* To sell or get by questionable or aggressive means. ▸*n.* Energetic activity; drive. [< MDu. *hustelen.*] —**hus′tler** *n.*

hut (hŭt) ▸*n.* A crude or makeshift dwelling; shack. [Fr. *hutte*, of Gmc. orig.]

hutch (hŭch) ▸*n.* **1.** A coop for small animals, esp. rabbits. **2.** A cupboard with drawers and usu. open shelves on top. **3.** A hut. [< Med.Lat. *hūtica*, chest.]

Hutch•in•son (hŭch′ĭn-sən), **Anne.** 1591–1643. English-born Amer. colonist and religious leader.

Hu•tu (ho͞o′to͞o′) ▸*n., pl.* **-tu, -tus.** A member of a Bantu people inhabiting Rwanda and Burundi.

Hux•ley (hŭks′lē), **Aldous Leonard.** 1894–1963. British writer.

Huxley, Thomas Henry. 1825–95. British biologist.

huz•zah also **huz•za** (hə-zä′) ▸*interj.* Used to express joy, encouragement, or triumph. —**huz•zah′** *n.*

Hwang Ho (hwäng′ hō′) See **Huang He.**

hwy ▸*abbr.* highway

hy•a•cinth (hī′ə-sĭnth) ▸*n.* **1.** A bulbous plant having narrow leaves and variously colored, usu. fragrant flowers. **2.** A similar or related plant. [< Gk. *huakinthos.*]

hy•brid (hī′brĭd) ▸*n.* **1.** The offspring of genetically dissimilar parents, esp. of different varieties or species. **2.** Something of mixed origin or composition. [Lat. *hybrida.*] —**hy′brid** *adj.* —**hy′brid•ism** *n.*

hy•brid•ize (hī′brĭ-dīz′) ▸*v.* **-ized, -iz•ing.** To produce or cause to produce hybrids; crossbreed. —**hy′brid•i•za′tion** *n.*

Hyde Park (hīd) A public park in W-central London, England.

Hy•der•a•bad (hī′dər-ə-băd′, -bäd′) **1.** A city of S-central India ESE of Mumbai. Pop. 2,964,638. **2.** A city of S Pakistan on the Indus R. Pop. 751,529.

hy•dra (hī′drə) ▸*n.* A small freshwater polyp having a cylindrical body and a mouth surrounded by tentacles. [< Gk. *Hudra*, a many-headed monster.]

hy•dran•gea (hī-drān′jə, -drăn′-) ▸*n.* A shrub having large rounded clusters of white, pink, or blue flowers. [Gk. *hudro-*, HYDRO– + *angeion*, vessel.]

hy•drant (hī′drənt) ▸*n.* A fire hydrant.

hy•drate (hī′drāt′) ▸*n.* A solid compound containing water molecules combined in a definite ratio as an integral part of the crystal. ▸*v.* **-drat•ed, -drat•ing 1.** To rehydrate. **2.** To become a hydrate. —**hy•dra′tion** *n.* —**hy′dra′tor** *n.*

hy•drau•lic (hī-drô′lĭk) ▸*adj.* **1.** Of, involving, or operated by a fluid, esp. water, under pressure. **2.** Able to set and harden under water, as Portland cement. **3.** Of or relating to hydraulics. [< Gk. *hudraulis*, water organ : *hudro-*, HYDRO– + *aulos*, flute.] —**hy•drau′li•cal•ly** *adv.*

hy•drau•lics (hī-drô′lĭks) ▸*n. (takes sing. v.)* The physical science and technology of the static and dynamic behavior of fluids.

hydro– or **hydr–** ▸*pref.* **1a.** Water: *hydroelectric.* **b.** Fluid: *hydrodynamics.* **2.** Hydrogen: *hydrocarbon.* [< Gk. *hudōr*, water.]

hy•dro•car•bon (hī′drə-kär′bən) ▸*n.* An organic compound, such as benzene or methane, that contains only carbon and hydrogen. —**hy′dro•car′bo•na′ceous** (-bə-nā′shəs), **hy′dro•car•bon′ic** (-bŏn′ĭk) *adj.*

hy•dro•ceph•a•lus (hī′drō-sĕf′ə-ləs) also **hy•dro•ceph•a•ly** (-lē) ▸*n.* A congenital defect in which accumulation of fluid in the cerebral ventricles causes enlargement of the skull and compression of the brain. [HYDRO– + Gk. *kephalē*, head.] —**hy′dro•ce•phal′ic** (-sə-făl′ĭk), **hy′dro•ceph′a•loid′**, **hy′dro•ceph′a•lous** *adj.*

hy•dro•chlo•ric acid (hī′drə-klôr′ĭk, -klōr′-) ▸*n.* A clear, fuming, poisonous, highly acidic aqueous solution of hydrogen chloride, HCl, used in petroleum production, food processing, pickling, and metal cleaning.

hy•dro•cor•ti•sone (hī′drə-kôr′tĭ-sōn′, -zōn′) ►*n.* **1.** A steroid hormone, $C_{21}H_{30}O_5$, produced by the adrenal cortex, that regulates carbohydrate metabolism and maintains blood pressure. **2.** A preparation of this hormone used to treat inflammations and adrenal failure.

hy•dro•dy•nam•ics (hī′drō-dī-năm′ĭks) ►*n.* **1.** *(takes sing. v.)* The branch of science that deals with the dynamics of fluids, esp. incompressible fluids, in motion. **2.** *(takes pl. v.)* The dynamics of fluids in motion. —**hy′dro•dy•nam′i•cist** *n.*

hy•dro•e•lec•tric (hī′drō-ĭ-lĕk′trĭk) ►*adj.* Of or relating to electricity generated by conversion of the energy of running water. —**hy′dro•e•lec•tric′i•ty** (-ĭ-lĕk-trĭs′ĭ-tē) *n.*

hy•dro•foil (hī′drə-foil′) ►*n.* **1.** A winglike structure on the hull of a boat that raises the hull out of the water for efficient high-speed operation. **2.** A boat with hydrofoils.

hy•dro•gen (hī′drə-jən) ►*n. Symbol* **H** A colorless, highly flammable gaseous element, the most abundant element in the universe and present in most organic compounds. At. no. 1. See table at **element.** —**hy•drog′e•nous** (-drŏj′ə-nəs) *adj.*

hy•dro•gen•ate (hī′drə-jə-nāt′, hī-drŏj′ə-) ►*v.* **-at•ed, -at•ing.** To combine with or subject to the action of hydrogen.

hydrogen bomb ►*n.* A bomb whose explosive power is caused by the fusion of hydrogen nuclei into helium nuclei.

hydrogen peroxide ►*n.* A colorless, strongly oxidizing liquid, H_2O_2, used esp. as an antiseptic, bleaching agent, oxidizing agent, and laboratory reagent.

hy•drol•y•sis (hī-drŏl′ĭ-sĭs) ►*n.* Decomposition of a chemical compound by reaction with water. —**hy′dro•lyte′** (-līt′) *n.* —**hy′dro•lyt′ic** (-drə-lĭt′ĭk) *adj.* —**hy′dro•ly•za′tion** (hī′drə-lĭ-zā′shən) *n.* —**hy′dro•lyze′** *v.*

hy•drom•e•ter (hī-drŏm′ĭ-tər) ►*n.* An instrument used to determine the specific gravity of a fluid. —**hy′dro•met′ric** (hī′drə-mĕt′rĭk), **hy′dro•met′ri•cal** *adj.* —**hy•drom′e•try** *n.*

hy•dro•pho•bi•a (hī′drə-fō′bē-ə) ►*n.* **1.** Fear of water. **2.** Rabies. —**hy′dro•pho′bic** *adj.*

hy•dro•plane (hī′drə-plān′) ►*n.* **1.** See **seaplane. 2.** A motorboat designed to skim the water's surface at high speeds. **3.** See **hydrofoil** 2. ►*v.* **-planed, -plan•ing 1.** To drive or ride in a hydroplane. **2a.** To skim along on the surface of the water. **b.** To lose control by skimming along the surface of a wet road. Used of a motor vehicle.

hy•dro•pon•ics (hī′drə-pŏn′ĭks) ►*n.* *(takes sing. v.)* Cultivation of plants in nutrient solution rather than in soil. [HYDRO– + Gk. *ponein*, to work.] —**hy′dro•pon′ic** *adj.* —**hy′dro•pon′i•cal•ly** *adv.*

hy•dro•stat•ics (hī′drə-stăt′ĭks) ►*n.* *(takes sing. v.)* The physics of fluids at rest and under pressure. —**hy′dro•stat′ic, hy′dro•stat′i•cal** *adj.* —**hy′dro•stat′i•cal•ly** *adv.*

hy•dro•ther•a•py (hī′drə-thĕr′ə-pē) ►*n., pl.* **-pies.** External use of water in the treatment of diseases.

hy•drous (hī′drəs) ►*adj.* Containing water, esp. water of crystallization or hydration.

hy•drox•ide (hī-drŏk′sīd′) ►*n.* A chemical compound containing the univalent group OH.

hy•e•na (hī-ē′nə) ►*n.* Any of several carnivorous mammals of Africa and Asia feeding chiefly on carrion. [< Gk. *huaina*, feminine of *hus*, swine.]

hy•giene (hī′jēn′) ►*n.* **1.** The science of the promotion and preservation of health. **2.** Conditions and practices that promote or preserve health. [< Gk. *hugiēs*, healthy.] —**hy′gi•en′ic** (-jē-ĕn′ĭk, -jĕn′-) *adj.* —**hy′gi•en′i•cal•ly** *adv.* —**hy•gien′ist** (hī-jē′nĭst, -jĕn′ĭst) *n.*

hy•grom•e•ter (hī-grŏm′ĭ-tər) ►*n.* Any of several instruments that measure atmospheric humidity. [Gk. *hugros*, wet + –METER.] —**hy′gro•met′ric** (hī′grə-mĕt′rĭk) *adj.* —**hy•grom′e•try** *n.*

hy•ing (hī′ĭng) ►*v.* Pr.part. of **hie.**

hy•men (hī′mən) ►*n.* A membranous fold of tissue closing the external vaginal orifice. [< Gk. *humēn*, membrane.] —**hy′men•al** *adj.*

hy•me•ne•al (hī′mə-nē′əl) ►*adj.* Of a wedding or marriage. [< Gk. *humēn*, HYMEN.]

hymn (hĭm) ►*n.* A song of praise or thanksgiving, esp. to God. [< Gk. *humnos.*]

hym•nal (hĭm′nəl) ►*n.* A book or collection of church hymns. [< Med.Lat. *hymnāle.*]

hype[1] (hīp) ►*n. Slang* **1.** Excessive publicity. **2.** Extravagant claims made esp. in advertising. [< *hype*, a swindle.] —**hype** *v.*

hype[2] (hīp) *Slang* ►*n.* A hypodermic injection or syringe. ►*v.* **hyped, hyp•ing.** To stimulate with or as if with a hypodermic injection. [< HYPODERMIC.]

hy•per (hī′pər) ►*adj. Slang* **1.** Excitable; high-strung. **2.** Manic; frenzied. [< HYPERACTIVE.]

hyper– ►*pref.* **1.** Over; above; beyond: *hypersonic.* **2.** Excessive; excessively: *hypercritical.* [< Gk. *huper.*]

hy•per•ac•tive (hī′pər-ăk′tĭv) ►*adj.* Highly or excessively active. —**hy′per•ac′tive•ly** *adv.* —**hy′per•ac•tiv′i•ty** *n.*

hy•per•bo•la (hī-pûr′bə-lə) ►*n., pl.* **-las** or **-lae** (-lē) *Math.* A plane curve having two branches, formed by the intersection of a plane with both halves of a right circular cone at an angle parallel to the axis of the cone. [< Gk. *huperbolē*, excess. See HYPERBOLE.]

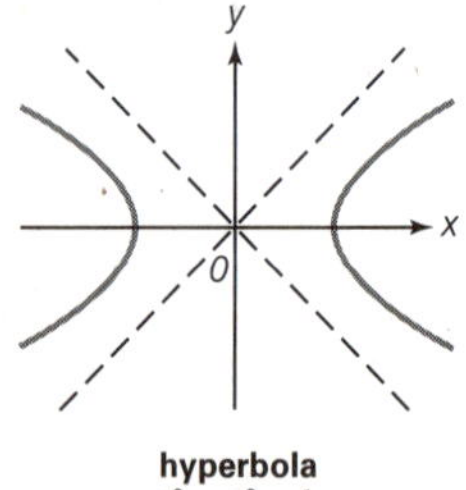

hyperbola
$x^2 - y^2 = 1$

hy•per•bo•le (hī-pûr′bə-lē) ►*n.* A figure of speech in which exaggeration is used for emphasis or effect, as in *I could sleep for a year.* [< Gk. *huperbolē*, excess : HYPER– + *ballein*, throw.]

hy•per•bol•ic (hī′pər-bŏl′ĭk) also **hy•per•bol•i•cal** (-ĭ-kəl) ►*adj.* **1.** Of or employing hyperbole. **2.** *Math.* Of or shaped like a hyperbola. —**hy′per•bol′i•cal•ly** *adv.*

hy•per•crit•i•cal (hī′pər-krĭt′ĭ-kəl) ►*adj.* Excessively critical; captious. —**hy′per•crit′i•cal•ly** *adv.*

hy•per•gly•ce•mi•a (hī′pər-glī-sē′mē-ə) ►*n.* An excess of glucose in the blood. [HYPER– + Gk. *glukus*, sweet + –EMIA.] —**hy′per•gly•ce′mic** *adj.*

hy•per•link (hī′pər-lĭngk′) *Comp. Sci.* ►*n.* See **link** 3. ►*v.* To follow a hypertext link to an electronic document.

hy•per•sen•si•tive (hī′pər-sĕn′sĭ-tĭv) ►*adj.* Abnormally sensitive. —**hy′per•sen′si•tive•ness, hy′per•sen′si•tiv′i•ty** *n.*

hy•per•son•ic (hī′pər-sŏn′ĭk) ►*adj.* Of or relating to speed equal to or exceeding five times the speed of sound. —**hy′per•son′i•cal•ly** *adv.*

hy•per•ten•sion (hī′pər-tĕn′shən) ►*n.* **1.** Abnormally high arterial blood pressure. **2.** High emotional tension. —**hy′per•ten′sive** *adj. & n.*

hy•per•text (hī′pər-tĕkst′) ►*n.* A computer-based text retrieval system that provides access to particular locations in webpages or other electronic documents by clicking on embedded links.

hy•per•thy•roid•ism (hī′pər-thī′roi-dĭz′əm) ►*n.* **1.** Pathologically excessive production of thyroid hormones. **2.** The condition resulting from such production.

hy•per•tro•phy (hī-pûr′trə-fē) ►*n., pl.* **-phies.** A nontumorous enlargement of an organ or a tissue. [HYPER– + Gk. *trophē*, food.] —**hy′per•tro′phic** (-trō′fĭk, -trŏf′ĭk) *adj.* —**hy•per′tro•phy** *v.*

hy•per•ven•ti•late (hī′pər-vĕn′tl-āt′) ►*v.* **-lat•ed, -lat•ing 1.** To breathe so as to effect hyperventilation. **2.** To breathe fast or deeply, as from excitement or anxiety.

hy•per•ven•ti•la•tion (hī′pər-vĕn′tl-ā′shən) ►*n.* Fast or deep respiration resulting in abnormally low levels of carbon dioxide in the blood.

hy•phen (hī′fən) ►*n.* A punctuation mark (-) used between the parts of a compound word or between the syllables of a word, esp. when divided at the end of a line of text. [< Gk. *huph' hen*, in one.]

hy•phen•ate (hī′fə-nāt′) ►*v.* **-at•ed, -at•ing.** To divide or connect with a hyphen. —**hy′phen•a′tion** *n.*

hyp•no•sis (hĭp-nō′sĭs) ►*n., pl.* **-ses** (-sēz). An induced sleeplike state in which the subject may experience forgotten or suppressed memories, hallucinations, and heightened suggestibility. [Gk. *hupnos*, sleep + –OSIS.]

hyp•not•ic (hĭp-nŏt′ĭk) ►*adj.* **1.** Of or relating to hypnosis. **2.** Inducing or tending to induce sleep. ►*n.* An agent that causes sleep. [< Gk. *hupnōtikos*, inducing sleep < *hupnos*, sleep.] —**hyp•not′i•cal•ly** *adv.*

hyp•no•tism (hĭp′nə-tĭz′əm) ►*n.* **1.** The theory, practice, or act of inducing hypnosis. **2.** Hypnosis. —**hyp′no•tist** *n.*

hyp•no•tize (hĭp′nə-tīz′) ►*v.* **-tized, -tiz•ing 1.** To put into a state of hypnosis. **2.** To fascinate; mesmerize. —**hyp′no•ti•za′tion** *n.* —**hyp′no•tiz′er** *n.*

hy•po (hī′pō) ►*n., pl.* **-pos** *Informal* A hypodermic syringe or injection.

hypo– or **hyp–** ►*pref.* **1.** Below; beneath; under: *hypodermic.* **2.** Lower than normal: *hypothermia.* [< Gk. *hupo*, beneath.]

hy•po•al•ler•gen•ic (hī′pō-ăl′ər-jĕn′ĭk) ►*adj.* Having a decreased tendency to provoke an allergic reaction: *hypoallergenic cosmetics.*

hy•po•chon•dri•a (hī′pə-kŏn′drē-ə) ►*n.* The neurosis that one is or is becoming ill. [< Gk. *hupokhondrion*, abdomen.] —**hy′po•chon′dri•ac′** *adj. & n.*

hy•poc•ri•sy (hĭ-pŏk′rĭ-sē) ►*n., pl.* **-sies.** The professing of beliefs or virtues one does not possess. [< Gk. *hupokrisis*, pretense.]

hyp•o•crite (hĭp′ə-krĭt′) ►*n.* A person given to hypocrisy. [< Gk. *hupocritēs*, actor.] —**hyp′o•crit′i•cal** *adj.* —**hyp′o•crit′i•cal•ly** *adv.*

hy•po•der•mic (hī′pə-dûr′mĭk) ►*adj.* Injected beneath the skin. ►*n.* **1.** A hypodermic injection. **2.** A hypodermic needle or syringe. —**hy′po•der′mi•cal•ly** *adv.*

hypodermic needle ►*n.* **1.** A hollow needle used with a hypodermic syringe. **2.** A hypodermic syringe with its needle.

hypodermic syringe ►*n.* A syringe fitted with a hypodermic needle for giving injections.

hy•po•gly•ce•mi•a (hī′pō-glī-sē′mē-ə) ►*n.* An abnormally low level of glucose in the blood. [< HYPO– + Gk. *glukus*, sweet + –EMIA.] —**hy′po•gly•ce′mic** *adj.*

hy•pot•e•nuse (hī-pŏt′n-o͞os′, -yo͞os′) ►*n.* *Math.* The side of a right triangle opposite the right angle. [< Gk. *hupoteinousa.*]

hy•po•thal•a•mus (hī′pō-thăl′ə-məs) ►*n.* The part of the brain that lies below the thalamus and regulates bodily temperature, certain metabolic processes, and other autonomic activities. —**hy′po•tha•lam′ic** (-thə-lăm′ĭk) *adj.*

hy•po•ther•mi•a (hī′pə-thûr′mē-ə) ►*n.* Abnormally low body temperature. —**hy′po•ther′mic** *adj.*

hy•poth•e•sis (hī-pŏth′ĭ-sĭs) ►*n., pl.* **-ses** (-sēz′). A tentative explanation that accounts for a set of facts and can be tested by further investigation. [< Gk. *hupothesis.*] —**hy•poth′e•size** *v.*

hy•po•thet•i•cal (hī′pə-thĕt′ĭ-kəl) also **hy•po•thet•ic** (-thĕt′ĭk) ►*adj.* **1.** Of or based on a hypothesis. See Syns at **theoretical. 2.** Suppositional; uncertain. See Syns at **supposed.** [< Gk. *hupothetikos.*] —**hy′po•thet′i•cal** *n.* —**hy′po•thet′i•cal•ly** *adv.*

hy•po•thy•roid•ism (hī′pō-thī′roi-dĭz′əm) ►*n.* **1.** Insufficient production of thyroid hormones, marked by lack of energy and a slowed metabolism. **2.** A pathological condition resulting from such an insufficiency.

hy•rax (hī′răks′) ►*n., pl.* **-rax•es** or **-ra•ces** (-rə-sēz′). An herbivorous mammal of Africa and adjacent Asia, resembling the woodchuck but more closely related to hoofed mammals. [Gk. *hurax*, shrew mouse.]

hys•sop (hĭs′əp) ►*n.* A woody plant having spikes of small blue flowers and aromatic leaves. [< Gk. *hussōpos.*]

hys•ter•ec•to•my (hĭs′tə-rĕk′tə-mē) ►*n., pl.* **-mies.** Surgical removal of the uterus. [Gk. *hustera*, womb + –ECTOMY.]

hys•ter•i•a (hĭ-stĕr′ē-ə, -stîr′-) ►*n.* **1.** A neurosis marked by a physical ailment with no organic cause, such as sleepwalking or amnesia. **2.** Excessive or uncontrollable emotion, such as fear or panic. [< Gk. *hustera*, womb.]

hys•ter•ic (hĭ-stĕr′ĭk) ►*n.* **1.** A person suffering from hysteria. **2. hysterics** *(takes sing. or*

pl. v.) **a.** A fit of laughing or crying. **b.** An attack of hysteria. ►*adj.* Hysterical. [< Gk. *hustera*, womb.]
hys•ter•i•cal (hĭ-stĕr′ĭ-kəl) ►*adj.* **1.** Marked by or due to hysteria. **2.** Having or prone to having hysterics. **3.** *Informal* Extremely funny. —**hys•ter′i•cal•ly** *adv.*
Hz ►*abbr.* hertz

I

i[1] or **I** (ī) ►*n., pl.* **i's** or **I's** also **is** or **Is.** The 9th letter of the English alphabet.
i[2] ► The symbol for **imaginary unit.**
I[1] (ī) ►*pron.* Used to refer to oneself as speaker or writer. ►*n.* The self; the ego. [< OE *ic.*]
Usage: The nominative forms of pronouns should be used in formal speech and writing in such sentences as *John and she* (not *her*) *will be giving the talk.* • *Between you and I,* a construction in which the pronouns occur as the objects of a preposition, is widely regarded as a marker of grammatical ignorance; use *between you and me.*
I[2] ► **1.** The symbol for the element **iodine** 1. **2.** The symbol for **current** 3.
IA or **Ia.** ►*abbr.* Iowa
–ia[1] ►*suff.* **1.** Disease; disorder: *dyslexia.* **2.** Territory; country: *suburbia.* [< Lat. and Gk.]
–ia[2] ►*suff.* Things derived from or relating to: *marginalia.* [< Lat. and Gk.]
–ial ►*suff.* Of, relating to, or characterized by: *axial.* [< Lat. *-iālis.*]
i•amb (ī′ămb′, ī′ăm′) ►*n., pl.* **i•ambs.** A metrical foot in which a stressed syllable follows an unstressed syllable. [< Gk. *iambos.*] —**i•am′bic** *adj. & n.*
–ian ►*suff.* **1.** Of, relating to, or resembling: *Devonian.* **2.** One relating to, belonging to, or resembling: *tragedian.* [< Lat. *-iānus.*]
–iana ►*suff.* Var. of **–ana.**
Ia•şi (yäsh, yä′shē) A city of NE Romania NNE of Bucharest. Pop. 337,643.
–iatric ►*suff.* Of or relating to a specified kind of medical practice: *pediatric.* [< Gk. *iatros*, physician.]
–iatrics ►*suff.* Medical treatment: *pediatrics.*
–iatry ►*suff.* Medical treatment: *psychiatry.* [< Gk. *iatros*, physician.]
ib. ►*abbr.* ibidem
I•ba•dan (ē-bäd′n, ē-bä′dän) A city of SW Nigeria NNW of Lagos. Pop. 1,009,400.
I•be•ri•a (ī-bîr′ē-ə) **1.** An ancient country of Transcaucasia roughly equivalent to E Georgia. **2.** See **Iberian Peninsula.** —**I•be′ri•an** *adj. & n.*
Iberian Peninsula also **Iberia.** A peninsula of SW Europe occupied by Spain and Portugal.
i•bex (ī′bĕks′) ►*n., pl.* **ibex** or **i•bex•es.** A wild goat native to Eurasia and N Africa and having long curving horns. [Lat.]
ibid. ►*abbr.* ibidem
i•bi•dem (ĭb′ĭ-dĕm′, ĭ-bī′dəm) ►*adv.* In the same place, as in a book cited before. [Lat. *ibīdem.*]
i•bis (ī′bĭs) ►*n., pl.* **ibis** or **i•bis•es.** Any of a family of storklike wading birds having a long, downward-curving bill. [< Gk.]
I•bi•za (ē-bē′sə) A Spanish island of the Balearic Is. in the W Mediterranean SW of Majorca.
–ible ►*suff.* Var. of **–able.**
Ibn Sa•ud (ĭb′ən sä-o͞od′), **Abdul Aziz.** 1880?–1953. Arab leader; founder and first king of Saudi Arabia (1932–53).

Iberian Peninsula

I•bo (ē′bō) ►*n., pl.* **Ibo** or **I•bos 1.** A member of a people of SE Nigeria. **2.** The language of the Ibo.
Ib•sen (ĭb′sən, ĭp′-), **Henrik.** 1828–1906. Norwegian playwright.
i•bu•pro•fen (ī′byo͞o-prō′fən) ►*n.* An anti-inflammatory medication used esp. to treat arthritis and for its analgesic and antipyretic properties. [< the chemical name *i(so)bu(tyl)phen(yl) pro(pionic acid).*]
–ic ►*suff.* **1.** Of, relating to, or characterized by: *seismic.* **2.** Having a valence higher than corresponding *–ous* compounds: *ferric.* [< Lat. *-icus* and Gk. *-ikos.*]
ICBM ►*abbr.* intercontinental ballistic missile
ICC ►*abbr.* Interstate Commerce Commission
ice (īs) ►*n.* **1.** Water frozen solid. **2.** A dessert consisting of sweetened and flavored crushed ice. **3.** *Slang* Diamonds. **4.** Extreme unfriendliness or reserve. —***idiom:*** **on ice** In reserve or readiness. ►*v.* **iced, ic•ing 1a.** To form ice; freeze. **b.** To coat with ice. **2.** To chill or freeze. **3.** To cover or decorate with icing. **4.** *Slang* To ensure of victory; clinch. [< OE *īs.*]
ice age ►*n.* **1.** A cold period marked by episodes of extensive glaciation. **2. Ice Age** The most recent glacial period.
ice bag ►*n.* See **ice pack** 2.
ice•berg (īs′bûrg′) ►*n.* A massive floating body of ice broken away from a glacier. [< MDu. *ijsbergh.*]
ice•boat (īs′bōt′) ►*n.* **1.** A boatlike vehicle with sharp runners, used for sailing on ice. **2.** See **icebreaker** 1. —**ice′boat′er** *n.* —**ice′boat′ing** *n.*
ice•bound (īs′bound′) ►*adj.* Locked in or covered over by ice.
ice•box (īs′bŏks′) ►*n.* A refrigerator.
ice•break•er (īs′brā′kər) ►*n.* **1.** A ship built for breaking a passage through icebound waters. **2a.** Something done or said to relax an unduly formal situation. **b.** A start. —**ice′break′ing** *n.*

icebreaker

ice•cap or **ice cap** (īs′kăp′) ►*n.* An extensive perennial cover of ice and snow.

ice cream ►*n.* A sweet frozen food prepared from milk products and flavorings.

ice hockey ►*n.* A game played on ice in which two teams of skaters use curved sticks to drive a puck into the opponent's goal.

ice•house (īs′hous′) ►*n.* A place where ice is made, stored, or sold.

Ice•land (īs′lənd) An island country in the North Atlantic near the Arctic Circle. Cap. Reykjavík. Pop. 266,000. —**Ice′land•er** *n.*

Ice•land•ic (īs-lăn′dĭk) ►*adj.* Of or relating to Iceland or its people or language. ►*n.* The Germanic language of Iceland.

ice milk ►*n.* A frozen dessert prepared from milk products, containing less butterfat than ice cream.

ice pack ►*n.* **1.** A floating mass of compacted ice fragments. **2.** A sac filled with crushed ice and applied to sore or swollen parts of the body.

ice pick ►*n.* An awl for chipping or breaking ice.

ice skate ►*n.* A boot with a metal blade fitted to the sole, used for skating on ice. —**ice′-skate′** *v.* —**ice skater** *n.*

ice storm ►*n.* A storm in which snow or rain freezes on contact.

ichthyo– or **ichthy–** ►*pref.* Fish: *ichthyology.* [< Gk. *ikhthus*, fish.]

ich•thy•ol•o•gy (ĭk′thē-ŏl′ə-jē) ►*n.* The branch of zoology that studies fishes. —**ich′thy•o•log′ic** (-ə-lŏj′ĭk), **ich′thy•o•log′i•cal** *adj.* —**ich′thy•ol′o•gist** *n.*

ich•thy•o•saur (ĭk′thē-ə-sôr′) also **ich•thy•o•sau•rus** (ĭk′thē-ə-sôr′əs) ►*n.* An extinct fishlike marine reptile of the Mesozoic Era having an elongated, toothed snout. [ICHTHYO– + Gk. *sauros*, lizard.]

–ician ►*suff.* One who practices; a specialist: *beautician.* [< OFr. *-icien.*]

i•ci•cle (ī′sĭ-kəl) ►*n.* **1.** A tapering spike of ice formed by the freezing of dripping water. **2.** *Informal* An aloof person. [ME *isikel.*]

ic•ing (ī′sĭng) ►*n.* A sweet glaze used on cakes and cookies.

i•con (ī′kŏn′) ►*n.* **1.** An image or representation. **2.** A religious painting, usu. on wood, venerated in some Christian churches. **3.** *Comp. Sci.* A picture on a screen that represents a specific file, directory, window, or program. [< Gk. *eikōn*, likeness.]

i•con•o•clast (ī-kŏn′ə-klăst′) ►*n.* **1.** One who attacks traditional ideas or institutions. **2.** One who destroys sacred images. [< Med.Gk. *eikonoklastēs.*] —**i•con′o•clasm′** *n.* —**i•con′o•clas′tic** *adj.* —**i•con′o•clas′ti•cal•ly** *adv.*

–ics ►*suff.* **1.** Study; knowledge; skill: *graphics.* **2.** Actions, activities, or practices of: *athletics.* **3.** Qualities or operations of: *mechanics.* [< –IC.]

ic•tus (ĭk′təs) ►*n.*, *pl.* **-tus** or **-tus•es** *Medic.* A sudden seizure. [Lat., stroke.]

ICU ►*abbr.* intensive care unit

ic•y (ī′sē) ►*adj.* **-i•er, -i•est 1.** Containing or covered with ice. **2.** Bitterly cold; freezing. See Syns at **cold. 3.** Chilling in manner: *an icy smile.* —**ic′i•ly** *adv.* —**ic′i•ness** *n.*

id (ĭd) ►*n.* In psychoanalysis, the part of the psyche that is the source of instinctual impulses and demands for satisfaction of primitive needs. [< Lat., it.]

ID[1] (ī′dē′) *Informal* ►*n.* A form of identification, such as a card or passport. ►*v.* **ID′ed, ID′•ing.** To check the identification of; card.

ID[2] ►*abbr.* **1.** also **Id.** Idaho **2.** identification

id. ►*abbr.* idem

I'd (īd) ► **1.** I had. **2.** I would. **3.** I should.

I•da (ī′də), **Mount.** A peak, 2,457.7 m (8,058 ft), of central Crete.

I•da•ho (ī′də-hō′) A state of the NW US. Cap. Boise. Pop. 1,011,986. —**I′da•ho′an** *adj. & n.*

–ide ►*suff.* **1.** Chemical compound: *chloride.* **2.** Chemical element with properties similar to another: *lanthanide.* [< (OX)IDE.]

i•de•a (ī-dē′ə) ►*n.* **1.** Something, such as a thought, that exists in the mind as a product of mental activity. **2.** An opinion, conviction, or principle. **3.** A plan, scheme, or method. **4.** A general meaning or purport. [< Gk.]

i•de•al (ī-dē′əl, ī-dēl′) ►*n.* **1.** A concept of something as perfect. **2.** A standard of perfection or excellence. **3.** An ultimate objective; goal. **4.** An honorable or worthy principle. ►*adj.* **1.** Of or embodying an ideal. **2.** Considered the best of its kind. **3.** Completely satisfactory. **4.** Existing only in the mind; imaginary. [< LLat. *ideālis* < Lat. *idea.*] —**i•de′al•ly** *adv.*

i•de•al•ism (ī-dē′ə-lĭz′əm) ►*n.* **1.** The practice of envisioning things in an ideal form. **2.** Pursuit of one's ideals. **3.** *Philos.* The theory that things, in themselves or as perceived, consist of ideas. —**i•de′al•ist** *n.* —**i•de′al•is′tic** *adj.* —**i•de′al•is′ti•cal•ly** *adv.*

i•de•al•ize (ī-dē′ə-līz′) ►*v.* **-ized, -iz•ing.** To regard, envision, or represent as ideal. —**i•de′al•i•za′tion** *n.* —**i•de′al•iz′er** *n.*

i•de•ate (ī′dē-āt′) ►*v.* **-at•ed, -at•ing.** To form an idea (of). —**i′de•a′tion** *n.* —**i′de•a′tion•al** *adj.*

i•dem (ī′dĕm′) ►*pron.* Something mentioned previously. [Lat. *īdem* < *id*, it.]

i•den•ti•cal (ī-dĕn′tĭ-kəl) ►*adj.* **1.** Being the same. **2.** Exactly equal and alike. **3.** *Biol.* Of or relating to a twin or twins developed from the same ovum. [< Med.Lat. *identicus.*] —**i•den′ti•cal•ly** *adv.* —**i•den′ti•cal•ness** *n.*

i•den•ti•fi•ca•tion (ī-dĕn′tə-fĭ-kā′shən) ►*n.* **1.** The act of identifying. **2.** The state of being identified. **3.** Proof of identity. **4.** *Psychol.* A person's association with the characteristics or views of another person.

i•den•ti•fy (ī-dĕn′tə-fī′) ►*v.* **-fied, -fy•ing 1.** To establish the identity of. **2.** To ascertain the origin, nature, or characteristics of. **3.** To equate. **4.** To associate (oneself) closely with a person or group. [Med.Lat. *identificāre*, make the same as.] —**i•den′ti•fi′a•ble** *adj.* —**i•den′ti•fi′a•bly** *adv.*

i•den•ti•ty (ī-dĕn′tĭ-tē) ►*n., pl.* **-ties 1.** The collective aspect of the set of characteristics by which a thing is definitively recognizable or known. **2.** The set of characteristics by which an individual is recognizable. **3.** The quality or condition of being the same as something else. **4.** *Math.* An equation satisfied by any number that replaces the letter for which the equation is defined. [< LLat. *identitās.*]

identity element ►*n. Math.* The element of a set of numbers that when combined with another number in an operation leaves that number unchanged: *Zero is the identity element under addition for the real numbers.*

ideo– ►*pref.* Idea: *ideogram.* [< Gk. *idea*, idea.]

id•e•o•gram (ĭd′ē-ə-grăm′, ī′dē-) ►*n.* **1.** A character or symbol representing an idea or a thing without expressing the pronunciation of a particular word or words for it. **2.** A graphic symbol, such as &, $, or @. —**id′e•o•gram•mat′ic** (-grə-măt′ĭk) *adj.* —**id′e•o•gram•mat′i•cal•ly** *adv.*

i•de•o•logue (ī′dē-ə-lôg′, -lŏg′, ĭd′ē-) ►*n.* An advocate of a particular ideology. [Fr. *idéologue* < *idéologie*, ideology.]

i•de•ol•o•gy (ī′dē-ŏl′ə-jē, ĭd′ē-) ►*n., pl.* **-gies 1.** The body of ideas reflecting the social needs and aspirations of an individual, group, class, or culture. **2.** A systematic set of doctrines or beliefs. —**i′de•o•log′i•cal** (ī′dē-ə-lŏj′ĭ-kəl, ĭd′ē-) *adj.* —**i′de•o•log′i•cal•ly** *adv.* —**i′de•ol′o•gist** *n.*

ides (īdz) ►*pl.n. (takes sing. or pl. v.)* The 15th day of March, May, July, or October or the 13th day of the other months in the ancient Roman calendar. [< Lat. *īdūs.*]

id•i•o•cy (ĭd′ē-ə-sē) ►*n., pl.* **-cies 1.** Extreme folly or stupidity. **2.** The condition of profound mental retardation. [< IDIOT.]

id•i•om (ĭd′ē-əm) ►*n.* **1.** An expression having a meaning that cannot be understood from the individual meanings of its elements, as in *hand over fist.* **2.** The specific grammatical, syntactic, and structural character of a given language. **3.** Regional speech or dialect. [< Gk. *idiōma* < *idios*, one's own.] —**id′i•o•mat′ic** (-ə-măt′ĭk) *adj.* —**id′i•o•mat′i•cal•ly** *adv.*

id•i•op•a•thy (ĭd′ē-ŏp′ə-thē) ►*n.* A disease of unknown cause. [Gk. *idios*, one's own + –PATHY.] —**id′i•o•path′ic** (-ə-păth′ĭk) *adj.*

id•i•o•syn•cra•sy (ĭd′ē-ō-sĭng′krə-sē) ►*n., pl.* **-sies.** A structural or behavioral peculiarity; eccentricity. [Gk. *idiosunkrasia.*] —**id′i•o•syn•crat′ic** (-sĭn-krăt′ĭk) *adj.* —**id′i•o•syn•crat′i•cal•ly** *adv.*

id•i•ot (ĭd′ē-ət) ►*n.* **1.** A foolish or stupid person. **2.** A person of profound mental retardation, gen. unable to learn connected speech or guard against common dangers. No longer in use. [< Gk. *idiōtēs*, layman < *idios*, private.] —**id′i•ot′ic** (-ŏt′ĭk) *adj.* —**id′i•ot′i•cal•ly** *adv.*

i•dle (īd′l) ►*adj.* **i•dler, i•dlest 1a.** Not employed or busy. **b.** Avoiding work or employment; lazy. See Syns at **lazy. c.** Not in use or operation. **2.** Lacking substance or basis. See Syns at **baseless, vain.** ►*v.* **i•dled, i•dling 1.** To pass time without working. **2.** To move lazily. **3.** To run or cause to run at a slow speed or out of gear. [< OE *īdel.*] —**i′dle•ness** *n.* —**i′dler** *n.* —**i′dly** *adv.*

i•dol (īd′l) ►*n.* **1.** An image used as an object of worship. **2.** One that is adored. [< Gk. *eidōlon*, image < *eidos*, form.]

i•dol•a•try (ī-dŏl′ə-trē) ►*n., pl.* **-tries 1.** Worship of idols. **2.** Excessive devotion. [Ult. < Gk. *eidōlolatria* : *eidōlon*, IDOL + *latreia*, service.] —**i•dol′a•ter** *n.* —**i•dol′a•trous** *adj.* —**i•dol′a•trous•ly** *adv.*

i•dol•ize (īd′l-īz′) ►*v.* **-ized, -iz•ing 1.** To regard with excessive admiration or devotion. **2.** To worship as an idol. —**i′dol•i•za′tion** *n.* —**i′dol•iz′er** *n.*

i•dyll also **i•dyl** (īd′l) ►*n.* **1.** A short poem idealizing rural life. **2.** A scene or event of a simple and tranquil nature. **3.** A romantic interlude. [< Gk. *eidullion*, dim. of *eidos*, form.] —**i•dyl′lic** (ī-dĭl′ĭk) *adj.* —**i•dyl′li•cal•ly** *adv.*

IE ►*abbr.* **1.** Indo-European **2.** industrial engineer **3.** industrial engineering

i.e. ►*abbr. Lat.* id est (that is)

–ie ►*suff.* Var. of **–y³**.

if (ĭf) ►*conj.* **1a.** In the event that: *If I were to go, I would be late.* **b.** Granting that: *If that is true, what can we do?* **c.** On the condition that: *She will sing only if she is paid.* **2.** Even though: *a handsome if useless trinket.* **3.** Whether: *Ask if he plans to come.* **4.** Used to introduce an exclamatory clause, indicating a wish: *If only he were here!* ►*n.* A possibility, condition, or stipulation: *no ifs, ands, or buts.* [< OE *gif.*]

Usage: In spoken English there is a growing tendency to use *would have* in place of the subjunctive in contrary-to-fact clauses, as in *if I would have been the President,* but this usage is still widely considered incorrect.

IF ►*abbr.* intermediate frequency

if•fy (ĭf′ē) ►*adj.* **-fi•er, -fi•est** *Informal.* Doubtful; uncertain: *an iffy proposition.* —**if′fi•ness** *n.*

–ify ►*suff.* Var. of **–fy.**

Ig ►*abbr.* immunoglobulin

IG ►*abbr.* inspector general

ig•loo (ĭg′lo͞o) ►*n., pl.* **-loos.** An Inuit or Eskimo dwelling, esp. one built of blocks of packed snow. [Inuit *iglu*, house.]

Ig•na•tius of Loy•o•la (ĭg-nā′shəs, loi-ō′lə), Saint. 1491–1556. Spanish ecclesiastic who founded the Jesuits.

ig•ne•ous (ĭg′nē-əs) ►*adj.* **1.** Of or relating to fire. **2.** *Geol.* Formed by solidification from a molten state. [< Lat. *igneus* < *ignis*, fire.]

ig•nis fat•u•us (ĭg′nĭs făch′o͞o-əs) ►*n., pl.* **ig•nes fat•u•i** (ĭg′nēz făch′o͞o-ī′) **1.** A phosphorescent light that hovers over swampy ground at night. **2.** An illusion. [Med.Lat., foolish fire.]

ig•nite (ĭg-nīt′) ►*v.* **-nit•ed, -nit•ing 1.** To set fire to or catch fire. **2.** To excite; kindle. [< Lat. *ignis*, fire.]

ig•ni•tion (ĭg-nĭsh′ən) ►*n.* **1.** An act or instance of igniting. **2.** An electrical system that provides the spark to ignite the fuel mixture in an internal-combustion engine.

ig•no•ble (ĭg-nō′bəl) ►*adj.* **1.** Not noble in quality or purpose; base or mean. **2.** Not of the nobility; common. [< Lat. *ignōbilis.*] —**ig′no•bil′i•ty** *n.* —**ig•no′bly** *adv.*

ig•no•min•y (ĭg′nə-mĭn′ē, -mə-nē) ►*n., pl.* **-ies 1.** Great personal dishonor or humiliation. **2.** Shameful or disgraceful action, conduct, or character. [< Lat. *ignōminia.*] —**ig′no•min′i•**

ous *adj.* —**ig′no•min′i•ous•ly** *adv.*

ig•no•ra•mus (ĭg′nə-rā′məs) ▸*n., pl.* **-mus•es.** An ignorant person. [< Lat. *ignōrāmus*, we do not know.]

ig•no•rant (ĭg′nər-ənt) ▸*adj.* **1.** Lacking education or knowledge. **2.** Demonstrating a lack of education or knowledge. **3.** Unaware or uninformed. [< Lat. *ignōrāre*, not know.] —**ig′nor•ance** *n.* —**ig′no•rant•ly** *adv.*

ig•nore (ĭg-nôr′, -nōr′) ▸*v.* **-nored, -nor•ing.** To refuse to pay attention to; disregard. [< Lat. *ignōrāre*, not know.] —**ig•nor′a•ble** *adj.* —**ig•nor′er** *n.*

I•gua•zú (ē′gwə-zo͞o′) also **I•gua•çú** (-so͞o′). A river, about 1,199 km (745 mi), of S Brazil flowing to the Paraná R. at the Argentina–Paraguay–Brazil border. Just above the border it forms **Iguazú Falls,** about 61 m (200 ft).

i•gua•na (ĭ-gwä′nə) ▸*n.* A large tropical American lizard. [< Arawak *iwana.*]

ihp or **i.hp.** ▸*abbr.* indicated horsepower

Ijs•sel or **IJs•sel** (ī′səl). A river, about 113 km (70 mi), of E Netherlands flowing from the Lower Rhine R. N to the Ijsselmeer.

Ijs•sel•meer or **IJs•sel•meer** (ī′səl-mâr′, -mär′). A lake of NW Netherlands formed by the diking of Zuider Zee.

IL ▸*abbr.* Illinois

il– ▸*pref.* Var. of **in–**[1].

–ile ▸*suff.* Of, relating to, or capable of: *infantile.* [< Lat. *-ilis.*]

il•e•i•tis (ĭl′ē-ī′tĭs) ▸*n.* Inflammation of the ileum. [ILE(UM) + –ITIS.]

il•e•um (ĭl′ē-əm) ▸*n., pl.* **-e•a** (-ē-ə). The portion of the small intestine extending from the jejunum to the cecum. [LLat. *īleum*, groin.] —**il′e•al** *adj.*

ILGWU ▸*abbr.* International Ladies' Garment Workers' Union

il•i•um (ĭl′ē-əm) ▸*n., pl.* **-i•a** (-ē-ə). The uppermost of the three fused bones constituting either half of the pelvis. [LLat. *īlium*, groin, flank.] —**il′i•ac′** (-ăk′) *adj.*

ilk (ĭlk) ▸*n.* Type or kind: *a remark of that ilk.* [< OE *ilca*, same.]

ill (ĭl) ▸*adj.* **worse** (wûrs), **worst** (wûrst) **1a.** Not healthy; sick. **b.** Unsound; bad: *ill health.* **2.** Resulting in suffering; distressing. **3.** Hostile or unfriendly. **4.** Not favorable; unpropitious: *ill omen.* **5.** Not measuring up to standard: *ill treatment.* ▸*adv.* **worse, worst 1.** In a sickly manner; not well. **2.** Scarcely or with difficulty. ▸*n.* **1.** Evil. **2.** Disaster or harm. **3.** Something that causes suffering. [< ON *illr*, bad.]

Ill. ▸*abbr.* Illinois

I'll (īl) ▸ **1.** I will. **2.** I shall.

ill-ad•vised (ĭl′əd-vīzd′) ▸*adj.* Done without wise counsel or careful deliberation. —**ill′-ad•vis′ed•ly** (-vī′zĭd-lē) *adv.*

Il•lam•pu (ē-yäm′po͞o) A peak, 6,366.3 m (20,873 ft), in the Andes of W Bolivia NW of La Paz.

ill at ease ▸*adj.* Nervously uncomfortable.

ill-bred (ĭl′brĕd′) ▸*adj.* Badly brought up; impolite and crude.

ill-con•sid•ered (ĭl′kən-sĭd′ərd) ▸*adj.* Unwise; foolish.

il•le•gal (ĭ-lē′gəl) ▸*adj.* **1.** Prohibited by law. **2.** *Sports & Games* Prohibited by official rules. **3.** *Comp. Sci.* Not performable by a computer. ▸*n.* An illegal immigrant. —**il′le•gal′i•ty** (ĭl′ē-găl′ĭtē) *n.* —**il•le′gal•ly** *adv.*

il•leg•i•ble (ĭ-lĕj′ə-bəl) ▸*adj.* Not legible. —**il•leg′i•bil′i•ty** *n.* —**il•leg′i•bly** *adv.*

il•le•git•i•mate (ĭl′ĭ-jĭt′ə-mĭt) ▸*adj.* **1.** Illegal. **2.** Born out of wedlock. **3.** Incorrectly deduced; illogical. —**il′le•git′i•ma•cy** *n.* —**il′le•git′i•mate•ly** *adv.*

ill-fat•ed (ĭl′fā′tĭd) ▸*adj.* **1.** Destined for misfortune; doomed. **2.** Disastrous; unlucky. See Syns at **unfortunate.**

ill-fa•vored (ĭl′fā′vərd) ▸*adj.* **1.** Ugly or unattractive. See Syns at **ugly. 2.** Objectionable; offensive.

ill-found•ed (ĭl′foun′dĭd) ▸*adj.* Having no factual basis.

ill-got•ten (ĭl′gŏt′n) ▸*adj.* Obtained by dishonest or immoral means: *ill-gotten gains.*

ill-hu•mored (ĭl′hyo͞o′mərd) ▸*adj.* Irritable; surly. —**ill′-hu′mored•ly** *adv.*

il•lib•er•al (ĭ-lĭb′ər-əl) ▸*adj.* Narrow-minded; bigoted. —**il•lib′er•al′i•ty** (-ə-răl′ĭ-tē), **il•lib′er•al•ness** *n.*

il•lic•it (ĭ-lĭs′ĭt) ▸*adj.* Not permitted by custom or law; unlawful. —**il•lic′it•ly** *adv.*

il•lim•it•a•ble (ĭ-lĭm′ĭ-tə-bəl) ▸*adj.* Limitless. See Syns at **infinite.** —**il•lim′it•a•bly** *adv.*

Il•li•nois[1] (ĭl′ə-noi′) ▸*n., pl.* **-nois 1.** A member of a Native American confederacy formerly inhabiting parts of Wisconsin, Illinois, Iowa, and Missouri. **2.** The Algonquian language of the Illinois.

Il•li•nois[2] (ĭl′ə-noi′) A state of the N-central US. Cap. Springfield. Pop. 11,466,682. —**Il′li•nois′an** (-noi′ən) *adj. & n.*

il•lit•er•ate (ĭ-lĭt′ər-ĭt) ▸*adj.* **1.** Having little or no formal education, esp. unable to read and write. **2.** Unfamiliar with language and literature. **3.** Ignorant of the fundamentals of a given art or branch of knowledge. —**il•lit′er•a•cy** *n.* —**il•lit′er•ate** *n.*

ill-man•nered (ĭl′măn′ərd) ▸*adj.* Lacking good manners; rude.

ill-na•tured (ĭl′nā′chərd) ▸*adj.* Surly; disagreeable. —**ill′-na′tured•ly** *adv.*

ill•ness (ĭl′nĭs) ▸*n.* Sickness.

il•log•i•cal (ĭ-lŏj′ĭ-kəl) ▸*adj.* Contradicting or disregarding the principles of logic. —**il•log′i•cal′i•ty** (-kăl′ĭ-tē) *n.* —**il•log′i•cal•ly** *adv.*

ill-starred (ĭl′stärd′) ▸*adj.* Ill-fated; unlucky. See Syns at **unfortunate.**

ill-tem•pered (ĭl′tĕm′pərd) ▸*adj.* Having a bad temper; irritable. —**ill′-tem′pered•ly** *adv.*

ill-treat (ĭl′trēt′) ▸*v.* To treat unkindly or harshly; maltreat. —**ill′-treat′ment** *n.*

il•lu•mi•nate (ĭ-lo͞o′mə-nāt′) ▸*v.* **-nat•ed, -nat•ing 1.** To provide or brighten with light. **2.** To make understandable; clarify. **3.** To enable to understand; enlighten. **4.** To adorn (a page of a book) with designs in brilliant colors. [< Lat. *illūmināre.*] —**il′lu•mi•na′tion** *n.* —**il•lu′mi•na′tor** *n.*

il•lu•mine (ĭ-lo͞o′mĭn) ▸*v.* **-mined, -min•ing.** To give light to; illuminate. [< Lat. *illūmināre.*]

ill-us•age (ĭl′yo͞o′sĭj, -zĭj) ▸*n.* Bad treatment; ill-use.

ill-use (ĭl′yo͞oz′) ▸*v.* To treat badly or unjustly; maltreat. —**ill′-use′** (ĭl′yo͞os′) *n.*

il•lu•sion (ĭ-lo͞o′zhən) ▸*n.* **1a.** An erroneous perception of reality. **b.** An erroneous concept or belief. **2.** Illusionism. **3.** A misleading visual image. [< Lat. *illūdere, illūs-*, to mock.] —**il•lu′sion•al, il•lu′sion•ar′y** (-zhə-nĕr′ē) *adj.*

il•lu•sion•ism (ĭ-lo͞o′zhə-nĭz′əm) ▸*n.* The use of techniques such as foreshortening to produce the illusion of reality, esp. in visual art. —**il•lu′sion•ist** *n.* —**il•lu′sion•is′tic** *adj.*

il•lu•sive (ĭ-lo͞o′sĭv) ▸*adj.* Illusory. —**il•lu′sive•ly** *adv.* —**il•lu′sive•ness** *n.*

il•lu•so•ry (ĭ-lo͞o′sə-rē, -zə-rē) ▸*adj.* Produced by or based on an illusion; deceptive.

il•lus•trate (ĭl′ə-strāt′, ĭ-lŭs′trāt′) ▸*v.* **-trat•ed, -trat•ing 1a.** To clarify, as by use of examples. **b.** To serve as an instructive example of. **2.** To provide (a publication) with explanatory or decorative graphic features. [Lat. *illūstrāre.*] —**il′lus•tra′tor** *n.*

il•lus•tra•tion (ĭl′ə-strā′shən) ▸*n.* **1a.** The act of illustrating. **b.** The state of being illustrated. **2.** Material used to clarify; example. **3.** Visual matter used to explain or decorate a text.

il•lus•tra•tive (ĭ-lŭs′trə-tĭv, ĭl′ə-strā′tĭv) ▸*adj.* Acting or serving as an illustration.

il•lus•tri•ous (ĭ-lŭs′trē-əs) ▸*adj.* Highly distinguished; eminent. See Syns at **noted.** [< Lat. *illūstris*, shining.] —**il•lus′tri•ous•ly** *adv.* —**il•lus′tri•ous•ness** *n.*

ill will ▸*n.* Unfriendly feeling; enmity.

Il•lyr•i•a (ĭ-lîr′ē-ə) An ancient region of the Balkan Peninsula on the Adriatic coast. —**Il•lyr′i•an** *adj. & n.*

ILO ▸*abbr.* International Labor Organization

ILS ▸*abbr.* instrument landing system

im–[1] ▸*pref.* Var. of **in–**[1].

im–[2] ▸*pref.* Var. of **in–**[2].

I'm (īm) ▸ I am.

im•age (ĭm′ĭj) ▸*n.* **1.** A reproduction of the form of a person or object, esp. a sculptured likeness. **2.** *Phys.* An optically formed duplicate of an object, esp. one formed by a lens or mirror. **3.** One that closely resembles another. **4.** An outward impression of character, esp. one projected to the public. **5.** A personification: *the image of good health.* **6.** A mental picture of something not real or present. **7a.** A vivid description or representation. **b.** A figure of speech. **c.** A concrete representation evocative of something else: *night as an image of death.* ▸*v.* **-aged, -ag•ing 1.** To make a likeness of. **2.** To mirror or reflect. **3.** To picture mentally; imagine. **4.** To describe, esp. vividly. [< Lat. *imāgō, imāgin-.*]

im•age•ry (ĭm′ĭj-rē) ▸*n., pl.* **-ries 1.** Mental images. **2.** The use of vivid or figurative language to represent objects, actions, or ideas.

i•mag•i•na•ble (ĭ-măj′ə-nə-bəl) ▸*adj.* Capable of being imagined. —**i•mag′i•na•bly** *adv.*

i•mag•i•nar•y (ĭ-măj′ə-nĕr′ē) ▸*adj.* **1.** Having existence only in the imagination. **2.** *Math.* Of or being an imaginary number.

imaginary number ▸*n. Math.* A complex number in which the real part is zero and the coefficient of the imaginary unit is not zero.

imaginary unit ▸*n. Symbol* **i** The square root of −1.

i•mag•i•na•tion (ĭ-măj′ə-nā′shən) ▸*n.* **1.** The formation of a mental image of something not real or present. **2.** Creative power. **3.** Resourcefulness. —**i•mag′i•na•tive** (ĭ-măj′ə-nə-tĭv, -nā′tĭv) *adj.* —**i•mag′i•na•tive•ly** *adv.* —**i•mag′i•na•tive•ness** *n.*

i•mag•ine (ĭ-măj′ĭn) ▸*v.* **-ined, -in•ing 1.** To form a mental image of. **2.** To think; conjecture. **3.** To fancy. [< Lat. *imāginārī.*]

i•ma•go (ĭ-mā′gō, ĭ-mä′-) ▸*n., pl.* **-goes** or **-gi•nes** (-gə-nēz′). An insect in its sexually mature adult stage. [Lat. *imāgō*, image.]

i•mam also **I•mam** (ĭ-mäm′) ▸*n. Islam* The caliph who is successor to Muhammad as the leader of the Islamic community. [Ar. *'imām.*]

im•bal•ance (ĭm-băl′əns) ▸*n.* A lack of balance, as in distribution. —**im•bal′anced** *adj.*

im•be•cile (ĭm′bə-sĭl, -səl) ▸*n.* **1.** A stupid or silly person. **2.** *Psychol.* A person of moderate to severe mental retardation. No longer in use. [< Lat. *imbēcillus.*] —**im′be•cil′ic** *adj.* —**im′be•cil′i•ty** *n.*

im•bed (ĭm-bĕd′) ▸*v.* Var. of **embed.**

im•bibe (ĭm-bīb′) ▸*v.* **-bibed, -bib•ing 1.** To drink. **2.** To absorb or take in as if by drinking. [< Lat. *imbibere*, drink in.] —**im•bib′er** *n.*

im•bro•glio (ĭm-brōl′yō) ▸*n., pl.* **-glios 1a.** A difficult or intricate situation. **b.** A confused or complicated disagreement. **2.** A confused heap; tangle. [Ital.]

im•bue (ĭm-byo͞o′) ▸*v.* **-bued, -bu•ing 1.** To permeate or invade. See Syns at **charge. 2.** To stain or dye deeply. [< Lat. *imbuere.*]

IMF ▸*abbr.* International Monetary Fund

im•i•tate (ĭm′ĭ-tāt′) ▸*v.* **-tat•ed, -tat•ing 1a.** To copy the actions, appearance, mannerisms, or speech of. **b.** To copy or use the style of. **2.** To copy exactly; reproduce. **3.** To appear like; resemble. [Lat. *imitārī.*] —**im′i•ta•ble** *adj.* —**im′i•ta′tor** *n.*

im•i•ta•tion (ĭm′ĭ-tā′shən) ▸*n.* **1.** The act of imitating. **2.** Something derived or copied from an original. —**im′i•ta′tion** *adj.*

im•i•ta•tive (ĭm′ĭ-tā′tĭv) ▸*adj.* **1.** Of or involving imitation. **2.** Not original; derivative. **3.** Tending to imitate. **4.** Onomatopoeic. —**im′i•ta′tive•ly** *adv.*

im•mac•u•late (ĭ-măk′yə-lĭt) ▸*adj.* **1.** Impeccably clean. See Syns at **clean. 2.** Free from stain or blemish; pure. **3.** Free from fault or error. [< Lat. *immaculātus.*] —**im•mac′u•late•ly** *adv.* —**im•mac′u•late•ness** *n.*

im•ma•nent (ĭm′ə-nənt) ▸*adj.* **1.** Existing or remaining within; inherent. **2.** Restricted entirely to the mind; subjective. [< LLat. *immanēre*, remain in.] —**im′ma•nence, im′ma•nen•cy** *n.* —**im′ma•nent•ly** *adv.*

im•ma•te•ri•al (ĭm′ə-tîr′ē-əl) ▸*adj.* **1.** Of no importance; inconsequential. See Syns at **irrelevant. 2.** Having no material body or form. —**im′ma•te′ri•al•ly** *adv.*

Syns: *immaterial, incorporeal, insubstantial, spiritual* ***Ant:*** *material* **adj.**

im•ma•ture (ĭm′ə-tyo͝or′, -to͝or′, -cho͝or′) ▸*adj.* **1.** Not fully grown or developed. **2.** Marked by or suggesting a lack of normal maturity. —**im′ma•ture′ly** *adv.* —**im′ma•tur′i•ty** *n.*

im•meas•ur•a•ble (ĭ-mĕzh′ər-ə-bəl) ▸*adj.* **1.** Impossible to measure. See Syns at **incalculable. 2.** Vast; limitless. —**im•meas′ur•a•bil′i•ty, im•meas′ur•a•ble•ness** *n.* —**im•meas′ur•a•bly** *adv.*

im•me•di•a•cy (ĭ-mē′dē-ə-sē) ▸*n., pl.* **-cies 1.** Directness. **2.** Urgency.

im•me•di•ate (ĭ-mē′dē-ĭt) ▸*adj.* **1.** Occurring at once; instant. **2.** Of or near the present time: *in the immediate future.* **3.** Close at hand; near:

in the immediate vicinity. See Syns at **close. 4.** Next in line: *an immediate successor.* **5.** Occurring without interposition; direct. [< LLat. *immediātus.*] —**im•me′di•ate•ly** *adv.*

im•me•mo•ri•al (ĭm′ə-môr′ē-əl, -mōr′-) ▸*adj.* Reaching beyond the limits of memory, tradition, or history. —**im′me•mo′ri•al•ly** *adv.*

im•mense (ĭ-mĕns′) ▸*adj.* **1.** Extremely large; huge. **2.** Of immeasurable size or extent. **3.** *Informal* Excellent. [< Lat. *immēnsus.*] —**im•mense′ly** *adv.* —**im•men′si•ty** *n.*

im•merse (ĭ-mûrs′) ▸*v.* **-mersed, -mers•ing 1.** To cover completely in a liquid. **2.** To baptize by submerging in water. **3.** To engage deeply; absorb. [< Lat. *immergere.*] —**im•mer′sion** *n.*

im•mesh (ĭm-mĕsh′) ▸*v.* Var. of **enmesh.**

im•mi•grant (ĭm′ĭ-grənt) ▸*n.* **1.** One who immigrates. **2.** A plant or animal that establishes itself in a new area or habitat.

im•mi•grate (ĭm′ĭ-grāt′) ▸*v.* **-grat•ed, -grat•ing.** To enter and settle in a foreign country. See Usage Note at **migrate.** [Lat. *immigrāre.*] —**im′mi•gra′tion** *n.*

im•mi•nent (ĭm′ə-nənt) ▸*adj.* About to occur. [< Lat. *imminēre*, hang over.] —**im′mi•nence** *n.* —**im′mi•nent•ly** *adv.*

im•mo•bile (ĭ-mō′bəl, -bēl′, -bīl′) ▸*adj.* **1.** Immovable; fixed. **2.** Not moving; motionless. —**im′mo•bil′i•ty** (-bĭl′ĭ-tē) *n.*

im•mo•bi•lize (ĭ-mō′bə-līz′) ▸*v.* **-lized, -liz•ing.** To render immobile. —**im•mo′bi•li•za′tion** *n.*

im•mod•er•ate (ĭ-mŏd′ər-ĭt) ▸*adj.* Extreme; excessive. —**im•mod′er•ate•ly** *adv.* —**im•mod′er•ate•ness, im•mod′er•a′tion** *n.*

im•mod•est (ĭ-mŏd′ĭst) ▸*adj.* **1.** Lacking modesty. **2.** Indecent or offensive. —**im•mod′est•ly** *adv.* —**im•mod′es•ty** *n.*

im•mo•late (ĭm′ə-lāt′) ▸*v.* **-lat•ed, -lat•ing 1.** To kill as a sacrifice. **2.** To kill (oneself) by fire. **3.** To destroy. [Lat. *immolāre*, sprinkle with meal.] —**im′mo•la′tion** *n.* —**im′mo•la′tor** *n.*

im•mor•al (ĭ-môr′əl, -mŏr′-) ▸*adj.* Contrary to established moral principles. —**im′mor•al′i•ty** *n.* —**im•mor′al•ly** *adv.*

im•mor•tal (ĭ-môr′tl) ▸*adj.* **1.** Not subject to death. **2.** Having enduring fame; undying. [< Lat. *immortālis.*] —**im•mor′tal** *n.* —**im′mor•tal′i•ty** *n.* —**im•mor′tal•ize′** *v.* —**im•mor′tal•ly** *adv.*

im•mov•a•ble (ĭ-mo͞o′və-bəl) ▸*adj.* **1a.** Impossible to move. **b.** Incapable of movement. **2.** Unyielding; steadfast. **3.** Impassive; insensitive. —**im•mov′a•bil′i•ty** *n.* —**im•mov′a•bly** *adv.*

im•mune (ĭ-myo͞on′) ▸*adj.* **1.** Exempt. **2.** Resistant to infection by a specific pathogen. [< Lat. *immūnis.*] —**im•mun′i•ty** *n.*

immune response ▸*n.* An integrated bodily response to an antigen, esp. one mediated by lymphocytes and involving recognition of antigens by specific antibodies or previously sensitized lymphocytes.

immune system ▸*n.* The integrated body system of organs, tissues, cells, and cell products such as antibodies that differentiates self from nonself and neutralizes potentially pathogenic organisms or substances.

im•mu•nize (ĭm′yə-nīz′) ▸*v.* **-nized, -niz•ing.** To render immune. —**im′mu•ni•za′tion** *n.*

immuno– ▸*pref.* Immune; immunity: *immunology.* [< IMMUNE.]

im•mu•no•de•fi•cien•cy (ĭm′yə-nō-dĭ-fĭsh′ən-sē, ĭ-myo͞o′-) ▸*n., pl.* **-cies.** An inability to develop a normal immune response. —**im′mu•no•de•fi′cient** *adj.*

im•mu•no•glob•u•lin (ĭm′yə-nō-glŏb′yə-lĭn, ĭ-myo͞o′-) ▸*n.* Any of a group of proteins that function as antibodies in the body's immune response.

im•mu•nol•o•gy (ĭm′yə-nŏl′ə-jē) ▸*n.* The branch of medicine dealing with the immune system. —**im′mu•no•log′ic** (-nə-lŏj′ĭk), **im′mu•no•log′i•cal** *adj.* —**im′mu•no•log′i•cal•ly** *adv.* —**im′mu•nol′o•gist** *n.*

im•mu•no•sup•pres•sion (ĭm′yə-nō-sə-prĕsh′ən, ĭ-myo͞o′-) ▸*n.* Suppression of the immune response, as by drugs or radiation. —**im′mu•no•sup•pres′sant** (-prĕs′ənt) *n.* —**im′mu•no•sup•pres′sive** *adj.*

im•mure (ĭ-myo͝or′) ▸*v.* **-mured, -mur•ing 1.** To confine within or as if within walls; imprison. **2.** To build into or entomb within a wall. [Med.Lat. *immūrāre* < Lat. *mūrus*, wall.]

im•mu•ta•ble (ĭ-myo͞o′tə-bəl) ▸*adj.* Not susceptible to change. —**im•mu′ta•bil′i•ty** *n.* —**im•mu′ta•bly** *adv.*

imp (ĭmp) ▸*n.* **1.** A mischievous child. **2.** A small demon. [< OE *impa*, young shoot, ult. < Gk. *emphuein*, implant : EN–[2] + *phuein*, make grow.] —**imp′ish** *adj.* —**imp′ish•ly** *adv.* —**imp′ish•ness** *n.*

im•pact (ĭm′păkt′) ▸*n.* **1.** A collision. **2.** The force transmitted by a collision. **3.** The effect or impression of one thing on another. ▸*v.* (ĭm-păkt′) **1.** To pack firmly together. **2.** To strike forcefully. **3.** To affect or change. [< Lat. *impāctus*, p.part. of *impingere*, push against.] —**im•pac′tion** *n.*

Usage: Despite being in use since the 1930s, the verb *impact* meaning "to affect" has not lost its association with bureaucratic jargon. Fully 95 percent of the Usage Panel disapproves of the verb in phrases like *techniques that have a potential for impacting our health.*

im•pact•ed (ĭm-păk′tĭd) ▸*adj.* Wedged inside the gum in a manner prohibiting eruption into a normal position: *an impacted tooth.*

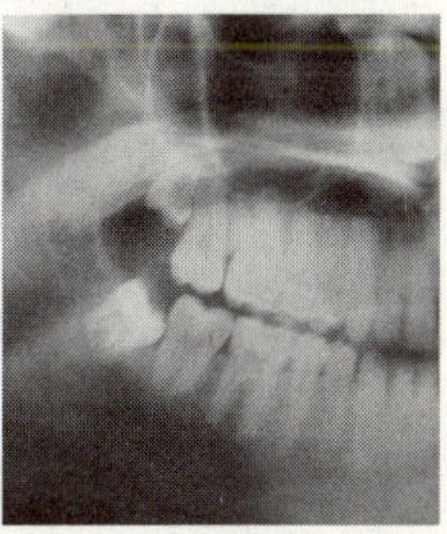

impacted
x-ray of an impacted wisdom tooth in the lower jaw

im•pair (ĭm-pâr′) ▸*v.* To diminish in strength, value, or quality; damage: *The storm impaired communications.* [< VLat. *impēiōrāre*, make worse < Lat. *pēior*, worse.] —**im•pair′ment** *n.*

im•paired (ĭm-pârd′) ►*adj.* **1.** Diminished; weakened: *structurally impaired.* **2.** Functioning poorly or incompetently: *an impaired driver.* **3.** Having a physical or mental disability: *learning-impaired.* ►*n.* People who have a physical or mental disability considered as a group: *the visually impaired.*

im•pa•la (ĭm-pä′lə) ►*n.* An African antelope noted for its leaping ability. [Zulu *im-pala.*]

im•pale (ĭm-pāl′) ►*v.* **-paled, -pal•ing 1.** To pierce with or as if with a sharp point. **2.** To torture or kill by impaling. [Med.Lat. *impālāre* < Lat. *pālus*, stake.] —**im•pale′ment** *n.* —**im•pal′er** *n.*

im•pal•pa•ble (ĭm-păl′pə-bəl) ►*adj.* **1.** Not perceptible to the touch; intangible. **2.** Difficult for the mind to grasp. —**im•pal′pa•bil′i•ty** *n.* —**im•pal′pa•bly** *adv.*

im•pan•el (ĭm-păn′əl) also **em•pan•el** (ĕm-) ►*v.* **-eled, -el•ing** or **-elled, -el•ling.** To enroll (a jury) upon a panel or list. —**im•pan′el•ment** *n.*

im•part (ĭm-pärt′) ►*v.* **1.** To grant a share of; bestow. **2.** To make known; disclose. [< Lat. *impartīre*, share with.]

im•par•tial (ĭm-pär′shəl) ►*adj.* Not partial or biased; unprejudiced. —**im′par•ti•al′i•ty** (-shē-ăl′ĭ-tē) *n.* —**im•par′tial•ly** *adv.*

im•pass•a•ble (ĭm-păs′ə-bəl) ►*adj.* Impossible to pass or cross. —**im•pass′a•bil′i•ty** *n.* —**im•pass′a•bly** *adv.*

im•passe (ĭm′păs′) ►*n.* **1.** A road or passage having no exit. **2.** A situation allowing for no further progress; stalemate. *reached an impasse in the negotiations.* [Fr.]

im•pas•si•ble (ĭm-păs′ə-bəl) ►*adj.* **1.** Not subject to suffering or pain. **2.** Unfeeling.

im•pas•sioned (ĭm-păsh′ənd) ►*adj.* Filled with passion; fervent.

im•pas•sive (ĭm-păs′ĭv) ►*adj.* **1.** Revealing no emotion; expressionless. **2.** Not susceptible to emotion. —**im•pas′sive•ly** *adv.* —**im•pas′sive•ness, im′pas•siv′i•ty** *n.*

im•pa•tiens (ĭm-pā′shənz, -shəns) ►*n.* Any of various plants of a genus which includes the jewelweed. [Lat. *impatiēns*, impatient.]

im•pa•tient (ĭm-pā′shənt) ►*adj.* **1.** Unable to wait patiently or tolerate delay; restless. **2.** Unable to endure opposition; intolerant. **3.** Restively eager or desirous; anxious: *impatient to begin.* —**im•pa′tience** *n.* —**im•pa′tient•ly** *adv.*

im•peach (ĭm-pēch′) ►*v.* **1.** To charge (a public official) with improper conduct in office before a proper tribunal. **2.** To try to discredit; challenge: *impeach a witness's credibility.* [< LLat. *impedicāre*, entangle : IN–[2] + Lat. *pedica*, fetter.] —**im•peach′a•ble** *adj.* —**im•peach′er** *n.* —**im•peach′ment** *n.*

Usage: The verb *impeach* often occurs in popular usage with the meaing "to remove from office," but this use does not accord with the legal meaning of the word, which is limited to the formal accusation of wrongdoing. In strict usage, an official is impeached (accused), tried, and then convicted or acquitted. An official can be impeached and, if acquitted, still remain in office.

im•pec•ca•ble (ĭm-pĕk′ə-bəl) ►*adj.* **1.** Having no flaws. See Syns at **perfect. 2.** Incapable of sin. [Lat. *impeccābilis* : IN–[1] + *peccāre*, to sin.] —**im•pec′ca•bil′i•ty** *n.* —**im•pec′ca•bly** *adv.*

im•pe•cu•ni•ous (ĭm′pĭ-kyo͞o′nē-əs) ►*adj.* Lacking money; penniless. [< IN–[1] + Lat. *pecūnia*, money.] —**im′pe•cu′ni•ous•ly** *adv.* —**im′pe•cu′ni•ous•ness** *n.*

im•ped•ance (ĭm-pēd′ns) ►*n.* *Symbol* **Z** A measure of the total opposition to current flow in an alternating current circuit.

im•pede (ĭm-pēd′) ►*v.* **-ped•ed, -ped•ing.** To retard or obstruct the progress of. [Lat. *impedīre.*] —**im•ped′er** *n.*

im•ped•i•ment (ĭm-pĕd′ə-mənt) ►*n.* **1.** Something that impedes; hindrance or obstruction. **2.** A speech defect preventing clear articulation. [< Lat. *impedīmentum* < *impedīre*, IMPEDE.]

im•ped•i•men•ta (ĭm-pĕd′ə-mĕn′tə) ►*pl.n.* Objects, such as baggage, that impede or encumber. [Lat. *impedīmenta.*]

im•pel (ĭm-pĕl′) ►*v.* **-pelled, -pel•ling 1.** To urge to action. **2.** To drive forward; propel. [< Lat. *impellere*, drive against.]

im•pel•ler (ĭm-pĕl′ər) ►*n.* A rotor or rotor blade.

im•pend (ĭm-pĕnd′) ►*v.* **1.** To be about to take place. **2.** To threaten to happen; menace. [Lat. *impendēre*, hang over.]

im•pen•e•tra•ble (ĭm-pĕn′ĭ-trə-bəl) ►*adj.* **1.** Impossible to penetrate or enter. **2.** Impossible to understand. —**im•pen′e•tra•bil′i•ty** *n.* —**im•pen′e•tra•bly** *adv.*

im•pen•i•tent (ĭm-pĕn′ĭ-tənt) ►*adj.* Not repentant. —**im•pen′i•tence** *n.* —**im•pen′i•tent** *n.* —**im•pen′i•tent•ly** *adv.*

im•per•a•tive (ĭm-pĕr′ə-tĭv) ►*adj.* **1.** Expressing a command or plea. **2.** Having the authority to command or control. **3.** *Gram.* Of or relating to the mood that expresses a command. **4.** Pressing; urgent. [< Lat. *imperāre*, to command.] —**im•per′a•tive** *n.* —**im•per′a•tive•ly** *adv.*

im•per•cep•ti•ble (ĭm′pər-sĕp′tə-bəl) ►*adj.* **1.** Impossible or difficult to perceive. **2.** Insignificantly small or slight. —**im′per•cep′ti•bil′i•ty** *n.* —**im′per•cep′ti•bly** *adv.*

im•per•fect (ĭm-pûr′fĭkt) ►*adj.* **1.** Not perfect. **2.** *Gram.* Of or being a verb tense expressing a past action or condition as incomplete or continuous. ►*n.* *Gram.* **1.** The imperfect tense. **2.** A verb in the imperfect tense. —**im•per′fect•ly** *adv.*

im•per•fec•tion (ĭm′pər-fĕk′shən) ►*n.* **1.** The quality or condition of being imperfect. **2.** A defect; flaw.

im•pe•ri•al (ĭm-pîr′ē-əl) ►*adj.* **1.** Of or relating to an empire, emperor, or empress. **2.** Ruling over extensive territories or over colonies or dependencies. **3.** Regal; majestic. [< Lat. *imperium*, rule.] —**im•pe′ri•al•ly** *adv.*

im•pe•ri•al•ism (ĭm-pîr′ē-ə-lĭz′əm) ►*n.* The policy of extending a nation's authority by economic and political means over other nations. —**im•pe′ri•al•ist** *adj. & n.* —**im•pe′ri•al•is′tic** *adj.* —**im•pe′ri•al•is′ti•cal•ly** *adv.*

im•per•il (ĭm-pĕr′əl) ►*v.* **-iled, -il•ing** or **-illed, -il•ling.** To put into peril. See Syns at **endanger.** —**im•per′il•ment** *n.*

im•pe•ri•ous (ĭm-pîr′ē-əs) ►*adj.* **1.** Arrogantly domineering or overbearing: *lectured in an imperious tone.* **2.** Urgent; pressing. [< Lat. *imperium*, absolute rule.] —**im•pe′ri•ous•ly**

adv. —**im•pe′ri•ous•ness** *n.*
im•per•ish•a•ble (ĭm-pĕr′ĭ-shə-bəl) ▸*adj.* Not perishable. —**im•per′ish•a•bil′i•ty** *n.* —**im•per′ish•a•bly** *adv.*
im•per•ma•nent (ĭm-pûr′mə-nənt) ▸*adj.* Not lasting; transient. —**im•per′ma•nence** *n.* —**im•per′ma•nent•ly** *adv.*
im•per•me•a•ble (ĭm-pûr′mē-ə-bəl) ▸*adj.* Impossible to permeate. —**im•per′me•a•bil′i•ty** *n.* —**im•per′me•a•bly** *adv.*
im•per•mis•si•ble (ĭm′pər-mĭs′ə-bəl) ▸*adj.* Forbidden. —**im′per•mis′si•bil′i•ty** *n.*
im•per•son•al (ĭm-pûr′sə-nəl) ▸*adj.* **1.** Not being a person: *an impersonal force.* **2.** Showing no emotion: *an impersonal manner.* **3.** Having no personal reference or connection. —**im•per′son•al′i•ty** (-sə-năl′ĭ-tē) *n.* —**im•per′son•al•ly** *adv.*
im•per•son•ate (ĭm-pûr′sə-nāt′) ▸*v.* **-at•ed, -at•ing.** To assume the character or appearance of. —**im•per′son•a′tion** *n.* —**im•per′son•a′tor** *n.*
im•per•ti•nent (ĭm-pûr′tn-ənt) ▸*adj.* **1.** Impudent; insolent. **2.** Not pertinent. See Syns at **irrelevant.** —**im•per′ti•nence** *n.* —**im•per′ti•nent•ly** *adv.*
im•per•turb•a•ble (ĭm′pər-tûr′bə-bəl) ▸*adj.* Unshakably calm and collected. —**im′per•turb′a•bil′i•ty** *n.* —**im′per•turb′a•bly** *adv.*
im•per•vi•ous (ĭm-pûr′vē-əs) ▸*adj.* **1.** Incapable of being penetrated, as by water. **2.** Incapable of being affected: *impervious to fear.* —**im•per′vi•ous•ly** *adv.* —**im•per′vi•ous•ness** *n.*
im•pe•ti•go (ĭm′pĭ-tī′gō) ▸*n.* A contagious bacterial skin infection marked by pustules. [< Lat. *impetīgō* < *impetere*, to attack.]
im•pet•u•ous (ĭm-pĕch′o͞o-əs) ▸*adj.* Marked by sudden and forceful energy or emotion; impulsive. [< Lat. *impetus*, IMPETUS.] —**im•pet′u•os′i•ty** (ĭm-pĕch′o͞o-ŏs′ĭ-tē) *n.* —**im•pet′u•ous•ly** *adv.* —**im•pet′u•ous•ness** *n.*
im•pe•tus (ĭm′pĭ-təs) ▸*n.*, *pl.* **-tus•es 1.** An impelling force; impulse. **2.** The force or energy associated with a moving body. **3.** Something that incites; stimulus. [< Lat. *impetere*, go towards, attack.]
im•pi•e•ty (ĭm-pī′ĭ-tē) ▸*n.*, *pl.* **-ties 1.** The quality or state of being impious. **2.** An impious act.
im•pinge (ĭm-pĭnj′) ▸*v.* **-pinged, -ping•ing 1.** To collide or strike. **2.** To encroach; trespass. [Lat. *impingere*, fasten on.] —**im•pinge′ment** *n.* —**im•ping′er** *n.*
im•pi•ous (ĭm′pē-əs, ĭm-pī′-) ▸*adj.* Lacking reverence; not pious. —**im′pi•ous•ly** *adv.* —**im′pi•ous•ness** *n.*
im•plac•a•ble (ĭm-plăk′ə-bəl, -plā′kə-) ▸*adj.* Impossible to reconcile or appease: *implacable foes.* —**im•plac′a•bil′i•ty** *n.* —**im•plac′a•bly** *adv.*
im•plant (ĭm-plănt′) ▸*v.* **1.** To set or fix firmly. **2.** To establish securely, as in the mind; instill. **3.** *Medic.* To insert or embed (a tissue or device) surgically. **4.** To become attached to the uterine lining. Used of a fertilized egg. —**im′plant′** *n.* —**im′plan•ta′tion** *n.*
im•plau•si•ble (ĭm-plô′zə-bəl) ▸*adj.* Difficult to believe; not plausible. —**im•plau′si•bil′i•ty** *n.* —**im•plau′si•bly** *adv.*
im•ple•ment (ĭm′plə-mənt) ▸*n.* A tool or utensil. ▸*v.* (-mĕnt′). To put into effect. [< Lat. *implēre*, fill up.] —**im′ple•men•ta′tion** *n.*
im•pli•cate (ĭm′plĭ-kāt′) ▸*v.* **-cat•ed, -cat•ing 1.** To involve, esp. incriminatingly. **2.** To imply. [< Lat. *implicāre.*] —**im′pli•ca′tion** *n.*
im•plic•it (ĭm-plĭs′ĭt) ▸*adj.* **1.** Implied or understood though not directly expressed. **2.** Contained in the nature of something though not readily apparent. **3.** Having no reservations; unquestioning: *implicit trust.* [Lat. *implicitus* < *implicāre*, implicate.] —**im•plic′it•ly** *adv.* —**im•plic′it•ness** *n.*
im•plode (ĭm-plōd′) ▸*v.* **-plod•ed, -plod•ing.** To burst inward. [IN–[2] + (EX)PLODE.] —**im•plo′sion** (-plō′zhən) *n.*
im•plore (ĭm-plôr′, -plōr′) ▸*v.* **-plored, -plor•ing.** To appeal to; beseech. [Lat. *implōrāre*, weep for.] —**im•plor′ing•ly** *adv.*
im•ply (ĭm-plī′) ▸*v.* **-plied, -ply•ing 1.** To involve by logical necessity; entail. **2.** To express or indicate indirectly. See Usage Note at **infer.** [< Lat. *implicāre*, implicate.]
im•po•lite (ĭm′pə-līt′) ▸*adj.* Not polite; discourteous. —**im′po•lite′ly** *adv.* —**im′po•lite′ness** *n.*
im•pol•i•tic (ĭm-pŏl′ĭ-tĭk) ▸*adj.* Not wise or expedient. —**im•pol′i•tic•ly** *adv.*
im•pon•der•a•ble (ĭm-pŏn′dər-ə-bəl) ▸*adj.* That cannot undergo precise evaluation. —**im•pon′der•a•ble** *n.* —**im•pon′der•a•bil′i•ty** *n.* —**im•pon′der•a•bly** *adv.*
im•port (ĭm-pôrt′, -pōrt′, ĭm′pôrt′, -pōrt′) ▸*v.* **1.** To bring in from an outside source, esp. from a foreign country, for sale. **2.** *Comp. Sci.* To receive (data) from one program into another. **3.** To signify. **4.** To be significant. See Syns at **count[1].** ▸*n.* (ĭm′pôrt′, -pōrt′) **1.** Something imported. **2.** The occupation of importing goods or materials. **3.** Signification. See Syns at **meaning. 4.** Importance; significance. [< Lat. *importāre.*] —**im•port′er** *n.*
im•por•tant (ĭm-pôr′tnt) ▸*adj.* **1.** Strongly affecting the course of events. **2.** Having or suggesting an air of authority; authoritative. [< Lat. *importāre*, be significant.] —**im•por′tance** *n.* —**im•por′tant•ly** *adv.*
im•por•ta•tion (ĭm′pôr-tā′shən, -pōr-) ▸*n.* **1.** The act or business of importing. **2.** Something imported.
im•por•tu•nate (ĭm-pôr′chə-nĭt) ▸*adj.* Troublesomely urgent or persistent. —**im•por′tu•nate•ly** *adv.* —**im•por′tu•nate•ness** *n.*
im•por•tune (ĭm′pôr-to͞on′, -tyo͞on′, ĭm-pôr′chən) ▸*v.* **-tuned, -tun•ing.** To beset with insistent requests. [< Lat. *importūnus*, inopportune.] —**im′por•tune′ly** *adv.* —**im′por•tun′er** *n.* —**im′por•tu′ni•ty** *n.*
im•pose (ĭm-pōz′) ▸*v.* **-posed, -pos•ing 1.** To establish as compulsory; levy: *impose a tax.* **2.** To apply by or as if by authority: *impose a settlement.* See Syns at **dictate. 3.** To force (oneself) on others. **4.** To pass off on others. **5.** To take unfair advantage: *imposing on their generosity.* [< Lat. *impōnere*, place upon.] —**im•pos′er** *n.* —**im′po•si′tion** (ĭm′pə-zĭsh′ən) *n.*
im•pos•ing (ĭm-pō′zĭng) ▸*adj.* Impressive, as in size or power. —**im•pos′ing•ly** *adv.*
im•pos•si•ble (ĭm-pŏs′ə-bəl) ▸*adj.* **1.** Incapable of existing or occurring. **2.** Not capable of

being accomplished. **3.** Unacceptable. **4.** Extremely difficult to deal with or tolerate: *an impossible situation.* —**im•pos′si•bil′i•ty** *n.* —**im•pos′si•bly** *adv.*

im•post (ĭm′pōst′) ►*n.* A tax or duty. [< Med. Lat. *impostum* < Lat. *impōnere*, place upon.]

im•pos•tor (ĭm-pŏs′tər) ►*n.* One who deceives under an assumed identity. [< LLat.]

im•pos•ture (ĭm-pŏs′chər) ►*n.* The act or instance of engaging in deception under an assumed identity. [< LLat. *impostūra* < Lat. *impōnere*, IMPOSE.]

im•po•tent (ĭm′pə-tənt) ►*adj.* **1.** Lacking physical strength or vigor. **2.** Lacking in power; helpless. **3.** *Physiol.* Incapable of penile erection. —**im′po•tence** *n.* —**im′po•tent•ly** *adv.*

im•pound (ĭm-pound′) ►*v.* **1.** To confine in or as if in a pound: *impound stray dogs.* **2.** To seize and retain in legal custody. **3.** To set aside in a fund rather than spend as prescribed. **4.** To accumulate and store (water) in a reservoir. —**im•pound′age, im•pound′ment** *n.*

im•pov•er•ish (ĭm-pŏv′ər-ĭsh) ►*v.* **1.** To reduce to poverty. **2.** To deprive of natural richness or strength. [< OFr. *empovrir* < *povre*, poor.] —**im•pov′er•ish•ment** *n.*

im•prac•ti•ca•ble (ĭm-prăk′tĭ-kə-bəl) ►*adj.* Impossible to do or carry out. See Usage Note at **practicable.** —**im•prac′ti•ca•bil′i•ty** *n.* —**im•prac′ti•ca•bly** *adv.*

im•prac•ti•cal (ĭm-prăk′tĭ-kəl) ►*adj.* **1.** Unwise to implement or maintain in practice. **2.** Unable to deal efficiently with practical matters. **3.** Impracticable. See Usage Note at **practicable.** —**im•prac′ti•cal′i•ty** (-kăl′ĭ-tē), **im•prac′ti•cal•ness** *n.*

im•pre•ca•tion (ĭm′prĭ-kā′shən) ►*n.* A curse. [< Lat. *imprecārī*, to curse.]

im•pre•cise (ĭm′prĭ-sīs′) ►*adj.* Not precise. —**im′pre•cise′ly** *adv.* —**im′pre•ci′sion** (-sĭzh′ən) *n.*

im•preg•na•ble (ĭm-prĕg′nə-bəl) ►*adj.* **1.** Impossible to capture or enter by force. **2.** Beyond challenge or refutation. [< OFr. *imprenable.*]

im•preg•nate (ĭm-prĕg′nāt) ►*v.* **-nat•ed, -nat•ing 1.** To make pregnant; inseminate. **2.** To fertilize (an ovum). **3.** To fill throughout; saturate. **4.** To permeate or imbue. See Syns at **charge.** [Prob. < LLat. *impraegnātus*, pregnant < Lat. *praegnāns.*] —**im′preg•na′tion** *n.* —**im•preg′na′tor** *n.*

im•pre•sa•ri•o (ĭm′prĭ-sär′ē-ō′, -sâr′-) ►*n.*, *pl.* **-os.** One who sponsors or produces entertainment, esp. the director of an opera company. [Ital. < *impresa*, undertaking.]

im•press[1] (ĭm-prĕs′) ►*v.* **1.** To affect strongly, often favorably. **2.** To produce vivid impression of. **3.** To mark or stamp with or as if with pressure. **4.** To apply with pressure. ►*n.* (ĭm′prĕs′) **1.** The act of impressing. **2.** A mark or pattern produced by or as if by impressing. **3.** A stamp or seal to be impressed. [< Lat. *imprimere*, *impress-*, imprint.] —**im•press′i•bil′i•ty** *n.* —**im•press′i•ble** *adj.*

im•press[2] (ĭm-prĕs′) ►*v.* **1.** To compel (a person) to serve in a military force. **2.** To confiscate (property). [IN–[2] + *press*, force into service.] —**im•press′ment** *n.*

im•pres•sion (ĭm-prĕsh′ən) ►*n.* **1.** An effect, feeling, or image retained after an experience. **2.** A vague notion, remembrance, or belief. **3.** A mark produced on a surface by pressure. **4.** *Print.* **a.** All the copies of a publication printed at one time from the same set of type. **b.** A single copy of such a printing. **5.** A humorous imitation esp. of a famous person.

im•pres•sion•a•ble (ĭm-prĕsh′ə-nə-bəl) ►*adj.* Readily or easily influenced; suggestible. —**im•pres′sion•a•bil′i•ty, im•pres′sion•a•ble•ness** *n.*

im•pres•sion•ism (ĭm-prĕsh′ə-nĭz′əm) ►*n.* A style of painting marked by concentration on the immediate visual impression produced by a scene and by the use of unmixed primary colors and small strokes to simulate actual reflected light. —**im•pres′sion•ist** *n.* —**im•pres′sion•is′tic** *adj.* —**im•pres′sion•is′ti•cal•ly** *adv.*

im•pres•sive (ĭm-prĕs′ĭv) ►*adj.* Making a strong or vivid impression; remarkable: *an impressive achievement.* —**im•pres′sive•ly** *adv.* —**im•pres′sive•ness** *n.*

im•pri•ma•tur (ĭm′prə-mä′to͝or, -mā′tər) ►*n.* **1.** Official approval or license to print or publish. **2.** Official approval; sanction. [NLat. *imprimātur*, let it be printed.]

im•print (ĭm-prĭnt′) ►*v.* **1.** To produce (a mark or pattern) on a surface. **2.** To impart a strong impression of. **3.** To fix firmly, as in the mind. ►*n.* (ĭm′prĭnt′) **1.** A mark or pattern produced by imprinting. **2.** A distinguishing influence or effect: *the imprint of Islamic rule.* **3.** A publisher's name, often with the date, address, and edition, printed at the bottom of a title page. [< OFr. *empreinte*, impression.]

im•pris•on (ĭm-prĭz′ən) ►*v.* To put in or as if in prison. [< OFr. *emprisoner.*] —**im•pris′on•a•ble** *adj.* —**im•pris′on•ment** *n.*

im•prob•a•ble (ĭm-prŏb′ə-bəl) ►*adj.* Unlikely to happen or be true. —**im•prob′a•bil′i•ty** *n.* —**im•prob′a•bly** *adv.*

im•promp•tu (ĭm-prŏmp′to͞o, -tyo͞o) ►*adj.* **1.** Prompted by the occasion rather than being planned in advance. **2.** Extemporaneous. [< Lat. *in prōmptū*, in readiness.] —**im•promp′tu** *adv. & n.*

im•prop•er (ĭm-prŏp′ər) ►*adj.* **1.** Not suited to circumstances or needs; unsuitable. **2.** Not in keeping with conventional mores; indecorous. **3.** Not consistent with fact; incorrect. —**im•prop′er•ly** *adv.*

improper fraction ►*n.* A fraction in which the numerator is larger than or equal to the denominator.

im•pro•pri•e•ty (ĭm′prə-prī′ĭ-tē) ►*n.*, *pl.* **-ties 1.** The quality of being improper. **2.** An improper act or expression.

im•prove (ĭm-pro͞ov′) ►*v.* **-proved, -prov•ing 1.** To make or become better. **2.** To increase the productivity or value of (property). [ME *improwen*, to enclose (land) for cultivation.]

im•prove•ment (ĭm-pro͞ov′mənt) ►*n.* **1a.** The act or process of improving. **b.** The state of being improved. **2.** A change or addition that improves.

im•prov•i•dent (ĭm-prŏv′ĭ-dənt) ►*adj.* Not providing for the future; thriftless. —**im•prov′i•dence** *n.* —**im•prov′i•dent•ly** *adv.*

im•pro•vise (ĭm′prə-vīz′) ►*v.* **-vised, -vis•ing 1.** To invent, compose, or recite without preparation. **2.** To make or provide from available materials: *improvised a hasty dinner.* [<

Lat. *imprōvīsus*, unforeseen : IN–[1] + *prōvidēre*, foresee; see PROVIDE.] —**im•prov′i•sa′tion** (ĭm-prŏv′ĭ-zā′shən) *n.* —**im′pro•vis′er** *n.*

im•pru•dent (ĭm-pro͞od′nt) ▸*adj.* Unwise or indiscreet; not prudent. —**im•pru′dence** *n.* —**im•pru′dent•ly** *adv.*

im•pu•dent (ĭm′pyə-dənt) ▸*adj.* Brashly bold; insolent; impertinent. [< Lat. *impudēns*, immodest.] —**im′pu•dence** *n.* —**im′pu•dent•ly** *adv.*

im•pugn (ĭm-pyo͞on′) ▸*v.* To attack as false or questionable; challenge. [< Lat. *impugnāre*, fight against.] —**im•pugn′a•ble** *adj.* —**im•pugn′er** *n.*

im•pulse (ĭm′pŭls′) ▸*n.* **1a.** An impelling force. **b.** The motion produced by such a force. **2.** A sudden wish or urge that prompts an unpremeditated act. **3.** A motivating force. **4.** *Physiol.* The electrochemical transmission of a signal along a nerve fiber that produces a response at a target tissue. [Lat. *impulsus* < p.part. of *impellere*, impel.]

im•pul•sive (ĭm-pŭl′sĭv) ▸*adj.* **1.** Inclined to act on impulse rather than thought. **2.** Resulting from impulse; spontaneous. **3.** Having power to impel. —**im•pul′sive•ly** *adv.* —**im•pul′sive•ness** *n.*

im•pu•ni•ty (ĭm-pyo͞o′nĭ-tē) ▸*n.* Exemption from punishment or penalty. [< Lat. *impūne*, without punishment.]

im•pure (ĭm-pyo͝or′) ▸*adj.* **1.** Not clean; contaminated. **2.** Immoral or sinful. **3.** Mixed with another substance; adulterated. —**im•pure′ly** *adv.* —**im•pure′ness** *n.* —**im•pu′ri•ty** *n.*

im•pute (ĭm-pyo͞ot′) ▸*v.* **-put•ed, -put•ing 1.** To charge with the fault or responsibility for. **2.** To attribute; credit. [< Lat. *imputāre*, reckon in.] —**im•put′a•ble** *adj.* —**im′pu•ta′tion** *n.*

in[1] (ĭn) ▸*prep.* **1.** Within the limits, bounds, or area of. **2.** From the outside to the inside of; into: *threw it in the wastebasket.* **3.** To or at a situation or condition of: *in love.* **4.** Having the activity, occupation, or function of: *a life in politics.* **5.** By means of: *paid in cash.* **6.** With reference to: *six inches in depth.* ▸*adv.* **1.** To or toward the inside. **2.** To or toward a place. **3.** Within a place, as of business or residence. ▸*adj.* **1.** Located inside; inner. **2.** Incoming. **3.** Holding office; having power. **4.** *Informal* Currently fashionable. See Syns at **fashionable.** ▸*n.* **1.** One with position, influence, or power. **2.** *Informal* Influence. [< OE.]

in[2] or **in.** ▸*abbr.* inch

In ▸ The symbol for the element **indium.**

IN ▸*abbr.* Indiana

in–[1] or **il–** or **im–** or **ir–** ▸*pref.* Not: *inarticulate.* [< Lat.]

in–[2] or **im–** or **ir–** ▸*pref.* **1.** In; into; within: *irradiate.* **2.**Var. of **en–**[1]. [< Lat. *in* and OE *in.*]

–in ▸*suff.* **1.** Neutral chemical compound: *globulin.* **2.** Enzyme: *pepsin.* **3.** A pharmaceutical: *niacin.* **4.** An antibiotic: *penicillin.* **5.**Var. of **–ine**[2] 1. [Var. of –INE[2].]

in•a•bil•i•ty (ĭn′ə-bĭl′ĭ-tē) ▸*n.* Lack of ability or means.

in ab•sen•tia (ĭn ăb-sĕn′shə, -shē-ə) ▸*adv.* While or although not present. [Lat. *in absentiā.*]

in•ac•ces•si•ble (ĭn′ăk-sĕs′ə-bəl) ▸*adj.* Not accessible; unapproachable. —**in′ac•ces′si•bil′i•ty** *n.* —**in′ac•ces′si•bly** *adv.*

in•ac•cu•rate (ĭn-ăk′yər-ĭt) ▸*adj.* Mistaken or incorrect; not accurate. —**in•ac′cu•ra•cy** *n.* —**in•ac′cu•rate•ly** *adv.*

in•ac•tion (ĭn-ăk′shən) ▸*n.* Lack or absence of action.

in•ac•ti•vate (ĭn-ăk′tə-vāt′) ▸*v.* **-vat•ed, -vat•ing.** To render inactive. —**in•ac′ti•va′tion** *n.*

in•ac•tive (ĭn-ăk′tĭv) ▸*adj.* **1.** Not active or functioning; idle. **2.** Retired from duty or service. —**in•ac′tive•ly** *adv.* —**in′ac•tiv′i•ty, in•ac′tive•ness** *n.*

in•ad•e•quate (ĭn-ăd′ĭ-kwĭt) ▸*adj.* Not adequate; insufficient. —**in•ad′e•qua•cy** *n.* —**in•ad′e•quate•ly** *adv.*

in•ad•mis•si•ble (ĭn′əd-mĭs′ə-bəl) ▸*adj.* Not admissible. —**in′ad•mis′si•bil′i•ty** *n.* —**in′ad•mis′si•bly** *adv.*

in•ad•ver•tent (ĭn′əd-vûr′tnt) ▸*adj.* **1.** Not duly attentive. **2.** Unintentional. [< Med.Lat. *inadvertentia*, inadvertence.] —**in′ad•ver′tence** *n.* —**in′ad•ver′tent•ly** *adv.*

in•ad•vis•a•ble (ĭn′əd-vī′zə-bəl) ▸*adj.* Not recommended; unwise. —**in′ad•vis′a•bil′i•ty** *n.*

in•al•ien•a•ble (ĭn-āl′yə-nə-bəl, -ā′lē-ə-) ▸*adj.* That cannot be transferred to another. —**in•al′ien•a•bil′i•ty** *n.* —**in•al′ien•a•bly** *adv.*

in•ane (ĭn-ān′) ▸*adj.* **-an•er, -an•est.** Lacking sense or substance. [Lat. *inānis.*] —**in•ane′ly** *adv.* —**in•an′i•ty** (ĭ-năn′ĭ-tē) *n.*

in•an•i•mate (ĭn-ăn′ə-mĭt) ▸*adj.* Lacking the qualities of active, living organisms; not animate. —**in•an′i•mate•ly** *adv.* —**in•an′i•mate•ness** *n.*

in•a•ni•tion (ĭn′ə-nĭsh′ən) ▸*n.* Exhaustion, as from lack of nourishment or vitality. [< Lat. *inānīre*, make empty < *inānis*, empty.]

in•ap•pli•ca•ble (ĭn-ăp′lĭ-kə-bəl, ĭn′ə-plĭk′ə-) ▸*adj.* Not applicable. —**in•ap′pli•ca•bil′i•ty** *n.*

in•ap•pre•cia•ble (ĭn′ə-prē′shə-bəl) ▸*adj.* Too small to be noticed; negligible. —**in′ap•pre′cia•bly** *adv.*

in•ap•pro•pri•ate (ĭn′ə-prō′prē-ĭt) ▸*adj.* Unsuitable or improper; not appropriate. —**in′ap•pro′pri•ate•ly** *adv.* —**in′ap•pro′pri•ate•ness** *n.*

in•apt (ĭn-ăpt′) ▸*adj.* Inappropriate. —**in•apt′ly** *adv.* —**in•apt′ness** *n.*

in•ar•tic•u•late (ĭn′är-tĭk′yə-lĭt) ▸*adj.* **1.** Uttered without the use of normal words or syllables. **2.** Unable to speak; speechless. **3.** Unable to speak with clarity or eloquence. **4.** Going unexpressed: *inarticulate sorrow.* —**in′ar•tic′u•late•ly** *adv.* —**in′ar•tic′u•late•ness** *n.*

in•as•much as (ĭn′əz-mŭch′) ▸*conj.* Because of the fact that; since.

in•at•ten•tion (ĭn′ə-tĕn′shən) ▸*n.* Lack of attention, notice, or regard. —**in′at•ten′tive** *adj.* —**in′at•ten′tive•ly** *adv.* —**in′at•ten′tive•ness** *n.*

in•au•di•ble (ĭn-ô′də-bəl) ▸*adj.* Impossible to hear. —**in•au′di•bil′i•ty** *n.* —**in•au′di•bly** *adv.*

in•au•gu•ral (ĭn-ô′gyər-əl) ▸*adj.* **1.** Of or relating to an inauguration. **2.** Initial; first. ▸*n.* An inaugural speech.

in•au•gu•rate (ĭn-ô′gyə-rāt′) ▸*v.* **-rat•ed, -rat•ing 1.** To induct into office by a formal ceremony. **2.** To begin, esp. formally. **3.** To open with a ceremony; dedicate. [Lat. *inaugurāre* : IN–[2] + *augur*, seer.] —**in•au′gu•ra′tor** *n.*

in•au•gu•ra•tion (ĭn-ô′gyə-rā′shən) ►*n.* **1.** Formal induction into office. **2.** A formal beginning or introduction.

in•aus•pi•cious (ĭn′ô-spĭsh′əs) ►*adj.* Not favorable; not auspicious. —**in′aus•pi′cious•ly** *adv.* —**in′aus•pi′cious•ness** *n.*

in•board (ĭn′bôrd′, -bōrd′) ►*adj.* **1.** Within the hull of a vessel. **2.** Close to the fuselage of an aircraft: *the inboard engines.* —**in′board′** *adv.*

in•born (ĭn′bôrn′) ►*adj.* Hereditary; innate.

in•bound (ĭn′bound′) ►*adj.* Incoming: *inbound traffic.*

in•bred (ĭn′brĕd′) ►*adj.* **1.** Produced by inbreeding. **2.** Innate; deep-seated.

in•breed (ĭn′brēd′) ►*v.* To breed by the continued mating of closely related individuals. —**in′breed′er** *n.*

Inc. ►*abbr.* incorporated

In•ca (ĭng′kə) ►*n., pl.* **-ca** or **-cas** **1.** A member of a Quechuan people who established an empire centered in highland Peru before the Spanish conquest. **2.** A ruler of the Inca empire. —**In′can** *adj.*

in•cal•cu•la•ble (ĭn-kăl′kyə-lə-bəl) ►*adj.* **1.** Impossible to calculate, esp. too great to be conceived. **2.** Unforeseeable; unpredictable. —**in•cal′cu•la•bly** *adv.*

Syns: *incalculable, countless, immeasurable, inestimable, infinite, innumerable* ***Ant:*** *calculable* ***adj.***

in•can•des•cent (ĭn′kən-dĕs′ənt) ►*adj.* **1.** Emitting visible light as a result of being heated. **2.** Shining brilliantly; very bright. [< Lat. *incandēscere*, to glow.] —**in′can•des′cence** *n.* —**in′can•des′cent•ly** *adv.*

incandescent lamp ►*n.* An electric lamp in which a filament is heated to incandescence by an electric current.

in•can•ta•tion (ĭn′kăn-tā′shən) ►*n.* **1.** Ritual recitation of verbal charms or spells to produce a magic effect. **2.** A charm or spell used in ritual recitation. [< Lat. *incantāre*, enchant.] —**in′can•ta′tion•al** *adj.* —**in•can′ta•to′ry** (-tə-tôr′ē, -tōr′ē) *adj.*

in•ca•pa•ble (ĭn-kā′pə-bəl) ►*adj.* Lacking the necessary ability, capacity, or power to perform adequately. —**in•ca′pa•bil′i•ty, in•ca′pa•ble•ness** *n.* —**in•ca′pa•bly** *adv.*

in•ca•pac•i•tate (ĭn′kə-păs′ĭ-tāt′) ►*v.* **-tat•ed, -tat•ing.** To deprive of strength or ability; disable. —**in′ca•pac′i•ta′tion** *n.*

in•ca•pac•i•ty (ĭn′kə-păs′ĭ-tē) ►*n., pl.* **-ties.** Inadequate capacity, strength, or ability.

in•car•cer•ate (ĭn-kär′sə-rāt′) ►*v.* **-at•ed, -at•ing** **1.** To imprison. **2.** To confine. [Med. Lat. *incarcerāre* < Lat. *carcer*, prison.] —**in•car′cer•a′tion** *n.*

in•car•nate (ĭn-kär′nĭt) ►*adj.* **1.** Invested with bodily nature and form. **2.** Personified: *evil incarnate.* ►*v.* (-nāt′) **-nat•ed, -nat•ing** **1.** To give bodily, esp. human, form to. **2.** To personify; embody. [< LLat. *incarnātus*, p.part. of *incarnāre*, make flesh.]

in•car•na•tion (ĭn′kär-nā′shən) ►*n.* **1.** The act of incarnating or condition of being incarnated. **2. Incarnation** The Christian doctrine that God the Son became man. **3.** One who personifies something.

in•case (ĭn-kās′) ►*v.* Var. of **encase.**

in•cau•tious (ĭn-kô′shəs) ►*adj.* Not cautious; rash. —**in•cau′tious•ly** *adv.* —**in•cau′tious•ness** *n.*

in•cen•di•ar•y (ĭn-sĕn′dē-ĕr′ē) ►*adj.* **1.** Producing intensely hot fire, as a military weapon. **2.** Of or involving arson. **3.** Tending to inflame; inflammatory. [< Lat. *incendium*, fire.] —**in•cen′di•ar′y** *n.*

in•cense[1] (ĭn-sĕns′) ►*v.* **-censed, -cens•ing.** To cause to be extremely angry; infuriate. [< Lat. *incendere, incēns-*, set on fire.]

in•cense[2] (ĭn′sĕns′) ►*n.* **1.** An aromatic substance burned to produce a pleasant odor. **2.** The smoke or odor produced by the burning of incense. [< Lat. *incēnsum.*]

in•cen•tive (ĭn-sĕn′tĭv) ►*n.* Something, such as a punishment or reward, that induces action. [< LLat. *incentīvus*, inciting.]

in•cep•tion (ĭn-sĕp′shən) ►*n.* The beginning of something. [< Lat. *incipere, incept-*, take up, begin.] —**in•cep′tive** *adj.*

in•cer•ti•tude (ĭn-sûr′tĭ-to͞od′, -tyo͞od′) ►*n.* **1.** Uncertainty. **2.** Insecurity or instability.

in•ces•sant (ĭn-sĕs′ənt) ►*adj.* Continuing without interruption. [< LLat. *incessāns*, unceasing.] —**in•ces′san•cy** *n.* —**in•ces′sant•ly** *adv.*

in•cest (ĭn′sĕst′) ►*n.* Sexual relations between persons so closely related that their marriage is illegal or forbidden by custom. [< Lat. *incestus*, unchaste.] —**in•ces′tu•ous** (ĭn-sĕs′cho͞o-əs) *adj.* —**in•ces′tu•ous•ly** *adv.* —**in•ces′tu•ous•ness** *n.*

inch (ĭnch) ►*n.* **1.** See table at **measurement.** **2.** A very small degree or amount: *won't budge an inch.* ►*v.* To move or cause to move slowly or by small degrees. —***idiom:*** **every inch** In every respect; entirely. [< Lat. *uncia*, twelfth part.]

in•cho•ate (ĭn-kō′ĭt) ►*adj.* In an initial or early stage; incipient. [< Lat. *inchoāre*, begin.] —**in•cho′ate•ly** *adv.* —**in•cho′ate•ness** *n.*

In•chon (ĭn′chŏn′) A city of NW South Korea on an inlet of the Yellow Sea SW of Seoul. Pop. 2,116,794.

inch•worm (ĭnch′wûrm′) ►*n.* See **measuring worm.**

in•ci•dence (ĭn′sĭ-dəns) ►*n.* Extent or frequency of occurrence.

in•ci•dent (ĭn′sĭ-dənt) ►*n.* **1.** An occurrence; event. **2.** An event that causes a crisis. ►*adj.* **1.** Tending to arise or occur as a result. **2.** *Phys.* Striking a surface: *incident radiation.* [< Lat. *incidere*, happen.]

in•ci•den•tal (ĭn′sĭ-dĕn′tl) ►*adj.* **1.** Occurring or likely to occur as a minor consequence. **2.** Of a minor or casual nature: *incidental expenses.* ►*n.* A minor accompanying item or expense. —**in′ci•den′tal•ly** *adv.*

in•cin•er•ate (ĭn-sĭn′ə-rāt′) ►*v.* **-at•ed, -at•ing.** To consume by fire; burn to ashes. [Med. Lat. *incinerāre* < Lat. *cinis*, ashes.] —**in•cin′er•a′tion** *n.*

in•cin•er•a•tor (ĭn-sĭn′ə-rā′tər) ►*n.* An apparatus for burning waste.

in•cip•i•ent (ĭn-sĭp′ē-ənt) ►*adj.* Beginning to exist or appear. [< Lat. *incipere*, begin.] —**in•cip′i•en•cy, in•cip′i•ence** *n.* —**in•cip′i•ent•ly** *adv.*

in•cise (ĭn-sīz′) ►*v.* **-cised, -cis•ing** **1.** To cut

into or mark with a sharp instrument. **2.** To engrave (e.g., designs) into a surface; carve. [< Lat. *incīdere*, *incīs-*.]
in•ci•sion (ĭn-sĭzh′ən) ►*n.* **1.** The act of incising. **2.** A cut, esp. a surgical cut into soft tissue.
in•ci•sive (ĭn-sī′sĭv) ►*adj.* Penetrating, clear, and sharp: *incisive comments.* —**in•ci′sive•ly** *adv.* —**in•ci′sive•ness** *n.*
in•ci•sor (ĭn-sī′zər) ►*n.* A tooth adapted for cutting or gnawing, located at the apex of the dental arch.
in•cite (ĭn-sīt′) ►*v.* **-cit•ed, -cit•ing.** To provoke to action; stir up: *incite a mob.* [< Lat. *incitāre*, urge forward.] —**in•cite′ment** *n.* —**in•cit′er** *n.*
in•ci•vil•i•ty (ĭn′sĭ-vĭl′ĭ-tē) ►*n.*, *pl.* **-ties.** Rudeness.
incl. ►*abbr.* **1.** including **2.** inclusive
in•clem•ent (ĭn-klĕm′ənt) ►*adj.* **1.** Stormy: *inclement weather.* **2.** Unmerciful. —**in•clem′en•cy** *n.* —**in•clem′ent•ly** *adv.*
in•cli•na•tion (ĭn′klə-nā′shən) ►*n.* **1.** A bend or tilt. **2a.** A slant: *the inclination of the roof.* **b.** An incline; slope. **3.** A tendency or disposition toward something.
in•cline (ĭn-klīn′) ►*v.* **-clined, -clin•ing 1.** To deviate or cause to deviate from the horizontal or vertical. See Syns at **slant. 2.** To dispose or be disposed; tend. **3.** To lower or bend (the head or body), as in a nod or bow. ►*n.* (ĭn′klīn′). An inclined surface; slope. [< Lat. *inclīnāre* : IN-[2] + *-clīnāre*, lean.] —**in•clin′er** *n.*
Syns: *incline, dispose, predispose* ***Ant:*** *disincline* **v.**
in•clined plane (ĭn-klīnd′) ►*n.* A plane set at an angle to the horizontal, esp. a simple machine used in raising or lowering loads.
in•close (ĭn-klōz′) ►*v.* Var. of **enclose.**
in•clude (ĭn-klo͞od′) ►*v.* **-clud•ed, -clud•ing 1.** To have as a part, element, or member; contain. See Usage Note at **comprise. 2.** To place into a group, class, or total. [< Lat. *inclūdere.*] —**in•clu′sion** *n.* —**in•clu′sive** *adj.* —**in•clu′sive•ly** *adv.* —**in•clu′sive•ness** *n.*
in•cog•ni•to (ĭn′kŏg-nē′tō, ĭn-kŏg′nĭ-tō′) ►*adv. & adj.* With one's identity disguised or concealed. [Ital. < Lat. *incognitus*, unknown.]
in•co•her•ent (ĭn′kō-hîr′ənt) ►*adj.* **1.** Lacking cohesion; not coherent. **2.** Unable to express one's thoughts in an orderly manner. —**in′co•her′ence** *n.* —**in′co•her′ent•ly** *adv.* —**in′co•her′ent•ness** *n.*
in•com•bus•ti•ble (ĭn′kəm-bŭs′tə-bəl) ►*adj.* Incapable of burning. —**in′com•bus′ti•bil′i•ty** *n.* —**in′com•bus′ti•ble** *n.* —**in′com•bus′ti•bly** *adv.*
in•come (ĭn′kŭm′) ►*n.* The amount of money or its equivalent received in exchange for labor or services, from the sale of goods or property, or as profit from investments.
income tax ►*n.* A tax levied on net income.
in•com•ing (ĭn′kŭm′ĭng) ►*adj.* Coming in or about to come in.
in•com•men•su•rate (ĭn′kə-mĕn′sər-ĭt, -shər-) ►*adj.* **1.** Not commensurate; disproportionate. **2.** Inadequate. —**in′com•men′su•rate•ly** *adv.*
in•com•mode (ĭn′kə-mōd′) ►*v.* **-mod•ed, -mod•ing.** To inconvenience; disturb.
in•com•mu•ni•ca•do (ĭn′kə-myo͞o′nĭ-kä′dō) ►*adv. & adj.* Without the means or right of communicating with others. [Sp. *incomunicado*, p.part. of *incomunicar*, deny communication to.]
in•com•pa•ra•ble (ĭn-kŏm′pər-ə-bəl) ►*adj.* **1.** Being such that comparison is impossible. **2.** Beyond comparison; unsurpassed. —**in•com′pa•ra•bil′i•ty, in•com′pa•ra•ble•ness** *n.* —**in•com′pa•ra•bly** *adv.*
in•com•pat•i•ble (ĭn′kəm-păt′ə-bəl) ►*adj.* **1.** Not compatible; not in harmony or agreement. **2.** Inconsistent. —**in′com•pat′i•bil′i•ty** *n.* —**in′com•pat′i•bly** *adv.*
in•com•pe•tent (ĭn-kŏm′pĭ-tənt) ►*adj.* Not competent. —**in•com′pe•tence, in•com′pe•ten•cy** *n.* —**in•com′pe•tent** *n.* —**in•com′pe•tent•ly** *adv.*
in•com•plete (ĭn′kəm-plēt′) ►*adj.* Not complete. —**in′com•plete′ly** *adv.* —**in′com•plete′ness, in′com•ple′tion** *n.*
in•com•pre•hen•si•ble (ĭn′kŏm-prĭ-hĕn′sə-bəl, ĭn-kŏm′-) ►*adj.* Impossible to understand; unintelligible. —**in′com•pre•hen′si•bil′i•ty** *n.* —**in′com•pre•hen′si•bly** *adv.* —**in′com•pre•hen′sion** *n.*
in•com•press•i•ble (ĭn′kəm-prĕs′ə-bəl) ►*adj.* Impossible to compress. —**in′com•press′i•bil′i•ty** *n.*
in•con•ceiv•a•ble (ĭn′kən-sē′və-bəl) ►*adj.* **1.** Impossible to comprehend or grasp fully. **2.** Implausible; incredible. —**in′con•ceiv′a•bil′i•ty** *n.* —**in′con•ceiv′a•bly** *adv.*
in•con•clu•sive (ĭn′kən-klo͞o′sĭv) ►*adj.* Not conclusive. —**in′con•clu′sive•ly** *adv.* —**in′con•clu′sive•ness** *n.*
in•con•gru•ent (ĭn-kŏng′gro͞o-ənt, ĭn′kŏn-gro͞o′ənt) ►*adj.* Not congruent. —**in•con′gru•ence** *n.* —**in•con′gru•ent•ly** *adv.*
in•con•gru•ous (ĭn-kŏng′gro͞o-əs) ►*adj.* **1.** Lacking in harmony; incompatible. **2.** Not in keeping with what is correct, proper, or logical; inappropriate. —**in′con•gru′i•ty** (ĭn′kŏn-gro͞o′ĭ-tē) *n.* —**in•con′gru•ous•ly** *adv.* —**in•con′gru•ous•ness** *n.*
in•con•se•quen•tial (ĭn-kŏn′sĭ-kwĕn′shəl, ĭn′kŏn-) ►*adj.* Lacking importance. —**in•con′se•quence** (-kwəns) *n.* —**in•con′se•quen′ti•al′i•ty** (-kwĕn′shē-ăl′ĭ-tē) *n.* —**in•con′se•quen′tial•ly** *adv.*
in•con•sid•er•a•ble (ĭn′kən-sĭd′ər-ə-bəl) ►*adj.* Trivial. —**in′con•sid′er•a•bly** *adv.*
in•con•sid•er•ate (ĭn′kən-sĭd′ər-ĭt) ►*adj.* **1.** Thoughtless of others. **2.** Ill-considered. —**in′con•sid′er•ate•ly** *adv.* —**in′con•sid′er•ate•ness** *n.*
in•con•sis•tent (ĭn′kən-sĭs′tənt) ►*adj.* Displaying a lack of consistency, esp. erratic, contradictory, or incompatible. —**in′con•sis′ten•cy** *n.* —**in′con•sis′tent•ly** *adv.*
in•con•sol•a•ble (ĭn′kən-sō′lə-bəl) ►*adj.* Impossible to console; forlorn. —**in′con•sol′a•bil′i•ty** *n.* —**in′con•sol′a•bly** *adv.*
in•con•spic•u•ous (ĭn′kən-spĭk′yo͞o-əs) ►*adj.* Not readily noticeable. —**in′con•spic′u•ous•ly** *adv.* —**in′con•spic′u•ous•ness** *n.*
in•con•stant (ĭn-kŏn′stənt) ►*adj.* **1.** Changing, esp. often and erratically. **2.** Fickle. —**in•con′stan•cy** *n.* —**in•con′stant•ly** *adv.*
in•con•test•a•ble (ĭn′kən-tĕs′tə-bəl) ►*adj.* Beyond dispute; unquestionable. —**in′con•test′a•bil′i•ty** *n.* —**in′con•test′a•bly** *adv.*
in•con•ti•nent (ĭn-kŏn′tə-nənt) ►*adj.* **1.** Not

restrained. **2.** Lacking normal voluntary control of excretory functions. —**in•con′ti•nence** *n.* —**in•con′ti•nent•ly** *adv.*

in•con•tro•vert•i•ble (ĭn-kŏn′trə-vûr′tə-bəl, ĭn′kŏn-) ▸*adj.* Impossible to dispute; unquestionable. —**in•con′tro•vert′i•bil′i•ty** *n.* —**in•con′tro•vert′i•bly** *adv.*

in•con•ven•ience (ĭn′kən-vēn′yəns) ▸*n.* **1.** The state or quality of being inconvenient. **2.** Something inconvenient. ▸*v.* **-ienced, -ienc•ing.** To cause inconvenience to.

in•con•ven•ient (ĭn′kən-vēn′yənt) ▸*adj.* Not convenient, esp.: **a.** Not accessible. **b.** Not suited to one's purpose or needs. **c.** Inopportune. —**in′con•ven′ient•ly** *adv.*

in•cor•po•rate (ĭn-kôr′pə-rāt′) ▸*v.* **-rat•ed, -rat•ing 1.** To unite or combine (one thing) with something else. **2.** To form or cause to form into a legal corporation. **3.** To give material form to; embody. [< LLat. *incorporāre*, form into a body < *corpus*, body.] —**in•cor′po•ra′tion** *n.* —**in•cor′po•ra′tive** *adj.* —**in•cor′po•ra′tor** *n.*

in•cor•po•re•al (ĭn′kôr-pôr′ē-əl, -pōr′-) ▸*adj.* Lacking material form or substance. See Syns at **immaterial.** —**in′cor•po′re•al′i•ty** (-ăl′ĭ-tē) *n.*

in•cor•rect (ĭn′kə-rĕkt′) ▸*adj.* **1.** Not correct; erroneous. **2.** Improper; inappropriate. —**in′cor•rect′ly** *adv.* —**in′cor•rect′ness** *n.*

in•cor•ri•gi•ble (ĭn-kôr′ĭ-jə-bəl, -kŏr′-) ▸*adj.* Incapable of being corrected or reformed. [< Lat. *incorrigibilis.*] —**in•cor′ri•gi•bil′i•ty, in•cor′ri•gi•ble•ness** *n.* —**in•cor′ri•gi•bly** *adv.*

in•cor•rupt•i•ble (ĭn′kə-rŭp′tə-bəl) ▸*adj.* **1.** Incapable of being morally corrupted. **2.** Not subject to decay. —**in′cor•rupt′i•bil′i•ty** *n.* —**in′cor•rupt′i•bly** *adv.*

in•crease (ĭn-krēs′) ▸*v.* **-creased, -creas•ing 1.** To make or become greater or larger. **2.** To multiply; reproduce. ▸*n.* (ĭn′krēs′) **1.** The act of increasing. **2.** The amount or rate by which something is increased. [< Lat. *incrēscere.*] —**in•creas′ing•ly** *adv.*

in•cred•i•ble (ĭn-krĕd′ə-bəl) ▸*adj.* **1.** So implausible as to elicit disbelief. **2.** Astonishing. —**in•cred′i•bil′i•ty, in•cred′i•ble•ness** *n.* —**in•cred′i•bly** *adv.*

in•cred•u•lous (ĭn-krĕj′ə-ləs) ▸*adj.* **1.** Skeptical; disbelieving. **2.** Expressive of disbelief. —**in′cre•du′li•ty** (ĭn′krĭ-do͞o′lĭ-tē, -dyo͞o′-) *n.* —**in•cred′u•lous•ly** *adv.* —**in•cred′u•lous•ness** *n.*

in•cre•ment (ĭn′krə-mənt, ĭng′-) ▸*n.* **1.** The process of increasing. **2.** Something added or gained, esp. one of a series of regular, usu. small additions. [< Lat. *incrēmentum.*] —**in′cre•men′tal** (-mĕn′tl) *adj.* —**in′cre•men′tal•ly** *adv.*

in•crim•i•nate (ĭn-krĭm′ə-nāt′) ▸*v.* **-nat•ed, -nat•ing.** To accuse of or implicate in a crime or other wrongful act. [LLat. *incrīmināre.*] —**in•crim′i•na′tion** *n.* —**in•crim′i•na•to′ry** (-nə-tôr′ē, -tōr′ē) *adj.*

in•crust (ĭn-krŭst′) ▸*v.* Var. of **encrust.**

in•cu•bate (ĭn′kyə-bāt′, ĭng′-) ▸*v.* **-bat•ed, -bat•ing 1.** To warm (eggs) esp. with the body to promote hatching. **2.** To maintain at optimal environmental conditions for development. [Lat. *incubāre*, lie down on.] —**in′cu•ba′tion** *n.*

in•cu•ba•tor (ĭn′kyə-bā′tər, ĭng′-) ▸*n.* **1.** An apparatus in which environmental conditions, such as temperature and humidity, can be controlled, used for incubating or culturing. **2.** An apparatus for maintaining a young or premature infant in an environment of controlled temperature, humidity, and oxygen.

in•cu•bus (ĭn′kyə-bəs, ĭng′-) ▸*n., pl.* **-bus•es** or **-bi** (-bī′) **1.** An evil spirit believed to violate sleeping women. **2.** An oppressive nightmare. [< LLat.]

in•cul•cate (ĭn-kŭl′kāt′, ĭn′kŭl-) ▸*v.* **-cat•ed, -cat•ing.** To teach or impress by frequent instruction or repetition; instill. [Lat. *inculcāre*, force upon < *calcāre*, trample.] —**in′cul•ca′tion** *n.* —**in•cul′ca′tor** *n.*

in•cul•pa•ble (ĭn-kŭl′pə-bəl) ▸*adj.* Free of guilt; blameless.

in•cul•pate (ĭn-kŭl′pāt′, ĭn′kŭl-) ▸*v.* **-pat•ed, -pat•ing.** To incriminate. [Lat. *inculpāre.*] —**in′cul•pa′tion** *n.*

in•cum•bent (ĭn-kŭm′bənt) ▸*adj.* **1.** Imposed as an obligation or duty; obligatory. **2.** Lying, leaning, or resting on something else. **3.** Currently holding a specified office. ▸*n.* A person who holds an office. [< Lat. *incumbere*, lean upon.] —**in•cum′ben•cy** *n.*

in•cu•nab•u•lum (ĭn′kyə-năb′yə-ləm, ĭng′-) ▸*n., pl.* **-la** (-lə). A book printed before 1501. [< Lat. *incūnābula*, cradle.]

in•cur (ĭn-kûr′) ▸*v.* **-curred, -cur•ring 1.** To acquire or come into; sustain: *incurred substantial losses.* **2.** To become liable or subject to as a result of one's actions; bring upon oneself. [< Lat. *incurrere*, run into.]

in•cur•a•ble (ĭn-kyo͝or′ə-bəl) ▸*adj.* **1.** Impossible to cure. **2.** Inveterate: *an incurable optimist.* —**in•cur′a•bil′i•ty** *n.* —**in•cur′a•ble** *n.* —**in•cur′a•bly** *adv.*

in•cu•ri•ous (ĭn-kyo͝or′ē-əs) ▸*adj.* Lacking curiosity. —**in•cu′ri•ous•ly** *adv.*

in•cur•sion (ĭn-kûr′zhən, -shən) ▸*n.* A raid or invasion. [< Lat. *incurrere*, run at.]

in•cus (ĭng′kəs) ▸*n., pl.* **in•cu•des** (ĭng-kyo͞o′dēz). An anvil-shaped bone in the middle ear. [Lat. *incūs*, anvil.]

Ind. ▸*abbr.* **1.** Indian **2.** Indiana **3.** Indies

in•debt•ed (ĭn-dĕt′ĭd) ▸*adj.* Obligated to another; beholden. —**in•debt′ed•ness** *n.*

in•de•cent (ĭn-dē′sənt) ▸*adj.* **1.** Offensive to good taste. **2.** Morally offensive. —**in•de′cen•cy** *n.* —**in•de′cent•ly** *adv.*

in•de•ci•pher•a•ble (ĭn′dĭ-sī′fər-ə-bəl) ▸*adj.* Impossible to decipher. —**in′de•ci′pher•a•bil′i•ty** *n.* —**in′de•ci′pher•a•bly** *adv.*

in•de•ci•sion (ĭn′dĭ-sĭzh′ən) ▸*n.* Inability to make up one's mind; irresolution.

in•de•ci•sive (ĭn′dĭ-sī′sĭv) ▸*adj.* **1.** Marked by indecision. **2.** Inconclusive. —**in′de•ci′sive•ly** *adv.* —**in′de•ci′sive•ness** *n.*

in•dec•o•rous (ĭn-dĕk′ər-əs) ▸*adj.* Lacking propriety or good taste. —**in•dec′o•rous•ly** *adv.* —**in•dec′o•rous•ness** *n.*

in•deed (ĭn-dēd′) ▸*adv.* **1.** Without a doubt; certainly. **2.** In fact; in reality. ▸*interj.* Used to express surprise, skepticism, or irony. [ME *in dede*, in fact.]

indef. ▸*abbr.* indefinite

in•de•fat•i•ga•ble (ĭn′dĭ-făt′ĭ-gə-bəl) ▸*adj.* Incapable of being fatigued; untiring. See Syns at **tireless.** [< Lat. *indēfatīgābilis* < *dēfatīgāre*, tire out.] —**in′de•fat′i•ga•**

bil′i•ty *n.* —**in′de•fat′i•ga•bly** *adv.*

in•de•fen•si•ble (ĭn′dĭ-fĕn′sə-bəl) ▸*adj.* **1.** Inexcusable; unpardonable. **2.** Invalid; untenable. **3.** Not capable of being defended. —**in′de•fen′si•bly** *adv.*

in•de•fin•a•ble (ĭn′dĭ-fī′nə-bəl) ▸*adj.* Impossible to define, describe, or analyze. See Syns at **unspeakable.** —**in′de•fin′a•bil′i•ty** *n.* —**in′de•fin′a•bly** *adv.*

in•def•i•nite (ĭn-dĕf′ə-nĭt) ▸*adj.* **1.** Unclear; vague. **2.** Lacking precise limits. **3.** Uncertain; undecided. —**in•def′i•nite•ly** *adv.* —**in•def′i•nite•ness** *n.*

indefinite article ▸*n.* An article, such as English *a* or *an,* that does not fix the identity of the noun modified.

in•del•i•ble (ĭn-dĕl′ə-bəl) ▸*adj.* **1.** Impossible to remove, erase, or wash away. **2.** Making a mark not easily erased or washed away. [Lat. *indēlēbilis* < *dēlēre,* wipe out.] —**in•del′i•bil′i•ty** *n.* —**in•del′i•bly** *adv.*

in•del•i•cate (ĭn-dĕl′ĭ-kĭt) ▸*adj.* **1.** Offensive to propriety; improper. **2.** Tasteless. **3.** Tactless. —**in•del′i•ca•cy** *n.* —**in•del′i•cate•ly** *adv.*

in•dem•ni•fy (ĭn-dĕm′nə-fī′) ▸*v.* **-fied, -fy•ing 1.** To protect against damage or loss; insure. **2.** To compensate for damage suffered. [< Lat. *indemnis,* uninjured.] —**in•dem′ni•fi•ca′tion** *n.* —**in•dem′ni•fi′er** *n.*

in•dem•ni•ty (ĭn-dĕm′nĭ-tē) ▸*n., pl.* **-ties 1.** Security against damage or injury. **2.** A legal exemption from liability for damages. **3.** Compensation for damage, loss, or injury suffered. [< Lat. *indemnis,* uninjured.]

in•dent¹ (ĭn-dĕnt′) ▸*v.* **1.** To set (the first line of a paragraph) in from the margin. **2.** To notch or serrate the edge of; make jagged. ▸*n.* (ĭn-dĕnt′, ĭn′dĕnt′). An indentation. [< Med.Lat. *indentāre,* to notch < Lat. *dēns, dent-,* tooth.]

in•dent² (ĭn-dĕnt′) ▸*v.* **1.** To make a dent in. **2.** To impress; stamp.

in•den•ta•tion (ĭn′dĕn-tā′shən) ▸*n.* **1.** The act of indenting or condition of being indented. **2.** The blank space between a margin and the beginning of an indented line. **3.** A notch or jagged cut in an edge. **4.** A recess, as in a border or coastline.

in•den•ture (ĭn-dĕn′chər) ▸*n.* **1.** often **indentures** A contract binding one party into the service of another for a specified term. **2.** A deed or legal contract. ▸*v.* **-tured, -tur•ing.** To bind by indenture. [< AN *endenter,* INDENT¹.]

In•de•pen•dence (ĭn′dĭ-pĕn′dəns) A city of W MO, a suburb of Kansas City. Pop. 112,301.

Independence Day ▸*n.* July 4, celebrated in the US to commemorate the adoption in 1776 of the Declaration of Independence.

in•de•pen•dent (ĭn′dĭ-pĕn′dənt) ▸*adj.* **1.** Not governed by a foreign power. **2.** Free from the influence, guidance, or control of others; self-reliant. **3.** Not contingent. **4.** Not committed to any one political party. **5a.** Financially self-sufficient. **b.** Providing or being sufficient income to enable one to live without working. ▸*n.* One that is independent, esp. a voter not committed to any one party. —**in′de•pen′dence** *n.* —**in′de•pen′dent•ly** *adv.*

independent living ▸*n.* A living arrangement that maximizes the independence and self-determination of disabled persons.

in-depth (ĭn′dĕpth′) ▸*adj.* Detailed; thorough.

in•de•scrib•a•ble (ĭn′dĭ-skrī′bə-bəl) ▸*adj.* **1.** Impossible to describe. **2.** Beyond description. See Syns at **unspeakable.** —**in′de•scrib′a•bly** *adv.*

in•de•struc•ti•ble (ĭn′dĭ-strŭk′tə-bəl) ▸*adj.* Impossible to destroy. —**in′de•struc′ti•bil′i•ty** *n.* —**in′de•struc′ti•bly** *adv.*

in•de•ter•mi•nate (ĭn′dĭ-tûr′mə-nĭt) ▸*adj.* **1a.** Not precisely determined. **b.** Not precisely fixed. **2.** Lacking clarity or precision; vague. —**in′de•ter′mi•na•cy** *n.* —**in′de•ter′mi•nate•ly** *adv.*

in•dex (ĭn′dĕks′) ▸*n., pl.* **-dex•es** or **-di•ces** (-dĭ-sēz′) **1.** An alphabetized list of names, places, and subjects treated in a printed work. **2.** Something that reveals or indicates; sign. **3.** *Print.* A character (☞) used in printing to call attention to a particular paragraph. **4.** *Math.* A number or symbol, often a subscript or superscript to a mathematical expression, that indicates a specific element of a set or sequence. **5.** A number derived from a formula, used to characterize a set of data: *the cost-of-living index.* ▸*v.* **1.** To furnish with or enter in an index. **2.** To indicate or signal. [< Lat., forefinger.] —**in′dex′er** *n.*

index finger ▸*n.* The finger next to the thumb.

index of refraction ▸*n.* The ratio of the speed of light in a vacuum to the speed of light in a medium under consideration.

In•di•a (ĭn′dē-ə) **1.** A peninsula and subcontinent of S Asia S of the Himalayas, comprising India, Nepal, Bhutan, Sikkim, Pakistan, and Bangladesh. **2.** A country of S Asia. Cap. New Delhi. Pop. 918,570,000.

In•di•an (ĭn′dē-ən) ▸*n.* **1.** A native or inhabitant of India or of the East Indies. **2.** See **Native American.** See Usage Note at **Native American. 3.** Any of the languages of the Native Americans. —**In′di•an** *adj.*

In•di•an•a (ĭn′dē-ăn′ə) A state of the N-central US. Cap. Indianapolis. Pop. 5,564,228. —**In′di•an′an, In′di•an′i•an** *adj. & n.*

In•di•an•ap•o•lis (ĭn′dē-ə-năp′ə-lĭs) The capital of IN, in the central part SSW of Fort Wayne. Pop. 741,952.

Indian corn ▸*n.* See **corn¹** 1.

Indian Ocean. A body of water extending from S Asia to Antarctica and from E Africa to SE Australia.

Indian pipe ▸*n.* A waxy white woodland plant with scalelike leaves and a nodding flower.

Indian summer ▸*n.* A period of mild weather occurring in late autumn.

Indian Territory. A former territory of the S-central US, mainly in present-day OK.

In•dic (ĭn′dĭk) ▸*n.* A branch of Indo-European that comprises the languages of the Indian subcontinent and Sri Lanka. —**In′dic** *adj.*

indic. ▸*abbr.* indicative

in•di•cate (ĭn′dĭ-kāt′) ▸*v.* **-cat•ed, -cat•ing 1.** To show the way to or point out. **2.** To serve as a sign, symptom, or token of; signify. **3.** To suggest the necessity or advisability of. **4.** To state or express briefly. [Lat. *indicāre* < *index, indic-,* forefinger.] —**in′di•ca′tion** *n.* —**in′di•ca′tor** *n.*

Syns: *indicate, argue, attest, bespeak, betoken, testify, witness* **v.**

in•dic•a•tive (ĭn-dĭk′ə-tĭv) ▸*adj.* **1.** Serving to indicate. **2.** *Gram.* Of or being the mood of the verb used in ordinary objective statements. ▸*n. Gram.* **1.** The indicative mood. **2.** A verb in the indicative mood. —**in•dic′a•tive•ly** *adv.*

in•di•ces (ĭn′dĭ-sēz′) ▸*n.* Pl. of **index.**

in•dict (ĭn-dīt′) ▸*v.* **1.** To accuse of wrongdoing. **2.** *Law* To make a formal accusation against (a party) by the findings of a grand jury. [< ME *enditen,* INDITE.] —**in•dict′a•ble** *adj.* —**in′dict•ee′** (ĭn′dī-tē′) *n.* —**in•dict′er, in•dict′or** *n.* —**in•dict′ment** *n.*

In•dies (ĭn′dēz) **1.** See **East Indies. 2.** See **West Indies.**

in•dif•fer•ent (ĭn-dĭf′ər-ənt, -dĭf′rənt) ▸*adj.* **1.** Not partial; unbiased. **2.** Not mattering one way or the other. **3.** Having no marked feeling for or against. **4.** Having no particular interest in or concern for; apathetic. **5.** Neither good nor bad; mediocre. —**in•dif′fer•ence** *n.* —**in•dif′fer•ent•ly** *adv.*

in•dig•e•nous (ĭn-dĭj′ə-nəs) ▸*adj.* Originating and living or occurring naturally in an area or environment; native. [< Lat. *indigena,* a native.] —**in•dig′e•nous•ly** *adv.*

in•di•gent (ĭn′dĭ-jənt) ▸*adj.* Lacking the means of subsistence; impoverished. [< Lat. *indigēre,* be in need of.] —**in′di•gence** *n.* —**in′di•gent** *n.* —**in′di•gent•ly** *adv.*

in•di•gest•i•ble (ĭn′dĭ-jĕs′tə-bəl, -dī-) ▸*adj.* Difficult or impossible to digest. —**in′di•gest′i•bil′i•ty** *n.* —**in′di•gest′i•bly** *adv.*

in•di•ges•tion (ĭn′dĭ-jĕs′chən, -dī-) ▸*n.* **1.** Inability to properly digest food. **2.** Discomfort or illness resulting from indigestion.

in•dig•nant (ĭn-dĭg′nənt) ▸*adj.* Feeling or expressing indignation. See Syns at **angry.** [< Lat. *indignus,* unworthy.] —**in•dig′nant•ly** *adv.*

in•dig•na•tion (ĭn′dĭg-nā′shən) ▸*n.* Anger aroused by something unjust or mean. [< Lat. *indignārī,* deem unworthy.]

in•dig•ni•ty (ĭn-dĭg′nĭ-tē) ▸*n., pl.* **-ties 1.** Humiliating or degrading treatment. **2.** A source of offense, as to a person's pride or sense of dignity; affront.

in•di•go (ĭn′dĭ-gō′) ▸*n., pl.* **-gos** or **-goes 1.** A plant that yields a blue dyestuff. **2.** A blue dye obtained from this plant or produced synthetically. **3a.** A dark to purplish blue. **b.** The hue of the visible spectrum lying between blue and violet. [< Gk. *Indikon (pharmakon),* Indian (dye).]

indigo bunting ▸*n.* A small New World finch, the male of which has deep blue plumage.

in•di•rect (ĭn′dĭ-rĕkt′, -dī-) ▸*adj.* **1.** Diverging from a direct course; roundabout. **2a.** Not proceeding straight to the point. **b.** Not forthright and candid; devious. **3.** Not directly planned for; secondary: *indirect benefits.* —**in′di•rec′tion** *n.* —**in′di•rect′ly** *adv.* —**in′di•rect′ness** *n.*

indirect object ▸*n.* An object indirectly affected by the action of a verb, as *me* in *Sing me a song.*

in•dis•cern•i•ble (ĭn′dĭ-sûr′nə-bəl, -zûr′-) ▸*adj.* Impossible to perceive; imperceptible. —**in′dis•cern′i•bly** *adv.*

in•dis•creet (ĭn′dĭ-skrēt′) ▸*adj.* Lacking discretion; injudicious: *an indiscreet remark.* —**in′dis•creet′ly** *adv.* —**in′dis•creet′ness** *n.* —**in′dis•cre′tion** (ĭn′dĭ-skrĕsh′ən) *n.*

in•dis•crim•i•nate (ĭn′dĭ-skrĭm′ə-nĭt) ▸*adj.* **1.** Not making or based on careful distinctions; unselective. **2.** Widespread; wholesale: *indiscriminate violence.* **3.** Random; haphazard. **4.** Confused; chaotic. —**in′dis•crim′i•nate•ly** *adv.*

in•dis•pens•a•ble (ĭn′dĭ-spĕn′sə-bəl) ▸*adj.* Not to be dispensed with; essential. —**in′dis•pens′a•bil′i•ty, in′dis•pens′a•ble•ness** *n.* —**in′dis•pens′a•bly** *adv.*

Syns: *indispensable, essential, necessary, needful, requisite* **adj.**

in•dis•posed (ĭn′dĭ-spōzd′) ▸*adj.* **1.** Mildly ill. **2.** Averse; disinclined. —**in•dis′po•si′tion** (ĭn-dĭs′pə-zĭsh′ən) *n.*

in•dis•put•a•ble (ĭn′dĭ-spyōō′tə-bəl) ▸*adj.* Beyond doubt; undeniable. —**in′dis•put′a•ble•ness** *n.* —**in′dis•put′a•bly** *adv.*

in•dis•sol•u•ble (ĭn′dĭ-sŏl′yə-bəl) ▸*adj.* Impossible to dissolve, disintegrate, or undo. —**in′dis•sol′u•bil′i•ty** *n.* —**in′dis•sol′u•bly** *adv.*

in•dis•tinct (ĭn′dĭ-stĭngkt′) ▸*adj.* **1.** Not clearly or sharply delineated. **2.** Hazy, vague. —**in′dis•tinct′ly** *adv.* —**in′dis•tinct′ness** *n.*

in•dis•tin•guish•a•ble (ĭn′dĭ-stĭng′gwĭ-shə-bəl) ▸*adj.* **1.** Impossible to differentiate or tell apart. **2.** Impossible to discern; imperceptible. —**in′dis•tin′guish•a•bly** *adv.*

in•dite (ĭn-dīt′) ▸*v.* **-dit•ed, -dit•ing.** To write; compose. [< VLat. **indictāre.*]

in•di•um (ĭn′dē-əm) ▸*n. Symbol* **In** A soft, malleable, silvery-white metallic element used as a plating over silver in making mirrors and in compounds for making transistors. At. no. 49. See table at **element.** [IND(IGO) + -IUM.]

in•di•vid•u•al (ĭn′də-vĭj′ōō-əl) ▸*adj.* **1a.** Of or relating to a single human. **b.** By or for one person: *an individual portion.* **2.** Existing singly; separate: *individual words.* **3.** Distinguished by particular attributes; distinctive: *an individual way of dressing.* ▸*n.* **1.** A human or organism considered by itself. **2.** A particular person. [< Lat. *indīviduus,* indivisible, single.] —**in′di•vid′u•al•ly** *adv.*

in•di•vid•u•al•ism (ĭn′də-vĭj′ōō-ə-lĭz′əm) ▸*n.* **1.** Belief in the primary importance of the individual and personal independence. **2.** The doctrine that the interests of the individual should take precedence over those of the state. **3.** Individuality.

in•di•vid•u•al•ist (ĭn′də-vĭj′ōō-ə-lĭst) ▸*n.* **1.** A person of independent thought and action. **2.** An advocate of individualism. —**in′di•vid′u•al•is′tic** *adj.*

in•di•vid•u•al•i•ty (ĭn′də-vĭj′ōō-ăl′ĭ-tē) ▸*n.* **1.** The aggregate of qualities that distinguish one individual from another. **2.** The quality of being individual.

in•di•vid•u•al•ize (ĭn′də-vĭj′ōō-ə-līz′) ▸*v.* **-ized, -iz•ing 1.** To give individuality to. **2.** To consider or treat individually. **3.** To modify to suit a particular individual. —**in′di•vid′u•al•i•za′tion** *n.*

individual retirement account ▸*n.* A personal investment account in which contributions and interest are tax-deferred until retirement.

in•di•vis•i•ble (ĭn′də-vĭz′ə-bəl) ▸*adj.* Incapable of division. —**in′di•vis′i•bly** *adv.*

In•do•chi•na (ĭn′dō-chī′nə) **1.** A peninsula of SE Asia comprising Vietnam, Laos, Cambodia, Thailand, Myanmar (Burma), and the mainland territory of Malaysia. **2.** The former French colonial empire in SE Asia, including much of the E part of the Indochinese peninsula. —**In'do·chi'nese'** (-nēz', -nēs') *adj. & n.*

in·doc·tri·nate (ĭn-dŏk'trə-nāt') ►*v.* **-nat·ed, -nat·ing 1.** To instruct in a body of doctrine. **2.** To imbue with a partisan point of view. —**in·doc'tri·na'tion** *n.*

In·do-Eu·ro·pe·an (ĭn'dō-yo͝or'ə-pē'ən) ►*n.* **1a.** A family of languages consisting of most of the languages of Europe as well as those of Iran, the Indian subcontinent, and other parts of Asia. **b.** Proto-Indo-European. **2.** A member of any of the peoples speaking an Indo-European language. —**In'do-Eu'ro·pe'an** *adj.*

In·do-I·ra·ni·an (ĭn'dō-ĭ-rā'nē-ən) ►*n.* **1.** A subfamily of the Indo-European language family that comprises the Indic and Iranian branches. **2.** A member of any of the peoples speaking an Indo-Iranian language. —**In'do-I·ra'ni·an** *adj.*

in·do·lent (ĭn'də-lənt) ►*adj.* Disinclined to work; habitually lazy. See Syns at **lazy.** [LLat. *indolēns*, painless.] —**in'do·lence** *n.* —**in'do·lent·ly** *adv.*

in·dom·i·ta·ble (ĭn-dŏm'ĭ-tə-bəl) ►*adj.* Impossible to overcome; unconquerable. [LLat. *indomitābilis.*] —**in·dom'i·ta·bly** *adv.*

In·do·ne·sia (ĭn'də-nē'zhə, -shə, -dō-) A country of SE Asia in the Malay Archipelago comprising Sumatra, Java, Sulawesi, the Moluccas, parts of Borneo, New Guinea, and Timor, and many smaller islands. Cap. Jakarta, on Java. Pop. 192,217,000.

In·do·ne·sian (ĭn'də-nē'zhən, -shən) ►*n.* **1.** A native or inhabitant of Indonesia. **2.** A subfamily of Austronesian that includes Malay, Tagalog, and the languages of Indonesia. —**In'do·ne'sian** *adj.*

in·door (ĭn'dôr', -dōr') ►*adj.* Of, situated in, or intended for use in the interior of a building.

in·doors (ĭn-dôrz', -dōrz') ►*adv.* In or into a building.

In·dore (ĭn-dôr', -dōr') A city of W-central India NNE of Mumbai (Bombay). Pop. 1,091,674.

in·dorse (ĭn-dôrs') ►*v.* Var. of **endorse.**

in·du·bi·ta·ble (ĭn-do͞o'bĭ-tə-bəl, -dyo͞o'-) ►*adj.* Too apparent to be doubted; unquestionable. [LLat. *indubitābilis.*] —**in·du'bi·ta·bly** *adv.*

in·duce (ĭn-do͞os', -dyo͞os') ►*v.* **-duced, -duc·ing 1.** To persuade or move to action; influence. **2.** To bring about the occurrence of; cause: *a drug used to induce labor.* [< Lat. *indūcere.*] —**in·duc'i·ble** *adj.* —**in·duce'ment** *n.*

in·duct (ĭn-dŭkt') ►*v.* **1.** To place formally in office; install. **2.** To admit as a member; initiate. **3.** To take into military service. [< Lat. *indūcere*, lead in.] —**in'duc·tee'** *n.*

in·duc·tance (ĭn-dŭk'təns) ►*n.* A circuit element in which electromotive force is generated by electromagnetic induction.

in·duc·tion (ĭn-dŭk'shən) ►*n.* **1.** The act of inducting or the process of being inducted. **2.** *Elect.* **a.** The generation of electromotive force in a closed circuit by a varying magnetic flux through the circuit. **b.** The charging of an isolated conducting object by momentarily grounding it while a charged body is nearby. **3.** *Logic* The process of deriving general principles from particular facts or instances.

in·duc·tive (ĭn-dŭk'tĭv) ►*adj.* **1.** Of or using logical induction. **2.** *Elect.* Of or arising from inductance. —**in·duc'tive·ly** *adv.* —**in·duc'tive·ness** *n.*

in·dulge (ĭn-dŭlj') ►*v.* **-dulged, -dulg·ing 1.** To yield to the desires and whims of; humor. **2a.** To yield to; gratify: *indulge a craving for chocolate.* **b.** To allow (oneself) a special pleasure. [Lat. *indulgēre.*] —**in·dulg'er** *n.*

in·dul·gence (ĭn-dŭl'jəns) ►*n.* **1.** The act of indulging or state of being indulgent. **2.** Something indulged in. **3.** Liberal or lenient treatment; tolerance. **4.** Something granted as a favor or privilege. **5.** *Rom. Cath. Ch.* The remission of temporal punishment due for a sin that has been absolved.

in·dul·gent (ĭn-dŭl'jənt) ►*adj.* Showing, characterized by, or given to indulgence; lenient. —**in·dul'gent·ly** *adv.*

in·du·rate (ĭn'də-rāt', -dyə-) ►*v.* **-rat·ed, -rat·ing 1.** To make or become hard; harden. **2.** To inure, as to hardship or ridicule. [Lat. *indūrāre*, harden.] —**in'dur·a'tion** *n.*

in·du·ra·tion (ĭn'də-rā'shən, -dyə-) ►*n.* **1.** The quality or condition of being hardened. **2.** The act or process of becoming hardened. **3.** *Pathol.* The hardening of a normally soft tissue or organ, especially the skin, because of inflammation, infiltration of a neoplasm, or an accumulation of blood.

In·dus (ĭn'dəs) A river of S-central Asia rising in SW Xizang (Tibet) and flowing about 3,057 km (1,900 mi) through N India and Pakistan to the Arabian Sea.

in·dus·tri·al (ĭn-dŭs'trē-əl) ►*adj.* **1.** Of or relating to industry. **2.** Having highly developed industries. **3.** Used in industry: *industrial diamonds.* —**in·dus'tri·al·ly** *adv.*

in·dus·tri·al·ist (ĭ-dŭs'trē-ə-lĭst) ►*n.* One who owns or has a financial interest in an industrial enterprise.

in·dus·tri·al·ize (ĭn-dŭs'trē-ə-līz') ►*v.* **-ized, -iz·ing.** To make or become industrial. —**in·dus'tri·al·i·za'tion** *n.*

industrial park ►*n.* An area, usu. on the outskirts of a city, zoned for industries and businesses.

in·dus·tri·ous (ĭn-dŭs'trē-əs) ►*adj.* Hard-working; diligent. —**in·dus'tri·ous·ly** *adv.* —**in·dus'tri·ous·ness** *n.*

in·dus·try (ĭn'də-strē) ►*n., pl.* **-tries 1.** Commercial production and sale of goods. **2.** A specific branch of manufacture and trade. **3.** The sector of an economy made up of manufacturing enterprises. **4.** Hard work; diligence. [< Lat. *industria*, diligence.]

-ine[1] ►*suff.* **1.** Of or relating to: *Benedictine.* **2.** Made of; resembling: *opaline.* [< Lat. *-īnus* and Gk. *-inos.*]

-ine[2] ►*suff.* **1.** also **-in** A chemical substance, esp.: **a.** Halogen: *bromine.* **b.** Basic compound: *amine.* **c.** Alkaloid: *quinine.* **2.** Amino acid: *glycine.* **3.** A mixture of compounds: *gasoline.* **4.** Commercial material: *glassine.* [< Lat. *-īna.*]

in·e·bri·ate (ĭn-ē'brē-āt') ►*v.* **-at·ed, -at·ing.** To make drunk; intoxicate. ►*n.* (-ĭt). An intoxicated person. [Lat. *inēbriāre* < *ēbrius*, drunk.] —**in·e'bri·a'tion** *n.*

in·ed·i·ble (ĭn-ĕd'ə-bəl) ►*adj.* Not edible. —**in·ed'i·bil'i·ty** *n.* —**in·ed'i·bly** *adv.*

in•ef•fa•ble (ĭn-ĕf′ə-bəl) ▸ *adj.* **1.** Incapable of being expressed; indescribable. See Syns at **unspeakable. 2.** Not to be uttered; taboo. [< Lat. *ineffābilis.*] —**in•ef′fa•bly** *adv.*

in•ef•face•a•ble (ĭn′ĭ-fā′sə-bəl) ▸ *adj.* Impossible to efface; indelible.

in•ef•fec•tive (ĭn′ĭ-fĕk′tĭv) ▸ *adj.* **1.** Not effective; ineffectual. **2.** Incompetent. —**in′ef•fec′tive•ly** *adv.* —**in′ef•fec′tive•ness** *n.*

in•ef•fec•tu•al (ĭn′ĭ-fĕk′cho͞o-əl) ▸ *adj.* **1.** Not having a desired effect; vain. **2.** Lacking forcefulness; weak. —**in′ef•fec′tu•al•ly** *adv.*

in•ef•fi•cient (ĭn′ĭ-fĭsh′ənt) ▸ *adj.* Not efficient; wasteful of time, energy, or materials. —**in′ef•fi′cien•cy** *n.* —**in′ef•fi′cient•ly** *adv.*

in•el•e•gant (ĭn-ĕl′ĭ-gənt) ▸ *adj.* Lacking refinement; not elegant. —**in•el′e•gance** *n.* —**in•el′e•gant•ly** *adv.*

in•el•i•gi•ble (ĭn-ĕl′ĭ-jə-bəl) ▸ *adj.* Disqualified by law or rule. —**in•el′i•gi•bil′i•ty** *n.* —**in•el′i•gi•bly** *adv.*

in•e•luc•ta•ble (ĭn′ĭ-lŭk′tə-bəl) ▸ *adj.* Not to be avoided or escaped; inevitable. [Lat. *inēluctābilis.*] —**in′e•luc′ta•bly** *adv.*

in•ept (ĭn-ĕpt′) ▸ *adj.* **1.** Not apt or fitting; inappropriate. **2.** Lacking judgment or sense; foolish. **3.** Bungling or clumsy; incompetent. [Lat. *ineptus.*] —**in•ept′ly** *adv.* —**in•ept′ness, in•ep′ti•tude′** (-ĕp′tĭ-to͞od′, -tyo͞od′) *n.*

in•e•qual•i•ty (ĭn′ĭ-kwŏl′ĭ-tē) ▸ *n., pl.* **-ties 1.** The condition of being unequal. **2.** Social or economic disparity. **3.** Lack of regularity; unevenness. **4.** A mathematical statement that two quantities are not equal.

in•eq•ui•ta•ble (ĭn-ĕk′wĭ-tə-bəl) ▸ *adj.* Not equitable; unfair. —**in•eq′ui•ta•bly** *adv.*

in•eq•ui•ty (ĭn-ĕk′wĭ-tē) ▸ *n., pl.* **-ties 1.** Injustice; unfairness. **2.** An instance of unfairness.

in•er•ran•cy (ĭn-ĕr′ən-sē) ▸ *n.* Freedom from error or untruths; infallibility.

in•ert (ĭn-ûrt′) ▸ *adj.* **1.** Unable to move or act. **2.** Sluggish in action or motion; lethargic. **3.** *Chem.* Not readily reactive with other elements; forming few or no chemical compounds. [Lat. *iners, inert-,* inactive.] —**in•ert′ly** *adv.* —**in•ert′ness** *n.*

in•er•tia (ĭ-nûr′shə) ▸ *n.* **1.** *Phys.* The tendency of a body to remain at rest or stay in motion unless acted on by an outside force. **2.** Resistance to motion, action, or change. [Lat., idleness.] —**in•er′tial** *adj.*

in•es•cap•a•ble (ĭn′ĭ-skā′pə-bəl) ▸ *adj.* Impossible to escape; inevitable. See Syns at **certain.** —**in′es•cap′a•bly** *adv.*

in•es•ti•ma•ble (ĭn-ĕs′tə-mə-bəl) ▸ *adj.* **1.** Impossible to estimate or compute. See Syns at **incalculable. 2.** Of immeasurable worth; invaluable. —**in•es′ti•ma•bly** *adv.*

in•ev•i•ta•ble (ĭn-ĕv′ĭ-tə-bəl) ▸ *adj.* **1.** Impossible to avoid or prevent. See Syns at **certain. 2.** Predictable. [LLat. *inēvītābilis* : IN–[1] + *ēvītāre,* shun.] —**in•ev′i•ta•bil′i•ty** *n.* —**in•ev′i•ta•bly** *adv.*

in•ex•act (ĭn′ĭg-zăkt′) ▸ *adj.* Not accurate or precise; not exact. —**in′ex•act′ly** *adv.* —**in′ex•act′ness** *n.*

in•ex•cus•a•ble (ĭn′ĭk-skyo͞o′zə-bəl) ▸ *adj.* Impossible to excuse; unpardonable. —**in′ex•cus′a•bly** *adv.*

in•ex•haust•i•ble (ĭn′ĭg-zô′stə-bəl) ▸ *adj.* **1.** That cannot be used up. **2.** Never wearying; tireless. —**in′ex•haust′i•bil′i•ty, in′ex•haust′i•ble•ness** *n.* —**in′ex•haust′i•bly** *adv.*

in•ex•o•ra•ble (ĭn-ĕk′sər-ə-bəl) ▸ *adj.* Not capable of being persuaded by entreaty; relentless. [Lat. *inexōrābilis.*] —**in•ex′o•ra•bil′i•ty** *n.* —**in•ex′o•ra•bly** *adv.*

in•ex•pen•sive (ĭn′ĭk-spĕn′sĭv) ▸ *adj.* Not costly; cheap. —**in′ex•pen′sive•ly** *adv.*

in•ex•pe•ri•ence (ĭn′ĭk-spîr′ē-əns) ▸ *n.* Lack of experience. —**in′ex•pe′ri•enced** *adj.*

in•ex•pert (ĭn-ĕk′spûrt′) ▸ *adj.* Not expert; unskilled. —**in•ex′pert′ly** *adv.*

in•ex•pli•ca•ble (ĭn-ĕk′splĭ-kə-bəl, ĭn′ĭk-splĭk′ə-bəl) ▸ *adj.* Impossible to explain or account for. —**in•ex′pli•ca•bly** *adv.*

in•ex•press•i•ble (ĭn′ĭk-sprĕs′ə-bəl) ▸ *adj.* Impossible to express; indescribable. See Syns at **unspeakable.** —**in′ex•press′i•bly** *adv.*

in•ex•tin•guish•a•ble (ĭn′ĭk-stĭng′gwĭ-shə-bəl) ▸ *adj.* Difficult or impossible to extinguish.

in ex•tre•mis (ĭn ĕk-strē′mĭs) ▸ *adv.* At the point of death. [Lat. *in extrēmīs,* at the end.]

in•ex•tri•ca•ble (ĭn-ĕk′strĭ-kə-bəl, ĭn′ĭk-strĭk′ə-bəl) ▸ *adj.* **1.** Difficult or impossible to disentangle or untie. **2.** Too involved or complicated to solve. —**in•ex′tri•ca•bil′i•ty** *n.* —**in•ex′tri•ca•bly** *adv.*

inf. ▸ *abbr.* **1.** inferior **2.** infinitive

in•fal•li•ble (ĭn-făl′ə-bəl) ▸ *adj.* **1.** Incapable of erring. **2.** Incapable of failing; certain: *an infallible antidote.* —**in•fal′li•bil′i•ty** *n.* —**in•fal′li•bly** *adv.*

in•fa•mous (ĭn′fə-məs) ▸ *adj.* **1.** Having an exceedingly bad reputation; notorious. **2.** Causing or deserving infamy. —**in′fa•mous•ly** *adv.* —**in′fa•mous•ness** *n.*

in•fa•my (ĭn′fə-mē) ▸ *n., pl.* **-mies 1.** Evil fame or reputation. **2.** The condition of being infamous. **3.** An infamous act. [< Lat. *īnfāmia.*]

in•fan•cy (ĭn′fən-sē) ▸ *n., pl.* **-cies 1.** The state or period of being an infant. **2.** An early stage of existence.

in•fant (ĭn′fənt) ▸ *n.* **1.** A child in the earliest period of life; baby. **2.** *Law* A minor. [< Lat. *īnfāns,* not speaking.] —**in′fant** *adj.*

in•fan•ti•cide (ĭn-făn′tĭ-sīd′) ▸ *n.* **1.** The killing of an infant. **2.** One who kills an infant.

in•fan•tile (ĭn′fən-tīl′, -tĭl) ▸ *adj.* **1.** Of or relating to infants or infancy. **2.** Immature; childish.

infantile paralysis ▸ *n.* See **poliomyelitis.**

in•fan•try (ĭn′fən-trē) ▸ *n., pl.* **-tries.** The combat arm made up of units trained to fight on foot. [< OItal. *infanteria* < *infante,* youth.] —**in′fan•try•man** *n.*

in•farct (ĭn′färkt′, ĭn-färkt′) ▸ *n.* A necrotic area of tissue due to the obstruction of local blood supply. [< Lat. *infarcīre,* cram in.] —**in•farct′ed** *adj.* —**in•farc′tion** *n.*

in•fat•u•ate (ĭn-făch′o͞o-āt′) ▸ *v.* **-at•ed, -at•ing.** To inspire with unreasoning love or attachment. [Lat. *īnfatuāre* < *fatuus,* foolish.] —**in•fat′u•at′ed** *adj.* —**in•fat′u•a′tion** *n.*

in•fea•si•ble (ĭn-fē′zə-bəl) ▸ *adj.* Not feasible; impracticable.

in•fect (ĭn-fĕkt′) ▸ *v.* **1.** To contaminate with a pathogenic microorganism. **2.** To communicate a disease to. **3.** To contaminate or corrupt:

a land infected by hate. [< Lat. *īnficere, īnfect-,* to stain.] —**in•fec′tion** *n.*

in•fec•tious (ĭn-fĕk′shəs) ►*adj.* **1.** Capable of causing infection. **2.** Caused or transmitted by infection. **3.** Easily or readily communicated, as laughter. —**in•fec′tious•ly** *adv.*

infectious mononucleosis ►*n.* An acute infectious disease caused by Epstein-Barr virus and marked by fever, swollen lymph nodes, sore throat, and lymphocyte abnormalities.

in•fe•lic•i•tous (ĭn′fĭ-lĭs′ĭ-təs) ►*adj.* Inappropriate or ill-chosen, as a remark. —**in′fe•lic′i•tous•ly** *adv.* —**in′fe•lic′i•ty** *n.*

in•fer (ĭn-fûr′) ►*v.* **-ferred, -fer•ring 1.** To conclude from evidence or premises. **2.** To lead to as a result or conclusion. [Lat. *īnferre* : IN–[2] + *ferre*, bring.]

Usage: When we say that a speaker or sentence implies something, we mean that it is conveyed or suggested without being stated outright: *She implied by her smile that we had won the award.* Inference, on the other hand, is the activity performed by a reader or interpreter in deriving conclusions that are not explicit in what is said: *We inferred from her smile that we had won the award.*

in•fer•ence (ĭn′fər-əns) ►*n.* **1.** The act or process of inferring. **2.** Something inferred.

in•fe•ri•or (ĭn-fîr′ē-ər) ►*adj.* **1.** Low or lower in order, degree, rank, quality, or estimation. **2.** Situated under or beneath. [< Lat. *īnferior* < *īnferus*, low.] —**in•fe′ri•or** *n.* —**in•fe′ri•or′i•ty** (-ôr′ĭ-tē, -ŏr′-) *n.*

in•fer•nal (ĭn-fûr′nəl) ►*adj.* **1.** Of or relating to hell. **2.** Fiendish; diabolical. **3.** Abominable; awful. [< Lat. *īnfernus*, lower.] —**in•fer′nal•ly** *adv.*

in•fer•no (ĭn-fûr′nō) ►*n., pl.* **-nos 1.** Hell. **2.** A place of fiery heat or destruction. [Ital. < LLat. *īnfernus*, INFERNAL.]

in•fer•tile (ĭn-fûr′tl) ►*adj.* Not fertile; unproductive or barren. —**in′fer•til′i•ty** (-fər-tĭl′ĭ-tē) *n.*

in•fest (ĭn-fĕst′) ►*v.* To inhabit or overrun in numbers large enough to be harmful or obnoxious. [< Lat. *īnfestus*, hostile.] —**in′fes•ta′tion** *n.*

in•fi•del (ĭn′fĭ-dəl, -dĕl′) ►*n.* **1.** An unbeliever with respect to a particular religion, esp. Christianity or Islam. **2.** One with no religious beliefs. [< Lat. *īnfidēlis*, unfaithful.]

in•fi•del•i•ty (ĭn′fĭ-dĕl′ĭ-tē) ►*n., pl.* **-ties 1.** Lack of fidelity or loyalty, esp. to a spouse. **2.** Lack of religious belief.

in•field (ĭn′fēld′) ►*n. Baseball* **1.** The area of the field within the baselines. **2.** The defensive positions of first base, second base, third base, and shortstop. —**in′field′er** *n.*

in•fight•ing (ĭn′fī′tĭng) ►*n.* **1.** Contentious rivalry within an organization. **2.** *Sports* Fighting at close range. —**in′fight′er** *n.*

in•fil•trate (ĭn-fĭl′trāt′, ĭn′fĭl-) ►*v.* **-trat•ed, -trat•ing 1.** To pass, enter, or join gradually or surreptitiously. **2.** To pass or cause (a liquid or gas) to pass into. —**in′fil•tra′tion** *n.* —**in•fil′tra•tor** *n.*

infin. ►*abbr.* infinitive

in•fi•nite (ĭn′fə-nĭt) ►*adj.* **1.** Having no boundaries or limits. **2.** Immeasurably great or large: *infinite patience.* See Syns at **incalculable. 3.** *Math.* **a.** Being beyond or greater than any arbitrarily large value. **b.** Spatially unlimited. —**in′fin•ite** *n.* —**in′fi•nite•ly** *adv.*

Syns: *infinite, boundless, eternal, illimitable*
Ant: *finite* **adj.**

in•fin•i•tes•i•mal (ĭn′fĭn-ĭ-tĕs′ə-məl) ►*adj.* **1.** Immeasurably or incalculably small. **2.** *Math.* Capable of having values approaching zero as a limit. [< Lat. *īnfīnītus*, infinite.] —**in′fin•i•tes′i•mal•ly** *adv.*

in•fin•i•tive (ĭn-fĭn′ĭ-tĭv) ►*n.* A verb form that in English is often preceded by *to* and may be followed by an object or complement, as *be* in *I want to be president.* [< Lat. *īnfīnītus*, infinite.]

in•fin•i•tude (ĭn-fĭn′ĭ-to͞od′, -tyo͞od′) ►*n.* **1.** The state or quality of being infinite. **2.** An immeasurably large quantity, number, or extent.

in•fin•i•ty (ĭn-fĭn′ĭ-tē) ►*n., pl.* **-ties 1.** The quality or condition of being infinite. **2.** Unbounded space, time, or quantity. **3.** An indefinitely large number or amount.

in•firm (ĭn-fûrm′) ►*adj.* **1.** Weak in body, esp. from old age or disease; feeble. **2.** Not strong or stable; shaky. —**in•firm′ly** *adv.*

in•fir•ma•ry (ĭn-fûr′mə-rē) ►*n., pl.* **-ries.** A place for the care of the sick or injured.

in•fir•mi•ty (ĭn-fûr′mĭ-tē) ►*n., pl.* **-ties 1.** A bodily ailment or weakness. **2.** Frailty; feebleness. **3.** A defect in a person's character.

in•flame (ĭn-flām′) ►*v.* **-flamed, -flam•ing 1.** To arouse to strong feeling or action. **2.** To intensify. **3.** To produce or be affected by an inflammation. **4.** To set on fire; kindle.

in•flam•ma•ble (ĭn-flăm′ə-bəl) ►*adj.* **1.** Easily ignited and capable of burning rapidly; flammable. See Usage Note at **flammable. 2.** Quickly aroused to strong emotion. [< Lat. *īnflammāre*, set afire.] —**in•flam′ma•bil′i•ty** *n.* —**in•flam′ma•ble** *n.*

in•flam•ma•tion (ĭn′flə-mā′shən) ►*n.* A localized reaction of tissue to irritation, injury, or infection, characterized by pain, redness, heat, and swelling.

in•flam•ma•to•ry (ĭn-flăm′ə-tôr′ē, -tōr′ē) ►*adj.* **1.** Arousing strong emotion, esp. anger. **2.** Marked or caused by inflammation.

in•flate (ĭn-flāt′) ►*v.* **-flat•ed, -flat•ing 1.** To fill and swell with air or gas. **2.** To raise or expand abnormally or improperly. See Syns at **exaggerate. 3.** To cause (e.g., wages) to undergo inflation. [< Lat. *īnflāre*, blow in.] —**in•fla′tor, in•flat′er** *n.*

in•fla•tion (ĭn-flā′shən) ►*n.* **1.** The act of inflating or the state of being inflated. **2.** A persistent increase in prices or a persistent decline in the purchasing power of money. —**in•fla′tion•ar′y** (-shə-nĕr′ē) *adj.*

in•flect (ĭn-flĕkt′) ►*v.* **1.** To alter (the voice) in tone or pitch; modulate. **2.** *Gram.* To alter (a word) by inflection. **3.** To turn from a course; bend. [< Lat. *īnflectere*, bend down.] —**in•flec′tive** *adj.*

in•flec•tion (ĭn-flĕk′shən) ►*n.* **1.** Alteration in pitch or tone of the voice. **2a.** A change in the form of a word in accordance with grammar, syntax, or meaning, as in *near, nearer* or *man, men's.* **b.** The paradigm of a word. **c.** A pattern of forming paradigms, as of nouns or verbs. —**in•flec′tion•al** *adj.* —**in•flec′tion•al•ly** *adv.*

in•flex•i•ble (ĭn-flĕk′sə-bəl) ►*adj.* **1.** Not easily bent; rigid. **2.** Incapable of being changed; unalterable. **3.** Unyielding. —**in•flex′i•bil′i•ty** *n.* —**in•flex′i•bly** *adv.*

in•flict (ĭn-flĭkt′) ►*v.* **1.** To mete out (e.g., punishment); impose. **2.** To afflict. [Lat. *īnflīgere, īnflīct-*.] —**in•flict′er, in•flic′tor** *n.* —**in•flic′tion** *n.*

in•flo•res•cence (ĭn′flə-rĕs′əns) ►*n.* A characteristic arrangement of flowers on a stem or in a cluster. [< LLat. *īnflōrēscere*, begin to flower.] —**in′flo•res′cent** *adj.*

inflorescence
clockwise from top left: umbel, corymb, raceme, and panicle

in•flow (ĭn′flō′) ►*n.* A flowing in or into.

in•flu•ence (ĭn′flo͞o-əns) ►*n.* **1.** A power indirectly or intangibly affecting a person or course of events. **2a.** Power to sway or affect based on prestige, wealth, ability, or position. **b.** One exercising such power. ►*v.* **-enced, -enc•ing 1.** To affect or sway. **2.** To modify. —***idiom:* under the influence** Intoxicated, esp. with alcohol. [< Lat. *īnfluere*, flow in.] —**in′flu•en′tial** (-ĕn′shəl) *adj.* —**in′flu•en′tial•ly** *adv.*

in•flu•en•za (ĭn′flo͞o-ĕn′zə) ►*n.* An acute viral infection marked by inflammation of the respiratory tract and by fever, chills, and pain. [< Med.Lat. *īnfluentia*, influence. See INFLUENCE.]

in•flux (ĭn′flŭks′) ►*n.* A flowing in. [LLat. *īnflūxus* < Lat. *īnfluere*, flow in.]

in•fo (ĭn′fō) ►*n. Informal* Information.

in•fold (ĭn-fōld′) ►*v.* **1.** To fold inward. **2.** To enfold.

in•form (ĭn-fôrm′) ►*v.* **1.** To impart information to. **2.** To imbue with a quality. **3.** To give or disclose information. [< Lat. *īnfōrmāre*, give form to.]

in•for•mal (ĭn-fôr′məl) ►*adj.* **1.** Not formal or ceremonious; casual. **2.** Not in accord with prescribed regulations. **3.** Suited for everyday use: *informal clothes.* —**in′for•mal′i•ty** (-măl′ĭ-tē) *n.* —**in•for′mal•ly** *adv.*

in•for•mant (ĭn-fôr′mənt) ►*n.* **1.** One that gives information. **2.** An informer.

in•for•ma•tion (ĭn′fər-mā′shən) ►*n.* **1.** Knowledge derived from study or experience. **2.** Knowledge of an event or situation; intelligence. **3.** A collection of facts or data. **4.** Informing or being informed; communication of knowledge. **5.** *Comp. Sci.* Processed, stored, or transmitted data. —**in′for•ma′tion•al** *adj.*

in•for•ma•tive (ĭn-fôr′mə-tĭv) ►*adj.* Providing or disclosing information; instructive. —**in•for′ma•tive•ly** *adv.*

in•formed (ĭn-fôrmd′) ►*adj.* **1.** Possessing or based on reliable information. **2.** Knowledgeable; educated: *the informed consumer.*

in•form•er (ĭn-fôr′mər) ►*n.* An informant, esp. one who informs against others.

infra– ►*pref.* Inferior to, below, or beneath: *infrasonic.* [< Lat. *īnfrā*, beneath.]

in•frac•tion (ĭn-frăk′shən) ►*n.* The act or an instance of infringing; violation. [< Lat. *īnfringere, īnfrāct-*, infringe.]

in•fra•red (ĭn′frə-rĕd′) ►*adj.* Of or relating to the range of invisible radiation wavelengths longer than red in the visible spectrum and on the border of the microwave region.

in•fra•son•ic (ĭn′frə-sŏn′ĭk) ►*adj.* Generating or using waves or vibrations with frequencies below that of audible sound.

in•fra•struc•ture (ĭn′frə-strŭk′chər) ►*n.* **1.** An underlying base esp. for an organization or system. **2.** The basic facilities, services, and installations needed for a community or society.

in•fre•quent (ĭn-frē′kwənt) ►*adj.* **1.** Not occurring regularly; rare. **2.** Situated at wide intervals in time or space. —**in•fre′quence, in•fre′quen•cy** *n.* —**in•fre′quent•ly** *adv.*

in•fringe (ĭn-frĭnj′) ►*v.* **-fringed, -fring•ing 1.** To transgress; violate. **2.** To encroach; trespass. [Lat. *īnfringere*, break.] —**in•fringe′ment** *n.* —**in•fring′er** *n.*

in•fu•ri•ate (ĭn-fyo͝or′ē-āt′) ►*v.* **-at•ed, -at•ing.** To make furious; enrage. [Med.Lat. *īnfuriāre* < Lat. *furia*, rage.] —**in•fu′ri•at′ing•ly** *adv.*

in•fuse (ĭn-fyo͞oz′) ►*v.* **-fused, -fus•ing 1.** To put into as if by pouring. **2.** To fill; imbue. **3.** To steep or soak without boiling. [< Lat. *īnfundere, īnfūs-*, pour in.] —**in•fus′er** *n.* —**in•fus′i•ble** *adj.* —**in•fu′sion** *n.*

-ing¹ ►*suff.* **1.** Used to form the present participle of verbs: *seeing.* **2.** Used to form adjectives resembling present participles but not derived from verbs: *swashbuckling.* [< OE *-ende*.]

-ing² ►*suff.* **1.** Action, process, or art: *dancing.* **2.** Something necessary to perform an action or process: *mooring.* **3.** The result of an action or process: *drawing.* **4.** Something connected with a specified thing or concept: *siding.* [< OE *-ung*.]

Inge (ĭnj), **William.** 1913–73. Amer. playwright.

in•gen•ious (ĭn-jēn′yəs) ►*adj.* **1.** Marked by inventive skill; creative. **2.** Imaginative and resourceful; clever. [< Lat. *ingenium*, talent, skill.] —**in•gen′ious•ly** *adv.* —**in•gen′ious•ness** *n.*

in•gé•nue (ăɴ′zhə-no͞o′) ►*n.* **1.** An artless, innocent girl or young woman. **2.** An actress playing an ingenue. [Fr.]

in•ge•nu•i•ty (ĭn′jə-no͞o′ĭ-tē, -nyo͞o′-) ►*n., pl.* **-ties.** Inventive skill or imagination; cleverness. [Lat. *ingenuitās*, frankness.]

in•gen•u•ous (ĭn-jĕn′yo͞o-əs) ►*adj.* **1.** Unsophisticated; artless. **2.** Straightforward; candid. [< Lat. *ingenuus*, honest.] —**in•gen′u•ous•ly** *adv.* —**in•gen′u•ous•ness** *n.*

in•gest (ĭn-jĕst′) ►*v.* To take into the body by or as if by swallowing. See Syns at **eat.** [Lat. *ingerere, ingest-*.] —**in•ges′tion** *n.*

In•gle•wood (ĭng′gəl-wo͝od′) A city of S CA, a suburb of Los Angeles. Pop. 109,602.

in•glo•ri•ous (ĭn-glôr′ē-əs, -glōr′-) ►*adj.* **1.** Ignominious; disgraceful. **2.** Not famous or renowned. —**in•glo′ri•ous•ly** *adv.*

in•got (ĭng′gət) ►*n.* A mass of metal cast in a shape, such as a bar, for convenient storage or shipment. [ME, mold for casting metal.]

in•grain (ĭn-grān′) ►*v.* To fix deeply or indelibly, as in the mind. ►*n.* (ĭn′grān′). Yarn or fiber dyed before manufacture. [IN–[2] + GRAIN, dye (obs.).]

in•grained (ĭn-grānd′) ►*adj.* **1.** Firmly established; deep-seated: *ingrained prejudice.* **2.** Worked deeply into the fiber: *ingrained dirt.*

in•grate (ĭn′grāt′) ►*n.* An ungrateful person. [< Lat. *ingrātus*, ungrateful.]

in•gra•ti•ate (ĭn-grā′shē-āt′) ►*v.* **-at•ed, -at•ing.** To bring (oneself) into the favor of another. [< Lat. *in grātiam*, into favor.]

in•grat•i•tude (ĭn-grăt′ĭ-to͞od′, -tyo͞od′) ►*n.* Lack of gratitude; ungratefulness.

in•gre•di•ent (ĭn-grē′dē-ənt) ►*n.* An element in a mixture or compound; constituent. See Syns at **element.** [< Lat. *ingredī*, enter.]

In•gres (ăN′grə), **Jean Auguste Dominique.** 1780–1867. French painter.

in•gress (ĭn′grĕs′) ►*n.* **1.** A going in or entering. **2.** A means of entering. [< Lat. *ingredī*, step in.]

in-group (ĭn′gro͞op′) ►*n.* A clique.

in•grown (ĭn′grōn′) ►*adj.* **1.** Grown abnormally into the flesh. **2.** Inbred; innate: *ingrown habits.*

in•gui•nal (ĭng′gwə-nəl) ►*adj.* Relating to or located in the groin. [< Lat. *inguen*, groin.]

in•hab•it (ĭn-hăb′ĭt) ►*v.* To live or reside in. [< Lat. *inhabitāre.*] —**in•hab′it•a•bil′i•ty** *n.* —**in•hab′it•a•ble** *adj.*

in•hab•i•tant (ĭn-hăb′ĭ-tənt) ►*n.* A permanent resident.

in•ha•lant (ĭn-hā′lənt) ►*n.* A medication to be inhaled.

in•ha•la•tor (ĭn′hə-lā′tər) ►*n.* **1.** See **respirator** 1. **2.** See **inhaler** 2.

in•hale (ĭn-hāl′) ►*v.* **-haled, -hal•ing.** To draw into the lungs by breathing. [Lat. *inhālāre.*] —**in′ha•la′tion** (-hə-lā′shən) *n.*

in•hal•er (ĭn-hā′lər) ►*n.* **1.** One that inhales. **2.** A device that produces a vapor to ease breathing.

in•here (ĭn-hîr′) ►*v.* **-hered, -her•ing.** To be inherent or innate. [Lat. *inhaerēre.*] —**in•her′ence** (-hîr′əns, -hĕr′-), **in•her′en•cy** *n.*

in•her•ent (ĭn-hîr′ənt, -hĕr′-) ►*adj.* Existing as an essential constituent or characteristic; intrinsic. —**in•her′ent•ly** *adv.*

in•her•it (ĭn-hĕr′ĭt) ►*v.* **1.** To receive by legal succession or will. **2.** *Biol.* To receive from one's parents by genetic transmission. [< LLat. *inhērēditāre.*] —**in•her′it•a•bil′i•ty** *n.* —**in•her′it•a•ble** *adj.* —**in•her′i•tor** *n.*

in•her•i•tance (ĭn-hĕr′ĭ-təns) ►*n.* **1.** Something inherited or to be inherited. **2.** Something regarded as a heritage. See Syns at **heritage.**

in•hib•it (ĭn-hĭb′ĭt) ►*v.* **1.** To hold back; restrain. **2.** To prohibit; forbid. [< Lat. *inhibēre.*] —**in•hib′i•tive, in•hib′i•to′ry** (-tôr′ē, -tōr′ē) *adj.*

in•hi•bi•tion (ĭn′hə-bĭsh′ən, ĭn′ə-) ►*n.* **1.** The act of inhibiting or the state of being inhibited. **2.** *Psychol.* Restraint of a behavioral process, desire, or impulse.

in•hib•i•tor also **in•hib•it•er** (ĭn-hĭb′ĭ-tər) ►*n.* One that inhibits, as a substance that retards or stops a chemical reaction.

in•hos•pi•ta•ble (ĭn-hŏs′pĭ-tə-bəl, ĭn′hŏ-spĭt′ə-bəl) ►*adj.* **1.** Displaying no hospitality; unfriendly. **2.** Unfavorable to life or growth; hostile. —**in•hos′pi•ta•ble•ness** *n.* —**in•hos′pi•ta•bly** *adv.*

in-house (ĭn′hous′) ►*adj.* Conducted or being within an organization or firm.

in•hu•man (ĭn-hyo͞o′mən) ►*adj.* **1a.** Lacking kindness or pity; cruel. **b.** Deficient in emotional warmth; cold. **2.** Not suited for human needs. **3.** Not of ordinary human form; monstrous. —**in•hu′man•ly** *adv.*

in•hu•mane (ĭn′hyo͞o-mān′) ►*adj.* Lacking pity or compassion. —**in′hu•mane′ly** *adv.*

in•hu•man•i•ty (ĭn′hyo͞o-măn′ĭ-tē) ►*n.*, *pl.* **-ties 1.** Lack of pity or compassion; cruelty. **2.** An inhuman or cruel act.

in•im•i•cal (ĭ-nĭm′ĭ-kəl) ►*adj.* **1.** Injurious or harmful. **2.** Unfriendly; hostile. [< Lat. *inimīcus*, enemy.] —**in•im′i•cal•ly** *adv.*

in•im•i•ta•ble (ĭ-nĭm′ĭ-tə-bəl) ►*adj.* Defying imitation; matchless. —**in•im′i•ta•bly** *adv.*

in•iq•ui•ty (ĭ-nĭk′wĭ-tē) ►*n.*, *pl.* **-ties 1.** Wickedness; sinfulness. **2.** A wicked sin. [< Lat. *inīquus*, unjust.] —**in•iq′ui•tous** *adj.*

in•i•tial (ĭ-nĭsh′əl) ►*adj.* Of or occurring at the beginning; first. ►*n.* The first letter of a name or word. ►*v.* **-tialed, -tial•ing** also **-tialled, -tial•ling.** To mark or sign with initials, esp. as authorization or approval. [< Lat. *initium*, beginning.] —**in•i′tial•ly** *adv.*

in•i•tial•ize (ĭ-nĭsh′ə-līz′) ►*v.* **-ized, -iz•ing** *Comp. Sci.* **1.** To set to a starting position or value. **2.** To prepare (e.g., a printer) for use. —**in•i′tial•i•za′tion** *n.*

in•i•ti•ate (ĭ-nĭsh′ē-āt′) ►*v.* **-at•ed, -at•ing 1.** To begin or originate. **2.** To introduce to a new field, interest, skill, or activity. **3.** To admit into membership, as with ceremonies or ritual. ►*n.* (-ĭt). One who has been initiated. [Lat. *initiāre.*] —**in•i′ti•a′tion** *n.* —**in•i′ti•a′tor** *n.* —**in•i′ti•a•to′ry** (-ə-tôr′ē, -tōr′ē) *adj.*

in•i•tia•tive (ĭ-nĭsh′ə-tĭv) ►*n.* **1.** The ability to begin or follow through with a plan or task; enterprise. **2.** A first step: *took the initiative in breaking the deadlock.* **3.** The right and procedure by which citizens can propose a law by petition and ensure its submission to the electorate.

in•ject (ĭn-jĕkt′) ►*v.* **1.** To force or drive (a fluid) into. **2.** To introduce into conversation or consideration: *injected a note of humor.* **3.** To place into an orbit, trajectory, or stream. [Lat. *inicere, iniect-*, throw in.] —**in•jec′tion** *n.* —**in•jec′tor** *n.*

in•ju•di•cious (ĭn′jo͞o-dĭsh′əs) ►*adj.* Showing a lack of judgment or discretion; unwise. —**in′ju•di′cious•ly** *adv.*

in•junc•tion (ĭn-jŭngk′shən) ►*n.* **1.** A command, directive, or order. **2.** A court order prohibiting or requiring a specific action. [< Lat. *iniungere*, enjoin.] —**in•junc′tive** *adj.*

in•jure (ĭn′jər) ►*v.* **-jured, -jur•ing 1.** To cause harm or damage to. **2.** To commit an injustice or offense against. [< Lat. *iniūriārī.*]

in•ju•ri•ous (ĭn-jo͝or′ē-əs) ►*adj.* Causing injury; harmful. —**in•ju′ri•ous•ly** *adv.*

in•ju•ry (ĭn′jə-rē) ►*n.*, *pl.* **-ries 1.** An act that harms or damages. **2.** A wound or other particular form of hurt, damage, or loss. **3.** Injustice. [< Lat. *iniūria*, injustice.]

in•jus•tice (ĭn-jŭs′tĭs) ►*n.* **1.** Violation of another's rights or of what is right; lack of justice. **2.** An unjust act; wrong.

ink (ĭngk) ►*n.* **1.** A pigmented liquid or paste used esp. for writing or printing. **2.** A dark liquid ejected for protection, as by the squid and octopus. ►*v.* To cover or stain with ink. [< LLat. *encaustum*, purple ink.] —**ink′y** *adj.*

ink•blot (ĭngk′blŏt′) ►*n.* **1.** A blotted pattern of spilled ink. **2.** A pattern resembling an inkblot that is used in inkblot tests.

inkblot test ►*n.* A psychological test in which a subject's interpretation of inkblots is analyzed.

ink-jet printer (ĭngk′jĕt′) ►*n.* A printer that directs electrically charged ink streams onto a page.

in•kling (ĭng′klĭng) ►*n.* **1.** A slight hint or indication. **2.** A vague idea or notion. [Prob. < ME *ningkiling*, suggestion.]

ink•well (ĭngk′wĕl′) ►*n.* A small reservoir for ink.

in•laid (ĭn′lād′) ►*v.* P.t. and p.part. of **inlay.** ►*adj.* Decorated with a pattern set into a surface.

in•land (ĭn′lənd) ►*adj.* **1.** Of or located in the interior part of a country. **2.** *Chiefly Brit.* Operating or applying within a country; domestic. —**in′land** *adv. & n.*

Inland Passage. See **Inside Passage.**

Inland Sea. An arm of the Pacific in S Japan between Honshu, Shikoku, and Kyushu.

in-law (ĭn′lô′) ►*n.* A relative by marriage.

in•lay (ĭn′lā′, ĭn-lā′) ►*v.* **-laid** (-lād′), **-lay•ing.** To set into a surface to form a design. ►*n.* **1.** An inlaid object, design, or decoration. **2.** A solid filling, as of gold, fitted and cemented to a tooth.

in•let (ĭn′lĕt′, -lĭt) ►*n.* **1.** A stream or bay leading inland, as from the ocean; estuary. **2.** A narrow passage of water, as between two islands.

in-line skate (ĭn′līn′) ►*n.* A roller skate whose wheels are arranged in a straight line.

in-line skate

in•mate (ĭn′māt′) ►*n.* An occupant of a communal dwelling, esp. a person confined to an institution such as a prison or hospital.

in me•di•as res (ĭn mē′dē-əs rās′) ►*adv.* In or into the middle of a sequence of events. [Lat. *in mediās rēs.*]

in me•mo•ri•am (ĭn′ mə-môr′ē-əm, -mōr′-) ►*prep.* In memory of. [Lat.]

inn (ĭn) ►*n.* **1.** A hotel. **2.** A tavern. [< OE.]

in•nards (ĭn′ərdz) ►*pl.n. Informal* **1.** Internal bodily organs; viscera. **2.** The inner parts, as of a machine. [Alteration of *inwards*, entrails.]

in•nate (ĭ-nāt′, ĭn′āt′) ►*adj.* **1.** Possessed at birth; inborn. **2.** Possessed as an essential characteristic; inherent. [< Lat. *innātus*, p.part. of *innāscī*, be born in.] —**in•nate′ly** *adv.*

in•ner (ĭn′ər) ►*adj.* **1.** Located farther inside: *an inner room.* **2.** Of or relating to the mind or spirit. **3.** More exclusive, influential, or important: *the inner circles of government.* [< OE *innera.*] —**in′ner•ness** *n.*

inner city ►*n.* The usu. older central part of a city, esp. when crowded, neglected, and decaying. —**in′ner-cit′y** *adj.*

in•ner-di•rect•ed (ĭn′ər-dĭ-rĕk′tĭd, -dī-) ►*adj.* Guided, as in behavior, by one's own set of values rather than external standards.

inner ear ►*n.* The part of the vertebrate ear that includes the semicircular canals, vestibule, and cochlea.

Inner Hebrides. See **Hebrides.**

Inner Mongolia. See **Nei Monggol.**

in•ner•most (ĭn′ər-mōst′) ►*adj.* **1.** Situated farthest within. **2.** Most intimate.

inner planet ►*n.* Any of the four planets, Mercury, Venus, Earth, and Mars, whose orbits are closest to the sun.

inner tube ►*n.* A flexible, airtight hollow ring, usu. made of rubber, inserted into the casing of a pneumatic tire for holding compressed air.

in•ning (ĭn′ĭng) ►*n.* A division of a baseball game in which each team has a turn at bat.

inn•keep•er (ĭn′kē′pər) ►*n.* One who owns or manages an inn or hotel.

in•no•cent (ĭn′ə-sənt) ►*adj.* **1.** Uncorrupted by evil, malice, or wrongdoing; sinless. **2.** Not guilty of a specific crime or offense; legally blameless. **3.** Not dangerous or harmful; innocuous. **4a.** Not experienced or worldly; naive. **b.** Without deception or guile; artless. [< Lat. *innocēns, innocent-*, harmless.] —**in′no•cence** *n.* —**in′no•cent** *n.* —**in′no•cent•ly** *adv.*

Innocent III. 1161–1216. Pope (1198–1216).

in•noc•u•ous (ĭ-nŏk′yo͞o-əs) ►*adj.* **1.** Having no adverse effect; harmless. **2.** Not likely to provoke strong emotion; insipid. [< Lat. *innocuus.*] —**in•noc′u•ous•ly** *adv.* —**in•noc′u•ous•ness** *n.*

in•nom•i•nate (ĭ-nŏm′ə-nĭt) ►*adj.* **1.** Having no name. **2.** Anonymous. [LLat. *innōminātus.*]

in•no•vate (ĭn′ə-vāt′) ►*v.* **-vat•ed, -vat•ing 1.** To begin or introduce (something new). **2.** To be creative. [< Lat. *innovāre*, renew < *novus*, new.] —**in′no•va′tive** *adj.* —**in′no•va′tor** *n.*

in•no•va•tion (ĭn′ə-vā′shən) ►*n.* **1.** The act of innovating. **2.** Something, such as a method or product, newly introduced. —**in′no•va′tion•al** *adj.*

Inns•bruck (ĭnz′bro͝ok′, ĭns′-) A city of SW Austria WSW of Salzburg. Pop. 118,112.

in•nu•en•do (ĭn′yo͞o-ĕn′dō) ►*n., pl.* **-does.** An indirect or subtle, usu. derogatory insinuation. [< Lat. *innuere*, nod to.]

in•nu•mer•a•ble (ĭ-no͞o′mər-ə-bəl, ĭ-nyo͞o′-) ►*adj.* Too numerous to be counted. See Syns at **incalculable.**

in•oc•u•late (ĭ-nŏk′yə-lāt′) ►*v.* **-lat•ed, -lat•ing.** To introduce a serum, vaccine, or antigenic substance into, esp. to produce or boost immunity to a specific disease. [< Lat. *inoculāre, inoculāt-*, engraft.] —**in•oc′u•la′tion** *n.*

in•oc•u•lum (ĭ-nŏk′yə-ləm) ►*n., pl.* **-la** (-lə) or **-lums.** The material used in an inoculation.

in•of•fen•sive (ĭn′ə-fĕn′sĭv) ►*adj.* Giving no offense; unobjectionable.

in•op•er•a•ble (ĭn-ŏp′ər-ə-bəl, -ŏp′rə-) ►*adj.* **1.** Not working; inoperative. **2.** Not able to be treated surgically.

in•op•er•a•tive (ĭn-ŏp′ər-ə-tĭv, -ŏp′rə-) ►*adj.* **1.** Not working or functioning. **2.** Not in force.

in•op•por•tune (ĭn-ŏp′ər-to͞on′, -tyo͞on′) ►*adj.* Inappropriate or ill-timed. —**in•op′-**

por•tune′ly *adv.* —**in•op′por•tune′ness** *n.*

in•or•di•nate (ĭn-ôr′dn-ĭt) ►*adj.* **1.** Exceeding reasonable limits; immoderate. **2.** Not regulated; disorderly. [< Lat. *inōrdinātus.*] —**in•or′di•nate•ly** *adv.*

in•or•gan•ic (ĭn′ôr-găn′ĭk) ►*adj.* **1a.** Involving neither organic life nor the products of organic life. **b.** Not composed of organic matter. **2.** *Chem.* Of or relating to compounds not usu. classified as organic. —**in′or•gan′i•cal•ly** *adv.*

in•pa•tient (ĭn′pā′shənt) ►*n.* A patient who is admitted to a hospital for treatment.

in•put (ĭn′po͝ot′) ►*n.* **1.** Something put in. **2.** Energy, work, or power put into a system or machine. **3.** Information put into a computer system for processing. **4.** *Informal* **a.** Contribution of information, comments, or viewpoint to a common effort. **b.** Information in general. —**in′put′** *v.*

in•quest (ĭn′kwĕst′) ►*n.* **1.** A judicial inquiry, usu. held before a jury. **2.** An investigation. See Syns at **inquiry.** [< Lat. *inquīrere, inquīsīt-,* inquire.]

in•quire (ĭn-kwīr′) also **en•quire** (ĕn-) ►*v.* **-quired, -quir•ing 1.** To ask or ask about. **2.** To make an inquiry or investigation. [< Lat. *inquīrere.*] —**in•quir′er** *n.* —**in•quir′ing•ly** *adv.*

in•quir•y (ĭn-kwīr′ē, ĭn′kwə-rē) also **en•quir•y** (ĕn-kwīr′ē, ĕn′kwə-rē) ►*n., pl.* **-ies 1.** The act or process of inquiring. **2.** A question; query. **3.** A close examination of a matter in a search for information or truth.

Syns: *inquiry, inquest, investigation, probe, research* **n.**

in•qui•si•tion (ĭn′kwĭ-zĭsh′ən, ĭng′-) ►*n.* **1.** An investigation, such as an inquest. **2. Inquisition** A former Roman Catholic tribunal established to suppress heresy. **3.** A rigorous interrogation or scrutiny. [< Lat. *inquīrere, inquīsīt-,* inquire.] —**in•quis′i•tor** (-kwĭz′ĭ-tər) *n.* —**in•quis′i•to′ri•al** (-kwĭz′ĭ-tôr′ē-əl, -tōr′-) *adj.*

in•quis•i•tive (ĭn-kwĭz′ĭ-tĭv) ►*adj.* **1.** Unduly curious. **2.** Eager for knowledge. —**in•quis′i•tive•ly** *adv.* —**in•quis′i•tive•ness** *n.*

in re (ĭn rā′, rē′) ►*prep. Law* In the matter or case of; in regard to. [Lat. *in rē.*]

in•road (ĭn′rōd′) ►*n.* **1.** A hostile invasion; raid. **2.** An advance, esp. at another's expense; encroachment. [IN[1] + ROAD, raid (obs.).]

in•rush (ĭn′rŭsh′) ►*n.* A sudden influx.

ins. ►*abbr.* **1.** inches **2.** inspector

in•sa•lu•bri•ous (ĭn′sə-lo͞o′brē-əs) ►*adj.* Not promoting health; unwholesome.

in•sane (ĭn-sān′) ►*adj.* **1a.** Of, exhibiting, or afflicted with mental disorder. **b.** Characteristic of or associated with persons who are insane. **2.** Very foolish; absurd. —**in•sane′ly** *adv.* —**in•san′i•ty** (-săn′ĭ-tē) *n.*

in•sa•tia•ble (ĭn-sā′shə-bəl, -shē-ə-) ►*adj.* Impossible to satiate or satisfy. —**in•sa′tia•bil′i•ty, in•sa′tia•ble•ness** *n.* —**in•sa′tia•bly** *adv.*

in•scribe (ĭn-skrīb′) ►*v.* **-scribed, -scrib•ing 1.** To write, print, carve, or engrave (words or letters) on or in a surface. **2.** To mark or engrave with words or letters. **3.** To enter (a name) on a list. **4.** To dedicate to someone. **5.** *Math.* To draw (one figure) within another figure so that every vertex of the enclosed figure touches the outer figure. [Lat. *īnscrībere.*] —**in•scrib′er** *n.* —**in•scrip′tion** (-skrĭp′shən) *n.*

in•scru•ta•ble (ĭn-skro͞o′tə-bəl) ►*adj.* Difficult to fathom or understand. [< LLat. *īnscrūtābilis.*] —**in•scru′ta•bil′i•ty, in•scru′ta•ble•ness** *n.* —**in•scru′ta•bly** *adv.*

in•seam (ĭn′sēm′) ►*n.* The inside seam of a pant leg.

in•sect (ĭn′sĕkt′) ►*n.* Any of a class of small, usu. winged invertebrate animals, such as flies, beetles, and moths, having three pairs of legs and a three-segmented body. [Lat. *īnsectum* < *īnsecāre,* cut up.]

in•sec•ti•cide (ĭn-sĕk′tĭ-sīd′) ►*n.* A substance used to kill insects. —**in•sec′ti•cid′al** *adj.*

in•sec•ti•vore (ĭn-sĕk′tə-vôr′, -vōr′) ►*n.* An insect-eating organism. —**in′sec•tiv′o•rous** (-tĭv′ər-əs) *adj.*

in•se•cure (ĭn′sĭ-kyo͝or′) ►*adj.* **1.** Inadequately guarded or protected; unsafe. **2.** Not firm or fixed; shaky. **3.** Lacking self-confidence. —**in′se•cure′ly** *adv.* —**in′se•cu′ri•ty** *n.*

in•sem•i•nate (ĭn-sĕm′ə-nāt′) ►*v.* **-nat•ed, -nat•ing.** To introduce or inject semen into the reproductive tract of (a female). [Lat. *īnsēmināre,* implant < *sēmen,* seed.] —**in•sem′i•na′tion** *n.* —**in•sem′i•na′tor** *n.*

in•sen•sate (ĭn-sĕn′sāt′, -sĭt) ►*adj.* **1a.** Inanimate. **b.** Unconscious. **2.** Lacking sensibility; unfeeling. **3.** Lacking sense; foolish.

in•sen•si•ble (ĭn-sĕn′sə-bəl) ►*adj.* **1.** Imperceptible; inappreciable. **2a.** Unconscious. **b.** Inanimate. **c.** Insensitive; numb. **3a.** Unaware. **b.** Callous; indifferent. —**in•sen′si•bil′i•ty** *n.* —**in•sen′si•bly** *adv.*

in•sen•si•tive (ĭn-sĕn′sĭ-tĭv) ►*adj.* **1.** Not physically sensitive; numb. **2.** Unresponsive to or unaffected by the feelings of others; unfeeling. —**in•sen′si•tive•ly** *adv.* —**in•sen′si•tiv′i•ty** *n.*

in•sen•tient (ĭn-sĕn′shənt) ►*adj.* Devoid of sensation or consciousness. —**in•sen′tience** *n.*

in•sep•a•ra•ble (ĭn-sĕp′ər-ə-bəl, -sĕp′rə-) ►*adj.* **1.** Impossible to separate. **2.** Very closely associated. —**in•sep′a•ra•bil′i•ty** *n.* —**in•sep′a•ra•bly** *adv.*

in•sert (ĭn-sûrt′) ►*v.* **1.** To put, place, or set into: *inserted a key in a lock.* **2.** To interpolate. ►*n.* (ĭn′sûrt′). Something inserted or intended for insertion, as a chart into a text. [Lat. *īnserere.*] —**in•ser′tion** *n.*

in•set (ĭn′sĕt′, ĭn-sĕt′) ►*v.* To set in; insert. —**in′set′** *n.*

in•shore (ĭn′shôr′, -shōr′) ►*adv.* & *adj.* Close to or coming toward a shore.

in•side (ĭn-sīd′, ĭn′sīd′) ►*n.* **1.** An inner or interior part. **2.** An inner side or surface. **3. insides** *Informal* **a.** The inner organs; entrails. **b.** The inner parts or workings: *the insides of a TV set.* ►*adv.* Into or in the interior; within. ►*prep.* **1.** Within: *inside an hour.* **2.** Into the interior of: *going inside the house.* —***idioms:*** **inside of** Within: *inside of an hour.* **inside out 1.** With the inner surface turned out. **2.** *Informal* Thoroughly; completely: *knew the city inside out.* **on the inside** In a position of confidence or influence. —**in•side′** *adj.*

Inside Passage also **Inland Passage.** A natural protected waterway extending about 1,529 km (950 mi) from Puget Sound to Skagway, AK.

in•sid•er (ĭn-sī′dər) ►*n.* **1.** An accepted member of a group. **2.** One who has special knowledge or access to confidential information.

inside track ►*n.* *Informal* An advantageous position, as in a competition.

in•sid•i•ous (ĭn-sĭd′ē-əs) ►*adj.* **1.** Working or spreading harmfully in a subtle or stealthy manner. **2.** Intended to entrap; treacherous. **3.** Beguiling but harmful. [< Lat. *īnsidēre*, lie in wait < *sedēre*, sit.] —**in•sid′i•ous•ly** *adv.* —**in•sid′i•ous•ness** *n.*

in•sight (ĭn′sīt′) ►*n.* The capacity to discern the true nature of a situation; penetration. —**in′sight′ful** *adj.* —**in•sight′ful•ness** *n.*

in•sig•ni•a (ĭn-sĭg′nē-ə) ►*n., pl.* **-ni•a** or **-ni•as.** A distinguishing badge of office, rank, membership, or nationality; emblem. [< Lat. *īnsignis*, marked.]

in•sig•nif•i•cant (ĭn′sĭg-nĭf′ĭ-kənt) ►*adj.* **1.** Lacking in importance; trivial. **2.** Small in size, power, value, or amount. **3.** Having little or no meaning. —**in′sig•nif′i•cance** *n.* —**in′sig•nif′i•cant•ly** *adv.*

in•sin•cere (ĭn′sĭn-sîr′) ►*adj.* Not sincere; hypocritical. —**in′sin•cere′ly** *adv.* —**in′sin•cer′i•ty** (-sĕr′ĭ-tē) *n.*

in•sin•u•ate (ĭn-sĭn′yo͞o-āt′) ►*v.* **-at•ed, -at•ing 1.** To introduce (e.g., a thought) gradually and insidiously. **2.** To introduce or insert (oneself) by subtle and artful means. **3.** To hint. [Lat. *īnsinuāre* < *sinus*, curve.] —**in•sin′u•a′tion** *n.*

in•sip•id (ĭn-sĭp′ĭd) ►*adj.* **1.** Lacking flavor or zest; not tasty. **2.** Lacking excitement or interest; dull. [< LLat. *īnsipidus*.] —**in•sip′id•ly** *adv.*

in•sist (ĭn-sĭst′) ►*v.* **1.** To be firm in one's demand or course. **2.** To assert or demand (something) vehemently and persistently. [Lat. *īnsistere*, persist < *sistere*, stand.] —**in•sis′tence, in•sis′ten•cy** *n.* —**in•sis′tent** *adj.* —**in•sis′tent•ly** *adv.*

in si•tu (ĭn sī′to͞o, sē′-) ►*adv.* & *adj.* In the original position. [Lat. *in situ*.]

in•so•far as (ĭn′sō-fär′) ►*conj.* To the extent that.

in•sole (ĭn′sōl′) ►*n.* **1.** The inner sole of a shoe or boot. **2.** An extra strip of material put inside a shoe for comfort or protection.

in•so•lent (ĭn′sə-lənt) ►*adj.* Disrespectfully arrogant; impertinent; rude. [< Lat. *īnsolēns*.] —**in′so•lence** *n.* —**in′so•lent•ly** *adv.*

in•sol•u•ble (ĭn-sŏl′yə-bəl) ►*adj.* **1.** Incapable of being dissolved. **2.** Difficult or impossible to solve or explain. —**in•sol′u•bil′i•ty** *n.* —**in•sol′u•bly** *adv.*

in•sol•vent (ĭn-sŏl′vənt) ►*adj.* Unable to pay one's debts. —**in•sol′ven•cy** *n.*

in•som•ni•a (ĭn-sŏm′nē-ə) ►*n.* Chronic inability to sleep. [< Lat. *īnsomnis*, sleepless < *somnus*, sleep.] —**in•som′ni•ac′** (-ăk′) *adj.* & *n.*

in•so•much as (ĭn′sō-mŭch′) ►*conj.* Inasmuch as; since.

in•sou•ci•ant (ĭn-so͞o′sē-ənt) ►*adj.* Blithely unconcerned. [Fr.] —**in•sou′ci•ance** *n.*

in•spect (ĭn-spĕkt′) ►*v.* **1.** To examine carefully and critically, esp. for flaws. **2.** To review or examine officially. [Lat. *īnspicere*, *īnspect-* < *specere*, look at.] —**in•spec′tion** *n.* —**in•spec′tor** *n.*

inspector general ►*n., pl.* **inspectors general.** An officer with general investigative powers within a civil, military, or other organization.

in•spi•ra•tion (ĭn′spə-rā′shən) ►*n.* **1a.** Stimulation of the mind or emotions to a high level of feeling or activity. **b.** The condition of being so stimulated. **2.** One that inspires. **3.** Something that is inspired. **4.** Inhalation. —**in′spi•ra′tion•al** *adj.* —**in′spi•ra′tion•al•ly** *adv.*

in•spire (ĭn-spīr′) ►*v.* **-spired, -spir•ing 1.** To fill with noble or reverent emotion; exalt. **2.** To stimulate creativity or action. **3.** To elicit or create in another. **4.** To inhale. [< Lat. *īnspīrāre*.] —**in•spir′er** *n.*

in•spir•it (ĭn-spĭr′ĭt) ►*v.* To instill courage or life into; animate. See Syns at **encourage.**

inst. ►*abbr.* **1.** institute **2.** institution

in•sta•bil•i•ty (ĭn′stə-bĭl′ĭ-tē) ►*n., pl.* **-ties.** Lack of stability.

in•stall also **in•stal** (ĭn-stôl′) ►*v.* **-stalled, -stall•ing 1.** To set in position and connect or adjust for use. **2.** To induct into an office, rank, or position. **3.** To put or place. [< Med.Lat. *īnstallāre*.] —**in′stal•la′tion** (-stə-lā′shən) *n.* —**in•stall′er** *n.*

in•stall•ment also **in•stal•ment** (ĭn-stôl′mənt) ►*n.* **1.** One of a number of successive payments of a debt. **2.** A portion of something, such as a publication, issued at intervals.

in•stance (ĭn′stəns) ►*n.* **1.** A case or example. **2.** An occurrence or occasion. **3.** A suggestion or request: *called at the instance of his attorney.* ►*v.* **-stanced, -stanc•ing.** To offer as an example; cite. [< Lat. *īnstantia*, presence < *īnstāns*, present. See INSTANT.]

in•stant (ĭn′stənt) ►*n.* **1.** A very brief space of time; moment. **2.** A particular point in time. ►*adj.* **1.** Immediate. **2.** Imperative; urgent: *an instant need.* **3.** Designed, prepared, or processed for quick preparation: *instant coffee.* [< Lat. *īnstāns*, present < *īnstāre*, approach < *stāre*, stand.]

in•stan•ta•ne•ous (ĭn′stən-tā′nē-əs) ►*adj.* **1.** Occurring or completed without perceptible delay: *Relief was instantaneous.* **2.** Present or occurring at a specific instant. —**in′stan•ta′ne•ous•ly** *adv.* —**in′stan•ta′ne•ous•ness** *n.*

in•stant•ly (ĭn′stənt-lē) ►*adv.* At once.

in•stead (ĭn-stĕd′) ►*adv.* In the place of that previously mentioned. —***idiom:* instead of** In place of; rather than.

in•step (ĭn′stĕp′) ►*n.* The arched middle part of the human foot between the toes and ankle.

in•sti•gate (ĭn′stĭ-gāt′) ►*v.* **-gat•ed, -gat•ing 1.** To urge on. **2.** To incite. [Lat. *īnstīgāre*.] —**in′sti•ga′tion** *n.* —**in′sti•ga′tor** *n.*

in•still also **in•stil** (ĭn-stĭl′) ►*v.* **-stilled, -still•ing 1.** To introduce gradually; implant. **2.** To pour in (e.g., medicine) drop by drop. [< Lat. *īnstīllāre*, drip in.] —**in′stil•la′tion** (-stə-lā′shən) *n.* —**in•still′er** *n.*

in•stinct (ĭn′stĭngkt′) ►*n.* **1.** An inner pattern of behavior that is not learned and results in complex animal responses such as building of nests and nursing of young. **2.** A powerful motivation or impulse. **3.** A natural capability or aptitude. [< Lat. *īnstinguere*, *īnstīnct-*, impel.] —**in•stinc′tive** *adj.* —**in•stinc′tive•ly** *adv.* —**in•stinc′tu•al** (-stĭngk′cho͞o-əl) *adj.*

in•sti•tute (ĭn′stĭ-to͞ot′, -tyo͞ot′) ►*v.* **-tut•ed,**

-tut•ing 1. To establish, organize, and set in operation. **2.** To initiate; begin. See Syns at **found**[1]. ►*n.* **1.** Something instituted, esp. an authoritative rule. **2.** An organization founded to promote a cause. **3.** An educational institution. **4.** A seminar or workshop. [< Lat. *īnstituere* : IN–[2] + *statuere*, set up.]

in•sti•tu•tion (ĭn′stĭ-to͞o′shən, -tyo͞o′-) ►*n.* **1.** The act of instituting. **2.** An established custom, practice, or relationship in a society. **3a.** An organization or foundation, esp. one dedicated to education, public service, or culture. **b.** The building housing such an organization. **c.** A place for care of the disabled or mentally ill. —**in′sti•tu′tion•al** *adj.* —**in′sti•tu′tion•al•ly** *adv.*

in•sti•tu•tion•al•ize (ĭn′stĭ-to͞o′shə-nə-līz′, -tyo͞o′-) ►*v.* **-ized, -iz•ing 1.** To make into an institution. **2.** To (confine) in an institution. —**in′sti•tu′tion•al•i•za′tion** *n.*

in•struct (ĭn-strŭkt′) ►*v.* **1.** To teach; educate. **2.** To give orders to; direct. [< Lat. *īnstruere*, *īnstrūct-*, prepare.] —**in•struc′tive** *adj.* —**in•struc′tive•ly** *adv.*

in•struc•tion (ĭn-strŭk′shən) ►*n.* **1.** The act, practice, or profession of instructing. **2a.** Something learned. **b.** A lesson. **3.** *Comp. Sci.* A sequence of bits that tells a central processing unit to perform a particular operation. **4a.** An authoritative direction; order. **b. instructions** Detailed directions on procedure. —**in•struc′tion•al** *adj.*

in•struc•tor (ĭn-strŭk′tər) ►*n.* One who instructs, esp. a college teacher ranking below assistant professor. —**in•struc′tor•ship′** *n.*

in•stru•ment (ĭn′strə-mənt) ►*n.* **1.** A means by which something is done; agency. **2.** An implement used to facilitate work. **3.** A device for recording or measuring, esp. one functioning as part of a control system. **4.** A device for playing or producing music. **5.** A legal document. ►*v.* (-mĕnt′). To provide with instruments. [< Lat. *īnstrūmentum*, tool.]

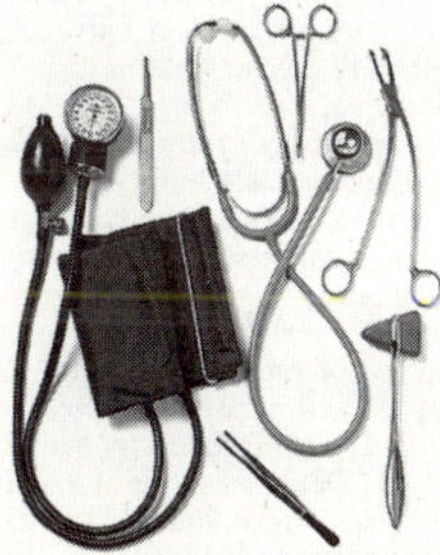

instrument
medical instruments

in•stru•men•tal (ĭn′strə-mĕn′tl) ►*adj.* **1.** Serving as a means or agency. **2.** *Mus.* Performed on or written for an instrument as opposed to a voice or voices. —**in′stru•men′tal•ly** *adv.*

in•stru•men•tal•ist (ĭn′strə-mĕn′tl-ĭst) ►*n.* One who plays a musical instrument.

in•stru•men•tal•i•ty (ĭn′strə-mĕn-tăl′ĭ-tē) ►*n., pl.* **-ties.** A means; agency.

in•stru•men•ta•tion (ĭn′strə-mĕn-tā′shən) ►*n.* **1.** The application or use of instruments. **2.** The arrangement of music for instruments.

instrument landing ►*n.* An aircraft landing made by means of instruments and ground-based radio equipment only.

in•sub•or•di•nate (ĭn′sə-bôr′dn-ĭt) ►*adj.* Not submissive to authority. —**in′sub•or′di•nate•ly** *adv.* —**in′sub•or′di•na′tion** *n.*

in•sub•stan•tial (ĭn′səb-stăn′shəl) ►*adj.* **1.** Lacking substance or reality. See Syns at **immaterial. 2.** Not firm or solid; flimsy. —**in′sub•stan′ti•al′i•ty** (-shē-ăl′ĭ-tē) *n.*

in•suf•fer•a•ble (ĭn-sŭf′ər-ə-bəl, -sŭf′rə-) ►*adj.* Impossible to endure; intolerable. —**in•suf′fer•a•bly** *adv.*

in•suf•fi•cient (ĭn′sə-fĭsh′ənt) ►*adj.* Not sufficient; inadequate. —**in′suf•fi′cien•cy** *n.* —**in′suf•fi′cient•ly** *adv.*

in•su•lar (ĭn′sə-lər, ĭns′yə-) ►*adj.* **1.** Of or constituting an island. **2a.** Isolated. **b.** Narrow-minded. [< Lat. *īnsula*, island.] —**in′su•lar′i•ty** *n.*

in•su•late (ĭn′sə-lāt′, ĭns′yə-) ►*v.* **-lat•ed, -lat•ing 1.** To detach. See Syns at **isolate. 2.** To prevent the passage of heat, electricity, or sound into or out of, esp. by surrounding with a nonconducting material. [< Lat. *īnsula*, island.] —**in′su•la′tion** *n.* —**in′su•la′tor** *n.*

in•su•lin (ĭn′sə-lĭn) ►*n.* **1.** A pancreatic hormone that regulates the metabolism of carbohydrates and fats by controlling blood glucose levels. **2.** A pharmaceutical preparation containing this hormone. [Lat. *īnsula*, island + -IN.]

insulin shock ►*n.* Acute hypoglycemia usu. resulting from excessive insulin in the blood.

in•sult (ĭn-sŭlt′) ►*v.* To speak to or treat with disrespect or contempt. ►*n.* (ĭn′sŭlt′). An offensive or disrespectful action or remark. [< Lat. *īnsultāre*.]

in•su•per•a•ble (ĭn-so͞o′pər-ə-bəl) ►*adj.* Impossible to overcome; insurmountable. —**in•su′per•a•bil′i•ty** *n.* —**in•su′per•a•bly** *adv.*

in•sup•port•a•ble (ĭn′sə-pôr′tə-bəl, -pōr′-) ►*adj.* **1.** Not endurable; intolerable. **2.** Unjustifiable. —**in′sup•port′a•bly** *adv.*

in•sur•ance (ĭn-sho͝or′əns) ►*n.* **1.** The act of insuring or state of being insured. **2.** The business of insuring persons or property. **3a.** A contract binding a company to indemnify an insured party against specified loss. **b.** The sum for which something is insured. **4.** A protective measure or device.

in•sure (ĭn-sho͝or′) ►*v.* **-sured, -sur•ing 1.** To cover with insurance. **2.** To make sure, certain, or secure. See Usage Note at **assure.** [< OFr. *enseurer*, assure.] —**in•sur′a•ble** *adj.* —**in•sur′er** *n.*

in•sured (ĭn-sho͝ord′) ►*n.* One that is covered by insurance.

in•sur•gent (ĭn-sûr′jənt) ►*adj.* Rising in revolt; rebellious. ►*n.* **1.** One who revolts against civil authority. **2.** A member of a political party who rebels against its leadership. [< Lat. *īnsurgere*, rise up.] —**in•sur′gence, in•sur′gen•cy** *n.*

in•sur•mount•a•ble (ĭn′sər-moun′tə-bəl) ►*adj.* Impossible to surmount; insuperable. —**in′sur•mount′a•bil′i•ty** *n.* —**in′sur•mount′a•bly** *adv.*

in•sur•rec•tion (ĭn′sə-rĕk′shən) ►*n.* The act

or an instance of open revolt against civil authority or a constituted government. [< Lat. *īnsurgere, īnsurrēct-*, rise up.] —**in′sur•rec′tion•ist** *n.*

int. ▸*abbr.* **1.** interest **2.** intermediate **3.** international **4.** intransitive

in•tact (ĭn-tăkt′) ▸*adj.* Not impaired in any way. [< Lat. *intāctus*, untouched.] —**in•tact′ness** *n.*

in•ta•glio (ĭn-tăl′yō, -täl′-) ▸*n., pl.* **-glios.** A figure or design carved deeply into the surface of hard metal or stone. [Ital. < *intagliare*, engrave.]

in•take (ĭn′tāk′) ▸*n.* **1.** An opening by which a fluid enters a container or pipe. **2a.** The act of taking in. **b.** The quantity taken in.

in•tan•gi•ble (ĭn-tăn′jə-bəl) ▸*adj.* **1.** Incapable of being perceived by the senses; lacking physical substance. **2.** Incapable of being realized or defined. ▸*n.* Something intangible. —**in•tan′gi•bil′i•ty, in•tan′gi•ble•ness** *n.* —**in•tan′gi•bly** *adv.*

in•te•ger (ĭn′tĭ-jər) ▸*n.* A member of the set of positive whole numbers (1, 2, 3, . . .), negative whole numbers (–1, –2, –3, . . .), and zero (0). [< Lat., whole.]

in•te•gral (ĭn′tĭ-grəl, ĭn-tĕg′rəl) ▸*adj.* **1.** Essential or necessary for completeness; constituent. **2.** Whole; entire. **3.** (ĭn′tĭ-grəl) *Math.* Expressed or expressible as or in terms of integers. ▸*n.* A complete unit; whole. [< Lat. *integer*, whole.]

integral calculus ▸*n. Math.* The study of integration and its use in finding volumes, areas, and solutions of differential equations.

in•te•grate (ĭn′tĭ-grāt′) ▸*v.* **-grat•ed, -grat•ing 1.** To make into a whole; unify. **2.** To join with something else; unite. **3.** To open to people of all races or ethnic groups without restriction; desegregate. [< Lat. *integer*, whole.] —**in′te•gra′tion** *n.* —**in′te•gra′tion•ist** *adj. & n.* —**in′te•gra′tive** *adj.*

in•te•grat•ed circuit (ĭn′tĭ-grā′tĭd) ▸*n.* A complex set of electronic components and their interconnections that are etched or imprinted on a chip.

in•teg•ri•ty (ĭn-tĕg′rĭ-tē) ▸*n.* **1.** Steadfast adherence to a strict moral or ethical code. **2.** Soundness. **3.** Completeness; unity. [< Lat. *integer*, whole.]

in•teg•u•ment (ĭn-tĕg′yo͞o-mənt) ▸*n.* A natural outer covering, such as the skin or a seed coat. [Lat. *integumentum* : IN–[2] + *tegere*, cover.]

in•tel•lect (ĭn′tl-ĕkt′) ▸*n.* **1a.** The ability to learn, reason, and understand. **b.** The ability to think abstractly or profoundly. **2.** A person of great intellectual ability. [< Lat. *intellegere, intellēct-*, perceive.]

in•tel•lec•tu•al (ĭn′tl-ĕk′cho͞o-əl) ▸*adj.* **1a.** Of, engaging, or requiring use of the intellect. **b.** Rational. **2a.** Having a superior intellect. **b.** Given to abstract or philosophical thought. ▸*n.* An intellectual person. —**in′tel•lec′tu•al•ly** *adv.*

in•tel•lec•tu•al•ize (ĭn′tl-ĕk′cho͞o-ə-līz′) ▸*v.* **-ized, -iz•ing 1.** To make rational. **2.** *Psychol.* To analyze (an emotional problem) intellectually, esp. so as to avoid a more direct confrontation. —**in′tel•lec′tu•al•i•za′tion** *n.*

in•tel•li•gence (ĭn-tĕl′ə-jəns) ▸*n.* **1a.** The capacity to acquire and apply knowledge. **b.** The faculty of thought and reason. **c.** Superior powers of mind. **2.** Information; news. See Syns at **news. 3a.** Secret information, esp. about an enemy. **b.** The work of gathering such information; espionage.

intelligence quotient ▸*n.* The ratio of tested mental age to chronological age, usu. expressed as a quotient multiplied by 100.

in•tel•li•gent (ĭn-tĕl′ə-jənt) ▸*adj.* **1.** Having intelligence: *intelligent life.* **2.** Having a high degree of intelligence. **3.** Showing intelligence: *an intelligent act.* [< Lat. *intellegere*, perceive.] —**in•tel′li•gent•ly** *adv.*

in•tel•li•gent•si•a (ĭn-tĕl′ə-jĕnt′sē-ə, -gĕnt′-) ▸*n.* The intellectual elite of a society. [Russ. *intelligentsiya.*]

in•tel•li•gi•ble (ĭn-tĕl′ĭ-jə-bəl) ▸*adj.* Capable of being understood; comprehensible. [< Lat. *intellegere*, perceive.] —**in•tel′li•gi•bil′i•ty** *n.* —**in•tel′li•gi•bly** *adv.*

in•tem•per•ance (ĭn-tĕm′pər-əns, -prəns) ▸*n.* Lack of temperance, esp. in the drinking of alcoholic beverages. —**in•tem′per•ate** *adj.* —**in•tem′per•ate•ly** *adv.*

in•tend (ĭn-tĕnd′) ▸*v.* **1.** To have in mind; plan. **2.** To design for a specific purpose. **3.** To signify or mean. [< Lat. *intendere.*]

in•tend•ed (ĭn-tĕn′dĭd) ▸*adj.* **1.** Deliberate; intentional. **2.** Prospective; future. ▸*n. Informal* One engaged to be married.

in•tense (ĭn-tĕns′) ▸*adj.* **-tens•er, -tens•est 1.** Displaying a distinctive feature to an extreme degree. **2.** Extreme in degree, strength, or size. **3.** Involving or showing great concentration or strain. **4.** Deeply felt; profound. [< Lat. *intēnsus*, p.part. of *intendere*, intend.] —**in•tense′ly** *adv.* —**in•tense′ness** *n.*

Syns: *intense, fierce, vehement, violent* **adj.**

in•ten•si•fy (ĭn-tĕn′sə-fī′) ▸*v.* **-fied, -fy•ing.** To make or become intense or more intense. —**in•ten′si•fi•ca′tion** *n.*

in•ten•si•ty (ĭn-tĕn′sĭ-tē) ▸*n., pl.* **-ties 1.** Exceptionally great concentration, power, or force. **2.** Degree; strength. **3.** *Phys.* The amount or degree of strength of electricity, light, heat, or sound per unit area or volume.

in•ten•sive (ĭn-tĕn′sĭv) ▸*adj.* **1.** Relating to or marked by intensity: *intensive training.* **2.** *Gram.* Adding emphasis. ▸*n. Gram.* A word or word element, such as the adverb *awfully,* that adds emphasis but no new meaning. —**in•ten′sive•ly** *adv.*

in•tent (ĭn-tĕnt′) ▸*n.* **1.** An aim or purpose. **2.** *Law* The state of one's mind at the time one carries out an action. **3.** Meaning or significance. ▸*adj.* **1.** Firmly fixed; concentrated. **2.** Engrossed. **3.** Determined on a specific purpose. [< Lat. *intendere*, intend.] —**in•tent′ly** *adv.* —**in•tent′ness** *n.*

in•ten•tion (ĭn-tĕn′shən) ▸*n.* **1.** A plan of action; design. **2.** An aim that guides action; objective.

in•ten•tion•al (ĭn-tĕn′shə-nəl) ▸*adj.* Done deliberately; intended. —**in•ten′tion•al′i•ty** (-năl′ĭ-tē) *n.* —**in•ten′tion•al•ly** *adv.*

in•ter (ĭn-tûr′) ▸*v.* **-terred, -ter•ring.** To place in a grave; bury. [< Med.Lat. *interrāre* < Lat. *terra*, earth.]

inter– ▸*pref.* **1.** Between; among: *international.* **2.** Mutual; reciprocal: *interdependent.* [< Lat. *inter*, among.]

in•ter•act (ĭn′tər-ăkt′) ▸*v.* To act on each

other: *students interacting before class.*

in•ter•ac•tion (ĭn′tər-ăk′shən) ►*n.* **1.** The act or process of interacting. **2.** *Phys.* Any of four ways that elementary particles and bodies can influence each other, classified as strong, weak, electromagnetic, and gravitational.

in•ter•ac•tive (ĭn′tər-ăk′tĭv) ►*adj.* **1.** Acting on each other. **2.** *Comp. Sci.* Of or relating to a program that responds to user activity. **3.** Of a form of television entertainment in which the viewer can affect events on the screen. —**in′ter•ac′tive•ly** *adv.*

in•ter a•li•a (ĭn′tər ā′lē-ə, ä′lē-ə) ►*adv.* Among other things. [Lat.]

in•ter•breed (ĭn′tər-brēd′) ►*v.* **1.** To crossbreed. **2.** To breed or cause to breed within a narrow range; inbreed.

in•ter•ca•lar•y (ĭn-tûr′kə-lĕr′ē, ĭn′tər-kăl′ə-rē) ►*adj.* **1.** Inserted in the calendar, as an extra day or month. **2.** Inserted between other elements or parts; interpolated. [Lat. *intercalārius* < Lat. *calāre*, proclaim.]

in•ter•cede (ĭn′tər-sēd′) ►*v.* **-ced•ed, -ced•ing 1.** To plead on another's behalf. **2.** To mediate. [Lat. *intercēdere*, intervene.]

in•ter•cel•lu•lar (ĭn′tər-sĕl′yə-lər) ►*adj. Biol.* Located among or between cells.

in•ter•cept (ĭn′tər-sĕpt′) ►*v.* **1.** To stop or interrupt the progress of. **2.** *Math.* To include or bound (a part of a space or curve) between two points or lines. [< Lat. *intercipere, intercept-.*] —**in′ter•cept′** *n.* —**in′ter•cep′tion** *n.* —**in′ter•cep′tor** *n.*

in•ter•ces•sion (ĭn′tər-sĕsh′ən) ►*n.* **1.** A prayer or petition to God in behalf of another. **2.** Mediation. [< Lat. *intercēdere*, intervene.] —**in′ter•ces′sion•al** *adj.* —**in′ter•ces′sor** *n.* —**in′ter•ces′so•ry** *adj.*

in•ter•change (ĭn′tər-chānj′) ►*v.* **1.** To switch each into the place of the other. **2.** To exchange. **3.** To alternate. ►*n.* (ĭn′tər-chānj′) **1.** An exchange. **2.** A highway intersection allowing traffic to move freely from one road to another without crossing another line of traffic. —**in′ter•change′a•ble** *adj.* —**in′ter•change′a•bly** *adv.*

in•ter•col•le•giate (ĭn′tər-kə-lē′jĭt, -jē-ĭt) ►*adj.* Involving two or more colleges.

in•ter•com (ĭn′tər-kŏm′) ►*n.* An electronic two-way communication system, as between two rooms. [< INTERCOMMUNICATION.]

in•ter•com•mu•ni•cate (ĭn′tər-kə-myo͞o′nĭ-kāt′) ►*v.* **1.** To communicate with each other. **2.** To be connected or adjoined, as rooms or passages. —**in′ter•com•mu′ni•ca′tion** *n.* —**in′ter•com•mu′ni•ca′tive** *adj.*

in•ter•con•nect (ĭn′tər-kə-nĕkt′) ►*v.* To connect or be connected with each other. —**in′ter•con•nec′tion** *n.*

in•ter•con•ti•nen•tal (ĭn′tər-kŏn′tə-nĕn′tl) ►*adj.* **1.** Taking place between continents. **2.** Traveling from one continent to another.

in•ter•cos•tal (ĭn′tər-kŏs′təl) ►*adj.* Located or occurring between the ribs. [< INTER– + Lat. *costa*, rib.]

in•ter•course (ĭn′tər-kôrs′, -kōrs′) ►*n.* **1.** Social interchange; communication. **2.** Sexual intercourse. [< Lat. *intercurrere, intercurs-*, mingle with.]

in•ter•de•pen•dent (ĭn′tər-dĭ-pĕn′dənt) ►*adj.* Mutually dependent. —**in′ter•de•pen′dence** *n.*

in•ter•dict (ĭn′tər-dĭkt′) ►*v.* **1.** To prohibit or forbid, esp. authoritatively. See Syns at **forbid. 2.** To confront and halt the activities or entry of: *interdicted the suspected spies at the border.* [< Lat. *interdīcere, interdict-.*] —**in′ter•dict′** *n.* —**in′ter•dic′tion** *n.*

in•ter•dis•ci•pli•nar•y (ĭn′tər-dĭs′ə-plə-nĕr′ē) ►*adj.* Of or involving two or more usu. distinct academic disciplines.

in•ter•est (ĭn′trĭst, -tər-ĭst, -trĕst′) ►*n.* **1a.** A state of curiosity or concern about or attention to something. **b.** Something that evokes this mental state. **2.** often **interests** Advantage or benefit. **3.** A right, claim, or legal share in something: *an interest in the will.* **4.** A charge for a loan, usu. a percentage of the amount loaned. ►*v.* **1.** To arouse interest in. **2.** To cause to become involved or concerned. [< Lat., it is of importance.]

in•ter•est•ed (ĭn′trĭ-stĭd, -tər-ĭ-stĭd, -tə-rĕs′tĭd) ►*adj.* **1.** Having or showing interest. **2.** Possessing a right, claim, or share. See Usage Note at **disinterested.**

interest group ►*n.* A group of persons strongly supporting a particular cause, such as an item of legislation.

in•ter•est•ing (ĭn′trĭ-stĭng, -tər-ĭ-stĭng, -tə-rĕs′tĭng) ►*adj.* Arousing or holding the attention; absorbing. —**in′ter•est•ing•ly** *adv.*

in•ter•face (ĭn′tər-fās′) ►*n.* **1.** A surface forming a common boundary between adjacent regions. **2.** A point at which independent systems or diverse groups interact. **3.** *Comp. Sci.* The point of interaction or communication between a computer and another entity, such as a printer or human operator. —**in′ter•face′** *v.* —**in′ter•fa′cial** (-fā′shəl) *adj.*

in•ter•fere (ĭn′tər-fîr′) ►*v.* **-fered, -fer•ing 1.** To hinder or impede. **2.** *Sports* To impede illegally the catching of a pass or the playing of a ball or puck. **3.** To intervene or intrude in the affairs of others; meddle. **4.** To inhibit or prevent clear reception of broadcast signals. [< OFr. *entreferer*, meddle.] —**in′ter•fer′ence** *n.* —**in′ter•fer′er** *n.*

in•ter•fe•rom•e•ter (ĭn′tər-fə-rŏm′ĭ-tər) ►*n.* An instrument that uses interference phenomena between waves to make measurements, as of wavelengths or very small distances. —**in′ter•fe•rom′e•try** *n.*

in•ter•fer•on (ĭn′tər-fîr′ŏn′) ►*n.* A cellular protein produced in response to and acting to prevent replication of an infectious viral form within an infected cell. [< INTERFERE.]

in•ter•ga•lac•tic (ĭn′tər-gə-lăk′tĭk) ►*adj.* Between galaxies.

in•ter•im (ĭn′tər-ĭm) ►*n.* A period between two events. ►*adj.* Serving or taking place during an interim. See Syns at **temporary.** [< Lat., in the meantime.]

in•te•ri•or (ĭn-tîr′ē-ər) ►*adj.* **1.** Of or located on the inside; inner. **2.** Inland. ►*n.* **1.** The internal portion or area; inside. **2.** One's mental or spiritual life. **3.** The inland part of a geographic area. **4.** A representation of the inside of a building or room. [< Lat., comp. of *inter*, between.]

interior decoration ►*n.* The arrangement, furnishing, and decoration of an architectural interior. —**interior decorator** *n.*

interj. ►*abbr.* interjection

in•ter•ject (ĭn′tər-jĕkt′) ►*v.* To insert between

elements; interpose. [< Lat. *intericere.*] —**in′ter•jec′to•ry** *adj.*

in•ter•jec•tion (ĭn′tər-jĕk′shən) ▸*n.* **1.** An exclamation. **2.** A part of speech usu. expressing emotion and capable of standing alone grammatically, such as *Ugh!* or *Wow!*

in•ter•lard (ĭn′tər-lärd′) ▸*v.* To insert something foreign or different into. [< OFr. *entrelarder*, mix fat into.]

in•ter•leu•kin (ĭn′tər-lo͞o′kĭn) ▸*n.* Any of a group of proteins produced by the immune system that regulate the body's immune response. [INTER– + Gk. *leukos*, white + –IN.]

in•ter•lin•ing (ĭn′tər-lī′nĭng) ▸*n.* An extra lining between the outer fabric and regular lining of a garment.

in•ter•lock (ĭn′tər-lŏk′) ▸*v.* **1.** To unite or join closely. **2.** To connect together (e.g., parts of a mechanism) so that the operating parts affect one another.

in•ter•loc•u•tor (ĭn′tər-lŏk′yə-tər) ▸*n.* One who takes part in a conversation or dialogue, often officially. [< Lat. *interloquī, interlocūt-*, interrupt.]

in•ter•loc•u•to•ry (ĭn′tər-lŏk′yə-tôr′ē, -tōr′ē) ▸*adj.* Of or relating to a temporary decree made during the course of a trial or suit.

in•ter•lop•er (ĭn′tər-lō′pər) ▸*n.* One who interferes; meddler. [INTER– + MDu. *lopen*, run.] —**in′ter•lope′** *v.*

in•ter•lude (ĭn′tər-lo͞od′) ▸*n.* **1.** An intervening episode, feature, or period of time. **2.** An entertainment between the acts of a play. **3.** *Mus.* A short piece inserted between the parts of a longer composition. [< Med.Lat. *interlūdium*, dramatic entertainment.]

in•ter•mar•ry (ĭn′tər-măr′ē) ▸*v.* **1.** To marry a member of another religion, nationality, race, or group. **2.** To be bound together by the marriages of members. **3.** To marry within one's own group. —**in′ter•mar′riage** *n.*

in•ter•me•di•ar•y (ĭn′tər-mē′dē-ĕr′ē) ▸*adj.* **1.** In between; intermediate. **2.** Acting as a mediator. ▸*n., pl.* **-ies 1.** A mediator; go-between. **2.** An intermediate state or stage.

in•ter•me•di•ate (ĭn′tər-mē′dē-ĭt) ▸*adj.* Lying or occurring between two extremes; in between. ▸*n.* **1.** One that is intermediate. **2.** An intermediary. [< Lat. *intermedius.*] —**in′ter•me′di•ate•ly** *adv.*

in•ter•ment (ĭn-tûr′mənt) ▸*n.* The act or ritual of interring or burying.

in•ter•mez•zo (ĭn′tər-mĕt′sō, -mĕd′zō) ▸*n., pl.* **-zos** or **-zi** (-sē, -zē) *Mus.* **1.** A short movement separating the major sections of a lengthy composition or work. **2.** A short independent instrumental composition. [Ital. < Lat. *intermedius*, intermediate.]

in•ter•mi•na•ble (ĭn-tûr′mə-nə-bəl) ▸*adj.* Tiresomely long. —**in•ter′mi•na•bly** *adv.*

in•ter•min•gle (ĭn′tər-mĭng′gəl) ▸*v.* To mix or become mixed together.

in•ter•mis•sion (ĭn′tər-mĭsh′ən) ▸*n.* A temporary suspension of activity, esp. the period between the acts of a theatrical or musical performance. See Syns at **pause.** [< Lat. *intermittere, intermiss-*, interrupt.]

in•ter•mit•tent (ĭn′tər-mĭt′nt) ▸*adj.* Stopping and starting at intervals. [< Lat. *intermittere*, suspend.] —**in′ter•mit′tent•ly** *adv.*

in•tern also **in•terne** (ĭn′tûrn′) ▸*n.* An advanced student or a recent graduate, as of a medical school, undergoing supervised practical training. ▸*v.* **1.** To train or serve as an intern. **2.** (*also* ĭn-tûrn′). To detain or confine, esp. in wartime. [< Lat. *internus*, internal.] —**in•tern′ment** *n.* —**in′tern•ship′** *n.*

in•ter•nal (ĭn-tûr′nəl) ▸*adj.* **1.** Inner; interior. **2.** Intrinsic; inherent. **3.** Located, acting, or effective within the body. **4.** Of or relating to the domestic affairs of a nation, group, or business. [< Lat. *internus.*] —**in•ter′nal•ly** *adv.*

in•ter•nal-com•bus•tion engine (ĭn-tûr′-nəl-kəm-bŭs′chən) ▸*n.* An engine in which fuel is burned within the engine.

in•ter•nal•ize (ĭn-tûr′nə-līz′) ▸*v.* **-ized, -iz•ing.** To make internal, personal, or subjective. —**in•ter′nal•i•za′tion** *n.*

internal medicine ▸*n.* The branch of medicine dealing with diseases affecting the internal organs, esp. in adults.

in•ter•na•tion•al (ĭn′tər-năsh′ə-nəl) ▸*adj.* Of or involving two or more nations or nationalities. —**in′ter•na′tion•al•ly** *adv.*

International Date Line ▸*n.* An imaginary line through the Pacific Ocean roughly corresponding to 180° longitude, to the east of which, by international agreement, the calendar date is one day earlier than to the west.

in•ter•na•tion•al•ism (ĭn′tər-năsh′ə-nə-lĭz′-əm) ▸*n.* A policy of cooperation among nations, esp. in politics and economics. —**in′ter•na′tion•al•ist** *n.*

in•ter•na•tion•al•ize (ĭn′tər-năsh′ə-nə-līz′) ▸*v.* **-ized, -iz•ing.** To put under international control. —**in′ter•na′tion•al•i•za′tion** *n.*

international law ▸*n.* A set of rules gen. accepted as binding between nations.

in•ter•nec•ine (ĭn′tər-nĕs′ēn′, -ĭn, -nē′sīn′) ▸*adj.* **1.** Relating to struggle within a nation, organization, or group. **2.** Mutually destructive. [< Lat. *internecāre*, to slaughter.]

in•tern•ee (ĭn′tûr-nē′) ▸*n.* One who is interned, esp. in wartime.

In•ter•net (ĭn′tər-nĕt′) ▸*n.* An interconnected system of networks that connects computers around the world.

in•ter•nist (ĭn-tûr′nĭst) ▸*n.* A physician specializing in internal medicine.

in•ter•of•fice (ĭn′tər-ô′fĭs, -ŏf′ĭs) ▸*adj.* Transmitted or taking place between offices, esp. of an organization.

in•ter•per•son•al (ĭn′tər-pûr′sə-nəl) ▸*adj.* Relating to or occurring among several people. —**in′ter•per′son•al•ly** *adv.*

in•ter•plan•e•tar•y (ĭn′tər-plăn′ĭ-tĕr′ē) ▸*adj.* Existing or occurring between planets.

in•ter•play (ĭn′tər-plā′) ▸*n.* Reciprocal action and reaction; interaction. —**in′ter•play′** *v.*

in•ter•po•late (ĭn-tûr′pə-lāt′) ▸*v.* **-lat•ed, -lat•ing 1.** To insert or introduce between other elements or parts. **2.** To change (a text) by introducing new or false material. [Lat. *interpolāre*, touch up.] —**in•ter′po•la′tion** *n.* —**in•ter′po•la′tor** *n.*

in•ter•pose (ĭn′tər-pōz′) ▸*v.* **-posed, -pos•ing 1a.** To insert or introduce between parts. **b.** To place (oneself) between. **2.** To introduce or interject into a discourse or conversation. **3.** To intervene. [< Lat. *interpōnere.*] —**in′ter•pos′er** *n.* —**in′ter•po•si′tion** (-pə-zĭsh′ən) *n.*

in•ter•pret (ĭn-tûr′prĭt) ▸*v.* **1.** To explain or clarify the meaning of. **2.** To conceive the significance of; construe. **3.** To perform or present according to one's artistic understanding. **4.** To serve as translator for speakers of different languages. [< Lat. *interpretārī* < *interpres*, negotiator.] —**in•ter′pret•a•ble** *adj.* —**in•ter′pret•er** *n.*

in•ter•pre•ta•tion (ĭn-tûr′prĭ-tā′shən) ►*n.* **1.** An explanation. **2.** A concept of a work of art as expressed by its representation or performance. —**in•ter′pre•ta′tion•al** *adj.*

in•ter•pre•tive (ĭn-tûr′prĭ-tĭv) also **in•ter•pre•ta•tive** (-tā′tĭv) ►*adj.* Marked by interpretation; explanatory. —**in•ter′pre•tive•ly** *adv.*

in•ter•ra•cial (ĭn′tər-rā′shəl) ►*adj.* Of or between different races.

in•ter•reg•num (ĭn′tər-rĕg′nəm) ►*n.*, *pl.* **-nums** or **-na** (-nə) **1.** The interval of time between two successive reigns or governments. **2.** A gap in continuity. [Lat.] —**in′ter•reg′nal** *adj.*

in•ter•re•late (ĭn′tər-rĭ-lāt′) ►*v.* To place in or come into mutual relationship. —**in′ter•re•la′tion** *n.* —**in′ter•re•la′tion•ship′** *n.*

interrog. ►*abbr.* interrogative

in•ter•ro•gate (ĭn-tĕr′ə-gāt′) ►*v.* **-gat•ed, -gat•ing.** To question formally. [< Lat. *interrogāre.*] —**in•ter′ro•ga′tion** *n.* —**in•ter′ro•ga′tion•al** *adj.* —**in•ter′ro•ga′tor** *n.*

in•ter•rog•a•tive (ĭn′tə-rŏg′ə-tĭv) ►*adj.* **1.** Of the nature of a question. **2.** *Gram.* Used to ask a question: *an interrogative pronoun.* —**in′ter•rog′a•tive** *n.* —**in′ter•rog′a•tive•ly** *adv.*

in•ter•rog•a•to•ry (ĭn′tə-rŏg′ə-tôr′ē, -tōr′ē) ►*adj.* Interrogative. ►*n.*, *pl.* **-ries** *Law.* A formal question, as to a witness, usu. answered under oath. —**in′ter•rog′a•to′ri•ly** *adv.*

in•ter•rupt (ĭn′tə-rŭpt′) ►*v.* **1.** To break the continuity or uniformity of. **2.** To stop (someone) by breaking in on. **3.** To break in on another's speech or action. [< Lat. *interrumpere*, break off.] —**in′ter•rupt′er** *n.* —**in′ter•rup′tion** *n.* —**in′ter•rup′tive** *adj.*

in•ter•sect (ĭn′tər-sĕkt′) ►*v.* **1.** To cut across or through. **2.** To form an intersection (with); cross. [Lat. *intersecāre*, *intersect-*.]

in•ter•sec•tion (ĭn′tər-sĕk′shən) ►*n.* **1.** The act or result of intersecting. **2.** A place where things intersect, esp. where roads cross. **3.** *Math.* The point or locus of points common to two or more geometric figures.

in•ter•sperse (ĭn′tər-spûrs′) ►*v.* **-spersed, -spers•ing 1.** To distribute randomly among other things. **2.** To supply or diversify with things distributed randomly. [< Lat. *interspergere*, *interspers-*.] —**in′ter•sper′sion** (-spûr′zhən, -shən) *n.*

in•ter•state (ĭn′tər-stāt′) ►*adj.* Involving, between, or connecting two or more states. ►*n.* One of a system of highways connecting the major cities of the 48 contiguous US states.

in•ter•stel•lar (ĭn′tər-stĕl′ər) ►*adj.* Between the stars.

in•ter•stice (ĭn-tûr′stĭs) ►*n.*, *pl.* **-stic•es** (-stĭ-sēz′, -sĭz). A small or narrow space between things or parts. [< Lat. *interstitium* < *intersistere*, make a break : INTER– + *sistere*, set up.] —**in′ter•sti′tial** (ĭn′tər-stĭsh′əl) *adj.*

in•ter•twine (ĭn′tər-twīn′) ►*v.* To join or become joined by twining together.

in•ter•ur•ban (ĭn′tər-ûr′bən) ►*adj.* Relating to, between, or connecting urban areas.

in•ter•val (ĭn′tər-vəl) ►*n.* **1.** A space between two objects or points. **2.** A period of time between two events. **3.** *Math.* The set of all numbers that lie between two given numbers, sometimes including either or both of the given numbers. **4.** *Mus.* The difference, usu. expressed in the number of steps, between two pitches. [< Lat. *intervallum.*]

in•ter•vene (ĭn′tər-vēn′) ►*v.* **-vened, -ven•ing 1.** To come or occur between two things, events, or points of time. **2a.** To come in or between so as to hinder or alter an action: *intervened to prevent a fight.* **b.** To interfere, usu. through force, in the affairs of another nation. [Lat. *intervenīre* : INTER– + *venīre*, come.] —**in′ter•ven′tion** (-vĕn′shən) *n.*

in•ter•view (ĭn′tər-vyo͞o′) ►*n.* **1.** A formal face-to-face meeting, esp. one conducted for the assessment of an applicant. **2.** A conversation between a reporter and one from whom facts or statements are elicited. [< OFr. *entrevoir*, see : INTER– + *voir*, see (< Lat. *vidēre*).] —**in′ter•view′** *v.* —**in′ter•view•ee′** *n.* —**in′ter•view′er** *n.*

in•ter•weave (ĭn′tər-wēv′) ►*v.* **1.** To weave together. **2.** To intertwine.

in•tes•tate (ĭn-tĕs′tāt′, -tĭt) ►*adj.* **1.** Having made no legal will. **2.** Not disposed of by a legal will. [< Lat. *intestātus.*]

in•tes•tine (ĭn-tĕs′tĭn) ►*n.* often **intestines.** The portion of the alimentary canal extending from the outlet of the stomach to the anus. [< Lat. *intestīnus*, internal.] —**in•tes′ti•nal** *adj.* —**in•tes′ti•nal•ly** *adv.*

in•ti (ĭn′tē) ►*n.* See table at **currency.** [< Quechua, sun.]

in•ti•fa•da (ĭn′tə-fä′də) ►*n.* A late 20th-cent. Palestinian uprising in protest of Israeli occupation. [Ar. *intifāḍa*, shudder, uprising.]

in•ti•mate[1] (ĭn′tə-mĭt) ►*adj.* **1.** Marked by close acquaintance, association, or familiarity. **2.** Essential; innermost. **3.** Comfortably private: *an intimate café.* **4.** Very personal. **5.** Of or involving a sexual relationship. ►*n.* A close friend or confidant. [Lat. *intimātus*, p.part. of *intimāre*, INTIMATE[2].] —**in′ti•ma•cy** *n.* —**in′ti•mate•ly** *adv.*

in•ti•mate[2] (ĭn′tə-māt′) ►*v.* **-mat•ed, -mat•ing.** To imply subtly. [Lat. *intimāre* < *intimus*, innermost.] —**in′ti•ma′tion** *n.*

in•tim•i•date (ĭn-tĭm′ĭ-dāt′) ►*v.* **-dat•ed, -dat•ing 1.** To make timid; fill with fear. **2.** To coerce, inhibit, or discourage by or as if by threats. [Med.Lat. *intimidāre* < Lat. *timidus*, timid.] —**in•tim′i•dat′ing•ly** *adv.* —**in•tim′i•da′tion** *n.* —**in•tim′i•da′tor** *n.*

intl. ►*abbr.* international

in•to (ĭn′to͞o) ►*prep.* **1.** To the inside of. **2.** To the activity or occupation of: *go into banking.* **3.** To the condition or form of. **4.** So as to be in or within. **5.** *Informal* Interested in or involved with: *into vegetarianism.* **6.** To a time or place in the course of: *well into the week.* **7.** Toward: *pointed into the sky.* **8.** Against: *crashed into a tree.*

in•tol•er•a•ble (ĭn-tŏl′ər-ə-bəl) ►*adj.* Unbearable: *intolerable agony.* —**in•tol′er•a•bly** *adv.*

in•tol•er•ant (ĭn-tŏl′ər-ənt) ►*adj.* **1.** Not tolerant of differences in beliefs of others; bigoted. **2.** Unable to endure: *intolerant of certain* *drugs.* —**in•tol′er•ance** *n.* —**in•tol′er•ant•ly** *adv.*

in•to•na•tion (ĭn′tə-nā′shən, -tō-) ►*n.* **1.** The act of intoning or chanting. **2.** A manner of producing musical tones, esp. with regard to pitch. **3.** The way in which the voice rises and falls in pitch to convey meaning: *a questioning intonation.* **4.** A use of pitch characteristic of a speaker or dialect.

in•tone (ĭn-tōn′) ►*v.* **-toned, -ton•ing.** To recite in a singing or chanting voice. [< Med.Lat. *intonāre* < Lat. *tonus*, tone.]

in to•to (ĭn tō′tō) ►*adv.* Totally; altogether. [Lat. *in tōtō.*]

in•tox•i•cate (ĭn-tŏk′sĭ-kāt′) ►*v.* **-cat•ed, -cat•ing 1.** To make drunk. **2.** To stimulate or excite. [< Med.Lat. *intoxicāre* < Lat. *toxicum*, poison.] —**in•tox′i•cant** (-kənt) *adj. & n.* —**in•tox′i•ca′tion** *n.*

intr. ►*abbr.* intransitive

intra– ►*pref.* Within: *intracellular.* [< Lat. *intrā.*]

in•tra•cel•lu•lar (ĭn′trə-sĕl′yə-lər) ►*adj.* Occurring or situated within a cell or cells.

in•trac•ta•ble (ĭn-trăk′tə-bəl) ►*adj.* Difficult to manage or govern; stubborn. —**in•trac′ta•bil′i•ty** *n.* —**in•trac′ta•bly** *adv.*

in•tra•mu•ral (ĭn′trə-myŏŏr′əl) ►*adj.* Existing or carried on within an institution, esp. a school. [< INTRA– + Lat. *mūrus*, wall.]

in•tra•net (ĭn′trə-nĕt′) ►*n.* A restricted-access computer network, as within an organization.

in•tran•si•gent (ĭn-trăn′sə-jənt, -zə-) ►*adj.* Refusing to moderate a position, esp. an extreme one; uncompromising. [< IN–[1] + Lat. *trānsigere*, reach agreement (TRANS– + *agere*, drive).] —**in•tran′si•gence, in•tran′si•gen•cy** *n.* —**in•tran′si•gent** *n.* —**in•tran′si•gent•ly** *adv.*

in•tran•si•tive (ĭn-trăn′sĭ-tĭv, -zĭ-) ►*adj.* Designating a verb that does not require a direct object to complete its meaning. ►*n.* An intransitive verb. —**in•tran′si•tive•ly** *adv.* —**in•tran′si•tive•ness, in•tran′si•tiv′i•ty** *n.*

in•tra•oc•u•lar (ĭn′trə-ŏk′yə-lər) ►*adj.* Within the eyeball.

in•tra•state (ĭn′trə-stāt′) ►*adj.* Existing within the boundaries of a state.

in•tra•u•ter•ine (ĭn′trə-yōō′tər-ĭn, -tə-rīn′) ►*adj.* Within the uterus.

intrauterine device ►*n.* A birth control device inserted into the uterus to prevent implantation.

in•tra•ve•nous (ĭn′trə-vē′nəs) ►*adj.* Within or administered into a vein. —**in′tra•ve′nous•ly** *adv.*

in•trep•id (ĭn-trĕp′ĭd) ►*adj.* Resolutely courageous; fearless. [Lat. *intrepidus.*] —**in•trep′id•ness** —**in•trep′id•ly** *adv.*

in•tri•cate (ĭn′trĭ-kĭt) ►*adj.* **1.** Having many complexly arranged elements. See Syns at **elaborate. 2.** Comprehensible only with painstaking effort. [< Lat. *intrīcāre*, entangle.] —**in′tri•ca•cy** (-kə-sē) *n.* —**in′tri•cate•ly** *adv.*

in•trigue (ĭn′trēg′, ĭn-trēg′) ►*n.* **1.** A secret or underhand scheme; plot. **2.** A secret love affair. ►*v.* (ĭn-trēg′) **-trigued, -trigu•ing 1.** To engage in or effect by secret scheming or plotting. **2.** To arouse the interest or curiosity of. [< Lat. *intrīcāre*, entangle.] —**in•trigu′er** *n.*

in•trin•sic (ĭn-trĭn′zĭk, -sĭk) ►*adj.* Relating to the essential nature of a thing; inherent. [< LLat. *intrīnsecus*, inward.] —**in•trin′si•cal•ly** *adv.*

in•tro (ĭn′trō′) ►*n., pl.* **-tros** *Informal* An introduction.

intro– ►*pref.* Inward: *introvert.* [Lat. *intrō-*.]

in•tro•duce (ĭn′trə-dōōs′, -dyōōs′) ►*v.* **-duced, -duc•ing 1.** To identify and present, esp. to make (strangers) acquainted. **2.** To bring forward (e.g., a plan) for consideration. See Syns at **broach. 3.** To inform (someone) of something for the first time. **4.** To originate. **5.** To put into; insert or inject. **6.** To preface. [< Lat. *intrōdūcere*, bring in.] —**in′tro•duc′tion** (-dŭk′shən) *n.*

in•tro•duc•to•ry (ĭn′trə-dŭk′tə-rē) ►*adj.* Serving to introduce. See Syns at **preliminary.**

in•tro•spec•tion (ĭn′trə-spĕk′shən) ►*n.* Contemplation of one's own thoughts and feelings; self-examination. [< Lat. *intrōspicere*, look within : INTRO– + *specere*, look.] —**in′tro•spect′** *v.* —**in′tro•spec′tive** *adj.*

in•tro•vert (ĭn′trə-vûrt′) ►*n.* One whose thoughts and feelings are directed inward. [INTRO– + Lat. *vertere*, turn.] —**in′tro•ver′sion** *n.*

in•trude (ĭn-trōōd′) ►*v.* **-trud•ed, -trud•ing.** To put or force in without being wanted or asked; barge in. [< Lat. *intrūdere*, thrust in.] —**in•trud′er** *n.* —**in•tru′sion** *n.* —**in•tru′sive** *adj.* —**in•tru′sive•ly** *adv.*

in•trust (ĭn-trŭst′) ►*v.* Var. of **entrust.**

in•tu•it (ĭn-tōō′ĭt, -tyōō′-) ►*v.* To know intuitively. [< INTUITION.]

in•tu•i•tion (ĭn′tōō-ĭsh′ən, -tyōō-) ►*n.* **1a.** The faculty of knowing as if by instinct without conscious reasoning. **b.** A perception based on this faculty. **2.** Sharp insight; impression. [< Lat. *intuērī*, *intuit-*, contemplate.] —**in′tu•i′tion•al** *adj.* —**in•tu′i•tive** (ĭn-tōō′ĭ-tĭv, -tyōō′-) *adj.* —**in•tu′i•tive•ly** *adv.* —**in•tu′i•tive•ness** *n.*

In•u•it (ĭn′yōō-ĭt) ►*n., pl.* **-it** or **-its 1.** A member of a group of Eskimoan peoples inhabiting the Arctic from N Alaska eastward to E Greenland. **2.** Any of the Eskimoan languages of the Inuit.

in•un•date (ĭn′ŭn-dāt′) ►*v.* **-dat•ed, -dat•ing.** To cover or overwhelm with or as if with a flood. [Lat. *inundāre* : IN–[2] + *unda*, wave.] —**in′un•da′tion** *n.*

in•ure (ĭn-yŏŏr′) ►*v.* **-ured, -ur•ing.** To make used to something undesirable; harden. [< ME *in ure*, customary.] —**in•ure′ment** *n.*

in u•ter•o (ĭn yōō′tə-rō) ►*adv. & adj.* In the uterus. [Lat. *in uterō.*]

in•vade (ĭn-vād′) ►*v.* **-vad•ed, -vad•ing 1.** To enter by force in order to conquer. **2.** To trespass or intrude on; violate. **3.** To overrun or infest. **4.** To enter and permeate, esp. harmfully. [< Lat. *invādere.*] —**in•vad′er** *n.*

in•va•lid[1] (ĭn′və-lĭd) ►*n.* One incapacitated by a chronic illness or injury. ►*adj.* Incapacitated by illness or injury. [< INVALID[2].]

in•val•id[2] (ĭn-văl′ĭd) ►*adj.* **1.** Not legally valid; null. **2.** Falsely based or reasoned; unjustified. [Lat. *invalidus*, weak.] —**in′va•lid′i•ty** (-və-lĭd′ĭ-tē) *n.* —**in•val′id•ly** *adv.*

in•val•i•date (ĭn-văl′ĭ-dāt′) ►*v.* **-dat•ed, -dat•ing.** To make invalid; nullify. —**in•val′i•da′tion** *n.* —**in•val′i•da′tor** *n.*

in•val•u•a•ble (ĭn-văl′yōō-ə-bəl) ►*adj.* Of inestimable value; priceless. —**in•val′u•a•bly** *adv.*

in•var•i•a•ble (ĭn-vâr′ē-ə-bəl) ▶*adj.* Not changing or subject to change; constant. —**in•var′i•a•bil′i•ty, in•var′i•a•ble•ness** *n.* —**in•var′i•a•bly** *adv.*

in•va•sion (ĭn-vā′zhən) ▶*n.* **1.** The act of invading, esp. entrance by force. **2.** A large-scale onset of something harmful, such as a disease. **3.** An intrusion or encroachment: *invasion of privacy.*

in•va•sive (ĭn-vā′sĭv) ▶*adj.* **1.** Of or engaging in armed aggression. **2.** Tending to spread, esp. into healthy tissue.

in•vec•tive (ĭn-vĕk′tĭv) ▶*n.* Harsh and insulting language used to attack or denounce. [< Lat. *invehī*, *invect-*, inveigh against.]

in•veigh (ĭn-vā′) ▶*v.* To protest or disapprove vehemently. [Lat. *invehī*.]

in•vei•gle (ĭn-vā′gəl, -vē′-) ▶*v.* **-gled, -gling 1.** To win over or lead astray by guile or deception. **2.** To obtain by deception or flattery. [< OFr. *aveugler*, to blind.] —**in•vei′gle•ment** *n.* —**in•vei′gler** *n.*

in•vent (ĭn-vĕnt′) ▶*v.* **1.** To conceive of or produce first; originate. **2.** To make up; fabricate: *invent a likely excuse.* [Lat. *invenīre*, *invent-*, find : IN–[2] + *venīre*, come.] —**in•ven′tor** *n.*

in•ven•tion (ĭn-vĕn′shən) ▶*n.* **1.** The act or process of inventing. **2.** A new device, method, or process developed from study and experimentation. **3.** A mental fabrication, esp. a falsehood. **4.** Skill in inventing.

in•ven•tive (ĭn-vĕn′tĭv) ▶*adj.* **1.** Of or characterized by invention. **2.** Skillful at inventing. —**in•ven′tive•ly** *adv.* —**in•ven′tive•ness** *n.*

in•ven•to•ry (ĭn′vən-tôr′ē, -tōr′ē) ▶*n., pl.* **-ries 1a.** A detailed list of things, esp. a periodic survey of all goods and materials in stock. **b.** The process of making such a list. **c.** The items so listed. **2.** The supply of goods on hand; stock. —**in′ven•to′ry** *v.*

in•verse (ĭn-vûrs′, ĭn′vûrs′) ▶*adj.* Reversed in order, nature, or effect. ▶*n.* (ĭn′vûrs′, ĭn-vûrs′). Something opposite, as in sequence, effect, or character; reverse. [< Lat. *inversus*, p.part. of *invertere*, invert.] —**in•verse′ly** *adv.*

in•ver•sion (ĭn-vûr′zhən, -shən) ▶*n.* **1.** The act of inverting or the state of being inverted. **2.** A reversal of position or order in a sequence. **3.** *Meteorol.* An atmospheric condition in which the air temperature rises with increasing altitude, holding surface air down along with its pollutants.

in•vert (ĭn-vûrt′) ▶*v.* **1.** To turn inside out or upside down. **2.** To reverse the position, order, or condition of. [Lat. *invertere*.] —**in•vert′er** *n.* —**in•vert′i•ble** *adj.*

in•ver•te•brate (ĭn-vûr′tə-brĭt, -brāt′) ▶*adj.* Lacking a backbone or spinal column; not vertebrate. —**in•ver′te•brate** *n.*

in•vest (ĭn-vĕst′) ▶*v.* **1.** To commit (money or capital) in order to gain a financial return. **2.** To spend or devote (time or effort) for future benefit. **3.** To endow with authority or power. **4.** To install in office; inaugurate. **5.** To surround or envelop. [< Lat. *investīre*, surround.] —**in•ves′tor** *n.*

in•ves•ti•gate (ĭn-vĕs′tĭ-gāt′) ▶*v.* **-gat•ed, -gat•ing.** To observe or inquire into in detail; examine systematically. [Lat. *investīgāre* < *vestīgium*, footprint.] —**in•ves′ti•ga′tive** *adj.* —**in•ves′ti•ga′tor** *n.*

in•ves•ti•ga•tion (ĭn-vĕs′tĭ-gā′shən) ▶*n.* **1.** The act or process of investigating. **2.** A detailed inquiry or systematic examination. See Syns at **inquiry.**

in•ves•ti•ture (ĭn-vĕs′tə-cho͝or′, -chər) ▶*n.* The act or ceremony of conferring the authority and symbols of a high office. [< Lat. *investīre*, clothe.]

in•vest•ment (ĭn-vĕst′mənt) ▶*n.* **1.** The act of investing or the conditon of being invested. **2.** An amount invested. **3.** Property acquired for future income. **4.** Investiture.

in•vet•er•ate (ĭn-vĕt′ər-ĭt) ▶*adj.* **1.** Firmly and long established. **2.** Persisting in an ingrained habit: *an inveterate liar.* See Syns at **chronic.** [< Lat. *inveterārī*, grow old < *vetus*, old.] —**in•vet′er•a•cy** (-ər-ə-sē), **in•vet′er•ate•ness** *n.* —**in•vet′er•ate•ly** *adv.*

in•vid•i•ous (ĭn-vĭd′ē-əs) ▶*adj.* **1.** Tending to rouse ill will or envy. **2.** Containing or implying a slight. [< Lat. *invidia*, envy.] —**in•vid′i•ous•ly** *adv.* —**in•vid′i•ous•ness** *n.*

in•vig•or•ate (ĭn-vĭg′ə-rāt′) ▶*v.* **-at•ed, -at•ing.** To impart vigor or vitality to; animate. —**in•vig′or•at′ing•ly** *adv.* —**in•vig′or•a′tion** *n.* —**in•vig′or•a′tive** *adj.*

in•vin•ci•ble (ĭn-vĭn′sə-bəl) ▶*adj.* Unconquerable. [< Lat. *invincibilis* < *vincere*, conquer.] —**in•vin′ci•bil′i•ty** *n.* —**in•vin′ci•bly** *adv.*

in•vi•o•la•ble (ĭn-vī′ə-lə-bəl) ▶*adj.* **1.** Secure from violation or profanation. **2.** Impregnable. —**in•vi′o•la•bil′i•ty** *n.* —**in•vi′o•la•bly** *adv.*

in•vi•o•late (ĭn-vī′ə-lĭt) ▶*adj.* Not violated or profaned; intact. —**in•vi′o•late•ly** *adv.* —**in•vi′o•late•ness** *n.*

in•vis•i•ble (ĭn-vĭz′ə-bəl) ▶*adj.* **1.** Incapable of being seen. **2.** Hidden from view. **3.** Inconspicuous. —**in•vis′i•bil′i•ty** *n.* —**in•vis′i•bly** *adv.*

in•vi•ta•tion (ĭn′vĭ-tā′shən) ▶*n.* **1.** The act of inviting. **2.** A request for someone's presence or participation. **3.** An allurement or enticement. —**in′vi•ta′tion•al** *adj. & n.*

in•vite (ĭn-vīt′) ▶*v.* **-vit•ed, -vit•ing 1.** To request the presence or participation of. **2.** To request formally. **3.** To welcome: *the speakers invited questions.* **4.** To tend to bring on; provoke. **5.** To entice; lure. ▶*n.* (ĭn′vīt′) *Informal* An invitation. [< Lat. *invītāre*.]

in•vit•ing (ĭn-vī′tĭng) ▶*adj.* Attractive; tempting. —**in•vit′ing•ly** *adv.*

in vi•tro (ĭn vē′trō) ▶*adv. & adj.* In an artificial environment outside the living organism. [NLat. *in vitrō*, in glass.]

in vi•vo (vē′vō) ▶*adv. & adj.* Within a living organism. [NLat. *in vīvō*.]

in•vo•ca•tion (ĭn′və-kā′shən) ▶*n.* **1.** The act of invoking, esp. an appeal to a higher power. **2.** A prayer or other formula used in invoking. [< Lat. *invocāre*, call upon.]

in•voice (ĭn′vois′) ▶*n.* **1.** A list of goods shipped or services rendered, detailing all costs. **2.** The goods or services so itemized. [< obsolete *invoyes* < Fr. *envoi*, shipment. See ENVOY[1].] —**in′voice′** *v.*

in•voke (ĭn-vōk′) ▶*v.* **-voked, -vok•ing 1.** To call on (a higher power) for help or inspiration. **2.** To appeal to; petition. **3.** To call for earnestly. **4.** To conjure. **5.** To use or apply: *in-*

voked the veto power. [< Lat. *invocāre.*] —**in•vok′er** *n.*

in•vol•un•tar•y (ĭn-vŏl′ən-tĕr′ē) ▸*adj.* **1.** Performed against one's will. **2.** Not subject to control: *an involuntary twitch.* —**in•vol′un•tar′i•ly** (-târ′ə-lē) *adv.* —**in•vol′un•tar′i•ness** *n.*

in•vo•lu•tion (ĭn′və-lo͞o′shən) ▸*n.* **1.** The act of involving or the state of being involved. **2.** Something, such as a long grammatical construction, that is intricate or complex. **3.** *Math.* The multiplying of a quantity by itself a specified number of times; raising to a power. [< Lat. *involvere, involūt-*, enwrap.]

in•volve (ĭn-vŏlv′) ▸*v.* **-volved, -volv•ing 1.** To contain as a part; include. **2.** To have as a necessary feature or consequence. **3.** To engage or draw in; embroil. **4.** To engross. **5.** To make complex; complicate. [< Lat. *involvere*, enwrap.] —**in•volve′ment** *n.*

in•vul•ner•a•ble (ĭn-vŭl′nər-ə-bəl) ▸*adj.* **1.** Immune to attack; impregnable. **2.** Impossible to damage or injure. —**in•vul′ner•a•bil′i•ty** *n.* —**in•vul′ner•a•bly** *adv.*

in•ward (ĭn′wərd) ▸*adj.* **1.** Located inside; inner. **2.** Directed or moving toward the interior. **3.** Existing in the mind. ▸*adv.* **1.** Toward the inside or center. **2.** Toward the mind or the self. —**in′wards** *adv.*

in•ward•ly (ĭn′wərd-lē) ▸*adv.* **1.** On or in the inside; within. **2.** To oneself; privately.

I/O ▸*abbr.* input/output

i•o•dide (ī′ə-dīd′) ▸*n.* A binary compound of iodine with a more electropositive atom or group.

i•o•dine (ī′ə-dīn′, -dĭn, -dēn′) ▸*n.* **1.** *Symbol* **I** A grayish-black, corrosive, poisonous element having radioactive isotopes used as tracers and in thyroid disease diagnosis and therapy, and compounds used as germicides, antiseptics, and dyes. At. no. 53. See table at **element. 2.** A liquid containing iodine dissolved in ethyl alcohol, used as an antiseptic for wounds. [< Gk. *ioeidēs*, violet-colored + -INE[2].]

i•o•dize (ī′ə-dīz′) ▸*v.* **-dized, -diz•ing.** To treat or combine with iodine or an iodide.

iodo– or **iod–** ▸*pref.* Iodine: *iodize.* [< Fr. *iode*, iodine.]

i•on (ī′ən, ī′ŏn′) ▸*n.* An atom or molecule having a net electric charge acquired by gaining or losing one or more electrons from an initially neutral configuration. [Gk., something that goes.] —**i•on′ic** (-ŏn′ĭk) *adj.*

–ion ▸*suff.* **1a.** Action or process: *completion.* **b.** Result of an action or process: *invention.* **2.** State or condition: *dehydration.* [< Lat. *-iō, -iōn-.*]

Io•nes•co (ē′ə-nĕs′kō, yə-), **Eugène.** 1912–94. Romanian-born French dramatist.

I•o•ni•a (ī-ō′nē-ə) An ancient region of W Asia Minor along the Aegean coast. —**I•o′ni•an** *adj. & n.*

Ionian Islands. A chain of islands of W Greece in the Ionian Sea.

Ionian Sea. An arm of the Mediterranean between W Greece and S Italy.

ionic bond ▸*n.* A chemical bond formed by the complex transfer of one or more electrons from one kind of atom to another.

Ionic order ▸*n. Archit.* A classical order marked by two opposed volutes in the column capital.

i•on•ize (ī′ə-nīz′) ▸*v.* **-ized, -iz•ing.** To convert or be converted totally or partially into ions. —**i′on•i•za′tion** *n.*

i•on•o•sphere (ī-ŏn′ə-sfîr′) ▸*n.* An electrically conducting set of layers of the earth's atmosphere, extending from altitudes of 70 km (43 mi) to 400 km (250 mi).

i•o•ta (ī-ō′tə) ▸*n.* **1.** The 9th letter of the Greek alphabet. **2.** A very small amount; bit. [< Gk. *iōta.*]

IOU (ī′ō-yo͞o′) ▸*n.* A usu. written promise to pay a debt.

–ious ▸*suff.* Characterized by or full of: *bilious.* [< Lat. *-ius* and *-iōsus.*]

I•o•wa[1] (ī′ə-wə) ▸*n., pl.* **-wa** or **-was 1.** A member of a Native American people formerly of Iowa and SW Minnesota, later in Nebraska, Kansas, and Oklahoma. **2.** The Siouan language of the Iowa.

I•o•wa[2] (ī′ə-wə) A state of the N-central US. Cap. Des Moines. Pop. 2,787,424. —**I′o•wan** *adj. & n.*

IPA ▸*abbr.* International Phonetic Alphabet

ip•e•cac (ĭp′ĭ-kăk′) ▸*n.* A preparation made from the roots of a tropical American shrub, used to induce vomiting. [< Tupi *ipekaaguéne.*]

IPO ▸*abbr. Bus.* initial public offering

ip•so fac•to (ĭp′sō făk′tō) ▸*adv.* By the fact itself; by that very fact. [< Lat. *ipsō factō.*]

IQ ▸*abbr.* intelligence quotient

I•qal•u•it (ĭ-kăl′o͞o-ĭt, ē-kä′lo͞o-ēt) The capital of Nunavut, Canada, on Baffin Island.

Ir ▸ The symbol for the element **iridium.**

ir–[1] ▸*pref.* Var. of **in–**[1].

ir–[2] ▸*pref.* Var. of **in–**[2].

IRA ▸*abbr.* **1.** individual retirement account **2.** Irish Republican Army

I•ran (ĭ-răn′, ĭ-rän′). Formerly **Per•sia** (pûr′zhə, -shə). A country of SW Asia. Cap. Tehran. Pop. 59,778,000.

I•ra•ni•an (ĭ-rā′nē-ən, ĭ-rä′-) ▸*n.* **1.** A native or inhabitant of Iran. **2.** A branch of the Indo-European language family that includes Persian, Kurdish, and Pashto. —**I•ra′ni•an** *adj.*

I•raq (ĭ-răk′, ĭ-räk′) A country of SW Asia. Pop. 19,925,000. —**I•ra′qi** (-răk′ē, -rä′kē) *adj. & n.*

i•ras•ci•ble (ĭ-răs′ə-bəl, ī-răs′-) ▸*adj.* Prone to outbursts of temper; easily angered. [< Lat. *īrāscī*, be angry < *īra*, anger.] —**i•ras′ci•bil′i•ty** *n.* —**i•ras′ci•bly** *adv.*

i•rate (ī-rāt′, ī′rāt′) ▸*adj.* Extremely angry; enraged. See Syns at **angry.** [Lat. *īrātus* < *īra*, anger.] —**i•rate′ly** *adv.*

Ir•bil (îr′bĭl) See **Arbil.**

ire (īr) ▸*n.* Anger; wrath. [< Lat. *īra.*]

ire•ful (īr′fəl) ▸*adj.* Full of ire. See Syns at **angry.** —**ire′ful•ly** *adv.*

Ire•land[1] (īr′lənd) An island in the N Atlantic W of Great Britain.

Ire•land[2] (īr′lənd) also **Eire.** A country occupying most of the island of Ireland. Cap. Dublin. Pop. 3,571,000.

Ireland, Northern. See **Northern Ireland.**

ir•i•des•cent (ĭr′ĭ-dĕs′ənt) ▸*adj.* Producing a display of lustrous, rainbowlike colors: *an iridescent oil slick.* [Gk. *iris, irid-*, rainbow + -ESCENT.] —**ir′i•des′cence** *n.*

i•rid•i•um (ĭ-rĭd′ē-əm) ▸*n. Symbol* **Ir** A hard, brittle, exceptionally corrosion-resistant whitish-yellow metallic element used as an alloy with platinum. At. no. 77. See table at **ele-**

ment. [Gk. *iris, irid-*, rainbow + -IUM.]

i•ris (ī′rĭs) ►*n., pl.* **i•ris•es** or **i•ri•des** (ī′rĭ-dēz′, ĭr′ĭ-) **1.** The pigmented, round, contractile membrane of the eye, situated between the cornea and lens and perforated by the pupil. **2.** A plant having narrow sword-shaped leaves and showy, variously colored flowers. [< Gk.]

I•rish (ī′rĭsh) ►*adj.* Of or relating to Ireland or its people or language. ►*n.* **1.** The people of Ireland. **2a.** See **Irish Gaelic. b.** English as spoken by the Irish. **3.** *Informal* Fieriness of temper or passion. —**I′rish•man** *n.* —**I′rish•wom′an** *n.*

Irish bull ►*n.* A statement containing an incongruity or a logical absurdity, usu. unbeknown to the speaker.

Irish Gaelic ►*n.* The Celtic language of Ireland.

Irish moss ►*n.* An edible North Atlantic seaweed that yields carrageenan.

Irish Sea. An arm of the N Atlantic between Ireland and Great Britain.

Irish setter ►*n.* A setter having a silky reddish-brown coat.

irk (ûrk) ►*v.* To annoy; irritate. [ME *irken.*]

irk•some (ûrk′səm) ►*adj.* Annoying; bothersome; tedious. —**irk′some•ly** *adv.* —**irk′some•ness** *n.*

Ir•kutsk (îr-ko͝otsk′) A city of S-central Russia near S Lake Baikal. Pop. 629,747.

i•ron (ī′ərn) ►*n.* **1.** *Symbol* **Fe** A silvery-white, malleable, magnetic or magnetizable metallic element used alloyed in many important structural materials. At. no. 26. See table at **element. 2.** An implement made of iron alloy or similar metal, esp. a bar heated for use in branding or curling hair. **3.** Great hardness or strength: *a will of iron.* **4.** A golf club with a metal head. **5.** An appliance with a weighted flat bottom, used when heated to press fabric. **6. irons** Fetters; shackles. ►*adj.* Of or like iron. ►*v.* To press and smooth with a heated iron. —***phrasal verb:*** **iron out** To discuss and settle; work out. [< OE *īren.*] —**i′ron•er** *n.* —**i′ron•ing** *n.*

Iron Age ►*n.* The period of human culture succeeding the Bronze Age, marked by the introduction of iron metallurgy and in Europe beginning around the 8th cent. B.C.

i•ron•clad (ī′ərn-klăd′) ►*adj.* **1.** Covered with iron plates for protection. **2.** Rigid; fixed: *an ironclad rule.*

iron curtain or **Iron Curtain** ►*n.* The military, political, and ideological barrier existing between the Soviet bloc and western Europe from 1945 until 1990.

i•ron•ic (ī-rŏn′ĭk) also **i•ron•i•cal** (-ĭ-kəl) ►*adj.* **1.** Marked by or constituting irony. **2.** Given to the use of irony. —**i•ron′i•cal•ly** *adv.* —**i•ron′i•cal•ness** *n.*

iron lung ►*n.* A tank that encloses all of the body except the head and forces the lungs to inhale and exhale through regulated changes in air pressure.

i•ron•stone (ī′ərn-stōn′) ►*n.* **1.** A hard white pottery. **2.** An iron ore.

i•ron•ware (ī′ərn-wâr′) ►*n.* Iron utensils and other products made of iron.

i•ron•work (ī′ərn-wûrk′) ►*n.* Work in iron, such as gratings and rails.

i•ron•work•er (ī′ərn-wûr′kər) ►*n.* **1.** A construction worker who builds steel structures. **2.** One who makes iron articles.

i•ron•works (ī′ərn-wûrks′) ►*pl.n. (takes sing. or pl. v.)* A building or establishment where iron is smelted or iron products are made.

i•ro•ny (ī′rə-nē, ī′ər-) ►*n., pl.* **-nies 1.** The use of words to convey the opposite of their literal meaning. **2.** Incongruity between what might be expected and what actually occurs. [< Gk. *eirōneia*, feigned ignorance.] —**i′ro•nist** *n.*

Ir•o•quoi•an (îr′ə-kwoi′ən) ►*n.* **1.** A family of Native American languages of E North America. **2.** A member of an Iroquoian-speaking people. —**Ir′o•quoi′an** *adj.*

Ir•o•quois (ĭr′ə-kwoi′) ►*n., pl.* **-quois** (-kwoi′, -kwoiz′) **1.** A member of a Native American confederacy of New York State composed of the Mohawk, Oneida, Onondaga, Cayuga, Seneca, and later the Tuscarora peoples. **2.** Any of the languages of the Iroquois.

ir•ra•di•ate (ĭ-rā′dē-āt′) ►*v.* **-at•ed, -at•ing 1.** To expose to or treat with radiation. **2.** To shed light on; illuminate. **3.** To emit in or as if in rays; radiate. [Lat. *irradiāre*, shine on < *radius*, ray.] —**ir•ra′di•a′tion** *n.* —**ir•ra′di•a′tive** *adj.* —**ir•ra′di•a′tor** *n.*

ir•ra•tion•al (ĭ-răsh′ə-nəl) ►*adj.* **1a.** Not endowed with reason. **b.** Incoherent, as from shock. **c.** Illogical: *an irrational dislike.* See Syns at **unreasonable. 2.** *Math.* Relating to an irrational number. —**ir•ra′tion•al′i•ty** (-ə-năl′ĭ-tē) *n.* —**ir•ra′tion•al•ly** *adv.*

irrational number ►*n.* Any real number that cannot be expressed as a ratio between two integers.

Ir•ra•wad•dy (îr′ə-wŏd′ē, -wô′dē) A river of Myanmar (Burma) flowing about 1,609 km (1,000 mi) to the Bay of Bengal and the Andaman Sea.

ir•rec•on•cil•a•ble (ĭ-rĕk′ən-sī′lə-bəl, ĭ-rĕk′ən-sī′-) ►*adj.* Impossible to reconcile. —**ir•rec′on•cil′a•bil′i•ty** *n.* —**ir•rec′on•cil′a•bly** *adv.*

ir•re•cov•er•a•ble (ĭr′ĭ-kŭv′ər-ə-bəl) ►*adj.* Impossible to recover; irreparable: *irrecoverable losses.* —**ir′re•cov′er•a•ble•ness** *n.* —**ir′re•cov′er•a•bly** *adv.*

ir•re•deem•a•ble (ĭr′ĭ-dē′mə-bəl) ►*adj.* **1.** That cannot be bought back or paid off. **2.** Not convertible into coin. **3.** Impossible to redeem or reform. —**ir′re•deem′a•bly** *adv.*

ir•re•den•tist (ĭr′ĭ-dĕn′tĭst) ►*n.* One who advocates the recovery of territory culturally or historically related to one's nation but now subject to a foreign government. [< Ital. *irredenta*, unredeemed.] —**ir′re•den′tism** *n.*

ir•re•duc•i•ble (ĭr′ĭ-do͞o′sə-bəl, -dyo͞o′-) ►*adj.* Impossible to reduce to a simpler or smaller form or amount. —**ir′re•duc′i•bil′i•ty** *n.* —**ir′re•duc′i•bly** *adv.*

ir•ref•u•ta•ble (ĭ-rĕf′yə-tə-bəl, ĭr′ĭ-fyo͞o′-) ►*adj.* Impossible to refute or disprove: *irrefutable evidence of guilt.* —**ir•ref′u•ta•bil′i•ty** *n.* —**ir•ref′u•ta•bly** *adv.*

irreg. ►*abbr.* irregular

ir•re•gard•less (ĭr′ĭ-gärd′lĭs) ►*adv. Nonstandard* Regardless.

Usage: *Irregardless* is a form that many people mistakenly believe to be a correct usage in formal style but that in fact has no legitimate antecedents in either standard or nonstandard varieties of English.

ir•reg•u•lar (ĭ-rĕg′yə-lər) ►*adj.* **1.** Contrary to

rule, accepted order, or general practice. **2.** Not straight, uniform, or symmetrical. **3.** Of uneven rate, occurrence, or duration. **4.** Deviating from a type; atypical. **5.** Not up to standard or specification; imperfect. **6.** *Gram.* Departing from the usual pattern of inflection. **7.** Not belonging to a permanent, organized military force. ▶*n.* **1.** One that is irregular. **2.** A guerrilla. —**ir•reg′u•lar′i•ty** (-yə-lăr′ĭ-tē) *n.* —**ir•reg′u•lar•ly** *adv.*

ir•rel•e•vant (ĭ-rĕl′ə-vənt) ▶*adj.* Unrelated to the matter at hand. —**ir•rel′e•vance, ir•rel′e•van•cy** *n.* —**ir•rel′e•vant•ly** *adv.*
Syns: *irrelevant, extraneous, immaterial, impertinent* **Ant:** *relevant* **adj.**

ir•re•li•gious (ĭr′ĭ-lĭj′əs) ▶*adj.* Hostile or indifferent to religion. —**ir′re•li′gious•ly** *adv.* —**ir′re•li′gious•ness** *n.*

ir•re•me•di•a•ble (ĭr′ĭ-mē′dē-ə-bəl) ▶*adj.* Impossible to remedy, correct, or repair. —**ir′re•me′di•a•bly** *adv.*

ir•rep•a•ra•ble (ĭ-rĕp′ər-ə-bəl) ▶*adj.* Impossible to repair, rectify, or amend. —**ir•rep′a•ra•bil′i•ty, ir•rep′a•ra•ble•ness** *n.* —**ir•rep′a•ra•bly** *adv.*

ir•re•place•a•ble (ĭr′ĭ-plā′sə-bəl) ▶*adj.* Impossible to replace.

ir•re•press•i•ble (ĭr′ĭ-prĕs′ə-bəl) ▶*adj.* Impossible to control or hold back. —**ir′re•press′i•bil′i•ty** *n.* —**ir′re•press′i•bly** *adv.*

ir•re•proach•a•ble (ĭr′ĭ-prō′chə-bəl) ▶*adj.* Being beyond reproach: *irreproachable conduct.* —**ir′re•proach′a•bly** *adv.*

ir•re•sis•ti•ble (ĭr′ĭ-zĭs′tə-bəl) ▶*adj.* **1.** Impossible to resist. **2.** Overwhelming. —**ir′re•sis′ti•bil′i•ty, ir′re•sis′ti•ble•ness** *n.* —**ir′re•sis′ti•bly** *adv.*

ir•res•o•lute (ĭ-rĕz′ə-lo͞ot′) ▶*adj.* **1.** Unsure of how to act or proceed; undecided. **2.** Lacking in resolution; indecisive. —**ir•res′o•lute′ly** *adv.* —**ir•res′o•lute′ness, ir•res′o•lu′tion** *n.*

ir•re•spec•tive of (ĭr′ĭ-spĕk′tĭv) ▶*prep.* Without consideration of; regardless of.

ir•re•spon•si•ble (ĭr′ĭ-spŏn′sə-bəl) ▶*adj.* **1.** Marked by a lack of responsibility: *irresponsible accusations.* **2.** Unreliable. —**ir′re•spon′si•bil′i•ty, ir′re•spon′si•ble•ness** *n.* —**ir′re•spon′si•bly** *adv.*

ir•re•triev•a•ble (ĭr′ĭ-trē′və-bəl) ▶*adj.* Impossible to retrieve or recover. —**ir′re•triev′a•ble•ness, ir′re•triev′a•bil′i•ty** *n.* —**ir′re•triev′a•bly** *adv.*

ir•rev•er•ence (ĭ-rĕv′ər-əns) ▶*n.* **1.** Lack of reverence or due respect. **2.** A disrespectful act or remark. —**ir•rev′er•ent** *adj.* —**ir•rev′er•ent•ly** *adv.*

ir•re•vers•i•ble (ĭr′ĭ-vûr′sə-bəl) ▶*adj.* Impossible to reverse. —**ir′re•vers′i•bil′i•ty** *n.* —**ir′re•vers′i•bly** *adv.*

ir•rev•o•ca•ble (ĭ-rĕv′ə-kə-bəl) ▶*adj.* Impossible to retract or revoke. —**ir•rev′o•ca•bil′i•ty, ir•rev′o•ca•ble•ness** *n.* —**ir•rev′o•ca•bly** *adv.*

ir•ri•gate (ĭr′ĭ-gāt′) ▶*v.* **-gat•ed, -gat•ing 1.** To supply land or crops with water by means of ditches, pipes, or streams. **2.** *Medic.* To wash out with water or a medicated fluid. [Lat. *irrigāre.*] —**ir′ri•ga•ble** (ĭr′ĭ-gə-bəl) *adj.* —**ir′ri•ga′tion** *n.* —**ir′ri•ga′tion•al** *adj.* —**ir′ri•ga′tor** *n.*

ir•ri•ta•ble (ĭr′ĭ-tə-bəl) ▶*adj.* **1.** Easily irritated or annoyed. **2.** *Pathol.* Abnormally sensitive. **3.** *Physiol.* Responsive to stimuli. [< Lat. *irrītāre,* irritate.] —**ir′ri•ta•bil′i•ty, ir′ri•ta•ble•ness** *n.* —**ir′ri•ta•bly** *adv.*

ir•ri•tant (ĭr′ĭ-tənt) ▶*adj.* Causing irritation, esp. physical irritation. ▶*n.* A source of irritation.

ir•ri•tate (ĭr′ĭ-tāt′) ▶*v.* **-tat•ed, -tat•ing 1.** To make impatient or angry; annoy. **2.** To chafe or inflame. [Lat. *irrītāre.*] —**ir′ri•ta′tion** *n.* —**ir′ri•ta′tor** *n.*

ir•rupt (ĭ-rŭpt′) ▶*v.* To break or burst in; invade. [Lat. *irrumpere, irrupt-.*] —**ir•rup′tion** *n.* —**ir•rup′tive** *adj.*

IRS ▶*abbr.* Internal Revenue Service

Ir•tysh or **Ir•tish** (ĭr-tĭsh′). A river of NW China, E Kazakhstan, and central Russia flowing about 4,264 km (2,650 mi) to the Ob R.

Ir•vine (ûr′vīn′) A city of S CA SE of Santa Ana. Pop. 110,330.

Ir•ving (ûr′vĭng) A town of NE TX, a suburb of Dallas. Pop. 155,037.

Irving, Washington. 1783–1859. Amer. writer.

is (ĭz) ▶*v.* 3rd pers. sing. pr. indic. of **be.**

Is. ▶*abbr.* island

I•saac (ī′zək). In the Bible, the son of Abraham.

Is•a•bel•la I (ĭz′ə-bĕl′ə). "Isabella the Catholic." 1451–1504. Queen of Castile (1474–1504).

Isabella I
detail from a c. 1500 retable

I•sa•iah (ī-zā′ə, ī-zī′ə) ▶*n.* **1.** A Hebrew prophet of the 8th cent. B.C. **2.** See table at **Bible.**

ISBN ▶*abbr.* International Standard Book Number

is•che•mi•a (ĭ-skē′mē-ə) ▶*n.* A decrease in the blood supply to a bodily organ or part caused by constriction or obstruction of the blood vessels. [< Gk. *iskhaimos,* stopping of the blood.] —**i•sche′mic** *adj.*

ISDN ▶*abbr.* Integrated Services Digital Network

Is•fa•han (ĭs′fə-hän′) See **Esfahan.**

-ish ▶*suff.* **1.** Of, relating to, or being: *Swedish.* **2a.** Characteristic of: *girlish.* **b.** Having the qualities of: *childish.* **3.** Approximately; somewhat: *greenish.* **4.** Tending toward; preoccupied with: *selfish.* [< OE *-isc.*]

Ish•er•wood (ĭsh′ər-wo͝od′), **Christopher William Bradshaw.** 1904–86. British-born Amer. writer.

i•sin•glass (ī′zən-glăs′, ī′zĭng-) ▶*n.* **1.** A transparent gelatin prepared from the air bladder esp. of the sturgeon. **2.** Mica in thin, transparent sheets. [< obsolete Du. *huizenblas*.]

I•sis (ī′sĭs) ▸*n. Myth.* An ancient Egyptian goddess of fertility, the sister and wife of Osiris.

Isl. ▸*abbr.* island

Is•lam (ĭs-läm′, ĭs′läm′, ĭz′-) ▸*n.* **1.** A monotheistic religion marked by the profession of submission to God and to Muhammad as the chief and last prophet of God. **2.** The people or nations that practice Islam; the Muslim world. —**Is•lam′ic** *adj.*

Is•lam•a•bad (ĭs-lä′mə-bäd′) The capital of Pakistan, in the NE. Pop. 201,000.

Islamic calendar ▸*n.* The lunar calendar used by Muslims, reckoned from the year of the Hegira in A.D. 622. See table at **calendar.**

is•land (ī′lənd) ▸*n.* **1.** A land mass, esp. one smaller than a continent, surrounded by water. **2.** Something that is completely isolated or surrounded. [< OE *īegland* : *īeg* + *land*, land.] —**is′land•er** *n.*

isle (īl) ▸*n.* An island, esp. a small one. [< Lat. *īnsula*.]

is•let (ī′lĭt) ▸*n.* A very small island.

ism (ĭz′əm) ▸*n. Informal* A distinctive doctrine, system, or theory. [< –ISM.]

–ism ▸*suff.* **1.** Action, process; practice: *terrorism.* **2.** Characteristic behavior or quality: *heroism.* **3a.** State; condition; quality: *pauperism.* **b.** State or condition resulting from an excess of something specified: *strychninism.* **4.** Distinctive or characteristic trait: *Latinism.* **5a.** Doctrine; theory; system of principles: *pacifism.* **b.** An attitude of prejudice against a given group: *racism.* [< Gk. *-ismos*, n. suff.]

is•n't (ĭz′ənt) ▸ Is not.

iso– or **is–** ▸*pref.* **1.** Equal; uniform: *isobar.* **2.** Isomeric: *isopropyl.* [< Gk. *isos*, equal.]

i•so•bar (ī′sə-bär′) ▸*n.* A line on a weather map connecting points of equal barometric pressure. [ISO– + Gk. *baros*, weight.] —**i′so•bar′ic** (-bär′ĭk, -băr′-) *adj.*

i•so•gon (ī′sə-gŏn′) ▸*n.* A polygon whose angles are equal. —**i′so•gon′ic** *adj.*

i•so•late (ī′sə-lāt′) ▸*v.* **-lat•ed, -lat•ing 1.** To set apart or cut off from a group or whole. **2.** To place in quarantine. [< Lat. *īnsula*, island.] —**i′so•la′tion** *n.* —**i′so•la′tor** *n.*

Syns: *isolate, insulate, seclude, segregate, sequester* **v.**

i•so•la•tion•ism (ī′sə-lā′shə-nĭz′əm) ▸*n.* A national policy of abstaining from political or economic entanglements with other countries. —**i′so•la′tion•ist** *n.*

i•so•mer (ī′sə-mər) ▸*n.* **1.** *Chem.* A compound having the same elements in the same proportions as another but differing in chemical or physical properties. **2.** *Phys.* An atom whose nucleus can exist in any of several bound excited states for a measurable period. —**i′so•mer′ic** (-mĕr′ĭk) *adj.*

i•so•met•ric (ī′sə-mĕt′rĭk) also **i•so•met•ri•cal** (-rĭ-kəl) ▸*adj.* **1.** Exhibiting equality in dimensions or measurements. **2.** *Physiol.* Involving muscular contraction against resistance in which the length of the muscle remains the same. ▸*n.* A line connecting isometric points. [< Gk. *isometros*, having equal measure.]

i•so•met•rics (ī′sə-mĕt′rĭks) ▸*n. (takes sing. or pl. v.)* Exercise in which isometric contraction is used to strengthen and tone muscles.

i•so•morph (ī′sə-môrf′) ▸*n.* An organism or substance exhibiting isomorphism.

i•so•mor•phism (ī′sə-môr′fĭz′əm) ▸*n.* Similarity of form, as in organisms of different ancestry, or of structure, as in chemical substances. —**i′so•mor′phic** *adj.*

i•so•pro•pyl alcohol (ī′sə-prō′pəl) ▸*n.* A clear, colorless, flammable mobile liquid used in antifreeze compounds, lotions, cosmetics, and as a solvent.

i•sos•ce•les (ī-sŏs′ə-lēz′) ▸*adj.* Having two equal sides: *an isosceles triangle.* [< Gk. *isoskelēs* : ISO– + *skelos*, leg.]

i•so•therm (ī′sə-thûrm′) ▸*n.* A line on a weather map linking all points of equal or constant temperature. [< ISO– + Gk. *thermē*, heat.] —**i′so•ther′mal** *adj.*

i•so•tope (ī′sə-tōp′) ▸*n.* One of two or more atoms whose nuclei have the same number of protons but different numbers of neutrons. [ISO– + Gk. *topos*, place.] —**i′so•top′ic** (-tŏp′ĭk) *adj.* —**i′so•top′i•cal•ly** *adv.*

i•so•tro•pic (ī′sə-trō′pĭk, -trŏp′ĭk) ▸*adj.* Invariant with respect to direction; identical in all directions. —**i•sot′ro•py** (ī-sŏt′rə-pē), **i•sot′ro•pism** (-pĭz′əm) *n.*

Is•ra•el[1] (ĭz′rē-əl) ▸*n.* **1a.** In the Bible, Jacob. **b.** The descendants of Jacob. **2.** *Judaism* The Hebrew people, past, present, and future.

Is•ra•el[2] (ĭz′rē-əl) **1.** An ancient kingdom of the Hebrews founded by Saul c. 1025 B.C. **2.** A country of SW Asia on the E Mediterranean. Cap. Jerusalem. Pop. 5,383,000.

Is•rae•li (ĭz-rā′lē) ▸*adj.* Of or relating to modern-day Israel or its people. ▸*n., pl.* **-lis.** A citizen of modern-day Israel.

Is•ra•el•ite (ĭz′rē-ə-līt′) ▸*n.* **1.** A native or inhabitant of ancient Israel. **2.** A Jew.

is•sue (ĭsh′o͞o) ▸*n.* **1.** The act or an instance of flowing, passing, or giving out. **2a.** Something produced, published, or offered, as stamps or coins. **b.** A single copy of a periodical. **3.** The final result of an action. **4.** Proceeds from estates or fines. **5.** Something proceeding from a specified source. **6.** Offspring; progeny. **7.** A point of discussion. **8.** An outlet. **9.** *Pathol.* A discharge, as of blood. ▸*v.* **-sued, -su•ing 1.** To go or come out. **2.** To be born or be descended. **3.** To publish or be published. **4.** To circulate, as coins. **5.** To come forth or cause to come forth. See Syns at **stem**[1]. **6.** To end or result. —***idioms:*** **at issue** In dispute. **take issue** To disagree. [< VLat. **exūta* < Lat. *exīre*, go out.] —**is′su•ance** *n.* —**is′su•er** *n.*

–ist ▸*suff.* **1a.** One that performs a specified action: *lobbyist.* **b.** One that produces, operates, or is connected with a specified thing: *novelist.* **2.** A specialist in a specified field: *biologist.* **3.** An adherent or advocate of a specified doctrine, theory, or school of thought: *anarchist.* **4.** One characterized by a specified trait or quality: *romanticist.* [< Gk. *-istēs*, agent n. suff.]

Is•tan•bul (ĭs′tăn-bo͝ol′, -tän-, ĭ-stän′bo͝ol). Formerly **Con•stan•ti•no•ple** (kŏn′stăn-tə-nō′pəl). The largest city of Turkey, in the NW part on the Bosporus at its entrance into the Sea of Marmara. Pop. 7,615,500.

Isth. ▸*abbr.* isthmus

isth•mus (ĭs′məs) ▸*n.* **1.** A narrow strip of land connecting two larger masses of land. **2.** *Anat.* **a.** A narrow strip of tissue joining two larger organs or parts of an organ. **b.** A narrow passage connecting two larger cavities. [< Gk. *isthmos.*] —**isth′mi•an** *adj.*

it (ĭt) ▸*pron.* **1.** Used to refer to a nonhuman entity, an animal or human whose sex is unknown or irrelevant, a group of persons, or an abstraction. **2.** Used as the subject of an impersonal verb: *It is snowing.* **3.** Used to refer to a general condition or state of affairs: *She couldn't stand it.* ▸*n. Games* A player, as in tag, who attempts to find or catch the other players. [< OE *hit.*]

It. or **Ital.** ▸*abbr.* Italian

ital. ▸*abbr.* **1.** italic **2.** italics

I•tal•ian (ĭ-tăl′yən) ▸*adj.* Of or relating to Italy or its people or language. ▸*n.* **1a.** A native or inhabitant of Italy. **b.** A person of Italian descent. **2.** The Romance language of the Italians and parts of Switzerland.

Italian sandwich ▸*n. Regional* See **submarine** 2. See Regional Note at **submarine.**

I•tal•ic (ĭ-tăl′ĭk, ī-tăl′-) ▸*adj.* **1.** Of or relating to ancient Italy. **2.** Of or relating to Italic. **3. italic** Of or being a style of printing type with the letters slanting to the right: *This sentence is in italic type.* ▸*n.* **1.** A branch of Indo-European that includes Latin. **2.** often **italics** Italic print or typeface. [< Lat. *Italia*, Italy.]

i•tal•i•cize (ĭ-tăl′ĭ-sīz′, ī-tăl′-) ▸*v.* **-cized, -ciz•ing.** To print in italic type. —**i•tal′i•ci•za′tion** *n.*

It•a•ly (ĭt′l-ē) **1.** A peninsula of S Europe projecting into the Mediterranean between the Tyrrhenian and Adriatic seas. **2.** A country of S Europe comprising the peninsula of Italy, Sardinia, Sicily, and several smaller islands. Cap. Rome. Pop. 57,193,000.

itch (ĭch) ▸*n.* **1.** A skin sensation causing a desire to scratch. **2.** A skin disorder marked by intense irritation and itching. **3.** A restless desire or craving. [< OE *gicce.*] —**itch** *v.* —**itch′i•ness** *n.* —**itch′y** *adj.*

-ite[1] ▸*suff.* **1.** Native or resident of: *urbanite.* **2.** Adherent or follower of: *Trotskyite.* **3.** A part of an organ or body: *dendrite.* **4a.** Rock; mineral: *graphite.* **b.** Fossil: *trilobite.* **5a.** Product: *metabolite.* **b.** A commercial product: *ebonite.* [< Gk. *-itēs.*]

-ite[2] ▸*suff.* A salt or ester of an acid named with an adjective ending in *-ous: sulfite.* [Alteration of -ATE[2].]

i•tem (ī′təm) ▸*n.* **1.** A single article or unit in a group, series, or list. **2a.** A bit of information. **b.** A short piece in a newspaper or magazine. [< Lat., also.]

Syns: *item, detail, particular* **n.**

i•tem•ize (ī′tə-mīz′) ▸*v.* **-ized, -iz•ing.** To set down by item; list. —**i′tem•i•za′tion** *n.* —**i′tem•iz′er** *n.*

it•er•ate (ĭt′ə-rāt′) ▸*v.* **-at•ed, -at•ing.** To say or perform again. See Syns at **repeat.** [< Lat. *iterum*, again.] —**it′er•a′tion** *n.*

I•thá•ki (ē-thä′kē) also **Ith•a•ca** (ĭth′ə-kə). An island of W Greece in the Ionian Is.

i•tin•er•ant (ī-tĭn′ər-ənt, ĭ-tĭn′-) ▸*adj.* Traveling from place to place, esp. to perform work. ▸*n.* An itinerant person. [< LLat. *itinerārī*, travel < Lat. *iter, itiner-*, journey.] —**i•tin′er•an•cy, i•tin′er•a•cy** *n.*

i•tin•er•ar•y (ī-tĭn′ə-rĕr′ē, ĭ-tĭn′-) ▸*n., pl.* **-ies** **1.** A route or proposed route of a journey. **2.** An account or record of a journey. **3.** A traveler's guidebook. [< Lat. *iter, itiner-*, journey.]

-itis ▸*suff.* Inflammation or disease of: *laryngitis.* [Gk., n. suff.]

it'll (ĭt′l) ▸ **1.** It will. **2.** It shall.

its (ĭts) ▸*adj.* The possessive form of **it.** Used as a modifier before a noun: *The airline canceled its early flight to Atlanta.*

Usage: *Its,* the possessive form of the pronoun *it,* is never written with an apostrophe. The contraction *it's* (for *it is* or *it has*) is always written with an apostrophe.

it's (ĭts) ▸ **1.** It is. **2.** It has.

it•self (ĭt-sĕlf′) ▸*pron.* **1.** That one identical with it. Used: **a.** Reflexively as the direct or indirect object of a verb or the object of a preposition: *The cat scratched itself.* **b.** For emphasis: *The trouble is in the machine itself.* **2.** Its normal condition or state: *The car is acting itself again since the oil change.*

-ity ▸*suff.* State; quality: *abnormality.* [< Lat. *-itās.*]

IU ▸*abbr.* international unit

IUD ▸*abbr.* intrauterine device

-ium ▸*suff.* Chemical element or group: *iridium.* [Alteration of Lat. *-um*, neuter suff.]

IV ▸*abbr.* intravenous

I•van III Va•sil•ie•vich (ī′vən, ē-vän′; və-sĭl′yə-vĭch′). "the Great." 1440–1505. Grand duke of Muscovy (1462–1505).

Ivan IV Vasilievich. "the Terrible." 1530–84. The first czar of Russia (1547–84).

-ive ▸*suff.* Performing or tending toward a specified action: *demonstrative.* [< Lat. *-īvus.*]

I've (īv) ▸ I have.

Ives (īvz), **Charles Edward.** 1874–1954. Amer. composer.

i•vo•ry (ī′və-rē, īv′rē) ▸*n., pl.* **-ries** **1.** A hard, smooth, yellowish-white substance that forms the tusks of certain animals, esp. the elephant. **2.** An article made of ivory. **3.** A substance resembling ivory. **4.** A yellowish white. **5.** often **ivories** **a.** Piano keys. **b.** Dice. **c.** *Slang* The teeth. [< Lat. *ebur*, of Egypt. orig.] —**i′vo•ry** *adj.*

Ivory Coast. See **Côte d'Ivoire.**

ivory tower ▸*n.* A place or attitude of retreat, esp. preoccupation with intellectual considerations rather than practical life.

i•vy (ī′vē) ▸*n., pl.* **i•vies.** Any of a genus of climbing or trailing plants having lobed evergreen leaves. [< OE *īfig.*]

I•wo Ji•ma (ē′wə jē′mə, ē′wō) The largest of the Volcano Is. of Japan, in the NW Pacific E of Taiwan.

I•yar also **Iy•yar** (ē-yär′, ē′yär′) ▸*n.* A month in the Jewish calendar. See table at **calendar.** [Heb. *'iyyār.*]

-ization ▸*suff.* Action, process, or result of doing or making: *colonization.*

-ize ▸*suff.* **1a.** To cause to be or become: *dramatize.* **b.** To cause to conform to or resemble: *Hellenize.* **c.** To treat as: *idolize.* **2a.** To treat or affect with: *anesthetize.* **b.** To subject to: *tyrannize.* **3.** To treat according to or practice the method of: *pasteurize.* **4.** To become; become like: *materialize.* **5.** To perform, engage in, or produce: *botanize.* [< Gk. *-izein*, v. suff.]

I•zhevsk (ē-zhĕfsk′) A city of W-central Russia NE of Kazan. Pop. 652,424.

Iz•mir (ĭz-mîr′). Formerly **Smyrna.** A city of W Turkey on the Aegean. Pop. 1,985,300.

J

j or **J** (jā) ►*n.*, *pl.* **j's** or **J's** also **js** or **Js.** The 10th letter of the English alphabet.

J or **j** ►*abbr.* joule

J. ►*abbr.* **1.** Japanese **2.** judge

JA ►*abbr.* judge advocate

jab (jăb) ►*v.* **jabbed, jab•bing 1.** To poke abruptly, esp. with something sharp. **2.** To punch with short blows. ►*n.* A quick stab or blow. [ME *jobben.*]

Jab•al•pur (jŭb′əl-po͝or′) A city of central India SSE of Delhi. Pop. 741,927.

jab•ber (jăb′ər) ►*v.* To talk rapidly, unintelligibly, or idly. [ME *javeren.*] —**jab′ber** *n.*

ja•bot (zhă-bō′, jăb′ō) ►*n.* A cascade of ruffles down the front of a shirt. [Fr., bird's crop.]

jabot

jac•a•ran•da (jăk′ə-răn′də) ►*n.* **1.** A tropical American tree having purple flowers. **2.** The wood of this tree. [Port. and Am.Sp.]

jack (jăk) ►*n.* **1.** often **Jack** *Informal* A man; fellow. **2.** *Games* A playing card showing the figure of a knave and ranking below a queen. **3.** *Games* **a. jacks** *(takes sing. or pl. v.)* A game played with a set of small six-pointed metal pieces and a rubber ball, the object being to pick up the pieces in various combinations. **b.** One of the metal pieces so used. **4.** A usu. portable device for raising heavy objects. **5.** A small flag flown at the bow of a ship, usu. to indicate nationality. **6.** The male of certain animals, esp. the ass. **7.** A socket that accepts a plug at one end and attaches to electric circuitry at the other. ►*v.* **1.** To hoist with a jack. **2.** To raise: *jack up prices.* [< the name *Jack.*]

jack•al (jăk′əl, -ôl′) ►*n.* A doglike mammal of Africa and S Asia. [< Skt. *śṛgālaḥ.*]

jack•ass (jăk′ăs′) ►*n.* **1.** A male ass or donkey. **2.** A foolish or stupid person.

jack•boot (jăk′bo͞ot′) ►*n.* A stout military boot extending above the knee.

jack•daw (jăk′dô′) ►*n.* A Eurasian crow. [JACK + *daw*, jackdaw.]

jack•et (jăk′ĭt) ►*n.* **1.** A short coat usu. extending to the hips. **2.** An outer covering or casing. [< OFr. *jaque*, short jacket.] —**jack′et•ed** *adj.*

jack•ham•mer (jăk′hăm′ər) ►*n.* A hand-held pneumatic machine for drilling rock and breaking up pavement. —**jack′ham′mer** *v.*

jack-in-the-box (jăk′ĭn-*thə*-bŏks′) ►*n.*, *pl.* **-box•es** or **jacks-in-the-box** (jăks′-). A clownlike puppet that springs out of a box when the lid is raised.

jack-in-the-pul•pit (jăk′ĭn-*thə*-po͝ol′pĭt, -pŭl′-) ►*n.*, *pl.* **-pits.** A plant having a leaflike spathe enclosing a clublike spadix.

jack•knife (jăk′nīf′) ►*n.* **1.** A large clasp knife. **2.** A dive in which one bends at the waist, touches the toes, and then straightens out. ►*v.* To fold or double like a jackknife.

jack-of-all-trades (jăk′əv-ôl′trādz′) ►*n.*, *pl.* **jacks-of-all-trades** (jăks′-). One who can do many kinds of work.

jack-o′-lan•tern (jăk′ə-lăn′tərn) ►*n.* A lantern made from a hollowed pumpkin with a carved face.

jack•pot (jăk′pŏt′) ►*n.* A cumulative pool or top prize in various games.

jack•rab•bit (jăk′răb′ĭt) ►*n.* A large, long-eared hare. [JACK(ASS) + RABBIT.]

jack•screw (jăk′skro͞o′) ►*n.* A jack operated by a screw.

Jack•son (jăk′sən) The capital of MS, in the W-central part. Pop. 196,637.

Jackson, Andrew. "Old Hickory." 1767–1845. The 7th US President (1829–37).

Jackson, Jesse Louis. b. 1941. Amer. civil rights leader and politician.

Andrew Jackson
1845 portrait

Jesse Jackson

Jackson, Thomas Jonathan. "Stonewall." 1824–63. Amer. Confederate general.

Jack•son•ville (jăk′sən-vĭl′) A city of NE FL near the Atlantic and the GA border. Pop. 672,971.

Ja•cob (jā′kəb). In the Bible, the son of Isaac and grandson of Abraham.

Jac•o•be•an (jăk′ə-bē′ən) ►*adj.* Relating to the reign of James I of England or his times. [< Lat. *Iacōbus*, James.] —**Jac′o•be′an** *n.*

Jac•o•bin (jăk′ə-bĭn) ►*n.* **1.** A radical leftist. **2.** A radical republican during the French Revolution. [After the *Jacobin* friars, in whose convent the Jacobins first met.]

Ja•cob's ladder (jā′kəbz) ►*n.* **1.** *Naut.* A rope or chain ladder with rigid rungs. **2.** A plant having blue flowers and compound leaves with numerous leaflets. [From the ladder seen by Jacob.]

Ja•cuz•zi (jə-ko͞o′zē, jă-) ► A trademark for a whirlpool bath.

jade[1] (jād) ►*n.* Either of two distinct minerals, nephrite and jadeite, that are gen. pale green and used mainly as gemstones. [< Sp. *(piedra de) ijada*, (stone of the) flank.]

jade[2] (jād) ►*v.* **jad•ed, jad•ing 1.** To wear out, as by overuse. **2.** To become weary or spiritless. ►*n.* **1.** A broken-down horse; nag. **2.** A disreputable woman. [ME, cart horse.]

jad•ed (jā′dĭd) ▸*adj.* **1.** Worn out; wearied. **2.** Dulled by surfeit; sated. **3.** Cynically callous. —**jad′ed•ly** *adv.* —**jad′ed•ness** *n.*

jade•ite (jā′dīt′) ▸*n.* A rare, usu. emerald to light green but sometimes white, auburn, buff, or violet jade, $NaAlSi_2O_6$.

Jaf•fa (jăf′ə, yä′fə) See **Yafo.**

jag[1] (jăg) ▸*n.* A sharp point; barb. [ME *jagge.*]

jag[2] (jăg) ▸*n. Slang* A period of overindulgence; spree. See Syns at **binge.** [?]

JAG ▸*abbr.* judge advocate general

jag•ged (jăg′ĭd) ▸*adj.* Having sharp or ragged projections. —**jag′ged•ly** *adv.* —**jag′ged•ness** *n.*

jag•uar (jăg′wär′, jăg′yo͞o-är′) ▸*n.* A large leopardlike mammal of Central and South America. [< Guarani *jaguá*, dog.]

jai a•lai (hī′ lī′, hī′ ə-lī′, hī′ ə-lī′) ▸*n.* A fast court game in which players use a long handshaped basket to propel the ball against a wall. [< Basque.]

jail (jāl) ▸*n.* A place for the confinement of persons in lawful detention; prison. ▸*v.* To put in jail; imprison. [< OFr. *jaiole.*]

jail•bird (jāl′bûrd′) ▸*n. Informal* A prisoner or ex-convict.

jail•break (jāl′brāk′) ▸*n.* An escape from jail.

jail•er also **jail•or** (jā′lər) ▸*n.* The keeper of a jail.

Jai•pur (jī′po͝or′) A city of NW India SSW of Delhi. Pop. 1,458,483.

Ja•kar•ta or **Dja•kar•ta** (jə-kär′tə). The capital of Indonesia, on the NE coast of Java. Pop. 8,259,266.

ja•la•pe•ño (hä′lə-pān′yō) ▸*n., pl.* **-ños.** A cultivated variety of capsicum pepper having a pungent green or red fruit used in cooking. [After *Jalapa*, Mexico.]

ja•lop•y (jə-lŏp′ē) ▸*n., pl.* **-ies** *Informal.* An old dilapidated automobile. [?]

jal•ou•sie (jăl′ə-sē) ▸*n.* A blind or shutter having adjustable horizontal slats. [< Fr., jealousy.]

jam[1] (jăm) ▸*v.* **jammed, jam•ming 1.** To drive or squeeze into a tight position. **2.** To activate or apply suddenly. **3.** To lock or cause to lock into an unworkable position. **4.** To fill to excess; cram. **5.** To block or clog. **6.** To interfere electronically with the reception of (broadcast signals). **7.** *Mus.* To play improvisations. ▸*n.* **1.** The act of jamming or the condition of being jammed. **2.** A crush or congestion. **3.** A predicament. [?] —**jam′mer** *n.*

jam[2] (jăm) ▸*n.* A preserve made from fruit boiled with sugar. [Perh. < JAM[1].]

Ja•mai•ca (jə-mā′kə) An island country in the Caribbean Sea S of Cuba. Cap. Kingston. Pop. 2,496,600. —**Ja•mai′can** *adj. & n.*

jamb (jăm) ▸*n.* One of the vertical posts of a door or window frame. [< LLat. *gamba*, horse's hock.]

jam•ba•lay•a (jŭm′bə-lī′ə) ▸*n.* A spicy Creole dish of rice and meat or seafood. [< Prov. *jambalaia.*]

jam•bo•ree (jăm′bə-rē′) ▸*n.* **1.** A noisy celebration. **2.** A large assembly, as of Boy Scouts or Girl Scouts. [?]

James (jāmz) ▸*n.* See table at **Bible.**

James[1], Saint. "the Great." d. A.D. 44. One of the 12 Apostles.

James[2], Saint. "the Less." d. c. A.D. 62. Traditionally regarded as the brother of Jesus.

James[3], Saint. fl. 1st cent. A.D. One of the 12 Apostles.

James I. 1566–1625. King of England (1603–25) and of Scotland as James VI (1567–1625).

James II. 1633–1701. King of England, Scotland, and Ireland (1685–88).

James, Henry. 1843–1916. Amer. writer and critic.

James, William. 1842–1910. Amer. psychologist and philosopher.

James Bay. The S arm of Hudson Bay, between NE Ontario and W Quebec, Canada.

James River 1. A river rising in central ND and flowing about 1,142 km (710 mi) across SD to the Missouri R. **2.** A river, about 547 km (340 mi), rising in central VA and flowing to Chesapeake Bay.

James•town (jāmz′toun′) **1.** The capital of St. Helena, in the S Atlantic. Pop. 1,516. **2.** A former village of SE VA; first permanent English settlement in America (1607).

jam session ▸*n.* An informal gathering of musicians to play improvised or unrehearsed music.

Jan. ▸*abbr.* January

jan•gle (jăng′gəl) ▸*v.* **-gled, -gling 1.** To make or cause to make a harsh metallic sound. **2.** To grate on or jar (the nerves). [< OFr. *jangler.*] —**jan′gle** *n.* —**jan′gler** *n.*

jan•i•tor (jăn′ĭ-tər) ▸*n.* One employed to maintain and clean a building. [Lat. *iānitor*, doorkeeper.] —**jan′i•to′ri•al** (-tôr′ē-əl, -tōr′-) *adj.*

Jan•u•ar•y (jăn′yo͞o-ĕr′ē) ▸*n., pl.* **-ies.** The 1st month of the Gregorian calendar. See table at **calendar.** [< Lat. *Iānuārius (mēnsis)*, (month) of Janus.]

Ja•nus (jā′nəs) ▸*n. Rom. Myth.* The god of gates and doorways, depicted with two faces looking in opposite directions.

ja•pan (jə-păn′) ▸*n.* A black enamel used to produce a durable glossy finish. [< JAPAN.] —**ja•pan′** *v.*

Japan. A country of Asia on an archipelago off the NE coast of the mainland. Cap. Tokyo. Pop. 124,961,000.

Japan, Sea of. An enclosed arm of the W Pacific between Japan and the Asian mainland.

Japan Current ▸*n.* A warm ocean current flowing NE from the Philippine Sea past SE Japan to the North Pacific.

Jap•a•nese (jăp′ə-nēz′, -nēs′) ▸*adj.* Of or relating to Japan or its people or language. ▸*n., pl.* **-nese 1a.** A native or inhabitant of Japan. **b.** A person of Japanese ancestry. **2.** The language of the Japanese.

Japanese beetle ▸*n.* A metallic-green beetle that is a plant pest in North America.

jape (jāp) ▸*v.* **japed, jap•ing.** To joke or quip. ▸*n.* A joke or quip. [< OFr. *japer*, to chatter.] —**jap′er** *n.* —**jap′er•y** *n.*

jar[1] (jär) ▸*n.* A cylindrical glass or earthenware vessel with a wide mouth. [< Ar. *jarra*, earthen vessel.] —**jar′ful′** *n.*

jar[2] (jär) ▸*v.* **jarred, jar•ring 1.** To make or utter a harsh sound. **2.** To disturb or irritate; grate. **3.** To shake from impact. **4.** To clash or conflict. **5.** To bump or cause to move from impact. ▸*n.* **1.** A jolt. **2.** A harsh sound. [Perh. imit.] —**jar′ring•ly** *adv.*

jar•di•nière (jär′dn-îr′, zhär′dn-yâr′) ▸*n.* A large decorative stand or pot for plants or flowers. [Fr. < OFr. *jardin*, GARDEN.]

jar•gon (jär′gən) ▶*n.* **1.** Nonsensical or incoherent talk. **2.** The specialized or technical language of a trade or profession. [< OFr.]

Jarls•berg (yärlz′bûrg′) ▶ A trademark for a mild, pale-yellow, hard Norwegian cheese.

jas•mine (jăz′mĭn) also **jes•sa•mine** (jĕs′ə-mĭn) ▶*n.* Any of a genus of vines or shrubs having fragrant white or yellow flowers. [< Pers. *yasmīn*.]

jas•per (jăs′pər) ▶*n.* An opaque red, yellow, or brown quartz. [< Gk. *iaspis*.]

ja•to (jā′tō) ▶*n., pl.* **-tos.** An aircraft takeoff aided by an auxiliary rocket. [*j(et-)a(ssisted) t(ake)o(ff)*.]

jaun•dice (jôn′dĭs, jän′-) ▶*n.* Yellowish discoloration of the eyes and tissues caused by deposition of bile salts. ▶*v.* **-diced, -dic•ing 1.** To affect with jaundice. **2.** To affect with envy, prejudice, or hostility. See Syns at **bias.** [< OFr. *jaunice*, yellowness.]

jaunt (jônt, jänt) ▶*n.* A short trip or excursion. [?] —**jaunt** *v.*

jaun•ty (jôn′tē, jän′-) ▶*adj.* **-ti•er, -ti•est 1.** Having a buoyant or self-confident air. **2.** Dapper in appearance. [< OFr. *gentil*, noble. See GENTLE.] —**jaun′ti•ly** *adv.* —**jaun′ti•ness** *n.*

ja•va (jä′və, jăv′ə) ▶*n. Informal* Brewed coffee. [< JAVA.]

Java. An island of Indonesia separated from Borneo by the **Java Sea,** an arm of the Pacific. —**Jav′a•nese′** *adj. & n.*

jave•lin (jăv′lĭn, jăv′ə-) ▶*n.* **1.** A light spear, thrown as a weapon. **2.** A metal or metal-tipped spear, used in contests of distance throwing. [< OFr. *javeline*, of Celt. orig.]

jaw (jô) ▶*n.* **1.** Either of two bony or cartilaginous structures that in most vertebrates form the framework of the mouth and hold the teeth. **2.** Either of two opposed hinged parts in a mechanical device. **3. jaws** A dangerous situation. **4.** *Slang* **a.** Back talk. **b.** A chat. ▶*v. Slang* To talk; converse. [ME *jawe*.] —**jaw′less** *adj.*

jaw•bone (jô′bōn′) ▶*n.* A bone of the jaw, esp. of the lower jaw. ▶*v.* **-boned, -bon•ing** *Slang.* To try to influence or pressure through strong persuasion.

jaw•break•er (jô′brā′kər) ▶*n.* **1.** A very hard candy. **2.** *Slang* A word difficult to pronounce.

jay (jā) ▶*n.* Any of various often crested birds gen. having a loud harsh call. [< LLat. *gāius*.]

Jay, John. 1745–1829. Amer. diplomat and first chief justice of the US Supreme Court (1789–95).

jay•walk (jā′wôk′) ▶*v.* To cross a street in violation of traffic regulations. [< *jay*, inexperienced person.] —**jay′walk′er** *n.*

jazz (jăz) ▶*n.* **1.** A style of American music marked by a strong but flexible rhythmic understructure with solo and ensemble improvisations and a highly sophisticated harmonic idiom. **2.** *Slang* **a.** Animation; enthusiasm. **b.** Nonsense. **c.** Miscellaneous, unspecified things. ▶*v. Slang* To exaggerate or lie (to): *Don't jazz me.* —***phrasal verb:* jazz up** *Slang* To make more interesting; enliven. [?]

jazz•y (jăz′ē) ▶*adj.* **-i•er, -i•est 1.** Of or resembling jazz. **2.** *Slang* Showy; flashy. —**jazz′i•ly** *adv.* —**jazz′i•ness** *n.*

JCS ▶*abbr.* Joint Chiefs of Staff

jct. ▶*abbr.* junction

JD ▶*abbr.* **1.** *Lat.* Juris Doctor (Doctor of Law) **2.** Justice Department **3.** juvenile delinquent

jeal•ous (jĕl′əs) ▶*adj.* **1.** Fearful of losing affection or position. **2.** Resentful or bitter in rivalry; envious. **3.** Arising from feelings of envy, apprehension, or bitterness. **4.** Vigilant in guarding something. [< VLat. **zēlōsus* < LLat. *zēlus*, ZEAL.] —**jeal′ous•ly** *adv.* —**jeal′ous•y, jeal′ous•ness** *n.*

Syns: *jealous, covetous, envious* **adj.**

jean (jēn) ▶*n.* **1.** A heavy cotton. **2. jeans** Pants made of jean or denim. [< OFr. *Genes*, Genoa.]

jeep (jēp) ▶*n.* A small durable US Army motor vehicle with four-wheel drive. [< *GP* < the manufacturer's parts-numbering system.]

jeer (jîr) ▶*v.* To speak or shout derisively. [?] —**jeer** *n.* —**jeer′er** *n.*

Jef•fer•son (jĕf′ər-sən), **Thomas.** 1743–1826. The 3rd US President (1801–09). —**Jef′fer•so′ni•an** *adj. & n.*

Thomas Jefferson
1805 portrait

Jefferson City. The capital of MO, in the central part on the Missouri R. Pop. 35,481.

Je•hosh•a•phat (jə-hŏsh′ə-făt′, -hŏs′-). 9th cent. B.C. King of Judah.

Je•ho•vah (jĭ-hō′və) ▶*n.* In the Old Testament, God. [Blend of consonants of YAHWEH and vowels of Heb. *'ădônāy*, my lord.]

je•june (jə-jo͞on′) ▶*adj.* **1.** Not interesting. **2.** Lacking maturity; childish. **3.** Lacking in nutrition. [< Lat. *iēiūnus*, dry, fasting.] —**je•june′ly** *adv.* —**je•june′ness** *n.*

je•ju•num (jə-jo͞o′nəm) ▶*n., pl.* **-na** (-nə). The section of the small intestine between the duodenum and the ileum. [< Med.Lat. *iēiūnum (intestīnum)*, fasting (intestine).]

jell (jĕl) ▶*v.* **1.** To make or become firm or gelatinous. **2.** To take shape; crystallize. [Prob. < JELLY.]

jel•ly (jĕl′ē) ▶*n., pl.* **-lies 1.** A soft semisolid food typically made by the boiling and setting of fruit juice, sugar, and pectin or gelatin. **2.** Something having the consistency of jelly. ▶*v.* **-lied, -ly•ing.** To make into or become jelly. [< Lat. *gelāre*, freeze.]

jel•ly•bean (jĕl′ē-bēn′) ▶*n.* A small chewy candy.

jel•ly•fish (jĕl′ē-fĭsh′) ▶*n.* **1.** A gelatinous, free-swimming marine animal often having a bell-shaped stage as the dominant phase of its life cycle. **2.** *Informal* A weakling.

jel•ly•roll (jĕl′ē-rōl′) ▶*n.* A thin sheet of sponge cake layered with jelly and then rolled up.

Jen•ghis Khan (jĕn′gĭz kän′, -gĭs, jĕng′-). See **Genghis Khan.**

jen•ny (jĕn′ē) ►*n., pl.* **-nies 1.** The female of certain animals, esp. the donkey and wren. **2.** A spinning jenny. [< the name *Jenny.*]

jeop•ard•ize (jĕp′ər-dīz′) ►*v.* **-ized, -iz•ing.** To expose to loss or injury. See Syns at **endanger.**

jeop•ard•y (jĕp′ər-dē) ►*n., pl.* **-ies.** Risk of loss or injury; danger. [< OFr. *jeu parti*, even game.]

jer•bo•a (jər-bō′ə) ►*n.* A small nocturnal leaping rodent of Asia and Africa. [< Ar. *jarbū'.*]

jer•e•mi•ad (jĕr′ə-mī′əd) ►*n.* A bitter lament or righteous prophecy of doom. [Fr. *jérémiade* < *Jérémie*, Jeremiah.]

Jer•e•mi•ah (jĕr′ə-mī′ə) ►*n.* **1.** A Hebrew prophet of the 7th and 6th cent. B.C. **2.** See table at **Bible.**

Jer•i•cho (jĕr′ĭ-kō′) An ancient city of Palestine near the NW shore of the Dead Sea.

jerk[1] (jûrk) ►*v.* **1.** To give a sudden quick thrust, pull, or twist to. **2.** To move in sudden abrupt motions. ►*n.* **1.** A sudden yank, twist, or jolt. **2.** A muscle spasm. **3.** *Slang* A stupid or foolish person. [?] —**jerk′i•ly** *adv.* —**jerk′i•ness** *n.* —**jerk′y** *adj.*

Syns: *jerk, snap, twitch, wrench, yank* **v.**

jerk[2] (jûrk) ►*v.* To cut (meat) into long strips and sun-dry or cure by smoking. [< JERKY.]

jer•kin (jûr′kĭn) ►*n.* A close-fitting sleeveless jacket. [?]

jerk•wa•ter (jûrk′wô′tər, -wŏt′ər) ►*adj. Informal* Remote and insignificant.

jerk•y (jûr′kē) ►*n.* Meat cured by jerking. [< Quechua *ch'arki.*]

jer•o•bo•am (jĕr′ə-bō′əm) ►*n.* A wine bottle holding ⅘ gal. (3.03 l). [After *Jeroboam I* (died c. 901 B.C.).]

jer•ry-build (jĕr′ē-bĭld′) ►*v.* **-built, -build•ing.** To build shoddily and cheaply. [< dial. *jerry*, defective.]

jer•sey (jûr′zē) ►*n., pl.* **-seys 1a.** A soft, plain-knitted fabric. **b.** A garment made of jersey. **2.** often **Jersey** A breed of fawn-colored dairy cattle. [< JERSEY.]

Jersey. The largest of the Channel Is. in the English Channel.

Jersey City. A city of NE NJ on the Hudson R. opposite Lower Manhattan. Pop. 228,537.

Je•ru•sa•lem (jə-ro͞o′sə-ləm, -zə-) The capital of Israel, in the E-central part. Pop. 561,900.

jes•sa•mine (jĕs′ə-mĭn) ►*n.* Var. of **jasmine.**

Jes•se (jĕs′ē). In the Bible, King David's father.

jest (jĕst) ►*n.* **1.** A playful remark or act. **2.** A frivolous mood. **3.** An object of ridicule. ►*v.* **1.** To act or speak playfully. **2.** To ridicule. [ME *geste*, tale < Lat. *gesta*, deeds.] —**jest′ing•ly** *adv.*

jest•er (jĕs′tər) ►*n.* One who jests, esp. a paid fool at medieval courts.

Jes•u•it (jĕzh′o͞o-ĭt, jĕz′o͞o-, -yo͞o-) ►*n. Rom. Cath. Ch.* A member of the Society of Jesus, an order founded by Saint Ignatius of Loyola in 1534.

Je•sus (jē′zəs) ►*n.* The founder of Christianity, regarded by Christians as the Son of God and the Christ.

jet[1] (jĕt) ►*n.* **1.** A dense black coal that takes a high polish and is used for jewelry. **2.** A deep black. [< Gk. *gagatēs*, after *Gagas*, a town of Lycia.] —**jet** *adj.*

jet[2] (jĕt) ►*n.* **1a.** A high-velocity fluid stream forced under pressure out of a small-diameter opening. **b.** An outlet for emitting such a stream. **c.** Something emitted in or as if in such a stream. **2.** A jet-propelled vehicle, esp. an aircraft. ►*v.* **jet•ted, jet•ting 1.** To travel by jet aircraft. **2.** To squirt. [< Lat. *iactāre*, throw out.]

jet engine ►*n.* **1.** An engine that develops thrust by ejecting a jet of gaseous combustion products. **2.** An engine that obtains the oxygen needed from the atmosphere, used esp. to propel aircraft.

jet lag ►*n.* A disruption of bodily rhythms caused by high-speed air travel across time zones. —**jet′-lagged′** *adj.*

jet-pro•pelled (jĕt′prə-pĕld′) ►*adj.* Driven by one or more jet engines. —**jet propulsion** *n.*

jet•sam (jĕt′səm) ►*n.* **1.** Cargo or equipment thrown overboard to lighten a ship in distress. **2.** Discarded odds and ends. [< ME *jetteson*, throwing overboard. See JETTISON.]

jet set ►*n.* An international social set made up of wealthy people who travel from one fashionable place to another. —**jet′-set′** *adj.* —**jet setter** *n.*

jet stream ►*n.* A high-speed, meandering wind current that gen. flows westerly at altitudes of 15 to 25 km (10 to 15 mi).

jet•ti•son (jĕt′ĭ-sən, -zən) ►*v.* **1.** To cast overboard or off. **2.** *Informal* To discard: *jettisoned the whole marketing plan.* [< VLat. **iectātiō*, a throwing.]

jet•ty (jĕt′ē) ►*n., pl.* **-ties 1.** A structure that projects into a body of water to influence the current or to protect a harbor. **2.** A wharf. [< OFr. *jetee* < *jeter*, to project.]

Jew (jo͞o) ►*n.* **1.** An adherent of Judaism. **2.** A member of the people descended from the ancient Hebrews and marked by adherence to Judaism.

jew•el (jo͞o′əl) ►*n.* **1a.** A precious stone; gem. **b.** A small natural or artificial gem used as a bearing in a watch. **2.** A costly ornament of precious metal or gems. **3.** One that is treasured or esteemed. ►*v.* **-eled, -el•ing** or **-elled, -el•ling.** To adorn or fit with jewels. [< AN *juel.*] —**jew′el•ry** *n.*

jewel box ►*n.* **1.** A usu. lined box for holding jewelry. **2.** A hinged plastic case for holding a compact disk and usu. a printed insert.

jewel box

jew•el•er also **jew•el•ler** (jo͞o′ə-lər) ►*n.* One who makes, repairs, or deals in jewelry.

jew•el•weed (jo͞o′əl-wēd′) ►*n.* Any of several plants having yellowish spurred flowers and dehiscent seed pods.

Jew•ess (jo͞o′ĭs) ►*n.* *Offensive* A Jewish woman or girl.

Jew•ish (jo͞o′ĭsh) ►*adj.* Of or relating to the Jews or their culture or religion. —**Jew′ish•ness** *n.*

Jew•ry (jo͞o′rē) ►*n.* The Jewish people.

Jew's-harp or **jew's-harp** (jo͞oz′härp′) ►*n.* A small musical instrument consisting of a lyre-shaped metal frame held between the teeth and a steel tongue that is plucked to produce a soft twanging sound.

jez•e•bel (jĕz′ə-bĕl′, -bəl) ►*n.* A wicked, scheming woman. [After JEZEBEL.]

Jez•e•bel (jĕz′ə-bĕl′). fl. 9th cent. B.C. Phoenician princess and queen of Israel.

jib (jĭb) ►*n.* A triangular sail set forward of the mast of a sailing vessel. [?]

jibe[1] (jīb) ►*v.* **jibed, jib•ing.** To shift a fore-and-aft sail from one side of a vessel to the other while sailing before the wind. [< obsolete Du. *gijben.*]

jibe[2] (jīb) ►*v.* **jibed, jib•ing** *Informal.* To be in accord; agree. [?]

jibe[3] (jīb) ►*v. & n.* Var. of **gibe.**

Jid•da (jĭd′ə) A city of W-central Saudi Arabia on the Red Sea. Pop. 1,300,000.

jif•fy (jĭf′ē) ►*n., pl.* **jif•fies** *Informal.* A moment. [?]

jig (jĭg) ►*n.* **1.** Any of various lively dances in triple time. **2.** A fishing lure with one or more hooks. **3.** A device for guiding a tool or for holding work in place. ►*v.* **jigged, jig•ging 1.** To dance a jig. **2.** To bob or jerk rapidly. **3.** To operate a jig. [?]

jig•ger (jĭg′ər) ►*n.* A small measure for liquor, usu. holding 1½ oz.

jig•gle (jĭg′əl) ►*v.* **-gled, -gling.** To move or cause to move jerkily up and down or to and fro. [Frequentative of JIG.] —**jig′gle** *n.* —**jig′gly** *adj.*

jig•saw (jĭg′sô′) ►*n.* A saw with a narrow vertical blade, used to cut sharp curves.

jigsaw puzzle ►*n.* A puzzle consisting of irregularly shaped pieces that form a picture when fitted together.

ji•had (jĭ-häd′) ►*n.* A Muslim holy war against infidels. [Ar. *jihād.*]

Ji•lin (jē′lĭn′) **1.** A province of NE China bordering on North Korea. **2.** A city of NE China E of Changchun. Pop. 2,251,848.

jilt (jĭlt) ►*v.* To drop (a lover) suddenly or callously. [Poss. < obsolete *jilt*, harlot.]

Jim Crow (jĭm) ►*n.* *Slang* The practice of discriminating against and segregating Black people. [From the title of a 19th-cent. song.] —**Jim′-Crow′** *adj.*

jim•my (jĭm′ē) ►*n., pl.* **-mies.** A short crowbar with curved ends. ►*v.* **-mied, -my•ing.** To pry (something) open with or as if with a jimmy. [Prob. < *Jimmy.*]

jim•son•weed (jĭm′sən-wēd′) ►*n.* A coarse poisonous plant having large, trumpet-shaped white or violet flowers. [*Jamestown weed.*]

Ji•nan also **Tsi•nan** (jē′nän′). A city of E China on the Huang He (Yellow R.) S of Tianjin. Pop. 2,403,946.

jin•gle (jĭng′gəl) ►*v.* **-gled, -gling.** To make or cause to make a tinkling or ringing metallic sound. ►*n.* **1.** A jingling sound. **2.** A catchy, often musical advertising slogan. [ME *ginglen.*] —**jin′gly** *adj.*

jin•go•ism (jĭng′gō-ĭz′əm) ►*n.* Extreme nationalism marked esp. by a belligerent foreign policy. [< the phrase *by jingo*, used in a bellicose British song.] —**jin′go•ist** *n.* —**jin′go•is′tic** *adj.*

jin•ni (jĭn′ē, jĭ-nē′) ►*n., pl.* **jinn** (jĭn). In Muslim legend, a supernatural spirit. [Ar. *jinnī.*]

jin•rik•sha (jĭn-rĭk′shô′) ►*n.* A small, two-wheeled carriage drawn by one or two persons; ricksha. [J. *jinrikisha.*]

jinx (jĭngks) *Informal* ►*n.* **1.** A person or thing believed to bring bad luck. **2.** A period of bad luck. ►*v.* **jinxed, jinx•ing.** To bring bad luck to. [Poss. < Gk. *iunx*, a bird used in magic.]

jit•ney (jĭt′nē) ►*n., pl.* **-neys.** A small motor vehicle that transports passengers on a route for a low fare. [?]

jit•ter (jĭt′ər) ►*v.* To be nervous or uneasy; fidget. ►*n.* **jitters.** A fit of nervousness. [?] —**jit′ter•i•ness** *n.* —**jit′ter•y** *adj.*

jit•ter•bug (jĭt′ər-bŭg′) ►*n.* A lively dance consisting of various two-step patterns embellished with twirls and acrobatic maneuvers. —**jit′ter•bug′** *v.*

jive (jīv) ►*n.* **1a.** Jazz or swing music. **b.** The jargon of jazz musicians. **2.** *Slang* Deceptive, nonsensical, or glib talk. [?] —**jive** *v. & adj.* —**jiv′er** *n.* —**jiv′ey, jiv′y** *adj.*

jnr. ►*abbr.* junior

Joan of Arc (jōn), Saint. 1412?–31. French military leader and heroine.

job (jŏb) ►*n.* **1.** A regular activity performed for payment. **2.** A position in which one is employed. **3a.** A task that must be done. **b.** A specified duty or responsibility. **4.** A specific piece of work to be done for a set fee. **5.** *Informal* A criminal act, esp. a robbery. ►*v.* **jobbed, job•bing 1.** To work by the piece or at odd jobs. **2.** To act as a jobber. **3.** To subcontract. [Perh. < obsolete *jobbe*, piece.] —**job′less** *adj.* —**job′less•ness** *n.*

Job (jōb) ►*n.* **1.** In the Bible, an upright man tested by God. **2.** See table at **Bible.**

job action (jŏb) ►*n.* A temporary action, such as a strike or slowdown, by workers to protest or make demands.

job•ber (jŏb′ər) ►*n.* **1.** One who buys merchandise from manufacturers and sells it to retailers. **2.** One who works by the piece.

job•hold•er (jŏb′hōl′dər) ►*n.* One who has a regular job.

job lot ►*n.* Miscellaneous merchandise sold in one lot.

job-share (jŏb′shâr′) ►*v.* To share one job in alternation with one or more part-time workers.

jock[1] (jŏk) ►*n.* **1.** A jockey. **2.** A disc jockey.

jock[2] (jŏk) ►*n.* **1.** An athletic supporter. **2.** An athlete. [< JOCKSTRAP.]

jock•ey (jŏk′ē) ►*n., pl.* **-eys.** One who rides horses in races, esp. as a profession. ►*v.* **1.** To ride (a horse) as jockey. **2.** To direct or maneuver by cleverness or skill. **3.** To maneuver for a certain position or advantage. [Dim. of Sc. *Jock*, nickname for *John.*]

jock•strap (jŏk′străp′) ►*n.* An athletic supporter. [*jock*, male genitals + STRAP.]

jo•cose (jō-kōs′) ►*adj.* Given to joking; merry. [Lat. *iocōsus* < *iocus*, joke.] —**jo•cose′ly** *adv.* —**jo•cose′ness, jo•cos′i•ty** (-kŏs′ĭ-tē) *n.*

joc•u•lar (jŏk′yə-lər) ►*adj.* Given to or marked by joking. [Lat. *iocularis* < *iocus*, joke.] —**joc′u•lar′i•ty** (-lăr′ĭ-tē) *n.* —**joc′u•lar•ly** *adv.*

joc•und (jŏk′ənd, jō′kənd) ►*adj.* Lighthearted; merry. [< Lat. *iūcundus*.] —**jo•cun′di•ty** (jō-kŭn′dĭ-tē) *n.* —**joc′und•ly** *adv.*

Jodh•pur (jŏd′pər, jōd′po͝or′) A city of W India SW of Delhi. Pop. 666,279.

jodh•purs (jŏd′pərz) ►*pl.n.* Wide-hipped riding pants of heavy cloth, fitting tightly from knee to ankle. [< JODHPUR.]

Jo•el (jō′əl) ►*n.* See table at **Bible.**

jo•ey (jō′ē) ►*n., pl.* **-eys** *Australian.* A young animal, esp. a baby kangaroo. [?]

jog[1] (jŏg) ►*v.* **jogged, jog•ging 1.** To jar or move by shoving, bumping, or jerking. **2.** To nudge. **3.** To run or ride at a steady slow trot, esp. for exercise or sport. **4.** To proceed in a leisurely manner. ►*n.* **1.** A slight nudge. **2.** A slow steady trot. [?] —**jog′ger** *n.*

jog[2] (jŏg) ►*n.* **1.** A protruding or receding part in a surface or line. **2.** An abrupt change in direction. [Var. of JAG[1].] —**jog** *v.*

jog•gle (jŏg′əl) ►*v.* **-gled, -gling.** To jar slightly. [Poss. frequentative of JOG[1].] —**jog′gle** *n.*

Jo•han•nes•burg (jō-hăn′ĭs-bûrg′, -hä′nĭs-) A city of NE South Africa NW of Durban. Pop. 703,980.

John[1] (jŏn). 1167?–1216. King of England (1199–1216).

John[2] (jŏn) ►*n.* See table at **Bible.**

John, Saint. fl. 1st cent. A.D. One of the 12 Apostles.

John XXIII. 1881–1963. Pope (1958–63).

John Doe ►*n.* **1.** Used as a name in legal proceedings to designate a fictitious or unidentified man. **2.** An average man.

john•ny•cake (jŏn′ē-kāk′) ►*n. Regional* A flat cornmeal bread usu. fried on a griddle. [Perh. < *jonakin.*]

John of Gaunt (gônt, gänt). Duke of Lancaster. 1340–99. English soldier.

John Paul I. 1912–78. Pope (1978).

John Paul II. b. 1920. Pope (since 1978).

John•son (jŏn′sən), **Andrew.** 1808–75. The 17th US President (1865–69).

Johnson, Lyndon Baines. 1908–73. The 36th US President (1963–69).

Andrew Johnson

Lyndon B. Johnson

Johnson, Samuel. 1709–84. British writer and lexicographer.

John the Baptist, Saint. 1st cent. B.C. Jewish prophet who in the Bible baptized Jesus.

joie de vi•vre (zhwä′ də vē′vrə) ►*n.* Carefree enjoyment of life. [Fr.]

join (join) ►*v.* **1.** To put or bring together. **2.** To put or bring into close association or relationship. **3.** To connect, as with a straight line. **4.** To meet and merge with. **5.** To become a part or member of. **6.** To come or act together. **7.** To take part; participate. [< Lat. *iungere.*]

join•er (joi′nər) ►*n.* **1.** A carpenter, esp. a cabinetmaker. **2.** *Informal* A person given to joining groups.

joint (joint) ►*n.* **1.** A place or part at which two or more things are joined. **2.** *Anat.* A point of articulation between two or more bones, esp. one that allows motion. **3.** A cut of meat for roasting. **4.** *Slang* A cheap or disreputable gathering place. **5.** *Slang* A marijuana cigarette. ►*adj.* **1.** Shared by or common to two or more. **2.** Formed or marked by cooperation or united action. ►*v.* **1.** To provide with joints. **2.** To separate (meat) at the joints. —***idiom:* out of joint 1.** Dislocated, as a bone. **2.** *Informal* **a.** Not harmonious. **b.** Out of order; unsatisfactory. **c.** In bad humor. [< OFr., p.part. of *joindre*, JOIN.] —**joint′ly** *adv.*

joist (joist) ►*n.* Any of the parallel horizontal beams set from wall to wall or across girders to support a floor or ceiling. [< OFr. *giste.*]

jo•jo•ba (hə-hō′bə, hō-) ►*n.* A shrub of the SW US and N Mexico having leathery leaves and edible seeds that contain a valuable oil. [Am.Sp.]

joke (jōk) ►*n.* **1.** Something said or done to evoke laughter, esp. an amusing story with a punch line. **2.** A mischievous trick. **3.** A ludicrous incident or situation. **4.** *Informal* A laughingstock. ►*v.* **joked, jok•ing 1.** To tell or play jokes. **2.** To speak in fun; be facetious. [Lat. *iocus.*] —**jok′ing•ly** *adv.*

jok•er (jō′kər) ►*n.* **1a.** One who tells or plays jokes. **b.** *Informal* A person, esp. an annoying one. **2.** A playing card used in certain games as the highest-ranking card or as a wild card. **3.** A minor clause in a document that voids or changes its original or intended purpose.

Jo•liot-Cu•rie (zhô-lyō′ kyo͝or′ē, -kyo͞o-rē′), **Irène.** 1897–1956. French physicist; shared a 1935 Nobel Prize with her husband, **Frédéric Joliot-Curie** (1900–58).

Jol•li•et also **Jo•li•et** (jō′lē-ĕt′, jō′lē-ĕt′, zhô-lyā′), **Louis.** 1645–1700. French-Canadian explorer.

jol•li•fi•ca•tion (jŏl′ə-fĭ-kā′shən) ►*n.* Festivity; revelry.

jol•li•ty (jŏl′ĭ-tē) ►*n.* Merriment; mirth.

jol•ly (jŏl′ē) ►*adj.* **-li•er, -li•est 1.** Full of good humor. **2.** Merry: *a jolly tune.* ►*adv. Chiefly Brit.* Very: *a jolly good cook.* [< OFr. *joli.*] —**jol′li•ly** *adv.* —**jol′li•ness** *n.*

jolt (jōlt) ►*v.* **1.** To shake or jar with or as if with a sudden hard blow. **2.** To move or cause to move jerkily. ►*n.* **1.** A hard jarring or jerking. **2.** A sudden shock, as of surprise. [?] —**jolt′y** *adj.*

Jo•nah (jō′nə) ►*n.* **1.** In the Bible, a prophet swallowed by a great fish and disgorged unharmed. **2.** See table at **Bible. 3.** One thought to bring bad luck.

Jones (jōnz), **John Paul.** 1747–92. Scottish-born Amer. naval officer.

jon•quil (jŏng′kwəl, jŏn′-) ►*n.* An ornamental plant with short-tubed, fragrant yellow flowers. [Sp. *junquilla.*]

Jon•son (jŏn′sən), **Benjamin.** "Ben." 1572–1637. English actor and writer.

Jop•lin (jŏp′lĭn), **Scott.** 1868–1917. Amer. composer.

Jor•dan (jôr′dn) A country of SW Asia in NW Arabia. Cap. Amman. Pop. 5,198,000. —**Jor•da′ni•an** (jôr-dā′nē-ən) *adj. & n.*

Jordan, Michael. b. 1963. Amer. basketball player.

Michael Jordan

Jordan River. A river of SW Asia rising in Syria and flowing about 322 km (200 mi) through the Sea of Galilee to the Dead Sea.

Jo•seph[1] (jō′zəf, -səf). In the Bible, the older son of Jacob and Rachel.

Jo•seph[2] (jō′zəf, -səf). "Chief Joseph." 1840?–1904. Nez Percé leader.

Joseph[2]
1878 portrait

Joseph, Saint. fl. first century A.D. In the Bible, the husband of Mary, mother of Jesus.

Jo•se•phine (jō′zə-fēn′, -sə-). See Josephine de **Beauharnais.**

Joseph of Ar•i•ma•the•a (ăr′ə-mə-thē′ə). fl. 1st cent. A.D. In the Bible, the disciple who buried Jesus.

Jo•se•phus (jō-sē′fəs), **Flavius.** A.D. 37–100? Jewish general and historian.

josh (jŏsh) ►*v.* To tease good-humoredly. See Syns at **banter.** [?] —**josh′er** *n.*

Josh•u•a (jŏsh′o͞o-ə) ►*n.* **1.** In the Bible, a Hebrew leader. **2.** See table at **Bible.**

jos•tle (jŏs′əl) ►*v.* **-tled, -tling 1.** To come in rough contact (with); push and shove. **2.** To make one's way by pushing or elbowing. **3.** To vie (with) for advantage or position. [< OFr. *juster,* JOUST.] —**jos′tle** *n.* —**jos′tler** *n.*

jot (jŏt) ►*n.* The smallest bit; iota. ►*v.* **jot•ted, jot•ting.** To write down briefly or hastily. [< Gk. *iōta,* iota.] —**jot′ting** *n.*

joule (jo͞ol, joul) ►*n.* A unit of electrical energy equal to the work done when a current of 1 ampere is passed through a resistance of 1 ohm for 1 second. [After James P. *Joule* (1818–89).]

jounce (jouns) ►*v.* **jounced, jounc•ing.** To move with bumps and jolts; bounce. [ME *jouncen.*] —**jounce** *n.* —**jounc′y** *adj.*

jour•nal (jûr′nəl) ►*n.* **1a.** A personal record of experiences and reflections; diary. **b.** An official record of daily proceedings, as of a legislative body. **2.** A newspaper. **3.** A specialized periodical. **4.** The part of a shaft or axle supported by a bearing. [< LLat. *diurnālis,* daily.]

jour•nal•ese (jûr′nə-lēz′, -lēs′) ►*n.* A slick, superficial style of writing often deemed typical of newspapers and magazines.

jour•nal•ism (jûr′nə-lĭz′əm) ►*n.* **1.** The collecting, writing, editing, and presentation of news in print or electronic media. **2.** Written material of current interest or popular appeal. —**jour′nal•ist** *n.* —**jour′nal•is′tic** *adj.* —**jour′nal•is′ti•cal•ly** *adv.*

jour•ney (jûr′nē) ►*n., pl.* **-neys.** Travel from one place to another; trip. ►*v.* To travel. [< VLat. **diurnāta,* day's travel < Lat. *diurnus,* of a day.] —**jour′ney•er** *n.*

jour•ney•man (jûr′nē-mən) ►*n.* **1.** One who has served an apprenticeship in a trade and works in another's employ. **2.** A competent worker.

joust (joust, jŭst, jo͞ost) ►*n.* A combat between two mounted knights using lances. ►*v.* To engage in a joust. [< OFr. *juste,* ult. < Lat. *iūxtā,* close together.] —**joust′er** *n.*

Jove (jōv) ►*n. Rom. Myth.* See **Jupiter** 1.

jo•vi•al (jō′vē-əl) ►*adj.* Mirthful; jolly. [< Lat. *Iovis,* Jupiter.] —**jo′vi•al′i•ty** (-ăl′ĭ-tē) *n.* —**jo′vi•al•ly** *adv.*

jowl[1] (joul) ►*n.* **1.** The jaw, esp. the lower jaw. **2.** The cheek. [< OE *ceafl.*]

jowl[2] (joul) ►*n.* The flesh under the lower jaw, esp. when plump or flabby. [< ME *cholle.*]

joy (joi) ►*n.* **1.** Intense or elated happiness. **2.** A source of great pleasure. ►*v.* To rejoice. [< Lat. *gaudia.*] —**joy′less** *adj.* —**joy′less•ly** *adv.* —**joy′less•ness** *n.*

Joyce (jois), **James.** 1882–1941. Irish writer. —**Joyc′e•an** *adj.*

joy•ful (joi′fəl) ►*adj.* Feeling, causing, or showing joy. —**joy′ful•ly** *adv.* —**joy′ful•ness** *n.*

joy•ous (joi′əs) ►*adj.* Joyful. —**joy′ous•ly** *adv.* —**joy′ous•ness** *n.*

joy ride ►*n. Slang* An often reckless automobile ride taken for fun and thrills.

joy•stick (joi′stĭk′) ►*n. Slang* **1.** A control stick. **2.** A manual control lever, as for a video game.

JP ►*abbr.* justice of the peace

jr. or **Jr.** ►*abbr.* junior

JSD ►*abbr. Lat.* Juris Scientiae Doctor (Doctor of Juristic Science)

Juan Car•los (wän kär′ləs, -lōs, hwän). b. 1938. Spanish king (since 1975).

Juan de Fu•ca (də fo͞o′kə, fyo͞o′-), **Strait of.** A strait between NW WA and Vancouver I., British Columbia, Canada.

Juá•rez (wär′ĕz, hwä′rĕs), **Benito Pablo.** 1806–72. Mexican revolutionary leader and politician.

ju•bi•lant (jo͞o′bə-lənt) ►*adj.* Exultingly joyful. [< Lat. *iūbilāre,* shout for joy.] —**ju′bi•lance** *n.* —**ju′bi•lant•ly** *adv.*

ju•bi•la•tion (jo͞o′bə-lā′shən) ►*n.* **1.** The act of rejoicing. **2.** A joyful celebration.

ju•bi•lee (jōō′bə-lē′, jōō′bə-lē′) ►*n.* **1.** A special anniversary, esp. a 50th anniversary. **2.** A season or occasion of joyful celebration. **3.** Jubilation; rejoicing. [< Heb. *yôbēl*, ram's horn, the Jewish year of jubilee.]

Ju•dah[1] (jōō′də). In the Bible, a son of Jacob and Leah.

Ju•dah[2] (jōō′də) An ancient kingdom of S Palestine between the Mediterranean and the Dead Sea.

Ju•da•ic (jōō-dā′ĭk) also **Ju•da•i•cal** (-ĭ-kəl) ►*adj.* Of or relating to Jews or Judaism.

Ju•da•ism (jōō′dē-ĭz′əm) ►*n.* The monotheistic religion of the Jews, having its spiritual and ethical principles embodied chiefly in the Hebrew Scriptures and the Talmud.

Ju•das (jōō′dəs) ►*n.* One who betrays another under the guise of friendship. [After JUDAS ISCARIOT.]

Judas Is•car•i•ot (ĭ-skăr′ē-ət). d. c. A.D. 30. In the Bible, one of the 12 Apostles and the betrayer of Jesus.

Jude (jōōd) ►*n.* See table at **Bible.**

Jude, Saint. fl. 1st cent. A.D. One of the 12 Apostles.

Ju•de•a also **Ju•dae•a** (jōō-dē′ə, -dā′ə). An ancient region of S Palestine comprising present-day S Israel and SW Jordan. —**Ju•de′an** *adj. & n.*

judge (jŭj) ►*v.* **judged, judg•ing 1.** To form an opinion (of). **2.** To hear and decide on in a court of law; try. **3.** To determine or declare after deliberation. **4.** *Informal* To think; suppose. ►*n.* **1.** One who makes estimates as to worth, quality, or fitness. **2.** A public official who hears and decides cases brought before a court of law. **3.** One appointed to decide the winners of a contest or competition. **4. Judges** *(takes sing. v.)* See table at **Bible.** [< Lat. *iūdex*, a judge.] —**judge′ship′** *n.*

judg•ment also **judge•ment** (jŭj′mənt) ►*n.* **1.** The act or process of judging. **2.** The mental ability to form an opinion, distinguish relationships, or draw sound conclusions. **3.** An opinion or estimate formed after due consideration: *awaited the judgment of the umpire.* **4.** A judicial decision.

judg•men•tal (jŭj-mĕn′tl) ►*adj.* **1.** Of or relating to judgment. **2.** Inclined to make judgments, esp. moral or personal ones. —**judg•men′tal•ly** *adv.*

Judgment Day ►*n.* In Judeo-Christian and Muslim traditions, the day when God judges all humans.

ju•di•ca•ture (jōō′dĭ-kə-chŏŏr′) ►*n.* **1.** Administration of justice. **2.** A system of courts of law. [< Lat. *iūdicāre*, to judge < *iūdex*, judge.]

ju•di•cial (jōō-dĭsh′əl) ►*adj.* **1a.** Of or proper to courts of law or the administration of justice. **b.** Decreed by or proceeding from a court of justice. **2.** Marked by or expressing judgment. [< Lat. *iūdicium*, judgment < *iūdex*, a judge.] —**ju•di′cial•ly** *adv.*

ju•di•ci•ar•y (jōō-dĭsh′ē-ĕr′ē, -dĭsh′ə-rē) ►*n., pl.* **-ies 1.** The judicial branch of government. **2a.** A system of courts of law. **b.** The judges of these courts.

ju•di•cious (jōō-dĭsh′əs) ►*adj.* Having or exhibiting sound judgment. —**ju•di′cious•ly** *adv.* —**ju•di′cious•ness** *n.*

Ju•dith (jōō′dĭth) ►*n.* See table at **Bible.**

ju•do (jōō′dō) ►*n.* A sport using principles of balance and leverage adapted from jujitsu. [J. *jūdō.*]

jug (jŭg) ►*n.* **1.** An often earthenware or glass vessel with a small mouth, a handle, and usu. a stopper or cap. **2.** *Slang* A jail. [ME *jugge.*]

jug band ►*n.* A musical group that uses unconventional instruments, such as jugs, kazoos, and washboards.

jug•ger•naut (jŭg′ər-nôt′) ►*n.* An overwhelming advancing force that crushes everything in its path. [< Skt. *jagannāthaḥ*, title of Krishna : *jagat*, world (< *jigāti*, goes) + *nāthaḥ*, lord.]

jug•gle (jŭg′əl) ►*v.* **-gled, -gling 1.** To keep (two or more objects) in the air at one time by alternately tossing and catching them. **2.** To keep (more than two activities) in progress at one time. **3.** To manipulate (e.g., figures) in order to deceive. [< Lat. *ioculārī*, to jest.] —**jug′gler** *n.*

jug•u•lar (jŭg′yə-lər) ►*adj.* Of or located in the neck or throat. ►*n.* A jugular vein. [< Lat. *iugulum*, collarbone < *iugum*, yoke.]

juice (jōōs) ►*n.* **1a.** A fluid naturally contained in plant or animal tissue. **b.** A bodily secretion. **2.** *Slang* **a.** Electric current. **b.** Fuel for an engine. ►*v.* **juiced, juic•ing.** To extract the juice from. [< Lat. *iūs.*]

juic•er (jōō′sər) ►*n.* An appliance used to extract juice from fruits and vegetables.

juic•y (jōō′sē) ►*adj.* **-i•er, -i•est 1.** Full of juice. **2.** Interesting, racy, or titillating. **3.** Rewarding or gratifying: *a juicy raise.* —**juic′i•ly** *adv.* —**juic′i•ness** *n.*

ju•jit•su also **ju•jut•su** (jōō-jĭt′sōō) ►*n.* An art of weaponless self-defense developed in China and Japan that uses throws, holds, and blows and derives added power from the attacker's own weight and strength. [J. *jūjitsu.*]

ju•jube (jōō′jōōb′, -jōō-bē′) ►*n.* A fruit-flavored, usu. chewy candy. [< Gk. *zizuphon*, a fruit tree.]

juke (jōōk) *Regional* ►*n.* A roadside tavern offering music for dancing. ►*v.* **juked, juk•ing.** To dance. [Of Western African orig.]

Regional Note: Gullah, which retains a number of words from the Western African languages brought over by slaves, contains the word *juke,* "bad, wicked, disorderly," the probable source of the English word *juke.* Used chiefly in the Southeastern states, *juke* means a roadside tavern. "To juke" is to dance, particularly to a jukebox.

juke•box (jōōk′bŏks′) ►*n.* A coin-operated phonograph. See Regional Note at **juke.**

ju•lep (jōō′lĭp) ►*n.* A mint julep. [< Pers. *gulāb*, rosewater.]

Jul•ian (jōōl′yən). A.D. 331?–363. Emperor of Rome (361–363).

Ju•li•an•a (jōō′lē-ăn′ə). b. 1909. Queen of the Netherlands (1948–80); abdicated.

ju•li•enne (jōō′lē-ĕn′, zhü-lyĕn′) ►*adj.* Cut into long thin strips: *julienne potatoes.* [Fr.]

Ju•ly (jōō-lī′) ►*n.* The 7th month of the Gregorian calendar. See table at **calendar.** [< Lat. *Iūlius*, of Julius (Caesar).]

Ju•ma•da (jōō-mä′dä) ►*n.* Either the 5th or the 6th month of the Muslim calendar. See table at **calendar.** [Ar. *jumādā.*]

jum•ble (jŭm′bəl) ►*v.* **-bled, -bling 1.** To mix in a confused way. **2.** To confuse. [?] —**jum′ble** *n.*

jum•bo (jŭm′bō) ►*n., pl.* **-bos.** An unusually large person, animal, or thing. [After *Jumbo*, an elephant exhibited by P.T. Barnum.] —**jum′bo** *adj.*

Jum•na (jŭm′nə) See **Yamuna.**

jump (jŭmp) ►*v.* **1.** To spring off the ground or from some other base by a muscular effort of the legs and feet. **2.** To move involuntarily, as in surprise. **3.** To react quickly: *jump at a bargain.* **4.** To enter eagerly into an activity. **5.** To form an opinion hastily. **6.** To spring upon in sudden attack. **7.** To rise suddenly and markedly. **8.** To move discontinuously; skip: *jumps from one subject to another.* **9.** To be displaced suddenly from (e.g., a track). **10.** To move over (an opponent's playing piece) in a board game. **11.** *Slang* To be lively; bustle. ►*n.* **1.** The act of jumping; leap. **2.** *Informal* An initial advantage; head start. **3.** A sudden rise, as in price. **4.** A sudden transition. **5a.** An involuntary nervous movement. **b. jumps** A condition of nervousness. —***idiom:*** **jump the gun** To start something too soon. [Perh. < ME *jumpen.*]

jump•er[1] (jŭm′pər) ►*n.* **1.** One that jumps. **2.** *Elect.* A short length of wire used temporarily to complete or bypass a circuit.

jump•er[2] (jŭm′pər) ►*n.* **1.** A sleeveless dress worn over a blouse or sweater. **2.** A loose protective smock or coat. **3. jumpers** A child's overalls. [Prob. < *jump*, short coat.]

jump shot ►*n. Basketball* A shot made by a player at the highest point of a jump.

jump suit ►*n.* **1.** A parachutist's uniform. **2.** A one-piece garment consisting of a blouse or shirt with attached slacks or shorts.

jump•y (jŭm′pē) ►*adj.* **-i•er, -i•est.** On edge; nervous. —**jump′i•ness** *n.*

jun. ►*abbr.* junior

jun•co (jŭng′kō) ►*n., pl.* **-cos** or **-coes.** A small North American bird having predominantly gray plumage. [Sp., reed < Lat. *iuncus.*]

junc•tion (jŭngk′shən) ►*n.* **1.** The act of joining or the condition of being joined. **2.** A place where two things join or meet. [< Lat. *iungere, iūnct-*, join.]

junc•ture (jŭngk′chər) ►*n.* **1.** The act of joining or the condition of being joined. **2.** A place where two things are joined; joint. **3.** A point in time, esp. a critical point. See Syns at **crisis.** [< Lat. *iungere, iūnct-*, join.]

June (jo͞on) ►*n.* The 6th month of the Gregorian calendar. See table at **calendar.** [< Lat. *Iūnius (mēnsis)*, (month of) Juno.]

Ju•neau (jo͞o′nō′) The capital of AK, in the SE part. Pop. 26,751.

June beetle or **June bug** ►*n.* A North American beetle appearing in late spring and having larvae that often destroy crops.

Jung (yo͝ong), **Carl Gustav.** 1875–1961. Swiss psychiatrist. —**Jung′i•an** *adj. & n.*

jun•gle (jŭng′gəl) ►*n.* **1.** Land densely overgrown with tropical vegetation. **2.** A dense thicket or growth. **3.** A bewildering complex or maze. **4.** A place of ruthless competition or struggle for survival. [< Skt. *jaṅgala-*, desert, waste.] —**jun′gly** (-glē) *adj.*

jungle gym ►*n.* A structure of poles and bars for children to climb and play on.

jun•ior (jo͞on′yər) ►*adj.* **1.** Younger. Used to distinguish a son from his father when they have the same given name. **2.** Intended for youthful persons: *junior fashions.* **3.** Lower in rank or shorter in length of tenure. **4.** Of the third year of a US high school or college. **5.** Lesser in scale than the usual. ►*n.* **1.** A person who is younger than another. **2.** A person lesser in rank or time of service. **3.** A third-year student in a US high school or college. [< Lat. *iūnior*, younger.]

junior college ►*n.* A school offering a two-year course that is the equivalent of the first two years of a four-year college.

junior high school ►*n.* A school including the 7th, 8th, and sometimes 9th grades.

ju•ni•per (jo͞o′nə-pər) ►*n.* An evergreen tree or shrub with scalelike leaves and aromatic, bluish-gray, berrylike cones. [< Lat. *iūniperus.*]

junk[1] (jŭngk) ►*n.* **1.** Discarded material that may be reused in some form. **2.** *Informal* **a.** Cheap or shoddy material. **b.** Something worthless or meaningless. **3.** *Slang* Heroin. ►*v.* To throw away or discard as useless. [ME *jonk*, an old rope.] —**junk′y** *adj.*

junk[2] (jŭngk) ►*n.* A Chinese flat-bottomed sailing ship. [< Javanese *djong.*]

junk[2]

junk bond ►*n.* A corporate bond having a high yield and high risk.

jun•ket (jŭng′kĭt) ►*n.* **1.** A dessert made from flavored milk and rennet. **2.** A party or outing. **3.** A trip taken by a public official or businessperson at public or corporate expense. [ME *jonket*, rush basket.] —**jun′ket** *v.* —**jun′ket•er** *n.*

junk food ►*n.* A high-calorie food that is low in nutritional value.

junk•ie also **junk•y** (jŭng′kē) ►*n., pl.* **-ies** *Slang* **1.** A narcotics addict, esp. one using heroin. **2.** One who has an insatiable devotion or interest: *a sports junkie.*

junk mail ►*n.* Third-class mail, such as advertisements, mailed indiscriminately in large quantities.

junk•yard (jŭngk′yärd′) ►*n.* A yard or lot used to store junk.

Ju•no (jo͞o′nō) ►*n. Rom. Myth.* The principal goddess of the pantheon, wife and sister of Jupiter.

jun•ta (ho͝on′tə, jŭn′-) ►*n.* A group of military officers ruling a country after seizing power. [Sp. < Lat. *iungere, iūnct-*, join.]

Ju•pi•ter (jo͞o′pĭ-tər) ►*n.* **1.** *Rom. Myth.* The supreme god, brother and husband of Juno. **2.** *Astron.* The largest of the planets and the 5th from the sun, at a mean distance of 777 million km (483 million mi), having a diameter of approx. 138,000 km (86,000 mi).

Ju•ra Mountains (jo͝or′ə, zhü-rä′) A range extending about 241 km (150 mi) along the border between France and Switzerland.

Ju•ras•sic (jo͝o-răs′ĭk) *Geol.* ▸*adj.* Of or being the 2nd period of the Mesozoic Era, marked by the appearance of the earliest birds. ▸*n.* The Jurassic Period. [After the JURA (MOUNTAINS).] —**Ju•ras′sic** *n.*

ju•rid•i•cal (jo͝o-rĭd′ĭ-kəl) also **ju•rid•ic** (-ĭk) ▸*adj.* Of or relating to the law and its administration. [< Lat. *iūridicus.*] —**ju•rid′i•cal•ly** *adv.*

ju•ris•dic•tion (jo͝or′ĭs-dĭk′shən) ▸*n.* **1.** The right and power to interpret and apply the law. **2a.** Authority or control. **b.** The extent of authority or control: *a matter beyond the school's jurisdiction.* **3.** The territorial range of authority or control. [< Lat. *iūrisdictiō.*] —**ju′ris•dic′tion•al** *adj.*

ju•ris•pru•dence (jo͝or′ĭs-pro͞od′ns) ▸*n.* **1.** The philosophy or science of law. **2.** A division or department of law. [LLat. *iūrisprūdentia.*] —**ju′ris•pru•den′tial** (-pro͞o-dĕn′shəl) *adj.*

ju•rist (jo͝or′ĭst) ▸*n.* One skilled in the law, esp. a judge or legal scholar. [< Lat. *iūs, iūr-*, law.]

ju•ris•tic (jo͝o-rĭs′tĭk) also **ju•ris•ti•cal** (-tĭ-kəl) ▸*adj.* **1.** Of or relating to a jurist or to jurisprudence. **2.** Of law or legality.

ju•ror (jo͝or′ər, -ôr′) ▸*n.* A member of a jury.

ju•ry (jo͝or′ē) ▸*n., pl.* **-ries 1.** A body of persons summoned by law and sworn to hear and hand down a verdict upon a case presented in court. **2.** A committee to select winners or award prizes. [< AN *jurer*, swear < Lat. *iūrāre.*]

just (jŭst) ▸*adj.* **1.** Honorable and fair in one's dealings and actions. **2.** Consistent with what is morally right: *a just cause.* **3.** Properly due or merited: *just deserts.* **4.** Lawful; legitimate. **5.** Suitable; fitting. **6.** Based on sound reason; well-founded. ▸*adv.* (jəst, jĭst; jŭst *when stressed*) **1.** Exactly: *just enough salt.* **2.** Only a moment ago. **3.** By a narrow margin. **4.** At a little distance. **5.** Merely; only. **6.** Simply: *It's just beautiful!* —***idiom:*** **just the same** Nevertheless. [< Lat. *iūstus.*] —**just′ly** *adv.* —**just′ness** *n.*

jus•tice (jŭs′tĭs) ▸*n.* **1.** The quality of being just; fairness. **2.** The principle of moral rightness; equity. **3.** The upholding of what is just, esp. fair treatment and due reward in accordance with honor, standards, or law. **4.** The administration and procedure of law. **5.** Conformity to fact or sound reason. **6.** A judge. —***idiom:*** **do justice to** To treat adequately, fairly, or with full appreciation. [< Lat. *iūstitia* < *iūstus*, just.]

justice of the peace ▸*n.* A local magistrate authorized to act on minor offenses, perform marriages, and administer oaths.

jus•ti•fi•ca•tion (jŭs′tə-fĭ-kā′shən) ▸*n.* **1.** The act of justifying or the condition of being justified. **2.** Something, such as a fact or circumstance, that justifies.

jus•ti•fy (jŭs′tə-fī′) ▸*v.* **-fied, -fy•ing 1.** To demonstrate to be just, right, or valid. **2.** To declare free of blame; absolve. **3.** To demonstrate sufficient legal reason for (an action taken). **4.** *Print.* To adjust the spacing within (a line or lines) so as to end evenly at a straight margin. [< Lat. *iūstificāre*, act justly toward.] —**jus′ti•fi′a•ble** *adj.* —**jus′ti•fi′a•bly** *adv.*

Jus•tin•i•an I (jŭ-stĭn′ē-ən). A.D. 483–565. Byzantine emperor (527–565).

jut (jŭt) ▸*v.* **jut•ted, jut•ting.** To extend outward or upward; project. See Syns at **bulge.** [< ME *gete*, JETTY.] —**jut** *n.*

jute (jo͞ot) ▸*n.* **1.** Either of two Asian plants yielding a fiber used for sacking and cordage. **2.** The fiber obtained from these plants. [< Skt. *jūṭaḥ*, twisted hair.]

Jute ▸*n.* A member of a Germanic people who migrated to Britain in the 5th and 6th cent. A.D.

Jut•land (jŭt′lənd) A peninsula of N Europe comprising mainland Denmark and N Germany.

Ju•ve•nal (jo͞o′və-nəl). A.D. 60?–140? Roman satirist.

ju•ve•nile (jo͞o′və-nīl′, -nəl) ▸*adj.* **1.** Not fully grown; young. **2.** Intended for or appropriate to children or young people. **3.** Immature; childish. ▸*n.* **1a.** A young person; child. **b.** A young animal that has not reached sexual maturity. **2.** An actor who plays children. [< Lat. *iuvenis*, young.] —**ju′ve•nile′ly** *adv.* —**ju′ve•nile′ness** *n.*

juvenile delinquent ▸*n.* A juvenile guilty of antisocial or criminal behavior. —**juvenile delinquency** *n.*

jux•ta•pose (jŭk′stə-pōz′) ▸*v.* **-posed, -pos•ing.** To place side by side. [Fr. *juxtaposer* : Lat. *iūxtā*, next to + Fr. *poser*, to place; see POSE.] —**jux′ta•po•si′tion** (-pə-zĭsh′ən) *n.*

JV ▸*abbr.* junior varsity

K

k[1] or **K** (kā) ▸*n., pl.* **k's** or **K's** also **ks** or **Ks.** The 11th letter of the English alphabet.

k[2] ▸*abbr.* karat

K[1] ▸ The symbol for the element **potassium.** [< *kali*, alkali.]

K[2] ▸*abbr.* **1.** kelvin **2.** kilobyte **3.** kindergarten **4.** *Games* king

K2 (kā′to͞o′). Also **Mount Godwin Austen.** A peak, 8,616.3 m (28,250 ft), in the Karakoram Range of N Kashmir.

kab•ba•lah or **ca•ba•la** (kăb′ə-lə, kə-bä′lə) ▸*n.* **1.** often **Kabbalah** A body of mystical teachings of rabbinical origin, often based on an esoteric interpretation of the Hebrew Scriptures. **2.** A secret or esoteric doctrine. [< Heb. *qabbālâ*, tradition.] —**kab′ba•lism** *n.* —**kab′ba•list** *n.* —**kab′ba•list′ic** *adj.*

ka•bob (kə-bŏb′) ▸*n.* Var. of **kebab.**

ka•bu•ki (kə-bo͞o′kē) ▸*n.* A type of popular Japanese drama in which elaborately costumed performers use stylized movements, dances, and songs. [J.]

Ka•bul (kä′bo͝ol, kə-bo͞ol′) The capital of Afghanistan, in the E part near the border with Pakistan on the **Kabul River,** about 483 km (300 mi). Pop. 1,424,400.

ka•chi•na (kə-chē′nə) ▸*n.* **1.** A deified ancestral spirit of the Pueblo peoples. **2.** A carved doll in the costume of such a spirit. [Hopi *katsina.*]

Ká•dar (kä′där), **János.** 1912–89. Hungarian politician.

Kad•dish (kä′dĭsh) ►*n. Judaism* A prayer recited in the daily synagogue services and by mourners after the death of a close relative. [Aram. *qaddîš*.]

Kaf•ka (käf′kə, -kä), **Franz.** 1883–1924. Austrian writer. —**Kaf′ka•esque′** *adj.*

kaf•tan (kăf′tăn′, -tən, kăf-tăn′) ►*n.* Var. of **caftan.**

Ka•go•shi•ma (kä′gô-shē′mə) A port city of S Kyushu, Japan. Pop. 539,911.

Kai•ser (kī′zər) ►*n.* Any of the emperors of the Holy Roman Empire (962–1806), of Austria (1806–1918), or of Germany (1871–1918). [< Lat. *Caesar*, Caesar.]

Kai•ser•in (kī′zər-ĭn) ►*n.* The wife of a Kaiser.

kale (kāl) ►*n.* A variety of cabbage having spreading crinkled leaves that do not form a compact head. [< Lat. *caulis*, cabbage.]

ka•lei•do•scope (kə-lī′də-skōp′) ►*n.* **1.** A tube-shaped optical instrument that is rotated to produce a succession of symmetrical designs by means of mirrors reflecting the constantly changing patterns made by bits of colored objects at one end of the tube. **2.** A constantly changing set of colors. **3.** A series of changing events. [Gk. *kalos*, beautiful + *eidos*, form + -SCOPE.] —**ka•lei′do•scop′ic** (-skŏp′ĭk) *adj.* —**ka•lei′do•scop′i•cal•ly** *adv.*

ka•lim•ba (kə-lĭm′bə) ►*n.* A musical instrument consisting of a box or gourd set with tuned metal bars that are plucked. [Of Bantu orig.]

kalimba

Ka•li•nin•grad (kə-lē′nĭn-grăd′) A city of extreme W Russia near the Polish border. Pop. 413,491.

Kam•chat•ka (kăm-chăt′kə) A peninsula of E Russia between the Sea of Okhotsk and the Bering Sea.

Ka•me•ha•me•ha I (kə-mā′ə-mā′ə). 1758–1819. King of the Hawaiian Is. (1795–1819).

Ka•met (kŭm′āt′) A mountain, 7,761.3 m (25,447 ft), in the NW Himalayas on the India-China border.

ka•mi•ka•ze (kä′mĭ-kä′zē) ►*n.* **1.** A Japanese pilot trained in World War II to make a suicidal crash attack. **2.** An airplane loaded with explosives for such an attack. [J.]

Kam•pa•la (käm-pä′lə) The capital of Uganda, in the S part on Lake Victoria. Pop. 458,503.

ka•na (kä′nə) ►*n., pl.* **kana** or **-nas.** Japanese syllabic writing. [J.]

Ka•nan•ga (kə-näng′gə) A city of S-central Congo (formerly Zaire) ESE of Kinshasa. Pop. 298,693.

Kan•chen•jun•ga (kŭn′chən-jŭng′gə, -jŏŏng′-, kän′-) A mountain, 8,603.4 m (28,208 ft), in the Himalayas on the Sikkim-Nepal border.

Kan•din•sky or **Kan•din•ski** (kăn-dĭn′skē), **Wassily.** 1866–1944. Russian abstract painter.

kan•ga•roo (kăng′gə-ro͞o′) ►*n., pl.* **-roo** or **-roos.** Any of various large Australian marsupials having short forelimbs, large hind limbs adapted for leaping, and a long tapered tail. [Guugu Yimidhirr (Australian) *gaŋgurru*.]

kangaroo court ►*n.* A court set up in violation of established legal procedure, typically marked by dishonesty or incompetence.

Ka•no (kä′nō) A city of N-central Nigeria NE of Lagos. Pop. 475,000.

Kan•pur (kän′po͝or) A city of N India on the Ganges R. SE of Delhi. Pop. 1,874,409.

Kan•sas (kăn′zəs) A state of the central US. Cap. Topeka. Pop. 2,485,600. —**Kan′san** *adj. & n.*

Kansas City 1. A city of NE KS on the Missouri R. adjacent to Kansas City, MO. Pop. 149,767. **2.** A city of W MO on the Missouri R. WNW of St. Louis. Pop. 435,146.

Kant (kănt, känt), **Immanuel.** 1724–1804. German philosopher. —**Kant′i•an** *adj. & n.*

Kao•hsiung (kou′shyo͝ong′, gou′-) A city of SW Taiwan on Taiwan Strait. Pop. 1,248,175.

ka•o•lin also **ka•o•line** (kā′ə-lĭn) ►*n.* A fine clay used esp. in ceramics and refractories. [< Mandarin *gāo lĭng*, an area in China.]

ka•pok (kā′pŏk′) ►*n.* A silky fiber obtained from the fruit of the silk-cotton tree and used esp. for padding. [Malay.]

Ka•po•si's sarcoma (kə-pō′sēz, kăp′ə-) ►*n.* A cancer endemic to equatorial Africa that often occurs in people with AIDS and is characterized by bluish-red nodules on the skin. [After Moritz *Kaposi* (1837–1902).]

kap•pa (kăp′ə) ►*n.* The 10th letter of the Greek alphabet. [Gk.]

ka•put also **ka•putt** (kä-po͝ot′, -po͞ot′, kə-) ►*adj. Informal* **1.** Destroyed; wrecked. **2.** Incapacitated. [Ger. *kaputt* < Fr. *capot*, not having won a trick at cards.]

Ka•ra•chi (kə-rä′chē) A city of S Pakistan on the Arabian Sea. Pop. 5,180,562.

Ka•ra•ko•ram Range (kăr′ə-kôr′əm, -kōr′-) A mountain system of N Pakistan and India and SW China.

kar•a•kul (kăr′ə-kəl) ►*n.* **1.** Any of a breed of Central Asian sheep having a wide tail and wool that is curled and glossy in the young but wiry and coarse in the adult. **2.** Fur made from the pelt of a karakul lamb. [After *Kara Kul*, a lake of S Tadzhikistan.]

kar•a•o•ke (kâr′ē-ō′kē) ►*n.* A music entertainment system providing prerecorded accompaniment to songs that a performer sings live. [J. : *kara*, empty + *oke(sutora)*, ORCHESTRA.]

kar•at also **car•at** (kăr′ət) ►*n.* A unit of measure for the fineness of gold, equal to 1/24 part; for example, gold that is 50 percent pure is 12 karat. [Var. of CARAT.]

ka•ra•te (kə-rä′tē) ►*n.* A Japanese art of self-defense in which sharp blows and kicks are administered to an opponent. [J.]

Karls•ru•he (kärlz′ro͞o′ə, kärls′-) A city of SW Germany on the Rhine R. WNW of Stuttgart. Pop. 277,998.

kar•ma (kär′mə) ►*n.* **1.** *Hinduism & Buddhism* The effect of a person's actions during the successive phases of the person's existence, regarded as determining the person's destiny. **2.** Fate; destiny. **3.** *Informal* A distinctive aura or feeling. [Skt. *karma*, a doing.] —**kar′mic** (-mĭk) *adj.*

Kar•roo also **Ka•roo** (kə-ro͞o′). A semiarid plateau region of SW South Africa.

karst (kärst) ▸*n.* A limestone region marked by fissures, sinkholes, underground streams, and caverns. [Ger.]

kar•y•o•type (kăr′ē-ə-tīp′) ▸*n.* The characterization of the chromosomal complement of an individual or a species according to the number, form, and size of the chromosomes. [Gk. *karuon*, nut, kernel + TYPE.]

Kash•mir (kăsh′mîr′, kăsh-mîr′) A historical region of NW India and NE Pakistan. —**Kash•mir′i** *adj. & n.*

ka•ta•ka•na (kä′tä-kä′nä) ▸*n.* An angular kana used for writing foreign words or official documents. [J.]

Kath•man•du also **Kat•man•du** (kăt′măn-do͞o′). The capital of Nepal, in the central part in the E Himalayas. Pop. 235,160.

Ka•to•wi•ce (kä′tə-vēt′sə) A city of S Poland WNW of Krakow. Pop. 366,465.

Kat•te•gat (kăt′ĭ-găt′) A strait of the North Sea between SW Sweden and E Jutland, Denmark.

ka•ty•did (kā′tē-dĭd′) ▸*n.* A green insect related to the grasshopper, the male of which produces a shrill sound. [Imit. of its sound.]

Kau•ai (kou′ī′) An island of HI NW of Oahu.

Kau•nas (kou′nəs, -näs) A city of central Lithuania NW of Vilnius. Pop. 421,600.

ka•va (kä′və) ▸*n.* **1.** A shrub native to the Pacific islands. **2.** A narcotic beverage made from the roots of this plant. [Tongan.]

Ka•wa•sa•ki (kä′wə-sä′kē) A city of E-central Honshu, Japan, a suburb of Tokyo on Tokyo Bay. Pop. 1,199,707.

kay•ak (kī′ăk′) ▸*n.* **1.** A watertight Inuit or Eskimo canoe covered with skins except for a single or double opening in the center. **2.** A similar lightweight canoe. [Canadian Eskimo and Inuit *qajaq*.] —**kay′ak′** *v.* —**kay′ak′er** *n.*

kay•o (kā-ō′, kā′ō′) ▸*n., pl.* **-os.** A knockout in boxing. [< *KO* < K(NOCK)O(UT).] —**kay′o** *v.*

Ka•zakh (kä′zäk′, kə-zäk′) ▸*n., pl.* **-zakh** or **-zakhs 1.** A member of a Turkic people living in Kazakhstan and NW China. **2.** The language of this people.

Ka•zakh•stan (kä′zäk-stän′, kə-zäk′-) A region and republic S of Russia and NE of the Caspian Sea. Cap. Astana. Pop. 17,027,000.

Ka•zan (kə-zăn′, -zän′) A city of W-central Russia on the Volga R. E of Moscow. Pop. 1,085,944.

ka•zoo (kə-zo͞o′) ▸*n., pl.* **-zoos.** A toy musical instrument in which a paper membrane is vibrated by the performer's voice. [Imit.]

kc ▸*abbr.* kilocycle

KC ▸*abbr.* **1.** King's Counsel **2.** Knight of Columbus

kcal ▸*abbr.* kilocalorie

Keats (kēts), **John.** 1795–1821. British poet. —**Keats′i•an** *adj.*

ke•bab or **ke•bob** also **ka•bob** (kə-bŏb′) ▸*n.* Shish kebab.

kedge (kĕj) ▸*n.* A light anchor used for warping a vessel. ▸*v.* **kedged, kedg•ing.** To move (a vessel) by means of a line attached to a kedge. [Poss. < ME *caggen*, to tie.]

keel (kēl) ▸*n.* **1a.** The principal structural member of a ship, running lengthwise along the center line from bow to stern, to which the frames are attached. **b.** A corresponding structure on an aircraft. **2.** The breastbone of a bird. **3.** A pair of united petals in certain flowers, as those of the pea. ▸*v.* To capsize. —***phrasal verb:*** **keel over** To collapse or fall, as from death or fainting. [< ON *kjølr*.]

keel•boat (kēl′bōt′) ▸*n.* A riverboat with a keel, used for carrying freight.

keel•haul (kēl′hôl′) ▸*v.* To punish by dragging under the keel of a ship. [< Du. *kielhalen*.]

Kee•lung (kē′lo͝ong′) See **Chi-lung.**

keen¹ (kēn) ▸*adj.* **-er, -est 1.** Having a fine sharp edge or point. **2.** Intellectually acute. **3.** Acutely sensitive: *a keen ear.* **4.** Sharp; vivid. **5.** Intense; piercing: *a keen wind.* **6.** Pungent; acrid. **7a.** Ardent; enthusiastic. **b.** Eagerly desirous: *keen on going.* **8.** *Slang* Great; splendid. [< OE *cēne*, brave.] —**keen′ly** *adv.* —**keen′ness** *n.*

keen² (kēn) ▸*n.* A loud wailing lament for the dead. [< Ir.Gael. *caoineadh*.] —**keen** *v.* —**keen′er** *n.*

keep (kēp) ▸*v.* **kept** (kĕpt), **keep•ing 1.** To retain possession of. **2.** To provide (e.g., a family) with maintenance and support. **3.** To put customarily; store. **4.** To raise: *keep chickens.* **5.** To maintain: *keep a diary.* **6.** To manage or have charge of. **7.** To remain fresh or unspoiled. **8.** To continue or cause to continue in a state or condition. **9a.** To detain: *was kept after school.* **b.** To prevent: *kept them from entering.* **10.** To refrain from divulging: *keep a secret.* **11.** To save; reserve. **12.** To adhere to: *keep oneÕs word.* **13.** To celebrate; observe. **14.** To continue: *keep talking.* —***phrasal verbs:*** **keep down** To prevent from accomplishing or succeeding. **keep up 1.** To maintain in good condition. **2.** To persevere in. **3.** To continue at the same level or pace. ▸*n.* **1.** Care; charge. **2.** A means of support: *earn oneÕs keep* **3a.** The stronghold of a castle. **b.** A jail. —***idiom:*** **for keeps 1.** For an indefinitely long period. **2.** Permanently: *WeÕre separating for keeps.* [< OE *cēpan*, observe.] —**keep′er** *n.*

keep•sake (kēp′sāk′) ▸*n.* Something given or kept as a reminder; memento.

keg (kĕg) ▸*n.* A small barrel. [< ON *kaggi*.]

Kel•ler (kĕl′ər), **Helen Adams.** 1880–1968. Amer. memoirist and lecturer.

Helen Keller
with her tutor Anne Sullivan

Kel•logg (kĕl′ôg′, -ŏg′), **Frank Billings.** 1856–1937. Amer. public official; 1929 Nobel Peace Prize.

Kel•ly (kĕl′lē), **Grace Patricia.** Princess Grace. 1929–82. Amer. actress.

kelp (kĕlp) ►*n.* Any of various brown, often large seaweeds. [ME *culp.*]

kel•vin (kĕl′vĭn) ►*n.* A unit of the absolute temperature scale, the zero point of which equals – 273.16°C. [After 1st Baron KELVIN.]

Kelvin, 1st Baron. 1824–1907. British physicist.

Ke•mal At•a•türk (kə-mäl′ ăt′ə-tûrk′). 1881–1938. Turkish national leader.

ken (kĕn) ►*n.* **1.** Perception; understanding. **2.** Range of vision; view. ►*v.* **kenned** or **kent** (kĕnt), **ken•ning** *Scots.* To know. [< OE *cennan*, declare.]

Ken•ne•dy (kĕn′ĭ-dē), **Cape.** See Cape **Canaveral.**

Kennedy, John Fitzgerald. 1917–63. The 35th US President (1961–63); assassinated.

John F. Kennedy
detail from a 1966 portrait, from a 1962 life sketch

Kennedy, Robert Francis. 1925–68. Amer. politician; assassinated.

ken•nel (kĕn′əl) ►*n.* **1.** A shelter for a dog. **2.** An establishment where dogs are bred, trained, or boarded. [< VLat. **canīle* < Lat. *canis*, dog.] —**ken′nel** *v.*

Ken•ny (kĕn′ē), **Elizabeth.** 1880?–1952. Australian nurse who developed a treatment for the paralysis caused by polio.

ken•te (kĕn′tā) ►*n.* **1.** A brightly patterned, hand-woven ceremonial cloth of the Ashanti. **2.** A durable machine-woven fabric resembling this cloth. [Twi, cloth.]

Ken•tuck•y (kən-tŭk′ē) A state of the E-central US. Cap. Frankfort. Pop. 3,698,969. —**Ken•tuck′i•an** *adj. & n.*

Ken•ya (kĕn′yə, kēn′-) A country of E-central Africa bordering on the Indian Ocean. Cap. Nairobi. Pop. 29,292,000. —**Ken′yan** *adj. & n.*

Kenya, Mount. An extinct volcano, 5,202.7 m (17,058 ft), in central Kenya.

Ken•yat•ta (kĕn-yä′tə), **Jomo.** 1893?–1978. First president of independent Kenya (1964–78).

Ke•ogh plan (kē′ō) ►*n.* A retirement plan for the self-employed. [After E.J. *Keogh* (b. 1907).]

ke•pi (kā′pē, kĕp′ē) ►*n., pl.* **-pis.** A French military cap with a flat circular top and a visor. [< Ger. dial. *Kappi* < Ger. *Kappe*, cap.]

Kep•ler (kĕp′lər), **Johannes.** 1571–1630. German astronomer and mathematician.

kept (kĕpt) ►*v.* P.t. and p.part. of **keep.**

ker•a•tin (kĕr′ə-tĭn) ►*n.* A tough insoluble protein that is the chief constituent of hair, nails, horns, and hoofs. [Gk. *keras*, *kerat-*, horn + –IN.] —**ke•rat′i•nous** (kə-răt′n-əs) *adj.*

kerb (kûrb) ►*n. Chiefly Brit.* Var. of **curb** 1.

ker•chief (kûr′chĭf, -chēf′) ►*n., pl.* **-chiefs** also **-chieves** (-chĭvz, -chēvz) **1.** A woman's square scarf, often worn as a head covering. **2.** A handkerchief. [< AN *courchief.*]

Ke•ren•sky (kə-rĕn′skē), **Aleksandr Feodorovich.** 1881–1970. Russian revolutionary.

kerf (kûrf) ►*n.* A groove or notch made by a cutting tool, such as a saw. [< OE *cyrf*, a cutting.]

ker•nel (kûr′nəl) ►*n.* **1.** A grain or seed, as of a cereal grass. **2.** The inner, usu. edible seed of a nut or fruit stone. **3.** The central part; core. [< OE *cyrnel.*]

ker•o•sene (kĕr′ə-sēn′, kĕr′ə-sēn′) ►*n.* A thin oil distilled from petroleum or shale oil, used as a fuel and as a denaturant for alcohol. [Gk. *kēros*, wax + –ENE.]

Ker•ou•ac (kĕr′o͞o-ăk′), **Jack.** 1922–69. Amer. writer.

kes•trel (kĕs′trəl) ►*n.* Any of various small falcons noted for their habit of hovering. [< OFr. *cresserele.*]

ketch (kĕch) ►*n.* A two-masted fore-and-aft-rigged sailing vessel with a smaller mast aft of the mainmast but forward of the rudder. [ME *cache.*]

ketch•up (kĕch′əp, kăch′-) also **catch•up** (kăch′əp, kĕch′-) or **cat•sup** (kăt′səp, kăch′əp, kĕch′-) ►*n.* A thick, smooth, spicy sauce usu. made from tomatoes. [Prob. < Malay *kicap*, fish sauce.]

ke•tone (kē′tōn′) ►*n.* Any of a class of organic compounds having the group –OH– linked to two hydrocarbon radicals. [Ger. *Keton* < *Aketon*, acetone.]

ket•tle (kĕt′l) ►*n.* A metal pot or container for boiling or stewing. [< ON *ketill* and OE *cetel.*]

ket•tle•drum (kĕt′l-drŭm′) ►*n.* A large copper or brass drum with a parchment head that can be tuned by adjusting the tension.

key¹ (kē) ►*n., pl.* **keys 1a.** A notched, usu. metal implement that is turned to open or close a lock. **b.** A similar device used for opening or winding. **2.** A means of access, control, or possession. **3a.** A crucial element. **b.** A set of answers to a test. **c.** A table, gloss, or cipher for decoding or explaining. **4.** A device, such as a pin, inserted to lock together mechanical or structural parts. **5a.** A button or lever that is pressed to operate a machine. **b.** A button that is depressed to cause a character or function to be typed or executed by a typewriter or to be accepted as input by a computer. **c.** *Mus.* A button or lever that is pressed to produce or modulate the sound of an instrument. **6.** *Mus.* A tonal system consisting of seven tones in fixed relationship to a tonic; tonality. **7.** The pitch of a voice or other sound. **8.** A characteristic tone or level of intensity. ►*adj.* Of crucial importance; significant. ►*v.* **1.** *Mus.* To regulate the pitch of. **2.** To bring into harmony; adjust or adapt. **3.** To supply an explanatory key for. **4a.** To operate (a device) by means of a keyboard. **b.** To enter (data) into a computer by means of a keyboard. —***phrasal verb:*** **key up** To make intense, excited, or nervous. [< OE *cēg*.]

key² (kē) ▸*n.*, *pl.* **keys.** A low offshore island or reef; cay. [< Sp. *cayo*, cay.]

Key, Francis Scott. 1779–1843. Amer. lawyer and poet.

key•board (kē′bôrd′, -bōrd′) ▸*n.* **1.** A set of keys, as on a computer terminal or piano. **2.** *Mus.* Any of various, often electronic instruments played by means of a set of pianolike keys. ▸*v. Comp. Sci.* To enter (text or data) by means of a keyboard. —**key′board′er** *n.*

key•card (kē′kärd′) ▸*n.* A plastic card with a magnetically coded strip that is scanned to operate a mechanism such as an automated teller machine.

key•hole (kē′hōl′) ▸*n.* The hole in a lock into which a key fits.

Key Largo. A narrow island off S FL, the largest of the Florida Keys.

Keynes (kānz), **John Maynard.** 1st Baron of Tilton. 1883–1946. British economist.

key•note (kē′nōt′) ▸*n.* **1.** The tonic of a musical key. **2.** A prime element or theme.

keynote address ▸*n.* An opening address, as at a political convention.

key•pad (kē′păd′) ▸*n.* A computer input device consisting of a set of number and function keys.

key•punch (kē′pŭnch′) ▸*n.* A keyboard machine used to punch holes in cards or tapes for data-processing systems. ▸*v.* To process on a keypunch. —**key′punch′er** *n.*

key signature ▸*n. Mus.* The group of sharps or flats placed to the right of the clef on a staff to identify the key.

key•stone (kē′stōn′) ▸*n.* **1.** The central wedge-shaped stone of an arch that locks its parts together. **2.** A basic or fundamental element.

key•stroke (kē′strōk′) ▸*n.* A stroke of a key, as on a computer keyboard.

Key West. A city of extreme S FL on the island of **Key West,** westernmost of the Florida Keys in the Gulf of Mexico. Pop. 24,832.

kg ▸*abbr.* kilogram

KGB (kā′jē-bē′) ▸*n.* The intelligence and internal security agency of the former Soviet Union. [Russ. < *K(omitet) G(osudarstvennoĭ) B(ezopasnosti)*, committee for state security.]

Kha•ba•rovsk (kə-bär′əfsk, KHə-) A city of SE Russia on the Amur R. near the Chinese border. Pop. 607,669.

khak•i (kăk′ē, kä′kē) ▸*n.* **1.** A light yellow brown. **2a.** A sturdy cloth of this color. **b.** **khakis** A uniform or garment of this cloth. [< Pers. *khāk*, dust.] —**khak′i** *adj.*

Kha•lid (kä-lēd′, KHä-). Khalid ibn Abd al-Aziz Al Saud. 1913–82. King of Saudi Arabia (1975–82).

khan (kän, kăn) ▸*n.* **1.** A ruler, official, or important person in India and some central Asian countries. **2.** A medieval ruler of a Mongol, Tartar, or Turkish tribe. [< Turk. *khān*.]

Khar•kiv (kär′kôf′) A city of NE Ukraine E of Kiev. Pop. 1,621,600.

Khar•toum (kär-to͞om′) The capital of Sudan, in the E-central part at the confluence of the Blue Nile and the White Nile. Pop. 924,505.

Kher•son (kĕr-sôn′) A city of S-central Ukraine on the Dnieper R. ENE of Odessa. Pop. 368,300.

Khmer (kmâr) ▸*n.*, *pl.* **Khmer** or **Khmers 1.** A member of a people of Cambodia. **2.** The official language of Cambodia.

Khoi•san (koi′sän′) ▸*n.* A family of languages of S Africa.

Kho•mei•ni (kō-mā′nē, KHō-), Ayatollah **Ruholla.** 1900–89. Iranian Shiite leader and head of state (1979–89).

khoum (ko͞om, ko͝om) ▸*n.* See table at **currency.** [Indigenous word in Mauritania.]

Khru•shchev (kro͞osh′chĕf, -chôf), **Nikita Sergeyevich.** 1894–1971. Soviet politician.

Khul•na (ko͞ol′nə) A city of SW Bangladesh near the Ganges River delta. Pop. 545,849.

Khy•ber Pass (kī′bər) A narrow pass, about 53 km (33 mi), through mountains on the border between W Afghanistan and N Pakistan.

kib•butz (kĭ-bo͝ots′, -bo͞ots′) ▸*n.*, *pl.* **kib•but•zim** (kĭb′o͝ot-sēm′, -o͞ot-). A collective farm or settlement in modern Israel. [Heb. *qibbūṣ*, gathering.]

kib•itz (kĭb′ĭts) ▸*v. Informal* **1.** To look on and offer unwanted advice. **2.** To chat. [Yiddish *kibitsen*.] —**kib′itz•er** *n.*

ki•bosh (kī′bŏsh′, kĭ-bŏsh′) ▸*n. Informal* A checking or restraining element: *put the kibosh on a plan.* [?]

kick (kĭk) ▸*v.* **1.** To strike or strike out with the foot. **2.** *Sports* To score or gain ground by kicking a ball. **3.** To recoil, as a gun when fired. **4.** *Informal* To object vigorously; complain or protest. —***phrasal verbs:*** **kick around 1.** *Informal* To treat badly; abuse. **2.** To move from place to place. **kick in** *Informal* To contribute (one's share). **kick off 1.** To begin or resume play with a kickoff. **2.** *Informal* To begin; start. **kick out** *Slang* To throw out; eject or expel. ▸*n.* **1.** A vigorous blow or motion with the foot or feet. **2.** A jolting recoil, as of a gun. **3.** *Slang* A complaint; protest. **4.** *Slang* Power; force. **5.** *Slang* **a.** A feeling of pleasurable stimulation: *got a kick out of the show.* **b.** **kicks** Fun: *just for kicks.* **6.** *Slang* Temporary, often obsessive interest. **7a.** The act or an instance of kicking a ball. **b.** A kicked ball. **c.** The distance spanned by a kicked ball. —***idioms:*** **kick the bucket** *Slang* To die. **kick the habit** *Slang* To free oneself of an addiction. [ME *kiken*.]

Kick•a•poo (kĭk′ə-po͞o′) ▸*n.*, *pl.* **-poo** or **-poos 1.** A member of a Native American people formerly of S Wisconsin and N Illinois, now chiefly in Kansas and Oklahoma. **2.** Their Algonquian language.

kick•back (kĭk′băk′) ▸*n.* **1.** A sharp reaction; repercussion. **2.** *Slang* A secret payment to one who has influenced or facilitated a profitable deal.

kick•er (kĭk′ər) ▸*n.* **1.** One that kicks. **2.** *Informal* A sudden surprising turn of events.

kick•off (kĭk′ôf′, -ŏf′) ▸*n.* **1.** A place kick in football or soccer with which play is begun. **2.** *Informal* A beginning.

kid (kĭd) ▸*n.* **1.** A young goat. **2.** Kidskin. **3.** *Informal* A child. ▸*adj.* **1.** Made of kidskin. **2.** *Informal* Younger than oneself: *my kid brother.* ▸*v.* **kid•ded, kid•ding 1.** To mock playfully. See Syns at **banter. 2.** To deceive in fun; fool. [< ON *kidh*.] —**kid′der** *n.* —**kid′ding•ly** *adv.*

Kidd (kĭd), **William.** "Captain Kidd." 1645?–1701. British pirate.

kid•nap (kĭd′năp′) ▸*v.* **-napped, -nap•ping**

or **-naped, -nap•ing.** To seize and detain unlawfully and usu. for ransom. [KID + *nap*, to snatch.] —**kid′nap′per, kid′nap′er** *n.*

kid•ney (kĭd′nē) ►*n.*, *pl.* **-neys 1.** Either of a pair of organs in the vertebrate abdominal cavity functioning to maintain proper water balance and to filter the blood of metabolic wastes for excretion. **2.** Kind; sort. [ME *kidenei.*]

kidney bean ►*n.* A bean cultivated in many forms for its edible pods and seeds.

kid•skin (kĭd′skĭn′) ►*n.* Soft leather made from the skin of a young goat.

Kiel (kēl) A city of N Germany on **Kiel Bay,** an arm of the Baltic Sea. Pop. 248,931.

kiel•ba•sa (kĭl-bä′sə, kēl-) ►*n.* A spicy smoked Polish sausage. [Pol. *kie·basa.*]

Kiel Canal. An artificial waterway, 98.1 km (61 mi), of N Germany connecting the North Sea with the Baltic Sea.

Kier•ke•gaard (kîr′kĭ-gärd′, -gôr′), **Søren Aaby.** 1813–55. Danish religious philosopher.

Ki•ev (kē′ĕf, -ĕv) The capital of Ukraine, in the N-central part on the Dnieper R. Pop. 2,642,700.

Ki•ga•li (kĭ-gä′lē, kē-) The capital of Rwanda, in the central part. Pop. 156,700.

Ki•ku•yu (kĭ-ko͞o′yo͞o) ►*n.*, *pl.* **-yu** or **-yus 1.** A member of a people of central and S Kenya. **2.** The Bantu language of the Kikuyu.

Kil•i•man•ja•ro (kĭl′ə-mən-jär′ō), **Mount.** The highest mountain in Africa, in NE Tanzania near the Kenya border, rising to 5,898.7 m (19,340 ft).

kill[1] (kĭl) ►*v.* **1a.** To put to death. **b.** To deprive of life. **2a.** To put an end to; extinguish. **b.** To veto: *kill a congressional bill.* **3.** To cause to cease operating: *killed the motor.* **4.** To use up: *kill time.* **5.** To cause extreme discomfort to: *My shoes are killing me.* **6.** To delete. **7.** *Informal* To overwhelm, esp. with hilarity. —***phrasal verb:*** **kill off** To destroy in such large numbers as to render extinct. ►*n.* **1.** The act of killing. **2.** One that is killed, as an animal in hunting. **3.** An enemy aircraft, vessel, or missile that has been destroyed. [ME *killen.*] —**kill′er** *n.*

kill[2] (kĭl) ►*n.* *Regional* A creek. See Regional Note at **run.** [< MDu. *kille.*]

kill•deer (kĭl′dîr′) ►*n.*, *pl.* **-deer** or **-deers.** A New World plover having a distinctive noisy cry. [Imit. of its call.]

killer whale ►*n.* A black and white predatory whale feeding esp. on large fish and squid.

kill•ing (kĭl′ĭng) ►*n.* **1.** Murder; homicide. **2.** A large profit. ►*adj.* **1.** Fatal. **2.** Thoroughly exhausting. **3.** *Informal* Hilarious.

kill•joy (kĭl′joi′) ►*n.* One who spoils the enthusiasm or fun of others.

kiln (kĭln, kĭl) ►*n.* An oven for hardening, firing, or drying. [< Lat. *culīna*, stove.]

ki•lo (kē′lō) ►*n.*, *pl.* **-los.** A kilogram.

kilo– ►*pref.* One thousand (10^3): *kilowatt.* [< Gk. *khilioi*, thousand.]

kil•o•byte (kĭl′ə-bīt′) ►*n.* A unit of computer memory equal to 1,024 (2^{10}) bytes.

kil•o•cal•o•rie (kĭl′ə-kăl′ə-rē) ►*n.* See **calorie** 1.

kil•o•cy•cle (kĭl′ə-sī′kəl) ►*n.* Kilohertz.

kil•o•gram (kĭl′ə-grăm′) ►*n.* See table at **measurement.**

kil•o•hertz (kĭl′ə-hûrts′) ►*n.* A unit of frequency equal to 1,000 hertz.

kil•o•li•ter (kĭl′ə-lē′tər) ►*n.* See table at **measurement.**

kil•o•me•ter (kĭ-lŏm′ĭ-tər, kĭl′ə-mē′tər) ►*n.* See table at **measurement.** —**kil′o•met′ric** (kĭl′ə-mĕt′rĭk) *adj.*

kil•o•ton (kĭl′ə-tŭn′) ►*n.* **1.** A unit of weight equal to 1,000 tons. **2.** An explosive force equivalent to that of 1,000 metric tons of TNT.

kil•o•watt (kĭl′ə-wŏt′) ►*n.* A unit of power equal to 1,000 watts.

kil•o•watt-hour (kĭl′ə-wŏt-our′) ►*n.* A unit of electric power equal to the work done by one kilowatt acting for one hour.

kilt (kĭlt) ►*n.* A knee-length pleated skirt, usu. of a tartan wool, traditionally worn by men in the Scottish Highlands. [< ME *kilten*, tuck up, of Scand. orig.]

kil•ter (kĭl′tər) ►*n.* Good condition; proper form: *out of kilter.* [?]

kim•chi (kĭm′chē) ►*n.*, *pl.* **-chis.** A Korean dish made of salted, fermented vegetables. [Korean *kimchÕi* of Chin. orig.]

ki•mo•no (kə-mō′nə, -nō) ►*n.*, *pl.* **-nos 1.** A long, wide-sleeved Japanese robe worn with an obi. **2.** A loose robe worn chiefly by women. [J.]

kimono

kin (kĭn) ►*n.* **1.** *(takes pl. v.)* One's relatives. **2.** A family member. ►*adj.* Related; akin. [< OE *cyn.*]

–kin ►*suff.* Little one: *napkin.* [ME, prob. < MDu.]

ki•na (kē′nə) ►*n.*, *pl.* **-na** or **-nas.** See table at **currency.** [Indigenous word in Papua New Guinea.]

kind[1] (kīnd) ►*adj.* **-er, -est 1.** Of a generous or warm-hearted nature. **2.** Showing sympathy or understanding. **3.** Humane: *kind to animals.* [< OE *gecynde*, natural.] —**kind′ness** *n.*

kind[2] (kīnd) ►*n.* **1.** A group of individuals linked by traits held in common. **2.** A particular variety; a sort. —***idioms:*** **in kind 1.** With produce or commodities rather than with money. **2.** In the same manner. **kind of** *Informal* Rather; somewhat. [< OE *gecynd*, race, kind.]

kin•der•gar•ten (kĭn′dər-gär′tn, -dn) ►*n.* A class for four- to six-year-old children. [Ger.] —**kin′der•gart′ner, kin′der•gar′ten•er** *n.*

kind•heart•ed (kīnd′här′tĭd) ►*adj.* Having or proceeding from a kind heart. —**kind′heart′ed•ly** *adv.* —**kind′heart′ed•ness** *n.*

kin•dle (kĭn′dl) ►*v.* **-dled, -dling 1.** To start (a fire); ignite. **2.** To glow or cause to glow. **3.** To arouse; stir up. [Prob. < ON *kynda.*]

kin•dling (kĭnd′lĭng) ►*n.* Easily ignited material, used to start a fire.

kind•ly (kīnd′lē) ►*adj.* **-li•er, -li•est.** Of a sympathetic, helpful, or benevolent nature. ►*adv.* **1.** In a kind manner. **2.** In an accommodating manner: *Would you kindly close the door?* —**kind′li•ness** *n.*

kin•dred (kĭn′drĭd) ►*n.* **1.** A group of related persons. **2.** *(takes pl. v.)* Kinfolk. ►*adj.* Being similar or related. [< OE *cynrǣde.*]

kine (kīn) ►*n. Archaic* Pl. of **cow**[1]. [< OE *cȳna.*]

kin•e•mat•ics (kĭn′ə-măt′ĭks) ►*n. (takes sing. v.) Phys.* The study of motion without regard to the influence of mass or force. [< Gk. *kinēma, kinēmat-,* motion.] —**kin′e•mat′ic** *adj.* —**kin′e•mat′i•cal•ly** *adv.*

kin•e•scope (kĭn′ĭ-skōp′, kī′nĭ-) ►*n.* **1.** See **picture tube. 2.** A film of a transmitted television program. [Originally a trademark.]

ki•net•ic (kə-nĕt′ĭk, kī-) ►*adj.* Of or produced by motion. [Gk. *kinētikos.*] —**ki•net′i•cal•ly** *adv.*

kinetic energy ►*n.* The energy possessed by a body because of its motion.

ki•net•ics (kə-nĕt′ĭks, kī-) ►*n. (takes sing. v.)* **1.** See **dynamics** 1. **2.** The branch of chemistry concerned with the rates of change of reactants in a chemical reaction.

kin•folk (kĭn′fōk′) also **kins•folk** (kĭnz′-) or **kin•folks** (kĭn′fōks′) ►*pl.n.* One's relatives; kindred.

king (kĭng) ►*n.* **1.** A male sovereign. **2.** One that is preeminent in a group, category, or sphere. **3a.** A playing card bearing the figure of a king. **b.** The principal chess piece. **c.** A piece in checkers that has been crowned. **4. Kings** *(takes sing. v.)* See table at **Bible.** [< OE *cyning.*] —**king′li•ness** *n.* —**king′ly** *adj. & adv.* —**king′ship′** *n.*

King, Coretta Scott. b. 1927. Amer. civil rights leader.

King, Martin Luther, Jr. 1929–68. Amer. cleric and civil rights leader; assassinated. Won 1964 Nobel Peace Prize.

Martin Luther King, Jr.
photographed in 1966

King, William Lyon Mackenzie. 1874–1950. Canadian prime minister (1921–26, 1926–30, and 1935–48).

king•bolt (kĭng′bōlt′) ►*n.* A vertical bolt that joins the body of a wagon or other vehicle to its front axle and usu. acts as a pivot.

king crab ►*n.* A large edible crab of coastal waters of Alaska, Japan, and Siberia.

king•dom (kĭng′dəm) ►*n.* **1.** A land ruled by a king or queen. **2.** An area in which one thing is dominant. **3.** One of the three main divisions (animal, vegetable, and mineral) of the natural world. **4.** *Biol.* The highest taxonomic classification into which organisms are grouped, based on fundamental similarities and common ancestry.

king•fish•er (kĭng′fĭsh′ər) ►*n.* Any of a family of crested, large-billed birds that feed on fish.

King James Bible ►*n.* An English translation of the Bible published in 1611.

king•pin (kĭng′pĭn′) ►*n.* **1.** The foremost or central pin in bowling. **2.** The most important person or element. **3.** See **kingbolt.**

King's English (kĭngz) ►*n.* English speech or usage that is deemed standard or accepted.

king-size (kĭng′sīz′) or **king-sized** (-sīzd′) ►*adj.* **1.** Larger or longer than the usual size. **2.** Very large.

King•ston (kĭng′stən) The capital of Jamaica, in the SE part on the Caribbean Sea. Pop. 103,962.

Kings•town (kĭngz′toun′) The capital of St. Vincent and the Grenadines, West Indies, on the SW coast of St. Vincent I. Pop. 18,378.

kink (kĭngk) ►*n.* **1.** A tight curl or twist in a length of thin material. **2.** A muscle cramp. **3.** A difficulty that is likely to impede operation. **4.** A mental peculiarity; quirk. ►*v.* To form a kink (in). [Du., a twist in rope.]

kink•a•jou (kĭng′kə-jo͞o′) ►*n.* A furry long-tailed arboreal mammal of tropical America. [Fr. *quincajou,* wolverine, of Algonquian orig.]

kink•y (kĭng′kē) ►*adj.* **-i•er, -i•est 1.** Tightly twisted or curled. **2.** *Slang* Of or relating to eccentric sexual practices. —**kink′i•ness** *n.*

kins•folk (kĭnz′fōk′) ►*pl.n.* Var. of **kinfolk.**

Kin•sha•sa (kĭn-shä′sə) The capital of Congo, in the W part on the Congo R. Pop. 2,654,309.

kin•ship (kĭn′shĭp′) ►*n.* **1.** Connection by blood, marriage, or adoption; family relationship. **2.** Likeness; affinity.

kins•man (kĭnz′mən) ►*n.* A male relative.

kins•wom•an (kĭnz′wo͝om′ən) ►*n.* A female relative.

ki•osk (kē′ŏsk′, kē-ŏsk′) ►*n.* A small, usu. freestanding structure used as a newsstand or booth. [< Turk. *köşk.*]

Ki•o•wa (kī′ə-wô′, -wä′, -wā′) ►*n., pl.* **-wa** or **-was 1.** A member of a Native American people formerly inhabiting the S Great Plains, now chiefly in SW Oklahoma. **2.** The Tanoan language of the Kiowa.

Kiowa Apache ►*n.* A member of an Athabaskan-speaking Native American people closely associated with the Kiowa.

kip (kĭp) ►*n., pl.* **kip.** See table at **currency.** [Thai.]

Kip•ling (kĭp′lĭng), **(Joseph) Rudyard.** 1865–1936. British writer; 1907 Nobel.

kip•per (kĭp′ər) ►*n.* A split, salted, and smoked herring or salmon. [< OE *cypera,* spawning male salmon.] —**kip′per** *v.*

Kir•ghiz (kîr-gēz′) ►*n.* Var. of **Kyrgyz.**

Ki•ri•ba•ti (kēr′ə-bä′tē, kîr′ə-băs′) An island country of the W-central Pacific near the equator. Cap. Tarawa. Pop. 56,213.

kir•i•ga•mi (kĭr′ĭ-gä′mē) ►*n.* The Japanese art of cutting and folding paper into ornamental objects or designs. [J.]

kirk (kûrk) ►*n. Scots* A church. [< OE *cirice*, CHURCH.]

Ki•rov (kē′rôf′) A city of W-central Russia ENE of Moscow. Pop. 490,964.

kirsch (kîrsh) ►*n.* A cherry brandy. [< Ger. *Kirschwasser* : *Kirsch*, cherry + *Wasser*, water (< OHGer. *wassar*).]

Ki•san•ga•ni (kē′sän-gä′nē) A city of N Congo on the Congo R. NE of Kinshasa. Pop. 317,581.

Ki•shi•nev (kĭsh′ə-nĕf′, -nôf′) See **Chişinău.**

Kis•lev (kĭs′ləv, kēs-lĕv′) ►*n.* A month of the Jewish calendar. See table at **calendar.** [Heb. *kislēw.*]

kis•met (kĭz′mĕt′, -mĭt) ►*n.* Fate; fortune. [Turk.]

kiss (kĭs) ►*v.* **1.** To touch or caress with the lips, as in affection or greeting. **2.** To touch lightly or gently. ►*n.* **1.** A caress or touch with the lips. **2.** A slight touch. **3.** A small piece of candy, esp. of chocolate. [< OE *cyssan.*]

kiss•er (kĭs′ər) ►*n.* **1.** One that kisses. **2.** *Slang* The mouth. **3.** *Slang* The face.

Kis•sin•ger (kĭs′ĭn-jər), **Henry Alfred.** b. 1923. German-born Amer. diplomat; 1973 Nobel Peace Prize.

kit (kĭt) ►*n.* **1a.** A set of articles or implements: *a shaving kit.* **b.** A container for such a set. **2.** A set of parts to be assembled: *a model airplane kit.* **3.** A packaged set of related materials: *a sales kit.* —***idiom:* the (whole) kit and caboodle** The entire collection or lot. [ME *kitte*, wooden tub.]

Ki•ta•kyu•shu (kē-tä′kyo͞o-sho͞o) A city of N Kyushu, Japan. Pop. 1,019,996.

kitch•en (kĭch′ən) ►*n.* **1.** A room or area for preparing and cooking food. **2.** A staff that prepares, cooks, and serves food. [< LLat. *coquīna.*]

Kitch•e•ner (kĭch′-nər, kĭch′ə-nər) A city of S Ontario, Canada, WSW of Toronto. Pop. 168,282.

kitch•en•ette (kĭch′ə-nĕt′) ►*n.* A small kitchen.

kitchen police ►*n.* **1.** Enlisted military personnel assigned to work in a kitchen. **2.** Military duty assisting cooks.

kitch•en•ware (kĭch′ən-wâr′) ►*n.* Utensils for use in a kitchen.

kite (kīt) ►*n.* **1.** A light framework covered with cloth, plastic, or paper, designed to be flown in the wind at the end of a long string. **2.** Any of various predatory birds having a long, often forked tail and long pointed wings. [< OE *cyta*, bird of prey.]

kith and kin (kĭth) ►*pl.n.* One's acquaintances and relatives. [< OE *cȳth*, kinsfolk.]

kitsch (kĭch) ►*n.* Art or artwork marked by sentimental, often pretentious bad taste. [Ger.] —**kitsch′y** *adj.*

kit•ten (kĭt′n) ►*n.* A young cat. [ME *kitoun.*]

kit•ten•ish (kĭt′n-ĭsh) ►*adj.* Playfully coy and frisky. —**kit′ten•ish•ly** *adv.*

kit•ty[1] (kĭt′ē) ►*n., pl.* **-ties.** A pool of money, esp. one to which a number of people have contributed. [Prob. < KIT.]

kit•ty[2] (kĭt′ē) ►*n., pl.* **-ties.** A cat or kitten.

Kitty Hawk. A village on a sandy peninsula of NE NC, site of the Wright brothers' first two successful flights (December 17, 1903).

Ki•twe (kē′twā′) A city of N-central Zambia N of Lusaka. Pop. 338,207.

ki•va (kē′və) ►*n.* A usu. underground ceremonial chamber in a Pueblo village. [Hopi *kiva.*]

ki•wi (kē′wē) ►*n., pl.* **-wis 1.** A flightless New Zealand bird having vestigial wings and a long slender bill. **2a.** A woody Chinese vine having fuzzy fruit with an edible pulp. **b.** The fruit of this plant. [Maori.]

KKK ►*abbr.* Ku Klux Klan

Klam•ath (klăm′əth) ►*n., pl.* **-ath** or **-aths 1.** A member of a Native American people of S-central Oregon and N California. **2.** The Penutian language of the Klamath.

Klee (klā), **Paul.** 1879–1940. Swiss artist.

Kleen•ex (klē′nĕks′) ► A trademark for a soft facial tissue.

klep•to•ma•ni•a (klĕp′tə-mā′nē-ə, -mān′yə) ►*n.* An obsessive impulse to steal regardless of economic need. [Gk. *kleptein*, steal + -MANIA.] —**klep′to•ma′ni•ac′** *n.*

klieg light (klēg) ►*n.* A powerful lamp used esp. in making movies. [After J.H. *Kliegl* (1869–1959) and A.T. *Kliegl* (1872–1927).]

Klon•dike (klŏn′dīk′) A region of Yukon Terr., Canada, E of AK.

klutz (klŭts) ►*n. Slang* A clumsy or inept person. [Yiddish *klots.*] —**klutz′i•ness** *n.* —**klutz′y** *adj.*

km ►*abbr.* kilometer

kmph ►*abbr.* kilometers per hour

knack (năk) ►*n.* **1.** A clever, expedient way of doing something. **2.** A specific talent for something. See Syns at **art**[1]. [< MDu. *cnacken*, to crack.]

knack•wurst or **knock•wurst** (nŏk′wûrst′, -wo͝orst′) ►*n.* A short, thick, highly seasoned sausage. [Ger.]

knap•sack (năp′săk′) ►*n.* A sturdy bag with shoulder straps for carrying articles on the back. [LGer. *Knappsack.*]

knave (nāv) ►*n.* **1.** An unprincipled, crafty fellow. **2.** See **jack** 2. [< OE *cnafa*, boy.] —**knav′er•y** *n.* —**knav′ish** *adj.* —**knav′ish•ly** *adv.* —**knav′ish•ness** *n.*

knead (nēd) ►*v.* **1.** To mix and work into a uniform mass, esp. with the hands: *kneading dough.* **2.** To massage. [< OE *cnedan.*]

knee (nē) ►*n.* The joint between the thigh and the lower leg. ►*v.* **kneed, knee•ing.** To strike with the knee. [< OE *cnēo.*]

knee•cap (nē′kăp′) ►*n.* See **patella.**

kneel (nēl) ►*v.* **knelt** (nĕlt) or **kneeled, kneel•ing.** To go down or rest on one or both knees. [< OE *cnēowlian.*]

knell (nĕl) ►*v.* **1.** To ring slowly and solemnly, esp. for a funeral; toll. **2.** To signal or proclaim by or as if by tolling. ►*n.* **1.** A solemn or mournful toll. **2.** A signal of disaster or destruction. [< OE *cnyllan.*]

knew (no͞o, nyo͞o) ►*v.* P.t. of **know.**

knick•ers (nĭk′ərz) ►*pl.n.* **1.** Full breeches gathered and banded just below the knee. **2.** *Chiefly Brit.* Panties. [< *knickerbockers.*]

knick•knack (nĭk′năk′) ►*n.* A small ornamental article; trinket. [< KNACK.]

knife (nīf) ►*n., pl.* **knives** (nīvz) **1.** A cutting instrument consisting of a sharp blade attached to a handle. **2.** A cutting edge; blade. ►*v.* **knifed, knif•ing 1.** To use a knife on, esp. to stab. **2.** *Informal* To betray. —***idiom:*** **under the knife** *Informal* Undergoing surgery. [< ON *knífr.*]

knight (nīt) ▸*n.* **1a.** A medieval gentleman-soldier. **b.** A man holding a nonhereditary title conferred by a sovereign. **2.** A member of certain fraternal orders. **3.** A noble defender or champion. **4.** A chess piece, usu. in the shape of a horse's head. ▸*v.* To raise (a person) to knighthood. [< OE *cniht.*] —**knight′ly** *adj.*

knight-errant (nīt′ĕr′ənt) ▸*n., pl.* **knights-errant** (nīts′-). A knight who wanders in search of adventures to prove his chivalry.

knight•hood (nīt′ho͝od′) ▸*n.* **1.** The rank or vocation of a knight. **2.** Knights collectively.

knish (kə-nĭsh′) ▸*n.* A piece of dough stuffed with potato, meat, or cheese and baked or fried. [Yiddish < Ukrainian *knysh.*]

knit (nĭt) ▸*v.* **knit** or **knit•ted, knit•ting 1.** To make (a fabric or garment) by intertwining yarn or thread in a series of connected loops. **2.** To join closely. **3.** To draw (the brows) together in wrinkles; furrow. ▸*n.* A fabric or garment made by knitting. [< OE *cnyttan*, tie in a knot.] —**knit′ter** *n.*

knob (nŏb) ▸*n.* **1.** A rounded protuberance. **2a.** A rounded handle. **b.** A rounded control switch or dial. [ME *knobbe.*] —**knobbed** *adj.* —**knob′by** *adj.*

knock (nŏk) ▸*v.* **1.** To strike with a hard or sharp blow. **2.** To collide or cause to collide. **3.** To produce by hitting: *knocked a hole in the wall.* **4.** *Slang* To disparage; criticize. **5.** To make the rattling noise of a misfiring engine. —***phrasal verbs:*** **knock around** (or **about) 1.** To be rough or brutal with. **2.** To wander from place to place. **knock down 1.** To fell; topple. **2.** To disassemble into parts. **3.** To declare sold at an auction. **4.** *Informal* To reduce in price. **knock off 1.** *Informal* To stop an activity; quit. **2.** *Informal* To produce in routine fashion. **3.** *Slang* To kill. **4.** *Slang* To hold up or rob. **knock out 1.** To render unconscious. **2.** To defeat (a boxing opponent) by a knockout. **3.** To render useless. **4.** *Slang* To overwhelm or amaze. —***idiom:*** **knock dead** *Slang* To affect strongly and positively. [< OE *cnocian.*] —**knock** *n.*

knock•down (nŏk′doun′) ▸*adj.* **1.** Strong enough to knock down or overwhelm: *a knockdown blow.* **2.** Easily assembled or disassembled: *knockdown furniture.*

knock•er (nŏk′ər) ▸*n.* A hinged fixture used for knocking on a door.

knock-knee (nŏk′nē′) ▸*n.* A deformity of the legs in which the knees are abnormally close together. —**knock′-kneed′** *adj.*

knock•out (nŏk′out′) ▸*n.* **1.** A victory in boxing in which one's opponent is unable to rise from the canvas within a specified time. **2.** *Slang* A strikingly attractive or impressive person or thing.

knock•wurst (nŏk′wûrst′, -wo͝orst′) ▸*n.* Var. of **knackwurst.**

knoll (nōl) ▸*n.* A small rounded hill; hillock. [< OE *cnoll.*]

Knos•sos (nŏs′əs) An ancient city of N Crete.

knot (nŏt) ▸*n.* **1a.** A compact intersection of interlaced material, such as rope. **b.** A fastening made by tying together lengths of material. **2.** A decorative bow. **3.** A unifying bond, esp. a marriage bond. **4.** A tight cluster of persons or things. **5.** A feeling of tightness: *a knot in my stomach.* **6.** A complex problem. **7a.** A hard node on a tree trunk at a point from which a branch grows. **b.** The round, often darker cross section of such a node in cut lumber. **8.** A protuberant growth or swelling in a tissue. **9.** A unit of speed, one nautical mile per hour. ▸*v.* **knot•ted, knot•ting 1.** To tie in or fasten with a knot. **2.** To make or become snarled or entangled. [< OE *cnotta.*] —**knot′ti•ness** *n.* —**knot′ty** *adj.*

Usage: In nautical usage *knot* is a unit of speed, not of distance, and has a built-in meaning of "per hour." Therefore, a ship would strictly be said to travel at ten knots (not ten knots per hour).

knot•hole (nŏt′hōl′) ▸*n.* A hole in a piece of lumber where a knot once was.

know (nō) ▸*v.* **knew** (no͞o, nyo͞o), **known** (nōn), **know•ing 1.** To perceive directly with the mind or senses. **2.** To regard as true beyond doubt. **3.** To be capable of or skilled in: *knows how to cook.* **4.** To have learned: *knows her Latin verbs.* **5.** To have experience of. **6a.** To recognize: *I know that face.* **b.** To be acquainted with. **7.** To be able to distinguish: *knows right from wrong.* —***idiom:*** **in the know** Possessing special or secret information. [< OE *cnāwan.*] —**know′a•ble** *adj.* —**know′er** *n.*

know-how (nō′hou′) ▸*n.* Practical knowledge or skill. See Syns at **art**[1].

know•ing (nō′ĭng) ▸*adj.* **1.** Possessing knowledge, information, or understanding. **2.** Clever; shrewd. **3.** Suggestive of private knowledge: *a knowing glance.* **4.** Deliberate; conscious. —**know′ing•ly** *adv.*

knowl•edge (nŏl′ĭj) ▸*n.* **1.** The state or fact of knowing. **2.** Familiarity, awareness, or understanding gained through experience or study. **3.** The sum or range of what has been perceived, discovered, or learned. **4.** Learning; erudition. [ME *knowleche.*] —**knowl′edge•a•ble** *adj.* —**knowl′edge•a•bly** *adv.*

Knox (nŏks), **Henry.** 1750–1806. Amer. Revolutionary soldier.

Knox, John. 1514?–72. Scottish religious reformer.

Knox•ville (nŏks′vĭl′, -vəl) A city of E TN on the Tennessee R. NE of Chattanooga. Pop. 165,121.

Knt. ▸*abbr.* knight

knuck•le (nŭk′əl) ▸*n.* The rounded prominence of a joint, esp. of one of the joints connecting the fingers to the hand. ▸*v.* **-led, -ling.** To press, rub, or hit with the knuckles. —***phrasal verbs:*** **knuckle down** To apply oneself earnestly. **knuckle under** To yield to pressure; give in. [ME *knokel.*]

knuck•le•bone (nŭk′əl-bōn′) ▸*n.* A knobbed bone, as of a knuckle or joint.

knurl (nûrl) ▸*n.* **1.** A knob or knot. **2.** One of a set of small ridges, as on a thumbscrew, to aid in gripping. [Prob. < ME *knor*, a swelling.] —**knurled** *adj.* —**knurl′y** *adj.*

KO (kā′ō′) *Slang* ▸*v.* **KO'd, KO'ing.** To knock out in boxing. ▸*n.* (kā-ō′, kā′ō′). A knockout in boxing.

ko•a•la (kō-ä′lə) ▸*n.* A furry, bearlike arboreal Australian marsupial. [Dharuk (Australian) *gulawan*ʸ.]

Ko•be (kō′bē′, -bā′) A city of S Honshu, Japan,

SSW of Kyoto. Pop. 1,509,395.

Ko•di•ak bear (kō′dē-ăk′) ►*n.* A brown bear inhabiting islands and coastal areas of Alaska. [After KODIAK (ISLAND).]

Kodiak Island. An island of S AK in the Gulf of Alaska E of the Alaska Peninsula.

Koest•ler (kĕst′lər, kĕs′-), **Arthur.** 1905–83. Hungarian-born British writer.

K of C ►*abbr.* Knights of Columbus.

kohl (kōl) ►*n.* A cosmetic preparation used to darken the rims of the eyelids. [Ar. *kuḥl.*]

kohl•ra•bi (kōl-rä′bē, -răb′ē) ►*n., pl.* **-bies.** A plant whose thick basal stem is eaten as a vegetable. [< Ital. *cavoli rape.*]

ko•la (kō′lə) ►*n.* Var. of **cola[3].**

Kola Peninsula. A peninsula of NW Russia projecting eastward from Scandinavia between the White Sea and the Barents Sea.

Ko•ly•ma (kə-lē′mə, kə-lē-mä′) A river of NE Russia rising in the Kolyma Mts. and flowing about 2,148 km (1,335 mi) to the East Siberian Sea.

Kolyma Mountains. A range of NE Russia extending about 1,126 km (700 mi) E of the Kolyma R.

kook (ko͝ok) ►*n. Slang* An eccentric or crazy person. [Poss. < CUCKOO.] —**kook′i•ness** *n.* —**kook′y** *adj.*

kook•a•bur•ra (ko͝ok′ə-bûr′ə, -bŭr′ə) ►*n.* A large kingfisher of S and E Australia, having a call like raucous laughter. [Wiradhuri (Australian) *gugubarra*, of imit. orig.]

kookaburra

Koo•te•nay River also **Koo•te•nai River** (ko͞ot′n-ā′). A river, about 655 km (407 mi), flowing from SE British Columbia, Canada, through NW Montana, N Idaho, and back into British Columbia, where it forms **Kootenay Lake** before joining the Columbia R.

ko•peck or **ko•pek** (kō′pĕk) ►*n.* A coin equal to 1/100 of the Russian ruble. [Russ. *kopeĭka.*]

Ko•ran or **Qur•'an** (kə-răn′, -rän′, kô-, kō-) ►*n.* The sacred text of Islam, considered by Muslims to contain the revelations of God to Muhammad. [Ar. *qurʾān.*] —**Ko•ran′ic** *adj.*

Ko•re•a (kə-rē′ə, kô-, kō-) A peninsula and former country of E Asia between the Yellow Sea and the Sea of Japan.

Korea Bay. An inlet of the Yellow Sea between NE China and W North Korea.

Ko•re•an (kə-rē′ən, kô-, kō-) ►*n.* **1.** A native or inhabitant of Korea. **2.** The language of the Koreans. —**Ko•re′an** *adj.*

ko•ru•na (kôr′ə-nä′) ►*n.* See table at **currency.** [Czech.]

Kos also **Cos** (kŏs, kôs). An island of SE Greece, one of the Dodecanese Is. in the Aegean Sea off the SW coast of Turkey.

Kos•ci•us•ko (kŏs′ē-ŭs′kō, kŏs′kē-), **Mount.** A peak, 2,231.4 m (7,316 ft), of SW Australia in the Australian Alps; highest point in continent.

Kosciusko, Thaddeus. 1746–1817. Polish general and patriot in the American Revolution.

ko•sher (kō′shər) ►*adj.* **1.** Conforming to or prepared in accordance with Jewish dietary laws. **2.** *Slang* Legitimate; permissible. [< Heb. *kāšēr*, proper.]

Ko•ši•ce (kō′shĭ-tsĕ) A city of E Slovakia NE of Budapest, Hungary. Pop. 236,984.

Ko•so•vo (kô′sə-vō′, kō′-) A province of S Yugoslavia in the Serbian republic. —**Ko′so•var′** (-vär′) *adj. & n.*

Kos•suth (kŏs′o͞oth′), **Lajos.** 1802–94. Hungarian revolutionary leader.

Ko•sy•gin (kə-sē′gən), **Aleksei Nikolayevich.** 1904–80. Soviet premier (1964–80).

Kow•loon (kou′lo͞on′) A city of SE China on **Kowloon Peninsula** opposite Hong Kong I. Pop. 799,123.

kow•tow (kou-tou′, kou′tou′) ►*v.* **1.** To kneel and touch the forehead to the ground in expression of deep respect, worship, or submission. **2.** To show servile deference. See Syns at **fawn[1].** [Mandarin *kòu tóu.*] —**kow′tow′** *n.*

KP ►*abbr.* kitchen police

Kr ► The symbol for the element **krypton.**

kraal (krôl, kräl) ►*n. South African* **1.** A rural village. **2.** An enclosure for livestock. [Afr. < Port. *curral*, pen.]

Kra•ka•tau (krăk′ə-tou′, krä′kə-) or **Kra•ka•to•a** (-tō′ə). A volcanic island of Indonesia between Sumatra and Java.

Kra•ków (krăk′ou, krä′kou, -ko͞of) A city of S Poland on the Vistula R. SSE of Warsaw. Pop. 750,588.

Kras•no•dar (krăs′nə-där′) A city of SW Russia in the N Caucasus S of Rostov. Pop. 635,856.

Kras•no•yarsk (krăs′nə-yärsk′) A city of south-central Russia on the upper Yenisey R. E of Novosibirsk. Pop. 916,525.

Krem•lin (krĕm′lĭn) ►*n.* **1.** The citadel of Moscow, housing the offices of the Russian and formerly the Soviet government. **2.** The government of Russia and formerly that of the Soviet Union. [< ORuss. *kremlĭnŭ*, separate.]

Krem•lin•ol•o•gy (krĕm′lə-nŏl′ə-jē) ►*n.* The study of the policies of the Soviet or Russian government. —**Krem′lin•ol′o•gist** *n.*

krill (krĭl) ►*n., pl.* **krill.** Small marine crustaceans that are the principal food of baleen whales. [Norw. *kril*, young fry of fish.]

Krish•na (krĭsh′nə) ►*n. Hinduism* The 8th and principal avatar of Vishnu.

kro•na[1] (krō′nə) ►*n., pl.* **-nur** (-nər). See table at **currency.** [Icel. *króna.*]

kro•na[2] (krō′nə) ►*n., pl.* **-nor** (-nôr′, -nər). See table at **currency.** [Swed.]

kro•ne[1] (krō′nə) ►*n., pl.* **-ner** (-nər). See table at **currency.** [Norw.]

kro•ne[2] (krō′nə) ►*n., pl.* **-ner** (-nər). See table at **currency.** [Dan.]

kroon (krōn) ►*n., pl.* **kroon•i** (krō′nē). See table at **currency.** [Estonian.]

kryp•ton (krĭp′tŏn′) ►*n. Symbol* **Kr** A whitish, largely inert gaseous element used chiefly in fluorescent lamps. At. no. 36. See table at **ele-**

ment. [< Gk. *kruptos*, hidden.]

KS ▶ *abbr.* **1.** Kansas **2.** Kaposi's sarcoma

Kt ▶ *abbr.* knight (chess)

kt. ▶ *abbr.* **1.** karat **2.** *Naut.* knot

Kt. ▶ *abbr.* knight (title)

Kua•la Lum•pur (kwä′lə lo͝om-po͝or′) The capital of Malaysia, on the SW Malay Peninsula NW of Singapore. Pop. 1,145,075.

Ku•blai Khan (ko͞o′blī kän′) also **Ku•bla Khan** (-blə). 1215–94. Mongol emperor (1260–94) and founder of the Mongol dynasty in China.

ku•dos (ko͞o′dōz′, -dōs′, -dŏs′, kyo͞o′-) ▶ *n.* Acclaim or praise for exceptional achievement. [Gk.]

Usage: Since it comes from a Greek singular noun, kudos should be viewed as a singular. Correctness requires *Kudos is* (not *are*) *due her for her brilliant work on the score.* However, use of the plural form, as in *She received many kudos for her work,* is common.

ku•du (ko͞o′do͞o) ▶ *n., pl.* **-du** or **-dus.** A large striped African antelope with spirally curved horns in the male. [< Xhosa *i-qudu.*]

kud•zu (ko͝od′zo͞o) ▶ *n.* A fast-growing vine native to E Asia and grown for fodder, forage, and erosion control. [J. *kuzu.*]

ku•lak (ko͞o-lăk′, ko͞o′lăk′, -läk′) ▶ *n.* A prosperous landed peasant in czarist Russia. [Russ.]

Ku•ma•si (ko͞o-mä′sē) A city of S-central Ghana NW of Accra. Pop. 348,880.

kum•quat (kŭm′kwŏt′) ▶ *n.* **1.** A tree or shrub bearing small edible orangelike fruit. **2.** The fruit itself. [Cantonese *kamkwat.*]

ku•na (ko͞o′nə) ▶ *n.* See table at **currency.** [Serbo-Croatian.]

kung fu (kŭng′ fo͞o′, ko͝ong′) ▶ *n.* The Chinese martial arts, esp. those forms similar to karate. [Cantonese.]

Kun•lun (ko͞on′lo͞on′) A mountain system of W China extending from the Karakoram Range along the N edge of the Xizang (Tibet) plateau.

Kun•ming (ko͞on′mĭng′) A city of S China SW of Chongqing. Pop. 1,611,969.

Ku•ra (ko͞o-rä′) A river of NE Turkey and S Azerbaijan flowing about 1,514 km (941 mi) to the Caspian Sea S of Baku.

Kurd (kûrd, ko͝ord) ▶ *n.* A member of a people inhabiting the transnational region of Kurdistan.

Kurd•ish (kûr′dĭsh, ko͝or′-) ▶ *n.* The Iranian language of the Kurds. —**Kurd′ish** *adj.*

Kurd•i•stan (kûr′dĭ-stăn′, ko͝or′dĭ-stän′) An extensive plateau region of SW Asia.

Ku•ril Islands also **Ku•rile Islands** (ko͝or′ĭl, ko͞o-rēl′). An island chain of extreme E Russia extending about 1,207 km (750 mi) in the Pacific between Kamchatka Peninsula and N Hokkaido, Japan. —**Ku•ril′i•an** *adj.*

Ku•ro•sa•wa (ko͝or′ə-sä′wə), **Akira.** 1910–98. Japanese filmmaker.

Kursk (ko͝orsk) A city of W Russia SSW of Moscow. Pop. 433,991.

Ku•wait (ko͞o-wāt′) **1.** A country of NE Arabia at the head of the Persian Gulf. Cap. Kuwait (city of). Pop. 1,620,000. **2.** The capital of Kuwait, in the E-central part on the Persian Gulf. Pop. 151,060. —**Ku•wait′i** (-wā′tē) *adj. & n.*

Kuz•netsk Basin (ko͞oz-nĕtsk′) A coal-producing region of W-central Russia extending from Tomsk to Novokuznetsk.

kW ▶ *abbr.* kilowatt

kwa•cha (kwä′chə) ▶ *n.* See table at **currency.** [Indigenous word in Zambia.]

Kwa•ki•u•tl (kwä′kē-o͞ot′l) ▶ *n., pl.* **-tl** or **-tls** **1.** A member of a Native American people of coastal British Columbia and Vancouver Island. **2.** Their language.

Kwang•chow (kwäng′chō′) See **Guangzhou.**

kwan•za (kwän′zə) ▶ *n., pl.* **-za** or **-zas.** See table at **currency.** [Bantu or Swahili.]

Kwan•zaa also **Kwan•za** (kwän′zə) ▶ *n.* An African-American cultural festival celebrated from Dec. 26 to Jan. 1. [Poss. < Swahili *kwanzaa*, first fruit of the harvest.]

kwa•shi•or•kor (kwä′shē-ôr′kôr′) ▶ *n.* Severe protein malnutrition, esp. in children, marked by anemia, potbelly, reduced pigmentation, and growth retardation. [Indigenous word in Ghana.]

Kwei•yang (kwā′yäng′) See **Guiyang.**

kWh ▶ *abbr.* kilowatt-hour

KY or **Ky.** ▶ *abbr.* Kentucky

kyat (chät) ▶ *n.* See table at **currency.** [Burmese.]

Kyo•to (kē-ō′tō, kyō′-) A city of W-central Honshu, Japan, NNE of Osaka. Pop. 1,452,240.

Kyr•gyz or **Kir•ghiz** (kîr-gēz′) ▶ *n., pl.* **-gyz** or **-gyz•es** or **-ghiz** or **-ghiz•es** **1.** A member of a traditionally nomadic people living principally in Kyrgyzstan. **2.** The language of this people.

Kyr•gyz•stan (kîr′gē-stän′) A region and republic of W-central Asia bordering on NW China. Cap. Bishkek. Pop. 4,596,000.

Kyu•shu (kē-o͞o′sho͞o, kyo͞o′-) An island of SW Japan on the East China Sea and the Pacific.

Ky•zyl Kum (kĭ-zĭl′ ko͞om′) A desert of N-central Uzbekistan and S-central Kazakhstan SE of the Aral Sea.

L

l[1] or **L** (ĕl) ▶ *n., pl.* **l's** or **L's** also **ls** or **Ls.** The 12th letter of the English alphabet.

l[2] ▶ *abbr.* **1.** length **2.** liter

L[1] also **l** ▶ The symbol for the Roman numeral 50.

L[2] ▶ *abbr.* **1.** large **2.** left

l. ▶ *abbr.* **1.** line **2.** lira

L. ▶ *abbr.* **1.** lake **2.** Latin

la (lä) ▶ *n.* *Mus.* The 6th tone of the diatonic scale. [< Med.Lat.]

La ▶ The symbol for the element **lanthanum.**

LA ▶ *abbr.* **1.** Los Angeles **2.** also **La.** Louisiana

lab (lăb) ▶ *n.* A laboratory.

la•bel (lā′bəl) ▶ *n.* **1.** Something, such as a small piece of paper or cloth, attached to an article to identify its owner, contents, or destination. **2.** A descriptive term; epithet. ►*v.* **-beled, -bel•ing** or **-belled, -bel•ling 1.** To attach a label to. **2.** To identify or classify. See Syns at **mark**[1]. [< OFr., strip of cloth.] —**la′bel•er, la′bel•ler** *n.*

la•bi•al (lā′bē-əl) ►*adj.* **1.** Of the lips or labia. **2.** *Ling.* Articulated mainly with the lips, as (b), (m), or (w). ►*n. Ling.* A labial consonant. [< Lat. *labium*, lip.] —**la′bi•al•ly** *adv.*

la•bi•um (lā′bē-əm) ►*n., pl.* **-bi•a** (-bē-ə) *Anat.* Any of four folds of tissue of the female external genitalia. [Lat., lip.]

la•bor (lā′bər) ►*n.* **1.** Physical or mental exertion. **2.** A specific task. **3.** Work for wages. **4a.** Workers collectively. **b.** The trade union movement. **5.** The physical efforts of childbirth. ►*v.* **1.** To work; toil. **2.** To strive painstakingly. **3.** To proceed with effort; plod. **4.** To suffer from distress or a disadvantage: *labored under a misconception.* [< Lat.] —**la′bor•er** *n.*

lab•o•ra•to•ry (lăb′rə-tôr′ē, -tōr′ē) ►*n., pl.* **-ries 1.** A place equipped for scientific experimentation, research, or testing. **2.** A place where drugs and chemicals are manufactured.

laboratory

Labor Day ►*n.* The 1st Monday in Sep., observed as a holiday in honor of working people.

la•bored (lā′bərd) ►*adj.* **1.** Produced or done with effort. **2.** Lacking natural ease; strained.

la•bo•ri•ous (lə-bôr′ē-əs, -bōr′-) ►*adj.* Marked by or requiring hard or tedious work. —**la•bo′ri•ous•ly** *adv.* —**la•bo′ri•ous•ness** *n.*

labor union ►*n.* An organization of workers formed to promote the members' interests with respect to wages and working conditions.

Lab•ra•dor (lăb′rə-dôr′) The mainland territory of Newfoundland, Canada, on NE Labrador Peninsula. —**Lab′ra•dor′e•an, Lab′ra•dor′i•an** *adj. & n.*

Labrador Current ►*n.* A cold ocean current flowing S from Baffin Bay along the coast of Labrador.

Labrador Peninsula. A peninsula of E Canada between Hudson Bay and the Atlantic.

la•bret (lā′brĭt) ►*n.* An ornament inserted into a perforation of the lip.

la•bur•num (lə-bûr′nəm) ►*n.* A tree or shrub cultivated for its drooping clusters of yellow flowers. [< Lat.]

lab•y•rinth (lăb′ə-rĭnth′) ►*n.* **1.** An intricate structure of interconnecting passages through which it is difficult to find one's way; maze. **2.** **Labyrinth** *Gk. Myth.* The maze in which the Minotaur was confined. [< Gk. *laburinthos.*] —**lab′y•rin′thine** (-rĭn′thĭn, -thēn′) *adj.*

lac (lăk) ►*n.* A resinous secretion of an Asian insect, used in making shellac. [< Hindi *lākh* < Skt. *lākṣā*, resin.]

lace (lās) ►*n.* **1.** A cord used to draw and tie together two opposite edges, as of a shoe. **2.** A delicate fabric woven in an open weblike pattern. ►*v.* **laced, lac•ing 1.** To draw together and tie the laces of. **2.** To intertwine: *lace garlands through a trellis.* **3.** To add a touch of liquor to. [< OFr. *las*, noose < Lat. *laqueus.*] —**lac′er** *n.* —**lac′y** *adj.*

lac•er•ate (lăs′ə-rāt′) ►*v.* **-at•ed, -at•ing 1.** To rip or tear (e.g., the skin). **2.** To wound. [< Lat. *lacer*, torn.] —**lac′er•a′tion** *n.*

lach•ry•mal also **lac•ri•mal** (lăk′rə-məl) ►*adj.* Of tears or the tear-producing glands. [< Lat. *lacrima*, tear.]

lach•ry•mose (lăk′rə-mōs′) ►*adj.* Tearful. [Lat. *lacrimōsus.*] —**lach′ry•mose′ly** *adv.*

lack (lăk) ►*n.* A deficiency or absence. ►*v.* **1.** To be without any or much of. **2.** To be wanting or deficient. [ME.]

lack•a•dai•si•cal (lăk′ə-dā′zĭ-kəl) ►*adj.* Lacking spirit, liveliness, or interest; languid. [< *lackaday*, an exclamation of regret.] —**lack′a•dai′si•cal•ly** *adv.* —**lack′a•dai′si•cal•ness** *n.*

lack•ey (lăk′ē) ►*n., pl.* **-eys 1.** A footman. **2.** A servile follower; toady. [< OFr. *laquais.*]

lack•lus•ter (lăk′lŭs′tər) ►*adj.* Lacking brightness, luster, or vitality. See Syns at **dull.**

la•con•ic (lə-kŏn′ĭk) ►*adj.* Using few words; terse. [< Gk. *Lakōnikos*, Spartan.] —**la•con′i•cal•ly** *adv.*

La Co•ru•ña (lä′ kə-ro͞on′yə) A city of NW Spain on the Atlantic. Pop. 248,293.

lac•quer (lăk′ər) ►*n.* Any of various clear or colored synthetic or resinous coatings used to impart a high gloss to surfaces. [< Ar. *lakk*, LAC.] —**lac′quer** *v.*

la•crosse (lə-krôs′, -krŏs′) ►*n.* A game of Native American origin played on a field by two teams using long-handled sticks with webbed pouches to maneuver a ball into the opposing team's goal. [< Fr. *(jeu de) la crosse*, (game of) the hooked stick.]

lac•tate (lăk′tāt′) ►*v.* **-tat•ed, -tat•ing.** To secrete or produce milk. —**lac•ta′tion** *n.*

lac•tic (lăk′tĭk) ►*adj.* Of or derived from milk.

lactic acid ►*n.* A syrupy liquid, $C_3H_6O_3$, present in sour milk, molasses, various fruits, and wines.

lacto– or **lact–** ►*pref.* Milk: *lactate.* [< Lat. *lac, lact-*, milk.]

lac•tose (lăk′tōs′) ►*n.* A white crystalline sugar, $C_{12}H_{22}O_{11}$, obtained from whey and used in infant foods, bakery products, confections, and pharmaceuticals.

la•cu•na (lə-kyo͞o′nə) ►*n., pl.* **-nae** (-nē) or **-nas 1.** An empty space; gap. **2.** *Anat.* A cavity or depression. [Lat. *lacūna*, pool.] —**la•cu′nal** *adj.*

lad (lăd) ►*n.* A boy or young man. [ME *ladde.*]

lad•der (lăd′ər) ►*n.* **1.** A structure consisting of two long sides crossed by parallel rungs, used to climb up and down. **2.** A series of ranked stages or levels. [< OE *hlǣder.*]

lad•der-back (lăd′ər-băk′) ►*n.* A chair back

made of two upright posts connected by horizontal slats.

ladder-back

lade (lād) ►*v.* **lad•ed, lad•en** (lād′n) or **lad•ed, lad•ing 1.** To load or be loaded with or as if with cargo. **2.** To burden; weigh down. [< OE *hladan.*] —**lad′en** *adj.*

lad•ing (lā′dĭng) ►*n.* Cargo; freight.

La•di•no (lə-dē′nō) ►*n.* A Romance language with Hebrew elements, spoken by Sephardic Jews esp. in the Balkans. [Sp. < Lat. *Latīnus.*]

la•dle (lād′l) ►*n.* A long-handled spoon with a deep bowl for serving liquids. [< OE *hlædel.*] —**la′dle** *v.* —**la′dler** *n.*

Lad•o•ga (lä′də-gə), **Lake.** A lake of NW Russia NE of St. Petersburg.

la•dy (lā′dē) ►*n., pl.* **-dies 1.** A woman of superior social position. **2.** A well-mannered woman. **3.** A woman who is the head of a household. **4.** A woman. **5. Lady** *Chiefly Brit.* A general feminine title of nobility and other rank. [< OE *hlǣfdige.*] —**la′dy•like′** *adj.*

la•dy•bird (lā′dē-bûrd′) ►*n.* See **ladybug.**

la•dy•bug (lā′dē-bŭg′) ►*n.* A small, rounded, usu. brightly colored beetle, often reddish with black spots.

la•dy•fin•ger (lā′dē-fĭng′gər) ►*n.* A small finger-shaped sponge cake.

lady in waiting ►*n., pl.* **ladies in waiting.** A lady appointed to attend a queen or princess.

la•dy•ship also **La•dy•ship** (lā′dē-shĭp′) ►*n.* Used with *Your* or *Her* as a title for a woman holding the rank of lady.

la•dy's slipper (lā′dēz) ►*n.* An orchid having flowers with an inflated pouchlike lip.

La•fay•ette (lăf′ē-ĕt′, lä′fē-), Marquis de. 1757–1834. French soldier and politician.

La Fon•taine (lə fŏn-tān′, lä fôɴ-tĕn′), **Jean de.** 1621–95. French writer.

lag (lăg) ►*v.* **lagged, lag•ging 1.** To fail to keep up a pace; straggle. **2.** To weaken or slacken gradually. ►*n.* **1.** The act of lagging. **2.** The extent or duration of lagging. [< *lag*, last person.] —**lag′ger** *n.*

la•ger (lä′gər) ►*n.* A beer aged from six weeks to six months to allow sedimentation. [< Ger. *Lagerbier* < *lagern*, to store.]

lag•gard (lăg′ərd) ►*n.* One that lags; straggler. —**lag′gard•ly** *adv.* —**lag′gard•ness** *n.*

la•gniappe (lăn′yəp, lăn-yăp′) ►*n. Regional* An extra item or amount; bonus. [< Am.Sp. *(la) ñapa*, (the) gift, poss. < Quechua *yapay*, give more.]

Regional Note: *Lagniappe,* which derives from Spanish and ultimately Quechua, came into the rich Creole dialect mixture of New Orleans and there acquired a French spelling. It is still used in the Gulf states, especially southern Louisiana, to denote a little bonus added to a purchase.

la•goon (lə-go͞on′) ►*n.* A shallow body of water, esp. one separated from a sea by sandbars or coral reefs. [< Lat. *lacūna*, pool.]

La•gos (lā′gŏs′, lä′gōs) The largest city of Nigeria, in the SW part on the Gulf of Guinea. Pop. 1,404,000.

La•hore (lə-hôr′, -hōr′) A city of NE Pakistan SE of Rawalpindi. Pop. 2,952,689.

laid (lād) ►*v.* P.t. and p.part. of **lay**[1]**.**

laid-back (lād′băk′) ►*adj. Informal* Relaxed and casual; easygoing.

lain (lān) ►*v.* P.part. of **lie**[1]**.**

lair (lâr) ►*n.* The den or dwelling of a wild animal. [< OE *leger.*]

lais•sez faire also **lais•ser faire** (lĕs′ā fâr′) ►*n.* Noninterference, esp. an economic doctrine that opposes governmental involvement in commerce. [< Fr., let (people) do (as they choose).] —**lais′sez-faire′** *adj.*

la•i•ty (lā′ĭ-tē) ►*n.* **1.** Laypeople collectively. **2.** Nonprofessionals.

lake (lāk) ►*n.* **1.** A large inland body of water. **2.** A large pool of liquid. [< Lat. *lacus.*]

La•ko•ta (lə-kō′tə) ►*n., pl.* **-ta** or **-tas.** See **Teton.**

lam (lăm) *Slang* ►*v.* **lammed, lam•ming.** To escape, as from prison. ►*n.* Flight, esp. from the law: *on the lam.* [?]

la•ma (lä′mə) ►*n.* A Buddhist monk of Tibet or Mongolia. [Tibetan *bla-ma.*]

La•ma•ism (lä′mə-ĭz′əm) ►*n.* Tibetan Buddhism. —**La′ma•ist** *n.* —**La′ma•is′tic** *adj.*

La•marck (lə-märk′, lä-), Chevalier de **Jean Baptiste Pierre Antoine de Monet.** 1744–1829. French naturalist.

lamb (lăm) ►*n.* **1a.** A young sheep. **b.** The flesh of a young sheep used as meat. **2.** A sweet, mild-mannered person. [< OE.]

Lamb, Charles. "Elia." 1775–1834. British critic and essayist.

lam•baste (lăm-bāst′) ►*v.* **-bast•ed, -bast•ing** *Informal* **1.** To give a thrashing to. See Syns at **beat. 2.** To scold sharply; berate. [Perh. *lam*, beat + BASTE[3].]

lamb•da (lăm′də) ►*n.* The 11th letter of the Greek alphabet. [Gk.]

lam•bent (lăm′bənt) ►*adj.* **1.** Flickering or glowing gently. **2.** Effortlessly light or brilliant: *lambent wit.* [< Lat. *lambere*, lick.] —**lam′ben•cy** *n.* —**lam′bent•ly** *adv.*

lamb•skin (lăm′skĭn′) ►*n.* The hide of a lamb or a fine leather made from it.

lame (lām) ►*adj.* **lam•er, lam•est 1.** Disabled so that movement, esp. walking, is difficult. **2.** Weak and ineffectual: *a lame excuse.* ►*v.* **lamed, lam•ing.** To make lame. [< OE *lama.*] —**lame′ly** *adv.* —**lame′ness** *n.*

la•mé (lă-mā′) ►*n.* A fabric woven with metallic threads. [Fr., ult. < Lat. *lamina*, thin plate.]

lame duck ►*n.* **1.** An elected officeholder continuing in office during the period between the election and inauguration of a successor. **2.** An ineffective person. —**lame′-duck′** *adj.*

la•mel•la (lə-mĕl′ə) ►*n., pl.* **-mel•lae** (-mĕl′ē′) or **-mel•las.** A thin scale, plate, or layer. [Lat. *lāmella*.] —**la•mel′lar, la•mel′late′** (lə-mĕl′āt′, lăm′ə-lāt′) *adj.*

la•ment (lə-mĕnt′) ►*v.* **1.** To express grief for or about; mourn. See Syns at **grieve. 2.** To regret deeply; deplore. ►*n.* **1.** An expression of grief; lamentation. **2.** A dirge or elegy. [< Lat. *lāmentārī*.] —**la•men′ta•ble** *adj.* —**la•men′ta•bly** *adv.* —**la•ment′er** *n.*

lam•en•ta•tion (lăm′ən-tā′shən) ►*n.* **1.** The act of lamenting. **2.** A lament. **3. Lamentations** *(takes sing. v.)* See table at **Bible.**

lam•i•na (lăm′ə-nə) ►*n., pl.* **-nae** (-nē′) or **-nas.** A thin plate, sheet, or layer. [Lat. *lāmina*.] —**lam′i•nar, lam′i•nal** *adj.*

lam•i•nate (lăm′ə-nāt′) ►*v.* **-nat•ed, -nat•ing 1.** To form into a thin sheet. **2.** To divide into thin layers. **3.** To bond together in layers. ►*adj.* (-nĭt, -nāt′) also **lam•i•nat•ed** (-nā′tĭd). Consisting of thin layers. —**lam′i•na′tion** *n.* —**lam′i•na′tor** *n.*

lamp (lămp) ►*n.* **1.** A device that generates light, heat, or therapeutic radiation. **2.** A vessel containing oil or alcohol burned through a wick for illumination. [< Gk. *lampas*, torch.]

lamp•black (lămp′blăk′) ►*n.* Fine soot used as a pigment and in matches, explosives, and fertilizers.

lam•poon (lăm-po͞on′) ►*n.* A written attack ridiculing a person, group, or institution. [Poss. < Fr. *lampons*, let us drink.] —**lam•poon′** *v.* —**lam•poon′er, lam•poon′ist** *n.*

lam•prey (lăm′prē) ►*n., pl.* **-preys.** A primitive elongated fish having a jawless sucking mouth. [< Med.Lat. *lampreda*.]

LAN (lăn) ►*n.* A system that links computers and related equipment to form a network, as within an office. [*l(ocal) a(rea) n(etwork)*.]

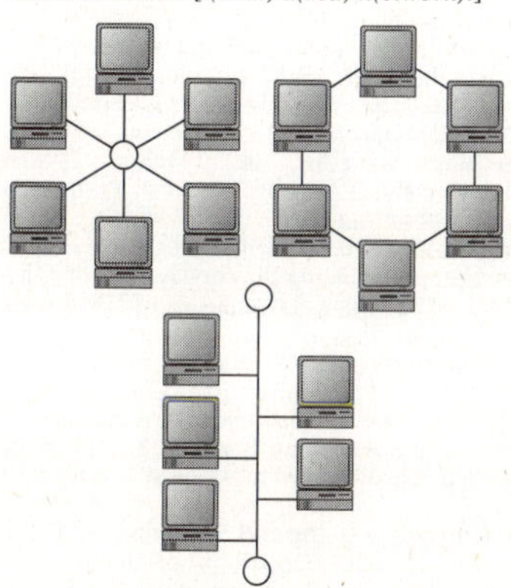

LAN
top: star and ring configurations
bottom: bus configuration

la•nai (lə-nī′) ►*n., pl.* **-nais.** A veranda or patio: See Regional Note at **ukulele.** [Hawaiian.]

Lanai. An island of central HI W of Maui.

lance (lăns) ►*n.* **1.** A thrusting weapon with a long shaft and a sharp metal head. **2.** A similar implement for spearing fish. **3.** *Medic.* See **lancet.** ►*v.* **lanced, lanc•ing 1.** To pierce with a lance. **2.** *Medic.* To make a surgical incision in; cut into: *lance a boil.* [< Lat. *lancea*.]

lance corporal ►*n.* A rank in the US Marine Corps below corporal.

Lan•ce•lot (lăn′sə-lət, -lŏt′, län′-) ►*n.* In Arthurian legend, a Knight of the Round Table whose love affair with Queen Guinevere resulted in a war with King Arthur.

lanc•er (lăn′sər) ►*n.* A cavalryman armed with a lance.

lan•cet (lăn′sĭt) ►*n.* A surgical knife with a short, wide, pointed double-edged blade.

Lan•chow (län′jō′) See **Lanzhou.**

land (lănd) ►*n.* **1.** The solid ground of the earth. **2.** A distinct area or region: *desert land.* **3.** A nation, country, or realm. **4.** Public or private landed property; real estate. ►*v.* **1.** To put or arrive on land after traveling by water or air. **2.** *Informal* To arrive or cause to arrive in a place or condition: *land in jail.* **3.** To catch by or as if by fishing. **4.** To come to rest; alight. [< OE.]

land•ed (lăn′dĭd) ►*adj.* **1.** Owning land. **2.** Consisting of land.

land•fall (lănd′fôl′) ►*n.* **1.** The act or an instance of sighting or reaching land. **2.** The land sighted or reached.

land•fill (lănd′fĭl′) ►*n.* A method of solid waste disposal in which refuse is buried between layers of dirt in low-lying ground. —**land′fill′** *v.*

land grant ►*n.* A government grant of public land for a railroad, highway, or state college.

land•hold•er (lănd′hōl′dər) ►*n.* One who owns land. —**land′hold′ing** *n.*

land•ing (lăn′dĭng) ►*n.* **1.** The act or site of coming to land or rest. **2.** A platform at the top, bottom, or between flights of stairs.

landing gear ►*n.* The structure supporting an aircraft on the ground.

landing strip ►*n.* An aircraft runway without airport facilities.

land•la•dy (lănd′lā′dē) ►*n.* A woman who owns and rents land, buildings, or dwelling units.

land•locked (lănd′lŏkt′) ►*adj.* **1.** Surrounded or almost surrounded by land. **2.** Confined to inland waters, as certain salmon.

land•lord (lănd′lôrd′) ►*n.* One who owns and rents land, buildings, or dwelling units.

land•lub•ber (lănd′lŭb′ər) ►*n.* A person unfamiliar with the sea or seamanship. [LAND + *lubber*, clumsy person.] —**land′lub′ber•ly** *adj.*

land•mark (lănd′märk′) ►*n.* **1.** A prominent identifying feature of a landscape. **2.** A fixed marker indicating a boundary line. **3.** A historically significant event or site.

land•mass (lănd′măs′) ►*n.* A large area of land.

land mine ►*n.* An explosive mine laid usu. just below the surface of the ground.

land-of•fice business (lănd′ô′fĭs, -ŏf′ĭs) ►*n.* A thriving or rapidly moving volume of trade.

land-poor (lănd′po͝or′) ►*adj.* Owning much land but lacking the capital to improve it.

land•scape (lănd′skāp′) ►*n.* **1.** A view or vista of scenery on land. **2.** A picture depicting such a view. ►*v.* **-scaped, -scap•ing.** To improve (a section of ground) by contouring and decorative planting. [< MDu. *landscap*, region.] —**land′scap′er** *n.*

land•slide (lănd′slīd′) ►*n.* **1.** The downward sliding of a mass of earth and rock. **2.** An overwhelming victory, esp. in an election.

land•ward (lănd′wərd) ►*adv. & adj.* To or toward land. —**land′wards** *adv.*

lane (lān) ►*n.* **1.** A narrow way or road. **2.** A set passage or course, as for vehicles or ships. [< OE.]

Lang•ley (lăng′lē), **Samuel Pierpoint.** 1834–1906. Amer. astronomer and aviation pioneer.

lan•guage (lăng′gwĭj) ►*n.* **1a.** Communication of thoughts and feelings through a system of arbitrary signals, such as voice sounds, gestures, or written symbols. **b.** Such a system, including rules for combining components, such as words. **c.** Such a system used by a particular group or community. **2.** *Comp. Sci.* A system of symbols and rules used for communication with or between computers. **3.** The special vocabulary of a scientific, professional, or other group. **4.** A particular style of speech or writing: *poetic language.* **5.** Communication between nonhumans. [< OFr. *langue*, tongue < Lat. *lingua.*]

Lan•gue•doc (läng-dôk′, läɴg-) A former province of S-central France on an arm of the Mediterranean Sea W of the Rhone R.

lan•guid (lăng′gwĭd) ►*adj.* **1.** Lacking energy or vitality; weak. **2.** Apathetic; listless. **3.** Lacking force; slow. [< Lat. *languidus.*] —**lan′guid•ly** *adv.* —**lan′guid•ness** *n.*

lan•guish (lăng′gwĭsh) ►*v.* **1.** To lose strength or vigor. **2.** To exist in miserable conditions; be neglected. **3.** To become downcast; pine. **4.** To affect a wistful or languid air. [< Lat. *languēre.*]

lan•guor (lăng′gər, lăng′ər) ►*n.* **1.** Lack of physical or mental energy; lethargy. **2.** A dreamy, lazy mood or quality. [< Lat. < *languēre*, languish.] —**lan′guor•ous** *adj.* —**lan′guor•ous•ly** *adv.*

La Ni•ña (lä nēn′yä) ►*n.* A periodic cooling of the ocean surface off the W coast of South America that affects Pacific and other weather patterns. [Am.Sp., the girl (to distinguish it from El Niño).]

lank (lăngk) ►*adj.* **-er, -est 1.** Long and lean. **2.** Long, straight, and limp: *lank hair.* [< OE *hlanc.*] —**lank′ly** *adv.* —**lank′ness** *n.*

lank•y (lăng′kē) ►*adj.* **-i•er, -i•est.** Tall, thin, and ungainly. —**lank′i•ly** *adv.* —**lank′i•ness** *n.*

lan•o•lin (lăn′ə-lĭn) ►*n.* A fatty substance obtained from wool and used in soaps, cosmetics, and ointments. [< Lat. *lāna*, wool.]

Lan•sing (lăn′sĭng) The capital of MI, in the S-central part NW of Detroit. Pop. 127,321.

lan•tern (lăn′tərn) ►*n.* An often portable case with transparent or translucent sides for holding and protecting a light. [< Gk. *lamptēr.*]

lan•tha•nide (lăn′thə-nīd′) ►*n.* See **rare-earth element.** [LANTHAN(UM) + -IDE.]

lan•tha•num (lăn′thə-nəm) ►*n. Symbol* **La** A soft, silvery-white rare-earth element used esp. in glass manufacture. At. no. 57. See table at **element.** [< Gk. *lanthanein*, escape notice.]

lan•yard also **lan•iard** (lăn′yərd) ►*n.* **1.** *Naut.* A short rope used for securing rigging. **2.** A cord worn around the neck for carrying something, such as a whistle. [< OFr. *laniere*, strap.]

Lan•zhou also **Lan•chow** (län′jō′). A city of central China on the Huang He (Yellow R.) N of Chengdu. Pop. 1,617,761.

Lao (lou) ►*n., pl.* **Lao** or **Laos** (louz) **1.** A member of a Buddhist people of Laos and Thailand. **2.** The Tai language of the Lao.

La•os (lous, lā′ŏs′) A country of SE Asia. Cap. Vientiane. Pop. 4,742,000. —**La•o′tian** (lā-ō′shən, lou′shən) *adj. & n.*

Lao Tzu also **Lao-tse** (lou′dzŭ′). fl. 6th cent. B.C. Chinese philosopher.

lap[1] (lăp) ►*n.* **1.** The front area from the waist to the knees of a seated person. **2.** The portion of a garment that covers the lap. [< OE *læppa*, flap of a garment.] —**lap′ful′** *n.*

lap[2] (lăp) ►*v.* **lapped, lap•ping 1.** To place or lay (something) so as to overlap another. **2.** To fold or wrap or wind around (something); encircle. **3.** To get ahead of (an opponent) in a race by one or more laps. ►*n.* **1.** A part that overlaps. **2.** One complete round or circuit, esp. of a racetrack. **3.** A segment or stage, as of a trip. [ME *lappen* < *lappe*, LAP[1].]

lap[3] (lăp) ►*v.* **lapped, lap•ping 1.** To take in (a liquid or food) with the tongue. **2.** To wash against with soft liquid sounds: *waves lapping the shore.* —***phrasal verb:* lap up** To receive eagerly. [< OE *lapian.*] —**lap** *n.*

La Paz (lə päz′, lä päs′) The administrative capital of Bolivia, in the W part. Pop. 784,976.

lap belt ►*n.* A seat belt that fastens across the lap.

lap•board (lăp′bôrd′, -bōrd′) ►*n.* A flat board held on the lap and used as a table or desk.

lap dog ►*n.* A small, easily held pet dog.

la•pel (lə-pĕl′) ►*n.* The part of a garment that is an extension of the collar and folds back against the breast. [< LAP[1].] —**la•peled′, la•pelled′** *adj.*

lap•i•dar•y (lăp′ĭ-dĕr′ē) ►*n., pl.* **-ies.** One who cuts and polishes gems. ►*adj.* **1.** Of precious stones or the art of working with them. **2.** Concise and polished: *lapidary prose.* [< Lat. *lapis*, *lapid-*, stone.]

lap•in (lăp′ĭn, lä-păɴ′) ►*n.* Rabbit fur. [Fr.]

lap•is laz•u•li (lăp′ĭs lăz′ə-lē, -yə-, lăzh′ə-) ►*n.* An opaque blue semiprecious gemstone. [< Med.Lat. *lapis lazulī.*]

La•place (lə-pläs′, lä-), Marquis **Pierre Simon de.** 1749–1827. French mathematician and astronomer.

Lap•land (lăp′lănd′, -lənd) A region of extreme N Europe including N Norway, Sweden, and Finland and the Kola Peninsula of NW Russia. —**Lap′land•er** *n.*

La Pla•ta (lä plä′tä) A city of E-central Argentina SE of Buenos Aires. Pop. 520,647.

Lapp (lăp) ►*n.* **1.** A member of a nomadic herding people inhabiting Lapland. **2.** Any of the Finnic languages of the Lapps. —**Lap′pish** *adj.*

lapse (lăps) ►*v.* **lapsed, laps•ing 1.** To fall from a previous standard, as of quality. **2.** To pass or come to an end, esp. gradually. **3.** To be no longer valid or active; expire. ►*n.* **1.** A minor or temporary failure; slip. **2.** A deterioration or decline. **3.** A period of time; interval. **4.** *Law* The termination of a right or privilege through disuse, neglect, or death. [< Lat. *lābī*, *lāps-*.] —**laps′er** *n.*

lap•top (lăp′tŏp′) ►*n.* A portable computer small enough to use on one's lap.

lap•wing (lăp′wĭng′) ►*n.* Any of several crested Old World birds related to the plovers. [< OE *hlēapewince.*]

La Ra•za (lä rä′sä) ►*n.* Mexicans or Mexican Americans considered as a group. [Am.Sp., the people.]

lar•board (lär′bərd) ►*n. Naut.* See **port²**. [< ME *laddebord.*] —**lar′board** *adj.*

lar•ce•ny (lär′sə-nē) ►*n., pl.* **-nies.** The stealing of another's personal property; theft. [< Lat. *latrōcinium* < *latrō*, robber.] —**lar′ce•nous** (-nəs) *adj.*

larch (lärch) ►*n.* A deciduous, cone-bearing tree having needlelike leaves and heavy durable wood. [< Lat. *larix.*]

lard (lärd) ►*n.* The white rendered fat of a hog. ►*v.* **1.** To insert strips of fat in (meat) before cooking. **2.** To embellish throughout: *larded the report with quotations.* [< Lat. *lārdum.*] —**lard′y** *adj.*

lar•der (lär′dər) ►*n.* A place, such as a pantry, where food is stored.

La•re•do (lə-rā′dō) A city of S TX SSW of San Antonio. Pop. 122,899.

large (lärj) ►*adj.* **larg•er, larg•est 1.** Of greater than average size or amount; big. **2.** Broad; comprehensive. **3.** Tolerant; liberal. —***idiom:* at large 1.** Not in captivity; at liberty. **2.** As a whole; in general. **3.** Not representing a particular country, state, or district. [< Lat. *largus.*] —**large′ness** *n.*
Syns: *large, big, great* ***Ant:*** *small* ***adj.***

large calorie ►*n.* See **calorie** 1.

large intestine ►*n.* The portion of the intestine from the ileum to the anus.

large•ly (lärj′lē) ►*adv.* **1.** For the most part; mainly. **2.** On a large scale; amply.

large-scale (lärj′skāl′) ►*adj.* **1.** Large in scope or extent. **2.** Drawn or made large to show detail.

lar•gess also **lar•gesse** (lär-zhĕs′, -jĕs′, lär′jĕs′) ►*n.* **1.** Liberality in giving. **2.** Money or gifts bestowed. [< OFr. *largesse.*]

lar•go (lär′gō) ►*adv. & adj. Mus.* In a slow, solemn tempo. [Ital.] —**lar′go** *n.*

la•ri (lä′rē) ►*n.* See table at **currency.** [Georgian.]

lar•i•at (lăr′ē-ət) ►*n.* See **lasso.** [Sp. *la reata*, the lariat.]

lark¹ (lärk) ►*n.* **1.** Any of various chiefly Old World birds with a sustained, melodious song. **2.** Any of several similar birds. [< OE *lāwerce.*]

lark² (lärk) ►*n.* A carefree adventure or prank. ►*v.* To engage in fun or pranks. [Perh. < ON *leikr*, play.] —**lark′er** *n.* —**lark′ish** *adj.*

lark•spur (lärk′spûr′) ►*n.* See **delphinium.**

La Roche•fou•cauld (lä rōsh-fo͞o-kō′), Duc **François de.** 1613–80. French writer.

lar•va (lär′və) ►*n., pl.* **-vae** (-vē) or **-vas 1.** The newly hatched, wingless, often wormlike form of many insects. **2.** The newly hatched stage of any of various animals that differ markedly in appearance from the adult. [Lat. *lārva*, specter, mask.] —**lar′val** *adj.*

lar•yn•gi•tis (lăr′ĭn-jī′tĭs) ►*n.* Inflammation of the larynx. —**lar′yn•git′ic** (-jĭt′ĭk) *adj.*

lar•ynx (lăr′ĭngks) ►*n., pl.* **la•ryn•ges** (lə-rĭn′jēz) or **lar•ynx•es.** The part of the respiratory tract between the pharynx and the trachea, containing the vocal cords. [< Gk. *larunx.*] —**la•ryn′ge•al** (lə-rĭn′jē-əl) *adj.*

la•sa•gna also **la•sa•gne** (lə-zän′yə) ►*n.* Flat wide noodles, usu. baked in layers with sauce and cheese. [Ital.]

La Salle (lə săl′, lä), Sieur de. Title of Robert Cavelier 1643–87. French explorer in North America.

las•civ•i•ous (lə-sĭv′ē-əs) ►*adj.* **1.** Lustful; lecherous. **2.** Lewd; salacious. [< Lat. *lascīvus.*] —**las•civ′i•ous•ly** *adv.* —**las•civ′i•ous•ness** *n.*

la•ser (lā′zər) ►*n.* Any of several devices that convert incident electromagnetic radiation of mixed frequencies to one or more discrete frequencies of highly amplified and coherent radiation. [*l(ight) a(mplification by) s(timulated) e(mission of) r(adiation).*]

laser disk ►*n.* See **optical disk.**

laser printer ►*n.* A printer that uses a laser to produce an image on a rotating drum before electrostatically transferring the image to paper.

lash¹ (lăsh) ►*n.* **1.** A stroke or blow with or as if with a whip. **2.** A whip or its thong. **3.** An eyelash. ►*v.* **1.** To strike with or as if with a whip. **2.** To strike against with force or violence: *sleet lashing the roof.* **3.** To beat or swing rapidly; thrash. **4.** To attack verbally: *lashed out at her critics.* **5.** To goad; sting. [ME.] —**lash′er** *n.*

lash² (lăsh) ►*v.* To secure or bind, as with a rope. [< Lat. *laqueāre*, ensnare.]

Las Pal•mas (läs päl′mäs) The chief city of the Canary Is. of Spain. Pop. 359,611.

lass (lăs) ►*n.* **1.** A girl or young woman. **2.** A sweetheart. [ME *las.*]

las•sie (lăs′ē) ►*n.* A lass.

las•si•tude (lăs′ĭ-to͞od′, -tyo͞od′) ►*n.* A state of weariness, lethargy, or listlessness. [< Lat. *lassus*, weary.]

las•so (lăs′ō, lă-so͞o′) ►*n., pl.* **-sos** or **-soes.** A long rope with a noose at one end, used esp. to catch horses and cattle. [Sp. *lazo.* See LACE.] —**las′so** *v.* —**las′so•er** *n.*

last¹ (lăst) ►*adj.* **1.** Being, coming, or placed after all others; final. **2.** Most recent; latest. **3.** Most authoritative or conclusive. **4.** Least likely or expected: *the last person we would have suspected.* ►*adv.* **1.** After all others. **2.** Most recently. **3.** At the end; finally. ►*n.* **1.** One that is last. **2.** The end. —***idiom:* at last** Finally. [< OE *latost.*] —**last′ly** *adv.*

last² (lăst) ►*v.* **1.** To continue in existence; go on. **2.** To remain adequate or sufficient. [< OE *lǣstan.*]

last³ (lăst) ►*n.* A foot-shaped block or form used in making or repairing shoes. [< OE *lǣst*, sole of the foot.]

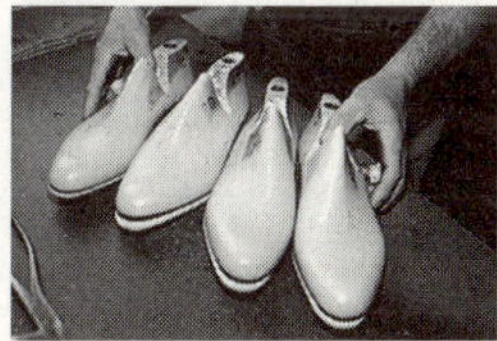

last³

last-ditch (lăst′dĭch′) ►*adj.* Done as a final recourse; desperate.

last-in, first-out (lăst′ĭn′ fûrst′out′) ►*n.* A method of inventory accounting in which the most recently acquired items are assumed to have been the first sold.

last•ing (lăs′tĭng) ►*adj.* Continuing or remaining for a long time; enduring. —**last′ing•ly** *adv.* —**last′ing•ness** *n.*

Last Judgment ▸ *n. Theol.* The final judgment by God of all humankind.

last rites ▸ *pl.n.* Rites performed for one in danger of dying or for a burial.

last straw ▸ *n.* The last of a series of annoyances or setbacks that leads to a final loss of patience or hope.

Last Supper ▸ *n.* Jesus's supper with his disciples on the night before his crucifixion.

Las Ve•gas (läs vā′gəs) A city of SE NV near the CA and AZ borders. Pop. 258,295.

lat. ▸ *abbr.* latitude

Lat. ▸ *abbr.* Latin

latch (lăch) ▸ *n.* **1.** A fastening or lock, as for a door or gate, typically consisting of a movable bar that fits into a notch. **2.** A spring lock opened by a key. ▸ *v.* To close with a latch. —***idiom:*** **latch on to** (or **onto**) **1.** To get hold of; obtain. **2.** To cling to. [< OE *læccan*, seize.]

late (lāt) ▸ *adj.* **lat•er, lat•est 1.** Coming, occurring, or remaining after the proper or expected time. See Syns at **tardy. 2.** Occurring at an advanced hour. **3.** Of or toward the end. **4.** Recent. **5.** Recently deceased: *in memory of the late explorer.* ▸ *adv.* **later, latest 1.** After the expected or usual time. **2.** At or into an advanced period or stage. **3.** Recently. —***idiom:*** **of late** Recently. [< OE *læt.*] —**late′ness** *n.*

Usage: It is technically correct to use a phrase such as *our late treasurer* to refer to a person who is still alive but who no longer holds the relevant post, but the use of *former* in this context will ensure that no embarrassing misunderstanding is created.

late•com•er (lāt′kŭm′ər) ▸ *n.* **1.** One that arrives late. **2.** A recent arrival or participant.

Late Greek ▸ *n.* Greek in late antiquity and the early Byzantine period.

Late Latin ▸ *n.* Latin from the 3rd to the 7th cent. A.D.

late•ly (lāt′lē) ▸ *adv.* Not long ago; recently.

la•tent (lāt′nt) ▸ *adj.* Present or potential but not evident or active. [< Lat. *latēre*, lie hidden.] —**la′ten•cy** *n.* —**la′tent•ly** *adv.*

lat•er•al (lăt′ər-əl) ▸ *adj.* Of or situated at or on the side. ▸ *n. Football* A pass thrown sideways or backward. [< Lat. *latus, later-*, side.] —**lat′er•al** *v.* —**lat′er•al•ly** *adv.*

la•tex (lā′tĕks′) ▸ *n.* **1.** The milky sap of certain plants that coagulates on exposure to air. **2.** An emulsion of rubber or plastic globules in water, used in paints, adhesives, and various synthetic rubber products. [Lat., fluid.] —**la′tex′** *adj.*

lath (lăth) ▸ *n., pl.* **laths** (lă*th*z, lăths) **1.** A thin strip of wood or metal, usu. nailed in rows as a substructure for plaster, shingles, or tiles. **2.** A similarly used building material. [< OE *lætt.*]

lathe (lā*th*) ▸ *n.* A machine on which a piece of material, such as wood or metal, is spun and shaped against a fixed cutting tool. [ME.] —**lathe** *v.*

lath•er (lă*th*′ər) ▸ *n.* **1.** A foam formed esp. by soap agitated in water. **2.** Frothy sweat. **3.** *Informal* An agitated state; dither. ▸ *v.* To produce or coat with lather. [< OE *lēthran*, to lather.] —**lath′er•er** *n.* —**lath′er•y** *adj.*

Lat•in (lăt′n) ▸ *n.* **1.** The Indo-European language of the ancient Romans. **2.** A member of a Latin people, esp. a native or inhabitant of Latin America. ▸ *adj.* **1.** Relating to ancient Rome or its language or culture. **2.** Relating to the Romance languages or to the peoples that speak them. **3.** Relating to Latinos or their culture. **4.** Relating to the Roman Catholic Church. [< Lat. *Latīnus.*]

La•ti•na (lə-tē′nə, lă-) ▸ *n.* A Latino woman or girl. See Usage Note at **Hispanic.**

Latin America. The countries of the Western Hemisphere S of the US, esp. those speaking Spanish, Portuguese, or French. —**Latin American** *n.* —**Lat′in-A•mer′i•can** *adj.*

La•ti•no (lə-tē′nō, lă-) ▸ *n., pl.* **-nos 1.** A Latin American. **2.** A person of Latin-American descent, esp. one living in the US. See Usage Note at **Hispanic.** —**La•ti′no** *adj.*

lat•i•tude (lăt′ĭ-to͞od′, -tyo͞od′) ▸ *n.* **1a.** The angular distance north or south of the equator, measured in degrees along a meridian. **b.** A region considered in relation to this distance. **2.** Freedom from limitations. See Syns at **room. 3.** Extent; breadth. [< Lat. *lātitūdō* < *lātus*, wide.] —**lat′i•tu′din•al** *adj.* —**lat′i•tu′di•nal•ly** *adv.*

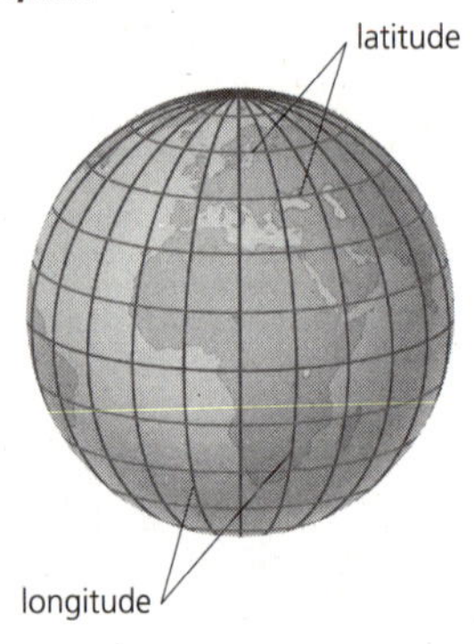

latitude

lat•i•tu•di•nar•i•an (lăt′ĭ-to͞od′n-âr′ē-ən, -tyo͞od′-) ▸ *adj.* Holding or expressing tolerant views, esp. in religious matters. —**lat′i•tu′di•nar′i•an** *n.* —**lat′i•tu′di•nar′i•an•ism** *n.*

La•ti•um (lā′shē-əm, -shəm) An ancient country of W-central Italy bordering on the Tyrrhenian Sea.

lat•ke (lät′kə) ▸ *n.* A pancake, esp. one made of grated potato. [Yiddish.]

La Tour (lə to͝or′, lä to͝or′), **Georges de.** 1593–1652. French painter.

la•trine (lə-trēn′) ▸ *n.* A communal toilet. [< Lat. *lavātrīna*, bath.]

lats (läts) ▸ *n., pl.* **la•ti** (lä′tē′). See table at **currency.** [Latvian.]

lat•te (lä′tā) ▸ *n.* A caffe latte.

lat•ter (lăt′ər) ▸ *adj.* **1.** Being the second of two persons or things mentioned. **2.** Near the end. [< OE *lætra.*] —**lat′ter•ly** *adv.*

lat•ter-day (lăt′ər-dā′) ▸ *adj.* Belonging to present or recent times; modern.

Latter-day Saint ▸ *n.* See **Mormon.**

lat•tice (lăt′ĭs) ▸ *n.* **1a.** An open framework made of interwoven strips, as of metal or wood. **b.** A structure, such as a window, made of or containing a lattice. **2.** *Phys.* A regular, periodic configuration of points throughout an area or space. [< OFr. *lattis.*] —**lat′ticed** *adj.* —**lat′tice•work′** *n.*

Lat•vi•a (lăt′vē-ə) A country of N Europe on the Baltic Sea. Cap. Riga. Pop. 2,548,000.

Lat•vi•an (lăt′vē-ən) ►*n.* **1.** A native or inhabitant of Latvia. **2.** The Baltic language of the Latvians. —**Lat′vi•an** *adj.*

laud (lôd) ►*v.* To praise highly. ►*n.* Praise. [< Lat. *laudāre.*] —**laud•a′tion** *n.* —**laud′er** *n.*

laud•a•ble (lô′də-bəl) ►*adj.* Praiseworthy; commendable. —**laud′a•bil′i•ty, laud′a•ble•ness** *n.* —**laud′a•bly** *adv.*

lau•da•num (lôd′n-əm) ►*n.* A tincture of opium, formerly used as a drug. [NLat.]

laud•a•to•ry (lô′də-tôr′ē, -tōr′ē) ►*adj.* Expressing or conferring praise.

laugh (lăf) ►*v.* **1.** To express mirth, delight, or derision by a series of unarticulated sounds. **2.** To affect by laughter: *laughed them off the stage.* ►*n.* **1.** The sound or act of laughing. **2.** *Informal* Something amusing or absurd. **3.** often **laughs** *Informal* Fun; amusement. [< OE *hlæhhan.*] —**laugh′ing•ly** *adv.*

laugh•a•ble (lăf′ə-bəl) ►*adj.* Causing or deserving laughter or derision. —**laugh′a•ble•ness** *n.* —**laugh′a•bly** *adv.*

laugh•ing•stock (lăf′ĭng-stŏk′) ►*n.* An object of jokes or ridicule; a butt.

laugh•ter (lăf′tər) ►*n.* The act or sound of laughing. [< OE *hleahtor.*]

launch[1] (lônch, länch) ►*v.* **1a.** To propel with force; hurl. **b.** To set or thrust in motion: *launch a rocket.* **2.** To put (a boat) into the water. **3.** To set going; initiate. [< Lat. *lanceāre*, wield a lance < *lancea*, lance.] —**launch** *n.* —**launch′er** *n.*

launch[2] (lônch, länch) ►*n.* An open motorboat. [< Malay *lancha.*]

launch pad or **launch•ing pad** (lôn′chĭng, län′-) ►*n.* The base or platform from which a rocket or space vehicle is launched.

laun•der (lôn′dər, län′-) ►*v.* **1.** To wash or wash and iron (clothes or linens). **2.** To disguise the source or nature of (money) by channeling through an intermediate agent. [< Lat. *lavandāria*, things to be washed < *lavāre*, wash.] —**laun′der•er** *n.* —**laun′dress** (-drĭs) *n.*

Laun•dro•mat (lôn′drə-măt′, län′-) ► A service mark for a commercial establishment with washing machines and dryers.

laun•dry (lôn′drē, län′-) ►*n., pl.* **-dries 1.** Soiled or laundered clothes. **2.** A place where laundering is done.

lau•re•ate (lôr′ē-ĭt, lŏr′-) ►*n.* One awarded a prize for great achievements esp. in the arts or sciences. [< Lat. *laureātus*, adorned with laurel.] —**lau′re•ate** *adj.* —**lau′re•ate•ship′** *n.*

lau•rel (lôr′əl, lŏr′-) ►*n.* **1.** A Mediterranean evergreen tree having aromatic leaves. **2.** Any of several similar shrubs or trees, such as the mountain laurel. **3.** often **laurels a.** A wreath of laurel conferred as a mark of honor. **b.** Honor and glory. [< Lat. *laurus.*]

Lau•ren•tian Mountains (lô-rĕn′shən) A range of S Quebec, Canada, N of the St. Lawrence and Ottawa rivers.

Laurentian Plateau. A plateau region of E Canada from the Great Lakes and the St. Lawrence R. to the Arctic.

Lau•sanne (lō-zăn′, -zän′) A city of W Switzerland on the N shore of Lake Geneva. Pop. 117,303.

la•va (lä′və, lăv′ə) ►*n.* **1.** Molten rock that reaches the earth's surface through a volcano or fissure. **2.** Rock formed by the cooling and solidifying of lava. [Ital.]

lav•age (lăv′ĭj, lä-väzh′) ►*n.* A washing, esp. of a hollow bodily organ. [< Lat. *lavāre*, wash.]

La•val (lə-văl′, lä-väl′) A city of S Quebec, Canada, on an island opposite Montreal. Pop. 314,398.

lav•a•liere (lăv′ə-lîr′) ►*n.* A pendant worn on a chain around the neck. [Fr. *lavallière*, type of necktie, after the Duchesse de *la Vallière* (1644–1710).]

la•vash (lə-văsh′) ►*n.* A thin leavened bread of Armenian origin. [Ult. < Turk. *lavaç.*]

lav•a•to•ry (lăv′ə-tôr′ē, -tōr′ē) ►*n., pl.* **-ries 1.** A room equipped with washing and toilet facilities; bathroom. **2.** A flush toilet. [< LLat. *lavātōrium* < Lat. *lavāre*, wash.]

lave (lāv) ►*v.* **laved, lav•ing.** To wash; bathe. [< Lat. *lavāre.*]

lav•en•der (lăv′ən-dər) ►*n.* **1.** Any of a genus of aromatic plants having small purplish flowers. **2.** A pale to light purple. [< Med.Lat. *lavendula.*] —**lav′en•der** *adj.*

lav•ish (lăv′ĭsh) ►*adj.* **1.** Extravagant. See Syns at **profuse. 2.** Immoderate in giving. ►*v.* To give or bestow in abundance; shower. [< OFr. *lavasse*, downpour < *laver*, LAVE.] —**lav′ish•er** *n.* —**lav′ish•ly** *adv.* —**lav′ish•ness** *n.*

La•voi•sier (lə-vwä′zē-ā′, lä-vwä-zyā′), **Antoine Laurent.** 1743–94. French chemist.

law (lô) ►*n.* **1a.** A rule of conduct established by custom, agreement, or authority. **b.** A body of such rules. **2.** A piece of enacted legislation. **3.** A judicial system or its workings. **4.** The science and study of law; jurisprudence. **5. Law** *Judaism* The Pentateuch. **6.** Something having unquestioned authority. **7.** A code of ethics or behavior. **8.** A formulation or generalization based on observed phenomena or consistent experience. [< OE *lagu.*]

law-a•bid•ing (lô′ə-bī′dĭng) ►*adj.* Adhering to the law.

law•break•er (lô′brā′kər) ►*n.* One that breaks the law.

law•ful (lô′fəl) ►*adj.* Allowed or recognized by law. —**law′ful•ly** *adv.* —**law′ful•ness** *n.*

law•less (lô′lĭs) ►*adj.* **1.** Unrestrained by or contrary to the law. **2.** Not governed by law. —**law′less•ly** *adv.* —**law′less•ness** *n.*

law•mak•er (lô′mā′kər) ►*n.* One who drafts laws; a legislator. —**law′mak′ing** *n.*

lawn[1] (lôn) ►*n.* A plot of grass, usu. tended or mowed. [< OFr. *launde*, pasture.]

lawn[2] (lôn) ►*n.* A fine light cotton or linen. [After *Laon*, France.]

Law•rence (lôr′əns, lŏr-), **D(avid) H(erbert).** 1885–1930. British writer.

Lawrence, Sir **Thomas.** 1769–1830. British painter.

Lawrence, T(homas) E(dward). "Lawrence of Arabia." 1888–1935. Welsh-born British soldier, adventurer, and writer.

law•ren•ci•um (lô-rĕn′sē-əm, lō-) ►*n. Symbol* **Lr** A short-lived, synthetic radioactive element. At. no. 103. See table at **element.** [After E.O. *Lawrence* (1901–58).]

law•suit (lô′so͞ot′) ►*n.* A case brought before a court for settlement.

law•yer (lô′yər) ►*n.* One who gives legal advice to clients and represents them in court. [ME *lauier* < *law*, LAW.] —**law′yer•ly** *adv.*

lax (lăks) ►*adj.* **-er, -est 1.** Lacking due care or concern. See Syns at **negligent. 2.** Not strict; lenient. **3.** Not taut; slack. See Syns at **loose.** [< Lat. *laxus*, loose.] —**lax•a′tion** *n.* —**lax′i•ty, lax′ness** *n.* —**lax′ly** *adv.*

lax•a•tive (lăk′sə-tĭv) ►*n.* A food or drug that stimulates evacuation of the bowels. [< Lat. *laxāre*, relax.] —**lax′a•tive** *adj.*

lay[1] (lā) ►*v.* **laid** (lād), **lay•ing 1.** To cause to lie down. **2.** To place in or bring to a specified condition. **3.** To bury. **4.** To put or set down: *lay railroad track.* **5.** To produce and deposit (eggs). **6.** To put against: *laid an ear to the door.* **7.** To put forward or impose: *lay the blame on us.* **8.** To devise; contrive. **9.** To spread: *lay paint on a canvas.* **10.** To prepare: *lay the table for lunch.* **11.** To present; submit: *laid the case before us.* —***phrasal verbs:* lay aside 1.** To give up; abandon. **2.** To save for the future. **lay away** To reserve for the future; save. **lay by** To save. **lay down 1.** To give up; surrender. **2.** To specify: *laid down the rules.* **lay in** To store for future use. **lay off 1.** To dismiss or suspend from a job. **2.** *Slang* To cease; quit. **lay out 1.** To make a plan for. **2.** To knock to the ground. **3.** To spend (money). **lay over** To make a stopover. **lay up 1.** To store for future needs. **2.** *Informal* To confine with an illness or injury. —***idioms:* lay of the land** The nature, arrangement, or disposition of something. **lay waste** To destroy. [< OE *lecgan.*]

lay[2] (lā) ►*adj.* **1.** Of or relating to the laity. **2.** Nonprofessional. [< Gk. *laos*, the people.]

lay[3] (lā) ►*n.* **1.** A narrative poem, such as one sung by medieval minstrels; ballad. **2.** A song; tune. [< OFr. *lai.*]

lay[4] (lā) ►*v.* P.t. of **lie**[1].

lay•a•way (lā′ə-wā′) ►*n.* A payment plan in which merchandise is reserved with a down payment until the balance is paid in full.

lay•er (lā′ər) ►*n.* **1.** One that lays, esp. a hen. **2.** A single thickness, coating, or level of material. ►*v.* To divide or form into layers.

lay•ette (lā-ĕt′) ►*n.* Clothing and other supplies for a newborn child. [Fr. < OFr. *laie*, box.]

lay•man (lā′mən) ►*n.* **1.** A man who is not a cleric. **2.** A man who is a nonprofessional. See Usage Note at **man.**

lay•off (lā′ôf′, -ŏf′) ►*n.* **1.** Dismissal of employees, esp. for lack of work. **2.** A period of temporary inactivity or rest.

lay•out (lā′out′) ►*n.* **1.** An arrangement or plan. **2.** *Print.* The overall design of a page, spread, or book.

lay•o•ver (lā′ō′vər) ►*n.* A short stop in a journey.

lay•per•son (lā′pûr′sən) ►*n.* A layman or laywoman. See Usage Note at **man.** —**lay′peo′ple** *n.*

lay•wom•an (lā′wo͝om′ən) ►*n.* **1.** A woman who is not a cleric. **2.** A woman who is a nonprofessional. See Usage Note at **man.**

Laz•a•rus (lăz′ər-əs). In the Bible, the brother of Mary and Martha.

Lazarus, Emma. 1849–87. Amer. writer.

laze (lāz) ►*v.* **lazed, laz•ing.** To be lazy; loaf.

la•zy (lā′zē) ►*adj.* **-zi•er, -zi•est 1.** Resistant to work or exertion; slothful. **2.** Slow-moving; sluggish. [Prob. of LGer. orig.] —**la′zi•ly** *adv.* —**la′zi•ness** *n.*

Syns: *lazy, idle, indolent, slothful* **adj.**

lazy Su•san (so͞o′zən) ►*n.* A revolving tray for condiments or food.

lb. ►*abbr.* **1.** libra (ancient Roman weight) **2.** pound (modern weight)

lc ►*abbr.* lowercase

L/C ►*abbr.* letter of credit

lcd ►*abbr.* least common denominator

LCD ►*abbr.* liquid-crystal display

lcm ►*abbr.* least common multiple

LCpl ►*abbr.* lance corporal

Ld. ►*abbr.* **1a.** limited **b.** limited company **2.** lord (title)

LDL (ĕl′dē-ĕl′) ►*n.* A complex of lipids and proteins that transports cholesterol in the blood, high levels of which may increase the risk of heart disease. [*l(ow-)d(ensity) l(ipoprotein).*]

L-do•pa (ĕl-dō′pə) ►*n.* A drug used to treat Parkinson's disease.

lea (lē, lā) ►*n.* A meadow. [< OE *lēah.*]

leach (lēch) ►*v.* To remove or be removed from by the action of a percolating liquid. [< OE **lece*, muddy stream.] —**leach′er** *n.*

lead[1] (lēd) ►*v.* **led** (lĕd), **lead•ing 1.** To guide, conduct, escort, or direct. See Syns at **guide. 2.** To influence; induce. **3.** To be ahead or be at the head of: *My name led the list.* **4.** To pursue; live: *lead an independent life.* **5.** To begin or open with, as in games: *led an ace.* **6.** To tend toward a certain goal or result: *policies that led to disaster.* —***phrasal verbs:* lead off** To begin; start. **lead on** To lure; entice. **lead up to** To proceed toward (a main topic) with preliminary remarks. ►*n.* **1.** The first or foremost position. **2.** The margin by which one is ahead. **3.** A clue. **4.** Command; leadership. **5.** An example; precedent. **6.** The principal role in a play. **7.** *Games* **a.** The prerogative or turn to make the first play. **b.** A card played first in a round. **8.** A leash. [< OE *lǣdan.*] —**lead′er** *n.* —**lead′er•ship′** *n.*

lead[2] (lĕd) ►*n.* **1.** *Symbol* **Pb** A malleable, bluish-white, dense metallic element used in solder, radiation shields, and alloys. At. no. 82. See table at **element. 2.** A weight used to make soundings. **3.** Bullets; shot. **4.** *Print.* A thin strip of metal used to separate lines of type. **5.** A thin stick of graphitic composition, used in pencils. ►*v.* **1.** To cover, line, weight, or fill with lead. **2.** To secure (window glass) with lead. **3.** To treat (e.g., gasoline or paint) with lead. [< OE *lēad.*] —**lead** *adj.*

lead•en (lĕd′n) ►*adj.* **1.** Made of lead. **2.** Heavy and inert. **3.** Downcast; depressed: *leaden spirits.* **4.** Dark gray: *a leaden sky.* —**lead′en•ly** *adv.* —**lead′en•ness** *n.*

lead•ing[1] (lē′dĭng) ►*adj.* **1.** In the first or front position. **2.** Chief; principal. **3.** Performing a lead in a theatrical production. **4.** Encouraging a desired response: *a leading question.*

lead•ing[2] (lĕd′ĭng) ►*n.* **1.** A border of lead, as around a windowpane. **2.** *Print.* The spacing between lines.

lead-time (lēd′tīm′) ►*n.* The time between the initial stage of a project and the appearance of results.

leaf (lēf) ►*n., pl.* **leaves** (lēvz) **1.** A usu. green, flattened plant structure attached to a stem and functioning as a principal organ of photosynthesis. **2.** A leaflike part. **3.** Leaves collectively; foliage. **4.** Any of the sheets of paper bound in a book. **5.** A very thin sheet of metal. **6.** A hinged or removable section for a table top. **7.** A movable section of a folding door, shutter, or gate. ►*v.* **1.** To produce leaves. **2.** To turn pages: *leafed through the catalog.* [< OE *lēaf.*] —**leaf′i•ness** *n.* —**leaf′less** *adj.* —**leaf′y** *adj.*

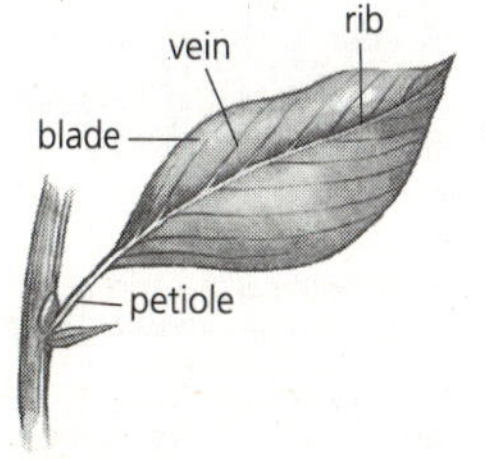

leaf

leaf•age (lē′fĭj) ►*n.* Foliage.

leaf•let (lē′flĭt) ►*n.* **1.** A small leaf or leaflike part. **2.** A printed handbill or flier. ►*v.* To hand out leaflets (to).

leaf spring ►*n.* A spring consisting of several layers of flexible metallic strips.

leaf•stalk or **leaf stalk** (lēf′stôk′) ►*n.* See **petiole.**

league[1] (lēg) ►*n.* **1.** An association or alliance for common action. **2.** An association of sports teams. **3.** A level of competition. [< Lat. *ligāre,* tie together.] —**league** *v.*

league[2] (lēg) ►*n.* A unit of distance equal to 3.0 mi (4.8 km). [< Lat. *leuga,* a unit of distance, of Celt. orig.]

League of Nations. A world organization (1920–46) to promote international cooperation and peace.

Le•ah (lē′ə). In the Bible, the first wife of Jacob.

leak (lēk) ►*v.* **1.** To escape or permit the escape of something through a breach or flaw. **2.** *Informal* To disclose or become known through a breach of secrecy. ►*n.* **1.** A crack or flaw that permits something to escape from or enter a container or conduit. **2a.** The act or instance of leaking. **b.** An amount leaked. **3.** *Informal* A disclosure of confidential information. [ME *leken.*] —**leak′er** *n.* —**leak′i•ness** *n.* —**leak′y** *adj.*

leak•age (lē′kĭj) ►*n.* **1.** The process of leaking. **2.** An amount that escapes by leaking.

lean[1] (lēn) ►*v.* **1.** To bend or cause to bend away from the vertical. See Syns at **slant. 2.** To incline one's weight so as to be supported. **3.** To rely for assistance or support. **4.** To have a tendency or preference. **5.** *Informal* To exert pressure. [< OE *hleonian.*]

lean[2] (lēn) ►*adj.* **-er, -est 1.** Not fleshy or fat; thin. **2.** Containing little or no fat: *a lean steak.* **3.** Not productive or prosperous; meager: *lean years* ►*n.* Meat with little or no fat. [< OE *hlǣne.*] —**lean′ly** *adv.* —**lean′ness** *n.*

lean•ing (lē′nĭng) ►*n.* A tendency; preference. See Syns at **predilection.**

lean-to (lēn′to͞o′) ►*n., pl.* **-tos 1.** A structure with a single-pitch roof attached to the side of a building. **2.** A shelter resembling this.

leap (lēp) ►*v.* **leaped** or **leapt** (lĕpt, lēpt), **leap•ing 1a.** To spring upward, as from the ground; jump. **b.** To jump over. **2.** To act quickly, abruptly, or impulsively. ►*n.* **1.** The act of leaping; jump. **2.** An abrupt transition. [< OE *hlēapan.*] —**leap′er** *n.*

leap•frog (lēp′frôg′, -frŏg′) ►*n.* A game in which a player bends over while the next in line leaps over him or her. —**leap′frog′** *v.*

leap year ►*n.* A year having 366 days, with Feb. 29 being the extra day.

Lear (lîr), **Edward.** 1812–88. British artist and writer.

learn (lûrn) ►*v.* **learned** also **learnt** (lûrnt), **learn•ing 1.** To gain knowledge, comprehension, or mastery of through experience or study. **2.** To memorize. **3.** To become informed. See Syns at **discover.** [< OE *leornian.*] —**learn′er** *n.*

learn•ed (lûr′nĭd) ►*adj.* Possessing systematic knowledge. —**learn′ed•ly** *adv.* —**learn′ed•ness** *n.*

Syns: *learned, erudite, scholarly* ***adj.***

learn•ing (lûr′nĭng) ►*n.* Acquired knowledge or skill.

learning curve ►*n.* A graph that depicts rate of learning, esp. a graph of progress in the mastery of a skill against the time required for such mastery.

learning disability ►*n.* Any of various cognitive disorders that impede the ability to learn. —**learn′ing-dis•a′bled** *adj.*

lease (lēs) ►*n.* A contract granting use or occupation of property during a specified period for a specified rent. ►*v.* **leased, leas•ing 1.** To grant use of by lease. **2.** To hold under lease. [< Lat. *laxāre,* let go.]

lease•hold (lēs′hōld′) ►*n.* **1.** Possession by lease. **2.** Property held by lease. —**lease′hold′er** *n.*

leash (lēsh) ►*n.* A restraining chain, rope, or strap attached to the collar or harness of an animal. [< Lat. *laxāre,* let go.] —**leash** *v.*

least (lēst) ►*adj.* Superl. of **little. 1.** Lowest in importance or rank. **2.** Smallest. ►*adv.* Superl. of **little.** To or in the lowest or smallest degree. ►*n.* The lowest or smallest. —***idioms:*** **at least 1.** Not less than. **2.** In any event. **in the least** At all. [< OE *lǣst.*]

least common denominator ►*n.* The least common multiple of the denominators of a set of fractions.

least common multiple ►*n.* The smallest quantity exactly divisible by two or more given quantities.

leath•er (lĕ*th*′ər) ►*n.* The dressed or tanned hide of an animal, usu. with the hair removed. [< OE *lether-.*] —**leath′er** *adj.* —**leath′er•y** *adj.*

leath•er•neck (lĕ*th*′ər-nĕk′) ►*n.* *Slang* A US Marine.

leave[1] (lēv) ►*v.* **left** (lĕft), **leav•ing 1.** To go out of or away (from). **2a.** To go without taking: *left my book on the bus.* **b.** To omit: *left out the best part.* **3.** To have as a remainder or result. **4.** To allow to remain in a specified state. **5.** To bequeath. **6.** To abandon; forsake. —***phrasal verb:*** **leave off** To stop; cease. [< OE *lǣfan.*]

leave[2] (lēv) ►*n.* **1.** Permission. See Syns at **permission. 2.** Official permission to be absent from work or duty. **3.** Departure; farewell. [< OE *lēaf.*]

leav•en (lĕv′ən) ►*n.* **1.** An agent, such as yeast, that causes batter or dough to rise, esp. by fermentation. **2.** An element that lightens or enlivens. ►*v.* **1.** To add a rising agent to. **2.** To lighten or enliven. [< Lat. *levāre*, raise.] —**leav′en** *adj.*

leav•en•ing (lĕv′ə-nĭng) ►*n.* A rising agent; leaven.

leaves (lēvz) ►*n.* Pl. of **leaf.**

leave-tak•ing (lēv′tā′kĭng) ►*n.* A departure or farewell.

leav•ings (lē′vĭngz) ►*pl.n.* Scraps or remains; residue.

Leb•a•non (lĕb′ə-nən, -nŏn′) A country of SW Asia on the Mediterranean Sea. Cap. Beirut. Pop. 2,915,000. —**Leb′a•nese′** (-nēz′, -nēs′) *adj. & n.*

lech•er (lĕch′ər) ►*n.* A man given to lewd or lascivious behavior. [< OFr. *lechier*, lick.] —**lech′er•ous** *adj.* —**lech′er•ous•ly** *adv.* —**lech′er•y** *n.*

lec•i•thin (lĕs′ə-thĭn) ►*n.* Any of a group of fatty compounds found in plant and animal tissues and used in the processing of foods, cosmetics, and plastics. [< Gk. *lekithos*, egg yolk + -IN.]

Le Cor•bu•sier (lə kôr-bo͞o-zyā′, -bü-). Charles Édouard Jeanneret. 1887–1965. Swiss-born French architect and writer.

lec•tern (lĕk′tərn) ►*n.* A reading stand for a public speaker. [< Med.Lat. *lēctrīnum.*]

lec•ture (lĕk′chər) ►*n.* **1.** A speech on a given subject delivered before an audience or class, as for the purpose of instruction. **2.** A solemn scolding or admonition. [< Lat. *legere, lēct-*, read.] —**lec′ture** *v.*

lec•tur•er (lĕk′chər-ər) ►*n.* **1.** One who delivers lectures. **2.** A member of the faculty of a college or university, usu. without rank or tenure.

led (lĕd) ►*v.* P.t. and p.part. of **lead**[1].

LED (ĕl′ē-dē′, lĕd) ►*n.* A semiconductor diode that converts electrical energy to light and is used in digital displays, as of a calculator. [*l(ight-)e(mitting) d(iode).*]

ledge (lĕj) ►*n.* **1.** A shelflike projection on a wall or cliff. **2.** A reef. [ME, crossbar.]

ledg•er (lĕj′ər) ►*n.* A book in which the monetary transactions of a business are posted. [ME *legger*, breviary.]

lee (lē) ►*n.* **1.** *Naut.* The side away from the wind; the sheltered side. **2.** Cover; shelter. [< OE *hlēo*, shelter.]

Lee, Ann. "Mother Ann." 1736–84. British-born founder (1776) of the Shakers in America.

Lee, Henry. "Lighthorse Harry." 1756–1818. Amer. Revolutionary politician and soldier.

Lee, Robert Edward. 1807–70. Amer. Confederate general.

leech (lēch) ►*n.* **1.** Any of various aquatic bloodsucking worms, of which one species was formerly used by physicians to bleed patients. **2.** One that preys on others; parasite. **3.** *Archaic* A physician. [< OE *lǣce.*] —**leech** *v.*

Leeds (lēdz) A borough of N-central England NE of Manchester. Pop. 724,524.

leek (lēk) ►*n.* An edible plant related to the onion, having a white slender bulb and dark-green leaves. [< OE *lēac.*]

Robert E. Lee

leer (lîr) ►*v.* To give a lewd or malicious look. [< OE *hlēor*, cheek.] —**leer** *n.* —**leer′ing•ly** *adv.*

leer•y (lîr′ē) ►*adj.* **-i•er, -i•est.** Suspicious; wary. —**leer′i•ly** *adv.* —**leer′i•ness** *n.*

lees (lēz) ►*pl.n.* Dregs. [< Med.Lat. *lia.*]

Leeu•wen•hoek (lā′vən-ho͝ok′), **Anton van.** 1632–1723. Dutch microscopy pioneer.

lee•ward (lo͞o′ərd, lē′wərd) ►*adv. & adj. Naut.* Away from the wind. —**lee′ward** *n.*

Lee•ward Islands (lē′wərd) **1.** The N group of the Lesser Antilles in the West Indies, from the Virgin Is. SE to Guadeloupe. **2.** A chain of small islets of HI in the central Pacific WNW of the main islands.

lee•way (lē′wā′) ►*n.* **1.** The drift of a ship or aircraft to leeward of the course being steered. **2.** A margin of freedom or variation; latitude. See Syns at **room.**

left[1] (lĕft) ►*adj.* **1.** Of, located on, or corresponding to the side of the body to the north when one is facing east. **2.** often **Left** Of or belonging to the political left. ►*n.* **1a.** The direction or position on the left side. **b.** The left side or hand. **c.** A turn in this direction: *make a left.* **2.** often **Left** The people and groups who pursue liberal or egalitarian political goals. ►*adv.* Toward or on the left. [ME.]

left[2] (lĕft) ►*v.* P.t. and p.part. of **leave**[1].

left field ►*n.* **1.** *Baseball* The third of the outfield to the left, looking from home plate. **2.** *Informal* A position far from the mainstream, as of opinion. —**left fielder** *n.*

left-hand (lĕft′hănd′) ►*adj.* **1.** Of or on the left. **2.** Designed for or done with the left hand.

left-hand•ed (lĕft′hăn′dĭd) ►*adj.* **1.** Using the left hand more skillfully or easily than the right. **2.** Done with or made for the left hand. **3.** Awkward; clumsy. **4.** Counterclockwise. ►*adv.* With the left hand. —**left′-hand′ed•ly** *adv.* —**left′-hand′ed•ness** *n.*

left-hand•er (lĕft′hăn′dər) ►*n.* One who is left-handed.

left•ism also **Left•ism** (lĕf′tĭz′əm) ►*n.* The ideology of the political left. —**left′ist** *adj. & n.*

left•o•ver (lĕft′ō′vər) ►*adj.* Remaining as an unused portion. ►*n.* **1.** A remnant or unused portion. **2. leftovers** Food remaining from a previous meal.

left wing ►*n.* **1.** The leftist faction of a group. **2.** See **left**[1] 2. —**left′-wing′** *adj.* —**left′-wing′er** *n.*

left•y (lĕf′tē) ►*n., pl.* **-ies** *Informal* A left-handed person.

leg (lĕg) ►*n.* **1.** A limb or appendage used for locomotion or support. **2.** A part resembling a leg in shape or function. **3.** The part of a pair of trousers that covers the leg. **4.** A stage of a journey or course. ►*v.* **legged, leg•ging** *Informal.* To go on foot; walk or run: *legged it home.* [< ON *leggr.*]

leg•a•cy (lĕg′ə-sē) ►*n., pl.* **-cies 1.** Money or property bequeathed to another by will. **2.** Something handed down from an ancestor or predecessor. See Syns at **heritage.** [< Lat. *lēgāre*, bequeath.]

le•gal (lē′gəl) ►*adj.* **1.** Of or relating to law or lawyers. **2a.** Authorized by or based on law. **b.** Established by law; statutory. **3.** In conformity with or permitted by law. [< Lat. *lēx*, *lēg-*, law.] —**le•gal′i•ty** (lē-găl′ĭ-tē) *n.* —**le′gal•i•za′tion** *n.* —**le′gal•ize′** *v.* —**le′gal•ly** *adv.*

le•gal•ism (lē′gə-lĭz′əm) ►*n.* Strict, literal adherence to law. —**le′gal•ist** *n.* —**le′gal•is′tic** *adj.* —**le′gal•is′ti•cal•ly** *adv.*

leg•ate (lĕg′ĭt) ►*n.* An official emissary, esp. of the pope. [< Lat. *lēgātus*, p.part. of *lēgāre*, depute.]

leg•a•tee (lĕg′ə-tē′) ►*n.* The inheritor of a legacy.

le•ga•tion (lĭ-gā′shən) ►*n.* A diplomatic mission in a foreign country ranking below an embassy. —**le•ga′tion•ar•y** *adj.*

le•ga•to (lĭ-gä′tō) ►*adv. & adj. Mus.* In a smooth, even style. [Ital.]

leg•end (lĕj′ənd) ►*n.* **1.** An unverified popular story, esp. one believed to be historical. **2.** One of great fame or popular renown. **3.** An inscription on an object. **4.** An explanatory caption. [< Med.Lat. *(lectiō) legenda*, (lesson) to be read.] —**leg′en•dar′y** *adj.*

leg•er•de•main (lĕj′ər-də-mān′) ►*n.* Sleight of hand. [< OFr. *leger de main*, light of hand.]

leg•ged (lĕg′ĭd, lĕgd) ►*adj.* Having a specified kind or number of legs.

leg•ging (lĕg′ĭng) ►*n.* **1.** A leg covering usu. extending from the ankle to the knee. **2. leggings** Close-fitting knit trousers.

leg•gy (lĕg′ē) ►*adj.* **-gi•er, -gi•est.** Having long slender legs. —**leg′gi•ness** *n.*

leg•horn or **Leg•horn** (lĕg′hôrn′, -ərn) ►*n.* Any of a breed of hardy domestic fowl noted for prolific production of eggs.

Leghorn. See **Livorno.**

leg•i•ble (lĕj′ə-bəl) ►*adj.* Possible to read or decipher. [< Lat. *legere*, read.] —**leg′i•bil′i•ty, leg′i•ble•ness** *n.* —**leg′i•bly** *adv.*

le•gion (lē′jən) ►*n.* **1.** A unit of the Roman army consisting of 3,000 to 6,000 infantry and 100 to 200 cavalry. **2.** A large number; multitude. [< Lat. *legere*, gather.] —**le′gion•ar′y** *adj. & n.* —**le′gion•naire′** *n.*

leg•is•late (lĕj′ĭ-slāt′) ►*v.* **-lat•ed, -lat•ing 1.** To create or pass laws. **2.** To bring about by legislation. [< Lat. *lēgis lātor*, proposer of a law.] —**leg′is•la′tor** *n.* —**leg′is•la•to′ri•al** (-lə-tôr′ē-əl, -tōr′-) *adj.*

leg•is•la•tion (lĕj′ĭ-slā′shən) ►*n.* **1.** The act or process of legislating; lawmaking. **2.** A proposed or enacted law or group of laws.

leg•is•la•tive (lĕj′ĭ-slā′tĭv) ►*adj.* **1.** Of or relating to the enactment of laws. **2.** Having the power to create laws.

leg•is•la•ture (lĕj′ĭ-slā′chər) ►*n.* A body of people empowered to make laws.

le•git•i•mate (lə-jĭt′ə-mĭt) ►*adj.* **1.** Lawful. **2.** Being in accordance with accepted standards. **3.** Reasonable: *a legitimate doubt.* **4.** Authentic; genuine. **5.** Born of legally married parents. ►*v.* (-māt′) **-mat•ed, -mat•ing.** To make legitimate. [< Lat. *lēgitimus* < *lēx*, law.] —**le•git′i•ma•cy** (-mə-sē) *n.* —**le•git′i•mate•ly** *adv.*

le•git•i•mize (lə-jĭt′ə-mīz′) ►*v.* **-mized, -miz•ing.** To legitimate. —**le•git′i•mi•za′tion** *n.*

leg•ume (lĕg′yo͞om′, lə-gyo͞om′) ►*n.* **1.** A pod, such as that of a pea or bean, that splits in two when mature. **2.** A plant of or related to the pea family. [< Lat. *legūmen*, bean.] —**le•gu′mi•nous** *adj.*

leg•work (lĕg′wûrk′) ►*n. Informal* Work, such as collecting information, that involves walking or traveling about.

Le Ha•vre (lə hä′vrə, häv′) A city of N France on the English Channel WNW of Paris. Pop. 195,932.

lei[1] (lā, lā′ē) ►*n., pl.* **leis.** A garland of flowers, esp. one worn around the neck. See Regional Note at **ukulele.** [Hawaiian.]

lei[2] (lā) ►*n.* Pl. of **leu.**

Leib•niz or **Leib•nitz** (līb′nĭts, līp′-), Baron **Gottfried Wilhelm von.** 1646–1716. German philosopher and mathematician.

Leices•ter (lĕs′tər) A borough of central England ENE of Birmingham. Pop. 289,286.

Lei•den also **Ley•den** (līd′n). A city of SW Netherlands NE of The Hague. Pop. 114,365.

Leip•zig (līp′sĭg, -sĭk) A city of E-central Germany SSW of Berlin. Pop. 490,851.

lei•sure (lē′zhər, lĕzh′ər) ►*n.* Freedom from time-consuming duties or activities. —***idiom:* at (one's) leisure** At one's convenience. [< OFr. *leisir*, be permitted.] —**lei′sured** *adj.*

lei•sure•ly (lē′zhər-lē, lĕzh′ər-) ►*adj.* Done without haste; unhurried. ►*adv.* In an unhurried manner. —**lei′sure•li•ness** *n.*

leit•mo•tif also **leit•mo•tiv** (līt′mō-tēf′) ►*n.* **1.** *Mus.* A melodic passage or phrase associated with a specific character or element. **2.** A dominant and recurring theme, as in a novel. [Ger. *Leitmotiv.*]

lek (lĕk) ►*n.* See table at **currency.** [Albanian, after *Lek* Dukagjin.]

lem•ming (lĕm′ĭng) ►*n.* A small rodent inhabiting northern regions and known for periodic mass migrations. [Norw.]

Lem•nos (lĕm′nŏs) An island of NE Greece in the Aegean Sea off the coast of Turkey.

lem•on (lĕm′ən) ►*n.* **1a.** A spiny evergreen citrus tree cultivated for its yellow, egg-shaped fruit. **b.** The tart juicy fruit of this tree. **2.** *Informal* One that is unsatisfactory or defective. [< Pers. *līmūn.*] —**lem′on•y** *adj.*

lem•on•ade (lĕm′ə-nād′) ►*n.* A drink made of lemon juice, water, and sugar.

lem•pi•ra (lĕm-pîr′ə) ►*n.* See table at **currency.** [After *Lempira* (1497–1537), Honduran leader.]

le•mur (lē′mər) ►*n.* A small arboreal African primate having large eyes and a long tail. [< Lat. *lemurēs*, ghosts.]

Le•na (lē′nə, lyĕ′-) A river of E Russia rising near Lake Baikal and flowing about 4,296 km (2,670 mi) to the Laptev Sea.

lend (lĕnd) ►*v.* **lent** (lĕnt), **lend•ing 1.** To give or allow the use of temporarily. **2.** To provide (money) temporarily, usu. at interest. **3.**

To contribute; impart. **4.** To be suitable for. [< OE *lǣnan.*] —**lend'er** *n.*

L'En•fant (län-fänt', läN-fäN'), **Pierre Charles.** 1754–1825. French-born architect.

length (lĕngkth, lĕngth, lĕnth) ►*n.* **1.** The measurement of something along its greatest dimension. **2.** Measured distance or dimension. **3.** Extent or duration: *the length of a journey.* **4.** often **lengths** The degree to which an action or policy is carried. —***idiom:* at length** **1.** Eventually. **2.** Fully. [< OE *lengthu.*] —**length'y** *adj.*

length•en (lĕngk'thən, lĕng'-, lĕn'-) ►*v.* To make or become long or longer.

length•ways (lĕngkth'wāz', lĕngth'-, lĕnth'-) ►*adv.* Lengthwise.

length•wise (lĕngkth'wīz', lĕngth'-, lĕnth'-) ►*adv. & adj.* Along the direction of the length.

le•ni•ent (lē'nē-ənt, lēn'yənt) ►*adj.* Not harsh or strict; merciful or indulgent. [< Lat. *lēnīre*, pacify < *lēnis*, soft.] —**le'ni•en•cy, le'ni•ence** *n.* —**le'ni•ent•ly** *adv.*

Le•nin (lĕn'ĭn), **Vladimir Ilich.** 1870–1924. Russian revolutionary leader and first head of the USSR (1917–24).

Vladimir Lenin

Len•in•grad (lĕn'ĭn-grăd') See **Saint Petersburg.**

Len•in•ism (lĕn'ə-nĭz'əm) ►*n.* The theory and practice of proletarian revolution as developed by Lenin. —**Len'in•ist** *adj. & n.*

lens (lĕnz) ►*n., pl.* **lens•es 1.** A piece of glass or other transparent material with opposite surfaces either or both of which are curved, by means of which light rays converge or diverge to form an image. **2.** A combination of two or more such pieces used to form an image for viewing or photographing. **3.** A transparent part of the eye that focuses light rays to form an image on the retina. [< Lat. *lēns*, lentil.]

lent (lĕnt) ►*v.* P.t. and p.part. of **lend.**

Lent ►*n.* The 40 weekdays from Ash Wednesday until Easter, observed by Christians as a season of penitence. [< OE *lencten*, spring.]

len•til (lĕn'təl) ►*n.* The round, flattened, edible seed of a pealike Old World plant. [< Lat. *lenticula*, dim. of *lēns*, lentil.]

len•to (lĕn'tō) ►*adv. & adj. Mus.* In a slow tempo. [Ital. < Lat. *lentus.*]

Le•o (lē'ō) ►*n.* **1.** A constellation in the Northern Hemisphere. **2.** The 5th sign of the zodiac. [< Lat. *leō*, LION.]

Leo I, Saint. "Leo the Great." A.D. 400?–461. Pope (440–461).

Leo III, Saint. d. 816. Pope (795–816).

Leo X. 1475–1521. Pope (1513–21).

Le•ón (lā-ōn') **1.** A region and former kingdom of NW Spain. **2.** A city of central Mexico ENE of Guadalajara. Pop. 593,002.

Le•o•nar•do da Vin•ci (lē'ə-när'dō də vĭn'-chē, dä, lā'-). 1452–1519. Italian painter, engineer, musician, and scientist.

le•one (lē-ōn') ►*n.* See table at **currency.** [< SIERRA LEONE.]

le•o•nine (lē'ə-nīn') ►*adj.* Of or characteristic of a lion. [< Lat. *leō*, *leōn*-, LION.]

leop•ard (lĕp'ərd) ►*n.* **1.** A large wild cat of Africa and S Asia, having either tawny and black-spotted or all-black fur. **2.** The pelt of this animal. [< Gk. *leopardos.*]

Le•o•pold II (lē'ə-pōld'). 1835–1909. King of Belgium (1865–1909) and the Congo Free State (later Zaire, now Congo) (1876–1904).

le•o•tard (lē'ə-tärd') ►*n.* **1.** A snug one-piece garment that covers the torso, worn esp. by dancers. **2. leotards** Tights. [After Jules *Léotard* (1830–70).] —**le'o•tard'ed** *adj.*

lep•er (lĕp'ər) ►*n.* **1.** A person affected by leprosy. **2.** A pariah; outcast. [< Gk. *lepros*, scaly.]

lep•i•dop•ter•ist (lĕp'ĭ-dŏp'tər-ĭst) ►*n.* An entomologist specializing in the study of butterflies and moths. [< Gk. *lepis*, scale.]

lep•re•chaun (lĕp'rĭ-kŏn', -kôn') ►*n.* An elf in Irish folklore. [Ir.Gael. *luprachán.*]

lep•ro•sy (lĕp'rə-sē) ►*n.* A chronic, mildly contagious disease marked by ulcers of the skin, bone, and viscera and leading to paralysis, gangrene, and deformation. [ME *lepruse* < *leprus*, leprous.] —**lep'rous** *adj.*

lep•tin (lĕp'tĭn') ►*n.* A neurotransmitter involved in appetite regulation. [Gk. *leptos*, thin + –IN.]

lep•ton (lĕp'tŏn') ►*n.* Any of a family of elementary particles, including the electrons and neutrinos, that take part in the weak interaction. [Gk. *leptos*, thin + –ON[1].]

les•bi•an (lĕz'bē-ən) ►*n.* A woman whose sexual orientation is to women. [After *Lesbos*, Gk. island.] —**les'bi•an** *adj.* —**les'bi•an•ism** *n.*

le•sion (lē'zhən) ►*n.* **1.** A wound or injury. **2.** A diseased patch of skin. [< Lat. *laesiō.*]

Le•so•tho (lə-sō'tō, -so͞o'to͞o) A country of S Africa forming an enclave within E-central South Africa. Cap. Maseru. Pop. 1,996,000.

less (lĕs) ►*adj.* Comp. of **little. 1.** Not as great in amount or quantity. **2.** Lower in importance, esteem, or rank. **3.** Consisting of a smaller number. See Usage Note at **few.** ►*adv.* Comp. of **little.** To a smaller extent, degree, or frequency. ►*n.* A smaller amount. —***idiom:* less than** not at all: *a less than favorable review.* [< OE *lǣssa* and *lǣs.*]

–less ►*suff.* **1.** Without; lacking: *blameless.* **2.** Unable to act or be acted on in a specified way: *dauntless.* [< OE *lēas*, without.]

les•see (lĕ-sē') ►*n.* One that holds a lease. [< AN < p.part. of *lesser*, to let out, lease; see LEASE.]

less•en (lĕs'ən) ►*v.* To make or become less.

Les•seps (lĕs'əps, lĕ-sĕps'), Vicomte **Ferdinand Marie de.** 1805–94. French diplomat and engineer.

less•er (lĕs'ər) ►*adj.* Comp. of **little.** Smaller in size or importance.

Lesser Antilles. An island group of the E West

Indies extending in an arc from Curaçao to the Virgin Is.

les•son (lĕs′ən) ►*n.* **1.** Something to be learned. **2a.** A period of instruction. **b.** An instructional exercise. **3.** An edifying experience or example. **4.** A rebuke or reprimand. **5.** A reading from a sacred text as part of a religious service. [< Lat. *lēctiō*, a reading.]

les•sor (lĕs′ôr′, lĕ-sôr′) ►*n.* One that lets property under a lease. [< AN *lesser*, LEASE.]

lest (lĕst) ►*conj.* For fear that: *tiptoed lest they should hear.* [< OE *thӯ lǣs the*, so that not.]

let[1] (lĕt) ►*v.* **let, let•ting 1.** To give permission or opportunity to; allow: *I let them borrow the car.* **2.** To cause to; make: *Let the news be known.* **3.** Used as an auxiliary in the imperative to express: **a.** A command, request, or proposal: *Let's finish the job!* **b.** A warning or threat: *Just let her try!* **4.** To release or give forth: *let out a yelp.* **5.** To rent or lease. —***phrasal verbs:* let down 1.** To lower. **2.** To disappoint. **let on** To allow to be known; admit. **let out 1.** To come to a close. **2.** To reveal: *Who let the story out?* **let up** To diminish: *The rain let up.* [< OE *lǣtan*.]

let[2] (lĕt) ►*n.* **1.** Something that hinders; obstacle. **2.** *Sports* An invalid stroke in tennis and other net games that must be repeated. [< OE *lettan*, hinder.]

-let ►*suff.* **1.** Small: *booklet.* **2.** Something worn on: *armlet.* [< OFr. *-elet*.]

let•down (lĕt′doun′) ►*n.* **1.** A decrease, decline, or relaxation, as of effort or energy. **2.** A disappointment.

le•thal (lē′thəl) ►*adj.* Causing or capable of causing death. [< Lat. *lētum*, death.] —**le•thal′i•ty** (lē-thăl′ĭ-tē) *n.* —**le′thal•ly** *adv.*

leth•ar•gy (lĕth′ər-jē) ►*n., pl.* **-gies.** A state of sluggishness, inactivity, and apathy. [< Gk. *lēthargos*, forgetful : *lēthē*, forgetfulness + *argos*, idle (A–[1] + *ergon*, work).] —**le•thar′gic** (lə-thär′jĭk) *adj.* —**le•thar′gi•cal•ly** *adv.*

le•the (lē′thē) ►*n.* **1. Lethe** *Gk. Myth.* The river of forgetfulness in Hades. **2.** Forgetfulness; oblivion. [Gk. *lēthē*.]

let's (lĕts) ► Let us.

Lett (lĕt) ►*n.* A member of a Baltic people constituting the main population of Latvia.

let•ter (lĕt′ər) ►*n.* **1.** A written character representing a speech sound and being a unit of an alphabet. **2.** A written or printed communication. **3.** Literal meaning. **4. letters** *(takes sing. v.)* Learning or knowledge, esp. of literature. ►*v.* To write letters on. [< Lat. *littera*.] —**let′ter•er** *n.*

let•tered (lĕt′ərd) ►*adj.* **1.** Literate. **2.** Learned. **3.** Inscribed with letters.

let•ter•head (lĕt′ər-hĕd′) ►*n.* **1.** Stationery with a printed or engraved heading. **2.** The heading itself.

let•ter•ing (lĕt′ər-ĭng) ►*n.* **1.** The act of forming letters. **2.** Letters inscribed, as on a sign.

let•ter-per•fect (lĕt′ər-pûr′fĭkt) ►*adj.* Correct to the last detail.

let•ter•press (lĕt′ər-prĕs′) ►*n.* The process of printing from a raised inked surface.

let•ter-qual•i•ty (lĕt′ər-kwŏl′ĭ-tē) ►*adj.* Of or producing printed characters similar in clarity to those produced by a typewriter.

Let•tish (lĕt′ĭsh) ►*n.* See **Latvian** 2.

let•tuce (lĕt′əs) ►*n.* **1.** A plant cultivated for its edible leaves, eaten esp. as a salad or garnish. **2.** *Slang* Paper money. [< Lat. *lactūca*.]

let•up (lĕt′ŭp′) ►*n.* **1.** A reduction; slowdown. **2.** A pause.

le•u (lĕ′o͝o) ►*n., pl.* **lei** (lā). See table at **currency.** [Rom. < Lat. *leō*, LION.]

leu•ke•mi•a (lo͞o-kē′mē-ə) ►*n.* Any of various acute or chronic diseases in which unrestrained proliferation of white blood cells occurs. —**leu•ke′mic** *adj. & n.*

leuko– or **leuk–** also **leuco–** or **leuc–** ►*pref.* **1.** White; colorless: *leukocyte.* **2.** Leukocyte: *leukemia.* [< Gk. *leukos*.]

leu•ko•cyte also **leu•co•cyte** (lo͞o′kə-sīt′) ►*n.* A white blood cell. —**leu′ko•cyt′ic** (-sĭt′ĭk) *adj.*

lev (lĕf) ►*n., pl.* **lev•a** (lĕv′ə). See table at **currency.** [Bulgarian, ult. < Lat. *leō*, LION.]

Le•vant (lə-vănt′) The countries bordering on the E Mediterranean Sea. —**Le′van•tine′** (lĕv′ən-tīn′, -tēn′, lə-văn′-) *adj. & n.*

lev•ee (lĕv′ē) ►*n.* **1.** An embankment raised to prevent a river from overflowing. **2.** A landing place on a river. [< OFr. *lever*, raise.]

lev•el (lĕv′əl) ►*n.* **1.** Relative position or rank on a scale. **2.** A natural or proper position, place, or stage. **3.** Position along a vertical axis; height or depth. **4a.** A horizontal line or plane at right angles to the plumb. **b.** The position or height of such a line or plane. **5.** A flat horizontal surface. **6.** A land area of uniform elevation. **7.** An instrument for ascertaining whether a surface is horizontal. ►*adj.* **1.** Having a flat smooth surface. **2.** Horizontal. **3.** At the same height or position as another; even. **4.** Consistent: steady. **5.** Rational; sensible. **6.** Filled evenly to the top. ►*v.* **-eled, -el•ing** or **-elled, -el•ling 1.** To make horizontal, flat, or even. **2.** To tear down; raze. **3.** To equalize. **4.** To aim or direct. See Syns at **aim. 5.** To direct emphatically toward someone: *leveled charges of dishonesty.* **6.** *Informal* To be frank and open. —***phrasal verbs:* level off** To move toward stability or consistency. **on the level** *Informal* Without deception; honest. [< VLat. **lībellum*, leveling tool < *lībra*, a balance.] —**lev′el•er** *n.* —**lev′el•ly** *adv.* —**lev′el•ness** *n.*

lev•el•head•ed (lĕv′əl-hĕd′ĭd) ►*adj.* Characteristically self-composed and sensible. —**lev′el•head′ed•ness** *n.*

lev•er (lĕv′ər, lē′vər) ►*n.* **1.** A simple machine consisting of a rigid bar pivoted on a fixed point and used to transmit force. **2.** A projecting handle used to adjust or operate a mecha-

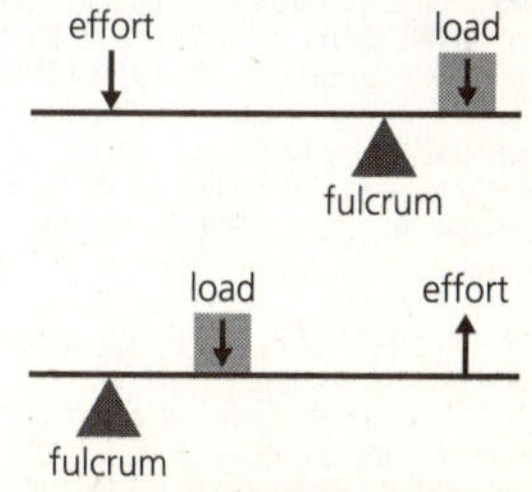

lever
top: first-class model
bottom: second-class model

nism. **3.** A means of accomplishing; tool. ►*v.* To move or lift with or as if with a lever. [< OFr. *lever*, raise < Lat. *levāre.*]

lev•er•age (lĕv′ər-ĭj, lē′vər-) ►*n.* **1.** The action or mechanical advantage of a lever. **2.** Positional advantage. **3.** The use of credit or borrowed funds to improve one's speculative capacity. —**lev′er•age** *v.*

Le•vi (lē′vī′). In the Bible, a son of Jacob and Leah.

le•vi•a•than (lə-vī′ə-thən) ►*n.* **1.** Something unusually large of its kind. **2.** *Bible* A monstrous sea creature in the Hebrew Bible. [< Heb. *liwyātān*, a sea monster.]

Le•vi's (lē′vīz′) ► A trademark for denim trousers.

Lé•vi-Strauss (lā′vē-strous′), **Claude.** b. 1908. French social anthropolgist.

lev•i•tate (lĕv′ĭ-tāt′) ►*v.* **-tat•ed, -tat•ing.** To rise or raise into the air and float in apparent defiance of gravity. [Lat. *levis*, light + (GRAVI)TATE.] —**lev′i•ta′tion** *n.*

Le•vit•i•cus (lə-vĭt′ĭ-kəs) ►*n.* See table at **Bible.**

lev•i•ty (lĕv′ĭ-tē) ►*n., pl.* **-ties.** Lightness of manner or speech; frivolity. [< Lat. *levitās.*]

lev•y (lĕv′ē) ►*v.* **-ied, -y•ing 1.** To impose or collect (a tax). **2.** To draft into military service. **3.** To wage (a war). **4.** To confiscate property. ►*n., pl.* **-ies 1.** The act or process of levying. **2.** Money, property, or troops levied. [< OFr. *lever*, raise. See LEVER.] —**lev′i•er** *n.*

lewd (lo͞od) ►*adj.* **-er, -est 1.** Lustful. **2.** Obscene; indecent. [< OE *lǣwede*, ignorant.] —**lewd′ly** *adv.* —**lewd′ness** *n.*

Lew•is (lo͞o′ĭs), **Carl.** b. 1961. Amer. athlete.

Lewis, C(live) S(taples). 1898–1963. British writer and critic.

Lewis, (Harry) Sinclair. 1885–1951. Amer. novelist; 1930 Nobel.

Lewis, John Llewellyn. 1880–1969. Amer. labor leader.

Lewis, Meriwether. 1774–1809. Amer. soldier and explorer.

Lew•is•ton (lo͞o′ĭ-stən) A city of SW ME N of Portland. Pop. 39,757.

lex•i•cog•ra•phy (lĕk′sĭ-kŏg′rə-fē) ►*n.* The work of writing or compiling a dictionary. —**lex′i•cog′ra•pher** *n.* —**lex′i•co•graph′ic** (-kə-grăf′ĭk), **lex′i•co•graph′i•cal** *adj.*

lex•i•con (lĕk′sĭ-kŏn′) ►*n.* **1.** A dictionary. **2.** A specialized vocabulary. [< Gk. *lexikon (biblion)*, (book) of words.] —**lex′i•cal** *adj.*

Lex•ing•ton (lĕk′sĭng-tən) **1.** A city of NE-central KY ESE of Louisville. Pop. 204,165. **2.** A town of NE MA; site of first battle of the American Revolution (Apr. 19, 1775). Pop. 28,974.

Ley•den (līd′n) See **Leiden.**

Ley•te (lā′tē, -tĕ) An island of the E-central Philippines in the Visayan group N of Mindanao.

lf ►*abbr.* lightface

LF ►*abbr.* **1.** left field **2.** low frequency

lg. ►*abbr.* **1.** large **2.** long

Lha•sa (lä′sə, lăs′ə) A city of SW China, the capital of Xizang (Tibet). Pop. 139,822.

Li ► The symbol for the element **lithium.**

li•a•bil•i•ty (lī′ə-bĭl′ĭ-tē) ►*n., pl.* **-ties 1.** Something for which one is liable; an obligation, responsibility, or debt. **2.** Something that holds one back; handicap. **3.** Likelihood.

li•a•ble (lī′ə-bəl) ►*adj.* **1.** Legally obligated; responsible. **2.** Subject; susceptible. **3.** Likely; apt. [Prob. < OFr. *lier*, bind.]

li•ai•son (lē′ā-zŏn′, lē-ā′-) ►*n.* **1a.** Communication between groups or units. **b.** One that maintains communication. **2.** A love affair. [< Lat. *ligātiō*, binding < *ligāre*, bind.]

li•an•a (lē-ä′nə, -ăn′ə) ►*n.* Any climbing, woody, usu. tropical vine. [< Fr. *liane*, prob. < *lier*, bind.]

Liao He (lyou′ hə′) A river of NE China flowing about 1,448 km (900 mi) to the Gulf of Liaodong.

li•ar (lī′ər) ►*n.* One that tells lies.

li•ba•tion (lī-bā′shən) ►*n.* **1.** The ritual pouring of a liquid offering or the liquid so poured. **2.** *Informal* An alcoholic drink. [< Lat. *lībāre*, pour out as an offering.]

li•bel (lī′bəl) ►*n.* **1.** A written, printed, or pictorial statement that maliciously damages a person's reputation. **2.** The act or offense of publishing a libel. ►*v.* **-beled, -bel•ing** or **-belled, -bel•ling.** To make or publish a libel about. [< Lat. *libellus*, petition < *liber*, book.] —**li′bel•er, li′bel•ist** *n.* —**li′bel•ous** *adj.* —**li′bel•ous•ly** *adv.*

lib•er•al (lĭb′ər-əl, lĭb′rəl) ►*adj.* **1a.** Open-minded; tolerant. See Syns at **broad-minded. b.** Favoring civil and political liberties, democratic reforms, and protection from arbitrary authority. **2a.** Tending to give freely; generous. **b.** Abundant; ample. **3.** Not strict or literal; approximate. **4.** Of or based on the traditional arts and sciences of a college or university curriculum: *a liberal education.* ►*n.* A person with liberal ideas or opinions. [< Lat. *līber*, free.] —**lib′er•al•ism** *n.* —**lib′er•al′i•ty** (lĭb′ə-răl′ĭ-tē) *n.* —**lib′er•al•i•za′tion** *n.* —**lib′er•al•ize′** *v.* —**lib′er•al•ly** *adv.*

Syns: *liberal, bounteous, bountiful, freehanded, generous, handsome, munificent, openhanded* ***Ant:*** *stingy* **adj.**

lib•er•ate (lĭb′ə-rāt′) ►*v.* **-at•ed, -at•ing.** To set free, as from oppression, confinement, or foreign control. [Lat. *līberāre* < *līber*, free.] —**lib′er•a′tion** *n.* —**lib′er•a′tion•ist** *n.* —**lib′er•a′tor** *n.*

Li•be•ri•a (lī-bîr′ē-ə) A country of W Africa on the Atlantic. Cap. Monrovia. Pop. 2,700,000. —**Li•be′ri•an** *adj. & n.*

lib•er•tar•i•an (lĭb′ər-târ′ē-ən) ►*n.* One who advocates maximizing individual rights and minimizing the role of the state. [< LIBERTY.] —**lib′er•tar′i•an•ism** *n.*

lib•er•tine (lĭb′ər-tēn′) ►*n.* A dissolute or licentious person. [< Lat. *līber*, free.] —**lib′er•tine′** *adj.* —**lib′er•tin•ism′** *n.*

lib•er•ty (lĭb′ər-tē) ►*n., pl.* **-ties 1a.** The condition of being free from restriction or control; freedom. **b.** The right to act or believe as one chooses. **2.** Permission; authorization. **3.** often **liberties a.** Undue familiarity. **b.** Latitude; license: *took liberties with the truth.* **4.** Authorized leave from naval duty. [< Lat. *lībertās* < *līber*, free.]

li•bi•do (lĭ-bē′dō, -bī′-) ►*n., pl.* **-dos 1.** The psychic and emotional energy associated with biological drives. **2.** Sexual desire. [Lat. *libīdō*, desire.] —**li•bid′i•nal** (-bĭd′n-əl) *adj.* —**li•bid′i•nous** *adj.*

Li•bra (lē′brə, lī′-) ►*n.* **1.** A constellation in the

Southern Hemisphere near Scorpius and Virgo. **2.** The 7th sign of the zodiac. [< Lat. *lībra*, scales.]

li•brar•i•an (lī-brâr′ē-ən) ►*n.* A specialist in library work. —**li•brar′i•an•ship′** *n.*

li•brar•y (lī′brĕr′ē) ►*n.*, *pl.* **-ies 1.** A place where written or recorded materials, such as books, periodicals, tapes, or films, are kept for reading, reference, or lending. **2.** A collection of such materials. [< Lat. *librārium*, bookcase.]

li•bret•to (lĭ-brĕt′ō) ►*n.*, *pl.* **-bret•tos** or **-bret•ti** (-brĕt′ē). The text of a dramatic musical work, such as an opera. [Ital., dim. of *libro*, book.] —**lib•bret′tist** *n.*

Li•bre•ville (lē′brə-vĭl′, -vēl′) The capital of Gabon, in the NW part on the Gulf of Guinea. Pop. 235,700.

Lib•y•a (lĭb′ē-ə) A country of N Africa on the Mediterranean Sea. Cap. Tripoli. Pop. 4,899,000. —**Lib′y•an** *adj. & n.*

lice (līs) ►*n.* Pl. of **louse** 1.

li•cense (lī′səns) ►*n.* **1a.** Official or legal permission to do or own a specified thing. See Syns at **permission. b.** Proof of permission granted, usu. in the form of a document, card, plate, or tag. **2.** Deviation from normal rules, practices, or methods. **3.** Latitude of action, esp. in behavior or speech. **4.** Excessive freedom. ►*v.* **-censed, -cens•ing 1.** To give permission to or for. **2.** To grant a license to or for. See Syns at **authorize.** [< Lat. *licentia*, permission < *licēre*, be permitted.] —**li′cens•a•ble** *adj.* —**li′cens•ee′** *n.* —**li′cens•er** *n.*

li•censed practical nurse (lī′sənst) ►*n.* A nurse who has completed a practical nursing program and is licensed by a state to provide routine patient care under the direction of a registered nurse or a physician.

li•cen•tious (lī-sĕn′shəs) ►*adj.* Lacking moral, esp. sexual restraint. [< Lat. *licentia*, LICENSE.] —**li•cen′tious•ly** *adv.* —**li•cen′tious•ness** *n.*

li•chee (lē′chē) ►*n.* Var. of **litchi.**

li•chen (lī′kən) ►*n.* A fungus that grows symbiotically with algae, resulting in a composite organism that forms a crustlike or branching growth on rocks or tree trunks. [< Gk. *leikhēn.*] —**li′chen•ous** *adj.*

lic•it (lĭs′ĭt) ►*adj.* Legal. [< Lat. *licēre*, be permitted.] —**lic′it•ly** *adv.* —**lic′it•ness** *n.*

lick (lĭk) ►*v.* **1.** To pass the tongue over or along. **2.** To lap up. **3.** To touch lightly: *waves licked the shore.* **4.** *Slang* To thrash; defeat. ►*n.* **1.** The act of licking. **2.** A small quantity. **3.** A deposit of exposed natural salt licked by passing animals. **4.** A blow. [< OE *liccian.*] —**lick′er** *n.*

lick•e•ty-split (lĭk′ĭ-tē-splĭt′) ►*adv.* *Informal* With great speed. [< LICK, fast + SPLIT.]

lick•ing (lĭk′ĭng) ►*n.* *Slang* **1.** A beating or spanking. **2.** A severe loss or defeat.

lic•o•rice (lĭk′ər-ĭs, -ĭsh) ►*n.* **1.** A plant having a sweet, distinctively flavored root. **2.** A candy made from or flavored with this root. [< Gk. *glukurrhiza* : *glukus*, sweet + *rhiza*, root.]

lid (lĭd) ►*n.* **1.** A removable cover for a hollow receptacle. **2.** An eyelid. [< OE *hlid.*]

li•do•caine (lī′də-kān′) ►*n.* A synthetic drug used chiefly as a local anesthetic. [*(acetani)lide*, a compound + (CO)CAINE.]

lie[1] (lī) ►*v.* **lay** (lā), **lain** (lān), **ly•ing** (lī′ĭng) **1.** To be or place oneself at rest in a flat, horizontal, or recumbent position; recline. **2.** To be or remain in a specified condition. **3.** To occupy a position or place. **4.** To extend. ►*n.* The position in which something lies. —***idiom:*** **lie** (or **lay**) **low** To keep oneself or one's plans hidden. [< OE *licgan.*]

lie[2] (lī) ►*n.* A false statement deliberately presented as true. ►*v.* **lied, ly•ing** (lī′ĭng) **1.** To tell a lie. **2.** To convey a false image or impression: *Appearances often lie.* [< OE *lyge.*]

Lie (lē), **Trygve Halvden.** 1896–1968. Norwegian politician; first secretary-general of the United Nations (1946–53).

Liech•ten•stein (lĭk′tən-stīn′, lĭKH′tən-shtīn′) A small Alpine principality in central Europe between Austria and Switzerland. Cap. Vaduz. Pop. 31,000.

lied (lēt) ►*n.*, *pl.* **lie•der** (lē′dər). A German lyric song. [< OHGer. *liod.*]

lie detector ►*n.* A machine used to detect possible deception during an interrogation.

lief (lēf) ►*adv.* **-er, -est.** Readily; willingly. [< OE *lēof*, dear.]

liege (lēj) ►*n.* **1.** A feudal lord. **2.** A vassal. ►*adj.* Loyal; faithful. [< LLat. *lœticus*, of a serf < *lœtus*, serf.]

Li•ège (lē-āzh′, lyĕzh) A city of E Belgium near the Dutch and German borders. Pop. 195,201.

lien (lēn, lē′ən) ►*n.* The right to take and hold or sell the property of a debtor as security or payment for a debt. [< Lat. *ligāmen*, bond.]

lieu (lo͞o) ►*n.* *Archaic* Place; stead. —***idiom:*** **in lieu of** In place of; instead of. [< OFr.]

lieut. ►*abbr.* lieutenant

lieu•ten•ant (lo͞o-tĕn′ənt) ►*n.* **1a.** A rank, as in the US Navy, above lieutenant junior grade and below lieutenant commander. **b.** A first lieutenant. **c.** A second lieutenant. **2.** An officer in a police or fire department ranking below a captain. **3.** One who acts in place of a superior. See Syns at **assistant.** [< OFr., deputy.] —**lieu•ten′an•cy** *n.*

lieutenant colonel ►*n.* A rank, as in the US Army, above major and below colonel.

lieutenant commander ►*n.* A rank, as in the US Navy, above lieutenant and below commander.

lieutenant general ►*n.* A rank, as in the US Army, above major general and below general.

lieutenant governor ►*n.* An elected official ranking just below the governor of a state in the US.

lieutenant junior grade ►*n.*, *pl.* **lieutenants junior grade.** A rank, as in the US Navy, above ensign and below lieutenant.

life (līf) ►*n.*, *pl.* **lives** (līvz) **1.** *Biol.* The quality that distinguishes living organisms from dead organisms and inanimate matter, manifested in functions such as metabolism, growth, reproduction, and response to stimuli. **2.** Living organisms collectively: *marine life.* **3.** A living being. **4.** The interval between birth and death. **5.** A biography. **6.** Human existence, relationships, or activities: *everyday life.* **7.** A manner of living: *led a hard life.* **8.** Liveliness; animation. [< OE *līf.*] —**life′less** *adj.* —**life′less•ly** *adv.* —**life′less•ness** *n.*

life•blood (līf′blŭd′) ►*n.* An indispensable or vital part.

life•boat (līf′bōt′) ►*n.* A boat used for abandoning ship or for rescue services.

life buoy ►*n.* A buoyant device, such as a cork or polystyrene ring, used as a life preserver.

life care ►*n.* The provision of services, such as housing and social activities, for the elderly.

life•guard (līf′gärd′) ►*n.* An expert swimmer employed to safeguard other swimmers.

life insurance ►*n.* Insurance that guarantees a specific sum of money to a designated beneficiary upon the death of the insured.

life•like (līf′līk′) ►*adj.* Accurately representing real life. See Syns at **graphic.**

life•line (līf′līn′) ►*n.* **1.** A line thrown to someone falling or drowning. **2.** A means or route by which necessary supplies are transported.

life•long (līf′lông′, -lŏng′) ►*adj.* Continuing for a lifetime.

life preserver ►*n.* A buoyant device designed to keep a person afloat in the water.

life-size (līf′sīz′) also **life-sized** (-sīzd′) ►*adj.* Being of the same size as an original.

life•style also **life-style** or **life style** (līf′stīl′) ►*n.* A way of life that reflects the attitudes and values of a person or group.

life-sup•port (līf′sə-pôrt′, -pōrt′) ►*adj.* Relating to the methods, equipment, or conditions needed to sustain life. —**life support** *n.*

life•time (līf′tīm′) ►*n.* The period of time during which an individual is alive.

life•work (līf′wûrk′) ►*n.* The chief or entire work of a person's lifetime.

LIFO (lī′fō) ►*n.* See **last-in, first-out.**

lift (lĭft) ►*v.* **1a.** To elevate; raise. **b.** To ascend; rise. **2a.** To revoke; rescind. **b.** To bring an end to. **3.** To elate. **4.** *Informal* To steal. **5.** To pay off (a debt). —***phrasal verb:* lift off** To begin flight. ►*n.* **1.** The act or process of rising or raising. **2.** Power or force available for raising. **3.** A load. **4.** The extent or height to which something is raised or rises. **5.** An elevation of the spirits. **6.** A machine or device designed to raise or carry something. **7.** *Chiefly Brit.* An elevator. **8.** A ride in a vehicle given to help someone. **9.** The component of the total aerodynamic force acting on an aircraft, perpendicular to the relative wind and normally exerted in an upward direction. [< ON *lypta.*] —**lift′a•ble** *adj.* —**lift′er** *n.*

lift•off (lĭft′ôf′, -ŏf′) ►*n.* The moment in which a rocket or other craft leaves the ground.

lig•a•ment (lĭg′ə-mənt) ►*n.* A sheet or band of tough, fibrous tissue connecting bones or cartilages at a joint or supporting an organ. [< Med. Lat. *ligāmentum.*]

lig•a•ture (lĭg′ə-cho͝or′, -chər) ►*n.* **1.** The act of tying or binding. **2.** A cord, wire, or bandage used for binding. **3.** A character, such as *æ,* combining two or more letters. **4.** *Mus.* A slur. [< Lat. *ligāre,* bind.]

light[1] (līt) ►*n.* **1.** Electromagnetic radiation that may be perceived by the human eye. **2.** The sensation of perceiving light; brightness. **3a.** A source of light, esp. a lamp or electric fixture. **b.** The illumination derived from such a source. **4a.** Daylight. **b.** Dawn; daybreak. **5.** A source of fire, such as a match or cigarette lighter. **6.** A state of awareness or understanding. **7.** Public attention. **8.** A way of looking at or considering a matter; aspect. **9.** A prominent person. ►*v.* **light•ed** or **lit** (lĭt), **light•ing 1.** To set or be set on fire; ignite. **2.** To cause to give out light: *lit a lamp.* **3.** To illuminate. ►*adj.* **-er, -est 1.** Not dark; bright. **2.** Not dark in color: *light hair.* —***idiom:* in (the) light of** In consideration of. [< OE *lēoht.*] —**light′ness** *n.*

Usage: *Lighted* and *lit* are equally acceptable as past tense and past participle of *light.* Both forms are well established as adjectives also: *a lit* (or *lighted*) *cigarette.*

light[2] (līt) ►*adj.* **-er, -est 1a.** Not heavy. **b.** Of relatively low density. **2.** Having less force, quantity, intensity, or volume than normal. **3a.** Consuming moderate amounts. **b.** Not severe: *a light punishment.* **4.** Not serious or profound. **5.** Free from worries or troubles; blithe. **6.** Liable to change; fickle. **7.** Mildly dizzy. **8.** Moving easily and quickly; nimble. **9.** Easily disturbed: *a light sleeper.* **10.** Low in a potentially harmful ingredient, such as alcohol, fat, or sodium. ►*adv.* **-er, -est 1.** Lightly. **2.** With little weight and few burdens: *traveling light.* ►*v.* **light•ed** or **lit** (lĭt), **light•ing 1.** To get down; alight. **2.** To land. —***phrasal verbs:* light into** *Informal* To assail. **light out** *Informal* To leave hastily. [< OE *lēoht.*] —**light′ly** *adv.* —**light′ness** *n.*

light bulb ►*n.* An incandescent lamp or its glass housing.

light-e•mit•ting diode (līt′ĭ-mĭt′ĭng) ►*n.* LED.

light•en[1] (līt′n) ►*v.* To make or become light or lighter; illuminate or brighten.

light•en[2] (līt′n) ►*v.* **1.** To make or become less heavy. **2.** To make or become less oppressive, troublesome, or severe.

light•er[1] (lī′tər) ►*n.* **1.** One that ignites. **2.** A device for lighting a cigarette, cigar, or pipe.

light•er[2] (lī′tər) ►*n.* A barge used to deliver goods to or from a cargo ship. [ME.] —**light′er** *v.*

light•face (līt′fās′) ►*n.* A typeface with relatively thin, light lines. —**light′faced′** *adj.*

light•head•ed (līt′hĕd′ĭd) ►*adj.* **1.** Faint, giddy, or delirious. **2.** Frivolous; silly. —**light′head′ed•ly** *adv.* —**light′head′ed•ness** *n.*

light•heart•ed (līt′här′tĭd) ►*adj.* Happy and carefree. —**light′heart′ed•ly** *adv.* —**light′heart′ed•ness** *n.*

light heavyweight ►*n.* A boxer weighing from 161 to 175 lbs., between a middleweight and a heavyweight.

light•house (līt′hous′) ►*n.* A tall structure topped by a powerful light that guides ships.

light•ing (lī′tĭng) ►*n.* **1.** The state of being lighted; illumination. **2.** The method or equipment used to provide artificial illumination. **3.** The act or process of igniting.

light•ning (līt′nĭng) ►*n.* An abrupt, powerful natural electric discharge in the atmosphere, accompanied by a flash of light. ►*adj.* Very fast or sudden. [ME < *lightnen,* light up.] —**light′ning** *v.*

lightning bug ►*n.* See **firefly.**

Regional Note: *Lightning bug* is the term used by 80 percent of those interviewed by the *Dictionary of American Regional English.* A mere 30 percent use *firefly* (including those who said both). Only in the northernmost states and along the Pacific coast does the less colloquial term *firefly* hold its own with *lightning bug.*

lightning rod ►*n.* A metal rod placed high on a structure to prevent damage by conducting lightning to the ground.

light•weight (līt′wāt′) ▸*n.* **1.** One that weighs relatively little or less than average. **2.** A boxer weighing from 127 to 135 lbs., between a featherweight and a welterweight. **3.** A person of little intelligence, influence, or importance. —**light′weight′** *adj.*

light-year also **light year** (līt′yîr′) ▸*n.* **1.** The distance that light travels in a vacuum in one year, approx. 9.46 trillion km or 5.88 trillion mi. **2.** often **light-years** *Informal* A long way.

lig•nin (lĭg′nĭn) ▸*n.* A complex polymer that hardens and strengthens the cell walls of plants. [Lat. *lignum*, wood + -IN.]

lig•nite (lĭg′nīt′) ▸*n.* A soft, brownish-black coal. [Lat. *lignum*, wood + -ITE[1].] —**lig•nit′ic** (-nĭt′ĭk) *adj.*

lig•num vi•tae (lĭg′nəm vī′tē) ▸*n., pl.* **-taes** **1.** A tropical American tree having very heavy, durable wood. **2.** The wood of this tree. [NLat. *lignum vītae*, wood of life.]

lig•ro•in (lĭg′rō-ĭn) ▸*n.* A volatile, flammable fraction of petroleum, obtained by distillation and used as a solvent. [Ger.]

Li•gu•ri•a (lĭ-gyo͝or′ē-ə) A region of NW Italy on the **Ligurian Sea,** an arm of the Mediterranean Sea between NW Italy and Corsica. —**Li•gu′ri•an** *adj. & n.*

lik•a•ble also **like•a•ble** (lī′kə-bəl) ▸*adj.* Pleasing; attractive. —**lik′a•ble•ness** *n.*

like[1] (līk) ▸*v.* **liked, lik•ing** **1.** To find pleasant; enjoy. **2.** To want, wish, or prefer. **3.** To feel about; regard. ▸*n.* Something that is liked; preference. [< OE *līcian*, please.]

like[2] (līk) ▸*prep.* **1.** Resembling closely; similar to. **2.** In the typical manner of: *It's not like you.* **3.** Inclined to: *felt like running away.* **4.** Indicative of: *looks like rain.* **5.** Such as: *saved things like old newspapers.* ▸*adj.* **1.** Similar. **2.** Alike. ▸*adv.* As if: *ran like crazy.* ▸*n.* One similar to or like another: *bolts, screws, and the like.* ▸*conj. Informal* **1.** In the same way that; as: *To dance like she does takes practice.* **2.** As if: *It looks like we'll finish on time.* —***idiom:*** **be like** *Informal* To say: *And he's like, "Leave me alone!"* See Usage Note at **go[1].** [< OE *gelīc*, similar.]

Usage: Writers since Chaucer's time have used *like* as a conjunction, but this usage has received so much criticism that many people prefer to restrict *like* to its function as a preposition, at least in formal writing, thus requiring *The dogs howled as* (not *like*) *we expected them to.* The use of *like* as a conjunction when the following verb is not expressed, as in *He took to politics like a duck to water,* is less likely to provoke objections, in part because it so closely resembles a preposition in these instances.

-like ▸*suff.* Resembling or characteristic of: *ladylike.* [< LIKE[2].]

like•li•hood (līk′lē-ho͝od′) ▸*n.* **1.** The state of being probable; probability. **2.** Something probable.

like•ly (līk′lē) ▸*adj.* **-li•er, -li•est** **1.** Having a tendency or likelihood: *They are likely to win.* **2.** Credible; plausible: *a likely excuse.* **3.** Apparently suitable: *a likely candidate for the job.* **4.** Promising: *a likely topic for investigation.* ▸*adv. Informal* Probably.

like-mind•ed (līk′mīn′dĭd) ▸*adj.* Of the same turn of mind.

lik•en (lī′kən) ▸*v.* To see, mention, or show as similar: *likened the branches to fingers.*

like•ness (līk′nĭs) ▸*n.* **1.** Similarity; resemblance. **2.** An imitative appearance; semblance. **3.** A copy or picture of something; image.

like•wise (līk′wīz′) ▸*adv.* **1.** In the same way; similarly. **2.** As well; also.

lik•ing (lī′kĭng) ▸*n.* **1.** A feeling of attraction; fondness. **2.** Preference or taste.

li•lac (lī′lək, -lŏk, -lăk) ▸*n.* **1.** A shrub widely cultivated for its clusters of fragrant purplish or white flowers. **2.** A pale purple. [< Ar. *līlak*, ult. < Skt. *nīla-*, dark blue.] —**li′lac** *adj.*

li•lan•ge•ni (lĭ-läng′gĕ-nē) ▸*n., pl.* **em•a•lan•ge•ni** (ĕm′ə-läng-gĕn′ē). See table at **currency.** [Of Bantu orig.]

Li•li•u•o•ka•la•ni (lē-lē′o͞o-ō-kä-lä′nē), **Lydia Kamekeha Paki.** 1838–1917. Queen of the Hawaiian Islands (1891–93).

Liliuokalani
photographed c. 1891

Li•long•we (lĭ-lông′wā) The capital of Malawi, in the S-central part. Pop. 233,973.

lilt (lĭlt) ▸*n.* **1.** A cheerful or lively manner of speaking. **2.** A light, happy tune or song. [< ME *lilten*, sound an alarm.]

lil•y (lĭl′ē) ▸*n., pl.* **-ies** **1.** Any of a genus of plants having variously colored, often trumpet-shaped flowers. **2.** A similar plant, such as the day lily. [< Lat. *līlium.*]

lil•y-liv•ered (lĭl′ē-lĭv′ərd) ▸*adj.* Cowardly.

lily of the valley ▸*n., pl.* **lilies of the valley.** A plant having a cluster of small, fragrant, bell-shaped white flowers.

lily pad ▸*n.* One of the floating leaves of a water lily.

Li•ma (lē′mə) The capital of Peru, in the west-central part. Pop. 6,414,500.

li•ma bean (lī′mə) ▸*n.* **1.** A plant having flat pods containing large, light green, edible seeds. **2.** The seed of this plant. [After LIMA, Peru.]

limb (lĭm) ▸*n.* **1.** A large tree branch. **2.** One of the jointed appendages of an animal, such as an arm, leg, wing, or flipper. [< OE *lim.*]

lim•ber (lĭm′bər) ▸*adj.* **1.** Bending or flexing readily; pliable. **2.** Capable of moving, bending, or contorting easily; supple. ▸*v.* To make or become limber: *limbered up before the game.* [?] —**lim′ber•ness** *n.*

lim•bic system (lĭm′bĭk) ▸*n.* A group of deep brain structures in mammals associated with primitive brain functions. [< Lat. *limbus*, border.] —**lim′bic** *adj.*

lim•bo[1] (lĭm′bō) ▸*n., pl.* **-bos** **1.** often **Limbo** In the Roman Catholic Church, the abode of souls excluded from heaven but not condemned to further punishment. **2.** A region or condition of oblivion, neglect, or prolonged uncertainty. [< Lat. *limbus*, border.]

lim•bo² (lĭm′bō) ►*n.*, *pl.* **-bos.** A West Indian dance in which the dancers bend over backward and pass under a pole lowered slightly each time. [Prob. ult. of African orig.]

Lim•burg•er (lĭm′bûr′gər) ►*n.* A soft white cheese with a very strong odor and flavor. [After *Limburg*, Belgium.]

lime¹ (līm) ►*n.* **1.** A spiny evergreen citrus tree cultivated for its green, egg-shaped fruit. **2.** The fruit of this tree. [Prob. < Ar. *līmūn*, lemon.]

lime² (līm) ►*n.* See **linden.** [< OE *lind.*]

lime³ (līm) ►*n.* **1.** Calcium oxide. **2.** Birdlime. ►*v.* **limed, lim•ing.** To treat with lime. [< OE *līm*, birdlime.] —**lim′y** *adj.*

lime•light (līm′līt′) ►*n.* **1.** A focus of public attention. **2.** An early type of stage light in which lime was heated to incandescence producing brilliant illumination.

lim•er•ick (lĭm′ər-ĭk) ►*n.* A humorous or nonsensical verse of five anapestic lines usu. with the rhyme scheme *aabba.* [After *Limerick*, Ireland.]

lime•stone (līm′stōn′) ►*n.* A common sedimentary rock consisting mostly of calcium carbonate.

lim•it (lĭm′ĭt) ►*n.* **1.** The point, edge, or line beyond which something cannot or may not proceed. **2. limits** A boundary; bounds: *within city limits.* **3.** The greatest or least amount or number allowed. ►*v.* To confine or restrict within a boundary. [< Lat. *līmes*, *līmit-*.] —**lim′it•a•ble** *adj.* —**lim′i•ta′tion** *n.* —**lim′it•er** *n.* —**lim′it•less** *adj.*

lim•it•ed (lĭm′ĭ-tĭd) ►*adj.* **1.** Confined within certain limits. **2.** Mediocre or qualified: *a limited success.* **3.** Designating trains or buses that make few stops. —**lim′i•ted•ly** *adv.*

limn (lĭm) ►*v.* **limned, limn•ing 1.** To describe. **2.** To depict by painting or drawing. See Syns at **represent.** [< Lat. *lūmināre*, illuminate.] —**limn′er** (lĭm′nər) *n.*

lim•o (lĭm′ō) ►*n.*, *pl.* **lim•os** *Informal.* A limousine.

lim•ou•sine (lĭm′ə-zēn′, lĭm′ə-zēn′) ►*n.* **1.** A large, luxurious passenger vehicle, esp. one driven by a chauffeur. **2.** A small bus used to carry passengers esp. to airports and hotels. [After *Limousin*, a region of France.]

limp (lĭmp) ►*v.* **1.** To walk lamely, favoring one leg. **2.** To proceed haltingly. ►*n.* An irregular, jerky, or awkward gait. ►*adj.* **-er, -est 1.** Lacking rigidity. **2.** Weak or spiritless. [Prob. < OE *lempheal*t, lame.] —**limp′ly** *adv.* —**limp′ness** *n.*

Syns: *limp, flabby, flaccid, floppy* ***Ant:*** *firm* ***adj.***

lim•pet (lĭm′pĭt) ►*n.* A marine gastropod mollusk having a conical shell and adhering to rocks of tidal areas. [Poss. ME *lempet.*]

lim•pid (lĭm′pĭd) ►*adj.* Crystal clear; transparent. See Syns at **clear.** [Lat. *limpidus.*] —**lim•pid′i•ty, lim′pid•ness** *n.* —**lim′pid•ly** *adv.*

Lim•po•po (lĭm-pō′pō) A river of SE Africa rising near Johannesburg in NE South Africa and flowing about 1,770 km (1,100 mi) to the Indian Ocean in S Mozambique.

lin•age also **line•age** (lī′nĭj) ►*n.* The number of lines of printed or written material.

linch•pin (lĭnch′pĭn′) ►*n.* **1.** A locking pin inserted in the end of a shaft, as in an axle, to prevent a wheel from slipping off. **2.** A central cohesive element. [< OE *lynis*, linchpin + PIN.]

Lin•coln (lĭng′kən) The capital of NE, in the SE part SW of Omaha. Pop. 191,972.

Lincoln, Abraham. 1809–65. The 16th US President (1861–65); assassinated.

Abraham Lincoln
photographed c. 1864

Lincoln, Mary Todd. 1818–82. First Lady of the US (1861–65) as the wife of President Abraham Lincoln.

Lind•bergh (lĭnd′bûrg′, lĭn′-), **Anne Spencer Morrow.** b. 1906. Amer. aviator and writer.

Lindbergh, Charles Augustus. 1902–74. Amer. pioneer aviator.

lin•den (lĭn′dən) ►*n.* A shade tree having heart-shaped leaves and drooping clusters of yellowish, often fragrant flowers. [< OE *lind.*]

Lind•say (lĭn′zē), **(Nicholas) Vachel.** 1879–1931. Amer. poet.

line¹ (līn) ►*n.* **1.** A geometric figure formed by a point moving along a fixed direction and the reverse direction. **2.** A thin continuous mark, as that made by a pen, pencil, or brush. **3.** A crease in the skin; wrinkle. **4.** A border or boundary. **5.** A contour or outline. **6.** A cable, rope, string, cord, or wire. **7.** An electric-power transmission cable. **8.** A telephone connection. **9.** A system of transportation, esp. a company owning such a system. **10.** A course of progress or movement: *a line of flight.* **11.** A general manner or course of procedure: *different lines of thought.* **12.** An official policy: *the party line.* **13.** Alignment: *brought the front wheels into line.* **14a.** One's trade or occupation. **b.** Range of competence: *not in my line.* **15.** Merchandise of a similar nature: *a line of small tools.* **16.** A group of persons or things arranged in a row: *long lines at the box office.* **17.** A horizontal row of printed or written words or symbols. **18.** A brief letter; note. **19a.** A unit of verse ending in a textual or typographic break. **b.** often **lines** The dialogue of a theatrical presentation, such as a play. **20.** *Informal* Glib or insincere talk. **21.** *Football* **a.** A line of scrimmage. **b.** The linemen. ►*v.* **lined, lin•ing 1.** To mark with lines. **2.** To place in a series or row. **3.** To form a bordering line along. —***phrasal verb:*** **line up 1.** To form a line. **2.** *Football* To take one's position in a formation before a snap or kickoff. **3.** To organize: *line up support.* —***idioms:*** **down the line 1.** Throughout. **2.** In the future. **in line for** Next in order for. **on the line 1.** Ready for immediate payment. **2.** In jeopardy. **out of line**

1. Uncalled for; improper. 2. Out of control. [< Lat. *līnum*, linen, thread.]

line² (līn) ►*v.* **lined, lin•ing 1.** To fit or sew a covering to the inside surface of. **2.** To cover the inner surface of. [< OE *līn*, flax < Lat. *līnum*.]

lin•e•age¹ (lĭn′ē-ĭj) ►*n.* Direct descent from a particular ancestor; ancestry. [< OFr. *lignage* < *ligne*, LINE¹.]

line•age² (lī′nĭj) ►*n.* Var. of **linage**.

lin•e•al (lĭn′ē-əl) ►*adj.* **1.** In the direct line of descent from an ancestor. **2.** Linear. —**lin′e•al•ly** *adv.*

lin•e•a•ment (lĭn′ē-ə-mənt) ►*n.* A distinctive shape, contour, or line, esp. of the face. [< Lat. *līnea*, LINE¹.]

lin•e•ar (lĭn′ē-ər) ►*adj.* **1.** Of or resembling a line; straight. **2.** Having only one dimension. [< Lat. *līnea*, LINE¹.] —**lin′e•ar•ly** *adv.*

linear equation ►*n.* An algebraic equation involving only terms of the first degree.

line•back•er (līn′băk′ər) ►*n.* *Football* A defensive player positioned behind the ends and tackles.

line drive ►*n.* *Baseball* A batted ball hit sharply in a roughly straight line.

line-i•tem veto (līn′ī′təm) ►*n.* Authority, as of a government executive, to reject individual provisions of a bill.

line•man (līn′mən) ►*n.* **1.** One who installs or repairs telephone, telegraph, or electric power lines. **2.** *Football* A player positioned on the forward line.

lin•en (lĭn′ən) ►*n.* **1.** Thread or cloth made from flax. **2.** also **linens** Household articles made from linen or other cloth; bed sheets and tablecloths. [< OE *līnen*, flaxen, ult. < Lat. *līnum*, flax.] —**lin′en** *adj.*

line of scrimmage ►*n.* *Football* Either of two imaginary lines parallel to the goal line at the ends of the ball as it rests prior to being snapped and at which each team lines up for a new play.

line printer ►*n.* A high-speed printer that prints each line of type as a unit instead of printing each character individually.

lin•er¹ (lī′nər) ►*n.* **1.** One that makes lines. **2.** A large commercial ship or airplane, esp. one carrying passengers on a regular route.

lin•er² (lī′nər) ►*n.* **1.** One who puts in linings. **2.** Material used as a lining.

lines•man (līnz′mən) ►*n.* **1a.** *Football* An official who marks the downs and the position of the ball. **b.** *Sports* An official in various court games who calls shots that fall out of bounds. **2.** See **lineman** 1.

line•up also **line-up** (līn′ŭp′) ►*n.* **1.** A line of people formed for inspection or identification. **2.** *Sports* **a.** The members of a team chosen to start a game. **b.** A list of such players.

-ling ►*suff.* **1.** One connected with: *hireling.* **2.** One having a specified quality: *underling.* **3.** One that is young, small, or inferior: *duckling.* [< OE.]

lin•ger (lĭng′gər) ►*v.* **1.** To be slow in leaving, esp. out of reluctance; tarry. **2.** To persist: *an aftertaste that lingers.* **3.** To procrastinate. [ME *lengeren* < *lengen*, prolong.] —**lin′ger•er** *n.* —**lin′ger•ing•ly** *adv.*

lin•ge•rie (län′zhə-rā′, län′zhə-rē) ►*n.* Women's underwear. [< OFr. < *linge*, linen.]

lin•go (lĭng′gō) ►*n., pl.* **-goes 1.** Unintelligible or unfamiliar language. **2.** Specialized language; jargon. [< Lat. *lingua*, language.]

lin•gua fran•ca (lĭng′gwə frăng′kə) ►*n., pl.* **lingua fran•cas** (-kəz). A medium of communication between peoples of different languages. [Ital.]

lin•gual (lĭng′gwəl) ►*adj.* Of or pronounced with the tongue. [< Lat. *lingua*, tongue.] —**lin′gual** *n.* —**lin′gual•ly** *adv.*

lin•gui•ne also **lin•gui•ni** (lĭng-gwē′nē) ►*n.* Pasta in long, flat, thin strands. [Ital., pl. dim. of *lingua*, tongue.]

lin•guist (lĭng′gwĭst) ►*n.* **1.** A specialist in linguistics. **2.** A polyglot. [Lat. *lingua*, language + -IST.]

lin•guis•tics (lĭng-gwĭs′tĭks) ►*n.* *(takes sing. v.)* The study of the nature and structure of human speech. —**lin•guis′tic** *adj.* —**lin•guis′ti•cal•ly** *adv.*

lin•i•ment (lĭn′ə-mənt) ►*n.* A medicinal fluid rubbed into the skin. [< LLat. *linīmentum* < Lat. *linere*, anoint.]

lin•ing (lī′nĭng) ►*n.* A covering or coating for an inside surface.

link (lĭngk) ►*n.* **1.** One of the rings or loops forming a chain. **2a.** One of a connected series of units: *links of sausage.* **b.** A unit in a transportation or communications system. **c.** A tie or bond. **3.** *Comp. Sci.* A text segment or graphical item that serves as a cross-reference, as between or within hypertext documents. ►*v.* To connect or become connected with or as if with a link. [ME *linke*, of Scand. orig.]

link•age (lĭng′kĭj) ►*n.* **1.** The act or process of linking or the condition of being linked. **2.** A system of connected elements.

link•ing verb (lĭng′kĭng) ►*n.* See **copula**.

links (lĭngks) ►*pl.n.* A golf course. [< OE *hlinc*, ridge.]

Lin•nae•us (lĭ-nē′əs, -nā′-), **Carolus.** 1707–78. Swedish botanist.

lin•net (lĭn′ĭt) ►*n.* A small brownish Old World finch. [< OFr. *linette* < *lin*, flax.]

li•no•le•um (lĭ-nō′lē-əm) ►*n.* A durable, washable material made in sheets, used as a covering esp. for floors. [Orig. a trademark.]

lin•seed (lĭn′sēd′) ►*n.* The seed of flax, esp. when used as the source of linseed oil. [< OE *līnsǣd*.]

lint (lĭnt) ►*n.* Clinging bits of fiber and fluff; fuzz. [< Lat. *linteum*, linen.] —**lint′y** *adj.*

lin•tel (lĭn′tl) ►*n.* The horizontal beam over the top of a window or door. [< VLat. **līmitāris*, of a threshold.]

Linz (lĭnts) A city of N Austria on the Danube R. W of Vienna. Pop. 203,044.

li•on (lī′ən) ►*n.* **1.** A large wild cat of Africa and NW India, having a short tawny coat and, in the male, a long heavy mane. **2.** A celebrity. —***idiom:*** **lion's share** The greatest or best part. [< Gk. *leōn*.]

li•on•ess (lī′ə-nĭs) ►*n.* A female lion.

li•on•heart•ed (lī′ən-här′tĭd) ►*adj.* Extraordinarily courageous.

li•on•ize (lī′ə-nīz′) ►*v.* **-ized, -iz•ing.** To treat (a person) as a celebrity. —**li′on•i•za′tion** *n.*

lip (lĭp) ►*n.* **1.** Either of two fleshy folds that surround the opening of the mouth. **2a.** A structure or part that encircles an orifice. **b.** A protruding part of certain flowers. **3a.** The tip of a pouring spout, as on a pitcher. **b.** A rim.

4. *Slang* Insolent talk. [< OE *lippa.*]

Li•petsk (lē′pĕtsk′) A city of W-central Russia SSE of Moscow. Pop. 465,753.

lip•id (lĭp′ĭd) ►*n.* Any of a group of organic compounds that includes fats, oils, waxes, sterols, and triglycerides. [LIPO– + –IDE.] —**lip•id′ic** *adj.*

lipo– or **lip–** ►*pref.* **1.** Fat: *liposuction.* **2.** Lipid: *lipoprotein.* [< Gk. *lipos*, fat.]

lip•o•pro•tein (lĭp′ō-prō′tēn′, -tē-ĭn, lī′pō-) ►*n.* A lipid-protein complex by which lipids are transported in the bloodstream.

lip•o•suc•tion (lĭp′ō-sŭk′shən, lī′pō-) ►*n.* A surgical procedure that uses suction to remove excess fat from an area of the body.

Lip•pi (lĭp′ē), Fra **Filippo.** 1406?–69? Italian Renaissance painter.

lip reading ►*n.* A technique for understanding unheard speech by interpreting the lip and facial movements of the speaker. —**lip′-read′** *v.* —**lip reader** *n.*

lip service ►*n.* Insincere agreement or allegiance; hypocritical respect.

lip•stick (lĭp′stĭk′) ►*n.* A small stick of waxy lip coloring enclosed in a cylindrical case.

lip-synch also **lip-sync** (lĭp′sĭngk′) ►*v.* **-synched, -synch•ing** also **-synced, -sync•ing.** To move the lips in synchronization with recorded speech or song.

liq•ue•fy also **liq•ui•fy** (lĭk′wə-fī′) ►*v.* To make or become liquid. [< Lat. *liquefacere.*] —**liq′ue•fac′tion** (-făk′shən) *n.*

li•queur (lĭ-kûr′, -kyŏŏr′) ►*n.* A strongly flavored alcoholic beverage, usu. served after dinner. [Fr. LIQUOR.]

liq•uid (lĭk′wĭd) ►*n.* A substance capable of flowing or of being poured. ►*adj.* **1.** Of or being a liquid. **2.** Liquefied, esp.: **a.** Melted by heating: *liquid wax.* **b.** Condensed by cooling: *liquid oxygen.* **3.** Readily convertible into cash: *liquid assets.* [< Lat. *liquēre*, be liquid.] —**liq′uid•ness** *n.*

liq•ui•date (lĭk′wĭ-dāt′) ►*v.* **-dat•ed, -dat•ing 1a.** To pay off (e.g., a debt); settle. **b.** To settle the affairs of (e.g., a business). **2.** To convert (assets) into cash. **3.** To put an end to; abolish or kill. See Syns at **eliminate.** —**liq′ui•da′tion** *n.* —**liq′ui•da′tor** *n.*

li•quid•i•ty (lĭ-kwĭd′ĭ-tē) ►*n.* **1.** The state of being liquid. **2.** The quality of being readily convertible into cash.

liq•uor (lĭk′ər) ►*n.* **1.** An alcoholic beverage made by distillation rather than by fermentation. **2.** A liquid substance or solution. [< Lat., a liquid.]

li•ra (lîr′ə, lē′rä) ►*n., pl.* **li•re** (lîr′ā, lē′rĕ) or **li•ras.** See table at **currency.** [< Lat. *lībra*, pound.]

Lis•bon (lĭz′bən) The capital of Portugal, in the W part on the Tagus R. estuary. Pop. 663,315.

lisle (līl) ►*n.* A fine, smooth, tightly twisted thread spun from long-stapled cotton. [After *Lisle* (Lille), France.]

lisp (lĭsp) ►*n.* A speech defect or mannerism in which the sounds (s) and (z) are pronounced as (th) and (*th*). [< OE *wlisp.*] —**lisp** *v.* —**lisp′er** *n.*

lis•some also **lis•som** (lĭs′əm) ►*adj.* Limber; supple; lithe. [Alteration of LITHESOME.] —**lis′some•ly** *adv.* —**lis′some•ness** *n.*

list[1] (lĭst) ►*n.* A series of names, words, or other items written, printed, or imagined one after the other. ►*v.* **1.** To make a list of; itemize. **2.** To enter in a list. **3.** To have a stated list price. [< OItal. *lista.*]

list[2] (lĭst) ►*n.* An inclination to one side, as of a ship; tilt. [?] —**list** *v.*

lis•ten (lĭs′ən) ►*v.* **1.** To make an effort to hear something. **2.** To pay attention. [< OE *hlysnan.*] —**lis′ten•er** *n.*

Lis•ter (lĭs′tər), **Joseph.** First Baron Lister. 1827–1912. British surgeon.

list•ing (lĭs′tĭng) ►*n.* **1.** An entry in a list. **2.** A list. **3.** *Comp. Sci.* A printout of a program or data set.

list•less (lĭst′lĭs) ►*adj.* Lacking energy or enthusiasm; lethargic. [Poss. ME *liste*, desire + –NESS.] —**list′less•ly** *adv.* —**list′less•ness** *n.*

list price ►*n.* A basic published price, often subject to discount.

list•serv•er (lĭst′sûr′vər) ►*n.* A file server used in the management of e-mail for members of a discussion group.

Liszt (lĭst), **Franz.** 1811–86. Hungarian composer and pianist.

lit[1] (lĭt) ►*v.* P.t. and p.part. of **light**[1]**.** See Usage Note at **light**[1]**.**

lit[2] (lĭt) ►*v.* P.t. and p.part. of **light**[2]**.**

lit. ►*abbr.* **1.** liter **2a.** literal **b.** literally **3.** literary **4.** literature

lit•a•ny (lĭt′n-ē) ►*n., pl.* **-nies 1.** A prayer consisting of petitions recited by a leader alternating with responses by the congregation. **2.** A repetitive recital. [< Gk. *litaneia*, entreaty.]

lit•as (lĭt′äs) ►*n.* See table at **currency.** [Lithuanian.]

li•tchi also **li•chee** (lē′chē) ►*n.* **1.** A Chinese tree that bears edible fruit. **2.** The nutlike fruit of this tree. [Mandarin *lì zhī.*]

li•ter (lē′tər) ►*n.* See table at **measurement.** [< Gk. *litra*, a unit of weight.]

lit•er•a•cy (lĭt′ər-ə-sē) ►*n.* The ability to read and write.

lit•er•al (lĭt′ər-əl) ►*adj.* **1.** Conforming or limited to the simplest, nonfigurative, or most obvious meaning of a word or words. **2.** Word for word; verbatim: *a literal translation.* **3.** Avoiding exaggeration or embellishment; prosaic. **4.** Consisting of or expressed by letters: *literal notation.* [< Lat. *littera*, letter.] —**lit′er•al•ly** *adv.* —**lit′er•al•ness** *n.*

lit•er•ar•y (lĭt′ə-rĕr′ē) ►*adj.* **1.** Of or relating to literature. **2a.** Found in or appropriate to literature: *a literary style.* **b.** Bookish; pedantic: *literary language.* [Lat. *litterārius.*] —**lit′er•ar′i•ly** (-râr′ə-lē) *adv.* —**lit′er•ar′i•ness** *n.*

lit•er•ate (lĭt′ər-ĭt) ►*adj.* **1.** Able to read and write. **2.** Knowledgeable; well-read. **3.** Well-written. [< Lat. *litterātus*, lettered.] —**lit′er•ate** *n.* —**lit′er•ate•ly** *adv.*

lit•er•a•ti (lĭt′ə-rä′tē) ►*pl.n.* The literary intelligentsia. [Lat. *litterāti*, lettered people.]

lit•er•a•ture (lĭt′ər-ə-chŏŏr′, -chər) ►*n.* **1.** Imaginative or creative writing. **2.** The body of written works of a particular language, period, or culture. **3.** Printed material of any kind, as for a political campaign. [< Lat. *litterātūra.*]

–lith ►*suff.* Rock; stone: *megalith.* [< Gk. *lithos*, stone.]

lithe (līth) ►*adj.* **lith•er, lith•est 1.** Readily bent; supple. **2.** Graceful. [< OE *līthe.*] —**lithe′ly** *adv.* —**lithe′ness** *n.*

lithe•some (līth′səm) ►*adj.* Lithe; lissome.

-lithic ▶*suff.* Stone Age: *Paleolithic.* [Gk. *lithos*, stone + -IC.]

lith•i•um (lĭth′ē-əm) ▶*n. Symbol* **Li** A light, silvery, highly reactive metallic element used in ceramics, alloys, and thermonuclear weapons. At. no. 3. See table at **element.**

litho- or **lith-** ▶*pref.* Stone: *lithography.* [< Gk. *lithos*, stone.]

lith•o•graph (lĭth′ə-grăf′) ▶*n.* A print produced by lithography. —**lith′o•graph′** *v.* —**li•thog′raph•er** (lĭ-thŏg′rə-fər) *n.* —**lith′o•graph′ic, lith′o•graph′i•cal** *adj.*

li•thog•ra•phy (lĭ-thŏg′rə-fē) ▶*n.* A printing process in which the image is rendered on a flat surface and treated to retain ink while the nonimage areas are treated to repel ink.

lith•o•sphere (lĭth′ə-sfîr′) ▶*n.* The outer part of the earth; the earth's crust and upper mantle.

Lith•u•a•ni•a (lĭth′o͞o-ā′nē-ə) A country of N Europe on the Baltic Sea. Cap. Vilna. Pop. 3,721,000.

Lith•u•a•ni•an (lĭth′o͞o-ā′nē-ən) ▶*n.* **1.** A native or inhabitant of Lithuania. **2.** The Baltic language of the Lithuanians. —**Lith′u•a′ni•an** *adj.*

lit•i•gant (lĭt′ĭ-gənt) ▶*n.* A party in a lawsuit.

lit•i•gate (lĭt′ĭ-gāt′) ▶*v.* **-gat•ed, -gat•ing.** To engage in or subject to legal proceedings. [Lat. *lītigāre, lītigāt-* : *līs, līt-*, lawsuit + *agere*, pursue.] —**lit′i•ga′tion** *n.* —**lit′i•ga′tor** *n.*

li•ti•gious (lĭ-tĭj′əs) ▶*adj.* **1.** Of or marked by litigation. **2.** Tending to engage in lawsuits. —**li•ti′gious•ly** *adv.* —**li•ti′gious•ness** *n.*

lit•mus (lĭt′məs) ▶*n.* A water-soluble blue powder derived from lichens that changes to red with increasing acidity and to blue with increasing basicity. [Of Scand. orig.]

litmus paper ▶*n.* White paper impregnated with litmus and used as a pH or acid-base indicator.

litmus test ▶*n.* **1.** A test for chemical acidity or basicity using litmus paper. **2.** A test that uses a single indicator to prompt a decision.

li•tre (lē′tər) ▶*n. Chiefly Brit.* Var. of **liter.**

lit•ter (lĭt′ər) ▶*n.* **1a.** A disorderly accumulation; pile. **b.** Carelessly discarded refuse, such as wastepaper. **2.** The offspring produced at one birth by a mammal. **3a.** Straw or other material used as bedding for animals. **b.** A material used to absorb an animal's excretions. **4.** A couch mounted on shafts, used to carry a passenger. **5.** A stretcher for carrying a disabled or dead person. ▶*v.* **1.** To make untidy by discarding rubbish carelessly. **2.** To scatter about; strew. [< Med.Lat. *lectāria* < Lat. *lectus*, bed.] —**lit′ter•er** *n.*

lit•ter•bug (lĭt′ər-bŭg′) ▶*n. Informal* One who litters public areas.

lit•tle (lĭt′l) ▶*adj.* **-tler** or **less** (lĕs) also **less•er** (lĕs′ər), **-tlest** or **least** (lēst) **1.** Small in size, quantity, or degree. See Syns at **small. 2.** Short in extent or duration; brief: *little time.* **3.** Unimportant; trivial. **4.** Narrow; petty. **5.** Without much power or influence. **6.** Young. ▶*adv.* **less, least.** Not much: *slept little.* ▶*n.* A small quantity: *Give me a little.* —***idiom:*** **little by little** Gradually. [< OE *lȳtel.*] —**lit′tle•ness** *n.*

Little Bighorn River. A river, about 145 km (90 mi), rising in N WY and flowing to S MT.

Little Dipper ▶*n.* Ursa Minor.

Little Rock. The capital of Arkansas, in the central part on the Arkansas R. Pop. 175,795.

lit•to•ral (lĭt′ər-əl) ▶*adj.* Of or on a shore, esp. a seashore. ▶*n.* A coastal region; shore. [< Lat. *lītus, lītor-*, shore.]

lit•ur•gy (lĭt′ər-jē) ▶*n., pl.* **-gies 1.** A prescribed form for public worship. **2.** often **Liturgy** The Christian Eucharist. [< Gk. *leitourgia*, public service : *lēiton*, town hall + *ergon*, work.] —**li•tur′gi•cal** (lĭ-tûr′jĭ-kəl) *adj.*

liv•a•ble also **live•a•ble** (lĭv′ə-bəl) ▶*adj.* **1.** Suitable to live in; habitable. **2.** Endurable. —**liv′a•ble•ness** *n.*

live[1] (lĭv) ▶*v.* **lived, liv•ing 1.** To be alive; exist. **2.** To continue to be alive. **3.** To subsist. **4.** To reside. **5.** To conduct one's life in a particular manner: *lived frugally.* **6.** To remain in memory or usage: *an event that lives on in our minds.* —***phrasal verbs:*** **live down** To overcome the shame or effect of over time. **live with** To resign oneself to. [< OE *libban.*]

live[2] (līv) ▶*adj.* **1.** Having life; alive. **2.** Of current interest. **3.** Glowing; burning. **4.** Not yet exploded: *live ammunition.* **5.** Carrying an electric current. **6.** Broadcast while being performed. [Alteration of ALIVE.]

live-in (lĭv′ĭn′) ▶*adj.* **1.** Residing in the place where one is employed. **2.** Residing together with another, esp. in sexual intimacy. —**live′-in′** *n.*

live•li•hood (līv′lē-ho͝od′) ▶*n.* Means of support; subsistence. [< OE *līflād*, course of life.]

live•long (lĭv′lông′, -lŏng′) ▶*adj.* Complete; whole: *the livelong day.* [ME : OE *lēof*, dear + LONG[1].]

live•ly (līv′lē) ▶*adj.* **-li•er, -li•est 1.** Full of life and energy; vigorous. **2.** Full of spirit; animated: *a lively tune.* **3.** Marked by animated intelligence: *a lively discussion.* **4.** Effervescent; sparkling. ▶*adv.* With energy or vigor: *Step lively!* —**live′li•ly** *adv.* —**live′li•ness** *n.*

li•ven (lī′vən) ▶*v.* To make or become more lively.

live oak (līv) ▶*n.* Any of several American evergreen oaks.

liv•er (lĭv′ər) ▶*n.* A large, reddish-brown, glandular vertebrate organ that secretes bile and is active in the formation of certain blood proteins and in the metabolism of carbohydrates, fats, and proteins. [< OE *lifer.*]

Liv•er•pool (lĭv′ər-po͞ol′) A borough of NW England on the Mersey R. Pop. 476,969.

liver spot ▶*n.* A benign brownish patch on the skin, often occurring in old age in fair-skinned people.

liv•er•wort (lĭv′ər-wûrt′, -wôrt′) ▶*n.* Any of a class of small, green, nonvascular plants related to the mosses.

liv•er•wurst (lĭv′ər-wûrst′, -wo͝orst′) ▶*n.* A sausage made of or containing ground liver.

liv•er•y (lĭv′ə-rē, lĭv′rē) ▶*n., pl.* **-ies 1.** A distinctive uniform worn by the male servants of a household. **2a.** The boarding and care of horses for a fee. **b.** The hiring out of horses and carriages. [< OFr. *livree*, delivery.] —**liv′er•ied** *adj.* —**liv′er•y•man** *n.*

lives (līvz) ▶*n.* Pl. of **life.**

live•stock (līv′stŏk′) ▶*n.* Domestic animals, such as cattle or horses, raised for home use or for profit.

live wire (līv) ▶*n.* **1.** A wire carrying electric current. **2.** *Informal* A vivacious, alert, or energetic person.

liv•id (lĭv′ĭd) ▸*adj.* **1.** Discolored, as from a bruise; black-and-blue. **2.** Ashen or pallid. **3.** Extremely angry. [< Lat. *līvidus.*] —**li•vid′i•ty, liv′id•ness** *n.* —**liv′id•ly** *adv.*

liv•ing (lĭv′ĭng) ▸*adj.* **1.** Possessing life; alive. **2.** In active function or use: *a living language.* **3.** True to life; realistic. ▸*n.* **1.** The condition or action of maintaining life. **2.** A manner or style of life. **3.** A livelihood.

living room ▸*n.* A room in a private residence intended for social and leisure activities.

Liv•ing•stone (lĭv′ĭng-stən), **David.** 1813–73. Scottish missionary and explorer.

living will ▸*n.* A will in which the signer requests not to be kept alive by medical life-support systems in the event of a terminal illness.

Li•vo•ni•a (lĭ-vō′nē-ə, -vōn′yə) **1.** A region comprising N Latvia and Estonia. **2.** A city of SE MI, a suburb of Detroit. Pop. 100,850. —**Li•vo′ni•an** *adj. & n.*

Li•vor•no (lē-vôr′nō) or **Leg•horn** (lĕg′hôrn′, -ərn). A city of NW Italy on the Ligurian Sea. Pop. 167,445.

li•vre (lē′vər, -vrə) ▸*n.* See table at **currency.** [Fr.]

Liv•y (lĭv′ē). 59 B.C.–A.D.17. Roman historian.

liz•ard (lĭz′ərd) ▸*n.* **1.** Any of numerous reptiles having a scaly elongated body, movable eyelids, four legs, and a tapering tail. **2.** Leather made from the skin of a lizard. [< Lat. *lacerta.*]

Lju•blja•na (lo͞o′blē-ä′nə) The capital of Slovenia, on the Sava R. WNW of Zagreb, Croatia. Pop. 281,821.

ll. ▸*abbr.* lines

lla•ma (lä′mə) ▸*n.* A South American mammal related to the camel, raised for its soft fleecy wool and used as a beast of burden. [< Quechua.]

Lloyd George (loid′ jôrj′), **David.** 1863–1945. British prime minister (1916–22).

lm ▸*abbr. Phys.* lumen

LNG ▸*abbr.* liquefied natural gas

lo (lō) ▸*interj.* Used to attract attention or to show surprise. [< OE *lā.*]

load (lōd) ▸*n.* **1a.** A supported weight or mass. **b.** The force to which a structure is subjected. **2.** Something carried, as by a vehicle, person, or animal. **3.** The share of work allocated to or required of a person, machine, group, or organization. **4.** A heavy responsibility; burden. **5.** often **loads** *Informal* A great number or amount. ▸*v.* **1.** To put (something) into or onto a structure or conveyance. **2.** To fill nearly to overflowing. **3.** To weigh down; burden. **4.** To charge (a firearm) with ammunition. **5.** To insert material into: *loaded the camera with film.* **6.** *Games* To make (dice) heavier on one side. **7.** To charge with meanings or implications. **8.** To dilute. **9.** *Comp. Sci.* To transfer (data) from storage into a computer's memory. [< OE *lād.*] —**load′er** *n.*

load•ed (lō′dĭd) ▸*adj.* **1.** Carrying a load. **2.** Heavy with meaning or emotional import: *a loaded question.* **3.** *Slang* Intoxicated; drunk. **4.** *Slang* Rich.

loaf¹ (lōf) ▸*n., pl.* **loaves** (lōvz). A shaped mass of bread or other food baked in one piece. [< OE *hlāf.*]

loaf² (lōf) ▸*v.* To pass time idly. [< obsolete *land-loafer,* vagabond.] —**loaf′er** *n.*

loam (lōm) ▸*n.* A fine soil composed of a mixture of sand, clay, silt, and organic matter. [< OE *lām,* clay.] —**loam′y** *adj.*

loan (lōn) ▸*n.* **1.** Something lent for temporary use. **2.** A sum of money lent at interest. ▸*v.* To lend (money or goods). [< ON *lān.*] —**loan′er** *n.*

loan•word (lōn′wûrd′) ▸*n.* A word, such as *honcho,* adopted from another language and at least partly naturalized.

loath (lōth, lō*th*) ▸*adj.* Unwilling or reluctant. [< OE *lāth,* loathsome.]

loathe (lō*th*) ▸*v.* **loathed, loath•ing.** To dislike greatly; abhor. [< OE *lāthian.*]

loath•ing (lō′*th*ĭng) ▸*n.* Great dislike; abhorrence. —**loath′ing•ly** *adv.*

loath•some (lō*th*′səm, lōth′-) ▸*adj.* Arousing loathing; abhorrent. See Syns at **offensive.** —**loath′some•ness** *n.*

lob (lŏb) ▸*v.* **lobbed, lob•bing.** To hit, throw, or propel in a high arc. [ME, lout.] —**lob** *n.*

lob•by (lŏb′ē) ▸*n., pl.* **-bies 1.** A hall, foyer, or waiting room at or near the entrance to a building, such as a hotel. **2.** A group of persons engaged in trying to influence legislators. ▸*v.* **-bied, -by•ing.** To try to influence public officials for or against a specific cause. [Med.Lat. *lobia,* cloister, of Gmc. orig.] —**lob′by•er, lob′by•ist** *n.*

lobe (lōb) ▸*n.* A rounded part or projection, esp. of an organic structure: *the lobe of an ear.* [< Gk. *lobos.*] —**lobed** *adj.*

lo•bot•o•my (lə-bŏt′ə-mē, lō-) ▸*n., pl.* **-mies.** Surgery on the frontal lobe of the brain to sever one or more nerve tracts.

lob•ster (lŏb′stər) ▸*n.* **1.** A large edible marine crustacean having five pairs of legs, the first pair of which is modified into large pincers. **2.** Any of several related crustaceans. [< OE *loppestre.*]

lo•cal (lō′kəl) ▸*adj.* **1.** Of or relating to a particular place: *a local custom.* **2.** Not widespread: *local outbreaks of flu.* **3.** Of or affecting a specific part of the body: *a local infection; local anesthetic.* **4.** Making many stops on a route: *a local train.* ▸*n.* **1.** A public conveyance that stops at all stations. **2.** A local chapter or branch of an organization, esp. of a labor union. **3.** *Informal* A person from a particular locality. [< Lat. *locus,* place.] —**lo′cal•ly** *adv.*

lo•cale (lō-kăl′) ▸*n.* A place, esp. with reference to an event. [< OFr. *local,* LOCAL.]

lo•cal•i•ty (lō-kăl′ĭ-tē) ▸*n., pl.* **-ties.** A particular neighborhood, place, or district.

lo•cal•ize (lō′kə-līz′) ▸*v.* **-ized, -iz•ing 1.** To make local. **2.** To confine or restrict to a locality. —**lo′cal•i•za′tion** *n.*

lo•cate (lō′kāt′, lō-kāt′) ▸*v.* **-cat•ed, -cat•ing 1.** To determine the position of. **2.** To find by searching. **3.** To place; situate. **4.** To become established; settle. [Lat. *locāre,* to place.] —**lo′cat′er, lo′cat′or** *n.*

lo•ca•tion (lō-kā′shən) ▸*n.* **1.** The act or process of locating. **2.** A place where something is located. **3.** A site away from a studio at which part or all of a movie is shot. —**lo•ca′tion•al** *adj.*

loc. cit. ▸*abbr. Lat.* loco citato (in the place cited)

loch (lŏKH, lŏk) ▸*n. Scots* **1.** A lake. **2.** An arm of the sea similar to a fjord. [< Sc.Gael. *loch.*]

lo•ci (lō′sī′, -kē, -kī′) ▸*n.* Pl. of **locus.**

lock¹ (lŏk) ▸*n.* **1.** A device operated by a key,

combination, or keycard and used, as on a door, for holding, closing, or securing. **2.** A section of a canal closed off with gates for raising or lowering the water level. **3.** A mechanism in a firearm for exploding the charge. ►*v.* **1.** To fasten or become fastened with a lock. **2.** To confine or exclude by or as if by means of a lock. **3.** To clasp or link firmly: *lock arms.* **4.** To bind in close struggle or battle. **5.** To become entangled; interlock. **6.** To become rigid or immobile. [< OE *loc*, bolt, bar.] —**lock′a•ble** *adj.*

lock[1]
Miraflores Locks, Panama Canal

lock[2] (lŏk) ►*n.* A length or curl of hair; tress. [< OE *locc*.]

Locke (lŏk), **John.** 1632–1704. English philosopher.

lock•er (lŏk′ər) ►*n.* **1.** A small, usu. metal compartment that can be locked, esp. one at a public place for the safekeeping of clothing and valuables. **2.** A flat trunk for storage. **3.** A refrigerated cabinet or room for storing frozen foods.

locker room ►*n.* A room with lockers and usu. showers, as in a gymnasium, in which to change clothes and store equipment.

lock•et (lŏk′ĭt) ►*n.* A small ornamental case for a keepsake, usu. worn as a pendant.

lock•jaw (lŏk′jô′) ►*n.* **1.** See **tetanus. 2.** A symptom of tetanus, in which the jaw is held tightly closed by a spasm of muscles.

lock•out (lŏk′out′) ►*n.* The closing down of a workplace by an employer during a labor dispute.

lock•smith (lŏk′smĭth′) ►*n.* One who makes or repairs locks.

lock•step (lŏk′stĕp′) ►*n.* A way of marching in which the marchers follow each other closely.

lo•co (lō′kō) ►*adj. Slang* Mad; insane. [Sp.]

lo•co•mo•tion (lō′kə-mō′shən) ►*n.* The act of moving or ability to move from place to place. [Lat. *locus*, place + MOTION.]

lo•co•mo•tive (lō′kə-mō′tĭv) ►*n.* A self-propelled vehicle, usu. electric or diesel-powered, that moves railroad cars. ►*adj.* Of or involved in locomotion.

lo•co•mo•tor (lō′kə-mō′tər) ►*adj.* Locomotive.

lo•co•weed (lō′kō-wēd′) ►*n.* Any of several plants of the western and central US that are poisonous to livestock.

lo•cus (lō′kəs) ►*n., pl.* **-ci** (-sī′, -kē, -kī′) **1.** A place. **2.** *Math.* The set of all points that satisfy specified conditions. [Lat.]

lo•cust (lō′kəst) ►*n.* **1.** A grasshopper that travels in destructive swarms that devour vegetation and crops. **2.** The periodical cicada. **3.** A North American tree having compound leaves, clusters of fragrant white flowers, and durable hard wood. [< Lat. *locusta*.]

lo•cu•tion (lō-kyōō′shən) ►*n.* **1.** A particular word, phrase, or expression. **2.** Style of speaking; phraseology. [< Lat. *loquī*, *locūt-*, speak.]

lode (lōd) ►*n.* A vein of mineral ore deposited between layers of rock. [< OE *lād*, way.]

lo•den (lōd′n) ►*n.* **1.** A durable, water-repellent, coarse woolen fabric. **2.** A deep olive green. [Ger., coarse fabric.]

lode•star (lōd′stär′) ►*n.* **1.** A star, esp. Polaris, used as a point of reference. **2.** A guiding principle or ambition. [ME *lodesterre*.]

lode•stone (lōd′stōn′) ►*n.* A magnetized piece of magnetite. [Obsolete *lode*, course + STONE.]

lodge (lŏj) ►*n.* **1a.** A cottage or cabin, often rustic, used as a temporary abode or shelter: *a ski lodge.* **b.** An inn. **2.** Any of various Native American dwellings, such as a hogan, wigwam, or longhouse. **3a.** A local chapter of certain fraternal organizations. **b.** The meeting hall of such a chapter. **4.** The den of certain animals, such as the dome-shaped one built by beavers. ►*v.* **lodged, lodg•ing 1.** To provide with or rent quarters temporarily, esp. for sleeping. **2.** To live in a rented room or rooms. **3.** To register (e.g., a complaint) before an authority. **4.** To vest (authority). **5.** To be or become embedded. [< OFr. *loge*.]

lodg•er (lŏj′ər) ►*n.* One that lodges, esp. one who rents and lives in a furnished room.

lodg•ing (lŏj′ĭng) ►*n.* **1.** Sleeping accommodations. **2.** Rented rooms.

Łódź (lŏdz, wōōch) A city of central Poland WSW of Warsaw. Pop. 846,514.

lo•ess (lō′əs, lĕs, lŭs) ►*n.* A windblown deposit of fine-grained silt or clay. [Ger. *Löss*.]

loft (lôft, lŏft) ►*n.* **1a.** A large, usu. unpartitioned floor in a commercial building. **b.** A loft converted into an apartment or studio. **2.** An open space under a roof; attic. **3.** A gallery or balcony, as in a church. **4.** A high arc given to a struck or thrown object, such as a golf ball or baseball. ►*v.* **1.** To put, store, or keep in a loft. **2.** To propel in a high arc. [< ON *lopt*, upstairs room.]

loft•y (lôf′tē, lŏf′-) ►*adj.* **-i•er, -i•est 1.** Of imposing height. **2.** Exalted; noble. **3.** Arrogant; haughty. —**loft′i•ly** *adv.* —**loft′i•ness** *n.*

log[1] (lôg, lŏg) ►*n.* **1.** A section of a trunk or limb of a fallen or felled tree. **2.** A device trailed from a ship to determine its speed through water. **3.** A record of a ship's or aircraft's speed, progress, and navigation. **4.** A regularly kept record; journal. ►*v.* **logged, log•ging 1a.** To cut down timber (on). **b.** To cut (trees) into logs. **2.** To enter in a ship's or aircraft's log. **3.** To travel (a specified distance, time, or speed). —***phrasal verbs:*** **log in** (or **on**) To enter into a computer the information required to begin a session. **log out** (or **off**) To enter into a computer the command to end a session. [ME *logge*.] —**log′ger** *n.*

log[2] (lôg, lŏg) ►*n. Math.* A logarithm.

Lo•gan (lō′gən) A city of N UT N of Ogden. Pop. 32,762.

lo•gan•ber•ry (lō′gən-bĕr′ē) ►*n.* An edible blackberrylike red fruit. [After James H. *Logan* (1841–1928).]

log•a•rithm (lôg′ə-rĭth′əm, lŏg′ə-) ►*n.* The power to which a fixed number, the base, must be raised to produce a given number. [Gk. *logos*, reason + *arithmos*, number.] —**log′a•rith′mic, log′a•rith′mi•cal** *adj.* —**log′a•rith′mi•cal•ly** *adv.*

loge (lōzh) ►*n.* **1.** A small compartment, esp. a box in a theater. **2.** The front rows of the mezzanine in a theater. [< OFr., lodge.]

log•ger•head (lô′gər-hĕd′, lŏg′ər-) ►*n.* A marine turtle having a large beaked head. —***idiom:* at loggerheads** Engaged in a head-on dispute. [Prob. dial. *logger*, wooden block + HEAD.]

log•ic (lŏj′ĭk) ►*n.* **1.** The study of the principles of reasoning. **2.** Valid reasoning, esp. as distinguished from invalid or irrational argumentation. **3.** The mathematical operations performed by a computer, such as sorting and comparing, that involve yes-no decisions. [< Gk. *logos*, reason.] —**lo•gi′cian** (lō-jĭsh′ən) *n.*

log•i•cal (lŏj′ĭ-kəl) ►*adj.* **1.** Of, using, or in accordance with logic. **2.** Reasonable. **3.** Showing consistency of reasoning. —**log′i•cal•ly** *adv.* —**log′i•cal•ness** *n.*

Syns: *logical, analytic, ratiocinative, rational* ***Ant:*** *illogical* **adj.**

log•in (lôg′ĭn′, lŏg′-) also **log•on** (-ŏn′, -ôn′) ►*n.* The process of identifying oneself to a computer, as by entering one's username and password.

lo•gis•tics (lō-jĭs′tĭks, lə-) ►*n.* *(takes sing. or pl. v.)* The procurement, distribution, maintenance, and replacement of materiel and personnel. [< Gk. *logistikos*, skilled in calculating.] —**lo•gis′tic, lo•gis′ti•cal** *adj.* —**lo•gis′ti•cal•ly** *adv.*

log•jam (lôg′jăm′, lŏg′-) ►*n.* **1.** An immovable mass of floating logs crowded together. **2.** A deadlock; impasse.

lo•go (lō′gō′) ►*n.*, *pl.* **-gos.** A distinctive name, symbol, or trademark of a company designed for easy recognition. [< LOGOTYPE.]

lo•go•type (lô′gə-tīp′, lŏg′ə-) ►*n.* **1.** A piece of type bearing two or more usu. separate elements. **2.** A logo. [< Gk. *logos*, word.]

log•roll•ing (lôg′rō′lĭng, lŏg′-) ►*n.* The trading of influence or votes among legislators to achieve passage of projects of interest to one another. —**log′roll′er** *n.*

-logue or **-log** ►*suff.* Speech; discourse: *travelogue.* [< Gk. *-logos* < *legein*, speak.]

lo•gy (lō′gē) ►*adj.* **-gi•er, -gi•est.** Lethargic; sluggish. [Perh. < Du. *log*, heavy.]

-logy ►*suff.* **1.** Discourse; expression: *phraseology.* **2.** Science; theory; study: *geology.* [< Gk. *-logia* < *legein*, speak.]

loin (loin) ►*n.* **1a.** *Anat.* The part of the side and back between the ribs and pelvis. **b.** A cut of meat from this part of an animal. **2. loins a.** The region of the thighs and groin. **b.** The genitals. [< VLat. **lumbea*, of the loin < Lat. *lumbus*, loin.]

loin•cloth (loin′klôth′, -klŏth′) ►*n.* A strip of cloth worn around the loins.

Loire (lwär) A river, about 1,014 km (630 mi), rising in SE France and flowing to the Bay of Biscay.

loi•ter (loi′tər) ►*v.* **1.** To stand idly about; linger aimlessly. **2.** To proceed slowly or with many stops. **3.** To delay or dawdle. [Prob. < MDu. *loteren*, be loose.] —**loi′ter•er** *n.*

loll (lŏl) ►*v.* **1.** To recline in an indolent or relaxed way. **2.** To hang or droop laxly. [Prob. < MDu. *lollen*, doze.] —**loll′er** *n.*

lol•li•pop also **lol•ly•pop** (lŏl′ē-pŏp′) ►*n.* A piece of hard candy on the end of a small stick. [Perh. dial. *lolly*, tongue + POP[1].]

Lom•bar•dy (lŏm′bər-dē, lŭm′-) A region of N Italy bordering on Switzerland. —**Lom′bard** *adj. & n.*

Lo•mé (lō-mā′) The capital of Togo, in the S part on the Gulf of Guinea. Pop. 369,926.

lo mein (lō′ mān′) ►*n.* A Chinese dish of wheat noodles boiled then seasoned and stir-fried. [Cantonese.]

Lon•don (lŭn′dən) **1.** A city of SE Ontario, Canada, SW of Toronto. Pop. 303,165. **2.** The capital of the United Kingdom, on the Thames R. in SE England. Pop. 6,904,600.

London, John Griffith. "Jack." 1876–1916. Amer. writer.

lone (lōn) ►*adj.* **1.** Solitary: *a lone tree.* **2.** Isolated; unfrequented: *the lone prairie.* **3.** Sole: *the lone school in town.* [< ALONE.]

lone•ly (lōn′lē) ►*adj.* **-li•er, -li•est 1.** Without companions; solitary. **2.** Unfrequented by people; desolate. **3a.** Sad at being alone. **b.** Producing such sadness. —**lone′li•ness** *n.*

lon•er (lō′nər) ►*n.* One who avoids the company of other people.

lone•some (lōn′səm) ►*adj.* **1.** Sad at feeling alone. **2.** Offering solitude; secluded. —**lone′some•ly** *adv.* —**lone′some•ness** *n.*

long[1] (lông, lŏng) ►*adj.* **-er, -est 1.** Having great length. **2.** Of relatively great duration: *a long time.* **3.** Of a specified length or duration: *a mile long; an hour long.* **4.** Concerned with distant issues; far-reaching: *a long view of the plan.* **5.** Risky; chancy: *long odds.* **6.** Having an abundance or excess: *long on hope.* **7.** Of or being a vowel sound of comparatively great duration, such as those in *made* or *feed.* ►*adv.* **1.** For an extended period of time. **2.** For or throughout a specified period: *all night long.* **3.** At a distant point of time: *long before we were born.* ►*n.* A long time. —***idioms:* any longer** For more time: *can't wait any longer.* **as (**or **so) long as** Inasmuch as; since. **no longer** Not now as formerly: *We no longer smoke.* [< OE *lang.*]

long[2] (lông, lŏng) ►*v.* To have an earnest desire; yearn. [< OE *langian.*]

long. ►*abbr.* longitude

Long Beach. A city of S CA on an arm of the Pacific SE of Los Angeles. Pop. 429,433.

long•bow (lông′bō′, lŏng′-) ►*n.* A wooden, hand-drawn bow, often 6 ft. or longer.

long distance ►*n.* Telephone service between distant points. —**long′-dis′tance** *adj. & adv.*

lon•gev•i•ty (lŏn-jĕv′ĭ-tē, lôn-) ►*n.* **1.** Long life. **2.** Long duration. [< Lat. *longaevus*, ancient.]

Long•fel•low (lông′fĕl′ō, lŏng′-), **Henry Wadsworth.** 1807–82. Amer. writer.

long•hair (lông′hâr′, lŏng′-) ►*n.* *Informal* **1.** One dedicated to the arts and esp. to classical music. **2.** One having long hair, esp. a hippie. —**long′hair′, long′haired′** *adj.*

long•hand (lông′hănd′, lŏng′-) ►*n.* Cursive writing.

long•horn (lông′hôrn′, lŏng′-) ►*n.* Any of a breed of cattle with long horns, formerly bred in the SW US.

long•house (lông′hous′) ►*n.* A long communal dwelling, esp. of certain Native American, Polynesian, and Indonesian peoples.

long•ing (lông′ĭng, lŏng′-) ►*n.* A persistent yearning or desire. —**long′ing** *adj.* —**long′ing•ly** *adv.*

Long Island. An island of SE NY separated from CT by **Long Island Sound,** an arm of the Atlantic.

lon•gi•tude (lŏn′jĭ-to͞od′, -tyo͞od′, lôn′-) ►*n.* Angular distance east or west, measured with respect to the prime meridian at Greenwich, England. [< Lat. *longitūdō* < *longus*, long.] —**lon′gi•tu′di•nal** *adj.* —**lon′gi•tu′di•nal•ly** *adv.*

long jump ►*n.* A jump in track and field made for distance, usu. from a moving start.

long-lived (lông′līvd′, -lĭvd′, lŏng′-) ►*adj.* Having a long life. —**long′-lived′ness** *n.*

long-play•ing (lông′plā′ĭng, lŏng′-) ►*adj.* Of or being a phonograph record that turns at 33⅓ revolutions per minute.

long-range (lông′rānj′, lŏng′-) ►*adj.* **1.** Of or designed for great distances: *long-range missiles.* **2.** Involving an extended span of time: *long-range planning.*

long•shore•man (lông′shôr′mən, -shōr′-, lŏng′-) ►*n.* A dock worker who loads and unloads ships.

long shot ►*n.* An entry, as in a horserace, with only a slight chance of winning.

long-stand•ing (lông′stăn′dĭng, lŏng′-) ►*adj.* Of long duration or existence.

long-suf•fer•ing (lông′sŭf′ər-ĭng, lŏng′-) ►*adj.* Patiently enduring pain or difficulties.

long-term (lông′tûrm′, lŏng′-) ►*adj.* Involving or being in effect for a long time.

long ton ►*n.* See table at **measurement.**

Lon•gueil (lông-gāl′) A city of S Quebec, Canada, on the St. Lawrence R. opposite Montreal. Pop. 129,874.

long-wind•ed (lông′wĭn′dĭd, lŏng′-) ►*adj.* Wearisomely talkative. See Syns at **wordy.** —**long′-wind′ed•ly** *adv.* —**long′-wind′ed•ness** *n.*

loo•fa (lo͞o′fə) ►*n.* **1.** A tropical vine having cylindrical fruit with a fibrous interior. **2.** The interior of this fruit, used esp. as a sponge. [Ar. *lūfa.*]

look (lo͝ok) ►*v.* **1.** To use the eyes to see. **2.** To search. **3.** To focus one's gaze or attention: *look toward the river.* **4.** To seem or appear to be: *look ripe.* See Syns at **seem. 5.** To face in a specified direction. **6.** To have an appearance of conformity with: *look one's age.* —***phrasal verbs:*** **look after** To take care of. **look into** To investigate. **look on 1.** To be a spectator. **2.** To consider; regard. **look out** To be on guard. **look over** To inspect, esp. in a casual way. **look up 1.** To search for and find, as in a reference book. **2.** To visit: *look up an old friend.* **3.** To improve. ►*n.* **1.** The act or instance of looking; *gaze or glance.* **2.** Appearance or aspect. **3. looks** Physical appearance, esp. when pleasing. —***idioms:*** **look down on** To regard with contempt or condescension. **look up to** To admire. [< OE *lōcian.*] —**look′er** *n.*

look•ing glass (lo͝ok′ĭng) ►*n.* See **mirror** 1.

look•out (lo͝ok′out′) ►*n.* **1.** The act of observing or keeping watch. **2.** A high place commanding a wide view for observation. **3.** One who keeps watch.

loom¹ (lo͞om) ►*v.* **1.** To come into view as a massive, distorted, or indistinct image. **2.** To appear imminent and usu. theatening. [Perh. of Scand. orig.]

loom² (lo͞om) ►*n.* An apparatus for making thread or yarn into cloth by weaving strands together at right angles. [< OE *gelōma*, tool.]

loon¹ (lo͞on) ►*n.* A diving bird having mottled plumage and an eerie, laughlike cry. [Of Scand. orig.]

loon² (lo͞on) ►*n. Informal* One who is crazy or simple-minded. [ME *louen*, rogue.]

loon•y or **loon•ey** (lo͞o′nē) ►*adj.* **-i•er, -i•est** *Informal* **1.** Extremely foolish or silly. **2.** Crazy; insane. —**loon′i•ness** *n.* —**loon′y** *n.*

loop (lo͞op) ►*n.* **1.** A length of line, ribbon, or other thin material doubled over and joined at the ends. **2.** Something having a shape, order, or path of motion that is circular or curved over on itself. **3.** *Comp. Sci.* A sequence of instructions that repeats either a specified number of times or until a particular condition is met. ►*v.* **1.** To form, or form into, a loop. **2.** To fasten, join, or encircle with a loop or loops. [ME *loupe.*]

loop•hole (lo͞op′hōl′) ►*n.* **1.** A means of evasion. **2.** A small hole or slit in a wall, esp. one through which small arms may be fired. [ME *loupe* + HOLE.]

loop•y (lo͞o′pē) ►*adj.* **-i•er, -i•est.** Offbeat; crazy.

loose (lo͞os) ►*adj.* **loos•er, loos•est 1.** Not tightly fastened or secured. **2.** Not tightly stretched, taut, or fixed. **3.** Free from confinement. **4.** Not tight-fitting. **5.** Not bound, bundled, or gathered together. **6.** Lacking restraint or responsibility: *loose talk.* **7.** Licentious; immoral. **8.** Not literal or exact: *a loose translation.* ►*adv.* In a loose manner. ►*v.* **loosed, loos•ing 1.** To set free; release. **2.** To undo, untie, or unwrap. **3.** To make less tight, firm, or compact; loosen. **4.** To let fly; discharge: *loosed an arrow.* **5.** To relax. [< ON *lauss.*] —**loose′ly** *adv.* —**loose′ness** *n.*

Syns: *loose, lax, slack* ***Ant:*** *tight* **adj.**

loos•en (lo͞o′sən) ►*v.* **1.** To make or become loose or looser. **2.** To free from restraint, pressure, or strictness.

loot (lo͞ot) ►*n.* **1.** Valuables pillaged in war; spoils. **2.** Goods stolen or illicitly obtained. ►*v.* To pillage; plunder. [Hindi *lūṭ* < Skt. *lotram*, plunder.] —**loot′er** *n.*

lop (lŏp) ►*v.* **lopped, lop•ping 1.** To cut off (a part) from, esp. with a single swift blow. **2.** To cut off branches or twigs from; trim. [Perh. < ME *loppe*, small branches.]

lope (lōp) ►*v.* **loped, lop•ing.** To run or ride with a steady, easy gait. ►*n.* A steady, easy gait. [< ON *hlaupa*, leap.] —**lop′er** *n.*

lop•sid•ed (lŏp′sī′dĭd) ►*adj.* Heavier, larger, or higher on one side than on the other. —**lop′sid′ed•ly** *adv.* —**lop′sid′ed•ness** *n.*

lo•qua•cious (lō-kwā′shəs) ►*adj.* Very talkative. [< Lat. *loquāx*, *loquāc-* < *loquī*, speak.] —**lo•qua′cious•ly** *adv.* —**lo•qua′cious•ness, lo•quac′i•ty** (-kwăs′ĭ-tē) *n.*

lord (lôrd) ►*n.* **1.** The owner of a feudal estate. **2. Lord** *Chiefly Brit.* The general masculine title of nobility and other rank. **3. Lord a.** God. **b.** *Christianity* Jesus. **4.** A man of renowned power, authority, or mastery in a given field or activity. ►*v.* To domineer: *always lording it* *over their subordinates.* [< OE *hlāford.*]

lord•ly (lôrd′lē) ►*adj.* **-li•er, -li•est 1.** Of or characteristic of a lord. **2.** Dignified and noble. **3.** Arrogant and overbearing. —**lord′li•ness** *n.*

lord•ship (lôrd′shĭp′) ►*n.* **1.** often **Lordship** Used with *Your, His,* or *Their* as a title for a man holding the rank of lord. **2.** The position or domain of a lord.

Lord's Prayer (lôrdz prâr) ►*n.* The prayer taught by Jesus to his disciples.

lore (lôr, lōr) ►*n.* Accumulated facts, traditions, or beliefs about a specific subject. [< OE *lār.*]

lor•gnette (lôrn-yĕt′) ►*n.* Eyeglasses or opera glasses with a short handle. [< OFr. < *lorgne,* squinting.]

lorgnette

lorn (lôrn) ►*adj.* Bereft; forlorn. [< OE *-loren,* p.part. of *-lēosan,* lose.]

Lor•raine (lō-rān′, lô-, lô-rĕn′) A region and former province of NE France.

lor•ry (lôr′ē, lŏr′ē) ►*n., pl.* **-ries** *Chiefly Brit.* A motor truck. [?]

Los An•ge•les (lôs ăn′jə-ləs, -lēz′, ăng′gə-ləs) A city of S CA on the Pacific. Pop. 3,485,398.

lose (lo͞oz) ►*v.* **lost** (lôst, lŏst), **los•ing 1.** To be unable to find; mislay. **2.** To be deprived of: *lost a friend.* **3.** To be unable to maintain or keep. **4.** To fail to win; be defeated. **5.** To fail to take advantage of. **6.** To let (oneself) become engrossed. **7.** To rid oneself of: *lost five pounds.* **8.** To cause the loss of: *Politics lost her the job.* **9.** To suffer loss. —***phrasal verb:*** **lose out** To fail or be defeated. [< OE *losian,* be lost.] —**los′er** *n.*

loss (lôs, lŏs) ►*n.* **1.** The act or an instance of losing or having lost. **2.** One that is lost. **3.** **losses** People killed, wounded, or captured in wartime; casualties. —***idiom:*** **at a loss** Perplexed; puzzled. [< OE *los.*]

loss leader ►*n.* A commodity offered at or below cost to attract customers.

lost (lôst, lŏst) ►*v.* P.t. and p.part. of **lose.** ►*adj.* **1.** Unable to find one's way: strayed or missing. **2a.** No longer in one's possession or control. **b.** No longer known or practiced: *a lost art.* **3.** Unable to function; helpless; bewildered. **4.** Absorbed or rapt.

lot (lŏt) ►*n.* **1.** An object used in making a determination at random. **2.** The use of lots for selection. **3.** One's fate in life. **4.** A number of associated people or things. **5.** *Informal* A large amount or number. **6.** A piece of land having fixed boundaries. [< OE *hlot.*]

lo•ti (lō′tē) ►*n., pl.* **ma•lo•ti** (mä-). See table at **currency.** [Sotho.]

lo•tion (lō′shən) ►*n.* A liquid medicine or cosmetic applied to the skin. [< Lat. *lōtiō,* a washing < *lavere,* wash.]

lot•ter•y (lŏt′ə-rē) ►*n., pl.* **-ies.** A contest in which winners are selected in a drawing of lots. [Prob. < Du. *loterije* < MDu. *lot,* lot.]

lo•tus (lō′təs) ►*n.* **1a.** An Asian water lily having large leaves and pinkish flowers. **b.** Any of several similar or related plants. **2.** *Gk. Myth.* A fruit said to produce a drugged, indolent state in those who ate it. [< Gk. *lōtos,* name of several plants.]

lotus position ►*n.* A cross-legged sitting position used in yoga.

loud (loud) ►*adj.* **-er, -est 1.** Marked by high volume and intensity of sound. **2.** Producing or capable of producing sound of high volume and intensity. **3.** Offensively bright; flashy. See Syns at **gaudy.** [< OE *hlūd.*] —**loud, loud′ly** *adv.* —**loud′ness** *n.*

Syns: *loud, earsplitting, stentorian, strident*
Ant: *soft* ***adj.***

loud•mouth (loud′mouth′) ►*n. Informal* One given to loud, irritating, or indiscreet talk. —**loud′mouthed′** (-mouthd′, -moutht′) *adj.*

loud•speak•er (loud′spē′kər) ►*n.* A device that converts electric signals to sound and projects it.

Louis XIV. "the Sun King." 1638–1715. King of France (1643–1715).

Louis XV. 1710–74. King of France (1715–74).

Louis XVI. 1754–93. King of France (1774–92); executed.

Louis XVIII. 1755–1824. King of France (1814–24).

Lou•ise (lo͞o-ēz′), **Lake.** A lake of SW Alberta, Canada, in the Rocky Mts.

Lou•i•si•an•a (lo͞o-ē′zē-ăn′ə, lo͞o′zē-) A state of the S US on the Gulf of Mexico. Cap. Baton Rouge. Pop. 4,238,216.

Louisiana French ►*n.* French as spoken by the descendants of the original French settlers of Louisiana.

Louisiana Purchase. A territory of the W US from the Mississippi R. to the Rocky Mts. between the Gulf of Mexico and the Canadian border; purchased from France in 1803.

Lou•is Phi•lippe (lo͞o′ē fĭ-lēp′, lo͞o-ē′ fē-lēp′). "the Citizen King." 1773–1850. King of France (1830–48).

Lou•is•ville (lo͞o′ē-vĭl′, -ə-vəl) A city of N-central KY on the Ohio R. W of Lexington. Pop. 269,063.

lounge (lounj) ►*v.* **lounged, loung•ing.** To stand, sit, or lie in a lazy, relaxed way. ►*n.* **1.** A comfortably furnished waiting room, as in a hotel or theater. **2.** A bar serving cocktails. **3.** A long couch. [Perh. < Fr. *s'allonger,* stretch out.] —**loung′er** *n.*

lour (lour) ►*v. & n.* Var. of **lower**[1].

Lourdes (lo͝ord, lo͝ordz) A town of SW France at the foot of the Pyrenees. Pop. 16,581.

louse (lous) ►*n.* **1.** *pl.* **lice** (līs) Any of numerous small wingless insects parasitic on various animals, including humans. **2.** *pl.* **lous•es** *Slang* A mean or despicable person. ►*v.* **loused, lous•ing** *Slang.* To bungle: *louse up a deal.* [< OE *lūs.*]

lous•y (lou′zē) ►*adj.* **-i•er, -i•est 1.** Infested with lice. **2.** Mean; nasty. **3.** Inferior or worthless. **4.** Very bad or painful: *a lousy headache.* —**lous′i•ly** *adv.* —**lous′i•ness** *n.*

lout (lout) ►*n.* An awkward, stupid person; oaf. See Syns at **boor.** [Perh. < OE *lūtan,* bend.]

—**lout′ish** *adj.* —**lout′ish•ly** *adv.*

lou•ver also **lou•vre** (lo͞o′vər) ▸*n.* **1.** An opening fitted with fixed or movable horizontal slats for admitting air and light and shedding rain. **2.** One of the slats of a louver. [< OFr. *lover*, skylight.] —**lou′vered** *adj.*

louver

love (lŭv) ▸*n.* **1.** Deep affection and warm feeling for another. **2.** The emotion of sex and romance; strong sexual desire for another person. **3.** A beloved person. **4.** A strong fondness or enthusiasm. **5.** *Sports* A zero score in tennis. ▸*v.* **loved, lov•ing 1.** To feel love (for). **2.** To like or desire enthusiastically. —***idiom:* in love** Feeling love; enamored. [< OE *lufu.*] —**lov′a•ble, love′a•ble** *adj.* —**love′less** *adj.*

love•bird (lŭv′bûrd′) ▸*n.* A small parrot often kept as a cage bird.

Love•lace (lŭv′lās′), **Richard.** 1618–57? English Cavalier poet.

love•lorn (lŭv′lôrn′) ▸*adj.* Deprived of love or one's lover.

love•ly (lŭv′lē) ▸*adj.* **-li•er, -li•est 1.** Having pleasing or attractive qualities; beautiful. **2.** Enjoyable; delightful. —**love′li•ness** *n.*

love•mak•ing (lŭv′mā′kĭng) ▸*n.* **1.** Sexual activity between lovers. **2.** Courtship.

lov•er (lŭv′ər) ▸*n.* **1.** One who loves another, esp. one who feels sexual love. **2. lovers** A couple in love with each other. **3.** A sexual partner. **4.** One who is fond of or devoted to something. —**lov′er•ly** *adv. & adj.*

love seat ▸*n.* A small sofa that seats two.

love•sick (lŭv′sĭk′) ▸*adj.* **1.** Pining with love. **2.** Exhibiting or expressing a lover's yearning. —**love′sick′ness** *n.*

lov•ing (lŭv′ĭng) ▸*adj.* Feeling or showing love; affectionate. —**lov′ing•ly** *adv.*

loving cup ▸*n.* A large ornamental vessel, usu. with two or more handles, often given as an award in sporting contests.

low[1] (lō) ▸*adj.* **-er, -est 1.** Having little height. **2.** Of less than the usual height or depth. **3.** Humble or inferior in status. **4.** Morally base. **5.** Emotionally or mentally depressed; sad. **6.** Below average or standard in degree, intensity, or amount. **7.** Of small value or quality. **8.** Having a pitch corresponding to a relatively small number of sound-wave cycles per second. **9.** Not loud; soft or hushed. **10.** Depreciatory; disparaging: *a low opinion.* ▸*adv.* **1.** At, in, or to a low position, level, or space. **2.** Softly; quietly: *speak low.* **3.** With or at a low pitch. ▸*n.* **1.** A low level, position, or degree. **2.** *Meteorol.* A region of atmospheric air that exerts less pressure than the air around it. **3.** The gear configuration that produces the lowest range of output speeds, as in an automotive transmission. [< ON *lāgr.*] —**low′ness** *n.*

low[2] (lō) ▸*n.* A moo. [< OE *hlōwan.*] —**low** *v.*

low beam ▸*n.* The beam of a vehicle's headlight that provides short-range illumination.

low•born (lō′bôrn′) ▸*adj.* Of humble birth.

low•boy (lō′boi′) ▸*n.* A low tablelike chest of drawers.

low•bred (lō′brĕd′) ▸*adj.* Coarse; vulgar.

low•brow (lō′brou′) ▸*n.* One having uncultivated tastes. —**low′brow′** *adj.*

low-cal (lō′kăl′) ▸*adj.* Having fewer calories than what is typical: *low-cal foods.*

Low Countries. Belgium, the Netherlands, and Luxembourg.

low•down (lō′doun′) ▸*n.* *Slang* All the facts; the whole truth.

low-down (lō′doun′) ▸*adj.* Despicable; mean.

Low•ell (lō′əl), **Amy.** 1874–1925. Amer. poet.

Lowell, James Russell. 1819–91. Amer. editor, poet, and diplomat.

Lowell, Robert Traill Spence, Jr. 1917–77. Amer. poet.

low•er[1] (lou′ər, lour) also **lour** (lour) ▸*v.* **1.** To look angry; scowl. See Syns at **frown. 2.** To appear dark or threatening, as the sky. [ME *louren.*] —**low′er** *n.*

low•er[2] (lō′ər) ▸*adj.* Comp. of **low**[1]. **1.** Below another in rank, position, or authority. **2. Lower** *Geol. & Archaeol.* Being an earlier division of the period named. **3.** Denoting the larger and usu. more representative house of a bicameral legislature. ▸*v.* **1.** To let, bring, or move something down to a lower level. **2.** To make or become less; reduce or diminish.

Lower California. See **Baja California.**

low•er•case or **low•er-case** (lō′ər-kās′) ▸*adj.* Of or relating to small letters as distinguished from capital letters. —**low′er•case′** *n. & v.*

low•er class (lō′ər) ▸*n.* The socioeconomic class or classes of lower than middle rank in a society. —**low′er-class′** *adj.*

low•est common denominator (lō′ĭst) ▸*n.* See **least common denominator.**

low frequency ▸*n.* A radio-wave frequency in the range from 30 to 300 kilohertz.

Low German ▸*n.* **1.** The German dialects of northern Germany. **2.** The continental Scandinavian and Germanic languages except High German.

low-grade (lō′grād′) ▸*adj.* **1.** Of inferior quality. **2.** Reduced in degree or intensity: *a low-grade fever.*

low-key (lō′kē′) also **low-keyed** (-kēd′) ▸*adj.* Restrained, as in style or quality.

low•land (lō′lənd) ▸*n.* An area of relatively low land. —**low′land** *adj.* —**low′land•er** *n.*

low•ly (lō′lē) ▸*adj.* **-li•er, -li•est 1.** Having a low rank or position. **2.** Humble or meek in manner. —**low′li•ness** *n.* —**low′ly** *adv.*

low-mind•ed (lō′mīn′dĭd) ▸*adj.* Exhibiting a coarse, vulgar character. —**low′-mind′ed•ly** *adv.* —**low′-mind′ed•ness** *n.*

low profile ▸*n.* Unobtrusive, restrained behavior or activity.

low relief ▸*n.* Sculptural relief that projects very little from the background; bas-relief.

low road ▸*n.* Deceitful, immoral behavior or practice.

low-tech (lō′tĕk′) ▸ *adj.* Relating to technology that does not involve highly advanced systems or devices.

low tide ▸ *n.* **1.** The lowest level of the tide. **2.** The time of this level.

lox[1] (lŏks) ▸ *n., pl.* **lox** or **-es.** Smoked salmon. [Yiddish *laks* < OHGer. *lahs*, salmon.]

lox[2] (lŏks) ▸ *n.* Liquid oxygen, esp. when used in rocket fuel. [L(IQUID) + OX(YGEN).]

loy•al (loi′əl) ▸ *adj.* **1.** Steadfast in allegiance, as to one's homeland. **2.** Faithful, as to a person, ideal, cause, or duty. [< Lat. *lēgālis*, LEGAL.] —**loy′al•ly** *adv.* —**loy′al•ty** *n.*

loy•al•ist (loi′ə-lĭst) ▸ *n.* One who maintains loyalty to the lawful government during a revolt.

Lo•yang (lō′yäng′) See **Luoyang.**

loz•enge (lŏz′ĭnj) ▸ *n.* **1.** A small medicated candy dissolved slowly in the mouth to soothe irritated throat tissues. **2.** A flat diamond-shaped figure. [< OFr. *losenge.*]

LP (ĕl′pē′) ▸ *n.* A long-playing record.

LPN ▸ *abbr.* licensed practical nurse

Lr ▸ The symbol for the element **lawrencium.**

LSAT ▸ *abbr.* Law School Admissions Test

LSD (ĕl′ĕs-dē′) ▸ *n.* A powerful drug, lysergic acid diethylamide, $C_{20}H_{25}N_3O$, that induces hallucinations.

lt. ▸ *abbr.* light

Lt. or **LT** ▸ *abbr.* lieutenant

LTC or **Lt Col** ▸ *abbr.* lieutenant colonel

ltd. or **Ltd.** ▸ *abbr.* limited

LTG or **Lt Gen** ▸ *abbr.* lieutenant general

Lt. Gov. ▸ *abbr.* lieutenant governor

Lu ▸ The symbol for the element **lutetium.**

Lu•an•da (lo͞o-ăn′də) The capital of Angola, in the NW part on the Atlantic. Pop. 1,200,000.

lu•au (lo͞o-ou′, lo͞o′ou′) ▸ *n.* A traditional Hawaiian feast. See Regional Note at **ukulele.** [Hawaiian *lū′au.*]

Lub•bock (lŭb′ək) A city of NW TX S of Amarillo. Pop. 186,206.

lube (lo͞ob) *Informal* ▸ *v.* **lubed, lub•ing.** To lubricate (e.g., a car's joints). ▸ *n.* A lubricant, esp. one applied to machinery.

Lü•beck (lo͞o′bĕk′, lü′-) A city of N-central Germany NE of Hamburg. Pop. 217,269.

lu•bri•cant (lo͞o′brĭ-kənt) ▸ *n.* A substance, such as grease or oil, that reduces friction when applied as a surface coating to moving parts. —**lu′bri•cant** *adj.*

lu•bri•cate (lo͞o′brĭ-kāt′) ▸ *v.* **-cat•ed, -cat•ing.** To apply a lubricant to. [< Lat. *lūbricus*, slippery.] —**lu′bri•ca′tion** *n.*

lu•bri•cious (lo͞o-brish′əs) also **lu•bri•cous** (lo͞o′brĭ-kəs) ▸ *adj.* **1.** Slippery. **2.** Shifty or tricky. **3a.** Lewd; wanton. **b.** Salacious. [< Lat. *lūbricus.*] —**lu•bri′cious•ness** *n.* —**lu•bric′i•ty** (-brĭs′ĭ-tē) *n.*

Lu•bum•ba•shi (lo͞o′bo͝om-bä′shē) A city of SE Congo (formerly Zaire) near the Zambia border. Pop. 543,268.

Luce (lo͞os), **Clare Boothe.** 1902–87. Amer. writer and public official.

Luce, Henry Robinson. 1898–1967. Amer. editor and publisher.

Lu•cerne (lo͞o-sûrn′, -sĕrn′) A city of central Switzerland on the N shore of the **Lake of Lucerne.** Pop. 61,000.

lu•cid (lo͞o′sĭd) ▸ *adj.* **1.** Easily understood; intelligible: *a lucid explanation.* **2.** Clear-minded; rational. **3.** Translucent. See Syns at **clear.** [Lat. *lūcidus* < *lūcēre*, shine.] —**lu•cid′i•ty, lu′cid•ness** *n.* —**lu′cid•ly** *adv.*

Lu•ci•fer (lo͞o′sə-fər) ▸ *n.* In Christian tradition, the archangel cast from heaven for leading the revolt of the angels; Satan.

Lu•cite (lo͞o′sīt′) ▸ A trademark for a transparent thermoplastic acrylic resin.

luck (lŭk) ▸ *n.* **1.** The chance happening of good or bad events; fortune. **2.** Good fortune; success. ▸ *v.* To gain success or something desirable by chance: *lucked into a good apartment.* [< MDu. *gheluc.*]

luck•less (lŭk′lĭs) ▸ *adj.* Unlucky. See Syns at **unfortunate.**

luck•y (lŭk′ē) ▸ *adj.* **-i•er, -i•est.** Having, bringing, or attended by good luck. See Syns at **happy.** —**luck′i•ly** *adv.* —**luck′i•ness** *n.*

lu•cra•tive (lo͞o′krə-tĭv) ▸ *adj.* Producing wealth; profitable. [< Lat. *lucrārī*, make a profit.] —**lu′cra•tive•ly** *adv.*

lu•cre (lo͞o′kər) ▸ *n.* Money or profits. [< Lat. *lucrum.*]

Lu•cre•tius (lo͞o-krē′shəs, -shē-əs). 96?–55? B.C. Roman philosopher and poet. —**Lu•cre′tian** (-shən) *adj.*

lu•cu•brate (lo͞o′kyo͞o-brāt′) ▸ *v.* **-brat•ed, -brat•ing.** To write or study laboriously. [Lat. *lūcubrāre*, work by lamplight.]

Lü•da (lo͞o′dä′, lü′-) A city of NE China on Korea Bay. Pop. 3,473,832.

lu•di•crous (lo͞o′dĭ-krəs) ▸ *adj.* Laughable because of obvious absurdity or incongruity. [< Lat. *lūdicrus*, playful.] —**lu′di•crous•ly** *adv.* —**lu′di•crous•ness** *n.*

lug[1] (lŭg) ▸ *n.* **1.** A stubby handle or projection, used as a hold or support or to provide traction. **2.** A lug nut. **3.** *Slang* A clumsy fool. [ME *lugge*, earflap.]

lug[2] (lŭg) ▸ *v.* **lugged, lug•ging.** To drag or haul with difficulty. [ME *luggen.*]

luge (lo͞ozh) ▸ *n. Sports* A racing sled for one or two people lying supine. [< Med.Lat. *sludia.*]

lug•gage (lŭg′ĭj) ▸ *n.* Baggage, esp. suitcases. [Prob. LUG[2] + (BAG)GAGE.]

lug nut ▸ *n.* A heavy rounded nut that fits over a bolt.

lu•gu•bri•ous (lo͞o-go͞o′brē-əs, -gyo͞o′-) ▸ *adj.* Mournful or gloomy, esp. to a ludicrous degree. [< Lat. *lūgubris* < *lūgēre*, mourn.] —**lu•gu′bri•ous•ly** *adv.* —**lu•gu′bri•ous•ness** *n.*

Lu•hans′k (lo͞o-hänsk′) A city of W Ukraine in the Donets Basin SE of Kharkov. Pop. 505,100.

Luke (lo͝ok) ▸ *n.* See table at **Bible.**

Luke, Saint. 1st cent. A.D. Companion of Saint Paul and author of the third Gospel of the Bible.

luke•warm (lo͞ok′wôrm′) ▸ *adj.* **1.** Mildly warm; tepid. **2.** Half-hearted: *lukewarm support for the candidate.* [ME *leukwarm.*] —**luke′warm′ly** *adv.* —**luke′warm′ness** *n.*

lull (lŭl) ▸ *v.* **1.** To cause to sleep or rest; soothe. **2.** To deceive into trustfulness. ▸ *n.* A relatively calm or inactive interval or period. [ME *lullen.*]

lull•a•by (lŭl′ə-bī′) ▸ *n., pl.* **-bies.** A soothing song with which to lull a child to sleep. [< ME *lullen*, to lull + (GOOD)BY(E).]

lum•ba•go (lŭm-bā′gō) ▸ *n.* A painful condition of the lower back, as one resulting from muscle strain or a slipped disk. [LLat. *lumbāgō.*]

lum•bar (lŭm′bər, -bär′) ▸*adj.* Of, near, or situated in the part of the back and sides between the lowest ribs and the hips. [< Lat. *lumbus*, loin.]

lum•ber¹ (lŭm′bər) ▸*n.* **1.** Timber sawed into boards and planks. **2.** Something useless or cumbersome. ▸*v.* To cut down (trees) and prepare as marketable timber. [Perh. < LUMBER².] —**lum′ber•er** *n.*

lum•ber² (lŭm′bər) ▸*v.* To walk or move with heavy clumsiness. See Syns at **blunder.** [ME *lomeren.*]

lum•ber•jack (lŭm′bər-jăk′) ▸*n.* One who fells trees and transports the timber to a mill.

lum•ber•yard (lŭm′bər-yärd′) ▸*n.* An establishment that sells lumber and other building materials from a yard.

lu•men (lo͞o′mən) ▸*n., pl.* **-mens** or **-mi•na** (-mə-nə) *Anat.* The inner open space or cavity of a tubular organ. [Lat., light, an opening.] —**lu′men•al, lu′min•al** *adj.*

lu•mi•nar•i•a (lo͞o′mə-nâr′ē-ə) ▸*n.* A votive candle set into a paper bag weighted with sand and placed in a row with others as a holiday decoration. [Sp.]

lu•mi•nar•y (lo͞o′mə-nĕr′ē) ▸*n., pl.* **-ies 1.** An object, such as a celestial body, that gives light. **2.** A notable person in a specific field. See Syns at **celebrity.** [< Lat. *lūmen*, light.] —**lu′mi•nar′y** *adj.*

lu•mi•nes•cence (lo͞o′mə-nĕs′əns) ▸*n.* **1.** The production of light without heat, as in fluorescence. **2.** The light so produced. [< Lat. *lūmen*, light.] —**lu′mi•nes′cent** *adj.*

lu•mi•nous (lo͞o′mə-nəs) ▸*adj.* **1.** Emitting light, esp. self-generated light. **2.** Full of light; illuminated. **3.** Easily comprehended; clear. [< Lat. *lūmen*, *lūmin-*, light.] —**lu′mi•nos′i•ty** (-nŏs′ĭ-tē), **lu′mi•nous•ness** *n.* —**lu′mi•nous•ly** *adv.*

luminous flux ▸*n.* The rate of flow of light per unit of time.

lum•mox (lŭm′əks) ▸*n. Informal* An oaf; lout. [?]

lump¹ (lŭmp) ▸*n.* **1.** An irregularly shaped mass or piece. **2.** *Pathol.* A swelling or small palpable mass in a part of the body. **3. lumps** *Informal* Punishment or criticism: *take one's lumps.* ▸*adj.* **1.** Formed into lumps: *lump sugar.* **2.** Not divided into parts: *a lump payment.* ▸*v.* To put together in a single group or pile. —***idiom:*** **a lump in (one's) throat** A feeling of constriction in the throat caused by emotion. [ME *lumpe.*] —**lump′i•ness** *n.* —**lump′y** *adj.*

lump² (lŭmp) ▸*v.* To tolerate: *like it or lump it.* [Perh. < dial. *lump*, look sullen.]

lump•ec•to•my (lŭm-pĕk′tə-mē) ▸*n., pl.* **-mies.** Surgical excision of a tumor from the breast.

lump•ish (lŭm′pĭsh) ▸*adj.* **1.** Stupid or dull. **2.** Clumsy or cumbersome. —**lump′ish•ly** *adv.* —**lump′ish•ness** *n.*

lu•na•cy (lo͞o′nə-sē) ▸*n., pl.* **-cies 1.** Insanity. **2.** Foolish conduct. [< LUNATIC.]

lu•nar (lo͞o′nər) ▸*adj.* **1.** Of, involving, caused by, or affecting the moon. **2.** Measured in reference to the revolution of the moon: *a lunar month.* [< Lat. *lūna*, moon.]

lu•na•tic (lo͞o′nə-tĭk) ▸*adj.* **1.** Insane. **2.** Of or for the insane. **3.** Wildly or giddily foolish. [< Lat. *lūnāticus* < *lūna*, moon.] —**lu′na•tic** *n.*

lunch (lŭnch) ▸*n.* A meal eaten at midday. [Short for LUNCHEON.] —**lunch** *v.*

lunch•eon (lŭn′chən) ▸*n.* A lunch, esp. a party at which lunch is served. [Poss. < ME *nonshench*, a drink at noon.]

lunch•eon•ette (lŭn′chə-nĕt′) ▸*n.* A small restaurant that serves simple meals.

lung (lŭng) ▸*n.* Either of two spongy, saclike thoracic organs in most vertebrates, functioning to remove carbon dioxide from the blood and provide it with oxygen. [< OE *lungen*, lungs.]

lunge (lŭnj) ▸*n.* **1.** A sudden thrust or pass, as with a sword. **2.** A sudden forward movement. ▸*v.* **lunged, lung•ing.** To move with a lunge. [< OFr. *alongier*, lengthen.] —**lung′er** *n.*

lung•fish (lŭng′fĭsh′) ▸*n.* Any of several tropical freshwater fishes that have lunglike organs as well as gills.

Luo•yang (lwō′yäng′) also **Lo•yang** (lō′-). A city of E-central China ENE of Xi'an. Pop. 1,202,192.

lu•pine also **lu•pin** (lo͞o′pən) ▸*n.* A plant having tall spikes of variously colored flowers. [< Lat. *lupīnus*, wolflike.]

lu•pus (lo͞o′pəs) ▸*n.* An autoimmune disease of the connective tissue, usu. involving multiple organ systems. [< Lat., wolf.]

lurch¹ (lûrch) ▸*v.* **1.** To stagger. See Syns at **blunder. 2.** To roll or pitch suddenly, as a ship. [?] —**lurch** *n.* —**lurch′ing•ly** *adv.*

lurch² (lûrch) ▸*n.* A difficult position. [Perh. < ME *lurching*, total victory in a game.]

lure (lo͝or) ▸*n.* **1.** Something that tempts or attracts with the promise of pleasure or reward. **2.** An artificial bait used in catching fish. [< AN, of Gmc. orig.] —**lure** *n.*

lu•rid (lo͝or′ĭd) ▸*adj.* **1.** Horrible; gruesome. **2.** Marked by sensationalism or violence. [Lat. *lūridus*, pale.] —**lu′rid•ly** *adv.* —**lu′rid•ness** *n.*

lurk (lûrk) ▸*v.* **1.** To lie in wait, as in ambush. **2.** To move furtively; sneak. **3.** To read but not contribute to the discussion in a newsgroup or chatroom. [ME *lurken*, poss. of Scand. orig.]

Lu•sa•ka (lo͞o-sä′kə) The capital of Zambia, in the S-central part. Pop. 982,362.

lus•cious (lŭsh′əs) ▸*adj.* **1.** Sweet and pleasant to taste or smell. See Syns at **delicious. 2.** Sensually appealing. [ME *lucius.*] —**lus′cious•ly** *adv.* —**lus′cious•ness** *n.*

lush¹ (lŭsh) ▸*adj.* **-er, -est 1a.** Marked by luxuriant growth or vegetation. **b.** Abundant; plentiful. See Syns at **profuse. 2.** Luxurious; opulent. [ME *lush*, soft.] —**lush′ly** *adv.* —**lush′ness** *n.*

lush² (lŭsh) ▸*n. Slang* A drunkard. [?]

lust (lŭst) ▸*n.* **1.** Intense, excessive, or unrestrained sexual desire. **2.** An overwhelming craving. **3.** Intense eagerness or enthusiasm. ▸*v.* To have an intense desire, esp. sexual desire. [< OE, desire.] —**lust′ful** *adj.* —**lust′ful•ly** *adv.* —**lust′ful•ness** *n.*

lus•ter (lŭs′tər) ▸*n.* **1.** Soft reflected light; sheen. **2.** Brilliance or radiance. **3.** Glory, distinction, or splendor. [< Lat. *lūstrāre*, brighten.] —**lus′trous** (-trəs) *adj.* —**lus′trous•ly** *adv.* —**lus′trous•ness** *n.*

lus•tre (lŭs′tər) ▸*n. Chiefly Brit.* Var. of **luster.**

lust•y (lŭs′tē) ▸*adj.* **-i•er, -i•est.** Full of vigor; robust. —**lust′i•ly** *adv.* —**lust′i•ness** *n.*

lute (lo͞ot) ►*n.* A stringed instrument having a fretted fingerboard and a body shaped like half a pear. [< Ar. *al-'ud.*] —**lu′te•nist, lu′ta•nist** (lo͞ot′n-ĭst), **lut′ist** *n.*

lute

lu•te•ti•um also **lu•te•ci•um** (lo͞o-tē′shē-əm) ►*n. Symbol* **Lu** A silvery-white rare-earth element. At. no. 71. See table at **element.** [< Lat. *Lutetia*, ancient name of Paris.]

Lu•ther (lo͞o′thər), **Martin.** 1483–1546. German theologian and Reformation leader.

Lu•ther•an (lo͞o′thər-ən) ►*adj.* Of or relating to the branch of the Protestant Church adhering to the views of Martin Luther. —**Lu′ther•an** *n.* —**Lu′ther•an•ism** *n.*

Lux•em•bourg also **Lux•em•burg** (lŭk′səm-bûrg′) **1.** A country of NW Europe. Cap. the city of Luxembourg. Pop. 401,000. **2.** Also **Luxembourg City.** The capital of Luxembourg, in the S part. Pop. 75,833.

Lux•em•burg (lŭk′səm-bûrg′), **Rosa.** 1870–1919. German socialist; murdered.

lux•u•ri•ant (lŭg-zho͝or′ē-ənt, lŭk-sho͝or′-) ►*adj.* **1a.** Marked by rich or profuse growth. **b.** Producing or yielding in abundance. See Syns at **profuse. 2.** Excessively elaborate; ornate. —**lux•u′ri•ance** *n.* —**lux•u′ri•ant•ly** *adv.*

lux•u•ri•ate (lŭg-zho͝or′ē-āt′, lŭk-sho͝or′-) ►*v.* **-at•ed, -at•ing.** To take luxurious pleasure.

lux•u•ry (lŭg′zhə-rē, lŭk′shə-) ►*n., pl.* **-ries 1.** Something inessential, usu. expensive, that provides pleasure and comfort. **2.** Sumptuous living or surroundings. [< Lat. *luxuria* < *luxus.*] —**lux•u′ri•ous** (-zho͝or′ēəs, -sho͝or′-) *adj.* —**lux•u′ri•ous•ly** *adv.*

Syns: *luxury, extravagance, frill* **n.**

Lu•zon (lo͞o-zŏn′) An island of the NW Philippines at the N end of the archipelago.

L′viv (lə-vĭv′, -vĭf′) or **L′vov** (lə-vôv′, -vôf′). A city of W-central Ukraine near the Polish border. Pop. 742,000.

-ly[1] ►*suff.* **1.** Like; having the characteristics of: *sisterly.* **2.** Recurring at a specified interval of time: *hourly.* [< OE *-līc.*]

-ly[2] ►*suff.* **1.** In a specified way; in the manner of: *gradually.* **2.** At a specified interval: *weekly.* **3.** With respect to: *partly.* [< OE *-līce.*]

Ly•all•pur (lī′əl-po͝or′) See **Faisalabad.**

ly•ce•um (lī-sē′əm) ►*n.* **1.** A hall in which public lectures, concerts, etc. are presented. **2.** An organization sponsoring such programs. [< Gk. *Lukeion*, Aristotle's school.]

Ly•ci•a (lĭsh′ē-ə, lĭsh′ə) An ancient country and Roman province of SW Asia Minor on the Aegean Sea. —**Ly′ci•an** *adj. & n.*

Lyd•i•a (lĭd′ē-ə) An ancient country of W-central Asia Minor on the Aegean Sea. —**Lyd′i•an** *adj. & n.*

lye (lī) ►*n.* **1.** The liquid obtained by leaching wood ashes. **2.** See **potassium hydroxide. 3.** See **sodium hydroxide.** [< OE *lēag.*]

Lyme disease (līm) ►*n.* An inflammatory disease that is caused by a spirochete transmitted by ticks. [After *Lyme*, Connecticut.]

lymph (lĭmf) ►*n.* A clear watery fluid that contains white blood cells and acts to remove bacteria and certain proteins from the tissues, transport fat from the small intestine, and supply mature lymphocytes to the blood. [Lat., water < Gk. *numphē*, water spirit.]

lym•phat•ic (lĭm-făt′ĭk) ►*adj.* **1.** Of or relating to lymph or the lymphatic system. **2.** Lacking energy or vitality; sluggish. ► *n.* A vessel that conveys lymph.

lymphatic system ►*n.* The system of spaces and vessels between tissues and organs by which lymph is circulated.

lymph node ►*n.* Any of numerous oval or round bodies that supply lymphocytes to the bloodstream and remove bacteria and foreign particles from the lymph.

lym•pho•cyte (lĭm′fə-sīt′) ►*n.* A white blood cell formed in lymphoid tissue.

lym•phoid (lĭm′foid′) ►*adj.* Of lymph, lymphatic tissue, or the lymphatic system.

lynch (lĭnch) ►*v.* To execute without due process of law, esp. to hang by a mob. [After William *Lynch* (d. 1830).] —**lynch′ing** *n.*

lynx (lĭngks) ►*n., pl.* **lynx** or **-es.** A wildcat with soft thick fur, a short tail, and tufted ears. [< Gk. *lunx.*]

lynx-eyed (lĭngks′īd′) ►*adj.* Keen of vision.

Ly•on or **Ly•ons** (lē-ōN′, lyôN). A city of E-central France at the confluence of the Rhone and Saône rivers. Pop. 415,479.

lyre (līr) ►*n.* A stringed instrument of the harp family used esp. in ancient Greece. [< Gk. *lura.*]

lyr•ic (lĭr′ĭk) ►*adj.* **1.** Of or relating to poetry that expresses subjective thoughts and feelings, often in a songlike style or form. **2.** Lyrical. ►*n.* **1.** A lyric poem. **2.** often **lyrics** The words of a song. [< Gk. *lurikos*, of a lyre.] —**lyr′i•cism** (-sĭz′əm) *n.*

lyr•i•cal (lĭr′ĭ-kəl) ►*adj.* **1.** Expressing deep personal emotion or observations. **2.** Highly enthusiastic; rhapsodic. **3.** Lyric. —**lyr′i•cal•ly** *adv.*

lyr•i•cist (lĭr′ĭ-sĭst) ►*n.* A writer of song lyrics.

ly•ser•gic acid (lĭ-sûr′jĭk, lī-) ►*n.* A crystalline alkaloid, $C_{16}H_{16}N_2O_2$, derived from ergot and used in medical research. [< Gk. *lusis*, loosening + ERG(OT) + -IC.]

lysergic acid di•eth•yl•am•ide (dī′ĕth-əl-ăm′īd′) ►*n.* See **LSD.**

ly•sin (lī′sĭn) ►*n.* An antibody that acts to destroy red blood cells, bacteria, or other cellular elements. [< Gk. *lusis*, a loosening.]

ly•sis (lī′sĭs) ►*n., pl.* **-ses** (-sēz) **1.** The dissolution or destruction of cells. **2.** The gradual subsiding of the symptoms of an acute disease. [< Gk. *lusis*, a loosening.]

-lysis ►*suff.* Decomposition; dissolving: *hydrolysis.* [< Gk. *lusis*, a loosening.]

-lyte ►*suff.* A substance that can be decomposed by a specified process: *electrolyte.* [< Gk. *lutos*, soluble < *luein*, loosen.]

M

m[1] or **M** (ĕm) ►*n., pl.* **m's** or **M's** also **ms** or **Ms.** The 13th letter of the English alphabet.

m[2] ►*abbr.* **1.** *Gram.* masculine **2.** *Phys.* mass **3.** meter (measurement)

M[1] also **m** ► The symbol for the Roman numeral 1,000.

M[2] ►*abbr.* **1.** *Print.* em **2.** Mach number **3.** male **4.** medium **5.** metal **6.** Monday **7.** month

m. ►*abbr.* **1.** married **2.** meridian **3.** mile

M. ►*abbr.* **1.** master **2.** Monsieur

mA ►*abbr.* milliampere

MA ►*abbr.* **1.** *Lat.* Magister Artium (Master of Arts) **2.** Massachusetts

ma'am (măm) ►*n.* Used as a form of polite address for a woman: *Is that all, ma'am?* [< MADAM.]

Maas (mäs) A section of the Meuse R. flowing through the S Netherlands to the Rhine.

ma•ca•bre (mə-kä'brə, mə-käb', -kä'bər) ►*adj.* Suggesting the horror of death and decay; gruesome; ghastly. [< OFr. *(danse) Macabre*, (dance) of death.]

mac•ad•am (mə-kăd'əm) ►*n.* Pavement made of layers of compacted broken stone, now usu. bound with tar or asphalt. [After J.L. *McAdam* (1756–1836).] —**mac•ad'am•ize** *v.*

Ma•cao also **Ma•cau** (mə-kou'). An administrative region of SE China. Cap. the city of **Macao.** Pop. 398,000.

ma•caque (mə-kăk', -käk') ►*n.* A short-tailed monkey of Asia, Japan, Gibraltar, and N Africa. [Of Bantu orig.]

mac•a•ro•ni (măk'ə-rō'nē) ►*n., pl.* **-ni.** Pasta in any of various hollow shapes, especially short curved tubes. [Ital. dial. *maccaroni.*]

mac•a•roon (măk'ə-ro͞on') ►*n.* A chewy cookie made with sugar, egg whites, and almond paste or coconut. [< Ital. dial. *maccarone*, dumpling.]

Mac•Ar•thur (mĭk-är'thər), **Douglas.** 1880–1964. Amer. general.

Ma•cau•lay (mə-kô'lē), **Thomas Babington.** First Baron Macaulay. 1800–59. British historian, writer, and politician.

ma•caw (mə-kô') ►*n.* A large, usu. brilliantly colored tropical American parrot. [Port. *macaú.*]

Mac•ca•bees (măk'ə-bēz') ►*pl.n. Bible* **1.** A family of Jewish patriots of the 2nd and 1st cent. B.C. **2.** See table at **Bible.** —**Mac'ca•be'an** *adj.*

Mac•don•ald (mĭk-dŏn'əld), Sir **John Alexander.** 1815–91. Canadian prime minister (1867–73 and 1878–91).

MacDonald, (James) Ramsay. 1866–1937. British prime minister (1924 and 1929–35).

mace[1] (mās) ►*n.* **1.** A ceremonial staff used as a symbol of authority. **2.** A heavy medieval war club with a spiked head. [< OFr.]

mace[2] (mās) ►*n.* An aromatic spice made from the dried seed covering of the nutmeg. [< Gk. *makir*, a kind of spice.]

Mace ► A trademark for a temporarily disabling liquid sprayed into the face of an attacker.

Mac•e•do•ni•a (măs'ĭ-dō'nē-ə, -dōn'yə) **1.** Also (-dən, -dŏn'). An ancient kingdom of N Greece. **2.** A historical region of SE Europe on the Balkan Peninsula. **3.** A republic of the S-central Balkan Peninsula. Cap. Skopje. Pop. 2,142,000.

Mac•e•do•ni•an (măs'ĭ-dō'nē-ən) ►*adj.* Of or relating to ancient or modern Macedonia. ►*n.* **1.** A native or inhabitant of ancient or modern Macedonia. **2.** The language of ancient Macedonia, of uncertain affiliation within Indo-European. **3.** The Slavic language of modern Macedonia, closely related to Bulgarian.

mac•er•ate (măs'ə-rāt') ►*v.* **-at•ed, -at•ing 1.** To soften or separate by soaking or steeping. **2.** To emaciate, usu. by starvation. [Lat. *mācerāre.*] —**mac'er•a'tion** *n.*

Mach also **mach** (mäk) ►*n.* Mach number.

Mach (mäk, mäKH), **Ernst.** 1838–1916. Austrian physicist and philosopher.

ma•chet•e (mə-shĕt'ē, -chĕt'ē) ►*n.* A large, broad-bladed knife used for cutting and as a weapon. [Sp., ult. < VLat. **mattea*, mace.]

Ma•chi•a•vel•li (măk'ē-ə-vĕl'ē, mä'kyä-), **Niccolò.** 1469–1527. Italian political theorist.

Ma•chi•a•vel•li•an (măk'ē-ə-vĕl'ē-ən) ►*adj.* Of or relating to the political doctrine of Machiavelli, which holds that craft and deceit are justified in pursuing and maintaining political power. —**Ma'chi•a•vel'li•an** *n.* —**Ma'chi•a•vel'li•an•ism** *n.*

mach•i•na•tion (măk'ə-nā'shən, măsh'-) ►*n.* A scheme or secret plot usu. meant to achieve an evil end. —**mach'i•nate'** *v.*

ma•chine (mə-shēn') ►*n.* **1a.** A device or system consisting of fixed and moving parts that alters, directs, or modifies mechanical energy and transmits it to accomplish a specific objective. **b.** A simple device, such as a lever, pulley, or screw, that alters an applied force. **2.** A system or device, such as a computer, that performs or assists with a human task. **3.** An automaton. **4.** An organized political group under the control of a strong leader or faction. **5.** An answering machine: *left a message on her machine.* ►*v.* **-chined, -chin•ing.** To shape or finish by machine. [< Gk. *mēkhanē.*]

machine code ►*n.* See **machine language.**

machine gun ►*n.* A gun, often mounted, that fires rapidly and repeatedly. —**ma•chine'-gun** *v.* —**machine gunner** *n.*

machine language ►*n.* A set of coded instructions that a computer can use directly without further translation.

ma•chin•er•y (mə-shē'nə-rē, -shēn'rē) ►*n., pl.* **-ies 1.** Machines or machine parts collectively. **2.** The working parts of a particular machine. **3.** A system of related elements that operate together: *diplomatic and political machinery.*

ma•chin•ist (mə-shē'nĭst) ►*n.* One who makes, operates, or repairs machines.

ma•chis•mo (mä-chēz'mō) ►*n.* A strong or exaggerated sense of masculinity. [Sp. < *macho*, MACHO.]

Mach number also **mach number** (mäk) ►*n.* The ratio of the speed of an object to the speed of sound in the surrounding medium. [After Ernst MACH.]

ma•cho (mä'chō) ►*adj.* Marked by machismo. ►*n., pl.* **-chos 1.** Machismo. **2.** A macho person. [Sp., male < Lat. *masculus.*]

Ma•chu Pic•chu (mä′cho͞o pēk′cho͞o, pē′-) An ancient Inca fortress city in the Andes NW of Cuzco, Peru.

Mac•ken•zie River (mə-kĕn′zē) A river of NW Canada flowing about 1,802 km (1,120 mi) to **Mackenzie Bay,** an arm of the Beaufort Sea.

mack•er•el (măk′ər-əl, măk′rəl) ►*n., pl.* **-el** or **-els.** Any of several widely distributed marine food fishes. [< OFr. *maquerel.*]

Mack•i•nac Island (măk′ə-nô′) An island of N MI in the **Straits of Mackinac,** a passage connecting Lakes Huron and Michigan between the Upper and Lower peninsulas.

mack•i•naw (măk′ə-nô′) ►*n.* A short double-breasted coat of heavy, usu. plaid, woolen material. [< *Mackinaw City,* Michigan.]

mack•in•tosh also **mac•in•tosh** (măk′ĭn-tŏsh′) ►*n. Chiefly Brit.* A raincoat. [After Charles *Macintosh* (1766–1843).]

Mac•Leish (mĭk-lēsh′), **Archibald.** 1892–1982. Amer. poet and playwright.

Mac•mil•lan (mĭk-mĭl′ən), **(Maurice) Harold.** 1894–1986. British prime minister (1957–63).

Ma•con (mā′kən) A city of central GA SE of Atlanta. Pop. 106,612.

mac•ra•mé (măk′rə-mā′) ►*n.* Coarse lace work made by weaving and knotting cords. [< Ar. *miqrama,* embroidered veil.]

mac•ro (măk′rō′) ►*n., pl.* **-ros** *Comp. Sci.* A single, user-defined command that is part of an application and executes a series of commands. [< MACROINSTRUCTION.]

macro– or **macr–** ►*pref.* **1.** Large: *macroscopic.* **2.** Long: *macrobiotics.* **3.** Inclusive: *macroeconomics.* [< Gk. *makros,* large.]

mac•ro•bi•ot•ics (măk′rō-bī-ŏt′ĭks) ►*n. (takes sing. v.)* The theory or practice of promoting well-being and longevity esp. by means of a diet chiefly of whole grains and beans. —**mac′ro•bi•ot′ic** *adj.*

mac•ro•ceph•a•ly ►*n.* Abnormal largeness of the head. —**mac′ro•ce•phal′ic** (-sə-făl′ĭk), **mac′ro•ceph′a•lous** *adj.*

mac•ro•cosm (măk′rə-kŏz′əm) ►*n.* **1.** The entire world; universe. **2.** A system that contains subsystems. [Med.Lat. *macrocosmus.*] —**mac′ro•cos′mic** *adj.*

mac•ro•ec•o•nom•ics (măk′rō-ĕk′ə-nŏm′ĭks, -ē′kə-) ►*n. (takes sing. v.)* The study of the overall workings of a national economy. —**mac′ro•e•con′o•mist** *n.*

mac•ro•in•struc•tion (măk′rō-ĭn-strŭk′shən) ►*n.* A macro.

ma•cron (mā′krŏn′, -krən, măk′rŏn′) ►*n.* A mark (ˉ) placed above a vowel to indicate a long sound, as the (ā) in *make.* [< Gk. *makros,* long.]

mac•ro•phage (măk′rə-fāj′) ►*n.* A large phagocytic cell.

mac•ro•scop•ic (măk′rə-skŏp′ĭk) also **mac•ro•scop•i•cal** (-ĭ-kəl) ►*adj.* Large enough to be seen or examined by the unaided eye.

mad (măd) ►*adj.* **mad•der, mad•dest 1.** Feeling anger or resentment. See Syns at **angry. 2.** Suffering from a disorder of the mind; insane. **3.** Lacking restraint, reason, or judgment. **4.** Feeling or showing strong liking or enthusiasm: *mad about sports.* **5.** Marked by extreme excitement, confusion, or agitation; frantic: *a mad scramble for the bus.* **6.** Affected by rabies; rabid. [< OE *gemǣd,* insane.] —**mad′ly** *adv.* —**mad′man** *n.* —**mad′ness** *n.* —**mad′wom′an** *n.*

Mad•a•gas•car (măd′ə-găs′kər) An island country in the Indian Ocean off SE Africa. Cap. Antananarivo. Pop. 14,303,000. —**Mad′a•gas′can** *adj. & n.*

Mad•am (măd′əm) ►*n.* **1.** *pl.* **Mes•dames** (mā-dăm′, -däm′) Used formerly as a courtesy title before a woman's given name. **2.** Used as a salutation in a letter. **3. madam** Used as a form of polite address for a woman. **4. madam** A woman who manages a house of prostitution. [< OFr. *ma dame* : *ma,* my + *dame,* lady (< Lat. *domina*).]

Ma•dame (mə-dăm′, măd′əm) ►*n., pl.* **Mes•dames** (mā-dăm′, -däm′). A French courtesy title for a woman. [Fr.]

mad•cap (măd′kăp′) ►*adj.* Behaving or acting impulsively or rashly. [MAD + CAP, head.] —**mad′cap′** *n.*

mad•den (măd′n) ►*v.* **1.** To make or become angry. **2.** To make frantic or insane.

mad•der (măd′ər) ►*n.* **1.** A SW Asian plant having small yellow flowers and a fleshy red root. **2.** A red dye obtained from the roots of the madder. [< OE *mædere.*]

made (mād) ►*v.* P.t. and p.part. of **make.**

Ma•dei•ra[1] (mə-dîr′ə, -dĕr′ə) A river of NW Brazil flowing about 3,315 km (2,060 mi) to the Amazon R.

Ma•dei•ra[2] (mə-dîr′ə) ►*n.* A fortified dessert wine, esp. from the Madeira Is.

Madeira Islands. An archipelago of Portugal in the NE Atlantic W of Morocco. —**Ma•dei′ran** *adj. & n.*

Mad•e•moi•selle (măd′ə-mə-zĕl′, măd-mwä-zĕl′) ►*n., pl.* **Mad•e•moi•selles** (-zĕlz) or **Mes•de•moi•selles** (mād′mwä-zĕl′). A French courtesy title for a girl or young woman. [< OFr. *ma demoiselle* : *ma,* my + *damisele,* young lady; see DAMSEL.]

made-to-or•der (mād′to͞o-ôr′dər) ►*adj.* **1.** Made according to particular instructions. **2.** Very suitable.

made-up (mād′ŭp′) ►*adj.* **1.** Fictitious: *a made-up story.* **2.** Wearing makeup.

mad•house (măd′hous′) ►*n.* **1.** Formerly, an insane asylum. **2.** *Informal* A place of disorder and confusion.

Mad•i•son (măd′ĭ-sən) The capital of WI, in the S-central part. Pop. 191,262.

Madison, Dolley Payne Todd. 1768–1849. First Lady of the US (1809–17) as the wife of President James Madison.

Madison, James. 1751–1836. The 4th US President (1809–17). —**Mad′i•so′ni•an** (-sō′nē-ən) *adj.*

Dolley Madison
1804 portrait

James Madison
c. 1830 portrait

Ma•don•na (mə-dŏn′ə) ►*n.* The Virgin Mary. [Ital. : *ma*, my + *donna*, lady (< Lat. *domina*).]

mad•ras (măd′rəs, mə-drăs′, -dräs′) ►*n.* A fine cotton cloth, usu. with a plaid, striped, or checked pattern. [< MADRAS.]

Ma•dras (mə-drăs′, -dräs′) See **Chennai.**

Ma•dre de Di•os (mä′drā dā dē-ōs′) A river, about 1,126 km (700 mi), of SE Peru and NW Bolivia.

Ma•drid (mə-drĭd′) The capital of Spain, in the central part. Pop. 2,976,064.

mad•ri•gal (măd′rĭ-gəl) ►*n.* **1.** An unaccompanied vocal composition for two or three voices in simple harmony. **2.** A polyphonic song written for four to six voices and usu. unaccompanied. [Ital. *madrigale.*]

ma•dro•ña (mə-drō′nyə) also **ma•dro•ño** (-drō′nyō) or **ma•dro•ne** (-drō′nə) ►*n., pl.* **-ñas** also **-ños** or **-nes.** An evergreen tree of W North America, having scaly bark and orange or red edible berries. [Am.Sp.]

Ma•du•rai (mä′də-rī′, măd′yo͞o-rī′) A city of S India SSW of Chennai (Madras). Pop. 940,989.

mael•strom (māl′strəm) ►*n.* **1.** A violent or turbulent situation. **2.** A large and violent whirlpool. [Obsolete Du. : Du. *malen*, grind + *stroom*, stream.]

maes•tro (mīs′trō) ►*n., pl.* **-tros** or **-tri** (-trē). A master in an art, esp. a composer, conductor, or music teacher. [< Lat. *magister*, master.]

Mae•ter•linck (mā′tər-lĭngk′, mĕt′ər-), Count **Maurice.** 1862–1949. Belgian writer; 1911 Nobel.

Ma•fi•a (mä′fē-ə) ►*n.* **1.** A secret terrorist organization in Sicily. **2.** A criminal organization believed active, esp. in Italy and the US. [Ital.]

Ma•fi•o•so (mä′fē-ō′sō) ►*n., pl.* **-si** (-sē) or **-sos.** A member of the Mafia. [Ital.]

mag•a•zine (măg′ə-zēn′, măg′ə-zēn′) ►*n.* **1.** A periodical containing articles, stories, pictures, or other features. **2.** A place where goods are stored, esp. ammunition. **3.** A usu. detachable compartment in some types of firearms, in which cartridges are held. **4.** A compartment in a camera for holding film. [< Ar. *maḫzan*, storehouse.]

Mag•da•le•na (măg′də-lā′nə) A river rising in SW Colombia and flowing about 1,601 km (1,000 mi) to the Caribbean Sea.

Mag•de•burg (măg′də-bûrg′, mäg′-) A city of central Germany on the Elbe R. WSW of Berlin. Pop. 270,546.

Ma•gel•lan (mə-jĕl′ən), **Ferdinand.** 1480?–1521. Portuguese navigator.

Magellan, Strait of. A channel separating South America from Tierra del Fuego and connecting the Atlantic and Pacific.

ma•gen•ta (mə-jĕn′tə) ►*n.* A vivid purplish red. [After *Magenta*, Italy.] —**ma•gen′ta** *adj.*

mag•got (măg′ət) ►*n.* The legless, soft-bodied larva of any of various flies, often found in decaying matter. [ME *magot.*] —**mag′got•y** *adj.*

ma•gi (mā′jī′) ►*n.* Pl. of **magus.**

mag•ic (măj′ĭk) ►*n.* **1.** The art that purports to control or forecast natural events, effects, or forces by invoking the supernatural through the use of charms, spells, or rituals. **2.** The exercise of sleight of hand or conjuring for entertainment. **3.** A mysterious quality of enchantment. [< Gk. *magos*, MAGUS.] —**mag′ic, mag′i•cal** *adj.* —**mag′i•cal•ly** *adv.* —**ma•gi′cian** (mə-jish′ən) *n.*

mag•is•te•ri•al (măj′ĭ-stîr′ē-əl) ►*adj.* **1a.** Authoritative; commanding. **b.** Dogmatic; overbearing. **2.** Of a magistrate or a magistrate's official functions. [< Lat. *magister*, master.] —**mag′is•te′ri•al•ly** *adv.*

mag•is•trate (măj′ĭ-strāt′, -strĭt) ►*n.* A civil officer with power to administer the law. [< Lat. *magistrātus.*]

mag•ma (măg′mə) ►*n., pl.* **-ma•ta** (-mä′tə) or **-mas.** The molten rock material under the earth's crust that cools and hardens to form igneous rock. [< Gk., unguent.] —**mag•mat′ic** (-măt′ĭk) *adj.*

Mag•na Car•ta or **Mag•na Char•ta** (măg′nə kär′tə) ►*n.* The charter of English political and civil liberties granted by King John in 1215.

mag•nan•i•mous (măg-năn′ə-məs) ►*adj.* Generous and noble, esp. in forgiving. [< Lat. *magnanimus.*] —**mag′na•nim′i•ty** (-nə-nĭm′ĭ-tē) *n.* —**mag•nan′i•mous•ly** *adv.*

mag•nate (măg′nāt′, -nĭt) ►*n.* A powerful or influential person, esp. in business or industry. [< LLat. *magnās, magnāt-.*]

mag•ne•sia (măg-nē′zhə, -shə) ►*n.* A white powdery compound, MgO, used in refractories, electric insulation, and as a laxative and antacid. [< Gk. *Magnēsia*, ancient city-state in Asia Minor.]

mag•ne•si•um (măg-nē′zē-əm, -zhəm) ►*n.* *Symbol* **Mg** A light, silvery, moderately hard metallic element that burns with a brilliant white flame, used in lightweight structural alloys. At. no. 12. See table at **element.** [< MAGNESIA.]

mag•net (măg′nĭt) ►*n.* **1.** An object that is surrounded by a magnetic field and attracts iron or steel. **2.** An electromagnet. **3.** A person, place, or object that attracts. [< Gk. *Magnēs (lithos)*, (stone) of Magnesia.]

mag•net•ic (măg-nĕt′ĭk) ►*adj.* **1a.** Of or relating to magnetism or magnets. **b.** Having the properties of a magnet. **c.** Capable of being magnetized or attracted by a magnet. **2.** Relating to the magnetic poles of the earth. **3.** Exerting attraction: *a magnetic personality.* —**mag•net′i•cal•ly** *adv.*

magnetic disk ►*n.* *Comp. Sci.* A memory device, such as a hard disk, covered with a magnetic coating on which digital information is stored by magnetization of microscopically small needles.

magnetic field ►*n.* A detectable force that exists at every point in the region around a magnet or electric current.

magnetic needle ►*n.* A slender bar of magnetized steel, usu. suspended in a magnetic compass to indicate the direction of the earth's magnetic poles.

magnetic north ►*n.* The direction of the earth's magnetic pole, to which the north-seeking pole of a magnetic needle points.

magnetic pole ►*n.* **1.** Either of two limited regions in a magnet at which the magnet's field is strongest. **2.** Either of two variable points on the earth, close to but not coinciding with the geographic poles, where the earth's magnetic field is most intense.

magnetic resonance imaging ►*n.* The use of nuclear magnetic resonance to produce images of atoms and molecules in solids, esp.

human cells, tissues, and organs.

magnetic tape ►*n.* A plastic tape coated with iron oxide for use in magnetic recording.

mag•net•ism (măg′nĭ-tĭz′əm) ►*n.* **1.** The properties and effects associated with a magnetic field. **2.** The study of magnets and their effects. **3.** The force exerted by a magnetic field. **4.** Unusual power to attract or influence: *the magnetism of money.*

mag•net•ite (măg′nĭ-tīt′) ►*n.* A magnetic black iron ore, Fe_3O_4.

mag•net•ize (măg′nĭ-tīz′) ►*v.* **-ized, -iz•ing** **1.** To make magnetic. **2.** To attract. —**mag′net•i•za′tion** *n.* —**mag′net•iz′er** *n.*

mag•ne•to (măg-nē′tō) ►*n., pl.* **-tos.** A small generator of alternating current that works by means of permanent magnets, used in the ignition systems of some internal-combustion engines. [Short for *magnetoelectric machine.*]

mag•ne•tom•e•ter (măg′nĭ-tŏm′ĭ-tər) ►*n.* A device that measures the strength and direction esp. of the earth's magnetic field.

magnet school ►*n.* A public school for students of high ability that attracts its student body from all parts of a city.

mag•nif•i•cent (măg-nĭf′ĭ-sənt) ►*adj.* **1.** Splendid in appearance; grand: *a magnificent palace.* **2.** Grand or noble in thought or deed; exalted. **3.** Outstanding or exceptional; superlative: *a magnificent place for sailing.* [< Lat. *magnificus.*] —**mag•nif′i•cence** *n.* —**mag•nif′i•cent•ly** *adv.*

mag•ni•fy (măg′nə-fī′) ►*v.* **-fied, -fy•ing** **1.** To make greater in size, extent, or effect; enlarge. **2.** To cause to appear greater or more important. See Syns at **exaggerate. 3.** To increase the apparent size of, esp. by means of a lens. **4.** To glorify or praise. [< Lat. *magnificāre.*] —**mag′ni•fi•ca′tion** *n.* —**mag′ni•fi′er** *n.*

mag•ni•fy•ing glass (măg′nə-fī′ĭng) ►*n.* A lens or system of lenses that enlarges the image of an object.

Mag•ni•to•gorsk (măg-nē′tə-gôrsk′) A city of SW Russia in the Ural Mts. SSW of Chelyabinsk. Pop. 438,808.

mag•ni•tude (măg′nĭ-to͞od′, -tyo͞od′) ►*n.* **1.** Greatness, esp. in size or extent. **2.** Greatness in significance or influence. **3.** *Astron.* The relative brightness of a celestial body designated on a numerical scale. [< Lat. *magnus*, great.]

mag•no•lia (măg-nōl′yə) ►*n.* A tree having large, usu. white, pink, or purple flowers. [After Pierre *Magnol* (1638–1715).]

mag•num (măg′nəm) ►*n.* A bottle for wine or liquor holding approx. ⅖ gal. [< Lat., neuter of *magnus*, great.]

magnum opus ►*n.* The greatest single work of an artist, writer, or composer. [Lat.]

mag•pie (măg′pī′) ►*n.* **1.** A long-tailed, loud-voiced, chiefly black and white bird related to the crows and jays. **2.** A person who chatters constantly. [*Mag*, a nickname for Margaret + *pie*, magpie.]

Ma•gritte (mä-grēt′), **René.** 1898–1967. Belgian painter.

ma•guey (mə-gā′, măg′wā) ►*n., pl.* **-gueys** **1.** Any of various agaves or related plants. **2.** The fiber obtained from a maguey. [Sp., of Cariban orig.]

ma•gus (mā′gəs) ►*n., pl.* **ma•gi** (mā′jī′) **1.** **Magus** In the New Testament, one of the three wise men from the East who paid homage to the infant Jesus. **2.** A sorcerer; magician. [< Pers. *maguš.*]

Mag•yar (măg′yär′, mäg′-) ►*n.* **1.** An ethnic Hungarian. **2.** See **Hungarian** 2. [Hung.] —**Mag′yar** *adj.*

ma•ha•ra•jah or **ma•ha•ra•ja** (mä′hə-rä′jə, -zhə) ►*n.* A king or prince in India ranking above a rajah. [< Skt. *mahārājaḥ.*]

ma•ha•ra•ni or **ma•ha•ra•nee** (mä′hə-rä′nē) ►*n., pl.* **-nis** or **-nees** **1.** The wife of a maharajah. **2.** A princess in India ranking above a rani. [< Skt. *mahārājñī.*]

ma•ha•ri•shi (mä′hə-rē′shē, mə-här′ə-shē) ►*n., pl.* **-shis** *Hinduism.* A teacher of spiritual knowledge. [Skt. *mahārṣiḥ.*]

Ma•hat•ma (mə-hät′mə, -hăt′-) ►*n. Hinduism* Used as a title of respect for a person renowned for spirituality and high-mindedness. [Skt. *mahātmā.*]

Mah•di (mä′dē) ►*n., pl.* **-dis** *Islam.* The messiah expected to appear at the world's end and establish a reign of peace. [Ar. *mahdī*, rightly guided (one), Mahdi.] —**Mah′dism** *n.* —**Mah′dist** *n.*

Ma•hi•can (mə-hē′kən) also **Mo•hi•can** (mō-, mə-) ►*n., pl.* **-can** or **-cans** **1.** A member of a Native American confederacy formerly inhabiting the upper Hudson R. valley, now in Oklahoma and Wisconsin. **2.** The Algonquian language of the Mahican.

mah•jong also **mah•jongg** (mä′zhŏng′, -zhông′) ►*n.* A Chinese game usu. played by four persons with rectangular tiles bearing various designs. [Mandarin *má jiàng.*]

Mah•ler (mä′lər), **Gustav.** 1860–1911. Austrian composer.

ma•hog•a•ny (mə-hŏg′ə-nē) ►*n., pl.* **-nies** **1a.** Any of a genus of tropical American trees valued for their hard, reddish-brown wood. **b.** The wood of such a tree. **2.** Any of several similar trees or their wood. [?]

ma•hout (mə-hout′) ►*n.* The keeper and driver of an elephant. [Hindi *mahāut.*]

maid (mād) ►*n.* **1.** An unmarried girl or woman. **2.** A woman servant. [< OE *mægden.*]

maid•en (mād′n) ►*n.* An unmarried girl or woman. ►*adj.* **1.** Of or befitting a maiden. **2.** First or earliest: *a maiden voyage.* [< OE *mægden.*] —**maid′en•hood′** *n.*

maid•en•hair fern (mād′n-hâr′) ►*n.* A fern having feathery fronds with fan-shaped leaflets. [From the fineness of its stems.]

maiden name ►*n.* A woman's family name if different from her married name.

maid of honor ►*n., pl.* **maids of honor.** The chief unmarried woman attendant of a bride.

Mai•du (mī′do͞o) ►*n., pl.* **-du** or **-dus** **1.** A member of a Native American people inhabiting NE California. **2.** The Penutian language of the Maidu.

mail[1] (māl) ►*n.* **1a.** Materials, such as letters and packages, handled in a postal system. **b.** Postal material for a specific person or organization. **2.** often **mails** A postal system. **3.** *Comp. Sci.* Messages sent electronically; e-mail. ►*v.* To send by mail. [< OFr. *male*, bag, of Gmc. orig.] —**mail′er** *n.*

mail[2] (māl) ►*n.* Flexible armor composed of small overlapping metal rings, loops of chain, or scales. [< Lat. *macula*, mesh.] —**mailed** *adj.*

mail•box (māl′bŏks′) ►*n.* **1.** A public container for deposit of outgoing mail. **2.** A private box for the delivery of mail. **3.** A computer file for collecting and storing e-mail.

Mail•er (mā′lər), **Norman.** b. 1923. Amer. writer.

Mail•lol (mä-yôl′), **Aristide.** 1861–1944. French sculptor.

mail•man (māl′măn′, -mən) ►*n.* A man who carries and delivers mail.

mail order ►*n.* An order for goods to be shipped through the mail.

mail-or•der house (māl′ôr′dər) ►*n.* A business that promotes, receives, and fills requests for merchandise through the mail.

maim (mām) ►*v.* **1.** To disable, mutilate, or cripple. See Syns at **batter**[1]. **2.** To impair. [< OFr. *mahaignier.*] —**maim′er** *n.*

Mai•mon•i•des (mī-mŏn′ĭ-dēz′). Moses Ben Maimon. 1135–1204. Spanish-born Jewish philosopher and physician.

main (mān) ►*adj.* **1.** Most important; principal; chief. **2.** Exerted to the utmost; sheer: *by main strength.* **3.** Relating to or being the principal clause or verb of a complex sentence. ►*n.* **1.** The chief or largest part: *ideas that are in the main, impractical.* **2.** The principal pipe or conduit in a system for conveying water, gas, oil, or other utility. **3.** Physical strength: *fought with might and main.* [< OE *mægen*, strength.] —**main′ly** *adv.*

Main (mān, mīn) A river rising in E Germany and flowing about 499 km (310 mi) to the Rhine R. at Mainz.

Maine (mān) A state of the NE US. Cap. Augusta. Pop. 1,233,323.

main•frame (mān′frām′) ►*n.* A large, powerful computer, often serving many connected terminals.

main•land (mān′lănd′, -lənd) ►*n.* The principal landmass of a country or continent.

main•line (mān′līn′) ►*v.* **-lined, -lin•ing** *Slang.* To inject narcotics into a vein.

main•mast (mān′məst, -măst′) ►*n.* The principal mast of a sailing ship.

main•sail (mān′səl, -sāl′) ►*n.* The principal sail of a sailing ship.

main•spring (mān′sprĭng′) ►*n.* **1.** The principal spring mechanism in a device, esp. a timepiece. **2.** The chief motivating force.

main•stay (mān′stā′) ►*n.* **1.** A chief support. **2.** A rope that steadies and supports the mainmast of a sailing ship.

main•stream (mān′strēm′) ►*n.* The prevailing current or direction of a movement, influence, or activity. ►*v.* **1.** To integrate (a disadvantaged student) into regular classes. **2.** To incorporate into the mainstream. —**main′stream′** *adj.*

main•tain (mān-tān′) ►*v.* **1.** To carry on; continue. **2.** To preserve or retain. **3.** To keep in good repair. **4.** To provide for; support. **5.** To defend against criticism. **6.** To declare to be true. [< Lat. *manū tenēre*, hold in the hand.] —**main•tain′a•ble** *adj.* —**main′te•nance** (-tə-nəns) *n.*

Mainz (mīnts) A city of W-central Germany at the confluence of the Rhine and Main rivers WSW of Frankfurt. Pop. 185,487.

mai•tre d′ (mā′trə dē′, mā′tər) ►*n., pl.* **mai•tre d′s** (dēz′) *Informal.* A maitre d'hôtel.

maî•tre d'hô•tel (mā′trə dō-tĕl′) ►*n., pl.* **maî•tres d'hôtel** (-trə) **1.** A headwaiter. **2.** A head steward; major-domo. [Fr.]

maize (māz) ►*n.* See **corn**[1] 1. [< Cariban *mahiz.*]

Maj. or **Maj** or **MAJ** ►*abbr.* major

maj•es•ty (măj′ĭ-stē) ►*n., pl.* **-ties 1.** The greatness and dignity of a sovereign. **2.** Supreme authority or power. **3. Majesty** Used with *His, Her,* or *Your* as a title for a sovereign. **4.** Regal splendor, magnificence, or grandeur. [< Lat. *māiestās.*] —**ma•jes′tic** (mə-jĕs′tĭk) *adj.* —**ma•jes′ti•cal•ly** *adv.*

Maj Gen ►*abbr.* major general

ma•jor (mā′jər) ►*adj.* **1.** Greater in importance, rank, or extent. **2.** Of great concern; very serious: *a major illness.* **3.** *Mus.* Of or based on a major scale. ►*n.* **1.** A rank, as in the US Army, above captain and below lieutenant colonel. **2a.** A field of study chosen as an academic specialty. **b.** A student specializing in such studies. ►*v.* To pursue studies in a major field. [< Lat. *māior.*]

Major, John. b. 1943. British prime minister (1990–97).

Ma•jor•ca (mə-jôr′kə, -yôr′-) An island of Spain in the W Mediterranean off the E-central coast of the mainland. —**Ma•jor′can** *adj. & n.*

ma•jor-do•mo (mā′jər-dō′mō) ►*n., pl.* **-mos.** A head steward or butler. [< Lat. *māior*, chief + *domus*, house.]

major general ►*n.* A rank, as in the US Army, above brigadier general and below lieutenant general.

ma•jor•i•ty (mə-jôr′ĭ-tē, -jŏr′-) ►*n., pl.* **-ties 1.** A number more than half of the total number of a given group. **2.** The amount by which the greater number of votes cast, as in an election, exceeds the total number of remaining votes. **3.** The status of legal age.

major league ►*n.* A league of principal importance in professional sports, esp. baseball. —**ma′jor-league′** *adj.*

major medical ►*n.* Insurance that covers all or most medical bills for major illnesses.

major scale ►*n.* *Mus.* A diatonic scale having half steps between the 3rd and 4th and the 7th and 8th degrees.

Mak•a•lu (mŭk′ə-lo͞o′) A mountain, 8,476 m (27,790 ft), in the Himalayas of NE Nepal.

Ma•kar•i•os III (mä-kä′rē-ôs). 1913–77. Cypriot prelate and president of Cyprus (1959–77).

make (māk) ►*v.* **made** (mād), **mak•ing 1.** To bring about; create. **2.** To form or construct: *made a dress.* **3.** To cause to be or become: *made him happy.* **4a.** To cause to act in a specified manner. **b.** To compel: *made him leave.* **5.** To prepare; fix. **6.** To carry out; perform. **7.** To achieve or attain: *make peace.* **8.** To arrive at. **9.** To gain or earn. **10.** To develop into: *made a great teacher.* **11.** To constitute. **12.** To act or behave in a specified manner. **13.** To proceed. —***phrasal verbs:*** **make out 1.** To see, esp. with difficulty. **2.** To understand. **3.** To write out or draw up. **4.** To fare: *made out well on the deal.* **5.** *Informal* To neck; pet. **make up 1.** To put together; construct or compose. **2.** To constitute. **3.** To apply cosmetics. **4.** To invent: *made up an excuse.* **5.** To compensate, as for an omission. **6.** To resolve a quarrel. ►*n.* **1.** The style or manner in which a thing is made. **2.** A specific line of manufactured goods.

—***idioms:*** **make believe** To pretend. **make do** To get along with the means available. **make good 1.** To carry out successfully. **2.** To pay back. **make it** To be successful. **make light of** To treat as unimportant. **make love 1.** To court; woo. **2.** To engage in sexual intercourse. **make no bones about** To be completely frank about. **make the most of** To use to the greatest advantage. **make time** To move or travel fast. **make way** To give room for passage. [< OE *macian.*] —**mak′er** *n.*

make-be•lieve (māk′bĭ-lēv′) ►*n.* Playful or fanciful pretense. —**make′-be•lieve′** *adj.*

make•shift (māk′shĭft′) ►*n.* A temporary expedient or substitute. —**make′shift′** *adj.*

Syns: *makeshift, expedient, resort, stopgap* ***n.***

make•up or **make-up** (māk′ŭp′) ►*n.* **1.** The way in which something is composed, constructed, or arranged. **2.** The qualities or temperament that constitute a personality. **3.** Cosmetics applied esp. to the face.

mak•ings (mā′kĭngz) ►*pl.n.* The material or ingredients needed for making something.

Ma•ki•yiv•ka (mə-kē′əv-kə) A city of E Ukraine NE of Donetsk. Pop. 425,600.

ma•ko (mä′kō) ►*n., pl.* **-kos.** A shark having a large heavy body and a nearly symmetrical tail. [Maori.]

mal– ►*pref.* Bad; badly: *malformation.* [< Lat. *malus*, bad, and *male*, badly.]

Mal•a•bar Coast (măl′ə-bär′) A region of SW India on the Arabian Sea.

Mal•a•bo (măl′ə-bō′, mä-lä′bō) The capital of Equatorial Guinea, on Bioko I. in the Gulf of Guinea. Pop. 30,710.

Ma•lac•ca (mə-lăk′ə, -lä′kə), **Strait of.** A channel between Sumatra and the Malay Peninsula connecting the Andaman Sea with the South China Sea.

Mal•a•chi (măl′ə-kī′) ►*n.* **1.** A Hebrew prophet of the 6th cent. B.C. **2.** See table at **Bible.**

mal•a•chite (măl′ə-kīt′) ►*n.* A green carbonate mineral used as a source of copper and for ornamental stoneware. [< Gk. *molokhitis* < *malakhē*, mallow.]

mal•ad•just•ment (măl′ə-jŭst′mənt) ►*n.* Faulty or poor adjustment. —**mal′ad•just′ed** *adj.*

mal•a•droit (măl′ə-droit′) ►*adj.* Marked by a lack of dexterity; clumsy; inept. —**mal′a•droit′ly** *adv.* —**mal′a•droit′ness** *n.*

mal•a•dy (măl′ə-dē) ►*n., pl.* **-dies.** A disease, disorder, or ailment. [< Lat. *male habitus*, in poor condition.]

Má•la•ga (măl′ə-gə, mä′lä-gä′) A city of S Spain NE of Gibraltar. Pop. 523,450.

Mal•a•gas•y (măl′ə-găs′ē) ►*n., pl.* **-gas•y** or **-gas•ies 1.** A native or inhabitant of Madagascar. **2.** The Austronesian language of the Malagasy. —**Mal′a•gas′y** *adj.*

mal•aise (mă-lāz′, -lĕz′) ►*n.* A vague feeling of illness or depression. [< OFr.]

Mal•a•mud (măl′ə-məd), **Bernard.** 1914–86. Amer. writer.

mal•a•mute (măl′ə-myo͞ot′) ►*n.* A powerful dog developed in Alaska as a sled dog and having a thick coat and a bushy tail. [< *Malemute*, an Alaskan Eskimo people.]

mal•a•prop•ism (măl′ə-prŏp-ĭz′əm) ►*n.* A ludicrous or humorous misuse of a word. [After Mrs. *Malaprop*, a character in *The Rivals*, a play by Richard B. Sheridan.]

mal•a•pro•pos (măl′ăp-rə-pō′) ►*adj.* Out of place; inappropriate; inopportune. [Fr. *mal à propos.*] —**mal′a•pro•pos′** *adv.*

ma•lar•i•a (mə-lâr′ē-ə) ►*n.* An infectious disease marked by cycles of chills, fever, and sweating, transmitted by the bite of an infected mosquito. [Ital. < *mal' aria*, foul air.] —**ma•lar′i•al** *adj.*

ma•lar•key also **ma•lar•ky** (mə-lär′kē) ►*n.* *Slang* Exaggerated or foolish talk, usu. intended to deceive. [?]

Mal•a•thi•on (măl′ə-thī′ŏn′) ► A trademark for the organic compound $C_{10}H_{19}O_6PS_2$, used as an insecticide.

Ma•la•wi (mə-lä′wē) A country of SE Africa. Cap. Lilongwe. Pop. 9,461,000. —**Ma•la′wi•an** *adj. & n.*

Ma•lay (mə-lā′, mā′lā′) ►*n.* **1.** A member of a people inhabiting Malaysia, the N Malay Peninsula, and parts of the W Malay Archipelago. **2.** The Austronesian language of the Malays. —**Ma•lay′an, Ma•lay′** *adj. & n.*

Mal•a•ya•lam (măl′ə-yä′ləm) ►*n.* A Dravidian language spoken in SW India.

Malay Archipelago. An island group of SE Asia between Australia and the Asian mainland.

Malay Peninsula also **Ma•la•ya** (mə-lā′ə, mā-). A peninsula of SE Asia comprising SW Thailand, W Malaysia, and the island of Singapore.

Ma•lay•sia (mə-lā′zhə, -shə) A country of SE Asia consisting of the S Malay Peninsula and the N part of Borneo. Cap. Kuala Lumpur. Pop. 19,489,000. —**Ma•lay′sian** *adj. & n.*

Mal•colm X (măl′kəm ĕks′). 1925–65. Amer. activist; assassinated.

Malcolm X
photographed c. 1964

mal•con•tent (măl′kən-tĕnt′) ►*adj.* Discontented. ►*n.* A discontented person.

Mal•dives (môl′dīvz, -dēvz, măl′-) An island country in the Indian Ocean SW of Sri Lanka. Cap. Male. Pop. 246,000. —**Mal•div′i•an** (-dĭv′ē-ən), **Mal•di′van** *adj. & n.*

male (māl) ►*adj.* **1a.** Of or being the sex that has organs to produce spermatozoa for fertilizing ova. **b.** Consisting of members of this sex. **2.** *Bot.* **a.** Of or being an organ, as an anther, that produces gametes capable of fertilizing those produced by female organs. **b.** Bearing stamens but not pistils. **3.** Made for insertion into a fitted bore or socket. ►*n.* A member of the male sex. [< Lat. *masculus.*] —**male′ness** *n.*

Ma•le (mä′lē) The capital of the Maldives, on **Male,** the chief atoll of the island country. Pop. 46,334.

Mal•e•cite (măl′ə-sīt′) or **Mal•i•seet** (-sēt′) ►*n., pl.* **-cite** or **-cites** or **-seet** or **-seets 1.** A member of a Native American people inhabiting New Brunswick and NE Maine. **2.** The Algonquian language of the Malecite.

mal•e•dic•tion (măl′ĭ-dĭk′shən) ►*n.* A curse. [< Lat. *maledīcere*, to curse.]

mal•e•fac•tor (măl′ə-făk′tər) ►*n.* **1.** A criminal. **2.** An evildoer. [< Lat. < *malefacere*, do wrong.] —**mal′e•fac′tion** *n.*

ma•lef•ic (mə-lĕf′ĭk) ►*adj.* **1.** Exerting a malignant influence. **2.** Malicious. [Lat. *maleficus.*]

ma•lef•i•cence (mə-lĕf′ĭ-səns) ►*n.* **1.** The doing of evil or harm; mischief. **2.** Harmful or evil nature or quality. [Lat. *maleficentia.*] —**ma•lef′i•cent** *adj.*

ma•lev•o•lence (mə-lĕv′ə-ləns) ►*n.* **1.** The quality or state of being malevolent. **2.** Malicious behavior. [ME < OFr. *malivolence* < Lat. *malevolentia* < *malevolēns*, *malevolent-*, malevolent : *male*, badly + *volēns*, pr.part. of *velle*, to want.]

ma•lev•o•lent (mə-lĕv′ə-lənt) ►*adj.* Having or exhibiting ill will; malicious. [Lat. *malevolēns*, *malevolent-*.] —**ma•lev′o•lence** *n.* —**ma•lev′o•lent•ly** *adv.*

mal•fea•sance (măl-fē′zəns) ►*n. Law* Misconduct or wrongdoing, esp. by a public official. [AN *malfaisance* < Lat. *malefacere*, do wrong.]

mal•for•ma•tion (măl′fôr-mā′shən) ►*n.* An abnormal or irregular formation or structure; deformity. —**mal•formed′** *adj.*

mal•func•tion (măl-fŭngk′shən) ►*v.* To fail to function normally. —**mal•func′tion** *n.*

Ma•li (mä′lē) A country of W Africa. Cap. Bamako. Pop. 10,462,000. —**Ma′li•an** *adj. & n.*

mal•ice (măl′ĭs) ►*n.* A desire to harm others or to see others suffer; spite. [< Lat. *malitia* < *malus*, bad.] —**ma•li′cious** (mə-lĭsh′əs) *adj.* —**ma•li′cious•ly** *adv.* —**ma•li′cious•ness** *n.*

ma•lign (mə-līn′) ►*v.* To speak evil of; defame. ►*adj.* **1.** Evil or harmful in influence or effect; injurious. **2.** Malevolent. [< Lat. *malignus*, evil, harmful.] —**ma•lign′er** *n.*

ma•lig•nant (mə-lĭg′nənt) ►*adj.* **1.** Showing great malevolence. **2.** Highly injurious; pernicious. **3.** *Pathol.* Relating to an abnormal growth that tends to spread. —**ma•lig′nan•cy** *n.* —**ma•lig′nant•ly** *adv.*

ma•lig•ni•ty (mə-lĭg′nĭ-tē) ►*n., pl.* **-ties 1a.** Intense ill will or hatred; great malice. **b.** An act or feeling of great malice. **2.** The condition of being evil or injurious.

ma•lin•ger (mə-lĭng′gər) ►*v.* To feign illness or other incapacity to avoid work. [< Fr. *malingre*, sickly.] —**ma•lin′ger•er** *n.*

mall (môl, măl) ►*n.* **1.** A large, often enclosed shopping complex with stores, businesses, and restaurants. **2.** A street lined with shops and closed to vehicles. **3.** A shady public walk or promenade. **4.** *Regional* See **median strip.** See Regional Note at **neutral ground.** [After *The Mall*, London.]

mal•lard (măl′ərd) ►*n., pl.* **-lard** or **-lards.** A wild duck with a green head and neck in the male. [< OFr. *mallart*, perh. < *male*, MALE.]

Mal•lar•mé (măl′är-mā′), **Stéphane.** 1842–98. French poet.

mal•le•a•ble (măl′ē-ə-bəl) ►*adj.* **1.** Capable of being shaped or formed; pliable. **2.** Easily controlled; tractable. [< Lat. *malleus*, hammer.] —**mal′le•a•bil′i•ty, mal′le•a•ble•ness** *n.* —**mal′le•a•bly** *adv.*

mal•let (măl′ĭt) ►*n.* **1.** A short-handled hammer, usu. with a cylindrical head of wood. **2.** *Sports* A similar long-handled implement used to strike a ball, as in croquet and polo. [< OFr. *maillet*, dim. of *mail*, MAUL.]

mal•le•us (măl′ē-əs) ►*n., pl.* **-le•i** (-ē-ī′). A hammer-shaped bone that is the largest bone in the middle ear. [Lat., hammer.]

mal•low (măl′ō) ►*n.* A plant having showy pink or white flowers. [< Lat. *malva.*]

Mal•mö (măl′mō) A city of S Sweden, opposite Copenhagen. Pop. 236,684.

mal•nour•ished (măl-nûr′ĭsht, -nŭr′-) ►*adj.* Affected by improper or poor nutrition.

mal•nu•tri•tion (măl′no͞o-trĭsh′ən, -nyo͞o-) ►*n.* Insufficient or unhealthy nutrition.

mal•oc•clu•sion (măl′ə-klo͞o′zhən) ►*n.* Faulty closure between the upper and lower teeth.

mal•o•dor (măl-ō′dər) ►*n.* A bad odor. See Syns at **stench.** —**mal•o′dor•ous** *adj.* —**mal•o′dor•ous•ly** *adv.* —**mal•o′dor•ous•ness** *n.*

Mal•o•ry (măl′ə-rē), Sir **Thomas.** fl. 1470. English writer.

ma•lo•ti (mä-lō′tē) ►*n.* Pl. of **loti.**

mal•prac•tice (măl-prăk′tĭs) ►*n.* Improper, negligent, or unethical conduct or treatment, esp. by a physician or lawyer. —**mal′prac•ti′tion•er** *n.*

Mal•raux (măl-rō′, mäl-), **André.** 1901–76. French writer and politician.

malt (môlt) ►*n.* **1.** Grain, usu. barley, that has been allowed to sprout, used chiefly in brewing and distilling. **2.** An alcoholic beverage, such as beer, brewed from malt. **3.** See **malted milk** 2. [< OE *mealt.*] —**malt** *v.* —**malt′y** *adj.*

Mal•ta (môl′tə) An island country in the Mediterranean S of Sicily. Cap. Valletta. Pop. 364,000. —**Mal•tese′** *adj. & n.*

malt•ed milk (môl′tĭd) ►*n.* **1.** A soluble powder made of dried milk, malted barley, and wheat flour. **2.** A beverage made by mixing milk with this powder and often ice cream and flavoring; malt.

Mal•thus (măl′thəs), **Thomas Robert.** 1766–1834. British economist. —**Mal•thu′sian** (-tho͞o′zhən, -zē-ən) *adj. & n.*

mal•tose (môl′tōs′, -tōz′) ►*n.* A crystalline sugar formed in the digestion of starch.

mal•treat (măl-trēt′) ►*v.* To treat in a rough or cruel way; abuse. —**mal•treat′ment** *n.*

ma•ma or **mam•ma** (mä′mə, mə-mä′) ►*n. Informal* Mother. [Of baby-talk orig.]

mam•ba (mäm′bə) ►*n.* A venomous snake of tropical Africa. [Zulu *í-mâmbà.*]

mam•bo (mäm′bō) ►*n., pl.* **-bos.** A dance of Latin-American origin, resembling the rumba. [Am.Sp.] —**mam′bo** *v.*

mam•mal (măm′əl) ►*n.* Any of various warm-blooded vertebrate animals, including humans, marked by a covering of hair on the skin and, in the female, milk-producing glands. [< Lat. *mamma*, breast.] —**mam•ma′li•an** (mă-mā′lē-ən) *adj.* & *n.*

mam•mal•o•gy (mă-măl′ə-jē, -mŏl′-) ►*n.* The branch of zoology that deals with mammals. —**mam•mal′o•gist** *n.*

mam•ma•ry (măm′ə-rē) ►*adj.* Of or relating to a breast or milk-producing organ. [< Lat. *mamma*, breast.]

mam•mo•gram (măm′ə-grăm′) ►*n.* An x-ray image produced by mammography.

mam•mog•ra•phy (mă-mŏg′rə-fē) ►*n.*, *pl.* **-phies.** X-ray examination of the breasts for detection of tumors. [< Lat. *mamma*, breast.]

Mam•mon or **mam•mon** (măm′ən) ►*n.* Material wealth regarded as having an evil influence. [< Aram. *māmonā*, riches.]

mam•moth (măm′əth) ►*n.* An extinct elephant once widespread in the Northern Hemisphere. ►*adj.* Of enormous size; huge. [Obsolete Russ. *mamut.*]

mam•my (măm′ē) ►*n.*, *pl.* **-mies 1.** A mother. **2.** *Offensive* A Black nursemaid, esp. formerly in the S US. [< Dialectal *mam*, var. of MAMA.]

Ma•mo•ré (mä-mə-rā′) A river, about 965 km (600 mi), of N Bolivia flowing partly along the Brazilian border.

man (măn) ►*n.*, *pl.* **men** (mĕn) **1.** An adult male human. **2.** A human regardless of sex or age; person. **3.** The human race: *man's quest for peace.* **4.** A male human having qualities considered characteristic of manhood. **5.** *Informal* A husband, lover, or sweetheart. **6.** *Games* A piece used in a board game, such as chess or checkers. ►*v.* **manned, man•ning 1.** To supply with men or persons: *man a ship.* **2.** To take one's station at; attend or operate. —***idiom:* to a man** Without exception. [< OE *mann.*]

Usage: The use of *man* to mean "a human, regardless of sex" has a long history, but many feel that the sense of "male" is predominant over that of "person." Accordingly, many occupational titles in which *man* occurs as an element are being replaced, sometimes officially, by terms that are neutral. For example, *firefighter* is often used instead of *fireman, Member of Congress* instead of *Congressman,* and *chair* or *chairperson* instead of *chairman.* In addition, compounds formed with *woman,* as in *businesswoman, policewoman,* and *chairwoman,* are increasingly used as parallel terms to the corresponding compounds formed with *man.* See Usage Note at **-ess.**

Man, Isle of. An island of Great Britain in the Irish Sea off NW England.

Man. ►*abbr.* Manitoba

man about town ►*n.*, *pl.* **men about town.** A sophisticated, socially active man who frequents fashionable places.

man•a•cle (măn′ə-kəl) ►*n.* **1.** A device for shackling the hands; handcuff. **2.** Something that confines or restrains. ►*v.* **-cled, -cling.** To restrain with or as if with manacles. See Syns at **hamper**[1]. [< Lat. *manicula* < *manus*, hand.]

man•age (măn′ĭj) ►*v.* **-aged, -ag•ing 1.** To direct, control, or handle. **2.** To make submissive. **3.** To direct business affairs (of). **4.** To contrive or arrange. **5.** To get along; get by. [Ital. *maneggiare*, ult. < Lat. *manus*, hand.] —**man′age•a•bil′i•ty, man′age•a•ble•ness** *n.* —**man′age•a•bly** *adv.*

man•aged care (măn′ĭjd) ►*n.* A health care arrangement in which an organization, such as an HMO, acts as an intermediate between patient and physician.

man•age•ment (măn′ĭj-mənt) ►*n.* **1.** The act, manner, or practice of managing. **2.** The person or persons who manage an organization. **3.** Executive ability.

man•ag•er (măn′ĭ-jər) ►*n.* **1.** One who manages. **2.** One in charge of the training and performance of an athlete or team. —**man′a•ge′ri•al** (-ĭ-jîr′ē-əl) *adj.* —**man′a•ger′ri•al•ly** *adv.* —**man′ag•er•ship′** *n.*

Ma•na•gua (mä-nä′gwä) The capital of Nicaragua, in the W part on **Lake Managua.** Pop. 644,588. —**Ma•na′guan** *adj.* & *n.*

Ma•na•ma (mə-năm′ə, -nä′mə) The capital of Bahrain, on the Persian Gulf. Pop. 136,999.

ma•ña•na (mä-nyä′nə) ►*adv.* **1.** Tomorrow. **2.** At some future time. [Sp., morning, tomorrow < Lat. *māne.*] —**ma•ña′na** *n.*

ma•nat (mä-nät′) ►*n.* See table at **currency.** [Azerbaijani and Turkmen.]

man•a•tee (măn′ə-tē′) ►*n.* An aquatic, primarily tropical mammal. [Sp. *manatí* < Cariban.]

Ma•naus (mə-nous′, mä-) A city of NW Brazil on the Río Negro near its junction with the Amazon R. Pop. 1,010,544.

Man•ches•ter (măn′chĕs′tər, -chĭ-stər) **1.** A borough of NW England ENE of Liverpool. Pop. 432,038. **2.** A city of SE NH N of Nashua. Pop. 99,567.

Man•chu (măn′cho͞o, măn-cho͞o′) ►*n.*, *pl.* **-chu** or **-chus 1.** A member of a people native to Manchuria who ruled China during the Qing dynasty (1644–1912). **2.** The Tungusic language of the Manchu. —**Man′chu** *adj.*

Man•chu•ri•a (măn-cho͝or′ē-ə) A region of NE China. —**Man•chu′ri•an** *adj.* & *n.*

man•da•la (mŭn′də-lə) ►*n.* Any of various ritualistic geometric designs used in Hinduism and Buddhism as an aid to meditation. [Skt. *maṇḍalam*, circle.]

Man•da•lay (măn′dl-ā′) A city of central Myanmar (Burma) on the Irrawaddy R. N of Yangon. Pop. 532,949.

man•da•mus (măn-dā′məs) ►*n.* A writ issued by a superior court ordering a public official or body or a lower court to perform a duty. [Lat. *mandāmus*, we order.]

Man•dan (măn′dăn′) ►*n.*, *pl.* **-dan** or **-dans 1.** A member of a Native American people formerly living along the Missouri R. in S-central North Dakota, now in W-central North Dakota. **2.** Their Siouan language.

man•da•rin (măn′də-rĭn) ►*n.* **1.** A high-ranking public official in the Chinese Empire. **2. Mandarin** The official standard language of China, based on the dialect of Beijing. **3.** A mandarin orange. [< Skt. *mantrin-*, counselor < *mantraḥ*, counsel.] —**man′da•rin** *adj.*

mandarin collar ►*n.* A narrow upright collar usu. divided in front.

mandarin orange ►*n.* A small, loose-skinned, orange citrus fruit. [Fr. *mandarine* < Sp. *mandarín*, MANDARIN.]

man•date (măn′dāt′) ►*n.* **1.** An authoritative command or instruction. **2a.** A commission from the League of Nations authorizing a member nation to administer a territory. **b.** A region under administration. [< Lat. *mandāre*, to order.] —**man′date′** *v.*

man•da•to•ry (măn′də-tôr′ē, -tōr′ē) ▸*adj.* **1.** Required or obligatory. **2.** Of or containing a mandate.

Man•de•la (măn-dĕl′ə), **Nelson Rolihlahla.** b. 1918. South African political leader and president (1994–99); 1993 Nobel Peace Prize.

Man•del•stam (män′dəl-stəm), **Osip Emilyevich.** 1892–1938? Russian poet and critic.

man•di•ble (măn′də-bəl) ▸*n.* **1.** The lower jaw of a vertebrate animal. **2.** Either part of a bird's beak. **3.** A jawlike part of an insect. [< LLat. *mandibula* < *mandere*, chew.] —**man•dib′u•lar** (-dĭb′yə-lər) *adj.*

Man•din•go (măn-dĭng′gō) ▸*n., pl.* **-gos** or **-goes 1.** A member of any of various peoples inhabiting a large area of the upper Niger R. valley of W Africa. **2.** A group of related languages in W Africa.

man•do•lin (măn′də-lĭn′, măn′dl-ĭn) ▸*n.* A stringed musical instrument with a usu. pear-shaped body and a fretted neck. [< Ital. *mandola*, lute < Gk. *pandoura.*]

man•drake (măn′drāk′) ▸*n.* **1.** A S European plant having a branched root thought to resemble the human body, once widely believed to have magical powers. **2.** See **May apple.** [< Gk. *mandragoras.*]

man•drel or **man•dril** (măn′drəl) ▸*n.* **1.** A spindle or axle used to secure or support material being machined. **2.** A metal rod or bar around which material, such as metal or glass, may be shaped. [Poss. < Fr. *mandrin*, lathe.]

man•drill (măn′drəl) ▸*n.* A large African baboon having brilliant facial markings in the adult male. [MAN + *drill*, a baboon.]

mane (mān) ▸*n.* **1.** The long hair growing from the neck of certain animals, such as the horse and male lion. **2.** A long thick growth of human hair. [< OE *manu.*]

ma•nège also **ma•nege** (mă-nĕzh′) ▸*n.* The art of training or riding horses. [Fr. < Ital. *maneggio* < *maneggiare*, MANAGE.]

ma•nes or **Ma•nes** (mā′nēz′, mä′nās′) ▸*pl.n.* In ancient Roman religion, the spirits of the dead. [< Lat. *mānēs.*]

Ma•net (mə-nā′, mă-), **Edouard.** 1832–83. French painter.

ma•neu•ver (mə-no͞o′vər, -nyo͞o′-) ▸*n.* **1a.** A strategic or tactical military or naval movement. **b.** often **maneuvers** A large-scale tactical exercise that simulates combat. **2.** A physical movement involving skill and dexterity. **3.** An adroit, clever, and artful move or action; stratagem. ▸*v.* **1.** To carry out a military maneuver. **2.** To use stratagems in gaining an end. **3.** To manipulate or guide adroitly to a desired position or goal. See Syns at **manipulate.** [< Lat. *manū operārī*, work by hand.] —**ma•neu′ver•a•bil′i•ty** *n.* —**ma•neu′ver•a•ble** *adj.*

man•ful (măn′fəl) ▸*adj.* Courageous; resolute. —**man′ful•ly** *adv.* —**man′ful•ness** *n.*

man•ga•nese (măng′gə-nēz′, -nēs′) ▸*n. Symbol* **Mn** A brittle metallic element used chiefly in making alloys of steel. At. no. 25. See table at **element.** [< Ital. < Med.Lat. *magnēsia*, MAGNESIA.]

mange (mānj) ▸*n.* A chronic skin disease esp. of domestic animals, marked by itching and loss of hair. [< OFr. *manjue* < *mangier*, eat. See MANGER.] —**mang′y** *adj.*

man•ger (mān′jər) ▸*n.* A trough or an open box in which feed for livestock is placed. [< Lat. *mandūcāre*, eat.]

man•gle¹ (măng′gəl) ▸*v.* **-gled, -gling 1.** To mutilate or disfigure by battering or hacking. See Syns at **batter¹. 2.** To ruin or botch. [< AN *mangler.*] —**man′gler** *n.*

man•gle² (măng′gəl) ▸*n.* A laundry machine for pressing fabrics. [Du. *mangel.*]

man•go (măng′gō) ▸*n., pl.* **-goes** or **-gos 1.** A tropical Asian evergreen tree cultivated for its edible fruit. **2.** The sweet juicy fruit of the mango. [< Tamil *mānkāy.*]

man•grove (măn′grōv′, măng′-) ▸*n.* A tropical evergreen tree or shrub having stiltlike roots and stems and forming dense thickets in tidal regions. [< Taino *mangue.*]

man•han•dle (măn′hăn′dəl) ▸*v.* **1.** To handle roughly. **2.** To effect by physical effort.

Man•hat•tan¹ (măn-hăt′n) A borough of New York City in SE NY, mainly on **Manhattan Island.** —**Man•hat′tan•ite′** (-īt′) *n.*

Man•hat•tan² (măn-hăt′n, mən-) ▸*n.* A cocktail made of sweet vermouth and whiskey. [< MANHATTAN¹.]

man•hole (măn′hōl′) ▸*n.* A hole, usu. with a cover, through which an underground structure, such as a sewer, can be entered.

man•hood (măn′ho͝od′) ▸*n.* **1.** The state of being an adult male. **2.** The qualities, such as courage and vigor, often thought to be appropriate to a man. **3.** Men collectively.

man-hour (măn′our′) ▸*n.* An industrial unit of production equal to the work one person can produce in one hour.

man•hunt (măn′hŭnt′) ▸*n.* An organized search esp. for a fugitive criminal.

ma•ni•a (mā′nē-ə, mān′yə) ▸*n.* **1.** An excessively intense enthusiasm or desire; craze. **2.** A mental disorder characterized by excessive physical activity and emotional excitement. **3.** Violent abnormal behavior. [< Gk.]

-mania ▸*suff.* An exaggerated desire or enthusiasm for: *pyromania.* [< MANIA.]

ma•ni•ac (mā′nē-ăk′) ▸*n.* **1.** An insane person. **2.** One with an excessive enthusiasm for something. [< Gk. *maniakos*, mad < *mania*, madness.] —**ma′ni•ac′, ma•ni′a•cal** (mə-nī′ə-kəl) *adj.*

man•ic (măn′ĭk) ▸*adj.* Of, affected by, or marked by mania.

man•ic-de•pres•sive (măn′ĭk-dĭ-prĕs′ĭv) *Psychiat.* ▸*adj.* Bipolar. ▸*n.* A person with bipolar disorder.

man•i•cot•ti (măn′ĭ-kŏt′ē) ▸*n.* A dish of large pasta tubes with a filling, as of meat or cheese. [Ital.]

man•i•cure (măn′ĭ-kyo͝or′) ▸*n.* A cosmetic treatment of the fingernails. ▸*v.* **-cured, -curing 1.** To give a manicure to. **2.** To trim evenly. [Fr.] —**man′i•cur′ist** *n.*

man•i•fest (măn′ə-fĕst′) ▸*adj.* Clearly apparent to the sight or understanding; obvious. See Syns at **apparent.** ▸*v.* To show plainly; reveal. ▸*n.* A list of cargo or passengers. [< Lat. *manifestus.*] —**man′i•fest′ly** *adv.*

man•i•fes•ta•tion (măn′ə-fĕ-stā′shən) ▸*n.* An indication of the existence or presence of something.

man•i•fes•to (măn′ə-fĕs′tō) ▸*n., pl.* **-toes** or **-tos.** A public declaration of principles or intentions, esp. political ones. [Ital. MANIFEST.]

man•i•fold (măn′ə-fōld′) ▸*adj.* **1.** Of many

and diverse kinds. **2.** Having many features or forms. ▸*n.* A pipe having several openings for making multiple connections.

man•i•kin or **man•ni•kin** (măn′ĭ-kĭn) ▸*n.* **1.** A man short in stature. **2.** A mannequin. [< MDu. *mannekijn*, little man.]

Ma•nil•a (mə-nĭl′ə) The capital of the Philippines, on **Manila Bay,** an inlet of the South China Sea. Pop. 1,728,441.

Manila hemp ▸*n.* The fiber of the abaca, a Philippine plant related to the banana, used to make rope, cordage, and paper.

Manila paper ▸*n.* A strong paper or thin cardboard, usu. buff in color.

man•i•oc (măn′ē-ŏk′) ▸*n.* See **cassava.** [< Tupi *mandioca*.]

ma•nip•u•late (mə-nĭp′yə-lāt′) ▸*v.* **-lat•ed, -lat•ing 1.** To operate or control by skilled use of the hands; handle. **2.** To influence or manage shrewdly or deviously. **3.** To tamper with or falsify for personal gain. [< Lat. *manipulus*, handful.] —**ma•nip′u•la′tion** *n.* —**ma•nip′u•la′tive** *adj.* —**ma•nip′u•la′tor** *n.* —**ma•nip′u•la•to′ry** (-lə-tôr′ē, -tōr′ē) *adj.*

Syns: *manipulate, exploit, maneuver* ***v.***

Man•i•to•ba (măn′ĭ-tō′bə) A province of S-central Canada. Cap. Winnipeg. Pop. 1,026,241. —**Man′i•to′ban** *adj. & n.*

man•i•tou (măn′ĭ-to͞o′) ▸*n., pl.* **-tous.** In Algonquian religious belief, a supernatural power that permeates the world. [< Ojibwa *manitoo*.]

man•kind (măn′kīnd′) ▸*n.* **1.** The human race. **2.** Men as opposed to women.

man•ly (măn′lē) ▸*adj.* **-li•er, -li•est 1.** Having qualities traditionally attributed to a man. **2.** Of a man; masculine. ▸*adv.* In a manly manner. —**man′li•ness** *n.*

man-made or **man•made** (măn′mād′) ▸*adj.* Made by humans; synthetic.

Mann (măn), **Horace.** 1796–1859. Amer. educator.

Mann (măn, män), **Thomas.** 1875–1955. German writer; 1929 Nobel.

man•na (măn′ə) ▸*n.* **1.** In the Bible, the food miraculously provided for the Israelites in the wilderness during their flight from Egypt. **2.** Something of value that comes unexpectedly. [< Heb. *mān*.]

manned (mănd) ▸*adj.* Transporting or operated by a human: *a manned spacecraft.*

man•ne•quin (măn′ĭ-kĭn) ▸*n.* **1.** A life-size representation of the human body, used to fit or display clothes; dummy. **2.** One who models clothes. [Fr. < MDu. *mannekijn*, manikin.]

man•ner (măn′ər) ▸*n.* **1.** A way of doing something or the way in which a thing is done or happens. **2.** A way of acting; bearing or behavior. **3. manners a.** Socially proper behavior. **b.** The prevailing customs of a society or period, esp. as the subject of a literary work. **4.** Practice, style, or method in the arts. **5.** Kind; sort. —***idiom:*** **in a manner of speaking** In a way; so to speak. [< Lat. *manuārius*, of the hand.]

man•nered (măn′ərd) ▸*adj.* **1.** Having manners of a specific kind: *ill-mannered.* **2.** Artificial or affected. **3.** Of or exhibiting mannerisms.

man•ner•ism (măn′ə-rĭz′əm) ▸*n.* **1.** A distinctive behavioral trait. **2.** Exaggerated or affected style or habit.

man•ner•ly (măn′ər-lē) ▸*adj.* Having good manners. —**man′ner•li•ness** *n.*

Mann•heim (măn′hīm′, män′-) A city of SW Germany at the confluence of the Rhine and Neckar rivers. Pop. 318,025.

man•ni•kin (măn′ĭ-kĭn) ▸*n.* Var. of **manikin.**

man•nish (măn′ĭsh) ▸*adj.* Resembling or suggestive of a man rather than a woman: *a mannish stride.* —**man′nish•ly** *adv.* —**man′nish•ness** *n.*

man-of-war (măn′ə-wôr′) ▸*n., pl.* **men-of-war** (mĕn′-) **1.** See **warship. 2.** A Portuguese man-of-war.

ma•nom•e•ter (mă-nŏm′ĭ-tər) ▸*n.* An instrument for measuring the pressure of liquids and gases. [Gk. *manos*, sparse + -METER.] —**man′o•met′ric** (măn′ə-mĕt′rĭk), **man′o•met′ri•cal** *adj.* —**ma•nom′e•try** *n.*

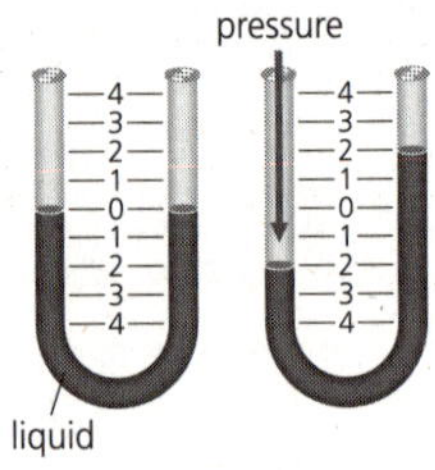

manometer
To calculate pressure in a U-tube manometer, add the sum of the readings above and below zero. This diagram shows a reading of 4.

man•or (măn′ər) ▸*n.* **1a.** A landed estate. **b.** The main house on an estate. **2.** The district over which a feudal lord had domain. [< Lat. *manēre*, dwell.] —**ma•no′ri•al** (mə-nôr′ē-əl, -nōr′-) *adj.*

man•pow•er (măn′pou′ər) ▸*n.* **1.** The power of human physical strength. **2.** Power in terms of the workers available, as for a particular task.

man•qué (mäɴ-kā′) ▸*adj.* Unfulfilled; frustrated: *an artist manqué.* [Fr. < Lat. *mancus*, maimed.]

man•sard (măn′särd′) ▸*n.* A four-sided roof having a double slope on all sides, with the lower slope much steeper than the upper. [After François *Mansart* (1598–1666).]

manse (măns) ▸*n.* A cleric's house and land, esp. the residence of a Presbyterian minister. [< Med.Lat. *mānsa*, dwelling < Lat. *manēre*, dwell.]

man•sion (măn′shən) ▸*n.* A large stately house. [< Lat. *mānsiō*, dwelling.]

man-sized (măn′sīzd′) also **man-size** (-sīz′) ▸*adj. Informal* Very large.

man•slaugh•ter (măn′slô′tər) ▸*n.* The unlawful killing of one human by another without express or implied intent to do injury.

man•ta (măn′tə) ▸*n.* A large ray of tropical and subtropical seas having winglike pectoral fins and two hornlike fins on the head. [Sp., blanket.]

Man•te•gna (män-tān′yə, -tĕ′nyä), **Andrea.** 1431–1506. Italian painter.

man•tel also **man•tle** (măn′tl) ▸*n.* **1.** An ornamental facing around a fireplace. **2.** The protruding shelf over a fireplace. [ME < var. of MANTLE.]

man•tel•piece (măn′tl-pēs′) ►*n.* *Regional* See **mantel.**

man•til•la (măn-tē′yə, -tĭl′ə) ►*n.* A lace or silk scarf worn over the head and shoulders by women in Spain and Latin America. [Sp.]

man•tis (măn′tĭs) ►*n.*, *pl.* **-es** or **-tes** (-tēz). A predatory insect having two pairs of walking legs and powerful grasping forelimbs. [Gk., seer.]

man•tis•sa (măn-tĭs′ə) ►*n.* The decimal part of a logarithm. [Lat., counterweight.]

man•tle (măn′tl) ►*n.* **1.** A loose sleeveless outer garment; cloak. **2.** Something that covers, envelops, or conceals. **3.** Var. of **mantel. 4.** A device in gas lamps consisting of a sheath of threads that glows brightly when heated by the flame. **5.** The layer of the earth between the crust and the core. ►*v.* **-tled, -tling.** To cover with or as if with a mantle. [< Lat. *mantellum.*]

man•tra (măn′trə, mŭn′-) ►*n.* **1.** *Hinduism* A sacred verbal formula repeated in prayer, meditation, or incantation. **2.** A commonly repeated word or phrase. [Skt. *mantraḥ.*] —**man′tric** *adj.*

Man•tu•a (măn′cho͞o-ə, -to͞o-ə) A city of N Italy SSW of Verona. Pop. 60,932

man•u•al (măn′yo͞o-əl) ►*adj.* **1.** Of or relating to the hands. **2.** Done by or operated with the hands. **3.** Employing human rather than mechanical energy: *manual labor.* ►*n.* **1.** A small reference book, esp. one giving instructions. **2.** An organ keyboard. **3.** Prescribed movements in the handling of a weapon. [< Lat. *manus,* hand.] —**man′u•al•ly** *adv.*

manual alphabet ►*n.* An alphabet used by hearing-impaired people in which finger positions represent the letters.

man•u•fac•to•ry (măn′yə-făk′tə-rē) ►*n.*, *pl.* **-ries.** A factory.

man•u•fac•ture (măn′yə-făk′chər) ►*v.* **-tured, -tur•ing 1.** To make or process from raw materials, esp. by means of a large-scale industrial operation. **2.** To make up; fabricate. ►*n.* **1.** The act or process of manufacturing. **2.** A manufactured product. [< Med.Lat. *manūfactūra,* making by hand.] —**man′u•fac′tur•er** *n.*

man•u•mit (măn′yə-mĭt′) ►*v.* **-mit•ted, -mit•ting.** To free from slavery or bondage. [< Lat. *manūmittere.*] —**man′u•mis′sion** (-mĭsh′ən) *n.*

ma•nure (mə-no͝or′, -nyo͝or′) ►*n.* Material, esp. dung, used to fertilize soil. ►*v.* **-nured, -nur•ing.** To fertilize (soil) by applying manure. [< AN *mainouverer,* cultivate. See MANEUVER.]

man•u•script (măn′yə-skrĭpt′) ►*n.* **1.** A book or other composition written by hand. **2.** A typewritten or handwritten version of a text prepared and submitted for publication. **3.** Handwriting. [< Med.Lat. *manūscrīptus,* written by hand.]

Manx (măngks) ►*n.*, *pl.* **Manx 1.** The people of the Isle of Man. **2.** The extinct Celtic language of the Manx. —**Manx** *adj.* —**Manx′man** *n.* —**Manx′wom′an** *n.*

man•y (mĕn′ē) ►*adj.* **more** (môr, mōr), **most** (mōst). Amounting to or being one of a large indefinite number: *many friends; many a day.* ►*n.* *(takes pl. v.)* A large indefinite number. ►*pron.* *(takes pl. v.)* A large number of persons or things. [< OE *manig.*]

man•y-sid•ed (mĕn′ē-sī′dĕd) ►*adj.* **1.** Having many sides. **2.** Having many aspects or talents. See Syns at **versatile.**

man•za•ni•ta (măn′zə-nē′tə) ►*n.* A small evergreen tree of the Pacific coast of North America. [Sp. < *manzana,* apple.]

Mao•ism (mou′ĭz′əm) ►*n.* Marxism-Leninism developed in China chiefly by Mao Zedong. —**Mao′ist** *adj.* & *n.*

Mao•ri (mou′rē) ►*n.*, *pl.* **-ri** or **-ris 1.** A member of a people of New Zealand, of Polynesian-Melanesian descent. **2.** Their Austronesian language. —**Mao′ri** *adj.*

Mao Ze•dong (mou′ dzə′dŏng′) also **Mao Tse-tung** (tsə′-to͝ong′). 1893–1976. Chinese Communist leader and theorist.

Mao Zedong

map (măp) ►*n.* **1.** A representation, usu. on a plane surface, of a region. **2.** Something resembling a map, as in schematic representation. ►*v.* **mapped, map•ping 1.** To make a map of. **2.** To plan in detail: *map out the future.* [< Lat. *mappa.*] —**map′mak′er** *n.* —**map′pa•ble** *adj.* —**map′per** *n.*

MAP ►*abbr.* modified American plan

ma•ple (mā′pəl) ►*n.* **1.** Any of a genus of deciduous trees or shrubs having palmate leaves and long-winged fruits borne in pairs. **2.** The wood of a maple. **3.** The flavor of maple sugar or syrup. [< OE *mapul.*]

maple sugar ►*n.* A sugar made by boiling down maple syrup.

maple syrup ►*n.* A sweet syrup made from the sap of the sugar maple.

Ma•pu•to (mə-po͞o′tō) The capital of Mozambique, in the extreme S part. Pop. 882,601.

mar (mär) ►*v.* **marred, mar•ring.** To damage, disfigure, or spoil. [< OE *mierran,* impede.]

mar. ►*abbr.* **1.** maritime **2.** married

Mar. ►*abbr.* March

mar•a•bou (măr′ə-bo͞o′) ►*n.* **1.** A large African stork that scavenges for carrion. **2.** The soft white down of the marabou, used esp. in trimming garments. [< Ar. *murābiṭ,* Muslim hermit.]

ma•ra•ca (mə-rä′kə) ►*n.* A percussion instrument consisting of a hollow gourd containing pebbles or beans. [Port. *maracá.*]

Ma•ra•cai•bo (mä′rä-kī′bō) A city of NW Venezuela on **Lake Maracaibo,** the largest lake of South America. Pop. 1,207,513.

Ma•ra•ñón (mä′rä-nyōn′) A river flowing about 1,609 km (1,000 mi) from W-central to NE Peru, where it joins the Amazon.

mar•a•schi•no (măr′ə-skē′nō, -shē′-) ►*n., pl.* **-nos.** A cordial made from the fermented juice and crushed pits of a bitter cherry. [Ital. < *marasca*, sour cherry.]

maraschino cherry ►*n.* A cherry preserved in a syrup flavored with maraschino.

Ma•rat (mə-rä′, mä-), **Jean Paul.** 1743–93. Swiss-born French revolutionary.

Ma•ra•thi (mə-rä′tē, -răt′ē) ►*n.* The principal Indic language of the state of Maharashtra, India.

mar•a•thon (măr′ə-thŏn′) ►*n.* **1.** A cross-country footrace of 26 mi, 385 yd (41.3 km). **2.** A test or contest of endurance. [After *Marathon*, Greece.] —**mar′a•thon′er** *n.*

ma•raud (mə-rôd′) ►*v.* To rove and raid in search of plunder. [Fr. *marauder.*] —**ma•raud′er** *n.*

mar•ble (mär′bəl) ►*n.* **1.** A metamorphic, often streaked rock formed by alteration of limestone or dolomite, used esp. in architecture and sculpture. **2.** Something resembling marble, as in being very hard, smooth, or cold. **3a.** A small hard ball, usu. of glass, used in children's games. **b. marbles** *(takes sing. v.)* A game played with marbles. **4. marbles** *Slang* Common sense; sanity: *lost his marbles.* [< Gk. *marmaros.*] —**mar′ble** *adj.* —**mar′bly** *adj.*

mar•bled (mär′bəld) ►*adj.* **1.** Made of or covered with marble. **2.** Mottled or streaked: *meat marbled with fat.* —**mar′bling** *n.*

mar•ca•site (mär′kə-sīt′, -zīt′) ►*n.* **1.** A mineral with the same composition as pyrite, FeS_2, but differing in crystal structure. **2.** An ornament of pyrite, polished steel, or white metal. [< Aram. *marqəšītā.*]

march[1] (märch) ►*v.* **1.** To walk or cause to walk steadily and rhythmically forward, usu. in step with others. **2a.** To proceed directly and purposefully. **b.** To advance steadily: *Time marches on.* **3.** To participate in an organized walk. ►*n.* **1.** The act of marching. **2.** Steady forward movement or progression. **3.** A measured, even step. **4.** The distance covered by marching: *a week's march.* **5.** *Mus.* A composition in usu. duple meter that is appropriate for marching. **6.** An organized walk, as for a public cause. —***idiom:* on the march** Advancing steadily. [< OFr. *marchier*, of Gmc. orig.] —**march′er** *n.*

march[2] (märch) ►*n.* A border region; frontier. [< OFr. *marche*, of Gmc. origin.]

March (märch) ►*n.* The 3rd month of the Gregorian calendar. See table at **calendar.** [< Lat. *Mārtius (mēnsis)*, (month) of Mars.]

mar•chio•ness (mär′shə-nĭs, mär′shə-nĕs′) ►*n.* **1.** The wife or widow of a marquis. **2.** A noblewoman ranking above a countess and below a duchess. [Med.Lat. *marchiōnissa.*]

Mar•co•ni (mär-kō′nē), **Guglielmo.** 1874–1937. Italian engineer and inventor; 1909 Nobel.

Mar•cos (mär′kōs), **Ferdinand Edralin.** 1917–89. Philippine president (1965–86).

Mar•cus Au•re•li•us An•to•ni•nus (mär′kəs ô-rē′lē-əs ăn′tə-nī′nəs). A.D. 121–180. Roman philosopher and emperor (161–180).

Mar del Pla•ta (mär′ dĕl plä′tä) A city of E-central Argentina on the Atlantic SSE of Buenos Aires. Pop. 519,707.

Mar•di Gras (mär′dē grä′) ►*n.* The day before Ash Wednesday, celebrated in many places with carnivals and parades of costumed merrymakers. [Fr.]

mare[1] (mâr) ►*n.* A female horse or related animal. [< OE **mēre.*]

ma•re[2] (mä′rā) ►*n., pl.* **-ri•a** (-rē-ə). Any of the large dark areas on the moon or planets, esp. Mars. [Lat., sea.]

Mar•gar•et of Anjou (mär′gə-rət, -grət). 1430–82. Queen of Henry VI of England.

mar•ga•rine (mär′jər-ĭn) ►*n.* A fatty solid butter substitute consisting of hydrogenated vegetable oils mixed with emulsifiers, vitamins, and coloring matter. [Fr.]

mar•ga•ri•ta (mär′gə-rē′tə) ►*n.* A cocktail made with tequila, an orange-flavored liqueur, and lemon or lime juice. [Sp.]

mar•gin (mär′jĭn) ►*n.* **1.** An edge and the area immediately adjacent to it; border. **2.** The blank space bordering the written or printed area on a page. **3.** An allowance beyond what is needed: *a margin of safety.* See Syns at **room. 4.** A measure or degree of difference: *a margin of 500 votes.* **5.** The difference between cost and selling price, as of securities. [< Lat. *margō, margin-.*]

mar•gin•al (mär′jə-nəl) ►*adj.* **1.** Of, at, or constituting a margin. **2.** Barely within a lower standard or limit: *marginal writing ability.* —**mar′gin•al•ly** *adv.*

mar•gi•na•li•a (mär′jə-nā′lē-ə) ►*pl.n.* Notes in the margin or margins of a book. [< Med.Lat. *marginālis*, marginal.]

Mar•gre•the II (mär-grā′tə). b. 1940. Queen of Denmark (since 1972).

ma•ri•a•chi (mä′rē-ä′chē) ►*n., pl.* **-chis.** A street band in Mexico. [Am.Sp., perh. < Fr. *marriage*, marriage.]

Mar•i•an•a Islands (măr′ē-ăn′ə, mâr′-) A US-administered island group in the W Pacific E of the Philippines, comprising Guam, an independent commonwealth, and the **Northern Mariana Islands.**

Ma•ri•a The•re•sa (mə-rē′ə tə-rā′sə, -zə). 1717–80. Queen of Hungary and Bohemia (1740–80).

Ma•rie An•toi•nette (mə-rē′ ăn′twə-nĕt′). 1755–93. Queen of France (1774–93) as the wife of Louis XVI; executed.

Marie Antoinette
detail of a 1786 portrait

Marie de Mé•di•cis (də mā′dē-sēs′). 1573–1642. Queen of France as the wife (1600–10) of Henry IV and regent (1610–17) for her son Louis XIII.

mar•i•gold (măr′ĭ-gōld′, mâr′-) ►*n.* Any of various American plants cultivated for their showy yellow or orange flowers. [ME.]

mar•i•jua•na also **mar•i•hua•na** (măr′ə-wä′nə) ►*n.* **1.** The cannabis plant. **2.** A preparation made from the dried flower clusters and leaves of the cannabis plant, smoked or eaten to induce euphoria. [Sp. *marihuana.*]

ma•rim•ba (mə-rĭm′bə) ►*n.* A large wooden percussion instrument with resonators, resembling a xylophone. [Of Bantu orig.]

Mar•in (măr′ĭn), **John.** 1870–1953. Amer. painter.

ma•ri•na (mə-rē′nə) ►*n.* A boat basin that has docks, moorings, and supplies for small boats. [< Lat. *marīnus*, MARINE.]

mar•i•nade (măr′ə-nād′) ►*n.* A spiced liquid in which food is soaked before cooking. [Fr. < *mariner*, MARINATE.]

mar•i•nate (măr′ə-nāt′) ►*v.* **-nat•ed, -nat•ing.** To soak (e.g., meat) in a marinade. [Fr. *mariner* < *marine*, sea water, brine (obs.). See MARINE.]

ma•rine (mə-rēn′) ►*adj.* **1.** Of or relating to the sea: *marine exploration.* **2.** Of shipping or maritime affairs. **3.** Of sea navigation. See Syns at **nautical.** ►*n.* **1a.** A soldier serving on a ship. **b. Marine** A member of the US Marine Corps. **2.** A picture of the sea. [< Lat. *mare*, sea.]

Marine Corps ►*n.* A branch of the US armed forces composed chiefly of amphibious troops.

mar•i•ner (măr′ə-nər) ►*n.* A sailor.

mar•i•o•nette (măr′ē-ə-nĕt′) ►*n.* A jointed puppet manipulated by strings. [Fr. *marionnette.*]

mar•i•tal (măr′ĭ-tl) ►*adj.* Of or relating to marriage. [< Lat. *marītus*, married.] —**mar′i•tal•ly** *adv.*

mar•i•time (măr′ĭ-tīm′) ►*adj.* **1.** Of or adjacent to the sea. **2.** Of marine shipping or navigation. See Syns at **nautical.** [Lat. *maritimus* < *mare*, sea.]

Maritime Provinces. The Canadian provinces of Nova Scotia, New Brunswick, and Prince Edward Island. —**Mar′i•tim′er** *n.*

Ma•ri•u•pol′ (mä′rē-o͞o′pŏl′) A city of SE Ukraine on the Sea of Azov. Pop. 522,900.

Mar•i•us (mâr′ē-əs, măr′-), **Gaius.** 155?–86 B.C. Roman general and politician.

mar•jo•ram (mär′jər-əm) ►*n.* Any of several aromatic plants having opposite leaves used as seasoning. [< Med.Lat. *maiorana.*]

mark[1] (märk) ►*n.* **1.** A visible trace or impression, such as a line or spot. **2.** A written or printed symbol: *a punctuation mark.* **3a.** An academic grade. **b.** often **marks** An appraisal; rating: *earned high marks.* **4.** A name, stamp, or seal placed on merchandise to signify ownership or origin. **5a.** A distinctive trait or property: *a mark of good breeding.* **b.** A lasting effect: *The experience had left its mark.* **6.** A recognized standard of quality. **7.** Importance; note. **8.** A target. **9.** An aim or goal. **10.** An object or a point that serves as a guide. **11.** *Slang* An intended victim. ►*v.* **1a.** To make a mark (on). **b.** To form, make, or depict by making a mark. **2a.** To single out or identify by or as if by a mark. **b.** To distinguish or characterize. **3.** To set off or separate, as with a line: *marked off the property.* **4.** To grade (academic work). —***phrasal verbs:*** **mark down** To reduce in price. **mark up 1.** To deface by covering with marks. **2.** To increase the price of. —***idiom:*** **mark time 1.** To move the feet in a marching rhythm without advancing. **2.** To suspend progress. [< OE *mearc.*] —**mark′er** *n.*

Syns: *mark, brand, label, tag, ticket* **v.**

mark[2] (märk) ►*n.* The deutsche mark. [< OE *marc*, unit of weight.]

Mark (märk) ►*n.* See table at **Bible.**

Mark, Saint. Author of the second Gospel in the Bible and disciple of Saint Peter.

mar•ka (mär′kä) ►*n.* See table at **currency.** [Serbo-Croatian.]

Mark An•to•ny (ăn′tə-nē) or **Mark An•tho•ny** (ăn′thə-nē). 83?–30 B.C. Roman orator, politician, and soldier.

mark•down (märk′doun′) ►*n.* A reduction in price.

marked (märkt) ►*adj.* **1.** Having a distinguishing mark. **2.** Clearly defined; noticeable. **3.** Singled out, esp. for a dire fate: *a marked man.* —**mark′ed•ly** (mär′kĭd-lē) *adv.*

mar•ket (mär′kĭt) ►*n.* **1.** A public gathering held for buying and selling merchandise. **2.** A place where goods are sold. **3.** A shop that sells a particular type of merchandise: *a meat market.* **4a.** The business of buying and selling a specified commodity: *the soybean market.* **b.** A geographic region considered as a place for sales. **c.** A specific group of buyers: *the student market.* **5.** The extent of demand for merchandise: *a big market for gourmet foods.* ►*v.* **1.** To offer for sale. **2.** To sell. [< Lat. *mercārī*, *mercāt-*, buy.] —**mar′ket•a•bil′i•ty** *n.* —**mar′ket•a•ble** *adj.* —**mar′ket•er** *n.*

mar•ket•place (mär′kĭt-plās′) ►*n.* **1.** An open area in which a public market is set up. **2.** The world of business and commerce.

market price ►*n.* The prevailing price at which a commodity is sold.

market value ►*n.* The amount a seller may expect to obtain in the open market.

Mark•ham (mär′kəm), **Beryl.** 1903–86. British aviation pioneer.

mark•ing (mär′kĭng) ►*n.* **1.** An act or result of marking. **2.** The characteristic pattern of coloration of a plant or animal.

mark•ka (mär′kä′) ►*n.*, *pl.* **-kaa.** See table at **currency.** [Finn. < Swed. *mark*, mark.]

marks•man (märks′mən) ►*n.* A man skilled in shooting. —**marks′man•ship′** *n.*

marks•wom•an (märks′wo͝om′ən) ►*n.* A woman skilled in shooting.

mark•up (märk′ŭp′) ►*n.* **1.** A raise in price. **2.** An amount added to a cost price in calculating a selling price. **3a.** The set of typesetting instructions written on a manuscript. **b.** *Comp. Sci.* The set of tags describing an electronic document's formatting specifications.

markup language ►*n.* A coding system, such as HTML, used to structure and link text files.

marl (märl) ►*n.* Clay containing calcium carbonate, used as fertilizer. [< Med.Lat. *margila* < Lat. *marga.*] —**marl′y** *adj.*

mar•lin (mär′lĭn) ►*n.* A large saltwater game fish, having an elongated spearlike upper jaw. [< MARLINESPIKE.]

mar•line•spike also **mar•lin•spike** (mär′lĭn-spīk′) ►*n.* A pointed metal spike, used to separate strands of rope in splicing. [*marline*, two-strand rope + SPIKE[1].]

Mar•lowe (mär′lō), **Christopher.** 1564–93. English playwright and poet.

mar•ma•lade (mär′mə-lād′) ►*n.* A preserve made from the pulp and rind esp. of citrus fruits. [< Gk. *melimēlon*, a kind of apple.]

Mar•ma•ra (mär′mər-ə), **Sea of.** A sea of NW Turkey between Europe and Asia.

mar•mo•re•al (mär-môr′ē-əl, -mōr′-) ►*adj.* Resembling marble, as in smoothness or hardness. [< Lat. *marmoreus* < *marmor*, marble.]

mar•mo•set (mär′mə-sĕt′, -zĕt′) ►*n.* Any of various small tropical American monkeys having soft fur, tufted ears, and long tails. [< OFr. *marmouset*, grotesque figurine.]

mar•mot (mär′mət) ►*n.* Any of various stocky, short-legged burrowing rodents of the Northern Hemisphere. [Fr. *marmotte*.]

Marne (märn) A river, about 523 km (325 mi), of NE France flowing to the Seine R. near Paris.

ma•roon[1] (mə-ro͞on′) ►*v.* **1.** To abandon on a deserted island or coast. **2.** To leave helpless. [< Fr. *marron*, fugitive slave.]

ma•roon[2] (mə-ro͞on′) ►*n.* A dark purplish red. [< Ital. *marrone*.] —**ma•roon′** *adj.*

Mar•quand (mär-kwŏnd′), **John Phillips.** 1893–1960. Amer. writer.

mar•quee (mär-kē′) ►*n.* **1.** A large, often open-sided tent used chiefly for outdoor entertainment. **2.** A rooflike structure, often bearing a signboard, projecting over an entrance, as to a theater. [Fr. *marquise*, marquise.]

Mar•que•sas Islands (mär-kā′zəz, -səz, -səs) A volcanic archipelago in the S Pacific, part of French Polynesia. —**Mar•que′san** *adj. & n.*

mar•que•try (mär′kĭ-trē) ►*n.*, *pl.* **-tries.** Material, such as wood, inlaid into a veneer in an intricate design. [< OFr. *marqueter*, to checker, of Gmc. orig.]

Mar•quette (mär-kĕt′), Père **Jacques.** 1637–75. French missionary and explorer.

mar•quis (mär′kwĭs, mär-kē′) or **mar•quess** (mär′kwĭs) ►*n.*, *pl.* **-quis•es** (-kwĭ-sĭz) or **-quis** (-kēz′) or **-quess•es** (-kwĭ-sĭz). A nobleman ranking below a duke and above an earl or count. [< OFr. *marche*, border country, of Gmc. orig.]

mar•quise (mär-kēz′) ►*n.* See **marchioness** 2. [Fr.]

mar•qui•sette (mär′kĭ-zĕt′, -kwĭ-) ►*n.* A sheer fabric used for clothing, curtains, and mosquito nets.

Mar•ra•kesh or **Mar•ra•kech** (măr′ə-kĕsh′, mə-rä′kĕsh). A city of W-central Morocco in the Atlas Mts. foothills. Pop. 602,000.

mar•riage (măr′ĭj) ►*n.* **1a.** The legal union of a man and woman as husband and wife. **b.** Wedlock. **2.** A wedding. **3.** A close union. —**mar′riage•a•ble** *adj.*

mar•row (măr′ō) ►*n.* **1.** The soft fatty tissue that fills most bone cavities and is the source of red and many white blood cells. **2.** The inmost, choicest, or most important part. [< OE *mearg*.]

mar•ry (măr′ē) ►*v.* **-ried, -ry•ing 1a.** To join as spouses by exchanging vows. **b.** To take as a spouse. **c.** To give in marriage. **2.** To obtain by marriage: *marry money.* **3.** To unite in a close, usu. permanent way. [< Lat. *marītus*, married.] —**mar′ried** *adj.*

Mars (märz) ►*n.* **1.** *Rom. Myth.* The god of war. **2.** The 4th planet from the sun, at a mean distance of 227.8 million km (141.6 million mi) and a mean diameter of approx. 6,726 km (4,180 mi).

Mar•seille (mär-sā′) or **Mar•seilles.** A city of SE France on the Mediterranean Sea. Pop. 800,309.

marsh (märsh) ►*n.* A grassy or reedy wetland. [< OE *mersc*.] —**marsh′y** *adj.*

mar•shal (mär′shəl) ►*n.* **1.** A military officer of the highest rank in some countries. **2a.** A US federal or city officer who carries out court orders. **b.** The head esp. of a fire department. **3.** A person in charge of a parade or ceremony. **4.** A high official in a royal court. ►*v.* **-shaled, -shal•ing** also **-shalled, -shal•ling 1.** To place or set in position or order. See Syns at **arrange. 2.** To enlist and organize: *marshal public support.* **3.** To guide ceremoniously; usher. [< OFr. *mareschal*, military commander.]

Mar•shall (mär′shəl), **George Catlett.** 1880–1959. Amer. soldier, diplomat, and politician; 1953 Nobel Peace Prize.

Marshall, John. 1755–1835. Amer. jurist and politician; the chief justice of the US Supreme Court (1801–35).

Marshall, Thurgood. 1908–93. Amer. jurist; US Supreme Court justice (1967–91).

Thurgood Marshall

Marshall Islands. A self-governing island group in the central Pacific. Pop. 58,363.

marsh•mal•low (märsh′mĕl′ō, -măl′ō) ►*n.* **1.** A light spongy confection made of corn syrup, gelatin, sugar, and starch. **2.** often **marsh mallow** A perennial wetland plant having showy pink flowers and a root sometimes used in confectionery.

marsh marigold ►*n.* A wetland plant having bright yellow flowers; cowslip.

mar•su•pi•al (mär-so͞o′pē-əl) ►*n.* Any of an order of mammals, including kangaroos, opossums, and wombats, found esp. in Australia and the Americas and marked by an abdominal pouch in the female in which the newly born young are sheltered and fed. [< Gk. *marsipion*, pouch.]

mart (märt) ►*n.* A market. [Ult. < VLat. **marcātus*, MARKET.]

mar•ten (mär′tn) ►*n.*, *pl.* **-ten** or **-tens 1.** A weasellike, chiefly arboreal mammal of northern forests. **2.** The fur of the marten. [< OFr. *martre* and Med.Lat. *martrīna*, both of Gmc. orig.]

Mar•tha's Vineyard (mär′thəz) An island of SE MA off the SW coast of Cape Cod.

Mar•tí (mär-tē′), **José Julian.** 1853–95. Cuban revolutionary leader and poet.

mar•tial (mär′shəl) ►*adj.* **1.** Of or suggestive of war. **2.** Of or connected with military life. [< Lat. *Mārs*, Mars.] —**mar′tial•ly** *adv.*

Martial. fl. 1st cent. B.C. Roman poet.

martial art ►*n.* Any of several arts of combat or self-defense, such as karate or judo.

martial law ►*n.* Rule by military authorities, imposed on a civilian population esp. in time of war or when civil authority has broken down.

Mar•tian (mär′shən) ►*adj.* Of or relating to the planet Mars. ►*n.* A hypothetical inhabitant of the planet Mars.

mar•tin (mär′tn) ►*n.* Any of several birds of the swallow family. [Prob. < *Martin.*]

mar•ti•net (mär′tn-ĕt′) ►*n.* A rigid disciplinarian. [After Jean *Martinet* (d. 1672).]

mar•ti•ni (mär-tē′nē) ►*n.*, *pl.* **-nis.** A cocktail of gin or vodka and dry vermouth. [?]

Mar•ti•nique (mär′tĭ-nēk′, -tn-ēk′) An island and overseas department of France in the Windward Is. of the West Indies. Cap. Fort-de-France. Pop. 375,000.

Martin Luther King Day ►*n.* The 3rd Monday in Jan., observed in the US in commemoration of the birthday of Martin Luther King, Jr.

mar•tyr (mär′tər) ►*n.* **1.** One who chooses to suffer death rather than renounce religious principles. **2.** One who makes great sacrifices for a cause. **3.** One who endures great suffering. [< Gk. *martus*, *martur-*, witness.] —**mar′tyr** *v.* —**mar′tyr•dom** *n.*

mar•vel (mär′vəl) ►*n.* One that evokes surprise, admiration, or wonder. See Syns at **wonder.** ►*v.* **-veled, -vel•ing** also **-velled, -vel•ling.** To become filled with wonder. [< Lat. *mīrābilis*, wonderful.]

Mar•vell (mär′vəl), **Andrew.** 1621–78. English metaphysical poet.

mar•vel•ous also **mar•vel•lous** (mär′və-ləs) ►*adj.* **1.** Causing wonder or astonishment. **2.** Miraculous. **3.** Excellent; superb. —**mar′vel•ous•ly** *adv.* —**mar′vel•ous•ness** *n.*

Marx (märks), **Karl.** 1818–83. German philosopher, economist, author, and revolutionary. —**Marx′i•an** *adj. & n.*

Marx•ism (märk′sĭz′əm) ►*n.* The political and economic ideas of Karl Marx and Friedrich Engels that society inevitably develops through class struggle from oppression under capitalism to eventual classlessness. —**Marx′ist** *n. & adj.*

Marx•ism-Len•in•ism (märk′sĭz′əm-lĕn′ĭ-nĭz′əm) ►*n.* The expansion of Marxism to include the concepts of Leninism. —**Marx′ist-Len′in•ist** *adj. & n.*

Mar•y (mâr′ē). In the Bible, the mother of Jesus.

Mary I or **Mary Tu•dor** (to͞o′dər, tyo͞o′-). "Bloody Mary." 1516–58. Queen of England and Ireland (1553–58).

Mary II. 1662–94. Queen of England, Scotland, and Ireland (1689–94) with her husband William III.

Mar•y•land (mĕr′ə-lənd) A state of the E-central US. Cap. Annapolis. Pop. 4,798,622. —**Mar′y•land•er** *n.*

Mary Mag•da•lene (măg′də-lən, -lēn′). In the Bible, a woman whom Jesus cured of evil spirits; also identified with the repentent prostitute who washed Jesus' feet.

Mary Queen of Scots. Mary Stuart 1542–87. Queen of Scotland (1542–67); executed.

mar•zi•pan (mär′zə-păn′, märt′sə-pän′) ►*n.* A confection made of ground almonds, egg whites, and sugar. [< Ital. *marzapane.*]

Ma•sai (mä-sī′, mä′sī) ►*n.*, *pl.* **-sai** or **-sais 1.** A member of a people of Kenya and parts of Tanzania. **2.** The Nilotic language of this people. —**Ma•sai′** *adj.*

Mas•a•ryk (măs′ə-rĭk, mä′sä-), **Tomáš Garrigue.** 1850–1937. Czechoslovakian politician; first president of independent Czechoslovakia (1918–35).

masc. ►*abbr.* masculine

mas•car•a (mă-skăr′ə) ►*n.* A cosmetic applied to darken the eyelashes. [Prob. < Sp. *máscara*, MASK.]

mas•cot (măs′kŏt′, -kət) ►*n.* A person, animal, or object believed to bring good luck. [< Prov. *mascoto*, fetish < Med.Lat. *masca*, mask.]

mas•cu•line (măs′kyə-lĭn) ►*adj.* **1.** Of or relating to men or boys. **2.** Marked by qualities gen. attributed to a man. **3.** *Gram.* Of or being the gender of words referring to things classified as male. ►*n.* *Gram.* **1.** The masculine gender. **2.** A word belonging to this gender. [< Lat. *masculus* < *mās.*] —**mas′cu•line•ly** *adv.* —**mas′cu•line•ness** *n.* —**mas′cu•lin′i•ty** *n.*

Mase•field (mās′fēld′), **John.** 1878–1967. British writer.

ma•ser (mā′zər) ►*n.* Any of several devices that amplify or generate electromagnetic waves, esp. microwaves. [*m(icrowave) a(mplification by) s(timulated) e(mission of) r(adiation).*]

Mas•er•u (măz′ə-ro͞o′) The capital of Lesotho, in the W part. Pop. 14,686.

mash (măsh) ►*n.* **1.** A fermentable starchy mixture from which alcohol can be distilled. **2.** A mixture of ground grain and nutrients fed to livestock and fowl. **3.** A soft pulpy mixture or mass. ►*v.* **1.** To convert (malt or grain) into mash. **2.** To convert into a soft pulpy mixture: *mash potatoes.* **3.** To crush or grind. See Syns at **crush.** [< OE **mǣsc.*] —**mash′er** *n.*

MASH ►*abbr.* Mobile Army Surgical Hospital

Mash•had (mə-shăd′, mäsh-häd′) also **Me•shed** (mĕ-shĕd′). A city of NE Iran near the Turkmenistan and Afghanistan borders. Pop. 1,964,489.

mask (măsk) ►*n.* **1.** A covering worn on the face to conceal one's identity. **2.** A figure of a head worn by actors in Greek and Roman drama. **3a.** A protective covering for the face or head. **b.** A covering for the nose and mouth that is used for inhaling oxygen or an anesthetic. **4.** A mold of a person's face. **5.** The facial markings of certain animals. **6.** Something that disguises or conceals. **7.**Var. of **masque.** ►*v.* **1.** To cover with a mask. **2.** To make indistinct or blurred to the senses. **3.** To conceal, protect, or disguise. See Syns at **disguise.** [< Med.Lat. *masca*, specter, witch, mask.]

mas•och•ism (măs′ə-kĭz′əm) ►*n.* **1.** A psychological disorder in which sexual gratification is derived from abuse or physical pain. **2.** The deriving of pleasure from being dominated or mistreated. [After Leopold von Sacher-*Masoch* (1836–1895).] —**mas′och•ist** *n.* —**mas′och•is′tic** *adj.* —**mas′och•is′ti•cal•ly** *adv.*

ma•son (mā′sən) ►*n.* **1.** One who builds or works with stone or brick. **2. Mason** A Freemason. [< OFr. *masson.*]

Ma•son-Dix•on Line (mā′sən-dĭk′sən) The boundary between PA and MD, regarded as the division between free and slave states before the Civil War.

Ma•son•ic (mə-sŏn′ĭk) ►*adj.* Of or relating to Freemasonry.

Mason jar ►*n.* A wide-mouthed glass jar with a screw top, used for preserving food. [After John L. *Mason* (1832–1902).]

ma•son•ry (mā′sən-rē) ►*n., pl.* **-ries 1.** The trade or work of a mason. **2.** Stonework or brickwork. **3. Masonry** Freemasonry.

masque also **mask** (măsk) ►*n.* **1.** An allegorical dramatic entertainment, popular in the 16th and early 17th cent. **2.** See **masquerade** 1. [Fr. See MASK.]

mas•quer•ade (măs′kə-rād′) ►*n.* **1.** A costume party or ball at which masks are worn. **2.** A disguise or false outward show; pretense. ►*v.* **-ad•ed, -ad•ing 1.** To wear a mask or disguise. **2.** To have a deceptive appearance. [< Ital. *mascherata* < *maschera,* MASK.] —**mas′quer•ad′er** *n.*

mass (măs) ►*n.* **1.** A unified body of matter with no specific shape. **2.** A large but nonspecific amount or number. **3.** The principal part; majority. **4.** The physical volume or bulk of a solid body. **5.** *Phys.* The quantity of matter that a body contains, not dependent on gravity and therefore different from but proportional to its weight. **6. masses** The body of common people. ►*v.* To gather or form into a mass. [< Gk. *maza.*]

Mass also **mass** ►*n.* In certain Christian churches, the celebration of the Eucharist. [< LLat. *missa.*]

Mass. ►*abbr.* Massachusetts

Mas•sa•chu•sett also **Mas•sa•chu•set** (măs′ə-cho͞o′sĭt, -zĭt) ►*n., pl.* **-sett** or **-setts** also **-set** or **-sets 1.** A member of a Native American people formerly located along Massachusetts Bay from Plymouth N to Salem. **2.** Their Algonquian language.

Mas•sa•chu•setts (măs′ə-cho͞o′sĭts) A state of the NE US. Cap. Boston. Pop. 6,029,051.

mas•sa•cre (măs′ə-kər) ►*n.* **1.** The act of killing many humans indiscriminately and cruelly. **2.** *Informal* A severe defeat, as in sports. [< OFr. *macecre,* butchery.] —**mas′sa•cre** *v.*

mas•sage (mə-säzh′, -säj′) ►*n.* The rubbing or kneading of parts of the body to aid circulation or relax the muscles. [Fr. < Ar. *masaḥa,* to stroke, or *massa,* touch.] —**mas•sage′** *v.*

Mas•sa•soit (măs′ə-soit′). 1580?–1661. Wampanoag leader.

Mas•se•net (măs′ə-nā′), **Jules émile Frédéric.** 1842–1912. French composer.

mas•seur (mă-sûr′, mə-) ►*n.* A man who gives massages professionally. [Fr. < *masser,* to massage.]

mas•seuse (mă-sœz′) ►*n.* A woman who gives massages professionally. [Fr. < *masser,* to massage.]

Mas•sif Cen•tral (mă-sēf′ säɴ-träl′) A mountainous plateau of S-central France.

mas•sive (măs′ĭv) ►*adj.* **1.** Consisting of or making up a large mass. **2.** Imposing, as in quantity or scale. —**mas′sive•ly** *adv.*

mass-mar•ket (măs′mär′kĭt) ►*adj.* Of or produced for consumption by large numbers of people.

mass medium ►*n., pl.* **mass media.** A means of public communication reaching a large audience.

mass number ►*n.* The sum of the number of neutrons and protons in an atomic nucleus.

mass-pro•duce (măs′prə-do͞os′, -dyo͞os′) ►*v.* To manufacture in large quantities, often by or as if by assembly-line techniques. —**mass production** *n.*

mast (măst) ►*n.* **1.** A tall vertical spar that rises from the keel of a sailing vessel to support the sails and rigging. **2.** A vertical pole. [< OE *mæst.*]

mas•tec•to•my (mă-stĕk′tə-mē) ►*n., pl.* **-mies.** Surgical removal of all or part of a breast. [Gk. *mastos,* breast + -ECTOMY.]

mas•ter (măs′tər) ►*n.* **1.** One having control or authority over another or others. **2.** The captain of a merchant ship. **3.** A male teacher or tutor. **4.** One who holds a master's degree. **5.** An artist or performer of great skill. **6.** An expert. **7. Master** Used as a courtesy title for a boy not considered old enough to be addressed as Mister. **8.** An original audio recording from which copies can be made. ►*v.* **1.** To make oneself a master of: *master a language.* **2.** To overcome or defeat. [< Lat. *magister.*]

master chief petty officer ►*n.* The highest noncommissioned rank in the US Navy or Coast Guard.

mas•ter•ful (măs′tər-fəl) ►*adj.* **1.** Domineering; imperious. **2.** Skillful; expert. —**mas′ter•ful•ly** *adv.* —**mas′ter•ful•ness** *n.*

master gunnery sergeant ►*n.* A rank in the US Marine Corps equivalent to sergeant major.

master key ►*n.* A key that opens every one of a set of locks.

mas•ter•ly (măs′tər-lē) ►*adj.* Showing the knowledge or skill of a master. ►*adv.* With the skill of a master. —**mas′ter•li•ness** *n.*

mas•ter•mind (măs′tər-mīnd′) ►*n.* One who plans and directs a difficult project. —**mas′ter•mind′** *v.*

master of ceremonies ►*n., pl.* **masters of ceremonies.** One who acts as host at a formal event or program of varied entertainment.

mas•ter•piece (măs′tər-pēs′) ►*n.* **1.** An outstanding work of art or craft. **2.** Something superlative of its kind.

Mas•ters (măs′tərz), **Edgar Lee.** 1869–1950. Amer. poet.

mas•ter's degree (măs′tərz) ►*n.* An academic degree conferred upon those who complete at least one year of study beyond the bachelor's degree.

master sergeant ►*n.* **1.** A rank in the US Army and Marine Corps below sergeant major. **2.** A rank in the US Air Force below senior master sergeant.

mas•ter•stroke (măs′tər-strōk′) ►*n.* A masterly achievement or action. See Syns at **feat.**

mas•ter•work (măs′tər-wûrk′) ►*n.* A masterpiece.

mas•ter•y (măs′tə-rē) ►*n., pl.* **-ies 1.** Possession of consummate skill. **2.** The status of master. **3.** Full command of a subject.

mast•head (măst′hĕd′) ►*n.* **1.** *Nautical* The top of a ship's mast. **2.** The listing in a newspaper or periodical containing information about its staff, operation, and circulation.

mas•tic (măs′tĭk) ►*n.* A pastelike cement, esp. one made with powdered lime or brick and tar. [< Gk. *mastikhē*, chewing gum.]

mas•ti•cate (măs′tĭ-kāt′) ►*v.* **-cat•ed, -cat•ing.** To chew. [< Gk. *mastikhan*, grind one's teeth.] —**mas′ti•ca′tion** *n.*

mas•tiff (măs′tĭf) ►*n.* A large dog with a short brownish coat. [< Lat. *mānsuētus*, tamed.]

mas•ti•tis (mă-stī′tĭs) ►*n.* Inflammation of the breast or udder. [< Gk. *mastos*, breast.]

mas•to•don (măs′tə-dŏn′) ►*n.* An extinct elephantlike mammal. [Gk. *mastos*, nipple + Gk. *odōn*, tooth.]

mas•toid (măs′toid′) ►*n.* The mastoid process. [Gk. *mastos*, breast + -OID.]

mastoid process ►*n.* The rear portion of the temporal bone behind the ear.

mas•tur•bate (măs′tər-bāt′) ►*v.* **-bat•ed, -bat•ing.** To excite one's own or another's genitals by means other than intercourse. [Lat. *māsturbārī*.] —**mas′tur•ba′tion** *n.* —**mas′tur•ba′tor** *n.* —**mas′tur•ba•to′ry** *adj.*

mat[1] (măt) ►*n.* **1.** A flat piece of material used as a floor covering. **2.** A floor pad to protect athletes, as in wrestling. **3.** A thickly tangled mass. ►*v.* **mat•ted, mat•ting 1.** To cover or protect with a mat. **2.** To form into a tangled mass. [< LLat. *matta*.]

mat[2] (măt) ►*n.* **1.** A border placed around a picture to serve as a frame or provide contrast between the picture and the frame. **2.** also **matte** A dull, often rough finish, as of paint, glass, or paper. ►*adj.* also **matte.** Having a dull finish. [< Fr., dull.] —**mat** *v.*

mat•a•dor (măt′ə-dôr′) ►*n.* A bullfighter who performs the final passes and kills the bull. [Sp. < *matar*, kill.]

match[1] (măch) ►*n.* **1.** One equal or similar to another. **2.** A pair, each one of which harmonizes with the other. **3.** *Sports* A game or contest. **4.** A marriage or arrangement of marriage. ►*v.* **1.** To be or make similar or equal to. **2.** To harmonize with. **3.** To join in marriage. **4.** To place in competition with. [< OE *gemæcca*, mate.] —**match′er** *n.*

match[2] (măch) ►*n.* A narrow strip of flammable material coated on one end with a compound that ignites easily. [< Gk. *muxa*, lamp wick.]

match•book (măch′bo͝ok′) ►*n.* A small cardboard folder containing safety matches.

match•less (măch′lĭs) ►*adj.* Having no equal.

match•lock (măch′lŏk′) ►*n.* A gunlock in which powder is ignited by a match.

match•mak•er (măch′mā′kər) ►*n.* **1.** One who arranges marriages. **2.** *Sports* One who arranges athletic competitions. —**match′mak′ing** *n.*

match•up (măch′ŭp′) ►*n.* The pairing of two people or things, as for athletic competition or for comparison.

mate[1] (māt) ►*n.* **1.** One of a matched pair: *the mate to this glove.* **2.** A spouse. **3.** Either of a pair of breeding animals. **4.** A close associate. **5.** A deck officer on a merchant ship ranking below the master. ►*v.* **mat•ed, mat•ing 1.** To join closely; pair. **2.** To unite in marriage. **3.** To pair for breeding. [< MLGer., messmate.]

mate[2] (māt) ►*n.* A checkmate. ►*v.* **mat•ed, mat•ing.** To checkmate. [< Ar. *māt*, dead.]

ma•té (mä′tā, mä-tĕ′) ►*n.* A tealike beverage made from the leaves of a South American tree. [< Quechua *mate*, hollow gourd.]

ma•te•ri•al (mə-tîr′ē-əl) ►*n.* **1.** The substance out of which a thing is or can be made. **2. materials** Tools or apparatus for the performance of a given task. **3.** Cloth; fabric. ►*adj.* **1.** Of or composed of matter. **2.** Of or affecting physical well-being. **3.** Of or concerned with the physical rather than the intellectual or spiritual. **4.** Relevant: *testimony material to the inquiry.* [< Lat. *māteria*, matter.] —**ma•te′ri•al•ly** *adv.*

ma•te•ri•al•ism (mə-tîr′ē-ə-lĭz′əm) ►*n.* **1.** *Philos.* The theory that physical matter is the only reality and that everything can be explained in terms of matter and physical phenomena. **2.** Excessive regard for worldly concerns. —**ma•te′ri•al•ist** *n.* —**ma•te′ri•al•is′tic** *adj.*

ma•te•ri•al•ize (mə-tîr′ē-ə-līz′) ►*v.* **-ized, -iz•ing 1.** To cause to become real or actual. **2.** To take physical form or shape. **3.** To appear, esp. suddenly. —**ma•te′ri•al•i•za′tion** *n.*

ma•te•ri•el or **ma•té•ri•el** (mə-tîr′ē-ĕl′) ►*n.* The equipment and supplies of a military force or other organization. See Syns at **equipment.** [< Fr. *matériel*, MATERIAL.]

ma•ter•nal (mə-tûr′nəl) ►*adj.* **1.** Relating to or characteristic of a mother or motherhood; motherly. **2.** Inherited from or related through one's mother. [< Lat. *māternus* < *māter*, mother.] —**ma•ter′nal•ism** *n.* —**ma•ter′nal•ly** *adv.*

ma•ter•ni•ty (mə-tûr′nĭ-tē) ►*n.* The state of being a mother; motherhood.

math (măth) ►*n.* Mathematics.

math•e•mat•ics (măth′ə-măt′ĭks) ►*n.* *(takes sing. v.)* The study of the measurement, properties, and relationships of quantities and sets, using numbers and symbols. [< Gk. *mathēma*, science.] —**math′e•mat′i•cal** *adj.* —**math′e•mat′i•cal•ly** *adv.* —**math′e•ma•ti′cian** (-mə-tĭsh′ən) *n.*

Math•er (măth′ər). **Increase** (1639–1723) and **Cotton** (1663–1728). Amer. clerics and writers.

mat•i•nee or **mat•i•née** (măt′n-ā′) ►*n.* An entertainment, such as a dramatic performance or movie, given in the afternoon. [< Lat. *mātūtīnus*, of the morning.]

mat•ins (măt′nz) ►*n.* *(takes sing. or pl. v.)* *Eccles.* The office that formerly constituted the first of the seven canonical hours. [< Med.Lat. *mātūtīnus*, of morning.]

Ma•tisse (mə-tēs′, mä-), **Henri.** 1869–1954. French artist.

matri– ►*pref.* Mother; maternal: *matrilineal.* [< Lat. *māter*, *mātr-*.]

ma•tri•arch (mā′trē-ärk′) ►*n.* **1.** A woman who rules a family, clan, or tribe. **2.** A leading or venerable woman. —**ma′tri•ar′chal, ma′tri•ar′chic** *adj.*

ma•tri•ar•chy (mā′trē-är′kē) ►*n.*, *pl.* **-chies.** A social system in which the mother is head of the family.

mat•ri•cide (măt′rĭ-sīd′) ►*n.* **1.** The act of killing one's mother. **2.** One who kills one's mother. —**mat′ri•cid′al** *adj.*

ma•tric•u•late (mə-trĭk′yə-lāt′) ►*v.* **-lat•ed, -lat•ing.** To admit or be admitted into a group, esp. a college or university. [< LLat. *mātrīcula*, list < *mātrīx*, MATRIX.] —**ma•tric′u•la′tion** *n.*

mat•ri•lin•e•al (măt′rə-lĭn′ē-əl) ▶*adj.* Based on or tracing ancestral descent through the maternal line. —**mat′ri•lin′e•al•ly** *adv.*

mat•ri•mo•ny (măt′rə-mō′nē) ▶*n., pl.* **-nies.** The act or state of being married. [< Lat. *mātrimōnium.*] —**mat′ri•mo′ni•al** *adj.*

ma•trix (mā′trĭks) ▶*n., pl.* **ma•tri•ces** (mā′trĭ-sēz′, măt′rĭ-) or **ma•trix•es 1.** A situation or surrounding substance within which something else originates, develops, or is contained. **2.** A mold or die. [< Lat. *mātrīx*, breeding animal < *māter*, mother.]

ma•tron (mā′trən) ▶*n.* **1.** A married woman or widow, esp. a woman in middle age or older. **2.** A woman who acts as a supervisor in a public institution, such as a school or prison. [< Lat. *mātrōna.*] —**ma′tron•li•ness** *n.* —**ma′tron•ly** *adv. & adj.*

matron of honor ▶*n., pl.* **matrons of honor.** A married woman serving as chief attendant of the bride at a wedding.

Mat•su (mät′so͞o′) An island in the East China Sea off the SE coast of China.

matte (măt) ▶*n.* Var. of **mat**[2] 2. ▶*adj.* Var. of **mat**[2].

mat•ter (măt′ər) ▶*n.* **1a.** Something that occupies space and can be perceived by the senses; a physical substance or the physical universe as a whole. **b.** *Phys.* Something that has mass and exists as a solid, liquid, or gas. **2.** A specific type of substance: *inorganic matter.* **3.** The substance of thought or expression. **4.** A subject of concern or action. **5.** Trouble or difficulty: *What's the matter?* **6.** An approximated quantity: *a matter of years.* **7.** Something printed or written. ▶*v.* To be of importance. See Syns at **count**[1]. —***idioms:* as a matter of fact** In fact; actually. **no matter** Regardless of. [< Lat. *māteria.*]

Mat•ter•horn (măt′ər-hôrn′) A mountain, 4,481.1 m (14,692 ft), in the Pennine Alps on the Italian-Swiss border.

mat•ter-of-fact (măt′ər-əv-făkt′) ▶*adj.* Relating or adhering to facts; literal. —**mat′ter-of-fact′ly** *adv.* —**mat′ter-of-fact′ness** *n.*

Mat•thew (măth′yo͞o) ▶*n.* See table at **Bible.**

Matthew, Saint. 1st cent. A.D. One of the 12 Apostles and the traditionally accepted author of the first Gospel.

mat•ting (măt′ĭng) ▶*n.* A coarse fabric used esp. for covering floors.

mat•tock (măt′ək) ▶*n.* A digging tool with a flat blade set at right angles to the handle. [< OE *mattuc.*]

mat•tress (măt′rĭs) ▶*n.* A pad of heavy cloth filled with soft material used as or on a bed. [< Ar. *maṭraḥ*, mat, cushion.]

ma•ture (mə-tyo͝or′, -to͝or′, -cho͝or′) ▶*adj.* **-tur•er, -tur•est 1.** Fully grown or developed. **2.** In a desired or final condition; ripe. **3.** Worked out fully by the mind; considered. **4.** Payable; due: *a mature bond.* ▶*v.* **-tured, -tur•ing 1.** To bring or come to full development; ripen. **2.** To become due. [< Lat. *mātūrus.*] —**mat′u•ra′tion** (măch′ə-rā′shən) *n.* —**ma•ture′ly** *adv.* —**ma•tur′i•ty, ma•ture′ness** *n.*

Syns: *mature, age, develop, ripen* ***v.***

mat•zo also **mat•zoh** (mät′sə, -sō) ▶*n., pl.* **-zos** also **-zohs** (-səz, -səs, -sōs′). A brittle, flat piece of unleavened bread, eaten esp. during Passover. [< Heb. *maṣṣâ.*]

maud•lin (môd′lĭn) ▶*adj.* Effusively or tearfully sentimental. See Syns at **sentimental.** [< Mary *Magdalene.*]

Maugham (môm), **W(illiam) Somerset.** 1874–1965. British writer.

Mau•i (mou′ē) An island of HI NW of Hawaii I.

maul (môl) ▶*n.* A heavy, long-handled hammer used to drive stakes, piles, or wedges. ▶*v.* **1.** To injure by or as if by beating. See Syns at **batter**[1]. **2.** To handle roughly. [< Lat. *malleus.*] —**maul′er** *n.*

mau-mau (mou′mou′) ▶*v. Informal* To attack or denounce vociferously, esp. so as to intimidate. [After the *Mau Mau*, terrorists in Kenya in the 1950s.]

Mau•na Ke•a (mou′nə kā′ə) An active volcano, about 4,208 m (13,796 ft), of N-central Hawaii I.

Mauna Lo•a (lō′ə) An active volcano, 4,172.4 m (13,680 ft), of S-central Hawaii I.

maun•der (môn′dər, män′-) ▶*v.* **1.** To talk incoherently or aimlessly. **2.** To move or act aimlessly or vaguely. [Prob. < MEANDER.]

Mau•pas•sant (mō′pə-sänt′, mō-pä-säN′), **(Henri René Albert) Guy de.** 1850–93. French writer.

Mau•re•ta•ni•a (môr′ĭ-tā′nē-ə) An ancient Roman district in present-day Morocco and Algeria. —**Mau′re•ta′ni•an** *adj. & n.*

Mau•riac (môr-yäk′), **François.** 1885–1970. French writer; 1952 Nobel.

Mau•ri•ta•ni•a (môr′ĭ-tā′nē-ə) A country of NW Africa bordering on the Atlantic. Cap. Nouakchott. Pop. 2,211,000. —**Mau′ri•ta′ni•an** *adj. & n.*

Mau•ri•tius (mô-rĭsh′əs, -ē-əs) An island country in the SW Indian Ocean. Cap. Port Louis. Pop. 1,104,000. —**Mau•ri′tian** *adj. & n.*

Mau•rois (môr-wä′), **André.** Émile Herzog. 1885–1967. French writer.

mau•so•le•um (mô′sə-lē′əm, -zə-) ▶*n., pl.* **-le•ums** or **-le•a** (-lē′ə). A large stately tomb or a building housing such a tomb or tombs. [After *Mausōlos* (d. 353 B.C.).]

mauve (mōv) ▶*n.* A grayish to reddish purple. [< Lat. *malva*, mallow.] —**mauve** *adj.*

ma•ven (mā′vən) ▶*n.* An expert. [< Heb. *mēbîn.*]

mav•er•ick (măv′ər-ĭk, măv′rĭk) ▶*n.* **1.** An unbranded range calf or colt. **2.** One that resists adherence to a group. [Poss. after Samuel A. *Maverick* (1803–1870).] —**mav′er•ick** *adj.*

maw (mô) ▶*n.* **1.** The mouth or gullet of a voracious animal. **2.** The opening into something deemed insatiable. [< OE *maga.*]

mawk•ish (mô′kĭsh) ▶*adj.* Excessively and objectionably sentimental. See Syns at **sentimental.** [< ME *mawke*, maggot.] —**mawk′ish•ly** *adv.* —**mawk′ish•ness** *n.*

max. ▶*abbr.* maximum

max•il•la (măk-sĭl′ə) ▶*n., pl.* **-lae** (-ē) or **-las.** *Anat.* Either of two bones forming the upper jaw. [Lat., jaw bone.] —**max′il•lar′y** (-sə-lĕr′ē) *adj. & n.*

max•im (măk′sĭm) ▶*n.* A succinct formulation of a fundamental principle or rule of conduct. [< Med.Lat. *(prōpositiō) maxima*, greatest (premise).]

max•i•mal (măk′sə-məl) ▶*adj.* Of or being a maximum. —**max′i•mal•ly** *adv.*

Max•i•mil•ian (măk′sə-mĭl′yən). 1832–67. Austrian archduke and emperor of Mexico (1864–67).

Maximilian I. 1459–1519. King of Germany (1486–1519) and Holy Roman emperor (1493–1519).

max•i•mize (măk′sə-mīz′) ▸*v.* **-mized, -miz•ing.** To make as great as possible. —**max′i•mi•za′tion** *n.* —**max′i•miz′er** *n.*

max•i•mum (măk′sə-məm) ▸*n., pl.* **-mums** or **-ma** (-mə) **1.** The greatest possible quantity, degree, or number. **2.** An upper limit permitted by law or other authority. ▸*adj.* The greatest or highest possible or permitted. [< Lat. *maximus*, greatest.]

Max•well (măks′wĕl′, -wəl), **James Clerk.** 1831–79. British physicist.

may (mā) ▸*aux.v. P.t.* **might** (mīt) **1.** To be allowed to: *May I go? Yes, you may.* **2.** Used to indicate possibility: *It may rain.* **3.** Used to express a fervent wish: *Long may he live!* **4.** Used to express contingency, purpose, or result in clauses introduced by *that* or *so that*: *displayed so that all may see.* See Usage Note at **can**[1]. [< OE *magan*, be able.]

May ▸*n.* The 5th month in the Gregorian calendar. See table at **calendar.** [< Lat. *Maia*, an Italic goddess.]

May, Cape. A peninsula of S NJ between the Atlantic and Delaware Bay.

Ma•ya (mä′yə) ▸*n., pl.* **-ya** or **-yas 1.** A member of an American Indian people of SE Mexico, Guatemala, and Belize, whose civilization reached its height around A.D. 300–900. **2.** Any of the Mayan languages.

Ma•yan (mä′yən) ▸*adj.* **1.** Of or relating to the Maya. **2.** Of the Mayan linguistic stock. ▸*n.* **1.** A Maya. **2.** A linguistic stock of Central America that includes Maya.

Mayan
detail from a Mayan codex

May apple ▸*n.* A North American plant having a single white flower, oval yellow fruit, and poisonous roots, leaves, and seeds.

may•be (mā′bē) ▸*adv.* Perhaps; possibly.

may•day (mā′dā′) ▸*n.* An international radiotelephone signal word used by aircraft and ships in distress. [< Fr. *m'aidez*, help me!]

May Day ▸*n.* **1.** May 1, a traditional holiday in celebration of spring. **2.** May 1, a holiday in some countries in honor of labor.

may•flow•er (mā′flou′ər) ▸*n.* Any of various plants that bloom in May, esp. the trailing arbutus.

may•fly (mā′flī′) ▸*n.* A winged insect that lives in the adult stage for only a few days.

may•hem (mā′hĕm′, mā′əm) ▸*n.* **1.** *Law* The crime of willfully maiming or crippling a person. **2.** Infliction of wanton destruction. **3.** A state of violent disorder or riotous confusion; havoc. [< OFr. *mahaignier*, maim.]

may•n't (mā′ənt, mānt) ▸ May not.

may•on•naise (mā′ə-nāz′, mā′ə-nāz′) ▸*n.* A dressing made of egg yolk, oil, lemon juice or vinegar, and seasonings. [Fr.]

may•or (mā′ər, mâr) ▸*n.* The head of government of a city, town, or borough. [< Lat. *māior*, superior.] —**may′or•al** *adj.* —**may′or•al•ty** *n.* —**may′or•ship′** *n.*

May•pole also **may•pole** (mā′pōl′) ▸*n.* A pole decorated with streamers that May Day celebrants hold while dancing.

Mays (māz), **Willie Howard, Jr.** b. 1931. Amer. baseball player.

Maz•a•rin (măz′ə-răN′), **Jules.** 1602–61. Italian-born French cardinal and minister to Louis XIV.

maze (māz) ▸*n.* **1.** An intricate, usu. confusing network of interconnecting pathways, as in a garden; labyrinth. **2.** Something made up of many confused or conflicting elements; tangle. [< OE *āmasian*, bewilder.]

ma•zur•ka (mə-zûr′kə, -zo͝or′-) ▸*n.* **1.** A lively Polish dance. **2.** Music for a mazurka.

Maz•zi•ni (mät-sē′nē), **Giuseppe.** 1805–72. Italian patriot.

MB ▸*abbr.* **1.** Manitoba **2.** megabyte

MBA ▸*abbr.* Master of Business Administration

Mba•bane (əm-bä-bän′, -bä′nē) The capital of Swaziland, in the NW part. Pop. 38,290.

MC (ĕm′sē′) ▸*n.* A master of ceremonies.

Mc•Clel•lan (mə-klĕl′ən), **George Brinton.** 1826–85. Amer. Union general.

Mc•Cor•mick (mə-kôr′mĭk), **Cyrus Hall.** 1809–84. Amer. inventor.

Mc•Cul•lers (mə-kŭl′ərz), **Carson Smith.** 1917–67. Amer. writer.

Mc•Kin•ley (mə-kĭn′lē), **Mount.** Also **De•na•li** (də-nä′lē). The highest mountain in North America, rising to 6,197.6 m (20,320 ft) in the Alaska Range of S-central AK.

McKinley, William. 1843–1901. The 25th US President (1897–1901); assassinated.

William McKinley
detail of an 1892 portrait

Md ▸ The symbol for the element **mendelevium.**

MD ▸*abbr.* **1.** also **Md.** Maryland **2.** *Lat.* Medicinae Doctor (Doctor of Medicine) **3.** muscular distrophy

Mdm. ▸*abbr.* Madam

me (mē) ▸*pron. The objective case of* **I**[1]. Used as: **a.** The direct object of a verb: *He saw me.* **b.** The indirect object of a verb: *They gave me a ride.* **c.** The object of a preposition: *It's for me.* See Usage Note at **I**[1]. [< OE *mē*.]

ME ▸*abbr.* **1.** also **Me.** Maine **2.** mechanical engineering **3.** Middle English

mead (mēd) ▸*n.* An alcoholic beverage made from fermented honey. [< OE *meodu*.]

Mead, Lake. A reservoir of SE NV and NW AZ formed by Hoover Dam on the Colorado R.

Mead, Margaret. 1901–78. Amer. anthropologist.

Margaret Mead

Meade (mēd), **George Gordon.** 1815–72. Amer. Union general.

mead•ow (mĕd′ō) ▸*n.* A tract of grassland used as pasture or for growing hay. [< OE *mǣd*.] —**mead′ow•y** *adj.*

mead•ow•lark (mĕd′ō-lärk′) ▸*n.* A North American songbird having brownish plumage and a yellow breast.

mea•ger also **mea•gre** (mē′gər) ▸*adj.* **1.** Deficient in quantity, fullness, or extent. **2.** Thin; lean. [< Lat. *macer*.] —**mea′ger•ly** *adv.* —**mea′ger•ness** *n.*

meal[1] (mēl) ▸*n.* **1.** Coarsely ground edible grain. **2.** Any granular substance. [< OE *melu*.] —**meal′i•ness** *n.* —**meal′y** *adj.*

meal[2] (mēl) ▸*n.* The food served and eaten in one sitting. [< OE *mǣl*.]

meal•time (mēl′tīm′) ▸*n.* The usual time for eating a meal.

meal•y-mouthed (mē′lē-mouthd′, -moutht′) ▸*adj.* Unwilling to speak simply and directly.

mean[1] (mēn) ▸*v.* **meant** (mĕnt), **mean•ing** **1a.** To be defined as; denote. **b.** To act as a symbol of; represent. **2.** To intend to convey or indicate. **3.** To have as a consequence: *Friction means heat.* **4.** To be of a specified importance: *She meant so much to me.* [< OE *mǣnan*, tell of.]

mean[2] (mēn) ▸*adj.* **-er, -est 1.** Spiteful and petty; unkind. **2.** Ignoble; base. **3.** Miserly. **4a.** Low in quality or grade. **b.** Low in value or amount. **5.** Low in social status. **6.** *Informal* Ill-tempered. **7.** *Slang* Hard to cope with. [< OE *gemǣne*, common.] —**mean′ly** *adv.* —**mean′ness** *n.*

mean[3] (mēn) ▸*n.* **1.** Something midway between extremes; a medium. **2.** *Math.* The average value of a set of numbers. **3. means** *(takes sing. or pl. v.)* A course of action or instrument by which an end can be achieved. **4. means** *(takes pl. v.)* Money, property, or other wealth. ▸*adj.* Occupying a middle position between two extremes. —***idioms:*** **by all means** Without fail; certainly. **by no means** In no sense; certainly not. [< Lat. *mediānus* < *medius*, middle.]

Usage: In the sense of "financial resources," *means* takes a plural verb: *His means are more than adequate.* In the sense of "a way to an end," *means* is singular when referring to a particular strategy or method but plural when it refers to a group of strategies or methods: *Every means was tried. There are several means at our disposal.*

me•an•der (mē-ăn′dər) ▸*v.* **1.** To follow a winding and turning course. **2.** To move aimlessly and idly. ▸*n.* **meanders** Circuitous windings, as of a stream or path. [< Gk. *Maiandros*, a river in Phrygia.]

mean•ing (mē′nĭng) ▸*n.* **1.** Something signified; sense. **2.** Something one wishes to convey, esp. by language. **3.** Intent; end. —**mean′ing•ful** *adj.* —**mean′ing•ful•ly** *adv.* —**mean′ing•less** *adj.*

Syns: *meaning, acceptation, import, sense, significance, signification* **n.**

mean•time (mēn′tīm′) ▸*n.* The time between two occurrences. ▸*adv.* Meanwhile.

mean•while (mēn′hwīl′, -wīl′) ▸*n.* The intervening time. ▸*adv.* In the intervening time.

mea•sles (mē′zəlz) ▸*n. (takes sing. or pl. v.)* **1.** An acute, contagious viral disease, marked by red spots on the skin, fever, and coughing. **2.** Any of several milder diseases similar to measles. [Of MLGer. orig.]

mea•sly (mēz′lē) ▸*adj.* **-sli•er, -sli•est.** *Slang* Contemptibly small: *a measly tip.*

meas•ure (mĕzh′ər) ▸*n.* **1.** Dimensions, quantity, or capacity ascertained by a standard. **2.** A reference used for the quantitative comparison of properties. **3.** A unit specified by a scale, such as an inch, or by variable conditions, such as a day's march. **4.** A device used for measuring. **5.** The act of measuring. **6.** A basis of comparison. See Syns at **standard. 7.** Extent or degree. **8.** A limited amount or degree. **9.** often **measures** An action taken as a means to an end. **10.** A legislative bill or enactment. **11.** Poetic meter. **12.** *Mus.* The metric unit between two bars on the staff; bar. ▸*v.* **-ured, -ur•ing 1.** To ascertain the dimensions, quantity, or capacity of. **2.** To lay out dimensions by measuring: *measure off an area.* **3.** To compare: *measured our strength against theirs.* **4.** To consider or choose with care; weigh: *He measures his words.* —***phrasal verb:*** **measure up 1.** To be the equal of. **2.** To have the necessary qualifications. —***idiom:*** **for good measure** In addition to the required amount. [< Lat. *mēnsūra*.] —**meas′ur•a•ble** *adj.* —**meas′ur•a•bly** *adv.* —**meas′ure•ment** *n.* —**meas′ur•er** *n.*

meas•ure•ment (mĕzh′ər-mənt) ▸*n.* **1.** The act of measuring or the process of being measured. **2.** A system of measuring. See table pp. 526-527. **3.** The dimension, quantity, or capacity determined by measuring: *the measurements of a room.*

meas•ur•ing worm (mĕzh′ə-rĭng) ▸*n.* A caterpillar that moves in alternate contractions and expansions suggestive of measuring.

meat (mēt) ▸*n.* **1.** The edible flesh of animals,

esp. mammals. **2.** The edible part, as of a piece of fruit. **3.** The essence, substance, or gist: *the meat of the editorial.* **4.** Food. [< OE *mete*, food.] —**meat′i•ness** *n.* —**meat′y** *adj.*

meat•ball (mēt′bôl′) ►*n.* **1.** A ball of cooked ground meat. **2.** *Slang* A stupid person.

mec•ca (mĕk′ə) ►*n.* A center of interest or attraction: *a mecca for tourists.*

Mecca. A city of W Saudi Arabia near the coast of the Red Sea; birthplace of Muhammad. Pop. 689,010.

me•chan•ic (mĭ-kăn′ĭk) ►*n.* A worker skilled in making, using, or repairing machines.

me•chan•i•cal (mĭ-kăn′ĭ-kəl) ►*adj.* **1.** Of or relating to machines or tools. **2.** Operated or produced by a machine. **3.** Of or relating to mechanics. **4.** Performed in a machinelike manner; automatic: *a mechanical task.* [< Gk. *mēkhanē*, machine.] —**me•chan′i•cal•ly** *adv.*

mechanical drawing ►*n.* **1.** Drafting. **2.** A drawing that enables measurements to be interpreted.

me•chan•ics (mĭ-kăn′ĭks) ►*n.* **1.** *(takes sing. v.)* The branch of physics concerned with the analysis of the action of forces on matter or material systems. **2.** *(takes sing. or pl. v.)* Design, construction, and use of machinery or mechanical structures. **3.** *(takes pl. v.)* The functional and technical aspects of an activity: *the mechanics of football.*

mech•a•nism (mĕk′ə-nĭz′əm) ►*n.* **1a.** A machine or mechanical appliance. **b.** The arrangement of connected parts in a machine. **2.** A system of parts that operate or interact like those of a machine. **3.** A means or process by which something is done or comes into being. **4.** *Philos.* The doctrine that all natural phenomena are explicable by material causes and mechanical principles.

mech•a•nis•tic (mĕk′ə-nĭs′tĭk) ►*adj.* **1.** *Philos.* Of or relating to the philosophy of mechanism. **2.** Automatic and impersonal. —**mech′a•nis′ti•cal•ly** *adv.*

mech•a•nize (mĕk′ə-nīz′) ►*v.* **-nized, -niz•ing 1.** To equip with machinery. **2.** To make automatic or routine. —**mech′a•ni•za′tion** *n.*

med•al (mĕd′l) ►*n.* **1.** A flat piece of metal stamped with a design commemorating an event or person, often given as an award. **2.** A piece of metal stamped with a religious device. [< Ital. *medaglia.*]

med•al•ist (mĕd′l-ĭst) ►*n.* **1.** A recipient of a medal. **2.** One who designs medals.

me•dal•lion (mĭ-dăl′yən) ►*n.* **1.** A large medal. **2.** An emblem of registration for a taxicab. **3.** Something resembling a large medal. [< Ital. *medaglione.*]

Me•dan (mā-dän′) A city of Indonesia on N Sumatra NNW of Padang. Pop. 1,378,955.

med•dle (mĕd′l) ►*v.* **-dled, -dling.** To intrude into other people's affairs; interfere. [< VLat. **misculāre*, mix up.] —**med′dler** (mĕd′lər, mĕd′l-ər) *n.* —**med′dle•some** *adj.*

Mede (mēd) ►*n.* A member of an Iranian people inhabiting ancient Media.

Me•del•lín (mĕ′dĕ-yēn′) A city of NW-central Colombia NW of Bogotá. Pop. 1,473,351.

med•e•vac (mĕd′ĭ-văk′) ►*n.* Air transport of persons to a place where they can receive medical care. [*med(ical) evac(uation).*]

me•di•a (mē′dē-ə) ►*n.* Pl. of **medium.** See Usage Note at **medium.**

Media. An ancient country of SW Asia in NW Iran. —**Me′di•an** *adj. & n.*

me•di•ae•val (mē′dē-ē′vəl, mĕd′ē-) ►*adj.* Var. of **medieval.**

me•di•al (mē′dē-əl) ►*adj.* Of or situated in the middle; median. [< Lat. *medius*, middle.] —**me′di•al•ly** *adv.*

medial strip ►*n.* *Regional* See **median strip.** See Regional Note at **neutral ground.**

me•di•an (mē′dē-ən) ►*adj.* **1.** Of or located in the middle. **2.** *Statistics* Of or being the middle value in a distribution. ►*n.* **1a.** A median point, plane, line, or part. **b.** See **median strip.** See Regional Note at **neutral ground. 2.** *Statistics* The middle value in a distribution, above and below which lie an equal number of values. **3.** *Math.* A line that joins a vertex of a triangle to the midpoint of the opposite side. [< Lat. *medius*, middle.]

median strip ►*n.* A paved or landscaped strip that divides opposing traffic lanes of a highway. See Regional Note at **neutral ground.**

me•di•ate (mē′dē-āt′) ►*v.* **-at•ed, -at•ing 1.** To resolve or seek to resolve (differences) by working with all conflicting parties. **2.** To act as intermediary. [LLat. *mediāre*, be in the middle.] —**me′di•a′tion** *n.* —**me′di•a′tor** *n.*

med•ic (mĕd′ĭk) ►*n.* **1.** A member of a military medical corps. **2.** A physician or surgeon. [Lat. *medicus*, physician.]

Med•i•caid also **med•i•caid** (mĕd′ĭ-kād′) ►*n.* A US government program that pays for medical care for people who cannot finance their own medical expenses.

med•i•cal (mĕd′ĭ-kəl) ►*adj.* Of or relating to the study or practice of medicine. [< Lat. *medicus*, physician.] —**med′i•cal•ly** *adv.*

me•dic•a•ment (mĭ-dĭk′ə-mənt, mĕd′ĭ-kə-) ►*n.* A medicine. [Lat. *medicāmentum.*]

Med•i•care also **med•i•care** (mĕd′ĭ-kâr′) ►*n.* A US government program that pays for medical care for people over 65.

med•i•cate (mĕd′ĭ-kāt′) ►*v.* **-cat•ed, -cat•ing 1.** To treat with medicine. **2.** To add a medicinal substance to. [Lat. *medicāre.*]

med•i•ca•tion (mĕd′ĭ-kā′shən) ►*n.* **1.** A medicine. **2.** The act of medicating.

Med•i•ci (mĕd′ə-chē′, mĕ′dē-). Italian noble family including **Cosimo** (1389–1464) and **Lorenzo** (1449–92). —**Med′i•ce′an** (-chē′ən, -sē′-) *adj.*

med•i•cine (mĕd′ĭ-sĭn) ►*n.* **1a.** The science of diagnosing, treating, or preventing disease or bodily injury. **b.** The branch of this science encompassing treatment by means other than surgery. **2.** An agent used to treat disease. **3.** Something serving as a remedy or corrective. **4.** Shamanistic practices or beliefs. [< Lat. *medicīna* < *medicus*, physician.] —**me•di′ci•nal** (mĭ-dĭs′ə-nəl) *adj.* —**me•di′ci•nal•ly** *adv.*

medicine man ►*n.* A male shaman, esp. among Native American peoples.

medicine woman ►*n.* A female shaman, esp. among Native American peoples.

med•i•co (mĕd′ĭ-kō′) ►*n.*, *pl.* **-cos** *Informal.* A doctor or medical student. [< Lat. *medicus.*]

me•di•e•val also **me•di•ae•val** (mē′dē-ē′vəl, mĕd′ē-, mĭ-dē′vəl) ►*adj.* **1.** Of or belonging to the Middle Ages. **2.** *Informal* Old-fashioned; unenlightened. [< Lat. *medius*, middle +

MEASUREMENT TABLE

Conversion between Metric and US Customary Units

From Metric to US Customary

WHEN YOU KNOW	MULTIPLY BY	TO FIND
millimeters	0.04	inches
centimeters	0.39	inches
meters	3.28	feet
	1.09	yards
kilometers	0.62	miles
milliliters	0.03	fluid ounces
liters	1.06	quarts
	0.26	gallons
cubic meters	35.31	cubic feet
grams	0.035	ounces
kilograms	2.20	pounds
metric tons (1,000 kg)	1.10	short tons
square centimeters	0.155	square inches
square meters	1.20	square yards
square kilometers	0.39	square miles
hectares	2.47	acres

From US Customary to Metric

WHEN YOU KNOW	MULTIPLY BY	TO FIND
inches	2.54	centimeters
feet	30.48	centimeters
yards	0.91	meters
miles	1.61	kilometers
fluid ounces	29.57	milliliters
cups	0.24	liters
pints	0.47	liters
quarts	0.95	liters
gallons	3.79	liters
cubic feet	0.028	cubic meters
ounces	28.35	grams
pounds	0.45	kilograms
short tons (2,000 lbs)	0.91	metric tons
square inches	6.45	square centimeters
square feet	0.09	square meters
square yards	0.84	square meters
square miles	2.59	square kilometers
acres	0.40	hectares

Temperature Conversion between Celsius and Fahrenheit

$$^{\circ}C = (\,^{\circ}F - 32\,) \div 1.8$$
$$^{\circ}F = (\,^{\circ}C \times 1.8\,) + 32$$

Metric Prefixes

A multiple of a unit in the metric system is formed by adding a prefix to its name. The prefixes change the magnitude of the unit by orders of ten. Those for 10^9 to 10^{-9} are given below.

PREFIX	SYMBOL	MULTIPLYING FACTOR
giga-	G	10^9 = 1,000,000,000
mega-	M	10^6 = 1,000,000
kilo-	k	10^3 = 1,000
hecto-	h	10^2 = 100
deca-	da	10 = 10
deci-	d	10^{-1} = 0.1
centi-	c	10^{-2} = 0.01
milli-	m	10^{-3} = 0.001
micro-	m	10^{-6} = 0.000,001
nano-	n	10^{-9} = 0.000,000,001

MEASUREMENT TABLE, continued

US Customary System

Unit	Relation to Other US Customary Units	Metric Equivalent
Length		
inch	1/12 foot	2.54 centimeters
foot	12 inches or 1/3 yard	0.305 meter
yard	36 inches or 3 feet	0.91 meter
rod	16 1/2 feet or 5 1/2 yards	5.03 meters
furlong	220 yards or 1/8 mile	0.20 kilometer
mile (statute)	5,280 feet or 1,760 yards	1.61 kilometers
mile (nautical)	6,076 feet or 2,025 yards	1.852 kilometers
Volume or Capacity (Liquid Measure)		
ounce	1/16 pint	29.574 milliliters
gill	4 ounces	0.12 liter
cup	8 ounces	0.24 liter
pint	16 ounces	0.47 liter
quart	2 pints or 1/4 gallon	0.95 liter
gallon	128 ounces or 8 pints	3.79 liters
barrel (wine)	31 1/2 gallons	119.24 liters
barrel (beer)	36 gallons	136.27 liters
barrel (oil)	42 gallons	158.99 liters
Volume or Capacity (Dry Measure)		
cup	1/2 pint	0.275 liter
pint	2 cups or 1/2 quart	0.55 liter
quart	4 cups or 2 pints	1.10 liters
peck	8 quarts or 1/4 bushel	8.81 liters
bushel	4 pecks	35.239 liters
Weight		
grain	1/7000 pound	64.799 milligrams
dram	1/16 ounce	1.772 grams
ounce	16 drams	28.350 grams
pound	16 ounces	453.6 grams
ton (short)	2,000 pounds	907.18 kilograms
ton (long)	2,240 pounds	1,016.0 kilograms
Geographic Area		
acre	43,560 square feet or 4,840 square yards	4,047 square meters

British Imperial System

Unit	Relation to Other British Imperial Units	Conversion to US Customary Units	Conversion to Metric Units
Volume or Capacity (Liquid Measure)			
pint	1/2 quart	1.20 pints	0.57 liter
quart	2 pints = 1/4 gallon	1.20 quarts	1.14 liters
gallon	8 pints = 4 quarts	1.20 gallons	4.55 liters
Volume or Capacity (Dry Measure)			
peck	1/4 bushel	1.03 pecks	9.09 liters
bushel	4 pecks	1.03 bushels	36.37 liters

aevum, age.] —**me′di•e′val•ist** *n.* —**me′di•e′val•ly** *adv.*

Medieval Greek ►*n.* The Greek language from about 800 to about 1500.

Medieval Latin ►*n.* The Latin language from about 700 to about 1500.

Med•i•gap (mĕd′ĭ-găp′) ►*n.* Private health insurance designed to supplement Medicare. [MEDI(CARE) and MEDI(CAID) + GAP.]

Me•di•na (mĭ-dē′nə) A city of W Saudi Arabia N of Mecca. Pop. 290,000.

me•di•o•cre (mē′dē-ō′kər) ►*adj.* Moderate to inferior in quality; ordinary. [< Lat. *mediocris* : *medius*, middle + *ocris*, rugged mountain.] —**me′di•oc′ri•ty** (-ŏk′rĭ-tē) *n.*

med•i•tate (mĕd′ĭ-tāt′) ►*v.* **-tat•ed, -tat•ing** **1.** To reflect on; contemplate. **2a.** *Buddhism & Hinduism* To train or empty the mind, as by focusing on a single object. **b.** To engage in prayer. [Lat. *meditārī.*] —**med′i•ta′tion** *n.* —**med′i•ta•tion•al** *adj.* —**med′i•ta′tive** *adj.* —**med′i•ta′tive•ly** *adv.* —**med′i•ta′tor** *n.*

Med•i•ter•ra•ne•an (mĕd′ĭ-tə-rā′nē-ən) The region surrounding the Mediterranean Sea. —**Med′i•ter•ra′ne•an** *adj. & n.*

Mediterranean fruit fly ►*n.* A black and white two-winged fly, the larvae of which destroy fruit crops.

Mediterranean Sea. An inland sea surrounded by Europe, Asia, Asia Minor, the Near East, and Africa.

me•di•um (mē′dē-əm) ►*n., pl.* **-di•a** (-dē-ə) or **-di•ums** **1.** A position, condition, or course of action midway between extremes. **2.** An intervening substance through which something else is transmitted or carried on. **3.** An agency by which something is accomplished, conveyed, or transferred. **4.** *pl.* **media** *Usage Problem* **a.** A means of mass communication. **b. media** *(takes sing. or pl. v.)* The communications industry or profession. **5.** *pl.* **mediums** A person thought to have the power to communicate with the spirits of the dead. **6.** *pl.* **media** An environment in which something functions and thrives. **7.** A means of expression as determined by the materials or the creative methods involved. ►*adj.* Midway between extremes; intermediate: *broil a medium steak.* [Lat. < *medius*, middle.]

Usage: The plural form *media* is often used as a singular to refer to a particular means of communication, as in *This is the most exciting new media since television.* However, many people prefer *medium* in such contexts. *Media* is standard when used as a collective term for journalists and broadcasters, as in *The media has ignored the issue.*

med•ley (mĕd′lē) ►*n., pl.* **-leys** **1.** A jumbled assortment. **2.** A musical arrangement of several melodies. [< AN *medler*, MEDDLE.]

me•dul•la (mĭ-dŭl′ə) ►*n., pl.* **-las** or **-dul•lae** (-dŭl′ē) **1.** The inner core of certain organs or body structures, such as the marrow of bone. **2.** The medulla oblongata. [< Lat.] —**me•dul′lar, med′ul•lar′y** (mĕd′l-ĕr′ē, mə-dŭl′ə-rē) *adj.*

medulla ob•lon•ga•ta (ŏb′lông-gä′tə) ►*n., pl.* **-tas** or **medullae ob•lon•ga•tae** (-tē). The lowermost portion of the vertebrate brain that controls respiration, circulation, and certain other bodily functions. [NLat. *medulla oblongāta*, oblong medulla.]

meek (mēk) ►*adj.* **-er, -est** **1.** Showing patience and humility. **2.** Submissive; passive. [ME *meke*, of Scand. orig.] —**meek′ly** *adv.* —**meek′ness** *n.*

meer•kat (mîr′kăt′) ►*n.* An African burrowing mammal related to the mongoose, having grayish fur and a long tail. [< MDu. *meercatte*, sea cat, monkey (since monkeys came from overseas).]

meer•schaum (mîr′shəm, -shôm′) ►*n.* **1.** A claylike mineral used esp. to make tobacco pipes. **2.** A pipe made of meerschaum. [Ger. : *Meer*, sea (< OHGer. *mari*) + *Schaum*, foam.]

meet[1] (mēt) ►*v.* **met** (mĕt), **meet•ing** **1.** To come upon. **2.** To be present at the arrival of: *met the train.* **3.** To be introduced to. **4.** To come into conjunction with. **5.** To come into the company of, as for a conference. **6.** To come to the notice of: *more than meets the eye.* **7.** To cope effectively with. **8.** To fulfill. See Syns at **satisfy. 9.** To come together: *Let's meet tonight.* ►*n.* A meeting or contest. [< OE *mētan.*]

meet[2] (mēt) ►*adj.* Fitting; proper. [< OE *gemǣte.*] —**meet′ly** *adv.*

meet•ing (mē′tĭng) ►*n.* **1.** A coming together. **2.** An assembly or gathering.

mega– ►*pref.* **1.** Large: *megalith.* **2.** One million (10^6): *megaton.* [< Gk. *megas*, great.]

meg•a•byte (mĕg′ə-bīt′) ►*n.* A unit of computer memory equal to 1,048,576 (2^{20}) bytes.

meg•a•cy•cle (mĕg′ə-sī′kəl) ►*n.* See **megahertz.**

meg•a•fau•na (mĕg′ə-fô′nə) ►*n. (takes sing. or pl. v.)* Large animals, as of a particular period, considered as a group.

meg•a•hertz (mĕg′ə-hûrts′) ►*n.* One million cycles per second.

meg•a•lith (mĕg′ə-lĭth′) ►*n.* A very large stone used in various prehistoric structures or monuments. —**meg′a•lith′ic** *adj.*

megalith
c. 1800 B.C. standing stones at Callanish, Isle of Lewis, Scotland

megalo– ►*pref.* Exaggeratedly large: *megalomania.* [< Gk. *megas*, *megal-*, great.]

meg•a•lo•ma•ni•a (mĕg′ə-lō-mā′nē-ə, -mān′yə) ►*n.* A mental disorder characterized by delusions of wealth, power, or omnipotence. —**meg′a•lo•ma′ni•ac′** *n.*

meg•a•lop•o•lis (mĕg′ə-lŏp′ə-lĭs) ►*n.* **1.** A very large city. **2.** An urban complex made up of several large cities and their surrounding areas. [MEGALO– + Gk. *polis*, city.]

meg•a•phone (mĕg′ə-fōn′) ►*n.* A funnel-shaped device used to amplify the voice.

meg•a•ton (mĕg′ə-tŭn′) ▸*n.* A unit of explosive force equal to that of one million metric tons of TNT. —**meg′a•ton′nage** (-tŭn′ĭj) *n.*

meg•a•vi•ta•min (mĕg′ə-vī′tə-mĭn) ▸*n.* A dose of a vitamin greatly exceeding the amount required to maintain health.

meg•a•watt (mĕg′ə-wŏt′) ▸*n.* One million watts. —**meg′a•watt′age** *n.*

mei•o•sis (mī-ō′sĭs) ▸*n., pl.* **-ses** (-sēz′). Cell division in sexually reproducing organisms that reduces the number of chromosomes in reproductive cells. [Gk. *meiōsis,* diminution.] —**mei•ot′ic** (-ŏt′ĭk) *adj.* —**mei•ot′i•cal•ly** *adv.*

Me•ir (mĭ′ər, mā-ēr′), **Golda.** 1898–1978. Russian-born Israeli politician.

meit•ner•i•um (mīt-nûr′ē-əm) ▸*n. Symbol* **Mt** A short-lived synthetic radioactive element. At. no. 109. See table at **element.** [After Lise *Meitner* (1878–1968).]

Me•kong (mā′kông′, -kŏng′) A river of SE Asia flowing about 4,183 km (2,600 mi) from SE China to the South China Sea through S Vietnam.

mel•an•cho•li•a (mĕl′ən-kō′lē-ə) ▸*n.* A mental disorder marked by severe depression and apathy. [LLat. MELANCHOLY.]

mel•an•chol•ic (mĕl′ən-kŏl′ĭk) ▸*adj.* **1.** Affected with melancholy. **2.** Of or relating to melancholia. —**mel′an•chol′ic** *n.* —**mel′an•chol′i•cal•ly** *adv.*

mel•an•chol•y (mĕl′ən-kŏl′ē) ▸*n.* **1.** Sadness; depression. **2.** Pensive reflection. ▸*adj.* **1.** Gloomy; sad. **2.** Pensive; thoughtful. [< Gk. *melankholia.*]

Mel•a•ne•sia (mĕl′ə-nē′zhə, -shə) A division of Oceania in the SW Pacific comprising the islands NE of Australia and S of the equator.

Mel•a•ne•sian (mĕl′ə-nē′zhən, -shən) ▸*adj.* Of Melanesia or its peoples, languages, or cultures. ▸*n.* **1.** A native or inhabitant of Melanesia. **2.** A subfamily of the Austronesian languages spoken in Melanesia.

mé•lange also **me•lange** (mā-läɴzh′) ▸*n.* A mixture. [< OFr. *meslance* < *mesler,* MEDDLE.]

mel•a•nin (mĕl′ə-nĭn) ▸*n.* A dark pigment found esp. in skin, hair, fur, and feathers.

mel•a•nism (mĕl′ə-nĭz′əm) ▸*n.* **1.** See **melanosis.** **2.** Dark coloration due to a high concentration of melanin. —**mel′a•nis′tic** *adj.*

melano– or **melan–** ▸*pref.* Black; dark: *melanism.* [< Gk. *melas, melan-.*]

mel•a•no•ma (mĕl′ə-nō′mə) ▸*n., pl.* **-mas** or **-ma•ta** (-mə-tə). A dark-pigmented malignant tumor usu. occurring in the skin.

mel•a•no•sis (mĕl′ə-nō′sĭs) ▸*n.* Abnormally dark pigmentation resulting from a disorder of pigment metabolism. —**mel′a•not′ic** (-nŏt′ĭk) *adj.*

mel•a•to•nin (mĕl′ə-tō′nĭn) ▸*n.* A neurotransmitter involved in sleep, aging, and reproduction in mammals. [Gk. *melas,* black + TON(E) + -IN.]

Mel•ba toast (mĕl′bə) ▸*n.* Very thinly sliced crisp toast. [After Dame Nellie *Melba* (1861–1931).]

Mel•bourne (mĕl′bərn) A city of SE Australia SW of Canberra. Met. area pop. 3,189,200.

meld[1] (mĕld) ▸*v.* To declare or display (a card or combination of cards) for inclusion in one's score in various card games. [Prob. < Ger. *melden,* announce.] —**meld** *n.*

meld[2] (mĕld) ▸*v.* To merge or become merged; blend. [Perh. blend of MELT and WELD.]

me•lee (mā′lā′, mā-lā′) also **mê•lée** (mĕ-lā′) ▸*n.* **1.** Confused, hand-to-hand fighting. See Syns at **brawl.** **2.** A tumultuous mingling. [< OFr. *meslee* < *mesler,* MEDDLE.]

mel•io•rate (mēl′yə-rāt′, mē′lē-ə-) ▸*v.* **-rat•ed, -rat•ing.** To make or become better; improve. [< Lat. *melior,* better.] —**mel′io•ra•ble** (-rə-bəl) *adj.* —**mel′io•ra′tion** *n.*

mel•lif•lu•ous (mə-lĭf′lo͞o-əs) ▸*adj.* Flowing in a smooth or sweet manner. [< LLat. *mellifluus.*] —**mel•lif′lu•ous•ly** *adv.*

mel•low (mĕl′ō) ▸*adj.* **-er, -est 1.** Soft, sweet, and full-flavored because of ripeness. **2.** Rich and soft in quality: *a mellow wine.* **3.** Having the gentleness often associated with maturity. **4.** Relaxed; easygoing. **5.** *Slang* Slightly and pleasantly intoxicated. ▸*v.* To make or become mellow. [ME *melwe.*] —**mel′low•ly** *adv.* —**mel′low•ness** *n.*

me•lo•de•on (mə-lō′dē-ən) ▸*n.* A small harmonium. [Alteration of *melodium* < MELODY.]

me•lo•di•ous (mə-lō′dē-əs) ▸*adj.* **1.** Tuneful. **2.** Agreeable to hear. —**me•lo′di•ous•ly** *adv.* —**me•lo′di•ous•ness** *n.*

mel•o•dra•ma (mĕl′ə-drä′mə, -drăm′ə) ▸*n.* **1.** A dramatic work marked by exaggerated emotions, stereotypical characters, and interpersonal conflicts. **2.** Behavior or events having melodramatic characteristics. [< Fr. *mélodrame,* musical drama.]

mel•o•dra•mat•ic (mĕl′ə-drə-măt′ĭk) ▸*adj.* **1.** Having the emotional appeal of melodrama. **2.** Exaggeratedly emotional or sentimental. —**mel′o•dra•mat′i•cal•ly** *adv.*

mel•o•dy (mĕl′ə-dē) ▸*n., pl.* **-dies 1.** A pleasing succession or arrangement of sounds. **2.** A rhythmic sequence of single tones organized so as to make up a musical phrase. [< Gk. *melōidia.*] —**me•lod′ic** (mə-lŏd′ĭk) *adj.* —**me•lod′i•cal•ly** *adv.*

mel•on (mĕl′ən) ▸*n.* Any of several fruits, as cantaloupe or watermelon, having a hard rind and juicy flesh. [< Gk. *mēlopepōn.*]

melt (mĕlt) ▸*v.* **1.** To change or be changed from a solid to a liquid state by application of heat or pressure or both. **2.** To dissolve: *Sugar melts in water.* **3.** To disappear or cause to disappear gradually. **4.** To pass imperceptibly into something else. **5.** To become softened in feeling. [< OE *meltan.*] —**melt′a•ble** *adj.* —**melt′ing•ly** *adv.*

melt•down (mĕlt′doun′) ▸*n.* Severe overheating of a nuclear reactor core, resulting in escape of radiation.

melt•ing point (mĕl′tĭng) ▸*n.* The temperature at which a solid becomes a liquid at standard atmospheric pressure.

melting pot ▸*n.* A place where immigrants of different cultures or races form an integrated society.

Mel•ville (mĕl′vĭl), **Herman.** 1819–91. Amer. writer. —**Mel•vil′le•an** *adj.*

Melville Island. An island of N Northwest Terrs., Canada, N of Victoria I.

mem•ber (mĕm′bər) ▸*n.* **1.** A distinct part of a whole. **2.** A part or an organ of a human or animal body. **3.** One that belongs to a group or organization. [< Lat. *membrum.*]

mem•ber•ship (mĕm′bər-shĭp′) ▸*n.* **1.** The state of being a member. **2.** All the members in

a group: *a growing membership.*
mem•brane (mĕm′brān′) ►*n.* **1.** A thin pliable layer of plant or animal tissue covering or separating structures or organs. **2.** A thin sheet of natural or synthetic material that is permeable to substances in solution, as in osmosis. [Lat. *membrāna*, skin.] —**mem′bra•nal** (-brə-nəl), **mem′bra•nous** *adj.*
me•men•to (mə-mĕn′tō) ►*n., pl.* **-tos** or **-toes.** A reminder of the past; keepsake. [< Lat. *mementō*, imper. of *meminisse*, remember.]
Mem•ling (mĕm′lĭng), **Hans.** 1430?–94. Flemish painter.
mem•o (mĕm′ō) ►*n., pl.* **-os** *Informal.* A memorandum.
mem•oir (mĕm′wär′, -wôr′) ►*n.* **1.** often **memoirs** An autobiography or biography. **2. memoirs** The report of the proceedings of a learned society. [< Fr. *mémoire*, memory.] —**mem′oir•ist** *n.*
mem•o•ra•bil•i•a (mĕm′ər-ə-bĭl′ē-ə, -bĭl′yə) ►*pl.n.* **1.** Objects valued for their historical significance. **2.** Events or experiences worthy of remembrance. [< Lat. *memorābilis*, MEMORABLE.]
mem•o•ra•ble (mĕm′ər-ə-bəl) ►*adj.* Worth being remembered or noted. [< Lat. *memor*, mindful.] —**mem′o•ra•bil′i•ty, mem′o•ra•ble•ness** *n.* —**mem′o•ra•bly** *adv.*
mem•o•ran•dum (mĕm′ə-răn′dəm) ►*n., pl.* **-dums** or **-da** (-də) **1.** A short note written as a reminder. **2.** A written record or communication, as in a business office. [Lat., thing to be remembered.]
me•mo•ri•al (mə-môr′ē-əl, -mōr′-) ►*n.* **1.** Something, such as a monument or holiday, intended to honor the memory of a person or event. **2.** A written statement of facts or a formal petition. ►*adj.* Commemorative. —**me•mo′ri•al•ize′** *v.* —**me•mo′ri•al•ly** *adv.*
Memorial Day ►*n.* May 30, a US holiday commemorating members of the armed forces killed in war, officially observed on the last Monday in May.
mem•o•rize (mĕm′ə-rīz′) ►*v.* **-rized, -riz•ing.** To commit to memory; learn by heart. —**mem′o•ri•za′tion** *n.* —**mem′o•riz′er** *n.*
mem•o•ry (mĕm′ə-rē) ►*n., pl.* **-ries 1.** The mental faculty of retaining and recalling past experience. **2.** The act of remembering; recollection. **3.** All that a person can remember. **4.** Something remembered: *childhood memories.* **5.** The period of time covered by remembrance or recollection. **6.** *Comp. Sci.* **a.** A unit of a computer that preserves data for retrieval. **b.** Capacity for storing information. [< Lat. *memoria* < *memor*, mindful.]
Mem•phis (mĕm′fĭs) **1.** An ancient city of Egypt S of Cairo. **2.** A city of SW TN on the Mississippi R. Pop. 610,337.
mem•sa•hib (mĕm′sä′ĭb) ►*n.* Used formerly as a respectful address for a European woman in colonial India. [MA'AM + SAHIB.]
men (mĕn) ►*n.* Pl. of **man.**
men•ace (mĕn′ĭs) ►*n.* **1.** A threat. **2.** A troublesome or annoying person. ►*v.* **-aced, -ac•ing.** To threaten. [< Lat. *minān*, *mināc-*, threatening < *minārī*, threaten.] —**men′ac•er** *n.* —**men′ac•ing•ly** *adv.*
mé•nage (mā-näzh′) ►*n.* A household. [< OFr. < *maneir*, REMAIN.]
me•nag•er•ie (mə-năj′ə-rē, -năzh′-) ►*n.* A collection of wild animals on exhibition. [Fr. *ménagerie* < OFr. *menage*, MÉNAGE.]
Me•nan•der (mə-năn′dər). 342–292 B.C. Greek dramatist.
me•nar•che (mə-när′kē) ►*n.* The first menstrual period, usu. occurring during puberty. [Gk. *mēn*, month + *arkhē*, beginning.] —**me•nar′che•al** *adj.*
Menck•en (mĕng′kən), **H(enry) L(ouis).** 1880–1956. Amer. editor and critic.
mend (mĕnd) ►*v.* **1.** To make repairs or restoration to; fix. **2.** To reform or correct. **3.** To improve in health; heal. ►*n.* A mended place. —***idiom:* on the mend** Improving, esp. in health. [< ME *amenden*, AMEND.] —**mend′a•ble** *adj.* —**mend′er** *n.*
men•da•cious (mĕn-dā′shəs) ►*adj.* **1.** Lying; untruthful. **2.** False; untrue. [< Lat. *mendāx*, *mendāc-*.] —**men•da′cious•ly** *adv.* —**men•dac′i•ty** (-dăs′ĭ-tē) *n.*
Men•del (mĕn′dl), **Gregor Johann.** 1822–84. Austrian botanist.
Men•de•le•ev (mĕn′də-lā′əf), **Dmitri Ivanovich.** 1834–1907. Russian chemist.
men•de•le•vi•um (mĕn′də-lē′vē-əm) ►*n.* *Symbol* **Md** A synthetic radioactive element. At. no. 101. See table at **element.** [After Dmitri Ivanovich MENDELEEV.]
Men•dels•sohn (mĕn′dl-sən, -zōn′), **Felix.** 1809–47. German composer, pianist, and conductor.
men•di•cant (mĕn′dĭ-kənt) ►*adj.* Depending on alms for a living. ►*n.* **1.** A beggar. **2.** A friar. [< Lat. *mendīcāre*, beg.]
Men•e•la•us (mĕn′ə-lā′əs) ►*n.* *Gk. Myth.* The king of Sparta at the time of the Trojan War.
men•ha•den (mĕn-hād′n) ►*n., pl.* **-den** or **-dens.** A fish of American Atlantic and Gulf waters, used as fertilizer and bait. [Of Algonquian orig.]
men•hir (mĕn′hîr′) ►*n.* See **standing stone.** [Fr. < Breton, long stone.]
me•ni•al (mē′nē-əl, mēn′yəl) ►*adj.* **1.** Of or relating to work regarded as servile. **2.** Of or appropriate for a servant. ►*n.* A domestic servant. [< AN *meignee*, household.] —**me′ni•al•ly** *adv.*
men•in•gi•tis (mĕn′ĭn-jī′tĭs) ►*n.* Inflammation of the meninges of the brain and the spinal cord.
me•ninx (mē′nĭngks) ►*n., pl.* **me•nin•ges** (mə-nĭn′jēz). Any of the three membranes enclosing the brain and spinal cord in vertebrates. [Gk. *mēninx*, membrane.] —**me•nin′ge•al** (mə-nĭn′jē-əl)
me•nis•cus (mə-nĭs′kəs) ►*n., pl.* **-nis•ci** (-nĭs′ī, -kī, -kē) or **-es 1.** A crescent-shaped body. **2.** The curved upper surface of a liquid in a container. [< Gk. *mēniskos*, crescent.]
men•o•pause (mĕn′ə-pôz′) ►*n.* The cessation of menstruation, occurring usu. between the ages of 45 and 55. [Gk. *mēn*, month + PAUSE.] —**men′o•paus′al** *adj.*
me•no•rah (mə-nôr′ə, -nōr′ə) ►*n.* *Judaism* A nine-branched candelabrum used in celebration of Hanukkah. [Heb. *mənôrâ*.]
Me•not•ti (mə-nŏt′ē), **Gian Carlo.** b. 1911. Italian-born Amer. composer.
men•ses (mĕn′sēz) ►*pl.n.* *(takes sing. or pl. v.)* The monthly flow of blood and cellular debris from the uterus that begins at puberty in women

and the females of other primates. [Lat. *mēnsēs*, pl. of *mēnsis*, month.]

men•stru•al (mĕn′stro͞o-əl) ▸*adj.* Relating to menstruation. [< Lat. *mēnstruus.*]

men•stru•ate (mĕn′stro͞o-āt′) ▸*v.* **-at•ed, -at•ing.** To undergo menstruation. [< Lat. *mēnstrua*, menses.]

men•stru•a•tion (mĕn′stro͞o-ā′shən) ▸*n.* The process of discharging the menses.

men•su•ra•ble (mĕn′sər-ə-bəl, -shər-) ▸*adj.* That can be measured. [< Lat. *mēnsūra*, measure.] —**men′su•ra•bil′i•ty** *n.*

men•su•ra•tion (mĕn′sə-rā′shən, -shə-) ▸*n.* The act, process, or art of measuring.

-ment ▸*suff.* Product, means, action, or state: *curtailment.* [< Lat. *-mentum*, n. suff.]

men•tal (mĕn′tl) ▸*adj.* **1.** Of the mind. **2.** Executed or performed by the mind. [< Lat. *mēns*, mind.] —**men′tal•ly** *adv.*

mental age ▸*n.* A measure of mental development as determined by intelligence tests, gen. restricted to children and expressed as the age of which that level is typical.

men•tal•i•ty (mĕn-tăl′ĭ-tē) ▸*n.*, *pl.* **-ties 1.** Cast or turn of mind. **2.** Intellectual capabilities or endowment.

mental retardation ▸*n.* Subnormal intellectual development or functioning resulting from congenital causes, brain injury, or disease and marked by impaired learning ability.

men•thol (mĕn′thôl′) ▸*n.* A white crystalline organic compound used in perfumes, flavorings, and inhalants. [< Lat. *mentha*, mint + -OL.] —**men′tho•lat′ed** *adj.*

men•tion (mĕn′shən) ▸*v.* To refer to, esp. incidentally. See Syns at **refer.** [< Lat. *mentiō*, reference.] —**men′tion** *n.* —**men′tion•a•ble** *adj.*

men•tor (mĕn′tôr′, -tər) ▸*n.* A wise and trusted counselor or teacher. [< Gk. *Mentōr*, counselor of Odysseus.]

men•u (mĕn′yo͞o) ▸*n.* **1.** A list of dishes to be served or available for a meal. **2.** A list or display of options, esp. as displayed on a computer screen. [< OFr. *menut*, small. See MINUTE[2].]

men•u-driv•en (mĕn′yo͞o-drĭv′ən) ▸*adj.* *Comp. Sci.* Relating to a GUI in which commands are issued by making selections from menus.

me•ow (mē-ou′) ▸*n.* *Informal* The cry of a cat. [Imit.] —**me•ow′** *v.*

me•phi•tis (mə-fī′tĭs) ▸*n.* **1.** An offensive smell; stench. **2.** A foul-smelling gas emitted from the earth. [Lat. *mephītis.*] —**me•phit′ic** (-fĭt′ĭk) *adj.*

mer. ▸*abbr.* meridian

-mer ▸*suff.* Part; segment: *monomer.* [< Gk. *meros*, part.]

mer•can•tile (mûr′kən-tēl′, -tīl′, -tĭl) ▸*adj.* Of or relating to merchants or trade. [< Ital. < *mercante*, MERCHANT.]

Mer•ca•tor (mər-kā′tər), **Gerhardus.** 1512–94. Flemish cartographer.

mer•ce•nar•y (mûr′sə-nĕr′ē) ▸*adj.* **1.** Motivated by a desire for monetary or material gain. **2.** Hired for service in a foreign army. [< Lat. *mercēnārius* < *mercēs*, wages.] —**mer′ce•nar′y** *n.*

mer•cer (mûr′sər) ▸*n.* *Chiefly Brit.* A dealer in textiles. [< Lat. *merx*, *merc-*, merchandise.]

mer•cer•ize (mûr′sə-rīz′) ▸*v.* **-ized, -iz•ing.** To treat (cotton thread) with sodium hydroxide so as to shrink the fiber and increase its luster and affinity for dye. [After John *Mercer* (1791–1866).]

mer•chan•dise (mûr′chən-dīz′, -dīs′) ▸*n.* Goods bought and sold in business; commercial wares. ▸*v.* (-dīz′) **-dised, -dis•ing 1.** To buy and sell (goods). **2.** To promote merchandise sales. [< OFr. *marchand*, MERCHANT.] —**mer′chan•dis′er** *n.*

mer•chant (mûr′chənt) ▸*n.* **1.** One whose occupation is buying and selling goods for profit. **2.** A shopkeeper. [< Lat. *mercārī*, to trade.]

mer•chant•man (mûr′chənt-mən) ▸*n.* A ship used in commerce.

merchant marine ▸*n.* **1.** A nation's commercial ships. **2.** The personnel of the merchant marine.

Mer•ci•a (mûr′shē-ə, -shə) An Anglo-Saxon kingdom of central England (about A.D. 500–874). —**Mer′ci•an** *adj.* & *n.*

mer•ci•ful (mûr′sĭ-fəl) ▸*adj.* Full of mercy; compassionate. See Syns at **humane.** —**mer′ci•ful•ly** *adv.* —**mer′ci•ful•ness** *n.*

mer•cu•ri•al (mər-kyo͝or′ē-əl) ▸*adj.* **1.** Containing or caused by the action of the element mercury. **2.** Quick and changeable in temperament; volatile. [< Lat. *Mercurius*, Mercury.] —**mer•cu′ri•al•ly** *adv.*

mer•cu•ric (mər-kyo͝or′ĭk) ▸*adj.* Relating to or containing bivalent mercury.

mer•cu•rous (mər-kyo͝or′əs, mûr′kyər-əs) ▸*adj.* Of or containing monovalent mercury.

mer•cu•ry (mûr′kyə-rē) ▸*n.* **1.** *Symbol* **Hg** A silvery-white poisonous metallic element, liquid at room temperature, used in thermometers and batteries. At. no. 80. See table at **element.** **2.** Temperature: *The mercury fell overnight.* [< Lat. *Mercurius*, Mercury.]

Mercury ▸*n.* **1.** *Rom. Myth.* A god that served as messenger to the other gods and was himself the god of commerce, travel, and thievery. **2.** The smallest of the planets and the one nearest the sun, at a mean distance of 58.3 million km (36.2 million mi) and a mean radius of approx. 2,414 km (1,500 mi).

mer•cy (mûr′sē) ▸*n.*, *pl.* **-cies 1.** Compassionate treatment, esp. of those under one's power. **2.** A disposition to be kind and forgiving. **3.** A blessing. [< Lat. *mercēs*, reward.] —**mer′ci•less** *adj.* —**mer′ci•less•ly** *adv.* —**mer′ci•less•ness** *n.*

mere (mîr) ▸*adj.* *Superl.* **mer•est 1.** Being no more than what is specified: *a mere 50 cents.* **2.** Considered apart from anything else: *shocked by the mere idea.* [< Lat. *merus*, pure.] —**mere′ly** *adv.*

Mer•e•dith (mĕr′ĭ-dĭth), **George.** 1828–1909. British writer.

Meredith, James Howard. b. 1933. Amer. civil rights advocate.

me•ren•gue (mə-rĕng′gā) ▸*n.* A ballroom dance of Dominican and Haitian origin, marked by a sliding step. [< Sp., meringue.]

mer•e•tri•cious (mĕr′ĭ-trĭsh′əs) ▸*adj.* Attracting attention in a vulgar manner. [< Lat. *meretrīx*, prostitute.] —**mer′e•tri′cious•ly** *adv.* —**mer′e•tri′cious•ness** *n.*

mer•gan•ser (mər-găn′sər) ▸*n.* A fish-eating diving duck having a slim hooked bill. [Lat. *mergus*, diver + *ānser*, goose.]

merge (mûrj) ▸*v.* **merged, merg•ing.** To

blend together or cause to be absorbed, esp. in gradual stages. [Lat. *mergere*, plunge.]

merg•er (mûr′jər) ►*n.* The act or an instance of merging, esp. the union of two or more commercial interests or corporations.

Mé•ri•da (mĕ′rē-dä) A city of SE Mexico on the Yucatán Peninsula. Pop. 400,142.

me•rid•i•an (mə-rĭd′ē-ən) ►*n.* **1a.** A great circle on the earth's surface passing through the North and South geographic poles. **b.** Either half of such a circle from pole to pole. **2.** *Astron.* A great circle passing through the two poles of the celestial sphere and the point directly overhead. **3.** The highest point or stage; zenith. **4.** *Regional* See **median strip.** See Regional Note at **neutral ground.** [< Lat. *merīdiēs*, midday.]

me•ringue (mə-răng′) ►*n.* A dessert topping or pastry shell made from stiffly beaten egg whites and sugar. [Fr. *méringue.*]

me•ri•no (mə-rē′nō) ►*n., pl.* **-nos 1.** A breed of sheep having long fine wool. **2.** A soft lightweight fabric made of fine wool. [Sp.]

mer•it (mĕr′ĭt) ►*n.* **1.** Superior quality or worth; excellence. **2.** often **merits** An aspect of character or behavior deserving approval or disapproval. **3. merits a.** *Law* A party's strict legal rights. **b.** The factual content of a matter. ►*v.* To earn; deserve. See Syns at **earn.** [< Lat. *meritus*, p.part. of *merēre*, deserve.] —**mer′it•less** *adj.*

mer•i•to•ri•ous (mĕr′ĭ-tôr′ē-əs, -tōr′-) ►*adj.* Deserving reward or praise; having merit. [< Lat. *meritōrius*, earning money.] —**mer′i•to′ri•ous•ly** *adv.*

mer•maid (mûr′mād′) ►*n.* A legendary sea creature having the head and upper body of a woman and the tail of a fish. [ME : OE *mere*, sea + MAID.]

mer•man (mûr′măn′, -mən) ►*n.* A legendary sea creature having the head and upper body of a man and the tail of a fish. [MER(MAID) + MAN.]

mer•ry (mĕr′ē) ►*adj.* **-ri•er, -ri•est 1.** Full of high-spirited gaiety. **2.** Marked by fun and festivity. [< OE *mirige.*] —**mer′ri•ly** *adv.* —**mer′ri•ment** *n.* —**mer′ri•ness** *n.*

mer•ry-go-round (mĕr′ē-gō-round′) ►*n.* **1.** A revolving circular platform fitted with seats, often in the form of animals, ridden for amusement. **2.** A busy round; whirl.

mer•ry•mak•ing (mĕr′ē-mā′kĭng) ►*n.* **1.** Participation in festive activities. **2.** A festivity; revelry. —**mer′ry•mak′er** *n.*

Mer•sey (mûr′zē) A river of NW England flowing about 113 km (70 mi) to the Irish Sea at Liverpool.

Mer•ton (mûr′tn), **Thomas.** 1915–68. Amer. Trappist monk and writer.

me•sa (mā′sə) ►*n.* A flat-topped elevation with steep sides. [Sp. < Lat. *mēnsa*, table.]

Me•sa (mā′sə) A city of S-central AZ E of Phoenix. Pop. 288,091.

Me•sa•bi Range (mə-sä′bē) A series of low hills in NE MN.

mes•cal (mĕs-kăl′) ►*n.* **1.** See **peyote** 1. **2.** A Mexican liquor distilled from fermented agave juice. **3.** See **maguey** 1. [< Nahuatl *mexcalli*, liquor made from agave.]

mes•ca•line (mĕs′kə-lēn′, -lĭn) ►*n.* A hallucinogenic alkaloid drug, obtained from peyote buttons.

mesa
Arizona landscape

mes•clun (mĕs′klən) ►*n.* A mixture of young leafy greens used as salad. [Provençal *mesclom*, mixture.]

Mes•dames (mā-däm′, -dăm′) ►*n.* **1.** Pl. of **Madam** 1. **2.** Pl. of **Madame.**

Mes•de•moi•selles (mād′mwä-zĕl′) ►*n.* Pl. of **Mademoiselle.**

mes•en•ceph•a•lon (mĕz′ĕn-sĕf′ə-lŏn′, mĕs′-) ►*n.* The midbrain. —**mes′en•ce•phal′ic** (-sə-făl′ĭk) *adj.*

mesh (mĕsh) ►*n.* **1.** Any of the open spaces in a net or network. **2.** A net or network: *a screen made of wire mesh.* **3.** The engagement of gear teeth. ►*v.* **1.** To ensnare. **2.** To engage or cause (gear teeth) to become engaged. **3.** To fit together harmoniously; be coordinated. [Prob. < MDu. *maesche.*]

Me•shed (mĕ-shĕd′) See **Mashhad.**

mes•mer•ize (mĕz′mə-rīz′, mĕs′-) ►*v.* **-ized, -iz•ing.** To hypnotize. [After Franz *Mesmer* (1734–1815).] —**mes′mer•ism′** *n.* —**mes′mer•ist** *n.* —**mes′mer•iz′er** *n.*

meso– or **mes–** ►*pref.* Middle: *mesosphere.* [< Gk. *mesos.*]

Mes•o•a•mer•i•ca (mĕz′ō-ə-mĕr′ĭ-kə, mĕs′-) A region extending S and E from central Mexico to include parts of Guatemala, Belize, Honduras, and Nicaragua. —**Mes′o•a•mer′i•can** *adj. & n.*

Mes•o•lith•ic (mĕz′ə-lĭth′ĭk, mĕs′-) ►*adj.* Of or being the Stone Age period between the Paleolithic and Neolithic, marked by the appearance of microlithic tools and weapons. ►*n.* The Mesolithic Period.

mes•on (mĕz′ŏn′, mĕs′-) ►*n.* Any of a family of subatomic particles that participate in strong interactions and are composed of a quark and an antiquark.

Mes•o•po•ta•mi•a (mĕs′ə-pə-tā′mē-ə) An ancient region of SW Asia between the Tigris and Euphrates rivers in modern-day Iraq. —**Mes′o•po•ta′mi•an** *adj. & n.*

mes•o•sphere (mĕz′ə-sfîr′, mĕs′-) ►*n.* The portion of the atmosphere from about 30 to 80 km (20 to 50 mi) above the earth's surface. —**mes′o•spher′ic** (-sfîr′ĭk, -sfĕr′-) *adj.*

Mes•o•zo•ic (mĕz′ə-zō′ĭk, mĕs′-) ►*adj.* Of or being the 3rd geologic era, including the Cretaceous, Jurassic, and Triassic periods and marked esp. by the appearance and extinction of dinosaurs. ►*n.* The Mesozoic Era.

mes•quite (mĕ-skēt′, mə-) ►*n.* A small spiny shrub native to hot dry regions of North America. [< Nahuatl *mizquitl.*]

Mes•quite (mə-skēt′, mĕ-) A city of NE TX, a suburb of Dallas. Pop. 101,484.

mess (měs) ►*n.* **1.** A disorderly or dirty accumulation, heap, or jumble. **2.** A confused or troubling condition. **3.** An unspecified amount of food, as for a meal: *a mess of fish.* **4a.** A group, as of soldiers, that regularly eats meals together. **b.** Food served to such a group. ►*v.* **1.** To make disorderly or soiled. **2.** To botch; bungle. **3.** To interfere: *messing in our affairs.* [< Lat. *missus*, course of meal.]

mes•sage (měs′ĭj) ►*n.* **1.** A usu. short communication transmitted from one person or group to another. **2.** A lesson or moral. [< Med.Lat. *missāticum* < Lat. *missus*, sent.]

mes•sen•ger (měs′ən-jər) ►*n.* One that carries messages or performs errands. [< OFr. *messagier* < *message*, MESSAGE.]

Mes•si•ah (mĭ-sī′ə) ►*n.* **1.** also **Mes•si•as** (mĭ-sī′əs) The anticipated deliverer and king of the Jews. **2.** also **Messias** *Christianity* Jesus. **3. messiah** An expected savior or liberator. [< Aram. *məšiḥā* or Heb. *māšîaḥ*, anointed.] —**Mes′si•an′ic** (měs′ē-ăn′ĭk) *adj.*

Mes•sieurs (mā-syœ′) ►*n.* Pl. of **Monsieur.**

Mes•si•na (mĭ-sē′nə, mě-) A city of NE Sicily, Italy, on the **Strait of Messina,** a channel separating Sicily from Italy. Pop. 255,890.

Messrs.[1] (měs′ərz) ►*n.* Pl. of **Mr.**

Messrs.[2] ►*abbr.* Messieurs

mess•y (měs′ē) ►*adj.* **-i•er, -i•est 1.** Disorderly and dirty. **2.** Unpleasantly difficult to settle or resolve: *a messy court case.* —**mess′i•ly** *adv.* —**mess′i•ness** *n.*

mes•ti•zo (měs-tē′zō) ►*n., pl.* **-zos** or **-zoes.** A person of mixed racial ancestry, esp. of European and Native American ancestry. [< LLat. *mixtīcius*, mixed.]

met (mět) ►*v.* P.t. and p.part. of **meet**[1]**.**

meta– or **met–** ►*pref.* **1.** Change; transformation: *metastasis.* **2.** Situated behind: *metacarpus.* [< Gk. *meta*, beside, after.]

me•tab•o•lism (mĭ-tăb′ə-lĭz′əm) ►*n.* **1.** The physical and chemical processes occurring within a living cell or organism that are necessary for life. **2.** The functioning of a specific substance within the body: *iodine metabolism.* [< Gk. *metabolē*, change.] —**met′a•bol′ic** (mĕt′ə-bŏl′ĭk) *adj.* —**met′a•bol′i•cal•ly** *adv.* —**me•tab′o•lize′** *v.*

me•tab•o•lite (mĭ-tăb′ə-līt′) ►*n.* A substance produced by metabolism. [METABOL(ISM) + –ITE[1].]

met•a•car•pus (mĕt′ə-kär′pəs) ►*n., pl.* **-pi** (-pī) **1.** The part of the human hand that includes the five bones between the fingers and the wrist. **2.** The corresponding part of the forefoot of a quadruped.

Met•a•com (mĕt′ə-kŏm′). d. 1676. Wampanoag leader.

met•al (mĕt′l) ►*n.* **1.** Any of a category of elements that usu. have a shiny surface, are gen. good conductors of heat and electricity, and can be melted or fused, hammered into thin sheets, or drawn into wires. **2.** An alloy of two or more metals. **3.** Basic character; mettle. **4.** *Mus.* Heavy metal. [< Gk. *metallon.*] —**me•tal′lic** (mə-tăl′ĭk) *adj.* —**me•tal′li•cal•ly** *adv.*

metallic bond ►*n.* The chemical bond characteristic of metals, in which mobile valence electrons are shared among atoms in a usu. stable crystalline structure.

met•al•lur•gy (mĕt′l-ûr′jē) ►*n.* The science that deals with extracting metals from their ores and creating useful objects from them. [< Gk. *metallourgos*, miner : *metallon*, metal + *ergon*, work.] —**met′al•lur′gic, met′al•lur′gi•cal** *adj.* —**met′al•lur′gist** *n.*

met•al•work (mĕt′l-wûrk′) ►*n.* Work done in metal. —**met′al•work′er** *n.*

met•a•mor•phic (mĕt′ə-môr′fĭk) ►*adj.* **1.** also **met•a•mor•phous** (-fəs) Of metamorphosis. **2.** *Geol.* Changed in structure or composition as a result of metamorphism.

met•a•mor•phism (mĕt′ə-môr′fĭz′əm) ►*n.* *Geol.* The process by which rocks are altered in composition, texture, or structure by heat, pressure, and chemical action.

met•a•mor•phose (mĕt′ə-môr′fōz′, -fōs′) ►*v.* **-phosed, -phos•ing.** To change by metamorphosis. See Syns at **convert.**

met•a•mor•pho•sis (mĕt′ə-môr′fə-sĭs) ►*n., pl.* **-ses** (-sēz′) **1.** A transformation, as by magic or sorcery. **2.** A marked change in appearance, character, condition, or function. **3.** *Biol.* A change in form and often habits during development after the embryonic stage, as in insects. [< Gk. *metamorphōsis.*]

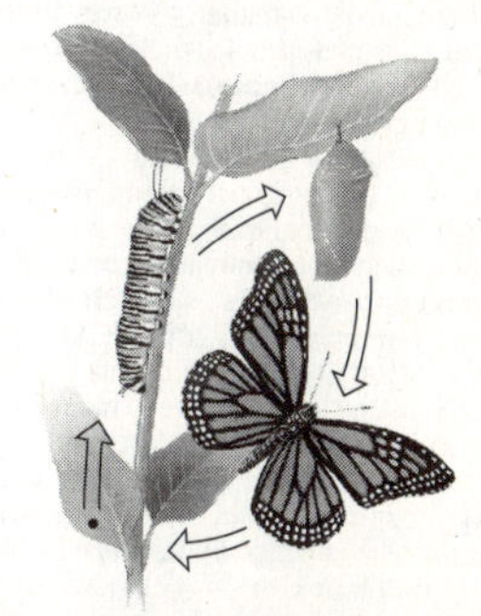

metamorphosis
development of a monarch butterfly

met•a•phor (mĕt′ə-fôr′, -fər) ►*n.* A figure of speech in which a word or phrase that ordinarily designates one thing is used to designate another, thus making an implicit comparison, as in *the evening of life.* [< Gk. *metaphora* : META– + *pherein*, carry.] —**met′a•phor′ic** (-fôr′ĭk, -fŏr′-), **met′a•phor′i•cal** *adj.* —**met′a•phor′i•cal•ly** *adv.*

met•a•phys•i•cal (mĕt′ə-fĭz′ĭ-kəl) ►*adj.* **1.** Of or relating to metaphysics. **2.** Based on speculative or abstract reasoning. **3.** Abstruse. —**met′a•phys′i•cal•ly** *adv.*

met•a•phys•ics (mĕt′ə-fĭz′ĭks) ►*n.* *(takes sing. v.)* The branch of philosophy that examines the nature of reality and the relationship between mind and matter. [< Med.Gk. *metaphusika*, title of Artistotle's treatise on the subject.] —**met′a•phy•si′cian** (-fĭ-zĭsh′ən) *n.*

me•tas•ta•sis (mə-tăs′tə-sĭs) ►*n., pl.* **-ses** (-sēz′). The spreading of a disease from an original site to one or more sites elsewhere in the body. —**me•tas′ta•size′** *v.* —**met′a•stat′ic** (mĕt′ə-stăt′ĭk) *adj.* —**met′a•stat′i•cal•ly** *adv.*

met•a•tar•sus (mĕt′ə-tär′səs) ►*n., pl.* **-si** (-sī, -sē). The middle part of the foot, composed of the five bones between the toes and tarsus, that forms the instep. —**met′a•tar′sal** *adj.*

mete (mēt) ►*v.* **met•ed, met•ing.** To dole; allot: *mete out punishment.* [< OE *metan.*]

me•tem•psy•cho•sis (mə-tĕm′sĭ-kō′sĭs, mĕt′əm-sī-) ►*n., pl.* **-ses** (-sēz). Reincarnation. [< Gk. *metempsukhōsis.*]

me•te•or (mē′tē-ər, -ôr′) ►*n.* A bright trail or streak that appears in the sky when a meteoroid is heated to incandescence by friction with the earth's atmosphere. [< Gk. *meteōros*, high in the air.]

me•te•or•ic (mē′tē-ôr′ĭk, -ŏr′-) ►*adj.* **1.** Of or formed by a meteoroid. **2.** Similar to a meteor in speed or brilliance: *a meteoric rise to fame.* —**me′te•or′i•cal•ly** *adv.*

me•te•or•ite (mē′tē-ə-rīt′) ►*n.* A stony or metallic mass of matter that has fallen to the earth's surface from outer space. —**me′te•or•it′ic** (-ə-rĭt′ĭk), **me′te•or•it′i•cal** *adj.*

me•te•or•oid (mē′tē-ə-roid′) ►*n.* A solid body, moving in space, that is smaller than an asteroid and at least as large as a speck of dust.

me•te•or•ol•o•gy (mē′tē-ə-rŏl′ə-jē) ►*n.* The science that deals with the phenomena of the atmosphere, esp. weather. —**me′te•or•o•log′i•cal** (-ər-ə-lŏj′ĭ-kəl), **me′te•or•o•log′ic** *adj.* —**me′te•or•o•log′i•cal•ly** *adv.* —**me′te•or•ol′o•gist** *n.*

me•ter[1] (mē′tər) ►*n.* **1a.** The measured arrangement of words in poetry, as by accentual rhythm. **b.** A particular arrangement of words in a poem, such as iambic pentameter. **2.** *Mus.* **a.** Division into measures or bars. **b.** A specific rhythm in a measure. [ME, ult. < Gk. *metron.*]

me•ter[2] (mē′tər) ►*n.* See table at **measurement.** [Fr. *mètre* < Gk. *metron*, measure.]

me•ter[3] (mē′tər) ►*n.* Any of various devices that measure or indicate and record or regulate. ►*v.* **1.** To measure or regulate with a meter. **2.** To imprint with postage by means of a postage meter or similar device. [< -METER.]

-meter ►*suff.* Measuring device: *thermometer* [< Gk. *metron*, measure.]

me•ter-kil•o•gram-sec•ond (mē′tər-kĭl′ə-grăm-sĕk′ənd) ►*adj.* Of or relating to a system of units for mechanics, using the meter, the kilogram, and the second as basic units of length, mass, and time.

meth•a•done (mĕth′ə-dōn′) ►*n.* A potent synthetic narcotic drug, $C_{21}H_{27}NO$, used in addiction treatment programs.

meth•am•phet•a•mine (mĕth′ăm-fĕt′ə-mēn′, -mĭn) ►*n.* An amine derivative of amphetamine used in the form of its crystalline hydrochloride as a stimulant.

meth•ane (mĕth′ān′) ►*n.* An odorless, colorless, flammable gas, CH_4, the major constituent of natural gas, used as a fuel and an important source of organic compounds. [METH(YL) + -ANE.]

meth•a•nol (mĕth′ə-nôl′, -nōl′, -nŏl′) ►*n.* A colorless, toxic, flammable liquid, CH_3OH, used as an antifreeze, solvent, fuel, and denaturant for ethyl alcohol.

meth•od (mĕth′əd) ►*n.* **1.** A systematic means or manner of procedure. **2.** Orderly arrangement of parts or steps to accomplish an end. [< Gk. *methodos.*] —**me•thod′i•cal** (mə-thŏd′ĭ-kəl), **me•thod′ic** *adj.* —**me•thod′i•cal•ly** *adv.*

Meth•od•ist (mĕth′ə-dĭst) ►*n.* A member of an evangelical Protestant church founded on the principles of John and Charles Wesley. —**Meth′od•ism** *n.* —**Meth′od•is′tic** *adj.*

meth•od•ol•o•gy (mĕth′ə-dŏl′ə-jē) ►*n., pl.* **-gies 1.** A body of practices, procedures, and rules used in a discipline. **2.** The branch of logic that deals with the general principles of the formation of knowledge. —**meth′od•o•log′i•cal** (-ə-də-lŏj′ĭ-kəl) *adj.* —**meth′od•o•log′i•cal•ly** *adv.*

Me•thu•se•lah (mə-thōō′zə-lə). A biblical patriarch said to have lived 969 years.

meth•yl (mĕth′əl) ►*n.* The univalent hydrocarbon radical, CH_3^-. [Ult. < Gk. *methu*, wine.] —**me•thyl′ic** (mə-thĭl′ĭk) *adj.*

methyl alcohol ►*n.* See **methanol.**

meth•yl•at•ed spirit (mĕth′ə-lā′tĭd) ►*n.* A denatured alcohol consisting of a mixture of ethanol and methanol. Often used in the plural.

met•i•cal (mĕt′ĭ-kăl′, mĕt′ĭ-käl′) ►*n.* See table at **currency.** [< Ar. *miṯqāl*, a unit of weight.]

me•tic•u•lous (mĭ-tĭk′yə-ləs) ►*adj.* Extremely or excessively careful and precise. [< Lat. *metīculōsus*, timid < *metus*, fear.] —**me•tic′u•los′i•ty** (-lŏs′ĭ-tē), **me•tic′u•lous•ness** *n.* —**me•tic′u•lous•ly** *adv.*

mé•tier (mĕ-tyā′, mā-) ►*n.* **1.** A trade or profession. **2.** One's specialty. See Syns at **forte**[1]. [< Lat. *ministērium*, ministry.]

me•ton•y•my (mə-tŏn′ə-mē) ►*n., pl.* **-mies.** A figure of speech in which one word or phrase is substituted for another with which it is closely associated, as in the use of *Washington* for *the US government.* [Gk. *metōnumia.*] —**met′o•nym′** (mĕt′ə-nĭm′) *n.* —**met′o•nym′ic, met′o•nym′i•cal** *adj.*

me•tre (mē′tər) ►*n. Chiefly Brit.* **1.**Var. of **meter**[1]. **2.**Var. of **meter**[2].

met•ric (mĕt′rĭk) ►*adj.* Of or relating to the metric system.

met•ri•cal (mĕt′rĭ-kəl) ►*adj.* **1.** Of or composed in poetic meter: *metrical verse.* **2.** Of or relating to measurement. [< Gk. *metrikos.*] —**met′ri•cal•ly** *adv.*

met•ri•ca•tion (mĕt′rĭ-kā′shən) ►*n.* Conversion to the metric system of weights and measures.

met•rics (mĕt′rĭks) ►*n.* *(takes sing. v.)* The study of poetic meter; prosody.

metric system ►*n.* A decimal system of units based on the meter as a unit length, the kilogram as a unit mass, and the second as a unit time. See table at **measurement.**

metric ton ►*n.* See table at **measurement.**

met•ro•nome (mĕt′rə-nōm′) ►*n. Mus.* An adjustable device used to mark time at precise intervals. [Gk. *metron*, measure + *nomos*, division.] —**met′ro•nom′ic** (mĕt′rə-nŏm′ĭk) *adj.*

me•trop•o•lis (mĭ-trŏp′ə-lĭs) ►*n.* **1.** A major city, esp. the chief city of a country or region. **2.** A city or an urban area regarded as the center of a specific activity. [< Gk. *mētropolis*, mother city.] —**met′ro•pol′i•tan** (mĕt′rə-pŏl′ĭ-tən) *adj. & n.*

-metry ►*suff.* Process or science of measuring: *photometry.* [< Gk. *metron*, measure.]

Met•ter•nich (mĕt′ər-nĭk, -nĭKH), Prince **Klemens Wenzel Nepomuk Lothar von.** 1773–1859. Austrian politician.

met•tle (mĕt′l) ►*n.* **1.** Courage and fortitude; spirit. **2.** Quality of character and temperament.

[< METAL.] —**met′tle•some** *adj.*

Meuse (myo͞oz, mœz) A river of W Europe flowing about 901 km (560 mi) from NE France through S Belgium and the SE Netherlands to the North Sea.

MeV ►*abbr.* **1.** mega-electron volt **2.** or **mev** million electron volts

mew (myo͞o) ►*v.* To make the cry of a cat; meow. [ME *meuen.*] —**mew** *n.*

mews (myo͞oz) ►*pl.n. (takes sing. or pl. v.)* A small street or alley orig. with private stables, often converted into residential apartments. [< OFr. *mue* < *muer*, molt.]

Mex. ►*abbr.* **1.** Mexican **2.** Mexico

Mex•i•cal•i (mĕk′sĭ-kăl′ē) A city of NW Mexico near the CA border E of Tijuana. Pop. 341,559.

Mexican American ►*n.* A US citizen or resident of Mexican descent. —**Mex′i•can-A•mer′i•can** *adj.*

Mex•i•co (mĕk′sĭ-kō′) A country of S-central North America. Cap. Mexico City. Pop. 93,008,000. —**Mex′i•can** (-kən) *adj. & n.*

Mexico, Gulf of. An arm of the Atlantic in SE North America bordering on E Mexico, the SE US, and Cuba.

Mexico City. The capital of Mexico, at the S end of the central plateau. Pop. 8,235,744.

Mey•er•beer (mī′ər-bîr′), **Giacomo.** 1791–1864. German composer of French operas.

mez•za•nine (mĕz′ə-nēn′, mĕz′ə-nēn′) ►*n.* **1.** A partial story between two main stories of a building. **2.** The lowest balcony in a theater or its first few rows. [< Ital. *mezzanino* < Lat. *mediānus*, in the middle.]

mez•zo-so•pran•o (mĕt′sō-sə-prăn′ō, -prä′nō, mĕd′zō-) ►*n., pl.* **-os 1.** A woman's singing voice having a range between soprano and contralto. **2.** A woman having a mezzo-soprano voice. [Ital.]

MFA ►*abbr.* Master of Fine Arts

mfg. ►*abbr.* manufacturing

mg ►*abbr.* milligram

Mg ► Symbol for the element **magnesium.**

mgt. ►*abbr.* management

MHz ►*abbr.* megahertz

mi (mē) ►*n. Mus.* The 3rd tone of the diatonic scale. [< Med.Lat.]

MI ►*abbr.* **1.** Michigan **2.** military intelligence **3.** myocardial infarction

mi. or **mi** ►*abbr.* mile

MIA (ĕm′ī-ā′) ►*n.* A member of the armed services reported missing in action. [*m(issing) i(n) a(ction).*]

Mi•am•i (mī-ăm′ē, -ăm′ə) A city of SE FL on Biscayne Bay S of Fort Lauderdale. Pop. 358,548.

Miami Beach. A city of SE FL across from Miami on an island between Biscayne Bay and the Atlantic. Pop. 92,639.

mi•as•ma (mī-ăz′mə, mē-) ►*n., pl.* **-mas** or **-ma•ta** (-mə-tə) **1.** A noxious atmosphere or influence. **2.** A poisonous vapor formerly thought to rise from swamps and putrid matter and cause disease. [Gk. < *miainein*, pollute.] —**mi•as′mal, mi•as′mic** *adj.*

mi•ca (mī′kə) ►*n.* Any of a group of chemically and physically related silicate minerals, common in igneous and metamorphic rocks. [< Lat. *mīca*, grain.]

Mi•cah (mī′kə) also **Mi•che•as** (mī-kē′əs) ►*n.* **1.** A Hebrew prophet of the 8th cent. B.C. **2.** See table at **Bible.**

mice (mīs) ►*n.* Pl. of **mouse.**

Mich. ►*abbr.* Michigan

Mi•chel•an•ge•lo Buo•nar•ro•ti (mī′kəl-ăn′jə-lō′ bwôn′ə-rô′tē, mĭk′-, mē′kĕl-än′jĕ-lō bwō′är-rō′tē). 1475–1564. Italian sculptor, painter, architect, and poet.

Mich•i•gan (mĭsh′ĭ-gən) A state of the N-central US. Cap. Lansing. Pop. 9,328,784.

Michigan, Lake. The third largest of the Great Lakes, between WI and MI.

Mic•mac (mĭk′măk′) ►*n., pl.* **-mac** or **-macs 1.** A member of a Native American people of E Canada. **2.** The Algonquian language of the Micmac.

mi•cra (mī′krə) ►*n.* Pl. of **micron.**

mi•cro (mī′krō) ►*adj.* Basic or small-scale: *the economy's performance at the micro level.* [< MICRO–.]

micro– or **micr–** ►*pref.* **1a.** Small: *microcircuit.* **b.** Abnormally small: *microcephaly.* **c.** Requiring or involving microscopy: *microsurgery.* **2.** One-millionth (10^{-6}): *microsecond.* [< Gk. *mikros*, small.]

mi•crobe (mī′krōb′) ►*n.* A microorganism. [Fr. : MICRO– + Gk. *bios*, life.] —**mi•cro′bi•al** (-krō′bē-əl) *adj.*

mi•cro•bi•ol•o•gy (mī′krō-bī-ŏl′ə-jē) ►*n.* The branch of biology that deals with microorganisms. —**mi′cro•bi′o•log′i•cal** (-bī′ə-lŏj′ĭ-kəl) *adj.* —**mi′cro•bi′o•log′i•cal•ly** *adv.* —**mi′cro•bi•ol′o•gist** *n.*

mi•cro•brew (mī′krō-bro͞o′) ►*n.* A beer or ale brewed in a microbrewery.

mi•cro•brew•e•ry (mī′krō-bro͞o′ə-rē, -bro͝or′ē) ►*n.* A small brewery, often selling its products on the premises. —**mi′cro•brew′** *n.* —**mi′cro•brew′er** *n.*

mi•cro•bus (mī′krō-bŭs′) ►*n.* A station wagon in the shape of a small bus.

mi•cro•ceph•a•ly (mī′krō-sĕf′ə-lē) ►*n.* Abnormal smallness of the head. [MICRO– + Gk. *kephalē*, head + –Y[2].] —**mi′cro•ce•phal′ic** (-sə-făl′ĭk) *adj. & n.* —**mi′cro•ceph′a•lous** *adj.*

mi•cro•chip (mī′krə-chĭp′) ►*n. Comp. Sci.* See **chip** 4a.

mi•cro•cir•cuit (mī′krō-sûr′kĭt) ►*n.* An electric circuit consisting of miniaturized components. —**mi′cro•cir′cuit•ry** *n.*

mi•cro•com•put•er (mī′krō-kəm-pyo͞o′tər) ►*n.* A personal computer.

mi•cro•cosm (mī′krə-kŏz′əm) ►*n.* A small, representative system having analogies to a larger system in constitution, configuration, or development. [< Gk. *mikros kosmos*, small world.] —**mi′cro•cos′mic** (-kŏz′mĭk), **mi′cro•cos′mi•cal** *adj.*

mi•cro•dot (mī′krə-dŏt′) ►*n.* A copy or photograph reduced to an extremely small size.

mi•cro•ec•o•nom•ics (mī′krō-ĕk′ə-nŏm′ĭks, -ēk′ə-) ►*n. (takes sing. v.)* The study of specific components of a national economy, such as individual firms, households, and consumers. —**mi′cro•ec′o•nom′ic** *adj.*

mi•cro•e•lec•tron•ics (mī′krō-ĭ-lĕk-trŏn′ĭks) ►*n. (takes sing. v.)* The branch of electronics that deals with miniature components. —**mi′cro•e•lec•tron′ic** *adj.*

mi•cro•fiche (mī′krō-fēsh′) ►*n., pl.* **-fiche** or **-fich•es.** A sheet of microfilm containing rows of pages in reduced form. [Fr.]

mi•cro•film (mī′krə-fĭlm′) ►*n.* A film on which printed materials are photographed greatly reduced in size. —**mi′cro•film′** *v.*

mi•cro•lith (mī′krō-lĭth′) ►*n.* *Archaeol.* A very small blade made of flaked stone. —**mi′cro•lith′ic** (-lĭth′ĭk) *adj.*

mi•cro•man•age (mī′krō-măn′ĭj) ►*v.* To direct or control in a detailed, often meddlesome manner.

mi•crom•e•ter (mī-krŏm′ĭ-tər) ►*n.* A device for measuring very small distances.

mi•cron (mī′krŏn′) ►*n.*, *pl.* **-crons** or **-cra** (-krə). A unit of length equal to one millionth (10^{-6}) of a meter. No longer in technical use. [< Gk. *mikros*, small.]

Mi•cro•ne•si•a (mī′krō-nē′zhə, -shə) The islands of the W Pacific, E of the Philippines and N of the equator.

Mi•cro•ne•sian (mī′krə-nē′zhən, -shən) ►*n.* **1.** A member of any of the peoples inhabiting Micronesia. **2.** A subfamily of the Austronesian language family. —**Mi′cro•ne′sian** *adj.*

mi•cro•or•gan•ism (mī′krō-ôr′gə-nĭz′əm) ►*n.* An organism of microscopic size, esp. a bacterium or protozoan.

mi•cro•phone (mī′krə-fōn′) ►*n.* An instrument that converts sound waves into an electric current, usu. fed into an amplifier, recorder, or broadcast transmitter.

mi•cro•proc•es•sor (mī′krō-prŏs′ĕs-ər) ►*n.* An integrated circuit that contains the entire central processing unit of a computer on a single chip.

mi•cro•scope (mī′krə-skōp′) ►*n.* An optical instrument that uses a combination of lenses to produce magnified images of small objects, esp. of objects too small to be seen by the unaided eye.

mi•cro•scop•ic (mī′krə-skŏp′ĭk) also **mi•cro•scop•i•cal** (-ĭ-kəl) ►*adj.* **1.** Relating to microscopes. **2a.** So small as to require a microscope for viewing. **b.** Tiny; minute. —**mi′cro•scop′i•cal•ly** *adv.*

mi•cros•co•py (mī-krŏs′kə-pē) ►*n.* **1.** The study or use of microscopes. **2.** Investigation employing a microscope.

mi•cro•sec•ond (mī′krō-sĕk′ənd) ►*n.* One millionth (10^{-6}) of a second.

mi•cro•sur•ger•y (mī′krō-sûr′jə-rē) ►*n.* Surgery on minute body structures or cells performed with the aid of microscopes. —**mi′cro•sur′gi•cal** *adj.*

mi•cro•wave (mī′krə-wāv′, -krō-) ►*n.* **1.** An electromagnetic wave intermediate between infrared and short-wave radio wavelengths. **2.** *Informal* A microwave oven. —**mi′cro•wav′a•ble, mi′cro•wave′a•ble** *adj.* —**mi′cro•wave′** *v.*

microwave oven ►*n.* An oven in which microwaves cook the food.

mid (mĭd) ►*adj.* Middle; central. [< OE *midd.*]

mid– ►*pref.* Middle: *midsummer.* [< MID.]

mid•air (mĭd′âr′) ►*n.* A point or region in the air. —**mid′air′** *adj.*

Mi•das (mī′dəs) ►*n.* A fabled king who turned all that he touched to gold.

mid•day (mĭd′dā′) ►*n.* Noon. —**mid′day′** *adj.*

mid•den (mĭd′n) ►*n.* A refuse heap. [ME *midding*, of Scand. orig.]

mid•dle (mĭd′l) ►*adj.* **1.** Equally distant from extremes or limits. **2.** Intermediate; in-between. **3.** Intervening between an earlier and a later period of time. ►*n.* **1.** An area or a point equidistant between extremes. **2.** The waist. [< OE *middel.*]

middle age ►*n.* The time of human life gen. between 40 and 60. —**mid′dle-aged′** *adj.*

Middle Ages ►*pl.n.* The period in European history between antiquity and the Renaissance, often dated from A.D. 476 to 1453.

Middle America ►*n.* **1.** That part of the US middle class thought of as being conservative in values and attitudes. **2.** The American heartland thought of as being made up of small towns, small cities, and suburbs.

middle class ►*n.* The members of society occupying a socioeconomic position between the lower working classes and the wealthy.

Middle Dutch ►*n.* Dutch from the middle of the 12th through the 15th cent.

middle ear ►*n.* The space between the eardrum and the inner ear that contains the malleus, incus, and stapes.

Middle East also **Mid•east** (mĭd-ēst′). An area comprising the countries of SW Asia and NE Africa. —**Middle Eastern** *adj.* —**Middle Easterner** *n.*

Middle English ►*n.* English from about 1100 to 1500.

middle ground ►*n.* A point of view midway between extremes.

Middle High German ►*n.* High German from the 11th through the 15th cent.

Middle Low German ►*n.* Low German from the mid-13th through the 15th cent.

mid•dle•man (mĭd′l-măn′) ►*n.* **1.** A trader who buys from producers and sells to retailers or consumers. **2.** A go-between.

middle management ►*n.* A group of persons occupying intermediate managerial positions. —**middle manager** *n.*

mid•dle-of-the-road (mĭd′l-əv-thə-rōd′) ►*adj.* Pursuing a course of action midway between extremes, esp. in politics.

middle school ►*n.* A school typically including grades five or six through eight.

mid•dle•weight (mĭd′l-wāt′) ►*n.* A boxer weighing from 148 to 160 lbs., between a welterweight and a light heavyweight.

Middle West. See **Midwest.** —**Middle Western** *adj.* —**Middle Westerner** *n.*

mid•dling (mĭd′lĭng, -lĭn) ►*adj.* **1.** Of medium size, position, or quality. **2.** Mediocre. ►*adv.* *Informal* Fairly; moderately. [ME *midlin.*] —**mid′dling•ly** *adv.*

mid•dy (mĭd′ē) ►*n.*, *pl.* **-dies 1.** A midshipman. **2.** A loose blouse with a sailor collar.

Mid•east (mĭd-ēst′) See **Middle East.** —**Mid•east′ern** *adj.* —**Mid•east′ern•er** *n.*

midge (mĭj) ►*n.* A gnatlike fly. [< OE *mycg.*]

midg•et (mĭj′ĭt) ►*n.* **1.** *Offensive* An unusually small or short person of otherwise normal proportions. **2.** A miniature version of something. —**midg′et** *adj.*

MIDI (mĭd′ē) ►*n.* A standard for representing musical information in a digital format. [*M(usical) I(nstrument) D(igital) I(nterface).*]

mid•land (mĭd′lənd) ►*n.* The middle part of a country or region. —**mid′land** *adj.*

Mid•lands (mĭd′ləndz) A region of central England.

mid•line (mĭd′līn′) ►*n.* A medial line, esp. the medial line of the body.

mid•night (mĭd′nīt′) ►*n.* The middle of the night; 12 o'clock at night. See Usage Note at **ante meridiem.**

midnight sun ►*n.* The sun as seen at midnight during the summer within the Arctic and Antarctic regions.

mid•point (mĭd′point′) ►*n.* A point or position at or near the middle.

mid•riff (mĭd′rĭf) ►*n.* **1.** See **diaphragm** 1. **2.** The outer part of the human body from below the breast to the waist. [< OE *midhrif.*]

mid•ship•man (mĭd′shĭp′mən, mĭd-shĭp′mən) ►*n.* A student at a naval academy training to be a commissioned officer.

midst (mĭdst, mĭtst) ►*n.* **1.** The middle position or part; center. **2.** The condition of being surrounded by something: *the midst of chaos.* ►*prep.* Among. [< ME *middes.*]

mid•sum•mer (mĭd′sŭm′ər) ►*n.* **1.** The middle of the summer. **2.** The summer solstice, about Jun. 21. —**mid′sum′mer** *adj.*

mid•term (mĭd′tûrm′) ►*n.* **1.** The middle esp. of an academic or political term. **2.** An examination given at the middle of a school term. —**mid′term′** *adj.*

mid•town (mĭd′toun′) ►*n.* A central portion of a city. —**mid′town′** *adj.*

mid•way (mĭd′wā′) ►*n.* The area of a fair, carnival, or circus where sideshows and other amusements are located. ►*adv.* In the middle; halfway. —**mid′way′** *adj.*

Midway Islands. Two small islands and a surrounding coral atoll in the central Pacific NW of Honolulu.

mid•week (mĭd′wēk′) ►*n.* The middle of the week. —**mid′week′** *adj.* —**mid′week′ly** *adj. & adv.*

Mid•west (mĭd-wĕst′) or **Middle West.** A region of the N-central US around the Great Lakes and the upper Mississippi Valley. —**Mid•west′ern** *adj.* —**Mid•west′ern•er** *n.*

mid•wife (mĭd′wīf′) ►*n., pl.* **-wives** (-wīvz′). A person, usu. a woman, trained to assist women in childbirth. [ME *midwif* : prob. *mid,* with + *wif,* woman.] —**mid•wife′ry** (-wĭf′ə-rē, mĭd′wīf′rē) *n.*

mid•win•ter (mĭd′wĭn′tər) ►*n.* **1.** The middle of the winter. **2.** The winter solstice, about Dec. 22. —**mid′win′ter** *adj.*

mid•year (mĭd′yîr′) ►*n.* **1.** The middle of the calendar or academic year. **2.** An examination given in the middle of a school year. —**mid′-year′** *adj.*

mien (mēn) ►*n.* Bearing or manner; appearance. [< ME *demeine,* DEMEANOR.]

miff (mĭf) ►*v.* To offend; annoy. [?]

might[1] (mīt) ►*n.* **1.** The power or force held by a person or group. **2.** Physical strength. [< OE *miht.*]

might[2] (mīt) ►*aux.v.* P.t. of **may.** Used to indicate a condition contrary to fact, a possibility weaker than *may,* or to express a higher degree of politeness than *may.* [< OE *magan,* be able.]

might•y (mī′tē) ►*adj.* **-i•er, -i•est 1.** Having great power. **2.** Imposing or awesome. ►*adv. Regional* Very: *a mighty hard job.* —**might′i•ly** *adv.* —**might′i•ness** *n.*

mi•graine (mī′grān′) ►*n.* A severe, recurring headache, usu. affecting only one side of the head. [< Gk. *hēmikrania,* pain in half the head.]

mi•grant (mī′grənt) ►*n.* **1.** One that migrates. **2.** A worker who travels from one area to another in search of work. —**mi′grant** *adj.*

mi•grate (mī′grāt′) ►*v.* **-grat•ed, -grat•ing 1.** To move from one country or region and settle in another. **2.** To move periodically from one region or climate to another. [Lat. *migrāre.*] —**mi•gra′tion** *n.* —**mi′gra•to′ry** (-grə-tôr′ē, -tōr′ē) *adj.*

Usage: *Migrate* sometimes implies a lack of permanent settlement, especially as a result of seasonal or periodic movement. *Emigrate* and *immigrate* imply a permanent move, generally across a political boundary. *Emigrate* describes the move relative to the point of departure, while *immigrate* describes the move relative to the destination.

mi•ka•do (mĭ-kä′dō) ►*n., pl.* **-dos.** An emperor of Japan. [J.]

mike (mīk) *Informal* ►*n.* A microphone. ►*v.* **miked, mik•ing.** To supply with or transmit through a microphone.

mil (mĭl) ►*n.* A unit of length equal to one thousandth (10^{-3}) of an inch. [< Lat. *mīllēsimus,* thousandth < *mīlle,* thousand.]

Mi•lan (mĭ-lăn′, -län′) A city of N Italy NE of Genoa. Pop. 1,371,008. —**Mil′a•nese′** (mĭl′ə-nēz′, -nēs′) *adj. & n.*

mild (mīld) ►*adj.* **-er, -est 1.** Gentle or kind in disposition or behavior. **2.** Not harsh, severe, or strong; moderate. [< OE *milde.*] —**mild′ly** *adv.* —**mild′ness** *n.*

mil•dew (mĭl′do͞o′, -dyo͞o′) ►*n.* Any of various fungi that form a usu. whitish growth on plants and materials such as cloth and paper. [< OE *mildēaw.*] —**mil′dew′** *v.*

mile (mīl) ►*n.* **1.** See table at **measurement. 2.** A nautical mile. **3.** An air mile. [< Lat. *mīlia (passuum),* a thousand (paces).]

mile•age (mī′lĭj) ►*n.* **1.** Distance measured or expressed in miles. **2.** Service or wear estimated by miles used or traveled. **3.** An allowance for travel expenses established at a specified rate per mile.

mile•post (mīl′pōst′) ►*n.* A post indicating distance in miles, as along a highway.

mil•er (mī′lər) ►*n.* One who competes in one-mile races.

mile•stone (mīl′stōn′) ►*n.* **1.** A stone milepost. **2.** A turning point.

Mi•le•tus (mī-lē′təs) An ancient Ionian city of W Asia Minor in present-day Turkey.

mi•lieu (mĭl-yo͞o′, mē-lyœ′) ►*n., pl.* **-lieus** or **-lieux** (-lyœ′). An environment; setting. [< OFr., center.]

mil•i•tant (mĭl′ĭ-tənt) ►*adj.* **1.** Fighting or warring. **2.** Combative or aggressive esp. for a cause. ►*n.* A militant person or party. [< Lat. *mīlitāre,* serve as a soldier.] —**mil′i•tance, mil′i•tan•cy** *n.* —**mil′i•tant•ly** *adv.*

mil•i•ta•rism (mĭl′ĭ-tə-rĭz′əm) ►*n.* **1.** Glorification of the ideals of a professional military class. **2.** Predominance of the armed forces in state policies. —**mil′i•ta•rist** *n.* —**mil′i•ta•ris′tic** *adj.*

mil•i•ta•rize (mĭl′ĭ-tə-rīz′) ►*v.* **-rized, -riz•ing 1.** To equip, train, or prepare for war. **2.** To imbue with militarism. —**mil′i•ta•ri•za′tion** *n.*

mil•i•tar•y (mĭl′ĭ-tĕr′ē) ►*adj.* Of or relating to the armed forces or war. ►*n., pl.* **-y** also **-ies.** Armed forces. [< Lat. *mīles, mīlit-,* soldier.]

—**mil′i•tar′i•ly** (-târ′ə-lē) *adv.*

mil•i•tate (mĭl′ĭ-tāt′) ►*v.* **-tat•ed, -tat•ing.** To bring about an effect or change. [Lat. *mīlitāre*, serve as a soldier.]

mi•li•tia (mə-lĭsh′ə) ►*n.* An army composed of ordinary citizens rather than professional soldiers, on call for service in an emergency. [Lat. *mīlitia*, military service.] —**mi•li′tia•man** *n.*

milk (mĭlk) ►*n.* **1.** A nourishing whitish liquid produced by the mammary glands of female mammals after they have given birth and used to feed their young. **2.** The milk of cows or other animals, used as food by humans. **3.** A liquid that resembles milk: *coconut milk.* ►*v.* **1.** To draw milk from (a female mammal). **2.** To draw or extract a liquid from as if by milking. **3.** *Informal* To obtain from: *milked the witness for information.* [< OE *milc.*] —**milk′er** *n.* —**milk′i•ness** *n.* —**milk′y** *adj.*

milk•maid (mĭlk′mād′) ►*n.* A girl or woman who milks cows.

milk•man (mĭlk′măn′) ►*n.* A man who sells or delivers milk to customers.

milk of magnesia ►*n.* A milky white liquid suspension of magnesium hydroxide, $Mg(OH)_2$, used as an antacid and laxative.

milk shake ►*n.* A whipped beverage made of milk, flavoring, and usu. ice cream.

Regional Note: To most Americans, a milk shake includes ice cream. To a person living in Rhode Island or the adjoining part of Massachussetts, a milk shake consists of milk shaken up with flavored syrup; if ice cream is included, the drink is called a *cabinet* or, farther north, a *velvet* or a *frappe.*

milk tooth ►*n.* Any of the temporary first teeth of a young mammal.

milk•weed (mĭlk′wēd′) ►*n.* A plant having milky juice and pods that split open to release downy seeds.

Milky Way ►*n.* The galaxy containing the solar system, visible as a broad band of faint light in the night sky.

mill[1] (mĭl) ►*n.* **1.** A building equipped with machinery for grinding grain. **2.** A device for crushing or grinding. **3.** A building equipped with machinery for processing materials; factory. **4.** A place that turns out something routinely in the manner of a factory: *a diploma mill.* ►*v.* **1.** To grind or crush in or as if in a mill. **2.** To move around in churning confusion. [< LLat. *molīna.*] —**mill′er** *n.*

mill[2] (mĭl) ►*n.* A monetary unit equal to ¹⁄₁₀₀₀ of a US dollar. [< Lat. *mīllēsimus.* See MIL.]

Mill, James. 1773–1836. Scottish philosopher and economist.

Mill, John Stuart. 1806–73. British philosopher and economist.

Mil•lay (mĭ-lā′), **Edna Saint Vincent.** 1892–1950. Amer. poet.

mill•dam (mĭl′dăm′) ►*n.* A dam to make a millpond.

mil•len•ni•um (mə-lĕn′ē-əm) ►*n., pl.* **-ni•ums** or **-ni•a** (ē-ə) **1.** A span of 1,000 years. **2.** In the New Testament, a thousand-year period in which Jesus is to rule on earth. **3.** A hoped-for period of joy, serenity, and justice. [< Lat. *mīlle*, thousand + *annus*, year.] —**mil•len′ni•al** (-əl) *adj.* —**mil•len′ni•al•ism** *n.* —**mil•len′ni•al•ist** *n.* —**mil•len′ni•al•ly** *adv.*

mil•le•pede (mĭl′ə-pēd′) ►*n.* Var. of **millipede.**

Mil•ler (mĭl′ər), **Arthur.** b. 1915. Amer. playwright.

mil•let (mĭl′ĭt) ►*n.* **1.** A grass grown for its edible white grain and for hay. **2.** The grain itself. [< OFr. *mil* < Lat. *milium.*]

Mil•let (mĭ-lā′, mē-), **Jean François.** 1814–1875. French painter.

milli– ►*pref.* One thousandth (10^{-3}): *millisecond.* [< Lat. *mīlle*, thousand.]

mil•liard (mĭl′yərd, -yärd′, mĭl′ē-ärd′) ►*n.* *Chiefly Brit.* A billion. [Fr.]

mil•li•bar (mĭl′ə-bär′) ►*n.* A unit of atmospheric pressure equal to 100 newtons per square meter.

mil•li•gram (mĭl′ĭ-grăm′) ►*n.* See table at **measurement.**

mil•li•li•ter (mĭl′ə-lē′tər) ►*n.* See table at **measurement.**

mil•li•me•ter (mĭl′ə-mē′tər) ►*n.* See table at **measurement.**

mil•li•ner (mĭl′ə-nər) ►*n.* One who makes or sells esp. women's hats. [< ME *Milener*, a native of Milan.] —**mil′li•ner′y** (-nĕr′ē) *n.*

mil•lion (mĭl′yən) ►*n., pl.* **-lion** or **-lions.** The cardinal number equal to 10^6. [< OItal. *milione* < Lat. *mīlle*, thousand.] —**mil′lion** *adj. & pron.*

mil•lion•aire (mĭl′yə-nâr′) ►*n.* A person whose wealth amounts to at least a million dollars, pounds, or the equivalent in other currency. [Fr. *millionnaire.*]

mil•lionth (mĭl′yənth) ►*n.* **1.** The ordinal number matching the number million in a series. **2.** One of a million equal parts. —**mil′lionth** *adv. & adj.*

mil•li•pede or **mil•le•pede** (mĭl′ə-pēd′) ►*n.* A crawling, plant-eating myriapod having a long segmented body with two pairs of legs attached to most of its body segments. [Lat. *mīlipeda*, a kind of insect : *mīlle*, thousand + *pēs*, *ped-*, foot.]

mil•li•sec•ond (mĭl′ĭ-sĕk′ənd) ►*n.* One thousandth (10^{-3}) of a second.

mill•pond (mĭl′pŏnd′) ►*n.* A pond formed by a dam to provide power for turning a mill wheel.

mill•race (mĭl′rās′) ►*n.* **1.** The fast stream of water that drives a mill wheel. **2.** The channel in which this stream flows.

mill•stone (mĭl′stōn′) ►*n.* **1.** One of a pair of large circular stones used for grinding grain. **2.** A heavy burden.

mill•stream (mĭl′strēm′) ►*n.* The rapid stream of water in a millrace.

mill wheel ►*n.* A wheel, typically driven by water, that powers a mill.

Milne (mĭln), **A(lan) A(lexander).** 1882–1956. British writer.

Mi•losz (mē′lŏsh′, -wŏsh′), **Czeslaw.** b. 1911. Polish-born Amer. writer; 1980 Nobel.

milque•toast (mĭlk′tōst′) ►*n.* One who has a timid, unassertive nature. [After Caspar *Milquetoast*, a comic-strip character.]

milt (mĭlt) ►*n.* Fish sperm. [< MDu. *milte.*]

Mil•ton (mĭl′tən), **John.** 1608–74. English poet and scholar.

Mil•wau•kee (mĭl-wô′kē) A city of SE WI on Lake Michigan. Pop. 628,088.

mime (mīm) ►*n.* **1.** Pantomime. **2.** A modern performer who specializes in silent comic mimicry. ►*v.* **mimed, mim•ing 1.** To mimic. **2.** To pantomime. [< Gk. *mimos*, actor, mimic.] —**mim′er** *n.*

MIME ▸*abbr.* Multipurpose Internet Mail Extensions

mim•e•o•graph (mĭm′ē-ə-grăf′) ▸*n.* A duplicator that makes copies of written, drawn, or typed material from a stencil fitted around an inked drum. [Originally a trademark.] —**mim′e•o•graph′** *v.*

mi•me•sis (mĭ-mē′sĭs, mī-) ▸*n.* The representation of aspects of the sensible world, esp. human actions, in literature and art. [Gk. *mimēsis*, mimicry < *mimeisthai*, imitate.]

mi•met•ic (mĭ-mĕt′ĭk, mī-) ▸*adj.* Of or exhibiting mimicry. [< Gk. *mimēsis*, mimicry. See MIMESIS.] —**mi•met′i•cal•ly** *adv.*

mim•ic (mĭm′ĭk) ▸*v.* **-icked, -ick•ing 1.** To imitate closely, as in speech or gesture; ape. **2.** To ridicule by imitating; mock. **3.** To resemble closely; simulate. ▸*n.* One who mimics. ▸*adj.* Of mimicry. [< Gk. *mimikos*, of mimicry < *mimos*, mime.] —**mim′ick•er** *n.*

mim•ic•ry (mĭm′ĭ-krē) ▸*n., pl.* **-ries.** The act or practice of mimicking; imitation.

mi•mo•sa (mĭ-mō′sə, -zə) ▸*n.* Any of various shrubs or trees having ball-like clusters of small flowers. [< Lat. *mīmus*, MIME.]

min. ▸*abbr.* **1.** minimum **2. Min.** minister **3.** minor **4.** minute

min•a•ret (mĭn′ə-rĕt′) ▸*n.* A tall slender tower attached to a mosque, from which a muezzin calls the faithful to prayer. [< Ar. *manāra*, lamp.]

minaret
Selimiye Mosque, Edirne, Turkey

min•a•to•ry (mĭn′ə-tôr′ē, -tōr′ē) also **min•a•to•ri•al** (-tôr′ē-əl, -tōr′-) ▸*adj.* Menacing or threatening. [< Lat. *minārī*, threaten.]

mince (mĭns) ▸*v.* **minced, minc•ing 1.** To cut into very small pieces. **2.** To pronounce in an affected way. **3.** To moderate (words) for the sake of politeness or decorum; euphemize. **4.** To walk with exaggerated primness. [< VLat. **minūtiāre* < Lat. *minūtus*, MINUTE[2].] —**minc′er** *n.* —**minc′ing** *adj.*

mince•meat (mĭns′mēt′) ▸*n.* A mixture, as of finely chopped apples, raisins, spices, and rum or brandy, used esp. as a pie filling. —***idiom:* make mincemeat of** To destroy utterly.

mind (mīnd) ▸*n.* **1.** The human consciousness that originates in the brain and is manifested esp. in thought, perception, emotion, will, memory, and imagination. **2.** Intelligence; intellect. **3.** A person of great mental ability. **4.** Memory; recollection. **5.** Opinion or sentiment. **6.** Sanity. ▸*v.* **1.** To obey. **2.** To attend to; heed. See Syns at **tend[2]**. **3.** To be careful about. **4.** To care or be concerned about. **5.** To object (to); dislike. [< OE *gemynd*.]

Min•da•na•o (mĭn′də-nä′ō, -nou′) An island of the S Philippines NE of Borneo.

mind-blow•ing (mīnd′blō′ĭng) ▸*adj. Informal* **1.** Producing hallucinatory effects. **2.** Mind-boggling. —**mind′blow′er** *n.*

mind-bog•gling (mīnd′bŏg′lĭng) ▸*adj. Informal* Intellectually or emotionally overwhelming. —**mind′-bog′gler** *n.*

mind-ex•pand•ing (mīnd′ĭk-spăn′dĭng) ▸*adj.* Psychedelic.

mind•ful (mīnd′fəl) ▸*adj.* Attentive; heedful. See Syns at **careful.** —**mind′ful•ness** *n.*

mind•less (mīnd′lĭs) ▸*adj.* **1.** Lacking intelligence or sense. **2.** Careless; heedless. —**mind′less•ly** *adv.* —**mind′less•ness** *n.*

Min•do•ro (mĭn-dôr′ō, -dōr′ō) An island of the W-central Philippines S of Luzon.

mind•set or **mind-set** (mīnd′sĕt′) ▸*n.* A fixed mental attitude that determines one's responses to and interpretations of situations.

mine[1] (mīn) ▸*n.* **1.** An excavation from which ore or minerals are extracted. **2.** A deposit of ore or minerals. **3.** An abundant source. **4a.** A tunnel dug under an enemy position. **b.** An explosive device, often buried or submerged and designed to be detonated by contact or a time fuse. ▸*v.* **mined, min•ing 1.** To extract (ore or minerals) from the earth. **2.** To dig a mine in. **3.** To lay explosive mines in or under. **4.** To undermine; subvert. [< VLat. **mīna*, of Celt. orig.] —**min′a•ble, mine′a•ble** *adj.* —**min′er** *n.*

mine[2] (mīn) ▸*pron. (takes sing. or pl. v.)* Used to indicate the one or ones belonging to me: *The green gloves are mine.* [< OE *mīn*.]

mine•field (mīn′fēld′) ▸*n.* An area in which explosive mines have been placed.

min•er•al (mĭn′ər-əl) ▸*n.* **1.** A natural inorganic substance having a definite chemical composition and characteristic crystalline structure. **2a.** An element, such as gold or silver. **b.** An organic derivative, such as coal or petroleum. **3.** A substance that is neither animal nor vegetable; inorganic matter. **4.** A nutritionally important inorganic element, such as calcium or zinc. **5.** An ore. [< Med.Lat. *minerāle*, of a mine.] —**min′er•al** *adj.* —**min′er•al•ize′** *v.*

min•er•al•o•gy (mĭn′ə-rŏl′ə-jē, -răl′-) ▸*n.* The study of minerals. —**min′er•a•log′i•cal** (-ər-ə-lŏj′ĭ-kəl) *adj.* —**min′er•a•log′i•cal•ly** *adv.* —**min′er•al′o•gist** *n.*

mineral oil ▸*n.* Any of various oils, esp. a distillate of petroleum used as a laxative.

mineral water ▸*n.* Water that contains dissolved mineral salts or gases.

mineral wool ▸*n.* A fibrous insulating material made by steam blasting and cooling molten glass or rock.

Mi•ner•va (mĭ-nûr′və) ▸*n. Rom. Myth.* The goddess of wisdom, the arts, and warfare. [Lat.]

min•e•stro•ne (mĭn′ĭ-strō′nē, -strōn′) ▸*n.* A thick soup containing vegetables, beans, and pasta. [Ital. < *minestrare*, serve.]

mine•sweep•er (mīn′swē′pər) ▸*n.* A ship equipped for detecting, removing, or neutralizing marine mines.

min•gle (mĭng′gəl) ▸*v.* **-gled, -gling.** To mix together in close association. [< OE *mengan*, mix.] —**min′gler** *n.*

min•i (mĭn′ē) ▸*n., pl.* **min•is 1.** Something that is distinctively smaller than others of its class. **2.** A miniskirt. —**min′i** *adj.*

mini– ►*pref.* Small; miniature: *minibike.* [< MINIATURE and MINIMUM.]

min•i•a•ture (mĭn′ē-ə-cho͝or′, -chər, mĭn′ə-) ►*n.* **1.** A very small copy or model. **2.** A very small, detailed painting. ►*adj.* Very small. See Syns at **small.** [Ital. *miniatura,* illumination of manuscripts.] —**min′i•a•tur′ist** *n.* —**min′i•a•tur•i•za′tion** *n.* —**min′i•a•tur•ize′** *v.*

min•i•bike (mĭn′ē-bīk′) ►*n.* A small motorbike. [Originally a trademark.]

min•i•bus (mĭn′ē-bŭs′) ►*n.* A small bus.

min•i•com•put•er (mĭn′ē-kəm-pyo͞o′tər) ►*n.* A mid-sized computer, usu. fitting within a single cabinet about the size of a refrigerator, that has less memory than a mainframe.

min•im (mĭn′əm) ►*n.* **1.** A unit of fluid measure equal to 1/60 of a fluid dram. **2.** A small portion. [< Lat. *minimus,* least.]

min•i•mal (mĭn′ə-məl) ►*adj.* Smallest in amount or degree. —**min′i•mal•ly** *adv.*

min•i•mal•ism (mĭn′ə-mə-lĭz′əm) ►*n.* Use of the fewest and barest essentials or elements, as in the arts, literature, or design.

min•i•mal•ist (mĭn′ə-mə-lĭst) ►*n.* **1.** One who advocates a moderate or conservative policy. **2.** A practitioner of minimalism. —**min′i•mal•ist** *adj.*

min•i•mize (mĭn′ə-mīz′) ►*v.* **-mized, -miz•ing.** To reduce to or represent as having minimal importance or value. —**min′i•mi•za′tion** *n.* —**min′i•miz′er** *n.*

min•i•mum (mĭn′ə-məm) ►*n., pl.* **-mums** or **-ma** (-mə) **1.** The least possible quantity or degree. **2.** The lowest quantity reached or permitted. [Lat., neuter of *minimus,* least.] —**min′i•mum** *adj.*

minimum wage ►*n.* The lowest wage, determined by law or contract, that can be paid for a specified job.

min•ion (mĭn′yən) ►*n.* An obsequious follower or dependent. [< OFr. *mignot,* darling.]

min•i•se•ries (mĭn′ē-sîr′ēz) ►*n.* **1.** A televised drama shown in a number of episodes. **2.** A short series of athletic contests.

min•i•skirt (mĭn′ē-skûrt′) ►*n.* A very short skirt. —**min′i•skirt′ed** *adj.*

min•is•ter (mĭn′ĭ-stər) ►*n.* **1.** One authorized to perform religious functions in a Christian church. **2.** The head of a governmental department. **3.** A diplomat ranking below an ambassador. **4.** A person serving as an agent for another. ►*v.* To attend to the wants and needs of others. See Syns at **tend².** [< Lat., servant.] —**min′is•te′ri•al** (-stîr′ē-əl) *adj.* —**min′is•te′ri•al•ly** *adv.* —**min′is•trant** *n.* —**min′is•tra′tion** *n.* —**min′is•tra′tive** *adj.*

min•is•try (mĭn′ĭ-strē) ►*n., pl.* **-tries 1.** The act of serving; ministration. **2a.** The profession and services of a minister. **b.** The clergy. **c.** The period of service of a minister. **3a.** A governmental department presided over by a minister. **b.** The building in which it is housed. **c.** The duties, functions, or term of a governmental minister.

min•i•van (mĭn′ē-văn′) ►*n.* A small passenger van, typically with removable rear seats.

mink (mĭngk) ►*n., pl.* **mink** or **minks 1.** A semiaquatic weasellike mammal having soft, thick, lustrous brown fur. **2.** The fur of the mink. [ME, mink fur.]

Minn. ►*abbr.* Minnesota

Min•ne•ap•o•lis (mĭn′ē-ăp′ə-lĭs) A city of SE MN on the Mississippi R. adjacent to St. Paul. Pop. 368,383.

Min•ne•so•ta (mĭn′ĭ-sō′tə) A state of the N US bordering on Lake Superior and Canada. Cap. St. Paul. Pop. 4,387,029. —**Min′ne•so′tan** *adj. & n.*

Minnesota River. A river, about 534 km (332 mi), of S MN flowing to the Mississippi R. near St. Paul.

min•now (mĭn′ō) ►*n., pl.* **-now** or **-nows.** Any of various small freshwater fishes widely used as bait. [ME *meneu.*]

Mi•no•an (mĭ-nō′ən) ►*adj.* Of or relating to the Bronze Age culture in Crete from about 3000 to 1100 B.C. [< Gk. *Minōs,* Minos, Crete.] —**Mi•no′an** *n.*

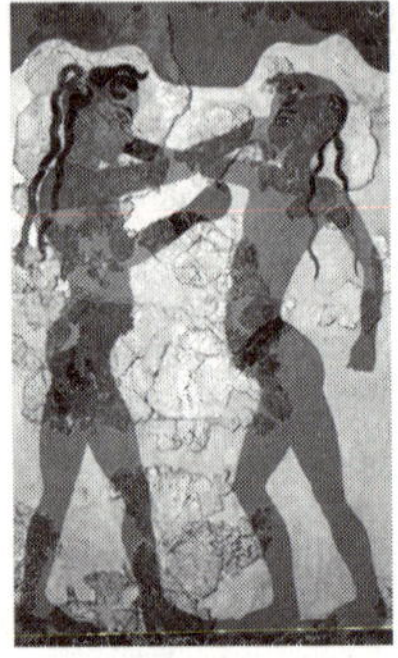

Minoan
detail of a fresco depicting young men boxing

mi•nor (mī′nər) ►*adj.* **1.** Lesser or smaller in amount, size, or importance. **2.** Lesser in seriousness or danger. **3.** *Law* Being under legal age. **4.** *Mus.* Of or being a minor scale. ►*n.* **1.** *Law* One who is under legal age. **2a.** A secondary area of academic study. **b.** One studying a minor: *She is a chemistry minor.* **3.** *Mus.* A minor key, scale, or interval. **4. minors** *Sports* The minor leagues. ►*v.* To pursue academic studies in a minor field. [< Lat.]

Mi•nor•ca (mĭ-nôr′kə) A Spanish island in the Balearics of the W Mediterranean Sea. —**Mi•nor′can** *adj. & n.*

mi•nor•i•ty (mə-nôr′ĭ-tē, -nŏr′-, mī-) ►*n., pl.* **-ties 1.** The smaller of two groups forming a whole. **2a.** A racial, religious, or other group different from the larger group of which it is part. **b.** A member of such a group. **3.** The state or period of being under legal age.

minor league ►*n.* A league of professional sports clubs not belonging to the major leagues. —**mi′nor-league′** *adj.*

minor scale ►*n. Mus.* A diatonic scale having a half step between the 2nd and 3rd degrees.

Min•o•taur (mĭn′ə-tôr′, mī′nə-) ►*n. Gk. Myth.* A monster who was half man and half bull.

Minsk (mĭnsk) The capital of Belarus, in the central part. Pop. 1,654,800.

min•ster (mĭn′stər) ►*n. Chiefly Brit.* A monastery church. [< VLat. **monistērium,* MONASTERY.]

min•strel (mĭn′strəl) ►*n.* **1.** A medieval traveling entertainer. **2.** A performer in a minstrel show. [< LLat. *ministeriālis*, official in the imperial household.]

minstrel show ▶*n.* A comic variety show presenting jokes, songs, dances, and skits, usually by white actors in blackface.

mint[1] (mĭnt) ▶*n.* **1.** A place where money is manufactured by a government. **2.** An abundant amount, esp. of money. ▶*v.* **1.** To produce (money) by stamping metal. **2.** To invent or fabricate (e.g., a phrase). ▶*adj.* New or as if new: *mint condition.* [< Lat. *monēta*, coin.] —**mint′er** *n.*

mint[2] (mĭnt) ▶*n.* **1.** Any of various related plants, many of which yield an aromatic oil used for flavoring. **2.** A candy flavored with mint. [< Lat. *menta.*] —**mint′y** *adj.*

mint julep ▶*n.* A drink made of bourbon, sugar, crushed mint leaves, and shaved ice.

min•u•end (mĭn′yo͞o-ĕnd′) ▶*n.* The quantity from which another quantity is to be subtracted. [< Lat. *minuendum*, thing to be diminished.]

min•u•et (mĭn′yo͞o-ĕt′) ▶*n.* **1.** A stately dance in 3/4 time originating in 17th-cent. France. **2.** Music for a minuet. [< OFr., dainty < *menu*, MINUTE[2].]

Min•u•it (mĭn′yo͞o-ĭt), **Peter.** 1580–1638. Dutch colonial administrator.

mi•nus (mī′nəs) ▶*prep.* **1.** *Math.* Reduced by; less: *Nine minus three is six.* **2.** *Informal* Without: *I went to work minus my briefcase.* ▶*adj.* **1.** *Math.* Negative or on the negative part of a scale: *a minus value.* **2.** Ranking on the lower end of a designated scale: *a grade of A minus.* ▶*n.* **1.** *Math.* **a.** The minus sign (–). **b.** A negative quantity. **2.** A deficiency or defect. [< Lat. < *minor*, less.]

min•us•cule (mĭn′ə-skyo͞ol′, mĭ-nŭs′kyo͞ol′) ▶*adj.* Very small; tiny. See Syns at **small.** [< Lat. *minusculus*, very small.]

minus sign ▶*n. Math.* The symbol –, as in 4 – 2 = 2, used to indicate subtraction or a negative quantity.

min•ute[1] (mĭn′ĭt) ▶*n.* **1.** A unit of time equal to $\frac{1}{60}$ of an hour or 60 seconds. **2.** A unit of angular measurement equal to $\frac{1}{60}$ of a degree or 60 seconds. **3.** A moment. **4.** A specific point in time. **5. minutes** An official record of the proceedings at a meeting. [< Lat. *minūtus*, small. See MINUTE[2].]

mi•nute[2] (mī-no͞ot′, -nyo͞ot′, mĭ-) ▶*adj.* **1.** Exceptionally small; tiny. See Syns at **small. 2.** Beneath notice; insignificant. **3.** Marked by careful examination; detailed. [< Lat. *minūtus*, p.part. of *minuere*, lessen.] —**mi•nute′ly** *adv.* —**mi•nute′ness** *n.*

min•ute•man (mĭn′ĭt-măn′) ▶*n.* An armed man ready to fight on a minute's notice during the American Revolutionary War.

mi•nu•ti•a (mĭ-no͞o′shē-ə, -shə, -nyo͞o′-) ▶*n.*, *pl.* **-ti•ae** (-shē-ē′). A small or trivial detail. [< LLat. *minūtiae*, petty details.]

minx (mĭngks) ▶*n.* An impudent young woman. [?] —**minx′ish** *adj.*

Mi•o•cene (mī′ə-sēn′) *Geol.* ▶*adj.* Of or being the 4th epoch of the Tertiary Period, marked by the development of grasses and grazing mammals. ▶*n.* The Miocene Epoch. [Gk. *meiōn*, less + -CENE.]

mir•a•cle (mĭr′ə-kəl) ▶*n.* **1.** An event inexplicable by the laws of nature and so held to be supernatural in origin or an act of God. **2.** A marvel. See Syns at **wonder.** [< Lat. *mīrāculum.*] —**mi•rac′u•lous** (mĭ-răk′yə-ləs) *adj.* —**mi•rac′u•lous•ly** *adv.*

mi•rage (mĭ-räzh′) ▶*n.* **1.** An optical phenomenon that creates the illusion of water, often with inverted reflections of distant objects. **2.** Something illusory or insubstantial. [Fr. < Lat. *mīrārī*, wonder at.]

mire (mīr) ▶*n.* **1.** A bog. **2.** Deep slimy soil or mud. ▶*v.* **mired, mir•ing 1.** To sink or stick in or as if in mire. **2.** To soil with mud. [< ON *mȳrr.*] —**mir′y** *adj.*

mir•in (mĭr′ĭn) ▶*n.* A sweet Japanese rice wine, used esp. in cooking. [Jap.]

Mi•ró (mē-rō′), **Joan.** 1893–1983. Spanish artist.

mir•ror (mĭr′ər) ▶*n.* **1.** A surface capable of reflecting sufficient undiffused light to form a virtual image of an object in front of it. **2.** Something that gives a true picture of something else. ▶*v.* To reflect in or as in a mirror. [< OFr. *mireor* < *mirer*, look at.]

mirth (mûrth) ▶*n.* Gladness and gaiety. [< OE *myrgth.*] —**mirth′ful** *adj.* —**mirth′ful•ly** *adv.* —**mirth′ful•ness** *n.*

mis– ▶*pref.* **1.** Bad; badly; wrong; wrongly: *misconduct.* **2.** Failure; lack: *misfire.* [< OE and OFr. *mes-.*]

mis•ad•ven•ture (mĭs′əd-vĕn′chər) ▶*n.* A misfortune; mishap.

mis•al•li•ance (mĭs′ə-lī′əns) ▶*n.* An unsuitable marriage.

mis•an•thrope (mĭs′ən-thrōp′, mĭz′-) also **mis•an•thro•pist** (mĭs-ăn′thrə-pĭst, mĭz′-) ▶*n.* One who hates humankind. [< Gk. *misanthrōpos*, hating people.] —**mis′an•throp′ic** (-thrŏp′ĭk) *adj.* —**mis′an•throp′i•cal•ly** *adv.* —**mis•an′thro•py** *n.*

mis•ap•pre•hend (mĭs-ăp′rĭ-hĕnd′) ▶*v.* To misunderstand. —**mis•ap′pre•hen′sion** *n.*

mis•be•got•ten (mĭs′bĭ-gŏt′n) ▶*adj.* **1.** Of illegitimate birth. **2.** Of dubious origin.

misc. ▶*abbr.* miscellaneous

mis•car•riage (mĭs′kăr′ĭj, mĭs-kăr′-) ▶*n.* **1.** Premature expulsion of a nonviable fetus from the uterus. **2.** Mismanagement.

mis•car•ry (mĭs′kăr′ē, mĭs-kăr′ē) ▶*v.* **1.** To have a miscarriage. **2.** To go wrong.

mis•ceg•e•na•tion (mĭ-sĕj′ə-nā′shən, mĭs′ĭ-jə-) ▶*n.* Cohabitation, sexual relations, or marriage between persons of different races. [< Lat. *miscēre*, mix + *genus*, race.]

mis•cel•la•ne•ous (mĭs′ə-lā′nē-əs) ▶*adj.* Made up of a variety of parts or ingredients. [< Lat. *miscellāneus* < *miscēre*, mix.] —**mis′cel•la′ne•ous•ly** *adv.*

mis•cel•la•ny (mĭs′ə-lā′nē) ▶*n.*, *pl.* **-nies 1.** A collection of various items or ingredients. **2.** A collection of diverse literary works.

mis•chance (mĭs-chăns′) ▶*n.* **1.** A mishap. **2.** Bad luck.

mis•chief (mĭs′chĭf) ▶*n.* **1.** A cause of discomfiture or annoyance. **2.** An inclination to play pranks. **3.** Damage caused by a specific person. [< OFr. *meschief*, misfortune.]

mis•chie•vous (mĭs′chə-vəs) ▶*adj.* **1.** Causing mischief. **2.** Playful in a naughty or teasing way. —**mis′chie•vous•ly** *adv.* —**mis′chie•vous•ness** *n.*

mis•ci•ble (mĭs′ə-bəl) ▶*adj. Chem.* That can be mixed in all proportions. [< Lat. *miscēre*, mix.] —**mis′ci•bil′i•ty** *n.*

mis•con•ceive (mĭs′kən-sēv′) ►*v.* To misunderstand. —**mis′con•cep′tion** *n.*

mis•con•duct (mĭs-kŏn′dŭkt) ►*n.* **1.** Improper or immoral behavior. **2.** Dishonest or bad management. ►*v.* (mĭs′kən-dŭct′) **1.** To mismanage. **2.** To behave (oneself) badly.

mis•con•strue (mĭs′kən-stro͞o′) ►*v.* To misinterpret. —**mis′con•struc′tion** *n.*

mis•cre•ant (mĭs′krē-ənt) ►*n.* A wrongdoer or offender; villain. [< OFr. *mescroire*, disbelieve : MIS– + *croire*, believe (< Lat. *crēdere*).]

mis•cue (mĭs-kyo͞o′) ►*n.* A mistake. —**mis•cue′** *v.*

mis•deed (mĭs-dēd′) ►*n.* A wrongdoing.

mis•de•mean•or (mĭs′dĭ-mē′nər) ►*n.* **1.** A misdeed. **2.** *Law* An offense less serious than a felony.

mise en scène (mēz′ äN sĕn′) ►*n., pl.* **mise en scènes** (sĕn′). The arrangement and setting for a play or film. [Fr., putting on stage.]

mi•ser (mī′zər) ►*n.* A stingy person, esp. one who hoards money. [< Lat., wretched.] —**mi′ser•li•ness** *n.* —**mi′ser•ly** *adj.*

mis•er•a•ble (mĭz′ər-ə-bəl, mĭz′rə-) ►*adj.* **1.** Very unhappy; wretched. **2.** Causing discomfort or distress. **3.** Wretchedly poor; squalid. **4.** Of poor quality. [< Lat. *miserābilis*, pitiable < *miser*, wretched.] —**mis′er•a•bly** *adv.*

mis•er•y (mĭz′ə-rē) ►*n., pl.* **-ies 1.** Great physical or emotional suffering. **2.** An affliction or trial. [< Lat. *miseria.*]

mis•fire (mĭs-fīr′) ►*v.* **1.** To fail to ignite, fire, or discharge when expected. **2.** To fail to achieve an anticipated result. —**mis′fire′** *n.*

mis•fit (mĭs′fĭt′, mĭs-fĭt′) ►*n.* **1.** A poor fit. **2.** A maladjusted person.

mis•for•tune (mĭs-fôr′chən) ►*n.* **1.** Bad fortune. **2.** A mishap.

mis•giv•ing (mĭs-gĭv′ĭng) ►*n.* A feeling of doubt or distrust.

mis•guide (mĭs-gīd′) ►*v.* To lead in the wrong direction; lead astray. —**mis•guid′ance** *n.* —**mis•guid′ed** *adj.* —**mis•guid′ed•ly** *adv.*

mis•han•dle (mĭs-hăn′dl) ►*v.* To deal with clumsily or inefficiently.

mis•hap (mĭs′hăp′, mĭs-hăp′) ►*n.* An unfortunate accident.

mish•mash (mĭsh′măsh′) ►*n.* A hodgepodge.

mis•in•ter•pret (mĭs′ĭn-tûr′prĭt) ►*v.* To interpret or explain inaccurately. —**mis′in•ter′pre•ta′tion** *n.* —**mis′in•ter′pret•er** *n.*

Mis•ki•to (mĭ-skē′tō) ►*n., pl.* **-to** or **-tos 1.** A member of an American Indian people of the Caribbean coast of NE Nicaragua and SE Honduras. **2.** Their language.

mis•lay (mĭs-lā′) ►*v.* To put in a place that is afterward forgotten; lose.

mis•lead (mĭs-lēd′) ►*v.* **1.** To lead in the wrong direction. **2.** To lead into error.

mis•like (mĭs-līk′) ►*v.* To dislike. ►*n.* Dislike.

mis•no•mer (mĭs-nō′mər) ►*n.* A wrong or inappropriate name. [< OFr. *mesnomer*, call by a wrong name.]

mi•so (mē′sō) ►*n., pl.* **-sos.** A thick fermented paste made of cooked soybeans, salt, and often rice or barley. [J.]

mi•sog•a•my (mĭ-sŏg′ə-mē) ►*n.* Hatred of marriage. [Gk. *misein*, to hate + –GAMY.] —**mi•sog′a•mist** *n.*

mi•sog•y•ny (mĭ-sŏj′ə-nē) ►*n.* Hatred of women. [< Gk. *misein*, to hate + *gunē*, woman.] —**mi•sog′y•nist** *n.* —**mi•sog′y•nis′tic, mi•sog′y•nous** *adj.*

mis•place (mĭs-plās′) ►*v.* **1a.** To put in a wrong place. **b.** To mislay. **2.** To bestow (e.g., confidence) on an unsuitable or unworthy person. —**mis•place′ment** *n.*

mis•play (mĭs-plā′, mĭs′plā′) ►*n. Sports & Games* A mistaken play. —**mis•play′** *v.*

mis•read (mĭs-rēd′) ►*v.* **1.** To read inaccurately. **2.** To misinterpret.

mis•rep•re•sent (mĭs-rĕp′rĭ-zĕnt′) ►*v.* To give a false or misleading representation of. —**mis•rep′re•sen•ta′tion** *n.*

miss[1] (mĭs) ►*v.* **1.** To fail to hit, reach, catch, meet, or make contact with. **2.** To fail to perceive or understand. **3.** To fail to achieve or attain. **4.** To fail to attend or perform. **5.** To omit. **6.** To avoid. **7.** To discover or feel the absence of. **8.** To misfire. ►*n.* **1.** A failure to hit or succeed. **2.** A misfire. [< OE *missan.*]

mis′ad•dress′ *v.*
mis′ad•vise′ *v.*
mis′a•ligned′ *adj.*
mis′a•lign′ment *n.*
mis•al′lo•cate′ *v.*
mis′al•ly′ *v.*
mis′ap•ply′ *v.*
mis′ap•pro′pri•ate′ *v.*
mis′at•trib′ute *v.*
mis′be•have′ *v.*
mis′be•hav′ior *n.*
mis′be•lieve′ *v.*
mis•cal′cu•late′ *v.*
mis•call′ *v.*
mis•cast′ *v.*
mis•char′ac•ter•ize′ *v.*
mis•clas′si•fy′ *v.*
mis′com•mu′ni•ca′tion *n.*
mis•count′ *v.*
mis′count′ *n.*
mis•date′ *v.*
mis•deal′ *v.*
mis•di′ag•nose′ *v.*
mis•di′ag•no′sis *n.*
mis•di′al *v.*
mis′di•rect′ *v.*
mis′di•rec′tion *n.*
mis•do′ing *n.*
mis•ed′u•cate′ *v.*
mis•es′ti•mate′ *v.*
mis•file′ *v.*
mis•gov′ern *v.*
mis•hear′ *v.*
mis′i•den′ti•fy *v.*
mis′im•pres′sion *n.*
mis′in•form′ *v.*
mis•in′for•ma′tion *n.*
mis•judge′ *v.*
mis•judg′ment *n.*
mis•la′bel *v.*
mis•man′age *v.*
mis•man′age•ment *n.*
mis•match′ *v.*
mis′match′ *n.*
mis•mate′ *v.*
mis•name′ *v.*
mis′per•ceive′ *v.*
mis′per•cep′tion *n.*
mis′print′ *n.*
mis•print′ *v.*
mis′pro•nounce′ *v.*
mis•quote′ *v.*
mis•reck′on *v.*
mis′re•mem′ber *v.*
mis′re•port′ *v. & n.*
mis•rule′ *n. & v.*
mis•shape′ *v.*
mis•shap′en *adj.*
mis•shap′en•ly *adv.*
mis•spell′ *v.*
mis•spel′ling *n.*
mis•spend′ *v.*
mis•state′ *v.*
mis•time′ *v.*
mis′trans•late′ *v.*
mis•val′ue *v.*
mis•word′ *v.*
mis•write′ *v.*

miss² (mĭs) ►*n.* **1. Miss** Used as a courtesy title for a young woman or girl. **2.** Used as a polite address for a girl or young woman. [< MISTRESS.]

Miss. ►*abbr.* Mississippi

mis•sal (mĭs′əl) ►*n. Rom. Cath. Ch.* A book containing all the prayers and responses necessary for celebrating the Mass. [< Med.Lat. *missālis*, of the Mass.]

mis•sile (mĭs′əl, -īl′) ►*n.* **1.** An object or weapon fired or projected at a target. **2.** A guided missile. **3.** A ballistic missile. [< Lat. *missilis*, throwable < *mittere*, let go.] —**mis′sile•ry** *n.*

miss•ing (mĭs′ĭng) ►*adj.* Absent; lost; lacking.

mis•sion (mĭsh′ən) ►*n.* **1a.** A body of envoys to a foreign country. **b.** A permanent diplomatic office abroad. **2.** A body of missionaries, or the building housing them. **3.** A special assignment given to a person or group. **4.** A vocation. [< Lat. *mittere*, *miss-*, send off.]

mission
San Xavier del Bac Mission, Tucson, Arizona

mis•sion•ar•y (mĭsh′ə-nĕr′ē) ►*n.*, *pl.* **-ies 1.** A propagandist for a belief or cause. **2.** One who attempts to convert others to a particular doctrine or set of principles. —**mis′sion•ar′y** *adj.*

Mis•sis•sip•pi (mĭs′ĭ-sĭp′ē) A state of the SE US. Cap. Jackson. Pop. 2,586,443. —**Mis′sis•sip′pi•an** *adj. & n.*

Mis•sis•sip•pi•an (mĭs′ĭ-sĭp′ē-ən) *Geol.* ►*adj.* Of or being the 5th period of the Paleozoic Era, marked by widespread shallow seas. ►*n.* The Mississippian Period.

Mississippi River. The chief river of the US, rising in N MN and flowing about 3,781 km (2,350 mi) to the Gulf of Mexico.

mis•sive (mĭs′ĭv) ►*n.* A written message. [< Med.Lat. *(littere) missīve*, (letter) sent.]

Mis•sou•ri¹ (mĭ-zo͝or′ē) ►*n.*, *pl.* **-ri** or **-ris 1.** A member of a Native American people formerly of N-central Missouri, now in Oklahoma. **2.** Their Siouan language.

Mis•sou•ri² (mĭ-zo͝or′ē, -zo͝or′ə) A state of the central US. Cap. Jefferson City. Pop. 5,137,804. —**Mis•sou′ri•an** *adj. & n.*

Missouri River. A river of the US rising in the Rocky Mts. and flowing about 4,127 km (2,565 mi) to the Mississippi R. N of St. Louis, MO.

mis•speak (mĭs-spēk′) ►*v.* To speak mistakenly, inappropriately, or rashly.

mis•step (mĭs-stĕp′) ►*n.* **1.** A misplaced step. **2.** A social or procedural blunder.

mist (mĭst) ►*n.* **1.** A mass of fine droplets of water in the atmosphere. **2.** Water vapor condensed on and clouding a surface. **3.** Fine drops of a liquid sprayed into the air. **4.** Something that dims or conceals. ►*v.* To become obscured or misty. [< OE.]

mis•take (mĭ-stāk′) ►*n.* **1.** An error or fault. **2.** A misconception or misunderstanding. [< ON *mistaka*, take in error.] —**mis•tak′a•ble** *adj.* —**mis•take′** *v.*

mis•tak•en (mĭ-stā′kən) ►*adj.* **1.** Wrong in opinion, understanding, or perception. **2.** Based on error. —**mis•tak′en•ly** *adv.*

Mis•ter (mĭs′tər) ►*n.* **1.** Used as a courtesy title for a man, usu. written in its abbreviated form *Mr.* **2. mister** *Informal* Used in addressing a man. [Alteration of MASTER.]

mis•tle•toe (mĭs′əl-tō′) ►*n.* A plant growing as a parasite on trees and having leathery evergreen leaves and waxy white berries. [< OE *misteltān*, sprig of mistletoe.]

mis•treat (mĭs-trēt′) ►*v.* To treat roughly or wrongly; abuse. —**mis•treat′ment** *n.*

mis•tress (mĭs′trĭs) ►*n.* **1.** A woman in a position of authority, control, or ownership. **2.** Something personified as female that has supremacy or control: *a country that is mistress of the seas.* **3.** A woman who has a continuing sexual relationship with a man who is not her husband. **4. Mistress** Used formerly as a courtesy title for a woman. [< OFr. *maistresse*, feminine of *maistre*, MASTER.]

mis•tri•al (mĭs′-trī′əl, -trīl′, mĭs-trī′əl, -trīl′) ►*n.* **1.** A trial declared invalid because of a procedural error. **2.** An inconclusive trial.

mis•trust (mĭs-trŭst′) ►*n.* Lack of trust; suspicion. ►*v.* To regard with suspicion or doubt. —**mis•trust′ful** *adj.*

mist•y (mĭs′tē) ►*adj.* **-i•er, -i•est 1.** Consisting of or resembling mist. **2.** Obscured or clouded by or as if by mist. **3.** Vague or hazy. —**mist′i•ly** *adv.* —**mist′i•ness** *n.*

mis•un•der•stand (mĭs′-ŭn-dər-stănd′) ►*v.* To understand incorrectly; misinterpret.

mis•un•der•stand•ing (mĭs′-ŭn-dər-stăn′-dĭng) ►*n.* **1.** A failure to understand correctly. **2.** A disagreement or quarrel.

mis•use (mĭs-yo͞os′) ►*n.* Improper, unlawful, or incorrect use. ►*v.* (-yo͞oz′) **1.** To use incorrectly. **2.** To mistreat or abuse.

mite¹ (mīt) ►*n.* Any of various small, often parasitic arachnids. [< MDu.]

mite² (mīt) ►*n.* **1.** A very small contribution or amount of money. **2.** A tiny object or amount. [< MDu. *mīte*, a small coin.]

mi•ter (mī′tər) ►*n.* **1.** *Eccles.* A tall pointed hat with peaks in front and back, worn esp. by bishops. **2.** A miter joint. ►*v.* To fit together with or meet in a miter joint. [< Gk. *mitra*, headdress.]

miter joint ►*n.* A joint made by fitting together two beveled edges to form a 90° corner.

mit•i•gate (mĭt′ĭ-gāt′) ►*v.* **-gat•ed, -gat•ing.** To make or become less in force or intensity; moderate. [< Lat. *mītigāre* : *mītis*, soft + *agere*, do.] —**mit′i•ga•ble** (-gə-bəl) *adj.* —**mit′i•ga′tion** *n.* —**mit′i•ga′tive, mit′i•ga•to′ry** (-gə-tôr′ē, -tōr′ē) *adj.*

mi•to•chon•dri•on (mī′tə-kŏn′drē-ən) ►*n.*, *pl.* **-dri•a** (-drē-ə). A microscopic structure in nearly all living cells, containing genetic material and enzymes important for cell metabolism. [< Gk. *mitos*, warp thread + *khondrion*, granule.] —**mi′to•chon′dri•al** *adj.*

mi•to•sis (mī-tō′sĭs) ►*n. Biol.* **1.** The process in cell division by which the nucleus divides, normally resulting in two new nuclei, each of which contains a complete copy of the parental chromosomes. **2.** The entire process of cell division including division of the nucleus and the cytoplasm. [Gk. *mitos*, thread + -OSIS.] —**mi•tot′ic** (-tŏt′ĭk) *adj.* —**mi•tot′i•cal•ly** *adv.*

mi•tre (mī′tər) ►*n. & v. Chiefly Brit.* Var. of **miter.**

mitt (mĭt) ►*n.* **1.** A woman's glove that extends over the hand and only partially covers the fingers. **2.** A mitten. **3.** A baseball glove, esp. one used by catchers and first basemen. **4.** *Slang* A hand. [< MITTEN.]

mit•ten (mĭt′n) ►*n.* A covering for the hand that encases the thumb separately and the four fingers together. [< OFr. *mitaine*.]

Mit•ter•rand (mē′tə-rănd′, -räN′), **François Maurice.** 1916–96. French president (1981–95).

mitz•vah (mĭts′və) ►*n., pl.* **-voth** (-vōt′, -vōs′) or **-vahs** **1.** A commandment of the Jewish law. **2.** A worthy deed. [Heb. *miṣwâ* < *ṣiwwâ*, to command.]

mix (mĭks) ►*v.* **1a.** To combine or blend so that the constituent parts are indistinguishable. **b.** To create or form by blending. **2.** To combine or join: *mix joy with sorrow.* **3.** To associate socially. **4.** To crossbreed. **5a.** To combine (audio tracks or channels) to make an audio recording. **b.** To make in this manner. —***phrasal verb:*** **mix up 1.** To confuse. **2.** To involve: *got mixed up in the scandal.* **3.** To throw into disorder; jumble. ►*n.* A mixture, esp. of ingredients packaged and sold commercially. [< Lat. *miscēre*, *mixt-*.] —**mix′a•ble** *adj.*

mixed bag (mĭkst) ►*n.* A varied assortment.

mixed drink ►*n.* A drink made of one or more kinds of liquor combined with other ingredients, usu. shaken or stirred.

mixed number ►*n.* A number, such as 7¼, consisting of an integer and a fraction or decimal.

mix•er (mĭk′sər) ►*n.* **1.** One that mixes, esp. a device that mixes substances or ingredients. **2.** A sociable person. **3.** A party affording people an opportunity to get acquainted. **4.** A nonalcoholic beverage, such as soda water, used in mixed drinks.

Mix•tec (mēs′tĕk) ►*n., pl.* **-tec** or **-tecs** **1.** A member of a Mesoamerican Indian people of S Mexico whose civilization was overthrown by the Aztecs in the 16th cent. **2.** The language of this people.

mix•ture (mĭks′chər) ►*n.* **1.** The act of mixing or the state of being mixed. **2.** Something made by mixing. **3.** One that consists of diverse elements. **4.** *Chem.* A blend of substances not chemically bound to each other. [< Lat. *mixtūra* < *miscēre*, mix.]

mix-up also **mix•up** (mĭks′ŭp′) ►*n.* A state or instance of confusion; muddle.

miz•zen or **miz•en** (mĭz′ən) ►*n.* **1.** A fore-and-aft sail set on the mizzenmast. **2.** A mizzenmast. [Ult. < Lat. *mediānus*, middle.] —**miz′zen** *adj.*

miz•zen•mast or **miz•en•mast** (mĭz′ən-məst, -măst′) ►*n.* The third mast aft on sailing ships carrying three or more masts.

mks ►*abbr.* meter-kilogram-second

mL also **ml** ►*abbr.* milliliter

MLA ►*abbr.* Modern Language Association

Mlle. ►*abbr.* Mademoiselle

Mlles. ►*abbr.* Mesdemoiselles

mm ►*abbr.* millimeter

Mme. ►*abbr.* Madame

Mmes. ►*abbr.* Mesdames

Mn ► The symbol for the element **manganese.**

MN ►*abbr.* **1.** magnetic north **2.** Minnesota

mne•mon•ic (nĭ-mŏn′ĭk) ►*adj.* Assisting or intended to assist the memory. ►*n.* A device, such as a formula or rhyme, used as a mnemonic aid. [< Gk. *mnēmōn*, mindful.] —**mne•mon′i•cal•ly** *adv.*

Mo ► The symbol for the element **molybdenum.**

MO ►*abbr.* **1.** mail order **2.** also **Mo.** Missouri **3.** modus operandi **4.** money order

mo. ►*abbr.* month

Mo•ab (mō′ăb) An ancient kingdom E of the Dead Sea in SW Jordan. —**Mo′ab•ite′** *adj. & n.*

moan (mōn) ►*n.* **1.** A low, sustained, mournful cry, as of sorrow or pain. **2.** A whining complaint. [ME *mone*.] —**moan** *v.* —**moan′er** *n.*

moat (mōt) ►*n.* A deep wide ditch, usu. filled with water, esp. one surrounding a medieval town, fortress, or castle as a defense. [< OFr. *mote*, mound.]

mob (mŏb) ►*n.* **1.** A large disorderly throng. See Syns at **crowd. 2.** The mass of common people. **3.** *Informal* An organized gang of criminals. ►*v.* **mobbed, mob•bing 1.** To crowd around and jostle, annoy, or attack. **2.** To crowd into (a place). [< Lat. *(vulgus) mōbile*, fickle (crowd).]

mo•bile (mō′bəl, -bēl′, -bīl′) ►*adj.* **1.** Capable of moving or of being moved readily. **2.** Changing quickly from one condition to another. ►*n.* (mō′bēl′). A sculpture consisting of parts that move, esp. in response to air currents. [< Lat. *mōbilis*.] —**mo•bil′i•ty** (-bĭl′ĭ-tē) *n.*

Mo•bile (mō-bēl′, mō′bēl′) A city of SW AL on **Mobile Bay,** an arm of the Gulf of Mexico. Pop. 196,278.

mobile home ►*n.* A house trailer installed on a site and used as a home.

mo•bi•lize (mō′bə-līz′) ►*v.* **-lized, -liz•ing 1.** To make mobile or capable of movement. **2.** To assemble and prepare for or as if for war. —**mo′bi•li•za′tion** *n.*

mob•ster (mŏb′stər) ►*n. Informal* A member of a criminal gang.

moc•ca•sin (mŏk′ə-sĭn) ►*n.* **1.** A soft leather slipper or shoe. **2.** A water moccasin. [Of Virginia Algonquian orig.]

mo•cha (mō′kə) ►*n.* **1.** A rich, pungent Arabian coffee. **2.** A flavoring of coffee mixed with chocolate. **3.** A dark olive brown. [After *Mocha*, Yemen.]

mock (mŏk) ►*v.* **1.** To treat with ridicule or contempt; deride. **2.** To mimic, as in sport or derision. ►*adj.* Simulated; sham. [< OFr. *mocquer*.] —**mock′er** *n.* —**mock′er•y** *n.* —**mock′ing•ly** *adv.*

mock-he•ro•ic (mŏk′hĭ-rō′ĭk) ►*n.* A satirical imitation or burlesque of the heroic manner or style. —**mock′-he•ro′ic** *adj.*

mock•ing•bird (mŏk′ĭng-bûrd′) ►*n.* A gray and white songbird of the E US that mimics the sounds of other birds.

mock orange ►*n.* Any of numerous deciduous shrubs having white, usu. fragrant flowers.

mock•up also **mock-up** (mŏk′ŭp′) ►*n.* A usu.

full-sized scale model of a machine or structure, used for demonstration or testing.

mod (mŏd) ▶*n.* Fashionable style of dress. ▶*adj.* Fashionably up-to-date. [< MODERN.]

mode (mōd) ▶*n.* **1a.** A manner, way, or method of doing or acting. **b.** A particular form, variety, or manner. **c.** A given condition of functioning; status. **2.** The current fashion or style. **3.** *Mus.* Any of certain arrangements of the diatonic tones of an octave. **4.** *Statistics* The number in a distribution that occurs the most frequently. [< Lat. *modus.*] —**mod′al** *adj.*

mod•el (mŏd′l) ▶*n.* **1.** A small representation of an existing object, usu. built to scale. **2.** A preliminary pattern. **3.** A schematic description of a system or theory that accounts for its known properties. **4.** A style or design. **5.** An example to be emulated. **6.** One who poses for an artist. **7.** One who models clothes. ▶*v.* **-eled, -el•ing** also **-elled, -el•ling 1.** To plan or construct a model (of). **2.** To display (clothes) by wearing or posing. **3.** To serve or work as a model. ▶*adj.* **1.** Being or used as a model. **2.** Worthy of imitation; exemplary. [< Lat. *modus*, measure.] —**mod′el•er** *n.*

mo•dem (mō′dəm) ▶*n.* A device for transmitting data over telephone wires by modulating the data into an audio signal to send it and demodulating an audio signal into data to receive it. [*mo(dulator-)dem(odulator).*]

mod•er•ate (mŏd′ər-ĭt) ▶*adj.* **1.** Not excessive or extreme. **2.** Temperate. **3.** Average or mediocre. **4.** Opposed to radical views or measures. ▶*n.* One who holds moderate views or opinions. ▶*v.* (mŏd′ə-rāt′) **-at•ed, -at•ing 1.** To make or become less violent, severe, or extreme. **2.** To preside over as a moderator. [< Lat. *moderātus*, p.part. of *moderārī*, to moderate.] —**mod′er•ate•ly** *adv.* —**mod′er•a′tion** *n.*

Syns: *moderate, qualify, temper* ***v.***

mod•er•a•tor (mŏd′ə-rā′tər) ▶*n.* **1.** One that moderates. **2.** A presiding officer.

mod•ern (mŏd′ərn) ▶*adj.* **1.** Of or relating to recent times or the present. **2.** Characteristic of the present; up-to-date. [< LLat. *modernus.*] —**mod′ern** *n.* —**mod•ern′i•ty** (mŏ-dûr′nĭ-tē, mō-) *n.* —**mod′ern•i•za′tion** *n.* —**mod′ern•ize′** *v.*

Modern English ▶*n.* English since about 1500.

Modern Greek ▶*n.* Greek since the early 16th cent.

Modern Hebrew ▶*n.* The Hebrew language as used in Israel from 1948 on.

mod•ern•ism (mŏd′ər-nĭz′əm) ▶*n.* **1.** A theory, practice, or belief that is peculiar to modern times. **2.** often **Modernism** The use of innovative forms of expression that distinguish many styles in the arts and literature of the 20th cent. —**mod′ern•ist** *n.* —**mod′ern•is′tic** *adj.*

mod•est (mŏd′ĭst) ▶*adj.* **1.** Having or showing a moderate estimation of oneself. **2.** Retiring; shy. **3.** Observing conventional proprieties; decent. **4.** Free from ostentation. See Syns at **plain. 5.** Not extreme; moderate: *a modest price.* [Lat. *modestus.*] —**mod′est•ly** *adv.* —**mod′es•ty** *n.*

Mo•des•to (mə-dĕs′tō) A city of central CA SE of Stockton. Pop. 164,730.

mod•i•cum (mŏd′ĭ-kəm) ▶*n.* A small or token amount. [< Lat. *modicus*, moderate.]

mod•i•fy (mŏd′ə-fī′) ▶*v.* **-fied, -fy•ing 1.** To change or become changed; alter. **2.** To make or become less extreme, severe, or strong. **3.** *Gram.* To qualify or limit the meaning of. [< Lat. *modificāre*, to limit.] —**mod′i•fi•ca′tion** *n.* —**mod′i•fi′er** *n.*

Mo•di•glia•ni (mō-dē′lē-ä′nē, mō′dē-lyä′nē), **Amedeo.** 1884–1920. Italian painter and sculptor.

mod•ish (mō′dĭsh) ▶*adj.* Conforming to the current fashion. See Syns at **fashionable.** —**mod′ish•ly** *adv.* —**mod′ish•ness** *n.*

mo•diste (mō-dēst′) ▶*n.* One who produces, designs, or deals in women's fashions. [Fr.]

mod•u•late (mŏj′ə-lāt′) ▶*v.* **-lat•ed, -lat•ing 1.** To regulate or temper. **2.** To change or vary the pitch, intensity, or tone of. **3.** *Mus.* To pass from one tonality to another by harmonic progression. **4.** *Electron.* To vary the frequency, amplitude, phase, or other characteristic of (electromagnetic waves). [< Lat. *modulus*, measure.] —**mod′u•la′tion** *n.* —**mod′u•la′tor** *n.*

mod•ule (mŏj′o͞ol) ▶*n.* **1.** A standard or unit of measurement. **2.** A standardized unit or component of a system designed for easy assembly or flexible use. **3.** *Electron.* A self-contained assembly of electronic components and circuitry. **4.** A self-contained unit of a spacecraft that performs a specific task. [Lat. *modulus*, dim. of *modus*, measure.] —**mod′u•lar** *adj.*

mo•dus op•er•an•di (mō′dəs ŏp′ə-răn′dē, -dī′) ▶*n.*, *pl.* **mo•di operandi** (mō′dē, -dī). A method of operating or functioning. [NLat.]

Mo•ga•di•shu (mō′gə-dē′sho͞o, -dĭsh′o͞o, mô′-) The capital of Somalia, on the Indian Ocean. Pop. 400,000.

mo•gul (mō′gəl) ▶*n.* A hard mound or bump on a ski slope. [Prob. of Scand. orig.]

Mo•gul (mō′gəl, mō-gŭl′) ▶*n.* **1.** also **Mo•ghul** (mo͞o-gŭl′) **a.** A member of the force that under Baber conquered India in 1526. **b.** A member of the Muslim dynasty founded by Baber that ruled India until 1857. **2.** A Mongol or Mongolian. **3. mogul** A rich or powerful person. [< Mongolian *Mongul.*]

mo•hair (mō′hâr′) ▶*n.* **1.** The long silky hair of the Angora goat. **2.** Fabric made with yarn from this hair. [< Ar. *muḫayyar.*]

Mo•ham•med (mō-hăm′ĭd, -hä′mĭd, mo͞o-). See **Muhammad.**

Mo•ham•med•an (mō-hăm′ĭ-dən) ▶*n.* Var. of **Muhammadan.** —**Mo•ham′med•an•ism′** *n.*

Mo•ha•ve Desert (mō-hä′vē) See **Mojave Desert.**

Mo•hawk (mō′hôk′) ▶*n.*, *pl.* **-hawk** or **-hawks 1.** A member of a Native American people formerly of NE New York, now in S Ontario and extreme N New York. **2.** The Iroquoian language of the Mohawk.

Mo•he•gan (mō-hē′gən) ▶*n.*, *pl.* **-gan** or **-gans 1.** A member of a Native American people formerly of E Connecticut, now in SE Connecticut and Wisconsin. **2.** The Algonquian language of the Mohegan.

Mo•hen•jo-Da•ro (mō-hĕn′jō-där′ō) A ruined prehistoric city of Pakistan in the Indus River valley NE of Karachi.

Mo•hi•can (mō-hē′kən, mə-) ▶*n.* Var. of **Mahican.**

Mohs scale (mōz) ►*n.* A scale for determining the hardness of a mineral ranging from 1 for the softest to 10 for the hardest. [After Friedrich *Mohs* (1773–1839).]

moi•e•ty (moiʹĭ-tē) ►*n., pl.* **-ties 1.** A half. **2.** A portion or share. [< LLat. *medietās.*]

moil (moil) ►*v.* To work hard; toil. [< OFr. *moillier,* moisten.] —**moil** *n.* —**moilʹer** *n.*

moi•ré (mwä-rāʹ, mô-) ►*n.* **1.** Fabric, esp. silk, with a wavy or rippled pattern. **2.** A similar pattern pressed on cloth by engraved rollers. [Fr. < p.part. of *moirer,* to water.] —**moi•réʹ** *adj.*

moist (moist) ►*adj.* **-er, -est.** Slightly wet; damp. [< Lat. *mūcidus,* moldy.] —**moisʹten** (moiʹsən) *v.* —**moistʹly** *adv.* —**moistʹness** *n.*

mois•ture (moisʹchər) ►*n.* Diffused or condensed liquid; dampness. —**moisʹtur•izeʹ** *v.* —**moisʹtur•izʹer** *n.*

Mo•ja•ve Desert also **Mo•ha•ve Desert** (mō-häʹvē). An arid region of S CA SE of the Sierra Nevada.

mo•jo (mōʹjōʹ) ►*n., pl.* **-jos** or **-joes 1.** A magic charm or spell. **2.** An amulet worn by adherents of hoodoo or voodoo. **3.** Personal magnetism; charm. [Perh. of African orig.]

mol (mōl) ►*n.* Var. of **mole⁴**.

mol. ►*abbr.* **1.** molecular **2.** molecule

mo•lal (mōʹləl) ►*adj.* Being a solution having one mole of solute in 1,000 grams of solvent. —**mo•lalʹi•ty** (mō-lălʹĭ-tē) *n.*

mo•lar (mōʹlər) ►*n.* A tooth with a broad crown for grinding food, located behind the bicuspids. [< Lat. *molāris,* of a mill, grinding.] —**moʹlar** *adj.*

mo•las•ses (mə-lăsʹĭz) ►*n.* A thick brownish syrup produced in refining raw sugar. [< LLat. *mellāceum,* must.]

mold¹ (mōld) ►*n.* **1.** A hollow form or matrix for shaping a fluid or plastic substance. **2.** A frame or model for forming or shaping something. **3.** Something made in or shaped on a mold. **4.** General shape or form. **5.** Distinctive shape, character, or type. ►*v.* To shape in or on a mold. [< Lat. *modulus,* dim. of *modus,* measure.] —**moldʹa•ble** *adj.* —**moldʹer** *n.*

mold² (mōld) ►*n.* **1.** Any of various fungi that cause disintegration of organic matter. **2.** The growth of such fungi. ►*v.* To become moldy. [ME *moulde.*]

mold³ (mōld) ►*n.* Loose soil rich in humus and fit for planting. [< OE *molde.*]

Mol•da•vi•a (mŏl-dāʹvē-ə, -dāvʹyə) **1.** A historical region of E Romania E of Transylvania. **2.** See **Moldova.** —**Mol•daʹvi•an** *adj. & n.*

mold•er (mōlʹdər) ►*v.* To decay or crumble into dust. [Poss. < MOLD³.]

mold•ing (mōlʹdĭng) ►*n.* **1.** The act or process of molding. **2.** Something molded. **3.** An ornamental strip, as of wood, used to decorate or finish a surface, such as a wall or door.

Mol•do•va (mŏl-dōʹvə, môl-). Formerly **Mol•da•vi•a** (-dāʹvē-ə, -dāvʹyə). A country of E Europe bordering on Romania. Cap. Kishinev. Pop. 4,350,000. —**Mol•doʹvan** *adj. & n.*

mold•y (mōlʹdē) ►*adj.* **-i•er, -i•est 1.** Covered with or containing mold. **2.** Musty or stale, as from decay. —**moldʹi•ness** *n.*

mole¹ (mōl) ►*n.* A small congenital growth on the human skin, usu. dark and slightly raised. [< OE *māl.*]

mole² (mōl) ►*n.* A small burrowing mammal having silky fur, rudimentary eyes, a narrow snout, and strong forefeet for digging. [ME *molle.*]

mole³ (mōl) ►*n.* A massive jetty or breakwater built to protect a harbor. [< Lat. *mōlēs.*]

mole⁴ or **mol** (mōl) ►*n.* The amount of a substance that contains Avogadro's number of atoms, molecules, or other elementary units. [Ger. *Mol.*]

molecular biology ►*n.* The branch of biology dealing with the structure and function of essential molecules, such as nucleic acids, and esp. their role in heredity.

molecular weight ►*n.* The sum of the atomic weights of the atoms in a molecule.

mol•e•cule (mŏlʹĭ-kyōōlʹ) ►*n.* **1.** The smallest particle into which an element or compound can be divided without changing its chemical and physical properties. **2.** A small particle; tiny bit. [< Lat. *mōlēs,* mass.] —**mo•lecʹu•lar** *adj.*

mole•hill (mōlʹhĭlʹ) ►*n.* A small mound of loose earth raised by a burrowing mole.

mole•skin (mōlʹskĭnʹ) ►*n.* **1.** The fur of a mole. **2.** A heavy-napped cotton fabric.

mo•lest (mə-lĕstʹ) ►*v.* **1.** To disturb or annoy. **2.** To subject to unwanted or improper sexual activity. [< Lat. *molestāre.*] —**moʹles•taʹtion** (mōʹlĕ-stāʹshən) *n.* —**mo•lestʹer** *n.*

Mo•lière (mōl-yârʹ), **Jean Baptiste Poquelin.** 1622–73. French playwright.

moll (mŏl) ►*n. Slang* A woman companion of a gangster. [< *Moll,* nickname for *Mary.*]

mol•li•fy (mŏlʹə-fīʹ) ►*v.* **-fied, -fy•ing 1.** To placate; soothe. **2.** To soften or ease. [< LLat. *mollificāre,* make soft.] —**molʹli•fi•caʹtion** *n.*

mol•lusk also **mol•lusc** (mŏlʹəsk) ►*n.* Any of a phylum of chiefly marine invertebrates typically having a soft body and a protective shell and including the edible shellfish and the snails. [< Lat. *molluscus,* thin-shelled < *mollis,* soft.]

mol•ly•cod•dle (mŏlʹē-kŏdʹl) ►*v.* **-dled, -dling.** To spoil by pampering. ►*n.* A pampered person. [*molly,* milksop + CODDLE.]

Mo•lo•kai (mŏlʹə-kīʹ, mōʹlə-) An island of central HI between Oahu and Maui.

Mo•lo•tov cocktail (mŏlʹə-tôfʹ, môlʹ-, mōʹlə-) ►*n.* A makeshift incendiary bomb made of a bottle filled with flammable liquid and a usu. rag wick. [After V.M. *Molotov* (1890–1986).]

molt (mōlt) ►*v.* To periodically shed an outer covering, such as feathers or skin, for replacement by a new growth. ►*n.* The act of molting. [< Lat. *mūtāre,* to change.]

mol•ten (mōlʹtən) ►*adj.* Made liquid and glowing by heat; melted. [P.part. of MELT.]

Mo•luc•cas (mə-lŭkʹəz) A group of islands of E Indonesia between Sulawesi and New Guinea. —**Mo•lucʹcan** *adj. & n.*

mol. wt. ►*abbr.* molecular weight

mo•lyb•de•num (mə-lĭbʹdə-nəm) ►*n. Symbol* **Mo** A hard, silvery-white metallic element used to toughen alloy steels and soften steel alloys. At. no. 42. See table at **element.** [< Gk. *molubdos,* lead.]

mom (mŏm) ►*n. Informal* Mother. [< MAMA.]

Mom•ba•sa (mŏm-băsʹə, -bäʹsä) A city of SE Kenya mainly on **Mombasa Island,** in the Indian Ocean. Pop. 425,600.

mo•ment (mō′mənt) ▶*n.* **1.** A brief interval of time. **2.** A specific point in time: *not here at the moment.* **3.** A particular period of importance or excellence. **4.** Importance. [< Lat. *mōmentum* < *movēre*, move.]

mo•men•tar•i•ly (mō′mən-târ′ə-lē) ▶*adv.* **1.** For a moment. **2.** In a moment; shortly.

mo•men•tar•y (mō′mən-tĕr′ē) ▶*adj.* **1.** Lasting for only a moment. **2.** Occurring or present at every moment. —**mo′men•tar′i•ness** *n.*

mo•ment•ly (mō′mənt-lē) ▶*adv.* From moment to moment.

mo•men•tous (mō-mĕn′təs) ▶*adj.* Of utmost importance or significance. —**mo•men′tous•ly** *adv.* —**mo•men′tous•ness** *n.*

mo•men•tum (mō-mĕn′təm) ▶*n., pl.* **-ta** (-tə) or **-tums 1.** The product of a body's mass and velocity. **2.** Impetus. [Lat. *mōmentum*, movement < *movēre*, move.]

mom•my ▶*n., pl.* **-mies** *Informal* A mother. [Alteration of MAMMY.]

mommy track ▶*n.* A career path in which mothers relinquish certain professional opportunities in favor of benefits such as shorter or flexible hours.

Mon. ▶*abbr.* Monday

mon– ▶*pref.* Var. of **mono–.**

Mon•a•co (mŏn′ə-kō′, mə-nä′kō) A principality on the Mediterranean Sea consisting of an enclave in SE France. Cap. **Monaco** or **Monaco-Ville.** Pop. 27,063. —**Mon′a•can** *adj. & n.*

mon•arch (mŏn′ərk, -ärk′) ▶*n.* **1.** A hereditary sovereign, such as a king or queen. **2.** One that presides over or rules. **3.** A large orange and black butterfly. [< Gk. *monarkhos.*] —**mo•nar′chal** (mə-när′kəl), **mo•nar′chic** *adj.*

mon•ar•chism (mŏn′ər-kĭz′əm, -är′-) ▶*n.* **1.** The system or principles of monarchy. **2.** Belief in or advocacy of monarchy. —**mon′ar•chist** *n.* —**mon′ar•chis′tic** *adj.*

mon•ar•chy (mŏn′ər-kē, -är′-) ▶*n., pl.* **-chies 1.** Government by a monarch. **2.** A state ruled or headed by a monarch.

mon•as•ter•y (mŏn′ə-stĕr′ē) ▶*n., pl.* **-ries.** The dwelling place of a community of monks. [< LGk. *monastērion* < Gk. *monazein*, live alone.] —**mon′as•te′ri•al** (-stîr′ē-əl, -stĕr′-) *adj.*

mo•nas•tic (mə-năs′tĭk) also **mo•nas•ti•cal** (-tĭ-kəl) ▶*adj.* **1.** Of a monastery. **2.** Characteristic of life in a monastery or convent, esp.: **a.** Secluded and contemplative. **b.** Strictly disciplined. **c.** Self-abnegating; austere. [< LGk. *monastikos.*] —**mo•nas′ti•cal•ly** *adv.* —**mo•nas′ti•cism** *n.*

mon•au•ral (mŏn-ôr′əl) ▶*adj.* **1.** Of or designating sound reception by one ear. **2.** Using a single channel to record or reproduce sound; monophonic. —**mon•au′ral•ly** *adv.*

Mön•chen•glad•bach (mŭn′kən-glät′bäk) A city of W-central Germany WSW of Düsseldorf. Pop. 265,312.

Mon•dale (mŏn′dāl′), **Walter Frederick.** b. 1928. Vice President of the US (1977–81).

Mon•day (mŭn′dē, -dā′) ▶*n.* The 2nd day of the week. [< OE *Mōnandæg.*]

Mon•dri•an (môn′drē-än′, mŏn′-), **Piet.** 1872–1944. Dutch painter.

Mo•net (mō-nā′, mô-), **Claude.** 1840–1926. French painter.

mon•e•ta•rism (mŏn′ĭ-tə-rĭz′əm, mŭn′-) ▶*n.* A policy of regulating an economy by altering the money supply, esp. by increasing it moderately but steadily. —**mon′e•ta•rist** *adj. & n.*

mon•e•tar•y (mŏn′ĭ-tĕr′ē, mŭn′-) ▶*adj.* **1.** Of or relating to money. **2.** Of or relating to a nation's currency or coinage. [< Lat. *monēta*, money.] —**mon′e•tar′i•ly** *adv.*

mon•e•tize (mŏn′ĭ-tīz′, mŭn′-) ▶*v.* **-tized, -tiz•ing 1.** To establish as legal tender. **2.** To coin (money). —**mon′e•ti•za′tion** *n.*

mon•ey (mŭn′ē) ▶*n., pl.* **-eys** or **-ies 1.** A commodity that is legally established as an exchangeable equivalent of all other commodities and used as a measure of their comparative market value. **2.** The official currency issued by a government. **3.** Assets and property considered in terms of monetary value; wealth. **4.** Profit or loss: *made money on the sale.* **5.** often **moneys** or **monies** Sums of money; funds: *state tax monies.* [< Lat. *monēta.*]

mon•eyed also **mon•ied** (mŭn′ēd) ▶*adj.* **1.** Wealthy. See Syns at **rich. 2.** Representing or arising from money or wealth.

mon•ey•lend•er (mŭn′ē-lĕn′dər) ▶*n.* One that lends money at an interest rate.

mon•ey•mak•ing (mŭn′ē-mā′kĭng) ▶*n.* Acquisition of money. ▶*adj.* **1.** Engaged in acquiring wealth. **2.** Profitable. —**mon′ey•mak′er** *n.*

money market ▶*n.* **1.** The trade in short-term, low-risk securities, such as certificates of deposit and US Treasury notes. **2.** A mutual fund that sells its shares in order to purchase short-term securities.

money order ▶*n.* An order for the payment of a specified amount of money, usu. issued and payable at a bank or post office.

mon•ger (mŭng′gər, mŏng′-) ▶*n.* A dealer. [< Lat. *mangō.*]

Mon•gol (mŏng′gəl, -gōl′, mŏn′-) ▶*n.* **1.** A member of any of the traditionally nomadic peoples of Mongolia. **2.** See **Mongolian** 4. **3.** *Anthro.* A member of the Mongoloid racial division. —**Mon′gol** *adj.*

Mon•go•li•a (mŏng-gō′lē-ə, -gōl′yə, mŏn-) **1.** An ancient region of E-central Asia comprising modern-day Nei Monggol (Inner Mongolia) and the country of Mongolia. **2.** A country of N-central Asia between Russia and China. Cap. Ulaanbaatar. Pop. 2,363,000.

Mon•go•li•an (mŏng-gō′lē-ən, -gōl′yən, mŏn-) ▶*n.* **1.** A native or inhabitant of Mongolia. **2.** A Mongol. **3.** *Anthro.* A member of the Mongoloid racial division. **4a.** A subfamily of the Altaic language family including Mongolian. **b.** Any of the languages of the Mongols.

Mon•gol•ic (mŏng-gŏl′ĭk, mŏn-) ▶*adj.* *Anthro.* Of the Mongoloid racial division.

mon•gol•ism also **Mon•gol•ism** (mŏng′gə-lĭz′əm, mŏn′-) ▶*n.* *Offensive* Down syndrome.

Mon•gol•oid (mŏng′gə-loid′, mŏn′-) ▶*adj.* **1.** *Anthro.* Of or being a purported human racial classification distinguished by yellowish-brown skin color and straight black hair and including peoples indigenous to central and E Asia. Not in scientific use. **2.** Of or like a Mongol. **3.** also **mongoloid** *Offensive* Relating to Down syndrome. —**Mon′gol•oid′** *n.*

mon•goose (mŏng′go͞os′, mŏn′-) ▶*n., pl.* **-goos•es.** Any of various weasellike, chiefly African or Asian mammals noted for their ability to kill venomous snakes. [Marathi *mangūs.*]

mon•grel (mŭng′grəl, mŏng′-) ►*n.* A plant or animal, esp. a dog, of mixed breed. ►*adj.* Of mixed origin or character. [Prob. < ME *mong*, mixture.]

mon•ied (mŭn′ēd) ►*adj.* Var. of **moneyed.**

mon•ies (mŭn′ēz) ►*n.* Pl. of **money.**

mon•i•ker or **mon•ick•er** (mŏn′ĭ-kər) ►*n.* *Slang* A nickname. [< Ir. dial. *munik.*]

mo•nism (mō′nĭz′əm, mŏn′ĭz′əm) ►*n.* The view in metaphysics that all reality is composed of and reducible to one substance. —**mo′nist** *n.* —**mo•nis′tic** (mō-nĭs′tĭk, mŏ-) *adj.*

mo•ni•tion (mō-nĭsh′ən, mə-) ►*n.* A warning or admonition. [< Lat. *monēre, monit-*, warn.]

mon•i•tor (mŏn′ĭ-tər) ►*n.* **1.** A pupil who assists a teacher. **2a.** A usu. electronic device used to record or control a process or system. **b.** A screen used to check the picture being broadcast or picked up by a camera. **c.** *Comp. Sci.* A device that accepts video signals from a computer and displays information on a screen. ►*v.* To check, watch, or keep track of, often by means of an electronic device. [Lat., one who warns < *monēre*, warn.]

mon•i•to•ry (mŏn′ĭ-tôr′ē, -tōr′ē) ►*adj.* Conveying an admonition or warning.

monk (mŭngk) ►*n.* A man who is a member of a religious community living in a monastery. [< LGk. *monakhos* < Gk. *monos*, single.] —**monk′ish** *adj.* —**monk′ish•ly** *adv.*

mon•key (mŭng′kē) ►*n.*, *pl.* **-keys.** Any of various long-tailed, medium-sized primates including the macaques, baboons, capuchins, and marmosets and excluding apes and prosimians. ►*v.* *Informal* To play or tamper with something. [?]

monkey business ►*n.* *Slang* Mischievous or deceitful behavior.

mon•key•shine (mŭng′kē-shīn′) ►*n.* *Slang* A prank. Often used in the plural.

monkey wrench ►*n.* **1.** A hand tool with adjustable jaws for turning nuts. **2.** *Informal* Something that hinders or disrupts.

monks•hood (mŭngks′ho͝od′) ►*n.* **1.** See **aconite. 2.** A poisonous perennial plant whose dried leaves and roots yield aconite.

Mon•mouth (mŏn′məth), Duke of. James Scott 1649–85. English pretender to the throne.

mon•o[1] (mŏn′ō) ►*n.* *Informal* Infectious mononucleosis.

mon•o[2] (mŏn′ō) ►*adj.* *Informal* Monaural.

mono– or **mon–** ►*pref.* One; single; alone: *monofilament.* [< Gk. *monos*, single.]

mon•o•chro•mat•ic (mŏn′ə-krō-măt′ĭk) ►*adj.* **1.** Of only one color. **2.** Of or composed of radiation of only one wavelength. —**mon′o•chro•mat′i•cal•ly** *adv.*

mon•o•chrome (mŏn′ə-krōm′) ►*n.* **1.** A painting or drawing done in different shades of a single color. **2.** The technique of executing a monochrome. [< Gk. *monokhrōmos*, of one color.] —**mon′o•chro′mic** *adj.*

mon•o•cle (mŏn′ə-kəl) ►*n.* An eyeglass for one eye. [< LLat. *monoculus*, one-eyed.]

mon•o•cline (mŏn′ə-klīn′) ►*n.* A geologic structure in which all layers are inclined in the same direction. —**mon′o•cli′nal** *adj.*

mon•o•clo•nal (mŏn′ə-klō′nəl) ►*adj.* Of, forming, or derived from a single clone: *a monoclonal antibody.*

mon•o•cot•y•le•don (mŏn′ə-kŏt′l-ēd′n) also **mon•o•cot** (mŏn′ə-kŏt′) ►*n.* A plant having a single embryonic seed leaf that appears at germination. —**mon′o•cot′y•le′don•ous** *adj.*

mo•noc•u•lar (mŏ-nŏk′yə-lər, mə-) ►*adj.* **1.** Having one eye. **2.** Of or intended for use by only one eye.

mon•o•cul•ture (mŏn′ə-kŭl′chər) ►*n.* **1.** The cultivation of a single crop in an area or region. **2.** A single homogeneous society or culture. —**mon′o•cul′tur•al** *adj.*

mon•o•dy (mŏn′ə-dē) ►*n.*, *pl.* **-dies.** An ode or elegy. [< Gk. *monōidia.*] —**mo•nod′ic** (mə-nŏd′ĭk) *adj.* —**mon′o•dist** *n.*

mon•o•fil•a•ment (mŏn′ə-fĭl′ə-mənt) ►*n.* A single strand of untwisted synthetic fiber used esp. for fishing line.

mo•nog•a•my (mə-nŏg′ə-mē) ►*n.* **1.** The condition or practice of being sexually faithful to one partner during a relationship. **2.** Marriage to only one person at a time. —**mo•nog′a•mist** *n.* —**mo•nog′a•mous** *adj.* —**mo•nog′a•mous•ly** *adv.*

mon•o•gram (mŏn′ə-grăm′) ►*n.* A design composed of one or more initials of a name. ►*v.* **-grammed, -gram•ming** also **-gramed, -gram•ing.** To mark with a monogram. —**mon′o•gram•mat′ic** (-grə-măt′ĭk) *adj.*

mon•o•graph (mŏn′ə-grăf′) ►*n.* A scholarly book or article on a specific, often limited subject. —**mon′o•graph′ic** *adj.*

mon•o•lin•gual (mŏn′ə-lĭng′gwəl) ►*adj.* Using or knowing only one language. —**mon′o•lin′gual** *n.* —**mon′o•lin′gual•ism** *n.*

mon•o•lith (mŏn′ə-lĭth′) ►*n.* **1.** A large block of stone, esp. one used in architecture or sculpture. **2.** A large organization that acts as a powerful unit. —**mon′o•lith′ic** *adj.*

mon•o•logue also **mon•o•log** (mŏn′ə-lôg′, -lŏg′) ►*n.* **1.** A soliloquy. **2.** A series of jokes delivered by a comedian. **3.** A long speech by one person, often monopolizing a conversation. —**mon′o•logu′ist, mo•nol′o•gist** (mə-nŏl′ə-jĭst, mŏn′ə-lôg′ĭst, -lŏg′-) *n.*

mon•o•ma•ni•a (mŏn′ə-mā′nē-ə, -mān′yə) ►*n.* **1.** Obsession with one idea. **2.** Intent concentration on one subject. —**mon′o•ma′ni•ac′** *n.* —**mon′o•ma•ni′a•cal** (-mə-nī′ə-kəl) *adj.*

mon•o•mer (mŏn′ə-mər) ►*n.* A molecule that can be chemically bound to form a polymer. —**mon′o•mer′ic** (-mĕr′ĭk) *adj.*

mo•no•mi•al (mŏ-nō′mē-əl, mə-) ►*n.* **1.** An algebraic expression consisting of only one term. **2.** *Biol.* A taxonomic name consisting of a single word. [MON(O)– + (BIN)OMIAL.] —**mo•no′mi•al** *adj.*

Mo•non•ga•he•la River (mə-nŏng′gə-hē′lə, -hā′-) A river rising in N WV and flowing about 206 km (128 mi) to join the Allegheny R. and form the Ohio R.

mon•o•nu•cle•o•sis (mŏn′ō-no͞o′klē-ō′sĭs, -nyo͞o-) ►*n.* Infectious mononucleosis.

mon•o•phon•ic (mŏn′ə-fŏn′ĭk) ►*adj.* Monaural. —**mon′o•phon′i•cal•ly** *adv.*

mon•o•plane (mŏn′ə-plān′) ►*n.* An airplane with only one pair of wings.

mo•nop•o•lize (mə-nŏp′ə-līz′) ►*v.* **-lized, -liz•ing 1.** To acquire or maintain a monopoly of. **2.** To dominate by excluding others: *mo-*

nopolized the conversation. —**mo•nop′o•li•za′tion** *n.* —**mo•nop′o•liz′er** *n.*

Syns: *monopolize, absorb, consume, engross, preoccupy* **v.**

mo•nop•o•ly (mə-nŏp′ə-lē) ►*n., pl.* **-lies 1.** Exclusive control or ownership, as of a commodity or service. **2a.** A company or group having such control. **b.** A commodity or service so controlled. [< Gk. *monopōlion*, sole selling rights.] —**mo•nop′o•list** *n.* —**mo•nop′o•lis′tic** *adj.*

mon•o•rail (mŏn′ə-rāl′) ►*n.* A railway system using a single rail.

monorail

mon•o•sac•cha•ride (mŏn′ə-săk′ə-rīd′, -rĭd) ►*n.* A carbohydrate that cannot be decomposed by hydrolysis; simple sugar.

mon•o•so•di•um glu•ta•mate (mŏn′ə-sō′dē-əm glo͞o′tə-māt′) ►*n.* A white crystalline compound used as a flavor enhancer.

mon•o•syl•la•ble (mŏn′ə-sĭl′ə-bəl) ►*n.* A word of one syllable. —**mon′o•syl•lab′ic** (-sĭ-lăb′ĭk) *adj.*

mon•o•the•ism (mŏn′ə-thē-ĭz′əm) ►*n.* The belief that there is only one God. —**mon′o•the′ist** *n.* —**mon′o•the•is′tic** *adj.*

mon•o•tone (mŏn′ə-tōn′) ►*n.* A succession of sounds or words uttered in a single tone of voice or sung at a single pitch.

mo•not•o•nous (mə-nŏt′n-əs) ►*adj.* **1.** Unvarying in tone or pitch. **2.** Repetitiously dull. —**mo•not′o•nous•ly** *adv.* —**mo•not′o•nous•ness** *n.* —**mo•not′o•ny** *n.*

mon•o•type (mŏn′ə-tīp′) ►*n. Biol.* The sole member of its group, such as a single species that constitutes a genus. —**mon′o•typ′ic** (-tĭp′ĭk) *adj.*

mon•o•un•sat•u•rat•ed (mŏn′ō-ŭn-săch′ə-rā′tĭd) ►*adj.* Being an unsaturated fat composed esp. of fatty acids having only one double bond in the carbon chain.

mon•o•va•lent (mŏn′ə-vā′lənt) ►*adj.* Univalent. —**mon′o•va′lence, mon′o•va′len•cy** *n.*

mon•ox•ide (mə-nŏk′sīd′) ►*n.* An oxide with each molecule containing one oxygen atom.

mon•o•zy•got•ic (mŏn′ō-zī-gŏt′ĭk) ►*adj.* Derived from a single fertilized ovum. Used esp. of identical twins.

Mon•roe (mən-rō′), **James.** 1758–1831. The 5th US President (1817–25).

Monroe, Marilyn. Norma Jean Baker. 1926–62. Amer. actress.

Mon•ro•vi•a (mən-rō′vē-ə) The capital of Liberia, in the NW. Pop. 421,053.

Mon•sieur (mə-syœ′) ►*n., pl.* **Mes•sieurs** (mā-syœ′, mĕs′ərz). A French courtesy title for a man. [< OFr., my lord.]

Mon•si•gnor also **mon•si•gnor** (mŏn-sēn′yər) ►*n. Rom. Cath. Ch.* A title and office conferred on a cleric by the Pope. [Ital. < Fr. *Monseigneur*.]

James Monroe
detail of a c. 1820 portrait

mon•soon (mŏn-so͞on′) ►*n.* A wind system that influences large climatic regions and reverses direction seasonally, esp. the Asiatic system producing dry and wet seasons in India and S Asia. [< Ar. *mawsim*, season.]

mon•ster (mŏn′stər) ►*n.* **1.** A creature having a strange or frightening appearance. **2.** An animal or plant having gross defects or deformities. **3.** Something unusually large. **4.** One who inspires horror or disgust. [< Lat. *mōnstrum*, portent < *monēre*, warn.] —**mon•stros′i•ty** (-strŏs′ĭ-te) *n.* —**mon′strous** *adj.* —**mon′strous•ly** *adv.* —**mon′strous•ness** *n.*

mon•strance (mŏn′strəns) ►*n. Rom. Cath. Ch.* A receptacle in which the host is held. [< Lat. *mōnstrāre*, show < *mōnstrum*, MONSTER.]

Mont. ►*abbr.* Montana

mon•tage (mŏn-täzh′, môN-) ►*n.* **1.** A single pictorial composition made by juxtaposing several pictures or designs. **2.** A rapid succession of scenes or images, as in a movie, that exhibits different aspects of the same idea or situation. [Fr. < *monter*, MOUNT[1].]

Mon•tag•nais (mŏn′tən-yā′) ►*n., pl.* **-nais 1.** A member of a Native American people inhabiting Quebec and Labrador. **2.** The Algonquian language of the Montagnais.

Mon•taigne (mŏn-tān′), **Michel Eyquem de.** 1533–92. French essayist.

Mon•tan•a (mŏn-tăn′ə) A state of the NW US bordering on Canada. Cap. Helena. Pop. 803,655. —**Mon•tan′an** *adj. & n.*

mon•tane (mŏn-tān′, mŏn′tān′) ►*adj.* Of, growing in, or inhabiting mountain areas. [Lat. *montānus*.]

Mont•calm de Saint-Ve•ran (mŏnt-käm′ də săN′vā-räN′, môN-kälm′), Marquis **Louis Joseph de.** 1712–59. French commander in Canada.

Mon•te Car•lo (mŏn′tē kär′lō) A resort town of Monaco on the Mediterranean Sea and the French Riviera. Pop. 13,150.

Mon•te•neg•ro (mŏn′tə-nĕg′rō, -nē′grō) A constituent republic of Yugoslavia in the SW part, bordering on the Adriatic Sea. Cap. Podgorica. Pop. 616,327. —**Mon′te•neg′rin** *adj. & n.*

Mon•te•rey (mŏn′tə-rā′) A city of W CA S of San Francisco on **Monterey Bay,** an inlet of the Pacific. Pop. 31,954.

Monterey jack ►*n.* A mild semisoft cheese with a high moisture content. [After MONTEREY.]

Mon•ter•rey (mŏn′tə-rā′, môn′tĕ-) A city of NE Mexico E of Matamoros. Pop. 1,090,099.

Mon•tes•quieu (mŏn′tə-skyōō′). Baron de la Brede et de Montesquieu. Title of Charles de Secondat. 1689–1755. French philosopher and jurist.

Mon•tes•so•ri (mŏn′tĭ-sôr′ē, -sōr′ē), **Maria.** 1870–1952. Italian physician and educator.

Montessori method ►*n.* A method of educating children that stresses development of a child's own initiative.

Mon•te•vi•de•o (mŏn′tə-vĭ-dā′ō) The capital of Uruguay, in the S part on the Río de la Plata estuary. Pop. 1,360,258.

Mon•te•zu•ma II (mŏn′tĭ-zōō′mə). 1466?–1520. Aztec emperor in Mexico (1502–20).

Mont•gom•er•y (mŏnt-gŭm′ə-rē, -gŭm′rē) The capital of AL, in the SE-central part SSE of Birmingham. Pop. 187,106.

Montgomery, Sir **Bernard Law.** 1887–1976. British army officer.

month (mŭnth) ►*n.* **1.** The period during which the moon passes once through its phases, equal to about 30 days or 4 weeks. **2.** One of the usu. 12 divisions of a calendar year. See table at **calendar. 3.** A period extending from a date in one calendar month to the corresponding date in the next month. [< OE *mōnath.*]

month•ly (mŭnth′lē) ►*adj.* **1.** Occurring, appearing, or payable every month. **2.** Continuing or lasting for a month. ►*adv.* Once a month; every month. ►*n., pl.* **-lies.** A publication appearing once each month.

Mont•pel•ier (mŏnt-pēl′yər) The capital of VT, in the N-central part. Pop. 8,247.

Mon•tre•al (mŏn′trē-ôl′) A city of S Quebec, Canada, on **Montreal Island** in the St. Lawrence R. Pop. 1,017,666.

Mont-Saint-Mi•chel (môN-săN-mē-shĕl′) A small island off the coast of NW France in an arm of the English Channel.

Mont•ser•rat (mŏnt′sə-răt′) An island in the Leeward Is. of the British West Indies NW of Guadaloupe.

mon•u•ment (mŏn′yə-mənt) ►*n.* **1.** A structure erected as a memorial. **2.** A tombstone. **3.** Something preserved for its historic or aesthetic significance. **4a.** An outstanding or enduring achievement. **b.** An exceptional example. [< Lat. *monumentum* < *monēre*, remind.]

mon•u•men•tal (mŏn′yə-mĕn′tl) ►*adj.* **1.** Of or serving as a monument. **2.** Impressively large and sturdy. **3.** Of outstanding significance. **4.** Astounding: *monumental cowardice.* —**mon′u•men′tal•ly** *adv.*

moo (mōō) ►*v.* To emit the deep bellowing sound made by a cow. [Imit.] —**moo** *n.*

mooch (mōōch) ►*v. Slang* To obtain free; beg. See Syns at **cadge.** [< OFr. *muchier*, skulk.] —**mooch′er** *n.*

mood[1] (mōōd) ►*n.* **1.** A state of mind or emotion. **2.** Inclination; disposition. [< OE *mōd.*]

mood[2] (mōōd) ►*n.* A set of verb forms or inflections used to indicate the factuality or likelihood of the action or condition expressed. [< MODE.]

mood•y (mōō′dē) ►*adj.* **-i•er, -i•est 1.** Given to changeable moods; temperamental. **2.** Subject to periods of depression; gloomy. —**mood′i•ly** *adv.* —**mood′i•ness** *n.*

moon (mōōn) ►*n.* **1.** often **Moon** The natural satellite of Earth, approx. 221,600 miles distant at perigee and 252,950 miles at apogee, and having a mean diameter of 2,160 miles, mass approx. one eightieth that of Earth, and an average period of revolution around Earth of 29 days 12 hours 44 minutes. **2.** A natural satellite revolving around a planet. **3.** The moon as it appears at a particular phase: *the full moon.* **4.** A month. **5.** A disk, globe, or crescent resembling the moon. ►*v.* To wander about or pass time in a dreamy or aimless way. [< OE *mōna.*] —**moon′y** *adj.*

moon•beam (mōōn′bēm′) ►*n.* A ray of moonlight.

moon•light (mōōn′līt′) ►*n.* The light of the moon. ►*v. Informal* To work at a second job, often at night. —**moon′light′er** *n.*

moon•lit (mōōn′lĭt′) ►*adj.* Lighted by moonlight.

moon•shine (mōōn′shīn′) ►*n.* **1.** Moonlight. **2.** *Informal* Foolish talk; nonsense. **3.** Illegally distilled whiskey. —**moon′shin′er** *n.*

moon•stone (mōōn′stōn′) ►*n.* A form of feldspar valued for its pearly translucence.

moon•struck (mōōn′strŭk′) ►*adj.* **1.** Dazed or distracted with romantic sentiment. **2.** Mentally unbalanced; crazed. [From the belief that the moon caused insanity.]

moor[1] (mŏŏr) ►*v.* To secure in place with or as if with lines, cables, or anchors. See Syns at **fasten.** [ME *moren.*] —**moor′age** *n.*

moor[2] (mŏŏr) ►*n.* A broad area of open, often boggy land, usu. covered with low shrubs. [< OE *mōr.*]

Moor ►*n.* **1.** A member of a Muslim people of mixed Berber and Arab descent, now living chiefly in NW Africa. **2.** One of the Muslims who invaded Spain in the 8th cent. [< Gk. *Mauros.*] —**Moor′ish** *adj.*

Moore (mŏŏr, môr), **Henry.** 1898–1986. British sculptor.

Moore, Marianne Craig. 1887–1972. Amer. poet.

moor•ing (mŏŏr′ĭng) ►*n.* **1.** A place at which a vessel or aircraft can be moored. **2.** often **moorings** Elements providing stability or security.

moose (mōōs) ►*n., pl.* **moose.** A large deer of N North America, having broad flattened antlers in the male. [Of Algonquian orig.]

moot (mōōt) ►*v.* To bring up as a subject for discussion or debate. See Syns at **broach.** ►*adj.* **1.** Subject to debate; arguable. **2.** *Law* Without legal significance. **3.** Irrelevant. [< OE *mōt*, assembly.]

moot court ►*n.* A mock court where hypothetical cases are tried by law students as an exercise.

mop (mŏp) ►*n.* **1.** A household implement made of absorbent material attached to a handle and used for cleaning floors. **2.** A tangled mass, esp. of hair. ►*v.* **mopped, mop•ping.** To wash or wipe with or as if with a mop. —***phrasal verb:*** **mop up 1.** To clear (an area) of remaining enemy troops after a victory. **2.** To conclude a project or activity. [ME *mappe.*] —**mop′per** *n.*

mope (mōp) ►*v.* **moped, mop•ing.** To be gloomy or dejected. See Syns at **brood.** [?] —**mop′er** *n.* —**mop′ish•ly** *adv.*

mo•ped (mō′pĕd′) ►*n.* A motorbike that can be pedaled as well as driven by a low-powered gasoline engine.

mop•pet (mŏp′ĭt) ►*n.* A young child. [< ME *moppe*, child.]

mop-up (mŏp′ŭp′) ►*n.* The act of disposing of final or remaining details.

mo•raine (mə-rān′) ►*n.* An accumulation of boulders, stones, or other debris carried and deposited by a glacier. [Fr.]

mor•al (môr′əl, mŏr′-) ►*adj.* **1.** Of or concerned with the judgment or instruction of goodness or badness of character and behavior. **2.** Conforming to established standards of good behavior. **3.** Arising from conscience. **4.** Having psychological rather than tangible effects. **5.** Based on likelihood rather than evidence. ►*n.* **1.** The principle taught by a story or event. **2. morals** Rules or habits of conduct, esp. of sexual conduct. [< Lat. *mōrālis* < *mōs*, *mōr-*, custom.] —**mor′al•ly** *adv.*

mo•rale (mə-răl′) ►*n.* The state of mind of a person or group as exhibited by confidence, cheerfulness, and discipline. [Fr.]

Syns: *morale, esprit, esprit de corps* **n.**

mor•al•ist (môr′ə-lĭst, mŏr′-) ►*n.* **1.** A teacher or student of ethics. **2.** One who follows a system of moral principles. —**mor′a•lis′tic** *adj.* —**mor′a•lis′ti•cal•ly** *adv.*

mo•ral•i•ty (mə-răl′ĭ-tē, mô-) ►*n., pl.* **-ties 1.** The quality of being moral. **2.** A system of ideas of right and wrong conduct. **3.** Virtuous conduct.

mor•al•ize (môr′ə-līz′, mŏr′-) ►*v.* **-ized, -iz•ing.** To think about or discuss moral issues. —**mor′al•i•za′tion** *n.* —**mor′al•iz′er** *n.*

mo•rass (mə-răs′, mô-) ►*n.* **1.** An area of low-lying, soggy ground. **2.** A difficult, perplexing, or overwhelming situation. [< OFr. *marais*.]

mor•a•to•ri•um (môr′ə-tôr′ē-əm, -tōr′-, mŏr′-) ►*n., pl.* **-to•ri•ums** or **-to•ri•a** (-tôr′ē-ə, -tōr′-) **1.** *Law* An authorization to a debtor permitting temporary suspension of payments. **2.** A suspension or delay of any action or activity. [< LLat. *morātōrius*, delaying < Lat. *mora*, delay.]

Mo•ra•vi•a (mə-rā′vē-ə, mō-) A region of central and E Czech Republic. —**Mo•ra′vi•an** *adj. & n.*

mo•ray (môr′ā, mə-rā′) ►*n.* Any of numerous chiefly tropical marine eels that are ferocious fighters. [< Gk. *muraina*.]

mor•bid (môr′bĭd) ►*adj.* **1.** Of or caused by disease. **2.** Marked by preoccupation with unwholesome matters. **3.** Gruesome; grisly. [Lat. *morbidus* < *morbus*, disease.] —**mor′bid•ly** *adv.* —**mor′bid•ness** *n.*

mor•bid•i•ty (môr-bĭd′ĭ-tē) ►*n., pl.* **-ties 1.** The condition or quality of being morbid. **2.** The rate of incidence of a disease.

mor•da•cious (môr-dā′shəs) ►*adj.* **1.** Given to biting. **2.** Caustic; sarcastic. [< Lat. *mordāx*, *mordāc-* < *mordēre*, bite.] —**mor•da′cious•ly** *adv.* —**mor•dac′i•ty** (-dăs′ĭ-tē) *n.*

mor•dant (môr′dnt) ►*adj.* **1.** Bitingly sarcastic. **2.** Incisive and trenchant. [< Lat. *mordēre*, bite.] —**mor′dan•cy** *n.* —**mor′dant•ly** *adv.*

more (môr, mōr) ►*adj.* Comp. of **many, much. 1a.** Greater in number. **b.** Greater in size, amount, extent, or degree. **2.** Additional; extra: *She needs some more time.* ►*n.* A greater or additional quantity, number, degree, or amount. ►*pron. (takes pl. v.)* A greater or additional number of persons or things. ►*adv.* Comp. of **much. 1a.** To or in a greater extent or degree: *loved him even more.* **b.** Used to form the comparative of many adjectives and adverbs: *more difficult; more softly.* **2.** In addition: *phoned twice more.* —***idiom:*** **more or less 1.** About; approximately. **2.** To an undetermined degree. [< OE *māra*.]

More, Sir **Thomas.** 1478–1535. English politician, scholar, and writer.

mo•rel (mə-rĕl′, mô-) ►*n.* An edible mushroom having a brownish spongelike cap. [< OFr. *morille*.]

more•o•ver (môr-ō′vər, mōr-, môr′ō′vər, mōr′-) ►*adv.* Furthermore; besides.

mo•res (môr′āz′, -ēz, mōr′-) ►*pl.n.* The accepted customs and rules of a particular social group. [Lat. *mōrēs*, customs.]

Mor•gan (môr′gən), **John Pierpont.** 1837–1913. Amer. financier and philanthropist.

morgue (môrg) ►*n.* **1.** A place in which the bodies of persons found dead are temporarily kept. **2.** A reference file in a newspaper or magazine office. [Fr.]

mor•i•bund (môr′ə-bŭnd′, mŏr′-) ►*adj.* At the point of death. [Lat. *moribundus* < *morī*, die.] —**mor′i•bun′di•ty** *n.* —**mor′i•bund′ly** *adv.*

Mo•ri•sot (mô-rē-zō′), **Berthe.** 1841–95. French impressionist painter.

Mor•mon (môr′mən) ►*n.* A member of the Mormon Church. —**Mor′mon** *adj.* —**Mor′mon•ism** *n.*

Mormon Church ►*n.* A church founded by Joseph Smith in 1830 and having its headquarters in Salt Lake City, Utah.

morn (môrn) ►*n.* Morning. [< OE *morgen*.]

morn•ing (môr′nĭng) ►*n.* The first or early part of the day, esp. from sunrise to noon.

morning glory ►*n.* Any of various twining vines having funnel-shaped flowers that close late in the day.

mo•roc•co (mə-rŏk′ō) ►*n., pl.* **-cos.** A soft fine leather of goatskin. [< MOROCCO.]

Morocco. A country of NW Africa on the Mediterranean and the Atlantic. Cap. Rabat. Pop. 26,590,000. —**Mo•roc′can** *adj. & n.*

mo•ron (môr′ŏn′, mōr′-) ►*n.* **1.** A stupid person. **2.** *Psychol.* A person of mild mental retardation having a mental age of from 7 to 12 years. Not in scientific use. [< Gk. *mōros*, stupid.] —**mo•ron′ic** (mə-rŏn′ĭk, mô-) *adj.*

Mo•ro•ni (mə-rō′nē, mô-) The capital of the Comoros, on Grand Comoro I. at the N end of the Mozambique Channel. Pop. 20,112.

mo•rose (mə-rōs′, mô-) ►*adj.* Sullenly melancholy; gloomy. [Lat. *mōrōsus*, peevish.] —**mo•rose′ly** *adv.* —**mo•rose′ness** *n.*

morph (môrf) ►*v.* **1.** To transform (an image) by computer: *morphed the villain into a snake.* **2.** To be transformed. [< METAMORPHOSE.]

-morph ►*suff.* **1.** Form; shape; structure: *isomorph.* **2.** Morpheme: *allomorph.* [< Gk. *morphē*, shape.]

mor•pheme (môr′fēm′) ►*n.* A linguistic unit, such as *man*, or *-ed* in *walked*, that has meaning and cannot be divided into smaller meaningful parts. [Fr. *morphème*.] —**mor•phem′ic** *adj.* —**mor•phem′i•cal•ly** *adv.*

mor•phine (môr′fēn′) ►*n.* A powerfully addictive narcotic drug extracted from opium, used in medicine as an anesthetic or sedative. [Fr. < Lat. *Morpheus*, god of dreams.]

morpho– or **morph–** ►*pref.* **1.** Form; shape; structure: *morphogenesis.* **2.** Morpheme: *morphology.* [< Gk. *morphē*, shape.]

mor•pho•gen•e•sis (môr′fō-jĕn′ĭ-sĭs) ►*n.* Evolutionary or embryological development of the structure of an organism or part. —**mor′pho•ge•net′ic** (-jə-nĕt′ĭk), **mor′pho•gen′ic** *adj.*

mor•phol•o•gy (môr-fŏl′ə-jē) ►*n., pl.* **-gies 1.** The biological study of the form and structure of organisms. **2.** *Ling.* The study of word formation, including inflection, derivation, and compounds. —**mor′pho•log′i•cal** (-fə-lŏj′ĭ-kəl), **mor′pho•log′ic** *adj.* —**mor′pho•log′i•cal•ly** *adv.* —**mor•phol′o•gist** *n.*

mor•ris (môr′ĭs, mŏr′-) ►*n.* An English folk dance in which a story is enacted by costumed dancers. [< ME *moreys*, Moorish.]

Morris, Gouverneur. 1752–1816. Amer. political leader and diplomat.

Morris, Robert. 1734–1806. Amer. Revolutionary politician and financier.

Morris, William. 1834–96. British poet, artist, and social reformer.

Morris chair ►*n.* A large easy chair with an adjustable back and removable cushions. [After William MORRIS.]

Morris Jes•up (jĕs′əp), **Cape.** A cape of N Greenland on the Arctic Ocean; the world's northernmost point of land.

Mor•ris•on (môr′ĭ-sən, mŏr′-), **Toni.** b. 1931. Amer. writer; 1993 Nobel.

Toni Morrison

mor•row (môr′ō, mŏr′ō) ►*n.* The following day. [ME *morwe* < OE *morgen.*]

Morse (môrs), **Samuel Finley Breese.** 1791–1872. Amer. painter and inventor.

Morse code ►*n.* A code, used esp. in telegraphy, in which letters of the alphabet and numbers are represented by various sequences of dots and dashes or short and long signals. [After Samuel F. B. MORSE.]

mor•sel (môr′səl) ►*n.* **1.** A small piece of food. **2.** A tasty tidbit. **3.** A bit or item: *a morsel of wisdom.* [< Lat. *mordēre*, to bite.]

mor•tal (môr′tl) ►*adj.* **1.** Liable or subject to death. **2.** Of or accompanying death. **3.** Causing death; fatal. **4a.** Fought to the death: *mortal combat.* **b.** Unrelentingly antagonistic: *mortal foes.* **5.** Of great intensity or severity; dire: *mortal terror.* ►*n.* A human. [< Lat. *mors, mort-*, death.] —**mor′tal•ly** *adv.*

mor•tal•i•ty (môr-tăl′ĭ-tē) ►*n.* **1.** The condition of being mortal. **2.** Death rate.

mor•tar (môr′tər) ►*n.* **1.** A vessel in which substances are crushed or ground with a pestle. **2.** A muzzleloading cannon used to fire shells in high trajectories. **3.** A bonding material used in building, esp. a mixture of cement or lime with sand and water. [< Lat. *mortārium.*]

A	B	C	D
.-	-...	-.-.	-..
E	F	G	H
.	..-.	--.	....
I	J	K	L
..	.---	-.-	.-..
M	N	O	P
--	-.	---	.--.
Q	R	S	T
--.-	.-.	...	-
U	V	W	X
..-	...-	.--	-..-
Y	Z		
-.--	--..		

Morse code
international Morse code

mor•tar•board (môr′tər-bôrd′, -bōrd′) ►*n.* **1.** A square board with a handle used for holding and carrying mortar. **2.** An academic cap topped by a flat square and a tassel.

mort•gage (môr′gĭj) ►*n.* **1.** A legal pledge of property to a creditor as security for the payment of a loan or other debt. **2.** A contract or deed specifying the terms of a mortgage. ►*v.* **-gaged, -gag•ing.** To pledge (property) by means of a mortgage. [< OFr.] —**mort′ga•gee′** (-gĭ-jē′) *n.* —**mort′ga•gor′** (-jôr′, -jər) *n.*

mor•ti•cian (môr-tĭsh′ən) ►*n.* See **funeral director.** [Lat. *mors, mort-*, death + –ICIAN.]

mor•ti•fy (môr′tə-fī′) ►*v.* **-fied, -fy•ing 1.** To shame; humiliate. **2.** To discipline (one's body and appetites) by self-denial. [< Lat. *mortificāre*, cause to die.] —**mor′ti•fi•ca′tion** *n.*

mor•tise (môr′tĭs) ►*n.* A usu. rectangular cavity in a piece of wood, stone, or other material, prepared to receive a tenon and thus form a joint. [< OFr. *mortaise.*]

mort•main (môrt′mān′) ►*n.* **1.** *Law* Perpetual ownership of real estate by institutions such as churches that cannot transfer or sell it. **2.** The often oppressive influence of the past on the present. [< OFr. *mortemain.*]

mor•tu•ar•y (môr′cho͞o-ĕr′ē) ►*n., pl.* **-ies.** A place where dead bodies are kept before burial or cremation. [< Lat. *mortuus*, dead.]

mos. ►*abbr.* months

mo•sa•ic (mō-zā′ĭk) ►*n.* A picture or decorative design made by setting small colored pieces, as of stone, glass, or tile, into a surface. [< Med.Lat. *mūsāicus*, of the Muses < *Musa*, MUSE.]

Mos•cow (mŏs′kou, -kō) The capital of Russia, in the W-central part. Pop. 8,526,750.

Mo•selle (mō-zĕl′) also **Mo•sel** (mō′zəl). A river rising in the Vosges Mts. of NE France and flowing about 547 km (340 mi) to the Rhine R. in W Germany.

Mos•es (mō′zĭz, -zĭs). In the Bible, the Hebrew prophet and lawgiver who led the Israelites out of Egypt. —**Mo•sa′ic** (mō-zā′ĭk) *adj.*

Moses, Anna Mary Robertson. "Grandma

Moses." 1860–1961. Amer. painter.

mo•sey (mō′zē) ►*v. Informal* To move in a leisurely manner; saunter. [?]

mosh (mŏsh) ►*v.* To knock against others intentionally while dancing at a rock concert; slam-dance. [Perh. alteration of MASH.]

mosh pit ►*n.* An area in front of a concert stage in which audience members mosh.

Mos•lem (mŏz′ləm, mŏs′-) ►*n. & adj.* Var. of **Muslim.**

mosque (mŏsk) ►*n.* A Muslim house of worship. [< Ar. *masjid* < *sajada*, to worship.]

mos•qui•to (mə-skē′tō) ►*n., pl.* **-toes** or **-tos.** Any of various two-winged insects of which the females suck blood and in some species transmit diseases. [< Lat. *musca*, fly.]

Mosquito ►*n., pl.* **-to** or **-tos.** See **Miskito.**

moss (môs, mŏs) ►*n.* Any of various small, green, nonflowering plants often forming a dense matlike growth. [< OE *mos*, bog, and Med.Lat. *mossa*, moss (of Gmc. orig.).] —**moss′i•ness** *n.* —**moss′y** *adj.*

most (mōst) ►*adj.* Superl. of **many, much. 1a.** Greatest in number. **b.** Greatest in amount, extent, or degree. **2.** In the greatest number of instances: *Most fish have fins.* ►*n.* The greatest amount or degree: *She has the most to gain.* ►*pron. (takes sing. or pl. v.)* The greatest part or number: *Most of the town was destroyed.* ►*adv.* Superl. of **much. 1.** In or to the highest degree, quantity, or extent. Used with many adjectives and adverbs to form the superlative: *most honest; most impatiently.* **2.** Very: *a most impressive book.* **3.** *Informal* Almost: *Most everyone agrees.* —***idiom:* at (the) most** At the maximum: *two miles at most.* [< OE *mǣst.*]

-most ►*suff.* **1.** Most: *innermost.* **2.** Nearest to: *endmost.* [< OE *-mest.*]

most•ly (mōst′lē) ►*adv.* **1.** For the greatest part; mainly. **2.** Generally; usually.

Mo•sul (mō-so͞ol′, mō′səl) A city of N Iraq on the Tigris R. Pop. 664,221.

mot (mō) ►*n.* A short witty saying or remark. [< OFr., word, saying.]

mote (mōt) ►*n.* A speck, esp. of dust. [< OE *mot.*]

mo•tel (mō-tĕl′) ►*n.* A hotel for motorists providing rooms usu. having direct access to an open parking area. [Blend of MOTOR and HOTEL.]

mo•tet (mō-tĕt′) ►*n. Mus.* A polyphonic composition based on a religious text. [< OFr. < *mot*, word.]

moth (môth, mŏth) ►*n., pl.* **moths** (mô*th*z, mŏ*th*z, môths, mŏths). Any of numerous insects related to and resembling butterflies but gen. night-flying and having hairlike or feathery antennae. [< OE *moththe.*]

moth•ball (môth′bôl′, mŏth′-) ►*n.* **1.** A marble-sized ball, orig. of camphor but now of naphthalene, stored with clothes to repel moths. **2. mothballs** Protective storage: *put the battleship into mothballs.*

moth•er (mŭ*th*′ər) ►*n.* **1.** A female parent. **2.** A woman having some of the authority or responsibility of a mother: *a den mother.* **3.** A creative source; origin: *Philosophy is the mother of the sciences.* ►*adj.* **1.** Being a mother: *a mother hen.* **2.** Characteristic of a mother: *mother love.* **3.** Native: *one's mother language.* ►*v.* **1.** To give birth to; create and produce. **2.** To watch over, nourish, and protect; care for. [< OE *mōdor.*] —**moth′er•hood′** *n.* —**moth′er•less** *adj.* —**moth′er•li•ness** *n.* —**moth′er•ly** *adj.*

moth•er•board (mŭ*th*′ər-bôrd′, -bōrd′) ►*n.* The main board of a computer, usu. containing the circuitry for the central processing unit, keyboard, and monitor.

moth•er-in-law (mŭ*th*′ər-ĭn-lô′) ►*n., pl.* **moth•ers-in-law** (-ərz-). The mother of one's spouse.

moth•er•land (mŭ*th*′ər-lănd′) ►*n.* **1.** One's native land. **2.** The land of one's ancestors.

moth•er-of-pearl (mŭ*th*′ər-əv-pûrl′) ►*n.* The pearly internal layer of certain mollusk shells, used to make decorative objects.

mother superior ►*n., pl.* **mothers superior** or **mother superiors.** A woman in charge of a religious community of women.

moth•proof (môth′pro͞of′, mŏth′-) ►*adj.* Resistant to damage by moth larvae. —**moth′proof′** *v.*

mo•tif (mō-tēf′) ►*n.* A recurrent thematic element in a musical, artistic, or literary work. See Syns at **figure.** [< OFr. MOTIVE.]

mo•tile (mōt′l, mō′tīl′) ►*adj. Biol.* Moving or having the power to move spontaneously. [Lat. *movēre, mōt-*, move + -ILE.] —**mo•til′i•ty** (mō-tĭl′ĭ-tē) *n.*

mo•tion (mō′shən) ►*n.* **1.** The act or process of changing position or place. **2.** A meaningful or expressive change in the position of a part of the body; gesture. **3.** A formal proposal put to the vote under parliamentary procedures. ►*v.* **1.** To signal to or direct by making a gesture. **2.** To gesture meaningfully: *motioned to her to enter.* [< Lat. *movēre, mōt-*, move.] —**mo′tion•less** *adj.* —**mo′tion•less•ly** *adv.* —**mo′tion•less•ness** *n.*

motion picture ►*n.* **1.** A movie. **2. motion pictures** The movie industry. —**mo′tion-pic′ture** *adj.*

motion sickness ►*n.* Nausea and dizziness caused by motion, as in travel by aircraft, car, or ship.

mo•ti•vate (mō′tə-vāt′) ►*v.* **-vat•ed, -vat•ing.** To provide with an incentive; move to action; impel. —**mo′ti•va′tion** *n.* —**mo′ti•va′tion•al** *adj.* —**mo′ti•va′tor** *n.*

mo•tive (mō′tĭv) ►*n.* An emotion, desire, need, or similar impulse that causes one to act in a particular way. ►*adj.* Causing or able to cause motion. [< LLat. *mōtīvus*, of motion < Lat. *movēre*, move.]

mot•ley (mŏt′lē) ►*adj.* **1.** Having elements of great variety; heterogenous; varied. **2.** Multicolored. [ME *motlei.*]

mo•to•cross (mō′tō-krôs′, -krŏs′) ►*n.* A cross-country motorcycle race. [Fr. *motocross* : *moto*, motorcycle + CROSS(-COUNTRY).]

mo•tor (mō′tər) ►*n.* **1.** Something that produces or imparts motion. **2.** A device that converts any other energy into mechanical energy, esp. an internal-combustion engine or a device that converts electric current into mechanical power. ►*adj.* **1.** Causing or producing motion. **2.** Driven by or having a motor. **3.** Of or for motors or motor vehicles: *motor oil.* **4.** *Physiol.* Relating to movements of the muscles. ►*v.* To travel in a motor vehicle. [< Lat. *mōtor.*] —**mo′tor•i•za′tion** *n.* —**mo′tor•ize′** *v.*

mo•tor•bike (mō′tər-bīk′) ►*n.* **1.** A lightweight motorcycle. **2.** A pedal bicycle that is also powered by an attached motor.

mo•tor•boat (mō′tər-bōt′) ►*n.* A boat propelled by an internal-combustion engine.

mo•tor•cade (mō′tər-kād′) ►*n.* A procession of motor vehicles. [< CAVALCADE.]

mo•tor•car (mō′tər-kär′) ►*n.* See **automobile.**

motor court ►*n.* See **motel.**

mo•tor•cy•cle (mō′tər-sī′kəl) ►*n.* A two-wheeled vehicle resembling a heavy bicycle, propelled by a gasoline engine. —**mo′tor•cy′cle** *v.* —**mo′tor•cy′clist** *n.*

motor home ►*n.* A large motor vehicle having self-contained living quarters, used for recreational travel.

motor inn ►*n.* An urban motel usu. having several stories and a guest parking lot.

mo•tor•ist (mō′tər-ĭst) ►*n.* One who drives or rides in an automobile.

motor lodge ►*n.* See **motel.**

mo•tor•man (mō′tər-mən) ►*n.* One who drives a streetcar or subway train.

motor scooter ►*n.* A small two-wheeled vehicle with a low-powered gasoline engine.

motor vehicle ►*n.* A self-propelled wheeled vehicle that does not run on rails.

Mott (mŏt), **Lucretia Coffin.** 1793–1880. Amer. feminist and social reformer.

mot•tle (mŏt′l) ►*v.* **-tled, -tling.** To mark with spots or blotches of different shades or colors. [Prob. < MOTLEY.]

mot•to (mŏt′ō) ►*n., pl.* **-toes** or **-tos.** A brief statement used to express a principle, goal, or ideal. [Ital. < VLat. **mōttum*, utterance.]

moue (mo͞o) ►*n.* A grimace; pout. [Fr.]

mould[1] (mōld) ►*n. & v. Chiefly Brit.* Var. of **mold**[1].

mould[2] (mōld) ►*n. & v. Chiefly Brit.* Var. of **mold**[2].

Moul•mein (mo͞ol-mān′, mōl-) A city of S Myanmar (Burma) E of Yangon. Pop. 219,991.

mound (mound) ►*n.* **1.** A raised mass, as of earth, sand, or rocks. **2.** A natural elevation, such as a small hill. **3.** A pile; heap. See Syns at **heap. 4.** *Baseball* The slightly elevated pitcher's area in the center of the diamond. [?] —**mound** *v.*

Mound Builder ►*n.* A Native American culture flourishing from the 5th cent. B.C. to the 16th cent. A.D. esp. in the Ohio and Mississippi valleys, known for its large burial and effigy mounds.

mount[1] (mount) ►*v.* **1.** To climb or ascend. **2.** To get up on: *mount a horse.* **3.** To increase in amount, extent, or intensity. **4a.** To fix securely to a support: *mount an engine in a car.* **b.** To place or fix in an appropriate setting for display, study, or use. **5.** To prepare and set in motion. **6.** To set (guns) in position. ►*n.* **1.** A horse or other animal on which to ride. **2.** An object to which another is affixed for accessibility, display, or use. [< VLat. **montāre* < Lat. *mōns, mont-*, hill.] —**mount′a•ble** *adj.*

mount[2] (mount) ►*n.* A mountain or hill: *Mount Rainier.* [< Lat. *mōns, mont-*.]

moun•tain (moun′tən) ►*n.* A natural elevation of the earth's surface greater in height than a hill. [< VLat. **montānea*.]

mountain ash ►*n.* Any of various deciduous trees having clusters of small white flowers and bright orange-red berries.

mountain bike ►*n.* A bicycle with wide tires and horizontal handlebars, often used for off-road cycling. —**mountain biking** *n.*

moun•tain•eer (moun′tə-nîr′) ►*n.* **1.** An inhabitant of a mountainous area. **2.** One who climbs mountains for sport. ►*v.* To climb mountains for sport.

mountain goat ►*n.* A hoofed mammal of the NW North American mountains, having short curved black horns and shaggy yellowish-white hair and beard.

mountain laurel ►*n.* An evergreen shrub of E North America, having leathery poisonous leaves and pink or white flowers.

mountain lion ►*n.* A large wild cat of mountainous regions of the Western Hemisphere, having an unmarked tawny body.

moun•tain•ous (moun′tə-nəs) ►*adj.* **1.** Having many mountains. **2.** Massive; huge.

mountain range ►*n.* A series of mountain ridges alike in form, direction, and origin.

moun•tain•side (moun′tən-sīd′) ►*n.* The sloping side of a mountain.

moun•tain•top (moun′tən-tŏp′) ►*n.* The summit of a mountain.

Mount•bat•ten (mount-băt′n), **Louis.** 1st Earl Mountbatten of Burma. 1900–79. British naval officer.

moun•te•bank (moun′tə-băngk′) ►*n.* **1.** A peddler of quack medicines. **2.** An impostor or swindler. [< Ital. *monta im banco*, he gets up onto the bench.]

Mount•ie also **Mount•y** (moun′tē) ►*n., pl.* **-ies** *Informal.* A member of the Royal Canadian Mounted Police.

mount•ing (moun′tĭng) ►*n.* A supporting structure or frame: *a mounting for a gem.*

Mount Ver•non (vûr′nən) An estate of NE VA on the Potomac R.; home of George Washington (1752–99).

Mount Vernon

mourn (môrn, mōrn) ►*v.* To feel or express grief or sorrow (for). See Syns at **grieve.** [< OE *murnan.*] —**mourn′er** *n.*

mourn•ful (môrn′fəl, mōrn′-) ►*adj.* **1.** Feeling or expressing grief. **2.** Causing or suggesting sadness. —**mourn′ful•ly** *adv.* —**mourn′ful•ness** *n.*

mourn•ing (môr′nĭng, mōr′-) ►*n.* **1.** Expression of grief. **2.** Outward signs of grief for the dead, such as wearing black clothes. **3.** The period during which a death is mourned.

mourning dove ►*n.* A wild dove of North America, noted for its mournful call.

mouse (mous) ►*n., pl.* **mice** (mīs) **1.** Any of numerous small, usu. long-tailed rodents, some living in or near human dwellings. **2.** A hand-held, button-activated input device that controls the movement of an indicator on a computer screen, allowing the user to select operations or manipulate text or graphics. ▸*v.* (mouz) **moused, mous•ing.** To hunt or catch mice. [< OE *mūs.*] —**mous′er** (mou′zər, -sər) *n.*

mouse•pad (mous′păd′) ▸*n. Comp. Sci.* A flat pad that provides a surface on which to use a mouse.

mouse•trap (mous′trăp′) ▸*n.* A trap for catching mice.

mous•sa•ka (mo͞o-sä′kə, mo͞o′sä-kä′) ▸*n.* A Greek baked dish of ground meat, sliced eggplant, and cheese. [< Ar. dial. *musaqqa'a.*]

mousse (mo͞os) ▸*n.* **1.** A chilled dessert made with whipped cream, gelatin, eggs, and flavoring. **2.** A foam for styling the hair. [< OFr., foam.]

mous•tache (mŭs′tăsh′, mə-stăsh′) ▸*n.* Var. of **mustache.**

mous•y (mou′sē, -zē) ▸*adj.* **-i•er, -i•est 1.** Of a drab, mouselike color. **2.** Timid or shy. —**mous′i•ness** *n.*

mouth (mouth) ▸*n., pl.* **mouths** (mou*th*z) **1.** The body opening and related organs through which food is taken in, chewed, and swallowed and sounds and speech are articulated. **2.** A natural opening, as the part of a river that empties into a larger body of water or the entrance to a harbor, valley, or cave. **3.** The opening by which a container is filled or emptied. ▸*v.* (mou*th*) **1.** To declare in a pompous manner; declaim. **2.** To put, take, or move around in the mouth. —***phrasal verb:* mouth off** *Slang* To criticize, brag, or talk back loudly. [< OE *mūth.*] —**mouth′ful′** *n.*

mouth organ ▸*n.* See **harmonica.**

mouth•part (mouth′pärt′) ▸*n.* Any of the parts of the mouth of an insect or other arthropod.

mouth•piece (mouth′pēs′) ▸*n.* **1.** A part, as of a musical instrument, used in or near the mouth. **2.** A protective device worn over the teeth by athletes. **3.** A spokesperson.

mouth-to-mouth resuscitation (mouth′tə-mouth′) ▸*n.* A technique of artificial resuscitation in which the rescuer's mouth is placed over the victim's and air is forced into the victim's lungs.

mouth•wash (mouth′wŏsh′, -wôsh′) ▸*n.* A flavored, usu. antiseptic solution used for cleaning the mouth and freshening the breath.

mouth•wa•ter•ing or **mouth-wa•ter•ing** (mouth′wô′tər-ĭng) ▸*adj.* Appealing to the sense of taste; appetizing.

mouth•y (mou′*th*ē, -thē) ▸*adj.* **-i•er, -i•est.** Annoyingly talkative; bombastic. —**mouth′i•ness** *n.*

move (mo͞ov) ▸*v.* **moved, mov•ing 1.** To change in position from one point to another. **2.** To settle in a new place. **3.** To change hands commercially: *Woolens move slowly in the summer.* **4.** To take action; act. **5.** To stir the emotions (of). **6.** To make a formal motion in parliamentary procedure. **7.** To evacuate (the bowels). **8.** To transfer (a piece) in a board game. ▸*n.* **1.** The act of moving. **2.** A change of residence or place of business. **3a.** The act of transferring a piece in board games. **b.** A player's turn to move a piece. **4.** A calculated action taken to achieve an end. —***idioms:* get a move on** *Informal* To get going. **move in on** To attempt to seize control of. **on the move** Busily moving about or making progress. [< Lat. *movēre.*] —**mov′a•bil′i•ty, mov′a•ble•ness** *n.* —**mov′a•ble, move′a•ble** *adj.*

move•ment (mo͞ov′mənt) ▸*n.* **1.** The act of moving or a change in position. **2.** A change in the location of troops, ships, or aircraft for strategic purposes. **3.** A large-scale organized effort: *the labor movement.* **4.** Activity, esp. in business or commerce. **5.** An evacuation of the bowels. **6.** *Mus.* A self-contained section of an extended composition. **7.** A mechanism, such as the works of a watch, that produces or transmits motion.

mov•er (mo͞o′vər) ▸*n.* **1.** One that moves. **2.** One that transports furnishings as an occupation.

mov•ie (mo͞o′vē) ▸*n.* **1a.** A sequence of filmed images projected onto a screen in rapid succession to create the illusion of motion and continuity; motion picture. **b.** A cinematic narrative represented in this form; film. **2. movies** The movie industry. [< MOVING PICTURE.]

mov•ing (mo͞o′vĭng) ▸*adj.* **1.** Of or causing motion or transfer. **2.** Arousing deep emotion. —**mov′ing•ly** *adv.*

moving picture ▸*n.* A movie.

mow¹ (mou) ▸*n.* A place, usu. a barn, where hay or grain is stored. [< OE *mūga.*]

mow² (mō) ▸*v.* **mowed, mowed** or **mown** (mōn), **mow•ing 1.** To cut down (grass or grain) with a scythe or machine. **2.** To cut (grass or grain) from. —***phrasal verb:* mow down** To destroy in great numbers, as in battle. [< OE *māwan.*] —**mow′er** *n.*

mox•ie (mŏk′sē) ▸*n. Slang* Courage in adversity. [< *Moxie*, a trademark for a soft drink.]

Mo•zam•bique (mō′zəm-bēk′, -zăm-) A country of SE Africa. Cap. Maputo. Pop. 16,614,000. —**Mo′zam•bi′can** (-bē′kən) *adj. & n.*

Mozambique Channel. An arm of the Indian Ocean between Madagascar and SE Africa.

Mo•zart (mōt′särt), **Wolfgang Amadeus.** 1756–91. Austrian composer.

moz•za•rel•la (mŏt′sə-rĕl′ə, mōt′-) ▸*n.* A mild white Italian cheese, often melted, as on pizza. [Ital. < *mozzare*, slice off.]

MP ▸*abbr.* **1.** member of Parliament **2.** military police **3.** nounted police

MP3 (ĕm′pē-thrē′) ▸*n.* **1.** An MPEG standard used esp. for digitally transmitting music over the Internet. **2.** An audio file with data encoded using this standard. [< *MP(EG-1 layer) 3.*]

MPEG (ĕm′pĕg′) ▸*n.* **1.** A set of standards for the compression of digital video and audio data. **2.** A video or audio data file that has been so compressed. [*m(oving) p(ictures) e(xperts) g(roup).*]

mpg ▸*abbr.* miles per gallon

mph ▸*abbr.* miles per hour

Mr. (mĭs′tər) ▸*n., pl.* **Messrs.** (mĕs′ərz). Used as a courtesy title before the surname or full name of a man. [< MASTER.]

MRI ▸*abbr.* magnetic resonance imaging

Mrs. (mĭs′ĭz) ▸*n., pl.* **Mmes.** (mā-däm′, -dăm′). Used as a courtesy title for a married or widowed woman. [< MISTRESS.]

ms ▸*abbr.* **1.** or **ms.** manuscript **2.** millisecond

MS ▸*abbr.* **1.** *Lat.* Magister Scientiae (Master of Science) **2.** Mississippi **3.** multiple sclerosis

Ms. also **Ms** (mĭz) ▸*n., pl.* **Mses.** also **Mss.** (mĭz′ĭz). Used as a courtesy title before the full name or surname of a woman or girl. [Blend of

Miss, form of address and MRS.]

MSG ▸*abbr.* **1.** master sergeant **2.** monosodium glutamate

Msgr. ▸*abbr.* Monsignor

MSGT or **MSgt** ▸*abbr.* master sergeant

mss or **mss.** ▸*abbr.* manuscripts

MST ▸*abbr.* Mountain Standard Time

Mt ▸ The symbol for the element **meitnerium.**

MT ▸*abbr.* **1.** megaton **2.** metric ton **3.** Montana **4.** Mountain Time

Mt. ▸*abbr.* **1.** mount **2.** mountain

Mts. ▸*abbr.* mountains

mu (myo͞o, mo͞o) ▸*n.* The 12th letter of the Greek alphabet. [Gk.]

Mu•bar•ak (mo͞o-bär′ək), **Hosni.** b. 1929. Egyptian politician and diplomat.

much (mŭch) ▸*adj.* **more** (môr, mōr), **most** (mōst). Great in quantity, degree, or extent: *not much rain.* ▸*n.* **1.** A large quantity or amount. **2.** Something great or remarkable: *I've never been much to look at.* ▸*adv.* **more, most 1.** To a great degree or extent: *much smarter.* **2.** Just about; almost: *much the same.* [< OE *mycel.*]

mu•ci•lage (myo͞o′sə-lĭj) ▸*n.* A sticky substance used as an adhesive. [< Lat. *mūcus*, mucus.] —**mu′ci•lag′i•nous** (-lăj′ə-nəs) *adj.*

muck (mŭk) ▸*n.* **1.** A moist sticky mixture, esp. of mud and filth. **2.** Moist farmyard dung. **3.** Dark fertile soil that is rich in humus. ▸*v.* To soil or make dirty with or as if with muck. —***phrasal verb:*** **muck up** *Informal* To botch. [ME *muk*, of Scand. orig.] —**muck′y** *adj.*

muck•rake (mŭk′rāk′) ▸*v.* **-raked, -rak•ing.** To search for and expose misconduct in public life. —**muck′rak′er** *n.*

mu•co•sa (myo͞o-kō′sə) ▸*n., pl.* **-sae** (-sē) or **-sas.** See **mucous membrane.** [< Lat. *mūcōsus*, mucous.]

mu•cous (myo͞o′kəs) ▸*adj.* Containing or secreting mucus. [< Lat. *mūcōsus.*]

mucous membrane ▸*n.* A membrane lining all body passages that communicate with the air, the glands of which secrete mucus.

mu•cus (myo͞o′kəs) ▸*n.* The viscous substance secreted as a protective lubricant coating by glands of the mucous membranes. [Lat. *mūcus.*]

mud (mŭd) ▸*n.* **1.** Wet, sticky, soft earth. **2.** Slanderous or defamatory charges. [ME *mudde.*] —**mud′di•ly** *adv.* —**mud′di•ness** *n.* —**mud′dy** *adj. & v.*

mud•dle (mŭd′l) ▸*v.* **-dled, -dling 1.** To make turbid or muddy. **2.** To mix confusedly; jumble. **3.** To befuddle (the mind), as with alcohol. See Syns at **confuse. 4.** To botch; bungle. —***phrasal verb:*** **muddle through** To persist successfully in a disorganized, blundering way. ▸*n.* A mess or jumble. [Poss. < MDu. *moddelen.*] —**mud′dler** *n.*

mud•guard (mŭd′gärd′) ▸*n.* A shield over or behind a vehicle's wheel.

mud•sling•er (mŭd′slĭng′ər) ▸*n.* One who makes malicious charges in hopes of discrediting an opponent. —**mud′sling′ing** *n.*

mues•li (myo͞oz′lē) ▸*n.* A mixture of rolled oats, nuts, and dried fruit, often used as a breakfast cereal. [Ger. dialectal, dim. of Ger. *Mus*, mash.]

mu•ez•zin (myo͞o-ĕz′ĭn, mo͞o-) ▸*n. Islam* The crier who calls the faithful to prayer five times a day. [< Ar. *mu'aḏḏin.*]

muff[1] (mŭf) ▸*v.* To perform clumsily; bungle. See Syns at **botch.** [?] —**muff** *n.*

muff[2] (mŭf) ▸*n.* A small, cylindrical, usu. fur cover, open at both ends, used to keep the hands warm. [< Med.Lat. *muffula.*]

muf•fin (mŭf′ĭn) ▸*n.* A small, cup-shaped bread, often sweetened. [Poss. < LGer. *Muffen*, cakes.]

muf•fle (mŭf′əl) ▸*v.* **-fled, -fling 1.** To wrap up snugly for warmth, protection, or secrecy. **2.** To wrap or pad in order to deaden a sound. **3.** To deaden (a sound). **4.** To suppress; stifle: *muffle political opposition.* [ME *muflen*, poss. < OFr. *mofle*, MUFF[2].]

muf•fler (mŭf′lər) ▸*n.* **1.** A heavy scarf worn around the neck for warmth. **2.** A device that absorbs noise, esp. one used with an internal-combustion engine.

muf•ti (mŭf′tē) ▸*n.* Civilian dress, esp. when worn by one usu. in uniform. [Prob. < Ar. *muftī*, judge.]

mug[1] (mŭg) ▸*n.* A heavy cylindrical drinking cup usu. having a handle. [Perh. of Scand. orig.]

mug[2] (mŭg) ▸*n.* **1.** *Informal* **a.** The human face. **b.** A grimace. **2.** A hoodlum. ▸*v.* **mugged, mug•ging 1.** *Informal* To take a photograph of for police files. **2.** To waylay and assault with intent to rob. **3.** To grimace, esp. for humorous effect. [Prob. < MUG[1].] —**mug′ger** *n.*

Mu•ga•be (mo͞o-gä′bē), **Robert Gabriel.** b. 1924. Zimbabwean political leader.

mug•gy (mŭg′ē) ▸*adj.* **-gi•er, -gi•est.** Warm and extremely humid. [Prob. < ME *mugen*, to drizzle.] —**mug′gi•ness** *n.*

mug shot ▸*n. Informal* A photograph of a person's face, esp. for police files.

Mu•ham•mad (mo͞o-hăm′ĭd, -hä′mĭd) also **Mo•ham•med** (mō-, mo͞o-). 570?–632. Arab prophet of Islam.

Mu•ham•mad•an (mo͞o-hăm′ĭ-dən) or **Mo•ham•med•an** (mō-) ▸*adj.* Of or relating to Muhammad or Islam; Muslim. ▸*n. Offensive* A Muslim.

Mu•ham•mad•an•ism (mo͞o-hăm′ĭ-də-nĭz′əm) also **Mo•ham•med•an•ism** (mō-) ▸*n. Offensive* Islam.

Mu•har•ram (mo͞o-hăr′əm) ▸*n.* The 1st month of the Muslim calendar. See table at **calendar.** [Ar. *Muḥarram.*]

Muir (myo͝or), **John.** 1838–1914. British-born Amer. naturalist.

mu•ja•hi•deen also **mu•ja•he•deen** or **mu•ja•hi•din** (mo͞o-jä′hĕ-dēn′) ▸*pl.n.* Muslim guerrilla warriors engaged in a jihad. [< Ar. *jihād*, jihad.]

muk•luk (mŭk′lŭk′) ▸*n.* **1.** A soft Eskimo boot made of reindeer skin or sealskin. **2.** A slipper similar to a mukluk. [Yupik *maklak*, bearded seal.]

mu•lat•to (mo͞o-lăt′ō, -lä′tō, myo͞o-) ▸*n., pl.* **-tos** or **-toes 1.** A person having one white and one Black parent. **2.** A person of mixed white and Black ancestry. [Sp. *mulato*, person of mixed race.]

mul•ber•ry (mŭl′bĕr′ē, -bə-rē) ▸*n.* **1.** A tree bearing sweet reddish or purplish berrylike fruit. **2.** The fruit itself. [< OE *mōrberie.*]

mulch (mŭlch) ►*n.* A protective covering, as of leaves or hay, placed around plants to prevent evaporation of moisture, freezing of roots, and growth of weeds. ►*v.* To cover with mulch. [Prob. < ME *melsh*, soft.]

mulct (mŭlkt) ►*n.* A penalty such as a fine. ►*v.* **1.** To penalize by fining. **2.** To defraud or swindle. [< Lat. *mulcta*.]

mule[1] (myo͞ol) ►*n.* **1.** The sterile hybrid offspring of a male donkey and female horse. **2.** *Informal* A stubborn person. [< Lat. *mūlus*.] —**mul′ish** *adj.* —**mul′ish•ly** *adv.* —**mul′ish•ness** *n.*

mule[2] (myo͞ol) ►*n.* An open slipper or shoe that leaves the heel bare. [Ult. < Lat. *mulleus (calceus)*, reddish-purple (shoe).]

mule[1]

mule[2]

mule deer ►*n.* A long-eared deer of W North America, having a black-tipped tail.

mule•skin•ner (myo͞ol′skĭn′ər) ►*n. Informal* A driver of mules.

mu•le•teer (myo͞o′lə-tîr′) ►*n.* A driver of mules. [< OFr. *mulet*, mule.]

mull[1] (mŭl) ►*v.* To heat and spice (e.g., wine). [?]

mull[2] (mŭl) ►*v.* To ponder or ruminate: *mull over a plan.* [?]

mul•lah also **mul•la** (mŭl′ə, mo͝ol′ə) ►*n. Islam* A religious teacher or leader, esp. one trained in law. [< Ar. *mawlā*, master.]

mul•lein (mŭl′ən) ►*n.* Any of various tall plants having closely clustered yellow flowers and downy leaves. [< AN *moleine*.]

mul•let (mŭl′ĭt) ►*n., pl.* **-let** or **-lets.** Any of various saltwater and freshwater edible fishes of tropical and temperate waters. [Ult. < Gk. *mullos*.]

mul•li•ga•taw•ny (mŭl′ĭ-gə-tô′nē) ►*n., pl.* **-nies.** An East Indian soup made with meat or chicken and curry. [Tamil *miḷagutaṇṇī*.]

mul•lion (mŭl′yən) ►*n.* A vertical strip, as of wood or stone, dividing the panes of a window. [< AN *moynel*, perh. < Lat. *mediānus*, middle.] —**mul′lioned** *adj.*

Mul•ro•ney (mŭl-rō′nē, -ro͞o′-), **(Martin) Brian.** b. 1939. Canadian prime minister (1984–1993).

multi– ►*pref.* **1.** Many; much; multiple: *multicolored.* **2a.** More than one: *multiparous.* **b.** More than two: *multilateral.* [< Lat. *multus*, much, many.]

mul•ti•cel•lu•lar (mŭl′tē-sĕl′yə-lər, -tī-) ►*adj.* Having many cells. —**mul′ti•cel′lu•lar′i•ty** (-lăr′ĭ-tē) *n.*

mul•ti•col•ored (mŭl′tĭ-kŭl′ərd) also **mul•ti•col•or** (-kŭl′ər) ►*adj.* Having many colors.

mul•ti•cul•tur•al (mŭl′tē-kŭl′chər-əl, -tī-) ►*adj.* Of or including several cultures or ethnic groups.

mul•ti•cul•tur•al•ism (mŭl′tē-kŭl′chər-ə-lĭz′əm, -tī-) ►*n.* The belief that a society should respect and promote all the various cultures or ethnic groups of which it is composed.

mul•ti•di•men•sion•al (mŭl′tĭ-dĭ-mĕn′shə-nəl) ►*adj.* Having several dimensions. —**mul′ti•di•men′sion•al′i•ty** (-shə-năl′ĭ-tē) *n.*

mul•ti•di•rec•tion•al (mŭl′tē-dĭ-rĕk′shə-nəl, -dī-, -tī-) ►*adj.* Reaching out or operating in several directions.

mul•ti•dis•ci•pli•nar•y (mŭl′tē-dĭs′ə-plə-nĕr′ē, -tī-) ►*adj.* Involving or making use of several academic disciplines at once.

mul•ti•eth•nic (mŭl′tē-ĕth′nĭk, -tī-) ►*adj.* Of or including a variety of ethnic groups.

mul•ti•fac•et•ed (mŭl′tē-făs′ĭ-tĭd, -tī-) ►*adj.* Having many facets or aspects. See Syns at **versatile.**

mul•ti•fam•i•ly (mŭl′tē-făm′ə-lē, -tī-) ►*adj.* Of or intended for use by several families.

mul•ti•far•i•ous (mŭl′tə-fâr′ē-əs) ►*adj.* Having great variety. See Syns at **versatile.** [< LLat. *multifārius*.] —**mul′ti•far′i•ous•ly** *adv.* —**mul′ti•far′i•ous•ness** *n.*

mul•ti•form (mŭl′tə-fôrm′) ►*adj.* Occurring in or having many forms or shapes. —**mul′ti•for′mi•ty** *n.*

mul•ti•lane (mŭl′tē-lān′, -tī-) ►*adj.* Having several lanes: *a multilane highway.*

mul•ti•lat•er•al (mŭl′tĭ-lăt′ər-əl) ►*adj.* **1.** Having many sides. **2.** Involving more than two nations or parties. —**mul′ti•lat′er•al•ly** *adv.*

mul•ti•lay•ered (mŭl′tē-lā′ərd, -tī-) ►*adj.* Consisting of several layers or levels.

mul•ti•lev•el (mŭl′tə-lĕv′əl) ►*adj.* Having several levels: *a multilevel parking garage.*

mul•ti•lin•gual (mŭl′tē-lĭng′gwəl, -tī-) ►*adj.* **1.** Of, including, or expressed in several languages. **2.** Fluent in several languages.

mul•ti•me•di•a (mŭl′tē-mē′dē-ə, -tī-) ►*pl.n. (takes sing. v.)* **1.** The combined use of several media, such as slides and music. **2.** The use of several mass media, such as television and print, as for advertising. ►*adj.* **1.** Relating to the combined use of media. **2.** *Comp. Sci.* Relating to an application that can integrate text, graphics, video, and sound.

mul•ti•mil•lion•aire (mŭl′tē-mĭl′yə-nâr′, -tī-) ►*n.* A person whose wealth amounts to two or more million dollars, pounds, or the equivalent in other currency.

mul•ti•na•tion•al (mŭl′tē-năsh′ə-nəl, -năsh′nəl, -tī-) ►*adj.* Of or involving more than two countries.

mul•tip•a•rous (mŭl-tĭp′ər-əs) ►*adj.* **1.** Having given birth two or more times. **2.** Giving birth to more than one offspring at a time.

mul•ti•ple (mŭl′tə-pəl) ►*adj.* Of, having, or consisting of more than one individual, element, or part. ►*n. Math.* A number into which another number may be divided with no remainder. [< Lat. *multipulus*.]

mul•ti•ple-choice (mŭl′tə-pəl-chois′) ►*adj.* Offering several answers from which the correct one is to be chosen.

multiple fruit ►*n.* A fruit, such as a fig or pineapple, derived from several flowers that are combined into one structure.

multiple personality ►*n.* A highly disputed psychological disorder in which a person exhibits two or more disassociated personalities, each functioning as a distinct entity.

multiple sclerosis ▶*n.* A degenerative disease of the central nervous system causing muscular weakness, loss of coordination, and speech and visual disturbances.

multiple star ▶*n.* Three or more stars that appear as one to the naked eye.

mul•ti•plex (mŭl′tə-plĕks′) ▶*adj.* **1.** Multiple; manifold. **2.** Of or being a system of simultaneous communication of two or more messages on the same wire or radio channel. ▶*n.* A movie theater or dwelling with multiple separate units. [Lat.] —**mul′ti•plex′** *v.*

mul•ti•pli•cand (mŭl′tə-plĭ-kănd′) ▶*n.* A number to be multiplied by another. [Lat. *multiplicandum*, thing to be multiplied.]

mul•ti•pli•ca•tion (mŭl′tə-plĭ-kā′shən) ▶*n.* **1.** The act of multiplying or the condition of being multiplied. **2.** The reproduction of plants and animals. **3.** *Math.* The operation of adding a number to itself a certain number of times. —**mul′ti•pli′ca•tive** *adj.*

multiplication sign ▶*n.* The sign used to indicate multiplication, either a times sign (×) or a centered dot (·).

mul•ti•plic•i•ty (mŭl′tə-plĭs′ĭ-tē) ▶*n., pl.* **-ties 1.** The state of being various or multiple. **2.** A large number. [< LLat. *multiplicitās.*]

mul•ti•pli•er (mŭl′tə-plī′ər) ▶*n.* The number by which another number is multiplied.

mul•ti•ply (mŭl′tə-plī′) ▶*v.* **-plied, -ply•ing 1.** To increase in amount, number, or degree. **2.** *Math.* To perform multiplication (on). **3.** To breed; reproduce. [< Lat. *multiplicāre.*]

mul•ti•pur•pose (mŭl′tē-pûr′pəs, -tī-) ▶*adj.* Designed or used for several purposes.

mul•ti•ra•cial (mŭl′tē-rā′shəl, -tī-) ▶*adj.* **1.** Made up of, involving, or acting on behalf of various races: *a multiracial society.* **2.** Having ancestors of several or various races.

mul•ti•stage (mŭl′tĭ-stāj′) ▶*adj.* Functioning by stages: *a multistage rocket.*

mul•ti•sto•ry (mŭl′tĭ-stôr′ē, -stōr′ē) ▶*adj.* Having several stories: *a multistory hotel.*

mul•ti•task•ing (mŭl′tē-tăs′kĭng, -tī-) ▶*n.* The concurrent operation by one central processing unit of two or more processes. —**mul′ti•task′** *v.*

mul•ti•tude (mŭl′tĭ-to͞od′, -tyo͞od′) ▶*n.* A very great number. [< Lat. *multitūdō* < *multus*, many.] —**mul′ti•tu′di•nous** *adj.* —**mul′ti•tu′di•nous•ly** *adv.*

mul•ti•va•lent (mŭl′tĭ-vā′lənt, mŭl-tĭv′ə-lənt) ▶*adj.* Polyvalent. —**mul′ti•va′lence** *n.*

mul•ti•vi•ta•min (mŭl′tə-vī′tə-mĭn) ▶*adj.* Containing many vitamins. ▶*n.* A preparation containing many vitamins.

mum[1] (mŭm) ▶*adj.* Not talking. [ME.]

mum[2] (mŭm) ▶*n.* A chrysanthemum.

Mum•bai (mŭm′bī′). Formerly **Bom•bay** (bŏm-bā′). A city of W-central India. Pop. 9,925,891.

mum•ble (mŭm′bəl) ▶*v.* **-bled, -bling.** To speak or utter indistinctly by lowering the voice or partially closing the mouth. [< MDu. *mommelen.*] —**mum′ble** *n.* —**mum′bler** *n.* —**mum′bly** *adj.*

mum•bo jum•bo (mŭm′bō jŭm′bō) ▶*n.* **1.** Confusing or incomprehensible language or activity. **2.** An obscure ritual or incantation. [Perh. of Mandingo origin.]

mum•mer (mŭm′ər) ▶*n.* One who acts or plays in a mask or costume. [< OFr. *momer*, to pantomime.] —**mum′mer•y** *n.*

mum•my (mŭm′ē) ▶*n., pl.* **-mies.** A body embalmed after death, as by the ancient Egyptians. [< Ar. *mūmīya*, embalmed body < *mūm*, wax.] —**mum′mi•fi•ca′tion** *n.* —**mum′mi•fy** *v.*

mumps (mŭmps) ▶*pl.n. (takes sing. or pl. v.)* A contagious viral disease marked by painful swelling esp. of the salivary glands and sometimes of the ovaries or testes. [< dial. *mump*, grimace.]

munch (mŭnch) ▶*v.* To chew (food) noisily or with pleasure. [ME *monchen.*]

mun•dane (mŭn-dān′, mŭn′dān′) ▶*adj.* **1.** Of this world; worldly. **2.** Of or concerned with the ordinary. [< LLat. *mundānus* < *mundus*, world.] —**mun•dane′ly** *adv.*

mung bean (mŭng) ▶*n.* An Asian plant cultivated for its edible seeds and pods and the chief source of bean sprouts. [< Skt. *mudgaḥ.*]

Mu•nich (myo͞o′nĭk) A city of SE Germany SE of Augsburg. Pop. 1,255,623.

mu•nic•i•pal (myo͞o-nĭs′ə-pəl) ▶*adj.* **1.** Of or typical of a municipality. **2.** Having local self-government. [< Lat. *mūnicipium*, town.] —**mu•nic′i•pal•ly** *adv.*

municipal bond ▶*n.* An often tax-exempt bond, such as one issued by a city or county, for financing public projects.

mu•nic•i•pal•i•ty (myo͞o-nĭs′ə-păl′ĭ-tē) ▶*n., pl.* **-ties.** A political unit, such as a city or town, that is incorporated for local self-government.

mu•nif•i•cent (myo͞o-nĭf′ĭ-sənt) ▶*adj.* Extremely liberal in giving; very generous. See Syns at **liberal.** [Lat. *mūnificēns* < *mūnus*, gift.] —**mu•nif′i•cence** *n.* —**mu•nif′i•cent•ly** *adv.*

mu•ni•tions (myo͞o-nĭsh′ənz) ▶*pl.n.* War materiel. [< Lat. *mūnīre*, *mūnīt-*, defend.]

Mu•ñoz Ma•rín (mo͞o-nyōs′ mä-rēn′), **Luis.** 1898–1980. Puerto Rican politician; the first elected governor of Puerto Rico (1948–64).

Luis Muñoz Marín
photographed in 1961

Mun•ro (mən-rō′), **Hector Hugh.** Saki. 1870–1916. British writer.

Mün•ster (mo͝on′stər, mŭn′-, mün′-) A city of W-central Germany NNE of Cologne. Pop. 267,367.

mu•on (myo͞o′ŏn′) ▶*n.* An elementary particle in the lepton family having a mass 209 times that of the electron. [< *mu meson.*]

mu•ral (myo͝or′əl) ▶*n.* A painting or photograph applied directly to a wall or ceiling. [<

Lat. *mūrus*, wall.] —**mu′ral•ist** *n.*

Mu•ra•sa•ki Shi•ki•bu (mo͞o′rä-sä′kē shē′-kē-bo͞o′), Baroness. 978?–1031? Japanese writer.

Mu•rat (myo͞o-rä′, mü-), **Joachim.** 1767?–1815. French marshal; king of Naples (1808–15).

Mur•cia (mûr′shə, -shē-ə) A region and former kingdom of SE Spain on the Mediterranean Sea.

mur•der (mûr′dər) ►*n.* The unlawful killing of one human by another, esp. with premeditated malice. ►*v.* **1.** To kill (a human) unlawfully. **2.** To mar or spoil by ineptness: *murder the English language.* **3.** *Slang* To defeat decisively. [< OE *morthor*.] —**mur′der•er** *n.* —**mur′der•ess** *n.*

mur•der•ous (mûr′dər-əs) ►*adj.* **1.** Capable of, guilty of, or intending murder. **2.** Characteristic of murder; brutal. **3.** *Informal* Very difficult or dangerous: *a murderous exam.* —**mur′der•ous•ly** *adv.* —**mur′der•ous•ness** *n.*

mu•rex (myo͝or′ĕks) ►*n., pl.* **mu•ri•ces** (myo͝or′ĭ-sēz′) or **mu•rex•es.** Any of various tropical marine gastropods having rough spiny shells. [< Lat. *mūrex*, mollusk yielding purple dye.]

murk (mûrk) ►*n.* Partial or total darkness; gloom. [< ON *myrkr* or OE *mirce*.] —**murk′i•ly** *adv.* —**murk′i•ness** *n.* —**murk′y** *adj.*

Mur•mansk (mo͝or-mänsk′) A city of extreme NW Russia. Pop. 453,590.

mur•mur (mûr′mər) ►*n.* **1.** A low, indistinct, continuous sound. **2.** A grumbled complaint. **3.** *Medic.* An abnormal sound, usu. in the heart. [< Lat.] —**mur′mur** *v.* —**mur′mur•er** *n.* —**mur′mur•ous** *adj.*

Mur•ray River (mûr′ē) A river of SE Australia rising in the Australian Alps and flowing about 2,589 km (1,609 mi) to the Indian Ocean S of Adelaide.

Mur•rum•bidg•ee (mûr′əm-bĭj′ē) A river of SE Australia rising in the Australian Alps and flowing about 1,689 km (1,050 mi) to the Murray R.

mus•cat (mŭs′kăt′, -kət) ►*n.* A sweet white grape used for making wine or raisins. [< LLat. *muscus*, MUSK.]

Muscat. The capital of Oman, in the N on the Gulf of Oman. Pop. 30,000.

mus•ca•tel (mŭs′kə-tĕl′) ►*n.* A rich sweet wine made from muscat grapes. [ME *muscadelle* < LLat. *muscus*, MUSK.]

mus•cle (mŭs′əl) ►*n.* **1.** A tissue composed of fibers capable of contracting and relaxing to effect bodily movement. **2.** A contractile organ consisting of muscle tissue. **3.** Muscular strength. **4.** *Informal* Power or authority. ►*v.* **-cled, -cling** *Informal.* To force one's way. [< Lat. *mūsculus*, dim. of *mūs*, mouse.]

mus•cle•bound also **mus•cle-bound** (mŭs′əl-bound′) ►*adj.* Having stiff, overdeveloped muscles, usu. from excessive exercise.

Mus•co•vite (mŭs′kə-vīt′) ►*adj.* A native or resident of Moscow or Muscovy. —**Mus′co•vite′** *adj.*

Mus•co•vy (mŭs′kə-vē) A former principality of W-central Russia.

mus•cu•lar (mŭs′kyə-lər) ►*adj.* **1.** Of or consisting of muscle. **2.** Having well-developed muscles. **3.** Strong; forceful: *muscular prose.* [< Lat. *mūsculus*, MUSCLE.] —**mus′cu•lar′i•ty** (-lăr′ĭ-tē) *n.* —**mus′cu•lar•ly** *adv.*

Syns: *muscular, athletic, brawny, burly, sinewy* **adj.**

muscular dystrophy ►*n.* A chronic noncontagious genetic disease in which gradual irreversible muscle deterioration results in complete incapacitation.

mus•cu•la•ture (mŭs′kyə-lə-cho͝or′) ►*n.* The system of muscles in a body or a body part. [Fr. < Lat. *mūsculus*, MUSCLE.]

muse (myo͞oz) ►*v.* **mused, mus•ing.** To ponder, consider, or deliberate at length. [< OFr. *muser*.] —**mus′er** *n.*

Muse ►*n.* **1.** *Gk. Myth.* Any of the nine daughters of Zeus, each of whom presided over a different art or science. **2. muse** A source of inspiration, esp. of a poet. [< Gk. *Mousa*.]

mu•se•um (myo͞o-zē′əm) ►*n.* A place devoted to the acquisition, study, and exhibition of objects of scientific, historical, or artistic value. [< Gk. *Mouseion*, shrine of the Muses < *Mousa*, MUSE.]

mush[1] (mŭsh) ►*n.* **1.** Cornmeal boiled in water or milk. **2.** Something thick, soft, and pulpy. **3.** *Informal* Mawkish sentimentality. [Prob. alteration of MASH.]

mush[2] (mŭsh) ►*v.* To drive (a team of dogs) over snow. [Poss. < Fr. *marchons*, let's go.]

mush•room (mŭsh′ro͞om′, -ro͝om′) ►*n.* Any of various fleshy fungi having an umbrella-shaped cap borne on a stalk. ►*v.* To grow or spread rapidly. [< Med.Lat. *musariō*.]

mush•y (mŭsh′ē, mo͝osh′ē) ►*adj.* **-i•er, -i•est** **1.** Thick, soft, and pulpy. **2.** *Informal* Marked by maudlin sentimentality. See Syns at **sentimental.** —**mush′i•ness** *n.*

mu•sic (myo͞o′zĭk) ►*n.* **1.** The art of arranging sounds in time to produce a composition that elicits an aesthetic response in a listener. **2.** Vocal or instrumental sounds having some degree of melody, harmony, or rhythm. **3.** A musical composition. **4.** Aesthetically pleasing or harmonious sound or combination of sounds. [< Gk. *(hē) mousikē (tekhnē)*, (the art) of the Muses < *Mousa*, MUSE.]

mu•si•cal (myo͞o′zĭ-kəl) ►*adj.* **1.** Of or producing music. **2.** Melodious. **3.** Set to or accompanied by music. **4.** Devoted to or skilled in music. ►*n.* **1.** A play or movie having musical numbers. **2.** A musical comedy. —**mu′si•cal•ly** *adv.*

musical comedy ►*n.* A comedic play in which dialogue is interspersed with songs and dances.

mu•si•cale (myo͞o′zĭ-kăl′) ►*n.* A program of music performed at a social gathering. [Fr. < *(soirée) musicale*, musical (evening).]

music box ►*n.* A box containing a mechanical device that produces music.

mu•si•cian (myo͞o-zĭsh′ən) ►*n.* One who composes, conducts, or performs music. —**mu•si′cian•ship′** *n.*

mu•si•col•o•gy (myo͞o′zĭ-kŏl′ə-jē) ►*n.* The historical and scientific study of music. —**mu′si•col′o•gist** *n.*

musk (mŭsk) ►*n.* An odorous substance secreted by an Asian deer or produced synthetically, used in perfumes. [< Pers. *mušk*.] —**musk′i•ness** *n.* —**musk′y** *adj.*

mus•keg (mŭs′kĕg′) ►*n.* A peaty bog of N North America. [Cree *maskek*.]

mus•kel•lunge (mŭs′kə-lŭnj′) ►*n., pl.* **-lunge**

or **-lung•es.** A large pike of the N US and S Canada. [< Ojibwa *maashkinoozhe.*]

mus•ket (mŭs′kĭt) ►*n.* A smoothbore shoulder gun used from the late 16th through the 18th cent. [< Ital. *moschetto* < Lat. *musca,* fly.] —**mus′ket•eer** *n.*

mus•ket•ry (mŭs′kĭ-trē) ►*n.* **1.** Muskets collectively. **2.** Musketeers collectively.

musk•mel•on (mŭsk′mĕl′ən) ►*n.* Any of several edible melons, such as the cantaloupe, having a rough rind and juicy flesh.

Mus•ko•ge•an (mŭs-kō′gē-ən) ►*n.* A family of Native American languages of the SE US that includes Choctaw, Chickasaw, and Creek.

Mus•ko•gee (mŭs-kō′gē) ►*n.* See **Creek.**

musk•ox or **musk ox** (mŭsk′ŏks′) ►*n.* A large ox of N Canada and Greenland, having broad, flat, downward-curving horns and a shaggy coat.

musk•rat (mŭs′krăt′) ►*n., pl.* **-rat** or **-rats 1.** A large aquatic rodent of North America. **2.** The dense brown fur of the muskrat.

Mus•lim (mŭz′ləm, mo͝oz′-, mŭs′-, mo͝os′-) or **Mos•lem** (mŏz′ləm, mŏs′-) ►*n.* A believer or adherent of Islam. —**Mus′lim** *adj.*

mus•lin (mŭz′lĭn) ►*n.* Any of various sturdy cotton fabrics of plain weave, used esp. for sheets. [< Ital. *mussolina,* of Mosul, Iraq.]

muss (mŭs) ►*v.* To make messy or untidy; rumple. ►*n.* A state of disorder; a mess. [Prob. < MESS.] —**muss′i•ly** *adv.* —**muss′i•ness** *n.* —**muss′y** *adj.*

mus•sel (mŭs′əl) ►*n.* Any of various narrow-shelled bivalve mollusks, esp. an edible marine species. [< Med.Lat. *mūscula* < Lat. *mūsculus,* muscle.]

Mus•so•li•ni (mo͞o′sə lē′nē), **Benito.** "Il Duce." 1883–1945. Italian Fascist dictator and prime minister (1922–43).

Mus•sorg•sky (mə-zôrg′skē, -sôrg′-), **Modest Petrovich.** 1839–81. Russian composer.

must[1] (mŭst) ►*aux.v.* Used to indicate: **a.** Necessity or obligation: *Citizens must register in order to vote.* **b.** Insistence: *You must not go there alone.* **c.** Inevitability or certainty: *We all must die.* **d.** Probability: *It must be almost midnight.* ►*n.* An absolute requirement. [< OE *mōste,* p.t. of *mōtan,* be allowed.]

must[2] (mŭst) ►*n.* Staleness. [< MUSTY.]

must[3] (mŭst) ►*n.* Unfermented or fermenting fruit juice, usu. grape. [< Lat. *mustum.*]

mus•tache also **mous•tache** (mŭs′tăsh′, mə-stăsh′) ►*n.* The hair growing on the human upper lip. [< Gk. *mustax.*]

mus•ta•chio (mə-stăsh′ō, -stăsh′ē-ō′) ►*n., pl.* **-chios.** A mustache, esp. a luxuriant one. [< Ital. dial. *mustaccio,* MUSTACHE.]

mus•tang (mŭs′tăng′) ►*n.* A small, hardy wild horse of the W North American plains. [Am.Sp. *mesteño,* stray animal.]

mus•tard (mŭs′tərd) ►*n.* **1.** Any of various plants having yellow flowers and often pungent seeds. **2.** A condiment made from mustard seeds. [< OFr. *mustarde* < Lat. *mustum,* new wine.] —**mus′tard•y** *adj.*

mustard gas ►*n.* An oily volatile liquid used in warfare as a blistering agent.

mus•ter (mŭs′tər) ►*v.* **1.** To summon or assemble (troops). **2.** To gather or summon up: *mustering up her strength for the ordeal.* See Syns at **call.** —***phrasal verbs:*** **muster in** To enlist (someone) in military service. **muster out** To discharge (someone) from military service. ►*n.* A gathering, esp. of troops, for service, inspection, or roll call. [< Lat. *mōnstrāre,* show < *mōnstrum,* portent. See MONSTER.]

must•n't (mŭs′ənt) ► Must not.

must•y (mŭs′tē) ►*adj.* **-i•er, -i•est.** Stale or moldy in odor or taste. [Alteration of obsolete *moisty* < MOIST.] —**must′i•ness** *n.*

mu•ta•ble (myo͞o′tə-bəl) ►*adj.* **1.** Subject to change. **2.** Fickle. —**mu′ta•bil′i•ty, mu′ta•ble•ness** *n.* —**mu′ta•bly** *adv.*

mu•ta•gen (myo͞o′tə-jən, -jĕn′) ►*n.* An agent, such as ultraviolet light or a radioactive element, that can induce mutation in an organism. —**mu′ta•gen′ic** *adj.*

mu•tant (myo͞ot′nt) ►*n.* An organism or a new genetic character differing from the parental strain as a result of mutation. —**mu′tant** *adj.*

mu•tate (myo͞o′tāt, myo͞o-tāt′) ►*v.* **-tat•ed, -tat•ing.** To undergo or cause to undergo mutation. [Lat. *mūtāre.*] —**mu′ta′tive** (-tā′tĭv, -tə-tĭv) *adj.*

mu•ta•tion (myo͞o-tā′shən) ►*n.* **1.** A change, as in nature, form, or quality. **2.** Any heritable alteration of an organism.

mute (myo͞ot) ►*adj.* **mut•er, mut•est 1.** Incapable of producing speech or vocal sound. **2.** Unable to speak. **3.** Expressed without speech; unspoken. ►*n.* **1.** *Often Offensive* One who is incapable of speech. **2.** *Mus.* A device used to muffle or soften the tone of an instrument. ►*v.* **mut•ed, mut•ing.** To soften the sound, color, or shade of. [< Lat. *mūtus.*] —**mute′ly** *adv.* —**mute′ness** *n.*

Usage: In reference to people who are unable to speak, *mute* and *deaf-mute* are now often considered objectionable. These terms imply that a person who is incapable of oral speech is necessarily deprived of the use of language. In fact, many deaf people communicate fully through the use of a sign language.

mu•ti•late (myo͞ot′l-āt′) ►*v.* **-lat•ed, -lat•ing 1.** To deprive of a limb or an essential part. **2.** To disfigure by damaging irreparably. See Syns at **batter**[1]. [< Lat. *mutilus,* maimed.] —**mu′ti•la′tion** *n.* —**mu′ti•la′tive** *adj.* —**mu′ti•la′tor** *n.*

mu•ti•ny (myo͞ot′n-ē) ►*n., pl.* **-nies.** Open rebellion against constituted authority, esp. by military personnel against superior officers. [< VLat. **movita,* a revolt.] —**mu′ti•neer′** *n.* —**mu′ti•nous** *adj.* —**mu′ti•nous•ly** *adv.* —**mu′ti•ny** *v.*

mutt (mŭt) ►*n. Informal* A mongrel dog. [< *muttonhead,* fool.]

mut•ter (mŭt′ər) ►*v.* **1.** To speak or utter indistinctly in low tones. **2.** To complain or grumble. ►*n.* A low, indistinct utterance. [ME *muttren.*] —**mut′ter•er** *n.*

mut•ton (mŭt′n) ►*n.* The flesh of a fully grown sheep. [< OFr. *moton.*]

mut•ton•chops (mŭt′n-chŏps′) ►*pl.n.* Side whiskers narrow at the temple and broad along the lower jawline.

mu•tu•al (myo͞o′cho͞o-əl) ►*adj.* **1.** Having the same relationship each to the other: *mutual predators.* **2.** Given and received in equal amount: *mutual respect.* **3.** Possessed in common: *mutual interests.* [< Lat. *mūtuus,* borrowed.] —**mu′tu•al′i•ty** (-ăl′ĭ-tē) *n.* —**mu′tu•al•ly** *adv.*

mutual fund ►*n.* An investment company that

by the sale of its shares acquires funds to invest in diversified securities.

muu•muu (mo͞o′mo͞o′) ▶ *n.* A long loose dress. See Regional Note at **ukulele.** [Hawaiian *mu'umu'u.*]

Mu•zak (myo͞o′zăk′) ▶ A trademark for recorded background music transmitted by wire on a subscription basis.

muz•zle (mŭz′əl) ▶ *n.* **1.** The usu. projecting nose and jaws of certain animals; snout. **2.** A device fitted over an animal's snout to prevent biting or eating. **3.** The front end of the barrel of a firearm. ▶ *v.* **-zled, -zling 1.** To put a muzzle on (an animal). **2.** To restrain from expressing opinions. [< Med.Lat. *mūsellum* < Lat. *mūsum.*]

muz•zle•load•er (mŭz′əl-lō′dər) ▶ *n.* A firearm loaded at the muzzle. —**muz′zle•load′ing** *adj.*

mV ▶ *abbr.* millivolt

MV ▶ *abbr.* **1.** mean variation **2.** megavolt

MVP ▶ *abbr.* most valuable player

mW ▶ *abbr.* milliwatt

MW ▶ *abbr.* megawatt

my (mī) ▶ *adj.* The possessive form of **I**[1]. Used as a modifier before a noun: *my boots; my brother.* ▶ *interj.* Used as an exclamation of surprise, pleasure, or dismay: *Oh, my! What a day!* [< OE *mīn.*]

my•al•gi•a (mī-ăl′jē-ə, -jə) ▶ *n.* Muscular pain or tenderness, esp. when diffuse and nonspecific. [Gk. *mus*, muscle + -ALGIA.] —**my•al′gic** (-jĭk) *adj.*

Myan•mar (myän-mär′) A country of SE Asia on the Bay of Bengal and the Andaman Sea. Cap. Yangon (formerly Rangoon). Pop. 45,555,000.

my•as•the•ni•a grav•is (mī′əs-thē′nē-ə grăv′ĭs) ▶ *n.* A disease marked by progressive muscular weakness and fatigue caused by impaired transmission of nerve impulses. [Gk. *mus*, muscle + Gk. *asthenia*, weakness + Lat. *gravis*, serious.]

my•ce•li•um (mī-sē′lē-əm) ▶ *n., pl.* **-li•a** (-lē-ə). The vegetative part of a fungus, consisting of a mass of branching, threadlike filaments that forms its main growing structure. [MYC(O)– + Gk. *hēlos*, wart.] —**my•ce′li•al** *adj.*

My•ce•nae (mī-sē′nē) An ancient Greek city in the NE Peloponnesus. —**My′ce•nae′an** (-sə-nē′ən) *adj.* & *n.*

–mycin ▶ *suff.* A substance derived from a bacterium in the order Actinomycetales: *streptomycin.* [MYC(O)– + –IN.]

myco– or **myc–** ▶ *pref.* Fungus: *mycology.* [< Gk. *mukēs.*]

my•col•o•gy (mī-kŏl′ə-jē) ▶ *n.* The branch of botany that deals with fungi. —**my′co•log′i•cal** (-kə-lŏj′ĭ-kəl) *adj.* —**my•col′o•gist** *n.*

my•co•tox•in (mī′kō-tŏk′sĭn) ▶ *n.* A toxin produced by a fungus.

my•e•lin (mī′ə-lĭn) also **my•e•line** (-lĭn, -lēn′) ▶ *n.* A white fatty material that encloses certain axons and nerve fibers.

my•e•li•tis (mī′ə-lī′tĭs) ▶ *n.* Inflammation of the spinal column or bone marrow.

myelo– or **myel–** ▶ *pref.* **1.** Spinal cord: *myelitis.* **2.** Bone marrow: *myeloma.* [< Gk. *muelos*, marrow, poss. < *mus*, muscle.]

my•e•lo•ma (mī′ə-lō′mə) ▶ *n., pl.* **-mas** or **-ma•ta** (-mə-tə). A malignant tumor formed by the cells of the bone marrow.

My•ko•la•yiv (mĭk′ə-lä′yĭv, -yĭf) A city of S Ukraine NE of Odessa. Pop. 515,400.

my•na or **my•nah** (mī′nə) ▶ *n.* An Asian starling, certain species of which can mimic human speech. [Hindi *mainā*, perh. < Skt. *madana-*, joyful.]

my•o•car•di•um (mī′ō-kär′dē-əm) ▶ *n., pl.* **-di•a** (-dē-ə). The muscular tissue of the heart. [Gk. *mus*, muscle + *kardia*, heart.] —**my′o•car′di•al** *adj.*

my•o•pi•a (mī-ō′pē-ə) ▶ *n.* **1.** A visual defect in which distant objects appear blurred because their images are focused in front of the retina rather than on it; nearsightedness. **2.** Shortsightedness in thinking or planning. [< Gk. *muōps*, nearsighted.] —**my•op′ic** (-ŏp′ĭk, -ō′pĭk) *adj.* —**my•op′i•cal•ly** *adv.*

my•o•sin (mī′ə-sĭn) ▶ *n.* The commonest protein in muscle cells. [Gk. *muos*, genitive of *mus*, muscle + –IN.]

myr•i•ad (mĭr′ē-əd) ▶ *adj.* Constituting a very large, indefinite number. ▶ *n.* A vast number. [Gk. *murias*, *muriad-*, ten thousand.]

myr•i•a•pod (mĭr′ē-ə-pŏd′) ▶ *n.* Any of several arthropods, such as the centipede, having at least nine pairs of legs. [Gk. *murias*, ten thousand + –POD.]

My•ron (mī′rən). 5th cent. B.C. Greek sculptor.

myrrh (mûr) ▶ *n.* An aromatic gum resin obtained from several Asian or African trees and shrubs and used in perfume and incense. [< Gk. *murrha.*]

myr•tle (mûr′tl) ▶ *n.* **1.** An Old World shrub having pink or white flowers and blackish berries. **2.** See **periwinkle**[2]. [< Gk. *murtos.*]

my•self (mī-sĕlf′) ▶ *pron.* **1.** That one identical with me. Used: **a.** Reflexively: *I hurt myself.* **b.** For emphasis: *I myself was certain of the facts.* **2.** My normal or healthy state: *I'm feeling myself again.* [< OE *mē selfum.*]

My•sore (mī-sôr′, -sōr′) A city of S India SW of Bangalore. Pop. 480,692.

mys•ter•y (mĭs′tə-rē) ▶ *n., pl.* **-ies 1.** Something that cannot be explained or fully understood. **2.** The quality that is associated with the unexplained, secret, or unknown. **3.** A work of fiction or drama dealing with a puzzling crime. **4.** A religious truth that is knowable only through divine revelation. [< Gk. *mustērion*, secret rite.] —**mys•te′ri•ous** (mĭ-stîr′ē-əs) *adj.* —**mys•te′ri•ous•ly** *adv.* —**mys•te′ri•ous•ness** *n.*

mystery play ▶ *n.* A medieval drama based on episodes in the life of Jesus. [< Med.Lat. *misterium*, craft guild or < MYSTERY.]

mys•tic (mĭs′tĭk) ▶ *adj.* **1.** Of or relating to religious mysteries or occult rites and practices. **2.** Of or relating to mysticism or mystics. **3.** Mysterious or enigmatic. **4.** Mystical. ▶ *n.* One who practices or believes in mysticism. [< Gk. *mustikos* < *mustērion*, MYSTERY.]

mys•ti•cal (mĭs′tĭ-kəl) ▶ *adj.* **1.** Spiritually significant. **2.** Of or relating to mystics, mysticism, or mystic rites or practices. —**mys′ti•cal•ly** *adv.* —**mys′ti•cal•ness** *n.*

mys•ti•cism (mĭs′tĭ-sĭz′əm) ▶ *n.* Consciousness of transcendent reality or of God through deep meditation or contemplation.

mys•ti•fy (mĭs′tə-fī′) ▶ *v.* **-fied, -fy•ing 1.** To perplex or bewilder. **2.** To make obscure or mysterious. [Fr. *mystifier.*] —**mys′ti•fi•ca′-**

tion *n.* —**mys′ti•fy′ing•ly** *adv.*

mys•tique (mĭ-stēk′) ▸*n.* An aura of mystery or reverence surrounding a particular person, thing, or idea. [Fr. < Lat. *mysticus*, MYSTIC.]

myth (mĭth) ▸*n.* **1.** A traditional, typically ancient story dealing with supernatural beings, ancestors, or heroes that serves as a primordial type in the world view of a people. **2.** A fiction or half-truth. **3.** A fictitious story, person, or thing. [< Gk. *muthos.*] —**myth′i•cal, myth′ic** *adj.* —**myth′i•cal•ly** *adv.*

myth•mak•er (mĭth′mā′kər) ▸*n.* One that creates myths or mythical situations. —**myth′mak•ing** *n.*

my•thol•o•gy (mĭ-thŏl′ə-jē) ▸*n.*, *pl.* **-gies 1.** A body of myths about the origin, history, deities, ancestors, and heroes of a people. **2.** The study of myths. —**myth′o•log′i•cal** (mĭth′ə-lŏj′ĭ-kəl) *adj.* —**myth′o•log′i•cal•ly** *adv.* —**my•thol′o•gist** *n.* —**my•thol′o•gize′** *v.*

N

n[1] or **N** (ĕn) ▸*n.*, *pl.* **n's** or **N's** also **ns** or **Ns.** The 14th letter of the English alphabet.

n[2] ▸*abbr.* **1.** *Gram.* neuter **2.** neutron **3.** also **N** *Chem.* normal

N[1] ▸ The symbol for the element **nitrogen.**

N[2] ▸*abbr.* **1.** *Print.* en **2.** knight (chess) **3.** newton **4a.** north **b.** northern

n. ▸*abbr.* noun

Na ▸ The symbol for the element **sodium.** [< NLat. *natrium*, ult. < Gk. *nitron*, NITER.]

NA ▸*abbr.* **1.** North America **2.** also **n/a** not applicable

NAACP ▸*abbr.* National Association for the Advancement of Colored People

nab (năb) ▸*v.* **nabbed, nab•bing** *Informal* **1.** To seize; arrest. **2.** To grab; snatch. [Perh. var. of dial. *nap*, seize.]

Nab•a•tae•a (năb′ə-tē′ə) An ancient kingdom of Arabia in present-day Jordan.

na•bob (nā′bŏb′) ▸*n.* A person of wealth and prominence. [< Ar. *nuwwāb*, deputies.]

Na•bo•kov (nə-bô′kəf, nä′bə-kôf′), **Vladimir Vladimirovich.** 1899–1977. Russian-born Amer. writer.

na•celle (nə-sĕl′) ▸*n.* A streamlined enclosure on an aircraft for housing the crew or an engine. [< LLat. *nāvicella*, boat.]

na•cho (nä′chō′) ▸*n.*, *pl.* **-chos.** A piece of tortilla topped with cheese or chili-pepper sauce and broiled. [Am.Sp.]

na•cre (nā′kər) ▸*n.* See **mother-of-pearl.** [< Ar. *naqqāra*, drum.]

Na-De•ne also **Na•Dé•né** (nä-dā′nē, -dā-nā′) ▸*n.* A North American Indian language family including Athabaskan and Tlingit.

Na•der (nā′dər), **Ralph.** b. 1934. Amer. lawyer and consumer advocate.

na•dir (nā′dər, -dîr′) ▸*n.* **1.** A point on the celestial sphere diametrically opposite the zenith. **2.** The lowest point. [< Ar. *naẓīr (as-samt)*, opposite (the zenith).]

NAFTA ▸*abbr.* North American Free Trade Agreement

nag[1] (năg) ▸*v.* **nagged, nag•ging 1.** To annoy by constant scolding, complaining, or urging. **2.** To torment persistently, as with anxiety or pain. **3.** To scold, complain, or find fault constantly: *nagging at the children.* ▸*n.* One who nags. [Prob. of Scand. orig.] —**nag′ger** *n.* —**nag′ging•ly** *adv.*

nag[2] (năg) ▸*n.* A horse, esp. an old or worn-out horse. [ME *nagge.*]

Na•ga•sa•ki (nä′gə-sä′kē) A city of W Kyushu, Japan, on **Nagasaki Bay,** an inlet of the East China Sea. Pop. 441,308.

Na•go•ya (nə-goi′ə, nä′gô-yä′) A city of central Honshu, Japan, E of Kyoto. Pop. 2,116,350.

Na•hua•tl (nä′wät′l) ▸*n.*, *pl.* **-tl** or **-tls 1.** A member of any of various Indian peoples of central Mexico, esp. the Aztecs. **2.** The Uto-Aztecan language of the Nahuatl.

Na•hum (nā′həm, nā′əm) ▸*n.* **1.** A Hebrew prophet of the 7th cent. B.C. who predicted the fall of Nineveh. **2.** See table at **Bible.**

nai•ad (nā′əd, -ăd′, nī′-) ▸*n.*, *pl.* **-a•des** (-ə-dēz′) or **-ads** *Gk. Myth.* One of the nymphs living in brooks, springs, and fountains. [< Gk. *naias.*]

nail (nāl) ▸*n.* **1.** A slim, pointed piece of metal hammered into material as a fastener. **2a.** A thin, horny, transparent plate covering the upper surface of the tip of each finger and toe. **b.** A claw or talon. ▸*v.* **1.** To fasten with or as if with a nail. **2.** To cover, enclose, or shut by fastening with nails: *nail up a window.* **3.** *Slang* To seize; catch: *nail a suspect.* **4.** *Slang* To strike or hit. —***phrasal verb:* nail down** To settle conclusively. [< OE *nægl*, fingernail, toenail.]

Nai•paul (nī′pôl), Sir **V(idiahar) S(urajprasad).** b. 1932. Trinidadian - born British writer.

nai•ra (nī′rə) ▸*n.* See table at **currency.** [Alteration of NIGERIA.]

Nai•ro•bi (nī-rō′bē) The capital of Kenya, in the S-central part. Pop. 1,162,189.

na•ive or **na•ïve** (nī-ēv′, nä-) also **na•if** or **na•ïf** (-ēf′) ▸*adj.* **1.** Lacking worldliness and sophistication. **2.** Simple and credulous; ingenuous. [< Lat. *nātīvus*, native, rustic.] —**na•ive′ly** *adv.* —**na•ive′ness** *n.*

na•ive•té or **na•ïve•té** (nī′ēv-tā′, nä′-, nī-ē′-vĭ-tā′, nä-) ▸*n.* **1.** The state of being naive. **2.** A naive statement or act. [Fr. *naïveté.*]

na•ked (nā′kĭd) ▸*adj.* **1.** Without clothing; nude. **2.** Having no covering; bare. **3.** Being without addition, disguise, or embellishment: *naked ambition.* [< OE *nacod.*] —**na′ked•ly** *adv.* —**na′ked•ness** *n.*

naked eye ▸*n.* The eye unassisted by an optical instrument.

nak•fa (näk′fä′) ▸*n.* See table at **currency.** [Tigré (Ethiopian) *naqfa.*]

nam•by-pam•by (năm′bē-păm′bē) ▸*adj.* **1.** Insipid and sentimental. **2.** Indecisive; spineless. [From *Namby-Pamby*, satire on Ambrose Philips (1674–1749) by Henry Carey (1687?–1743).] —**nam′by-pam′by** *n.*

name (nām) ▸*n.* **1.** A word or words by which an entity is designated. **2.** A disparaging designation: *called me names.* **3.** Appearance rather than reality: *a democracy in name only.* **4a.** General reputation: *a bad name.* **b.** Renown. **5.**

An illustrious person. See Syns at **celebrity.** ►*v.* **named, nam•ing 1.** To give a name to. **2.** To mention, specify, or cite by name. **3.** To nominate or appoint. See Syns at **appoint. 4.** To specify or fix: *name the time and date.* ►*adj. Informal* Well-known by a name: *a name performer.* —***idioms:* in the name of** By the authority of. **to (one's) name** Belonging to one. [< OE *nama.*] —**nam'a•ble, name'a•ble** *adj.* —**nam'er** *n.*

name day ►*n.* The feast day of the saint after whom one is named.

name-drop (nām'drŏp') ►*v.* To mention casually the names of illustrious or famous people as a means of self-promotion. —**name'-drop'per** *n.* —**name'-drop'ping** *n.*

name•less (nām'lĭs) ►*adj.* **1.** Having no name. **2.** Unknown by name; obscure. **3.** Anonymous: *a nameless benefactor.* **4.** Defying description; inexpressible: *nameless horror.* —**name'-less•ly** *adv.* —**name'less•ness** *n.*

name•ly (nām'lē) ►*adv.* That is to say; specifically.

name•sake (nām'sāk') ►*n.* One who is named after another.

Na•mib•i•a (nə-mĭb'ē-ə) A country of SW Africa on the Atlantic. Cap. Windhoek. Pop. 1,500,000. —**Na•mib'i•an** *adj. & n.*

Nan•chang (nän'chäng') A city of SE China SE of Wuhan. Pop. 1,262,031.

Nan•ga Par•bat (nŭng'gə pûr'bət) A peak, 8,131.3 m (26,660 ft) of the Himalayas in NW Kashmir.

Nan•jing (nän'jĭng') also **Nan•king** (năn'-kĭng', nän'-). A city of E-central China on the Chang Jiang (Yangtze R.) NW of Shanghai. Pop. 2,610,594.

nan•keen (năn-kēn') also **nan•kin** (-kēn', -kĭn') ►*n.* A sturdy yellow or buff cotton cloth. [< NANJING.]

nan•ny (năn'ē) ►*n., pl.* **-nies.** A children's nurse. [Alteration of *nana.*]

nanny goat ►*n.* A female goat. [< *Nanny,* nickname for *Anne.*]

nano– ►*pref.* **1.** One-billionth (10^{-9}): *nanosecond.* **2.** Extremely small: *nanotube.* [< Gk. *nanos,* dwarf.]

nan•o•sec•ond (năn'ə-sĕk'ənd) ►*n.* One billionth (10^{-9}) of a second.

nan•o•tech•nol•o•gy (năn'ə-tĕk-nŏl'ə-jē) ►*n.* The science of building electronic circuits and devices from single atoms and molecules.

nan•o•tube (năn'ə-to͞ob', -tyo͞ob') ►*n.* An elongated fullerene having a cylindrical configuration.

Nan•sen (năn'sən, nän'-), **Fridtjof.** 1861–1930. Norwegian explorer, zoologist, and politician; 1922 Nobel Peace Prize.

Nantes (nănts, näNT) A city of W France on the Loire R. W of Tours. Pop. 244,514.

Nan•tuck•et (năn-tŭk'ĭt) An island of SE MA S of Cape Cod. —**Nan•tuck'et•er** *n.*

nap¹ (năp) ►*n.* A brief sleep, often during the day. ►*v.* **napped, nap•ping 1.** To take a nap. **2.** To be unaware of imminent danger or trouble. [< OE *hnappian,* doze.]

nap² (năp) ►*n.* A soft or fuzzy surface on fabric or leather. [< MDu. *noppe.*]

na•palm (nā'päm') ►*n.* A highly incendiary jelly used in bombs and flamethrowers. [*na(phthenate)* + *palm(itate),* substances used in its composition.] —**na'palm'** *v.*

nape (nāp, năp) ►*n.* The back of the neck. [ME.]

na•per•y (nā'pə-rē) ►*n.* Household linen, esp. table linen. [< OFr. *nape,* tablecloth.]

naph•tha (năf'thə, năp'-) ►*n.* A highly volatile, flammable liquid distilled esp. from petroleum and used as a fuel or solvent and in making chemicals. [< Gk.]

naph•tha•lene (năf'thə-lēn', năp'-) ►*n.* A white crystalline compound, $C_{10}H_8$, used in dyes, moth repellents, and explosives and as a solvent. [NAPHTH(A) + AL(COHOL) + -ENE.]

Na•pi•er (nā'pē-ər, nə-pîr'), **John.** 1550–1617. Scottish mathematician.

nap•kin (năp'kĭn) ►*n.* **1.** A piece of cloth or absorbent paper used at table to protect the clothes or wipe the lips and fingers. **2.** A cloth or towel. [< OFr. *nape,* tablecloth.]

Na•ples (nā'pəlz) A city of S-central Italy on the **Bay of Naples,** an arm of the Tyrrhenian Sea. Pop. 1,054,601.

Na•po•le•on I (nə-pō'lē-ən, -pōl'yən). Napoleon Bonaparte. 1769–1821. Emperor of the French (1804–14). —**Na•po'le•on'ic** (-ŏn'ĭk) *adj.*

Napoleon I
Napoleon I at Malmaison in 1804
by François Gerard

Napoleon III. Charles Louis Napoleon Bonaparte. 1808–73. Emperor of the French (1852–71).

narc (närk) ►*n. Slang* A narcotics agent.

nar•cis•sism (när'sĭ-sĭz'əm) ►*n.* Excessive love or admiration of oneself. See Syns at **conceit.** [< NARCISSUS.] —**nar'cis•sist** *n.* —**nar'cis•sis'tic** *adj.*

nar•cis•sus (när-sĭs'əs) ►*n., pl.* **-es** or **-cis•si** (-sĭs'ī', -sĭs'ē). Any of a genus of plants that includes the daffodil and jonquil. [< Gk. *narkissos.*]

Narcissus ►*n. Gk. Myth.* A youth who fell in love with his own image in a pool of water and was transformed into a flower.

nar•co•lep•sy (när'kə-lĕp'sē) ►*n.* A disorder marked by sudden and uncontrollable, often brief, attacks of deep sleep. [Gk. *narkē,* numbness + *lēpsis,* seizure.] —**nar'co•lep'tic** (-lĕp'tĭk) *adj. & n.*

nar•co•sis (när-kō'sĭs) ►*n., pl.* **-ses** (-sēz). Deep stupor or unconsciousness produced by a drug. [< Gk. *narkōsis,* a numbing.]

nar•cot•ic (när-kŏt'ĭk) ►*n.* An addictive drug that reduces pain, alters mood and behavior, and usu. induces sleep or stupor. [< Gk. *narkōtikos*, numbing.] —**nar•cot′ic** *adj.*

nar•co•tism (när′kə-tĭz′əm) ▸*n.* **1.** Addiction to narcotics. **2.** Narcosis.

nar•co•tize (när′kə-tīz′) ▸*v.* **-tized, -tiz•ing 1.** To place under the influence of a narcotic. **2.** To put to sleep. **3.** To dull; deaden.

nar•co•traf•fick•ing (när′kō-trăf′ĭ-kĭng) ▸*n.* The smuggling and distribution of illegal drugs. [NARCO(TIC) + TRAFFICKING.]

nar•is (nâr′ĭs) ▸*n.*, *pl.* **-es** (-ēz). A nostril. [Lat. *nāris.*]

Nar•ra•gan•sett (năr′ə-găn′sĭt) ▸*n.*, *pl.* **-sett** or **-setts 1.** A member of a Native American people inhabiting parts of Rhode Island. **2.** Their Algonquian language.

Narragansett Bay. A deep inlet of the Atlantic in E RI.

nar•rate (năr′āt′, nă-rāt′) ▸*v.* **-rat•ed, -rat•ing 1.** To give an account of; tell. See Syns at **describe. 2.** To supply a descriptive commentary for a movie or performance. [Lat. *narrāre.*] —**nar•ra′tion** *n.* —**nar′ra′tor** *n.*

nar•ra•tive (năr′ə-tĭv) ▸*n.* **1.** A narrated account; story. **2.** The act or process of narrating. —**nar′ra•tive** *adj.*

nar•row (năr′ō) ▸*adj.* **-er, -est 1.** Of small or limited width. **2.** Limited in area or scope; cramped. **3.** Lacking flexibility; rigid: *narrow opinions.* **4.** Barely sufficient; close: *a narrow margin of victory.* **5.** Painstakingly thorough; meticulous: *narrow scrutiny.* ▸*v.* To reduce in width or extent; make narrower. ▸*n.* **narrows** *(takes sing. or pl. v.)* A narrow body of water that connects two larger ones. [< OE *nearu.*] —**nar′row•ly** *adv.* —**nar′row•ness** *n.*

nar•row-mind•ed (năr′ō-mīn′dĭd) ▸*adj.* Lacking tolerance or breadth of view; petty. —**nar′row-mind′ed•ly** *adv.* —**nar′row-mind′ed•ness** *n.*

nar•thex (när′thĕks′) ▸*n.* A portico or lobby to the nave of a church. [LGk. *narthēx.*]

nar•whal (när′wəl) ▸*n.* An Arctic whale marked in the male by a long spirally twisted ivory tusk. [< ON *nāhvalr.*]

nar•y (nâr′ē) ▸*adj.* Not one. [< *ne'er a.*]

NASA (năs′ə) ▸*abbr.* National Aeronautics and Space Administration

na•sal (nā′zəl) ▸*adj.* **1.** Of or relating to the nose. **2.** Marked by or resembling a resonant sound produced through the nose: *a nasal whine.* [< Lat. *nāsus*, nose.] —**na•sal′i•ty** (nā-zăl′ĭ-tē) *n.* —**na′sal•ly** *adv.*

nas•cent (năs′ənt, nā′sənt) ▸*adj.* Coming into existence; emergent. [< Lat. *nāscī*, be born.] —**nas′cence** *n.*

Nash (năsh), **Ogden.** 1902–71. Amer. writer.

Nash•u•a (năsh′o͞o-ə) A city of S NH S of Manchester. Pop. 79,662.

Nash•ville (năsh′vĭl′) The capital of TN, in the N-central part NE of Memphis. Pop. 488,374.

Nas•sau (năs′ô′) The capital of the Bahamas, on the NE coast of New Providence I. Pop. 172,196.

Nas•ser (năs′ər, nä′sər), **Gamal Abdel.** 1918–70. Egyptian army officer and politician.

nas•tur•tium (nə-stûr′shəm, nă-) ▸*n.* A plant having pungent juice, edible round leaves, and usu. yellow, orange, or red irregular flowers. [< Lat., a kind of cress.]

nas•ty (năs′tē) ▸*adj.* **-ti•er, -ti•est 1.** Disgustingly dirty; foul. **2.** Offensive; indecent. See Syns at **offensive. 3.** Malicious. **4.** Very unpleasant: *nasty weather.* **5.** Painful or dangerous: *a nasty accident.* [ME *nasti.*] —**nas′ti•ly** *adv.* —**nas′ti•ness** *n.*

na•tal (nāt′l) ▸*adj.* **1.** Of or accompanying birth. **2.** Of the time or place of one's birth. [< Lat. *nātus*, p.part. of *nāscī*, be born.]

na•tal•i•ty (nā-tăl′ĭ-tē, nə-) ▸*n.* See **birthrate.**

Natch•ez (năch′ĭz) ▸*n.*, *pl.* **Natchez 1.** A member of an extinct Native American people formerly living along the lower Mississippi R. **2.** The language of the Natchez.

Na•tick (nā′tĭk) ▸*n.* A dialect of Massachusett.

na•tion (nā′shən) ▸*n.* **1.** A relatively large group of people organized under a single government. **2.** A people; nationality. **3.** A federation or tribe. [< Lat. *nātiō* < *nāscī*, be born.] —**na′tion•hood′** *n.*

Nation, Carry Amelia Moore. 1846–1911. Amer. temperance crusader.

na•tion•al (năsh′ə-nəl, năsh′nəl) ▸*adj.* **1.** Of or belonging to a nation. **2.** Characteristic of the people of a nation: *a national trait.* ▸*n.* A citizen of a particular nation. See Syns at **citizen.** —**na′tion•al•ly** *adv.*

National Guard ▸*n.* The military reserve units controlled by each US state and subject to the call of either the federal or the state government.

na•tion•al•ism (năsh′ə-nə-lĭz′əm, năsh′nə-) ▸*n.* **1.** Devotion to the interests or culture of a particular nation. **2.** Aspirations for national independence. —**na′tion•al•ist** *n.* —**na′tion•al•is′tic** *adj.* —**na′tion•al•is′ti•cal•ly** *adv.*

na•tion•al•i•ty (năsh′ə-năl′ĭ-tē, năsh-năl′-) ▸*n.*, *pl.* **-ties 1.** The status of belonging to a particular nation by origin, birth, or naturalization. **2.** A people having common origins or traditions and often constituting a nation.

na•tion•al•ize (năsh′ə-nə-līz′, năsh′nə-) ▸*v.* **-ized, -iz•ing 1.** To convert from private to governmental ownership and control. **2.** To make national in character or scope. —**na′tion•al•i•za′tion** *n.*

national monument ▸*n.* A landmark or site of historic interest set aside by a national government for public enjoyment.

national park ▸*n.* A tract of public land maintained by a national government for recreational and cultural use.

na•tion•wide (nā′shən-wīd′) ▸*adv.* & *adj.* Throughout a whole nation.

na•tive (nā′tĭv) ▸*adj.* **1.** Inborn; innate: *native ability.* **2.** Being such by birth or origin: *a native Scot.* **3.** Being one's own by birth: *our native land.* **4.** Originating or produced in a certain place; indigenous. ▸*n.* **1a.** One born in a specified place. **b.** An original or lifelong inhabitant of a place. **2.** An animal or plant that originated in a particular place. [< Lat. *nātīvus* < *nāscī*, be born.]

Usage: When used to refer to a member of an indigenous people, the noun *native,* like its synonym *aborigine,* can evoke unwelcome stereotypes of cultural backwardness. But, as is often the case with words that categorize people, the adjectival forms of these words are acceptable. Thus, *the peoples native to northern Europe* or *the aboriginal inhabitants of the South Pacific* is preferable to *the natives of northern Europe* or *the aborigines of the South Pacific.*

Native Alaskan ►*n.* See **Alaska Native.**

Native American ►*n.* A member of any of the peoples indigenous to the Western Hemisphere before European contact. —**Native American** *adj.*

Usage: Many people now prefer *Native American* to Columbus's misnomer *Indian* in referring to the earliest inhabitants of the Western Hemisphere. However, it should not be assumed that the latter is necessarily offensive or out of date. *Indian* is often used in combinations, such as *American Indian* or *Pueblo Indian,* that cannot reasonably be formed with *Native American.* Of the two terms, only *Native American* is customarily held to include the Eskimo and Aleut peoples. See Usage Note at **color.**

Native Hawaiian ►*n.* A member or descendant of the indigenous Polynesian people of the Hawaiian Islands.

na•tiv•i•ty (nə-tĭv′ĭ-tē, nā-) ►*n., pl.* **-ties 1.** Birth, esp. the conditions or circumstances of being born. **2. Nativity a.** The birth of Jesus. **b.** Christmas. [< Lat. *nātīvitās.*]

natl. ►*abbr.* national

NATO (nā′tō) ►*abbr.* North Atlantic Treaty Organization

nat•ty (năt′ē) ►*adj.* **-ti•er, -ti•est.** Neat, trim, and smart; dapper. [Perh. < ME *net,* good.] —**nat′ti•ly** *adv.* —**nat′ti•ness** *n.*

nat•u•ral (năch′ər-əl, năch′rəl) ►*adj.* **1.** Present in or produced by nature. **2.** Of or relating to nature. **3.** Conforming to the usual course of nature: *a natural death.* **4a.** Not acquired; inherent. **b.** Having a particular character by nature: *a natural leader.* **5.** Free from affectation or inhibitions. **6.** Not altered or treated: *natural coloring.* **7.** Expected and accepted. **8.** *Math.* Of or relating to positive integers. **9.** *Mus.* Not sharped or flatted. ►*n.* **1.** One especially suited by nature or qualifications: *a natural for the job.* **2.** *Mus.* The sign (♮) placed before a note to cancel a preceding sharp or flat. —**nat′u•ral•ness** *n.*

natural gas ►*n.* A mixture of hydrocarbon gases, chiefly methane, occurring with petroleum deposits and used esp. as a fuel.

natural history ►*n.* The study of organisms and natural objects, esp. their origins, evolution, and relationships.

nat•u•ral•ism (năch′ər-ə-lĭz′əm, năch′rə-) ►*n.* **1.** Factual or realistic representation in art or literature. **2.** The view that all phenomena can be explained in terms of natural causes and laws.

nat•u•ral•ist (năch′ər-ə-lĭst, năch′rə-) ►*n.* **1.** One versed in natural history, esp. in zoology or botany. **2.** An adherent of naturalism.

nat•u•ral•is•tic (năch′ər-ə-lĭs′tĭk, năch′rə-) ►*adj.* Lifelike; realistic. —**nat′u•ral•is′ti•cal•ly** *adv.*

nat•u•ral•ize (năch′ər-ə-līz′, năch′rə-) ►*v.* **-ized, -iz•ing 1.** To grant full citizenship to. **2.** To adopt into general use. **3.** To adapt or acclimate (a plant or animal) to a new environment. —**nat′u•ral•i•za′tion** *n.*

nat•u•ral•ly (năch′ər-ə-lē, năch′rə-) ►*adv.* **1.** In a natural manner. **2.** By nature; inherently. **3.** Without a doubt; surely.

natural resource►*n.* A material source of wealth, such as timber, fresh water, or a mineral deposit, that occurs in a natural state.

natural science ►*n.* A science, such as biology, chemistry, or physics, that deals with the objects, phenomena, or laws of nature and the physical world.

natural selection ►*n.* The process in nature by which only the organisms best adapted to their environment tend to survive and transmit their genetic characters to succeeding generations.

na•ture (nā′chər) ►*n.* **1.** The material world and its phenomena. **2.** The forces that produce and control such phenomena: *the laws of nature.* **3.** The world of living things and the outdoors. **4.** A primitive state of existence. **5.** A kind or sort. **6.** The essential character of a person or thing. **7.** Disposition; temperament: *a sweet nature.* [< Lat. *nātūra* < *nāscī,* be born.] —**na′tured** *adj.*

na•tur•op•a•thy (nā′chə-rŏp′ə-thē) ►*n., pl.* **-thies.** A system of therapy that relies on natural remedies, such as sunlight, diet, and massage, to treat illness. —**na′tur•o•path′** (nā′chər-ə-păth′, nə-cho͝or′-) *n.* —**na′tur•o•path′ic** *adj*

naught also **nought** (nôt) ►*n.* **1.** Nonexistence; nothingness. **2.** The figure 0; zero. [< OE *nāwiht,* not a thing.]

naugh•ty (nô′tē) ►*adj.* **-ti•er, -ti•est 1.** Disobedient; mischievous. **2.** Indecent; improper. —**naugh′ti•ly** *adv.* —**naugh′ti•ness** *n.*

Na•u•ru (nä-o͞o′ro͞o) An island country of the central Pacific S of the equator and W of Kiribati. Cap. Yaren. Pop. 11,000. —**Na•u′ru•an** *adj. & n.*

nau•se•a (nô′zē-ə, -zhə, -sē-ə, -shə) ►*n.* **1.** A feeling of sickness in the stomach marked by an urge to vomit. **2.** Strong aversion; disgust. [< Gk. *nausiē,* seasickness.]

nau•se•ate (nô′zē-āt′, -zhē-, -sē-, -shē-) ►*v.* **-at•ed, -at•ing.** To feel or cause to feel nausea. See Syns at **disgust.** —**nau′se•at′ing•ly** *adv.* —**nau′se•a′tion** *n.*

nau•seous (nô′shəs, -zē-əs) ►*adj.* **1.** Causing nausea; sickening. **2.** Affected with nausea.

nau•ti•cal (nô′tĭ-kəl) ►*adj.* Of or characteristic of ships, shipping, sailors, or navigation. [< Gk. *nautēs,* sailor.] —**nau′ti•cal•ly** *adv.*

Syns: *nautical, marine, maritime, naval* **adj.**

nautical mile ►*n.* A unit of length used in sea and air navigation, usu. equal to 1,852 m (about 6,076 ft).

nau•ti•lus (nôt′l-əs) ►*n., pl.* **-es** or **-li** (-lī′). A cephalopod mollusk having a partitioned spiral shell. [< Gk. *nautilos,* sailor.]

nautilus

Nav•a•jo also **Nav•a•ho** (năv′ə-hō′, nä′və-) ►*n., pl.* **-jo** or **-jos** also **-ho** or **-hos 1.** A member of a Native American people inhabiting reservation lands in Arizona, New Mexico, and SE Utah. **2.** The Athabaskan language of the Navajo. —**Nav′a•jo′** *adj.*

na•val (nā′vəl) ►*adj.* **1.** Of or relating to ships or shipping. See Syns at **nautical. 2.** Of or relating to a navy.

Na•varre (nə-vär′, nä-) A former kingdom of SW Europe in the Pyrenees of N Spain and SW France.

nave (nāv) ►*n.* The central part of a church, extending from the narthex to the chancel and flanked by the aisles. [< Lat. *nāvis*, ship.]

na•vel (nā′vəl) ►*n.* The mark on the abdomen of mammals where the umbilical cord was attached during gestation. [< OE *nafela.*]

navel orange ►*n.* A usu. seedless orange having at its apex a navellike formation enclosing an underdeveloped fruit.

nav•i•ga•ble (năv′ĭ-gə-bəl) ►*adj.* **1.** Sufficiently deep or wide to provide passage for vessels. **2.** That can be steered. —**nav′i•ga•bil′i•ty, nav′i•ga•ble•ness** *n.*

nav•i•gate (năv′ĭ-gāt′) ►*v.* **-gat•ed, -gat•ing 1.** To control the course of a ship or aircraft. **2.** To voyage over water in a boat or ship; sail. **3.** To make one's way (through). [Lat. *nāvigāre* : *nāvis*, ship + *agere*, drive.] —**nav′i•ga′tion** *n.* —**nav′i•ga′tion•al** *adj.* —**nav′i•ga′tor** *n.*

Nav•ra•ti•lo•va (năv′rə-tĭ-lō′və, nä′vrə-), **Martina.** b. 1956. Czechoslovakian-born Amer. tennis player.

na•vy (nā′vē) ►*n., pl.* **-vies 1.** All of a nation's warships. **2.** A nation's entire military organization for sea warfare and defense. **3.** Navy blue. [< Lat. *nāvigia*, ships.]

navy bean ►*n.* A variety of the kidney bean cultivated for its edible white seeds.

navy blue ►*n.* A dark grayish blue. [From the color of the British naval uniform.]

nay (nā) ►*adv.* **1.** No: *voted nay.* **2.** And moreover: *He was ill-favored, nay, hideous.* ►*n.* **1.** A denial or refusal. **2.** A negative vote or voter. [< ON *nei.*]

Naz•a•reth (năz′ər-əth) A town of N Israel SE of Haifa. Pop. 46,300.

Na•zi (nät′sē, năt′-) ►*n., pl.* **-zis.** A member of the fascist political party that held power (1933–45) in Germany under Adolf Hitler. —**Na′zi** *adj.* —**Na′zism, Na′zi•ism** *n.*

Nb ► The symbol for the element **niobium.**

NB ►*abbr.* **1.** also **N.B.** New Brunswick **2.** nota bene

NBA ►*abbr.* National Basketball Association

NbE ►*abbr.* north by east

NbW ►*abbr.* north by west

NC or **N.C.** ►*abbr.* North Carolina

NCAA ►*abbr.* National Collegiate Athletic Association

NCC ►*abbr.* National Council of Churches

NCO ►*abbr.* noncommissioned officer

Nd ► The symbol for the element **neodymium.**

ND or **N.D.** ►*abbr.* North Dakota

n.d. ►*abbr.* no date

N'Dja•me•na (ən-jä′mə-nə) The capital of Chad, in the SW part. Pop. 303,000.

Ne ► The symbol for the element **neon.**

NE ►*abbr.* **1.** Nebraska **2.** New England **3a.** northeast **b.** northeastern

NEA ►*abbr.* **1.** National Education Association **2.** National Endowment for the Arts

Ne•an•der•thal (nē-ăn′dər-thôl′, -tôl′, nā-ăn′dər-täl′) ►*adj.* **1.** Of or being an extinct species or subspecies of humans of the late Pleistocene Epoch, esp. in Europe. **2.** *Slang* Crude, boorish, or slow-witted. —**Ne•an′der•thal′** *n.*

neap tide (nēp) ►*n.* A tide occuring during the first and third quarters of the moon, when the difference between high and low tides is least. [< OE *nēp(flōd)*, neap (tide).]

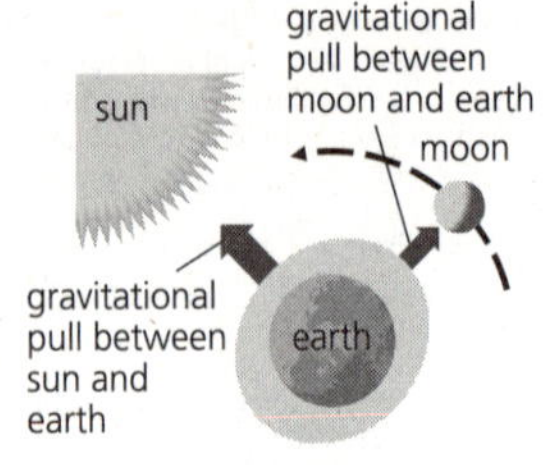

neap tide

Neap tides occur when the sun, moon, and earth form a right angle and the gravitational pull of the sun counteracts the pull of the moon.

near (nîr) ►*adv.* **-er, -est 1.** To, at, or within a short distance or interval in space or time. **2.** Almost; nearly: *was near exhausted from the work.* **3.** With or in a close relationship. ►*adj.* **-er, -est 1.** Close in time, space, position, or degree: *near equals.* **2.** Closely related. See Syns at **close. 3.** Nearly so: *a near victory.* **4.** Closely resembling an original. **5.** Closer of two or more. ►*prep.* Close to: *an inn near Tokyo.* ►*v.* To come close or closer to; draw near. [< OE *nēar*, comp. of *nēah.*] —**near′ness** *n.*

near•by (nîr′bī′) ►*adj.* Located a short distance away. See Syns at **close.** ►*adv.* Not far away.

Near East. A region of SW Asia generally thought to include the countries of the E Mediterranean, the Arabian Peninsula, and, sometimes, NE Africa. —**Near Eastern** *adj.*

near•ly (nîr′lē) ►*adv.* Almost but not quite.

near•sight•ed (nîr′sī′tĭd) ►*adj.* Unable to see distant objects clearly; myopic. —**near′sight′ed•ly** *adv.* —**near′sight′ed•ness** *n.*

neat (nēt) ►*adj.* **-er, -est 1.** Clean and tidy. **2.** Orderly and precise; systematic. **3.** Marked by ingenuity and skill; adroit: *a neat turn of phrase.* **4.** Not diluted: *neat whiskey.* **5.** *Slang* Wonderful; terrific: *a neat party.* [< Lat. *nitidus*, elegant.] —**neat′ly** *adv.* —**neat′ness** *n.*

neat•en (nēt′n) ►*v.* To make neat or tidy.

neath or **'neath** (nēth) ►*prep.* Beneath.

neat's-foot oil (nēts′fo͝ot′) ►*n.* A light yellow oil obtained from the feet and shinbones of cattle, used chiefly to dress leather. [< *neat*, cow < OE *nēat.*]

neb (nĕb) ►*n.* **1a.** A beak of a bird. **b.** A nose. **2.** A projecting part, esp. a nib. [< OE.]

neb•bish (nĕb′ĭsh) ►*n.* A weak-willed or timid person. [< Yiddish *nebekh*, poor.]

NEbE ►*abbr.* northeast by east

NEbN ►*abbr.* northeast by north

Ne•bras•ka (nə-brăs′kə) A state of the central US in the Great Plains. Cap. Lincoln. Pop.

1,584,617. —**Ne•bras′kan** *adj. & n.*

Neb•u•chad•nez•zar II (nĕb′ə-kəd-nĕz′ər, nĕb′yə-). 630?–562 B.C. King of Babylonia (605–562).

neb•u•la (nĕb′yə-lə) ▸*n., pl.* **-lae** (-lē′) or **-las** **1.** A diffuse mass of interstellar dust or gas. **2.** See **galaxy** 1. [< Lat., cloud.] —**neb′u•lar** *adj.*

neb•u•lize (nĕb′yə-līz′) ▸*v.* **-lized, -liz•ing.** To convert (a liquid) to a fine spray; atomize. —**neb′u•li•za′tion** *n.* —**neb′u•liz′er** *n.*

neb•u•los•i•ty (nĕb′yə-lŏs′ĭ-tē) ▸*n., pl.* **-ties** **1.** The quality or condition of being nebulous. **2.** A nebula.

neb•u•lous (nĕb′yə-ləs) ▸*adj.* **1.** Cloudy, misty, or hazy. **2.** Lacking definite form or limits; vague. **3.** Of or like a nebula. —**neb′u•lous•ly** *adv.* —**neb′u•lous•ness** *n.*

nec•es•sar•i•ly (nĕs′ĭ-sâr′ə-lē, -sĕr′-) ▸*adv.* Of necessity; inevitably.

nec•es•sar•y (nĕs′ĭ-sĕr′ē) ▸*adj.* **1.** Absolutely essential; indispensable. See Syns at **indispensable. 2.** Unavoidably determined; inevitable. **3.** Required, as by obligation, compulsion, or convention. ▸*n., pl.* **-ies.** Something indispensable. [< Lat. *necesse.*]

ne•ces•si•tate (nə-sĕs′ĭ-tāt′) ▸*v.* **-tat•ed, -tat•ing.** To make necessary or unavoidable. —**ne•ces′si•ta′tion** *n.*

ne•ces•si•tous (nə-sĕs′ĭ-təs) ▸*adj.* **1.** Needy; indigent. **2.** Urgent.

ne•ces•si•ty (nə-sĕs′ĭ-tē) ▸*n., pl.* **-ties 1a.** The condition or quality of being necessary. **b.** Something necessary. **2.** The force exerted by circumstance. **3.** Pressing or urgent need. [< Lat. *necessitās.*]

neck (nĕk) ▸*n.* **1.** The part of the body joining the head to the trunk. **2.** The part of a garment around or near the neck. **3.** A narrow elongation, projection, or connecting part: *a neck of land; the neck of a flask.* **4.** A narrow margin: *won by a neck.* ▸*v. Informal* To kiss and caress amorously. —***idiom:* neck and neck** Very close together, as in a race. [< OE *hnecca.*] —**necked** *adj.*

neck•er•chief (nĕk′ər-chĭf, -chēf′) ▸*n.* A kerchief worn around the neck.

neck•lace (nĕk′lĭs) ▸*n.* An ornament worn around the neck.

neck•line (nĕk′līn′) ▸*n.* The line formed by the edge of a garment at the neck.

neck•tie (nĕk′tī′) ▸*n.* A narrow fabric band worn around the neck and tied in a knot or bow close to the throat.

necro– or **necr–** ▸*pref.* Death; the dead: *necrosis.* [< Gk. *nekros*, corpse.]

ne•crol•o•gy (nə-krŏl′ə-jē, nĕ-) ▸*n., pl.* **-gies** **1.** A list of people who have died, esp. in the recent past. **2.** An obituary. —**nec′ro•log′ic** (nĕk′rə-lŏj′ĭk), **nec′ro•log′i•cal** *adj.* —**ne•crol′o•gist** *n.*

nec•ro•man•cy (nĕk′rə-măn′sē) ▸*n.* **1.** The art that professes to communicate with the spirits of the dead so as to predict the future. **2.** Black magic; sorcery. [NECRO– + Gk. *manteia*, divination.] —**nec′ro•man′cer** *n.*

ne•crop•o•lis (nə-krŏp′ə-lĭs, nĕ-) ▸*n., pl.* **-lis•es** or **-leis** (-lās′). A cemetery, esp. a large and elaborate one in an ancient city. [Gk. *nekropolis* : NECRO– + *polis*, city.]

ne•cro•sis (nə-krō′sĭs, nĕ-) ▸*n., pl.* **-ses** (-sēz′). Death of cells or tissues through injury or disease. —**ne•crot′ic** (-krŏt′ĭk) *adj.*

nec•tar (nĕk′tər) ▸*n.* **1.** A sweet liquid secreted by flowers. **2.** *Gk. & Rom. Myth.* The drink of the gods. **3.** A delicious or invigorating drink. [< Gk. *nektar.*]

nec•tar•ine (nĕk′tə-rēn′) ▸*n.* A variety of peach having a smooth waxy skin. [< obsolete *nectarine*, sweet as nectar.]

née also **nee** (nā) ▸*adj.* Born. [Fr., feminine p.part. of *naître*, be born.]

need (nēd) ▸*n.* **1.** A lack of something required or desirable. **2.** Something required or wanted; requisite. **3.** Necessity; obligation. **4.** Poverty or misfortune: *in dire need.* ▸*v.* **1.** To have need of; require: *The family needs money.* **2.** To be in need or want. —*aux.* To be under the necessity of or the obligation to: *They need not come.* [< OE *nēod*, necessity.]

need•ful (nēd′fəl) ▸*adj.* Necessary; required. See Syns at **indispensable.** —**need′ful•ly** *adv.* —**need′ful•ness** *n.*

nee•dle (nēd′l) ▸*n.* **1a.** A small slender implement used for sewing, made usu. of steel and having an eye at one end through which a thread is passed. **b.** A similarly shaped implement, such as one used in knitting. **2.** A stylus used to transmit vibrations from the grooves of a phonograph record. **3.** A slender pointer or indicator, as on a dial. **4.** A hypodermic needle. **5.** A narrow stiff leaf, as those of conifers. **6.** A fine sharp projection, as a spine of a sea urchin. ▸*v.* **-dled, -dling.** *Informal* To goad, provoke, or tease. [< OE *nǣdl.*]

nee•dle•point (nēd′l-point′) ▸*n.* Decorative needlework on canvas.

need•less (nēd′lĭs) ▸*adj.* Not needed or wished for; unnecessary. —**need′less•ly** *adv.*

nee•dle•work (nēd′l-wûrk′) ▸*n.* Work, such as embroidery, that is done with a needle.

need•n't (nēd′nt) ▸ Need not.

needs (nēdz) ▸*adv.* Of necessity; necessarily: *We must needs go.* [< OE *nēde.*]

need•y (nē′dē) ▸*adj.* **-i•er, -i•est.** Being in need; impoverished. —**need′i•ness** *n.*

ne'er (nâr) ▸*adv.* Never.

ne'er-do-well (nâr′do͞o-wĕl′) ▸*n.* An idle, irresponsible person. —**ne'er′-do-well′** *adj.*

ne•far•i•ous (nə-fâr′ē-əs) ▸*adj.* Extremely wicked. [< Lat. *nefās*, crime.] —**ne•far′i•ous•ly** *adv.* —**ne•far′i•ous•ness** *n.*

Nef•er•ti•ti (nĕf′ər-tē′tē). 14th cent. B.C. Queen of Egypt as the wife of Akhenaton.

Nefertiti
14th century B.C. limestone bust

neg. ►*abbr.* Negative.

ne•gate (nĭ-gāt′) ►*v.* **-gat•ed, -gat•ing 1.** To make ineffective or invalid; nullify. **2.** To rule out; deny. See Syns at **deny.** [Lat. *negāre*, deny.] —**ne•ga′tion** *n.*

neg•a•tive (nĕg′ə-tĭv) ►*adj.* **1a.** Expressing negation, refusal, or denial. **b.** Indicating opposition or resistance: *a negative reaction.* **2.** Not positive or constructive: *negative criticism.* **3.** *Medic.* Not indicating the presence of a disease or specific condition. **4.** *Math.* **a.** Of or being a quantity less than zero. **b.** Of or being a quantity, number, angle, velocity, or direction in a sense opposite to another understood to be positive. **5.** *Phys.* Of or being an electric charge of the same sign as that of an electron, indicated by the symbol (–). ►*n.* **1.** A negative word, statement, or act. See Usage Note at **double negative. 2.** A feature or aspect that is not positive or affirmative. **3.** A statement that is highly critical of another: *a political ad based solely on negatives.* **4.** The side in a debate that opposes the question being debated. **5a.** An image in which the light areas of the object rendered appear dark and the dark areas appear light. **b.** A film, plate, or other photographic material containing such an image. ►*v.* **-tived, -tiv•ing 1.** To veto. **2.** To deny. —**neg′a•tive•ly** *adv.* —**neg′a•tive•ness, neg′a•tiv′i•ty** (-tĭv′ĭ-tē) *n.*

neg•a•tiv•ism (nĕg′ə-tĭ-vĭz′əm) ►*n.* A habitual attitude of skepticism or resistance to the suggestions, orders, or instructions of others. —**neg′a•tiv•ist** *n.* —**neg′a•tiv•is′tic** *adj.*

neg•a•tron (nĕg′ə-trŏn′) ►*n.* An electron with a negative charge, as contrasted with a positron. [NEGA(TIVE) + (ELEC)TRON.]

Ne•gev (nĕg′ĕv) A hilly desert region of S Israel.

ne•glect (nĭ-glĕkt′) ►*v.* **1.** To ignore; disregard. **2.** To fail to care for or attend to properly: *neglects her appearance.* **3.** To fail to do through carelessness or oversight. ►*n.* **1.** The act or an instance of neglecting something. **2.** The state of being neglected. [Lat. *neglegere*, *neglēct-*.] —**ne•glect′er** *n.*

ne•glect•ful (nĭ-glĕkt′fəl) ►*adj.* Marked by neglect. See Syns at **negligent.** —**ne•glect′ful•ly** *adv.* —**ne•glect′ful•ness** *n.*

neg•li•gee also **neg•li•gée** (nĕg′lĭ-zhā′, nĕg′lĭ-zhā′) ►*n.* A woman's loose dressing gown. [Fr. *négligée*.]

neg•li•gence (nĕg′lĭ-jəns) ►*n.* **1.** The state or quality of being negligent. **2.** *Law* Failure to exercise the degree of care considered reasonable under the circumstances.

neg•li•gent (nĕg′lĭ-jənt) ►*adj.* **1.** Marked by or inclined to neglect. **2.** Careless or casual. **3.** *Law* Guilty of negligence. [< Lat. *neglegere*, neglect.] —**neg′li•gent•ly** *adv.*

Syns: *negligent, derelict, lax, neglectful, remiss, slack* **adj.**

neg•li•gi•ble (nĕg′lĭ-jə-bəl) ►*adj.* Not worth considering; trifling. —**neg′li•gi•bil′i•ty** *n.* —**neg′li•gi•bly** *adv.*

ne•go•tia•ble (nĭ-gō′shə-bəl, -shē-ə-) ►*adj.* **1.** Capable of being negotiated. **2.** Transferable from one person to another by delivery or endorsement: *negotiable securities.* —**ne•go′tia•bil′i•ty** *n.*

ne•go•ti•ant (nĭ-gō′shē-ənt, -shənt) ►*n.* One that negotiates.

ne•go•ti•ate (nĭ-gō′shē-āt′) ►*v.* **-at•ed, -at•ing 1.** To confer with another in order to come to terms. **2.** To arrange or settle by agreement: *negotiate a contract.* **3.** To transfer title to or ownership of (e.g., a promissory note) to another party in return for value received. **4.** To succeed in coping with: *negotiate a sharp curve.* [< Lat. *negōtium*, business.] —**ne•go′ti•a′tion** *n.* —**ne•go′ti•a′tor** *n.*

Ne•gress (nē′grĭs) ►*n.* *Offensive* A Black woman or girl.

ne•gri•tude or **Ne•gri•tude** (nē′grĭ-to͞od′, -tyo͞od′, nĕg′rĭ-) ►*n.* Awareness of and pride in Black culture. [Fr. *négritude*.]

Ne•gro (nē′grō) ►*n.*, *pl.* **-groes** *Often Offensive* A Black person. See Usage Note at **black.** [< Sp. and Port. *negro*, black < Lat. *niger*.] —**Ne′gro** *adj.*

Ne•gro (nĕ′grō, -gro͞o), **Río 1.** A river rising in S Brazil and flowing about 805 km (500 mi) to the Uruguay R. in central Uruguay. **2.** A river of NW South America flowing about 2,253 km (1,400 mi) from E Colombia to the Amazon R. near Manaus, Brazil.

Ne•groid (nē′groid′) ►*adj.* *Anthro.* Of or being a purported human racial classification distinguished by brown to black pigmentation and often tightly curled hair and including peoples indigenous to sub-Saharan Africa. Not in scientific use. —**Ne′groid′** *n.*

Ne•he•mi•ah (nē′hə-mī′ə, nē′ə-) ►*n.* **1.** A Hebrew leader of the 5th cent. B.C. **2.** See table at **Bible.**

Neh•ru (nā′ro͞o), **Jawaharlal.** 1889–1964. Indian prime minister (1947–64.)

neigh (nā) ►*n.* The long, high-pitched sound made by a horse. [< OE *hnǣgan*, to neigh.] —**neigh** *v.*

neigh•bor (nā′bər) ►*n.* **1.** One that lives or is located near another. **2.** A fellow human. ►*v.* **1.** To lie close to or border on. **2.** To live or be situated close by. [< OE *nēahgebūr* : *nēah*, near + *gebūr*, dweller.]

neigh•bor•hood (nā′bər-ho͝od′) ►*n.* **1.** A district or area with distinctive characteristics. **2.** The people who live in a particular district. **3.** The surrounding area; vicinity. **4.** *Informal* Approximate amount or range: *in the neighborhood of a million dollars.*

neigh•bor•ly (nā′bər-lē) ►*adj.* Having or exhibiting the qualities of a friendly neighbor. —**neigh′bor•li•ness** *n.*

Nei Mong•gol (nā′ mŏn′gōl′, mŏng′-) also **Inner Mongolia.** An autonomous region of NE China. Pop. 21,456,798.

nei•ther (nē′*th*ər, nī′-) ►*adj.* Not one or the other; not either: *Neither shoe feels comfortable.* ►*pron.* Not either one: *Neither of them fits.* ►*conj.* **1.** Not either. Used with *nor*: *I got neither the gift nor the card.* **2.** Also not: *If he won't go, neither will she.* [< OE *nāhwæther*.]

Usage: As a conjunction *neither* is properly followed by *nor*, not *or*, in formal style: *Neither prayers nor curses did any good.*

nel•son (nĕl′sən) ►*n.* A wrestling hold in which the user places an arm under the opponent's arm and presses the wrist or the palm of the hand against the opponent's neck. [Poss. < the name *Nelson*.]

Nelson, Horatio. Viscount Nelson. 1758–1805. British admiral.

nem•a•tode (nĕm′ə-tōd′) ►*n.* Any of several

often parasitic worms having unsegmented cylindrical bodies. [Gk. *nēma*, thread + –OID.]

Ne•me•a (nē′mē-ə) A valley of N Argolis in ancient Greece. —**Ne′me•an** *adj. & n.*

nem•e•sis (nĕm′ĭ-sĭs) ►*n.*, *pl.* **-ses** (-sēz′) **1.** A source of downfall or ruin. **2.** An implacable or unbeatable foe. **3.** One that inflicts just retribution; avenger. **4. Nemesis** *Gk. Myth.* The goddess of retributive justice or vengeance. [Gk., retribution.]

neo– ►*pref.* New; recent: *Neolithic.* [< Gk. *neos*, new.]

ne•o•clas•si•cism also **Ne•o•clas•si•cism** (nē′ō-klăs′ĭ-sĭz′əm) ►*n.* A revival of classical aesthetics and forms, esp. in art, architecture, or music. —**ne′o•clas′sic, ne′o•clas′si•cal** *adj.* —**ne′o•clas′si•cist** *n.*

ne•o•co•lo•ni•al•ism (nē′ō-kə-lō′nē-ə-lĭz′əm) ►*n.* A policy whereby a major power uses economic and political means to perpetuate or extend its influence over other nations. —**ne′o•co•lo′ni•al** *adj.* —**ne′o•co•lo′ni•al•ist** *n.*

ne•o•dym•i•um (nē′ō-dĭm′ē-əm) ►*n. Symbol* **Nd** A bright, silvery rare-earth element used esp. for coloring glass. At. no. 60. See table at **element.** [NEO– + *(di)dymium*, a mixture of rare-earth elements.]

Ne•o•lith•ic (nē′ə-lĭth′ĭk) ►*adj.* Of or being the Stone Age period beginning in the Middle East around 10,000 B.C., marked by the development of agriculture and the making of polished stone implements. ►*n.* The Neolithic Period.

ne•ol•o•gism (nē-ŏl′ə-jĭz′əm) ►*n.* A new word, expression, or usage.

ne•on (nē′ŏn′) ►*n. Symbol* **Ne** A rare, inert gaseous element that glows red in an electric discharge and is used in display and television tubes. At. no. 10. See table at **element.** [< Gk. *neos*, new.]

ne•o•nate (nē′ə-nāt′) ►*n.* A newborn infant. [NEO– + Lat. *nātus*, born.] —**ne′o•na′tal** *adj.*

Ne•o-Pa•gan (nē′ō-pā′gən) ►*adj.* Of or relating to a religious movement combining worship of pagan nature deities, particularly of the earth, with benign witchcraft. ►*n.* An adherent of such a religion. —**Ne•o-Pa•gan•ism** *n.*

ne•o•phyte (nē′ə-fīt′) ►*n.* **1.** A recent convert. **2.** A beginner or novice. [< Gk. *neophutos* : NEO– + *-phutos*, planted (< *phuein*, bring forth).]

ne•o•plasm (nē′ə-plăz′əm) ►*n.* An abnormal new growth of tissue; tumor. —**ne′o•plas′tic** *adj.*

ne•o•prene (nē′ə-prēn′) ►*n.* A tough synthetic rubber used esp. in weather-resistant products, adhesives, shoe soles, paints, and rocket fuels. [NEO– + *(chloro)prene.*]

Ne•pal (nə-pôl′, -päl′, nā-) A country of central Asia in the Himalayas between India and SW China. Cap. Kathmandu. Pop. 21,360,000. —**Nep′al•ese′** (nĕp′ə-lēz′, -lēs′), **Ne•pal′i** *adj. & n.*

ne•pen•the (nĭ-pĕn′thē) ►*n.* **1.** A legendary drug of ancient times, used as a remedy for grief. **2.** Something that eases sorrow or pain. [< Gk. *nēpenthes (pharmakon)*, grief-banishing (drug).]

neph•ew (nĕf′yo͞o) ►*n.* A son of one's brother or sister or of the brother or sister of one's spouse. [< Lat. *nepōs.*]

neph•rite (nĕf′rīt′) ►*n.* A white to dark green variety of jade. [Gk. *nephros*, kidney + –ITE[1].]

ne•phrit•ic (nə-frĭt′ĭk) ►*adj.* **1.** Of the kidneys. **2.** Of or affected with nephritis.

ne•phri•tis (nə-frī′tĭs) ►*n.* Inflammation of the kidneys.

nephro– or **nephr–** ►*pref.* Kidney: *nephritis.* [< Gk. *nephros.*]

nep•o•tism (nĕp′ə-tĭz′əm) ►*n.* Favoritism shown or patronage granted to relatives. [< Lat. *nepōs*, nephew.] —**nep′o•tist** *n.*

Nep•tune (nĕp′to͞on′, -tyo͞on′) ►*n.* **1.** *Rom. Myth.* The god of the sea. **2.** The 8th planet from the sun, at a mean distance of 4.5 billion km (2.8 billion mi) and with a mean radius of 24,000 km (15,000 mi). —**Nep•tu′ni•an** *adj.*

nep•tu•ni•um (nĕp-to͞o′nē-əm, -tyo͞o′-) ►*n. Symbol* **Np** A naturally radioactive metallic element found in trace quantities in uranium ores. At. no. 93. See table at **element.** [< NEPTUNE.]

nerd (nûrd) ►*n. Slang* An unpopular or socially inept person, esp. one regarded as excessively studious. [Perhaps after *Nerd*, a character in *If I Ran the Zoo* by Theodor Seuss Geisel.] —**nerd′y** *adj.*

Ne•ro (nîr′ō, nē′rō). A.D. 37–68. Emperor of Rome (54–68). —**Ne•ro′ni•an** *adj.*

Ne•ru•da (nĕ-ro͞o′də), **Pablo.** Ricardo Eliezer Neftali Reyes. 1904–73. Chilean poet; 1971 Nobel.

Pablo Neruda

nerve (nûrv) ►*n.* **1.** Any of the cordlike bundles of fibers made up of neurons through which sensory stimuli and motor impulses pass between the central nervous system and other parts of the body. **2.** The sensitive tissue in the pulp of a tooth. **3.** A sore point: *The criticism touched a nerve.* **4a.** Courage: *lost my nerve.* **b.** Fortitude; stamina. **c.** Brazen boldness; cheek. **5. nerves** Nervous agitation caused by fear, anxiety, or stress. ►*v.* **nerved, nerv•ing.** To give strength or courage to. [< Lat. *nervus.*]

nerve cell ►*n.* See **neuron.**

nerve center ►*n.* A source of power or control.

nerve gas ►*n.* A poisonous gas used in war that attacks the nervous system.

nerve•less (nûrv′lĭs) ►*adj.* **1.** Lacking strength or energy. **2.** Lacking courage. **3.** Calm and controlled. —**nerve′less•ly** *adv.* —**nerve′less•ness** *n.*

nerve-rack•ing or **nerve-wrack•ing** (nûrv′răk′ĭng) ►*adj.* Intensely distressing.

nerv•ous (nûr′vəs) ►*adj.* **1.** Of or affecting the

nerves or nervous system. **2.** High-strung; jumpy. **3.** Uneasy; apprehensive. **4.** Restless; lively: *nervous energy.* —**nerv′ous•ly** *adv.* —**nerv′ous•ness** *n.*

nervous breakdown ►*n.* An episode of severe or incapacitating emotional disorder.

nervous system ►*n.* The system of cells, tissues, and organs that regulates the body's responses to internal and external stimuli.

nerv•y (nûr′vē) ►*adj.* **-i•er, -i•est 1.** Arrogantly impudent; brazen. **2.** Bold; daring. **3.** *Chiefly Brit.* Jumpy; nervous.

Ness (nĕs), **Loch.** A lake of N-central Scotland.

-ness ►*suff.* State; quality; condition; degree: *brightness.* [< OE *-nes.*]

nest (nĕst) ►*n.* **1a.** A shelter made by a bird to hold its eggs and young. **b.** A similar structure built by fish, insects, or other animals. **2.** A snug, cozy place. **3.** A hotbed: *a nest of criminal activity.* **4.** A set of objects that can be stacked together: *a nest of tables.* ►*v.* **1.** To build or occupy a nest. **2.** To fit or stack snugly together. [< OE.]

nest egg ►*n.* A reserve sum of money.

nes•tle (nĕs′əl) ►*v.* **-tled, -tling 1.** To settle snugly and comfortably. **2.** To lie in a sheltered location. **3.** To snuggle. [< OE *nestlian*, make a nest.] —**nes′tler** *n.*

nest•ling (nĕst′lĭng, nĕs′-) ►*n.* A bird too young to leave its nest.

net[1] (nĕt) ►*n.* **1.** An openwork meshed fabric. **2.** Something made of net, as a device used to capture animals or act as a barrier: *a fishing net; a mosquito net.* **3.** A barrier strung between two posts to divide a court in half, as in tennis. **4.** Something that entraps. ►*v.* **net•ted, net•ting.** To catch or ensnare in or as if in a net. [< OE.] —**net′ting** *n.*

net[2] (nĕt) ►*adj.* **1.** Remaining after all deductions or adjustments have been made: *net profit.* **2.** Ultimate; final: *the net result.* ►*n.* A net amount. ►*v.* **net•ted, net•ting.** To bring in as profit. [ME < OFr. NEAT.]

Net ►*n.* The Internet.

neth•er (nĕ*th*′ər) ►*adj.* Located beneath or below. [< OE *neother*, down.]

Neth•er•lands (nĕ*th*′ər-ləndz). Often called **Holland.** A country of NW Europe on the North Sea. Caps. Amsterdam and The Hague. Pop. 15,380,000. —**Neth′er•land′ish** *adj.*

Netherlands Antilles. An autonomous territory of the Netherlands consisting of several islands in the Caribbean Sea. Cap. Willemstad. Pop. 192,056.

net•i•quette (nĕt′ĭ-kĕt′, -kĭt) ►*n.* Etiquette advocated in communication over a computer network. [Blend of (INTER)NET and ETIQUETTE.]

net•tle (nĕt′l) ►*n.* A plant with toothed leaves and stinging hairs. ►*v.* **-tled, -tling.** To irritate; vex. [< OE *netele.*] —**net′tle•some** *adj.*

net•work (nĕt′wûrk′) ►*n.* **1.** An openwork fabric or structure in which cords, threads, or wires cross at regular intervals. **2.** A complex, interconnected group or system: *a spy network.* **3.** A chain of radio or television broadcasting stations with shared or coordinated programming. **4.** A system of computers interconnected so as to share information. ►*v.* **1.** To interact with others for mutual assistance or support. **2.** *Comp. Sci.* To connect (computers) into a network.

Ne•tza•hual•có•yotl (nĕ-tsä′wäl-kō′yōt′l) A city of S-central Mexico, a suburb of Mexico City. Pop. 1,341,230.

neu•ral (no͝or′əl, nyo͝or′-) ►*adj.* Of or relating to a nerve or the nervous system.

neu•ral•gia (no͞o-răl′jə, nyo͞o-) ►*n.* Intense pain extending along a nerve. [< NEUR(O)– + Gk. *algos*, pain.] —**neu•ral′gic** *adj.*

neu•ras•the•ni•a (no͝or′əs-thē′nē-ə, nyo͝or′-) ►*n.* A neurotic disorder marked by chronic fatigue and weakness, loss of memory, and generalized aches and pains. [NEUR(O)– + Gk. *asthenia*, weakness.] —**neu′ras•then′ic** (-thĕn′ĭk) *adj.* & *n.*

neu•ri•tis (no͞o-rī′tĭs, nyo͞o-) ►*n.* Inflammation of a nerve. —**neu•rit′ic** (-rĭt′ĭk) *adj.*

neuro– or **neur–** ►*pref.* Nerve; nervous system: *neuritis.* [< Gk. *neuron*, sinew, string.]

neu•rol•o•gy (no͞o-rŏl′ə-jē, nyo͞o-) ►*n.* The medical science that deals with the nervous system and disorders affecting it. —**neu′ro•log′ic** (no͝or′ə-lŏj′ĭk, nyo͝or′-), **neu′ro•log′i•cal** (-ĭ-kəl) *adj.* —**neu′ro•log′i•cal•ly** *adv.* —**neu•rol′o•gist** *n.*

neu•ron (no͝or′ŏn′, nyo͝or′-) also **neu•rone** (-ōn′) ►*n.* Any of the cells that make up the nervous system, consisting of a nucleated cell body with dendrites and a single axon. [Gk., sinew, nerve.] —**neu•ron′ic** *adj.*

neu•ro•sis (no͞o-rō′sĭs, nyo͞o-) ►*n.*, *pl.* **-ses** (-sēz). Any of various mental or emotional disorders, such as hypochondria, not due to any organic cause.

neu•ro•sur•ger•y (no͝or′ō-sûr′jə-rē, nyo͝or′-) ►*n.* Surgery on a part of the nervous system. —**neu′ro•sur′geon** *n.* —**neu′ro•sur′gi•cal** *adj.*

neu•rot•ic (no͞o-rŏt′ĭk, nyo͞o-) ►*adj.* Of or affected with a neurosis. ►*n.* A neurotic person. —**neu•rot′i•cal•ly** *adv.*

neu•ro•trans•mit•ter (no͝or′ō-trăns′mĭt-ər, -trănz′-, nyo͝or′-) ►*n.* A chemical substance, such as dopamine, that transmits nerve impulses across a synapse.

neut. ►*abbr.* **1.** neuter **2.** neutral

neu•ter (no͞o′tər, nyo͞o′-) ►*adj.* **1.** *Gram.* Neither masculine nor feminine in gender. **2.** Having undeveloped sexual organs or parts. ►*n.* **1.** *Gram.* **a.** The neuter gender. **b.** A neuter word. **2.** A castrated or spayed animal. **3.** A sexually undeveloped insect, such as a worker bee. **4.** A plant without stamens or pistils. ►*v.* To castrate or spay. [< Lat., neither.]

neu•tral (no͞o′trəl, nyo͞o′-) ►*adj.* **1.** Not aligned with or supporting a side in a war, dispute, or contest. **2.** Belonging to neither kind or side. **3.** *Chem.* Neither acidic nor alkaline. **4.** *Phys.* Having a net electric charge of zero. **5.** Of or indicating a color that lacks hue; achromatic. ►*n.* **1.** A neutral nation or person. **2.** A neutral color. **3.** A position in which a set of gears is disengaged. [< Lat. *neutrālis*, grammatically neutral.] —**neu′tral•ly** *adv.*

neutral ground ►*n.* See **median strip.**

Regional Note: The strip of grass dividing the opposing lanes of an avenue or highway is known by a variety of terms in the United States. The most common term is *median strip* or *median.* Regional terms are *mall* (upstate New York), *medial strip* (Pennsylvania), *meridian* or *boulevard* (Upper Midwest), and *neutral ground* (Louisiana and S Mississippi).

neu•tral•ism (no͞o′trə-lĭz′əm, nyo͞o′-) ►*n.* Neutrality. —**neu′tral•ist** *adj. & n.*

neu•tral•i•ty (no͞o-trăl′ĭ-tē, nyo͞o-) ►*n.* The state or policy of being neutral, esp. in war.

neu•tral•ize (no͞o′trə-līz′, nyo͞o′-) ►*v.* **-ized, -iz•ing 1.** To make neutral. **2.** To render ineffective. —**neu′tral•i•za′tion** *n.* —**neu′tral•iz′er** *n.*

neutral spirits ►*pl.n. (takes sing. or pl. v.)* Ethyl alcohol distilled at or above 190 proof and used in blended alcoholic beverages.

neu•tri•no (no͞o-trē′nō, nyo͞o-) ►*n., pl.* **-nos.** Any of three electrically neutral elementary particles in the lepton family. [Ital.]

neu•tron (no͞o′trŏn′, nyo͞o′-) ►*n.* An electrically neutral subatomic particle, stable when bound in an atomic nucleus and having a mean lifetime of about 12 minutes as a free particle. [NEUTR(AL) + -ON[1].]

neutron bomb ►*n.* A nuclear bomb that would produce many neutrons but little blast and thus destroy life but spare property.

Nev. ►*abbr.* Nevada

Ne•va (nē′və) A river of NW Russia flowing about 74 km (46 mi) from Lake Ladoga to the Gulf of Finland.

Ne•vad•a (nə-văd′ə, -vä′də) A state of the W US. Cap. Carson City. Pop. 1,206,152. —**Ne•vad′an, Ne•vad′i•an** *adj. & n.*

Nev•el•son (nĕv′əl-sən), **Louise.** 1899–1988. Russian-born Amer. sculptor.

nev•er (nĕv′ər) ►*adv.* **1.** Not ever; at no time. **2.** Not at all; in no way. [< OE *nǣfre.*]

nev•er•more (nĕv′ər-môr′, -mōr′) ►*adv.* Never again.

nev•er•the•less (nĕv′ər-*th*ə-lĕs′) ►*adv.* In spite of that; however.

ne•vus (nē′vəs) ►*n., pl.* **-vi** (-vī′). A congenital growth or mark on the skin, such as a mole. [Lat. *naevus.*]

new (no͞o, nyo͞o) ►*adj.* **-er, -est 1.** Not old; recent. **2.** Never used or worn before: *a new car.* **3.** Just found or learned: *new information.* **4.** Unfamiliar. **5.** Different from the former or the old. **6.** Recently arrived or established: *a new president.* **7.** Rejuvenated. **8.** Currently fashionable. **9. New** In the most recent form, period, or development. ►*adv.* Freshly; recently. [< OE *nīwe.*] —**new′ness** *n.*

New Age ►*adj.* **1.** Relating to a complex of spiritual and consciousness-raising movements originating in the 1980s. **2.** Of or being a style of modern music marked esp. by quiet harmonies and drones.

New Amsterdam. A settlement estab. by the Dutch on S Manhattan I. in 1624 and renamed New York after its capture by the English in 1664.

New•ark (no͞o′ərk, nyo͞o′-) A city of NE NJ on **Newark Bay,** an inlet of the Atlantic. Pop. 275,221.

new•bie (no͞o′bē, nyo͞o′-) ►*n.* One that is new to something, esp. a novice at using computer technology or the Internet. [< NEW.]

new•born (no͞o′bôrn′, nyo͞o′-) ►*adj.* **1.** Very recently born. **2.** Born anew. ►*n.* A neonate.

New Brunswick. A province of E Canada on the Gulf of St. Lawrence. Cap. Fredericton. Pop. 696,405.

New•cas•tle or **New•cas•tle upon Tyne** (no͞o′kăs′əl, nyo͞o′-). A borough of NE England on the Tyne R. N of Leeds. Pop. 285,310.

new•com•er (no͞o′kŭm′ər, nyo͞o′-) ►*n.* One who has only recently arrived.

New Deal ►*n.* The programs and policies to promote economic recovery and social reform introduced in the 1930s by President Franklin Roosevelt. —**New Dealer** *n.*

New Delhi. The capital of India, in the N-central part S of Delhi. Pop. 301,297.

new•el (no͞o′əl, nyo͞o′-) ►*n.* **1.** A vertical support at the center of a circular staircase. **2.** A post for a handrail at the bottom or landing of a staircase. [< Lat. *nōdulus*, little knot, nodule.]

newel

New England. A region of the NE US comprising ME, NH, VT, MA, CT, and RI. —**New Eng′land•er** *n.*

Newf. ►*abbr.* Newfoundland

new•fan•gled (no͞o′făng′gəld, nyo͞o′-) ►*adj.* New and often needlessly novel. [< ME *neufangel*, fond of novelty.]

new•found (no͞o′found′, nyo͞o′-) ►*adj.* Recently discovered.

New•found•land (no͞o′fən-lənd, -lănd′, -fənd-, nyo͞o′-) A province of E Canada including the island of **Newfoundland** and nearby islands and Labrador. Cap. St. John's. Pop. 567,681. —**New′found•land•er** *n.*

New France. The possessions of France in North America from the 16th cent. until the Treaty of Paris (1763), including much of SE Canada, the Great Lakes region, and the Mississippi Valley.

New Guinea. An island in the SW Pacific N of Australia; divided politically between Indonesia and Papua New Guinea. —**New Guinean** *adj. & n.*

New Hamp•shire (hămp′shər, -shîr′, hăm′-) A state of the NE US between VT and ME. Cap. Concord. Pop. 1,113,915. —**New Hamp′shir•ite′** *n.*

New Haven. A city of S CT NE of Bridgeport. Pop. 130,474.

New Hebrides. See **Vanuatu.**

New Jersey. A state of the E-central US on the Atlantic. Cap. Trenton. Pop. 7,748,634. —**New Jer′sey•ite′** *n.*

New Latin ►*n.* Latin as used since about 1500.

new•ly (no͞o′lē, nyo͞o′-) ►*adv.* **1.** Not long ago; recently. **2.** Once more; anew. **3.** In a new or different way; freshly.

new•ly•wed (no͞o′lē-wĕd′, nyo͞o′-) ►*n.* A person recently married.

New•man (no͞o′mən, nyo͞o′-), **John Henry.** 1801–90. British prelate and theologian.

new math ►*n.* Mathematics taught in elementary and secondary schools that is based on set theory.

New Mexico. A state of the SW US on the

Mexican border. Cap. Santa Fe. Pop. 1,521,729. —**New Mexican** *adj. & n.*

new moon ▸*n.* The phase of the moon occurring when it passes between the earth and the sun and is invisible or visible only as a thin crescent at sunset.

New Neth•er•land (nĕ*th*′ər-lənd) A Dutch colony in North America along the Hudson and lower Delaware rivers; renamed New York in 1664.

New Or•leans (no͞o ôr′lē-ənz, ôr′lənz, ôr-lēnz′, ô′lənz, nyo͞o, nô′lənz) A city of SE LA on the Mississippi R. Pop. 496,938.

New•port News (no͞o′pôrt′, -pōrt′, nyo͞o′-) An independent city of SE VA NNW of Norfolk. Pop. 170,045.

New Providence. An island of the Bahamas in the West Indies.

news (no͞oz, nyo͞oz) ▸*pl.n. (takes sing. v.)* **1a.** Information about recent events. **b.** A presentation of such information, as in a newspaper. **2.** New information of any kind.

Syns: *news, intelligence, tidings, word* **n.**

news•cast (no͞oz′kăst′, nyo͞oz′-) ▸*n.* A radio or television broadcast of the news. [NEWS + (BROAD)CAST.] —**news′cast′er** *n.*

news•group (no͞oz′gro͞op′, nyo͞oz′-) ▸*n.* An area on a computer network, esp. the Internet, devoted to discussion of a specified topic.

news•let•ter (no͞oz′lĕt′ər, nyo͞oz′-) ▸*n.* A printed report giving news or information of interest to a special group.

New Spain. The former Spanish possessions in the New World, including South America (except Brazil), Central America, Mexico, the West Indies, Florida, and much of the land W of the Mississippi R.

news•pa•per (no͞oz′pā′pər, nyo͞oz′-) ▸*n.* **1.** A publication, usu. issued daily or weekly, containing current news, editorials, feature articles, and advertising. **2.** See **newsprint.** —**news′pa′per•man** *n.* —**news′pa′per•wom′an** *n.*

news•print (no͞oz′prĭnt′, nyo͞oz′-) ▸*n.* Inexpensive paper used esp. for newspapers.

news•reel (no͞oz′rēl′, nyo͞oz′-) ▸*n.* A short film dealing with recent events.

news•stand (no͞oz′stănd′, nyo͞oz′-) ▸*n.* A stand at which newspapers and periodicals are sold.

news•wor•thy (no͞oz′wûr′*th*ē, nyo͞oz′-) ▸*adj.* Interesting or important enough to warrant news coverage. —**news′wor′thi•ness** *n.*

news•y (no͞o′zē, nyo͞o′-) ▸*adj.* **-i•er, -i•est** *Informal* Full of news; informative.

newt (no͞ot, nyo͞ot) ▸*n.* Any of several small semiaquatic salamanders. [< ME *an eute*, an eft < *evete*, EFT.]

New Testament ▸*n.* The Gospels, Acts, Epistles, and the Book of Revelation. See table at **Bible.**

new•ton (no͞ot′n, nyo͞ot′n) ▸*n.* A unit of force equal to the force needed to accelerate a mass of 1 kilogram 1 meter per second per second. [After Sir Isaac NEWTON.]

Newton, Sir **Isaac.** 1642–1727. English mathematician and scientist. —**New•to′ni•an** *adj.*

New World. The Western Hemisphere.

New Year's Day ▸*n.* Jan. 1, the first day of the year in the Gregorian calendar, celebrated as a holiday in many countries.

New Year's Eve ▸*n.* The eve of New Year's Day, celebrated with merrymaking.

New York 1. A state of the NE US. Cap. Albany. Pop. 18,044,505. **2.** or **New York City** A city of S NY at the mouth of the Hudson R. Pop. 7,322,564. —**New York′er** *n.*

New Zea•land (zē′lənd) An island country in the S Pacific SE of Australia. Cap. Wellington. Pop. 3,493,000. —**New Zea′land•er** *n.*

next (nĕkst) ▸*adj.* **1.** Nearest in space or position; adjacent. **2.** Immediately following, as in time or sequence. ▸*adv.* **1.** In the time, order, or place nearest or immediately following. **2.** On the first subsequent occasion: *when next I write.* ▸*n.* The next person or thing. —***idiom:*** **next to 1.** Adjacent to. **2.** Almost; practically. [< OE *nīehsta*, superl. of *nēah*, near.]

nex•us (nĕk′səs) ▸*n., pl.* **-us** or **-us•es 1.** A means of connection; link or tie. **2.** A connected series or group. **3.** The core or center. [Lat. < *nectere*, bind.]

Nez Perce (nĕz′ pûrs′, nĕs′) ▸*n., pl.* **Nez Perce** or **-ces** (pûr′sĭz) **1.** A member of a Native American people inhabiting W Idaho and NE Washington. **2.** The language of the Nez Perce.

NF ▸*abbr.* **1.** Newfoundland **2.** or **n/f** no funds

NFL ▸*abbr.* National Football League

Nfld. ▸*abbr.* Newfoundland

NGO ▸*abbr.* nongovernmental organization

ngul•trum (əng-gŭl′trəm) ▸*n.* See table at **currency.** [Bhutanese.]

NH or **N.H.** ▸*abbr.* New Hampshire

NHL ▸*abbr.* National Hockey League

Ni ▸ The symbol for the element **nickel** 1.

ni•a•cin (nī′ə-sĭn) ▸*n.* A white crystalline acid that is a component of the vitamin B complex. [< NICOTINIC ACID.]

Ni•ag•a•ra Falls (nī-ăg′rə, -ər-ə) Falls in the Niagara R. between W NY and Ontario, Canada.

Niagara River. A river flowing about 55 km (34 mi) from Lake Erie to Lake Ontario.

Nia•mey (nē-ä′mā, nyä-mā′) The capital of Niger, in the SW part on the Niger R. Pop. 399,100.

nib (nĭb) ▸*n.* The point of a pen. [Alteration of NEB.]

nib•ble (nĭb′əl) ▸*v.* **-bled, -bling 1.** To bite at gently and repeatedly. **2.** To take small or hesitant bites. ▸*n.* A morsel. [ME *nebyllen.*]

Ni•cae•a (nī-sē′ə) An ancient city of NW Asia Minor. —**Ni•cae′an** *adj.*

Nic•a•ra•gua (nĭk′ə-rä′gwə) A country of Central America on the Caribbean Sea and the Pacific. Cap. Managua. Pop. 4,401,000. —**Ni′ca•ra′guan** *adj. & n.*

Nicaragua, Lake. The largest lake of Central America, in SW Nicaragua.

nice (nīs) ▸*adj.* **nic•er, nic•est 1.** Pleasing; agreeable. **2.** Pleasant; attractive. **3.** Courteous; polite. **4.** Of good character; respectable. **5.** Fastidious; fussy. **6.** Showing or requiring sensitive discernment; subtle. **7.** Done with skill. [< Lat. *nescius*, ignorant.] —**nice′ly** *adv.* —**nice′ness** *n.*

Nice (nēs) A city of SE France on the Mediterranean Sea NE of Cannes. Pop. 342,903.

ni•ce•ty (nī′sĭ-tē) ▸*n., pl.* **-ties 1.** Precision or accuracy. **2.** Delicacy of character; scrupulousness. **3.** A fine point or subtle distinction. **4.** An elegant or refined feature.

niche (nĭch, nēsh) ▸*n.* **1.** A recess in a wall, as

for holding a statue. **2.** A situation or activity specially suited to one's interests or abilities. [< Lat. *nīdus*, nest.]

Nich•o•las (nĭk′ə-ləs), Saint. 4th cent. A.D. Bishop of Myra in Asia Minor; often associated with Santa Claus.

Nicholas II. 1868–1918. The last czar of Russia (1894–1917); executed.

Nicholas II
photographed c. 1905 with his family

nick (nĭk) ►*n.* A shallow notch, cut, or chip on an edge or surface. ►*v.* **1.** To cut a nick or notch in. **2.** To cut short; check. —***idiom:* in the nick of time** Just at the critical moment. [ME *nik.*]

nick•el (nĭk′əl) ►*n.* **1.** *Symbol* **Ni** A silvery, hard, ductile, ferromagnetic metallic element used in alloys, in corrosion-resistant surfaces and batteries, and for electroplating. At. no. 28. See table at **element. 2.** A US coin worth five cents. [< Ger. *Kupfernickel*, a nickel ore.]

nick•el•o•de•on (nĭk′ə-lō′dē-ən) ►*n.* **1.** An early movie theater charging an admission of five cents. **2.** A player piano. **3.** A jukebox. [NICKEL + *(Mel)odeon*, music hall.]

nick•er (nĭk′ər) ►*v.* To neigh softly. [Perh. < *neigher* < *neigh.*]

Nick•laus (nĭk′ləs), **Jack William.** b. 1940. Amer. golfer.

nick•name (nĭk′nām′) ►*n.* **1.** A descriptive name added to or replacing the actual name of a person, place, or thing. **2.** A familiar or shortened form of a proper name. ►*v.* To give a nickname to. [< ME *an ekename*, an additional name : OE *ēaca*, addition + NAME.]

Nic•o•bar Islands (nĭk′ə-bär′) An island group in the Bay of Bengal NW of Sumatra.

Nic•o•si•a (nĭk′ə-sē′ə) The capital of Cyprus, in the N-central part. Pop. 186,400.

nic•o•tine (nĭk′ə-tēn′) ►*n.* A colorless, poisonous alkaloid, $C_{10}H_{14}N_2$, derived from the tobacco plant and used as an insecticide. [Fr., after Jean *Nicot* (1530?–1600).]

nic•o•tin•ic acid (nĭk′ə-tĭn′ĭk, -tē′nĭk) ►*n.* See **niacin.**

nic•ti•tate (nĭk′tĭ-tāt′) ►*v.* **-tat•ed, -tat•ing.** To wink. [Med.Lat. *nictitāre.*] —**nic′ti•ta′tion** *n.*

Nie•buhr (nē′bo͝or′, -bər), **Reinhold.** 1892–1971. Amer. theologian.

niece (nēs) ►*n.* The daughter of one's brother or sister or of the brother or sister of one's spouse. [< Lat. *neptis.*]

Nie•tzsche (nē′chə, -chē), **Friedrich Wilhelm.** 1844–1900. German philosopher. —**Nie′tzsche•an** *adj. & n.*

nif•ty (nĭf′tē) ►*adj.* **-ti•er, -ti•est** *Slang* First-rate; great. [?]

Ni•ger (nī′jər, nē-zhâr′) A country of W-central Africa. Cap. Niamey. Pop. 8,846,000.

Ni•ger-Con•go (nī′jər-kŏng′gō) ►*n.* A large language family of sub-Saharan Africa.

Ni•ge•ri•a (nī-jîr′ē-ə) A country of W Africa on the Gulf of Guinea. Cap. Abuja. Pop. 108,467,000. —**Ni•ge′ri•an** *adj. & n.*

Niger River. A river of W Africa rising in Guinea and flowing about 4,183 km (2,600 mi) through Mali, Niger, and Nigeria to the Gulf of Guinea.

nig•gard (nĭg′ərd) ►*n.* A stingy person; miser. ►*adj.* Stingy; miserly. [ME *nigard*, of Scand. orig.]

nig•gard•ly (nĭg′ərd-lē) ►*adj.* **1.** Grudging and petty; stingy. **2.** Scanty; meager. —**nig′gard•li•ness** *n.* —**nig′gard•ly** *adv.*

nig•gling (nĭg′lĭng) ►*adj.* **1.** Petty; trifling: *niggling details.* **2.** Overly concerned with details; fussy. [?] —**nig′gling•ly** *adv.*

nigh (nī) ►*adv.* **-er, -est 1.** Near in time, place, or relationship. **2.** Nearly; almost: *talked for nigh onto two hours.* ►*adj.* **-er, -est.** Close; near. ►*prep.* Near. [< OE *nēah.*]

night (nīt) ►*n.* **1.** The period between sunset and sunrise, esp. the hours of darkness. **2.** Nightfall. **3.** Darkness. **4.** A time or condition of gloom, obscurity, ignorance, or despair. [< OE *niht.*]

night blindness ►*n.* Abnormally weak vision at night or in dim light. —**night′blind′** *adj.*

night•cap (nīt′kăp′) ►*n.* **1.** A usu. alcoholic drink taken just before bedtime. **2.** A cloth cap worn esp. in bed.

night•clothes (nīt′klōz′, -klō*thz*′) ►*pl.n.* Clothes, such as pajamas, worn in bed.

night•club (nīt′klŭb′) ►*n.* An establishment that stays open late at night and provides food, drink, and entertainment.

night crawler ►*n.* An earthworm that crawls out from the ground at night.

night•dress (nīt′drĕs′) ►*n.* See **nightgown.**

night•fall (nīt′fôl′) ►*n.* The approach of night.

night•gown (nīt′goun′) ►*n.* A loose garment worn in bed by women and girls.

night•hawk (nīt′hôk′) ►*n.* **1.** An insectivorous, chiefly nocturnal bird having mottled grayish-brown feathers. **2.** *Informal* A night owl.

night•ie or **night•y** (nī′tē) ►*n., pl.* **-ies** *Informal* A nightgown.

night•in•gale (nīt′n-gāl′, nī′tĭng-) ►*n.* A brownish European songbird noted for the melodious song of the male at night. [< OE *nihtegale* : *niht*, NIGHT + *galan*, sing.]

Nightingale, Florence. 1820–1910. British nursing pioneer.

night•life (nīt′līf′) ►*n.* Social activities or entertainment available in the evening.

night•ly (nīt′lē) ►*adj.* Of or occurring during the night or every night. —**night′ly** *adv.*

night•mare (nīt′mâr′) ►*n.* **1.** An extremely frightening dream. **2.** An event or experience that is intensely distressing. [ME, female incubus : NIGHT + *mare*, goblin.] —**night′mar′ish** *adj.*

night owl ►*n.* *Informal* A person who habitually stays up late at night.

night school ►*n.* A school that holds classes in the evening.

night•shade (nīt′shād′) ►*n.* Any of several related, sometimes poisonous plants, such as belladonna. [< OE *nihtscada.*]

night•shirt (nīt′shûrt′) ►*n.* A long loose shirt worn in bed.

night•stick (nīt′stĭk′) ►*n.* A club carried by a police officer.

night•time (nīt′tīm′) ►*n.* The time between sunset and sunrise.

ni•hil•ism (nī′ə-lĭz′əm, nē′-) ►*n.* **1.** A doctrine holding that all values are baseless and that nothing can be known or communicated. **2.** The belief that destruction of existing political or social institutions is necessary for future improvement. [< Lat. *nihil,* nothing.] —**ni′hil•ist** *n.* —**ni′hil•is′tic** *adj.*

Ni•jin•sky (nĭ-zhĭn′skē, -jĭn′-), **Vaslav.** 1890–1950. Russian-born dancer and choreographer.

–nik ►*suff.* One associated with or characterized by: *beatnik.* [Of Slav. orig.]

Ni•ke (nī′kē) ►*n. Gk. Myth.* The goddess of victory.

nil (nĭl) ►*n.* Nothing; zero. [Lat. *nihil, nīl.*] —**nil** *adj.*

Nile (nīl) The longest river in the world, flowing about 6,677 km (4,150 mi) through E Africa from its sources in Burundi to a delta on the Mediterranean Sea in NE Egypt.

Ni•lo-Sa•har•an (nī′lō-sə-hăr′ən, -hä′rən) ►*n.* A language family of sub-Saharan Africa.

Ni•lot•ic (nī-lŏt′ĭk) ►*n.* A subfamily within the Nilo-Saharan languages.

Nils•son (nĭl′sən), **Birgit.** b. 1918. Swedish operatic soprano.

nim•ble (nĭm′bəl) ►*adj.* **-bler, -blest 1.** Quick and light in movement or action; deft. **2.** Quick and clever in devising or understanding. [< OE *nǣmel* and *numol.*] —**nim′ble•ness** *n.* —**nim′bly** *adv.*

nim•bus (nĭm′bəs) ►*n., pl.* **-bi** (-bī′) or **-es 1.** A radiant light usu. in the form of a halo about or over the head in a representation, as of a deity or saint. **2.** A uniformly gray rain cloud. [Lat., cloud.]

NIMBY ►*abbr.* not in my backyard

Nim•itz (nĭm′ĭts), **Chester Williams.** 1885–1966. Amer. admiral.

nin•com•poop (nĭn′kəm-po͞op′, nĭng′-) ►*n.* A silly or foolish person. [?]

nine (nīn) ►*n.* **1.** The cardinal number equal to 8 + 1. **2.** The 9th in a set or sequence. [< OE *nigon.*] —**nine** *adj. & pron.*

nine•teen (nīn-tēn′) ►*n.* **1.** The cardinal number equal to 18 + 1. **2.** The 19th in a set or sequence. —**nine•teen′** *adj. & pron.*

nine•teenth (nīn-tēnth′) ►*n.* **1.** The ordinal number matching the number 19 in a series. **2.** One of 19 equal parts. —**nine•teenth′** *adv. & adj.*

nine•ti•eth (nīn′tē-ĭth) ►*n.* **1.** The ordinal number matching the number 90 in a series. **2.** One of 90 equal parts. —**nine′ti•eth** *adv. & adj.*

nine•ty (nīn′tē) ►*n., pl.* **-ties.** The cardinal number equal to 9 × 10. —**nine′ty** *adj. & pron.*

Nin•e•veh (nĭn′ə-və) An ancient city of Assyria on the Tigris R. opposite the site of present-day Mosul, Iraq.

nin•ja (nĭn′jə) ►*n., pl.* **-ja** or **-jas.** A 14th-cent. Japanese mercenary trained in the martial arts. [J.]

nin•ny (nĭn′ē) ►*n., pl.* **-nies.** A fool; simpleton. [Perh. < alteration of INNOCENT.]

ninth (nīnth) ►*n.* **1.** The ordinal number matching the number 9 in a series. **2.** One of nine equal parts. —**ninth** *adv. & adj.*

ni•o•bi•um (nī-ō′bē-əm) ►*n. Symbol* **Nb** A silvery, soft, ductile metallic element used in steel alloys, arc welding, and superconductivity research. At. no. 41. See table at **element.** [< *Niobe,* in Greek myth.]

nip[1] (nĭp) ►*v.* **nipped, nip•ping 1.** To seize and pinch or bite. **2.** To sever by pinching or snipping. **3.** To sting with the cold. **4.** To check the growth or development of. See Syns at **blast. 5.** *Slang* **a.** To snatch up hastily. **b.** To steal. ►*n.* **1.** A small pinch or bite. **2.** A small amount. **3.** Sharp stinging cold. [Perh. < MDu. *nipen.*]

nip[2] (nĭp) ►*n.* A small amount of liquor. ►*v.* **nipped, nip•ping.** To sip (liquor) in small amounts. [Prob. of Du. or LGer. orig.]

nip•per (nĭp′ər) ►*n.* **1.** often **nippers** A tool, such as pliers or pincers, used for grasping or nipping. **2.** A pincerlike claw, as of a crab. **3.** *Chiefly Brit.* A small boy.

nip•ple (nĭp′əl) ►*n.* **1.** The small projection of a mammary gland containing the outlets of the milk ducts. **2.** Something resembling a nipple, esp. the rubber cap on a baby's bottle. [< obsolete *neble,* dim. of NEB.]

nip•py (nĭp′ē) ►*adj.* **-pi•er, -pi•est 1.** Sharp or biting. **2.** Bitingly cold.

nir•va•na (nîr-vä′nə, nər-) ►*n.* **1.** often **Nirvana** *Buddhism* The ineffable ultimate in which one has attained disinterested wisdom and compassion. **2.** An ideal condition of harmony, stability, or joy. [Skt. *nirvāṇam.*]

Ni•san (nĭs′ən, nē-sän′) ►*n.* A month of the Jewish calendar. See table at **calendar.** [Heb. *nîsān.*]

Ni•sei (nē-sā′, nē′sā′) ►*n., pl.* **-sei** or **-seis.** A person born in America of parents who emigrated from Japan. [J.]

nit (nĭt) ►*n.* The egg or young of a parasitic insect, such as a louse. [< OE *hnitu.*] —**nit′ty** *adj.*

ni•ter (nī′tər) ►*n.* A white or gray mineral of potassium nitrate, used in making gunpowder. [< Gk. *nitron,* soda, of Semitic orig.]

nit•pick (nĭt′pĭk′) ►*v.* To be concerned with insignificant details. See Syns at **quibble.** —**nit′pick′er** *n.*

ni•trate (nī′trāt′, -trĭt) ►*n.* **1.** The univalent radical NO_3 or a compound containing it, as a salt of nitric acid. **2.** Fertilizer consisting of sodium nitrate or potassium nitrate. ►*v.* **-trat•ed, -trat•ing.** To treat with nitric acid or a nitrate, usu. to change (an organic compound) into a nitrate. —**ni•tra′tion** *n.*

ni•tre (nī′tər) ►*n. Chiefly Brit.* Var. of **niter.**

ni•tric acid (nī′trĭk) ►*n.* A transparent, corrosive liquid, HNO_3, used in the production of fertilizers, explosives, and rocket fuels.

ni•tride (nī′trīd′) ►*n.* A compound containing nitrogen with another more electropositive element.

ni•tri•fy (nī′trə-fī′) ►*v.* **-fied, -fy•ing 1.** To oxidize (an ammonia compound) into nitric or nitrous acids or salts, esp. by the action of nitrobacteria. **2.** To treat or combine with nitrogen or compounds containing nitrogen. —**ni′tri•fi•ca′tion** *n.*

ni•trite (nī′trīt′) ► *n.* The univalent radical NO_2 or a compound containing it.

nitro– or **nitr–** ► *pref.* **1.** Nitrate; niter: *nitric acid.* **2a.** Nitrogen: *nitrify.* **b.** Containing the univalent group NO_2: *nitrite.* [< Gk. *nitron,* NITER.]

ni•tro•bac•te•ri•um (nī′trō-băk-tîr′ē-əm) ► *n., pl.* **-te•ri•a** (-tîr′ē-ə). Any of various soil bacteria that oxidize ammonium compounds into nitrites or nitrites into nitrates.

ni•tro•cel•lu•lose (nī′trō-sĕl′yə-lōs′, -lōz′) ► *n.* A cottonlike substance derived from cellulose treated with sulfuric and nitric acids and used in explosives and plastics.

ni•tro•gen (nī′trə-jən) ► *n. Symbol* **N** A colorless, odorless, almost inert gaseous element that constitutes nearly four fifths of the air by volume. At. no. 7. See table at **element.** —**ni•tric** (nī′trĭk) *adj.* —**ni•trog′e•nous** (nī-trŏj′ə-nəs) *adj.* —**ni•trous** (nī′trəs) *adj.*

ni•tro•glyc•er•in also **ni•tro•glyc•er•ine** (nī′trō-glĭs′ər-ĭn, -trə-) ► *n.* A thick, pale yellow, explosive liquid, used in dynamite and as a vasodilator in medicine.

ni•trous oxide (nī′trəs) ► *n.* A colorless, sweet-tasting gas, N_2O, used as a mild anesthetic.

nit•ty-grit•ty (nĭt′ē-grĭt′ē) ► *n. Informal* The specific or practical details. [?]

nit•wit (nĭt′wĭt′) ► *n.* A stupid, silly person.

nix (nĭks) *Slang* ► *n.* Nothing. ► *adv.* No. ► *v.* To forbid; veto. [Ger. dial.]

Nix•on (nĭk′sən), **Richard Milhous.** 1913–94. The 37th US President (1969–74); resigned.

Richard M. Nixon

Nizh•niy Nov•go•rod (nĭzh′nē nŏv′gə-rŏd′, -rət) or **Gor•ky** (gôr′kē). A city of W Russia on the Volga R.. Pop. 1,425,316.

NJ or **N.J.** ► *abbr.* New Jersey

Nkru•mah (ən-kro͞o′mə, əng-), **Kwame.** 1909–72. Ghanaian politician.

NL ► *abbr.* **1.** National League **2.** New Latin

NLRB ► *abbr.* National Labor Relations Board

nm ► *abbr.* **1.** nanometer **2.** nautical mile

NM or **N.M.** ► *abbr.* New Mexico

NMR ► *abbr.* nuclear magnetic resonance

NNE ► *abbr.* north-northeast

NNW ► *abbr.* north-northwest

no[1] (nō) ► *adv.* **1.** Used to express refusal, denial, disbelief, or disagreement. **2.** Not at all. Used with the comparative: *no better.* **3.** Not: *whether or no.* ► *n., pl.* **noes** (nōz). A negative response or vote. [< OE *nā.*]

no[2] (nō) ► *adj.* **1.** Not any; not one. **2.** Not at all: *He is no child.* [< OE *nān,* none.]

No[1] also **Noh** (nō) ► *n.* The classical drama of Japan, with elaborate costumes and highly stylized music and dance. [J. *nō.*]

No[2] ► The symbol for the element **nobelium.**

no. or **No.** ► *abbr.* **1a.** north **b.** northern **2.** number

No•ah (nō′ə). In the Bible, the patriarch who was chosen by God to build an ark to save human and animal life from a flood.

No•bel (nō-bĕl′), **Alfred Bernhard.** 1833–96. Swedish chemist and philanthropist.

no•bel•i•um (nō-bĕl′ē-əm) ► *n. Symbol* **No** A radioactive element artificially produced in trace amounts. At. no. 102. See table at **element.** [After Alfred Bernhard NOBEL.]

Nobel Prize ► *n.* Any of the international prizes awarded annually by the Nobel Foundation for outstanding achievements in physics, chemistry, physiology or medicine, literature, economics, and for the promotion of world peace. —**No•bel′ist** *n.*

no•bil•i•ty (nō-bĭl′ĭ-tē) ► *n., pl.* **-ties 1.** A class of persons distinguished by high birth or rank. **2.** Noble rank or status. **3.** High moral character. [< Lat. *nōbilitās.*]

no•ble (nō′bəl) ► *adj.* **-bler, -blest 1.** Of or belonging to the nobility. **2a.** Having or showing high moral character. **b.** Lofty; exalted: *a noble ideal.* **3.** Majestic; grand. **4.** *Chem.* Inert. ► *n.* A member of the nobility. [< Lat. *nōbilis.*] —**no′ble•ness** *n.* —**no′bly** *adv.*

no•ble•man (nō′bəl-mən) ► *n.* A man of noble rank.

no•blesse o•blige (nō-blĕs′ ō-blēzh′) ► *n.* Benevolent, honorable behavior considered to be the duty of persons of high birth or rank. [Fr., nobility is an obligation.]

no•ble•wom•an (nō′bəl-wo͝om′ən) ► *n.* A woman of noble rank.

no•bod•y (nō′bŏd′ē, -bŭd′ē, -bə-dē) ► *pron.* No person; not anyone. ► *n., pl.* **-ies.** A person of no importance or influence.

no-brain•er (nō′brā′nər) ► *n. Informal* Something so simple as to require no thought.

noc•tur•nal (nŏk-tûr′nəl) ► *adj.* **1.** Of or occurring in the night. **2.** Most active at night: *nocturnal animals.* [< Lat. *nocturnus* < *nox,* night.] —**noc•tur′nal•ly** *adv.*

noc•turne (nŏk′tûrn′) ► *n.* **1.** A painting of a night scene. **2.** A musical composition of a pensive, dreamy mood, esp. one for the piano. [Fr. < OFr. NOCTURNAL.]

nod (nŏd) ► *v.* **nod•ded, nod•ding 1.** To lower and raise the head quickly, as in agreement or acknowledgment. **2.** To express with a nod: *nodded agreement.* **3.** To let the head fall forward when sleepy. **4.** To be momentarily inattentive. **5.** To sway or bend, as flowers in the wind. ► *n.* A nodding movement. [ME *nodden.*]

node (nōd) ► *n.* **1.** A protuberance or swelling. **2a.** *Bot.* The point on a stem where a leaf is attached. **b.** See **knot** 7. **3.** *Phys.* A point or region of virtually zero amplitude in a periodic system. [< Lat. *nōdus,* knot.] —**nod′al** *adj.*

nod•ule (nŏj′o͞ol) ► *n.* A small knotlike lump or growth. —**nod′u•lar** (nŏj′ə-lər) *adj.*

No•ël also **No•el** (nō-ĕl′) ► *n.* **1.** Christmas. **2. noël** also **noel** A Christmas carol. [< Lat. *nātālis (diēs),* (day) of birth.]

noes (nōz) ► *n.* Pl. of **no**[1].

no-fault (nō′fôlt′) ► *adj.* **1.** Of or indicating a system of motor vehicle insurance in which accident victims are compensated by their insurance companies without assignment of blame. **2.** Of or indicating a type of divorce in which blame is assigned to neither party.

no-fly zone (nō′flī′) ▸ *n.* Airspace in which certain, esp. military, aircraft are forbidden to fly.

nog•gin (nŏg′ĭn) ▸ *n.* **1.** A small mug or cup. **2.** A unit of liquid measure equal to ¼ pint. **3.** *Slang* The human head. [?]

Noh (nō) ▸ *n.* Var. of **No**[1].

noise (noiz) ▸ *n.* **1a.** Sound or a sound that is loud, unpleasant, or unexpected. **b.** Sound of any kind. **2.** A loud outcry or commotion. **3.** *Phys.* A usu. persistent disturbance that obscures or reduces the clarity of a signal. ▸ *v.* **noised, nois•ing.** To spread the rumor or report of. [< OFr., poss. < Lat. *nausea.*] —**noise′less** *adj.* —**noise′less•ly** *adv.* —**nois′i•ly** *adv.* —**nois′i•ness** *n.* —**nois′y** *adj.*

noise•mak•er (noiz′mā′kər) ▸ *n.* One that makes noise, esp. a device such as a horn used to make noise at a party.

noi•some (noi′səm) ▸ *adj.* **1.** Offensive; foul. **2.** Harmful or dangerous. [ME *noiesom.*] —**noi′some•ly** *adv.* —**noi′some•ness** *n.*

no•lo con•ten•de•re (nō′lō kən-tĕn′də-rē) ▸ *n.* A plea made by the defendant in a criminal action that is equivalent to an admission of guilt but permits denial of the alleged facts in other proceedings. [Lat. *nōlō contendere*, I do not wish to contest.]

no•mad (nō′măd′) ▸ *n.* **1.** A member of a group of people who have no fixed home and move or migrate from place to place. **2.** A wanderer. [< Gk. *nomas*, wandering in search of pasture.] —**no•mad′ic** *adj.*

no man's land ▸ *n.* **1.** Land under dispute by two opposing entrenched armies. **2.** An area of uncertainty or ambiguity. **3.** An unclaimed or unowned piece of land.

nom de guerre (nŏm′ də gâr′) ▸ *n., pl.* **noms de guerre** (nŏm′). A fictitious name; pseudonym. [Fr., war name.]

nom de plume (plo͞om′) ▸ *n., pl.* **noms de plume.** See **pen name.** [Fr.]

Nome (nōm) A city of W AK on Seward Peninsula. Pop. 3,500.

no•men•cla•ture (nō′mən-klā′chər, nō-mĕn′klə-) ▸ *n.* A system of names used in an art or science. [Lat. *nōmenclātūra.*]

nom•i•nal (nŏm′ə-nəl) ▸ *adj.* **1.** Of or like a name or names. **2.** Existing in name only. **3.** *Gram.* Of or relating to a noun. **4.** Trifling: *a nominal sum.* [< Lat. *nōmen*, name.] —**nom′i•nal•ly** *adv.*

nom•i•nate (nŏm′ə-nāt′) ▸ *v.* **-nat•ed, -nat•ing 1.** To propose as a candidate, esp. for election. **2.** To name or appoint, as to an office. See Syns at **appoint.** [Lat. *nōmināre*, to name.] —**nom′i•na′tion** *n.* —**nom′i•na′tor** *n.*

nom•i•na•tive (nŏm′ə-nə-tĭv) ▸ *adj.* Of or belonging to a grammatical case that usu. indicates the subject of a verb. ▸ *n.* The nominative case.

nom•i•nee (nŏm′ə-nē′) ▸ *n.* One who has been nominated. [NOMIN(ATE) + -EE[1].]

-nomy ▸ *suff.* A system of laws governing or a body of knowledge about a specified field: *astronomy.* [< Gk. *nomos*, law.]

non– ▸ *pref.* Not: *nonfat.* [< Lat. *nōn.*]

non•age (nŏn′ĭj, nō′nĭj) ▸ *n.* **1.** Legal minority. **2.** A period of immaturity. [< OFr. *nonaage* : NON– + *aage*, AGE.]

non•a•ge•nar•i•an (nŏn′ə-jə-nâr′ē-ən, nō′nə-) ▸ *n.* A person between 90 and 100 years of age. [< Lat. *nōnāgēnārius.*] —**non′a•ge•nar′i•an** *adj.*

non•a•gon (nŏn′ə-gŏn′, nō′nə-) ▸ *n.* A polygon with 9 sides.

non•a•ligned (nŏn′ə-līnd′) ▸ *adj.* Not allied with any other nation or bloc; neutral. —**non′a•lign′ment** *n.*

nonce (nŏns) ▸ *n.* The present or particular occasion: *for the nonce.* [< ME *for then anes*, for the one.]

non•cha•lant (nŏn′shə-länt′) ▸ *adj.* Seeming to be coolly unconcerned or indifferent. [< OFr. *nonchaloir*, be unconcerned.] —**non′cha•lance′** *n.* —**non′cha•lant′ly** *adv.*

non•com (nŏn′kŏm′) ▸ *n.* *Informal* A noncommissioned officer.

non•com•bat•ant (nŏn′kəm-băt′nt, -kŏm′bə-tnt) ▸ *n.* **1.** A member of the armed forces

non′ab•ra′sive *adj.*
non′ab•sorb′ent *adj. & n.*
non′ac•a•dem′ic *adj.*
non•ac′id *n.*
non′ad•dict′ing *adj.*
non′ad•her′ence *n.*
non′ad•he′sive *adj.*
non′ad•just′a•ble *adj.*
non′ag•gres′sion *n.*
non′ag•ri•cul′tur•al *adj.*
non′al•co•hol′ic *adj.*
non′an•a•lyt′ic *adj.*
non′a•pol′•o•get′ic *adj.*
non′ap•pear′ance *n.*
non′as•ser′tive *adj.*
non′be•liev′er *n.*
non•bind′ing *adj.*
non′ca•lor′ic *adj.*
non•car′bon•at′ed *adj.*
non′car•niv′o•rous *adj.*
non′cat•e•gor′i•cal *adj.*
non-Cath′o•lic *adj. & n.*
non′-Cau•ca′sian *adj. & n.*
non•caus′al *adj. & n.*
non•cit′i•zen *n.*
non•com′bat′ *adj.*
non′com•mer′cial *adj.*
non′com•mu′ni•ca•ble *adj.*
non′com•mu′ni•ca•tive *adj.*
non′com•pet′i•tive *adj.*
non′com•pli′ance *n.*
non′com•pli′ant *adj. & n.*
non′con•clu′sive *adj.*
non′con•cur′rent *adj.*
non′con•fi•den′tial *adj.*
non′con•sec′u•tive *adj.*
non′con•ta′gious *adj.*
non′con•tig′u•ous *adj.*
non′con•tin′u•ous *adj.*
non′co•op′er•a′tion *n.*
non′co•op′er•a•tive *adj.*
non′cor•ro′sive *adj. & n.*
non•crim′i•nal *adj. & n.*
non•cur′rent *adj.*
non•dair′y *adj.*
non′de•duct′i•ble *adj.*
non′de•struc′tive *adj.*
non′•di•gest′i•ble *adj.*
non′dis•crim′i•na•to′ry *adj.*
non•drink′er *n.*
non•du′ra•ble *adj.*
non•ed′i•ble *adj. & n.*
non′ed•u•ca′tion•al *adj.*
non′ef•fec′tive *adj.*
non′e•las′tic *adj.*
non′e•lect′ed *adj.*
non•el′i•gi•ble *adj.*
non′en•force′a•ble *adj.*
non′en•force′ment *n.*
non′es•sen′tial *adj.*
non′-Eu•clid′e•an *adj.*
non′ex•ist′ence *n.*
non′ex•ist′ent *adj.*
non′ex•pend′a•ble *adj.*
non′ex•per′i•men′tal *adj.*
non′ex•plo′sive *adj. & n.*
non′ex•tinct′ *adj.*
non•fac′tu•al *adj.*
non•fas′cist *adj. & n.*
non•fer′rous *adj.*
non•fic′tion *n.*

whose duties lie outside combat. **2.** A civilian in wartime.

non•com•mis•sioned officer (nŏn′kə-mĭsh′ənd) ▶*n.* An enlisted member of the armed forces, such as a corporal or sergeant, appointed to a rank over other enlisted personnel.

non•com•mit•tal (nŏn′kə-mĭt′l) ▶*adj.* Refusing commitment to a particular opinion or course of action.

non com•pos men•tis (nŏn kŏm′pəs mĕn′tĭs) ▶*adj. Law* Not of sound mind and hence not legally responsible. [Lat. *nōn compos mentis*, not in control of the mind.]

non•con•duc•tor (nŏn′kən-dŭk′tər) ▶*n.* A material that conducts little or no electricity, heat, or sound.

non•con•form•ist (nŏn′kən-fôr′mĭst) ▶*n.* One who does not conform to accepted beliefs, customs, or practices. —**non′con•form′i•ty** *n.*

non•de•script (nŏn′dĭ-skrĭpt′) ▶*adj.* Lacking distinctive qualities. [NON– + Lat. *dēscrīptus*, p.part. of *dēscrībere*, DESCRIBE.] —**non′de•script′** *n.*

none (nŭn) ▶*pron.* **1.** No one; nobody. **2.** Not any. **3.** No part: *none of your business.* ▶*adv.* Not at all; in no way. [< OE *nān.*]

Usage: Although *none* often occurs as a singular pronoun, as in *None of the pizza was left,* it can sometimes be used with either a singular or plural verb: *None of the conspirators has* (or *have*) *been brought to trial.* When modified by *almost, none* must have a plural verb: *Almost none of the officials agree with you. None* can only be plural in sentences such as *None but his most loyal supporters believe his story.*

non•en•ti•ty (nŏn-ĕn′tĭ-tē) ▶*n., pl.* **-ties 1.** A person of no importance or significance. **2.** Something that does not exist or that exists only in the imagination.

nones (nōnz) ▶*pl.n.* In the ancient Roman calendar, the 7th day of March, May, July, or October and the 5th day of the other months. [< Lat. *nōnus*, ninth.]

none•such (nŭn′sŭch′) ▶*n.* A person or thing without equal. —**none′such′** *adj.*

none•the•less (nŭn′*thə*-lĕs′) ▶*adv.* Nevertheless; however.

non•e•vent (nŏn′ĭ-vĕnt′) ▶*n. Informal* An anticipated event that does not occur or proves anticlimactic.

non•fat (nŏn′făt′) ▶*adj.* Lacking fat solids or having the fat content removed.

non•fea•sance (nŏn-fē′zəns) ▶*n. Law* Failure to perform an official duty or legal requirement. [< *misfeasance*, legal term.]

no•nil•lion (nō-nĭl′yən) ▶*n.* **1.** The cardinal number equal to 10^{30}. **2.** *Chiefly Brit.* The cardinal number equal to 10^{54}. [Fr. < Lat. *nōnus*, ninth.] —**no•nil′lion** *adj.* —**no•nil′lionth** *n. & adj.*

non•in•ter•ven•tion (nŏn′ĭn-tər-vĕn′shən) ▶*n.* Failure or refusal to intervene, esp. in the affairs of another nation. —**non′in•ter•ven′tion•ist** *n.*

non•met•al (nŏn-mĕt′l) ▶*n.* Any of a number of elements, such as oxygen or sulfur, that lack the properties of metals. —**non′me•tal′lic** (-mə-tăl′ĭk) *adj.*

no-no (nō′nō′) ▶*n., pl.* **-noes** *Informal* Something unacceptable or impermissible.

non•pa•reil (nŏn′pə-rĕl′) ▶*adj.* Having no equal; peerless. ▶*n.* **1.** One that has no equal. **2.** A small flat chocolate drop covered with white pellets of sugar. [< OFr.]

non•per•son (nŏn-pûr′sən) ▶*n.* A person whose obliteration from the memory of the public is sought, esp. for political reasons.

non•plus (nŏn-plŭs′) ▶*v.* **-plused, -plus•ing** also **-plussed, -plus•sing.** To put at a loss; bewilder. [< Lat. *nōn plūs*, no more.]

non•pro•lif•er•a•tion (nŏn′prə-lĭf′ə-rā′shən) ▶*adj.* Of or calling for an end to the proliferation of nuclear weapons.

non•rep•re•sen•ta•tion•al (nŏn-rĕp′rĭ-zĕn-tā′shə-nəl) ▶*adj.* Not representing natural objects realistically.

non•re•stric•tive (nŏn′rĭ-strĭk′tĭv) ▶*adj. Gram.* Of or being a subordinate clause or phrase that describes but does not identify or restrict the meaning of the modified term. See Usage Note at **that.**

non•flam′ma•ble *adj.*
non•flex′i•ble *adj.*
non•fluc′tu•at′ing *adj.*
non′food′ *adj.*
non•haz′ard•ous *adj.*
non′he•red′i•tar′y *adj.*
non•hu′man *adj. & n.*
non′i•den′ti•cal *adj.*
non′in•crim′i•nat′ing *adj.*
non′in•duc′tive *adj.*
non′in•dus′tri•al *adj.*
non′in•fect′ed *adj.*
non′in•form′a•tive *adj.*
non′in•hab′it•a•ble *adj.*
non′in•stinc′tive *adj.*
non′judg•men′tal *adj.*
non•lin′e•ar *adj.*
non′mag•net′ic *adj.*
non′ma•li′•cious *adj.*
non•mar′ket•a•ble *adj.*
non•meas′ur•a•ble *adj.*
non•med′i•cal *adj.*
non•mem′ber *n.*
non•mil′i•tar′y *adj.*
non′ne•go′tia•ble *adj.*
non•nu′cle•ar *adj.*
non′ob•ser′vant *adj.*
non′•par′ti•san *adj.*
non′pa•ter′nal *adj.*
non•per′ma•nent *adj.*
non•per′me•a•ble *adj.*
non′per•sis′tent *adj.*
non•poi′son•ous *adj.*
non′pre•scrip′tion *adj.*
non′pro•duc′tive *adj.*
non′pro•fes′sion•al *n. & adj.*
non•prof′it *adj.*
non′pro•tec′tive *adj.*
non′ra•di•o•ac′tive *adj.*
non•read′er *n.*
non′re•cov′er•a•ble *adj.*
non′re•lig′ious *adj.*
non′re•sem′blance *n.*
non•res′i•dent *n.*
non′re•sis′tance *n.*
non′re•sis′tant *adj.*
non′re•solv′a•ble *adj.*
non′re•turn′a•ble *adj. & n.*
non•rig′id *adj.*
non•ru′ral *adj.*
non′sec•tar′i•an *adj.*
non•seg′re•gat′ed *adj.*
non•sex′ist *adj.*
non′sig•nif′i•cance *n.*
non′sig•nif′i•cant *adj.*
non′skid′ *adj.*
non′smok′er *n.*
non′smok′ing *adj.*
non•spher′i•cal *adj.*
non′ste•roi′dal *adj. & n.*
non′stick′ *adj.*
non′sub•mis′sive *adj.*
non•talk′a•tive *adj.*
non•ten′ured *adj.*
non•think′ing *adj.*
non•triv′i•al *adj.*
non•u′ni•fied′ *adj.*
non•ur′ban *adj.*
non•us′er *n.*
non•vot′er *n.*
non•ze′ro *adj.*

non•self (nŏn-sĕlf′) ▸*n.* That which the immune system identifies as foreign to the body.
non•sense (nŏn′sĕns′, -səns) ▸*n.* **1.** Foolish or absurd language or behavior. **2.** Matter of little or no importance or use. —**non•sen′si•cal** *adj.* —**non•sen′si•cal•ly** *adv.*
non se•qui•tur (nŏn sĕk′wĭ-tər, -to͝or′) ▸*n.* A statement that does not follow logically from what preceded it. [Lat. *nōn sequitur*, it does not follow.]
non•stan•dard also **non-stan•dard** (nŏn-stăn′dərd) ▸*adj.* **1.** Varying from or not adhering to the standard. **2.** *Ling.* Associated with a language variety used by uneducated speakers or socially disfavored groups.
non•stop (nŏn′stŏp′) ▸*adj.* Made or done without a stop. —**non′stop′** *adv.*
non•suit (nŏn-so͞ot′) ▸*n.* A judgment against a plaintiff for failure to prosecute the case or to introduce sufficient evidence.
non•sup•port (nŏn′sə-pôrt′, -pōrt′) ▸*n.* Failure to provide for the maintenance of one's dependents.
non trop•po (nŏn trô′pō, nōn) ▸*adv. & adj.* *Mus.* In moderation. [Ital., not too much.]
non•un•ion (nŏn-yo͞on′yən) ▸*adj.* **1.** Not belonging to a labor union. **2.** Not recognizing a labor union or employing union members.
non•vi•o•lence (nŏn-vī′ə-ləns) ▸*n.* The doctrine or practice of rejecting violence in favor of peaceful tactics as a means of gaining political objectives. —**non•vi′o•lent** *adj.* —**non•vi′o•lent•ly** *adv.*
non•white (nŏn′hwīt′, -wīt′) ▸*n.* A person who is not white. —**non′white′** *adj.*

Usage: Many people object to the term *nonwhite* for referring to people by what they are not rather than what they are. The term *person of color* is often preferable.

noo•dle[1] (no͞od′l) ▸*n.* A narrow ribbonlike strip of dried dough, usu. made of flour, eggs, and water. [Ger. *Nudel*.]
noo•dle[2] (no͞od′l) ▸*n.* *Slang* The human head. [Alteration of *noddle*, back of head.]
nook (no͝ok) ▸*n.* **1.** A small corner or recess in a room. **2.** A hidden or secluded spot. [ME *nok*, prob. of Scand. orig.]
noon (no͞on) ▸*n.* Twelve o'clock in the daytime; midday. See Usage Note at **ante meridiem.** [< OE *nōn*, ninth hour after sunrise < Lat. *nōnus*, ninth.]
noon•day (no͞on′dā′) ▸*n.* Midday; noon.
no one ▸*pron.* No person; nobody.
noon•time (no͞on′tīm′) ▸*n.* Noon.
noose (no͞os) ▸*n.* A loop formed in a rope by a slipknot so that it binds tighter as the rope is pulled. [ME *nose*.]
Noot•ka (no͞ot′kə, no͝ot′-) ▸*n.*, *pl.* **-ka** or **-kas** **1.** A member of a Native American people inhabiting Vancouver Island in British Columbia and an adjacent area in NW Washington. **2.** Their language.
no-par (nō′pär′) ▸*adj.* Being without face or par value: *a no-par stock certificate.*
nope (nōp) ▸*adv.* *Informal* No. [Alteration of NO[1].]
nor (nôr; nər *when unstressed*) ▸*conj.* And not; or not; not either: *has neither phoned nor written us.* [ME.]

Usage: When a noun phrase of the type *this or that* is introduced by *no, or* is more common than *nor: He has no experience or interest. Or* is also more common than *nor* when such a noun phrase, adjective phrase, or adverb phrase is introduced by *not: He is not a philosopher or a statesman.* See Usage Note at **neither.**

Nor. ▸*abbr.* **1.** Norman **2.** north
Nor•dic (nôr′dĭk) ▸*adj.* **1.** Scandinavian. **2.** Of a human physical type exemplified by the light-skinned, blond-haired peoples of Scandinavia. **3.** Of a ski competition featuring ski jumping and cross-country racing. [< Fr. *nord*, NORTH.] —**Nor′dic** *n.*
Nor•folk (nôr′fək, -fôk) An independent city of SE VA SE of Richmond. Pop. 261,229.
Nor•gay (nôr′gā), **Tenzing.** 1914–86. Sherpa guide; with Sir Edmund Hillary made the first ascent of Mount Everest (1953).

Tenzing Norgay
photographed in 1953

norm (nôrm) ▸*n.* A standard, model, or pattern regarded as typical. [< Lat. *norma*, carpenter's square.]
nor•mal (nôr′məl) ▸*adj.* **1.** Conforming to a norm or standard; typical: *normal room temperature.* **2a.** Of average intelligence or development. **b.** Free from physical or emotional disorder. ▸*n.* **1.** A norm. **2.** The usual state, amount, or degree. —**nor′mal•cy** *n.* —**nor•mal′i•ty** (-măl′ĭ-tē) *n.* —**nor′mal•ly** *adv.*
normal curve ▸*n.* See **bell curve.**
nor•mal•ize (nôr′mə-līz′) ▸*v.* **-ized, -iz•ing.** To make normal or regular. —**nor′mal•i•za′tion** *n.* —**nor′mal•iz′er** *n.*
normal school ▸*n.* A school that trains teachers, chiefly for the elementary grades.
Nor•man (nôr′mən) ▸*n.* **1a.** A member of a Scandinavian people who settled in N France in the 10th cent. **b.** A member of a people of Norman and French blood who invaded England in 1066. **2.** A native or inhabitant of Normandy. —**Nor′man** *adj.*
Nor•man•dy (nôr′mən-dē) A historical region and former province of NW France on the English Channel.
Norman French ▸*n.* The dialect of Old French used in medieval Normandy.
nor•ma•tive (nôr′mə-tĭv) ▸*adj.* Of or prescribing a norm or standard. —**nor′ma•tive•ly** *adv.* —**nor′ma•tive•ness** *n.*
Norse (nôrs) ▸*adj.* **1.** Of or relating to medieval Scandinavia. **2.** Norwegian. **3.** Of or relating to the branch of the Germanic languages that includes Norwegian, Icelandic, and Faeroese. —**Norse** *n.*
Norse•man (nôrs′mən) ▸*n.* A member of any of the peoples of medieval Scandinavia.

north (nôrth) ▸*n.* **1a.** The direction along a meridian 90° counterclockwise from east. **b.** The compass point located at 0°. **2.** often **North a.** The northern part of the earth. **b.** The northern part of a region or country. ▸*adj.* **1.** To, toward, of, or in the north. **2.** Coming from the north: *a north wind.* ▸*adv.* In, from, or toward the north. [< OE.] —**north′ward** *adj. & adv.* —**north′ward•ly** *adj. & adv.* —**north′wards** *adv.*

North, Frederick. 2nd Earl of Guilford. "Lord North." 1732–92. British prime minister (1770–82).

North Africa. A region of N Africa usu. considered to include Morocco, Algeria, Tunisia, and Libya. —**North African** *adj. & n.*

North America. The N continent of the Western Hemisphere, extending northward from the Colombia-Panama border and including Central America, Mexico, the islands of the Caribbean Sea, the US, Canada, the Arctic Archipelago, and Greenland. —**North American** *adj. & n.*

North Atlantic Ocean. The N part of the Atlantic Ocean, extending from the equator to the Arctic Ocean.

North Car•o•li•na (kăr′ə-lī′nə) A state of the SE US bordering on the Atlantic. Cap. Raleigh. Pop. 6,657,630. —**North Car•o•lin′i•an** (-lĭn′ē-ən) *adj. & n.*

North Dakota. A state of the N-central US bordering on Canada. Cap. Bismarck. Pop. 641,364. —**North Dakotan** *adj. & n.*

north•east (nôrth-ēst′, nôr-ēst′) ▸*n.* **1.** The direction halfway between due north and due east. **2.** An area or region lying in the northeast. —**north•east′** *adj. & adv.* —**north•east′er•ly** *adj. & adv.* —**north•east′ern** *adj.* —**north•east′ward** *adj. & adv.* —**north•east′ward•ly** *adj. & adv.* —**north•east′wards** *adv.*

north•east•er (nôrth-ē′stər, nôr-ē′-) ▸*n.* A storm or gale blowing from the northeast.

north•er•ly (nôr′*th*ər-lē) ▸*adj.* **1.** In or toward the north. **2.** Coming from the north: *northerly winds.* —**north′er•ly** *adv.*

north•ern (nôr′*th*ərn) ▸*adj.* **1.** Of, in, or toward the north. **2.** From the north: *northern breezes.*

north•ern•er also **North•ern•er** (nôr′*th*ər-nər) ▸*n.* A native or inhabitant of a northern region.

Northern Hemisphere ▸*n.* The half of the earth north of the equator.

Northern Ireland. A division of the United Kingdom in the NE section of the island of Ireland. Cap. Belfast. Pop. 1,488,077.

northern lights ▸*pl.n.* See **aurora borealis.**

Northern Mariana Islands. See **Mariana Islands.**

northern oriole ▸*n.* A species of American songbird composed of two subspecies, the Baltimore and Bullock's orioles.

North Frigid Zone. See **Frigid Zone.**

North Island. An island of New Zealand separated from South I. by Cook Strait.

North Korea. A country of NE Asia on the Korean Peninsula. Cap. Pyongyang. Pop. 23,904,000. —**North Korean** *adj. & n.*

North Pacific Ocean. The N part of the Pacific Ocean, extending from the equator to the Arctic Ocean.

North Polar Region. See **Polar Regions.**

North Pole ▸*n.* **1.** The northern end of the earth's axis of rotation. **2.** The celestial zenith of the heavens as viewed from the south terrestrial pole.

North Sea. An arm of the Atlantic between Great Britain and NW Europe.

North Star ▸*n.* See **Polaris.**

North Temperate Zone. See **Temperate Zone.**

North•um•bri•a (nôr-thŭm′brē-ə) An Anglo-Saxon kingdom of N England. —**North•um′bri•an** *adj. & n.*

North Vietnam. A former country (1954–75) of SE Asia; now part of Vietnam. —**North Vietnamese** *adj. & n.*

north•west (nôrth-wĕst′, nôr-wĕst′) ▸*n.* **1.** The direction halfway between due north and due west. **2.** An area or region lying in the northwest. —**north•west′** *adj. & adv.* —**north•west′er•ly** *adj. & adv.* —**north•west′ern** *adj.* —**north•west′ward** *adj. & adv.* —**north•west′ward•ly** *adj. & adv.* —**north•west′wards** *adv.*

Northwest Passage. A water route from the Atlantic to the Pacific through the Arctic Archipelago of N Canada and along the N coast of AK.

Northwest Territories. A territory of N Canada between Yukon Territory and Nunavut including islands of the W Arctic Archipelago. Cap. Yellowknife. Pop. 45,741.

Northwest Territory. A historical region of the N-central US from the Ohio and Mississippi rivers to the Great Lakes.

North Yemen. The former country of Yemen (1962–90).

Nor•way (nôr′wā′) A country of N Europe in the W part of the Scandinavian Peninsula. Cap. Oslo. Pop. 4,325,000.

Nor•we•gian (nôr-wē′jən) ▸*n.* **1.** A native or inhabitant of Norway. **2.** Either of the Germanic languages of the Norwegians. —**Nor•we′gian** *adj.*

Norwegian Sea. A section of the Atlantic off the coast of Norway N of the North Sea.

nos. or **Nos.** ▸*abbr.* numbers

nose (nōz) ▸*n.* **1.** The part of the face that contains the nostrils and organs of smell and forms the beginning of the respiratory tract. **2.** The sense of smell. **3.** The ability to detect, as if by smell: *has a nose for gossip.* **4.** Something, such as the forward end of an aircraft, that resembles a nose. ▸*v.* **nosed, nos•ing 1.** To find out by or as if by smell. **2.** To touch with the nose; nuzzle. **3.** To move or advance carefully. **4.** *Informal* To snoop or pry. —***idioms:*** **on the nose** Exactly; precisely. **under (someone's) nose** In plain view. [< OE *nosu.*]

nose•bleed (nōz′blēd′) ▸*n.* Bleeding from the nose.

nose cone ▸*n.* The forwardmost, usu. separable section of a rocket or guided missile.

nose•dive (nōz′dīv′) ▸*n.* **1.** A very steep dive of an aircraft. **2.** A sudden plunge. —**nose′dive′** *v.*

nose•gay (nōz′gā′) ▸*n.* A small bouquet of flowers. [ME.]

nosh (nŏsh) ▸*v.* *Informal* To eat a snack or light meal. [Yiddish *nash, naschen,* to nibble.] —**nosh** *n.* —**nosh′er** *n.*

nos•tal•gi•a (nŏ-stăl′jə, nə-) ►*n.* **1.** A bittersweet longing for the past. **2.** Homesickness. [Gk. *nostos*, a return home + -ALGIA.] —**nos•tal′gic** *adj.* —**nos•tal′gi•cal•ly** *adv.*

Nos•tra•da•mus (nŏs′trə-dā′məs, -dä′-, nō′strə-). 1503–66. French physician and astrologer.

nos•tril (nŏs′trəl) ►*n.* Either of the external openings of the nose. [< OE *nosthyrl.*]

nos•trum (nŏs′trəm) ►*n.* A quack medicine or remedy. [Lat. *nostrum (remedium)*, our (remedy).]

nos•y or **nos•ey** (nō′zē) ►*adj.* **-i•er, -i•est** *Informal.* Prying; inquisitive. [< NOSE.] —**nos′i•ly** *adv.* —**nos′i•ness** *n.*

not (nŏt) ►*adv.* In no way; to no degree. Used to express negation, denial, refusal, or prohibition: *I will not go. You may not have any.* [ME, alteration of *naught*, NAUGHT.]

Usage: In formal writing the *not only . . . but also* construction should be used in such a way that each of its elements is followed by a construction of the same type. Instead of *She not only bought a new car but a new lawnmower,* write *She bought not only a new car but a new lawnmower.*

no•ta be•ne (nō′tə bĕn′ē, bē′nē) ► Used to direct attention to something particularly important. [Lat. *notā bene*, note well.]

no•ta•ble (nō′tə-bəl) ►*adj.* **1.** Worthy of note or notice; remarkable. **2.** Distinguished; eminent. See Syns at **noted.** ►*n.* A person of distinction. See Syns at **celebrity.** —**no′ta•bil′i•ty** *n.* —**no′ta•bly** *adv.*

no•ta•rize (nō′tə-rīz′) ►*v.* **-rized, -riz•ing.** To certify or attest to as a notary public. —**no′ta•ri•za′tion** *n.*

no•ta•ry (nō′tə-rē) ►*n., pl.* **-ries.** A notary public. [< Lat. *notārius*, stenographer.]

notary public ►*n., pl.* **notaries public.** A person legally empowered to witness and certify the validity of documents and to take affidavits and depositions.

no•ta•tion (nō-tā′shən) ►*n.* **1a.** A system of figures or symbols used to represent numbers, quantities, tones, or values. **b.** The act or process of using such a system. **2.** A brief note; annotation.

notch (nŏch) ►*n.* **1.** A V-shaped cut. **2.** A narrow pass between mountains. **3.** *Informal* A level or degree. ►*v.* **1.** To cut a notch in. **2.** To record by or as if by making notches. [Prob. < *an otch < OFr. *oche* < *ochier*, to notch.]

note (nōt) ►*n.* **1.** A brief written record. **2.** A brief informal letter. **3.** A formal written diplomatic or official communication. **4.** A comment or explanation, as on a passage in a text. **5a.** A piece of paper currency. **b.** A promissory note. **6.** *Mus.* **a.** A tone of definite pitch. **b.** A symbol for such a tone. **7.** The vocal sound made by a songbird or other animal. **8.** The sign of a particular quality or emotion: *a note of despair.* **9.** Importance; consequence. **10.** Notice; observation: *took note of the scene.* ►*v.* **not•ed, not•ing 1.** To observe carefully; notice. **2.** To make a note of; write down. **3.** To make mention of; remark. [< Lat. *nota*, a mark.]

note•book (nōt′bo͝ok′) ►*n.* **1.** A book of blank pages for notes. **2.** A portable computer, gen. thinner than a laptop.

not•ed (nō′tĭd) ►*adj.* Well-known; famous.

Syns: *noted, celebrated, eminent, famous, illustrious, notable, preeminent, renowned* ***Ant:*** *obscure* ***adj.***

note•wor•thy (nōt′wûr′*th*ē) ►*adj.* Deserving notice or attention; notable. —**note′wor′thi•ness** *n.*

noth•ing (nŭth′ĭng) ►*pron.* **1.** No thing; not anything. **2.** No part; no portion: *Nothing remains of the old house.* **3.** One of no consequence or interest. ►*n.* **1.** Absence of anything perceptible; nonexistence. **2.** Zero. **3.** A nonentity. ►*adv.* Not at all: *She looks nothing like me.* [< OE *nāthing*.]

Usage: According to the traditional rule, *nothing* is invariably treated as a singular, even when followed by an exception phrase containing a plural noun: *Nothing except your fears stops* (not *stop*) *you.*

noth•ing•ness (nŭth′ĭng-nĭs) ►*n.* **1.** The condition or quality of being nothing; nonexistence. **2.** Empty space; void.

no•tice (nō′tĭs) ►*n.* **1.** Observation; attention. **2.** Respectful attention or consideration. **3.** A written or printed announcement. **4.** A formal announcement or warning. **5.** A critical review. ►*v.* **-ticed, -tic•ing 1.** To observe. **2.** To comment on. [< Lat. *nōtitia*, knowledge < *nōscere*, come to know.]

no•tice•a•ble (nō′tĭ-sə-bəl) ►*adj.* **1.** Evident; observable. **2.** Worthy of notice; significant. —**no′tice•a•bly** *adv.*

no•ti•fy (nō′tə-fī′) ►*v.* **-fied, -fy•ing 1.** To give notice to; inform. **2.** *Chiefly Brit.* To make known; proclaim. [< Lat. *nōtificāre.*] —**no′ti•fi•ca′tion** *n.* —**no′ti•fi′er** *n.*

no•tion (nō′shən) ►*n.* **1.** A belief or opinion. **2.** An idea or conception. **3.** A fanciful impulse; whim. **4. notions** Small lightweight items for household use, such as needles, buttons, and thread. [< Lat. *nōtiō* < *nōscere*, come to know.] —**no′tion•al** *adj.*

no•to•ri•ous (nō-tôr′ē-əs, -tōr′-) ►*adj.* Known widely and usu. unfavorably; infamous. [< Med.Lat. *nōtōrius* < Lat. *nōtus*, known.] —**no′to•ri′e•ty** (-tə-rī′ĭ-tē) *n.* —**no•to′ri•ous•ly** *adv.*

Not•ting•ham (nŏt′ĭng-əm) A borough of central England N of Leicester. Pop. 282,590.

not•with•stand•ing (nŏt′wĭth-stăn′dĭng, -wĭ*th*-) ►*prep.* In spite of. ►*adv.* All the same; nevertheless. ►*conj.* Although.

Nouak•chott (nwäk-shŏt′) The capital of Mauritania, in the W part on the Atlantic Ocean. Pop. 150,000.

nou•gat (no͞o′gət) ►*n.* A candy made from a sugar or honey paste and nuts. [< Prov.]

nought (nôt) ►*n.* Var. of **naught.**

noun (noun) ►*n.* A word used to name a person, place, thing, quality, or action. [< Lat. *nōmen*, name.]

nour•ish (nûr′ĭsh, nŭr′-) ►*v.* **1.** To provide with food or other substances necessary for life and growth. **2.** To foster the development of; promote. [< Lat. *nūtrīre.*] —**nour′ish•ing** *adj.* —**nour′ish•ment** *n.*

nou•veau riche (no͞o′vō rēsh′) ►*n., pl.* **nou•veaux riches** (no͞o′vō rēsh′). One who has recently become rich. [Fr., new rich.]

Nov. ►*abbr.* November

no•va (nō′və) ►*n., pl.* **-vae** (-vē) or **-vas.** A star that suddenly becomes much brighter and then returns to its original brightness over a period of weeks to years. [< Lat. *novus*, new.]

Nova Sco•tia (skō′shə) A province of E Canada comprising a mainland peninsula and the adjacent Cape Breton I. Cap. Halifax. Pop. 847,442. —**No′va Sco′tian** *adj. & n.*

nov•el[1] (nŏv′əl) ▶*n.* A fictional prose narrative of considerable length, typically having a plot that is unfolded by the actions, speech, and thoughts of the characters. [< VLat. **novella*, new things < Lat. *novellus*, NOVEL[2].] —**nov′el•is′tic** *adj.*

nov•el[2] (nŏv′əl) ▶*adj.* Strikingly new, unusual, or different. [< Lat. *novellus*, dim. of *novus*, new.] —**nov′el•ly** *adv.*

nov•el•ette (nŏv′ə-lĕt′) ▶*n.* A short novel.

nov•el•ist (nŏv′ə-lĭst) ▶*n.* A writer of novels.

nov•el•ize (nŏv′ə-līz′) ▶*v.* **-ized, -iz•ing.** To convert into a novelistic format. —**nov′el•i•za′tion** *n.*

no•vel•la (nō-vĕl′ə) ▶*n.* A short novel. [Ital. NOVEL[1].]

nov•el•ty (nŏv′əl-tē) ▶*n.*, *pl.* **-ties 1.** The quality of being novel; newness. **2.** Something new and unusual. **3.** A small mass-produced article, such as a trinket.

No•vem•ber (nō-vĕm′bər) ▶*n.* The 11th month of the Gregorian calendar. See table at **calendar.** [< Lat., ninth month.]

no•ve•na (nō-vē′nə) ▶*n.* *Rom. Cath. Ch.* A recitation of devotions for nine consecutive days. [Med.Lat. < Lat. *novem*, nine.]

Nov•go•rod (nŏv′gə-rŏd′) A city of NW Russia SSE of St. Petersburg. Pop. 232,534.

nov•ice (nŏv′ĭs) ▶*n.* **1.** A beginner. **2.** One who has entered a religious order but has not yet taken vows. [< Med.Lat. *novīcius*.]

no•vi•ti•ate (nō-vĭsh′ē-ĭt, -āt′) ▶*n.* **1.** The period of being a religious novice. **2.** A place where novices live. **3.** See **novice** 2. [< Med. Lat. *novīcius*, novice.]

No•vo•cain (nō′və-kān′) ▶ A trademark for an anesthetic preparation of procaine.

No•vo•kuz•netsk (nō′və-ko͝oz-nĕtsk′) A city of S-central Russia SE of Novosibirsk. Pop. 597,483.

No•vo•si•birsk (nō′və-sə-bîrsk′) A city of S-central Russia on the Ob R. E of Omsk. Pop. 1,423,860.

now (nou) ▶*adv.* **1.** At the present time. **2.** At once: *Stop now.* **3.** Very recently: *left the room just now.* **4.** At this point in the series of events; then. **5.** In these circumstances; as things are. **6.** Used to introduce a command, reproof, or request: *Now pay attention.* ▶*conj.* Seeing that; since. ▶*n.* The present time or moment. ▶*adj.* **1.** Current. **2.** *Slang* Fashionable; trendy. [< OE *nū*.]

NOW ▶*abbr.* National Organization for Women

now•a•days (nou′ə-dāz′) ▶*adv.* During the present time; now. [ME *nouadaies*.]

no•way (nō′wā′) also **no•ways** (-wāz′) ▶*adv.* *Informal* Nowise.

no•where (nō′hwâr′, -wâr′) ▶*adv.* **1.** Not anywhere. **2.** To no place or result. ▶*n.* A remote or unknown place.

no•wise (nō′wīz′) ▶*adv.* In no way, manner, or degree; not at all.

nox•ious (nŏk′shəs) ▶*adj.* Injurious to health or morals. [< Lat. *noxius* < *noxa*, damage.] —**nox′ious•ly** *adv.*

noz•zle (nŏz′əl) ▶*n.* A projecting part with an opening for regulating a flow of fluid. [Dim. of NOSE.]

Np ▶ The symbol for the element **neptunium.**

NP ▶*abbr.* notary public

NRA ▶*abbr.* **1.** National Recovery Administration **2.** National Rifle Association

NRC ▶*abbr.* Nuclear Regulatory Commission

ns ▶*abbr.* nanosecond

NS ▶*abbr.* **1.** also **N.S.** Nova Scotia **2.** nuclear ship

n/s ▶*abbr.* not sufficient

NSC ▶*abbr.* National Security Council

NSE ▶*abbr.* National Stock Exchange

NSPCA ▶*abbr.* National Society for the Prevention of Cruelty to Animals

NT ▶*abbr.* **1.** New Testament **2.** Northwest Territories

nth (ĕnth) ▶*adj.* **1.** Relating to an unspecified ordinal number. **2.** Highest; utmost: *to the nth degree.*

nt. wt. ▶*abbr.* net weight

nu (no͞o, nyo͞o) ▶*n.* The 13th letter of the Greek alphabet. [Gk.]

nu•ance (no͞o′äns′, nyo͞o′-) ▶*n.* A subtle or slight degree of difference, as in meaning or feeling; gradation. [< OFr. *nuer*, to shade < VLat. **nūba*, cloud.] —**nu•anced′** *adj.*
Syns: nuance, gradation, shade ***n.***

nub (nŭb) ▶*n.* **1.** A lump or knob. **2.** The essence; core. [< MLGer. *knubbe*.] —**nub′by** *adj.*

Nu•bi•a (no͞o′bē-ə, nyo͞o′-) A desert region and ancient kingdom in the Nile valley of S Egypt and N Sudan. —**Nu′bi•an** *adj. & n.*

Nubian Desert. A desert region of NE Sudan extending E of the Nile R. to the Red Sea.

nu•bile (no͞o′bĭl, -bīl′, nyo͞o′-) ▶*adj.* Of marriageable age or condition. [< Lat. *nūbere*, take a husband.]

nu•cle•ar (no͞o′klē-ər, nyo͞o′-) ▶*adj.* **1.** *Biol.* Of or forming a nucleus. **2.** *Phys.* Of or relating to atomic nuclei. **3.** Of, using, or derived from nuclear energy.

nuclear energy ▶*n.* The energy released by a nuclear reaction, esp. by fission or fusion.

nuclear family ▶*n.* A family unit consisting of a mother and father and their children.

nuclear magnetic resonance ▶*n.* The absorption of electromagnetic radiation of a specific frequency by an atomic nucleus placed in a strong magnetic field.

nuclear reaction ▶*n.* A reaction, as in fission, that alters the energy, composition, or structure of an atomic nucleus.

nuclear reactor ▶*n.* A device in which a nuclear chain reaction is initiated and controlled.

nu•cle•ate (no͞o′klē-ĭt, nyo͞o′-) ▶*adj.* Having a nucleus or nuclei. ▶*v.* (-āt′) **-at•ed, -at•ing 1.** To bring together into or form a nucleus. **2.** To act as a nucleus for. —**nu′cle•a′tion** *n.*

nu•cle•ic acid (no͞o-klē′ĭk, -klā′-, nyo͞o-) ▶*n.* Any of a group of complex compounds that are found in all living cells and viruses and that control cellular function and heredity.

nucleo– or **nucle–** ▶*pref.* **1.** Nucleus: *nucleon.* **2.** Nucleic acid: *nucleotide.* [< NUCLEUS.]

nu•cle•o•lus (no͞o-klē′ə-ləs, nyo͞o-) ▶*n.*, *pl.* **-li** (-lī′). A small granular body composed of protein and RNA in the nucleus of a cell. [Lat., dim. of *nucleus*, NUCLEUS.] —**nu•cle′o•lar** (-lər) *adj.*

nu•cle•on (no͞o′klē-ŏn′, nyo͞o′-) ▶*n.* A proton

or a neutron. —**nu′cle•on′ic** *adj.*

nu•cle•on•ics (no͞o′klē-ŏn′ĭks, nyo͞o′-) ►*n.* *(takes sing. v.)* The study of the behavior of nucleons or atomic nuclei.

nu•cle•o•tide (no͞o′klē-ə-tīd′, nyo͞o′-) ►*n.* Any of various compounds that form the basic constituents of DNA and RNA. [Alteration of *nucleoside*.]

nu•cle•us (no͞o′klē-əs, nyo͞o′-) ►*n.*, *pl.* **-cle•i** (-klē-ī′) or **-es 1.** A central or essential part around which other parts are gathered or grouped; core. **2.** *Biol.* A membrane-bound structure within a living cell that contains the cell's hereditary material and controls its metabolism, growth, and reproduction. **3.** *Phys.* The positively charged central region of an atom, composed of protons and neutrons and containing almost all of the mass of the atom. [Lat., kernel < *nux*, nut.]

nu•clide (no͞o′klīd′, nyo͞o′-) ►*n.* A type of atom specified by its atomic number, atomic mass, and energy state. —**nu•clid′ic** (no͞o-klĭd′ĭk, nyo͞o-) *adj.*

nude (no͞od, nyo͞od) ►*adj.* **nud•er, nud•est.** Being without clothing; naked. ►*n.* **1.** An unclothed human figure, esp. in artistic representation. **2.** The condition of being unclothed. [Lat. *nūdus*.] —**nu′di•ty** *n.*

nudge (nŭj) ►*v.* **nudged, nudg•ing.** To push against gently, esp. in order to gain attention. [Prob. of Scand. orig.] —**nudge** *n.*

nud•ism (no͞o′dĭz′əm, nyo͞o′-) ►*n.* The belief in or practice of going nude, esp. for reasons of health. —**nud′ist** *adj. & n.*

Nue•vo La•re•do (no͞o-ā′vō lə-rā′dō) A city of NE Mexico across the Rio Grande from Laredo, TX. Pop. 201,731.

nu•ga•to•ry (no͞o′gə-tôr′ē, -tōr′ē, nyo͞o′-) ►*adj.* **1.** Insignificant; trifling. **2.** Hollow. See Syns at **vain.** [< Lat. *nūgae*, jokes.]

nug•get (nŭg′ĭt) ►*n.* A small solid lump, esp. of gold. [< dial. *nug*, lump.]

nui•sance (no͞o′səns, nyo͞o′-) ►*n.* One that is inconvenient, annoying, or vexatious; bother. [< OFr., ult. < Lat. *nocēre*, to harm.]

nuke (no͞ok, nyo͞ok) *Slang* ►*n.* **1.** A nuclear device or weapon. **2.** A nuclear power plant. ►*v.* **nuked, nuk•ing.** To attack with nuclear weapons.

Nu•ku•′a•lo•fa (no͞o′ko͞o-ə-lô′fə) The capital of Tonga, in the SW Pacific. Pop. 21,745.

null (nŭl) ►*adj.* **1.** Having no legal force; invalid. **2.** Of no consequence; insignificant. **3.** Amounting to nothing. ►*n.* Zero; nothing. [< Lat. *nūllus*.] —**nul′li•ty** *n.*

null character ►*n.* *Comp. Sci.* A data control character used as a filler between blocks of data.

nul•li•fy (nŭl′ə-fī′) ►*v.* **-fied, -fy•ing 1.** To make null; invalidate. **2.** To counteract the force or effectiveness of. —**nul′li•fi•ca′tion** *n.*

numb (nŭm) ►*adj.* **-er, -est 1.** Unable to feel or move normally. **2.** Stunned, as from shock. [< ME *nomin*, seized.] —**numb** *v.* —**numb′ly** *adv.* —**numb′ness** *n.*

num•ber (nŭm′bər) ►*n.* **1.** *Math.* **a.** A member of the set of positive integers. **b.** A member of any of the further sets of objects that can be derived from the positive integers. **2. numbers** Arithmetic. **3.** A numeral or series of numerals used for reference or identification: *a telephone number.* **4.** One item in a sequence or series. **5.** A total; sum. **6.** An indefinite quantity: *a number of people.* **7. numbers** A multitude. **8.** *Gram.* The indication of the singularity or plurality of a linguistic form. **9. Numbers** *(takes sing. v.)* See table at **Bible. 10.** An item in a program of entertainment. ►*v.* **1.** To assign a number to. **2.** To count or enumerate. **3.** To add up to. **4.** To include in a group or category. **5.** To limit in number. [< Lat. *numerus*.]

Usage: As a collective noun *number* may take either a singular or a plural verb. It takes a singular verb when it is preceded by *the: The number of skilled workers is small.* It takes a plural verb when preceded by *a: A number of the workers are unskilled.*

num•ber•less (nŭm′bər-lĭs) ►*adj.* Innumerable; countless.

numbers game ►*n.* A lottery in which bets are made on an unpredictable number, such as a daily stock quote.

nu•mer•a•ble (no͞o′mər-ə-bəl, nyo͞o′-) ►*adj.* That can be counted; countable.

nu•mer•al (no͞o′mər-əl, nyo͞o′-) ►*n.* A symbol or mark used to represent a number. [< Lat. *numerus*, number.] —**nu′mer•al** *adj.*

nu•mer•ate (no͞o′mə-rāt′, nyo͞o′-) ►*v.* **-at•ed, -at•ing.** To enumerate. [Lat. *numerāre* < *numerus*, number.] —**nu′mer•a′tion** *n.*

nu•mer•a•tor (no͞o′mə-rā′tər, nyo͞o′-) ►*n.* The expression written above the line in a common fraction to indicate the number of parts.

nu•mer•i•cal (no͞o-mĕr′ĭ-kəl, nyo͞o-) also **nu•mer•ic** (-mĕr′ĭk) ►*adj.* Of, represented by, or being a number or numbers. [< Lat. *numerus*, number.] —**nu•mer′i•cal•ly** *adv.*

nu•mer•ol•o•gy (no͞o′mə-rŏl′ə-jē, nyo͞o′-) ►*n.* The study of occult meanings of numbers. [< Lat. *numerus*, number.] —**nu′mer•ol′o•gist** *n.*

nu•mer•ous (no͞o′mər-əs, nyo͞o′-) ►*adj.* Amounting to a large number; many. [< Lat. *numerōsus*.] —**nu′mer•ous•ly** *adv.* —**nu′mer•ous•ness** *n.*

Nu•mid•i•a (no͞o-mĭd′ē-ə, nyo͞o-) An ancient country of NW Africa corresponding roughly to present-day Algeria. —**Nu•mid′i•an** *adj. & n.*

nu•mi•nous (no͞o′mə-nəs, nyo͞o′-) ►*adj.* **1.** Filled with a sense of a supernatural presence. **2.** Spiritually elevated; sublime. [< Lat. *nūmen*, *nūmin-*, spirit.]

nu•mis•mat•ics (no͞o′mĭz-măt′ĭks, -mĭs-, nyo͞o′-) ►*n.* *(takes sing. v.)* The study or collection of money, coins, and medals. [< Gk. *nomisma*, coin in circulation.] —**nu′mis•mat′ic** *adj.* —**nu•mis′ma•tist** (-mĭz′mə-tĭst, -mĭs′-) *n.*

num•skull also **numb•skull** (nŭm′skŭl′) ►*n.* A stupid person. [NUM(B) + SKULL.]

nun (nŭn) ►*n.* A woman who belongs to a religious order. [< LLat. *nonna*.]

Nu•na•vut (no͞o′nə-vo͞ot′) A territory of N Canada including part of the mainland W of Hudson Bay and N of latitude 60° N, islands in the Hudson Bay, and most of the Arctic Archipelago. Cap. Iqaluit. Pop. 24,730.

nun•ci•o (nŭn′sē-ō′, no͞on′-) ►*n.*, *pl.* **-os.** A papal ambassador or representative. [Ital. < Lat. *nūntius*, messenger.]

nun•ner•y (nŭn′ə-rē) ►*n.*, *pl.* **-ies.** A convent of nuns.

nup•tial (nŭp′shəl, -chəl) ► *adj.* Of marriage or the wedding ceremony. ► *n.* often **nuptials** A wedding ceremony. [< Lat. *nūptiae*, wedding < *nūbere*, take a husband.]

Nu•rem•berg (no͝or′əm-bûrg′, nyo͝or′-) A city of SE Germany NNW of Munich. Pop. 498,945.

Nu•re•yev (no͝or′ĭ-yĕf, no͞o-rā′-), **Rudolf.** 1938–93. Russian-born ballet dancer and choreographer.

nurse (nûrs) ► *n.* **1.** A person trained to care for the sick or disabled. **2a.** A wet nurse. **b.** A nursemaid. ► *v.* **nursed, nurs•ing 1.** To serve as a nurse for. **2.** To suckle. **3.** To treat: *nurse a cough.* **4.** To take special care of. **5.** To assist; attend. See Syns at **nurture. 6.** To bear privately in the mind: *nursing a grudge.* **7.** To consume slowly: *nurse a drink.* [< Lat. *nūtrīx*, wet nurse.]

nurse•maid (nûrs′mād′) ► *n.* A woman employed to take care of children.

nurse practitioner ► *n.* A registered nurse with special training for providing primary health care.

nurs•er•y (nûr′sə-rē, nûrs′rē) ► *n., pl.* **-ies 1.** A room set apart for children. **2a.** A place for the temporary care of children. **b.** A nursery school. **3.** A place where plants are grown, esp. for sale.

nursery school ► *n.* A school for children, usu. between the ages of three and five.

nurs•ing (nûr′sĭng) ► *n.* The profession or tasks of a nurse.

nursing home ► *n.* A residential establishment that provides care for the elderly or the chronically ill.

nurs•ling (nûrs′lĭng) ► *n.* A nursing infant or young animal.

nur•ture (nûr′chər) ► *n.* **1.** Something that nourishes. **2.** Upbringing; rearing. ► *v.* **-tured, -tur•ing 1.** To nourish; feed. **2.** To educate; train. **3.** To foster; cultivate. [< Lat. *nūtrīre*, suckle.] —**nur′tur•er** *n.*

Syns: *nurture, cultivate, foster, nurse* **v.**

nut (nŭt) ► *n.* **1a.** A fruit or seed with a hard shell and an inner kernel. **b.** The kernel itself. **2.** *Slang* **a.** A crazy or eccentric person. **b.** An enthusiast: *a movie nut.* **3.** *Mus.* A ridge of wood at the top of the fingerboard or neck of a stringed instrument, over which the strings pass. **4.** A small block of metal or wood with a central threaded hole that is designed to fit around and secure a bolt or screw. [< OE *hnutu.*]

nut•crack•er (nŭt′krăk′ər) ► *n.* An implement used to crack nuts.

nut•meat (nŭt′mēt′) ► *n.* The edible kernel of a nut.

nut•meg (nŭt′mĕg′) ► *n.* The hard aromatic seed of an East Indian tree, grated or ground as a spice. [Prob. < OFr. *nois mugede.*]

nu•tri•a (no͞o′trē-ə, nyo͞o′-) ► *n.* **1.** A beaverlike South American rodent. **2.** Its thick brownish fur. [Sp. < VLat., var. of Lat. *lutra.*]

nu•tri•ent (no͞o′trē-ənt, nyo͞o′-) ► *n.* A source of nourishment. ► *adj.* Providing nourishment. [< Lat. *nūtrīre*, nourish.]

nu•tri•ment (no͞o′trə-mənt, nyo͞o′-) ► *n.* A source of nourishment, esp. food.

nu•tri•tion (no͞o-trĭsh′ən, nyo͞o-) ► *n.* **1.** The process of nourishing or being nourished, esp. the process by which a living organism assimilates and uses food. **2.** The study of food and nourishment. [< Lat. *nūtrīre*, nourish.] —**nu•tri′tion•al** *adj.* —**nu•tri′tion•al•ly** *adv.* —**nu•tri′tion•ist** *n.* —**nu′tri•tive** (-trĭ-tĭv) *adj.*

nu•tri•tious (no͞o-trĭsh′əs, nyo͞o-) ► *adj.* Providing nourishment or nutrition. [< Lat. *nūtrīx*, nurse.] —**nu•tri′tious•ly** *adv.* —**nu•tri′tious•ness** *n.*

nuts (nŭts) *Slang* ► *adj.* **1.** Crazy; insane. **2.** Extremely enthusiastic. ► *interj.* Used to express contempt, disappointment, or refusal. [< NUT.]

nut•shell (nŭt′shĕl′) ► *n.* The shell of a nut. —***idiom:* in a nutshell** In a few words.

nut•ty (nŭt′ē) ► *adj.* **-ti•er, -ti•est 1.** Full of or tasting like nuts. **2.** *Slang* Crazy: *a nutty idea.* —**nut′ti•ly** *adv.* —**nut′ti•ness** *n.*

nuz•zle (nŭz′əl) ► *v.* **-zled, -zling 1.** To rub or push against gently with the nose or snout. **2.** To nestle together. [< NOSE.]

NV ► *abbr.* Nevada

NW ► *abbr.* **1.** northwest **2.** northwestern

NWbN ► *abbr.* northwest by north

NWbW ► *abbr.* northwest by west

NWT or **N.W.T.** ► *abbr.* Northwest Territories

n. wt. ► *abbr.* net weight

NY or **N.Y.** ► *abbr.* New York

Ny•as•a (nī-ăs′ə), **Lake.** A lake of SE-central Africa between Tanzania, Mozambique, and Malawi.

NYC ► *abbr.* New York City

ny•lon (nī′lŏn′) ► *n.* **1a.** Any of a family of high-strength, resilient synthetic resins. **b.** Cloth or yarn made from nylon. **2. nylons** Stockings made of nylon. [Coined by E.I. Du Pont de Nemours and Co., Inc.]

nymph (nĭmf) ► *n.* **1.** *Gk. & Rom. Myth.* Any of numerous female spirits dwelling in woodlands and waters. **2.** The larval form of certain insects, usu. resembling the adult form but smaller and lacking fully developed wings. [< Gk. *numphē.*]

nym•pho•ma•ni•a (nĭm′fə-mā′nē-ə, -mān′yə) ► *n.* Abnormal or excessive sexual desire in a female. [Gk. *numphē*, nymph + -MANIA.] —**nym′pho•ma′ni•ac** (-nē-ăk) *n.*

NYSE ► *abbr.* New York Stock Exchange

NZ ► *abbr.* New Zealand

O

o or **O** (ō) ► *n., pl.* **o's** or **O's** also **os** or **Os 1.** The 15th letter of the English alphabet. **2.** A zero. **3. O** A type of blood in the ABO system.

O[1] (ō) ► *interj.* **1.** Used before the name of a person or thing being formally addressed. **2.** Used to express surprise or strong emotion.

O[2] ► The symbol for the element **oxygen.**

O[3] ► *abbr.* **1.** *Baseball* out **2.** outstanding

O. ► *abbr.* **1.** ocean **2.** Ohio

oaf (ōf) ► *n.* A stupid, clumsy person. [ON *alfr*, elf.] —**oaf′ish** *adj.* —**oaf′ish•ly** *adv.* —**oaf′ish•ness** *n.*

O•a•hu (ō-ä′ho͞o) An island of central HI between Molokai and Kauai.

oak (ōk) ▸*n.* **1.** Any of numerous trees bearing acorns as fruit. **2.** The durable wood of these trees. [< OE *āc.*] —**oak′en** *adj.*

Oak•land (ōk′lənd) A city of W CA on San Francisco Bay opposite San Francisco. Pop. 372,242.

Oak•ley (ōk′lē), **Annie.** 1860–1926. Amer. sharpshooter.

oa•kum (ō′kəm) ▸*n.* Loose hemp or jute fiber, sometimes treated with tar, used chiefly for caulking ships. [< OE *ācumba.*]

oar (ôr, ōr) ▸*n.* **1.** A long pole with a blade at one end, used to row or steer a boat. **2.** One who rows a boat. [< OE *ār.*]

oar•lock (ôr′lŏk′, ōr′-) ▸*n.* A U-shaped metal hoop used to hold an oar in place.

oars•man (ôrz′mən, ōrz′-) ▸*n.* A rower, esp. in a racing crew.

OAS ▸*abbr.* Organization of American States

o•a•sis (ō-ā′sĭs) ▸*n., pl.* **-ses** (-sēz). A fertile or green spot in a desert. [< Gk.]

oat (ōt) ▸*n.* often **oats** *(takes sing. or pl. v.)* **1.** A cereal grass widely cultivated for its edible grains. **2.** The grain of this plant. [< OE *āte.*] —**oat′en** *adj.*

oat•cake (ōt′kāk′) ▸*n.* A flattened cake of baked oatmeal.

Oates (ōts), **Joyce Carol.** b. 1938. Amer. writer.

Joyce Carol Oates

oath (ōth) ▸*n., pl.* **oaths** (ō*th*z, ōths) **1.** A formal promise to fulfill a pledge, often calling on God or a god as witness. **2.** A blasphemous use of a sacred name. [< OE *āth.*]

oat•meal (ōt′mēl′) ▸*n.* **1.** Meal made from oats; rolled or ground oats. **2.** A porridge made from rolled or ground oats.

Ob (ŏb, ôb) A river, about 3,700 km (2,300 mi), of W and central Russia flowing to the **Gulf of Ob,** an arm of the Arctic Ocean.

O•ba•di•ah (ō′bə-dī′ə) ▸*n.* **1.** A Hebrew prophet of the 6th cent. B.C. **2.** See table at **Bible.**

ob•bli•ga•to (ŏb′lĭ-gä′tō) ▸*n., pl.* **-tos** or **-ti** (-tē) *Mus.* An accompaniment that is an indispensable part of a piece. [Ital.]

ob•du•rate (ŏb′do͞o-rĭt, -dyo͞o-) ▸*adj.* Hardened against influence or feeling; intractable. [< LLat. *obdūrāre*, harden.] —**ob′du•ra•cy** *n.* —**ob′du•rate•ly** *adv.*

o•be•di•ent (ō-bē′dē-ənt) ▸*adj.* Dutifully complying with the orders or instructions of one in authority. [< Lat. *oboedīre*, obey.] —**o•be′di•ence** *n.* —**o•be′di•ent•ly** *adv.*

o•bei•sance (ō-bā′səns, ō-bē′-) ▸*n.* **1.** A gesture or body movement expressing deference. **2.** An attitude of deference. [< OFr. *obeir, obeiss-*, OBEY.] —**o•bei′sant** *adj.*

ob•e•lisk (ŏb′ə-lĭsk) ▸*n.* **1.** A tall, four-sided shaft of stone, usu. tapered, that rises to a pointed pyramidal top. **2.** *Print.* The dagger sign (†), used esp. as a reference mark. [< Gk. *obeliskos.*]

o•bese (ō-bēs′) ▸*adj.* Extremely fat; grossly overweight. [Lat. *obēsus* < p.part. of **obedere*, devour.] —**o•bese′ly** *adv.* —**o•be′si•ty, o•bese′ness** *n.*

o•bey (ō-bā′) ▸*v.* **1.** To carry out the command of. **2.** To comply with (a command). [< Lat. *oboedīre.*] —**o•bey′er** *n.*

ob•fus•cate (ŏb′fə-skāt′, ŏb-fŭs′kāt′) ▸*v.* **-cat•ed, -cat•ing 1.** To make so confused as to be difficult to understand. **2.** To render indistinct or dim. [Lat. *obfuscāre.*] —**ob′fus•ca′tion** *n.* —**ob•fus′ca•to′ry** (ŏb-fŭs′kə-tôr′ē, -tōr′ē, əb-) *adj.*

o•bi (ō′bē) ▸*n.* A wide sash worn by Japanese women as part of the traditional dress. [J.]

o•bit (ō′bĭt, ō-bĭt′) ▸*n. Informal* An obituary.

o•bi•ter dic•tum (ō′bĭ-tər dĭk′təm) ▸*n., pl.* **obiter dic•ta** (dĭk′tə) **1.** *Law* An incidental, nonbinding opinion voiced by a judge. **2.** An incidental remark or observation. [Lat., something said in passing.]

o•bit•u•ar•y (ō-bĭch′o͞o-ĕr′ē) ▸*n., pl.* **-ies.** A published notice of a death, usu. with a brief biography of the deceased. [Med.Lat. *obituārius*, (report) of death.]

ob•ject (ŏb′jĭkt, -jĕkt′) ▸*n.* **1.** Something perceptible by the senses; a material thing. **2.** A focus of attention or action. **3.** The purpose of a specific action. **4.** *Gram.* A noun that receives or is affected by the action of a verb or that follows and is governed by a preposition. **5.** *Comp. Sci.* A discrete item that can be selected and maneuvered, such as an onscreen graphic. ▸*v.* (əb-jĕkt′) **1.** To present a dissenting or opposing argument. **2.** To feel or express disapproval. [< Lat. *obiectus*, p.part. of *obicere*, to put forward, oppose.] —**ob•jec′tion** *n.* —**ob•jec′tor** *n.*

ob•jec•tion•a•ble (əb-jĕk′shə-nə-bəl) ▸*adj.* Arousing disapproval; offensive. —**ob•jec′tion•a•bil′i•ty** *n.* —**ob•jec′tion•a•bly** *adv.*

ob•jec•tive (əb-jĕk′tĭv) ▸*adj.* **1.** Of or having to do with a material object. **2.** Having actual existence. **3a.** Uninfluenced by emotions or personal prejudices. **b.** Based on observable phenomena. **4.** *Gram.* Of or being the case of a noun or pronoun that serves as the object of a verb. ▸*n.* **1.** Something worked toward or striven for; goal. **2.** *Gram.* The objective case or a noun or pronoun in the objective case. **3.** The lens in an optical instrument that first receives light rays from the object. —**ob•jec′tive•ly** *adv.* —**ob•jec′tive•ness** *n.* —**ob′jec•tiv′i•ty** (ŏb′jĕk-tĭv′ĭ-tē) *n.*

object lesson ▸*n.* A concrete illustration of a moral or principle.

ob•jet d'art (ôb′zhĕ där′) ▸*n., pl.* **ob•jets d'art** (ôb′zhĕ där′). An object of artistic merit. [Fr.]

ob•jur•gate (ŏb′jər-gāt′, ŏb-jûr′gāt′) ▸*v.*

-gat•ed, -gat•ing. To rebuke sharply; berate. [Lat. *obiūrgāre.*] —**ob′jur•ga′tion** *n.*

ob•late (ŏb′lāt′, ŏ-blāt′) ▶*adj.* Flattened at the poles: *an oblate spheroid.* [NLat. *oblātus.*] —**ob′late′ly** *adv.* —**ob′late′ness** *n.*

ob•la•tion (ə-blā′shən, ō-blā′-) ▶*n.* The act of offering something to a deity. [< Lat. *offerre, oblāt-*, to offer.] —**ob•la′tion•al, ob′la•to′ry** (ŏb′lə-tôr′ē, -tōr′ē) *adj.*

ob•li•gate (ŏb′lĭ-gāt′) ▶*v.* **-gat•ed, -gat•ing.** To bind, compel, or constrain by a social, legal, or moral tie. [Lat. *obligāre.*]

ob•li•ga•tion (ŏb′lĭ-gā′shən) ▶*n.* **1.** The act of binding oneself by a social, legal, or moral tie. **2.** A requirement, such as a contract or promise, that compels one to a particular course of action. **3.** The constraining power of a promise, contract, law, or sense of duty. **4.** The fact or condition of being indebted to another for a favor received.

o•blig•a•to•ry (ə-blĭg′ə-tôr′ē, -tōr′ē, ŏb′lĭ-gə-) ▶*adj.* **1.** Morally or legally binding. **2.** Compulsory. —**o•blig′a•to′ri•ly** *adv.*

o•blige (ə-blīj′) ▶*v.* **o•bliged, o•blig•ing 1.** To constrain. **2.** To make indebted or grateful. **3.** To do a service or favor (for). [< Lat. *obligāre.*] —**o•blig′ing** *adj.* —**o•blig′ing•ly** *adv.* —**o•blig′ing•ness** *n.*

Syns: *oblige, accommodate, favor* ***Ant:*** *disoblige* ***v.***

o•blique (ō-blēk′, ə-blēk′) ▶*adj.* **1a.** Slanting or sloping. **b.** *Math.* Neither parallel nor perpendicular. **2.** Indirect or evasive. **3.** *Gram.* Designating any noun case except the nominative or vocative. ▶*n.* Something oblique. ▶*adv.* (ō-blīk′, ə-blīk′). At an angle of 45°. [< Lat. *oblīquus.*] —**o•blique′ly** *adv.* —**o•blique′ness, o•bliq′ui•ty** (ō-blĭk′wĭ-tē, ə-blĭk′-) *n.*

o•blit•er•ate (ə-blĭt′ə-rāt′, ō-blĭt′-) ▶*v.* **-at•ed, -at•ing 1.** To do away with completely. **2.** To wipe out or erase. [Lat. *oblitterāre*, erase.] —**o•blit′er•a′tion** *n.* —**o•blit′er•a′tive** (-ə-rā′tĭv, -ər-ə-tĭv) *adj.*

o•bliv•i•on (ə-blĭv′ē-ən) ▶*n.* **1.** The condition of being completely forgotten. **2.** Forgetfulness. [< Lat. *oblīvīscī*, forget.]

o•bliv•i•ous (ə-blĭv′ē-əs) ▶*adj.* **1.** Lacking all memory; forgetful. **2.** Unaware. —**o•bliv′i•ous•ly** *adv.* —**o•bliv′i•ous•ness** *n.*

Usage: A majority of the Usage Panel accepts the use of both *of* and *to* with *oblivious: The party appeared oblivious to* (or *of*) *the mounting pressures for political reform.*

ob•long (ŏb′lông′, -lŏng′) ▶*adj.* **1a.** Deviating from a square, circular, or spherical form by being elongated in one direction. **b.** Rectangular or elliptical. **2.** *Bot.* Elongated. [< Lat. *oblongus.*] —**ob′long′** *n.*

ob•lo•quy (ŏb′lə-kwē) ▶*n., pl.* **-quies 1.** Abusively detractive language. **2.** Disgrace; ill repute. [< Lat. *obloquī*, speak against.]

ob•nox•ious (ŏb-nŏk′shəs, əb-) ▶*adj.* Very objectionable; odious. [< Lat. *obnoxius*, punishable.] —**ob•nox′ious•ly** *adv.* —**ob•nox′ious•ness** *n.*

o•boe (ō′bō) ▶*n.* A woodwind instrument with a conical bore and a double reed mouthpiece. [< Fr. *hautbois.*] —**o′bo•ist** *n.*

ob•scene (ŏb-sēn′, əb-) ▶*adj.* **1.** Offensive to accepted standards of decency. **2.** Inciting lust; lewd. **3.** Offensive to the senses. **4.** Outrageous: *obscene prices.* [Lat. *obscēnus.*] —**ob•scene′ly** *adv.* —**ob•scen′i•ty** (-sĕn′ĭ-tē) *n.*

ob•scur•ant•ism (ŏb-skyo͝or′ən-tĭz′əm, əb-, ŏb′skyo͝o-răn′-) ▶*n.* **1.** The practice of deliberate abstruseness. **2.** A policy of withholding information from the public. —**ob•scur′ant•ist** *n.*

ob•scure (ŏb-skyo͝or′, əb-) ▶*adj.* **-scur•er, -scur•est 1.** Dim; dark. **2.** Indistinctly heard or perceived. **3.** Out of sight; hidden. **4.** Of undistinguished station or reputation. **5.** Ambiguous or vague; unclear. ▶*v.* **-scured, -scur•ing 1.** To make dim or unclear. See Syns at **block. 2.** To conceal or cover. [< Lat. *obscūrus.*] —**ob•scure′ly** *adv.* —**ob•scure′ness, ob•scu′ri•ty** *n.*

ob•se•qui•ous (ŏb-sē′kwē-əs, əb-) ▶*adj.* Full of or exhibiting servile compliance. [< Lat. *obsequī*, comply.] —**ob•se′qui•ous•ly** *adv.* —**ob•se′qui•ous•ness** *n.*

ob•se•quy (ŏb′sĭ-kwē) ▶*n., pl.* **-quies.** A funeral rite or ceremony. [< Lat. *obsequium*, compliance.]

ob•ser•vance (əb-zûr′vəns) ▶*n.* **1.** The act or practice of complying with a law, custom, command, or rule. **2.** The custom of celebrating a holiday or other ritual occasion. **3.** A customary rite or ceremony.

ob•ser•vant (əb-zûr′vənt) ▶*adj.* **1.** Quick to perceive or apprehend; alert. See Syns at **careful. 2.** Diligent in observing a law, custom, or principle. —**ob•ser′vant•ly** *adv.*

ob•ser•va•tion (ŏb′zər-vā′shən) ▶*n.* **1.** The act of observing or the fact of being observed. **2.** The act of noting and recording something with instruments. **3.** A comment or remark. See Syns at **comment.** —**ob′ser•va′tion•al** *adj.* —**ob′ser•va′tion•al•ly** *adv.*

ob•ser•va•to•ry (əb-zûr′və-tôr′ē, -tōr′ē) ▶*n., pl.* **-ries.** A place designed for making observations of astronomical, meteorological, or other natural phenomena.

ob•serve (əb-zûrv′) ▶*v.* **-served, -serv•ing 1.** To be or become aware of, esp. through careful attention; notice. **2.** To watch attentively. **3.** To make a systematic or scientific observation of. **4.** To say casually; remark. **5.** To adhere to or abide by. **6.** To keep or celebrate (e.g., a holiday). [< Lat. *observāre*, abide by.] —**ob•serv′a•ble** *adj.* —**ob•serv′a•bly** *adv.* —**ob•serv′er** *n.*

ob•sess (əb-sĕs′, ŏb-) ▶*v.* To preoccupy the mind of excessively. [Lat. *obsidēre, obsess-* : *ob-*, on + *sedēre*, sit.]

ob•ses•sion (əb-sĕsh′ən, ŏb-) ▶*n.* **1.** Compulsive preoccupation with a fixed idea or unwanted emotion. **2.** A compulsive, often unreasonable idea or emotion. —**ob•ses′sion•al** *adj.* —**ob•ses′sive** *adj.* —**ob•ses′sive•ly** *adv.* —**ob•ses′sive•ness** *n.*

ob•sid•i•an (ŏb-sĭd′ē-ən) ▶*n.* A hard, usu. black or banded volcanic glass formed in rapid cooling of lava. [Lat. *obsidiānus.*]

ob•so•les•cent (ŏb′sə-lĕs′ənt) ▶*adj.* Becoming obsolete. [< Lat. *obsolēscere*, go out of use.] —**ob′so•les′cence** *n.* —**ob′so•les′cent•ly** *adv.*

ob•so•lete (ŏb′sə-lēt′, ŏb′sə-lēt′) ▶*adj.* **1.** No longer in use or in effect. **2.** Outmoded in style or construction. [Lat. *obsolētus*, p.part. of *obsolēscere*, fall into disuse.] —**ob′so•lete′ly** *adv.* —**ob′so•lete′ness** *n.* —**ob′so•let′ism** *n.*

ob•sta•cle (ŏb′stə-kəl) ▶*n.* One that opposes,

stands in the way of, or holds up progress. [< Lat. *obstāculum* < *obstāre*, impede : *ob-*, against + *stāre*, stand.]

ob•ste•tri•cian (ŏb′stĭ-trĭsh′ən) ►*n.* A physician who specializes in obstetrics.

ob•stet•rics (ŏb-stĕt′rĭks, əb-) ►*n. (takes sing. or pl. v.)* The branch of medicine that deals with the care of women during and after pregnancy and childbirth. [< Lat. *obstetrīx*, midwife : *ob-*, opposite + *stāre*, stand.] —**ob•stet′ric, ob•stet′ri•cal** *adj.*

ob•sti•nate (ŏb′stə-nĭt) ►*adj.* **1.** Stubbornly adhering to an attitude or course of action. **2.** Difficult to manage, control, or subdue. [< Lat. *obstināre*, persist.] —**ob′sti•na•cy** (-nə-sē) *n.* —**ob′sti•nate•ly** *adv.*

ob•strep•er•ous (ŏb-strĕp′ər-əs, əb-) ►*adj.* Noisily and stubbornly defiant. [< Lat. *obstrepere*, make a noise against.] —**ob•strep′er•ous•ly** *adv.* —**ob•strep′er•ous•ness** *n.*

ob•struct (əb-strŭkt′, ŏb-) ►*v.* **1.** To block (a passage) with obstacles. See Syns at **block. 2.** To impede; retard. **3.** To get in the way of; hide from sight. [Lat. *obstruere, obstrūct-*, pile up against.] —**ob•struct′er, ob•struc′tor** *n.* —**ob•struc′tive** *adj.* —**ob•struc′tive•ly** *adv.* —**ob•struc′tive•ness** *n.*

ob•struc•tion (əb-strŭk′shən, ŏb-) ►*n.* **1.** An obstacle. **2.** The act or an instance of obstructing. **3.** The causing of a delay.

ob•struc•tion•ist (əb-strŭk′shə-nĭst, ŏb-) ►*n.* One who systematically blocks or delays a process. —**ob•struc′tion•ism** *n.* —**ob•struc′tion•is′tic** *adj.*

ob•tain (əb-tān′, ŏb-) ►*v.* **1.** To succeed in gaining possession of; acquire. **2.** To be accepted or customary. [< Lat. *obtinēre*.] —**ob•tain′a•ble** *adj.* —**ob•tain′er** *n.*

ob•trude (ŏb-tro͞od′, əb-) ►*v.* **-trud•ed, -trud•ing 1.** To impose (oneself or one's ideas) on others. **2.** To thrust out; push forward. [Lat. *obtrūdere*.] —**ob•trud′er** *n.* —**ob•tru′sion** (-tro͞o′zhən) *n.* —**ob•tru′sive** (-tro͞o′sĭv, -zĭv) *adj.* —**ob•tru′sive•ly** *adv.*

ob•tuse (ŏb-to͞os′, -tyo͞os′, əb-) ►*adj.* **-tus•er, -tus•est 1.** Lacking quickness of perception or intellect. **2.** Not sharp, pointed, or acute in form; blunt. [< Lat. *obtūsus*, p.part. of *obtundere*, to blunt.] —**ob•tuse′ly** *adv.* —**ob•tuse′ness** *n.*

obtuse angle ►*n.* An angle greater than 90° and less than 180°.

ob•verse (ŏb-vûrs′, əb-, ŏb′vûrs′) ►*adj.* **1.** Facing the observer. **2.** Serving as a counterpart or complement. ►*n.* (ŏb′vûrs′, ŏb-vûrs′, əb-) **1.** The side of a coin or medal that bears the principal stamp or design. **2.** A counterpart or complement. [Lat. *obversus*, p.part. of *obvertere*, turn toward.] —**ob•verse′ly** *adv.*

ob•vi•ate (ŏb′vē-āt′) ►*v.* **-at•ed, -at•ing.** To prevent or render unnecessary by anticipatory measures. [Lat. *obviāre*, hinder.] —**ob′vi•a′tion** *n.* —**ob′vi•a′tor** *n.*

ob•vi•ous (ŏb′vē-əs) ►*adj.* Easily perceived or understood; apparent. See Syns at **apparent.** [< Lat. *obviam*, in the way.] —**ob′vi•ous•ly** *adv.* —**ob′vi•ous•ness** *n.*

oc•a•ri•na (ŏk′ə-rē′nə) ►*n.* A small bulb-shaped wind instrument with finger holes and a mouthpiece. [< Ital. *oca*, goose.]

OCAS ►*abbr.* Organization of Central American States

O'Ca•sey (ō-kā′sē), **Sean.** 1880–1964. Irish playwright.

oc•ca•sion (ə-kā′zhən) ►*n.* **1.** An event or happening, esp. a significant event. **2.** The time at which an event occurs. **3.** A favorable time; opportunity. **4.** Something that brings on an action. **5.** A reason; ground. **6.** An important social gathering. ►*v.* To provide occasion for. —***idiom:* on occasion** From time to time. [< Lat. *occidere*, fall down.]

oc•ca•sion•al (ə-kā′zhə-nəl) ►*adj.* **1.** Occurring from time to time. **2.** Created for a special occasion. —**oc•ca′sion•al•ly** *adv.*

oc•ci•dent (ŏk′sĭ-dənt, -dĕnt′) ►*n.* **1.** The west. **2. Occident** Europe and the Western Hemisphere. [< Lat. *occidere*, to set.] —**oc′ci•den′tal, Oc′ci•den′tal** *adj. & n.*

oc•cip•i•tal (ŏk-sĭp′ĭ-tl) ►*adj.* Of the occiput or the occipital bone. ►*n.* The occipital bone.

occipital bone ►*n.* A cranial bone that forms the lower posterior part of the skull.

oc•ci•put (ŏk′sə-pŭt′, -pət) ►*n., pl.* **oc•cip•i•ta** (ŏk-sĭp′ĭ-tə) or **-puts.** The back part of the head or skull. [< Lat.]

oc•clude (ə-klo͞od′) ►*v.* **-clud•ed, -clud•ing 1.** To close or shut off; obstruct. **2.** *Chem.* To absorb or adsorb and retain (a substance). **3.** To close so that the opposing tooth surfaces fit together. [Lat. *occlūdere*.] —**oc•clu′sion** *n.*

oc•cult (ə-kŭlt′, ŏk′ŭlt′) ►*adj.* **1.** Of or relating to supernatural influences, agencies, or phenomena. **2.** Beyond human comprehension. **3.** Available only to the initiate; secret. [< Lat. *occulere*, conceal.] —**oc•cult′** *n.* —**oc•cult′ly** *adv.* —**oc•cult′ness** *n.*

oc•cult•ism (ə-kŭl′tĭz′əm, ŏk′ŭl-) ►*n.* **1.** The study of the supernatural. **2.** A belief in supernatural powers. —**oc•cult′ist** *n.*

oc•cu•pan•cy (ŏk′yə-pən-sē) ►*n., pl.* **-cies 1.** The act of occupying or the condition of being occupied. **2.** The period during which one occupies a place or position. —**oc′cu•pant** *n.*

oc•cu•pa•tion (ŏk′yə-pā′shən) ►*n.* **1.** An activity that serves as one's regular source of livelihood. **2.** The act or process of holding a place. **3.** Invasion, conquest, and control of a nation or territory by foreign armed forces. —**oc′cu•pa′tion•al** *adj.*

occupational therapy ►*n.* The use of productive or creative activity in the treatment of disabled people. —**occupational therapist** *n.*

oc•cu•py (ŏk′yə-pī′) ►*v.* **-pied, -py•ing 1.** To fill up (time or space). **2.** To dwell or reside in. **3.** To hold or fill (an office or position). **4.** To seize possession of and maintain control over by or as if by conquest. **5.** To engage or busy (oneself). [< Lat. *occupāre*, seize.] —**oc′cu•pi′er** *n.*

oc•cur (ə-kûr′) ►*v.* **-curred, -cur•ring 1.** To take place. See Syns at **happen. 2.** To be found to exist or appear. **3.** To come to mind. [Lat. *occurrere*, run toward.] —**oc•cur′rence** *n.*

o•cean (ō′shən) ►*n.* **1.** The entire body of salt water that covers more than 70 percent of the earth's surface. **2.** often **Ocean** Any of the principal divisions of the ocean: *the Indian Ocean.* **3.** A great expanse or amount. [< Gk. *Ōkeanos*, a great river encircling the earth.] —**o′ce•an′ic** (ō′shē-ăn′ĭk) *adj.*

o•cean•ar•i•um (ō′shə-nâr′ē-əm) ►*n., pl.* **-i•ums** or **-i•a** (-ē-ə). A large aquarium for the study or display of marine life.

O•ce•an•i•a (ō′shē-ăn′ē-ə, -ā′nē-ə, -ä′nē-ə) The islands of the S, W, and central Pacific, including Melanesia, Micronesia, Polynesia, and sometimes Australia, New Zealand, and the Malay Archipelago. —**O′ce•an′i•an** *adj. & n.*

o•cean•og•ra•phy (ō′shə-nŏg′rə-fē) ▸*n.* The exploration and scientific study of the ocean. —**o′cean•og′ra•pher** *n.* —**o′cean•o•graph′ic** (-nə-grăf′ĭk) *adj.*

O•cean•side (ō′shən-sīd′) A city of S CA NNW of San Diego. Pop. 128,398.

oc•e•lot (ŏs′ə-lŏt′, ō′sə-) ▸*n.* A spotted wildcat of the SW US and Central and South America. [< Nahuatl *ocelotl.*]

o•cher or **o•chre** (ō′kər) ▸*n.* **1.** Any of several earthy mineral oxides of iron occurring in yellow, brown, or red and used as pigments. **2.** A moderate orange yellow. [< Gk. *ōkhros*, pale yellow.] —**o′cher•ous, o′cher•y** (ō′krē) *adj.*

o′clock (ə-klŏk′) ▸*adv.* Of or according to the clock: *three o'clock.* [< *of the clock.*]

O′Con•nor (ō-kŏn′ər), **Flannery.** 1925–64. Amer. writer.

O′Connor, Sandra Day. b. 1930. Amer. jurist; first woman associate justice of the US Supreme Court (appointed 1981).

OCR ▸*abbr.* **1.** optical character reader **2.** optical character recognition

OCS ▸*abbr.* Officer Candidate School

Oct. ▸*abbr.* October

oc•ta•gon (ŏk′tə-gŏn′) ▸*n.* A polygon with 8 sides. —**oc•tag′o•nal** (ŏk-tăg′ə-nəl) *adj.*

oc•ta•he•dron (ŏk′tə-hē′drən) ▸*n., pl.* **-drons** or **-dra** (-drə). A polyhedron with 8 surfaces.

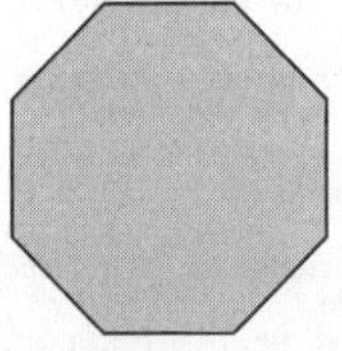

octagon octahedron

oc•tal (ŏk′təl) ▸*adj.* Of or based on the number 8.

oc•tane (ŏk′tān′) ▸*n.* **1.** Any of various hydrocarbons with the formula C_8H_{18}. **2.** An octane number.

octane number ▸*n.* A numerical representation of the antiknock properties of motor fuel compared with a standard reference fuel with a rating of 100.

oc•tant (ŏk′tənt) ▸*n.* One eighth of a circle. [Lat. *octāns.*] —**oc•tan′tal** (ŏk-tăn′təl) *adj.*

oc•tave (ŏk′tĭv, -tāv′) ▸*n.* **1.** *Mus.* The interval of eight diatonic degrees between two tones of the same name. **2.** A group or series of eight. [< Lat. *octāvus*, eighth.]

Oc•ta•vi•an (ŏk-tā′vē-ən). See **Augustus.**

oc•ta•vo (ŏk-tā′vō, -tä′-) ▸*n., pl.* **-vos** *Print.* **1.** The page size, from 5 by 8 inches to 6 by 9½ inches, of a book composed of printer's sheets folded into eight leaves. **2.** A book composed of octavo pages. [< Lat. *octāvus*, eighth.]

oc•tet (ŏk-tĕt′) ▸*n.* **1.** *Mus.* A composition written for eight voices or eight instruments. **2.** A group of eight. [Ital. *ottetto.*]

oc•til•lion (ŏk-tĭl′yən) ▸*n.* **1.** The cardinal number equal to 10^{27}. **2.** *Chiefly Brit.* The cardinal number equal to 10^{48}. [OCT(O)– + (M)ILLION.] —**oc•til′lion** *adj.* —**oc•til′lionth** *n. & adj.*

octo– or **octa–** or **oct–** ▸*pref.* Eight: *octagon.* [< Gk. *oktō* and Lat. *octō-*, eight.]

Oc•to•ber (ŏk-tō′bər) ▸*n.* The 10th month of the Gregorian calendar. See table at **calendar.** [< Lat. *Octōber*, eighth month.]

oc•to•ge•nar•i•an (ŏk′tə-jə-nâr′ē-ən) ▸*n.* A person between 80 and 90 years of age. [< Lat. *octōgēnārius*, containing eighty.]

oc•to•pus (ŏk′tə-pəs) ▸*n., pl.* **-pus•es** or **-pi** (-pī′). A marine mollusk with a soft rounded body and eight sucker-bearing tentacles. [< Gk. *oktōpous*, eight-footed : *oktō*, eight + *pous*, foot.]

oc•tu•plet (ŏk-tŭp′lĭt, -to͞o′plĭt, -tyo͞o′-) ▸*n.* One of eight offspring born in a single birth. [*octu(ple)*, multiply by eight + (TRI)PLET.]

oc•u•lar (ŏk′yə-lər) ▸*adj.* **1.** Of or relating to the eye. **2.** Visual. ▸*n.* The eyepiece of an optical instrument. [< Lat. *oculus*, eye.]

oc•u•list (ŏk′yə-lĭst) ▸*n.* **1.** An ophthalmologist. **2.** An optometrist. [< Lat. *oculus*, eye.]

OD[1] (ō′dē′) *Slang* ▸*n.* **1.** An overdose of a drug. **2.** One who has taken an overdose. ▸*v.* **OD′ed, OD′•ing.** To overdose.

OD[2] ▸*abbr.* **1.** Doctor of Optometry **2.** also **o/d** overdraft **3.** overdrawn

odd (ŏd) ▸*adj.* **-er, -est 1.** Strange or peculiar. **2.** In excess of a given number: *invited 30-odd guests.* **3.** Being one of an incomplete pair or set. **4.** *Math.* Designating an integer not divisible by 2. [< ON *oddi*, odd number.] —**odd′ly** *adv.* —**odd′ness** *n.*

odd•ball (ŏd′bôl′) ▸*n.* *Informal* An eccentric person.

odd•i•ty (ŏd′ĭ-tē) ▸*n., pl.* **-ties 1.** One that is odd. **2.** The state of being odd.

odd job ▸*n.* A usu. temporary unskilled or menial job.

odd•ment (ŏd′mənt) ▸*n.* Something left over.

odds (ŏdz) ▸*pl.n.* **1.** An advantage given to a weaker side in a contest to equalize the chances of all participants. **2.** A ratio expressing the probability of an outcome. **3.** Chances: *The odds are that it will rain.* —***idiom:*** **at odds** In disagreement.

odds and ends ▸*pl.n.* Miscellaneous items.

odds-on (ŏdz′ŏn′, -ôn′) ▸*adj.* *Informal* More likely than others to win.

ode (ōd) ▸*n.* A lyric poem, often in the form of an address and having an elevated style and formal structure. [< Gk. *aoidē*, song.]

–ode ▸*suff.* **1.** Way; path: *electrode.* **2.** Electrode: *diode.* [< Gk. *hodos.*]

O•den•se (ōd′n-sə, o͞od′-) A city of S Denmark near the **Odense Fjord,** an arm of the Kattegat. Pop. 180,799.

O•der (ō′dər) A river of central Europe flowing about 904 km (562 mi) from NE Czech Republic through Poland and Germany to the Baltic Sea.

O•des•sa (ō-dĕs′ə) A city of S Ukraine on **Odessa Bay,** an arm of the Black Sea. Pop. 1,095,800.

O•dets (ō-dĕts′), **Clifford.** 1906–63. Amer. playwright.

O•din (ō′dĭn) ▸*n.* *Myth.* The Norse god of wisdom, war, art, culture, and the dead.

o•di•ous (ō′dē-əs) ►*adj.* Arousing strong dislike or intense displeasure. —**o′di•ous•ly** *adv.* —**o′di•ous•ness** *n.*

o•di•um (ō′dē-əm) ►*n.* **1.** The state or quality of being odious. **2.** Disgrace resulting from hateful conduct. [Lat., hatred.]

o•dom•e•ter (ō-dŏm′ĭ-tər) ►*n.* An instrument that indicates distance traveled by a vehicle. [Fr. *odomètre*.]

o•don•tol•o•gy (ō′dŏn-tŏl′ə-jē) ►*n.* The study of the structure and abnormalities of the teeth. [Gk. *odous*, *odont-*, tooth + -LOGY.] —**o•don′to•log′i•cal** (-tə-lŏj′ĭ-kəl) *adj.* —**o′don•tol′o•gist** *n.*

o•dor (ō′dər) ►*n.* **1.** The property or quality of a thing perceived by the sense of smell. See Syns at **smell. 2.** Esteem; repute. [< Lat.] —**o′dor•less** *adj.* —**o′dor•less•ly** *adv.* —**o′dor•ous** *adj.* —**o′dor•ous•ly** *adv.* —**o′dor•ous•ness** *n.*

o•dor•if•er•ous (ō′də-rĭf′ər-əs) ►*adj.* Having or giving off an odor. —**o′dor•if′er•ous•ly** *adv.* —**o′dor•if′er•ous•ness** *n.*

O•dys•seus (ō-dĭs′yo͞os′, ō-dĭs′ē-əs) ►*n. Gk. Myth.* The hero of Homer's *Odyssey.*

od•ys•sey (ŏd′ĭ-sē) ►*n., pl.* **-seys.** A long adventurous voyage. [< ODYSSEUS.]

Oed•i•pus (ĕd′ə-pəs, ē′də-) ►*n. Gk. Myth.* A Theban prince who unwittingly killed his father and then married his mother.

Oedipus complex ►*n. Psychiat.* A subconscious sexual desire in a child, esp. a male child, for the parent of the opposite sex. —**oed′i•pal** *adj.*

oe•nol•o•gy (ē-nŏl′ə-jē) ►*n.* **enology.**

o′er (ôr, ōr) ►*prep. & adv.* Over.

oeu•vre (œ′vrə) ►*n., pl.* **oeu•vres** (œ′vrə) **1.** A work of art. **2.** The lifework of an artist. [Fr. < Lat. *opera*, works.]

of (ŭv, ŏv; əv *when unstressed*) ►*prep.* **1.** Derived or coming from. **2.** Owing to: *died of cholera.* **3.** Away from. **4.** So as to be separated from: *robbed of one's dignity.* **5.** From the total or group comprising. **6.** Composed or made from. **7.** Associated with. **8.** Belonging or connected to. **9.** Possessing: *a person of honor.* **10.** Containing or carrying. **11.** Specified as: *a depth of ten feet; the Garden of Eden.* **12.** Centering on; directed toward. **13.** Produced by. **14.** Characterized or identified by. **15.** With reference to; about. **16.** Set aside for: *a day of rest.* **17.** Before: *five minutes of two.* **18.** During or on: *of recent years.* [< OE.]

Usage: The so-called double genitive construction, as in *a friend of my father's* or *a book of mine,* is well supported by literary precedent, and serves a useful purpose.

off (ôf, ŏf) ►*adv.* **1.** From a place or position. **2.** At a certain distance in space or time. **3.** So as to be no longer operating or functioning. **4.** So as to be smaller, fewer, or less. **5.** So as to be away from work or duty. ►*adj.* **1.** Remote. **2.** Not on, attached, or connected. **3.** Not operating or operational. **4.** No longer taking place; canceled. **5.** Inferior. **6.** Incorrect. **7.** Going. **8.** Absent or away from work or duty: *He's off every Tuesday.* ►*prep.* **1.** So as to be removed or distant from. **2.** Away or relieved from: *off duty.* **3a.** By consuming: *living off honey.* **b.** With the means provided by: *living off my pension.* **4.** Extending or branching out from. **5.** Not up to the usual standard of: *off her game.* **6.** So as to abstain from. **7.** To seaward of: *a mile off Sandy Hook.* ►*v. Slang* To murder. —***idiom:*** **off and on** Intermittently. [< OE *of.*]

Usage: In Modern English the compound preposition *off of* is generally regarded as informal and is best avoided in formal speech and writing: *He stepped off* (not *off of*) *the platform.*

of•fal (ô′fəl, ŏf′əl) ►*n.* **1.** Waste parts, esp. of a butchered animal. **2.** Rubbish. [ME.]

off•beat (ôf′bēt′, ŏf′-) ►*n. Mus.* An unaccented beat in a measure. ►*adj.* (ôf′bēt′, ŏf′-) *Slang* Unconventional.

off chance ►*n.* A remote or slight chance: *made other plans on the off chance it would rain.*

off-col•or (ôf′kŭl′ər, ŏf′-) ►*adj.* **1.** Risqué: *an off-color joke.* **2.** Varying from the expected or required color.

Of•fen•bach (ô′fən-bäk′, ŏf′ən-), **Jacques.** 1819–80. French composer.

of•fend (ə-fĕnd′) ►*v.* **1.** To cause anger, resentment, or wounded feelings in. **2.** To be displeasing or disagreeable to. **3.** To violate; transgres. [< Lat. *offendere.*] —**of•fend′er** *n.*

of•fense (ə-fĕns′) ►*n.* **1.** The act of offending. **2.** A violation of a moral or social code. **3.** A crime. **4.** (ŏf′ĕns′). The act of attacking or assaulting. **5.** (ŏf′ĕns′) *Sports* A team in possession of the ball or puck. [< Lat. *offendere, offēns-*, offend.]

of•fen•sive (ə-fĕn′sĭv) ►*adj.* **1.** Disagreeable to the senses. **2.** Causing anger, resentment, or affront. **3.** Making an attack. **4.** (ŏf′ĕn-) *Sports* Relating to the offense. —**of•fen′sive•ly** *adv.* —**of•fen′sive•ness** *n.*

Syns: *offensive, disgusting, loathsome, nasty, repellent, repulsive, revolting* **adj.**

of•fer (ô′fər, ŏf′ər) ►*v.* **1.** To present for acceptance or rejection. **2.** To present for sale. **3.** To present as payment; bid. **4.** To present as an act of worship. **5.** To put up; mount. **6.** To produce or introduce on the stage. [< Lat. *offerre* : *ob-*, to + *ferre*, bring.] —**of′fer** *n.* —**of′fer•er, of′fer•or** *n.*

of•fer•ing (ô′fər-ĭng, ŏf′ər-) ►*n.* **1.** The act of making an offer. **2.** Something offered. **3.** A presentation made to a deity as an act of worship.

of•fer•to•ry (ô′fər-tôr′ē, -tōr′ē, ŏf′ər-) ►*n., pl.* **-ries 1.** often **Offertory** The part of the Eucharist at which bread and wine are offered to God. **2.** A collection of offerings at a religious service. [< Lat. *offerre*, OFFER.]

off-guard (ôf′gärd′, ŏf′-) ►*adj.* Off one's guard; unprepared.

off•hand (ôf′hănd′, ŏf′-) ►*adv. & adj.* Without preparation or forethought. —**off′hand′ed•ly** *adv.* —**off′hand′ed•ness** *n.*

of•fice (ô′fĭs, ŏf′ĭs) ►*n.* **1a.** A place in which business, clerical, or professional activities are conducted. **b.** The staff working in such a place. **2.** A duty or function assigned to or assumed by someone. See Syns at **function. 3.** A position of authority given to a person, as in a government or corporation. **4.** A subdivision of a governmental department. **5.** A public position: *seek office.* **6.** often **offices** A favor or beneficial act. **7.** *Eccles.* A service, esp. liturgical prayer. [< Lat. *officium*, duty.]

of•fice•hold•er (ô′fĭs-hōl′dər, ŏf′ĭs-) ► *n.* One who holds public office.

of•fi•cer (ô′fĭ-sər, ŏf′ĭ-) ► *n.* **1.** One who holds an office of authority or trust in an organization. **2.** One who holds a commission in the armed forces. **3.** A person licensed in the merchant marine as master, mate, chief engineer, or assistant engineer. **4.** A police officer.

of•fi•cial (ə-fĭsh′əl) ► *adj.* **1.** Of or relating to an office of authority. **2.** Authorized by a proper authority. **3.** Holding office in a public capacity. **4.** Formal: *an official banquet.* ► *n.* **1.** One who holds an office or a position. **2.** *Sports* A referee or umpire. —**of•fi′cial•dom** *n.* —**of•fi′cial•ly** *adv.*

of•fi•cial•ism (ə-fĭsh′ə-lĭz′əm) ► *n.* Rigid adherence to official forms and procedures.

of•fi•ci•ate (ə-fĭsh′ē-āt′) ► *v.* **-at•ed, -at•ing** **1.** To perform the functions of an office or position of authority, esp. at a religious service. **2.** *Sports* To serve as a referee or umpire. —**of•fi′ci•a′tor** *n.*

of•fi•cious (ə-fĭsh′əs) ► *adj.* Overly eager in offering unwanted services or advice. [Lat. *officiōsus*, obliging, dutiful.] —**of•fi′cious•ly** *adv.* —**of•fi′cious•ness** *n.*

off•ing (ô′fĭng, ŏf′ĭng) ► *n.* The near future: *new developments in the offing.*

off•ish (ô′fĭsh, ŏf′ĭsh) ► *adj.* Distant; aloof. —**off′ish•ly** *adv.* —**off′ish•ness** *n.*

off-key (ôf′-kē′, ŏf′-) ► *adj.* **1.** *Mus.* Out of tune; sharp or flat. **2.** Inappropriate; improper. —**off′key′** *adv.*

off-lim•its (ôf-lĭm′ĭts, ŏf-) ► *adj.* Forbidden to a designated group.

off•line or **off-line** (ôf′līn′, ŏf′-) ► *adj.* Not connected to or controlled by a computer.

off•load or **off-load** (ôf′lōd′, ŏf′-) ► *v.* **1.** To unload (e.g., a vehicle). **2.** *Comp. Sci.* To transfer (data) to a peripheral device.

off•print (ôf′prĭnt′, ŏf′-) ► *n.* A reproduction of an article from a publication. —**off′print′** *v.*

off-road (ôf′rōd′, ŏf′-) ► *adj.* Taking place or designed for use off public roads. —**off′-road′** *adv.*

off-sea•son (ôf′-sē′zən, ŏf′-) ► *n.* A part of the year marked by a cessation or lessening of activity. —**off′-sea′son** *adv. & adj.*

off•set (ôf′sĕt′, ŏf′-) ► *n.* **1.** One that balances, counteracts, or compensates. **2.** *Archit.* A ledge or recess in a wall. **3.** A bend made in a pipe or bar to allow it to pass around an obstruction. **4.** Printing by indirect image transfer. ► *v.* (ôf′sĕt′, ŏf′-, ôf-sĕt′, ŏf-) **-set, -set•ting** **1.** To counterbalance or compensate for. **2.** To produce by offset printing. **3.** To make or form an offset in (a wall, bar, or pipe). —**off′set′** *adv. & adj.*

off•shoot (ôf′shōōt′, ŏf′-) ► *n.* Something that branches out or derives its origin from a particular source, as a shoot from a plant stem. See Syns at **branch.**

off•shore (ôf′shôr′, -shōr′, ŏf′-) ► *adj.* **1.** Away from the shore. **2.** At a distance from the shore. —**off′shore′** *adv.*

off•side (ôf′sīd′, ŏf′-) also **off•sides** (-sīdz′) ► *adv. & adj. Sports* Illegally ahead of the ball or puck.

off•spring (ôf′sprĭng′, ŏf′-) ► *n., pl.* **-spring** **1.** Progeny; young. **2.** A result; product. [< OE *ofspring.*]

off•stage (ôf′stāj′, ŏf′-) ► *adj. & adv.* Away from the area of a stage visible to the audience.

off-the-cuff (ôf′*th*ə-kŭf′, ŏf′-) ► *adv. & adj.* Without preparation; impromptu.

off-the-rec•ord (ôf′*th*ə-rĕk′ərd, ŏf′-) ► *adv. & adj.* Not for publication or attribution.

off-the-wall (ôf′*th*ə-wôl′, ŏf′-) ► *adj. Informal* Very unconventional or unusual.

off-track betting (ôf′trăk′, ŏf′-) ► *n.* A system of placing bets away from a racetrack.

off-white (ôf′hwīt′, -wīt′, ŏf′-) ► *n.* A grayish or yellowish white. —**off′-white′** *adj.*

off year ► *n.* **1.** A year in which no major political elections occur. **2.** A year of reduced activity or production.

oft (ôft, ŏft) ► *adv.* Often. [< OE.]

of•ten (ô′fən, ŏf′ən, ôf′tən, ŏf′-) ► *adv.* Many times; frequently. [< OE *oft.*]

of•ten•times (ô′fən-tīmz′, ôf′tən-, ŏf′ən-, ŏf′tən-) also **oft•times** (ôf′tīmz′, ŏf′-) ► *adv.* Often.

Og•bo•mo•sho (ŏg′bə-mō′shō) A city of SW Nigeria NNE of Ibadan. Pop. 514,400.

O•gla•la (ō-glä′lə) ► *n., pl.* **-la** or **-las.** A member of a Teton Sioux people inhabiting SW South Dakota.

o•gle (ō′gəl, ô′gəl) ► *v.* **o•gled, o•gling.** To stare at, esp. impertinently or flirtatiously. [Poss. < LGer. *oegeln.*] —**o′gler** *n.*

O•gle•thorpe (ō′gəl-thôrp′), **James Edward.** 1696–1785. English philanthropist and colonizer.

o•gre (ō′gər) ► *n.* **1.** A fabled giant that eats humans. **2.** A brutish or cruel person. [Fr.] —**o′gre•ish** (ō′gər-ĭsh, ō′grĭsh) *adj.*

o•gress (ō′grĭs) ► *n.* **1.** A female ogre. **2.** A brutish or cruel woman.

oh (ō) ► *interj.* **1.** Used to express strong emotion, such as surprise, fear, anger, or pain. **2.** Used to indicate understanding.

OH ► *abbr.* Ohio

O. Henry. See William Sydney **Porter.**

O•hi•o (ō-hī′ō) A state of the N-central US. Cap. Columbus. Pop. 10,887,325. —**O•hi′o•an** *adj. & n.*

Ohio River. A river formed by the confluence of the Allegheny and Monongahela rivers in W Pennsylvania and flowing about 1,578 km (981 mi) to the Mississippi R. in S IL.

ohm (ōm) ► *n.* A unit of electrical resistance equal to that of a conductor in which a current of one ampere is produced by a potential of one volt across its terminals. [After Georg S. *Ohm* (1787–1854), German physicist.] —**ohm′ic** *adj.*

ohm•me•ter (ōm′mē′tər) ► *n.* An instrument for measurement in ohms of the resistance of a conductor.

-oid ► *suff.* Resembling; having the appearance of: *humanoid.* [< Gk. *eidos*, shape.]

oil (oil) ► *n.* **1.** Any of numerous mineral, vegetable, and synthetic substances and animal and vegetable fats that are gen. slippery, combustible, viscous, liquid or liquefiable at room temperatures, soluble in various organic solvents such as ether but not in water, and used in a great variety of products, esp. lubricants and fuels. **2.** Petroleum. **3.** A substance with an oily consistency. **4.** Oil paint. **5.** An oil painting. ► *v.* To lubricate, supply, or cover with oil. [< Gk. *elaion*, olive oil.] —**oil′er** *n.*

oil•cloth (oil′klôth′, -klŏth′) ► *n.* Fabric treated with clay and oil to make it waterproof.

oil color ▸ *n.* See **oil paint.**
oil field ▸ *n.* An area with reserves of recoverable petroleum.
oil paint ▸ *n.* A paint in which the vehicle is a drying oil.
oil painting ▸ *n.* **1.** A painting done in oil paints. **2.** The art of painting with oils.
oil shale ▸ *n.* A black or dark brown shale containing hydrocarbons that yield petroleum by distillation.
oil•skin (oil′skĭn′) ▸ *n.* **1.** Cloth treated with oil to make it waterproof. **2.** A garment made of oilskin.
oil slick ▸ *n.* A layer of oil on water.
oil well ▸ *n.* A hole drilled or dug in the earth from which petroleum flows or is pumped.
oil•y (oi′lē) ▸ *adj.* **-i•er, -i•est 1.** Of or relating to oil. **2.** Impregnated with oil; greasy. **3.** Unctuous. See Syns at **unctuous.** —**oil′i•ly** *adv.* —**oil′i•ness** *n.*
oink (oingk) ▸ *n.* The characteristic grunting noise of a hog. [Imit.] —**oink** *v.*
oint•ment (oint′mənt) ▸ *n.* A highly viscous or semisolid substance used on the skin as a cosmetic or salve. [< Lat. *unguentum.*]
Oise (wäz) A river rising in S Belgium and flowing about 299 km (186 mi) to the Seine R. in N France.
O•jib•wa (ō-jĭb′wā′, -wə) also **O•jib•way** (-wā′) ▸ *n., pl.* **-wa** or **-was** also **-way** or **-ways 1.** A member of a Native American people inhabiting a region of the US and Canada around Lake Superior. **2.** The Algonquian language of the Ojibwa.
OK[1] or **o•kay** (ō-kā′) *Informal* ▸ *n.* Approval; agreement. ▸ *v.* **OK′ed** or **OK′d** or **o•kayed, OK′•ing** or **o•kay•ing.** To approve of or agree to; authorize. ▸ *interj.* Used to express approval or agreement. [Abbr. of *oll korrect,* slang respelling of *all correct.*] —**OK** *adv. & adj.*
OK[2] ▸ *abbr.* Oklahoma
O•ka (ō-kä′) A river, about 1,488 km (925 mi), of W Russia flowing to the Volga R. near Gorky.
O•ka•van•go (ō′kə-văng′gō) A river of SW-central Africa flowing about 1,609 km (1,000 mi) from central Angola to N Botswana.
O•ka•ya•ma (ō′kä-yä′mä) A city of W Honshu, Japan, on an inlet of the Inland Sea. Pop. 604,513.
O•kee•cho•bee (ō′kĭ-chō′bē), **Lake.** A lake of SE FL N of the Everglades.
O'Keeffe (ō-kēf′), **Georgia.** 1887–1986. Amer. painter.
O•ke•fe•no•kee Swamp (ō′kə-fə-nō′kē, -kē-) A large swampy area of SE GA and NE FL.
O•khotsk (ō-kŏtsk′), **Sea of.** An arm of the NW Pacific W of the Kamchatka Peninsula and Kuril Is.
O•ki•na•wa (ō′kĭ-nä′wə, -nou′-) An island and island group of the central Ryukyu Is. in the W Pacific SW of Japan.
O•kla•ho•ma (ō′klə-hō′mə) A state of the S-central US. Cap. Oklahoma City. Pop. 3,157,604. —**O′kla•ho′man** *adj. & n.*
Oklahoma City. The capital of OK, in the central part. Pop. 444,719.
o•kra (ō′krə) ▸ *n.* **1.** A tall tropical Asian plant cultivated for its edible green pods. **2.** The pods of this plant, used esp. in soups. **3.** See **gumbo** 2. See Regional Note at **goober.** [Of West African orig.]
-ol ▸ *suff.* An alcohol or phenol: *glycerol.* [< (ALCOH)OL.]
O•laf II (ō′läf, ō′ləf, o͞o′läf) or **O•lav II** (ō′läv). Saint Olaf. 995?–1030. Patron saint and king of Norway (1016–28).
old (ōld) ▸ *adj.* **-er, -est 1.** Having lived or existed for a long time; far advanced in years or life. **2.** Made or acquired long ago; not new. **3.** Wise; mature. **4.** Having a specified age. **5.** Belonging to or being of an earlier time: *her old classmates.* **6.** Known through long acquaintance: *an old friend.* **7.** Used as an intensive or to express affection: *any old time; good old Fido.* ▸ *n.* **1.** An individual of a specified age: *a five-year-old.* See Usage Note at **elder**[1]. **2.** Old people collectively. **3.** Former times; yore: *days of old.* [< OE *eald.*] —**old′ness** *n.*
old•en (ōl′dən) ▸ *adj.* Old. [ME.]
Old English ▸ *n.* English from the middle of the 5th to the beginning of the 12th cent.
old-fash•ioned (ōld′făsh′ənd) ▸ *adj.* Outdated. ▸ *n.* A cocktail made of whiskey, bitters, and fruit.
Old French ▸ *n.* French from the 9th to the early 16th cent.
old guard ▸ *n.* A conservative, often reactionary element of a class or group.
old hand ▸ *n.* One with skill derived from long experience.
old hat ▸ *adj.* **1.** Old-fashioned. **2.** Trite.
Old High German ▸ *n.* High German from the middle of the 9th to the late 11th cent.
old•ie (ōl′dē) ▸ *n.* Something old, esp. a song that was once popular.
Old Irish ▸ *n.* Irish from 725 to about 950.
Old Italian ▸ *n.* Italian until the middle of the 16th cent.
old-line (ōld′līn′) ▸ *adj.* **1.** Conservative; reactionary. **2.** Long established.
old master ▸ *n.* **1.** A distinguished European artist from about 1500 to the early 1700s. **2.** A work by such an artist.
Old Norse ▸ *n.* The Germanic language of the Scandinavians until the mid-14th cent.
Old North French ▸ *n.* The northern dialects of Old French.
Old Persian ▸ *n.* An ancient Iranian language attested in inscriptions dating from the 6th to the 5th cent. B.C.
Old Provençal ▸ *n.* Provençal before the middle of the 16th cent.
old school ▸ *n.* A group committed to traditional ideas or practices.
Old Spanish ▸ *n.* Spanish before the middle of the 16th cent.
old•ster (ōld′stər) ▸ *n.* *Informal* An elderly person.
Old Testament ▸ *n.* *Bible* The first of the two main divisions of the Christian Bible, corresponding to the Hebrew Scriptures. See table at **Bible.**
old-tim•er (ōld′tī′mər) ▸ *n.* *Informal* **1a.** An oldster. **b.** One with long tenure or experience. **2.** Something very old.
Ol•du•vai Gorge (ōl′də-vī′, ôl′do͝o-) A ravine in N Tanzania W of Mt. Kilimanjaro.
old wives' tale ▸ *n.* A superstitious belief.
Old World. The Eastern Hemisphere; often used to refer to Europe.
o•le•ag•i•nous (ō′lē-ăj′ə-nəs) ▸ *adj.* **1.** Of or

relating to oil. **2.** Unctuous. [< Lat. *oleāginus*, of the olive tree.]

o•le•an•der (ō′lē-ăn′dər, ō′lē-ăn′dər) ►*n.* A poisonous Eurasian shrub having fragrant white, rose, or purple flowers. [Med.Lat.]

o•le•ic acid (ō-lē′ĭk) ►*n.* An oily liquid occurring in animal and vegetable oils.

o•le•o (ō′lē-ō′) ►*n., pl.* **-os.** Margarine. [< OLEOMARGARINE.]

oleo– or **ole–** ►*pref.* Oil: *oleomargarine.* [< Lat. *oleum.*]

o•le•o•mar•ga•rine (ō′lē-ō-mär′jə-rĭn, -rēn′) ►*n.* Margarine.

ol•fac•tion (ŏl-făk′shən, ōl-) ►*n.* **1.** The sense of smell. **2.** The act of smelling. [< Lat. *olfacere*, to smell.]

ol•fac•to•ry (ŏl-făk′tə-rē, -trē, ōl-) ►*adj.* Of or relating to the sense of smell. [Lat. *olfactōrius.*]

ol•i•gar•chy (ŏl′ĭ-gär′kē, ō′lĭ-) ►*n., pl.* **-chies 1a.** Government by a few. **b.** Those making up such a government. **2.** A state governed by oligarchy. —**ol′i•garch′** *n.* —**ol′i•gar′chic, ol′i•gar′chi•cal** *adj.*

oligo– or **olig–** ►*pref.* Few: *oligarchy.* [< Gk. *oligos.*]

Ol•i•go•cene (ŏl′ĭ-gō-sēn′, ō′lĭ-) *Geol.* ►*adj.* Of or being the 3rd epoch of the Tertiary Period, marked by the rise of true carnivores. ►*n.* The Oligocene Epoch.

ol•ive (ŏl′ĭv) ►*n.* **1.** A Mediterranean evergreen tree having fragrant white flowers, leathery leaves, and edible fruit. **2.** The small ovoid fruit of the olive, an important food and source of oil. **3.** A dull yellowish green. [< Gk. *elaia.*] —**ol′ive** *adj.*

olive branch ►*n.* A branch of an olive tree regarded as an emblem of peace.

Ol•ives (ŏl′ivz), **Mount of.** Also **Ol•i•vet** (ŏl′ə-vĕt′). A ridge of hills in the West Bank E of Jerusalem.

ol•la (ŏl′ə, ō′yä) ►*n. Regional* A rounded earthenware pot, used esp. for cooking or to hold water. [Sp., ult. < Lat. *aula*, jar.]

olla
Cibola pottery, Chaco Canyon, Arizona

Ol•mec (ŏl′mĕk, ōl′-) ►*n., pl.* **-mec** or **-mecs 1.** An early Mesoamerican Indian civilization of SE Mexico that flourished around 1300–400 B.C. **2.** A member of a people sharing the Olmec culture.

O•lym•pi•a[1] (ō-lĭm′pē-ə, ə-lĭm′-) A plain of S Greece in the NW Peleponnesus.

O•lym•pi•a[2] (ō-lĭm′pē-ə, ə-lĭm′-) The capital of WA, in the W part on the S end of Puget Sound. Pop. 33,840.

O•lym•pi•an (ō-lĭm′pē-ən) ►*adj.* **1.** *Gk. Myth.* Of or relating to the gods and goddesses of Mount Olympus. **2.** Surpassing all others in scope. ►*n.* **1.** *Gk. Myth.* One of the gods or goddesses of Mount Olympus. **2.** A contestant in the ancient or modern Olympic Games.

O•lym•pic Games (ō-lĭm′pĭk) ►*pl.n.* **1.** A group of modern international athletic contests held every four years. **2.** An ancient Greek festival of athletic games and contests of choral poetry and dance. —**O•lym′pic** *adj.*

O•lym•pics (ō-lĭm′pĭks) ►*pl.n.* See **Olympic Games** 1.

O•lym•pus (ə-lĭm′pəs, ō-lĭm′-) A range of N Greece near the Aegean coast; rises to 2,918.9 m (9,570 ft) at **Mount Olympus,** home of the mythical Greek gods.

Om (ōm) ►*n. Hinduism & Buddhism* A sacred Sanskrit syllable uttered as a mantra. [Skt.]

–oma ►*suff.* Tumor: *melanoma.* [< Gk. *-ōma*, n. suff.]

O•ma•ha[1] (ō′mə-hô′, -hä′) ►*n., pl.* **-ha** or **-has 1.** A member of a Native American people inhabiting NE Nebraska. **2.** The Siouan language of the Omaha.

O•ma•ha[2] (ō′mə-hô′, -hä′) A city of E NE on the Missouri R. Pop. 335,795.

O•man (ō-män′) A sultanate of the SE Arabian Peninsula on the **Gulf of Oman,** an arm of the Arabian Sea. Cap. Muscat. Pop. 2,077,000. —**O•man′i** *adj. & n.*

O•mar Khay•yám (ō′mär kī-yäm′, -ăm′). 1050?–1123. Persian poet, mathematician, and astronomer.

OMB ►*abbr.* Office of Management and Budget

om•buds•man (ŏm′bŭdz′mən, -bədz-, -bo͝odz′-) ►*n.* One who investigates complaints, as from consumers, and mediates grievances and disputes. [< ON *umbodhsmadhr*, deputy.] —**om′buds′man•ship′** *n.*

Om•dur•man (ŏm′do͝or-män′) A city of NE-central Sudan on the Nile opposite Khartoum. Pop. 526,287.

o•me•ga (ō-mĕg′ə, ō-mē′gə, ō-mā′-) ►*n.* The 24th letter of the Greek alphabet. [Gk. *ō mega*, large o.]

o•me•ga-3 fatty acid (ō-mĕg′ə-thrē′, -mē′gə-, -mā′-) ►*n.* Any of several polyunsaturated fatty acids found in leafy green vegetables, vegetable oils, and fish.

om•e•let also **om•e•lette** (ŏm′ə-lĭt, ŏm′lĭt) ►*n.* A dish of beaten eggs cooked and folded, often around a filling. [< Lat. *lāmella*, thin metal plate.]

o•men (ō′mən) ►*n.* Something believed to be a sign of future good or evil. [Lat. *ōmen.*]

om•i•cron (ŏm′ĭ-krŏn′, ō′mĭ-) ►*n.* The 15th letter of the Greek alphabet. [Gk. *o mikron*, small o.]

om•i•nous (ŏm′ə-nəs) ►*adj.* **1.** Menacing; threatening. **2.** Of or being an evil omen. [Lat. *ōminōsus.*] —**om′i•nous•ly** *adv.* —**om′i•nous•ness** *n.*

o•mit (ō-mĭt′) ►*v.* **o•mit•ted, o•mit•ting 1.** To fail to include or mention; leave out. **2a.** To pass over; neglect. **b.** To desist or fail in doing. [< Lat. *omittere.*] —**o•mis′si•ble** *adj.* —**o•mis′sion** (ō-mĭsh′ən) *n.*

omni– ►*pref.* All: *omnidirectional.* [< Lat. *omnis.*]

om•ni•bus (ŏm′nĭ-bŭs′, -bəs) ►*n.* A bus. ►*adj.*

Covering many things or classes: *an omnibus trade bill.* [< Lat., for all.]
om•ni•di•rec•tion•al (ŏm′nē-dĭ-rĕk′shə-nəl, -dī-) ►*adj.* Capable of transmitting or receiving signals in all directions.
om•nip•o•tent (ŏm-nĭp′ə-tənt) ►*adj.* Having unlimited power, authority, or force. ►*n.* **Omnipotent.** God. —**om•nip′o•tence** *n.*
om•ni•pres•ent (ŏm′nĭ-prĕz′ənt) ►*adj.* Present everywhere. —**om′ni•pres′ence** *n.*
om•nis•cient (ŏm-nĭsh′ənt) ►*adj.* Having total knowledge; knowing everything. [Med. Lat. *omnisciēns* : OMNI– + Lat. *scīre*, know.] —**om•nis′cience** *n.* —**om•nis′cient•ly** *adv.*
om•ni•um-gath•er•um (ŏm′nē-əm-găth′ər-əm) ►*n.* A miscellaneous collection; hodgepodge. [< Lat. *omnium*, of all.]
om•niv•o•rous (ŏm-nĭv′ər-əs) ►*adj.* **1.** Eating both animal and vegetable foods. **2.** Taking in everything available: *an omnivorous mind.* —**om′ni•vore′** (ŏm′nə-vôr′, -vōr′) *n.* —**om•niv′o•rous•ly** *adv.*
Omsk (ômsk) A city of S-central Russia at the confluence of the Irtysh and Om rivers. Pop. 1,163,885.
on (ŏn, ôn) ►*prep.* **1.** Used to indicate: **a.** Position above. **b.** Contact with. **c.** Location at or along. **d.** Proximity. **e.** Attachment to or suspension from. **2.** Used to indicate motion toward or against. **3.** Used to indicate: **a.** Occurrence during: *on July 3rd.* **b.** The particular occasion or circumstance: *On entering the room, she saw him.* **4.** Used to indicate: **a.** The object affected by an action: *The spotlight fell on the actress.* **b.** The agent or agency of a specified action: *cut my foot on the broken glass.* **5.** Used to indicate a source or basis: *live on bread and water.* **6.** Used to indicate: **a.** The state or process of: *on leave; on fire.* **b.** The purpose of: *travel on business.* **c.** A means of conveyance: *ride on a train.* **d.** Availability by means of: *beer on tap.* **7.** Used to indicate belonging: *a nurse on the hospital staff.* **8.** Used to indicate addition or repetition: *heaped error on error.* **9.** Concerning: *a book on dogs.* **10.** *Informal* With: *I haven't a cent on me.* **11.** At the expense of: *drinks on the house.* ►*adv.* **1.** In or into a position of being in contact with something: *Put the coffee on.* **2.** In or into a position of covering something: *Put your clothes on.* **3.** In the direction of something: *He looked on while the ship docked.* **4.** Toward a point lying ahead in space or time: *The play moved on to the next city.* **5.** In a continuous course. **6.** In or into performance or operation. [< OE.]
Usage: In constructions where *on* is an adverb attached to a verb, it should not be joined with *to* to form the single word *onto: move on to* (not *onto*) *new subjects.*
ON ►*abbr.* Ontario
-on¹ ►*suff.* **1.** Subatomic particle: *baryon.* **2.** Unit; quantum: *photon.* [< ION.]
-on² ►*suff.* Inert gas: *radon.* [< (ARG)ON.]
once (wŭns) ►*adv.* **1.** One time only: *once a day.* **2.** At one time in the past; formerly. **3.** At any time; ever. ►*n.* A single occurrence; one time: *You can go this once.* ►*conj.* As soon as; when. —***idiom:* at once 1.** All at one time; simultaneously. **2.** Immediately. [ME *ones* < OE *ān*, one.]
once-o•ver (wŭns′ō′vər) ►*n.* A quick but comprehensive survey or performance.
on•co•gene (ŏn′kə-jēn, ŏng′-) ►*n.* A gene that causes the transformation of normal cells into cancerous tumor cells, esp. a viral gene. [Gk. *onkos*, mass, tumor + GENE.] —**on′co•gen′ic** (-jĕn′ĭk) *adj.* —**on′co•ge•nic′i•ty** (-jə-nĭs′ĭ-tē) *n.*
on•co•gen•e•sis (ŏn′kō-jĕn′ĭ-sĭs, ŏng′-) ►*n.* The formation and development of tumors. [Gk. *onkos*, mass, tumor + –GENESIS.]
on•col•o•gy (ŏn-kŏl′ə-jē, ŏng-) ►*n.* The scientific study of tumors. [Gk. *onkos*, mass, tumor + –LOGY.] —**on′co•log′i•cal** (-kə-lŏj′ĭ-kəl), **on′co•log′ic** *adj.* —**on•col′o•gist** *n.*
on•com•ing (ŏn′kŭm′ĭng, ôn′-) ►*adj.* Approaching.
one (wŭn) ►*adj.* **1.** Being a single entity, unit, object, or living being; not two or more. **2.** United: *They spoke with one voice.* **3.** Being a single member of a group, category, or kind: *I'm just one player on the team.* ►*n.* **1.** The cardinal number, represented by the symbol 1, designating the first such unit in a series. **2.** A single person or thing: *This is the one I like best.* ►*pron.* **1.** An indefinitely specified individual: *met one of the crew.* **2.** An unspecified individual; anyone. [< OE *ān*.] —**one′ness** *n.*
Usage: When a construction headed by *one* appears as the subject of a sentence or relative clause, there may be a question whether the verb should be singular or plural, as in *One of every ten rotors was found defective.* In an earlier survey, a large majority of the Usage Panel preferred a singular verb in such cases. Constructions using *one or more* or *one or two* take a plural verb: *One or more cars were usually parked in front of his house. One or two students from our department have won prizes.*
O•nei•da (ō-nī′də) ►*n., pl.* **-da** or **-das 1.** A member of Native American people formerly inhabiting central New York, now in Wisconsin, New York, and Ontario. **2.** The Iroquoian language of the Oneida.
O'Neill (ō-nēl′), **Eugene Gladstone.** 1888–1953. Amer. playwright; 1936 Nobel.
on•er•ous (ŏn′ər-əs, ō′nər-) ►*adj.* Troublesome or oppressive; burdensome. [< Lat. *onerōsus.*] —**on′er•ous•ly** *adv.*
one•self (wŭn-sĕlf′) also **one's self** (wŭn sĕlf′, wŭnz sĕlf′) ►*pron.* **1.** One's own self. Used: **a.** Reflexively: *One can congratulate oneself on one's victories.* **b.** In an absolute construction: *When in charge oneself, one may do as one pleases.* **2.** One's normal or healthy condition or state.
one-shot (wŭn′shŏt′) ►*adj.* *Informal* **1.** Effective after only one attempt. **2.** Being the only one and unlikely to be repeated.
one-sid•ed (wŭn′-sī′dĭd) ►*adj.* **1.** Biased: *a one-sided view.* **2.** Unequal: *a one-sided contest.* —**one′-sid′ed•ness** *n.*
one•time (wŭn′tīm′) ►*adj.* Former: *a onetime boxing champion.*
one-time (wŭn′tīm′) ►*adj.* Only once: *a one-time winner in 1970.*
one-to-one (wŭn′tə-wŭn′) ►*adj.* Allowing the pairing of each member of a class uniquely with a member of another class.
one-track (wŭn′trăk′) ►*adj.* Obsessed with a single idea or purpose.
one-up (wŭn′ŭp′) ►*v.* **-upped, -up•ping** *Informal.* To practice one-upmanship on.

one-up•man•ship (wŭn-ŭp′mən-shĭp′) ►*n.* The art of outdoing or showing up a rival.

one-way (wŭn′wā′) ►*adj.* Moving or permitting movement in one direction only: *a one-way street; a one-way ticket.*

on•go•ing (ŏn′gō′ĭng, ôn′-) ►*adj.* Currently taking place.

on•ion (ŭn′yən) ►*n.* **1.** A bulbous plant widely cultivated as a vegetable. **2.** The pungent bulb of this plant. [< Lat. *uniō.*]

on•ion•skin (ŭn′yən-skĭn′) ►*n.* A thin, strong, translucent paper.

on•line (ŏn′līn′, ôn′-) ►*adj.* **1.** *Comp. Sci.* **a.** Controlled by a central computer. **b.** Connected to a computer network. **c.** Accessible via a computer. **2.** Ongoing: *online editorial projects.*

on•look•er (ŏn′lo͝ok′ər, ôn′-) ►*n.* A spectator.

on•ly (ōn′lē) ►*adj.* Alone in kind or class; sole. ►*adv.* **1.** Without anyone or anything else; alone. **2a.** At the very least. **b.** And nothing else or more. **3.** Exclusively; solely. ►*conj.* But; except. [< OE *ānlīc.*]

Usage: Generally the adverb *only* should adjoin the word or words that it limits. Variation in the placement of *only* can change the meaning of the sentence, as the following examples show: *Dictators respect only force; they are not moved by words. Dictators only respect force; they do not worship it.* See Usage Note at **not.**

on•o•mat•o•poe•ia (ŏn′ə-măt′ə-pē′ə, -mä′tə-) ►*n.* The formation or use of words such as *buzz* or *murmur* that imitate the sounds associated with the objects or actions they refer to. [< Gk. *onomatopoiia.*] —**on′o•mat′o•poe′ic, on′o•mat′o•po•et′ic** (-pō-ĕt′ĭk) *adj.* —**on′o•mat′o•poe′i•cal•ly, on′o•mat′o•po•et′i•cal•ly** *adv.*

On•on•da•ga (ŏn′ən-dô′gə, -dä′-, -dā′-) ►*n., pl.* **-ga** or **-gas 1.** A member of a Native American people inhabiting W-central New York, now also in SE Ontario. **2.** Their Iroquoian language. —**On′on•da′gan** *adj.*

on•rush (ŏn′rŭsh′, ôn′-) ►*n.* **1.** A forward rush. **2.** An assault. —**on′rush′ing** *adj.*

on•set (ŏn′sĕt′, ôn′-) ►*n.* **1.** An onslaught. **2.** A beginning.

on•shore (ŏn′shôr′, -shōr′, ôn′-) ►*adj.* **1.** Moving or directed toward the shore. **2.** Located on the shore. —**on′shore′** *adv.*

on•slaught (ŏn′slôt′, ôn′-) ►*n.* A violent attack. [< Du. *aanslag*, a striking at.]

Ont. ►*abbr.* Ontario

On•tar•i•o (ŏn-târ′ē-ō′) **1.** A province of E-central Canada. Cap. Toronto. Pop. 8,625,107. **2.** A city of S CA E of Los Angeles. Pop. 133,179.

Ontario, Lake. The smallest of the Great Lakes, between SE Ontario, Canada, and NW NY.

on•to (ŏn′to͞o′, -tə, ôn′-) ►*prep.* **1.** On top of; upon. See Usage Note at **on. 2.** *Informal* Aware of: *I'm onto your plans.*

onto– or **ont–** ►*pref.* **1.** Existence; being: *ontology.* **2.** Organism: *ontogeny.* [< Gk. *ōn, ont-*, pr.part. of *einai*, to be.]

on•tog•e•ny (ŏn-tŏj′ə-nē) ►*n., pl.* **-nies.** The origin and development of an individual organism. —**on′to•ge•net′ic** (ŏn′tō-jə-nĕt′ĭk) *adj.* —**on′to•ge•net′i•cal•ly** *adv.*

on•tol•o•gy (ŏn-tŏl′ə-jē) ►*n.* The branch of metaphysics that deals with the nature of being. —**on′to•log′i•cal** (ŏn′tə-lŏj′ĭ-kəl) *adj.* —**on′to•log′i•cal•ly** *adv.* —**on•tol′o•gist** *n.*

o•nus (ō′nəs) ►*n.* **1.** A burden. **2.** Blame. [Lat.]

on•ward (ŏn′wərd, ôn′-) ►*adv.* also **on•wards** (-wərdz). In a direction or toward a position that is ahead. —**on′ward** *adj.*

–onym ►*suff.* Word; name: *acronym.* [< Gk. *onuma*, name.]

on•yx (ŏn′ĭks) ►*n.* A chalcedony that occurs in bands of different colors. [< Gk. *onux.*]

oo– ►*pref.* Egg; ovum: *oogenesis.* [< Gk. *ōion*, egg.]

o•o•cyte (ō′ə-sīt′) ►*n.* A cell from which an egg or ovum develops by meiosis; a female germ cell.

oo•dles (o͞od′lz) ►*pl.n. Informal* A great amount. [?]

o•o•gen•e•sis (ō′ə-jĕn′ĭ-sĭs) ►*n.* The formation, development, and maturation of an ovum. —**o′o•ge•net′ic** (-jə-nĕt′ĭk) *adj.*

o•o•go•ni•um (ō′ə-gō′nē-əm) ►*n., pl.* **-ni•a** (-nē-ə) or **-ni•ums 1.** A cell that differentiates into an oocyte in the ovary. **2.** A female reproductive structure in certain fungi. [oo– + Gk. *gonos*, seed.]

o•o•lite (ō′ə-līt′) ►*n.* **1.** A small round calcareous grain found esp. in limestones. **2.** Rock, usu. limestone, composed of oolites. [< Gk. *lithos*, stone.] —**o′o•lit′ic** (-lĭt′ĭk) *adj.*

o•ol•o•gy (ō-ŏl′ə-jē) ►*n.* The branch of ornithology that deals with the study of eggs. —**o′o•log′ic** (ō′ə-lŏj′ĭk), **o′o•log′i•cal** *adj.* —**o′o•log′i•cal•ly** *adv.* —**o•ol′o•gist** *n.*

oomph (o͝omf) ►*n. Slang* **1.** Spirited vigor. **2.** Sex appeal. [Of expressive orig.]

oops (o͝ops) ►*interj.* Used to acknowledge a minor accident or mistake.

ooze¹ (o͞oz) ►*v.* **oozed, ooz•ing 1.** To flow or leak out slowly. **2.** To disappear or ebb slowly. [< OE *wōs*, juice.] —**ooze** *n.* —**ooz′i•ness** *n.* —**ooz′y** *adj.*

ooze² (o͞oz) ►*n.* Soft mud or slime, as on the floor of oceans and lakes. [< OE *wāse.*] —**ooz′i•ness** *n.* —**ooz′y** *adj.*

o•pal (ō′pəl) ►*n.* A translucent mineral of hydrated silica, often used as a gem. [< Skt. *upalaḥ.*] —**o′pal•ine′** (ō′pə-līn′, -lēn′) *adj.*

o•pal•es•cent (ō′pə-lĕs′ənt) ►*adj.* Exhibiting a milky iridescence like that of an opal. —**o′pal•esce′** *v.* —**o′pal•es′cence** *n.*

o•paque (ō-pāk′) ►*adj.* **1a.** Impenetrable by light. **b.** Not reflecting light; dull. **2.** Unintelligible. **3.** Obtuse; dense. [< Lat. *opācus*, dark.] —**o•pac′i•ty** (ō-păs′ĭ-tē), **o•paque′ness** *n.* —**o•paque′ly** *adv.*

op art also **Op Art** (ŏp) ►*n.* Abstract art marked by the use of geometric shapes and brilliant colors to create optical illusions.

op. cit. ►*abbr. Lat.* opere citato (in the work cited)

OPEC (ō′pĕk′) ►*abbr.* Organization of Petroleum Exporting Countries

op-ed page (ŏp′ĕd′) ►*n.* A newspaper page, usu. opposite the editorial page, with articles expressing personal viewpoints.

o•pen (ō′pən) ►*adj.* **1.** Affording unobstructed entrance and exit; not shut or closed. **2.** Having no protecting cover. **3.** Not sealed, tied, or folded. **4.** Having gaps, spaces, or intervals. **5.** Accessible to all; unrestricted. **6.** Susceptible;

vulnerable. **7.** Available; obtainable. **8.** Ready to transact business. **9.** Not filled, engaged, or in use. **10.** Frank; candid. ►*v.* **1.** To release from a closed or fastened position. **2.** To remove obstructions from; clear. **3.** To make or force an opening in. **4.** To remove the cover or wrapping from; undo. **5.** To spread out or apart. **6.** To get (something) going; initiate; commence. **7.** To make available. **8.** To make or become more responsive or understanding. **9.** To reveal the secrets of. **10.** To come into view; become revealed. —***phrasal verb:*** **open up** *Informal* To speak freely and candidly. ►*n.* **1.** The outdoors. **2.** A tournament or contest for both professional and amateur players. [< OE.] —**o′pen•er** *n.* —**o′pen•ly** *adv.* —**o′pen•ness** *n.*

o•pen-air (ō′pən-âr′) ►*adj.* Outdoor: *an open-air concert.*

o•pen-and-shut (ō′pən-ən-shŭt′) ►*adj.* Easily settled or determined.

o•pen-end (ō′pən-ĕnd′) ►*adj.* Unlimited.

o•pen-end•ed (ō′pən-ĕn′dĭd) ►*adj.* **1.** Not limited; open-end. **2.** Allowing for change. **3.** Inconclusive or indefinite.

o•pen-eyed (ō′pən-īd′) ►*adj.* **1.** Having the eyes wide open. **2.** Watchful and alert.

o•pen•hand•ed (ō′pən-hăn′dĭd) ►*adj.* Giving freely; generous. See Syns at **liberal.** —**o′pen•hand′ed•ly** *adv.* —**o′pen•hand′ed•ness** *n.*

o•pen-hearth (ō′pən-härth′) ►*adj.* Of a process for producing high-quality steel in a furnace with a heat-reflecting roof.

open house ►*n.* **1.** A social event with a general invitation to all. **2.** An occasion when an institution is open for visiting by the public.

o•pen•ing (ō′pə-nĭng) ►*n.* **1.** The act of becoming open or being made to open. **2.** An open space. **3.** A breach; aperture. **4.** The first part or stage. **5.** The first performance. **6.** *Games* A series of beginning moves, esp. in chess. **7.** An opportunity. **8.** An unfilled job or position.

o•pen-mind•ed (ō′pən-mīn′dĭd) ►*adj.* Receptive to new ideas or to reason. See Syns at **broad-minded.** —**o′pen-mind′ed•ly** *adv.* —**o′pen-mind′ed•ness** *n.*

open shop ►*n.* A business employing both union and nonunion workers.

o•pen•work (ō′pən-wûrk′) ►*n.* Ornamental or structural work containing numerous openings, usu. in set patterns.

op•er•a[1] (ŏp′ər-ə, ŏp′rə) ►*n.* **1.** A theatrical presentation in which a dramatic performance is set to music. **2.** A theater designed primarily for operas. [< Lat., work.] —**op′er•at′ic** (ŏp′ə-răt′ĭk) *adj.* —**op′er•at′i•cal•ly** *adv.*

o•pe•ra[2] (ō′pər-ə, ŏp′ər-ə) ►*n.* Pl. of **opus.**

op•er•a•ble (ŏp′ər-ə-bəl, ŏp′rə-) ►*adj.* **1.** Capable of or suitable for use. **2.** Treatable by surgery. [< OPERATE.] —**op′er•a•bil′i•ty** *n.* —**op′er•a•bly** *adv.*

op•er•a glasses (ŏp′ər-ə, ŏp′rə) ►*pl.n.* Small binoculars for use esp. at the theater.

op•er•and (ŏp′ər-ənd) ►*n.* *Math.* A quantity on which an operation is performed. [< Lat. *operandum.*]

op•er•ate (ŏp′ə-rāt′) ►*v.* **-at•ed, -at•ing 1.** To perform a function; work. **2.** To perform surgery. **3.** To exert an influence. **4.** To control the functioning of. [Lat. *operāre, operāt-.*]

op•er•at•ing system (ŏp′ə-rā′tĭng) ►*n.* Software designed to control the hardware of a specific computer system in order to allow users and application programs to make use of it.

op•er•a•tion (ŏp′ə-rā′shən) ►*n.* **1.** The act or process of operating. **2.** The state of being operative. **3.** *Medic.* A surgical procedure for remedying an injury or ailment. **4.** *Math.* A process, such as addition, performed in accordance with specific rules. **5.** *Comp. Sci.* An action resulting from a single instruction. **6.** A military action or campaign. —**op′er•a′tion•al** *adj.* —**op′er•a′tion•al•ly** *adv.*

op•er•a•tive (ŏp′ər-ə-tĭv, -ə-rā′tĭv, ŏp′rə-) ►*adj.* **1.** Being in effect; having force. **2.** Functioning effectively. **3.** Of or relating to a surgical operation. ►*n.* **1.** A skilled worker, esp. in industry. **2a.** A spy. **b.** A private detective. —**op′er•a•tive•ly** *adv.*

op•er•a•tor (ŏp′ə-rā′tər) ►*n.* **1.** One who operates a machine or system. **2.** The owner or manager of a business. **3.** *Informal* A person adept at accomplishing goals shrewdly or unscrupulously. **4.** *Math.* A symbol that represents an operation.

op•e•ret•ta (ŏp′ə-rĕt′ə) ►*n.* A theatrical production that has elements of opera but is lighter and more popular in subject and style. [Ital.]

oph•thal•mic (ŏf-thăl′mĭk, ŏp-) ►*adj.* Of or relating to the eye.

ophthalmo– or **ophthalm–** ►*pref.* Eye: *ophthalmology.* [< Gk. *ophthalmos*, eye.]

oph•thal•mol•o•gy (ŏf′thəl-mŏl′ə-jē, -thăl-, ŏp′-) ►*n.* The branch of medicine that deals with the anatomy, functions, pathology, and treatment of the eye. —**oph•thal′mo•log′ic** (-thăl′mə-lŏj′ĭk), **oph•thal′mo•log′i•cal** *adj.* —**oph′thal•mol′o•gist** *n.*

o•pi•ate (ō′pē-ĭt, -āt′) ►*n.* **1.** A narcotic containing opium or one of its derivatives. **2.** A narcotic. **3.** Something that dulls the senses and induces relaxation. ►*adj.* **1.** Containing opium or an opium derivative. **2.** Inducing sleep or sedation. [< Lat. *opium*, OPIUM.]

o•pine (ō-pīn′) ►*v.* **o•pined, o•pin•ing.** To hold or state as an opinion. [< Lat. *opīnārī*, suppose.]

o•pin•ion (ə-pĭn′yən) ►*n.* **1.** A belief or conclusion held with confidence but not substantiated by proof. **2.** A judgment based on special knowledge. **3.** A judgment or estimation. [< Lat. *opīniō.*]

o•pin•ion•at•ed (ə-pĭn′yə-nā′tĭd) ►*adj.* Holding stubbornly to one's opinions.

o•pi•um (ō′pē-əm) ►*n.* A bitter, yellowish-brown, addictive narcotic drug prepared from the pods of an Old World poppy. [< Gk. *opion.*]

O•por•to (ō-pôr′tō, -pōr′-) A city of NW Portugal near the mouth of the Douro R. N of Lisbon. Pop. 302,467.

o•pos•sum (ə-pŏs′əm, pŏs′əm) ►*n., pl.* **-sum** or **-sums.** Any of various nocturnal, usu. arboreal marsupials of the Western Hemisphere. [Of Virginia Algonquian orig.]

Op•pen•hei•mer (ŏp′ən-hī′mər), **J(ulius) Robert.** 1902–67. Amer. physicist.

op•po•nent (ə-pō′nənt) ►*n.* One that opposes another or others. See Syns at **enemy.** [< Lat. *oppōnere*, OPPOSE.] —**op•po′nent** *adj.*

op•por•tune (ŏp′ər-tōōn′, -tyōōn′) ►*adj.* Occurring at a fitting or advantageous time. [<

Lat. *opportūnus.*] —**op′por•tune′ly** *adv.* —**op′por•tune′ness** *n.*

op•por•tun•ist (ŏp′ər-to͞o′nĭst, -tyo͞o′-) ►*n.* One who takes advantage of any opportunity to achieve an end, often with no regard for principles or consequences. —**op′por•tun′ism** *n.* —**op′por•tun•is′tic** *adj.*

op•por•tu•ni•ty (ŏp′ər-to͞o′nĭ-tē, -tyo͞o′-) ►*n., pl.* **-ties.** A favorable or advantageous circumstance or combination of circumstances.

op•pose (ə-pōz′) ►*v.* **-posed, -pos•ing 1.** To be in contention or conflict with. **2.** To be resistant to. **3.** To place opposite, esp. in contrast or counterbalance. [< Lat. *oppōnere, oppōs-*, set against.] —**op•pos′a•bil′i•ty** *n.* —**op•pos′a•ble** *adj.* —**op′po•si′tion** (ŏp′ə-zĭsh′ən) *n.* —**op′po•si′tion•al** *adj.* —**op•pos′er** *n.*

op•po•site (ŏp′ə-zĭt) ►*adj.* **1.** Placed or located directly across from. **2.** Facing or moving away from each other. **3.** Sharply contrasting: *opposite views.* ►*n.* One that is opposite or contrary to another. ►*adv.* In an opposite position. ►*prep.* Across from or facing. [< Lat. *oppositus*, p.part. of *oppōnere*, OPPOSE.] —**op′po•site•ly** *adv.* —**op′po•site•ness** *n.*

op•press (ə-prĕs′) ►*v.* **1.** To keep down by unjust use of force or authority. **2.** To weigh heavily on the mind or spirit of. [< Lat. *opprimere, oppress-*, press against.] —**op•pres′sion** *n.* —**op•pres′sor** *n.*

op•pres•sive (ə-prĕs′ĭv) ►*adj.* **1.** Difficult to bear; burdensome. **2.** Tyrannical. **3.** Weighing heavily on the mind or spirit. —**op•pres′sive•ly** *adv.* —**op•pres′sive•ness** *n.*

op•pro•bri•ous (ə-prō′brē-əs) ►*adj.* **1.** Expressing contemptuous reproach. **2.** Shameful or infamous. —**op•pro′bri•ous•ly** *adv.*

op•pro•bri•um (ə-prō′brē-əm) ►*n.* **1.** Disgrace arising from shameful conduct. **2.** Scorn; contempt. **3.** A cause of shame. [Lat. < *opprobrāre*, reproach : *ob-*, intensive pref. + *probrum*, a reproach.]

-opsy ►*suff.* Examination: *biopsy.* [< Gk. *opsis*, sight.]

opt (ŏpt) ►*v.* To choose. [< Lat. *optāre.*]

op•tic (ŏp′tĭk) ►*adj.* Of or relating to the eye or vision. [< Gk. *optikos.*]

op•ti•cal (ŏp′tĭ-kəl) ►*adj.* **1.** Of or relating to sight. **2.** Designed to assist sight. **3.** Of or relating to optics. —**op′ti•cal•ly** *adv.*

optical art ►*n.* Op art.

optical disk ►*n. Comp. Sci.* A plastic-coated disk that stores digital data as tiny pits etched into the surface and is read with a laser scanning the surface; laser disk.

optical illusion ►*n.* A deceptive visual image.

op•ti•cian (ŏp-tĭsh′ən) ►*n.* One that makes or sells lenses, eyeglasses, and other optical instruments.

op•tics (ŏp′tĭks) ►*n. (takes sing. v.)* The scientific study of light and vision.

op•ti•mal (ŏp′tə-məl) ►*adj.* Most favorable or desirable. —**op′ti•mal•ly** *adv.*

op•ti•mism (ŏp′tə-mĭz′əm) ►*n.* **1.** A tendency to expect the best possible outcome or dwell on the most hopeful aspects of a situation. **2.** *Philos.* The doctrine that this world is the best of all possible worlds. [< Lat. *optimus*, best.] —**op′ti•mist** *n.* —**op′ti•mis′tic** *adj.* —**op′ti•mis′ti•cal•ly** *adv.*

op•ti•mize (ŏp′tə-mīz′) ►*v.* **-mized, -miz•ing 1.** To make as perfect or effective as possible. **2.** To make the most of. —**op′ti•mi•za′tion** *n.*

op•ti•mum (ŏp′tə-məm) ►*n., pl.* **-ma** (-mə) or **-mums.** The point at which the condition, degree, or amount of something is the most favorable. [Lat., best.] —**op′ti•mum** *adj.*

op•tion (ŏp′shən) ►*n.* **1.** The act of choosing; choice. **2.** The power or freedom to choose. **3.** The right to buy or sell something within a specified time at a set price. **4.** Something available as a choice. [Lat. *optiō.*] —**op′tion•al** *adj.* —**op′tion•al•ly** *adv.*

op•tom•e•try (ŏp-tŏm′ĭ-trē) ►*n.* The profession of examining eyes and prescribing corrective lenses or other treatments for visual defects. [Gk. *optos*, visible + -METRY.] —**op′to•met′ric** (ŏp′tə-mĕt′rĭk) *adj.* —**op•tom′e•trist** *n.*

op•u•lent (ŏp′yə-lənt) ►*adj.* **1.** Possessing great wealth. **2.** Lavish. [Lat. *opulentus.*] —**op′u•lence** *n.* —**op′u•lent•ly** *adv.*

o•pus (ō′pəs) ►*n., pl.* **o•pe•ra** (ō′pər-ə, ŏp′ər-ə) or **o•pus•es.** A creative work, esp. a musical composition. [Lat.]

or (ôr; ər *when unstressed*) ►*conj.* Used to indicate: **a.** An alternative. **b.** The second of two alternatives: *either right or wrong.* **c.** A synonymous or equivalent expression: *acrophobia, or fear of heights.* **d.** Indefiniteness: *two or three.* [< OE *oththe.*]

Usage: When all the elements in a series connected by *or* are singular, the verb they govern is singular: *Tom or Jack is coming.* When all the elements are plural, the verb is plural. When the elements do not agree in number, some grammarians have suggested that the verb be governed by the element to which it is nearer: *Tom or his sisters are coming.* Other grammarians, however, have argued that substitute constructions be found: *Either Tom is coming or his sisters are.* See Usage Notes at **neither, nor.**

OR ►*abbr.* **1.** operating room **2.** Oregon

-or[1] ►*suff.* One that performs a specified action: *detector.* [< Lat.]

-or[2] ►*suff.* State; activity: *behavior.* [< Lat.]

or•a•cle (ôr′ə-kəl, ŏr′-) ►*n.* **1a.** A shrine consecrated to a prophetic deity. **b.** A priest or priestess at such a shrine. **c.** A prophecy made known at such a shrine. **2.** A wise person. [< Lat. *ōrāculum.*] —**o•rac′u•lar** (ô-răk′yə-lər, ō-) *adj.*

o•ral (ôr′əl, ōr′-) ►*adj.* **1.** Spoken rather than written. See Usage Note at **verbal. 2.** Of the mouth: *oral surgery.* **3.** Used in or taken through the mouth. **4.** Relating to the first stage of psychosexual development in psychoanalytic theory. [< Lat. *ōs, ōr-*, mouth.] —**o′ral•ly** *adv.*

O•ran (ō-rän′, ô-räɴ′) A city of NW Algeria on the **Gulf of Oran,** an inlet of the Mediterranean Sea. Pop. 409,788.

or•ange (ôr′ĭnj, ŏr′-) ►*n.* **1a.** Any of several citrus trees having white flowers and round, reddish-yellow fruit. **b.** The sectioned pulpy fruit of an orange, having a sweetish acidic juice. **2.** The hue of the visible spectrum lying between red and yellow. [< Skt. *nāraṅgaḥ.*] —**or′ange** *adj.*

Orange. A city of S CA NNE of Santa Ana. Pop. 110,658.

or•ange•ade (ôr′ĭn-jād′, ŏr′-) ►*n.* A beverage of orange juice, sugar, and water.

Orange River. A river, about 2,092 km (1,300 mi), of Lesotho, South Africa, and Namibia flowing to the Atlantic Ocean.

o•rang•u•tan (ô-răng′ə-tăn′, ō-răng′-, ə-răng′-) also **o•rang•ou•tang** (-ə-tăng′) ►*n.* An arboreal anthropoid ape having a shaggy reddish-brown coat and very long arms. [Malay *ōrang hūtan.*]

o•rate (ô-rāt′, ō-rāt′, ôr′āt′, ŏr′-) ►*v.* **o•rat•ed, o•rat•ing.** To speak in a formal, often pompous manner. [Lat. *ōrāre.*]

o•ra•tion (ô-rā′shən, ō-rā′-) ►*n.* A formal speech. [< Lat. *ōrāre*, speak.]

or•a•tor (ôr′ə-tər, ŏr′-) ►*n.* **1.** One who delivers an oration. **2.** An eloquent and skilled public speaker. —**or′a•tor′i•cal** (-tôr′ĭ-kəl, -tŏr′-) —**or′a•tor′i•cal•ly** *adv.*

or•a•to•ri•o (ôr′ə-tôr′ē-ō′, -tōr′-, ŏr′-) ►*n., pl.* **-os** *Mus.* A composition for voices and orchestra, usu. on a religious theme, without costumes, scenery, or dramatic action. [After the *Oratorio*, the Oratory of Saint Philip Neri at Rome.]

or•a•to•ry[1] (ôr′ə-tôr′ē, -tōr′ē, ŏr′-) ►*n.* **1.** The art of public speaking. **2.** Eloquence or skill in making public speeches.

or•a•to•ry[2] (ôr′ə-tôr′ē, -tōr′ē, ŏr′-) ►*n., pl.* **-ries.** A small private chapel. [< Lat. *ōrāre*, pray.]

orb (ôrb) ►*n.* **1.** A sphere. **2.** A celestial body. **3.** An eye or eyeball. [< Lat. *orbis.*] —**or•bic′u•lar** (ôr-bĭk′yə-lər) *adj.*

or•bit (ôr′bĭt) ►*n.* **1.** The path of a celestial body or artificial satellite as it revolves around another body. **2.** The path of a body in a field of force surrounding another body. **3.** A range of activity or influence. See Syns at **range. 4.** An eye socket. ►*v.* **1.** To put into an orbit. **2.** To revolve around (a body or center of attraction). [< Lat. *orbita.*] —**or′bi•tal** *adj.* —**or′bit•er** *n.*

or•ca (ôr′kə) ►*n.* See **killer whale.** [< Lat. *orca*, whale.]

or•chard (ôr′chərd) ►*n.* **1.** An area of land devoted to the cultivation of fruit or nut trees. **2.** The trees cultivated in an orchard. [< OE *ortgeard.*]

or•ches•tra (ôr′kĭ-strə, -kĕs′trə) ►*n.* **1.** A group of musicians who play together on various instruments. **2a.** The front section of seats nearest the stage in a theater. **b.** The entire main floor of a theater. [< Gk. *orkhēstra*, space in front of a stage.] —**or•ches′tral** (-kĕs′trəl) *adj.* —**or•ches′tral•ly** *adv.*

or•ches•trate (ôr′kĭ-strāt′) ►*v.* **-trat•ed, -trat•ing 1.** To compose or arrange (music) for an orchestra. **2.** To arrange or organize; direct. —**or′ches•tra′tion** *n.* —**or′ches•tra′tor** *n.*

or•chid (ôr′kĭd) ►*n.* **1a.** Any of a large family of chiefly tropical plants with lipped, three-petaled flowers. **b.** The flower itself. **2.** A light reddish purple. [< Gk. *orkhis.*] —**or′chid** *adj.*

or•dain (ôr-dān′) ►*v.* **1.** To install as a minister, priest, or rabbi. **2.** To order by or as if by decree. **3.** To predestine. See Syns at **dictate.** [< Lat. *ōrdināre*, organize.] —**or•dain′er** *n.* —**or•dain′ment** *n.*

or•deal (ôr-dēl′) ►*n.* A difficult or painful experience. See Syns at **trial.** [< OE *ordāl.*]

or•der (ôr′dər) ►*n.* **1.** A condition of logical or comprehensible arrangement among the separate elements of a group. **2.** The condition or state of something: *a machine in good working order.* **3a.** The established system of social organization. **b.** A condition in which freedom from disorder is maintained through established authority. **4.** A sequence or arrangement of successive things. **5.** The prescribed form or customary procedure. **6.** A command or direction. **7.** A commission or instruction to buy, sell, or supply something. **8.** A request made by a customer at a restaurant for food. **9.** *Eccles.* **a.** Any of several grades of the Christian ministry. **b.** often **orders** Ordination. **10.** A group of persons living under a religious rule. **11.** A group of people upon whom a government or sovereign has formally conferred honor: *the Order of the Garter.* **12.** Degree of quality or importance; rank. **13.** *Archit.* Any of several classical styles marked by the type of column employed. **14.** *Biol.* The category ranking below a class and above a family in the hierarchy of taxonomic classification. ►*v.* **1.** To issue a command or instruction. **2.** To request to be supplied with. **3.** To put into a systematic arrangement. See Syns at **arrange.** —***idioms:* in order to** For the purpose of. **on the order of** Similar to; like. **to order** According to the buyer's specifications. [< Lat. *ōrdō.*] —**or′der•er** *n.*

or•der•ly (ôr′dər-lē) ►*adj.* **1.** Having a systematic arrangement; neat. **2.** Devoid of disruption; peaceful. ►*n., pl.* **-lies 1.** An attendant in a hospital. **2.** A soldier assigned to attend a superior officer. —**or′der•li•ness** *n.*

or•di•nal (ôr′dn-əl) ►*adj.* Being of a specified position in a numbered series. [< Lat. *ōrdō, ōrdin-*, order.]

ordinal number ►*n.* A number, such as *second* or *tenth,* indicating position in a series.

or•di•nance (ôr′dn-əns) ►*n.* **1.** An authoritative command or order. **2.** A municipal statute or regulation. [< Lat. *ōrdināre*, ordain.]

or•di•nar•i•ly (ôr′dn-âr′ə-lē, ôr′dn-ĕr′-) ►*adv.* As a general rule; usually.

or•di•nar•y (ôr′dn-ĕr′ē) ►*adj.* **1.** Commonly encountered; usual. **2.** Of no exceptional ability, degree, or quality; average. [< Lat. *ōrdinārius.*] —**or′di•nar′i•ness** *n.*

or•di•nate (ôr′dn-ĭt, -āt′) ►*n. Symbol* **y** *Math.* The plane Cartesian coordinate representing the distance from a specified point to the *x*-axis, measured parallel to the *y*-axis. [< Lat. *ōrdinātus*, ordered.]

or•di•na•tion (ôr′dn-ā′shən) ►*n.* The act or ceremony of ordaining, as to the ministry.

ord•nance (ôrd′nəns) ►*n.* **1.** Military materiel, such as weapons and ammunition. **2.** Cannon; artillery. [< Lat. *ordināre*, put in order.]

Or•do•vi•cian (ôr′də-vĭsh′ən) *Geol.* ►*adj.* Of or being the 2nd period of the Paleozoic Era, marked by the appearance of primitive fishes. ►*n.* The Ordovician Period. [< Lat. *Ordovicēs*, an ancient Welsh tribe.]

or•dure (ôr′jər) ►*n.* Excrement; dung. [< Lat. *horridus*, frightful.]

ore (ôr, ōr) ►*n.* A mineral or rock from which a valuable constituent, esp. a metal, can be mined or extracted. [< OE *ōra.*]

Ore. ►*abbr.* Oregon

o•re•ad (ôr′ē-ăd′, ōr′-) ►*n. Gk. Myth.* Any of

various mountain nymphs. [< Gk. *Oreias*.]

o•reg•a•no (ə-rĕg′ə-nō′, ô-rĕg′-) ►*n.* An herb having aromatic leaves used as a seasoning. [< Gk. *origanon*.]

Or•e•gon (ôr′ĭ-gən, -gŏn′, ŏr′-) A state of the NW US in the Pacific Northwest. Cap. Salem. Pop. 2,853,733. —**Or′e•go′ni•an** (-gō′nē-ən) *adj. & n.*

O•rel (ô-rĕl′, ō-rĕl′) A city of W Russia on the Oka R. S of Moscow. Pop. 342,846.

or•gan (ôr′gən) ►*n.* **1.** A musical instrument consisting of a number of pipes that sound tones when supplied with air and a keyboard that operates a mechanism controlling the flow of air to the pipes; pipe organ. **2.** An instrument resembling or suggestive of a pipe organ. **3.** *Biol.* A differentiated part of an organism that performs a specific function. **4.** An instrument or agency performing specified functions: *a government organ.* **5.** A periodical. [< Gk. *organon*, instrument.]

or•gan•dy (ôr′gən-dē) ►*n., pl.* **-dies.** A stiff transparent fabric of cotton or silk, used for curtains and light apparel. [Fr. *organdi*.]

or•gan•elle (ôr′gə-nĕl′) ►*n.* A differentiated structure within a cell, such as a vacuole, that performs a specific function. [NLat. *organella*, small organ.]

or•gan•ic (ôr-găn′ĭk) ►*adj.* **1.** Of or affecting an organ of the body. **2.** Of or derived from living organisms. **3.** Cultivated or raised without the use of synthetic chemicals, such as pesticides, or drugs, such as hormones. **4.** Resembling a living organism in organization or development: *an organic whole.* **5.** Constituting an integral part of a whole; fundamental. **6.** *Chem.* Of or designating carbon compounds. —**or•gan′i•cal•ly** *adv.* —**or′gan•ic′i•ty** (ôr′gə-nĭs′ĭ-tē) *n.*

or•gan•ism (ôr′gə-nĭz′əm) ►*n.* **1.** A living being. **2.** A system similar to a living body: *the social organism.*

or•gan•ist (ôr′gə-nĭst) ►*n.* One who plays the organ.

or•gan•i•za•tion (ôr′gə-nĭ-zā′shən) ►*n.* **1.** The act of organizing or process of being organized. **2.** Something organized into an ordered whole. **3.** A group of persons organized for a particular purpose; association. —**or′gan•i•za′tion•al** *adj.*

or•gan•ize (ôr′gə-nīz′) ►*v.* **-ized, -iz•ing 1.** To put together into an orderly, functional, structured whole. **2.** To arrange in a coherent form; systematize. **3.** To arrange systematically for united action. See Syns at **arrange. 4.** To establish as an organization. See Syns at **found**[1]. **5.** To persuade to form or join a labor union. [< Lat. *organum*, instrument. See ORGAN.] —**or′gan•iz′er** *n.*

or•gan•za (ôr-găn′zə) ►*n.* A sheer stiff fabric of silk or synthetic material. [Prob. < *Organzi* (Urgench), Uzbekistan.]

or•gasm (ôr′găz′əm) ►*n.* The highest point of sexual excitement; climax. [< Gk. *orgasmos*.] —**or•gas′mic, or•gas′tic** *adj.*

or•gy (ôr′jē) ►*n., pl.* **-gies 1.** A revel involving unrestrained indulgence, esp. sexual activity. **2.** Uncontrolled indulgence in an activity. See Syns at **binge.** [< Gk. *orgia*.] —**or′gi•ast** *n.* —**or′gi•as′tic** *adj.* —**or′gi•as′ti•cal•ly** *adv.*

o•ri•el (ôr′ē-əl, ōr′-) ►*n.* A projecting bay window supported by a bracket. [< Med.Lat. *oriolum*, porch.]

o•ri•ent (ôr′ē-ənt, -ĕnt′, ōr′-) ►*n.* **Orient** The countries of Asia, esp. of E Asia. ►*v.* (ôr′ē-ĕnt′, ōr′-) **1.** To locate or place in a particular relation to the points of the compass. **2.** To make familiar with or adjusted to a situation. [< Lat. *oriēns*, pr.part. of *orīrī*, rise.] —**o′ri•en•tate′** *v.* —**o′ri•en•ta′tion** *n.*

O•ri•en•tal also **o•ri•en•tal** (ôr′ē-ĕn′tl, ōr′-) ►*adj.* Of or designating the Orient. ►*n. Often Offensive* An Asian person. See Usage Note at **Asian.**

or•i•fice (ôr′ə-fĭs, ŏr′-) ►*n.* An opening, esp. to a cavity or passage of the body. [< LLat. *ōrificium*.] —**or′i•fi′cial** (-fĭsh′əl) *adj.*

o•ri•ga•mi (ôr′ĭ-gä′mē) ►*n.* The Japanese art of folding paper. [J.]

or•i•gin (ôr′ə-jĭn, ŏr′-) ►*n.* **1.** The point at which something comes into existence. **2.** Ancestry. **3.** The fact of originating. **4.** *Math.* The point of intersection of coordinate axes. [< Lat. *orīgō* < *orīrī*, arise.]

o•rig•i•nal (ə-rĭj′ə-nəl) ►*adj.* **1.** Preceding all others; first. **2.** Fresh and unusual; new. **3.** Inventive. ►*n.* **1.** A first form from which other forms are made or developed. **2.** An authentic work of art. —**o•rig′i•nal′i•ty** (-năl′ĭ-tē) *n.* —**o•rig′i•nal•ly** *adv.*

o•rig•i•nate (ə-rĭj′ə-nāt′) ►*v.* **-nat•ed, -nat•ing.** To come or bring into being. See Syns at **stem**[1]. —**o•rig′i•na′tion** *n.* —**o•rig′i•na′tor** *n.*

O•ri•no•co (ôr′ə-nō′kō, ōr′-) A river rising in SE Venezuela and flowing more than 2,414 km (1,500 mi) to the Atlantic.

o•ri•ole (ôr′ē-ōl′, ōr′-) ►*n.* A songbird with black and bright yellow or orange plumage. [< Lat. *aureolus*, golden.]

O•ri•on (ō-rī′ən, ə-rī′-) ►*n.* A constellation in the celestial equator near Gemini and Taurus.

or•i•son (ôr′ĭ-sən, -zən, ŏr′-) ►*n.* A prayer. [< LLat. *ōrātiō*, a speech.]

Ork•ney Islands (ôrk′nē) An archipelago in the Atlantic Ocean and the North Sea off the NE coast of Scotland.

Or•lan•do (ôr-lăn′dō) A city of central FL ENE of Tampa. Pop. 164,693.

Or•lé•ans (ôr-lā-äɴ′) A city of N-central France on the Loire R. SSW of Paris. Pop. 105,099.

Or•lon (ôr′lŏn′) ► A trademark for an acrylic fiber.

Or•mazd (ôr′məzd) ►*n.* The chief deity of Zoroastrianism. [< OPers. *Auramazda*.]

or•mo•lu (ôr′mə-lo͞o′) ►*n.* An alloy resembling gold, used to ornament furniture. [Fr. *or moulu*, ground gold.]

Or•muz (ôr′mŭz′, ôr-mo͞oz′), **Strait of.** See Strait of **Hormuz.**

or•na•ment (ôr′nə-mənt) ►*n.* Something that decorates or adorns; embellishment. ►*v.* (-mĕnt′). To decorate. [< Lat. *ōrnāre*, adorn.] —**or′na•men′tal** *adj.* —**or′na•men′tal•ly** *adv.* —**or′na•men•ta′tion** *n.*

or•nate (ôr-nāt′) ►*adj.* **1.** Elaborately, often excessively ornamented. **2.** Showy or florid in style; flowery. [< Lat. *ōrnātus*, adorned.] —**or•nate′ly** *adv.* —**or•nate′ness** *n.*

or•ner•y (ôr′nə-rē) ►*adj.* **-i•er, -i•est.** Mean and stubborn; cantankerous. [< ORDINARY.] —**or′ner•i•ness′** *n.*

or•ni•thol•o•gy (ôr′nə-thŏl′ə-jē) ►*n.* The branch of zoology that deals with the study of birds. [< Gk. *ornis, ornith-*, bird.] —**or′ni•tho•log′ic** (-thə-lŏj′ĭk), **or′ni•tho•log′i•cal** *adj.* —**or′ni•thol′o•gist** *n.*

o•rog•e•ny (ô-rŏj′ə-nē) ►*n.* The process of mountain formation, esp. by a folding of the earth's crust. [Gk. *oros*, mountain + -GENY.]

o•ro•tund (ôr′ə-tŭnd′, ōr′-) ►*adj.* **1.** Pompous and bombastic. **2.** Sonorous. [< Lat. *ōre rotundō*, with a round mouth.]

or•phan (ôr′fən) ►*n.* A child whose parents are dead. [< Gk. *orphanos*, orphaned.] —**or′phan** *v.* —**or′phan•hood′** *n.*

or•phan•age (ôr′fə-nĭj) ►*n.* An institution for the care of orphans.

Or•phe•us (ôr′fē-əs, -fyo͞os′) ►*n. Gk. Myth.* A poet and musician who almost succeeded in rescuing his wife Eurydice from Hades. —**Or′phic** *adj.*

Or•te•ga y Gas•set (ôr-tā′gə ē gä-sĕt′), **José.** 1883–1955. Spanish philosopher.

ortho– or **orth–** ►*pref.* **1.** Straight; correct: *orthodontics.* **2.** Perpendicular: *orthogonal.* [< Gk. *orthos*, straight.]

or•tho•don•tia (ôr′thə-dŏn′shə) or **or•tho•don•ture** (-dŏn′chər) ►*n.* Orthodontics.

or•tho•don•tics (ôr′thə-dŏn′tĭks) ►*n. (takes sing. v.)* The dental specialty and practice of correcting irregularities of the teeth. —**or′tho•don′tic** *adj.* —**or′tho•don′tist** *n.*

or•tho•dox (ôr′thə-dŏks′) ►*adj.* **1.** Adhering to an accepted or established doctrine. **2.** often **Orthodox** Of or relating to the most conservative or traditional form of a religion, philosophy, or ideology. **3. Orthodox** Of or relating to the Eastern Orthodox Church. **4.** Commonly accepted; customary. [< LGk. *orthodoxos.*] —**or′tho•dox′ly** *adv.* —**or′tho•dox′y** *n.*

or•thog•o•nal (ôr-thŏg′ə-nəl) ►*adj. Math.* Relating to or composed of right angles. —**or•thog′o•nal•ly** *adv.*

or•thog•ra•phy (ôr-thŏg′rə-fē) ►*n., pl.* **-phies 1.** Correct spelling. **2.** A method of representing the sounds of a language by letters and diacritics. —**or′tho•graph′ic** (ôr′thə-grăf′ĭk) *adj.* —**or′tho•graph′i•cal•ly** *adv.*

or•tho•pe•dics (ôr′thə-pē′dĭks) ►*n. (takes sing. v.)* The branch of medicine that deals with injuries or disorders of the skeletal system. [< ORTHO– + Gk. *pais, paid-*, child.] —**or′tho•pe′dic** *adj.* —**or′tho•pe′di•cal•ly** *adv.* —**or′tho•pe′dist** *n.*

or•thot•ics (ôr-thŏt′ĭks) ►*n. (takes sing. v.)* The science that deals with the use of specialized mechanical devices to support or supplement impaired joints or limbs. [< Gk. *orthōsis, orthōt-*, straightening.] —**or•thot′ic** *adj. & n.* —**or•thot′ist** (ôr-thŏt′ĭst, ôr′thə-tĭst) *n.*

ORV ►*abbr.* off-road vehicle

Or•well (ôr′wĕl′, -wəl), **George.** Eric Arthur Blair. 1903–50. British writer.

-ory ►*suff.* **1.** Of, relating to, or characterized by: *advisory.* **2.** A place or thing used for or connected with: *crematory.* [< Lat. *-ōrius*, adj. suff., and *-ōrium*, n. suff.]

o•ryx (ôr′ĭks, ōr′-, ŏr′-) ►*n., pl.* **oryx** or **-es.** An African antelope having slightly curved horns. [< Gk. *orux*, pickax, gazelle.]

oryx
Arabian oryx

Os ► The symbol for the element **osmium.**

OS ►*abbr.* ordinary seaman

O•sage (ō′sāj′, ō-sāj′) ►*n., pl.* **O•sage** or **O•sag•es 1.** A member of a Native American people formerly inhabiting W Missouri, now in N-central Oklahoma. **2.** Their Siouan language. —**O′sage′** *adj.*

O•sa•ka (ō-sä′kə) A city of S Honshu, Japan, on **Osaka Bay,** an inlet of the Pacific. Pop. 2,588,989.

Os•ce•o•la (ŏs′ē-ō′lə, ō′sē-). 1804?–38. Seminole leader.

Osceola
1838 portrait

os•cil•late (ŏs′ə-lāt′) ►*v.* **-lat•ed, -lat•ing 1.** To swing back and forth steadily. **2.** To waver; vacillate. **3.** *Phys.* To vary between alternate extremes, usu. within a definable period of time. [< Lat. *ōscillum*, a swing.] —**os′cil•la′tion** *n.* —**os′cil•la′tor** *n.*

os•cil•lo•scope (ə-sĭl′ə-skōp′) ►*n.* An electronic instrument that produces an instantaneous trace on the screen of a cathode-ray tube corresponding to oscillations of voltage and current. [OSCILL(ATION) + -SCOPE.] —**os•cil′lo•scop′ic** (-skŏp′ĭk) *adj.*

os•cu•late (ŏs′kyə-lāt′) ►*v.* **-lat•ed, -lat•ing 1.** To kiss. **2.** To come together; contact. [< Lat. *ōsculum*, a kiss.] —**os′cu•la′tion** *n.*

-ose[1] ►*suff.* Possessing; having the characteristics of: *comatose.* [< Lat. *-ōsus.*]

-ose[2] ►*suff.* Carbohydrate: *fructose.* [< GLUCOSE.]

o•sier (ō′zhər) ►*n.* **1.** A willow having long rodlike twigs used in basketry. **2.** A twig of such a willow. [< Med.Lat. *osera.*]

O•si•ris (ō-sī′rĭs) ►*n. Myth.* The ancient Egyptian god of the underworld, the brother and husband of Isis.

-osis ►*suff.* **1.** Condition; process; action: *osmosis.* **2.** Diseased or abnormal condition: *cyanosis.* [< Gk. *-ōsis*, n. suff.]

Os•lo (ŏz′lō, ŏs′-) The capital of Norway, in the SE part. Pop. 473,454.

os•mi•um (ŏz′mē-əm) ►*n. Symbol* **Os** A bluish-white, hard, dense metallic element used as a platinum hardener and in phonograph needles. At. no. 76. See table at **element.** [< Gk. *osmē*, odor.]

os•mo•sis (ŏz-mō′sĭs, ŏs-) ►*n.* **1.** Diffusion of fluid through a semipermeable membrane until there is an equal concentration of fluid on both sides of the membrane. **2.** A gradual process of assimilation or absorption. [< Gk. *ōsmos*, a push.] —**os•mot′ic** (-mŏt′ĭk) *adj.* —**os•mot′i•cal•ly** *adv.*

os•prey (ŏs′prē, -prā) ►*n., pl.* **-preys.** A large fish-eating hawk having dark plumage on the back and white below. [< Med.Lat. *avis prede*, bird of prey : Lat. *avis*, bird + Lat. *praeda*, prey.]

os•si•fy (ŏs′ə-fī′) ►*v.* **-fied, -fy•ing 1.** To change into bone. **2.** To become set in a rigidly conventional pattern. [Lat. *os*, bone + –FY.] —**os•sif′ic** (ŏ-sĭf′ĭk) *adj.* —**os′si•fi•ca′tion** *n.*

os•te•i•tis (ŏs′tē-ī′tĭs) ►*n.* Inflammation of bone or bony tissue.

os•ten•si•ble (ŏ-stĕn′sə-bəl) ►*adj.* Represented or appearing as such; apparent. [< Lat. *ostendere*, *ostēns-*, show.] —**os•ten′si•bly** *adv.*

os•ten•ta•tion (ŏs′tĕn-tā′shən, -tən-) ►*n.* Pretentious display. [< Lat. *ostentāre*, show off.]

os•ten•ta•tious (ŏs′tĕn-tā′shəs, -tən-) ►*adj.* Pretentious. See Syns at **showy.** —**os′ten•ta′tious•ly** *adv.*

osteo– or **oste–** ►*pref.* Bone: *osteopathy.* [< Gk. *osteon*, bone.]

os•te•op•a•thy (ŏs′tē-ŏp′ə-thē) ►*n.* A system that emphasizes manipulation esp. of the bones for treating disease. —**os′te•o•path′** (ŏs′tē-ə-păth′) *n.* —**os′te•o•path′ic** *adj.* —**os′te•o•path′i•cal•ly** *adv.*

os•te•o•po•ro•sis (ŏs′tē-ō-pə-rō′sĭs) ►*n.* A disease in which the bones become extremely porous, occurring esp. in women following menopause. [OSTEO– + Gk. *poros*, pore + –OSIS.] —**os′te•o•po•rot′ic** (-rŏt′ĭk) *adj.*

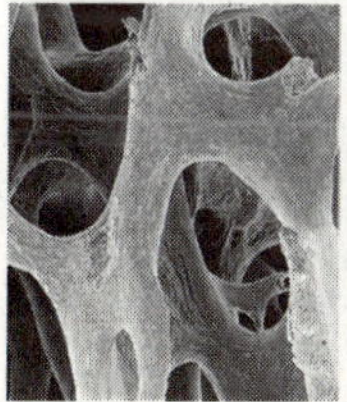
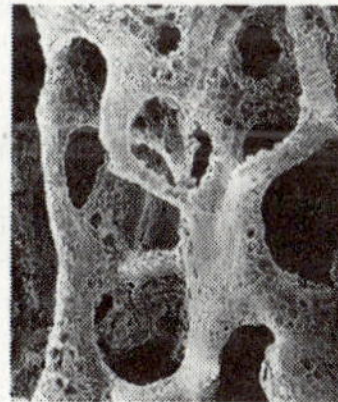

osteoporosis
left to right: normal and diseased bone

Os•ti•a (ŏs′tē-ə) An ancient city of W-central Italy at the mouth of the Tiber R.

os•tra•cize (ŏs′trə-sīz′) ►*v.* **-cized, -ciz•ing.** To banish or exclude from a group. See Syns at **blackball.** [Gk. *ostrakizein.*] —**os′tra•cism** *n.*

Os•tra•va (ō′strä-vä) A city of NE Czech Republic near the Oder R. Pop. 327,159.

os•trich (ŏs′trĭch, ôs′-) ►*n., pl.* **-trich** or **-trich•es.** A large, swift-running flightless bird of Africa, having a long bare neck and two-toed feet. [< Lat. *avis*, bird + Gk. *strouthos*, ostrich.]

Os•tro•goth (ŏs′trə-gŏth′) ►*n.* One of a tribe of eastern Goths that conquered and ruled Italy from A.D. 493 to 555.

OT ►*abbr.* **1.** occupational therapy **2.** Old Testament **3.** overtime

OTB ►*abbr.* off-track betting

OTC ►*abbr.* over-the-counter

oth•er (ŭ*th*′ər) ►*adj.* **1a.** Being the remaining one of two or more. **b.** Being the remaining ones of several. **2.** Different from that or those implied or specified. **3.** Additional; extra. **4.** Opposite; reverse. **5.** Alternate; second: *every other day.* **6.** Of the recent past: *the other day.* ►*n.* **1a.** The remaining one of two or more. **b. others** The remaining ones of several. **2a.** A different one: *one storm after the other.* **b.** An additional one: *How many others will come later?* ►*pron.* A different person or thing. ►*adv.* In another way. [< OE *ōther.*]

oth•er•wise (ŭ*th*′ər-wīz′) ►*adv.* **1.** In another way; differently. **2.** Under other circumstances. **3.** In other respects: *an otherwise logical mind.* ►*adj.* Other than supposed; different: *The facts are otherwise.*

oth•er•world•ly (ŭ*th*′ər-wûrld′lē) ►*adj.* **1.** Of or characteristic of another world, esp. a mystical world. **2.** Concerned with intellectual or imaginative things. —**oth′er•world′li•ness** *n.*

–otic ►*suff.* **1.** Of or characterized by a specified condition or process: *mitotic.* **2.** Having a specified disease or abnormality: *sclerotic.* [< Gk. *-ōtikos*, adj. suff.]

o•ti•ose (ō′shē-ōs′, ō′tē-) ►*adj.* **1.** Lazy. **2.** Of no use. **3.** Futile. See Syns at **vain.** [Lat. *otiōsus.*]

O•tis (ō′tĭs), **James.** 1725–83. Amer. Revolutionary leader.

o•ti•tis (ō-tī′tĭs) ►*n.* Inflammation of the ear. [Gk. *ous*, *ōt-*, ear + –ITIS.]

OTS ►*abbr.* Officers' Training School

Ot•ta•wa[1] (ŏt′ə-wə, -wä′, -wô′) ►*n., pl.* **-wa** or **-was 1.** A member of a Native American people of S Ontario and N Michigan. **2.** The Ojibwa dialect spoken by the Ottawa.

Ot•ta•wa[2] (ŏt′ə-wə) The capital of Canada, in SE Ontario on the Ottawa R. Pop. 313,987.

Ottawa River. A river, about 1,126 km (700 mi), rising in SW Quebec, Canada, and flowing to the St. Lawrence R. near Montreal.

ot•ter (ŏt′ər) ►*n., pl.* **-ter** or **-ters 1.** Any of several aquatic carnivorous mammals having webbed feet and thick brown fur. **2.** The fur of an otter. [< OE *otor.*]

Ot•to I (ŏt′ō, ôt′ō). "Otto the Great." 912–973. King of Germany (936–973) and first Holy Roman emperor (962–973).

ot•to•man (ŏt′ə-mən) ►*n., pl.* **-mans 1.** A backless upholstered sofa. **2.** An upholstered footstool. [< Fr. *ottoman*, Turk.]

Ottoman ►*n., pl.* **-mans.** A Turk, esp. of the Ottoman Empire. ►*adj.* **1.** Of the Ottoman Empire. **2.** Turkish.

Ottoman Empire. A Turkish sultanate (1299?–1919) of SW Asia, NE Africa, and SE Europe.

Oua•ga•dou•gou (wä′gə-dōō′gōō) The capital of Burkina Faso, in the central part. Pop. 634,479.

ouch (ouch) ►*interj.* Used to express sudden pain.
ought[1] (ôt) ►*aux.v.* Used to indicate: **a.** Obligation or duty: *You ought to work harder than that.* **b.** Advisability or prudence: *You ought to wear a raincoat.* **c.** Desirability: *You ought to have been there.* **d.** Probability or likelihood: *She ought to finish by next week.* [< OE *āhte*, p.t. of *āgan*, to possess.]
ought[2] (ôt) ►*pron. & adv.* Var. of **aught**[1].
ought[3] (ôt) ►*n.* Var. of **aught**[2].
ou•gui•ya (o͞o-gē′yə) ►*n.* See table at **currency.** [Indigenous word in Mauritania.]
ounce (ouns) ►*n.* **1a.** See table at **measurement. b.** A unit of apothecary weight, equal to 480 grains (31.104 grams). **2.** A fluid ounce. **3.** A tiny bit. [< Lat. *ūncia*, a twelfth.]
our (our) ►*adj.* The possessive form of **we.** Used as a modifier before a noun: *our deeds; our hometown.* [< OE *ūre*.]
ours (ourz) ►*pron. (takes sing. or pl. v.)* Used to indicate the one or ones belonging to us: *The victory is ours. If your car doesn't start, take ours.* [< OE *ūre*, our.]
our•self (our-sĕlf′, är-) ►*pron.* Myself. Used as a reflexive, as in a royal proclamation.
our•selves (our-sĕlvz′, är-) ►*pron.* **1.** Those ones identical with us. Used: **a.** Reflexively as a direct or indirect object or the object of a preposition: *We bought ourselves a new camera.* **b.** For emphasis. **2.** Our normal or healthy condition: *We're feeling ourselves again.*
-ous ►*suff.* **1.** Possessing; full of: *joyous.* **2.** Having a valence lower than in compounds or ions named with adjectives ending in *-ic*: *ferrous.* [< Lat. *-ōsus*.]
oust (oust) ►*v.* To eject; force out. [< Lat. *obstāre*, to hinder.]
oust•er (ous′tər) ►*n.* Eviction; expulsion. [< AN, to oust.]
out (out) ►*adv.* **1.** Away from the inside. **2.** Away from the center or middle. **3.** Away from a usual place. **4.** Outside: *went out to play.* **5a.** To exhaustion or depletion: *The supplies have run out.* **b.** Into extinction: *The fire has gone out.* **c.** To a finish or conclusion: *Play the game out.* **6.** In or into a state of unconsciousness: *The drug put him out for hours.* **7.** Into view: *The moon came out.* **8.** Into distribution: *giving out free passes.* **9.** Into disuse. **10.** *Baseball* So as to be retired. **11.** On strike. ►*adj.* **1.** Exterior; external. **2.** Outgoing: *the out doorway.* **3.** Not operating or operational: *The power was out.* **4.** Not to be considered or permitted: *A taxi is out, because I don't have any money.* **5.** No longer fashionable. **6.** No longer existing in one's possession or supplies: *We're out of coffee.* **7.** *Baseball* Retired. **8.** *Informal* Openly gay, lesbian, or bisexual. ►*prep.* **1.** Forth from; through. **2.** Within the area of: *a house with a garden out back.* ►*n.* **1.** One that is out, esp. one who is out of power. **2.** A means of escape. **3.** *Baseball* A play in which a batter or base runner is retired. ►*v.* **1.** To be disclosed or revealed: *Truth will out.* **2.** To expose (someone) as being gay, lesbian, or bisexual. —***idiom:*** **on the outs** *Informal* Not on friendly terms. [< OE *ūt*.]
out– ►*pref.* In a way that surpasses or exceeds: *outdistance.* [< OUT.]
out•age (ou′tĭj) ►*n.* A temporary suspension of operation, esp. of electric power.
out-and-out (out′n-out′) ►*adj.* Complete; thoroughgoing.
out•back (out′băk′) ►*n.* The wild, remote part esp. of Australia or New Zealand.
out•bid (out-bĭd′) ►*v.* To bid higher than.
out•board (out′bôrd′, -bōrd′) ►*adj.* **1.** Situated outside the hull of a vessel. **2.** Situated toward or nearer the end of an aircraft wing. —**out′board′** *adv.*
out•bound (out′bound′) ►*adj.* Outward bound.
out•break (out′brāk′) ►*n.* A sudden eruption.
out•build•ing (out′bĭl′dĭng) ►*n.* A building separate from but associated with a main building.
out•burst (out′bûrst′) ►*n.* A sudden violent display, as of activity or emotion.
out•cast (out′kăst′) ►*n.* One that has been excluded from a society. —**out′cast′** *adj.*
out•class (out-klăs′) ►*v.* To surpass decisively, so as to appear of a higher class.
out•come (out′kŭm′) ►*n.* A result; consequence.
out•crop (out′krŏp′) ►*n.* A portion of bedrock protruding through the soil level. [< *crop*, appear on the surface.] —**out•crop′** *v.*
out•cry (out′krī′) ►*n.* **1.** A loud cry or clamor. **2.** A strong protest.
out•dat•ed (out-dā′tĭd) ►*adj.* Out-of-date; old-fashioned.
out•dis•tance (out-dĭs′təns) ►*v.* To surpass by a wide margin.
out•do (out-do͞o′) ►*v.* To do better than.
out•door (out′dôr′, -dōr′) also **out-of-door** (out′əv-dôr′, -dōr′) ►*adj.* Located in, done in, or suited to the open air.
out•doors (out-dôrz′, -dōrz′) also **out-of-doors** (out′əv-dôrz′, -dōrz′) ►*n.* The open air; the area away from buildings. ►*adv.* In or into the outdoors.
out•er (ou′tər) ►*adj.* **1.** Located on the outside. **2.** Farther from the center or middle.
outer ear ►*n.* See **external ear.**
out•er•most (ou′tər-mōst′) ►*adj.* Farthest out.
outer planet ►*n.* Any of the five planets, Jupiter, Saturn, Uranus, Neptune, and Pluto, with orbits outside that of Mars.
outer space ►*n.* Space beyond the limits of a celestial body or system.
out•face (out-fās′) ►*v.* **1.** To overcome with a bold or self-assured look. **2.** To defy.
out•fall (out′fôl′) ►*n.* The place where a sewer, drain, or stream discharges.
out•field (out′fēld′) ►*n.* *Baseball* The playing area extending outward from the diamond. —**out′field′er** *n.*
out•fit (out′fĭt′) ►*n.* **1.** Clothing or equipment for a specialized purpose. See Syns at **equipment. 2.** *Informal* An association of persons who work together. ►*v.* To provide with an outfit. —**out′fit′ter** *n.*
out•flank (out-flăngk′) ►*v.* **1.** To maneuver around the flank of (an opposing force). **2.** To gain a tactical advantage over.
out•flow (out′flō′) ►*n.* **1.** The act of flowing out. **2.** Something that flows out.
out•fox (out-fŏks′) ►*v.* To outsmart.
out•go (out′gō′) ►*n., pl.* **-goes.** Something that goes out, esp. money.
out•go•ing (out′gō′ĭng) ►*adj.* **1.** Going out; departing. **2.** Sociable; friendly.

out•grow (out-grō′) ►*v.* **1.** To grow too large for. **2.** To grow too mature for: *outgrow childish games.* **3.** To surpass in growth.
out•growth (out′grōth′) ►*n.* **1.** A product of growing out; offshoot. **2.** A consequence.
out•guess (out-gĕs′) ►*v.* To anticipate correctly the actions of.
out•house (out′hous′) ►*n.* **1.** A toilet housed in a small outdoor structure. **2.** An outbuilding.
out•ing (ou′tĭng) ►*n.* **1.** An excursion. **2.** A walk outdoors. **3.** The exposing of someone as being gay, lesbian, or bisexual.
out•land (out′lănd′, -lənd) ►*n.* **1.** A foreign land. **2. outlands** The outlying areas of a country. —**out′land′** *adj.* —**out′land′er** *n.*
out•land•ish (out-lăn′dĭsh) ►*adj.* **1.** Conspicuously unconventional; bizarre. **2.** Strikingly unfamiliar. —**out•land′ish•ly** *adv.* —**out•land′ish•ness** *n.*
out•last (out-lăst′) ►*v.* To last longer than.
out•law (out′lô′) ►*n.* **1.** A fugitive from the law. **2.** A person excluded from normal legal protection and rights. ►*v.* **1.** To declare illegal. **2.** To deprive of the protection of the law. —**out′law′** *adj.* —**out′law′ry** *n.*
out•lay (out′lā′) ►*n.* **1.** The spending or disbursement of money. **2.** An amount spent.
out•let (out′lĕt′, -lĭt) ►*n.* **1a.** A passage for escape or exit; vent. **b.** A means of release or gratification, as for energies or desires. **2.** A commercial market for goods or services. **3.** A receptacle connected to a power supply and having a socket for a plug.
out•line (out′līn′) ►*n.* **1a.** A line marking the outer boundaries of an object or figure. **b.** Shape; contour. **2.** A style of drawing in which objects are delineated in contours without shading. **3.** A short description, account, or summary. ►*v.* **-lined, -lin•ing 1.** To draw an outline of. **2.** To summarize.
Syns: *outline, contour, profile, silhouette* **n.**
out•live (out-lĭv′) ►*v.* To live longer than.
out•look (out′lo͝ok′) ►*n.* **1.** A point of view; attitude. **2.** Expectation for the future; prospect. **3a.** A place where something can be viewed. **b.** The view seen.
out•ly•ing (out′lī′ĭng) ►*adj.* Relatively distant or remote from a center.
out•ma•neu•ver (out′mə-no͞o′vər, -nyo͞o′-) ►*v.* **1.** To overcome by more artful maneuvering. **2.** To excel in maneuverability.
out•mod•ed (out-mō′dĭd) ►*adj.* **1.** Not in fashion. **2.** Obsolete.
out•num•ber (out-nŭm′bər) ►*v.* To be more numerous than.
out of ►*prep.* **1a.** From within to the outside of: *got out of the car.* **b.** From a given condition: *came out of her trance.* **c.** From a source or cause: *made out of wood.* **2a.** In a position or situation beyond the range, boundaries, or sphere of: *flew out of sight.* **b.** In a state away from the expected or usual: *out of practice.* **3.** From among: *five out of six votes.* **4.** Because of: *did it out of spite.* **5.** In a condition of no longer having: *We're out of coffee.*
out-of-bounds (out′əv-boundz′) ►*adv. & adj.* Beyond the designated boundaries or limits.
out-of-date (out′əv-dāt′) ►*adj.* Out of style.
out-of-door (out′əv-dôr′, -dōr′) ►*adj.* Var. of **outdoor.**
out-of-doors (out′əv-dôrz′, -dōrz′) ►*adv. & n.* Var. of **outdoors.**
out-of-pock•et (out′əv-pŏk′ĭt) ►*adj.* **1.** Calling for the spending of cash: *out-of-pocket expenses.* **2.** Lacking funds.
out-of-the-way (out′əv-*th*ə-wā′) ►*adj.* **1.** Remote; secluded. **2.** Unusual.
out•pace (out-pās′) ►*v.* To surpass; outstrip.
out•pa•tient (out′pā′shənt) ►*n.* A patient who receives treatment at a hospital but does not require an overnight stay.
out•place•ment (out′plās′mənt) ►*n.* The process by which an employer helps a terminated employee find a new job.
out•play (out-plā′) ►*v.* To play better than.
out•post (out′pōst′) ►*n.* **1a.** A detachment of troops stationed at a distance from a main force. **b.** The station occupied by such troops. **2.** An outlying settlement.
out•pour•ing (out′pôr′ĭng, -pōr′-) ►*n.* Something that pours out or is poured out: *an outpouring of lava; an outpouring of grief.*
out•put (out′po͝ot′) ►*n.* **1.** An amount produced or manufactured during a certain time. **2a.** The energy, power, or work produced by a system. **b.** *Comp. Sci.* The information produced by a program or process from a specific input. —**out′put′** *v.*
output device ►*n.* A device, such as a printer or speaker, that presents computer data.
out•rage (out′rāj′) ►*n.* **1.** An act of extreme violence or viciousness. **2.** An act grossly offensive to decency or good taste. **3.** Resentful anger. ►*v.* **-raged, -rag•ing 1.** To commit an outrage on. **2.** To produce anger or indignity in. [< OFr. *outre,* OUTRÉ.]
out•ra•geous (out-rā′jəs) ►*adj.* **1a.** Grossly offensive. **b.** Beyond the bounds of good taste. **2.** Extravagant; immoderate. —**out•ra′geous•ly** *adv.* —**out•ra′geous•ness** *n.*
out•rank (out-răngk′) ►*v.* To rank higher than.
ou•tré (o͞o-trā′) ►*adj.* Eccentric; bizarre. [< Lat. *ultrā,* beyond.]
out•reach (out-rēch′) ►*v.* **1.** To surpass in reach. **2.** To exceed. ►*n.* (out′rēch′) **1.** Extent of reach. **2.** A systematic attempt to provide services to a community.
out•rid•er (out′rī′dər) ►*n.* A mounted attendant.
out•rig•ger (out′rĭg′ər) ►*n.* **1.** A long thin float attached parallel to a seagoing canoe to prevent it from capsizing. **2.** A vessel fitted with an outrigger.
out•right (out′rīt′, -rīt′) ►*adv.* **1.** Without reservation or qualification. **2.** Completely; wholly. **3.** At once; straightway. ►*adj.* (out′rīt′) **1.** Unqualified: *an outright gift.* **2.** Thoroughgoing; out-and-out.
out•run (out-rŭn′) ►*v.* **1.** To run faster than. **2.** To exceed.
out•sell (out-sĕl′) ►*v.* To surpass in sales or selling.
out•set (out′sĕt′) ►*n.* Beginning; start.
out•shine (out-shīn′) ►*v.* **1.** To shine brighter than. **2.** To outdo.
out•side (out-sīd′, out′sīd′) ►*n.* **1.** The outer surface or side; exterior. **2.** The space beyond a boundary or limit. **3.** The utmost limit; maximum: *We'll be leaving in ten days at the outside.* ►*adj.* **1.** Of, restricted to, or situated on the outer side; external: *an outside door lock.* **2.** Acting, occurring, originating, or being at a place beyond certain limits: *outside assistance.* **3.** Extreme; uttermost: *exceeded even our out-*

side estimates. **4.** Unlikely; remote: *an outside chance.* ▸*adv.* **1.** On or to the outer side. **2.** Outdoors. ▸*prep.* **1.** On or to the outer side of. **2.** Beyond the limits of: *outside the city.* **3.** Except: *no information outside the figures given.*

out•sid•er (out-sī′dər) ▸*n.* One who is not part of a group or community.

out•size (out′sīz′) ▸*n.* An unusual size, esp. a very large size. —**out′size′, out′sized′** *adj.*

out•skirts (out′skûrts′) ▸*pl.n.* The peripheral parts, as of a city.

out•smart (out-smärt′) ▸*v.* To outwit.

out•spend (out-spĕnd′) ▸*v.* **1.** To spend beyond the limits of. **2.** To outdo in spending.

out•spo•ken (out-spō′kən) ▸*adj.* **1.** Spoken without reserve; candid. **2.** Frank in speech. —**out•spo′ken•ly** *adv.* —**out•spo′ken•ness** *n.*

out•spread (out-sprĕd′) ▸*v.* To spread out; extend. —**out′spread′** *adj.*

out•stand•ing (out-stăn′dĭng, out′stăn′-) ▸*adj.* **1.** Prominent. **2.** Superior; distinguished. **3.** Projecting upward or outward. **4.** Not settled or resolved. —**out•stand′ing•ly** *adv.*

out•stretch (out-strĕch′) ▸*v.* To extend.

out•strip (out-strĭp′) ▸*v.* **1.** To leave behind; outrun. **2.** To exceed; surpass.

out•take (out′tāk′) ▸*n.* A shot or scene, as of a movie, that is filmed but not used in the final version.

out•ward (out′wərd) ▸*adj.* **1.** Of or moving toward the outside or exterior. **2.** Purely external; superficial. ▸*adv.* also **out•wards** (-wərdz) Toward the outside. —**out′ward•ly** *adv.*

out•wear (out-wâr′) ▸*v.* To outlast.

out•weigh (out-wā′) ▸*v.* **1.** To weigh more than. **2.** To be more significant than.

out•wit (out-wĭt′) ▸*v.* **-wit•ted, -wit•ting.** To best or defeat by cleverness or cunning.

out•work (out-wûrk′) ▸*v.* To work better or faster than.

ou•zo (o͞o′zō) ▸*n.* A Greek liqueur flavored with anise. [Mod.Gk.]

o•va (ō′və) ▸*n.* Pl. of **ovum.**

o•val (ō′vəl) ▸*adj.* **1.** Egg-shaped. **2.** Shaped like an ellipse; elliptical. [< Lat. *ōvum*, egg.] —**o′val** *n.*

o•va•ry (ō′və-rē) ▸*n., pl.* **-ries 1.** The usu. paired female reproductive organ that produces ova. **2.** *Bot.* The ovule-bearing part of a pistil. [< Lat. *ōvum*, egg.] —**o•var′i•an** (ō-vâr′ē-ən) *adj.*

o•vate (ō′vāt′) ▸*adj.* Oval. —**o′vate′ly** *adv.*

o•va•tion (ō-vā′shən) ▸*n.* Enthusiastic, prolonged applause. [< Lat. *ovāre*, rejoice.]

ov•en (ŭv′ən) ▸*n.* A compartment for heating or baking food, as in a stove. [< OE *ofen.*]

o•ver (ō′vər) ▸*prep.* **1.** Above. **2.** Above and across. **3.** On the other side of. **4.** Upon. **5.** All through. **6.** So as to cover. **7.** Higher than. **8.** Through the duration of. **9.** More than. **10.** With reference to: *an argument over methods.* ▸*adv.* **1.** Above. **2a.** Across to another or opposite side. **b.** Across the edge or brim. **3.** Across an intervening distance. **4.** To a different opinion or allegiance. **5.** To a different person, condition, or title: *sign the property over.* **6.** So as to be completely enclosed or covered: *The river froze over.* **7.** Completely through; thoroughly: *Think the problem over.* **8a.** From an upright position. **b.** From an upward position to an inverted or reversed position. **9.** Again. **10.** In repetition: *ten times over.* **11.** In addition or excess. **12.** At an end: *The war is over.* ▸*adj.* **1.** External; outer. **2.** Excessive; extreme. **3a.** Not yet used up. **b.** Extra; surplus. —***idioms:*** **over against** Contrasted with. **over and above** In addition to; besides. [< OE *ofer.*]

o•ver•act (ō′vər-ăkt′) ▸*v.* To act with unnecessary exaggeration.

o•ver•age¹ (ō′vər-ĭj) ▸*n.* A surplus; excess.

o•ver•age² (ō′vər-āj′) ▸*adj.* Beyond the proper or required age.

o•ver•all (ō′vər-ôl′) ▸*adj.* **1.** From one end to the other. **2.** Including everything; comprehensive: *the overall cost.* ▸*adv.* (ō′vər-ôl′). Generally. ▸*n.* **overalls** Loose-fitting trousers with a bib front and shoulder straps.

o•ver•arm (ō′vər-ärm′) ▸*adj. Sports* Executed with the arm raised above the shoulder.

o•ver•awe (ō′vər-ô′) ▸*v.* To control or subdue by inspiring awe.

o•ver•bear (ō′vər-bâr′) ▸*v.* **1.** To crush or press down on with physical force. **2.** To prevail over; dominate.

o•ver•bear•ing (ō′vər-bâr′ĭng) ▸*adj.* Domineering and arrogant.

o•ver•bite (ō′vər-bīt′) ▸*n.* A condition of the teeth in which the front upper incisors and canines project over the lower.

o•ver•blown (ō′vər-blōn′) ▸*adj.* **1.** Excessive; overdone. **2.** Inflated; exaggerated.

o•ver•board (ō′vər-bôrd′, -bōrd′) ▸*adv.* Over the side of a boat or ship. —***idiom:*** **go overboard** To go to extremes.

o•ver•build (ō′vər-bĭld′) ▸*v.* To build beyond the demand or need of (an area).

o•ver•cast (ō′vər-kăst′, ō′vər-kăst′) ▸*adj.* **1.**

o′ver•a•bun′dance *n.*
o′ver•a•bun′dant *adj.*
o′ver•ac′tive *adj.*
o′ver•ag•gres′sive *adj.*
o′ver•am•bi′tion *n.*
o′ver•am•bi′tious *adj.*
o′ver•anx′ious *adj.*
o′ver•bid′ *v.*
o′ver•bur′den *v.*
o′ver•buy′ *v.*
o′ver•ca•pac′i•ty *n.*
o′ver•cap′i•tal•ize′ *v.*
o′ver•cau′tious *adj.*
o′ver•com′pen•sate′ *v.*
o′ver•con′fi•dence *n.*
o′ver•con′fi•dent *adj.*
o′ver•crit′i•cal *adj.*
o′ver•crowd′ *v.*
o′ver•de•vel′op *v.*
o′ver•de•vel′op•ment *n.*
o′ver•dress′ *v.*
o′ver•ea′ger *adj.*
o′ver•eat′ *v.*
o′ver•eat′er *n.*
o′ver•em′pha•sis *n.*
o′ver•em′pha•size′ *v.*
o′ver•es′ti•mate′ *v.*
o′ver•ex•ert′ *v.*
o′ver•ex•tend′ *v.*
o′ver•fed′ *adj.*
o′ver•feed′ *v.*
o′ver•fill′ *v.*
o′ver•graze′ *v.*
o′ver•in•dulge′ *v.*
o′ver•in•dul′gence *n.*
o′ver•load′ *v.*
o′ver•load′ *n.*
o′ver•long′ *adj. & adv.*
o′ver•med′i•cate′ *v.*
o′ver•med′i•ca′tion *n.*
o′ver•op′ti•mism *n.*
o′ver•op′ti•mis′tic *adj.*
o′ver•pay′ *v.*
o′ver•pop′u•late′ *v.*
o′ver•pop′u•lat′ed *adj.*

overalls

Clouded over. **2.** Gloomy; melancholy. **3.** Sewn with long overlying stiches.

o•ver•charge (ō′vər-chärj′) ►*v.* **1.** To charge too much. **2.** To fill too full. —**o′ver•charge′** *n.*

o•ver•coat (ō′vər-kōt′) ►*n.* A heavy coat worn over ordinary clothing.

o•ver•come (ō′vər-kŭm′) ►*v.* **1.** To defeat; conquer. **2.** To prevail over; surmount. **3.** To overpower, as with emotion.

o•ver•do (ō′vər-do͞o′) ►*v.* **1.** To do or use to excess; exaggerate. **2.** To cook too long.

o•ver•dose (ō′vər-dōs′) ►*v.* To take or cause to take too large a dose. —**o′ver•dose′** *n.*

o•ver•draft (ō′vər-drăft′) ►*n.* **1.** The act of overdrawing a bank account. **2.** The amount overdrawn.

o•ver•draw (ō′vər-drô′) ►*v.* **1.** To draw against (a bank account) in excess of credit. **2.** To exaggerate or overstate.

o•ver•drive (ō′vər-drīv′) ►*n.* An automotive transmission gear that transmits to the drive shaft a speed greater than engine speed.

o•ver•due (ō′vər-do͞o′, -dyo͞o′) ►*adj.* **1.** Being unpaid when due. **2.** Past due; late. See Syns at **tardy.**

o•ver•ex•pose (ō′vər-ĭk-spōz′) ►*v.* **-posed, -pos•ing.** To expose too long or too much. —**o′ver•ex•po′sure** *n.*

o•ver•flow (ō′vər-flō′) ►*v.* **1.** To flow over the top, brim, or banks (of). **2.** To spread or cover over. **3.** To teem; abound. See Syns at **teem.** ►*n.* (ō′vər-flō′) **1.** A flood. **2.** An excess; surplus: *received an overflow of mail.* **3.** An outlet through which excess liquid may escape.

o•ver•grow (ō′vər-grō′, ō′vər-grō′) ►*v.* **1.** To grow over with foliage. **2.** To grow too large for. **3.** To grow beyond normal size. —**o′ver•grown′** *adj.* —**o′ver•growth′** *n.*

o•ver•hand (ō′vər-hănd′) also **o•ver•hand•ed** (ō′vər-hăn′dĭd) ►*adj.* Executed with the hand above the level of the shoulder. —**o′ver•hand′** *adv. & n.*

o•ver•hang (ō′vər-hăng′) ►*v.* **1.** To project or extend beyond. See Syns at **bulge. 2.** To loom over. —**o′ver•hang′** *n.*

o•ver•haul (ō′vər-hôl′, ō′vər-hôl′) ►*v.* **1a.** To examine carefully. **b.** To repair thoroughly. **2.** To overtake. —**o′ver•haul′** *n.*

o•ver•head (ō′vər-hĕd′) ►*adj.* **1.** Located or functioning from above. **2.** Of or relating to the operating expenses of a business. ►*n.* The operating expenses of a business, including rent, utilities, and taxes. —**o′ver•head′** *adv.*

o•ver•hear (ō′vər-hîr′) ►*v.* To hear without the speaker's awareness or intent.

o•ver•joy (ō′vər-joi′) ►*v.* To fill with joy; delight. —**o′ver•joyed′** (-joid′) *adj.*

o•ver•kill (ō′vər-kĭl′) ►*n.* **1.** Destructive nuclear capacity exceeding the amount needed to destroy an enemy. **2.** An excess response.

o•ver•land (ō′vər-lănd′, -lənd) ►*adj.* Over or across land. —**o′ver•land′** *adv.*

o•ver•lap (ō′vər-lăp′) ►*v.* **1.** To extend over and cover part of. **2.** To have something in common with. —**o′ver•lap′** *n.*

o•ver•lay (ō′vər-lā′) ►*v.* To lay or spread over or on. —**o′ver•lay′** *n.*

o•ver•look (ō′vər-lo͝ok′) ►*v.* **1.** To look over from above. **2.** To afford a view over. **3.** To fail to notice or consider. **4.** To ignore deliberately or indulgently; disregard. **5.** To look over; examine. **6.** To oversee. See Syns at **supervise.** ►*n.* (ō′vər-lo͝ok′). An elevated spot that affords a broad view.

o•ver•lord (ō′vər-lôrd′) ►*n.* A lord having supremacy over other lords.

o•ver•ly (ō′vər-lē) ►*adv.* Excessively.

o•ver•mas•ter (ō′vər-măs′tər) ►*v.* To overcome.

o•ver•match (ō′vər-măch′) ►*v.* **1.** To be more than a match for. **2.** To match with a superior opponent.

o•ver•much (ō′vər-mŭch′) ►*adj.* Too much. ►*adv.* In excess.

o•ver•night (ō′vər-nīt′) ►*adj.* **1.** Lasting for or remaining during a night. **2.** Sudden: *an overnight success.* ►*adv.* (ō′vər-nīt′) **1.** During or

o′ver•pop′u•la′tion *n.*
o′ver•pow′er•ful *adj.*
o′ver•praise′ *v.*
o′ver•pre•scribe′ *v.*
o′ver•price′ *v.*
o′ver•pro•duce′ *v.*
o′ver•pro•duc′tion *n.*
o′ver•pro•tect′ *v.*
o′ver•pro•tec′tion *n.*
o′ver•pro•tec′tive *adj.*
o′ver•rate′ *v.*
o′ver•re•act′ *v.*
o′ver•re•ac′tion *n.*
o′ver•re•fine′ *v.*
o′ver•reg′u•late *v.*
o′ver•reg′u•la′tion *n.*
o′ver•rep′re•sent′ed *adj.*
o′ver•ripe′ *adj.*
o′ver•rip′en *v.*
o′ver•sell′ *v.*
o′ver•sen′si•tive *adj.*
o′ver•sim′pli•fi•ca′tion *n.*
o′ver•sim′pli•fy′ *v.*
o′ver•sized′ *adv.*
o′ver•spe′cial•ize′ *v.*
o′ver•spend′ *v.*
o′ver•staff′ *v.*
o′ver•stock′ *v.*
o′ver•strain′ *v.*
o′ver•stress′ *v.*
o′ver•stretch′ *v.*
o′ver•sup•ply′ *n.*
o′ver•sup•ply′ *v.*
o′ver•tax′ *v.*
o′ver•tax•a′tion *n.*
o′ver•use′ *v. & n.*
o′ver•val′u•a′tion *n.*
o′ver•val′ue *v.*
o′ver•wea′ry *adj. & v.*
o′ver•weight′ *adj.*
o′ver•wind′ *v.*
o′ver•work′ *v.*
o′ver•writ′ten *adj.*
o′ver•zeal′ous *adj.*

for the length of the night. **2.** Suddenly. —**o′ver•night′** *n.*

o•ver•pass (ō′vər-păs′) ►*n.* A roadway or bridge that crosses above another.

o•ver•play (ō′vər-plā′) ►*v.* **1.** To overact. **2.** To overestimate the strength of (one's position).

o•ver•pow•er (ō′vər-pou′ər) ►*v.* **1.** To overcome by superior force. **2.** To overwhelm.

o•ver•qual•i•fied (ō′vər-kwŏl′ə-fīd′) ►*adj.* Educated or skilled beyond what is necessary for a particular job.

o•ver•rate (ō′vər-rāt′) ►*v.* To overestimate the merits of.

o•ver•reach (ō′vər-rēch′) ►*v.* **1.** To reach or extend over or beyond. **2.** To miss by reaching too far or attempting too much. **3.** To defeat (oneself) by going too far. —**o′ver•reach′** *n.* —**o′ver•reach′er** *n.*

o•ver•ride (ō′vər-rīd′) ►*v.* **1.** To ride across. **2.** To trample on. **3.** To prevail over. **4.** To declare null and void; set aside.

o•ver•rid•ing (ō′vər-rī′dĭng) ►*adj.* More important than all others: *an overriding concern.* —**o′ver•rid′ing•ly** *adv.*

o•ver•rule (ō′vər-ro͞ol′) ►*v.* **1.** To rule against. **2.** To nullify or reverse.

o•ver•run (ō′vər-rŭn′) ►*v.* **1.** To spread or swarm over destructively. **2.** To spread swiftly throughout. **3.** To overflow. **4.** To run or extend beyond; exceed. ►*n.* (ō′vər-rŭn′) **1.** An act of overrunning. **2.** The amount by which something overruns.

o•ver•scale (ō′vər-skāl′) or **o•ver•scaled** (-skāld′) ►*adj.* Unusually large or extensive.

o•ver•seas (ō′vər-sēz′, ō′vər-sēz′) ►*adv.* Beyond the sea; abroad. —**o′ver•seas′** *adj.*

o•ver•see (ō′vər-sē′) ►*v.* **1.** To watch over and direct. See Syns at **supervise. 2.** To examine or inspect. —**o′ver•se′er** *n.*

o•ver•sexed (ō′vər-sĕkst′) ►*adj.* Having an excessive sexual appetite.

o•ver•shad•ow (ō′vər-shăd′ō) ►*v.* **1.** To cast a shadow over. **2.** To surpass; dominate.

o•ver•shoe (ō′vər-sho͞o′) ►*n.* An outer shoe worn as protection from water or snow.

o•ver•shoot (ō′vər-sho͞ot′) ►*v.* **1.** To shoot or go over or beyond. **2.** To miss by or as if by shooting or going too far.

o•ver•sight (ō′vər-sīt′) ►*n.* **1.** An unintentional omission or mistake. **2.** Supervision.

o•ver•size (ō′vər-sīz′) also **o•ver•sized** (-sīzd′) ►*adj.* Larger in size than usual.

o•ver•skirt (ō′vər-skûrt′) ►*n.* A skirt worn over another.

o•ver•sleep (ō′vər-slēp′) ►*v.* To sleep beyond one's intended time for waking.

o•ver•state (ō′vər-stāt′) ►*v.* To exaggerate. See Syns at **exaggerate.** —**o′ver•state′ment** *n.*

o•ver•stay (ō′vər-stā′) ►*v.* To stay beyond the limits or duration of.

o•ver•step (ō′vər-stĕp′) ►*v.* To go beyond.

o•ver•stuff (ō′vər-stŭf′) ►*v.* **1.** To stuff too much into. **2.** To upholster thickly.

o•ver•sub•scribe (ō′vər-səb-skrīb′) ►*v.* To subscribe for in excess of available supply. —**o′ver•sub•scrip′tion** (-skrĭp′shən) *n.*

o•vert (ō-vûrt′, ō′vûrt′) ►*adj.* Open and observable; not concealed. [< OFr., p.part. of *ovrir*, to open.] —**o•vert′ly** *adv.* —**o•vert′ness** *n.*

o•ver•take (ō′vər-tāk′) ►*v.* To catch up with.

o•ver-the-count•er (ō′vər-*th*ə-koun′tər) ►*adj.* **1.** Not listed or available on an officially recognized stock exchange. **2.** Sold legally without a doctor's prescription.

o•ver-the-top (ō′vər-*th*ə-tŏp′) ►*adj.* Exceeding the normal bounds; extravagant.

o•ver•throw (ō′vər-thrō′) ►*v.* **1.** To overturn. **2.** To bring about the downfall of; topple. **3.** To throw over and beyond. —**o′ver•throw′** *n.*

Syns: *overthrow, overturn, subvert, topple, upset* **v.**

o•ver•time (ō′vər-tīm′) ►*n.* **1.** Working hours in addition to those of a regular schedule. **2.** Payment for such work. **3.** *Sports* A period of playing time added after the expiration of the set time limit.

o•ver•tone (ō′vər-tōn′) ►*n.* **1.** often **overtones** An implication; hint: *overtones of jealousy.* **2.** See **harmonic** 1.

o•ver•top (ō′vər-tŏp′) ►*v.* **1.** To tower above. **2.** To take precedence over.

o•ver•ture (ō′vər-cho͝or′) ►*n.* **1.** *Mus.* **a.** An instrumental introduction to an extended work. **b.** An independent instrumental composition of similar form. **2.** A first offer or proposal. [< Lat. *apertūra*, opening.]

o•ver•turn (ō′vər-tûrn′) ►*v.* **1.** To turn over; upset. **2.** To overthrow. See Syns at **overthrow.**

o•ver•view (ō′vər-vyo͞o′) ►*n.* A comprehensive view; survey.

o•ver•ween•ing (ō′vər-wē′nĭng) ►*adj.* **1.** Arrogant; overbearing. **2.** Immoderate.

o•ver•weigh (ō′vər-wā′) ►*v.* **1.** To outweigh. **2.** To overburden.

o•ver•whelm (ō′vər-hwĕlm′, -wĕlm′) ►*v.* **1.** To submerge; engulf. **2.** To defeat completely. **3.** To turn over; upset.

o•ver•wrought (ō′vər-rôt′) ►*adj.* **1.** Nervous or excited. **2.** Extremely elaborate.

ovi– or **ovo–** or **ov–** ►*pref.* Egg; ovum: *oviduct.* [< Lat. *ōvum*, egg.]

Ov•id (ŏv′ĭd). 43 B.C.–A.D. 17. Roman poet.

o•vi•duct (ō′vĭ-dŭkt′) ►*n.* A tube through which ova pass from an ovary.

o•vip•a•rous (ō-vĭp′ər-əs) ►*adj.* Producing eggs that hatch outside the body.

o•void (ō′void′) also **o•voi•dal** (ō-void′l) ►*adj.* Egg-shaped. —**o′void** *n.*

o•vo•vi•vip•a•rous (ō′vō-vī-vĭp′ər-əs) ►*adj.* Producing eggs that hatch within the female's body.

o•vu•late (ō′vyə-lāt′, ŏv′yə-) ►*v.* **-lat•ed, -lat•ing.** To produce or discharge ova. [< OVULE.] —**o′vu•la′tion** *n.*

o•vule (ō′vyo͞ol, ŏv′yo͞ol) ►*n.* A minute structure in seed plants that develops into a seed after fertilization. [< Lat. *ōvum*, egg.] —**o′vu•lar** (ō′vyə-lər, ŏv′yə-) *adj.*

o•vum (ō′vəm) ►*n.*, *pl.* **o•va** (ō′və). The female reproductive cell of animals. [Lat. *ōvum*, egg.]

owe (ō) ►*v.* **owed, ow•ing 1.** To have to pay or repay: *He owes me five dollars.* **2.** To be in debt to. **3.** To have a moral obligation to: *I owe them an apology.* **4.** To be indebted for. [< OE *āgan*, possess.]

Ow•en (ō′ĭn), **Robert.** 1771–1858. Welsh-born British manufacturer and reformer.

Ow•ens (ō′ĭnz), **James Cleveland.** "Jesse." 1913–80. Amer. athlete.

ow•ing (ō′ĭng) ►*adj.* Still to be paid; due.

Jesse Owens
photographed in 1936

owl (oul) ►*n.* Any of various usu. nocturnal birds of prey having large heads, short hooked beaks, and large eyes set forward. [< OE *ūle.*] —**owl'ish** *adj.*

owl•et (ou'lĭt) ►*n.* A young owl.

own (ōn) ►*adj.* Of or belonging to oneself. ►*n.* That which belongs to one. ►*v.* **1.** To have or possess. **2.** To admit or acknowledge. —***idiom:* on (one's) own** Completely independent. [< OE *āgen.*] —**own'er** *n.* —**own'er•ship'** *n.*

ox (ŏks) ►*n., pl.* **ox•en** (ŏk'sən) **1.** An adult castrated bull. **2.** A bovine mammal. [< OE *oxa.*]

ox•al•ic acid (ŏk-săl'ĭk) ►*n.* A poisonous, crystalline organic acid used as a bleach and rust remover. [< Lat. *oxalis*, a plant.]

ox•blood red (ŏks'blŭd') ►*n.* A deep reddish brown.

ox•bow (ŏks'bō') ►*n.* **1.** A U-shaped collar for an ox. **2.** A U-shaped bend in a river.

ox•ford (ŏks'fərd) ►*n.* **1.** A low shoe that laces over the instep. **2.** A cotton cloth used primarily for shirts.

Oxford. A borough of S-central England on the Thames R. WNW of London. Pop. 131,967.

ox•i•dant (ŏk'sĭ-dənt) ►*n.* An oxidizing agent.

ox•i•da•tion (ŏk'sĭ-dā'shən) ►*n.* **1.** The combination of a substance with oxygen. **2.** A reaction in which the atoms in an element lose electrons and the element's valence is correspondingly increased. —**ox'i•da'tive** *adj.* —**ox'i•da'tive•ly** *adv.*

ox•ide (ŏk'sīd') ►*n.* A binary compound of an element or radical with oxygen. —**ox•id'ic** (ŏk-sĭd'ĭk) *adj.*

ox•i•dize (ŏk'sĭ-dīz') ►*v.* **-dized, -diz•ing 1.** To combine with oxygen. **2.** To increase the positive charge or valence of (an element) by removing electrons. **3.** To coat with oxide. —**ox'i•di•za'tion** *n.* —**ox'i•diz'er** *n.*

Ox•nard (ŏks'närd') A city of S CA WNW of Los Angeles. Pop. 142,216.

Ox•o•ni•an (ŏk-sō'nē-ən) ►*adj.* Of or relating to Oxford or Oxford University. [< Med.Lat. *Oxōnia*, Oxford.] —**Ox•o'ni•an** *n.*

oxy– ►*pref.* Oxygen, esp. additional oxygen: *oxyacetylene.* [< OXYGEN.]

ox•y•a•cet•y•lene (ŏk'sē-ə-sĕt'l-ĭn, -ēn') ►*adj.* Of or using a mixture of acetylene and oxygen: *an oxyacetylene torch.*

ox•y•gen (ŏk'sĭ-jən) ►*n. Symbol* **O** A gaseous element that constitutes 21 percent of the atmosphere by volume, is essential for plant and animal respiration, and is required for nearly all combustion. At. no. 8. See table at **element.** [Fr. *oxygène* : Gk. *oxus*, acid + -GEN.] —**ox'y•gen'ic** (-jĕn'ĭk) *adj.* —**ox•yg'e•nous** (ŏk-sĭj'ə-nəs) *adj.*

ox•y•gen•ate (ŏk'sĭ-jə-nāt') ►*v.* **-at•ed, -at•ing.** To treat, combine, or infuse with oxygen. —**ox'y•gen•a'tion** *n.*

oxygen mask ►*n.* A masklike device placed over the mouth and nose and through which oxygen is supplied from an attached tank.

oxygen tent ►*n.* A canopy placed usu. over the head and shoulders of a patient to provide oxygen at a higher level than normal.

ox•y•mo•ron (ŏk'sē-môr'ŏn', -mōr'-) ►*n., pl.* **-mo•ra** (-môr'ə, -mōr'ə) or **-rons.** A rhetorical figure in which incongruous or contradictory terms are combined, as in *a deafening silence.* [Gk. *oxumōron* : *oxus*, sharp + *mōros*, dull.] —**ox'y•mo•ron'ic** (-mə-rŏn'ĭk) *adj.*

oys•ter (oi'stər) ►*n.* Any of several edible bivalve mollusks that have a rough, irregularly shaped shell. [< Gk. *ostreon.*]

oz also **oz.** ►*abbr.* ounce

oz. ap. ►*abbr.* apothecaries' ounce

O•zark Plateau or **O•zark Mountains** (ō'zärk'). An upland region of the S-central US in SW MO, NW AR, and E OK.

oz. av. ►*abbr.* avoirdupois ounce

o•zone (ō'zōn') ►*n.* **1.** A blue gaseous allotrope of oxygen, O_3, formed naturally from diatomic oxygen by electric discharge or exposure to ultraviolet radiation, used to purify water and as a bleach. **2.** *Informal* Fresh, pure air. [< Gk. *ozein*, to smell.]

ozone hole ►*n.* An area of the ozone layer periodically depleted of ozone, gen. occurring over the Polar Regions.

ozone layer ►*n.* A region of the upper atmosphere, between about 15 and 30 km (10 and 20 mi) in altitude, containing a relatively high concentration of ozone that absorbs solar ultraviolet radiation.

o•zo•no•sphere (ō-zō'nə-sfîr') ►*n.* See **ozone layer.**

oz. t. ►*abbr.* troy ounce

P

p[1] or **P** (pē) ►*n., pl.* **p's** or **P's** also **ps** or **Ps.** The 16th letter of the English alphabet.

p[2] ►*abbr.* proton

P[1] ► The symbol for the element **phosphorus.**

P[2] ►*abbr.* **1.** pawn (chess) **2.** *Phys.* pressure

p. ►*abbr.* **1.** page **2.** part **3.** participle **4.** past **5.** penny **6.** peseta **7.** peso **8.** pint

Pa ► The symbol for the element **protactinium.**

PA ►*abbr.* **1.** or **Pa.** Pennsylvania **2.** physician's assistant **3.** power of attorney **4.** prosecuting attorney **5.** public-address system

pa. ▸*abbr.* per annum

pa'an•ga (päng'gə, pä-äng'-) ▸*n.* See table at **currency.** [Tongan.]

PABA (pä'bə) ▸*n.* A compound used in sunscreens to absorb ultraviolet light. [*p(ara)-a(mino)b(enzoic) a(cid).*]

pab•u•lum (păb'yə-ləm) ▸*n.* A substance that gives nourishment, esp. a soft food. [Lat. *pābulum.*]

PAC ▸*abbr.* political action committee

pace (pās) ▸*n.* **1.** A step made in walking. **2.** The distance spanned by such a step. **3.** Rate of movement or progress. **4.** A manner of walking or running: *a jaunty pace.* **5.** A gait of a horse in which both feet on one side leave and return to the ground together. ▸*v.* **paced, pac•ing 1.** To walk or stride back and forth. **2.** To measure by counting the number of steps needed to cover a distance. **3.** To set or regulate the rate of speed for. **4.** To train (a horse) in a particular gait, esp. the pace. [< Lat. *passus.*] —**pac'er** *n.*

pace•mak•er (pās'mā'kər) ▸*n.* **1.** One who sets the pace in a race. **2.** A leader in a field. **3a.** A part of the body, esp. of the heart, that sets the pace or rhythm of physiological activity. **b.** A surgically implanted electronic device used to regulate the heartbeat. —**pace'mak'ing** *adj. & n.*

pach•y•derm (păk'ĭ-dûrm') ▸*n.* A large, thick-skinned, hoofed mammal such as the elephant or rhinoceros. [< Gk. *pakhudermos*, thick-skinned.]

pach•y•san•dra (păk'ĭ-săn'drə) ▸*n.* A low-growing plant with evergreen leaves, cultivated as a ground cover. [< Gk. *pakhus*, thick + Gk. *aner, andr-*, man, male.]

pa•cif•ic (pə-sĭf'ĭk) ▸*adj.* **1.** Tending to diminish conflict. **2.** Of a peaceful nature; tranquil. —**pa•cif'i•cal•ly** *adv.*

Pacific Islander ▸*n.* A native or inhabitant of any of the islands of Oceania.

Pacific Islands, Trust Territory of the. A group of islands and islets of the NW Pacific administered by the US from 1947 to 1978.

Pacific Northwest. A region of the NW US including WA and OR and sometimes SW British Columbia, Canada.

Pacific Ocean. The largest of the world's oceans, divided into the **North Pacific** and the **South Pacific** and extending from the W Americas to E Asia and Australia.

pac•i•fi•er (păs'ə-fī'ər) ▸*n.* A rubber or plastic nipple for a baby to suck or chew on.

pac•i•fism (păs'ə-fĭz'əm) ▸*n.* Opposition to war or violence as a means of resolving disputes. —**pac'i•fist** *n.* —**pac'i•fis'tic** *adj.*

pac•i•fy (păs'ə-fī') ▸*v.* **-fied, -fy•ing 1.** To ease the anger or agitation of. **2.** To end fighting or violence in. [< Lat. *pāx, pāc-*, peace.] —**pac'i•fi•ca'tion** *n.*

pack (păk) ▸*n.* **1a.** A collection of items tied up or wrapped; bundle. **b.** A container made to be carried on the back. **2.** A small package containing a standard number of identical or similar items: *a pack of matches.* **3.** A complete set of related items: *a pack of cards.* **4a.** A group of animals, such as wolves. **b.** A gang or group of people. **5.** A material, such as gauze, that is applied to the body for therapeutic purposes. ▸*v.* **1.** To fold, roll, or combine into a bundle. **2a.** To put into a receptacle for transporting or storing. **b.** To fill up with items: *pack one's trunk.* **3a.** To crowd together tightly. **b.** To fill up tight; cram. **4.** To wrap tightly, as for protection. **5.** To press together; compact firmly. **6.** *Informal* To carry: *pack a pistol.* **7.** To send unceremoniously: *packed the children off to bed.* **8.** To rig (a voting panel) to be favorable to one's purposes. [ME.]

pack•age (păk'ĭj) ▸*n.* **1.** A wrapped or boxed object; parcel. **2.** A proposition or an offer composed of several items: *a benefits package.* ▸*v.* **-aged, -ag•ing.** To place or make into a package.

package store ▸*n.* A store that sells sealed bottles of alcoholic beverages for consumption off the premises.

pack•ag•ing (păk'ə-jĭng) ▸*n.* **1.** Material used for making packages. **2.** The manner in which something is presented to the public.

pack animal ▸*n.* An animal, such as a mule, used to carry loads.

pack•er (păk'ər) ▸*n.* **1.** One that packs. **2.** One who processes and packs goods, usu. meat products.

pack•et (păk'ĭt) ▸*n.* **1.** A small package or bundle. **2.** A regularly scheduled passenger and cargo boat.

pack•ing (păk'ĭng) ▸*n.* **1.** The processing and packaging of manufactured products, esp. food products. **2.** Material used to prevent breakage or seepage.

pack rat ▸*n.* **1.** Any of various small North American rodents that collect a great variety of small objects. **2.** *Slang* A collector of miscellaneous objects.

pack•sad•dle (păk'săd'l) ▸*n.* A saddle on which loads can be secured.

pact (păkt) ▸*n.* A formal agreement; treaty. [< Lat. *pactum.*]

pad[1] (păd) ▸*n.* **1.** Soft material used esp. to fill, give shape, or protect against injury. **2.** A number of sheets of paper glued together at one end; tablet. **3.** The broad, floating leaf of an aquatic plant such as the water lily. **4.** The cushionlike flesh on the underpart of the feet of many animals. **5.** A launch pad. **6.** *Slang* One's apartment or room. ▸*v.* **pad•ded, pad•ding 1.** To line or stuff with soft material. **2.** To lengthen or fill out with extraneous material. [?]

pad[2] (păd) ▸*v.* **pad•ded, pad•ding.** To go about quietly on foot. [Prob. of LGer. orig.]

pad•ding (păd'ĭng) ▸*n.* Material that is used to pad.

pad•dle[1] (păd'l) ▸*n.* **1.** A wooden implement having a blade at one end or at both ends, used to propel a canoe or small boat. **2.** Any of various implements resembling a paddle, used esp. for stirring, mixing, or beating. **3.** A light wooden racket used in playing table tennis. **4.** A board on a paddle wheel. ▸*v.* **-dled, -dling 1.** To move or propel through water with or as if with a paddle. **2.** To stir or beat with a paddle. [ME *padell*, cleaning implement.] —**pad'dler** *n.*

pad•dle[2] (păd'l) ▸*v.* **-dled, -dling.** To dabble about in shallow water; splash gently with the hands or feet. [Perh. of LGer. orig.]

pad•dle•board (păd'l-bôrd', -bōrd') ▸*n.* A long, narrow, floatable board used esp. in surfing.

paddle wheel ► *n.* A wheel with boards or paddles around its rim, used to propel a ship.

pad•dock (păd′ək) ► *n.* **1.** A fenced area, usu. near a stable, used chiefly for grazing horses. **2.** An enclosure at a racetrack where horses are saddled and paraded before a race. [< OE *pearroc.*]

pad•dy (păd′ē) ► *n., pl.* **-dies.** An irrigated or flooded field where rice is grown. [Malay *padi.*]

paddy wagon ► *n. Slang* A van used by police for taking suspects into custody. [?]

Pa•de•rew•ski (păd′ə-rĕf′skē, -rĕv′-, pä′də-), **Ignace Jan.** 1860–1941. Polish pianist and politician.

pad•lock (păd′lŏk′) ► *n.* A lock with a U-shaped bar that is passed through the staple of a hasp or a link in a chain and then snapped shut. [ME *padlok.*] —**pad′lock′** *v.*

pad thai (păd′ tī′, päd′) ► *n.* A Thai dish of stir-fried rice noodles, egg, peanuts, and other ingredients. [Thai *phàd thaj*, Thai fried dish.]

Pad•u•a (păj′o͞o-ə, păd′yo͞o-ə) A city of NE Italy W of Venice. Pop. 215,025.

pae•an (pē′ən) ► *n.* A song of joyful praise or exultation. [< Gk. *Paian*, Apollo.]

pa•el•la (pä-ĕl′ə, pä-ā′yä) ► *n.* A Spanish dish made with rice, vegetables, meat, and seafood. [< Lat. *patella*, pan.]

Paes•tum (pĕs′təm, pē′stəm) An ancient city of S Italy on the Gulf of Salerno.

pa•gan (pā′gən) ► *n.* One who is not a Christian, Muslim, or Jew. [< Lat. *pāgānus*, country dweller.] —**pa′gan** *adj.* —**pa′gan•ism** *n.*

Pa•ga•ni•ni (păg′ə-nē′nē, pä′gä-), **Niccolò.** 1782–1840. Italian violinist and composer.

page[1] (pāj) ► *n.* **1.** A sheet of paper or one side of a sheet, as of a book, letter, or manuscript. **2.** *Comp. Sci.* A webpage. ► *v.* **paged, pag•ing** **1.** To number the pages of. **2.** To turn the pages of. [< Lat. *pāgina.*]

page[2] (pāj) ► *n.* **1.** A youth in attendance at court. **2.** One who is employed to run errands, carry messages, or act as a guide, as in a hotel. ► *v.* **paged, pag•ing.** To summon or call (a person) by name. [< OFr.]

pag•eant (păj′ənt) ► *n.* **1.** An elaborate public spectacle depicting a historical event. **2.** A spectacular procession or celebration. **3.** Colorful, showy display. [< Med.Lat. *pāgina*, mystery play.] —**pag′eant•ry** *n.*

page•boy (pāj′boi′) ► *n.* A hairstyle, usu. shoulder-length, with the ends of the hair curled under smoothly.

pag•i•na•tion (păj′ə-nā′shən) ► *n.* **1.** The system by which pages are numbered. **2.** The arrangement and number of pages in a book. —**pag′i•nate** *v.*

pa•go•da (pə-gō′də) ► *n.* A many-storied Buddhist tower, erected as a memorial or shrine. [Port. *pagode.*]

Pa•go Pa•go also **Pan•go Pan•go** (päng′ō päng′ō, päng′gō päng′gō). The capital of American Samoa, on S Tutuila I. Pop. 3,519.

Pah•la•vi (pä′lə-vē′), **Muhammad Reza.** 1919–80. Shah of Iran from 1941 to 1979.

paid (pād) ► *v.* P.t. and p.part. of **pay.**

pail (pāl) ► *n.* A watertight cylindrical vessel with a handle; bucket. [ME *paile.*]

pain (pān) ► *n.* **1.** An unpleasant sensation occurring as a consequence of injury, disease, or emotional disorder. **2.** Suffering or distress. **3.**

pagoda

pains Great care or effort: *take pains with one's work.* **4.** *Informal* A source of annoyance; nuisance. ► *v.* To cause or suffer pain. —***idiom:* on** (or **under) pain of** Subject to the penalty of a specified punishment, such as death. [< Gk. *poinē*, penalty.] —**pain′ful** *adj.* —**pain′ful•ly** *adv.* —**pain′less** *adj.* —**pain′less•ly** *adv.*

Syns: *pain, ache, pang, throe, twinge* **n.**

Paine (pān), **Thomas.** 1737–1809. British-born Amer. Revolutionary leader.

pain•kill•er (pān′kĭl′ər) ► *n.* An agent, such as an analgesic drug, that relieves pain. —**pain′kill′ing** *adj.*

pains•tak•ing (pānz′tā′kĭng) ► *adj.* Taking pains; very careful and diligent. —**pains′tak′ing•ly** *adv.*

paint (pānt) ► *n.* **1a.** A liquid mixture, usu. of a solid pigment in a liquid vehicle, used as a decorative or protective coating. **b.** The dry film formed by such a mixture when applied to a surface. **2.** Makeup. **3.** See **pinto.** ► *v.* **1a.** To represent with paints. **b.** To depict vividly in words. **2.** To coat or decorate with paint. **3.** To apply cosmetics to (e.g., the face). **4.** To practice the art of painting. [< Lat. *pingere*, to paint.] —**paint′er** *n.*

paint•brush (pānt′brŭsh′) ► *n.* A brush for applying paint.

Paint•ed Desert (pān′tĭd) A plateau region of N-central AZ E of the Colorado and Little Colorado rivers.

paint•ing (pān′tĭng) ► *n.* **1.** The process, art, or occupation of working with paint. **2.** A picture or design in paint.

pair (pâr) ► *n., pl.* **pair** or **pairs** **1.** Two corresponding persons or items similar in form or function: *a pair of shoes.* **2.** One object composed of two joined, similar parts: *a pair of pliers.* **3.** Two persons or animals considered together. ► *v.* **1.** To arrange in sets of two; couple. **2.** To form pairs or a pair. [< Lat. *paria*, equals.]

pais•ley (pāz′lē) ► *adj.* **1.** Made of a soft wool fabric with a colorful swirled pattern of curved shapes. **2.** Marked with this pattern. [After *Paisley*, Scotland.]

Pai•ute (pī′yo͞ot′) ► *n., pl.* **-ute** or **-utes.** A member of either of two distinct Native American peoples, the Northern Paiute and the Southern Paiute, of the Great Basin.

pa•ja•mas (pə-jä′məz, -jăn′əz) ► *pl.n.* A loose-fitting garment consisting of trousers and a jacket, worn for sleeping or lounging. [Hindi *pāijāma*, loose-fitting trousers.]

Pak•i•stan (păk′ĭ-stăn′, pä′kĭ-stän′) A country of S Asia on the Arabian Sea. Cap. Islamabad. Pop. 126,610,000. —**Pak′i•stan′i** (-stăn′ē, -stä′nē) *adj. & n.*

pal (păl) *Informal* ►*n.* A friend; chum. ►*v.* **palled, pal•ling.** To spend time with a friend. [Romany *phral, phal.*]

pal•ace (păl′ĭs) ►*n.* **1.** The official residence of a royal personage. **2.** A large or splendid residence. [< Lat. *Palātium*, Palatine Hill, Rome.]

pal•a•din (păl′ə-dĭn) ►*n.* A paragon of chivalry; heroic champion. [< LLat. *palātīnus*, palatine.]

pal•an•quin (păl′ən-kēn′) ►*n.* A covered litter carried on poles on the shoulders of four or more bearers. [< Skt. *palyaṅkaḥ*, couch.]

pal•at•a•ble (păl′ə-tə-bəl) ►*adj.* **1.** Agreeable to the taste. **2.** Acceptable to the mind or sensibilities: *a palatable solution.*

pal•ate (păl′ĭt) ►*n.* **1.** The roof of the mouth, consisting of the hard palate and the soft palate. **2.** The sense of taste. [< Lat. *palātum.*] —**pal′a•tal** *adj.*

pa•la•tial (pə-lā′shəl) ►*adj.* **1.** Of or suitable for a palace. **2.** Of the nature of a palace, as in spaciousness or ornateness. [< Lat. *Palātium*, imperial residence.]

pa•lat•i•nate (pə-lăt′n-āt′, -ĭt) ►*n.* The office or territory of a palatine.

pal•a•tine (păl′ə-tīn′) ►*n.* **1.** A title for various officials of the late Roman and Byzantine empires. **2.** A feudal lord exercising sovereign power over his lands. ►*adj.* **1.** Belonging to or fit for a palace. **2.** Of a palatine or palatinate. [< Lat. *Palātium*, imperial residence.]

Pa•lau (pä-lou′, pə-) A group of volcanic islands in the Caroline Is. of the W Pacific.

pa•lav•er (pə-lăv′ər, -lä′vər) ►*n.* Long and idle chatter. [< LLat. *parabola*, speech, parable.] —**pa•lav′er** *v.*

pale[1] (pāl) ►*n.* **1.** A stake or pointed stick; picket. **2.** A fence enclosing an area. **3.** The area enclosed by a fence or boundary. —***idiom:* beyond the pale** Beyond safe or acceptable limits. [< Lat. *pālus.*]

pale[2] (pāl) ►*adj.* **pal•er, pal•est 1.** Whitish in complexion; pallid. **2.** Of a low intensity of color; light. **3.** Of a low intensity of light; dim or faint. [< Lat. *pallēre*, be pale.] —**pale** *v.* —**pale′ness** *n.*

Pa•lem•bang (pä′ləm-bäng′, -lĕm-) A city of Indonesia on SE Sumatra I. Pop. 787,187.

paleo– or **pale–** ►*pref.* Ancient or prehistoric: *paleography.* [< Gk. *palaios*, ancient.]

pa•le•o•bi•ol•o•gy (pā′lē-ō-bī-ŏl′ə-jē) ►*n.* The study of ancient organisms by means of their fossils. —**pa′le•o•bi•ol′o•gist** *n.*

Pa•le•o•cene (pā′lē-ə-sēn′) *Geol.* ►*adj.* Of or being the 1st epoch of the Tertiary Period, marked by the appearance of placental mammals. ►*n.* The Paleocene Epoch.

pa•le•og•ra•phy (pā′lē-ŏg′rə-fē) ►*n.* The study of ancient written documents. —**pa′le•og′ra•pher** *n.* —**pa′le•o•graph′ic** (-ə-grăf′ĭk), **pa′le•o•graph′i•cal** *adj.*

Pa•le•o•lith•ic (pā′lē-ə-lĭth′ĭk) ►*adj.* Of or being the Stone Age period beginning with the earliest chipped stone tools, about 750,000 years ago, until the beginning of the Mesolithic, about 15,000 years ago. ►*n.* The Paleolithic Period.

pa•le•on•tol•o•gy (pā′lē-ŏn-tŏl′ə-jē) ►*n.* The study of the forms of life existing in prehistoric or geologic times. —**pa′le•on′to•log′ic** (-ŏn′tə-lŏj′ĭk), **pa′le•on′to•log′i•cal** *adj.* —**pa′le•on•tol′o•gist** *n.*

Pa•le•o•zo•ic (pā′lē-ə-zō′ĭk) ►*adj.* Of or being the 2nd geologic era, including the Cambrian, Ordovician, Silurian, Devonian, Mississippian, Pennsylvanian, and Permian periods. ►*n.* The Paleozoic Era.

Pa•ler•mo (pə-lâr′mō, pä-lĕr′-) A city of NW Sicily, Italy, on the Tyrrhenian Sea. Pop. 697,162.

Pal•es•tine (păl′ĭ-stīn′) A region of SW Asia on the E Mediterranean shore, roughly coextensive with modern Israel and the West Bank. —**Pal′es•tin′i•an** (-stĭn′ē-ən) *adj. & n.*

pal•ette (păl′ĭt) ►*n.* **1.** A board, usu. with a hole for the thumb, on which the artist mixes colors. **2.** The range of colors on a palette. [< OFr., small spade.]

pal•i•mo•ny (păl′ə-mō′nē) ►*n. Informal* An allowance for support made under court order and given by one partner to the other after they have separated.

pal•imp•sest (păl′ĭmp-sĕst′) ►*n.* A manuscript, usu. of papyrus or parchment, that has been written on more than once, with the earlier writing incompletely erased. [< Gk. *palimpsēstos*, scraped again.]

pal•in•drome (păl′ĭn-drōm′) ►*n.* A word, phrase, verse, or sentence that reads the same backward or forward, as *A man, a plan, a canal, Panama!* [< Gk. *palindromos*, running back again.]

pal•ing (pā′lĭng) ►*n.* **1.** A pale; picket. **2.** A fence made of pales or pickets.

pal•i•sade (păl′ĭ-sād′) ►*n.* A fence of pales forming a defense barrier or fortification. [< OProv. *palissa*, stake.]

Pal•i•sades (păl′ĭ-sādz′) A row of cliffs in NE NJ along the W bank of the Hudson R.

pall[1] (pôl) ►*n.* **1.** A cover for a coffin, bier, or tomb, often made of velvet. **2.** A coffin. **3.** A covering that darkens or obscures: *a pall of smoke.* [< Lat. *pallium*, cloak.]

pall[2] (pôl) ►*v.* **1.** To become insipid, boring, or wearisome. **2.** To cloy; satiate. [ME *pallen*, grow feeble.]

Pal•la•dio (pə-lä′dē-ō), **Andrea.** 1508–80. Italian architect. —**Pal•la′di•an** (-lā′dē-ən) *adj.*

pal•la•di•um (pə-lā′dē-əm) ►*n. Symbol* **Pd** A steel-white, tarnish-resistant, metallic element alloyed for use in electric contacts, jewelry, watch parts, and surgical instruments. At. no. 46. See table at **element.** [< the asteroid *Pallas.*]

pall•bear•er (pôl′bâr′ər) ►*n.* One carrying or attending a coffin at a funeral.

pal•let[1] (păl′ĭt) ►*n.* A portable platform used for storing or moving cargo or freight. [< OFr. *palete*, small spade.]

pal•let[2] (păl′ĭt) ►*n.* A narrow, hard bed or straw-filled mattress. [< LLat. *palea*, straw.]

pal•li•ate (păl′ē-āt′) ►*v.* **-at•ed, -at•ing 1.** To make (e.g., a crime) seem less serious; extenuate. **2.** To mitigate. **3.** To soothe without curing. [< Lat. *pallium*, cloak.] —**pal′li•a′tion** *n.* —**pal′li•a′tive** *adj. & n.*

Syns: *palliate, extenuate, gloss, gloze, whitewash* **v.**

pal•lid (păl′ĭd) ►*adj.* **1.** Pale or wan in color or

complexion. **2.** Lacking in vitality; dull. [Lat. *pallidus* < *pallēre*, be pale.]

pal•lor (păl′ər) ▶*n.* Extreme or unnatural paleness. [< Lat. < *pallēre*, be pale.]

palm¹ (päm) ▶*n.* The inner surface of the hand, extending from the wrist to the base of the fingers. ▶*v.* To conceal (something) in the palm of the hand. —***phrasal verb:*** **palm off** To dispose of or pass off by deception. [< Lat. *palma.*]

palm² (päm) ▶*n.* **1.** Any of various chiefly tropical evergreen trees, shrubs, or woody vines usu. having unbranched trunks with a crown of large pinnate or palmate leaves. **2.** An emblem of victory, success, or joy. **3.** Triumph; victory. [< Lat. *palma.*]

Pal•ma (päl′mä) A city of W Majorca I., Spain. Pop. 298,971.

pal•mate (păl′māt′, päl′-, pä′māt′) also **pal•mat•ed** (-mā′tĭd) ▶*adj.* **1.** Shaped like a hand with the fingers extended. **2.** *Zool.* Webbed. —**pal′mate′ly** *adv.*

Pal•mer•ston (pä′mər-stən, päl′-), 3rd Viscount. 1784–1865. British prime minister (1855–58 and 1859–65).

pal•met•to (păl-mĕt′ō) ▶*n.*, *pl.* **-tos** or **-toes.** Any of several small, mostly tropical palms having fan-shaped leaves. [Sp. *palmito.*]

palm•is•try (pä′mĭ-strē) ▶*n.* The practice or art of telling fortunes from the patterns on the palms of the hands. —**palm′ist** *n.*

Palm Springs. A resort city of SE CA. Pop. 40,181.

Palm Sunday ▶*n.* The Sunday before Easter, observed by Christians in commemoration of Jesus's entry into Jerusalem.

palm•top (päm′tŏp′) ▶*n.* A computer that fits in the palm of one's hand. [PALM¹ + (LAP)TOP.]

palm•y (pä′mē) ▶*adj.* **-i•er, -i•est 1.** Of, relating to, or covered with palm trees. **2.** Prosperous; flourishing.

Pal•o•mar (păl′ə-mär′), **Mount.** A peak, 1,868.4 m (6,126 ft), of S CA NE of San Diego.

pal•o•mi•no (păl′ə-mē′nō) ▶*n.*, *pl.* **-nos.** A horse with a golden or tan coat and a white or cream-colored mane and tail. [< Sp., young dove.]

pal•pa•ble (păl′pə-bəl) ▶*adj.* **1.** Capable of being touched or felt; tangible. **2.** Easily perceived; obvious. [< LLat. *palpāre*, touch.] —**pal′pa•bly** *adv.*

pal•pate (păl′pāt′) ▶*v.* **-pat•ed, -pat•ing.** To examine by touching (an area of the body). [Lat. *palpāre*, touch.] —**pal•pa′tion** *n.*

pal•pi•tate (păl′pĭ-tāt′) ▶*v.* **-tat•ed, -tat•ing 1.** To tremble, shake, or quiver. **2.** To beat with excessive rapidity; throb. [< Lat. *palpāre*, touch.] —**pal′pi•ta′tion** *n.*

pal•sy (pôl′zē) ▶*n.*, *pl.* **-sies.** Complete or partial muscle paralysis. [< OFr. *paralisie*, PARALYSIS.] —**pal′sied** *adj.*

pal•try (pôl′trē) ▶*adj.* **-tri•er, -tri•est 1.** Lacking in importance or worth; trivial. **2.** Wretched or contemptible. [< obsolete *paltry*, trash.] —**pal′tri•ness** *n.*

Pa•mir (pə-mîr′, pä-) A mountainous region of S-central Asia mostly in Tajikistan with extensions in N Afghanistan, N Kashmir, and W China.

pam•pa (păm′pə) ▶*n.*, *pl.* **-pas** (-pəz, -pəs). In South America, a treeless grassland area. [< Quechua, flat field.]

pam•per (păm′pər) ▶*v.* To treat with excessive indulgence. [ME *pamperen.*]

pam•phlet (păm′flĭt) ▶*n.* An unbound printed work, usu. with a paper cover. [< *Pamphilus*, a short Latin poem of the 12th century.] —**pam′phlet•eer′** (-flĭ-tîr′) *n.*

Pam•plo•na (păm-plō′nə, päm-plō′nä) A city of N Spain. Pop. 181,349.

pan¹ (păn) ▶*n.* **1.** A shallow, wide, open container, usu. of metal and used for holding liquids, cooking, and other domestic purposes. **2.** A vessel similar in form to a pan. **3a.** A basin or depression in the earth. **b.** Hardpan. ▶*v.* **panned, pan•ning 1.** To wash (e.g., gravel) in a pan for gold or other precious metal. **2.** *Informal* To criticize or review harshly. —***phrasal verb:*** **pan out** To turn out well; be successful. [< OE *panne.*]

pan² (păn) ▶*v.* **panned, pan•ning.** To move (a movie or television camera) to follow an object or create a panoramic effect.

Pan ▶*n.* *Gk. Myth.* The god of woods, fields, and flocks.

pan– ▶*pref.* All: *panchromatic.* [Gk. < *pas*, all.]

pan•a•ce•a (păn′ə-sē′ə) ▶*n.* A remedy for all diseases, evils, or difficulties; cure-all. [< Gk. *panakēs*, all-healing.]

pa•nache (pə-năsh′, -näsh′) ▶*n.* **1.** Dash; verve. **2.** A bunch of feathers or a plume, esp. on a helmet. [< Ital. *pinnacchio*, plume.]

Pan•a•ma (păn′ə-mä′) **1.** A country of SE Central America. Cap. Panama. Pop. 2,583,000. **2.** Also **Panama City.** The capital of Panama, in the central part. Pop. 445,902. —**Pan′a•ma′ni•an** (-mā′nē-ən) *adj. & n.*

Panama, Isthmus of. An isthmus of Central America connecting North and South America and separating the Pacific from the Caribbean Sea.

Panama Canal. A ship canal, about 82 km (51 mi), crossing the Isthmus of Panama between the Caribbean Sea and the Pacific.

Panama Canal Zone. See **Canal Zone.**

Panama hat ▶*n.* A natural-colored hat made from leaves of a palmlike tropical plant of South and Central America.

Pan-A•mer•i•can (păn′ə-mĕr′ĭ-kən) ▶*adj.* Of North, South, and Central America.

pan•a•tel•a (păn′ə-tĕl′ə) ▶*n.* A long, slender cigar. [Sp.]

Pa•nay (pə-nī′, pä-) An island of the central Philippines in the Visayan Is.

pan-broil (păn′broil′) ▶*v.* To cook over direct heat in an uncovered, usu. ungreased skillet.

pan•cake (păn′kāk′) ▶*n.* A thin cake made of batter that is cooked on both sides.

pan•chro•mat•ic (păn′krō-măt′ĭk) ▶*adj.* Sensitive to all colors, as film.

pan•cre•as (păng′krē-əs, păn′-) ▶*n.* A long, irregularly shaped gland that produces insulin and secretes pancreatic juice into the intestine. [Gk. *pankreas.*] —**pan′cre•at′ic** (păng′krē-ăt′ĭk, păn′-) *adj.*

pan•cre•a•ti•tis (păng′krē-ə-tī′tĭs, păn′-) ▶*n.* Inflammation of the pancreas.

pan•da (păn′də) ▶*n.* **1.** A bearlike black and white mammal of the mountains of China and Tibet. **2.** A small, raccoonlike mammal of NE Asia. [Fr.]

pan•dem•ic (păn-dĕm′ĭk) ▶*adj.* **1.** Widespread; general. **2.** Epidemic over a wide geographic area. ►*n.* A pandemic disease. [< Gk. *pandēmos*, of all the people.]

pan•de•mo•ni•um (păn′də-mō′nē-əm) ►*n.* Wild uproar or noise. [< *Pandæmonium*, capital of Hell in Milton's *Paradise Lost.*]

pan•der (păn′dər) ►*v.* **1.** To act as a go-between or liaison in sexual intrigues. **2.** To cater to the lower tastes and desires of others or exploit their weaknesses. [< *Pandare*, character in Chaucer's *Troilus and Criseyde.*] —**pan′der, pan′der•er** *n.*

P and L ►*abbr.* profit and loss

Pan•do•ra (păn-dôr′ə, -dōr′ə) ►*n. Gk. Myth.* The first woman, who opened a box containing all the evils of human life.

pan•dow•dy (păn-dou′dē) ►*n., pl.* **-dies.** Sliced fruit baked with sugar and spices in a deep dish, with a thick top crust.

pane (pān) ►*n.* **1.** A framed, glass-filled division of a window or door. **2.** The glass itself. [< Lat. *pannus*, cloth.]

pan•e•gyr•ic (păn′ə-jĭr′ĭk, -jī′rĭk) ►*n.* **1.** A speech or written composition of commendation or praise. **2.** Elaborate praise; encomium. [< Gk. *panēguris*, public assembly.] —**pan′e•gyr′i•cal** *adj.* —**pan′e•gyr′ist** *n.*

pan•el (păn′əl) ►*n.* **1.** A flat, usu. rectangular piece forming a raised, recessed, or framed part of the surface in which it is set. **2.** A vertical section of fabric. **3.** A thin wooden board, used as a painting surface. **4.** A board with switches or buttons to control an electric device. **5.** A list or group of persons for jury duty. **6.** A group of people gathered to discuss a topic, judge a contest, or act as a team on a quiz program. ►*v.* **-eled, -el•ing** or **-elled, -el•ling 1.** To cover, decorate, or furnish with panels. **2.** To separate into panels. [< Lat. *pannus*, cloth.]

pan•el•ing (păn′ə-lĭng) ►*n.* A section of panels or paneled wall.

pan•el•ist (păn′ə-lĭst) ►*n.* A member of a panel.

panel truck ►*n.* A small delivery truck with a fully enclosed body.

pang (păng) ►*n.* **1.** A sudden sharp spasm of pain. See Syns at **pain. 2.** A sudden, sharp feeling of emotional distress. [?]

Pan•gae•a (păn-jē′ə) ►*n.* A hypothetical landmass comprising all the earth's continents in the late Paleozoic Era. [PAN– + Gk. *gaia*, earth.]

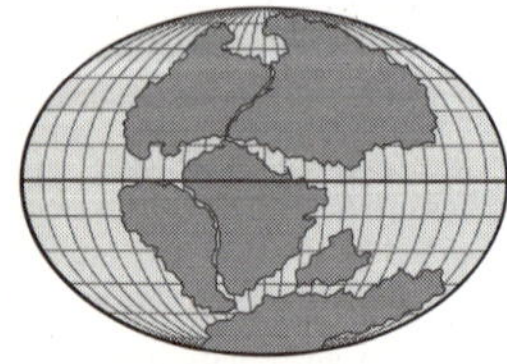

Pangaea

Pan•go Pan•go (päng′ō päng′ō, päng′gō päng′gō) See **Pago Pago.**

pan•han•dle[1] (păn′hăn′dl) ►*v.* **-dled, -dling** *Informal.* To beg for money or food. See Syns at **cadge.** —**pan′han′dler** *n.*

pan•han•dle[2] (păn′hăn′dl) ►*n.* A narrow strip of territory projecting from a larger, broader area.

pan•ic (păn′ĭk) ►*n.* A sudden, overpowering terror, often affecting many people at once. [< Gk. *Panikos*, of Pan (a source of terror, as in flocks or herds).] —**pan′ic** *v.* —**pan′ick•y** *adj.*

pan•i•cle (păn′ĭ-kəl) ►*n.* A branched cluster of flowers in which the branches are racemes. [Lat. *pānicula.*] —**pan′i•cled** *adj.*

Pan•ja•bi (pŭn-jä′bē, -jăb′ē) ►*n. & adj.* Var. of **Punjabi.**

Pank•hurst (păngk′hûrst′), **Emmeline Goulden.** 1858–1928. British suffrage leader.

pan•nier (păn′yər, păn′ē-ər) ►*n.* **1.** A large wicker basket, esp. one carried on the back. **2.** One of a pair of baskets or packs carried on either side of an animal or vehicle, such as a bicycle. [< Lat. *pānārium*, breadbasket.]

pan•o•ply (păn′ə-plē) ►*n., pl.* **-plies 1.** A splendid or striking array. See Syns at **display. 2.** Something that covers and protects. **3.** The complete arms and armor of a warrior. [Gk. *panoplia.*]

pan•o•ram•a (păn′ə-răm′ə, -rä′mə) ►*n.* **1.** An unbroken view of a wide area. **2.** A picture or series of pictures representing a continuous scene. [PAN– + Gk. *horama*, sight.] —**pan′o•ram′ic** *adj.*

pan•pipe (păn′pīp′) ►*n.* A wind instrument consisting of a series of pipes or reeds of graduated length bound together.

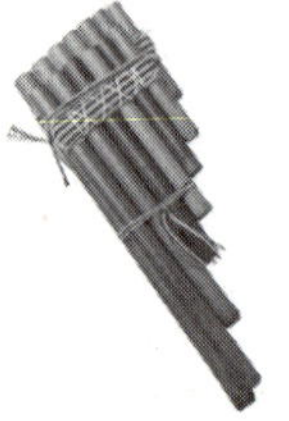

panpipe

pan•sy (păn′zē) ►*n., pl.* **-sies.** Any of various plants having flowers with velvety petals of various colors. [< OFr. *pensee*, thought, pansy.]

pant (pănt) ►*v.* **1.** To breathe rapidly in short gasps, as after exertion. **2.** To utter hurriedly or breathlessly. **3.** To long demonstratively; yearn. ►*n.* A short, labored breath; gasp. [ME *panten.*] —**pant′ing•ly** *adv.*

pan•ta•loon (păn′tə-lo͞on′) ►*n.* often **pantaloons.** Trousers, esp. tight trousers extending from waist to ankle. [< OItal. *Pantalone*, a comic character portrayed as an old man in tight trousers.]

pan•the•ism (păn′thē-ĭz′əm) ►*n.* A doctrine identifying the deity with the universe. —**pan′the•ist** *n.* —**pan′the•is′tic** *adj.*

pan•the•on (păn′thē-ŏn′, -ən) ►*n.* **1.** A temple dedicated to all gods. **2.** All the gods of a people. **3.** A public building commemorating and dedicated to the heroes and heroines of a nation. [< Gk. *Pantheion.*]

pan•ther (păn′thər) ►*n.* **1.** The leopard, esp. in its black, unspotted form. **2.** See **mountain lion.** [< Gk. *panthēr.*]

pant•ies (păn′tēz) ►*pl.n.* Short underpants for women or children.

pan•to•mime (păn′tə-mīm′) ►*n.* **1.** Communication by means of gesture and facial expression. **2.** A play, dance, or other theatrical performance presented in pantomime. [< Gk. *pantomimos*, pantomimic actor.] —**pan′to•mime** *v.* —**pan′to•mim′ic** (-mĭm′ĭk) *adj.* —**pan′to•mim′ist** (-mī′mĭst) *n.*

pan•try (păn′trē) ►*n., pl.* **-tries.** A small room or closet where food, tableware, linens, and similar items are stored. [< OFr. *paneterie*, bread closet.]

pants (pănts) ►*pl.n.* **1.** Trousers. **2.** Underpants. [< PANTALOON.]

pant•suit also **pants suit** (pănt′so͞ot′) ►*n.* A woman's suit having trousers instead of a skirt.

pant•y•hose or **pant•y hose** (păn′tē-hōz′) ►*pl.n.* A woman's one-piece undergarment consisting of underpants and stockings.

pant•y•waist (păn′tē-wāst′) ►*n. Slang* A sissy.

pap (păp) ►*n.* **1.** Soft or semiliquid food, as for infants. **2.** Material lacking real value or substance. [ME < Lat. *pappa*.]

pa•pa (pä′pə, pə-pä′) ►*n. Informal* Father. [Fr.]

pa•pa•cy (pā′pə-sē) ►*n., pl.* **-cies 1.** The office and jurisdiction of a pope. **2.** The period of time during which a pope is in office. **3. Papacy** The system of church government headed by the pope. [< LLat. *pāpa*, POPE.]

Pa•pa•go (păp′ə-gō′, pä′pə-) ►*n., pl.* **-go** or **-gos 1.** A member of a Native American people inhabiting S Arizona and NW Mexico. **2.** Their Uto-Aztecan language.

pa•pal (pā′pəl) ►*adj.* Of or issued by a pope. [< LLat. *pāpa*, POPE.]

Papal States. A group of territories in central Italy ruled by the popes (754–1870).

pa•paw also **paw•paw** (pô′pô′) ►*n.* **1.** A deciduous North American tree having fleshy edible fruit. **2.** The fruit of this tree. **3.** See **papaya.** [< Sp. *papaya*, PAPAYA.]

pa•pa•ya (pə-pä′yə) ►*n.* **1.** An evergreen tropical American tree having large, yellow, edible fruit. **2.** The fruit of this tree. [Sp., of Cariban orig.]

Pa•pe•e•te (pä′pē-ā′tā, pə-pē′tē) The capital of French Polynesia, on the NW coast of Tahiti in the S Pacific. Pop. 23,496.

pa•per (pā′pər) ►*n.* **1.** A material made of cellulose pulp, derived mainly from wood, rags, and certain grasses, processed into flexible sheets or rolls, and used for writing, printing, drawing, wrapping, and covering walls. **2.** A sheet of this material. **3.** A written work such as an essay or a treatise. **4.** often **papers** An official document, esp. one establishing the identity of the bearer. **5.** A newspaper. **6.** Wallpaper. ►*v.* To cover, wrap, or line with paper. [< Gk. *papuros*, papyrus.] —**pa′per•er** *n.* —**pa′per•y** *adj.*

pa•per•back (pā′pər-băk′) ►*n.* A book having a flexible paper binding.

pa•per•board (pā′pər-bôrd′, -bōrd′) ►*n.* Cardboard; pasteboard.

pa•per•bound (pā′pər-bound′) ►*adj.* Bound in paper; paperback.

pa•per•hang•er (pā′pər-hăng′ər) ►*n.* One whose occupation is hanging wallpaper.

pa•per•less (pā′pər-lĭs) ►*adj.* Not requiring paper to record, convey, and store information.

paper tiger ►*n.* One that is seemingly dangerous and powerful but is in fact weak.

paper trail ►*n. Informal* Documentary evidence of one's actions.

pa•per•weight (pā′pər-wāt′) ►*n.* A small, heavy object for holding down papers.

pa•per•work (pā′pər-wûrk′) ►*n.* Work involving the handling of reports, letters, and forms.

pa•pier-mâ•ché (pā′pər-mə-shā′, pă-pyā′-) ►*n.* A material, made from paper pulp or shreds of paper mixed with glue or paste, that can be molded into various shapes when wet. [Fr.] —**pa′pier-mâ•ché′** *adj.*

pa•pil•la (pə-pĭl′ə) ►*n., pl.* **-pil•lae** (-pĭl′ē). A small nipplelike projection, such as a protuberance on the tongue. [Lat., nipple.] —**pap′il•lar′y** (păp′ə-lĕr′ē, pə-pĭl′ə-rē) *adj.*

pa•pist (pā′pĭst) ►*n. Offensive* A Roman Catholic. [< LLat. *pāpa*, POPE.] —**pa′pist•ry** *n.*

pa•poose (pă-po͞os′, pə-) ►*n.* A Native American infant or very young child. [Narragansett *papoòs*.]

pa•pri•ka (pă-prē′kə, pə-, păp′rĭ-kə) ►*n.* A mild, powdered seasoning made from sweet red peppers. [Hung., ult. < Gk. *peperi*, pepper.]

Pap smear ►*n.* A test for cancer, esp. of the female genital tract. [After George *Papanicolaou* (1883–1962).]

Pap•u•a New Guinea (păp′yo͞o-ə, pä′po͞o-ä′) An island country of the SW Pacific comprising the E half of the island of New Guinea and adjacent islands. Cap. Moresby. Pop. 3,997,000. —**Pap′u•an** *adj. & n.* —**Pap′u•a New Guin′e•an** *adj. & n.*

pa•py•rus (pə-pī′rəs) ►*n., pl.* **-rus•es** or **-ri** (-rī′) **1.** A tall, aquatic, grasslike plant of Northern Africa. **2.** A material on which to write made from the pith or the stems of this plant. [< Gk. *papuros*.]

par (pär) ►*n.* **1.** An amount or a level considered to be average; standard. **2.** An equality of status, level, or value; equal footing. **3.** The established value of a monetary unit of a country. **4.** The face value of a stock or bond. **5.** The number of golf strokes considered necessary to complete a hole or course. [< Lat. *pār*, equal.]

par. ►*abbr.* **1.** paragraph **2.** parallel **3.** parish

para– or **par–** ►*pref.* **1.** Beside; near: *parathyroid gland.* **2.** Beyond: *paranormal.* **3.** Subsidiary; assistant: *paralegal.* [< Gk. *para*, beside.]

par•a•ble (păr′ə-bəl) ►*n.* A simple story illustrating a moral or religious lesson. [< Gk. *parabolē*.]

pa•rab•o•la (pə-răb′ə-lə) ►*n.* A plane curve formed by the intersection of a right circular cone and a plane parallel to an element of the cone. [< Gk. *parabolē*.] —**par′a•bol′ic** (păr′ə-bŏl′ĭk) *adj.*

Par•a•cel•sus (păr′ə-sĕl′səs), **Philippus Aureolus.** 1493–1541. German-Swiss alchemist and physician.

par•a•chute (păr′ə-sho͞ot′) ►*n.* A light, usu. hemispherical apparatus used to retard free fall from an aircraft. ►*v.* **-chut•ed, -chut•ing.** To drop by means of a parachute. [Fr.] —**par′a•chut′ist** *n.*

pa•rade (pə-rād′) ►*n.* **1.** An organized public procession on a festive or ceremonial occasion. **2.** A ceremonial review of troops. **3.** An extended, usu. showy succession. **4.** An ostentatious show; exhibition: *a parade of wealth.* See Syns at **display.** ►*v.* **-rad•ed, -rad•ing 1.** To take part or cause to take part in a parade. **2.** To assemble for a ceremonial military review. **3.**

To stroll in public; promenade. **4.** To exhibit ostentatiously; flaunt. [< Lat. *parāre*, prepare.]

par•a•digm (păr′ə-dīm′, -dĭm′) ►*n.* **1.** An example that serves as a pattern or a model. **2.** A list of all the inflectional forms of a word taken as an illustrative example. [< Gk. *paradeigma*.] —**par′a•dig•mat′ic** (-dĭg-măt′ĭk) *adj.*

par•a•dise (păr′ə-dīs′, -dīz′) ►*n.* **1.** often **Paradise** Heaven. **2.** A place of ideal beauty or loveliness. [< Avestan (ancient Iranian language) *pairi-daēza-*, enclosure.] —**par′a•di•si′a•cal** (-dĭ-sī′ə-kəl, -zī′-) *adj.*

par•a•dox (păr′ə-dŏks′) ►*n.* **1.** A seemingly contradictory statement that may nonetheless be true. **2.** One exhibiting inexplicable or contradictory aspects. [< Gk. *paradoxos*, conflicting with expectation.] —**par′a•dox′i•cal** *adj.* —**par′a•dox′i•cal•ly** *adv.*

par•af•fin (păr′ə-fĭn) ►*n.* **1.** A waxy, white or colorless, solid hydrocarbon mixture used to make candles, wax paper, lubricants, and sealing materials. **2.** *Chiefly Brit.* Kerosene. [< Lat. *parum*, little + Lat. *affīnis*, associated with.] —**par′af•fin′ic** *adj.*

par•a•foil (păr′ə-foil′) ►*n.* A nonrigid, parachutelike airfoil of ribbed or cellular construction. [PARA(CHUTE) + (AIR)FOIL.]

par•a•glid•er (păr′ə-glī′dər) ►*n.* A recreational aircraft consisting of a large parafoil from which a harnessed rider hangs. [PARA(FOIL) + GLIDER.]

par•a•gon (păr′ə-gŏn′, -gən) ►*n.* A model of excellence or perfection. [< OItal. *paragonare*, test on a touchstone.]

par•a•graph (păr′ə-grăf′) ►*n.* **1.** A distinct division of written or printed matter that consists of one or more sentences and typically deals with a single thought or topic. **2.** A mark (¶) used to indicate where a new paragraph should begin. **3.** A brief article, notice, or announcement, as in a newspaper. ►*v.* To divide or arrange into paragraphs. [< Gk. *paragraphein*, write beside : PARA– + *graphein*, write.]

Par•a•guay (păr′ə-gwī′, -gwā′) A country of S-central South America. Cap. Asunción. Pop. 4,700,000. —**Par′a•guay′an** *adj. & n.*

Pa•ra•í•ba (păr′ə-ē′bə, pä′rä-ē′bä) also **Paraíba do Sul** (do͝o so͞ol′). A river, about 1,046 km (650 mi), of southeast Brazil.

par•a•keet (păr′ə-kēt′) ►*n.* Any of various small slender parrots, usu. having long tapering tails. [Sp. *periquito*.]

par•a•le•gal (păr′ə-lē′gəl) ►*adj.* Relating to or being a person with specialized training who assists an attorney. —**par′a•le′gal** *n.*

par•al•lax (păr′ə-lăks′) ►*n.* An apparent change in the direction of an object, caused by a change in the viewer's position. [< Gk. *parallassein*, change direction.]

par•al•lel (păr′ə-lĕl′) ►*adj.* **1.** Being an equal distance apart everywhere and never intersecting. **2a.** Having comparable parts or analogous aspects. **b.** Having the same tendency or direction. ►*adv.* In a parallel relationship or manner. ►*n.* **1.** *Math.* One of a set of parallel geometric figures, such as lines or planes. **2a.** One that closely resembles or is analogous to another. **b.** A comparison indicating likeness; analogy. **3.** Any of the imaginary lines representing degrees of latitude that encircle the earth parallel to the plane of the equator. **4.** *Electron.* An arrangement of components in a circuit that splits the current into two or more paths. ►*v.* **-leled, -lel•ing** also **-lelled, -lel•ling 1.** To make parallel. **2.** To be or extend parallel to. **3.** To be similar or analogous to. [< Gk. *parallēlos*.] —**par′al•lel•ism** *n.*

parallel bars ►*pl.n.* An apparatus for gymnastic exercises consisting of two bars set parallel to each other in adjustable upright supports.

par•al•lel•e•pi•ped (păr′ə-lĕl′ə-pī′pĭd, -pĭp′ĭd) ►*n.* A solid with 6 faces, each a parallelogram and each being parallel to the opposite face. [Gk. *parallēlepipedon* : *parallēlos*, parallel + *epipedon*, plane surface : EPI– + *pedon*, ground.]

par•al•lel•o•gram (păr′ə-lĕl′ə-grăm′) ►*n.* A four-sided plane figure with opposite sides parallel.

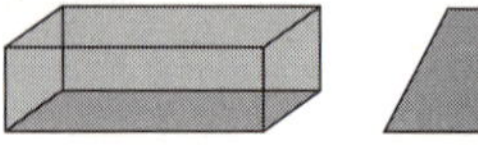

parallelepiped **parallelogram**

pa•ral•y•sis (pə-răl′ĭ-sĭs) ►*n., pl.* **-ses** (-sēz′) **1a.** Loss or impairment of the ability to move a body part. **b.** Loss of sensation over a region of the body. **2.** Total stoppage or severe impairment of activity. [< Gk. *paralusis*.] —**par′a•lyt′ic** (păr′ə-lĭt′ĭk) *adj. & n.*

par•a•lyze (păr′ə-līz′) ►*v.* **-lyzed, -lyz•ing 1.** To affect with paralysis. **2.** To make inoperative or powerless.

Par•a•mar•i•bo (păr′ə-măr′ə-bō′) The capital of Suriname, on the Suriname R. near its mouth on the Atlantic. Pop. 67,905.

par•a•me•ci•um (păr′ə-mē′shē-əm, -sē-əm) ►*n., pl.* **-ci•a** (-shē-ə, -sē-ə) or **-ci•ums.** Any of various freshwater, usu. oval protozoans that move by means of cilia. [< Gk. *paramēkēs*, oblong.]

par•a•med•ic (păr′ə-mĕd′ĭk) ►*n.* A person who is trained to give emergency medical treatment or assist medical professionals. —**par′a•med′i•cal** *adj.*

pa•ram•e•ter (pə-răm′ĭ-tər) ►*n.* **1.** *Math.* A constant in an equation that can be varied to represent a family of curves or surfaces, such as the radius in a family of concentric circles. **2.** A measurable factor, such as temperature, that helps define a system and its behavior. **3.** *Informal* A limiting or restrictive factor. —**par′a•met′ric** (păr′ə-mĕt′rĭk) *adj.*

par•a•mil•i•tar•y (păr′ə-mĭl′ĭ-tĕr′ē) ►*adj.* Of or being a group of civilians organized in a military fashion.

par•a•mount (păr′ə-mount′) ►*adj.* **1.** Of chief concern or importance. **2.** Supreme in rank or power. [AN *paramont*, above.]

par•a•mour (păr′ə-mo͝or′) ►*n.* A lover, esp. one in an adulterous relationship. [< AN *par amour*, by way of love.]

Pa•ra•ná (păr′ə-nä′, pä′rä-) A river rising in E-central Brazil and flowing about 3,282 km (2,040 mi) to E Argentina.

par•a•noi•a (păr′ə-noi′ə) ►*n.* A psychotic disorder characterized by delusions of persecution or grandeur. [Gk., madness.] —**par′a•noi′ac′** (-ăk′, -ĭk) *n.* —**par′a•noid′** *adj. & n.*

par•a•nor•mal (păr′ə-nôr′məl) ►*adj.* Beyond the range of normal experience or scientific explanation.

par•a•pet (păr′ə-pĭt, -pĕt′) ►*n.* **1.** A low protective wall or railing along the edge of a raised structure such as a roof or balcony. **2.** An embankment protecting soldiers from enemy fire. [< Ital. *parapetto.*]

par•a•pher•na•lia (păr′ə-fər-nāl′yə, -fə-nāl′yə) ►*pl.n. (takes sing. or pl. v.)* **1.** Personal belongings. **2.** The articles used in a particular activity. See Syns at **equipment.** [< Gk. *parapherna*, a married woman's property exclusive of her dowry : PARA– + *phernē*, dowry.]

par•a•phrase (păr′ə-frāz′) ►*n.* A restatement of a text or passage in another form or other words, often to clarify meaning. [< Gk. *paraphrasis.*] —**par′a•phrase′** *v.*

par•a•ple•gi•a (păr′ə-plē′jē-ə, -jə) ►*n.* Paralysis of the lower half of the body including both legs. [< Gk. *paraplēssein*, strike on one side.] —**par′a•ple′gic** (-jĭk) *adj. & n.*

par•a•pro•fes•sion•al (păr′ə-prə-fĕsh′ə-nəl) ►*n.* One trained to assist a professional.

par•a•psy•chol•o•gy (păr′ə-sī-kŏl′ə-jē) ►*n.* The study of paranormal phenomena, such as telepathy and clairvoyance.

par•a•quat (păr′ə-kwŏt′) ►*n.* A colorless compound, $C_{12}H_{14}Cl_2N_2$, or a related yellow compound, $C_{12}H_{14}N_2(CH_3SO_4)_2$, used as a herbicide. [PARA– + *quat(ernary)*, bonded to four carbon atoms.]

par•a•site (păr′ə-sīt′) ►*n.* **1.** An organism that grows and feeds on or in a different organism while contributing nothing to the survival of its host. **2.** One who habitually takes advantage of the generosity of others. [< Gk. *parasitos.*] —**par′a•sit•ism** (-sĭ-tĭz′əm, -sī-) *n.* —**par′a•sit•ize′** (-sĭ-tīz′, -sī-) *v.*

par•a•sit•ic (păr′ə-sĭt′ĭk) also **par•a•sit•i•cal** (-ĭ-kəl) ►*adj.* **1.** Of or characteristic of a parasite. **2.** Caused by a parasite.

par•a•si•tol•o•gy (păr′ə-sĭ-tŏl′ə-jē, -sī-) ►*n.* The scientific study of parasites or parasitic populations. —**par′a•si•tol′o•gist** *n.*

par•a•sol (păr′ə-sôl′, -sŏl′) ►*n.* A light, usu. small umbrella carried as protection from the sun. [< Ital. *parasole.*]

par•a•sym•pa•the•tic nervous system (păr′ə-sĭm′pə-thĕt′ĭk) ►*n.* The part of the autonomic nervous system that inhibits or opposes the physiological effects of the sympathetic nervous system.

par•a•thy•roid gland (păr′ə-thī′roid) ►*n.* Any of four small kidney-shaped glands that lie in pairs near or within the thyroid gland and secrete a hormone necessary for the metabolism of calcium and phosphorus.

par•a•troops (păr′ə-tro͞ops′) ►*pl.n.* Infantry trained and equipped to parachute. —**par′a•troop′er** *n.*

par•a•ty•phoid fever (păr′ə-tī′foid′) ►*n.* An acute food poisoning, similar to typhoid fever but less severe.

par•boil (pär′boil′) ►*v.* To cook partially by boiling for a brief period. [< LLat. *perbullīre*, boil thoroughly.]

par•cel (pär′səl) ►*n.* **1.** Something wrapped up or packaged; package. **2.** A plot of land, usu. a division of a larger area. **3.** A quantity of merchandise offered for sale. **4.** A group or company; pack. ►*v.* **-celed, -cel•ing** also **-celled, -cel•ling 1.** To divide into parts and distribute. **2.** To make into a parcel; package. [< Lat. *particula*, portion.]

parcel post ►*n.* A postal service or department that handles and delivers packages.

parch (pärch) ►*v.* **1.** To make or become extremely dry, esp. by exposure to heat. See Syns at **dry. 2.** To make or become thirsty. [ME *parchen.*]

parch•ment (pärch′mənt) ►*n.* **1.** The skin of a sheep or goat prepared as a material on which to write or paint. **2.** A written text or drawing on a sheet of this material. [< Lat. *pergamēna.*]

par•don (pär′dn) ►*v.* **1.** To release (a person) from punishment. **2.** To let (an offense) pass without punishment. **3.** To forgive; excuse. ►*n.* **1.** Exemption of a convicted person from the penalties of an offense or a crime. **2.** Allowance or forgiveness for an offense or a discourtesy. [< VLat. **perdōnāre*, give wholeheartedly : PER– + Lat. *dōnāre*, give (< *dōnum*, gift).] —**par′don•a•ble** *adj.* —**par′don•er** *n.*

pare (pâr) ►*v.* **pared, par•ing 1.** To remove the outer covering or skin of: *pare apples.* **2.** To reduce by or as if by cutting off outer parts; trim: *pare expenses.* [< Lat. *parāre*, prepare.] —**par′er** *n.*

par•e•gor•ic (păr′ə-gôr′ĭk, -gŏr′-) ►*n.* A camphorated tincture of opium, taken internally for the relief of diarrhea and intestinal pain. [< Gk. *parēgoros*, consoling.]

par•ent (pâr′ənt, păr′-) ►*n.* **1.** A father or mother. **2.** An ancestor; progenitor. **3.** An organism that produces or generates offspring. **4.** A source or cause; origin. ►*v.* To act as a parent (to). [< Lat. *parēns*, *parent-* < Lat. *parere*, give birth.] —**par′ent•age** *n.* —**pa•ren′tal** (pə-rĕn′tl) *adj.* —**par′ent•hood′** *n.*

pa•ren•the•sis (pə-rĕn′thĭ-sĭs) ►*n.*, *pl.* **-ses** (-sēz′) **1.** Either or both of the upright curved lines, ( ), used to mark off explanatory or qualifying remarks or enclose a mathematical expression. **2.** A qualifying or amplifying word, phrase, or sentence inserted within a passage. [< Gk., insertion.] —**par′en•thet′i•cal** (păr′ən-thĕt′ĭ-kəl), **par′en•thet′ic** (-ĭk) *adj.*

pa•re•sis (pə-rē′sĭs, păr′ĭ-sĭs) ►*n.* Slight or partial paralysis. [Gk.] —**pa•ret′ic** (pə-rĕt′ĭk) *adj. & n.*

pa•re•ve (pä′rə-və) also **par•ve** (pär′və) ►*adj.* Prepared without meat or milk and thus permissible to be eaten with both meat and dairy dishes according to Jewish dietary laws. [Yiddish *páreve.*]

par ex•cel•lence (pär ĕk-sə-läɴs′) ►*adj.* Being of the highest degree; quintessential. [Fr.]

par•fait (pär-fā′) ►*n.* **1.** A dessert made of cream, eggs, sugar, and flavoring. **2.** A dessert made of several layers of different flavors of ice cream or ices, variously garnished. [< Lat. *perfectus*, perfect.]

par•he•li•on (pär-hē′lē-ən, -hēl′yən) ►*n.*, *pl.* **-he•li•a** (-hē′lē-ə, -hēl′yə). A bright spot appearing on either side of the sun, often on a luminous ring or halo. [< Gk. *parēlios*, beside the sun.]

pa•ri•ah (pə-rī′ə) ►*n.* **1.** A social outcast. **2.** An Untouchable. [Tamil *paṛaiyar.*]

pa•ri•e•tal (pə-rī′ĭ-təl) ►*adj.* **1.** *Anat.* **a.** Relating to or forming the wall of a body part, organ, or cavity. **b.** Of or located in the region of the sides of the skull. **2.** Dwelling within or having authority within the walls or buildings of a college. [< Lat. *pariēs*, wall.]

par•i-mu•tu•el (păr′ĭ-myōō′chōō-əl) ►*n.* A system of betting on races whereby the winners divide the total amount bet, after deducting management expenses, in proportion to the sums they have wagered individually. [Fr. *pari-mutuel.*]

par•ing (pâr′ĭng) ►*n.* Something, such as a peel, that has been pared off.

pa•ri pas•su (păr′ē păs′ōō) ►*adv.* At an equal pace; side by side. [Lat. *parī passū.*]

Par•is[1] (păr′ĭs) ►*n. Gk. Myth.* The prince of Troy whose abduction of Helen provoked the Trojan war.

Par•is[2] (păr′ĭs) The capital of France, in the N-central part on the Seine R. Pop. 2,152,329.

par•ish (păr′ĭsh) ►*n.* **1a.** An administrative part of a diocese that has its own church. **b.** The members of such a parish. **2.** An administrative subdivision in Louisiana that corresponds to a county in other US states. [< LGk. *paroikia*, diocese < Gk. *paroikos*, neighboring.]

pa•rish•ion•er (pə-rĭsh′ə-nər) ►*n.* A member of a parish.

par•i•ty (păr′ĭ-tē) ►*n., pl.* **-ties 1.** Equality, as in amount, status, or value. **2.** The equivalent in value of a sum of money in a different currency at a fixed rate of exchange. **3.** A level for farm-product prices maintained by governmental support. [< Lat. *pār*, equal.]

park (pärk) ►*n.* **1.** An area of land set aside for public use, as for recreation. **2.** *Sports* A stadium or an enclosed playing field: *a baseball park.* **3.** An area in or near a town designed and usu. zoned for a certain purpose: *a commercial park.* **4.** A place for parking vehicles; parking lot. ►*v.* **1.** To put or leave (a vehicle) for a time in a certain location. **2.** *Informal* To place or leave temporarily. [< OFr. *parc*, enclosure.]

Park, Mungo. 1771–1806. Scottish explorer in Africa.

par•ka (pär′kə) ►*n.* **1.** A hooded fur pullover outer garment worn in the Arctic. **2.** A coat or jacket with a hood and usu. a warm lining. [Alaskan Russ., pelt.]

Par•ker (pär′kər), **Dorothy Rothschild.** 1893–1967. Amer. writer.

Par•kin•son's disease (pär′kĭn-sənz) ►*n.* A progressive nervous disease chiefly of later life, marked by muscular tremor and slowing of movement. [After James *Parkinson* (1755–1824).]

Park•man (pärk′mən), **Francis.** 1823–93. Amer. historian.

Parks (pärks), **Rosa.** b. 1913. Amer. civil rights leader.

park•way (pärk′wā′) ►*n.* A broad landscaped highway.

par•lance (pär′ləns) ►*n.* A particular manner of speaking; idiom: *legal parlance.* [< OFr. *parler*, speak. See PARLEY.]

par•lay (pär′lā′, -lē) ►*n.* A bet comprising the sum of a prior wager plus its winnings or a series of bets made in such a manner. [< Fr. *paroli.*] —**par′lay′** *v.*

par•ley (pär′lē) ►*n., pl.* **-leys.** A discussion or conference, esp. between opponents. ►*v.* To have a discussion, esp. with an opponent. [< LLat. *parabolāre*, speak.]

par•lia•ment (pär′lə-mənt) ►*n.* **1.** A national legislative body. **2. Parliament** The national legislature of various countries, esp. the United Kingdom. [< OFr. *parler*, talk.] —**par′lia•men′ta•ry** (-mən′tə-rē, -men′trē) *adj.*

Rosa Parks
1990 bronze bust by Artis Lane

par•lia•men•tar•i•an (pär′lə-mĕn-târ′ē-ən) ►*n.* **1.** One who is expert in parliamentary procedures, rules, or debate. **2.** A member of a parliament.

par•lor (pär′lər) ►*n.* **1.** A room in a private home set apart for the entertainment of visitors. **2.** A business establishment: *a funeral parlor.* [< OFr. *parlur* < *parler*, to talk.]

par•lous (pär′ləs) ►*adj.* Perilous; dangerous. [ME < *perilous*, PERILOUS.]

Par•ma (pär′mə) A city of N-central Italy SE of Milan. Pop. 168,905.

Par•me•san (pär′mə-zän′, -zăn′, -zən) ►*n.* A hard, sharp, dry Italian cheese usu. served grated as a garnish. [< Ital. *parmigiano*, of Parma.]

par•mi•gia•na (pär′mĭ-zhä′nə, -jä′-) ►*adj.* Made or covered with Parmesan cheese: *eggplant parmigiana.*

Par•na•í•ba (pär′nə-ē′bə, -nä-ē′bä) A river, about 1,287 km (800 mi), of NE Brazil flowing to the Atlantic.

Par•nas•sus (pär-năs′əs) A mountain, about 2,458 m (8,060 ft), of central Greece N of the Gulf of Corinth.

Par•nell (pär-nĕl′, pär′nəl), **Charles Stewart.** 1846–91. Irish nationalist leader.

pa•ro•chi•al (pə-rō′kē-əl) ►*adj.* **1.** Of, supported by, or located in a parish. **2.** Narrowly restricted in scope or outlook; provincial: *parochial attitudes.* [< LLat. *parochia*, diocese. See PARISH.] —**pa•ro′chi•al•ism** *n.* —**pa•ro′chi•al•ly** *adv.*

parochial school ►*n.* A school supported by a church parish.

par•o•dy (păr′ə-dē) ►*n., pl.* **-dies 1.** A satirical imitation, as of a literary work. **2.** Travesty: *a parody of justice.* [< Gk. *parōidia.*] —**par′o•dist** *n.* —**par′o•dy** *v.*

pa•role (pə-rōl′) ►*n.* **1.** The release of a prisoner whose term has not yet expired on condition of good behavior. **2.** Word of honor. ►*v.* **-roled, -rol•ing.** To release on parole. [Fr., promise.] —**pa•rol′ee′** *n.*

pa•rot•id gland (pə-rŏt′ĭd) ►*n.* Either of the pair of salivary glands situated below and in front of each ear. [< Gk. *parōtis*, tumor near the ear : PARA– + *ous*, *ōt*-, ear.]

-parous ►*suff.* Giving birth to; bearing: *mul-*

tiparous. [< Lat. *parere*, give birth.]

par•ox•ysm (păr′ək-sĭz′əm) ►*n.* **1.** A sudden outburst, as of emotion. **2a.** A sudden attack or intensification of a disease. **b.** A spasm or fit; convulsion. [< Gk. *paroxusmos* : PARA– + *oxunein*, sharpen, goad (< *oxus*, sharp).] —**par′ox•ys′mal** (-ək-sĭz′məl) *adj.*

par•quet (pär-kā′) ►*n.* **1.** A floor made of parquetry. **2.** The art or process of making parquetry. **3a.** The part of the main floor of a theater in front of the balcony. **b.** The entire main floor of a theater. [< OFr. *parc*, enclosure.]

par•quet•ry (pär′kĭ-trē) ►*n.*, *pl.* **-ries.** Inlay of wood, often of different colors, that is used esp. for floors.

Parr (pär), **Catherine.** 1512–48. Queen of England as the sixth wife of Henry VIII.

par•ri•cide (păr′ĭ-sīd′) ►*n.* **1.** The murdering of one's father, mother, or other near relative. **2.** One who commits such a murder. [Lat. *parricīda.*] —**par′ri•cid′al** (-sīd′l) *adj.*

par•rot (păr′ət) ►*n.* **1.** Any of numerous tropical and semitropical birds, marked by a short hooked bill, brightly colored plumage, and, in some species, the ability to mimic human speech. **2.** One who imitates the words or actions of another, esp. without understanding them. ►*v.* To repeat or imitate, esp. without understanding. [Prob. < Fr. dial. *Perrot*, dim. of *Pierre*, Peter.]

parrot fever ►*n.* See **psittacosis.**

par•ry (păr′ē) ►*v.* **-ried, -ry•ing 1.** To deflect or ward off. **2.** To evade skillfully; avoid. [< Ital. *parare*, defend.] —**par′ry** *n.*

parse (pärs) ►*v.* **parsed, pars•ing 1.** To provide a grammatical description of a word, group of words, or sentence. **2.** *Comp. Sci.* To analyze or separate (e.g., input) into more easily processed components. **3.** To examine or analyze closely. [< Lat. *pars*, part (of speech).] —**pars′er** *n.*

par•sec (pär′sĕk′) ►*n.* A unit of astronomical length equal to 3.258 light-years. [PAR(ALLAX) + SEC(OND)[1].]

par•si•mo•ny (pär′sə-mō′nē) ►*n.* Unusual or excessive frugality; stinginess. [< Lat. *parcere*, *pars-*, spare.] —**par′si•mo′ni•ous** *adj.* —**par′si•mo′ni•ous•ly** *adv.*

pars•ley (pär′slē) ►*n.* An herb having flat or curled leaves that are used for seasoning or as a garnish. [< Gk. *petroselinon.*]

pars•nip (pär′snĭp) ►*n.* **1.** A strong-scented plant cultivated for its long, white, edible root. **2.** Its root. [< Lat. *pastināca.*]

par•son (pär′sən) ►*n.* **1.** An Anglican cleric in charge of a parish. **2.** A Protestant minister. [< Lat. *persōna*, character.]

par•son•age (pär′sə-nĭj) ►*n.* The official residence provided by a church for its parson.

part (pärt) ►*n.* **1.** A portion, division, or segment of a whole. **2.** A component of a system; detachable piece: *spare parts for cars.* **3.** A role, as in a play. **4.** One's responsibility, duty, or obligation; share. **5.** often **parts** A region, area, land, or territory. **6.** A side in a dispute or controversy. **7.** The line where the hair on the head is parted. **8.** *Mus.* **a.** The music or score for a particular instrument. **b.** One of the melodic divisions or voices of a composition. ►*v.* **1.** To divide or break into separate parts. **2.** To break up (a relationship) by separating the elements involved: *parted company.* **3.** To put or keep apart. **4.** To comb (e.g., hair) into a part. **5.** To go apart from one another; separate: *parted as friends.* **6.** To go away; depart. —***phrasal verb:*** **part with** To give up or let go of; relinquish. ►*adv.* Partially; in part. ►*adj.* Not full or complete; partial. —***idioms:*** **in part** To some extent; partly. **take part** To join in. [< Lat. *pars.*]

part. ►*abbr.* participle

par•take (pär-tāk′) ►*v.* **-took** (-to͝ok′), **-tak•en** (-tā′kən), **-tak•ing 1.** To take or have a part or share; participate. **2.** To take or be given part or portion. [< ME *part-taker*, one who takes part.] —**par•tak′er** *n.*

par•terre (pär-târ′) ►*n.* A flower garden whose beds form a pattern. [< OFr. *par terre*, on the ground : *par*, on + *terre*, ground (< Lat. *terra*, earth).]

par•the•no•gen•e•sis (pär′thə-nō-jĕn′ĭ-sĭs) ►*n.* Reproduction in which an unfertilized egg develops into a new individual. [< Gk. *parthenos*, virgin.] —**par′the•no•ge•net′ic** (-jə-nĕt′ĭk) *adj.*

Par•thi•a (pär′thē-ə) An ancient country of SW Asia corresponding to modern NE Iran. —**Par′thi•an** *adj. & n.*

par•tial (pär′shəl) ►*adj.* **1.** Not total; incomplete. **2.** Favoring one person or side over another or others; biased. **3.** Particularly fond: *partial to detective novels.* [< Lat. *pars*, part.] —**par′tial•ly** *adv.*

par•ti•al•i•ty (pär′shē-ăl′ĭ-tē, pär-shăl′-) ►*n.*, *pl.* **-ties 1.** The state of being partial. **2.** Favorable prejudice or bias. **3.** A special fondness. See Syns at **predilection.**

par•tic•i•pate (pär-tĭs′ə-pāt′) ►*v.* **-pat•ed, -pat•ing.** To take part or share in something. [< Lat. *particeps*, partaker.] —**par•tic′i•pant** (pənt), **par•tic′i•pa′tor** *n.* —**par•tic′i•pa′tion** *n.* —**par•tic′i•pa•to′ry** (pə-tŏr′ē, tōr′ē) *adj.*

par•ti•ci•ple (pär′tĭ-sĭp′əl) ►*n.* A form of a verb that can function independently as an adjective and can be used with an auxiliary verb to indicate tense, aspect, or voice. [< Lat. *participium.*] —**par′ti•cip′i•al** (-ē-əl) *adj.*

Usage: The "dangling participle" is common in speech, where it often passes unremarked; but its use in writing can lead to unintentional absurdities, as in *He watched his horse take a turn around the track carrying a racing sheet under his arm.* Sometimes the solution lies in moving the participial phrase to be adjacent to the noun or pronoun it logically modifies. In this case, moving the phrase to the start of the sentence would work. In other cases, such as *Turning the corner, the view was quite different,* the sentence must be recast in different form: *When we turned the corner, the view was quite different.*

par•ti•cle (pär′tĭ-kəl) ►*n.* **1.** A very small piece or part; speck. **2.** A very small or the smallest possible amount. **3.** A subatomic particle. **4.** *Ling.* A word (e.g., a preposition) that has little meaning but specifies, connects, or limits the meanings of other words. [< Lat. *particula*, small part.]

par•ti-col•ored (pär′tē-kŭl′ərd) ►*adj.* Having parts or sections colored differently from each other. [< OFr. *parti*, divided, striped.]

par•tic•u•lar (pər-tĭk′yə-lər, pə-tĭk′-) ►*adj.* **1.** Belonging to or associated with a specific person, group, thing, or category. **2.** Separate and distinct from others; specific. **3.** Worthy of note; exceptional. **4.** Attentive to or concerned with details, often excessively so; fussy. ►*n.* An individual item, fact, or detail. See Syns at **item.** [< Lat. *particula*, small part.] —**par•tic′u•lar′i•ty** (lăr′ĭ-tē) *n.* —**par•tic′u•lar•ly** *adv.*

par•tic•u•lar•ize (pər-tĭk′yə-lə-rīz′, pə-tĭk-) ►*v.* **-ized, -iz•ing 1.** To mention, describe, or treat individually; itemize or specify. **2.** To go into or give details or particulars.

par•tic•u•late (pər-tĭk′yə-lĭt, -lāt′, pär-) ►*adj.* Of or formed of separate particles. —**par•tic′u•late** *n.*

part•ing (pär′tĭng) ►*n.* **1.** The act or process of separating or dividing. **2.** A departure or leave-taking. ►*adj.* Given, received, or done on departing or separating.

par•ti•san (pär′tĭ-zən) ►*n.* **1.** A strong supporter of a party, cause, faction, person, or idea. **2.** A guerrilla. [< OItal. *parte*, PART.] —**par′ti•san** *adj.* —**par′ti•san•ship′** *n.*

par•tite (pär′tīt′) ►*adj.* Divided into parts. [< Lat. *partīre*, divide.]

par•ti•tion (pär-tĭsh′ən) ►*n.* **1a.** The act or process of dividing something into parts. **b.** The state of being so divided. **2.** Something that divides or separates, as a wall dividing one room or cubicle from another. **3.** A part or section into which something has been divided. ►*v.* **1.** To divide into parts, pieces, or sections. **2.** To divide or separate by means of a partition.

part•ly (pärt′lē) ►*adv.* In part or in some degree; not completely.

part•ner (pärt′nər) ►*n.* **1.** One associated with another in an activity or a sphere of common interest. **2.** A member of a business partnership. **3a.** A spouse. **b.** A domestic partner. **4.** Either of two persons dancing together. **5.** One of a pair or team in a sport or game. [< AN *parcen*, partition.] —**part′ner•ship′** *n.*

part of speech ►*n.*, *pl.* **parts of speech.** Any of the traditional grammatical classes of words according to their functions in context, including the noun, verb, and adjective.

par•took (pär-to͝ok′) ►*v.* P.t. of **partake.**

par•tridge (pär′trĭj) ►*n.*, *pl.* **-tridge** or **-tridg•es.** Any of several plump-bodied game birds. [< Gk. *perdix*.]

part-time (pärt′tīm′) ►*adj.* For or during less than the customary or standard time: *a part-time job.* —**part′-time′** *adv.*

par•tu•ri•tion (pär′tyo͞o-rĭsh′ən, -to͞o-, pär′chə-) ►*n.* The act of giving birth; childbirth. [< Lat. *parturīre*, be in labor.]

part•way (pärt′wā′) ►*adv.* *Informal* To a certain degree or distance; in part.

par•ty (pär′tē) ►*n.*, *pl.* **-ties 1a.** A social gathering. **b.** A group of people who have gathered to participate in a specific task or activity. See Syns at **band**[2]. **2.** A political group organized to promote and support its principles and candidates. **3a.** A participant or accessory: *I refuse to be a party to your scheme.* **b.** A person or group involved in a legal proceeding. ►*adj.* **1.** Of or relating to a political organization. **2.** Of or for use at a social gathering. ►*v.* **-tied, -ty•ing** *Informal* To celebrate or carouse at or as if at a party. [< OFr. *parti*, divided.]

party line ►*n.* **1.** A telephone circuit connecting two or more subscribers with the same exchange. **2.** One or more of the policies of a political party to which loyal members are expected to adhere.

par•ve (pär′və) ►*adj.* Var. of **pareve.**

par•ve•nu (pär′və-no͞o′, -nyo͞o′) ►*n.* A person who has suddenly risen to a higher social and economic class and has not yet gained acceptance by others in that class. [Fr. < *parvenir*, arrive : *par*, along + *venir*, come (< Lat. *venīre*).]

pas (pä) ►*n.*, *pl.* **pas** (pä). A step or dance. [Fr. < Lat. *passus*, step.]

Pas•a•de•na (păs′ə-dē′nə) **1.** A city of S CA NE of Los Angeles. Pop. 131,591. **2.** A city of SE TX. Pop. 119,363.

Pas•cal (pă-skăl′, pä-skäl′), **Blaise.** 1623–62. French philosopher and mathematician.

pas de deux (də dœ) ►*n.*, *pl.* **pas de deux.** A dance for two, esp. in ballet. [Fr.]

pa•sha (pä′shə, păsh′ə, pə-shä′) ►*n.* Used formerly as a title for military and civil officers, esp. in Turkey and N Africa. [Turk. *paşa*.]

Pash•to (pŭsh′tō) also **Push•tu** (pŭsh′to͞o) ►*n.* An Iranian language of Afghanistan and W Pakistan.

pass (păs) ►*v.* **1.** To move on or ahead; proceed. **2.** To extend; run: *The river passes through town.* **3.** To move by or past. **4.** To elapse or allow to elapse. **5.** To cause to move: *passed her hand over the curtain.* **6a.** To hand over to someone else: *pass the bread.* **b.** To transfer or be transferred from one to another. **c.** To transfer (a ball or puck) to a teammate. **7.** To be communicated or exchanged. **8.** To come to an end. **9.** To happen; take place. **10.** To be allowed to happen without challenge: *let the remark pass.* **11.** *Games* To decline one's turn to play or bid. **12.** To undergo or cause to undergo a course or test with favorable results. **13.** To serve as a barely acceptable substitute. **14.** To approve or be approved, as by a legislature. **15.** *Law* To pronounce an opinion or judgment. **16.** To discharge (bodily wastes); excrete; void. —***phrasal verbs:* pass away** To end or die. **pass out** To lose consciousness. **pass up** To reject; turn down. ►*n.* **1.** The act of passing. **2.** A narrow passage between mountains; way. **3.** A permit, ticket, or authorization to come or go at will or without charge. **4.** A sweep or run by a military aircraft over a target area. **5.** A complete cycle of operations, as by a computer program. **6.** A critical situation; predicament. See Syns at **crisis. 7.** A sexual invitation or overture. —***idiom:* pass the buck** *Slang* To shift blame to another. [< Lat. *passus*, step.] —**pass′er** *n.*

Usage: The past tense and past participle of *pass* is *passed*: *They passed* (or *have passed*) *our home. Past* is the corresponding adjective (*in centuries past*), adverb (*drove past*), preposition (*past midnight; past the crisis*), and noun (*lived in the past*).

pass. ►*abbr.* passive

pass•a•ble (păs′ə-bəl) ►*adj.* **1.** That can be passed, traversed, or crossed; navigable. **2.** Satisfactory but not outstanding; adequate. —**pass′a•bly** *adv.*

pas•sage (păs′ĭj) ►*n.* **1.** The act or process of passing. **2.** A journey, esp. by air or water. **3.** The right to travel as a passenger, esp. on a ship. **4a.** A path, channel, or duct through, over, or along which something may pass. **b.** A corridor. **5.** Enactment into law of a legislative measure. **6.** A segment of a written work or musical composition.

pas•sage•way (păs′ĭj-wā′) ▶*n.* A corridor.

Pas•sa•ma•quod•dy (păs′ə-mə-kwŏd′ē) ▶*n., pl.* **-dy** or **-dies** **1.** A member of a Native American people inhabiting parts of coastal Maine and New Brunswick. **2.** The Algonquian language of the Passamaquoddy.

pass•book (păs′bo͝ok′) ▶*n.* See **bankbook.**

pas•sé (pă-sā′) ▶*adj.* **1.** No longer current or in fashion; out-of-date. **2.** Past the prime; faded or aged. [Fr. < *passer*, PASS.]

pas•sen•ger (păs′ən-jər) ▶*n.* A person who travels in a conveyance, such as a car or train. [< OFr. *passageor.*]

passe-par•tout (păs-pär-to͞o′) ▶*n.* Something, such as a master key, that permits one to pass or go at will. [Fr.]

pas•ser•by (păs′ər-bī′, -bī′) ▶*n., pl.* **pas•sers•by** (păs′ərz-). A person who passes by, esp. casually or by chance.

pas•ser•ine (păs′ə-rīn′) ▶*adj.* Of the order of birds that includes perching birds and songbirds. [< Lat. *passer*, sparrow.]

pass-fail (păs′fāl′) ▶*adj.* Of or being a system of grading in which a student simply passes or fails instead of receiving a letter grade.

pas•sim (păs′ĭm) ▶*adv.* Throughout or frequently; used to indicate that a word, a passage, or an idea occurs frequently in the work cited. [Lat.]

pass•ing (păs′ĭng) ▶*adj.* **1.** Moving by; going past. **2.** Of brief duration; transitory: *a passing fancy.* **3.** Cursory or superficial; casual: *a passing glance.* **4.** Satisfactory: *a passing grade.* ▶*n.* **1.** The act of one that passes. **2.** Death. —**pass′ing•ly** *adv.*

pas•sion (păsh′ən) ▶*n.* **1.** A powerful emotion, such as love or anger. **2a.** Ardent love. **b.** Strong sexual desire; lust. **c.** The object of such love or desire. **3a.** Boundless enthusiasm: *a passion for sports.* **b.** The object of such enthusiasm. **4. Passion** The sufferings of Jesus after the Last Supper, including the Crucifixion. [< Lat. *patī, pass-*, suffer.] —**pas′sion•ate** (ə-nĭt) *adj.* —**pas′sion•ate•ly** *adv.* —**pas′sion•less** *adj.*

pas•sive (păs′ĭv) ▶*adj.* **1.** Receiving or subjected to an action without acting in return. **2.** Accepting or submitting without resistance; compliant. **3.** Not participating, acting, or operating; inactive. **4.** *Gram.* Of or being a verb form or voice used to indicate that the grammatical subject is the object of the action. ▶*n.* *Gram.* **1.** The passive voice. **2.** A verb or construction in the passive voice. [< Lat. *patī, pass-*, suffer.] —**pas′sive•ly** *adv.* —**pas′sive•ness** *n.* —**pas•siv′i•ty** *n.*

passive restraint ▶*n.* An automatic safety device, such as an air bag, in a motor vehicle that protects a person during a crash.

pass•key (păs′kē′) ▶*n.* **1.** See **master key. 2.** See **skeleton key.**

Pass•o•ver (păs′ō′vər) ▶*n.* *Judaism* A holiday celebrated in the spring to commemorate the exodus of the Jews from Egypt.

pass•port (păs′pôrt′, -pōrt′) ▶*n.* An official government document that certifies one's identity and citizenship and permits a citizen to travel abroad. [Fr. *passeport.*]

pass•word (păs′wûrd′) ▶*n.* **1.** A secret word or phrase that one uses to gain admittance or access to information. **2.** A sequence of characters that one must input to access a file, application, or computer system.

past (păst) ▶*adj.* **1.** No longer current; over. **2.** Having existed or occurred in an earlier time; bygone. **3a.** Earlier than the present time; ago: *40 years past.* **b.** Just gone by or elapsed: *in the past few days.* **4.** Having served formerly in a given capacity: *a past president.* **5.** *Gram.* Of or being a verb tense or form used to express an action or a condition prior to the time it is expressed. ▶*n.* **1.** The time before the present. **2.** Previous background, experiences, and activities. **3.** *Gram.* **a.** The past tense. **b.** A verb form in the past tense. ▶*adv.* So as to pass by or go beyond: *He waved as he walked past.* ▶*prep.* **1.** Beyond in time, position, extent, or amount. **2.** Beyond in position; farther than. See Usage Note at **pass.** [ME < p.part. of *passen*, PASS.]

pas•ta (päs′tə) ▶*n.* **1.** Unleavened dough, made of wheat flour, water, and sometimes eggs, molded into any of a variety of shapes and boiled. **2.** A prepared dish of pasta. [Ital. < LLat.]

paste (pāst) ▶*n.* **1.** A smooth viscous mixture, as of flour and water, that is used as an adhesive. **2.** A soft, smooth, thick mixture, as: **a.** A smooth dough used in making pastry. **b.** A food that has been pounded until smooth: *anchovy paste.* **3.** The moist clay or clay mixture used in making porcelain or pottery. **4.** A hard, brilliant glass used in making artificial gems. ▶*v.* **past•ed, past•ing** **1.** To cause to adhere by or as if by applying paste. **2.** *Comp. Sci.* To insert (e.g., text or a graphic) into a document or file. [< LLat. *pasta.*]

paste•board (pāst′bôrd′, -bōrd′) ▶*n.* A thin, firm board made of sheets of paper pasted together or pressed paper pulp.

pas•tel (pă-stĕl′) ▶*n.* **1a.** A drawing medium of dried paste made of ground pigments and a water-based binder. **b.** A crayon of this material. **2a.** A picture or sketch drawn with this type of crayon. **b.** The art of drawing with pastels. **3.** A soft, delicate hue; a pale color. [< LLat. *pastellus*, woad dye < *pasta*, paste.] —**pas•tel′** *adj.*

pas•tern (păs′tərn) ▶*n.* The part of a horse's foot between the fetlock and hoof. [< OFr. *pasturon* < *pasture*, pasture.]

Pas•ter•nak (păs′tər-năk′), **Boris Leonidovich.** 1890–1960. Russian writer; forced to decline a 1958 Nobel.

Pas•teur (păs-tûr′, pä-stœr′), **Louis.** 1822–95. French chemist. —**Pas•teur′i•an** *adj.*

pas•teur•i•za•tion (păs′chər-ĭ-zā′shən, păs′tər-) ▶*n.* The process of heating a beverage or other food, such as milk or beer, in order to kill microorganisms that could cause disease, spoilage, or undesired fermentation. [After Louis PASTEUR.] —**pas′teur•ize′** *v.* —**pas′teur•iz′er** *n.*

pas•tiche (pă-stēsh′, pä-) ▶*n.* A dramatic, literary, or musical piece openly imitating the works of other artists. [< Ital. *pasticcio.*]

pas•tille (pă-stēl′) also **pas•til** (păs′tĭl) ▶*n.* **1.** A small medicated or flavored tablet. **2.** A tablet containing aromatic substances that is burned to fumigate or deodorize the air. [< Lat. *pastillus.*]

pas•time (păs′tīm′) ►*n.* An activity that occupies one's spare time pleasantly.
pas•tor (păs′tər) ►*n.* A Christian minister or priest who is the leader of a congregation. [< Lat. *pāstor*, shepherd.]
pas•tor•al (păs′tər-əl) ►*adj.* **1.** Of or relating to shepherds or herders. **2a.** Of or relating to rural life. **b.** Charmingly simple and serene; idyllic. **3.** Of or relating to a pastor or the duties of a pastor. ►*n.* A literary or other artistic work that portrays or evokes rural life, usu. in an idealized manner. —**pas′tor•al•ly** *adv.*
pas•to•rale (păs′tə-räl′, -răl′, pä′stə-) ►*n.* A musical composition with a pastoral theme. [Ital.]
past participle ►*n.* A verb form indicating past or completed action or time that is used as an adjective and with auxiliaries to form the passive voice or perfect and pluperfect tenses.
past perfect ►*n.* See **pluperfect** 1.
pas•tra•mi (pə-strä′mē) ►*n.* A highly seasoned smoked cut of beef, usu. from the shoulder. [< Rom. *pastrámă.*]
pas•try (pā′strē) ►*n.*, *pl.* **-tries 1.** Dough or paste of flour, water, and shortening that is baked and used as a crust for foods such as pies. **2a.** Baked foods made with pastry. **b.** One of these foods.
pas•tur•age (păs′chər-ĭj) ►*n.* **1.** The grass or other vegetation eaten by grazing animals. **2.** Land suitable for grazing animals.
pas•ture (păs′chər) ►*n.* **1.** Grass or other vegetation eaten by grazing animals. **2.** Ground set aside for use by grazing animals. ►*v.* **-tured, -tur•ing 1.** To herd (animals) into a pasture to graze. **2.** To graze. [< Lat. *pāscere*, *pāst-*, feed.]
past•y (pā′stē) ►*adj.* **-i•er, -i•est 1.** Resembling paste in consistency. **2.** Having a pale, lifeless appearance; pallid.
pat[1] (păt) ►*v.* **pat•ted, pat•ting 1a.** To tap gently with the open hand or with something flat. **b.** To stroke lightly as a gesture of affection. **2.** To mold by tapping gently with the hands or a flat implement. ►*n.* **1.** A light stroke or tap. **2.** The sound made by a pat. **3.** A small mass: *a pat of butter.* —***idiom:*** **pat on the back** A word or gesture of praise or approval. [< ME, a blow.]
pat[2] (păt) ►*adj.* **1.** Trite or glib: *pat answer.* **2a.** Timely or opportune. **b.** Suitable; fitting. ►*adv.* *Informal* Completely, exactly, or perfectly: *has the lesson down pat.* [< PAT[1].] —**pat′ly** *adv.* —**pat′ness** *n.*
pat. ►*abbr.* patent
pa•ta•ca (pə-tä′kə) ►*n.* See table at **currency.** [Port. < Ar. *'abū ṭāqa*, having a window.]
Pat•a•go•ni•a (păt′ə-gō′nē-ə, -gōn′yə) A region of South America in S Argentina and Chile extending from the Río Colorado to the Straits of Magellan and from the Andes to the Atlantic. —**Pat′a•go′ni•an** *adj. & n.*
patch (păch) ►*n.* **1a.** A small piece of material affixed to another, larger piece to conceal, reinforce, or repair a worn area, hole, or tear. **b.** A small piece of cloth used for patchwork. **2.** A cloth badge affixed to a garment as a decoration or an insignia, as of a military unit. **3a.** A dressing or covering applied to a wound. **b.** A pad or shield of cloth, esp. one worn over an injured eye. **4a.** A small area that differs from the whole. **b.** A small plot or piece of land: *a bean patch.* **5.** A temporary, removable electronic connection. ►*v.* **1.** To put a patch or patches on. **2.** To make by sewing scraps of material together: *patch a quilt.* **3.** To mend, repair, or put together, esp. hastily. **4.** *Electron.* To connect temporarily. —***phrasal verb:*** **patch up** To settle: *patch up a quarrel.* [ME *pacche.*]
patch test ►*n.* A test for allergic sensitivity in which a suspected allergen is applied to the skin on a small surgical pad.
patch•work (păch′wûrk′) ►*n.* Needlework consisting of varicolored patches of material sewn together, as in a quilt.
patch•y (păch′ē) ►*adj.* **-i•er, -i•est 1.** Made up of or marked by patches. **2.** Uneven in quality or performance: *patchy work.* —**patch′i•ness** *n.*
pate (pāt) ►*n.* The human head, esp. the top of the head. [ME.]
pâ•té (pä-tā′) ►*n.* A meat paste. [< OFr. *paste*, PASTE.]
pa•tel•la (pə-tĕl′ə) ►*n.*, *pl.* **-tel•lae** (-tĕl′ē). A flat triangular bone located at the front of the knee joint. [Lat.] —**pa•tel′lar** *adj.*
pat•en (păt′n) ►*n.* **1.** A plate used to hold the host during the celebration of the Eucharist. **2.** A thin disk of or resembling metal. [< Gk. *patanē*, platter.]
pat•ent (păt′nt) ►*n.* **1.** A grant made by a government that confers upon the creator of an invention the sole right to make, use, and sell that invention for a set period of time. **2.** An invention protected by such a grant. ►*adj.* **1a.** Protected or conferred by a patent. **b.** Of or relating to patents: *patent law.* **2.** (*also* pāt′nt). Obvious; plain. See Syns at **apparent. 3.** (*also* pāt′nt) *Archaic* Open to general inspection: *letters patent.* ►*v.* **1.** To obtain a patent on. **2.** To grant a patent to. [< Lat. *patēns*, open.] —**pat′ent•ee′** *n.* —**pat′ent•ly** *adv.*
patent leather ►*n.* Black leather finished to a hard, glossy surface. [So called because it is made by a once-patented process.]
pa•ter•fa•mil•i•as (pā′tər-fə-mĭl′ē-əs, pä′-) ►*n.*, *pl.* **pa•tres•fa•mil•i•as** (pā′trēz-, pä′-). A man who is the head of a household or the father of a family. [Lat. *paterfamiliās* : *pater*, father + *familiās*, of the family.]
pa•ter•nal (pə-tûr′nəl) ►*adj.* **1.** Relating to or characteristic of a father or fatherhood; fatherly. **2.** Inherited from or related through one's father. [< Lat. *pater*, father.] —**pa•ter′nal•ly** *adv.*
pa•ter•nal•ism (pə-tûr′nə-lĭz′əm) ►*n.* A policy or practice of treating or governing people in a fatherly manner, esp. by providing for their needs without giving them rights or responsibilities. —**pa•ter′nal•is′tic** *adj.*
pa•ter•ni•ty (pə-tûr′nĭ-tē) ►*n.* The state of being a father; fatherhood.
pa•ter•nos•ter also **Pa•ter•nos•ter** (pā′tər-nŏs′tər, pä′-, păt′ər-) ►*n.* The Lord's Prayer. [< LLat. : Lat. *pater*, father + *noster*, our.]
Pat•er•son (păt′ər-sən) A city of NE NJ N of Newark. Pop. 140,891.
path (păth) ►*n.*, *pl.* **paths** (păthz, păths) **1.** A trodden track or way. **2.** A course; route. [< OE *pæth.*]
pa•thet•ic (pə-thĕt′ĭk) ►*adj.* **1.** Arousing sympathetic sadness and compassion. **2.** Arousing scornful pity. [< Gk. *pathos*, suffering.] —**pa•thet′i•cal•ly** *adv.*

path•find•er (păth′fīn′dər, päth′-) ►*n.* One that discovers a new course or way, esp. through or into unexplored regions.

path•name (păth′nām′, päth′-) ►*n.* The full name of a computer file, including its position in the directory structure.

patho– or **path–** ►*pref.* Disease; suffering: *pathogen.* [< Gk. *pathos*, suffering.]

path•o•gen (păth′ə-jən) ►*n.* An agent that causes disease, esp. a living microorganism such as a bacterium or fungus. —**path′o•gen′ic** (-jĕn′ĭk) *adj.* —**path′o•ge•nic′i•ty** (-jə-nĭs′ĭ-tē) *n.*

path•o•gen•e•sis (păth′ə-jĕn′ĭ-sĭs) ►*n.* The development of a diseased or morbid condition.

pa•thol•o•gy (pă-thŏl′ə-jē) ►*n., pl.* **-gies 1.** The scientific study of the nature of disease. **2.** The anatomic or functional manifestations of a disease. **3.** A departure or deviation from a normal condition. —**path′o•log′i•cal** (păth′ə-lŏj′ĭ-kəl) *adj.* —**path′o•log′i•cal•ly** *adv.* —**pa•thol′o•gist** *n.*

pa•thos (pā′thŏs′, -thôs′) ►*n.* A quality, as of an experience or a work of art, that arouses feelings of pity, sympathy, tenderness, or sorrow. [Gk., suffering.]

path•way (păth′wā′, päth′-) ►*n.* A path.

–pathy ►*suff.* **1.** Feeling; perception: *telepathy.* **2a.** Disease: *idiopathy.* **b.** A system of treating disease: *homeopathy.* [< Gk. *pathos*, suffering.]

pa•tience (pā′shəns) ►*n.* **1.** The capacity, quality, or fact of being patient. **2.** *Chiefly Brit.* The game solitaire.

pa•tient (pā′shənt) ►*adj.* **1.** Enduring pain or difficulty with calmness. **2.** Tolerant; understanding. **3.** Persevering; constant. **4.** Capable of calmly awaiting an outcome; not hasty or impulsive. ►*n.* One who receives medical treatment. [< Lat. *patī*, endure.] —**pa′tient•ly** *adv.*

pat•i•na (păt′n-ə, pə-tē′nə) ►*n.* **1.** A thin greenish layer that forms on copper or copper alloys as a result of corrosion. **2.** The sheen on any surface, produced by age and use. [< Lat., plate.]

pat•i•o (păt′ē-ō′) ►*n., pl.* **-os 1.** An outdoor space for dining or recreation that adjoins a residence and is often paved. **2.** A roofless inner courtyard. [< OSpan.]

Pat•na (pŭt′nə) A city of NE India on the Ganges R. NW of Calcutta. Pop. 917,243.

pat•ois (păt′wä′, pă-twä′) ►*n., pl.* **pat•ois** (păt′wäz′, pă-twä′) **1.** A regional dialect. **2a.** A creole language. **b.** Nonstandard speech. **3.** Jargon; cant. [< OFr.]

Pa•ton (pāt′n), **Alan Stewart.** 1903–88. South African writer.

patri– or **patr–** ►*pref.* Father, paternal: *patrilineal.* [< Lat. *pater* and Gk. *patēr*, father.]

pa•tri•arch (pā′trē-ärk′) ►*n.* **1.** A man who rules a family, clan, or tribe. **2.** A leading or venerable man. **3.** A bishop of high rank, esp. in an eastern Christian church. —**pa′tri•ar′chal, pa′tri•ar′chic** *adj.*

pa•tri•ar•chy (pā′trē-är′kē) ►*n., pl.* **-chies.** A social system in which the father is the head of the family.

pa•tri•cian (pə-trĭsh′ən) ►*n.* A person of high rank; aristocrat. —**pa•tri′cian** *adj.*

pat•ri•cide (păt′rĭ-sīd′) ►*n.* **1.** The act of murdering one's father. **2.** One who commits this act. —**pat′ri•cid′al** (-sīd′l) *adj.*

Pat•rick (păt′rĭk), Saint. A.D. 389?–461? Christian missionary and patron saint of Ireland.

pat•ri•lin•e•al (păt′rə-lĭn′ē-əl) ►*adj.* Relating to, based on, or tracing ancestral descent through the paternal line.

pat•ri•mo•ny (păt′rə-mō′nē) ►*n., pl.* **-nies.** An inheritance, esp. from a father or other ancestor. [< Lat. *patrimōnium* < *pater*, father.] —**pat′ri•mo′ni•al** *adj.*

pa•tri•ot (pā′trē-ət, -ŏt′) ►*n.* One who loves, supports, and defends one's country. [< Gk. *patrios*, of one's fathers < *patēr*, father.] —**pa′tri•ot′ic** (-ŏt′ĭk) *adj.* —**pa′tri•ot′i•cal•ly** *adv.* —**pa′tri•ot•ism** (-ə-tĭz′əm) *n.*

pa•tris•tic (pə-trĭs′tĭk) also **pa•tris•ti•cal** (-tĭ-kəl) ►*adj.* Of or relating to the fathers of the early Christian church or their writings.

pa•trol (pə-trōl′) ►*n.* **1.** The act of moving about an area for observation, inspection, or security. **2.** A person or group of persons who perform such an act. **3.** A military unit sent out on a reconnaissance or combat mission. ►*v.* **-trolled, -trol•ling.** To engage in a patrol (of). [< OFr. *patouiller*, paddle about in mud.]

pa•trol•man (pə-trōl′mən) ►*n.* A policeman who patrols or polices an assigned area.

patrol wagon ►*n.* An enclosed police truck used to convey prisoners.

pa•trol•wom•an (pə-trōl′wo͝om′ən) ►*n.* A policewoman who patrols or polices an assigned area.

pa•tron (pā′trən) ►*n.* **1.** One that supports, protects, or champions someone or something; sponsor or benefactor. **2.** A customer, esp. a regular customer. [< Lat. *patrōnus* < *pater*, father.]

pa•tron•age (pā′trə-nĭj, păt′rə-) ►*n.* **1.** Support from a patron. **2.** The trade given to a commercial establishment by its customers. **3.** Customers considered as a group; clientele. **4.** The power to appoint people to political positions.

pa•tron•ess (pā′trə-nĭs) ►*n.* A woman who supports, protects, or champions someone or something; sponsor or benefactor.

pa•tron•ize (pā′trə-nīz′, păt′rə-) ►*v.* **-ized, -iz•ing 1.** To act as a patron to; support or sponsor. **2.** To go to as a customer, esp. on a regular basis. **3.** To treat in a condescending manner. —**pa′tron•iz′ing•ly** *adv.*

patron saint ►*n.* A saint who is regarded as the advocate in heaven of a nation, place, craft, activity, class, or person.

pat•ro•nym•ic (păt′rə-nĭm′ĭk) ►*n.* A name derived from the name of one's father or a paternal ancestor. [< Gk. *patrōnumos*, named after one's father : *patēr*, father + *onuma*, name.] —**pat′ro•nym′ic** *adj.*

pa•troon (pə-tro͞on′) ►*n.* A landholder in New York under Dutch colonial rule who was granted proprietary rights to a large tract of land. [Du. < Fr. *patron*, PATRON.]

pat•sy (păt′sē) ►*n., pl.* **-sies** *Slang* A person easily taken advantage of, blamed, or ridiculed. [?]

pat•ter[1] (păt′ər) ►*v.* To make a quick succession of light, soft tapping sounds. ►*n.* A quick succession of light, soft tapping sounds. [< PAT[1].]

pat•ter[2] (păt′ər) ►*v.* To speak or chatter glibly or mechanically. ►*n.* **1.** The jargon of a particular group; cant. **2.** Glib, rapid speech, as of an auctioneer. [ME *patren.*]

pat•tern (păt′ərn) ►*n.* **1a.** A model or an original used as an archetype. **b.** A person or thing considered worthy of imitation. **2.** A plan, diagram, or model to be followed in making things. **3.** A representative sample; specimen or ideal. **4.** An artistic or decorative design. See Syns at **figure. 5.** A composite of traits or features. ►*v.* To make, mold, or design by following a pattern. [< OFr. *patron*, PATRON.]

Pat•ton (păt′n), **George Smith, Jr.** 1885–1945. Amer. general.

pat•ty (păt′ē) ►*n., pl.* **-ties 1.** A small rounded, flattened cake of food, esp. chopped food. **2.** A small pie. [Fr. *pâté*, PÂTÉ.]

pau•ci•ty (pô′sĭ-tē) ►*n.* **1.** Smallness of number. **2.** Scarcity. [< Lat. *paucus*, few.]

Paul (pôl), Saint. A.D. 5?–67? Apostle to the Gentiles. —**Paul′ine** (-īn, -ēn) *adj.*

Paul III. 1468–1549. Pope (1534–49).

Paul VI. 1897–1978. Pope (1963–78).

Pau•ling (pô′lĭng), **Linus Carl.** 1901–94. Amer. chemist; 1954 Nobel.

paunch (pônch, pänch) ►*n.* **1.** The belly, esp. a protuding one; potbelly. **2.** See **rumen.** [< Lat. *pantex.*] —**paunch′y** *adj.*

pau•per (pô′pər) ►*n.* One who is extremely poor, esp. one on public charity. [< Lat., poor.] —**pau′per•ism** *n.* —**pau′per•ize** *v.*

pause (pôz) ►*v.* **paused, paus•ing.** To cease or suspend an action temporarily; linger or hesitate. ►*n.* **1.** A temporary cessation. **2.** A hesitation. **3.** *Mus.* A sign indicating that a note or rest is to be held. **4.** Reason for hesitation. [< Gk. *pausis*, a pause.]

Syns: *pause, intermission, recess, respite, suspension* ***n.***

pave (pāv) ►*v.* **paved, pav•ing.** To cover with pavement. —***idiom:* pave the way** To make progress easier. [< Lat. *pavīre*, tread down.]

pave•ment (pāv′mənt) ►*n.* **1.** A hard smooth surface, esp. of a thoroughfare, that will bear travel. **2.** The material with which such a surface is made.

pa•vil•ion (pə-vĭl′yən) ►*n.* **1.** An ornate tent. **2.** A light, often open structure, used for amusement or shelter. **3.** An annex of a building. **4.** One of a group of related buildings forming a complex. [< Lat. *pāpiliō.*]

pav•ing (pā′vĭng) ►*n.* **1.** The act or technique of laying pavement. **2.** Pavement.

Pav•lov (păv′lôv′, päv′ləf), **Ivan Petrovich.** 1849–1936. Russian physiologist; 1904 Nobel. —**Pav•lo′vi•an** (păv-lō′vē-ən, -lô′-) *adj.*

Pav•lo•va (păv-lō′və, păv′lə-, päv′-), **Anna.** 1882–1931. Russian ballerina.

paw (pô) ►*n.* **1.** The clawed foot esp. of a quadruped animal. **2.** *Informal* A human hand. ►*v.* **1.** To strike with the paw. **2.** To scrape (e.g., the ground) with a paw or foot. **3.** To handle clumsily, rudely, or with too much familiarity. [< OFr. *powe.*]

pawl (pôl) ►*n.* A hinged or pivoted device adapted to fit into a notch of a ratchet wheel to impart forward motion or prevent backward motion. [Prob. < Du. *pal.*]

pawn[1] (pôn) ►*n.* **1.** Something given as security for a loan; a pledge or guarantee. **2.** The condition of being held as a pledge. ►*v.* To give or deposit (personal property) as security for money borrowed. [< OFr. *pan.*]

Anna Pavlova
photographed c. 1910

pawn[2] (pôn) ►*n.* **1.** A chess piece of lowest value. **2.** One used to further the purposes of another. [< Med.Lat. *pedō*, foot soldier < Lat. *pēs*, foot.]

pawn•bro•ker (pôn′brō′kər) ►*n.* One that lends money at interest in exchange for personal property deposited as security.

Paw•nee (pô-nē′) ►*n., pl.* **-nee** or **-nees 1.** A member of a Native American people formerly of Kansas and Nebraska, now of Oklahoma. **2.** Their Caddoan language.

pawn•shop (pôn′shŏp′) ►*n.* The shop of a pawnbroker.

paw•paw (pô′pô) ►*n.* Var. of **papaw.**

pay (pā) ►*v.* **paid** (pād), **pay•ing 1.** To recompense for goods or services. **2.** To discharge or settle (a debt or obligation). **3.** To requite. **4.** To bear (a cost or penalty): *pay the price for nonconformity.* **5.** To yield as a return. **6.** To give or bestow: *pay compliments.* **7.** To make (a visit or call). **8.** To be profitable or worthwhile: *Crime doesn't pay.* —***phrasal verb:* pay off 1.** To pay the full amount on (a debt). **2.** To be profitable. **3.** *Informal* To bribe. ►*adj.* Requiring payment to operate: *a pay telephone.* ►*n.* **1.** The act of paying or state of being paid. **2.** Something paid, as a salary or wages. —***idiom:* pay the piper** To bear the consequences of something. [< LLat. *pācāre*, appease < Lat. *pāx*, peace.] —**pay′a•ble** *adj.* —**pay•ee′** *n.* —**pay′er** *n.*

pay•check (pā′chĕk′) ►*n.* **1.** A check issued to an employee in payment of salary or wages. **2.** Salary or wages.

pay dirt ►*n.* **1.** Earth, ore, or gravel that is profitable to mine. **2.** *Informal* A profitable discovery or venture.

pay•load (pā′lōd′) ►*n.* **1.** The revenue-producing part of a cargo. **2.** The total weight of passengers and cargo that can be carried by an aircraft or spacecraft. **3.** The warhead of a missile.

pay•mas•ter (pā′măs′tər) ►*n.* A person in charge of paying wages and salaries.

pay•ment (pā′mənt) ►*n.* **1.** The act of paying. **2.** An amount paid.

pay•off (pā′ôf′, -ŏf′) ►*n.* **1.** Full payment of a salary or wages. **2.** *Informal* **a.** A final settlement or reckoning. **b.** The climax of a narrative or sequence of events. **3.** Final retribution or revenge. **4.** *Informal* A bribe or inducement.

pay•roll (pā′rōl′) ►*n.* **1.** A list of employees with the wages due to each. **2.** The total sum of wages paid during a pay period.

Pb ► The symbol for the element **lead**² 1. [Lat. *plumbum*, lead.]

PBS ►*abbr.* Public Broadcasting Service

PBX ►*abbr.* private branch exchange

PC ►*abbr.* **1.** personal computer **2.** politically correct

p.c. ►*abbr.* **1.** percent **2.** *Lat.* post cibum (after meals)

p/c or **P/C** ►*abbr.* **1.** petty cash **2.** prices current

PCB (pē′sē-bē′) ►*n.* An industrial compound and environmental pollutant. [*p(oly)c(hlorinated) b(iphenyl).*]

PCP (pē′sē-pē′) ►*n.* A drug, $C_{17}H_{25}N$, used in veterinary medicine as an anesthetic and illegally as a hallucinogen. [*p(henyl)c(yclohexyl)p(iperidine).*]

pct. ►*abbr.* percent

Pd ► The symbol for the element **palladium.**

pd. ►*abbr.* paid

p.d. ►*abbr.* per diem

PDT ►*abbr.* Pacific Daylight Time

PE ►*abbr.* **1.** physical education **2.** Prince Edward Island **3.** *Statistics* probable error

pea (pē) ►*n.* **1.** A vine having edible seeds enclosed in green pods. **2.** The round seed of this plant. **3.** Any of several related or similar plants. [< Gk. *pison.*]

peace (pēs) ►*n.* **1.** The absence of war or other hostilities. **2.** An agreement or treaty to end hostilities. **3.** Freedom from quarrels and disagreement; harmony. **4.** Public security and order: *disturbing the peace.* **5.** Serenity: *peace of mind.* [< Lat. *pāx.*] —**peace′a•ble, peace′ful** *adj.* —**peace′a•bly, peace′ful•ly** *adv.* —**peace′ful•ness** *n.*

peace•keep•ing (pēs′kē′pĭng) ►*n.* The preservation of peace, esp. the supervision by international forces of a truce between hostile nations. —**peace′keep′ing** *adj.*

peace•mak•er (pēs′mā′kər) ►*n.* One who makes peace, esp. by settling disputes. —**peace′mak′ing** *adj.* & *n.*

peace officer ►*n.* A law enforcement officer responsible for maintaining civil peace.

peace pipe ►*n.* A calumet.

Peace River. A river, about 1,521 km (945 mi), of British Columbia and Alberta, Canada.

peace•time (pēs′tīm′) ►*n.* A time free from war. —**peace′time′** *adj.*

peach (pēch) ►*n.* **1.** A small tree having pink flowers and edible fruit. **2.** The soft juicy fruit of this tree, having yellow flesh and downy, red-tinted yellow skin. [< Lat. *persicus*, Persian.] —**peach′y** *adj.*

pea•cock (pē′kŏk′) ►*n.* A male peafowl, having brilliant blue or green plumage and long back feathers that can be spread in a fanlike form. [< Lat. *pāvō*, peacock + COCK¹.]

pea•fowl (pē′foul′) ►*n.* A large Asian pheasant. [PEA(COCK) + FOWL.]

pea•hen (pē′hĕn′) ►*n.* A female peafowl.

pea jacket ►*n.* A short, warm, double-breasted coat of heavy wool. [Prob. < Du. *pijjekker.*]

peak (pēk) ►*n.* **1.** A tapering, projecting point. **2a.** The pointed summit of a mountain. **b.** The mountain itself. **3.** The point of greatest development, value, or intensity. ►*v.* **1.** To bring to or form a peak. **2.** To achieve a maximum of development or intensity. [Prob. ME *pike.*]

peak•ed (pē′kĭd) ►*adj.* Having a sickly appearance. [< *peak*, become sickly.]

peal (pēl) ►*n.* **1.** A ringing of bells. **2.** A set of tuned bells. **3.** A loud burst of noise: *peals of laughter.* ►*v.* To ring, as bells. [< ME *apel*, appeal.]

Peale (pēl), **Charles Wilson.** 1741–1827. Amer. painter.

pea•nut (pē′nŭt′) ►*n.* **1.** A widely cultivated plant having seed pods that ripen underground. **2.** The edible, nutlike, oily seed of this plant. **3. peanuts** *Informal* A very small amount of money.

peanut butter ►*n.* A paste made from ground roasted peanuts.

pear (pâr) ►*n.* **1.** A widely cultivated tree having white flowers and edible fruit. **2.** The fruit of this tree, spherical at the base and narrow at the stem. [< Lat. *pirum.*]

pearl (pûrl) ►*n.* **1.** A smooth, lustrous, variously colored deposit formed in the shells of certain mollusks and valued as a gem. **2.** Mother-of-pearl. **3.** One highly valued or esteemed. **4.** A yellowish white. [< Lat. *perna*, seashell.] —**pearl′y** *adj.*

Pearl Harbor. An inlet of the Pacific on the S coast of Oahu, HI, W of Honolulu.

Pear•son (pîr′sən), **Lester Bowles.** 1897–1972. Canadian prime minister (1963–68); 1957 Nobel Peace Prize.

Pea•ry (pîr′ē), **Robert Edwin.** 1856–1920. Amer. naval officer and Arctic explorer.

Robert E. Peary
photographed in 1909

peas•ant (pĕz′ənt) ►*n.* **1.** A member of a class made up of agricultural workers, including small or tenant farmers and laborers on the land. **2.** A country person; rustic. **3.** An uncouth, crude, or ill-bred person; boor. [< LLat. *pāgēnsis*, inhabitant of a district.] —**peas′ant•ry** *n.*

peat (pēt) ►*n.* Partially carbonized vegetable matter, usu. mosses, found in bogs and used as fertilizer and fuel. [ME *pete.*]

peat moss ►*n.* Any of various wetland mosses used as mulch and plant food.

peb•ble (pĕb′əl) ►*n.* A small stone, esp. one worn smooth by erosion. ►*v.* **-bled, -bling 1.** To pave with pebbles. **2.** To impart a rough grainy surface to (leather or paper). [< OE *papol-*.] —**peb′bly** *adj.*

pe•can (pĭ-kän′, -kăn′, pē′kăn) ▸*n.* **1.** A tree of the central and S US, having deeply furrowed bark and edible nuts. **2.** The smooth oval nut of this tree. [< Illinois *pakani.*]

pec•ca•dil•lo (pĕk′ə-dĭl′ō) ▸*n., pl.* **-loes** or **-los.** A minor sin or fault. [< Lat. *peccātum*, sin.]

pec•ca•ry (pĕk′ə-rē) ▸*n., pl.* **-ries.** Any of several piglike American mammals having long, dark, dense bristles. [< Carib *pakira.*]

peck[1] (pĕk) ▸*v.* **1.** To strike or make strokes with the beak or a pointed instrument. **2.** To pick up with the beak. **3.** *Informal* To kiss briefly and casually. **4.** To eat sparingly: *pecked at his dinner.* ▸*n.* **1.** A stroke or mark made with the beak. **2.** *Informal* A light, quick kiss. [ME *pecken.*]

peck[2] (pĕk) ▸*n.* **1.** See table at **measurement. 2.** A unit of dry volume or capacity equal to 8 qt. or approx. 554.8 cu. in. [ME.]

peck•ing order (pĕk′ĭng) ▸*n.* **1.** A hierarchy among a group, as of people, classes, or nations. **2.** The social hierarchy in a flock of domestic fowl in which each bird pecks subordinate birds and submits to being pecked by dominant birds.

Pe•cos (pā′kəs) A river of E NM and W TX flowing about 1,490 km (926 mi) to the Rio Grande.

Pécs (pāch) A city of SW Hungary SSW of Budapest. Pop. 171,870.

pec•tin (pĕk′tĭn) ▸*n.* Any of a group of water-soluble colloids found in ripe fruits and used to jell various foods, drugs, and cosmetics. [< Gk. *pēktos*, coagulated.] —**pec′tic, pec′tin•ous** *adj.*

pec•to•ral (pĕk′tər-əl) ▸*adj.* Of or situated in the breast or chest. [< Lat. *pectus*, breast.]

pec•u•late (pĕk′yə-lāt′) ▸*v.* **-lat•ed, -lat•ing.** To embezzle. [< Lat. *pecūlium*, private property.] —**pec′u•la′tion** *n.*

pe•cu•liar (pĭ-kyo͞ol′yər) ▸*adj.* **1.** Unusual or eccentric; odd. **2.** Distinct from all others. **3.** Belonging distinctively to one person, group, or kind; unique. [< Lat. *pecūlium*, private property.] —**pe•cu′li•ar′i•ty** (-kyo͞o′lē-ăr′ĭ-tē, -kyo͞ol-yăr′-) *n.*

pe•cu•ni•ar•y (pĭ-kyo͞o′nē-ĕr′ē) ▸*adj.* Of or relating to money. [< Lat. *pecūnia*, wealth.]

ped– ▸*pref.* Var. of **pedo–.**

–ped or **–pede** ▸*suff.* Foot: *biped.* [< Lat. *pēs*, foot.]

ped•a•gogue (pĕd′ə-gŏg′, -gôg′) ▸*n.* A schoolteacher; educator. [< Gk. *paidagōgos* : *pais*, child + *agōgos*, leader (< *agein*, to lead).]

ped•a•go•gy (pĕd′ə-gō′jē, -gŏj′ē) ▸*n.* The art or profession of teaching. —**ped′a•gog′ic** (-gŏj′ĭk, -gō′jĭk), **ped′a•gog′i•cal** *adj.* —**ped′a•gog′i•cal•ly** *adv.*

ped•al (pĕd′l) ▸*n.* A foot-operated lever, as on a piano or bicycle. ▸*adj.* Of or relating to a foot or footlike part. ▸*v.* **-aled, -al•ing** or **-alled, -al•ling 1.** To use or operate a pedal or pedals. **2.** To ride a bicycle. [< Lat. *pēs*, *ped-*, foot.]

ped•ant (pĕd′nt) ▸*n.* **1.** One who stresses trivial details of learning. **2.** One who exhibits his or her learning ostentatiously. [Prob. < Gk. *paideuein*, instruct.]

pe•dan•tic (pə-dăn′tĭk) ▸*adj.* Marked by a narrow, often ostentatious concern for book learning and formal rules. —**pe•dan′ti•cal•ly** *adv.* —**ped′ant•ry** (pĕd′n-trē) *n.*

Syns: *pedantic, academic, bookish, scholastic* **adj.**

ped•dle (pĕd′l) ▸*v.* **-dled, -dling.** To travel about selling (wares). [< ME *pedlere*, peddler < Lat. *pēs*, foot.] —**ped′dler** *n.*

ped•er•ast (pĕd′ə-răst′) ▸*n.* A man who has sexual relations with a boy. [Gk. *paiderastēs.*] —**ped′er•as′ty** *n.*

ped•es•tal (pĕd′ĭ-stəl) ▸*n.* A support or base, as for a column or statue. [< Ital. *piedestallo.*]

pe•des•tri•an (pə-dĕs′trē-ən) ▸*n.* A person traveling on foot. ▸*adj.* **1.** Going or performed on foot. **2.** Dull; ordinary: *pedestrian prose.* See Syns at **dull.** [< Lat. *pedester*, going on foot < *pēs*, foot.]

pe•di•at•rics (pē′dē-ăt′rĭks) ▸*n. (takes sing. v.)* The branch of medicine that deals with the care of infants and children and the treatment of their diseases. —**pe′di•at′ric** *adj.* —**pe′di•a•tri′cian** (-ə-trĭsh′ən) *n.*

ped•i•cure (pĕd′ĭ-kyo͝or′) ▸*n.* A cosmetic treatment of the feet and toenails. [Fr. *pédicure* : Lat. *pēs*, foot + *cūra*, care.] —**ped′i•cur′ist** *n.*

ped•i•gree (pĕd′ĭ-grē′) ▸*n.* **1.** A line of ancestors; ancestry or lineage. **2.** A list of ancestors, as of a purebred animal. [< AN *pe de grue*, crane's foot (from the shape of the lines on a family tree).] —**ped′i•greed′** *adj.*

ped•i•ment (pĕd′ə-mənt) ▸*n.* A gablelike, usu. triangular architectural or decorative element, as above a façade. [Prob. < PYRAMID.]

pedo– or **ped–** ▸*pref.* Child; children: *pediatrics.* [< Gk. *pais*, *paid-*, child.]

pe•dom•e•ter (pĭ-dŏm′ĭ-tər) ▸*n.* An instrument that gauges the approximate distance traveled on foot by registering the number of steps taken. [Lat. *pēs*, *ped-*, foot + –METER.]

pe•dun•cle (pĭ-dŭng′kəl, pē′dŭng′kəl) ▸*n.* **1.** *Bot.* A stalk bearing a flower. **2.** *Zool.* A stalklike part or structure. [NLat. *pedunculus*, dim. of Lat. *pēs*, foot.]

peek (pēk) ▸*v.* **1.** To glance quickly. **2.** To look or peer furtively, as from a place of concealment. [ME *piken.*] —**peek** *n.*

peel (pēl) ▸*n.* The skin or rind of certain fruits and vegetables. ▸*v.* **1.** To strip or cut away the skin, rind, or bark from; pare. **2.** To strip away; pull off. **3.** To lose or shed skin, bark, or other covering. **4.** To come off in thin strips or pieces, as paint. [< Lat. *pilāre*, deprive of hair.] —**peel′er** *n.*

Peel, Sir **Robert.** 1788–1850. British politician.

peen (pēn) ▸*n.* The end of a hammerhead opposite the flat striking surface, often wedge-shaped or ball-shaped. [Prob. of Scand. orig.]

peep[1] (pēp) ▸*v.* To cheep or chirp, as a frog or baby bird. [ME **pepen*, to peep. See PIPE.] —**peep** *n.* —**peep′er** *n.*

peep[2] (pēp) ▸*v.* **1.** To peek furtively, as through a small aperture. **2.** To become partly visible. ▸*n.* **1.** A quick or furtive look. **2.** A first glimpse or appearance: *the peep of dawn.* [ME *pepen.*] —**peep′er** *n.*

peep•hole (pēp′hōl′) ▸*n.* A small hole or crevice through which one may peep.

peer[1] (pîr) ▸*v.* **1.** To look intently, searchingly, or with difficulty. **2.** To be partially visible; show. [ME *piren.*]

peer² (pîr) ►*n.* **1.** One who has equal standing with another. **2a.** A nobleman. **b.** A British duke, marquis, earl, viscount, or baron. [< Lat. *pār*, equal.]

peer•age (pîr′ĭj) ►*n.* The rank or title of a peer or peeress.

peer•ess (pîr′ĭs) ►*n.* A British duchess, marchioness, countess, viscountess, or baroness.

peer•less (pîr′lĭs) ►*adj.* Having no match or equal; incomparable. —**peer′less•ly** *adv.*

peeve (pēv) ►*v.* **peeved, peev•ing.** To annoy or vex. ►*n.* **1.** A vexation; grievance. **2.** A resentful mood. [< PEEVISH.]

pee•vish (pē′vĭsh) ►*adj.* **1.** Querulous or discontented. **2.** Ill-tempered. [ME *pevish.*] —**pee′vish•ly** *adv.* —**pee′vish•ness** *n.*

pee•wee (pē′wē) ►*n. Informal* One that is relatively or unusually small. [Prob. reduplication of WEE.]

peg (pĕg) ►*n.* **1a.** A small cylindrical or tapered pin, as of wood, used to fasten things or plug a hole. **b.** A projection used as a support or boundary marker. **2.** A degree or notch. **3.** A straight throw of a ball. **4.** A pretext or occasion. ►*v.* **pegged, peg•ging 1.** To fasten or plug with a peg or pegs. **2.** To mark with a peg or pegs. **3.** To fix (a price) at a certain level. **4.** *Informal* To classify; categorize. **5.** To throw. **6.** To work steadily; plug. [< MDu. *pegge.*]

peg•ma•tite (pĕg′mə-tīt′) ►*n.* A coarse-grained granite. [< Gk. *pēgma*, solid mass.]

Pei (pā), **I(eoh) M(ing).** b. 1917. Chinese-born Amer. architect.

P.E.I. ►*abbr.* Prince Edward Island

pei•gnoir (pān-wär′, pĕn-) ►*n.* A woman's loose-fitting dressing gown. [Fr.]

pe•jor•a•tive (pĭ-jôr′ə-tĭv, -jŏr′-, pĕj′ə-rā′tĭv) ►*adj.* **1.** Tending to make or become worse. **2.** Disparaging; belittling. ►*n.* A disparaging word or expression. [< Lat. *peior*, worse.] —**pe•jor′a•tive•ly** *adv.*

Pe•king (pē′kĭng′, pā′-) See **Beijing.**

Pe•king•ese (pē′kĭng-ēz′, -ēs′) also **Pe•kin•ese** (pē′kə-nēz′, -nēs′) ►*n., pl.* **-ese 1.** A native or resident of Peking (Beijing). **2.** The Chinese dialect of Peking. **3.** (pē′kə-nēz′, -nēs′). A small, short-legged, long-haired dog with a flat nose.

pe•koe (pē′kō) ►*n.* Black tea made of the leaves around the buds. [Chin. dial. *pek ho.*]

pe•lag•ic (pə-lăj′ĭk) ►*adj.* Of or relating to open oceans or seas. [< Gk. *pelagos*, sea.]

Pe•lé (pā′lā). Edson Arantes do Nascimento. b. 1940. Brazilian soccer player.

Pe•lée (pə-lā′), **Mount.** A volcano, about 1,373 m (4,500 ft), on N Martinique in the French West Indies.

pelf (pĕlf) ►*n.* Wealth or riches. [< OFr. *pelfre*, booty.]

pel•i•can (pĕl′ĭ-kən) ►*n.* A large, web-footed bird with an expandable pouch under the lower bill used for catching and holding fish. [< Gk. *pelekan.*]

pel•lag•ra (pə-lăg′rə, -lā′grə, -lä′-) ►*n.* A disease caused by a deficiency of niacin and protein in the diet and marked by skin eruptions and digestive and nervous system disturbances. [Ital.] —**pel•lag′rous** *adj.*

pel•let (pĕl′ĭt) ►*n.* **1.** A small, solid or densely packed ball or mass, as of medicine. **2.** A bullet or piece of small shot. [< Lat. *pila*, ball.]

pell-mell also **pell•mell** (pĕl′mĕl′) ►*adv.* **1.** In a jumbled, confused manner. **2.** In frantic, disorderly haste; headlong. [< OFr. *pesle mesle.*]

pel•lu•cid (pə-lo͞o′sĭd) ►*adj.* **1.** Transparent or translucent. See Syns at **clear. 2.** Very clear in style or meaning. [< Lat. *pellūcēre*, shine through.] —**pel•lu′cid•ly** *adv.*

Pel•o•pon•ne•sus (pĕl′ə-pə-nē′səs) A peninsula forming the S part of Greece S of the Gulf of Corinth. —**Pel′o•pon•ne′sian** (-nē′zhən, -shən) *adj. & n.*

pelt¹ (pĕlt) ►*n.* The skin of an animal with the fur or hair still on it. [ME.]

pelt² (pĕlt) ►*v.* To strike repeatedly with or as if with blows or missiles. [ME *pelten.*]

pel•vis (pĕl′vĭs) ►*n., pl.* **-vis•es** or **-ves** (-vēz). A basin-shaped structure of the vertebrate skeleton that rests on the lower limbs and supports the spinal column. [Lat. *pēlvis*, basin.] —**pel′vic** *adj.*

pem•mi•can also **pem•i•can** (pĕm′ĭ-kən) ►*n.* A food prepared from dried meat that is pounded into paste and mixed with fat. [Cree *pimihkaam.*]

pen¹ (pĕn) ►*n.* An instrument for writing or drawing with ink. ►*v.* **penned, pen•ning.** To write, esp. with a pen. [< Lat. *penna*, feather.]

pen² (pĕn) ►*n.* **1.** A fenced enclosure for animals. **2.** A confining room or space. ►*v.* **penned** or **pent** (pĕnt), **pen•ning.** To confine in or as if in a pen. See Syns at **enclose.** [< OE *penn.*]

pen³ (pĕn) ►*n. Informal* A prison.

pe•nal (pē′nəl) ►*adj.* Of or relating to punishment, esp. for breaking the law. [< Gk. *poinē*, penalty.] —**pe′nal•ly** *adv.*

pe•nal•ize (pē′nə-līz′, pĕn′ə-) ►*v.* **-ized, -iz•ing 1.** To subject to a penalty. **2.** To hinder; handicap. —**pe′nal•i•za′tion** *n.*

pen•al•ty (pĕn′əl-tē) ►*n., pl.* **-ties 1.** A punishment for a crime or offense. **2.** Something, esp. a sum of money, required as a forfeit for an offense. **3.** *Sports* A punishment, handicap, or loss of advantage imposed for infraction of a rule.

penalty kick ►*n.* In soccer, a free kick on the goal awarded when the defense has committed a foul in the penalty area.

pen•ance (pĕn′əns) ►*n.* **1.** A voluntary act of contrition for a sin or other wrongdoing. **2.** A sacrament in some Christian churches for the forgiveness of one's sins. [< Lat. *paenitēns*, PENITENT.]

Pe•nang (pə-năng′, pē′näng′) See **George Town.**

Pe•na•tes (pə-nā′tēz, -nä′-) ►*pl.n.* The ancient Roman gods of the household.

pence (pĕns) ►*n. Chiefly Brit.* Pl. of **penny.**

pen•chant (pĕn′chənt) ►*n.* A definite liking; strong inclination. See Syns at **predilection.** [Fr. < *pencher*, incline.]

pen•cil (pĕn′səl) ►*n.* **1.** A writing or drawing implement consisting of a thin rod esp. of graphite encased in wood or held in a mechanical holder. **2.** Something shaped or used like a pencil: *an eyebrow pencil.* ►*v.* **-ciled, -cil•ing** also **-cilled, -cil•ling.** To write, draw, or mark with a pencil. [< Lat. *pēniculus*, small brush.]

pen•dant also **pen•dent** (pĕn′dənt) ►*n.* Something suspended from something else, esp. an ornament. ►*adj.* Var. of **pendent.** [< Lat. *pendēre*, hang.]

pen•dent also **pen•dant** (pĕn′dənt) ▸*adj.* **1.** Hanging down; dangling. **2.** Projecting; overhanging. **3.** Awaiting settlement; pending. ▸*n.* Var. of **pendant.** [< Lat. *pendēre*, hang.]

pend•ing (pĕn′dĭng) ▸*adj.* **1.** Not yet decided or settled. **2.** Impending; imminent. ▸*prep.* **1.** While in the process of; during. **2.** While awaiting; until. [< Fr. *pendant*, during.]

pen•du•lar (pĕn′jə-lər, pĕn′dyə-, -də-) ▸*adj.* Swinging back and forth like a pendulum.

pen•du•lous (pĕn′jə-ləs, pĕn′dyə-, -də-) ▸*adj.* Hanging loosely; sagging. [< Lat. *pendēre*, hang.]

pen•du•lum (pĕn′jə-ləm, pĕn′dyə-, pĕn′də-) ▸*n.* A body suspended from a fixed support so that it swings freely back and forth under the influence of gravity, used esp. in regulating clocks. [< Lat. *pendulus*, hanging.]

pe•ne•plain also **pe•ne•plane** (pē′nə-plān′) ▸*n.* A nearly flat land surface resulting from long erosion. [Lat. *paene*, almost + PLAIN.]

pen•e•trate (pĕn′ĭ-trāt′) ▸*v.* **-trat•ed, -trat•ing 1.** To enter or force a way into; pierce. **2.** To permeate. **3.** To grasp the inner significance of; understand. **4.** To see through. **5.** To affect deeply. [Lat. *penetrāre.*] —**pen′e•tra•ble** (-trə-bəl) *adj.* —**pen′e•trant** (-trənt) *n.* —**pen′e•tra′tion** *n.*

pen•e•trat•ing (pĕn′ĭ-trā′tĭng) ▸*adj.* **1.** Able or seeming to penetrate; piercing. **2.** Keenly perceptive or understanding; acute: *a penetrating mind.* —**pen′e•trat′ing•ly** *adv.*

pen•guin (pĕng′gwĭn, pĕn′-) ▸*n.* Any of various stout flightless marine birds of cool regions of the Southern Hemisphere, having flipperlike wings, webbed feet, and gen. black-and-white plumage. [Poss. < Welsh *pen gwyn*, white head : *pen*, chief, head + *gwynn*, white.]

pen•i•cil•lin (pĕn′ĭ-sĭl′ĭn) ▸*n.* Any of a group of antibiotic drugs obtained from molds or produced synthetically and used in the treatment of various infections and diseases. [< Lat. *pēnicillus*, small brush.]

pen•in•su•la (pə-nĭn′syə-lə, -sə-lə) ▸*n.* A piece of land that projects into a body of water. [Lat. *paenīnsula.*] —**pen•in′su•lar** *adj.*

pe•nis (pē′nĭs) ▸*n., pl.* **-nis•es** or **-nes** (-nēz). The male organ of copulation and, in mammals, of urination. [Lat. *pēnis.*] —**pe′nile′** (-nīl′, -nəl) *adj.*

pen•i•tence (pĕn′ĭ-təns) ▸*n.* The condition or quality of being penitent.

Syns: *penitence, compunction, contrition, remorse, repentance* **n.**

pen•i•tent (pĕn′ĭ-tənt) ▸*adj.* Feeling or expressing remorse for one's misdeeds or sins. ▸*n.* One who is penitent. [< Lat. *paenitēre*, repent.] —**pen′i•ten′tial** (-tĕn′shəl) *adj.* —**pen′i•tent•ly** *adv.*

pen•i•ten•tia•ry (pĕn′ĭ-tĕn′shə-rē) ▸*n., pl.* **-ries.** A prison for those convicted of major crimes. ▸*adj.* Of or resulting in imprisonment in a penitentiary.

pen•knife (pĕn′nīf′) ▸*n.* A small pocketknife.

pen•man (pĕn′mən) ▸*n.* **1.** A copyist; scribe. **2.** An expert in penmanship. **3.** An author.

pen•man•ship (pĕn′mən-shĭp′) ▸*n.* The art, skill, or style of handwriting.

Penn (pĕn), **William.** 1644–1718. English Quaker colonizer in America.

Penn. ▸*abbr.* Pennsylvania

pen name also **pen•name** (pĕn′nām′) ▸*n.* A pseudonym used by a writer.

pen•nant (pĕn′ənt) ▸*n.* **1.** A long, tapering, usu. triangular flag, used on ships for signaling or identification. **2.** A flag or emblem similar to a pennant. **3.** *Sports* A flag that symbolizes the championship of a league. [Blend of PENDANT and PENNON.]

pen•ne (pĕn′ā) ▸*n., pl.* **penne.** Pasta in small short tubes with diagonally cut ends. [Ital., pl. of *penna*, feather.]

pen•ni•less (pĕn′ē-lĭs, pĕn′ə-) ▸*adj.* Entirely without money; very poor.

Pen•nine Alps (pĕn′īn′) A range of the Alps extending along the Swiss-Italian border.

Pen•nines (pĕn′īnz′) also **Pennine Chain.** A range of hills extending about 257 km (160 mi) from S Scotland to central England.

pen•non (pĕn′ən) ▸*n.* A long narrow banner borne on a lance. [< Lat. *penna*, feather.]

Penn•syl•va•nia (pĕn′səl-vān′yə, -vā′nē-ə) A state of the E US. Cap. Harrisburg. Pop. 11,924,710.

Pennsylvania Dutch ▸*n.* **1.** The descendants of German and Swiss immigrants who settled in Pennsylvania in the 17th and 18th cent. **2.** The dialect of High German spoken by the Pennsylvania Dutch. [< Ger. *Deutsch*, German.]

Penn•syl•va•nian (pĕn′səl-vān′yən, -vā′nē-ən) *Geol.* ▸*adj.* Of or being the 6th period of the Paleozoic Era, marked by the formation of coal-bearing rock. ▸*n.* The Pennsylvanian Period.

pen•ny (pĕn′ē) ▸*n., pl.* **-nies 1.** See table at **currency. 2.** A US or Canadian coin worth one cent. **3.** Any of various coins of small denomination. —***idiom:*** **pretty penny** A considerable sum of money. [< OE *penig*, a coin.]

penny pincher ▸*n.* *Informal* A very stingy person. —**pen′ny-pinch′ing** *adj. & n.*

pen•ny•roy•al (pĕn′ē-roi′əl) ▸*n.* Either of two plants whose leaves yield an aromatic oil.

pen•ny•weight (pĕn′ē-wāt′) ▸*n.* A unit of troy weight equal to 24 grains, $\frac{1}{20}$ of a troy ounce or approx. 1.555 grams.

pen•ny-wise (pĕn′ē-wīz′) ▸*adj.* Careful in dealing with small sums of money or small matters.

Pe•nob•scot (pə-nŏb′skət, -skŏt′) ▸*n., pl.* **-scot** or **-scots 1.** A member of a Native American people inhabiting central Maine. **2.** Their Algonquian language.

pe•nol•o•gy (pē-nŏl′ə-jē) ▸*n.* The study, theory, and practice of prison management and criminal rehabilitation. [Lat. *poena*, penalty + -LOGY.] —**pe•nol′o•gist** *n.*

pen pal ▸*n.* A person with whom one becomes acquainted through correspondence.

pen•sion (pĕn′shən) ▸*n.* A sum of money paid regularly, esp. as a retirement benefit. ▸*v.* To grant a pension to. [< Lat. *pēnsiō*, payment.]

pen•sion•er (pĕn′shə-nər) ▸*n.* One who receives a pension.

pen•sive (pĕn′sĭv) ▸*adj.* Deeply, often wistfully or dreamily thoughtful. [< Lat. *pēnsāre*, think over.] —**pen′sive•ness** *n.*

pent (pĕnt) ▸*v.* P.t. and p.part of **pen**[2]**.** ▸*adj.* Penned or shut up; closely confined.

penta– or **pent–** ▸*pref.* Five: *pentameter.* [< Gk. *pente*, five.]

pen•ta•cle (pĕn′tə-kəl) ▸*n.* A five-pointed star formed by five straight lines connecting the vertices of a pentagon. [Med.Lat. **pentăculum*](#) < Gk. *pente*, five.]

pen•ta•gon (pĕn′tə-gŏn′) ►*n.* **1.** A polygon having five sides. **2. Pentagon** The US military establishment. —**pen•tag′o•nal** (pĕn-tăg′ə-nəl) *adj.*

pen•tam•e•ter (pĕn-tăm′ĭ-tər) ►*n.* A line of verse composed of five metrical feet.

Pen•ta•teuch (pĕn′tə-to͞ok′, -tyo͞ok′) ►*n.* The first five books of the Hebrew Scriptures. [< Gk. *Pentateukhos* : PENTA– + *teukhos*, scroll case.]

pen•tath•lon (pĕn-tăth′lən, -lŏn′) ►*n.* An athletic contest in which each participant competes in five track and field events. [Gk. : PENTA– + *athlon*, contest.]

Pen•te•cost (pĕn′tĭ-kôst′, -kŏst′) ►*n.* A Christian festival celebrated the 7th Sunday after Easter to commemorate the descent of the Holy Spirit upon the disciples. [< Gk. *pentēkostē (hēmera)*, fiftieth (day) < *pentēkonta*, fifty.]

pent•house (pĕnt′hous′) ►*n.* **1.** An apartment or dwelling on the top floor or roof of a building. **2.** A shed or sloping roof attached to the side of a building or wall. [< OFr. *apendre*, be attached to.]

pent-up (pĕnt′ŭp′) ►*adj.* Not given expression; repressed: *pent-up emotions.*

pe•nul•ti•mate (pĭ-nŭl′tə-mĭt) ►*adj.* Next to last. [< Lat. *paenultimus*.] —**pe•nul′ti•mate** *n.*

pe•num•bra (pĭ-nŭm′brə) ►*n.*, *pl.* **-brae** (-brē) or **-bras.** A partial shadow, as in an eclipse, between regions of complete shadow and complete illumination. [< Lat. *paene*, almost + *umbra*, shadow.]

pe•nu•ri•ous (pə-no͝or′ē-əs, -nyo͝or′-) ►*adj.* **1.** Miserly; stingy. **2.** Poverty-stricken.

pen•u•ry (pĕn′yə-rē) ►*n.* Extreme poverty; destitution. [< Lat. *pēnūria*.]

Pe•nu•ti•an (pə-no͞o′tē-ən, -shən) ►*n.* A proposed stock of North American Indian languages spoken in Pacific coastal areas.

Pen•za (pĕn′zə, pyĕn′-) A city of W-central Russia SSW of Kazan. Pop. 547,623.

pe•on (pē′ŏn′, pē′ən) ►*n.* **1a.** An unskilled laborer or farm worker, esp. of Latin America. **b.** Such a worker bound in servitude to a landlord creditor. **2.** A menial worker. [< Med.Lat. *pedō*, foot soldier. See PIONEER.] —**pe′on•age** (-ə-nĭj) *n.*

pe•o•ny (pē′ə-nē) ►*n.*, *pl.* **-nies.** A garden plant having large, variously colored flowers. [< Gk. *paiōnia*.]

peo•ple (pē′pəl) ►*n.*, *pl.* **-ple 1.** Humans collectively. **2.** A body of persons living in the same country under one national government; nationality. **3.** *pl.* **-ples** A body of persons sharing a common religion, culture, language, or inherited condition of life. **4. the people a.** The mass of ordinary persons; populace. **b.** The citizens of a political unit; electorate. **5.** Family, relatives, or ancestors. ►*v.* **-pled, -pling.** To populate. [< Lat. *populus*.]

Pe•or•i•a (pē-ôr′ē-ə, -ōr′-) A city of NW-central IL on the Illinois R. N of Springfield. Pop. 113,504.

pep (pĕp) *Informal* ►*n.* Energy; vim. ►*v.* **pepped, pep•ping.** To impart pep to; invigorate. [< PEPPER.] —**pep′py** *adj.*

Pep•in the Short (pĕp′ĭn). 714?–768. King of the Franks (751–768).

pep•per (pĕp′ər) ►*n.* **1a.** A tropical Asian vine bearing small berrylike fruit. **b.** A peppercorn. **c.** A pungent spice made from whole or ground peppercorns. **2a.** Any of several tropical American plants, such as the bell pepper, having podlike, variously colored fruit. **b.** The mild to pungent fruit of any of these plants. ►*v.* **1.** To season or sprinkle with or as if with pepper. **2.** To shower with or as if with small missiles. See Syns at **barrage.** [< Skt. *pippalī*.]

pep•per•corn (pĕp′ər-kôrn′) ►*n.* The small, dark, berrylike fruit of the pepper vine.

pep•per•mint (pĕp′ər-mĭnt′) ►*n.* **1.** An aromatic plant having leaves that yield a pungent oil. **2.** A candy flavored with this oil.

pep•per•y (pĕp′ə-rē) ►*adj.* **1.** Of, containing, or like pepper; pungent. **2.** Sharp-tempered; feisty. **3.** Fiery: *a peppery speech.*

pep•sin (pĕp′sĭn) ►*n.* **1.** A digestive enzyme found in gastric juice that catalyzes the breakdown of protein to peptides. **2.** A substance containing pepsin and used as a digestive aid. [< Gk. *pepsis*, digestion.]

pep talk ►*n.* *Informal* A speech meant to instill enthusiasm or bolster morale.

pep•tic (pĕp′tĭk) ►*adj.* **1.** Of or assisting digestion. **2.** Induced by or associated with the action of digestive secretions: *a peptic ulcer.* [< Gk. *peptein*, digest.]

pep•tide (pĕp′tīd′) ►*n.* Any of various natural or synthetic compounds consisting of two or more amino acids linked end to end. [< Gk. *peptein*, digest.]

Pepys (pēps, pĕp′ĭs), **Samuel.** 1633–1703. English diarist. —**Pepys′i•an** *adj.*

Pe•quot (pē′kwŏt′) ►*n.*, *pl.* **-quot** or **-quots 1.** A member of a Native American people of E Connecticut. **2.** The Algonquian language of the Pequot.

per (pûr) ►*prep.* **1.** To, for, or by each. **2.** According to. **3.** By means of; through. [Lat.]

per– ►*pref.* Containing a large or the largest possible proportion of an element: *peroxide.* [< Lat. *per*, through.]

per•am•bu•late (pə-răm′byə-lāt′) ►*v.* **-lat•ed, -lat•ing.** To walk about; stroll. [Lat. *perambulāre*.] —**per•am′bu•la′tion** *n.*

per•am•bu•la•tor (pə-răm′byə-lā′tər) ►*n.* *Chiefly Brit.* A baby carriage.

per an•num (pər ăn′əm) ►*adv.* By the year; annually. [Lat.]

per•cale (pər-kāl′) ►*n.* A closely woven cotton fabric used for sheets and clothing. [< Pers. *pargālah*, rag.]

per cap•i•ta (pər kăp′ĭ-tə) ►*adv.* & *adj.* Per person. [Med.Lat., by heads.]

per•ceive (pər-sēv′) ►*v.* **-ceived, -ceiv•ing 1.** To become aware of through the senses. **2.** To achieve understanding of; apprehend. [< Lat. *percipere*.] —**per•ceiv′a•ble** *adj.*

per•cent also **per cent** (pər-sĕnt′) ►*adv.* Out of each hundred; per hundred. ►*n.*, *pl.* **percent** also **per cent 1.** One part in a hundred. **2.** A percentage or portion. [< Lat. *per centum*, by the hundred.]

per•cent•age (pər-sĕn′tĭj) ►*n.* **1.** A fraction or ratio with 100 understood as the denominator. **2.** A proportion or share in relation to a whole; part. **3.** *Informal* Advantage.

Usage: *Percentage,* when preceded by *the,* takes a singular verb: *The percentage of unskilled workers is small.* When preceded by *a,* it takes either a singular or plural verb, depending on the number of the noun in the prepositional phrase that follows: *A small percentage of the workers are unskilled. A large percentage of the crop has spoiled.*

per•cen•tile (pər-sĕn′tīl′) ►*n.* One of a set of points on a scale arrived at by dividing a group into parts in order of magnitude.

per•cep•ti•ble (pər-sĕp′tə-bəl) ►*adj.* Capable of being perceived. —**per•cep′ti•bil′i•ty** *n.*

per•cep•tion (pər-sĕp′shən) ►*n.* **1.** The process, act, or result of perceiving. **2a.** Insight or knowledge gained by perceiving. **b.** The capacity for such insight. [< Lat. *percipere, percept-*, perceive.]

per•cep•tive (pər-sĕp′tĭv) ►*adj.* **1.** Of or relating to perception. **2a.** Having the ability to perceive. **b.** Marked by discernment; insightful. —**per•cep′tive•ly** *adv.*

per•cep•tu•al (pər-sĕp′cho͞o-əl) ►*adj.* Of or involving perception.

perch[1] (pûrch) ►*n.* **1.** A rod or branch serving as a roost for a bird. **2a.** A place for resting or sitting. **b.** A secure position. [< Lat. *pertica*, stick, pole.] —**perch** *v.*

perch[2] (pûrch) ►*n., pl.* **perch** or **-es 1.** An edible freshwater fish. **2.** Any of various similar or related fishes. [< Gk. *perkē*.]

per•chance (pər-chăns′) ►*adv.* Perhaps.

per•cip•i•ent (pər-sĭp′ē-ənt) ►*adj.* Having the power of perceiving. [< Lat. *percipere*, perceive.] —**per•cip′i•ence** *n.*

per•co•late (pûr′kə-lāt′) ►*v.* **-lat•ed, -lat•ing 1.** To pass or cause to pass through a porous substance. **2.** To make (coffee) in a percolator. [Lat. *percōlāre*.] —**per′co•la′tion** *n.*

per•co•la•tor (pûr′kə-lā′tər) ►*n.* A coffeepot in which boiling water is filtered repeatedly through a basket of ground coffee.

per•cus•sion (pər-kŭsh′ən) ►*n.* **1.** The striking together of two bodies, esp. when noise is produced. **2.** The sound, vibration, or shock caused by percussion. **3.** The act of detonating a percussion cap in a firearm. **4.** *Mus.* Percussion instruments or their players. [< Lat. *percutere, percuss-*, strike hard.] —**per•cus′sive** *adj.*

percussion cap ►*n.* A thin metal cap containing gunpowder or another detonator that explodes on being struck.

percussion instrument ►*n.* An instrument, such as a drum, piano, or maraca, in which sound is produced by one object striking another or by being scraped or shaken. —**per•cus′sion•ist** *n.*

per di•em (pər dē′əm, dī′əm) ►*adv.* Per day. ►*n.* An allowance for daily expenses. [Lat., by the day.]

per•di•tion (pər-dĭsh′ən) ►*n.* **1.** Eternal damnation. **2.** Hell. [< Lat. *perdere*, lose : *per-*, completely + *dare*, give.]

per•e•gri•nate (pĕr′ĭ-grə-nāt′) ►*v.* **-nat•ed, -nat•ing.** To journey or travel from place to place. [< Lat. *peregrīnus*, foreigner.] —**per′e•gri•na′tion** *n.*

per•e•grine falcon (pĕr′ə-grĭn, -grēn′) ►*n.* A large, widely distributed falcon much used in falconry.

per•emp•to•ry (pə-rĕmp′tə-rē) ►*adj.* **1.** Precluding further debate or action: *a peremptory decree.* **2.** Not allowing contradiction or refusal; imperative. **3.** Imperious; dictatorial. [Lat. *perēmptōrius*.] —**per•emp′to•ri•ly** *adv.* —**per•emp′to•ri•ness** *n.*

per•en•ni•al (pə-rĕn′ē-əl) ►*adj.* **1.** Lasting through the year or many years. **2a.** Lasting indefinitely; enduring. **b.** Recurring regularly. **3.** *Bot.* Living three or more years. ►*n. Bot.* A perennial plant. [< Lat. *perennis*.] —**per•en′ni•al•ly** *adv.*

per•fect (pûr′fĭkt) ►*adj.* **1.** Lacking nothing essential. **2.** Being without defect or blemish: *a perfect specimen.* **3.** Completely suited for a particular purpose; ideal. **4.** Accurate; exact. **5.** Complete; utter: *a perfect fool.* **6.** *Gram.* Of or constituting a verb form expressing action completed prior to a fixed point of reference in time. ►*n. Gram.* **1.** The perfect tense. **2.** A verb in this tense. ►*v.* (pər-fĕkt′). To bring to perfection or completion. [< Lat. *perfectus*, p.part. of *perficere*, finish.] —**per•fect′i•bil′i•ty** *n.* —**per•fect′i•ble** *adj.* —**per′fect•ly** *adv.* —**per′fect•ness** *n.*

Syns: *perfect, consummate, faultless, flawless, impeccable* **Ant:** *imperfect* **adj.**

Usage: *Perfect* has often been described as an absolute term, hence not allowing modification by *quite* and other qualifiers of degree. But the qualification of *perfect* has numerous reputable precedents. *Perfect* freely allows comparison in examples such as *There could be no more perfect spot for the picnic,* where it is used to mean "ideal for the purposes."

per•fec•tion (pər-fĕk′shən) ►*n.* **1.** The quality or condition of being perfect. **2.** The act or process of perfecting. **3.** One considered perfect.

per•fec•tion•ism (pər-fĕk′shə-nĭz′əm) ►*n.* A propensity for being displeased with anything not perfect or not meeting very high standards. —**per•fec′tion•ist** *adj. & n.*

per•fi•dy (pûr′fĭ-dē) ►*n., pl.* **-dies.** Deliberate breach of faith; treachery. [< Lat. *perfidus*, treacherous.] —**per•fid′i•ous** (pər-fĭd′ē-əs) *adj.* —**per•fid′i•ous•ly** *adv.*

per•fo•rate (pûr′fə-rāt′) ►*v.* **-rat•ed, -rat•ing 1.** To pierce, punch, or bore a hole or holes in. **2.** To pierce or stamp with rows of holes to allow easy separation. [Lat. *perforāre*.] —**per′fo•ra′tion** *n.*

per•force (pər-fôrs′, -fōrs′) ►*adv.* By necessity; by force of circumstance.

per•form (pər-fôrm′) ►*v.* **1.** To begin and carry through to completion; do. **2.** To carry out; fulfill. **3.** To give a public performance (of). [< OFr. *parfornir*.] —**per•form′er** *n.*

per•for•mance (pər-fôr′məns) ►*n.* **1.** The act or manner of performing. **2.** A presentation, as of a play or dance, before an audience. **3.** Something performed; accomplishment.

per•fume (pûr′fyo͞om′, pər-fyo͞om′) ►*n.* **1.** A fragrant substance, esp. a volatile liquid distilled from flowers or prepared synthetically. **2.** A pleasing scent or odor. See Syns at **fragrance.** ►*v.* (pər-fyo͞om′) **-fumed, -fum•ing.** To fill with fragrance. [< OItal. *parfumare*, fill with smoke.]

per•fum•er•y (pər-fyo͞o′mə-rē) ►*n., pl.* **-ies 1.** Perfumes. **2.** An establishment that makes or sells perfume.

per•func•to•ry (pər-fŭngk′tə-rē) ►*adj.* Done routinely and with little care. [< Lat. *perfungī*, get through with.] —**per•func′to•ri•ly** *adv.* —**per•func′to•ri•ness** *n.*

Per•ga•mum (pûr′gə-məm) An ancient Greek

city and kingdom of W Asia Minor.

per•go•la (pûr′gə-lə) ►*n.* An arbor or passageway of columns supporting a roof of trelliswork. [< Lat. *pergula.*]

per•haps (pər-hăps′) ►*adv.* Maybe; possibly.

peri– ►*pref.* **1.** Around; about; enclosing: *periodontal.* **2.** Near: *perigee.* [< Gk. *peri*, around, near.]

per•i•anth (pĕr′ē-ănth′) ►*n.* The outer envelope of a flower. [PERI– + Gk. *anthos*, flower.]

per•i•car•di•um (pĕr′ĭ-kär′dē-əm) ►*n., pl.* **-di•a** (-dē-ə). The membranous sac that encloses the heart. [PERI– + Gk. *kardia*, heart.] —**per′i•car′di•al** *adj.*

Per•i•cles (pĕr′ĭ-klēz′). d. 429 B.C. Athenian leader. —**Per′i•cle′an** *adj.*

per•i•gee (pĕr′ə-jē) ►*n.* The point nearest the earth's center in the orbit of the moon or a satellite. [PERI– + Gk. *gē*, earth.]

per•i•he•li•on (pĕr′ə-hē′lē-ən, -hēl′yən) ►*n., pl.* **-he•li•a** (-hē′lē-ə, -hēl′yə). The point nearest the sun in the orbit of a planet or other celestial body. [PERI– + Gk. *hēlios*, sun.]

per•il (pĕr′əl) ►*n.* **1.** Danger. **2.** Something that endangers or involves risk. [< Lat. *perīculum.*] —**per′il•ous** *adj.*

pe•rim•e•ter (pə-rĭm′ĭ-tər) ►*n.* **1.** *Math.* A closed curve bounding a plane area. **2.** The outer limits of an area. See Syns at **circumference.**

per•i•ne•um (pĕr′ə-nē′əm) ►*n., pl.* **-ne•a** (-nē′ə). The portion of the body extending from the anus to the genitals. [< Gk. *perinaion* : PERI– + *inan*, excrete.]

pe•ri•od (pîr′ē-əd) ►*n.* **1.** An interval of time characterized by the occurrence of a certain condition or event. **2.** An interval regarded as a distinct evolutionary or developmental phase. **3.** *Geol.* A unit of time, longer than an epoch and shorter than an era. **4.** An arbitrary unit of time, as of an academic day. **5.** An instance of menstruation. **6.** A point at which something is ended; completion. **7.** The full pause at the end of a spoken sentence. **8.** A punctuation mark (.) indicating a full stop, placed esp. at the end of declarative sentences. ►*adj.* Of or representing a historical time. [< Gk. *periodos*, circuit.]

pe•ri•od•ic (pîr′ē-ŏd′ĭk) ►*adj.* **1.** Having or marked by repeated cycles. **2.** Happening or appearing at regular intervals. **3.** Occasional; intermittent. —**pe′ri•od′i•cal•ly** *adv.* —**pe′ri•o•dic′i•ty** (-ə-dĭs′ĭ-tē) *n.*

pe•ri•od•i•cal (pîr′ē-ŏd′ĭ-kəl) ►*adj.* **1.** Periodic. **2a.** Published at regular intervals of more than one day. **b.** Of a publication issued at such intervals. ►*n.* A periodical publication.

periodical cicada ►*n.* A cicada of the E US whose 17- or 13-year life cycle consists almost entirely of a nymphal stage spent underground.

periodic table ►*n.* A tabular arrangement of the elements according to their atomic numbers.

per•i•o•don•tal (pĕr′ē-ə-dŏn′tl) ►*adj.* Of or being tissue and structures surrounding and supporting teeth. —**per′i•o•don′tist** *n.*

per•i•pa•tet•ic (pĕr′ə-pə-tĕt′ĭk) ►*adj.* Walking about from place to place. [< Gk. *peripatein*, walk about.]

pe•riph•er•al (pə-rĭf′ər-əl) ►*adj.* **1.** Of or on an outer boundary or periphery. **2.** Of minor relevance or importance. ►*n. Comp. Sci.* An auxiliary device, such as a printer or modem, that works in conjunction with a computer. —**pe•riph′er•al•ly** *adv.*

pe•riph•er•y (pə-rĭf′ə-rē) ►*n., pl.* **-ies 1.** A line that forms the boundary of an area; perimeter. See Syns at **circumference. 2a.** The outermost part or region within a precise boundary. **b.** A zone constituting an imprecise boundary. [< Gk. *periphereia* : PERI– + *pherein*, carry.]

pe•riph•ra•sis (pə-rĭf′rə-sĭs) ►*n., pl.* **-ses** (-sēz′). Circumlocution. [< Gk.] —**per′i•phras′tic** (pĕr′ə-frăs′tĭk) *adj.*

per•i•scope (pĕr′ĭ-skōp′) ►*n.* An optical instrument in which mirrors or prisms allow observation of objects not in a direct line of sight. —**per′i•scop′ic** (-skŏp′ĭk) *adj.*

per•ish (pĕr′ĭsh) ►*v.* **1.** To die, esp. in a violent or untimely manner. **2.** To disappear gradually. [< Lat. *perīre.*]

per•ish•a•ble (pĕr′ĭ-shə-bəl) ►*adj.* Subject to decay or spoilage. ►*n.* Something, esp. foodstuff, that is perishable. —**per′ish•a•bil′i•ty** *n.* —**per′ish•a•bly** *adv.*

per•i•stal•sis (pĕr′ĭ-stôl′sĭs, -stăl′-) ►*n., pl.* **-ses** (-sēz). The wavelike muscular contractions of the alimentary canal or other tubular structures by which contents are forced onward toward the opening. [< Gk. *peristellein*, wrap around.] —**per′i•stal′tic** *adj.*

per•i•style (pĕr′ĭ-stīl′) ►*n.* A series of columns surrounding a building or enclosing a court. [< Gk. *peristulon* : PERI– + *stulos*, pillar.]

per•i•to•ne•um (pĕr′ĭ-tn-ē′əm) ►*n., pl.* **-to•ne•a** (-tn-ē′ə). The membrane that lines the walls of the abdominal cavity. [< Gk. *peritonaios*, stretched across.]

per•i•to•ni•tis (pĕr′ĭ-tn-ī′tĭs) ►*n.* Inflammation of the peritoneum.

per•i•wig (pĕr′ĭ-wĭg′) ►*n.* A wig; peruke. [< OFr. *perruque*, PERUKE.]

per•i•win•kle[1] (pĕr′ĭ-wĭng′kəl) ►*n.* A small, often edible marine snail having a cone-shaped shell. [Prob. < OE *pīnewincle.*]

per•i•win•kle[2] (pĕr′ĭ-wĭng′kəl) ►*n.* A trailing evergreen plant having glossy, dark green leaves and blue flowers. [< Lat. *pervinca.*]

per•jure (pûr′jər) ►*v.* **-jured, -jur•ing** *Law* To deliberately testify falsely under oath. [< Lat. *periūrāre.*] —**per′jur•er** *n.* —**per′ju•ry** *n.*

perk[1] (pûrk) ►*v.* To raise (e.g., the head or ears) smartly or attentively. —***phrasal verb:* perk up 1.** To regain or cause to regain one's good spirits or liveliness. **2.** To add to or refresh the appearance of. [Poss. < ME *perken*, to perch.] —**perk′i•ness** *n.* —**perk′y** *adj.*

perk[2] (pûrk) ►*n. Informal* A perquisite.

perk[3] (pûrk) ►*v.* To percolate.

Per•kins (pûr′kĭnz), **Frances.** 1882–1965. Amer. social reformer and public official.

per•lite (pûr′līt′) ►*n.* A natural volcanic glass used in a fluffy heat-expanded form for fire-resistant insulation and in soil for potting plants. [< Fr. *perle* or Ger. *Perle*, pearl.]

Perl•man (pûrl′mən), **Itzhak.** b. 1945. Israeli-born Amer. violinist.

perm (pûrm) *Informal* ►*n.* A permanent. ►*v.* To give (hair) a permanent.

Perm (pĕrm) A city of W-central Russia in the foothills of the Ural Mts. Pop. 1,091,056.

per•ma•frost (pûr′mə-frôst′, -frŏst′) ►*n.* Permanently frozen subsoil occurring in perennially frigid areas.

per•ma•nent (pûr′mə-nənt) ►*adj.* Lasting or fixed. ►*n.* A long-lasting hair wave. [< Lat. *permanēre*, endure.] —**per′ma•nence, per′ma•nen•cy** *n.* —**per′ma•nent•ly** *adv.*

permanent press ►*n.* A chemical process in which fabrics are permanently shaped and treated for wrinkle resistance. —**per′ma•nent-press′** *adj.*

per•me•a•ble (pûr′mē-ə-bəl) ►*adj.* Capable of being permeated, esp. by liquids or gases. —**per′me•a•bil′i•ty** *n.*

per•me•ate (pûr′mē-āt′) ►*v.* **-at•ed, -at•ing 1.** To spread or flow throughout; pervade. See Syns at **charge. 2.** To pass through openings or small gaps of. [Lat. *permeāre*.] —**per′me•a′tion** *n.* —**per′me•a′tive** *adj.*

Per•mi•an (pûr′mē-ən, pĕr′-) *Geol.* ►*adj.* Of or being the 7th and last period of the Paleozoic Era, ending with the largest known mass extinction in the history of life. ►*n.* The Permian Period. [After *Perm*, Russia.]

per•mis•si•ble (pər-mĭs′ə-bəl) ►*adj.* Permitted or allowable. —**per•mis′si•bil′i•ty, per•mis′si•ble•ness** *n.*

per•mis•sion (pər-mĭsh′ən) ►*n.* Consent, esp. formal consent. [< Lat. *permittere*, permit.]

Syns: *permission, authorization, consent, leave, license, sanction* **Ant:** *prohibition* **n.**

per•mis•sive (pər-mĭs′ĭv) ►*adj.* Granting permission; tolerant or lenient. —**per•mis′sive•ly** *adv.* —**per•mis′sive•ness** *n.*

per•mit (pər-mĭt′) ►*v.* **-mit•ted, -mit•ting 1.** To allow the doing of; consent to. **2.** To afford opportunity or possibility (for). ►*n.* (pûr′mĭt, pər-mĭt′). A document or certificate granting permission. [< Lat. *permittere*.] —**per′mit•tee′** *n.* —**per•mit′ter** *n.*

per•mu•ta•tion (pûr′myo͞o-tā′shən) ►*n.* **1.** A transformation. **2.** The act of altering a given set of objects in a group. **3.** *Math.* An ordered arrangement of the elements of a set. [< Lat. *permūtāre*, change completely.] —**per′mu•ta′tion•al** *adj.*

per•ni•cious (pər-nĭsh′əs) ►*adj.* **1.** Deadly. **2.** Destructive. [< Lat. *perniciēs*, destruction.] —**per•ni′cious•ness** *n.*

pernicious anemia ►*n.* A severe anemia caused by failure to absorb vitamin B_{12} and marked by abnormally large red blood cells and gastrointestinal disturbances.

Pe•rón (pə-rōn′, pĕ-). Argentinian popular and political leaders, including **Juan Domingo** (1895–1974), **(Maria) Eva Duarte de Perón** ("Evita"; 1919–52), and **Maria Estela Martínez de Perón** ("Isabelita"; b. 1931).

per•o•rate (pĕr′ə-rāt′) ►*v.* **-rat•ed, -rat•ing 1.** To conclude a speech, esp. with a formal recapitulation. **2.** To speak at great length; declaim. [Lat. *perōrāre*, speak at length.] —**per′o•ra′tion** *n.*

per•ox•ide (pə-rŏk′sīd′) ►*n.* **1.** A compound containing oxygen that yields hydrogen peroxide when treated with an acid. **2.** Hydrogen peroxide. ►*v.* **-id•ed, -id•ing.** To treat or bleach with peroxide.

per•pen•dic•u•lar (pûr′pən-dĭk′yə-lər) ►*adj.* **1.** *Math.* Intersecting at or forming right angles. **2.** Being at right angles to the horizontal; vertical. [< Lat. *perpendiculum*, plumb line.] —**per′pen•dic′u•lar** *n.* —**per′pen•dic′u•lar′i•ty** (-lăr′ĭ-tē) *n.*

per•pe•trate (pûr′pĭ-trāt′) ►*v.* **-trat•ed, -trat•ing.** To be guilty of or responsible for; commit. [Lat. *perpetrāre*, accomplish < *patrāre*, bring about < *pater*, father.] —**per′pe•tra′tion** *n.* —**per′pe•tra′tor** *n.*

per•pet•u•al (pər-pĕch′o͞o-əl) ►*adj.* **1.** Lasting for eternity. **2.** Lasting for an indefinitely long time. **3.** Continuing without interruption. [< Lat. *perpetuus*, continuous.] —**per•pet′u•al•ly** *adv.*

per•pet•u•ate (pər-pĕch′o͞o-āt′) ►*v.* **-at•ed, -at•ing 1.** To make perpetual. **2.** To prolong the existence of. —**per•pet′u•ance, per•pet′u•a′tion** *n.* —**per•pet′u•a′tor** *n.*

per•pe•tu•i•ty (pûr′pĭ-to͞o′ĭ-tē, -tyo͞o′-) ►*n.*, *pl.* **-ties.** The quality or condition of being perpetual. —***idiom:*** **in perpetuity** Always.

per•plex (pər-plĕks′) ►*v.* To confuse or puzzle; bewilder. [< Lat. *perplexus*, confused.] —**per•plex′ing•ly** *adv.* —**per•plex′•i•ty** *n.*

per•qui•site (pûr′kwĭ-zĭt) ►*n.* **1.** A payment or profit received in addition to a regular wage or salary. **2.** A tip; gratuity. **3.** Something claimed as an exclusive right. [< Lat. *perquīrere*, search for.]

Per•ry (pĕr′ē), **Matthew Calbraith.** 1794–1858. Amer. naval officer.

Perry, Oliver Hazard. 1785–1819. Amer. naval officer.

pers. ►*abbr.* person

per se (pər sā′, sē′) ►*adv.* In or by itself or oneself; as such. [Lat. *per sē*.]

per•se•cute (pûr′sĭ-kyo͞ot′) ►*v.* **-cut•ed, -cut•ing 1.** To oppress or harass with ill-treatment, esp. because of race, religion, or beliefs. **2.** To annoy persistently. [< Lat. *persequī*, *persecūt-*, pursue.] —**per′se•cu′tion** *n.* —**per′se•cu′tor** *n.*

Per•sep•o•lis (pər-sĕp′ə-lĭs) An ancient city of Persia in present-day SW Iran.

per•se•vere (pûr′sə-vîr′) ►*v.* **-vered, -ver•ing.** To persist in or remain constant to a purpose, idea, or task in spite of obstacles. [< Lat. *persevērus*, very serious.] —**per′se•ver′ance** *n.*

Per•shing (pûr′shĭng, -zhĭng), **John Joseph.** "Black Jack." 1860–1948. Amer. general.

Per•sia (pûr′zhə, -shə) **1.** Also **Persian Empire.** An ancient empire of SW Asia. **2.** See **Iran.**

Per•sian (pûr′zhən, -shən) ►*n.* **1.** A native or inhabitant of Persia or Iran. **2.** Any of the W Iranian dialects or languages of ancient or medieval Persia and modern Iran.

Persian cat ►*n.* A domestic cat having long silky fur and short legs.

Persian Gulf. An arm of the Arabian Sea between Arabia and SW Iran.

Persian lamb ►*n.* The glossy, tightly curled fur of a young lamb of the karakul sheep of Asia.

per•si•flage (pûr′sə-fläzh′) ►*n.* Light good-natured talk; banter. [Fr. < *persifler*, to banter.]

per•sim•mon (pər-sĭm′ən) ►*n.* **1.** A tropical tree having hard wood and orange-red fruit edible only when fully ripe. **2.** The fruit of a persimmon tree. [Of Algonquian orig.]

per•sist (pər-sĭst′, -zĭst′) ►*v.* **1.** To be obstinately repetitious, insistent, or tenacious. **2.** To hold firmly and steadfastly to a purpose or undertaking despite obstacles. **3.** To continue in existence; last. [Lat. *persistere* < *sistere*, stand.] —**per•sis′tence** *n.* —**per•sis′tent** *adj.* —**per•sis′tent•ly** *adv.*

per•snick•e•ty (pər-snĭk′ĭ-tē) ►*adj.* Very particular about details; fastidious. [?]

per•son (pûr′sən) ►*n.* **1.** A human. See Usage Note at **man. 2.** An individual of specified character: *a person of importance.* **3.** The personality of a human; self. **4.** The living body of a human. **5.** *Gram.* Any of three groups of pronouns with corresponding verb inflections that distinguish the speaker (first person), the individual addressed (second person), and the individual or thing spoken of (third person). [< Lat. *persōna*, mask, role, person.]

per•so•na (pər-sō′nə) ►*n., pl.* **-nas** or **-nae** (-nē) **1.** A voice or character representing the speaker or narrator in a literary work. **2.** *pl.* **-nas** One's public image or personality. [Lat. *persōna*, mask, role, person.]

per•son•a•ble (pûr′sə-nə-bəl) ►*adj.* Pleasing in personality or appearance. —**per′son•a•ble•ness** *n.* —**per′son•a•bly** *adv.*

per•son•age (pûr′sə-nĭj) ►*n.* A person of distinction. See Syns at **celebrity.**

per•son•al (pûr′sə-nəl) ►*adj.* **1.** Of a particular person; private. **2.** Done in person: *a personal appearance.* **3.** Aimed pointedly at an individual, esp. in a critical or hostile manner. **4.** Of the body or physical being. **5.** *Law* Relating to a person's movable property. **6.** Indicating grammatical person. ►*n.* A personal item or notice in a newspaper. —**per′son•al•ly** *adv.*

personal computer ►*n.* A computer built around a microprocessor for use by an individual.

personal effects ►*pl.n.* Privately owned items, such as keys or a wallet or watch, regularly worn or carried on one's person.

per•son•al•i•ty (pûr′sə-năl′ĭ-tē) ►*n., pl.* **-ties 1.** The quality or condition of being a person. **2.** The totality of distinctive traits of a specific person. **3.** The personal traits that make one socially appealing. **4.** *Informal* A celebrity.

per•son•al•ize (pûr′sə-nə-līz) ►*v.* **-ized, -iz•ing 1.** To personify. **2.** To have printed, engraved, or monogrammed with one's name or initials. —**per′son•al•i•za′tion** *n.*

personal property ►*n. Law* Temporary or movable property.

personal watercraft ►*n. (takes pl. v.)* A motorized recreational water vehicle usu. ridden by straddling a seat.

personal watercraft

persona non gra•ta (nŏn grä′tə, grăt′ə) ►*adj.* Unacceptable or unwelcome, esp. to a foreign government. [Lat. *persōna nōn grāta*, unacceptable person.]

per•son•i•fy (pər-sŏn′ə-fī′) ►*v.* **-fied, -fy•ing 1.** To think of or represent (e.g., an inanimate object) as a person. **2.** To be the embodiment or perfect example of. —**per•son′i•fi•ca′tion** *n.* —**per•son′i•fi′er** *n.*

per•son•nel (pûr′sə-nĕl′) ►*n.* **1.** The body of persons employed by or active in an organization, business, or service. **2.** An administrative division of an organization concerned with this body of persons. [Fr.]

per•spec•tive (pər-spĕk′tĭv) ►*n.* **1.** The technique of representing three-dimensional objects and depth relationships on a two-dimensional surface. **2a.** The relationship of aspects of a subject to each other and to a whole. **b.** A point of view. [< Lat. *perspicere*, inspect : *per-*, through + *specere*, look.] —**per•spec′tive•ly** *adv.*

per•spi•cac•i•ty (pûr′spĭ-kăs′ĭ-tē) ►*n.* Acuteness of perception or understanding. [< Lat. *perspicere*, see through.] —**per•spi•ca′cious** (-kā-shəs) *adj.*

per•spic•u•ous (pər-spĭk′yo͞o-əs) ►*adj.* Clearly expressed or presented; easy to understand; lucid. [< Lat. *perspicere*, see through.] —**per′spi•cu′i•ty** (-kyo͞o′ĭ-tē) *n.* —**per•spic′u•ous•ness** *n.*

per•spi•ra•tion (pûr′spə-rā′shən) ►*n.* **1.** The saline moisture excreted through the pores of the skin by the sweat glands; sweat. **2.** The act or process of perspiring.

per•spire (pər-spīr′) ►*v.* **-spired, -spir•ing.** To excrete through the pores of the skin. [< Lat. *perspīrāre*, breathe through.]

per•suade (pər-swād′) ►*v.* **-suad•ed, -suad•ing.** To induce to undertake a course of action or embrace a point of view by means of argument, reasoning, or entreaty. [Lat. *persuādēre* < *suādēre*, urge.] —**per•suad′a•ble** *adj.* —**per•suad′er** *n.* —**per•sua′sive** *adj.* —**per•sua′sive•ly** *adv.* —**per•sua′sive•ness** *n.*

per•sua•sion (pər-swā′zhən) ►*n.* **1.** The act of persuading or state of being persuaded. **2.** The ability to persuade. **3.** A strongly held opinion. **4.** A body of religious beliefs.

pert (pûrt) ►*adj.* **-er, -est 1.** Trim and stylish; jaunty. **2.** High-spirited. **3.** Impudently bold. [< Lat. *apertus*, p.part. of *aperīre*, to open.] —**pert′ly** *adv.* —**pert′ness** *n.*

per•tain (pər-tān′) ►*v.* **1.** To have reference; relate. **2.** To belong as an adjunct or accessory. **3.** To be suitable. [< Lat. *pertinēre*.]

Perth (pûrth) A city of SW Australia near the Indian Ocean. Pop. 1,018,702.

per•ti•na•cious (pûr′tn-ā′shəs) ►*adj.* **1.** Holding tenaciously to a purpose, belief, opinion, or course of action. **2.** Stubbornly persistent. [< Lat. *pertināx*.] —**per′ti•na′cious•ly** *adv.* —**per′ti•na′cious•ness** *n.* —**per′ti•nac′i•ty** (-ăs′ĭ-tē) *n.*

per•ti•nent (pûr′tn-ənt) ►*adj.* Relating to a specific matter; relevant. [< Lat. *pertinēre*, pertain.] —**per′ti•nence, per′ti•nen•cy** *n.*

per•turb (pər-tûrb′) ►*v.* To disturb greatly; make uneasy or anxious. [< Lat. *perturbāre*.] —**per•turb′a•ble** *adj.* —**per•tur•ba′tion** *n.*

per•tus•sis (pər-tŭs′ĭs) ►*n.* See **whooping cough.** [Lat. *per-*, intensive pref. + *tussis*, cough.] —**per•tus′sal** *adj.*

Pe•ru (pə-ro͞o′) A country of W South America on the Pacific. Cap. Lima. Pop. 23,088,000. —**Pe•ru′vi•an** (-vē-ən) *adj. & n.*

pe•ruke (pə-ro͞ok′) ►*n.* A wig, esp. one worn

by men in the 17th and 18th cent.; periwig. [< OItal. *perrucca.*]

pe•ruse (pə-ro͞oz′) ►*v.* **-rused, -rus•ing.** To read or examine, esp. with great care. [ME *perusen,* use up.] —**pe•rus′al** *n.*

per•vade (pər-vād′) ►*v.* **-vad•ed, -vad•ing.** To spread throughout; permeate. See Syns at **charge.** [Lat. *pervādere.*] —**per•va′sion** (-vā′zhən) *n.* —**per•va′sive** (-vā′sĭv, -zĭv) *adj.* —**per•va′sive•ness** *n.*

per•verse (pər-vûrs′, pûr′vûrs′) ►*adj.* **1.** Directed away from what is right or good; perverted. **2.** Obstinately persisting in an error or fault. **3.** Cranky; peevish. [< Lat. *perversus,* p.part. of *pervertere,* pervert.] —**per•verse′ness, per•ver′si•ty** *n.*

per•ver•sion (pər-vûr′zhən, -shən) ►*n.* **1.** The act of perverting or the state of being perverted. **2.** A sexual practice considered deviant.

per•vert (pər-vûrt′) ►*v.* **1.** To corrupt or debase. **2.** To misuse. See Syns at **corrupt. 3.** To interpret incorrectly. ►*n.* (pûr′vûrt′). One who practices sexual perversion. [< Lat. *pervertere.*] —**per•vert′ed** *adj.*

per•vi•ous (pûr′vē-əs) ►*adj.* **1.** Open to passage; permeable. **2.** Open to arguments, ideas, or change. [< Lat. *pervius.*] —**per′vi•ous•ly** *adv.* —**per′vi•ous•ness** *n.*

pe•se•ta (pə-sā′tə) ►*n.* See table at **currency.** [Sp., dim. of *peso,* PESO.]

pes•ky (pĕs′kē) ►*adj.* **-ki•er, -ki•est** *Informal.* Troublesome; annoying. [Prob. < PEST.] —**pes′ki•ly** *adv.* —**pes′ki•ness** *n.*

pe•so (pā′sō) ►*n., pl.* **-sos.** See table at **currency.** [Sp. < Lat. *pēnsum,* weight.]

pes•si•mism (pĕs′ə-mĭz′əm) ►*n.* **1.** A tendency to take the gloomiest possible view of a situation. **2.** The doctrine or belief that the evil in the world outweighs the good. [< Lat. *pessimus,* worst.] —**pes′si•mist** *n.* —**pes′si•mis′tic** *adj.*

pest (pĕst) ►*n.* **1.** An annoying person or thing; nuisance. **2.** An injurious plant or animal. [< Lat. *pestis,* plague.]

pes•ter (pĕs′tər) ►*v.* To harass with petty annoyances; bother. [Prob. < OFr. *empestrer,* hobble.] —**pes′ter•er** *n.*

pes•ti•cide (pĕs′tĭ-sīd′) ►*n.* A chemical used to kill pests, esp. insects.

pes•tif•er•ous (pĕ-stĭf′ər-əs) ►*adj.* **1.** Producing, causing, or contaminated with an infectious disease. **2.** Bothersome or annoying. [< Lat. *pestis,* plague.] —**pes•tif′er•ous•ly** *adv.* —**pes•tif′er•ous•ness** *n.*

pes•ti•lence (pĕs′tə-ləns) ►*n.* A usu. fatal epidemic disease, esp. bubonic plague.

pes•ti•lent (pĕs′tə-lənt) ►*adj.* **1.** Tending to cause death. **2.** Likely to cause an epidemic disease. [< Lat. *pestis,* plague.] —**pes′ti•len′tial** (-lĕn′shəl) *adj.*

pes•tle (pĕs′əl, pĕs′təl) ►*n.* A club-shaped, hand-held tool for grinding or mashing substances in a mortar. [< Lat. *pistillum.*]

pes•to (pĕs′tō) ►*n.* A sauce made of usu. fresh basil, garlic, pine nuts, olive oil, and grated cheese. [Ital. < *pistare,* pound.]

pet[1] (pĕt) ►*n.* **1.** An animal kept for amusement or companionship. **2.** An object of the affections. **3.** A favorite: *the teacher's pet.* ►*adj.* **1.** Kept as a pet. **2.** Particularly cherished or indulged. ►*v.* **pet•ted, pet•ting 1.** To stroke or caress gently. See Syns at **caress. 2.** To engage in amorous fondling and caressing. [< OIr. *peata.*] —**pet′ter** *n.*

pet[2] (pĕt) ►*n.* Bad temper or pique. [?]

Pé•tain (pā-tăN′), **Henri Philippe.** 1856–1951. French soldier and politician.

pet•al (pĕt′l) ►*n.* A segment of a flower corolla, usu. showy and colored. [< Gk. *petalon,* leaf.] —**pet′aled, pet′alled** *adj.*

pe•tard (pĭ-tärd′) ►*n.* A small bell-shaped bomb used to breach a gate or wall. [< OFr. *peter,* break wind.]

pet•cock (pĕt′kŏk′) ►*n.* A small valve used to drain pipes. [Perh. PET[1] + COCK[1].]

pe•ter (pē′tər) ►*v.* **1.** To come to an end slowly; diminish: *Their enthusiasm soon petered out.* **2.** To become exhausted. [?]

Peter ►*n.* See table at **Bible.**

Peter, Saint. d. c. A.D. 67. The chief of the 12 Apostles.

Peter I. "Peter the Great." 1672–1725. Russian czar (1682–1725).

Peter Principle ►*n.* The theory that an employee within an organization will advance to his or her level of incompetence and remain there. [After L.J. *Peter* (1919–1990).]

pet•i•ole (pĕt′ē-ōl′) ►*n. Bot.* The stalk by which a leaf is attached to a stem; leafstalk. [Prob. < Lat. *pediculus,* little foot.]

pet•it also **pet•ty** (pĕt′ē) ►*adj. Law* Lesser; minor: *petit larceny.* [< OFr.]

pe•tite (pə-tēt′) ►*adj.* Small, slender, and trim. See Syns at **small.** [Fr.]

petit four ►*n., pl.* **pe•tits fours** or **pet•it fours** (pĕt′ē). A small, square-cut, frosted tea cake. [Fr.]

pe•ti•tion (pə-tĭsh′ən) ►*n.* **1.** A solemn request; entreaty. **2.** A formal document containing such a request. ►*v.* **1.** To address a petition to: *petitioned the king for an audience.* **2.** To request formally. **3.** To make a request, esp. formally: *petitioned for retrial.* [< Lat. *petere, petīt-,* request.] —**pe•ti′tion•ar′y** (-tĭsh′ə-nĕr′ē) *adj.* —**pe•ti′tion•er** *n.*

petit jury also **petty jury** ►*n.* A jury that sits at civil and criminal trials.

petit mal (mäl, măl) ►*n.* A mild form of epilepsy marked by frequent but transient lapses of consciousness and only rare spasms or falling. [Fr.]

petit point ►*n.* Needlepoint done with a small stitch. [Fr.]

Pe•tra (pē′trə, pĕt′rə) An ancient ruined city of Edom in present-day SW Jordan.

Pe•trarch (pē′trärk′, pĕt′rärk′), **Francesco.** 1304–74. Italian poet, scholar, and humanist. —**Pe•trarch′an** (pĭ-trär′kən) *adj.*

pe•tri dish (pē′trē) ►*n.* A shallow dish with a loose cover, used to culture microorganisms. [After J.R. *Petri* (1852–1921).]

pet•ri•fy (pĕt′rə-fī′) ►*v.* **-fied, -fy•ing 1.** To convert (wood or other organic matter) into a stony replica by structural impregnation with dissolved minerals. **2.** To cause to become stonelike; deaden. **3.** To stun or paralyze with terror. [< Gk. *petra,* rock.] —**pet′ri•fac′tion** (-făk′shən), **pet′ri•fi•ca′tion** *n.*

petro– or **petri–** or **petr–** ►*pref.* **1.** Rock; stone: *petroglyph.* **2.** Petroleum: *petrochemical.* [< Gk. *petros,* stone.]

pet•ro•chem•i•cal (pĕt′rō-kĕm′ĭ-kəl) ►*n.* A chemical derived from petroleum or natural gas. —**pet′ro•chem′i•cal** *adj.*

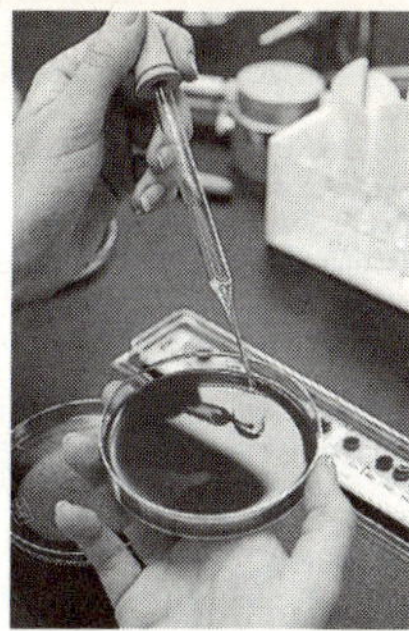

petri dish

pet•ro•glyph (pĕt′rə-glĭf′) ►*n. Archaeol.* A carving or line drawing on rock, esp. one made by prehistoric people. [< Gk. *gluphē*, carving.] —**pet′ro•glyph′ic** *adj.*

petroglyph
Newspaper Rock State Historical Monument, Indian Creek Canyon, Utah

pe•trog•ra•phy (pə-trŏg′rə-fē) ►*n.* The description and classification of rocks. —**pe•trog′ra•pher** *n.*

pet•rol (pĕt′rəl) ►*n. Chiefly Brit.* Gasoline. [Fr. *(essence de) pétrole*, (essence of) petroleum.]

pet•ro•la•tum (pĕt′rə-lā′təm, -lä′təm) ►*n.* See **petroleum jelly.** [< PETROL.]

pe•tro•le•um (pə-trō′lē-əm) ►*n.* A thick, flammable, yellow-to-black liquid hydrocarbon mixture that occurs naturally beneath the earth's surface and is processed for fractions including natural gas, gasoline, naphtha, kerosene, paraffin wax, and asphalt. [< Med.Lat. *petrōleum.*]

petroleum jelly ►*n.* A colorless-to-amber gelatinous semisolid, obtained from petroleum and used in lubricants and medicinal ointments.

pe•trol•o•gy (pə-trŏl′ə-jē) ►*n.* The study of the origin, composition, structure, and alteration of rocks. —**pe•trol′o•gist** *n.*

pet•ti•coat (pĕt′ē-kōt′) ►*n.* A woman's slip or underskirt. [ME *peticote.*]

pet•ti•fog•ger (pĕt′ē-fŏg′ər, -fô′gər) ►*n.* A petty, quibbling, unscrupulous lawyer. —**pet′ti•fog′** *v.* —**pet′ti•fog′ger•y** *n.*

pet•tish (pĕt′ĭsh) ►*adj.* Petulant or ill-tempered. [Prob. < PET[2].]

pet•ty (pĕt′ē) ►*adj.* **-ti•er, -ti•est 1.** Of small importance; trivial. **2.** Marked by narrowness of mind or views. **3.** Marked by meanness; spiteful. **4.** Secondary in importance or rank. **5.** *Law* Var. of **petit.** [< OFr. *petit*, small.] —**pet′ti•ly** *adv.* —**pet′ti•ness** *n.*

petty cash ►*n.* A small fund of money for incidental expenses, as in an office.

petty jury ►*n.* Var. of **petit jury.**

petty officer ►*n.* A noncommissioned naval officer, esp. in the three lower ranks.

pet•u•lant (pĕch′ə-lənt) ►*adj.* Unreasonably irritable or ill-tempered; peevish. [Lat. *petulāns.*] —**pet′u•lance, pet′u•lan•cy** *n.* —**pet′u•lant•ly** *adv.*

pe•tu•nia (pĭ-to͞on′yə, -tyo͞on′-) ►*n.* A garden plant having funnel-shaped, variously colored flowers. [Of Tupi-Guarani orig.]

pew (pyo͞o) ►*n.* A bench for the congregation in a church. [< Lat. *podium*, balcony.]

pe•wee (pē′wē) ►*n.* A small brownish North American flycatcher. [Imit. of its call.]

pew•ter (pyo͞o′tər) ►*n.* An alloy of tin with various amounts of antimony, copper, and lead, used for kitchen utensils and tableware. [< VLat. **peltrum.*] —**pew′ter** *adj.*

pe•yo•te (pā-ō′tē) ►*n.* **1.** A spineless, dome-shaped cactus of Mexico and the SW US, having buttonlike tubercles that are the source of mescaline. **2.** See **mescaline.** [< Nahuatl *peyotl.*]

pfen•nig (fĕn′ĭg) ►*n., pl.* **-nigs** or **pfen•ni•ge** (fĕn′ĭ-gə). A coin equal to 1/100 of the deutsche mark. [Ger.]

PG (pē′jē′) ► A trademark for a movie rating granting admission to persons of all ages but advising parental guidance for children.

pg. ►*abbr.* page

PG-13 (pē′jē′thûr-tēn′) ► A trademark for a movie rating granting admission to persons of all ages but advising parental guidance in the case of children under 13.

PGA ►*abbr.* Professional Golfers' Association

pH (pē′āch′) ►*n.* A measure of the acidity or alkalinity of a solution, numerically equal to 7 for neutral solutions, increasing with increasing alkalinity and decreasing with increasing acidity. [*p(otential of) h(ydrogen).*]

pha•e•ton (fā′ĭ-tn) ►*n.* A light, four-wheeled open carriage, usu. drawn by a pair of horses. [Fr. *phaéton.*]

-phage ►*suff.* One that eats: *bacteriophage.* [< Gk. *phagein*, to eat.]

phago– ►*pref.* Eating; consuming: *phagocyte.* [< Gk. *phagein*, eat.]

phag•o•cyte (făg′ə-sīt′) ►*n.* A cell, such as a white blood cell, that engulfs and absorbs foreign bodies in the bloodstream and tissues. —**phag′o•cyt′ic** (-sĭt′ĭk) *adj.*

pha•lanx (fā′lăngks′, făl′ăngks′) ►*n., pl.* **-es** or **pha•lan•ges** (fə-lăn′jēz, fā-) **1.** A compact or close-knit group. **2.** A formation of infantry carrying overlapping shields and long spears, developed in Greece in the 4th cent. B.C. **3.** *pl.* **phalanges** *Anat.* A bone of a finger or toe. [< Gk.]

phal•a•rope (făl′ə-rōp′) ►*n.* Any of several small wading shore birds. [< Gk. *phalaris*, coot + *pous*, foot.]

phal•lus (făl′əs) ►*n., pl.* **phal•li** (făl′ī′) or **-es 1.** The penis. **2.** A representation or symbol of it. [< Gk. *phallos.*] —**phal′lic** *adj.*

Phan•e•ro•zo•ic (făn′ər-ə-zō′ĭk) ►*n.* Of or being the geologic time period from approx. 570 million years ago to the present, including the Paleozoic, Mesozoic, and Cenozoic eras. [Gk. *phaneros*, visible + –ZOIC.]

phan•tasm (făn′tăz′əm) ►*n.* A phantom. [< Gk. *phantasma.*] —**phan•tas′mal** (făn-tăz′məl), **phan•tas′mic** (-tăz′mĭk) *adj.*

phan•tas•ma•go•ri•a (făn-tăz′mə-gôr′ē-ə, -gōr′-) ►*n.* A fantastic sequence of haphazardly associative imagery, as in dreams. [Poss. OFr. *fantasme*, PHANTASM + *allegorie*, ALLEGORY.] —**phan•tas′ma•gor′ic** *adj.*

phan•tom (făn′təm) ►*n.* **1.** Something apparently seen, heard, or sensed, but having no physical reality; a ghost or apparition. **2.** An illusory mental image. ►*adj.* Resembling or being a phantom; illusive. [< Gk. *phantasma.*]

Phar•aoh also **phar•aoh** (fâr′ō, fā′rō) ►*n.* A king of ancient Egypt. —**Phar′a•on′ic** (fâr′ā-ŏn′ĭk) *adj.*

phar•i•see (făr′ĭ-sē) ►*n.* **1. Pharisee** A member of an ancient Jewish group that emphasized strict interpretation and observance of the Mosaic law. **2.** A hypocritical, self-righteous person. [< Aram. *pərišayyā*, pl. of *pəriš*, separate.] —**phar′i•sa′ic** (-sā′ĭk) *adj.*

phar•ma•ceu•ti•cal (fär′mə-so͞o′tĭ-kəl) also **phar•ma•ceu•tic** (-tĭk) ►*adj.* Of pharmacy or pharmacists. ►*n.* A medicinal drug. [< Gk. *pharmakeutikos.*]

phar•ma•cist (fär′mə-sĭst) ►*n.* A person trained in pharmacy; druggist.

pharmaco– ►*pref.* Drug: *pharmacology.* [< Gk. *pharmakon*, drug.]

phar•ma•col•o•gy (fär′mə-kŏl′ə-jē) ►*n.* The science of drugs, including their composition, uses, and effects. —**phar′ma•co•log′ic** (-kə-lŏj′ĭk), **phar′ma•co•log′i•cal** *adj.* —**phar′ma•col′o•gist** *n.*

phar•ma•co•poe•ia also **phar•ma•co•pe•ia** (fär′mə-kə-pē′ə) ►*n.* **1.** A book containing an official list of medicinal drugs together with articles on their preparation and use. **2.** A collection or stock of drugs. [PHARMACO– + Gk. *poiein*, make.]

phar•ma•cy (fär′mə-sē) ►*n.*, *pl.* **-cies 1.** The art of preparing and dispensing drugs. **2.** A drugstore; apothecary. [< Gk. *pharmakeia*, use of drugs.]

pharyngo– or **pharyng–** ►*pref.* Pharynx: *pharyngoscope.* [< Gk. *pharunx.*]

phar•yn•gol•o•gy (făr′ĭn-gŏl′ə-jē, făr′ĭng-) ►*n.* The medical study of the pharynx and its diseases.

pha•ryn•go•scope (fə-rĭng′gə-skōp′) ►*n.* An instrument used in examining the pharynx. —**phar′yn•gos′co•py** (făr′ĭn-gŏs′kə-pē) *n.*

phar•ynx (făr′ĭngks) ►*n.*, *pl.* **pha•ryn•ges** (fə-rĭn′jēz) or **-ynx•es.** The section of the alimentary canal that extends from the nasal cavities to the larynx, where it becomes continuous with the esophagus. [< Gk. *pharunx.*] —**pha•ryn′ge•al** (fə-rĭn′jē-əl, făr′ĭn-jē′əl) *adj.*

phase (fāz) ►*n.* **1.** A distinct stage of development. **2.** A temporary pattern of behavior: *just a passing phase.* **3.** An aspect or facet; part: *every phase of the operation.* **4.** One of the cyclically recurring apparent forms of the moon or a planet. ►*v.* **phased, phas•ing.** To plan or carry out systematically in phases. —***phrasal verbs:* phase in** To introduce in stages. **phase out** To eliminate in stages. [< Gk. *phasis*, appearance.] —**pha′sic** (fā′zĭk) *adj.*

phase-in (fāz′ĭn′) ►*n.* A gradual introduction.

phase•out (fāz′out′) ►*n.* A gradual discontinuation.

PhD ►*abbr. Lat.* Philosophiae Doctor (Doctor of Philosophy)

pheas•ant (fĕz′ənt) ►*n.*, *pl.* **-ants** or **-ant.** Any of various chickenlike birds having long tails and, in the males, often brilliantly colored plumage. [< Gk. *phasianos*, of the Phasis River in the Caucasus.]

phe•nix (fē′nĭks) ►*n.* Var. of **phoenix.**

pheno– or **phen–** ►*pref.* **1.** Showing; displaying: *phenotype.* **2.** Derived from benzene: *phenol.* [< Gk. *phainein*, show.]

phe•no•bar•bi•tal (fē′nō-bär′bĭ-tôl′, -tăl′) ►*n.* A shiny white crystalline compound, $C_{12}H_{12}N_2O_3$, used medicinally as a sedative, hypnotic, and anticonvulsant.

phe•nol (fē′nôl′, -nōl′, -nŏl′) ►*n.* A caustic, poisonous, white crystalline compound, C_6H_5OH, derived from benzene and used in plastics, disinfectants, and drugs. —**phe•no′lic** (-nô′lĭk, -nō′-, -nŏl′ĭk) *adj.*

phe•nom•e•non (fĭ-nŏm′ə-nŏn′, -nən) ►*n.*, *pl.* **-na** (-nə) **1.** An occurrence or fact that is perceptible by the senses. **2.** *pl.* **-nons a.** An unusual fact or occurrence; marvel. **b.** A remarkable or outstanding person; paragon. See Syns at **wonder.** [< Gk. *phainomenon.*] —**phe•nom′e•nal** *adj.* —**phe•nom′e•nal•ly** *adv.*

Usage: *Phenomenon* is the only singular form of this noun; *phenomena* is the usual plural. *Phenomenons* may also be used as the plural in nonscientific writing when the meaning is "extraordinary things, occurrences, or persons": *They were phenomenons in the history of music.*

phe•no•type (fē′nə-tīp′) ►*n.* **1.** The environmentally and genetically determined visible appearance of an organism. **2.** An individual or group of organisms exhibiting a particular phenotype. —**phe′no•typ′ic** (-tĭp′ĭk), **phe′no•typ′i•cal** *adj.*

pher•o•mone (fĕr′ə-mōn′) ►*n.* A chemical secreted by an animal that influences the behavior or development of others of the same species. [Gk. *pherein*, carry + (HOR)MONE.]

phi (fī) ►*n.* The 21st letter of the Greek alphabet. [< Gk. *phei.*]

phi•al (fī′əl) ►*n.* A vial. [< Gk. *phialē*, shallow vessel.]

Phi Beta Kappa ►*n.* An honorary society, founded in 1776, of college students and graduates whose members are chosen on the basis of high academic standing. [< the initials of the Gk. motto *philosophia biou kubernētēs*, philosophy the guide of life.]

Phid•i•as (fĭd′ē-əs). fl. 5th cent. B.C. Athenian sculptor.

Phil•a•del•phi•a (fĭl′ə-dĕl′fē-ə) A city of SE PA on the Delaware R. Pop. 1,585,577. —**Phil′a•del′phi•an** *adj. & n.*

phi•lan•der (fĭ-lăn′dər) ►*v.* To engage in love affairs frivolously or casually. [< Gk. *philandros*, loving men.] —**phi•lan′der•er** *n.*

phil•an•throp•ic (fĭl′ən-thrŏp′ĭk) also **phil•an•throp•i•cal** (-ĭ-kəl) ►*adj.* **1.** Marked by philanthropy; humanitarian. **2.** Providing charitable assistance. See Syns at **benevolent.** —**phil′an•throp′i•cal•ly** *adv.*

phi•lan•thro•py (fĭ-lăn′thrə-pē) ►*n.*, *pl.* **-pies**

1. The effort to increase the well-being of humankind, as by charitable donations. **2.** Love of humankind in general. **3.** A charitable activity or institution. [< Gk. *philanthrōpos*, loving humankind.] —**phi•lan′thro•pist** *n.*

phi•lat•e•ly (fĭ-lăt′l-ē) ▸*n.* The collection and study of postage stamps, postmarks, and related materials. [Fr. *philatélie.*] —**phil′a•tel′ic** (fĭl′ə-tĕl′ĭk) *adj.* —**phi•lat′e•list** *n.*

–phile or **–phil** ▸*suff.* One that loves or has a strong affinity or preference for: *audiophile.* [< Gk. *philos*, loving.]

Phi•le•mon (fĭ-lē′mən, fī-) ▸*n.* See table at **Bible.**

phil•har•mon•ic (fĭl′här-mŏn′ĭk, fĭl′ər-) ▸*n.* A symphony orchestra or group that supports it.

–philia ▸*suff.* Tendency toward: *hemophilia.* [< Gk. *philos*, loving.]

Phil•ip (fĭl′ĭp). See **Metacom.**

Philip, Prince. Duke of Edinburgh. b. 1921. Husband of Elizabeth II of Great Britain.

Philip, Saint. fl. 1st cent. A.D. One of the 12 Apostles.

Philip II[1]. 382–336 B.C. King of Macedon (359–336).

Philip II[2]. 1165–1223. King of France (1180–1223).

Philip II[3]. 1527–98. King of Spain (1556–98), of Naples and Sicily (1554–98), and of Portugal (1580–98) as Philip I.

Philip IV. 1268–1314. King of France (1285–1314) and of Navarre (1284–1305) as the husband of Joan I of Navarre (1273–1305).

Phi•lip•pi (fĭ-lĭp′ī) An ancient town of NE Greece, near the Aegean Sea. —**Phi•lip′pi•an** (-lĭp′ē-ən) *adj. & n.*

Phi•lip•pi•ans (fĭ-lĭp′ē-ənz) ▸*pl.n. (takes sing. v.)* See table at **Bible.**

phi•lip•pic (fĭ-lĭp′ĭk) ▸*n.* A passionate speech intended to arouse opposition; tirade. [After PHILIP II[1].]

Phil•ip•pines (fĭl′ə-pēnz′, fĭl′ə-pēnz′) A country of E Asia consisting of the **Philippine Islands,** an archipelago in the W Pacific. Cap. Manila. Pop. 67,038,000. —**Phil′ip•pine′** *adj.*

Philippine Sea. A section of the W Pacific E of the Philippines and W of the Marianas.

Phil•is•tine (fĭl′ĭ-stēn′, fĭ-lĭs′tĭn, -tēn′) ▸*n.* **1.** A member of an ancient people in Palestine. **2.** often **philistine** One who is indifferent or antagonistic to artistic and cultural values. ▸*adj.* **1.** Of the ancient Philistines. **2.** often **philistine** Boorish or uncultured.

phil•o•den•dron (fĭl′ə-dĕn′drən) ▸*n., pl.* **-drons** or **-dra** (-drə). Any of various climbing tropical American plants often grown as houseplants. [< Gk. *philodendros*, fond of trees.]

phi•lol•o•gy (fĭ-lŏl′ə-jē) ▸*n.* **1.** Literary study or classical scholarship. **2.** The study of linguistic change over time. [< Gk. *philologos*, fond of learning or of words.] —**phil′o•log′i•cal** (fĭl′ə-lŏj′ĭ-kəl) *adj.* —**phil′o•log′i•cal•ly** *adv.* —**phi•lol′o•gist** *n.*

phi•los•o•pher (fĭ-lŏs′ə-fər) ▸*n.* **1.** A specialist in philosophy. **2.** One who lives by a particular philosophy. **3.** One who takes a calm and rational approach toward life. [< Gk. *philosophos*, lover of wisdom.]

phi•los•o•phize (fĭ-lŏs′ə-fīz′) ▸*v.* **-phized, -phiz•ing.** To speculate in a philosophical manner. —**phi•los′o•phiz′er** *n.*

phi•los•o•phy (fĭ-lŏs′ə-fē) ▸*n., pl.* **-phies 1a.** Investigation of the nature, causes, or principles of reality, knowledge, or values, based on logical reasoning rather than empirical methods. **b.** A system of thought based on or involving such inquiry. **2.** The sciences and liberal arts, except medicine, law, and theology. **3.** A system of values by which one lives. **4.** A basic theory concerning a particular subject. —**phil′o•soph′i•cal** (fĭl′ə-sŏf′ĭ-kəl), **phil′o•soph′ic** *adj.*

phil•ter also **phil•tre** (fĭl′tər) ▸*n.* **1.** A love potion. **2.** A magic potion or charm. [< Gk. *philtron* < *philein*, to love.]

phle•bi•tis (flĭ-bī′tĭs) ▸*n.* Inflammation of a vein. —**phle•bit′ic** (-bĭt′ĭk) *adj.*

phlebo– or **phleb–** ▸*pref.* Vein: *phlebotomy.* [< Gk. *phleps, phleb-*, blood vessel.]

phle•bot•o•my (flĭ-bŏt′ə-mē) ▸*n., pl.* **-mies.** The therapeutic practice of opening a vein by incision or puncture to draw blood.

phlegm (flĕm) ▸*n.* Thick, sticky, stringy mucus produced in the respiratory tract. [< Gk. *phlegma*, humor caused by heat.]

phleg•mat•ic (flĕg-măt′ĭk) also **phleg•mat•i•cal** (-ĭ-kəl) ▸*adj.* Having or suggesting a calm, stolid temperament; unemotional. [< Gk. *phlegma*, the humor phlegm.]

phlo•em (flō′ĕm′) ▸*n.* The food-conducting tissue of vascular plants. [< Gk. *phloios*, bark.]

phlox (flŏks) ▸*n., pl.* **phlox** or **-es.** A plant having clusters of white, red, pink, or purple flowers. [< Gk., wallflower.]

Phnom Penh (pə-nôm′ pĕn′, nŏm′) The capital of Cambodia, in the SW part on the Mekong R. Pop. 400,000.

–phobe ▸*suff.* One who fears or detests a specified thing: *xenophobe.* [< Gk. *phobos*, fear.]

pho•bi•a (fō′bē-ə) ▸*n.* A persistent, abnormal, or irrational fear of a specific thing or situation. [< Gk. *phobos*, fear.] —**pho′bic** (-bĭk) *adj.*

–phobia ▸*suff.* An intense, abnormal, or illogical fear: *claustrophobia.* [< Gk. *phobos*, fear.]

phoe•be (fē′bē) ▸*n.* A medium-sized North American flycatcher. [Imit. of its song.]

Phoe•ni•cia (fĭ-nĭsh′ə, -nē′shə) An ancient maritime country of SW Asia consisting of city-states along the E Mediterranean.

Phoe•ni•cian (fĭ-nĭsh′ən, -nē′shən) ▸*n.* **1.** A native or inhabitant of ancient Phoenicia. **2.** The Semitic language of ancient Phoenicia.

phoe•nix also **phe•nix** (fē′nĭks) ▸*n.* A bird in Egyptian mythology that consumed itself by

phoenix
Phoenix, a 1952 serigraph with handpainted watercolor by Ben Shahn

fire after 500 years and rose renewed from its ashes. [< Gk. *phoinix*.]

Phoenix. The capital of AZ, in the S-central part NW of Tucson. Pop. 983,403.

phone (fōn) *Informal* ►*n.* A telephone. ►*v.* **phoned, phon•ing.** To telephone.

-phone ►*suff.* **1.** Sound: *homophone.* **2.** Device that receives or emits sound: *megaphone.* **3.** Speaker of a language: *Anglophone.* [< Gk. *phōnē*, sound, voice.]

phone card ►*n.* A prepaid or credit card used to pay for telephone calls.

pho•neme (fō′nēm′) ►*n.* The smallest unit of speech that is capable of conveying a distinction in meaning, as the *m* of *mat* and the *b* of *bat* in English. [< Gk. *phōnēma*, utterance.] —**pho•ne′mic** (fə-nē′mĭk, fō-) *adj.* —**pho•ne′mi•cal•ly** *adv.*

pho•net•ic (fə-nĕt′ĭk) ►*adj.* **1.** Of or relating to phonetics. **2.** Representing the sounds of speech with a set of distinct symbols, each designating a single sound. [< Gk. *phōnētos*, to be spoken.] —**pho•net′i•cal•ly** *adv.*

pho•net•ics (fə-nĕt′ĭks) ►*n.* *(takes sing. v.)* The branch of linguistics that deals with the study of the sounds of speech. —**pho′ne•ti′cian** (fō′nĭ-tĭsh′ən) *n.*

phon•ic (fŏn′ĭk) ►*adj.* Of or relating to sound, esp. speech sounds.

phon•ics (fŏn′ĭks) ►*n.* *(takes sing. v.)* **1.** A method of teaching reading and spelling based on phonetics. **2.** Phonetics.

phono– or **phon–** ►*pref.* Sound; voice; speech: *phonology.* [< Gk. *phōnē*.]

pho•no•graph (fō′nə-grăf′) ►*n.* A machine that reproduces sound recorded on a grooved disk. —**pho′no•graph′ic** *adj.*

pho•nol•o•gy (fə-nŏl′ə-jē, fō-) ►*n.* The study of the distribution and pronunciation of speech sounds in a language. —**pho′no•log′ic** (fō′nə-lŏj′ĭk), **pho′no•log′i•cal** *adj.* —**pho•nol′o•gist** *n.*

pho•ny also **pho•ney** (fō′nē) ►*adj.* **-ni•er, -ni•est 1.** Not genuine or real; fake. **2.** Insincere or hypocritical. [< Ir.Gael. *fáinne*, gilt brass ring.] —**pho′ni•ness** *n.* —**pho′ny** *n.*

-phony ►*suff.* Sound: *telephony.* [Gk. *-phōnia*.]

-phore ►*suff.* Bearer; carrier: *semaphore.* [< Gk. *pherein*, carry.]

-phoresis ►*suff.* Transmission: *electrophoresis.* [< Gk. *phorēsis*, a carrying < *pherein*, carry.]

phos•gene (fŏs′jēn′, fŏz′-) ►*n.* A colorless volatile liquid or gas, $COCl_2$, used as a poison gas and in making glass, dyes, resins, and plastics. [< Gk. *phōs*, light.]

phos•phate (fŏs′fāt′) ►*n.* **1.** A salt or ester of phosphoric acid. **2.** A fertilizer containing phosphorus compounds. —**phos•phat′ic** (-făt′ĭk) *adj.*

phos•pho•lip•id (fŏs′fō-lĭp′ĭd) ►*n.* Any of various lipids that contain a phosphate group and one or more fatty acids.

phos•phor (fŏs′fər, -fôr′) ►*n.* **1.** A substance that exhibits phosphorescence. **2.** The phosphorescent coating on the inside of the screen of a cathode-ray tube. [< PHOSPHORUS.]

phos•pho•res•cence (fŏs′fə-rĕs′əns) ►*n.* Persistent emission of light following exposure to and removal of incident radiation. —**phos′pho•resce′** *v.* —**phos′pho•res′cent** *adj.* —**phos′pho•res′cent•ly** *adv.*

phosphoric acid ►*n.* A clear colorless liquid, H_3PO_4, used in fertilizers, detergents, and food flavorings.

phos•pho•rus (fŏs′fər-əs) ►*n.* **1.** *Symbol* **P** A highly reactive, poisonous, nonmetallic element used in safety matches, pyrotechnics, incendiary shells, and fertilizers. At. no. 15. See table at **element. 2.** A phosphorescent substance. [< Gk. *phōsphoros*, light-bearing : *phōs*, light + *pherein*, carry.] —**phos•phor′ic** (fŏs-fôr′ĭk, -fŏr′-) *adj.* —**phos′pho•rous** (fŏs′fər-əs, fŏs-fôr′əs, -fŏr′-) *adj.*

pho•tic (fō′tĭk) ►*adj.* **1.** Of or relating to light. **2.** Penetrated by light, esp. by sunlight: *the photic zone of the ocean.*

pho•to (fō′tō) ►*n.*, *pl.* **-tos** *Informal* A photograph. —**pho′to** *v.*

photo– or **phot–** ►*pref.* **1.** Light: *photosynthesis.* **2.** Photographic: *photomontage.* **3.** Photoelectric: *photoemission.* [< Gk. *phōs*, light.]

pho•to•cell (fō′tō-sĕl′) ►*n.* A photoelectric cell.

pho•to•chem•is•try (fō′tō-kĕm′ĭ-strē) ►*n.* The study of the effects of light on chemical reactions. —**pho′to•chem′i•cal** *adj.*

pho•to•com•po•si•tion (fō′tō-kŏm′pə-zĭsh′ən) ►*n.* The preparation of manuscript for printing by the projection of images of type characters on photographic film. —**pho′to•com•pose′** *v.* —**pho′to•com•pos′er** *n.*

pho•to•cop•y (fō′tə-kŏp′ē) ►*v.* To make a photographic reproduction of (printed or pictorial material), esp. by xerography. ►*n.* A photographic reproduction. —**pho′to•cop′i•er** *n.*

pho•to•du•pli•cate (fō′tō-do͞o′plĭ-kāt′, -dyo͞o′-) ►*v.* To photocopy. —**pho′to•du′pli•cate** (-kĭt) *n.* —**pho′to•du′pli•ca′tion** *n.*

pho•to•e•lec•tric (fō′tō-ĭ-lĕk′trĭk) also **pho•to•e•lec•tri•cal** (-trĭ-kəl) ►*adj.* Of or relating to electric effects, esp. increased conductivity, caused by light. —**pho′to•e•lec′tri•cal•ly** *adv.*

photoelectric cell ►*n.* An electronic device having an electrical output that varies in response to the intensity of incident radiation; electric eye.

pho•to•e•lec•tron (fō′tō-ĭ-lĕk′trŏn′) ►*n.* An electron that is released in photoemission.

pho•to•e•mis•sion (fō′tō-ĭ-mĭsh′ən) ►*n.* Emission of photoelectrons from a metallic surface exposed to light or similar radiation.

pho•to•en•grav•ing (fō′tō-ĕn-grā′vĭng) ►*n.* **1.** The process of reproducing graphic material by photographing it on a metal plate and then etching the plate for printing. **2.** A reproduction made by this process. —**pho′to•en•grave′** *v.* —**pho′to•en•grav′er** *n.*

pho•to-es•say (fō′tō-ĕs′ā′) ►*n.* A story told chiefly through photographs usu. supplemented by a written commentary.

photo finish ►*n.* A race so closely contested that the winner must be determined by a photograph taken at the finish.

pho•to•flash (fō′tō-flăsh′) ►*n.* See **flashbulb.**

pho•to•gen•ic (fō′tə-jĕn′ĭk) ►*adj.* Attractive as a subject for photography.

pho•to•graph (fō′tə-grăf′) ►*n.* An image, esp. a positive print, recorded by a camera and reproduced chemically on a photosensitive surface. ►*v.* **1.** To take a photograph of. **2.** To be the subject for photographs. —**pho•tog′ra•pher** (fə-tŏg′rə-fər) *n.*

pho•to•graph•ic (fō′tə-grăf′ĭk) also **pho•to•graph•i•cal** (-ĭ-kəl) ►*adj.* **1.** Of or relating to photography or a photograph. **2.** Used in photography. **3.** Like a photograph, esp. in representing with accuracy and detail. —**pho′to•graph′i•cal•ly** *adv.*

pho•tog•ra•phy (fə-tŏg′rə-fē) ►*n.* **1.** The art or process of producing images on light-sensitive surfaces. **2.** The art, practice, or profession of taking and printing photographs.

pho•to•gra•vure (fō′tə-grə-vyo͝or′) ►*n.* The process of printing from an intaglio plate, etched according to a photographic image.

pho•to•jour•nal•ism (fō′tō-jûr′nə-lĭz′əm) ►*n.* Journalism in which pictorial matter, esp. photographs, takes precedence over written copy. —**pho′to•jour′nal•ist** *n.*

pho•tom•e•try (fō-tŏm′ĭ-trē) ►*n.* Measurement of the properties of light, esp. luminous intensity. —**pho′to•met′ric** (fō′tə-mĕt′rĭk), **pho′to•met′ri•cal** *adj.*

pho•to•mi•cro•graph (fō′tō-mī′krə-grăf′) ►*n.* A photograph made through a microscope. —**pho′to•mi′cro•graph′** *v.* —**pho′to•mi•crog′ra•phy** (-krŏg′rə-fē) *n.*

pho•to•mon•tage (fō′tō-mŏn-täzh′, -môn-) ►*n.* **1.** The technique of making a picture by assembling pieces of photographs, often with other graphic material. **2.** A composite picture produced by this technique.

pho•ton (fō′tŏn′) ►*n.* The quantum of electromagnetic energy, usu. regarded as a discrete particle having zero mass and no electric charge. —**pho•ton′ic** *adj.*

pho•ton•ics (fō-tŏn′ĭks) ►*n.* *(takes sing. v.)* The study or application of electromagnetic energy whose basic unit is the photon, including optics and information storage and processing.

pho•to•play (fō′tə-plā′) ►*n.* A play filmed or arranged for filming as a movie.

pho•to•re•cep•tor (fō′tō-rĭ-sĕp′tər) ►*n.* A nerve ending, cell, or group of cells specialized to sense or receive light.

pho•to•re•con•nais•sance (fō′tō-rĭ-kŏn′ə-səns, -zəns) ►*n.* Photographic aerial reconnaissance esp. of military targets.

pho•to•sen•si•tive (fō′tō-sĕn′sĭ-tĭv) ►*adj.* Sensitive to light. —**pho′to•sen′si•tiv′i•ty** *n.*

pho•to•sphere (fō′tə-sfîr′) ►*n.* The visible outer layer of a star, esp. of the sun.

Pho•to•stat (fō′tə-stăt′) ► A trademark for a device used to make positive or negative copies of graphic matter.

pho•to•syn•the•sis (fō′tō-sĭn′thĭ-sĭs) ►*n.* The process by which chlorophyll-containing cells in green plants use light as an energy source to synthesize carbohydrates from carbon dioxide and water. —**pho′to•syn′the•size** *v.* —**pho′to•syn•thet′ic** (-sĭn-thĕt′ĭk) *adj.* —**pho′to•syn•thet′i•cal•ly** *adv.*

pho•tot•ro•pism (fō-tŏt′rə-pĭz′əm, fō′tō-trō′-) ►*n.* *Biol.* Growth or movement in response to light. —**pho′to•tro′pic** (fō′tə-trō′pĭk) *adj.*

pho•to•type•set•ting (fō′tō-tīp′sĕt′ĭng) ►*n.* See **photocomposition.**

pho•to•vol•ta•ic (fō′tō-vŏl-tā′ĭk, -vōl-) ►*adj.* Capable of producing a voltage when exposed to radiant energy, esp. light.

photovoltaic cell ►*n.* See **solar cell.**

phrase (frāz) ►*n.* **1.** A sequence of words intended to have meaning. **2.** A brief, cogent expression. **3.** *Gram.* Two or more words in sequence that form a syntactic unit that is less than a complete sentence. **4.** *Mus.* A short passage, often consisting of four measures or forming part of a larger unit. ►*v.* **phrased, phras•ing 1.** To express orally or in writing. **2.** *Mus.* To render in phrases. [< Gk. *phrasis,* diction.] —**phras′al** *adj.*

phra•se•ol•o•gy (frā′zē-ŏl′ə-jē) ►*n.*, *pl.* **-gies.** The way in which words and phrases are used in speech or writing; style. —**phra′se•o•log′i•cal** (-ə-lŏj′ĭ-kəl) *adj.*

phre•net•ic (frə-nĕt′ĭk) or **phre•net•i•cal** (-ĭ-kəl) ►*adj.* Vars. of **frenetic.**

-phrenia ►*suff.* Mental disorder: *schizophrenia.* [< Gk. *phrēn,* mind.]

phre•nol•o•gy (frĭ-nŏl′ə-jē) ►*n.* The study of the shape and irregularities of the human skull, based on the now discredited belief that they reveal character and mental capacity. [< Gk. *phrēn,* mind.] —**phren′o•log′ic** (frĕn′ə-lŏj′ĭk, frē′nə-), **phren′o•log′i•cal** *adj.* —**phre•nol′o•gist** *n.*

Phryg•i•a (frĭj′ē-ə) An ancient region of central Asia Minor in modern-day central Turkey. —**Phryg′i•an** *adj. & n.*

phy•la (fī′lə) ►*n.* Pl. of **phylum.**

phy•lac•ter•y (fĭ-lăk′tə-rē) ►*n.*, *pl.* **-ies.** *Judaism* Either of two small leather boxes containing quotations from the Hebrew Scriptures, worn strapped to the forehead and the left arm esp. by orthodox Jewish men during weekday morning worship. [< Gk. *phulaktērion,* safeguard.]

phyl•lo•tax•y (fĭl′ə-tăk′sē) also **phyl•lo•tax•is** (fĭl′ə-tăk′sĭs) ►*n.*, *pl.* **-tax•ies** also **-tax•es.** The arrangement of leaves on a stem. [Gk. *phyllon,* leaf + *taxis,* arrangement.]

phy•log•e•ny (fī-lŏj′ə-nē) ►*n.*, *pl.* **-nies.** The evolutionary development of an animal or plant species. [Gk. *phulon,* race + –GENY.] —**phy′lo•ge•net′ic** (fī′lō-jə-nĕt′ĭk), **phy′lo•gen′ic** (-jĕn′ĭk) *adj.*

phy•lum (fī′ləm) ►*n.*, *pl.* **-la** (-lə) **1.** *Biol.* The category ranking below a kingdom and above a class in the hierarchy of taxonomic classification. **2.** *Ling.* A large division of possibly genetically related families of languages or linguistic stocks. [< Gk. *phulon,* class.]

phys– ►*pref.* Var. of **physio–.**

physi– ►*pref.* Var. of **physio–.**

phys•ic (fĭz′ĭk) ►*n.* A medicine or drug, esp. a cathartic. ►*v.* **-icked, -ick•ing 1.** To act on as a cathartic. **2.** To cure or heal. [< Gk. *phusikē,* natural science < *phusis,* nature.]

phys•i•cal (fĭz′ĭ-kəl) ►*adj.* **1.** Of or relating to the body. See Syns at **bodily. 2.** Of material things. **3.** Of or relating to matter and energy or the sciences dealing with them, esp. physics. ►*n.* A physical examination. —**phys′i•cal•ly** *adv.*

physical education ►*n.* Education in the care and development of the human body, stressing athletics and including hygiene.

physical examination ►*n.* A medical examination to determine the condition of a person's health or physical fitness.

physical geography ►*n.* The study of the natural features, structure, and phenomena of the earth's surface, esp. in its current aspects.

physical science ►*n.* Any of the sciences, such as physics, chemistry, astronomy, and geology, that analyze the nature and properties of energy and nonliving matter.

physical therapy ►*n.* The treatment of disease and injury by mechanical means such as exercise, heat, light, and massage. —**physical therapist** *n.*

phy•si•cian (fĭ-zĭsh′ən) ►*n.* A medical doctor.

phys•i•cist (fĭz′ĭ-sĭst) ►*n.* A scientist who specializes in physics.

phys•ics (fĭz′ĭks) ►*n.* **1.** *(takes sing. v.)* The science of matter and energy and of interactions between the two. **2.** *(takes pl. v.)* Physical properties, processes, or laws.

physio– or **physi–** or **phys–** ►*pref.* **1.** Nature: *physiography.* **2.** Physical: *physiotherapy.* [< Gk. *phusis*, nature.]

phys•i•og•no•my (fĭz′ē-ŏg′nə-mē, -ŏn′ə-mē) ►*n., pl.* **-mies 1.** The art of judging human character from facial features. **2.** Facial features; the face. [< Gk. *phusiognōmonia.*]

phys•i•og•ra•phy (fĭz′ē-ŏg′rə-fē) ►*n.* See **physical geography.** —**phys′i•og′ra•pher** *n.* —**phys′i•o•graph′ic** (-ə-grăf′ĭk), **phys′i•o•graph′i•cal** *adj.*

phys•i•ol•o•gy (fĭz′ē-ŏl′ə-jē) ►*n.* **1.** The biological science of the functions, activities, and processes of living organisms. **2.** All the functions of an organism. —**phys′i•o•log′i•cal** (-ə-lŏj′ĭ-kəl) *adj.* —**phys′i•o•log′i•cal•ly** *adv.* —**phys′i•ol′o•gist** *n.*

phys•i•o•ther•a•py (fĭz′ē-ō-thĕr′ə-pē) ►*n.* See **physical therapy.** —**phys′i•o•ther′a•peu′tic** (-ə-pyo͞o′tĭk) *adj.* —**phys′i•o•ther′a•pist** *n.*

phys•i•o•type (fĭz′ē-ō-tīp′) ►*n.* The physical characteristics or features that distinguish a person or other organism.

phy•sique (fĭ-zēk′) ►*n.* The body considered with reference to its proportions, muscular development, and appearance. [Fr., physical, physique < Gk. *phusis*, nature.] —**phy•siqued′** *adj.*

–phyte ►*suff.* A plant with a specified character or habitat: *epiphyte.* [< Gk. *phuton*, plant.]

phyto– or **phyt–** ►*pref.* Plant: *phytochemical.* [< Gk. *phuton.*]

phy•to•chem•i•cal (fī′tō-kĕm′ĭ-kəl) ►*adj.* Relating to plant chemistry. ►*n.* A nonnutritive plant substance thought to have health benefits.

phy•to•plank•ton (fī′tō-plăngk′tən) ►*n.* Minute, free-floating aquatic plants.

pi[1] (pī) ►*n.* **1.** The 16th letter of the Greek alphabet. **2.** *Math.* A transcendental number, approx. 3.14159, expressing the ratio of the circumference to the diameter of a circle. [< Gk. *pei.*]

pi[2] also **pie** (pī) ►*n., pl.* **pis** also **pies** *Print.* Jumbled type. [?]

pi•a•nis•si•mo (pē′ə-nĭs′ə-mō′) ►*adv. & adj. Mus.* In a very soft or quiet tone. [Ital.]

pi•an•ist (pē-ăn′ĭst, pē′ə-nĭst) ►*n.* One who plays the piano.

pi•an•o[1] (pē-ăn′ō, pyăn′ō) ►*n., pl.* **-os.** A keyboard musical instrument with hammers that strike wire strings. [Ital. < *pianoforte*, PIANOFORTE.]

pi•a•no[2] (pē-ä′nō, pyä′-) ►*adv. & adj. Mus.* In a soft or quiet tone. [Ital.]

pi•an•o•for•te (pē-ăn′ō-fôr′tā, -tē, pē-ăn′ō-fôrt′) ►*n.* A piano. [Ital. < *piano (e) forte*, soft (and) loud.]

pi•az•za (pē-ăz′ə, -ä′zə) ►*n.* **1.** (*also* pē-ät′sə, pyät′sä). A public square in an Italian town. **2.** *Regional* A verandah; porch. [Ital. < Gk. *plateia*, broad.]

pi•ca (pī′kə) ►*n. Print.* **1.** A printer's unit of type size, equal to 12 points or about ⅙ of an inch. **2.** A type size for typewriters, providing 10 characters to the inch. [Prob. < Med.Lat. *pīca*, list of church services.]

pic•a•dor (pĭk′ə-dôr′) ►*n.* A horseman in a bullfight who lances the bull's neck muscles so as to weaken them. [Sp. < *picar*, to prick.]

Pic•ar•dy (pĭk′ər-dē) A historical region of N France on the English Channel.

pic•a•resque (pĭk′ə-rĕsk′, pē′kə-) ►*adj.* Of or involving clever rogues or adventurers, esp. in prose fiction. [< Sp. *pícaro*, rogue.]

Pi•cas•so (pĭ-kä′sō, -kăs′ō), **Pablo.** 1881–1973. Spanish artist.

Pablo Picasso
photographed in 1950

pic•a•yune (pĭk′ə-yo͞on′) ►*adj.* **1.** Of little value or importance; paltry. **2.** Petty; mean. [< Prov. *picaioun*, small coin.]

pic•co•lo (pĭk′ə-lō′) ►*n., pl.* **-los.** A small flute pitched an octave above a regular flute. [Ital.]

pick[1] (pĭk) ►*v.* **1.** To select from a group. **2.** To gather in or from; harvest. **3a.** To remove the outer covering of; pluck. **b.** To tear off bit by bit. **4.** To poke at with the fingers. **5.** To break up, separate, or detach with a sharp instrument. **6.** To pierce with a sharp instrument. **7.** To steal the contents of (a pocket or purse). **8.** To open (a lock) without the use of a key. **9.** To provoke: *pick a fight.* **10.** *Mus.* To pluck (a string or stringed instrument). —***phrasal verbs:*** **pick on** To tease or bully. **pick out** To choose or select. **pick up 1.** To take on (e.g., passengers or freight). **2.** To learn without great effort. **3.** To receive or intercept: *pick up a radio signal.* **4.** *Informal* To take into custody; arrest. **5.** *Informal* To improve in condition or activity. ►*n.* **1.** The act of selecting; choice. **2.** The best or choicest part. —***idioms:*** **pick and choose** To select or decide with great care. **pick (one's) way** To make one's way carefully. [< VLat. **piccāre*, to pierce.] —**pick′er** *n.*

pick[2] (pĭk) ►*n.* **1.** A tool for breaking hard surfaces, consisting of a curved bar sharpened at both ends and fitted to a long handle. **2.** *Mus.* A plectrum. [ME *pik.*]

pick•ax or **pick•axe** (pĭk′ăks′) ►*n.* A pick,

esp. with one end of the head pointed and the other end with a chisel edge. [< OFr. *picois*.]

pick•er•el (pĭk′ər-əl, pĭk′rəl) ▸*n.*, *pl.* **-el** or **-els.** A North American freshwater fish related to the pike. [ME *pikerel*, dim. of *pike*, PIKE[2].]

pick•et (pĭk′ĭt) ▸*n.* **1.** A pointed stake driven into the ground to support a fence, secure a tent, tether animals, mark surveying points, or serve as a defense. **2.** A detachment of one or more troops, ships, or aircraft on guard against an enemy's approach. **3.** A person or persons stationed outside a place of employment, usu. during a strike, to express grievance or protest. ▸*v.* **1.** To enclose, secure, mark out, or fortify with pickets. **2.** *Military* To guard with a picket. **3.** To post a picket or pickets at a strike or demonstration. **4.** To act or serve as a picket. [< OFr. *piquet*.] —**pick′et•er** *n.*

picket fence ▸*n.* A fence of pointed pickets.

picket line ▸*n.* A line or procession of people picketing a place of business or otherwise staging a public protest.

Pick•ett (pĭk′ĭt), **George Edward.** 1825–75. Amer. Confederate general.

pick•ing (pĭk′ĭng) ▸*n.* **1. pickings** Something that is or may be picked. **2.** often **pickings a.** Leftovers. **b.** A share of spoils.

pick•le (pĭk′əl) ▸*n.* **1.** An edible product, such as a cucumber, preserved and flavored in a solution of brine or vinegar. **2.** A solution of brine or vinegar, often spiced, for preserving and flavoring food. **3.** *Informal* A disagreeable, difficult, or troublesome situation; plight. ▸*v.* **-led, -ling.** To preserve or flavor in a solution of brine or vinegar. [Prob. < MDu. *pekel*, brine.]

pick-me-up (pĭk′mē-ŭp′) ▸*n.* *Informal* A usu. alcoholic drink taken as a stimulant.

pick•pock•et (pĭk′pŏk′ĭt) ▸*n.* One who steals from pockets or purses.

pick•up (pĭk′ŭp′) ▸*n.* **1.** The act or process of picking up. **2.** Ability to accelerate rapidly. **3.** One that is picked up. **4.** A pickup truck. **5.** *Electron.* **a.** A device that converts the oscillations of a phonograph needle into electrical impulses for subsequent conversion into sound. **b.** The tone arm of a record player. **6a.** The reception of light or sound waves for conversion to electrical impulses. **b.** The apparatus used for such reception. **c.** A telecast originating outside a studio. **d.** The apparatus for transmitting a broadcast to a broadcasting station from outside.

pickup truck ▸*n.* A light truck with an open body and low sides.

pick•y (pĭk′ē) ▸*adj.* **-i•er, -i•est** *Informal* Meticulous; fussy.

pic•nic (pĭk′nĭk) ▸*n.* **1.** A meal eaten outdoors, as on an excursion. **2.** *Slang* An easy task. ▸*v.* **-nicked, -nick•ing.** To go on a picnic. [Fr. *piquenique*.] —**pic′nick•er** *n.*

pi•cot (pē′kō, pē-kō′) ▸*n.* A small embroidered loop forming an edging, as on ribbon. [< OFr.]

pic•to•graph (pĭk′tə-grăf′) ▸*n.* **1.** A hieroglyph. **2.** A pictorial representation of numerical data or relationships. [< Lat. *pictus*, painted.] —**pic′to•graph′ic** *adj.*

pic•to•ri•al (pĭk-tôr′ē-əl, -tōr′-) ▸*adj.* **1.** Of or composed of pictures. **2.** Illustrated by pictures. ▸*n.* An illustrated periodical. [< Lat. *pictor*, painter.] —**pic•to′ri•al•ly** *adv.*

pic•ture (pĭk′chər) ▸*n.* **1.** A visual representation or image painted, drawn, photographed, or otherwise rendered on a flat surface. **2.** A vivid verbal description. **3.** One that bears a marked resemblance to another. **4.** One that typifies or embodies an emotion, state of mind, or mood. **5.** The chief circumstances of an event or time; situation. **6.** A movie. **7.** An image or series of images on a television or movie screen. ▸*v.* **-tured, -tur•ing 1.** To make a picture of. **2.** To visualize. **3.** To describe vividly in words. See Syns at **represent.** [< Lat. *pictūra* < *pingere*, *pict-*, to paint.]

pic•tur•esque (pĭk′chə-rĕsk′) ▸*adj.* **1.** Of or suggesting a picture. **2.** Unusually or quaintly attractive. **3.** Strikingly expressive or vivid: *picturesque language.* —**pic′tur•esque′ly** *adv.* —**pic′tur•esque′ness** *n.*

picture tube ▸*n.* A cathode-ray tube in a television receiver that translates received electrical signals into a visible picture on a luminescent screen.

picture window ▸*n.* A large, usu. single-paned window that provides a broad view.

pid•dling (pĭd′lĭng) ▸*adj.* Trifling or trivial. [?]

pidg•in (pĭj′ən) ▸*n.* A simplified mixture of two or more languages, used for communication between groups speaking different languages. [< PIDGIN ENGLISH.]

Pidgin English ▸*n.* Any of several pidgins based on English and now spoken mostly in the Pacific islands. [Perh. < *business English*.]

pie[1] (pī) ▸*n.* A baked pastry shell filled with fruit or other ingredients, and usu. covered with a crust. —***idiom:*** **pie in the sky** An empty wish or promise. [ME.]

pie[2] (pī) ▸*n.* *Print.* Var. of **pi**[2].

pie•bald (pī′bôld′) ▸*adj.* Spotted or patched in color, esp. in black and white. ▸*n.* A piebald animal, esp. a horse. [*pie*, magpie + BALD.]

piece (pēs) ▸*n.* **1.** A unit or element of a larger quantity or class; portion. **2.** An artistic or musical work. **3.** An instance; specimen. **4.** One's opinions or findings: *speak one's piece.* **5.** A coin or counter. **6.** A counter or figure used in a game. **7.** *Slang* A firearm, esp. a rifle. **8.** *Informal* A given distance: *down the road a piece.* ▸*v.* **pieced, piec•ing 1.** To mend by adding a piece to. **2.** To join the pieces of. —***idiom:*** **of a piece** Of the same class or kind. [< VLat. **pettia*.]

pièce de ré•sis•tance (pyĕs də rā-zē-stäɴs′) ▸*n.*, *pl.* **pièces de résistance** (pyĕs) **1.** An outstanding accomplishment. **2.** The principal dish of a meal. [Fr.]

piece goods ▸*pl.n.* Fabrics made and sold in standard lengths.

piece•meal (pēs′mēl′) ▸*adv.* By a small amount at a time; in stages. ▸*adj.* Made or done in stages. [ME *pecemeale*.]

piece of eight ▸*n.*, *pl.* **pieces of eight.** An old Spanish silver coin.

piece•work (pēs′wûrk′) ▸*n.* Work paid for by number of units made. —**piece′work′er** *n.*

pie chart ▸*n.* A circular graph divided into sectors proportional to the relative size of the quantities represented.

pied (pīd) ▸*adj.* Patchy in color; piebald. [< ME *pie*, magpie.]

pied-à-terre (pyā-dä-târ′) ▸*n.*, *pl.* **pieds-à-terre** (pyā-dä-târ′). A secondary or temporary place of lodging. [Fr.]

pied•mont (pēd′mŏnt′) ▸*n.* An area of land at

the foot of a mountain or mountain range.

Piedmont 1. A historical region of NW Italy bordering on France and Switzerland. **2.** A plateau region of the E US extending from NY to AL between the Appalachian Mts. and the Atlantic coastal plain. —**Pied′mon•tese′** (-tēz′, -tēs′) *adj. & n.*

pier (pîr) ►*n.* **1.** A platform extending from a shore over water, used to secure, protect, and provide access to ships or boats. **2.** A supporting structure for the spans of a bridge. **3.** *Archit.* Any of various vertical supporting or reinforcing structures. [< OFr. *puier*, support, and ONFr. *piere*, breakwater.]

pierce (pîrs) ►*v.* **pierced, pierc•ing 1.** To cut or pass through with or as if with a sharp instrument. **2.** To perforate. **3.** To make a way through. [< Lat. *pertundere, pertūs-*, bore through.] —**pierc′ing•ly** *adv.*

Pierce, Franklin. 1804–69. The 14th US President (1853–57).

Franklin Pierce

pier glass ►*n.* A tall mirror, esp. one placed between windows.

Pie•ro del•la Fran•ce•sca (pyâr′ō dĕl′ə frăn-chĕs′kə, frän-). 1420?–92. Italian painter.

Pierre (pîr) The capital of SD, in the central part on the Missouri R. Pop. 12,906.

pi•e•ty (pī′ĭ-tē) ►*n., pl.* **-ties 1.** Devotion and reverence, esp. to God and family. **2.** A pious act or thought. [< Lat. *pietās.*]

pi•e•zo•e•lec•tric•i•ty (pī-ē′zō-ĭ-lĕk-trĭs′ĭ-tē, -ē′lĕk-, pē-ā′zō-) ►*n.* Electricity or polarity induced in certain crystals, such as quartz, by mechanical stress. [Gk. *piezein*, squeeze + ELECTRICITY.] —**pi•e′zo•e•lec′tric, pi•e′zo•e•lec′tri•cal** *adj.*

pif•fle (pĭf′əl) ►*v.* **-fled, -fling.** To talk or act in a foolish, feeble, or futile way. ►*n.* Nonsense. [?]

pig (pĭg) ►*n.* **1.** A mammal having short legs, cloven hooves, bristly hair, and a blunt snout used for digging, esp. one of a kind raised for meat. **2.** *Informal* A slovenly, greedy, or gross person. **3.** A crude oblong block of metal, chiefly iron or lead, poured from a smelting furnace. **4.** *Offensive Slang* A police officer. ►*v.* **pigged, pig•ging.** To bear pigs; farrow. —***phrasal verb:* pig out** *Slang* To eat ravenously; gorge. [ME *pigge.*]

pi•geon (pĭj′ən) ►*n.* **1.** Any of various doves having a deep-chested body, small head, and short legs, esp. a common, often domesticated species. **2.** *Slang* One easily swindled; dupe. [< LLat. *pīpiō*, young chirping bird.]

pi•geon•hole (pĭj′ən-hōl′) ►*n.* A small compartment, as in a desk. ►*v.* **-holed, -hol•ing 1.** To place or file in a pigeonhole. **2.** To categorize. **3.** To put aside and ignore.

pi•geon-toed (pĭj′ən-tōd′) ►*adj.* Having the toes turned inward.

pig•gish (pĭg′ĭsh) ►*adj.* **1.** Greedy. **2.** Pigheaded. **3.** Dirty; slovenly.

pig•gy (pĭg′ē) *Informal* ►*n., pl.* **-gies.** A little pig. ►*adj.* Piggish.

pig•gy•back (pĭg′ē-băk′) ►*adv. & adj.* **1.** On the shoulders or back. **2.** By or of a method of transportation in which truck trailers are carried on trains. [< *pickaback.*]

piggy bank ►*n.* A coin bank shaped like a pig.

pig•head•ed (pĭg′hĕd′ĭd) ►*adj.* Stubborn. —**pig′head′ed•ness** *n.*

pig iron ►*n.* Crude iron cast in blocks.

pig Latin ►*n.* A jargon formed by the transposition of the initial consonant to the end of the word and the suffixion of an additional syllable, as *igpay atinlay* for *pig Latin.*

pig•let (pĭg′lĭt) ►*n.* A young pig.

pig•ment (pĭg′mənt) ►*n.* **1.** A coloring substance or matter, usu. a powder to be mixed with water, oil, or other base. **2.** A substance, such as chlorophyll or melanin, that produces a characteristic color in plant or animal tissue. [< Lat. *pigmentum.*] —**pig′men•tar′y** (-mən-tĕr′ē) *adj.*

pig•men•ta•tion (pĭg′mən-tā′shən) ►*n.* Coloration of animal or plant tissues by pigment.

Pig•my (pĭg′mē) ►*n. & adj.* Var. of **Pygmy.**

pig•pen (pĭg′pĕn′) ►*n.* **1.** A pen for pigs. **2.** *Slang* A dirty or very untidy place.

Pigs (pĭgz), **Bay of.** A small inlet of the Caribbean Sea on the S coast of W Cuba.

pig•skin (pĭg′skĭn′) ►*n.* **1.** The skin of a pig or leather made from it. **2.** *Sports* A football.

pig•sty (pĭg′stī′) ►*n.* A pigpen.

pig•tail (pĭg′tāl′) ►*n.* A plait of braided hair. —**pig′tailed′** *adj.*

pi•ka (pī′kə, pē′-) ►*n.* A small, tailless, furry mammal of the mountains of North America and Eurasia. [Evenki (Siberia) *piika.*]

pike[1] (pīk) ►*n.* A long spear formerly used by infantry. [< *piquer*, to prick.] —**piked** *adj.*

pike[2] (pīk) ►*n., pl.* **pike** or **pikes.** A freshwater game and food fish having a narrow body and long snout. [ME.]

pike[3] (pīk) ►*n.* A turnpike.

pike[4] (pīk) ►*n.* A spike or sharp point. [< OE *pīc.*]

pik•er (pī′kər) ►*n. Slang* A petty or stingy person. [?]

Pikes Peak (pīks) A mountain, 4,303.6 m (14,110 ft), in the Rocky Mts. of central CO.

pi•laf or **pi•laff** (pĭ-läf′, pē′läf′) ►*n.* A steamed rice dish with bits of meat, shellfish, or vegetables. [< Turk. *pilâv.*]

pi•las•ter (pĭ-lăs′tər) ►*n.* A rectangular column projecting slightly from a wall as an ornamental motif. [< Med.Lat. *pīlaster.*]

Pi•late (pī′lət), **Pontius.** fl. 1st cent. A.D. Roman prefect who ordered the crucifixion of Jesus.

pil•chard (pĭl′chərd) ►*n.* A small edible marine fish related to the herring. [?]

pile[1] (pīl) ►*n.* **1.** A quantity of objects heaped or thrown together in a stack. See Syns at **heap. 2.** *Informal* A large accumulation or quantity. **3.** A funeral pyre. **4.** A nuclear reactor. ►*v.* **piled, pil•ing 1a.** To stack in or form a pile. **b.** To load with a pile: *pile a plate with food.* **2.**

To move in a disorderly mass or group: *pile into a car.* [< Lat. *pīla*, pillar.]

pile² (pīl) ►*n.* A heavy timber, concrete, or steel beam driven into the earth as a structural support. [< Lat. *pīlum*, spear.]

pile³ (pīl) ►*n.* Cut or uncut loops of yarn forming the surface of certain fabrics, such as velvet and carpeting. [< Lat. *pilus*, hair.] —**piled** *adj.*

pi•le•at•ed woodpecker (pī′lē-ā′tĭd) ►*n.* A large North American woodpecker having black and white plumage and a red crest. [< Lat. *pīleus*, felt cap.]

pile driver ►*n.* A machine that drives piles into the ground.

piles (pīlz) ►*pl.n.* See **hemorrhoid** 2. [< Lat. *pila*, ball.]

pile•up or **pile-up** (pīl′ŭp′) ►*n. Informal* A serious collision of several motor vehicles.

pil•fer (pĭl′fər) ►*v.* To steal or filch. [< OFr. *pelfre*, spoils.] —**pil′fer•age** (-ĭj) *n.*

pil•grim (pĭl′grəm) ►*n.* **1.** One who goes on a pilgrimage. **2.** A traveler. **3. Pilgrim** One of the English Puritans who migrated to New England in 1620. [< Lat. *peregrīnus*, foreigner.]

pil•grim•age (pĭl′grə-mĭj) ►*n.* **1.** A journey to a sacred place. **2.** A long journey or search, esp. one of exalted purpose.

pil•ing (pī′lĭng) ►*n.* A number of piles supporting a structure.

Pil•i•pi•no (pĭl′ə-pē′nō) ►*n.* The Filipino language.

pill (pĭl) ►*n.* **1.** A small pellet or tablet of medicine. **2. the pill** *Informal* An oral contraceptive. **3.** Something both distasteful and necessary. **4.** *Slang* An ill-natured person. [< Lat. *pilula*, little ball.]

pil•lage (pĭl′ĭj) ►*v.* **-laged, -lag•ing.** To rob of goods by force; plunder. ►*n.* **1.** The act of pillaging. **2.** Spoils. [< OFr. *piller.*]

pil•lar (pĭl′ər) ►*n.* **1.** A slender, freestanding, vertical support; column. **2.** One occupying a central or responsible position. [< Lat. *pīla.*]

pill•box (pĭl′bŏks′) ►*n.* **1.** A small box for pills. **2.** A low-roofed concrete emplacement, esp. for a machine gun or antitank gun.

pil•lion (pĭl′yən) ►*n.* A seat for an extra rider behind the saddle on a horse or motorcycle. [< Sc.Gael. *pillean.*]

pil•lo•ry (pĭl′ə-rē) ►*n., pl.* **-ries.** A wooden framework with holes for the head and hands, in which offenders were formerly locked to be exposed to public scorn as punishment. ►*v.* **-ried, -ry•ing 1.** To expose to ridicule and abuse. **2.** To put in a pillory as punishment. [< OFr. *pilori.*]

pil•low (pĭl′ō) ►*n.* **1.** A cloth case stuffed with soft material and used to cushion the head, esp. during sleep. **2.** A decorative cushion. ►*v.* To serve as a pillow for. [< Lat. *pulvīnus.*] —**pil′low•y** *adj.*

pil•low•case (pĭl′ō-kās′) ►*n.* A removable covering for a pillow.

pil•low•slip (pĭl′ō-slĭp′) ►*n.* See **pillowcase.**

pillow talk ►*n.* Intimate conversation between lovers, esp. while in bed.

pi•lose (pī′lōs) also **pi•lous** (-ləs) ►*adj.* Covered with fine soft hair. [< Lat. *pilus*, hair.] —**pi•los′i•ty** (-lŏs′ĭ-tē) *n.*

pi•lot (pī′lət) ►*n.* **1.** One who flies or is licensed to fly an aircraft. **2a.** A licensed specialist who conducts a ship in and out of port or through dangerous waters. **b.** A ship's helmsman. **3.** A guide or leader. **4.** A television program produced as a prototype of a prospective series. ►*v.* **1.** To serve as the pilot of. **2.** To steer or control the course of. See Syns at **guide.** ►*adj.* **1.** Serving as a small-scale experimental model. **2.** Serving or leading as guide. [< OItal. *pilota* < Gk. *pēdon*, steering oar.] —**pi′lot•age** (-lə-tĭj) *n.*

pilot fish ►*n.* A small slender marine fish that often swims with larger fishes, esp. sharks and mantas.

pi•lot•house (pī′lət-hous′) ►*n. Naut.* An enclosed area, usu. on the bridge of a vessel, from which the vessel is controlled.

pilot light ►*n.* A small jet of gas kept burning in order to ignite a gas burner, as in a stove.

pilot whale ►*n.* Any of several large, usu. black dolphins having an outward-curving globular forehead.

pils•ner (pĭlz′nər, pĭls′-) ►*n.* **1.** A light lager with a strong hops flavor. **2.** A tall, thin, footed beer glass. [Ger.]

Pilt•down man (pĭlt′doun′) ►*n.* An early species of human postulated from a skull allegedly found about 1912 but proved in 1953 to be a fake. [After *Piltdown* Common in southeast England.]

Pi•ma (pē′mə) ►*n., pl.* **-ma** or **-mas 1.** A member of a Native American people of S Arizona. **2.** The Uto-Aztecan language of the Pima. —**Pi′man** *adj.*

pi•men•to (pĭ-mĕn′tō) ►*n., pl.* **-tos 1.** See **allspice. 2.** Var. of **pimiento.** [< LLat. *pigmentum*, pigment.]

pi•mien•to (pĭ-mĕn′tō, -myĕn′tō) also **pi•men•to** (-mĕn′tō) ►*n., pl.* **-tos.** A capsicum pepper having a mild-flavored red fruit. [Sp. See PIMENTO.]

pimp (pĭmp) ►*n.* One who procures customers for a prostitute. ►*v.* To be a pimp. [?]

pim•per•nel (pĭm′pər-nĕl′, -nəl) ►*n.* A plant having small red, purple, or white flowers. [< LLat. *pimpinella.*]

pim•ple (pĭm′pəl) ►*n.* A small inflamed swelling of the skin, usu. caused by acne. [ME.] —**pim′pled, pim′ply** *adj.*

pin (pĭn) ►*n.* **1.** A short, straight, stiff piece of wire with a blunt head and a sharp point, used esp. for fastening. **2.** Something, such as a safety pin or hairpin, that resembles a pin in shape or use. **3.** A slender, usu. cylindrical piece of wood or metal for holding, fastening, or supporting. **4.** An ornament fastened to clothing by means of a clasp. **5.** One of the clubs at which the ball is aimed in bowling. **6.** The pole bearing a pennant to mark a hole in golf. **7. pins** *Informal* The legs. ►*v.* **pinned, pin•ning 1.** To fasten or secure with or as if with a pin. **2.** To make completely dependent: *pinning all our hopes on winning.* **3.** To hold fast; immobilize. —***phrasal verbs:* pin down 1.** To fix or establish clearly. **2.** To oblige to make a definite response. **pin on** To attribute (a wrongdoing or crime) to. [< OE *pinn.*]

PIN ►*abbr.* personal identification number

pin•a•fore (pĭn′ə-fôr′, -fōr′) ►*n.* A sleeveless apronlike garment. [PIN + *afore*, in front.]

pi•ña•ta (pēn-yä′tə) ►*n.* A decorated container filled with candy and toys and hung from a

piñata

height to be broken by blindfolded children with sticks. [Sp.]

pin•ball (pĭn′bôl′) ► *n.* A game in which the player operates a plunger to shoot a ball down or along a slanted surface having obstacles and targets.

pince-nez (păns′nā′, pĭns′-) ► *n., pl.* **pince-nez** (-nāz′, -nā′). Eyeglasses clipped to the bridge of the nose. [Fr.]

pin•cers (pĭn′sərz) also **pinch•ers** (pĭn′chərz) ► *pl.n. (takes sing. or pl. v.)* **1.** A grasping tool having a pair of jaws and handles pivoted together to work in opposition. **2.** The articulated, prehensile claws of certain arthropods, such as the lobster. [< OFr. *pincier*, pinch.]

pinch (pĭnch) ► *v.* **1.** To squeeze between the thumb and a finger, the jaws of a tool, or other edges. **2.** To squeeze or bind (a part of the body) painfully. **3.** To wither or shrivel. **4.** To be miserly. **5.** *Slang* To steal. **6.** *Slang* To take into custody; arrest. ► *n.* **1.** The act or an instance of pinching. **2.** An amount that can be held between thumb and forefinger. **3.** A difficult or straitened circumstance. **4.** An emergency. [< OFr. *pincier*.] —**pinch′er** *n.*

pinch-hit (pĭnch′hĭt′) ► *v.* **1.** *Baseball* To bat in place of a scheduled player. **2.** *Informal* To substitute for another. —**pinch hitter** *n.*

pin•cush•ion (pĭn′ko͝osh′ən) ► *n.* A cushion into which pins are stuck when not in use.

Pin•dar (pĭn′dər). 522?–443? B.C. Greek lyric poet. —**Pin•dar′ic** (-dăr′ĭk) *adj.*

pine[1] (pīn) ► *n.* **1.** Any of various cone-bearing evergreen trees having needle-shaped leaves in clusters. **2.** The wood of any of these trees. [< Lat. *pīnus*.]

pine[2] (pīn) ► *v.* **pined, pin•ing 1.** To feel longing; yearn. **2.** To wither away from longing or grief. [< Gk. *poinē*, punishment.]

pin•e•al gland (pĭn′ē-əl, pī′nē-) ► *n.* A small, cone-shaped organ in the brain of most vertebrates whose function in mammals is unclear. [< Lat. *pīnea*, pine cone.]

pine•ap•ple (pīn′ăp′əl) ► *n.* **1.** A tropical American plant having swordlike leaves and a large, fleshy, edible fruit. **2.** The fruit of the pineapple. [ME *pinappel*, pine cone.]

pine needle ► *n.* The needle-shaped leaf of a pine tree.

pine nut ► *n.* The edible seed of certain pines.

pine•y (pī′nē) ► *adj.* Var. of **piny.**

pin•feath•er (pĭn′fĕth′ər) ► *n.* A growing feather, esp. one that is just emerging.

ping (pĭng) ► *n.* **1.** A sharp, high-pitched sound, as that made by a bullet striking metal. **2.** Engine knock. [Imit.] —**ping** *v.*

Ping-Pong (pĭng′pông′, -pŏng′) ► A trademark for table tennis.

pin•head (pĭn′hĕd′) ► *n.* **1.** The head of a pin. **2.** Something small or insignificant. **3.** *Slang* A stupid person. —**pin′head′ed** *adj.*

pin•hole (pĭn′hōl′) ► *n.* A tiny puncture made by or as if by a pin.

pin•ion[1] (pĭn′yən) ► *n.* A bird's wing. ► *v.* **1.** To restrain or immobilize by binding the wings or arms. **2.** To bind fast, hold down, or fix in one place. [< Lat. *pinna*, feather.]

pin•ion[2] (pĭn′yən) ► *n.* A small cogwheel that engages or is engaged by a larger cogwheel or a rack. [< Lat. *pecten*, comb.]

pink[1] (pĭngk) ► *n.* **1.** A light or pale red. **2.** Any of various plants related to the carnation, often cultivated for their showy, fragrant flowers. **3.** The highest degree of excellence: *in the pink of health.* [?] —**pink** *adj.* —**pink′ish** *adj.*

pink[2] (pĭngk) ► *v.* **1.** To stab lightly; prick. **2.** To decorate with a perforated pattern. **3.** To cut with pinking shears. [ME *pinken*.]

pink•eye (pĭngk′ī′) ► *n.* An acute, very contagious form of conjunctivitis.

pink•ie also **pink•y** (pĭng′kē) ► *n., pl.* **-ies** *Informal* The little finger. [Prob. < Du. *pinkje*.]

pink•ing shears (pĭng′kĭng) ► *pl.n.* Shears with notched blades, used to finish edges of cloth with a zigzag cut for decoration or to prevent raveling or fraying.

pin money ► *n.* Money for incidental expenses.

pin•na•cle (pĭn′ə-kəl) ► *n.* **1.** A small turret or spire on a roof or buttress. **2.** A tall, pointed formation. **3.** The highest point; acme. [< LLat. *pinnāculum*, dim. of Lat. *pinna*, feather.]

pin•nate (pĭn′āt′) ► *adj.* Featherlike, as a compound leaf with leaflets along each side of a stalk. [< Lat. *pinna*, feather.]

pi•noch•le or **pi•noc•le** (pē′nŭk′əl, -nŏk′əl) ► *n.* A card game for two to four persons, played with a deck of 48 cards. [Perh. < Ger. dial. *Binokel*, card game.]

pi•ñon also **pin•yon** (pĭn′yōn′, -yən) ► *n.* Any of several pine trees bearing edible, nutlike seeds. [< Lat. *pīnea*, pine cone.]

pin•point (pĭn′point′) ► *n.* An extremely small thing or spot; particle. ► *v.* To locate, identify, or target with precision.

pin•prick (pĭn′prĭk′) ► *n.* **1.** A slight puncture made by or as if by a pin. **2.** A minor annoyance.

pins and needles (pĭnz) ► *pl.n.* Tingling felt in a part of the body numbed from lack of circulation. —***idiom:* on pins and needles** In a state of tense anticipation.

pin•stripe (pĭn′strīp′) ► *n.* **1.** A thin stripe, esp. on a fabric. **2.** A fabric with pinstripes.

pint (pīnt) ► *n.* **1.** See table at **measurement.** **2.** A unit of volume or capacity used in dry and liquid measure, equal to 0.568 liter. [< VLat. **pīncta*, mark on a container.]

Pin•ter (pĭn′tər), **Harold.** b. 1930. British playwright. —**Pin′ter•esque′** *adj.*

pin•to (pĭn′tō) ► *n., pl.* **-tos** or **-toes.** A horse with patchy spots or markings. [Sp.]

pinto bean ► *n.* A form of the common string bean having mottled seeds.

pint•size (pīnt′sīz′) also **pint•sized** (-sīzd′) ► *adj. Informal* Diminutive.

pin•up (pĭn′ŭp′) ► *n.* A picture that is intended to be displayed on a wall, esp. of a sexually attractive person. —**pin′up′** *adj.*

pin•wheel (pĭn′hwēl′, -wēl′) ►*n.* **1.** A toy consisting of vanes of colored paper or plastic pinned to a stick so that they revolve when blown on. **2.** A firework that forms a rotating wheel of colored flames.

pin•worm (pĭn′wûrm′) ►*n.* Any of various small parasitic nematode worms, esp. one that infests the human intestines and rectum.

pin•y also **pine•y** (pī′nē) ►*adj.* **-i•er, -i•est.** Of or abounding in pines.

Pin•yin or **pin•yin** (pĭn′yĭn′, -yĭn) ►*n.* A system for transliterating Chinese characters into the Roman alphabet.

pin•yon (pĭn′yōn′, -yən) ►*n.* Var. of **piñon.**

pi•on (pī′ŏn′) ►*n.* A semistable subatomic particle in the meson family that exists in neutral, positively charged, or negatively charged forms. [< *pi meson.*]

pi•o•neer (pī′ə-nîr′) ►*n.* **1.** One who ventures into unknown or unclaimed territory to settle. **2.** An innovator, esp. in research and development. [< OFr. *peonier*, foot soldier < Lat. *pēs, ped-*, foot.] —**pi′o•neer′** *v.*

pi•ous (pī′əs) ►*adj.* **1.** Reverently observant of religion; devout. **2.** Marked by false devoutness; solemnly hypocritical: *a pious fraud.* **3.** Devotional: *pious readings.* **4.** High-minded. **5.** Commendable. [< Lat. *pius.*] —**pi′ous•ly** *adv.* —**pi′ous•ness** *n.*

pip[1] (pĭp) ►*n.* A small fruit seed, as that of an apple or orange. [< PIPPIN.]

pip[2] (pĭp) ►*n.* **1.** A dot indicating numerical value on dice or dominoes. **2.** See **blip** 1. [?]

pip[3] (pĭp) ►*n.* **1.** A disease of birds. **2.** *Slang* A minor, unspecified human ailment. [< Lat. *pītuīta.*]

pipe (pīp) ►*n.* **1.** A hollow cylinder or tube used to conduct a liquid, gas, or finely divided solid. **2.** A device for smoking, consisting of a tube of wood, clay, or other material with a small bowl at one end and a mouthpiece at the other. **3.** *Informal* **a.** A tubular part or organ of the body. **b. pipes** The human respiratory system. **4a.** A tubular musical wind instrument, such as a fife. **b.** Any of the tubes in an organ. **5. pipes a.** A small wind instrument, consisting of tubes of different lengths bound together. **b.** A bagpipe. ►*v.* **piped, pip•ing 1.** To convey or transmit by or as if by pipes. **2.** To play (a tune) on a pipe or pipes. **3.** To make a shrill sound. —***phrasal verbs:*** **pipe down** *Slang* To be quiet. **pipe up** To speak up. [< Lat. *pīpāre*, chirp.] —**pip′er** *n.*

pipe dream ►*n.* A fantastic notion or vain hope. [From opium fantasies.]

pipe fitter ►*n.* One that installs and repairs piping systems.

pipe•line (pīp′līn′) ►*n.* **1.** A conduit of pipe for the conveyance of water, gas, or petroleum products. **2.** A channel by which information is privately transmitted. **3.** A line of supply.

pipe organ ►*n. Mus.* See **organ** 1.

pipe•stone (pīp′stōn′) ►*n.* A red or pink clay stone used by Native American peoples for making tobacco pipes.

pi•pette also **pi•pet** (pī-pĕt′) ►*n.* A glass tube open at both ends and usu. graduated, used for transferring or measuring liquids.

pipe wrench ►*n.* A wrench with two serrated jaws, one adjustable, for gripping and turning pipe.

pip•ing (pī′pĭng) ►*n.* **1.** A system of pipes. **2.** Music made by a pipe or pipes. **3.** A narrow band of material, used for trimming a fabric. —***idiom:*** **piping hot** Very hot.

pip•pin (pĭp′ĭn) ►*n.* Any of several varieties of apple. [< OFr. *pepin.*]

pip-squeak (pĭp′skwēk′) ►*n. Informal* One that is small or insignificant.

pi•quant (pē′kənt, -känt′, pē-känt′) ►*adj.* **1.** Pleasantly pungent; spicy. **2.** Appealingly provocative. [< OFr. *piquer*, to prick.] —**pi′quan•cy, pi′quant•ness** *n.*

pique (pēk) ►*n.* Resentment or vexation from wounded pride; huff. ►*v.* **piqued, piqu•ing 1.** To cause to feel resentment. **2.** To provoke; arouse: *The box piqued her curiosity.* [< OFr. *piquer*, to prick.]

pi•qué (pĭ-kā′, pē-) ►*n.* A fabric with various patterns of wales. [< OFr. *piquer*, to prick.]

Pi•rae•us (pī-rē′əs, pĭ-rā′-) A city of E-central Greece SW of Athens. Pop. 196,389.

Pi•ran•del•lo (pîr′ən-dĕl′ō, pē′rän-dĕl′lō), **Luigi.** 1867–1936. Italian writer; 1934 Nobel.

pi•ra•nha also **pi•ra•ña** (pĭ-rän′yə, -răn′yə) ►*n.* A sharp-toothed tropical American freshwater fish that often attacks and destroys living animals. [< Tupi.]

pi•rate (pī′rĭt) ►*n.* **1.** One who robs at sea or plunders the land from the sea. **2.** One who makes use of or reproduces the work of another illicitly or without authorization. [< Gk. *peiratēs.*] —**pi′ra•cy** *n.* —**pi′rate** *v.* —**pi•rat′ic** (-răt′ĭk), **pi•rat′i•cal** *adj.*

pi•rogue (pĭ-rōg′, pîr′ō) ►*n.* A canoe made from a hollowed tree trunk. [< Carib *piragua.*]

pir•ou•ette (pĭr′o͞o-ĕt′) ►*n.* A full turn of the body on the tip of the toe or the ball of the foot, esp. in ballet. [< OFr. *pirouet*, spinning top.] —**pir′ou•ette′** *v.*

Pi•sa (pē′zə, -zä) A city of W Italy on the Arno R. near the Tyrrhenian Sea. Pop. 98,006. —**Pi′san** *adj. & n.*

pis•ca•to•ri•al (pĭs′kə-tôr′ē-əl, -tōr′-) ►*adj.* Relating to fish or fishing. [< Lat. *piscis*, fish.]

Pi•sces (pī′sēz) ►*pl.n. (takes sing. v.)* **1.** A constellation in the equatorial region of the Northern Hemisphere. **2.** The 12th sign of the zodiac.

Pi•sis•tra•tus (pī-sĭs′trə-təs, pĭ-). d. 527 B.C. Athenian tyrant (560–527).

pis•mire (pĭs′mīr′, pĭz′-) ►*n.* An ant. [ME *pissemyre.*]

Pis•sar•ro (pĭ-sär′ō, pē-), **Camille.** 1830–1903. French impressionist painter.

pis•ta•chi•o (pĭ-stăsh′ē-ō′, -stä′shē-ō′) ►*n., pl.* **-os 1.** An Asian tree bearing hard-shelled edible nuts with a green kernel. **2.** The nut of this tree. [< Gk. *pistakē.*]

pis•til (pĭs′təl) ►*n.* The seed-bearing reproductive organ of a flower. [< Lat. *pistillum*, pestle.]

pis•tol (pĭs′təl) ►*n.* A firearm designed to be held and fired with one hand. [< Czech *pišt′ala*, pipe.]

pis•tol-whip (pĭs′təl-hwĭp′, -wĭp′) ►*v.* To beat with a pistol.

pis•ton (pĭs′tən) ►*n.* A solid cylinder or disk that fits snugly into a cylinder and moves back and forth under fluid pressure. [< Ital. *pistone*, large pestle.]

pit[1] (pĭt) ►*n.* **1.** A relatively deep hole in the ground. **2.** A trap or pitfall. **3a.** Hell. **b. the**

pits *Slang* The worst. **4a.** A natural depression in the body or an organ. **b.** A small indented scar left in the skin by disease or injury; pockmark. **5.** An enclosed area in which animals are placed for fighting. **6.** The musicians' section directly in front of the stage of a theater. **7.** The section of an exchange where trading in a specific commodity is carried on. **8.** A refueling area beside an auto racecourse. ►*v.* **pit•ted, pit•ting 1.** To mark or scar with pits. **2.** To set in opposition: *pitted brother against brother.* [< OE *pytt.*]

pit² (pĭt) ►*n.* The single, hard-shelled seed of certain fruits, such as a peach or cherry; stone. ►*v.* **pit•ted, pit•ting.** To extract the pit from (a fruit). [< MDu.]

pi•ta (pē′tə) ►*n.* A round, flat bread that opens to form a pocket for filling. [Mod.Gk., bread.]

pit•a•pat (pĭt′ə-păt′) ►*v.* **-pat•ted, -pat•ting.** To make a repeated tapping sound. ►*n.* A series of quick steps, taps, or beats. [Imit.]

Pit•cairn Island (pĭt′kârn′) A volcanic island of the S Pacific ESE of Tahiti.

pitch¹ (pĭch) ►*n.* Any of various thick, dark, sticky substances obtained from the distillation residue of coal tar, wood tar, or petroleum and used for waterproofing, roofing, caulking, and paving. [< Lat. *pix.*]

pitch² (pĭch) ►*v.* **1.** To throw, usu. with careful aim. **2.** To throw (a baseball) from the mound to the batter. **3.** To put up or in position: *pitched a tent; pitch camp.* **4.** To set firmly; implant. **5.** To fix the level of. **6.** *Mus.* To set at a specified pitch or key. **7.** To hit (a golf ball) in a high arc with backspin. **8.** To fall headlong; plunge. **9.** To dip bow and stern alternately, as a ship in rough seas. —***phrasal verb:* pitch in** *Informal* To set to work vigorously, esp. in cooperation with others. ►*n.* **1.** The act or an instance of pitching. **2a.** A downward slant. **b.** The degree of such a slant, as of the angle of a roof. **3.** A level or degree, as of intensity or development. **4.** Lowness or highness of a complex sound, such as a musical tone, that is dependent primarily on frequency. **5.** *Informal* A line of talk designed to persuade. [ME *pichen.*]

pitch-black (pĭch′blăk′) ►*adj.* Extremely black.

pitch•blende (pĭch′blĕnd′) ►*n.* A brownish-black mineral, the principal ore of uranium. [< Ger. *Pechblende.*]

pitch-dark (pĭch′därk′) ►*adj.* Extremely dark.

pitched roof (pĭcht) ►*n.* A two-sided sloped roof having a gable at both ends.

pitch•er¹ (pĭch′ər) ►*n.* *Baseball* The player who pitches.

pitch•er² (pĭch′ər) ►*n.* A container for liquids, usu. having a handle and a lip or spout for pouring. [< Med.Lat. *bicārium*, drinking cup.]

pitcher plant ►*n.* Any of various insectivorous plants having pitcherlike leaves that attract and trap insects.

pitch•fork (pĭch′fôrk′) ►*n.* A large, long-handled fork with widely spaced prongs for lifting and pitching hay. [< ME *pikforke.*]

pitch pipe ►*n.* A small pipe sounded to give the pitch for a piece of music or for tuning an instrument.

pit•e•ous (pĭt′ē-əs) ►*adj.* Demanding or arousing pity; pathetic: *a piteous appeal for help.* —**pit′e•ous•ness** *n.*

pitchfork

pit•fall (pĭt′fôl′) ►*n.* **1.** An unapparent difficulty or danger. **2.** A concealed hole in the ground that serves as a trap.

pith (pĭth) ►*n.* **1.** The soft, spongelike substance in the center of stems and branches of many plants. **2.** The essential or central part; heart. See Syns at **substance. 3.** Strength; force. [< OE *pitha.*]

pith helmet ►*n.* A lightweight hat of dried pith worn for protection from the sun.

pith•y (pĭth′ē) ►*adj.* **-i•er, -i•est 1.** Precise and meaningful. **2.** Of or resembling pith. —**pith′i•ly** *adv.* —**pith′i•ness** *n.*

pit•i•a•ble (pĭt′ē-ə-bəl) ►*adj.* Arousing pity. —**pit′i•a•ble•ness** *n.* —**pit′i•a•bly** *adv.*

pit•i•ful (pĭt′ĭ-fəl) ►*adj.* **1.** Inspiring, arousing, or deserving pity. **2.** Arousing contemptuous pity, as through ineptitude, inadequacy, or inferiority. —**pit′i•ful•ly** *adv.* —**pit′i•ful•ness** *n.*

pit•i•less (pĭt′ĭ-lĭs) ►*adj.* Having no pity; merciless. —**pit′i•less•ness** *n.*

pi•ton (pē′tŏn′) ►*n.* A spike with an eye or ring for securing a support rope in mountain climbing. [< OFr., nail.]

pit stop ►*n.* **1.** A stop at a pit for refueling or service during an automobile race. **2.** *Informal* A rest stop during a trip.

Pitt¹ (pĭt), **William.** 1st Earl of Chatham. 1708–78. British political leader and orator.

Pitt² (pĭt), **William.** 2nd Earl of Chatham. 1759–1806. British prime minister (1783–1801 and 1804–06).

pit•tance (pĭt′ns) ►*n.* A small amount or portion, esp. of money. [< Med.Lat. *pīetantia*, handout to the poor.]

pit•ter-pat•ter (pĭt′ər-păt′ər) ►*n.* Repeated light, tapping sounds. [Imit.]

Pitts•burgh (pĭts′bûrg′) A city of SW PA at the point where the confluence of the Allegheny and Monongahela rivers forms the Ohio R. Pop. 369,879.

pi•tu•i•tar•y (pĭ-to͞o′ĭ-tĕr′ē, -tyo͞o′-) ►*n.*, *pl.* **-ies.** A small oval endocrine gland attached to the base of the vertebrate brain, the secretions of which control the other endocrine glands and influence growth, metabolism, and maturation. [< Lat. *pītuīta*, phlegm.] —**pi•tu′i•tar′y** *adj.*

pit viper ►*n.* Any of various venomous snakes, such as the rattlesnake, having a small sensory pit below each eye.

pit•y (pĭt′ē) ►*n.*, *pl.* **-ies 1.** Sympathy and sorrow aroused by the misfortune or suffering of another. **2.** A matter of regret: *It's a pity she can't go.* ▸*v.* **-ied, -y•ing.** To feel pity (for). [< Lat. *pietās*, piety.]

Pi•us V (pī′əs), Saint. 1504–72. Pope (1566–72).

Pius IX. 1792–1878. Pope (1846–78).

Pius X, Saint. 1835–1914. Pope (1903–14).

Pius XI. 1857–1939. Pope (1922–39).

Pius XII. 1876–1958. Pope (1939–58).

piv•ot (pĭv′ət) ▸*n.* **1.** A short rod or shaft on which a related part rotates or swings. **2.** One that determines the direction or effect of something. **3.** The act of turning on or as if on a pivot. ▸*v.* To turn or cause to turn on or as if on a pivot. [< OFr.] —**piv′ot•al** *adj.* —**piv′ot•al•ly** *adv.*

pix (pĭks) ▸*n.* Var. of **pyx.**

pix•el (pĭk′səl, -sĕl′) ▸*n.* The basic compositional unit of an image on a television screen or computer monitor. [PIC(TURE) + EL(EMENT).]

pix•ie or **pix•y** (pĭk′sē) ▸*n., pl.* **-ies.** A fairylike or elfin creature. [?] —**pix′y•ish** *adj.*

Pi•zar•ro (pĭ-zär′ō, -sär′-), **Francisco.** 1475?–1541. Spanish explorer.

piz•za (pēt′sə) ▸*n.* An Italian baked pie consisting of a crust covered usu. with seasoned tomato sauce and cheese. [Ital.]

piz•zazz or **piz•zaz** (pĭ-zăz′) ▸*n. Slang* **1.** Dazzling style; flamboyance. **2.** Energy or excitement. [?]

piz•ze•ri•a (pēt′sə-rē′ə) ▸*n.* A place where pizzas are made and sold.

piz•zi•ca•to (pĭt′sĭ-kä′tō) ▸*adj. Mus.* Played by plucking the strings. [Ital.] —**piz′zi•ca′to** *adv.*

pk. ▸*abbr.* **1.** park **2.** also **Pk.** peak **3.** peck

pkg. ▸*abbr.* package

pl. ▸*abbr.* **1.** or **Pl.** place **2.** plural

plac•ard (plăk′ärd′, -ərd) ▸*n.* **1.** A sign or notice for public display. **2.** A nameplate, as on a door. [< OFr., official document.] —**plac′ard** *v.*

pla•cate (plā′kāt′, plăk′āt′) ▸*v.* **-cat•ed, -cat•ing.** To allay the anger of; appease. [Lat. *plācāre.*] —**plac′a•ble** *adj.* —**pla•ca′tion** *n.*

place (plās) ▸*n.* **1.** An area with or without definite boundaries; a portion of space. **2.** An area occupied by or allocated to a person or thing. **3.** A definite location. **4.** often **Place** A public square or short street in a town. **5.** A table setting. **6.** A position regarded as belonging to someone or something else; stead: *She was chosen in his place.* **7.** Relative position in a series; standing: *fourth place.* ▸*v.* **placed, plac•ing 1.** To put in or as if in a particular position; set. **2.** To put or rank in a specified relation, order, or sequence. **3.** To appoint to a post. **4a.** To give an order for: *place a bet.* **b.** To arrange for; make: *place a telephone call.* **5.** To arrive among the first three finishers in a race, esp. to finish second. —***idiom:*** **in place of** Instead of. [< Gk. *plateia (hodos)*, broad (street).]

pla•ce•bo (plə-sē′bō) ▸*n., pl.* **-bos** or **-boes 1.** A substance containing no medication, administered for its psychological effect on a patient. **2.** An inactive substance used as a control in an experiment. [< LLat. *placēbō*, I shall please.]

place kick ▸*n. Football* A kick, as for a field goal, for which the ball is held or propped up in a fixed position. —**place′kick′** *v.*

place mat ▸*n.* A protective table mat for a single setting of dishes and flatware.

place•ment (plās′mənt) ▸*n.* **1a.** The act of placing or arranging. **b.** The state of being placed or arranged. **2.** The finding of jobs, lodgings, or other positions for applicants.

pla•cen•ta (plə-sĕn′tə) ▸*n., pl.* **-tas** or **-tae** (-tē). A membranous vascular organ that develops in female mammals during pregnancy, lining the uterine wall and partially enveloping the fetus, to which it is attached by the umbilical cord. [< Lat., flat cake.] —**pla•cen′tal** *adj.*

plac•er (plăs′ər) ▸*n.* A sand or gravel deposit left by a river or glacier, containing particles of valuable minerals. [Sp. < Med.Lat. *placea*, PLACE.]

plac•id (plăs′ĭd) ▸*adj.* Undisturbed by tumult or disorder; calm or composed. [< Lat. *placēre*, please.] —**pla•cid′i•ty** (plə-sĭd′ĭ-tē), **plac′id•ness** *n.* —**plac′id•ly** *adv.*

plack•et (plăk′ĭt) ▸*n.* A slit in a dress, blouse, or skirt. [?]

pla•gia•rize (plā′jə-rīz′) ▸*v.* **-rized, -riz•ing.** To use and pass off as one's own (the ideas or writings of another). [< Lat. *plagiārius*, kidnapper.] —**pla′gia•rism, pla′gia•ry** *n.* —**pla′gia•rist, pla′gia•riz′er** *n.*

plague (plāg) ▸*n.* **1.** A widespread affliction or calamity. **2.** A cause of annoyance; nuisance. **3.** A highly infectious, usu. fatal epidemic disease, esp. bubonic plague. ▸*v.* **plagued, plagu•ing.** To harass, pester, or annoy. [< Lat. *plāga*, blow, calamity.]

plaid (plăd) ▸*n.* **1.** A rectangular woolen scarf of a checked or tartan pattern worn over the left shoulder by Scottish Highlanders. **2.** A pattern of this kind, esp. in cloth. [Sc.Gael. *plaide.*] —**plaid** *adj.*

plain (plān) ▸*adj.* **-er, -est 1.** Free from obstructions; open to view; clear. **2.** Easily understood; clearly evident. See Syns at **apparent. 3.** Uncomplicated; simple. **4.** Straightforward. **5.** Not mixed with other substances; pure. **6.** Common in rank or station; ordinary. **7.** Not pretentious or affected. **8.** Having little or no ornamentation or decoration. **9.** Unattractive. ▸*n.* An extensive, level, usu. treeless area of land. ▸*adv. Informal* Clearly; simply. [< Lat. *plānus*, flat.] —**plain′ly** *adv.* —**plain′ness** *n.*

Syns: *plain, modest, simple, unostentatious, unpretentious* **Ant:** *ornate* **adj.**

plain•clothes (plān′klōz′, -klōthz′) ▸*adj.* Wearing civilian clothes while on duty to avoid being identified as police or security.

plain•clothes man or **plain•clothes•man** (plān′klōz′mən, -klōthz′-) ▸*n.* A member of a police force, esp. a detective, who wears civilian clothes on duty.

Plains Indian (plānz) ▸*n.* A member of any of the Native American peoples inhabiting the Great Plains of North America.

plain•song (plān′sông′, -sŏng′) ▸*n.* Medieval liturgical music traditionally sung without accompaniment.

plain•spo•ken (plān′spō′kən) ▸*adj.* Frank; straightforward. —**plain′spo′ken•ness** *n.*

plaint (plānt) ▸*n.* **1.** A complaint. **2.** A lamentation. [< Lat. *plangere, plānct-*, lament.]

plain•tiff (plān′tĭf) ▸*n. Law* The party instituting a suit in a court. [< OFr. *plaintif*, aggrieved.]

plain•tive (plān′tĭv) ►*adj.* Expressing sorrow; mournful or melancholy. —**plain′tive•ly** *adv.* —**plain′tive•ness** *n.*

plait (plāt, plăt) ►*n.* A braid, esp. of hair. ►*v.* To braid. [< Lat. *plicāre*, fold.]

plan (plăn) ►*n.* **1.** A detailed scheme or method for the accomplishment of an objective. **2.** A proposed or tentative project or goal. **3.** An outline or sketch, esp. a drawing or diagram made to scale. ►*v.* **planned, plan•ning 1.** To formulate, draw up, or make a plan or plans. **2.** To intend. [< Lat. *plantāre*, to plant.] —**plan′ner** *n.*

Syns: *plan, blueprint, design, project, scheme, strategy* **n.**

pla•nar (plā′nər, -när′) ►*adj.* **1.** Of or in a plane. **2.** Flat. —**pla•nar′i•ty** (plā-năr′ĭ-tē) *n.*

Planck (plängk), **Max Karl Ernst Ludwig.** 1858–1947. German physicist; 1918 Nobel.

plane¹ (plān) ►*n.* **1.** A surface containing all the straight lines that connect any two points on it. **2.** A flat or level surface. **3.** A level of development. **4.** An airplane. **5.** A supporting surface of an airplane. ►*adj.* Of or being a figure lying in a plane. [Lat. *plānum*.]

plane² (plān) ►*n.* A carpenter's tool for smoothing and leveling wood. [< Lat. *plānus*, flat.] —**plane** *v.* —**plan′er** *n.*

plane³ (plān) ►*n.* A plane tree. [< Gk. *platanos*.]

plane geometry ►*n.* The geometry of two-dimensional figures.

plan•et (plăn′ĭt) ►*n.* A nonluminous celestial body that revolves around a star. [< Gk. *planētēs*, wanderer.]

plan•e•tar•i•um (plăn′ĭ-târ′ē-əm) ►*n., pl.* **-i•ums** or **-i•a** (-ē-ə) **1.** An apparatus or model representing the solar system. **2a.** A device for projecting images of celestial bodies onto the inner surface of a dome. **b.** A building housing such a device.

plan•e•tar•y (plăn′ĭ-tĕr′ē) ►*adj.* **1.** Of or resembling a planet. **2.** Worldwide; global.

plane tree ►*n.* A sycamore or related tree having ball-shaped seed clusters and usu. bark that flakes off in patches.

plan•gent (plăn′jənt) ►*adj.* **1.** Loud and resounding. **2.** Plaintive. [< Lat. *plangere*, strike.] —**plan′gen•cy** *n.*

plank (plăngk) ►*n.* **1.** A thick piece of lumber. **2.** One of the articles of a political platform. ►*v.* **1.** To cover with planks. **2.** To bake or broil and serve (fish or meat) on a board. **3.** To put or set down with force. [< LLat. *plancus*, flat.]

plank•ton (plăngk′tən) ►*n.* Small or microscopic plant or animal organisms that float in bodies of water. [< Gk. *planktos*, wandering.] —**plank•ton′ic** (-tŏn′ĭk) *adj.*

Pla•no (plā′nō) A city of NE TX, a suburb of Dallas. Pop. 128,713.

plant (plănt) ►*n.* **1.** *Bot.* **a.** An organism characteristically having cellulose cell walls, growing by synthesis of inorganic substances, and lacking the power of locomotion. **b.** A plant having no permanent woody stem, as distinguished from a tree or shrub. **2.** A factory. **3.** The buildings, equipment, and fixtures of an institution. ►*v.* **1.** To place in the ground to grow. **2.** To sow or supply with or as if with seeds or plants. **3.** To fix or set firmly in position. **4.** To establish or found. **5.** To implant in the mind. **6.** To (place) for the purpose of spying, deception, or influencing behavior. [< Lat. *planta*, shoot.] —**plant′a•ble** *adj.*

plan•tain¹ (plăn′tən) ►*n.* A weedy plant with a dense spike of small greenish or whitish flowers. [< Lat. *plantāgō*.]

plan•tain² (plăn′tən) ►*n.* A bananalike tropical plant or its fruit. [Sp. *plátano*, plane tree.]

plan•ta•tion (plăn-tā′shən) ►*n.* **1.** A group of cultivated trees or plants. **2.** A large estate or farm on which crops are raised and harvested, often by resident workers.

plant•er (plăn′tər) ►*n.* **1.** One that plants. **2.** The owner or manager of a plantation. **3.** A decorative container for a plant.

plaque (plăk) ►*n.* **1.** An ornamented or engraved plate, slab, or disk used for decoration or on a monument for information. **2.** A small ornament or badge of membership. **3.** A deposit that builds up on a tooth or the inner lining of a blood vessel. [< OFr., metal plate.]

plash (plăsh) ►*n.* A light splash or the sound it makes. [Poss. < OE *plæsc*, pool of water.]

-plasm ►*suff.* Material forming cells or tissue: *cytoplasm.* [< PLASMA.]

plas•ma (plăz′mə) ►*n.* **1.** The clear yellowish fluid portion of blood, lymph, or intramuscular fluid in which cells are suspended. **2.** Protoplasm or cytoplasm. **3.** Whey. **4.** *Phys.* An electrically neutral, highly ionized gas composed of ions, electrons, and neutral particles. [< Gk., image.] —**plas•mat′ic** (-măt′ĭk), **plas′mic** *adj.*

plas•min (plăz′mĭn) ►*n.* An enzyme in plasma that dissolves fibrin and other blood clotting factors.

plasmo– or **plasm–** ►*pref.* Plasma: *plasmin.*

plas•mol•y•sis (plăz-mŏl′ĭ-sĭs) ►*n., pl.* **-ses** (-sēz′). Shrinkage or contraction of the protoplasm in a cell, esp. a plant cell, caused by loss of water through osmosis. —**plas′mo•lyt′ic** (-mə-lĭt′ĭk) *adj.*

plas•ter (plăs′tər) ►*n.* **1.** A paste that hardens to a smooth solid and is used for coating walls and ceilings. **2.** Plaster of Paris. **3.** A pastelike mixture applied to a part of the body, as for healing. ►*v.* **1.** To cover with or as if with plaster. **2.** To cover conspicuously or to excess. [< Gk. *emplastron*, medical dressing.] —**plas′ter•er** *n.*

plas•ter•board (plăs′tər-bôrd′, -bōrd′) ►*n.* A rigid board made of layers of fiberboard or paper bonded to a plaster core, used in construction to form walls.

plaster of Paris ►*n.* A quick-setting paste of white gypsum powder and water, used esp. for casts and statuary molds.

plas•tic (plăs′tĭk) ►*adj.* **1.** Capable of being shaped or formed: *plastic material such as clay.* **2.** Relating to or dealing with shaping or modeling. **3.** Made of a plastic. ►*n.* **1.** Any of various complex organic compounds produced by polymerization, capable of being molded, extruded, cast into various shapes and films, or drawn into filaments used as textile fibers. **2.** *Informal* A credit card or credit cards. [< Gk. *plassein*, mold.] —**plas′ti•cal•ly** *adv.* —**plas•tic′i•ty** (plăs-tĭs′ĭ-tē) *n.* —**plas′ti•cize** (-tĭ-sīz′) *v.*

plastic explosive ►*n.* A versatile explosive substance in the form of a moldable doughlike solid.

plastic surgery ►*n.* Surgery to remodel, repair, or restore injured or defective tissue or body parts. —**plastic surgeon** *n.*

plas•tid (plăs′tĭd) ►*n.* Any of several pigmented organelles found in plant cells and having various functions, such as the synthesis and storage of food. [< Gk. *plastos*, molded.]

plas•tique (plă-stēk′) ►*n.* See **plastic explosive.** [Fr.]

plat. ►*abbr.* **1.** plateau **2.** platoon

Pla•ta (plä′tə, -tä), **Río de la.** A wide estuary of SE South America between Argentina and Uruguay formed by the Paraná and Uruguay rivers.

plate (plāt) ►*n.* **1.** A smooth, flat, relatively thin, rigid body of uniform thickness. **2a.** A sheet of hammered, rolled, or cast metal. **b.** A flat piece of metal on which something is engraved. **3.** *Print.* **a.** A sheet of material converted into a printing surface, such as an electrotype. **b.** An impression taken from such a surface. **c.** A full-page book illustration, often in color. **4.** A light-sensitive sheet of glass or metal on which a photographic image can be recorded. **5.** A thin metallic or plastic support fitted to the gums to anchor artificial teeth. **6.** *Baseball* Home plate. **7.** A shallow dish from which food is served or eaten. **8.** Service and food for one person at a meal. **9.** Household articles or utensils made of or with a precious metal. **10.** *Geol.* In plate tectonics, one of the large sections into which the earth's crust is divided. ►*v.* **plat•ed, plat•ing 1.** To cover with a thin layer of metal. **2.** To armor. [< Gk. *platus*, flat.] —**plat′ed** *adj.*

pla•teau (plă-tō′) ►*n.*, *pl.* **-teaus** or **-teaux** (-tōz′) **1.** An elevated, level expanse of land; tableland. **2.** A stable level, period, or state. [< OFr. *platel*, platter.]

plate glass ►*n.* A strong rolled and polished glass used for mirrors and large windows.

plate•let (plāt′lĭt) ►*n.* A protoplasmic disk found in the blood plasma of mammals that promotes blood clotting.

plat•en (plăt′n) ►*n.* **1.** The roller on a typewriter or computer printer. **2.** A flat metal plate in a printing press that positions the paper and holds it against the inked type. [< OFr. *platine*, metal plate.]

plate tectonics ►*n.* A theory that the earth's crust is made up of semirigid sections whose movement has resulted in seismic and volcanic activity and continental drift.

plat•form (plăt′fôrm′) ►*n.* **1.** A horizontal surface higher than an adjacent area. **2.** A formal declaration of the policy of a group, as of a political party. **3.** The basic technology of a computer system's hardware and software that defines how a computer is operated. [< OFr. *plate-forme*, diagram.]

Plath (plăth), **Sylvia.** 1932–63. Amer. writer.

plat•ing (plā′tĭng) ►*n.* **1.** A thin layer or coating of metal, such as gold or silver. **2.** A covering or layer of metal plates.

plat•i•num (plăt′n-əm) ►*n.* **1.** *Symbol* **Pt** A malleable, silver-white, corrosion-resistant metallic element used in electrical components, jewelry, and dentistry. At. no. 78. See table at **element. 2.** A medium to light gray. [< Sp. *platina* < *plata*, silver.]

plat•i•tude (plăt′ĭ-to͞od′, -tyo͞od′) ►*n.* A trite remark or idea. See Syns at **cliché.** [Fr. < *plat*, flat.] —**plat′i•tu′di•nous** *adj.*

Pla•to (plā′tō). 427?–347? B.C. Greek philosopher.

Pla•ton•ic (plə-tŏn′ĭk, plā-) ►*adj.* **1.** Of or characteristic of Plato or his philosophy. **2.** often **platonic** Transcending physical desire; spiritual. —**Pla•ton′i•cal•ly** *adv.*

pla•toon (plə-to͞on′) ►*n.* **1.** A subdivision of a military company usu. consisting of two or more squads. **2.** A group of people working together. [< OFr. *peloton.*]

Platte (plăt) A river, about 499 km (310 mi), of central NE flowing to the Missouri R. at the IA border.

plat•ter (plăt′ər) ►*n.* **1.** A large shallow dish or plate. **2.** *Slang* A phonograph record. [< OFr. *plate*, PLATE.]

plat•y•pus (plăt′ĭ-pəs) ►*n.*, *pl.* **-pus•es.** A semiaquatic, egg-laying Australian mammal with webbed feet and a snout like a duck's bill. [< Gk. *platupous*, flat-footed : *platus*, flat + *pous*, foot.]

platypus

plau•dit (plô′dĭt) ►*n.* An expression of praise or approval. [< Lat. *plaudere*, applaud.]

plau•si•ble (plô′zə-bəl) ►*adj.* Apparently true or likely. [< Lat. *plaudere*, *plaus-*, applaud.] —**plau′si•bil′i•ty, plau′si•ble•ness** *n.*

Syns: *plausible, believable, credible* ***Ant:*** *implausible* ***adj.***

Plau•tus (plô′təs), **Titus Maccius.** 254?–184 B.C. Roman comic playwright.

play (plā) ►*v.* **1.** To occupy oneself in amusement, sport, or other recreation. **2.** To act in jest. **3.** To behave carelessly; toy. See Syns at **flirt. 4.** To act in a specified way: *play fair.* **5a.** To engage in (a game or sport). **b.** To compete against in a game or sport. **c.** To occupy (a position) in a game or sport. **d.** To use (a card, piece, or ball) in a game or sport. **6a.** To act or perform (a role). **b.** To pretend to be: *play cowboy.* **7.** To be performed, as a theatrical work. **8.** *Mus.* **a.** To perform on (an instrument). **b.** To perform (a piece). **9.** To perform or put into effect: *play a joke.* **10.** To manipulate: *played the rivals against each other.* **11.** To cause (e.g., a recorded tape) to emit sound. **12.** To move lightly or irregularly: *The breeze played on the water.* **13.** To bet or wager. —***phrasal verbs:*** **play back** To replay (e.g., a recorded tape). **play down** To minimize the importance of. **play on** (or **upon**) To take advantage of (another's feelings). **play up** To emphasize or publicize. ►*n.* **1a.** A literary work for the stage. **b.** The performance of such a work. **2.** Activity engaged in for enjoyment or recreation. **3.** Fun. **4.** The act or manner of playing a game or sport. **5.** A move in a game: *a close play.* **6.** Manner or conduct: *fair play.* **7.** Action or use:

the play of the imagination. **8.** Freedom for action; scope. See Syns at **room. 9.** Free movement, as of mechanical parts. —***idioms:* in play** *Sports* In a position to be legitimately played. **play ball** *Slang* To cooperate. **play both ends against the middle** To set opponents against one another so as to advance one's goals. **play fast and loose** To behave irresponsibly or deceitfully. **play up to** To curry favor with. **play with fire** To take part in a dangerous or risky undertaking. [< OE *plegian.*] —**play′a•ble** *adj.*

pla•ya (plī′ə) ►*n.* A flat area at the bottom of a desert basin, sometimes temporarily covered with water. [Sp. < LLat. *plagia*, shore.]

play-act (plā′ăkt′) ►*v.* **1.** To play a role in a dramatic performance. **2.** To make believe. **3.** To behave affectedly or artificially.

play•back (plā′băk′) ►*n.* The act or process of replaying a recording.

play•bill (plā′bĭl′) ►*n.* A poster announcing a theatrical performance.

play•boy (plā′boi′) ►*n.* A man devoted to the pursuit of pleasure.

play-by-play (plā′bī-plā′) ►*adj.* Being a detailed running commentary, as of the action of a sports event. —**play′-by-play′** *n.*

play•er (plā′ər) ►*n.* **1.** One who participates in a game or sport. **2.** An actor. **3.** A musician. **4.** A device for reproducing recorded sound or images: *a CD player.*

player piano ►*n.* A mechanically operated piano that uses a perforated paper roll to actuate and control the keys.

play•ful (plā′fəl) ►*adj.* **1.** Full of fun; frolicsome. **2.** Humorous; jesting. —**play′ful•ly** *adv.* —**play′ful•ness** *n.*

play•girl (plā′gûrl′) ►*n.* A woman devoted to the pursuit of pleasure.

play•go•er (plā′gō′ər) ►*n.* One who attends the theater. —**play′go′ing** *n.*

play•ground (plā′ground′) ►*n.* An outdoor area for recreation and play.

play•ing card (plā′ĭng) ►*n.* A card marked with its rank and suit belonging to a deck and used in playing various games.

play•mate (plā′māt′) ►*n.* A companion in play.

play•off also **play-off** (plā′ôf′, -ŏf′) ►*n.* A final game or series of games played to determine a championship or break a tie.

play•pen (plā′pĕn′) ►*n.* A portable enclosure in which a baby can be left to play.

play•room (plā′ro͞om′, -ro͝om′) ►*n.* A room designed for recreation or play.

play•thing (plā′thĭng′) ►*n.* A toy.

play•wright (plā′rīt′) ►*n.* One who writes plays.

pla•za (plä′zə, plăz′ə) ►*n.* **1.** A public square or similar open area in a town or city. **2.** A parking or service area next to a highway. **3.** A shopping center. [< Lat. *platea*, broad street. See PLACE.]

plea (plē) ►*n.* **1.** An earnest request; appeal. **2.** An excuse; pretext. **3.** *Law* The answer of the accused to a charge or indictment. [< LLat. *placitum*, decree.]

plea-bar•gain (plē′bär′gən) ►*v.* *Law* To make an agreement to plead guilty to a lesser charge so as to avoid being tried for a more serious one. —**plea′-bar′gain•ing** *n.*

plead (plēd) ►*v.* **plead•ed** or **pled** (plĕd), **plead•ing 1.** To appeal earnestly; beg. **2.** To argue for or against something. **3.** To put forward a plea in a court of law. **4.** To assert or submit as an excuse or defense. **5.** To argue or present (a case) in a court of law. [< LLat. *placitum*, decree.] —**plead′er** *n.* —**plead′ing•ly** *adv.*

Usage: In strict legal usage, one is said to *plead guilty* or *plead not guilty* but not to *plead innocent.* In nonlegal contexts, however, *plead innocent* is well established.

pleas•ant (plĕz′ənt) ►*adj.* **-er, -est 1.** Pleasing or agreeable; delightful. **2.** Pleasing in manner; amiable. —**pleas′ant•ness** *n.*

pleas•ant•ry (plĕz′ən-trē) ►*n.*, *pl.* **-ries.** A pleasant or humorous remark.

please (plēz) ►*v.* **pleased, pleas•ing 1.** To give enjoyment or satisfaction (to). **2.** To be the will or desire of: *may it please the court.* **3.** To be willing to. **4.** To like; wish. [< Lat. *placēre.*] —**pleas′ing** *adj.*

Syns: *please, delight, gladden, gratify, tickle*
Ant: *displease* **v.**

pleas•ur•a•ble (plĕzh′ər-ə-bəl) ►*adj.* Agreeable; gratifying. —**pleas′ur•a•bly** *adv.*

pleas•ure (plĕzh′ər) ►*n.* **1.** Enjoyment or satisfaction. **2.** A source of enjoyment. **3.** One's preference, wish, or choice.

pleat (plēt) ►*n.* A fold in cloth made by doubling the material upon itself. [< PLAIT.] —**pleat** *v.*

plebe (plēb) ►*n.* A freshman at a military academy. [Prob. < PLEBEIAN.]

ple•be•ian (plĭ-bē′ən) ►*adj.* Common or vulgar: *plebeian tastes.* ►*n.* One who is common and crude. [< Lat. *plēbs*, common people.]

pleb•i•scite (plĕb′ĭ-sīt′, -sĭt) ►*n.* A direct vote by the entire electorate on an important issue. [< Lat. *plēbiscītum.*]

plebs (plĕbz) ►*n.*, *pl.* **ple•bes** (plē′bēz) **1.** The common people of ancient Rome. **2.** The populace. [Lat. *plēbs.*]

plec•trum (plĕk′trəm) ►*n.*, *pl.* **-trums** or **-tra** (-trə). A thin piece of metal, plastic, or similar material, used to pluck the strings of certain musical instruments, such as the guitar or harpsichord. [< Gk. *plēktron.*]

pled (plĕd) ►*v.* P.t. and p.part of **plead.**

pledge (plĕj) ►*n.* **1.** A formal promise. **2.** Something considered as security to guarantee payment of a debt or obligation. **3.** One who has been accepted for membership in a club, fraternity, or sorority. ►*v.* **pledged, pledg•ing 1.** To promise solemnly. See Syns at **promise. 2.** To bind by or as if by a pledge. **3.** To deposit as security. **4.** To promise to join (e.g., a club). [Prob. < LLat. *plevium.*] —**pledg′er** *n.*

Ple•ia•des (plē′ə-dēz′, plī′-) ►*pl.n.* An open star cluster in the constellation Taurus, consisting of several hundred stars, of which six are visible to the naked eye.

Pleis•to•cene (plī′stə-sēn′) *Geol.* ►*adj.* Of or being the 1st epoch of the Quaternary Period, marked by the appearance of humans. ►*n.* The Pleistocene Epoch. [Gk. *pleistos*, most + -CENE.]

ple•na•ry (plē′nə-rē, plĕn′ə-) ►*adj.* **1.** Unlimited or full: *a diplomat with plenary powers.* **2.** Fully attended by all qualified members. [< Lat. *plēnus*, full.] —**ple′na•ri•ly** *adv.*

plen•i•po•ten•ti•ar•y (plĕn′ə-pə-tĕn′shē-ĕr′-

ē, -shə-rē) ▸*adj.* Invested with full powers. ▸*n., pl.* **-ies.** A diplomatic agent fully authorized to represent his or her government. [< LLat. *plēnipotēns.*]

plen•i•tude (plĕn′ĭ-to͞od′, -tyo͞od′) ▸*n.* An abundance; fullness. [< Lat. *plēnus*, full.]

plen•te•ous (plĕn′tē-əs) ▸*adj.* **1.** Abundant; copious. **2.** Producing or yielding in abundance. See Syns at **plentiful.**

plen•ti•ful (plĕn′tĭ-fəl) ▸*adj.* **1.** Existing in great quantity or ample supply. **2.** Providing or producing an abundance. —**plen′ti•ful•ly** *adv.* —**plen′ti•ful•ness** *n.*

Syns: *plentiful, abundant, ample, copious, plenteous* ***Ant:*** *scant* ***adj.***

plen•ty (plĕn′tē) ▸*n.* **1.** A full or more than adequate amount: *plenty of time; goods in plenty.* **2.** A condition of general abundance or prosperity. ▸*adv. Informal* Sufficiently: *It's plenty hot.* [< Lat. *plēnitās.*]

ple•si•o•saur (plē′sē-ə-sôr′, plē′zē-) also **ple•si•o•sau•rus** (plē′sē-ə-sôr′əs, plē′zē-) ▸*n.* A large extinct marine reptile of the Mesozoic Era having paddlelike limbs. [Gk. *plēsios*, near to + *sauros*, lizard.]

pleth•o•ra (plĕth′ər-ə) ▸*n.* A superabundance; excess. [< Gk. *plēthōra.*]

pleu•ri•sy (plo͝or′ĭ-sē) ▸*n.* Inflammation of the membranous sacs that enclose the lungs. [< Gk. *pleura*, rib, side.]

Plex•i•glas (plĕk′sĭ-glăs′) ▸ A trademark for a light, transparent, strong thermoplastic.

plex•us (plĕk′səs) ▸*n., pl.* **-us** or **-us•es.** A structure in the form of a network, esp. of nerves, blood vessels, or lymphatics. [< Lat. *plectere, plect-*, plait.]

plf. ▸*abbr.* plaintiff

pli•a•ble (plī′ə-bəl) ▸*adj.* **1.** Easily bent or shaped. **2.** Easily influenced, persuaded, or swayed. [< OFr. *plier*, bend.] —**pli′a•bil′i•ty, pli′a•ble•ness** *n.* —**pli′a•bly** *adv.*

pli•ant (plī′ənt) ▸*adj.* **1.** Easily bent or flexed. **2.** Receptive to change; adaptable. [< OFr. *plier*, fold, bend.] —**pli′an•cy** *n.*

pli•ers (plī′ərz) ▸*pl.n.* A tool having a pair of pivoted jaws, used for holding, bending, or cutting.

plight[1] (plīt) ▸*n.* A difficult or adverse situation. [< Lat. *plicitum*, a wrinkle.]

plight[2] (plīt) ▸*v.* To promise or bind by a solemn pledge, esp. to betroth. [< OE *pliht*, risk.] —**plight′er** *n.*

plinth (plĭnth) ▸*n.* A block or slab on which a pedestal, column, or statue is placed. [< Gk. *plinthos*, tile.]

Plin•y[1] (plĭn′ē). "the Elder." A.D. 23–79. Roman scholar and naturalist.

Plin•y[2] (plĭn′ē). "the Younger." A.D. 62?–113? Roman consul and writer.

Pli•o•cene (plī′ə-sēn′) *Geol.* ▸*adj.* Of or being the 5th and last epoch of the Tertiary Period, marked by the appearance of modern animals. ▸*n.* The Pliocene Epoch. [Gk. *pleiōn*, more + –CENE.]

PLO ▸*abbr.* Palestine Liberation Organization

plod (plŏd) ▸*v.* **plod•ded, plod•ding 1.** To walk heavily or laboriously; trudge. **2.** To work or act in a persevering or monotonous way; drudge. [Perh. imit.] —**plod′der** *n.*

plop (plŏp) ▸*v.* **plopped, plop•ping 1.** To fall with a sound like that of an object falling into water without splashing. **2.** To drop or set heavily. [Imit.] —**plop** *n. & adv.*

plot (plŏt) ▸*n.* **1.** A small piece of ground. **2.** The pattern of events or main story in a narrative or drama. **3.** A secret plan; scheme. ▸*v.* **plot•ted, plot•ting 1.** To represent graphically, as on a chart. **2.** To conspire. [< OE.] —**plot′ter** *n.*

plough (plou) ▸*n. & v.* Var. of **plow.**

Plov•div (plôv′dĭf′) A city of S-central Bulgaria SE of Sofia. Pop. 341,374.

plov•er (plŭv′ər, plō′vər) ▸*n., pl.* **-er** or **-ers.** Any of various smallish, short-billed wading birds. [< Lat. *pluvia*, rain < *pluere*, to rain.]

plow also **plough** (plou) ▸*n.* **1.** A farm implement used for breaking up soil and cutting furrows. **2.** An implement of similar function, such as a snowplow. ▸*v.* **1.** To break and turn over (earth) with a plow. **2.** To move or progress with driving force: *plowed through the crowd.* —***phrasal verbs:*** **plow back** To reinvest (e.g., profits) in one's business. **plow into** *Informal* To strike with force. **plow under** To overwhelm. [< OE *plōh*, plow, plowland.] —**plow′a•ble** *adj.* —**plow′er** *n.*

plow•share (plou′shâr′) ▸*n.* The cutting blade of a plow.

ploy (ploi) ▸*n.* A strategem to gain an advantage. [?]

pluck (plŭk) ▸*v.* **1.** To pull off or out; pick. **2.** To pull out the hair or feathers of. **3.** *Mus.* To sound (the strings of an instrument) by pulling and releasing them. ▸*n.* **1.** The act or an instance of plucking. **2.** Resourceful courage; spirit. [< OE *pluccian.*]

pluck•y (plŭk′ē) ▸*adj.* **-i•er, -i•est.** Courageous; brave. —**pluck′i•ness** *n.*

plug (plŭg) ▸*n.* **1.** An object used to fill a hole tightly; stopper. **2a.** A fitting, usu. with metal prongs for insertion in a fixed socket, used to make electrical connections. **b.** A spark plug. **3.** A hydrant. **4.** A piece of chewing tobacco. **5.** *Informal* A favorable public mention, esp. of a person or product. **6.** *Slang* An old, worn-out horse. **7.** An artificial fishing lure. ▸*v.* **plugged, plug•ging 1.** To fill (a hole) tightly with or as if with a plug. **2.** *Slang* To hit with a bullet. **3.** *Informal* To make favorable public mention of (e.g., a product). **4.** *Informal* To work doggedly and persistently. —***phrasal verb:*** **plug in** To connect to an electrical outlet by means of a plug. [< MDu. *plugge.*]

plug-in (plŭg′ĭn′) ▸*n.* See **add-in** 2.

plum (plŭm) ▸*n.* **1a.** A smooth-skinned, fleshy, edible fruit with a hard-shelled pit. **b.** A tree bearing such fruit. **2.** An especially desirable position, assignment, or reward. [< Lat. *prūnum.*] —**plum′my** *adj.*

plum•age (plo͞o′mĭj) ▸*n.* The feathers of a bird.

plumb (plŭm) ▸*n.* **1.** A weight on the end of a line, used to determine water depth. **2.** Such a device used to establish true vertical. ▸*adv.* **1.** Straight up and down. **2.** *Informal* Directly; squarely. **3.** *Informal* Utterly; completely: *plumb worn out.* ▸*adj.* **1.** Exactly vertical. **2.** *Informal* Utter; sheer: *a plumb fool.* ▸*v.* **1.** To determine the depth of; sound. **2.** To test the alignment or angle of with a plumb. [< Lat. *plumbum*, lead.] —**plumb′a•ble** *adj.*

plumb•er (plŭm′ər) ▸*n.* One who installs and repairs pipes and plumbing.

plumb•ing (plŭm′ĭng) ▸*n.* **1.** The pipes, fixtures, and other apparatus of a water or sewage system in a building. **2.** The work or trade of a plumber.

plumb line ▸*n.* A line from which a weight is suspended to determine verticality or depth.

plume (plo͞om) ▸*n.* **1.** A feather, esp. a large and showy one. **2.** Something that resembles a long feather: *a plume of smoke.* ▸*v.* **plumed, plum•ing 1.** To decorate with or as if with plumes. **2.** To pride (oneself) in a self-satisfied way. [< Lat. *plūma.*]

plum•met (plŭm′ĭt) ▸*v.* To fall or drop straight down. [< Lat. *plumbum,* lead.]

plump[1] (plŭmp) ▸*adj.* **-er, -est.** Well-rounded and full in form; chubby. ▸*v.* To make or become plump. [Prob. < MLGer. *plomp,* thick.] —**plump′ness** *n.*

plump[2] (plŭmp) ▸*v.* **1.** To drop abruptly or heavily. **2.** To give full support or praise. ▸*n.* **1.** A heavy or abrupt fall. **2.** The sound of such a fall. ▸*adv.* **1.** With a heavy or abrupt drop. **2.** Straight down. [< MLGer. *plumpen.*]

plun•der (plŭn′dər) ▸*v.* To rob of goods by force, esp. in time of war; pillage. ▸*n.* Property stolen by fraud or force. [< MLGer., household goods.] —**plun′der•er** *n.*

plunge (plŭnj) ▸*v.* **plunged, plung•ing 1.** To thrust or throw forcefully into a substance or place. **2.** To enter or cast suddenly into a given state, situation, or activity. **3.** To descend steeply or suddenly. **4.** To speculate or gamble extravagantly. [< VLat. **plumbicāre,* heave a sounding lead.] —**plunge** *n.*

plung•er (plŭn′jər) ▸*n.* **1.** A device consisting of a rubber suction cup attached to the end of a stick, used to unclog drains and pipes. **2.** A machine part that operates with a thrusting or plunging movement.

plunk (plŭngk) ▸*v.* **1.** To throw, place, or drop heavily or abruptly. **2.** To strum or pluck (a stringed instrument). **3.** To emit a hollow, twanging sound. [Imit.] —**plunk** *n.*

plu•per•fect (plo͞o-pûr′fĭkt) ▸*adj.* Of or relating to a verb tense used to express action completed before a specified or implied past time. ▸*n.* **1.** The pluperfect tense. **2.** A verb or form in this tense. [< Lat. *plūs quam perfectum,* more than perfect.]

plu•ral (plo͝or′əl) ▸*adj.* Of or being a grammatical form that designates more than one of the things specified. ▸*n.* **1.** The plural number or form. **2.** A word or term in the plural form. [ME *plurel* < OFr. < Lat. *plūrālis* < *plūs, plūr-,* more.] —**plu′ral•ize′** *v.* —**plu′ral•i•za′tion** *n.*

plu•ral•ism (plo͝or′ə-lĭz′əm) ▸*n.* A condition of society in which numerous distinct ethnic, religious, or cultural groups coexist within one nation. —**plu′ral•ist** *n.* —**plu′ral•is′tic** *adj.*

plu•ral•i•ty (plo͞o-răl′ĭ-tē) ▸*n., pl.* **-ties 1a.** In a contest of more than two choices, the number of votes cast for the winner if this number is not more than one half of the total votes cast. **b.** The number by which the vote of a winning choice in such a contest exceeds that of the closest opponent. **2.** The larger or greater part.

plus (plŭs) ▸*conj.* **1.** *Math.* Increased by: *Two plus two is four.* **2.** Added to; along with. ▸*adj.* **1.** Positive or on the positive part of a scale. **2.** Added or extra: *a plus value.* ▸*n., pl.* **plus•es** or **plus•ses 1.** *Math.* A symbol (+) used to indicate addition or a positive quantity. **2.** A favorable condition or factor. [Lat. *plūs,* more.]

Usage: When mathematical equations are pronounced as English sentences, the verb is usually in the singular: *Two plus two* is (or *equals*) *four.* • The use of *plus* introducing an independent clause, as in *She has a lot of talent, plus she is willing to work hard,* is limited chiefly to informal contexts.

plush (plŭsh) ▸*n.* A fabric having a thick, deep pile. ▸*adj.* **-er, -est.** Luxurious. [< OFr. *peluchier,* pluck.] —**plush′i•ly, plush′ly** *adv.* —**plush′i•ness, plush′ness** *n.* —**plush′y** *adj.*

Plu•tarch (plo͞o′tärk′). A.D. 46?–120? Greek biographer and philosopher.

Plu•to (plo͞o′tō) ▸*n.* **1.** *Gk. Myth.* The god of the dead and the ruler of the underworld. **2.** The 9th and usu. farthest planet from the sun, 4.5 billion km (2.8 billion mi) distant at perihelion and 7.4 billion km (4.6 billion mi) at aphelion, with a diameter less than half that of Earth. [< Gk. *ploutos,* wealth.]

plu•toc•ra•cy (plo͞o-tŏk′rə-sē) ▸*n., pl.* **-cies 1.** Government by the wealthy. **2.** A wealthy class that controls a government. [Gk. *ploutos,* wealth + -CRACY.] —**plu′to•crat′** (plo͞o′tə-krăt′) *n.* —**plu′to•crat′ic, plu′to•crat′i•cal** *adj.*

plu•ton•ic (plo͞o-tŏn′ĭk) ▸*adj.* Of deep igneous or magmatic origin: *plutonic rocks.*

plu•to•ni•um (plo͞o-tō′nē-əm) ▸*n. Symbol* **Pu** A naturally radioactive, silvery metallic element used as a reactor fuel and in nuclear weapons. At. no. 94. See table at **element.**

plu•vi•al (plo͞o′vē-əl) ▸*adj.* Of or caused by rain. [< Lat. *pluvia,* rain < *pluere,* to rain.]

ply[1] (plī) ▸*v.* **plied** (plīd), **ply•ing 1.** To join together, as by molding or twisting. **2.** To double over (e.g., cloth). ▸*n., pl.* **plies 1.** A layer, as of cloth or wood. **2.** One of the strands twisted together to make yarn, rope, or thread. [< Lat. *plicāre,* fold.]

ply[2] (plī) ▸*v.* **plied** (plīd), **ply•ing 1.** To use diligently; wield. **2.** To engage in (e.g., a trade); practice. **3.** To traverse or sail over regularly. **4.** To continue supplying: *plied their guests with food.* [< APPLY.]

Plym•outh (plĭm′əth) **1.** A borough of SW England on **Plymouth Sound,** an inlet of the English Channel. Pop. 259,040. **2.** A town of SE MA on **Plymouth Bay,** an inlet of the Atlantic SE of Boston; founded (1620) by Pilgrims from the *Mayflower.* Pop. 45,608

ply•wood (plī′wo͝od′) ▸*n.* A structural material made of layers of wood glued together.

Pm ▸ The symbol for the element **promethium.**

P.M. also **p.m.** or P.M. ▸*abbr.* post meridiem See Usage Note at **ante meridiem.**

PMS ▸*abbr.* premenstrual syndrome

p.n. or **P/N** ▸*abbr.* promissory note

pneu•mat•ic (no͞o-măt′ĭk, nyo͞o-) also **pneu•mat•i•cal** (-ĭ-kəl) ▸*adj.* **1.** Of or relating to air or other gases. **2.** Filled with or operated by compressed air. [< Gk. *pneuma,* wind.]

pneu•mo•coc•cus (no͞o′mə-kŏk′əs, nyo͞o′-) ▸*n., pl.* **-coc•ci** (-kŏk′sī′, -kŏk′ī′). A bacterium that causes pneumonia. [Gk. *pneuma,* breath + -COCCUS.] —**pneu′mo•coc′cal** *adj.*

pneu•mo•nia (no͞o-mōn′yə, nyo͞o-) ▸*n.* An acute or chronic disease marked by inflammation of the lungs and caused by viruses, bacteria, and physical and chemical irritants. [< Gk. *pleumōn*, lung.] —**pneu•mon′ic** (-mŏn′ĭk) *adj.*

Po[1] (pō) A river of N Italy flowing about 652 km (405 mi) to the Adriatic Sea.

Po[2] ▸ The symbol for the element **polonium.**

PO ▸*abbr.* **1.** petty officer **2.** postal order **3.** post office

poach[1] (pōch) ▸*v.* To cook in a simmering liquid. [< OFr. *pochier*, put in pockets.]

poach[2] (pōch) ▸*v.* **1.** To trespass on another's property in order to take fish or game. **2.** To take (fish or game) illegally. [< OFr. *pochier*, poke, gouge.] —**poach′er** *n.*

Po•ca•hon•tas (pō′kə-hŏn′təs). 1595?–1617. Powhatan princess.

Pocahontas
1616 portrait

Po•ca•tel•lo (pō′kə-tĕl′ō, -tĕl′ə) A city of SE ID SSW of Idaho Falls. Pop. 46,080.

pock (pŏk) ▸*n.* **1.** A pustule caused by smallpox or a similar eruptive disease. **2.** A mark or scar left in the skin by such a pustule; pockmark. [< OE *pocc.*] —**pock** *v.*

pock•et (pŏk′ĭt) ▸*n.* **1.** A pouch with an open edge sewn into or onto a garment and used to carry small items. **2.** A receptacle or cavity. **3.** Financial means. **4.** A small isolated or protected area or group. ▸*adj.* **1.** Suitable for being carried in one's pocket. **2.** Small; miniature. ▸*v.* **1.** To place in or as if in a pocket. **2.** To take possession of for oneself, esp. dishonestly. [< ONFr. *poke*, bag, of Gmc. orig.] —**pock′et•ful′** *n.*

pock•et•book (pŏk′ĭt-bo͝ok′) ▸*n.* **1.** A wallet; billfold. **2.** A handbag. **3.** Financial means.

pock•et•knife (pŏk′ĭt-nīf′) ▸*n.* A small knife with a blade or blades that fold into the handle when not in use.

pocket veto ▸*n.* An executive's indirect veto of a bill by retaining the bill unsigned until the legislature adjourns.

pock•mark (pŏk′märk′) ▸*n.* A pitlike scar left on the skin by smallpox or another eruptive disease. —**pock′mark′** *v.*

po•co (pō′kō) ▸*adv. Mus.* To a slight degree; somewhat. [Ital. < Lat. *paucus*, little.]

pod[1] (pŏd) ▸*n.* **1.** *Bot.* A seed vessel, as of the pea, that splits open. **2.** An external or detachable housing, as for instruments or personnel, forming part of a vehicle. [?]

pod[2] (pŏd) ▸*n.* A school of marine mammals, such as seals or whales. [?]

-pod or **-pode** ▸*suff.* Foot; footlike part: *gastropod.* [< Gk. *pous*, foot.]

Pod•go•ri•ca (pŏd′gə-rēt′sə). Formerly **Ti•to•grad** (tē′tō-grăd′, -gräd′). The capital of Montenegro, in the SE part. Pop. 118,059.

po•di•a•try (pə-dī′ə-trē) ▸*n.* The branch of medicine that deals with diseases of the foot. [Gk. *pous*, *pod-*, foot + -IATRY.] —**po′di•at′ric** (pō′dē-ăt′rĭk) *adj.* —**po•di′a•trist** *n.*

po•di•um (pō′dē-əm) ▸*n., pl.* **-di•a** (-dē-ə) or **-di•ums.** An elevated platform, as for a speaker or orchestra conductor. [< Gk. *podion*, base, dim. of *pous*, foot.]

Poe (pō), **Edgar Allan.** 1809–49. Amer. writer.

POE ▸*abbr.* port of entry

po•em (pō′əm) ▸*n.* A verbal composition characterized by the use of condensed language chosen for its sound and suggestive power and by the use of literary techniques such as meter and metaphor. [< Gk. *poiēma*, a creation.]

po•e•sy (pō′ĭ-zē, -sē) ▸*n.* Poetry. [< Gk. *poiēsis*, creation.]

po•et (pō′ĭt) ▸*n.* A writer of poems. [< Gk. *poiētēs*, maker.]

po•et•as•ter (pō′ĭt-ăs′tər) ▸*n.* An inferior poet. [POET + Lat. *-aster*, pejorative suff.]

po•et•ess (pō′ĭ-tĭs) ▸*n.* A woman who writes poems. See Usage Note at **-ess.**

po•et•ic (pō-ĕt′ĭk) also **po•et′i•cal** ▸*adj.* Of or characteristic of poetry or poets.

poetic justice ▸*n.* The rewarding of virtue and the punishment of vice, often in an appropriate or ironic manner.

poetic license ▸*n.* The liberty taken by an artist or a writer in deviating from conventional form or fact to achieve a desired effect.

poet laureate ▸*n., pl.* **poets laureate** or **poet laureates 1.** A poet appointed for life by a British monarch as chief poet of the kingdom. **2.** A poet appointed to a similar honorary position.

po•et•ry (pō′ĭ-trē) ▸*n.* **1.** The art or work of a poet. **2a.** Poems regarded as forming a division of literature. **b.** The poetic works of a given author, group, or kind.

po•grom (pə-grŏm′, pō′grəm) ▸*n.* An organized massacre of a minority group, esp. Jews. [Russ.]

Po Hai (bō′ hī′) See **Bo Hai.**

poi (poi) ▸*n.* A food made from cooked taro root pounded to a paste and fermented. See Regional Note at **ukulele.** [Hawaiian.]

poign•ant (poin′yənt) ▸*adj.* **1.** Keenly distressing to the mind or feelings: *poignant anxiety.* **2.** Profoundly moving; touching: *a poignant memory.* [< Lat. *pungere*, to prick.] —**poign′ance, poign′an•cy** *n.*

poi•kil•o•therm (poi-kĭl′ə-thûrm′) ▸*n.* An organism, such as a reptile, having a body temperature that varies with the temperature of its surroundings. [Gk. *poikilos*, various + *thermē*, heat.] —**poi′ki•lo•ther′mic** (-kə-lō-thûr′mĭk) *adj.*

poin•ci•an•a (poin′sē-ăn′ə, -ä′nə) ▸*n.* A tropical and semitropical tree having scarlet flowers and long pods. [From M. De *Poinci*, 17th-cent. governor, French West Indies.]

poin•set•ti•a (poin-sĕt′ē-ə, -sĕt′ə) ▸*n.* A tropical American shrub that has showy, usu. scarlet bracts beneath the small yellow flowers. [After J.R. *Poinsett* (1779–1851).]

point (point) ▸*n.* **1a.** A sharp or tapered end. **b.** A mark formed by or as if by a sharp end. **2.** A tapering extension of land projecting into water. **3.** *Math.* A dimensionless geometric object having no properties except location. **4.** A place or position. **5.** A specified degree, condition, or limit. **6.** A specific moment in time. **7.** An objective or purpose to be achieved. **8.** A significant or outstanding idea or suggestion. **9.** A distinctive quality or characteristic. **10.** A single unit, as in counting, rating, or measuring. **11.** An electrical contact, esp. one in the distributor of an automobile engine. ►*v.* **1.** To direct or aim. See Syns at **aim. 2.** To bring to notice: *point out an error.* **3.** To indicate the position or direction of. **4.** To give emphasis to; stress: *pointed up the difference between them.* —***idioms:*** **beside the point** Irrelevant. **in point of** With reference to. **stretch a point** To make an exception. **to the point** Closely concerning the matter at hand. [< Lat. *pūnctus*, p.part. of *pungere*, to prick.] —**point′y** *adj.*

point-and-click (point′ənd-klĭk′) ►*adj.* Allowing the activation of a selected computer command by clicking a pointing device.

point-blank (point′blăngk′) ►*adj.* **1a.** Aiming straight at a target. **b.** So close that missing the target is unlikely. **2.** Straightforward; blunt. —**point′-blank′** *adv.*

point•ed (poin′tĭd) ►*adj.* **1.** Having a point. **2.** Sharp; incisive. **3.** Obviously directed at a particular thing: *a pointed comment.* **4.** Clearly evident; marked: *a pointed lack of interest.* —**point′ed•ly** *adv.*

point•er (poin′tər) ►*n.* **1.** An indicator, as on a watch or scale. **2.** A long, tapered stick for indicating objects, as on a chart or blackboard. **3.** A usu. short-haired hunting dog bred to indicate game with an immobile stance. **4.** A piece of advice; suggestion.

poin•til•lism (pwăN′tē-ĭz′-əm, point′l-ĭz′-) ►*n.* A painting technique characterized by the application of paint in small dots and brush strokes. [< OFr. *point*, dot.] —**poin′til•list** *adj. & n.* —**poin′til•lis′tic** *adj.*

point•ing device (poin′tĭng) ►*n. Comp. Sci.* An input device, such as a mouse, for manipulating a cursor or pointer on a GUI.

point•less (point′lĭs) ►*adj.* Meaningless; irrelevant. —**point′less•ness** *n.*

point-of-sale (point′əv-sāl′) ►*adj.* Of or being the place where an item is purchased.

point of view ►*n.* **1.** A manner of viewing things; attitude. **2.** A position from which something is observed or considered.

poise (poiz) ►*v.* **poised, pois•ing.** To balance or be balanced. ►*n.* **1.** Balance; stability. **2.** Composure. **3.** Dignity of manner. [< Lat. *pēnsāre.*]

poi•son (poi′zən) ►*n.* A substance that causes injury, illness, or death, esp. by chemical means. ►*v.* **1.** To kill or harm with poison. **2.** To put poison on or into. **3a.** To pollute. See Syns at **contaminate. b.** To have a harmful influence on; corrupt. [< Lat. *pōtiō*, a drink.] —**poi′son•er** *n.* —**poi′son•ous** *adj.* —**poi′son•ous•ly** *adv.*

poison hemlock ►*n.* A deadly poisonous European plant, widely naturalized in North America, having small white flowers.

poison ivy ►*n.* **1.** A North American plant having compound leaves with three leaflets and causing a rash on contact. **2.** The rash itself.

poison oak ►*n.* **1.** Either of two plants of the SE and W US related to poison ivy and causing a rash on contact. **2.** The rash itself.

poison sumac ►*n.* **1.** A swamp shrub of the SE US, having compound leaves and causing a rash on contact. **2.** The rash itself.

poke[1] (pōk) ►*v.* **poked, pok•ing 1.** To push or jab at, as with a finger; prod. **2.** To make (a hole or pathway) by or as if by prodding or jabbing. **3.** To push; thrust. **4.** To pry or meddle. **5.** To search curiously; rummage. ►*n.* A push, thrust, or jab. —***idiom:*** **poke fun at** To ridicule; tease. [ME *poken.*]

poke[2] (pōk) ►*n. Regional* A sack. [Prob. < ONFr. See POCKET.]

pok•er[1] (pō′kər) ►*n.* A metal rod used to stir a fire.

pok•er[2] (pō′kər) ►*n.* Any of various card games played by two or more players who bet on the value of their hands. [?]

poke•weed (pōk′wēd′) ►*n.* A tall North American plant having small white flowers, blackish-red berries and a poisonous root. [< dial. *pocan*, of Algonquian orig.]

po•key also **po•ky** (pō′kē) ►*n., pl.* **-keys** also **-kies** *Slang.* A jail. [?]

pok•y also **poke•y** (pō′kē) ►*adj.* **-i•er, -i•est** *Informal* Dawdling; slow. [< POKE[1].] —**pok′i•ly** *adv.* —**pok′i•ness** *n.*

pol (pôl) ►*n. Informal* A politician.

Po•land (pō′lənd) A country of central Europe bordering on the Baltic Sea. Cap. Warsaw. Pop. 38,544,000.

po•lar (pō′lər) ►*adj.* **1.** Of, measured from, or referred to a pole. **2.** Of or near the North or South Pole. **3.** Occupying or characterized by opposite extremes.

polar bear ►*n.* A large white bear of Arctic regions.

Po•lar•is (pə-lăr′ĭs) ►*n.* A star at the end of the handle of the Little Dipper and almost at the north celestial pole.

po•lar•i•ty (pō-lăr′ĭ-tē, pə-) ►*n., pl.* **-ties 1.** Intrinsic polar separation, alignment, or orientation, esp. of a physical property. **2.** An indicated polar extreme. **3.** The manifestation of two opposing tendencies.

po•lar•ize (pō′lə-rīz′) ►*v.* **-ized, -iz•ing 1.** To impart polarity to. **2.** To acquire polarity. **3.** To cause to concentrate about two conflicting positions. —**po′lar•i•za′tion** *n.*

Po•lar•oid (pō′lə-roid′) ► **1.** A trademark for a transparent plastic capable of polarizing light, used in glare-reducing optical devices. **2.** A trademark for an instant camera.

Polar Regions. The lands and waters surrounding the North and South Poles, known respectively as the **North Polar Region** and the **South Polar Region.**

pole[1] (pōl) ►*n.* **1.** Either extremity of an axis through a sphere. **2.** *Geog.* The North Pole or the South Pole. **3.** *Phys.* A magnetic pole. **4.** Either of two oppositely charged terminals, as in an electric cell or battery. **5.** Either of two opposing forces. [< Gk. *polos*, axis.]

pole[2] (pōl) ►*n.* A long slender piece of wood or other material. ►*v.* **poled, pol•ing 1.** To propel (e.g., a boat) with a pole. **2.** To use ski poles to maintain or gain speed. [< Lat. *pālus*, stake.]

Pole ►*n.* **1.** A native or inhabitant of Poland. **2.** A person of Polish descent.

pole•ax or **pole•axe** (pōl′ăks′) ►*n.* A long-handled battle-ax. [ME *pollax.*]

pole•cat (pōl′kăt′) ▸*n.* **1.** A weasellike European mammal. **2.** See **skunk** 1. [ME *polcat.*]
po•lem•ic (pə-lĕm′ĭk) ▸*n.* **1.** A controversy or refutation. **2. polemics** *(takes sing. or pl. v.)* The art or practice of debate or controversy. [< Gk. *polemos*, war.] —**po•lem′ic, po•lem′i•cal** *adj.* —**po•lem′i•cist** *n.*
po•len•ta (pō-lĕn′tə) ▸*n.* A thick mush made of coarse cornmeal. [Ital. < Lat., barley meal.]
pole•star (pōl′stär′) ▸*n.* See **Polaris.**
pole vault ▸*n.* A field event in which the contestant jumps or vaults over a high crossbar with the aid of a long pole. —**pole′-vault′** *v.* —**pole′-vault′er** *n.*
po•lice (pə-lēs′) ▸*n., pl.* **-lice 1.** The governmental department established to maintain order, enforce the law, and detect and prevent crime. **2a.** A body of persons making up such a department. **b.** A body of persons having similar organization and function: *campus police.* **3.** The soldiers assigned to a specified maintenance duty. ▸*v.* **-liced, -lic•ing 1.** To regulate, control, or keep in order with or as if with police. **2.** To make (e.g., a military area) neat in appearance. [< Lat. *polītīa*, the State.]
police dog ▸*n.* **1.** A guard dog. **2.** See **German shepherd.**
police force ▸*n.* See **police** 2.
po•lice•man (pə-lēs′mən) ▸*n.* A man who is a member of a police force. See Usage Note at **man.**
police state ▸*n.* A state in which the government exercises rigid and repressive controls, esp. by means of a secret police force.
police station ▸*n.* The headquarters of a police force.
po•lice•wom•an (pə-lēs′wo͝om′ən) ▸*n.* A woman who is a member of a police force. See Usage Note at **man.**
pol•i•cy[1] (pŏl′ĭ-sē) ▸*n., pl.* **-cies 1.** A plan or course of action, as of a government or business, intended to influence and determine decisions, actions, and other matters. **2.** Prudence or sagacity in practical matters. [< Gk. *politeia*, government.]
pol•i•cy[2] (pŏl′ĭ-sē) ▸*n., pl.* **-cies.** A written contract or certificate of insurance. [< Gk. *apodeixis*, proof.] —**pol′i•cy•hol′der** *n.*
pol•i•cy•mak•ing (pŏl′ĭ-sē-mā′kĭng) ▸*n.* High-level development of policy, esp. government policy. —**pol′i•cy•mak′er** *n.*
po•li•o (pō′lē-ō′) ▸*n.* Poliomyelitis.
po•li•o•my•e•li•tis (pō′lē-ō-mī′ə-lī′tĭs) ▸*n.* An infectious viral disease that chiefly affects children and in its acute forms attacks the central nervous system, leading to paralysis, muscular atrophy, and often deformity. [Gk. *polios*, gray + MYELITIS.] —**po′li•o•my′e•lit′ic** (-lĭt′ĭk) *adj.*
pol•ish (pŏl′ĭsh) ▸*v.* **1.** To make smooth and shiny by rubbing or chemical action. **2.** To remove the outer layers from (grains of rice). **3.** To free from coarseness; refine. —***phrasal verb:*** **polish off** *Informal* To finish or dispose of quickly. ▸*n.* **1.** Smoothness or shininess of surface. **2.** A substance used to shine a surface. **3.** Elegance of style or manner. [< Lat. *polīre.*] —**pol′ish•er** *n.*
Po•lish (pō′lĭsh) ▸*adj.* Of or relating to Poland or its people or language. ▸*n.* The Slavic language of the Poles.
pol•it•bu•ro (pŏl′ĭt-byo͝or′ō, pə-lĭt′-) ▸*n., pl.* **-ros.** The chief political and executive committee of a Communist party. [Russ.]
po•lite (pə-līt′) ▸*adj.* **-lit•er, -lit•est 1.** Marked by consideration, tact, and courtesy. **2.** Refined; elegant. [< Lat. *polītus*, polished.] —**po•lite′ly** *adv.* —**po•lite′ness** *n.*
pol•i•tesse (pŏl′ĭ-tĕs′, pô′lē-) ▸*n.* Courteous formality. [Fr.]
pol•i•tic (pŏl′ĭ-tĭk) ▸*adj.* **1.** Shrewd; artful. **2.** Prudent; judicious. [< Gk. *politēs*, citizen.]
po•lit•i•cal (pə-lĭt′ĭ-kəl) ▸*adj.* **1.** Of or relating to the affairs of government, politics, or the state. **2.** Characteristic of politics, parties, or politicians. —**po•lit′i•cal•ly** *adv.*
politically correct ▸*adj.* Of or relating to broad social, political, and educational change, esp. to redress historical injustices in matters such as race and gender. —**political correctness** *n.*
political science ▸*n.* The study of the processes, principles, and structure of government and political institutions.
pol•i•ti•cian (pŏl′ĭ-tĭsh′ən) ▸*n.* **1.** One actively involved in politics. **2.** One who holds or seeks a political office.
po•lit•i•cize (pə-lĭt′ĭ-sīz′) ▸*v.* **-cized, -ciz•ing.** To make political. —**po•lit′i•ci•za′tion** *n.*
pol•i•tick (pŏl′ĭ-tĭk) ▸*v.* To engage in or discuss politics. —**pol′i•tick′er** *n.*
po•lit•i•co (pə-lĭt′ĭ-kō′) ▸*n., pl.* **-cos.** A politician. [< Ital. and Sp. *político.*]
pol•i•tics (pŏl′ĭ-tĭks) ▸*n.* **1.** *(takes sing. v.)* The art or science of government or governing. **2.** *(takes sing. or pl. v.)* The activities or affairs engaged in by a government. **3.** *(takes sing. or pl. v.)* Intrigue or maneuvering within a group: *office politics.* **4.** *(takes sing. or pl. v.)* Political positions.
pol•i•ty (pŏl′ĭ-tē) ▸*n., pl.* **-ties.** An organized society, such as a nation, having a specific form of government. [< LLat. *polītīa*, government.]
Polk (pōk), **James Knox.** 1795–1849. The 11th US President.

James K. Polk
detail of an 1846 portrait

pol•ka (pōl′kə, pō′kə) ▸*n.* **1.** A lively dance performed by couples. **2.** Music for this dance, having duple meter. [Prob. < Pol.] —**pol′ka** *v.*
polka dot ▸*n.* One of a number of dots forming a pattern on cloth.
poll (pōl) ▸*n.* **1.** The casting and registering of votes in an election. **2.** The number of votes cast or recorded. **3.** often **polls** The place where votes are cast and registered. **4.** A survey of the public or of a sample of public opinion to

acquire information. ►*v.* **1.** To receive (a given number of votes). **2.** To receive or record the votes of. **3.** To question in a survey; canvass. **4.** To cut off or trim (e.g., hair or horns). [< MLGer. or MDu. *polle*, head.] —**poll′er** *n.*

pol•lack (pŏl′ək) also **-lock** ►*n., pl.* **-lack** or **-lacks** also **-lock** or **-locks.** A marine food fish of N Atlantic waters. [< Sc. *podlok.*]

pol•len (pŏl′ən) ►*n.* The powderlike material produced by the anthers of seed plants and functioning as the male agent in fertilization. [Lat., fine flour.]

pol•li•nate (pŏl′ə-nāt′) ►*v.* **-li•nat•ed, -li•nat•ing.** To fertilize by transferring pollen from an anther to the stigma of (a flower). —**pol′li•na′tion** *n.* —**pol′li•na′tor** *n.*

pol•li•no•sis (pŏl′ə-nō′sĭs) ►*n.* See **hay fever.**

pol•li•wog also **pol•ly•wog** (pŏl′ē-wŏg′, -wôg′) ►*n.* See **tadpole.** [< ME *polwigle.*]

Pol•lock (pŏl′ək), **Jackson.** 1912–56. Amer. artist.

poll•ster (pōl′stər) ►*n.* One that takes public-opinion surveys.

poll tax ►*n.* A tax levied on people rather than on property, often as a voting requirement.

pol•lute (pə-lo͞ot′) ►*v.* **-lut•ed, -lut•ing 1.** To make unfit for or harmful to living things, esp. by the addition of waste matter. See Syns at **contaminate. 2.** To render impure; corrupt. [< Lat. *polluere*, *pollūt-*.] —**pol•lut′ant** *n.* —**pol•lut′er** *n.* —**pol•lu′tion** *n.*

Pol•lux (pŏl′əks) ►*n.* A bright star in the constellation Gemini.

po•lo (pō′lō) ►*n.* A game played by two teams on horseback equipped with long-handled mallets for driving a wooden ball. [Of Tibeto-Burman orig.]

Polo, Marco. 1254–1324. Venetian traveler in Asia.

pol•o•naise (pŏl′ə-nāz′, pō′lə-) ►*n.* **1.** A stately Polish dance in triple meter. **2.** Music for this dance. [Fr. < Med.Lat. *Polonia*, Poland.]

po•lo•ni•um (pə-lō′nē-əm) ►*n. Symbol* **Po** A radioactive metallic element that occurs naturally as a product of radium decay and is also produced artificially. At. no. 84. See table at **element.** [< Med.Lat. *Polōnia*, Poland.]

polo shirt ►*n.* A knitted pullover sport shirt.

pol•ter•geist (pōl′tər-gīst′) ►*n.* A noisy, usu. mischievous ghost. [Ger.]

pol•troon (pŏl-tro͞on′) ►*n.* A base coward. [< OItal. *poltrone.*] —**pol•troon′er•y** *n.*

poly– ►*pref.* **1.** More than one; many; much: *polyatomic.* **2.** More than usual; excessive; abnormal: *polydipsia.* **3.** Polymer; polymeric: *polyethylene.* [< Gk. *polus*, many.]

pol•y•an•dry (pŏl′ē-ăn′drē) ►*n.* The condition or practice of having more than one husband at one time. —**pol′y•an′drous** *adj.*

pol•y•chrome (pŏl′ē-krōm′) ►*adj.* Having or decorated in many colors. —**pol′y•chro•mat′ic** (-krō-măt′ĭk), **pol′y•chro′mic, pol′y•chro′mous** *adj.*

pol•y•clin•ic (pŏl′ē-klĭn′ĭk) ►*n.* A clinic that treats various diseases and injuries.

pol•y•dip•si•a (pŏl′ē-dĭp′sē-ə) ►*n.* Excessive or abnormal thirst. [< POLY– + Gk. *dipsa*, thirst.] —**pol′y•dip′sic** *adj.*

pol•y•es•ter (pŏl′ē-ĕs′tər, pŏl′ē-ĕs′tər) ►*n.* Any of numerous synthetic resins used esp. in textile fibers, adhesives, and molded parts.

pol•y•eth•yl•ene (pŏl′ē-ĕth′ə-lēn′) ►*n.* A synthetic resin, used esp. in the form of films and sheets.

po•lyg•a•my (pə-lĭg′ə-mē) ►*n.* The condition or practice of having more than one spouse at one time. —**po•lyg′a•mist** *n.* —**po•lyg′a•mous** *adj.* —**po•lyg′a•mous•ly** *adv.*

pol•y•glot (pŏl′ē-glŏt′) ►*n.* One with a speaking, reading, or writing knowledge of several languages. [POLY– + Gk. *glōtta*, tongue.]

pol•y•gon (pŏl′ē-gŏn′) ►*n.* A closed plane figure bounded by three or more line segments. —**po•lyg′o•nal** (pə-lĭg′ə-nəl) *adj.*

pol•y•graph (pŏl′ē-grăf′) ►*n.* An instrument that records changes in physiological processes such as heartbeat, blood pressure, and respiration, often used as a lie detector.

po•lyg•y•ny (pə-lĭj′ə-nē) ►*n.* The condition or practice of having more than one wife at one time. [< POLY– + Gk. *gunē*, woman.] —**po•lyg′y•nous** *adj.*

pol•y•he•dron (pŏl′ē-hē′drən) ►*n., pl.* **-drons** or **-dra** (-drə). A solid whose faces are polygons. —**pol′y•he′dral** *adj.*

pol•y•math (pŏl′ē-măth′) ►*n.* A person of great or varied learning. [Gk. *polumathēs.*] —**pol′y•math′, pol′y•math′ic** *adj.*

pol•y•mer (pŏl′ə-mər) ►*n.* Any of numerous natural and synthetic compounds of usu. high molecular weight consisting of repeated linked units, each a relatively light and simple molecule. —**pol′y•mer′ic** (-mĕr′ĭk) *adj.*

pol•y•mer•ase (pŏl′ə-mə-rās′, -rāz′) ►*n.* Any of various enzymes that catalyze the formation of DNA or RNA.

pol•y•mer•ize (pŏl′ə-mə-rīz′, pə-lĭm′ə-) ►*v.* **-ized, -iz•ing.** To bond two or more monomers to form a polymer. —**po•lym′er•i•za′tion** *n.*

Pol•y•ne•sia (pŏl′ə-nē′zhə, -shə) A division of Oceania including islands of the central and S Pacific roughly between New Zealand, Hawaii, and Easter I.

Pol•y•ne•sian (pŏl′ə-nē′zhən, -shən) ►*n.* **1.** A native or inhabitant of Polynesia. **2.** A subfamily of the Austronesian language family spoken in Polynesia.

pol•y•no•mi•al (pŏl′ē-nō′mē-əl) ►*adj.* Of or consisting of more than two names or terms. ►*n. Math.* An algebraic function of one or more summed terms, each term consisting of a constant multiplier and one or more variables raised to integral powers. [POLY– + (BI)NOMIAL.]

pol•yp (pŏl′ĭp) ►*n.* **1.** An organism, such as a hydra or coral, having a cylindrical body and an oral opening usu. surrounded by tentacles. **2.** *Pathol.* A growth protruding from the mucous lining of an organ. [< Gk. *polupous*, cuttlefish.] —**pol′yp•oid′** *adj.*

pol•y•pep•tide (pŏl′ē-pĕp′tīd′) ►*n.* A peptide containing many molecules of amino acids.

po•lyph•o•ny (pə-lĭf′ə-nē) ►*n., pl.* **-nies.** Music with two or more independent melodic parts sounded together. —**pol′y•phon′ic** (pŏl′ē-fŏn′ĭk), **po•lyph′o•nous** *adj.*

pol•y•sac•cha•ride (pŏl′ē-săk′ə-rīd′) ►*n.* Any of a class of carbohydrates, such as starch and cellulose, consisting of a number of monosaccharides.

pol•y•sty•rene (pŏl′ē-stī′rēn) ►*n.* A rigid,

clear thermoplastic polymer used esp. in molded parts or as an insulating foam. [< Lat. *styrax*, a tree.]

pol•y•syl•la•ble (pŏl′ē-sĭl′ə-bəl) ►*n.* A word of more than three syllables. —**pol′y•syl•lab′ic** (-sĭ-lăb′ĭk) *adj.*

pol•y•tech•nic (pŏl′ē-tĕk′nĭk) ►*adj.* Offering or dealing with instruction in many industrial arts and applied sciences. ►*n.* A school specializing in such subjects.

pol•y•the•ism (pŏl′ē-thē-ĭz′əm, pŏl′ē-thē′ĭz-əm) ►*n.* The worship of or belief in more than one god. —**pol′y•the′ist** *n.*

pol•y•un•sat•u•rat•ed (pŏl′ē-ŭn-săch′ə-rā′tĭd) ►*adj.* Relating to long-chain carbon compounds, esp. fats, having many unsaturated bonds.

pol•y•u•re•thane (pŏl′ē-yo͝or′ə-thān′) ►*n.* Any of various resins used in tough chemical-resistant coatings, adhesives, and foams. [< POLY– + UR(O)– + ETH(YL).]

pol•y•va•lent (pŏl′ē-vā′lənt) ►*adj.* **1.** Involving more than one kind of antigen, antibody, toxin, or microorganism. **2.** *Chem.* **a.** Having more than one valence. **b.** Having a valence of 3 or higher. —**pol′y•va′lence, pol′y•va′len•cy** *n.*

pol•y•vi•nyl chloride (pŏl′ē-vī′nəl) ►*n.* PVC.

po•made (pō-măd′, pŏ-) ►*n.* A perfumed hair ointment. [< LLat. *pōmum*, apple.] —**po′made** *v.*

pome•gran•ate (pŏm′grăn′ĭt, pŏm′ĭ-) ►*n.* **1.** A shrub or small tree widely cultivated for its edible fruit. **2.** The fruit of this tree, having a tough reddish rind and many seeds. [< OFr. *pome grenate* : *pome*, apple + *grenate*, having many seeds (< Lat. *grānum*, grain, seed).]

Pom•er•a•ni•a (pŏm′ə-rā′nē-ə, -rān′yə) A historical region of N-central Europe bordering on the Baltic Sea in present-day NW Poland and NE Germany.

Pom•er•a•ni•an (pŏm′ə-rā′nē-ən, -rān′yən) ►*adj.* Of or relating to Pomerania or its people. ►*n.* **1.** A native or inhabitant of Pomerania. **2.** Any of a breed of small dog having long silky hair and a foxlike face.

pom•mel (pŭm′əl, pŏm′-) ►*v.* **-meled, -mel•ing** also **-melled, -mel•ling.** To beat; pummel. ►*n.* **1.** The upper front part of a saddle. **2.** A knob on the hilt of a sword. [< Lat. *pōmum*, fruit.]

pommel horse ►*n.* A padded apparatus for gymnastic exercises having two handles on top and adjustable legs.

pommel horse

Po•mo•na (pə-mō′nə) A city of S CA, a suburb of Los Angeles. Pop. 131,723.

pomp (pŏmp) ►*n.* **1.** Magnificent display; splendor. **2.** Ostentatious display. See Syns at **display.** [< Gk. *pompē*, procession.]

pom•pa•dour (pŏm′pə-dôr′, -dōr′) ►*n.* A hairstyle formed by sweeping the hair up from the forehead.

Pompadour, Marquise de. Jeanne Antoinette Poisson. 1721–64. The lover of Louis XV of France.

pom•pa•no (pŏm′pə-nō′) ►*n., pl.* **-no** or **-nos.** A food fish of tropical and temperate Atlantic waters. [< Lat. *pampinus*, vine tendril.]

Pom•pe•ii (pŏm-pā′, -pā′ē) An ancient city of S Italy SE of Naples; destroyed by an eruption of Mount Vesuvius (A.D. 79). —**Pom•pe′ian, Pom•pei′ian** *adj. & n.*

Pom•pey (pŏm′pē). 106–48 B.C. Roman general and political leader.

pom•pon (pŏm′pŏn′) also **pom•pom** (-pŏm′) ►*n.* **1.** A tuft or ball of wool, feathers, or other material used as a decoration. **2.** A buttonlike flower of some chrysanthemums and dahlias. [Fr.]

pom•pous (pŏm′pəs) ►*adj.* **1.** Self-important; pretentious. **2.** Marked by pomp or stately display. —**pom•pos′i•ty** (-pŏs′ĭ-tē), **pom′pous•ness** *n.* —**pom′pous•ly** *adv.*

Pon•ce (pōn′sā, -sĕ) A city of S Puerto Rico SW of San Juan. Pop. 189,317.

Ponce de Le•ón (pŏns′ də lē-ŏn′, pōn′sĕ), **Juan.** 1460–1521. Spanish explorer.

pon•cho (pŏn′chō) ►*n., pl.* **-chos 1.** A blanketlike cloak having a hole in the center for the head. **2.** A similar hooded garment used as a raincoat. [Am.Sp.]

pond (pŏnd) ►*n.* A still body of water smaller than a lake. [< OE *pund-*, enclosure.]

pon•der (pŏn′dər) ►*v.* **1.** To weigh carefully in the mind. **2.** To reflect on; meditate. [< Lat. *ponderāre*.] —**pon′der•a•ble** *adj.*

pon•der•o•sa pine (pŏn′də-rō′sə) ►*n.* A tall timber tree of W North America, having long, dark green needles. [< Lat. *ponderōsus*, massive.]

pon•der•ous (pŏn′dər-əs) ►*adj.* **1.** Having great weight. **2.** Lacking fluency; dull. [< Lat. *pondus*, *ponder-*, weight.] —**pon′der•ous•ly** *adv.* —**pon′der•ous•ness, pon′der•os′i•ty** (-ŏs′ĭ-tē) *n.*

pone (pōn) ►*n. Regional* See **johnnycake.** [< Virginia Algonquian *poan*.]

Regional Note: *Pone,* "a bread made by Native Americans from flat cakes of cornmeal dough baked in ashes," is one of several American English borrowings (including *hominy* and *tomahawk*) from Virginia Algonquian. *Pone,* usually *cornpone,* is now used mainly in the South, where it means cakes of cornbread baked on a griddle or in hot ashes.

pon•gee (pŏn-jē′, pŏn′jē) ►*n.* A soft thin silk cloth. [Mandarin *běn zhī* : *běn*, one's own + *zhī*, to weave, spin.]

pon•iard (pŏn′yərd) ►*n.* A dagger. [Fr. *poignard* < Lat. *pugnus*, fist.]

pons (pŏnz) ►*n., pl.* **pon•tes** (pŏn′tēz). A slender tissue joining two parts of an organ. [Lat. *pōns*, bridge.]

Pon•ta Del•ga•da (pŏn′tə dĕl-gä′də) A city of SW São Miguel I. in the Azores. Pop. 21,187.

Pon•ti•ac (pŏn′tē-ăk′). 1720?–69. Ottawa leader.

pon•tiff (pŏn′tĭf) ►*n.* **1.** The pope. **2.** A bishop.

[< Lat. *pontifex*, high priest.]

pon•tif•i•cal (pŏn-tĭf′ĭ-kəl) ► *adj.* **1.** Of or suitable for a pontiff. **2.** Pompously dogmatic; pretentious. ► *n.* **pontificals** The vestments and insignia of a pontiff.

pon•tif•i•cate (pŏn-tĭf′ĭ-kĭt, -kāt′) ► *n.* The office or term of office of a pontiff. ► *v.* (-kāt′) **-cat•ed, -cat•ing 1.** To express opinions or judgments in a dogmatic way. **2.** To administer the office of a pontiff. —**pon•tif′i•ca′tion** *n.*

pon•toon (pŏn-to͞on′) ► *n.* **1.** A flat-bottomed boat or other structure used to support a floating bridge. **2.** A float on a seaplane. [< Lat. *pontō*, floating bridge.]

pontoon

Pon•tus (pŏn′təs) An ancient country of NE Asia Minor along the S coast of the Black Sea. —**Pon′tic** *adj.*

po•ny (pō′nē) ► *n., pl.* **-nies 1.** A small horse. **2.** A word-for-word translation of a foreign language text, esp. one used secretly in studying or test-taking. [Prob. < obsolete Fr. *poulenet*, foal.]

po•ny•tail (pō′nē-tāl′) ► *n.* A hairstyle in which the hair is drawn back and fastened so as to hang down like a horse's tail.

pooch (po͞och) ► *n. Slang* A dog. [?]

poo•dle (po͞od′l) ► *n.* A dog bred in various sizes and having thick curly hair. [< LGer. *pūdel*, puddle.]

pooh (po͞o) ► *interj.* Used to express disdain.

Pooh-Bah or **pooh-bah** (po͞o′bä′) ► *n.* **1.** A pompous ineffectual official. **2.** A person in high office. [After the character in Gilbert and Sullivan's *The Mikado*.]

pooh-pooh (po͞o′po͞o′) ► *v. Informal* To express contempt for; make light of.

pool[1] (po͞ol) ► *n.* **1.** A small pond. **2.** A puddle. **3.** A deep or still place in a stream. **4.** A swimming pool. [< OE *pōl*.] —**pool** *v.*

pool[2] (po͞ol) ► *n.* **1.** A fund containing all the money bet in a game of chance or on the outcome of an event. **2.** A grouping of resources for the common advantage of the participants. **3.** An agreement between competing business concerns to establish certain controls for common profit. **4.** Any of several games played on a six-pocket billiard table. ► *v.* **1.** To put into a fund for use by all. **2.** To join or form a pool. [Fr. *poule*, hen, stakes.]

pool•room (po͞ol′ro͞om′, -ro͝om′) ► *n.* A place for the playing of pool or billiards.

pool table ► *n.* A six-pocket billiards table on which pool is played.

Poo•na (po͞o′nə) See **Pune.**

poop[1] (po͞op) ► *n. Naut.* **1.** A superstructure at the stern of a ship. **2.** A poop deck. [< Lat. *puppis*.]

poop[2] (po͞op) ► *v. Slang* To become or cause to become fatigued. [?]

poop[3] (po͞op) ► *n. Slang* Inside information. [?]

poop deck ► *n.* The aftermost deck of a ship.

poor (po͝or) ► *adj.* **-er, -est 1.** Having little or no wealth. **2.** Lacking a specified resource or quality. **3.** Inferior: *a poor performance.* **4.** Lacking in value; insufficient: *poor wages.* **5.** Humble. **6.** Pitiable. [< Lat. *pauper*.] —**poor′ly** *adv.* —**poor′ness** *n.*

poor box ► *n.* A box in a church used for collecting alms.

poor boy ► *n. Regional* See **submarine** 2. See Regional Note at **submarine.**

poor•house (po͝or′hous′) ► *n.* An establishment maintained at public expense as housing for the homeless.

poor•mouth (po͝or′mouth′, -mou*th*′) ► *v.* To claim poverty as an excuse or defense.

pop[1] (pŏp) ► *v.* **popped, pop•ping 1.** To make or cause to make a short, sharp, explosive sound. **2.** To burst open with such a sound. **3.** To appear abruptly. **4.** To open wide suddenly. **5.** To shoot a firearm, such as a pistol. **6.** To put or thrust suddenly. ► *n.* **1.** A sudden sharp, explosive sound. **2.** A shot with a firearm. **3.** *Regional* See **soft drink.** See Regional Note at **tonic.** [ME *poppen*.]

pop[2] (pŏp) ► *n. Informal* Father. [< PAPA.]

pop[3] (pŏp) ► *adj. Informal* **1.** Of or for the general public; popular: *pop psychology.* **2.** Of or specializing in popular music: *a pop singer.* **3.** Suggestive of pop art. —**pop** *n.*

pop. ► *abbr.* population

pop art ► *n.* A form of art that depicts objects from everyday life and employs techniques of commercial art.

pop art
Campbell's Soup (Tomato), 1968,
by Andy Warhol

pop•corn (pŏp′kôrn′) ► *n.* A variety of corn having hard kernels that burst to form small white puffs when heated.

pope (pōp) ► *n.* often **Pope** The bishop of Rome and head of the Roman Catholic Church. [< Gk. *pappas*, father.]

Pope, Alexander. 1688–1744. English writer.

pop•eyed (pŏp′īd′) ► *adj.* **1.** Having bulging eyes. **2.** Amazed.

pop fly ► *n. Baseball* A short high fly ball.

pop•gun (pŏp′gŭn′) ► *n.* A toy gun that makes a popping noise.

pop•in•jay (pŏp′ĭn-jā′) ► *n.* A vain, talkative person. [< Ar. *babaġā'*, parrot.]

pop•lar (pŏp′lər) ►*n.* **1.** Any of several trees having unisexual flowers borne in catkins. **2.** See **tulip tree.** [< Lat. *pōpulus.*]

pop•lin (pŏp′lĭn) ►*n.* A ribbed fabric used in making clothing and upholstery. [Poss. < OProv. *papalin*, papal.]

Po•po•ca•té•petl (pō′pə-kăt′ə-pĕt′l, -pô-kä-tĕ′-) A volcano, 5,455.5 m (17,887 ft), in central Mexico W of Puebla.

pop•o•ver (pŏp′ō′vər) ►*n.* A very light, hollow muffin made with eggs, milk, and flour.

pop•py (pŏp′ē) ►*n., pl.* **-pies.** Any of numerous plants having showy red, orange, or white flowers and a milky juice. [< Lat. *papāver.*]

pop•py•cock (pŏp′ē-kŏk′) ►*n.* Senseless talk. [Du. dial. *pappekak.*]

pop-top (pŏp′tŏp′) ►*adj.* Having a tab that can be pulled up or off to make an opening in a container. —**pop′-top′** *n.*

pop•u•lace (pŏp′yə-lĭs) ►*n.* **1.** The general public; masses. **2.** A population. [< Ital. *popolaccio*, rabble.]

pop•u•lar (pŏp′yə-lər) ►*adj.* **1.** Widely liked or appreciated. **2.** Of, representing, or carried on by the people at large. **3.** Accepted by or prevalent among the people in general. [< Lat. *populus*, the people.] —**pop′u•lar′i•ty** (-lăr′ĭ-tē) *n.* —**pop′u•lar•ly** *adv.*

popular front ►*n.* A political coalition of leftist parties against fascism.

pop•u•lar•ize (pŏp′yə-lə-rīz′) ►*v.* **-ized, -iz•ing.** To make popular. —**pop′u•lar•i•za′tion** *n.* —**pop′u•lar•iz′er** *n.*

pop•u•late (pŏp′yə-lāt′) ►*v.* **-lat•ed, -lat•ing 1.** To supply with inhabitants. **2.** To inhabit. [< Lat. *populus*, the people.]

pop•u•la•tion (pŏp′yə-lā′shən) ►*n.* **1.** All of the people inhabiting a specified area. **2.** *Ecol.* All the organisms of the same kind living in a specified habitat. **3.** The set of individuals, items, or data from which a statistical sample is taken.

population explosion ►*n.* Great expansion of a biological population, esp. the unchecked growth in human population resulting from a decrease in infant mortality and an increase in longevity.

pop•u•lism (pŏp′yə-lĭz′əm) ►*n.* A political philosophy opposing the concentration of power in the hands of corporations, the government, and the rich. —**pop′u•list** *n.*

pop•u•lous (pŏp′yə-ləs) ►*adj.* Containing many inhabitants; having a large population. —**pop′u•lous•ness** *n.*

pop-up (pŏp′ŭp′) ►*n.* **1.** A device or illustration that pops up. **2.** *Baseball* See **pop fly.**

por•ce•lain (pôr′sə-lĭn, pōr′-) ►*n.* **1.** A hard white translucent ceramic. **2.** An object made of porcelain. [< OItal. *porcellana.*]

porch (pôrch, pōrch) ►*n.* **1.** A covered platform, usu. having a separate roof, at an entrance to a building. **2.** An open or enclosed gallery or room attached to the outside of a building. [< Lat. *porticus*, portico.]

por•cine (pôr′sīn′) ►*adj.* Of or resembling swine or a pig. [< Lat. *porcus*, pig.]

por•cu•pine (pôr′kyə-pīn′) ►*n.* Any of various rodents having long sharp quills. [< OFr. *porc espin*, spiny pig.]

pore[1] (pôr, pōr) ►*v.* **pored, por•ing 1.** To read or study carefully and attentively: *pored over the report.* **2.** To gaze intently; stare. **3.** To meditate deeply. [ME *pouren.*]

pore[2] (pôr, pōr) ►*n.* A minute opening, as in an animal's skin or a plant leaf, for the passage of fluid. [< Gk. *poros*, passage.]

pork (pôrk, pōrk) ►*n.* The flesh of a pig or hog used as food. [< Lat. *porcus*, pig.]

pork barrel ►*n. Slang* A government project or appropriation that benefits a specific locale and a legislator's constituents.

pork•er (pôr′kər, pōr′-) ►*n.* A fattened young pig.

porn (pôrn) also **por•no** (pôr′nō) ►*n. Slang* Pornography. —**porn** *adj.*

por•nog•ra•phy (pôr-nŏg′rə-fē) ►*n.* Pictures, writing, or other material that is sexually explicit and intended to cause sexual arousal. [< LGk. *pornē*, prostitute + -GRAPHY.] —**por•nog′ra•pher** *n.* —**por′no•graph′ic** (-nə-grăf′ĭk) *adj.*

po•rous (pôr′əs, pōr′-) ►*adj.* **1.** Full of or having pores. **2.** Admitting the passage of gas or liquid through pores or interstices. —**po•ros′i•ty** (pə-rŏs′ĭ-tē) *n.* —**po′rous•ly** *adv.* —**po′rous•ness** *n.*

por•phy•ry (pôr′fə-rē) ►*n., pl.* **-ries.** A fine-grained igneous rock containing relatively large crystals, esp. of feldspar. [< Gk. *porphura*, purple.]

por•poise (pôr′pəs) ►*n., pl.* **-poise** or **-pois•es.** Any of several toothed whales of oceanic waters, characterized by a blunt snout and a triangular dorsal fin. [< OFr. *porpeis.*]

por•ridge (pôr′ĭj, pŏr′-) ►*n.* A soft food made by boiling oatmeal or another meal in water or milk. [< POTTAGE.]

por•rin•ger (pôr′ĭn-jər, pŏr′-) ►*n.* A shallow cup or bowl with a handle. [< OFr. *potager.*]

porringer

port[1] (pôrt, pōrt) ►*n.* **1.** A city or town on a waterway with facilities for loading and unloading ships. **2.** A harbor. **3.** *Comp. Sci.* A connection point for a peripheral device. [< Lat. *portus.*]

port[2] (pôrt, pōrt) ►*n.* The left-hand side of a ship or aircraft facing forward. ►*adj.* Of or relating to the port. [Prob. < PORT[1].]

port[3] (pôrt, pōrt) ►*n.* **1.** A porthole. **2.** An opening, as in a cylinder, for the passage of steam or fluid. [< Lat. *porta*, gate.]

port[4] also **Port** (pôrt, pōrt) ►*n.* A rich sweet fortified wine. [< OPORTO.]

Port. ►*abbr.* Portuguese

por•ta•ble (pôr′tə-bəl, pōr′-) ►*adj.* Carried or moved with ease. [< Lat. *portāre*, carry.] —**por′ta•bil′i•ty, por′ta•ble•ness** *n.* —**por′ta•ble** *n.* —**por′ta•bly** *adv.*

port•age (pôr′tĭj, pōr′-, pôr-täzh′) ►*n.* **1.** The carrying of boats and supplies overland between two waterways. **2.** A track or route used for such carrying. ►*v.* **-aged, -ag•ing.** To transport or travel by portage. [< Lat. *portāre*, carry.]

por•tal (pôr′tl, pōr′-) ►*n.* **1.** A doorway or entrance, esp. a large and imposing one. **2.** *Comp. Sci.* A website considered as an entry point to other websites, often by being or providing access to a search engine. [< Med.Lat. *portāle*, city gate.]

portal tomb ►*n.* A Neolithic tomb consisting of two or more upright stones with a capstone.

Port-au-Prince (pôrt′ō-prĭns′, pōrt′-) The capital of Haiti, in the SW part. Pop. 690,168.

port•cul•lis (pôrt-kŭl′ĭs, pōrt-) ►*n.* A grating suspended in the gateway of a fortified place and lowered to block passage. [< OFr. *porte coleice*, sliding gate.]

porte-co•chère or **porte-co•chere** (pôrt′kō-shâr′, pōrt′-) ►*n.* An enclosure over a driveway at the entrance of a building to provide shelter. [Fr. *porte cochère*, coach door.]

Port Elizabeth. A city of SE South Africa on an inlet of the Indian Ocean. Pop. 303,353.

por•tend (pôr-tĕnd′, pōr-) ►*v.* **1.** To serve as an omen or warning of; presage. **2.** To indicate; forecast. [< Lat. *portendere.*]

por•tent (pôr′tĕnt′, pōr′-) ►*n.* **1.** An indication of something about to occur; omen. **2.** Something amazing; prodigy. [Lat. *portentum.*]

por•ten•tous (pôr-tĕn′təs, pōr-) ►*adj.* **1.** Of or constituting a portent. **2.** Exciting wonder and awe. **3.** Pompous; pretentiously weighty. —**por•ten′tous•ness** *n.*

por•ter[1] (pôr′tər, pōr′-) ►*n.* **1.** A person employed to carry travelers' baggage. **2.** A railroad employee who waits on passengers. **3.** A maintenance worker. [< LLat. *portātor* < Lat. *portāre*, carry.]

por•ter[2] (pôr′tər, pōr′-) ►*n. Chiefly Brit.* One in charge of a gate or door. [< LLat. *portārius* < Lat. *porta*, gate.]

por•ter[3] (pôr′tər, pōr′-) ►*n.* A dark beer made from browned or charred malt. [< *porter's ale.*]

Porter, Cole Albert. 1891?–1964. Amer. composer and lyricist.

Porter, Katherine Anne. 1890–1980. Amer. writer.

Porter, William Sydney. O. Henry. 1862–1910. Amer. writer.

por•ter•house (pôr′tər-hous′, pōr′-) ►*n.* A cut of beef having a T-bone and a sizable piece of tenderloin.

port•fo•li•o (pôrt-fō′lē-ō′, pōrt-) ►*n., pl.* **-os** **1.** A portable case for holding loose papers or drawings. **2.** The office or post of a cabinet member or minister of state. **3.** A group of investments. [Ital. *portafoglio.*]

port•hole (pôrt′hōl′, pōrt′-) ►*n.* A small, usu. circular window in a ship's side.

por•ti•co (pôr′tĭ-kō′, pōr′-) ►*n., pl.* **-coes** or **-cos.** A porch or walkway with a roof supported by columns, often leading to the entrance of a building. [< Lat. *porticus.*]

por•tière or **por•tiere** (pôr-tyâr′, pōr-) ►*n.* A heavy curtain hung across a doorway. [Fr.]

por•tion (pôr′shən, pōr′-) ►*n.* **1.** A part of a whole. **2.** A part allotted to a person or group. **3.** A person's lot or fate. ►*v.* **1.** To distribute in portions. **2.** To provide with a share. [< Lat. *portiō.*]

Port•land (pôrt′lənd, pōrt′-) **1.** A city of SW ME S of Lewiston. Pop. 64,348. **2.** A city of NW OR near the Columbia R. Pop. 437,319. —**Port′land•er** *n.*

Portland cement or **portland cement** ►*n.* A hydraulic cement made by heating and pulverizing a mixture of limestone and clay. [After *Portland*, England.]

Port Lou•is (lo͞o′ĭs, lo͞o′ē, lo͞o-ē′) The capital of Mauritius, in the NW part. Pop. 143,509.

port•ly (pôrt′lē, pōrt′-) ►*adj.* **-li•er, -li•est.** Comfortably stout; corpulent. [< *port*, bearing.] —**port′li•ness** *n.*

port•man•teau (pôrt-măn′tō, pōrt-, pôrt′măn-tō′, pōrt′-) ►*n., pl.* **-teaus** or **-teaux** (-tōz, -tōz′). A large leather suitcase with two hinged compartments. [Fr. *portemanteau.*]

Port Mores•by (môrz′bē, mōrz′-) The capital of Papua New Guinea, on SE New Guinea. Pop. 173,500.

Pôr•to A•le•gre (pôr′to͝o ə-lĕ′grə) A city of SE Brazil. Pop. 1,263,239.

port of call ►*n.* A port where ships dock in the course of voyages to load or unload cargo, obtain supplies, or undergo repairs.

port of entry ►*n.* A place where travelers or goods may enter or leave a country under official supervision.

Port of Spain or **Port-of-Spain** (pôrt′əv-spān′, pōrt′-). The capital of Trinidad and Tobago, on the NW coast of Trinidad on an arm of the Atlantic. Pop. 50,878.

Por•to-No•vo (pôr′tō-nō′vō, pōr′-) The capital of Benin, in the SE part on an inlet of the Gulf of Guinea. Pop. 179,138.

por•trait (pôr′trĭt, -trāt′, pōr′-) ►*n.* **1.** A likeness of a person, esp. one showing the face, created by a painter or photographer. **2.** A verbal picture or description, esp. of a person. [< OFr. *portraire*, portray.] —**por′trait•ist** *n.*

por•trai•ture (pôr′trĭ-cho͝or′, pōr′-) ►*n.* The art or practice of making portraits.

por•tray (pôr-trā′, pōr-) ►*v.* **1.** To depict pictorially. **2.** To describe in words. **3.** To represent dramatically, as on the stage. See Syns at **represent.** [< OFr. *portraire.*] —**por•tray′al** *n.* —**por•tray′er** *n.*

Port Sa•id (sä-ēd′) A city of NE Egypt on the Mediterranean at the N entrance to the Suez Canal. Pop. 460,000.

Ports•mouth (pôrt′sməth, pōrt′-) **1.** A borough of S England on the English Channel opposite the I. of Wight. Pop. 189,073. **2.** A city of SE VA opposite Norfolk. Pop. 103,907.

Port Stanley. See **Stanley.**

Port Sudan. A city of NE Sudan on the Red Sea NE of Khartoum. Pop. 305,385.

Por•tu•gal (pôr′chə-gəl, pōr′-) A country of SW Europe on the W Iberian Peninsula. Cap. Lisbon. Pop. 9,830,000.

Por•tu•guese (pôr′chə-gēz′, -gēs′, pōr′-) ►*n., pl.* **-guese** **1.** A native or inhabitant of Portugal. **2.** The Romance language of Portugal and Brazil. —**Por′tu•guese′** *adj.*

Portuguese man-of-war ►*n.* A complex marine organism of warm seas, having a bluish, bladderlike float from which hang numerous long stinging tentacles.

por•tu•lac•a (pôr′chə-lăk′ə, pōr′-) ►*n.* A fleshy South American plant having showy flowers. [< Lat. *portulāca*, purslane.]

Port-Vi•la (pôrt′vē′lə, pōrt′-, pôr-vē-lä′) The capital of Vanuatu, on Efate I. in the SW Pacific. Pop. 13,067.

pose (pōz) ►*v.* **posed, pos•ing 1.** To assume or cause to assume a particular position or posture, as in sitting for a portrait. **2.** To affect a particular attitude. **3.** To represent oneself falsely. **4.** To place in a specific position. **5.** To put forward; present: *pose a threat.* ►*n.* **1.** A bodily attitude or position, esp. one assumed for an artist. See Syns at **posture. 2.** A studied attitude assumed for effect. [< Lat. *pausa*, PAUSE.] —**pos′a•ble** *adj.*

Po•sei•don (pō-sīd′n, pə-) ►*n. Gk. Myth.* The god of the sea and brother of Zeus.

pos•er[1] (pō′zər) ►*n.* One who poses.

pos•er[2] (pō′zər) ►*n.* A baffling problem.

po•seur (pō-zœr′) ►*n.* One who affects a particular attitude or manner to impress others. [Fr. < *poser*, pose.]

posh (pŏsh) ►*adj.* Fashionable. See Syns at **fashionable.** [Perh. < Romany *pāšh*, money.] —**posh′ly** *adv.* —**posh′ness** *n.*

pos•it (pŏz′ĭt) ►*v.* To affirm or assume the existence of; postulate. [< Lat. *pōnere, posit-*, place.]

po•si•tion (pə-zĭsh′ən) ►*n.* **1.** A place or location. **2.** The right or appropriate place. **3.** The way in which something or someone is placed. **4.** A situation relative to circumstances: *in a position to bargain.* **5.** A point of view. **6.** Status; rank. **7.** A post of employment; job. ►*v.* To put in position. [< Lat. *pōnere, posit-*, place.] —**po•si′tion•al** *adj.* —**po•si′tion•er** *n.*

pos•i•tive (pŏz′ĭ-tĭv) ►*adj.* **1.** Marked by or displaying certainty or affirmation: *a positive answer.* **2.** Explicitly expressed: *a positive demand.* **3.** Admitting of no doubt; irrefutable. **4.** Very sure; confident. **5.** Real. **6.** *Math.* Of or designating: **a.** A quantity greater than zero. **b.** A quantity, number, angle, or direction opposite to another designated as negative. **7.** *Phys.* Of or designating electric charge of a sign opposite to that of an electron. **8.** Having the areas of light and dark in their original and normal relationship, as in a photographic print. **9.** *Gram.* Of or being the simple uncompared degree of an adjective or adverb. ►*n.* **1.** A photographic image in which the lights and darks appear as they do in nature. **2.** *Gram.* The positive degree of an adjective or adverb. [< Lat. *positīvus*, formally laid down.] —**pos′i•tive•ly** *adv.* —**pos′i•tive•ness, pos′i•tiv′i•ty** *n.*

pos•i•tron (pŏz′ĭ-trŏn′) ►*n.* The antiparticle of the electron. [POSI(TIVE) + (ELEC)TRON.]

pos•se (pŏs′ē) ►*n.* A group of people summoned by a sheriff to aid in law enforcement. [< Lat. *posse comitātūs*, power of the county.]

pos•sess (pə-zĕs′) ►*v.* **1.** To have as property; own. **2.** To have as an attribute. **3.** To exert influence or control over; dominate. [< Lat. *possidēre* : *pos-*, as master + *sedēre*, sit.] —**pos•ses′sor** *n.*

pos•sessed (pə-zĕst′) ►*adj.* **1.** Controlled by or as if by a spirit or other force. **2.** Calm; collected.

pos•ses•sion (pə-zĕsh′ən) ►*n.* **1a.** The act or fact of possessing. **b.** The state of being possessed. **2.** Something owned or possessed. **3. possessions** Wealth or property. **4.** A territory subject to foreign control. **5.** Self-control. **6.** The state of being dominated by evil spirits. **7.** *Sports* Physical control of the ball or puck.

pos•ses•sive (pə-zĕs′ĭv) ►*adj.* **1.** Having or manifesting a desire to control or dominate: *a possessive parent.* **2.** *Gram.* Of or being a noun or pronoun case that indicates possession. ►*n. Gram.* **1.** The possessive case. **2.** A possessive form or construction. —**pos•ses′sive•ly** *adv.* —**pos•ses′sive•ness** *n.*

pos•si•ble (pŏs′ə-bəl) ►*adj.* **1.** Capable of happening, existing, or being true. **2.** Capable of occurring or being done. **3.** Potential. [< Lat. *possibilis.*] —**pos′si•bil′i•ty** *n.* —**pos′si•bly** *adv.*

pos•sum (pŏs′əm) ►*n.* An opossum.

post[1] (pōst) ►*n.* **1.** A stake set upright into the ground to serve as a marker or support. **2.** Something similar to a post. **3.** *Comp. Sci.* An electronic message sent to a newsgroup. ►*v.* **1.** To display in a place of public view. **2.** To announce by or as if by posters. **3.** To put up signs on (property) warning against trespassing. **4.** To publish (a name) on a list. **5.** *Comp. Sci.* To send (an electronic message) to a newsgroup. [< Lat. *postis.*]

post[2] (pōst) ►*n.* **1.** A military base. **2.** An assigned station, as of a sentry. **3.** A position of employment. **4.** A trading post. ►*v.* **1.** To assign to a position or station. **2.** To put forward; present: *post bail.* [< Lat. *positum*, p.part. of *pōnere*, place.]

post[3] (pōst) ►*n.* **1.** A delivery of mail. **2.** *Chiefly Brit.* **a.** A governmental system for transporting and delivering the mail. **b.** A post office. ►*v.* **1.** To mail (a letter or package). **2.** To inform of the latest news. **3.** To make entries in (a ledger). **4.** To travel with speed. [< OItal. *posta*, relay station, ult. < Lat. *pōnere*, place.]

post– ►*pref.* **1.** After; later: *postdate.* **2.** Behind; posterior to: *postnasal.* [< Lat. *post*, after.]

post•age (pō′stĭj) ►*n.* The charge for mailing an item.

post•al (pō′stəl) ►*adj.* Of or relating to a post office or mail service. —**post′al•ly** *adv.*

postal card ►*n.* An unadorned card printed with the image of a postage stamp, issued by a government.

post card also **post•card** (pōst′kärd′) ►*n.* **1.** A commercially printed card used for sending a short message through the mail. **2.** See **postal card.**

post chaise ►*n.* A closed, four-wheeled, horse-drawn carriage.

post•date (pōst-dāt′, pōst′-) ►*v.* **1.** To put a date on (e.g., a check) that is later than the actual date. **2.** To occur later than.

post•doc•tor•al (pōst-dŏk′tər-əl) also **post•doc•tor•ate** (-ĭt) ►*adj.* Of or engaged in academic study beyond the doctorate.

post•er (pō′stər) ►*n.* A large, usu. printed placard, bill, or announcement posted to advertise or publicize something.

pos•te•ri•or (pŏ-stîr′ē-ər, pō-) ►*adj.* **1.** Located behind a part or toward the rear of a structure. **2.** Relating to the hind or back part of a body. **3.** Following in time; subsequent. ►*n.* The buttocks. [Lat. < *posterus*, coming after.] —**pos•te′ri•or•ly** *adv.*

pos•ter•i•ty (pŏ-stĕr′ĭ-tē) ►*n.* **1.** Future generations. **2.** All of a person's descendants. [< Lat. *posterus*, coming after.]

pos•tern (pō′stərn, pŏs′tərn) ►*n.* A rear gate, esp. in a fort or castle. [< LLat. *posterula.*]

Post Exchange ► A service mark for a store on a military base that sells goods to military personnel and their families.

post•grad•u•ate (pōst-grăj′o͞o-ĭt, -āt′) ▸*adj.* Of or relating to advanced study after graduation from college. ▸*n.* One engaged in postgraduate study.

post•haste (pōst′hāst′) ▸*adv.* With great speed; rapidly. [< *post, haste,* a direction on letters.]

post•hu•mous (pŏs′chə-məs) ▸*adj.* **1.** Occurring or continuing after one's death. **2.** Published after the writer's death. [< Lat. *postumus.*] —**post′hu•mous•ly** *adv.*

post•hyp•not•ic suggestion (pōst′hĭp-nŏt′ĭk) ▸*n.* A suggestion made to a hypnotized person that specifies an action to be performed after awakening.

pos•til•ion also **pos•til•lion** (pō-stĭl′yən, pŏ-) ▸*n.* One who rides the near horse of the leaders to guide the horses drawing a coach. [< Ital. *postiglione.*]

Post-It (pōst′ĭt′) ▸ A trademark for a slip of notepaper with an adhesive edge.

post•lude (pōst′lo͞od′) ▸*n.* An organ voluntary played at the end of a church service. [POST– + (PRE)LUDE.]

post•man (pōst′mən) ▸*n.* See **mailman.**

post•mark (pōst′märk′) ▸*n.* An official mark stamped on mail that cancels the stamp and records the date and place of mailing. —**post′mark′** *v.*

post•mas•ter (pōst′măs′tər) ▸*n.* A man in charge of a post office.

postmaster general ▸*n., pl.* **postmasters general.** The executive head of a national postal service.

post me•rid•i•em (mə-rĭd′ē-əm) ▸*adv. & adj.* After noon. Used chiefly in the abbreviated form to specify the hour: *10:30 P.M.; a P.M. appointment.* See Usage Note at **ante meridiem.** [Lat. *post merīdiem.*]

post•mis•tress (pōst′mĭs′trĭs) ▸*n.* A woman in charge of a post office.

post•mor•tem (pōst-môr′təm) ▸*adj.* **1.** Occurring or done after death. **2.** Of or relating to a postmortem. ▸*n.* **1.** See **autopsy. 2.** *Informal* An analysis or review of a completed event. [Lat. *post mortem,* after death.] —**post mor′tem** *adv.*

post•na•sal (pōst-nā′zəl) ▸*adj.* Located or occurring posterior to the nose.

post•na•tal (pōst-nāt′l) ▸*adj.* Of or occurring after birth. —**post•na′tal•ly** *adv.*

post office ▸*n.* **1.** The public department responsible for the transportation and delivery of the mails. **2.** A local office where mail is processed and stamps are sold.

post•op•er•a•tive (pōst-ŏp′ər-ə-tĭv, -ŏp′rə-, -ŏp′ə-rā′-) ▸*adj.* Happening or done after surgery. —**post•op′er•a•tive•ly** *adv.*

post•paid (pōst′pād′) ▸*adj.* With the postage paid in advance.

post•par•tum (pōst-pär′təm) ▸*adj.* Of or occurring after childbirth. [Lat. *post partum,* after birth.]

post•pone (pōst-pōn′, pōs-pōn′) ▸*v.* **-poned, -pon•ing.** To delay until a future time; put off. See Syns at **defer¹.** [Lat. *postpōnere.*] —**post•pone′ment** *n.*

post•script (pōst′skrĭpt′, pōs′skrĭpt′) ▸*n.* A message added to a letter after the writer's signature. [< Lat. *postscrīptum.*]

pos•tu•lant (pŏs′chə-lənt) ▸*n.* A candidate for admission into a religious order. [< Lat. *postulāre,* request.] —**pos′tu•lan•cy** *n.*

pos•tu•late (pŏs′chə-lāt′) ▸*v.* **-lat•ed, -lat•ing.** To assume or assert the truth or reality of, esp. as a basis of an argument. ▸*n.* (pŏs′chə-lĭt, -lāt′). Something assumed without proof as being self-evident or generally accepted. [< Lat. *postulāre,* request.] —**pos′tu•la′tion** *n.*

pos•ture (pŏs′chər) ▸*n.* **1a.** A position or attitude of the body or of body parts. **b.** An attitude; pose: *assumed a posture of defiance.* **2.** A stance with regard to something. **3.** A frame of mind; attitude. ▸*v.* **-tured, -tur•ing.** To assume an exaggerated or unnatural pose or mental attitude. [< Lat. *positūra,* position.] —**pos′tur•al** *adj.* —**pos′tur•er, pos′tur•ist** *n.*

Syns: *posture, attitude, carriage, pose, stance* ***n.***

po•sy (pō′zē) ▸*n., pl.* **-sies.** A flower or bunch of flowers. [< POESY.]

pot¹ (pŏt) ▸*n.* **1.** A round cooking vessel with a handle. **2.** Something resembling a pot in appearance or function. **3.** *Games* The total amount staked by all the players in one hand at cards. See Syns at **bet. 4.** *Informal* A common fund. ▸*v.* **pot•ted, pot•ting 1.** To place or plant in a pot. **2.** To cook or preserve in a pot. [< VLat. *pottus.*]

pot² (pŏt) ▸*n. Slang* Marijuana. [?]

po•ta•ble (pō′tə-bəl) ▸*adj.* Fit to drink. [< Lat. *pōtāre,* drink.]

pot•ash (pŏt′ăsh′) ▸*n.* **1.** See **potassium carbonate. 2.** See **potassium hydroxide. 3.** Any of several compounds containing potassium, esp. soluble compounds used chiefly in fertilizers. [< obsolete *pot ashes.*]

po•tas•si•um (pə-tăs′ē-əm) ▸*n. Symbol* **K** A soft, silver-white, highly or explosively reactive metallic element found naturally only in compounds and used in fertilizers and soaps. At. no. 19. See table at **element.** [< POTASH.] —**po•tas′sic** *adj.*

potassium bromide ▸*n.* A white crystalline solid or powder, KBr, used as a sedative and in lithography.

potassium carbonate ▸*n.* A granular powder used in making glass, enamels, and soaps.

potassium cyanide ▸*n.* An extremely poisonous white compound used in electroplating, photography, and as an insecticide.

potassium hydroxide ▸*n.* A caustic white solid used as a bleach and in making soaps, dyes, and alkaline batteries; lye.

potassium nitrate ▸*n.* A white crystalline compound used to pickle meat and in making explosives and fertilizers; saltpeter.

po•ta•tion (pō-tā′shən) ▸*n.* **1.** The act of drinking. **2.** A drink, esp. an alcoholic beverage. [< Lat. *pōtāre,* drink.]

po•ta•to (pə-tā′tō) ▸*n., pl.* **-toes 1.** A South American plant widely cultivated for its starchy edible tubers. **2.** A tuber of this plant. [< Taino *batata.*]

potato chip ▸*n.* A thin slice of potato fried in deep fat until crisp and then salted.

Pot•a•wat•o•mi (pŏt′ə-wŏt′ə-mē) ▸*n., pl.* **-mi** or **-mis 1.** A member of a Native American people with populations in Oklahoma, Kansas, Michigan, and Ontario. **2.** The Algonquian language of the Potawatomi.

pot•bel•ly (pŏt′bĕl′ē) ▸*n.* A protruding belly. —**pot′bel′lied** *adj.*

pot•boil•er (pŏt′boi′lər) ▸*n.* A literary or artistic work of poor quality, produced quickly for profit.

pot cheese ► *n.* See **cottage cheese.**

po•tent (pōt′nt) ► *adj.* **1.** Possessing strength; powerful. **2.** Exerting or capable of exerting strong effects. **3.** Able to perform sexual intercourse. Used of a male. [< Lat. *potēns*.] —**po′ten•cy** *n.* —**po′tent•ly** *adv.*

po•ten•tate (pōt′n-tāt′) ► *n.* One who has the power and position to rule over others; monarch. [< Lat. *potentātus*, power.]

po•ten•tial (pə-tĕn′shəl) ► *adj.* Capable of being but not yet in existence; latent. ► *n.* **1.** Capacity for growth, development, or coming into being. **2.** *Symbol* **V** *Elect.* The potential energy of a unit charge measured with respect to a specified reference point; voltage. —**po•ten′ti•al′i•ty** (-shē-ăl′ĭ-tē) *n.* —**po•ten′tial•ly** *adv.*

potential energy ► *n.* The energy of a body or system derived from position or condition rather than motion.

pot•head (pŏt′hĕd′) ► *n. Slang* One who habitually smokes marijuana.

poth•er (pŏ*th*′ər) ► *n.* **1.** A commotion; disturbance. **2.** A fuss. [?]

pot•hold•er (pŏt′hōl′dər) ► *n.* A small fabric pad used to handle hot cooking utensils.

pot•hole (pŏt′hōl′) ► *n.* A large hole, esp. in a road surface. —**pot′holed′** *adj.*

po•tion (pō′shən) ► *n.* A liquid dose, esp. of medicinal, magic, or poisonous content. [< Lat. *pōtiō*.]

pot•luck (pŏt′lŭk′) ► *n.* **1.** Whatever food happens to be available for a meal. **2.** A meal at which each guest brings food that is then shared by all.

Po•to•mac River (pə-tō′mək) A river of the E-central US rising in NE WV and flowing about 459 km (285 mi) to Chesapeake Bay.

pot•pie (pŏt′pī′) ► *n.* Meat or poultry and vegetables covered with a pastry crust and baked in a deep dish.

pot•pour•ri (pō′po͞o-rē′) ► *n., pl.* **-ris 1.** A combination of incongruous things. **2.** A mixture of dried flower petals and spices. [Fr. *pot pourri*.]

pot roast ► *n.* Beef that is browned and then cooked until tender in a covered pot.

Pots•dam (pŏts′dăm′) A city of NE Germany on the Havel R. near Berlin. Pop. 139,262.

pot•sherd (pŏt′shûrd′) also **pot•shard** (-shärd′) ► *n.* A fragment of broken pottery.

pot•shot also **pot shot** (pŏt′shŏt′) ► *n.* **1.** A random or easy shot. **2.** A criticism made without careful thought and aimed at a handy target.

pot•tage (pŏt′ĭj) ► *n.* A thick soup or stew of vegetables and sometimes meat. [< OFr. *potage*.]

pot•ted (pŏt′ĭd) ► *adj.* **1.** Placed or grown in a pot. **2.** *Slang* Intoxicated; drunk.

pot•ter[1] (pŏt′ər) ► *n.* A maker of pottery.

pot•ter[2] (pŏt′ər) ► *v. Chiefly Brit.* Var. of **putter**[2].

Potter, Beatrix. 1866–1943. British writer and illustrator.

pot•ter•y (pŏt′ə-rē) ► *n., pl.* **-ies 1.** Ware, such as vases, pots, bowls, or plates, shaped from moist clay and hardened by heat. **2.** The craft or occupation of a potter. **3.** The place where a potter works.

pouch (pouch) ► *n.* **1.** A small bag used esp. for carrying loose items. **2.** A bag used to carry mail or diplomatic dispatches. **3.** A sealed container used in packaging frozen or dehydrated food. **4.** *Zool.* A saclike structure, such as the external abdominal pocket in which marsupials carry their young. [< OFr., of Gmc. orig.]

poul•tice (pōl′tĭs) ► *n.* A soft, moist, usu. heated mass spread on cloth and applied to a sore or inflamed part of the body. [< Med.Lat. *pultēs*, thick paste.] —**poul′tice** *v.*

poul•try (pōl′trē) ► *n.* Domestic fowls, such as chickens, turkeys, ducks, or geese, raised for meat or eggs. [< OFr. *pouletrie*.]

pounce (pouns) ► *v.* **pounced, pounc•ing.** To spring or swoop suddenly so as to seize someone or something. [< ME, hawk's talon.] —**pounce** *n.* —**pounc′er** *n.*

pound[1] (pound) ► *n., pl.* **pound** or **pounds 1a.** See table at **measurement. b.** A unit of apothecary weight equal to 12 oz. (373.242 gr). **2.** A unit of weight differing in various countries and times. **3.** See table at **currency.** [< Lat. *pondō*, by weight.]

pound[2] (pound) ► *v.* **1.** To strike repeatedly and forcefully. See Syns at **beat. 2.** To beat to a powder or pulp; pulverize or crush. **3.** To instill by persistent, emphatic repetition. **4.** To pulsate rapidly and heavily. [< OE *pūnian*.] —**pound′er** *n.*

pound[3] (pound) ► *n.* A public enclosure for confining stray animals. [< OE *pund-*.]

Pound, Ezra Loomis. 1885–1972. Amer. writer.

pound•age (poun′dĭj) ► *n.* Weight measured in pounds.

pound cake ► *n.* A rich yellow cake containing eggs, flour, butter, and sugar.

pound sign ► *n.* **1.** The symbol (£) for a unit of currency, esp. the pound sterling. **2.** The symbol (#) for a pound as a unit of weight.

pour (pôr, pōr) ► *v.* **1.** To flow or cause to flow in a steady stream. **2.** To send forth or produce copiously, as if in a stream or flood. **3.** To rain heavily. [ME *pouren*.] —**pour′er** *n.*

pout (pout) ► *v.* **1.** To exhibit displeasure or disappointment; sulk. **2.** To protrude the lips in an expression of displeasure. [ME *pouten*.] —**pout** *n.* —**pout′y** *adj.*

POV ► *abbr.* point of view

pov•er•ty (pŏv′ər-tē) ► *n.* **1.** The state of being poor; lack of money or material goods. **2.** Deficiency in amount; scantiness. **3.** Unproductiveness. [< Lat. *paupertās*.]

pov•er•ty-strick•en (pŏv′ər-tē-strĭk′ən) ► *adj.* Destitute; miserably poor.

POW (pē′ō-dŭb′əl-yo͞o, -yo͞o) ► *n.* A prisoner of war.

pow•der (pou′dər) ► *n.* **1.** A substance consisting of ground, pulverized, or otherwise finely dispersed solid particles. **2.** Any of various preparations in the form of powder, as certain cosmetics and medicines. **3.** An explosive mixture, such as gunpowder. **4.** Light dry snow. ► *v.* **1.** To pulverize. **2.** To dust or cover with or as if with powder. [< Lat. *pulvis*, *pulver-*.] —**pow′der•y** *adj.*

powder keg ► *n.* **1.** A small cask for holding gunpowder or other explosives. **2.** A potentially explosive situation.

powder puff ► *n.* A soft pad for applying powder to the skin.

powder room ►*n.* A lavatory for women.

pow•er (pou′ər) ►*n.* **1.** The ability or capacity to perform or act effectively. **2.** often **powers** A specific capacity, faculty, or aptitude: *her powers of concentration.* **3.** Strength or force exerted or capable of being exerted; might. **4.** The ability or official capacity to exercise control; authority. **5.** A person, group, or nation having influence or control over others. **6.** Forcefulness; effectiveness. **7.** The energy or motive force by which a physical system or machine is operated. **8.** Electricity. **9.** *Phys.* The rate at which work is done, commonly measured in units such as the watt and horsepower. **10.** *Math.* See **exponent** 2. **11.** A measure of the magnification of an optical instrument. ►*v.* To supply with power, esp. mechanical power. [< VLat. **potēre*, be able.] —**pow′er•ful** *adj.* —**pow′er•ful•ly** *adv.* —**pow′er•ful•ness** *n.* —**pow′er•less** *adj.* —**pow′er•less•ly** *adv.*

pow•er•boat (pou′ər-bōt′) ►*n.* See **motorboat.**

pow•er•house (pou′ər-hous′) ►*n.* **1.** See **power plant** 2. **2.** One that possesses great force or energy.

power of attorney ►*n.* A legal instrument authorizing one to act as another's attorney or agent.

power plant ►*n.* **1.** All the equipment that constitutes a unit power source. **2.** A complex of structures and machinery for generating electric energy from another source of energy.

power shovel ►*n.* A large earthmoving machine used for excavating.

power train ►*n.* An assembly of gears and associated parts by which power is transmitted from an engine to a driving axle.

Pow•ha•tan[1] (pou′ə-tăn′, pou-hăt′n). 1550?–1618. Algonquian leader.

Pow•ha•tan[2] (pou′ə-tăn′, pou-hăt′n) ►*n., pl.* **-tan** or **-tans 1.** A member of a confederacy of Native American peoples formerly inhabiting E Virginia. **2.** The Algonquian language of the Powhatan.

pow•wow (pou′wou′) ►*n.* **1.** A council or meeting with or of Native Americans. **2.** A ceremony during which a shaman performs healing or hunting rituals. **3.** *Informal* A conference or gathering. [< Narragansett *powwaw*, shaman.] —**pow′wow′** *v.*

pox (pŏks) ►*n.* A disease such as smallpox, marked by purulent skin eruptions. [< POCK.]

Poz•nań (pōz′nän′) A city of W-central Poland W of Warsaw. Pop. 590,087.

pp. ►*abbr.* **1.** pages **2.** prepaid **3.** postpaid

p.p. ►*abbr.* **1.** parcel post **2.** past participle

PPO ►*abbr.* preferred provider organization

PQ ►*abbr.* Quebec

Pr ► The symbol for the element **praseodymium.**

PR ►*abbr.* **1.** public relations **2.** or **P.R.** Puerto Rico

pr. ►*abbr.* **1.** pair **2.** present **3a.** printed **b.** printing **4.** pronoun

prac•ti•ca•ble (prăk′tĭ-kə-bəl) ►*adj.* **1.** Capable of being effected, done, or put into practice; feasible. **2.** Usable. —**prac′ti•ca•bil′i•ty** *n.* —**prac′ti•ca•bly** *adv.*

Usage: *Practicable* means "feasible" as well as "usable" and hence overlaps in meaning to some extent with *practical,* which can mean "useful." *Practicable* shares no other senses with *practical.*

prac•ti•cal (prăk′tĭ-kəl) ►*adj.* **1.** Of or acquired through practice or action, rather than theory or speculation: *practical experience.* **2.** Manifested in or involving practice: *practical applications.* **3.** Capable of being used or put into effect; useful. See Usage Note at **practicable. 4.** Intended to serve a purpose without elaboration: *practical shoes.* **5.** Level-headed, efficient, and unspeculative. **6.** Being almost actually so; virtual. [< Gk. *praktikos.*] —**prac′ti•cal′i•ty** (-kăl′ĭ-tē), **prac′ti•cal•ness** *n.*

practical joke ►*n.* A prank played on a person, esp. one that embarrasses the victim.

prac•ti•cal•ly (prăk′tĭk-lē) ►*adv.* **1.** In a practical way. **2.** Nearly; almost.

practical nurse ►*n.* A licensed practical nurse.

prac•tice (prăk′tĭs) ►*v.* **-ticed, -tic•ing 1.** To do or perform habitually or customarily; make a habit of: *practice restraint.* **2.** To do or perform repeatedly in order to acquire or polish a skill. **3.** To work at, esp. as a profession: *practice law.* **4.** To carry out; observe. ►*n.* **1.** A habitual or customary action or way of doing something. **2a.** Repeated performance of an activity in order to learn or perfect a skill. **b.** Proficiency gained through repeated exercise. **3.** The act or process of doing something; performance. **4.** Exercise of an occupation or profession. **5.** The business of a professional person. **6.** A habitual action. [< Gk. *praktikos*, practical.] —**prac′tic•er** *n.*

Syns: *practice, exercise, rehearse* **v.**

prac•ti•tion•er (prăk-tĭsh′ə-nər) ►*n.* One who practices an occupation, profession, or technique. [< OFr. *practicien.*]

prae•tor (prē′tər) ►*n.* An ancient Roman magistrate below a consul. [< Lat.] —**prae•to′ri•an** (-tôr′ē-ən, -tōr′-) *adj. & n.*

prag•mat•ic (prăg-măt′ĭk) ►*adj.* **1.** Concerned with facts or actual events; practical. **2.** Relating to pragmatism. [< Gk. *pragma*, deed.] —**prag•mat′i•cal•ly** *adv.*

prag•ma•tism (prăg′mə-tĭz′əm) ►*n.* A practical, matter-of-fact way of approaching or assessing situations or of solving problems. —**prag′ma•tist** *n.*

Prague (präg) The capital of Czech Republic, in the W part. Pop. 1,216,513.

Prai•a (prī′ə) The capital of Cape Verde, on the SE coast of São Tiago I. Pop. 61,644.

prai•rie (prâr′ē) ►*n.* An extensive area of flat or rolling grassland, esp. in central North America. [< Lat. *prāta*, meadow.]

prairie dog ►*n.* A burrowing rodent of W-central North America, having light brown fur and a barklike call.

prairie schooner ►*n.* A covered wagon used by pioneers crossing the North American plains.

praise (prāz) ►*n.* **1.** Expression of approval, commendation, or admiration. **2.** The extolling or exaltation of a deity, ruler, or hero. [< LLat. *pretiāre*, to prize.] —**praise** *v.*

praise•wor•thy (prāz′wûr′*thē*) ►*adj.* Meriting praise; highly commendable.

pra•line (prä′lēn′, prā′-) ►*n.* A crisp confection made of nut kernels stirred in boiling sugar syrup. [After the Comte du Plessis-*Praslin* (1598–1675).]

pram (prăm) ►*n. Chiefly Brit.* A perambulator.
prance (prăns) ►*v.* **pranced, pranc•ing 1.** To spring forward on the hind legs, as a spirited horse. **2.** To walk or move about in a spirited manner; strut. [ME *prauncen.*] —**pranc′er** *n.* —**pranc′ing•ly** *adv.*
prank (prăngk) ►*n.* A mischievous trick. [?] —**prank′ster** *n.*
pra•se•o•dym•i•um (prā′zē-ō-dĭm′ē-əm, prā′sē-) ►*n. Symbol* **Pr** A soft, silvery, malleable, rare-earth element used to color glass yellow and in metallic alloys. At. no. 59. See table at **element.** [Gk. *prasios*, leek-green + E. *didymium*, a metal mixture.]
prate (prāt) ►*v.* **prat•ed, prat•ing.** To talk idly and at length; chatter. [< MDu. *prāten.*]
prat•fall (prăt′fôl′) ►*n.* A fall on the buttocks. [*prat*, buttocks + FALL.]
prat•tle (prăt′l) ►*v.* **-tled, -tling.** To talk idly; babble. [< PRATE.] —**prat′tle** *n.*
prawn (prôn) ►*n.* An edible crustacean similar to but larger than the shrimps. [ME *praine.*]
prax•is (prăk′sĭs) ►*n., pl.* **-es** (-sēz′). Practical application of a branch of learning. [< Gk. < *prassein*, do.]
Prax•it•e•les (prăk′sĭt′l-ēz′). fl. 4th cent. B.C. Greek sculptor.
pray (prā) ►*v.* **1.** To address a prayer to a deity. **2.** To make a fervent request for something. **3.** To beseech; implore. [< Lat. *precārī.*] —**pray′er** (prā′ər) *n.*
prayer (prâr) ►*n.* **1.** A reverent petition made to a deity. **2.** An act of praying. **3.** A specially worded form of praying. **4. prayers** A religious observance in which praying predominates. **5.** A fervent request. **6.** The slightest chance or hope. [< Med.Lat. *precāria.*]
prayer•ful (prâr′fəl) ►*adj.* **1.** Inclined to praying frequently. **2.** Typical of prayer, as a mannerism. —**prayer′ful•ly** *adv.*
prayer rug (prâr) ►*n.* A small rug used by Muslims to kneel upon during devotions.
prayer wheel ►*n.* A revolving cylinder inscribed with prayers and used in devotions, esp. by Tibetan Buddhists.

prayer wheel

pray•ing mantis (prā′ĭng) ►*n.* A green or brownish predatory insect that while at rest folds its front legs as if in prayer.
pre– ►*pref.* **1a.** Earlier; before: *prehistoric.* **b.** Preparatory; preliminary: *premedical.* **c.** In advance: *prepay.* **2.** Anterior; in front of: *premolar.* [< Lat. *prae*, before.]
preach (prēch) ►*v.* **1.** To proclaim or deliver in a sermon. **2.** To advocate or urge: *preach tolerance.* **3.** To give moral instruction, esp. in a tedious manner. [< Lat. *praedicāre*, proclaim.] —**preach′er** *n.* —**preach′y** *adj.*
pre•ad•o•les•cence (prē′ăd-l-ĕs′əns) ►*n.* The period between childhood and puberty. —**pre′ad•o•les′cent** *adj. & n.*
pre•am•ble (prē′ăm′bəl, prē-ăm′-) ►*n.* A preliminary statement, esp. to a formal document, explaining its purpose. [< Med.Lat. *praeambulus*, walking in front.] —**pre•am′bu•lar′y** (-byə-lĕr′ē) *adj.*
pre•am•pli•fi•er (prē-ăm′plə-fī′ər) ►*n.* An electronic circuit or device that detects and strengthens weak signals, as from a radio receiver, for subsequent amplification.
pre•ap•prove (prē′ə-pro͞ov′) ►*v.* To approve or qualify (e.g., an application) without formalities.
preb•end (prĕb′ənd) ►*n.* **1.** A cleric's stipend drawn from the endowment or revenues of an Anglican cathedral or church. **2.** The property or tithe providing a prebend. [< Lat. *praebēre*, to grant.]
preb•en•dar•y (prĕb′ən-dĕr′ē) ►*n., pl.* **-ies.** An Anglican cleric who receives a prebend.
Pre•cam•bri•an (prē-kăm′brē-ən) ►*adj.* Of or being the 1st geologic era and oldest and largest division of geologic time, marked by the appearance of early forms of life. ►*n.* The Precambrian Era.
pre•car•i•ous (prĭ-kâr′ē-əs) ►*adj.* **1.** Dangerously lacking in stability. **2.** Subject to chance or unknown conditions. [< Lat. *precārius*, obtained by entreaty.] —**pre•car′i•ous•ly** *adv.* —**pre•car′i•ous•ness** *n.*
pre•cau•tion (prĭ-kô′shən) ►*n.* An action taken to protect against possible danger or failure. [< Lat. *praecavēre*, guard against.] —**pre•cau′tion•ar′y** (-shə-nĕr′ē) *adj.*
pre•cede (prĭ-sēd′) ►*v.* **-ced•ed, -ced•ing.** To come or be before in time, place, or rank. [< Lat. *praecēdere*, go before.]
prec•e•dence (prĕs′ĭ-dəns, prĭ-sēd′ns) ►*n.* The fact, state, or right of preceding; priority.
prec•e•dent (prĕs′ĭ-dənt) ►*n.* **1.** An act or instance that may be used as an example in dealing with later similar instances. **2.** Convention or custom. ►*adj.* (prĭ-sēd′nt, prĕs′ĭ-dənt). Preceding.
pre•ced•ing (prĭ-sē′dĭng) ►*adj.* Existing or coming before; previous.
pre•cen•tor (prĭ-sĕn′tər) ►*n.* A cleric who directs the choir of a church. [< Lat. *praecinere*, *praecent-*, sing before.]
pre•cept (prē′sĕpt′) ►*n.* A rule or principle prescribing a particular course of action or conduct. [< Lat. *praeceptum.*]
pre•cep•tor (prĭ-sĕp′tər, prē′sĕp′tər) ►*n.* A teacher; instructor. —**pre′cep•to′ri•al** (prē′-sĕp-tôr′ē-əl, -tōr′-) *adj.*
pre•cinct (prē′sĭngkt′) ►*n.* **1.** A district of a city patrolled by a specific unit of its police force. **2.** An election district of a city or town. **3.** often **precincts** A place or enclosure marked off by definite limits. **4. precincts** Neighborhood; environs. [< Lat. *praecingere*, encircle.]
pre•ci•os•i•ty (prĕsh′ē-ŏs′ĭ-tē, prĕs′-) ►*n., pl.* **-ties.** Extreme meticulousness or overrefinement.
pre•cious (prĕsh′əs) ►*adj.* **1.** Of high cost or worth; valuable. **2.** Dear; beloved. **3.** Affectedly dainty or overrefined. [< Lat. *pretiōsus.*] —**pre′cious•ness** *n.*
prec•i•pice (prĕs′ə-pĭs) ►*n.* **1.** An overhanging or extremely steep cliff. **2.** The brink of a dangerous situation. [< Lat. *praeceps*, headlong.]
pre•cip•i•tant (prĭ-sĭp′ĭ-tənt) ►*adj.* **1.** Rushing or falling headlong. **2.** Impulsive in thought or action; rash. **3.** Abrupt or unexpected.

—**pre•cip′i•tance, pre•cip′i•tan•cy** *n.*

pre•cip•i•tate (prĭ-sĭp′ĭ-tāt′) ►*v.* **-tat•ed, -tat•ing 1.** To hurl downward. **2.** To cause to happen, esp. suddenly or prematurely. **3.** To condense and fall as rain or snow. **4.** *Chem.* To cause (a solid substance) to be separated from a solution. ►*adj.* (-tĭt) **1.** Moving rapidly and heedlessly. **2.** Impetuous; reckless. **3.** Occurring suddenly or unexpectedly. ►*n.* (-tāt′, -tĭt). *Chem.* A solid or solid phase separated from a solution. [< Lat. *praeceps*, headlong.] —**pre•cip′i•tate•ly** (-tĭt-lē) *adv.* —**pre•cip′i•tate•ness** *n.* —**pre•cip′i•ta′tive** *adj.* —**pre•cip′i•ta′tor** *n.*

pre•cip•i•ta•tion (prĭ-sĭp′ĭ-tā′shən) ►*n.* **1.** A headlong fall or rush. **2.** Abrupt or impulsive haste. **3a.** Water that falls as rain or snow. **b.** The quantity of such water falling in a specific area within a specific period. **4.** *Chem.* The production of precipitation.

pre•cip•i•tous (prĭ-sĭp′ĭ-təs) ►*adj.* **1.** Resembling a precipice; extremely steep. See Syns at **steep**[1]. **2.** Having precipices: *a precipitous bluff.* **3.** *Informal* Headlong, precipitate. —**pre•cip′i•tous•ly** *adv.* —**pre•cip′i•tous•ness** *n.*

pré•cis (prā′sē, prā-sē′) ►*n., pl.* **pré•cis** (prā′sēz, prā-sēz′). A concise summary of a text. [< OFr. *precis*, condensed.] —**pré′cis** *v.*

pre•cise (prĭ-sīs′) ►*adj.* **1.** Clearly expressed or delineated; definite. **2.** Exact, as in performance or amount; correct. **3.** Strictly distinguished from others; very: *at that precise moment.* **4.** Conforming strictly to rule or proper form. [< Lat. *praecīsus*, p.part. of *praecīdere*, cut short.] —**pre•cise′ly** *adv.* —**pre•cise′ness** *n.*

pre•ci•sion (prĭ-sĭzh′ən) ►*n.* The state or quality of being precise.

pre•clude (prĭ-klo͞od′) ►*v.* **-clud•ed, -clud•ing 1.** To make impossible; prevent. **2.** To exclude; debar. [Lat. *praeclūdere.*] —**pre•clu′sion** (-klo͞o′zhən) *n.* —**pre•clu′sive** (-klo͞o′sĭv, -zĭv) *adj.* —**pre•clu′sive•ly** *adv.*

pre•co•cious (prĭ-kō′shəs) ►*adj.* Marked by unusually early development or maturity, esp. in mental aptitude. [< Lat. *praecox*, premature.] —**pre•co′cious•ly** *adv.* —**pre•coc′ity** (-kŏs′ĭ-tē), **pre•co′cious•ness** *n.*

pre•cog•ni•tion (prē′kŏg-nĭsh′ən) ►*n.* Knowledge of something before it occurs; clairvoyance. —**pre•cog′ni•tive** *adj.*

pre-Co•lum•bi•an (prē′kə-lŭm′bē-ən) ►*adj.* Of or originating in the Americas before the arrival of Columbus.

pre•con•ceive (prē′kən-sēv′) ►*v.* **-ceived, -ceiv•ing.** To form an opinion or a conception of before having adequate knowledge. —**pre′con•cep′tion** (-sĕp′shən) *n.*

pre•con•di•tion (prē′kən-dĭsh′ən) ►*n.* A prerequisite. ►*v.* To condition, train, or accustom in advance.

pre•cur•sor (prĭ-kûr′sər, prē′kûr′sər) ►*n.* **1.** One that precedes and indicates or announces another. **2.** One that precedes another; predecessor. [< Lat. *praecursor.*]

pre•da•cious (prĭ-dā′shəs) ►*adj.* Predatory. [< Lat. *praedārī*, plunder.]

pre•date (prē-dāt′) ►*v.* Antedate.

pre•da•tion (prĭ-dā′shən) ►*n.* **1.** The act of plundering or marauding. **2.** The capturing of prey as a means of maintaining life. [< Lat. *praedārī*, plunder.]

pred•a•to•ry (prĕd′ə-tôr′ē, -tōr′ē) ►*adj.* **1.** Living by preying on other organisms. **2.** Of or marked by plundering or marauding. [< Lat. *praedārī*, plunder.] —**pred′a•tor** (-tər, -tôr′) *n.* —**pred′a•to′ri•ness** *n.*

pred•e•ces•sor (prĕd′ĭ-sĕs′ər, prē′dĭ-) ►*n.* One who precedes another, esp. in an office or position. [< LLat. *praedēcessor.*]

pre•des•ti•na•tion (prē-dĕs′tə-nā′shən) ►*n.* **1.** *Theol.* **a.** The doctrine that God has foreordained all things. **b.** The divine decree foreordaining all souls to either salvation or damnation. **2.** Destiny; fate.

pre•des•tine (prē-dĕs′tĭn) ►*v.* To decide or decree in advance.

pre•de•ter•mine (prē′dĭ-tûr′mĭn) ►*v.* To determine or decide in advance. —**pre′de•ter′mi•nate** (-mə-nĭt) *adj.* —**pre′de•ter′mi•na′tion** *n.*

pred•i•ca•ble (prĕd′ĭ-kə-bəl) ►*adj.* That can be stated or predicated.

pre•dic•a•ment (prĭ-dĭk′ə-mənt) ►*n.* A troublesome or unpleasant situation. [< LLat. *praedicāmentum.*]

pred•i•cate (prĕd′ĭ-kāt′) ►*v.* **-cat•ed, -cat•**

pre′a•dapt′ *v.*
pre′ag•ri·cul′tur·al *adj.*
pre′ar•range′ *v.*
pre′ar•range′ment *n.*
pre′built′ *adj.*
pre•can′cer•ous *adj.*
pre-Chris′tian *adj.*
pre′co•lo′ni•al *adj.*
pre•con′scious *adj. & n.*
pre•cook′ *v.*
pre•cool′ *v.*
pre′cut′ *adj.*
pre′dawn′ *n. & adj.*
pre′de•cease′ *v.*
pre•des′ig•nate′ *v.*
pre′flight′ *adj.*
pre•gla′cial *adj.*
pre•heat′ *v.*
pre•hom′i•nid *n. & adj.*
pre′in•dus′tri•al *adj.*
pre•judge′ *v.*
pre•judg′ment *n.*
pre′launch′ *adj.*
pre•mar′i•tal *adj.*
pre′men•o•paus′al *adj.*
pre′mi•gra′tion *n.*
pre′mix′ *n. & v.*
pre•mod′ern *adj.*
pre•na′tal *adj.*
pre′no•ti•fi•ca′tion *n.*
pre•no′ti•fy *v.*
pre•nup′tial *adj.*
pre′or•dain′ *v.*
pre•or′di•na′tion *n.*
pre•owned′ *adj.*
pre•pay′ *v.*
pre•pay′ment *n.*
pre′pro•fes′sion•al *adj.*
pre•pro′gram′ *v.*
pre•pu′ber•ty *n.*
pre′pu•bes′cence *n.*
pre′pu•bes′cent *adj. & n.*
pre•pub′li•ca′tion *adj.*
pre′re•cord′ *v.*
pre•reg′is•ter *v.*
pre′reg•is•tra′tion *n.*
pre′re•lease′ *n. & adj.*
pre′re•tire′ment *adj. & n.*
pre′sci•en•tif′ic *adj.*
pre•screen′ *v.*
pre′sea′son *n.*
pre′se•lect′ *v.*
pre•set′ *v.*
pre•sig′ni•fy′ *v.*
pre•sort′ *v.*
pre•treat′ *v.*
pre•treat′ment *n.*
pre•tri′al *n.*
pre′war′ *adj.*

ing 1. To base or establish: *predicate an argument on the facts.* **2.** To affirm as an attribute or quality: *predicate the perfectibility of humankind.* ▸*n.* (-kĭt). *Gram.* The part of a sentence or clause, including the verb, that expresses what the subject is or does. [< Lat. *praedicāre,* proclaim.] —**pred′i•ca′tion** *n.* —**pred′i•ca′tive** *adj.*

pre•dict (prĭ-dĭkt′) ▸*v.* To state, tell about, or make known in advance; foretell. [Lat. *praedīcere,* foretell.] —**pre•dict′a•bil′i•ty** *n.* —**pre•dict′a•ble** *adj.* —**pre•dic′tion** *n.* —**pre•dic′tive** *adj.* —**pre•dic′tor** *n.*

pre•di•gest (prē′dī-jĕst′, -dĭ-) ▸*v.* To subject to partial digestion. —**pre′di•ges′tion** *n.*

pred•i•lec•tion (prĕd′l-ĕk′shən, prēd′-) ▸*n.* A disposition in favor of something; preference. [< Med.Lat. *praedīligere,* prefer.]

Syns: *predilection, bias, leaning, partiality, penchant, prejudice, proclivity, propensity* **n.**

pre•dis•pose (prē′dĭ-spōz′) ▸*v.* **-posed, -pos•ing 1.** To make (someone) inclined to something in advance. See Syns at **incline. 2.** To make susceptible or liable. —**pre′dis•po•si′tion** (-dĭs-pə-zĭsh′ən) *n.*

pre•dom•i•nant (prĭ-dŏm′ə-nənt) ▸*adj.* **1.** Having greatest importance or authority. **2.** Most common or conspicuous; prevalent. —**pre•dom′i•nance, pre•dom′i•nan•cy** *n.* —**pre•dom′i•nant•ly** *adv.*

pre•dom•i•nate (prĭ-dŏm′ə-nāt′) ▸*v.* **-nat•ed, -nat•ing 1.** To have controlling power or influence; prevail. **2.** To be of or have greater quantity or importance. [Med.Lat. *praedominārī, praedomināt-* : PRE– + Lat. *dominus,* master.] —**pre•dom′i•nate•ly** (-nĭt-lē) *adv.* —**pre•dom′i•na′tion** *n.* —**pre•dom′i•na′tor** *n.*

pree•mie (prē′mē) ▸*n. Informal* A prematurely born infant. [< PREMATURE.]

pre•em•i•nent or **pre-em•i•nent** (prē-ĕm′ə-nənt) ▸*adj.* Superior to all others; outstanding. See Syns at **noted.** [< Lat. *praeēminēre,* excel.] —**pre•em′i•nence** *n.* —**pre•em′i•nent•ly** *adv.*

pre•empt or **pre-empt** (prē-ĕmpt′) ▸*v.* **1.** To appropriate or seize for oneself before others. See Syns at **appropriate. 2.** To take the place of; displace. **3.** To settle on (public land) so as to obtain the right to buy before others. [PRE– + Lat. *emere, ēmpt-,* buy.] —**pre•emp′tion** *n.* —**pre•emp′tive** *adj.* —**pre•emp′tor′** (-ĕmp′tôr′) *n.*

preen (prēn) ▸*v.* **1.** To smooth or clean (feathers) with the beak or bill. **2.** To dress or groom (oneself) with care; primp. **3.** To take great pride or satisfaction in (oneself). [ME *preinen.*]

pre•ex•ist or **pre-ex•ist** (prē′ĭg-zĭst′) ▸*v.* To exist before. —**pre′ex•is′tence** *n.* —**pre′ex•is′tent** *adj.*

pref. ▸*abbr.* **1.** preface **2.** prefix

pre•fab (prē′făb′) ▸*n. Informal* Something prefabricated, esp. a building or section of a building. —**pre′fab′** *adj. & v.*

pre•fab•ri•cate (prē-făb′rĭ-kāt′) ▸*v.* To manufacture in advance, esp. in standard sections that can be easily shipped and assembled. —**pre•fab′ri•ca′tion** *n.*

pref•ace (prĕf′ĭs) ▸*n.* A preliminary statement introducing a book, usu. written by the author. ▸*v.* **-aced, -ac•ing.** To introduce by or provide with a preface. [< Lat. *praefātiō.*]

pref•a•to•ry (prĕf′ə-tôr′ē, -tōr′ē) ▸*adj.* Of or being a preface; introductory. [< Lat. *praefārī, praefāt-,* say before.]

pre•fect (prē′fĕkt′) ▸*n.* **1.** A high administrative official, as in ancient Rome. **2.** A student monitor, esp. in a private school. [< Lat. *praefectus.*] —**pre′fec′ture** *n.*

pre•fer (prĭ-fûr′) ▸*v.* **-ferred, -fer•ring 1.** To choose as more desirable. **2.** *Law* To file before a legal authority: *prefer charges.* [< Lat. *praeferre* : PRE– + *ferre,* carry.]

pref•er•a•ble (prĕf′ər-ə-bəl, prĕf′rə-) ▸*adj.* More desirable. —**pref′er•a•bly** *adv.*

pref•er•ence (prĕf′ər-əns, prĕf′rəns) ▸*n.* **1.** The exercise of choice. **2.** One so chosen. **3.** The state of being preferred. —**pref′er•en′tial** (-ə-rĕn′shəl) *adj.*

pre•fer•ment (prĭ-fûr′mənt) ▸*n.* Selection for promotion or favored treatment.

pre•fig•ure (prē-fĭg′yər) ▸*v.* **1.** To presage; foreshadow. **2.** To imagine in advance. —**pre•fig′ur•a•tive** (-fĭg′yər-ə-tĭv) *adj.* —**pre•fig′ure•ment** *n.*

pre•fix (prē′fĭks′) ▸*v.* To put or attach before. ▸*n. Gram.* An affix attached to the front of a word to produce a derivative word or an inflected form. [< OFr. *prefixer.*]

pre•fron•tal (prē-frŭn′tl) ▸*adj.* Of or situated in the anterior part of the frontal lobe.

preg•na•ble (prĕg′nə-bəl) ▸*adj.* Vulnerable to seizure or capture: *a pregnable fort.* [< OFr. *prendre, pregn-,* seize.] —**preg′na•bil′i•ty** *n.*

preg•nant (prĕg′nənt) ▸*adj.* **1.** Carrying developing offspring within the body. **2.** Weighty or significant; full of meaning. [< Lat. *praegnāns.*] —**preg′nan•cy** *n.*

pre•hen•sile (prē-hĕn′səl, -sīl′) ▸*adj.* Adapted for seizing or holding, esp. by wrapping around: *a prehensile tail.* [< Lat. *prehendere, prehēns-,* grasp.] —**pre′hen•sil′i•ty** (-sĭl′ĭ-tē) *n.*

pre•his•tor•ic (prē′hĭ-stôr′ĭk, -stŏr′-) also **pre•his•tor•i•cal** (-ĭ-kəl) ▸*adj.* Of or belonging to an era before recorded history. —**pre•his′to•ry** (-hĭs′tə-rē) *n.*

prej•u•dice (prĕj′ə-dĭs) ▸*n.* **1.** An adverse judgment or opinion formed beforehand without knowledge of the facts. See Syns at **predilection. 2.** Irrational suspicion or hatred of a particular group, race, or religion. **3.** Harm or injury. ▸*v.* **-diced, -dic•ing 1.** To cause (someone) to have a prejudice. **2.** To do harm to: *a mistake that prejudiced the outcome.* See Syns at **bias.** [< Lat. *praeiūdicium.*] —**prej′u•di′cial** (-dĭsh′əl) *adj.*

prel•ate (prĕl′ĭt) ▸*n.* A high-ranking member of the clergy, esp. a bishop. [< Med.Lat. *praelātus.*] —**prel′a•cy** (-ə-sē) *n.*

pre•lim•i•nar•y (prĭ-lĭm′ə-nĕr′ē) ▸*adj.* Prior to the main matter, action, or business; introductory. ▸*n., pl.* **-ies.** Something that precedes, prepares for, or introduces the main matter or action. [< PRE– + Lat. *līmen,* threshold.] —**pre•lim′i•nar′i•ly** (-nâr′ə-lē) *adv.*

Syns: *preliminary, introductory, preparatory* **adj.**

prel•ude (prĕl′yo͞od′, prā′lo͞od′, prē′-) ▸*n.* **1.** An introductory performance, event, or action. **2.** *Mus.* A piece or movement serving as an introduction to another section or composition.

[< Lat. *praelūdere*, play beforehand.]

pre•mar•i•tal (prē-măr′ĭ-tl) ▸*adj.* Taking place or existing before marriage.

pre•ma•ture (prē′mə-tyo͝or′, -to͝or′, -cho͝or′) ▸*adj.* Occurring, growing, or existing before the customary, correct, or assigned time; early. —**pre′ma•ture′ly** *adv.*

pre•med (prē′mĕd′) *Informal* ▸*adj.* Premedical. ▸*n.* A premedical student.

pre•med•i•cal (prē-mĕd′ĭ-kəl) ▸*adj.* Preparing for or leading to the study of medicine.

pre•med•i•tate (prē-mĕd′ĭ-tāt′) ▸*v.* To plan, arrange, or plot in advance. —**pre•med′i•ta′tion** *n.* —**pre•med′i•ta′tive** *adj.*

pre•men•stru•al (prē-mĕn′stro͞o-əl) ▸*adj.* Of or occurring in the period just before menstruation. —**pre•men′stru•al•ly** *adv.*

pre•mier (prĭ-mîr′, -myîr′, prē′mîr) ▸*adj.* **1.** First in status or importance; chief. **2.** First to occur or exist; earliest. ▸*n.* (prĭ-mîr′). A prime minister. [< Lat. *prīmārius.*] —**pre•mier′ship′** *n.*

pre•miere or **pre•mière** (prĭ-mîr′, -myâr′) ▸*n.* The first public performance, as of a play. ▸*v.* **-miered, -mier•ing** or **-mièred, -mièr•ing.** To present or receive a first public performance. [Fr.]

prem•ise (prĕm′ĭs) ▸*n.* **1.** A proposition upon which an argument is based or from which a conclusion is drawn. **2. premises** Land and the buildings on it. [< Lat. *praemittere, praemiss-*, set in front.] —**prem′ise** *v.*

pre•mi•um (prē′mē-əm) ▸*n.* **1.** A prize or award. **2.** A sum of money paid in addition to a regular amount. **3.** The amount paid, often in installments, for an insurance policy. **4.** An unusual or high value: *put a premium on honesty.* ▸*adj.* Of superior quality or value: *premium gasoline.* —***idiom:* at a premium** More valuable than usual, as from scarcity. [Lat. *praemium*, reward.]

pre•mo•lar (prē-mō′lər) ▸*n.* One of eight bicuspid teeth located in pairs between the canines and molars. —**pre•mo′lar** *adj.*

pre•mo•ni•tion (prē′mə-nĭsh′ən, prĕm′ə-) ▸*n.* **1.** A presentiment of the future; foreboding. **2.** An advance warning; forewarning. [< Lat. *praemonēre*, forewarn : PRE– + *monēre*, warn.] —**pre•mon′i•to′ry** (-mŏn′ĭ-tôr′ē, -tōr′ē) *adj.*

pre•na•tal (prē-nāt′l) ▸*adj.* Existing or occurring before birth. —**pre•na′tal•ly** *adv.*

pre•oc•cu•py (prē-ŏk′yə-pī′) ▸*v.* **1.** To occupy completely the mind or attention of; engross. See Syns at **monopolize. 2.** To occupy or take possession of in advance or before another. —**pre•oc′cu•pa′tion** (-pā′shən) *n.*

pre•op•er•a•tive (prē-ŏp′ər-ə-tĭv, -ŏp′rə-, -ŏp′ə-rā′-) ▸*adj.* Happening or done before surgery. —**pre•op′er•a•tive•ly** *adv.*

prep. ▸*abbr.* preposition

pre•pack•age (prē-păk′ĭj) ▸*v.* To wrap or package (a product) before marketing.

prep•a•ra•tion (prĕp′ə-rā′shən) ▸*n.* **1.** The act or process of preparing. **2.** Readiness. **3.** often **preparations** A preliminary measure or measures. **4.** A prepared substance, such as a medicine.

pre•par•a•to•ry (prĭ-păr′ə-tôr′ē, -tōr′ē, -pâr′-, prĕp′ər-ə-) ▸*adj.* Serving to make ready or prepare. See Syns at **preliminary.**

preparatory school ▸*n.* A usu. private secondary school that prepares students for college.

pre•pare (prĭ-pâr′) ▸*v.* **-pared, -par•ing 1.** To make ready. **2.** To put together by combining various elements or ingredients. **3.** To fit out; equip. [< Lat. *praeparāre.*]

pre•par•ed•ness (prĭ-pâr′ĭd-nĭs) ▸*n.* The state of being prepared, esp. for combat.

pre•pon•der•ate (prĭ-pŏn′də-rāt′) ▸*v.* **-at•ed, -at•ing.** To be greater than something else, as in power, weight, or importance. [Lat. *praeponderāre.*] —**pre•pon′der•ance** *n.* —**pre•pon′der•ant** *adj.*

prep•o•si•tion (prĕp′ə-zĭsh′ən) ▸*n.* In some languages, a word placed before a substantive indicating its relation to a verb, an adjective, or another substantive, as English *at, by, in, to, from,* and *with.* [< Lat. *praepōnere, praeposit-*, put in front.] —**prep′o•si′tion•al** *adj.*

Usage: In spite of the rule that a preposition may not be used to end a sentence, sentences ending with prepositions can be found in the works of most of the great writers. English syntax allows final placement of the preposition, as in *I asked her which course she had signed up for,* and efforts to rewrite such sentences by placing the preposition elsewhere can have stilted and even comical results.

pre•pos•sess (prē′pə-zĕs′) ▸*v.* **1.** To influence beforehand; prejudice. **2.** To impress favorably in advance.

pre•pos•sess•ing (prē′pə-zĕs′ĭng) ▸*adj.* Serving to impress favorably; pleasing: *a prepossessing appearance.*

pre•pos•ter•ous (prĭ-pŏs′tər-əs) ▸*adj.* Contrary to reason or common sense; absurd. [< Lat. *praeposterus*, topsy-turvy.] —**pre•pos′ter•ous•ness** *n.*

prep•py or **prep•pie** (prĕp′ē) ▸*n., pl.* **-pies** *Informal* A student of a preparatory school. —**prep′pi•ness** *n.* —**prep′py** *adj.*

prep school ▸*n. Informal* A preparatory school.

pre•puce (prē′pyo͞os′) ▸*n.* See **foreskin.** [< Lat. *praepūtium.*] —**pre•pu′tial** (-pyo͞o′shəl) *adj.*

pre•re•cord (prē′rĭ-kôrd′) ▸*v.* To record (a radio or television program) for later presentation or use.

pre•req•ui•site (prē-rĕk′wĭ-zĭt) ▸*adj.* Required as a prior condition. —**pre•req′ui•site** *n.*

pre•rog•a•tive (prĭ-rŏg′ə-tĭv) ▸*n.* An exclusive right or privilege. [< Lat. *praerogāre*, ask before.]

pres. ▸*abbr.* **1.** present **2.** or **Pres.** president

pres•age (prĕs′ĭj) ▸*n.* **1.** An indication or warning of a future occurrence; omen. **2.** A presentiment; foreboding. ▸*v.* (prĭ-sāj′, prĕs′ĭj) **-saged, -sag•ing 1.** To indicate or warn of in advance; portend. **2.** To have a presentiment of. [< Lat. *praesāgium.*]

pres•by•ter (prĕz′bĭ-tər, prĕs′-) ▸*n.* **1.** A priest in various hierarchical churches. **2.** An elder in the Presbyterian Church. [< Gk. *presbuteros*, elder.]

pres•by•te•ri•an (prĕz′bĭ-tîr′ē-ən, prĕs′-) ▸*adj.* **1.** Relating to ecclesiastical government by presbyters. **2. Presbyterian** Of or relating to a Protestant church governed by presbyters and traditionally Calvinist in doctrine. ▸*n.* **Presbyterian** A member of a Presbyterian

Church. —**pres′by•te′ri•an•ism** *n.*

pres•by•ter•y (prĕz′bĭ-tĕr′ē, prĕs′-) ▶*n., pl.* **-ies 1.** A court composed of Presbyterian Church ministers and representative elders of a particular locality. **2.** The section of a church reserved for the clergy.

pre•school (prē′sko͞ol′) ▶*adj.* Of or intended for the years of childhood that precede elementary school. —**pre′school′er** *n.*

pre•science (prĕsh′əns, -ē-əns, prē′shəns, -shē-əns) ▶*n.* Knowledge of actions or events before they occur. [< Lat. *praescīre*, know before.] —**pre′scient** *adj.*

Pres•cott (prĕs′kət, -kŏt′), **William Hickling.** 1796–1859. Amer. historian.

pre•scribe (prĭ-skrīb′) ▶*v.* **-scribed, -scrib•ing 1.** To set down as a rule or guide. See Syns at **dictate. 2.** To order the use of (a medicine or other treatment). [< Lat. *praescrībere.*] —**pre•scrib′er** *n.* —**pre•scrip′tive** (-skrĭp′tĭv) *adj.* —**pre•scrip′tive•ness** *n.*

pre•scrip•tion (prĭ-skrĭp′shən) ▶*n.* **1.** The act of prescribing. **2a.** A written order, esp. by a physician, for the preparation and administration of a medicine. **b.** A prescribed medicine.

pres•ence (prĕz′əns) ▶*n.* **1.** The state or fact of being present. **2.** The area immediately surrounding someone. **3.** A person who is present. **4a.** A person's bearing. **b.** The quality of self-assurance and effectiveness.

pres•ent[1] (prĕz′ənt) ▶*n.* **1.** A moment or period in time intermediate between past and future; now. **2.** *Gram.* The present tense. **3. presents** *Law* The document or instrument in question. ▶*adj.* **1.** Existing or happening now: *present trends.* **2.** Being at hand. **3.** *Gram.* Designating a verb tense or form that expresses current time. [< Lat. *praesēns*, pr.part. of *praeesse*, be present.] —**pres′ent•ness** *n.*

pre•sent[2] (prĭ-zĕnt′) ▶*v.* **1.** To introduce, esp. formally. **2.** To bring before the public. **3a.** To make a gift or award of. **b.** To make a gift to. **4.** To offer for examination or consideration. **5.** To salute with (a weapon). **6.** *Law* To bring a charge or indictment against. ▶*n.* **pres•ent** (prĕz′ənt). Something presented; gift. [< Lat. *presentāre.*] —**pre•sent′a•ble** *adj.* —**pres′en•tation** (prĕz′ən-tā′shən, prē′zən-) *n.*

pres•ent-day (prĕz′ənt-dā′) ▶*adj.* Current.

pre•sen•tient (prē-sĕn′shənt, -shē-ənt) ▶*adj.* Having a presentiment. [Lat. *praesentiēns*, *praesentient-*, pr.part. of *praesentīre*, to feel beforehand; see PRESENTIMENT.]

pre•sen•ti•ment (prĭ-zĕn′tə-mənt) ▶*n.* A sense that something is about to occur; premonition. [< Lat. *praesentīre*, feel beforehand.]

pres•ent•ly (prĕz′ənt-lē) ▶*adv.* **1.** In a short time; soon. **2.** Currently.

Usage: An original meaning of *presently,* "at the present time; currently," has survived in popular use, but it is often frowned upon. The sentence *General Walters is . . . presently the United States Ambassador to the United Nations* was acceptable to only 50 percent of the Usage Panel in the late 1980s.

pres•ent participle (prĕz′ənt) ▶*n.* A participle expressing present action, in English formed by adding *-ing* to the infinitive and used to express present action, to form progressive tenses, and to function as a verbal adjective.

present per•fect (pûr′fĭkt) ▶*n.* The verb tense expressing action completed at the present time, formed in English by combining the present tense of *have* with a past participle, as in *He has spoken.*

pres•er•va•tion•ist (prĕz′ər-vā′shə-nĭst) ▶*n.* One who advocates preservation, esp. of natural areas or endangered species. —**pres′er•va′tion•ism** *n.*

pre•ser•va•tive (prĭ-zûr′və-tĭv) ▶*n.* Something used to preserve, esp. a chemical added to foods to inhibit spoilage. —**pre•ser′va•tive** *adj.*

pre•serve (prĭ-zûrv′) ▶*v.* **-served, -serv•ing 1.** To protect from injury or peril. **2.** To keep or maintain intact. **3.** To treat fruit or other foods so as to prevent decay. ▶*n.* **1.** often **preserves** Fruit cooked with sugar to protect against decay or fermentation. **2.** An area maintained for the protection of wildlife or natural resources. [< Med.Lat. *praeservāre.*] —**pres′er•va′tion** (prĕz′ər-vā′shən) *n.* —**pre•serv′er** *n.*

pre•shrunk also **pre-shrunk** (prē′shrŭngk′) ▶*adj.* Shrunk during manufacture to minimize subsequent shrinkage.

pre•side (prĭ-zīd′) ▶*v.* **-sid•ed, -sid•ing 1.** To hold the position of authority; act as chairperson. **2.** To possess or exercise authority or control. [< Lat. *praesidēre* : PRE– + *sedēre*, sit.]

pres•i•dent (prĕz′ĭ-dənt, -dĕnt′) ▶*n.* **1.** One appointed or elected to preside over an assembly or meeting. **2.** often **President** The chief executive of a republic, esp. of the US. **3.** The chief officer of an organization, as a corporation. —**pres′i•den•cy** *n.* —**pres′i•den′tial** (-dĕn′shəl) *adj.* —**pres′i•dent•ship′** *n.*

Pres•i•dents' Day (prĕz′ĭ-dənts, -dĕnts) ▶*n.* The 3rd Monday in Feb., a US legal holiday commemorating the birthdays of George Washington and Abraham Lincoln.

press (prĕs) ▶*v.* **1.** To exert steady weight or force against; bear down on. **2.** To squeeze the juice or other contents from. **3a.** To reshape or make compact by applying steady force. **b.** To iron (e.g., clothing). **4.** To try to influence, as by insistent arguments. **5.** To place in trying circumstances; harass. **6.** To advance or carry on vigorously. **7.** To put forward insistently. **8.** To assemble in large numbers; crowd. ▶*n.* **1.** Any of various machines or devices that apply pressure. **2.** A printing press. **3.** A place or establishment where matter is printed. **4.** The art, method, or business of printing. **5a.** The collecting and publishing or broadcasting of news; journalism in general. **b.** The entirety of media that collect, publish, transmit, or broadcast the news. **c.** The people involved in the media, as news reporters and broadcasters. **6.** A large gathering; throng. See Syns at **crowd. 7.** The act of applying pressure. **8.** The urgency of business or matters. **9.** The set of proper creases in a garment or fabric, formed by ironing. [< Lat. *premere, press-*.]

press agent ▶*n.* A person employed to arrange advertising and publicity, as for a performer or business. —**press a′gent•ry** *n.*

press conference ▶*n.* An interview held for news reporters by a political figure or famous person.

press•ing (prĕs′ĭng) ▶*adj.* Demanding immediate attention; urgent. —**press′ing•ly** *adv.*

press•room (prĕs′ro͞om′, -ro͝om′) ▶*n.* The

room in a printing or newspaper publishing establishment that contains the presses.

pres•sure (prĕsh′ər) ►*n.* **1.** The act of pressing or the condition of being pressed. **2.** The application of continuous force by one body on another that it is touching. **3.** *Phys.* Force applied uniformly over a surface, measured as force per unit of area. **4.** A constraining influence: *pressure to conform.* **5.** Urgent claim or demand: *under the pressure of business.* ►*v.* **-sured, -sur•ing.** To exert pressure on. [< Lat. *premere*, press.]

pressure group ►*n.* A group that endeavors to influence public policy.

pressure suit ►*n.* A garment worn in high-altitude aircraft or in spacecraft to compensate for low-pressure conditions.

pres•sur•ize (prĕsh′ə-rīz′) ►*v.* **-ized, -iz•ing.** To maintain normal air pressure in (an enclosure, as an aircraft or submarine). —**pres′sur•i•za′tion** *n.* —**pres′sur•iz′er** *n.*

pres•ti•dig•i•ta•tion (prĕs′tĭ-dĭj′ĭ-tā′shən) ►*n.* Sleight of hand. [Fr.] —**pres′ti•dig′i•ta′tor** *n.*

pres•tige (prĕ-stēzh′, -stēj′) ►*n.* **1.** The level of respect at which one is regarded by others; standing. **2.** Prominence, honor, or distinction. [< Lat. *praestīgiae*, tricks.] —**pres•ti′gious** (-stē′jəs, -stĭj′əs) *adj.*

pres•to (prĕs′tō) ►*adv.* **1.** *Mus.* In rapid tempo. **2.** Suddenly; right away. [Ital.] —**pres′to** *adj.*

pre•sume (prĭ-zo͞om′) ►*v.* **-sumed, -sum•ing 1.** To take for granted; assume. **2.** To act overconfidently; take liberties. **3.** To take unwarranted advantage of something. [< LLat. *praesūmere*, anticipate.] —**pre•sum′a•ble** *adj.* —**pre•sum′a•bly** *adv.*

pre•sump•tion (prĭ-zŭmp′shən) ►*n.* **1.** Behavior or attitude that is boldly arrogant or offensive; effrontery. **2.** Belief based on reasonable evidence; assumption or supposition. **3.** A condition or basis for accepting or presuming. —**pre•sump′tive** *adj.*

pre•sump•tu•ous (prĭ-zŭmp′cho͞o-əs) ►*adj.* Going beyond what is right or proper; excessively forward. —**pre•sump′tu•ous•ly** *adv.* —**pre•sump′tu•ous•ness** *n.*

pre•sup•pose (prē′sə-pōz′) ►*v.* **-posed, -pos•ing 1.** To believe or suppose in advance. **2.** To require or involve necessarily as an antecedent condition. —**pre•sup′po•si′tion** (-sŭp′ə-zĭsh′ən) *n.*

pre•teen (prē′tēn′) ►*adj.* Of or designed for preadolescent children. —**pre′teen′** *n.*

pre•tend (prĭ-tĕnd′) ►*v.* **1.** To give a false appearance of; feign. **2.** To claim or allege insincerely or falsely; profess. **3.** To make believe. **4.** To make pretensions: *pretends to gourmet tastes.* [< Lat. *praetendere*.] —**pre•tend′er** *n.*

pre•tense (prē′tĕns′, prĭ-tĕns′) ►*n.* **1.** A false appearance or action intended to deceive. **2.** A studied show; affectation. **3.** A feigned reason or excuse; pretext. **4.** An outward appearance. **5.** A claim, esp. one without foundation. **6.** Pretentiousness; ostentation. [< Lat. *praetendere*, assert.]

pre•ten•sion (prĭ-tĕn′shən) ►*n.* **1.** A specious allegation; pretext. **2.** A claim, esp. one without foundation. **3.** Ostentation; pretentiousness.

pre•ten•tious (prĭ-tĕn′shəs) ►*adj.* **1.** Claiming or demanding distinction or merit, esp. when unjustified. **2.** Extravagantly showy; ostentatious. See Syns at **showy.** —**pre•ten′tious•ly** *adv.* —**pre•ten′tious•ness** *n.*

pret•er•it or **pret•er•ite** (prĕt′ər-ĭt) ►*adj.* Of or being the verb tense that describes a past action or state. [< Lat. *praeterīre*, go by.] —**pret′er•it** *n.*

pre•ter•nat•u•ral (prē′tər-năch′ər-əl, -năch′rəl) ►*adj.* **1.** Beyond the normal course of nature. **2.** Supernatural. [< Lat. *praeter nātūrām*, beyond nature.] —**pre′ter•nat′u•ral•ly** *adv.* —**pre′ter•nat′u•ral•ness** *n.*

pre•text (prē′tĕkst′) ►*n.* An ostensible or professed purpose; excuse. [Lat. *praetextum* < *praetexere*, disguise : PRE– + *texere*, weave.]

Pre•to•ri•a (prĭ-tôr′ē-ə, -tōr′-) The administrative capital of South Africa, in the NE part N of Johannesburg. Pop. 435,100.

pret•ti•fy (prĭt′ĭ-fī′) ►*v.* **-fied, -fy•ing.** To make pretty. —**pret′ti•fi•ca′tion** *n.*

pret•ty (prĭt′ē) ►*adj.* **-ti•er, -ti•est 1.** Pleasing or attractive in a graceful or delicate way. **2.** Clever; adroit: *a pretty maneuver.* **3.** Very bad; terrible: *in a pretty predicament.* **4.** Superficially attractive but lacking substance: *full of pretty phrases.* **5.** *Informal* Considerable in size or extent: *a pretty fortune.* ►*adv.* To a fair degree; moderately: *a pretty good student.* ►*v.* **-tied, -ty•ing.** To make pretty. [< OE *prættig*, cunning.] —**pret′ti•ly** *adv.* —**pret′ti•ness** *n.*

pret•zel (prĕt′səl) ►*n.* A glazed, often salted biscuit usu. baked in the form of a loose knot or stick. [Ger.]

pre•vail (prĭ-vāl′) ►*v.* **1.** To be victorious; triumph. **2.** To win out. **3.** To be most common or frequent. **4.** To use persuasion or inducement successfully. [< Lat. *praevalēre*, be stronger.] —**pre•vail′er** *n.* —**pre•vail′ing** *adj.* —**pre•vail′ing•ly** *adv.*

prev•a•lent (prĕv′ə-lənt) ►*adj.* Widely or commonly occurring or practiced. [< Lat. *praevalēre*, be stronger.] —**prev′a•lence** *n.*

pre•var•i•cate (prĭ-văr′ĭ-kāt′) ►*v.* **-cat•ed, -cat•ing.** To stray from or evade the truth; equivocate. [Lat. *praevāricārī*.] —**pre•var′i•ca′tion** *n.* —**pre•var′i•ca′tor** *n.*

pre•vent (prĭ-vĕnt′) ►*v.* **1.** To keep from happening: *took steps to prevent the strike.* **2.** To keep (someone) from doing something; impede: *prevented us from winning.* [< Lat. *praevenīre*, *praevent-* : PRE– + *venīre*, come.] —**pre•vent′a•ble, pre•vent′i•ble** *adj.* —**pre•ven′tion** *n.*

pre•ven•tive (prĭ-vĕn′tĭv) also **pre•ven•ta•tive** (-tə-tĭv) ►*adj.* **1.** Intended or used to prevent or hinder; acting as an obstacle. **2.** Preventing or slowing the course of illness or disease; prophylactic. —**pre•ven′tive** *n.*

pre•view also **pre•vue** (prē′vyo͞o′) ►*n.* **1.** An advance showing, as of a movie, before public presentation begins. **2.** The presentation of several scenes advertising a forthcoming movie. **3.** An introductory sample or overview; foretaste. —**pre′view′** *v.*

pre•vi•ous (prē′vē-əs) ►*adj.* Existing or occurring before something else; prior. [< Lat. *praevius*, going before.] —**pre′vi•ous•ly** *adv.* —**pre′vi•ous•ness** *n.*

pre•vi•sion (prĭ-vĭzh′ən) ►*n.* **1.** A knowing in advance; foresight. **2.** A prediction.

prey (prā) ►*n.* **1.** An animal hunted or caught

for food; quarry. **2.** A victim. **3.** The act or practice of preying. ►*v.* **1.** To hunt, catch, or eat as prey. **2.** To victimize. **3.** To exert an injurious effect. [< Lat. *praeda.*]

price (prīs) ►*n.* **1.** The sum of money asked or given for something. **2.** The cost at which something is obtained. **3.** The cost of bribing someone: *everyone has a price.* ►*v.* **priced, pric•ing 1.** To fix or establish a price for. **2.** To find out the price of. [< Lat. *pretium.*]

Price, (Mary) Leontyne. b. 1927. Amer. operatic soprano.

price•less (prīs′lĭs) ►*adj.* Of inestimable worth; invaluable.

price support ►*n.* Maintenance of prices, as of a raw material, at a certain level usu. through government intervention.

price war ►*n.* A period of intense competition in which each competitor tries to cut retail prices below those of the others.

pric•ey also **pric•y** (prī′sē) ►*adj.* **-i•er, -i•est** *Informal* Expensive.

prick (prĭk) ►*n.* **1a.** The act of pricking. **b.** The sensation of being pricked. **2.** A small mark or puncture made by a pointed object. **3.** A pointed object, such as a thorn. ►*v.* **1.** To puncture lightly. **2.** To affect with a mental or emotional pang, as of remorse. **3.** To mark or delineate on a surface by means of small punctures. —***idiom:* prick up (one's) ears** To listen with attentive interest. [< OE *prica*, puncture.]

prick•er (prĭk′ər) ►*n.* A prickle or thorn.

prick•le (prĭk′əl) ►*n.* **1.** A small sharp spine or thorn. **2.** A tingling sensation. ►*v.* **-led, -ling 1.** To prick, as with a thorn. **2.** To tingle. [< OE *pricel.*]

prick•ly (prĭk′lē) ►*adj.* **-li•er, -li•est 1.** Having prickles. **2.** Marked by tingling. **3.** Causing trouble; thorny. —**prick′li•ness** *n.*

prickly heat ►*n.* See **heat rash.**

prickly pear ►*n.* **1.** Any of various cacti having bristly, flattened or cylindrical joints and showy, usu. yellow flowers. **2.** The edible fruit of a prickly pear.

pride (prīd) ►*n.* **1.** A sense of one's proper dignity or value; self-respect. **2.** Pleasure or satisfaction taken in achievement, possession, or association. **3.** Arrogance; conceit. **4.** The best of a group or class. **5.** A group of lions. ►*v.* **prid•ed, prid•ing.** To indulge (oneself) in a feeling of satisfaction. [< OE *prūd*, PROUD.] —**pride′ful** *adj.* —**pride′ful•ly** *adv.* —**pride′ful•ness** *n.*

prie-dieu (prē-dyœ′) ►*n.*, *pl.* **-dieus** or **-dieux** (-dyœz′). A narrow, desklike kneeling bench for use at prayer. [Fr. *prie-Dieu.*]

priest (prēst) ►*n.* **1.** In many Christian churches, a member of the clergy ranking below a bishop but above a deacon. **2.** A person having the authority to perform and administer religious rites. [< OE *prēost.*] —**priest′hood′** *n.* —**priest′li•ness** *n.* —**priest′ly** *adj.*

priest•ess (prē′stĭs) ►*n.* A woman who presides over rites, esp. in paganism.

Priest•ley (prēst′lē), **Joseph.** 1733–1804. British chemist.

prig (prĭg) ►*n.* A smugly proper or prudish person. [?] —**prig′ger•y** *n.* —**prig′gish** *adj.* —**prig′gish•ness** *n.*

prim (prĭm) ►*adj.* **prim•mer, prim•mest.** Precise or proper to the point of affectation. [?] —**prim′ly** *adv.* —**prim′ness** *n.*

pri•ma•cy (prī′mə-sē) ►*n.*, *pl.* **-cies 1.** The state of being first or foremost. **2.** *Eccles.* The office or rank of primate. [< Med.Lat. *prīmātia*, office of primate.]

pri•ma don•na (prē′mə dŏn′ə, prĭm′ə) ►*n.* **1.** The leading woman soloist in an opera company. **2.** A temperamental, conceited person. [Ital.]

pri•ma fa•cie (prī′mə fā′shē, -shē-ē, fā′shə) ►*adv.* At first sight; before closer inspection. [< Lat. *prīmā faciē.*] —**pri′ma fa′cie** *adj.*

pri•mal (prī′məl) ►*adj.* **1.** Being first in time; original. **2.** Of first importance; primary.

pri•mar•i•ly (prī-mâr′ə-lē, -mĕr′-) ►*adv.* **1.** Chiefly; mainly. **2.** At first; originally.

pri•mar•y (prī′mĕr′ē, -mə-rē) ►*adj.* **1.** First in rank, quality, or importance. **2.** Occurring first in time or sequence; earliest. **3.** Being the first of a kind. **4.** Being an essential component; basic. **5.** Immediate; direct. ►*n.*, *pl.* **-ies 1.** One that is first in time, order, or importance. **2.** A preliminary election in which voters nominate candidates for office. [< Lat. *prīmārius.*]

primary care ►*n.* Medical care received upon first contact with the health care system, before referral elsewhere within the system.

primary color ►*n.* Any of a group of colors, such as red, yellow, and blue, which can be regarded as generating all colors.

primary school ►*n.* **1.** A school including the first three or four grades and sometimes kindergarten. **2.** See **elementary school.**

pri•mate (prī′mĭt, -māt′) ►*n.* **1.** (prī′māt′) One of the group of mammals which includes monkeys, apes, and humans. **2.** A bishop of highest rank in a province or country. [< Lat. *prīmus*, first.]

prime (prīm) ►*adj.* **1.** First in quality, importance, rank, or time. **2.** *Math.* Of or being a prime number. ►*n.* **1.** The earliest or beginning stage of something. **2.** Springtime. **3.** The period or phase of ideal or peak condition. See Syns at **bloom. 4.** *Math.* A prime number. ►*v.* **primed, prim•ing 1.** To make ready; prepare. **2.** To load (a gun or mine) for firing. **3.** To prepare for operation, as by pouring water into a pump. **4.** To prepare (a surface) for painting by covering with an undercoat. **5.** To instruct beforehand; coach. [< Lat. *prīmus.*] —**prime′ness** *n.*

prime meridian ►*n.* The zero meridian from which longitude east and west is measured. It passes through Greenwich, England.

prime minister ►*n.* **1.** A chief minister appointed by a ruler. **2.** The chief executive of a parliamentary democracy. —**prime ministership, prime ministry** *n.*

prime number ►*n.* A positive integer that has itself and one as its only factors.

prim•er[1] (prĭm′ər) ►*n.* **1.** An elementary reading textbook. **2.** A book that covers the basic elements of a subject. [< Lat. *prīmārius*, first.]

prim•er[2] (prī′mər) ►*n.* **1.** A device used to detonate an explosive charge. **2.** An undercoat of paint or size applied to prepare a surface.

prime rate ►*n.* The lowest rate of interest on bank loans at a given time and place, offered to preferred borrowers.

prime time ►*n.* The hours between 7 and 11 P.M., when the largest television audience is available. —**prime′-time′** *adj.*

pri•me•val (prī-mē′vəl) ►*adj.* Belonging to

the first or earliest age or ages; original. [< Lat. *prīmaevus*, early in life.]

prim•i•tive (prĭm′ĭ-tĭv) ▶*adj.* **1.** Of or relating to an earliest or original stage or state; primeval. **2.** Simple or crude; unsophisticated. See Syns at **rude. 3.** *Anthro.* Of a nonindustrial, often tribal culture. **4.** Of or created by an artist without formal training. ▶*n.* **1.** *Anthro.* A person belonging to a nonindustrial society. **2a.** A self-taught artist. **b.** A work of art by a primitive artist. [< Lat. *prīmitus*, at first.] —**prim′i•tive•ly** *adv.* —**prim′i•tive•ness** *n.*

prim•i•tiv•ism (prĭm′ĭ-tĭ-vĭz′əm) ▶*n.* The style characteristic of a primitive artist. —**prim′i•tiv•ist** *adj. & n.*

pri•mo•gen•i•tor (prī′mō-jĕn′ĭ-tər) ▶*n.* The earliest ancestor. [LLat. *prīmōgenitor.*]

pri•mo•gen•i•ture (prī′mō-jĕn′ĭ-cho͝or′) ▶*n.* **1.** The state of being the firstborn or eldest child of the same parents. **2.** *Law* The right of the eldest child, esp. a son, to inherit the entire estate of one or both parents. [LLat. *prīmōgenitūra.*]

pri•mor•di•al (prī-môr′dē-əl) ▶*adj.* Being or happening first in sequence of time; original. [< Lat. *prīmōrdium*, origin.] —**pri•mor′di•al•ly** *adv.*

primp (prĭmp) ▶*v.* To dress or groom (oneself) with excessive care. [Perh. < PRIM.]

prim•rose (prĭm′rōz′) ▶*n.* Any of numerous plants having tubular, variously colored flowers. [< Med.Lat. *prīma rosa*, first rose.]

prince (prĭns) ▶*n.* **1.** A boy or man in a royal family. **2.** A hereditary ruler; king. **3.** An outstanding man in a group or class: *a merchant prince.* [< Lat. *prīnceps.*] —**prince′dom** *n.* —**prince′li•ness** *n.* —**prince′ly** *adj.*

Prince Edward Island. A province of SE Canada consisting of **Prince Edward Island** in the S Gulf of St. Lawrence. Cap. Charlottetown. Pop. 122,506.

prin•cess (prĭn′sĭs, -sĕs′, prĭn-sĕs′) ▶*n.* **1.** A female member of a royal family. **2.** The wife of a prince.

prin•ci•pal (prĭn′sə-pəl) ▶*adj.* First or foremost in importance; chief. ▶*n.* **1.** The head of an elementary school or high school. **2.** A main participant. **3.** A person having a leading or starring role. **4a.** The capital of a financial holding as distinguished from the revenue from it. **b.** A sum of money owed as a debt, upon which interest is calculated. **5.** *Law* **a.** A person who empowers another to act as his or her representative. **b.** One primarily responsible for an obligation. [< Lat. *prīnceps*, prince.] —**prin′ci•pal•ly** *adv.* —**prin′ci•pal•ship′** *n.*

Usage: *Principal* and *principle* have no meanings in common. *Principle* is only a noun, and most of its senses refer to that which is basic or to rules and standards. *Principal* is both a noun and an adjective. As a noun it generally denotes a person who holds a high position or plays an important role. As an adjective it has the sense of "chief" or "leading."

prin•ci•pal•i•ty (prĭn′sə-păl′ĭ-tē) ▶*n., pl.* **-ties.** A territory, position, or jurisdiction of a prince.

principal parts ▶*pl.n.* In traditional grammars, the forms of the verb from which all other forms are derived.

prin•ci•ple (prĭn′sə-pəl) ▶*n.* **1.** A basic truth, law, or assumption. **2a.** A rule or standard, esp. of good behavior. **b.** Moral or ethical standards or judgments. **3.** A fixed or predetermined policy. **4.** A rule or law concerning the functioning of natural phenomena or mechanical processes. **5.** A basic source. See Usage Note at **principal.** [< Lat. *prīncipium.*]

prin•ci•pled (prĭn′sə-pəld) ▶*adj.* Based on, marked by, or manifesting principle.

prink (prĭngk) ▶*v.* To primp. [Prob. < *prank*, adorn.] —**prink′er** *n.*

print (prĭnt) ▶*n.* **1.** A mark or impression made by pressure. **2.** Something marked with an impression. **3a.** Lettering or other impressions produced in ink. **b.** Matter so produced; printed material. **c.** Printed state or form. **4.** A design or picture reproduced by printing. **5.** A photographic image transferred to a surface, usu. from a negative. **6.** A copy of a film made from a negative. **7.** A fabric with a stamped dyed pattern. ▶*v.* **1.** To press (e.g., a mark or design) onto a surface. **2.** To make an impression on or in (a surface). **3.** To produce by means of pressed type, an electronic printer, or similar means, on a paper surface. **4.** To publish. **5.** To write in characters similar to those commonly used in print. **6.** To produce a photographic image from by passing light through film onto sensitized paper. [< Lat. *premere*, press.]

print•a•ble (prĭn′tə-bəl) ▶*adj.* **1.** Capable of being printed or of producing a print. **2.** Fit for publication.

print•ed circuit (prĭn′tĭd) ▶*n.* An electric circuit in which the conducting connections have been printed in predetermined patterns on an insulating base.

print•er (prĭn′tər) ▶*n.* **1.** One whose occupation is printing. **2.** A device that prints text or graphics on paper.

print•ing (prĭn′tĭng) ▶*n.* **1.** The art, process, or business of producing printed material. **2.** Matter that is printed. **3.** All the copies of a publication, such as a book, that are printed at one time.

printing press ▶*n.* A machine that transfers images onto paper or similar material.

print•mak•ing (prĭnt′mā′kĭng) ▶*n.* The artistic design and making of prints, such as woodcuts. —**print′mak′er** *n.*

print•out (prĭnt′out′) ▶*n. Comp. Sci.* Printed output.

pri•or[1] (prī′ər) ▶*adj.* **1.** Preceding in time or order. **2.** Preceding in importance or value. [Lat.]

pri•or[2] (prī′ər) ▶*n.* A monastic officer in charge of a priory. [< Lat., superior.]

pri•or•ess (prī′ər-ĭs) ▶*n.* A nun in charge of a priory.

pri•or•i•tize (prī-ôr′ĭ-tīz′, -ŏr′-) ▶*v.* **-tized, -tiz•ing.** To arrange or deal with in order of importance. [PRIORIT(Y) + -IZE.] —**pri•or′i•ti•za′tion** *n.*

Usage: Although *prioritize* is often criticized for being associated with corporate or bureaucratic jargon, resistance to this verb appears to be waning, probably because it offers a useful way of saying "arrange according to priority." In 1997, 53 percent of the Usage Panel approved the word in the sentence *Overwhelmed with work, the lawyer was forced to prioritize his caseload.*

pri•or•i•ty (prī-ôr′ĭ-tē, -ŏr′-) ▶*n., pl.* **-ties 1.** Precedence, esp. by order of importance. **2.** An established right to precedence. **3.** Something deserving prior attention.

prior to ▶*prep.* Before.

pri•or•y (prī′ə-rē) ▶*n., pl.* **-ies.** A monastery governed by a prior or a convent governed by a prioress.

prism (prĭz′əm) ▶*n.* **1.** A polyhedron with parallel, congruent polygons as ends and parallelograms as sides. **2.** A transparent solid, usu. with triangular ends, used for separating white light passed into a spectrum. **3.** A cut-glass object, such as a pendant of a chandelier. [< Gk. *prisma.*] —**pris•mat′ic** (prĭz-măt′ĭk) *adj.* —**pris•mat′i•cal•ly** *adv.*

pris•on (prĭz′ən) ▶*n.* A place where persons convicted or accused of crimes are confined; jail. [< Lat. *prēnsiō*, a seizing.]

pris•on•er (prĭz′ə-nər, prĭz′nər) ▶*n.* **1.** A person held in custody or captivity, esp. in a prison. **2.** One deprived of freedom of expression or action.

prisoner of war ▶*n., pl.* **prisoners of war.** A person taken by or surrendering to enemy forces in wartime.

pris•sy (prĭs′ē) ▶*adj.* **-si•er, -si•est.** Excessively prim and proper. [Perh. blend of PRI(M) and (SI)SSY.] —**pris′si•ness** *n.*

Priš•ti•na (prĭsh′tə-nä′) A city of S Yugoslavia, the chief city of the Kosovo region. Pop. 155,000.

pris•tine (prĭs′tēn′, prĭ-stēn′) ▶*adj.* **1.** Remaining in a pure state; uncorrupted. **2.** Of or typical of the earliest time or condition; primitive or original. [Lat. *prīstinus.*]

prith•ee (prĭ*th*′ē, prĭth′ē) ▶*interj. Archaic* Please. [< *(I) pray thee.*]

pri•va•cy (prī′və-sē) ▶*n.* **1.** The condition of being secluded from others. **2.** Secrecy.

pri•vate (prī′vĭt) ▶*adj.* **1.** Secluded from the sight, presence, or intrusion of others. **2.** Of or confined to the individual; personal. **3.** Not available for public use, control, or participation. **4.** Belonging to a particular person or persons. **5.** Not holding an official or public position. **6.** Intimate; secret. ▶*n.* Any of the lowest enlisted ranks, as in the US Army. [< Lat. *prīvātus*, not in public life.] —**pri′vate•ly** *adv.* —**pri′vate•ness** *n.*

private enterprise ▶*n.* Business activities unregulated by state ownership or control.

pri•va•teer (prī′və-tîr′) ▶*n.* **1.** A ship privately owned and manned but authorized to attack and capture enemy vessels. **2.** Such a ship's commander or one of its crew.

pri•va•tion (prī-vā′shən) ▶*n.* **1.** Lack of the basic necessities or comforts of life. **2.** The condition resulting from such lack. [< Lat. *prīvāre*, deprive.]

pri•va•tize (prī′və-tīz′) ▶*v.* **-tized, -tiz•ing.** To change (e.g., an industry) from governmental or public ownership or control to private enterprise. —**pri′va•ti•za′tion** *n.*

priv•et (prĭv′ĭt) ▶*n.* A shrub having opposite leaves and clusters of white flowers, widely used for hedges. [?]

priv•i•lege (prĭv′ə-lĭj, prĭv′lĭj) ▶*n.* A special advantage, immunity, or benefit granted to or enjoyed by an individual, class, or caste. ▶*v.* **-leged, -leg•ing.** To grant a privilege to. [< Lat. *prīvilēgium.*]

priv•i•leged (prĭv′ə-lĭjd, prĭv′lĭjd) ▶*adj.* **1.** Having privileges. **2.** Confined to a chosen group of individuals: *privileged information.*

priv•y (prĭv′ē) ▶*adj.* **1.** Made a participant in something secret. **2.** Belonging to a person, such as the British sovereign, in a private rather than official capacity. ▶*n., pl.* **-ies.** An outhouse. [< Lat. *prīvātus*, private.]

prize[1] (prīz) ▶*n.* **1.** Something offered or won as an award for superiority or victory, as in a contest or competition. **2.** Something worth striving for or aspiring to. ▶*adj.* **1.** Offered or given as a prize. **2.** Given or worthy of a prize. **3.** Outstanding. ▶*v.* **prized, priz•ing.** To value highly; esteem. [< ME *pris*, PRICE.]

prize[2] (prīz) ▶*n.* Something, esp. an enemy ship captured during wartime. [< OFr. *prise.*]

prize[3] (prīz) ▶*v.* **prized, priz•ing.** To move with a lever; pry. [< ME *prise*, instrument for prying.]

prize•fight (prīz′fīt′) ▶*n.* A match fought between professional boxers for money. —**prize′fight′er** *n.* —**prize′fight′ing** *n.*

prize•win•ner (prīz′wĭn′ər) ▶*n.* One that wins a prize. —**prize′win′ning** *adj.*

pro[1] (prō) ▶*n., pl.* **pros 1.** An argument in favor of something. **2.** One who takes an affirmative position. ▶*adv.* In favor; affirmatively. [< Lat. *prō*, for.]

pro[2] (prō) *Informal* ▶*n., pl.* **pros 1.** A professional. **2.** An expert. ▶*adj.* Professional.

pro–[1] ▶*pref.* **1.** Acting in place of: *pronoun.* **2.** Supporting; favoring: *prorevolutionary.* [< Lat. *prō*, for.]

pro–[2] ▶*pref.* **1.** Precursor of: *procaine* **2.** Anterior; in front of: *prognathous.* [< Gk. *pro.*]

prob•a•bil•i•ty (prŏb′ə-bĭl′ĭ-tē) ▶*n., pl.* **-ties 1.** The quality or condition of being probable; likelihood. **2.** A probable situation, condition, or event. **3.** *Statistics* A number expressing the likelihood that a specific event will occur.

prob•a•ble (prŏb′ə-bəl) ▶*adj.* **1.** Likely to happen or to be true. **2.** Likely but uncertain; plausible. [< Lat. *probāre*, prove.] —**prob′a•bly** *adv.*

pro•bate (prō′bāt′) *Law* ▶*n.* The process of establishing the validity of a will. ▶*v.* **-bat•ed, -bat•ing.** To establish the validity of (a will). [< Lat. *probāre*, prove.]

pro•ba•tion (prō-bā′shən) ▶*n.* **1.** A trial period in which a person's fitness, as for membership in a group, is tested. **2.** *Law* The release of a convicted offender on the condition of good behavior. [< Lat. *probāre*, test.] —**pro•ba′tion•al** *adj.* —**pro•ba′tion•ar′y** *adj.*

pro•ba•tion•er (prō-bā′shə-nər) ▶*n.* A person on probation.

pro•ba•tive (prō′bə-tĭv) ▶*adj.* **1.** Serving to test or prove. **2.** Furnishing evidence or proof.

probe (prōb) ▶*n.* **1.** An exploratory action, expedition, or device, esp. one designed to investigate an unknown region. **2.** A slender, flexible instrument used to explore a wound or body cavity. **3.** A thorough examination or investigation. See Syns at **inquiry.** ▶*v.* **probed, prob•ing 1.** To explore with or as if with a probe. **2.** To delve into; investigate. [< Lat. *probāre*, test.]

pro•bi•ty (prō′bĭ-tē) ▶*n.* Integrity; honesty. [< Lat. *probus*, upright.]

prob•lem (prŏb′ləm) ▶*n.* **1.** A question to be considered, solved, or answered. **2.** A situation, matter, or person that presents perplexity or difficulty. ▶*adj.* Difficult to deal with or control:

a problem child. [< Gk. *problēma.*]

prob•lem•at•ic (prŏb′lə-măt′ĭk) also **prob•lem•at•i•cal** (-ĭ-kəl) ▸*adj.* **1.** Posing a problem. **2.** Open to doubt; dubious or unsettled. —**prob′lem•at′i•cal•ly** *adv.*

pro bo•no (prō bō′nō) ▸*adj.* Done for the public good without compensation. [Lat. *prō bonō (publicō)*, for the (public) good.]

pro•bos•cis (prō-bŏs′ĭs) ▸*n., pl.* **-cis•es** or **-bos•ci•des** (-bŏs′-ĭ-dēz′). A long flexible snout or trunk, as of an elephant. [< Gk. *proboskis.*]

pro•caine (prō′kān′) ▸*n.* A white crystalline powder, $C_{13}H_{20}N_2O_2$, used chiefly in its hydrochloride form as a local anesthetic. [PRO–[2] + (CO)CAINE.]

pro•ce•dure (prə-sē′jər) ▸*n.* **1.** A way of doing something. **2.** A series of steps to an end. **3.** A set of established forms or methods for conducting legal or business affairs. [< OFr. *proceder,* PROCEED.] —**pro•ce′dur•al** *adj.* —**pro•ce′dur•al•ly** *adv.*

pro•ceed (prō-sēd′, prə-) ▸*v.* **1.** To continue, esp. after an interruption. **2.** To begin to carry on an action or a process. **3.** To progress in an orderly manner. **4.** To come from a source; originate. See Syns at **stem**[1]. **5.** To institute and conduct legal action. ▸*n.* **pro•ceeds** (prō′sēdz′). The amount of money derived from a commercial or fundraising venture. [< Lat. *prōcēdere.*]

pro•ceed•ing (prō-sē′dĭng, prə-) ▸*n.* **1.** A course of action; procedure. **2. proceedings a.** Events; doings. **b.** A record of business carried on by an organization. **3.** often **proceedings** Legal action; litigation.

proc•ess[1] (prŏs′ĕs′, prō′sĕs′) ▸*n.* **1.** A series of actions, changes, or functions bringing about a result. **2.** Progress; passage: *the process of time.* **3.** *Law* **a.** The entire course of a judicial proceeding. **b.** A summons or writ ordering a defendant to appear in court. **4.** *Biol.* An outgrowth of tissue: *a bony process.* ▸*v.* **1.** To put through the steps of a prescribed procedure. **2.** To prepare, treat, or convert by subjecting to a special process. **3.** *Comp. Sci.* To perform operations on (data). [< Lat. *prōcēdere, prōcess-,* advance.]

pro•cess[2] (prə-sĕs′) ▸*v.* To move along in or as if in a procession. [< PROCESSION.]

pro•ces•sion (prə-sĕsh′ən) ▸*n.* A group of persons, vehicles, or objects moving along in an orderly, formal manner.

pro•ces•sion•al (prə-sĕsh′ə-nəl) ▸*n.* Music intended to be played or sung during a procession, esp. a church procession.

proc•es•sor (prŏs′ĕs′ər, prō′sĕs′-) ▸*n.* **1.** One that processes, esp. an apparatus for preparing, treating, or converting material. **2.** *Comp. Sci.* **a.** A computer. **b.** A central processing unit.

pro-choice (prō-chois′) ▸*adj.* Favoring the legal right of women to choose whether or not to continue a pregnancy to term.

pro•claim (prō-klām′, prə-) ▸*v.* To announce officially and publicly; declare. See Syns at **announce.** [< Lat. *prōclāmāre.*] —**proc′la•ma′tion** (prŏk′lə-mā′shən) *n.*

pro•cliv•i•ty (prō-klĭv′ĭ-tē) ▸*n., pl.* **-ties.** A natural propensity or inclination. See Syns at **predilection.** [< Lat. *prōclīvis,* inclined : PRO–[1] + *clīvus,* slope.]

pro•con•sul (prō-kŏn′səl) ▸*n.* **1.** An ancient Roman provincial governor of consular rank. **2.** A high administrator in certain modern colonial empires. [< Lat. *prō cōnsule,* in place of the consul.] —**pro•con′su•lar** (-sə-lər) *adj.*

pro•cras•ti•nate (prō-krăs′tə-nāt′, prə-) ▸*v.* **-nat•ed, -nat•ing.** To put off doing something, esp. out of habitual carelessness or laziness. [Lat. *prōcrāstināre.*] —**pro•cras′ti•na′tion** *n.* —**pro•cras′ti•na′tor** *n.*

pro•cre•ate (prō′krē-āt′) ▸*v.* **-at•ed, -at•ing.** To beget offspring; reproduce. [Lat. *prōcreāre.*] —**pro′cre•a′tion** *n.* —**pro′cre•a′tive** *adj.* —**pro′cre•a′tor** *n.*

Pro•crus•te•an also **pro•crus•te•an** (prō-krŭs′tē-ən) ▸*adj.* Showing no regard for individual differences or special circumstances; ruthlessly inflexible. [After *Procrustes,* a mythical Greek giant.]

proc•tor (prŏk′tər) ▸*n.* A dormitory and examination supervisor in a school. ▸*v.* To supervise (an examination). [< Lat. *prōcūrātor,* PROCURATOR.] —**proc•to′ri•al** (-tôr′ē-əl, -tōr′-) *adj.*

proc•u•ra•tor (prŏk′yə-rā′tər) ▸*n.* An administrator, esp. a civil or provincial administrator of ancient Rome. [< Lat. *prōcūrāre,* take care of.]

pro•cure (prō-kyo͝or′, prə-) ▸*v.* **-cured, -cur•ing 1.** To get by special effort; obtain or acquire. **2.** To bring about; effect. **3.** To obtain (a sexual partner) for another. [< Lat. *prōcūrāre,* manage.] —**pro•cur′a•ble** *adj.* —**pro•cure′ment** *n.* —**pro•cur′er** *n.*

prod (prŏd) ▸*v.* **prod•ded, prod•ding 1.** To jab or poke, as with a pointed object. **2.** To goad to action; incite. ▸*n.* **1.** A pointed object used to prod. **2.** An incitement; stimulus. [?] —**prod′der** *n.*

prod•i•gal (prŏd′ĭ-gəl) ▸*adj.* **1.** Rashly or wastefully extravagant. **2.** Profuse; lavish. See Syns at **profuse.** [< Lat. *prōdigus* : *prō-,* forth + *agere,* drive.] —**prod′i•gal** *n.* —**prod′i•gal′i•ty** (-găl′ĭ-tē) *n.* —**prod′i•gal•ly** *adv.*

pro•di•gious (prə-dĭj′əs) ▸*adj.* **1.** Impressively great in size, force, or extent; enormous. **2.** Extraordinary; marvelous. —**pro•di′gious•ly** *adv.*

prod•i•gy (prŏd′ə-jē) ▸*n., pl.* **-gies 1.** A person with exceptional talents or powers. **2.** Something extraordinary or rare; marvel. See Syns at **wonder.** [< Lat. *prōdigium,* portent.]

pro•duce (prə-do͞os′, -dyo͞os′, prō-) ▸*v.* **-duced, -duc•ing 1.** To bring forth; yield. **2a.** To create by physical or mental effort. **b.** To manufacture. **3.** To cause; give rise to. **4.** To bring forth; exhibit. **5.** To supervise and finance the making of: *produce a play.* **6.** *Math.* To extend (an area or volume) or lengthen (a line). ▸*n.* (prŏd′o͞os, prō′do͞os). Something produced, esp. fresh farm products. [< Lat. *prōdūcere.*] —**pro•duc′er** *n.*

Syns: *produce, bear, yield* ***v.***

prod•uct (prŏd′əkt) ▸*n.* **1.** Something produced naturally or by human effort. **2.** A direct result; consequence. **3.** *Math.* The result obtained by performing multiplication. [< Lat. *prōductus,* p.part of *prōdūcere,* produce.]

pro•duc•tion (prə-dŭk′shən, prō-) ▸*n.* **1.** The act or process of producing. **2.** Something produced; product. **3.** An amount or quantity produced; output. **4.** A presentation of a theatrical work.

pro•duc•tive (prə-dŭk′tĭv, prō-) ▸*adj.* **1.** Producing or capable of producing. **2.** Producing abundantly. See Syns at **fertile.** —**pro•duc′tive•ly** *adv.* —**pro′duc•tiv′i•ty** (prō′dŭk-tĭv′ĭ-tē, prŏd′ək-), **pro•duc′tive•ness** *n.*

pro•em (prō′ĕm′) ▸*n.* An introduction; preface. [< Gk. *prooimion.*]

pro•fane (prō-fān′, prə-) ▸*adj.* **1.** Marked by contempt or irreverence for what is sacred. **2.** Nonreligious; secular. **3.** Vulgar; coarse. ▸*v.* **-faned, -fan•ing 1.** To treat with irreverence. **2.** To put to an improper, unworthy, or degrading use; abuse. [< Lat. *profānus.*] —**prof′a•na′tion** (prŏf′ə-nā′shən) *n.* —**pro•fan′a•to′ry** (-făn′ə-tôr′ē, -tōr′ē) *adj.* —**pro•fane′ness** *n.*

pro•fan•i•ty (prō-făn′ĭ-tē, prə-) ▸*n., pl.* **-ties 1.** The condition or quality of being profane. **2.** Obscene or irreverent language.

pro•fess (prə-fĕs′, prō-) ▸*v.* **1.** To affirm openly; declare. **2.** To make a pretense of. **3.** To claim skill in or knowledge of. **4.** To affirm belief in. [< Lat. *profitērī.*] —**pro•fess′ed•ly** *adv.*

pro•fes•sion (prə-fĕsh′ən) ▸*n.* **1.** An occupation requiring training and specialized study. **2.** The body of qualified persons in an occupation or field: *the teaching profession.* **3.** An act of professing; declaration. **4.** An avowal of faith or belief.

pro•fes•sion•al (prə-fĕsh′ə-nəl) ▸*adj.* **1.** Of or engaged in a profession. **2.** Engaging in a given activity as a source of livelihood. ▸*n.* A person following a profession. —**pro•fes′sion•al•ly** *adv.*

pro•fes•sion•al•ism (prə-fĕsh′ə-nə-lĭz′əm) ▸*n.* Professional status, methods, character, or standards.

pro•fes•sion•al•ize (prə-fĕsh′ə-nə-līz′) ▸*v.* **-ized, -iz•ing.** To make professional. —**pro•fes′sion•al•i•za′tion** *n.*

pro•fes•sor (prə-fĕs′ər) ▸*n.* **1.** A college or university teacher of the highest rank. **2.** A teacher or instructor. —**pro′fes•so′ri•al** (prō′fĭ-sôr′ē-əl, -sōr′-, prŏf′ĭ-) *adj.* —**pro′fes•so′ri•al•ly** *adv.* —**pro•fes′sor•ship′** *n.*

prof•fer (prŏf′ər) ▸*v.* To offer for acceptance. [< OFr. *profrir.*] —**prof′fer** *n.*

pro•fi•cient (prə-fĭsh′ənt) ▸*adj.* Expert in an art, vocation, or area of learning. [< Lat. *prōficere*, progress.] —**pro•fi′cien•cy** *n.*

pro•file (prō′fīl′) ▸*n.* **1.** A side view of an object or a structure, esp. of the human head. **2.** An outline; silhouette. See Syns at **outline. 3.** Degree of exposure to public notice; visibility: *kept a low profile.* **4.** A brief biographical essay. [< Ital. *profilare*, draw in outline.] —**pro′file** *v.*

prof•it (prŏf′ĭt) ▸*n.* **1.** An advantageous gain or return; benefit. **2.** often **profits** The return received on an investment or a business undertaking after all charges or expenses have been paid. ▸*v.* **1.** To make a gain or profit. **2.** To derive advantage; benefit. See Syns at **benefit.** [< Lat. *prōfectus.*] —**prof′it•a•bil′i•ty** *n.* —**pro′it•a•ble** *adj.* —**prof′it•a•bly** *adv.*

prof•it•eer (prŏf′ĭ-tîr′) ▸*n.* One who makes excessive profits on goods in short supply. —**prof′it•eer′** *v.*

prof•li•gate (prŏf′lĭ-gĭt, -gāt′) ▸*adj.* **1.** Given over to immorality; dissolute. **2.** Recklessly wasteful; extravagant. ▸*n.* A profligate person. [< Lat. *prōflīgāre*, to ruin.] —**prof′li•ga•cy** (-gə-sē) *n.*

pro for•ma (prō fôr′mə) ▸*adj.* Done as a formality; perfunctory. [NLat. *prō formā.*]

pro•found (prə-found′, prō-) ▸*adj.* **-er, -est 1.** Extending to or coming from a great depth; deep. **2.** Coming as if from the depths of one's being: *profound contempt.* **3.** Thoroughgoing; far-reaching. **4.** Penetrating beyond what is superficial or obvious. **5.** Unqualified: *a profound silence.* [< Lat. *profundus.*] —**pro•found′ly** *adv.* —**pro•fun′di•ty** (fŭn′dĭ-tē) *n.*

pro•fuse (prə-fyo͞os′, prō-) ▸*adj.* **1.** Plentiful; copious. **2.** Giving or given freely and abundantly; extravagant. [< Lat. *profūsus*, p.part. of *profundere*, pour forth.] —**pro•fuse′ly** *adv.* —**pro•fuse′ness** *n.* —**pro•fu′sion** (-fyo͞o′zhən) *n.*

Syns: *profuse, exuberant, lavish, lush, luxuriant, prodigal, riotous* ***Ant:*** *spare* ***adj.***

pro•gen•i•tor (prō-jĕn′ĭ-tər) ▸*n.* **1.** A direct ancestor. See Syns at **ancestor. 2.** An originator of a line of descent. **3.** An originator; founder. [< Lat. *prōgenitor.*]

prog•e•ny (prŏj′ə-nē) ▸*n.* Offspring or descendants. [< Lat. *prōgeniēs.*]

pro•ges•ter•one (prō-jĕs′tə-rōn′) ▸*n.* A steroid hormone secreted by the ovary before implantation of the fertilized ovum. [PRO–[1] + GES(TATION) + STER(OL) + *-one*, suff.]

prog•na•thous (prŏg′nə-thəs, prŏg-nā′-) ▸*adj.* Having jaws that project forward to a marked degree. [< PRO–[2] + Gk. *gnathos*, jaw.] —**prog′na•thism** *n.*

prog•no•sis (prŏg-nō′sĭs) ▸*n., pl.* **-ses** (-sēz). A prediction, esp. of the probable course and outcome of a disease. [< Gk.]

prog•nos•tic (prŏg-nŏs′tĭk) ▸*adj.* Of or useful in prognosis. ▸*n.* **1.** A forecast or prediction. **2.** A portent; omen. [< Gk. *prognōstikos*, foreknowing.]

prog•nos•ti•cate (prŏg-nŏs′tĭ-kāt′) ▸*v.* **-cat•ed, -cat•ing.** To predict according to present indications or signs; foretell. —**prog•nos′ti•ca′tion** *n.* —**prog•nos′ti•ca′tor** *n.*

pro•gram (prō′grăm′, -grəm) ▸*n.* **1a.** A listing of the order of events and other information for a public presentation. **b.** The presentation itself. **2.** A scheduled radio or television show. **3.** An ordered list of events or procedures to be followed; schedule. **4.** *Comp. Sci.* A set of coded instructions that enables a machine, especially a computer, to perform a desired sequence of operations. ▸*v.* **-grammed, -gram•ming** or **-gramed, -gram•ing 1.** To include or schedule in a program. **2.** To design a program for. **3.** To provide (a computer) with a set of instructions. [< Gk. *programma*, public notice : PRO–[2] + *graphein*, write.] —**pro′gram′ma•ble** *adj.* —**pro′gram•mat′ic** (-grə-măt′ĭk) *adj.*

pro•gramme (prō′grăm′, -grəm) ▸*n.* & *v.* *Chiefly Brit.* Var. of **program.**

pro•gram•mer or **pro•gram•er** (prō′grăm′ər) ▸*n.* One who programs, esp. one who writes computer programs.

pro•gram•ming language (prō′grăm′ĭng, -grə-mĭng) ▸*n.* An artificial language that can be translated into machine language and executed by a computer.

prog•ress (prŏg′rĕs′, -rəs, prō′grĕs′) ▸*n.* **1.** Movement, as toward a goal. **2.** Development or growth. **3.** Steady improvement, as of a society or civilization. ►*v.* **pro•gress** (prə-grĕs′) **1.** To advance; proceed. **2.** To move toward a higher or better stage. [< Lat. *prōgressus*.]

pro•gres•sion (prə-grĕsh′ən) ►*n.* **1.** Movement forward; advance. **2.** A continuous series; sequence. **3.** *Math.* A series of numbers or quantities in which there is always the same relation between each quantity and the one succeeding it.

pro•gres•sive (prə-grĕs′ĭv) ►*adj.* **1.** Moving forward; advancing. **2.** Proceeding in steps. **3.** Favoring progress toward better conditions or new policies. **4.** Increasing in rate as the taxable amount increases. **5.** *Pathol.* Tending to spread or become more severe. **6.** *Gram.* Designating a verb form that expresses an action or condition in progress. ►*n.* A person who favors progress toward better conditions. —**pro•gres′sive•ly** *adv.* —**pro•gres′sive•ness** *n.* —**pro′gres•siv′i•ty** (prō′grĕ-sĭv′ĭ-tē, prŏg′rə-) *n.*

pro•hib•it (prō-hĭb′ĭt) ►*v.* **1.** To forbid by authority. See Syns at **forbid. 2.** To prevent; preclude. [< Lat. *prohibēre, prohibit-*.]

pro•hi•bi•tion (prō′ə-bĭsh′ən) ►*n.* **1.** The act of prohibiting. **2.** The forbidding by law of making, transporting, or selling alcoholic beverages. —**pro′hi•bi′tion•ist** *n.*

pro•hib•i•tive (prō-hĭb′ĭ-tĭv) also **pro•hib•i•to•ry** (-tôr′ē, -tōr′ē) ►*adj.* **1.** Prohibiting; forbidding. **2.** So high or burdensome as to discourage purchase or use. —**pro•hib′i•tive•ly** *adv.*

proj•ect (prŏj′ĕkt′, -ĭkt) ►*n.* **1.** A plan or proposal; scheme. See Syns at **plan. 2.** An undertaking requiring concerted effort. ►*v.* **pro•ject** (prə-jĕkt′) **1.** To thrust or extend outward or forward. See Syns at **bulge. 2.** To throw forward; hurl. **3.** To cause (light or an image) to appear on a surface. **4.** To direct (one's voice) so as to be heard clearly at a distance. **5.** To estimate based on present data: *project next year's expenses.* [< Lat. *prōiectus*, p.part. of *prōicere*, throw out.] —**pro•jec′tion** *n.*

pro•jec•tile (prə-jĕk′təl, -tīl′) ►*n.* **1.** A fired, thrown, or otherwise propelled object, such as a bullet. **2.** A self-propelled missile, such as a rocket.

pro•jec•tor (prə-jĕk′tər) ►*n.* A machine for projecting an image onto a screen. —**pro•jec′tion•ist** *n.*

pro•kar•y•ote (prō-kăr′ē-ōt′) ►*n.* A single-celled organism that lacks a nuclear membrane, such as a bacterium. [< PRO–[2] + Gk. *karuon*, kernel.] —**pro•kar′y•ot′ic** (-ŏt′ĭk) *adj.*

Pro•kof•iev (prə-kô′fē-ĕf, -kôf′yĭf), **Sergei Sergeyevich.** 1891–1953. Russian composer.

pro•lapse (prō-lăps′) ►*v.* **-lapsed, -laps•ing** *Medic.* To fall or slip out of place, as a bodily organ. [Lat. *prōlābī, prōlāps-*, fall down.] —**pro′lapse′** *n.*

pro•le•gom•e•non (prō′lĭ-gŏm′ə-nŏn′, -nən) ►*n., pl.* **-na** (-nə). An introductory essay or remark. [Gk.]

pro•le•tar•i•an (prō′lĭ-târ′ē-ən) ►*n.* A member of the proletariat. [< Lat. *prōlētārius*, of the lowest class of Roman citizens.] —**pro′le•tar′i•an** *adj.* —**pro′le•tar′i•an•ism** *n.*

pro•le•tar•i•at (prō′lĭ-târ′ē-ĭt) ►*n.* The class of industrial wage earners who must earn their living by selling their labor. [Fr. *prolétariat*.]

pro-life (prō-līf′) ►*adj.* Advocating full legal protection of human embryos or fetuses, esp. by opposing legalized abortion. —**pro-lif′er** *n.*

pro•lif•er•ate (prə-lĭf′ə-rāt′) ►*v.* **-at•ed, -at•ing 1.** To grow or multiply by rapidly producing new parts, cells, or offspring. **2.** To increase or spread. [< Fr. *prolifère*, procreative.] —**pro•lif′er•a′tion** *n.*

pro•lif•ic (prə-lĭf′ĭk) ►*adj.* **1.** Producing offspring or fruit in abundance. **2.** Producing abundant works or results. See Syns at **fertile.** [< Lat. *prōlēs*, offspring.]

pro•lix (prō-lĭks′, prō′lĭks′) ►*adj.* Tediously long and wordy. See Syns at **wordy.** [< Lat. *prōlixus*, abundant.] —**pro•lix′i•ty** *n.*

pro•logue (prō′lôg′, -lŏg′) ►*n.* An introduction or preface, as to a play. [< Gk. *prologos*.]

pro•long (prə-lông′, -lŏng′) ►*v.* **1.** To lengthen in duration; protract. **2.** To lengthen in extent. [< LLat. *prōlongāre*.] —**pro′lon•ga′•tion** (prō′lông-gā′shən, -lŏng-) *n.*

prom (prŏm) ►*n.* A formal dance held for a high-school or college class. [< PROMENADE.]

prom•e•nade (prŏm′ə-nād′, -näd′) ►*n.* **1a.** A leisurely walk; stroll. **b.** A public place for such walking. **2.** A march of all the guests at the opening of a ball. [< Fr. *promener*, take for a walk.] —**prom′e•nade′** *v.*

Pro•me•the•us (prə-mē′thē-əs, -thyo͞os′) ►*n.* *Gk. Myth.* A Titan who stole fire from Olympus and gave it to humankind.

pro•me•thi•um (prə-mē′thē-əm) ►*n.* *Symbol* **Pm** A radioactive rare-earth element. At. no. 61. See table at **element.** [< PROMETHEUS.]

prom•i•nence (prŏm′ə-nəns) ►*n.* **1.** The quality or condition of being prominent. **2.** Something prominent; projection.

prom•i•nent (prŏm′ə-nənt) ►*adj.* **1.** Projecting outward or upward. **2.** Immediately noticeable; conspicuous. **3.** Widely known; eminent. [< Lat. *prōminēre*, jut out.]

pro•mis•cu•ous (prə-mĭs′kyo͞o-əs) ►*adj.* **1.** Indiscriminate in the choice of sexual partners. **2.** Lacking standards of selection; indiscriminate. **3.** Consisting of miscellaneous parts or members. [< Lat. *prōmiscuus*.] —**prom′is•cu′i•ty** (prŏm′ĭs-kyo͞o′ĭ-tē, prō′mĭ-) *n.* —**pro•mis′cu•ous•ly** *adv.*

prom•ise (prŏm′ĭs) ►*n.* **1a.** A declaration assuring that one will or will not do something; vow. **b.** Something promised. **2.** Indication of something favorable to come, esp. future excellence or success. ►*v.* **-ised, -is•ing 1.** To commit oneself by a promise to do or give; pledge. **2.** To afford a basis for expecting: *clouds that promise rain.* [< Lat. *prōmittere, prōmiss-*, promise.] —**prom′is•er** *n.*

Syns: *promise, pledge, swear, vow* **v.**

prom•is•ing (prŏm′ĭ-sĭng) ►*adj.* Likely to develop favorably. —**prom′is•ing•ly** *adv.*

prom•is•so•ry (prŏm′ĭ-sôr′ē, -sōr′ē) ►*adj.* Containing or involving a promise.

promissory note ►*n.* A written promise to pay or repay a specified sum of money at a stated time or on demand.

prom•on•to•ry (prŏm′ən-tôr′ē, -tōr′ē) ►*n., pl.* **-ries.** A high ridge of land or rock jutting out into a body of water. [Lat. *prōmontorium*.]

pro•mote (prə-mōt′) ►*v.* **-mot•ed, -mot•ing 1.** To raise in position or rank. **2.** To contribute to the progress or growth of; further. See Syns at **advance.** **3.** To advocate: *promote a constitutional amendment.* **4.** To attempt to sell or popularize: *promote a new product.* [< Lat. *prōmovēre, prōmōt-.*] —**pro•mo′tion** *n.* —**pro•mo′tion•al** *adj.*

pro•mot•er (prə-mō′tər) ►*n.* **1.** An active supporter or advocate. **2.** A financial and publicity organizer, as of a boxing match.

prompt (prŏmpt) ►*adj.* **-er, -est 1.** On time; punctual. **2.** Done without delay. ►*v.* **1.** To move to act; spur or incite. **2.** To give rise to; inspire. **3.** To give a cue to, as in a theatrical performance. ►*n.* **1.** A reminder or cue. **2.** *Comp. Sci.* A symbol that appears on a monitor to indicate that the computer is ready to receive input. [< Lat. *prōmptus*, ready.] —**prompt′er** *n.* —**promp′ti•tude′** (prŏmp′tĭ-to͞od′, -tyo͞od′), **prompt′ness** *n.*

prom•ul•gate (prŏm′əl-gāt′, prō-mŭl′gāt′) ►*v.* **-gat•ed, -gat•ing 1.** To make known (e.g., a decree) by public declaration. See Syns at **announce.** **2.** To put (a law) into effect by formal public announcement. [Lat. *prōmulgāre.*] —**prom′ul•ga′tion** *n.* —**prom′ul•ga′tor** *n.*

pron. ►*abbr.* **1.** pronoun **2.** pronunciation

prone (prōn) ►*adj.* **1.** Lying with the front or face downward. **2.** Having a tendency; inclined. [< Lat. *prōnus*, leaning forward.] —**prone** *adv.* —**prone′ness** *n.*

prong (prông, prŏng) ►*n.* **1.** A thin, pointed, projecting part. **2.** A branch or division. [ME *pronge*, forked instrument.]

prong•horn (prông′hôrn′, prŏng′-) ►*n., pl.* **-horn** or **-horns.** A small mammal resembling an antelope and having small forked horns, found on W North American plains.

pro•noun (prō′noun′) ►*n.* One of a class of words that function as substitutes for nouns or noun phrases.

pro•nounce (prə-nouns′) ►*v.* **-nounced, -nounc•ing 1.** To utter or articulate (a word or speech sound). **2.** To declare officially or formally. [< Lat. *prōnūntiāre.*] —**pro•nounce′a•ble** *adj.* —**pro•nun′ci•a′tion** (-nŭn′sē-ā′shən) *n.*

pro•nounced (prə-nounst′) ►*adj.* Strongly marked; distinct: *a pronounced limp.* —**pro•nounc′ed•ly** (-noun′sĭd-lē) *adv.*

pro•nounce•ment (prə-nouns′mənt) ►*n.* A formal or authoritative declaration or statement.

pron•to (prŏn′tō) ►*adv. Informal* Without delay; quickly. [Sp. < Lat. *prōmptus.*]

pro•nun•ci•a•men•to (prō-nŭn′sē-ə-mĕn′tō) ►*n., pl.* **-tos** or **-toes.** An official declaration; proclamation. [Sp.]

proof (pro͞of) ►*n.* **1.** The evidence or argument that establishes an assertion as true. **2.** Convincing demonstration of something. **3.** Determination of the quality of something by testing; trial. **4.** The alcoholic strength of a liquor, expressed as twice the percentage of alcoholic content. **5a.** A trial sheet of printed material. **b.** A trial impression, as of an engraved plate. **6.** A trial photographic print. ►*adj.* **1.** Fully resistant; impervious: *proof against temptation; bulletproof.* **2.** Of standard alcoholic strength. ►*v.* **1.** To make a trial impression of. **2.** To proofread (copy). [< LLat. *proba.*]

proof•read (pro͞of′rēd′) ►*v.* To read (copy or proof) in order to find errors and mark corrections. —**proof′read′er** *n.*

prop[1] (prŏp) ►*n.* A support, esp. one placed under or against something to keep it from falling. [ME *proppe.*] —**prop** *v.*

prop[2] (prŏp) ►*n.* A theatrical property.

prop[3] (prŏp) ►*n. Informal* A propeller.

prop•a•gan•da (prŏp′ə-găn′də) ►*n.* **1.** The systematic propagation of a doctrine or cause. **2.** Material disseminated by the advocates of a doctrine or cause. [< Lat. *prōpāgāre*, propagate.] —**prop′a•gan′dist** *n.* —**prop′a•gan′dize′** *v.*

prop•a•gate (prŏp′ə-gāt′) ►*v.* **-gat•ed, -gat•ing 1.** To reproduce or cause to reproduce; breed. **2.** To make known; publicize. **3.** *Phys.* To cause (e.g., a wave) to move in some direction or through a medium. [Lat. *prōpāgāre.*] —**prop′•a•ga′tion** *n.* —**prop′a•ga′tive** *adj.* —**prop′a•ga′tor** *n.*

pro•pane (prō′pān′) ►*n.* A colorless gas, C_3H_8, found in natural gas and petroleum and widely used as a fuel.

pro•pel (prə-pĕl′) ►*v.* **-pelled, -pel•ling.** To cause to move forward or onward. See Syns at **push.** [< Lat. *prōpellere.*]

pro•pel•lant also **pro•pel•lent** (prə-pĕl′ənt) ►*n.* Something, such as an explosive charge or a rocket fuel, that propels. —**pro•pel′lant** *adj.*

pro•pel•ler also **pro•pel•lor** (prə-pĕl′ər) ►*n.* A machine for propelling an aircraft or boat, consisting of a revolving power-driven shaft with radiating blades.

pro•pen•si•ty (prə-pĕn′sĭ-tē) ►*n., pl.* **-ties.** An innate inclination; tendency. See Syns at **predilection.** [< Lat. *prōpendēre*, be inclined.]

prop•er (prŏp′ər) ►*adj.* **1.** Suitable; appropiate. **2.** Called for by rules or conventions; correct. **3.** Strictly following rules or conventions; seemly. **4.** Characteristically belonging to a person or thing: *regained its proper shape.* **5.** Strictly speaking: *the city proper.* [< Lat. *proprius*, one's own.] —**prop′er•ly** *adv.* —**prop′er•ness** *n.*

proper fraction ►*n.* A fraction in which the numerator is less than the denominator.

proper noun ►*n.* A noun that is the name of a particular person, place, or thing.

prop•er•tied (prŏp′ər-tēd) ►*adj.* Owning land or securities as a principal source of revenue.

prop•er•ty (prŏp′ər-tē) ►*n., pl.* **-ties 1a.** Something owned; a possession. **b.** A piece of real estate. **2.** The right of ownership; title. **3.** An article, except costumes and scenery, that is used in a play or movie. **4.** A characteristic trait, quality, or attribute. [< Lat. *proprietās*, ownership.]

proph•e•cy (prŏf′ĭ-sē) ►*n., pl.* **-cies 1.** An inspired utterance of a prophet. **2.** A prediction. [< Gk. *prophēteia.*]

proph•e•sy (prŏf′ĭ-sī′) ►*v.* **-sied, -sy•ing 1.** To reveal by divine inspiration. **2.** To predict. See Syns at **foretell.** [< OFr. *prophecie*, PROPHECY.] —**proph′e•si′er** *n.*

proph•et (prŏf′ĭt) ►*n.* **1.** A person who speaks by or as if by divine inspiration. **2.** A predictor; soothsayer. **3.** The chief spokesperson of a movement or cause. **4. Prophets.** See table at **Bible.** **5. Prophet** *Islam* Muhammad. Used with *the.* [< Gk. *prophētēs.*]

proph•et•ess (prŏf′ĭ-tĭs) ►*n.* **1.** A woman who speaks by or as if by divine inspiration. **2.** A woman predictor. **3.** The chief spokeswoman of a movement or cause.

pro•phet•ic (prə-fĕt′ĭk) also **pro•phet•i•cal** (-ĭ-kəl) ►*adj.* Of or characteristic of a prophet or prophecy. —**pro•phet′i•cal•ly** *adv.*

pro•phy•lac•tic (prō′fə-lăk′tĭk, prŏf′ə-) ►*adj.* Acting to defend against or prevent something, esp. disease; protective. ►*n.* A prophylactic agent or device, such as a condom. [< Gk. *prophulaktikos.*] —**pro′phy•lac′ti•cal•ly** *adv.*

pro•phy•lax•is (prō′fə-lăk′sĭs, prŏf′ə-) ►*n., pl.* **-lax•es** (-lăk′sēz′). Prevention of or protective treatment for disease. [< Gk. *prophulaktikos*, prophylactic.]

pro•pin•qui•ty (prə-pĭng′kwĭ-tē) ►*n.* Proximity; nearness. [< Lat. *propinquus*, near.]

pro•pi•ti•ate (prō-pĭsh′ē-āt′) ►*v.* **-at•ed, -at•ing.** To conciliate; appease. [Lat. *propitiāre.*] —**pro•pi′ti•a′tion** *n.* —**pro•pi′ti•a′tor** *n.* —**pro•pi′ti•a•to′ry** (-ə-tôr′ē, -tōr′ē) *adj.*

pro•pi•tious (prə-pĭsh′əs) ►*adj.* **1.** Favorable; auspicious. **2.** Kindly; gracious. [< Lat. *propitius.*] —**pro•pi′tious•ly** *adv.*

pro•po•nent (prə-pō′nənt) ►*n.* One who argues in support of something; advocate. [< Lat. *prōpōnere*, propose.]

pro•por•tion (prə-pôr′shən, -pōr′-) ►*n.* **1.** A part considered in relation to the whole. **2.** A relationship between things or parts of things with respect to comparative magnitude, quantity, or degree. **3.** A relationship between quantities such that if one varies then another varies as a multiple of the first. **4.** Harmonious relation; symmetry. **5.** often **proportions** Dimensions; size. ►*v.* **1.** To adjust so that proper relations between parts are attained. **2.** To form with symmetry. [< Lat. *prōportiō.*] —**pro•por′tion•al** *adj.* —**pro•por′tion•al•ly** *adv.* —**pro•por′tion•ate** *adj.*

pro•pose (prə-pōz′) ►*v.* **-posed, -pos•ing 1.** To put forward for consideration; suggest. **2.** To nominate (a person) for a position, office, or membership. **3.** To offer (a toast to be drunk). **4.** To make known as one's intention. **5.** To make an offer, esp. of marriage. [< Lat. *prōpōnere.*] —**pro•pos′al** *n.*

prop•o•si•tion (prŏp′ə-zĭsh′ən) ►*n.* **1.** A plan suggested for acceptance; proposal. **2.** *Informal* A matter to be dealt with; task. **3.** *Informal* An offer of a private bargain, esp. a request for sexual relations. **4.** A subject for discussion or analysis. —**prop′o•si′tion•al** *adj.*

pro•pound (prə-pound′) ►*v.* To put forward for consideration; set forth. [< Lat. *prōpōnere.*]

pro•pri•e•tar•y (prə-prī′ĭ-tĕr′ē) ►*adj.* **1.** Of or befitting a proprietor. **2.** Exclusively owned; private. **3.** Owned by a private individual or corporation under a trademark or patent: *a proprietary drug.* [< LLat. *proprietārius.*] —**pro•pri′e•tar′i•ly** *adv.*

pro•pri•e•tor (prə-prī′ĭ-tər) ►*n.* An owner, as of a business. —**pro•pri′e•tor•ship′** *n.*

pro•pri•e•tress (prə-prī′ĭ-trĭs) ►*n.* A woman who is an owner, as of a business.

pro•pri•e•ty (prə-prī′ĭ-tē) ►*n., pl.* **-ties 1.** The quality of being proper; appropriateness. **2.** Conformity to prevailing customs and usages. **3. proprieties** The usages and customs of polite society. [< OFr. *propriete*, property.]

pro•pul•sion (prə-pŭl′shən) ►*n.* **1.** The process of driving or propelling. **2.** A driving or propelling force. [< Lat. *prōpellere*, drive forward.] —**pro•pul′sive** *adj.*

pro ra•ta (prō rā′tə, răt′ə, rä′tə) ►*adv.* In proportion. [Lat. *prō ratā (parte)*, according to the calculated (share).]

pro•rate (prō-rāt′, prō′rāt′) ►*v.* **-rat•ed, -rat•ing.** To divide, distribute, or assess proportionately. [< PRO RATA.] —**pro•ra′tion** *n.*

pro•rogue (prō-rōg′) ►*v.* **-rogued, -rogu•ing.** To discontinue a session of (e.g., a parliament). [< Lat. *prōrogāre*, postpone.] —**pro′ro•ga′tion** *n.*

pro•sa•ic (prō-zā′ĭk) ►*adj.* **1.** Matter-of-fact; straightforward. **2.** Lacking in imagination and spirit; dull. [LLat. *prōsaīcus*, in prose.] —**pro•sa′i•cal•ly** *adv.*

pro•sce•ni•um (prō-sē′nē-əm, prə-) ►*n.* The area of a modern theater located between the curtain and the orchestra. [< Gk. *proskēnion.*]

pro•sciut•to (prō-shōō′tō) ►*n., pl.* **-ti** (-tē), **-tos.** An aged, dry-cured, spiced Italian ham. [Ital. < VLat. **perexsūctus*, thoroughly dried out.]

pro•scribe (prō-skrīb′) ►*v.* **-scribed, -scrib•ing 1.** To denounce or condemn. **2.** To prohibit. See Syns at **forbid. 3.** To outlaw (a person). [< Lat. *prōscrībere.*] —**pro•scrip′tion** (-skrĭp′shən) *n.*

prose (prōz) ►*n.* Ordinary speech or writing, without metrical structure. [< Lat. *prōsa (ōrātiō)*, straightforward (discourse).]

pros•e•cute (prŏs′ĭ-kyōōt′) ►*v.* **-cut•ed, -cut•ing 1.** To initiate court action against. **2.** To pursue (e.g., a task) until completion. [< Lat. *prōsequī, prōsecūt-*, follow up.] —**pros′e•cu′tion** *n.* —**pros′e•cu′tor** *n.*

pros•e•lyte (prŏs′ə-līt′) ►*n.* A new convert to a doctrine or religion. ►*v.* **-lyt•ed, -lyt•ing.** To proselytize. [< Gk. *prosēlutos.*]

pros•e•ly•tize (prŏs′ə-lĭ-tīz′) ►*v.* **-tized, -tiz•ing.** To convert (a person) from one belief or faith to another. —**pros′e•ly•ti•za′tion** *n.* —**pros′e•ly•tiz′er** *n.*

pro•sim•i•an (prō-sĭm′ē-ən) ►*adj.* Of or belonging to a suborder of primates that includes the lemurs.

pros•o•dy (prŏs′ə-dē) ►*n.* The study of the metrical structure of verse. [< Gk. *prosōidia*, song sung to music.] —**pro•sod′ic** (prə-sŏd′ĭk) *adj.*

pros•pect (prŏs′pĕkt′) ►*n.* **1.** Something expected; possibility. **2. prospects** Chances, esp. of success. **3a.** A potential customer or purchaser. **b.** A candidate likely to succeed. **4.** The direction in which an object faces. **5.** Something presented to the eye; scene. ►*v.* To search about or explore (a region) for mineral deposits or oil. [< Lat. *prōspectus*, view : *prō-*, forward + *specere*, look at.] —**pros′pec′tor** *n.*

pro•spec•tive (prə-spĕk′tĭv) ►*adj.* Likely to happen or become. —**pro•spec′tive•ly** *adv.*

pro•spec•tus (prə-spĕk′təs) ►*n.* A formal summary of a proposed venture or project, sent out to prospective buyers, investors, or participants. [Lat. *prōspectus*, view. See PROSPECT.]

pros•per (prŏs′pər) ►*v.* To be successful, esp. financially. [< Lat. *prosperāre.*]

pros•per•i•ty (prŏ-spĕr′ĭ-tē) ►*n.* The condition of being prosperous.

pros•per•ous (prŏs′pər-əs) ▶*adj.* **1.** Successful. **2.** Well-to-do; well-off. **3.** Propitious; favorable. —**pros′per•ous•ly** *adv.*

pros•tate (prŏs′tāt′) ▶*n.* A gland in male mammals at the base of the bladder that controls release of urine and secretes a fluid which is a major constituent of semen. [< Gk. *prostatēs* : *pro-*, in front + *histanai*, set, place.]

pros•the•sis (prŏs-thē′sĭs) ▶*n., pl.* **-ses** (-sēz). An artificial device used to replace a missing body part, such as a limb. [Gk., addition.] —**pros•thet′ic** (-thĕt′ĭk) *adj.*

prosthesis

pros•ti•tute (prŏs′tĭ-to͞ot′, -tyo͞ot′) ▶*n.* One who solicits and accepts payment for sex acts. ▶*v.* **-tut•ed, -tut•ing 1.** To offer (oneself or another) for sexual hire. **2.** To sell (oneself or one's talent) for an unworthy purpose. [Lat. *prōstitūta* : *prō-*, in front + *statuere*, cause to stand.] —**pros′ti•tu′tion** *n.*

pros•trate (prŏs′trāt′) ▶*adj.* **1.** Lying face down, as in submission or adoration. **2.** Stretched at full length. **3.** Physically or emotionally incapacitated; overcome. ▶*v.* **-trat•ed, -trat•ing 1.** To place (oneself) in a prostrate position. **2.** To throw down flat. **3.** To crush or enervate; overcome. [< Lat. *prōstrātus*, p.part. of *prōsternere*, throw down.] —**pros•tra′tion** *n.*

pros•y (prō′zē) ▶*adj.* **-i•er, -i•est 1.** Prosaic. **2.** Dull; commonplace. —**pros′i•ness** *n.*

Prot. ▶*abbr.* Protestant

prot– ▶*pref.* Var. of **proto–.**

pro•tac•tin•i•um (prō′tăk-tĭn′ē-əm) ▶*n. Symbol* **Pa** A rare radioactive element chemically similar to uranium. At. no. 91. See table at **element.** [< PROT(O)–.]

pro•tag•o•nist (prō-tăg′ə-nĭst) ▶*n.* **1.** The main character in a drama or other literary work. **2.** A leading or principal figure, as of a cause. [Gk. *prōtagōnistēs* : PROT(O)– + *agōnistēs*, actor (< *agein*, to drive, lead).]

Pro•tag•o•ras (prō-tăg′ər-əs). fl. 5th cent. B.C. Greek philosopher. —**Pro•tag′o•re′an** (-ə-rē′ən) *adj.*

pro•te•an (prō′tē-ən, prō-tē′-) ▶*adj.* Readily taking on varied shapes, forms, or meanings. [< PROTEUS.]

pro•tect (prə-tĕkt′) ▶*v.* To keep from damage, attack, theft, or injury. [< Lat. *prōtegere.*] —**pro•tec′tive** *adj.*

pro•tec•tion (prə-tĕk′shən) ▶*n.* **1.** The act of protecting or the condition of being protected. **2.** One that protects. **3.** A system of tariffs protecting domestic producers from foreign competition.

pro•tec•tion•ism (prə-tĕk′shə-nĭz′əm) ▶*n.* The protection of domestic producers by impeding or limiting, as by tariffs, the importation of foreign goods and services. —**pro•tec′tion•ist** *n.*

pro•tec•tor (prə-tĕk′tər) ▶*n.* **1.** One that protects; guard or guardian. **2. Protector** One who rules a kingdom during the minority of a sovereign. —**pro•tec′tor•ship′** *n.*

pro•tec•tor•ate (prə-tĕk′tər-ĭt) ▶*n.* **1a.** A relationship of protection and partial control by a superior power over a dependent country or region. **b.** The protected country or region. **2. Protectorate** The government, office, or term of a protector.

pro•té•gé (prō′tə-zhā′, prō′tə-zhā′) ▶*n.* One whose welfare, training, or career is promoted by an influential person. [Fr. < p.part. of *protéger*, protect.]

pro•tein (prō′tēn′, -tē-ĭn) ▶*n.* Any of a group of complex organic compounds that are composed of amino acids, occur in all living cells, and are essential for the growth and repair of animal tissue. [< LGk. *prōteios*, of the first quality.]

pro tem (prō tĕm′) ▶*adv.* Pro tempore.

pro tem•po•re (tĕm′pə-rē) ▶*adv.* For the time being. [Lat. *prō tempore.*]

pro•test (prə-tĕst′, prō-, prō′tĕst′) ▶*v.* **1.** To object to, esp. in a formal statement. **2.** To promise or affirm with earnest solemnity. ▶*n.* (prō′tĕst′) **1.** A formal declaration of disapproval or objection issued by a person or group. **2.** An individual or collective display of disapproval. [< Lat. *prōtestārī.*] —**prot′es•ta′tion** (prŏt′ĭ-stā′shən, prō′tĭ-) *n.* —**pro•test′er** *n.*

Prot•es•tant (prŏt′ĭ-stənt) ▶*n.* **1.** A Christian belonging to a denomination descending from those that broke away from the Roman Catholic Church in the 16th cent. **2.** (*also* prə-tĕs′tənt) **protestant** One who makes a declaration or avowal. —**Prot′es•tant•ism** *n.*

Pro•te•us (prō′tē-əs, -tyo͞os′) ▶*n. Gk. Myth.* A sea god able to change his shape at will.

proto– or **prot–** ▶*pref.* Earliest; original: *prototype.* [< Gk. *prōtos*, first.]

pro•to•col (prō′tə-kôl′, -kōl′, -kŏl′) ▶*n.* **1a.** The forms of ceremony and etiquette observed by diplomats and heads of state. **b.** A code of correct conduct. **2.** The first copy of a treaty or other such document before its ratification. **3.** A preliminary draft or record of a transaction. **4.** The plan for a course of medical treatment or for a scientific experiment. **5.** A standard procedure for regulating data transmission between computers. [< LGk. *prōtokollon*, table of contents.]

Pro•to-In•do-Eur•o•pe•an (prō′tō-ĭn′dō-yo͝or′ə-pē′ən) ▶*n.* The earliest reconstructed stage of Indo-European.

pro•ton (prō′tŏn′) ▶*n.* A stable, positively charged subatomic particle found in all atomic nuclei. [Gk. *prōton.*]

pro•to•plasm (prō′tə-plăz′əm) ▶*n.* The complex, semifluid substance that constitutes the living matter of plant and animal cells. —**pro′to•plas′mic** (-plăz′mĭk) *adj.*

pro•to•type (prō′tə-tīp′) ▶*n.* An original type or form that serves as a model on which later stages or examples are based or judged.

—**pro′to•typ′al** (-tī′pəl), **pro′to•typ′ic** (-tĭp′ĭk), **pro′to•typ′•i•cal** *adj.*

pro•to•zo•an (prō′tə-zō′ən) ▸*n., pl.* **-zo•ans** or **-zo•a** (-zō′ə). Any of a large group of single-celled, usu. microscopic organisms, such as amoebas. —**pro′to•zo′an, pro′to•zo′ic** *adj.*

pro•tract (prō-trăkt′, prə-) ▸*v.* To draw out or lengthen; prolong. [Lat. *prōtrahere, prōtract-.*] —**pro•trac′tion** *n.*

pro•trac•tile (prō-trăk′təl, -tīl′, prə-) ▸*adj.* That can be protracted; extensible.

pro•trac•tor (prō-trăk′tər, prə-) ▸*n.* A semicircular instrument for measuring and constructing angles.

pro•trude (prō-trōōd′) ▸*v.* **-trud•ed, -trud•ing.** To push or jut outward; project. See Syns at **bulge.** [Lat. *prōtrūdere.*] —**pro•tru′sion** *n.* —**pro•tru′sive** *adj.*

pro•tu•ber•ance (prō-tōō′bər-əns, -tyōō′-, prə-) ▸*n.* Something, such as a bulge, knob, or swelling, that protrudes. [< Lat. *prōtūberāre,* swell out.] —**pro•tu′ber•ant** *adj.*

proud (proud) ▸*adj.* **-er, -est 1.** Feeling pleasurable satisfaction. **2.** Occasioning pride. **3.** Feeling or showing self-respect. **4.** Filled with or showing excessive self-esteem. **5.** Of great dignity; honored. **6.** Majestic; magnificent. [< LLat. *prōde,* advantageous.] —**proud′ly** *adv.* —**proud′ness** *n.*

Prou•dhon (prōō-dôN′), **Pierre Joseph.** 1809–65. French anarchist.

Proust (prōōst), **Marcel.** 1871–1922. French writer. —**Proust′i•an** *adj.*

Prov. ▸*abbr.* province

prove (prōōv) ▸*v.* **proved** or **prov•en** (prōō′vən), **prov•ing 1.** To establish the truth or validity of by argument or evidence. **2.** To determine the quality of by testing; try out. **3.** To be shown to be such; turn out. [< Lat. *probāre,* test.] —**prov′a•ble** *adj.*

Usage: Both *proved* and *proven* are now well established in written English as participles: *He has proved* (or *proven*) *his point. Proven* is more common as an adjective before a noun: *a proven talent.*

prov•e•nance (prŏv′ə-nəns, -näns′) ▸*n.* Place of origin. [< Lat. *prōvenīre,* originate : *prō-,* forth + *venīre,* come.]

Pro•ven•çal (prō′vən-säl′, -vän-, prŏv′ən-) ▸*n.* **1.** A native or inhabitant of Provence. **2.** The Romance language of Provence. —**Pro′ven•çal′** *adj.*

Pro•vence (prə-väns′, prô-väNs′) A historical region and former province of SE France bordering the Mediterranean Sea.

prov•en•der (prŏv′ən-dər) ▸*n.* **1.** Dry food, such as hay, for livestock. **2.** Food or provisions. [< LLat. *praebenda,* stipend.]

pro•ve•nience (prə-vēn′yəns, -vē′nē-əns) ▸*n.* A source or origin. [< PROVENANCE.]

prov•erb (prŏv′ûrb′) ▸*n.* **1.** A short pithy saying in widespread use that expresses a basic truth or practical precept. **2. Proverbs** *(takes sing. v.)* See table at **Bible.** [< Lat. *prōverbium.*] —**pro•ver′bi•al** (prə-vûr′bē-əl) *adj.*

pro•vide (prə-vīd′) ▸*v.* **-vid•ed, -vid•ing 1.** To furnish; supply. **2.** To make available; afford. **3.** To set down as a stipulation. **4.** To take measures in preparation: *provide against emergencies.* **5.** To supply means of subsistence: *She provides for her family by writing screenplays.* [< Lat. *prōvidēre,* provide for : *prō-,* forward + *vidēre,* see.] —**pro•vid′er** *n.*

pro•vid•ed (prə-vī′dĭd) ▸*conj.* On the condition; if.

prov•i•dence (prŏv′ĭ-dəns, -dĕns′) ▸*n.* **1.** Care or preparation in advance; foresight. **2.** Prudent management; economy. **3.** Divine care and guardianship. **4. Providence** God.

Providence. The capital of RI, in the NE part on Narragansett Bay. Pop. 160,728.

prov•i•dent (prŏv′ĭ-dənt, -dĕnt′) ▸*adj.* **1.** Providing for future needs or events. **2.** Frugal; economical. —**prov′i•dent•ly** *adv.*

prov•i•den•tial (prŏv′ĭ-dĕn′shəl) ▸*adj.* **1.** Of or resulting from divine providence. **2.** Fortunate; opportune.

pro•vid•ing (prə-vī′dĭng) ▸*conj.* On the condition; provided.

prov•ince (prŏv′ĭns) ▸*n.* **1.** A territory governed as an administrative or political unit of a country or empire. **2. provinces** Areas of a country situated away from the capital or population center. **3.** A comprehensive area of knowledge, activity, or interest. See Syns at **field.** [< Lat. *prōvincia.*]

pro•vin•cial (prə-vĭn′shəl) ▸*adj.* **1.** Of or relating to a province. **2.** Limited in perspective; narrow and self-centered. —**pro•vin′cial•ism** *n.* —**pro•vin′cial•ly** *adv.*

prov•ing ground (prōō′vĭng) ▸*n.* A place for testing new devices or theories.

pro•vi•sion (prə-vĭzh′ən) ▸*n.* **1.** The act of supplying or fitting out. **2.** Something provided. **3.** A preparatory action or measure. **4. provisions** A stock of necessary supplies, esp. food. **5.** A stipulation or qualification, esp. a clause in a document. ▸*v.* To supply with provisions. [< Lat. *prōvidēre, prōvīs-,* PROVIDE.] —**pro•vi′sion•er** *n.*

pro•vi•sion•al (prə-vĭzh′ə-nəl) ▸*adj.* Provided or serving only for the time being. See Syns at **temporary.**

pro•vi•so (prə-vī′zō) ▸*n., pl.* **-sos** or **-soes.** A clause in a document making a qualification, condition, or restriction. [< Med.Lat. *prōvīsō (quod),* provided (that).]

Pro•vo (prō′vō) A city of N-central UT SSE of Salt Lake City. Pop. 86,835.

prov•o•ca•tion (prŏv′ə-kā′shən) ▸*n.* **1.** The act of provoking or inciting. **2.** Something that provokes.

pro•voc•a•tive (prə-vŏk′ə-tĭv) ▸*adj.* Tending to provoke. —**pro•voc′a•tive•ness** *n.*

pro•voke (prə-vōk′) ▸*v.* **-voked, -vok•ing 1.** To incite to anger or resentment. **2.** To stir to action or feeling. [< Lat. *prōvocāre,* call out.]

pro•vo•lo•ne (prō′və-lō′nē) ▸*n.* A hard, usu. smoked Italian cheese. [Ital.]

pro•vost (prō′vōst′, -vəst, prŏv′əst) ▸*n.* A high administrative officer, as of a university. [< Lat. *praepositus,* superintendent.]

pro•vost marshal (prō′vō) ▸*n.* The head of a unit of military police.

prow (prou) ▸*n.* The forward part of a ship's hull; bow. [< Gk. *prōira.*]

prow•ess (prou′ĭs) ▸*n.* **1.** Superior skill or ability. **2.** Superior strength and courage, esp. in battle. [< OFr. *prou,* brave.]

prowl (proul) ▸*v.* To roam (through) stealthily, as in search of prey. [ME *prollen.*] —**prowl** *n.* —**prowl′er** *n.*

prowl car ▸*n.* See **squad car.**

prox•i•mate (prŏk′sə-mĭt) ▸*adj.* **1.** Close in

space, time, or order; near. **2.** Approximate. [< Lat. *proximāre*, come near.]

prox•im•i•ty (prŏk-sĭm′ĭ-tē) ▸*n.* Nearness; closeness. [< Lat. *proximus*, nearest.]

prox•y (prŏk′sē) ▸*n.*, *pl.* **-ies 1.** A person authorized to act for another. **2.** Authority or written authorization to act for another. [< Med. Lat. *prōcūrātia*.]

Pro•zac (prō′zăk′) ▸ A trademark for a brand of antidepressant.

prude (pro͞od) ▸*n.* One who is too concerned with being or seeming to be proper, modest, or righteous. [< OFr. *prude femme*, virtuous woman.] —**prud′er•y** *n.* —**prud′ish** *adj.* —**prud′ish•ly** *adv.* —**prud′ish•ness** *n.*

pru•dent (pro͞od′nt) ▸*adj.* **1.** Wise in practical matters. **2.** Careful for one's own interests; provident. **3.** Careful about one's conduct; circumspect. [< Lat. *prūdēns*.] —**pru′dence** *n.* —**pru•den′•tial** (pro͞o-dĕn′shəl) *adj.* —**pru′dent•ly** *adv.*

prune[1] (pro͞on) ▸*n.* A partially dried plum. [< Lat. *prūnum*, plum.]

prune[2] (pro͞on) ▸*v.* **pruned, prun•ing 1.** To cut off parts or branches of (a plant) to improve shape or growth. **2.** To remove or cut out as superfluous. [< OFr. *proignier*.]

pru•ri•ent (pro͝or′ē-ənt) ▸*adj.* Appealing to or arousing immoderate sexual desire. [< Lat. *prūrīre*, itch.] —**pru′ri•ence** *n.*

Prus•sia (prŭsh′ə) A historical region and former kingdom of N-central Europe including present-day N Germany and Poland. —**Prus′sian** *adj.* & *n.*

pry[1] (prī) ▸*v.* **pried** (prīd), **pry•ing.** To look or inquire closely or curiously; snoop. [ME *prien*.] —**pry′ing•ly** *adv.*

pry[2] (prī) ▸*v.* **pried** (prīd), **pry•ing 1.** To raise, move, or force open with a lever. **2.** To obtain with difficulty. ▸*n.*, *pl.* **pries** (prīz). A tool, as a crowbar, for prying. [< PRIZE[3].]

PS ▸*abbr.* **1.** postscript **2.** public school

psalm (säm) ▸*n.* **1.** A sacred song; hymn. **2. Psalms** *(takes sing. v.)* See table at **Bible.** [< Gk. *psalmos*.] —**psalm′ist** *n.*

psalm•o•dy (sä′mə-dē, săl′mə-) ▸*n.*, *pl.* **-dies 1.** The singing of psalms in divine worship. **2.** A collection of psalms. [< Gk. *psalmōidia*, singing to the harp : *psalmos*, psalm + *ōidē*, *aoidē*, SONG.]

Psal•ter also **psal•ter** (sôl′tər) ▸*n.* A book containing the Book of Psalms or a particular version of, musical setting for, or selection from it. [< Gk. *psaltērion*, harp.]

pseudo– or **pseud–** ▸*pref.* False; deceptive; sham: *pseudonym.* [< Gk. *pseudēs*, false.]

pseu•do•nym (so͞od′n-ĭm′) ▸*n.* A fictitious name assumed by an author; pen name. —**pseu•don′y•mous** (so͞o-dŏn′ə-məs) *adj.*

psf ▸*abbr.* pounds per square foot

psi[1] (sī, psī) ▸*n.* The 23rd letter of the Greek alphabet. [< Gk. *psei*.]

psi[2] ▸*abbr.* pounds per square inch

psit•ta•co•sis (sĭt′ə-kō′sĭs) ▸*n.* An infectious disease of parrots and related birds that is communicable to humans. [< Gk. *psittakos*, parrot + –OSIS.]

pso•ri•a•sis (sə-rī′ə-sĭs) ▸*n.* A skin disease marked by recurring inflammation and scaly patches. [Gk. *psōriasis*.]

PST ▸*abbr.* Pacific Standard Time

psych (sīk) *Informal* ▸*n.* Psychology. ▸*v.* **1.** To put into the right frame of mind. **2.** To undermine psychologically.

psy•che (sī′kē) ▸*n.* **1.** The spirit or soul. **2.** In psychoanalysis, the mind functioning as the center of thought, emotion, and behavior. [< Gk. *psukhē*.]

psy•che•del•ic (sī′kĭ-dĕl′ĭk) ▸*adj.* Marked by or generating hallucinations and distortions of perception. [< PSYCHE + Gk. *dēloun*, make visible.] —**psy′che•del′ic** *n.*

psy•chi•a•try (sĭ-kī′ə-trē, sī-) ▸*n.* The branch of medicine that deals with the diagnosis, treatment, and prevention of mental and emotional disorders. —**psy′chi•at′ric** (sī′kē-ăt′rĭk) *adj.* —**psy•chi′a•trist** *n.*

psy•chic (sī′kĭk) ▸*n.* See **medium** 5. ▸*adj.* **1.** Of the human mind or psyche: *psychic trauma.* **2.** Of or possessing extraordinary mental powers, such as ESP or mental telepathy. —**psy′chi•cal•ly** *adv.*

psycho– or **psych–** ▸*pref.* Mind; mental: *psychology.* [< Gk. *psukhē*, spirit.]

psy•cho•ac•tive (sī′kō-ăk′tĭv) ▸*adj.* Affecting the mind or mental processes.

psy•cho•a•nal•y•sis (sī′kō-ə-năl′ĭ-sĭs) ▸*n.* **1.** A method of psychiatric therapy in which free association, dream interpretation, and analysis of feelings and behavior are used to investigate mental and emotional disorders. **2.** Psychiatric treatment incorporating the techniques of psychoanalysis. —**psy′cho•an′a•lyst** (-ăn′ə-lĭst) *n.* —**psy′cho•an′a•lyt′ic** (-ăn′ə-lĭt′ĭk), **psy′cho•an′a•lyt′i•cal** *adj.* —**psy′cho•an′a•lyze′** (-līz′) *v.*

psy•cho•dra•ma (sī′kə-drä′mə, -drăm′ə) ▸*n.* A psychotherapeutic and analytic technique in which people are assigned roles to be played spontaneously in a drama.

psy•cho•gen•ic (sī′kə-jĕn′ĭk) ▸*adj.* Originating in the mind or in mental or emotional processes. —**psy′cho•gen′i•cal•ly** *adv.*

psy•chol•o•gist (sī-kŏl′ə-jĭst) ▸*n.* A person trained and educated to perform psychological research, testing, and therapy.

psy•chol•o•gy (sī-kŏl′ə-jē) ▸*n.*, *pl.* **-gies 1.** The science that deals with mental processes and behavior. **2.** The emotional and behavioral characteristics of an individual or group. —**psy′cho•log′i•cal** (sī′kə-lŏj′ĭ-kəl) *adj.* —**psy′cho•log′i•cal•ly** *adv.*

psy•cho•met•rics (sī′kə-mĕt′rĭks) ▸*n.* *(takes sing. v.)* The branch of psychology that deals with testing and measuring psychological variables such as intelligence.

psy•chom•e•try (sī-kŏm′ĭ-trē) ▸*n.* See **psychometrics.**

psy•cho•mo•tor (sī′kō-mō′tər) ▸*adj.* Of or relating to movement or muscular activity associated with mental processes.

psy•cho•path (sī′kə-păth′) ▸*n.* A person with an antisocial personality disorder, esp. one manifested in aggressive, perverted, or criminal behavior. —**psy′cho•path′ic** *adj.* —**psy′cho•path′i•cal•ly** *adv.* —**psy•chop′a•thy** (sī-kŏp′ə-thē) *n.*

psy•cho•pa•thol•o•gy (sī′kō-pə-thŏl′ə-jē, -pă-) ▸*n.* The study of the origin, growth, and symptoms of mental or behavioral disorders. —**psy′cho•path′o•log′i•cal** (-păth′ə-lŏj′ĭ-kəl), **psy′cho•path′o•log′ic** *adj.* —**psy′cho•pa•thol′o•gist** *n.*

psy•cho•phar•ma•col•o•gy (sī′kō-fär′mə-kŏl′ə-jē) ►*n.* The branch of pharmacology that deals with psychoactive drugs. —**psy′cho•phar′ma•col′o•gist** *n.*

psy•cho•phys•i•ol•o•gy (sī′kō-fĭz′ē-ŏl′ə-jē) ►*n.* The study of correlations between the mind, behavior, and bodily mechanisms. —**psy′cho•phys′i•o•log′i•cal** (-fĭz′ē-ə-lŏj′ĭ-kəl), **psy′cho•phys′i•o•log′ic** *adj.* —**psy′cho•phys′i•ol′o•gist** *n.*

psy•cho•sex•u•al (sī′kō-sĕk′shōō-əl) ►*adj.* Of or relating to the mental and emotional aspects of sexuality.

psy•cho•sis (sī-kō′sĭs) ►*n., pl.* **-ses** (-sēz). A mental disorder marked by derangement of personality, loss of contact with reality, and deterioration of normal social functioning. —**psy•chot′ic** (-kŏt′ĭk) *adj. & n.*

psy•cho•so•mat•ic (sī′kō-sō-măt′ĭk) ►*adj.* **1.** Of or relating to a disorder having physical symptoms but originating from mental or emotional causes. **2.** Of or concerned with the influence of the mind on the body, esp. with respect to disease.

psy•cho•ther•a•py (sī′kō-thĕr′ə-pē) ►*n.* The treatment of mental and emotional disorders through the use of psychological techniques. —**psy′cho•ther′a•peu′tic** (-pyōō′tĭk) *adj.* —**psy′cho•ther′a•pist** *n.*

psy•cho•tro•pic (sī′kə-trō′pĭk, -trŏp′ĭk) ►*adj.* Having an altering effect on perception, emotion, or behavior. Used esp. of a drug.

Pt ► The symbol for the element **platinum** 1.

PT ►*abbr.* **1.** Pacific Time **2.** physical therapy

pt. ►*abbr.* **1.** part **2.** pint **3.** point **4.** also **Pt.** port

PTA ►*abbr.* Parent Teacher Association

ptar•mi•gan (tär′mĭ-gən) ►*n., pl.* **-gan** or **-gans.** A grouse of northern regions having feathered legs and feet and plumage that changes from brown to white in winter. [< Sc.Gael. *tarmachan.*]

PT boat (pē-tē′) ►*n.* A fast, lightly armed vessel used to torpedo enemy shipping. [P(ATROL) + *t(orpedo) boat.*]

pter•o•dac•tyl (tĕr′ə-dăk′təl) ►*n.* An extinct flying reptile. [Gk. *pteron*, feather, wing + *daktulos*, finger.]

pter•o•saur (tĕr′ə-sôr′) ►*n.* Any of an order of extinct flying reptiles that includes the pterodactyls. [Gk. *pteron*, wing + *sauros*, lizard.]

Ptol•e•ma•ic system (tŏl′ə-mā′ĭk) ►*n.* The astronomical system of Ptolemy, in which Earth is at the center of the universe.

Ptol•e•my[1] (tŏl′ə-mē). An Egyptian dynasty of Macedonian kings (323–30 B.C.), including **Ptolemy I** (367?–283?) and **Ptolemy XV** (47–30).

Ptol•e•my[2] (tŏl′ə-mē). fl. 2nd cent. A.D. Alexandrian astronomer, mathematician, and geographer.

pto•maine (tō′mān′, tō-mān′) ►*n.* A basic nitrogenous organic compound produced by bacterial putrefaction of protein. [< Gk. *ptōma*, corpse.]

ptomaine poisoning ►*n.* Food poisoning, erroneously ascribed to ptomaine ingestion.

Pu ► The symbol for the element **plutonium.**

pub (pŭb) ►*n.* A tavern; bar. [< PUBLIC HOUSE.]

pu•ber•ty (pyōō′bər-tē) ►*n.* The stage of adolescence in which an individual becomes physiologically capable of sexual reproduction. [< Lat. *pūbertās.*] —**pu′ber•tal** *adj.*

pu•bes•cent (pyōō-bĕs′ənt) ►*adj.* **1.** Reaching or having reached puberty. **2.** Covered with short hairs or soft down. [< Lat. *pūbēscere*, reach puberty.] —**pu•bes′cence** *n.*

pu•bic (pyōō′bĭk) ►*adj.* Of or located in the region of the pubis or the pubes.

pu•bis (pyōō′bĭs) ►*n., pl.* **-bes** (-bēz). The forward portion of either of the hipbones, at the juncture forming the front arch of the pelvis. [< Lat. *pūbēs*, groin.]

pub•lic (pŭb′lĭk) ►*adj.* **1.** Of or affecting the community or the people. **2.** Maintained for or used by the people or community. **3.** Participated in or attended by the people or community: *a public worship.* **4.** Connected with or acting on behalf of the people, community, or government: *a public office.* **5.** Generally or widely known. **6.** Noncommercial: *public television.* ►*n.* **1.** The community or the people as a whole. **2.** A group of people sharing a common interest: *the reading public.* See Usage Note at **collective noun.** [< Lat. *pūblicus.*] —**pub′lic•ly** *adv.*

pub•lic-ad•dress system (pŭb′lĭk-ə-drĕs′) ►*n.* An electronic amplification apparatus used for broadcasting in public areas.

pub•li•can (pŭb′lĭ-kən) ►*n.* **1.** *Chiefly Brit.* The keeper of a public house or tavern. **2.** A tax collector in the Roman Empire. [< Lat. *pūblicānus*, tax collector.]

pub•li•ca•tion (pŭb′lĭ-kā′shən) ►*n.* **1.** The act or process of publishing. **2.** An issue of printed material.

public defender ►*n.* An attorney, usu. publicly appointed, responsible for the defense of those unable to afford legal assistance.

public domain ►*n.* **1.** Land owned and controlled by the state or federal government. **2.** The status of publications, products, and processes unprotected by patent or copyright.

public house ►*n.* *Chiefly Brit.* A licensed tavern or bar.

pub•li•cist (pŭb′lĭ-sĭst) ►*n.* One who publicizes, esp. a press or publicity agent.

pub•lic•i•ty (pŭ-blĭs′ĭ-tē) ►*n.* **1.** Information disseminated to attract public notice. **2.** Public interest, notice, or notoriety.

pub•li•cize (pŭb′lĭ-sīz′) ►*v.* **-cized, -ciz•ing.** To give publicity to.

public relations ►*pl.n.* **1.** The methods and activities employed to establish a favorable relationship with the public. **2.** *(takes sing. or pl. v.)* The degree of success obtained in achieving favor with the public.

public school ►*n.* **1.** A tax-supported school in the US providing free education for children of a community or district. **2.** A private boarding school in Great Britain for pupils between the ages of 13 and 18.

pub•lic-spir•it•ed (pŭb′lĭk-spĭr′ĭ-tĭd) ►*adj.* Motivated by or showing devotion to the public welfare.

pub•lish (pŭb′lĭsh) ►*v.* **1.** To prepare and issue (printed material) for public distribution or sale. **2.** To bring to the public attention; announce. See Syns at **announce.** [< Lat. *pūblicāre*, make public.] —**pub′lish•a•ble** *adj.* —**pub′lish•er** *n.*

Puc•ci•ni (pōō-chē′nē), **Giacomo.** 1858–1924. Italian operatic composer.

puck (pŭk) ►*n.* A hard rubber disk used in ice hockey. [Perh. < dial. *puck*, strike.]

Puck ►*n.* A mischievous sprite in English folklore.
puck•er (pŭk′ər) ►*v.* To gather into small wrinkles or folds. ►*n.* A wrinkle or fold. [Prob. < dial. *pock*, bag.]
puck•ish (pŭk′ĭsh) ►*adj.* Mischievous.
pud•ding (po͝od′ĭng) ►*n.* A sweet dessert, usu. with a soft smooth consistency, that has been boiled, steamed, or baked. [< OFr. *boudin*, sausage.]
pud•dle (pŭd′l) ►*n.* A small pool of liquid, esp. rainwater. [< OE *pudd*, ditch.]
pud•dling (pŭd′lĭng) ►*n.* Purification of impure metal, esp. pig iron, by heating and stirring in an oxidizing atmosphere.
pu•den•dum (pyo͞o-dĕn′dəm) ►*n.*, *pl.* **-da** (-də). The human external genitalia, esp. of a woman. [Lat. < *pudēre*, be ashamed.]
pudg•y (pŭj′ē) ►*adj.* **-i•er, -i•est.** Short and fat; chubby. [< *pudge*, something thick and short.] —**pudg′i•ness** *n.*
Pueb•la (pwĕb′lä) A city of E-central Mexico ESE of Mexico City. Pop. 835,759.
Pueb•lo[1] (pwĕb′lō) ►*n.*, *pl.* **Pueblo** or **-los 1.** A member of certain Native American peoples, such as the Hopi or Zuni, living in pueblos in N and W New Mexico and NE Arizona. **2. pueblo,** *pl.* **-los** A permanent community of a Pueblo people, typically consisting of multilevel adobe dwellings built around a central plaza. [< Lat. *populus*, people.]

pueblo
Taos Pueblo, New Mexico

Pueblo[2]**.** A city of SE-central CO SSE of Colorado Springs. Pop. 98,640.
pu•er•ile (pyo͞o′ər-əl, pyo͝or′əl, -īl′) ►*adj.* Immature; childish. [< Lat. *puer*, boy.] —**pu′er•il′i•ty** (-ĭl′ĭ-tē) *n.*
pu•er•per•al (pyo͞o-ûr′pər-əl) ►*adj.* Relating to or occurring during or immediately after childbirth. [< Lat. *puerper*, a woman in childbed.]
Puer•to Ri•co (pwĕr′tə rē′kō, pôr′tə, pōrt′ə, pwĕr′tō) A self-governing US commonwealth in the Caribbean Sea E of Hispaniola. Cap. San Juan. Pop. 3,646,000. —**Puer′to Ri′can** *adj. & n.*
puff (pŭf) ►*n.* **1a.** A short forceful discharge, as of air or smoke. **b.** A short sibilant sound produced by a puff. **2.** An act of drawing in and expelling the breath, as in smoking tobacco. **3.** A swelling or rounded protuberance. **4.** A light flaky pastry. **5.** A soft pad for applying powder or lotion. **6.** An expression of exaggerated praise. ►*v.* **1.** To blow in puffs. **2.** To breathe forcefully and rapidly. **3.** To emit puffs. **4.** To take puffs on smoking material. **5.** To swell or seem to swell. **6.** To fill with pride or conceit. **7.** To publicize with exaggerated praise. [< OE *pyff.*] —**puff′i•ness** *n.* —**puff′y** *adj.*
puff•ball (pŭf′bôl′) ►*n.* A ball-shaped fungus that when pressed or struck releases the enclosed spores in puffs of dust.
puff•er (pŭf′ər) ►*n.* Any of various prickly, often poisonous, chiefly marine fishes capable of puffing up with water or air.
puff•er•y (pŭf′ə-rē) ►*n.* Flattering, often exaggerated praise and publicity.
puf•fin (pŭf′ĭn) ►*n.* A black and white sea bird of northern regions having a flattened triangular bill. [ME *poffoun.*]
pug[1] (pŭg) ►*n.* **1.** A small dog having a snub nose, a wrinkled face, and a curled tail. **2.** A short, turned-up nose. [?]
pug[2] (pŭg) ►*n.* *Slang* A boxer. [< PUGILIST.]
Pu•get Sound (pyo͞o′jĭt) A deep inlet of the Pacific in W WA.
pu•gi•lism (pyo͞o′jə-lĭz′əm) ►*n.* *Sports* Boxing. [< Lat. *pugil*, pugilist.] —**pu′gi•list** *n.* —**pu′gi•lis′tic** *adj.*
pug•na•cious (pŭg-nā′shəs) ►*adj.* Combative in nature; belligerent. [< Lat. *pugnus*, fist.] —**pug•na′cious•ness, pug•nac′i•ty** (-năs′ĭ-tē) *n.*
puis•sance (pwĭs′əns, pyo͞o′ĭ-səns) ►*n.* Power; might. [< OFr.] —**puis′sant** *adj.*
puke (pyo͞ok) ►*v.* **puked, puk•ing** *Slang* To vomit. [Perh. imit.] —**puke** *n.*
pu•la (po͞o′lä) ►*n.* See table at **currency.** [Tswana.]
Pu•las•ki (po͞o-lăs′kē, pə-), **Casimir** or **Kazimierz.** 1747–79. Polish patriot and general in the American Revolution.
pul•chri•tude (pŭl′krĭ-to͞od′, -tyo͞od′) ►*n.* Physical beauty. [< Lat. *pulcher*, beautiful.] —**pul′chri•tu′di•nous** (-to͞od′n-əs, -tyo͞od′-) *adj.*
pule (pyo͞ol) ►*v.* **puled, pul•ing.** To whine; whimper. [Perh. < Fr. *piauler.*] —**pul′er** *n.*
Pu•lit•zer (po͝ol′ĭt-sər, pyo͞o′lĭt-), **Joseph.** 1847–1911. Hungarian-born Amer. newspaper publisher.
pull (po͝ol) ►*v.* **1.** To apply force to so as to cause motion toward the source of the force. **2.** To remove from a fixed position; extract. **3.** To tug at; jerk or tweak. **4.** To rip or tear; rend. **5.** To stretch (e.g., taffy) repeatedly. **6.** To strain (e.g., a muscle) injuriously. **7.** *Informal* To attract; draw: *pull a large crowd.* **8.** *Slang* To draw out (a weapon). **9.** *Informal* To remove. **10.** To row a boat. —***phrasal verbs:* pull off** *Informal* To do or accomplish in spite of difficulties. **pull out** To leave or depart. **pull through** To come or bring successfully through difficulty. **pull up** To bring or come to a halt. ►*n.* **1.** The act or process of pulling. **2.** Force exerted in pulling. **3.** Something, such as a knob, that is used for pulling. **4.** A deep inhalation or draft, as of smoke or liquor. **5.** *Slang* A means of gaining special advantage; influence. **6.** *Informal* Ability to draw or attract; appeal. [< OE *pullian.*] —**pull′er** *n.*
Syns: *pull, drag, draw, haul, tow, tug* ***Ant:*** *push* **v.**
pull•back (po͝ol′băk′) ►*n.* An orderly troop withdrawal.
pul•let (po͝ol′ĭt) ►*n.* A young domestic hen. [< Lat. *pullus.*]
pul•ley (po͝ol′ē) ►*n.*, *pl.* **-leys 1.** A simple machine consisting essentially of a wheel with a

grooved rim in which a pulled rope or chain can run to change the direction of the pull and thereby lift a load. **2.** A wheel turned by or driving a belt. [< OFr. *polie.*]

Pull•man (pŏŏl′mən) ▸*n.* **1.** A railroad parlor car or sleeping car. **2.** A large suitcase. [After G.M. *Pullman* (1831–97).]

pull•out (pŏŏl′out′) ▸*n.* A withdrawal, esp. of troops.

pull•o•ver (pŏŏl′ō′vər) ▸*n.* A garment that is put on by being drawn over the head.

pul•mo•nar•y (pŏŏl′mə-nĕr′ē, pŭl′-) ▸*adj.* Of or involving the lungs. [< Lat. *pulmō*, lung.]

pulp (pŭlp) ▸*n.* **1.** A soft, moist, shapeless mass of matter. **2.** The soft, moist part of a vegetable or fruit. **3.** A mixture of cellulose material, such as wood, paper, and rags, ground up and moistened to make paper. **4.** The soft inner structure of a tooth, containing nerves and blood vessels. **5.** A publication, such as a magazine, containing lurid subject matter. ▸*v.* To reduce to pulp. See Syns at **crush.** [< Lat. *pulpa.*] —**pulp′i•ness** *n.* —**pulp′y** *adj.*

pul•pit (pŏŏl′pĭt, pŭl′-) ▸*n.* An elevated platform, lectern, or stand used in preaching or conducting a religious service. [< Lat. *pulpitum*, platform.]

pulp•wood (pŭlp′wŏŏd′) ▸*n.* Soft wood used in making paper.

pul•sar (pŭl′sär′) ▸*n.* Any of several celestial radio sources emitting short intense bursts, as of radio waves or x-rays. [< PULSE.]

pul•sate (pŭl′sāt′) ▸*v.* **-sat•ed, -sat•ing 1.** To expand and contract rhythmically; beat. **2.** To quiver; vibrate. [Lat. *pulsāre.*] —**pul•sa′tion** *n.*

pulse (pŭls) ▸*n.* **1.** The rhythmical throbbing of arteries produced by the regular contractions of the heart. **2.** *Phys.* A brief sudden change in a normally constant quantity: *a pulse of current.* ▸*v.* **pulsed, puls•ing.** To pulsate. [< Lat. *pulsus* < *pellere*, beat.]

pul•ver•ize (pŭl′və-rīz′) ▸*v.* **-ized, -iz•ing 1.** To reduce or be reduced to a powder or dust. **2.** To demolish. [< Lat. *pulvis*, dust.]

pu•ma (pyŏŏ′mə, pŏŏ′-) ▸*n.* See **mountain lion.** [< Quechua.]

pum•ice (pŭm′ĭs) ▸*n.* A light porous lava, used in solid form as an abrasive and in powdered form as a polish. [< Lat. *pūmex.*] —**pum′ice** *v.*

pum•mel (pŭm′əl) ▸*v.* **-meled, -mel•ing** also **-melled, -mel•ling.** To beat, as with the fists; pommel. See Syns at **beat.** [< POMMEL.]

pump[1] (pŭmp) ▸*n.* A device for raising, compressing, or transferring fluids. ▸*v.* **1.** To raise or cause to flow by means of a pump. **2.** To draw, deliver, or pour forth as if with a pump. **3.** To remove the water from. **4.** To cause to move with the up-and-down motion of a pump handle. **5.** To propel, eject, or insert with or as if with a pump. **6.** To question closely or persistently. —***phrasal verb:* pump up 1.** To inflate with gas by means of a pump. **2.** *Slang* To fill with enthusiasm and energy. —***idiom:* pump iron** To lift weights. [ME *pumpe.*] —**pump′er** *n.*

pump[2] (pŭmp) ▸*n.* A low-cut woman's shoe with no fastenings. [?]

pum•per•nick•el (pŭm′pər-nĭk′əl) ▸*n.* A dark coarse rye bread. [Ger.]

pump•kin (pŭmp′kĭn, pŭm′-, pŭng′-) ▸*n.* **1.** A trailing vine cultivated for its fruit. **2.** The large round fruit of this plant, having a thick, orange-yellow rind and numerous seeds. [< Gk. *pepōn*, ripe melon.]

pun (pŭn) ▸*n.* A play on words, sometimes on different senses of the same word and sometimes on the similar sense or sound of different words. [?] —**pun** *v.*

punch[1] (pŭnch) ▸*n.* **1.** A tool for piercing or stamping. **2.** A tool for forcing a pin, bolt, or rivet in or out of a hole. [< PUNCHEON[1].] —**punch** *v.*

punch[2] (pŭnch) ▸*v.* **1.** To hit with a sharp blow of the fist. **2a.** To poke or prod with a stick. **b.** To herd (cattle). **3.** To depress (e.g., a key or button). ▸*n.* **1.** A blow with the fist. **2.** Vigor or drive. See Syns at **vigor.** [ME *punchen.*] —**punch′er** *n.*

punch[3] (pŭnch) ▸*n.* A beverage of fruit juices, often spiced and mixed with wine or liquor. [Perh. < Skt. *pañca*, five.]

punch card ▸*n.* A card punched with holes or notches to represent data for a computer.

pun•cheon[1] (pŭn′chən) ▸*n.* **1.** A short wooden upright used in structural framing. **2.** A piece of broad, roughly dressed timber. [< Lat. *pungere*, *pūnct-*, to prick.]

pun•cheon[2] (pŭn′chən) ▸*n.* A cask with a capacity of from 72 to 120 gal. (273 to 454 l). [< OFr. *poinçon*, cask.]

punch line ▸*n.* The climax of a joke or humorous story.

punch•y (pŭn′chē) ▸*adj.* **-i•er, -i•est 1.** Marked by vigor or drive. **2.** Groggy or dazed from or as if from a blow.

punc•til•i•o (pŭngk-tĭl′ē-ō′) ▸*n., pl.* **-os 1.** A fine point of etiquette. **2.** Precise observance of formalities. [Obsolete Italian *punctiglio.*] —**punc•til′i•ous** *adj.* —**punc•til′i•ous•ly** *adv.* —**punc•til′i•ous•ness** *n.*

punc•tu•al (pŭngk′chŏŏ-əl) ▸*adj.* Acting or arriving exactly at the time appointed; prompt. [< Lat. *pūnctum*, point.] —**punc′tu•al′i•ty** (-ăl′ĭ-tē) *n.* —**punc′tu•al•ly** *adv.*

punc•tu•ate (pŭngk′chŏŏ-āt′) ▸*v.* **-at•ed, -at•ing 1.** To provide (a text) with punctuation marks. **2.** To interrupt periodically. **3.** To emphasize. [< Lat. *pūnctum*, point.]

punc•tu•a•tion (pŭngk′chŏŏ-ā′shən) ▸*n.* **1.** The use of standard marks and signs in writing and printing to separate words into sentences, clauses, and phrases in order to clarify meaning. **2.** The marks so used.

punc•ture (pŭngk′chər) ▸*v.* **-tured, -tur•ing 1.** To pierce with a pointed object. **2.** To deflate by or as if by piercing. ▸*n.* **1.** The act or an instance of puncturing. **2.** A hole made by a sharp object. [< LLat. *pūnctūra*, a pricking.]

pun•dit (pŭn′dĭt) ▸*n.* A learned person; authority. [< Skt. *paṇḍitaḥ.*]

Pu•ne or **Poo•na** (pŏŏ′nə). A city of W-central India ESE of Mumbai (Bombay). Pop. 1,203,351.

pun•gent (pŭn′jənt) ▸*adj.* **1.** Having a sharp, acrid taste or smell. **2.** Penetrating, biting, or caustic: *pungent satire.* [< Lat. *pungere*, sting.] —**pun′gen•cy** *n.* —**pun′gent•ly** *adv.*

Pu•nic (pyŏŏ′nĭk) ▸*adj.* Of or relating to ancient Carthage. ▸*n.* The dialect of Phoenician spoken in Carthage.

pun•ish (pŭn′ĭsh) ▸*v.* **1.** To subject to a penalty for an offense or fault. **2.** To inflict a penalty for (an offense). **3.** To handle roughly; hurt. [< Lat. *poenīre.*] —**pun′ish•a•ble** *adj.*

pun•ish•ment (pŭn′ĭsh-mənt) ►*n.* **1a.** The act of punishing. **b.** The condition of being punished. **2.** A penalty for wrongdoing. **3.** Rough handling; mistreatment.

pu•ni•tive (pyo͞o′nĭ-tĭv) ►*adj.* Inflicting or aiming to inflict punishment. [< Lat. *pūnīre,* punish.]

Pun•jab (pŭn′jăb′, pŭn-jăb′) A historical region of NW India and N Pakistan.

Pun•ja•bi also **Pan•ja•bi** (pŭn-jä′bē, -jăb′ē) ►*n., pl.* **-bis 1.** A native or inhabitant of the Punjab. **2.** An Indic language spoken in the Punjab. —**Pun•ja′bi** *adj.*

punk (pŭngk) ►*n.* **1.** *Slang* **a.** A young hoodlum or tough. **b.** An inexperienced young man. **2.** *Mus.* **a.** Punk rock. **b.** A punk rocker. **3.** Dry decayed wood, used as tinder. **4.** A substance that smolders when ignited. ►*adj. Slang* **1.** Of or relating to punk rock. **2.** Of poor quality; worthless. [?]

punk rock ►*n.* A form of hard-driving rock 'n' roll marked by harsh, often angry lyrics. —**punk rocker** *n.*

pun•ster (pŭn′stər) ►*n.* A maker of puns.

punt[1] (pŭnt) ►*n.* An open, flat-bottomed boat with squared ends, propelled by a long pole. ►*v.* To propel (a boat) with a pole. [< Lat. *pontō,* PONTOON.]

punt[2] (pŭnt) ►*n. Football* A kick in which the ball is dropped from the hands and kicked before it touches the ground. [?] —**punt** *v.*

pu•ny (pyo͞o′nē) ►*adj.* **-ni•er, -ni•est.** Of inferior size, strength, or significance; weak. [< OFr. *puisne,* second-rank.]

pup (pŭp) ►*n.* **1.** A puppy. **2.** The young of certain other animals, such as the seal.

pu•pa (pyo͞o′pə) ►*n., pl.* **-pae** (-pē) or **-pas.** The nonfeeding stage between the larva and adult in the metamorphosis of an insect. [Lat., girl, doll.] —**pu′pal** *adj.*

pu•pil[1] (pyo͞o′pəl) ►*n.* A student under the supervision of a teacher or professor. [< Lat. *pūpillus,* little boy.]

pu•pil[2] (pyo͞o′pəl) ►*n.* The dark circular opening in the center of the iris of the eye. [< Lat. *pūpilla,* little doll.]

pup•pet (pŭp′ĭt) ►*n.* **1.** A figure of a person or animal that can be animated by a performer, esp. a small figure designed to fit over the hand. **2.** A marionette. **3.** A doll. **4.** One whose behavior is determined by the will of others. [ME *poppet,* doll.]

pup•pet•eer (pŭp′ĭ-tîr′) ►*n.* One who operates and entertains with puppets. —**pup′pet•ry** *n.*

pup•py (pŭp′ē) ►*n., pl.* **-pies.** A young dog; pup. [ME *popi.*]

pur•blind (pûr′blīnd′) ►*adj.* **1.** Nearly or partly blind. **2.** Slow in understanding or discernment; dull. [ME *pur blind,* totally blind.] —**pur′blind′ness** *n.*

pur•chase (pûr′chĭs) ►*v.* **-chased, -chas•ing.** To obtain in exchange for money or its equivalent; buy. ►*n.* **1a.** The act or an instance of buying. **b.** Something bought. **2.** A secure grasp or hold. **3.** A position or device affording means to move or secure a weight. [< OFr. *purchacier,* hunt down.] —**pur′chas•a•ble** *adj.* —**pur′chas•er** *n.*

pur•dah (pûr′də) ►*n.* The Hindu or Muslim system of sex segregation, esp. of keeping women in seclusion. [< Pers. *pardah,* veil.]

pure (pyo͝or) ►*adj.* **pur•er, pur•est 1.** Having a uniform composition; not mixed: *pure oxygen.* **2.** Free from adulterants or impurities. **3.** Free of dirt, defilement, or pollution. **4.** Complete; utter: *pure folly.* **5.** Having no faults; perfect. **6.** Chaste; virgin. **7.** Of unmixed blood or ancestry. **8.** Theoretical: *pure science.* [< Lat. *pūrus.*] —**pure′ly** *adv.* —**pu′ri•ty** *n.*

Syns: *pure, absolute, sheer, simple, unadulterated* **adj.**

pure•bred (pyo͝or′brĕd′) ►*adj.* Of a strain established by breeding many generations of unmixed stock. —**pure′bred′** *n.*

pu•rée (pyo͝o-rā′, pyo͝or′ā) ►*v.* **-réed, -rée•ing.** To rub (food) through a strainer or process in a blender to a thick pulpy consistency. ►*n.* Food prepared by puréeing. [< OFr. *purer,* strain.]

pur•ga•tion (pûr-gā′shən) ►*n.* The act of purging or purifying.

pur•ga•tive (pûr′gə-tĭv) ►*adj.* Tending to cleanse or purge, esp. causing evacuation of the bowels. —**pur′ga•tive** *n.*

pur•ga•to•ry (pûr′gə-tôr′ē, -tōr′ē) ►*n., pl.* **-ries 1.** In certain Christian doctrines, a temporary state in which the souls of those who have died in grace must expiate their sins. **2.** A place or condition of suffering, expiation, or remorse. —**pur′ga•to′ri•al** (-tôr′ē-əl, -tōr′-) *adj.*

purge (pûrj) ►*v.* **purged, purg•ing 1.** To purify, esp. of sin, guilt, or defilement. **2.** To rid of undesirable people. See Syns at **eliminate. 3.** To undergo or cause evacuation of (the bowels). ►*n.* **1.** The act of purging. **2.** Something that purges, esp. a medicinal purgative. [< Lat. *pūrgāre.*]

pu•ri•fy (pyo͝or′ə-fī′) ►*v.* **-fied, -fy•ing.** To make or become pure. [< Lat. *pūrificāre.*] —**pu′ri•fi•ca′tion** *n.* —**pu′ri•fi′er** *n.*

Pu•rim (po͝or′ĭm, po͝o-rēm′) ►*n. Judaism* The 14th of Adar, observed in commemoration of Esther's deliverance of the Jews of Persia from massacre. [Heb. *pûrîm.*]

pu•rine (pyo͝or′ēn′) ►*n.* **1.** A colorless crystalline organic base, $C_5H_4N_4$. **2.** Any of a group of organic compounds derived from or structurally related to purine, including uric acid and guanine. [Ger. *Purin.*]

pur•ism (pyo͝or′ĭz′əm) ►*n.* Strict observance of correctness, esp. of language. —**pur′ist** *n.* —**pu•ris′tic** *adj.*

Pu•ri•tan (pyo͝or′ĭ-tn) ►*n.* **1.** A member of a group of English Protestants who in the 16th and 17th cent. advocated strict discipline and simplification of religious ceremonies. **2. puritan** One who regards pleasure or luxury as sinful. [< LLat. *pūritās,* purity.] —**pu′ri•tan′i•cal** (-tăn′ĭ-kəl) *adj.*

purl[1] (pûrl) ►*v.* To flow or ripple with a murmuring sound. ►*n.* The sound made by rippling water. [Prob. of Scand. orig.]

purl[2] (pûrl) ►*n.* An inverted knitting stitch. [?] —**purl** *v.*

pur•lieu (pûrl′yo͞o, pûr′lo͞o) ►*n.* **1.** An outlying or neighboring area. **2. purlieus** Outskirts; environs. [< OFr. *poraler,* traverse.]

pur•loin (pər-loin′, pûr′loin′) ►*v.* To commit theft; steal. [< AN *purloigner,* remove.]

pur•ple (pûr′pəl) ►*n.* **1.** Any of a group of colors with a hue between violet and red. **2.** Purple cloth worn as a symbol of royalty or high office. ►*adj.* **1.** Of the color purple. **2.** Elaborate and ornate: *purple prose.* [< Gk. *porphura*, a shellfish yielding purple dye.] —**pur′ple** *v.* —**pur′plish** *adj.*

pur•port (pər-pôrt′, -pōrt′) ►*v.* To profess to be, often falsely. ►*n.* (pûr′pôrt′, -pōrt′) **1.** Meaning; import. See Syns at **substance. 2.** Intention; purpose. [< AN *purporter*.]

pur•pose (pûr′pəs) ►*n.* **1.** An aim or goal. **2.** A result or effect that is intended or desired; intention. **3.** Determination; resolution: *a man of purpose.* ►*v.* **-posed, -pos•ing.** To intend or resolve to perform or accomplish. —***idiom:* on purpose** Intentionally; deliberately. [< AN *purposer*, intend.] —**pur′pose•ful** *adj.* —**pur′pose•less** *adj.* —**pur′pose•ly** *adv.*

purr (pûr) ►*n.* A soft vibrant sound like that made by a contented cat. [Imit.] —**purr** *v.*

purse (pûrs) ►*n.* **1.** A woman's bag for carrying personal items; handbag. **2.** A small bag or pouch for carrying money. **3.** Available wealth or resources; money. **4.** A sum of money collected as a present or offered as a prize. ►*v.* **pursed, purs•ing.** To pucker. [< LLat. *bursa.* See BURSA.]

purs•er (pûr′sər) ►*n.* The officer in charge of money matters on board a ship or commercial aircraft.

purs•lane (pûrs′lĭn, -lān′) ►*n.* A trailing Asian weed having small yellow flowers and fleshy leaves that are cooked as a vegetable or used in salads. [< Lat. *portulāca*.]

pur•su•ance (pər-so͞o′əns) ►*n.* A carrying out or putting into effect.

pur•su•ant to (pər-so͞o′ənt) ►*prep.* In accordance with.

pur•sue (pər-so͞o′) ►*v.* **-sued, -su•ing 1.** To follow so as to overtake or capture. **2.** To strive to accomplish. **3.** To proceed along the course of; follow: *pursue a course.* **4.** To be engaged in (e.g., a hobby). [< Lat. *prōsequī*, prosecute.] —**pur•su′er** *n.*

pur•suit (pər-so͞ot′) ►*n.* **1.** The act of pursuing. **2.** An activity, such as a hobby, engaged in regularly. [< AN *pursuite*.]

pu•ru•lent (pyo͝or′ə-lənt, pyo͝or′yə-) ►*adj.* Containing or secreting pus. [< Lat. *pūrulentus*.] —**pu′ru•lence** *n.*

pur•vey (pər-vā′, pûr′vā′) ►*v.* To supply (e.g., food); furnish. [< Lat. *prōvidēre*, PROVIDE.] —**pur•vey′ance** *n.* —**pur•vey′or** *n.*

pur•view (pûr′vyo͞o′) ►*n.* **1.** The extent of function, power, or competence; scope. See Syns at **range. 2.** Range of vision, comprehension, or experience; outlook. [< AN *purveu*, provided.]

pus (pŭs) ►*n.* A usu. viscous, yellowish-white fluid formed in infected tissue, consisting of white blood cells, cellular debris, and necrotic tissue. [Lat. *pūs*.]

Pu•san (po͞o′sän′) A city of extreme SE South Korea on Korea Strait SE of Seoul. Pop. 3,814,000.

push (po͝osh) ►*v.* **1.** To apply pressure against for the purpose of moving. **2.** To move (an object) by exerting force against it; thrust or shove. **3.** To force (one's way). **4.** To urge forward insistently; pressure: *push a child to study harder.* **5.** To bear hard upon; press. **6.** *Slang* **a.** To promote or sell (a product). **b.** To sell (a narcotic) illegally. ►*n.* **1.** The act of pushing; thrust. **2.** A vigorous or insistent effort; drive. See Syns at **campaign. 3.** A provocation to action; stimulus. [< Lat. *pulsāre*.]

Syns: *push, propel, shove, thrust* **v.**

push•but•ton or **push button** (po͝osh′bŭt′n) ►*n.* A small button that activates an electric circuit when pushed.

push-but•ton (po͝osh′bŭt′n) ►*adj.* Equipped with or operated by a push button.

push•cart (po͝osh′kärt′) ►*n.* A light cart pushed by hand.

push•er (po͝osh′ər) ►*n.* *Slang* One who sells drugs illegally.

Push•kin (po͝osh′kĭn, po͝osh′-), **Aleksandr Sergeyevich.** 1799–1837. Russian writer.

Aleksandr S. Pushkin

push•o•ver (po͝osh′ō′vər) ►*n.* **1.** One easily defeated or deceived. **2.** Something easily done. See Syns at **breeze.**

Push•tu (pŭsh′to͞o) ►*n.* Var. of **Pashto.**

push•up (po͝osh′ŭp′) ►*n.* An exercise performed by lying face down with the palms on the floor and pushing the body up and down with the arms.

push•y (po͝osh′ē) ►*adj.* **-i•er, -i•est.** Disagreeably aggressive or forward. —**push′i•ly** *adv.* —**push′i•ness** *n.*

pu•sil•lan•i•mous (pyo͞o′sə-lăn′ə-məs) ►*adj.* Lacking courage; cowardly. [< LLat. *pusillanimis*.] —**pu′sil•lan′i•mous•ly** *adv.* —**pu′sil•la•nim′i•ty** (-lə-nĭm′ĭ-tē) *n.*

puss[1] (po͝os) ►*n.* *Informal* A cat. [Prob. of Gmc. orig.]

puss[2] (po͝os) ►*n.* *Slang* The human face. [< Middle Irish *bus*, lip.]

puss•y[1] (po͝os′ē) ►*n.*, *pl.* **-ies** *Informal* A cat.

pus•sy[2] (pŭs′ē) ►*adj.* **-si•er, -si•est.** Containing or resembling pus.

puss•y•cat (po͝os′ē-kăt′) ►*n.* **1.** A cat. **2.** *Informal* An easygoing, amiable person.

puss•y•foot (po͝os′ē-fo͝ot′) ►*v.* **1.** To move stealthily or cautiously. **2.** *Informal* To avoid committing oneself.

puss•y willow (po͝os′ē) ►*n.* A North American shrub or small tree with silky catkins.

pus•tule (pŭs′cho͞ol, pŭs′tyo͞ol) ►*n.* A small inflammation of the skin filled with pus. [< Lat. *pūstula*.] —**pus′tu•lar** *adj.*

put (po͝ot) ►*v.* **put, put•ting 1.** To place in a specified position; set. **2.** To cause to be in a specified condition. **3.** To subject: *put him to a lot of trouble.* **4.** To attribute: *put a false interpretation on events.* **5.** To estimate: *put the time at five o'clock.* **6.** To impose or levy (a tax). **7.** To hurl with an overhand pushing motion: *put the shot.* **8.** To bring up for consideration or judgment: *put a question.* **9.** To express; state.

10. To render in a specified language; translate. **11.** To adapt. **12.** To apply: *put our minds to it.* **13.** To proceed: *The ship put into the harbor.* —***phrasal verbs:*** **put across** To state so as to be understood or accepted. **put down 1.** To write down. **2.** To suppress: *put down a rebellion.* **3.** *Slang* To criticize or belittle. **put off 1.** To delay or postpone. **2.** To offend or repel. **put on 1.** To clothe oneself with. **2.** *Slang* To tease or mislead. **put out 1.** To extinguish. **2.** To inconvenience. **3.** To anger or irritate. —***idiom:*** **put up with** To endure. [ME *putten.*]

pu•ta•tive (pyōō′tə-tĭv) ► *adj.* Generally regarded as such. See Syns at **supposed.** [< Lat. *putāre*, think.]

put•down (pŏŏt′doun′) ► *n. Slang* A critical or slighting remark.

put-on (pŏŏt′ŏn′, -ôn′) ► *adj.* Pretended; feigned. ► *n. Slang* **1.** The act of teasing or misleading someone, esp. for amusement. **2.** Something intended as a hoax or joke.

pu•tre•fy (pyōō′trə-fī′) ► *v.* **-fied, -fy•ing 1.** To decay or cause to decay and have a foul odor. **2.** To make or become gangrenous. [< Lat. *puter*, rotten.] —**pu′tre•fac′tion** (-făk′shən) *n.* —**pu′tre•fac′tive** (-făk′tĭv) *adj.*

pu•tres•cent (pyōō-trĕs′ənt) ► *adj.* Becoming putrid; putrefying. [< Lat. *puter*, rotten.] —**pu•tres′cence** *n.*

pu•trid (pyōō′trĭd) ► *adj.* **1.** Decomposed and foul-smelling. **2.** Vile; corrupt. **3.** Extremely objectionable. [< Lat. *putridus.*] —**pu•trid′i•ty** (-trĭd′ĭ-tē), **pu′trid•ness** *n.*

putsch (pŏŏch) ► *n.* A sudden attempt by a group to overthrow a government. [Ger.]

putt (pŭt) ► *n.* A light golf stroke made in an effort to place the ball into the hole. [Var. of PUT.] —**putt** *v.*

put•tee (pŭ-tē′, pŭt′ē) ► *n.* **1.** A strip of cloth wound spirally around the lower leg. **2.** A gaiter covering the lower leg. [< Skt. *paṭṭikā.*]

put•ter[1] (pŭt′ər) ► *n.* A short golf club used for putting.

put•ter[2] (pŭt′ər) ► *v.* To occupy oneself in an aimless or ineffective manner. [< POTTER[2].]

put•ty (pŭt′ē) ► *n., pl.* **-ties 1.** A doughlike cement made by mixing whiting and linseed oil, used to fill holes in woodwork and secure panes of glass. **2.** A substance with a similar consistency or function. [< OFr. *potee*, a potful.] —**put′ty** *v.*

Pu•tu•ma•yo (pōō′tə-mī′ō, -tōō-mä′yō) A river of NW South America rising in SW Colombia and flowing about 1,609 km (1,000 mi) to the Amazon R. in NW Brazil.

puz•zle (pŭz′əl) ► *v.* **-zled, -zling 1.** To baffle or confuse by presenting a difficult problem or matter. **2.** To clarify or solve by reasoning or study: *puzzled out the answer.* **3.** To ponder over a problem in an effort to solve or understand it. ► *n.* **1.** Something, such as a toy or game, that tests one's ingenuity. **2.** Something that baffles or confuses. **3.** Bewilderment. [?] —**puz′zle•ment** *n.*

PVC (pē′vē-sē′) ► *n.* A common thermoplastic resin, used in a wide variety of manufactured products. [P(OLY)V(INYL) C(HLORIDE).]

PVT or **Pvt.** ► *abbr.* private

Pyg•my also **Pig•my** (pĭg′mē) ► *n., pl.* **-mies 1.** also **pygmy** A member of any of several African or Asian peoples of gen. short stature. **2. pygmy** One of unusually small size or of little importance. [< Gk. *pugmē*, cubit.] —**Pyg′my, pyg′my** *adj.*

py•ja•mas (pə-jä′məz, -jăm′əz) ► *pl.n. Chiefly Brit.* Var. of **pajamas.**

py•lon (pī′lŏn′) ► *n.* **1.** A steel tower supporting high-tension wires. **2.** A monumental gateway, esp. a pair of truncated pyramids serving as the entrance to an Egyptian temple. [Gk. *pulōn*, gateway.]

Pym (pĭm), **John.** 1584–1643. English Parliamentarian.

Pyong•yang (pyŭng′yäng′, -yăng′, pyông′-) The capital of North Korea, in the SW-central part. Pop. 2,355,000.

py•or•rhe•a or **py•or•rhoe•a** (pī′ə-rē′ə) ► *n.* **1.** Inflammation of the gums and tooth sockets, often leading to loosening of the teeth. **2.** A discharge of pus. [Gk. *puon*, pus + *rhein*, flow.]

pyr•a•mid (pĭr′ə-mĭd) ► *n.* **1.** A solid figure with a polygonal base and triangular faces that meet at a common point. **2a.** A massive monument of ancient Egypt having a rectangular base and four triangular faces meeting at an apex, built over or around a tomb. **b.** A flat-topped Mesoamerican temple of similar shape. ► *v.* **1.** To place or build in the shape of a pyramid. **2.** To increase rapidly and on a widening base. [< Gk. *puramis.*] —**py•ram′i•dal** (pĭ-răm′ĭ-dl) *adj.*

pyre (pīr) ► *n.* A combustible pile for burning a corpse as a funeral rite. [< Gk. *pur*, fire.]

Pyr•e•nees (pîr′ə-nēz′) A mountain range of SW Europe extending from the Bay of Biscay to the Mediterranean. —**Pyr′e•ne′an** *adj.*

py•re•thrum (pī-rē′thrəm, -rĕth′rəm) ► *n.* **1.** Any of several Old World plants cultivated for their showy flowers. **2.** An insecticide made from the dried flowers of these plants. [< Gk. *purethron*, a kind of plant.]

Py•rex (pī′rĕks′) ► A trademark for any of various types of heat-resistant and chemical-resistant glass.

py•rim•i•dine (pī-rĭm′ĭ-dēn′, pĭ-) ► *n.* **1.** A crystalline organic base, $C_4H_4N_2$. **2.** Any of several basic compounds derived from or structurally related to pyrimidine, esp. uracil, cytosine, and thymine.

py•rite (pī′rīt′) ► *n.* A brass-colored mineral, FeS_2, used as an iron ore and in producing sulfuric acid. [< Lat. *pyrītēs*, flint.] —**py•rit′ic** (-rĭt′ĭk) *adj.*

py•ri•tes (pī-rī′tēz, pī′rīts′) ► *n., pl.* **pyrites.** Any of various natural metallic sulfide minerals, esp. of iron. [< Gk. *puritēs (lithos)*, fire (stone).]

pyro– or **pyr–** ► *pref.* Fire; heat: *pyromania.* [< Gk. *pur*, fire.]

py•rol•y•sis (pī-rŏl′ĭ-sĭs) ► *n.* Decomposition or transformation of a compound caused by heat. —**py′ro•lyt′ic** (-rə-lĭt′ĭk) *adj.*

py•ro•ma•ni•a (pī′rō-mā′nē-ə, -mān′yə) ► *n.* An uncontrollable impulse to start fires. —**py′ro•ma′ni•ac′** (-mā′nē-ăk′) *n.*

py•rom•e•ter (pī-rŏm′ĭ-tər) ► *n.* A thermometer used for measuring high temperatures.

py•ro•tech•nics (pī′rə-tĕk′nĭks) ► *n. (takes sing. v.)* **1.** A fireworks display. **2.** A brilliant display, as of wit. —**py′ro•tech′nic, py′ro•tech′ni•cal** *adj.*

Pyr•rhic victory (pĭr′ĭk) ► *n.* A victory offset

by excessive losses. [From the victory of *Pyrrhus* (319–272 B.C.) over the Romans in 279 B.C.]

Py•thag•o•ras (pĭ-thăg′ər-əs). fl. 6th cent. B.C. Greek philosopher and mathematician.

Py•thag•o•re•an theorem (pĭ-thăg′ə-rē′ən) ▸*n.* The theorem that the sum of the squares of the lengths of the sides of a right triangle is equal to the square of the length of the hypotenuse. [After PYTHAGORAS.]

py•thon (pī′thŏn′, -thən) ▸*n.* Any of various nonvenomous snakes found chiefly in Asia, Africa, and Australia, that coil around and suffocate their prey. [< Lat. *Pȳthōn*, mythical serpent.]

py•tho•ness (pī′thə-nĭs, pĭth′ə-) ▸*n.* **1.** *Gk. Myth.* A priestess of Apollo at Delphi. **2.** A prophetess. [< Gk. *Pūthōn.*]

pyx also **pix** (pĭks) ▸*n.* **1a.** A container in which wafers for the Eucharist are kept. **b.** A container in which the Eucharist is carried to the sick. **2.** A chest in a mint for specimen coins awaiting assay. [< Gk. *puxis*, box.]

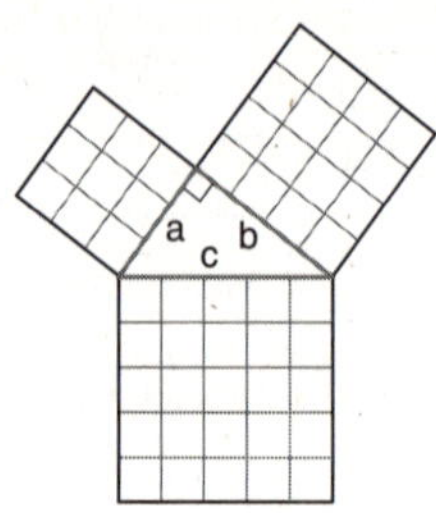

Pythagorean theorem
$a^2 + b^2 = c^2$

Q

q[1] or **Q** (kyo͞o) ▸*n., pl.* **q's** or **Q's** also **qs** or **Qs.** The 17th letter of the English alphabet.

q[2] ▸ *Phys.* The symbol for **charge** 11.

Q ▸*abbr.* **1.** quarter (of a year) **2.** *Games* queen

q. ▸*abbr.* **1.** quart **2.** also **Q.** quarto **3.** question

Qad•da•fi (kə-dä′fē), **Muammar al-.** b. 1942. Libyan political leader.

Q and A ▸*abbr.* question and answer

Qa•tar (kä′tär′, KHŭt′ər) A country of E Arabia on a peninsula in the SW Persian Gulf. Pop. 540,000. —**Qa•tar′i** *adj. & n.*

QED ▸*abbr. Lat.* quod erat demonstrandum (which was to be demonstrated)

Qing•dao (chĭng′dou′) also **Tsing•tao** (tsĭng′tou′). A city of E China on the Yellow Sea NNW of Shanghai. Pop. 2,060,000.

Qi•qi•har (chē′chē′här′) also **Tsi•tsi•har** (tsē′tsē′-). A city of NE China in Manchuria NW of Harbin. Pop. 1,400,591.

QM ▸*abbr.* quartermaster

Qom (kōm) also **Qum** (ko͞om). A city of W-central Iran SSW of Tehran. Pop. 780,453.

qt. or **qt** ▸*abbr.* quart

qto. ▸*abbr.* quarto

qty. ▸*abbr.* quantity

quack[1] (kwăk) ▸*n.* The characteristic sound of a duck. [ME *quek.*] —**quack** *v.*

quack[2] (kwăk) ▸*n.* **1.** An untrained person who pretends to have medical knowledge. **2.** A charlatan. [< obsolete Du. *quacksalver.*] —**quack′er•y** *n.*

quad[1] (kwŏd) ▸*n.* A quadrangle.

quad[2] (kwŏd) ▸*n.* A quadruplet.

quad•ran•gle (kwŏd′răng′gəl) ▸*n.* **1.** A quadrilateral. **2.** A rectangular area surrounded on all four sides by buildings. [< LLat. *quadrangulum.*]

quad•rant (kwŏd′rənt) ▸*n.* **1.** *Math.* **a.** A circular arc of 90°; one fourth of the circumference of a circle. **b.** The plane area bounded by such an arc and two perpendicular radii. **c.** Any of the four areas into which a plane is divided by the reference axes in a Cartesian coordinate system. **2.** An early instrument for measuring altitude of celestial bodies. [< Lat. *quadrāns*, quarter.]

quad•ra•phon•ic also **quad•ri•phon•ic** (kwŏd′rə-fŏn′ĭk) ▸*adj.* Of or for a four-channel sound system.

quad•rat•ic (kwŏ-drăt′ĭk) ▸*adj. Math.* Of, relating to, or containing quantities of the second degree. [< Lat. *quadrum*, square.] —**quad•rat′ic** *n.*

quad•ren•ni•al (kwŏ-drĕn′ē-əl) ▸*adj.* **1.** Happening once in four years. **2.** Lasting for four years. [< Lat. *quadrennium*, period of four years.] —**quad•ren′ni•al•ly** *adv.*

quadri– or **quadru–** or **quadr–** ▸*pref.* Four: *quadrilateral.* [< Lat.]

quad•ri•ceps (kwŏd′rĭ-sĕps′) ▸*n.* The large four-part extensor muscle at the front of the thigh. [QUADRI– + (BI)CEPS.]

quad•ri•lat•er•al (kwŏd′rə-lăt′ər-əl) ▸*n.* A plane figure with four sides and four angles. ▸*adj.* Having four sides.

qua•drille (kwŏ-drĭl′, kwə-, kə-) ▸*n.* **1.** A square dance performed by four couples. **2.** Music for this dance. [< Sp. *cuadrilla*, squad of horsemen < Lat. *quadrum*, square.]

quad•ril•lion (kwŏ-drĭl′yən) ▸*n.* **1.** The cardinal number equal to 10^{15}. **2.** *Chiefly Brit.* The cardinal number equal to 10^{24}. [QUADR(I)– + (M)ILLION.] —**quad•ril′lion** *adj.* —**quad•ril′lionth** *n. & adj.*

quad•ri•par•tite (kwŏd′rə-pär′tīt′) ▸*adj.* **1.** Consisting of or divided into four parts. **2.** Involving four participants.

quad•ri•ple•gi•a (kwŏd′rə-plē′jē-ə, -jə) ▸*n.* Complete paralysis of the body from the neck down. [QUADRI– + (PARA)PLEGIA.] —**quad′ri•ple′gic** *adj. & n.*

quad•ru•ped (kwŏd′rə-pĕd′) ▸*n.* A four-footed animal. ▸*adj.* Four-footed.

quad•ru•ple (kwŏ-dro͞o′pəl, -drŭp′əl, kwŏd′ro͞o-pəl) ▸*adj.* **1.** Having four parts. **2.** Four times as many or as much. ▸*n.* A fourfold amount or number. ▸*v.* **-pled, -pling.** To multiply or be multiplied by four. [< Lat. *quadruplus*, fourfold.]

quad•ru•plet (kwŏ-drŭp′lĭt, -dro͞o′plĭt, kwŏd′rə-plĭt) ▸*n.* **1.** One of four offspring born in a single birth. **2.** A group of four.

quad•ru•pli•cate (kwŏ-dro͞o′plĭ-kĭt) ►*adj.* **1.** Multiplied by four; quadruple. **2.** Fourth in a group of four identical things. ►*n.* One of a group of four identical items. ►*v.* (-kāt′) **-cat•ed, -cat•ing.** To quadruple. [< Lat. *quadruplicāre*, multiply by four.] —**quad•ru′pli•ca′tion** *n.*

quaff (kwŏf, kwăf, kwôf) ►*v.* To drink heartily. [?] —**quaff** *n.* —**quaff′er** *n.*

quag•mire (kwăg′mīr′, kwŏg′-) ►*n.* **1.** Land with a soft muddy surface. **2.** A difficult or precarious situation; predicament. [*quag*, marsh + MIRE.]

qua•hog (kō′hôg′, -hŏg′, kwô′-, kwō′-) ►*n.* An edible clam of the Atlantic coast of North America, having a hard rounded shell. [Narragansett *poquaûhock.*]

quail[1] (kwāl) ►*n., pl.* **quail** or **quails.** Any of various small chickenlike game birds having brown plumage and a short tail. [Perh. < VLat. **coacula.*]

quail[2] (kwāl) ►*v.* To shrink back in fear; cower. [ME *quailen*, give way.]

quaint (kwānt) ►*adj.* **-er, -est 1.** Odd, esp. in an old-fashioned way. **2.** Unfamiliar or unusual; strange. [< Lat. *cognitus*, p.part. of *cognōscere*, learn.] —**quaint′ly** *adv.* —**quaint′ness** *n.*

quake (kwāk) ►*v.* **quaked, quak•ing 1.** To shake or tremble. **2.** To shiver, as with cold or from fear. ►*n.* **1.** An instance of quaking. **2.** An earthquake. [< OE *cwacian.*] —**quak′y** *adj.*

Quak•er (kwā′kər) ►*n.* A member of the Society of Friends. —**Quak′er•ism** *n.*

qual•i•fi•ca•tion (kwŏl′ə-fĭ-kā′shən) ►*n.* **1.** The act of qualifying or the condition of being qualified. **2.** A quality or an ability that makes a person suitable for a particular position or task. **3.** A restriction or modification.

qual•i•fy (kwŏl′ə-fī′) ►*v.* **-fied, -fy•ing 1.** To describe; characterize. **2.** To make competent or eligible for an office, position, or task. **3.** To declare competent or capable; certify. **4.** To modify, limit, or restrict. **5.** To make less harsh or severe. See Syns at **moderate. 6.** *Gram.* To modify the meaning of (e.g., a noun.) [< Med. Lat. *quālificāre*, attribute a quality to.] —**qual′i•fi′er** *n.*

qual•i•ta•tive (kwŏl′ĭ-tā′tĭv) ►*adj.* Of or concerning quality. —**qual′i•ta′tive•ly** *adv.*

qual•i•ty (kwŏl′ĭ-tē) ►*n., pl.* **-ties 1.** A trait or characteristic; property. **2.** Essential character; nature. **3.** Degree or grade of excellence. **4.** High social position. [< Lat. *quālis*, of what kind.] —**qual′i•ty** *adj.*

qualm (kwäm, kwôm) ►*n.* **1.** A sudden feeling of sickness, faintness, or nausea. **2.** A sudden disturbing feeling. **3.** A pang of conscience about a course of action. [?]

quan•da•ry (kwŏn′də-rē, -drē) ►*n., pl.* **-ries.** A state of uncertainty or perplexity. [?]

quan•ti•fy (kwŏn′tə-fī′) ►*v.* **-fied, -fy•ing.** To determine or express the quantity of. [< Lat. *quantus*, how much.] —**quan′ti•fi′a•ble** *adj.*

quan•ti•ta•tive (kwŏn′tĭ-tā′tĭv) ►*adj.* Relating to or expressed as a quantity. —**quan′ti•ta′tive•ly** *adv.*

quan•ti•ty (kwŏn′tĭ-tē) ►*n., pl.* **-ti•ties 1.** A specified or indefinite number or amount. **2.** A considerable amount or number. [< Lat. *quantus*, how much.]

quan•tum (kwŏn′təm) ►*n., pl.* **-ta** (-tə) **1.** A quantity or amount. **2.** *Phys.* A discrete quantity of electromagnetic radiation. [< Lat. *quantus*, how much.]

quantum physics ►*n.* *(takes sing. v.)* The branch of physics that uses quantum theory to describe and predict the properties of a physical system.

quantum theory ►*n.* *Phys.* The theory that radiant energy is transmitted in the form of discrete units.

quar•an•tine (kwôr′ən-tēn′, kwŏr′-) ►*n.* **1a.** A period of time during which one suspected of carrying a contagious disease is detained. **b.** A place for such detention. **2.** A condition of enforced isolation. ►*v.* **-tined, -tin•ing.** To isolate in or as if in quarantine. [< Lat. *quadrāgintā*, forty.] —**quar′an•tin′a•ble** *adj.*

quark (kwôrk, kwärk) ►*n.* Any of a group of hypothetical elementary particles with fractional electric charges, regarded as constituents of all hadrons. [Coined by Murray Gell-Mann (b. 1929).]

quar•rel (kwôr′əl, kwŏr′-) ►*n.* **1.** An angry dispute; altercation. **2.** A cause of a dispute or argument. ►*v.* **-reled, -rel•ing** or **-relled, -rel•ling 1.** To engage in a quarrel; argue. **2.** To find fault. [< Lat. *querēla*, complaint.] —**quar′rel•er, quar′rel•ler** *n.*

quar•rel•some (kwôr′əl-səm, kwŏr′-) ►*adj.* Given to quarreling; contentious. See Syns at **argumentative.**

quar•ry[1] (kwôr′ē, kwŏr′ē) ►*n., pl.* **-ries 1.** A hunted animal; prey. **2.** An object of pursuit. [< OFr. *cuiriee*, entrails of a deer given to hounds < Lat. *cor*, heart.]

quar•ry[2] (kwôr′ē, kwŏr′ē) ►*n., pl.* **-ries.** An open excavation or pit from which stone is obtained. [< Lat. *quadrum*, square.] —**quar′ri•er** *n.* —**quar′ry** *v.*

quart (kwôrt) ►*n.* **1.** A unit of volume or capacity in both liquid and dry measure. See table at **measurement. 2.** A container having a capacity of one quart. [< Lat. *quārtus*, fourth.]

quar•ter (kwôr′tər) ►*n.* **1.** One of four equal parts. **2.** A coin equal to one fourth of the dollar of the US and Canada. **3.** One fourth of an hour; 15 minutes. **4a.** One fourth of a year; three months: *Sales were up in the second quarter.* **b.** An academic term lasting approximately three months. **5.** One leg of an animal's carcass. **6. quarters** A place of residence. **7.** often **Quarter** A specific district or section, as of a city. **8.** often **quarters** An unspecified direction, person, or group: *information from the highest quarters.* **9.** Mercy or clemency. ►*adj.* Equal to or being a quarter. ►*v.* **1.** To divide into four equal or equivalent parts. **2.** To dismember (a human body) into four parts. **3.** To furnish with housing. [< Lat. *quārtārius* < *quārtus*, fourth.]

quar•ter•back (kwôr′tər-băk′) ►*n.* *Football* The offensive backfield player who usu. calls the signals for the plays. —**quar′ter•back′** *v.*

quar•ter•deck (kwôr′tər-dĕk′) ►*n.* The after part of the upper deck of a ship.

quarter horse ►*n.* One of a breed of strong saddle horses developed in the W US. [From its formerly being trained for quarter-mile races.]

quar•ter•ly (kwôr′tər-lē) ►*adj.* Occurring at three-month intervals: *a quarterly magazine; a quarterly payment.* ►*n., pl.* **-lies.** A publication issued regularly every three months.

quar•ter•mas•ter (kwôr′tər-măs′tər) ►*n.* **1.** An officer responsible for the food, clothing, and equipment of troops. **2.** A petty officer responsible for the navigation of a ship.

quarter note ►*n. Mus.* A note having one-fourth the time value of a whole note.

quar•tet also **quar•tette** (kwôr-tĕt′) ►*n.* **1.** *Mus.* A composition for four voices or instruments. **2.** A group or set of four. [< Lat. *quārtus*, fourth.]

quar•tile (kwôr′tīl′, -tĭl) ►*n. Statistics* The portion of a frequency distribution containing one fourth of the total sample. [< Lat. *quārtus*, fourth.]

quar•to (kwôr′tō) ►*n., pl.* **-tos 1.** The page size obtained by folding a whole sheet into four leaves. **2.** A book composed of pages of this size. [< Lat. *quārtus*, fourth.]

quartz (kwôrts) ►*n.* A hard mineral composed of silica, SiO_2, found worldwide in many different types of rocks, including sandstone and granite. [Ger. *Quarz.*]

quartz•ite (kwôrt′sīt′) ►*n.* A rock formed from the metamorphism of quartz sandstone.

qua•sar (kwā′zär′, -sär′, -zər, -sər) ►*n.* A starlike object that emits powerful blue light and often radio waves. [QUAS(I) + (ST)AR.]

quash[1] (kwŏsh) ►*v.* To set aside or annul, esp. by judicial action. [< Med.Lat. *cassare.*]

quash[2] (kwŏsh) ►*v.* To put down or suppress (e.g., a rebellion). [< Med.Lat. *quassāre*, shatter.]

qua•si (kwā′zī′, -sī′, kwä′zē, -sē) ►*adj.* Resembling: *a quasi success.* [< Lat., as if.]

quasi– ►*pref.* Almost; somewhat: *quasi-stellar object.* [Lat. *quasi*, as if.]

qua•si-stel•lar object (kwā′zī-stĕl′ər, -sī′-, kwä′zē-, -sē-) ►*n.* A quasar.

Quaternary (kwŏt′ər-nĕr′ē, kwə-tûr′nə-rē) *Geol.* ►*adj.* Of or being the 2nd period of the Cenozoic Era, including the Pleistocene and Holocene epochs. ►*n.* The Quaternary Period. [< Lat. *quater*, four times.]

quat•rain (kwŏt′rān′, kwŏ-trān′) ►*n.* A stanza or poem of four lines. [< Lat. *quattuor*, four.]

quat•re•foil (kăt′ər-foil′, kăt′rə-) ►*n.* **1.** A representation of a flower with four petals or a leaf with four leaflets. **2.** *Archit.* Tracery or an ornament with four lobes. [< OFr. *quatre*, four; see QUATRAIN + *foil*, leaf.]

quatrefoil

qua•ver (kwā′vər) ►*v.* **1.** To quiver, as from weakness; tremble. **2.** To speak in a shaky or tremulous voice. [ME *quaveren.*] —**qua′ver** *n.* —**qua′ver•y** *adj.*

quay (kē, kā) ►*n.* A wharf. [< ONFr. *cai.*]

Quayle (kwāl), **James Danforth.** b. 1947. Vice President of the US (1989–1993).

quea•sy (kwē′zē) ►*adj.* **-si•er, -si•est 1.** Experiencing nausea; nauseated. **2.** Uneasy; troubled. **3.** Ill at ease; squeamish. [ME *coisy.*] —**quea′si•ly** *adv.* —**quea′si•ness** *n.*

Que•bec (kwĭ-bĕk′) or **Qué•bec** (kā-) **1.** A province of E Canada. Cap. Quebec. Pop. 6,438,403. **2.** also **Quebec City.** The capital of Quebec, Canada, in the S part on the St. Lawrence R. Pop. 167,517. —**Que•beck′er, Que•bec′er** *n.*

Qué•be•cois (kā′bĕ-kwä′) ►*n., pl.* **-cois.** A native or inhabitant of Quebec, esp. a French-speaking one. —**Qué′be•cois′** *adj.*

Quech•ua (kĕch′wə, -wä′) ►*n., pl.* **-ua** or **-uas 1.** The Quechuan language of the Inca empire, now widely spoken in the Andes highlands. **2.** A speaker of the Quechua language.

Quech•uan (kĕch′wən) ►*n.* A subgroup of languages, the most important being Quechua. ►*adj.* Of the Quechua or their language or culture.

queen (kwēn) ►*n.* **1a.** The wife or widow of a king. **b.** A woman sovereign. **2.** Something eminent or supreme in a given domain and personified as a woman: *Paris is the queen of cities.* **3.** *Games* **a.** The most powerful chess piece. **b.** A playing card bearing the figure of a queen. **4.** The fertile, fully developed female in a colony of social bees, ants, or termites. [< OE *cwēn.*] —**queen′li•ness** *n.* —**queen′ly** *adj.*

queen mother ►*n.* A dowager queen who is the mother of a reigning monarch.

Queens (kwēnz) A borough of New York City in SE NY on W Long I. Pop. 1,951,598.

Queen's English ►*n.* English speech or usage that is considered standard or accepted.

queer (kwîr) ►*adj.* **-er, -est 1.** Deviating from the expected or normal; strange. **2.** Eccentric. **3.** *Offensive Slang* Gay; homosexual. ►*n. Offensive Slang* A gay or homosexual person. ►*v. Slang* To ruin or thwart. [Poss. of LGer. orig.] —**queer′ly** *adv.* —**queer′ness** *n.*

quell (kwĕl) ►*v.* **1.** To put down forcibly; suppress. **2.** To pacify; quiet. [< OE *cwellan*, kill.]

Que•moy (kĭ-moi′) An island off SE China in Taiwan Strait; administered by Taiwan.

quench (kwĕnch) ►*v.* **1.** To put out; extinguish. **2.** To suppress; squelch. **3.** To slake (thirst). **4.** To cool (hot metal) by thrusting into liquid. [< OE *ācwencan.*] —**quench′a•ble** *adj.*

quer•u•lous (kwĕr′ə-ləs, kwĕr′yə-) ►*adj.* **1.** Given to complaining; peevish. **2.** Expressing a complaint or grievance. [< Lat. *querulus.*] —**quer′u•lous•ly** *adv.* —**quer′u•lous•ness** *n.*

que•ry (kwîr′ē) ►*n., pl.* **-ries 1.** A question; inquiry. **2.** A doubt in the mind; reservation. **3.** A notation, usu. a question mark. ►*v.* **-ried, -ry•ing.** To question. [< Lat. *quaerere*, ask.]

que•sa•dil•la (kā′sə-dē′yə) ►*n.* A flour tortilla folded over a filling, then fried or toasted. [Am.Sp., ult. < Lat. *cāseus*, cheese.]

quest (kwĕst) ►*n.* **1.** The act or an instance of seeking; search. **2.** An expedition undertaken in medieval romance by a knight. ►*v.* To search; seek. [< Lat. *quaerere*, *quaest-*, seek.] —**quest′er** *n.*

ques•tion (kwĕs′chən) ►*n.* **1.** An expression of inquiry that invites or calls for a reply. **2.** A subject open to controversy; issue. **3.** A difficult matter; problem: *a question of ethics.* **4.** A point or subject under discussion or consideration. **5.** Uncertainty; doubt. ►*v.* **1.** To put a question to; ask. **2.** To examine (e.g., a witness); interrogate. **3.** To express doubt about; dispute. —***idiom:* out of the question** Not to be considered; impossible. [< Lat. *quaerere*, *quaest-*, ask.] —**ques′tion•er** *n.* —**ques′tion•ing•ly** *adv.*

ques•tion•a•ble (kwĕs′chə-nə-bəl) ►*adj.* **1.** Open to doubt; uncertain. **2.** Of dubious morality or respectability. —**ques′tion•a•bil′i•ty** *n.* —**ques′tion•a•bly** *adv.*

question mark ►*n.* A punctuation symbol (?) written at the end of a sentence or phrase to indicate a direct question.

ques•tion•naire (kwĕs′chə-nâr′) ►*n.* A set of questions usu. intended to gather information for a survey. [Fr.]

quet•zal (kĕt-säl′) ►*n.*, *pl.* **-zals** or **-za•les** (-sä′lās) **1.** A Central American bird with brilliant bronze-green and red plumage. **2.** See table at **currency.** [< Nahuatl *quetzalli*, large brilliant tail feather.]

queue (kyo͞o) ►*n.* **1.** A line of waiting people or vehicles. **2.** A long braid of hair worn hanging down the back of the neck. **3.** *Comp. Sci.* A sequence of stored data awaiting processing. ►*v.* **queued, queu•ing.** To get in line: *queue up for tickets.* [< Lat. *cauda*, tail.]

Que•zon City (kā′sôn′, -sōn′) A city of central Luzon, Philippines, adjoining Manila. Pop. 1,676,644.

Quezon y Mo•li•na (ē mə-lē′nə), **Manuel Luis.** 1878–1944. Philippine politician.

Manuel Quezon y Molina

quib•ble (kwĭb′əl) ►*v.* **-bled, -bling.** To raise trivial distinctions and objections, esp. so as to evade an issue. [Prob. < obsolete *quib*, equivocation.] —**quib′ble** *n.* —**quib′bler** *n.*

Syns: *quibble, carp, cavil, nitpick* **v.**

quiche (kēsh) ►*n.* A rich unsweetened custard pie, often with other ingredients. [< Ger. *Kuchen*, cake.]

quick (kwĭk) ►*adj.* **-er, -est 1.** Moving or functioning rapidly; speedy. **2.** Learning, thinking, or understanding with speed and dexterity; bright. **3.** Hasty or sharp in reacting. **4.** Occurring or achieved in a brief period of time. ►*n.* **1.** Sensitive flesh, as under the fingernails. **2.** The most sensitive aspect: *an insult that cut to the quick.* **3.** The living. **4.** The vital core; essence. ►*adv.* Quickly. [< OE *cwicu*, alive.] —**quick′ly** *adv.* —**quick′ness** *n.*

quick•en (kwĭk′ən) ►*v.* **1.** To make more rapid; accelerate. **2.** To come or bring to life; revive. **3.** To excite and stimulate; stir.

quick•ie (kwĭk′ē) ►*n.* *Informal* Something made or done rapidly.

quick•lime (kwĭk′līm′) ►*n.* Calcium oxide.

quick•sand (kwĭk′sănd′) ►*n.* A bed of loose sand mixed with water forming a soft shifting mass that yields easily to pressure and tends to engulf any object resting on its surface.

quick•sil•ver (kwĭk′sĭl′vər) ►*n.* See **mercury** 1. [< OE *cwicseolfor* : *cwicu*, alive + *seolfor*, silver.]

quick•step (kwĭk′stĕp′) ►*n.* A march for accompanying quick time.

quick-tem•pered (kwĭk′tĕm′pərd) ►*adj.* Easily aroused to anger.

quick time ►*n.* A military marching pace of 120 steps per minute.

quick-wit•ted (kwĭk′wĭt′ĭd) ►*adj.* Mentally alert and sharp; keen. —**quick′-wit′ted•ly** *adv.*

quid[1] (kwĭd) ►*n.* A cut, as of chewing tobacco. [< OE *cwidu*, cud.]

quid[2] (kwĭd) ►*n.*, *pl.* **quid** or **quids** *Chiefly Brit.* A pound sterling. [Poss. < Lat., something.]

quid pro quo (kwĭd′ prō kwō′) ►*n.* An equal exchange or substitution. [Lat. *quid prō quō*, what for what?]

qui•es•cent (kwē-ĕs′ənt, kwī-) ►*adj.* Still or dormant; inactive. [< Lat. *quiēscere*, be quiet.] —**qui•es′cence** *n.* —**qui•es′cent•ly** *adv.*

qui•et (kwī′ĭt) ►*adj.* **-er, -est 1.** Making no noise; silent. **2.** Unmoving; still. **3.** Peaceful; untroubled. **4.** Understated; restrained. ►*n.* The quality or condition of being quiet. ►*v.* To become or cause to become quiet. [< Lat. *quiētus.*] —**qui′et•ly** *adv.* —**qui′et•ness** *n.*

qui•e•tude (kwī′ĭ-to͞od′, -tyo͞od′) ►*n.* Tranquillity.

qui•e•tus (kwī-ē′təs) ►*n.* **1.** Death. **2.** A final discharge, as of a debt. [< Lat. *quiētus (est)*, (he is) at rest.]

quill (kwĭl) ►*n.* **1.** The hollow main shaft of a feather. **2.** A large stiff feather. **3.** A writing pen made from a quill. **4.** A sharp hollow spine, as of a porcupine. [ME *quil.*]

quilt (kwĭlt) ►*n.* A coverlet made by stitching two layers of fabric with padding in between. [< Lat. *culcita*, mattress.] —**quilt** *v.* —**quilt′ed** *adj.* —**quilt′er** *n.* —**quilt′ing** *n.*

quince (kwĭns) ►*n.* A tree with white flowers and hard applelike fruit that is edible only when cooked. [< Lat. *cotōneum.*]

qui•nine (kwī′nīn′) ►*n.* A bitter, colorless, amorphous powder or crystalline alkaloid derived from certain cinchona barks and used to treat malaria. [< Sp. *quina*, cinchona bark.]

quin•quen•ni•al (kwĭn-kwĕn′ē-əl, kwĭng-) ►*adj.* **1.** Happening once every five years. **2.** Lasting for five years. [< Lat. *quīnquennium*, period of five years.] —**quin•quen′ni•al** *n.* —**quin•quen′ni•al•ly** *adv.*

quin•sy (kwĭn′zē) ►*n.* Acute inflammation of the tonsils and the surrounding tissue. [< Gk. *kunankhē*, dog collar.]

quint (kwĭnt) ►*n.* A quintuplet.

quin•tal (kwĭnt′l) ►*n.* **1.** A metric unit of mass equal to 100 kg. **2.** See **hundredweight** 2. [< Ar. *qinṭār*, a unit of weight < Lat. *centēnārius*, of a hundred.]

quin•tes•sence (kwĭn-tĕs′əns) ►*n.* **1.** The purest, most essential element of a thing. **2.**

The purest or most typical instance. [< Med. Lat. *quīnta essentia*, fifth essence.] —**quin′tes•sen′tial** (kwĭn′tə-sĕn′shəl) *adj.*

quin•tet also **quin•tette** (kwĭn-tĕt′) ► *n.* **1.** *Mus.* A composition for five voices or instruments. **2.** A group or set of five. [< Lat. *quīntus*, fifth.]

quin•tile (kwĭn′tīl′, kwĭnt′l) ► *n. Statistics* The portion of a frequency distribution containing one fifth of the total sample. [< Lat. *quīntus*, fifth.]

Quin•til•ian (kwĭn-tĭl′yən, -ē-ən). 1st cent. A.D. Roman rhetorician.

quin•til•lion (kwĭn-tĭl′yən) ► *n.* **1.** The cardinal number equal to 10^{18}. **2.** *Chiefly Brit.* The cardinal number equal to 10^{30}. [Lat. *quīntus*, fifth + (M)ILLION.] —**quin•til′lion** *adj.* —**quin•til′lionth** *n. & adj.*

quin•tu•ple (kwĭn-to͞o′pəl, -tyo͞o′-, -tŭp′əl, kwĭn′tə-pəl) ► *adj.* **1.** Consisting of five parts. **2.** Five times as much or as many. ► *n.* A fivefold amount or number. ► *v.* **-pled, -pling.** To multiply by five. [< Lat. *quīntus*, fifth.]

quin•tu•plet (kwĭn-tŭp′lĭt, -to͞o′plĭt, -tyo͞o′-, kwĭn′tə-plĭt) ► *n.* **1.** One of five offspring born in a single birth. **2.** A group or combination of five.

quin•tu•pli•cate (kwĭn-to͞o′plĭ-kĭt, -tyo͞o′-) ► *adj.* **1.** Multiplied by five; fivefold. **2.** Fifth in a group of five identical things. ► *n.* One of a set of five identical things. ► *v.* (-kāt′) **-cat•ed, -cat•ing.** To quintuple. [< Lat. *quīntus*, fifth; see QUINTUPLE + (QUADRU)PLICATE.]

quip (kwĭp) ► *n.* A clever, witty, often sarcastic remark. ► *v.* **quipped, quip•ping.** To make quips or a quip. [Perh. < Lat. *quippe*, indeed.]

quire (kwīr) ► *n.* A set of 24 or sometimes 25 sheets of paper of the same size and stock. [< Lat. *quaternī*, set of four < *quater*, four times.]

quirk (kwûrk) ► *n.* **1.** A peculiarity of behavior; idiosyncrasy. **2.** A sudden sharp turn or twist. [?] —**quirk′i•ness** *n.* —**quirk′y** *adj.*

quirt (kwûrt) ► *n.* A riding whip with a short handle and a lash of braided rawhide. [Prob. < Am.Sp. *cuarta*, whip. See QUART.]

quis•ling (kwĭz′lĭng) ► *n.* A traitor who serves as the puppet of the enemy occupying his or her country. [After Vidkun *Quisling* (1887–1945).]

quit (kwĭt) ► *v.* **quit** or **quit•ted, quit•ting 1.** To depart from; leave. **2.** To give up; relinquish. **3.** To cease performing an action. See Syns at **stop.** [< Lat. *quiētus*, at rest.]

quit•claim (kwĭt′klām′) ► *n. Law* The transfer of a title, right, or claim to another. [< AN *quiteclamer*, release.] —**quit′claim′** *v.*

quite (kwīt) ► *adv.* **1.** Altogether; completely. **2.** Actually; really. **3.** To a degree; rather: *quite tasty.* [< Lat. *quiētus*, freed.]

Qui•to (kē′tō) The capital of Ecuador, in the N-central part. Pop. 890,355.

quits (kwĭts) ► *adj.* On even terms with, as by payment. [Prob. < Lat. *quiētus*, at rest.]

quit•tance (kwĭt′ns) ► *n.* **1.** Release from a debt or an obligation. **2.** Something given as recompense. [< OFr. *quiter*, to free.]

quit•ter (kwĭt′ər) ► *n.* One who gives up easily.

quiv•er[1] (kwĭv′ər) ► *v.* To shake with a tremulous movement. [ME *quiveren.*] —**quiv′er** *n.* —**quiv′er•y** *adj.*

quiv•er[2] (kwĭv′ər) ► *n.* A case for holding arrows. [< OFr. *cuivre*, of Gmc. orig.]

qui vive (kē vēv′) ► *n.* A sentinel's challenge. —***idiom:* on the qui vive** On the alert; vigilant. [Fr., (long) live who?]

quix•ot•ic (kwĭk-sŏt′ĭk) ► *adj.* **1.** Idealistic or romantic without regard to practicality. **2.** Capricious; impulsive. [After *Don Quixote*, hero of a romance by Miguel de Cervantes.] —**quix•ot′i•cal•ly** *adv.*

quiz (kwĭz) ► *v.* **quizzed, quiz•zing.** To question closely; interrogate. ► *n., pl.* **quiz•zes.** A short oral or written test. [?]

quiz•zi•cal (kwĭz′ĭ-kəl) ► *adj.* **1.** Suggesting puzzlement; questioning. **2.** Teasing; mocking. **3.** Eccentric; odd. —**quiz′zi•cal′i•ty** (-kăl′ĭ-tē) *n.* —**quiz′zi•cal•ly** *adv.*

Qum (ko͝om) See **Qom.**

quoin (koin, kwoin) ► *n.* **1a.** An exterior angle of a wall or building. **b.** A stone forming a quoin; cornerstone. **2.** A keystone. [Var. of COIN, corner.]

quoin

quoit (kwoit, koit) ► *n.* **1. quoits** *(takes sing. v.)* A game in which flat rings of iron or rope are pitched at a stake. **2.** One of the rings used in this game. [< Lat. *culcita*, cushion.]

quon•dam (kwŏn′dəm, -dăm′) ► *adj.* That once was; former. [Lat.]

quo•rum (kwôr′əm, kwōr′-) ► *n.* The minimum number of members of a committee or an organization needed for valid transaction of business. [< Lat. *quōrum*, of whom.]

quo•ta (kwō′tə) ► *n.* **1.** A proportional share; allotment. **2.** A production assignment. **3.** The maximum number, esp. of people, that may be admitted to a nation, group, or institution. [< Lat. *quotus*, of what number.]

quot•a•ble (kwō′tə-bəl) ► *adj.* Worth quoting.

quo•ta•tion (kwō-tā′shən) ► *n.* **1.** The act of quoting. **2.** A passage quoted. **3.** The quoting of current prices and bids for securities and goods.

quotation mark ► *n.* Either of a pair of punctuation marks (“ ” or ‘ ’) used to mark the beginning and end of a passage attributed to another and repeated word for word.

quote (kwōt) ► *v.* **quot•ed, quot•ing 1.** To repeat or copy the words of (another), usu. with acknowledgment of the source. **2.** To cite for illustration or proof. **3.** To state (a price) for securities, goods, or services. ► *n.* **1.** *Informal* A quotation. **2.** A quotation mark. [< Lat. *quotus*, of what number.] —**quot′er** *n.*

Usage: As a transitive verb *quote* is appropriately used to describe the use of an exact wording drawn from another source. When the original source is paraphrased or alluded to, the more general term *cite* is usually preferable.

quoth (kwōth) ► *v. Archaic* Uttered; said. [< OE *cwæth.*]

quo•tid•i•an (kwō-tĭd′ē-ən) ►*adj.* **1.** Everyday; commonplace: *a welcome change from the quotidian affairs of life.* **2.** Recurring daily. [< Lat. *quōtīdiānus.*]

quo•tient (kwō′shənt) ►*n.* The number obtained by dividing one quantity by another. [< Lat. *quotiēns*, how many times.]

Qur•'an (kə-răn′, -rän′, kô-, kō-) ►*n.* Var. of **Koran.**

q.v. ►*abbr. Lat.* quod vide (which see)

R

r[1] or **R** (är) ►*n., pl.* **r's** or **R's** also **rs** or **Rs.** The 18th letter of the English alphabet.

r[2] ►*abbr.* **1.** radius **2.** *Elect.* resistance

R[1] (är) ► A trademark for a movie rating granting admission only to persons of or over a certain age, usu. 17, unless accompanied by a parent or guardian.

R[2] ► *Chem.* The symbol for **radical.**

R[3] ►*abbr.* **1.** registered trademark **2.** Republican **3.** right **4.** or **r** roentgen **5.** rook (chess) **6.** *Baseball* run

r. ►*abbr.* **1.** retired **2.** rod (unit of length)

R. ►*abbr.* **1.** rabbi **2.** rector **3.** river

Ra[1] (rä) ►*n. Myth.* The ancient Egyptian sun god.

Ra[2] ► The symbol for the element **radium.**

RA ►*abbr.* residence assistant

Ra•bat (rə-bät′, rä-) The capital of Morocco, on the Atlantic NE of Casablanca. Pop. 1,220,000.

rab•bet (răb′ĭt) ►*n.* **1.** A cut or groove along or near the edge of a piece of wood that allows another piece to fit into it to form a joint. **2.** A joint so made. ►*v.* **1.** To cut a rabbet in. **2.** To join by a rabbet. [< *rabattre*, beat down.]

rab•bi (răb′ī) ►*n., pl.* **-bis 1.** A person ordained for leadership of a Jewish congregation. **2.** A scholar qualified to interpret Jewish law. [< Heb. *rabbî.*] —**rab•bin′i•cal** (rə-bĭn′ĭ-kəl), **rab•bin′ic** *adj.*

rab•bin•ate (răb′ə-nāt′, -nĭt) ►*n.* **1.** The office or function of a rabbi. **2.** Rabbis collectively.

rab•bit (răb′ĭt) ►*n., pl.* **-bits** or **-bit 1.** A long-eared, short-tailed, burrowing mammal with soft fur. **2.** A hare. **3.** The fur of a rabbit or hare. [ME *rabet.*]

rabbit punch ►*n.* A chopping blow to the back of the neck. —**rab′bit-punch′** *v.*

rab•ble (răb′əl) ►*n.* **1.** A tumultuous crowd; mob. **2.** The lowest or coarsest class of people. [ME.]

rab•ble-rous•er (răb′əl-rou′zər) ►*n.* One who stirs up the passions of the masses; demagogue.

Ra•be•lais (răb′ə-lā′), **François.** 1494?–1553. French writer. —**Rab′e•lai′si•an** (răb′ə-lā′zē-ən, -zhən) *adj.*

Ra•bi (rŭ′bē) also **Ra•bi•a** (rə-bē′ə) ►*n.* Either the 3rd or 4th month of the Muslim calendar. See table at **calendar.** [Ar. *rabī*ʻ, spring.]

rab•id (răb′ĭd) ►*adj.* **1.** Of or affected by rabies. **2.** Raging; uncontrollable: *rabid thirst.* **3.** Extremely zealous; fanatical. [Lat. *rabidus.*] —**ra•bid′i•ty** (rə-bĭd′ĭ-tē, ră-), **rab′id•ness** *n.* —**rab′id•ly** *adv.*

ra•bies (rā′bēz) ►*n.* An acute, infectious, often fatal viral disease of most mammals that attacks the central nervous system and is transmitted by the bite of infected animals. [Lat. *rabiēs*, rage < *rabere*, rave.]

rac•coon (ră-ko͞on′) ►*n., pl.* **-coons** or **-coon 1.** A carnivorous North American mammal having black masklike facial markings and a black-ringed bushy tail. **2.** The fur of this mammal. [Of Virginia Algonquian orig.]

race[1] (rās) ►*n.* **1.** A local geographic or global human population distinguished by genetically transmitted physical characteristics. **2.** A group of people united by a common history, nationality, or tradition. **3.** A genealogical line; lineage. **4.** A subspecies, breed, or strain of a plant or animal. [< OItal. *razza.*]

race[2] (rās) ►*n.* **1.** A competition of speed. **2.** A contest for supremacy: *the presidential race.* **3.** Rapid onward movement: *the race of time.* **4a.** A strong or swift current of water. **b.** The channel of such a current. ►*v.* **raced, rac•ing 1.** To compete in a race. **2.** To move rapidly or at top speed. **3.** To cause (an engine) to run rapidly, esp. too rapidly. [< ON *rās*, running.] —**rac′er** *n.*

race•course (rās′kôrs′, -kōrs′) ►*n.* A course laid out for racing.

race•horse (rās′hôrs′) ►*n.* A horse bred and trained to race.

ra•ceme (rā-sēm′, rə-) ►*n.* An inflorescence having flowers arranged singly along a common stem. [Lat. *racēmus*, bunch of grapes.]

race•track (rās′trăk′) ►*n.* A usu. oval course on which races are held.

race•way (rās′wā′) ►*n.* A racetrack.

Ra•chel (rā′chəl). In the Bible, the second wife of Jacob.

ra•chi•tis (rə-kī′tĭs) ►*n.* See **rickets.** [< Gk. *rhakhis*, spine.] —**ra•chit′ic** (-kĭt′ĭk) *adj.*

Rach•ma•ni•noff (räk-mä′nə-nôf′), **Sergei Vasilievich.** 1873–1943. Russian-born composer and pianist.

ra•cial (rā′shəl) ►*adj.* **1.** Of or determined by race. **2.** Between or among distinct human racial groups: *racial discrimination.* —**ra′cial•ly** *adv.*

ra•cial•ize (rā′shə-līz′) ►*v.* **1.** To categorize according to race. **2.** To impose a racial character or context on. —**ra′cial•i•za′tion** (-lĭ-zā′shən) *n.*

Ra•cine (rə-sēn′, ră-), **Jean Baptiste.** 1639–99. French playwright.

rac•ism (rā′sĭz′əm) ►*n.* **1.** The belief that a particular race is superior to others. **2.** Discrimination or prejudice based on race. —**rac′ist** *adj.* & *n.*

rack[1] (răk) ►*n.* **1.** A framework or stand in or on which to hold, hang, or display something. **2.** *Slang* A bed. **3.** A toothed bar that meshes with a gearwheel or pinion. **4.** An instrument of torture for slowly stretching the victim's body. ►*v.* **1.** To place (e.g., billiard balls) in a rack. **2.** To torment. See Syns at **afflict. 3.** To torture on a rack. **4.** To strain to the utmost: *rack one's brains.* —***phrasal verb:* rack up** *Informal* To accumulate or score: *rack up points.* [Prob. < MDu. *rec,* framework.]

rack² (răk) ▸*n.* A rib cut of lamb or veal. [Prob. < RACK¹.]

rack•et¹ also **rac•quet** (răk′ĭt) ▸*n.* **1.** A light bat with a tight network of strings stretched across an oval frame and a handle, used to strike a ball or shuttlecock. **2.** A table tennis paddle. [< Ar. *rāḥat,* palm.]

racket¹
top: tennis and racquetball rackets
bottom: squash racket

rack•et² (răk′ĭt) ▸*n.* **1.** A loud distressing noise. **2.** A fraudulent or dishonest business or practice. [?]

rack•et•eer (răk′ĭ-tîr′) ▸*n.* A person who engages in extortion or other illegal business activities. —**rack′et•eer′** *v.*

rac•on•teur (răk′ŏn-tûr′) ▸*n.* One who tells stories with skill and wit. [< OFr. *raconter,* relate.]

rac•quet•ball (răk′ĭt-bôl′) ▸*n.* **1.** A court game similar to handball but played with short-handled rackets and a softer, larger ball. **2.** The ball used in this game.

rac•y (rā′sē) ▸*adj.* **-i•er, -i•est 1.** Strong and sharp in flavor or odor. **2.** Risqué; ribald. [< RACE¹.] —**rac′i•ly** *adv.* —**rac′i•ness** *n.*

rad¹ (răd) ▸*n.* A unit of energy absorbed from ionizing radiation, equal to 0.01 joule per kilogram. [< RADIATION.]

rad² ▸*abbr.* radian

rad. ▸*abbr.* **1.** radical **2.** radius

ra•dar (rā′där) ▸*n.* A device used for detecting distant objects and determining such features as position or velocity by analysis of radio waves reflected from their surfaces. [*ra(dio) d(etecting) a(nd) r(anging).*]

ra•dar•scope (rā′där-skōp′) ▸*n.* The viewing screen of a radar receiver.

ra•di•al (rā′dē-əl) ▸*adj.* **1a.** Of or arranged like rays or radii. **b.** Having or marked by parts radiating from a common center. **2.** Moving or directed along a radius. [< Lat. *radius,* ray.] —**ra′di•al•ly** *adv.*

radial symmetry ▸*n.* Symmetrical arrangement of constituents, esp. of radiating parts, about a central point.

radial tire ▸*n.* A pneumatic tire in which the ply cords are laid at right angles to the center line of the tread.

ra•di•an (rā′dē-ən) ▸*n.* A unit of angular measure equal to approx. 57°17′44.6″. [< RADIUS.]

ra•di•ant (rā′dē-ənt) ▸*adj.* **1.** Emitting heat or light. **2.** Consisting of or emitted as radiation. **3a.** Filled with light; bright. **b.** Glowing; beaming. [< Lat. *radiāre,* RADIATE.] —**ra′di•ance, ra′di•an•cy** *n.*

radiant energy ▸*n.* Energy transferred by radiation, esp. by an electromagnetic wave.

ra•di•ate (rā′dē-āt′) ▸*v.* **-at•ed, -at•ing 1.** To send out or issue in rays or waves. **2.** To spread out in straight lines from a center. **3.** To irradiate. **4.** To manifest glowingly: *radiate confidence.* ▸*adj.* (-ĭt) **1.** *Bot.* Having rays or raylike parts. **2.** Marked by radial symmetry. [< Lat. *radius,* ray.] —**ra′di•a′tive** *adj.*

ra•di•a•tion (rā′dē-ā′shən) ▸*n.* **1.** The act or process of radiating. **2.** *Phys.* **a.** Emission of energy in the form of electromagnetic waves or photons. **b.** Energy traveling in this form. **c.** A stream of particles. **3.** Radiotherapy.

radiation sickness ▸*n.* An often fatal illness induced by overexposure to ionizing radiation, marked by nausea, diarrhea, and loss of hair and teeth.

ra•di•a•tor (rā′dē-ā′tər) ▸*n.* A device that radiates heat, esp.: **a.** A heating device through which steam or hot water is circulated. **b.** A cooling device that dissipates engine heat.

rad•i•cal (răd′ĭ-kəl) ▸*adj.* **1.** Fundamental; basic. **2.** Departing markedly from the usual; extreme. **3.** Advocating fundamental or revolutionary changes. ▸*n.* **1.** One who advocates fundamental or revolutionary changes. **2.** *Math.* The root of a quantity as indicated by the radical sign. **3.** *Symbol* **R** An atom or group of atoms with at least one unpaired electron. [< Lat. *rādīx,* root.] —**rad′i•cal•ness** *n.*

rad•i•cal•ism (răd′ĭ-kə-lĭz′əm) ▸*n.* The doctrines or practices of political radicals.

rad•i•cal•ize (răd′ĭ-kə-līz′) ▸*v.* **-ized, -iz•ing.** To make radical or more radical. —**rad′i•cal•i•za′tion** *n.*

radical sign ▸*n.* The sign $\sqrt{}$ placed before a quantity, indicating either the square root or the root designated by a raised integer.

ra•di•i (rā′dē-ī′) ▸*n.* Pl. of **radius.**

ra•di•o (rā′dē-ō) ▸*n., pl.* **-os 1.** The wireless transmission through space of electromagnetic waves in the radio frequency range. **2.** Communication of audible signals encoded in electromagnetic waves. **3.** An apparatus used to transmit or receive radio signals. **4.** Transmission of radio broadcast, esp. as an industry. ▸*v.* **1.** To transmit by radio. **2.** To communicate with by radio. [< *radiotelegraphy.*]

radio– or **radi–** ▸*pref.* **1.** Radiation; radiant energy: *radiometer.* **2.** Radioactive: *radiocarbon.* **3.** Radio: *radiotelephone.* [< RADIATION.]

ra•di•o•ac•tiv•i•ty (rā′dē-ō-ăk-tĭv′ĭ-tē) ▸*n.* **1.** Spontaneous emission of radiation, as from unstable atomic nuclei. **2.** The radiation, such as alpha particles, emitted by a radioactive source. —**ra′di•o•ac′tive** *adj.*

radio astronomy ▸*n.* The study of celestial objects and phenomena by observation and analysis of emitted or reflected radio waves. —**radio astronomer** *n.*

ra•di•o•car•bon (rā′dē-ō-kär′bən) ▸*n.* A radioactive isotope of carbon, esp. carbon 14.

radiocarbon dating ▸*n.* The estimation of the age of an ancient object, such as a fossil, by measuring its content of carbon 14.

radio frequency ▸*n.* A frequency in the range within which radio waves may be transmitted, from about 10 kilohertz to 300,000 megahertz.

ra•di•o•gram (rā′dē-ō-grăm′) ►*n.* A message transmitted by wireless telegraphy.

ra•di•o•graph (rā′dē-ō-grăf′) ►*n.* An image produced, as on photographic film, by radiation other than visible light, esp. by x-rays. ►*v.* To make a radiograph of. —**ra′di•og′ra•pher** (-ŏg′rə-fər) *n.* —**ra′di•o•graph′ic** *adj.* —**ra′di•og′ra•phy** *n.*

ra•di•o•i•so•tope (rā′dē-ō-ī′sə-tōp′) ►*n.* A radioactive isotope.

ra•di•o•lo•ca•tion (rā′dē-ō-lō-kā′shən) ►*n.* Detection of distant objects by radar.

ra•di•ol•o•gy (rā′dē-ŏl′ə-jē) ►*n.* The use of radioactive substances or ionizing radiation, esp. x-rays, in medicine. —**ra′di•o•log′i•cal** (-ə-lŏj′ĭ-kəl), **ra′di•o•log′ic** *adj.* —**ra′di•ol′o•gist** *n.*

ra•di•om•e•ter (rā′dē-ŏm′ĭ-tər) ►*n.* A device that measures the intensity of radiant energy. —**ra′di•om′e•try** *n.*

ra•di•o•paque (rā′dē-ō-pāk′) ►*adj.* Not allowing the passage of x-rays or other radiation. —**ra′di•o•pac′i•ty** (-ō-păs′ĭ-tē) *n.*

ra•di•o•phone (rā′dē-ō-fōn′) ►*n.* A radiotelephone. —**ra′di•o•phon′ic** (-fŏn′ĭk) *adj.*

ra•di•o•sonde (rā′dē-ō-sŏnd′) ►*n.* An instrument carried aloft, as by balloon, to gather and transmit meteorological data. [RADIO + Fr. *sonde*, sounding line.]

ra•di•o•tel•e•graph (rā′dē-ō-tĕl′ĭ-grăf′) ►*n.* Radio transmission of telegraphic messages. —**ra′di•o•tel′e•graph′ic** *adj.* —**ra′di•o•te•leg′ra•phy** (-tə-lĕg′rə-fē) *n.*

ra•di•o•tel•e•phone (rā′dē-ō-tĕl′ə-fōn′) ►*n.* A telephone that sends and receives messages by radio. —**ra′di•o•tel′e•phon′ic** (-fŏn′ĭk) *adj.* —**ra′di•o•te•leph′o•ny** (-tə-lĕf′ə-nē) *n.*

radio telescope ►*n.* A device used for detecting and recording radio waves coming from celestial objects.

ra•di•o•ther•a•py (rā′dē-ō-thĕr′ə-pē) ►*n.* Treatment of disease with radiation.

radio wave ►*n.* An electromagnetic wave within the range of radio frequencies.

rad•ish (răd′ĭsh) ►*n.* **1.** A Eurasian plant having an edible root. **2.** The pungent root of this plant. [< Lat. *rādīx*, root.]

ra•di•um (rā′dē-əm) ►*n.* *Symbol* **Ra** A rare, white, highly radioactive metallic element, used in cancer radiotherapy and as a neutron source. At. no. 88. See table at **element.** [< Lat. *radius*, ray.]

ra•di•us (rā′dē-əs) ►*n., pl.* **-di•i** (-dē-ī′) or **-es** **1a.** A line segment that joins the center of a circle with any point on its circumference. **b.** A line segment that joins the center of a sphere with any point on its surface. **c.** The length of any such line segment. **2.** A circular area measured by a given radius. **3.** The shorter and thicker of the two forearm bones. [Lat., ray.]

ra•don (rā′dŏn) ►*n.* *Symbol* **Rn** A radioactive, inert gaseous element formed by radium decay, used in radiotherapy. At. no. 86. See table at **element.** [< RADIUM.]

RAF ►*abbr.* Royal Air Force

raf•fi•a (răf′ē-ə) ►*n.* **1.** An African palm tree having large fibrous leaves. **2.** The leaf fibers of this plant, used esp. for mats and baskets. [Malagasy *rafia.*]

raff•ish (răf′ĭsh) ►*adj.* **1.** Vulgar; tawdry. **2.** Jaunty; rakish. [Prob. < ME *raf*, rubbish.] —**raff′ish•ly** *adv.* —**raff′ish•ness** *n.*

raf•fle (răf′əl) ►*n.* A lottery in which a number of persons buy chances to win a prize. ►*v.* **-fled, -fling.** To award as a prize in a raffle: *raffle off a new car.* [< OFr. *rafle*, act of seizing.]

raft[1] (răft) ►*n.* **1.** A floating platform, as of planks or logs fastened together, used for transport, travel, or recreation. **2.** A flat-bottomed inflatable boat. [< ON *raptr*, beam.] —**raft** *v.*

raft[2] (răft) ►*n.* *Informal* A great number or amount. [< ME *raf*, rubbish.]

raf•ter (răf′tər) ►*n.* One of the sloping beams that support a pitched roof. [< OE *ræfter.*]

rag[1] (răg) ►*n.* **1.** A scrap of cloth. **2. rags** Threadbare or tattered clothing. **3.** *Slang* A newspaper. [ME *ragge.*]

rag[2] (răg) ►*v.* **ragged, rag•ging** *Slang* **1.** To tease or taunt. See Syns at **banter. 2.** To scold. [?]

rag[3] (răg) ►*n.* A ragtime jazz composition.

rag•a•muf•fin (răg′ə-mŭf′ĭn) ►*n.* A dirty, shabbily clothed child. [ME *Ragamuffyn.*]

rage (rāj) ►*n.* **1.** Violent, explosive anger. **2.** Furious intensity. **3.** A fad or craze. ►*v.* **raged, rag•ing 1.** To speak or act in violent anger. **2.** To move or spread with violent force. [< LLat. *rabia.*]

rag•ged (răg′ĭd) ►*adj.* **1.** Tattered, frayed, or torn. **2.** Dressed in tattered clothes. **3.** Having an uneven surface or edge. **4.** Imperfect; uneven: *a ragged performance.* —**rag′ged•ness** *n.* —**rag′ged•y** *adj.*

rag•lan (răg′lən) ►*adj.* Having or being a sleeve with slanted seams and extending in one piece to the neckline. [After the First Baron *Raglan* (1788–1855).] —**rag′lan** *n.*

ra•gout (ră-go͞o′) ►*n.* A spicy meat or fish stew. [< Fr. *ragoûter*, revive the taste.]

rag•tag (răg′tăg′) ►*adj.* **1.** Unkempt; ragged. **2.** Diverse and disorderly.

rag•time (răg′tīm′) ►*n.* A style of jazz in which a syncopated melody is played against a steadily accented accompaniment.

rag•weed (răg′wēd′) ►*n.* Any of various weeds whose abundant pollen is one of the chief causes of hay fever.

raid (rād) ►*n.* A surprise attack, invasion, or forcible entry. ►*v.* To make a raid on. [< OE *rād*, a riding.] —**raid′er** *n.*

rail[1] (rāl) ►*n.* **1.** A bar extending horizontally between supports, as in a fence. **2.** A steel bar used as a track for railroad cars or other vehicles. **3.** The railroad: *goods transported by rail.* ►*v.* To supply or enclose with rails or a rail. [< Lat. *rēgula*, rod.]

rail[2] (rāl) ►*n.* A marsh bird having brownish plumage and short wings. [< OFr. *raale.*]

rail[3] (rāl) ►*v.* To complain bitterly or abusively. [< VLat. *ragulāre, bray.] —**rail′er** *n.*

rail•ing (rā′lĭng) ►*n.* A structure, such as a fence, made of rails and upright members.

rail•ler•y (rā′lə-rē) ►*n., pl.* **-ies.** Good-natured teasing or ridicule. [< OFr. *railler*, RAIL[3].]

rail•road (rāl′rōd′) ►*n.* **1.** A road composed of parallel steel rails supported by ties and providing a track for trains. **2.** A system of railroad track, together with the land, stations, rolling stock, and other assets. ►*v.* **1.** To transport by railroad. **2.** *Informal* **a.** To push through quickly in order to prevent careful consideration: *railroad a bill through Congress.* **b.** To convict without a fair trial or on false charges. —**rail′road′er** *n.*

rail•way (rāl′wā′) ►*n.* **1.** A railroad. **2.** A track providing a runway for wheeled equipment.

rai•ment (rā′mənt) ►*n.* Clothing; garments. [< OFr. *areement,* ARRAY.]

rain (rān) ►*n.* **1a.** Water condensed from atmospheric vapor and falling in drops. **b.** A rainfall. **2.** A heavy or abundant fall. ►*v.* **1.** To fall as or like rain. **2.** To release rain. —***phrasal verb:* rain out** To postpone or interrupt because of rain. [< OE *rēn.*] —**rain′i•ness** *n.* —**rain′y** *adj.*

rain•bow (rān′bō′) ►*n.* An arc of color appearing opposite the sun as a result of the refraction of sunlight in rain or mist.

rain check ►*n.* **1.** A ticket stub entitling the holder to admission to a future event if the scheduled event is canceled because of rain. **2.** An assurance that an offer will be honored or renewed at a later date.

rain•coat (rān′kōt′) ►*n.* A waterproof or water-resistant coat.

rain•drop (rān′drŏp′) ►*n.* A drop of rain.

rain•fall (rān′fôl′) ►*n.* **1.** A shower or fall of rain. **2.** The quantity of water that falls over a specified area during a given time.

rain forest ►*n.* A dense evergreen forest in a tropical region with an annual rainfall of at least 2.5 m (100 in.).

Rai•nier III (rā-nîr′, rə-, rĕ-nyā′). b. 1923. Prince of Monaco (since 1949).

Rai•nier (rə-nîr′, rā-), **Mount.** A peak, 4,395.1 m (14,410 ft), of the Cascade Range in W-central WA.

rain•mak•ing (rān′mā′kĭng) ►*n.* The process of producing or attempting to produce rain, as through magical or ritual actions. —**rain′mak′er** *n.*

rain•storm (rān′stôrm′) ►*n.* A storm accompanied by rain.

rain•wa•ter (rān′wô′tər, -wŏt′ər) ►*n.* Water that has fallen as rain.

raise (rāz) ►*v.* **raised, rais•ing 1.** To move to a higher position; elevate. **2.** To erect or build. **3.** To cause to arise or exist. **4.** To increase, as in size or worth. **5.** To improve in rank or status. **6a.** To grow or breed, esp. in quantity. **b.** To bring up; rear: *raise children.* **7.** To put forward for consideration. See Syns at **broach. 8.** To voice; utter: *raise a shout.* **9.** To arouse or stir up. **10.** To collect: *raise money.* **11.** To cause (dough) to puff up. **12.** To end (a siege). **13.** To bet more than (a preceding bettor in poker). ►*n.* **1.** The act of raising or increasing. **2.** An increase in salary. —***idioms:* raise Cain** To behave in a rowdy or disruptive fashion. **raise eyebrows** To cause surprise or mild disapproval. [< ON *reisa.*] —**rais′er** *n.*

rai•sin (rā′zĭn) ►*n.* A dried sweet grape. [< Lat. *racēmus,* bunch of grapes.]

rai•son d'ê•tre (rā′zōn dĕt′rə, rĕ-zôN) ►*n., pl.* **rai•sons d'être** (rā′zōn, rĕ-zôN). Reason for existing. [Fr.]

raj (räj) ►*n.* Dominion or rule, esp. the British rule over India (1757–1947). [< Skt. *rājā,* king.]

Raj•ab (rŭj′əb) ►*n.* The 7th month of the Muslim calendar. See table at **calendar.** [Ar.]

ra•jah or **ra•ja** (rä′jə) ►*n.* A prince or ruler in India or the East Indies. [< Skt. *rājā,* king.]

rake[1] (rāk) ►*n.* A long-handled tool with a row of projecting teeth at its head. ►*v.* **raked, rak•ing 1.** To gather, smooth, loosen, or move with or as if with a rake. **2.** *Informal* To acquire in abundance: *raking in money.* **3.** To conduct a thorough search: *raked through the files.* **4.** To aim heavy gunfire along the length of. —***phrasal verb:* rake up** To revive or bring to light: *rake up old gossip.* [< OE *raca.*] —**rak′er** *n.*

rake[2] (rāk) ►*n.* An immoral or dissolute person. [< *rakehell,* scoundrel.]

rake[3] (rāk) ►*v.* **raked, rak•ing.** To slant or cause to incline from the perpendicular. [?] —**rake** *n.*

rake-off (rāk′ôf′, -ŏf′) ►*n. Informal* A share of the profits of an enterprise, esp. one accepted as a bribe.

rak•ish[1] (rā′kĭsh) ►*adj.* **1.** Having a trim, streamlined appearance. **2.** Dashing or sporting; jaunty. [Prob. < RAKE[3].]

rak•ish[2] (rā′kĭsh) ►*adj.* Morally corrupt; dissolute.

Ra•leigh (rô′lē, rä′-) The capital of NC, in the E-central part SE of Durham. Pop. 207,951.

Raleigh (rô′lē, rä′-), Sir **Walter.** 1552?–1618. English navigator and colonizer.

ral•ly (răl′ē) ►*v.* **-lied, -ly•ing 1.** To call or come together for a common purpose; assemble. **2.** To restore to order. **3.** To rouse or recover from inactivity or decline. **4.** *Sports* To engage in a rally. ►*n., pl.* **-lies 1.** The act of rallying. **2.** A mass gathering, esp. to inspire enthusiasm: *a political rally.* **3.** A notable rise in stock market prices and trading volume after a decline. **4.** *Sports* **a.** An extended volley, as in tennis. **b.** A race in which vehicles are driven over public roads. [< OFr. *ralier,* reunite.]

ram (răm) ►*n.* **1.** A male sheep. **2.** A device used to drive, batter, or crush by forceful impact. ►*v.* **rammed, ram•ming 1.** To strike or drive against with a heavy impact. **2.** To force into place. **3.** To cram; stuff. [< OE *ramm.*]

RAM (răm) ►*abbr. Comp. Sci.* A memory device in which information can be accessed in any order. [R(ANDOM-)A(CCESS) M(EMORY).]

Ra•ma (rä′mə) ►*n. Hinduism* A deified hero worshiped as an incarnation of Vishnu.

Ram•a•dan (răm′ə-dän′, răm′ə-dän′) ►*n.* **1.** The 9th month of the Muslim calendar. See table at **calendar. 2.** The fast that is held from sunrise to sunset during this period. [Ar. *ramaḍān.*]

ram•ble (răm′bəl) ►*v.* **-bled, -bling 1.** To wander aimlessly. **2.** To digress at length. ►*n.* A leisurely stroll. [Prob. < MDu. **rammelen.*] —**ram′bler** *n.*

ram•bunc•tious (răm-bŭngk′shəs) ►*adj.* Boisterous and disorderly. [Prob. < *robustious,* ROBUST.] —**ram•bunc′tious•ness** *n.*

ra•men (rä′mən) ►*n.* **1.** A Japanese dish of noodles in broth. **2.** A thin white noodle. [Jap. *rāmen.*]

Ram•e•ses II also **Ram•es•ses II** (răm′ĭ-sēz′) or **Ram•ses II** (răm′sēz′). 14th–13th cent. B.C. King of Egypt (1304–1237 B.C.).

ram•ie (răm′ē, rā′mē) ►*n.* A flaxlike fiber obtained from the stem of a tropical Asian plant and used in textiles. [Malay *rami.*]

ram•i•fy (răm′ə-fī′) ►*v.* **-fied, -fy•ing 1.** To have complicating consequences or developments. **2.** To branch out; divide. [< Lat. *rāmus,* branch.] —**ram'i•fi•ca'tion** *n.*

ram•jet (răm'jĕt') ► *n.* A jet engine that propels aircraft by igniting fuel mixed with air taken in and compressed by the engine.

ramp (rămp) ► *n.* An inclined surface or roadway connecting different levels. [< OFr. *ramper*, rise up.]

ram•page (răm'pāj') ► *n.* A course of violent, frenzied action or behavior. ► *v.* (*also* răm-pāj') **-paged, -pag•ing.** To move about wildly or violently. [Sc.] —**ram•pa'geous** *adj.* —**ram•pag'er** *n.*

ram•pant (răm'pənt) ► *adj.* Growing or spreading unchecked. [< OFr. *ramper*, rear up.] —**ram'pan•cy** *n.* —**ram'pant•ly** *adv.*

ram•part (răm'pärt', -pərt) ► *n.* A defensive embankment, often with a parapet on top. [< OFr. *remparer*, fortify.]

ram•rod (răm'rŏd') ► *n.* **1.** A rod used to force the charge into a muzzleloading firearm. **2.** A rod used to clean the barrel of a firearm.

Ram•say (răm'zē), Sir **William.** 1852–1916. British chemist; 1904 Nobel.

Ram•ses II (răm'sēz'). See **Rameses II.**

ram•shack•le (răm'shăk'əl) ► *adj.* Poorly constructed; rickety. [< ME *ransaken*, RANSACK.]

ran (răn) ► *v.* P.t. of **run.**

ranch (rănch) ► *n.* **1.** A large farm, esp. one on which cattle, sheep, or horses are raised. **2.** A ranch house. ► *v.* To manage or work on a ranch. [< OFr. *se ranger*, be arranged.] —**ranch'er** *n.*

ranch house ► *n.* **1.** The main house on a ranch. **2.** A rectangular, one-story house with a low-pitched roof.

ran•cid (răn'sĭd) ► *adj.* Having the disagreeable odor or taste of decomposing oils or fats; rank. [Lat. *rancidus.*] —**ran•cid'i•ty, ran'cid•ness** *n.*

ran•cor (răng'kər) ► *n.* Bitter, long-lasting resentment. [< LLat., rancid smell.] —**ran'cor•ous** *adj.* —**ran'cor•ous•ly** *adv.*

rand (rănd, ränd) ► *n.* See table at **currency.** [Afr.]

R & B ► *abbr.* rhythm and blues

R & D ► *abbr.* research and development

Ran•dolph (răn'dŏlf'), **Edmund Jennings.** 1753–1813. Amer. Revolutionary leader.

ran•dom (răn'dəm) ► *adj.* **1.** Having no specific pattern or purpose. **2.** *Statistics* Of or relating to equal probability of selection or occurrence for each member of a group. [< OFr. *randon.*] —**ran'dom•ly** *adv.* —**ran'dom•ness** *n.*

ran•dom-ac•cess memory (răn'dəm-ăk'sĕs) ► *n.* RAM.

ran•dom•ize (răn'də-mīz') ► *v.* **-ized, -iz•ing.** To make random in arrangement. —**ran'dom•i•za'tion** *n.*

R & R ► *abbr.* rest and recreation

ran•dy (răn'dē) ► *adj.* **-di•er, -di•est.** Lascivious; lecherous. [?]

rang (răng) ► *v.* P.t. of **ring².**

range (rānj) ► *n.* **1a.** Extent of perception, knowledge, experience, or ability. **b.** The area or sphere of an activity or occurrence. **2.** An amount or extent of variation: *a wide price range.* **3.** The maximum extent or distance of operation, action, or effectiveness. **4.** A place for shooting at targets. **5.** Open land on which livestock wander and graze. **6.** The act of wandering or roaming. **7.** An extended group or series, esp. a chain of mountains. **8.** A stove for cooking. ► *v.* **ranged, rang•ing 1.** To arrange in a particular order, esp. in rows or lines. **2.** To classify. **3.** To determine the distance of (a target). **4.** To vary within limits. **5.** To extend in a direction. **6.** To wander freely; roam. [< OFr. *rangier*, put in a row.]

Syns: *range, ambit, compass, orbit, purview, reach, scope, sweep* **n.**

rang•er (rān'jər) ► *n.* **1.** A wanderer; rover. **2.** A warden employed to maintain and protect a forest or other natural area. **3. Ranger** A member of a group of US soldiers trained for making raids.

Ran•goon (răn-gōōn', răng-) See **Yangon.**

rang•y (rān'jē) ► *adj.* **-i•er, -i•est.** Having long slender limbs.

ra•ni also **ra•nee** (rä'nē) ► *n.*, *pl.* **-nis** also **-nees 1.** The wife of a rajah. **2.** A princess or queen in India or the East Indies. [< Skt. *rājñī.*]

rank¹ (răngk) ► *n.* **1a.** A relative position or status in a group. **b.** An official position or grade. **c.** High station or position. **2.** A row, line, or series. **3a.** A line esp. of soldiers standing side by side in close order. **b. ranks** Personnel, esp. enlisted military personnel. **4. ranks** A body of people classed together; numbers. ► *v.* **1.** To place in a row or rows. **2.** To classify. **3.** To take precedence over. **4.** To hold a particular rank: *ranked first in the class.* [< OFr. *renc.*]

rank² (răngk) ► *adj.* **-er, -est 1.** Growing profusely or with excessive vigor. **2.** Strong and offensive in odor or flavor. **3.** Absolute; complete: *a rank amateur.* [< OE *ranc*, strong.] —**rank'ly** *adv.* —**rank'ness** *n.*

rank and file ► *n.* **1.** The common soldiers of an army. **2.** The ordinary members of a group, excluding the leaders and officers.

Ran•kin (răng'kĭn), **Jeannette.** 1880–1973. Amer. reformer and politician.

Jeannette Rankin

rank•ing (răng'kĭng) ► *adj.* Of a high or the highest rank.

ran•kle (răng'kəl) ► *v.* **-kled, -kling 1.** To cause irritation or resentment. **2.** To become sore or inflamed; fester. [< OFr. *rancler.*]

ran•sack (răn'săk') ► *v.* **1.** To search thoroughly. **2.** To pillage. [< ON *rannsaka.*]

ran•som (răn'səm) ► *n.* **1.** The release of a captive in return for payment of a demanded price. **2.** The price demanded or paid for such release. [< Lat. *redēmptiō*, a buying back.] —**ran'som** *v.* —**ran'som•er** *n.*

rant (rănt) ► *v.* To speak violently or vehemently. [Prob. < Du. *ranten.*] —**rant'er** *n.*

rap¹ (răp) ►*v.* **rapped, rap•ping 1.** To hit sharply and swiftly. **2.** To utter sharply. **3.** To criticize or blame. ►*n.* **1.** A quick sharp blow. **2.** A knocking or tapping sound. **3.** *Slang* **a.** A reprimand. **b.** A prison sentence. [ME *rappen.*]

rap² (răp) ►*n.* **1.** *Slang* A talk or conversation. **2.** A form of popular music marked by spoken or chanted rhyming lyrics with a rhythmic accompaniment. ►*v.* **rap•ped, rap•ping 1.** *Slang* To discuss freely. **2.** To perform rap music. [Poss. < RAP¹.]

ra•pa•cious (rə-pā′shəs) ►*adj.* **1.** Greedy; ravenous. See Syns at **voracious. 2.** Subsisting on live prey. [< Lat. *rapāx.*] —**ra•pac′i•ty** (rə-păs′ĭ-tē), **ra•pa′cious•ness** *n.*

rape¹ (rāp) ►*n.* **1.** The crime of forcing a person to submit to sexual intercourse. **2.** Seizing and carrying off by force; abduction. **3.** Violation: *a rape of justice.* [< Lat. *rapere*, seize.] —**rape** *v.* —**rap′ist** *n.*

rape² (rāp) ►*n.* A plant cultivated as fodder and for its seed oil. [< Lat. *rāpa*, turnip.]

Raph•a•el (răf′ē-əl, rä′fē-ĕl′). 1483–1520. Italian painter.

rap•id (răp′ĭd) ►*adj.* **-er, -est.** Very fast; swift. ►*n.* often **rapids.** A fast-moving part of a river. [Lat. *rapidus.*] —**ra•pid′i•ty** (rə-pĭd′ĭ-tē), **rap′id•ness** *n.* —**rap′id•ly** *adv.*

Rapid City. A city of SW SD WSW of Pierre. Pop. 46,492.

rapid eye movement ►*n.* REM.

rapid transit ►*n.* An urban passenger rail system.

ra•pi•er (rā′pē-ər, rāp′yər) ►*n.* A long slender sword with a double-edged blade. [< OFr. *rapiere.*]

rap•ine (răp′ĭn) ►*n.* Forcible seizure of property; plunder. [< Lat. *rapīna.*]

rap•pel (ră-pĕl′) ►*v.* **-pelled, -pel•ling.** To descend from a steep height by means of a belayed rope that is passed under one thigh and over the opposite shoulder. [< OFr. *rapeler*, recall.] —**rap•pel′** *n.*

rap•port (ră-pôr′, -pōr′, rə-) ►*n.* A relationship, esp. one of mutual trust or affinity. [< OFr. *raporter*, bring back.]

rap•proche•ment (rä′prôsh-mäN′) ►*n.* **1.** The establishment of cordial relations, as between two countries. **2.** Cordial relations. [< Fr. *rapprocher*, bring together.]

rap•scal•lion (răp-skăl′yən) ►*n.* A rascal; scamp. [< RASCAL.]

rapt (răpt) ►*adj.* **1.** Deeply moved or delighted; enraptured. **2.** Deeply absorbed; engrossed. [< Lat. *raptus*, p.part. of *rapere*, seize.] —**rapt•ly** *adv.*

rap•tor (răp′tər) ►*n.* A bird of prey. [< Lat. *rapere*, seize.] —**rap•to′ri•al** (-tôr′ē-əl, -tōr′-) *adj.*

rap•ture (răp′chər) ►*n.* A state of ecstasy. [< Lat. *raptus*, RAPT.] —**rap′tur•ous** *adj.*

ra•ra a•vis (râr′ə ā′vĭs) ►*n.*, *pl.* **ra•ra a•vis•es** or **ra•rae a•ves** (râr′ē ā′vēz). A rare person or thing. [Lat. *rāra avis*, rare bird.]

rare¹ (râr) ►*adj.* **rar•er, rar•est 1.** Infrequently occurring; uncommon. **2.** Excellent; extraordinary. **3.** Thin in density; rarefied. [< Lat. *rārus.*] —**rare′ness** *n.* —**rar′i•ty** *n.*

rare² (râr) ►*adj.* **rar•er, rar•est.** Cooked a short time: *a rare steak.* [< OE *hrēr.*]

rare-earth element (râr′ûrth′) ►*n.* Any of the abundant metallic elements of atomic number 57 through 71, orig. thought to be rare.

rar•e•fied also **rar•i•fied** (râr′ə-fīd′) ►*adj.* **1.** Of or reserved for a small, select group; esoteric. **2.** Elevated in character; lofty.

rar•e•fy also **rar•i•fy** (râr′ə-fī′) ►*v.* **-fied, -fy•ing 1.** To make or become thin, less compact, or less dense. **2.** To purify or refine. [< Lat. *rārēfacere.*] —**rar′e•fac′tion** *n.* —**rar′e•fi′a•ble** *adj.*

rare•ly (râr′lē) ►*adv.* **1.** Not often; infrequently. **2.** With uncommon excellence. See Usage Note at **hardly.**

ras•cal (răs′kəl) ►*n.* **1.** One that is playfully mischievous. **2.** An unscrupulous person; scoundrel. [< OFr. *rascaille*, rabble.] —**ras•cal′i•ty** (-kăl′ĭ-tē) *n.*

rash¹ (răsh) ►*adj.* **-er, -est.** Imprudently hasty or bold. [ME *rasche*, active.] —**rash′ness** *n.*

rash² (răsh) ►*n.* **1.** A skin eruption. **2.** An outbreak of many instances within a brief period: *a rash of burglaries.* [Poss. < OFr. *raschier*, scratch.]

rash•er (răsh′ər) ►*n.* **1.** A thin slice of fried or broiled bacon. **2.** A serving of thin slices of bacon. [?]

rasp (răsp) ►*v.* **1.** To file or scrape with a coarse file having sharp projections. **2.** To utter in a grating voice. **3.** To grate on (e.g., nerves). [< OFr. *rasper.*] —**rasp** *n.*

rasp•ber•ry (răz′bĕr′ē) ►*n.* **1.** A shrubby, usu. prickly plant in the rose family that bears edible fruit. **2.** The fruit of this plant, consisting of many small, fleshy, usu. red drupelets. [Obsolete *raspis*, raspberry + BERRY.]

Ras•pu•tin (răs-pyo͞o′tĭn, rə-spo͞o′tyĭn), **Grigori Efimovich.** 1872?–1916. Russian mystic; assassinated.

Rasputin

rasp•y (răs′pē) ►*adj.* **-i•er, -i•est.** Rough; grating.

rat (răt) ►*n.* **1.** Any of various long-tailed rodents similar to but larger than mice. **2.** *Informal* A despicable person, esp. one who betrays or informs on associates. ►*v.* **rat•ted, rat•ting 1.** To hunt for or catch rats. **2.** *Slang* To betray one's associates by giving information. [< OE *ræt.*]

ra•ta•tou•ille (răt′ə-to͞o′ē, rä′tä-) ►*n.* A vegetable stew made with eggplant, tomatoes, zucchini, peppers, onions, and spices. [Fr.]

ratch•et (răch′ĭt) ►*n.* A mechanism consisting of a pawl that engages the sloping teeth of a wheel or bar, permitting motion in one direction only. ►*v.* To increase or decrease by increments. [< OFr. *rocquet*, head of a lance.]

rate¹ (rāt) ►*n.* **1.** A quantity measured with respect to another measured quantity. **2.** A measure of a part with respect to a whole; proportion. **3.** A charge or payment calculated in relation to a sum or quantity. **4.** Level of quality. ►*v.* **rat•ed, rat•ing 1.** To estimate the value of; appraise. **2.** To place or be placed in a rank or grade. **3.** To regard or consider. **4.** *Informal* To merit or deserve. See Syns at **earn. 5.** *Informal* To have status or importance. —***idiom:* at any rate 1.** Whatever the case may be. **2.** At least. [< Lat. *(prō) ratā (parte)*, (according to a) fixed (part).]

rate² (rāt) ►*v.* **rat•ed, rat•ing.** To berate. [ME *raten.*]

rate of exchange ►*n.* The ratio at which the unit of currency of one country may be exchanged for the unit of currency of another country.

rath•er (răth′ər, rä′thər) ►*adv.* **1.** Preferably. **2.** With more reason. **3.** More exactly or accurately. **4.** Somewhat: *rather cold.* **5.** On the contrary. [ME < OE *hrathor.*]

raths•kel•ler (rät′skĕl′ər, răt′-, răth′-) ►*n.* A restaurant, usu. below street level, that serves beer. [Ger., restaurant in the city hall basement.]

rat•i•fy (răt′ə-fī′) ►*v.* **-fied, -fy•ing.** To approve and give formal sanction to. [< Med.Lat. *ratificāre.*] —**rat′i•fi•ca′tion** *n.*

rat•ing (rā′tĭng) ►*n.* **1.** A position assigned on a scale; a standing. **2.** An evaluation of financial status.

ra•tio (rā′shō, rā′shē-ō′) ►*n., pl.* **-tios 1.** Relation in degree or number between two things. **2.** *Math.* The relation between two quantities expressed as the quotient of one divided by the other. [Lat. *ratiō*, calculation.]

ra•ti•oc•i•nate (răsh′ē-ŏs′ə-nāt′) ►*v.* **-nat•ed, -nat•ing.** To reason methodically and logically. [Lat. *ratiōcinārī.*] —**ra′ti•oc′i•na′tion** *n.* —**ra′ti•oc′i•na•tive** *adj.* —**ra′ti•oc′i•na′tor** *n.*

ra•tion (răsh′ən, rā′shən) ►*n.* **1.** A fixed portion, esp. of food. **2. rations** Food issued or available to group members. ►*v.* **1.** To supply with rations. **2.** To distribute as rations. [< Lat. *ratiō*, calculation.]

ra•tion•al (răsh′ə-nəl) ►*adj.* **1.** Having or exercising the ability to reason. **2.** Of sound mind; sane. **3.** Consistent with or based on reason. See Syns at **logical. 4.** *Math.* Capable of being expressed as a quotient of integers. [< Lat. *ratiō*, reason.] —**ra′tion•al•ly** *adv.* —**ra′tion•al•ness** *n.*

ra•tion•ale (răsh′ə-năl′) ►*n.* **1.** A fundamental reason; rational basis. **2.** An exposition of principles or reasons.

ra•tion•al•ism (răsh′ə-nə-lĭz′əm) ►*n.* Reliance on reason as the best guide for belief and action. —**ra′tion•al•ist** *n.*

ra•tion•al•i•ty (răsh′ə-năl′ĭ-tē) ►*n., pl.* **-ties.** The quality or condition of being rational.

ra•tion•al•ize (răsh′ə-nə-līz′) ►*v.* **-ized, -iz•ing 1.** To make rational. **2.** To interpret from a rational standpoint. **3.** To devise self-satisfying but false reasons for (one's behavior). —**ra′tion•al•i•za′tion** *n.*

rational number ►*n.* A number capable of being expressed as an integer or a quotient of integers, excluding zero as a denominator.

rat•line also **rat•lin** (răt′lĭn) ►*n.* Any of the small ropes fastened horizontally to the shrouds of a ship and forming a ladder for going aloft. [ME *rathelinge.*]

rat race ►*n. Informal* A frantic, often competitive activity or routine.

rat•tan (ră-tăn′, rə-) ►*n.* **1.** Any of various climbing palms of tropical Asia, having long, tough, slender stems. **2.** The stems of any of these palms, used to make wickerwork, canes, and furniture. [Malay *rōtan.*]

rat•tle (răt′l) ►*v.* **-tled, -tling 1.** To make or cause to make a quick succession of short percussive sounds. **2.** To speak rapidly, usu. at length and without much thought or effort. **3.** *Informal* To fluster; unnerve. See Syns at **embarrass.** ►*n.* **1.** A rapid succession of short percussive sounds. **2.** A device, such as a baby's toy, that rattles when shaken. **3.** The series of horny segments at the end of a rattlesnake's tail. [ME *ratelen.*]

rat•tler (răt′lər) ►*n.* **1.** One that rattles. **2.** A rattlesnake.

rat•tle•snake (răt′l-snāk′) ►*n.* Any of various venomous New World snakes having a series of horny segments at the end of the tail that can be vibrated to produce a rattling or buzzing sound.

rat•tle•trap (răt′l-trăp′) ►*n.* A rickety, worn-out vehicle.

rat•ty (răt′ē) ►*adj.* **-ti•er, -ti•est 1.** Characteristic of or infested with rats. **2.** Dilapidated; shabby.

rau•cous (rô′kəs) ►*adj.* **1.** Rough-sounding; harsh. **2.** Boisterous and disorderly. [< Lat. *raucus.*] —**rau′cous•ness** *n.*

raun•chy (rôn′chē, rän′-) ►*adj.* **-chi•er, -chi•est** *Slang* **1.** Obscene, lewd, or vulgar. **2.** Grimy; unkempt. [?] —**raun′chi•ly** *adv.* —**raun′chi•ness** *n.*

rav•age (răv′ĭj) ►*v.* **-aged, -ag•ing 1.** To destroy; devastate. **2.** To pillage; sack. ►*n.* **1.** The act or practice of ravaging. **2.** Grievous damage; havoc. [< OFr. *ravir*, RAVISH.]

rave (rāv) ►*v.* **raved, rav•ing 1.** To speak wildly or irrationally. **2.** To roar; rage. **3.** To speak with wild enthusiasm. ►*n.* **1.** The act or an instance of raving. **2.** *Informal* An extravagantly enthusiastic opinion or review. ►*adj. Informal* Extravagantly enthusiastic: *a rave review.* [< ONFr. *resver*, dream, wander.]

rav•el (răv′əl) ►*v.* **-eled, -el•ing** also **-elled, -el•ling 1.** To separate the fibers or threads of (e.g., cloth); unravel. **2.** To tangle or complicate. ►*n.* **1.** A raveling. **2.** A loose thread. **3.** A tangle. [< obsolete Du. *ravel*, loose thread.] —**rav′el•er** *n.*

Ra•vel (rə-vĕl′, rä-), **Maurice Joseph.** 1875–1937. French composer.

rav•el•ing also **rav•el•ling** (răv′ə-lĭng) ►*n.* A thread or fiber that has become separated from a woven material.

ra•ven (rā′vən) ►*n.* A large bird having black plumage and a croaking cry. ►*adj.* Black and shiny. [< OE *hræfn.*]

rav•en•ous (răv′ə-nəs) ►*adj.* **1.** Extremely hungry. **2.** Predatory. **3.** Greedy for gratification. See Syns at **voracious.** [< OFr. *raviner*, take by force.] —**rav′en•ous•ness** *n.*

ra•vine (rə-vēn′) ►*n.* A deep narrow valley, esp. one worn by running water. [< Lat. *rapīna*, rapine.]

rav•i•o•li (răv′ē-ō′lē) ►*n., pl.* **ravioli** or **-lis.** A small casing of pasta with a filling, such as chopped meat or cheese. [Ital.]

rav•ish (răv′ĭsh) ▸ *v.* **1.** To seize and carry away by force. **2.** To rape; violate. **3.** To overwhelm with emotion. See Syns at **enrapture.** [< Lat. *rapere*, seize.] —**rav′ish•er** *n.* —**rav′ish•ment** *n.*

rav•ish•ing (răv′ĭ-shĭng) ▸ *adj.* Extremely attractive; entrancing. —**rav′ish•ing•ly** *adv.*

raw (rô) ▸ *adj.* **-er, -est 1.** Uncooked: *raw meat.* **2a.** In a natural condition; not refined or finished: *raw wool.* See Syns at **rude. b.** Not subjected to adjustment, treatment, or analysis: *raw data.* **3.** Untrained and inexperienced. **4.** Having subcutaneous tissue exposed: *a raw wound.* **5.** Inflamed; sore. **6.** Unpleasantly damp and chilly: *raw weather.* **7.** Cruel and unfair: *a raw deal.* **8.** Outspoken; crude. —***idiom:* in the raw 1.** In a crude or unrefined state. **2.** Nude; naked. [< OE *hrēaw.*] —**raw′ness** *n.*

Ra•wal•pin•di (rä′wəl-pĭn′dē) A city of NE Pakistan NNW of Lahore. Pop. 794,843.

raw•boned (rô′bōnd′) ▸ *adj.* Having a lean, gaunt frame with prominent bones.

raw•hide (rô′hīd′) ▸ *n.* **1.** The untanned hide of cattle or other animals. **2.** A whip or rope made of rawhide.

Raw•lings (rô′lĭngz), **Marjorie Kinnan.** 1896–1953. Amer. writer.

ray[1] (rā) ▸ *n.* **1.** A thin line or narrow beam of light or other radiant energy. **2.** A small amount; trace: *a ray of hope.* **3a.** A straight line extending from a point. **b.** A structure or part having the form of such a line. [< Lat. *radius.*]

ray[2] (rā) ▸ *n.* Any of an order of marine fishes having horizontally flattened bodies and narrow tails. [< Lat. *raia.*]

ray•on (rā′ŏn) ▸ *n.* **1.** Any of several synthetic textile fibers produced by forcing a cellulose solution through fine spinnerets and solidifying the resulting filaments. **2.** A fabric woven or knit with this fiber. [Poss. < Fr. *rayon*, RAY[1].]

raze (rāz) ▸ *v.* **razed, raz•ing.** To level to the ground; demolish. [< VLat. **rāsāre*, scrape.]

ra•zor (rā′zər) ▸ *n.* A sharp-edged cutting instrument used esp. for shaving. [< OFr. *raser*, scrape. See RAZE.]

razor clam ▸ *n.* Any of various clams characteristically having long narrow shells.

razz (răz) ▸ *v. Slang* To deride, heckle, or tease. See Syns at **banter.** [< RASPBERRY.]

Rb ▸ The symbol for the element **rubidium.**

RBI ▸ *abbr. Baseball* runs batted in

RC ▸ *abbr.* **1.** Red Cross **2.** Roman Catholic

rd ▸ *abbr.* rod (unit of measure)

RD ▸ *abbr.* rural delivery

Rd. ▸ *abbr.* road

RDA ▸ *abbr.* recommended daily allowance

re[1] (rā) ▸ *n. Mus.* The 2nd tone of the diatonic scale. [< Med.Lat.]

re[2] (rē) ▸ *prep.* In reference to; concerning. [Lat. *rē*, ablative of *rēs*, thing.]

Re ▸ The symbol for the element **rhenium.**

RE ▸ *abbr.* real estate

re– ▸ *pref.* **1.** Again: *rebuild.* **2.** Back: *react.* **3.** Used as an intensive: *refine.* [< Lat.]

reach (rēch) ▸ *v.* **1.** To stretch out (a body part); extend. **2.** To touch or grasp by extending. **3.** To arrive at or get to. **4.** To succeed in communicating with. **5.** To extend or carry as far as. **6.** To aggregate or amount to. ▸ *n.* **1.** The act of stretching or thrusting out. **2.** The extent something can reach. See Syns at **range. 3.** An unbroken expanse. [< OE *rǣcan.*]

re•act (rē-ăkt′) ▸ *v.* **1.** To act in response to a stimulus or prompting. **2.** To act in opposition to a former condition or act. **3.** To undergo a chemical reaction.

re•ac•tance (rē-ăk′təns) ▸ *n. Symbol* **X** Opposition to the flow of alternating electric current caused by the inductance and capacitance in a circuit.

re•ac•tant (rē-ăk′tənt) ▸ *n.* A substance participating in a chemical reaction.

re•ac•tion (rē-ăk′shən) ▸ *n.* **1a.** A response to a stimulus. **b.** The state resulting from such a response. **2.** A reverse or opposing action. **3.** Opposition to progress or liberalism. **4.** A chemical change or transformation. **5.** A nuclear reaction.

re•ac•tion•ar•y (rē-ăk′shə-nĕr′ē) ▸ *adj.* Opposed to progress or liberalism. ▸ *n., pl.* **-ar•ies.** An opponent of progress or liberalism.

re•ac•tive (rē-ăk′tĭv) ▸ *adj.* **1.** Tending to be responsive or to react to a stimulus. **2.** Marked

re′ab•sorb′ *v.*
re′ab•sorp′tion *n.*
re•ac′ti•vate′ *v.*
re′ad•just′ *v.*
re′af•firm′ *v.*
re′a•lign′ *v.*
re•an′i•mate′ *v.*
re′ap•por′tion *v.*
re′ap•prais′al *n.*
re′ap•praise′ *v.*
re•arm′ *v.*
re•ar′ma•ment *n.*
re′ar•range′ *v.*
re′ar•range′ment *n.*
re′as•sem′ble *v.*
re′as•sign′ *v.*
re•broad′cast′ *v.* & *n.*
re•cal′cu•late′ *v.*
re•cap′i•tal•ize′ *v.*
re•cast′ *v.*
re•charge′ *v.*
re•charge′a•ble *adj.*
re′com•mis′sion *v.*
re′com•mit′ *v.*
re′com•mit′ment *n.*
re′com•pose′ *v.*
re′con•di′tion *v.*
re′con•duct′ *v.*
re′con•firm′ *v.*
re′con•vert′ *v.*
re•dec′o•rate′ *v.*
re•dec′o•ra′tion *n.*
re′de•liv′er *v.*
re′de•ploy′ *v.*
re′de•sign′ *v.*
re′di•rect′ *v.*
re′dis•trib′ute *v.*
re•do′ *v.*
re•dou′ble *v.*
re•ed′u•cate′ *v.*
re′e•lect′ *v.*
re′e•lec′tion *n.*
re′en•act′ *v.*
re′en•act′ment *n.*
re•en′ter *v.*
re•en′trance *n.*
re′ex•am′i•na′tion *n.*
re′ex•am′ine *v.*
re′fin•ance′ *v.*
re•fin′ish *v.*
re•fit′ *v.*
re•freeze′ *v.*
re•fry′ *v.*
re•fu′el *v.*
re•hear′ *v.*
re•hear′ing *n.*
re•house′ *v.*
re′im•port′ *v.*
re′im•press′ *v.*
re′im•pris′on *v.*
re′in•fect′ *v.*
re′in•fec′tion *n.*
re′in•sure′ *v.*
re•in′te•grate′ *v.*
re′in•ter′pret *v.*
re′in•vent′ *v.*
re′in•vest′ *v.*
re′in•vig′o•rate′ *v.*

by reaction. **3.** Tending to participate readily in chemical or physical reactions.

re•ac•tor (rē-ăk′tər) ▸*n.* **1.** One that reacts. **2.** *Electron.* A circuit element, such as a coil, used to introduce reactance. **3.** A nuclear reactor.

read (rēd) ▸*v.* **read** (rĕd), **read•ing 1.** To comprehend the meaning of (written or printed characters, words, or symbols). **2.** To speak aloud (written or printed material). **3.** To determine the intent or mood of. **4.** To attribute a certain interpretation or meaning to. **5.** To foretell or predict. **6.** To receive or comprehend (e.g., a radio message). **7.** To study: *read law.* **8.** To learn by reading. **9.** To indicate or register: *The dial reads 32°.* **10.** *Comp. Sci.* To obtain information from (a storage medium). **11.** To have a particular wording. **12.** To contain a specific meaning. —***idiom:* read between the lines** To perceive an implicit or unexpressed meaning. [< OE *rǣdan,* advise.] —**read′a•bil′i•ty, read′a•ble•ness** *n.* —**read′a•ble** *adj.* —**read′er** *n.* —**read′er•ship′** *n.*

read•i•ly (rĕd′ə-lē, rĕd′l-ē) ▸*adv.* **1.** Promptly. **2.** Willingly. **3.** Easily.

read•ing (rē′dĭng) ▸*n.* **1.** The act or activity of a reader. **2.** An official or public recitation of written material. **3.** The specific form of a particular passage in a text. **4.** A personal interpretation or appraisal. **5.** Written or printed material. **6.** The information indicated by a gauge.

read-on•ly memory (rēd′ōn′lē) ▸*n.* ROM.

read•out or **read-out** (rēd′out′) ▸*n.* Presentation of computer data, from calculations or storage.

read•y (rĕd′ē) ▸*adj.* **-i•er, -i•est 1.** Prepared or available for service or action. **2.** Inclined; willing. **3.** Prompt in apprehending or reacting. ▸*v.* **read•ied, read•y•ing.** To make ready. [< OE *rǣde.*] —**read′i•ness** *n.*

read•y-made (rĕd′ē-mād′) ▸*adj.* Already made or available: *ready-made clothes.*

Rea•gan (rā′gən), **Ronald Wilson.** b. 1911. The 40th US President (1981–89).

re•a•gent (rē-ā′jənt) ▸*n.* A substance used in a chemical reaction to detect, measure, examine, or produce other substances.

Ronald Reagan

re•al¹ (rē′əl, rēl) ▸*adj.* **1.** Being or occurring in fact or actuality; not imaginary or ideal. **2.** Genuine; not artificial. See Syns at **authentic.** **3.** Serious: *in real trouble.* **4.** *Law* Of or relating to stationary or fixed property. [< LLat. *reālis.*] —**real′ness** *n.*

re•al² (rā-äl′) ▸*n., pl.* **re•ais** (-īsh′). See table at **currency.** [Sp. *royal, real.*]

re•al estate (rē′əl, rēl) ▸*n.* Land, including all the natural resources and permanent buildings on it. —**re′al-es•tate′** *adj.*

re•al•ism (rē′ə-lĭz′əm) ▸*n.* **1.** An inclination toward objective truth and pragmatism. **2.** The representation in art or literature of objects, actions, or social conditions as they actually are. —**re′al•ist** *n.*

re•al•is•tic (rē′ə-lĭs′tĭk) ▸*adj.* **1.** Tending to or expressing an awareness of things as they are. **2.** Relating to the representation of objects, actions, or social conditions as they are: *a realistic novel.* See Syns at **graphic.** —**re′al•is′ti•cal•ly** *adv.*

re•al•i•ty (rē-ăl′ĭ-tē) ▸*n., pl.* **-ties 1.** The quality or state of being actual or true. **2.** One that exists objectively.

re•al•ize (rē′ə-līz′) ▸*v.* **-ized, -iz•ing 1.** To comprehend completely or correctly. **2.** To make real; fulfill. **3.** To obtain or achieve as gain or profit. —**re′al•iz′a•ble** *adj.* —**re′al•i•za′tion** *n.*

re•al•ly (rē′ə-lē′, rē′lē) ▸*adv.* **1.** In truth or fact. **2.** Truly; genuinely. **3.** Indeed.

re•is′sue *v. & n.*
re•kin′dle *v.*
re•line′ *v.*
re•lo′cate′ *v.*
re•lo•ca′tion *n.*
re•made′ *adj.*
re•make′ *v.*
re′match′ *n.*
re•mil′i•ta•rize′ *v.*
re•mon′e•tize′ *v.*
re•mount′ *v.*
re′ne•go′ti•ate′ *v.*
re•nom′i•nate′ *v.*
re•num′ber *v.*
re•or′gan•i•za′tion *n.*
re•or′gan•ize′ *v.*
re•pack′ *v.*
re•pack′age *v.*
re•pass′ *v.*
re•phrase′ *v.*
re•plant′ *v.*
re′print′ *n.*
re•proc′ess *v.*
re•pub′li•ca′tion *n.*
re•pub′lish *v.*
re•pur′chase *v.*
re•ra′di•ate′ *v.*
re′re•cord′ *v.*
re′sale′ *n.*
re•sched′ule *v.*
re•seg′re•gate′ *v.*
re•seg′re•ga′tion *n.*
re•set′ *v.*
re•shape′ *v.*
re•shuf′fle *v.*
re•sole′ *v.*
re•start′ *v.*
re•state′ *v.*
re•stock′ *v.*
re′strike′ *n.*
re•struc′ture *v.*
re′sup•ply′ *v. & n.*
re•sur′face *v.*
re′sur•vey′ *v.*
re•tell′ *v.*
re′test′ *v. & n.*
re•think′ *v.*
re•train′ *v.*
re′train•ee′ *n.*
re′trans•late′ *v.*
re′tri′al *n.*
re•try′ *v.*
re•u′ni•fy′ *v.*
re′u•nite′ *v.*
re•us′a•ble *adj. & n.*
re•use′ *v. & n.*
re•val′i•date′ *v.*
re•val′i•da′tion *n.*
re•val′u•ate′ *v.*
re•val′u•a′tion *n.*
re•val′ue *v.*
re•vis′it *v.*
re•vi′tal•i•za′tion *n.*
re•vi′tal•ize′ *v.*
re•wak′en *v.*
re•wind′ *v.*
re•wire′ *v.*
re•work′ *v.*
re•zone′ *v.*

realm (rĕlm) ►*n.* **1.** A kingdom. **2.** A field or sphere: *the realm of science.* See Syns at **field.** [< Lat. *regimen*, government.]

re•al number (rē′əl, rēl) ►*n.* A number that is rational or irrational, not imaginary.

re•al•po•li•tik (rā-äl′pō′lĭ-tēk′) ►*n.* Politics based upon practical, not theoretical or ethical, considerations. [Ger.]

re•al time (rē′əl, rēl) ►*n.* **1.** The actual time in which a physical process under computer study or control occurs. **2.** The time required for a computer to solve a problem.

Re•al•tor (rē′əl-tər, -tôr′) ► A service mark for a real-estate agent affiliated with the National Association of Realtors.

re•al•ty (rē′əl-tē) ►*n., pl.* **-ties.** Real estate.

ream[1] (rēm) ►*n.* **1.** A quantity of paper, usu. 500 or 516 sheets. **2.** often **reams** A large amount. [< Ar. *rizma*, bundle.]

ream[2] (rēm) ►*v.* **1.** To form, shape, taper, or enlarge (a hole) with or as if with a reamer. **2.** To remove (material) with a reamer. [Poss. < ME *remen*, make room.]

ream•er (rē′mər) ►*n.* A tool used to shape or enlarge holes.

reap (rēp) ►*v.* **1.** To cut and gather (grain or a similar crop). **2.** To harvest a crop (from). **3.** To obtain as a result of effort: *reap profits.* [< OE *rīpan.*]

reap•er (rē′pər) ►*n.* One that reaps, esp. a machine for harvesting grain.

rear[1] (rîr) ►*n.* **1.** A back or hind part. **2.** The part of a military deployment farthest from the fighting front. ►*adj.* Of, at, or located in the rear. [< ME *rerewarde*, rear guard.]

rear[2] (rîr) ►*v.* **1.** To care for (children or a child) during the early stages of life. **2.** To lift upright. **3.** To build; erect. **4.** To breed or raise: *reared cattle.* **5.** To rise on the hind legs, as a horse. [< OE *rǣran*, raise.]

rear admiral ►*n.* A rank, as in the US Navy, above commodore and below vice admiral.

rear guard ►*n.* A detachment of troops that protects the rear of a military force.

rear•most (rîr′mōst′) ►*adj.* Farthest in the rear; last.

rear•ward (rîr′wərd) also **rear•wards** (-wərdz) ►*adv.* Toward, to, or at the rear. —**rear′ward** *adj.*

rea•son (rē′zən) ►*n.* **1.** The basis or motive for an action, decision, or conviction. **2.** An underlying fact or cause that provides logical sense for a premise or occurrence. **3.** The capacity for logical, rational, and analytic thought. **4.** A normal mental state; sanity: *lost his reason.* ►*v.* **1.** To use the faculty of reason; think logically. **2.** To talk or argue logically and persuasively. **3.** To determine or conclude by logical thinking. —***idioms:* by reason of** Because of. **within reason** Within the bounds of good sense or practicality. [< Lat. *ratiō* < *rērī*, think.] —**rea′son•er** *n.* —**rea′son•ing** *n.*

rea•son•a•ble (rē′zə-nə-bəl) ►*adj.* **1.** Capable of reasoning; rational. **2.** In accordance with reason or sound thinking. **3.** Not excessive or extreme. —**rea′son•a•bil′i•ty, rea′son•a•ble•ness** *n.*

re•as•sure (rē′ə-shŏŏr′) ►*v.* **-sured, -sur•ing** **1.** To restore confidence to. **2.** To assure again. —**re′as•sur′ance** *n.*

re•bate (rē′bāt′) ►*n.* A deduction from an amount to be paid or a return of part of an amount paid. ►*v.* (rē′bāt′, rĭ-bāt′) **-bat•ed, -bat•ing.** To deduct or return (an amount) from a payment or bill. [< OFr. *rabattre*, reduce.] —**re′bat•er** *n.*

Re•bec•ca (rĭ-bĕk′ə). In the Bible, the wife of Isaac and the mother of Jacob and Esau.

re•bel (rĭ-bĕl′) ►*v.* **-belled, -bel•ling** **1.** To refuse allegiance to and oppose by force an established government or ruling authority. **2.** To resist or defy an authority or a convention. **3.** To feel or express strong unwillingness or repugnance. ►*n.* **reb•el** (rĕb′əl). One who rebels. [< Lat. *rebellāre* < *bellum*, war.]

re•bel•lion (rĭ-bĕl′yən) ►*n.* **1.** Open, armed, and organized resistance to a government. **2.** An act or a show of defiance toward an authority or convention. —**re•bel′lious** *adj.* —**re•bel′lious•ness** *n.*

re•birth (rē-bûrth′, rē′bûrth′) ►*n.* **1.** A second or new birth. **2.** A revival.

re•born (rē-bôrn′) ►*adj.* Born again; revived.

re•bound (rē′bound′, rĭ-) ►*v.* **1.** To spring or bounce back after hitting or colliding with something. **2.** To recover, as from disappointment. **3.** *Basketball* To retrieve the ball as it bounces off the backboard or rim after an unsuccessful shot. ►*n.* (rē′bound′, rĭ-bound′) **1.** A springing or bounding back; recoil. **2a.** A rebounding or caroming ball or hockey puck. **b.** *Basketball* The act or an instance of taking possession of a rebounding ball. **3.** A recovery, as from a disappointment.

re•buff (rĭ-bŭf′) ►*n.* A blunt or abrupt repulse or refusal. ►*v.* **1.** To reject bluntly, often disdainfully; snub. **2.** To repel or drive back. [< Ital. *ribuffo*, reprimand.]

re•buke (rĭ-byōōk′) ►*v.* **-buked, -buk•ing.** To criticize sharply; reprimand. [< ONFr. *rebuker.*] —**re•buke′** *n.*

re•bus (rē′bəs) ►*n., pl.* **-bus•es.** A representation of words in the form of pictures or symbols, often presented as a puzzle. [Lat. *rēbus*, by things, ablative pl. of *rēs*, thing.]

re•but (rĭ-bŭt′) ►*v.* **-but•ted, -but•ting.** To refute by offering opposing evidence or arguments. [< OFr. *rebouter.*] —**re•but′tal** *n.*

rec (rĕk) ►*n.* *Informal* Recreation.

re•cal•ci•trant (rĭ-kăl′sĭ-trənt) ►*adj.* Stubbornly resistant to and defiant of authority or guidance. [< LLat. *recalcitrāre*, be disobedient.] —**re•cal′ci•trance, re•cal′ci•tran•cy** *n.*

re•call (rĭ-kôl′) ►*v.* **1.** To ask or order to return; call back. **2.** To remember; recollect. See Syns at **remember. 3.** To cancel, take back, or revoke. **4.** To bring back; restore. ►*n.* (*also* rē′kôl′) **1.** The act of recalling. **2.** The ability to remember information or experiences. **3.** The act of revoking. **4.** The procedure by which a public official may be removed from office by popular vote.

re•cant (rĭ-kănt′) ►*v.* To make a formal denial of (e.g., an earlier statement). [Lat. *recantāre.*] —**re′can•ta′tion** *n.*

re•cap[1] (rē-kăp′) ►*v.* **1.** To cap again. **2.** To restore (a used automobile tire) by bonding new rubber onto the worn tread. ►*n.* (rē′kăp′). A recapped tire.

re•cap[2] (rē′kăp′) *Informal* ►*v.* **-capped, -cap•ping.** To recapitulate. ►*n.* A recapitulation.

re•ca•pit•u•late (rē′kə-pĭch′ə-lāt′) ►*v.* **-lat•ed, -lat•ing.** To repeat in concise form; summarize. [< Lat. *capitulum*, main point.] —**re′ca•pit′u•la′tion** *n.*

re•cap•ture (rē-kăp′chər) ►*v.* **1.** To capture again. **2.** To recall: *recapture the past.* —**re•cap′ture** *n.*

recd. ►*abbr.* received

re•cede (rĭ-sēd′) ►*v.* **-ced•ed, -ced•ing 1.** To move back or away from a limit or point. **2.** To slope backward. **3.** To become or seem to become more distant. [< Lat. *recēdere.*]

Syns: *recede, ebb, retract, retreat, retrograde* **Ant:** *advance* **v.**

re•ceipt (rĭ-sēt′) ►*n.* **1.** The act of receiving or being received. **2.** often **receipts** A quantity or amount received: *cash receipts.* **3.** A written acknowledgment that a specified article has been received. **4.** A recipe. ►*v.* **1.** To mark (a bill) as having been paid. **2.** To give a receipt for. [< Lat. *receptus*, received.]

re•ceiv•a•ble (rĭ-sē′və-bəl) ►*adj.* **1.** Suitable for being received. **2.** Awaiting or requiring payment. —**re•ceiv′a•ble** *n.*

re•ceive (rĭ-sēv′) ►*v.* **-ceived, -ceiv•ing 1.** To take or acquire (something given, offered, or transmitted); get. **2.** To meet with; experience. **3.** To hear or see: *receive bad news.* **4.** To take in, hold, or contain. **5.** To greet or welcome: *receive guests.* **6.** To convert incoming electromagnetic waves into visible or audible signals. [< Lat. *recipere.*]

re•ceiv•er (rĭ-sē′vər) ►*n.* **1.** One that receives something. **2.** A device, as part of a radio or telephone, that receives incoming electromagnetic signals and converts them to perceptible forms. **3.** A person appointed by a court to hold and administer the property of others pending litigation.

re•ceiv•er•ship (rĭ-sē′vər-shĭp′) ►*n.* *Law* **1.** The office or functions of a receiver. **2.** The state of being held by a receiver.

re•cent (rē′sənt) ►*adj.* **1.** Of or occurring at a time immediately before the present. **2.** Modern; new. [< Lat. *recēns*, fresh.] —**re′cen•cy, re′cent•ness** *n.* —**re′cent•ly** *adv.*

re•cep•ta•cle (rĭ-sĕp′tə-kəl) ►*n.* **1.** Something that holds or contains. **2.** *Electron.* A fitting connected to a power supply and equipped to receive a plug. [< Lat. *receptāculum.*]

re•cep•tion (rĭ-sĕp′shən) ►*n.* **1.** The act of receiving or of being received. **2.** A welcome or acceptance: *a friendly reception.* **3.** A social function: *a wedding reception.* **4a.** The receiving of electromagnetic signals. **b.** The quality of the waves or signals received. [< Lat. *receptiō.*]

re•cep•tion•ist (rĭ-sĕp′shə-nĭst) ►*n.* One employed chiefly to receive visitors and answer the telephone.

re•cep•tive (rĭ-sĕp′tĭv) ►*adj.* **1.** Capable of receiving. **2.** Ready or willing to receive favorably: *receptive to the proposal.* —**re′cep•tiv′i•ty, re•cep′tive•ness** *n.*

re•cep•tor (rĭ-sĕp′tər) ►*n.* **1.** A specialized cell or group of nerve endings that responds to sensory stimuli. **2.** A site on or in a cell that binds with substances such as drugs.

re•cess (rē′sĕs′, rĭ-sĕs′) ►*n.* **1a.** A temporary cessation of customary activities. **b.** The period of such cessation. See Syns at **pause. 2.** often **recesses** A remote, secret, or secluded place. **3a.** An indentation or hollow. **b.** A recess. ►*v.* **1.** To create a recess in: *recessed a portion of the wall.* **2.** To suspend (e.g., a session) for a recess. [< Lat. *recēdere, recess-*, recede.]

re•ces•sion (rĭ-sĕsh′ən) ►*n.* **1.** The act of withdrawing. **2.** An extended, moderate decline in general business activity. **3.** A ceremonial exit, esp. of clerics and choir members after a church service. [< Lat. *recēdere, recess-*, recede.]

re•ces•sion•al (rĭ-sĕsh′ə-nəl) ►*n.* A hymn that accompanies a church recession.

re•ces•sive (rĭ-sĕs′ĭv) ►*adj.* **1.** Tending to go backward or recede. **2.** *Genet.* Incapable of being manifested when occurring with a dominant form of a gene. —**re•ces′sive•ly** *adv.* —**re•ces′sive•ness** *n.*

re•cid•i•vism (rĭ-sĭd′ə-vĭz′əm) ►*n.* A tendency to lapse into a previous pattern of behavior, esp. a tendency to return to criminal activity. [< Lat. *recidere*, fall back.] —**re•cid′i•vist** *n.* —**re•cid′i•vis′tic, re•cid′i•vous** *adj.*

Re•ci•fe (rə-sē′fə) A city of NE Brazil on the Atlantic S of Natal. Pop. 1,296,995.

rec•i•pe (rĕs′ə-pē′) ►*n.* A set of directions for making or preparing something, esp. food. [Lat., imper. of *recipere*, take.]

re•cip•i•ent (rĭ-sĭp′ē-ənt) ►*adj.* Receptive. ►*n.* One that receives. [< Lat. *recipere*, receive.]

re•cip•ro•cal (rĭ-sĭp′rə-kəl) ►*adj.* **1.** Given or shown in return: *reciprocal trade concessions.* **2.** Performed or felt by both sides; mutual. **3.** Complementary. ►*n.* **1.** Something reciprocal to something else. **2.** *Math.* Either of a pair of numbers whose product is 1. [< Lat. *reciprocus*, alternating.] —**re•cip′ro•cal′i•ty** (-kăl′ĭ-tē), **re•cip′ro•cal•ness** *n.* —**re•cip′ro•cal•ly** *adv.*

re•cip•ro•cate (rĭ-sĭp′rə-kāt′) ►*v.* **-cat•ed, -cat•ing 1.** To give or take mutually; interchange. **2.** To show or give in return. **3.** To make a return for something given or done. —**re•cip′ro•ca′tion** *n.* —**re•cip′ro•ca′tive** *adj.* —**re•cip′ro•ca′tor** *n.*

Syns: *reciprocate, requite, return* **v.**

rec•i•proc•i•ty (rĕs′ə-prŏs′ĭ-tē) ►*n., pl.* **-ties 1.** A reciprocal condition or relationship. **2.** A mutual or cooperative interchange of favors, esp. the exchange of rights or privileges of trade between nations.

re•cit•al (rĭ-sīt′l) ►*n.* **1.** The act of reciting publicly. **2.** A detailed account of something. **3.** A performance of music or dance, esp. by a solo performer. —**re•ci′tal•ist** *n.*

rec•i•ta•tion (rĕs′ĭ-tā′shən) ►*n.* **1.** The act of reciting. **2.** Oral delivery of prepared lessons by a pupil.

rec•i•ta•tive (rĕs′ĭ-tə-tēv′, rĕch′-) ►*n.* **1.** A style used in operas, oratorios, and cantatas in which the text is declaimed in the rhythm of natural speech. **2.** A passage rendered in this style. [Ital. *recitativo.*]

re•cite (rĭ-sīt′) ►*v.* **-cit•ed, -cit•ing 1.** To repeat or utter aloud (something prepared or memorized), esp. before an audience. **2.** To relate in detail. See Syns at **describe.** [< Lat. *recitāre.*] —**re•cit′er** *n.*

reck•less (rĕk′lĭs) ►*adj.* **1.** Heedless or careless. **2.** Headstrong; rash. [< OE *rēcelēas.*] —**reck′less•ly** *adv.* —**reck′less•ness** *n.*

reck•on (rĕk′ən) ►*v.* **1.** To count or compute: *reckon the cost.* **2.** To regard as. **3.** *Informal* To think or assume. —***phrasal verb:* reckon with** To settle accounts with. [< OE *gerecenian*, recount.]

reck•on•ing (rĕk′ə-nĭng) ►*n.* **1.** The act of counting or computing. **2.** A statement of a sum due. **3.** A settlement of accounts: *a day of reckoning.* **4.** The calculation of the position of a ship or aircraft.

re•claim (rĭ-klām′) ►*v.* **1.** To make (e.g., land) suitable for cultivation or habitation. **2.** To procure (usable substances) from waste products. **3.** To reform. [< Lat. *reclāmāre*, entreat.] —**re•claim′a•ble** *adj.* —**re•claim′ant, re•claim′er** *n.* —**rec′la•ma′tion** (rĕk′lə-mā′shən) *n.*

re•cline (rĭ-klīn′) ►*v.* **-clined, -clin•ing.** To assume or cause to assume a leaning or prone position. [< Lat. *reclīnāre.*]

re•clin•er (rĭ-klī′nər) ►*n.* An armchair with an adjustable backrest and footrest.

re•cluse (rĕk′lo͞os′, rĭ-klo͞os′) ►*n.* One who lives in seclusion. [< Lat. *reclūsus*, p.part. of *reclūdere*, close off.] —**re•clu′sive** (-sĭ, -zĭv) *adj.* —**re•clu′sive•ness** *n.*

rec•og•ni•tion (rĕk′əg-nĭsh′ən) ►*n.* **1.** The act of recognizing or condition of being recognized. **2.** An acknowledgment, as of a claim. **3.** Attention or favorable notice.

re•cog•ni•zance (rĭ-kŏg′nĭ-zəns, -kŏn′ĭ-) ►*n.* *Law* An obligation of record that commits a person to perform a particular act, such as making a court appearance. —**re•cog′ni•zant** *adj.*

rec•og•nize (rĕk′əg-nīz′) ►*v.* **-nized, -niz•ing 1.** To know or identify from past experience or knowledge. **2.** To acknowledge or accept. **3.** To approve of or appreciate. [< Lat. *recognōscere.*] —**rec′og•niz′a•ble** *adj.*

re•coil (rĭ-koil′) ►*v.* **1.** To spring back, as a gun upon firing. **2.** To shrink back, as in fear. [< OFr. *reculer.*] —**re′coil′** (rē′koil′) *n.*

rec•ol•lect (rĕk′ə-lĕkt′) ►*v.* To recall to mind; remember. See Syns at **remember.** [< Lat. *recolligere*, gather up.] —**rec′ol•lec′tion** *n.*

re•com•bi•nant DNA (rē-kŏm′bə-nənt) ►*n.* Genetically engineered DNA prepared by transplanting or splicing genes from one species into the cells of a different species.

re•com•bi•na•tion (rē′kŏm-bə-nā′shən) ►*n.* The natural formation in offspring of genetic combinations not present in parents.

rec•om•mend (rĕk′ə-mĕnd′) ►*v.* **1.** To commend to another as worthy or desirable; endorse. **2.** To advise or counsel. See Syns at **advise.** [< Med.Lat. *recommendāre.*] —**rec′om•men•da′tion** *n.*

rec•om•pense (rĕk′əm-pĕns′) ►*v.* **-pensed, -pens•ing.** To award compensation to or for. ►*n.* **1.** Amends made, as for damage or loss. **2.** Payment in return for something. [< LLat. *recompēnsāre.*]

rec•on•cile (rĕk′ən-sīl′) ►*v.* **-ciled, -cil•ing 1.** To reestablish a close relationship between. **2.** To settle or resolve. **3.** To bring (oneself) to accept. **4.** To make compatible or consistent: *reconcile opposing views.* See Syns at **adapt.** [< Lat. *reconciliāre.*] —**rec′on•cil′a•bil′i•ty** *n.* —**rec′on•cil′a•ble** *adj.* —**rec′on•cile′ment, rec′on•cil′i•a′tion** (-sĭl′ē-ā′shən) *n.* —**rec′on•cil′er** *n.*

rec•on•dite (rĕk′ən-dīt′, rĭ-kŏn′dīt′) ►*adj.* **1.** Not easily understood; abstruse. **2.** Concealed; hidden. [Lat. *reconditus*, p.part. of *recondere*, put away.] —**rec′on•dite′ness** *n.*

re•con•nais•sance (rĭ-kŏn′ə-səns, -zəns) ►*n.* An inspection or exploration of an area, esp. to gather military information. [< OFr. *reconnoistre*, RECOGNIZE.]

re•con•noi•ter (rē′kə-noi′tər, rĕk′ə-) ►*v.* To make a preliminary inspection of, esp. to gather military information. [< OFr. *reconnoistre*, RECOGNIZE.] —**re′con•noi′ter•er** *n.*

re•con•sid•er (rē′kən-sĭd′ər) ►*v.* To consider again, esp. with intent to modify a previous decision. —**re′con•sid′er•a′tion** *n.*

re•con•struct (rē′kən-strŭkt′) ►*v.* To construct again; make over. —**re′con•struct′i•ble** *adj.* —**re′con•struc′tive** *adj.*

re•con•struc•tion (rē′kən-strŭk′shən) ►*n.* **1.** The act or result of reconstructing. **2. Reconstruction** The period (1865–77) during which the states of the Confederacy were controlled by the federal government before being readmitted to the Union.

re•cord (rĭ-kôrd′) ►*v.* **1.** To set down for preservation, esp. in writing. **2.** To register or indicate. **3.** To register (sound or images) in permanent form, as on a record or tape. ►*n.* **rec•ord** (rĕk′ərd) **1a.** A usu. written account of events or facts. **b.** Something on which such an account is made. **2.** Information on a particular subject collected and preserved: *the coldest day on record.* **3.** The known history of performance: *your academic record.* **4.** An unsurpassed measurement: *a world record in weightlifting.* **5.** A disk designed for a phonograph. —***idioms:* off the record** Not for publication. **on record** Known to have taken a certain position. [< Lat. *recordārī*, remember : RE– + *cor, cord-*, heart.]

re•cord•er (rĭ-kôr′dər) ►*n.* **1.** One that records: *a video recorder.* **2.** A flute with eight finger holes and a whistlelike mouthpiece.

re•cord•ing (rĭ-kôr′dĭng) ►*n.* **1.** Something on which sound or images have been recorded. **2.** A recorded sound or picture.

re•count (rĭ-kount′) ►*v.* To narrate the facts or particulars of. See Syns at **describe.** [< OFr. *reconter.*]

re-count (rē-kount′) ►*v.* To count again. ►*n.* (*also* rē′kount′). An additional count, as of votes.

re•coup (rĭ-ko͞op′) ►*v.* **1.** To receive an equivalent for (e.g., a loss). **2.** To reimburse. [< OFr. *recouper*, cut back.]

re•course (rē′kôrs′, -kōrs′, rĭ-kôrs′, -kōrs′) ►*n.* **1.** A turning or applying to a person or thing for aid or security: *have recourse to the courts.* **2.** One that is turned to for aid or security. [< Lat. *recursus*, a running back.]

re•cov•er (rĭ-kŭv′ər) ►*v.* **1.** To get back; regain. **2.** To regain a usual condition, as of health. **3.** To procure (usable substances) from unusable substances, such as waste. **4.** To receive a favorable judgment in a lawsuit. [< Lat. *recuperāre.*] —**re•cov′er•a•ble** *adj.* —**re•cov′er•y** *n.*

rec•re•ant (rĕk′rē-ənt) ►*adj.* **1.** Unfaithful or disloyal. **2.** Craven or cowardly. ►*n.* **1.** A faithless or disloyal person. **2.** A coward. [< OFr. < *recroire*, remember : RE– + Lat. *crēdere*, believe.] —**rec′re•ance, rec′re•an•cy** *n.*

re-cre•ate (rē′krē-āt′) ►*v.* To create anew. —**re′-cre•a′tion** *n.*

rec•re•a•tion (rĕk′rē-ā′shən) ▸*n.* Refreshment of one's mind or body through activity that amuses or stimulates; play. [< Lat. *recreāre*, refresh.] —**rec′re•ate′** *v.* —**rec′re•a′tion•al** *adj.*

recreational vehicle ▸*n.* A vehicle, such as a camper or motor home, used for traveling and recreation.

re•crim•i•nate (rĭ-krĭm′ə-nāt′) ▸*v.* **-nat•ed, -nat•ing.** To counter one accusation with another. [Med.Lat. *recrīmināri.*] —**re•crim′i•na′tion** *n.* —**re•crim′i•na′tive, re•crim′i•na•to′ry** (-nə-tôr′ē, -tōr′ē) *adj.*

re•cru•desce (rē′kro͞o-dĕs′) ▸*v.* **-desced, -desc•ing.** To break out anew, as after an inactive period. [Lat. *recrūdēscere.*] —**re′cru•des′cence** *n.* —**re′cru•des′cent** *adj.*

re•cruit (rĭ-kro͞ot′) ▸*v.* **1.** To seek out and engage (persons), as for work or military service. **2.** To strengthen or raise (an armed force) by enlistment. ▸*n.* A newly engaged member of a military force or other organization. [< OFr. *recroistre*, grow again.] —**re•cruit′er** *n.* —**re•cruit′ment** *n.*

rec•tal (rĕk′təl) ▸*adj.* Of or situated near the rectum. —**rec′tal•ly** *adv.*

rec•tan•gle (rĕk′tăng′gəl) ▸*n.* A parallelogram with four right angles. [< Med.Lat. *rēctangulum.*] —**rec•tan′gu•lar** *adj.* —**rec•tan′gu•lar′i•ty** (-lăr′ĭ-tē) *n.*

rec•ti•fy (rĕk′tə-fī′) ▸*v.* **-fied, -fy•ing.** To set right; correct. [< Lat. *rēctus*, right.] —**rec′ti•fi′a•ble** *adj.* —**rec′ti•fi•ca′tion** *n.*

rec•ti•lin•e•ar (rĕk′tə-lĭn′ē-ər) ▸*adj.* Moving in, bounded by, or characterized by a straight line or lines. [< LLat. *rēctilīneus.*]

rec•ti•tude (rĕk′tĭ-to͞od′, -tyo͞od′) ▸*n.* Moral uprightness. [< LLat. *rēctitūdō.*]

rec•to (rĕk′tō) ▸*n.*, *pl.* **-tos.** A right-hand page. [< Lat. *(foliō) rēctō*, (the leaf) being right.]

rec•tor (rĕk′tər) ▸*n.* **1.** A cleric in charge of a parish. **2.** A Roman Catholic priest serving as managerial and spiritual head of a church or other institution. **3.** The principal of certain schools, colleges, and universities. [< Lat. *rēctor*, director.]

rec•to•ry (rĕk′tə-rē) ▸*n.*, *pl.* **-ries.** The house in which a rector lives.

rec•tum (rĕk′təm) ▸*n.*, *pl.* **-tums** or **-ta** (-tə). The terminal portion of the large intestine, extending from the colon to the anal canal. [< Lat. *(intestīnum) rēctum*, straight (intestine).]

re•cum•bent (rĭ-kŭm′bənt) ▸*adj.* Lying down; reclining. [< Lat. *recumbere*, lie down.]

re•cu•per•ate (rĭ-ko͞o′pə-rāt′, -kyo͞o′-) ▸*v.* **-at•ed, -at•ing 1.** To return to health or strength; recover. **2.** To regain: *recuperate losses.* [Lat. *recuperāre.*] —**re•cu′per•a′tion** *n.* —**re•cu′per•a′tive** (-pə-rā′tĭv, -pər-ə-tĭv) *adj.*

re•cur (rĭ-kûr′) ▸*v.* **-curred, -cur•ring.** To happen, come up, or show up again or repeatedly. [Lat. *recurrere.*] —**re•cur′rence** *n.* —**re•cur′rent** *adj.* —**re•cur′rent•ly** *adv.*

re•curve (rē-kûrv′) ▸*v.* To curve backward or downward.

re•cy•cle (rē-sī′kəl) ▸*v.* **-cled, -cling 1.** To put or pass through a cycle again, as for further treatment. **2.** To reprocess and use again: *recycle aluminum cans.* —**re•cy′cla•ble** *adj.* & *n.* —**re•cy′cler** *n.*

red (rĕd) ▸*n.* **1a.** Any of a group of colors whose hue resembles that of blood. **b.** The hue of the long-wave end of the visible spectrum. **2.** often **Red** A revolutionary, esp. a Communist. ▸*adj.* **red•der, red•dest 1.** Of the color red. **2a.** Having a red or reddish color: *red hair.* **b.** Ruddy or flushed: *red with embarrassment.* **3.** often **Red** Communist. —***idiom:* in the red** Operating at a loss; in debt. [< OE *rēad.*] —**red′ness** *n.*

red blood cell ▸*n.* A cell in the blood of vertebrates that transports oxygen and carbon dioxide to and from the tissues.

red-blood•ed (rĕd′blŭd′ĭd) ▸*adj.* Strong and highly spirited.

red•breast (rĕd′brĕst′) ▸*n.* A bird, such as the robin, with a red or reddish breast.

red card ▸*n.* A red-colored card shown by a referee, esp. in soccer, to eject a player from the game. —**red′-card′** *v.*

Red Cloud. 1822–1909. Oglala Sioux leader.

Red Cloud

red•coat (rĕd′kōt′) ▸*n.* A British soldier, esp. during the American Revolution.

red•den (rĕd′n) ▸*v.* To make or become red.

red•dish (rĕd′ĭsh) ▸*adj.* Mixed or tinged with red; somewhat red. —**red′dish•ness** *n.*

re•deem (rĭ-dēm′) ▸*v.* **1.** To recover ownership of by paying a specified sum. **2.** To pay off (e.g., a promissory note). **3.** To turn in (e.g., coupons) and receive something in exchange. **4.** To set free; rescue. **5.** To save from sinfulness. **6.** To make up for: *redeem an earlier mistake.* [< Lat. *redimere.*] —**re•deem′a•ble** *adj.* —**re•deem′er** *n.*

re•demp•tion (rĭ-dĕmp′shən) ▸*n.* The act of redeeming or state of being redeemed. [< Lat. *redimere, redēmpt-*, buy back.] —**re•demp′tion•al, re•demp′tive** *adj.*

red-faced (rĕd′fāst′) ▸*adj.* Embarrassed.

red flag ▸*n.* **1.** A warning signal. **2.** Something that provokes an irritated reaction.

red giant ▸*n.* A star of great size and brightness with a relatively low surface temperature.

red-hand•ed (rĕd′hăn′dĭd) ▸*adv.* & *adj.* In the act of committing something wrong.

red•head (rĕd′hĕd′) ▸*n.* A person with red hair.

red herring ▸*n.* Something that draws attention away from the central issue.

red-hot (rĕd′hŏt′) ▸*adj.* **1.** Glowing hot; very hot. **2.** Very recent: *red-hot information.*

re•dis•trict (rē-dĭs′trĭkt) ▸*v.* To divide again into administrative or election districts.

red-let•ter (rĕd′lĕt′ər) ▸*adj.* Memorably happy: *a red-letter day.* [From marking in red the holy days in church calendars.]

red•line (rĕd′līn′) ▶*v.* **-lined, -lin•ing.** To refuse home mortgages or insurance to areas or neighborhoods deemed poor financial risks.

red•o•lent (rĕd′l-ənt) ▶*adj.* **1.** Strongly scented; aromatic. **2.** Suggestive; reminiscent: *a campaign redolent of machine politics.* [< Lat. *redolēre*, smell.] —**red′o•lence** *n.*

re•doubt (rĭ-dout′) ▶*n.* A small, often temporary defensive fortification. [< Med.Lat. *reductus*, concealed place.]

re•doubt•a•ble (rĭ-dou′tə-bəl) ▶*adj.* **1.** Arousing fear or awe; formidable. **2.** Worthy of respect or honor. [< OFr. *redouter*, to dread.] —**re•doubt′a•bly** *adv.*

re•dound (rĭ-dound′) ▶*v.* **1.** To have an effect or consequence. **2.** To contribute; accrue. [< Lat. *redundāre*, overflow. See REDUNDANT.]

red pepper ▶*n.* **1.** The pungent red fruit of certain pepper plants. **2.** See **cayenne pepper.**

re•dress (rĭ-drĕs′) ▶*v.* **1.** To set right; remedy or rectify. **2.** To make amends to or for. ▶*n.* (*also* rē′drĕs) **1.** Satisfaction for wrong or injury; reparation. **2.** Correction or reformation. [< OFr. *redrecier*, rearrange.]

Red River. A river of the S-central US rising in two branches in the Texas Panhandle and flowing about 1,638 km (1,018 mi) to the Mississippi R.

Red Sea. A sea between NE Africa and the Arabian Peninsula.

red•shift (rĕd′shĭft′) ▶*n.* An increase in the wavelength of radiation emitted by a celestial body due to the Doppler effect.

red snapper ▶*n.* Any of several marine food fishes with red or reddish bodies.

red tape ▶*n.* Official forms and procedures, esp. when oppressively complex and time consuming. [From its former use in tying British official documents.]

red tide ▶*n.* A reddish discoloration of coastal ocean waters caused by a proliferation of red, single-celled organisms that produce toxins harmful to fish and shellfish.

re•duce (rĭ-do͞os′, -dyo͞os′) ▶*v.* **-duced, -duc•ing 1.** To bring down, as in extent, amount, or degree; diminish. **2.** To bring to a humbler, weaker, or more difficult state or condition. **3.** To lower in rank or grade; demote. See Syns at **demote. 4.** To put in order systematically. **5.** To separate into orderly components by analysis. **6.** *Chem.* **a.** To decrease the valence of (an atom) by adding electrons. **b.** To remove oxygen from. **c.** To add hydrogen to. **d.** To change to a metallic state; smelt. **7.** *Math.* To simplify the form of (e.g., a fraction) without changing the value. **8.** To lose weight, as by dieting. [< Lat. *redūcere*, bring back.] —**re•duc′i•bil′i•ty** *n.* —**re•duc′i•ble** *adj.* —**re•duc′tion** (-dŭk′shən) *n.* —**re•duc′tive** *adj.*

re•dun•dan•cy (rĭ-dŭn′dən-sē) ▶*n.*, *pl.* **-cies 1.** The state of being redundant. **2.** An excess. **3.** Unnecessary repetition.

Usage: The usages that critics have condemned as redundancies fall into several classes. In some cases, such as *consensus of opinion,* the use of what is regarded as an unnecessary qualifier can be justified on the grounds that it in fact makes a semantic contribution. A *consensus of opinion* can be distinguished from a consensus of judgments or practice. In other cases the use of the qualifier is harder to defend. Thus there is no way to *revert* without *reverting back* and no *consensus* that is not *general.*

re•dun•dant (rĭ-dŭn′dənt) ▶*adj.* **1.** Exceeding what is necessary or natural; superfluous. **2.** Needlessly repetitive; verbose. [< Lat. *redundāre*, overflow : RE– + *unda*, wave.] —**re•dun′dant•ly** *adv.*

re•du•pli•cate (rĭ-do͞o′plə-kāt′, -dyo͞o′-) ▶*v.* **-cat•ed, -cat•ing 1.** To redouble. **2.** *Ling.* To double (the initial syllable or all of a root word) to form a new word. [LLat. *reduplicāre.*] —**re•du′pli•ca′tion** *n.*

red•wood (rĕd′wo͝od′) ▶*n.* **1.** A very tall evergreen coniferous tree of S Oregon and N California. **2.** Its soft reddish wood.

reed (rēd) ▶*n.* **1a.** Any of various tall, hollow-stemmed aquatic grasses. **b.** The stalk of a reed. **2a.** A flexible strip of cane or metal used in the mouthpiece of certain musical instruments to produce tone by vibrating in response to a stream of air. **b.** An instrument fitted with a reed. [< OE *hrēod.*] —**reed′i•ness** *n.* —**reed′y** *adj.*

Reed, John. 1887–1920. Amer. writer.

Reed, Walter. 1851–1902. Amer. physician and army surgeon.

reef[1] (rēf) ▶*n.* A strip or ridge of rocks, sand, or coral at or near the surface of a body of water. [Obsolete Du. *rif*, poss. < ON, ridge.]

reef[2] (rēf) ▶*n.* A portion of a sail rolled and tied down to lessen the area exposed to the wind. ▶*v.* To reduce the size of (a sail) by tucking in a part. [< ON *rif*, ridge.]

reef•er (rē′fər) ▶*n.* *Slang* Marijuana, esp. a marijuana cigarette. [?]

reek (rēk) ▶*v.* **1.** To smoke, steam, or fume. **2.** To be pervaded by something unpleasant. **3.** To give off a strong, unpleasant odor. ▶*n.* **1.** A stench. See Syns at **stench. 2.** Vapor; steam. [< OE *rēocan.*]

reel[1] (rēl) ▶*n.* **1.** A device, such as a spool, that turns on an axis and is used for winding rope, tape, film, or similar materials. **2.** A cylindrical device on a fishing rod for winding the line. **3.** The quantity of material wound on one reel. ▶*v.* **1.** To wind on a reel. **2.** To recover by winding on a reel: *reel in a fish.* —***phrasal verb:* reel off** To recite fluently: *reeled off a list of names.* [< OE *hrēol.*]

reel[1]
left to right: film and fishing reels

reel[2] (rēl) ▶*v.* **1.** To be thrown off balance or fall back. **2.** To stagger or sway, as from drunkenness. **3.** To feel dizzy, as with confusion. ▶*n.* **1.** A staggering or whirling movement. **2a.** A moderately fast dance of Scottish origin. **b.** The music for this dance. [ME *relen*, whirl about.]

re•en•try also **re-en•try** (rē-ĕn′trē) ▶*n.* **1.** The act of reentering. **2.** The return of a missile or spacecraft into Earth's atmosphere.

re•fec•to•ry (rĭ-fĕk′tə-rē) ▶*n.*, *pl.* **-ries.** A

room where meals are served. [< Lat. *reficere*, *refect-*, refresh.]

re•fer (rĭ-fûr′) ▸*v.* **-ferred, -fer•ring 1.** To direct to a source for help or information. **2.** To direct the attention of. **3.** To pertain; concern. **4.** To make mention or reference. **5.** To have recourse; turn: *refer to a dictionary.* [< Lat. *referre* : RE– + *ferre*, carry.] —**ref′er•a•ble** (rĕf′ər-ə-bəl, rĭ-fûr′-) *adj.* —**re•fer′ral** *n.*

Syns: *refer, advert, mention* ***v.***

ref•e•ree (rĕf′ə-rē′) ▸*n.* **1.** One to whom something is referred, esp. for settlement or decision. **2.** *Sports* An official who supervises play. ▸*v.* **-reed, -ree•ing.** To act as referee (at or for).

ref•er•ence (rĕf′ər-əns, rĕf′rəns) ▸*n.* **1.** An act of referring. **2.** Regard; respect: *with reference to.* **3.** A mention or an allusion. **4.** A note in a publication referring the reader to another passage or source. **5.** A work frequently used as a source. **6a.** A person who is in a position to recommend another, as for a job. **b.** A statement about a person's qualifications and character. —**ref′er•en′tial** (-ə-rĕn′shəl) *adj.*

ref•er•en•dum (rĕf′ə-rĕn′dəm) ▸*n., pl.* **-dums** or **-da** (-də) **1.** The submission of a proposed public measure or actual statute to a direct popular vote. **2.** Such a vote. [Lat., thing to be referred.]

re•fill (rē-fĭl′) ▸*v.* To fill again. ▸*n.* (rē′fĭl′) **1.** A replacement for the used contents of a container. **2.** An additional filling.

re•fine (rĭ-fīn′) ▸*v.* **-fined, -fin•ing 1.** To reduce to a pure state; purify. **2.** To free from coarse characteristics: *refined his manners.* —**re•fin′er** *n.*

re•fined (rĭ-fīnd′) ▸*adj.* **1.** Free from coarseness or vulgarity. **2.** Free of impurities. **3.** Precise to a fine degree.

re•fine•ment (rĭ-fīn′mənt) ▸*n.* **1.** The act of refining or the condition of being refined. **2.** An improvement. **3.** Fineness, as of expression or taste. **4.** A subtle distinction.

re•fin•er•y (rĭ-fī′nə-rē) ▸*n., pl.* **-ies.** An industrial plant for purifying a crude substance, such as petroleum or sugar.

re•flect (rĭ-flĕkt′) ▸*v.* **1.** To throw or bend back (e.g., light) from a surface. See Syns at **echo. 2.** To form an image of; mirror. **3.** To manifest; show: *Her work reflects intelligence.* **4.** To think seriously. [< Lat. *reflectere*, bend back.] —**re•flec′tion** *n.* —**re•flec′tive** *adj.* —**re•flec′tive•ly** *adv.*

re•flec•tor (rĭ-flĕk′tər) ▸*n.* Something, such as a surface, that reflects.

re•flex (rē′flĕks′) ▸*adj.* **1.** Bent, turned, or thrown back. **2.** Involuntary or automatic: *a reflex response.* ▸*n.* **1a.** Something reflected. **b.** An image produced by reflection. **2.** An involuntary, unlearned, or instinctive response to a stimulus. [< Lat. *reflexus*, p.part. of *reflectere*, bend back.]

re•flex•ive (rĭ-flĕk′sĭv) ▸*adj.* **1.** Directed back on itself. **2.** *Gram.* **a.** Of or being a verb having an identical subject and direct object, as *dressed* in the sentence *She dressed herself.* **b.** Of or being the pronoun used as the direct object of a reflexive verb, as *herself* in *She dressed herself.* **3.** Of or relating to a reflex. **4.** Elicited automatically; spontaneous. —**re•flex′ive** *n.* —**re•flex′ive•ly** *adv.* —**re•flex′ive•ness, re′flex•iv′i•ty** (rē′flĕk-sĭv′ĭ-tē) *n.*

re•for•est (rē-fôr′ĭst, -fŏr′ĭst) ▸*v.* To replant (an area) with trees. —**re′for•es•ta′tion** *n.*

re•form (rĭ-fôrm′) ▸*v.* **1.** To improve by correcting errors, or removing defects. **2.** To abolish abuse or malpractice in. **3.** To give up harmful or immoral practices. ▸*n.* **1.** A change for the better; an improvement. **2.** Action to improve social or economic conditions. ▸*adj.* **Reform.** Of a branch of Judaism that does not require strict observance of traditional religious law and ritual. [< Lat. *refōrmāre*.] —**re•form′a•ble** *adj.* —**re•for′ma•tive** *adj.* —**re•formed′** *adj.* —**re•form′er** *n.*

ref•or•ma•tion (rĕf′ər-mā′shən) ▸*n.* **1.** The act of reforming or the state of being reformed. **2. Reformation** A 16th-cent. movement in Western Europe for the reform of the Roman Catholic Church that resulted in the establishment of the Protestant and other churches. —**ref′or•ma′tion•al** *adj.*

re•for•ma•to•ry (rĭ-fôr′mə-tôr′ē, -tōr′ē) ▸*n., pl.* **-ries.** A penal institution for young offenders.

re•fract (rĭ-frăkt′) ▸*v.* To deflect from a straight path by refraction. [Lat. *refringere*, *refrăct-*, break up.]

re•frac•tion (rĭ-frăk′shən) ▸*n.* The turning or bending of wave when it passes from one medium into another of different density. —**re•frac′tion•al, re•frac′tive** *adj.* —**re•frac′tive•ly** *adv.* —**re•frac′tive•ness, re′frac•tiv′i•ty** (rē′frăk-tĭv′ĭ-tē) *n.*

re•frac•to•ry (rĭ-frăk′tə-rē) ▸*adj.* **1.** Resistant to authority or control; obstinate. **2.** Difficult to melt or work. ▸*n., pl.* **-ries.** A material that has a high melting point. —**re•frac′to•ri•ly** *adv.* —**re•frac′to•ri•ness** *n.*

re•frain[1] (rĭ-frān′) ▸*v.* To hold oneself back; forbear: *refrained from swearing.* [< Lat. *refrēnāre*, restrain.]

Syns: *refrain, abstain, forbear* ***v.***

re•frain[2] (rĭ-frān′) ▸*n.* A phrase or verse repeated at intervals throughout a song or poem. [< OFr. *refraindre*, repeat.]

re•fresh (rĭ-frĕsh′) ▸*v.* **1.** To revive with or as if with rest or food. **2.** To make cool, clean, or moist; freshen up. **3.** To renew by stimulation: *refresh one's memory.* **4.** To replenish: *refresh a drink.* —**re•fresh′er** *n.* —**re•fresh′ing** *adj.*

re•fresh•ment (rĭ-frĕsh′mənt) ▸*n.* **1.** The act of refreshing or the state of being refreshed. **2.** Something that refreshes. **3. refreshments** A snack or light meal.

re•frig•er•ant (rĭ-frĭj′ər-ənt) ▸*n.* A substance, such as air, ammonia, water, or carbon dioxide, used to provide cooling.

re•frig•er•ate (rĭ-frĭj′ə-rāt′) ▸*v.* **-at•ed, -at•ing 1.** To cool or chill (a substance). **2.** To preserve (food) by chilling. [Lat. *refrīgerāre*.] —**re•frig′er•a′tion** *n.*

re•frig•er•a•tor (rĭ-frĭj′ə-rā′tər) ▸*n.* A cabinet for storing food or other substances at a low temperature.

ref•uge (rĕf′yo͞oj) ▸*n.* **1.** Protection or shelter, as from danger or hardship. **2.** A place providing protection or shelter; sanctuary. [< Lat. *refugere*, flee.]

ref•u•gee (rĕf′yo͞o-jē′) ▸*n.* One who flees in search of refuge, as from war or political oppression.

re•ful•gent (rĭ-fo͝ol′jənt, -fŭl′-) ▸*adj.* Shining

radiantly; resplendent. [< Lat. *refulgēre*, flash back.] —**re•ful′gence** *n.*

re•fund (rĭ-fŭnd′, rē′fŭnd′) ▸*v.* To give back, (esp. money); repay. ▸*n.* (rē′fŭnd′) **1.** A repayment of funds. **2.** An amount repaid. [< Lat. *refundere*, pour back.] —**re•fund′a•ble** *adj.*

re•fur•bish (rē-fûr′bĭsh) ▸*v.* To make clean, bright, or fresh again; restore. —**re•fur′bish•ment** *n.*

re•fuse[1] (rĭ-fyo͞oz′) ▸*v.* **-fused, -fus•ing.** To decline to do, accept, give, or allow. [< VLat. **refūsāre.*] —**re•fus′al** *n.*

ref•use[2] (rĕf′yo͞os) ▸*n.* Anything discarded or rejected as useless or worthless; trash. [< OFr. *refus.*]

re•fute (rĭ-fyo͞ot′) ▸*v.* **-fut•ed, -fut•ing.** To prove to be false or erroneous. [Lat. *refūtāre.*] —**re•fut′a•ble** (rĭ-fyo͞o′tə-bəl, rĕf′yə-tə-) *adj.* —**re•fut′a•bly** *adv.* —**ref′u•ta′tion** *n.* —**re•fut′er** *n.*

reg. ▸*abbr.* **1.** regent **2.** regiment **3.** region **4.** registered **5.** registrar **6.** registry **7.** regular

re•gain (rē-gān′) ▸*v.* **1.** To recover possession of. **2.** To reach again.

re•gal (rē′gəl) ▸*adj.* Of a monarch; royal. [< Lat. *rēgālis.*] —**re′gal•ly** *adv.*

re•gale (rĭ-gāl′) ▸*v.* **-galed, -gal•ing 1.** To delight or entertain. **2.** To entertain sumptuously. [< OFr. *regal*, feast.]

re•ga•lia (rĭ-gāl′yə, -gā′lē-ə) ▸*pl.n.* *(takes sing. or pl. v.)* **1.** The emblems and symbols of royalty. **2.** The distinguishing symbols of a rank, office, order, or society. **3.** Magnificent attire; finery. [< Lat. *rēgālis*, regal.]

re•gard (rĭ-gärd′) ▸*v.* **1.** To look at attentively; observe. **2.** To look upon or consider: *I regard him as my best friend.* **3.** To hold in esteem or respect. **4.** To relate or refer to; concern. **5.** To take into account. ▸*n.* **1.** A look or gaze. **2.** Careful thought or attention; heed. **3a.** Respect, affection, or esteem. **b. regards** Good wishes: *Give her my regards.* **4.** Respect: *lucky in that regard.* **5.** Reference or relation: *in regard to her.* [< OFr. *regarder.*] —**re•gard′ful** *adj.*

Usage: *Regard* is traditionally used in the singular in the phrase *in regard to.*

re•gard•ing (rĭ-gär′dĭng) ▸*prep.* In reference to; concerning.

re•gard•less (rĭ-gärd′lĭs) ▸*adv.* In spite of everything; anyway. ▸*adj.* Heedless; unmindful. —**re•gard′less•ly** *adv.*

re•gat•ta (rĭ-gä′tə, -găt′ə) ▸*n.* A boat race or a series of boat races. [Ital.]

re•gen•cy (rē′jən-sē) ▸*n., pl.* **-cies 1.** A person or group governing in place of a monarch who is absent, disabled, or still in minority. **2.** The period during which a regent governs. **3.** The office, region, or government of regents or a regent.

re•gen•er•ate (rĭ-jĕn′ə-rāt′) ▸*v.* **-at•ed, -at•ing 1.** To reform spiritually or morally. **2.** To form, construct, or create anew. **3.** To give new life or energy to; revitalize. ▸*adj.* (-ər-ĭt) **1.** Spiritually or morally reformed. **2.** Formed or created anew. **3.** Refreshed or renewed. —**re•gen′er•a′tion** *n.* —**re•gen′er•a′tive** *adj.* —**re•gen′er•a′tor** *n.*

re•gent (rē′jənt) ▸*n.* **1.** One who rules during the minority, absence, or disability of a monarch. **2.** One acting as a ruler or governor. **3.** A member of a governing board of an institution, as a state university. [< Lat. *regere*, to rule.]

reg•gae (rĕg′ā) ▸*n.* Popular music of Jamaican origin having a strongly accentuated offbeat. [Jamaican E.]

reg•i•cide (rĕj′ĭ-sīd′) ▸*n.* **1.** The killing of a king. **2.** One who kills a king. [Lat. *rēx*, king + -CIDE.] —**reg′i•cid′al** *adj.*

re•gime (rā-zhēm′, rĭ-) ▸*n.* **1.** A government in power; administration. **2.** A regulated system, as of diet and exercise; regimen. [< Lat. *regimen.*]

reg•i•men (rĕj′ə-mən, -mĕn′) ▸*n.* **1.** Governmental rule or control. **2.** A system or course, as of diet or exercise. [< Lat.]

reg•i•ment (rĕj′ə-mənt) ▸*n.* A military unit of ground troops consisting of at least two battalions. ▸*v.* (rĕj′ə-mĕnt′) **1.** To put into order; systematize. **2.** To subject to uniformity and rigid order. [< LLat. *regimentum*, rule.] —**reg′i•men′tal** *adj.* —**reg′i•men•ta′tion** *n.*

Re•gi•na (rĭ-jī′nə) The capital of Saskatchewan, Canada, in the S part. Pop. 179,178.

re•gion (rē′jən) ▸*n.* **1.** A large, usu. continuous segment of a surface or space; area. **2.** A specified district or territory. **3.** An area of the body: *the abdominal region.* [< Lat. *regiō.*]

re•gion•al (rē′jə-nəl) ▸*adj.* **1.** Of or relating to a large geographic region. **2.** Of or characteristic of a particular region: *a regional accent.* —**re′gion•al•ly** *adv.*

reg•is•ter (rĕj′ĭ-stər) ▸*n.* **1a.** An official recording of items, names, or actions. **b.** A book for such entries. **2.** A device that automatically records a quantity or number. **3.** A grill-like device through which heated or cooled air is released into a room. **4.** A state of proper alignment or adjustment. **5.** *Mus.* The range or part of the range of an instrument or voice. ▸*v.* **1a.** To enter in an official register. **b.** To enroll; esp. in order to vote or attend classes. **2.** To indicate on an instrument or a scale. **3.** To reveal; express: *Her face registered surprise.* **4.** To cause (mail) to be officially recorded by payment of a fee. **5.** To make an impression in the mind: *The warning failed to register.* [< Lat. *regestus*, recorded.] —**reg′is•tra•ble** (-ĭ-strə-bəl) *adj.* —**reg′is•trant** *n.*

reg•is•tered nurse (rĕj′ĭ-stərd) ▸*n.* A graduate trained nurse who has passed a state registration examination and has been licensed to practice nursing.

reg•is•trar (rĕj′ĭ-strär′, rĕj′ĭ-strär′) ▸*n.* An official, as of a university or corporation, who is in charge of keeping records.

reg•is•tra•tion (rĕj′ĭ-strā′shən) ▸*n.* **1.** The act or process of registering. **2.** The number of persons registered; enrollment. **3.** A document certifying registering.

reg•is•try (rĕj′ĭ-strē) ▸*n., pl.* **-tries 1.** Registration. **2.** A place where official records are kept.

reg•nant (rĕg′nənt) ▸*adj.* Reigning; ruling. [< Lat. *rēgnāre*, reign.]

re•gress (rĭ-grĕs′) ▸*v.* **1.** To go back; move backward. **2.** To return to a previous, usu. worse or less developed state. [Lat. *regredī, regress-.*] —**re′gress′** *n.*

re•gres•sion (rĭ-grĕsh′ən) ▸*n.* **1.** Backward movement. **2.** Relapse to a less perfect or developed state.

re•gres•sive (rĭ-grĕs′ĭv) ▸*adj.* **1.** Tending to regress. **2.** Marked by regression. **3.** Decreasing proportionately as the amount taxed increases. —**re•gres′sive•ly** *adv.* —**re•gres′sive•ness** *n.*

re•gret (rĭ-grĕt′) ►*v.* **-gret•ted, -gret•ting 1.** To feel sorry, disappointed, or distressed about. **2.** To mourn. ►*n.* **1.** A sense of loss and longing for someone or something gone. **2.** Distress about something that one wishes could be different. **3. regrets** A courteous refusal of an invitation. [< OFr. *regreter*, lament.] —**re•gret′ful** *adj.* —**re•gret′ful•ly** *adv.* —**re•gret′ful•ness** *n.* —**re•gret′ta•ble** *adj.* —**re•gret′ta•bly** *adv.* —**re•gret′ter** *n.*

re•group (rē-gro͞op′) ►*v.* **1.** To arrange in a new grouping. **2.** To reorganize for renewed effort, as after a setback.

regt. ►*abbr.* regiment

reg•u•lar (rĕg′yə-lər) ►*adj.* **1.** Customary, usual, or normal. **2.** Orderly, even, or symmetrical. **3.** Conforming to a fixed procedure, principle, or discipline. **4.** Well-ordered; methodical. **5.** Occurring at fixed or normal intervals; periodic. **6.** Not varying; constant. **7.** Formally correct; proper. **8.** *Informal* Complete; thorough: *a regular scoundrel.* **9.** *Informal* Good; nice: *a regular guy.* **10.** *Gram.* Conforming to the usual pattern of inflection, derivation, or word formation. **11.** *Math.* **a.** Having equal sides and angles. **b.** Having faces that are congruent regular polygons and congruent polyhedral angles. **12.** Belonging to or constituting the permanent army of a nation. ►*n.* **1.** A soldier in a regular army. **2.** A dependable, loyal person. **3.** A habitual customer. [< Lat. *rēgula*, rule.] —**reg′u•lar′i•ty** (-lăr′ĭ-tē) *n.* —**reg′u•lar•ly** *adv.*

reg•u•lar•ize (rĕg′yə-lə-rīz′) ►*v.* **-ized, -iz•ing.** To make regular. —**reg′u•lar•i•za′tion** *n.*

reg•u•late (rĕg′yə-lāt′) ►*v.* **-lat•ed, -lat•ing 1.** To control or direct according to rule, principle, or law. **2.** To adjust to a specification or requirement: *regulate temperature.* **3.** To adjust for accurate and proper functioning. [< Lat. *rēgula*, rule.] —**reg′u•la′tive, reg′u•la•to′ry** (-lə-tôr′ē, -tōr′ē) *adj.* —**reg′u•la′tor** *n.*

reg•u•la•tion (rĕg′yə-lā′shən) ►*n.* **1.** The act of regulating or the state of being regulated. **2.** A principle, rule, or law for controlling or governing conduct. **3.** A governmental order having the force of law.

re•gur•gi•tate (rē-gûr′jĭ-tāt′) ►*v.* **-tat•ed, -tat•ing.** To vomit. [Med.Lat. *regurgitāre*, overflow.] —**re•gur′gi•ta′tion** *n.*

re•ha•bil•i•tate (rē′hə-bĭl′ĭ-tāt′) ►*v.* **-tat•ed, -tat•ing 1.** To restore to health or useful life, as through therapy and education. **2.** To restore the former rank, privileges, or good name of. [Med.Lat. *rehabilitāre.*] —**re′ha•bil′i•ta′tion** *n.* —**re′ha•bil′i•ta′tive** *adj.*

re•hash (rē-hăsh′) ►*v.* To repeat, rework, rewrite: *rehash old ideas.* —**re′hash′** *n.*

re•hears•al (rĭ-hûr′səl) ►*n.* **1.** The act of practicing in preparation for a public performance. **2.** A session of practice for a performance, as of a play.

re•hearse (rĭ-hûrs′) ►*v.* **-hearsed, -hears•ing 1.** To practice in preparation for a public performance. **2.** To perfect (an action) by repetition. See Syns at **practice. 3.** To retell or recite. [< OFr. *rehercier*, repeat.]

Rehn•quist (rĕn′kwĭst′), **William Hubbs.** b. 1924. Amer. jurist; associate justice of the US Supreme Court (1972–86) and chief justice (since 1986).

reign (rān) ►*n.* **1.** Exercise of sovereign power, as by a monarch. **2.** The period during which a monarch rules. **3.** Dominance or widespread influence. [< Lat. *rēgnum.*] —**reign** *v.*

re•im•burse (rē′ĭm-bûrs′) ►*v.* **-bursed, -burs•ing.** To pay back. [RE– + *imburse*, pay.] —**re′im•burs′a•ble** *adj.* —**re′im•burse′ment** *n.*

Reims (rēmz, răNs) See **Rheims.**

rein (rān) ►*n.* **1.** often **reins** A long, narrow leather strap attached to each end of the bit of a bridle and used by a rider or driver to control a horse or other animal. **2.** A means of restraint, check, or guidance. ►*v.* **1.** To check or hold back by or as if by the use of reins. **2.** To restrain or control. —***idiom:* give (free) rein to** To release from restraints. [< Lat. *retinēre*, retain.]

re•in•car•na•tion (rē′ĭn-kär-nā′shən) ►*n.* **1.** Rebirth of the soul in another body. **2.** A new embodiment. —**re′in•car′nate** *v.*

rein•deer (rān′dîr′) ►*n.*, *pl.* **-deer** or **-deers.** A large deer of arctic regions, having branched antlers. [ON *hreinn* + DEER.]

re•in•force (rē′ĭn-fôrs′, -fōrs′) ►*v.* **-forced, -forc•ing 1.** To strengthen or support. **2.** To strengthen with additional personnel or equipment. **3.** *Psychol.* To reward (e.g., a desired response) in order to encourage its repetition. [RE– + *inforce* (var. of ENFORCE).] —**re′in•force′ment** *n.* —**re′in•forc′er** *n.*

re•in•forced concrete (rē′ĭn-fôrst′, -fōrst′) ►*n.* Poured concrete containing steel bars or metal netting to increase strength.

re•in•state (rē′ĭn-stāt′) ►*v.* **-stat•ed, -stat•ing.** To restore to a previous condition or position. —**re′in•state′ment** *n.*

re•it•er•ate (rē-ĭt′ə-rāt′) ►*v.* **-at•ed, -at•ing.** To say again or repeatedly. See Syns at **repeat.** —**re•it′er•a′tion** *n.* —**re•it′er•a′tive** (-ə-rā′tĭv, -ər-ə-tĭv) *adj.*

re•ject (rĭ-jĕkt′) ►*v.* **1.** To refuse to accept, submit to, believe, or make use of. **2.** To refuse to consider or grant; deny. **3.** To discard as defective or useless. ►*n.* (rē′jĕkt). One that has been rejected. [< Lat. *rēicere*, *rēiect-*, throw back.] —**re•jec′tion** *n.*

re•joice (rĭ-jois′) ►*v.* **-joiced, -joic•ing.** To feel joyful or be delighted. [< OFr. *rejoir.*] —**re•joic′ing** *n.*

re•join¹ (rĭ-join′) ►*v.* To say in reply; answer. [< OFr. *rejoindre.*]

re•join² (rē-join′) ►*v.* To come or join together again.

re•join•der (rĭ-join′dər) ►*n.* An answer, esp. to a reply. [< OFr. *rejoindre*, answer.]

re•ju•ve•nate (rĭ-jo͞o′və-nāt′) ►*v.* **-nat•ed, -nat•ing.** To restore to youthful vigor or appearance. [< RE– + Lat. *iuvenis*, young.] —**re•ju′ve•na′tion** *n.* —**re•ju′ve•na′tor** (-tər) *n.*

re•lapse (rĭ-lăps′) ►*v.* **-lapsed, -laps•ing 1.** To fall or slide back into a former state. **2.** To regress after partial recovery from illness. ►*n.* (rē′lăps, rĭ-lăps′). A falling back into a former state, esp. after improvement. [< Lat. *relābī*, *relāps-*, slip back.]

re•late (rĭ-lāt′) ►*v.* **-lat•ed, -lat•ing 1.** To narrate or tell. See Syns at **describe. 2.** To bring into logical or natural association. **3.** To establish or demonstrate a connection between. **4.** To have connection, relation, or reference. **5.** To interact with others. [< Lat. *referre, relāt-*.] —**re•lat′a•ble** *adj.*

re•lat•ed (rĭ-lā′tĭd) ►*adj.* **1.** Connected; associated. **2.** Connected by kinship, common origin, or marriage. —**re•lat′ed•ness** *n.*

re•la•tion (rĭ-lā′shən) ►*n.* **1.** A logical or natural association between two or more things. **2.** The connection of people by blood or marriage; kinship. **3.** A relative. **4. relations a.** Mutual dealings or connections, as among persons, groups, or nations. **b.** Sexual intercourse. **5.** Reference; regard. **6.** The act of telling or narrating. —**re•la′tion•ship′** *n.*

rel•a•tive (rĕl′ə-tĭv) ►*adj.* **1.** Connected or related. **2.** Considered in comparison to or dependent on something else. See Syns at **dependent. 3.** *Gram.* Referring to or qualifying an antecedent, as the pronoun *who* in *the man who was on TV.* ►*n.* **1.** One related by kinship or marriage. **2.** Something related or connected to something else. —**rel′a•tive•ly** *adv.* —**rel′a•tive•ness** *n.*

relative clause ►*n.* A dependent clause introduced by a relative pronoun, as *which is downstairs* in *The dining room, which is downstairs, is too dark.*

relative humidity ►*n.* The ratio of the amount of water vapor in the air at a specific temperature to the maximum capacity of the air at that temperature.

rel•a•tiv•ism (rĕl′ə-tĭ-vĭz′əm) ►*n. Philos.* A theory that conceptions of truth and moral values are not absolute but are relative to the persons holding them.

rel•a•tiv•ist (rĕl′ə-tĭ-vĭst) ►*n.* **1.** *Philos.* A proponent of relativism. **2.** A physicist who specializes in the theories of relativity.

rel•a•tiv•i•ty (rĕl′ə-tĭv′ĭ-tē) ►*n.* **1.** The quality or state of being relative. **2.** *Phys.* **a.** Special relativity. **b.** General relativity.

re•lax (rĭ-lăks′) ►*v.* **1.** To make or become less tight. **2.** To make or become less severe or strict. **3.** To relieve from tension or strain. **4.** To take one's ease; rest. [< Lat. *relaxāre.*] —**re′lax•a′tion** (rē′lăk-sā′shən) *n.* —**re•lax′er** *n.*

re•lax•ant (rĭ-lăk′sənt) ►*n.* Something, such as a medicament, that relieves muscular or nervous tension. —**re•lax′ant** *adj.*

re•lay (rē′lā) ►*n.* **1.** An act of passing something along, as from one person to another. **2.** A relay race. **3.** *Electron.* A device that responds to a small current or voltage change by activating switches or other devices in an electric circuit. **4.** A fresh team or crew that relieves another. ►*v.* (rē′lā, rĭ-lā′) **1.** To pass or send along. **2.** To supply with fresh relays. [< OFr. *relai*, fresh team of hunting dogs.]

relay race ►*n.* A race between two or more teams in which each team member runs part of the race and is then relieved by a teammate.

re•lease (rĭ-lēs′) ►*v.* **-leased, -leas•ing 1.** To set free from confinement or restraint. **2.** To free or unfasten; let go. **3.** To dismiss, as from a job. **4.** To issue for performance, sale, publication, or distribution. **5.** To relinquish (e.g., a right.) ►*n.* **1.** An act of releasing. **2.** A device or catch for locking or releasing a mechanism. **3.** Something issued or made public. **4.** The document authorizing the relinquishment of a right or claim. [< Lat. *relaxāre*, relax.] —**re•leas′a•ble** *adj.* —**re•leas′er** *n.*

rel•e•gate (rĕl′ĭ-gāt′) ►*v.* **-gat•ed, -gat•ing 1.** To assign to an obscure place or position. **2.** To assign to a category; classify. **3.** To refer or assign (e.g., a task) for decision or action. **4.** To exile; banish. [< Lat. *relēgāre*, send away.] —**rel′e•ga′tion** *n.*

re•lent (rĭ-lĕnt′) ►*v.* To become more lenient or forgiving. [< AN *relenter.*]

re•lent•less (rĭ-lĕnt′lĭs) ►*adj.* **1.** Unyielding; pitiless. **2.** Steady and persistent. —**re•lent′less•ly** *adv.* —**re•lent′less•ness** *n.*

rel•e•vant (rĕl′ə-vənt) ►*adj.* Having to do with the matter at hand. [< *relevāre*, raise up.] —**rel′e•vance, rel′e•van•cy** *n.* —**rel′e•vant•ly** *adv.*

re•li•a•ble (rĭ-lī′ə-bəl) ►*adj.* Capable of being relied on; dependable. —**re•li′a•bil′i•ty, re•li′a•ble•ness** *n.* —**re•li′a•bly** *adv.*

Syns: *reliable, dependable, responsible, trustworthy, trusty* **adj.**

re•li•ant (rĭ-lī′ənt) ►*adj.* Having or exhibiting trust in or dependence on something. —**re•li′ance** *n.* —**re•li′ant•ly** *adv.*

rel•ic (rĕl′ĭk) ►*n.* **1.** Something that has survived from an extinct culture or bygone period. **2.** A memento; keepsake. **3.** An object of religious veneration. **4.** or **relics** A corpse; remains. [< Lat. *reliquus*, remaining.]

re•lief (rĭ-lēf′) ►*n.* **1.** The easing of a burden or distress. **2.** Something that alleviates pain or distress. **3.** Aid, as given to the needy or disaster victims. **4a.** Release from a post or duty. **b.** One who releases another by taking over a post or duty. **5.** The projection of figures or forms from a flat background, as in sculpture. **6.** The variations in elevation of an area of the earth's surface. [< OFr. *relever*, relieve.]

relief map ►*n.* A map that depicts land configuration, usu. with contour lines.

re•lieve (rĭ-lēv′) ►*v.* **-lieved, -liev•ing 1.** To lessen or alleviate. **2.** To free from pain, anxiety, or distress. **3.** To assist; aid. **4.** To free from a specified duty or obligation, esp. by providing a substitute. **5.** To make less tedious or unpleasant. **6.** To make distinct by contrast; set off. [< Lat. *relevāre*, lift up.] —**re•liev′er** *n.*

re•li•gion (rĭ-lĭj′ən) ►*n.* **1a.** Belief in and reverence for a supernatural power or powers regarded as creator or governor of the universe. **b.** A personal or institutionalized system grounded in such belief. **2.** A cause or activity pursued with zeal or conscientious devotion. [< Lat. *religiō.*]

re•li•gious (rĭ-lĭj′əs) ►*adj.* **1.** Having belief in and reverence for a deity. **2.** Of or relating to religion. **3.** Scrupulous or conscientious. ►*n., pl.* **-gious.** A member of a monastic order. —**re•li′gious•ly** *adv.* —**re•li′gious•ness** *n.*

re•lin•quish (rĭ-lĭng′kwĭsh) ►*v.* **1.** To retire from; give up or abandon. **2.** To put aside or desist from. **3.** To surrender. **4.** To release. [< Lat. *relinquere*, leave behind.] —**re•lin′quish•er** *n.* —**re•lin′quish•ment** *n.*

rel•i•quar•y (rĕl′ĭ-kwĕr′ē) ►*n., pl.* **-ies.** A receptacle for keeping or displaying sacred relics. [< LLat. *reliquiae*, relics.]

rel•ish (rĕl′ĭsh) ►*n.* **1.** An appetite for something. **2a.** Hearty enjoyment. See Syns at **zest. b.** Something that lends pleasure or zest. **3.** A spicy or savory condiment, as of chopped sweet pickles. **4.** The flavor of a food, esp. when appetizing. See Syns at **taste.** ▶*v.* **1.** To take keen or zestful pleasure in. **2.** To enjoy the flavor of. [< OFr. *relaissier*, leave behind. See RELEASE.]

re•live (rē-lĭv′) ▶*v.* To undergo or experience again, esp. in the imagination.

re•luc•tant (rĭ-lŭk′tənt) ▶*adj.* **1.** Unwilling; disinclined: *reluctant to help.* **2.** Hesitant; grudging: *a reluctant smile.* [< Lat. *reluctārī*, be reluctant.] —**re•luc′tance** *n.* —**re•luc′tant•ly** *adv.*

re•ly (rĭ-lī′) ▶*v.* **-lied, -ly•ing 1.** To depend: *relies on her parents for tuition.* **2.** To have faith or confidence: *relied on them to tell the truth.* [< Lat. *religāre*, bind fast.]

rem (rĕm) ▶*n. Phys.* The amount of ionizing radiation required to produce the same biological effect as one rad of high-penetration x-rays. [*r(oentgen) e(quivalent in) m(an).*]

REM (rĕm) ▶*n.* The rapid, periodic, jerky movement of the eyes during certain stages of the sleep cycle when dreaming takes place. [*r(apid) e(ye) m(ovement).*]

rem. ▶*abbr.* Remittance.

re•main (rĭ-mān′) ▶*v.* **1.** To continue in the same state, condition, or place. **2.** To be left after the removal, loss, passage, or destruction of others. **3.** To be left as still to be dealt with: *A cure remains to be found.* **4.** To endure or persist. [< Lat. *remanēre*, stay behind.]

re•main•der (rĭ-mān′dər) ▶*n.* **1.** Something left over after other parts have been taken away. **2a.** The number left over when one integer is divided by another. **b.** The number obtained when one number is subtracted from another; difference. **3.** A book that remains with a publisher after sales have fallen off. ▶*v.* To sell (books) as a remainder, usu. at a reduced price. [< OFr. *remaindre*, REMAIN.]

re•mains (rĭ-mānz′) ▶*pl.n.* **1.** All that is left after other parts have been taken away, used up, or destroyed. **2.** A corpse.

re•mand (rĭ-mănd′) ▶*v.* To send back to prison, to a lower court, or to another agency for further proceedings. [< LLat. *remandāre*, send back word.] —**re•mand′ment** *n.*

re•mark (rĭ-märk′) ▶*v.* **1.** To express briefly and casually as a comment. **2.** To take notice of; observe. ▶*n.* **1.** The act of noticing or observing. **2.** A casual or brief statement. See Syns at **comment.** [< Fr. *remarquer*, notice.]

re•mark•a•ble (rĭ-mär′kə-bəl) ▶*adj.* **1.** Worthy of notice. **2.** Unusual; extraordinary. —**re•mark′a•bly** *adv.*

Re•marque (rə-märk′), **Erich Maria.** 1898–1970. German-born Amer. writer.

Rem•brandt van Rijn or **Rem•brandt van Ryn** (rĕm′bränt′ vän rīn′, -bränt′). 1606–69. Dutch painter.

re•me•di•a•ble (rĭ-mē′dē-ə-bəl) ▶*adj.* Possible to remedy.

re•me•di•al (rĭ-mē′dē-əl) ▶*adj.* Intended to correct or improve something, esp. deficient skills. —**re•me′di•al•ly** *adv.*

rem•e•dy (rĕm′ĭ-dē) ▶*n., pl.* **-dies 1.** Something that relieves pain, cures disease, or corrects a disorder. **2.** Something that corrects an evil, a fault, or an error. ▶*v.* **-died, -dy•ing 1.** To relieve or cure. **2.** To set right; rectify. See Syns at **cure.** [< Lat. *remedium.*]

re•mem•ber (rĭ-mĕm′bər) ▶*v.* **1.** To recall to the mind; think of again. **2.** To retain in the memory. **3.** To keep (someone) in mind. **4.** To give greetings from. [< Lat. *rememorārī.*] —**re•mem′ber•a•ble** *adj.*

Syns: *remember, recall, recollect* ***Ant:*** *forget* **v.**

re•mem•brance (rĭ-mĕm′brəns) ▶*n.* **1.** The act of remembering or the state of being remembered. **2.** A memorial. **3.** The length of time over which one's memory extends. **4.** Something remembered. **5.** A souvenir.

re•mind (rĭ-mīnd′) ▶*v.* To cause (someone) to remember. —**re•mind′er** *n.*

Rem•ing•ton (rĕm′ĭng-tən), **Frederic.** 1861–1909. Amer. artist and journalist.

rem•i•nisce (rĕm′ə-nĭs′) ▶*v.* **-nisced, -nisc•ing.** To recollect and tell of the past. [< REMINISCENCE.]

rem•i•nis•cence (rĕm′ə-nĭs′əns) ▶*n.* **1.** The act or process of recalling the past. **2.** A memory. **3.** often **reminiscences** A narration of past experiences.

rem•i•nis•cent (rĕm′ə-nĭs′ənt) ▶*adj.* **1.** Of or containing reminiscence. **2.** Suggestive of something in the past. [< Lat. *reminīscī*, recollect.]

re•miss (rĭ-mĭs′) ▶*adj.* Lax in attending to duty. See Syns at **negligent.** [< Lat. *remissus*, slack.] —**re•miss′ness** *n.*

re•mis•si•ble (rĭ-mĭs′ə-bəl) ▶*adj.* Able to be forgiven. —**re•mis′si•bil′i•ty** *n.* —**re•mis′si•bly** *adv.*

re•mis•sion (rĭ-mĭsh′ən) ▶*n.* **1.** The act of remitting or the condition of being remitted. **2.** A lessening of intensity or seriousness, as of a disease.

re•mit (rĭ-mĭt′) ▶*v.* **-mit•ted, -mit•ting 1.** To transmit (money) in payment. **2a.** To cancel (e.g., a tax or penalty). **b.** To pardon; forgive. **3.** To slacken. **4.** To diminish; abate. [< Lat. *remittere*, send back.] —**re•mit′ta•ble** *adj.* —**re•mit′tal** *n.* —**re•mit′ter** *n.*

re•mit•tance (rĭ-mĭt′ns) ▶*n.* Credit or money sent to someone.

re•mit•tent (rĭ-mĭt′nt) ▶*adj.* Marked by temporary abatement in severity.

re•mix (rē-mĭks′) ▶*v.* To recombine recorded audio tracks or channels so as to produce a new recording. ▶*n.* (rē′mĭks′). A recording produced by remixing.

rem•nant (rĕm′nənt) ▶*n.* **1.** Something left over; remainder. **2.** A surviving trace or vestige. [< OFr. *remaindre*, REMAIN.]

re•mod•el (rē-mŏd′l) ▶*v.* To make over in structure or style; renovate. —**re•mod′el•er** *n.*

re•mon•strance (rĭ-mŏn′strəns) ▶*n.* The act or an instance of remonstrating.

re•mon•strate (rĭ-mŏn′strāt′) ▶*v.* **-strat•ed, -strat•ing.** To say or plead in protest, objection, or reproof. [Med.Lat. *remōnstrāre*, demonstrate.] —**re′mon•stra′tion** (rē′mŏn-strā′shən, rĕm′ən-) *n.* —**re•mon′stra•tive** (-strə-tĭv) *adj.* —**re•mon′stra′tor** *n.*

rem•o•ra (rĕm′ər-ə) ▶*n.* Any of a family of marine fishes having a sucking disk on the head with which they attach themselves to sharks, whales, sea turtles, or the hulls of ships. [Lat., delay.]

re•morse (rĭ-môrs′) ▶*n.* Bitter regret for past misdeeds. See Syns at **penitence.** [< Lat. *remordēre*, *remors-*, torment.] —**re•morse′ful**

adj. —**re•morse′ful•ly** *adv.* —**re•morse′ful•ness** *n.*

re•morse•less (rĭ-môrs′lĭs) ►*adj.* Having no pity or compassion. —**re•morse′less•ly** *adv.* —**re•morse′less•ness** *n.*

re•mote (rĭ-mōt′) ►*adj.* **-mot•er, -mot•est 1.** Located far away. **2.** Distant in time. **3.** Faint; slight: *a remote possibility.* **4.** Distantly related: *a remote cousin.* **5.** Distant in manner; aloof. **6.** Operating or controlled from a distance. ►*n.* **1.** A radio or television broadcast from outside a studio. **2.** Remote control. [< Lat. *remōtus*, p.part. of *removēre*, remove.] —**re•mote′ly** *adv.* —**re•mote′ness** *n.*

remote control ►*n.* **1.** The control of an activity, process, or machine from a distance, as by radioed instructions or coded signals. **2.** A device used to control an apparatus from a distance.

re•move (rĭ-mo͞ov′) ►*v.* **-moved, -mov•ing 1.** To move from a place or position occupied. **2.** To take off: *removed her jewelry.* **3.** To take away; eliminate. **4.** To dismiss from office. **5.** To change one's residence; move. ►*n.* **1.** The act of removing. **2.** Distance or degree of separation. [< Lat. *removēre.*] —**re•mov′a•ble** *adj.* —**re•mov′a•bly** *adv.* —**re•mov′al** *n.* —**re•mov′er** *n.*

re•moved (rĭ-mo͞ovd′) ►*adj.* **1.** Distant in space, time, or nature; remote. **2.** Separated in relationship by a given degree of descent: *first cousin once removed.*

re•mu•ner•ate (rĭ-myo͞o′nə-rāt′) ►*v.* **-at•ed, -at•ing.** To pay for goods provided, services rendered, or losses incurred. [Lat. *remūnerārī.*] —**re•mu′ner•a′tion** *n.* —**re•mu′ner•a•tive** (-nər-ə-tĭv, -nə-rā′tĭv) *adj.*

ren•ais•sance (rĕn′ĭ-säns′, -zäns′, rĭ-nā′səns) ►*n.* **1.** A rebirth or revival. **2. Renaissance a.** The humanistic revival of classical art, architecture, literature, and learning in Europe. **b.** The period of this revival, roughly the 14th through the 16th cent. **3.** often **Renaissance** A revival of intellectual or artistic achievement. [< OFr.]

re•nal (rē′nəl) ►*adj.* Relating to or near the kidneys. [< Lat. *rēnēs*, kidneys.]

re•nas•cent (rĭ-năs′ənt, -nā′sənt) ►*adj.* Showing renewed growth or vigor. [< Lat. *renāscī*, be born again.] —**re•nas′cence** *n.*

rend (rĕnd) ►*v.* **rent** (rĕnt) or **rend•ed, rend•ing 1.** To tear or split apart or into pieces violently. **2.** To tear away forcibly; wrest. **3.** To pierce or disturb with sound. **4.** To cause pain or distress to. [< OE *rendan.*]

ren•der (rĕn′dər) ►*v.* **1.** To submit or present. **2.** To give; provide: *render assistance.* **3.** To give what is due. **4.** To represent in verbal or artistic form; depict. **5.** To translate. **6.** To make: *The news rendered her speechless.* **7.** To liquefy (fat) by heating. [< OFr. *rendre* < Lat. *reddere* : RE– + *dare*, give.] —**ren′der•er** *n.*

ren•dez•vous (rän′dā-vo͞o′, -də-) ►*n., pl.* **-vous** (-vo͞oz′) **1.** A meeting at a set time and place. **2.** A set meeting place. **3.** A popular gathering place. ►*v.* To meet at a set time and place. [< OFr. *rendez vous*, present yourselves.]

ren•di•tion (rĕn-dĭsh′ən) ►*n.* **1.** The act of rendering. **2.** An interpretation or performance of a musical or dramatic work. **3.** A translation. [< OFr. *rendre*, RENDER.]

ren•e•gade (rĕn′ĭ-gād′) ►*n.* **1.** One who rejects a religion, cause, allegiance, or group for another; deserter. **2.** An outlaw. [< Med.Lat. *renegāre*, deny.] —**ren′e•gade′** *adj.*

re•nege (rĭ-nĭg′, -nĕg′) ►*v.* **-neged, -neg•ing 1.** To fail to carry out a promise or commitment. **2.** To fail to follow suit in card games when able and required to do so. [Med.Lat. *renegāre*, deny.] —**re•neg′er** *n.*

re•new (rĭ-no͞o′, -nyo͞o′) ►*v.* **1.** To make new or as if new again; restore. **2.** To take up again; resume. **3.** To repeat so as to reaffirm: *renew a promise.* **4.** To arrange for the extension of: *renew a contract.* —**re•new′a•ble** *adj.* —**re•new′al** *n.*

ren•net (rĕn′ĭt) ►*n.* A dried extract from the stomach lining of a ruminant, used in cheesemaking to curdle milk. [ME.]

ren•nin (rĕn′ĭn) ►*n.* A milk-coagulating enzyme produced from rennet.

Re•no (rē′nō′) A city of W NV near the CA border. Pop. 133,850.

Ren•oir (rĕn′wär′, rən-wär′), **Pierre Auguste.** 1841–1919. French painter.

re•nounce (rĭ-nouns′) ►*v.* **-nounced, -nounc•ing 1.** To give up, esp. by formal announcement. **2.** To reject; disown. [< Lat. *renūntiāre*, report.] —**re•nounce′ment** *n.*

ren•o•vate (rĕn′ə-vāt′) ►*v.* **-vat•ed, -vat•ing.** To restore to an earlier state. [Lat. *renovāre.*] —**ren′o•va′tion** *n.* —**ren′o•va′tor** *n.*

re•nown (rĭ-noun′) ►*n.* Widespread honor and acclaim; fame. [< AN *renomer*, make famous.] —**re•nowned′** *adj.*

rent¹ (rĕnt) ►*n.* Periodic payment made by a tenant in return for the right to use the property of another. ►*v.* **1.** To use (another's property) in return for regular payments. **2.** To be for rent. [< VLat. **rendita.*] —**rent′a•ble** *adj.* —**rent′er** *n.*

rent² (rĕnt) ►*v.* P.t. and p.part. of **rend.** ►*n.* An opening made by rending; rip.

rent•al (rĕn′tl) ►*n.* **1.** An amount paid out or taken in as rent. **2.** Property available for renting. **3.** The act of renting. —**rent′al** *adj.*

rent control ►*n.* Governmental regulation of the amounts charged for rented housing.

re•nun•ci•a•tion (rĭ-nŭn′sē-ā′shən) ►*n.* The act or an instance of renouncing. [< Lat. *renūntiāre*, renounce.] —**re•nun′ci•a′tive, re•nun′ci•a•to′ry** (-ə-tôr′ē, -tōr′ē) *adj.*

re•or•der (rē-ôr′dər) ►*v.* **1.** To order (the same goods) again. **2.** To rearrange. —**re•or′der** *n.*

rep¹ (rĕp) ►*n.* A ribbed or corded fabric. [< Fr. *reps* < E. *ribs.*]

rep² (rĕp) ►*n. Informal* A representative.

rep³ (rĕp) ►*n. Informal* Reputation.

rep⁴ (rĕp) ►*n. Informal* A repetition of an exercise movement.

Rep. ►*abbr.* **1.** representative **2.** republic **3.** Republican

re•pair¹ ►*v.* **1.** To restore to sound condition after damage or injury; fix. **2.** To set right; remedy. **3.** To renew or revitalize. ►*n.* **1.** The work or act of repairing. **2.** General condition after use or repairing: *in good repair.* [< Lat. *reparāre.*] —**re•pair′a•ble** *adj.* —**re•pair′man** *n.* —**re•pair′wom′an** *n.*

re•pair² (rĭ-pâr′) ►*v.* To betake oneself; go. [< LLat. *repatriāre*, return to one's country. See REPATRIATE.]

rep•a•ra•ble (rĕpʹər-ə-bəl) ▸*adj.* Possible to repair. —**repʹa•ra•bly** *adv.*
rep•a•ra•tion (rĕpʹə-rāʹshən) ▸*n.* **1.** The act or process of making amends. **2.** Something done or paid to make amends. **3. reparations** Compensation, esp. that required from a defeated nation as indemnity for war damages. [< Lat. *reparāre*, repair.] —**re•parʹa•tive** (rĭ-părʹə-tĭv), **re•parʹa•toʹry** (-tôrʹē, -tōrʹē) *adj.*
rep•ar•tee (rĕpʹər-tēʹ, -tāʹ, -är-) ▸*n.* **1.** A swift, witty reply. **2.** Conversation marked by witty retorts. [< OFr. *repartir*, to retort.]
re•past (rĭ-păstʹ) ▸*n.* A meal or the food eaten or provided at a meal. ▸*v.* To eat or feast. [< Lat. *repāscere*, feed.]
re•pa•tri•ate (rē-pāʹtrē-ātʹ) ▸*v.* **-at•ed, -at•ing.** To return (a person) to the country of birth, citizenship, or origin. ▸*n.* (-ĭt, -ātʹ). One who has been repatriated. [LLat. *repatriāre*, return to one's country : RE– + *patria*, native country; see EXPATRIATE.] —**re•paʹtri•aʹtion** *n.*
re•pay (rĭ-pāʹ) ▸*v.* **1.** To pay back: *repaid a debt.* **2.** To give in return for. —**re•payʹa•ble** *adj.* —**re•payʹment** *n.*
re•peal (rĭ-pēlʹ) ▸*v.* To revoke or rescind, esp. by an official or formal act. [< OFr. *rapeler.*] —**re•pealʹ** *n.* —**re•pealʹer** *n.*
re•peat (rĭ-pētʹ, rēʹpētʹ) ▸*v.* **1.** To say or do again. **2.** To tell to another. **3.** To manifest or express (oneself) in the same way or words. ▸*n.* **1.** An act of repeating. **2.** Something repeated. [< Lat. *repetere*, seek again.] —**re•peatʹa•ble** *adj.* —**re•peatʹer** *n.*
Syns: *repeat, iterate, reiterate* ***v.***
re•peat•ed (rĭ-pēʹtĭd) ▸*adj.* Said, done, or occurring again and again. —**re•peatʹed•ly** *adv.*
re•peat•ing decimal (rĭ-pēʹtĭng) ▸*n.* A decimal in which a pattern of one or more digits is repeated indefinitely.
re•pel (rĭ-pĕlʹ) ▸*v.* **-pelled, -pel•ling 1.** To ward off or keep away: *repel insects.* **2.** To drive back: *repel an invasion.* **3.** To cause aversion or distaste in. See Syns at **disgust.**See Usage Note at **repulse. 4.** To be incapable of absorbing or mixing with: *Oil repels water.* **5.** To present an opposing force to: *Electric charges of the same sign repel one another.* [< Lat. *repellere.*]
re•pel•lent also **re•pel•lant** (rĭ-pĕlʹənt) ▸*adj.* **1.** Serving or tending to repel. **2.** Repulsive. See Syns at **offensive. 3.** Resistant or impervious to a substance. ▸*n.* **1.** A substance used to repel insects. **2.** A substance for making a surface resistant to something. —**re•pelʹlence, re•pelʹlen•cy** *n.*
re•pent (rĭ-pĕntʹ) ▸*v.* **1.** To feel regret or self-reproach for what one has done or failed to do. **2.** To change for the better as a result of remorse or contrition for one's sins. [< OFr. *repentir.*] —**re•pentʹer** *n.*
re•pen•tance (rĭ-pĕnʹtəns) ▸*n.* Remorse or contrition for past conduct or sin. See Syns at **penitence.** —**re•penʹtant** *adj.* —**re•penʹtant•ly** *adv.*
re•per•cus•sion (rēʹpər-kŭshʹən, rĕpʹər-) ▸*n.* **1.** An often indirect effect of an event or action. **2.** A reciprocal motion after impact. **3.** A reflection, esp. of sound. [< Lat. *repercutere*, cause to rebound.] —**reʹper•cusʹsive** *adj.*
rep•er•toire (rĕpʹər-twärʹ) ▸*n.* **1.** The stock of songs, plays, or other works that a player or company is prepared to perform. **2.** The range of skills, aptitudes, or accomplishments of a person or group. [< LLat. *repertōrium.*]
rep•er•to•ry (rĕpʹər-tôrʹē, -tōrʹē) ▸*n.*, *pl.* **-ries 1.** A repertoire. **2.** A theater in which a resident company presents works from a specified repertoire, usu. in alternation. [LLat. *repertōrium.*] —**repʹer•toʹri•al** *adj.*
rep•e•tend (rĕpʹĭ-tĕndʹ, rĕpʹĭ-tĕndʹ) ▸*n.* The digit or group of digits that repeats infinitely in a repeating decimal. [< Lat. *repetendum*, thing to be repeated.]
rep•e•ti•tion (rĕpʹĭ-tĭshʹən) ▸*n.* **1.** The act or an instance of repeating. **2.** Something repeated. [< Lat. *repetere*, repeat.]
rep•e•ti•tious (rĕpʹĭ-tĭshʹəs) ▸*adj.* Filled esp. with needless repetition. —**repʹe•tiʹtious•ly** *adv.* —**repʹe•tiʹtious•ness** *n.*
re•pet•i•tive (rĭ-pĕtʹĭ-tĭv) ▸*adj.* Given to or marked by repetition. —**re•petʹi•tive•ly** *adv.* —**re•petʹi•tive•ness** *n.*
repetitive strain injury ▸*n.* Damage to soft tissue, esp. tendons or nerves, caused by excessive repetition of certain movements.
re•pine (rĭ-pīnʹ) ▸*v.* **-pined, -pin•ing.** To be discontented or low in spirits; fret. —**re•pinʹer** *n.*
re•place (rĭ-plāsʹ) ▸*v.* **1.** To put back in place. **2.** To take the place of. —**re•placeʹa•ble** *adj.* —**re•placeʹment** *n.* —**re•placʹer** *n.*
re•play (rē-plāʹ) ▸*v.* To play (e.g., a game or recording) over again. —**reʹplayʹ** *n.*
re•plen•ish (rĭ-plĕnʹĭsh) ▸*v.* To fill or make complete again. [< OFr. *replenir.*] —**re•plenʹish•er** *n.* —**re•plenʹish•ment** *n.*
re•plete (rĭ-plētʹ) ▸*adj.* **1.** Abundantly supplied; abounding: *a report replete with errors.* **2.** Filled to satiation; gorged. [< Lat. *replētus*, p.part. of *replēre*, refill.] —**re•pleʹtion, re•pleteʹness** *n.*
rep•li•ca (rĕpʹlĭ-kə) ▸*n.* A copy or close reproduction. [< LLat. *replicāre*, repeat.]
rep•li•cate (rĕpʹlĭ-kātʹ) ▸*v.* **-cat•ed, -cat•ing 1.** To duplicate, copy, reproduce, or repeat. **2.** To fold over or bend back. [< Lat. *replicāre*, fold back.] —**repʹli•caʹtion** *n.*
re•ply (rĭ-plīʹ) ▸*v.* **-plied, -ply•ing 1.** To say or give as an answer. **2.** To respond by an action or gesture. ▸*n.*, *pl.* **-plies.** A response; answer. [< Lat. *replicāre*, fold back.] —**re•pliʹer** *n.*
re•port (rĭ-pôrtʹ -pōrtʹ) ▸*n.* **1.** An account, esp. one presented formally and in detail. **2.** Common talk; rumor. **3.** Reputation: *a person of bad report.* **4.** An explosive noise. ▸*v.* **1.** To make or present an account of. **2.** To relate or present: *report one's findings.* See Syns at **describe. 3.** To make known, esp. to an authority: *reported the incident to the police.* **4.** To serve as a reporter. **5.** To present oneself: *report for duty.* [< Lat. *reportāre*, carry back.]
report card ▸*n.* A periodic report of a student's progress.
re•port•ed•ly (rĭ-pôrʹtĭd-lē, -pōrʹ-) ▸*adv.* By report; supposedly.
re•port•er (rĭ-pôrʹtər, -pōrʹ-) ▸*n.* A writer or investigator of news stories. —**repʹor•toʹri•al** (rĕpʹər-tôrʹē-əl, -tōrʹ-, rēʹpər-) *adj.*
re•pose[1] (rĭ-pōzʹ) ▸*n.* **1.** The act of resting or the state of being at rest. **2.** Calmness; tranquillity. ▸*v.* **-posed, -pos•ing 1.** To lie at rest;

relax. **2.** To lie supported by something. [< LLat. *repausāre*, make rest.] —**re•pose′ful** *adj.* —**re•pose′ful•ly** *adv.*

re•pose² (rĭ-pōz′) ▶*v.* **-posed, -pos•ing.** To put or place: *Reposed our hopes in a single man.* [< Lat. *repōnere*, *repos-*, put away.]

re•pos•i•to•ry (rĭ-pŏz′ĭ-tôr′ē, -tōr′ē) ▶*n., pl.* **-ries 1.** A place where things may be put esp. for safekeeping. **2.** One possessing or entrusted with something. [< Lat. *repōnere*, *reposit-*, put away.]

re•pos•sess (rē′pə-zĕs′) ▶*v.* To regain possession of (property). —**re′pos•ses′sion** *n.*

rep•re•hend (rĕp′rĭ-hĕnd′) ▶*v.* To reprove or blame; censure. [< Lat. *reprehendere*.] —**rep′re•hen′sion** *n.*

rep•re•hen•si•ble (rĕp′rĭ-hĕn′sə-bəl) ▶*adj.* Deserving rebuke or censure. See Syns at **blameworthy.** —**rep′re•hen′si•bil′i•ty** *n.* —**rep′re•hen′si•bly** *adv.*

rep•re•sent (rĕp′rĭ-zĕnt′) ▶*v.* **1.** To stand for; symbolize. **2.** To depict; portray. **3.** To describe (a person or thing) as having a specified quality. **4.** To serve as the delegate, spokesperson, or agent for. **5.** To serve as an example of. [< Lat. *repraesentāre*, show.] —**rep′re•sent′a•ble** *adj.*

Syns: *represent, delineate, depict, limn, picture, portray* **v.**

rep•re•sen•ta•tion (rĕp′rĭ-zĕn-tā′shən, -zən-) ▶*n.* **1.** The act of representing or the state of being represented. **2.** Something that represents. **3.** A statement, as of facts or arguments.

rep•re•sen•ta•tion•al (rĕp′rĭ-zĕn-tā′shə-nəl, -zən-) ▶*adj.* Of or relating to realistic graphic representation.

rep•re•sen•ta•tive (rĕp′rĭ-zĕn′tə-tĭv) ▶*n.* **1.** A typical example, esp. of a class or group. **2.** A delegate or agent acting on behalf of another. **3a.** A member of a legislative body chosen by popular vote. **b.** A member of the US House of Representatives or of the lower house of a state legislature. ▶*adj.* **1.** Of or based on political representation: *representative government.* **2.** Serving as a typical example. —**rep′re•sen′ta•tive•ly** *adv.* —**rep′re•sen′ta•tive•ness** *n.*

re•press (rĭ-prĕs′) ▶*v.* **1.** To hold back: *repress a laugh.* **2.** To put down by force: *repress a rebellion.* **3.** *Psychol.* To exclude from the conscious mind. [< Lat. *reprimere*, *repress-*.] —**re•press′i•ble** *adj.* —**re•pres′sion** *n.* —**re•pres′sive** *adj.* —**re•pres′sive•ly** *adv.* —**re•pres′sor** *n.*

re•prieve (rĭ-prēv′) ▶*v.* **-prieved, -priev•ing.** To postpone or cancel the punishment of. ▶*n.* **1.** Postponement or cancellation of a punishment. **2.** Temporary relief, as from pain. [< Lat. *reprehendere*, hold back.]

rep•ri•mand (rĕp′rə-mănd′) ▶*v.* To reprove severely; admonish. ▶*n.* A severe or formal rebuke. [< Lat. *reprimere*, restrain.]

re•print (rē′prĭnt′) ▶*n.* **1.** A new or additional printing of a book. **2.** A printed excerpt; offprint. —**re•print′** *v.* —**re•print′er** *n.*

re•pri•sal (rĭ-prī′zəl) ▶*n.* Retaliation for an injury with the intent of inflicting at least as much injury in return. [< OItal. *ripreso* < *riprendere*, take back. See REPREHEND.]

re•prise (rĭ-prēz′) ▶*n.* **1.** *Mus.* **a.** A repetition of a theme or verse. **b.** A return to an original theme. **2.** A recurrence of an action. [< OFr. *reprendre*, take back. See REPREHEND.]

re•proach (rĭ-prōch′) ▶*v.* To express disapproval or criticism. ▶*n.* **1.** Blame; rebuke. **2.** Disgrace; shame. [< OFr. *reprochier*.] —**re•proach′a•ble** *adj.* —**re•proach′ful** *adj.* —**re•proach′ful•ly** *adv.*

rep•ro•bate (rĕp′rə-bāt′) ▶*n.* A morally unprincipled person. [< LLat. *reprobāre*, disapprove.] —**rep′ro•bate′** *adj.* —**rep′ro•ba′tion** *n.*

re•pro•duce (rē′prə-do͞os′, -dyo͞os′) ▶*v.* **-duced, -duc•ing 1.** To produce a counterpart, image, or copy of. **2.** To produce offspring sexually or asexually. **3.** To produce again or anew; re-create. **4.** To undergo copying: *graphics that reproduce well.* —**re′pro•duc′er** *n.* —**re′pro•duc′i•ble** *adj.* —**re′pro•duc′tion** (-dŭk′shən) *n.* —**re′pro•duc′tive** (-dŭk′tĭv) *adj.* —**re′pro•duc′tive•ly** *adv.*

re•proof (rĭ-pro͞of′) ▶*n.* Censure; rebuke.

re•prove (rĭ-pro͞ov′) ▶*v.* **-proved, -prov•ing 1.** To voice or convey disapproval of; rebuke. **2.** To find fault with. [< LLat. *reprobāre*, disapprove.] —**re•prov′ing•ly** *adv.*

rep•tile (rĕp′tīl′, -tīl) ▶*n.* Any of various cold-blooded, usu. egg-laying vertebrates, such as a snake, crocodile, or turtle, having scales or horny plates. [< Lat. *rēptilis*, creeping < *rēpere*, creep.] —**rep•til′i•an** (-tĭl′ē-ən, -tĭl′yən) *adj. & n.*

re•pub•lic (rĭ-pŭb′lĭk) ▶*n.* **1.** A government whose head of state is not a monarch and is usu. a president. **2.** A country governed by the elected representatives of its people. [< Lat. *rēspūblica*.]

re•pub•li•can (rĭ-pŭb′lĭ-kən) ▶*adj.* **1.** Of or advocating a republic. **2. Republican** Of or belonging to the Republican Party. ▶*n.* **1.** One who favors a republican form of government. **2. Republican** A member of the Republican Party. —**re•pub′li•can•ism** *n.*

Republican Party ▶*n.* One of the two major US political parties.

re•pu•di•ate (rĭ-pyo͞o′dē-āt′) ▶*v.* **-at•ed, -at•ing 1.** To reject the validity of. **2.** To refuse to recognize, acknowledge, or pay. [Lat. *repudiāre*.] —**re•pu′di•a′tion** *n.*

re•pug•nant (rĭ-pŭg′nənt) ▶*adj.* **1.** Arousing disgust or aversion; repulsive. **2.** *Logic* Contradictory. [< Lat. *repugnāre*, fight against.] —**re•pug′nance** *n.*

re•pulse (rĭ-pŭls′) ▶*v.* **-pulsed, -puls•ing 1.** To drive back; repel. **2.** To reject with rudeness, coldness, or denial. **3.** *Informal* To cause repulsion in. ▶*n.* **1.** The act of repulsing. **2.** Rejection; refusal. [< Lat. *repellere*, *repuls-*.]

Usage: A number of critics have maintained that *repulse* should not be used to mean "to cause repulsion in." Reputable literary precedent exists for this usage, but writers who want to stay on the safe side may prefer to use only *repel* when the intended sense is "to cause repulsion in."

re•pul•sion (rĭ-pŭl′shən) ▶*n.* **1.** The act of repulsing. **2.** Extreme aversion.

re•pul•sive (rĭ-pŭl′sĭv) ▶*adj.* **1.** Causing repugnance or disgust. See Syns at **offensive. 2.** Tending to repel or drive off. —**re•pul′sive•ly** *adv.* —**re•pul′sive•ness** *n.*

rep•u•ta•ble (rĕp′yə-tə-bəl) ▶*adj.* Having a good reputation. —**rep′u•ta•bly** *adv.*

rep•u•ta•tion (rĕp′yə-tā′shən) ▶*n.* **1.** The

general estimation of a person or thing held by the public. **2.** The state of being held in high esteem.

re•pute (rĭ-pyo͞ot′) ▸*v.* **-put•ed, -put•ing.** To consider; suppose. ▸*n.* Reputation; esteem. [< Lat. *reputāre*, think over.]

re•put•ed (rĭ-pyo͞o′tĭd) ▸*adj.* Generally supposed. See Syns at **supposed.** —**re•put′ed•ly** *adv.*

re•quest (rĭ-kwĕst′) ▸*v.* **1.** To ask for. **2.** To ask (a person) to do something. ▸*n.* **1.** The act of asking. **2.** Something asked for. —***idiom:*** **on** (or **upon) request** When asked for: *References are available on request.* [< Lat. *requīrere*.]

req•ui•em (rĕk′wē-əm, rē′kwē-) ▸*n.* **1. Requiem** *Rom. Cath. Ch.* **a.** A mass for a deceased person. **b.** A musical composition for such a mass. **2.** A hymn, composition, or service for the dead. [< Lat. *requiēs*, rest.]

re•quire (rĭ-kwīr′) ▸*v.* **-quired, -quir•ing 1.** To need. **2.** To insist upon; demand. See Syns at **demand.** [< Lat. *requīrere.*] —**re•quire′ment** *n.*

re•quired (rĭ-kwīrd′) ▸*adj.* **1.** Needed; essential. **2.** Obligatory: *required reading.*

req•ui•site (rĕk′wĭ-zĭt) ▸*adj.* Required; essential. See Syns at **indispensable.** ▸*n.* A necessity. [< Lat. *requīsītus*, p.part. of *requīrere*, require.]

req•ui•si•tion (rĕk′wĭ-zĭsh′ən) ▸*n.* **1.** A formal request for something needed. **2.** The state of being needed or in use. ▸*v.* To demand, as for military needs.

re•quite (rĭ-kwīt′) ▸*v.* **-quit•ed, -quit•ing 1.** To make repayment or return for. See Syns at **reciprocate. 2.** To avenge. [RE– + ME *quiten*, pay.] —**re•quit′a•ble** *adj.* —**re•quit′al** *n.* —**re•quit′er** *n.*

re•run (rē′rŭn′) ▸*n.* A second or subsequent presentation of a movie or television program. —**re•run′** *v.*

re•scind (rĭ-sĭnd′) ▸*v.* To repeal or annul. [Lat. *rescindere.*] —**re•scind′a•ble** *adj.* —**re•scis′sion** (-sĭzh′ən) *n.*

res•cue (rĕs′kyo͞o) ▸*v.* **-cued, -cu•ing.** To save, as from danger. [< OFr. *rescourre.*] —**res′cue** *n.* —**res′cu•er** *n.*

re•search (rĭ-sûrch′, rē′sûrch′) ▸*n.* Careful investigation or study, esp. of a scholarly or scientific nature. See Syns at **inquiry.** [< OFr. *recercher*, search closely.] —**re•search′** *v.* —**re•search′er** *n.*

re•sec•tion (rĭ-sĕk′shən) ▸*n.* Surgical removal of part of an organ or structure.

re•sem•blance (rĭ-zĕm′bləns) ▸*n.* A similarity, esp. in appearance.

re•sem•ble (rĭ-zĕm′bəl) ▸*v.* **-bled, -bling.** To exhibit similarity or likeness to. [< OFr. *resembler.*]

re•sent (rĭ-zĕnt′) ▸*v.* To feel angry or bitter about. [< OFr. *resentir*, feel strongly.] —**re•sent′ful** *adj.* —**re•sent′ful•ly** *adv.* —**re•sent′ment** *n.*

res•er•va•tion (rĕz′ər-vā′shən) ▸*n.* **1.** The act of reserving. **2.** A limiting qualification or condition. **3.** A tract of public land set apart for a special purpose, esp. one for the use of a Native American people. **4.** An arrangement by which accommodations are secured in advance.

re•serve (rĭ-zûrv′) ▸*v.* **-served, -serv•ing 1.** To keep back, as for future use. **2.** To set apart for a particular person or use. **3.** To retain; defer: *reserve judgment.* ▸*n.* **1.** Something kept back, as for future use. **2.** The condition of being reserved: *funds held in reserve.* **3.** Self-restraint; reticence. **4.** A reservation of public land. **5.** An amount of a resource known to exist in a particular location: *oil reserves.* **6.** often **reserves** The part of a country's armed forces not on active duty but subject to call in an emergency. [< Lat. *reservāre*, keep back.] —**re•serv′a•ble** *adj.*

re•served (rĭ-zûrvd′) ▸*adj.* **1.** Set aside, as for a particular person or use. **2.** Marked by self-restraint and reticence. —**re•serv′ed•ly** (-zûr′vĭd-lē) *adv.* —**re•serv′ed•ness** *n.*

re•serv•ist (rĭ-zûr′vĭst) ▸*n.* A member of a military reserve.

res•er•voir (rĕz′ər-vwär′, -vwôr′, -vôr′) ▸*n.* **1.** A body of water stored for public use. **2.** A chamber for storing a fluid. **3.** A large or extra supply. [Fr. *réservoir.*]

re•side (rĭ-zīd′) ▸*v.* **-sid•ed, -sid•ing 1.** To live in a place; dwell. **2.** To be inherently present: *the power that resides in the electorate.* [< Lat. *residēre* : RE– + *sedēre*, sit.] —**re•sid′er** *n.*

res•i•dence (rĕz′ĭ-dəns, -dĕns′) ▸*n.* **1.** The place in which one lives. **2.** The act or a period of residing in a place.

res•i•den•cy (rĕz′ĭ-dən-sē, -dĕn′-) ▸*n., pl.* **-cies.** A period of specialized clinical training for a physician.

res•i•dent (rĕz′ĭ-dənt, -dĕnt′) ▸*n.* **1.** One who resides in a particular place. **2.** A physician serving a period of residency. —**res′i•dent** *adj.*

res•i•den•tial (rĕz′ĭ-dĕn′shəl) ▸*adj.* **1.** Of or having residence. **2.** Of or limited to homes: *residential zoning.* —**res′i•den′tial•ly** *adv.*

re•sid•u•al (rĭ-zĭj′o͞o-əl) ▸*adj.* Of or remaining as a residue. ▸*n.* **1.** A residue; remainder. **2.** A payment made, as to a performer, for each rerun of a television show. —**re•sid′u•al•ly** *adv.*

res•i•due (rĕz′ĭ-do͞o′, -dyo͞o′) ▸*n.* The remainder of something after removal of parts or a part. [< Lat. *residuus*, remaining < *residēre*, RESIDE.]

re•sign (rĭ-zīn′) ▸*v.* **1.** To submit (oneself) passively. **2.** To give up (a position); quit **3.** To relinquish (a privilege, right, or claim). [< Lat. *resignāre*, unseal.]

res•ig•na•tion (rĕz′ĭg-nā′shən) ▸*n.* **1.** The act of resigning. **2.** A formal statement that one is resigning. **3.** Acceptance; submission.

re•signed (rĭ-zīnd′) ▸*adj.* Acquiescent; accepting. —**re•sign′ed•ly** (-zī′nĭd-lē) *adv.*

re•sil•ient (rĭ-zĭl′yənt) ▸*adj.* **1.** Marked by the ability to recover readily, as from misfortune. **2.** Capable of returning to an original shape or position, as after having been compressed. [< Lat. *resilīre*, leap back.] —**re•sil′ience, re•sil′ien•cy** *n.* —**re•sil′ient•ly** *adv.*

res•in (rĕz′ĭn) ▸*n.* **1.** A viscous substance of plant origin, such as rosin or amber, used in varnishes, adhesives, synthetic plastics, and pharmaceuticals. **2.** Any of various synthetic substances similar to natural resins, used in plastics. ▸*v.* To treat with resin. [< Lat. *rēsīna.*] —**res′in•ous** *adj.*

re•sist (rĭ-zĭst′) ▸*v.* **1.** To strive or work against. **2.** To remain firm against; withstand.

[< Lat. *resistere* : RE– + *sistere*, place.] —**re•sist′er** *n.* —**re•sist′i•ble** *adj.*

re•sis•tance (rĭ-zĭs′təns) ▸*n.* **1.** The act of resisting or the capacity to resist. **2.** A force that opposes or retards motion. **3.** *Elect.* The opposition of a body or substance to current passing through it. —**re•sis′tant** *adj.*

re•sis•tor (rĭ-zĭs′tər) ▸*n.* A device used to provide resistance in an electric circuit.

res•o•lute (rĕz′ə-lo͞ot′, rĕz′ə-lo͞ot′) ▸*adj.* Firm or determined; unwavering. [Lat. *resolūtus*, p.part. of *resolvere*, resolve.] —**res′o•lute′ly** *adv.* —**res′o•lute′ness** *n.*

res•o•lu•tion (rĕz′ə-lo͞o′shən) ▸*n.* **1.** The state or quality of being resolute. **2.** A course of action determined or decided on. **3.** A formal statement of a decision, as by a legislature. **4.** An explanation, as of a problem; solution. **5.** The fineness of detail that can be distinguished in an image.

re•solve (rĭ-zŏlv′) ▸*v.* **-solved, -solv•ing 1.** To make a firm decision about. **2.** To decide or express by formal vote. **3.** To separate (something) into constituent parts. **4.** To find a solution to. See Syns at **solve. 5.** To dispel: *resolve a doubt.* ▸*n.* **1.** Firmness of purpose; resolution. **2.** A determination or decision. [< Lat. *resolvere*, untie, loosen.] —**re•solv′a•ble** *adj.*

res•o•nance (rĕz′ə-nəns) ▸*n.* **1.** The quality or condition of being resonant. **2.** *Phys.* The increase in amplitude of oscillation of an electric or mechanical system exposed to a periodic force whose frequency is equal or very close to the natural frequency of the system. **3.** Intensification of sound, esp. of a musical tone, by sympathetic vibration.

res•o•nant (rĕz′ə-nənt) ▸*adj.* **1a.** Strong and deep in tone; resounding. **b.** Continuing to sound; echoing: *resonant words.* **2.** Producing, exhibiting, or resulting from resonance. —**res′o•nant•ly** *adv.*

res•o•nate (rĕz′ə-nāt′) ▸*v.* **-nat•ed, -nat•ing 1.** To exhibit or produce resonance. **2.** To resound. [Lat. *resonāre*, resound.]

res•o•na•tor (rĕz′ə-nā′tər) ▸*n.* A hollow chamber designed to permit internal resonant oscillation of electromagnetic or acoustical waves of specific frequencies.

re•sort (rĭ-zôrt′) ▸*v.* **1.** To have recourse: *resorted to violence.* **2.** To go customarily or frequently. ▸*n.* **1.** A place frequented by people for relaxation or recreation. **2.** Recourse. **3.** One turned to for aid or relief. See Syns at **makeshift.** [< OFr. *resortir*, go out again.]

re•sound (rĭ-zound′) ▸*v.* **1.** To be filled with sound; reverberate. **2.** To sound loudly; ring. **3.** To send back (sound). See Syns at **echo.** [< Lat. *resonāre*.] —**re•sound′ing** *adj.* —**re•sound′ing•ly** *adv.*

re•source (rē′sôrs′, -sōrs′, -zôrs′, -zōrs′,) ▸*n.* **1.** A source of support or help. **2.** often **resources** An available supply. **3.** The ability to deal with a situation effectively. **4.** often **resources** Means; assets. **5.** A natural resource. [< Lat. *resurgere*, rise again.]

re•source•ful (rĭ-sôrs′fəl, -sōrs′-, -zôrs′-, -zōrs′-) ▸*adj.* Clever and imaginative, esp. in dealing with difficult situations. —**re•source′ful•ly** *adv.* —**re•source′ful•ness** *n.*

re•spect (rĭ-spĕkt′) ▸*v.* **1.** To have regard for; esteem. **2.** To avoid violation of. **3.** To concern. ▸*n.* **1.** High, often deferential regard; esteem. **2. respects** Expressions of consideration or deference: *pay one's respects.* **3.** A particular aspect, feature, or detail. **4.** Relation; reference. [< Lat. *respectus*, p.part. of *respicere*, regard : RE– + *specere*, look at.] —**re•spect′er** *n.* —**re•spect′ful** *adj.* —**re•spect′ful•ly** *adv.* —**re•spect′ful•ness** *n.*

re•spect•a•ble (rĭ-spĕk′tə-bəl) ▸*adj.* **1.** Meriting respect or esteem. **2.** Good or proper in behavior or conventional conduct. **3.** Of moderately good quality. **4.** Considerable in amount, number, or size: *a respectable sum of money.* **5.** Acceptable in appearance; presentable. —**re•spect′a•bil′i•ty** *n.* —**re•spect′a•bly** *adv.*

re•spec•tive (rĭ-spĕk′tĭv) ▸*adj.* Individual; particular: *They took their respective seats.*

re•spec•tive•ly (rĭ-spĕk′tĭv-lē) ▸*adv.* Singly in the order designated or mentioned.

res•pi•ra•tion (rĕs′pə-rā′shən) ▸*n.* **1.** The act or process of inhaling and exhaling. **2.** The act or process by which a cell or organism without lungs exchanges gases with its environment. —**res′pi•ra•to′ry** (-pər-ə-tôr′ē, -tōr′ē, rĭ-spīr′ə-) *adj.*

res•pi•ra•tor (rĕs′pə-rā′tər) ▸*n.* **1.** A device for artificial respiration. **2.** A screenlike device worn over the mouth and nose to protect the respiratory tract.

respiratory system ▸*n.* The system of organs involved in the intake and exchange of oxygen and carbon dioxide between an organism and the environment.

re•spire (rĭ-spīr′) ▸*v.* **-spired, -spir•ing 1.** To breathe in and out. **2.** To engage in respiration. [< Lat. *respīrāre*, breathe again.]

res•pite (rĕs′pĭt) ▸*n.* **1.** A short interval of rest or relief. See Syns at **pause. 2.** A reprieve. [< Lat. *respectus*, refuge. See RESPECT.]

re•splen•dent (rĭ-splĕn′dənt) ▸*adj.* Splendid or dazzling in appearance. [< Lat. *resplendēre*, shine brightly.] —**re•splen′dence, re•splen′den•cy** *n.* —**re•splen′dent•ly** *adv.*

re•spond (rĭ-spŏnd′) ▸*v.* **1.** To reply; answer. **2.** To act in return. **3.** To react positively or favorably. [< Lat. *respondēre*.]

re•spon•dent (rĭ-spŏn′dənt) ▸*n.* One who responds, esp. a defendant in a divorce or equity case. —**re•spon′dent** *adj.*

re•sponse (rĭ-spŏns′) ▸*n.* **1.** The act of responding. **2.** A reply; answer. **3.** A reaction to a specific stimulus. [< Lat. *respōnsum*.]

re•spon•si•bil•i•ty (rĭ-spŏn′sə-bĭl′ĭ-tē) ▸*n.*, *pl.* **-ties 1.** The state or fact of being responsible. **2.** Something for which one is responsible.

re•spon•si•ble (rĭ-spŏn′sə-bəl) ▸*adj.* **1.** Liable to be required to give account for something. **2.** Involving personal accountability: *a responsible position.* **3.** Being a source or cause. **4.** Dependable; reliable. See Syns at **reliable.** —**re•spon′si•ble•ness** *n.* —**re•spon′si•bly** *adv.*

re•spon•sive (rĭ-spŏn′sĭv) ▸*adj.* **1.** Readily reacting. **2.** Containing responses: *responsive liturgy.* —**re•spon′sive•ly** *adv.* —**re•spon′sive•ness** *n.*

rest¹ (rĕst) ▸*n.* **1.** Cessation or absence of work, motion, or activity. **2.** A period of inactivity, sleep, or quiet activity. **3.** *Mus.* **a.** An interval of silence having a specified length. **b.** The symbol indicating such a pause. **4.** A device used as a support: *a back rest.* ▶*v.* **1.** To stop motion or work. **2.** To lie down, esp. to sleep. **3.** To be or cause to be temporarily quiet or inactive. **4a.** To be supported or based: *The ladder rests against the wall.* **b.** To place, lay, or lean. **5.** To be imposed as a responsibility: *The decision rests with you.* **6.** To depend or rely. [< OE.] —**rest′er** *n.*

rest[1]
A. note
B. rest

rest[2] (rĕst) ▶*n.* **1.** Something left over; remainder. **2.** That or those remaining: *The rest are arriving later.* ▶*v.* To remain: *Rest assured that we'll be there.* [< Lat. *restāre*, stay behind : RE– + *stāre*, stand.]

rest area ▶*n.* A roaside area, often with public toilets, where motorists can stop to relax.

res•tau•rant (rĕs′tər-ənt, -tə-ränt′) ▶*n.* A place where meals are served to the public. [< Fr. *restaurer*, RESTORE.]

res•tau•ra•teur (rĕs′tər-ə-tûr′) also **res•tau•ran•teur** (-tə-rän-tûr′) ▶*n.* The manager or owner of a restaurant. [Fr.]

rest•ful (rĕst′fəl) ▶*adj.* Affording, marked by, or suggesting rest; tranquil. —**rest′ful•ly** *adv.* —**rest′ful•ness** *n.*

rest home ▶*n.* An establishment where the elderly or frail are housed and cared for.

res•ti•tu•tion (rĕs′tĭ-to͞o′shən, -tyo͞o′-) ▶*n.* **1.** The act of restoring something to the rightful owner. **2.** The act of compensating for loss, damage, or injury. [< Lat. *restituere*, restore : RE– + *statuere* set up.]

res•tive (rĕs′tĭv) ▶*adj.* **1.** Impatiently restless; uneasy. **2.** Difficult to control. [< Lat. *restāre*, keep back : RE– + *stāre*, stand.] —**res′tive•ly** *adv.* —**res′tive•ness** *n.*

Usage: *Restive* is properly applied to the impatience or uneasiness induced by external coercion or restriction and is not a general synonym for *restless: The atmosphere in the office was congenial, but she began to grow restless* (not *restive*).

rest•less (rĕst′lĭs) ▶*adj.* **1.** Marked by a lack of quiet, repose, or rest. **2.** Not able to rest, relax, or be still. **3.** Never still: *the restless sea.* See Usage Note at **restive.** —**rest′less•ly** *adv.* —**rest′less•ness** *n.*

res•to•ra•tion (rĕs′tə-rā′shən) ▶*n.* **1.** An act of restoring or the state of being restored. **2.** Something that has been restored.

re•stor•a•tive (rĭ-stôr′ə-tĭv, -stōr′-) ▶*adj.* Tending or having the power to restore. ▶*n.* Something that restores health or strength.

re•store (rĭ-stôr′, -stōr′) ▶*v.* **-stored, -stor•ing 1.** To bring back into existence or use. **2.** To bring back to an original condition. See Syns at **revive. 3.** To make restitution of; give back. [< Lat. *restaurāre.*] —**re•stor′er** *n.*

re•strain (rĭ-strān′) ▶*v.* **1.** To hold back. **2.** To deprive of freedom. **3.** To limit or restrict. [< Lat. *restringere*, bind back.] —**re•strain′a•ble** *adj.* —**re•strain′er** *n.*

re•straint (rĭ-strānt′) ▶*n.* **1.** The act of restraining or the condition of being restrained. **2.** Something that restrains. **3.** Control or repression of feelings.

re•strict (rĭ-strĭkt′) ▶*v.* To keep or confine within limits. [Lat. *restringere*, *restrict-*, bind up.] —**re•stric′tion** *n.*

re•stric•tive (rĭ-strĭk′tĭv) ▶*adj.* **1.** Tending or serving to restrict. **2.** *Gram.* Of or being a subordinate clause that restricts the meaning of the noun, phrase, or clause it modifies, as the clause *who live in glass houses* in *People who live in glass houses shouldn't throw stones.* See Usage Note at **that.** —**re•stric′tive•ly** *adv.* —**re•stric′tive•ness** *n.*

rest•room (rĕst′ro͞om′, -ro͝om′) ▶*n.* A room with toilets and sinks for public use.

re•sult (rĭ-zŭlt′) ▶*v.* **1.** To come about as a consequence. **2.** To end in a particular way. ▶*n.* **1.** A consequence; outcome. **2.** *Math.* The quantity or expression obtained by calculation. [< Lat. *resultāre*, leap back.] —**re•sul′tant** *adj. & n.*

re•sume (rĭ-zo͞om′) ▶*v.* **-sumed, -sum•ing 1.** To begin or take up again after interruption. **2.** To take or occupy again. [< Lat. *resūmere.*] —**re•sum′a•ble** *adj.* —**re•sump′tion** (-zŭmp′shən) *n.*

re•su•mé or **re•su•me** or **ré•su•mé** (rĕz′o͞o-mā′, rĕz′o͞o-mā′) ▶*n.* A summary of one's work experience and qualifications, often submitted when applying for a job. [Fr., summarized.]

re•sur•gent (rĭ-sûr′jənt) ▶*adj.* **1.** Experiencing or bringing about renewal or revival. **2.** Sweeping or surging back again. —**re•sur′gence** *n.*

res•ur•rect (rĕz′ə-rĕkt′) ▶*v.* **1.** To raise from the dead. **2.** To bring back, as into notice or use.

res•ur•rec•tion (rĕz′ə-rĕk′shən) ▶*n.* **1.** A revival; rebirth. **2. Resurrection** *Christianity* **a.** The rising of Jesus on the third day after the Crucifixion. **b.** The rising of the dead at the Last Judgment. [< Lat. *resurrēctus*, p.part. of *resurgere*, to rise again.]

re•sus•ci•tate (rĭ-sŭs′ĭ-tāt′) ▶*v.* **-tat•ed, -tat•ing.** To return or bring back to consciousness or life. See Syns at **revive.** [Lat. *resuscitāre.*] —**re•sus′ci•ta′tion** *n.* —**re•sus′ci•ta′tive** *adj.* —**re•sus′ci•ta′tor** *n.*

ret. ▶*abbr.* **1.** retired **2.** return

re•tail (rē′tāl′) ▶*n.* The sale of goods directly to consumers. [< OFr. *retaillier*, cut up.] —**re′tail′** *adj., adv. & v.* —**re′tail′er** *n.*

re•tain (rĭ-tān′) ▶*v.* **1.** To maintain possession of. **2.** To keep or hold in a particular place, condition, or position. **3.** To keep in mind; remember. **4.** To hire (e.g., a lawyer) by paying a fee. **5.** To keep in one's service or pay. [< Lat. *retinēre*, hold back.] —**re•tain′a•ble** *adj.* —**re•tain′ment** *n.*

re•tain•er[1] (rĭ-tā′nər) ▶*n.* **1.** One that retains. **2.** A servant or attendant, esp. in a noble or wealthy household.

re•tain•er[2] (rĭ-tā′nər) ▶*n.* A fee paid to retain a professional adviser.

re•take (rē-tāk′) ▶*v.* **1.** To take back or again. **2.** To recapture. **3.** To photograph, film, or record again. —**re′take′** *n.*

re•tal•i•ate (rĭ-tăl′ē-āt′) ▶*v.* **-at•ed, -at•ing.**

To return like for like; take revenge. [LLat. *re-tāliāre.*] —**re•tal′i•a′tion** *n.* —**re•tal′i•a′-tive, re•tal′i•a•to′ry** (-ə-tôr′ē, -tōr′ē) *adj.*

re•tard (rĭ-tärd′) ▸*v.* To cause to move or develop slowly; delay or impede. [< Lat. *retardāre.*]

re•tar•dant (rĭ-tär′dnt) ▸*adj.* Acting or tending to retard. —**re•tar′dant** *n.*

re•tar•da•tion (rē′tär-dā′shən) ▸*n.* **1.** The act or the state of being retarded. **2.** The extent to which something is held back or delayed. **3.** Mental retardation.

re•tard•ed (rĭ-tär′dĭd) ▸*adj. Often Offensive* Slow or arrested in mental, emotional, or physical development.

retch (rĕch) ▸*v.* To vomit or try to vomit. [< OE *hrǣcan.*] —**retch** *n.*

re•ten•tion (rĭ-tĕn′shən) ▸*n.* **1.** The act of retaining or the state of being retained. **2.** Capacity or power of retaining. [< Lat. *retentus*, p.part. of *retinēre*, retain.] —**re•ten′tive** *adj.* —**re•ten′tive•ness** *n.*

ret•i•cent (rĕt′ĭ-sənt) ▸*adj.* **1.** Inclined to keep one's personal affairs to oneself. **2.** Restrained or reserved in style. **3.** Reluctant; unwilling. [< Lat. *reticēre*, keep silent.] —**ret′i•cence** *n.* —**ret′i•cent•ly** *adv.*

ret•i•na (rĕt′n-ə) ▸*n., pl.* **-nas** or **-nae** (rĕt′n-ē′). A delicate, multilayered, light-sensitive membrane lining the inner eyeball and connected by the optic nerve to the brain. [< Med. Lat. *rētina.*] —**ret′i•nal** *adj.*

ret•i•nue (rĕt′n-o͞o′, -yo͞o′) ▸*n.* The attendants accompanying a high-ranking person. [< OFr. *retenir*, retain.]

re•tire (rĭ-tīr′) ▸*v.* **-tired, -tir•ing 1.** To withdraw, as for rest or seclusion. **2.** To go to bed. **3.** To withdraw from business or public life. **4.** To take out of use or circulation. **5.** *Baseball* To put out (a batter). [< OFr. *retirer*, draw back.] —**re•tire′ment** *n.*

re•tired (rĭ-tīrd′) ▸*adj.* **1.** Withdrawn from business or public life. **2.** Withdrawn; secluded.

re•tir•ee (rĭ-tīr′ē′) ▸*n.* One who has retired from active working life.

re•tir•ing (rĭ-tīr′ĭng) ▸*adj.* Shy and reserved; modest. —**re•tir′ing•ness** *n.*

re•tool (rē-to͞ol′) ▸*v.* **1.** To provide (e.g., a factory) with new machinery and tools. **2.** To revise and reorganize.

re•tort[1] (rĭ-tôrt′) ▸*v.* **1.** To reply or answer, esp. in a quick, caustic, or witty manner. **2.** To return in kind; pay back. ▸*n.* A quick, witty reply. [Lat. *retorquēre*, *retort-*, bend back.]

re•tort[2] (rĭ-tôrt′, rē′tôrt′) ▸*n.* A closed laboratory vessel with an outlet tube, used for distillation or decomposition by heat. [< Med.Lat. *retorta* < Lat. *retorquēre*, bend back.]

re•touch (rē-tŭch′) ▸*v.* **1.** To add new details or touches to. **2.** To improve or change (a photograph) as by removing flaws. —**re′-touch′** *n.*

re•trace (rē-trās′) ▸*v.* To trace again or back. —**re•trace′a•ble** *adj.*

re•tract (rĭ-trăkt′) ▸*v.* **1.** To take back. **2.** To draw back or in. See Syns at **recede.** [Lat. *retractāre*, revoke.] —**re•tract′a•ble, re•tract′i•ble** *adj.* —**re′trac′tion** *n.*

re•trac•tile (rĭ-trăk′tĭl, -tīl′) ▸*adj.* That can be drawn back or in.

re•tread (rē-trĕd′) ▸*v.* To fit (a worn tire) with a new tread. ▸*n.* (rē′trĕd′). A tire that has been retreaded.

re•treat (rĭ-trēt′) ▸*n.* **1.** The act or process of withdrawing, esp. from difficulty or danger. **2.** A place affording peace, privacy, or security. **3.** A period of retirement or solitude, esp. for prayer or meditation. **4a.** Withdrawal of a military force from an enemy attack. **b.** The signal for such withdrawal. **c.** A bugle call or drumbeat signaling the lowering of the flag at sunset. ▸*v.* To fall or draw back; withdraw. See Syns at **recede.** [< Lat. *retrahere*, draw back.]

re•trench (rĭ-trĕnch′) ▸*v.* **1.** To cut down; reduce. **2.** To curtail expenses; economize. [< OFr. *retrenchier.*] —**re•trench′ment** *n.*

ret•ri•bu•tion (rĕt′rə-byo͞o′shən) ▸*n.* Something given or demanded in repayment, esp. punishment. [< Lat. *retribuere*, pay back.] —**re•trib′u•tive** (rĭ-trĭb′yə-tĭv), **re•trib′u•to′ry** (-tôr′ē, -tōr′ē) *adj.*

re•trieve (rĭ-trēv′) ▸*v.* **-trieved, -triev•ing 1.** To get or bring back; regain. **2.** To find and carry back; fetch. [< OFr. *retrover.*] —**re•triev′a•ble** *adj.* —**re•triev′al** *n.*

re•triev•er (rĭ-trē′vər) ▸*n.* One that retrieves, esp. any of several breeds of dog developed and trained to retrieve game.

ret•ro (rĕt′rō) ▸*adj.* **1.** Retroactive. **2.** Involving or reminiscent of things past.

retro– ▸*pref.* Backward; back: *retroactive* [< Lat. *retrō.*]

ret•ro•ac•tive (rĕt′rō-ăk′tĭv) ▸*adj.* Applying to a period before enactment. —**ret′ro•ac′-tive•ly** *adv.*

ret•ro•fire (rĕt′rō-fīr′) ▸*v.* To fire (a retro-rocket).

ret•ro•fit (rĕt′rō-fĭt′) ▸*v.* To provide with parts or equipment unavailable at the time of original manufacture. —**ret′ro•fit′** *n.*

ret•ro•grade (rĕt′rə-grād′) ▸*adj.* **1.** Moving or tending backward. **2.** Reverting to an earlier or inferior condition. ▸*v.* **-grad•ed, -grad•ing 1.** To move backward. See Syns at **recede. 2.** To deteriorate; degenerate. [< Lat. *retrōgradī*, go back.]

ret•ro•gress (rĕt′rə-grĕs′, rĕt′rə-grĕs′) ▸*v.* **1.** To return to an earlier, inferior, or less complex condition. **2.** To go or move backward. [Lat. *retrōgradī*, *retrōgress-*, go backward.] —**ret′-ro•gres′sion** *n.* —**ret′ro•gres′sive** *adj.* —**re′tro•gres′sive•ly** *adv.*

ret•ro•rock•et (rĕt′rō-rŏk′ĭt) ▸*n.* A rocket used to retard, arrest, or reverse motion.

ret•ro•spect (rĕt′rə-spĕkt′) ▸*n.* A review or contemplation of things in the past. [< Lat. *retrōspicere*, look back at : RETRO– + *specere*, look at.] —**ret′ro•spec′tion** *n.* —**ret′ro•spec′tive** *n. & adj.*

ret•ro•vi•rus (rĕt′rō-vī′rəs, rĕt′rə-vī′-) ▸*n.* A virus, such as the one causing AIDS, that contains RNA and an enzyme that can create DNA using RNA as a template.

re•turn (rĭ-tûrn′) ▸*v.* **1.** To go or come back, as to an earlier condition or place. **2.** To answer or respond. **3.** To send, put, or carry back. **4.** To give in reciprocation. See Syns at **reciprocate. 5.** To yield (profit or interest). **6.** *Law* To deliver (e.g. a verdict) to a court of law. **7.** To reelect to an office. ▸*n.* **1.** The act of returning. **2.** Something returned. **3.** A periodic recurrence. **4.** Something exchanged for that received; repayment. **5.** A reply; response. **6.** A profit or yield. **7.** An official report: *a tax return.* ▶*adj.* **1.** Of or bringing about a return. **2.** Given, sent, or done in reciprocation: *return mail.* [< OFr. *retourner.*] —**re•turn′a•ble** *adj. & n.* —**re•turn′er** *n.*

re•turn•ee (rĭ-tûr′nē′) ▶*n.* One who returns, as from military duty overseas.

re•un•ion (rē-yo͞on′yən) ▶*n.* **1.** The act of reuniting or the state of being reunited. **2.** A gathering of the members of a group who have been separated.

Ré•un•ion (rē-yo͞on′yən, rā-ü-nyôN′) An island of France in the W Indian Ocean SW of Mauritius.

Reu•ther (ro͞o′thər), **Walter Philip.** 1907–70. Amer. labor leader.

rev (rĕv) *Informal* ▶*n.* A revolution, as of a motor. ▶*v.* **revved, rev•ving 1.** To increase the speed of (e.g., a motor). **2.** To make livelier or more productive.

rev. ▶*abbr.* **1.** revenue **2.** reverse **3.** review **4.** revision **5.** revolution

Rev. ▶*abbr.* Reverend

re•vamp (rē-vămp′) ▶*v.* To make over; revise. —**re•vamp′** *n.*

re•veal (rĭ-vēl′) ▶*v.* **1.** To make known. **2.** To bring to view; show. [< Lat. *revēlāre.*]

rev•eil•le (rĕv′ə-lē) ▶*n.* A signal, as on a bugle, given in the morning to awaken soldiers. [< OFr. *resveiller*, awaken.]

rev•el (rĕv′əl) ▶*v.* **-eled, -el•ing** also **-elled, -el•ling 1.** To take great pleasure or delight. **2.** To engage boisterous festivities. ▶*n.* A boisterous festivity or celebration. [< Lat. *rebellāre*, to rebel.] —**rev′el•er, rev′el•ler** *n.* —**rev′el•ry** *n.*

rev•e•la•tion (rĕv′ə-lā′shən) ▶*n.* **1a.** An act of revealing. **b.** Something revealed, esp. a dramatic disclosure. **2. Revelation.** See table at **Bible.** [< Lat. *revēlāre*, reveal.] —**rev′e•la•to′ry** (-lə-tôr′ē, -tōr′ē) *adj.*

re•venge (rĭ-vĕnj′) ▶*v.* **-venged, -veng•ing.** To inflict punishment in return for (injury or insult); avenge. ▶*n.* **1.** The act of revenging. **2.** A desire for revenge. **3.** An opportunity to retaliate or get even. [< OFr. *revengier.*] —**re•venge′ful** *adj.* —**re•veng′er** *n.*

rev•e•nue (rĕv′ə-no͞o, -nyo͞o) ▶*n.* **1.** The income of a government. **2.** Yield from property or investment. [< OFr. < Lat. *revenīre*, return : RE– + *venīre*, come.]

re•ver•ber•ate (rĭ-vûr′bə-rāt′) ▶*v.* **-at•ed, -at•ing.** To echo repeatedly; resound. See Syns at **echo.** [Lat. *reverberāre.*] —**re•ver′ber•a′tion** *n.*

re•vere (rĭ-vîr′) ▶*v.* **-vered, -ver•ing.** To regard with deference and devotion. [< Lat. *reverērī.*]

Revere, Paul. 1735–1818. Amer. Revolutionary hero.

rev•er•ence (rĕv′ər-əns) ▶*n.* **1.** Profound awe and respect. **2.** An act of respect, esp. a bow or curtsy. **3. Reverence** Used as a form of address for certain members of the Christian clergy. ▶*v.* **-enced, -enc•ing.** To consider or treat with reverence.

rev•er•end (rĕv′ər-ənd) ▶*adj.* **1.** Deserving reverence. **2. Reverend** A title of respect for certain Christian clerics. ▶*n. Informal* A cleric or minister. [< Lat. *reverendus.*]

rev•er•ent (rĕv′ər-ənt) ▶*adj.* Feeling or expressing reverence. —**rev′er•ent•ly** *adv.*

rev•er•en•tial (rĕv′ə-rĕn′shəl) ▶*adj.* **1.** Reverent. **2.** Inspiring reverence.

rev•er•ie (rĕv′ə-rē) ▶*n.* **1.** A state of abstracted musing. **2.** A daydream. [< OFr. *rever*, to dream.]

re•ver•sal (rĭ-vûr′səl) ▶*n.* **1.** The act or an instance of reversing. **2.** A usu. adverse change in fortune.

re•verse (rĭ-vûrs′) ▶*adj.* **1.** Turned backward in position, direction, or order. **2.** Moving, acting, or organized in a manner contrary to the usual. **3.** Causing backward movement: *a reverse gear.* ▶*n.* **1.** The opposite or contrary. **2.** The back or rear part. **3.** A change to an opposite position, condition, or direction esp. for the worse. **4.** A mechanism, such as a gear in a motor vehicle, used to reverse movement. ▶*v.* **-versed, -vers•ing 1.** To turn around to the opposite direction or position. **2.** To exchange the positions of; transpose. **3.** *Law* To revoke or annul. **4.** To turn or move in the opposite direction. **5.** To reverse the action of an engine. [< Lat. *revertere, revers-*, turn back.] —**re•vers′er** *n.* —**re•vers′i•ble** *adj. & n.*

reverse osmosis ▶*n.* A method of purifying water with a membrane across which salts or impurities cannot pass.

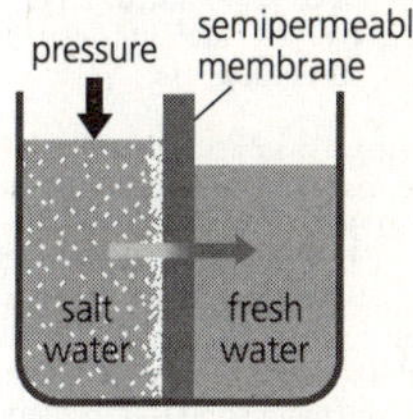

reverse osmosis

re•vert (rĭ-vûrt′) ▶*v.* **1.** To return to a former condition, practice, or belief. See Usage Note at **redundancy. 2.** *Law* To return to the former owner or to the rightful heirs. [< Lat. *revertere.*] —**re•ver′sion** *n.* —**re•ver′sion•ar•y** *adj.*

re•view (rĭ-vyo͞o′) ▶*v.* **1.** To look over, study, or examine again. **2.** To look back on. **3.** To examine critically or for correction. **4.** To write or give a critical report on. **5.** *Law* To reexamine judicially, esp. in a higher court. **6.** To subject to a formal inspection. ▶*n.* **1.** A reexamination or reconsideration. **2.** A restudying of subject matter. **3.** An inspection or examination for evaluation. **4a.** A critical estimate of a work or performance. **b.** A periodical devoted esp. to critical articles and essays. **5.** A formal military inspection. **6.** *Law* A judicial reexamination, esp. by a higher court. [< Lat. *revidēre* : RE– + *vidēre*, see.]

re•view•er (rĭ-vyo͞o′ər) ▶*n.* One who reviews, esp. one who writes critical reviews.

re•vile (rĭ-vīl′) ▶*v.* **-viled, -vil•ing.** To assail with or use abusive language. [< OFr. *reviler.*] —**re•vile′ment** *n.* —**re•vil′er** *n.*

re•vise (rĭ-vīz′) ▶*v.* **-vised, -vis•ing 1.** To prepare a new edition of (a text). **2.** To reconsider and modify. [Lat. *revīsere*, visit again : RE– + *vidēre, vīs-*, see.] —**re•vis′er, re•vi′sor** *n.* —**re•vi′sion** (-vĭzh′ən) *n.*

re•vi•sion•ism (rĭ-vĭzh′ə-nĭz′əm) ▶*n.* Advocacy of the revision of an accepted, usu. long-standing view, theory, or doctrine. —**re•vi′sion•ist** *adj. & n.*

re•viv•al (rĭ-vī′vəl) ▶*n.* **1.** The act of reviving or the state of being revived. **2.** A new presentation, as of a play. **3.** A meeting or series of meetings for reawakening religious faith.

re•vive (rĭ-vīv′) ▶*v.* **-vived, -viv•ing 1.** To return or bring back to life or consciousness. **2.** To impart new health, vigor, or spirit to. **3.** To restore to use, currency, or notice. **4.** To present (e.g., an old play) again. [< Lat. *revīvere*, live again : RE– + *vīvere*, live.] —**re•viv′a•ble** *adj.* —**re•viv′er** *n.*

Syns: *restore, resuscitate, revivify* **v.**

re•viv•i•fy (rē-vĭv′ə-fī′) ▶*v.* **-fied, -fy•ing.** To give new life to. See Syns at **revive.** —**re•viv′i•fi•ca′tion** *n.*

rev•o•ca•ble (rĕv′ə-kə-bəl) also **re•vok•a•ble** (rĭ-vō′-) ▶*adj.* That can be revoked.

re•voke (rĭ-vōk′) ▶*v.* **-voked, -vok•ing.** To void or annul by recalling or withdrawing. [< Lat. *revocāre*, call back.] —**rev′o•ca′tion** (rĕv′ə-kā′shən) *n.* —**re•vok′er** *n.*

re•volt (rĭ-vōlt′) ▶*v.* **1.** To attempt to overthrow the authority of the state; rebel. **2.** To oppose or refuse to accept something. **3.** To fill with disgust or abhorrence; repel. See Syns at **disgust.** ▶*n.* An uprising, esp. against state authority; rebellion. [< VLat. **revolvitāre*, overturn.]

re•volt•ing (rĭ-vōl′tĭng) ▶*adj.* Causing abhorrence or disgust. See Syns at **offensive.**

rev•o•lu•tion (rĕv′ə-lo͞o′shən) ▶*n.* **1a.** Orbital motion about a point, esp. as distinguished from axial rotation. **b.** A turning or rotation about an axis. **c.** A single complete cycle of such orbital or axial motion. **2.** The overthrow of one government and its replacement with another. **3.** A sudden or momentous change in a situation. [< Lat. *revolūtus*, p.part. of *revolvere*, turn over.]

rev•o•lu•tion•ar•y (rĕv′ə-lo͞o′shə-nĕr′ē) ▶*adj.* **1.** Of or relating to a revolution: *revolutionary war.* **2.** Marked by or resulting in radical change. ▶*n., pl.* **-ies.** One who supports or engages in revolution.

rev•o•lu•tion•ist (rĕv′ə-lo͞o′shə-nĭst) ▶*n.* A revolutionary. —**rev′o•lu′tion•ist** *adj.*

rev•o•lu•tion•ize (rĕv′ə-lo͞o′shə-nīz′) ▶*v.* **-ized, -iz•ing.** To bring about a radical change in.

re•volve (rĭ-vŏlv′) ▶*v.* **-volved, -volv•ing 1.** To orbit a central point. **2.** To turn on an axis; rotate. **3.** To recur periodically. [< Lat. *revolvere*, turn over.] —**re•volv′a•ble** *adj.*

re•volv•er (rĭ-vŏl′vər) ▶*n.* A pistol having a revolving cylinder with several cartridge chambers that may be fired in succession.

re•vue (rĭ-vyo͞o′) ▶*n.* A musical show consisting of often satirical skits, songs, and dances. [Fr. < OFr. REVIEW.]

re•vul•sion (rĭ-vŭl′shən) ▶*n.* **1.** A sudden strong feeling of disgust or loathing. **2.** A withdrawing or turning away from something. [< Lat. *revulsus*, p.part. of *revellere*, tear back.]

re•ward (rĭ-wôrd′) ▶*n.* **1.** Something given or received for worthy behavior. **2.** Money offered or given for some special service, such as the return of a lost article. ▶*v.* To give a reward to or for. [< AN.]

re•word (rē-wûrd′) ▶*v.* To state or express again in different words: *reword a memo.*

re•write (rē-rīt′) ▶*v.* To write again, esp. in a different or improved form. —**re′write′** *n.*

Rey•kja•vík (rā′kyə-vēk′, -vĭk′) The capital of Iceland, in the SW. Pop. 101,418.

Reyn•olds (rĕn′əldz), Sir **Joshua.** 1723–92. British painter.

Rf ▶ The symbol for the element **rutherfordium.**

RF ▶*abbr.* **1.** radio frequency **2.** right field

RFD ▶*abbr.* rural free delivery

Rh[1] (är′āch′) ▶*adj.* Of or relating to the Rh factor: *an Rh antigen.*

Rh[2] ▶ The symbol for the element **rhodium.**

Rhae•ti•a (rē′shē-ə, -shə) An ancient Roman province in present-day E Switzerland and W Austria. —**Rhae′tian** *adj. & n.*

Rhae•to-Ro•mance (rē′tō-rō-măns′) ▶*n.* A group of Romance dialects spoken in S Switzerland, N Italy, and the Tyrol.

rhap•so•dy (răp′sə-dē) ▶*n., pl.* **-dies 1.** Exalted or excessively enthusiastic expression of feeling. **2.** *Mus.* A usu. instrumental composition of irregular form, often incorporating improvisation. [< Gk. *rhapsōidein*, recite poems.] —**rhap•sod′ic** (-sŏd′ĭk) *adj.* —**rhap•sod′i•cal•ly** *adv.* —**rhap′so•dize** *v.*

rhe•a (rē′ə) ▶*n.* A flightless, three-toed South American bird resembling the ostrich. [< *Rhea*, a character in Roman myth.]

Rhee (rē), **Syngman.** 1875–1965. South Korean politician.

Rheims or **Reims** (rēmz, răɴs). A city of NE France ENE of Paris. Pop. 180,611.

rhe•ni•um (rē′nē-əm) ▶*n. Symbol* **Re** A rare, dense, silvery-white metallic element used for electrical contacts and high-temperature thermocouples. At. no. 75. See table at **element.** [< Lat. *Rhēnus*, the Rhine.]

rhe•o•stat (rē′ə-stăt′) ▶*n.* A variable electrical resistor used to regulate current. [< Gk. *rheos*, current.] —**rhe′o•stat′ic** *adj.*

rhe•sus monkey (rē′səs) ▶*n.* A brownish monkey of India, often used in scientific research. [< Gk. *Rhēsos*, a mythical king of Thrace.]

rhet•o•ric (rĕt′ər-ĭk) ▶*n.* **1.** The art or study of using language effectively and persuasively. **2.** A style of speaking or writing: *political rhetoric.* **3.** Language that is pretentious or insincere. [< Gk. *rhētōr*, public speaker.] —**rhe•tor′i•cal** (rĭ-tôr′ĭ-kəl, -tŏr′-) *adj.* —**rhe•tor′i•cal•ly** *adv.* —**rhet′o•ri′cian** (rĕt′ə-rĭsh′ən) *n.*

rhetorical question ▶*n.* A question to which no answer is expected.

rheum (ro͞om) ▶*n.* A watery mucous discharge from the eyes or nose. [< Gk. *rheuma.*] —**rheum′y** *adj.*

rheu•mat•ic (ro͞o-măt′ĭk) ▶*adj.* Of or suffering from rheumatism. ▶*n.* One who is affected by rheumatism.

rheumatic fever ▶*n.* A severe infectious disease occurring chiefly in children, marked by fever and painful inflammation of the joints and frequently resulting in permanent damage to the heart valves.

rheu•ma•tism (ro͞o′mə-tĭz′əm) ▶*n.* **1.** Any of several pathological conditions of the muscles, tendons, joints, bones, or nerves, marked by pain and disability. **2.** Rheumatoid arthritis. [< Gk. *rheuma*, RHEUM.]

rheu•ma•toid arthritis (ro͞o′mə-toid′) ►*n.* A chronic disease marked by stiffness, inflammation, and deformity of the joints.

Rh factor ►*n.* Any of several substances on the surface of red blood cells that induce a strong antigenic response in individuals lacking the substance. [< RH(ESUS MONKEY).]

Rhine (rīn) A river of W Europe rising in E Switzerland and flowing about 1,319 km (820 mi) through Germany and the Netherlands to the North Sea.

Rhine•land (rīn′lănd′, -lənd) A region along the Rhine R. in W Germany.

rhine•stone (rīn′stōn′) ►*n.* A colorless artificial gem of paste or glass. [From the *Rhine* River.] —**rhine′stoned′** *adj.*

rhi•ni•tis (rī-nī′tĭs) ►*n.* Inflammation of the nasal mucous membranes. [< Gk. *rhis, rhin-*, nose.]

rhi•no (rī′nō) ►*n., pl.* **-nos.** A rhinoceros.

rhi•noc•er•os (rī-nŏs′ər-əs) ►*n., pl.* **-os** or **-os•es.** A large, thick-skinned, herbivorous mammal of Africa and Asia, having one or two upright horns on the snout. [< Gk. *rhinokerōs.*]

rhi•zome (rī′zōm′) ►*n.* A horizontal, usu. underground stem that often sends out roots and shoots. [< Gk. *rhiza*, root.]

Rh-neg•a•tive (är′āch-nĕg′ə-tĭv) ►*adj.* Lacking an Rh factor.

rho (rō) ►*n.* The 17th letter of the Greek alphabet. [Gk. *rhō.*]

Rhode Island (rōd) A state of the NE US on the Atlantic. Cap. Providence. Pop. 1,005,984. —**Rhode Is′land•er** *n.*

Rhodes (rōdz) The largest of the Dodecanese Is. of SE Greece, in the Aegean off SW Turkey.

Rhodes, Cecil John. 1853–1902. British financier and colonizer.

Rho•de•sia (rō-dē′zhə) See **Zimbabwe.** —**Rho•de′sian** *adj. & n.*

rho•di•um (rō′dē-əm) ►*n. Symbol* **Rh** A hard, durable, silvery-white metallic element used to form high-temperature alloys with platinum. At. no. 45. See table at **element.** [< Gk. *rhodon*, rose.]

rho•do•den•dron (rō′də-dĕn′drən) ►*n.* A usu. evergreen ornamental shrub having clusters of variously colored, often bell-shaped flowers. [< Gk., oleander.]

rhom•boid (rŏm′boid′) ►*n.* A parallelogram with unequal adjacent sides.

rhom•bus (rŏm′bəs) ►*n., pl.* **-bus•es** or **-bi** (-bī). An equilateral parallelogram. [< Gk. *rhombos.*]

Rhone or **Rhône** (rōn). A river of SW Switzerland and SE France, flowing about 813 km (505 mi) to the Mediterranean Sea.

rhp ►*abbr.* rated horsepower

Rh-pos•i•tive (är′āch-pŏz′ĭ-tĭv) ►*adj.* Containing an Rh factor.

rhu•barb (ro͞o′bärb′) ►*n.* **1.** A plant with long reddish leafstalks that are edible when cooked. **2.** *Informal* A heated dispute; fray. [Prob. < LLat. *rhabarbarum*, foreign rhubarb.]

rhyme also **rime** (rīm) ►*n.* **1.** Correspondence of terminal sounds of words or of lines of verse. **2.** A poem or poems having such correspondence. **3.** A word that corresponds with another in terminal sound. ►*v.* **rhymed, rhym•ing** also **rimed, rim•ing 1.** To form a rhyme. **2.** To compose rhymes or verse. **3.** To use as a rhyme. [< OFr. *rime.*]

rhythm (rĭth′əm) ►*n.* **1.** Movement or action marked by the regular recurrence of different quantities or conditions. **2.** The patterned, recurring alternations of contrasting elements of sound. **3.** *Mus.* The pattern of musical movement through time. **4.** Metrical movement as regulated by the alternation of long and short or accented and unaccented syllables. [< Gk. *rhuthmos.*] —**rhyth′mic, rhyth′mi•cal** *adj.* —**rhyth′mi•cal•ly** *adv.*

rhythm and blues ►*pl.n. (takes sing. or pl. v.)* A kind of music that combines blues and jazz, marked by a strong backbeat.

rhythm method ►*n.* A birth-control method based on abstinence during ovulation.

RI or **R.I.** ►*abbr.* Rhode Island

ri•al (rē-ôl′, -äl′) ►*n.* See table at **currency.** [Pers. < Ar. *riyāl.*]

rib (rĭb) ►*n.* **1.** One of a series of long, curved bones extending from the spine to or toward the sternum in most vertebrates. **2.** Something similar to a rib and serving to shape or support. **3.** A cut of meat with one or more rib bones. **4.** A raised ridge or wale in fabric. ►*v.* **ribbed, rib•bing 1.** To shape, support, or provide with a rib or ribs. **2.** To make with ridges. **3.** *Informal* To tease or make fun of. See Syns at **banter.** [< OE *ribb.*]

rib•ald (rĭb′əld, rī′bôld′) ►*adj.* Marked by vulgar, lewd humor. ►*n.* A vulgar, lewdly funny person. [< OFr. *riber*, be wanton.] —**rib′ald•ry** *n.*

rib•bing (rĭb′ĭng) ►*n.* **1.** An arrangement of ribs, as in a boat. **2.** *Informal* The act or an instance of joking or teasing.

rib•bon (rĭb′ən) ►*n.* **1.** A narrow strip or band of fabric, finished at the edges and used for trimming or tying. **2.** Something resembling a ribbon in shape. **3. ribbons** Tattered or ragged strips. **4.** An inked band used for making an impression, as in a typewriter. [< OFr. *ruban*, prob. of Gmc. orig.]

rib cage ►*n.* The structure formed by the ribs and the bones to which they are attached.

ri•bo•fla•vin (rī′bō-flā′vĭn, -bə-) ►*n.* An orange-yellow crystalline compound, the principal growth-promoting factor in the vitamin B complex, found in milk, leafy vegetables, fresh meat, and egg yolks. [RIBO(SE) + Lat. *flāvus*, yellow.]

ri•bo•nu•cle•ic acid (rī′bō-no͞o-klē′ĭk, -klā′-, -nyo͞o-) ►*n.* See **RNA.** [RIBO(SE) + NUCLEIC ACID.]

ri•bose (rī′bōs′) ►*n.* A crystalline sugar, occurring as a component of riboflavin, nucleotides, and nucleic acids. [Ger.]

ri•bo•some (rī′bə-sōm′) ►*n.* A minute, round particle composed of RNA and protein found in cytoplasm and active in the synthesis of proteins. [RIBO(SE) + -SOME[3].] —**ri′bo•so′mal** *adj.*

Ri•car•do (rĭ-kär′dō), **David.** 1772–1823. British economist.

rice (rīs) ►*n.* **1.** A cereal grass cultivated extensively in warm climates. **2.** The starchy edible grain of this plant. [< Gk. *oruza.*]

rich (rĭch) ►*adj.* **-er, -est 1.** Possessing great material wealth. **2.** Having great worth or value: *a rich harvest.* **3.** Magnificent; sumptuous. **4a.** Abundant: *rich in ideas.* **b.** Abounding, esp. in natural resources: *a rich land.* **5.** Very productive: *rich soil.* **6a.** Containing a

large amount of choice ingredients, such as butter, sugar, or eggs. **b.** Strongly aromatic. **7a.** Pleasantly full and mellow. **b.** Warm and strong in color. **8.** Containing a large proportion of fuel to air: *a rich gas mixture.* **9.** *Informal* Highly amusing. [< OFr. *riche* and OE *rīce.*] —**rich'ly** *adv.* —**rich'ness** *n.*
Syns: *affluent, moneyed, wealthy* **adj.**

Rich•ard I (rĭch'ərd). "the Lion-Hearted." 1157–99. King of England (1189–99).

Richard II. 1367–1400. King of England (1377–99).

Richard III. 1452–85. King of England (1483–85).

Rich•ard•son (rĭch'ərd-sən), **Samuel.** 1689–1761. English writer.

Ri•che•lieu (rĭsh'ə-lo͞o', rē-shə-lyœ'), Duc de. 1585–1642. French prelate and politician.

rich•es (rĭch'ĭz) ►*pl.n.* Valuable or precious possessions. [< OFr. *richesse.*]

Rich•mond (rĭch'mənd) **1.** The capital of VA, in the E-central part on the James R. Pop. 203,056. **2.** See **Staten Island.**

Rich•ter scale (rĭk'tər) ►*n.* A logarithmic scale usu. ranging from 1 to 9, used to express an earthquake's magnitude. [After Charles F. *Richter* (1900–1985).]

rick (rĭk) ►*n.* A stack, as of hay or straw, esp. when covered. [< OE *hrēac.*]

rick•ets (rĭk'ĭts) ►*n.* *(takes sing. or pl. v.)* A disease occurring chiefly in children, resulting from a lack of vitamin D or calcium, and marked by defective bone growth. [?]

rick•et•y (rĭk'ĭ-tē) ►*adj.* **-i•er, -i•est 1.** Likely to break or fall apart; shaky. **2.** Of, having, or resembling rickets. [< RICKETS.] —**rick'et•i•ness** *n.*

rick•ey (rĭk'ē) ►*n., pl.* **-eys.** A drink of soda water, lime or lemon juice, sugar, and usu. gin. [Prob. < the name *Rickey.*]

Rick•o•ver (rĭk'ō'vər), **Hyman George.** 1900–86. Amer. admiral.

rick•sha or **rick•shaw** (rĭk'shô) ►*n.* A jinriksha.

ric•o•chet (rĭk'ə-shā', rĭk'ə-shā') ►*v.* **-cheted** (-shād'), **-chet•ing** (-shā'ĭng). To rebound from a surface. [Fr.] —**ric'o•chet'** *n.*

ri•cot•ta (rĭ-kŏt'ə) ►*n.* A soft Italian cheese that resembles cottage cheese. [Ital.]

rid (rĭd) ►*v.* **rid** or **rid•ded, rid•ding.** To free from. [< ON *rydhja*, clear land.] —**rid'dance** *n.*

rid•dle[1] (rĭd'l) ►*v.* **-dled, -dling 1.** To pierce with numerous holes; perforate. **2.** To spread throughout. [< OE *hriddel*, sieve.]

rid•dle[2] (rĭd'l) ►*n.* **1.** A puzzling question or statement requiring thought to answer or understand. **2.** One that is perplexing; enigma. ►*v.* **-dled, -dling.** To solve or explain. [< OE *rǣdels.*] —**rid'dler** *n.*

ride (rīd) ►*v.* **rode** (rōd), **rid•den** (rĭd'n), **rid•ing 1.** To be carried or conveyed, as in a vehicle or on horseback. **2.** To travel over a surface: *This car rides well.* **3.** To move on or as if on water. **4.** To be sustained or supported as on a pivot or an axle. **5.** To be contingent; depend. **6.** To continue without interference: *Let the matter ride.* **7.** To sit on and move in a given direction: *rode my bike to town.* **8.** To take part in or do by riding: *He rode his last race.* **9.** To cause to be carried. —***phrasal verb:*** **ride out** to survive or outlast: *rode out the storm.* ►*n.* **1.** The act or an instance of riding. **2.** A path made for riding. **3.** A device, as at an amusement park, that one rides for pleasure or excitement. **4.** A means of transportation: *waiting for my ride to come.* [< OE *rīdan.*]

Ride, Sally. b. 1951. Amer. astronaut; the first US woman in space (1983).

rid•er (rī'dər) ►*n.* **1.** One that rides. **2.** An amendment or addition, esp. a clause added to a legislative bill.

rid•er•ship (rī'dər-shĭp') ►*n.* The number of people who ride a public transport system.

ridge (rĭj) ►*n.* **1.** A long narrow upper section or crest: *the ridge of a wave.* **2.** A long narrow chain of hills or mountains. **3.** A long, narrow, or crested part of the body: *the ridge of the nose.* **4.** The horizontal line formed by the juncture of two sloping planes, esp. the line formed by the surfaces at the top of a roof. **5.** A narrow, raised strip, as in cloth or on plowed ground. ►*v.* **ridged, ridg•ing.** To mark with, form into, or provide with ridges. [< OE *hrycg.*]

ridge•pole (rĭj'pōl') ►*n.* A horizontal beam at the ridge of a roof to which the rafters are attached.

rid•i•cule (rĭd'ĭ-kyo͞ol') ►*n.* Words or actions intended to evoke contemptuous laughter at a person or thing. ►*v.* **-culed, -cul•ing.** To make fun of. [< Lat. *rīdiculus*, laughable.]

ri•dic•u•lous (rĭ-dĭk'yə-ləs) ►*adj.* Deserving or inspiring ridicule; absurd or preposterous. —**ri•dic'u•lous•ly** *adv.* —**ri•dic'u•lous•ness** *n.*

ri•el (rē-ĕl') ►*n.* See table at **currency.** [?]

rife (rīf) ►*adj.* **rif•er, rif•est 1.** Widespread; prevalent. **2.** Abounding; full. [< OE *rȳfe.*]

riff (rĭf) ►*n.* *Mus.* A short rhythmic phrase, esp. one repeated in improvisation. [?]

riff•raff (rĭf'răf') ►*n.* **1.** Disreputable or worthless people. **2.** Rubbish; trash. [< AN *rif et raf*, one and all.]

ri•fle[1] (rī'fəl) ►*n.* A firearm with a rifled bore, designed to be fired from the shoulder. ►*v.* **-fled, -fling.** To cut spiral grooves within. [< OFr. *rifler*, scratch.]

ri•fle[2] (rī'fəl) ►*v.* **-fled, -fling 1.** To search with intent to steal. **2.** To rob: *rifle a safe.* [< OFr. *rifler*, plunder.] —**ri'fler** *n.*

ri•fle•ry (rī'fəl-rē) ►*n.* The skill and practice of shooting a rifle.

ri•fling (rī'flĭng) ►*n.* Grooves cut in a rifle barrel.

rift (rĭft) ►*n.* **1.** A narrow fissure in rock. **2.** A break in friendly relations. ►*v.* To split or cause to split open. [ME, of Scand. orig.]

rig (rĭg) ►*v.* **rigged, rig•ging 1.** To equip; fit out. **2.** To equip (a ship) with rigging. **3.** *Informal* To dress, clothe, or adorn. **4.** To make or construct in a makeshift manner. **5.** To manipulate dishonestly for personal gain: *rig a prizefight.* ►*n.* **1.** The arrangement of masts, spars, and sails on a sailing vessel. **2.** Gear used for a particular purpose. **3a.** A truck, tractor, or tractor-trailer. **b.** A vehicle with its horses. [ME *riggen.*]

Ri•ga (rē'gə) The capital of Latvia, in the central part on the **Gulf of Riga,** an inlet of the Baltic Sea. Pop. 865,227.

rig•a•ma•role (rĭg'ə-mə-rōl') ►*n.* Var. of **rigmarole.**

rig•ging (rĭg'ĭng) ►*n.* **1.** The system of ropes, chains, and tackle used to support and control the masts, sails, and yards of a sailing vessel. **2.** The supporting material for construction work.

right (rīt) ►*adj.* **-er, -est 1.** Conforming with justice or morality. **2.** In accordance with fact, reason, or truth; correct. **3.** Fitting, proper, or appropriate. **4.** Favorable, desirable, or convenient. **5.** In or into a satisfactory state or condition. **6.** Intended to be worn or positioned facing outward: *the right side of the medallion.* **7.** Of, located on, or corresponding to the side of the body to the south when one is facing east. **8.** often **Right** Of or belonging to the political right. **9.** *Math.* **a.** Formed by or in reference to a line or plane that is perpendicular to another line or plane. **b.** Having a right angle: *a right triangle.* ►*n.* **1.** That which is just, morally good, legal, proper, or fitting. **2a.** The direction or position on the right side. **b.** A turn in this direction: *make a right.* **c.** The right side. **d.** The right hand. **3.** often **Right** The people and groups who pursue conservative or reactionary political goals. **4.** Something due to a person or governmental body by law, tradition, or nature. ►*adv.* **1.** Toward or on the right. **2.** In a straight line; directly. **3.** In the proper or desired manner. **4.** Exactly; just: *right over there.* **5.** Immediately: *right after dinner.* **6.** Used as an intensive: *kept right on going.* **7.** Used in titles: *The Right Reverend Pat Smith.* ►*v.* **1.** To put in or restore to an upright or proper position. **2.** To put in order or set right; correct. **3.** To redress: *right a wrong.* —***idioms:* by rights** In a just or proper manner; justly. **to rights** In a satisfactory or orderly condition. [< OE *riht.*] —**right′er** *n.* —**right′ness** *n.*

right angle ►*n.* An angle of 90° formed by two intersecting perpendicular lines. —**right′-an′gled** *adj.*

right•eous (rī′chəs) ►*adj.* Morally upright; just. [< OE *rihtwīs.*] —**right′eous•ly** *adv.* —**right′eous•ness** *n.*

right field ►*n. Baseball* The third of the outfield that is to the right as viewed from home plate. —**right field′er** *n.*

right•ful (rīt′fəl) ►*adj.* **1.** Right or proper; just. **2.** Having or held by a rightful claim. —**right′ful•ly** *adv.* —**right′ful•ness** *n.*

right-hand (rīt′hănd′) ►*adj.* **1.** Relating to or located on the right. **2.** Designed for or done with the right hand. **3.** Indispensible; reliable.

right-hand•ed (rīt′hăn′dĭd) ►*adj.* **1.** Using the right hand more skillfully or easily than the left. **2.** Done with or made for the right hand. **3.** Clockwise. ►*adv.* With the right hand. —**right′-hand′ed•ly** *adv.* —**right′-hand′ed•ness** *n.*

right-hand•er (rīt′hăn′dər) ►*n.* One who is right-handed.

right•ism also **Right•ism** (rī′tĭz′əm) ►*n.* The ideology of the political right. —**right′ist** *n.*

right•ly (rīt′lē) ►*adv.* **1.** In a correct manner; properly. **2.** With honesty; justly.

right of way also **right-of-way** (rīt′əv-wā′) ►*n., pl.* **rights of way** or **right of ways 1a.** The right to pass over property owned by another. **b.** The path or thoroughfare on which such passage is made. **2.** The strip of land over which facilities such as highways, railroads, or power lines are built. **3.** The customary or legal right of a person, vessel, or vehicle to pass in front of another.

right-on (rīt′ŏn′, -ôn′) ►*adj. Slang* **1.** Up-to-date and sophisticated. **2.** Absolutely right.

right-to-life (rīt′tə-līf′) ►*adj.* Pro-life. —**right′-to-lif′er** *n.*

right whale ►*n.* Any of several whales with a large head, whalebone plates in the mouth, and no dorsal fin.

right wing ►*n.* **1.** The conservative or reactionary faction of a group. **2.** See **right** 3. —**right′-wing′** *adj.* —**right′-wing′er** *n.*

rig•id (rĭj′ĭd) ►*adj.* **1.** Not flexible or pliant; stiff. **2.** Not moving; fixed. **3.** Rigorous and exacting. [Lat. *rigidus.*] —**rig′id•ly** *adv.* —**ri•gid′i•ty, rig′id•ness** *n.*

rig•ma•role (rĭg′mə-rōl′) also **rig•a•ma•role** (-ə-mə-rōl′) ►*n.* **1.** Confused or rambling discourse; nonsense. **2.** A complicated, petty procedure. [< ME *ragmane rolle,* scroll used in a game of chance.]

rig•or (rĭg′ər) ►*n.* **1.** Strictness or severity. **2.** A harsh or trying circumstance; hardship. See Syns at **difficulty. 3.** Shivering or trembling, as caused by a chill. [< Lat.] —**rig′or•ous** *adj.* —**rig′or•ous•ly** *adv.*

rigor mor•tis (môr′tĭs) ►*n.* Muscular stiffening after death. [Lat., stiffness of death.]

rile (rīl) ►*v.* **riled, ril•ing.** To stir to anger; irritate. [Var. of ROIL.]

Ril•ke (rĭl′kə), **Rainer Maria.** 1875–1926. German poet.

rill (rĭl) ►*n.* A small brook. [LGer. *rille.*]

rim (rĭm) ►*n.* **1.** The border or edge of an object. **2.** The circular outer part of a wheel. ►*v.* **rimmed, rim•ming.** To furnish with a rim. [< OE *rima.*]

rime[1] (rīm) ►*n.* Frost or a coating of granular ice, as on grass and trees. [< OE *hrīm.*] —**rime** *v.* —**rim′y** *adj.*

rime[2] (rīm) ►*n. & v.* Var. of **rhyme.**

Rim•ski-Kor•sa•kov (rĭm′skē-kôr′sə-kôf′), **Nikolai Andreyevich.** 1844–1908. Russian composer.

rind (rīnd) ►*n.* A tough outer covering such as bark or the skin of some fruits. [< OE.]

ring[1] (rĭng) ►*n.* **1.** A circular object, form, or arrangement with a vacant circular center. **2.** A small circular band, often of precious metal, worn on the finger. **3.** An enclosed area in which exhibitions or contests take place. **4.** A group of people acting to advance their interests. ►*v.* **1.** To surround with or as if with a ring; encircle. See Syns at **surround. 2.** To form into a ring or rings. [< OE *hring.*]

ring[2] (rĭng) ►*v.* **rang** (răng), **rung** (rŭng), **ring•ing 1.** To give forth a clear, resonant sound. **2.** To cause something to ring. **3.** To sound a bell to summon someone. **4.** To have a character suggestive of a particular quality: *a story that rings true.* **5.** To be filled with sound; resound. **6.** To hear a persistent humming or buzzing: *My ears were ringing from the blast.* **7.** To call (someone) on the telephone. —***phrasal verb:* ring up** To record, esp. by means of a cash register: *ring up a sale.* ►*n.* **1.** The sound created by or as if by a bell. **2.** A loud sound that is repeated or continued. **3.** A telephone call. **4.** A suggestion of a quality: *His offer has a suspicious ring.* —***idiom:* ring a bell** *Informal* To arouse an often indistinct memory. [< OE *hringan.*]

ring•er (rĭng′ər) ►*n.* **1.** One that rings, esp. one that sounds a bell or chime. **2.** *Slang* A contestant entered dishonestly into a competition. **3.**

Slang One who bears a striking resemblance to another.

ring•git (rĭng′gĭt) ►*n.* See table at **currency.** [Malay.]

ring•lead•er (rĭng′lē′dər) ►*n.* A leader, esp. of a group involved in illicit activities.

ring•let (rĭng′lĭt) ►*n.* **1.** A curled lock of hair. **2.** A small circle or ring.

ring•mas•ter (rĭng′măs′tər) ►*n.* A person in charge of the performances in a circus ring.

ring•side (rĭng′sīd′) ►*n.* The area or seats immediately outside an arena or a ring.

ring•worm (rĭng′wûrm′) ►*n.* A contagious skin disease caused by a fungi and marked by ring-shaped, scaly, itching patches.

rink (rĭngk) ►*n.* **1.** An area surfaced with smooth ice for skating. **2.** A smooth floor suited for roller-skating. [< OFr. *renc*, line, of Gmc. orig.]

rinse (rĭns) ►*v.* **rinsed, rins•ing 1.** To wash lightly, as with water. **2.** To remove (e.g., soap) by flushing with water. ►*n.* **1.** The act of rinsing. **2.** The liquid used in rinsing. **3.** A solution used in coloring or conditioning the hair. [< Lat. *recēns*, fresh.]

Ri•o de Ja•nei•ro (rē′ō dā zhə-nâr′ō, dē-) A city of SE Brazil on Guanabara Bay, an arm of the Atlantic. Pop. 5,473,909.

Ri•o Grande (rē′ō grănd′, grăn′dē) A river, about 3,033 km (1,885 mi), rising in SW CO and flowing to the Gulf of Mexico, forming much of the US-Mexican border.

ri•ot (rī′ət) ►*n.* **1.** A public uproar or disturbance. **2.** An unrestrained outbreak, as of laughter or passions. **3.** A profusion. **4.** *Slang* An irresistibly funny person or thing. ►*v.* **1.** To take part in a riot. **2.** To engage in uncontrolled revelry. [< OFr. *rioter*, quarrel.] —**ri′ot•er** *n.*

ri•ot•ous (rī′ət-əs) ►*adj.* **1.** Of or resembling a riot. **2.** Participating in or inciting to riot. **3.** Uproarious; boisterous. **4.** Dissolute; wanton. **5.** Abundant or luxuriant. See Syns at **profuse.** —**ri′ot•ous•ly** *adv.* —**ri′ot•ous•ness** *n.*

rip (rĭp) ►*v.* **ripped, rip•ping 1.** To tear apart or become torn apart esp. roughly or energetically. **2.** To split or saw (wood) along the grain. **3.** *Informal* To move quickly or violently. —***phrasal verb:* rip off** *Slang* **1.** to steal or steal from. **2.** To exploit, swindle, or defraud. ►*n.* **1.** The act of ripping. **2.** A torn or split place; tear. [< Flem. *rippen.*] —**rip′per** *n.*

RIP ►*abbr. Lat.* requiescat in pace (may he rest in peace; may she rest in peace.)

ri•par•i•an (rĭ-pâr′ē-ən) ►*adj.* Of or relating to the banks of a natural course of water. [< Lat. *rīpa*, bank.]

rip•cord (rĭp′kôrd′) ►*n.* A cord pulled to release a parachute from its pack.

ripe (rīp) ►*adj.* **rip•er, rip•est 1.** Fully developed; mature: *ripe peaches.* **2.** Fully prepared; ready. **3.** Sufficiently advanced; opportune. [< OE *rīpe.*] —**ripe′ly** *adv.* —**rip′en** *v.* —**ripe′ness** *n.*

rip-off (rĭp′ôf′, -ŏf′) ►*n. Slang* **1.** A theft. **2.** An act of exploitation. **3.** Something clearly imitative of or based on something else.

ri•poste (rĭ-pōst′) ►*n.* **1.** A quick thrust given after parrying an opponent's lunge in fencing. **2.** A retaliatory action or retort. [< Ital. *risposta*, an answer.] —**ri•poste** *v.*

rip•ple (rĭp′əl) ►*v.* **-pled, -pling 1.** To form or display small waves on the surface. **2.** To rise and fall gently in tone or volume. ►*n.* **1.** A small wave or wavelike motion. **2.** A sound like that made by rippling water: *a ripple of laughter.* [ME *ripplen*, wrinkle.]

rip•saw (rĭp′sô′) ►*n.* A coarse-toothed saw used for cutting wood along the grain.

rip tide ►*n.* A strong surface current flowing away from shore.

rise (rīz) ►*v.* **rose** (rōz), **ris•en** (rĭz′ən), **ris•ing 1.** To stand up after lying, sitting, or kneeling. **2.** To get out of bed. **3.** To move from a lower to a higher position. **4.** To increase in size, volume, or level. **5.** To increase in number, amount, or value. **6.** To increase in intensity, force, or speed. **7.** To increase in pitch or volume. **8.** To appear above the horizon. **9.** To slope or extend upward. **10.** To come into existence; originate. See Syns at **stem**[1]. **11.** To attain a higher status. **12.** To return to life. **13.** To rebel. ►*n.* **1.** The act of rising; ascent. **2.** The appearance of the sun or other celestial body above the horizon. **3.** An increase in height, as of the level of water. **4.** A gently sloped hill. **5.** An origin, beginning, or source. See Syns at **beginning. 6.** An increase in price, worth, quantity, or degree. **7.** An increase in intensity, volume, or pitch. **8.** Elevation in status, prosperity, or importance. **9.** *Informal* An angry or irritated reaction. [< OE *rīsan.*]

ris•er (rī′zər) ►*n.* **1.** One who rises, esp. from sleep. **2.** The vertical part of a stair step.

ris•i•bil•i•ty (rĭz′ə-bĭl′ĭ-tē) ►*n.* **1.** The ability or tendency to laugh. **2.** Laughter; hilarity.

ris•i•ble (rĭz′ə-bəl) ►*adj.* **1.** Eliciting laughter; ludicrous. **2.** Capable of laughing or inclined to laugh. [< Lat. *rīsus*, p.part. of *rīdēre*, laugh.] —**ris′i•bly** *adv.*

risk (rĭsk) ►*n.* **1.** The possibility of suffering harm or loss; danger. **2.** A factor, element, or course involving uncertain danger. ►*v.* **1.** To expose to a chance of loss or damage. **2.** To incur the risk of: *His action risked a sharp reprisal.* See Syns at **endanger.** [< Ital. *risco.*] —**risk′i•ness** *n.* —**risk′y** *adj.*

ri•sot•to (rē-zōt′tō) ►*n., pl.* **-tos.** A dish of rice cooked in broth, often flavored with saffron. [Ital. < *riso*, rice.]

ris•qué (rĭs-kā′) ►*adj.* Suggestive of or bordering on indelicacy or impropriety. [Fr. < *risquer*, risk.]

ri•stra (rē′strə) ►*n.* A string on which foodstuffs, such as chilies, are threaded for storage. [< Lat. *restis*, cord.]

rite (rīt) ►*n.* **1.** The prescribed form for conducting a religious or other solemn ceremony. **2.** A ceremonial act. [< Lat. *rītus.*]

rit•u•al (rĭch′o͞o-əl) ►*n.* **1.** The prescribed form of a ceremony. **2.** A system of ceremonies or rites. **3. rituals** A ceremonial act or a series of such acts. **4.** A customary or regular procedure. [< Lat. *rītuālis*, of rites.] —**rit′u•al•ism** *n.* —**rit′u•al•is′tic** *adj.* —**rit′u•al•ize′** *v.* —**rit′u•al•ly** *adv.*

ritz•y (rĭt′sē) ►*adj.* **-i•er, -i•est** *Informal.* Elegant; fancy. [After the *Ritz* hotels.]

ri•val (rī′vəl) ►*n.* **1.** One who attempts to equal or surpass another; competitor. **2.** One that equals another in a particular respect. ►*v.* **-valed, -val•ing** or **-valled, -val•ling 1.** To attempt to equal or surpass. **2.** To be the equal of; match. [Lat. *rīvālis*, one who shares a stream.] —**ri′val** *adj.* —**ri′val•ry** *n.*

rive (rīv) ► *v.* **rived riv•en** (rĭv′ən) also **rived riv•ing 1.** To rend or tear apart. **2.** To cleave or split into pieces. [< ON *rīfa.*]

riv•er (rĭv′ər) ► *n.* A large natural stream of water. [< Lat. *rīpāria.*]

Ri•ve•ra (rĭ-vĕr′ə, rē-vĕ′rä), **Diego.** 1886–1957. Mexican painter.

riv•er•boat (rĭv′ər-bōt′) ► *n.* A boat for use on a river.

riv•er•side (rĭv′ər-sīd′) ► *n.* The bank or area alongside a river. —**riv′er•side** *adj.*

Riv•er•side (rĭv′ər-sīd′) A city of S CA NE of Santa Ana. Population, 226,505.

riv•et (rĭv′ĭt) ► *n.* A metal bolt or pin having a head on one end, inserted through the pieces to be joined and then hammered on the plain end to form a second head. ► *v.* **1.** To fasten or secure with or as if with a rivet. **2.** To engross or hold (e.g., the attention). [< OFr. *river*, attach.] —**riv′et•er** *n.*

Riv•i•er•a (rĭv′ē-ĕr′ə, rē-vyĕ′rä) A coastal region between the Alps and the Mediterranean from SE France to NW Italy.

riv•u•let (rĭv′yə-lĭt) ► *n.* A small brook or stream. [< Lat. *rīvulus*, small stream.]

Ri•yadh (rē-yäd′) The capital of Saudi Arabia, in the E-central part. Pop. 1,400,000.

ri•yal (rē-ôl′, -äl′) ► *n.* See table at **currency.** [Ar. *riyāl.*]

rm. ► *abbr.* **1.** ream **2.** room

Rn ► The symbol for the element **radon.**

RN ► *abbr.* **1.** registered nurse **2.** Royal Navy

RNA (är′ĕn-ā′) ► *n.* A nucleic acid that is involved in protein synthesis, consisting of a long, usu. single-stranded chain of nucleotides. [R(IBO)N(UCLEIC) A(CID).]

roach[1] (rōch) ► *n., pl.* **roach** or **-es.** A freshwater fish of N Europe. [< OFr. *roche.*]

roach[2] (rōch) ► *n., pl.* **roach•es.** A cockroach.

road (rōd) ► *n.* **1.** An open, usu. public way for the passage of vehicles, people, and animals. **2.** A course or path. —***idiom:* on the road** Traveling. [< OE *rād*, a riding.]

road•bed (rōd′bĕd′) ► *n.* **1.** The foundation upon which railroad tracks are laid. **2.** The foundation and surface of a road.

road•block (rōd′blŏk′) ► *n.* **1.** A blockade set across a road. **2.** Something that prevents progress; obstacle.

road•house (rōd′hous′) ► *n.* An inn, restaurant, or nightclub located on a road outside a city.

road•kill (rōd′kĭl′) ► *n.* **1.** An animal or animals killed by a car. **2.** One that been utterly defeated.

road•run•ner (rōd′rŭn′ər) ► *n.* A swift-running, crested bird of SW North America, with streaked brownish plumage and a long tail.

road show ► *n.* A show presented by traveling performers.

road•side (rōd′sīd′) ► *n.* The area bordering a road. —**road′side′** *adj.*

road•ster (rōd′stər) ► *n.* An open automobile having a single seat in the front for two or three people.

Road Town. The capital of the British Virgin Is., on Tortola I. in the West Indies. Pop. 2,479.

road•way (rōd′wā′) ► *n.* A road, esp. the part over which vehicles travel.

road•work (rōd′wûrk′) ► *n.* **1.** Outdoor long-distance running as a form of exercise or conditioning. **2.** Highway construction.

roam (rōm) ► *v.* To move about without purpose; wander. [ME *romen.*] —**roam′er** *n.*

roan (rōn) ► *adj.* Having a chestnut, bay, or sorrel coat thickly sprinkled with white or gray: *a roan horse.* ► *n.* A roan animal. [< OSpan. *roano.*]

Ro•a•noke (rō′ə-nōk′) An independent city of SW VA WSW of Richmond. Population, 96,397.

Roanoke Island. An island off the NE coast of NC, where Sir Walter Raleigh attempted to found the first English settlement in North America (1585).

roar (rôr, rōr) ► *v.* **1.** To utter a loud, deep, prolonged sound, as in rage or excitement. See Syns at **shout. 2.** To laugh loudly or excitedly. [< OE *rārian.*] —**roar** *n.*

roast (rōst) ► *v.* **1.** To cook with dry heat, as in an oven. **2.** To expose to great or excessive heat. **3.** To heat (ores) in order to dehydrate, purify, or oxidize. **4.** *Informal* To ridicule or criticize harshly. ► *n.* **1.** A cut of meat suitable for roasting. **2.** An outing at which food is roasted. ► *adj.* Roasted. [< OFr. *rostir.*] —**roast′er** *n.*

rob (rŏb) ► *v.* **robbed, rob•bing 1.** To steal (from) esp. by using or threatening to use force. **2.** To deprive of something. [< OFr. *rober.*] —**rob′ber** *n.* —**rob′ber•y** *n.*

robe (rōb) ► *n.* **1.** A long, loose, flowing outer garment, esp. one worn to show office or rank. **2.** A dressing gown or bathrobe. **3.** A blanket or covering for the lap or legs. ► *v.* **robed, rob•ing.** To dress in or as if in a robe. [< OFr., of Gmc. orig.]

Rob•ert I (rŏb′ərt). "Robert the Bruce." 1274–1329. King of Scotland (1306–29).

Robe•son (rōb′sən), **Paul Bustill.** 1898–1976. Amer. actor and singer.

Robes•pierre (rōbz′pē-âr′), **Maximilien François Marie Isidore de.** 1758–94. French revolutionary; executed.

rob•in (rŏb′ĭn) ► *n.* **1.** A North American songbird having a rust-red breast and gray and black upper plumage. **2.** A small Old World bird having an orange breast and a brown back. [< the name *Robin.*]

Rob•in•son (rŏb′ĭn-sən), **Edwin Arlington.** 1869–1935. Amer. poet.

Robinson, Jack Roosevelt. "Jackie." 1919–72. Amer. baseball player.

Jackie Robinson

ro•bot (rō′bət, -bŏt′) ► *n.* **1.** A mechanical device, sometimes resembling a human, capable of performing often complex tasks. **2.** A device that operates automatically or by remote control. **3.** A person who works or follows orders mechanically. [Czech < *robota*, drudgery.] —**ro•bot′ic** *adj.*

ro•bot•ics (rō-bŏt′ĭks) ▸*n.* *(takes sing. v.)* The science and technology of robotic design.

ro•bust (rō-bŭst′, rō′bŭst′) ▸*adj.* **1.** Full of health and strength; vigorous. **2.** Marked by richness and fullness: *a robust wine.* [< Lat. *rōbus*, oak, strength.] —**ro•bust′ly** *adv.* —**ro•bust′ness** *n.*

Ro•cham•beau (rō′shăm-bō′, -shäN-), **Comte de.** 1725–1807. French army officer.

Roch•es•ter (rŏch′ĭ-stər, -ĕs′tər) A city of W NY ENE of Buffalo. Pop. 231,636.

rock[1] (rŏk) ▸*n.* **1.** Relatively hard, naturally formed mineral or petrified matter. **2.** A fragment or body of such material. **3.** A naturally formed aggregate of mineral matter making up much of the earth's crust. **4.** One that is stable, firm, or dependable. **5.** *Slang* A large gem, esp. a diamond. —***idiom:* on the rocks 1.** In a state of difficulty or ruin. **2.** Served over ice cubes. [< VLat. **rocca.*]

rock[2] (rŏk) ▸*v.* **1.** To move back and forth or from side to side, esp. gently or rhythmically. **2.** To shake or cause to shake violently. See Syns at **agitate. 3.** To play or dance to rock 'n' roll. ▸*n.* **1.** A rocking motion. **2.** Rock 'n' roll. [< OE *roccian.*]

rock-and-roll (rŏk′ən-rōl′) ▸*n.* Var. of **rock 'n' roll.**

rock bottom ▸*n.* The lowest possible level.

rock•bound also **rock-bound** (rŏk′bound′) ▸*adj.* Hemmed in by or bordered with rocks.

Rock•e•fel•ler (rŏk′ə-fĕl′ər). Amer. family of business executives, politicians, and philanthropists, including **John Davison** (1839–1937), **John Davison, Jr.** (1874–1960), and **Nelson Aldrich** (1908–79).

rock•er (rŏk′ər) ▸*n.* **1.** A rocking chair. **2.** One of the two curved pieces upon which something rocks. **3.** A rock 'n' roll song, fan, or musician. —***idiom:* off (one's) rocker** *Slang* Out of one's mind; crazy.

rock•et[1] (rŏk′ĭt) ▸*n.* **1.** An engine that propels by the ejection of matter, esp. by the high-velocity ejection of gaseous combustion products. **2.** A device, such as a craft or projectile weapon, propelled by one or more rocket engines. ▸*v.* To move swiftly and powerfully, as a rocket. [Ital. *rocchetta*, dim. of *rocca*, spindle.]

rock•et[2] (rŏk′ĭt) ▸*n.* A Mediterranean plant having yellowish flowers and leaves that are used in salads. [< Ital. *rochetta.*]

rock•et•ry (rŏk′ĭ-trē) ▸*n.* The science and technology of rocket design, construction, and flight.

rocket ship ▸*n.* A spacecraft propelled by rockets.

Rock•ford (rŏk′fərd) A city of N IL WNW of Chicago. Pop. 139,426.

rock•ing chair (rŏk′ĭng) ▸*n.* A chair mounted on rockers or springs.

Rock•ing•ham (rŏk′ĭng-əm, -həm), 2nd Marquis of. 1730–82. British prime minister (1765–66 and 1782).

rocking horse ▸*n.* A toy horse mounted on rockers or springs.

rock 'n' roll or **rock-and-roll** (rŏk′ən-rōl′) ▸*n.* A form of popular music arising esp. from rhythm and blues, country music, and gospel and marked by amplified instrumentation and a heavily accented beat.

rock salt ▸*n.* Common salt in large chunks.

Rock•ville (rŏk′vĭl′, -vəl) A city of central MD NNW of Washington DC. Pop. 43,811.

rock wool ▸*n.* See **mineral wool.**

rock•y[1] (rŏk′ē) ▸*adj.* **-i•er, -i•est 1.** Consisting of or abounding in rocks. **2.** Resembling or suggesting rock; unyielding. **3.** Marked by difficulties. —**rock′i•ness** *n.*

rock•y[2] (rŏk′ē) ▸*adj.* **-i•er, -i•est 1.** Inclined to sway or totter; unsteady or shaky. **2.** Weak, dizzy, or nauseated.

Rocky Mountains. A mountain system of W North America extending more than 4,827 km (3,000 mi) from NW Alaska to the Mexican border.

ro•co•co also **Ro•co•co** (rə-kō′kō, rō′kə-kō′) ▸*n.* A style of art, esp. architecture and decorative art, originating in France in the early 18th cent. and marked by elaborate and fanciful ornamentation. ▸*adj.* **1.** Of the rococo. **2.** Overly elaborate or complicated. [Fr.]

rod (rŏd) ▸*n.* **1.** A thin straight stick or bar, such as: **a.** A fishing rod. **b.** A lightning rod. **c.** A stick used for measuring. **2a.** A stick used to punish by whipping. **b.** Punishment. **3.** A scepter or wand symbolizing authority. **4.** See table at **measurement. 5.** A rod-shaped cell in the retina that responds to dim light. **6.** *Slang* A handgun. [< OE *rodd.*]

rode (rōd) ▸*v.* P.t. of **ride.**

ro•dent (rōd′nt) ▸*n.* Any of an order of mammals, such as a mouse, rat, squirrel, or beaver, with large incisors adapted for gnawing or nibbling. [< Lat. *rōdere*, gnaw.]

ro•de•o (rō′dē-ō′, rō-dā′ō) ▸*n.*, *pl.* **-os 1.** A competition or exhibition of skills such as riding broncos or roping calves. **2.** A cattle roundup. [Sp. < *rodear*, surround.]

Ro•din (rō-dăn′, -dăN′), **François Auguste René.** 1840–1917. French sculptor.

roe[1] (rō) ▸*n.* The eggs or the egg-laden ovary of a fish. [ME *row.*]

roe[2] (rō) ▸*n.*, *pl.* **roe** or **roes.** A rather small, delicately formed Eurasian deer. [< OE *rā.*]

roent•gen (rĕnt′gən, -jən, rŭnt′-) ▸*n.* A unit of exposure to ionizing radiation, such as x-rays or gamma rays. [After Wilhelm Konrad ROENTGEN.] —**roent′gen** *adj.*

Roentgen, Wilhelm Konrad. 1845–1923. German physicist; 1901 Nobel.

Roeth•ke (rĕt′kē, -kə, rĕth′-), **Theodore.** 1908–63. Amer. poet.

rog•er (rŏj′ər) ▸*interj.* Used esp. in radio communications to indicate receipt of a message. [< *Roger*, spoken representation of the letter *r*, short for RECEIVED.]

Ro•get (rō-zhā′, rō′zhā), **Peter Mark.** 1779–1869. British physician and scholar.

rogue (rōg) ▸*n.* **1.** An unprincipled person; scoundrel. **2.** One who is playfully mischievous. [?] —**rogu′er•y** *n.* —**rogu′ish** *adj.* —**rogu′ish•ness** *n.*

roil (roil) ▸*v.* **1.** To make muddy or cloudy by stirring up sediment. **2.** To displease or disturb; vex. [?]

role also **rôle** (rōl) ▸*n.* **1.** A character or part played by a performer. **2.** A function: *his role in the coup.* See Syns at **function.** [< OFr. *rolle*, roll of parchment.]

role model ►*n.* A person whose behavior serves as a model for another person.

roll (rōl) ►*v.* **1.** To move or cause to move by repeatedly turning over. **2.** To move or push on wheels or rollers. **3.** To start to move or operate: *The cameras were rolling.* **4.** To gain momentum: *The campaign is finally rolling.* **5.** To turn around; revolve or rotate. **6.** To advance with a rising and falling motion, as waves. **7.** To move or rock from side to side, as a ship. **8.** To make a deep rumbling sound, as thunder. **9.** To pronounce with a trill: *roll one's* r*'s.* **10.** To wrap something around itself or something else: *roll up a rug.* **11.** To envelop or enfold in a covering. **12.** To spread or flatten by applying pressure with a roller. **13.** *Games* To throw (dice), as in craps. —***phrasal verb:* roll back** To reduce (e.g., prices or wages) to a previous level. ►*n.* **1.** The act or an instance of rolling. **2.** Something rolled up: *a roll of tape.* **3.** A quantity, as of cloth, rolled into a cylinder. **4.** A piece of parchment or paper that can be or is rolled up; scroll. **5.** A list of names of persons belonging to a group. **6a.** A small rounded portion of bread. **b.** A portion of food shaped like a tube with a filling. **7.** A rolling, swaying, or rocking motion. **8.** A gentle undulation of a surface. **9.** A deep reverberation or rumble. **10.** A rapid succession of short sounds: *a drum roll.* —***idiom:* on a roll** *Informal* Having sustained success. [< Lat. *rotula*, small wheel.]

roll•back (rōl′băk′) ►*n.* A reduction, esp. in prices or wages, to a previous level.

roll call ►*n.* The reading aloud of a list of names to determine who is present.

roll•er (rō′lər) ►*n.* **1.** One that rolls. **2.** A small spokeless wheel, as on a caster. **3.** An elongated cylinder on which something is wound. **4.** A heavy cylinder used to level, crush, or smooth. **5.** A cylinder used to apply ink or paint to a surface. **6.** A heavy, breaking wave.

Rol•ler•blade (rō′lər-blād′) ► A trademark for an in-line skate.

roller coaster ►*n.* **1.** A steep, sharply banked elevated railway with open cars, operated as a ride. **2.** Something marked by abrupt, extreme changes.

roller skate ►*n.* A shoe or boot with two or four wheels attached to its sole for skating on hard surfaces. —**rol′ler-skate′** *v.*

rol•lick (rŏl′ĭk) ►*v.* To romp or frolic boisterously. [?] —**rol′lick•ing** *adj.*

roll•ing pin (rō′lĭng) ►*n.* A smooth cylinder used for rolling out dough.

Röl•vaag (rōl′väg′), **Ole Edvart.** 1876–1931. Norwegian-born Amer. writer.

ro•ly-po•ly (rō′lē-pō′lē) ►*adj.* Short and plump. [< ROLL.]

Rom (rōm) ►*n.* **1.** A Gypsy, esp. a Gypsy man or boy. **2.** *(takes pl. v.)* Gypsies considered as a group. [Romany, man.]

ROM (rŏm) ►*n.* *Comp. Sci.* Memory hardware that allows access to stored data but prevents modification of the data. [R(EAD-)O(NLY) M(EMORY).]

rom. ►*abbr.* *Print.* roman

Rom. ►*abbr.* **1.** Roman **2.** Romance (languages)

Ro•ma (rō′mə) ►*n.* *(takes pl. v.)* Gypsies considered as a group. [Romany, men.]

Ro•ma•gna (rō-män′yə, -mä′nyä) A historical region of N-central Italy.

ro•maine (rō-mān′) ►*n.* A variety of lettuce having a slender head of long leaves. [< Fr., Roman.]

Ro•man (rō′mən) ►*adj.* **1a.** Of or relating to Rome or its people or culture. **b.** Of the Roman Empire. **2.** Of or relating to Latin. **3.** Of the Roman Catholic Church. **4. roman** Of or being a style of printing type with upright letters having serifs. ►*n.* **1.** A native or inhabitant of ancient or modern Rome. **2. roman** Roman print or typestyle. **3. Romans** *(takes sing. v.)* See table at **Bible.**

Roman candle ►*n.* A cylindrical firework that emits balls of fire.

Roman Catholic ►*adj.* Relating to the Roman Catholic Church. ►*n.* A member of the Roman Catholic Church. —**Roman Catholicism** *n.*

Roman Catholic Church ►*n.* The Christian church having the Bishop of Rome as its head.

ro•mance (rō-măns′, rō′măns′) ►*n.* **1a.** A love affair. **b.** Romantic involvement; love. **2.** A mysterious or fascinating quality or appeal, as of something adventurous. **3a.** A medieval narrative telling of the adventures of chivalric heroes. **b.** A long fictitious tale of heroes and extraordinary or mysterious events. **4.** A story or film dealing with a love affair. **5. Romance** The Romance languages. ►*adj.* **Romance** Of or being any of the languages that developed from Latin, including Italian, French, Portuguese, Romanian, and Spanish. ►*v.* (rō-măns′) **-manced, -manc•ing.** *Informal* To have a love affair with; woo. [< OFr. *romans* < Lat. *Rōmānicus*, Roman.] —**ro•manc′er** *n.*

Roman Empire. An empire (27 B.C.–A.D. 395) stretching from Britain and Germany to North Africa and the Persian Gulf.

Ro•man•esque (rō′mə-nĕsk′) ►*adj.* Of or being a style of European architecture containing both Roman and Byzantine elements, prevalent esp. in the 11th and 12th cent. —**Ro′man•esque′** *n.*

Ro•ma•ni•a (rō-mā′nē-ə, -mān′yə) or **Ru•ma•ni•a** (ro͞o-). A country of SE Europe with a short coastline on the Black Sea. Cap. Bucharest. Pop. 22,736,000.

Ro•ma•ni•an (rō-mā′nē-ən, -mān′yən) also **Ru•ma•ni•an** (ro͞o-) ►*n.* **1.** A native or inhabitant of Romania. **2.** Their Romance language. —**Ro•ma′ni•an** *adj.*

Roman nose ►*n.* A nose with a high prominent bridge.

Roman numeral ►*n.* Any of the numerical symbols formed with the Roman letters I, V, X, L, C, D, and M, representing respectively the numbers 1, 5, 10, 50, 100, and 1000.

Ro•mansch also **Ro•mansh** (rō-mänsh′, -mănsh′) ►*n.* The Rhaeto-Romance dialect that is an official language of Switzerland.

ro•man•tic (rō-măn′tĭk) ►*adj.* **1.** Of or characteristic of romance. **2.** Given to thoughts or feelings of romance. See Syns at **sentimental.** **3.** Expressive of or conducive to love. **4.** Imaginative but impractical. **5.** often **Romantic** Of or relating to romanticism in the arts. ►*n.* **1.** A romantic person. **2.** often **Romantic** A follower or adherent of romanticism. —**ro•man′ti•cal•ly** *adv.*

ro•man•ti•cism (rō-măn′tĭ-sĭz′əm) ►*n.* often **Romanticism** An artistic and intellectual movement originating in Europe in the late 18th cent. and marked by emphasis on emotion and imagination, departure from classical forms, and rebellion against social conventions. —**ro•man′ti•cist** *n.*

ro•man•ti•cize (rō-măn′tĭ-sīz′) ►*v.* **-cized, -ciz•ing 1.** To view or interpret romantically. **2.** To think in a romantic way.

Rom•a•ny (rŏm′ə-nē, rō′mə-) ►*n., pl.* **-nies 1.** A Gypsy. **2.** The Indic language of the Gypsies. —**Rom′a•ny** *adj.*

Rom•berg (rŏm′bərg), **Sigmund.** 1887–1951. Hungarian-born Amer. composer.

Rome (rōm) The capital of Italy, in the W-central part. Pop. 2,693,383.

Ro•me•o (rō′mē-ō′) ►*n., pl.* **-os.** A man devoted to the pursuit of love. [After *Romeo*, in Shakespeare's *Romeo and Juliet.*]

romp (rŏmp) ►*v.* **1.** To play or frolic boisterously. **2.** *Slang* To win a race or game easily. [< OFr. *ramper*, rear up.] —**romp** *n.*

romp•er (rŏm′pər) ►*n.* **1.** One that romps. **2. rompers** A loosely fitted, one-piece garment worn esp. by small children for play.

ron•do (rŏn′dō, rŏn-dō′) ►*n., pl.* **-dos.** A musical work with a recurring main theme. [Ital. < Fr. *rondeau.*]

rood (ro͞od) ►*n.* **1.** A crucifix or cross. **2.** A measure of land equal to ¼ acre, or 40 square rods (0.10 hectare). [< OE *rōd.*]

roof (ro͞of, ro͝of) ►*n.* **1.** The exterior top surface of a building and its supporting structures. **2.** The top covering of something: *the roof of a car.* **3.** The upper surface of the mouth. **4.** The highest point or limit. ►*v.* To cover with a roof. [< OE *hrōf.*] —**roof′er** *n.*

roof•ing (ro͞o′fĭng, ro͝of′ĭng) ►*n.* **1.** Materials used in building a roof. **2.** A roof.

roof•tree (ro͞of′trē′, ro͝of′-) ►*n.* The ridgepole of a roof.

rook¹ (ro͝ok) ►*n.* An Old World bird resembling the crow. ►*v.* To swindle; cheat. [< OE *hrōc.*]

rook² (ro͝ok) ►*n.* A chess piece that may move in a rank or file over any number of empty squares. [< Pers. *rukh.*]

rook•er•y (ro͝ok′ə-rē) ►*n., pl.* **-ies 1.** A place where rooks nest or breed. **2.** The breeding ground of certain other birds or animals.

rook•ie (ro͝ok′ē) ►*n.* **1.** *Slang* **a.** An untrained or inexperienced recruit. **b.** A novice. **2.** A first-year professional athlete. [< RECRUIT.]

room (ro͞om, ro͝om) ►*n.* **1.** Space that is or can be occupied. **2a.** An interior area of a building set off by walls or partitions. **b.** The people present in such an area: *The whole room laughed.* **3. rooms** Living quarters. **4.** Opportunity or scope: *no room for error.* ►*v.* To occupy a room; lodge. [< OE *rūm.*] —**room′ful** *n.* —**room′y** *adj.*

Syns: *room, elbowroom, latitude, leeway, margin, play, scope* **n.**

room•er (ro͞o′mər, ro͝om′ər) ►*n.* A lodger.

room•ing house (ro͞o′mĭng, ro͝om′ĭng) ►*n.* A house where lodgers may rent rooms.

room•mate (ro͞om′māt′, ro͝om′-) ►*n.* A person with whom one shares a room or rooms.

room•y (ro͞o′mē, ro͝om′ē) ►*adj.* **-i•er, -i•est.** Having plenty of room; spacious. See Syns at **spacious.** —**room′i•ness** *n.*

Roo•se•velt (rō′zə-vĕlt′, ro͞o′-), **(Anna) Eleanor.** 1884–1962. Amer. diplomat, writer, and First Lady of the US (1933–45).

Roosevelt, Franklin Delano. 1882–1945. The 32nd US President (1933–45).

Eleanor Roosevelt

Franklin D. Roosevelt

Roosevelt, Theodore. 1858–1919. The 26th US President (1901–09); 1906 Nobel Peace Prize.

Theodore Roosevelt

roost (ro͞ost) ►*n.* **1.** A perch on which birds rest. **2.** A place where birds perch. ►*v.* To perch for the night. [< OE *hrōst.*]

roost•er (ro͞o′stər) ►*n.* An adult male chicken.

root¹ (ro͞ot, ro͝ot) ►*n.* **1.** The usu. underground portion of a plant that serves as support, draws minerals and water from the soil, and sometimes stores food. **2.** A similar underground plant part, such as a rhizome. **3.** The part of an organ or structure, such as a hair, that is embedded in other tissue. **4.** A base or support. **5.** An essential part; core. **6.** A source; origin. **7.** often **roots** The condition of belonging to a particular place or society. **8.** *Ling.* The element that carries the meaning in a word and provides the base for inflection. **9.** *Math.* A number that when multiplied by itself an indicated number of times forms a specified product. ►*v.* **1.** To grow roots or a root. **2.** To become firmly established or settled. **3.** To remove by or as if by the roots. [< ON *rōt.*] —**root′er** *n.* —**root′less** *adj.*

root² (ro͞ot, ro͝ot) ►*v.* **1.** To dig with or as if with the snout or nose. **2.** To rummage for something. [< OE *wrōtan.*] —**root′er** *n.*

root³ (ro͞ot, ro͝ot) ►*v.* To encourage by applause; cheer. See Syns at **applaud.** [Poss. alteration of *rout*, bellow.] —**root′er** *n.*

Root (ro͞ot), **Elihu.** 1845–1937. Amer. lawyer and public official; 1912 Nobel Peace Prize.

root beer ►*n.* A carbonated soft drink made from extracts of plant roots and herbs.

root canal ►*n.* **1.** A pulp-filled channel in the root of a tooth. **2.** A treatment in which diseased tissue from the root canal is removed.

root cellar ►*n.* An underground pit or cellar used for storing vegetables.

root•stock (ro͞ot′stŏk′, ro͝ot′-) ►*n.* **1.** See **rhi-**

zome. 2. A root used as a stock for plant propagation.

rope (rōp) ▶*n.* **1.** A flexible heavy cord of tightly intertwined hemp or other fiber. **2.** A string of items attached in one line by or as if by twisting or braiding: *a rope of onions.* **3. ropes** *Informal* Specialized procedures or details: *learn the ropes.* ▶*v.* **roped, rop•ing 1.** To tie or fasten with or as if with rope. **2.** To enclose with a rope: *rope off the area.* **3.** To lasso. —***idioms:* on the ropes** On the verge of defeat or collapse. **the end of (one's) rope** The limit of one's patience, endurance, or resources. [< OE *rāp.*]

Roque•fort (rōk′fərt) ▶ A trademark for a sheep's milk cheese ripened in caves.

ror•qual (rôr′kwəl) ▶*n.* Any of a family of baleen whales with a grooved throat and a small, pointed dorsal fin. [< Norw. *rørhval* : ON *raudhr*, red + *hvalr*, whale.]

Ror•schach test (rôr′shäk′, -shäKH′) ▶*n. Psychol.* A projective test in which a subject's interpretations of ten standard inkblots are used to measure emotional and intellectual functioning and integration. [After Hermann *Rorschach* (1884–1922).]

Ro•sa•ri•o (rō-zär′ē-ō′, -sär′-) A city of E-central Argentina on the Paraná R. NW of Buenos Aires. Population, 894,645.

ro•sa•ry (rō′zə-rē) ▶*n., pl.* **-ries** *Rom. Cath. Ch.* **1.** A series of prayers dedicated to the Virgin Mary. **2.** A string of beads on which these prayers are counted. [< Med.Lat. *rosārium.*]

rose[1] (rōz) ▶*n.* **1a.** Any of a genus of shrubs or vines having prickly stems and variously colored, often fragrant flowers. **b.** The flower of any of these plants. **2.** A rosette. **3.** A dark pink. [< Lat. *rosa.*] —**rose** *adj.*

rose[2] (rōz) ▶*v.* P.t. of **rise.**

ro•sé (rō-zā′) ▶*n.* A light pink wine made from purple grapes. [Fr.]

ro•se•ate (rō′zē-ĭt, -āt′) ▶*adj.* **1.** Rose-colored. **2.** Cheerful or bright; optimistic.

rose•bud (rōz′bŭd′) ▶*n.* The bud of a rose.

rose•bush (rōz′bo͝osh′) ▶*n.* A shrub that bears roses.

rose-col•ored (rōz′kŭl′ərd) ▶*adj.* Cheerfully, often unduly optimistic.

rose•mar•y (rōz′mâr′ē) ▶*n., pl.* **-ies.** An aromatic evergreen shrub having grayish-green leaves that are used in cooking and perfumery. [< Lat. *rōs marīnus*, sea dew.]

ro•sette (rō-zĕt′) ▶*n.* An ornament, as of ribbon or silk, that resembles a rose.

rose water ▶*n.* A fragrant preparation made by steeping or distilling rose petals in water, used in cosmetics and cookery.

rose window ▶*n.* A circular window with radiating tracery suggesting a rose.

rose•wood (rōz′wo͝od′) ▶*n.* **1.** Any of various tropical trees having hard reddish wood. **2.** The wood itself, used in cabinetwork.

Rosh Ha•sha•nah (rôsh′ hə-shô′nə, hä-shä-nä′) ▶*n.* The Jewish New Year, observed on the 1st or 1st and 2nd days of Tishri. [Heb. *rō'š haš-šānâ*, head of the year.]

Ro•si•cru•cian (rō′zĭ-kro͞o′shən, rŏz′ĭ-) ▶*n.* A member of an international organization devoted to the study of ancient mysticism and its application to modern life. —**Ro′si•cru′cian•ism** *n.*

ros•in (rŏz′ĭn) ▶*n.* A brownish translucent resin derived from pine sap, used on the bows of stringed instruments, to prevent slipping, and as an ingredient in varnishes, inks, and adhesives. ▶*v.* To coat or rub with rosin. [< RESIN.] —**ros′in•y** *adj.*

Ross (rôs, rŏs), **Betsy Griscom.** 1752–1836. Amer. patriot.

Ross, Sir **James Clark.** 1800–62. British polar explorer.

Ros•set•ti (rō-zĕt′ē). **Dante Gabriel** (1828–82) and **Christina Georgina Rossetti** (1830–94). British Pre-Raphaelite artists.

Ross Ice Shelf. A vast area in Antarctica bordering on **Ross Sea,** an arm of the S Pacific.

Ros•si•ni (rō-sē′nē), **Gioacchino Antonio.** 1792–1868. Italian composer.

Ros•tand (rôs-täN′), **Edmond.** 1868–1918. French playwright.

ros•ter (rŏs′tər, rô′stər) ▶*n.* **1.** A list of names. **2.** A list of military personnel enrolled for active duty. [Du. *rooster.*]

Ros•tock (rŏs′tŏk′, rôs′tôk′) A city of NE Germany near the Baltic Sea NNW of Berlin. Pop. 237,307.

Ros•tov (rə-stôf′) also **Ros•tov-on-Don** (-ŏn-dŏn′, -dôn′, -ôn-). A city of SW Russia on the Don R. Pop. 1,012,649.

ros•trum (rŏs′trəm, rô′strəm) ▶*n., pl.* **-trums** or **-tra** (-trə). An elevated platform for public speaking. [Lat. *rōstrum*, beak.]

ros•y (rō′zē) ▶*adj.* **-i•er, -i•est 1a.** Having a rose color. **b.** Flushed: *rosy cheeks.* **2.** Bright; optimistic. —**ros′i•ness** *n.*

rot (rŏt) ▶*v.* **rot•ted, rot•ting 1.** To decompose; decay. **2.** To languish: *rot in jail* ▶*n.* **1.** The process of rotting or the condition of being rotten. **2.** A plant or animal disease marked by the breakdown of tissue. **3.** Foolish talk; nonsense. [< OE *rotian.*]

ro•ta•ry (rō′tə-rē) ▶*adj.* Of, causing, or marked by rotation, esp. axial rotation. ▶*n., pl.* **-ries 1.** A rotary part or device. **2.** A traffic circle. [< Lat. *rota*, wheel.]

ro•tate (rō′tāt) ▶*v.* **-tat•ed, -tat•ing 1.** To turn on an axis. **2.** To alternate in sequence. [< Lat. *rota*, wheel.] —**ro′ta′tor** *n.* —**ro′ta•to′ry** (-tə-tŏr′ē, -tōr′ē) *adj.*

ro•ta•tion (rō-tā′shən) ▶*n.* **1a.** The act or process of turning around a center or an axis **b.** A single complete cycle of such motion. **2.** Regular and uniform variation in a sequence or series. —**ro•ta′tion•al** *adj.*

ROTC ▶*abbr.* Reserve Officer's Training Corps

rote (rōt) ▶*n.* **1.** Memorization through repetition, often without understanding. **2.** Mechanical routine. [ME.] —**rote** *adj.*

Roth IRA (rôth) ▶*n.* A modified IRA in which contributions are made from after-tax income, and withdrawals after age 59½ are untaxed. [After William Victor *Roth*, Jr. (b. 1921), US congressman.]

Roth•schild (rŏth′chīld, rŏths′-). German family of bankers, including **Mayer Amschal** (1743–1812), **Salomon** (1774–1855), and **Nathan Mayer** (1774–1836).

ro•tis•se•rie (rō-tĭs′ə-rē) ▶*n.* A device with a rotating spit on which meat or other food is roasted. [< OFr. *rostir*, roast.]

ro•to•gra•vure (rō′tə-grə-vyo͝or′) ▶*n.* **1.** An intaglio printing process in which the impression is transferred from an etched copper cylinder in a rotary press. **2.** Material produced by this process. [Lat. *rota*, wheel + GRAVURE.]

ro•tor (rō′tər) ►*n.* **1.** A rotating part of a machine or device. **2.** An assembly of rotating airfoils, as of a helicopter. [< ROTATOR.]

ro•to•till•er (rō′tə-tĭl′ər) ►*n.* A motorized rotary cultivator. [ROT(ARY) + TILLER[1].] **—ro′to•till′** *v.*

rot•ten (rŏt′n) ►*adj.* **-er, -est 1.** Being in a state of decay; decomposed. **2.** Having a foul odor; putrid. **3.** Morally corrupt or despicable. **4.** Very bad; wretched. [< ON *rotinn.*] **—rot′ten•ness** *n.*

Rot•ter•dam (rôt′ər-dăm′) A city of SW Netherlands on the Rhine-Meuse delta SSE of The Hague. Pop. 597,272.

rott•wei•ler (rŏt′wī′lər, rôt′-) ►*n.* A breed of dog having a stocky body, short black fur, and tan face markings. [After *Rottweil*, Germany.]

ro•tund (rō-tŭnd′) ►*adj.* Rounded in figure; plump. [Lat. *rotundus.*] **—ro•tun′di•ty** *n.*

ro•tun•da (rō-tŭn′də) ►*n.* **1.** A circular building, esp. one with a dome. **2.** A large, often round room with a high ceiling. [< Lat. *rotundus*, round.]

Rou•ault (ro͞o-ō′), **Georges.** 1871–1958. French artist.

rou•ble (ro͞o′bəl) ►*n.* Var. of **ruble.**

rou•é (ro͞o-ā′) ►*n.* A lecherous, dissipated man. [Fr. < *rouer*, break on a wheel.]

Rou•en (ro͞o-än′, -äɴ′) A city of N France WNW of Paris. Pop. 102,722.

rouge (ro͞ozh) ►*n.* **1.** A red or pink cosmetic for coloring the cheeks or lips. **2.** A reddish powder used to polish metals or glass. [< Lat. *rubeus*, red.] **—rouge** *v.*

rough (rŭf) ►*adj.* **-er, -est 1.** Having a bumpy or irregular surface; not smooth. **2.** Coarse or shaggy to the touch. **3.** Stormy; turbulent: *rough seas.* **4.** Marked by violence or force; harsh: *rough handling.* **5.** Difficult or unpleasant; taxing. **6.** Uncouth or rowdy: *a rough crowd.* **7.** Not polished or refined. See Syns at **rude. 8.** Harsh to the ear. **9.** Not complete, exact, or perfect: *a rough drawing.* ►*n.* **1a.** Rugged, overgrown terrain. **b.** The part of a golf course left unmowed and uncultivated. **2.** An unrefined or imperfect state: *a diamond in the rough.* **3.** A rowdy; tough. ►*v.* **1.** To roughen. **2.** To treat roughly or with physical violence. **3.** To prepare or make in an unfinished form: *rough out a house plan.* ►*adv.* In a rough manner. **—*idiom:* rough it** To live without comforts and conveniences. [< OE *rūh.*] **—rough′ly** *adv.* **—rough′ness** *n.*

rough•age (rŭf′ĭj) ►*n.* See **fiber** 6.

rough•en (rŭf′ən) ►*v.* To make or become rough.

rough-hew (rŭf′hyo͞o′) ►*v.* **1.** To hew or shape (e.g., timber) roughly, without finishing. **2.** To make in rough form. **—rough′hewn′** *adj.*

rough•house (rŭf′hous′) ►*n.* Rowdy, rough behavior. **—rough′house′** (-houz′) *v.*

rough•neck (rŭf′nĕk′) ►*n.* A rowdy; tough.

rough•shod (rŭf′shŏd′) ►*adj.* Shod with horseshoes having projecting points to prevent slipping. **—*idiom:* ride roughshod over** To treat with brutal force.

rou•lade (ro͞o-läd′) ►*n.* A slice of meat rolled around a filling and cooked. [Fr. < *rouler*, to roll.]

rou•lette (ro͞o-lĕt′) ►*n.* A gambling game in which the players bet on which slot of a rotating disk a small ball will come to rest in. [< OFr. *ruelete*, small wheel.]

round (round) ►*adj.* **-er, -est 1a.** Spherical; ball-shaped. **b.** Circular or curved. **c.** Cylindrical. **2.** Complete; full: *a round dozen.* **3.** *Math.* Expressed or designated as a whole number or integer; not fractional. **4.** Not exact; approximate: *a round estimate.* ►*n.* **1.** Something round, such as a circle, disk, globe, or ring. **2.** A cut of beef between the rump and the shank. **3a.** A complete course, succession, or series: *a round of negotiations.* **b.** often **rounds** A course of customary or prescribed actions, duties, or places: *physicians' rounds.* **4.** One drink for each person in a gathering. **5.** A single outburst, as of applause or cheering. **6a.** A single shot or volley. **b.** A single cartridge or shell. **7.** An interval of play or action in various sports and games. **8.** *Mus.* A composition in which the melody is repeated by successive overlapping voices. ►*v.* **1.** To make or become round. **2.** To surround. **3.** To fill out; make plump. **4.** To bring to completion or perfection; finish. **5.** To express as a round number. **6.** To go or pass around. **7.** To make a turn about or to the other side of: *rounded a bend in the road.* **—*phrasal verb:* round up 1.** To bring together. **2.** To herd (cattle) in a roundup. ►*adv. & prep.* Around. **—*idiom:* in the round 1.** With the stage in the center of the audience. **2.** Fully shaped and freestanding, as a sculpture. [< Lat. *rotundus.*] **—round′ish** *adj.* **—round′ness** *n.*

round•a•bout (round′ə-bout′) ►*adj.* Indirect; circuitous.

roun•de•lay (roun′də-lā′) ►*n.* A poem or song with a recurring refrain. [< OFr. *rondelet.*]

round•house (round′hous′) ►*n.* **1.** A circular building for housing and switching locomotives. **2.** *Slang* A sweeping sidearm punch.

round•ly (round′lē) ►*adv.* Fully; thoroughly.

round robin ►*n.* A tournament in which each contestant is matched in turn against every other contestant.

round•ta•ble (round′tā′bəl) ►*n.* **1.** often **round table** A conference or discussion involving several participants. **2. Round Table** In Arthurian legend, the circular table of King Arthur and his knights.

round-the-clock (round′*th*ə-klŏk′) ►*adj.* Twenty-four hours a day; continuous.

round•trip also **round trip** (round′trĭp′) ►*n.* A trip to a place and back.

round•up (round′ŭp′) ►*n.* **1.** A herding together of cattle. **2.** A gathering up, as of suspects by the police. **3.** A summary.

round•worm (round′wûrm′) ►*n.* See **nematode.**

rouse (rouz) ►*v.* **roused, rous•ing 1.** To arouse from sleep, apathy, or depression. **2.** To excite, as to anger or action; stir up. [ME *rousen*, shake the feathers.]

rous•ing (rou′zĭng) ►*adj.* Inducing enthusiasm or excitement; stirring.

Rous•seau (ro͞o-sō′), **Henri.** "Le Douanier Rousseau." 1844–1910. French painter.

Rousseau, Jean Jacques. 1712–78. Swiss philosopher and writer.

Rousseau, Théodore. 1812–67. French landscape painter.

roust (roust) ►*v.* To rout or drive energetically,

esp. out of bed. [Alteration of ROUSE.]

roust•a•bout (rous′tə-bout′) ▶*n.* An unskilled laborer, as in an oil field.

rout[1] (rout) ▶*n.* **1.** A disorderly retreat or flight following defeat. **2.** An overwhelming defeat. ▶*v.* **1.** To put to disorderly flight or retreat. **2.** To defeat overwhelmingly. [< VLat. **rupta* < Lat. *rumpere*, break.]

rout[2] (rout) ▶*v.* **1.** To dig with the snout; root. **2.** To rummage. **3.** To gouge out. **4.** To drive or force out: *rout out an informant.* [Var. of ROOT[2].] —**rout′er** *n.*

route (ro͞ot, rout) ▶*n.* **1.** A road or way from one place to another. **2.** A customary line of travel. **3.** A means of reaching a goal. ▶*v.* **rout•ed, rout•ing.** To send by a route. See Syns at **send.** [< OFr.]

rou•tine (ro͞o-tēn′) ▶*n.* **1.** A prescribed and detailed course of action. **2.** A set of customary and often mechanically performed procedures or activities. **3.** A set piece of entertainment. **4.** *Comp. Sci.* A set of programming instructions for a specific task. ▶*adj.* **1.** In accord with established procedure. **2.** Not special; ordinary. [Fr. < *route*, ROUTE.] —**rou•tine′ly** *adv.*

roux (ro͞o) ▶*n., pl.* **roux.** A mixture of flour and fat cooked together, used as a thickening. [Fr. *(beurre) roux*, browned (butter), ult. < Lat. *russus*, red.]

rove (rōv) ▶*v.* **roved, rov•ing.** To wander about at random; roam. [ME *roven*, shoot arrows at a mark.] —**rov′er** *n.*

row[1] (rō) ▶*n.* **1.** A series of objects or persons placed next to each other, usu. in a straight line. **2.** A continuous line of buildings along a street. [< OE *rāw*.]

row[2] (rō) ▶*v.* **1.** To propel (a boat) with oars. **2.** To travel or carry by rowboat. ▶*n.* A trip by rowboat. [< OE *rōwan*.] —**row′er** *n.*

row[3] (rou) ▶*n.* **1.** A noisy fight or quarrel. See Syns at **brawl. 2.** An uproar. [?] —**row** *v.*

row•boat (rō′bōt′) ▶*n.* A small boat propelled by oars.

row•dy (rou′dē) ▶*n., pl.* **-dies.** A rough, disorderly person. ▶*adj.* **-di•er, -di•est.** Disorderly; rough. [Prob. < ROW[3].] —**row′di•ly** *adv.* —**row′di•ness** *n.* —**row′dy•ism** *n.*

row•el (rou′əl) ▶*n.* A sharp-toothed wheel inserted into the end of the shank of a spur. [< OFr. *roelle*, little wheel.] —**row′el** *v.*

rowel

row house (rō) ▶*n.* One of a series of similar or identical houses built side by side and joined by common walls.

roy•al (roi′əl) ▶*adj.* **1.** Of or relating to a monarch. **2.** Befitting royalty; stately. [< Lat. *rēgālis* < *rēx*, king.] —**roy′al•ly** *adv.*

royal blue ▶*n.* A deep to strong blue. —**roy′al-blue′** *adj.*

roy•al•ist (roi′ə-lĭst) ▶*n.* A supporter of government by a monarch.

royal poinciana ▶*n.* A tree native to Madagascar and having clusters of large scarlet flowers.

roy•al•ty (roi′əl-tē) ▶*n., pl.* **-ties 1a.** A person of royal rank or lineage. **b.** Monarchs and their families collectively. **2.** The power, status, or authority of a monarch. **3.** Royal quality or bearing. **4a.** A share paid to a writer or composer out of the proceeds resulting from the sale or performance of his or her work. **b.** A share paid to an inventor or a proprietor for the right to use his or her invention or services.

rpm ▶*abbr.* revolutions per minute

RR ▶*abbr.* **1.** railroad **2.** rural route

-rrhea or **-rrhoea** ▶*suff.* Flow; discharge: *pyorrhea.* [< Gk. *rhoia*, a flowing < *rhein*, flow.]

rRNA ▶*abbr.* ribosomal RNA

RSI ▶*abbr.* repetitive strain injury

RSV ▶*abbr.* Revised Standard Version

RSVP ▶*abbr.* *French* répondez s'il vous plaît (please reply)

Rte. ▶*abbr.* route

Rt. Hon. ▶*abbr.* Right Honorable

Ru ▶ The symbol for the element **ruthenium.**

rub (rŭb) ▶*v.* **rubbed, rub•bing 1a.** To apply friction and pressure to (a surface), as with a back and forth motion. **b.** To move or cause to move along a surface with friction and pressure. **2a.** To irritate; annoy. **b.** To chafe. **3.** To be transferred: *Her luck rubbed off on me.* —***phrasal verbs:* rub down** To massage. **rub out 1.** To obliterate by or as if by rubbing. **2.** *Slang* To murder. ▶*n.* **1.** The act of rubbing. **2.** A difficulty or obstacle. [ME *rubben*.]

rub•ber[1] (rŭb′ər) ▶*n.* **1.** A yellowish elastic material obtained from the milky sap of various tropical plants and used in products such as electric insulation, elastic bands, and tires. **2.** Any of numerous synthetic materials similar to natural rubber. **3.** A low overshoe made of rubber. **4.** An eraser. **5.** *Slang* A condom. [< RUB.] —**rub•ber•y** *adj.*

rub•ber[2] (rŭb′ər) ▶*n.* *Games* **1.** A series of games of which a majority must be won to terminate the play. **2.** An odd game played to break a tie. [?]

rubber band ▶*n.* An elastic loop of rubber used to hold objects together.

rubber cement ▶*n.* An adhesive of nonvulcanized rubber.

rub•ber•ize (rŭb′ə-rīz′) ▶*v.* **-ized, -iz•ing.** To coat, treat, or impregnate with rubber.

rub•ber•neck (rŭb′ər-nĕk′) ▶*v.* *Slang* To stare or gawk. —**rub′ber•neck′er** *n.*

rubber stamp ▶*n.* A piece of rubber with raised letters or designs, used to make ink impressions.

rub•ber-stamp (rŭb′ər-stămp′) ▶*v.* To endorse or approve without question or deliberation.

rub•bing (rŭb′ĭng) ▶*n.* An image of a raised or indented surface made by placing paper over the surface and rubbing the paper gently with a marking agent.

rub•bish (rŭb′ĭsh) ▶*n.* **1.** Refuse; garbage. **2.** Foolish discourse; nonsense. [ME *robishe*.] —**rub′bish•y** *adj.*

rub•ble (rŭb′əl) ▶*n.* **1.** Fragments of rock or masonry. **2.** Irregular pieces of rock used in masonry. [ME *rubel*.] —**rub′bly** *adj.*

rub•down (rŭb′doun′) ▶*n.* A massage.

rube (ro͞ob) ▶*n.* *Slang* An unsophisticated rustic. [Prob. < *Rube*, nickname for *Reuben*.]

ru•bel (ro͞o′bəl) ►*n.* See table at **currency.** [Belarusian.]

ru•bel•la (ro͞o-bĕl′ə) ►*n.* A mild, contagious viral disease capable of producing congenital defects in infants born to mothers infected during early pregnancy. [< Lat. *rubellus*, reddish < *ruber*, red.]

Ru•bens (ro͞o′bənz), **Peter Paul.** 1577–1640. Flemish painter. —**Ru′ben•esque′** *adj.*

ru•bi•cund (ro͞o′bĭ-kənd) ►*adj.* Rosy in complexion; ruddy. [Lat. *rubicundus.*]

ru•bid•i•um (ro͞o-bĭd′ē-əm) ►*n. Symbol* **Rb** A soft, alkali metallic element used in photocells. At. no. 37. See table at **element.** [< Lat. *rūbidus*, red.]

Ru•bin•stein (ro͞o′bĭn-stīn′), **Anton Gregor.** 1829–94. Russian pianist and composer.

Rubinstein, Arthur or **Artur.** 1887–1982. Polish-born Amer. pianist.

ru•ble also **rou•ble** (ro͞o′bəl) ►*n.* See table at **currency.** [Russ. *rubl′.*]

ru•bric (ro͞o′brĭk) ►*n.* **1a.** A class or category. **b.** A title or heading, as of a chapter in a code of law. **2.** A heading or initial letter printed distinctively, usu. in red lettering. [< Lat. *rūbrīca*, red chalk < *ruber*, red.]

ru•by (ro͞o′bē) ►*n., pl.* **-bies 1.** A deep red, translucent corundum, highly valued as a precious stone. **2.** A deep purplish red. [< Lat. *rubeus*, red.] —**ru′by** *adj.*

ruck•sack (rŭk′săk′, ro͝ok′-) ►*n.* A knapsack. [Ger.]

ruck•us (rŭk′əs) ►*n.* A disturbance; commotion. [Blend of *ruction*, disturbance, and RUMPUS.]

rud•der (rŭd′ər) ►*n.* **1.** A vertically hinged plate mounted at the stern of a vessel or aircraft for steering. **2.** A controlling agent or influence. [< OE *rōther*, steering oar.]

rud•dy (rŭd′ē) ►*adj.* **-di•er, -di•est 1.** Having a healthy reddish color. **2.** Reddish; rosy. [< OE *rudig.*] —**rud′di•ness** *n.*

rude (ro͞od) ►*adj.* **rud•er, rud•est 1.** Relatively undeveloped; primitive. **2.** Crudely or roughly made. **3.** Ill-mannered; discourteous. **4.** Abrupt and unpleasant: *a rude shock.* [< Lat. *rudis.*] —**rude′ly** *adv.* —**rude′ness** *n.*

Syns: *crude, primitive, raw, rough* **adj.**

ru•di•ment (ro͞o′də-mənt) ►*n.* **1.** A fundamental element, principle, or skill. **2.** often **rudiments** Something in an incipient or undeveloped form. [< Lat. *rudis*, rough, unformed.] —**ru′di•men′ta•ry** (-mĕn′tə-rē, -mĕn′trē) *adj.*

Ru•dolf I (ro͞o′dŏlf). 1218–91. Holy Roman emperor (1273–91) and founder of the Hapsburg dynasty.

Ru•dolph (ro͞o′dŏlf), **Wilma Glodean.** 1940–94. Amer. athlete.

rue[1] (ro͞o) ►*v.* **rued, ru•ing.** To feel regret, remorse, or sorrow for. [< OE *hrēowian.*] —**rue′ful** *adj.* —**rue′ful•ness** *n.*

rue[2] (ro͞o) ►*n.* Any of various aromatic Eurasian plants that yield an acrid oil formerly used in medicine. [< Gk. *rhutē.*]

ruff (rŭf) ►*n.* **1.** A stiffly starched circular collar worn in the 16th and 17th cent. **2.** A collarlike projection around the neck, as of feathers on a bird. [Perh. < RUFFLE.] —**ruffed** *adj.*

ruf•fi•an (rŭf′ē-ən, rŭf′yən) ►*n.* A tough or rowdy person. [< OItal. *ruffiano.*]

ruf•fle (rŭf′əl) ►*n.* **1.** A strip of frilled or closely pleated fabric used for trimming or decoration. **2.** A ruff on a bird. **3.** A ripple. ►*v.* **-fled, -fling 1.** To disturb the smoothness or regularity of. **2.** To pleat or gather (fabric) into a ruffle. **3.** To erect (the feathers). **4.** To discompose; fluster. **5.** To annoy. [< ME *ruffelen*, roughen.]

ruff

ru•fi•yaa (ro͞o′fē-yä′) ►*n.* See table at **currency.** [< Hindi *rupiyā.*]

ru•fous (ro͞o′fəs) ►*adj.* Reddish to reddish-orange. [< Lat. *rūfus*, red.]

rug (rŭg) ►*n.* A heavy fabric used to cover a floor. [Of Scand. orig.]

Rug•by (rŭg′bē) ►*n.* A form of football in which forward passing, substitution of players, and time-outs are not permitted. [After *Rugby* School, England.]

rug•ged (rŭg′ĭd) ►*adj.* **1.** Having a rough, irregular surface. **2.** Strong and sturdy. **3.** Foul; stormy. **4.** Demanding great effort or endurance. [ME, shaggy, of Scand. orig.] —**rug′ged•ly** *adv.* —**rug′ged•ness** *n.*

Ruhr (ro͝or) A region of NW Germany along and N of the **Ruhr River,** which flows about 233 km (145 mi) to the Rhine R.

ru•in (ro͞o′ĭn) ►*n.* **1.** Total destruction or disintegration. **2.** A cause of such destruction. **3.** often **ruins** The remains of something destroyed, disintegrated, or decayed. ►*v.* **1.** To destroy completely; demolish. **2.** To harm irreparably. **3.** To reduce to poverty or bankruptcy. [< Lat. *ruīna.*] —**ru′in•a•ble** *adj.* —**ru′in•a′tion** *n.* —**ru′in•ous** *adj.*

rule (ro͞ol) ►*n.* **1.** Governing power; authority. **2.** An authoritative direction for conduct or procedure. **3.** A usual or customary course of action or behavior. **4.** A statement that describes what is true in most or all cases. **5.** A standard method or procedure. **6.** See **ruler** 2. ►*v.* **ruled, rul•ing 1.** To exercise control (over); govern. **2.** To dominate by powerful influence. **3.** To decide judicially; decree. **4.** To mark with straight parallel lines. —***phrasal verb:*** **rule out** To exclude. [< Lat. *rēgula*, ruler, straightedge.]

rule of thumb ►*n., pl.* **rules of thumb.** A useful principle having wide application but not intended to be strictly accurate.

rul•er (ro͞o′lər) ►*n.* **1.** One that rules or governs. **2.** A straightedged strip for drawing straight lines and measuring lengths.

rul•ing (ro͞o′lĭng) ►*adj.* **1.** Exercising control or authority. **2.** Predominant. ►*n.* An official decision: *a court ruling.*

rum (rŭm) ►*n.* An alcoholic liquor distilled from fermented molasses or sugar cane. [Prob. short for obsolete *rumbullion.*]

Ru•ma•ni•a (ro͞o-mā′nē-ə, -mān′yə) See **Romania.** —**Ru•ma′ni•an** *adj. & n.*

rum•ba (rŭm′bə, ro͝om′-, ro͞om′-) ►*n.* A complex rhythmical dance of Cuban origin. [Am.Sp.] —**rum′ba** *v.*

rum•ble (rŭm′bəl) ►*v.* **-bled, -bling 1.** To make a deep long rolling sound. **2.** To move or proceed with a rumble. **3.** *Slang* To engage in a gang fight. ►*n.* **1.** A deep long rolling sound. **2.** *Slang* **a.** Murmurous discontent. **b.** A gang fight. [ME *romblen.*] —**rum′bler** *n.* —**rum′bly** *adj.*

rumble seat ►*n.* An uncovered passenger seat that opens out from the rear of an automobile.

ru•men (ro͞o′mən) ►*n., pl.* **-mi•na** (-mə-nə) or **-mens.** The first division of the stomach of a ruminant. [Lat. *rūmen*, throat.] —**ru′mi•nal** *adj.*

ru•mi•nant (ro͞o′mə-nənt) ►*n.* Any of various hoofed, usu. horned mammals, such as cattle, sheep, and deer, having a divided stomach and chewing a cud. ►*adj.* **1.** Chewing cud. **2.** Meditative; contemplative.

ru•mi•nate (ro͞o′mə-nāt′) ►*v.* **-nat•ed, -nat•ing 1.** To consider a matter at length. **2.** To chew cud. [Lat. *rūmināre* < *rūmen*, throat.] —**ru′mi•na′tion** *n.* —**ru′mi•na′tive** *adj.* —**ru′mi•na′tor** *n.*

rum•mage (rŭm′ĭj) ►*v.* **-maged, -mag•ing.** To make a thorough, often disorderly search (of). [< OFr. *arumer*, stow.]

rummage sale ►*n.* A sale of assorted secondhand objects.

rum•my (rŭm′ē) ►*n.* A card game in which the object is to obtain sets of three or more cards of the same rank or suit. [?]

ru•mor (ro͞o′mər) ►*n.* A report of uncertain origin and accuracy; hearsay. [< Lat. *rūmor.*] —**ru′mor** *v.*

ru•mor•mon•ger (ro͞o′mər-mŭng′gər, -mŏng′-) ►*n.* One who spreads rumors. —**ru′mor•mon′ger** *v.*

rump (rŭmp) ►*n.* **1.** The fleshy hindquarters of an animal. **2.** A cut of beef from the rump. **3.** The buttocks. **4.** The last or inferior part. [ME *rumpe*, of Scand. orig.]

rum•ple (rŭm′pəl) ►*v.* **-pled, -pling.** To wrinkle or form into folds or creases. [Poss. < MDu *rumpelen.*] —**rum′ply** *adj.*

rum•pus (rŭm′pəs) ►*n.* A noisy ruckus. [?]

rumpus room ►*n.* A play or family room.

rum•run•ner (rŭm′rŭn′ər) ►*n.* One who illegally transports liquor across a border.

run (rŭn) ►*v.* **ran** (răn), **run, run•ning 1.** To move on foot at a pace faster than a walk. **2.** To flee. **3.** To move without hindrance or restraint. **4.** To make a short, quick trip. **5.** To cause to move quickly: *ran her finger along the keyboard.* **6.** To hurry; hasten. **7a.** To take part in a race. **b.** To compete for elected office: *ran for mayor.* **8.** To swim in large numbers, as in migrating. **9.** To move freely, as by rolling or sliding. **10a.** To function or cause to function. **b.** To control or manage. **11.** To cause to collide or penetrate. **12.** To go regularly. **13.** *Naut.* To sail or steer before the wind or on an indicated course. **14a.** To flow in a steady stream. **b.** To discharge or leak. **15.** To cause to flow: *run the water into the tub.* **16.** To spread and dissolve, as dye in fabric. **17.** To extend: *This road runs into the next town.* **18.** To spread or climb, as a vine. **19.** To spread rapidly, as a disease. **20.** To unravel, as a nylon stocking. **21.** To continue in effect or operation. **22.** To pass; elapse. **23.** To persist or recur. **24.** To accumulate or accrue. **25.** To have a particular form or expression. **26.** To tend or incline. **27.** To exist in a certain range: *sizes run from small to large.* **28.** To pass into a specified condition: *run into debt.* **29.** *Comp. Sci.* To process or execute (a program or instruction). —***phrasal verbs:* run along** To go away; leave. **run down 1.** To stop because of lack of force or power. **2.** To become tired. **3.** To collide with and knock down. **4.** To chase and capture. **5.** To trace the source of. **6.** To disparage. **run out** To become used up. **run over 1.** To collide with and knock down. **2.** To go beyond a limit. **run through 1.** To pierce. **2.** To use up. **3.** To examine or rehearse quickly. ►*n.* **1a.** A pace faster than a walk. **b.** A fast gallop. **2.** An act of running. **3.** A distance covered by or as if by running. **4.** A quick trip or visit. **5a.** A running race. **b.** A campaign for public office. **6.** *Baseball* A point scored by reaching home plate safely. **7.** The migration of fish, esp. in order to spawn. **8.** Unrestricted freedom or use: *the run of the library.* **9.** A continuous period of operation, as by a machine or factory. **10.** A movement or flow. **11a.** A conduit or channel. **b.** *Regional* See **creek. 12.** A continuous length or extent. **13.** The direction, configuration, or lie of something. **14.** An outdoor enclosure for domestic animals or poultry. **15.** A length of unraveled stitches in a knitted fabric. **16.** An unbroken series or sequence, as of theatrical performances. **17.** A series of unexpected and urgent demands, as by customers: *a run on a bank.* **18a.** A continuous set or sequence, as of playing cards. **b.** A successful sequence of shots or points. **19.** A sustained state or condition: *a run of good luck.* **20.** A trend or tendency. **21.** An average type or category: *the broad run of voters.* —***idioms:* in the long run** In the final analysis or outcome. **in the short run** In the immediate future. **on the run 1.** In rapid retreat. **2.** In hiding. **3.** Hurrying busily from place to place. **run out of** To exhaust the supply of. **run rings around** To be markedly superior to. [< OE *rinnan* and ON *rinna.*]

Regional Note: Terms for "a small, fast-flowing stream" vary throughout the United States. Regional terms are *run* (Virginia, West Virginia, Delaware, Maryland, and southern Pennsylvania), *kill* (New York state), *brook* (throughout the Northeast), *branch* (the South), and *crick*, a variant of *creek* (the North).

run•a•bout (rŭn′ə-bout′) ►*n.* A small open automobile, carriage, or motorboat.

run•a•round (rŭn′ə-round′) ►*n.* *Informal* Deception, usu. in the form of evasive excuses.

run•a•way (rŭn′ə-wā′) ►*n.* **1.** One who has run away. **2.** *Informal* An easy victory. ►*adj.* **1.** Escaping or having escaped confinement. **2.** Out of control. **3.** Easily won.

run•down (rŭn′doun′) ►*n.* A point-by-point summary. ►*adj.* also **run-down** (rŭn′doun′) **1a.** Weak or exhausted. **b.** Dirty and dilapidated. **2.** Unwound and not running.

rune (ro͞on) ►*n.* **1.** One of the letters of an al-

rune
detail from the 5th-century
Kylver Stone, Gotland, Sweden

phabet used by ancient Germanic peoples. **2.** A magic charm. [< OE *rūn*.]

rung¹ (rŭng) ►*n.* **1.** A bar forming a step of a ladder. **2.** A crosspiece between the legs of a chair. **3.** A spoke of a wheel. [< OE *hrung*.]

rung² (rŭng) ►*v.* P.part. of **ring²**.

run-in (rŭn′ĭn′) ►*n.* A quarrel or argument.

run•nel (rŭn′əl) ►*n.* **1.** A rivulet; brook. **2.** A narrow channel, as for water. [< OE *rynel*.]

run•ner (rŭn′ər) ►*n.* **1.** One who runs, as in a race. **2a.** *Baseball* One who runs the bases. **b.** *Football* One who carries the ball. **3.** A messenger. **4.** A smuggler. **5.** A vessel engaged in smuggling. **6.** A device in or on which a mechanism slides or moves, as the blade of a skate. **7.** A long narrow carpet. **8.** A slender creeping stem that roots at intervals along its length.

run•ner-up (rŭn′ər-ŭp′) ►*n., pl.* **run•ners-up** (rŭn′ərz-). One that takes second place.

run•ning (rŭn′ĭng) ►*n.* The act or sport of running. ►*adj.* Ongoing; continuous. ►*adv.* Consecutively.

running board ►*n.* A narrow footboard extending under and along the doors of some vehicles.

running light ►*n.* One of several lights on a ship or aircraft to indicate position and size.

run•ny (rŭn′ē) ►*adj.* **-ni•er, -ni•est.** Inclined to run or flow: *a runny nose*.

run•off (rŭn′ôf′, -ŏf′) ►*n.* **1.** An overflow of fluid. **2.** A competition held to break a tie.

run-of-the-mill (rŭn′əv-*th*ə-mĭl′) ►*adj.* Not special; average.

runt (rŭnt) ►*n.* **1.** An undersized animal, esp. the smallest of a litter. **2.** *Slang* A short person. [?] —**runt′y** *adj.*

run-through (rŭn′thro͞o′) ►*n.* A complete but rapid review or rehearsal.

run•way (rŭn′wā′) ►*n.* **1.** A usu. paved strip of level ground on which aircraft take off and land. **2.** A path, channel, or track over which something runs. **3.** A narrow walkway from a stage into an auditorium.

ru•pee (ro͞o-pē′, ro͞o′pē) ►*n.* See table at **currency.** [< Skt. *rūpya-*, silver.]

ru•pi•ah (ro͞o-pē′ə) ►*n., pl.* **-ah** or **-ahs.** See table at **currency.** [Hindi *rupiyā*, rupee.]

rup•ture (rŭp′chər) ►*n.* **1a.** The process of breaking open or bursting. **b.** The state of being broken. **2.** A hernia. [< Lat. *rumpere*, *rupt-*, break.] —**rup′ture** *v.*

ru•ral (ro͝or′əl) ►*adj.* Of or relating to the country as opposed to the city. [< Lat. *rūs*, *rūr-*, country.] —**ru′ral•ly** *adv.*

Rus. or **Russ.** ►*abbr.* Russian

ruse (ro͞os, ro͞oz) ►*n.* An action or device meant to mislead or confuse; deception. [< OFr. *ruser*, drive back.]

rush¹ (rŭsh) ►*v.* **1.** To move or cause to move swiftly; hurry. **2.** To attack suddenly. **3.** To perform with haste. **4.** To transport with urgent speed. ►*n.* **1.** A sudden forward motion. **2a.** Urgent movement to or from a place. **b.** A sudden generalized demand: *a rush for gold coins.* **3.** General haste or busyness. **4.** A sudden attack. **5.** A rapid, often noisy flow. See Syns at **flow. 6.** A sudden brief exhilaration. ►*adj.* Performed with or requiring great haste or urgency. [< Lat. *recūsāre*, reject.] —**rush′er** *n.*

rush² (rŭsh) ►*n.* **1.** A marsh plant having pliant hollow or pithy stems. **2.** The stem itself, used in wickerwork. [< OE *rysc*.]

Rush•more (rŭsh′môr′, -mōr′), **Mount.** A mountain, 1,708 m (5,600 ft), in the Black Hills of W SD; site of a national memorial.

rusk (rŭsk) ►*n.* Sweet raised bread dried and browned in an oven. [Sp. *rosca*, coil.]

Rus•kin (rŭs′kĭn), **John.** 1819–1900. British writer and art critic. —**Rus′kin′i•an** *adj.*

Rus•sell (rŭs′əl), **Bertrand Arthur William.** 3rd Earl Russell. 1872–1970. British philosopher and mathematician; 1950 Nobel.

rus•set (rŭs′ĭt) ►*n.* **1.** A reddish brown. **2.** A brown homespun cloth. **3.** A winter apple with a reddish-brown skin. [< Lat. *russus*, red.] —**rus′set** *adj.*

Rus•sia (rŭsh′ə) A region and republic of E Europe and N Asia extending from the Gulf of Finland to the Pacific and N to the Arctic Ocean. Cap. Moscow. Pop. 147,997,000.

Rus•sian (rŭsh′ən) ►*n.* **1.** A native or inhabitant of Russia. **2.** The Slavic language of the Russians. —**Rus′sian** *adj.*

rust (rŭst) ►*n.* **1.** Any of various reddish-brown oxides formed on iron and iron-containing materials by low-temperature oxidation in the presence of water. **2.** Any of various metallic coatings formed by corrosion. **3.** A plant disease caused by various fungi, marked by reddish or brownish spots on leaves and stems. **4.** A strong brown. ►*v.* **1.** To corrode. **2.** To deteriorate through inactivity or neglect. [< OE *rūst*.] —**rust** *adj.* —**rust′i•ness** *n.* —**rust′y** *adj.*

rus•tic (rŭs′tĭk) ►*adj.* **1.** Typical of country life. **2.** Unsophisticated; simple; crude. ►*n.* **1.** A rural person. **2.** A crude, coarse, or simple person. [< Lat. *rūs*, country.] —**rus•tic′i•ty** (-tĭs′ĭ-tē) *n.*

rus•ti•cate (rŭs′tĭ-kāt′) ►*v.* **-cat•ed, -cat•ing.** To go to or live in the country. —**rus′ti•ca′tion** *n.*

rus•tle (rŭs′əl) ►*v.* **-tled, -tling 1.** To move or cause to move with soft fluttering or crackling sounds. **2.** To obtain in an enterprising manner: *rustle up supper.* **3.** To steal (livestock). [ME *rustlen*.] —**rus′tler** *n.*

rut¹ (rŭt) ►*n.* **1.** A sunken track or groove made by the passage of vehicles. **2.** A fixed, usu. boring routine. ►*v.* **rut•ted, rut•ting.** To furrow. [Poss. < ROUTE.] —**rut′ty** *adj.*

rut² (rŭt) ►*n.* An annually recurring condition of sexual activity, as in male deer. [< Lat. *rūgīre*, roar.] —**rut** *v.*

ru•ta•ba•ga (ro͞o′tə-bā′gə, ro͝ot′ə-) ►*n.* A turniplike plant having a thick, bulbous, edible root. [Swed. dial. *rotabagge* : ON *rōt*, root + *baggi*, bag.]

Ruth (ro͞oth) ►*n.* See table at **Bible.**

Ruth, George Herman. "Babe." 1895–1948. Amer. baseball player.

Ru•the•nia (ro͞o-thēn′yə, -thē′nē-ə) A region of W Ukraine S of the Carpathian Mts. —**Ru•the′ni•an** *adj. & n.*

ru•the•ni•um (ro͞o-thē′nē-əm) ▸*n. Symbol* **Ru** A hard, white, acid-resistant metallic element used to harden platinum and palladium. At. no. 44. See table at **element.** [< Med.Lat. *Ruthenia*, Russia.]

Ruth•er•ford (rŭ*th*′ər-fərd, rŭth′-), **Ernest.** 1871–1937. New Zealand-born British physicist; 1908 Nobel.

ruth•er•for•di•um (rŭ*th*′ər-fôr′dē-əm, -fōr′-) ▸*n. Symbol* **Rf** A short-lived, synthetic radioactive element. At. no. 104. See table at **element.** [After Ernest RUTHERFORD.]

ruth•less (ro͞oth′lĭs) ▸*adj.* Having no compassion or pity. [< ME *ruthe*, compassion.] —**ruth′less•ly** *adv.* —**ruth′less•ness** *n.*

RV ▸*abbr.* **1.** recreational vehicle **2.** reentry vehicle **3.** Revised Version

R-val•ue (är′văl′yo͞o) ▸*n.* A measure of the capacity of a material, such as insulation, to impede heat flow. [*r(esistance) value.*]

Rwan•da (ro͞o-än′də) A country of E-central Africa. Cap. Kigali. Pop. 7,750,000. —**Rwan′dan** *adj. & n.*

rwy. ▸*abbr.* railway

Rx (är′ĕks′) ▸*n.* A medical prescription. [< ℞, symbol used in prescriptions, abbr. of Lat. *recipe*, take.]

-ry ▸*suff.* Var. of **-ery.**

rye (rī) ▸*n.* **1.** A widely cultivated cereal grass. **2.** The grain of this plant, used in making flour and whiskey and for livestock feed. **3.** Whiskey made from this grain. [< OE *ryge.*]

Ryu•kyu Islands (rē-o͞o′kyo͞o′, ryo͞o′-kyo͞o) An island group of SW Japan extending between Kyushu and Taiwan.

S

s[1] or **S** (ĕs) ▸*n., pl.* **s's** or **S's** also **ss** or **Ss.** The 19th letter of the English alphabet.

s[2] ▸*abbr.* **1.** second (unit of time) **2.** *Math.* second (of arc) **3.** stere

S[1] ▸ The symbol for the element **sulfur.**

S[2] ▸*abbr.* **1.** satisfactory **2.** small **3.** soprano **4.** south **5.** *Baseball* strike

s. ▸*abbr.* **1.** shilling **2.** singular **3.** son

S. ▸*abbr.* **1.** saint **2.** sea

-s[1] or **-es** ▸*suff.* Used to form plural nouns: *letters; ashes.* [< OE *-es, -as.*]

-s[2] or **-es** ▸*suff.* Used to form the 3rd person singular present tense of all regular and most irregular verbs: *looks; goes.* [< OE *-es, -as.*]

-s[3] ▸*suff.* Used to form adverbs: *caught unawares.* [< OE *-es*, genitive suff.]

-'s ▸*suff.* Used to form the possessive case: *nation's.* [< OE *-es*, genitive suff.]

Saar (sär, zär) A river, about 241 km (150 mi), flowing from NE France to the Moselle R. in W Germany.

Saar•land (sär′lănd′, zär′-) A region of SW Germany on the border with France.

Sab•bath (săb′əth) ▸*n.* **1.** The 7th day of the week, Saturday, observed as the day of rest and worship by Jews and some Christians. **2.** The 1st day of the week, Sunday, observed as the day of rest and worship by most Christians. [< Heb. *šabbāt.*]

sab•bat•i•cal year also **sab•bat•i•cal** (sə-băt′ĭ-kəl) ▸*n.* An often paid leave of absence, usu. granted every 7th year, as to a professor, for travel, research, or rest. [< Gk. *sabbatikos*, of the sabbath.]

sa•ber (sā′bər) ▸*n.* **1.** A heavy cavalry sword with a one-edged, slightly curved blade. **2.** A light dueling or fencing sword having a tapered flexible blade. [< Hung. *szablya.*]

Sa•bin (sā′bĭn), **Albert Bruce.** 1906–93. Amer. microbiologist and physician.

Sa•bine (sā′bīn′) ▸*n.* **1.** A member of an ancient people of central Italy. **2.** The Italic language of the Sabines. —**Sa′bine′** *adj.*

Sabin vaccine ▸*n.* An oral poliomyelitis vaccine consisting of live attenuated polio viruses. [After Albert B. SABIN.]

sa•ble (sā′bəl) ▸*n.* **1a.** A weasellike mammal of N Eurasia, having soft dark fur. **b.** The fur of this animal. **2a.** The color black. **b. sables** Black garments worn in mourning. [< ORuss. *sobol′.*] —**sa′ble** *adj.*

sab•o•tage (săb′ə-täzh′) ▸*n.* **1.** Destruction of property or obstruction of normal operations, as by civilians or enemy agents in time of war. **2.** Treacherous action to hinder an endeavor; deliberate subversion. [< OFr. *saboter*, bungle.] —**sab′o•tage′** *v.*

sab•o•teur (săb′ə-tûr′) ▸*n.* One who commits sabotage. [Fr.]

sa•bra (sä′brə) ▸*n.* A native-born Israeli. [Heb. *ṣābār*, prickly pear.]

sac (săk) ▸*n.* A pouchlike plant or animal structure. [< Lat. *saccus*, bag.]

Sac (săk, sôk) ▸*n.* Var. of **Sauk.**

SAC ▸*abbr.* Strategic Air Command

Sac•a•ga•we•a (săk′ə-gə-wē′ə, sä-kä′gä-wē′ä) or **Sac•a•ja•we•a** (săk′ə-jə-wē′ə). 1787?–1812. Shoshone guide and interpreter for the Lewis and Clark Expedition.

Sacagawea

sacchar- ▸*pref.* Sugar: *saccharine.* [< Gk. *sakkhar* < Skt. *śarkarā.*]

sac•cha•rin (săk′ər-ĭn) ▸*n.* A white crystalline powder, $C_7H_5NO_3S$, having a taste about 500 times sweeter than cane sugar, used as a calorie-free sweetener.

sac•cha•rine (săk′ər-ĭn, -ə-rēn′, -ə-rīn′) ▸*adj.* **1.** Of or characteristic of sugar or saccharin; sweet. **2.** Cloyingly sweet.

Sac•co (săk′ō, säk′kō), **Nicola.** 1891–1927. Italian-born Amer. anarchist; executed.

sac•er•do•tal (săs′ər-dōt′l, săk′-) ▸*adj.* Of or relating to priests or the priesthood. [< Lat. *sacerdōs*, priest.]

sa•chem (sā′chəm) ▸*n.* A chief of a Native American, esp. Algonquian tribe or confederation. [Of Massachusett orig.]

sa•chet (să-shā′) ▸*n.* A packet of perfumed powder used to scent clothes. [< OFr.]

sack[1] (săk) ▸*n.* **1a.** A large bag of strong coarse material. **b.** A similar container of paper or plastic. **2.** A short, loose-fitting garment. **3.** *Slang* Dismissal from employment. **4.** *Informal* A bed. ▸*v.* **1.** To place into a sack. **2.** *Slang* To dismiss; fire. See Syns at **dismiss.** [< Gk. *sakkos.*]

sack[2] (săk) ▸*v.* To plunder; pillage. [< Fr. *(mettre à) sac*, (put in) a sack.] —**sack** *n.*

sack•cloth (săk′klôth′, -klŏth′) ▸*n.* **1.** Sacking. **2a.** A rough coarse cloth. **b.** Garments made of sackcloth, worn as a symbol of mourning or penitence.

sack•ing (săk′ĭng) ▸*n.* A coarse woven cloth used for making sacks.

sa•cra (sā′krə, săk′rə) ▸*n.* Pl. of **sacrum.**

sac•ra•ment (săk′rə-mənt) ▸*n.* *Christianity* **1.** A rite instituted by Jesus that confers sanctifying grace. **2.** often **Sacrament** The consecrated elements of the Eucharist. [< Lat. *sacrāmentum*, oath.] —**sac′ra•men′tal** (-mĕn′tl) *n. & adj.*

Sac•ra•men•to (săk′rə-mĕn′tō) The capital of CA, in the N-central part on the Sacramento R. Pop. 369,365.

Sacramento River. A river of N CA flowing about 611 km (380 mi) to San Francisco Bay.

sa•cred (sā′krĭd) ▸*adj.* **1.** Dedicated to or set apart for worship. **2.** Worthy of religious veneration. **3.** Made or declared holy. **4.** Dedicated or devoted exclusively to a single use or person. **5.** Worthy of respect; venerable. **6.** Of or relating to religious objects or practices. [< Lat. *sacrāre*, consecrate.] —**sa′cred•ly** *adv.* —**sa′cred•ness** *n.*

sacred cow ▸*n.* One immune from criticism.

sac•ri•fice (săk′rə-fīs′) ▸*n.* **1.** The offering of something to a deity. **2a.** Forfeiture of something highly valued for the sake of one that is considered to have a greater value or claim. **b.** Something so forfeited. **3.** Relinquishment of something at less than its presumed value. ▸*v.* **-ficed, -fic•ing 1.** To offer as a sacrifice. **2.** To forfeit (one thing) for another thing considered of greater value. **3.** To sell or give away at a loss. [< Lat. *sacrificium.*] —**sac′ri•fic′er** *n.* —**sac′ri•fi′cial** (-fĭsh′əl) *adj.* —**sac′ri•fi′cial•ly** *adv.*

sac•ri•lege (săk′rə-lĭj) ▸*n.* Desecration, profanation, misuse, or theft of something sacred. [< Lat. *sacrilegium.*]

sac•ri•le•gious (săk′rə-lĭj′əs, -lē′jəs) ▸*adj.* Grossly irreverent toward what is sacred. —**sac′ri•le′gious•ly** *adv.*

Usage: *Sacrilegious,* the adjective of *sacrilege,* is often misspelled through confusion with *religious.*

sac•ris•tan (săk′rĭ-stən) ▸*n.* **1.** One in charge of a sacristy. **2.** A sexton. [ME, < Med.Lat. *sacristānus*, < *sacrista*, < Latin *sacer*, sacred.]

sac•ris•ty (săk′rĭ-stē) ▸*n., pl.* **-ties.** A room in a church housing the sacred vessels and vestments. [< Med.Lat. *sacristia.*]

sac•ro•il•i•ac (săk′rō-ĭl′ē-ăk′, sā′krō-) ▸*n.* The region of the lower back in which the sacrum and ilium join. [< SACRUM + ILIUM.] —**sac′ro•il′i•ac′** *adj.*

sac•ro•sanct (săk′rō-săngkt′) ▸*adj.* Inviolably sacred. [Lat. *sacrōsānctus*, consecrated with religious ceremonies.] —**sac′ro•sanc′ti•ty** *n.*

sa•crum (sā′krəm, săk′rəm) ▸*n., pl.* **sa•cra** (sā′krə, săk′rə). A triangular bone that forms the posterior section of the pelvis. [< LLat., sacred.] —**sa′cral** *adj.*

sad (săd) ▸*adj.* **sad•der, sad•dest 1.** Sorrowful; unhappy. **2.** Causing sorrow or gloom. **3.** Deplorable; sorry. [< OE *sæd*, sated, weary.] —**sad′ly** *adv.* —**sad′ness** *n.*

SAD ▸*abbr.* seasonal affective disorder

Sa•dat (sə-dăt′, -dät′), **Anwar el-.** 1918–81. Egyptian politician; 1978 Nobel Peace Prize.

sad•den (săd′n) ▸*v.* To make or become sad.

sad•dle (săd′l) ▸*n.* **1a.** A leather seat for a rider, secured on an animal's back. **b.** The seat of a bicycle or similar vehicle. **2.** A cut of meat consisting of part of the backbone and both loins. ▸*v.* **-dled, -dling 1.** To put a saddle onto. **2.** To load or burden; encumber. —***idiom:* in the saddle** In control; dominant. [< OE *sadol.*]

sad•dle•bag (săd′l-băg′) ▸*n.* **1.** A pouch that hangs across the back of a horse. **2.** A similar pouch on a motorcycle or bicycle.

Sad•du•cee (săj′ə-sē′, săd′yə-) ▸*n.* A member of a priestly Jewish sect (2nd cent. B.C.–1st cent. A.D.) that accepted only the written Mosaic law. —**Sad′du•ce′an** (-sē′ən) *adj.*

Sade (säd, săd), Comte **Donatien Alphonse François de.** "Marquis de Sade." 1740–1814. French writer.

sa•dism (sā′dĭz′əm, săd′ĭz′-) ▸*n.* **1.** *Psychol.* The association of sexual gratification with infliction of pain on others. **2.** Delight in cruelty. [After the Marquis de SADE.] —**sa′dist** *n.* —**sa•dis′tic** (sə-dĭs′tĭk) *adj.* —**sa•dis′ti•cal•ly** *adv.*

sa•do•mas•o•chism (sā′dō-măs′ə-kĭz′əm, săd′ō-) ▸*n.* *Psychol.* Deriving esp. sexual pleasure from both sadism and masochism. [SAD(ISM) + MASOCHISM.] —**sa′do•mas′o•chist** *n.* —**sa′do•mas′o•chis′tic** *adj.*

Sa•far also **Sa•phar** (sə-fär′) ▸*n.* The 2nd month of the Muslim calendar. See table at **calendar.** [Ar. *ṣafar.*]

sa•fa•ri (sə-fär′ē) ▸*n., pl.* **-ris.** An overland expedition, esp. in E Africa. [Ar. *safarīya*, journey.]

safe (sāf) ▸*adj.* **saf•er, saf•est 1.** Secure from danger, harm, or evil. **2.** Unhurt: *safe and sound.* **3.** Free from risk: *a safe bet.* **4.** Affording protection: *a safe place.* **5.** *Baseball* Reaching a base without being put out. ▸*n.* A strong container for storing valuables. [< Lat. *salvus*, healthy.] —**safe′ly** *adv.*

safe-con•duct (sāf′kŏn′dŭkt) ▸*n.* A document or an escort assuring unmolested passage, as through enemy territory.

safe•crack•er (sāf′krăk′ər) ▸*n.* One who breaks into safes. —**safe′crack′ing** *n.*

safe-de•pos•it box (sāf′dĭ-pŏz′ĭt) ▸*n.* A fireproof box, usu. in a bank vault, for the safe storage of valuables.

safe•guard (sāf′gärd′) ►*n.* A precautionary measure or device. ►*v.* To ensure the safety of; protect.

safe•keep•ing (sāf′kē′pĭng) ►*n.* Protection; care.

safe•light (sāf′līt′) ►*n.* A lamp that allows darkroom illumination without affecting photosensitive film or paper.

safe sex ►*n.* Sexual activity in which safeguards, such as the use of a condom, are taken to reduce the risk of acquiring or spreading a sexually transmitted disease. —**safe′-sex′** *adj.*

safe•ty (sāf′tē) ►*n., pl.* **-ties 1.** Freedom from danger, risk, or injury. **2.** A protective device, as a lock on a firearm. **3.** *Football* A play in which the offensive team downs the ball behind its own goal line, resulting in two points for the defensive team.

safety belt ►*n.* A strap or belt worn as a safety precaution, esp. a seat belt.

safety glass ►*n.* Glass that resists shattering, esp. a composite of two sheets of glass with an intermediate layer of plastic.

safety match ►*n.* A match that can be lighted only by being struck against a chemically prepared friction surface.

safety pin ►*n.* A pin in the form of a clasp, with a sheath to cover and hold the point.

safety razor ►*n.* A razor with guards around the blade to prevent deep cuts.

safety valve ►*n.* A valve, as in a steam boiler, that automatically opens when pressure reaches a dangerous level.

saf•flow•er (săf′lou′ər) ►*n.* A plant with flowers yielding a dyestuff and seeds that yield a cooking oil. [< Ar. *'aṣfar*, a yellow plant.]

saf•fron (săf′rən) ►*n.* **1.** The dried stigmas of a kind of crocus, used to color and flavor food and as a dye. **2.** A moderate or strong orange yellow. [< Ar. *za'farān.*]

sag (săg) ►*v.* **sagged, sag•ging 1.** To sink, droop, or settle from pressure or weight. **2.** To lose vigor, firmness, or resilience. **3.** To decline, as in value or price. [ME *saggen.*] —**sag** *n.*

sa•ga (sä′gə) ►*n.* **1.** An Icelandic prose narrative written between the 12th and 14th cent. **2.** A long heroic narrative. [ON.]

sa•ga•cious (sə-gā′shəs) ►*adj.* Shrewd and wise. [< Lat. *sagāx.*] —**sa•ga′cious•ly** *adv.* —**sa•gac′i•ty** (-găs′ĭ-tē) *n.*

sage[1] (sāj) ►*n.* A venerated, wise person. ►*adj.* **sag•er, sag•est.** Judicious; wise. [< VLat. **sapius* < Lat. *sapere*, be wise.] —**sage′ly** *adv.* —**sage′ness** *n.*

sage[2] (sāj) ►*n.* **1.** An aromatic plant with grayish-green leaves used as a seasoning. **2.** Sagebrush. [< Lat. *salvia.*]

sage•brush (sāj′brŭsh′) ►*n.* An aromatic shrub of arid regions of W North America.

Sag•it•tar•i•us (săj′ĭ-târ′ē-əs) ►*n.* **1.** A constellation in the Southern Hemisphere. **2.** The 9th sign of the zodiac in astrology.

sa•go (sā′gō) ►*n., pl.* **-gos.** A powdery edible starch obtained from the trunks of an Asian palm. [Malay *sagu*, mealy pith.]

sa•gua•ro (sə-gwär′ō, -wär′ō) also **sa•hua•ro** (sə-wär′ō) ►*n., pl.* **-ros 1.** A large branching cactus of the SW US and N Mexico. **2.** Its edible fruit. [Am.Sp.]

Sa•hap•tin (sä-hăp′tĭn) ►*n., pl.* **-tin** or **-tins 1.** A member of a Native American people of Idaho, Washington, and Oregon. **2.** The dialectally diverse language of the Sahaptin.

Sa•har•a (sə-hâr′ə, -hăr′ə, -hä′rə) A desert of N Africa extending from the Atlantic coast to the Nile Valley and S from the Atlas Mts. to the Sudan. —**Sa•har′an** *adj.*

Sa•hel (sə-hāl′, -hēl′) A semiarid region of N-central Africa S of the Sahara Desert. —**Sa•hel′i•an** *adj.*

sa•hib (sä′ĭb, -ēb, -hĭb) ►*n.* Used as a form of respectful address for a European man in colonial India. [Hindi *sāhab*, master.]

said (sĕd) ►*v.* P.t. and p.part. of **say.** ►*adj.* *Law* Aforementioned.

Usage: The adjective *said* is seldom appropriate to any but legal or business writing, where it is equivalent to *aforesaid*: *the said tenant* (named in a lease).

Sai•gon (sī-gŏn′) See **Ho Chi Minh City.**

sail (sāl) ►*n.* **1.** A piece of shaped fabric that catches the wind and propels or aids in maneuvering a vessel. **2.** A sailing vessel. **3.** A trip in a sailing craft. **4.** Something resembling a sail. ►*v.* **1a.** To move across the surface of water, esp. by means of a sail. **b.** To travel by water in a vessel. **c.** To start out on such a voyage. **2.** To navigate or manage (a vessel). **3.** To glide through the air. [< OE *segl.*]

sail•board (sāl′bôrd′, -bōrd′) ►*n.* A modified surfboard having a sail mounted on a pivoting mast, ridden while standing up. —**sail′board′** *v.* —**sail′board′er** *n.*

sail•boat (sāl′bōt′) ►*n.* A relatively small boat propelled by a sail or sails.

sail•fish (sāl′fĭsh′) ►*n.* A large marine fish with a high dorsal fin and a spearlike projection from the upper jaw.

sail•or (sā′lər) ►*n.* One who sails, esp. one who serves in a navy or works on a ship.

sail•plane (sāl′plān′) ►*n.* A light glider used esp. for soaring. —**sail′plane′** *v.*

saint (sānt) ►*n.* **1.** A person considered holy and worthy of public veneration, esp. one who has been canonized. **2.** An extremely virtuous person. [< Lat. *sānctus*, holy.] —**saint′dom** *n.* —**saint′ed** *adj.* —**saint′hood′** *n.* —**saint′li•ness** *n.* —**saint′ly** *adj.*

Saint Au•gus•tine (ô′gə-stēn′) A city of NE FL on the Atlantic; the oldest permanent European settlement in the US. Pop. 11,692.

Saint Ber•nard (bər-närd′) ►*n.* A large strong dog orig. used in the Swiss Alps to rescue lost travelers.

Saint Bernard

Saint Cath•a•rines (kăth′ə-rĭnz′, kăth′rĭnz) A

city of SE Ontario, Canada, ESE of Hamilton. Pop. 129,300.

Saint Chris•to•pher-Ne•vis (krĭs′tə-fər-nē′vĭs, -nĕv′ĭs) See **Saint Kitts and Nevis.**

Saint Croix (kroi) An island of the US Virgin Is. in the West Indies E of Puerto Rico.

Saint E•li•as (ĭ-lī′əs), **Mount.** A peak, 5,492.4 m (18,008 ft), in the **Saint Elias Mountains** between E AK and SW Yukon Terr., Canada.

Saint El•mo's fire (ĕl′mōz) ►*n.* A visible electric discharge on a pointed object during an electrical storm. [After *Saint Elmo*, 4th-cent. A.D. patron saint of sailors.]

Saint-Gau•dens (sānt-gôd′nz), **Augustus.** 1848–1907. Irish-born Amer. sculptor.

Saint George's (jôr′jəz) The capital of Grenada, on the SW coast. Pop. 7,500.

Saint George's Channel. A strait between W Wales and SE Ireland.

Saint Gott•hard (gŏt′ərd) A range of the central Alps in S-central Switzerland.

Saint He•le•na (hə-lē′nə) A volcanic island in the S Atlantic W of Angola; part of the British dependency of **Saint Helena.** Pop. 7,000.

Saint Hel•ens (hĕl′ənz), **Mount.** An active volcanic peak of the Cascade Range in SW WA.

Saint John's (jŏnz) **1.** The capital of Antigua and Barbuda, on the N coast of Antigua. Pop. 24,359. **2.** The capital of Newfoundland, Canada, on the SE coast. Pop. 175,909.

Saint John's wort ►*n.* Any of of genus of herbs or shrubs thought to have medicinal properties.

Saint Kitts and Ne•vis (kĭts; nē′vĭs, nĕv′ĭs) also **Saint Chris•to•pher-Ne•vis** (krĭs′tə-fər-nē′vĭs, -nĕv′ĭs). An island country in the Leeward Is. of the West Indies ESE of Puerto Rico comprising **Saint Kitts** and the islands of Nevis and Sombrero. Cap. Basseterre. Pop. 41,000.

Saint Lau•rent (săɴ lô-räɴ′), **Louis Stephen.** 1882–1973. Canadian prime minister (1948–57).

Saint Lawrence (sānt), **Gulf of.** An arm of the NW Atlantic off SE Canada between New Brunswick and Newfoundland.

Saint Lawrence River. A river of SE Canada flowing about 1,207 km (750 mi) from Lake Ontario to the Gulf of St. Lawrence.

Saint Lawrence Seaway. A waterway, about 3,781 km (2,350 mi), consisting of a system of canals, dams, and locks in the St. Lawrence R. and connecting channels through the Great Lakes.

Saint Lou•is (lo͞o′ĭs) A city of E MO on the Mississippi R. Pop. 396,685.

Saint Lu•cia (lo͞o′shə, lo͞o-sē′ə) An island country of the West Indies in the Windward Is. S of Martinique. Cap. Castries. Pop. 141,000.

Saint Mar•tin or **Saint Maar•ten** (mär′tn). An island of the West Indies in the W Leeward Is.

Saint Paul. The capital of MN, in the SE part on the Mississippi R. adjacent to Minneapolis. Pop. 272,235.

Saint Pe•ters•burg (pē′tərz-bûrg′) **1.** A city of W-central FL on Tampa Bay SSW of Tampa. Pop. 238,629. **2.** Formerly **Leningrad.** A city of NW Russia on the Neva R. Pop. 4,328,851.

Saint Pi•erre and Mi•que•lon (pîr′, pē-âr′; mĭk′ə-lŏn′) A French island group and overseas department in the N Atlantic Ocean S of Newfoundland, Canada.

Saint-Saëns (săɴ-säɴs′), **Charles Camille.** 1835–1921. French composer.

Saint Thomas (sānt) An island of the US Virgin Is. in the West Indies E of Puerto Rico.

Saint Valentine's Day ►*n.* Feb. 14, celebrated by the exchange of valentines.

Saint Vincent and the Grenadines. An island country in the central Windward Is. of the West Indies. Cap. Kingstown. Pop. 111,000.

Sai•pan (sī-păn′, -pän′, sī′păn) An island of the W Pacific in the S Mariana Is. —**Sai′pa•nese′** (-nēz′, -nēs′) *adj. & n.*

saith (sĕth, sā′ĭth) ►*v. Archaic* 3rd pers. sing. pr.t. of **say.**

Sa•kai (sä′kī′) A city of S Honshu, Japan, on Osaka Bay S of Osaka. Pop. 806,263.

sake[1] (sāk) ►*n.* **1.** Purpose: *for the sake of argument.* **2.** Advantage; good: *for the sake of your health.* [< OE *sacu.*]

sa•ke[2] also **sa•ki** (sä′kē, -kĕ) ►*n.* A Japanese liquor made from fermented rice. [J.]

Sa•kha•lin (săk′ə-lēn′) An island of SE Russia in the Sea of Okhotsk N of Hokkaido, Japan.

Sa•kha•rov (sä′kə-rôf′), **Andrei Dimitrievich.** 1921–89. Soviet physicist and dissident; 1975 Nobel Peace Prize.

sal (săl) ►*n.* Salt. [< Lat. *sāl.*]

sa•laam (sə-läm′) ►*n.* An act of deference or obeisance, esp. a low bow performed while placing the right palm on the forehead. [Ar. *salām*, peace.] —**sa•laam′** *v.*

sa•la•cious (sə-lā′shəs) ►*adj.* Prurient; lascivious. [< Lat. *salāx.*] —**sa•la′cious•ly** *adv.* —**sa•la′cious•ness** *n.*

sal•ad (săl′əd) ►*n.* A dish usu. made of leafy greens or raw vegetables served with a dressing. [< VLat. **salāta* < Lat. *sāl*, salt.]

Sal•a•din (săl′ə-dĭn). 1137?–93. Sultan of Egypt and Syria.

Sal•a•man•ca (săl′ə-măng′kə) A city of W-central Spain WNW of Madrid. Pop. 163,400.

sal•a•man•der (săl′ə-măn′dər) ►*n.* A small lizardlike amphibian. [< Gk. *salamandra.*]

sa•la•mi (sə-lä′mē) ►*n.* A highly spiced sausage. [< VLat. **salāmen* < Lat. *sāl*, salt.]

sal•a•ry (săl′ə-rē, săl′rē) ►*n.*, *pl.* **-ries.** Fixed compensation for services, paid to a person on a regular basis. [< Lat. *salārium*, money given to Roman soldiers to buy salt.] —**sal′a•ried** *adj.*

sale (sāl) ►*n.* **1.** The exchange of goods or services for money. **2.** An instance of selling. **3.** Availability for purchase. **4.** An auction. **5.** A special disposal of goods at lowered prices. [< ON *sala.*] —**sal′a•bil′i•ty** *n.* —**sal′a•ble, sale′a•ble** *adj.*

Sa•lem (sā′ləm) **1.** A city of NE MA NE of Boston; site of witchcraft trials (1692). Pop. 38,091. **2.** The capital of OR, in the NW part on the Willamette R. Pop. 107,786.

Sa•ler•no (sə-lûr′nō, -lĕr′-) A city of S Italy on the **Gulf of Salerno,** an inlet of the Tyrrhenian Sea. Pop. 153,436.

sales•clerk (sālz′klûrk′) ►*n.* One employed to sell goods in a store.

sales•man (sālz′mən) ►*n.* A man employed to sell merchandise in a store or designated territory. See Usage Note at **man.** —**sales′man•ship′** *n.*

sales•per•son (sālz′pûr′sən) ►*n.* A salesman or saleswoman. —**sales′peo′ple** *pl.n.*

sales tax (sālz) ►*n.* A tax levied on the price of goods and services.

sales•wom•an (sālz′wo͝om′ən) ▸*n.* A woman employed to sell merchandise in a store or territory. See Usage Note at **man.**

sal•i•cyl•ic acid (săl′ĭ-sĭl′ĭk) ▸*n.* A white crystalline acid used in making aspirin. [< Fr. *salicyle*, the radical of salicylic acid.]

sa•li•ent (sā′lē-ənt, sāl′yənt) ▸*adj.* **1.** Projecting or jutting beyond a line or surface. **2.** Strikingly conspicuous. [< Lat. *salīre*, leap.] —**sa′li•ence, sa′li•en•cy** *n.*

Sa•li•nas (sə-lē′nəs) A city of W CA ENE of Monterey. Pop. 108,777.

sa•line (sā′lēn′, -līn′) ▸*adj.* Of or containing salt. [Lat. *salīnus.*] —**sa•lin′i•ty** (sə-lĭn′ĭ-tē) *n.*

Sal•in•ger (săl′ĭn-jər), **J(erome) D(avid).** b. 1919. Amer. writer.

Salis•bur•y (sôlz′bĕr′ē, -brē) **1.** A municipal borough of S England on the edge of **Salisbury Plain,** the site of Stonehenge. Pop. 35,700. **2.** See **Harare.**

Sa•lish (sā′lĭsh) also **Sa•lish•an** (-lĭ-shən) ▸*n.* **1.** A family of Native American languages of the NW US and British Columbia. **2.** The group of Native American peoples speaking languages of this family. —**Sa′lish•an** *adj.*

sa•li•va (sə-lī′və) ▸*n.* The watery mixture of secretions from glands in the mouth that aids in swallowing and digestion. [Lat. *salīva.*] —**sal′i•var′y** (săl′ə-vĕr′ē) *adj.*

sal•i•vate (săl′ə-vāt′) ▸*v.* **-vat•ed, -vat•ing.** To secrete or produce saliva. —**sal′i•va′tion** *n.*

Salk (sôlk), **Jonas Edward.** 1914–95. Amer. microbiologist.

Salk vaccine ▸*n.* A vaccine consisting of inactivated polioviruses, used to immunize against poliomyelitis. [After Jonas SALK.]

sal•low (săl′ō) ▸*adj.* **-er, -est.** Of a sickly yellowish color. [< OE *salo.*] —**sal′low•ly** *adv.* —**sal′low•ness** *n.*

sal•ly (săl′ē) ▸*n., pl.* **-lies 1.** A sudden assault from a defensive position. **2.** A quick witticism; quip. **3.** A venturing forth; jaunt. [< Lat. *salīre*, leap.] —**sal′ly** *v.*

salm•on (săm′ən) ▸*n., pl.* **-on** or **-ons 1.** Any of various large food and game fishes of northern waters, usu. with pinkish flesh. **2.** A yellowish pink to reddish orange. [< Lat. *salmō.*] —**salm′on** *adj.*

sal•mo•nel•la (săl′mə-nĕl′ə) ▸*n., pl.* **-nel•lae** (-nĕl′ē) or **-las** or **-la.** Any of various rod-shaped bacteria, many of which cause food poisoning or other diseases in warm-blooded animals. [After Daniel E. *Salmon* (1850–1914).]

sa•lon (sə-lŏn′, să-lôN′) ▸*n.* **1.** A large room, such as a drawing room, used for receiving and entertaining guests. **2.** A periodic gathering of people of social or intellectual distinction. **3.** A commercial establishment offering a product or service related to fashion: *a beauty salon.* [< Ital. *sala*, hall.]

Sa•lo•ni•ka (sə-lŏn′ĭ-kə, săl′ə-nē′kə) See **Thessaloníki.**

sa•loon (sə-lo͞on′) ▸*n.* **1.** A bar; tavern. **2.** A large social lounge on a passenger ship. [Fr. *salon*, SALON.]

sal•sa (säl′sə) ▸*n.* **1.** A spicy sauce usu. made of tomatoes, onions, and chili peppers. **2.** A popular form of Latin-American dance music. [< Sp. SAUCE.]

salt (sôlt) ▸*n.* **1.** A colorless or white crystalline solid, chiefly sodium chloride, used extensively as a food seasoning and preservative. **2.** A chemical compound formed by replacing all or part of the hydrogen ions of an acid with metal ions or electropositive radicals. **3. salts** Any of various mineral salts used as laxatives or cathartics. **4.** An element that gives flavor or zest. **5.** Sharp, lively wit. **6.** *Informal* A veteran sailor. ▸*adj.* **1.** Salty. **2.** Preserved in salt. ▸*v.* **1.** To add salt to. **2.** To preserve with salt. —***phrasal verb:*** **salt away** To put aside; save. —***idiom:*** **worth (one's) salt** Efficient and capable. [< OE *sealt.*] —**salt′i•ly** *adv.* —**salt′i•ness** *n.* —**salt′y** *adj.*

SALT ▸*abbr.* Strategic Arms Limitation Talks

salt•cel•lar (sôlt′sĕl′ər) ▸*n.* A small dish for dispensing salt. [< ME *salt saler.*]

sal•tine (sôl-tēn′) ▸*n.* A thin salted cracker.

Salt Lake City. The capital of UT, in the N-central part near Great Salt Lake. Pop. 159,936.

salt lick ▸*n.* A block or deposit of exposed salt that animals lick.

salt marsh ▸*n.* Low coastal grassland frequently overflowed by the tide.

salt•pe•ter (sôlt′pē′tər) ▸*n.* **1.** See **potassium nitrate. 2.** See **sodium nitrate. 3.** See **niter.** [< Med.Lat. *sālpetrae.*]

salt•shak•er (sôlt′shā′kər) ▸*n.* A container for sprinkling table salt.

salt•wa•ter (sôlt′wô′tər, -wŏt′ər) ▸*adj.* Consisting of or inhabiting salt water.

sa•lu•bri•ous (sə-lo͞o′brē-əs) ▸*adj.* Conducive or favorable to health or well-being. [< Lat. *salūbris.*] —**sa•lu′bri•ty** (-brĭ-tē) *n.*

sal•u•tar•y (săl′yə-tĕr′ē) ▸*adj.* **1.** Beneficial; *salutary advice.* **2.** Wholesome. [< Lat. *salūs*, health.] —**sal′u•tar′i•ly** (-târ′ə-lē) *adv.* —**sal′u•tar′i•ness** *n.*

sal•u•ta•tion (săl′yə-tā′shən) ▸*n.* An expression of greeting, goodwill, or courtesy.

sa•lu•ta•to•ri•an (sə-lo͞o′tə-tôr′ē-ən, -tōr′-) ▸*n.* The student with the second highest academic rank in a class who delivers the opening address at graduation.

sa•lute (sə-lo͞ot′) ▸*v.* **-lut•ed, -lut•ing 1.** To greet. **2.** To recognize (a military superior) with a prescribed gesture. **3.** To honor formally. [< Lat. *salūtāre* < *salūs*, health.] —**sa•lute′** *n.*

Sal•va•dor (săl′və-dôr′) A city of E Brazil on the Atlantic SSW of Recife. Pop. 2,072,058.

Sal•va•do•ran (săl′və-dôr′ən, -dōr′-) or **Sal•va•do•ri•an** (-dôr′ē-ən, -dōr′-) ▸*n.* A native or inhabitant of El Salvador. —**Sal′va•do′ran, Sal′va•do′ri•an** *adj.*

sal•vage (săl′vĭj) ▸*n.* **1a.** The rescue of a ship. **b.** Compensation given to those who aid in such a rescue. **2a.** The act of saving imperiled property from loss. **b.** The property so saved. ▸*v.* **-vaged, -vag•ing.** To save from loss or destruction. [< LLat. *salvāre*, save.] —**sal′vage•a•ble** *adj.* —**sal′vag•er** *n.*

sal•va•tion (săl-vā′shən) ▸*n.* **1a.** Preservation or deliverance from difficulty or evil. **b.** A means or cause of such deliverance. **2.** Deliverance from sin; redemption. [< Lat. *salvāre*, save.] —**sal•va′tion•al** *adj.*

salve (săv, säv) ▸*n.* An ointment that soothes or heals. ▸*v.* **salved, salv•ing.** To soothe or heal with or as if with salve. [< OE *sealf.*]

sal•ver (săl′vər) ▸*n.* A serving tray. [< Sp. *salva*, tasting of food.]

sal•vi•a (săl′vē-ə) ▸*n.* Any of various plants having opposite leaves, a two-lipped corolla, and two stamens. [Lat., sage.]

sal•vo (săl′vō) ►*n., pl.* **-vos** or **-voes 1.** A simultaneous discharge of firearms. **2.** A sudden outburst. [Ital. *salva.*]

Sal•ween (săl′wēn′) A river of SE Asia rising in E Xizang (Tibet) and flowing about 2,816 km (1,750 mi) through Myanmar.

Salz•burg (sôlz′bûrg′) A city of W-central Austria SW of Linz. Pop. 143,973.

SAM ►*abbr.* surface-to-air missile

Sa•mar•a (sə-mâr′ə) A city of W Russia on the Volga R. ESE of Moscow. Pop. 1,231,653.

Sa•mar•i•a (sə-măr′ē-ə, -mâr′-) An ancient city of Palestine in present-day NW Jordan.

Sa•mar•i•tan (sə-măr′ĭ-tn) ►*n.* **1.** A native or inhabitant of Samaria. **2.** often **samaritan** A Good Samaritan. —**Sa•mar′i•tan** *adj.*

sa•mar•i•um (sə-mâr′ē-əm, -măr′-) ►*n. Symbol* **Sm** A silvery or pale gray metallic rare-earth element used in laser materials, in infrared absorbing glass, and as a neutron absorber. At. no. 62. See table at **element.** [After Colonel M. von *Samarski*, 19th-cent. Russian mining official.]

Sam•ar•qand (săm′ər-kănd′) A city of S Uzbekistan SW of Tashkent. Pop. 370,000.

sam•ba (săm′bə, säm′-) ►*n.* **1.** A Brazilian ballroom dance of African origin. **2.** Music for this dance. [Port.] —**sam′ba** *v.*

same (sām) ►*adj.* **1.** Being the very one; identical. **2.** Similar or corresponding. ►*adv.* In the same way. ►*pron.* **1.** One identical with another. **2.** The one previously mentioned. [< ON *samr.*] —**same′ness** *n.*

Usage: The expressions *same* and *the same* are sometimes used in place of pronouns such as *it* or *one,* as in *When you have filled out the form, please remit same to this office.* This usage is associated chiefly with commercial and legal language.

same-sex (sām′sĕks′) ►*adj.* **1.** Involving or restricted to members of the same sex: *same-sex schools.* **2.** Of or involving gay men or lesbians: *same-sex couples.*

Sa•mo•a[1] (sə-mō′ə) An island group of the S Pacific ENE of Fiji, divided between **Samoa,** a sovereign nation, and **American Samoa.** —**Sa•mo′an** *adj. & n.*

Sa•mo•a[2] (sə-mō′ə). Formerly **Western Samoa.** An island country of the S Pacific comprising the W Samoa Is. Cap. Apia. Pop. 209,360.

Sam•o•set (săm′ə-sĕt′). d. c. 1653. Native American leader and friend of the early colonists.

sam•o•var (săm′ə-vär′) ►*n.* A metal urn with a spigot, used to boil water for tea. [Russ.]

Sam•o•yed (săm′oi-ĕd′, sə-moi′ĭd) ►*n.* **1.** A member of a nomadic people of NW Siberia. **2.** The Uralic language of the Samoyed. **3.** A working dog of a breed orig. developed in N Eurasia. —**Sam′o•yed′** *adj.*

sam•pan (săm′păn′) ►*n.* A flat-bottomed Asian skiff. [Cantonese *saam-paán.*]

sam•ple (săm′pəl) ►*n.* **1.** A portion, piece, or segment representative of a whole. **2.** *Statistics* A set of elements drawn from and analyzed to estimate the characteristics of a population. ►*v.* **-pled, -pling.** To take a sample of, esp. in order to test or examine. [< Lat. *exemplum,* EXAMPLE.]

sam•pler (săm′plər) ►*n.* **1.** One employed to appraise samples. **2.** A piece of cloth embroidered with various designs.

sam•pling (săm′plĭng) ►*n.* See **sample** 2.

Sam•son (săm′sən). In the Bible, a warrior betrayed to the Philistines by Delilah.

Sam•u•el (săm′yo͞o-əl) ►*n.* **1.** Hebrew judge and prophet of the 11th cent. B.C. **2.** See table at **Bible.**

sam•u•rai (săm′ə-rī′) ►*n., pl.* **-rai** or **-rais.** The Japanese feudal military aristocracy or one of its members. [J., warrior.]

San (sän) ►*n., pl.* **San** or **Sans 1.** A member of a nomadic hunting people of SW Africa. **2.** Any of the Khoisan languages of the San.

Sa•na also **Sa•n′a** or **Sa•naa** (sä-nä′). The capital of Yemen, in the W part. Pop. 427,000.

San An•to•ni•o (săn ăn-tō′nē-ō′) A city of S-central TX SW of Austin. Pop. 935,933.

san•a•to•ri•um (săn′ə-tôr′ē-əm, -tōr′-) also **san•a•tar•i•um** (-târ′-) ►*n., pl.* **-to•ri•ums** or **-to•ri•a** (-tôr′ē-ə, -tōr′-) also **-tar•i•ums** or **-tar•i•a** (-târ′ē-ə) **1.** An institution for the treatment of chronic diseases. **2.** A resort for improvement of health, esp. for convalescents. [< Lat. *sānāre*, heal.]

San Ber•nar•di•no (bûr′nə-dē′nō, -nər-) A city of S CA E of Los Angeles. Pop. 164,164.

sanc•ti•fy (săngk′tə-fī′) ►*v.* **-fied, -fy•ing 1.** To set apart for sacred use; consecrate. **2.** To make holy; purify. [< Lat. *sānctus*, holy.] —**sanc′ti•fi•ca′tion** *n.*

sanc•ti•mo•ny (săngk′tə-mō′nē) ►*n.* Hypocritical piety. [< Lat. *sānctimōnia*, sacredness.] —**sanc′ti•mo′ni•ous** *adj.* —**sanc′ti•mo′ni•ous•ly** *adv.*

sanc•tion (săngk′shən) ►*n.* **1.** Authoritative permission or approval. See Syns at **permission. 2.** A penalty intended to enforce compliance or conformity. **3.** A coercive measure adopted usu. by several nations against a nation violating international law. ►*v.* To authorize, approve, or encourage. [< Lat. *sānctus*, holy.]

sanc•ti•ty (săngk′tĭ-tē) ►*n., pl.* **-ties 1.** Holiness of life; saintliness. **2.** Sacredness or inviolability. [< Lat. *sānctus*, sacred.]

sanc•tu•ar•y (săngk′cho͞o-ĕr′ē) ►*n., pl.* **-ies 1.** A sacred place, such as a church, temple, or mosque. **2.** A place of refuge, asylum, or protection. [< LLat. *sānctuārium.*]

sanc•tum (săngk′təm) ►*n., pl.* **-tums** or **-ta** (-tə) **1.** A sacred or holy place. **2.** A private room or study. [LLat. *sānctum.*]

sand (sănd) ►*n.* Small loose grains of worn or disintegrated rock, finer than a granule and coarser than silt. ►*v.* To polish or scrape with sand or sandpaper. [< OE.] —**sand′er** *n.* —**sand′i•ness** *n.* —**sand′y** *adj.*

Sand, George. Amandine Aurore Lucie Dupin, Baroness Dudevant. 1804–76. French writer.

George Sand

san•dal (săn′dl) ►*n.* **1.** A shoe consisting of a sole fastened to the foot by thongs or straps. **2.** A low-cut shoe with an ankle strap. [< Gk. *sandalon.*] —**san′daled** *adj.*

san•dal•wood (săn′dl-wo͝od′) ►*n.* **1.** An Asian tree with aromatic wood used in carving and perfumery. **2.** The wood of this tree. [< Ar. *ṣandal.*]

sand•bag (sănd′băg′) ►*n.* A bag filled with sand and used esp. to form protective walls. ►*v.* **1.** To put sandbags in or around. **2.** *Slang* **a.** To deal a heavy blow to. **b.** To coerce.

sand•bar (sănd′bär′) ►*n.* A ridge of sand formed in a river or along a shore.

sand•blast (sănd′blăst′) ►*n.* A blast of air carrying sand at high velocity, as for cleaning stone or glass. —**sand′blast′** *v.*

sand•box (sănd′bŏks′) ►*n.* A box filled with sand for children to play in.

Sand•burg (sănd′bûrg′, săn′-), **Carl.** 1878–1967. Amer. writer.

sand dollar ►*n.* Any of various thin circular echinoderms of sandy ocean bottoms of the N Atlantic and Pacific.

sand•hog (sănd′hôg′, -hŏg′) ►*n.* *Slang* One who works in a caisson, as in the construction of underwater tunnels.

San Di•e•go (dē-ā′gō) A city of S CA on **San Diego Bay,** an inlet of the Pacific near the Mexican border. Pop. 1,110,549.

S & L ►*abbr.* savings and loan association

sand•lot (sănd′lŏt′) ►*n.* A vacant lot used esp. by children for games. —**sand′lot′** *adj.*

sand•man (sănd′măn′) ►*n.* A character in folklore who puts children to sleep by sprinkling sand in their eyes.

sand•pa•per (sănd′pā′pər) ►*n.* Heavy paper coated on one side with an abrasive material, used for smoothing surfaces.

sand•pi•per (sănd′pī′pər) ►*n.* Any of various small, usu. long-billed shore birds.

sand•stone (sănd′stōn′) ►*n.* A sedimentary rock formed by the compaction of sand with a natural cement, such as silica.

sand•storm (sănd′stôrm′) ►*n.* A strong wind carrying clouds of sand and dust.

sand trap ►*n.* A sand-filled depression serving as a hazard on a golf course.

sand•wich (sănd′wĭch, săn′-) ►*n.* Two or more slices of bread with a filling placed between them. ►*v.* **1.** To insert (one thing) tightly between two other things. **2.** To make room or time for: *sandwich an errand between meetings.* [After the 4th Earl of *Sandwich* (1718–92).]

sane (sān) ►*adj.* **san•er, san•est 1.** Mentally healthy. **2.** Reasonable. [Lat. *sānus*, healthy.] —**sane′ly** *adv.* —**sane′ness** *n.*

San Fer•nan•do Valley (fər-năn′dō) A valley of S CA NW of central Los Angeles.

San Fran•cis•co (frən-sĭs′kō) A city of W CA on a peninsula between the Pacific and **San Francisco Bay,** an inlet of the Pacific. Pop. 723,959. —**San Fran•cis′can** *n.*

sang (săng) ►*v.* P.t. of **sing.**

Sang•er (săng′ər), **Margaret Higgins.** 1879–1966. Amer. nurse and social reformer.

sang-froid (säɴ-frwä′) ►*n.* Coolness and composure. [Fr.]

san•gri•a (săng-grē′ə, săn-) ►*n.* A cold drink usu. made of wine, brandy, sugar, fruit juice, and soda water. [< Sp. *sangría* < *sangre*, blood.]

Margaret Sanger
photographed in 1922

san•gui•nar•y (săng′gwə-nĕr′ē) ►*adj.* **1.** Accompanied by bloodshed. **2.** Bloodthirsty. —**san′gui•nar′i•ly** (-nâr′ə-lē) *adv.*

san•guine (săng′gwĭn) ►*adj.* **1a.** Of the color of blood; red. **b.** Ruddy: *a sanguine complexion.* **2.** Cheerful; optimistic. [< Lat. *sanguīs*, blood.] —**san′guine•ly** *adv.* —**san′guine•ness, san•guin′i•ty** *n.* —**san•guin′e•ous** *adj.*

san•i•tar•i•um (săn′ĭ-târ′ē-əm) ►*n.*, *pl.* **-i•ums** or **-i•a** (-ē-ə). See **sanatorium.** [< Lat. *sānitās*, health.]

san•i•tar•y (săn′ĭ-tĕr′ē) ►*adj.* **1.** Relating to health or the protection of health. **2.** Clean; hygienic. [< Lat. *sānitās*, health.] —**san′i•tar′i•ly** (-târ′ə-lē) *adv.*

sanitary landfill ►*n.* Rehabilitated land in which garbage and trash have been buried.

sanitary napkin ►*n.* A disposable pad of absorbent material worn to absorb menstrual flow.

san•i•ta•tion (săn′ĭ-tā′shən) ►*n.* **1.** Formulation and application of public health measures. **2.** Disposal of sewage and garbage.

san•i•tize (săn′ĭ-tīz′) ►*v.* **-tized, -tiz•ing 1.** To make sanitary. **2.** To remove unpleasant or offensive features from: *sanitized the language in the novel for television.*

san•i•ty (săn′ĭ-tē) ►*n.* The quality or condition of being sane.

San Joa•quin (wô-kēn′, wä-) A river of central CA flowing about 515 km (320 mi) through the **San Joaquin Valley** to the Sacramento R.

San Jo•se (hō-zā′) A city of W CA SE of San Francisco. Pop. 782,248.

San Jo•sé (sän′ hō-sĕ′) The capital of Costa Rica, in the central part. Pop. 315,909.

San Juan (săn wän′, hwän′) The capital of Puerto Rico, in the NE part on the Atlantic. Pop. 441,401.

sank (săngk) ►*v.* P.t. of **sink.**

San Lu•is Po•to•sí (sän lo͞o-ēs′ pō′tō-sē′) A city of central Mexico NE of León. Pop. 362,371.

San Ma•ri•no (săn mə-rē′nō) **1.** A country within N-central Italy in the Apennines. Cap. San Marino. Pop. 25,000. **2.** The capital of the country of San Marino. Pop. 2,792.

San Mi•guel de Tu•cu•mán (sän mĭ-gĕl′ də to͞o′kə-män′) or **Tucumán.** A city of N Argentina NNW of Córdoba. Pop. 470,604.

sans (sănz, säɴ) ►*prep.* Without. [< OFr.]

San Sal•va•dor (săn săl′və-dôr′) The capital of El Salvador, in the W-central part. Pop. 422,570.

San•skrit (săn′skrĭt′) ►*n.* An ancient Indic language that is the classical language of India. —**San′skrit′ist** *n.*

San•ta An•a[1] (săn′tə ăn′ə) **1.** A city of W El Salvador. Pop. 202,337. **2.** A city of S CA E of Long Beach. Pop. 293,742.

San•ta An•a[2] (săn′tə ăn′ə) ►*n.* A hot desert wind of S California blowing toward the Pacific coast usu. in winter. [After the *Santa Ana* Canyon of S California.]

San•ta An•na or **San•ta An•a** (săn′tə ăn′ə), **Antonio López de.** 1795?–1876. Mexican military and political leader.

Santa Clara (klăr′ə, klâr′ə) A city of central Cuba ESE of Havana. Pop. 172,652.

Santa Claus (klôz′) ►*n.* The personification of the spirit of Christmas, usu. represented as a jolly, fat old man with a white beard and red suit. [Prob. < Du. *Sinterklaas.*]

Santa Cruz (kro͞oz′) A city of central Bolivia NE of Sucre. Pop. 767,260.

Santa Cruz de Te•ne•ri•fe (də tĕn′ə-rē′fā) A city of the Canary Is. on the NE coast of Tenerife I. Pop. 202,112.

San•ta Fe (săn′tə fā′) The capital of NM, in the N-central part NE of Albuquerque. Pop. 55,859.

Santa Fe Trail. A trade route to the SW US extending about 1,287 km (800 mi) from Independence, MO, to Santa Fe, NM.

Santa Ro•sa (rō′zə) A city of W CA NNW of San Francisco. Pop. 113,313.

San•ta•ya•na (săn′tē-ăn′ə), **George.** 1863–1952. Spanish-born Amer. philosopher.

San•tee (săn-tē′) ►*n., pl.* **-tee** or **-tees.** A member of the eastern branch of the Sioux, with populations in Nebraska, Minnesota, the Dakotas, and Canada.

San•te•ri•a (săn′tə-rē′ə, sän′-) ►*n.* An African-based religion originating in Cuba and Brazil that combines worship of traditional Yoruban deities with worship of Roman Catholic saints. [Am.Sp. *santería*, worship of saints < Sp. *santo*, SAINT.]

San•ti•a•go (săn′tē-ä′gō, sän′-) **1.** The capital of Chile, in the central part ESE of Valparaiso. Pop. 4,385,481. **2.** Also **Santiago de los Ca•bal•le•ros** (dā′ lōs kä′bəl-yĕr′ōz). A city of N Dominican Republic NW of Santo Domingo. Pop. 690,000.

Santiago de Cu•ba (də kyo͞o′bə) A city of SE Cuba on the Caribbean Sea. Pop. 432,898.

San•to Do•min•go (săn′tō də-mĭng′gō) The capital of the Dominican Republic, in the SE part on the Caribbean Sea. Pop. 2,100,000.

São Fran•cis•co (souN frən-sĭs′kō) A river of E Brazil flowing about 2,896 km (1,800 mi) to the Atlantic.

Saône (sōn) A river, about 431 km (268 mi), rising in the Vosges Mts. of NE France and flowing to the Rhone R. at Lyon.

São Pau•lo (pou′lō) A city of SE Brazil WSW of Rio de Janeiro. Pop. 9,626,894.

São To•mé (tə-mā′) **1.** An island of São Tomé and Príncipe. **2.** The capital of São Tomé and Príncipe, in the SW part of the island of São Tomé. Pop. 43,420.

São Tomé and Prín•ci•pe (prĭn′sə-pə) An island country in the Gulf of Guinea off W Africa. Cap. São Tomé. Pop. 144,128.

sap[1] (săp) ►*n.* **1.** The watery fluid that circulates through a plant, carrying food and other substances to the tissues. **2.** Health and energy; vitality. **3.** *Slang* A gullible person; dupe. ►*v.* **sapped, sap•ping.** To drain of sap. [< OE *sæp.*]

sap[2] (săp) ►*v.* **sapped, sap•ping 1.** To undermine the foundations of (a fortification). **2.** To deplete or weaken gradually. [< LLat. *sappa*, hoe.]

Sa•phar (sə-fär′) ►*n.* Var. of **Safar.**

sa•pi•ent (sā′pē-ənt) ►*adj.* Wise and discerning. [< Lat. *sapere*, be wise.] —**sa′pi•ence** *n.* —**sa′pi•ent•ly** *adv.*

sap•ling (săp′lĭng) ►*n.* A young tree.

sap•o•dil•la (săp′ə-dĭl′ə, -dē′yə) ►*n.* **1.** An evergreen tree of Mexico and Central America having an edible fruit. **2.** The fruit of this plant. [< Nahuatl *tzapotl.*]

sa•pon•i•fi•ca•tion (sə-pŏn′ə-fĭ-kā′shən) ►*n.* A reaction in which an ester is heated with an alkali, producing a free alcohol and an acid salt, esp. alkaline hydrolysis of a fat or oil to make soap.

sa•pon•i•fy (sə-pŏn′ə-fī′) ►*v.* **-fied, -fy•ing 1.** To convert (an ester) by saponification. **2.** To convert (a fat or oil) into soap. [< Lat. *sāpō*, hair dye.]

sap•per (săp′ər) ►*n.* A military engineer.

sap•phire (săf′īr′) ►*n.* **1.** A clear, hard, usu. blue variety of corundum used as a gemstone. **2.** A corundum gem. **3.** Having the blue color of a gem sapphire. [Gk. *sapheiros*, of Semitic orig.]

Sap•pho (săf′ō). fl. c. 600 B.C. Greek lyric poet. —**Sap′phic** *adj.*

Sap•po•ro (sə-pôr′ō, -pōr′ō) A city of SW Hokkaido, Japan, near the head of Ishikari Bay. Pop. 1,731,670.

sap•py (săp′ē) ►*adj.* **-pi•er, -pi•est 1.** Full of sap; juicy. **2.** *Slang* Silly; foolish.

sap•ro•phyte (săp′rə-fīt′) ►*n.* An organism that grows on and derives its nourishment from dead or decaying organic matter. [Gk. *sapros*, rotten + -PHYTE.] —**sap′ro•phyt′ic** (-fĭt′ĭk) *adj.*

sap•suck•er (săp′sŭk′ər) ►*n.* A small American woodpecker that drills holes in trees to feed on sap and insects.

Sar•a•cen (săr′ə-sən) ►*n.* **1.** A member of a pre-Islamic nomadic people of the Syrian-Arabian deserts. **2.** An Arab. **3.** A Muslim, esp. of the time of the Crusades.

Sar•a•gos•sa (săr′ə-gŏs′ə) A city of NE Spain on the Ebro R. NE of Madrid. Pop. 598,078.

Sar•ah (sâr′ə) In the Bible, the wife of Abraham and mother of Isaac.

Sa•ra•je•vo (săr′ə-yā′vō) The capital of Bosnia and Herzegovina, in the S-central part. Pop. 415,631.

sa•ran (sə-răn′) ►*n.* Any of various thermoplastic resins used to make packaging films and in various heavy fabrics. [< *Saran*, a former US trademark.]

sa•ra•pe (sə-rä′pē, -răp′ē) ►*n.* Var. of **serape.**

Sa•ra•tov (sə-rä′təf) A city of SW Russia on the Volga R. NNE of Volgograd. Pop. 889,173.

Sa•ra•wak (sə-rä′wäk, -wä) A region of Malaysia on NW Borneo.

sar•casm (sär′kăz′əm) ►*n.* **1.** A cutting, often ironic remark. **2.** The use of sarcasm. [< Gk. *sarkasmos.*] —**sar•cas′tic** (-kăs′tĭk) *adj.* —**sar•cas′ti•cal•ly** *adv.*

sar•co•ma (sär-kō′mə) ►*n.*, *pl.* **-mas** also **-ma•ta** (-mə-tə). A malignant tumor arising from connective tissues. [< Gk. *sarkōma*, fleshy excrescence.]

sar•coph•a•gus (sär-kŏf′ə-gəs) ►*n.*, *pl.* **-gi** (-jī′) or **-gus•es.** A stone coffin. [< Gk. *sarkophagos*, coffin.]

sar•dine (sär-dēn′) ►*n.* A small herring or related fish, often canned in oil. [< Lat. *sardīna.*]

Sar•din•i•a (sär-dĭn′ē-ə) An island of Italy in the Mediterranean S of Corsica. —**Sar•din′i•an** *adj. & n.*

Sar•dis (sär′dĭs) An ancient city of W Asia Minor NE of modern-day Izmir, Turkey.

sar•don•ic (sär-dŏn′ĭk) ►*adj.* Scornfully mocking. [< Gk. *sardonios.*] —**sar•don′i•cal•ly** *adv.*

sar•gas•so (sär-găs′ō) ►*n.*, *pl.* **-sos.** See **gulfweed.** [Port. *sargaço.*]

Sar•gas•so Sea (sär-găs′ō) A part of the N Atlantic between the West Indies and the Azores.

Sar•gent (sär′jənt), **John Singer.** 1856–1925. Amer. painter.

Sar•gon II (sär′gŏn′). d. 705 B.C. Assyrian king (721–705).

sa•ri (sä′rē) ►*n.*, *pl.* **-ris.** A lightweight, wrapped outer garment worn chiefly by women of India and Pakistan. [< Skt. *śāṭī.*]

sari

Sar•ma•tia (sär-mā′shə, -shē-ə) An ancient region of E Europe NE of the Black Sea. —**Sar•ma′tian** *adj. & n.*

sa•rong (sə-rông′, -rŏng′) ►*n.* A length of brightly colored cloth wrapped about the waist, worn by men and women in Malaysia, Indonesia, and the Pacific islands. [Malay.]

Sa•roy•an (sə-roi′ən), **William.** 1908–81. Amer. writer.

sar•sa•pa•ril•la (săs′pə-rĭl′ə, särs′-) ►*n.* **1.** The dried roots of a tropical American plant, used as a flavoring. **2.** A sweet soft drink flavored with these roots. [Sp. *zarzaparrilla.*]

sar•to•ri•al (sär-tôr′ē-əl, -tōr′-) ►*adj.* Of or relating to tailors or tailoring. [< LLat. *sartor*, tailor.] —**sar•to′ri•al•ly** *adv.*

Sar•tre (sär′trə, särt), **Jean Paul.** 1905–80. French writer and philosopher; declined a 1957 Nobel.

SASE ►*abbr.* self-addressed stamped envelope

sash[1] (săsh) ►*n.* A band or ribbon worn about the waist as clothing or over the shoulder as a symbol of rank. [Ar. *šāš*, muslin.]

sarong

sash[2] (săsh) ►*n.* A frame in which the panes of a window or door are set. [< Fr. *châssis*, frame.]

sa•shay (să-shā′) ►*v.* *Informal* To strut or flounce in a showy manner. [< Fr. *chassé*, a dance step.]

Sask. ►*abbr.* Saskatchewan

Sas•katch•e•wan (să-skăch′ə-wän′, -wən) A province of S-central Canada. Cap. Regina. Pop. 968,313.

Saskatchewan River. A river of S-central Canada flowing E to Lake Winnipeg.

Sas•ka•toon (săs′kə-to͞on′) A city of S-central Saskatchewan, Canada, NW of Regina. Pop. 186,058.

Sas•quatch (săs′kwŏch, -kwăch) ►*n.* See **Bigfoot.**

sass (săs) ►*n.* *Informal* Impertinence; back talk. [< SASSY.] —**sass** *v.*

sas•sa•fras (săs′ə-frăs′) ►*n.* **1.** A North American tree with irregularly lobed leaves and aromatic bark. **2.** The dried root bark of this plant, used as a flavoring. [< LLat. *saxifragia.*]

sas•sy (săs′ē) ►*adj.* **-si•er, -si•est.** Rude and disrespectful; impudent. [< SAUCY.] —**sas′si•ly** *adv.* —**sas′si•ness** *n.*

sat (săt) ►*v.* P.t. and p.part. of **sit.**

SAT (ĕs′ā-tē′) ► A trademark used for a set of standardized college entrance examinations.

Sat. ►*abbr.* Saturday

Sa•tan (sāt′n) ►*n.* The Devil. [< Heb. *śāṭān.*]

sa•tan•ic (sə-tăn′ĭk, sā-) or **sa•tan•i•cal** (-ĭ-kəl) ►*adj.* **1.** Relating to or suggestive of Satan. **2.** Fiendishly cruel or evil. —**sa•tan′i•cal•ly** *adv.*

satch•el (săch′əl) ►*n.* A small bag for carrying books or clothing. [< LLat. *saccellus.*]

sate (sāt) ►*v.* **sat•ed, sat•ing 1.** To satisfy (an appetite) fully. **2.** To satisfy to excess. [< OE *sadian.*]

sa•teen (să-tēn′) ►*n.* A cotton fabric with a satinlike finish. [< SATIN.]

sat•el•lite (săt′l-īt′) ►*n.* **1.** *Astron.* A celestial body that orbits a planet; moon. **2.** An object launched to orbit a celestial body. **3.** A subservient follower; sycophant. **4.** A nation dominated politically and economically by another. **5.** A community located near a big city. [< Lat. *satelles*, attendant.]

satellite dish ►*n.* A dish antenna that receives and transmits satellite signals.

sa•ti•ate (sā′shē-āt′) ▸*v.* **-at•ed, -at•ing 1.** To satisfy fully. **2.** To satisfy to excess. ▸*adj.* (-ĭt). Filled to satisfaction. [< Lat. *satis*, sufficient.] —**sa′ti•a′tion** *n.*

sa•ti•e•ty (sə-tī′ĭ-tē) ▸*n.* The condition of being sated. [< Lat. *satietās*.]

sat•in (săt′n) ▸*n.* A smooth glossy fabric. [< OFr.] —**sat′in•y** *adj.*

sat•in•wood (săt′n-wo͝od′) ▸*n.* A tree of India and Sri Lanka with hard yellow wood.

sat•ire (săt′īr′) ▸*n.* **1.** An artistic work in which human vice or folly is attacked through irony, derision, or wit. **2.** Irony or caustic wit used to expose or attack human folly. [Lat. *satira*.] —**sa•tir′i•cal** (sə-tĭr′ĭ-kəl), **sa•tir′ic** *adj.* —**sa•tir′i•cal•ly** *adv.* —**sat′ir•ist** (săt′ər-ĭst) *n.*

sat•i•rize (săt′ə-rīz′) ▸*v.* **-rized, -riz•ing.** To ridicule or attack by satire.

sat•is•fac•tion (săt′ĭs-făk′shən) ▸*n.* **1a.** The gratification of a desire, need, or appetite. **b.** Pleasure derived from such gratification. **2.** Compensation for injury or loss; reparation.

sat•is•fac•to•ry (săt′ĭs-făk′tə-rē) ▸*adj.* Giving satisfaction; adequate. —**sat′is•fac′to•ri•ly** *adv.* —**sat′is•fac′to•ri•ness** *n.*

sat•is•fy (săt′ĭs-fī′) ▸*v.* **-fied, -fy•ing 1.** To gratify or fulfill (a need or desire). **2.** To free from doubt or question; assure. **3.** To fulfill or discharge (an obligation). **4.** To conform to the requirements of. **5.** To give satisfaction. [< Lat. *satisfacere*.]

Syns: *satisfy, answer, fill, fulfill, meet* **v.**

sa•trap (sā′trăp′, săt′răp′) ▸*n.* A subordinate ruler. [< OPers. *khshathrapāvā*, protector of the province.]

sat•u•rate (săch′ə-rāt′) ▸*v.* **-rat•ed, -rat•ing 1.** To imbue or impregnate thoroughly. See Syns at **charge. 2.** To soak, fill, or load to capacity. **3.** *Chem.* To cause (a substance) to unite with the greatest possible amount of another substance. ▸*adj.* (-rĭt). Saturated. [< Lat. *satur*, sated.] —**sat′u•ra•ble** (săch′ər-ə-bəl) *adj.* —**sat′u•ra′tion** *n.*

sat•u•rat•ed fat (săch′ə-rā′tĭd) ▸*n.* A fat, usu. of animal origin, composed predominantly of fatty acids having only single bonds in the carbon chain.

Sat•ur•day (săt′ər-dē, -dā′) ▸*n.* The 7th day of the week. [< OE *Sæternesdæg*.]

Saturday night special ▸*n.* *Informal* A cheap handgun easily obtained and concealed.

Sat•urn (săt′ərn) ▸*n.* **1.** *Rom. Myth.* The god of agriculture. **2.** The 2nd largest planet in the solar system and the 6th from the sun at a mean distance of about 1,425,000,000 km (886,000,000 mi), and having a mean diameter of approx. 119,000 km (74,000 mi).

sat•ur•nine (săt′ər-nīn′) ▸*adj.* Morose and sardonic.

sa•tyr (sā′tər, săt′ər) ▸*n.* **1.** often **Satyr** *Gk. Myth.* A woodland creature depicted as having the ears, legs, and horns of a goat. **2.** A lecher. [< Gk. *saturos*.]

sauce (sôs) ▸*n.* **1.** A liquid dressing served with food. **2.** Stewed fruit. **3.** *Informal* Impudence. **4.** *Slang* Alcoholic liquor. ▸*v.* **sauced, sauc•ing 1.** To flavor with sauce. **2.** To add zest to. **3.** *Informal* To be impudent to. [< Lat. *salsa*, salted.]

sauce•pan (sôs′păn′) ▸*n.* A deep cooking pan with a handle.

sau•cer (sô′sər) ▸*n.* **1.** A small shallow dish for holding a cup. **2.** An object resembling a saucer. [< OFr. *saussier*, sauce dish.]

sauc•y (sô′sē) ▸*adj.* **-i•er, -i•est 1.** Impertinent or disrespectful. **2.** Pert. —**sau′ci•ly** *adv.* —**sau′ci•ness** *n.*

Sau•di Arabia (sou′dē, sô′dē, sä-o͞o′dē) A country occupying most of the Arabian Peninsula. Cap. Riyadh. Pop. 17,451,000. —**Sau′di, Sau′di Arabian** *adj. & n.*

sau•er•bra•ten (sour′brät′n) ▸*n.* A pot roast of beef marinated in vinegar, water, wine, and spices before cooking. [Ger.]

sau•er•kraut (sour′krout′) ▸*n.* Shredded cabbage salted and fermented in its own juice. [Ger.]

Sauk (sôk) also **Sac** (săk, sôk) ▸*n., pl.* **Sauk** or **Sauks** also **Sac** or **Sacs 1.** A member of a Native American people formerly of Wisconsin, Illinois, and Iowa, now mainly in Oklahoma. **2.** Their Algonquian language.

Saul (sôl). fl. 11th cent. B.C. The first king of Israel.

Sault Sainte Ma•rie Canals (so͞o′ sānt′ mə-rē′). Popularly called **Soo Canals** (so͞o). Three ship canals between Lakes Superior and Huron.

sau•na (sô′nə, sou′-) ▸*n.* **1.** A steam bath in which the steam is produced by pouring water over heated rocks. **2.** A dry heat bath. [Finn.]

saun•ter (sôn′tər) ▸*v.* To walk at a leisurely pace. ▸*n.* A leisurely stroll. [Prob. < ME *santren*, muse.] —**saun′ter•er** *n.*

sau•sage (sô′sĭj) ▸*n.* Finely chopped and seasoned meat stuffed into a casing. [< LLat. *salsīcius*, prepared by salting.]

sau•té (sō-tā′, sô-) ▸*v.* **-téed, -té•ing.** To fry lightly in fat. [< Lat. *saltāre*, leap.]

Sau•ternes (sō-tûrn′, sô-) ▸*n., pl.* **-ternes.** A delicate, sweet white wine. [After *Sauternes*, France.]

sav•age (săv′ĭj) ▸*adj.* **1.** Not domesticated or cultivated; wild. **2.** Not civilized; barbaric. **3.** Ferocious; fierce. ▸*n.* **1.** A primitive or uncivilized person. **2.** A brutal person. **3.** A rude person. ▸*v.* **-aged, -ag•ing.** To assault ferociously. [< Lat. *silvāticus*, of the woods.] —**sav′age•ly** *adv.* —**sav′age•ry** *n.*

sa•van•na also **sa•van•nah** (sə-văn′ə) ▸*n.* A flat grassland of tropical or subtropical regions. [< Taino *zabana*.]

Sa•van•nah (sə-văn′ə) A city of SE GA near the mouth of the **Savannah River** (c. 505 km/314 mi). Pop. 137,560.

sa•vant (să-vänt′) ▸*n.* A learned person. [< OFr. < *savoir*, know.]

save[1] (sāv) ▸*v.* **saved, sav•ing 1a.** To rescue from danger. **b.** To deliver from sin. **2.** To preserve or safeguard. **3.** To prevent waste. **4.** To set aside for future use; store. **5.** To keep from harm; spare: *save one's eyesight.* **6.** *Comp. Sci.* To copy (a file) from main memory to a storage medium. [< LLat. *salvāre*.] —**sav′er** *n.*

save[2] (sāv) ▸*prep.* With the exception of; except. ▸*conj.* Except; but. [< Lat. *salvō*.]

sav•ing (sā′vĭng) ▸*n.* **1.** Preservation or rescue. **2.** Economy. **3. savings** Money saved. ▸*prep.* With the exception of. ▸*conj.* Except; save.

sav•ings account (sā′vĭngz) ▸*n.* A bank account that draws interest.

savings and loan association ▸*n.* A financial institution that invests deposits chiefly in home mortgage loans.

savings bank ► *n.* A bank that invests and pays interest on savings accounts.
sav•ior (sāv′yər) ► *n.* A person who rescues another from harm, danger, or loss. [< LLat. *salvātor.*]
sa•voir-faire (săv′wär-fâr′) ► *n.* Social skill or tact. [Fr.]
Sa•vo•na•ro•la (săv′ə-nə-rō′lə, sä′vō-nä-), **Girolamo.** 1452–98. Italian reformer.
sa•vor (sā′vər) ► *n.* **1.** Taste or aroma. **2.** A specific taste or smell. See Syns at **taste. 3.** A distinctive quality. ► *v.* **1.** To have a particular savor. **2.** To appreciate fully; relish. [< Lat. *sapor.*] —**sa′vor•er** *n.*
sa•vor•y[1] (sā′və-rē) ► *adj.* **1.** Appetizing to the taste or smell. **2.** Piquant, pungent, or salty to the taste. —**sa′vor•i•ness** *n.*
sa•vor•y[2] (sā′və-rē) ► *n., pl.* **-ies.** An aromatic herb used as a seasoning. [< Lat. *saturēia.*]
Sa•voy (sə-voi′) A historical region and former duchy of SE France, W Switzerland, and NW Italy. —**Sa•voy′ard** (sə-voi′ärd′, säv′oi-yärd′) *adj. & n.*
sav•vy (săv′ē) *Informal* ► *adj.* **-vi•er, -vi•est.** Well informed and perceptive; shrewd. ► *n.* Practical understanding. ► *v.* **sav•vied** (săv′ēd), **sav•vy•ing.** To understand. [< Sp. *sabe (usted),* (you) know.]
saw[1] (sô) ► *n.* A cutting tool having a thin metal blade or disk with a sharp-toothed edge. ► *v.* **sawed, sawed** or **sawn** (sôn), **saw•ing.** To cut or divide with a saw. [< OE *sagu.*] —**saw′er** *n.*
saw[2] (sô) ► *n.* A familiar and often trite saying. [< OE *sagu,* speech.]
saw[3] (sô) ► *v.* P.t. of **see**[1].
saw•buck (sô′bŭk′) ► *n.* A sawhorse, esp. one with x-shaped legs.
saw•dust (sô′dŭst′) ► *n.* The small waste particles that result from sawing.
sawed-off (sôd′ôf′, -ŏf′) ► *adj.* **1.** Having one end sawed off: *a sawed-off shotgun.* **2.** *Slang* Short; runty.
saw•fish (sô′fĭsh′) ► *n.* A fish related to the rays and skates and having a bladelike snout with teeth along both sides.
saw•horse (sô′hôrs′) ► *n.* A frame used to support pieces of wood being sawed.
saw•mill (sô′mĭl′) ► *n.* A mill where timber is sawed into boards.
sawn (sôn) ► *v.* P.part. of **saw**[1].
saw•yer (sô′yər) ► *n.* One employed in sawing wood. [ME *sawier.*]
sax (săks) ► *n.* A saxophone.
sax•i•frage (săk′sə-frĭj, -frāj′) ► *n.* Any of a genus of plants with flowers and leaves that often form a basal rosette. [< Lat. *saxifragus,* rock-breaking.]
Sax•on (săk′sən) ► *n.* **1.** A member of a Germanic tribal group that invaded Britain in the 5th cent. A.D. **2.** A native or inhabitant of Saxony. **3.** The Germanic language of any of the Saxons. —**Sax′on** *adj.*
Sax•ony (săk′sə-nē) A historical region of N Germany.
sax•o•phone (săk′sə-fōn′) ► *n.* A woodwind instrument with a single-reed mouthpiece and a usu. curved conical metal tube. [After the *Sax* family of 19th cent. Belgian instrument makers.] —**sax′o•phon′ist** *n.*
say (sā) ► *v.* **said** (sĕd), **say•ing 1.** To utter aloud. **2.** To express in words. **3.** To state; declare. **4.** To recite. **5.** To allege. **6.** To indicate; show: *The clock says noon.* **7.** To suppose; assume. ► *n.* A turn or chance to speak. ► *adv.* **1.** Approximately. **2.** For instance. [< OE *secgan.*] —**say′er** *n.*
Say•ers (sā′ərz), **Dorothy L(eigh).** 1893–1957. British writer.
say•ing (sā′ĭng) ► *n.* An adage or maxim.
sa•yo•na•ra (sī′ə-när′ə) ► *interj.* Good-bye. [J.]
say-so (sā′sō′) ► *n., pl.* **-sos** *Informal* **1.** An unsupported statement or assurance. **2.** An authoritative expression of permission or approval. **3.** The authority to decide.
Sb ► The symbol for the element **antimony.** [Lat. *stibium.*]
SB ► *abbr.* **1.** *Lat.* Scientiae Baccalaureus (Bachelor of Science) **2.** stolen base
SBA ► *abbr.* Small Business Administration
SbE ► *abbr.* south by east
SbW ► *abbr.* south by west
sc ► *abbr.* small capital
Sc ► The symbol for the element **scandium.**
SC ► *abbr.* **1.** Security Council **2.** or **S.C.** South Carolina **3.** Supreme Court
sc. ► *abbr.* **1.** scale **2.** scene **3.** scruple (unit of weight)
scab (skăb) ► *n.* **1.** A crust discharged from and covering a healing wound. **2.** A person who takes the place of a striking worker. ► *v.* **scabbed, scab•bing 1.** To become covered with a scab. **2.** To work as a scab. [< ON *skabb.*]
scab•bard (skăb′ərd) ► *n.* A sheath, as for a dagger or sword. [< OFr. *escauberc.*]
scab•by (skăb′ē) ► *adj.* **-bi•er, -bi•est 1.** Having or covered with scabs. **2.** Affected with scabies. —**scab′bi•ness** *n.*
sca•bies (skā′bēz) ► *n.* A contagious skin disease caused by a mite and characterized by intense itching. [< Lat. *scabiēs,* itch.] —**sca′bi•et′ic** (-ĕt′ĭk) *adj.*
scab•rous (skăb′rəs, skā′brəs) ► *adj.* Rough or harsh. [LLat. *scabrōsus.*]
scads (skădz) ► *pl.n. Informal* A large number or amount. [?]
scaf•fold (skăf′əld, -ōld′) ► *n.* **1.** A temporary platform on which workers perform tasks at heights above the ground. **2.** A platform used in the execution of condemned prisoners. [< Med.Lat. *scaffaldus.*]
sca•lar (skā′lər, -lär′) ► *n.* A quantity, such as length, that is completely specified by its magnitude and has no direction. [< Lat. *scālae,* ladder.]
scal•a•wag (skăl′ə-wăg′) ► *n. Informal* A scoundrel; rascal. [?]
scald (skôld) ► *v.* **1.** To burn with or as if with hot liquid or steam. **2.** To subject to or treat with boiling water. **3.** To heat (e.g., milk) almost to the boiling point. ► *n.* An injury caused by scalding. [< LLat. *excaldāre,* wash in hot water.]
scale[1] (skāl) ► *n.* **1a.** One of the small platelike structures forming the external covering of fishes, reptiles, and certain mammals. **b.** A similar structure or part. **2.** A dry thin flake of epidermis shed from the skin. **3.** A small thin piece. **4.** A scale insect. **5.** A flaky oxide film formed on a metal. ► *v.* **scaled, scal•ing 1.** To clear or strip of scale or scales: *scale and clean the fish.* **2.** To remove or come off in layers or scales. **3.** To become encrusted. [< OFr. *es-*

cale.] —**scal′i•ness** *n.* —**scal′y** *adj.*

scale² (skāl) ►*n.* **1a.** A system of ordered marks at fixed intervals used in measurement. **b.** An instrument or device bearing such marks. **2.** A progressive classification, as of size, importance, or rank. **3.** A relative level or degree. **4.** *Mus.* An ascending or descending series of tones proceeding by a specified scheme of intervals. ►*v.* **scaled, scal•ing 1.** To climb up or over; ascend. **2.** To make in accord with a particular proportion or scale. **3.** To adjust in calculated amounts: *scaled down their demands.* [< Lat. *scālae*, ladder.] —**scal′a•ble** *adj.*

scale³ (skāl) ►*n.* often **scales.** An instrument or machine for weighing. [< ON *skāl*, bowl.]

scale insect ►*n.* A destructive insect that sucks the juices of plants and secretes and remains under waxy scales on plant tissue.

sca•lene (skā′lēn′, skā-lēn′) ►*adj.* Having three unequal sides. Used of triangles. [< Gk. *skalēnos.*]

scal•lion (skăl′yən) ►*n.* A young onion before the development of the bulb. [< Lat. *(caepa) Ascalōnia*, (onion) of Ascalon, a city in Palestine.]

scal•lop (skŏl′əp, skăl′-) ►*n.* **1a.** A bivalve marine mollusk with a fan-shaped ridged shell. **b.** The edible muscle of a scallop. **2.** One of a series of curved projections forming an ornamental border. **3.** A thin, boneless slice of meat. ►*v.* **-loped, -lop•ing 1.** To edge (e.g., cloth) with scallops. **2.** To bake in a casserole with milk or a sauce and often with bread crumbs. [< OFr. *escalope*, shell.] —**scal′lop•er** *n.*

scalp (skălp) ►*n.* The skin covering the top of the human head. ►*v.* **1.** To cut or tear the scalp from. **2.** *Slang* To resell (tickets) at an excessively high price. [ME.] —**scalp′er** *n.*

scal•pel (skăl′pəl) ►*n.* A small surgical knife with a thin sharp blade. [Lat. *scalpellum.*]

scam (skăm) ►*n.* *Slang* A fraudulent business scheme; swindle. [?] —**scam** *v.*

scamp (skămp) ►*n.* A rogue; rascal. [< *scamp*, go about idly.]

scam•per (skăm′pər) ►*v.* To run nimbly. [Prob. < Flem. *schampeeren.*] —**scam′per** *n.* —**scam′per•er** *n.*

scan (skăn) ►*v.* **scanned, scan•ning 1.** To examine closely. **2.** To look over quickly. **3.** To analyze (verse) into metrical patterns. **4.** *Electron.* To move a finely focused beam of light or electrons in a systematic pattern over (a surface) to reproduce or sense and subsequently transmit an image. **5.** *Comp. Sci.* To search (stored data) automatically for specific data. **6.** *Medic.* To examine (e.g., a body part) with a scanner. [< Lat. *scandere*, climb.] —**scan** *n.*

scan•dal (skăn′dl) ►*n.* **1.** Public disgrace. **2.** A person, thing, or circumstance that causes disgrace or outrage. **3.** Malicious gossip. [< Gk. *skandalon*, snare.] —**scan′dal•ous** *adj.* —**scan′dal•ous•ly** *adv.*

scan•dal•ize (skăn′dl-īz′) ►*v.* **-ized, -iz•ing.** To offend the moral sensibilities of. —**scan′dal•i•za′tion** *n.* —**scan′dal•iz′er** *n.*

scandal sheet ►*n.* A newspaper that habitually prints scandalous stories.

Scan•di•na•vi•a (skăn′də-nā′vē-ə, -nāv′yə) A region of N Europe consisting of Norway, Sweden, and Denmark, and sometimes Finland, Iceland, and the Faeroe Is.

Scan•di•na•vi•an (skăn′də-nā′vē-ən, -nāv′yən) ►*n.* **1.** A native or inhabitant of Scandinavia. **2.** A subdivision of Germanic including Norwegian, Swedish, Danish, and Icelandic. —**Scan′di•na′vi•an** *adj.*

Scandinavian Peninsula. A peninsula of N Europe comprising Norway and Sweden.

scan•di•um (skăn′dē-əm) ►*n.* *Symbol* **Sc** A silvery-white metallic element found in various rare minerals and in certain uranium ores. At. no. 21. See table at **element.** [< Lat. *Scandia*, Scandinavia.]

scan•ner (skăn′ər) ►*n.* **1.** One that scans. **2.** A receiver that broadcasts signals from specified radio frequencies. **3.** A device that converts printed images and text into digital information stored as computer file. **4.** A device, such as a CAT scanner, for observing internal body structures.

scan•sion (skăn′shən) ►*n.* Analysis of verse into metrical patterns. [< Lat. *scandere*, *scāns-*, climb.]

scant (skănt) ►*adj.* **-er, -est 1.** Barely sufficient: *paid scant attention to me.* **2.** Falling just short of a specific measure. ►*v.* **1.** To skimp. **2.** To limit, as in amount; stint. [< ON *skamt*, short.] —**scant′ly** *adv.*

scant•y (skăn′tē) ►*adj.* **-i•er, -i•est 1.** Barely sufficient or adequate. **2.** Insufficient. —**scant′i•ly** *adv.* —**scant′i•ness** *n.*

scape•goat (skāp′gōt′) ►*n.* One bearing blame for others. ►*v.* To make a scapegoat of. [*(e)scape* + GOAT.]

scap•u•la (skăp′yə-lə) ►*n.*, *pl.* **-las** or **-lae** (-lē′). Either of two large, flat bones forming the back part of the shoulder; shoulder blade. [LLat.] —**scap′u•lar** *adj.*

scar (skär) ►*n.* **1.** A mark left on the skin after a surface injury or wound has healed. **2.** A lingering sign of damage or injury. ►*v.* **scarred, scar•ring.** To mark with or form a scar. [< Gk. *eskhara*, scab.]

scar•ab (skăr′əb) ►*n.* **1.** A large black beetle regarded as sacred by the ancient Egyptians. **2.** A representation of this beetle. [< Lat. *scarabaeus.*]

scarce (skârs) ►*adj.* **scarc•er, scarc•est 1.** Insufficient to meet a demand or requirement; short in supply. **2.** Hard to find; absent or rare. [< VLat. **excarpere*, *excarps-*, pluck out.] —**scarce′ness, scar′ci•ty** *n.*

scarce•ly (skârs′lē) ►*adv.* **1.** By a small margin; barely. **2.** Almost not; hardly. **3.** Certainly not.

Usage: *Scarcely* has the force of a negative and is therefore regarded as incorrectly used with another negative, as in *I couldn't scarcely believe it.* A clause following *scarcely* is correctly introduced by *when* or *before* but not by *than: The meeting had scarcely begun when* (or *before* but not *than*) *it was interrupted.* See Usage Notes at **double negative, hardly.**

scare (skâr) ►*v.* **scared, scar•ing.** To frighten or become frightened. ►*n.* **1.** A fright. **2.** A panic. [< ON *skjarr*, timid.]

scare•crow (skâr′krō′) ►*n.* A crude figure set up in a cultivated area to scare birds away.

scarf¹ (skärf) ►*n.*, *pl.* **scarfs** or **scarves** (skärvz) **1.** A piece of cloth worn about the head, neck, or shoulders. **2.** A runner, as for a bureau. [< ONFr. *escarpe*, sash.]

scarf² (skärf) ►*n.*, *pl.* **scarfs** (skärfs). A joint made by cutting the ends of two pieces correspondingly and strapping or bolting them together. [ME *skarf.*] —**scarf** *v.*

scar•i•fy (skăr′ə-fī′) ▸*v.* **-fied, -fy•ing 1.** To make shallow cuts in (the skin). **2.** To distress deeply, as with severe criticism. [< Gk. *skariphos*, pencil, stylus.] —**scar′i•fi•ca′tion** *n.*

scar•la•ti•na (skär′lə-tē′nə) ▸*n.* See **scarlet fever.** [< Ital. *scarlattina* < dim. of *scarlatto*, SCARLET.]

Scar•lat•ti (skär-lä′tē). **Alessandro** (1660–1725) and **Domenico** (1685–1757). Italian composers.

scar•let (skär′lĭt) ▸*n.* A strong to vivid red or reddish orange. [< Pers. *saqirlāt*, rich cloth.] —**scar′let** *adj.*

scarlet fever ▸*n.* An acute contagious bacterial disease occurring predominantly among children and marked by a scarlet skin eruption and high fever.

scarp (skärp) ▸*n.* An escarpment. [Ital. *scarpa*, slope.]

scar•y (skâr′ē) ▸*adj.* **-i•er, -i•est 1.** Frightening. **2.** Easily scared; very timid. —**scar′i•ly** *adv.* —**scar′i•ness** *n.*

scat[1] (skăt) ▸*v.* **scat•ted, scat•ting** *Informal.* To go away hastily. [?]

scat[2] (skăt) ▸*n.* Jazz singing in which improvised, meaningless syllables are sung to a melody. [?] —**scat** *v.*

scath•ing (skā′*th*ĭng) ▸*adj.* **1.** Harshly critical. **2.** Harmful or painful; injurious. [< ON *skadha.*] —**scath′ing•ly** *adv.*

sca•tol•o•gy (skă-tŏl′ə-jē, skə-) ▸*n.* An obsession with excrement or obscenity, esp. in literature. [< Gk. *skōr, skat-*, excrement.] —**scat′o•log′i•cal** (skăt′l-ŏj′ĭ-kəl), **scat′o•log′ic** *adj.*

scat•ter (skăt′ər) ▸*v.* **1.** To disperse. **2.** To distribute loosely by or as if by sprinkling; strew. **3.** *Phys.* To deflect (radiation or particles). [ME *scateren.*] —**scat′ter•er** *n.*

scat•ter•brain (skăt′ər-brān′) ▸*n.* A flighty or disorganized person. —**scat′ter•brained′** *adj.*

scatter rug ▸*n.* A small rug.

scat•ter•shot (skăt′ər-shŏt′) ▸*adj.* Wide-ranging and indiscriminate: *scattershot criticism.*

scav•en•ger (skăv′ən-jər) ▸*n.* **1.** One who searches, as through refuse, for food or useful material. **2.** An animal that feeds on dead or decaying matter. [< AN *scawage*, tax on the goods of foreign merchants.] —**scav′enge** *v.*

sce•nar•i•o (sĭ-nâr′ē-ō′, -när′-, -năr′-) ▸*n., pl.* **-os 1.** A script or outline of a motion picture. **2.** An outline of possible future events. [< Ital. *scena*, SCENE.] —**sce•nar′ist** *n.*

scene (sēn) ▸*n.* **1.** A prospect; view. **2.** The setting of an action. **3.** A subdivision of an act of a play. **4.** A shot or series of related shots in a movie. **5.** The scenery for a dramatic presentation. **6.** A public display of passion or temper. **7.** A sphere of activity: *the arts scene.* [< Gk. *skēnē*, tent, stage.]

scen•er•y (sē′nə-rē) ▸*n., pl.* **-ies 1.** A landscape. **2.** The painted backdrops on a theatrical stage. —**sce′nic** *adj.* —**sce′ni•cal•ly** *adv.*

sce•nog•ra•phy (sē-nŏg′rə-fē) ▸*n.* The art of representing objects in perspective, esp. in theatrical scenery. —**sce•nog′raph•er** *n.*

scent (sĕnt) ▸*n.* **1.** A distinctive odor. See Syns at **fragrance, smell. 2.** A perfume. **3.** The trail of a hunted animal or fugitive. ▸*v.* **1.** To smell, esp. to hunt by smell. **2.** To detect as if by smelling: *scented danger.* **3.** To fill with a scent. [< Lat. *sentīre*, feel.] —**scent′ed** *adj.*

scep•ter (sĕp′tər) ▸*n.* A staff held by a sovereign as an emblem of authority. [< Gk. *skēptron.*]

scep•tic (skĕp′tĭk) ▸*n.* Var. of **skeptic.**

scep•ti•cism (skĕp′tĭ-sĭz′əm) ▸*n.* Var. of **skepticism.**

sched•ule (skĕj′o͞ol, -o͞o-əl, skĕj′əl) ▸*n.* **1.** A timetable. **2.** A production plan. **3.** A list of items. **4.** A program of events or appointments. ▸*v.* **-uled, -ul•ing 1.** To enter on a schedule. **2.** To make up a schedule for. **3.** To plan for a certain time. [< LLat. *schedula*, small piece of paper.] —**sched′u•ler** *n.*

Schel•ling (shĕl′ĭng), **Friedrich Wilhelm Joseph von.** 1775–1854. German idealist philosopher.

sche•ma (skē′mə) ▸*n., pl.* **sche•ma•ta** (skē-mä′tə, skĭ-măt′ə) or **-mas.** A diagrammatic representation; outline; model. [< Gk. *skhēma.*]

sche•mat•ic (skē-măt′ĭk, skĭ-) ▸*adj.* Relating to or in the form of a scheme or diagram. ▸*n.* A structural diagram, esp. of an electrical or mechanical system. —**sche•mat′i•cal•ly** *adv.*

scheme (skēm) ▸*n.* **1.** A systematic plan or design. **2.** A plot. See Syns at **plan. 3.** An orderly combination of elements: *a color scheme.* ▸*v.* **schemed, schem•ing 1.** To contrive a plan or scheme for. **2.** To plot. [< Gk. *skhēma*, figure.] —**schem′er** *n.*

scher•zo (skĕr′tsō) ▸*n., pl.* **-zos** or **-zi** (-tsē) *Mus.* A lively movement commonly in 3/4 time. [Ital.]

Schick test (shĭk) ▸*n.* A skin test to determine immunity to diphtheria. [After Béla *Schick* (1877–1967).]

Schil•ler (shĭl′ər), **Johann Christoph Friedrich von.** 1759–1805. German writer.

schil•ling (shĭl′ĭng) ▸*n.* See table at **currency.** [Ger.]

schism (skĭz′əm, sĭz′-) ▸*n.* A separation or division into factions, esp. within a religious body. [< Gk. *skhisma.*] —**schis•mat′ic** *adj.* —**schis•mat′i•cal•ly** *adv.*

schist (shĭst) ▸*n.* A metamorphic rock composed of laminated, often flaky parallel layers. [< Gk. *skhistos*, split.]

schis•to•so•mi•a•sis (shĭs′tə-sə-mī′ə-sĭs) ▸*n.* A severe tropical disease caused by infestation with parasitic worms. [< *schistosome*, a parasitic worm.]

schizo– or **schiz–** ▸*pref.* **1.** Split: *schizophrenia.* **2.** Schizophrenia: *schizoid.* [< Gk. *skhizein*, split.]

schiz•oid (skĭt′soid′) ▸*adj.* **1.** Relating to a personality disorder marked by extreme shyness and reclusiveness. **2.** Schizophrenic. Not in scientific use. ▸*n.* A schizoid person.

schiz•o•phre•ni•a (skĭt′sə-frē′nē-ə, -frĕn′ē-ə) ▸*n.* A psychosis usu. marked by withdrawal from reality and by variable emotional, behavioral, or intellectual disturbances. —**schiz′o•phren′ic** (-frĕn′ĭk) *adj.* & *n.*

schle•miel (shlə-mēl′) ▸*n.* *Slang* A habitual bungler; dolt. [Yiddish *shlemíl.*]

schlep (shlĕp) ▸*v.* **schlepped, schlep•ping** *Slang* To carry clumsily or with difficulty; lug. [Yiddish *shlepn*, drag, pull.] —**schlep** *n.*

Schles•wig (shlĕs′wĭg) A historical region and

former duchy of N Germany and S Denmark in S Jutland.

Schlie•mann (shlē′män′), **Heinrich.** 1822–90. German archaeologist.

schlock (shlŏk) ►*n. Slang* Something that is inferior or shoddy. [Poss. < Yiddish *shlak*, stroke, nuisance.] —**schlock, shlock′y** *adj.*

schmaltz also **schmalz** (shmälts) ►*n. Informal* Excessively sentimental art or music. [Yiddish *shmalts*, animal fat.] —**schmaltz′y** *adj.*

Schmidt (shmĭt), **Helmut.** b. 1918. German politician.

schmuck (shmŭk) ►*n. Slang* An insignificant or contemptible person. [Yiddish *shmok*, penis, fool.]

schnapps (shnäps, shnăps) ►*n., pl.* **schnapps.** Any of various strong, often flavored liquors. [Ger. *Schnaps.*]

schnau•zer (shnou′zər, shnou′tsər) ►*n.* A dog with a wiry gray coat and blunt muzzle. [Ger. < *Schnauze*, snout.]

schol•ar (skŏl′ər) ►*n.* **1.** A learned person. **2.** A pupil or student. **3.** A student holding a scholarship. [< LLat. *scholāris*, of a school.] —**schol′ar•li•ness** *n.* —**schol′ar•ly** *adv.*

schol•ar•ship (skŏl′ər-shĭp′) ►*n.* **1.** The methods and attainments of a scholar. **2.** A grant awarded to a student.

scho•las•tic (skə-lăs′tĭk) ►*adj.* **1.** Of or relating to schools or scholarship. **2.** Showing narrow concern for scholarly detail. See Syns at **pedantic.** [< Gk. *skholastikos.*] —**scho•las′ti•cal•ly** *adv.*

Schön•berg (shûrn′bûrg, shœn′bĕrk′), **Arnold.** 1874–1951. Austrian composer.

school[1] (sko͞ol) ►*n.* **1.** An institution for instruction and learning. **2.** The student body of an educational institution. **3.** The process of being educated. **4.** A group of people under a common influence or sharing a unifying belief. ►*v.* **1.** To educate. **2.** To train or discipline. [< Gk. *skholē.*] —**school′boy′** *n.* —**school′girl′** *n.*

school[2] (sko͞ol) ►*n.* A large group of aquatic animals, esp. fish, swimming together. [< MDu. *scole.*] —**school** *v.*

school•ing (sko͞o′lĭng) ►*n.* **1.** Instruction given at school. **2.** Education obtained through experience.

school•marm (sko͞ol′märm′) ►*n.* A woman teacher, esp. a strict or old-fashioned one. [SCHOOL[1] + dial. *marm* (var. of MA'AM).]

school•mas•ter (sko͞ol′măs′tər) ►*n.* **1.** A man who teaches school. **2.** A headmaster.

school•mis•tress (sko͞ol′mĭs′trĭs) ►*n.* **1.** A woman who teaches school. **2.** A headmistress.

school•room (sko͞ol′ro͞om′, -ro͝om′) ►*n.* A classroom.

school•teach•er (sko͞ol′tē′chər) ►*n.* One who teaches in a school below the college level.

schoo•ner (sko͞o′nər) ►*n.* **1.** A fore-and-aft rigged sailing vessel with at least two masts. **2.** A large beer glass, usu. holding a pint or more. [?]

Scho•pen•hau•er (shō′pən-hou′ər), **Arthur.** 1788–1860. German philosopher.

Schrö•ding•er (shrō′dĭng-ər, shrœ′-), **Erwin.** 1887–1961. Austrian physicist; 1933 Nobel.

Schu•bert (sho͞o′bərt, -bĕrt′), **Franz Peter.** 1797–1828. Austrian composer.

Schu•mann (sho͞o′män′, -mən), **Robert.** 1810–56. German composer.

schuss (sho͝os, sho͞os) ►*v.* To ski a fast straight downhill course. [Ger., shot < OHGer. *scuz.*] —**schuss** *n.*

schwa (shwä) ►*n.* **1.** A neutral vowel sound typically occurring in unstressed syllables, as the final vowel of English *sofa.* **2.** The symbol (ə) used to represent schwa. [< Heb. *šəwā'.*]

Schweit•zer (shwīt′sər, shvīt′-), **Albert.** 1875–1965. French philosopher, physician, and musician; 1952 Nobel Peace Prize.

sci•at•i•ca (sī-ăt′ĭ-kə) ►*n.* Chronic neuralgic pain in the area of the hip or thigh. [< Med.Lat. *sciaticus*, of the hip.]

sci•ence (sī′əns) ►*n.* **1.** The observation, identification, description, experimental investigation, and theoretical explanation of phenomena. **2.** Methodological activity, discipline, or study. **3.** An activity regarded as requiring study and method. **4.** Knowledge gained through experience. [< Lat. *scientia*, knowledge.] —**sci′en•tif′ic** (sī′ən-tĭf′ĭk) *adj.* —**sci′en•tif′i•cal•ly** *adv.*

science fiction ►*n.* Fiction in which the plot is based on speculative scientific discoveries, drastic environmental changes, or space travel. —**sci′ence-fic′tion** *adj.*

scientific notation ►*n.* A method of writing or displaying numbers in terms of a decimal number between 1 and 10 multiplied by a power of 10.

sci•en•tist (sī′ən-tĭst) ►*n.* A person having expert knowledge of one or more sciences.

sci-fi (sī′fī′) ►*n. Informal* Science fiction.

scim•i•tar (sĭm′ĭ-tər, -tär′) ►*n.* A broad curved sword with the edge on the convex side. [Ital. *scimitarra.*]

scin•til•la (sĭn-tĭl′ə) ►*n.* A minute amount; trace. [Lat., spark.] —**scin′til•lant** *adj.*

scin•til•late (sĭn′tl-āt′) ►*v.* **-lat•ed, -lat•ing 1.** To throw off sparks; flash. **2.** To be animated and brilliant. [< Lat. *scintilla*, spark.] —**scin′til•la′tion** *n.*

sci•on (sī′ən) ►*n.* **1.** A descendant or heir. **2.** A detached plant shoot used in grafting. [< OFr. *cion.*]

Scip•io (sĭp′ē-ō′, skĭp′-), **Publius Cornelius.** "the Younger." 185?–129 B.C. Roman general.

Scipio Af•ri•ca•nus (ăf-rĭ-kā′nəs), **Publius Cornelius.** "the Elder." 236?–183? B.C. Roman general.

scis•sors (sĭz′ərz) ►*n. (takes sing. or pl. v.)* A cutting implement of two blades joined by a swivel pin that allows the cutting edges to be opened and closed. [< LLat. *cisorium*, cutting instrument.] —**scis′sor** *v.*

scissors kick ►*n.* A swimming kick in which the legs are opened and closed like scissors.

SCLC ►*abbr.* Southern Christian Leadership Conference

scle•ra (sklîr′ə) ►*n.* The tough fibrous tissue covering all of the eyeball except the cornea. [< Gk. *sklēros*, hard.] —**scle′ral** *adj.*

scle•ro•sis (sklə-rō′sĭs) ►*n., pl.* **-ses** (-sēz). A thickening or hardening of a body part, as of an artery, esp. from tissue overgrowth or disease. [< Gk. *sklēros*, hard.] —**scle•rot′ic** (-rŏt′ĭk) *adj.*

scoff (skŏf, skôf) ►*v.* To express derision or scorn: *scoffed at their threats.* [ME *scoffen.*] —**scoff** *n.* —**scoff′er** *n.*

scoff•law (skŏf′lô′, skôf′-) ►*n.* One who habitually violates the law.

scold (skōld) ►*v.* To reprimand harshly. ►*n.* A

persistent nag or critic. [< ME *scolde*, an abusive person.] —**scold′er** *n.*

sco•li•o•sis (skō′lē-ō′sĭs, skŏl′ē-) ►*n.* Abnormal lateral curvature of the spine. [< Gk. *skolios*, crooked.]

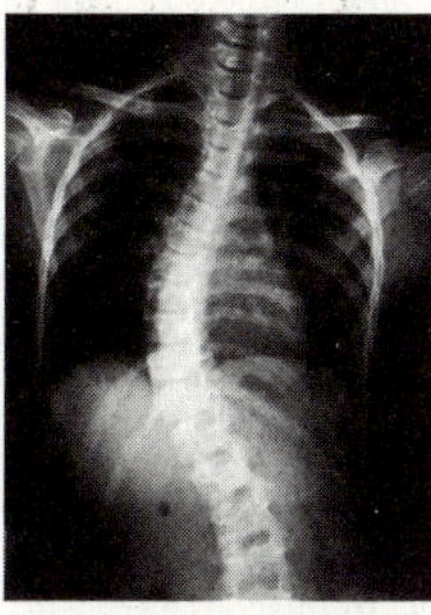

scoliosis
x-ray showing severe scoliosis of a human spine

sconce (skŏns) ►*n.* A wall bracket for candles or lights. [< Med.Lat. *scōnsa*, hiding place.]

scone (skōn, skŏn) ►*n.* A small, rich, biscuitlike pastry. [Perh. < Du. *schoonbrood*, fine white bread.]

scoop (sko͞op) ►*n.* **1.** A small shovellike serving utensil. **2.** The bucket or shovel, as of a dredge or backhoe. **3.** *Informal* An exclusive news story acquired by luck or initiative. ►*v.* **1.** To take up or dip into with or as if with a scoop. **2.** To hollow out. **3.** *Informal* To top or outmaneuver (a competitor) in acquiring a news story. [< MDu. *scope*.] —**scoop′er** *n.*

scoot (sko͞ot) ►*v.* To go suddenly and speedily. [Prob. of Scand. orig.]

scoot•er (sko͞o′tər) ►*n.* **1.** A child's vehicle consisting of a long footboard between two end wheels, controlled by an upright steering handle. **2.** A motor scooter.

scope (skōp) ►*n.* **1.** The range of one's perceptions, thoughts, or actions. **2.** Breadth or opportunity to function. See Syns at **room.** **3.** The area covered by a given activity or subject. See Syns at **range.** **4.** *Informal* A telescope. [< Gk. *skopos*, target, aim.]

-scope ►*suff.* An instrument for observing: *telescope.* [< Gk. *skopein*, see.]

Scopes (skōps), **John Thomas.** 1900–70. Amer. teacher; convicted (1925) for teaching evolution.

scor•bu•tic (skôr-byo͞o′tĭk) also **scor•bu•ti•cal** (-tĭ-kəl) ►*adj.* Of, resembling, or affected by scurvy. [< NLat. *scorbūtus*, scurvy.]

scorch (skôrch) ►*v.* **1.** To burn superficially. **2.** To wither or parch with intense heat. ►*n.* **1.** A slight burn. **2.** Discoloration caused by heat. [ME *scorchen*.] —**scorch′er** *n.*

score (skôr, skōr) ►*n.* **1.** A notch or incision. **2.** A record of points made in a competitive event. **3.** A result of a test or examination. **4.** A debt. **5.** A ground; reason. **6.** A group of 20 items. **7.** The written form of a musical composition. ►*v.* **scored, scor•ing 1.** To mark with lines or notches. **2.** To gain (a point) in a game or contest. **3.** To keep the score of a game or contest. **4.** To achieve; win. **5.** To evaluate and assign a grade to. **6.** *Mus.* **a.** To orchestrate. **b.** To arrange for a specific instrument. **7.** *Slang* To succeed in obtaining (e.g., an illegal drug). [< ON *skor*.] —**score′less** *adj.* —**scor′er** *n.*

sco•ri•a (skôr′ē-ə, skōr′-) ►*n.* **1.** *Geol.* Porous cinderlike fragments of dark lava. **2.** *Metall.* The refuse of a smelted metal or ore; slag. [< Gk. *skōr*, dung.]

scorn (skôrn) ►*n.* **1a.** Contempt or disdain. **b.** Derision. **2.** One spoken of or treated with contempt. ►*v.* **1.** To consider or treat as contemptible or unworthy. **2.** To reject or refuse with derision. See Syns at **despise.** [< OFr. *escarn*, of Gmc. orig.] —**scorn′ful** *adj.* —**scorn′ful•ly** *adv.* —**scorn′ful•ness** *n.*

Scor•pi•o (skôr′pē-ō′) ►*n.* **1.** Var. of **Scorpius.** **2.** The 8th sign of the zodiac.

scor•pi•on (skôr′pē-ən) ►*n.* Any of various arachnids with an erectile tail tipped with a venomous sting. [< Gk. *skorpios*.]

Scor•pi•us (skôr′pē-əs) also **Scor•pi•o** (-pē-ō′) ►*n.* A constellation in the Southern Hemisphere.

Scot (skŏt) ►*n.* **1.** A native or inhabitant of Scotland. **2.** A member of a Gaelic tribe that migrated to N Britain from Ireland in about the 6th cent. A.D.

scotch (skŏch) ►*v.* **1.** To put an abrupt end to. **2.** To injure so as to render harmless. **3.** To cut or score. [ME *scocchen*, cut.]

Scotch ►*n.* **1.** The people of Scotland. **2.** Scots English. **3.** Scotch whisky. ►*adj.* Scottish. —**Scotch′man** *n.* —**Scotch′wom′an** *n.*

Scotch-I•rish (skŏch′ī′rĭsh) ►*n.* The people of Scotland who settled in N Ireland or their descendants. —**Scotch′-I′rish** *adj.*

Scotch whisky ►*n.* A whiskey distilled in Scotland from malted barley.

scot-free (skŏt′frē′) ►*adv. & adj.* Free from obligation or penalty. [< ME *scot*, tax.]

Scot•land (skŏt′lənd) A constituent country of the United Kingdom, in N Great Britain. Pop. 5,149,500. —**Scots′man** *n.* —**Scots′wom′an** *n.*

Scott (skŏt), **Dred.** 1795?–1858. Amer. slave; subject of a US Supreme Court decision supporting slavery (1857).

Dred Scott
detail of an 1881 portrait, after an 1858 photograph

Scott, Robert Falcon. 1868–1912. British explorer.

Scott, Sir **Walter.** 1771–1832. British writer.

Scott, Winfield. Amer. general.

Scot•tish (skŏt′ĭsh) ►*adj.* Of or relating to Scotland or its people or language. ►*n.* **1.** Scots English. **2.** The people of Scotland.

Scottish Gaelic ►*n.* The Celtic language of Scotland.

Scotts•dale (skŏts′dāl′) A city of S-central AZ, a suburb of Phoenix. Pop. 130,069.

scoun•drel (skoun′drəl) ►*n.* A villain; rogue. [?] —**scoun′drel•ly** *adj.*

scour[1] (skour) ►*v.* **1.** To clean by scrubbing vigorously, as with an abrasive. **2.** To scrub something in order to clean or polish it. [< LLat. *excūrāre*, clean out.]

scour[2] (skour) ►*v.* **1.** To search through or over thoroughly. **2.** To move swiftly; scurry. [ME *scouren*, move swiftly.]

scourge (skûrj) ►*n.* **1.** A source of great suffering or harm. **2.** A means of inflicting severe suffering or punishment. **3.** A whip. ►*v.* **scourged, scourg•ing 1.** To devastate; ravage. **2.** To chastise severely. **3.** To whip or flog. [< OFr. *escorgier*, to whip.]

scout (skout) ►*v.* **1.** To reconnoiter. **2.** To observe and evaluate (a talented person) for possible hiring. ►*n.* **1.** One that is sent out to gather information. **2.** A sentinel. **3.** One who seeks out talented persons, esp. in sports and entertainment. **4.** often **Scout a.** A Boy Scout. **b.** A Girl Scout. [< Lat. *auscultāre*, listen.]

scout•mas•ter (skout′măs′tər) ►*n.* The adult leader of a troop of Boy Scouts.

scow (skou) ►*n.* A large flat-bottomed boat with square ends. [< MDu. *scouwe.*]

scowl (skoul) ►*v.* To wrinkle or contract the brow as in anger or disapproval. See Syns at **frown.** ►*n.* A look of anger or strong disapproval. [ME *scoulen.*] —**scowl′er** *n.* —**scowl′ing•ly** *adv.*

scr. ►*abbr.* scruple (unit of weight)

scrab•ble (skrăb′əl) ►*v.* **-bled, -bling 1.** To grope or scratch frantically. **2.** To struggle. **3.** To clamber. **4.** To scribble. [< MDu. *schrabben*, scrape.] —**scrab′ble** *n.*

scrag•gly (skrăg′lē) ►*adj.* **-gli•er, -gli•est.** Ragged; unkempt. [< *scrag*, a scrawny animal.]

scrag•gy (skrăg′ē) ►*adj.* **-gi•er, -gi•est 1.** Jagged; rough. **2.** Bony and lean. [< *scrag*, a scrawny animal.] —**scrag′gi•ness** *n.*

scram (skrăm) ►*v.* **scrammed, scram•ming** *Slang.* To leave at once. [< SCRAMBLE.]

scram•ble (skrăm′bəl) ►*v.* **-bled, -bling 1.** To move or climb hurriedly. **2.** To compete frantically. **3.** To mix haphazardly. **4.** To take off with all possible haste. Used of a warplane. **5.** To cook (beaten eggs) while stirring. **6.** *Electron.* To distort (a signal) so as to render it unintelligible without a special receiver. [Perh. blend of obsolete *scamble*, struggle for, and *cramble*, crawl.] —**scram′ble** *n.* —**scram′bler** *n.*

scrap[1] (skrăp) ►*n.* **1.** A small bit or fragment. **2.** **scraps** Leftover food. **3.** Discarded waste material, esp. metal suitable for reprocessing. ►*v.* **scrapped, scrap•ping 1.** To break down into parts for disposal or salvage. **2.** To discard as worthless; junk. [< ON *skrap*, trifles.] —**scrap′py** *adj.*

scrap[2] (skrăp) ►*v.* **scrapped, scrap•ping.** To fight, often with the fists. ►*n.* A fight or scuffle. [Perh. < SCRAPE.] —**scrap′per** *n.*

scrap•book (skrăp′bo͝ok′) ►*n.* A book with blank pages for mounting pictures, clippings, or other mementos.

scrape (skrāp) ►*v.* **scraped, scrap•ing 1.** To rub (a surface) with considerable pressure. **2.** To draw (a hard or abrasive object) forcefully over a surface. **3.** To abrade, smooth, injure, or remove by this procedure. **4.** To come into abrasive contact. **5.** To rub or move with a harsh grating noise. **6.** To amass or produce with difficulty: *scrape together some cash.* ►*n.* **1.** The act or sound of scraping. **2.** An abrasion on the skin. **3a.** A predicament. **b.** A scuffle. [< ON *skrapa.*] —**scrap′er** *n.*

scrap•py (skrăp′ē) ►*adj.* **-pi•er, -pi•est 1.** Quarrelsome; contentious. **2.** Full of fighting spirit. See Syns at **argumentative.** —**scrap′pi•ly** *adv.* —**scrap′pi•ness** *n.*

scratch (skrăch) ►*v.* **1.** To make a shallow cut or mark with something sharp. **2.** To use the nails or claws to dig or scrape at. **3.** To rub (the skin) to relieve itching. **4.** To strike out or cancel (e.g., a word) by or as if by drawing lines through. ►*n.* A mark or wound produced by scratching. ►*adj.* **1.** Done haphazardly or by chance. **2.** Assembled hastily or at random. —***idioms:* from scratch** From the very beginning. **up to scratch** *Informal* Meeting the requirements. [ME *scracchen.*] —**scratch′er** *n.* —**scratch′i•ly** *adv.* —**scratch′i•ness** *n.* —**scratch′y** *adj.*

scrawl (skrôl) ►*v.* To write hastily or illegibly: *scrawled a note.* [Perh. < obsolete *scrawl*, gesticulate.] —**scrawl** *n.* —**scrawl′y** *adj.*

scraw•ny (skrô′nē) ►*adj.* **-ni•er, -ni•est.** Gaunt and bony. [< dial. *scranny.*] —**scraw′ni•ness** *n.*

scream (skrēm) ►*v.* **1.** To utter a long loud piercing cry, as from pain or fear. **2.** To produce a startling effect. ►*n.* **1.** A long loud piercing cry or sound. **2.** *Informal* One that is hilariously or ridiculously funny. [ME *screamen.*] —**scream′er** *n.*

scree (skrē) ►*n.* Loose rock debris covering a slope. [Prob. < ON *skridha*, landslide.]

screech (skrēch) ►*n.* **1.** A high shrill cry. **2.** A similar sound, as of scraping metal. [< ME *scrichen*, to screech.] —**screech** *v.* —**screech′y** *adj.*

screech owl ►*n.* Any of various small North American owls with ear tufts and a quavering, whistlelike call.

screen (skrēn) ►*n.* **1.** Something serving to divide, conceal, or protect, such as a movable room partition. **2.** A coarse sieve. **3.** A window or door insertion of framed mesh used to keep out insects. **4a.** The surface on which a picture is projected for viewing. **b.** The movie industry. **5.** The phosphorescent surface on which an image is displayed in a cathode-ray tube. ►*v.* **1.** To provide with a screen. **2.** To conceal or protect. See Syns at **block. 3a.** To separate or sift out by means of a sieve or screen. **b.** To test or examine, as for suitability. **4.** To show (e.g., a movie) on a screen. [< MDu. *scherm*, shield.] —**screen′er** *n.*

screen•play (skrēn′plā′) ►*n.* The script for a movie.

screen saver ►*n.* A software program that protects a display screen from having an image etched onto its surface, as by displaying constantly shifting images.

screen test ►*n.* A brief movie sequence filmed to test the ability of an aspiring performer. —**screen′-test′** *v.*

screen•writ•er (skrēn′rī′tər) ►*n.* A writer of screenplays. —**screen′writ′ing** *n.*

screw (skrōō) ► *n.* **1.** A cylindrical rod with incised threads, having a slotted head so that it can be driven as a fastener by turning it with a screwdriver. **2.** A propeller. ► *v.* **1.** To fasten, tighten, or attach by or as if by means of a screw. **2.** To turn or twist. —***phrasal verb:*** **screw up** *Slang* To make a mess of. [< OFr. *escrove*, nut.]

screw•ball (skrōō′bôl′) ► *n.* **1.** *Baseball* A pitched ball curving in the direction opposite to a normal curve ball. **2.** *Slang* An eccentric or irrational person.

screw•driv•er (skrōō′drī′vər) ► *n.* **1.** A tool used for turning screws. **2.** A cocktail of vodka and orange juice.

screw•y (skrōō′ē) ► *adj.* **-i•er, -i•est** *Slang* **1.** Eccentric; crazy. **2.** Ludicrously odd.

scrib•ble (skrĭb′əl) ► *v.* **-bled, -bling.** To write hastily or carelessly. [< Lat. *scrībere*, write.] —**scrib′ble** *n.* —**scrib′bler** *n.*

scribe (skrīb) ► *n.* **1.** A public clerk. **2.** A professional copyist of manuscripts. **3.** A writer or journalist. [< LLat. *scrība* < Lat. *scrībere*, write.] —**scrib′al** *adj.*

scrim•mage (skrĭm′ĭj) ► *n.* **1.** *Football* The contest between two teams from the time the ball is snapped until it is declared dead. **2.** *Sports* A practice game. **3.** A rough-and-tumble struggle; tussle. [ME < *scrimish*, SKIRMISH.] —**scrim′mage** *v.*

scrimp (skrĭmp) ► *v.* To economize severely. [Perh. of Scand. orig.] —**scrimp′er** *n.*

scrim•shaw (skrĭm′shô′) ► *n., pl.* **-shaw** or **-shaws 1.** The art of carving on whalebone or whale ivory. **2.** An article made in this way. [?]

scrip[1] (skrĭp) ► *n.* Paper money issued for temporary emergency use. [Poss. < SCRIPT.]

scrip[2] (skrĭp) ► *n.* A provisional certificate entitling the holder to a fractional share of stock or of other property. [< *subscription receipt*, receipt for a portion of a loan.]

script (skrĭpt) ► *n.* **1a.** Handwriting. **b.** A style of writing in cursive. **2.** The text of a play, broadcast, or movie. **3.** *Comp. Sci.* A simple program, esp. in an application's proprietary language. ► *v.* To prepare (a text) for filming or broadcasting. [< Lat. *scrīptum*.] —**script′writ′er** *n.* —**script′writ′ing** *n.*

Scrip•ture (skrĭp′chər) ► *n.* **1a.** A sacred writing or book. **b.** A passage from such a writing or book. **2.** often **Scriptures** The Bible. **3. scripture** An authoritative statement. [< Lat. *scrīptūra*, writing.] —**Scrip′tur•al, scrip′tur•al** *adj.*

scriv•en•er (skrĭv′ə-nər, skrĭv′nər) ► *n.* A scribe or author. [< OFr. *escrivein*.]

scrod (skrŏd) ► *n., pl.* **scrod.** A young cod or haddock. [Poss. < obsolete Du. *schrood*, shred.]

scroll (skrōl) ► *n.* **1.** A roll, as of papyrus, used esp. for writing a document. **2.** Ornamentation that resembles a scroll. **3.** *Mus.* The curved head on an instrument, esp. a violin. ► *v. Comp. Sci.* To cause displayed text or graphics to move up, down, or across the screen. [< OFr. *escroue*, strip of parchment.]

Scrooge also **scrooge** (skrōōj) ► *n.* A mean-spirited miserly person; skinflint. [After Ebenezer *Scrooge*, a character in Dickens's *A Christmas Carol*.]

scro•tum (skrō′təm) ► *n., pl.* **-ta** (-tə) or **-tums.** The external sac of skin enclosing the testes. [Lat. *scrōtum*.] —**scro′tal** (skrōt′l) *adj.*

scroll
of a violin

scrounge (skrounj) ► *v.* **scrounged, scroung•ing** *Slang* **1.** To beg; mooch. **2.** To obtain by salvaging or foraging. [< dial. *scrunge*, steal.] —**scroung′er** *n.*

scrub[1] (skrŭb) ► *v.* **scrubbed, scrub•bing 1.** To rub hard in order to clean. **2.** To clean or wash something by hard rubbing. **3.** *Slang* To cancel. [< MDu. *schrobben*.] —**scrub** *n.* —**scrub′ber** *n.*

scrub[2] (skrŭb) ► *n.* **1.** A growth of stunted vegetation. **2.** An undersized, poorly developed plant or animal. **3.** *Sports* A player not on the first team. [ME.] —**scrub′by** *adj.*

scruff (skrŭf) ► *n.* The back of the neck; the nape. [< dial. *scuff*.]

scruff•y (skrŭf′ē) ► *adj.* **-i•er, -i•est.** Shabby; untidy. [< obsolete *scruff*, SCURF.] —**scruff′i•ly** *adv.* —**scruff′i•ness** *n.*

scrump•tious (skrŭmp′shəs) ► *adj.* Delicious; delectable. [Perh. < SUMPTUOUS.]

scrunch (skrŭnch, skrōōnch) ► *v.* **1.** To crush or crunch. **2.** To hunch. **3.** To make a crunching sound. [< CRUNCH.] —**scrunch** *n.*

scru•ple (skrōō′pəl) ► *n.* **1.** An uneasy feeling arising from conscience or principle. **2.** A unit of apothecary weight equal to about 1.3 grams, or 20 grains. [< Lat. *scrūpus*, rough stone.] —**scru′ple** *v.*

scru•pu•lous (skrōō′pyə-ləs) ► *adj.* **1.** Conscientious; painstaking. **2.** Having scruples; principled. —**scru′pu•los′i•ty** (-lŏs′ĭ-tē), **scru′pu•lous•ness** *n.* —**scru′pu•lous•ly** *adv.*

scru•ti•nize (skrōōt′n-īz′) ► *v.* **-nized, -niz•ing.** To examine carefully.

scru•ti•ny (skrōōt′n-ē) ► *n., pl.* **-nies.** A close, careful examination. [< Lat. *scrūtinium*.]

SCSI ► *abbr.* small computer system interface

scu•ba (skōō′bə) ► *n.* An apparatus containing compressed air and used for breathing under water. [*s(elf-)c(ontained) u(nderwater) b(reathing) a(pparatus)*.]

scud (skŭd) ► *v.* **scud•ded, scud•ding.** To skim along swiftly and easily: *dark clouds scudding by.* ► *n.* Wind-driven clouds, mist, or rain. [Poss. < ME *scut*, rabbit.]

scuff (skŭf) ► *v.* **1.** To scrape with the feet. **2.** To scrape and roughen the surface of. ► *n.* **1.** The act or sound of scuffing. **2.** A flat, backless slipper. [Prob. of Scand. orig.]

scuf•fle (skŭf′əl) ► *v.* **-fled, -fling 1.** To fight confusedly at close quarters. **2.** To shuffle. ► *n.* A disorderly struggle at close quarters. [Prob. < SCUFF.] —**scuf′fler** *n.*

scull (skŭl) ► *n.* **1.** An oar used for rowing a boat from the stern. **2.** One of a pair of short-handled oars used by a single rower. **3.** A small light boat for racing. [ME *sculle.*] —**scull** *v.* —**scull′er** *n.*

scul•ler•y (skŭl′ə-rē) ►*n., pl.* **-ies.** A room adjoining a kitchen for dishwashing and other chores. [< OFr. *escuele,* dish.]

sculpt (skŭlpt) ►*v.* To sculpture. [< Lat. *sculpere, sculpt-,* carve.]

sculp•tor (skŭlp′tər) ►*n.* One who sculptures.

sculp•tress (skŭlp′trĭs) ►*n.* A woman who sculptures. See Usage Note at **-ess.**

sculp•ture (skŭlp′chər) ►*n.* **1.** The art or practice of shaping three-dimensional figures or forms, as by chiseling marble, modeling clay, or casting in metal. **2.** A work of art created by sculpture. ►*v.* **-tured, -tur•ing 1.** To fashion (e.g., stone or clay) into sculpture. **2.** To represent in sculpture. **3.** To ornament with sculpture. [< Lat. *sculptūra.*] —**sculp′tur•al** *adj.*

scum (skŭm) ►*n.* **1.** A filmy layer of impure matter on the surface of a liquid. **2.** Refuse or worthless matter. **3.** *Slang* A worthless or disreputable person or element of society. [< MDu. *schūm.*] —**scum′my** *adj.*

scup•per (skŭp′ər) ►*n.* A deck-level opening in the side of a ship to allow water to run off. [ME *scoper.*]

scurf (skûrf) ►*n.* Scaly or shredded dry skin, such as dandruff. [ME, prob. of Scand. orig.] —**scurf′i•ness** *n.* —**scurf′y** *adj.*

scur•ri•lous (skûr′ə-ləs, skŭr′-) ►*adj.* Vulgar; abusive. [< Lat. *scurrīlis,* jeering.] —**scur′ri•lous•ly** *adv.* —**scur•ril′i•ty** (skə-rĭl′ĭ-tē), **scur′ri•lous•ness** *n.*

scur•ry (skûr′ē, skŭr′ē) ►*v.* **-ried, -ry•ing 1.** To scamper. **2.** To flurry or swirl about. [Prob. < *hurry-scurry.*]

scur•vy (skûr′vē) ►*n.* A disease caused by deficiency of vitamin C, marked by bleeding gums, subcutaneous bleeding, and weakness. ►*adj.* **-vi•er, -vi•est.** Contemptible. [< *scurf.*] —**scur′vi•ness** *n.*

scut•tle¹ (skŭt′l) ►*n.* A small hatch in a ship's deck or hull. ►*v.* **-tled, -tling 1.** To sink (a ship) by cutting or opening holes in the hull. **2.** To scrap; discard. [< OFr. *escoutille.*]

scut•tle² (skŭt′l) ►*n.* A metal pail for carrying coal. [< Lat. *scutella,* dish.]

scut•tle³ (skŭt′l) ►*v.* **-tled, -tling.** To run hastily; scurry. [ME *scottlen.*] —**scut′tle** *n.*

scut•tle•butt (skŭt′l-bŭt′) ►*n.* *Slang* Gossip; rumor. [SCUTTLE¹ + *butt,* cask.]

scythe (sīth) ►*n.* A tool with a long curved blade and a bent handle, used for mowing or reaping. [< OE *sīthe.*] —**scythe** *v.*

Scyth•i•a (sĭth′ē-ə, sĭth′-) An ancient region of SW Asia and SE Europe. —**Scyth′i•an** *adj.* & *n.*

SD ►*abbr.* **1.** or **S.D.** South Dakota **2.** special delivery **3.** standard deviation

Se ► The symbol for the element **selenium.**

SE ►*abbr.* **1.** southeast **2.** southeastern

sea (sē) ►*n.* **1a.** The continuous body of salt water covering most of the earth's surface. **b.** A tract of water within an ocean. **c.** A large body of water completely or partially enclosed by land. **2.** The condition of the ocean's surface: *a high sea.* **3.** Something that suggests the ocean in its vastness: *a sea of controversy.* —***idiom:* at sea 1.** On the ocean. **2.** At a loss; perplexed. [< OE *sǣ.*]

sea anemone ►*n.* Any of various marine organisms with a flexible cylindrical body and numerous tentacles.

sea anemone
white-spotted rose anemone

sea•board (sē′bôrd′, -bōrd′) ►*n.* **1.** A seacoast. **2.** Land near the sea. [SEA + obsolete *board,* border.]

sea•bor•gi•um (sē-bôr′gē-əm) ►*n.* *Symbol* **Sg** A synthetic radioactive element. At. no. 106. See table at **element.** [After Glenn Theodore *Seaborg* (1912–1999).]

sea•coast (sē′kōst′) ►*n.* Land bordering the sea.

sea•far•er (sē′fâr′ər) ►*n.* A sailor. —**sea′far′ing** *adj.*

sea•food (sē′fo͞od′) ►*n.* Edible fish or shellfish from the sea.

sea•go•ing (sē′gō′ĭng) ►*adj.* Made or used for ocean voyages.

sea•gull also **sea gull** (sē′gŭl′) ►*n.* A gull, esp. one found near coastal areas.

sea horse ►*n.* A small marine fish with a prehensile tail, a horselike head, and a body covered with bony plates.

seal¹ (sēl) ►*n.* **1a.** A die or signet with a raised or incised emblem used to stamp an impression on a substance such as wax or lead. **b.** The impression so made. **c.** A small disk or wafer bearing such an imprint and affixed to a document to prove authenticity or to secure it. **2.** Something that authenticates or confirms. **3.** A sealant. **4.** An airtight closure. **5.** A small decorative paper sticker. ►*v.* **1.** To affix a seal to, esp. in order to prove authenticity or attest to accuracy or quality. **2a.** To close with or as if with a seal. **b.** To apply sealant to. **3.** To determine irrevocably: *His fate was sealed.* [< Lat. *sigillum.*] —**seal′er** *n.*

seal² (sēl) ►*n.* **1.** Any of various aquatic mammals with a sleek, torpedo-shaped body and limbs in the form of flippers. **2.** The pelt or fur of a seal. ►*v.* To hunt seals. [< OE *seolh.*] —**seal′er** *n.*

sea-lane (sē′lān′) ►*n.* A sea route.

seal•ant (sē′lənt) ►*n.* A substance used to seal a surface to prevent passage of a liquid or gas.

sea level ►*n.* The level of the ocean's surface, esp. the level halfway between mean high and low tide.

sea lion ►*n.* A large seal of the N Pacific with relatively long neck and limbs.

seam (sēm) ►*n.* **1a.** A line formed by sewing together two pieces of material. **b.** A similar line, ridge, or groove. **2.** A line across a surface, as a crack or wrinkle. **3.** A thin layer or stratum, as of coal. ►*v.* **1.** To join with or as if with a seam. **2.** To mark with a wrinkle or crack: *a face seamed with age.* [< OE *sēam.*]

sea•man (sē′mən) ►*n.* **1.** A sailor. **2.** Any of

the three lowest ranks in the US Navy or Coast Guard.

sea•man•ship (sē′mən-shĭp′) ►*n.* Skill in navigating or managing a boat or ship.

seam•stress (sēm′strĭs) ►*n.* A woman who sews, esp. as an occupation.

seam•y (sē′mē) ►*adj.* **-i•er, -i•est 1.** Sordid; base. **2.** Having a seam. —**seam′i•ness** *n.*

sé•ance (sā′äns′) ►*n.* A meeting of people to receive spiritualistic messages. [< OFr. *seoir*, sit < Lat. *sedēre*.]

sea otter ►*n.* A large marine otter of N Pacific coastal waters.

sea•plane (sē′plān′) ►*n.* An aircraft equipped with floats for landing on or taking off from water.

sea•port (sē′pôrt′, -pōrt′) ►*n.* A port with facilities for seagoing ships.

sea power ►*n.* **1.** A nation having significant naval strength. **2.** Naval strength.

sea•quake (sē′kwāk′) ►*n.* An earthquake originating under the sea floor.

sear[1] (sîr) ►*v.* **1.** To scorch or burn the surface of. **2.** To wither or parch. [< OE *sēarian*.]

sear[2] (sîr) ►*adj.* Var. of **sere.**

search (sûrch) ►*v.* **1.** To make a thorough examination of in order to find something; explore. **2.** To look into or investigate; probe: *search one's conscience.* **3.** *Law* To make a thorough check of: *search a title.* [< Lat. *circāre*, go around.] —**search** *n.* —**search′er** *n.*

search engine ►*n.* A software program that searches a database for information about specified terms.

search•light (sûrch′līt′) ►*n.* **1.** A powerful light source with a reflector for projecting a high-intensity beam. **2.** The beam itself.

search warrant ►*n.* A warrant giving legal authorization for a search.

sea•scape (sē′skāp′) ►*n.* A view of the sea. [SEA + (LAND)SCAPE.]

sea•shell (sē′shĕl′) ►*n.* The shell of a marine mollusk.

sea•shore (sē′shôr′, -shōr′) ►*n.* Land by the sea.

sea•sick•ness (sē′sĭk′nĭs) ►*n.* Nausea and dizziness resulting from the motion of a vessel at sea. —**sea′sick′** *adj.*

sea•side (sē′sīd′) ►*n.* The seashore.

sea snake ►*n.* Any of various venomous tropical saltwater snakes.

sea•son (sē′zən) ►*n.* **1a.** One of the four natural divisions of the year, spring, summer, fall, and winter. **b.** The two divisions of the year, rainy and dry, in some tropical regions. **2.** A recurrent period marked by certain occurrences or festivities: *the holiday season; tomato season.* ►*v.* **1.** To enhance the flavor of (food) by adding salt or other flavorings. **2.** To add zest or interest to. **3.** To treat or dry (e.g., lumber) until usable; cure. **4.** To render competent through experience. **5.** To inure. See Syns at **harden.** [< Lat. *satiō*, act of sowing.]

sea•son•a•ble (sē′zə-nə-bəl) ►*adj.* **1.** In keeping with the time or the season. **2.** Occurring at the proper time. See Usage Note at **seasonal.** —**sea′son•a•bly** *adv.*

sea•son•al (sē′zə-nəl) ►*adj.* Of or dependent on a particular season. —**sea′son•al•ly** *adv.*

Usage: *Seasonal* applies to what depends on or is controlled by the season of the year: *a seasonal rise in employment.* The closely related word *seasonable* applies to what is appropriate to the season (*seasonable clothing*) or timely (*seasonable intervention in the dispute*).

sea•son•ing (sē′zə-nĭng) ►*n.* Something used to flavor food.

season ticket ►*n.* A ticket good for a specified period, as for a series of events.

seat (sēt) ►*n.* **1.** Something, such as a chair or bench, on which one may sit. **2.** A place in which one may sit. **3.** The part on which one rests in sitting: *a bicycle seat.* **4a.** The buttocks. **b.** The part of a garment covering the buttocks. **5a.** The place where something is located or based: *the seat of intelligence.* **b.** A center of authority; capital. See Syns at **center. 6.** Membership, as in a legislature. ►*v.* **1.** To place in or on a seat. **2.** To have or provide seats for. [< ON *sæti*.]

seat belt ►*n.* A safety strap that holds a person securely in a seat, as in a car.

seat•ing (sē′tĭng) ►*n.* **1.** The act of providing with seats. **2.** The seats so provided.

SEATO ►*abbr.* Southeast Asia Treaty Organization

Se•at•tle (sē-ăt′l) A city of W-central WA on Puget Sound. Pop. 516,259.

sea urchin ►*n.* Any of various marine organisms having a spiny globular shell.

sea•wall also **sea wall** (sē′wôl′) ►*n.* An embankment to prevent erosion of a shoreline.

sea•ward (sē′wərd) ►*adv. & adj.* Toward or at the sea. —**sea′wards** (-wərdz) *adv.*

sea•wa•ter (sē′wô′tər, -wŏt′ər) ►*n.* The salt water of the ocean.

sea•way (sē′wā′) ►*n.* **1.** A sea route. **2.** An inland waterway for ocean shipping.

sea•weed (sē′wēd′) ►*n.* Any of numerous marine algae, such as kelp or gulfweed.

sea•wor•thy (sē′wûr′*th*ē) ►*adj.* Fit to traverse the seas. —**sea′wor′thi•ness** *n.*

se•ba•ceous (sĭ-bā′shəs) ►*adj.* *Physiol.* Of or secreting oil. [< Lat. *sēbum*, tallow.]

SEbE ►*abbr.* southeast by east

seb•or•rhe•a also **seb•or•rhoe•a** (sĕb′ə-rē′ə) ►*n.* A disease of the sebaceous glands of the skin marked by excessive secretion of oil. [Lat. *sēbum*, fat, tallow + -RRHEA.] —**seb′or•rhe′ic** *adj.*

SEbS ►*abbr.* southeast by south

sec[1] (sĕk) ►*adj.* Dry. Used of wines. [Fr.]

sec[2] ►*abbr.* secant

SEC ►*abbr.* Securities and Exchange Commission

sec. ►*abbr.* **1.** second **2.** secretary **3.** section

se•cant (sē′kănt′, -kənt) ►*n.* The reciprocal of the cosine of an angle in a right triangle. [< Lat. *secāre*, cut.]

se•cede (sĭ-sēd′) ►*v.* **-ced•ed, -ced•ing.** To withdraw formally from membership in an organization, association, or alliance. [Lat. *sēcēdere*, withdraw.]

se•ces•sion (sĭ-sĕsh′ən) ►*n.* The act of seceding. [Lat. *sēcessiō*.] —**se•ces′sion•ism** *n.* —**se•ces′sion•ist** *n.*

se•clude (sĭ-klo͞od′) ►*v.* **-clud•ed, -clud•ing 1.** To set apart from others. See Syns at **isolate. 2.** To screen from view. [< Lat. *sēclūdere*, shut away.] —**se•clu′sion** *n.* —**se•clu′sive** *adj.*

sec•ond[1] (sĕk′ənd) ►*n.* **1.** A unit of time equal to $\frac{1}{60}$ of a minute. **2.** A brief interval of time. **3.** *Math.* A unit of angular measure equal to $\frac{1}{60}$ of a minute. [< Med.Lat. *(pars minūta) secunda,* second (small part).]

sec•ond² (sĕk′ənd) ▶*adj.* **1.** Coming next after the first. **2.** Inferior to another; subordinate. ▶*n.* **1a.** The ordinal number matching the number 2 in a series. **b.** One of two equal parts. **2.** One that is next after the first. **3.** often **seconds** Merchandise of inferior quality. **4.** The official attendant of a contestant in a duel or boxing match. See Syns at **assistant. 5.** The second lowest forward gear in a motor vehicle. ▶*v.* **1.** To attend as an aide or assistant. **2.** To promote or encourage. **3.** To endorse (a motion or nomination). [< Lat. *secundus.*] —**sec′ond, sec′ond•ly** *adv.*

sec•ond•ar•y (sĕk′ən-dĕr′ē) ▶*adj.* **1a.** Of the second rank; not primary. **b.** Inferior; minor. **2.** Derived from what is original: *a secondary source.* **3.** Of or relating to education between elementary school and college. ▶*n., pl.* **-ies.** One that acts in an auxiliary or subordinate capacity. —**sec′ond•ar′i•ly** (-dâr′ə-lē) *adv.* —**sec′ond•ar′i•ness** *n.*

secondary sex characteristic ▶*n.* Any of various genetically transmitted physiological or behavioral characteristics, such as growth of facial hair or breast development, that differentiate between the sexes without having a direct reproductive function.

second base ▶*n. Baseball* The 2nd base to be reached by a runner. —**second baseman** *n.*

second class ▶*n.* **1.** The class or category ranking below the first or best. **2.** A class of mail consisting of newspapers and periodicals. —**sec′ond-class′** *adj.*

sec•ond-de•gree burn (sĕk′ənd-dĭ-grē′) ▶*n.* A burn that blisters the skin.

second fiddle ▶*n. Informal* A secondary role.

sec•ond-gen•er•a•tion (sĕk′ənd-jĕn′ə-rā′shən) ▶*adj.* Of or relating to a person or persons whose parents are first-generation immigrants or citizens.

sec•ond-guess (sĕk′ənd-gĕs′) ▶*v.* **1.** To criticize (a decision) after an outcome is known. **2.** To outguess. —**sec′ond-guess′er** *n.*

sec•ond•hand (sĕk′ənd-hănd′) ▶*adj.* **1.** Previously used; not new. **2.** Dealing in used merchandise. **3.** Not primary or original. —**sec′ond•hand′** *adv.*

second lieutenant ▶*n.* The lowest commissioned rank, as in the US Army.

second nature ▶*n.* A deeply ingrained behavior or trait.

second person ▶*n.* The form of a pronoun or verb used in referring to the person addressed.

sec•ond-rate (sĕk′ənd-rāt′) ▶*adj.* Inferior.

sec•ond-string (sĕk′ənd-strĭng′) ▶*adj.* Of or being a substitute, as on a sports team.

second thought ▶*n.* A reconsideration of a decision or opinion.

second wind (wĭnd) ▶*n.* Restored energy or strength.

se•cre•cy (sē′krĭ-sē) ▶*n., pl.* **-cies 1.** The quality or condition of being secret. **2.** The ability or habit of keeping secrets.

se•cret (sē′krĭt) ▶*adj.* **1.** Concealed from knowledge or view. **2.** Operating covertly: *a secret agent.* **3.** Beyond ordinary understanding; mysterious. ▶*n.* **1.** Something concealed from others. **2.** Something beyond understanding or explanation; mystery. [< Lat. *sēcrētus.*] —**se′cret•ly** *adv.*

sec•re•tar•i•at (sĕk′rĭ-târ′ē-ĭt) ▶*n.* **1.** The department administered by a governmental secretary. **2.** The position of a governmental secretary. [Fr. *secrétariat.*]

sec•re•tar•y (sĕk′rĭ-tĕr′ē) ▶*n., pl.* **-ies 1.** One employed to handle correspondence and do clerical work. **2.** An officer in charge of records, minutes of meetings, and correspondence, as for a company. **3.** An official presiding over an administrative department of state. **4.** A desk with a small bookcase on top. [< Med.Lat. *sēcrētārius,* confidential officer.] —**sec′re•tar′i•al** (-târ′ē-əl) *adj.*

sec•re•tar•y-gen•er•al (sĕk′rĭ-tĕr′ē-jĕn′ər-əl) ▶*n., pl.* **sec•re•tar•ies-gen•er•al.** A principal executive officer, as in the United Nations.

se•crete¹ (sĭ-krēt′) ▶*v.* **-cret•ed, -cret•ing.** To generate and separate (a substance) from cells or bodily fluids. [< Lat. *sēcernere, sēcrēt-,* set aside.] —**se•cre′tion** *n.* —**se•cre′tion•ar′y** *adj.* —**se•cre′to•ry** *adj.*

se•crete² (sĭ-krēt′) ▶*v.* **-cret•ed, -cret•ing.** To conceal; hide. [Prob. < SECRET.] —**se•cre′tion** *n.*

se•cre•tive (sē′krĭ-tĭv, sĭ-krē′tĭv) ▶*adj.* Inclined to secrecy. —**se′cre•tive•ly** *adv.* —**se′cre•tive•ness** *n.*

secret service ▶*n.* **1.** A government agency engaged in intelligence-gathering activities. **2. Secret Service** A branch of the US Treasury Department concerned esp. with protection of the President.

sect (sĕkt) ▶*n.* **1.** A group of people forming a distinct unit within a larger group by virtue of common beliefs. **2.** A religious body, esp. one that has separated from a larger denomination. [< Lat. *sequī, sect-,* follow.]

–sect ▶*suff.* To cut; divide: *trisect.* [< Lat. *secāre, sect-,* cut.]

sec•tar•i•an (sĕk-târ′ē-ən) ▶*adj.* **1.** Of a sect. **2.** Partisan. **3.** Narrow-minded; parochial. ▶*n.* **1.** A member of a sect. **2.** One who is narrow-minded. —**sec•tar′i•an•ism** *n.*

sec•tion (sĕk′shən) ▶*n.* **1.** One of several components; a piece or part. **2.** Representation of a solid object as it would appear if cut by an intersecting plane, so that the internal structure is displayed. ▶*v.* To divide into parts. [< Lat. *secāre, sect-,* cut.]

sec•tion•al (sĕk′shə-nəl) ▶*adj.* **1.** Of or relating to a particular district. **2.** Composed of or divided into component sections. —**sec′tion•al•ly** *adv.*

sec•tion•al•ism (sĕk′shə-nə-lĭz′əm) ▶*n.* Excessive devotion to local interests and customs. —**sec′tion•al•ist** *n.*

sec•tor (sĕk′tər, -tôr′) ▶*n.* **1.** *Math.* The part of a circle bounded by two radii and the included arc. **2.** A military zone of action. **3.** A division, as of a city or economy. [< Lat., cutter.] —**sec•to′ri•al** (-tôr′ē-əl, -tōr′-) *adj.*

sec•u•lar (sĕk′yə-lər) ▶*adj.* **1.** Worldly rather than spiritual. **2.** Not related to religion. **3.** *Eccles.* Not belonging to a religious order. Used of the clergy. [< LLat. *saeculāris.*] —**sec′u•lar′i•ty** (-lăr′ĭ-tē) *n.* —**sec′u•lar•ly** *adv.*

sec•u•lar•ize (sĕk′yə-lə-rīz′) ▶*v.* **-ized, -iz•ing 1.** To transfer from ecclesiastical to civil use or ownership. **2.** To make secular. —**sec′u•lar•i•za′tion** *n.*

se•cure (sĭ-kyo͝or′) ► *adj.* **-cur•er, -cur•est 1.** Free from danger; safe. **2.** Free from fear or doubt. **3.** Reliable; dependable. **4.** Assured; certain. ► *v.* **-cured, -cur•ing 1.** To guard from danger or risk of loss. **2.** To make firm. See Syns at **fasten. 3.** To make certain; guarantee. **4.** To acquire. [Lat. *sēcūrus.*] —**se•cure′ly** *adv.* —**se•cure′ment** *n.*

se•cu•ri•ty (sĭ-kyo͝or′ĭ-tē) ► *n., pl.* **-ties 1.** Safety. **2.** Confidence. **3.** Something that gives or assures safety. **4.** Something deposited or given as assurance of the fulfillment of an obligation; pledge. **5.** A stock or bond. **6.** Measures adopted to guard against attack, theft, or disclosure.

se•dan (sĭ-dăn′) ► *n.* **1.** A closed car with two or four doors and a front and rear seat. **2.** also **sedan chair** An enclosed chair carried on poles by two bearers. [?]

se•date[1] (sĭ-dāt′) ► *adj.* Serenely deliberate in character or manner. [< Lat. *sēdāre*, settle.] —**se•date′ly** *adv.* —**se•date′ness** *n.*

se•date[2] (sĭ-dāt′) ► *v.* **-dat•ed, -dat•ing.** To administer a sedative to. [< SEDATIVE.] —**se•da′tion** *n.*

sed•a•tive (sĕd′ə-tĭv) ► *adj.* Having a soothing, calming, or tranquilizing effect. ► *n.* A sedative drug. [< Lat. *sēdāre*, settle, calm.]

sed•en•tar•y (sĕd′n-tĕr′ē) ► *adj.* Marked by or requiring little physical activity. [< Lat. *sedēns*, pr.part. of *sedēre*, sit.]

Se•der (sā′dər) ► *n. Judaism* The feast commemorating the exodus of the Jews from Egypt, celebrated on the first night or the first two nights of Passover. [Heb. *sēder.*]

sedge (sĕj) ► *n.* Any of numerous grasslike plants found esp. in wet places. [< OE *secg.*]

sed•i•ment (sĕd′ə-mənt) ► *n.* Material that settles to the bottom of a liquid; lees. [Lat. *sedimentum*, settling < *sedēre*, settle.] —**sed′i•men•ta′tion** *n.*

sed•i•men•ta•ry (sĕd′ə-mĕn′tə-rē, -mĕn′trē) ► *adj.* **1.** Of or resembling sediment. **2.** *Geol.* Of rocks formed from sediment.

se•di•tion (sĭ-dĭsh′ən) ► *n.* **1.** Conduct or language inciting rebellion against the state. **2.** Insurrection; rebellion. [< Lat. *sēditiō*, faction.] —**se•di′tious** *adj.* —**se•di′tious•ly** *adv.* —**se•di′tious•ness** *n.*

se•duce (sĭ-do͞os′, -dyo͞os′) ► *v.* **-duced, -duc•ing 1.** To lead away from proper conduct. **2.** To induce to engage in sex. **3.** To entice or beguile; win over. [< Lat. *sēdūcere*, lead away.] —**se•duc′er** *n.* —**se•duc′tion** (-dŭk′shən) *n.* —**se•duc′tive** *adj.*

sed•u•lous (sĕj′ə-ləs) ► *adj.* Persevering; assiduous. [< Lat. *sēdulus.*] —**sed′u•lous•ly** *adv.* —**sed′u•lous•ness** *n.*

see[1] (sē) ► *v.* **saw** (sô), **seen** (sēn), **see•ing 1.** To perceive with the eye. **2.** To understand; comprehend. **3.** To regard; view. **4.** To believe possible; imagine. **5.** To foresee. **6.** To undergo. **7.** To find out; ascertain. **8.** To take note of. **9.** To meet regularly, as in dating. **10a.** To visit socially. **b.** To visit for consultation: *see a doctor.* **11.** To escort; attend: *I'll see you home.* **12.** To make sure: *Please see that it gets done.* —***phrasal verb:*** **see through** To understand the true character of. [< OE *sēon.*]

see[2] (sē) ► *n.* The seat or jurisdiction of a bishop. [< Lat. *sēdēs*, seat.]

seed (sēd) ► *n., pl.* **seeds** or **seed 1.** A ripened plant ovule containing an embryo. **2.** Seeds collectively. **3.** A source or germ. **4.** Offspring. ► *v.* **1.** To plant seeds in. **2.** To remove seeds from. —***idiom:*** **go** (or **run**) **to seed 1.** To pass into the seed-bearing stage. **2.** To deteriorate. [< OE *sǣd.*]

seed•ling (sēd′lĭng) ► *n.* A young plant grown from a seed.

seed•pod (sēd′pŏd′) ► *n.* See **pod**[1] 1.

seed•y (sē′dē) ► *adj.* **-i•er, -i•est 1.** Having many seeds. **2.** Shabby; run-down. —**seed′i•ly** *adv.* —**seed′i•ness** *n.*

see•ing (sē′ĭng) ► *conj.* Inasmuch as.

seek (sēk) ► *v.* **sought** (sôt), **seek•ing 1.** To search for. **2.** To try to obtain or reach. **3.** To try; endeavor: *seek to do good.* [< OE *sēcan.*] —**seek′er** *n.*

seem (sēm) ► *v.* **1.** To give the impression of being. **2.** To appear to one's own mind. **3.** To appear to be true or evident. **4.** To appear to exist. [< ON *sœma*, conform to.]

Syns: *seem, appear, look* **v.**

seem•ing (sē′mĭng) ► *adj.* Apparent; ostensible. —**seem′ing** *n.* —**seem′ing•ly** *adv.*

seem•ly (sēm′lē) ► *adj.* **-li•er, -li•est 1.** Proper; suitable. **2.** Of pleasing appearance. [< ON *sœmiligr.*] —**seem′li•ness** *n.*

seen (sēn) ► *v.* P.part. of **see**[1].

seep (sēp) ► *v.* **1.** To pass slowly through small openings. **2.** To enter, depart, or spread gradually. [< dial. *sipe.*] —**seep′age** *n.*

seer (sîr) ► *n.* **1.** A clairvoyant. **2.** A prophet.

seer•suck•er (sîr′sŭk′ər) ► *n.* A light thin fabric with a crinkled surface and a usu. striped pattern. [< Pers. *shīroshakar*, milk and sugar.]

see•saw (sē′sô′) ► *n.* **1.** A long plank balanced on a central fulcrum so that with a person riding on each end, one end goes up as the other goes down. **2.** The game of riding a seesaw. **3.** A back-and-forth or up-and-down movement. [< SAW[1].] —**see′saw′** *v.*

seethe (sē*th*) ► *v.* **seethed, seeth•ing 1.** To churn and foam as if boiling. **2.** To be violently agitated. [< OE *sēothan.*]

seg•ment (sĕg′mənt) ► *n.* A part into which something can be divided; section. ► *v.* (sĕg-mĕnt′). To divide into segments. [Lat. *segmentum.*] —**seg•men′tal** *adj.* —**seg′men•ta′tion** *n.*

seg•re•gate (sĕg′rĭ-gāt′) ► *v.* **-gat•ed, -gat•ing 1.** To separate or isolate from others or from a main body or group. See Syns at **isolate. 2.** To impose the separation of (a race or class) from the rest of society. [Lat. *sēgregāre.*] —**seg′re•ga′tion** *n.* —**seg′re•ga′tion•ist** *adj. & n.* —**seg′re•ga′tor** *n.*

se•gue (sĕg′wā′, sā′gwā′) ► *v.* **-gued, -gue•ing 1.** *Mus.* To make a transition directly from one section or theme to another. **2.** To move smoothly from one situation or element to another. [< Ital., there follows.]

seign•ior (sān-yôr′, sān′yôr′) ► *n.* A feudal lord. [< VLat. **senior.*] —**sei•gnio′ri•al** *adj.*

seine (sān) ► *n.* A large fishing net made to hang vertically in the water by weights and floats. ► *v.* **seined, sein•ing.** To fish with a seine. [< Gk. *sagēnē.*] —**sein′er** *n.*

Seine (sān, sĕn) A river of N France flowing about 772 km (480 mi) to the English Channel near Le Havre.

seis•mic (sīz′mĭk) ► *adj.* **1.** Of or caused by an earthquake. **2.** Earthshaking. —**seis′mi•cal•**

ly *adv.* —**seis•mic′i•ty** (-mīs′ĭ-tē) *n.*
seismo– or **seism–** ▸*pref.* Earthquake: *seismograph.* [< *seismos.*]
seis•mo•graph (sīz′mə-grăf′) ▸*n.* An instrument for automatically detecting and recording the intensity and duration of ground movements, esp. of earthquakes. —**seis•mog′ra•pher** (-mŏg′rə-fər) *n.* —**seis′mo•graph′ic** *adj.* —**seis•mog′ra•phy** *n.*
seis•mol•o•gy (sīz-mŏl′ə-jē) ▸*n.* The geophysical science of earthquakes and the mechanical properties of the earth. —**seis′mo•log′ic** (-mə-lŏj′ĭk), **seis′mo•log′i•cal** *adj.* —**seis•mol′o•gist** *n.*
seis•mom•e•ter (sīz-mŏm′ĭ-tər) ▸*n.* A detecting device that receives seismic impulses.
sei•tan (sā′tăn′) ▸*n.* A chewy, protein-rich food made from wheat gluten and used as a meat substitute. [?]
seize (sēz) ▸*v.* **seized, seiz•ing 1.** To grasp suddenly and forcibly. **2.** To have a sudden forceful effect on. **3.** To take into custody; confiscate. [< OFr. *seisir.*]
sei•zure (sē′zhər) ▸*n.* **1.** The act of seizing or being seized. **2.** A sudden attack or spasm, as in epilepsy or another disorder.
sel•dom (sĕl′dəm) ▸*adv.* Not often; rarely. [< OE *seldan.*] —**sel′dom•ness** *n.*
se•lect (sĭ-lĕkt′) ▸*v.* To choose from among several; pick out. ▸*adj.* **1.** Singled out; chosen. **2.** Of special quality; choice. [Lat. *sēligere, sēlēct-.*] —**se•lec′tive** *adj.* —**se•lec′tive•ly** *adv.* —**se•lec′tiv′i•ty** *n.* —**se•lect′ness** *n.* —**se•lec′tor** *n.*
se•lect•ee (sĭ-lĕk′tē′) ▸*n.* One selected.
se•lec•tion (sĭ-lĕk′shən) ▸*n.* **1a.** The act of selecting or the fact of being selected. **b.** One selected. **2.** A carefully chosen collection. **3.** A literary or musical text chosen for reading or performance. **4.** *Biol.* A process that favors survival and perpetuation of one organism over others.
selective service ▸*n.* A system for calling up people for compulsory military service.
se•lect•man (sĭ-lĕkt′măn′, -mən) ▸*n.* One of a board of town officers chosen annually in New England communities. See Usage Note at **man.**
se•lect•wom•an (sĭ-lĕkt′wo͝om′ən) ▸*n.* A woman who is a selectman. See Usage Note at **man.**
se•le•ni•um (sĭ-lē′nē-əm) ▸*n. Symbol* **Se** A nonmetallic element resembling sulfur, used as a semiconductor and in photocells. At. no. 34. See table at **element.** [< Gk. *selēnē*, moon.]
Se•leu•ci•a (sĭ-lo͞o′shē-ə, -shə) An ancient city of Mesopotamia SSE of Baghdad.
Se•leu•cid (sĭ-lo͞o′-sĭd). A Hellenistic dynasty ruling much of Asia Minor (312–64 B.C.). —**Se•leu′cid** *adj.*
self (sĕlf) ▸*n., pl.* **selves** (sĕlvz) **1.** One's total being. **2.** Individuality. **3.** One's own interests or advantage. **4.** *Immunol.* That which the immune system identifies as belonging to the body. ▸*pron.* Myself, yourself, himself, or herself. [< OE, selfsame.]
self– ▸*pref.* **1.** Oneself: *self-control.* **2.** Automatic; automatically: *self-loading.* [< OE.]
self-ab•sorbed (sĕlf′əb-sôrbd′, -zôrbd′) ▸*adj.* Excessively self-involved. —**self′-ab•sorp′tion** *n.*
self-ad•dressed (sĕlf′ə-drĕst′) ▸*adj.* Addressed to oneself.
self-ap•point•ed (sĕlf′ə-poin′tĭd) ▸*adj.* Designated by oneself.
self-as•ser•tion (sĕlf′ə-sûr′shən) ▸*n.* Determined advancement of one's own personality, wishes, or views. —**self′-as•ser′tive** *adj.* —**self-as•ser′tive•ness** *n.*
self-as•sured (sĕlf′ə-sho͝ord′) ▸*adj.* Confident and poised. —**self′-as•sur′ance** *n.*
self-cen•tered (sĕlf′sĕn′tərd) ▸*adj.* Engrossed in oneself; selfish. —**self′-cen′tered•ly** *adv.* —**self′-cen′tered•ness** *n.*
self-con•scious (sĕlf′kŏn′shəs) ▸*adj.* **1.** Aware of oneself as an individual. **2.** Socially

self′-a•ban′don•ment *n.*
self′-a•base′ment *n.*
self′-ab•sorp′tion *n.*
self′-a•buse′ *n.*
self′-act′ing *adj.*
self′-ac′tu•al•i•za′tion *n.*
self′-ac′tu•al•ize′ *v.*
self′-ad•min′is•ter *v.*
self′-ad•min′i•stra′ting *adj.*
self′-ag•gran′dize•ment *n.*
self′-a•nal′y•sis *n.*
self′-ap•prov′al *n.*
self′-ap•proved *adj.*
self′-ap•prov′ing *adj.*
self′-as•sert′ing *adj.*
self′•a•ware′ *adj.*
self′-a•ware′ness *n.*
self′-clean′ing *adj.*
self′-com•pla′cen•cy *n.*
self′-com•pla′cent *adj.*
self′-con′cept *n.*
self′-con•cep′tion *n.*
self′-con•cern′ *n.*
self′-con•cerned′ *adj.*
self′-con•duct′ed *adj.*
self′-con•fessed′ *adj.*
self′-con′fi•dence *n.*
self′-con′fi•dent *adj.*
self′-con•tent′ *adj.* & *n.*
self′-con′tra•dic′tion *n.*
self′-con′tra•dic′to•ry *adj.*
self′-cor•rect′ing *adj.*
self′-crit′i•cal *adj.*
self′-crit′i•cal•ly *adv.*
self′-crit′i•cism *n.*
self′-de•ceit′ *n.*
self′-de•ceived′ *adj.*
self′-de•ceiv′ing *adj.*
self′-de•cep′tion *n.*
self′-de•cep′tive *adj.*
self′-de•cep′tive•ly *adv.*
self′-de•feat′ing *adj.*
self′-de•fin′ing *adj.*
self′-def′i•ni′tion *n.*
self′-dep′re•cat′ing *adj.*
self′-dep′re•ca•to′ry *adj.*
self′-de•vel′op•ment *n.*
self′-di′ag•no′sis *n.*
self′-di•rect′ed *adj.*
self′-di•rect′ing *adj.*
self′-di•rec′tion *n.*
self′-dis•cov′er•y *n.*
self′-dis•trust′ *n.*
self′-ed′u•cat′ed *adj.*
self′-ed′u•ca′tion *n.*
self′-e•lect′ed *adj.*
self′-em•ployed′ *adj.*
self′-em•ploy′ment *n.*
self′-en•rich′ment *n.*
self′-e•val′u•a′tion *n.*
self′-ex•am′i•na′tion *n.*
self′-ex′ile *n.*
self′-ex′iled *adj.*
self′-ex•plain′ing *adj.*
self′-fer′tile *adj.*
self′-fer′til•ized′ *adj.*
self′-fer′til•iz′ing *adj.*

awkward or ill at ease. —**self′-con′scious•ly** *adv.* —**self′-con′scious•ness** *n.*

self-con•tained (sĕlf′kən-tānd′) ►*adj.* **1.** Complete in itself. **2a.** Self-sufficient. **b.** Reserved. —**self′-con•tain′ment** *n.*

self-con•trol (sĕlf′kən-trōl′) ►*n.* Control of one's emotions, desires, or actions. —**self′-con•trolled′** *adj.*

self-de•fense (sĕlf′dĭ-fĕns′) ►*n.* **1.** Defense of oneself, one's property, or one's reputation. **2.** *Law* The right to protect oneself against violence or threatened violence with whatever means reasonably necessary.

self-de•ni•al (sĕlf′dĭ-nī′əl) ►*n.* Sacrifice of one's own desires or interests. —**self′-de•ny′ing** *adj.* —**self′-de•ny′ing•ly** *adv.*

self-de•struct (sĕlf′dĭ-strŭkt′) ►*n.* A mechanism for causing a device to destroy itself. ►*v.* To destroy oneself or itself.

self-de•struc•tion (sĕlf′dĭ-strŭk′shən) ►*n.* The act of destroying oneself, esp. suicide. —**self′-de•struc′tive** *adj.* —**self′-de•struc′tive•ly** *adv.* —**self′-de•struc′tive•ness** *n.*

self-de•ter•mi•na•tion (sĕlf′dĭ-tûr′mə-nā′shən) ►*n.* **1.** Determination of one's course of action without compulsion. **2.** Freedom of the people to determine their political status; independence.

self-dis•ci•pline (sĕlf′dĭs′ə-plĭn) ►*n.* Training and control of oneself, usu. for personal improvement.

self-ef•fac•ing (sĕlf′ĭ-fā′sĭng) ►*adj.* Not drawing attention to oneself; modest. —**self′-ef•face′ment** *n.*

self-es•teem (sĕlf′ĭ-stēm′) ►*n.* Confidence; self-respect.

self-ev•i•dent (sĕlf′ĕv′ĭ-dənt) ►*adj.* Requiring no proof or explanation. —**self′-ev′i•dence** *n.* —**self′-ev′i•dent•ly** *adv.*

self-ex•plan•a•to•ry (sĕlf′ĭk-splăn′ə-tôr′ē, -tōr′ē) ►*adj.* Needing no explanation.

self-ex•pres•sion (sĕlf′ĭk-sprĕsh′ən) ►*n.* Expression of one's own personality, as through speech or art. —**self′-ex•pres′sive** *adj.*

self-fer•til•i•za•tion (sĕlf′fûr′tl-ĭ-zā′shən) ►*n.* Fertilization of a plant or animal by itself.

self-ful•fill•ing (sĕlf′fo͝ol-fĭl′ĭng) ►*adj.* **1.** Achieving fulfillment as a result of having been expected or foretold: *a self-fulfilling prophecy.* **2.** Achieving self-fulfillment.

self-ful•fill•ment (sĕlf′fo͝ol-fĭl′mənt) ►*n.* Fulfillment of one's goals and potential.

self-gov•ern•ment (sĕlf′gŭv′ərn-mənt) ►*n.* **1.** Political independence; autonomy. **2.** Democracy. —**self′-gov′erned** *adj.* —**self′-gov′ern•ing** *adj.*

self-hard•en•ing (sĕlf′här′dn-ĭng) ►*adj.* Of or relating to materials that harden without special treatment.

self-im•age (sĕlf′ĭm′ĭj) ►*n.* One's conception of oneself.

self-im•por•tance (sĕlf′ĭm-pôr′tns) ►*n.* Excessively high regard for one's own importance. —**self′-im•por′tant** *adj.* —**self′-im•por′tant•ly** *adv.*

self-im•posed (sĕlf′ĭm-pōzd′) ►*adj.* Imposed by oneself on oneself; voluntarily assumed.

self-in•crim•i•na•tion (sĕlf′ĭn-krĭm′ə-nā′shən) ►*n.* Incrimination of oneself, esp. by one's own testimony in a criminal prosecution. —**self′-in•crim′i•nat′ing** *adj.* —**self′-in•crim′i•na•to′ry** (-nə-tôr′ē, -tōr′ē) *adj.*

self-in•duced (sĕlf′ĭn-do͞ost′, -dyo͞ost′) ►*adj.* **1.** Induced by oneself. **2.** *Elect.* Produced by self-induction.

self-in•duc•tion (sĕlf′ĭn-dŭk′shən) ►*n.* The generation by a changing current of an electromotive force in the same circuit. —**self′-in•duc′tive** *adj.*

self-in•dul•gence (sĕlf′ĭn-dŭl′jəns) ►*n.* Excessive indulgence of one's own appetites and desires. —**self′-in•dul′gent** *adj.* —**self′-in•dul′gent•ly** *adv.*

self-in•ter•est (sĕlf′ĭn′trĭst, -ĭn′tər-ĭst) ►*n.* **1.** Selfish regard for one's own advantage or in-

self′-giv′ing *adj.*
self′-gov′ern•ing *adj.*
self′-grat′i•fi•ca′tion *n.*
self′-guid′ance *n.*
self′-hate′ *n.*
self′-ha′tred *n.*
self′-heal′ *v.*
self′-heal′ing *adj.*
self′-help′ *n.*
self′-hyp•no′sis *n.*
self′-i•den′ti•fy′ *v.*
self′-i•den′ti•ty *n.*
self′-im•prove′ment *n.*
self′-in•flict′ed *adj.*
self′-in•struct′ed *adj.*
self′-in•volved′ *adj.*
self′-in•volve′ment *n.*
self′-knowl′edge *n.*
self′-lim′it•ed *adj.*
self′-lim′it•ing *adj.*
self′-load′ing *adj.*
self′-loath′ing *n.*
self′-lock′ing *adj.*
self′-mas′ter•y *n.*
self′-med′i•ca′tion *n.*
self′-ob′ser•va′tion *n.*
self′-or•dain′ed *adj.*
self′-per•cep′tion *n.*
self′-per•pet′u•at′ing *adj.*
self′-por′trait *n.*
self′-pow′ered *adj.*
self′-pro•mot′er *n.*
self′-pro•mo′tion *n.*
self′-pro•pelled′ *adj.*
self′-pro•pul′sion *n.*
self′-pro•tec′tion *n.*
self′-pro•tec′tive *adj.*
self′-pro•tec′tive•ly *adv.*
self′-pub′lished *adj.*
self′-re•cord′ing *adj.*
self′-ref′er•en′tial•ly *adv.*
self′-re•flec′tion *n.*
self′-re•gard′ *n.*
self′-reg′u•lat′ing *adj.*
self′-reg•u•la′tion *n.*
self′-re•li′ance *n.*
self′-re•li′ant *adj.*
self′-rep′li•cat′ing *adj.*
self′-rep′li•ca′tion *n.*
self′-re•proach′ *n.*
self′-re•proach′ful *adj.*
self′-re•straint′ *n.*
self′-re•veal′ing *adj.*
self′-rev′e•la′tion *n.*
self′-rule′ *n.*
self′-scru′ti•ny *n.*
self′-seal′ing *adj.*
self′-stud′y *n.*
self′-sup•port′ *n.*
self′-sup•port′ing *adj.*
self′-sus•tain′ing *adj.*
self′-sus•tain′ing•ly *adv.*
self′-taught′ *adj.*
self′-treat′ment *n.*
self′-trust′ *n.*
self′-un′der•stand′ing *n.*
self′-val′i•dat′ing *adj.*
self′-wind′ing *adj.*
self′-worth′ *n.*

terest. **2.** Personal advantage or interest. —**self′-in′ter•est•ed** *adj.*
self•ish (sĕl′fĭsh) ►*adj.* Concerned only with oneself. —**self′ish•ly** *adv.* —**self′ish•ness** *n.*
self•less (sĕlf′lĭs) ►*adj.* Having or exhibiting no concern for oneself; unselfish. —**self′less•ly** *adv.* —**self′less•ness** *n.*
self-love (sĕlf′lŭv′) ►*n.* Regard for one's self. —**self′-lov′ing** *adj.*
self-made (sĕlf′mād′) ►*adj.* Successful as a result of one's own efforts.
self-mail•er (sĕlf′mā′lər) ►*n.* A folder that can be mailed without being enclosed in an envelope. —**self′-mail′ing** *adj.*
self-pit•y (sĕlf′pĭt′ē) ►*n.* Exaggerated pity for oneself. —**self′-pit′y•ing** *adj.*
self-pol•li•na•tion (sĕlf′pŏl′ə-nā′shən) ►*n.* Transfer of pollen from an anther to a stigma of the same flower. —**self′-pol′li•nate′** *v.*
self-pos•ses•sion (sĕlf′pə-zĕsh′ən) ►*n.* Full command of one's faculties, feelings, and behavior. —**self′-pos•sessed′** *adj.*
self-pres•er•va•tion (sĕlf′prĕz′ər-vā′shən) ►*n.* Protection of oneself from harm or destruction.
self-pro•claimed (sĕlf′prō-klāmd′, -prə-) ►*adj.* Self-styled.
self-re•al•i•za•tion (sĕlf′rē′ə-lĭ-zā′shən) ►*n.* Complete development of one's own potential.
self-ref•er•en•tial (sĕlf′rĕf′ə-rĕn′shəl) ►*adj.* Referring to oneself. —**self′-ref′er•ence** *n.*
self-re•spect (sĕlf′rĭ-spĕkt′) ►*n.* Due respect for oneself. —**self′-re•spect′ing** *adj.*
self-right•eous (sĕlf′rī′chəs) ►*adj.* Piously sure of one's own righteousness; moralistic. —**self′-right′eous•ly** *adv.* —**self′-right′eous•ness** *n.*
self-ris•ing flour (sĕlf′rī′zĭng) ►*n.* A packaged mixture of flour and leavening.
self-sac•ri•fice (sĕlf′săk′rə-fīs′) ►*n.* Sacrifice of one's own interests or well-being for the sake of others. —**self′-sac′ri•fic′ing** *adj.*
self•same (sĕlf′sām′) ►*adj.* Being the very same; identical.
self-sat•is•fac•tion (sĕlf′săt′ĭs-făk′shən) ►*n.* Smug satisfaction with oneself. —**self′-sat′is•fied′** *adj.*
self-seal•ing (sĕlf′sē′lĭng) ►*adj.* **1.** Capable of sealing itself. **2.** Sealable without moisture: *a self-sealing envelope.*
self-search•ing (sĕlf′sûr′chĭng) ►*n.* Examination of one's feelings and actions and their motivation. —**self′-search′ing** *adj.*
self-seek•ing (sĕlf′sē′kĭng) ►*adj.* Pursuing only one's own ends or interests. —**self′-seek′ing** *n.*
self-ser•vice (sĕlf′sûr′vĭs) ►*adj.* Requiring customers or users to help themselves: *a self-service elevator.* —**self′-ser′vice** *n.*
self-serv•ing (sĕlf′sûr′vĭng) ►*adj.* Serving one's own interests, esp. without concern for others. —**self′-serv′ing•ly** *adv.*
self-start•er (sĕlf′stär′tər) ►*n.* One who displays an unusual amount of initiative. —**self′-start′ing** *adj.*
self-styled (sĕlf′stīld′) ►*adj.* As characterized by oneself, often without justification. See Usage Note at **so-called.**
self-suf•fi•cient (sĕlf′sə-fĭsh′ənt) ►*adj.* Able to provide for oneself without help. —**self′-suf•fi′cien•cy** *n.*
self-will (sĕlf′wĭl′) ►*n.* Willfulness; obstinacy. —**self′-willed′** *adj.*
Sel•juk (sĕl′jo͝ok′, sĕl-jo͝ok′). . A Turkish dynasty in central and W Asia (11th–13th cent.).
sell (sĕl) ►*v.* **sold** (sōld), **sell•ing 1.** To exchange for money or its equivalent. **2.** To offer for sale: *a firm that sells textiles.* **3.** To promote successfully. **4.** To convince: *They sold me on the idea.* **5.** To be sold or be on sale. —***phrasal verb:* sell out** *Slang* To betray. [< OE *sellan*, give.] —**sell′er** *n.*
sell•off (sĕl′ôf′, -ŏf′) ►*n.* The sale of a large number of stocks, bonds, or commodities that causes a sharp decline in prices.
sell•out (sĕl′out′) ►*n.* **1.** An event for which all the tickets are sold. **2.** *Slang* One who has betrayed one's principles.
selt•zer (sĕlt′sər) ►*n.* **1.** A natural effervescent spring water of high mineral content. **2.** See **soda water** 1. [< Ger. *Selterser (Wasser)*, (water) of Selters, Germany.]
sel•vage also **sel•vedge** (sĕl′vĭj) ►*n.* The edge of a fabric woven to prevent raveling. [ME.]
selves (sĕlvz) ►*n.* Pl. of **self.**
se•man•tic (sĭ-măn′tĭk) ►*adj.* Of or relating to meaning, esp. in language. [< Gk. *sēmantikos*, significant < *sēma*, sign.] —**se•man′ti•cal•ly** *adv.*
se•man•tics (sĭ-măn′tĭks) ►*n. (takes sing. or pl. v.)* The study of meaning in language.
sem•a•phore (sĕm′ə-fôr′, -fōr′) ►*n.* **1.** A visual signaling apparatus with flags, lights, or mechanically moving arms. **2.** A system for alphabetic signaling using hand-held flags. ►*v.* **-phored, -phor•ing.** To send (a message) by semaphore. [Gk. *sēma*, sign + –PHORE.]
Se•ma•rang (sə-mär′äng) A city of N Java, Indonesia, on the Java Sea E of Jakarta. Pop. 1,026,671.
sem•blance (sĕm′bləns) ►*n.* **1.** An outward or token appearance. **2.** A likeness. **3.** The barest trace. [< OFr. *sembler*, resemble.]
se•men (sē′mən) ►*n.* A whitish secretion of the male reproductive organs, containing spermatozoa. [< Lat. *sēmen*, seed.]
se•mes•ter (sə-mĕs′tər) ►*n.* One of two divisions of 15 to 18 weeks each of an academic year. [< Lat. *(cursus) sēmēstris*, (course) of six months.]
sem•i (sĕm′ī, sĕm′ē) ►*n.*, *pl.* **sem•is** *Informal* **1.** A semitrailer. **2.** A semifinal.
semi– ►*pref.* **1.** Half: *semicircle.* **2.** Partial; partially: *semiconscious.* **3.** Occurring twice during: *semimonthly.* See Usage Note at **bi** . [< Lat. *sēmi-*, half.]
sem•i•an•nu•al (sĕm′ē-ăn′yo͞o-əl, sĕm′ī-) ►*adj.* Occurring or issued twice a year. —**sem′i•an′nu•al•ly** *adv.*
sem•i•cir•cle (sĕm′ĭ-sûr′kəl) ►*n.* A half of a circle as divided by a diameter. —**sem′i•cir′cu•lar** (-kyə-lər) *adj.*
semicircular canal ►*n.* Any of three tubular and looped structures of the inner ear, together functioning in maintenance of the sense of balance in the body.
sem•i•co•lon (sĕm′ĭ-kō′lən) ►*n.* A mark of punctuation (;) used to connect independent clauses and indicating a closer relationship between the clauses than a period does.
sem•i•con•duc•tor (sĕm′ē-kən-dŭk′tər, sĕm′ī-) ►*n.* Any of various solid crystalline substances, such as germanium or silicon, hav-

ing electrical conductivity greater than insulators but less than good conductors. —**sem′i•con•duct′ing** *adj.*

sem•i•fi•nal (sĕm′ē-fī′nəl, sĕm′ī-) ▸*n.* A competition or examination that precedes the final one. —**sem′i•fi′nal** *adj.* —**sem′i•fi′nal•ist** *n.*

sem•i•month•ly (sĕm′ē-mŭnth′lē, sĕm′ī-) ▸*adj.* Occurring or issued twice a month. See Usage Note at **bi–.**

sem•i•nal (sĕm′ə-nəl) ▸*adj.* **1.** Of or relating to semen. **2.** Creative. **3.** Providing a basis or stimulus for further development: *seminal research in a new field.* [< Lat. *sēmen, sēmin-*, seed.] —**sem′i•nal•ly** *adv.*

sem•i•nar (sĕm′ə-när′) ▸*n.* **1.** A small group of advanced students engaged in original research or intensive study. **2.** A conference. [< Lat. *sēminārium*, seed plot.]

sem•i•nar•y (sĕm′ə-nĕr′ē) ▸*n., pl.* **-ies.** A school for the training of priests, ministers, or rabbis. —**sem′i•nar′i•an** (-nâr′ē-ən) *n.*

Sem•i•nole (sĕm′ə-nōl′) ▸*n., pl.* **-nole** or **-noles 1.** A member of a Native American people of primarily Creek origin, now living in Oklahoma and S Florida. **2.** Either of the Muskogean languages of the Seminole.

se•mi•ot•ics (sē′mē-ŏt′ĭks, sĕm′ē-, sē′mī-) ▸*n. (takes sing. v.)* The theory and study of signs and symbols, esp. as elements of language. [< Gk. *sēma*, sign.] —**se′mi•o•ti′cian** (-ə-tĭsh′ən) *n.*

sem•i•pre•cious stone (sĕm′ē-prĕsh′əs) ▸*n.* A gem, such as an opal, that is not as rare or expensive as a precious stone.

sem•i•pri•vate (sĕm′ē-prī′vĭt, sĕm′ī-) ▸*adj.* Shared with other hospital patients.

sem•i•pro (sĕm′ē-prō′, sĕm′ī-) ▸*adj. Informal* Semiprofessional. —**sem′i•pro′** *n.*

sem•i•pro•fes•sion•al (sĕm′ē-prə-fĕsh′ə-nəl, sĕm′ī-) ▸*adj. Sports* **1.** Playing a sport for pay but not on a full-time basis. **2.** Composed of or engaged in by semiprofessional players. —**sem′i•pro•fes′sion•al** *n.*

sem•i•skilled (sĕm′ē-skĭld′, sĕm′ī-) ▸*adj.* Possessing or requiring intermediate skills.

sem•i•sol•id (sĕm′ē-sŏl′ĭd, sĕm′ī-) ▸*adj.* Intermediate in properties, esp. in rigidity, between solids and liquids. ▸*n.* (sĕm′ē-sŏl′ĭd, sĕm′ī-). A semisolid substance.

Sem•ite (sĕm′īt′) ▸*n.* **1.** A member of a group of Semitic-speaking peoples of the Near East and N Africa, including the Arabs and Jews. **2.** A Jew.

Se•mit•ic (sə-mĭt′ĭk) ▸*adj.* **1.** Of or relating to the Semites. **2.** Of or relating to a subgroup of the Afro-Asiatic languages that includes Arabic and Hebrew. ▸*n.* **1.** The Semitic languages. **2.** Any of the Semitic languages.

Sem•i•tism (sĕm′ĭ-tĭz′əm) ▸*n.* Semitic traits or customs.

sem•i•tone (sĕm′ē-tōn′, sĕm′ī-) ▸*n. Mus.* An interval equal to a half tone in the standard diatonic scale. —**sem′i•ton′ic** (-tŏn′ĭk) *adj.*

sem•i•trail•er (sĕm′ē-trā′lər, sĕm′ī-) ▸*n.* A trailer having rear wheels only, with the forward portion supported by the truck tractor.

sem•i•vow•el (sĕm′ĭ-vou′əl) ▸*n.* A sound having the quality of a vowel but functioning as a consonant, as the initial sounds of *yell* and *well.*

sem•i•week•ly (sĕm′ē-wēk′lē, sĕm′ī-) ▸*adj.* Issued or occurring twice a week. See Usage Note at **bi–.**

sem•i•year•ly (sĕm′ē-yîr′lē, sĕm′ī-) ▸*adj.* Issued or occurring twice a year.

sem•o•li•na (sĕm′ə-lē′nə) ▸*n.* Gritty coarse particles of wheat left after bolting and used for pasta. [< Lat. *simila*, fine flour.]

sen•ate (sĕn′ĭt) ▸*n.* **1a.** often **Senate** The upper house in a bicameral legislature, such as the US Congress. **b.** The supreme council of state of the ancient Roman Republic and Empire. **2.** The building in which a senate meets. **3.** A governing or advisory body of some colleges. [< Lat. *senātus.*]

sen•a•tor (sĕn′ə-tər) ▸*n.* A member of a senate. —**sen′a•to′ri•al** (-tôr′ē-əl, -tōr′-) *adj.*

send (sĕnd) ▸*v.* **sent** (sĕnt), **send•ing 1.** To cause to be conveyed to a destination. **2a.** To direct to go on a mission. **b.** To enable to go. **3.** To emit. **4.** To direct or propel with force. **5.** To cause to take place or occur. **6a.** To put into a given state or condition. **b.** *Slang* To thrill: *That music really sends me.* [< OE *sendan.*] —**send′er** *n.*

Syns: *send, dispatch, forward, route, ship, transmit* **v.**

Sen•dai (sĕn-dī′) A city of NE Honshu, Japan, N of Tokyo. Pop. 950,893.

send•off (sĕnd′ôf′, -ŏf′) ▸*n.* A demonstration of affection and good wishes, as for a person beginning a journey.

Sen•e•ca (sĕn′ĭ-kə) ▸*n., pl.* **-ca** or **-cas 1.** A member of a Native American people of W New York, now also in SE Ontario. **2.** The Iroquoian language of the Seneca.

Seneca, Lucius Amaeus. "the Younger." 4 B.C.?–A.D. 65. Roman Stoic philosopher and writer.

Sen•e•gal (sĕn′ĭ-gôl′, -gäl′) A country of W Africa on the Atlantic. Cap. Dakar. Pop. 8,102,000. —**Sen′e•ga•lese′** (-gô-lēz′, -lēs′) *adj. & n.*

Senegal River. A river of W Africa rising in W Mali and flowing about 1,609 km (1,000 mi) to the Atlantic.

se•nes•cent (sĭ-nĕs′ənt) ▸*adj.* Growing old; aging. [< Lat. *senēscere*, grow old.] —**se•nes′cence** *n.*

se•nile (sē′nīl′, sĕn′īl′) ▸*adj.* **1.** Of or characteristic of old age. **2.** Relating to mental impairment associated with aging. [Lat. *senīlis.*] —**se′nile′ly** *adv.* —**se•nil′i•ty** (sĭ-nĭl′ĭ-tē) *n.*

sen•ior (sēn′yər) ▸*adj.* **1.** Of or being the older of two persons having the same name. **2.** Above others of the same set or class. **3.** Of the fourth and last year of a US high school or college. ▸*n.* **1.** A person who is older than another. **2.** A senior citizen. **3.** A fourth-year student in a US high school or college. [Lat., older.]

senior chief petty officer ▸*n.* A rank, as in the US Navy, below master chief petty officer.

senior citizen ▸*n.* A person of or over the age of retirement. —**sen′ior-cit′i•zen** *adj.*

senior high school ▸*n.* A high school usu. comprising grades 10, 11, and 12.

sen•ior•i•ty (sēn-yôr′ĭ-tē, -yŏr′-) ▸*n.* **1.** The state of being senior. **2.** Precedence over others because of length of service.

senior master sergeant ▸*n.* A rank in the US Air Force below chief master sergeant.

sen•na (sĕn′ə) ▸*n.* **1.** Any of various plants having compound leaves and yellow flowers.

2. The dried leaves of a senna, used as a cathartic. [< Ar. *sanā*.]

Sen•nach•er•ib (sĭ-năk′ər-ĭb). d. 681 B.C. King of Assyria (704–681).

se•ñor (sĕ-nyôr′) ▸*n.*, *pl.* **se•ño•res** (sĕ-nyō′rĕs). A Spanish courtesy title for a man. [< Lat. *senior*, senior.]

se•ño•ra (sĕ-nyō′rä) ▸*n.* A Spanish courtesy title for a married woman.

se•ño•ri•ta (sĕ′nyō-rē′tä) ▸*n.* A Spanish courtesy title for a girl or unmarried woman.

sen•sa•tion (sĕn-sā′shən) ▸*n.* **1.** A perception associated with stimulation of a sense organ. **2.** An indefinite, generalized body feeling. **3a.** A state of heightened interest or emotion. **b.** A cause of such interest and excitement. See Syns at **wonder.** —**sen•sa′tion•al** *adj.* —**sen•sa′tion•al•ly** *adv.*

sen•sa•tion•al•ism (sĕn-sā′shə-nə-lĭz′əm) ▸*n.* The use of lurid or exaggerated matter, esp. in writing, journalism, or politics. —**sen•sa′tion•al•ist** *n.* —**sen•sa′tion•al•is′tic** *adj.* —**sen•sa′tion•al•ize** *v.*

sense (sĕns) ▸*n.* **1.** Any of the faculties of hearing, sight, smell, touch, taste, and equilibrium. **2. senses** The faculties of sensation as means of providing physical gratification and pleasure. **3.** Intuitive or acquired perception. **4.** often **senses** Correct judgment. **5a.** A meaning; signification. **b.** One of the meanings of a word or phrase. See Syns at **meaning.** ▸*v.* **sensed, sens•ing 1.** To become aware of; perceive. **2.** To understand. **3.** To detect automatically: *sense radioactivity.* [< Lat. *sēnsus*.]

sense•less (sĕns′lĭs) ▸*adj.* **1.** Lacking sense or meaning; meaningless. **2.** Foolish. **3.** Unconscious. —**sense′less•ly** *adv.* —**sense′less•ness** *n.*

sen•si•ble (sĕn′sə-bəl) ▸*adj.* **1.** Perceptible by the senses or the mind. **2.** Readily perceived; appreciable. **3.** Able to feel or perceive. **4.** Aware; cognizant. **5.** Acting with or showing good sense: *a sensible choice.* —**sen′si•ble•ness** *n.* —**sen′si•bly** *adv.*

sen•si•tive (sĕn′sĭ-tĭv) ▸*adj.* **1.** Capable of perceiving. **2.** Responsive to external conditions or stimulation. **3.** Susceptible to the attitudes, feelings, or circumstances of others. **4.** Quick to take offense; touchy. **5.** Easily irritated. **6.** Readily altered: *film that is sensitive to light.* **7.** Registering very slight differences or changes. **8.** Of or relating to classified information. [< Lat. *sēnsus*, sense.] —**sen′si•tive•ly** *adv.* —**sen′si•tive•ness, sen′si•tiv′i•ty** *n.*

sen•si•tize (sĕn′sĭ-tīz′) ▸*v.* **-tized, -tiz•ing.** To make or become sensitive or more sensitive. —**sen′si•ti•za′tion** *n.*

sen•sor (sĕn′sər, -sôr′) ▸*n.* A device, such as a photoelectric cell, that receives and responds to a signal or stimulus.

sen•so•ry (sĕn′sə-rē) ▸*adj.* Of the senses.

sen•su•al (sĕn′shōō-əl) ▸*adj.* **1.** Of or affecting the senses. **2a.** Relating to gratification of the physical appetites. **b.** Suggesting sexuality. **c.** Physical rather than intellectual. —**sen′su•al•ness, sen′su•al′i•ty** (-ăl′ĭ-tē) *n.* —**sen′su•al•ize** *v.*

sen•su•ous (sĕn′shōō-əs) ▸*adj.* **1.** Of, derived from, or gratifying the senses. **2.** Highly appreciative of the pleasures of sensation. —**sen′su•os′i•ty** (-ŏs′ĭ-tē), **sen′su•ous•ness** *n.* —**sen′su•ous•ly** *adv.*

sent (sĕnt) ▸*v.* P.t. and p.part. of **send.**

sen•tence (sĕn′təns) ▸*n.* **1.** An independent grammatical unit that has a subject and a predicate with a finite verb. **2.** *Law* **a.** A court judgment, esp. a decision of the punishment to be inflicted on one found guilty. **b.** The penalty imposed. ▸*v.* **-tenced, -tenc•ing** *Law.* To pronounce sentence upon. See Syns at **condemn.** [< Lat. *sententia*, opinion.] —**sen•ten′tial** (sĕn-tĕn′shəl) *adj.* —**sen•ten′tial•ly** *adv.*

sen•ten•tious (sĕn-tĕn′shəs) ▸*adj.* **1.** Terse and energetic in expression; pithy. **2.** Given to pompous moralizing. [< Lat. *sententia*, opinion.] —**sen•ten′tious•ness** *n.*

sen•tient (sĕn′shənt, -shē-ənt) ▸*adj.* **1.** Having sense perception; conscious. **2.** Experiencing sensation. [< Lat. *sentīre*, feel.] —**sen′tience** *n.* —**sen′tient•ly** *adv.*

sen•ti•ment (sĕn′tə-mənt) ▸*n.* **1a.** A cast of mind; general mental disposition. **b.** An opinion about a specific matter; view. **2.** A thought or attitude based on emotion instead of reason. **3.** The emotional import of a passage. [< Lat. *sentīre*, feel.]

sen•ti•men•tal (sĕn′tə-mĕn′tl) ▸*adj.* **1a.** Characterized or swayed by sentiment. **b.** Affectedly or extravagantly emotional. **2.** Appealing to the sentiments, esp. to romantic feelings. —**sen′ti•men′tal•ism, sen′ti•men•tal′i•ty** (-tăl′ĭ-tē) *n.* —**sen′ti•men′tal•ize′** *v.* —**sen′ti•men′tal•ly** *adv.*

Syns: *sentimental, maudlin, mawkish, mushy, romantic* **adj.**

sen•ti•nel (sĕn′tə-nəl) ▸*n.* A guard; sentry. [< Ital. *sentinella*.]

sen•try (sĕn′trē) ▸*n.*, *pl.* **-tries 1.** A guard, esp. a soldier posted to prevent the passage of unauthorized persons. **2.** The duty of a sentry. [Perh. < obsolete *sentrinel*, var. of SENTINEL.]

Seoul (sōl) The capital and largest city of South Korea, in the NW part E of Inchon. Pop. 10,726,862.

se•pal (sē′pəl) ▸*n. Bot.* One of the leaflike segments of a calyx. [< Gk. *skepē*, covering.] —**se′paled, sep′a•lous** (sĕp′ə-ləs) *adj.*

sep•a•ra•ble (sĕp′ər-ə-bəl, sĕp′rə-) ▸*adj.* Possible to separate. —**sep′a•ra•bil′i•ty** *n.*

sep•a•rate (sĕp′ə-rāt′) ▸*v.* **-rat•ed, -rat•ing 1a.** To set, keep, or come apart; scatter; disunite. **b.** To sort. **2.** To differentiate between; distinguish. **3.** To remove from a mixture or combination; isolate. **4.** To stop living together as spouses. **5.** To part company; disperse. ▸*adj.* (sĕp′ər-ĭt, sĕp′rĭt) **1.** Set apart; disunited. **2.** Existing as an independent entity. **3.** Dissimilar; distinct. See Syns at **distinct. 4.** Not shared; individual: *separate rooms.* [< Lat. *sēparāre*.] —**sep′a•rate•ly** *adv.* —**sep′a•rate•ness** *n.*

sep•a•ra•tion (sĕp′ə-rā′shən) ▸*n.* **1a.** The act or process of separating. **b.** The condition of being separated. **2.** The place at which a division or parting occurs. **3.** *Law* A formal agreement terminating a spousal relationship.

sep•a•ra•tist (sĕp′ər-ə-tĭst, sĕp′rə-, sĕp′ə-rā′-) ▸*n.* One who advocates political or religious separation. —**sep′a•ra•tism** *n.* —**sep′a•ra•tist** *adj.*

sep•a•ra•tor (sĕp′ə-rā′tər) ▸*n.* One that separates, as a device for separating cream from milk.

Se•phar•di (sə-fär′dē) ▸*n.*, *pl.* **-dim** (-dĭm). A descendent of the Jews who lived in Spain and Portugal during the Middle Ages. —**Se•phar′dic** (-dĭk) *adj.*

se•pi•a (sē′pē-ə) ▸*n.* **1.** A dark brown pigment. **2.** A drawing or photograph in a brown tint. [< Gk. *sēpia*, cuttlefish.] —**se′pi•a** *adj.*

sep•pu•ku (sĕp′o͞o-ko͞o, sĕ-po͞o′-) ▸*n.* Ritual suicide by disembowelment. [J. : *setsu*, to cut + *fuku*, stomach.]

sep•sis (sĕp′sĭs) ▸*n.*, *pl.* **-ses** (-sēz). The presence of pathogenic organisms or their toxins in the blood or tissues. [Gk. *sēpsis*, putrefaction.]

Sept. ▸*abbr.* September

Sep•tem•ber (sĕp-tĕm′bər) ▸*n.* The 9th month of the Gregorian calendar. See table at **calendar.** [< Lat., the seventh month.]

sep•tic (sĕp′tĭk) ▸*adj.* Of or causing sespis. [< Gk. *sēptos*, rotten.]

sep•ti•ce•mi•a (sĕp′tĭ-sē′mē-ə) ▸*n.* A systemic disease resulting from sepsis of the bloodstream. —**sep′ti•ce′mic** (-mĭk) *adj.*

septic tank ▸*n.* A sewage-disposal tank in which waste material is decomposed by anaerobic bacteria.

sep•til•lion (sĕp-tĭl′yən) ▸*n.* **1.** The cardinal number equal to 10^{24}. **2.** *Chiefly Brit.* The cardinal number equal to 10^{42}. [Fr.] —**sep•til′lion** *adj.* —**sep•til′lionth** *n. & adj.*

Sep•tu•a•gint (sĕp′to͞o-ə-jĭnt′, sĕp-to͞o′ə-jənt, -tyo͞o′-) ▸*n.* A Greek translation of the Hebrew Bible made in the 3rd cent. B.C. [Lat. *septuāgintā*, seventy (from the traditional number of its translators).]

sep•tum (sĕp′təm) ▸*n.*, *pl.* **-ta** (-tə). A thin partition or membrane between two cavities or soft masses of tissue in an organism. [Lat. *saeptum*, partition.]

sep•tu•plet (sĕp-tŭp′lĭt, -to͞o′plĭt, -tyo͞o′-) ▸*n.* One of seven offspring born in a single birth. [*septu(ple)*, multiply by seven + (TRI)PLET.]

sep•ul•cher (sĕp′əl-kər) ▸*n.* **1.** A burial vault. **2.** A receptacle for sacred relics. ▸*v.* **-chered, -cher•ing.** To place into a sepulcher; inter. [< Lat. *sepulcrum.*] —**se•pul′chral** (sə-pŭl′krəl, -po͝ol′-) *adj.*

seq. ▸*abbr. Lat.* sequens (the following)

se•quel (sē′kwəl) ▸*n.* **1.** Something that follows; continuation. **2.** A literary work that continues an earlier narrative. **3.** A consequence. [< Lat. *sequēla.*]

se•quence (sē′kwəns, -kwĕns′) ▸*n.* **1.** A following of one thing after another; succession. **2.** An order of succession; arrangement. **3.** A related or continuous series. [< Lat. *sequēns*, following.] —**se′quence** *v.* —**se•quen′tial** (sĭ-kwĕn′shəl) *adj.* —**se•quen′tial•ly** *adv.*

se•ques•ter (sĭ-kwĕs′tər) ▸*v.* **1.** To cause to withdraw into seclusion. **2.** To set apart; segregate. See Syns at **isolate. 3.** *Law* To confiscate (property) as security against legal claims. [< Lat., trustee.] —**se′ques•tra′tion** *n.*

se•quin (sē′kwĭn) ▸*n.* A small shiny ornamental disk, usu. sewn on cloth; spangle. [< Ital. *zecchino*, a Venetian coin.] —**se′quined** *adj.*

se•quoi•a (sĭ-kwoi′ə) ▸*n.* See **redwood.** [After SEQUOYA.]

Se•quoy•a or **Se•quoy•ah** (sĭ-kwoi′ə). 1770?–1843. Cherokee scholar.

se•ra (sîr′ə) ▸*n.* Pl. of **serum.**

se•ra•glio (sə-răl′yō, -räl′-) ▸*n.*, *pl.* **-glios 1.** A harem. **2.** A sultan's palace. [Ital. *serraglio.*]

Sequoya

se•ra•pe also **sa•ra•pe** (sə-rä′pē, -răp′ē) ▸*n.* A long blanketlike shawl worn esp. by Mexican men. [Am.Sp. *sarape.*]

ser•aph (sĕr′əf) ▸*n.*, *pl.* **-a•phim** (-ə-fĭm) or **-aphs.** *Christianity* An angel of the highest order. [< Heb. *śārāp*, fiery serpent, seraph.] —**se•raph′ic** (sə-răf′ĭk), **se•raph′i•cal** *adj.*

Serb (sûrb) ▸*n.* A member of a southern Slavic people that is the principal ethnic group of Serbia.

Ser•bi•a (sûr′bē-ə) A constituent republic comprising most of Yugoslavia.

Ser•bi•an (sûr′bē-ən) ▸*n.* **1.** A native or inhabitant of Serbia. **2.** Serbo-Croatian as used by the Serbs. —**Ser′bi•an** *adj.*

Ser•bo-Cro•a•tian (sûr′bō-krō-ā′shən) ▸*n.* **1.** The Slavic language of the Serbs, Croats and other people. **2.** A native speaker of Serbo-Croatian. —**Ser′bo-Cro•a′tian** *adj.*

sere also **sear** (sîr) ▸*adj.* Withered; dry. [< OE *sēar.*]

ser•e•nade (sĕr′ə-nād′, sĕr′ə-nād′) ▸*n.* A musical performance given to honor or express love for someone. ▸*v.* **-nad•ed, -nad•ing.** To perform a serenade (for). [< Ital. *serenata.*] —**ser′e•nad′er** *n.*

ser•en•dip•i•ty (sĕr′ən-dĭp′ĭ-tē) ▸*n.* The faculty of making fortunate discoveries by accident. [After the Persian fairy tale *The Three Princes of Serendip.*] —**ser′en•dip′i•tous** *adj.* —**ser′en•dip′i•tous•ly** *adv.*

se•rene (sə-rēn′) ▸*adj.* **1.** Calm and unruffled; tranquil. **2.** Unclouded; fair. [< Lat. *serēnus.*] —**se•rene′ly** *adv.* —**se•rene′ness, se•ren′i•ty** (-rĕn′ĭ-tē) *n.*

serf (sûrf) ▸*n.* **1.** A member of a feudal class of people in Europe, bound to the land and owned by a lord. **2.** A slave. [< Lat. *servus*, slave.] —**serf′dom** *n.*

serge (sûrj) ▸*n.* A twilled cloth of worsted or worsted and wool. [< Lat. *sērica*, silken.]

ser•geant (sär′jənt) ▸*n.* **1.** Any of several ranks of noncommissioned officers, as in the US Army. **2.** A police officer ranking next below a captain, lieutenant, or inspector. [< LLat. *serviēns*, public official.]

sergeant at arms ▸*n.*, *pl.* **sergeants at arms.** An officer appointed to keep order within an organization, such as a legislature.

sergeant first class ▸*n.*, *pl.* **sergeants first class.** A rank in the US Army below master sergeant.

sergeant major ▸*n.*, *pl.* **sergeants major** or **sergeant majors 1.** Any of the highest noncommissioned ranks in the US Army and Marine Corps. **2.** *Chiefly Brit.* A noncommissioned officer of the highest rank.

se•ri•al (sîr′ē-əl) ▸*adj.* **1.** Of, forming, or arranged in a series. **2.** Published or produced in installments. ▸*n.* A work published or produced in installments. —**se′ri•al•i•za′tion** *n.* —**se′ri•al•ize′** *v.* —**se′ri•al•ly** *adv.*

se•ries (sîr′ēz) ▸*n., pl.* **series 1.** A number of objects or events arranged one after the other in succession; set. **2.** A succession of regularly aired radio or television programs. **3.** *Sports* A number of games played in succession by the same opposing teams. [Lat. *seriēs* < *serere*, join.]

Usage: When *series* has the singular sense of "one set," it takes a singular verb, even when followed by *of* and a plural noun: *A series of lectures is scheduled.* When *series* has the plural sense of "one or more sets," it takes a plural verb: *Two series of lectures are scheduled.*

ser•if (sĕr′ĭf) ▸*n. Print.* A fine line finishing off the main strokes of a letter. [Perh. < Du. *schreef*, line.]

se•ri•o•com•ic (sîr′ē-ō-kŏm′ĭk) ▸*adj.* Both serious and comic.

se•ri•ous (sîr′ē-əs) ▸*adj.* **1.** Grave in quality or manner. **2.** Carried out in earnest. **3.** Concerned with important rather than trivial matters. **4.** Causing great concern; critical. [< LLat. *sēriōsus.*] —**se′ri•ous•ly** *adv.* —**se′ri•ous•ness** *n.*

ser•mon (sûr′mən) ▸*n.* **1.** A homily delivered as part of a liturgy. **2.** A lengthy and tedious reproof or exhortation. [< Lat. *sermō*, discourse.] —**ser′mon•ize′** *v.* —**ser′mon•iz′er** *n.*

se•rol•o•gy (sĭ-rŏl′ə-jē) ▸*n.* The medical study of serum. —**se′ro•log′ic** (sîr′ə-lŏj′ĭk), **se′ro•log′i•cal** *adj.* —**se•rol′o•gist** *n.*

se•ro•neg•a•tive (sîr′ō-nĕg′ə-tĭv) ▸*adj.* Showing a negative reaction to a test on blood serum for a disease, esp. syphilis or AIDS.

se•ro•pos•i•tive (sîr′ō-pŏz′ĭ-tĭv) ▸*adj.* Showing a positive reaction to a test on blood serum for a disease.

se•ro•to•nin (sĕr′ə-tō′nĭn, sîr′-) ▸*n.* A hormone found in plants and animals that acts as a neurotransmitter and vasoconstrictor in humans. [SER(UM) + TON(E) + -IN.]

se•rous (sîr′əs) ▸*adj.* Containing, secreting, or resembling serum.

ser•pent (sûr′pənt) ▸*n.* A snake. [< Lat. *serpēns* < *serpere*, creep.]

ser•pen•tine (sûr′pən-tēn′, -tīn′) ▸*adj.* Of or like a serpent, as in form or movement.

ser•rate (sĕr′āt′) or **ser•rat•ed** (sĕr′ā′tĭd, sə-rā′-) ▸*adj.* Edged with sharp toothlike projections. [< Lat. *serra*, saw.] —**ser•ra′tion** (sə-rā′shən) *n.* —**ser′rate′** *v.*

ser•ried (sĕr′ēd) ▸*adj.* Pressed together in rows. [< Fr. *serrer*, to crowd.]

se•rum (sîr′əm) ▸*n., pl.* **se•rums** or **se•ra** (sîr′ə) **1.** The clear yellowish fluid obtained upon separating whole blood into its solid and liquid components. **2.** Blood serum from the tissues of immunized animals, used to transfer immunity to another individual. [Lat.]

ser•vant (sûr′vənt) ▸*n.* One employed to perform domestic services.

serve (sûrv) ▸*v.* **served, serv•ing 1.** To work for; be a servant to. **2.** To place food before (someone); wait on. **3.** To provide goods and services for (customers). See Usage Note at **service. 4.** To be of assistance to. **5.** To spend or complete (time). **6.** To undergo military service for. **7.** To give homage to. **8.** To requite. **9.** To meet the needs of; satisfy. **10.** *Law* To present (a writ or summons). **11.** *Sports* To put (a ball) in play, as in tennis. ▸*n. Sports* The right or act of serving in many court games. [< Lat. *servīre* < *servus*, slave.]

serv•er (sûr′vər) ▸*n.* **1.** One who serves. **2.** Something, as a tray, used in serving food and drink. **3.** *Comp. Sci.* **a.** A file server. **b.** A computer that processes HTML requests.

ser•vice (sûr′vĭs) ▸*n.* **1a.** Employment in work for another, esp. for a government. **b.** A government branch or department and its employees. **2.** The armed forces of a nation, or any branch thereof. **3.** The occupation or duties of a servant. **4.** Work done for others as an occupation. **5.** Installation or repairs provided by a dealer or manufacturer. **6.** A set of dishes or utensils. **7.** *Sports* A serve. ▸*v.* **-viced, -vic•ing 1.** To repair or maintain: *service a car.* **2.** To provide services to. [< Lat. *servitium*, slavery.]

Usage: *Service* is used principally in the sense "to repair or maintain": *service the electric dishwasher.* In the sense "to supply goods or services to," *serve* is the most frequent or only choice: *One radio network serves three states.*

ser•vice•a•ble (sûr′vĭ-sə-bəl) ▸*adj.* **1.** Ready for service; usable. **2.** Able to give long service; durable. —**ser′vice•a•bil′i•ty, ser′vice•a•ble•ness** *n.* —**ser′vice•a•bly** *adv.*

ser•vice•man (sûr′vĭs-măn′, -mən) ▸*n.* **1.** A man who is a member of the armed forces. **2.** also **service man** A man whose work is the maintenance and repair of equipment.

service mark ▸*n.* A mark used in the sale or advertising of services to identify and distinguish them.

service station ▸*n.* A retail establishment at which motor vehicles are refueled, serviced, and sometimes repaired.

ser•vice•wom•an (sûr′vĭs-wo͝om′ən) ▸*n.* A woman member of the armed forces.

ser•vile (sûr′vəl, -vīl′) ▸*adj.* Abjectly submissive; slavish. [< Lat. *servīlis* < *servus*, slave.] —**ser′vile•ly** *adv.* —**ser′vile•ness, ser•vil′i•ty** (sər-vĭl′ĭ-tē) *n.*

serv•ing (sûr′vĭng) ▸*n.* A helping of food or drink.

ser•vi•tor (sûr′vĭ-tər, -tôr′) ▸*n.* An attendant. [< Lat. *servītor.*]

ser•vi•tude (sûr′vĭ-to͞od′, -tyo͞od′) ▸*n.* **1.** Subjection to an owner or master. **2.** Forced labor imposed as a punishment. [< LLat. *servitūdō.*]

ser•vo (sûr′vō) ▸*n., pl.* **-vos 1.** A servomechanism. **2.** A servomotor.

ser•vo•mech•a•nism (sûr′vō-mĕk′ə-nĭz′əm) ▸*n.* A feedback system used in the automatic control of a mechanical device.

ser•vo•mo•tor (sûr′vō-mō′tər) ▸*n.* A motor that controls the action of the mechanical device in a servomechanism. [< Lat. *servus*, slave + MOTOR.]

ses•a•me (sĕs′ə-mē) ▸*n.* **1.** A tropical Asian plant bearing small, edible, oil-rich seeds. **2.** The seed of this plant. [< Gk. *sēsamē.*]

ses•qui•cen•ten•ni•al (sĕs′kwĭ-sĕn-tĕn′ē-əl) ▸*adj.* Relating to a period of 150 years. ▸*n.* A

150th anniversary or its celebration. [Lat. *sesqui-*, one and a half + CENTENNIAL.]

ses•qui•pe•da•lian (sĕs′kwĭ-pĭ-dāl′yən) ►*n.* A long word. ►*adj.* **1.** Given to the use of long words. **2.** Polysyllabic. [< Lat. *sesquipedālis*, of a foot and a half in length.]

ses•sile (sĕs′īl′, -əl) ►*adj.* **1.** *Bot.* Attached directly at the base: *sessile leaves.* **2.** *Zool.* Permanently attached, as a barnacle. [< Lat. *sedēre, sess-*, sit.]

ses•sion (sĕsh′ən) ►*n.* **1a.** A meeting of a legislative or judicial body. **b.** A series of such meetings. **c.** The duration of such a series of meetings. **2.** The part of a year or of a day during which a school holds classes. [< Lat. *sedēre, sess-*, sit.]

ses•tet (sĕ-stĕt′) ►*n.* The last six lines of a sonnet. [Ital. *sestetto.*]

set[1] (sĕt) ►*v.* **set, set•ting 1.** To put in a specified position or state. **2.** To put into a stable position; fix. **3.** To restore to a proper and normal state. **4.** To adjust for proper functioning. **5.** To arrange properly for use: *set a table.* **6.** To apply curlers and clips to (hair) in order to style. **7.** To arrange (type) into words and sentences preparatory to printing; compose. **8.** To prescribe or establish: *set a precedent.* **9.** To assign to a duty. **10.** To establish as a model: *set a good example.* **11.** To put in a mounting; mount. **12.** To cause to sit. **13.** To sit on eggs, as a hen. **14.** To determine (a price or value). **15.** To disappear below the horizon. **16.** To diminish or decline; wane. **17.** To become fixed; harden; coagulate. —***phrasal verbs:*** **set about** To begin. **set aside 1.** To reserve for a special purpose. **2.** To annul. **set back** To slow down the progress of. **set down** To put in writing. **set forth 1.** To present for consideration. **2.** To express in words. **3.** To begin a journey. **set off 1.** To cause to occur. **2.** To cause to explode. **3.** To distinguish. **4.** To direct attention to by contrast. **5.** To start a journey. **set out 1.** To start a journey. **2.** To undertake or begin something. **set up 1.** To place in an upright position. **2.** To invest with power. **3.** To assemble and erect. **4.** To establish; found. ►*adj.* **1.** Fixed or established. **2.** Established by convention. **3.** Fixed and rigid. **4.** Unwilling to change. **5.** Ready. ►*n.* **1.** The act or process of setting. **2.** The condition resulting from setting. —***idioms:*** **set sail** To begin a voyage on water. **set the stage for** To provide the basis for. [< OE *settan.*]

Usage: *Set* is now in most cases a transitive verb: *He sets the table. Sit* is generally an intransitive verb: *He sits at the table.* There are some exceptions: *The sun sets* (not *sits*). *A hen sets* (or *sits*) *on her eggs.*

set[2] (sĕt) ►*n.* **1.** A group of persons or things of the same kind that belong together: *a chess set.* **2.** A group of books or periodicals published as a unit. **3a.** The scenery constructed for a theatrical performance. **b.** The enclosure in which a movie is filmed. **4.** The receiving apparatus assembled to operate a radio or television. **5.** *Math.* A collection of distinct elements. **6.** *Sports* A group of tennis games constituting one division or unit of a match. [< Lat. *secta*, faction.]

set•back (sĕt′băk′) ►*n.* **1.** An unanticipated check in progress; reverse. **2.** A steplike recession, as in a wall or in the rise of a tall building.

Se•ton (sēt′n), Saint **Elizabeth Ann Bayley.** "Mother Seton." 1774–1821. Amer. religious leader.

Elizabeth Seton
c. 1805 portrait

set piece ►*n.* **1.** A piece of freestanding stage scenery. **2.** An artistic or literary work marked by a formal pattern. **3.** A carefully planned and executed military operation.

set•screw (sĕt′skro͞o′) ►*n.* A usu. headless screw used to hold two parts together.

set•tee (sĕ-tē′) ►*n.* **1.** A long wooden bench with a back. **2.** A small sofa. [Perh. < SETTLE, bench.]

set•ter (sĕt′ər) ►*n.* Any of several breeds of long-haired hunting dogs.

set theory ►*n. Math.* The study of the properties of sets.

set•ting (sĕt′ĭng) ►*n.* **1.** The position in which something, such as an automatic control, is set. **2.** A context or background. **3.** A mounting, as for a gem.

set•tle (sĕt′l) ►*v.* **-tled, -tling 1.** To put into order; arrange or fix definitely as desired. **2.** To establish residence (in). **3.** To restore calmness or comfort to. **4a.** To sink, become compact, or come to rest: *Dust settled on the road.* **b.** To cause (a liquid) to become clear by forming a sediment. **5.** To stabilize. **6a.** To make compensation for (a claim). **b.** To pay (a debt). **7.** To conclude (a dispute). **8.** To decide (a lawsuit) by mutual agreement without court action. [< OE *setlan* < *setl*, seat.] —**set′tler** *n.*

set•tle•ment (sĕt′l-mənt) ►*n.* **1.** The act or process of settling. **2a.** Establishment, as of a person in a business or of people in a new region. **b.** A newly colonized region. **3.** A small community. **4.** An adjustment or other understanding reached. **5.** also **settlement house** A center providing community services in an underprivileged area.

set-to (sĕt′to͞o′) ►*n., pl.* **-tos.** A brief, usu. heated conflict.

set•up (sĕt′ŭp′) ►*n.* **1.** An arrangement or plan, esp. an initial organization. **2.** often **setups** *Informal* The collective ingredients for serving alcoholic drinks. **3.** *Slang* **a.** A contest prearranged to result in an easy or faked victory. **b.** A deceptive scheme, such as a fraud.

Seu•rat (sə-rä′, sœ-), **Georges Pierre.** 1859–91. French painter.

Se•vas•to•pol (sə-văs′tə-pōl′, sĕv′ə-stō′pəl) A city of S Ukraine on the Black Sea W of Yalta. Pop. 371,400.

sev•en (sĕv′ən) ►*n.* **1.** The cardinal number equal to 6 + 1. **2.** The 7th in a set or sequence.

[< OE *seofon.*] —**sev′en** *adj. & pron.*
sev•en•teen (sĕv′ən-tēn′) ►*n.* **1.** The cardinal number equal to 16 + 1. **2.** The 17th in a set or sequence. [< OE *seofontīne.*] —**sev′en•teen′** *adj. & pron.*
sev•en•teenth (sĕv′ən-tēnth′) ►*n.* **1.** The ordinal number matching the number 17 in a series. **2.** One of 17 equal parts. —**sev′en•teenth′** *adv. & adj.*
sev•enth (sĕv′ənth) ►*n.* **1.** The ordinal number matching the number 7 in a series. **2.** One of seven equal parts. **3.** *Mus.* A tone seven degrees above or below a given tone in a diatonic scale. —**sev′enth** *adv. & adj.*
seventh heaven ►*n.* A state of great joy.
sev•en•ti•eth (sĕv′ən-tē-ĭth) ►*n.* **1.** The ordinal number matching the number 70 in a series. **2.** One of 70 equal parts. —**sev′en•ti•eth** *adv. & adj.*
sev•en•ty (sĕv′ən-tē) ►*n., pl.* **-ties.** The cardinal number equal to 7 × 10. [< OE *hundseofontig.*] —**sev′en•ty** *adj. & pron.*
sev•er (sĕv′ər) ►*v.* **1.** To divide or separate. **2.** To cut off (a part) from a whole. **3.** To break up (e.g., a relationship); dissolve. [< Lat. *sēparāre.*]
sev•er•al (sĕv′ər-əl, sĕv′rəl) ►*adj.* **1.** Being of a number more than two or three but not many. **2.** Respectively different; various: *They parted and went their several ways.* See Syns at **distinct.** ►*pron. (takes pl. v.)* An indefinite but small number; a few. [< Lat. *sēpar*, distinct.] —**sev′er•al•ly** *adv.*
sev•er•al•ty (sĕv′ər-əl-tē, sĕv′rəl-) ►*n., pl.* **-ties** *Law* **1.** A separate and individual right to possession or ownership. **2.** Property owned in severalty.
sev•er•ance (sĕv′ər-əns, sĕv′rəns) ►*n.* **1a.** The act or process of severing. **b.** The condition of being severed. **2.** Extra pay given an employee upon leaving a position.
se•vere (sə-vîr′) ►*adj.* **-ver•er, -ver•est 1.** Unsparing or harsh, as in treatment of others; strict. **2.** Marked by rigorous standards. **3.** Austere or dour; forbidding. **4.** Extremely plain in substance or style. **5.** Extremely violent or intense: *a severe storm.* **6.** Extremely difficult; trying: *a severe test of our loyalty.* [Lat. *sevērus.*] —**se•vere′ly** *adv.* —**se•vere′ness, se•ver′i•ty** (-vĕr′ĭ-tē) *n.*
Sev•ern River (sĕv′ərn) **1.** A river of NW Ontario, Canada, flowing about 676 km (420 mi) to Hudson Bay. **2.** A river of SW Great Britain rising in central Wales and flowing about 338 km (210 mi) to the Bristol Channel.
Se•ve•rus (sə-vîr′əs), **Lucius Septimius.** A.D. 146–211. Emperor of Rome (193–211).
Se•ville (sə-vĭl′) A city of SW Spain [north-northeast] of Cádiz. Pop. 678,902.
sew (sō) ►*v.* **sewed, sewn** (sōn) or **sewed, sew•ing 1.** To make, repair, or fasten by stitching, as with a needle and thread. **2.** To close, fasten, or attach with stitches. —***phrasal verb:* sew up** *Informal* **1.** To complete successfully. **2.** To monopolize. [< OE *seowian.*] —**sew′er** *n.*
sew•age (sōō′ĭj) ►*n.* Liquid and solid waste carried off in sewers or drains.
Sew•ard (sōō′ərd), **William Henry.** 1801–72. Amer. public official.
sew•er (sōō′ər) ►*n.* An artificial, usu. underground conduit for carrying off sewage or rainwater. [< VLat. *exaquāria : Lat. *ex-*, out + Lat. *aqua*, water.]
sew•er•age (sōō′ər-ĭj) ►*n.* **1.** A system of sewers. **2.** Removal of waste materials by sewers. **3.** Sewage.
sew•ing (sō′ĭng) ►*n.* **1.** The act of one who sews. **2.** An article being sewn.
sewing machine ►*n.* A machine for sewing usu. with attachments for special stitching.
sex (sĕks) ►*n.* **1a.** The property or quality by which organisms are classified on the basis of their reproductive organs. **b.** Either of the two divisions, designated female and male, of this classification. **2.** Females or males collectively. **3.** The condition or character of being female or male. See Usage Note at **gender. 4.** Sexual intercourse. [< Lat. *sexus.*]
sex•a•ge•nar•i•an (sĕk′sə-jə-nâr′ē-ən) ►*n.* A person between the ages of 60 and 70. [< Lat. *sexāgēnārius.*] —**sex′a•ge•nar′i•an** *adj.*
sex•a•ges•i•mal (sĕk′sə-jĕs′ə-məl) ►*adj.* Of or based on the number 60. [< Lat. *sexāgēsimus*, sixtieth.]
sex chromosome ►*n.* Either of a pair of chromosomes, usu. designated X or Y, in the germ cells of most animals and some plants, that combine to determine the sex of an individual, XX resulting in a female and XY in a male.
sex hormone ►*n.* Any of various hormones affecting the growth or function of the reproductive organs.
sex•ism (sĕk′sĭz′əm) ►*n.* Discrimination based on gender, esp. discrimination against women. —**sex′ist** *adj. & n.*
sex•less (sĕks′lĭs) ►*adj.* **1.** Lacking sexual characteristics; neuter. **2.** Lacking in sexual activity. —**sex′less•ness** *n.*
sex-linked (sĕks′lĭngkt′) ►*adj.* **1.** Carried by a sex chromosome, esp. an X chromosome: *a sex-linked gene.* **2.** Sexually determined. —**sex linkage** *n.*
sex•tant (sĕk′stənt) ►*n.* A navigational instrument used to measure the altitudes of celestial bodies. [< Lat. *sextāns*, sixth part.]

sextant

sex•tet (sĕk-stĕt′) ►*n.* **1a.** A group composed of six musicians. **b.** A composition written for six performers. **2.** A group of six persons or things. [Alteration of SESTET.]
sex•til•lion (sĕk-stĭl′yən) ►*n.* **1.** The cardinal number equal to 10^{21}. **2.** *Chiefly Brit.* The cardinal number equal to 10^{36}. [Fr.] —**sex•til′lion** *adj. & pron.* —**sex•til′lionth** *n. & adj.*
sex•ton (sĕk′stən) ►*n.* One responsible for the care and upkeep of church property. [< Med. Lat. *sacristānus.*]
Sexton, Anne. 1928–74. Amer. poet.
sex•tu•ple (sĕk-stōō′pəl, -styōō′-, -stŭp′əl) ►*v.* **-pled, -pling.** To multiply or be multiplied by six. ►*adj.* **1.** Having six parts or members. **2.** Multiplied by six; sixfold. ►*n.* A six-

fold amount or number. [Prob. Lat. *sextus*, sixth + (QUINT)UPLE.] —**sex•tu′ply** *adv.*

sex•tup•let (sĕk-stŭp′lĭt, -sto͞o′plĭt, -styo͞o′-) ►*n.* One of six offspring born in a single birth. [SEXTU(PLE) + (TRI)PLET.]

sex•u•al (sĕk′sho͞o-əl) ►*adj.* **1.** Of sex, sexuality, the sexes, or the sex organs and their functions. **2.** Implying or symbolizing erotic desires or activity. **3.** Of or involving the union of male and female gametes: *sexual reproduction.* —**sex′u•al•ly** *adv.*

sexual harassment ►*n.* The making of unwanted and offensive sexual advances, remarks, or acts, esp. by one in a supervisory position.

sexual intercourse ►*n.* Sexual union between humans, gen. involving physical union of the sexual organs.

sex•u•al•i•ty (sĕk′sho͞o-ăl′ĭ-tē) ►*n.* **1.** The condition of being characterized and distinguished by sex. **2.** Concern with sex. **3.** Sexual character or potency.

sexually transmitted disease ►*n.* Any of various diseases usu. contracted through intimate sexual contact.

sexual orientation ►*n.* The direction of one's sexual interest toward members of the same, opposite, or both sexes.

sex•y (sĕk′sē) ►*adj.* **-i•er, -i•est 1.** Arousing sexual desire or interest. **2.** *Slang* Highly appealing or interesting. —**sex′i•ly** *adv.* —**sex′i•ness** *n.*

Sey•chelles (sā-shĕl′, -shĕlz′) An island country in the W Indian Ocean N of Madagascar. Cap. Victoria. Pop. 74,000.

Sey•mour (sē′môr′, -mōr′), **Jane.** 1509?–37. Queen of England (1536–37) as the third wife of Henry VIII.

SF ►*abbr.* science fiction

Sg ► The symbol for the element **seaborgium.**

SGML (ĕs′jē-ĕm-ĕl′) ►*n.* A markup language for describing the logical structure of a computer document. [*S(tandard) G(eneralized) M(arkup) L(anguage).*]

Sgt. or **Sgt** or **SGT** ►*abbr.* sergeant

Sha'•ban also **Shaa•ban** (shə-bän′, shä-, shô-) ►*n.* The 8th month of the Muslim calendar. See table at **calendar.** [Ar. *ša'bān.*]

Shab•bat (shə-bät′, shä′bəs) ►*n.* *Judaism* The Sabbath. [Heb. *šabbāt.*]

shab•by (shăb′ē) ►*adj.* **-bi•er, -bi•est 1.** Wearing threadbare clothing. **2a.** Threadbare or worn-out. **b.** Dilapidated or deteriorated; seedy. **3.** Disgraceful; mean: *shabby treatment.* [< obsolete *shab*, scab.] —**shab′bi•ly** *adv.* —**shab′bi•ness** *n.*

shack (shăk) ►*n.* A small, crudely built cabin. [Poss. < Nahuatl *xacalli*, adobe hut.]

shack•le (shăk′əl) ►*n.* **1.** A metal fastening, usu. one of a pair, for encircling and confining the ankle or wrist of a prisoner or captive; fetter; manacle. **2.** Something that confines or restrains. ►*v.* **-led, -ling 1.** To confine with shackles. **2.** To restrict. See Syns at **hamper**[1]. [< OE *sceacel.*]

shad (shăd) ►*n.*, *pl.* **shad** or **shads.** A herringlike food fish that swims up streams from marine waters to spawn. [< OE *sceadd.*]

shade (shād) ►*n.* **1.** Light diminished in intensity; partial darkness. **2.** An area or space of partial darkness. **3.** Cover or shelter from the sun or its rays. **4.** Any of various devices used to screen light or heat. **5. shades** *Slang* Sunglasses. **6.** The degree to which a color is mixed with black or is decreasingly illuminated. **7.** A slight variation; nuance. See Syns at **nuance. 8.** A small amount; trace. **9.** A disembodied spirit; ghost. ►*v.* **shad•ed, shad•ing 1.** To screen from light or heat. **2.** To represent degrees of shade or shadow in. **3.** To vary by slight degrees. [< OE *sceadu.*]

shad•ow (shăd′ō) ►*n.* **1.** An area that is partially or totally unilluminated because of the interception of radiation by an opaque object. **2.** The rough image cast by an object blocking rays of illumination. **3.** A cause or feeling of gloom or unhappiness. **4.** A shaded area in a picture. **5.** A phantom; ghost. **6.** A constant companion. **7.** A faint indication. **8.** A remnant. **9.** A trace. ►*v.* **1.** To cast a shadow on; shade. **2.** To make gloomy or dark. **3.** To represent vaguely or mysteriously. **4.** To shade (a painting). **5.** To follow, esp. in secret; trail. ►*adj.* Not having official status: *a shadow cabinet.* [< OE *sceaduwe.*] —**shad′ow•er** *n.* —**shad′ow•i•ness** *n.* —**shad′ow•y** *adj.*

shad•ow•box (shăd′ō-bŏks′) ►*v.* To spar with an imaginary opponent. —**shad′ow•box′ing** *n.*

shad•y (shā′dē) ►*adj.* **-i•er, -i•est 1.** Full of shade. **2.** Of dubious character or honesty; questionable. —**shad′i•ly** *adv.* —**shad′i•ness** *n.*

shaft (shăft) ►*n.* **1a.** The long narrow body of a spear or arrow. **b.** A spear or arrow. **2.** A satirical barb. **3.** A ray or beam of light. **4.** A long handle, as of certain tools. **5.** A column or columnlike part. **6a.** A long cylindrical bar or pole. **b.** A drive shaft. **7.** A long, often vertical passage or duct: *an elevator shaft.* ►*v.* *Slang* To treat in a harsh, unfair way. [< OE *sceaft.*]

shag (shăg) ►*n.* **1.** A tangle or mass, esp. of matted hair. **2.** Cloth having a coarse, long nap. **3.** A rug with a thick, rough pile. [< OE *sceacga*, matted hair.]

shag•gy (shăg′ē) ►*adj.* **-gi•er, -gi•est 1.** Having long rough hair or wool. **2.** Bushy and matted: *shaggy hair.* **3.** Poorly groomed; unkempt. —**shag′gi•ness** *n.*

shah (shä) ►*n.* Used formerly as a title for the hereditary monarch of Iran. [Pers. *shāh.*]

Shah Ja•han (jə-hän′). 1592–1666. Mogul emperor of India (1628–58).

Shah Jahan
detail from a 1617 miniature

shake (shāk) ►*v.* **shook** (sho͝ok), **shak•en** (shā′kən), **shak•ing 1.** To move or cause to move to and fro with short jerky movements.

See Syns at **agitate. 2.** To tremble, vibrate, or rock. **3.** To cause to waver or become unstable. **4.** To remove or dislodge by or as if by jerky movements. **5.** To brandish or wave. **6.** To clasp (hands) in greeting or leave-taking or as a sign of agreement. —***phrasal verbs:* shake down** *Slang* **1.** To extort money from. **2.** *Slang* To make a thorough search of. **shake off** To free oneself from. **shake up 1.** To unnerve; shock. **2.** To rearrange drastically. ►*n.* **1.** The act or an instance of shaking. **2.** See **milk shake. 3. shakes** *Informal* Uncontrollable trembling. —***idioms:* no great shakes** *Slang* Unexceptional; ordinary. **shake a leg** *Informal* To hurry. [< OE *sceacan.*]

shake•down (shāk′doun′) ►*n.* **1.** *Slang* Extortion of money, as by blackmail. **2.** *Slang* A thorough search. **3.** A period of appraisal followed by adjustments to improve efficiency or functioning. ►*adj.* Serving to test performance: *a shakedown cruise.*

shak•er (shā′kər) ►*n.* **1.** One that impels or encourages action. **2.** A container used for shaking. **3. Shaker** A member of a Christian group practicing communal living and observing celibacy.

Shake•speare (shāk′spîr), **William.** 1564–1616. English playwright and poet. —**Shake•spear′e•an, Shake•spear′i•an** *adj. & n.*

shake•up (shāk′ŭp′) ►*n.* A thorough reorganization.

shak•o (shăk′ō, shā′kō, shä′-) ►*n., pl.* **-os** or **-oes.** A stiff cylindrical military dress hat with a short visor and a plume. [< Hung. *csákós (süveg),* pointed (cap).]

shak•y (shā′kē) ►*adj.* **-i•er, -i•est 1.** Trembling or quivering. **2.** Unsteady or weak. **3.** Precarious: *a shaky existence.* —**shak′i•ly** *adv.* —**shak′i•ness** *n.*

shale (shāl) ►*n.* A rock composed of layers of claylike, fine-grained sediments. [< OE *scealu.*] —**shal′ey** *adj.*

shale oil ►*n.* A crude oil obtained from oil shale by heating and distillation.

shall (shăl) ►*aux.v. p.t.* **should** (shŏŏd). Used before a verb in the infinitive to show: **a.** Simple futurity: *We shall arrive tomorrow.* **b.** An order, promise, or obligation: *You shall leave now.* **c.** Inevitability: *That day shall come.* [< OE *sceal.*]

Usage: The traditional rules require that *shall* be used with the first person to indicate simple futurity and that *will* be used for that same purpose with the second and third persons. These rules are rarely observed in American English, however, even at the most formal levels, and the widespread practice of using *will* to indicate futurity with all three persons is acceptable to a majority of the Usage Panel.

shal•lot (shăl′ət, shə-lŏt′) ►*n.* **1.** A type of onion with pear-shaped bulbs. **2.** The mild-flavored edible bulb of this plant. [< VLat. **escalōnia,* SCALLION.]

shal•low (shăl′ō) ►*adj.* **-er, -est 1.** Measuring little from bottom to top or surface; lacking physical depth. **2.** Lacking depth of intellect, emotion, or knowledge. ►*n.* often **shallows.** A part of a body of water of little depth; shoal. [ME *shalowe.*] —**shal′low•ly** *adv.* —**shal′low•ness** *n.*

sha•lom (shä-lōm′, shə-) ►*interj.* Used as a greeting or farewell. [Heb. *šālôm,* peace.]

shalt (shălt) ►*aux.v. Archaic* 2nd pers. sing. pr.t. of **shall.**

sham (shăm) ►*n.* **1.** Something false or empty purported to be genuine. **2.** One who assumes a false character; impostor. ►*adj.* Not genuine; fake. ►*v.* **shammed, sham•ming.** To put on a false appearance; feign. [Perh. < SHAME.]

sha•man (shä′mən, shā′-) ►*n.* A member of certain tribal societies who mediates between the visible and the spirit worlds for purposes of healing, divination, and control over natural events. [< Skt. *śramaṇaḥ,* Buddhist monk.] —**sha′man•ism** *n.* —**sha′man•is′tic** *adj.*

sham•ble (shăm′bəl) ►*v.* **-bled, -bling.** To walk in an awkward, lazy, or unsteady manner, shuffling the feet. [< *shamble,* ungainly.] —**sham′ble** *n.*

sham•bles (shăm′bəlz) ►*pl.n. (takes sing. v.)* A scene or condition of complete disorder or ruin. [< ME *shamel,* place where meat is butchered and sold.]

shame (shām) ►*n.* **1a.** A painful emotion caused by a strong sense of guilt, embarrassment, unworthiness, or disgrace. **b.** Capacity for such a feeling: *Have you no shame?* **2.** One that brings dishonor, disgrace, or condemnation. **3.** Disgrace; ignominy. **4.** A great disappointment. ►*v.* **shamed, sham•ing 1.** To cause to feel shame. **2.** To bring dishonor or disgrace on. **3.** To force by making ashamed: *He was shamed into an apology.* [< OE *sceamu.*] —**shame′ful** *adj.* —**shame′ful•ly** *adv.* —**shame′ful•ness** *n.*

shame•faced (shām′fāst′) ►*adj.* **1.** Indicative of shame: *a shamefaced excuse.* **2.** Shy; bashful. [< OE *sceamfæst.*] —**shame′fac′ed•ly** (-fā′sĭd-lē) *adv.* —**shame′fac′ed•ness** *n.*

shame•less (shām′lĭs) ►*adj.* **1.** Feeling no shame or disgrace. **2.** Brazen; blatant: *a shameless lie.* —**shame′less•ly** *adv.* —**shame′less•ness** *n.*

sham•my (shăm′ē) ►*n.* Var. of **chamois** 2.

sham•poo (shăm-pōō′) ►*n., pl.* **-poos 1.** A preparation of soap or detergent used to wash the hair and scalp. **2.** Any of various cleaning agents for rugs or upholstery. **3.** The act or process of washing or cleaning with shampoo. [< Hindi *cā̃pnā,* press.] —**sham•poo′** *v.*

sham•rock (shăm′rŏk′) ►*n.* A plant, such as a clover, having leaves with three leaflets, considered the national emblem of Ireland. [Ir. Gael. *seamróg.*]

Shan•dong (shän′dông′) also **Shan•tung** (shăn′tŭng′, shän′tŏŏng′). A province of E China bordered by the Bo Hai and the Yellow Sea. Pop. 84,392,827.

shang•hai (shăng-hī′, shăng′hī′) ►*v.* **-haied, -hai•ing 1.** To kidnap (a man) for service aboard a ship, esp. after drugging him. **2.** To compel (someone) to do something, esp. by fraud or force. [< SHANGHAI.]

Shang•hai (shăng-hī′, shäng′-) A city of E China at the mouth of the Chang Jiang R. SE of Nanjing. Pop. 8,205,598.

Shan•gri-la (shăng′grĭ-lä′) ►*n.* An imaginary, remote paradise on earth. [After *Shangri-La,* in James Hilton's *Lost Horizon.*]

shank (shăngk) ►*n.* **1.** The part of the human leg between the knee and ankle or the corresponding part in other vertebrates. **2.** A cut of meat from the leg of an animal. **3.** The section of a tool or instrument connecting the functioning part and handle. **4.** A long narrow part; shaft. [< OE *sceanca.*]

Shan•non (shăn′ən) A river, about 386 km (240 mi), rising in N-central Ireland and flowing to the Atlantic.

shan't (shănt, shänt) ► Shall not.

shan•ty (shăn′tē) ►*n., pl.* **-ties.** A shack. [Prob. < Canadian Fr. *chantier.*]

shape (shāp) ►*n.* **1.** The characteristic surface configuration of a thing; form. **2.** The contour of a person's body; figure. **3.** A definite, distinctive form. **4.** A form or condition in which something may exist or appear. ►*v.* **shaped, shap•ing 1.** To give a particular form to. **2.** To take a definite form; develop. —***phrasal verb:*** **shape up 1.** *Informal* To turn out; develop. **2.** To improve. [< OE *gesceap,* creation.] —**shaped** *adj.* —**shap′er** *n.*

shape•less (shāp′lĭs) ►*adj.* Lacking a definite shape. —**shape′less•ly** *adv.* —**shape′less•ness** *n.*

Syns: *shapeless, amorphous, formless, unformed* **adj.**

shape•ly (shāp′lē) ►*adj.* **-li•er, -li•est.** Having a pleasing shape. —**shape′li•ness** *n.*

shard (shärd) ►*n.* **1.** A piece of broken pottery, esp. one found in an archaeological dig. **2.** A fragment. [< OE *sceard,* notch.]

share[1] (shâr) ►*n.* **1.** A part or portion belonging to a person or group. **2.** An equitable portion. **3.** Any of the equal parts into which the capital stock of a corporation or company is divided. ►*v.* **shared, shar•ing 1.** To divide and parcel out in shares; apportion. **2.** To use or experience in common. [< OE *scearu.*] —**shar′er** *n.*

share[2] (shâr) ►*n.* A plowshare. [< OE *scēar.*]

share•crop•per (shâr′krŏp′ər) ►*n.* A tenant farmer who gives a share of the crops raised to the landlord as rent.

share•hold•er (shâr′hōl′dər) ►*n.* One that owns or holds shares of stock; stockholder. —**share′hold′ing** *n.*

share•ware (shâr′wâr′) ►*n.* Copyrighted software that is available free of charge on a trial basis.

shark (shärk) ►*n.* **1.** Any of numerous often large and voracious marine fishes having a cartilaginous skeleton and tough skin covered with small toothlike scales. **2.** A ruthless, greedy, or dishonest person. [?]

shark•skin (shärk′skĭn′) ►*n.* **1.** A shark's skin or leather made from it. **2.** A fabric having a smooth shiny surface.

sharp (shärp) ►*adj.* **-er, -est 1.** Having a thin edge or a fine point. **2a.** Having clear form and distinct detail. **b.** Not rounded or blunt; pointed: *a sharp nose.* **3.** Abrupt or acute: *a sharp turn.* **4.** Shrewd; astute. **5.** Crafty or deceitful. **6.** Alert: *a sharp eye.* **7.** Harsh or biting. **8.** Intense; severe: *a sharp pain.* **9.** Sudden and shrill. **10.** *Mus.* **a.** Raised in pitch by a semitone: *a C sharp.* **b.** Being above the proper pitch. **11.** *Informal* Attractive or stylish. See Syns at **fashionable.** ►*adv.* **1.** In a sharp manner. **2.** Punctually; exactly. **3.** *Mus.* Above the proper pitch. ►*n.* **1.** *Mus.* **a.** A note or tone raised one semitone above its normal pitch. **b.** A sign (♯) indicating this. **2.** A shrewd cheater. [< OE *scearp,* slope.] —**sharp′ly** *adv.* —**sharp′ness** *n.*

sharp•en (shär′pən) ►*v.* To make or become sharp or sharper. —**sharp′en•er** *n.*

sharp•shoot•er (shärp′sho͞o′tər) ►*n.* One who is highly proficient at shooting.

Shas•ta (shăs′tə), **Mount.** A volcanic peak, 4,319.4 m (14,162 ft), of the Cascade Range in N CA.

Shatt al Ar•ab or **Shatt-al-Ar•ab** (shăt′ ăl ăr′əb, shät′). A river channel, about 193 km (120 mi), of SE Iraq formed by the confluence of the Tigris and Euphrates rivers and flowing to the Persian Gulf.

shat•ter (shăt′ər) ►*v.* **1.** To break or burst suddenly into pieces, as with a violent blow. **2.** To disable or destroy. [< OE **sceaterian,* scatter.]

shat•ter•proof (shăt′ər-pro͞of′) ►*adj.* Resistant to shattering.

shave (shāv) ►*v.* **shaved, shaved** or **shav•en** (shā′vən), **shav•ing 1.** To remove the beard or other body hair (from) with a razor or shaver. **2.** To remove thin slices of or from. **3.** To come close to or graze in passing. See Syns at **brush**[1]. ►*n.* The act, process, or result of shaving. [< OE *sceafan.*]

shav•er (shā′vər) ►*n.* **1.** A device, esp. an electric razor, used in shaving. **2.** *Informal* A small child, esp. a boy.

shav•ing (shā′vĭng) ►*n.* A thin slice or sliver, as of wood.

Shaw (shô), **George Bernard.** 1856–1950. Irish-born British playwright; 1925 Nobel.

shawl (shôl) ►*n.* A piece of cloth worn as a covering for the head, neck, and shoulders. [< Pers. *shāl.*]

Shaw•nee (shô-nē′) ►*n., pl.* **-nee** or **-nees 1.** A member of a Native American people formerly of the central Ohio Valley, now in Oklahoma. **2.** Their Algonquian language.

Shaw•wal (shə-wäl′) ►*n.* The 10th month of the Muslim calendar. See table at **calendar.** [Ar. *šawwāl.*]

shay (shā) ►*n. Informal* A chaise. [< CHAISE.]

she (shē) ►*pron.* **1.** Used to refer to the female previously mentioned or implied. See Usage Note at **I**[1]. **2.** Used in place of *it* to refer to certain inanimate things, such as ships and nations. ►*n.* A female animal or person: *Is the cat a she?* [Prob. < OE *sēo,* feminine of *sē,* that one.]

sheaf (shēf) ►*n., pl.* **sheaves** (shēvz) **1.** A bound bundle of cut stalks, esp. of grain. **2.** A collection of items held or bound together. [< OE *scēaf.*]

shear (shîr) ►*v.* **sheared, sheared** or **shorn** (shôrn, shōrn), **shear•ing 1.** To remove (fleece or hair) by cutting or clipping. **2.** To remove the hair or fleece from. **3.** To cut with or as if with shears: *shear a hedge.* **4.** To divest or deprive. ►*n.* also **shears 1.** A pair of scissors. **2.** Any of various implements or machines that cut with a scissorlike action. [< OE *sceran.*] —**shear′er** *n.*

sheath (shēth) ►*n., pl.* **sheaths** (shē*th*z, shēths) **1a.** A case for a blade, as of a sword or knife. **b.** Any of various similar coverings. **2.** *Biol.* An enveloping tubular structure, as the base of a grass leaf. **3.** A close-fitting dress. [< OE *scēath.*] —**sheath** *v.*

sheathe (shē*th*) ►*v.* **sheathed, sheath•ing.** To insert into or provide with a sheath. [ME *shethen.*]

sheath•ing (shē′*th*ĭng) ►*n.* A layer esp. of boards applied to a building to serve as a base for weatherproof cladding.

she•bang (shə-băng′) ►*n. Slang* A situation or

organization: *ran the whole shebang.* [?]

She•bat (shə-bät′, -vät′) ► *n.* Var. of **Shevat.**

shed¹ (shĕd) ► *v.* **shed, shed•ding 1.** To pour forth: *shed tears.* **2.** To radiate; cast: *shed light.* **3.** To repel without allowing penetration: *shed water.* **4.** To lose by natural process: *a snake shedding its skin.* —***idiom:* shed blood** To kill. [< OE *scēadan*, divide.] —**shed′der** *n.*

shed² (shĕd) ► *n.* A small roofed structure for storage or shelter. [< ME *shadde.*]

she'd (shēd) ► **1.** She had. **2.** She would.

sheen (shēn) ► *n.* Glistening brightness; luster. [< OE *scīene.*]

sheep (shēp) ► *n., pl.* **sheep 1.** Any of various usu. horned ruminant mammals raised for wool, meat, or skin. **2.** One who is easily swayed or led. [< OE *scēap.*]

sheep•dog also **sheep dog** (shēp′dôg′, -dŏg′) ► *n.* A dog bred or trained to herd sheep.

sheep•ish (shē′pĭsh) ► *adj.* Embarrassed, as by consciousness of a fault: *a sheepish grin.* —**sheep′ish•ly** *adv.* —**sheep′ish•ness** *n.*

sheep•skin (shēp′skĭn′) ► *n.* **1.** The tanned skin of a sheep, with or without the fleece. **2.** *Informal* A diploma.

sheer¹ (shîr) ► *v.* To swerve from a course. [Prob. < LGer. *scheren.*] —**sheer** *n.*

sheer² (shîr) ► *adj.* **-er, -est 1.** Thin and transparent: *sheer curtains.* **2.** Undiluted; pure: *sheer happiness.* See Syns at **pure. 3.** Almost perpendicular: *a sheer cliff.* See Syns at **steep¹.** [< ME *shir*, clear, and *skir*, clean.]

sheet¹ (shēt) ► *n.* **1.** A rectangular piece of fabric serving as a basic article of bedding. **2.** A broad, thin, usu. rectangular piece, as of paper or metal. [< OE *scēte.*]

sheet² (shēt) ► *n. Naut.* **1.** A rope or chain attached to a lower corner of a sail, serving to move or extend it. **2. sheets** The spaces at either end of an open boat in front of and behind the seats. [< OE *scēata*, corner of a sail.]

sheet metal ► *n.* Metal rolled into a relatively thin sheet. —**sheet′-met′al** *adj.*

sheet music ► *n.* Musical compositions printed on unbound sheets of paper.

Sheet•rock (shēt′rŏk′) ► A trademark for plasterboard.

Shef•field (shĕf′ēld′) A borough of N-central England E of Manchester. Pop. 531,928.

sheik also **sheikh** (shēk, shāk) ► *n.* The leader of an Arab or Muslim tribe, village, or family. [Ar. *šayḫ*, old man.] —**sheik′dom** *n.*

shek•el (shĕk′əl) ► *n.* **1a.** Any of several ancient units of weight, esp. a Hebrew unit equal to about a half ounce. **b.** The chief silver coin of the ancient Hebrews. **2. shekels** *Slang* Money. [Heb. *šeqel.*]

shelf (shĕlf) ► *n., pl.* **shelves** (shĕlvz) **1.** A flat, usu. rectangular structure, as of wood or metal, fixed horizontally to a wall or in a frame and used to hold or store objects. **2.** Something, such as a projecting ledge of rock, that resembles a shelf. [ME.]

shelf life ► *n.* The length of time a product may be stored without deteriorating.

shell (shĕl) ► *n.* **1a.** The usu. hard outer covering that encases certain organisms, such as mollusks and insects. **b.** A similar outer covering on an egg, fruit, or nut. **2.** Something resembling a shell, esp.: **a.** An external, usu. hard, protective cover. **b.** A framework or exterior, as of a building. **c.** A thin layer of pastry. **3.** A long narrow racing boat propelled by rowers. **4.** A projectile or piece of ammunition. **5.** *Phys.* **a.** Any of the hypothetical spherical surfaces centered on the nucleus of an atom containing electrons. **b.** An analogous pattern of protons and neutrons within a nucleus. **6.** *Comp. Sci.* A program that works with the operating system as a command processor. ► *v.* **1.** To remove the shell of; shuck. **2.** To fire shells at; bombard. —***phrasal verb:* shell out** *Informal* To pay (money). [< OE *scell.*]

she'll (shēl) ► **1.** She will. **2.** She shall.

shel•lac (shə-lăk′) ► *n.* **1.** A purified lac formed into flakes and used in varnishes, paints, inks, and sealants. **2.** A thin varnish made by dissolving this substance in denatured alcohol. ► *v.* **-lacked, -lack•ing 1.** To coat or finish with shellac. **2.** *Slang* To defeat decisively. [SHEL(L) + LAC.]

Shel•ley (shĕl′ē), **Mary Wollstonecraft Godwin.** 1797–1851. British writer.

Shelley, Percy Bysshe. 1792–1822. British romantic poet.

Mary Shelley

Percy B. Shelley

shell•fire (shĕl′fīr′) ► *n.* The shooting of artillery shells.

shell•fish (shĕl′fĭsh′) ► *n.* An aquatic animal, such as a mollusk, having a shell or shell-like covering. —**shell′fish′ing** *n.*

shell shock ► *n.* Any of various acute neuroses due to trauma suffered under fire in modern warfare. —**shell′-shocked′** *adj.*

shel•ter (shĕl′tər) ► *n.* **1a.** Something that provides cover or protection, as from the weather. **b.** A refuge; haven. **c.** An establishment that provides temporary housing for homeless people. **2.** The state of being covered or protected. ► *v.* **1.** To provide shelter for. **2.** To take cover or refuge. [?]

shelve (shĕlv) ► *v.* **shelved, shelv•ing 1.** To place on a shelf. **2.** To put aside; postpone. See Syns at **defer¹.**

shelves (shĕlvz) ► *n.* Pl. of **shelf.**

shelv•ing (shĕl′vĭng) ► *n.* A set of shelves.

Shen•an•do•ah Valley (shĕn′ən-dō′ə) A valley of N VA between the Allegheny Mts. and the Blue Ridge.

she•nan•i•gan (shə-năn′ĭ-gən) ► *n. Informal* **1.** An underhanded act. **2.** often **shenanigans** Mischief. [?]

Shen•yang (shŭn′yăng′) A city of NE China ENE of Beijing. Pop. 4,655,280.

Shep•ard (shĕp′ərd), **Alan Bartlett, Jr.** 1923–98. First Amer. astronaut in space.

shep•herd (shĕp′ərd) ► *n.* One who herds, guards, and tends sheep. ► *v.* To guard or tend as or like a shepherd. See Syns at **guide.** [< OE *scēaphierde.*]

shep•herd•ess (shĕp′ər-dĭs) ► *n.* A girl or

woman who herds or guards sheep.

shep•herd's pie (shĕp′ərdz) ► *n.* A meat pie baked under a crust of mashed potatoes.

sheq•el (shĕk′əl) ► *n., pl.* **sheq•al•im** (shĕk′ə-lĭm). See table at **currency.** [Heb. *šeqel*, SHEKEL.]

sher•bet (shûr′bĭt) ► *n.* also **sher•bert** (-bûrt′) A frozen dessert made of fruit juice, sugar, and water with milk, egg white, or gelatin. [< Ar. *šarba*, drink.]

Sher•i•dan (shĕr′ĭ-dn), **Philip Henry.** 1831–88. Amer. Union general.

Sheridan, Richard Brinsley. 1751–1816. British playwright and politician.

sher•iff (shĕr′ĭf) ► *n.* The chief law enforcement officer in a US county. [< OE *scīrgerēfa*, royal representative in a shire.]

Sher•man (shûr′mən), **Roger.** 1721–93. Amer. Revolutionary patriot and politician.

Sherman, William Tecumseh. 1820–91. Amer. Union general.

Sher•pa (shûr′pə) ► *n., pl.* **-pa** or **-pas.** A member of a Tibetan people living in Nepal and Sikkim.

sher•ry (shĕr′ē) ► *n., pl.* **-ries.** A fortified Spanish wine. [From *Xeres* (Jerez), Spain.]

Sher•wood Forest (shŭr′wŏŏd′) A forest of central England; site of the legendary exploits of Robin Hood.

Shet•land (shĕt′lənd) ► *n.* A fine yarn made from the wool of sheep raised in the Shetland Islands.

Shetland Islands. An archipelago of N Scotland in the Atlantic NE of the Orkney Is.

Shetland pony ► *n.* A small sturdy pony of a breed originating in the Shetland Islands.

She•vat (shə-vät′) also **She•bat** (shə-bät′, -vät′) ► *n.* A month of the Jewish calendar. See table at **calendar.** [Heb. *šəbāṭ*.]

shi•at•su (shē-ät′sōō) ► *n.* Therapeutic massage with the thumbs and palms of those areas of the body used in acupuncture. [< J. *shiatsuryōhō*.]

shib•bo•leth (shĭb′ə-lĭth, -lĕth′) ► *n.* A word or phrase closely identified with a particular group or cause. [< Heb. *šibbōlet*.]

shied[1] (shīd) ► *v.* P.t. and p.part. of **shy**[1].

shied[2] (shīd) ► *v.* P.t. and p.part. of **shy**[2].

shield (shēld) ► *n.* **1.** A broad piece of armor strapped to the arm for protection against weapons. **2.** A protective device or structure. **3.** Something that resembles a shield. ► *v.* **1.** To protect or defend with or as if with a shield; guard. **2.** To cover up; conceal. [< OE *scield*.] —**shield′er** *n.*

shi•er (shī′ər) ► *adj.* Comp. of **shy**[1].

shi•est (shī′ĭst) ► *adj.* Superl. of **shy**[1].

shift (shĭft) ► *v.* **1.** To exchange (one thing) for another: *shifted assignments.* **2.** To move or transfer from one place or position to another. **3.** To change position, direction, or place. **4.** To change (gears), as in an automobile. **5.** To provide for one's own needs; get along. ► *n.* **1.** A change from one person or configuration to another; substitution. **2a.** A group of workers that relieve another on a regular schedule. **b.** The working period of such a group: *the night shift.* **3.** A change in direction or position. **4.** A gearshift. **5a.** A loosely fitting dress that hangs straight from the shoulder. **b.** A woman's undergarment; slip or chemise. [< OE *sciftan*, arrange.] —**shift′er** *n.*

shift•less (shĭft′lĭs) ► *adj.* Lacking ambition or purpose. —**shift′less•ness** *n.*

shift•y (shĭf′tē) ► *adj.* **-i•er, -i•est.** Suggestive of deceitful character; evasive or untrustworthy. —**shift′i•ly** *adv.* —**shift′i•ness** *n.*

Shi•ite also **Shi•′ite** (shē′īt′) ► *n.* A member of the branch of Islam that regards the caliph Ali and his descendants as the legitimate successors to Muhammad. —**Shi′ism** *n.* —**Shi′ite′** *adj.*

Shi•jia•zhuang (shœ′jyä′jwäng′) also **Shih•kia•chwang** (-kyä′chwäng′). A city of NE China SW of Beijing. Pop. 1,372,109.

Shi•ko•ku (shē-kô′kōō) An island of S Japan between SW Honshu and E Kyushu.

shill (shĭl) ► *n. Slang* One who poses as a satisfied customer to dupe bystanders into participating in a swindle. [?] —**shill** *v.*

shil•le•lagh (shə-lā′lē, -lə) ► *n.* A cudgel of oak or other hardwood. [After *Shillelagh*, Ireland.]

shil•ling (shĭl′ĭng) ► *n.* See table at **currency.** [< OE *scilling*.]

shil•ly-shal•ly (shĭl′ē-shăl′ē) ► *v.* **-lied** (-lēd), **-ly•ing 1.** To procrastinate; dawdle. **2.** To vacillate. [< *shall I*.] —**shil′ly-shal′li•er** *n.*

shim (shĭm) ► *n.* A thin piece or wedge used to make something level or to adjust something to fit properly. [?] —**shim** *v.*

shim•mer (shĭm′ər) ► *v.* To shine with a flickering light. ► *n.* A flickering or tremulous light; glimmer. [< OE *scimerian*.] —**shim′mer•ing•ly** *adv.* —**shim′mer•y** *adj.*

shim•my (shĭm′ē) ► *n., pl.* **-mies 1.** Abnormal vibration or wobbling, as of the wheels of an automobile. **2.** A chemise. ► *v.* **-mied, -my•ing.** To vibrate or wobble. [Prob. < CHEMISE.]

shin (shĭn) ► *n.* The front part of the leg between the knee and the ankle. ► *v.* **shinned, shin•ning.** To climb (e.g., a pole) by gripping and pulling alternately with the hands and legs. [< OE *scinu*.]

shin•dig (shĭn′dĭg′) ► *n.* A festive party or celebration. [Prob. < *shindy*, commotion.]

shine (shīn) ► *v.* **shone** (shōn) or **shined, shin•ing 1.** To emit light. **2.** To reflect light; glint or glisten. **3.** To distinguish oneself; excel. **4.** To aim or cast the beam of (a light). **5.** To make glossy or bright by polishing. ► *n.* **1.** Brightness; radiance. **2.** A shoeshine. **3.** Fair weather: *rain or shine.* —***idiom:*** **take a shine to** *Informal* To like spontaneously. [< OE *scīnan*.]

shin•er (shī′nər) ► *n.* **1.** *Slang* A black eye. **2.** Any of numerous small silvery fishes.

shin•gle[1] (shĭng′gəl) ► *n.* **1.** A thin oblong piece of material, such as wood, laid in overlapping rows to cover the roofs or sides of a house. **2.** *Informal* A small signboard, as one indicating a professional office. ► *v.* **1.** To cover (e.g., a roof) with shingles. **2.** To cut (hair) short and close to the head. [< Lat. *scandula*.] —**shin′gler** *n.*

shin•gle[2] (shĭng′gəl) ► *n.* **1.** Beach gravel consisting of large smooth pebbles. **2.** A beach covered with such gravel. [ME.]

shin•gles (shĭng′gəlz) ► *pl.n. (takes sing. or pl. v.)* An acute viral infection marked by skin eruption along a nerve path on one side of the body. [< Lat. *cingulum*, girdle.]

shin•ny (shĭn′ē) ► *v.* **-nied** (-nēd), **-ny•ing.** To shin: *shinny up a pole.* [< SHIN[1].]

Shin•to (shĭn′tō) ► *n.* A religion native to Japan, characterized by worship of nature spirits and ancestors. [J. *shintō*.] —**Shin′to** *adj.* —**Shin′to•ism** *n.* —**Shin′to•ist** *adj. & n.*

shin•y (shī′nē) ▸*adj.* **-i•er, -i•est.** Bright; glistening. —**shin′i•ness** *n.*

ship (shĭp) ▸*n.* **1.** A large vessel built for deep-water navigation. **2.** A sailing vessel having three or more square-rigged masts. **3.** An aircraft or spacecraft. ▸*v.* **shipped, ship•ping 1.** To place or receive on board a ship. **2.** To cause to be transported; send. See Syns at **send. 3.** To take in (water) over the side of a ship. [< OE *scip.*] —**ship′per** *n.*

-ship ▸*suff.* **1.** Quality or condition: *friendship.* **2.** Rank, status, or office: *professorship.* **3.** Art or skill: *penmanship.* [< OE *-scipe.*]

ship•board (shĭp′bôrd′, -bōrd′) ▸*n.* A ship.

ship•build•ing (shĭp′bĭl′dĭng) ▸*n.* The business of designing and constructing ships. —**ship′build′er** *n.*

ship•mas•ter (shĭp′măs′tər) ▸*n.* The officer in command of a merchant ship.

ship•mate (shĭp′māt′) ▸*n.* A fellow sailor.

ship•ment (shĭp′mənt) ▸*n.* **1.** The act of shipping goods. **2.** A quantity of goods or cargo shipped together.

ship•ping (shĭp′ĭng) ▸*n.* **1.** The act or business of transporting goods. **2.** The body of ships belonging to one port or country.

ship•shape (shĭp′shāp′) ▸*adj.* Orderly and neat; tidy. —**ship′shape′** *adv.*

ship•wreck (shĭp′rĕk′) ▸*n.* **1.** The destruction of a ship, as by storm or collision. **2.** The remains of a wrecked ship. ▸*v.* To cause to suffer shipwreck.

ship•yard (shĭp′yärd′) ▸*n.* A yard where ships are built or repaired.

Shi•raz (shē-räz′) A city of SW-central Iran SSE of Tehran. Pop. 1,042,801.

shire (shīr) ▸*n.* A division of Great Britain, equivalent to a county. [< OE *scīr*, district.]

shirk (shûrk) ▸*v.* To avoid or neglect (a duty or responsibility). [?] —**shirk′er** *n.*

shirr (shûr) ▸*v.* **1.** To gather (cloth) into parallel rows. **2.** To cook (eggs) by baking until set. [?]

shirt (shûrt) ▸*n.* **1.** A garment for the upper part of the body, usu. having a collar, sleeves, and a front opening. **2.** An undershirt. [< OE *scyrte*, skirt.]

shirt•waist (shûrt′wāst′) ▸*n.* A woman's blouse styled like a tailored shirt.

shish ke•bab also **shish ke•bob** or **shish ka•bob** (shĭsh′ kə-bŏb′) ▸*n.* A dish of pieces of seasoned meat and often vegetables roasted and served on skewers. [< Turk. *şiş kebabı.*]

Shi•va (shē′və) ▸*n.* A principal Hindu god, the destroyer and restorer of worlds.

shiv•er¹ (shĭv′ər) ▸*v.* To shake, as with cold or fear; tremble. [ME *chiveren.*] —**shiv′er** *n.* —**shiv′er•y** *adj.*

shiv•er² (shĭv′ər) ▸*v.* To break into fragments or splinters. [< ME *shivere*, splinter.]

Sho•ah (shō′ə) ▸*n.* The mass murder of European Jews by the Nazis during World War II. [Heb. *šô'â*, calamity.]

shoal¹ (shōl) ▸*n.* **1.** A shallow. **2.** A sandbank or sandbar. [< OE *sceald*, shallow.]

shoal² (shōl) ▸*n.* **1.** A large group; crowd. **2.** A large school of fish. [Prob. MLGer. or MDu. *schōle.*]

shoat (shōt) ▸*n.* A young pig. [ME *shote.*]

shock¹ (shŏk) ▸*n.* **1.** A violent collision or impact. **2.** A violent, unexpected disturbance of mental or emotional balance. **3.** A severe offense to one's sense of propriety or decency; outrage. **4.** A gen. temporary physiological reaction to severe trauma, usu. marked by loss of blood pressure and depression of vital processes. **5.** The sensation caused by an electric current passing through the body. ▸*v.* **1.** To strike with sudden forceful impact. **2.** To disgust; offend. **3.** To induce a state of shock in (a person). **4.** To subject to an electric shock. [< OFr. *chuquier*, collide with.]

shock² (shŏk) ▸*n.* **1.** A number of sheaves of grain stacked upright in a field for drying. **2.** A thick heavy mass: *a shock of white hair.* [ME *shok.*]

shock absorber ▸*n.* A device used to absorb mechanical shocks, esp. in a motor vehicle.

shock•er (shŏk′ər) ▸*n.* One that startles or horrifies, as a sensational story.

shock•ing (shŏk′ĭng) ▸*adj.* **1.** Highly disturbing emotionally. **2.** Highly offensive; distasteful. —**shock′ing•ly** *adv.*

shock therapy ▸*n.* A treatment for mental disorders in which a convulsion is induced by electric current or drugs.

shock troops ▸*pl.n.* Soldiers specially chosen, trained, and armed to lead an attack.

shock wave ▸*n.* A large-amplitude compression wave, as that produced by an explosion or by supersonic motion of a body in a medium.

shod•dy (shŏd′ē) ▸*adj.* **-di•er, -di•est 1.** Made of or containing inferior material. **2.** Dishonest or unscrupulous. **3.** Cheaply imitative. [?] —**shod′di•ly** *adv.* —**shod′di•ness** *n.*

shoe (shōō) ▸*n.* **1.** A durable covering for the human foot. **2.** A horseshoe. **3.** The casing of a pneumatic tire. **4.** The part of a brake that presses against the wheel or drum to retard motion. ▸*v.* **shod** (shŏd), **shod** or **shod•den** (shŏd′n), **shoe•ing.** To furnish or fit with shoes. [< OE *scōh.*]

shoe•horn (shōō′hôrn′) ▸*n.* A curved implement inserted at the heel to help put on a shoe. —**shoe′horn′** *v.*

shoe•lace (shōō′lās′) ▸*n.* A string or cord used for lacing and fastening shoes.

shoe•mak•er (shōō′mā′kər) ▸*n.* One that makes or repairs shoes. —**shoe′mak′ing** *n.*

shoe•string (shōō′strĭng′) ▸*n.* **1.** See **shoelace. 2.** A small sum of money or capital used to launch a venture. ▸*adj.* Cut long and slender: *shoestring potatoes.*

shoe•tree (shōō′trē′) ▸*n.* A form made of inflexible material inserted into a shoe to preserve its shape.

shoetree

sho•gun (shō′gən) ▸*n.* The hereditary commander of the Japanese army who until 1867 exercised absolute rule. [J. *shōgun*, general.]

shone (shōn) ▸*v.* P.t. and p.part. of **shine.**

shoo (sho͞o) ▸ *interj.* Used to frighten away animals. —**shoo** *v.*

shoo-in (sho͞o′ĭn′) ▸ *n. Informal* A sure winner.

shook (sho͝ok) ▸ *v.* P.t. of **shake.**

shook-up (sho͝ok-ŭp′) ▸ *adj. Slang* Emotionally upset; shaken.

shoot (sho͞ot) ▸ *v.* **shot** (shŏt), **shoot•ing 1.** To hit, wound, or kill with a missile. **2.** To fire (a missile) from a weapon. **3.** To discharge (a weapon). **4.** To send forth swiftly. **5.** To pass over or through swiftly: *shooting the rapids.* **6.** To record on film. **7.** To project or cause to project or protrude. **8.** To begin to grow or produce; put forth. **9.** *Sports & Games* To propel (e.g., a ball) toward its objective. **10.** *Informal* To spend, exhaust, or waste: *shot their savings on a new boat.* —***phrasal verb:* shoot up 1.** *Informal* To grow or get taller rapidly. **2.** *Slang* To inject a drug with a hypodermic syringe. ▸ *n.* **1.** The young growth arising from a germinating seed; sprout. **2.** An organized shooting activity, such as a hunt. [< OE *scēotan.*] —**shoot′er** *n.*

shoot•ing star (sho͞o′tĭng) ▸ *n.* See **meteor.**

shop (shŏp) ▸ *n.* **1.** A small retail store. **2.** A place for manufacturing or repairing goods or machinery. **3.** A commercial or industrial establishment. ▸ *v.* **shopped, shop•ping.** To visit stores to buy or examine goods. [< OE *sceoppa,* workshop.] —**shop′per** *n.*

shop•keep•er (shŏp′kē′pər) ▸ *n.* One who owns or manages a shop.

shop•lift (shŏp′lĭft′) ▸ *v.* To steal merchandise on display in a store. —**shop′lift′er** *n.* —**shop′lift′ing** *n.*

shop•ping center (shŏp′ĭng) ▸ *n.* A group of retail stores and other businesses having a common parking lot.

shopping mall ▸ *n.* **1.** An urban shopping area limited to pedestrians. **2.** A shopping center with stores facing enclosed walkways for pedestrians.

shop steward ▸ *n.* A union member elected to represent coworkers in dealings with management.

shop•talk (shŏp′tôk′) ▸ *n.* Talk or conversation concerning one's work or business.

shop•worn (shŏp′wôrn′, -wōrn′) ▸ *adj.* **1.** Frayed, faded, or defective from being on display in a store. **2.** Hackneyed; trite.

shore[1] (shôr, shōr) ▸ *n.* The land along the edge of an ocean, sea, lake, or river; coast. [< OE *scora.*]

shore[2] (shôr, shōr) ▸ *v.* **shored, shor•ing.** To support by or as if by a prop: *shore up a sagging wall.* [ME *shoren.*]

shore•line (shôr′līn′, shōr′-) ▸ *n.* The edge of a body of water.

shorn (shôrn, shōrn) ▸ *v.* P.part. of **shear.**

short (shôrt) ▸ *adj.* **-er, -est 1.** Having little length. **2.** Having little height. **3.** Lasting a brief time. **4.** Not lengthy; succinct. **5.** Rudely brief; abrupt. **6.** Inadequate; insufficient: *oil in short supply.* **7.** Lacking in length or amount. **8.** Containing shortening; flaky: *a short pie crust.* **9.** *Ling.* Of or being a speech sound of relatively brief duration, as the sound of (ă) in *pat.* ▸ *adv.* **1.** Abruptly; quickly. **2.** At a point before a given limit or goal. **3.** At a disadvantage: *caught short.* ▸ *n.* **1.** Anything short. **2a. shorts** Short trousers extending to the knee or above. **b. shorts** Men's undershorts. **3.** A short circuit. **4.** A short subject. ▸ *v.* To cause a short circuit in. [< OE *scort.*] —**short′ness** *n.*

short•age (shôr′tĭj) ▸ *n.* A deficiency in amount.

short•bread (shôrt′brĕd′) ▸ *n.* A cookie made with much butter or other shortening.

short•cake (shôrt′kāk′) ▸ *n.* A cake made with rich biscuit dough and usu. served with fruit.

short•change (shôrt′chānj′) ▸ *v.* **1.** To give less than the correct change to. **2.** *Informal* To treat deceitfully; cheat.

short circuit ▸ *n.* A low-resistance connection accidentally established between two points in an electric circuit. —**short′-cir′cuit** *v.*

short•com•ing (shôrt′kŭm′ĭng) ▸ *n.* A deficiency; flaw.

short•cut (shôrt′kŭt′) ▸ *n.* **1.** A more direct route than the customary one. **2.** A means of saving time or effort. —**short′cut′** *v.*

short•en (shôr′tn) ▸ *v.* To make or become short or shorter. —**short′en•er** *n.*

Syns: *shorten, abbreviate, abridge, curtail, truncate* ***Ant:*** *lengthen* **v.**

short•en•ing (shôr′tn-ĭng, shôrt′nĭng) ▸ *n.* A fat, such as butter or lard, used to make cake or pastry light and flaky.

short•fall (shôrt′fôl′) ▸ *n.* **1.** A shortage. **2.** The amount by which a supply falls short of expectation, need, or demand.

short•hand (shôrt′hănd′) ▸ *n.* A system of rapid handwriting employing symbols to represent words, phrases, and letters.

short-hand•ed (shôrt′hăn′dĭd) ▸ *adj.* Lacking the necessary number of workers.

short•list (shôrt′lĭst′) ▸ *n.* A list of preferable items or candidates selected for final consideration. —**short′-list′** *v.*

short-lived (shôrt′līvd′, -lĭvd′) ▸ *adj.* Living or lasting only a short time.

short•ly (shôrt′lē) ▸ *adv.* **1.** Soon. **2.** In a few words; concisely. **3.** Rudely; curtly.

short order ▸ *n.* Food prepared and served quickly. —**short′-or′der** *adj.*

short-range (shôrt′rānj′) ▸ *adj.* **1.** Designed for short distances: *a short-range missile.* **2.** Relating to the near future: *short-range goals.*

short shrift ▸ *n.* **1.** Careless treatment. **2.** Quick work.

short•sight•ed (shôrt′sī′tĭd) ▸ *adj.* **1.** Nearsighted; myopic. **2.** Lacking foresight. —**short′sight′ed•ness** *n.*

short•stop (shôrt′stŏp′) ▸ *n. Baseball* **1.** The field position between 2nd and 3rd base. **2.** The infielder who plays this position.

short story ▸ *n.* A relatively short piece of prose fiction, having few characters and aiming at unity of effect.

short subject ▸ *n.* A brief film shown before a feature-length film.

short-tem•pered (shôrt′tĕm′pərd) ▸ *adj.* Easily moved to anger.

short-term (shôrt′tûrm′) ▸ *adj.* **1.** Involving or lasting a relatively brief time. **2.** Payable or reaching maturity within a relatively brief time, such as a year.

short ton ▸ *n.* See table at **measurement.**

short wave ▸ *n.* An electromagnetic wave with a wavelength of approx. 200 m or less. —**short′wave′** *adj.*

Sho•sho•ne also **Sho•sho•ni** (shō-shō′nē) ▸ *n., pl.* **-ne** or **-nes** also **-ni** or **-nis 1.** A member of a Native American people inhabiting an area from W Wyoming and SE Idaho to S Nevada. **2.** Any of their languages. —**Sho•sho′ne•an** *adj.*

Shos•ta•ko•vich (shŏs′tə-kō′vĭch), **Dimitri.** 1906–75. Russian composer.

shot[1] (shŏt) ►*n.* **1.** The firing or discharge of a weapon. **2.** The distance over which something is shot; range. **3.** *Sports* A throw, hit, or drive in any of several games. **4.** *Informal* **a.** An attempt; try. **b.** A guess. **c.** An opportunity. **5.** *pl.* **shot a.** A projectile designed to be discharged from a gun. **b.** One of a group of pellets discharged esp. from a shotgun. **6.** *Sports* A shot put. **7a.** A photograph. **b.** A single cinematic take. **8.** A hypodermic injection. **9.** A drink of liquor. [< OE *scot.*]

shot[2] (shŏt) ►*v.* P.t. and p.part. of **shoot.**

shot•gun (shŏt′gŭn′) ►*n.* A smooth-bore gun that fires shot over short ranges.

shot put ►*n.* **1.** An athletic event in which a heavy metal ball is thrown for distance. **2.** The ball used in this competition. —**shot′-put′ter** *n.*

should (sho͝od) ►*aux.v.* P.t. of **shall.** Used to express obligation, necessity, probability, or contingency.

Usage: *Should have* is sometimes incorrectly written *should of* by writers who have mistaken the source of the spoken contraction *should've.*

shoul•der (shōl′dər) ►*n.* **1a.** The joint connecting the arm with the torso. **b.** The part of the human body between the neck and upper arm. **2.** often **shoulders** The area of the back from one shoulder to the other. **3.** The edge along either side of a roadway. ►*v.* **1.** To carry or place on the shoulders. **2.** To take on; assume. **3.** To push with or as if with the shoulder. [< OE *sculdor.*]

shoulder blade ►*n.* See **scapula.**

should•n't (sho͝od′nt) ► Should not.

shout (shout) ►*n.* A loud cry. ►*v.* To utter a shout. [ME *shoute.*] —**shout′er** *n.*

Syns: *shout, bawl, bellow, holler, howl, roar, whoop, yell* **v.**

shove (shŭv) ►*v.* **shoved, shov•ing 1.** To push forward or along. **2.** To push rudely or roughly. See Syns at **push.** —***phrasal verb:*** **shove off 1.** To push (a boat) away from shore in leaving. **2.** *Informal* To leave. [< OE *scūfan.*] —**shove** *n.* —**shov′er** *n.*

shov•el (shŭv′əl) ►*n.* **1.** A tool with a handle and scoop for digging and moving material, such as dirt or snow. **2.** A large mechanical device for heavy digging or excavation. ►*v.* **-eled, -el•ing** also **-elled, -el•ling 1.** To move or remove with a shovel. **2.** To convey roughly or hastily: *shoveled his food down.* [< OE *scofl.*]

show (shō) ►*v.* **showed, shown** (shōn) or **showed, show•ing 1.** To cause or allow to be seen; display. **2.** To conduct; guide. **3.** To point out. **4.** To manifest; reveal. **5.** To demonstrate by reasoning or procedure. **6.** To grant; bestow. **7.** To be visible or evident. **8.** *Sports* To finish third or better, as in a horserace. —***phrasal verb:*** **show off** To behave or display in an ostentatious or boasting manner. ►*n.* **1.** A display; manifestation. **2.** A false appearance; pretense. **3.** A striking display; spectacle. **4.** A public exhibition or entertainment. **5.** *Informal* An undertaking: *ran the whole show.* **6.** *Sports* Third place esp. in a horserace. [< OE *scēawian,* look at.]

show•boat (shō′bōt′) ►*n.* A river steamboat having a troupe of performers and a theater. ►*v.* To show off.

show business ►*n.* The entertainment industry.

show•case (shō′kās′) ►*n.* **1.** A display case, as in a store or museum. **2.** A setting for advantageous display. ►*v.* **-cased, -cas•ing.** To display or feature prominently.

show•down (shō′doun′) ►*n.* An event that forces an issue to a conclusion.

show•er (shou′ər) ►*n.* **1.** A brief fall of rain, hail, or sleet. **2.** An outpouring: *a shower of praise.* **3.** A party held to honor and present gifts to someone. **4.** A bath in which the water is sprayed on the bather. ►*v.* **1.** To pour down in a shower. **2.** To bestow abundantly or liberally. See Syns at **barrage. 3.** To take a shower. [< OE *scūr.*]

show•ing (shō′ĭng) ►*n.* **1.** A presentation or display. **2.** Performance: *a poor showing.*

show•man (shō′mən) ►*n.* **1.** A theatrical producer. **2.** One with a flair for dramatic behavior. —**show′man•ship′** *n.*

show•off (shō′ôf′, -ŏf′) ►*n.* **1.** The act of showing off. **2.** One who shows off.

show•piece (shō′pēs′) ►*n.* Something exhibited as an outstanding example of its kind.

show place also **show•place** (shō′plās′) ►*n.* A place viewed and frequented for its beauty or historical noteworthiness.

show room ►*n.* A large room in which merchandise is displayed.

show•stop•per (shō′stŏp′ər) ►*n. Informal* A performance that evokes so much applause from the audience that the show is temporarily interrupted.

show•y (shō′ē) ►*adj.* **-i•er, -i•est 1.** Making an imposing display; striking. **2.** Ostentatious; flashy. —**show′i•ly** *adv.* —**show′i•ness** *n.*

Syns: *showy, flamboyant, ostentatious, pretentious, splashy* **adj.**

shrank (shrăngk) ►*v.* P.t. of **shrink.**

shrap•nel (shrăp′nəl) ►*n., pl.* **-nel 1.** An artillery shell containing metal balls fused to explode in the air above enemy troops. **2.** Shell fragments from a high-explosive shell. [After Gen. Henry *Shrapnel* (1761–1842).]

shred (shrĕd) ►*n.* **1.** A long irregular strip cut or torn off. **2.** A small amount; particle: *not a shred of evidence.* ►*v.* **shred•ded** or **shred, shred•ding.** To cut or tear into shreds. [< OE *screāde.*] —**shred′der** *n.*

Shreve•port (shrēv′pôrt′, -pōrt′) A city of NW LA on the Red R. Pop. 198,525.

shrew (shro͞o) ►*n.* **1.** A small, mouselike, chiefly insectivorous mammal having a pointed snout. **2.** A nagging or scolding woman. [< OE *scrēawa.*] —**shrew′ish** *adj.* —**shrew′ish•ly** *adv.* —**shrew′ish•ness** *n.*

shrewd (shro͞od) ►*adj.* **-er, -est 1.** Marked by keen awareness and a sense of the practical. **2.** Artful; cunning. [< ME *shrew,* rascal.] —**shrewd′ly** *adv.* —**shrewd′ness** *n.*

shriek (shrēk) ►*n.* A shrill, often frantic cry. [ME *shriken,* to shriek.] —**shriek** *v.*

shrift (shrĭft) ►*n. Archaic* The act of shriving. [< OE *scrift* < Lat. *scrīptum,* something written.]

shrike (shrīk) ►*n.* A carnivorous bird having a strong hooked bill and often impaling its prey on thorns. [< OE *scrīc,* thrush.]

shrill (shrĭl) ▸*adj.* **-er, -est.** High-pitched and piercing. ▸*v.* To produce a shrill sound. [ME *shrille.*] —**shrill′ness** *n.* —**shril′ly** *adv.*

shrimp (shrĭmp) ▸*n., pl.* **shrimp** or **shrimps 1.** Any of various small, often edible marine crustaceans. **2.** *Slang* A small or unimportant person. [ME *shrimpe.*] —**shrimp′er** *n.*

shrine (shrīn) ▸*n.* **1.** A container for sacred relics. **2.** The tomb of a saint. **3.** A site or object revered for its associations. [< Lat. *scrīnium,* case for books or papers.]

shrink (shrĭngk) ▸*v.* **shrank** (shrăngk) or **shrunk** (shrŭngk), **shrunk** or **shrunk•en** (shrŭng′kən), **shrink•ing 1.** To contract from heat, moisture, or cold. **2.** To dwindle. **3.** To draw back; recoil. ▸*n. Slang* A psychotherapist. [< OE *scrincan.*] —**shrink′a•ble** *adj.* —**shrink′age** *n.* —**shrink′er** *n.*

shrink-wrap (shrĭngk′răp′) ▸*n.* A protective plastic film wound about articles of merchandise and then shrunk by heat to form a sealed package. —**shrink′-wrap′** *v.*

shrive (shrīv) ▸*v.* **shrove** (shrōv) or **shrived, shriv•en** (shrĭv′ən) or **shrived, shriv•ing.** To hear the confession of and give absolution to (a penitent). [< Lat. *scrībere,* write.]

shriv•el (shrĭv′əl) ▸*v.* **-eled, -el•ing** or **-elled, -el•ling 1.** To become or make shrunken and wrinkled, often by drying. **2.** To lose or cause to lose vitality. [?]

shroud (shroud) ▸*n.* **1.** A cloth used to wrap a body for burial. **2.** Something that conceals, protects, or screens. **3.** One of a set of ropes or cables stretched from the masthead to a vessel's sides to support the mast. ▸*v.* **1.** To wrap (a corpse) in burial clothing. **2.** To shut off from sight; screen. See Syns at **block.** [< OE *scrūd,* garment.]

shrub (shrŭb) ▸*n.* A low woody plant having several stems but no single trunk. [< OE *scrybb.*] —**shrub′bi•ness** *n.* —**shrub′by** *adj.*

shrub•ber•y (shrŭb′ə-rē) ▸*n., pl.* **-ies.** A group or planting of shrubs.

shrug (shrŭg) ▸*v.* **shrugged, shrug•ging.** To raise (the shoulders) as a gesture of doubt, disdain, or indifference. —***phrasal verb:*** **shrug off 1.** To minimize. **2.** To get rid of. [ME *shruggen.*] —**shrug** *n.*

shrunk (shrŭngk) ▸*v.* P.t. and p.part. of **shrink.**

shrunk•en (shrŭng′kən) ▸*v.* P.part. of **shrink.**

shuck (shŭk) ▸*n.* A husk or shell. ▸*v.* **1.** To remove the husk or shell from. **2.** *Informal* To cast off. ▸*interj.* **shucks** (shŭks). Used to express mild disappointment, disgust, or annoyance. [?] —**shuck′er** *n.*

shud•der (shŭd′ər) ▸*v.* **1.** To shiver convulsively, as from fear or revulsion. **2.** To vibrate; quiver. [ME *shodderen.*] —**shud′der** *n.* —**shud′der•ing•ly** *adv.*

shuf•fle (shŭf′əl) ▸*v.* **-fled, -fling 1.** To slide (the feet) along the floor or ground while walking. **2.** To move (something) from one place to another. **3.** To mix together; jumble. **4.** *Games* To mix together (playing cards, tiles, or dominoes) in random order. [ME *shovelen.*] —**shuf′fle** *n.* —**shuf′fler** *n.*

shuf•fle•board (shŭf′əl-bôrd′, -bōrd′) ▸*n.* A game in which disks are pushed along a smooth level surface toward numbered scoring areas. [< obsolete *shove-board.*]

shun (shŭn) ▸*v.* **shunned, shun•ning.** To avoid deliberately. [< OE *scunian,* abhor.]

shunt (shŭnt) ▸*n.* **1.** The act of turning aside or moving to an alternate course. **2.** A railroad switch. **3.** *Elect.* A low-resistance alternative path for a portion of the current. ▸*v.* **1.** To turn onto another course: *shunting traffic around an accident.* **2.** To evade by putting aside or ignoring. **3.** *Elect.* To provide or divert (current) by means of a shunt. [ME *shunten,* flinch.]

shush (shŭsh) ▸*interj.* Used to demand silence. ▸*v.* To silence by saying "shush".

shut (shŭt) ▸*v.* **shut, shut•ting 1.** To move or be moved so as to block an opening: *Shut the window. The door shut by itself.* **2.** To block entrance to or exit from. **3.** To confine. **4.** To stop or cause to stop operating: *shut down a club.* —***phrasal verbs:*** **shut off** To stop the flow of. **shut out 1.** To prevent (a team) from scoring any points or runs. **2.** To keep from entering. **shut up 1.** To become or cause to become silent. **2.** To confine. [< OE *scyttan.*]

shut•down (shŭt′doun′) ▸*n.* A cessation of operations, as at a factory.

shut•eye (shŭt′ī′) ▸*n. Slang* Sleep.

shut-in (shŭt′ĭn′) ▸*n.* One confined indoors by illness or disability. —**shut-in′** *adj.*

shut•out (shŭt′out′) ▸*n.* **1.** See **lockout. 2.** *Sports* A game in which one side does not score.

shut•ter (shŭt′ər) ▸*n.* **1.** A hinged cover or screen for a window. **2.** A device that opens and closes the lens aperture of a camera. ▸*v.* To furnish or close with shutters.

shut•ter•bug (shŭt′ər-bŭg′) ▸*n. Informal* An enthusiastic amateur photographer.

shut•tle (shŭt′l) ▸*n.* **1.** A device used in weaving to carry the woof thread back and forth. **2.** A device for holding the thread in tatting or in a sewing machine. **3.** A vehicle used for regular travel between two points. **4.** A space shuttle. ▸*v.* **-tled, -tling.** To move or travel back and forth by or as if by a shuttle. [< OE *scytel,* dart.]

shut•tle•cock (shŭt′l-kŏk′) ▸*n.* A small rounded piece of cork or rubber with a crown of feathers or plastic, used in badminton.

shy[1] (shī) ▸*adj.* **shi•er** (shī′ər), **shi•est** (shī′ĭst) or **shy•er, shy•est 1.** Easily startled; timid. **2.** Drawing back from contact with others; reserved. **3.** Distrustful; wary. **4.** Short; lacking. ▸*v.* **shied** (shīd), **shy•ing 1.** To move suddenly, as if startled. **2.** To draw back, as from fear. [< OE *scēoh.*] —**shy′ly** *adv.* —**shy′ness** *n.*

shy[2] (shī) ▸*v.* **shied** (shīd), **shy•ing.** To throw with a swift motion; fling. [Perh. < SHY[1].]

shy•ster (shī′stər) ▸*n. Slang* An unethical, unscrupulous practitioner, esp. of law. [Poss. < Ger. *Scheisser,* scoundrel.]

Si ▸ The symbol for the element **silicon.**

SI ▸*abbr. French* Système International [d'Unités] (International System [of Units])

Si•am (sī-ăm′) See **Thailand.** —**Si′a•mese′** (-ə-mēz, -mēs′) *adj. & n.*

Siamese cat ▸*n.* A short-haired cat having blue eyes and a pale coat with darker ears, tail, and feet.

Siamese twin ▸*n.* Either of a pair of twins born with their bodies joined at some point.

Si•an (sē′än′, shē′-) See **Xi'an.**

Siang Kiang (syäng′ kyäng′, shyäng′) See **Xiang Jiang.**

Si•be•li•us (sĭ-bā′lē-əs, -bāl′yəs), **Jean.** 1865–1957. Finnish composer.

Si•be•ri•a (sī-bîr′ē-ə) A region of central and E Russia stretching from the Urals to the Pacific. —**Si•be′ri•an** *adj. & n.*

sib•i•lant (sĭb′ə-lənt) *Ling.* ▸*adj.* Of or producing a hissing sound. ▸*n.* A sibilant speech sound, such as English (s) or (z). [< Lat. *sībilāre*, hiss.] —**sib′i•lance, sib′i•lan•cy** *n.* —**sib′i•lant•ly** *adv.*

sib•ling (sĭb′lĭng) ▸*n.* One of two or more individuals having one or both parents in common; a brother or sister. [< OE.]

sib•yl (sĭb′əl) ▸*n.* A woman prophet. [< Gk. *Sibulla.*]

sic[1] (sĭk) ▸*adv.* Thus; so. Used in written texts to indicate that a surprising or paradoxical word or fact is not a mistake and is to be read as it stands. [Lat. *sīc.*]

sic[2] also **sick** (sĭk) ▸*v.* **sicced, sic•cing** also **sicked, sick•ing.** To urge (e.g., a dog) to attack or chase. [Var. of SEEK.]

Si•chuan also **Sze•chwan** or **Sze•chuan** (sĕch′wän′). A province of S-central China. Pop. 107,218,173.

Si•ci•ly (sĭs′ə-lē) An island of S Italy in the Mediterranean off the S end of the Italian peninsula. —**Si•cil′ian** (sĭ-sĭl′yən) *adj. & n.*

sick (sĭk) ▸*adj.* **-er, -est 1a.** Suffering from a physical illness. **b.** Of or for sick persons: *sick wards.* **c.** Nauseated. **2a.** Mentally ill or disturbed. **b.** Unwholesome; morbid: *a sick joke.* **3.** Defective; unsound. **4a.** Deeply distressed; upset. **b.** Disgusted; revolted. **c.** Weary; tired: *sick of it all.* **d.** Pining; longing. [< OE *sēoc.*] —**sick′ness** *n.*

sick•bay (sĭk′bā′) ▸*n.* The hospital and dispensary of a ship.

sick•bed (sĭk′bĕd′) ▸*n.* A sick person's bed.

sick•en (sĭk′ən) ▸*v.* To make or become sick. See Syns at **disgust.**

sick•en•ing (sĭk′ə-nĭng) ▸*adj.* **1.** Revolting or disgusting. **2.** Causing sickness. —**sick′en•ing•ly** *adv.*

sick•le (sĭk′əl) ▸*n.* A tool having a curved blade attached to a short handle, used for cutting grain or tall grass. [< Lat. *sēcula.*]

sickle cell anemia ▸*n.* A hereditary, usu. fatal anemia marked by the presence of crescent-shaped red blood cells and by episodic pain in the joints, fever, leg ulcers, and jaundice.

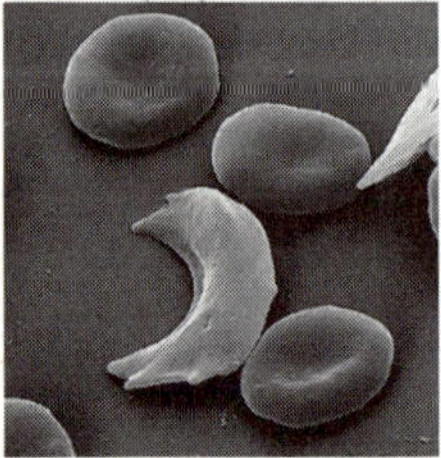

sickle cell anemia
one sickle cell and three normal red blood cells

sick•ly (sĭk′lē) ▸*adj.* **-li•er, -li•est 1.** Prone to sickness. **2.** Of or associated with sickness: *a sickly pallor.* **3.** Causing nausea; nauseating. **4.** Feeble or weak. —**sick′li•ness** *n.*

sick•out (sĭk′out′) ▸*n.* An organized job action in which employees absent themselves from work on the pretext of illness.

side (sīd) ▸*n.* **1.** A surface of an object, esp. a surface joining a top and bottom. **2.** Either of the two surfaces of a flat object, such as a piece of paper. **3.** The left or right half in reference to a vertical axis, as of the body. **4.** The space immediately next to someone or something: *stood at her father's side.* **5.** An area separated from another area by an intervening feature, such as a line or barrier: *on this side of the Atlantic.* **6.** One of two or more opposing individuals, groups, teams, or sets of opinions. **7.** A distinct aspect: *showed his kinder side.* **8.** Line of descent. ▸*adj.* **1.** Located on a side: *a side door.* **2.** From or to one side; oblique: *a side view.* **3.** Minor; incidental: *a side interest.* **4.** Supplementary: *a side benefit.* ▸*v.* **sid•ed, sid•ing.** To align oneself in a disagreement: *sided with the liberals.* —***idioms:* on the side** In addition to the main portion, occupation, or activity. **side by side** Next to each other. **this side of** *Informal* Verging on: *just this side of criminal.* [< OE *sīde.*]

side•arm (sīd′ärm′) ▸*adj.* Thrown with a sideways motion of the arm between shoulder and hip height. —**side′arm′** *adv.*

side arm ▸*n.* A small weapon, such as a pistol, carried at the side or waist.

side•board (sīd′bôrd′, -bōrd′) ▸*n.* A piece of dining room furniture having drawers for linens and tableware.

side•burns (sīd′bûrnz′) ▸*pl.n.* Growths of hair down the sides of a man's face in front of the ears. [After Ambrose E. *Burnside* (1824–81).]

side•car (sīd′kär′) ▸*n.* A one-wheeled passenger car attached to the side of a motorcycle.

side effect ▸*n.* A secondary, usu. undesirable effect, esp. of a drug or therapy.

side•kick (sīd′kĭk′) ▸*n.* *Slang* A close companion.

side•light (sīd′līt′) ▸*n.* Incidental information.

side•line (sīd′līn′) ▸*n.* **1.** *Sports* A line along either side of a playing court or field, marking its limits. **2.** A secondary job, activity, or line of merchandise. ▸*v.* *Informal* To remove from active participation.

side•long (sīd′lông′, -lŏng′) ▸*adj.* Directed to one side; sideways: *a sidelong glance.* —**side′long′** *adv.*

side•man (sīd′măn′) ▸*n.* A member of a jazz band who is not the leader.

si•de•re•al (sī dîr′ē-əl) ▸*adj.* **1.** Of or concerned with the stars. **2.** Measured in reference to the apparent motion of the stars: *sidereal time.* [< Lat. *sīdus*, *sīder-*, star.]

side•sad•dle (sīd′săd′l) ▸*n.* A saddle designed so that the rider sits with both legs on one side of the horse. —**side′sad•dle** *adv.*

side•show (sīd′shō′) ▸*n.* **1.** A minor show offered in addition to the main attraction. **2.** An incidental spectacle.

side•step (sīd′stĕp′) ▸*v.* **1.** To step out of the way of. **2.** To evade; skirt.

side•stroke (sīd′strōk′) ▸*n.* A swimming stroke in which a person swims on one side and thrusts the arms forward alternately while performing a scissors kick. —**side′stroke′** *v.*

side•swipe (sīd′swīp′) ▸*v.* To strike along the side in passing. ▸*n.* A glancing blow.

side•track (sīd′trăk′) ▸*v.* **1.** To divert from a

main issue or course. **2.** To switch (a railroad car) to a siding. ►*n.* A railroad siding.

side•walk (sīd′wôk′) ►*n.* A paved walkway along the side of a street.

side•wall (sīd′wôl′) ►*n.* A side surface of an automobile tire.

side•ways (sīd′wāz′) ►*adv. & adj.* **1.** Toward or from one side. **2.** With one side forward: *turned sideways to the camera.*

side•wind•er (sīd′wīn′dər) ►*n.* A small rattlesnake that moves by a lateral looping motion of its body.

sid•ing (sī′dĭng) ►*n.* **1.** Material, such as shingles, used for surfacing a frame building. **2.** A short section of railroad track connected by switches with a main track.

si•dle (sīd′l) ►*v.* **-dled, -dling 1.** To move sideways. **2.** To advance in a furtive or coy way. [< *sideling*, oblique.]

Sid•ney (sĭd′nē), Sir **Philip.** 1554–86. English poet and essayist.

Si•don (sīd′n) An ancient city of Phoenicia on the Mediterranean Sea in present-day SW Lebanon.

SIDS ►*abbr.* sudden infant death syndrome

siege (sēj) ►*n.* **1.** The surrounding and blockading of a city, town, or fortress by an army attempting to capture it. **2.** A prolonged period, as of illness. ►*v.* **sieged, sieg•ing.** To lay siege to. [< VLat. **sedicum*, a sitting < Lat. *sedēre*, sit.]

Si•en•a (sē-ĕn′ə, syĕ′nä) A city of W-central Italy S of Florence. Pop. 61,888. —**Si′e•nese′** (-nēz′, -nēs′) *adj. & n.*

si•er•ra (sē-ĕr′ə) ►*n.* A rugged range of mountains having a jagged profile. [Sp. < Lat. *serra*, saw.] —**si•er′ran** *adj.*

Sierra Le•one (lē-ōn′, -ō′nē) A country of W Africa on the Atlantic coast. Cap. Freetown. Pop. 4,402,000.

Sierra Ma•dre (mä′drā A mountain system of Mexico comprising three ranges: **Sierra Madre del Sur,** in the S along the Pacific; **Sierra Madre Occidental,** running parallel to the Pacific coastline; and **Sierra Madre Oriental,** roughly paralleling the Gulf of Mexico.

Sierra Nevada. A mountain range of E CA.

si•es•ta (sē-ĕs′tə) ►*n.* A rest after the midday meal. [Sp. < Lat. *sexta (hōra)*, sixth (hour).]

sieve (sĭv) ►*n.* A utensil of wire mesh or closely perforated metal, used for straining, sifting, or puréeing. [< OE *sife.*] —**sieve** *v.*

sift (sĭft) ►*v.* **1.** To put through a sieve to separate fine from coarse particles. **2.** To pass through or as if through a sieve. **3.** To examine and sort carefully: *sift the evidence.* [< OE *siftan.*] —**sift′er** *n.*

sigh (sī) ►*v.* **1.** To exhale audibly in a long deep breath, as in weariness or relief. **2.** To feel longing or grief. ►*n.* The act or sound of sighing. [< OE *sīcan.*] —**sigh′er** *n.*

sight (sīt) ►*n.* **1.** The ability to see. **2.** The act or fact of seeing. **3.** A view. **4.** Something worth seeing. **5.** *Informal* Something unsightly. **6.** A device used to assist aim by guiding the eye, as on a firearm. ►*v.* **1.** To perceive with the eyes: *sighted land after 40 days at sea.* **2.** To take aim (with). [< OE *sihth*, something seen.]

sight•ed (sī′tĭd) ►*adj.* Having sight.

sight•less (sīt′lĭs) ►*adj.* Unable to see; blind. —**sight′less•ly** *adv.* —**sight′less•ness** *n.*

sight•ly (sīt′lē) ►*adj.* **-li•er, -li•est.** Pleasing to see; attractive. —**sight′li•ness** *n.*

sight-read (sīt′rēd′) ►*v.* To read or perform (e.g., music) without preparation or prior acquaintance. —**sight′-read′er** *n.*

sight•see•ing (sīt′sē′ĭng) ►*n.* The act of visiting sights of interest.

sig•ma (sĭg′mə) ►*n.* The 18th letter of the Greek alphabet. [Gk.]

sign (sīn) ►*n.* **1.** Something that suggests the existence of a fact, condition, or quality. **2.** An act or gesture used to convey an idea. **3.** A posted notice bearing a designation, direction, or command. **4.** A figure or device that stands for a word, phrase, or operation: *a minus sign.* **5.** A portentous event; omen. **6.** One of the 12 divisions of the zodiac. ►*v.* **1.** To affix one's signature to. **2.** To write (one's signature). **3.** To approve or ratify (a document) by affixing a signature or seal. **4.** To hire by obtaining a signature on a contract. **5.** To relinquish or transfer title to by signature. **6.** To communicate with a sign or by sign language. —***phrasal verbs:* sign off** To stop broadcasting. **sign up** To enlist. [< Lat. *signum.*] —**sign′er** *n.*

sig•nal (sĭg′nəl) ►*n.* **1.** An indicator that serves as a means of communication: *a traffic signal; a smoke signal.* **2.** *Electron.* **a.** An impulse or fluctuating electric quantity whose variations represent coded information. **b.** The sound, image, or message transmitted by such coded information. ►*adj.* Notable; remarkable. ►*v.* **-naled, -nal•ing** or **-nalled, -nal•ling 1.** To make a signal (to). **2.** To relate or make known by signals: *signaled their approval.* [< LLat. *signālis*, of a sign.] —**sig′nal•er, sig′nal•ler** *n.* —**sig′nal•ly** *adv.*

sig•nal•ize (sĭg′nə-līz′) ►*v.* **-ized, -iz•ing 1.** To make remarkable or conspicuous. **2.** To point out particularly.

sig•na•to•ry (sĭg′nə-tôr′ē, -tōr′ē) ►*adj.* Bound by signed agreement. ►*n., pl.* **-ries.** One that has signed a treaty or document.

sig•na•ture (sĭg′nə-chər) ►*n.* **1.** One's name as written by oneself. **2.** A distinctive mark, characteristic, or sound. **3.** *Mus.* A sign used to indicate tempo or key. [< Lat. *signāre*, mark with a sign.]

sign•board (sīn′bôrd′, -bōrd′) ►*n.* A board bearing a sign.

sig•net (sĭg′nĭt) ►*n.* A seal, esp. one used officially to mark documents. [< OFr.]

sig•nif•i•cance (sĭg-nĭf′ĭ-kəns) ►*n.* **1.** The state or quality of being significant. **2.** The meaning of something; import. **3.** An implied meaning. See Syns at **meaning.**

sig•nif•i•cant (sĭg-nĭf′ĭ-kənt) ►*adj.* **1.** Having or expressing a meaning; meaningful. **2.** Insinuating; suggestive: *a significant glance.* See Syns at **expressive. 3.** Having a major effect; important. **4.** Fairly large; substantial: *significant losses.* [< Lat. *significāre*, SIGNIFY.] —**sig•nif′i•cant•ly** *adv.*

sig•ni•fi•ca•tion (sĭg′nə-fĭ-kā′shən) ►*n.* **1.** The established meaning of a word. See Syns at **meaning. 2.** The act of signifying; indication.

sig•ni•fy (sĭg′nə-fī′) ►*v.* **-fied, -fy•ing 1.** To denote; mean. **2.** To make known; signal. **3.** To be significant; matter. See Syns at **count**[1]. [< Lat. *significāre* < *signum*, sign.] —**sig′ni•fi′er** *n.*

sign language ►*n.* A language that uses a system of manual, facial, and other body movements as the means of communication.

sign•post (sīn′pōst′) ►*n.* **1.** A post supporting a sign. **2.** An indication; guide.

Sikh (sēk) ►*n.* An adherent of a monotheistic religion of India combining elements of Hinduism and Islam. —**Sikh** *adj.* —**Sikh′ism** *n.*

Sik•kim (sĭk′ĭm) A region and former kingdom of NE India in the E Himalayas between Nepal and Bhutan.

Si•kor•sky (sĭ-kôr′skē), **Igor Ivan.** 1889–1972. Russian-born Amer. aviation pioneer.

si•lage (sī′lĭj) ►*n.* Green fodder prepared by storing and fermenting in a silo.

si•lence (sī′ləns) ►*n.* **1.** The absence of sound; stillness. **2.** A period of time without speech or noise. **3.** Refusal or failure to speak out. ►*v.* **-lenced, -lenc•ing 1.** To make silent. **2.** To suppress.

si•lenc•er (sī′lən-sər) ►*n.* A device attached to a firearm to muffle the sound of firing.

si•lent (sī′lənt) ►*adj.* **1.** Marked by absence of sound; still. **2.** Not inclined to speak; reticent. **3.** Unable to speak. **4.** Not voiced or expressed; unspoken: *a silent prayer.* **5.** *Ling.* Unpronounced, as the *b* in *subtle.* [< Lat. *silēre*, be silent.] —**si′lent•ly** *adv.*

Si•le•sia (sī-lē′zhə, -shə, sĭ-) A region of central Europe mainly in SW Poland and N Czech Republic. —**Si•le′sian** *adj. & n.*

sil•hou•ette (sĭl′o͞o-ĕt′) ►*n.* **1.** A drawing consisting of the outline of something, esp. a human profile, filled in with a solid color. **2.** An outline. See Syns at **outline.** ►*v.* **-et•ted, -et•ting.** To cause to be seen as a silhouette; outline. [After Étienne de *Silhouette* (1709–67).]

sil•i•ca (sĭl′ĭ-kə) ►*n.* A crystalline compound, SiO_2, occurring abundantly as quartz, sand, and other minerals. [< Lat. *silex*, flint.] —**si•li′ceous** (sĭ-lĭsh′əs) *adj.*

sil•i•cate (sĭl′ĭ-kāt′, -kĭt) ►*n.* A compound containing silicon, oxygen, and a metal.

sil•i•con (sĭl′ĭ-kən, -kŏn′) ►*n. Symbol* **Si** A nonmetallic element occurring extensively in the earth's crust and used in glass, semiconductors, and concrete. At. no. 14. See table at **element.** [< SILICA.]

sil•i•cone (sĭl′ĭ-kōn′) ►*n.* Any of a group of semi-inorganic polymers containing chains of alternate silicon and oxygen atoms, characterized by wide-range thermal stability and used in adhesives, lubricants, protective coatings, and synthetic rubber.

sil•i•co•sis (sĭl′ĭ-kō′sĭs) ►*n.* A lung disease caused by continued inhalation of silica dust and marked by progressive fibrosis.

silk (sĭlk) ►*n.* **1a.** A fine lustrous fiber produced by a silkworm to form its cocoon. **b.** Thread or fabric made from this fiber. **2.** A silky, filamentous material, such as the webbing spun by spiders. [< OE *sioloc.*]

silk-cot•ton tree (sĭlk′kŏt′n) ►*n.* A spiny tropical tree cultivated for its leathery fruit that contain the silklike fiber kapok.

silk•en (sĭl′kən) ►*adj.* **1.** Made of silk. **2.** Smooth and lustrous. See Syns at **sleek.**

silk-screen also **silk•screen** (sĭlk′skrēn′) ►*n.* A stencil method in which ink is forced through a design-bearing screen of silk or other fine mesh onto the printing surface. —**silk′-screen′** *v.*

silk•worm (sĭlk′wûrm′) ►*n.* Any of various moth caterpillars that produce silk cocoons.

silk•y (sĭl′kē) ►*adj.* **-i•er, -i•est 1.** Resembling silk; lustrous. See Syns at **sleek. 2.** Silken. —**silk′i•ly** *adv.* —**silk′i•ness** *n.*

sill (sĭl) ►*n.* The horizontal member that bears the upright portion of a frame, esp. the base of a window. [< OE *syll*, threshold.]

sil•ly (sĭl′ē) ►*adj.* **-li•er, -li•est 1.** Lacking good sense; foolish. **2.** Frivolous. **3.** Dazed. [< OE *gesælig*, blessed.] —**sil′li•ness** *n.*

si•lo (sī′lō) ►*n., pl.* **-los 1.** A tall cylindrical structure in which fodder is stored. **2.** An underground shelter for a missile. [Sp.]

silt (sĭlt) ►*n.* A fine sediment intermediate in size between sand and clay. ►*v.* To fill or become filled with silt. [ME *cylte.*] —**silt•a′tion** *n.* —**silt′y** *adj.*

Si•lu•ri•an (sĭ-lo͝or′ē-ən, sī-) *Geol.* ►*adj.* Of or being the 3rd period of the Paleozoic Era, marked by the development of early invertebrate land animals. ►*n.* The Silurian Period.

sil•van (sĭl′vən) ►*adj.* Var. of **sylvan.**

sil•ver (sĭl′vər) ►*n.* **1.** *Symbol* **Ag** A lustrous white malleable metallic element highly valued for jewelry, tableware, and other ornamental use and used in coinage, photography, dental and soldering alloys, electrical contacts, and printed circuits. At. no. 47. See table at **element. 2.** Coins made of silver. **3.** Tableware and other articles made of or plated with silver. **4.** A lustrous medium gray. ►*adj.* **1.** Of the color silver. **2.** Eloquent: *a silver voice.* **3.** Of a 25th anniversary. ►*v.* **1.** To cover, plate, or adorn with silver or a silvery substance. **2.** To give a silver color to. [< OE *siolfor.*] —**sil′ver•i•ness** *n.* —**sil′ver•y** *adj.*

silver bromide ►*n.* A pale yellow crystalline compound, AgBr, used as the light-sensitive component on photographic film.

sil•ver•fish (sĭl′vər-fĭsh′) ►*n., pl.* **-fish** or **-fish•es.** A silvery wingless insect that often damages bookbindings and clothing.

silver iodide ►*n.* A yellow powder, AgI, used in photography, rainmaking, and medicine.

silver nitrate ►*n.* A poisonous colorless crystalline compound, $AgNO_3$, used in making photographic film, silvering mirrors, dyeing hair, plating silver, and medicine.

sil•ver•smith (sĭl′vər-smĭth′) ►*n.* One that makes or replates articles of silver.

sil•ver•ware (sĭl′vər-wâr′) ►*n.* Articles made of or plated with silver, esp. tableware.

Sim•birsk (sĭm-bîrsk′) A city of W Russia on the Volga R. ESE of Moscow. Pop. 664,025.

Sim•fer•o•pol (sĭm′fə-rō′pəl) A city of S Ukraine in the S Crimea NE of Sevastopol. Pop. 357,000.

sim•i•an (sĭm′ē-ən) ►*n.* An ape or monkey. [< Lat. *sīmia*, ape.] —**sim′i•an** *adj.*

sim•i•lar (sĭm′ə-lər) ►*adj.* Related in appearance or nature; alike though not identical. [< Lat. *similis*, like.] —**sim′i•lar•ly** *adv.*

sim•i•lar•i•ty (sĭm′ə-lăr′ĭ-tē) ►*n., pl.* **-ties.** The quality or condition of being similar.

sim•i•le (sĭm′ə-lē) ►*n.* A figure of speech in which two essentially unlike things are compared, often using *like* or *as*, as in *"eyes like stars."* [< Lat., like.]

si•mil•i•tude (sĭ-mĭl′ĭ-to͞od′, -tyo͞od′) ►*n.* Similarity; resemblance. [< Lat. *similis*, like.]

sim•mer (sĭm′ər) ►*v.* **1.** To be cooked gently

or remain just at or below the boiling point. **2.** To be filled with pent-up emotion; seethe. —***phrasal verb:* simmer down** To become calm after excitement or anger. [< ME *simpire.*] —**sim′mer** *n.*

si•mo•ny (sī′mə-nē, sĭm′ə-) ▶*n.* The buying or selling of ecclesiastical pardons or offices. [After *Simon* Magus, who tried to buy spiritual powers from the Apostle Peter.]

Si•mon Ze•lo•tes (sī′mən zē-lō′tēz). 1st cent. A.D. In the Bible, one of the 12 Apostles.

sim•pa•ti•co (sĭm-pä′tĭ-kō′, -păt′ĭ-) ▶*adj.* **1.** Compatible. **2.** Attractive; pleasing. [Ital.]

sim•per (sĭm′pər) ▶*v.* To smile in a silly or self-conscious manner. [Perh. of Scand. orig.] —**sim′per** *n.* —**sim′per•er** *n.*

sim•ple (sĭm′pəl) ▶*adj.* **-pler, -plest 1.** Having only one thing, element, or part. See Syns at **pure. 2.** Not involved or complicated; easy. **3.** Bare; mere: *a simple "yes" or "no."* **4.** Not embellished or adorned: *a simple dress.* **5.** Not elaborate or luxurious. See Syns at **plain. 6.** Unassuming or unpretentious. **7.** Simple-minded. **8.** Straightforward; sincere. **9.** Humble or lowly in condition or rank. **10.** Insignificant; trivial. [< Lat. *simplus.*] —**sim′ple•ness** *n.*

simple fraction ▶*n.* A fraction in which both the numerator and the denominator are whole numbers.

simple interest ▶*n.* Interest paid only on the original principal, not on the interest accrued.

sim•ple-mind•ed (sĭm′pəl-mīn′dĭd) ▶*adj.* **1.** Lacking in sophistication; naive. **2.** Stupid or silly. **3.** Mentally impaired. —**sim′ple-mind′ed•ly** *adv.* —**sim′ple-mind′ed•ness** *n.*

simple sentence ▶*n.* A sentence having only one clause, as *The cat purred.*

sim•ple•ton (sĭm′pəl-tən) ▶*n.* A person deficient in judgment or intelligence; fool.

sim•plic•i•ty (sĭm-plĭs′ĭ-tē) ▶*n., pl.* **-ties 1.** The property, condition, or quality of being simple. **2.** Absence of luxury or showiness; plainness. **3.** Absence of affectation or pretense. **4.** Foolishness. [< Lat. *simplicitās.*]

sim•pli•fy (sĭm′plə-fī′) ▶*v.* **-fied, -fy•ing.** To make simple or simpler. —**sim′pli•fi•ca′tion** *n.* —**sim′pli•fi′er** *n.*

sim•ply (sĭm′plē) ▶*adv.* **1.** In a plain and unadorned way. **2.** Merely; only. **3.** Absolutely; altogether: *simply delicious.*

sim•u•late (sĭm′yə-lāt′) ▶*v.* **-lat•ed, -lat•ing 1.** To take on the appearance or form of. **2.** To pretend; feign. **3.** To create a model of. [Lat. *simulāre.*] —**sim′u•la′tion** *n.* —**sim′u•la′tive** *adj.* —**sim′u•la′tor** *n.*

si•mul•cast (sī′məl-kăst′, sĭm′əl-) ▶*v.* To broadcast simultaneously by FM and AM radio or by radio and television. [SIMUL(TANEOUS) + (BROAD)CAST.] —**si′mul•cast′** *n.*

si•mul•ta•ne•ous (sī′məl-tā′nē-əs, sĭm′əl-) ▶*adj.* Happening, existing, or done at the same time. [Lat. *simul,* at the same time + (INSTAN)TANEOUS.] —**si′mul•ta′ne•ous•ly** *adv.* —**si′mul•ta′ne•ous•ness, si′mul•ta•ne′i•ty** (-tə-nē′ĭ-tē, -nā′-) *n.*

sin¹ (sĭn) ▶*n.* **1.** A transgression of a religious or moral law. **2.** Something shameful or wrong. [< OE *synn.*] —**sin** *v.* —**sin′ful** *adj.* —**sin′ful•ness** *n.* —**sin′ner** *n.*

sin² ▶*abbr.* sine

Si•nai (sī′nī′), **Mount.** A mountain, about 2,288 m (7,500 ft), of the S Sinai Peninsula.

Sinai Peninsula. A peninsula between the gulfs of Suez and Aqaba.

Sinai Peninsula

Si•na•tra (sə-nä′trə), **Francis Albert.** "Frank." 1915–98. Amer. singer and actor.

since (sĭns) ▶*adv.* **1.** From then until now or between then and now: *They left town and haven't been here since.* **2.** Before now; ago: *long since forgotten.* ▶*prep.* From the time of: *friends since school.* ▶*conj.* **1.** From the time when or after which: *hasn't worked since the accident.* **2.** Inasmuch as; because: *Since you asked, I'll tell you.* [OE *siththan.*]

sin•cere (sĭn-sîr′) ▶*adj.* **-cer•er, -cer•est.** Not feigned or affected; true. [Lat. *sincērus.*] —**sin•cer′i•ty** (-sĕr′ĭ-tē) *n.* —**sin•cere′ly** *adv.* —**sin•cere′ness** *n.*

Sin•clair (sĭn-klâr′), **Upton Beall.** 1878–1968. Amer. writer and reformer.

sine (sīn) ▶*n.* In a right triangle, the ratio of the side opposite an acute angle to the hypotenuse. [Med.Lat. *sinus.*]

si•ne•cure (sī′nĭ-kyo͝or′, sĭn′ĭ-) ▶*n.* A salaried position requiring little or no work. [< Med. Lat. *sine cūrā,* without care (of souls).]

si•ne di•e (sī′nī dī′ē, sĭn′ā dē′ā′) ▶*adv.* Without a future time specified; indefinitely. [Med. Lat. *sine diē,* without a day.]

si•ne qua non (sĭn′ĭ kwä nŏn′, nōn′, sī′nī) ▶*n.* An essential element or condition. [LLat. *sine quā nōn,* without which not.]

sin•ew (sĭn′yo͞o) ▶*n.* **1.** A tendon. **2.** Vigorous strength. [< OE *sinu.*]

sin•ew•y (sĭn′yo͞o-ē) ▶*adj.* **1.** Stringy and tough, as meat. **2.** Lean and muscular. See Syns at **muscular.**

sing (sĭng) ▶*v.* **sang** (săng) or **sung** (sŭng), **sung, sing•ing 1.** To utter a series of words or sounds in musical tones. **2.** To make melodious sounds. **3.** To bring to a specified state by singing: *sang the baby to sleep.* **4.** To proclaim or extol something in verse. **5.** *Slang* To give evidence against someone. ▶*n.* A gathering of people for group singing. [< OE *singan.*] —**sing′a•ble** *adj.* —**sing′er** *n.*

sing. ▶*abbr.* singular

Sin•ga•pore (sĭng′gə-pôr′, -pōr′, sĭng′ə-) A country of SE Asia comprising **Singapore Island** and adjacent smaller islands. Cap. the city of **Singapore.** Pop. 2,930,000. —**Sin′ga•por′e•an** *adj. & n.*

singe (sĭnj) ▶*v.* **singed, singe•ing 1.** To burn superficially; scorch. **2.** To burn off the feathers or bristles of (a bird or animal carcass). [< OE *sengan.*] —**singe** *n.*

Sing•er (sĭng′ər), **Isaac Bashevis.** 1904–91. Polish-born Amer. Yiddish writer; 1978 Nobel.

Sing•ha•lese (sĭng′gə-lēz′, -lēs′) ►*n. & adj.* Var. of **Sinhalese.**

sin•gle (sĭng′gəl) ►*adj.* **1.** Not accompanied by another or others; solitary. **2.** Consisting of one part or section. **3.** Separate; individual: *Every single one of you.* **4.** Designed to accommodate one person: *a single bed.* **5.** Unmarried. ►*n.* **1.** One that is separate and individual. **2.** An accommodation for one person, as in a hotel. **3.** An unmarried person. **4.** A one-dollar bill. **5.** *Baseball* A one-base hit. **6. singles** *Sports* A match between two players in tennis and other games. ►*v.* **-gled, -gling 1.** To choose or distinguish from others: *singled her out for praise.* **2.** *Baseball* To make a one-base hit. [< Lat. *singulus.*] —**sin′gle•ness** *n.*

sin•gle-breast•ed (sĭng′gəl-brĕs′tĭd) ►*adj.* Closing with a narrow overlap and fastened with a single row of buttons.

single file ►*n.* A line of people or things standing or moving one behind the other.

sin•gle-hand•ed (sĭng′gəl-hăn′dĭd) ►*adj.* **1.** Working or done without help; unassisted. **2.** Using only one hand. —**sin′gle-hand′ed•ly** *adv.* —**sin′gle-hand′ed•ness** *n.*

sin•gle-mind•ed (sĭng′gəl-mīn′dĭd) ►*adj.* **1.** Having one overriding purpose or goal. **2.** Steadfast; resolute. —**sin′gle-mind′ed•ly** *adv.* —**sin′gle-mind′ed•ness** *n.*

sin•gles bar (sĭng′gəlz) ►*n.* A bar patronized esp. by unmarried men and women.

sin•gly (sĭng′glē) ►*adv.* **1.** Alone. **2.** One by one; individually.

sing•song (sĭng′sông′, -sŏng′) ►*n.* A monotonous rising and falling of the voice. —**sing′song′** *adj.*

sin•gu•lar (sĭng′gyə-lər) ►*adj.* **1.** Being only one; individual. **2.** Unique. **3.** Being beyond what is usual; remarkable. **4.** Deviating from the expected; odd. **5.** *Gram.* Of or being a single person or thing or several entities considered as a unit. ►*n. Gram.* The singular number or a form designating it. [< Lat. *singulāris.*] —**sin′gu•lar′i•ty** (-lăr′ĭ-tē), **sin′gu•lar•ness** *n.* —**sin′gu•lar•ly** *adv.*

Sin•ha•lese (sĭn′hə-lēz′, -lēs′) or **Sing•ha•lese** (sĭng′gə-lēz′, -lēs′) ►*n., pl.* **-lese 1.** A member of a people constituting the majority of the population of Sri Lanka. **2.** The Indic language of the Sinhalese. —**Sin′ha•lese′** *adj.*

sin•is•ter (sĭn′ĭ-stər) ►*adj.* **1.** Suggesting or threatening evil. **2.** Presaging trouble; ominous. [< Lat., on the left.]

sink (sĭngk) ►*v.* **sank** (săngk) or **sunk** (sŭngk), **sunk, sink•ing 1a.** To descend to the bottom. **b.** To cause to descend beneath a surface. **2.** To fall or drop to a lower level. **3.** To force into or penetrate a substance. **4.** To dig or drill (e.g., a well) in the earth. **5.** To pass into a specified condition: *sank into a deep sleep.* **6.** To deteriorate in quality or condition. **7.** To diminish or decline. **8.** To become weaker, quieter, or less forceful. **9.** To become felt or understood: *The lesson sank in.* **10.** To invest. **11.** *Sports* To get (a ball) into a hole or basket. ►*n.* **1.** A basin fixed to a wall or floor and having a drainpipe and a piped water supply. **2.** A sinkhole. [< OE *sincan.*] —**sink′a•ble** *adj.*

sink•er (sĭng′kər) ►*n.* A weight used for sinking fishing lines or nets.

sink•hole (sĭngk′hōl′) ►*n.* A natural depression in a land surface, usu. occurring in limestone regions and formed by solution or collapse of a cavern roof.

sink•ing fund (sĭng′kĭng) ►*n.* A fund accumulated to pay off a corporate or public debt.

Sino– ►*pref.* Chinese: *Sinology.* [< Ar. *Sīn,* China.]

Si•nol•o•gy (sī-nŏl′ə-jē, sĭ-) ►*n.* The study of Chinese language, literature, or civilization. —**Si•nol′o•gist** *n.*

Si•no-Ti•bet•an (sī′nō-tĭ-bĕt′n, sĭn′ō-) ►*n.* A language family that includes Chinese and Tibeto-Burman. —**Si′no-Ti•bet′an** *adj.*

sin•u•ous (sĭn′yo͞o-əs) ►*adj.* **1.** Twisting; winding. **2.** Supple and lithe: *the sinuous grace of a dancer.* **3.** Not direct; devious. [< Lat. *sinus,* curve.] —**sin′u•os′i•ty** (-ŏs′ĭ-tē), **sin′u•ous•ness** *n.* —**sin′u•ous•ly** *adv.*

si•nus (sī′nəs) ►*n.* **1.** Any of various air-filled cavities in the bones of the skull, esp. one communicating with the nostrils. **2.** A bodily channel containing chiefly venous blood. [< Lat., curve, hollow.]

si•nus•i•tis (sī′nə-sī′tĭs) ►*n.* Inflammation of a sinus, esp. in the nasal region.

Si•on (sī′ən) ►*n.* Var. of **Zion.**

Siou•an (so͞o′ən) ►*n.* A large North American Indian language family spoken from Lake Michigan to the Rocky Mountains.

Sioux (so͞o) ►*n., pl.* **Sioux** (so͞o, so͞oz) **1.** A member of a group of Native American peoples of the N Great Plains, now mainly in North and South Dakota. **2.** Any of their Siouan languages. —**Sioux** *adj.*

Sioux Falls. A city of SE SD near the MN border. Pop. 100,814.

sip (sĭp) ►*v.* **sipped, sip•ping.** To drink in small quantities. ►*n.* **1.** The act of sipping. **2.** A small quantity of liquid sipped. [ME *sippen.*] —**sip′per** *n.*

si•phon also **sy•phon** (sī′fən) ►*n.* A bent tube through which a fluid can be drawn over the edge of one container into a lower container by means of air pressure. ►*v.* To draw off or drain with or as if with a siphon. [< Gk. *siphōn.*]

sir (sûr) ►*n.* **1. Sir** Used as an honorific title for baronets and knights. **2.** Used as a form of polite address for a man. **3.** Used as a salutation in a letter: *Dear Sir.* [< SIRE.]

sire (sīr) ►*n.* **1.** A father. **2.** *Archaic* Used as a form of address for a male superior, esp. a king. ►*v.* **sired, sir•ing.** To beget. [< Lat. *senior,* older.]

si•ren (sī′rən) ►*n.* A device for making a loud, usu. wailing sound as a signal or warning. [< OFr. *sereine,* SIREN.]

Siren ►*n.* **1.** *Gk. Myth.* One of a group of sea nymphs whose sweet singing lured mariners to destruction. **2. siren** A beautiful or alluring woman. [< Gk. *seirēn.*]

Sir•i•us (sĭr′ē-əs) ►*n.* A star in Canis Major, the brightest star in the sky.

sir•loin (sûr′loin′) ►*n.* A cut of meat from the upper part of the loin. [< OFr. *surlonge.*]

si•roc•co (sə-rŏk′ō) ►*n., pl.* **-cos.** A hot, humid southerly wind of S Europe originating in the Sahara. [< Ar. *šarq,* east.]

sir•up (sĭr′əp, sûr′-) ►*n.* Var. of **syrup.**

sis (sĭs) ►*n. Informal* Sister.

si•sal (sī′səl) ►*n.* The fiber of a Mexican and Central American plant, used for cordage and rope. [After *Sisal,* Mexico.]

sis•sy (sĭs′ē) ►*n., pl.* **-sies 1.** A boy or man

who does not fit the masculine stereotype. **2.** A timid person. [< SIS.] —**sis′sy•ish** *adj.*

sis•ter (sĭs′tər) ►*n.* **1.** A female having one or both parents in common with another person. **2.** A female who shares a common ancestry or allegiance with another, esp.: **a.** A kinswoman. **b.** A close female friend. **c.** A fellow African-American female. **3. Sister** A nun. ►*adj.* Closely related or associated: *sister ships.* [< OE *sweostor* and ON *systir.*] —**sis′ter•li•ness** *n.* —**sis′ter•ly** *adj.*

sis•ter•hood (sĭs′tər-ho͝od′) ►*n.* **1.** The relationship of being a sister or sisters. **2.** The quality of being sisterly. **3.** Association of women in a common cause.

sis•ter-in-law (sĭs′tər-ĭn-lô′) ►*n., pl.* **sis•ters-in-law** (-tərz-) **1.** The sister of one's husband or wife. **2.** The wife of one's brother. **3.** The wife of the brother of one's spouse.

sit (sĭt) ►*v.* **sat** (săt), **sit•ting 1.** To rest with the body supported on the buttocks or hindquarters. See Usage Note at **set**[1]. **2.** To perch, as a bird. **3.** To cover eggs for hatching; brood. **4.** To maintain a seated position on (a horse). **5.** To be situated or located. **6.** To pose for an artist or photographer. **7.** To be in session. **8.** To remain inactive or unused. **9.** To please: *The idea didn't sit well with me.* **10.** To baby-sit. —***phrasal verbs:*** **sit down** To take a seat. **sit in on** To attend as a visitor. **sit on** *Informal* To suppress: *sat on the evidence.* **sit up 1.** To rise to a sitting position. **2.** To become suddenly alert. —***idiom:*** **sit tight** *Informal* To patiently await the next move. [< OE *sittan.*] —**sit′ter** *n.*

si•tar (sĭ-tär′) ►*n.* A stringed instrument of India, having a track of 20 movable frets with 6 or 7 metal playing strings above and usu. 13 sympathetic resonating strings below. [< Pers. *sitār.*] —**si•tar′ist** *n.*

sit•com (sĭt′kŏm′) ►*n.* A situation comedy.

sit-down (sĭt′doun′) ►*n.* **1.** A work stoppage in which the workers refuse to leave their place of employment until their demands are met. **2.** An obstruction of normal activity by the act of a large group sitting down to express a grievance or protest.

site (sīt) ►*n.* **1.** The place where something was, is, or is to be located. **2.** A website. ►*v.* **sit•ed, sit•ing.** To situate or locate. [< Lat. *situs.*]

sit-in (sĭt′ĭn′) ►*n.* **1.** See **sit-down** 1. **2.** An organized protest in which participants sit down in a place and refuse to move.

sit•ting (sĭt′ĭng) ►*n.* **1.** A period during which one is seated and occupied with a single activity. **2.** A session, as of a legislature. ►*adj.* Incumbent: *a sitting governor.*

Sitting Bull. 1834?–90. Sioux leader.

sit•u•ate (sĭch′o͞o-āt′) ►*v.* **-at•ed, -at•ing.** To place in a certain spot; locate. [< Lat. *situs,* location.]

sit•u•a•tion (sĭch′o͞o-ā′shən) ►*n.* **1.** Position; location. **2.** A state of affairs. **3.** A job. —**sit′u•a′tion•al** *adj.*

situation comedy ►*n.* A humorous television series having a regular cast of characters.

sit-up (sĭt′ŭp′) ►*n.* A physical exercise in which one uses the abdominal muscles to raise the torso to a sitting position without moving the legs.

Si•van (sĭv′ən) ►*n.* A month of the Jewish calendar. See table at **calendar.** [Heb. *sīwān.*]

Sitting Bull
photographed in 1885

six (sĭks) ►*n.* **1.** The cardinal number equal to 5 + 1. **2.** The 6th in a set or sequence. [< OE.] —**six** *adj. & pron.*

six-gun (sĭks′gŭn′) ►*n.* A six-chambered revolver.

Six Nations ►*pl.n.* The Iroquois confederacy after the Tuscarora joined it in 1722.

six-pack (sĭks′păk′) ►*n.* Six units of a commodity, esp. six containers of a beverage sold in a pack.

six-shoot•er (sĭks′sho͞o′tər) ►*n.* A six-gun.

six•teen (sĭk-stēn′) ►*n.* **1.** The cardinal number equal to 15 + 1. **2.** The 16th in a set or sequence. —**six•teen′** *adj. & pron.*

six•teenth (sĭk-stēnth′) ►*n.* **1.** The ordinal number matching the number 16 in a series. **2.** One of 16 equal parts. —**six•teenth′** *adv. & adj.*

sixth (sĭksth) ►*n.* **1.** The ordinal number matching the number 6 in a series. **2.** One of six equal parts. **3.** *Mus.* A tone six degrees above or below a given tone in a diatonic scale. —**sixth** *adv. & adj.*

six•ti•eth (sĭk′stē-ĭth) ►*n.* **1.** The ordinal number matching the number 60 in a series. **2.** One of 60 equal parts. —**six′ti•eth** *adv. & adj.*

six•ty (sĭks′tē) ►*n., pl.* **-ties.** The cardinal number equal to 6 × 10. —**six′ty** *adj. & pron.*

siz•a•ble also **size•a•ble** (sī′zə-bəl) ►*adj.* Of considerable size; fairly large. —**siz′a•ble•ness** *n.* —**siz′a•bly** *adv.*

size[1] (sīz) ►*n.* **1.** The physical dimensions, magnitude, or extent of an object. **2.** Any of a series of graduated dimensions whereby manufactured articles are classified. ►*v.* **sized, siz•ing.** To arrange according to size. —***phrasal verb:*** **size up** To make an estimate or judgment of. [ME *sise.*]

size[2] (sīz) ►*n.* A gluey substance used as a glaze or filler for materials such as paper, cloth, or wall surfaces. [ME *sise.*] —**size** *v.*

siz•ing (sī′zĭng) ►*n.* A glaze or filler; size.

siz•zle (sĭz′əl) ►*v.* **-zled, -zling 1.** To make the hissing sound of frying fat. **2.** To seethe with anger. **3.** To be very hot. [< ME *sissen,* hiss.] —**siz′zle** *n.* —**siz′zling•ly** *adv.*

SJ ►*abbr.* Society of Jesus

Sjael•land (shĕl′än′) An island of E Denmark bounded by the Kattegat and the Baltic Sea.

SK ►*abbr.* Saskatchewan

ska (skä) ►*n.* Popular music of Jamaican origin having a fast tempo and a strongly accentuated offbeat. [Perh. < *Love Skavoovie,* greeting used by Cluet Johnson, early ska musician.]

Skag•er•rak also **Skag•er•ak** (skăg′ə-răk′). A strait between Norway and Denmark linking the North Sea and the Kattegat.

skate[1] (skāt) ►*n.* **1.** An ice skate. **2.** A roller skate. ►*v.* **skat•ed, skat•ing.** To glide along on or as if on skates. [< ONFr. *escache*, stilt.] —**skat′er** *n.*

skate[2] (skāt) ►*n.* A saltwater ray having a flattened body and winglike fins that extend around the head. [< ON *skata.*]

skate•board (skāt′bôrd′, -bōrd′) ►*n.* A short narrow board mounted on roller skate wheels and usu. ridden standing or crouching. —**skate′board′** *v.* —**skate′board′er** *n.*

skeet (skēt) ►*n.* A form of trapshooting in which clay targets are thrown from traps to simulate birds in flight. [< SHOOT.]

skein (skān) ►*n.* **1.** A length of thread or yarn wound in a loose long coil. **2.** A flock of geese in flight. [< OFr. *escaigne.*]

skel•e•ton (skĕl′ĭ-tn) ►*n.* **1a.** The internal supporting structure of a vertebrate, composed of bone and cartilage. **b.** The hard external supporting and protecting structure in many invertebrates, such as crustaceans. **2.** A supporting structure or framework. **3.** An outline or sketch. [< Gk. *skeletos*, dried up.] —**skel′e•tal** *adj.*

skeleton key ►*n.* A key designed or adapted to open many different locks.

skep•tic also **scep•tic** (skĕp′tĭk) ►*n.* **1.** One who habitually doubts, questions, or disagrees. **2.** One inclined to skepticism in religion or philosophy. [< Gk. *skeptesthai*, examine.] —**skep′ti•cal** *adj.* —**skep′ti•cal•ly** *adv.*

skep•ti•cism also **scep•ti•cism** (skĕp′tĭ-sĭz′əm) ►*n.* **1.** A doubting or questioning attitude. **2.** *Philos.* The doctrine that absolute knowledge is impossible. **3.** Doubt or disbelief esp. of religious tenets.

sketch (skĕch) ►*n.* **1.** A hasty or undetailed drawing or painting. **2.** A brief general account; outline. **3.** A short, often satirical scene or play; skit. ►*v.* To make a sketch (of). [< Ital. *schizzo.*] —**sketch′er** *n.* —**sketch′i•ly** *adv.* —**sketch′i•ness** *n.* —**sketch′y** *adj.*

skew (skyo͞o) ►*v.* **1.** To turn or place at an angle. **2.** To distort. ►*adj.* Turned to one side. ►*n.* A slant. [< ONFr. *eskiuer*, escape.]

skew•er (skyo͞o′ər) ►*n.* A long pointed rod for impaling and holding food during cooking. [ME *skuer.*] —**skew′er** *v.*

ski (skē) ►*n.*, *pl.* **skis.** One of a pair of long flat runners for gliding over snow or water. ►*v.* **skied, ski•ing.** To go or glide on skis, esp. as a sport. [< ON *skīdh.*] —**ski′a•ble** *adj.* —**ski′er** *n.* —**ski′ing** *n.*

skid (skĭd) ►*n.* **1.** The act of sliding or slipping over a surface. **2a.** A plank or log used for sliding or rolling heavy objects. **b.** A pallet for loading or handling goods. **3.** A device applying pressure to a wheel to brake a vehicle. **4.** A runner in the landing gear of certain aircraft, such as helicopters. **5. skids** *Slang* A path to ruin or failure: *His career hit the skids.* ►*v.* **skid•ded, skid•ding 1.** To slide sideways while moving due to loss of traction. **2.** To slide without revolving: *wheels skidding on oily pavement.* [?]

skid row (rō) ►*n.* *Slang* A squalid district inhabited by derelicts.

skiff (skĭf) ►*n.* A small, flat-bottomed open boat. [< OItal. *schifo*, of Gmc. orig.]

ski lift ►*n.* A power-driven conveyor used to carry skiers to the top of a slope.

skill (skĭl) ►*n.* **1.** Proficiency; dexterity. **2.** An art, trade, or technique, esp. one requiring use of the hands or body. [< ON *skil*, discernment.] —**skilled** *adj.*

skil•let (skĭl′ĭt) ►*n.* See **frying pan.** See Regional Notes at **andiron, frying pan.** [ME *skelet.*]

skill•ful also **skil•ful** (skĭl′fəl) ►*adj.* **1.** Possessing or exercising skill. **2.** Marked by or requiring skill. —**skill′ful•ly** *adv.* —**skill′ful•ness** *n.*

skim (skĭm) ►*v.* **skimmed, skim•ming 1a.** To remove floating matter from (a liquid). **b.** To remove (floating matter): *skimmed the cream off the milk.* **c.** To take away the choicest parts from. **2.** To glide or pass quickly and lightly over. See Syns at **brush**[1]. **3.** To read or glance through quickly or superficially. [ME *skimmen.*]

skim milk ►*n.* Milk from which the cream has been removed.

skimp (skĭmp) ►*v.* **1.** To deal with hastily or carelessly. **2.** To be stingy or sparing; scrimp. [Poss. < SCRIMP.]

skimp•y (skĭm′pē) ►*adj.* **-i•er, -i•est 1.** Inadequate in size or amount; scanty. **2.** Stingy or niggardly. —**skimp′i•ly** *adv.* —**skimp′i•ness** *n.*

skin (skĭn) ►*n.* **1.** The membranous tissue forming the outer covering of an animal. **2.** An animal hide or pelt. **3.** A usu. thin, closely adhering outer layer: *an avocado skin; the skin of an aircraft.* ►*v.* **skinned, skin•ning 1.** To remove skin from. **2.** To injure the skin of. **3.** *Slang* To cheat; swindle. —***idioms:* by the skin of (one's) teeth** By the smallest margin. **get under (one's) skin** To provoke. [< ON *skinn.*] —**skin′less** *adj.*

skin diving ►*n.* Underwater swimming, often with flippers, a face mask, and usu. a snorkel. —**skin′-dive′** *v.* —**skin diver** *n.*

skin•flint (skĭn′flĭnt′) ►*n.* A miser.

Skin•ner (skĭn′ər), **B(urrhus) F(rederick).** 1904–90. Amer. psychologist.

skin•ny (skĭn′ē) ►*adj.* **-ni•er, -ni•est.** Very thin. —**skin′ni•ness** *n.*

skin•ny-dip (skĭn′ē-dĭp′) ►*v.* *Informal* To swim in the nude. —**skin′ny-dip′ping** *n.*

skip (skĭp) ►*v.* **skipped, skip•ping 1a.** To move by stepping and hopping on one foot and then the other. **b.** To leap or jump lightly (over). **2.** To ricochet. **3.** To pass from point to point omitting what intervenes. **4.** To pass over, omit, or disregard. **5.** To be promoted beyond (the next grade or level). **6.** *Informal* To leave hastily: *skipped town.* ►*n.* **1.** A skipping gait. **2.** A gap or omission. [ME *skippen.*] —**skip′per** *n.*

skip•per (skĭp′ər) ►*n.* The master of a ship. [< MDu. *schipper.*] —**skip′per** *v.*

skir•mish (skûr′mĭsh) ►*n.* **1.** A minor battle in war. **2.** A minor conflict or dispute. [< OItal. *scaramuccia.*] —**skir′mish** *v.*

skirt (skûrt) ►*n.* **1.** The part of a garment, such as a dress or coat, that hangs from the waist down. **2.** A separate garment hanging from the waist down. ►*v.* **1.** To lie along the edge (of); border. **2.** To pass around the edge or border (of). **3.** To evade or avoid. [< ON *skyrta*, shirt.]

skit (skĭt) ►*n.* A short, usu. comic theatrical sketch. [?]

skit•ter (skĭt′ər) ►*v.* To skip, glide, or move rapidly or lightly along a surface. [Prob. < dial. *skite*, run rapidly.]

skit•tish (skĭt′ĭsh) ►*adj.* **1.** Excitable or nervous. **2.** Inconstant; capricious. [ME.] —**skit′tish•ly** *adv.* —**skit′tish•ness** *n.*

skoal (skōl) ►*interj.* Used as a drinking toast. [< ON *skāl*, bowl.]

Skop•je (skôp′yĕ) or **Skop•lje** (-lyĕ). The capital of Macedonia, SSE of Belgrade, Yugoslavia. Pop. 448,229.

skulk (skŭlk) ►*v.* **1.** To lie in hiding; lurk. **2.** To move about stealthily. [ME *skulken*, of Scand. orig.] —**skulk′er** *n.*

skull (skŭl) ►*n.* The bony framework of the head; cranium. [ME *skulle*.]

skull•cap (skŭl′kăp′) ►*n.* **1.** A light, close-fitting, brimless cap. **2.** A yarmulke.

skull•dug•ger•y or **skul•dug•ger•y** (skŭl-dŭg′ə-rē) ►*n.* Crafty deception or trickery. [Prob. < Sc. *sculduddery*, obscenity.]

skunk (skŭngk) ►*n.* **1.** A New World mammal having a bushy tail and black and white fur and ejecting a foul-smelling secretion if startled. **2.** *Slang* A despicable person. ►*v.* *Slang* To defeat overwhelmingly. [Of Massachusett orig.]

skunk cabbage ►*n.* A North American swamp plant having ill-smelling minute flowers in a mottled greenish or purplish spathe.

sky (skī) ►*n.*, *pl.* **skies** (skīz) **1.** The upper atmosphere, seen as a hemisphere above the earth. **2.** often **skies** Atmospheric conditions: *fair skies.* **3.** The celestial regions. [< ON *sky̅*, cloud.]

sky•cap (skī′kăp′) ►*n.* An airport porter.

sky•dive (skī′dīv′) ►*v.* To jump from an airplane, performing various maneuvers before opening a parachute. —**sky′div′er** *n.* —**sky′div′ing** *n.*

Skye (skī), **Isle of.** An island of NW Scotland in the Inner Hebrides.

sky-high (skī′hī′) ►*adv.* **1.** To a very high level: *garbage piled sky-high.* **2.** In or to pieces: *blew the bridge sky-high.* ►*adj.* Exorbitantly high in cost or value.

sky•jack (skī′jăk′) ►*v.* To hijack (an aircraft in flight). [SKY + (HI)JACK.] —**sky′jack′er** *n.* —**sky′jack′ing** *n.*

sky•lark (skī′lärk′) ►*n.* An Old World lark with brownish plumage, noted for its singing while in flight. ►*v.* To romp or frolic.

sky•light (skī′līt′) ►*n.* An overhead window, as in a roof, admitting daylight.

sky•line (skī′līn′) ►*n.* **1.** The horizon. **2.** An outline, as of buildings, against the sky.

sky•rock•et (skī′rŏk′ĭt) ►*n.* A firework that rises into the air and explodes brilliantly. ►*v.* To rise rapidly and suddenly.

sky•scrap•er (skī′skrā′pər) ►*n.* A very tall building.

sky•ward (skī′wərd) ►*adv.* & *adj.* At or toward the sky. —**sky′wards** *adv.*

sky•writ•ing (skī′rī′tĭng) ►*n.* The process of writing in the sky by releasing a visible vapor from a flying airplane. —**sky′writ′er** *n.*

slab (slăb) ►*n.* **1.** A broad, flat, thick piece or slice. **2.** An outside piece cut from a log when squaring it for lumber. [ME.]

slack (slăk) ►*adj.* **-er, -est 1.** Moving slowly; sluggish. **2.** Lacking in activity; not busy. **3.** Not tense, firm, or taut. See Syns at **loose. 4.** Lacking in diligence, care, or concern. See Syns at **negligent.** ►*v.* **1.** To make or become slack. **2.** To slake (lime). —***phrasal verb:*** **slack off** (or **up**) To decrease in activity or intensity. ►*n.* **1.** Something slack or loose. **2.** A period of little activity. **3. slacks** Trousers for informal wear. [< OE *slæc*.] —**slack′ly** *adv.* —**slack′ness** *n.*

slack•en (slăk′ən) ►*v.* To make or become slower, looser, or less intense or severe.

slack•er (slăk′ər) ►*n.* One who shirks work or duty, esp. military service in wartime.

slag (slăg) ►*n.* The glassy mass left after smelting metallic ore. [< MLGer. *slagge*.]

slain (slān) ►*v.* P.part. of **slay.**

slake (slāk) ►*v.* **slaked, slak•ing 1.** To cause to lessen or subside; moderate or quench. **2.** To combine (lime) chemically with water or moist air. [< OE *slacian*.]

sla•lom (slä′ləm) ►*n.* A skiing race along a downhill zigzag course. [Norw. *slalåm*.]

slam[1] (slăm) ►*v.* **slammed, slam•ming 1.** To shut with force and loud noise. **2.** To put, throw, or hit so as to produce a loud noise. ►*n.* **1.** A loud forceful impact. **2.** A noise so produced. [Perh. of Scand. orig.]

slam[2] (slăm) ►*n.* The winning of all the tricks or all but one during the play of one hand in bridge and other card games. [?]

slam dancing ►*n.* A style of dancing, usu. performed to punk rock, in which dancers intentionally collide. —**slam′-dance′** *v.*

slam dunk ►*n.* *Basketball* A dramatic forceful dunk. —**slam′-dunk′** *v.*

slam•mer (slăm′ər) ►*n.* *Slang* A jail. [< SLAM[1].]

slan•der (slăn′dər) ►*n.* A false and malicious, usu. oral statement injurious to a person's reputation. [< Lat. *scandalum*, SCANDAL.] —**slan′der** *v.* —**slan′der•er** *n.* —**slan′der•ous** *adj.* —**slan′der•ous•ly** *adv.*

slang (slăng) ►*n.* A vocabulary of casual or playful, often short-lived expressions used esp. for humor, irreverence, or striking effect. [?] —**slang′i•ness** *n.* —**slang′y** *adj.*

slant (slănt) ►*v.* **1.** To slope or cause to slope. **2.** To present in a way that conforms with a particular bias. ►*n.* **1.** A sloping plane, direction, or course. **2.** A particular bias. [< ME *slenten*.] —**slant′ing•ly** *adv.* —**slant′wise′** *adv.* & *adj.*

Syns: *slant, incline, lean, slope, tilt, tip* **v.**

slap (slăp) ►*n.* **1a.** A sharp blow made with the open hand or a flat object. **b.** The sound so made. **2.** An insult. ►*v.* **slapped, slap•ping 1.** To give a slap to. **2.** To strike or cause to strike sharply and loudly. **3.** To insult sharply. —***idiom:*** **slap on the wrist** A token punishment. [ME *slappe*.]

slap•dash (slăp′dăsh′) ►*adj.* Hasty and careless. —**slap′dash′** *adv.*

slap•hap•py (slăp′hăp′ē) ►*adj.* *Slang* Dazed, giddy, or silly, as if from blows to the head.

slap•stick (slăp′stĭk′) ►*n.* Comedy marked by loud and boisterous farce.

slash (slăsh) ►*v.* **1.** To cut with forceful sweeping strokes. **2.** To make a gash or slit in. **3.** To reduce drastically. ►*n.* **1a.** A sweeping stroke made with a sharp instrument. **b.** A cut made by slashing. **2.** A virgule. [Poss. < OFr. *esclater*, break.] —**slash′er** *n.*

slat (slăt) ►*n.* A flat narrow strip, as of metal or wood. [< OFr. *esclat*, splinter.]

slate (slāt) ►*n.* **1a.** A fine-grained rock that splits into thin, smooth-surfaced layers. **b.** A piece of this rock cut for use as roofing or surfacing material or as a writing surface. **2.** A list of the candidates of a political party running for various offices. **3.** A dark or bluish gray. ►*v.* **slat•ed, slat•ing 1.** To cover with slate. **2.** To schedule. [< OFr. *esclate*, splinter.] —**slat′y** *adj.*

slath•er (slăth′ər) ►*v.* *Informal* To spread thickly or lavishly. [?]

slat•tern (slăt′ərn) ►*n.* A slovenly woman. [Poss. < dial. *slatter*, to slop.] —**slat′tern•li•ness** *n.* —**slat′tern•ly** *adj.*

slaugh•ter (slô′tər) ►*n.* **1.** The killing of animals for food. **2.** The killing of a large number of people; massacre. ►*v.* **1.** To butcher (animals) for food. **2.** To kill brutally or in large numbers. [ME, of Scand. orig.] —**slaugh′ter•er** *n.*

slaugh•ter•house (slô′tər-hous′) ►*n.* A place where animals are butchered.

Slav (släv) ►*n.* A member of one of the Slavic-speaking peoples of E Europe.

slave (slāv) ►*n.* **1.** One bound in servitude as the property of a person or household. **2.** One who is abjectly subservient to a specified person, emotion, or influence. ►*v.* **slaved, slav•ing.** To work very hard or doggedly; toil. [< Lat. *Sclāvus*, Slav.]

slav•er[1] (slăv′ər) ►*v.* **1.** To slobber; drool. **2.** To fawn. See Syns at **fawn**[1]. [Prob. < ON *slafra.*] —**slav′er** *n.*

slav•er[2] (slā′vər) ►*n.* One, such as a person or ship, engaged in the trafficking of slaves.

slav•er•y (slā′və-rē, slāv′rē) ►*n.*, *pl.* **-ies 1.** The state of being a slave; bondage. **2.** The practice of owning slaves. **3.** A condition of hard work and subjection.

Slav•ic (slä′vĭk) ►*adj.* Of or relating to the Slavs or their languages. ►*n.* A branch of Indo-European including Bulgarian, Czech, Polish, Russian, Serbo-Croatian, Slovak, and Slovenian.

slav•ish (slā′vĭsh) ►*adj.* **1.** Of or like a slave; servile: *slavish devotion.* **2.** Showing no originality: *a slavish copy of the original.* —**slav′ish•ly** *adv.* —**slav′ish•ness** *n.*

Sla•vo•ni•a (slə-vō′nē-ə, -vōn′yə) A historical region of N Croatia. —**Sla•vo′ni•an** *adj. & n.*

Sla•von•ic (slə-vŏn′ĭk) ►*n.* Slavic. —**Sla•von′ic** *adj.*

slaw (slô) ►*n.* Coleslaw.

slay (slā) ►*v.* **slew** (slo͞o), **slain** (slān), **slay•ing.** To kill violently. [< OE *slēan.*] —**slay′er** *n.*

slea•zy (slē′zē) ►*adj.* **-zi•er, -zi•est 1a.** Shabby and dirty; tawdry. **b.** Dishonest or corrupt. **2.** Cheap or shoddy. [?] —**sleaze** *n.* —**slea′zi•ly** *adv.* —**slea′zi•ness** *n.*

sled (slĕd) ►*n.* **1.** A vehicle mounted on runners, used for moving over ice and snow. **2.** A light wooden frame on runners, used by children for coasting over snow or ice. ►*v.* **sled•ded, sled•ding.** To ride or convey by a sled. [< MDu. *sledde.*]

sledge (slĕj) ►*n.* A large sled drawn by work animals, used for transporting loads across ice and snow. [Du. dial. *sleedse.*]

sledge•ham•mer (slĕj′hăm′ər) ►*n.* A long heavy hammer usu. wielded with both hands. [< OE *slecg.*]

sleek (slēk) ►*adj.* **-er, -est 1.** Smooth and lustrous as if polished. **2.** Well-groomed and neatly tailored. **3.** Healthy or well-fed; thriving. **4.** Polished or smooth in behavior. [< SLICK.] —**sleek** *v.* —**sleek′ly** *adv.* —**sleek′ness** *n.*

Syns: *sleek, glossy, satiny, silken, silky, slick* ***adj.***

sleep (slēp) ►*n.* **1.** A natural, periodic state of rest in which consciousness is lost and bodily movement and responsiveness to external stimuli decrease. **2.** A state, as of inactivity or unconsciousness, similar to sleep. ►*v.* **slept** (slĕpt), **sleep•ing 1.** To be in or as if in a state of sleep. **2.** To pass by sleeping. —***phrasal verb:*** **sleep with** To have sexual relations with. [< OE *slǣp.*]

sleep•er (slē′pər) ►*n.* **1.** One that sleeps. **2.** A sleeping car. **3.** One that achieves unexpected recognition, popularity, or success.

sleep•ing bag (slē′pĭng) ►*n.* A lined, usu. zippered bag for sleeping, esp. outdoors.

sleeping car ►*n.* A railroad car having accommodations for sleeping.

sleeping pill ►*n.* A sedative in the form of a pill or capsule used to relieve insomnia.

sleeping sickness ►*n.* An often fatal infectious disease of tropical Africa transmitted by the tsetse fly and marked by fever and lethargy.

sleep•less (slēp′lĭs) ►*adj.* **1a.** Marked by a lack of sleep. **b.** Unable to sleep. **2.** Always alert or in motion. —**sleep′less•ly** *adv.* —**sleep′less•ness** *n.*

sleep•walk•ing (slēp′wô′kĭng) ►*n.* The act of walking or performing other activities while asleep or in a sleeplike state; somnambulism. —**sleep′walk′** *v.*

sleep•y (slē′pē) ►*adj.* **-i•er, -i•est 1.** Ready for sleep; drowsy. **2.** Inactive; quiet. —**sleep′i•ly** *adv.* —**sleep′i•ness** *n.*

sleet (slēt) ►*n.* **1.** Precipitation consisting of frozen or partially frozen raindrops. **2.** An icy glaze. ►*v.* To shower sleet. [ME *slete.*] —**sleet′y** *adj.*

sleeve (slēv) ►*n.* **1.** A part of a garment that covers the arm. **2.** A case into which an object fits. —***idiom:*** **up (one's) sleeve** Hidden but ready to be used. [< OE *slēf.*] —**sleeved** *adj.* —**sleeve′less** *adj.*

sleigh (slā) ►*n.* A light vehicle on runners, usu. drawn by a horse over snow or ice. [< MDu. *slēde.*] —**sleigh** *v.*

sleight (slīt) ►*n.* **1.** Dexterity. **2.** A trick or stratagem. [< ON *slægdh* < *slægr*, sly.]

sleight of hand ►*n.* **1.** A trick or set of tricks performed so quickly that the manner of execution cannot be observed; legerdemain. **2.** Performance of such tricks.

slen•der (slĕn′dər) ►*adj.* **-er, -est 1.** Having little width in proportion to height or length. **2.** Small in amount or extent; meager. [ME *sclendre.*] —**slen′der•ly** *adv.* —**slen′der•ness** *n.*

slen•der•ize (slĕn′də-rīz′) ►*v.* **-ized, -iz•ing.** To make or become slender.

slept (slĕpt) ►*v.* P.t. and p.part. of **sleep.**

sleuth (slo͞oth) ►*n.* A detective. [< SLEUTHHOUND.] —**sleuth** *v.*

sleuth•hound (slo͞oth′hound′) ►*n.* **1.** A dog used for tracking or pursuing. **2.** A detective. [< ME *sleuth*, track.]

slew[1] also **slue** (slōō) ▶*n. Informal* A large amount or number. [< OIr. *slúag*.]
slew[2] (slōō) ▶*v.* P.t. of **slay.**
slew[3] (slōō) ▶*v. & n.* Var. of **slue**[1].
slice (slīs) ▶*n.* **1.** A thin broad piece cut from a larger amount. **2.** A portion or share. **3.** *Sports* A stroke that causes a ball to curve off course to the right or, if the player is left-handed, to the left. ▶*v.* **sliced, slic•ing 1.** To cut or divide into slices. **2.** To cut or remove from a larger piece. **3.** *Sports* To hit (a ball) with a slice. [< OFr. *esclicier*, to splinter.] —**slice′a•ble** *adj.* —**slic′er** *n.*
slick (slĭk) ▶*adj.* **-er, -est 1.** Smooth, glossy, and slippery. See Syns at **sleek. 2.** Deftly executed; adroit. **3.** Shrewd; wily. **4.** Superficially attractive but lacking depth; glib. ▶*n.* A smooth or slippery surface or area: *an oil slick.* ▶*v.* To make smooth or glossy. [ME *slike*.] —**slick′ly** *adv.* —**slick′ness** *n.*
slick•er (slĭk′ər) ▶*n.* **1.** A long loose raincoat made of a glossy material. **2.** *Informal* A person with stylish clothing and manners.
slide (slīd) ▶*v.* **slid** (slĭd), **slid•ing 1.** To move over a surface while maintaining continuous contact. **2.** To pass smoothly and quietly; glide. **3.** To slip or skid. **4.** To return to a less favorable or worthy condition. ▶*n.* **1.** A sliding movement or action. **2.** A smooth surface or track for sliding. **3.** A playground apparatus for sliding down. **4.** A part that operates by sliding, as the bolt in a lock. **5.** A usu. photographic image on a transparent base for projection on a screen. **6.** A small glass plate for mounting specimens for a microscope. **7.** A fall of a mass of rock, earth, or snow down a slope. [< OE *slīdan*.]
slid•er (slī′dər) ▶*n.* **1.** One that slides. **2.** *Baseball* A fast pitch that breaks in the same direction as a curve ball at the last moment.
slide rule ▶*n.* A device consisting of two logarithmically scaled rules arranged to slide along each other, used in performing mathematical operations.
slid•ing scale (slī′dĭng) ▶*n.* A scale in which indicated prices, taxes, or wages vary in accordance with another factor, as wages with the cost-of-living index.
sli•er (slī′ər) ▶*adj.* Comp. of **sly.**
sli•est (slī′ĭst) ▶*adj.* Superl. of **sly.**
slight (slīt) ▶*adj.* **-er, -est 1.** Small in size, degree, or amount. **2.** Frail or delicate. **3.** Of small importance; trifling. ▶*v.* **1.** To treat as if of small importance. **2.** To snub or insult. **3.** To neglect. ▶*n.* An act of deliberate discourtesy or disrespect; snub. [ME, slender, poss. of Scand. orig.] —**slight′ly** *adv.* —**slight′ness** *n.*
slim (slĭm) ▶*adj.* **slim•mer, slim•mest 1.** Small in girth or thickness; slender. **2.** Scanty or meager. ▶*v.* **slimmed, slim•ming.** To make or become slim. [< MDu. *slimp*, bad, crooked.] —**slim′ly** *adv.* —**slim′ness** *n.*
slime (slīm) ▶*n.* **1.** A moist, foul, gen. slippery or sticky substance. **2.** A mucous secretion, as of fish or slugs. [< OE *slīm*.] —**slim′y** *adj.*
sling (slĭng) ▶*n.* **1.** A weapon made of a looped strap in which a stone is hurled. **2.** A looped belt, rope, strap, or chain for supporting, cradling, or hoisting loads. **3.** A cloth band suspended from the neck to support an injured arm or hand. ▶*v.* **slung** (slŭng), **sling•ing 1.** To hurl with a swinging motion; fling. **2.** To place, carry, or move in a sling: *sling cargo into a hold.* [ME *slinge*.] —**sling′er** *n.*
sling•shot (slĭng′shŏt′) ▶*n.* A Y-shaped stick having an elastic strap attached to the prongs, used for shooting stones or pellets.
slink (slĭngk) ▶*v.* **slunk** (slŭngk), **slink•ing.** To move furtively. [< OE *slincan*.]
slink•y (slĭng′kē) ▶*adj.* **-i•er, -i•est 1.** Stealthy; furtive. **2.** Sinuous and sleek.
slip[1] (slĭp) ▶*v.* **slipped, slip•ping 1.** To move quietly and stealthily. **2.** To slide involuntarily and lose one's balance. **3.** To slide out of place or from one's grasp. **4.** To leave or escape unnoticed. **5a.** To decline from a former or standard level; fall off. **b.** To make a mistake. **6.** To place or insert smoothly and quietly. **7.** To put on or remove easily or quickly: *slip on a sweater.* ▶*n.* **1.** The act of slipping. **2.** A slight error or oversight. **3.** A docking place for a ship between two piers. **4.** A woman's undergarment of dress length. **5.** A pillowcase. —***idioms:* give (someone) the slip** *Slang* To escape the company or pursuit of. **let slip** To say inadvertently or thoughtlessly. **slip one over on** *Informal* To hoodwink; trick. [ME *slippen*.] —**slip′page** *n.*
slip[2] (slĭp) ▶*n.* **1.** A plant cutting used for propagation. **2.** A slender, youthful person. **3.** A small piece of paper. [< MLGer. or MDu. *slippe*.]
slip•cov•er (slĭp′kŭv′ər) ▶*n.* A fitted, removable, usu. cloth cover for a piece of upholstered furniture. —**slip′cov′er** *v.*
slip•knot (slĭp′nŏt′) ▶*n.* A knot made with a loop so that it slips easily along the rope or cord around which it is tied.

slipknot

slipped disk (slĭpt) ▶*n.* An injury due to the shifting out of position of a cushioning disk between the spinal vertebrae.
slip•per (slĭp′ər) ▶*n.* A light low shoe that can be slipped on and off easily.
slip•per•y (slĭp′ə-rē) ▶*adj.* **-i•er, -i•est 1.** Causing or tending to cause sliding or slipping. **2.** Not trustworthy; elusive or tricky. [< OE *slipor*.] —**slip′per•i•ness** *n.*
slip•shod (slĭp′shŏd′) ▶*adj.* **1.** Careless; sloppy; slovenly. **2.** Shabby or seedy.
slip-up (slĭp′ŭp′) ▶*n.* An error; oversight.
slit (slĭt) ▶*n.* A long straight narrow cut or opening. [< OE *slītan*, cut up.] —**slit** *v.*
slith•er (slĭ*th*′ər) ▶*v.* **1.** To slip and slide. **2.** To move along by gliding, as a snake does. [< OE *slidrian*.] —**slith′er•y** *adj.*
sliv•er (slĭv′ər) ▶*n.* A thin sharp-ended piece; splinter. [< OE *slīfan*, split.] —**sliv′er** *v.*
slob (slŏb) ▶*n. Informal* A crude or slovenly person. [Ir.Gael. *slab*, mud.]
slob•ber (slŏb′ər) ▶*v.* **1.** To let saliva or food dribble from the mouth; drool. **2.** To express emotion effusively. [ME *sloberen*.] —**slob′ber** *n.* —**slob′ber•er** *n.*
sloe (slō) ▶*n.* **1.** See **blackthorn. 2.** The tart, blue-black, plumlike fruit of the blackthorn. [< OE *slā*.]

slog (slŏg) ▸*v.* **slogged, slog•ging 1.** To walk with a slow, labored gait. **2.** To work diligently for long hours; toil. [Perh. < SLUG[3].]

slo•gan (slō′gən) ▸*n.* **1.** A phrase expressing the aims or nature of an enterprise, team, or other group; motto. **2.** A catchword used in advertising or promotion. [< Sc. *slogorne*, battle cry.]

sloop (slo͞op) ▸*n.* A single-masted, fore-and-aft-rigged sailing boat with a mainsail and a jib. [Du. *sloep* < MDu. *slūpen*, glide.]

slop (slŏp) ▸*n.* **1.** Spilled or splashed liquid. **2.** Soft mud or slush. **3.** Unappetizing watery food. **4.** often **slops** Waste food used esp. to feed pigs. ▸*v.* **slopped, slop•ping 1.** To spill or splash messily. **2.** To feed slops to. [ME *sloppe*, muddy place.]

slope (slōp) ▸*v.* **sloped, slop•ing.** To incline upward or downward. See Syns at **slant.** ▸*n.* **1.** An inclined line, surface, plane, or stretch of ground. **2a.** A deviation from the horizontal. **b.** The amount of such deviation. [< ME *aslope*, sloping.]

slop•py (slŏp′ē) ▸*adj.* **-pi•er, -pi•est 1.** Untidy or messy. **2.** Carelessly done. **3.** Muddy or slushy. —**slop′pi•ly** *adv.* —**slop′pi•ness** *n.*

slosh (slŏsh) ▸*v.* **1.** To splash or flounder, as in water. **2.** To splash (a liquid) copiously. [Perh. < SLOP and SLUSH.] —**slosh′y** *adj.*

slot (slŏt) ▸*n.* **1.** A narrow groove or opening. **2.** A suitable place, position, or niche, as in a sequence. ▸*v.* **slot•ted, slot•ting 1.** To make a slot in. **2.** To put into or assign to a slot. [< OFr. *esclot*, hollow of the breastbone.]

sloth (slôth, slōth, slŏth) ▸*n.* **1.** Laziness or indolence. **2.** Any of a family of slow-moving, arboreal mammals of tropical America. [ME *slowth* < *slow*, SLOW.]

sloth•ful (slôth′fəl, slōth′-, slŏth′-) ▸*adj.* Indolent; lazy. See Syns at **lazy.** —**sloth′ful•ly** *adv.* —**sloth′ful•ness** *n.*

slot machine ▸*n.* A coin-operated vending or gambling machine.

slouch (slouch) ▸*n.* **1.** An awkward, drooping posture or gait. **2.** *Slang* A lazy or incompetent person. [?] —**slouch** *v.*

slough[1] (slo͞o, slou) ▸*n.* **1.** A hollow, usu. filled with mud. **2.** A stagnant swamp. **3.** A state of deep despair. [< OE *slōh.*]

slough[2] (slŭf) ▸*n.* **1.** Dead tissue separated from surrounding living tissue, as in a wound. **2.** An outer layer that is shed. ▸*v.* To shed or cast off. [ME *slughe.*]

Slo•vak (slō′väk′, -văk′) also **Slo•va•ki•an** (slō-vä′kē-ən, -văk′ē-ən) ▸*n.* **1.** A member of a Slavic people living in Slovakia. **2.** The Slavic language of the Slovaks. —**Slo′vak, Slo•va′ki•an** *adj.*

Slo•va•ki•a (slō-vä′kē-ə, -văk′ē-ə) A country of central Europe; formerly part of Czechoslovakia. Cap. Bratislava. Pop. 5,347,000.

slov•en (slŭv′ən) ▸*n.* One who is habitually untidy or careless. [ME *slovein.*]

Slo•vene (slō′vēn′) also **Slo•ve•ni•an** (slō-vē′nē-ən, -vēn′yən) ▸*n.* **1.** A member of a Slavic people living in Slovenia. **2.** The Slavic language of the Slovenes. —**Slo′vene, Slo•ve′ni•an** *adj.*

Slo•ve•ni•a (slō-vē′nē-ə, -vēn′yə) A republic of the NW Balkan Peninsula. Cap. Ljubljana. Pop. 1,942,000.

slov•en•ly (slŭv′ən-lē) ▸*adj.* **1.** Untidy or messy. **2.** Marked by carelessness; slipshod: *slovenly work.* —**slov′en•li•ness** *n.*

slow (slō) ▸*adj.* **-er, -est 1a.** Not moving or able to move quickly. **b.** Marked by a low speed or tempo: *a slow waltz.* **2.** Taking or requiring a long time. **3.** Registering a time or rate behind or below the correct one. **4.** Marked by low sales or activity. **5.** Dull or boring. **6.** Not having or showing mental quickness. ▸*adv.* **-er, -est.** Slowly. ▸*v.* **1.** To make or become slow or slower. **2.** To delay; retard. [< OE *slāw.*] —**slow′ly** *adv.* —**slow′ness** *n.*

Usage: *Slow* is often used adverbially in speech and informal writing, especially for brevity and forcefulness: *Drive slow! Slow* is also used with certain senses of common verbs: *The watch runs slow.* Otherwise, in formal writing *slowly* is generally preferred.

slow•down (slō′doun′) ▸*n.* A slackening of pace: *a production slowdown.*

slow motion ▸*n.* A filmmaking technique in which the action as projected is slower than the original action. —**slow′-mo′tion** *adj.*

slow•poke (slō′pōk′) ▸*n. Informal* One who moves, works, or acts slowly.

sludge (slŭj) ▸*n.* **1.** Semisolid material such as that precipitated by sewage treatment. **2.** Mud, mire, or ooze. [Perh. < dial. *slutch*, mire.] —**sludg′y** *adj.*

slue[1] also **slew** (slo͞o) ▸*v.* **slued, slu•ing** also **slewed, slew•ing.** To turn or twist to the side. ▸*n.* The act of sluing. [?]

slue[2] (slo͞o) ▸*n.* Var. of **slew[1].**

slug[1] (slŭg) ▸*n.* **1.** A round bullet larger than buckshot. **2.** *Informal* A shot of liquor. **3.** A small metal disk used in place of a coin. **4.** A lump of metal. [Perh. < SLUG[2].]

slug[2] (slŭg) ▸*n.* A terrestrial gastropod mollusk having a slow-moving elongated body with no shell. [ME *slugge*, sluggard.]

slug[3] (slŭg) ▸*v.* **slugged, slug•ging.** To strike heavily, esp. with the fist or a bat. [Poss. < SLUG[1].] —**slug** *n.* —**slug′ger** *n.*

slug•gard (slŭg′ərd) ▸*n.* A lazy person; idler. [ME *sluggart.*] —**slug′gard•ly** *adj.*

slug•gish (slŭg′ĭsh) ▸*adj.* **1.** Slow; inactive. **2.** Lazy or indolent. **3.** Slow to perform or respond. [Prob. ME *slugge*, lazy person.] —**slug′gish•ly** *adv.* —**slug′gish•ness** *n.*

sluice (slo͞os) ▸*n.* **1a.** An artificial channel for water, with a gate to regulate the flow. **b.** The gate itself. **2.** A sluiceway. **3.** A long inclined trough, as for floating logs or separating gold ore. ▸*v.* **sluiced, sluic•ing 1.** To wash with or as if with a sudden flow of water; flush. **2.** To draw off by a sluice. **3.** To send down a sluice. [< Lat. *exclūdere*, *exclūs-*, shut out.]

sluice•way (slo͞os′wā′) ▸*n.* An artificial channel, esp. one for carrying off excess water.

slum (slŭm) ▸*n.* A poor, squalid, densely populated urban area. ▸*v.* **slummed, slum•ming.** To visit a slum, esp. from curiosity. [?] —**slum′my** *adj.*

slum•ber (slŭm′bər) ▸*v.* **1.** To sleep or doze. **2.** To be dormant. [Prob. < OE *slūma*, sleep.] —**slum′ber** *n.* —**slum′ber•er** *n.*

slum•ber•ous (slŭm′bər-əs) or **slum•brous** (-brəs) ▸*adj.* **1.** Sleepy; drowsy. **2.** Quiet; tranquil. **3.** Causing or inducing sleep.

slum•lord (slŭm′lôrd′) ▸*n.* An owner of slum property, esp. one who allows the property to deteriorate.

slump (slŭmp) ▸*v.* **1.** To fall, decline, or sink

suddenly. **2.** To droop, as in sitting; slouch. [Prob. of Scand. orig.] —**slump** *n.*

slung (slŭng) ►*v.* P.t. and p.part. of **sling.**

slunk (slŭngk) ►*v.* P.t. and p.part. of **slink.**

slur (slûr) ►*v.* **slurred, slur•ring 1.** To pronounce indistinctly. **2.** To disparage. **3.** To pass over lightly or carelessly. **4.** *Mus.* To glide over (a series of notes) smoothly without a break. ►*n.* **1.** A disparaging remark; aspersion. **2.** A slurred sound. **3.** *Mus.* A curved line connecting notes to indicate that they are to be played or sung legato. [Prob. < ME *sloor*, mud.]

slurp (slûrp) ►*v.* To eat or drink noisily. [Du. *slurpen.*] —**slurp** *n.*

slush (slŭsh) ►*n.* **1.** Partially melted snow or ice. **2.** Soft mud; slop. **3.** Sentimental drivel. **4.** A drink made of flavored syrup and crushed ice. [Perh. of Scand. orig.] —**slush′i•ly** *adv.* —**slush′i•ness** *n.* —**slush′y** *adj.*

slush fund ►*n.* A fund for undesignated purposes, esp. one used to finance a corrupt practice, such as bribery.

slut (slŭt) ►*n.* **1a.** A sexually promiscuous woman. **b.** A prostitute. **2.** A slovenly woman. [ME *slutte.*] —**slut′tish** *adj.*

sly (slī) ►*adj.* **sli•er, sli•est** also **sly•er, sly•est 1.** Adept in craft or cunning. **2.** Secretive. **3.** Underhand or deceitful. **4.** Playfully mischievous. —***idiom:* on the sly** Secretly. [< ON *slægr.*] —**sly′ly** *adv.* —**sly′ness** *n.*

Sm ► The symbol for the element **samarium.**

SM ►*abbr.* service mark

smack[1] (smăk) ►*v.* **1.** To make a sound by pressing the lips together and pulling them apart quickly. **2.** To kiss or slap noisily. ►*n.* **1.** The loud sharp sound of smacking the lips. **2.** A noisy kiss. **3.** A sharp blow or loud slap. ►*adv.* Directly; straight: *was hit smack in the face.* [Perh. of MFlem. orig.]

smack[2] (smăk) ►*n.* **1.** A distinctive flavor. **2.** A suggestion or trace. ►*v.* **1.** To have a distinct flavor. **2.** To suggest: *This smacks of foul play.* [< OE *smæc.*]

smack[3] (smăk) ►*n.* A sloop-rigged boat used chiefly in fishing. [Du. or LGer. *smak.*]

smack[4] (smăk) ►*n.* *Slang* Heroin. [Prob. < Yiddish *shmek*, a sniff, smell.]

small (smôl) ►*adj.* **-er, -est 1.** Being below the average in size, quantity, or extent. **2.** Insignificant or trivial. **3.** Limited in degree or scope: *a small farmer.* **4.** Not fully grown. **5.** Narrow in outlook; petty: *a small mind.* **6.** Belittled; humiliated. **7.** Lacking force or volume: *a small voice.* ►*adv.* **1.** In small pieces: *Cut the meat up small.* **2.** Softly. **3.** In a small manner. ►*n.* Something smaller than the rest: *the small of the back.* [< OE *smæl.*] —**small′ness** *n.*

Syns: *small, diminutive, little, miniature, minuscule, minute, petite, tiny, wee* ***adj.***

small arm ►*n.* A firearm that can be carried in the hand.

small calorie ►*n.* See **calorie** 1.

small capital ►*n.* A letter having the form of a capital letter but smaller.

small fry ►*n.* **1.** Small children. **2.** Persons or things regarded as unimportant.

small intestine ►*n.* The part of the alimentary canal between the outlet of the stomach and the large intestine.

small-mind•ed (smôl′mīn′dĭd) ►*adj.* Having a narrow or petty attitude. —**small′-mind′ed•ly** *adv.* —**small′-mind′ed•ness** *n.*

small•pox (smôl′pŏks′) ►*n.* An acute, highly infectious viral disease marked by high fever and pustules that form pockmarks.

small talk ►*n.* Casual or light conversation.

small•time or **small-time** (smôl′tīm′) ►*adj.* *Informal* Insignificant or minor. —**small′-tim′er** *n.*

smarm•y (smär′mē) ►*adj.* **-i•er, -i•est.** Hypocritically or exaggeratedly earnest. See Syns at **unctuous.** [< *smarm*, smear.]

smart (smärt) ►*adj.* **-er, -est 1a.** Intelligent; bright. **b.** Amusingly clever; witty. **c.** Impertinent or insolent. **2.** Quick and energetic: *a smart pace.* **3.** Canny and sharp in dealings; shrewd. **4.** Fashionable; elegant: *a smart restaurant.* See Syns at **fashionable. 5.** Having a built-in computational ability: *a smart bomb.* ►*v.* **1.** To cause or feel a sharp stinging pain. **2.** To feel mental distress. [< OE *smeart*, stinging.] —**smart′ly** *adv.* —**smart′ness** *n.*

smart al•eck (ăl′ĭk) ►*n.* *Informal* One who is offensively arrogant. —**smart′-al′eck•y** *adj.*

smart•en (smär′tn) ►*v.* **1.** To make or become more brisk or lively. **2.** To make or become smart or smarter.

smash (smăsh) ►*v.* **1.** To break or be broken into pieces. **2.** To throw or dash violently so as to crush or shatter. See Syns at **crush. 3.** To strike with a heavy blow; hit. ►*n.* **1.** The act or sound of smashing or the condition of having been smashed. **2.** Total destruction; ruin. **3.** A collision or crash. **4.** *Sports* A powerful overhand stroke, as in tennis. **5.** *Informal* A resounding success. ►*adj.* *Informal* Very successful. [Prob. imit.] —**smash′er** *n.*

smash•up (smăsh′ŭp′) ►*n.* **1.** A total defeat. **2.** A serious collision between vehicles.

smat•ter•ing (smăt′ər-ĭng) ►*n.* **1.** Superficial or piecemeal knowledge. **2.** A small, scattered amount. [< *smatter*, dabble.]

smear (smîr) ►*v.* **1.** To spread, cover, or stain with a sticky dirty substance. **2.** To smudge or soil. **3.** To slander or vilify. ►*n.* **1.** A smudge or blot. **2.** Vilification or slander. **3.** A sample, as of blood, spread on a slide for microscopic examination. [< OE *smerian*, anoint.] —**smear′y** *adj.*

smell (smĕl) ►*v.* **smelled** or **smelt** (smĕlt), **smell•ing 1.** To perceive the odor of by the sense organs of the nose. **2.** To have or emit an odor. **3.** To suggest evil or corruption. ►*n.* **1.** The olfactory sense. **2.** The odor of something. **3.** The act of smelling. **4.** A distinctive quality; aura. [ME *smellen.*]

Syns: *smell, aroma, odor, scent* ***n.***

smell•ing salts (smĕl′ĭng) ►*pl.n.* A preparation based on an ammonia compound, sniffed esp. to relieve faintness.

smell•y (smĕl′ē) ►*adj.* **-i•er, -i•est** *Informal.* Having an unpleasant odor.

smelt[1] (smĕlt) ►*v.* To melt or fuse (ores) to separate the metallic constituents. [Du. or LGer. *smelten.*]

smelt[2] (smĕlt) ►*n., pl.* **smelts** or **smelt.** A small silvery food fish. [< OE.]

smelt[3] (smĕlt) ►*v.* P.t. and p.part. of **smell.**

smelt•er (smĕl′tər) ►*n.* **1.** also **smelt•er•y** (-tə-rē), *pl.* **-ies** An establishment for smelting. **2.** A worker who smelts ore.

smid•gen or **smid•gin** (smĭj′ən) ►*n.* A very small quantity or portion; bit. [Prob. < dial. *smitch*, particle.]

smi•lax (smī′lăks′) ►*n.* A slender, glossy-leaved climbing vine used in floral decoration. [< Gk.]

smile (smīl) ►*n.* A facial expression formed by an upward curving of the corners of the mouth and indicating pleasure, affection, or amusement. ►*v.* **smiled, smil•ing 1.** To have or form a smile. **2.** To express approval. **3.** To express with a smile. [< ME *smilen*, to smile.] —**smil′ing•ly** *adv.*

smil•ey (smī′lē) ►*n., pl.* **-eys.** An emoticon, esp. one indicating a smiling face [:-)].

smirch (smûrch) ►*v.* **1.** To soil or stain. **2.** To dishonor. [ME *smorchen.*] —**smirch** *n.*

smirk (smûrk) ►*v.* To smile in an affected, often offensively self-satisfied manner. [< OE *smercian*, smile.] —**smirk** *n.* —**smirk′er** *n.*

smite (smīt) ►*v.* **smote** (smōt), **smit•ten** (smĭt′n) or **smote, smit•ing 1.** To inflict a heavy blow on. **2.** To kill by or as if by blows. **3.** To afflict. [< OE *smītan*, smear.]

smith (smĭth) ►*n.* **1.** A metalworker, esp. one who works with hot metal. **2.** A blacksmith. [< OE.]

Smith, Adam. 1723–90. Scottish economist and philosopher.

Smith, Alfred Emanuel. 1873–1944. Amer. politician.

Smith, John. 1580?–1631. English colonist, explorer, and writer.

Smith, Joseph. 1805–44. Amer. founder (1830) of the Church of Jesus Christ of Latter-day Saints.

Smith, Margaret Chase. 1897–1995. Amer. politician.

smith•er•eens (smĭth′ə-rēnz′) ►*pl.n. Informal* Pieces; bits. [< Ir.Gael. *smidirīn.*]

Smith•son (smĭth′sən), **James.** 1765–1829. British chemist and philanthropist.

smith•y (smĭth′ē, smĭ*th*′ē) ►*n., pl.* **-ies.** A blacksmith's shop; forge. [< ON *smidhja.*]

smock (smŏk) ►*n.* A loose outer garment worn to protect the clothes. ►*v.* To decorate (fabric) with stitched gathers in a honeycomb pattern. [< OE *smoc.*]

smog (smŏg, smôg) ►*n.* **1.** Fog polluted with smoke. **2.** Air pollution produced when sunlight causes hydrocarbons and nitrogen oxides, esp. from automotive exhaust, to combine. [SM(OKE) + (F)OG.] —**smog′gy** *adj.*

smoke (smōk) ►*n.* **1.** The vapor made up of small particles of matter from incomplete burning of materials such as wood or coal. **2.** A cloud of fine particles. **3.** The act of smoking a form of tobacco. **4.** *Informal* A cigarette or cigar. ►*v.* **smoked, smok•ing 1.** To draw in and exhale smoke from a cigarette, cigar, or pipe. **2.** To emit smoke. **3.** To emit smoke excessively. **4.** To preserve (meat or fish) by exposure to smoke. **5.** To fumigate. **6.** *Slang* To perform at the utmost capacity. **7.** *Slang* To kill. —***phrasal verb:* smoke out** To force out of hiding by or as if by the use of smoke. [< OE *smoca.*] —**smoke′less** *adj.* —**smok′er** *n.* —**smok′i•ness** *n.* —**smok′y** *adj.*

smoke detector ►*n.* An alarm device that automatically detects the presence of smoke.

smoke•house (smōk′hous′) ►*n.* A structure where meat or fish is smoked.

smoke screen ►*n.* **1.** Dense smoke used to conceal military operations. **2.** Something used to conceal plans or intentions.

smoke•stack (smōk′stăk′) ►*n.* A large vertical pipe through which combustion gases and smoke are discharged.

smol•der also **smoul•der** (smōl′dər) ►*v.* **1.** To burn with little smoke and no flame. **2.** To exist in a suppressed state. ►*n.* Thick smoke resulting from a slow fire. [ME *smolderen*, suffocate.]

Smo•lensk (smō-lĕnsk′, smə-) A city of W Russia on the Dnieper R. Pop. 349,326.

Smol•lett (smŏl′ĭt), **Tobias George.** 1721–71. British writer.

smooch (smo͞och) *Slang* ►*n.* A kiss. ►*v.* To kiss. [Perh. of imit. orig.]

smooth (smo͞o*th*) ►*adj.* **-er, -est 1.** Free from irregularities, roughness, or projections. **2.** Having a fine texture or consistency. **3.** Having an even or gentle motion. **4.** Having no obstructions or difficulties. **5.** Ingratiating: *smooth talk.* ►*v.* **1.** To make or become smooth. **2.** To rid of obstructions, hindrances, or difficulties. **3.** To make calm; soothe. [< OE *smōth.*] —**smooth′er** *n.* —**smooth′ly** *adv.* —**smooth′ness** *n.*

smooth•bore (smo͞o*th*′bôr′, -bōr′) ►*adj.* Having no rifling within the barrel. Used of a firearm. —**smooth′bore′** *n.*

smor•gas•bord (smôr′gəs-bôrd′, -bōrd′) ►*n.* A buffet meal featuring a varied number of dishes. [Swed. *smörgåsbord.*]

smote (smōt) ►*v.* P.t. and p.part. of **smite.**

smoth•er (smŭ*th*′ər) ►*v.* **1.** To kill or extinguish by depriving of oxygen. **2.** To conceal or suppress. **3.** To cover thickly. [< ME *smorther*, dense smoke.]

smudge (smŭj) ►*v.* **smudged, smudg•ing.** To smear or blur. ►*n.* **1.** A blotch or smear. **2.** A smoky fire used to protect against insects or frost. [ME *smogen.*] —**smudg′y** *adj.*

smug (smŭg) ►*adj.* **smug•ger, smug•gest.** Self-satisfied or complacent. [< MLGer.] —**smug′ly** *adv.* —**smug′ness** *n.*

smug•gle (smŭg′əl) ►*v.* **-gled, -gling 1.** To import or export without paying lawful customs charges or duties. **2.** To convey illicitly or by stealth. [Prob. LGer. *smuggeln.*] —**smug′gler** *n.*

smut (smŭt) ►*n.* **1.** A particle of dirt. **2.** Obscene or pornographic speech or printed matter. **3.** Any of various plant diseases, esp. of cereal grasses, caused by fungi that form black powdery masses. [< ME *smotten*, defile.] —**smut′ti•ness** *n.* —**smut′ty** *adj.*

Smuts (smŭts, smœts), **Jan Christiaan.** 1870–1950. South African soldier and politician.

Smyr•na (smûr′nə) See **Izmir.**

Sn ► The symbol for the element **tin** 1. [< LLat. *stannum*, tin.]

snack (snăk) ►*n.* **1.** A light meal. **2.** Food eaten between meals. [< ME *snacche*, bite.] —**snack** *v.*

snaf•fle (snăf′əl) ►*n.* A jointed bit for a horse. [?]

sna•fu (snă-fo͞o′) ►*n., pl.* **-fus** *Slang* A chaotic or confused situation. [*s(ituation) n(ormal) a(ll) f(ouled) u(p).*]

snag (snăg) ►*n.* **1.** A sharp or jagged protuberance. **2.** A tree or limb that protrudes above a water surface. **3.** A break, pull, or tear in fabric. **4.** An unforeseen obstacle. ►*v.* **snagged, snag•ging 1.** To get caught by or as if by a snag. **2.** *Informal* To catch or get unexpectedly

snaffle
loose ring French training snaffle bit

or quickly. **3.** To hinder; impede. [Of Scand. orig.]

snail (snāl) ►*n.* An aquatic or terrestrial mollusk having a spirally coiled shell and distinct head. [< OE *snægl.*]

snail mail ►*n.* *Informal* Mail delivered by a postal system, as distinct from e-mail.

snake (snāk) ►*n.* **1.** Any of numerous scaly, legless, sometimes poisonous reptiles having a long, tapering, cylindrical body. **2.** A treacherous person. **3.** A long flexible wire used for cleaning drains and sewers. ►*v.* **snaked, snak•ing.** To move, drag, or pull in a snakelike manner. [< OE *snaca.*] —**snak′i•ly** *adv.* —**snak′y** *adj.*

snake oil ►*n.* A worthless preparation fraudulently peddled as a cure for many ills.

Snake River. A river of the NW US rising in NW WY and flowing about 1,670 km (1,038 mi) to the Columbia R. in SE WA.

snap (snăp) ►*v.* **snapped, snap•ping 1.** To make or cause to make a sharp cracking sound. **2.** To break suddenly with a sharp sound. **3.** To give way abruptly. **4.** To bite or seize with a snatching motion. **5.** To speak abruptly or sharply: *snapped at the child.* **6.** To move swiftly and smartly. See Syns at **jerk**[1]. **7.** To flash or sparkle. **8.** *Football* To pass the ball so as to initiate a play. **9.** To open or close with a click. **10a.** To take (a photograph). **b.** To photograph (a subject). ►*n.* **1.** A sharp cracking sound. **2.** A sudden breaking or release of something under pressure. **3.** A clasp, catch, or other fastening device. **4.** A sudden attempt to bite or snatch. **5.** A thin crisp cookie. **6.** *Informal* Briskness or energy. **7.** A spell of cold weather. **8.** Something accomplished without effort. See Syns at **breeze. 9.** *Football* The act of snapping the ball. [< MLGer. or MDu. *snappen*, seize.] —**snap′pish** *adj.* —**snap′py** *adj.*

snap bean ►*n.* A string bean cultivated for its crisp edible pods.

snap•drag•on (snăp′drăg′ən) ►*n.* A cultivated plant having showy clusters of two-lipped, variously colored flowers.

snap•per (snăp′ər) ►*n.* **1.** One that snaps. **2.** *pl.* **-per** or **-pers** Any of numerous marine fishes prized as food and game fishes.

snap•ping turtle (snăp′ĭng) ►*n.* Any of a family of freshwater turtles having a rough shell and powerful hooked jaws.

snap•shot (snăp′shŏt′) ►*n.* A photograph taken with a small camera.

snare[1] (snâr) ►*n.* **1.** A trap, often consisting of a noose, used for capturing birds and small animals. **2.** Something that entangles the unwary. ►*v.* **snared, snar•ing.** To trap with or as if with a snare. See Syns at **catch.** [< OE *snearu* and ON *snara.*]

snare[2] (snâr) ►*n.* Any of the wires or cords stretched across the lower head of a drum so as to vibrate against it and increase reverberation. [Prob. < Du. *snaar*, string.] —**snare drum** *n.*

snarl[1] (snärl) ►*v.* **1.** To growl while baring the teeth. **2.** To speak angrily or threateningly. [< obsolete *snar.*] —**snarl** *n.* —**snarl′er** *n.*

snarl[2] (snärl) ►*n.* A tangle. ►*v.* **1.** To tangle or knot. **2.** To confuse. [ME *snarle*, trap.]

snatch (snăch) ►*v.* **1.** To try to grasp or seize. **2.** To seize or grab. ►*n.* **1.** The act of snatching. **2.** A brief period. **3.** A bit or fragment: *a snatch of dialogue.* [ME *snacchen.*] —**snatch′er** *n.*

snaz•zy (snăz′ē) ►*adj.* **-zi•er, -zi•est** *Slang.* Fashionable and flashy or showy. [?]

sneak (snēk) ►*v.* **sneaked** also **snuck** (snŭk), **sneak•ing.** To move, give, or take in a quiet, stealthy way. ►*n.* **1.** One who is stealthy or underhanded. **2.** An instance of sneaking. [< OE *snīcan.*] —**sneak′i•ly** *adv.* —**sneak′i•ness** *n.* —**sneak′y** *adj.*

sneak•er (snē′kər) ►*n.* A sports shoe usu. made of canvas and having rubber soles.

sneer (snîr) ►*n.* A slight raising of one corner of the upper lip, expressive of contempt. [< OE *fnǣran*, breathe heavily.] —**sneer** *v.*

sneeze (snēz) ►*v.* **sneezed, sneez•ing.** To expel air forcibly from the mouth and nose in an explosive involuntary spasm. [< OE *fnēosan.*] —**sneeze** *n.*

snick•er (snĭk′ər) ►*v.* To utter a nasty, partly stifled laugh. [Perh. imit.] —**snick′er** *n.*

snide (snīd) ►*adj.* **snid•er, snid•est.** Slyly derogatory. [?] —**snide′ly** *adv.*

sniff (snĭf) ►*v.* **1.** To inhale a short audible breath through the nose. **2.** To indicate ridicule, contempt, or doubt. **3.** To detect by or as if by sniffing. [ME *sniffen.*] —**sniff** *n.* —**sniff′er** *n.*

snif•fle (snĭf′əl) ►*v.* **-fled, -fling 1.** To breathe audibly through a congested nose. **2.** To whimper. [< SNIFF.] —**snif′fle** *n.*

snif•ter (snĭf′tər) ►*n.* A pear-shaped goblet with a narrow top, used esp. in serving brandy. [< ME *sniften*, sniff.]

snig•ger (snĭg′ər) ►*v.* To snicker. [Perh. < SNICKER.] —**snig′ger** *n.*

snip (snĭp) ►*v.* **snipped, snip•ping.** To cut or clip with short quick strokes. ►*n.* **1a.** A small cut made with scissors or shears. **b.** A small piece clipped off. **2.** *Informal* A small person. [Du. or LGer. *snippen.*]

snipe (snīp) ►*n.* **1.** *pl.* **snipe** or **snipes** Any of various long-billed, brownish wading birds. **2.** A shot, esp. a gunshot, from a concealed place. ►*v.* **sniped, snip•ing 1.** To shoot at people from a concealed place. **2.** To make nasty remarks. [ME.] —**snip′er** *n.*

snip•pet (snĭp′ĭt) ►*n.* A tidbit or morsel.

snip•py (snĭp′ē) ►*adj.* **-pi•er, -pi•est** *Informal.* Sharp-tongued; impertinent.

snit (snĭt) ►*n.* *Informal* An agitated state. [?]

snitch (snĭch) ►*v.* *Slang* **1.** To steal. **2.** To turn informer. [?] —**snitch** *n.*

sniv•el (snĭv′əl) ►*v.* **-eled, -el•ing** or **-elled, -el•ling 1.** To complain or whine tearfully. **2.** To run at the nose, esp. while crying. [ME *snivelen.*] —**sniv′el** *n.*

snob (snŏb) ►*n.* One who affects an offensive air of superiority, as in matters of taste or intellect. [< *snob*, lower-class person.] —**snob′ber•y** *n.* —**snob′bish** *adj.* —**snob′bish•ly** *adv.*

snoop (sno͞op) ►*v.* To pry furtively. ►*n.* One who snoops. [Du. *snoepen*, eat on the sly.] —**snoop′er** *n.* —**snoop′i•ly** *adv.* —**snoop′i•ness** *n.* —**snoop′y** *adj.*

snoot (sno͞ot) ▸*n. Informal* A snout or nose.
snoot•y (sno͞o′tē) ▸*adj.* **-i•er, -i•est** *Informal.* Snobbishly aloof; haughty. —**snoot′i•ness** *n.*
snooze (sno͞oz) ▸*v.* **snoozed, snooz•ing.** To take a light nap; doze. [?] —**snooze** *n.*
snore (snôr, snōr) ▸*v.* **snored, snor•ing.** To breathe with harsh snorting noises while sleeping. [ME *snoren,* snort.] —**snore** *n.* —**snor′er** *n.*
snor•kel (snôr′kəl) ▸*n.* **1.** A breathing apparatus used by skin divers, consisting of a long tube held in the mouth. **2.** A retractable tube in a submarine that contains air-intake and exhaust pipes. [Ger. *Schnorchel.*] —**snor′kel** *v.*
snort (snôrt) ▸*n.* **1.** A loud rough sound made by breathing forcefully through the nostrils. **2.** *Slang* A drink of liquor, esp. a small one. ▸*v.* **1.** To make a snort. **2.** To make an abrupt noise expressive of scorn or anger. **3.** *Slang* To ingest (e.g., a drug) by sniffing. [< ME *snorten,* to snort.] —**snort′er** *n.*
snot (snŏt) ▸*n. Slang* **1.** Nasal mucus; phlegm. **2.** An annoying, arrogant, or impertinent person. [< OE *gesnot.*] —**snot′ti•ly** *adv.* —**snot′ti•ness** *n.* —**snot′ty** *adj.*
snout (snout) ▸*n.* **1.** The projecting nose or facial part of an animal's muzzle. **2.** *Slang* The human nose. [ME.]
snow (snō) ▸*n.* **1.** Frozen precipitation in the form of translucent ice crystals that fall in soft white flakes. **2.** A fall of snow. ▸*v.* **1.** To fall to the earth as snow. **2.** To cover or close off with snow. **3.** *Slang* To overwhelm with insincere talk, esp. with flattery. [< OE *snāw.*] —**snow′y** *adj.*
Snow, C(harles) P(ercy). 1905–80. British writer and scientist.
snow•ball (snō′bôl′) ▸*n.* A mass of soft wet snow packed into a ball. ▸*v.* **1.** To grow or cause to grow rapidly in significance, importance, or size. **2.** To throw snowballs (at).
snow blindness ▸*n.* A usu. temporary loss of vision caused by glare of light reflected from snow or ice.
snow•bound (snō′bound′) ▸*adj.* Confined in one place by heavy snow.
snow•drift (snō′drĭft′) ▸*n.* A mass or bank of snow piled up by the wind.
snow•drop (snō′drŏp′) ▸*n.* A bulbous plant having nodding white spring flowers.
snow•fall (snō′fôl′) ▸*n.* **1.** A fall of snow. **2.** The amount of snow that falls in a given period and area.
snow•flake (snō′flāk′) ▸*n.* A single flake or crystal of snow.
snow leopard ▸*n.* A large cat of central Asia, having grayish fur with dark markings.
snow•man (snō′măn′) ▸*n.* A figure of a person made from packed snow.
snow•mo•bile (snō′mō-bēl′, -mə-) ▸*n.* A small vehicle with skis in front and tanklike treads, used for traveling on snow.
snow pea ▸*n.* A variety of the common pea having a soft thick edible pod.
snow•plow (snō′plou′) ▸*n.* A plowlike device or vehicle used to remove snow.
snow•shoe (snō′sho͞o′) ▸*n.* A racket-shaped frame with interlaced strips attached to the shoe to prevent sinking into deep snow. —**snow′-shoe′** *v.*
snow•storm (snō′stôrm′) ▸*n.* A storm marked by heavy snowfall.

snowmobile

snow tire ▸*n.* A tire with a deep tread or studs for traction on snow-covered surfaces.
snub (snŭb) ▸*v.* **snubbed, snub•bing 1.** To ignore or behave coldly toward; slight. **2.** To dismiss or turn down in a decisive way. **3.** *Naut.* To check the movement of (e.g., a rope) by turning it quickly about a post. ▸*n.* A deliberate slight. [ME *snubben,* rebuke.]
snub-nosed (snŭb′nōzd′) ▸*adj.* Having a short, turned-up nose.
snuck (snŭk) ▸*v. Informal* P.t. and p.part. of **sneak.**
snuff¹ (snŭf) ▸*v.* **1.** To inhale audibly through the nose. **2.** To sniff (at). [ME *snoffen,* sniffle.]
snuff² (snŭf) ▸*v.* **1.** To put out; extinguish: *snuffed out the candles.* **2.** To cut off the charred portion of (a candlewick). [Poss. of LGer. orig.] —**snuff′er** *n.*
snuff³ (snŭf) ▸*n.* A preparation of finely pulverized tobacco for ingesting by sniffing. —***idiom:*** **up to snuff** *Informal* Up to standard. [< Du. *snuftabak.*]
snuf•fle (snŭf′əl) ▸*v.* **-fled, -fling 1.** To breathe noisily, as through a blocked nose. **2.** To sniffle. [Prob. < Du. *snuffelen,* sniff about.] —**snuf′fle** *n.* —**snuf′fler** *n.*
snug (snŭg) ▸*adj.* **snug•ger, snug•gest 1.** Comfortably sheltered; cozy. **2.** Small but well arranged: *a snug apartment.* **3.** Close-fitting; tight. [Of Scand. orig.] —**snug, snug′ly** *adv.* —**snug′ness** *n.*
snug•gle (snŭg′əl) ▸*v.* **-gled, -gling.** To nestle or cuddle. [< SNUG.]
so¹ (sō) ▸*adv.* **1.** In the manner expressed or indicated; thus: *Hold the brush so.* **2.** To such an extent: *She was so weary that she fell.* **3.** To a great extent: *It's so cold.* **4.** As a result; consequently. **5.** Afterward; then: *to the store and so home.* **6.** Thereabouts: *only $10 or so.* **7.** Likewise. **8.** Apparently; then: *So you think you've got troubles?* **9.** In truth; indeed. ▸*adj.* True or factual. ▸*conj.* **1.** With the result or consequence that: *He quit, so I took his place.* **2.** In order that: *I stayed so I could see you.* ▸*interj.* Used to express surprise or comprehension. —***idioms:*** **so as to** In order to: *Shop early so as to beat the rush.* **so that** In order that. [< OE *swā.*]

Usage: Many critics and grammarians have insisted that *so* must be followed by *that* in formal writing when used to introduce a clause giving the reason for or purpose of an action: *He stayed so that he could see the second feature.* But this rule is best regarded as a stylistic preference. • Both *so* and *so that* are acceptably used to introduce clauses that state a result or consequence: *The bridge was still closed, so* (or *so that*) *the drive took an hour.*

so² (sō) ►*n. Mus.* Var. of **sol¹**.

so. or **So.** ►*abbr.* **1.** south **2.** southern

soak (sōk) ►*v.* **1.** To make thoroughly wet by or as if by being immersed in liquid; steep. **2.** To absorb. **3.** To be immersed. **4.** To penetrate or permeate; seep. ►*n.* **1.** The act or process of soaking. **2.** *Slang* A drunkard. [< OE *socian.*] —**soak′er** *n.*

soap (sōp) ►*n.* **1.** A cleansing agent made from an alkali acting on natural oils and fats. **2.** A metallic salt of a fatty acid. **3.** *Slang* A soap opera. [< OE *sāpe.*] —**soap** *v.* —**soap′i•ly** *adv.* —**soap′i•ness** *n.* —**soap′y** *adj.*

soap•box (sōp′bŏks′) ►*n.* **1.** A box in which soap is packed. **2.** A temporary platform used for impromptu public speaking.

soap opera ►*n.* A serial drama, usu. performed on daytime television or radio, characterized by melodrama and sentimentality.

soap•stone (sōp′stōn′) ►*n.* A soft metamorphic rock composed mostly of talc.

soar (sôr, sōr) ►*v.* **1.** To rise, fly, or glide high in the air. **2.** To climb swiftly or powerfully. [< VLat. **exaurāre.*]

sob (sŏb) ►*v.* **sobbed, sob•bing.** To weep aloud with convulsive gasping. [ME *sobben.*] —**sob** *n.* —**sob′bing•ly** *adv.*

so•ba (sō′bə) ►*n.* A Japanese noodle made with buckwheat flour. [Jap.]

so•ber (sō′bər) ►*adj.* **-er, -est 1.** Abstemious or temperate. **2.** Not intoxicated. **3.** Devoid of frivolity, excess, or exaggeration. **4.** Serious; solemn. **5.** Marked by circumspection and self-restraint. ►*v.* To make or become sober. [< Lat. *sōbrius.*] —**so′ber•ly** *adv.* —**so′ber•ness** *n.*

so•bri•e•ty (sə-brī′ĭ-tē, sō-) ►*n.* **1.** Seriousness or gravity; solemnity. **2.** Absence of alcoholic intoxication.

so•bri•quet (sō′brĭ-kā′, -kĕt′) ►*n.* **1.** A nickname. **2.** An assumed name. [Fr.]

Soc. ►*abbr.* Socialist

so-called (sō′kôld′) ►*adj.* So named, called, or designated, often incorrectly.

Usage: Quotation marks are not used to set off descriptions that follow expressions such as *so-called* and *self-styled,* which themselves relieve the writer of responsibility for the attribution: *his so-called foolproof method* (not *"foolproof method"*).

soc•cer (sŏk′ər) ►*n.* A game in which two 11-member teams propel a ball into the opposing team's goal by kicking or butting or by using any part of the body except the arms and hands. [< *association football.*]

so•cia•ble (sō′shə-bəl) ►*adj.* **1.** Fond of the company of others. **2.** Marked by or affording occasion for agreeable conversation and conviviality. See Syns at **social. 3.** Pleasant and affable. See Syns at **gracious.** ►*n.* A social. [< Lat. *sociāre,* share.] —**so′cia•bil′i•ty, so′cia•ble•ness** *n.* —**so′cia•bly** *adv.*

so•cial (sō′shəl) ►*adj.* **1a.** Living together in communities or groups: *social insects.* **b.** Of or typical of communal or group living. **c.** Of or relating to human society and its organization: *social classes.* **2.** Of or in fashionable society. **3.** Seeking out or enjoying the company of others. **4.** Marked by friendly relations or companionship. **5.** Of or occupied with human welfare: *social programs.* ►*n.* An informal social gathering. [< Lat. *socius,* companion.] —**so′cial•ly** *adv.*

Syns: *social, companionable, convivial, gregarious, sociable* **Ant:** *antisocial* **adj.**

social disease ►*n.* A venereal disease.

so•cial•ism (sō′shə-lĭz′əm) ►*n.* A social system in which the means of producing and distributing goods are owned collectively and political power is exercised by the whole community. —**so′cial•ist** *n.* —**so′cial•is′tic** *adj.*

so•cial•ite (sō′shə-līt′) ►*n.* One prominent in fashionable society.

so•cial•ize (sō′shə-līz′) ►*v.* **-ized, -iz•ing 1.** To place under public ownership or control. **2.** To convert or adapt to social needs. **3.** To take part in social activities. —**so′cial•i•za′tion** *n.* —**so′cial•iz′er** *n.*

so•cial•ized medicine (sō′shə-līzd′) ►*n.* A system for providing medical and hospital care for all at nominal cost through government regulation of health services and tax subsidies.

social science ►*n.* A science, such as sociology, psychology, or anthropology, that studies society and individual relationships in and to society. —**social scientist** *n.*

social security ►*n.* A government program that provides monthly payments to the elderly and the disabled, financed by assessment of employers and employees.

social studies ►*pl.n. (takes sing. or pl. v.)* A course of study including geography, history, government, and sociology, taught in elementary and secondary schools.

social work ►*n.* Organized public work to aid the disadvantaged and counsel those with special problems. —**social worker** *n.*

so•ci•e•ty (sə-sī′ĭ-tē) ►*n., pl.* **-ties 1.** Humans collectively. **2.** A group of people having mutual interests, shared institutions, and a common culture. **3.** An association of people uniting in a common interest. **4.** The rich and fashionable social class. **5.** Companionship; company. **6.** *Biol.* A community of organisms. [< Lat. *societās,* fellowship.] —**so•ci′e•tal** *adj.*

Society Islands. An island group of French Polynesia in the S Pacific E of Samoa.

Society of Friends ►*n.* A Christian denomination, founded in the mid-17th cent. in England, that rejects ritual, formal sacraments, a formal creed, a priesthood, and violence; Quakers.

socio– ►*pref.* **1.** Society: *sociology.* **2.** Social: *socioeconomic.* [< Lat. *socius,* companion.]

so•ci•o•ec•o•nom•ic (sō′sē-ō-ĕk′ə-nŏm′ĭk, -ē′kə-, -shē-) ►*adj.* Both social and economic.

so•ci•ol•o•gy (sō′sē-ŏl′ə-jē, -shē-) ►*n.* The study of the origins, organization, institutions, and development of human society. —**so′ci•o•log′ic** (-ə-lŏj′ĭk), **so′ci•o•log′i•cal** *adj.* —**so′ci•o•log′i•cal•ly** *adv.* —**so′ci•ol′o•gist** *n.*

so•ci•o•path (sō′sē-ə-păth′, -shē-) ►*n.* One affected with a personality disorder marked by antisocial behavior. —**so′ci•o•path′ic** *adj.*

sock¹ (sŏk) ►*n., pl.* **socks** or **sox** (sŏks). A short stocking. [< Lat. *soccus,* a kind of shoe.]

sock² (sŏk) ►*v.* To strike forcefully; punch. [?] —**sock** *n.*

sock•et (sŏk′ĭt) ►*n.* An opening or cavity into which something fits. [< AN *soc,* plowshare.]

socket wrench ►*n.* A wrench with a usu. interchangeable socket to fit over a nut or bolt.

So•co•tra (sə-kō′trə) An island of Yemen in the

Indian Ocean at the mouth of the Gulf of Aden.

Soc•ra•tes (sŏk′rə-tēz′). 470?–399 B.C. Greek philosopher.

So•crat•ic (sə-krăt′ĭk, sō-) ►*adj.* Of Socrates or his method of trying to arrive at the truth by asking questions.

sod (sŏd) ►*n.* Grass-covered surface soil held together by matted roots. ►*v.* **sod•ded, sod•ding.** To cover with sod. [< MLGer. *sode.*]

so•da (sō′də) ►*n.* **1a.** Any of various forms of sodium carbonate. **b.** Chemically combined sodium. **2a.** Soda water. **b.** See **soft drink.** See Regional Note at **tonic. 3.** A drink made from carbonated water, ice cream, and usu. flavoring. [< OItal.]

soda fountain ►*n.* **1.** An apparatus for dispensing soda water. **2.** A counter where soft drinks, ice-cream dishes, or sandwiches are served.

soda pop ►*n.* See **soft drink.**

soda water ►*n.* **1.** Effervescent water charged under pressure with carbon dioxide; club soda. **2.** See **soft drink.**

sod•den (sŏd′n) ►*adj.* **1.** Thoroughly soaked; saturated. **2.** Soggy and heavy. **3.** Stupid or dull, esp. from drink. [ME *soden*, p.part. of *sethen*, to boil.] —**sod′den•ly** *adv.* —**sod′den•ness** *n.*

so•di•um (sō′dē-əm) ►*n. Symbol* **Na** A soft, light, extremely malleable metallic element that is naturally abundant in various compounds, esp. in common salt. At. no. 11. See table at **element.** [SOD(A) + –IUM.]

sodium bicarbonate ►*n.* See **baking soda.**

sodium chloride ►*n.* A colorless crystalline compound, NaCl, used in the manufacture of chemicals and as a food preservative and seasoning; salt.

sodium hydroxide ►*n.* An alkaline compound, NaOH, used in chemicals and soaps and in petroleum refining; lye.

sodium nitrate ►*n.* A white crystalline compound, $NaNO_3$, used in fertilizers, pyrotechnics, and glass.

Sod•om (sŏd′əm) A city of ancient Palestine.

sod•om•y (sŏd′ə-mē) ►*n.* Any of various forms of sexual intercourse held to be unnatural or abnormal, esp. anal intercourse or copulation with an animal. [< SODOM.] —**sod′o•mize′** (-mīz′) *v.*

so•fa (sō′fə) ►*n.* A long upholstered seat usu. with a back and arms; couch. [< Ar. *ṣuffa*, divan.]

So•fi•a (sō′fē-ə, sō-fē′ə) The capital of Bulgaria, in the W-central part. Pop. 1,114,476.

soft (sôft, sŏft) ►*adj.* **-er, -est 1.** Not hard or firm; yielding readily to pressure or weight. **2.** Out of condition; flabby. **3.** Smooth or fine to the touch. **4a.** Not loud, harsh, or irritating. **b.** Not brilliant or glaring; subdued. **5.** Mild; balmy: *a soft breeze.* **6a.** Of a gentle disposition; yielding. **b.** Affectionate. **c.** Not stern; lenient. **7.** *Informal* Simple; feeble. **8.** *Informal* Easy: *a soft job.* **9.** Apt to change, fluctuate, or devalue. **10.** Having low dissolved mineral content: *soft water.* ►*adv.* In a soft manner; gently. [< OE *sōfte*, pleasant.] —**soft′en** *v.* —**soft′en•er** *adv.* —**soft′ly** *adv.* —**soft′ness** *n.*

soft•ball (sôft′bôl′, sŏft′-) ►*n. Sports* **1.** A variation of baseball played with a larger, softer ball. **2.** The ball used in this game.

soft-boiled (sôft′boild′, sŏft′-) ►*adj.* Boiled in the shell to a soft consistency. Used of an egg.

soft coal ►*n.* See **bituminous coal.**

soft-core (sôft′kôr′, -kōr′, sŏft′-) ►*adj.* Being less explicit than hard-core material in depicting or describing sexual activity.

soft drink ►*n.* A sweetened, nonalcoholic carbonated beverage. See Regional Note at **tonic.**

soft•heart•ed (sôft′här′tĭd, sŏft′-) ►*adj.* Easily moved; tender; merciful. —**soft′heart′ed•ly** *adv.* —**soft′heart′ed•ness** *n.*

soft landing ►*n.* The landing of a space vehicle in such a way as to prevent damage.

soft palate ►*n.* The movable fold that hangs from the rear of the hard palate and closes off the nasal cavity from the oral cavity during swallowing.

soft-ped•al (sôft′pĕd′l, sŏft′-) ►*v. Informal* To make less emphatic or obvious.

soft sell ►*n. Informal* A subtly persuasive method of selling or advertising.

soft-shell clam (sôft′shĕl′, sŏft′-) ►*n.* An edible clam having a thin elongated shell.

soft soap ►*n. Informal* Flattery; cajolery. —**soft′-soap′** *v.*

soft•ware (sôft′wâr′, sŏft′-) ►*n. Comp. Sci.* The programs, routines, and symbolic languages that control the functioning of the hardware and direct its operation.

soft•wood (sôft′wo͝od′, sŏft′-) ►*n.* A coniferous tree or its wood.

soft•y or **soft•ie** (sôf′tē, sŏf′-) ►*n., pl.* **-ies** *Informal.* One who is overly sentimental, trusting, or lenient.

sog•gy (sŏg′ē, sô′gē) ►*adj.* **-gi•er, -gi•est.** Saturated with moisture; soaked. [< dial. *sog*, be soaked.] —**sog′gi•ly** *adv.* —**sog′gi•ness** *n.*

soil[1] (soil) ►*n.* **1.** The top layer of the earth's surface, suitable for the growth of plant life. **2.** A particular kind of earth or ground. **3.** Country; land: *one's native soil.* [< Lat. *solium*, seat.]

soil[2] (soil) ►*v.* **1.** To make or become dirty. **2.** To disgrace; tarnish. **3.** To corrupt; defile. ►*n.* **1a.** The state of being soiled. **b.** A stain. **2.** Manure, esp. human excrement, used as fertilizer. [< OFr. *souiller.*]

soi•ree also **soi•rée** (swä-rā′) ►*n.* An evening party or reception. [< OFr. *seir*, evening.]

so•journ (sō′jûrn′, sō-jûrn′) ►*v.* To stay for a time. ►*n.* A temporary stay. [< VLat. **subdiurnāre.*] —**so′journ′er** *n.*

sol[1] (sōl) also **so** (sō) ►*n. Mus.* The 5th tone of the diatonic scale. [< Med.Lat.]

sol[2] (sōl) ►*n., pl.* **so•les** (sō′lĕs). See table at **currency.** [Fr.]

sol•ace (sŏl′ĭs) ►*n.* **1.** Comfort in sorrow or distress; consolation. **2.** A source of comfort or consolation. ►*v.* **-aced, -ac•ing.** To comfort or console in time of trouble or sorrow. See Syns at **comfort.** [< Lat. *sōlācium* < *sōlārī*, console.]

so•lar (sō′lər) ►*adj.* **1.** Of or proceeding from the sun: *solar rays.* **2.** Powered by the energy of sunlight. **3.** Measured in reference to the sun: *a solar year.* [< Lat. *sōl*, sun.]

solar battery ►*n.* An electric battery consisting of a number of connected solar cells.

solar cell ►*n.* A semiconductor device that converts solar radiation to electric energy.

solar flare ►*n.* A temporary eruption of hydrogen gas from the sun's surface.

so•lar•i•um (sō-lâr′ē-əm, sə-) ►*n., pl.* **-i•a** (-ē-ə) or **-i•ums.** A room or glassed-in porch exposed to the sun. [Lat. *sōlārium.*]

solar plexus ►*n.* **1.** The large network of nerves located behind the stomach. **2.** The pit of the stomach.

solar system ►*n.* The sun together with the nine planets and all other celestial bodies that orbit the sun.

solar wind (wĭnd) ►*n.* The stream of charged atomic particles that radiates from the sun.

sold (sōld) ►*v.* P.t. and p.part. of **sell.**

sol•der (sŏd′ər) ►*n.* **1.** Any of various alloys, usu. tin and lead, used in the molten state to join metallic parts. **2.** Something that joins or cements. [< Lat. *solidāre*, make solid.] —**sol′der** *v.* —**sol′der•er** *n.*

sol•dier (sōl′jər) ►*n.* **1.** One who serves in an army. **2.** An enlisted person or a noncommissioned officer. **3.** An active follower. ►*v.* To be or serve as a soldier. [< AN *soldeier* < OFr. *sol*, pay.] —**sol′dier•ly** *adj.*

soldier of fortune ►*n.* One who will serve in any army for pay or love of adventure.

sol•dier•y (sōl′jə-rē) ►*n.* **1.** Soldiers collectively. **2.** The profession of soldiering.

sole[1] (sōl) ►*n.* **1.** The underside of the foot. **2.** The underside of a shoe or boot. ►*v.* **soled, sol•ing.** To furnish (a shoe or boot) with a sole. [< Lat. *solea*, sandal.]

sole[2] (sōl) ►*adj.* Being the only one; single. [< Lat. *sōlus.*] —**sole′ly** *adv.*

sole[3] (sōl) ►*n., pl.* **sole** or **soles.** Any of various chiefly marine flatfishes valued as food fishes. [< Lat. *solea*, sandal, flatfish.]

sol•e•cism (sŏl′ĭ-sĭz′əm, sō′lĭ-) ►*n.* **1.** A nonstandard usage or grammatical construction. **2.** A violation of etiquette. [< Gk. *soloikos*, speaking incorrectly.]

sol•emn (sŏl′əm) ►*adj.* **1.** Deeply earnest; grave. **2.** Performed with full ceremony. **3.** Gloomy; somber. [< Lat. *sollemnis*, customary.] —**so•lem′ni•ty** (sə-lĕm′nĭ-tē), **sol′emn•ness** *n.* —**sol′emn•ly** *adv.*

sol•em•nize (sŏl′əm-nīz′) ►*v.* **-nized, -niz•ing 1.** To celebrate or observe with dignity and gravity. **2.** To perform with formal ceremony. —**sol′em•ni•za′tion** *n.*

so•le•noid (sō′lə-noid′) ►*n.* A coil of insulated wire in which a magnetic field is established when an electric current passes through it. [< Gk. *sōlēnoeidēs*, pipe-shaped.]

so•lic•it (sə-lĭs′ĭt) ►*v.* **1.** To seek to obtain: *solicit votes.* **2.** To petition persistently; entreat. **3.** To entice or tempt. [< Lat. *sollicitāre*, to trouble.] —**so•lic′i•ta′tion** *n.*

so•lic•i•tor (sə-lĭs′ĭ-tər) ►*n.* **1.** One who solicits. **2.** The chief law officer of a city, town, or government department. **3.** *Chiefly Brit.* An attorney who is not a member of the bar and who may be heard only in the lower courts.

so•lic•i•tous (sə-lĭs′ĭ-təs) ►*adj.* **1.** Anxious or concerned; attentive. **2.** Eager. [< Lat. *sollicitus.*] —**so•lic′i•tous•ly** *adv.* —**so•lic′i•tous•ness** *n.*

so•lic•i•tude (sə-lĭs′ĭ-to͞od′, -tyo͞od′) ►*n.* The state of being solicitous.

sol•id (sŏl′ĭd) ►*adj.* **-er, -est 1a.** Of definite shape and volume; not liquid or gaseous. **b.** Firm or compact in substance. **2.** Not hollowed out. **3.** Being the same substance or color throughout. **4.** Of three-dimensional geometric figures or bodies. **5.** Of good quality and substance. **6.** Sound; reliable. **7.** Financially sound. **8.** Upstanding and dependable. **9.** Acting together; unanimous. ►*n.* **1.** A solid substance. **2.** A geometric figure having three dimensions. [< Lat. *solidus.*] —**so•lid′i•ty** (sə-lĭd′ĭ-tē), **sol′id•ness** *n.* —**sol′id•ly** *adv.*

sol•i•dar•i•ty (sŏl′ĭ-dăr′ĭ-tē) ►*n.* A unity of interests or sympathies among a group.

so•lid•i•fy (sə-lĭd′ə-fī′) ►*v.* **-fied, -fy•ing.** To make or become solid or united. —**so•lid′i•fi•ca′tion** *n.*

sol•id-state (sŏl′ĭd-stāt′) ►*adj.* **1.** Of or relating to the physical properties of solid materials, esp. crystalline solids. **2.** Based on or using transistors or other semiconducting materials or devices.

so•lil•o•quy (sə-lĭl′ə-kwē) ►*n., pl.* **-quies 1.** A dramatic discourse in which a character reveals his or her thoughts when alone or unaware of the presence of other characters. **2.** The act of speaking to oneself. [LLat. *sōliloquium.*] —**so•lil′o•quize′** *v.*

sol•ip•sism (sŏl′ĭp-sĭz′əm, sō′lĭp-) ►*n. Philos.* The theory that the self is the only reality. [Lat. *sōlus*, alone + *ipse*, self + –ISM.] —**sol′ip•sist** *n.* —**sol′ip•sis′tic** *adj.*

sol•i•taire (sŏl′ĭ-târ′) ►*n.* **1.** A gemstone set alone, as in a ring. **2.** A card game played by one person. [Fr. SOLITARY.]

sol•i•tar•y (sŏl′ĭ-tĕr′ē) ►*adj.* **1.** Existing or living alone. **2.** Happening or done alone. **3.** Remote or secluded. **4.** Single; sole. [< Lat. *sōlitās*, solitude.] —**sol′i•tar′i•ly** (-târ′ə-lē) *adv.* —**sol′i•tar′i•ness** *n.*

sol•i•tude (sŏl′ĭ-to͞od′, -tyo͞od′) ►*n.* **1.** The state of being alone; isolation. **2.** A lonely or secluded place. [< Lat. *sōlus*, alone.]

so•lo (sō′lō) ►*n., pl.* **-los 1.** *Mus.* A composition for an individual voice or instrument, with or without accompaniment. **2.** A performance or accomplishment by a single individual. ►*v.* To perform a solo. [Ital.] —**so′lo** *adj. & adv.* —**so′lo•ist** *n.*

Sol•o•mon (sŏl′ə-mən). fl. 10th cent. B.C. King of Israel famous for his wisdom.

Solomon Islands[1]. An island group of the W Pacific E of New Guinea divided between Papua New Guinea and the independent Solomon Is.

Solomon Islands[2]. A country comprising the Solomon Is. SE of Bougainville. Cap. Honiara. Pop. 366,000.

So•lon (sō′lən, -lŏn′). 638?–559? B.C. Athenian lawgiver and poet.

sol•stice (sŏl′stĭs, sōl′-, sôl′-) ►*n.* Either of two times of the year when the sun reaches an extreme of its northward or southward motion. [< Lat. *sōlstitium* : *sōl*, sun + *-stitium*, stoppage.] —**sol•sti′tial** (-stĭsh′əl) *adj.*

sol•u•ble (sŏl′yə-bəl) ►*adj.* **1.** Capable of being dissolved. **2.** Possible to solve or explain. [< Lat. *solvere*, loosen.] —**sol′u•bil′i•ty** *n.* —**sol′u•bly** *adv.*

sol•ute (sŏl′yo͞ot, sō′lo͞ot) ►*n.* A substance dissolved in another substance. ►*adj.* Being in solution; dissolved. [< Lat. *solūtus*, p.part. of *solvere*, loosen.]

so•lu•tion (sə-lo͞o′shən) ►*n.* **1a.** A homogeneous mixture of two or more substances, which may be solids, liquids, gases, or a combination of these. **b.** The process of forming such a mixture. **2.** The method or process of solving a problem. **3.** The answer to or disposition of a problem.

solve (sŏlv, sôlv) ▶*v.* **solved, solv•ing.** To find a solution to. [< Lat. *solvere*, loosen.] —**solv′a•ble** *adj.* —**solv′er** *n.*

Syns: *solve, decipher, resolve, unravel* **v.**

sol•vent (sŏl′vənt, sôl′-) ▶*adj.* **1.** Able to meet financial obligations. **2.** Capable of dissolving another substance. ▶*n.* A substance, usu. a liquid, capable of dissolving another substance. [< Lat. *solvere*, loosen.] —**sol′ven•cy** *n.*

Sol•zhe•ni•tsyn (sōl′zhə-nēt′sĭn), **Aleksandr Isayevich.** b. 1918. Soviet writer and dissident; 1970 Nobel.

som (sōm) ▶*n., pl.* **som.** See table at **currency.** [Kyrgyz.]

So•ma•li (sō-mä′lē) ▶*n., pl.* **-li** or **-lis 1.** A native or inhabitant of Somalia. **2.** The Cushitic language of Somalia. —**So•ma′li** *adj.*

So•ma•li•a (sō-mä′lē-ə, -mäl′yə) A country of extreme E Africa on the Gulf of Aden and the Indian Ocean. Cap. Mogadishu. Pop. 9,077,000. —**So•ma′li•an** *adj. & n.*

So•ma•li•land (sō-mä′lē-lănd′, sə-) A region of E Africa comprising present-day Somalia, Djibouti, and SE Ethiopia.

so•mat•ic (sō-măt′ĭk) ▶*adj.* Of the body, esp. as distinguished from a body part, the mind, or the environment; physical. See Syns at **bodily.** [< Gk. *sōma*, body.]

somatic cell ▶*n.* Any cell of a plant or animal other than a germ cell.

som•ber (sŏm′bər) ▶*adj.* **1.** Dark; gloomy. **2.** Melancholy; dismal. [< LLat. *subumbrāre*, cast a shadow.] —**som′ber•ly** *adv.*

som•bre (sŏm′bər) ▶*adj. Chiefly Brit.* Var. of **somber.**

som•bre•ro (sŏm-brâr′ō, səm-) ▶*n., pl.* **-ros.** A large, broad-brimmed hat. [Sp.]

sombrero

some (sŭm) ▶*adj.* **1.** Being an unspecified number or quantity: *some people; some sugar.* **2.** Unknown or unspecified by name: *Some man called.* **3.** *Informal* Remarkable: *She is some skier.* ▶*pron.* An indefinite or unspecified number, quantity, or portion. See Usage Note at **every.** ▶*adv.* **1.** Approximately; about. **2.** *Informal* Somewhat. [< OE *sum*, a certain one.]

-some[1] ▶*suff.* Characterized by a specified quality, condition, or action: *loathsome.* [< OE *-sum.*]

-some[2] ▶*suff.* A group of a specified number of members: *threesome.* [< OE *sum*, some.]

-some[3] ▶*suff.* Body: *centrosome.* [< Gk. *sōma.*]

some•bod•y (sŭm′bŏd′ē, -bŭd′ē, -bə-dē) ▶*pron.* An unspecified or unknown person. ▶*n. Informal* A person of importance.

some•day (sŭm′dā′) ▶*adv.* At an indefinite time in the future.

Usage: *Someday* (adverb) and *sometime* express future time indefinitely. This sense can also be conveyed by *some day* and *some time.* The two-word forms are always used when *some* is an adjective modifying and specifying a more particular *day* or *time: Come some day* (not *someday*) *soon.*

some•how (sŭm′hou′) ▶*adv.* In a way not specified, understood, or known.

some•one (sŭm′wŭn′, -wən) ▶*pron.* An unspecified or unknown person; somebody. ▶*n. Informal* A somebody.

some•place (sŭm′plās′) ▶*adv. & n.* Somewhere.

som•er•sault (sŭm′ər-sôlt′) ▶*n.* An acrobatic stunt in which the body rolls in a complete circle, heels over head. [< OFr. *sobresault.*] —**som′er•sault′** *v.*

some•thing (sŭm′thĭng) ▶*pron.* An unspecified or not definitely known thing. ▶*n. Informal* A remarkable or important thing or person. ▶*adv.* Somewhat. —***idiom:*** **something else** *Informal* One that is special or remarkable.

some•time (sŭm′tīm′) ▶*adv.* **1.** At an indefinite or unstated time. **2.** At an indefinite time in the future. See Usage Note at **someday.** ▶*adj.* Former.

some•times (sŭm′tīmz′) ▶*adv.* Now and then.

some•way (sŭm′wā′) also **some•ways** (-wāz′) ▶*adv.* In some way or another.

some•what (sŭm′hwŏt′, -wŏt′, -hwət, -wət) ▶*adv.* To some extent or degree; rather.

some•where (sŭm′hwâr′, -wâr′) ▶*adv.* **1.** At, in, or to a place not specified or known. **2.** To a place or state of further development or progress. ▶*n.* An unspecified place.

Somme (sŏm, sôm) A river, about 241 km (150 mi) of N France flowing to the English Channel.

som•me•lier (sŭm′əl-yā′, sô′mə-lyā′) ▶*n.* A restaurant employee who orders and maintains the wines sold in the restaurant. [Fr.]

som•nam•bu•late (sŏm-năm′byə-lāt′) ▶*v.* **-lat•ed, -lat•ing.** To walk while asleep. [Lat. *somnus*, sleep + *ambulāre*, walk.]

som•nam•bu•lism (sŏm-năm′byə-lĭz′əm) ▶*n.* See **sleepwalking.** —**som•nam′bu•list** *n.*

som•no•lent (sŏm′nə-lənt) ▶*adj.* Drowsy; sleepy. [< Lat. *somnolentus* < *somnus*, sleep.] —**som′no•lence** *n.* —**som′no•lent•ly** *adv.*

son (sŭn) ▶*n.* **1.** One's male child. **2.** A male descendant. **3.** A man considered as if in a relationship of child to parent: *a son of the soil.* [< OE *sunu.*] —**son′ly** *adj.*

so•nar (sō′när′) ▶*n.* A system or apparatus using transmitted and reflected sound waves to detect and locate underwater objects. [*so(und) na(vigation and) r(anging).*]

so•na•ta (sə-nä′tə) ▶*n. Mus.* A composition for one or more solo instruments, usu. written in three or four movements. [Ital.]

song (sông, sŏng) ▶*n.* **1a.** A brief composition written for singing. **b.** The act or art of singing: *broke into song.* **2.** A melodious utterance, as of a bird. **3a.** Poetry. **b.** A lyric poem. —***idiom:* for a song** *Informal* At a low price. [< OE *sang*.]

song•bird (sông′bûrd′, sŏng′-) ▶*n.* A bird having a melodious song or call.

Song•hua (so͝ong′hwä′) A river of NE China flowing about 1,850 km (1,150 mi) to the Amur R.

Song of Solomon ▶*n.* Song of Songs.

Song of Songs ▶*n.* See table at **Bible.**

song•ster (sông′stər, sŏng′-) ▶*n.* **1.** One who sings. **2.** See **songwriter.**

song•writ•er (sông′rī′tər, sŏng′-) ▶*n.* One who writes song lyrics or tunes.

son•ic (sŏn′ĭk) ▶*adj.* Of or relating to sound or its speed in air. [< Lat. *sonus*, sound.]

sonic barrier ▶*n.* The sudden sharp increase in aerodynamic drag experienced by aircraft approaching the speed of sound.

sonic boom ▶*n.* An explosive sound caused by the shock wave preceding an aircraft traveling at a supersonic speed.

son-in-law (sŭn′ĭn-lô′) ▶*n., pl.* **sons-in-law** (sŭnz′-). The husband of one's daughter.

son•net (sŏn′ĭt) ▶*n.* A 14-line poetic verse form usu. in iambic pentameter, with a fixed rhyme pattern. [< OProv. *sonet*.]

son•o•gram (sŏn′ə-grăm′, sō′nə-) ▶*n.* An image, as of an unborn fetus or an internal body organ, produced by ultrasonography.

son•o•rous (sŏn′ər-əs, sə-nôr′-, -nōr′-) ▶*adj.* **1.** Having or producing sound. **2.** Having or producing a full, deep, or rich sound. **3.** Impressive in style of speech: *a sonorous oration.* [< Lat. *sonor*, sound.] —**so•nor′i•ty** (sə-nôr′ĭ-tē, -nŏr′-) *n.* —**son′o•rous•ly** *adv.*

Soo Canals (so͞o) See **Sault Sainte Marie Canals.**

Soo•chow (so͞o′chou′, -jō′) See **Suzhou.**

soon (so͞on) ▶*adv.* **-er, -est 1.** In the near future. **2.** Within a short time; quickly. **3.** Early. **4.** Willingly; gladly: *I'd as soon leave right now.* —***idiom:* sooner or later** Eventually. [< OE *sōna*, immediately.]

Usage: *No sooner,* as a comparative adverb, should be followed by *than,* not *when,* as in: *No sooner had she left than he called.*

soot (so͝ot, so͞ot) ▶*n.* The fine black particles, chiefly carbon, produced by incomplete combustion of coal, oil, wood, or other fuel. [< OE *sōt*.] —**soot′i•ness** *n.* —**soot′y** *adj.*

sooth (so͞oth) ▶*n.* *Archaic* Truth; reality. [< OE *sōth*.]

soothe (so͞o*th*) ▶*v.* **soothed, sooth•ing 1.** To calm or quiet. **2.** To ease or relieve the pain of. [< OE *sōthian*, verify.] —**sooth′er** *n.* —**sooth′ing•ly** *adv.*

sooth•say•er (so͞oth′sā′ər) ▶*n.* One who foretells events; seer.

sop (sŏp) ▶*v.* **sopped, sop•ping 1.** To dip, soak, or drench in a liquid. **2.** To take up by absorption. ▶*n.* Something yielded to placate or soothe; bribe. [< OE *sopp*, bread dipped in liquid.] —**sop′py** *adj.*

SOP ▶*abbr.* standard operating procedure

soph. ▶*abbr.* sophomore

soph•ism (sŏf′ĭz′əm) ▶*n.* **1.** A plausible but fallacious argument. **2.** Deceptive or fallacious argumentation. [< Gk. *sophos*, clever.] —**soph′ist** *n.* —**so•phis′tic, so•phis′ti•cal** *adj.* —**so•phis′ti•cal•ly** *adv.*

so•phis•ti•cate (sə-fĭs′tĭ-kāt′) ▶*v.* **-cat•ed, -cat•ing 1.** To cause to become less naive and more worldly. **2.** To refine. ▶*n.* (-kĭt). A sophisticated person. —**so•phis′ti•ca′tion** *n.*

so•phis•ti•cat•ed (sə-fĭs′tĭ-kā′tĭd) ▶*adj.* **1.** Having acquired worldly knowledge or refinement. **2.** Very complex or complicated. **3.** Appealing to refined tastes.

soph•is•try (sŏf′ĭ-strē) ▶*n., pl.* **-tries.** Plausible but faulty or misleading argumentation.

Soph•o•cles (sŏf′ə-klēz′). 496?–406 B.C. Greek dramatist. —**Soph′o•cle′an** *adj.*

soph•o•more (sŏf′ə-môr′, -mōr′, sŏf′môr′, -mōr′) ▶*n.* A second-year student in a US high school or college. [< obsolete *sophom*, sophism.]

soph•o•mor•ic (sŏf′ə-môr′ĭk, -mōr′-, -mŏr′-) ▶*adj.* **1.** Of or like a sophomore. **2.** Exhibiting immaturity and lack of judgment.

sop•o•rif•ic (sŏp′ə-rĭf′ĭk, sō′pə-) ▶*adj.* **1.** Inducing sleep. **2.** Drowsy. ▶*n.* A drug that induces sleep. [< Lat. *sopor*, sleep.]

so•pran•o (sə-prăn′ō, -prä′nō) ▶*n., pl.* **-os 1.** The highest singing voice of a woman or young boy. **2.** The tonal range characteristic of a soprano. **3.** A singer, voice, or instrument having this range. [Ital. < Lat. *suprā*, above.]

sor•bi•tol (sôr′bĭ-tôl′, -tōl′, -tŏl′) ▶*n.* A white sweetish crystalline alcohol found in fruits, used esp. as a sugar substitute. [*sorb*, soak up + -IT(E)[2] + -OL.]

sor•cer•y (sôr′sə-rē) ▶*n.* Use of supernatural power over others through the assistance of spirits. [< Lat. *sors*, lot.] —**sor′cer•er** *n.* —**sor′cer•ess** *n.*

sor•did (sôr′dĭd) ▶*adj.* **1.** Filthy; foul. **2.** Depressingly squalid; wretched. **3.** Morally degraded; base. [< Lat. *sordēre*, be dirty.] —**sor′did•ly** *adv.* —**sor′did•ness** *n.*

sore (sôr, sōr) ▶*adj.* **sor•er, sor•est 1.** Painful or tender. **2.** Feeling pain; hurting. **3.** Causing sorrow or distress; grievous. **4.** *Informal* Angry; offended. ▶*n.* **1.** An open skin lesion, wound, or ulcer. **2.** A source of pain or distress. [< OE *sār*.] —**sore′ly** *adv.* —**sore′ness** *n.*

sor•ghum (sôr′gəm) ▶*n.* An Old World grass cultivated as grain and forage or as a source of syrup. [< Ital. *sorgo*.]

so•ror•i•ty (sə-rôr′ĭ-tē, -rŏr′-) ▶*n., pl.* **-ties 1.** A chiefly social organization of women college students. **2.** An association or society of women. [< Lat. *soror*, sister.]

sor•rel[1] (sôr′əl, sŏr′-) ▶*n.* Any of several plants with acid-flavored leaves. [< OFr. *sur*, sour.]

sor•rel[2] (sôr′əl, sŏr′-) ▶*n.* **1.** A yellowish to reddish brown. **2.** A sorrel-colored horse. [< OFr. *sor*, red-brown.]

sor•row (sŏr′ō, sôr′ō) ▶*n.* **1.** Mental suffering caused by loss or despair. **2.** Something causing sadness or grief. ▶*v.* To feel or express sorrow. See Syns at **grieve.** [< OE *sorg*.] —**sor′row•ful** *adj.* —**sor′row•ful•ly** *adv.* —**sor′row•ful•ness** *n.*

sor•ry (sŏr′ē, sôr′ē) ▶*adj.* **-ri•er, -ri•est 1.** Feeling or expressing sympathy or regret. **2.** Poor or wretched: *a sorry excuse.* **3.** Grievous or sad. [< OE *sār*, sore.] —**sor′ri•ness** *n.*

sort (sôrt) ▶*n.* **1.** A group of similar persons or things; kind. **2.** Type, character, or quality. **3.** A way of acting or behaving. ▶*v.* To arrange according to class, kind, or size. See Syns at **arrange.** —***idioms:* out of sorts 1.** Slightly ill. **2.** Irritable or cross. **sort of** *Informal*

Somewhat; rather. [< Lat. *sors*, lot.]

sor•tie (sôr′tē, sôr-tē′) ►*n.* **1.** An armed attack made from a place surrounded by enemy forces. **2.** A flight of a combat aircraft on a mission. [Fr. < OFr. *sortir*, go out.]

SOS (ĕs′ō-ĕs′) ►*n.* A call or signal for help or rescue. [From the international radiotelegraphic distress signal.]

so-so (sō′sō′) ►*adj.* Mediocre. —**so′-so′** *adv.*

sot (sŏt) ►*n.* A drunkard. [< OFr. *fool.*] —**sot′tish** *adj.* —**sot′tish•ly** *adv.*

sou•brette (so͞o-brĕt′) ►*n.* A saucy maid in comic drama or opera. [< Prov. *soubret*, conceited < *super*, above.]

souf•flé (so͞o-flā′) ►*n.* A light fluffy baked dish made with egg yolks and beaten egg whites. [< Lat. *sufflāre*, puff up.]

sough (sŭf, sou) ►*v.* To make a soft murmuring sound. [< OE *swōgan.*] —**sough** *n.*

sought (sôt) ►*v.* P.t. and p.part. of **seek.**

soul (sōl) ►*n.* **1.** The animating and vital principle in humans often conceived as an immaterial entity that survives death. **2.** A spirit or ghost. **3.** A human. **4.** The central or vital part of something. **5.** A person considered as the perfect embodiment of an intangible quality: *the very soul of discretion.* **6.** A person's emotional or moral nature. **7.** A sense of ethnic pride among African Americans. **8.** A strong, deeply felt emotion conveyed by a speaker, performer, or artist. [< OE *sāwol.*]

soul•ful (sōl′fəl) ►*adj.* Filled with or expressing deep feeling. —**soul′ful•ly** *adv.* —**soul′ful•ness** *n.*

sound¹ (sound) ►*n.* **1a.** A vibratory disturbance, with frequencies in the approximate range of 20 to 20,000 hertz, capable of being heard. **b.** The sensation stimulated in the organs of hearing by such a disturbance. **c.** Such sensations collectively. **2.** A distinctive noise. **3.** *Ling.* An articulation made by the vocal apparatus. **4.** A conveyed impression; implication. **5.** Auditory material that is recorded, as for a movie. ►*v.* **1.** To make or cause to make a sound. **2.** To convey an impression: *sounds reasonable.* **3.** To summon or signal by a sound. **4.** *Medic.* To examine by auscultation. [< Lat. *sonus.*] —**sound′er** *n.* —**sound′less** *adj.* —**sound′less•ly** *adv.*

sound² (sound) ►*adj.* **-er, -est 1.** Free from defect or damage. **2.** Solid. **3.** Financially secure or safe. **4.** Based on valid reasoning. **5.** Thorough; complete: *a sound thrashing.* **6.** Deep and undisturbed: *a sound sleep.* **7.** *Law* Legally valid: *sound title.* [< OE *gesund.*] —**sound′ly** *adv.* —**sound′ness** *n.*

sound³ (sound) ►*n.* A long body of water, wider than a strait, usu. connecting larger bodies of water. [< OE *sund*, sea.]

sound⁴ (sound) ►*v.* **1.** To measure the depth of (water). **2.** To try to learn the attitudes or opinions of. **3.** To dive swiftly downward, as a whale. [< OFr. *sonde*, sounding line.] —**sound′er** *n.* —**sound′ing** *n.*

sound barrier ►*n.* See **sonic barrier.**

sound box ►*n.* *Mus.* A hollow chamber, as of a violin or guitar, that intensifies resonance.

sound effect ►*n.* An imitative sound, as of thunder, produced for film, stage, or radio.

sound•ing board (soun′dĭng) ►*n.* **1.** A thin board forming the upper portion of the resonant chamber in an instrument, such as a violin or piano. **2.** A structure placed so as to amplify a speaker's voice. **3.** A means serving to spread or popularize opinions.

sound•proof (sound′pro͞of′) ►*adj.* Not penetrable by audible sound. —**sound′proof′** *v.*

sound•track (sound′trăk′) ►*n.* **1.** The narrow strip at one side of a movie film that carries the sound recording. **2.** A recording of the music from a movie.

soup (so͞op) ►*n.* **1.** A liquid food prepared from meat, fish, or vegetable stock combined with various other ingredients. **2.** Dense fog. —***phrasal verb:* soup up** *Slang* To modify so as to enhance power or performance. —***idiom:* in the soup** *Slang* In trouble or difficulties. [< OFr. *soupe*, of Gmc. orig.]

soup•çon (so͞op-sôɴ′, so͞op′sŏn′) ►*n.* A very small amount; trace. [< OFr. *sospeçon*, SUSPICION.]

soup kitchen ►*n.* A place where food is offered to the needy.

soup•y (so͞o′pē) ►*adj.* **-i•er, -i•est 1.** Having the appearance or consistency of soup. **2.** *Slang* Foggy.

sour (sour) ►*adj.* **-er, -est 1.** Having a sharp or acid taste. **2.** Spoiled or rancid. **3a.** Bad-tempered. **b.** Displeased, disagreeable, or disenchanted. ►*v.* To make or become sour. [< OE *sūr.*] —**sour′ish** *adj.* —**sour′ly** *adv.* —**sour′ness** *n.*

Syns: *sour, acid, tart* **adj.**

sour•ball (sour′bôl′) ►*n.* A round piece of hard tart candy.

source (sôrs, sōrs) ►*n.* **1.** A point of origin. **2.** The beginning of a stream of water, such as a spring or river. **3.** One that supplies information. [< OFr. *sourse* < *sourdre*, rise. See SURGE.]

sour cream ►*n.* Cream soured esp. by lactic-acid bacteria and used in cooking.

sour•dough (sour′dō′) ►*n.* Sour fermented dough used as leaven in making bread.

sour•sop (sour′sŏp′) ►*n.* A tropical American tree bearing spiny tart fruit.

Sou•sa (so͞o′zə, -sə), **John Philip.** 1854–1932. Amer. bandmaster and composer.

souse (sous) ►*v.* **soused, sous•ing 1.** To plunge into a liquid. **2.** To drench or become drenched. **3.** To steep. **4.** *Slang* To make intoxicated. ►*n.* **1.** The act or process of sousing. **2a.** Food steeped in pickle, esp. pork trimmings. **b.** Brine. **3.** *Slang* A drunkard. [< OFr. *sous*, pickled meat, of Gmc. orig.]

south (south) ►*n.* **1a.** The direction along a meridian 90° clockwise from east. **b.** The compass point 180° clockwise from north. **2.** often **South a.** The southern part of the earth. **b.** The southern part of a region or country. ►*adj.* **1.** To, toward, of, or in the south. **2.** Coming from the south: *a south wind.* ►*adv.* In, from, or toward the south. [< OE *sūth.*] —**south′ward** (south′wərd, sŭ*th*′ərd) *adj. & adv.* —**south′ward•ly** *adj. & adv.* —**south′wards** *adv.*

South Africa. A country of S Africa on the Atlantic and Indian oceans. Caps. Pretoria, Cape Town, and Bloemfontein. Pop. 40,436,000. —**South African** *adj. & n.*

South America. A continent of the S Western Hemisphere SE of North America between the Atlantic and Pacific oceans. —**South American** *adj. & n.*

South•amp•ton (south-hămp′tən, southămp′-) A borough of S-central England on an inlet of the English Channel. Pop. 209,192.

South Atlantic Ocean. The S part of the Atlantic, from the equator to Antarctica.

South Bend. A city of N IN near the MI border NW of Fort Wayne. Pop. 105,511.

South Car•o•li•na (kăr′ə-lī′nə) A state of the SE US bordering on the Atlantic. Cap. Columbia. Pop. 3,505,707. —**South Car′o•lin′i•an** (-lĭn′ē-ən) *adj. & n.*

South China Sea. An arm of the W Pacific bounded by SE China, Taiwan, the Philippines, Borneo, and Vietnam.

South Dakota. A state of the N-central US. Cap. Pierre. Pop. 699,999. —**South Dakotan** *adj. & n.*

south•east (south-ēst′, sou-ēst′) ▸*n.* **1.** The direction that is 45° clockwise from east and 45° counterclockwise from south. **2.** often **Southeast** An area or region lying to the southeast of a particular point. —**south•east′** *adj. & adv.* —**south•east′er•ly** *adj. & adv.* —**south•east′ern** *adj.* —**south•east′ward** *adv. & adj.* —**south•east′ward•ly** *adv. & adj.* —**south•east′wards** *adv.*

Southeast Asia. A region of Asia including Indochina, the Malay Peninsula, and the Malay Archipelago. —**Southeast Asian** *adj. & n.*

south•east•er (south-ē′stər, sou-ē′-) ▸*n.* A storm or gale blowing from the southeast.

south•east•er•ly (south-ē′stər-lē, sou-ē′-) ▸*adj.* **1.** Situated toward the southeast. **2.** Coming or being from the southeast. —**south•east′er•ly** *adv.*

south•er•ly (sŭ*th*′ər-lē) ▸*adj.* **1.** In or toward the south. **2.** From the south: *southerly winds.* —**south′er•ly** *adv.*

south•ern (sŭ*th*′ərn) ▸*adj.* **1.** Of, in, or toward the south. **2.** From the south: *southern breezes.* [< OE *sūtherne.*] —**south′ern•most′** *adj.*

Southern Alps. A mountain range of the W coast of South I., New Zealand.

south•ern•er also **South•ern•er** (sŭ*th*′ər-nər) ▸*n.* A native or inhabitant of a southern region.

Southern Hemisphere ▸*n.* The half of the earth south of the equator.

southern lights ▸*pl.n.* See **aurora australis.**

Southern Yemen. A former country of SW Asia on the Arabian Peninsula; united with North Yemen (1990) to form the new country of Yemen.

Sou•they (sou′*th*ē, sŭ*th*′ē), **Robert.** 1774–1843. British writer.

South Frigid Zone. See **Frigid Zone.**

South Island. An island of New Zealand SW of North I., from which it is separated by Cook Strait.

South Korea. A country of E Asia on the S Korean peninsula. Cap. Seoul. Pop. 44,453,000. —**South Korean** *adj. & n.*

South Pacific Ocean. The S part of the Pacific, from the equator to Antarctica.

south•paw (south′pô′) ▸*n. Slang* A left-handed person, esp. a left-handed baseball pitcher.

South Polar Region. See **Polar Regions.**

South Pole ▸*n.* **1.** The southern end of the earth's axis of rotation, a point in Antarctica. **2.** The celestial zenith of the heavens as viewed from the south terrestrial pole.

South Sea Islands. The islands of the S Pacific, roughly coextensive with Oceania. —**South Sea Islander** *n.*

South Seas. The oceans S of the equator, esp. the S Pacific.

South Temperate Zone. See **Temperate Zone.**

South Vietnam. A former country of SE Asia (1954–75); now part of Vietnam. —**South Vietnamese** *adj. & n.*

south•west (south-wĕst′, sou-wĕst′) ▸*n.* **1.** The direction 45° clockwise from south and 45° counterclockwise from west. **2.** often **Southwest** An area or region lying in the southwest. —**south•west′** *adj. & adv.* —**south•west′er•ly** *adj. & adv.* —**south•west′ern** *adj.* —**south•west′ward** *adv. & adj.* —**south•west′ward•ly** *adv. & adj.* —**south•west′wards** *adv.*

south•west•er (south-wĕs′tər, sou-wĕs′-) also **sou′•west•er** (sou-wĕs′-) ▸*n.* **1.** A storm or gale from the southwest. **2.** A waterproof hat with a broad brim in back.

sou•ve•nir (so͞o′və-nîr′, so͞o′və-nîr′) ▸*n.* A token of remembrance; memento. [< Lat. *subvenīre*, come to mind : *sub-*, under + *venīre*, come.]

sov•er•eign (sŏv′ər-ĭn, sŏv′rĭn) ▸*n.* **1.** The chief of state in a monarchy. **2.** A gold coin formerly used in Great Britain. ▸*adj.* **1.** Independent: *a sovereign state.* **2.** Having supreme rank or power. **3.** Paramount; supreme. **4a.** Excellent. **b.** Unmitigated: *sovereign contempt.* [< VLat. **superānus* < Lat. *super*, above.]

sov•er•eign•ty (sŏv′ər-ĭn-tē, sŏv′rĭn-) ▸*n., pl.* **-ties 1.** Supremacy of authority or rule. **2.** Royal rank, authority, or power. **3.** Complete independence and self-government.

so•vi•et (sō′vē-ĕt′, -ĭt, sŏv′ē-) ▸*n.* **1.** One of the popularly elected legislative assemblies of the former Soviet Union. **2. Soviets** The people and government of the former Soviet Union. [Russ. *sovet.*]

Soviet Union. See **Union of Soviet Socialist Republics.** —**Soviet** *adj.*

sow[1] (sō) ▸*v.* **sowed, sown** (sōn) or **sowed, sow•ing 1.** To plant (seeds) to produce a crop. **2.** To propagate or disseminate; spread. **3.** To scatter with or as if with seed. [< OE *sāwan.*] —**sow′er** *n.*

sow[2] (sou) ▸*n.* An adult female hog. [< OE *sugu, sū.*]

So•we•to (sə-wĕt′ō, -wā′tō) A city of NE South Africa SW of Johannesburg. Pop. 596,632.

sox (sŏks) ▸*n.* Pl. of **sock**[1].

soy (soi) ▸*n.* **1.** The soybean. **2.** A salty brown liquid condiment made from soybeans. [< J. *shō-yu*, soy sauce.]

soy•bean (soi′bēn′) ▸*n.* An Asian bean cultivated for forage and for its nutritious seeds.

So•yin•ka (shô-yĭng′kə), **Wole.** b. 1934. Nigerian writer; 1986 Nobel.

soy•milk (soi′mĭlk′) ▸*n.* A milk substitute made from soybeans, often supplemented with vitamins.

soy sauce ▸*n.* A salty brown sauce made by fermenting soybeans and wheat.

sp. ▸*abbr.* **1.** species **2.** specimen **3.** spelling

Sp. ▸*abbr.* Spanish

spa (spä) ▸*n.* **1.** A resort providing therapeutic baths. **2.** A resort area having mineral springs.

3. A fashionable hotel. [After *Spa*, Belgium.]

space (spās) ▶*n.* **1a.** *Math.* A set of elements or points satisfying specified geometric postulates. **b.** The infinite extension of the three-dimensional region in which all matter exists. **2a.** The expanse in which the solar system, stars, and galaxies exist; universe. **b.** The region of this expanse beyond Earth's atmosphere. **3.** A blank or empty area. **4.** A particular area, such as an accommodation on a train. **5a.** A period or interval of time. **b.** A little while. ▶*v.* **spaced, spac•ing 1.** To organize or arrange with spaces between. **2.** *Slang* To become disoriented from or as if from a drug: *space out.* [< Lat. *spatium.*] —**spac′er** *n.*

space bar ▶*n.* A bar of a typewriter or computer keyboard that when pressed introduces a blank space, as between words.

space•craft (spās′krăft′) ▶*n., pl.* **-craft.** A vehicle designed to be launched into space.

space heater ▶*n.* A small, usu. portable appliance that warms a small enclosed area.

space•ship (spās′shĭp′) ▶*n.* See **spacecraft.**

space shuttle ▶*n.* A reusable spacecraft designed to transport astronauts between Earth and an orbiting space station and to deploy and retrieve satellites.

space shuttle
Discovery landing at Edwards Air Force Base, California, October 3, 1988

space station ▶*n.* A large satellite equipped to support a human crew and designed to remain in extended orbit around Earth.

space suit ▶*n.* A protective pressure suit permitting an astronaut relatively free movement in space, esp. outside a spacecraft.

space-time (spās′tīm′) ▶*n. Phys.* The four-dimensional continuum of one temporal and three spatial coordinates in which any event or physical object is located.

space walk ▶*n.* Extravehicular activity. —**space walk** *v.* —**space walker** *n.*

spa•cious (spā′shəs) ▶*adj.* Large in range, extent, or scope. —**spa′cious•ly** *adv.* —**spa′cious•ness** *n.*

Syns: *spacious, ample, capacious, commodious, roomy* **adj.**

spac•y or **spac•ey** (spā′sē) ▶*adj.* **-i•er, -i•est** *Slang* **1.** Disoriented from or as if from drug use. **2.** Eccentric; offbeat.

spade[1] (spād) ▶*n.* A digging tool with a long handle and a flat blade. ▶*v.* **spad•ed, spad•ing.** To dig with a spade. [< OE *spadu.*]

spade[2] (spād) ▶*n.* Any of a suit of playing cards marked with a black, leaf-shaped figure. [< Gk. *spathē*, broad blade.]

spade•work (spād′wûrk′) ▶*n.* Preparatory work necessary for a project or activity.

spa•dix (spā′dĭks) ▶*n., pl.* **-di•ces** (-dĭ-sēz′). A clublike stalk bearing tiny flowers, usu. enclosed in a sheathlike spathe. [< Gk. *spadix*, broken-off palm branch.]

spa•ghet•ti (spə-gĕt′ē) ▶*n.* Pasta in long, often thick strands. [Ital., pl. dim. of *spago*, string.]

Spain (spān) A country of SW Europe comprising most of the Iberian Peninsula and the Balearic and Canary Is. Cap. Madrid. Pop. 39,143,000.

spake (spāk) ▶*v. Archaic* P.t. of **speak.**

spam (spăm) ▶*n.* Unsolicited e-mail, usu. of a commercial nature. ▶*v.* **spammed, spam•ming.** To send unsolicited e-mail to. [< *Spam*, trademark for a canned meat product.]

span[1] (spăn) ▶*n.* **1.** The distance or extent between two points or extremities. **2.** The distance between vertical supports of a horizontal structural part. **3.** The section between two intermediate supports of a bridge. **4.** A unit of measure equal to about 9 in. (23 cm). **5.** A period of time: *a span of life.* ▶*v.* **spanned, span•ning 1.** To measure by or as if by the extended hand. **2.** To extend across. [< OE *spann*, a unit of measurement.]

span[2] (spăn) ▶*n.* A pair of harnessed or matched animals, such as oxen. [< MDu. *spannen*, to harness.]

span•dex (spăn′dĕks) ▶*n.* An elastic synthetic fiber or fabric made from a polymer containing polyurethane. [< EXPAND.]

span•gle (spăng′gəl) ▶*n.* A small piece of shiny metal or plastic used esp. on garments for decoration. [< MDu. *spange*, clasp.] —**span′gle** *v.* —**span′gly** *adj.*

Span•iard (spăn′yərd) ▶*n.* A native or inhabitant of Spain.

span•iel (spăn′yəl) ▶*n.* A dog usu. having drooping ears, short legs, and a wavy, silky coat. [< OFr. *espaignol*, Spanish.]

Span•ish (spăn′ĭsh) ▶*n.* **1.** The Romance language of the largest part of Spain and most of Central and South America. **2.** The people of Spain. —**Span′ish** *adj.*

Spanish America. The former Spanish possessions in the New World.

Spanish American ▶*n.* **1.** A native or inhabitant of Spanish America. **2.** A US citizen or resident of Hispanic descent. See Usage Note at **Hispanic.** ▶*adj.* **Span•ish-A•mer•i•can** (spăn′ĭsh-ə-mĕr′ĭ-kən) **1.** Of Spanish America. **2.** Of Spain and America, esp. the United States.

Spanish moss ▶*n.* A plant of the SE US and tropical America that grows on trees in long gray tangled clusters.

Spanish Sahara. See **Western Sahara.**

spank (spăngk) ▶*v.* To slap on the buttocks with the open hand. [Perh. imit.] —**spank** *n.*

spank•ing (spăng′kĭng) ▶*adj.* **1.** *Informal* Exceptional; remarkable. **2.** Brisk and fresh: *a spanking breeze.* ▶*adv.* Used as an intensive: *a spanking clean shirt.* ▶*n.* A number of slaps on the buttocks in rapid succession. [Perh. of Scand. orig.]

spar[1] (spär) ▶*n.* A wooden or metal pole used to support sail rigging. [ME *sparre*, rafter.]

spar[2] (spär) ▶*v.* **sparred, spar•ring 1.** To box, esp. for practice. **2.** To bandy words about; wrangle. [ME *sparren*, strike rapidly.]

spare (spâr) ▶*v.* **spared, spar•ing 1.** To treat mercifully; deal with leniently. **2.** To refrain from harming or destroying. **3.** To save from experiencing or doing something; exempt. **4.** To use with restraint or frugality. **5.** To do without. ►*adj.* **spar•er, spar•est 1a.** Kept in reserve: *a spare part.* **b.** Extra: *spare cash.* See Syns at **superfluous. c.** Free for other use; unoccupied: *spare time.* **2a.** Without excess; meager. **b.** Lean and trim. **3.** Not profuse or copious. ►*n.* **1.** A replacement, esp. a tire, reserved for future need. **2.** The knocking down of all ten bowling pins with two successive rolls of the ball. [< OE *sparian.*] —**spare′ly** *adv.* —**spare′ness** *n.*

spare•ribs (spâr′rĭbz′) ►*pl.n.* Pork ribs with most of the meat trimmed off. [< MLGer. *ribbespēr.*]

spar•ing (spâr′ĭng) ►*adj.* Thrifty or frugal. —**spar′ing•ly** *adv.*

spark¹ (spärk) ►*n.* **1.** A glowing particle, esp. one thrown off from a burning substance or resulting from friction. **2a.** A brief flash of light, esp. one produced by electric discharge. **b.** A short pulse or flow of electric current. **3.** A quality or factor with latent potential; seed: *the spark of genius.* ►*v.* **1.** To give off sparks. **2.** To set in motion; spur: *spark a controversy.* [< OE *spearca.*]

spark² (spärk) ►*n.* **1.** A young dandy. **2.** A male suitor; beau. ►*v.* To court or woo. [Perh. of Scand. orig.] —**spark′er** *n.*

spar•kle (spär′kəl) ►*v.* **-kled, -kling 1.** To give off sparks. **2.** To give off or reflect flashes of light; glitter. **3.** To be brilliant or witty. **4.** To release gas bubbles; effervesce. [ME *sparklen.*] —**spar′kle** *n.* —**spar′kler** *n.*

spark plug ►*n.* A device in a cylinder of an internal-combustion engine that ignites the fuel mixture by an electric spark.

spar•row (spăr′ō) ►*n.* Any of various small brownish or grayish New World finches. [< OE *spearwa.*]

sparrow hawk ►*n.* **1.** A small Old World hawk that preys on small birds. **2.** A small North American falcon.

sparse (spärs) ►*adj.* **spars•er, spars•est.** Occurring, growing, or settled at widely spaced intervals. [Lat. *sparsus,* p.part. of *spargere,* scatter.] —**sparse′ly** *adv.* —**sparse′ness, spar′si•ty** *n.*

Spar•ta (spär′tə) A city-state of ancient Greece in the SE Peloponnesus.

Spar•ta•cus (spär′tə-kəs). d. 71 B.C. Thracian slave who led a revolt against Rome.

Spar•tan (spär′tn) ►*adj.* **1.** Of Sparta or its people. **2a.** Rigorously self-disciplined. **b.** Simple, frugal, or austere. ►*n.* **1.** A citizen of Sparta. **2.** One of Spartan character.

spasm (spăz′əm) ►*n.* **1.** A sudden involuntary muscular contraction. **2.** A sudden burst of energy, activity, or emotion. [< Gk. *spasmos.*] —**spas•mod′ic** (spăz-mŏd′ĭk) *adj.* —**spas•mod′i•cal•ly** *adv.*

spas•tic (spăs′tĭk) ►*adj.* Of or affected by muscular spasms. ►*n.* A person affected with chronic muscular spasms. [< Gk. *spastikos.*] —**spas′ti•cal•ly** *adv.*

spat¹ (spăt) ►*v.* P.t. and p.part. of **spit¹.**

spat² (spăt) ►*n., pl.* **spat** or **spats.** The larval stage of a bivalve mollusk, such as an oyster. [ME.]

spat³ (spăt) ►*n.* A gaiter covering the upper shoe and the ankle. [< *spatterdash.*]

spat⁴ (spăt) ►*n.* A brief quarrel. ►*v.* **spat•ted, spat•ting.** To engage in a spat. [?]

spate (spāt) ►*n.* A sudden flood, rush, or outpouring. [ME.]

spathe (spāth) ►*n. Bot.* A leaflike organ that encloses or spreads from the base of the spadix, as in the jack-in-the-pulpit and the calla lily. [< Gk. *spathē,* broad blade.]

spa•tial (spā′shəl) ►*adj.* Relating to space. [< Lat. *spatium,* space.] —**spa′tial•ly** *adv.*

spat•ter (spăt′ər) ►*v.* To scatter or be scattered in drops or small splashes; splatter. ►*n.* **1.** The act or sound of spattering. **2.** A drop or splash of something spattered. [Perh. of LGer. orig.]

spat•u•la (spăch′ə-lə) ►*n.* An implement with a flexible blade used esp. to mix, spread, or lift material. [< Gk. *spathē,* broad blade.]

spav•in (spăv′ĭn) ►*n.* A condition in which the hock joint becomes swollen or painful. [< OFr. *espavain,* swelling.] —**spav′ined** *adj.*

spawn (spôn) ►*n.* **1.** The eggs of aquatic animals such as fishes, oysters, or frogs. **2.** Offspring, esp. when produced in large numbers; brood. ►*v.* **1.** To produce offspring. **2.** To produce offspring in large numbers. **3.** To give rise to; engender. [< Lat. *expandere,* expand.]

spay (spā) ►*v.* To remove the ovaries of (an animal). [< AN *espeier,* cut with a sword.]

SPCA ►*abbr.* Society for the Prevention of Cruelty to Animals

speak (spēk) ►*v.* **spoke** (spōk), **spo•ken** (spō′kən), **speak•ing 1.** To utter words; talk. **2.** To converse. **3.** To deliver a public speech. **4.** To act as spokesperson. **5.** To converse in or be able to converse in (a language). —***phrasal verb:* speak out** (or **up**) To speak without fear or hesitation. [< OE *sprecan.*] —**speak′a•ble** *adj.*

speak•eas•y (spēk′ē′zē) ►*n., pl.* **-ies.** A place for the illegal sale and consumption of alcoholic drinks.

speak•er (spē′kər) ►*n.* **1.** One who speaks. **2.** One who delivers a public speech. **3.** The presiding officer of a legislative assembly. **4.** A loudspeaker.

spear¹ (spîr) ►*n.* **1.** A weapon consisting of a long shaft with a sharply pointed end. **2.** A barbed shaft for spearing fish. ►*v.* To pierce or stab with or as if with a spear. [< OE *spere.*]

spear² (spîr) ►*n.* A slender stalk, as of asparagus or grass. [< *spire,* whorl.]

spear•fish (spîr′fĭsh′) ►*v.* To fish with a spear or spear gun. —**spear′fish′er** *n.* —**spear′fish′ing** *n.*

spear gun ►*n.* A device for mechanically shooting a spearlike missile under water, as in spearfishing.

spear•head (spîr′hĕd′) ►*n.* **1.** The sharpened head of a spear. **2.** The leading forces in a military attack. **3.** The driving force in an action or endeavor. —**spear′head** *v.*

spear•mint (spîr′mĭnt′) ►*n.* A common mint yielding an oil used widely as a flavoring.

spe•cial (spĕsh′əl) ►*adj.* **1.** Surpassing what is common or usual; exceptional. **2.** Distinct among others of a kind; singular. **3.** Peculiar to a specific person or thing; particular. **4.** Having a limited or specific function, application, or scope. **5.** Additional or extra. ►*n.* **1.** One that is special. **2.** Something arranged, issued, or produced for a particular service or occasion: *a television special.* **3.** A featured attraction, such as a reduced price: *a special on salmon.* [< Lat.

speciēs, kind.] —**spe′cial•ly** *adv.*

special delivery ►*n.* Delivery of mail at an unscheduled time for an additional fee.

special education ►*n.* Instruction designed for students whose learning needs cannot be met by a standard school curriculum.

special effect ►*n.* A visual effect added to a movie or a taped television show during processing.

Special Forces ►*pl.n.* A division of the US Army composed of soldiers specially trained in guerrilla fighting.

spe•cial•ist (spĕsh′ə-lĭst) ►*n.* **1.** One who is devoted to a particular occupation or branch of study. **2.** A physician whose practice is limited to a particular branch of medicine or surgery. **3.** Any of several noncommissioned ranks in the US Army.

spe•cial•ize (spĕsh′ə-līz′) ►*v.* **-ized, -iz•ing 1.** To pursue a special activity, occupation, or field of study. **2.** *Biol.* To adapt or become adapted to a specific function or environment. —**spe′cial•i•za′tion** *n.*

special relativity ►*n.* The physical theory of space and time developed by Albert Einstein.

spe•cial•ty (spĕsh′əl-tē) ►*n., pl.* **-ties 1.** A special pursuit, occupation, aptitude, or skill. See Syns at **forte**[1]. **2.** A branch of medicine in which a physician specializes. **3.** A special feature; peculiarity.

spe•cie (spē′shē, -sē) ►*n.* Coined money; coin. [< Lat. *(in) speciē*, (in) kind.]

spe•cies (spē′shēz, -sēz) ►*n., pl.* **-cies 1.** *Biol.* **a.** The category ranking below a genus in the hierarchy of taxonomic classification, usu. the narrowest group to which an organism can be assigned. **b.** The group of organisms assigned to such a category. **2.** A kind, variety, or type. [< Lat. *speciēs*, kind, form.]

spe•cif•ic (spĭ-sĭf′ĭk) ►*adj.* **1.** Explicitly set forth; definite. See Syns at **explicit**. **2.** Of, characterizing, or distinguishing a species. **3.** Intended for or acting on a particular thing, esp. effective in the treatment of a particular disease. ►*n.* **1.** A remedy intended for a particular ailment or disorder. **2. specifics** Distinct items or details; particulars. [LLat. *specificus* < Lat. *speciēs*, kind.] —**spe•cif′i•cal•ly** *adv.* —**spec′i•fic′i•ty** (spĕs′ə-fĭs′ĭ-tē) *n.*

spec•i•fi•ca•tion (spĕs′ə-fĭ-kā′shən) ►*n.* **1.** Something that is specified. **2. specifications** A detailed statement of particulars, esp. one prescribing materials, dimensions, and quality of work for something to be built, installed, or manufactured.

specific gravity ►*n.* The ratio of the mass of a solid or liquid to the mass of an equal volume of distilled water at 4°C (39°F) or of a gas to an equal volume of air or hydrogen under prescribed conditions of temperature and pressure.

spec•i•fy (spĕs′ə-fī′) ►*v.* **-fied, -fy•ing.** To state explicitly, unambiguously, or in detail. [< LLat. *specificāre*. See SPECIFIC.]

spec•i•men (spĕs′ə-mən) ►*n.* An individual, item, or part representative of an entire set or whole; sample. [Lat., example < *specere*, look at.]

spe•cious (spē′shəs) ►*adj.* **1.** Seemingly true but actually fallacious: *a specious argument.* **2.** Deceptively attractive. [< Lat. *speciōsus*, attractive < *specere*, look at.] —**spe′cious•ly** *adv.* —**spe′cious•ness** *n.*

speck (spĕk) ►*n.* **1.** A small spot or mark. **2.** A tiny amount; bit. ►*v.* To mark with specks. [< OE *specca*.]

speck•le (spĕk′əl) ►*n.* A small spot, esp. a natural dot of color on skin, plumage, or foliage. [ME *spakle*.] —**speck′le** *v.* —**speck′led** *adj.*

spec•ta•cle (spĕk′tə-kəl) ►*n.* **1a.** A remarkable or impressive sight. **b.** A lavish public performance or display. **2. spectacles** A pair of eyeglasses. [< Lat. *spectāculum* < *spectāre*, watch < *specere*, look at.] —**spec′ta•cled** *adj.*

spec•tac•u•lar (spĕk-tăk′yə-lər) ►*adj.* Of the nature of a spectacle; sensational. ►*n.* A lavish spectacle. —**spec•tac′u•lar•ly** *adv.*

spec•ta•tor (spĕk′tā′tər) ►*n.* An observer of an event. [Lat. *spectātor* < *spectāre*, watch. See SPECTACLE.]

spec•ter (spĕk′tər) ►*n.* **1.** A ghostly apparition; phantom. **2.** A haunting or disturbing prospect: *the specter of nuclear war.* [< Lat. *spectrum*, apparition. See SPECTRUM.]

spec•tra (spĕk′trə) ►*n.* Pl. of **spectrum.**

spec•tral (spĕk′trəl) ►*adj.* **1.** Resembling a specter; ghostly. **2.** Of or produced by a spectrum.

spectro– ►*pref.* Spectrum: *spectrograph.* [< SPECTRUM.]

spec•tro•gram (spĕk′trə-grăm′) ►*n.* A graph or photograph of a spectrum.

spec•tro•graph (spĕk′trə-grăf′) ►*n.* **1.** A spectroscope equipped to photograph spectra. **2.** A spectrogram. —**spec′tro•graph′ic** *adj.* —**spec′tro•graph′i•cal•ly** *adv.* —**spec•trog′ra•phy** (-trŏg′rə-fē) *n.*

spec•trom•e•ter (spĕk-trŏm′ĭ-tər) ►*n.* A spectroscope equipped to measure wavelengths or indexes of refraction. —**spec′tro•met′ric** (-trə-mĕt′rĭk) *adj.* —**spec•trom′e•try** *n.*

spec•tro•scope (spĕk′trə-skōp′) ►*n.* An instrument for producing, observing, or recording spectra. —**spec′tro•scop′ic** (-skŏp′ĭk), **spec′tro•scop′i•cal** *adj.* —**spec•tros′co•pist** (-trŏs′kə-pĭst) *n.* —**spec•tros′co•py** *n.*

spec•trum (spĕk′trəm) ►*n., pl.* **-tra** (-trə) or **-trums 1.** *Phys.* The distribution of a characteristic of a physical system or phenomenon, esp. the distribution of energy emitted by a radiant source, as by an incandescent body, arranged in order of wavelengths. **2.** A broad range: *the whole spectrum of modern thought.* [Lat., appearance < *specere*, look at.]

spec•u•late (spĕk′yə-lāt′) ►*v.* **-lat•ed, -lat•ing 1.** To meditate on a subject; reflect. **2.** To engage in risky business ventures that offer the chance of large profits. [< *specula*, watchtower < *specere*, look at.] —**spec′u•la′tion** *n.* —**spec′u•la•tive** *adj.* —**spec′u•la′tor** *n.*

spec•u•lum (spĕk′yə-ləm) ►*n., pl.* **-la** (-lə) or **-lums 1.** A mirror used in optical instruments. **2.** An instrument for dilating a body cavity for medical examination. [< Lat., mirror < *specere*, look at.]

speech (spēch) ►*n.* **1a.** The act of speaking. **b.** The capacity to speak. **2.** Vocal communication; conversation. **3.** A talk or public address. **4.** One's manner of speaking. **5.** The language or dialect of a nation or region. [< OE *sprǣc*.]

speech•less (spēch′lĭs) ►*adj.* **1.** Lacking the faculty of speech. **2.** Temporarily unable to speak, as from astonishment. —**speech′less•ly** *adv.* —**speech′less•ness** *n.*

speed (spēd) ►*n.* **1.** The rate or a measure of the rate of motion. **2.** A rate of action, activity, or performance. **3a.** The act of moving rapidly. **b.** Rapidity or swiftness. See Syns at **haste. 4.** A transmission gear in a motor vehicle. **5.** *Slang* An amphetamine drug. ►*v.* **sped** (spĕd) or **speed•ed, speed•ing 1.** To move or cause to move rapidly. **2.** To increase the speed or rate of: *speed production.* **3.** To drive at a speed exceeding a legal limit. [< OE *spēd,* success.] —**speed′er** *n.* —**speed′i•ly** *adv.* —**speed′i•ness** *n.* —**speed′y** *adj.*

speed•boat (spēd′bōt′) ►*n.* A fast motorboat.

speed•om•e•ter (spĭ-dŏm′ĭ-tər, spē-) ►*n.* **1.** An instrument for indicating speed, as of an automobile. **2.** An odometer.

speed•up (spēd′ŭp′) ►*n.* Acceleration of production without an increase in pay.

speed•way (spēd′wā′) ►*n.* **1.** *Sports* A course for automobile or motorcycle racing. **2.** A road designed for fast-moving traffic.

speed•well (spēd′wĕl′) ►*n.* A plant with clusters of small, usu. blue flowers.

spell[1] (spĕl) ►*v.* **spelled** or **spelt** (spĕlt), **spell•ing 1.** To name or write in order the letters of (a word). **2.** To mean; signify: *an event that spells trouble.* —***phrasal verb:* spell out** To make explicit; specify. [< OFr. *espeller,* read letter by letter, of Gmc. orig.]

spell[2] (spĕl) ►*n.* **1.** A word or formula believed to have magic power. **2.** A bewitched state; trance. **3.** Allure; fascination. [< OE, tale.]

spell[3] (spĕl) ►*n.* **1.** A short, indefinite period of time. **2.** *Informal* A period of weather: *a cold spell.* **3.** One's turn at work; shift. **4.** *Informal* A period of illness or indisposition. ►*v.* To relieve (someone) from work temporarily. [< OE *spelian,* stand in for.]

spell•bind (spĕl′bīnd′) ►*v.* To hold under or as if under a spell; enchant. [Back-formation < *spellbound.*] —**spell′bind′er** *n.*

spell checker ►*n.* An application in a word processing program that checks for spelling errors. —**spell check** *v.*

spell•er (spĕl′ər) ►*n.* **1.** One who spells words. **2.** A book used to teach spelling.

spell•ing (spĕl′ĭng) ►*n.* **1.** The forming of words with letters in an accepted order. **2.** The way in which a word is spelled.

spe•lunk•er (spĭ-lŭng′kər, spē′lŭng′-) ►*n.* One who explores and studies caves; a caver. [< Gk. *spēlunx,* cave.] —**spe′lunk′ing** *n.*

Spen•cer (spĕn′sər), **Herbert.** 1820–1903. British philosopher.

spend (spĕnd) ►*v.* **spent** (spĕnt), **spend•ing 1.** To use up or put out; expend. **2.** To pay out (money); disburse. **3.** To wear out; exhaust. **4.** To pass (time). **5.** To waste or squander. [< Lat. *expendēre,* expend, and OFr. *despendre,* dispense.] —**spend′er** *n.*

spend•thrift (spĕnd′thrĭft′) ►*n.* One who spends money recklessly or wastefully. [SPEND + THRIFT, accumulated wealth (obs.).]

Spen•ser (spĕn′sər), **Edmund.** 1552?–1599. English poet. —**Spen•se′ri•an** (-sîr′ē-ən) *adj.*

spent (spĕnt) ►*v.* P.t. and p.part. of **spend.** ►*adj.* Depleted of energy, force, or strength; exhausted.

sperm (spûrm) ►*n., pl.* **sperm** or **sperms 1.** A spermatozoon. **2.** Semen. [< Gk. *sperma,* sperm.] —**sper•mat′ic** (spər-măt′ĭk) *adj.*

sper•ma•ce•ti (spûr′mə-sē′tē, -sĕt′ē) ►*n., pl.* **-tis.** A white waxy substance obtained from the sperm whale and used for making candles, ointments, and cosmetics. [< Med.Lat. *spermacētī* : LLat. *sperma,* SPERM + Lat. *cētī,* of a whale.]

sper•mat•o•zo•on (spər-măt′ə-zō′ŏn′, -ən, spûr′mə-tə-) ►*n., pl.* **-zo•a** (-zō′ə). The fertilizing gamete of a male animal. [*spermato-,* sperm + -ZOON.]

sper•mi•cide (spûr′mĭ-sīd′) ►*n.* A contraceptive agent that kills spermatozoa. —**sper′mi•cid′al** (-sīd′l) *adj.*

sperm whale ►*n.* A large toothed whale with a long narrow jaw and a massive head.

spew (spyo͞o) ►*v.* **1.** To force out in or as if in a stream. **2.** To vomit. [< OE *spīwan.*]

SPF ►*abbr.* sun protection factor

sp gr ►*abbr.* specific gravity

sphag•num (sfăg′nəm) ►*n.* Any of a genus of mosses whose decomposed remains form peat. [< Gk. *sphagnos,* a kind of shrub.]

sphere (sfîr) ►*n.* **1.** *Math.* A three-dimensional surface, all points of which are equidistant from a fixed point. **2.** A spherical object or figure; ball. **3.** A planet, star, or other heavenly body. **4.** An area of power, control, or influence; domain. See Syns at **field.** [< Gk. *sphaira.*] —**spher′i•cal** (sfîr′ĭ-kəl, sfĕr′-) *adj.* —**spher′i•cal•ly** *adv.*

spher•oid (sfîr′oid′, sfĕr′-) ►*n.* A three-dimensional geometric surface generated by revolving an ellipse around one of its axes. —**sphe•roi′dal** *adj.*

sphinc•ter (sfĭngk′tər) ►*n.* A ringlike muscle that normally maintains constriction of a body passage or orifice. [< Gk. *sphinktēr* < *sphingein,* bind tight.]

sphinx (sfĭngks) ►*n., pl.* **sphinx•es** or **sphin•ges** (sfĭn′jēz′) **1.** A figure in Egyptian myth having the body of a lion and the head of a man, ram, or hawk. **2.** A winged creature in Greek myth having the head of a woman and the body of a lion, noted for killing those who could not answer its riddle. **3.** A puzzling or mysterious person. [< Gk.]

sphinx
Great Sphinx of Giza, Egypt

spice (spīs) ►*n.* **1.** A pungent, aromatic plant substance, as nutmeg or pepper, used as flavoring. **2.** Something that adds zest or interest. [< LLat. *speciēs,* wares < Lat., kind. See SPECIES.] —**spice** *v.* —**spic′y** *adj.*

spick-and-span also **spic-and-span** (spĭk′ən-spăn′) ►*adj.* **1.** Neat and clean; spotless. **2.** Brand-new; fresh. [*spick,* spike + *spannew,* entirely new.]

spic•ule (spĭk′yo͞ol) ►*n. Biol.* A small needlelike structure or part. [Lat. *spīculum.*]

spi•der (spī′dər) ►*n.* **1.** Any of an order of eight-legged arachnids having a body divided into two parts and often spinning webs to trap insects. **2.** See **frying pan.** [< OE *spīthra.*] —**spi′der•y** *adj.*

spider monkey ►*n.* A tropical American monkey having long legs and a long prehensile tail and lacking a thumb.

spiel (spēl, shpēl) ►*n. Informal* A lengthy, usu. extravagant speech or argument intended to persuade. [Ger. *Spiel* or Yiddish *shpil*, play.] —**spiel** *v.*

spiff•y (spĭf′ē) ►*adj.* **-i•er, -i•est** *Informal* Smart in appearance or dress. [Poss. < dial. *spiff*, dandified.] —**spiff′i•ly** *adv.*

spig•ot (spĭg′ət) ►*n.* A faucet. See Regional Note at **andiron.** [ME.]

spike[1] (spīk) ►*n.* **1a.** A long, thick, sharp-pointed piece of wood or metal, such as one along the top of a fence or wall. **b.** A large heavy nail. **2.** A sharp-pointed projection such as one in the sole of a shoe for traction. ►*v.* **spiked, spik•ing 1.** To secure or provide with a spike. **2.** To pierce or injure with a spike. **3.** *Informal* To put an end to; block: *spike a rumor.* **4.** *Informal* To add liquor to. [< ON *spīk.*] —**spik′y** *adj.*

spike[2] (spīk) ►*n.* **1.** An ear of grain. **2.** *Bot.* A usu. elongated cluster of stalkless flowers. [< Lat. *spīca.*]

spike•let (spīk′lĭt) ►*n.* A small or secondary spike, characteristic of grasses and sedges.

spike•nard (spīk′närd′) ►*n.* An aromatic plant from which a fragrant ointment was obtained in ancient times.

spill (spĭl) ►*v.* **spilled** or **spilt** (spĭlt), **spill•ing 1.** To cause or allow to run, flow, or fall out. **2.** To shed (blood). **3.** To fall or cause to fall, as from a horse. ►*n.* **1.** The act or an instance of spilling. **2.** An amount spilled. **3.** A fall. [< OE *spillan*, kill.] —**spill′age** *n.*

spill•way (spĭl′wā′) ►*n.* A channel for an overflow of water, as from a reservoir.

spin (spĭn) ►*v.* **spun** (spŭn), **spin•ning 1a.** To draw out and twist (fibers) into thread. **b.** To form (thread or yarn) by spinning. **2.** To form (e.g., a web or cocoon) by extruding viscous threads. **3.** To tell, esp. imaginatively: *spin tales.* **4.** To rotate or cause to rotate swiftly; twirl. **5.** To reel; whirl. **6.** To ride or drive rapidly. **7.** To interpret or distort, esp. so as to sway public opinion. ►*n.* **1.** A swift whirling motion. **2.** A state of confusion. **3.** *Informal* A short drive in a vehicle. **4.** An interpretation or distortion. [< OE *spinnan.*] —**spin′ner** *n.*

spin•ach (spĭn′ĭch) ►*n.* A plant cultivated for its dark-green edible leaves. [< Pers. *aspanākh.*]

spi•nal (spī′nəl) ►*adj.* Of or near the spine or spinal cord. ►*n.* An anesthetic injected into the spinal cord. —**spi′nal•ly** *adv.*

spinal column ►*n.* The series of vertebrae encasing the spinal cord and forming the main support of the body; spine.

spinal cord ►*n.* The part of the central nervous system that extends from the brain through the spinal column.

spin•dle (spĭn′dl) ►*n.* **1.** A slender rod or pin on which fibers are twisted into thread and then wound. **2.** Any of various slender revolving mechanical parts. **3.** A dragonfly. See Regional Note at **dragonfly.** [< OE *spinel.*]

spin•dly (spĭnd′lē) ►*adj.* **-dli•er, -dli•est.** Slender, elongated, and often weak.

spin•drift (spĭn′drĭft′) ►*n.* Windblown sea spray. [< obsolete *spoon*, run before the wind + DRIFT.]

spine (spīn) ►*n.* **1.** The spinal column of a vertebrate. **2.** A sharp-pointed, projecting plant or animal part such as a thorn or quill. **3.** Courage or willpower; backbone. [< Lat. *spīna.*] —**spine′less** *adj.* —**spin′y** *adj.*

spin•et (spĭn′ĭt) ►*n.* **1.** A small upright piano. **2.** A small harpsichord with a single keyboard. [< Ital. *spinetta.*]

spin•na•ker (spĭn′ə-kər) ►*n.* A large triangular sail set on a spar that swings out opposite the mainsail. [Poss. < *Sphinx*, a racing yacht of the 1860s.]

spin•ner•et (spĭn′ə-rĕt′) ►*n.* A structure from which spiders and silkworms secrete silk threads to form webs or cocoons.

spin•ning jenny (spĭn′ĭng) ►*n.* An early spinning machine having several spindles.

spinning wheel ►*n.* A device for making yarn or thread, consisting of a foot-driven or hand-driven wheel and a single spindle.

spin•off or **spin-off** (spĭn′ôf′, -ŏf′) ►*n.* Something, such as a product or enterprise, derived from something larger or more complex; byproduct.

Spi•no•za (spĭ-nō′zə), **Baruch.** 1632–77. Dutch philosopher and theologian.

spin•ster (spĭn′stər) ►*n.* A woman who has remained single beyond the conventional age for marrying. [ME *spinnestere.*] —**spin′ster•hood′** *n.*

spir•a•cle (spĭr′ə-kəl, spī′rə-) ►*n.* **1.** A small respiratory opening, esp. in the exoskeleton of an insect. **2.** A blowhole. [< Lat. *spīrāculum* < *spīrāre*, breathe.]

spi•ral (spī′rəl) ►*n.* **1.** A curve on a plane that continuously winds around a fixed point at an increasing or decreasing distance. **2.** A three-dimensional curve that turns around an axis; helix. **3.** Something having the form of such a curve. ►*adj.* **1.** Of or resembling a spiral. **2.** Coiling in a constantly changing plane; helical. ►*v.* **-raled, -ral•ing** also **-ralled, -ral•ling 1.** To take or cause to take a spiral form or course. **2.** To rise or fall with steady acceleration. [< Gk. *speira*, coil.] —**spi′ral•ly** *adv.*

spiral galaxy ►*n.* A galaxy having a spiral structure.

spiral galaxy
NGC 6946 in Cepheus

spi•rant (spī′rənt) ►*n.* See **fricative.** [< Lat. *spīrāre*, breathe.] —**spi′rant** *adj.*

spire (spīr) ►*n.* **1.** A top part or point that tapers upward. **2.** A structure, such as a steeple, that tapers to a point. [< OE *spīr*.]

spi•re•a also **spi•rae•a** (spī-rē′ə) ►*n.* Any of various shrubs having clusters of white or pink flowers. [< Gk. *speiraia*, privet.]

spir•it (spĭr′ĭt) ►*n.* **1.** The animating force within living beings; soul. **2. Spirit** The Holy Spirit. **3.** A supernatural being; ghost. **4.** The part of a human associated with the mind, will, and feelings. **5.** A person as marked by a stated quality: *He is a proud spirit.* **6. spirits** A mood or emotional state. **7.** Vivacity, vigor, or courage. **8.** Strong loyalty or dedication. **9.** A predominant mood or attitude: *a spirit of rebellion.* **10.** The actual though unstated sense or significance of something: *the spirit of the law.* **11.** often **spirits** *(takes sing. v.)* An alcohol solution of an essential or volatile substance. **12. spirits** An alcoholic beverage. ►*v.* To carry off mysteriously or secretly. [< Lat. *spīritus*, breath.] —**spir′it•less** *adj.*

spir•it•ed (spĭr′ĭ-tĭd) ►*adj.* Marked by animation, vigor, or courage. —**spir′it•ed•ly** *adv.*

spir•i•tu•al (spĭr′ĭ-cho͞o-əl) ►*adj.* **1.** Relating to or consisting of spirit. See Syns at **immaterial. 2.** Ecclesiastical; sacred. ►*n.* A religious song of African-American origin. —**spir′i•tu•al′i•ty** (-ăl′ĭ-tē) *n.* —**spir′i•tu•al•ize′** *v.* —**spir′i•tu•al•ly** *adv.*

spir•i•tu•al•ism (spĭr′ĭ-cho͞o-ə-lĭz′əm) ►*n.* The belief that the dead communicate with the living, as through a medium. —**spir′i•tu•al•ist** *n.* —**spir′i•tu•al•is′tic** *adj.*

spir•i•tu•ous (spĭr′ĭ-cho͞o-əs) ►*adj.* Of or containing alcohol; alcoholic.

spi•ro•chete (spī′rə-kēt′) ►*n.* Any of an order of slender spiral microorganisms, including those causing syphilis. [< Gk. *speira*, coil + *khaitē*, long hair.]

spit[1] (spĭt) ►*n.* **1.** Saliva, esp. when expectorated. **2.** The act of spitting. ►*v.* **spat** (spăt) or **spit, spit•ting 1.** To eject (e.g., saliva) from the mouth. **2.** To eject as if by spitting. —***phrasal verb:*** **spit up** To vomit. [< OE *spittan*, to spit.]

spit[2] (spĭt) ►*n.* **1.** A slender pointed rod on which meat is impaled for roasting. **2.** A narrow point of land extending into a body of water. ►*v.* **spit•ted, spit•ting.** To impale on or as if on a spit. [< OE *spitu*.]

spit•ball (spĭt′bôl′) ►*n.* **1.** A chewed lump of paper to be used as a projectile. **2.** *Baseball* An illegal pitch in which the ball is moistened on one side, as if with saliva.

spite (spīt) ►*n.* Malicious ill will prompting an urge to hurt. ►*v.* **spit•ed, spit•ing.** To treat with malice. —***idiom:*** **in spite of** Regardless of; despite. [ME.] —**spite′ful** *n.* —**spite′ful•ly** *adv.* —**spite′ful•ness** *n.*

spit•tle (spĭt′l) ►*n.* Spit; saliva. [< OE *spātl*.]

spit•tle•bug (spĭt′l-bŭg′) ►*n.* Any of a family of insects whose nymphs form frothy masses of liquid on plant stems.

spit•toon (spĭ-to͞on′) ►*n.* A bowl-shaped vessel for spitting into; cuspidor. [< SPIT[1].]

splash (splăsh) ►*v.* **1.** To propel, dash, or scatter (a fluid) about in masses. **2.** To scatter fluid upon. **3.** To fall into or move through fluid with the sound of splashing. ►*n.* **1.** The act or sound of splashing. **2.** A flying mass of fluid. **3.** A mark made by or as if by splashing. **4.** A sensation; stir. [Prob. < PLASH.] —**splash′er** *n.*

splash•down (splăsh′doun′) ►*n.* The landing of a spacecraft or missile in water.

splash•y (splăsh′ē) ►*adj.* **-i•er, -i•est 1.** Making a splash or splashes. **2.** Ostentatious. See Syns at **showy.** —**splash′i•ness** *n.*

splat[1] (splăt) ►*n.* A slat of wood, as one in the middle of a chair back. [Perh. < ME *splatten*, split open.]

splat[2] (splăt) ►*n.* A smacking noise. [Imit.]

splat•ter (splăt′ər) ►*v.* To spatter. [Perh. blend of SPLASH and SPATTER.] —**splat′ter** *n.*

splay (splā) ►*adj.* **1.** Spread or turned out. **2.** Clumsy or awkward. ►*v.* **1.** To spread or be spread out or apart, esp. clumsily. **2.** To slant or slope or make slanting or sloping. [< ME *splayen*, display.] —**splay** *n.*

splay•foot (splā′fo͝ot′) ►*n.* A deformity marked by abnormally flat and turned-out feet. —**splay′foot′ed** *adj.*

spleen (splēn) ►*n.* **1.** A large lymphoid organ, lying on the left side of the human body below the diaphragm, that filters and stores blood and produces lymphocytes. **2.** Ill temper. [< Gk. *splēn*.]

splen•did (splĕn′dĭd) ►*adj.* **1.** Brilliant with light or color; radiant. **2.** Magnificent. **3.** Glorious; illustrious. **4.** Excellent. [< Lat. *splendēre*, shine.] —**splen′did•ly** *adv.*

splen•dif•er•ous (splĕn-dĭf′ər-əs) ►*adj.* Splendid. [< Med.Lat. *splendiferus*.]

splen•dor (splĕn′dər) ►*n.* **1.** Great light or luster; brilliance. **2.** Magnificent appearance or display. [< Lat. < *splendēre*, shine.]

splen•dour (splĕn′dər) ►*n.* *Chiefly Brit.* Var. of **splendor.**

sple•net•ic (splĭ-nĕt′ĭk) ►*adj.* **1.** Of the spleen. **2.** Ill-humored; irritable. [< Gk. *splēn*, spleen.]

splen•ic (splĕn′ĭk) ►*adj.* Of or near the spleen. [< Gk. *splēn*, spleen.]

splice (splīs) ►*v.* **spliced, splic•ing 1a.** To join (e.g., two pieces of film) at the ends. **b.** To join (e.g., ropes) by interweaving strands. **2.** To join (pieces of wood) by overlapping and binding. **3.** To join together or insert (segments of DNA or RNA) so as to form new genetic combinations. [< Du. *splissen*.] —**splice** *n.*

splint (splĭnt) ►*n.* **1.** A rigid device used to prevent motion of a joint or the ends of a fractured bone. **2.** A thin flexible wooden strip, such as one used in making baskets. [< MDu. or MLGer. *splinte*.] —**splint** *v.*

splin•ter (splĭn′tər) ►*n.* A sharp slender piece, as of wood or metal, split or broken off from a main body. ►*v.* To form or cause to form splinters. [< MDu.]

split (splĭt) ►*v.* **split, split•ting 1.** To divide or become divided, esp. into lengthwise sections. **2.** To break, burst, or rip apart with force; rend. **3.** To separate; disunite: *a quarrel that split the family.* **4.** To divide and share: *split a dessert.* **5.** To separate into layers or sections. **6.** *Slang* To leave, esp. abruptly. ►*n.* **1.** The act or a result of splitting. **2.** A breach or rupture in a group. [< MDu. *splitten*.] —**split′ter** *n.*

Split. A city of SW Croatia on the Dalmatian coast. Pop. 200,459.

split-lev•el (splĭt′lĕv′əl) ►*adj.* Having the floor levels of adjoining rooms separated by about half a story: *a split-level ranch house.*

split personality ►*n.* **1.** Multiple personality. **2.** Schizophrenia.

split second ►*n.* An instant; flash.

split•ting (splĭt′ĭng) ►*adj.* Very severe: *a splitting headache.*

splotch (splŏch) ►*n.* An irregularly shaped spot, stain, or blotch. [Perh. blend of SPOT and BOTCH.] —**splotch** *v.* —**splotch′y** *adj.*

splurge (splûrj) ►*v.* **splurged, splurg•ing.** To indulge in an extravagant expense or display. [?] —**splurge** *n.*

splut•ter (splŭt′ər) ►*v.* **1.** To make a spitting sound. **2.** To speak or utter incoherently, as when confused or angry. [Perh. < SPUTTER.] —**splut′ter** *n.*

Spock (spŏk), **Benjamin McLane.** 1903–98. Amer. pediatrician, educator, and writer.

spoil (spoil) ►*v.* **spoiled** or **spoilt** (spoilt), **spoil•ing 1.** To impair the value or quality of; damage. **2.** To impair the completeness, perfection, or unity of; disrupt; disturb. **3.** To overindulge (someone) so as to harm the character of. **4.** To become tainted or rotten; decay. **5.** To pillage or plunder. —***phrasal verb:* spoil for** To be eager for: *spoiling for a fight.* ►*n.* **spoils 1.** Goods or property seized by force; plunder. **2.** Political patronage enjoyed by a successful party or candidate. [< Lat. *spolium*, booty.] —**spoil′age** *n.* —**spoil′er** *n.*

spoil•sport (spoil′spôrt′, -spōrt′) ►*n.* One who spoils or mars the pleasure of others.

Spo•kane (spō-kăn′) A city of E WA near the ID border. Pop. 177,196.

spoke[1] (spōk) ►*n.* **1.** One of the rods connecting the hub and rim of a wheel. **2.** A rung of a ladder. [< OE *spāca.*]

spoke[2] (spōk) ►*v.* **1.** P.t. of **speak. 2.** *Archaic* P.part. of **speak.**

spo•ken (spō′kən) ►*v.* P.part. of **speak.**

spokes•man (spōks′mən) ►*n.* A man who speaks on behalf of another or others. See Usage Note at **man.**

spokes•per•son (spōks′pûr′sən) ►*n.* A spokesman or spokeswoman.

spokes•wom•an (spōks′wo͝om′ən) ►*n.* A woman who speaks on behalf of another or others. See Usage Note at **man.**

spo•li•a•tion (spō′lē-ā′shən) ►*n.* **1.** The act of plundering. **2.** The state of being plundered. [< Lat. *spoliāre*, despoil. See SPOIL.]

sponge (spŭnj) ►*n.* **1a.** A primitive marine animal with a porous skeleton. **b.** The flexible, absorbent skeleton of the sponge, used for bathing, cleaning, and other purposes. **c.** A material with similar qualities and uses. **2.** A gauze pad used to absorb blood and other fluids, as in surgery. ►*v.* **sponged, spong•ing 1.** To moisten, wipe, or clean with a sponge. **2.** *Informal* To live by relying on another's generosityl; freeload. [< Gk. *spongos.*] —**spong′er** *n.* —**spong′y** *adj.*

sponge cake ►*n.* A light, porous cake containing no shortening.

sponge rubber ►*n.* A soft porous rubber used in cushions, gaskets, and weather stripping.

spon•sor (spŏn′sər) ►*n.* **1.** One who assumes responsibility for another person or a group. **2.** A godparent. **3.** A business enterprise that pays for radio or television programming, usu. in return for advertising time. [LLat. *spōnsor.*] —**spon′sor** *v.* —**spon′sor•ship′** *n.*

spon•ta•ne•ous (spŏn-tā′nē-əs) ►*adj.* **1.** Happening or arising without apparent external cause; self-generated. **2.** Voluntary or unpremeditated: *spontaneous applause.* [< Lat. *sponte*, voluntarily.] —**spon′ta•ne′i•ty** (-tə-nē′ĭ-tē, -nā′-) *n.* —**spon•ta′ne•ous•ly** *adv.*

spontaneous abortion ►*n.* See **miscarriage** 1.

spontaneous combustion ►*n.* The breaking into flame of combustible material, such as oily rags or hay, due to heat generated within the material by slow oxidation.

spoof (spo͞of) ►*n.* **1.** A hoax. **2.** A gentle satirical imitation; light parody. [?] —**spoof** *v.*

spook (spo͝ok) ►*n.* **1.** *Informal* A ghost. **2.** *Slang* A secret agent; spy. ►*v.* *Informal* **1.** To haunt. **2.** To startle or frighten. [< MDu. *spooc.*] —**spook′i•ly** *adv.* —**spook′i•ness** *n.* —**spook′y** *adj.*

spool[1] (spo͞ol) ►*n.* **1.** A cylinder on which yarn, wire, thread, or string is wound. **2.** A reel for magnetic tape. [< MDu. and MLGer. *spoele.*] —**spool** *v.*

spool[2] (spo͞ol) ►*v.* To store (data sent to a printer) in a buffer. [*s(imultaneous) p(eripheral) o(perations) o(n) l(ine).*] —**spool′er** *n.*

spoon (spo͞on) ►*n.* **1.** A utensil consisting of a small shallow bowl on a handle, used in preparing, serving, or eating food. **2.** A shiny, curved, metallic fishing lure. ►*v.* **1.** To lift, scoop up, or carry with or as if with a spoon. **2.** To engage in amorous kissing or caressing. [< OE *spōn*, chip of wood.] —**spoon′ful′** *n.*

spoon•bill (spo͞on′bĭl′) ►*n.* Any of several long-legged wading birds having a long flat bill with a broad tip.

spoon•er•ism (spo͞o′nə-rĭz′əm) ►*n.* A transposition of sounds of two or more words, such as *Let me sew you to your sheet* for *Let me show you to your seat.* [After William A. *Spooner* (1844–1930).]

spoon-feed (spo͞on′fēd′) ►*v.* **1.** To feed (another) with a spoon. **2.** To treat (another) in a way that discourages independent thought or action.

spoor (spo͝or) ►*n.* The track or trail of an animal, esp. a wild animal. [Afr. < MDu.]

Spor•a•des (spôr′ə-dēz′, spô-rä′*th*ēs) Two island groups of Greece in the Aegean, the **Northern Sporades** off the central mainland and the **Southern Sporades** off Turkey.

spo•rad•ic (spə-răd′ĭk, spô-) ►*adj.* Occurring at irregular intervals; having no pattern in time. [< Gk. *sporas, sporad-*, scattered.] —**spo•rad′i•cal•ly** *adv.*

spore (spôr) ►*n.* A usu. one-celled reproductive body or resting stage, as of a fern, fungus, or bacterium. [Gk. *spora*, seed.]

spor•ran (spôr′ən, spŏr′-) ►*n.* A pouch worn at the front of the kilt by Scottish Highlanders. [< Middle Irish *sparán.*]

sport (spôrt) ►*n.* **1.** An activity usu. involving physical exertion and having a set form and body of rules; game. **2.** An active pastime; diversion. **3.** Light mockery. **4.** One known for the manner of one's acceptance of defeat or criticism: *a poor sport.* **5.** *Informal* One who lives a jolly, extravagant life. **6.** *Biol.* A mutation. ►*v.* **1.** To play or frolic. **2.** To joke or trifle. **3.** To display or show off. ►*adj.* also **sports.** Of or appropriate for sport: *sport fishing.* [< OFr. *desport*, pleasure.] —**sport′i•ness** *n.* —**sport′y** *adj.*

sport•ing (spôr′tĭng) ►*adj.* **1.** Used in or appropriate for sports: *sporting goods.* **2.** Marked by sportsmanship. **3.** Of or associated with gambling. —**sport′ing•ly** *adv.*

spor•tive (spôr′tĭv) ► *adj.* Playful or frolicsome. —**spor′tive•ly** *adv.* —**spor′tive•ness** *n.*

sports•cast (spôrts′kăst′) ► *n.* A radio or television broadcast of a sports event or of sports news. —**sports′cast′er** *n.*

sports•man (spôrts′mən) ► *n.* **1.** A man who is active in sports. **2.** One who exhibits sportsmanship. —**sports′man•like′** *adj.*

sports•man•ship (spôrts′mən-shĭp′) ► *n.* Conduct and attitude appropriate to sports, esp. fair play and courtesy.

sports•wom•an (spôrts′wo͝om′ən) ► *n.* A woman who is active in sports.

sports•writ•er (spôrts′rī′tər) ► *n.* One who writes about sports, esp. for a newspaper or magazine.

sport-u•til•i•ty vehicle (spôrt′yo͞o-tĭl′ĭ-tē, spōrt′-) ► *n.* A large four-wheel-drive vehicle designed for off-road travel.

spot (spŏt) ► *n.* **1.** A position; location. **2.** A mark, such as a stain, on a surface differing sharply in color from its surroundings. **3.** *Informal* A situation, esp. a troublesome one. ► *v.* **spot•ted, spot•ting 1.** To mark or become marked with spots. **2.** To locate precisely. **3.** To detect or discern, esp. visually. ► *adj.* Made, paid, or delivered immediately: *a spot sale.* —***idiom:* on the spot** Under pressure. [< OE.] —**spot′ted** *adj.*

spot check ► *n.* An inspection conducted at random or limited to a few instances. —**spot′-check′** *v.*

spot•less (spŏt′lĭs) ► *adj.* **1.** Perfectly clean. See Syns at **clean. 2.** Impeccable. —**spot′less•ly** *adv.* —**spot′less•ness** *n.*

spot•light (spŏt′līt′) ► *n.* **1a.** A strong beam of light that illuminates only a small area, used esp. on a stage. **b.** A lamp that produces such a light. **2.** Public attention, notoriety, or prominence. —**spot′light′** *v.*

spot•ter (spŏt′ər) ► *n.* One that looks for, locates, and reports something, esp. a military lookout.

spot•ty (spŏt′ē) ► *adj.* **-ti•er, -ti•est.** Lacking consistency; uneven, as in quality.

spou•sal (spou′zəl, -səl) ► *adj.* Of a spouse. ► *n.* often **spousals.** Marriage; nuptials. [< Lat. *spōnsālis.*]

spouse (spous, spouz) ► *n.* One's husband or wife; marriage partner. [< Lat. *spōnsus*, p.part. of *spondēre*, to pledge, betroth.]

spout (spout) ► *v.* **1.** To gush forth or discharge in a rapid stream or in spurts. **2.** *Informal* To utter loudly and pompously: *spout nonsense.* ► *n.* **1.** A tube, mouth, or pipe through which liquid is discharged. **2.** A continuous stream of liquid. [ME *spouten.*] —**spout′er** *n.*

spp. ► *abbr.* species (plural)

sprain (sprān) ► *n.* A painful wrenching or laceration of the ligaments of a joint. ► *v.* To cause a sprain to (a joint or ligament). [?]

sprang (sprăng) ► *v.* P.t. of **spring.**

sprat (sprăt) ► *n.* **1.** A small food fish of NE Atlantic waters, often canned as a sardine. **2.** A young herring. [< OE *sprot.*]

sprawl (sprôl) ► *v.* **1.** To sit or lie with the limbs spread out awkwardly. **2.** To spread out haphazardly: *suburbs sprawling in all directions.* [< OE *sprēawlian*, writhe.] —**sprawl** *n.*

spray[1] (sprā) ► *n.* **1.** Liquid moving in a mass of dispersed droplets or mist, as from a wave. **2a.** A fine jet of liquid discharged from a pressurized container. **b.** A pressurized container; atomizer. ► *v.* **1.** To disperse (a liquid) in a spray. **2.** To apply a spray to (a surface). [< MDu. *sprayen*, sprinkle.] —**spray′er** *n.*

spray[2] (sprā) ► *n.* A small branch bearing buds, flowers, or berries. [< OE **spræg.*]

spread (sprĕd) ► *v.* **spread, spread•ing 1.** To open or be extended more fully; stretch. **2.** To separate or become separated more widely; open out. **3.** To distribute over a surface in a layer; apply. **4.** To distribute widely: *The tornado spread destruction.* **5.** To become or cause to become widely known. ► *n.* **1.** The act or process of spreading. **2.** An open area of land; expanse. **3.** The extent or limit to which something is or can be spread; range. **4.** A cloth covering for a bed or table. **5.** *Informal* An abundant meal laid out on a table. **6.** A food to be spread on bread or crackers. **7.** Two facing pages of a magazine or newspaper, often with related matter extending across the fold. **8.** A difference, as between two figures or totals. **9.**Wingspread. [< OE *sprǣdan.*] —**spread′a•ble** *adj.* —**spread′er** *n.*

spread eagle ► *n.* **1.** The figure of an eagle with wings and legs spread. **2.** A posture or design resembling a spread eagle. —**spread′ea′gle** *adj.*

spread•sheet (sprĕd′shēt′) ► *n.* An accounting or bookkeeping program that displays data in rows and columns on a screen.

spree (sprē) ► *n.* Overindulgence in an activity. See Syns at **binge.** [Perh. < Sc. *spreath*, cattle raid.]

spri•er (sprī′ər) ► *adj.* Comp. of **spry.**

spri•est (sprī′ĭst) ► *adj.* Superl. of **spry.**

sprig (sprĭg) ► *n.* A small shoot or twig of a plant. [ME *sprigge.*]

spright•ly (sprīt′lē) ► *adj.* **-li•er, -li•est.** Lively and brisk; animated.

spring (sprĭng) ► *v.* **sprang** (sprăng) or **sprung** (sprŭng), **sprung, spring•ing 1.** To move upward or forward suddenly; leap. **2.** To move suddenly on or as if on a spring. **3.** To emerge suddenly. **4.** To arise from a source; develop. See Syns at **stem**[1]. **5.** To come loose, as parts of a mechanism. **6.** To release from a checked or held position; actuate: *spring a trap.* **7.** To present unexpectedly or suddenly: *spring a surprise.* ► *n.* **1.** An elastic device, esp. a coil of wire, that regains its original shape after being compressed or extended. **2.** Elasticity; resilience. **3.** The act of springing. **4.** A natural fountain or stream of water. **5.** A source or origin. **6.** The season of the year between winter and summer. [< OE *springan.*] —**spring′i•ly** *adv.* —**spring′i•ness** *n.* —**spring′y** *adj.*

spring•board (sprĭng′bôrd′, -bōrd′) ► *n.* **1.** A flexible board used by gymnasts. **2.** See **diving board.**

spring fever ► *n.* A feeling of languor or yearning brought on by the coming of spring.

Spring•field (sprĭng′fēld′) **1.** The capital of IL, in the central part. Pop. 105,227. **2.** A city of SW MA on the Connecticut R. Pop. 156,983. **3.** A city of SW MO SSW of Kansas City. Pop. 140,494.

spring-load•ed (sprĭng′lō′dĭd) ► *adj.* Secured

or loaded by means of a spring.
spring tide ►*n.* The exceptionally high and low tides that occur at the time of the new moon or the full moon.

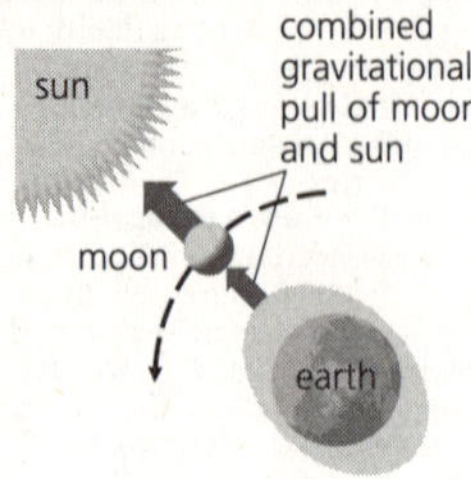

spring tide
Spring tides occur when the sun and moon are directly in line with the earth and their gravitational pulls reinforce each other.

spring•time (sprĭng′tīm′) ►*n.* The season of spring.
sprin•kle (sprĭng′kəl) ►*v.* **-kled, -kling.** To scatter or fall in drops or small particles. ►*n.* **1.** A light rainfall. **2.** A small amount. [ME *sprenklen.*] —**sprin′kler** *n.*
sprinkler system ►*n.* A network of overhead pipes that release water to extinguish fires.
sprin•kling (sprĭng′klĭng) ►*n.* A small or scattered amount.
sprint (sprĭnt) ►*n.* A short race at top speed. [Of Scand. orig.] —**sprint** *v.* —**sprint′er** *n.*
sprite (sprīt) ►*n.* **1.** An elf or pixie. **2.** A specter or ghost. [< Lat. *spīritus*, spirit.]
spritz•er (sprĭt′sər, shprĭt′-) ►*n.* A drink made of wine and carbonated water. [Ger. < *spritzen*, spray.]
sprock•et (sprŏk′ĭt) ►*n.* Any of various toothlike projections arranged on a wheel rim to engage the links of a chain. [?]
sprout (sprout) ►*v.* **1.** To begin to grow; give off shoots or buds. **2.** To emerge and develop rapidly. ►*n.* A young plant growth, such as a bud or shoot. [< OE *sprūtan.*]
spruce[1] (spro͞os) ►*n.* **1.** Any of various cone-bearing evergreen trees with short pointed needles and soft wood. **2.** The wood of a spruce. [< obsolete *Spruce fir*, Prussian fir.]
spruce[2] (spro͞os) ►*adj.* **spruc•er, spruc•est.** Neat and trim in appearance. ►*v.* **spruced, spruc•ing.** To neaten. [Perh. < obsolete *spruce leather*, Prussian leather.]
sprung (sprŭng) ►*v.* A p.t. and the p.part. of **spring.**
spry (sprī) ►*adj.* **spri•er** (sprī′ər), **spri•est** (sprī′ĭst) or **spry•er, spry•est.** Active; nimble. [Perh. of Scand. orig.] —**spry′ly** *adv.* —**spry′ness** *n.*
spud (spŭd) ►*n.* **1.** *Slang* A potato. **2.** A sharp spadelike tool. [ME *spudde*, short knife.]
spume (spyo͞om) ►*n.* Foam or froth on a liquid. [< Lat. *spūma.*] —**spu′mous, spum′y** *adj.*
spu•mo•ni or **spu•mo•ne** (spo͞o-mō′nē) ►*n.* Ice cream in layers of different colors or flavors, often with fruits and nuts. [Ital.]
spun (spŭn) ►*v.* P.t. and p.part. of **spin.**
spun glass ►*n.* See **fiberglass.**
spunk (spŭngk) ►*n.* *Informal* Spirit; pluck. [Sc.Gael. *spong*, tinder.] —**spunk′y** *adj.*

spur (spûr) ►*n.* **1.** A spiked device attached to a rider's heel and used to urge a horse forward. **2.** An incentive. **3.** A spurlike attachment or projection, as on the back of a bird's leg or on certain flowers. **4.** A lateral ridge projecting from a mountain or mountain range. **5.** A short side track connecting with the main railroad track. ►*v.* **spurred, spur•ring 1.** To urge (a horse) on by the use of spurs. **2.** To incite or stimulate. [< OE *spura.*]

spur
top to bottom: metal spurs and spurs on a long-spurred columbine

spurge (spûrj) ►*n.* Any of various plants with milky juice and small flowers. [< OFr. *espurgier*, purge (from its use as a purgative).]
spu•ri•ous (spyo͝or′ē-əs) ►*adj.* Lacking authenticity or validity; false. [< Lat. *spurius*, illegitimate.] —**spu′ri•ous•ly** *adv.* —**spu′ri•ous•ness** *n.*
spurn (spûrn) ►*v.* To reject or refuse disdainfully; scorn. [< OE *spurnan.*] —**spurn′er** *n.*
spurt (spûrt) ►*n.* **1.** A sudden forcible gush or jet. **2.** A sudden short burst of energy or activity. ►*v.* **1.** To gush forth. **2.** To make a brief intense effort. [?]
sput•nik (spŭt′nĭk, spo͞ot′nyĭk) ►*n.* A Soviet artificial earth satellite. [Russ. *sputnik (zemli)*, fellow traveler (of Earth).]
sput•ter (spŭt′ər) ►*v.* **1.** To spit out small particles in noisy bursts. **2.** To utter in an excited or confused manner. [Prob. of LGer. orig.] —**sput′ter** *n.* —**sput′ter•er** *n.*
spu•tum (spyo͞o′təm) ►*n., pl.* **-ta** (-tə). Expectorated matter including saliva and substances such as phlegm from the respiratory tract. [Lat. *spūtum* < *spuere*, to spit.]
spy (spī) ►*n., pl.* **spies** (spīz) **1.** An agent employed by a state to obtain secret information concerning its potential or actual enemies or rivals. **2.** One who secretly keeps watch on others. ►*v.* **spied** (spīd), **spy•ing 1.** To observe secretly with hostile intent. **2.** To catch sight of. **3.** To investigate intensively. [< OFr. *espier*, watch, of Gmc. orig.]
spy•glass (spī′glăs′) ►*n.* A small telescope.
sq. or **Sq.** ►*abbr.* square
squab (skwŏb) ►*n.* A young or unfledged pigeon. [Prob. of Scand. orig.]
squab•ble (skwŏb′əl) ►*v.* **-bled, -bling.** To engage in an argument, usu. over a trivial matter; wrangle. ►*n.* A noisy, usu. trivial quarrel. [Prob. of Scand. orig.]
squad (skwŏd) ►*n.* **1.** A small group of people

organized in a common activity. **2.** The smallest tactical military unit. **3.** A small police unit. **4.** An athletic team. [< VLat. **exquadra*, SQUARE.]

squad car ►*n.* A police automobile connected by radio with headquarters.

squad•ron (skwŏd′rən) ►*n.* **1.** A naval unit consisting of two or more divisions of a fleet. **2.** A basic tactical air force unit. [Ital. *squadrone*, augmentative of *squadra*, SQUAD.]

squal•id (skwŏl′ĭd) ►*adj.* **1.** Dirty and wretched. **2.** Morally repulsive; sordid. [Lat. *squālidus*.] —**squal′id•ly** *adv.* —**squal′id•ness** *n.*

squall[1] (skwôl) ►*n.* A loud harsh cry. [Prob. of Scand. orig.] —**squall** *v.*

squall[2] (skwôl) ►*n.* A brief sudden violent windstorm, often with rain or snow. [Prob. of Scand. orig.] —**squall′y** *adj.*

squal•or (skwŏl′ər) ►*n.* A filthy and wretched condition. [Lat. *squālor*.]

squa•mous (skwā′məs, skwä′-) ►*adj.* Covered with or resembling scales. [< Lat. *squāma*, scale.]

squan•der (skwŏn′dər) ►*v.* To spend or use extravagantly. See Syns at **waste.** [?]

Squan•to (skwŏn′tō). d. 1622. Native American who helped the English colonists in Massachusetts.

square (skwâr) ►*n.* **1.** A plane figure having four equal sides. **2.** Something having an equal-sided rectangular form. **3.** An instrument for drawing or testing right angles. **4.** *Math.* The product of a number or quantity multiplied by itself. **5a.** An open area at the intersection of two or more streets. **b.** A rectangular space enclosed by streets; block. **6.** *Slang* A dull, rigidly conventional person. ►*adj.* **squar•er, squar•est 1.** Having four equal sides and four right angles. **2.** Forming a right angle. **3a.** Expressed in units measuring area: *square feet.* **b.** Having a specified length in each of two equal dimensions. **4.** Like a square in form: *a square house.* **5.** Honest; direct: *a square answer.* **6.** Just; equitable: *a square deal.* **7.** Paid up; settled. **8.** Even; tied. **9.** *Slang* Rigidly conventional. ►*v.* **squared, squar•ing 1.** To cut to a square or rectangular shape. **2.** To conform; agree: *a story that did not square with the facts.* **3.** To bring into balance; settle: *square a debt.* **4.** *Math.* To multiply a number or quantity by itself. [< VLat. **exquadra* < Lat. *quadrum*, a square.] —**square′ly** *adv.* —**square′ness** *n.*

square bracket ►*n.* See **bracket** 3.

square dance ►*n.* A dance in which sets of four couples form squares. —**square′-dance′** *v.* —**square dancer** *n.*

square knot ►*n.* A double knot in which the loose ends are parallel to the standing parts, usu. used to join the ends of two lines.

square meal ►*n.* A substantial nourishing meal.

square-rigged (skwâr′rĭgd′) ►*adj. Naut.* Fitted with square sails as the principal sails.

square-rig•ger (skwâr′rĭg′ər) ►*n. Naut.* A square-rigged vessel.

square root ►*n. Math.* A divisor of a quantity that when squared gives the quantity.

squash[1] (skwŏsh, skwôsh) ►*n.* **1.** Any of various plants related to the pumpkins and gourds. **2.** The fleshy fruit of a squash, eaten as a vegetable. [< Narragansett *askútasquash*.]

squash[2] (skwŏsh, skwôsh) ►*v.* **1.** To beat, squeeze, or flatten into a pulp. See Syns at **crush. 2.** To suppress; quash. ►*n.* **1.** The impact or sound of squashing. **2.** A crush or press, as of people. **3.** A game played in a closed walled court with rackets and a hard rubber ball. [< OFr. *esquasser*.] —**squash′i•ness** *n.* —**squash′y** *adj.*

squat (skwŏt) ►*v.* **squat•ted, squat•ting 1.** To sit in a crouching position with the hams resting on or near the heels. **2.** To settle on unoccupied land without legal claim. **3.** To occupy a given piece of public land in order to acquire title to it. ►*adj.* **squat•ter, squat•test 1.** Short and thick. **2.** Crouched in a squatting position. ►*n.* The act or posture of squatting. [< OFr. *esquatir*, crush.] —**squat′ter** *n.*

squaw (skwô) ►*n. Offensive* A Native American woman. [Massachusett *squa*.]

squawk (skwôk) ►*v.* **1.** To utter a harsh cry; screech. **2.** *Informal* To complain noisily or peevishly. [Imit.] —**squawk** *n.*

squeak (skwēk) ►*v.* To utter or give forth a thin, high-pitched cry or sound. [ME *squeken*.] —**squeak** *n.* —**squeak′i•ly** *adv.* —**squeak′i•ness** *n.* —**squeak′y** *adj.*

squeal (skwēl) ►*v.* **1.** To utter with or produce a loud shrill cry or sound. **2.** *Slang* To turn informer. [ME *squelen*.] —**squeal** *n.* —**squeal′er** *n.*

squea•mish (skwē′mĭsh) ►*adj.* **1a.** Easily nauseated or sickened. **b.** Nauseated. **2.** Easily shocked or disgusted. **3.** Excessively fastidious. [< AN *escoymous*.] —**squea′mish•ly** *adv.* —**squea′mish•ness** *n.*

squee•gee (skwē′jē) ►*n.* A tool with a rubber or leather blade set perpendicular to a handle, used to remove water from a flat surface, as a window. [Poss. < alteration of SQUEEZE.] —**squee′gee** *v.*

squeeze (skwēz) ►*v.* **squeezed, squeez•ing 1.** To press together; compress. **2.** To press gently, as in affection: *squeezed her hand.* **3.** To exert pressure. **4.** To extract by applying pressure: *squeeze juice from a lemon.* **5.** To force by pressure; cram. ►*n.* **1.** An act of squeezing. **2.** An amount squeezed. [< OE *cwȳsan*.] —**squeez′er** *n.*

squelch (skwĕlch) ►*v.* **1.** To crush by or as if by trampling; squash. **2.** To put down or silence, as with a crushing retort. **3.** To produce a splashing, squishing, or sucking sound. [Prob. imit.] —**squelch** *n.*

squib (skwĭb) ►*n.* **1a.** A small firecracker. **b.** A firecracker that burns but does not explode. **2.** A brief witty writing or speech. [Prob. imit.]

squid (skwĭd) ►*n., pl.* **squids** or **squid.** A marine mollusk with a long body and ten arms surrounding the mouth. [?]

squig•gle (skwĭg′əl) ►*n.* A small wiggly mark or scrawl. ►*v.* **-gled, -gling.** To squirm and wriggle. [Perh. blend of SQUIRM and WIGGLE.] —**squig′gly** *adj.*

squint (skwĭnt) ►*v.* **1a.** To look with the eyes partly closed, as in bright sunlight. **b.** To close (the eyes) partly. **2.** To be affected with strabismus. [< ME *asquint*, looking sidelong.] —**squint** *n.* —**squint′y** *adj.*

squire (skwīr) ►*n.* **1.** A man who attends or escorts a woman; gallant. **2.** An English country gentleman. **3.** A judge or other local dignitary. **4.** A young nobleman attendant upon and

ranked next below a knight. ►*v.* **squired, squir•ing.** To attend as a squire; escort. [< OFr. *esquier*, ESQUIRE.]
squirm (skwûrm) ►*v.* **1.** To twist about in a wriggling motion; writhe. **2.** To feel or exhibit signs of humiliation or embarrassment. **3.** To fidget. [?] —**squirm** *n.* —**squirm′er** *n.* —**squirm′y** *adj.*
squir•rel (skwûr′əl, skwŭr′-) ►*n.* **1.** Any of various arboreal rodents with gray or reddish-brown fur and a long bushy tail. **2.** The fur of a squirrel. [< Gk. *skiouros.*]
squirt (skwûrt) ►*v.* To eject (liquid) in a thin swift stream or jet. ►*n.* **1.** A device for squirting. **2.** A squirted jet. **3.** A small or young person; pipsqueak. [ME *squirten.*]
squish (skwĭsh) ►*v.* **1.** To crush or squash. **2.** To emit the gurgling or sucking sound of soft mud being walked on. [Prob. < SQUASH².] —**squish** *n.* —**squish′y** *adj.*
Sr ► The symbol for the element **strontium.**
Sr. ►*abbr.* **1.** or **sr.** senior **2.** señor **3.** *Eccles.* sister (title)
Sri Lan•ka (srē läng′kə). Formerly **Cey•lon** (sĭ-lŏn′, sā-). An island country in the Indian Ocean off SE India. Cap. Colombo. Pop. 17,865,000. —**Sri Lan′kan** *adj. & n.*
SRO ►*abbr.* **1.** single room occupancy **2.** standing room only
SSA ►*abbr.* Social Security Administration
SSE ►*abbr.* south-southeast
SSN ►*abbr.* Social Security number
SSRI ►*abbr.* selective serotonin reuptake inhibitor
SSW ►*abbr.* south-southwest
ST ►*abbr.* standard time
st. ►*abbr.* **1.** statute **2.** stone (weight)
St. ►*abbr.* **1.** saint **2.** state **3.** strait **4.** street
-st ►*suff.* Var. of **-est².**
stab (stăb) ►*v.* **stabbed, stab•bing 1.** To pierce or wound with or as if with a pointed weapon. **2.** To thrust with or as if with a pointed weapon. ►*n.* **1.** An act of stabbing. **2.** A wound inflicted with a pointed weapon. **3.** A sudden piercing pain. **4.** An attempt; try. [ME *stabben.*]
sta•bi•lize (stā′bə-līz′) ►*v.* **-lized, -liz•ing 1.** To make or become stable. **2.** To maintain the stability of. —**sta′bi•li•za′tion** *n.* —**sta′bi•liz′er** *n.*
sta•ble¹ (stā′bəl) ►*adj.* **-bler, -blest 1a.** Resistant to change of position or condition. **b.** Maintaining equilibrium. **2.** Long-lasting; enduring. **3a.** Consistently dependable. **b.** Not subject to mental illness or irrationality. [< Lat. *stabilis.*] —**sta•bil′i•ty** *n.* —**sta′bly** *adv.*
sta•ble² (stā′bəl) ►*n.* **1.** A building for the shelter and feeding of domestic animals, esp. horses. **2.** All the racehorses of a single owner. ►*v.* **-bled, -bling.** To put or keep in a stable. [< Lat. *stabulum.*]
stac•ca•to (stə-kä′tō) ►*adj.* **1.** *Mus.* Cut short crisply; detached. **2.** Made up of short, sharp sounds: *staccato gunfire.* [Ital., p.part. of *staccare*, DETACH.] —**stac•ca′to** *n. & adv.*
stack (stăk) ►*n.* **1.** A large, usu. conical pile, as of straw. **2.** An orderly pile, esp. one arranged in layers. See Syns at **heap. 3.** A chimney or flue. **4.** A vertical exhaust pipe, as on a ship or locomotive. **5.** often **stacks** The area of a library in which most of the books are shelved. **6.** *Informal* A large quantity. ►*v.* **1.** To arrange in a stack; pile. **2.** *Games* To prearrange the order of (a deck of cards) so as to cheat. —***phrasal verb:* stack up** *Informal* To measure up or equal; compare. [< ON *stakkr.*] —**stack′er** *n.*
sta•di•um (stā′dē-əm) ►*n., pl.* **-di•ums** or **-di•a** (-dē-ə). A large, usu. open structure for sports events. [< Gk. *stadion*, unit of measure, racecourse.]
Staël (stäl), Madame de. Baronne Anne Louise Germaine Necker de Staël-Holstein. 1766–1817. French writer.
staff (stăf) ►*n., pl.* **staffs** or **staves** (stāvz) **1.** A stick or cane used as an aid in walking, as a weapon, or as a symbol of authority. **2.** *pl.* **staffs a.** A group of assistants to a person in authority. **b.** The personnel of an enterprise. **3.** A set of horizontal lines on which musical notes are written. ►*v.* To provide with a staff of employees. [< OE *stæf.*]
staff•er (stăf′ər) ►*n. Informal* A member of a staff.
staff sergeant ►*n.* A rank in the US Army, Air Force, and Marine Corps above sergeant.
stag (stăg) ►*n.* An adult male deer. ►*adj.* **1.** Of or for men only: *a stag party.* **2.** Pornographic: *stag films.* ►*adv.* Unaccompanied: *went to the dance stag.* [< OE *stagga.*]
stage (stāj) ►*n.* **1.** A raised and level floor or platform. **2a.** A raised platform on which theatrical performances are presented. **b.** The acting profession: *The stage is her life.* **3.** The scene of a noteworthy event. **4.** A resting place on a journey. **5.** A stagecoach. **6.** A level, degree, or period of time in the course of a process; step. **7.** One of the successive propulsion units of a rocket. ►*v.* **staged, stag•ing 1.** To exhibit or present on or as if on a stage. **2.** To produce or direct (a theatrical performance). **3.** To arrange and carry out: *stage an invasion.* —***idiom:* stage left** (or **right**) The area of a stage to one's left (or right) when facing the audience. [< VLat. **staticum* < Lat. *stāre*, stand.]
stage•coach (stāj′kōch′) ►*n.* A four-wheeled horse-drawn vehicle formerly used to transport mail and passengers.
stage•craft (stāj′krăft′) ►*n.* Skill in the techniques and devices of the theater.
stag•ger (stăg′ər) ►*v.* **1.** To move or cause to move unsteadily; totter. **2.** To cause to falter. **3.** To overwhelm, as with emotion or misfortune. **4.** To arrange in alternating or overlapping times or positions. ►*n.* A tottering or reeling motion. [< ON *stakra* < *staka*, push.] —**stag′ger•er** *n.* —**stag′ger•ing•ly** *adv.*
stag•ing (stā′jĭng) ►*n.* **1.** A temporary platform; scaffolding. **2.** The process of putting on a play.
stag•nant (stăg′nənt) ►*adj.* **1.** Not moving or flowing. **2.** Foul from standing: *stagnant ponds.* **3.** Lacking vitality; sluggish. **4.** Failing to change or develop. [< Lat. *stāgnāre*, STAGNATE.] —**stag′nan•cy** *n.* —**stag′nant•ly** *adv.*
stag•nate (stăg′nāt′) ►*v.* **-nat•ed, -nat•ing.** To be or become stagnant. [< Lat. *stāgnum*, swamp.] —**stag•na′tion** *n.*
stag•y also **stag•ey** (stā′jē) ►*adj.* **-i•er, -i•est.** Overly theatrical or dramatic. —**stag′i•ly** *adv.* —**stag′i•ness** *n.*
staid (stād) ►*adj.* **1.** Sedate and dignified; proper. **2.** Stodgy; stuffy. [< obsolete *staid*, p.part. of STAY¹.] —**staid′ly** *adv.*

stain (stān) ▸ *v.* **1.** To discolor, soil, or spot. **2.** To corrupt; taint. **3.** To color with a penetrating liquid dye or tint. ▸ *n.* **1.** A discolored or soiled spot or smudge. **2.** A blemish on one's character or reputation. **3.** A liquid substance, as a dye, used to stain. [< OFr. *desteindre*, deprive of color, and ON *steina*, paint.] —**stain′less** *adj.*
Syns: *stain, blot, brand, stigma, taint* **n.**

stained glass (stānd) ▸ *n.* Glass that is colored esp. for use in windows.

stainless steel ▸ *n.* Any of various steels alloyed with sufficient chromium to be resistant to corrosion or rusting.

stair (stâr) ▸ *n.* **1.** often **stairs** A staircase. **2.** One of a flight of steps. [< OE *stǣger*.]

stair•case (stâr′kās′) ▸ *n.* A flight of steps and its supporting structure.

stair•way (stâr′wā′) ▸ *n.* See **staircase.**

stair•well (stâr′wĕl′) ▸ *n.* A vertical shaft around which a staircase has been built.

stake (stāk) ▸ *n.* **1.** A pointed piece of wood or metal driven into the ground as a marker, barrier, or support. **2a.** A post to which an offender is bound for execution by burning. **b.** Execution by burning. **3.** often **stakes a.** Money or property risked in a wager or gambling game. See Syns at **bet. b.** The prize awarded the winner of a contest or race. **4.** A share or interest in an enterprise. ▸ *v.* **staked, stak•ing 1.** To mark the location or limits of with or as if with stakes. **2.** To fasten with or to a stake. **3.** To gamble; risk. **4.** To provide working capital for; finance. [< OE *staca*.]

stake•out (stāk′out′) ▸ *n.* Surveillance of an area, building, or person, esp. by police.

sta•lac•tite (stə-lăk′tīt′, stăl′ək-) ▸ *n.* An icicle-shaped mineral deposit hanging from the roof of a cavern. [< Gk. *stalaktos*, dripping.]

sta•lag•mite (stə-lăg′mīt′, stăl′əg-) ▸ *n.* A conical mineral deposit built up on the floor of a cavern. [< Gk. *stalagma*, a drop.]

stale (stāl) ▸ *adj.* **stal•er, stal•est 1.** Having lost freshness or flavor: *stale bread.* **2.** Lacking originality or spontaneity; trite. [ME, settled, clear (beer).] —**stale** *v.* —**stale′ly** *adv.* —**stale′ness** *n.*

stale•mate (stāl′māt′) ▸ *n.* A situation in which further action is blocked; deadlock. [Obsolete *stale* + MATE[2].] —**stale′mate′** *v.*

Sta•lin (stä′lĭn), **Joseph.** 1879–1953. Soviet politician. —**Sta′lin•ism** *n.* —**Stal′in•ist** *adj. & n.*

Joseph Stalin
photographed in 1936

Sta•lin•grad (stä′lĭn-grăd′) See **Volgograd.**

stalk[1] (stôk) ▸ *n.* A stem that supports a plant or plant part. [ME.]

stalk[2] (stôk) ▸ *v.* **1.** To walk with a stiff or haughty gait. **2.** To move threateningly or menacingly. **3.** To track (game). **4.** To pursue stealthily. [< OE *bestealcian*, move stealthily.] —**stalk′er** *n.*

stall[1] (stôl) ▸ *n.* **1.** A compartment for one animal in a barn or shed. **2a.** A booth or stand for selling wares. **b.** A small compartment: *a shower stall.* **3.** A pew in a church. ▸ *v.* **1.** To cause (an engine) accidentally to stop running. **2.** To come to a standstill: *Negotiations stalled.* [< OE *steall*, standing place.]

stall[2] (stôl) ▸ *v.* To employ delaying tactics (against). [< ME *stale*, decoy.] —**stall** *n.*

stal•lion (stăl′yən) ▸ *n.* An uncastrated adult male horse. [< AN *estaloun*, of Gmc. orig.]

stal•wart (stôl′wərt) ▸ *adj.* **1.** Physically strong; sturdy. **2.** Firm and resolute; stout. [< OE *stǣlwierthe*, serviceable.]

sta•men (stā′mən) ▸ *n., pl.* **-mens** or **sta•mi•na** (stā′mə-nə, stăm′ə-). The pollen-producing reproductive organ of a flower. [Lat. *stāmen*, thread.]

Stam•ford (stăm′fərd) A city of SW CT on Long Island Sound. Pop. 108,056.

stam•i•na (stăm′ə-nə) ▸ *n.* Physical or moral power of endurance. [Lat. *stāmina*, pl. of *stāmen*, thread, thread of life.]

sta•mi•nate (stā′mə-nĭt, -nāt′, stăm′ə-) ▸ *adj.* Having stamens but lacking pistils.

stam•mer (stăm′ər) ▸ *v.* To speak with involuntary pauses or repetitions. [< OE *stamerian*.] —**stam′mer** *n.* —**stam′mer•er** *n.*

stamp (stămp) ▸ *v.* **1.** To bring down (the foot) forcibly. **2.** To step on heavily, esp. so as to crush or extinguish. **3.** To shape or cut out with a mold, form, or die. **4.** To imprint or impress with a mark, design, or seal. **5.** To affix an adhesive stamp to. **6.** To mark; characterize. ▸ *n.* **1.** The act of stamping. **2a.** An implement or device used to stamp. **b.** The impression or shape stamped. **3.** A mark, design, or seal indicating ownership, approval, or completion. **4.** A postage stamp. **5.** A characterizing mark or quality. [ME *stampen*.]

stam•pede (stăm-pēd′) ▸ *n.* A sudden frenzied rush of panic-stricken animals or people. ▸ *v.* **-ped•ed, -ped•ing.** To participate in or cause a stampede. [Sp. *estampida*, uproar.]

stance (stăns) ▸ *n.* **1.** The position of a standing person or animal. See Syns at **posture. 2.** Point of view. [< VLat. **stantia* < Lat. *stāre*, stand.]

stanch[1] (stônch, stänch, stănch) also **staunch** (stônch, stänch) ▸ *v.* To stop or check the flow of a bodily fluid, esp. blood. See Usage Note at **staunch[1].** [< VLat. **stanticāre*, stop < Lat. *stāre*, stand.]

stanch[2] (stônch, stänch, stănch) ▸ *adj.* Var. of **staunch[1].** See Usage Note at **staunch[1].**

stan•chion (stăn′chən, -shən) ▸ *n.* An upright pole or post. [< OFr. *estanchon* < Lat. *stāre*, stand.]

stand (stănd) ▸ *v.* **stood** (sto͝od), **stand•ing 1.** To rise to an upright position. **2.** To assume or maintain an upright position. **3.** To place upright. **4.** To be placed or situated. **5.** To remain stable, valid, or intact. **6.** To be in a specific state or condition: *stands in awe of the achievement.* **7.** To remain motionless or inactive. **8.** To tolerate; endure. **9.** To undergo: *stand trial.* —***phrasal verbs:*** **stand for 1.** To represent; symbolize. **2.** To tolerate. **stand out** To be prominent or outstanding. **stand up** To remain valid, sound, or durable. ►*n.* **1.** The act of standing. **2.** A halt; standstill. **3.** A stop on a performance tour. **4.** A place designated for standing: *a witness stand.* **5.** A booth or counter for the display of goods for sale. **6.** A parking space reserved for taxis. **7.** A position or opinion one is prepared to uphold: *take a stand.* **8.** **stands** A grandstand; bleachers. **9.** A rack or prop for holding things upright. **10.** A growth of tall plants or trees. —***idioms:* stand up for** To side with; defend. **stand up to** To confront fearlessly. [< OE *standan.*]

stan•dard (stăn′dərd) ►*n.* **1.** A flag, banner, or ensign. **2.** An acknowledged basis for comparing or measuring; criterion. **3.** A degree or level of requirement, excellence, or attainment. **4.** A pedestal, stand, or base. [< OFr. *estandard*, rallying place, of Gmc. orig.] —**stan′dard** *adj.*

Syns: *standard, benchmark, criterion, gauge, measure, touchstone, yardstick* **n.**

stan•dard-bear•er (stăn′dərd-bâr′ər) ►*n.* One who is in the vanguard of a political or religious movement.

standard deviation ►*n.* A statistic used as a measure of the dispersion or variation in a distribution.

stan•dard•ize (stăn′dər-dīz′) ►*v.* **-ized, -iz•ing.** To cause to conform to a standard. —**stan′dard•i•za′tion** *n.*

standard of living ►*n.* A measure of the goods and services affordable by and available to a person or country.

standard time ►*n.* The time in any of 24 global time zones, usu. the mean solar time at the central meridian of each zone.

stand•by (stănd′bī′) ►*n.*, *pl.* **-bys 1.** One that can always be relied on, as in an emergency. **2.** One kept in readiness as a substitute. ►*adj.* Waiting to be assigned unfilled travel space, as on an airline. ►*adv.* On a standby basis: *flew standby to Seattle.*

stand•ee (stăn-dē′) ►*n.* One who stands, as in a theater.

stand-in (stănd′ĭn′) ►*n.* **1.** One who substitutes for a movie actor, as during technical adjustments. **2.** A substitute.

stand•ing (stăn′dĭng) ►*n.* **1.** A relative position in a group; rank. **2.** Status; reputation. **3.** Continuance in time; duration. ►*adj.* **1.** Remaining upright. **2.** Performed from a standing position: *a standing jump.* **3.** Permanent: *a standing army.* **4.** Remaining in force indefinitely: *a standing invitation.*

standing stone ►*n.* A prehistoric monument consisting of a single tall upright megalith.

Stan•dish (stăn′dĭsh′), **Miles** or **Myles.** 1584?–1656. English colonist in America.

stand•off (stănd′ôf′, -ŏf′) ►*n.* A tie or draw, as in a contest.

stand•off•ish (stănd-ô′fĭsh, -ŏf′ĭsh) ►*adj.* Aloof or reserved. —**stand•off′ish•ness** *n.*

stand•out (stănd′out′) ►*n.* *Informal* One that is outstanding or excellent.

stand•pipe (stănd′pīp′) ►*n.* A large vertical pipe into which water is pumped in order to produce a desired pressure.

stand•point (stănd′point′) ►*n.* A position from which things are considered; point of view. [Translation of Ger. *Standpunkt.*]

stand•still (stănd′stĭl′) ►*n.* A halt.

stand•up or **stand-up** (stănd′ŭp′) ►*adj.* **1.** Standing erect. **2.** Of or being a performer who works solo and without props: *a standup comedian.*

stank (stăngk) ►*v.* P.t. of **stink.**

Stan•ley or **Port Stan•ley** (stăn′lē). The administrative capital of the Falkland Is., in the E part. Pop. 1,557.

Stanley, Sir **Henry Morton.** 1841–1904. British journalist and explorer.

Stan•ton (stăn′tən), **Elizabeth Cady.** 1815–1902. Amer. feminist and social reformer.

Elizabeth Cady Stanton

stan•za (stăn′zə) ►*n.* One of the divisions of a poem, composed of two or more lines. [Ital.]

sta•pes (stā′pēz) ►*n.*, *pl.* **-pes** or **sta•pe•des** (stā′pĭ-dēz′). A small bone of the middle ear, shaped somewhat like a stirrup. [< Med.Lat. *stapēs*, stirrup.]

staph•y•lo•coc•cus (stăf′ə-lō-kŏk′əs) ►*n.*, *pl.* **-coc•ci** (-kŏk′sī, -kŏk′ī). A spherical parasitic bacterium usu. occurring in grapelike clusters and causing boils, septicemia, and other infections. [Gk. *staphulē*, bunch of grapes + -COCCUS.] —**staph′y•lo•coc′cal, staph′y•lo•coc•′cic** (-kŏk′sĭk, -kŏk′ĭk) *adj.*

sta•ple[1] (stā′pəl) ►*n.* **1.** A principal raw material or commodity. **2.** A major part, element, or feature. **3.** A basic dietary item. **4.** The fiber of cotton, wool, or flax, graded as to length and fineness. ►*adj.* **1.** Produced or stocked in large quantities. **2.** Principal; main. [Poss. < MDu. *stāpel*, emporium.]

sta•ple[2] (stā′pəl) ►*n.* **1.** A U-shaped metal loop with pointed ends, driven into a surface to hold something, as a bolt or wire. **2.** A thin piece of wire in the shape of a square bracket, used to fasten thin material, as paper. [< OE *stapol*, post.] —**sta′ple** *v.* —**sta′pler** *n.*

star (stär) ►*n.* **1a.** A luminous celestial body consisting of a mass of hot gas held together by its own gravity. **b.** A celestial body visible at night as a relatively stationary point of light. **2.** A graphic design having five or more radiating points. **3a.** An outstanding performer, esp. a leading actor or actress. **b.** A celebrity; luminary. **4.** An asterisk (*). **5.** **stars** The future; destiny. ►*v.* **starred, star•ring 1.** To ornament or mark with stars. **2.** To mark with an asterisk. **3.** To play the leading role in a theatrical or film production. [< OE *steorra.*] —**star′dom** *n.* —**star′ry** *adj.*

star•board (stär′bərd) ►*n.* The right-hand side of a ship or aircraft as one faces forward. [< OE

stēorbord.] —**star′board** *adj. & adv.*
starch (stärch) ►*n.* **1.** A nutrient carbohydrate, $(C_6H_{10}O_5)_n$, found notably in corn, potatoes, wheat, and rice and commonly prepared as a white tasteless powder. **2.** Any of various substances, such as natural starch, used to stiffen cloth, as in laundering. **3.** A food having a high starch content. ►*v.* To stiffen with starch. [< ME *sterchen*, stiffen.] —**starch′i•ness** *n.* —**starch′y** *adj.*
stare (stâr) ►*v.* **stared, star•ing.** To look directly and fixedly, often with a wide-eyed gaze. ►*n.* An intent gaze. [< OE *starian.*] —**star′er** *n.*
star•fish (stär′fĭsh′) ►*n.* Any of various, often spiny marine animals having five arms extending from a central disk.
star•gaze (stär′gāz′) ►*v.* **1.** To observe the stars. **2.** To daydream. —**star′gaz′er** *n.*
stark (stärk) ►*adj.* **-er, -est 1.** Bare; blunt: *stark truth.* **2.** Complete or utter; extreme: *stark poverty.* **3.** Harsh; grim. ►*adv.* Utterly: *stark naked.* [< OE *stearc*, severe.] —**stark′ly** *adv.* —**stark′ness** *n.*
star•let (stär′lĭt) ►*n.* A young film actress publicized as a future star.
star•light (stär′līt′) ►*n.* The light from the stars.
star•ling (stär′lĭng) ►*n.* An Old World bird with dark, often iridescent plumage, widely naturalized in North America. [< OE *stærlinc.*]
star•lit (stär′lĭt′) ►*adj.* Illuminated by starlight.
star•ry-eyed (stär′ē-īd′) ►*adj.* Naively enthusiastic, overoptimistic, or romantic.
Stars and Stripes (stärz) ►*n.* *(takes sing. or pl. v.)* The flag of the US.
start (stärt) ►*v.* **1.** To commence; begin. **2.** To move suddenly or involuntarily: *started at the noise.* **3.** To set into motion, operation, or activity. **4.** To introduce; originate. **5.** To enter in a race or game. **6.** To establish: *start a business.* ►*n.* **1.** A beginning. **2.** A place or time of beginning. **3.** A startled reaction or movement. [< OE **styrtan*, move suddenly.] —**start′er** *n.*
star•tle (stär′tl) ►*v.* **-tled, -tling 1.** To cause to make a quick involuntary movement, as in fright. **2.** To alarm or surprise. [< OE *steartlian*, kick.] —**star′tling•ly** *adv.*
start-up or **start•up** (stärt′ŭp′) ►*n.* **1.** The act of setting into operation or motion. **2.** A business that has recently begun operation.
starve (stärv) ►*v.* **starved, starv•ing 1.** To die or cause to die from prolonged lack of food. **2.** *Informal* To be hungry. **3.** To suffer from deprivation: *starving for love.* [< OE *steorfan*, die.] —**star•va′tion** *n.*
starve•ling (stärv′lĭng) ►*n.* One that is starving or being starved.
stash (stăsh) *Slang* ►*v.* To hide or store away in a secret place. ►*n.* A hidden or secret supply. [?]
-stasis ►*suff.* **1.** Stable state: *homeostasis.* **2.** Position: *metastasis.* [< Gk. *stasis*, standstill.]
stat. ►*abbr.* **1.** statistic **2.** statistics **3.** statuary **4.** statute
-stat ►*suff.* One that stabilizes: *rheostat.* [< Gk. *-statēs*, one that causes to stand.]
state (stāt) ►*n.* **1.** A condition of being. **2.** A mental or emotional condition. **3.** Social position or rank. **4.** The supreme public power within a sovereign political entity. **5.** A body politic, esp. one constituting a nation. **6.** One of the semiautonomous territorial and political subdivisions of a federated country, such as the US. ►*v.* **stat•ed, stat•ing.** To set forth in words; declare. [< Lat. *status.*] —**state′hood′** *n.*
state•craft (stāt′krăft′) ►*n.* The art of leading a country.
state•house (stāt′hous′) ►*n.* A building in which a state legislature holds sessions.
state•less (stāt′lĭs) ►*adj.* Not having citizenship in a state or nation.
state•ly (stāt′lē) ►*adj.* **-li•er, -li•est 1.** Dignified; formal. **2.** Majestic; lofty.
state•ment (stāt′mənt) ►*n.* **1.** The act of stating. **2.** Something stated. **3.** An abstract of a financial account. **4.** A monthly report sent to a debtor or bank depositor.
Stat•en Island (stăt′n). Formerly **Richmond.** A borough of New York City coextensive with **Staten Island** in New York Bay SW of Manhattan I. Pop. 378,977.
state•room (stāt′ro͞om′, -ro͝om′) ►*n.* A private compartment on a ship or train.
state•side (stāt′sīd′) ►*adj.* Of or in esp. the continental US. —**state′side′**
states•man (stāts′mən) ►*n.* **1.** A man who is a leader in national or international affairs. **2.** A man noted for disinterested public service. See Usage Note at **man.** —**states′man•like′** *adj.* —**states′man•ship′** *n.*
states•wom•an (stāts′wo͝om′ən) ►*n.* **1.** A woman who is a leader in national or international affairs. **2.** A woman noted for disinterested public service. See Usage Note at **man.**
stat•ic (stăt′ĭk) ►*adj.* **1.** Having no motion; being at rest. **2.** *Phys.* Relating to bodies at rest or forces that balance each other. **3.** Of or producing stationary electrical charges; electrostatic. **4.** Of or caused by random radio noise. ►*n.* **1.** Random noise, as crackling in a receiver or specks on a video screen, caused by atmospheric disturbance of the signal. **2.** *Informal* **a.** Interference. **b.** Angry criticism. [< Gk. *statos*, standing.] —**stat′i•cal•ly** *adv.*
sta•tion (stā′shən) ►*n.* **1.** The place where a person or thing stands or is assigned to stand; post. **2.** The place from which a service is provided or operations are directed: *a police station.* **3.** A stopping place along a route, esp. a depot. **4.** Social position; rank. **5.** An establishment equipped for radio or television transmission. ►*v.* To assign to a position. [< Lat. *statiō.*]
sta•tion•ar•y (stā′shə-nĕr′ē) ►*adj.* **1.** Not moving; fixed. **2.** Unchanging.
station break ►*n.* An intermission in a radio or television program for identification of the network or station.
sta•tion•er (stā′shə-nər) ►*n.* One who sells stationery. [Prob. < Lat. *statiō*, shop. See STATION.]
sta•tion•er•y (stā′shə-nĕr′ē) ►*n.* Writing materials, such as paper and envelopes.
station wagon ►*n.* An automobile having an extended interior with a third seat or luggage platform and a tailgate.
sta•tis•tic (stə-tĭs′tĭk) ►*n.* A numerical datum. —**sta•tis′ti•cal** *adj.* —**sta•tis′ti•cal•ly** *adv.*
sta•tis•tics (stə-tĭs′tĭks) ►*n.* **1.** *(takes sing. v.)* The mathematics of the collection, organization, and interpretation of numerical data. **2.** *(takes pl. v.)* Numerical data. [< Ger. *Statistik*, political science, ult. < Lat. *status*, state.] —**stat′is•ti′cian** (stăt′ĭ-stĭsh′ən) *n.*

stat•u•ar•y (stăch′o͞o-ĕr′ē) ►*n., pl.* **-ies.** Statues collectively.

stat•ue (stăch′o͞o) ►*n.* A form or likeness sculpted, modeled, or cast in material such as stone, clay, or bronze. [< Lat. *statuere*, set up. See STATUTE.]

stat•u•esque (stăch′o͞o-ĕsk′) ►*adj.* Suggestive of a statue, as in grace or dignity.

stat•u•ette (stăch′o͞o-ĕt′) ►*n.* A small statue.

stat•ure (stăch′ər) ►*n.* **1.** The natural height of a human or animal in an upright position. **2.** An achieved level; status. [< Lat. *statūra* < *stāre*, stand.]

stat•us (stăt′əs, stā′təs) ►*n.* **1.** Position relative to that of others; standing. **2.** High standing; prestige. **3.** The legal character or condition of a person or thing: *the status of a minor.* **4.** A state of affairs; situation. [Lat.]

status quo (kwō) ►*n.* The existing state of affairs. [Lat. *status quō*, state in which.]

stat•ute (stăch′o͞ot) ►*n.* **1.** A law enacted by a legislature. **2.** A bylaw or decree. [< Lat. *statuere*, *statūt-*, establish < *status*, position.]

statute mile ►*n.* The standard mile, 5,280 ft.

stat•u•to•ry (stăch′ə-tôr′ē, -tōr′ē) ►*adj.* Enacted, regulated, or authorized by statute.

staunch¹ (stônch, stänch) also **stanch** (stônch, stänch, stănch) ►*adj.* **-er, -est 1.** Firm and steadfast; true. **2.** Strong; solid. [< OFr. *estanchier*, STANCH¹.] —**staunch′ly** *adv.* —**staunch′ness** *n.*

Usage: *Staunch* is more common than *stanch* as the spelling of the adjective. *Stanch* is more common than *staunch* as the spelling of the verb.

staunch² (stônch, stänch) ►*v.* Var. of **stanch¹.**

stave (stāv) ►*n.* **1.** A narrow strip of wood forming part of the sides of a barrel, tub, or similar structure. **2.** A staff or cudgel. **3.** See **staff** 3. **4.** A stanza. ►*v.* **staved** or **stove** (stōv), **stav•ing 1.** To break in or puncture the staves of. **2.** To break or smash a hole in. —***phrasal verb:*** **stave off** To keep or hold off. [< STAVES.]

staves (stāvz) ►*n.* Pl. of **staff**.

stay¹ (stā) ►*v.* **1.** To continue to be in a place or condition. **2.** To stop moving; halt. **3.** To wait; pause. **4.** To endure or persist: *stay with a plan.* **5.** To postpone; delay. See Syns at **defer¹. 6.** To satisfy or appease temporarily. ►*n.* **1.** A stop or pause. **2.** A brief period of residence or visiting. [< Lat. *stāre*, stand.]

stay² (stā) ►*v.* To brace, support, or prop up. ►*n.* **1.** A support or brace. **2.** A strip of bone, plastic, or metal, used to stiffen a garment or part. **3. stays** A corset. [< OFr. *estaie*, a support, of Gmc. orig.]

STD ►*abbr.* sexually transmitted disease

std. ►*abbr.* standard

stead (stĕd) ►*n.* **1.** The place, position, or function of another person. **2.** Advantage: *stood them in good stead.* [< OE *stede.*]

stead•fast (stĕd′făst′, -fəst) ►*adj.* **1.** Fixed or unchanging; steady. **2.** Firmly loyal or constant. —**stead′fast′ly** *adv.* —**stead′fast′ness** *n.*

stead•y (stĕd′ē) ►*adj.* **-i•er, -i•est 1.** Firm in position or place; fixed. **2.** Direct and unfaltering; sure. **3.** Not changing or fluctuating; uniform: *steady work.* **4.** Not easily excited or upset. **5.** Reliable; dependable. ►*v.* **stead•ied, stead•y•ing.** To make or become steady. —**stead′i•ly** *adv.* —**stead′i•ness** *n.*

steak (stāk) ►*n.* **1.** A slice or slab of meat, esp. beef, usu. grilled or broiled. **2.** A thick slice of a large fish cut across the body. [< ON *steik.*]

steal (stēl) ►*v.* **stole** (stōl), **sto•len** (stō′lən), **steal•ing 1.** To take (the property of another) without right or permission. **2.** To get or effect surreptitiously or artfully: *steal a kiss.* **3.** To move, carry, or place stealthily. **4.** *Baseball* To advance safely to (another base) during the delivery of a pitch. ►*n.* **1.** The act of stealing. **2.** *Slang* A bargain. [< OE *stelan.*] —**steal′er** *n.*

stealth (stĕlth) ►*n.* **1.** The act of moving, proceeding, or acting in a covert way. **2.** Furtiveness. [ME *stelth.*] —**stealth′i•ly** *adv.* —**stealth′i•ness** *n.* —**stealth′y** *adj.*

steam (stēm) ►*n.* **1a.** The vapor phase of water. **b.** A mist of cooling water vapor. **2.** Pressurized water vapor used for heating, cooking, or to provide mechanical power. **3.** Power; energy. ►*v.* **1.** To produce or emit steam. **2.** To become or rise up as steam. **3.** To become misted or covered with steam. **4.** To move by means of steam power. **5.** *Informal* To become very angry; fume. **6.** To expose to steam, as in cooking. [< OE *stēam.*] —**steam′y** *adj.*

steam•boat (stēm′bōt′) ►*n.* A steamship.

steam engine ►*n.* An engine that converts the heat energy of pressurized steam into mechanical energy, esp. one in which steam drives a piston in a closed cylinder.

steam•er (stē′mər) ►*n.* **1.** A steamship. **2.** A container in which something is steamed. **3.** See **soft-shell clam.**

steam•fit•ter (stēm′fĭt′ər) ►*n.* One who installs and repairs heating, ventilating, refrigerating, and air-conditioning systems.

steam•roll•er (stēm′rō′lər) ►*n.* A machine equipped with a heavy roller for smoothing road surfaces. ►*v.* **1.** To smooth or level (a road) with a steamroller. **2.** To overwhelm or suppress ruthlessly; crush.

steam•ship (stēm′shĭp′) ►*n.* A large vessel propelled by steam-driven screws or paddles.

steam shovel ►*n.* **1.** A large, steam-driven machine for digging. **2.** See **power shovel.**

ste•a•tite (stē′ə-tīt′) ►*n.* See **soapstone.** [< Gk. *steatitis*, a precious stone.]

steed (stēd) ►*n.* A horse, esp. a spirited one. [< OE *stēda*, stallion.]

steel (stēl) ►*n.* **1.** A hard, strong, durable, malleable alloy of iron and carbon. **2.** Something, such as a sword, made of steel. **3.** A quality suggestive of steel: *nerves of steel.* ►*v.* **1.** To cover, plate, edge, or point with steel. **2.** To make hard or strong; brace. [< OE *stȳle.*] —**steel′i•ness** *n.* —**steel′y** *adj.*

steel drum ►*n.* A tuned metal percussion instrument fashioned from an oil barrel.

Steele (stēl), Sir **Richard.** 1672–1729. Irish-born English writer.

steel wool ►*n.* Fine fibers of steel matted or woven together to form an abrasive.

steep¹ (stēp) ►*adj.* **-er, -est 1.** Having a sharp inclination; precipitous. **2.** Excessive; stiff: *a steep price.* [< OE *stēap.*] —**steep′en** *v.* —**steep′ly** *adv.* —**steep′ness** *n.*

Syns: *steep, abrupt, precipitous, sheer* **adj.**

steep² (stēp) ►*v.* **1.** To soak or be soaked in liquid in order to cleanse, soften, or extract a given property from. **2.** To saturate: *steeped in history.* [ME *stepen.*]

stee•ple (stē′pəl) ►*n.* **1.** A tall tower rising from the roof of a building, such as a church. **2.** A spire. [< OE *stēpel.*]

stee•ple•chase (stē′pəl-chās′) ►*n.* A horse-race across open country or over an obstacle course. —**stee′ple•chas′er** *n.*

stee•ple•jack (stē′pəl-jăk′) ►*n.* A worker on very high structures, such as steeples.

steer[1] (stîr) ►*v.* **1.** To guide by a device such as a rudder or wheel. **2.** To direct the course or progress of. See Syns at **guide. 3.** To follow or move in a set course. [< OE *stēran.*] —**steer′er** *n.* —**steers′man** *n.*

steer[2] (stîr) ►*n.* A young ox, esp. one castrated before sexual maturity and raised for beef. [< OE *stēor.*]

steer•age (stîr′ĭj) ►*n.* **1.** The act or practice of steering. **2.** The section of a passenger ship providing the cheapest accommodations.

steg•o•saur (stĕg′ə-sôr′) also **steg•o•sau•rus** (stĕg′ə-sôr′əs) ►*n.* A herbivorous dinosaur having a double row of upright bony plates along the back. [Gk. *stegos*, roof + *sauros*, lizard.]

Stei•chen (stī′kən), **Edward Jean.** 1879–1973. Amer. photographer.

stein (stīn) ►*n.* A mug, esp. for beer. [Ger.]

Stein, Gertrude. 1874–1946. Amer. writer.

Stein•beck (stīn′bĕk′), **John Ernst.** 1902–68. Amer. writer; 1962 Nobel.

Stein•em (stī′nəm), **Gloria.** b. 1934. Amer. feminist, writer, and editor.

stel•lar (stĕl′ər) ►*adj.* **1.** Of or consisting of stars. **2a.** Of a star performer. **b.** Outstanding. [< Lat. *stēlla*, star.]

stem[1] (stĕm) ►*n.* **1a.** The main ascending axis of a plant; stalk. **b.** A stalk supporting another plant part, such as a leaf or flower. **2.** A connecting or supporting part, such as the tube of a tobacco pipe or the slender upright support of a wineglass. **3.** The main line of descent of a family. **4.** *Ling.* The main part of a word to which affixes are added. **5.** *Naut.* The prow. ►*v.* **stemmed, stem•ming 1.** To derive or originate. **2.** To make progress against (a force or flow). [< OE *stefn*, ship's stem.]

Syns: *stem, arise, derive, flow, issue, originate, proceed, rise, spring* **v.**

stem[2] (stĕm) ►*v.* **stemmed, stem•ming.** To stop or hold back by or as if by damming. [< ON *stemma.*]

stem•ware (stĕm′wâr′) ►*n.* Glassware mounted on a stem.

stench (stĕnch) ►*n.* A strong, foul odor; stink. [< OE *stenc*, odor.]

Syns: *stench, malodor, reek, stink* **n.**

sten•cil (stĕn′səl) ►*n.* A sheet, as of plastic, in which a letter or design has been cut so that ink or paint applied to the sheet will reproduce the pattern on the surface beneath. ►*v.* **-ciled, -cil•ing** or **-cilled, -cil•ling.** To mark or produce with a stencil. [< OFr. *estenceler*, adorn brightly.]

Sten•dhal (stĕn-däl′). Marie Henri Beyle. 1783–1842. French writer.

ste•nog•ra•phy (stə-nŏg′rə-fē) ►*n.* The art or process of writing or transcribing in shorthand. [< Gk. *stenos*, narrow.] —**ste•nog′ra•pher** *n.* —**sten′o•graph′ic** (stĕn′ə-grăf′ĭk) *adj.* —**sten′o•graph′i•cal•ly** *adv.*

sten•to•ri•an (stĕn-tôr′ē-ən, -tōr′-) ►*adj.* Extremely loud. See Syns at **loud.** [After *Stentor*, a loud herald in the *Iliad.*]

stencil
stencil (*left*) and painted motif

step (stĕp) ►*n.* **1a.** The single complete movement of raising one foot and putting it down in another spot, as in walking. **b.** A manner of walking; gait. **c.** A fixed rhythm or pace, as in marching. **2.** A short distance. **3a.** A rest for the foot in ascending or descending. **b. steps** Stairs. **4a.** One of a series of actions or measures taken to achieve a goal. **b.** A stage in a process. **5.** A degree in progress or a grade or rank in a scale. ►*v.* **stepped, step•ping 1.** To put or press the foot down. **2.** To shift or move by or as if by taking a step. **3.** To walk a short distance. **4.** To measure by pacing. —***phrasal verb:*** **step up 1.** To increase, esp. in stages: *step up production.* **2.** To come forward. —***idioms:*** **in step 1.** Moving in rhythm. **2.** In conformity with one's environment: *in step with the times.* **out of step 1.** Not moving in rhythm. **2.** Not in conformity with one's environment. [< OE *stæpe.*]

step– ►*pref.* Related through remarriage rather than by blood: *stepparent.* [< OE *stēop-.*]

step•broth•er (stĕp′brŭ*th*′ər) ►*n.* A son of one's stepparent.

step•child (stĕp′chīld′) ►*n.* A spouse's child by a previous marriage.

step•daugh•ter (stĕp′dô′tər) ►*n.* A spouse's daughter by a previous marriage.

step•fa•ther (stĕp′fä′*th*ər) ►*n.* The husband of one's mother and not one's natural father.

Ste•phen (stē′vən), Saint. d. c. A.D. 36. Christian martyr.

Stephen of Blois (blwä). 1097?–1154. King of England (1135–54).

step•lad•der (stĕp′lăd′ər) ►*n.* A portable ladder with a hinged supporting frame.

step•moth•er (stĕp′mŭ*th*′ər) ►*n.* The wife of one's father and not one's natural mother.

step•par•ent (stĕp′pâr′ənt, -păr′-) ►*n.* A stepfather or stepmother.

steppe (stĕp) ►*n.* A vast semiarid grass-covered plain, as found in SE Europe and Siberia. [< Russ. *step'.*]

step•ping•stone (stĕp′ĭng-stōn′) ►*n.* An advantageous position for advancement toward a goal.

step•sis•ter (stĕp′sĭs′tər) ►*n.* A daughter of one's stepparent.

step•son (stĕp′sŭn′) ►*n.* A spouse's son by a previous marriage.

ster. ►*abbr.* sterling

–ster ►*suff.* **1.** One that is associated with, participates in, makes, or does: *songster.* **2.** One that is: *youngster.* [< OE *-estre.*]

stere (stîr) ►*n.* A unit of volume equal to one cubic meter. [< Gk. *stereos*, solid.]

ster•e•o (stĕr′ē-ō′, stîr′-) ►*n., pl.* **-os 1.** A stereophonic sound-reproduction system. **2.** Stereophonic sound. —**ste′re•o′** *adj.*

stereo– ►*pref.* **1.** Solid: *stereotype.* **2.** Three-dimensional: *stereoscope.* [< Gk. *stereos.*]

ster•e•o•phon•ic (stĕr′ē-ə-fŏn′ĭk, stîr′-) ►*adj.* Of or used in a sound-reproduction system that uses two or more separate channels to give a more natural distribution of sound. —**ster′e•o•phon′i•cal•ly** *adv.*

ster•e•o•scope (stĕr′ē-ə-skōp′, stîr′-) ►*n.* An optical instrument with two eyepieces used to impart a three-dimensional effect to two photographs of the same scene taken at slightly different angles. —**ster′e•o•scop′ic** *adj.* —**ster′e•o•scop′i•cal•ly** *adv.*

stereoscope

ster•e•os•co•py (stĕr′ē-ŏs′kə-pē, stîr′-) ►*n.* The viewing of objects as three-dimensional.

ster•e•o•type (stĕr′ē-ə-tīp′, stîr′-) ►*n.* **1.** A conventional, oversimplified conception, opinion, or image. **2.** One regarded as embodying or conforming to a set image or type. **3.** A metal printing plate cast from a matrix that is molded from a raised printing surface. ►*v.* **1.** To make a stereotype of or from. **2.** To characterize by a conventional stereotype. —**ster′e•o•typ′ic** (-tĭp′ĭk), **ster′e•o•typ′i•cal** *adj.*

ster•ile (stĕr′əl, -īl′) ►*adj.* **1.** Incapable of producing offspring. **2.** Producing little or no vegetation. **3.** Free from microorganisms. **4.** Not productive or effective. [< Lat. *sterilis.*] —**ste•ril′i•ty** (stə-rĭl′ĭ-tē) *n.*

ster•il•ize (stĕr′ə-līz′) ►*v.* **-ized, -iz•ing.** To make sterile. —**ster′il•i•za′tion** *n.*

ster•ling (stûr′lĭng) ►*n.* **1.** British money. **2.** Sterling silver. ►*adj.* **1.** Of or consisting of British money. **2.** Made of sterling silver. **3.** Of the highest quality. [ME, silver penny.]

Sterling Heights. A city of SE MI, a suburb of Detroit. Pop. 117,810.

sterling silver ►*n.* An alloy of 92.5% silver with copper or another metal.

stern¹ (stûrn) ►*adj.* **-er, -est 1.** Hard or severe in manner or character. **2.** Firm or unyielding; uncompromising. **3.** Inexorable; relentless. [< OE *styrne.*] —**stern′ly** *adv.* —**stern′ness** *n.*

stern² (stûrn) ►*n.* The rear part of a ship or boat. [ME *sterne.*]

Sterne (stûrn), **Laurence.** 1713–68. British writer.

ster•num (stûr′nəm) ►*n., pl.* **-nums** or **-na** (-nə). A long flat bone that is situated along the center of the chest and articulates with the ribs; breastbone. [< Gk. *sternon.*]

ster•oid (stîr′oid′, stĕr′-) ►*n.* Any of numerous fat-soluble organic compounds having as a basis 17 carbon atoms arranged in 4 rings and including the sterols and many hormones. [STER(OL) + –OID.]

ster•ol (stîr′ôl′, stĕr′-) ►*n.* Any of a group of predominantly unsaturated solid alcohols of the steroid group, such as cholesterol, present in the fatty tissues of plants and animals. [< CHOLESTEROL.]

stet (stĕt) ►*v.* **stet•ted, stet•ting** *Print.* To nullify (a correction or deletion) in printed matter. [Lat., let it stand < *stāre*, stand.]

steth•o•scope (stĕth′ə-skōp′) ►*n.* An instrument used for listening to sounds produced within the body. [Gk. *stēthos*, chest + –SCOPE.]

Steu•ben (sto͞o′bən, styo͞o′-), Baron **Friedrich Wilhelm Ludolf Gerhard Augustin von.** 1730–94. Prussian-born Amer. Revolutionary leader.

ste•ve•dore (stē′vĭ-dôr′, -dōr′) ►*n.* A worker who loads or unloads ships. [Sp. *estibador* < *estibar*, stow.]

Ste•vens (stē′vənz), **Wallace.** 1879–1955. Amer. poet.

Ste•ven•son (stē′vən-sən), **Adlai Ewing.** 1835–1914. Vice President of the US (1893–97). His grandson **Adlai Ewing** (1900–65) was nominee for President (1952 and 1956).

Stevenson, Robert Louis Balfour. 1850–94. British writer.

stew (sto͞o, styo͞o) ►*v.* **1.** To cook (food) by simmering or boiling slowly. **2.** *Informal* To be in a state of anxiety or agitation. See Syns at **brood.** ►*n.* **1.** A dish, as of meat and vegetables, cooked by stewing. **2.** *Informal* Mental agitation. [< OFr. *estuver*, place in hot water.]

stew•ard (sto͞o′ərd, styo͞o′-) ►*n.* **1.** One who manages another's property, finances, or other affairs. **2.** One in charge of the household affairs of a large estate, club, hotel, or resort. **3.** A ship's officer in charge of provisions and dining arrangements. **4.** An attendant on a ship or airplane. [< OE *stigweard.*] —**stew′ard•ship′** *n.*

stew•ard•ess (sto͞o′ər-dĭs, styo͞o′-) ►*n.* A woman flight attendant. See Usage Note at **–ess.**

Stew•art (sto͞o′ərt, styo͞o′-), **James Maitland.** "Jimmy." 1908–97. Amer. actor.

stick (stĭk) ►*n.* **1.** A long slender piece of wood, esp. a branch cut from a tree or shrub. **2.** A sticklike implement, such as a cane or baton, used for a particular purpose. **3.** Something slender and often cylindrical in form: *a stick of dynamite.* **4.** A poke or thrust. **5. sticks** *Informal* A remote area; backwoods. **6.** *Informal* A stiff, boring, or spiritless person. ►*v.* **stuck** (stŭk), **stick•ing 1.** To pierce, puncture, or penetrate with a pointed instrument. **2.** To fasten by forcing an end or point into something. **3.** To fasten or attach with an adhesive, such as glue or tape. **4.** To fix or impale on a pointed object. **5.** To put, thrust, or push. **6.** To be or become fixed or embedded in place. **7.** To persist, endure, or persevere. **8.** To be or become blocked, checked, or obstructed: *stuck in the mud.* **9.** To confuse or puzzle. **10.** To project or protrude. —***phrasal verbs:*** **stick around** *Informal* To remain; linger. **stick up** To rob, esp. at gunpoint. [< OE *sticca.*]

stick•er (stĭk′ər) ►*n.* **1.** One that sticks, as an adhesive label. **2.** A thorn or prickle.

stick•ler (stĭk′lər) ►*n.* One who insists on something unyieldingly. [< ME *stightlen*, contend.]

stick shift ►*n.* An automotive transmission with a shift lever operated by hand.

stick-to-it•ive•ness (stĭk-to͞o′ĭ-tĭv-nĭs) ►*n.* *Informal* Unwavering tenacity.

stick•up (stĭk′ŭp′) ►*n.* *Slang* A robbery, esp. at gunpoint.

stick•y (stĭk′ē) ►*adj.* **-i•er, -i•est 1.** Sticking or tending to stick to a surface; adhesive. **2.** Warm and humid; muggy. **3.** *Informal* Painful or difficult: *a sticky situation.* —**stick′i•ly** *adv.* —**stick′i•ness** *n.*

stiff (stĭf) ►*adj.* **-er, -est 1.** Difficult to bend; rigid. **2.** Not moving or operating easily or freely: *stiff joints.* **3.** Drawn tightly; taut. **4a.** Rigidly formal. **b.** Lacking ease or grace. **5.** Not loose or fluid; thick: *stiff dough.* **6.** Blowing with strong steady force: *a stiff breeze.* **7.** Potent or strong: *a stiff drink.* **8.** Difficult; arduous. **9.** Harsh or severe: *a stiff penalty.* ►*n.* *Slang* A corpse. ►*v.* *Slang* To cheat (someone) of something owed. [< OE *stīf.*] —**stiff′en** *v.* —**stiff′ly** *adv.* —**stiff′ness** *n.*

stiff-necked (stĭf′nĕkt′) ►*adj.* Stubborn and arrogant or aloof.

sti•fle (stī′fəl) ►*v.* **-fled, -fling 1.** To extinguish or cut off: *stifle dissent.* **2.** To keep in or hold back; supress. **3.** To smother or suffocate. [ME *stifilen.*] —**sti′fling•ly** *adv.*

stig•ma (stĭg′mə) ►*n.*, *pl.* **stig•ma•ta** (stĭg-mä′tə, -măt′ə, stĭg′mə-) or **-mas 1.** A mark or token of infamy or disgrace. See Syns at **stain. 2. stigmata** Marks or sores corresponding to the crucifixion wounds of Jesus. **3.** *Bot.* The apex of a flower pistil, on which pollen is deposited. [< Gk., tattoo mark.] —**stig•mat′ic** (-măt′ĭk) *adj.*

stig•ma•tize (stĭg′mə-tīz′) ►*v.* **-tized, -tiz•ing 1.** To characterize as disgraceful; brand. **2.** To mark with stigmata or a stigma. —**stig′ma•ti•za′tion** *n.*

stile (stīl) ►*n.* A set or series of steps for crossing a fence or wall. [< OE *stigel.*]

sti•let•to (stĭ-lĕt′ō) ►*n.*, *pl.* **-tos** or **-toes.** A small dagger with a slender tapering blade. [Ital., dim. of *stilo*, dagger.]

still[1] (stĭl) ►*adj.* **-er, -est 1.** Free of sound. **2.** Low in sound; hushed or subdued. **3.** Not moving or in motion. **4.** Free from disturbance, agitation, or commotion. ►*n.* **1.** Silence; quiet. **2.** A still photograph, esp. one from a scene of a movie. ►*adv.* **1.** Without movement: *stand still.* **2.** Now as before; yet: *still unfinished.* **3.** In increasing amount or degree: *and still further complaints.* **4.** All the same; nevertheless. ►*v.* **1.** To make or become still. **2.** To allay; calm. [< OE *stille.*] —**still′ness** *n.*

still[2] (stĭl) ►*n.* **1.** An apparatus for distilling liquids, such as alcohols. **2.** A distillery. [< ME *distillen*, DISTILL.]

still•birth (stĭl′bûrth′) ►*n.* The birth of a dead child or fetus. —**still′born** *adj.*

still life ►*n.*, *pl.* **still lifes.** A painting, picture, or photograph of inanimate objects.

stilt (stĭlt) ►*n.* **1.** Either of a pair of long slender poles, each equipped with a raised footrest to enable the user to walk elevated above the ground. **2.** A tall supporting post, as for a dock. **3.** A long-billed American wading bird with black and white plumage. [ME *stilte.*]

stilt•ed (stĭl′tĭd) ►*adj.* Stiffly or artificially formal; stiff. —**stilt′ed•ly** *adv.*

stim•u•lant (stĭm′yə-lənt) ►*n.* **1.** An agent, esp. a drug, that temporarily arouses or accelerates physiological activity. **2.** A stimulus or incentive. **3.** An alcoholic drink. —**stim′u•lant** *adj.*

stim•u•late (stĭm′yə-lāt′) ►*v.* **-lat•ed, -lat•ing.** To rouse to activity or heightened action; excite. [< Lat. *stimulus*, goad.] —**stim′u•la′tion** *n.* —**stim′u•la′tive** *adj.*

stim•u•lus (stĭm′yə-ləs) ►*n.*, *pl.* **-li** (-lī′). Something that stimulates. [Latin, goad.]

sting (stĭng) ►*v.* **stung** (stŭng), **sting•ing 1.** To pierce or wound painfully with or as if with a sharp-pointed structure or organ. **2.** To cause to feel a sharp, smarting pain. **3.** To cause to suffer keenly. ►*n.* **1.** The act of stinging. **2.** The wound or pain caused by or as if by stinging. **3.** A sharp, piercing organ or part, as of a bee or wasp. [< OE *stingan.*] —**sting′er** *n.*

sting•ray (stĭng′rā′) ►*n.* A ray having a whiplike tail armed with one or more venomous spines.

stin•gy (stĭn′jē) ►*adj.* **-gi•er, -gi•est 1.** Giving or spending reluctantly. **2.** Scanty or meager. [Poss. < dial. *stingy*, stinging < STING.] —**stin′gi•ly** *adv.* —**stin′gi•ness** *n.*

stink (stĭngk) ►*v.* **stank** (stăngk) or **stunk** (stŭngk), **stunk, stink•ing 1.** To emit a strong foul odor. **2.** To be offensive or abhorrent. **3.** *Slang* To be extremely bad. ►*n.* **1.** A stench. See Syns at **stench. 2.** *Slang* A fuss; uproar. [< OE *stincan*, emit a smell.] —**stink′er** *n.*

stink•bug (stĭngk′bŭg′) ►*n.* Any of numerous insects that emit a foul odor.

stint (stĭnt) ►*v.* **1.** To restrict or limit, as in amount or number. **2.** To be frugal or sparing. ►*n.* **1.** A fixed or allotted amount of work. **2.** A limitation or restriction. **3.** A period of time spent in an activity. [< OE *styntan*, to blunt.] —**stint′er** *n.*

sti•pend (stī′pĕnd′, -pənd) ►*n.* A fixed and regular payment, such as a salary or allowance. [< Lat. *stīpendium*, soldier's pay.]

stip•ple (stĭp′əl) ►*v.* **-pled, -pling 1.** To draw, engrave, or paint in dots or short strokes. **2.** To apply (e.g., paint) in dots or short strokes. [< MDu. *stip*, dot.] —**stip′ple** *n.*

stip•u•late (stĭp′yə-lāt′) ►*v.* **-lat•ed, -lat•ing 1.** To lay down as a condition of an agreement. **2.** To guarantee or promise (something) in an agreement. [Lat. *stipulārī*, to bargain.] —**stip′u•la′tion** *n.*

stir[1] (stûr) ►*v.* **stirred, stir•ring 1.** To pass an implement through in circular motions so as to mix or cool the contents. **2.** To change or cause to change position slightly. **3a.** To rouse, as from indifference, and prompt to action. **b.** To provoke: *stir up trouble.* **4.** To excite strong feelings in. ►*n.* **1.** An act of stirring. **2.** A slight movement. **3.** A disturbance or commotion. [< OE *styrian*, agitate.] —**stir′rer** *n.*

stir[2] (stûr) ►*n.* *Slang* Prison. [?]

stir-fry (stûr′frī′) ►*v.* To fry quickly in a small amount of oil while stirring continuously.

stir•ring (stûr′ĭng) ►*adj.* **1.** Exciting; rousing. **2.** Active; lively. —**stir′ring•ly** *adv.*

stir•rup (stûr′əp, stĭr′-) ►*n.* A loop or ring hung

from either side of a horse's saddle to support the rider's foot. [< OE *stīgrāp*.]

stitch (stĭch) ►*n.* **1.** A link, loop, or knot formed by a threaded needle in sewing or surgical suturing. **2.** A single loop of yarn around a knitting needle. **3.** A method of sewing, knitting, or crocheting: *a purl stitch.* **4.** A sudden sharp pain. ►*v.* **1.** To fasten, join, or ornament with or as if with stitches. **2.** To sew. [< OE *stice*, a sting.] —**stitch′er** *n.* —**stitch′er•y** *n.*

stoat (stōt) ►*n.*, *pl.* **stoat** or **stoats** *Chiefly Brit.* The ermine, esp. in its brown color phase. [ME *stote*.]

sto•chas•tic (stō-kăs′tĭk) ►*adj. Math.* Involving or containing random variables. [< Gk. *stokhastēs*, diviner.]

stock (stŏk) ►*n.* **1.** A supply accumulated for future use; store. **2.** The total merchandise kept on hand by a commercial establishment. **3.** Domestic animals; livestock. **4a.** The capital or fund that a corporation raises through the sale of shares. **b.** The number of shares that each stockholder possesses. **5.** *Bot.* A trunk or main stem. **6a.** The original progenitor of a family line. **b.** The descendants of a common ancestor. **c.** Ancestry or lineage. **d.** A group of related languages. **7.** The raw material out of which something is made. **8.** The broth in which meat, fish, bones, or vegetables are simmered, used in preparing soup or sauces. **9.** A supporting structure, block, or frame: *a gun stock.* **10.** **stocks** A wooden device with holes for confining the ankles and sometimes the wrists, formerly used for punishment. **11.** A company of actors and technicians attached to a single theater and performing in repertory. **12.** Confidence or credence. ►*v.* **1.** To provide with stock. **2.** To keep and store for future sale or use. ►*adj.* **1.** Kept regularly in stock. **2.** Routine: *a stock answer.* [< OE *stocc*, tree trunk.]

stock•ade (stŏ-kād′) ►*n.* A defensive barrier made of strong posts or timbers driven upright side by side into the ground. [< Sp. *estaca*, stake, of Gmc. orig.]

stock•bro•ker (stŏk′brō′kər) ►*n.* One that acts as an agent in buying and selling stocks or other securities. —**stock′bro′ker•age** *n.*

stock car ►*n.* An automobile of a standard make modified for racing.

stock exchange ►*n.* **1.** A place where stocks, bonds, or other securities are bought and sold. **2.** An association of stockbrokers.

stock•hold•er (stŏk′hōl′dər) ►*n.* A shareholder.

Stock•holm (stŏk′hōlm′, -hōm′) The capital of Sweden, in the E part on the Baltic Sea. Pop. 684,576.

stock•ing (stŏk′ĭng) ►*n.* A close-fitting, usu. knitted covering for the foot and leg. [< ME *stokke*, leg covering.]

stocking cap ►*n.* A long tapering knitted cap.

stock market ►*n.* **1.** See **stock exchange.** **2.** The buying and selling of stocks.

stock•pile (stŏk′pīl′) ►*n.* A supply stored for future use. —**stock′pile′** *v.*

stock-still (stŏk′stĭl′) ►*adj.* Completely still; motionless.

Stock•ton (stŏk′tən) A city of central CA S of Sacramento. Pop. 210,943.

stock•y (stŏk′ē) ►*adj.* **-i•er, -i•est.** Solidly built; thickset. —**stock′i•ness** *n.*

stock•yard (stŏk′yärd′) ►*n.* A large enclosed yard in which livestock are kept until slaughtered or sold.

stodg•y (stŏj′ē) ►*adj.* **-i•er, -i•est 1a.** Dull, unimaginative, and commonplace. **b.** Prim or pompous; stuffy. See Syns at **dull.** **2.** Indigestible; heavy. [< *stodge*, to stuff.] —**stodg′i•ly** *adv.* —**stodg′i•ness** *n.*

sto•ic (stō′ĭk) ►*n.* **1.** One who is seemingly indifferent to or unaffected by pleasure or pain. **2. Stoic** A member of a Greek school of philosophy advocating the calm acceptance of all occurrences. ►*adj.* also **sto•i•cal** (-ĭ-kəl). Seemingly indifferent to or unaffected by pleasure or pain; impassive. [< Gk. *Stōikos* < *stoa (poikilē)*, (Painted) Porch, where Zeno taught.] —**sto′i•cal•ly** *adv.* —**sto′i•cism** *n.*

stoke (stōk) ►*v.* **stoked, stok•ing 1.** To stir up and feed (a fire or furnace). **2.** To tend a furnace, as on a steamship or steam locomotive. [< MDu. *stōken*, poke.] —**stok′er** *n.*

Stoke-on-Trent (stōk′ŏn-trĕnt′, -ôn-) A borough of W-central England S of Manchester. Pop. 252,914.

STOL ►*abbr.* short takeoff and landing

stole¹ (stōl) ►*n.* **1.** A long scarf worn by some members of the Christian clergy while officiating. **2.** A woman's long scarf of cloth or fur worn about the shoulders. [< Gk. *stolē*, garment.]

stole² (stōl) ►*v.* P.t. of **steal.**

sto•len (stō′lən) ►*v.* P.part. of **steal.**

stol•id (stŏl′ĭd) ►*adj.* **-er, -est.** Having or revealing little emotion; impassive. [Lat. *stolidus*, stupid.] —**sto•lid′i•ty** *n.*

sto•ma (stō′mə) ►*n.*, *pl.* **-ma•ta** (-mə-tə) or **-mas.** A small opening, esp. one of the minute pores in a leaf through which gases and water vapor pass. [< Gk., mouth.]

stom•ach (stŭm′ək) ►*n.* **1.** A large saclike digestive organ of the alimentary canal, located in vertebrates between the esophagus and the small intestine. **2.** The abdomen or belly. **3.** An appetite for food. **4.** Desire; inclination. ►*v.* To bear; tolerate. [< Gk. *stomakhos*.]

stom•ach•ache (stŭm′ək-āk′) ►*n.* Pain in the stomach or abdomen.

stom•ach•er (stŭm′ə-kər) ►*n.* A decorative garment formerly worn over the chest and stomach, esp. by women.

sto•mach•ic (stə-măk′ĭk) ►*adj.* Beneficial to or stimulating digestion in the stomach. —**sto•mach′ic** *n.*

stomp (stŏmp, stômp) ►*v.* To tread or trample heavily or violently (on). [< STAMP.]

stone (stōn) ►*n.* **1.** Hardened earthy or mineral matter; rock. **2.** A small piece of rock. **3.** A gem or precious stone. **4.** The hard covering enclosing the seed in certain fruits, such as the cherry. **5.** A mineral concretion in an organ, such as the kidney. **6.** *pl.* **stone** A unit of weight in Great Britain, 14 lbs. (6.4 kg). ►*v.* **stoned, ston•ing.** To pelt or kill with stones. [< OE *stān*.]

Stone, Lucy. 1818–93. Amer. feminist and reformer.

Stone Age ►*n.* **1.** The earliest known period of human culture, marked by the use of stone tools. **2.** *Slang* An extremely backward era or state.

stoned (stōnd) ►*adj. Slang* Drunk or intoxicated.

stone•wall (stōn′wôl′) ►*v. Informal* To refuse to answer or cooperate (with).

Lucy Stone

stone•ware (stōn′wâr′) ►*n.* A heavy, nonporous pottery.

ston•y (stō′nē) ►*adj.* **-i•er, -i•est 1.** Covered with or full of stones. **2.** Resembling stone. **3.** Cold; impassive: *a stony facial expression.* —**ston′i•ly** *adv.* —**ston′i•ness** *n.*

stood (stŏŏd) ►*v.* P.t. and p.part. of **stand.**

stooge (stōōj) ►*n.* **1.** The straight man to a comedian. **2.** A willing dupe. **3.** *Slang* A stool pigeon. [?]

stool (stōōl) ►*n.* **1.** A backless and armless single seat. **2.** A low bench or support for the feet. **3.** A toilet. **4.** Waste excreted from the bowel. [< OE *stōl.*]

stool pigeon ►*n.* **1.** *Slang* A person acting as a decoy or informer, esp. for the police. **2.** A pigeon used as a decoy.

stoop¹ (stōōp) ►*v.* **1.** To bend forward and down. **2.** To walk or stand with the head and upper back bent forward. **3a.** To lower or debase oneself. **b.** To condescend. ►*n.* The act, habit, or posture of stooping. [< OE *stūpian.*]

Syns: *stoop, condescend, deign* ***v.***

stoop² (stōōp) ►*n.* A small porch or staircase at the entrance of a house or building. [Du. *stoep*, front verandah.]

stop (stŏp) ►*v.* **stopped, stop•ping 1.** To close (an opening) by covering, filling in, or plugging up. **2.** To obstruct or prevent the flow or passage of. **3.** To bring or come to an end or halt. **4.** To desist from; cease. **5.** To restrain; prevent. **6.** To adjust a vibrating medium to produce a desired pitch. **7.** To make a brief halt, visit, or stay. ►*n.* **1.** The act of stopping or the condition of being stopped. **2.** A finish; end. **3.** A stay or visit. **4.** A place stopped at: *a bus stop.* **5.** A stopper. **6.** An f-stop. **7.** A mark of punctuation, esp. a period. **8a.** The act of stopping a string or hole on an instrument. **b.** A tuned set of pipes, as in an organ. [Prob. < VLat. **stuppāre*, to caulk < Gk. *stuppē*, tow.] —**stop′page** (stŏp′ĭj) *n.*

Syns: *stop, cease, desist, discontinue, halt, quit* ***Ant:*** *start* ***v.***

stop•cock (stŏp′kŏk′) ►*n.* A valve that regulates the flow of fluid through a pipe.

stop•gap (stŏp′găp′) ►*n.* A temporary expedient. See Syns at **makeshift.**

stop•light (stŏp′līt′) ►*n.* See **traffic light.**

stop•o•ver (stŏp′ō′vər) ►*n.* A place visited briefly in the course of a journey.

stop•per (stŏp′ər) ►*n.* A device, such as a plug, inserted to close an opening.

stop•watch (stŏp′wŏch′) ►*n.* A watch that can be instantly started and stopped by pushing a button and used to measure an exact duration of time.

stor•age (stôr′ĭj, stōr′-) ►*n.* **1a.** The act of storing or the state of being stored. **b.** A space for storing. **2.** The price charged for keeping goods stored.

storage battery ►*n.* A group of reversible or rechargeable electric cells acting as a unit.

store (stôr, stōr) ►*n.* **1.** A place where merchandise is offered for sale; shop. **2.** A stock or supply reserved for future use. **3. stores** Supplies, esp. of food, clothing, or arms. **4.** A storehouse. ►*v.* **stored, stor•ing 1.** To reserve or put away for future use. **2.** To fill, supply, or stock. **3.** To deposit in a storehouse for safekeeping. **4.** To copy (data) into memory or onto a storage device, such as a hard disk. [< Lat. *īnstaurāre*, restore.]

store•front (stôr′frŭnt′, stōr′-) ►*n.* **1.** The side of a store facing a street. **2.** A room in a commercial building at street level.

store•house (stôr′hous′, stōr′-) ►*n.* **1.** A building in which goods are stored; warehouse. **2.** An abundant source or supply.

store•keep•er (stôr′kē′pər, stōr′-) ►*n.* One who keeps a retail store or shop.

store•room (stôr′rōōm′, -rŏŏm′, stōr′-) ►*n.* A room in which things are stored.

sto•rey (stôr′ē, stōr′ē) ►*n.* *Chiefly Brit.* Var. of **story².**

sto•ried (stôr′ēd, stōr′-) ►*adj.* Celebrated or famous in history or story.

stork (stôrk) ►*n.* A large, chiefly Old World wading bird with long legs and a long straight bill. [< OE *storc.*]

storm (stôrm) ►*n.* **1.** An atmospheric disturbance with strong winds accompanied by rain, snow, or other precipitation. **2.** A violent disturbance or upheaval: *a storm of protest.* **3.** A sudden overwhelming attack. ►*v.* **1a.** To blow forcefully. **b.** To rain, snow, hail, or sleet. **2.** To be extremely angry. **3.** To move or rush violently or angrily: *stormed into the room.* **4.** To assault or overwhelm with sudden force. [< OE.] —**storm′i•ness** *n.* —**storm′y** *adj.*

sto•ry¹ (stôr′ē, stōr′ē) ►*n.*, *pl.* **-ries 1.** An account of an event or a series of events. **2.** A prose or verse narrative intended to entertain. **3.** A short story. **4.** A news report. **5.** An explanation: *What's the story on these bills?* **6.** A lie. [< Lat. *historia*, HISTORY.]

sto•ry² (stôr′ē, stōr′ē) ►*n.*, *pl.* **-ries 1.** A complete horizontal division of a building. **2.** The set of rooms on the same level of a building. [< Med.Lat. *historia*, picture, story < Lat. HISTORY.]

sto•ry•tell•er (stôr′ē-tĕl′ər, stōr′-) ►*n.* One who tells stories. —**sto′ry•tell′ing** *n.*

stoup (stōōp) ►*n.* A basin for holy water at a church. [< ON *staup*, cup.]

stout (stout) ►*adj.* **-er, -est 1.** Resolute or bold in character; valiant. **2.** Strong in body; sturdy. **3.** Substantial; solid. **4.** Thickset; fat. ►*n.* A strong, very dark beer or ale. [< OFr. *estout*, of Gmc. orig.] —**stout′ly** *adv.* —**stout′ness** *n.*

stout•heart•ed (stout′här′tĭd) ►*adj.* Brave; courageous. —**stout′heart′ed•ly** *adv.* —**stout′heart′ed•ness** *n.*

stove¹ (stōv) ►*n.* An apparatus in which electricity or a fuel is used to furnish heat, as for cooking or heating. [< MLGer. or MDu., heated room.]

stove² (stōv) ▸*v.* P.t. and p.part. of **stave.**

stove•pipe (stōv′pīp′) ▸*n.* **1.** A pipe used to conduct smoke from a stove into a chimney flue. **2.** A man's tall silk hat.

stow (stō) ▸*v.* **1.** To put or store away compactly. **2.** To fill by packing tightly. —***phrasal verb:* stow away** To be a stowaway. [< OE *stōw*, place.]

stow•a•way (stō′ə-wā′) ▸*n.* A person who hides aboard a vehicle, esp. a ship, to obtain free passage.

Stowe (stō), **Harriet (Elizabeth) Beecher.** 1811–96. Amer. writer.

STP ▸*abbr.* standard temperature and pressure

Str. ▸*abbr.* strait

stra•bis•mus (strə-bĭz′məs) ▸*n.* A visual defect in which one eye cannot focus with the other on an objective because of imbalance of the eye muscles. [< Gk. *strabizein*, squint.] —**stra•bis′mal, stra•bis′mic** *adj.*

strad•dle (străd′l) ▸*v.* **-dled, -dling 1.** To stand or sit with a leg on each side of. **2.** To appear to favor both sides of (an issue). [< STRIDE.] —**strad′dle** *n.* —**strad′dler** *n.*

strafe (strāf) ▸*v.* **strafed, straf•ing.** To attack with machine-gun fire from a low-flying aircraft. [< Ger. *strafen*, punish.]

strag•gle (străg′əl) ▸*v.* **-gled, -gling 1.** To stray or fall behind. **2.** To spread out in a scattered group. [ME *straglen*, wander.] —**strag′gler** *n.* —**strag′gly** *adj.*

straight (strāt) ▸*adj.* **-er, -est 1.** Extending continuously in the same direction without curving. **2.** Having no waves or bends. **3.** Erect; upright. **4.** Level or even. **5.** Direct and candid: *a straight answer.* **6a.** Honest; fair. **b.** Right; correct. **7.** Neatly arranged; orderly. **8.** Uninterrupted; consecutive: *five straight days.* **9.** Heterosexual. **10.** *Slang* Not being under the influence of alcohol or drugs. **11.** Not deviating from the normal or usual; conventional. **12.** Undiluted: *straight bourbon.* ▸*adv.* In a straight course or manner. ▸*n.* **1.** Something that is straight. **2.** A straightaway. **3.** *Games* A poker hand containing five cards of various suits in numerical sequence. **4a.** A conventional person. **b.** A heterosexual person. [ME < p.part. of *strecchen*, STRETCH.] —**straight′ly** *adv.* —**straight′ness** *n.*

straight angle ▸*n.* An angle of 180°.

straight•a•way (strāt′ə-wā′) ▸*n.* A straight course, stretch, or track, esp. the stretch of a racecourse from the last turn to the finish. ▸*adv.* (strāt′ə-wā′). At once; immediately.

straight•edge (strāt′ĕj′) ▸*n.* A rigid flat rectangular bar with a straight edge for testing or drawing straight lines.

straight•en (strāt′n) ▸*v.* To make or become straight or straighter. —***phrasal verb:* straighten out** To reform or correct. —**straight′en•er** *n.*

straight•for•ward (strāt-fôr′wərd) ▸*adj.* **1.** Direct. **2.** Honest; frank. ▸*adv.* In a direct or frank manner. —**straight•for′ward•ly** *adv.* —**straight•for′ward•ness** *n.*

straight man ▸*n.* An actor who serves as a foil for a comedian.

straight razor ▸*n.* A razor consisting of a blade hinged to a handle into which it slips when not in use.

straight•way (strāt′wā′, -wā′) ▸*adv.* At once.

strain¹ (strān) ▸*v.* **1.** To pull, draw, or stretch tight. **2.** To exert or tax to the utmost. **3.** To injure or impair by overuse or overexertion; wrench. **4.** To stretch or force beyond the proper or legitimate limit. **5.** To pass through a filtering agent such as a strainer. **6.** To strive hard. ▸*n.* **1.** The act of straining. **2a.** A great effort, force, or tension. **b.** A great pressure, demand, or stress. **3.** A deformation produced by stress. [< Lat. *stringere*, draw tight.]

strain² (strān) ▸*n.* **1.** The collective descendants of a common ancestor. **2.** Ancestry; lineage. **3.** *Biol.* A group of organisms of the same species, having distinctive characteristics but not usu. considered a separate breed or variety. **4.** A kind or sort. **5a.** An inborn tendency or character. **b.** A streak; trace. See Syns at **streak. 6.** often **strains** *Mus.* A tune or air. [< OE *strēon.*]

strain•er (strā′nər) ▸*n.* **1.** One that strains. **2.** A device, such as a filter or sieve, used to separate liquids from solids.

strainer

strait (strāt) ▸*n.* also **straits 1.** A narrow channel joining two larger bodies of water. **2.** A position of difficulty: *in desperate straits.* ▸*adj.* **1.** *Archaic* Narrow. **2.** Strict, rigid, or righteous. [< Lat. *strictus*, p.part. of *stringere*, draw tight.]

strait•en (strāt′n) ▸*v.* **1.** To make narrow or restricted. **2.** To put into difficulties.

strait•jack•et also **straight•jack•et** (strāt′jăk′ĭt) ▸*n.* A jacketlike garment used to bind the arms tightly as a means of restraining a violent patient or prisoner.

strait-laced (strāt′lāst′) ▸*adj.* Excessively strict in behavior, morality, or opinions.

strand¹ (strănd) ▸*n.* A shore; beach. ▸*v.* **1.** To drive or be driven aground. **2.** To bring into or leave in a difficult or helpless position. [< OE.]

strand² (strănd) ▸*n.* **1.** Any of a number of fibers or filaments that have been twisted together, as to form a cable or rope. **2.** A ropelike string, as of beads. [ME *strond.*]

strange (strānj) ▸*adj.* **strang•er, strang•est 1.** Not previously known; unfamiliar. **2.** Out of the ordinary; unusual or striking. **3.** Not of one's own locality or kind; exotic. See Syns at **foreign. 4.** Not comfortable or at ease. **5.** Not accustomed or conditioned. [< Lat. *extrāneus*, foreign.] —**strange′ly** *adv.* —**strange′ness** *n.*

strang•er (strān′jər) ▸*n.* **1.** One who is neither a friend nor an acquaintance. **2.** A foreigner, newcomer, or outsider.

stran•gle (străng′gəl) ▸*v.* **-gled, -gling 1a.**

To kill by choking or suffocating. **b.** To smother. **2.** To suppress or stifle. [< Gk. *strangalē*, halter.] —**stran′gler** *n.*

stran•gu•late (străng′gyə-lāt′) ►*v.* **-lat•ed, -lat•ing 1.** To strangle. **2.** *Pathol.* To constrict so as to cut off the flow of blood or other fluid. [Lat. *strangulāre*, STRANGLE.] —**stran′gu•la′tion** *n.*

strap (străp) ►*n.* A long narrow strip of pliant material, such as leather, often with a fastener for binding or securing objects. ►*v.* **strapped, strap•ping 1.** To fasten or secure with a strap. **2.** To beat with a strap. **3.** To strop (a razor). [< STROP.]

strap•less (străp′lĭs) ►*adj.* Having no strap or straps. ►*n.* A strapless garment.

strapped (străpt) ►*adj. Informal* In financial need.

strap•ping (străp′ĭng) ►*adj.* Tall and sturdy; robust.

Stras•bourg (sträs′bo͝org′, sträz-bo͝or′) A city of NE France near the German border. Pop. 252,274.

stra•ta (strā′tə, străt′ə) ►*n.* Pl. of **stratum.**

strat•a•gem (străt′ə-jəm) ►*n.* **1.** A maneuver designed to deceive or surprise an enemy. **2.** A scheme for achieving an objective. [< Gk. *stratēgēma* < *stratēgos*, general : *stratos*, army + *agein*, lead.]

strat•e•gy (străt′ə-jē) ►*n., pl.* **-gies 1.** The overall planning and conduct of large-scale military operations. **2.** A plan of action. See Syns at **plan. 3.** The art or skill of using stratagems, as in politics and business. —**stra•te′gic** (strə-tē′jĭk) *adj.* —**stra•te′gi•cal•ly** *adv.* —**strat′e•gist** *n.*

Strat•ford-up•on-Av•on (străt′fərd-ə-pŏn-ā′vən, -pôn-) also **Strat•ford-on-Av•on** (-ŏn-, -ôn-). A municipal borough of central England; birthplace of William Shakespeare. Pop. 21,100.

strat•i•fy (străt′ə-fī′) ►*v.* **-fied, -fy•ing 1.** To form, arrange, or deposit in layers. **2.** To arrange or separate into social levels. —**strat′i•fi•ca′tion** *n.*

strat•o•sphere (străt′ə-sfîr′) ►*n.* The region of the atmosphere above the troposphere and below the mesosphere. [Fr. *stratosphère.*] —**strat′o•spher′ic** (-sfîr′ĭk, -sfĕr′-) *adj.*

stra•tum (strā′təm, străt′əm) ►*n., pl.* **-ta** (-tə) or **-tums 1.** A horizontal layer of material, esp. one of several layers of sedimentary rock. **2.** A level of society composed of people with similar social or economic status. [< Lat. *sternere, strāt-*, spread.]

Usage: The standard singular form is *stratum;* the standard plural is *strata* (or sometimes *stratums*) but not *stratas.*

stra•tus (strā′təs, străt′əs) ►*n., pl.* **-ti** (-tī). A low-altitude cloud formation consisting of a horizontal layer of gray clouds. [< Lat. *strātus*, p.part. of *sternere*, spread.]

Strauss (strous, shtrous). **Johann** (1804–49), "the Elder," and **Johann** (1825–99), "the Younger." Austrian composers.

Strauss, Richard. 1864–1949. German composer.

Stra•vin•sky (strə-vĭn′skē), **Igor Fyodorovich.** 1882–1971. Russian-born composer.

straw (strô) ►*n.* **1a.** Stalks of threshed grain. **b.** A single stalk of threshed grain. **2.** A slender tube used for sucking up a liquid. **3.** Something of little value. [< OE *strēaw.*]

straw•ber•ry (strô′bĕr′ē) ►*n.* **1.** A low-growing plant having white flowers and red, fleshy, edible fruit. **2.** The fruit itself.

straw boss ►*n. Informal* A temporary boss or crew leader.

straw vote ►*n.* An unofficial vote or poll.

stray (strā) ►*v.* **1a.** To move away from or go beyond established limits. **b.** To become lost. **2.** To wander about; roam. **3.** To go morally astray; err. **4.** To digress. See Syns at **swerve.** ►*n.* One that has strayed, esp. a loose domestic animal. ►*adj.* **1.** Straying or having strayed; wandering or lost. **2.** Scattered or separate. [< OFr. *estraier.*]

streak (strēk) ►*n.* **1.** A line, mark, or band differentiated by color or texture from its surroundings. **2.** A slight contrasting element; trace. **3.** *Informal* An unbroken stretch; run. ►*v.* **1.** To mark with or form streaks. **2.** To move at high speed; rush. [< OE *strica.*] —**streak′er** *n.* —**streak′y** *adj.*

Syns: *streak, strain, vein* **n.**

stream (strēm) ►*n.* **1.** A flow of water in a channel or bed, as a brook. **2.** A steady current of a fluid. **3.** A steady flow or succession. See Syns at **flow.** ►*v.* **1.** To flow in or as if in a stream. **2.** To pour forth or give off a stream. **3.** To come or go in large numbers. **4.** To extend, wave, or float outward. **5.** To leave a continuous trail of light. [< OE *strēam.*]

stream•er (strē′mər) ►*n.* **1a.** A long narrow flag or banner. **b.** A long narrow strip of material. **2.** A newspaper headline that runs across a full page.

stream•line (strēm′līn′) ►*v.* **1.** To construct so as to offer the least resistance to fluid flow. **2.** To improve the efficiency of. —**stream′lined′** *adj.*

street (strēt) ►*n.* **1.** A public thoroughfare in a city or town. **2.** The people living, working, or gathering along a street. [< LLat. *strāta*, paved road < Lat. *sternere*, extend.]

street•car (strēt′kär′) ►*n.* A public vehicle operated on rails along the streets of a city.

street•walk•er (strēt′wô′kər) ►*n.* A prostitute.

strength (strĕngkth, strĕngth, strĕnth) ►*n.* **1.** The quality of being strong. **2.** The power to resist attack; impregnability. **3.** The power to resist strain or stress; durability. **4.** Moral or intellectual power. **5.** Capacity or potential for action. **6.** Power or force, as of an army. **7.** Degree of intensity, force, or potency. **8.** Effective or binding force: *the strength of an argument.* [< OE *strengthu.*]

strength•en (strĕngk′thən, strĕng′-, strĕn′-) ►*v.* To make or become strong or stronger. —**strength′en•er** *n.*

stren•u•ous (strĕn′yo͞o-əs) ►*adj.* **1.** Requiring great effort, energy, or exertion. **2.** Vigorously active. [< Lat. *strēnuus.*] —**stren′u•ous•ly** *adv.* —**stren′u•ous•ness** *n.*

strep throat (strĕp) ►*n.* A throat infection, often epidemic, caused by streptococci and characterized by fever and inflamed tonsils. [< STREPTOCOCCUS.]

strep•to•coc•cus (strĕp′tə-kŏk′əs) ►*n., pl.* **-coc•ci** (-kŏk′sī, -kŏk′ī). Any of various rounded bacteria that occur in pairs or chains and cause various diseases. [Gk. *streptos*, twisted + -COCCUS.] —**strep′to•coc′cal** *adj.*

strep•to•my•cin (strĕp′tə-mī′sĭn) ►*n.* An antibiotic used esp. to treat tuberculosis. [Gk. *streptos*, twisted + *mukēs*, fungus + -IN.]

stress (strĕs) ►*n.* **1.** Importance, significance, or emphasis placed on something. See Syns at **emphasis. 2.** The relative force with which a word or sound is spoken. **3.** *Mus.* Accent or a mark representing it. **4.** *Phys.* An applied force or system of forces that tends to strain or deform a body. **5.** A state of extreme difficulty, pressure, or strain. ►*v.* **1.** To place emphasis on. **2.** To pronounce with a stress. **3.** To subject to pressure or strain. **4.** To subject to mechanical stress. [< VLat. **strictia*, narrowness < Lat. *stringere*, draw tight.] —**stress′ful** *adj.*

stres•sor (strĕs′ər) ►*n.* An agent or condition that causes stress.

stretch (strĕch) ►*v.* **1.** To lengthen, widen, or distend. **2.** To cause to extend across a given space. **3.** To make taut; tighten. **4.** To reach or put forth; extend: *stretched out his hand.* **5.** To extend (oneself) to full length. **6.** To wrench or strain (e.g., a muscle). **7.** To extend or enlarge beyond the usual or proper limits. **8.** To increase the quantity of by admixture or dilution: *stretch a meal.* **9.** To prolong. ►*n.* **1.** The act of stretching or the state of being stretched. **2.** The extent to which something can be stretched. **3.** A continuous length, area, or expanse. **4.** A straight section of a racecourse or track. **5a.** A continuous period of time. **b.** *Slang* A term of imprisonment. ►*adj.* Made of an elastic material. [< OE *streccan.*] —**stretch′a•ble** *adj.* —**stretch′y** *adj.*

stretch•er (strĕch′ər) ►*n.* **1.** A litter used to transport the sick, wounded, or dead. **2.** One that stretches.

strew (stro͞o) ►*v.* **strewed, strewn** (stro͞on) or **strewed, strew•ing 1.** To spread here and there; scatter. **2.** To cover (a surface) with things scattered or sprinkled. **3.** To be or become dispersed over. [< OE *strēowian.*]

stri•a (strī′ə) ►*n., pl.* **stri•ae** (strī′ē) **1.** A thin narrow groove or channel. **2.** A thin line or band. [Lat.] —**stri′at′ed** (-ā′tĭd) *adj.* —**stri•a′tion** *n.*

strick•en (strĭk′ən) ►*v.* P.part. of **strike.** ►*adj.* **1.** Struck or wounded, as by a projectile. **2.** Afflicted, as with disease.

strict (strĭkt) ►*adj.* **-er, -est 1.** Precise; exact. **2.** Complete; absolute: *strict loyalty.* **3.** Kept within narrow limits: *a strict application of a law.* **4.** Rigorous in the imposition of discipline. **5.** Exacting; stringent. [< Lat. *strictus*, p.part. of *stringere*, draw tight.] —**strict′ly** *adv.* —**strict′ness** *n.*

stric•ture (strĭk′chər) ►*n.* **1.** A restraint, limit, or restriction. **2.** An adverse criticism. **3.** *Pathol.* An abnormal narrowing of a passage. [< LLat. *strictūra*, contraction.]

stride (strīd) ►*v.* **strode** (strōd), **strid•den** (strĭd′n), **strid•ing.** To walk with long steps. ►*n.* **1.** The act of striding. **2.** A single long step. **3.** often **strides** An advance. [< OE *strīdan.*] —**strid′er** *n.*

stri•dent (strīd′nt) ►*adj.* Loud, harsh, grating, or shrill. See Syns at **loud.** [< Lat. *strīdēre*, make harsh sounds.] —**stri′dence, stri′den•cy** *n.* —**stri′dent•ly** *adv.*

strife (strīf) ►*n.* **1.** Heated, often violent dissension; bitter conflict. **2.** A struggle, fight, or quarrel. **3.** Contention or competition between rivals. [< OFr. *estrif*, of Gmc. orig.]

strike (strīk) ►*v.* **struck** (strŭk), **struck** or **strick•en** (strĭk′ən), **strik•ing 1a.** To hit sharply, as with the hand, the fist, or a weapon. **b.** To inflict (a blow). **2.** To collide with or crash into. **3.** To attack or begin an attack. **4.** To afflict suddenly, as with a disease. **5.** To impress by stamping or printing. **6.** To produce by hitting some agent, as a key on a musical instrument. **7.** To indicate by a percussive sound: *The clock struck nine.* **8.** To produce (a flame or spark) by friction. **9.** To eliminate: *strike a statement from the records.* **10.** To discover. **11.** To reach; fall upon. **12.** To impress: *strikes me as a good idea.* **13.** To cause (an emotion) to penetrate deeply. **14a.** To make or conclude (a bargain). **b.** To achieve (a balance). **15.** To take on or assume (a pose). **16.** To set out: *strike out for new lands.* **17.** To engage in a strike against an employer. —***phrasal verbs:*** **strike out** *Baseball* **1.** To pitch three strikes to (a batter), putting the batter out. **2.** To be struck out. **strike up 1.** To start to play vigorously. **2.** To initiate or begin. ►*n.* **1.** An act of striking. **2.** An attack. **3.** A cessation of work by employees in support of demands made on their employer. **4.** A sudden achievement or discovery. **5.** *Baseball* A pitched ball counted against the batter, typically one swung at and missed or judged to have passed through the strike zone. **6.** The knocking down of all the pins in bowling with the first bowl of a frame. [< OE *strīcan*, stroke.] —**strik′er** *n.*

strike•break•er (strīk′brā′kər) ►*n.* A person who works or is hired during a strike.

strike•out (strīk′out′) ►*n. Baseball* An act of striking out.

strike zone ►*n. Baseball* The area over home plate through which a pitch must pass to be called a strike.

strik•ing (strī′kĭng) ►*adj.* Arrestingly or vividly impressive. —**strik′ing•ly** *adv.*

Strind•berg (strĭnd′bûrg), **(Johan) August.** 1849–1912. Swedish writer.

string (strĭng) ►*n.* **1.** A cord usu. made of fiber, used for fastening, tying, or lacing. **2.** Something shaped into a long thin line. **3.** A set of objects threaded together: *a string of beads.* **4.** A series; sequence. **5.** *Comp. Sci.* A set of consecutive characters. **6.** *Mus.* **a.** A cord stretched on an instrument and struck, plucked, or bowed to produce tones. **b.** also **strings** Stringed instruments collectively. **7.** also **strings** *Informal* A limiting or hidden condition. ►*v.* **strung** (strŭng), **string•ing 1.** To fit or furnish with strings or a string: *string a guitar.* **2.** To thread on a string. **3.** To arrange in a series. **4.** To fasten, tie, or hang with strings. **5.** To stretch out or extend. [< OE *streng.*] —**string′i•ness** *n.* —**string′y** *adj.*

string bean ►*n.* **1.** A tropical American plant having edible pods. **2.** The narrow green pod of this plant.

strin•gent (strĭn′jənt) ►*adj.* **1.** Imposing rigorous standards; severe. **2.** Constricted; tight. **3.** Characterized by scarcity of money or credit. [< Lat. *stringere*, draw tight.] —**strin′gen•cy** *n.* —**strin′gent•ly** *adv.*

string•er (strĭng′ər) ►*n.* **1.** One that strings. **2.** A heavy horizontal timber used as a support or connector. **3.** A part-time or freelance news correspondent.

strip[1] (strĭp) ▸*v.* **stripped, strip•ping 1a.** To remove the covering from. **b.** To undress. **2.** To deprive, as of honors or rank; divest. **3.** To remove all excess detail from. **4.** To dismantle piece by piece. **5.** To damage or break the threads of (e.g., a screw) or the teeth of (a gear). **6.** To rob or plunder. [< OE *bestrȳpan*, plunder.] —**strip′per** *n.*

strip[2] (strĭp) ▸*n.* **1.** A long narrow piece. **2.** A comic strip. **3.** An airstrip. **4.** A narrow space or area, as along a highway. [ME.]

stripe (strīp) ▸*n.* **1.** A long narrow band distinguished, as by color or texture, from the surrounding material or surface. **2.** A strip of cloth or braid worn on a uniform to indicate rank, awards received, or length of service. **3.** Sort; kind. ▸*v.* **striped, strip•ing.** To mark with stripes or a stripe. [Poss. < MDu. or MLGer. *strīpe*.]

strip•ling (strĭp′lĭng) ▸*n.* An adolescent youth. [ME.]

strip mall ▸*n.* A shopping complex containing a row of businesses that usu. open onto a common parking lot.

strip mine ▸*n.* An open mine, esp. a coal mine, whose seams are exposed by the removal of topsoil. —**strip′-mine′** *v.*

strip search ▸*n.* A bodily search in which a person is required to remove all clothing. —**strip′-search** *v.*

strip•tease (strĭp′tēz′) ▸*n.* A burlesque act in which a person slowly removes clothing, usu. to musical accompaniment.

strive (strīv) ▸*v.* **strove** (strōv), **striv•en** (strĭv′ən) or **strived, striv•ing 1.** To exert much effort or energy. **2.** To struggle; contend. [< OFr. *estriver* < *estrif*, STRIFE.]

strobe (strōb) ▸*n.* **1.** A strobe light. **2.** A stroboscope.

strobe light ▸*n.* A flash lamp that produces high-intensity short-duration light pulses. [< STROBOSCOPE.]

stro•bo•scope (strō′bə-skōp′) ▸*n.* Any of various instruments used to observe moving objects by making them appear stationary, as by pulsed illumination. [Gk. *strobos*, a whirling + -SCOPE.] —**stro′bo•scop′ic** (-skŏp′ĭk) *adj.*

strode (strōd) ▸*v.* P.t. of **stride.**

stroke[1] (strōk) ▸*n.* **1.** The act of striking; blow. **2.** A sudden occurrence or result. **3.** A sudden severe attack, as of paralysis. **4.** A sudden loss of brain function caused by a blockage or rupture of a blood vessel to the brain. **5.** An inspired or effective idea or act. **6a.** A single completed movement, as in swimming or rowing. **b.** A movement of a piston from one end of the limit of its motion to another. **7.** A single mark made by a writing implement, such as a pen. [ME.]

stroke[2] (strōk) ▸*v.* **stroked, strok•ing.** To rub lightly. ▸*n.* A light caressing movement. [< OE *strācian*.]

stroll (strōl) ▸*v.* To go for a leisurely walk. [Prob. Ger. dial. *strollen*.] —**stroll** *n.*

stroll•er (strō′lər) ▸*n.* **1.** One who strolls. **2.** A light four-wheeled carriage for transporting small children.

Strom•bo•li (strŏm′bə-lē, strōm′bō-) An island of S Italy off NE Sicily in the Tyrrhenian Sea.

strong (strông) ▸*adj.* **-er, -est 1.** Physically powerful. **2.** In good or sound health. **3.** Capable of withstanding force or wear. **4.** Having force or rapidity of motion: *a strong current.* **5.** Persuasive or forceful. **6.** Extreme; drastic. **7.** Intense in degree or quality. **8.** Having a specified number of members. **9.** Stressed or accented, as a word or syllable. [< OE *strang*.] —**strong′ly** *adv.*

strong-arm (strông′ärm′) ▸*adj. Informal* Coercive: *strong-arm tactics.*

strong•box (strông′bŏks′) ▸*n.* A stoutly made safe.

strong•hold (strông′hōld′) ▸*n.* A fortress.

strong interaction ▸*n.* A fundamental interaction between elementary particles that causes protons and neutrons to bind together in the atomic nucleus.

strong•man (strông′măn′) ▸*n.* A political figure who exercises control by force.

stron•ti•um (strŏn′chē-əm, -tē-əm, -shəm) ▸*n. Symbol* **Sr** A soft, silvery, easily oxidized metallic element, used in fireworks and various alloys. At. no. 38. See table at **element.** [< *Strontian*, Scotland.]

strontium 90 ▸*n.* A strontium isotope with a half-life of 28 years, present as a radiation hazard in nuclear fallout.

strop (strŏp) ▸*n.* A flexible strip of leather or canvas used to sharpen a razor. ▸*v.* **stropped, strop•ping.** To sharpen (a razor) on a strop. [< Gk. *strophos*, twisted cord.]

stro•phe (strō′fē) ▸*n.* A stanza of a poem. [Gk. *strophē*, a turning.] —**stro′phic** (strō′fĭk, strŏf′ĭk) *adj.*

strove (strōv) ▸*v.* P.t. of **strive.**

struck (strŭk) ▸*v.* P.t. and p.part. of **strike.** ▸*adj.* Affected or shut down by a labor strike.

struc•ture (strŭk′chər) ▸*n.* **1.** Something made up of parts that are put together in a particular way. **2.** The way in which parts are arranged or put together to form a whole. **3.** Something constructed, as a building. ▸*v.* **-tured, -tur•ing.** To give form or arrangement to. [< Lat. *struere*, *strūct-*, construct.] —**struc′tur•al** *adj.* —**struc′tur•al•ly** *adv.*

stru•del (strōōd′l) ▸*n.* A pastry made with fruit or cheese rolled up in layers of thin sheets of dough and baked. [Ger.]

strug•gle (strŭg′əl) ▸*v.* **-gled, -gling 1.** To make a strenuous effort; strive. **2.** To contend or compete. **3.** To progress with difficulty. ▸*n.* **1.** Strenuous effort. **2.** Combat; strife. [ME *struglen*.] —**strug′gler** *n.*

strum (strŭm) ▸*v.* **strummed, strum•ming.** To play (e.g., a guitar) by stroking or brushing the strings. [Perh. imit.] —**strum** *n.*

strum•pet (strŭm′pĭt) ▸*n.* A prostitute. [ME.]

strung (strŭng) ▸*v.* P.t. and p.part. of **string.**

strung-out (strŭng′out′) ▸*adj. Slang* Severely debilitated from long-term drug use.

strut (strŭt) ▸*v.* **strut•ted, strut•ting.** To walk in an exaggerated, self-important manner. ▸*n.* **1.** A strutting gait. **2.** A bar or rod used to brace a structure against forces applied from the side. [< OE *strūtian*, stand out stiffly.] —**strut′ter** *n.*

strych•nine (strĭk′nīn′, -nĭn, -nēn′) ▸*n.* A poisonous white crystalline alkaloid, $C_{21}H_{22}O_2N_2$, derived from plants and used as a poison and medicinally as a stimulant. [< Gk. *strukhnon*, a kind of nightshade.]

Stu•art (stōō′ərt, styōō′-), **Gilbert Charles.** 1755–1828. Amer. painter.

Stuart, James Ewell Brown. "Jeb." 1833–64. Amer. Confederate general.

stub (stŭb) ►*n.* **1.** A short blunt remaining end. **2a.** The part of a check or receipt retained as a record. **b.** The part of a ticket returned as a voucher of payment. ►*v.* **stubbed, stub•bing 1.** To strike (one's toe or foot) against something. **2.** To crush out (a lit cigarette). [< OE *stybb*, tree stump.]

stub•ble (stŭb′əl) ►*n.* **1.** The short stiff stalks, as of grain, that remain on a field after harvesting. **2.** Something, such as a short growth of beard, that resembles stubble. [< Lat. *stipula*, straw.] —**stub′bly** *adj.*

stub•born (stŭb′ərn) ►*adj.* **1.** Unreasonably determined to exert one's will; obstinate. **2.** Persistent. **3.** Difficult to treat or deal with. [ME *stuborn.*] —**stub′born•ly** *adv.* —**stub′born•ness** *n.*

stub•by (stŭb′ē) ►*adj.* **-bi•er, -bi•est.** Short and stocky. —**stub′bi•ness** *n.*

stuc•co (stŭk′ō) ►*n., pl.* **-coes** or **-cos.** A durable finish for exterior walls, usu. made of cement, sand, and lime. ►*v.* To finish or decorate with stucco. [Ital., of Gmc. orig.]

stuck (stŭk) ►*v.* P.t. and p.part. of **stick.**

stuck-up (stŭk′ŭp′) ►*adj. Informal* Snobbish; conceited.

stud[1] (stŭd) ►*n.* **1.** An upright post in the framework of a wall for supporting sheets of lath or wallboard. **2.** A small knob or rivet slightly projecting from a surface. **3a.** A small ornamental button mounted on a short post. **b.** A mounted buttonlike earring. ►*v.* **stud•ded, stud•ding 1.** To provide with studs. **2.** To strew: *Daisies studded the meadow.* [< OE *studu.*]

stud[2] (stŭd) ►*n.* **1.** A male animal, such as a bull or stallion, kept for breeding. **2.** *Slang* A virile man. [< OE *stōd*, breeding stable.]

stud•book (stŭd′bo͝ok′) ►*n.* A book registering the pedigrees of thoroughbred animals.

stu•dent (sto͞od′nt, styo͞od′-) ►*n.* **1.** One who attends a school, college, or university. **2.** One who makes a study of something. [< Med.Lat. *studiare*, STUDY.]

stud•ied (stŭd′ēd) ►*adj.* Carefully contrived; calculated.

stu•di•o (sto͞o′dē-ō, styo͞o′-) ►*n., pl.* **-os 1.** An artist's workroom. **2.** A place where an art is taught: *a dance studio.* **3.** A room or building for audio, movie, television, or radio productions. **4.** A studio apartment. [Ital.]

studio apartment ►*n.* A small apartment usu. consisting of one main living space, a kitchen, and a bathroom.

stu•di•ous (sto͞o′dē-əs, styo͞o′-) ►*adj.* **1.** Given to diligent study. **2.** Earnest; purposeful. —**stu′di•ous•ly** *adv.* —**stu′di•ous•ness** *n.*

stud•y (stŭd′ē) ►*n., pl.* **-ies 1.** The act or process of studying. **2.** Attentive scrutiny. **3.** A branch of knowledge. **4.** A room intended or equipped for studying or writing. ►*v.* **-ied, -y•ing 1.** To apply one's mind purposefully to the acquisition of knowledge or understanding of (a subject). **2.** To take (a course) at a school. **3.** To inquire into; investigate. **4.** To examine closely; scrutinize. [< Lat. *studium* < *studēre*, to study.]

stuff (stŭf) ►*n.* **1.** The material out of which something is made or formed; substance. **2.** *Informal* **a.** Unspecified material: *Put that stuff over there.* **b.** Worthless objects. **3.** *Slang* Foolish or empty words or ideas. **4.** *Chiefly Brit.* Woven material, esp. woolens. ►*v.* **1a.** To pack tightly. **b.** To block (a passage); plug. **2.** To fill with stuffing. **3.** To gorge: *stuffed myself on desserts.* [< OFr. *estoffer*, equip, of Gmc. orig.]

stuff•ing (stŭf′ĭng) ►*n.* **1.** Padding, as for cushions. **2.** Food used as a filling for meat or vegetables.

stuff•y (stŭf′ē) ►*adj.* **-i•er, -i•est 1.** Lacking sufficient ventilation. **2.** Blocked: *a stuffy nose.* **3.** Stodgy. —**stuff′i•ness** *n.*

stul•ti•fy (stŭl′tə-fī′) ►*v.* **-fied, -fy•ing 1.** To limit or stifle: *stultify free expression.* **2.** To cause to seem stupid or foolish. [< Lat. *stultus*, foolish.] —**stul′ti•fi•ca′tion** *n.*

stum•ble (stŭm′bəl) ►*v.* **-bled, -bling 1a.** To trip and almost fall. **b.** To proceed unsteadily; flounder. See Syns at **blunder. c.** To act or speak falteringly or clumsily. **2.** To make a mistake. **3.** To come upon accidentally. [ME *stumblen.*] —**stum′ble** *n.*

stum•bling block (stŭm′blĭng) ►*n.* An obstacle or impediment.

stump (stŭmp) ►*n.* **1.** The part of a tree trunk left in the ground after the tree has fallen or been felled. **2.** A part remaining after the main part has been cut off or worn away. **3.** A place or occasion used for political speeches. ►*v.* **1.** To clear stumps from. **2.** To traverse (a district) making political speeches. **3.** To walk in a stiff, heavy manner. **4.** To puzzle; baffle. [ME *stumpe.*] —**stump′er** *n.* —**stump′y** *adj.*

stun (stŭn) ►*v.* **stunned, stun•ning 1.** To daze or render senseless, as by a blow. **2.** To stupefy. See Syns at **daze.** [< OFr. *estoner.*]

stung (stŭng) ►*v.* P.t. and p.part. of **sting.**

stunk (stŭngk) ►*v.* P.t. and p.part. of **stink.**

stun•ning (stŭn′ĭng) ►*adj.* **1.** Strikingly attractive. **2a.** Impressive. **b.** Surprising. —**stun′ning•ly** *adv.*

stunt[1] (stŭnt) ►*v.* To check the growth or development of. [< OE *stunt*, short.]

stunt[2] (stŭnt) ►*n.* **1.** A feat displaying unusual skill or daring. **2.** Something unusual done for publicity. [?]

stu•pa (sto͞o′pə) ►*n.* A dome-shaped Buddhist shrine or monument. [Skt. *stūpaḥ.*]

stupa
Shwedagon Stupa, Yangon, Myanmar

stu•pe•fy (sto͞o′pə-fī′, styo͞o′-) ►*v.* **-fied, -fy•ing 1.** To dull the senses of. See Syns at **daze. 2.** To amaze; astonish. [< Lat. *stupēre*, be stunned.] —**stu′pe•fac′tion** (-făk′shən) *n.*

stu•pen•dous (sto͞o-pĕn′dəs, styo͞o-) ►*adj.* **1.** Of astounding force, volume, or degree. **2.** Amazingly large or great: *tremendous savings.* [< LLat. *stupendus*, stunning.] —**stu•pen′dous•ly** *adv.*

stu•pid (sto͞o′pĭd, styo͞o′-) ►*adj.* **-er, -est 1.** Slow to learn or understand. **2.** Lacking intelligence. **3.** In a dazed or stunned state. **4.** Pointless; worthless. [Lat. *stupidus*, stupefied.] —**stu•pid′i•ty** *n.* —**stu′pid•ly** *adv.* —**stu′pid•ness** *n.*

stu•por (sto͞o′pər, styo͞o′-) ►*n.* **1.** A state of reduced sensibility; daze. **2.** A state of mental numbness, as from shock. [< Lat. < *stupēre*, be stunned.] —**stu′por•ous** *adj.*

stur•dy (stûr′dē) ►*adj.* **-di•er, -di•est 1.** Substantially built; strong. **2.** Healthy and vigorous; robust. [< OFr. *estourdi*, stunned.] —**stur′di•ly** *adv.* —**stur′di•ness** *n.*

stur•geon (stûr′jən) ►*n.* Any of various large food fishes valued as a source of caviar. [< OFr. *estourgeon*, of Gmc. orig.]

stut•ter (stŭt′ər) ►*v.* To speak with a spasmodic repetition or prolongation of sounds. ►*n.* The act or habit of stuttering. [< ME *stutten.*] —**stut′ter•er** *n.*

Stutt•gart (sto͝ot′gärt′) A city of SW Germany on the Neckar R. Pop. 594,406.

Stuy•ve•sant (stī′vĭ-sənt), **Peter.** 1592?–1672. Dutch colonial administrator.

sty[1] (stī) ►*n., pl.* **sties** (stīz) **1.** An enclosure for swine. **2.** A filthy place. [< OE *stig*.]

sty[2] (stī) ►*n., pl.* **sties** (stīz). Inflammation of one or more sebaceous glands of an eyelid. [< OE *stīgan*, rise.]

style (stīl) ►*n.* **1.** The way in which something is said, done, expressed, or performed. **2.** Sort; type. **3.** Individuality expressed in one's actions and tastes. **4.** Elegance. **5a.** The fashion of the moment. **b.** A particular fashion. **6.** A customary manner of presenting printed material, including usage, punctuation, and spelling. **7.** A slender, pointed writing instrument. **8.** *Bot.* The usu. slender part of a pistil. ►*v.* **styled, styl•ing 1.** To call or name; designate. **2.** To make consistent with rules of style. **3.** To arrange or design. [< Lat. *stilus.*] —**sty•lis′tic** (stī-lĭs′tĭk) *adj.* —**sty•lis′ti•cal•ly** *adv.*

styl•ish (stī′lĭsh) ►*adj.* Conforming to the current fashion. See Syns at **fashionable.** —**styl′ish•ly** *adv.* —**styl′ish•ness** *n.*

styl•ist (stī′lĭst) ►*n.* **1.** One who cultivates an artful literary style. **2.** A designer of or consultant on styles. **3.** A hairdresser.

styl•ize (stī′līz′) ►*v.* **-ized, -iz•ing.** To restrict or make conform to a particular style.

sty•lus (stī′ləs) ►*n., pl.* **-lus•es** or **-li** (-lī) **1a.** A sharp, pointed instrument used for writing, marking, or engraving. **b.** *Comp. Sci.* A pointed instrument for use on a pressure-sensitive screen. **2.** A phonograph needle. [Lat.]

sty•mie (stī′mē) ►*v.* **-mied, -mie•ing.** To thwart; stump. [?]

styp•tic (stĭp′tĭk) ►*adj.* Contracting the tissues or blood vessels; astringent. [< Gk. *stuphein*, contract.] —**styp′tic** *n.*

Sty•ro•foam (stī′rə-fōm′) ► A trademark used for a light resilient polystyrene plastic.

suave (swäv) ►*adj.* **suav•er, suav•est.** Smoothly agreeable and courteous. [< Lat. *suāvis.*] —**suave′ly** *adv.* —**suave′ness, suav′i•ty** *n.*

sub[1] (sŭb) ►*n. Informal* A submarine. See Regional Note at **submarine.**

sub[2] (sŭb) *Informal* ►*n.* A substitute. ►*v.* **subbed, sub•bing.** To act as a substitute.

sub– ►*pref.* **1.** Below; beneath: *subsoil.* **2a.** Subordinate; secondary: *subhead.* **b.** Subdivision: *subatomic.* **3.** Less than; short of: *subnormal.* [< Lat. *sub*, under.]

sub•al•tern (sŭb-ôl′tərn, sŭb′əl-tûrn′) ►*n.* **1.** A subordinate. **2.** *Chiefly Brit.* An officer holding a military rank just below that of captain. [< LLat. *subalternus.*]

sub•a•tom•ic (sŭb′ə-tŏm′ĭk) ►*adj.* **1.** Of or relating to the constituents of the atom. **2.** Participating in reactions characteristic of these constituents.

subatomic particle ►*n.* Any of various units of matter below the size of an atom.

sub•com•mit•tee (sŭb′kə-mĭt′ē) ►*n.* A subordinate committee composed of members from a main committee.

sub•com•pact (sŭb-kŏm′păkt′) ►*n.* An automobile smaller than a compact.

sub•con•scious (sŭb-kŏn′shəs) ►*adj.* Beneath the threshold of conscious perception. ►*n.* The part of the mind below the level of conscious perception. —**sub•con′scious•ly** *adv.* —**sub•con′scious•ness** *n.*

sub•con•ti•nent (sŭb′kŏn′tə-nənt, sŭb-kŏn′-) ►*n.* A large landmass, such as India, that is part of a continent but is considered either geographically or politically separate.

sub•con•tract (sŭb-kŏn′trăkt′, sŭb′kŏn′trăkt) ►*n.* A contract that assigns some of the obligations of a prior contract to another party. —**sub•con′tract′** *v.* —**sub•con′trac′tor** *n.*

sub•cul•ture (sŭb′kŭl′chər) ►*n.* A cultural subgroup within a larger cultural group.

sub•cu•ta•ne•ous (sŭb′kyo͞o-tā′nē-əs) ►*adj.* Just beneath the skin. —**sub′cu•ta′ne•ous•ly** *adv.*

sub•di•vide (sŭb′dĭ-vīd′, sŭb′dĭ-vīd′) ►*v.* **1.** To divide into smaller parts. **2.** To divide into a number of parts, esp. to divide (land) into lots. —**sub′di•vid′er** *n.* —**sub′di•vi′sion** (-vĭzh′ən) *n.*

sub•due (səb-do͞o′, -dyo͞o′) ►*v.* **-dued, -du•ing 1.** To conquer and subjugate; vanquish. **2.** To quiet or bring under control. **3.** To make less intense. [< Lat. *subdūcere*, withdraw.] —**sub•du′er** *n.*

sub•head (sŭb′hĕd′) ►*n.* **1.** The heading or title of a subdivision of a printed subject. **2.** A subordinate heading or title.

subj. ►*abbr.* **1.** subject **2.** subjunctive

sub•ject (sŭb′jĭkt) ►*adj.* **1.** Under the power or authority of another. **2.** Prone; disposed: *subject to colds.* **3.** Likely to incur or receive: *subject to misinterpretation.* **4.** Contingent or dependent: *subject to approval.* See Syns at **dependent.** ►*n.* **1.** One who is under the rule of another, esp. one who owes allegiance to a government or ruler. See Syns at **citizen. 2a.** One about which something is said or done; topic. **b.** The main theme of a work of art. **3.** A course or area of study. **4a.** One that experiences or is subjected to something. **b.** One that is the object of study. **5.** *Gram.* The noun, noun phrase, or pronoun in a sentence or clause that denotes the doer of the action or what is described by the predicate. ▶*v.* (səb-jĕkt′) **1.** To expose to something. **2.** To cause to experience. **3.** To subjugate. [< Lat. *subiectus*, p.part. of *sūbicere*, to subject.] —**sub•jec′tion** (səb-jĕk′shən) *n.*

sub•jec•tive (səb-jĕk′tĭv) ▶*adj.* **1a.** Proceeding from or taking place within a person's mind such as to be unaffected by the external world. **b.** Particular to a given person; personal: *subjective experience.* **2.** *Gram.* Of or being the nominative case. —**sub•jec′tive•ly** *adv.* —**sub•jec′tive•ness, sub′jec•tiv′i•ty** (sŭb′-jĕk-tĭv′ĭ-tē) *n.*

sub•join (səb-join′) ▶*v.* To add at the end; append. [< Lat. *subiungere* : *sub-*, under + *iungere*, join.]

sub•ju•gate (sŭb′jə-gāt′) ▶*v.* **-gat•ed, -gat•ing 1.** To bring under control; conquer. **2.** To make subservient. [< Lat. *subiugāre* : *sub-*, under + *iugum*, yoke.] —**sub′ju•ga′tion** *n.* —**sub′ju•ga′tor** *n.*

sub•junc•tive (səb-jŭngk′tĭv) ▶*adj.* Of or being a mood of a verb used to express an uncertainty, a wish, or an unlikely condition. [< Lat. *subiungere*, *subiūnct-*, SUBJOIN.] —**sub•junc′tive** *n.*

sub•lease (sŭb′lēs′) ▶*n.* A lease of property granted by a lessee. —**sub′lease′** *v.*

sub•let (sŭb′lĕt′) ▶*v.* **1.** To rent (property one holds by lease) to another. **2.** To subcontract (work). ▶*n.* (sŭb′lĕt′). Property rented by one tenant to another.

sub•li•mate (sŭb′lə-māt′) ▶*v.* **-mat•ed, -mat•ing 1.** *Chem.* To change from a solid to a gaseous state or from a gaseous to a solid state without becoming a liquid. **2.** *Psychol.* To modify the natural expression of (an instinctual impulse) in a socially acceptable manner. [Lat. *sublīmāre*, elevate.] —**sub′li•ma′tion** *n.*

sub•lime (sə-blīm′) ▶*adj.* **1.** Of high spiritual, moral, or intellectual worth. **2.** Exalted; lofty. **3.** Inspiring awe; impressive. ▶*v.* **-limed, -lim•ing** *Chem.* To sublimate. [< Lat. *sublīmis*, uplifted.] —**sub•lime′ly** *adv.* —**sub•lime′ness, sub•lim′i•ty** (sə-blĭm′ĭ-tē) *n.*

sub•lim•i•nal (sŭb-lĭm′ə-nəl) ▶*adj. Psychol.* Below the threshold of conscious perception or awareness. [SUB– + Lat. *līmen*, threshold.] —**sub•lim′i•nal•ly** *adv.*

sub•lu•na•ry (sŭb-lo͞o′nə-rē, sŭb′lo͞o-nĕr′ē) ▶*adj.* **1.** Situated beneath the moon. **2.** Of this world; earthly. [LLat. *sublūnāris.*]

sub•ma•chine gun (sŭb′mə-shēn′) ▶*n.* A lightweight automatic or semiautomatic gun fired from the shoulder or hip.

sub•ma•rine (sŭb′mə-rēn′, sŭb′mə-rēn′) ▶*n.* **1.** A ship capable of operating under water. **2.** A large sandwich consisting of a long roll filled with layers of meat, cheese, tomatoes, lettuce, and condiments. ▶*adj.* Beneath the surface of the water; undersea.

Regional Note: The long sandwich featuring layers of meat and cheese on a crusty Italian roll or French bread goes by a variety of names. *Submarine* and *sub* are widespread. Localized terms are *hoagie* (Delaware Valley, including Philadelphia and southern New Jersey), *grinder* (New England and Sacramento, California), *Cuban sandwich* (Miami), *Italian sandwich* (Maine), and *poor boy* (New Orleans).

sub•merge (səb-mûrj′) ▶*v.* **-merged, -merg•ing 1.** To place under water. **2.** To cover with water. **3.** To go under or as if under

sub′ab•dom′i•nal *adj.*
sub′a•cute′ *adj.*
sub•a′gen•cy *n.*
sub•al′pine′ *adj.*
sub•ap′i•cal *adj.*
sub•ap′i•cal•ly *adv.*
sub•a′que•ous *adj.*
sub•arc′tic *adj.*
sub•ar′id *adj.*
sub′as•sem′bly *n.*
sub•av′er•age *adj.*
sub•ax′il•lar′y *adj.*
sub′base′ment *n.*
sub′branch′ *n.*
sub•cat•e•go′ry *n.*
sub′class′ *n.*
sub′class•si•fi•ca′tion *n.*
sub•class′i•fy′ *v.*
sub•clin′i•cal *adj.*
sub′com•mand′er *n.*
sub′com•mis′sion *n.*
sub′con′fer•ence *n.*
sub•coun′cil *n.*
sub•cra′ni•al *adj.*
sub•dea′con *n.*
sub•dean′ *n.*
sub′de•part′ment *n.*
sub′di•rec′tor *n.*
sub′di•rec′to•ry *n.*
sub′dis′ci•pline *n.*
sub′dis′trict *n.*
sub•dur′al *adj.*
sub′en′try *n.*
sub′fam′ily *n.*
sub′floor′ *n.*
sub′floor′ing *n.*
sub•freez′ing *adj.*
sub′gen′re *n.*
sub′ge′nus *n.*
sub•gla′cial *adj.*
sub′group′ *n.*
sub′head′ing *n.*
sub•hu′man *adj.*
sub•in′dex *n.*
sub′in′dus•try *n.*
sub′king′dom *n.*
sub•le′thal *adj.*
sub•le′thal•ly *adv.*
sub•lit′er•ate *adj.*
sub•mem′ber *n.*
sub•min′i•mal *adj.*
sub′min′i•mum *adj.*
sub′mo•lec′u•lar *adj.*
sub′o•ce•an′ic *adj.*
sub•of′fi•cer *n.*
sub•par′ *adj.*
sub′per•i•os′te•al *adj.*
sub′phy′lum *n.*
sub′pop•u•la′tion *n.*
sub•prin′ci•pal *n.*
sub′pro•fes′sion•al *n.*
sub′pro′gram *n.*
sub′re′gion *n.*
sub′-Sa•har′an *adj.*
sub′sam′ple *n. & v.*
sub′sec′tion *n.*
sub•seg′ment *n.*
sub•sense′ *n.*
sub•se′ries *n.*
sub•spe′cial•ist *n.*
sub•spe′cial•i•za′tion *n.*
sub′spe′cial•ize *v.*
sub′spe′cial•ty *n.*
sub′spe′cies *n.*
sub′stage′ *n.*
sub•strat′o•sphere′ *n.*
sub′sur′face *adj.*
sub′sys′tem *n.*
sub′teen′ *adj.*
sub•tem′per•ate *adj.*
sub•ten′ant *n.*
sub•thresh′old′ *adj.*
sub′top′ic *n.*
sub•treas′ur•y *n.*
sub′tribe′ *n.*
sub′type′ *n.*
sub′u′nit *n.*
sub•vo′cal *adj.*
sub•ze′ro *adj.*

water. [Lat. *submergere.*] —**sub•mer′gence** *n.* —**sub•mer′gi•ble** *adj.*

sub•merse (səb-mûrs′) ►*v.* **-mersed, -mers•ing.** To submerge. [< Lat. *submergere, submers-,* submerge.] —**sub•mer′sion** (-mûr′zhən, -shən) *n.*

sub•mers•i•ble (səb-mûr′sə-bəl) ►*adj.* Submergible. ►*n.* A vessel capable of operating under water.

sub•mi•cro•scop•ic (sŭb′mī-krə-skŏp′ĭk) ►*adj.* Too small to be resolved by an optical microscope.

sub•mit (səb-mĭt′) ►*v.* **-mit•ted, -mit•ting 1.** To yield or surrender (oneself) to the will or authority of another. **2.** To commit (something) to the consideration or judgment of another. **3.** To offer as a proposition or contention. **4.** To allow oneself to be subjected to something. [< Lat. *submittere,* set under.] —**sub•mis′sion** *n.* —**sub•mis′sive** *adj.* —**sub•mit′tal** *n.*

sub•nor•mal (sŭb-nôr′məl) ►*adj.* Less than normal; below the average. —**sub′nor•mal′i•ty** (-măl′ĭ-tē) *n.*

sub•or•bi•tal (sŭb-ôr′bĭ-tl) ►*adj.* Having a trajectory of less than one full orbit.

sub•or•di•nate (sə-bôr′dn-ĭt) ►*adj.* **1.** Of a lower or inferior class or rank. **2.** Subject to the authority or control of another. ►*n.* One that is subordinate. ►*v.* (sə-bôr′dn-āt′) **-nat•ed, -nat•ing 1.** To put in a lower or inferior rank or class. **2.** To make subservient. [< Med.Lat. *subōrdināre,* put in lower rank.] —**sub•or′di•nate•ly** *adv.* —**sub•or′di•na′tion** *n.* —**sub•or′di•na′tive** *adj.*

sub•orn (sə-bôrn′) ►*v.* To induce to commit an unlawful act, esp. perjury. [Lat. *subōrnāre.*] —**sub′or•na′tion** (sŭb′ôr-nā′shən) *n.* —**sub•orn′er** *n.*

sub•plot (sŭb′plŏt′) ►*n.* A plot subordinate to the main plot of a literary work or film.

sub•poe•na (sə-pē′nə) ►*n.* A writ requiring appearance in court to give testimony. ►*v.* To serve or summon with such a writ. [< Med.Lat., under a penalty.]

sub ro•sa (sŭb rō′zə) ►*adv.* In secret; privately. [Lat. *sub rosā,* under the rose.] —**sub-ro′sa** *adj.*

sub•rou•tine (sŭb′ro͞o-tēn′) ►*n. Comp. Sci.* A set of instructions that performs a specific task for a main routine.

sub-Sa•har•an (sŭb′sə-hâr′ən, -hăr′-, -här′-) ►*adj.* Of or relating to the region of Africa south of the Sahara.

sub•scribe (səb-scrīb′) ►*v.* **-scribed, -scrib•ing 1.** To pledge or contribute (a sum of money). **2.** To sign (one's name). **3.** To sign one's name to in testimony or consent: *subscribe a will.* **4.** To contract to receive and pay for a subscription, as to a publication. **5.** To express approval or agreement: *subscribe to a belief.* [< Lat. *subscrībere,* write under.] —**sub•scrib′er** *n.*

sub•script (sŭb′skrĭpt′) ►*n.* A character or symbol written directly beneath or next to and slightly below a letter or number. [< Lat. *subscrīptus,* p.part. of *subscrībere,* write under.]

sub•scrip•tion (səb-skrĭp′shən) ►*n.* **1.** A purchase made by signed order, as for issues of a periodical or a series of events. **2.** The signing of one's name, as to a document.

sub•se•quent (sŭb′sĭ-kwĕnt′, -kwənt) ►*adj.* Following in time or order; succeeding. [< Lat. *subsequī,* follow close after.] —**sub′se•quent′ly** *adv.*

sub•ser•vi•ent (səb-sûr′vē-ənt) ►*adj.* **1.** Subordinate. **2.** Obsequious; servile. [< Lat. *subservīre,* serve, support.] —**sub•ser′vi•ence** *n.* —**sub•ser′vi•ent•ly** *adv.*

sub•set (sŭb′sĕt′) ►*n.* A set contained within a set.

sub•side (səb-sīd′) ►*v.* **-sid•ed, -sid•ing 1.** To sink to a lower level. **2.** To sink to the bottom, as a sediment. **3.** To become less; abate. [Lat. *subsīdere* : *sub-,* down + *sīdere,* settle.] —**sub•si′dence** *n.*

sub•sid•i•ar•y (səb-sĭd′ē-ĕr′ē) ►*adj.* **1.** Serving to assist or supplement. **2.** Subordinate. **3.** Of or like a subsidy. ►*n., pl.* **-ar•ies.** One that is subsidiary to another, esp. a company owned by another company. —**sub•sid′i•ar′i•ly** (-âr′ə-lē) *adv.*

sub•si•dize (sŭb′sĭ-dīz′) ►*v.* **-dized, -diz•ing.** To assist or support with a subsidy. —**sub′si•di•za′tion** *n.*

sub•si•dy (sŭb′sĭ-dē) ►*n., pl.* **-dies.** Financial assistance given by one person or government to another. [< Lat. *subsidium,* support : *sub-,* behind + *sedēre,* sit.]

sub•sist (səb-sĭst′) ►*v.* **1.** To exist; be. **2.** To maintain life, esp. at a meager level: *subsisted on one meal a day.* [Lat. *subsistere,* support : *sub-,* behind + *sistere,* stand.]

sub•sis•tence (səb-sĭs′təns) ►*n.* **1.** The act or state of subsisting. **2.** A means of subsisting. **3.** Existence. —**sub•sis′tent** *adj.*

sub•soil (sŭb′soil′) ►*n.* The layer of earth beneath the topsoil.

sub•son•ic (sŭb-sŏn′ĭk) ►*adj.* **1.** Of less than audible frequency. **2.** Having a speed less than that of sound.

sub•stance (sŭb′stəns) ►*n.* **1a.** That which has mass and occupies space; matter. **b.** A material of a particular kind or constitution. **2.** The essence; gist. **3.** That which is solid and practical: *a plan without substance.* **4.** Density; body. **5.** Material possessions; wealth. [< Lat. *substāre,* be present : *sub-,* under + *stāre,* stand.]

Syns: *substance, burden, core, gist, pith, purport* **n.**

substance abuse ►*n.* Excessive use of addictive substances, esp. alcohol or narcotics.

sub•stan•dard (sŭb-stăn′dərd) ►*adj.* Failing to meet a standard; below standard.

sub•stan•tial (səb-stăn′shəl) ►*adj.* **1.** Of or having substance; material. **2.** Not imaginary; real. **3.** Solidly built; strong. **4.** Ample; sustaining. **5.** Considerable; large: *won by a substantial margin.* **6.** Possessing wealth; well-to-do. [< Lat. *substantia,* SUBSTANCE.] —**sub•stan′tial•ly** *adv.*

sub•stan•ti•ate (səb-stăn′shē-āt′) ►*v.* **-at•ed, -at•ing.** To support with proof or evidence. —**sub•stan′ti•a′tion** *n.*

sub•stan•tive (sŭb′stən-tĭv) ►*adj.* **1.** Substantial; considerable. **2.** Basic; essential. ►*n. Gram.* A word or group of words functioning as a noun. —**sub′stan•tive•ly** *adv.*

sub•sta•tion (sŭb′stā′shən) ►*n.* A branch station, as of a post office.

sub•sti•tute (sŭb′stĭ-to͞ot′, -tyo͞ot′) ►*n.* One that takes the place of another. ►*v.* **-tut•ed, -tut•ing 1.** To put or use in place of another. **2.** To take the place of another. [< Lat. *substituere,* stand in : *sub-,* in place of + *statuere,* cause to stand.] —**sub′sti•tu′tion** *n.*

sub•strate (sŭb′strāt′) ►*n.* **1.** The substance on which an enzyme acts. **2.** An underlying layer; substratum. [< SUBSTRATUM.]

sub•stra•tum (sŭb′strā′təm, -străt′əm) ►*n.* **1.** An underlying layer or foundation. **2.** Subsoil.

sub•struc•ture (sŭb′strŭk′chər) ►*n.* The supporting part of a structure; foundation.

sub•sume (səb-so͞om′) ►*v.* **-sumed, -sum•ing.** To place in a broader or more comprehensive category. [Med.Lat. *subsūmere.*] —**sub•sum′a•ble** *adj.*

sub•tend (səb-tĕnd′) ►*v. Math.* To be opposite to and delimit: *The hypotenuse subtends a right angle.* [Lat. *subtendere*, extend beneath.]

sub•ter•fuge (sŭb′tər-fyo͞oj′) ►*n.* A deceptive stratagem or device. [< Lat. *subterfugere*, flee secretly.]

sub•ter•ra•ne•an (sŭb′tə-rā′nē-ən) ►*adj.* **1.** Situated or operating beneath the earth's surface; underground. **2.** Hidden; secret. [Lat. *subterrāneus* : *sub-*, under + *terra*, earth.]

sub•text (sŭb′tĕkst′) ►*n.* The implicit meaning or theme of a literary text.

sub•ti•tle (sŭb′tīt′l) ►*n.* **1.** A secondary, usu. explanatory title, as of a literary work. **2.** A printed translation of the dialogue of a foreign-language film shown at the bottom of the screen. —**sub′ti′tle** *v.*

sub•tle (sŭt′l) ►*adj.* **-tler, -tlest 1a.** So slight as to be difficult to detect. **b.** Not obvious; abstruse. **2.** Able to make fine distinctions: *a subtle mind.* **3a.** Skillful; clever. **b.** Crafty. [< Lat. *subtīlis.*] —**sub′tle•ty, sub′tle•ness** *n.* —**sub′tly** *adv.*

sub•to•tal (sŭb′tōt′l) ►*n.* The total of part of a series of numbers. —**sub′to′tal** *v.*

sub•tract (səb-trăkt′) ►*v.* To take away or deduct, as one number from another. [Lat. *subtrahere, subtráct-.*] —**sub•trac′tion** *n.*

sub•tra•hend (sŭb′trə-hĕnd′) ►*n. Math.* A quantity to be subtracted from another. [Lat. *subtrahendum*, to be subtracted.]

sub•trop•i•cal (sŭb-trŏp′ĭ-kəl) ►*adj.* Of or being the geographic areas adjacent to the tropics.

sub•trop•ics (sŭb-trŏp′ĭks) ►*pl.n.* Subtropical regions.

sub•urb (sŭb′ûrb′) ►*n.* **1.** A usu. residential area near a city. **2. suburbs** The usu. residential region surrounding a major city. [< Lat. *suburbium.*] —**sub•ur′ban** (sə-bûr′bən) *adj.*

sub•ur•ban•ite (sə-bûr′bə-nīt′) ►*n.* One who lives in a suburb.

sub•ur•bi•a (sə-bûr′bē-ə) ►*n.* **1.** The suburbs. **2.** Suburbanites collectively.

sub•ven•tion (səb-vĕn′shən) ►*n.* An endowment or subsidy. [< Lat. *subvenīre*, come to help : *sub-*, behind + *venīre*, come.] —**sub•ven′tion•ar′y** *adj.*

sub•ver•sive (səb-vûr′sĭv, -zĭv) ►*adj.* Intended or serving to subvert, esp. an established government. ►*n.* One who advocates subversive means or policies. —**sub•ver′sive•ly** *adv.* —**sub•ver′sive•ness** *n.*

sub•vert (səb-vûrt′) ►*v.* **1.** To destroy completely; ruin. **2.** To undermine the character or morals of; corrupt. **3.** To overthrow completely. See Syns at **overthrow.** [< Lat. *subvertere.*] —**sub•ver′sion** (-vûr′zhən, -shən) *n.* —**sub•vert′er** *n.*

sub•way (sŭb′wā′) ►*n.* An underground railroad, usu. operated by electricity.

suc•ceed (sək-sēd′) ►*v.* **1.** To come next in time or succession, esp. to replace another in a position. **2.** To accomplish something attempted. [< Lat. *succēdere.*]

suc•cess (sək-sĕs′) ►*n.* **1.** The achievement of something attempted. **2.** The gaining of fame or prosperity. **3.** One that succeeds. [< Lat. *succēdere, success-*, succeed.] —**suc•cess′ful** *adj.* —**suc•cess′ful•ly** *adv.*

suc•ces•sion (sək-sĕsh′ən) ►*n.* **1.** The act of following in order. **2.** A group of people or things following in order; sequence. **3.** The sequence, right, or act of succeeding to a title, throne, or estate. —**suc•ces′sion•al** *adj.* —**suc•ces′sion•al•ly** *adv.*

suc•ces•sive (sək-sĕs′ĭv) ►*adj.* Following in uninterrupted order; consecutive. —**suc•ces′sive•ly** *adv.*

suc•ces•sor (sək-sĕs′ər) ►*n.* One that succeeds or follows another.

suc•cinct (sək-sĭngkt′) ►*adj.* Brief and clear in expression; concise. [< Lat. *succīnctus*, p.part. of *succingere*, gird from below.] —**suc•cinct′ly** *adv.* —**suc•cinct′ness** *n.*

suc•cor (sŭk′ər) ►*n.* Assistance in time of distress; relief. [< Lat. *succurrere*, run to the aid of.] —**suc′cor** *v.*

suc•co•tash (sŭk′ə-tăsh′) ►*n.* A stew of kernels of corn, lima beans, and tomatoes. [Narragansett *msíckquatash*, boiled whole-kernel corn.]

Suc•coth also **Suk•koth** (so͝ok′əs, so͞o-kôt′) ►*n.* A Jewish harvest festival celebrated in Tishri. [< Heb. *sukkâ*, booth.]

suc•cu•bus (sŭk′yə-bəs) ►*n., pl.* **-bus•es** or **-bi** (-bī′, -bē′). An evil spirit supposed to have sexual intercourse with a sleeping man. [< Lat. *succuba*, paramour.]

suc•cu•lent (sŭk′yə-lənt) ►*adj.* **1.** Full of juice or sap; juicy. **2.** Having thick fleshy leaves or stems. ►*n.* A succulent plant, such as a cactus. [Lat. *succulentus* < *succus*, juice.] —**suc′cu•lence** *n.* —**suc′cu•lent•ly** *adv.*

suc•cumb (sə-kŭm′) ►*v.* **1.** To submit or yield to something overwhelming. **2.** To die. [< Lat. *succumbere*, lie down before.]

such (sŭch) ►*adj.* Of this or that kind or extent. ►*adv.* **1.** To so extreme a degree; so: *such beautiful flowers.* **2.** Very; especially. ►*pron.* **1.** Such a one or ones. **2.** Someone or something implied or indicated: *Such are the fortunes of war.* **3.** The like: *pins, needles, and such.* —***idiom:* such as** For example. [< OE *swylc.*]

such•like (sŭch′līk′) ►*adj.* Similar. ►*pron.* One or ones of such a kind.

Sü•chow (so͞o′chou′, sü′jō′) See **Xuzhou.**

suck (sŭk) ►*v.* **1.** To draw (liquid) into the mouth by movements that create suction. **2.** To draw something in by or as if by suction. **3.** To suckle. ►*n.* The act or sound of sucking. [< OE *sūcan.*]

suck•er (sŭk′ər) ►*n.* **1.** One that sucks. **2.** *Informal* One who is easily deceived. **3.** A lollipop. **4.** A freshwater fish with a thick-lipped mouth adapted for feeding by suction. **5.** An organ or other structure adapted for sucking nourishment or for clinging by suction. **6.** *Bot.* A secondary shoot produced from the base or roots of a woody plant. ►*v. Informal* To trick; dupe.

suck•le (sŭk′əl) ► *v.* **-led, -ling 1.** To give or take milk at the breast or udder; nurse. **2.** To nourish; nurture. [ME *suclen.*]

suck•ling (sŭk′lĭng) ► *n.* A young unweaned mammal. [ME *suklinge.*] —**suck′ling** *adj.*

su•cre (so͞o′krā) ► *n.* See table at **currency.** [Am.Sp.]

Su•cre (so͞o′krā, -krĕ) The constitutional capital of Bolivia, in the S-central part SE of La Paz. Pop. 594,406.

su•crose (so͞o′krōs′) ► *n.* A sugar found in many plants, notably sugar cane and sugar beets. [Fr. *sucre*, sugar + -OSE[2].]

suc•tion (sŭk′shən) ► *n.* **1.** The act or process of sucking. **2.** A force that causes a fluid or solid to be drawn into a space or to adhere to a surface because of the difference between the external and internal pressures. [< Lat. *sūgere, sūct-*, suck.] —**suc′tion** *v.*

Su•dan (so͞o-dăn′) **1.** A region of N Africa S of the Sahara and N of the equator. **2.** A country of NE Africa S of Egypt. Cap. Khartoum. Pop. 28,947,000. —**Su′da•nese′** (so͞od′n-ēz′, -ēs′) *adj. & n.*

sud•den (sŭd′n) ► *adj.* **1.** Happening without warning; unforeseen. **2.** Hasty; abrupt. **3.** Rapid; swift. [< Lat. *subitus.*] —**sud′den•ly** *adv.* —**sud′den•ness** *n.*

sudden infant death syndrome ► *n.* A fatal syndrome of infants marked by sudden cessation of breathing.

Su•de•ten (so͞o-dā′tn, zo͞o-) A series of mountain ranges along the Czech-Polish border between the Elbe and Oder rivers.

Su•de•ten•land (so͞o-dāt′n-lănd′, zo͞o-) A historical region of N Czech Republic along the Polish border.

suds (sŭdz) ► *pl.n.* **1.** Soapy water. **2.** Foam; lather. **3.** *Slang* Beer. [Poss. < MDu. *sudse*, marsh.] —**sud′sy** *adj.*

sue (so͞o) ► *v.* **sued, su•ing 1.** To institute legal proceedings; bring suit against (a person) for redress of grievances. **2.** To make an appeal or entreaty: *sue for peace.* [< Lat. *sequī*, follow.] —**su′er** *n.*

suede also **suède** (swād) ► *n.* **1.** Leather with a soft napped surface. **2.** Fabric made to resemble suede. [< Fr. *Suède*, Sweden.]

su•et (so͞o′ĭt) ► *n.* The hard fat around the kidneys of cattle and sheep, used in cooking and making tallow. [< Lat. *sēbum.*]

Sue•to•ni•us (swē-tō′nē-əs). Gaius Suetonius Tranquillus. fl. 2nd cent. A.D. Roman historian.

Su•ez (so͞o-ĕz′, so͞o′ĕz′) A city of NE Egypt at the head of the **Gulf of Suez,** an arm of the Red Sea W of the Sinai Peninsula. Pop. 388,000.

Suez, Isthmus of. An isthmus of NE Egypt connecting Africa and Asia.

Suez Canal. A ship canal, about 166 km (103 mi), linking the Red Sea with the Mediterranean.

suff. ► *abbr.* suffix

suf•fer (sŭf′ər) ► *v.* **1.** To feel pain or distress; sustain loss or harm. **2.** To tolerate or endure: *suffered death for her beliefs.* **3.** To appear at a disadvantage: *suffer by comparison.* **4.** To endure or bear. **5.** To permit; allow. [< Lat. *sufferre* : *sub-*, under + *ferre*, carry.] —**suf′fer•a•ble** *adj.* —**suf′fer•a•bly** *adv.* —**suf′fer•er** *n.*

Usage: In general usage *suffer* is preferably used with *from,* rather than *with,* in constructions such as *He suffered from hypertension.*

Suez Canal

suf•fer•ance (sŭf′ər-əns, sŭf′rəns) ► *n.* **1.** Patient endurance. **2.** Sanction or permission implied by failure to prohibit; tacit consent.

suf•fer•ing (sŭf′ər-ĭng, sŭf′rĭng) ► *n.* Physical or mental pain or distress.

suf•fice (sə-fīs′) ► *v.* **-ficed, -fic•ing 1.** To be sufficient (for). **2.** To be capable or competent. [< Lat. *sufficere.*]

suf•fi•cient (sə-fĭsh′ənt) ► *adj.* Being as much as is needed. —**suf•fi′cien•cy** *n.* —**suf•fi′cient•ly** *adv.*

Syns: *sufficient, adequate, enough* **adj.**

suf•fix (sŭf′ĭks) ► *n.* An affix added to the end of a word or stem, serving to form a new word or an inflectional ending. [< Lat. *suffīxus*, p.part. of *suffīgere*, affix.] —**suf′fix** *v.* —**suf•fix′ion** (sə-fĭk′shən) *n.*

suf•fo•cate (sŭf′ə-kāt′) ► *v.* **-cat•ed, -cat•ing 1.** To kill or destroy by preventing access to oxygen. **2.** To suppress; stifle. [Lat. *suffōcāre.*] —**suf′fo•ca′tion** *n.*

suf•frage (sŭf′rĭj) ► *n.* **1.** The right or privilege of voting. **2.** A vote. [< Lat. *suffrāgium.*]

suf•fra•gette (sŭf′rə-jĕt′) ► *n. Chiefly Brit.* A woman advocating suffrage for women.

suf•fra•gist (sŭf′rə-jĭst) ► *n.* An advocate of the extension of voting rights, esp. to women. —**suf′fra•gism** *n.*

suf•fuse (sə-fyo͞oz′) ► *v.* **-fused, -fus•ing.** To spread through or over, as with liquid, color, or light. See Syns at **charge.** [Lat. *suffundere, suffūs-*.] —**suf•fu′sion** *n.* —**suf•fu′sive** *adj.*

Su•fi (so͞o′fē) ► *n. Islam* A Muslim mystic. —**Su′fism** (-fĭz′əm) *n.*

sug•ar (sho͝og′ər) ► *n.* **1.** Any of a class of water-soluble crystalline carbohydrates with a characteristically sweet taste. **2.** Crystalline or powdered sucrose, used as a sweetener; table sugar. ► *v.* **1.** To coat, cover, or sweeten with sugar. **2.** To make less distasteful. [< Skt. *śarkarā.*]

sugar beet ► *n.* A beet with fleshy white roots from which sugar is obtained.

sugar cane ► *n.* A tall tropical grass with thick stems that yield sugar.

sug•ar•coat (sho͝og′ər-kōt′) ► *v.* **1.** To cause to seem more appealing or pleasant. **2.** To cover with sugar.

sug•ar•less (sho͝og′ər-lĭs) ► *adj.* **1.** Containing no sugar. **2.** Sweetened with a substance other than sucrose.

sugar maple ► *n.* A maple tree of E North America, having hard wood and sap that is the source of maple syrup and maple sugar.

sug•ar•plum (sho͝og′ər-plŭm′) ▸*n.* A small ball of candy.

sug•ar•y (sho͝og′ə-rē) ▸*adj.* **-i•er, -i•est 1.** Tasting of or resembling sugar. **2.** Excessively or cloyingly sweet.

sug•gest (səg-jĕst′, sə-jĕst′) ▸*v.* **1.** To offer for consideration or action; propose. **2.** To bring or call to mind by association. **3.** To imply. [Lat. *suggerere, suggest-.*]

sug•gest•i•ble (səg-jĕs′tə-bəl, sə-jĕs′-) ▸*adj.* Readily influenced by suggestion.

sug•ges•tion (səg-jĕs′chən, sə-jĕs′-) ▸*n.* **1.** The act of suggesting. **2.** Something suggested. **3.** A hint or trace.

sug•ges•tive (səg-jĕs′tĭv, sə-jĕs′-) ▸*adj.* **1.** Tending to suggest thoughts or ideas; provocative. **2.** Tending to suggest something improper or indecent. —**sug•ges′tive•ly** *adv.* —**sug•ges′tive•ness** *n.*

Su•har•to (sə-här′tō, so͞o-). b. 1921. Indonesian military and political leader.

su•i•cide (so͞o′ĭ-sīd′) ▸*n.* **1.** The act or an instance of intentionally killing oneself. **2.** One who commits suicide. [Lat. *suī*, of oneself + -CIDE.] —**su′i•cid′al** *adj.*

su•i ge•ne•ris (so͞o′ī′ jĕn′ər-ĭs, so͞o′ē) ▸*adj.* Unique; singular. [Lat. *suī generis*, of its own kind.]

suit (so͞ot) ▸*n.* **1a.** A set of matching outer garments, esp. a coat with trousers or a skirt. **b.** A costume for a special activity: *a diving suit.* **2.** A group of related things. **3.** Any of the four sets of playing cards that constitute a deck. **4.** *Law* A proceeding to recover a right or claim. **5.** The act or an instance of courtship. ▸*v.* **1.** To meet the requirements of. **2.** To make appropriate; adapt. **3.** To be appropriate for; befit: *That color suits you.* **4.** To please; satisfy. [< VLat. **sequita*, following.]

suit•a•ble (so͞o′tə-bəl) ▸*adj.* Appropriate to a purpose or occasion. —**suit′a•bil′i•ty, suit′a•ble•ness** *n.* —**suit′a•bly** *adv.*

suit•case (so͞ot′kās′) ▸*n.* A usu. rectangular and flat piece of luggage.

suite (swēt) ▸*n.* **1.** A staff of attendants; retinue. **2.** (*also* so͞ot). A set of matching furniture. **3.** A series of connected rooms used as a unit. **4.** *Mus.* An instrumental composition consisting of a succession of dances. [< OFr. See SUIT.]

suit•or (so͞o′tər) ▸*n.* **1.** A man who is courting a woman. **2.** A petitioner.

Su•kar•no (so͞o-kär′nō). 1901–70. Indonesian politician.

su•ki•ya•ki (so͞o′kē-yä′kē) ▸*n.* A Japanese dish of sliced meat, bean curd, and vegetables fried together. [J.]

Suk•koth (so͝ok′əs, so͞o-kôt′) ▸*n.* Var. of **Succoth.**

Su•la•we•si (so͞o′lä-wā′sē) also **Cel•e•bes** (sĕl′ə-bēz′, sə-lē′bēz′, sĕ-lā′bĕs). An island of central Indonesia on the equator E of Borneo.

Su•lei•man I (so͞o′lā-män′, -lə-). 1494?–1566. Sultan of Turkey (1520–66).

sul•fa drug (sŭl′fə) ▸*n.* Any of a group of synthetic organic compounds used to inhibit bacterial growth and activity. [< SULFA(NILAMIDE).]

sul•fa•nil•a•mide (sŭl′fə-nĭl′ə-mīd′, -mĭd) ▸*n.* A white odorless compound used to treat various bacterial infections. [SULF(UR) + ANIL(INE) + *amide.*]

Suleiman I

sul•fate (sŭl′fāt′) ▸*n.* A chemical compound containing the bivalent group SO_4. [Fr. < Lat. *sulfur*, sulfur.]

sul•fide (sŭl′fīd′) ▸*n.* A compound of sulfur with another element, esp. a metal.

sul•fur also **sul•phur** (sŭl′fər) ▸*n. Symbol* **S** A pale yellow nonmetallic element occurring widely in nature and used in gunpowder, insecticides, pharmaceuticals, and compounds such as sulfuric acid. At. no. 16. See table at **element.** [< Lat. *sulfur.*]

sulfur dioxide ▸*n.* A colorless, extremely irritating gas or liquid, SO_2, used in the manufacture of sulfuric acid.

sul•fu•ric (sŭl-fyo͝or′ĭk) ▸*adj.* Of or containing sulfur.

sulfuric acid ▸*n.* A highly corrosive, dense oily liquid, H_2SO_4, used to manufacture a wide variety of chemicals and materials.

sul•fur•ous (sŭl′fər-əs, -fyər-, sŭl-fyo͝or′əs) ▸*adj.* **1.** Of or containing sulfur. **2.** Characteristic of burning sulfur, as in odor.

sulk (sŭlk) ▸*v.* **sulked, sulk•ing.** To be sullenly aloof or withdrawn. ▸*n.* A mood or display of sulking. [< SULKY[1].]

sulk•y[1] (sŭl′kē) ▸*adj.* **-i•er, -i•est.** Sullenly aloof. [Perh. < obsolete *sulke*, sluggish.] —**sulk′i•ly** *adv.* —**sulk′i•ness** *n.*

sulk•y[2] (sŭl′kē) ▸*n., pl.* **-ies.** A light two-wheeled vehicle carrying only the driver and drawn by one horse. [< SULKY[1].]

Sul•la (sŭl′ə), **Lucius Cornelius.** 138–78 B.C. Roman general and dictator (82–79).

sul•len (sŭl′ən) ▸*adj.* **-er, -est 1.** Showing a brooding ill humor or silent resentment. **2.** Gloomy or somber. [< Lat. *sōlus*, alone.] —**sul′len•ly** *adv.* —**sul′len•ness** *n.*

Sul•li•van (sŭl′ə-vən), Sir **Arthur Seymour.** 1842–1900. British composer.

Sullivan, Louis Henry or **Henri.** 1856–1924. Amer. architect.

sul•ly (sŭl′ē) ▸*v.* **-lied, -ly•ing 1.** To mar the cleanness or luster of. **2.** To defile; taint. [Prob. < OFr. *souiller.*]

sul•phur (sŭl′fər) ▸*n.* Var. of **sulfur.**

sul•tan (sŭl′tən) ▸*n.* A ruler of a Muslim country, esp. of the former Ottoman Empire. [< Ar. *sulṭān.*]

sul•tan•a (sŭl-tăn′ə, -tä′nə) ▸*n.* **1.** The wife, mother, sister, or daughter of a sultan. **2.** A small yellow seedless raisin.

sul•tan•ate (sŭl′tə-nāt′) ▸*n.* **1.** The office, power, or reign of a sultan. **2.** A country ruled by a sultan.

sul•try (sŭl′trē) ▸*adj.* **-tri•er, -tri•est 1a.**

Very humid and hot. **b.** Hot; torrid. **2.** Sensual; voluptuous. [Poss. < SWELTER.] —**sul′tri•ness** *n.*

Su•lu Sea (so͞o′lo͞o) An arm of the W Pacific between the Philippines and N Borneo.

sum[1] (sŭm) ►*n.* **1a.** The result obtained by addition. **b.** An arithmetic problem. **2.** The whole quantity; aggregate. **3.** An amount of money. **4.** A summary. **5.** The gist. ►*v.* **summed, sum•ming.** To add. —***phrasal verb:*** **sum up** To summarize. [< Lat. *summus*, highest.]

sum[2] (so͞om) ►*n.*, *pl.* **sum.** See table at **currency.** [Uzbek *sŭm.*]

su•mac also **su•mach** (so͞o′măk, sho͞o′-) ►*n.* Any of various shrubs or small trees with compound leaves, greenish flowers, and usu. red fruit. [< Ar. *summāq*, sumac tree.]

Su•ma•tra (so͝o-mä′trə) An island of W Indonesia in the Indian Ocean S of the Malay Peninsula. —**Su•ma′tran** *adj. & n.*

Su•mer (so͞o′mər) An ancient country of S Mesopotamia in present-day S Iraq. —**Su•me′ri•an** (-mîr′ē-ən, -mĕr′-) *adj. & n.*

sum•ma•rize (sŭm′ə-rīz′) ►*v.* **-rized, -riz•ing.** To make a summary of. —**sum′ma•ri•za′tion** *n.*

sum•ma•ry (sŭm′ə-rē) ►*adj.* **1.** Presented in condensed form; concise. **2.** Performed speedily and without ceremony: *summary justice.* ►*n.*, *pl.* **-ries.** A condensed statement of the substance or principal points of a larger work. [< Lat. *summa*, SUM[1].] —**sum•mar′i•ly** (sə-mĕr′ə-lē) *adv.*

sum•ma•tion (sə-mā′shən) ►*n.* A concluding statement summarizing the principal points, esp. of a case before a court of law.

sum•mer (sŭm′ər) ►*n.* The usu. warmest season of the year, occurring between spring and autumn. ►*v.* To pass the summer. [< OE *sumor.*] —**sum′mer•y** *adj.*

sum•mer•house (sŭm′ər-hous′) ►*n.* A small roofed structure in a park or garden.

sum•mer•time (sŭm′ər-tīm′) ►*n.* The summer season.

sum•mit (sŭm′ĭt) ►*n.* **1.** The highest point. **2.** The highest degree of achievement or status. **3.** A summit conference. [< Lat. *summus*, highest.]

summit conference ►*n.* A conference of leaders, esp. the highest-ranking officials of two or more governments.

sum•mon (sŭm′ən) ►*v.* **1.** To call together; convene. **2.** To request to appear; send for. See Syns at **call. 3.** To order to appear in court. **4.** To call forth; rouse or evoke. [< Lat. *summonēre*, remind privately : *sub-*, secretly + *monēre*, warn.]

sum•mons (sŭm′ənz) ►*n.*, *pl.* **-mons•es 1.** A call to appear or do something. **2.** *Law* A notice summoning a person to report to court. —**sum′mons** *v.*

Sum•ner (sŭm′nər), **Charles.** 1811–74. Amer. politician.

su•mo (so͞o′mō) ►*n.* A Japanese form of wrestling. [J. *sumō.*]

sump (sŭmp) ►*n.* **1.** A pit or hole that receives drainage. **2.** A cesspool. [ME *sompe*, marsh.]

sump•tu•ous (sŭmp′cho͞o-əs) ►*adj.* Of a size or splendor suggesting great expense; lavish. [< Lat. *sūmptus*, expense.] —**sump′tu•ous•ly** *adv.* —**sump′tu•ous•ness** *n.*

sun (sŭn) ►*n.* **1.** often **Sun** A star that is the center of the solar system, sustains life on Earth with its light and heat, and has a mean distance from Earth of about 150 million km (93 million mi). **2.** A star that is the center of a planetary system. **3.** The radiant energy, esp. heat and visible light, emitted by the sun; sunshine. ►*v.* **sunned, sun•ning.** To expose to or bask in the sun's rays. [< OE *sunne.*] —**sun′less** *adj.*

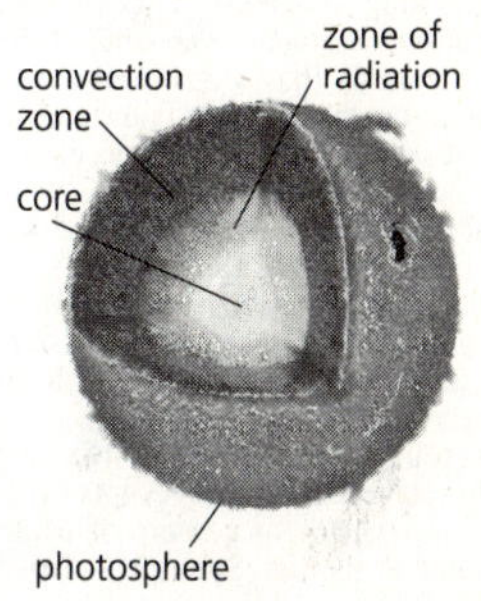

sun

Sun. ►*abbr.* Sunday

sun•baked (sŭn′bākt′) ►*adj.* Baked, dried, or hardened by exposure to sunlight.

sun•bathe (sŭn′bāth′) ►*v.* To expose the body to the sun. —**sun′bath′er** *n.*

sun•beam (sŭn′bēm′) ►*n.* A ray of sunlight.

Sun•belt also **Sun Belt** (sŭn′bĕlt′). The S and SW US

sun•block (sŭn′blŏk′) ►*n.* A sunscreen.

sun•bon•net (sŭn′bŏn′ĭt) ►*n.* A woman's wide-brimmed bonnet for shading the face and neck from the sun.

sun•burn (sŭn′bûrn′) ►*n.* Inflammation or blistering of the skin caused by overexposure to direct sunlight. —**sun′burn′** *v.*

sun•burst (sŭn′bûrst′) ►*n.* A design having a central sunlike disk with radiating spires.

sun•dae (sŭn′dē, -dā′) ►*n.* A dish of ice cream with a topping such as syrup, fruits, nuts, or whipped cream. [Poss. < SUNDAY.]

Sun•da Islands (sŭn′də, so͞on′-) A group of islands of the W Malay Archipelago between the South China Sea and the Indian Ocean.

Sun•day (sŭn′dē, -dā′) ►*n.* **1.** The 1st day of the week. **2.** The Sabbath for many Christians. [< OE *sunnandæg.*]

sun•der (sŭn′dər) ►*v.* To break or wrench apart; sever. [< OE *sundrian.*] —**sun′der•ance** *n.*

Sun•der•land (sŭn′dər-lənd) A borough of NE England on the North Sea ESE of Newcastle. Pop. 297,806.

sun•di•al (sŭn′dī′əl) ►*n.* An instrument that indicates the time of day by the shadow cast by a central projecting pointer on a calibrated dial.

sun•down (sŭn′doun′) ►*n.* Sunset.

sun•dries (sŭn′drēz) ►*pl.n.* Small miscellaneous items. [< SUNDRY.]

sun•dry (sŭn′drē) ►*adj.* Various; miscellaneous. [< OE *syndrig*, separate.]

sun•fish (sŭn′fĭsh′) ►*n.* **1.** Any of various flat-bodied North American freshwater fishes. **2.** Any of various large, round-bodied salt water fishes.

sun•flow•er (sŭn′flou′ər) ►*n.* Any of various plants with large yellow-rayed flower heads that produce edible seeds rich in oil.

sung (sŭng) ►*v.* A p.t. and the p.part. of **sing.**

sun•glass•es (sŭn′glăs′ĭz) ►*pl.n.* Eyeglasses with tinted lenses to protect the eyes from the sun's glare.

sunk (sŭngk) ►*v.* A p.t. and the p.part. of **sink.**

sunk•en (sŭng′kən) ►*adj.* **1.** Depressed, fallen in, or hollowed: *sunken cheeks.* **2.** Submerged: *a sunken reef.* **3.** Below a surrounding level.

sun•lamp or **sun lamp** (sŭn′lămp′) ►*n.* A lamp that radiates ultraviolet rays used in therapeutic and cosmetic treatments.

sun•light (sŭn′līt′) ►*n.* The light of the sun.

sun•lit (sŭn′lĭt′) ►*adj.* Illuminated by the sun.

Sun•na also **Sun•nah** (so͝on′ə) ►*n.* The way of life prescribed as normative in Islam, based on the teachings and practices of Muhammad and on the Koran. [Ar. *sunna.*]

Sun•ni (so͝on′ē) ►*n., pl.* **-ni** or **-nis.** A member of the branch of Islam that accepts the first four caliphs as rightful successors of Muhammad. [Ar. *sunnī* < *sunna*, Sunna.] —**Sun′ni** *adj.* —**Sun′nite′** *n.*

sun•ny (sŭn′ē) ►*adj.* **-ni•er, -ni•est 1.** Exposed to or abounding in sunshine. **2.** Cheerful; genial. —**sun′ni•ness** *n.*

Sun•ny•vale (sŭn′ē-vāl′) A city of W CA WNW of San Jose. Pop. 117,229.

sun•rise (sŭn′rīz′) ►*n.* The appearance of the sun above the eastern horizon.

sun•roof (sŭn′ro͞of′, -ro͝of′) ►*n.* A roof panel on a motor vehicle that can be slid back or raised.

sun•screen (sŭn′skrēn′) ►*n.* A preparation used to protect skin from the damaging rays of the sun.

sun•set (sŭn′sĕt′) ►*n.* The disappearance of the sun below the western horizon.

sun•shade (sŭn′shād′) ►*n.* Something, as a parasol, used as a protection from the sun.

sun•shine (sŭn′shīn′) ►*n.* **1.** The light or the direct rays from the sun. **2.** Cheerfulness; geniality. —**sun′shin′y** *adj.*

sun•spot (sŭn′spŏt′) ►*n.* Any of the relatively cool dark spots appearing in groups on the surface of the sun.

sun•stroke (sŭn′strōk′) ►*n.* Heat stroke caused by exposure to the sun.

sun•tan (sŭn′tăn′) ►*n.* A darkening of the skin resulting from exposure to the sun. —**sun′tanned′** *adj.*

sun•up (sŭn′ŭp′) ►*n.* The time of sunrise.

Sun Yat-sen (so͝on′ yät′sĕn′). 1866–1925. Chinese politician.

sup (sŭp) ►*v.* **supped, sup•ping.** To have supper; dine. [< OFr. *soupe*, SOUP.]

sup. ►*abbr.* **1.** superior **2.** superlative

su•per (so͞o′pər) *Informal* ►*n.* A superintendent in an apartment or office building. ►*adj.* **1.** Very large or great. **2.** Excellent.

super– ►*pref.* **1.** Above; over; upon: *superimpose.* **2.** Superior in size, quality, number, or degree: *superfine.* **3.** Exceeding a norm: *supersaturate.* [< Lat. *super*, over, above.]

su•per•a•ble (so͞o′pər-ə-bəl) ►*adj.* Possible to overcome; surmountable. [< Lat. *superāre*, overcome < *super*, over.]

su•per•a•bun•dant (so͞o′pər-ə-bŭn′dənt) ►*adj.* Abundant to excess. —**su′per•a•bun′dance** *n.*

su•per•an•nu•at•ed (so͞o′pər-ăn′yo͞o-ā′tĭd) ►*adj.* **1.** Retired or ineffective because of advanced age. **2.** Outmoded; obsolete. [< Med. Lat. *superannuātus*, over one year old : SUPER– + Lat. *annus*, year.]

su•perb (so͝o-pûrb′) ►*adj.* **1.** First-rate; excellent. **2.** Majestic; imposing. [Lat. *superbus.*] —**su•perb′ly** *adv.*

su•per•bug (so͞o′pər-bŭg′) ►*n.* A strain of bacteria resistant to all antibiotics.

su•per•car•go (so͞o′pər-kär′gō) ►*n., pl.* **-goes** or **-gos.** An officer on a merchant ship who has charge of the cargo. [< Sp. *sobrecargo* : SUPER– + *cargo*, CARGO.]

su•per•charge (so͞o′pər-chärj′) ►*v.* To increase the power of (e.g., an engine).

su•per•charg•er (so͞o′pər-chär′jər) ►*n.* A blower or compressor for supplying air under high pressure to the cylinders of an internal-combustion engine.

su•per•cil•i•ous (so͞o′pər-sĭl′ē-əs) ►*adj.* Feeling or showing haughty disdain. [< Lat. *supercilium*, eyebrow : SUPER– + *cilium*, lower eyelid.] —**su′per•cil′i•ous•ly** *adv.* —**su′per•cil′i•ous•ness** *n.*

su•per•col•lid•er (so͞o′pər-kə-līd′ər) ►*n.* A high-energy particle accelerator.

su•per•con•duc•tiv•i•ty (so͞o′pər-kŏn′dŭk-tĭv′ĭtē) ►*n.* The flow of electric current without resistance in certain metals, alloys, and ceramics, usu. at temperatures near absolute zero. —**su′per•con•duc′tive** *adj.* —**su′per•con•duc′tor** *n.*

su•per•cool (so͞o′pər-ko͞ol′) ►*v.* To cool (a liquid) below the freezing point without solidification.

su•per•e•go (so͞o′pər-ē′gō, -ĕg′ō) ►*n., pl.* **-gos.** In psychoanalysis, the part of the psyche formed through the internalization of moral standards of parents and society.

su•per•e•rog•a•to•ry (so͞o′pər-ĭ-rŏg′ə-tôr′ē, -tōr′ē) ►*adj.* Superfluous; unnecessary. [< LLat. *superērogāre*, overspend : SUPER– + *ērogāre*, spend.]

su•per•fi•cial (so͞o′pər-fĭsh′əl) ►*adj.* **1.** Of, affecting, or being on the surface. **2.** Concerned with or comprehending only the obvious; shallow. **3.** Apparent rather than actual or substantial. **4.** Trivial. [< Lat. *superficiēs*, surface : SUPER– + *faciēs*, face.] —**su′per•fi′ci•al′i•ty** (-fĭsh′ē-ăl′ĭ-tē) *n.* —**su′per•fi′cial•ly** *adv.*

su•per•fine (so͞o′pər-fīn′) ►*adj.* **1.** Of exceptional quality. **2.** Overly delicate or refined. **3.** Of extra fine texture.

su•per•flu•i•ty (so͞o′pər-flo͞o′ĭ-tē) ►*n., pl.* **-ties 1.** The quality or condition of being superfluous. **2.** Something superfluous. **3.** Overabundance; excess.

su•per•flu•ous (so͝o-pûr′flo͞o-əs) ►*adj.* Beyond what is required or sufficient. [< Lat. *superfluere*, overflow : SUPER– + *fluere*, flow.] —**su•per′flu•ous•ly** *adv.*

Syns: *superfluous, excess, extra, spare, supernumerary, surplus* **adj.**

su•per•gal•ax•y (so͞o′pər-găl′ək-sē) ►*n.* A very large group of galaxies.

su•per•gi•ant (so͞o′pər-jī′ənt) ►*n.* A very large star with a luminosity thousands of times that of the sun.

su•per•he•ro (so͞o′pər-hîr′ō) ►*n.* A figure, esp. in a comic strip or cartoon, of superhuman powers and usu. portrayed as fighting evil or crime.

su•per•high•way (sōō′pər-hī′wā′) ►*n.* A broad highway for high-speed traffic.

su•per•hu•man (sōō′pər-hyōō′mən) ►*adj.* **1.** Divine; supernatural. **2.** Beyond ordinary or normal human ability, power, or experience. —**su′per•hu′man•ly** *adv.*

su•per•im•pose (sōō′pər-ĭm-pōz′) ►*v.* **-posed, -pos•ing.** To lay or place on or over something else. —**su′per•im′po•si′tion** (-ĭm′pə-zĭsh′ən) *n.*

su•per•in•tend (sōō′pər-ĭn-tĕnd′, sōō′prĭn-) ►*v.* **1.** To oversee and direct; supervise. See Syns at **supervise. 2.** To take care of; manage. [SUPER– + Lat. *intendere*, INTEND.] —**su′per•in•ten′dence** *n.* —**su′per•in•ten′dent** *n.*

su•pe•ri•or (sōō-pîr′ē-ər) ►*adj.* **1.** High or higher in order, degree, rank, quality, or estimation. **2.** Situated above or over. **3.** Arrogant; haughty. **4.** Indifferent or immune. ►*n.* **1.** One who surpasses another in rank or quality. **2.** The head of a religious order or house. [< Lat. < *super*, over.] —**su•pe′ri•or′i•ty** (-ôr′ĭ-tē, -ŏr′-) *n.* —**su•pe′ri•or•ly** *adv.*

Superior, Lake. The largest of the Great Lakes, between the N-central US and S Ontario, Canada.

su•per•la•tive (sōō-pûr′lə-tĭv) ►*adj.* **1.** Of the highest order, quality, or degree. **2.** Excessive or exaggerated. **3.** *Gram.* Expressing or involving the extreme degree of comparison of an adjective or adverb. ►*n.* **1.** Something superlative. **2.** *Gram.* **a.** The superlative degree. **b.** An adjective, such as *biggest,* or adverb, such as *most highly,* expressing this degree. [< Lat. *superlātus*, exaggerated.] —**su•per′la•tive•ly** *adv.*

su•per•man (sōō′pər-măn′) ►*n.* A man with more than human powers.

su•per•mar•ket (sōō′pər-mär′kĭt) ►*n.* A large self-service retail market selling food and household goods.

su•per•nal (sōō-pûr′nəl) ►*adj.* **1.** Celestial; heavenly. **2.** Of or from the sky. [< Lat. *supernus.*] —**su•per′nal•ly** *adv.*

su•per•nat•u•ral (sōō′pər-năch′ər-əl) ►*adj.* **1.** Of or relating to existence outside the natural world. **2.** Attributed to divine power. —**su′per•nat′u•ral•ly** *adv.*

su•per•no•va (sōō′pər-nō′və) ►*n., pl.* **-vae** (-vē) or **-vas.** A rare celestial phenomenon in which a star explodes, resulting in an extremely bright, short-lived object.

su•per•nu•mer•ar•y (sōō′pər-nōō′mə-rĕr′ē, -nyōō′-) ►*adj.* **1.** Exceeding a fixed or prescribed number; extra. **2.** Superfluous. See Syns at **superfluous.** ►*n., pl.* **-ies 1.** One that is supernumerary. **2.** An actor or actress without a speaking part; extra. [Lat. *supernumerārius* : SUPER– + *numerus*, number.]

su•per•phos•phate (sōō′pər-fŏs′fāt′) ►*n.* **1.** An acid phosphate. **2.** A fertilizer made by the action of sulfuric acid on phosphate rock.

su•per•pow•er (sōō′pər-pou′ər) ►*n.* A powerful and dominant nation, esp. the leader of an international power bloc.

su•per•sat•u•rate (sōō′pər-săch′ə-rāt′) ►*v.* To cause (a chemical solution) to be more highly concentrated than is normally possible under given conditions of temperature and pressure. —**su′per•sat′u•ra′tion** *n.*

su•per•scribe (sōō′pər-skrīb′) ►*v.* **-scribed, -scrib•ing.** To write (something) on the outside or upper part, as of a letter. [SUPER– + Lat. *scrībere*, write.] —**su′per•scrip′tion** (-skrĭp′shən) *n.*

su•per•script (sōō′pər-skrĭpt′) ►*n.* A character placed above and immediately to one side of another. [Lat. *superscrīptus*, p.part. of *superscrībere*, SUPERSCRIBE.] —**su′per•script** *adj.*

su•per•sede (sōō′pər-sēd′) ►*v.* **-sed•ed, -sed•ing 1.** To take the place of; succeed. **2.** To displace; supplant. [< Lat. *supersedēre*, refrain from : SUPER– + *sedēre*, sit.]

su•per•son•ic (sōō′pər-sŏn′ĭk) ►*adj.* Of, caused by, or having a speed greater than the speed of sound. —**su′per•son′i•cal•ly** *adv.*

su•per•star (sōō′pər-stär′) ►*n.* A widely acclaimed star, as in movies or sports, who has great popular appeal.

su•per•sti•tion (sōō′pər-stĭsh′ən) ►*n.* **1.** A belief that an object, action, or circumstance not logically related to a course of events influences its outcome. **2.** A belief or practice irrationally maintained by ignorance or by faith in magic or chance. [< Lat. *superstes*, *superstit-*, standing over.] —**su′per•sti′tious** *adj.* —**su′per•sti′tious•ly** *adv.*

su•per•struc•ture (sōō′pər-strŭk′chər) ►*n.* A physical or conceptual structure built on top of something else, esp. a ship's structure above the main deck.

su•per•tank•er (sōō′pər-tăng′kər) ►*n.* A very large ship used esp. to transport oil.

su•per•vene (sōō′pər-vēn′) ►*v.* **-vened, -ven•ing.** To come or occur as something additional or unexpected. [Lat. *supervenīre* : SUPER– + *venīre*, come.]

su•per•vise (sōō′pər-vīz′) ►*v.* **-vised, -vis•ing.** To have the charge and direction of; superintend. [< Med.Lat. *supervidēre*, *supervīs-* : SUPER– + Lat. *vidēre*, see.] —**su′per•vi′sor** *n.* —**su′per•vi′so•ry** *adj.*

Syns: *supervise, boss, overlook, oversee, superintend* **v.**

su•per•vi•sion (sōō′pər-vĭzh′ən) ►*n.* The act or function of supervising. See Syns at **care.**

su•pine (sōō-pīn′, sōō′pīn′) ►*adj.* **1.** Lying on the back or having the face upward. **2.** Lethargic; passive. **3.** Cravenly submissive. [< Lat. *supīnus.*] —**su•pine′ly** *adv.*

sup•per (sŭp′ər) ►*n.* An evening meal, esp. a light meal when dinner is taken at midday. [< OFr. *souper*, SUP.]

sup•plant (sə-plănt′) ►*v.* To take the place of; supercede. [< Lat. *supplantāre*, trip up.]

sup•ple (sŭp′əl) ►*adj.* **-pler, -plest 1.** Readily bent; pliant. **2.** Agile; limber. **3.** Yielding readily; compliant or adaptable. [< Lat. *supplex*, suppliant.] —**sup′ple•ness** *n.* —**sup′ply, sup′ple•ly** *adv.*

sup•ple•ment (sŭp′lə-mənt) ►*n.* Something added to complete a thing or to make up for a deficiency. ►*v.* (-mĕnt′). To provide or form a supplement to. [< Lat. *supplēre*, to complete.] —**sup′ple•men′ta•ry** (-mĕn′tə-rē, -trē), **sup′ple•men′tal** *adj.* —**sup′ple•men•ta′tion** (-mĕn-tā′shən) *n.*

sup•pli•ant (sŭp′lē-ənt) ►*adj.* Asking humbly and earnestly; beseeching. ►*n.* A supplicant. [< Lat. *supplicāre*, SUPPLICATE.] —**sup′pli•ance** *n.* —**sup′pli•ant•ly** *adv.*

sup•pli•cant (sŭp′lĭ-kənt) ►*n.* One who beseeches or supplicates. ►*adj.* Supplicating.

sup•pli•cate (sŭp′lĭ-kāt′) ►*v.* **-cat•ed, -cat•**

ing 1. To make a humble, earnest petition; beg. **2.** To beseech. [< Lat. *supplicāre* < *supplex*, suppliant.] —**sup′pli•ca′tion** *n.*

sup•ply (sə-plī′) ►*v.* **-plied, -ply•ing 1.** To make available for use; provide. **2.** To furnish or equip with. **3.** To fill sufficiently; satisfy: *supply a need.* ►*n., pl.* **-plies 1.** The act of supplying. **2.** An amount available; stock. **3.** often **supplies** Materials or provisions stored and dispensed when needed. **4.** *Econ.* The amount of a commodity available for meeting a demand or for purchase at a given price. [< Lat. *supplēre*, to fill up.] —**sup•pli′er** *n.*

sup•port (sə-pôrt′, -pōrt′) ►*v.* **1.** To bear the weight of. **2.** To maintain in position; hold up. **3.** To be capable of bearing; withstand. **4.** To keep from weakening or failing. **5.** To provide for or maintain by supplying with money or necessities. **6.** To furnish corroborating evidence for. **7.** To aid the cause or interests of. ►*n.* **1.** The act of supporting or the condition of being supported. **2.** One that supports. **3.** Financial maintenance. [< Lat. *supportāre*, carry.] —**sup•port′a•ble** *adj.* —**sup•port′er** *n.* —**sup•por′tive** *adj.*

sup•pose (sə-pōz′) ►*v.* **-posed, -pos•ing 1.** To assume to be true for the sake of argument. **2a.** To believe, esp. on uncertain grounds. **b.** To consider to be probable or likely. **3.** To imply as an antecedent condition; presuppose. [< OFr. *supposer.*]

sup•posed (sə-pōzd′, -pō′zĭd) ►*adj.* Presumed or considered to be true, often mistakenly. —**sup•pos′ed•ly** *adv.*

Syns: *supposed, conjectural, hypothetical, putative, reputed* ***Ant:*** *certain* **adj.**

sup•pos•ing (sə-pō′zĭng) ►*conj.* Assuming that: *Supposing I'm right, what can we do?*

sup•po•si•tion (sŭp′ə-zĭsh′ən) ►*n.* **1.** The act of supposing. **2.** An assumption.

sup•pos•i•to•ry (sə-pŏz′ĭ-tôr′ē, -tōr′ē) ►*n., pl.* **-ries.** A small plug of medication designed to melt within a body cavity other than the mouth. [< Lat. *suppositus*, placed beneath.]

sup•press (sə-prĕs′) ►*v.* **1.** To put an end to forcibly; subdue. **2.** To keep from being revealed, published, or circulated. **3.** To inhibit the expression of; check: *suppress a smile.* [< Lat. *supprimere*, *suppress-*.] —**sup•press′ion** *n.* —**sup•press′ive** *adj.*

sup•pu•rate (sŭp′yə-rāt′) ►*v.* **-rat•ed, -rat•ing.** To form or discharge pus. [< Lat. *suppūrāre.*] —**sup′pu•ra′tion** *n.*

su•pra•na•tion•al (so͞o′prə-năsh′ə-nəl, -năsh′nəl) ►*adj.* Of or extending beyond the boundaries or authority of a nation. [Lat. *suprā*, beyond + NATIONAL.]

su•prem•a•cist (so͞o-prĕm′ə-sĭst) ►*n.* One who believes that a certain group is or should be supreme.

su•prem•a•cy (so͞o-prĕm′ə-sē) ►*n.* **1.** The quality or condition of being supreme. **2.** Supreme power.

su•preme (so͞o-prēm′) ►*adj.* **1.** Greatest in power, authority, or rank. **2.** Greatest in importance, degree, or achievement. **3.** Ultimate; final: *the supreme sacrifice.* [Lat. *suprēmus* < *super*, over.] —**su•preme′ly** *adv.* —**su•preme′ness** *n.*

Supreme Court ►*n.* **1.** The highest US federal court. **2. supreme court** The highest court in most US states.

Supt. ►*abbr.* superintendent

sur– ►*pref.* **1.** Over; above; upon: *surpass.* **2.** Additional: *surtax.* [< Lat. *super.*]

Su•ra•ba•ya also **Su•ra•ba•ja** (so͝or′ə-bä′yə). A city of NE Java, Indonesia, on the Java Sea. Pop. 2,027,913.

sur•cease (sûr′sēs′, sər-sēs′) ►*n.* Cessation. [< Lat. *supersedēre*, SUPERSEDE.]

sur•charge (sûr′chärj′) ►*n.* **1.** An additional sum added to the usual cost. **2.** An overcharge, esp. when unlawful. ►*v.* **1.** To charge an extra sum. **2.** To overcharge.

sure (sho͝or, shûr) ►*adj.* **sur•er, sur•est 1.** Impossible to doubt or dispute; certain. **2.** Strong; firm: *sure convictions.* **3.** Confident: *sure of victory.* **4a.** Bound to happen; inevitable: *sure defeat.* **b.** Destined: *sure to succeed.* See Syns at **certain. 5.** Trustworthy; reliable. —***idioms:*** **for sure** *Informal* Certainly; unquestionably. **make sure** Make certain. **to be sure** Indeed; certainly. [< Lat. *sēcūrus*, SECURE.] —**sure′ness** *n.*

sure-fire (sho͝or′fīr′) ►*adj. Informal* Bound to be successful.

sure-foot•ed or **sure•foot•ed** (sho͝or′fo͝ot′ĭd) ►*adj.* Not liable to stumble or fall. —**sure′foot′ed•ly** *adv.*

sure•ly (sho͝or′lē) ►*adv.* **1.** With confidence; unhesitatingly. **2.** Undoubtedly; certainly.

sur•e•ty (sho͝or′ĭ-tē) ►*n., pl.* **-ties 1.** The condition of being sure. **2.** Something beyond doubt. **3.** A guarantee or security. **4.** One who has contracted to be responsible for another. —**sur′e•ty•ship′** *n.*

surf (sûrf) ►*n.* The waves of the sea as they break upon a shore or reef. ►*v.* To engage in surfing. [?] —**surf′er** *n.*

sur•face (sûr′fəs) ►*n.* **1.** The outer or the topmost boundary of an object. **2.** The superficial or external aspect. ►*adj.* **1.** Of or on the surface. **2.** Superficial. ►*v.* **-faced, -fac•ing 1.** To form the surface of. **2.** To rise or come to the surface. **3.** To emerge from concealment. [Fr.]

surf•board (sûrf′bôrd′, -bōrd′) ►*n.* A narrow, somewhat rounded board used for surfing.

sur•feit (sûr′fĭt) ►*v.* To feed or supply to excess; satiate. ►*n.* **1a.** Overindulgence in food or drink. **b.** The result of such overindulgence; satiety or disgust. **2.** An excessive amount. [< OFr. *surfaire*, overdo.]

surf•ing (sûr′fĭng) ►*n.* The sport of riding on the crest or along the tunnel of a wave, esp. while on a surfboard.

surge (sûrj) ►*v.* **surged, surg•ing 1.** To move in a billowing or swelling manner. **2.** To increase suddenly. ►*n.* **1.** A swelling motion like that of great waves. **2.** A sudden onrush: *a surge of joy.* **3.** *Elect.* A sudden increase in current or voltage. [< Lat. *surgere*, rise.]

sur•geon (sûr′jən) ►*n.* A physician specializing in surgery. [< OFr. *cirurgie*, SURGERY.]

surge protector ►*n.* A device that protects equipment plugged into it from a surge in electric current.

sur•ger•y (sûr′jə-rē) ►*n., pl.* **-ies 1.** The diagnosis and treatment of injury, deformity, and disease by manual and instrumental means. **2.** A surgical procedure, esp. the removal of a diseased part. **3.** A surgical operating room or laboratory. [< Gk. *kheirourgos*, working by hand : *kheir*, hand + *ergon*, work.] —**sur′gi•cal** *adj.* —**sur′gi•cal•ly** *adv.*

Su•ri•na•me (so͝or′ə-nä′mə) also **Su•ri•nam** (so͝or′ə-năm′, -näm′). A country of NE South America on the Atlantic. Cap. Paramaribo. Pop. 418,000. —**Su′ri•na•mese′** (-nä-mēz′, -mēs′) *adj. & n.*

Suriname River also **Surinam River.** A river of Suriname flowing about 644 km (400 mi) to the Atlantic.

sur•ly (sûr′lē) ▸*adj.* **-li•er, -li•est.** Sullenly ill-humored; gruff. [ME *sirly*, lordly < *sir*, SIR.] —**sur′li•ly** *adv.* —**sur′li•ness** *n.*

sur•mise (sər-mīz′) ▸*v.* **-mised, -mis•ing.** To infer with little evidence; guess. ▸*n.* An idea or opinion based on little evidence; conjecture. [< OFr. *surmettre, surmis-*.]

sur•mount (sər-mount′) ▸*v.* **1.** To overcome; conquer: *surmount an obstacle.* **2.** To ascend to the top of. **3.** To be above or on top of. [< OFr. *surmonter.*] —**sur•mount′a•ble** *adj.* —**sur•mount′er** *n.*

sur•name (sûr′nām′) ▸*n.* A name shared in common to identify the members of a family; last name.

sur•pass (sər-păs′) ▸*v.* **1.** To be beyond the limit, powers, or capacity of; transcend: *surpass comprehension.* **2.** To be greater or better than; exceed.

sur•pass•ing (sər-păs′ĭng) ▸*adj.* Exceptional; exceeding. —**sur•pass′ing•ly** *adv.*

sur•plice (sûr′plĭs) ▸*n.* A loose-fitting white ecclesiastical gown worn over a cassock. [< Med.Lat. *superpellīcium* : SUPER– + Lat. *pellis*, skin.]

sur•plus (sûr′pləs, -plŭs′) ▸*adj.* Being in excess of what is needed. See Syns at **superfluous.** ▸*n.* A surplus amount or quantity. [< Med.Lat. *superplūs* : SUPER– + Lat. *plūs*, more.]

sur•prise (sər-prīz′) ▸*v.* **-prised, -pris•ing 1.** To encounter suddenly or unexpectedly. **2.** To attack or capture suddenly and without warning. **3.** To astonish by the unanticipated. ▸*n.* **1.** The act of surprising or the condition of being surprised. **2.** Something that surprises. [< OFr. *surprendre*, overcome.] —**sur•pris′ing** *adj.* —**sur•pris′ing•ly** *adv.*

sur•re•al•ism (sə-rē′ə-lĭz′əm) ▸*n.* A 20th-cent. literary and artistic movement that attempts to express the workings of the subconscious by fantastic imagery and incongruous juxtaposition of subject matter. —**sur•re′al, sur•re′al•is′tic** *adj.* —**sur•re′al•ist** *n.* —**sur•re′al•is′ti•cal•ly** *adv.*

sur•ren•der (sə-rĕn′dər) ▸*v.* **1.** To relinquish possession or control of to another because of demand or compulsion. **2.** To give (oneself) up, as to an emotion: *surrendered himself to grief.* **3.** To give oneself up to another. ▸*n.* The act of surrendering. [< OFr. *surrendre.*]

sur•rep•ti•tious (sûr′əp-tĭsh′əs) ▸*adj.* Secret and stealthy. [< Lat. *surripere*, take away secretly.] —**sur′rep•ti′tious•ly** *adv.*

sur•rey (sûr′ē, sŭr′ē) ▸*n., pl.* **-reys.** A four-wheeled horse-drawn carriage having two or four seats. [After *Surrey*, England.]

Surrey, Earl of. See Henry **Howard.**

sur•ro•gate (sûr′ə-gĭt, -gāt′, sŭr′-) ▸*n.* **1.** A substitute. **2.** *Law* A judge in some US states having jurisdiction over the settlement of estates. [< Lat. *surrogāre*, substitute.] —**sur′ro•gate** (-gĭt, gāt′) *adj.*

sur•round (sə-round′) ▸*v.* **1.** To extend on all sides of simultaneously; encircle. **2.** To enclose or confine on all sides. [< LLat. *superundāre*, inundate : SUPER– + *unda*, wave.]

Syns: *surround, circle, compass, encircle, encompass, gird, girdle, ring* **v.**

sur•round•ings (sə-roun′dĭngz) ▸*pl.n.* The external circumstances that surround one.

sur•tax (sûr′tăks′) ▸*n.* **1.** An additional tax. **2.** A tax levied after net income has exceeded a certain level.

sur•veil•lance (sər-vā′ləns) ▸*n.* Close observation of a person or group, esp. one under suspicion. [< OFr. *surveiller*, watch over.]

sur•vey (sər-vā′, sûr′vā′) ▸*v.* **1.** To examine or look at comprehensively. **2.** To determine the boundaries, area, or elevations of (part of the earth's surface) by means of measuring angles and distances. ▸*n.* (sûr′vā′) *pl.* **-veys 1.** A detailed inspection or investigation. **2.** A comprehensive view. **3a.** The process of surveying. **b.** A report on or map of what has been surveyed. [< Med.Lat. *supervidēre* : SUPER– + Lat. *vidēre*, look.] —**sur•vey′or** *n.*

sur•vey•ing (sər-vā′ĭng) ▸*n.* The act, practice, or occupation of a surveyor.

sur•vive (sər-vīv′) ▸*v.* **-vived, -viv•ing 1.** To remain alive or in existence; endure. **2.** To live longer than; outlive. [< Lat. *supervīvere* : SUPER– + *vīvere*, live.] —**sur•viv′a•ble** *adj.* —**sur•viv′al** *n.* —**sur•vi′vor** *n.*

sus•cep•ti•ble (sə-sĕp′tə-bəl) ▸*adj.* **1.** Easily influenced or affected. **2.** Likely to be affected with: *susceptible to colds.* **3.** Capable of accepting or permitting: *susceptible of proof.* [< Lat. *susceptus*, p.part. of *suscipere*, receive.] —**sus•cep′ti•bil′i•ty** *n.* —**sus•cep′ti•bly** *adv.*

su•shi (so͞o′shē) ▸*n.* Cold rice shaped into small pieces and topped with raw or cooked fish. [J.]

sushi

sus•pect (sə-spĕkt′) ▸*v.* **1.** To surmise to be true or probable; imagine. **2.** To distrust or doubt: *I suspect his motives.* **3.** To think guilty without proof. ▸*n.* (sŭs′pĕkt′). One who is suspected, esp. of a crime. ▸*adj.* (sŭs′pĕkt′, sə-spĕkt′). Open to or viewed with suspicion: *a suspect policy; suspect motives.* [< Lat. *suspectāre* : SUB– + *specere*, look at.]

sus•pend (sə-spĕnd′) ▸*v.* **1.** To bar for a period from a privilege, office, or position. **2.** To cause to stop for a period; interrupt. **3a.** To hold in abeyance; defer: *suspend judgment.* See Syns at **defer**[1]. **b.** To render temporarily ineffective: *suspend a jail sentence.* **4.** To hang so as to allow free movement. **5.** To support or keep from falling without apparent attachment. [< Lat. *suspendere*, hang up.]

sus•pend•ers (sə-spĕn′dərz) ▸*n.* A pair of

often elastic straps worn over the shoulders to support trousers.

sus•pense (sə-spĕns′) ▸*n.* **1.** The state or quality of being undecided. **2.** Anxiety or apprehension resulting from uncertainty. [< Lat. *suspēnsus*, p.part. of *suspendere*, suspend.] —**sus•pense′ful** *adj.*

sus•pen•sion (sə-spĕn′shən) ▸*n.* **1.** The act of suspending or the condition of being suspended, esp.: **a.** A temporary deferment. **b.** A postponement of judgment or decision. See Syns at **pause. 2.** A device from which a mechanical part is suspended. **3.** The system of springs and other devices that insulates the chassis of a vehicle from shocks. **4.** *Chem.* A relatively coarse, noncolloidal dispersion of solid particles in a liquid.

suspension bridge ▸*n.* A bridge having the roadway suspended from cables that are usu. supported at intervals by towers.

sus•pi•cion (sə-spĭsh′ən) ▸*n.* **1.** The act of suspecting something, esp. something wrong, on little evidence or proof. **2.** A hint or trace. [< Lat. *suspicere*, SUSPECT.]

sus•pi•cious (sə-spĭsh′əs) ▸*adj.* **1.** Arousing or apt to arouse suspicion; questionable. **2.** Tending to suspect; distrustful. **3.** Expressing suspicion. —**sus•pi′cious•ly** *adv.* —**sus•pi′cious•ness** *n.*

Sus•que•han•na River (sŭs′kwə-hăn′ə) A river of the NE US rising in central NY and flowing about 714 km (444 mi) through E PA and NE MD to Chesapeake Bay.

sus•tain (sə-stān′) ▸*v.* **1.** To keep in existence; maintain. **2.** To supply with necessities or nourishment. **3.** To keep from falling or sinking; prop. **4.** To support the spirits or resolution of; encourage. **5.** To endure or withstand: *sustain hardships.* **6.** To suffer: *sustained a fatal injury.* **7.** To affirm the validity of: *The judge sustained the objection.* **8.** To prove; confirm. [< Lat. *sustinēre*, hold up.] —**sus•tain′a•ble** *adj.*

sus•te•nance (sŭs′tə-nəns) ▸*n.* **1.** The act of sustaining or condition of being sustained. **2.** Something, esp. food, that sustains life or health. **3.** Means of livelihood. [< OFr. *sustenir*, SUSTAIN.]

Suth•er•land (sŭ*th*′ər-lənd), **Joan.** b. 1926. Australian operatic soprano.

su•tra (so͞o′trə) ▸*n.* **1.** *Hinduism* Any of various aphoristic doctrinal summaries recorded between 500 and 200 B.C. **2.** *Buddhism* A scriptural narrative, esp. a text regarded as a discourse of the Buddha. [Skt. *sūtram*, thread.]

su•ture (so͞o′chər) ▸*n.* **1a.** The act of joining together by or as if by sewing. **b.** The material used in this procedure. **2.** The line of junction or an immovable joint between two bones, esp. of the skull. ▸*v.* **-tured, -tur•ing.** To join by means of sutures. [< Lat. *sūtūra* < *suere*, sew.]

SUV ▸*abbr.* sport-utility vehicle

Su•va (so͞o′və, -vä) The capital of Fiji, on the SE coast of Viti Levu. Pop. 74,000.

su•ze•rain (so͞o′zər-ən, -zə-rān′) ▸*n.* **1.** A nation that controls another nation in international affairs but allows it domestic sovereignty. **2.** A feudal lord. [Fr.] —**su′ze•rain** *adj.* —**su′ze•rain•ty** *n.*

Su•zhou (so͞o′jō′) also **Soo•chow** (-chou′, -jō′). A city of E China WNW of Shanghai. Pop. 706,500.

svelte (svĕlt) ▸*adj.* **svelt•er, svelt•est.** Slender and graceful in figure or outline. [< Ital. *svelto*, stretched.]

Sverd•lovsk (sfĕrd-lôfsk′) See **Yekaterinburg.**

sw ▸*abbr.* short wave

SW ▸*abbr.* **1.** southwest **2.** southwestern

Sw. ▸*abbr.* Swedish

swab (swŏb) ▸*n.* **1.** Absorbent material attached to the end of a stick or wire and used for cleansing or applying medicine. **2.** A mop used for cleaning floors or decks. **3.** *Slang* A sailor. ▸*v.* **swabbed, swab•bing.** To clean or treat with a swab. [< MDu. *swabble*, mop.]

Swa•bi•a (swā′bē-ə) A historical region of SW Germany. —**Swa′bi•an** *adj. & n.*

swad•dle (swŏd′l) ▸*v.* **-dled, -dling 1.** To swathe. **2.** To wrap (a baby) in strips of cloth. [< OE *swathian.*]

swag (swăg) ▸*n. Slang* Stolen property; loot. [Prob. of Scand. orig.]

swag•ger (swăg′ər) ▸*v.* **1.** To walk or behave with an insolent air; strut. **2.** To brag. [Prob. of Scand. orig.] —**swag′ger** *n.*

swagger stick ▸*n.* A short cane carried esp. by military officers.

Swa•hi•li (swä-hē′lē) ▸*n., pl.* **-li** or **-lis 1.** A member of a predominantly Muslim people of the coast and islands of E Africa. **2.** The Bantu language of the Swahili, widely used as a lingua franca in E and E-central Africa.

swain (swān) ▸*n.* **1.** A country lad, esp. a young shepherd. **2.** A beau. [< ON *sveinn.*]

swal•low¹ (swŏl′ō) ▸*v.* **1.** To cause to pass through the mouth and throat into the stomach. **2.** To bear humbly or passively: *swallowed the insults.* **3.** To consume or devour. **4.** *Slang* To believe without question. ▸*n.* **1.** The act of swallowing. **2.** An amount swallowed. [< OE *swelgan.*]

swal•low² (swŏl′ō) ▸*n.* Any of a family of birds with long pointed wings and a usu. notched or forked tail. [< OE *swealwe.*]

swal•low•tail (swŏl′ō-tāl′) ▸*n.* **1.** A deeply forked tail, as of a swallow. **2.** Any of a family of butterflies with a taillike extension at the end of each hind wing.

swam (swăm) ▸*v.* P.t. of **swim.**

swa•mi (swä′mē) ▸*n., pl.* **-mis 1.** A Hindu religious teacher. **2.** A mystic. [< Skt. *svāmī.*]

swamp (swŏmp, swômp) ▸*n.* **1.** A wetland, esp. one that is forested and seasonally flooded. **2.** A tangle; morass. ▸*v.* **1.** To drench in or cover with liquid. **2.** To overwhelm: *I'm swamped with work.* **3.** To fill or sink (a ship) with water. [Perh. of Low Germ. orig.] —**swamp′i•ness** *n.* —**swamp′y** *adj.*

swan (swŏn) ▸*n.* Any of a family of large aquatic birds with webbed feet, a long slender neck, and usu. white plumage. [< OE.]

swan dive ▸*n.* A dive with the legs straight together, the back arched, and the arms stretched out from the sides.

swank (swăngk) ▸*adj.* **-er, -est 1.** Imposingly fashionable or elegant; grand. See Syns at **fashionable. 2.** Ostentatious. [Perh. akin to MHGer. *swanken*, swing.] —**swank′i•ness** *n.* —**swank′y** *adj.*

swan's-down also **swans•down** (swŏnz′doun′) ▸*n.* **1.** The soft down of a swan. **2.** A soft woolen fabric.

Swan•sea (swän′zē, -sē) A borough of S Wales WNW of Cardiff. Pop. 189,329.

swan dive

swan song ►*n.* A farewell appearance, action, or work.

swap (swŏp) *Informal* ►*v.* **swapped, swap•ping.** To trade one thing for another. ►*n.* An exchange; trade. [ME *swappen*, strike the hands together in closing a bargain.]

sward (swôrd) ►*n.* Land covered with grassy turf. [< OE *sweard*, skin.]

swarm (swôrm) ►*n.* **1.** A large number of insects or other small organisms, esp. when in motion. **2.** A multitude; throng. ►*v.* **1a.** To move in a swarm. **b.** To leave a hive as a swarm. Used of bees. **2.** To move or gather in large numbers. **3.** To be overrun; teem: *a riverbank swarming with insects.* See Syns at **teem.** [< OE *swearm.*]

swarth•y (swôr′*thē*) ►*adj.* **-i•er, -i•est.** Having a dark complexion or color. [< OE *sweart.*] —**swarth′i•ness** *n.*

swash (swŏsh, swôsh) ►*v.* To strike, move, or wash with a splashing sound. [Prob. imit.] —**swash** *n.*

swash•buck•ler (swŏsh′bŭk′lər, swôsh′-) ►*n.* A flamboyant soldier or adventurer. —**swash′buck′ling** *adj.*

swas•ti•ka (swŏs′tĭ-kə) ►*n.* **1.** The emblem of Nazi Germany. **2.** An ancient cosmic or religious symbol formed by a Greek cross with the ends of the arms bent at right angles. [Skt. *svastikaḥ*, sign of good luck.]

swat (swŏt) ►*v.* **swat•ted, swat•ting.** To deal a sharp blow to; slap. [< SQUAT, to squash (obs.).] —**swat** *n.* —**swat′ter** *n.*

swatch (swŏch) ►*n.* A sample strip cut from a piece of material. [?]

swath (swŏth, swôth) ►*n.* **1.** The width of a scythe stroke or a mowing-machine blade. **2.** A path left in mowing. —***idiom:* cut a swath** To create a great stir or impression. [< OE *swæth*, track.]

swathe (swŏ*th*, swô*th*, swā*th*) ►*v.* **swathed, swath•ing.** To wrap with or as if with bandages. [< OE *swathian.*] —**swathe** *n.*

sway (swā) ►*v.* **1.** To move or cause to move back and forth with a swinging motion. **2.** To incline or bend to one side. **3.** To vacillate. **4.** To exert influence on or control over. ►*n.* **1.** The act of swaying. **2.** Power; influence. **3.** Dominion or control. [ME *sweien.*]

sway•back (swā′băk′) ►*n.* Excessive inward or downward curvature of the spine. —**sway′-backed′** *adj.*

Swa•zi (swä′zē) ►*n., pl.* **-zi** or **-zis 1.** A member of a SE African people of Swaziland. **2.** The Bantu language of this people.

Swa•zi•land (swä′zē-lănd′) A country of SE Africa between South Africa and Mozambique. Cap. Mbabane. Pop. 832,000.

SWbS ►*abbr.* southwest by south

SWbW ►*abbr.* southwest by west

swear (swâr) ►*v.* **swore** (swôr, swōr), **sworn** (swôrn, swōrn), **swear•ing 1.** To make a solemn declaration. **2.** To promise; vow. See Syns at **promise. 3.** To use profane oaths; curse. **4.** To assert under oath. **5.** To declare or affirm with great conviction. **6.** To administer a legal oath to. —***phrasal verbs:* swear in** To administer an oath of office to. **swear off** *Informal* To renounce; give up. [< OE *swerian.*]

sweat (swĕt) ►*v.* **sweat•ed** or **sweat, sweat•ing 1.** To excrete perspiration through the pores in the skin; perspire. **2.** To exude or become moist with surface droplets. **3.** To condense atmospheric moisture. **4.** *Informal* To work or cause to work long and hard. **5.** *Informal* To fret or worry. —***phrasal verb:* sweat out** *Slang* To endure anxiously. ►*n.* **1.** Perspiration. **2.** Condensation of moisture in the form of droplets on a surface. **3.** The process of sweating or the condition of being sweated. **4.** *Informal* An anxious, fretful condition. [< OE *swǣtan.*] —**sweat′i•ness** *n.* —**sweat′y** *adj.*

sweat•er (swĕt′ər) ►*n.* A knitted or crocheted garment worn on the upper body.

sweat gland ►*n.* Any of the numerous small glands in the skin of humans that secrete perspiration externally through pores.

sweat•shirt (swĕt′shûrt′) ►*n.* A usu. long-sleeved pullover made usu. of heavy cotton jersey.

sweat•shop (swĕt′shŏp′) ►*n.* A shop or factory in which employees work long hours at low wages under poor conditions.

Swede (swēd) ►*n.* A native or inhabitant of Sweden.

Swe•den (swēd′n) A country of N Europe on the E Scandinavian Peninsula. Cap. Stockholm. Pop. 8,780,000.

Swe•den•borg (swēd′n-bôrg′), **Emanuel.** 1688–1772. Swedish scientist and theologian. —**Swe′den•bor′gi•an** *adj. & n.*

Swed•ish (swē′dĭsh) ►*adj.* Of or relating to Sweden, the Swedes, or their language. ►*n.* The Germanic language of Sweden.

sweep (swēp) ►*v.* **swept** (swĕpt), **sweep•ing 1.** To clean or clear with or as if with a broom or brush. **2.** To touch or brush lightly. **3.** To clear, drive, or convey with relentless force, as by wind or rain. **4.** To move swiftly or with great intensity: *The news swept through the country.* **5a.** To win all the stages of (a game or contest). **b.** To win overwhelmingly in. **6.** To extend gracefully, esp. in a long curve. ►*n.* **1.** An act or instance of sweeping. **2a.** A wide curving motion. **b.** The range or scope encompassed by sweeping. See Syns at **range. 3.** A broad reach or extent. **4.** A curve or contour. **5.** A chimney sweep. **6a.** The winning of all stages of a contest. **b.** An overwhelming victory. [ME *swepen.*] —**sweep′er** *n.*

sweep•ing (swē′pĭng) ►*adj.* **1.** Having wide-ranging influence or effect. **2.** Curving; contoured. ►*n.* **sweepings** Things swept up; refuse. —**sweep′ing•ly** *adv.*

sweep•stakes (swēp′stāks′) ►*pl.n.* *(takes sing. or pl. v.)* **1.** A lottery in which the participants' contributions form a fund awarded as a prize to one or several winners. **2.** An event or a contest, esp. a horserace, the result of which determines the winner of such a lottery.

sweet (swēt) ►*adj.* **-er, -est 1.** Having the taste of sugar. **2.** Pleasing to the senses, mind, or feelings. **3.** Having a pleasing disposition; lovable. **4.** Not saline or salted: *sweet butter.* **5.** Not spoiled, sour, or decaying. ►*n.* **1.** Something sweet to the taste. **2. sweets** Sweet foods, esp. candy. **3.** A dear or beloved person. [< OE *swēte.*] **—sweet′ly** *adv.* **—sweet′ness** *n.*

sweet alyssum ►*n.* A garden plant grown for its small, fragrant, varicolored flowers.

sweet•bread (swēt′brĕd′) ►*n.* The thymus gland or pancreas of a young animal used for food.

sweet•bri•er also **sweet•bri•ar** (swēt′brī′ər) ►*n.* A rose having prickly stems, fragrant leaves, and bright pink flowers.

sweet corn ►*n.* The common table corn, with kernels that are sweet when young.

sweet•en (swēt′n) ►*v.* **1.** To make sweet or sweeter. **2.** To make more valuable or agreeable. **—sweet′en•er** *n.*

sweet•en•ing (swēt′n-ĭng) ►*n.* **1.** The act or process of making sweet. **2.** Something that sweetens; sweetener.

sweet•heart (swēt′härt′) ►*n.* **1.** A beloved. **2.** *Informal* A generous or dear person.

sweet•meat (swēt′mēt′) ►*n.* A sweet delicacy, as a piece of candy or candied fruit.

sweet pea ►*n.* A climbing plant of the pea family, cultivated for its fragrant flowers.

sweet potato ►*n.* **1.** A tropical American vine cultivated for its fleshy, tuberous orange root. **2.** The root of this vine, eaten cooked as a vegetable.

sweet-talk (swēt′tôk′) ►*v. Informal* To coax or cajole with flattery. **—sweet talk** *n.*

sweet tooth ►*n. Informal* A fondness or craving for sweets.

sweet William ►*n.* A widely cultivated plant with flat-topped dense clusters of varicolored flowers.

swell (swĕl) ►*v.* **swelled, swelled** or **swol•len** (swō′lən), **swell•ing 1.** To increase in size or volume. **2.** To increase in force, size, number, or intensity. **3.** To bulge out, as a sail. **4.** To be or become filled or puffed up, as with pride. ►*n.* **1.** A swollen part. **2.** A long wave on water that moves continuously without breaking. **3.** *Informal* One who is fashionably dressed or socially prominent. ►*adj.* **-er, -est** *Informal* **1.** Fashionably elegant; stylish. **2.** Excellent; wonderful. [< OE *swellan.*]

swell•ing (swĕl′ĭng) ►*n.* **1.** The state of being swollen. **2.** Something swollen.

swel•ter (swĕl′tər) ►*v.* To suffer from oppressive heat. [< OE *sweltan*, perish.]

swept (swĕpt) ►*v.* P.t. and p.part. of **sweep.**

swerve (swûrv) ►*v.* **swerved, swerv•ing.** To turn aside or be turned aside from a straight course. ►*n.* The act of swerving. [< OE *sweorfan*, rub.]

Syns: *swerve, depart, deviate, digress, diverge, stray, veer* **v.**

swift (swĭft) ►*adj.* **-er, -est 1.** Moving or capable of moving with great speed; fast. **2.** Occurring or accomplished quickly. ►*n.* Any of various small dark birds noted for their long narrow wings and darting flight. [< OE.] **—swift′ly** *adv.* **—swift′ness** *n.*

Swift, Jonathan. 1667–1745. Irish-born English writer.

swig (swĭg) ►*n. Informal* A deep swallow or draft, esp. of liquor; gulp. [?] **—swig** *v.*

swill (swĭl) ►*v.* **1.** To drink greedily or grossly. **2.** To feed (animals) with swill. ►*n.* **1.** A mixture of liquid and solid food fed to animals, esp. pigs; slop. **2.** Kitchen waste; garbage. **3.** Nonsense; rubbish. [< OE *swilian*, wash out.]

swim (swĭm) ►*v.* **swam** (swăm), **swum** (swŭm), **swim•ming 1.** To move through water by means of the limbs, fins, or tail. **2.** To move as though gliding through water. **3.** To cross by swimming. **4.** To be covered with or as if with a liquid. **5.** To feel dizzy. **6.** To appear to spin or reel. ►*n.* The act or a period of swimming. **—*idiom:* in the swim** Active in the general current of affairs. [< OE *swimman.*] **—swim′mer** *n.*

swim•ming•ly (swĭm′ĭng-lē) ►*adv.* Splendidly; excellently.

swim•suit (swĭm′so͞ot′) ►*n.* A garment worn while swimming; bathing suit.

Swin•burne (swĭn′bûrn′), **Algernon Charles.** 1837–1909. British poet and critic.

swin•dle (swĭn′dl) ►*v.* **-dled, -dling.** To cheat or defraud of money or property. ►*n.* The act or an instance of swindling. [< Ger. *schwindeln*, be dizzy.] **—swin′dler** *n.*

swine (swīn) ►*n., pl.* **swine 1.** Any of various hoofed mammals of the family that includes pigs, hogs, and boars. **2.** A brutish or contemptible person. [< OE *swīn.*]

swing (swĭng) ►*v.* **swung** (swŭng), **swing•ing 1.** To move or cause to move back and forth. **2.** To hit at something with a sweeping motion. **3.** To turn in place, as on a hinge or pivot. **4.** To walk or move with a swaying motion. **5.** To hang freely. **6.** *Slang* To be put to death by hanging. **7.** *Informal* To manage or arrange successfully. **8.** To have a compelling or infectious rhythm. **9.** *Slang* **a.** To be lively, trendy, and exciting. **b.** To be sexually promiscuous. ►*n.* **1.** The act of swinging. **2.** The sweep or scope of something that swings. **3.** A seat suspended from above on which one can ride back and forth. **4.** A popular dance music based on jazz but usu. employing a larger band and simpler harmonic and rhythmic patterns. [< OE *swingan*, flog.]

swing•er (swĭng′ər) ►*n.* **1.** One that swings. **2.** *Slang* **a.** A sophisticated, socially active person. **b.** One who is sexually promiscuous.

swipe (swīp) ►*n.* **1.** A sweeping blow or stroke. **2.** *Informal* A critical remark. ►*v.* **swiped, swip•ing 1.** To hit with a sweeping motion. **2.** *Informal* To steal. [Perh. < SWEEP.]

swirl (swûrl) ►*v.* **1.** To move with a spinning or whirling motion. **2.** To arrange in a spiral or whorl. [< ME *swyrl*, eddy.] **—swirl** *n.* **—swirl′y** *adj.*

swish (swĭsh) ►*v.* **1.** To move with a hissing sound. **2.** To rustle. [Imit.] **—swish** *n.*

Swiss (swĭs) ►*n.* **1.** *pl.* **Swiss** A native or inhabitant of Switzerland. **2.** A firm white or pale yellow cheese with many holes. **—Swiss** *adj.*

Swiss chard ►*n.* A variety of beet having large succulent leaves used as a vegetable.

switch (swĭch) ►*n.* **1.** A slender flexible rod, stick, or twig. **2.** A blow given with a switch. **3.** A device used to break or open an electric circuit. **4.** A device used to transfer rolling stock from one track to another. **5.** A change or shift from one thing to another. ►*v.* **1.** To whip with or as if with a switch. **2.** To shift, transfer, or divert. **3.** To exchange: *switch seats.* **4.** To connect or disconnect by operating a switch. [Prob. of LGer. or Flem. orig.] —**switch′er** *n.*

switch•blade (swĭch′blād′) ►*n.* A pocketknife with a spring-operated blade.

switch•board (swĭch′bôrd′, -bōrd′) ►*n.* **1.** A panel with apparatus for operating electric circuits. **2.** See **telephone exchange.**

switch hitter ►*n. Baseball* A player who can bat either right-handed or left-handed.

switch•man (swĭch′mən) ►*n.* One who operates railroad switches.

Swit•zer•land (swĭt′sər-lənd) A country of W-central Europe. Cap. Bern. Pop. 6,995,000.

swiv•el (swĭv′əl) ►*n.* A link, pivot, or other fastening that permits free turning of attached parts. ►*v.* **-eled, -el•ing** or **-elled, -el•ling.** To turn or rotate on or as if on a swivel. [ME *swyvel.*]

swiz•zle stick (swĭz′əl) ►*n.* A small thin rod for stirring mixed drinks.

swol•len (swō′lən) ►*v.* P.part. of **swell.** ►*adj.* Puffed up; distended.

swoon (swo͞on) ►*v.* To faint. ►*n.* A fainting spell. [Prob. < OE **swōgan*, suffocate.]

swoop (swo͞op) ►*v.* To move in a sudden sweep, as a bird descending on its prey. [< OE *swāpan*, sweep.] —**swoop** *n.*

sword (sôrd) ►*n.* **1.** A weapon having a long blade with one or two cutting edges. **2.** An instrument of death or destruction. **3.** The use of force, as in war. [< OE *sweord.*]

sword•fish (sôrd′fĭsh′) ►*n.* A large marine food and game fish having a long swordlike extension of the upper jaw.

sword•play (sôrd′plā′) ►*n.* The act or art of using a sword.

swords•man (sôrdz′mən) ►*n.* One skilled in the use of swords. —**swords′man•ship′** *n.*

swore (swôr, swōr) ►*v.* P.t. of **swear.**

sworn (swôrn, swōrn) ►*v.* P.part. of **swear.**

swum (swŭm) ►*v.* P.part. of **swim.**

swung (swŭng) ►*v.* P.t. and p.part. of **swing.**

syb•a•rite (sĭb′ə-rīt) ►*n.* A person devoted to pleasure and luxury; voluptuary. [< *Sybaris*, an ancient Greek city in Italy.] —**syb′a•rit′ic** (-rĭt′ĭk) *adj.*

syc•a•more (sĭk′ə-môr′, -mōr′) ►*n.* **1.** A deciduous tree, esp. of North America, having palmately lobed leaves and ball-like fruit clusters. **2.** A Eurasian maple tree. [< Gk. *sukomoros*, a kind of fig tree.]

syc•o•phant (sĭk′ə-fənt, sī′kə-) ►*n.* A servile self-seeker who attempts to win favor by flattering influential people. [< Gk. *sukophantēs*, informer.] —**syc′o•phan•cy** *n.* —**syc′o•phan′tic** (-făn′tĭk) *adj.*

Syd•ney (sĭd′nē) A city of SE Australia on an inlet of the Tasman Sea. Met. area pop. 3,713,500.

syl•lab•i•fy (sĭ-lăb′ĭ-fī′) or **syl•lab•i•cate** (-kāt′) ►*v.* **-fied, -fy•ing** or **-cat•ed, -cat•ing.** To form or divide into syllables. —**syl•lab′i•fi•ca′tion, syl•lab′i•ca′tion** *n.*

syl•la•ble (sĭl′ə-bəl) ►*n.* **1.** A unit of spoken language consisting of a single uninterrupted sound forming a word, such as *wit*, or part of a word, such as *per-* in *person.* **2.** One or more letters or phonetic symbols representing a spoken syllable. [< Gk. *sullabē.*] —**syl•lab′ic** (sĭ-lăb′ĭk) *adj.* —**syl•lab′i•cal•ly** *adv.*

syl•la•bus (sĭl′ə-bəs) ►*n., pl.* **-bus•es** or **-bi** (-bī′). An outline or summary of the main points of a text, lecture, or course of study. [Prob. < Gk. *sillubos*, book label.]

syl•lo•gism (sĭl′ə-jĭz′əm) ►*n.* A form of deductive reasoning consisting of a major premise, a minor premise, and a conclusion. [< Gk. *sullogismos.*] —**syl′lo•gis′tic** *adj.* —**syl′lo•gis′ti•cal•ly** *adv.*

sylph (sĭlf) ►*n.* **1.** A slim graceful woman or girl. **2.** An imaginary being believed to inhabit the air. [NLat. *sylpha*, sylph (being).]

syl•van also **sil•van** (sĭl′vən) ►*adj.* **1.** Of or characteristic of woods or forest regions. **2.** Abounding in trees. [< Lat. *silva*, forest.]

sym•bi•o•sis (sĭm′bē-ō′sĭs, -bī-) ►*n. Biol.* A close association between two or more different organisms, esp. when mutually beneficial. [< Gk. *sumbios*, living together : *sun-*, together + *bios*, life.] —**sym′bi•ot′ic** (-ŏt′ĭk) *adj.* —**sym′bi•ot′i•cal•ly** *adv.*

sym•bol (sĭm′bəl) ►*n.* **1.** Something that represents something else by association, resemblance, or convention. **2.** A printed or written sign used to represent an operation, element, quantity, quality, or relation, as in mathematics or music. [< Gk. *sumbolon*, token for identification.] —**sym•bol′ic** (-bŏl′ĭk) *adj.* —**sym•bol′i•cal•ly** *adv.*

symbolic language ►*n.* A high-level programming language.

sym•bol•ism (sĭm′bə-lĭz′əm) ►*n.* The representation of things by means of symbols.

sym•bol•ize (sĭm′bə-līz′) ►*v.* **-ized, -iz•ing** **1.** To serve as a symbol of. **2.** To represent by a symbol. —**sym′bol•i•za′tion** *n.*

sym•me•try (sĭm′ĭ-trē) ►*n., pl.* **-tries** **1.** Exact correspondence of form and configuration on opposite sides of a dividing line or plane or about a center or axis. **2.** An arrangement with balanced or harmonious proportions. [< Gk. *summetros*, of like measure.] —**sym•met′ri•cal** (sĭ-mĕt′rĭ-kəl), **sym•met′ric** *adj.* —**sym•met′ri•cal•ly** *adv.*

sym•pa•thet•ic (sĭm′pə-thĕt′ĭk) ►*adj.* **1.** Of, expressing, feeling, or resulting from sympathy. **2.** Favorably inclined; agreeable. **3.** Produced in one body by transmission of vibrations of the same frequency from another body. —**sym′pa•thet′i•cal•ly** *adv.*

sympathetic nervous system ►*n.* The part of the autonomic nervous system that in general inhibits or opposes the parasympathetic nervous system, as by reducing digestive secretions, speeding up the heart, and contracting blood vessels.

sym•pa•thize (sĭm′pə-thīz′) ►*v.* **-thized, -thiz•ing** **1.** To feel or express compassion; commiserate. **2.** To share or understand the feelings or ideas of another. —**sym′pa•thiz′er** *n.*

sym•pa•thy (sĭm′pə-thē) ►*n., pl.* **-thies** **1a.** A relationship between people or things in which whatever affects one correspondingly affects the other. **b.** Mutual understanding or affection. **2.** A feeling or expression of pity or sorrow for the distress of another. **3.** Harmonious agreement; accord. [< Gk. *sumpathēs*, having like feelings.]

sym•phon•ic (sĭm-fŏn′ĭk) ►*adj.* **1.** Relating to or having the form of a symphony. **2.** Harmonious in sound. —**sym•phon′i•cal•ly** *adv.*

sym•pho•ny (sĭm′fə-nē) ►*n., pl.* **-nies 1.** An extended piece for a symphony orchestra. **2.** A symphony orchestra. **3.** Harmony, esp. of sound. [< Gk. *sumphōnos*, harmonious.]

symphony orchestra ►*n.* A large orchestra composed of string, wind, and percussion sections.

sym•po•si•um (sĭm-pō′zē-əm) ►*n., pl.* **-si•ums** or **-si•a** (-zē-ə) **1.** A meeting or conference for discussion of a particular topic. **2.** A collection of writings on a particular topic. [< Gk. *sumposion*, drinking party.]

symp•tom (sĭm′təm, sĭmp′-) ►*n.* **1.** An indication; sign. **2.** A sign or indication of disorder or disease, esp. a change from normal function, sensation, or appearance. [< Gk. *sumptōma*.] —**symp′to•mat′ic** *adj.* —**symp′to•mat′i•cal•ly** *adv.*

syn. ►*abbr.* synonym

syn•a•gogue (sĭn′ə-gŏg′, -gôg′) ►*n.* **1.** A building or place of meeting for worship and religious instruction in the Jewish faith. **2.** A congregation of Jews for the purpose of worship. [< Gk. *sunagōgē*, assembly : *sun-*, together + *agein*, bring.]

syn•apse (sĭn′ăps′, sĭ-năps′) ►*n.* The junction across which a nerve impulse passes to a neuron or other cell. ►*v.* **-apsed, -aps•ing.** To form a synapse. [Gk. *sunapsis*, point of contact.] —**syn•ap′tic** *adj.*

sync or **synch** (sĭngk) *Informal* ►*n.* **1.** Synchronization. **2.** Harmony; accord. ►*v.* To synchronize.

syn•chro•nize (sĭng′krə-nīz′, sĭn′-) ►*v.* **-nized, -niz•ing 1.** To occur or cause to occur at the same time. **2.** To operate in unison. **3.** To cause to agree exactly in time or rate. **4.** To arrange so as to indicate parallel occurrence. —**syn′chro•ni•za′tion** *n.* —**syn′chro•niz′er** *n.*

syn•chro•nous (sĭng′krə-nəs, sĭn′-) ►*adj.* **1.** Occurring or existing at the same time. **2.** Moving or operating at the same rate. [< Gk. *sunkhronos*.] —**syn′chro•nous•ly** *adv.* —**syn′chro•ny** *n.*

syn•co•pate (sĭng′kə-pāt′, sĭn′-) ►*v.* **-pat•ed, -pat•ing.** To modify (rhythm) by syncopation.

syn•co•pa•tion (sĭng′kə-pā′shən, sĭn′-) ►*n.* *Mus.* A shift of accent when a normally weak beat is stressed.

syn•co•pe (sĭng′kə-pē, sĭn′-) ►*n.* *Pathol.* A brief loss of consciousness; swoon. [< Gk. *sunkoptein*, cut short.]

syn•di•cate (sĭn′dĭ-kĭt) ►*n.* **1.** An association of people or firms authorized to undertake a duty or transact specific business. **2.** An agency that sells articles or photographs for publication in a number of newspapers or periodicals simultaneously. ►*v.* (-kāt′) **-cat•ed, -cat•ing 1.** To organize into a syndicate. **2.** To sell or publish through a syndicate. [< Gk. *sundikos*, public advocate.] —**syn′di•ca′tion** *n.*

syn•drome (sĭn′drōm′) ►*n.* A group of symptoms that collectively characterize a disease or disorder. [Gk. *sundromē*, concurrence of symptoms.]

syn•er•gy (sĭn′ər-jē) also **syn•er•gism** (-jĭz′əm) ►*n.* The interaction of two or more agents or forces so that their combined effect is greater than the sum of their individual effects. [< Gk. *sunergos*, working together : *sun-*, together + *ergon*, work.] —**syn′er•gist′ic** *adj.* —**syn′er•gist′ic•al•ly** *adv.*

syn•fu•el (sĭn′fyōō′əl) ►*n.* A fuel derived from coal, shale, or tar sand, or obtained by fermentation, as of grain. [SYN(THETIC) + FUEL.]

Synge (sĭng), **John Millington.** 1871–1909. Irish playwright.

syn•od (sĭn′əd) ►*n.* **1.** A council or assembly of Christian church officials. **2.** A council; assembly. [< Gk. *sunodos*, assembly.] —**syn•od′ic** (sĭ-nŏd′ĭk), **syn•od′i•cal** *adj.*

syn•o•nym (sĭn′ə-nĭm′) ►*n.* A word having the same or nearly the same meaning as another word in a language. [< Gk. *sunōnumon*.] —**syn′o•nym′i•ty** *n.* —**syn•on′y•mous** (sĭ-nŏn′ə-məs) *adj.* —**syn•on′y•mous•ly** *adv.*

syn•on•y•my (sĭ-nŏn′ə-mē) ►*n.* The quality of being synonymous.

syn•op•sis (sĭ-nŏp′sĭs) ►*n., pl.* **-ses** (-sēz). A brief outline or general view, as of a written work. [< Gk. *sunopsis*, general view.]

syn•tax (sĭn′tăks′) ►*n.* The way in which words or other elements of sentence structure are combined to form grammatical sentences. [< Gk. *suntassein*, put in order.] —**syn•tac′tic** (-tăk′tĭk), **syn•tac′ti•cal** *adj.* —**syn•tac′ti•cal•ly** *adv.*

syn•the•sis (sĭn′thĭ-sĭs) ►*n., pl.* **-ses** (-sēz′) **1.** The combining of separate elements or substances to form a coherent whole. **2.** The complex whole so formed. **3.** *Chem.* Formation of a compound from simpler compounds or elements. [< Gk. *synthesis* < *suntithenai*, put together.] —**syn′the•size′** *v.*

syn•the•siz•er (sĭn′thĭ-sī′zər) ►*n.* An electronic instrument that combines simple waveforms to produce more complex sounds, such as those of various other instruments.

syn•thet•ic (sĭn-thĕt′ĭk) ►*adj.* **1.** Of or produced by synthesis. **2.** Not natural or genuine; artificial. ►*n.* A synthetic chemical compound. [< Gk. *sunthetos*, combined.] —**syn•thet′i•cal•ly** *adv.*

syph•i•lis (sĭf′ə-lĭs) ►*n.* A chronic infectious disease caused by a spirochete, usu. transmitted in sexual intercourse, and progressing through three stages of increasing severity. [< *Syphilus*, protagonist of a 16th-cent. poem.] —**syph′i•lit′ic** *adj.*

sy•phon (sī′fən) ►*n. & v.* Var. of **siphon.**

Syr•a•cuse (sîr′ə-kyōōs′, -kyōōz′) A city of central NY ESE of Rochester. Pop. 163,860.

Sy•ri•a (sîr′ē-ə) A country of SW Asia on the E Mediterranean coast. Cap. Damascus. Pop. 13,844,000. —**Syr′i•an** *adj. & n.*

sy•ringe (sə-rĭnj′, sîr′ĭnj) ►*n.* **1.** A medical instrument used to inject fluids into the body or draw them from it. **2.** A hypodermic syringe. [< Gk. *surinx*, shepherd's pipe.]

syr•up also **sir•up** (sĭr′əp, sûr′-) ►*n.* **1.** A thick, sweet, sticky liquid consisting of sugar, flavorings, and water. **2.** The concentrated juice of a fruit or plant. [< Ar. *šarāb*.] —**syr′up•y** *adj.*

sys•tem (sĭs′təm) ►*n.* **1.** A group of interacting elements forming a complex whole. **2.** The human body regarded as a functional physiological unit. **3.** A network of structures and channels, as for communication. **4.** A condition of harmonious, orderly interaction. **5.** An organized method; procedure. [< Gk. *sustēma* :

sun-, together + *histanai*, set up.] —**sys′tem•at′ic** *adj.* —**sys′tem•at′i•cal•ly** *adv.*

sys•tem•a•tize (sĭs′tə-mə-tīz′) ►*v.* **-tized, -tiz•ing.** To formulate into or reduce to a system. See Syns at **arrange.** —**sys′tem•a•ti•za′tion** *n.*

sys•tem•ic (sĭ-stĕm′ĭk) ►*adj.* **1.** Of or relating to systems or a system. **2.** Of or affecting the entire body. —**sys•tem′i•cal•ly** *adv.*

sys•tem•ize (sĭs′tə-mīz′) ►*v.* **-ized, -iz•ing.** To systematize.

sys•tems analysis (sĭs′təmz) ►*n.* The study of an activity or procedure to determine the desired end and the most efficient method of obtaining it. —**systems analyst** *n.*

sys•to•le (sĭs′tə-lē) ►*n.* The rhythmic contraction of the heart, esp. of the ventricles. [Gk. *sustolē*,contraction.] —**sys•tol′ic** (sĭ-stŏl′ĭk) *adj.*

Szcze•cin (shchĕ′chēn′) A city of NW Poland on the Oder R. Pop. 413,561.

Sze•chuan or **Sze•chwan** (sĕch′wän′). See **Sichuan.**

Sze•ged (sĕg′ĕd′) A city of S Hungary near the Yugoslavian border. Pop. 178,690.

T

t[1] or **T** (tē) ►*n., pl.* **t's** or **T's** also **ts** or **Ts.** The 20th letter of the English alphabet. —***idiom:* to a T** Perfectly; precisely.

t[2] ►*abbr.* Troy (system of weights)

T ►*abbr.* **1.** temperature **2.** tenor **3.** Thursday **4.** Tuesday

t. ►*abbr.* **1.** tare **2.** teaspoon **3.** time **4.** transitive

T. ►*abbr.* tablespoon

Ta ► The symbol for the element **tantalum.**

tab[1] (tăb) ►*n.* A projection attached to an object to facilitate opening, handling, or identification.

tab[2] (tăb) ►*n.* **1.** *Informal* A bill or check. **2.** A key on a computer keyboard or typewriter used esp. in indenting text. —***idiom:* keep tabs on** *Informal* To observe carefully. [< TABLET or TABULATION. Sense 2 < TABULATOR.]

tab•bou•leh or **ta•bou•leh** (tə-bo͞o′lə) ►*n.* A Lebanese salad of bulgur, scallions, tomatoes, mint, and parsley.

tab•by (tăb′ē) ►*n., pl.* **-bies 1.** A domestic cat with black and grayish striped or mottled fur. **2.** A domestic cat, esp. a female. [< Ar. *'attābī.*]

tab•er•na•cle (tăb′ər-năk′əl) ►*n.* **1.** often **Tabernacle** The portable sanctuary in which the Jews carried the Ark of the Covenant through the desert. **2.** often **Tabernacle** A case or box on a church altar containing the consecrated elements of the Eucharist. **3.** A place of worship. [< LLat. *tabernāculum.*]

ta•ble (tā′bəl) ►*n.* **1.** An article of furniture having a flat horizontal surface supported by legs. **2.** An orderly display of data, usu. arranged in rows and columns. **3.** An abbreviated list, as of contents; synopsis. **4.** A slab or tablet bearing an inscription or a device. ►*v.* **-bled, -bling 1.** To put or place on a table. **2.** To postpone consideration of; shelve. [< Lat. *tabula*, board.]

tab•leau (tăb′lō′, tă-blō′) ►*n., pl.* **tab•leaux** or **tab•leaus** (tăb′lōz′, tă-blōz′) **1.** A vivid or graphic description. **2.** A stage technique in which the performers freeze in position simultaneously. **3.** A tableau vivant. [Fr.]

tableau vi•vant (vē-väɴ′) ►*n., pl.* **tab•leaux vi•vants** (tă-blō′vē-väɴ′). A scene presented on stage by costumed actors who remain silent and motionless as if in a picture. [Fr., living picture.]

ta•ble•cloth (tā′bəl-klôth′, -klŏth′) ►*n.* A cloth to cover a table, esp. during a meal.

ta•ble d'hôte (tä′bəl dōt′, tä′blə) ►*n., pl.* **ta•bles d'hôte** (tä′bəl, tä′blə). A full-course meal with limited choices, served at a fixed price in a restaurant or hotel. [Fr., host's table.]

ta•ble•land (tā′bəl-lănd′) ►*n.* A plateau or mesa.

ta•ble•spoon (tā′bəl-spo͞on′) ►*n.* **1.** A large spoon used for serving food. **2.** A household cooking measure equal to 3 teaspoons or ½ fl. oz. (15 ml). —**ta′ble•spoon•ful′** *n.*

tab•let (tăb′lĭt) ►*n.* **1.** A slab or plaque, as of stone or ivory, bearing an inscription. **2.** A pad of writing paper glued together along one edge. **3.** A small flat pellet of oral medication. [< OFr. *table*, TABLE.]

table tennis ►*n.* A game similar to lawn tennis, played on a table with wooden paddles and a small plastic ball.

ta•ble•top (tā′bəl-tŏp′) ►*n.* The flat surface of a table. ►*adj.* Designed or made for use on the top of a table.

ta•ble•ware (tā′bəl-wâr′) ►*n.* Dishes, glassware, and silverware used in setting a table for a meal.

tab•loid (tăb′loid′) ►*n.* A newspaper of small format giving the news in condensed form, often with sensational material. [< *Tabloid*, a trademark.]

ta•boo also **ta•bu** (tə-bo͞o′, tă-) ►*n., pl.* **-boos** also **-bus 1.** A ban attached to something by social custom. **2.** A prohibition, esp. among certain South Pacific peoples, excluding something from use, approach, or mention because of its sacred and inviolable nature. [Tongan *tabu*, prohibited.] —**ta•boo′** *adj.* —**ta•boo′** *v.*

ta•bor (tā′bər) ►*n.* A small drum used to accompany a fife. [< OFr. *tambur.*]

ta•bou•leh (tə-bo͞o′lə) ►*n.* Var. of **tabbouleh.**

Ta•briz (tə-brēz′, tä-) A city of NW Iran. Pop. 1,166,203.

tab•u•lar (tăb′yə-lər) ►*adj.* Organized as a table or list. [< Lat. *tabula*, board.]

tab•u•late (tăb′yə-lāt′) ►*v.* **-lat•ed, -lat•ing.** To arrange in tabular form; condense and list. [< Lat. *tabula*, writing.] —**tab′u•la′tion** *n.* —**tab′u•la′tor** *n.*

ta•chom•e•ter (tă-kŏm′ĭ-tər, tə-) ►*n.* An instrument used to measure speed, esp. rotational speed. [Gk. *takhos*, speed + –METER.] —**ta•chom′e•try** *n.*

tac•it (tăs′ĭt) ►*adj.* **1.** Not spoken: *tacit approval.* **2.** Implied by or inferred from actions or statements. [Lat. *tacitus*, silent.] —**tac′it•ly** *adv.* —**tac′it•ness** *n.*

tac•i•turn (tăs′ĭ-tûrn′) ►*adj.* Habitually untalkative or silent. [< Lat. *taciturnus.*] —**tac′i•tur′ni•ty** *n.* —**tac′i•turn•ly** *adv.*

Tac•i•tus (tăs′ĭ-təs), **Publius Cornelius.** A.D. 55?–120? Roman historian.

tack[1] (tăk) ►*n.* **1.** A short light nail with a sharp point and a flat head. **2.** The position of a vessel relative to the trim of its sails. **3.** A course of action. **4.** A loose, temporary stitch. ►*v.* **1.** To fasten or attach with a tack. **2.** To add as an extra item: *tacked on a hefty surcharge.* **3.** To change the course of a vessel. [< ONFr. *taque,* fastener.] —**tack′er** *n.*

tack[2] (tăk) ►*n.* The harness for a horse, including the bridle and saddle. [< TACKLE.]

tack•le (tăk′əl) ►*n.* **1.** The equipment used in a sport or occupation, esp. in fishing; gear. **2.** (tăk′əl, tā′kəl). A system of ropes and blocks for raising and lowering weights. **3.** *Sports* **a.** The act of stopping a player carrying the ball, esp. by forcing the player to the ground, as in football. **b.** The act of obstructing a player so as to cause loss of possession of the ball, as in soccer. **c.** In football, either of the two line players positioned between guard and end. ►*v.* **-led, -ling 1.** To take on and wrestle with (e.g., an opponent or problem). **2.** To stop or obstruct (an opponent) by means of a tackle. [ME *takel.*] —**tack′ler** *n.*

tack•y[1] (tăk′ē) ►*adj.* **-i•er, -i•est.** Gummy; sticky. [< TACK[1].] —**tack′i•ness** *n.*

tack•y[2] (tăk′ē) ►*adj.* **-i•er, -i•est** *Informal* **1.** Rundown; shabby. **2a.** Lacking style or good taste; *tacky clothes.* **b.** Vulgar; tasteless: *a tacky remark.* [< *tackey,* an inferior horse.] —**tack′i•ly** *adv.* —**tack′i•ness** *n.*

ta•co (tä′kō) ►*n., pl.* **-cos.** A corn tortilla folded around a filling, as of meat or cheese. [Am.Sp. < Sp., wad of bank notes.]

Ta•co•ma (tə-kō′mə) A city of W-central WA S of Seattle. Pop. 176,664.

tac•o•nite (tăk′ə-nīt′) ►*n.* A variety of chert mined as an iron ore. [After the *Taconic* Mountains in New York.]

tact (tăkt) ►*n.* Sensitivity in dealing with others. [< Lat. *tāctus,* sense of touch.] —**tact′ful** *adj.* —**tact′less** *adj.*

tac•tic (tăk′tĭk) ►*n.* **1.** An expedient for achieving a goal; maneuver. **2. tactics** *(takes sing. v.)* The military science of securing objectives set by strategy. [< Gk. *taktika,* tactics.] —**tac′ti•cal** *adj.* —**tac•ti′cian** (-tĭsh′ən) *n.*

tac•tile (tăk′təl, -tīl′) ►*adj.* Of, perceptible to, or proceeding from the sense of touch. [< Lat. *tangere, tāct-,* touch.] —**tac′tile•ly** *adv.* —**tac•til′i•ty** (-tĭl′ĭ-tē) *n.*

tad (tăd) ►*n. Informal* **1.** A small boy. **2.** A small amount or degree. [Perh. < TADPOLE.]

tad•pole (tăd′pōl′) ►*n.* The limbless aquatic larval stage of a frog or toad, with gills and a long flat tail. [ME *taddepol.*]

Tae•gu (tī-go͞o′) A city of SE South Korea NNW of Pusan. Pop. 2,031,000.

Tae•jon (tī-jôn′, -jŏn′) A city of central South Korea SSE of Seoul. Pop. 866,148.

tae kwon do (tī′ kwŏn′ dō′) ►*n.* A Korean art of self-defense. [Korean *t'aekwŏndo.*]

taf•fe•ta (tăf′ĭ-tə) ►*n.* A crisp, lustrous, plain-woven fabric of silk, rayon, or nylon. [< Pers. *tāftah,* silk or linen cloth.]

taf•fy (tăf′ē) ►*n., pl.* **-fies.** A sweet chewy candy of molasses or brown sugar. [?]

Taft (tăft), **William Howard.** 1857–1930. The 27th US President (1909–13); chief justice of the US Supreme Court (1921–30).

William Howard Taft

tag[1] (tăg) ►*n.* **1.** A strip of paper, metal, or plastic attached to something to identify, classify, or label. **2.** The plastic or metal tip at the end of a shoelace. **3.** A designation or epithet. **4.** *Comp. Sci.* A character sequence in a markup language that gives information, esp. formatting specifications. ►*v.* **tagged, tag•ging 1.** To label, identify, or recognize with or as with a tag. See Syns at **mark**[1]. **2.** To follow closely. **3.** To mark or vandalize (a surface) with graffiti. [ME *tagge,* dangling piece of cloth on a garment.] —**tag′ger** *n.*

tag[2] (tăg) ►*n.* **1.** A children's game in which one player pursues the others until he or she touches one of them, who in turn becomes the pursuer. **2.** *Baseball* The act of tagging a player out. ►*v.* **tagged, tag•ging 1.** To touch (another player) in the game of tag. **2.** *Baseball* To touch (a runner) with the ball in order to put that player out. [?]

Ta•ga•log (tə-gä′lôg, -ləg) ►*n., pl.* **-log** or **-logs 1.** A member of a people native to the Philippines. **2.** The Austronesian language of the Tagalog.

Ta•gore (tə-gôr′, -gōr′, tä-), Sir **Rabindranath.** 1861–1941. Indian writer; 1913 Nobel.

Ta•gus (tā′gəs) A river rising in E-central Spain and flowing about 941 km (585 mi) through central Portugal to the Atlantic.

ta•hi•ni (tə-hē′nē) ►*n.* A paste made from ground sesame seeds. [< Ar. *ṭaḥīna.*]

Ta•hi•ti (tə-hē′tē) An island of the S Pacific in the Society Is. of French Polynesia.

Ta•hi•tian (tə-hē′shən) ►*n.* **1.** A native or inhabitant of Tahiti. **2.** The Polynesian language of Tahiti. —**Ta•hi′tian** *adj.*

Ta•hoe (tä′hō), **Lake.** A lake on the CA-NV border W of Carson City, NV.

Tai (tī) ►*n., pl.* **Tai** or **Tais 1.** A family of languages of SE Asia and S China that includes Thai and Lao. **2.** A member of a Tai-speaking people. **3.** Thai. —**Tai** *adj.*

tai chi or **Tai Chi** (tī′ chē′, jē′) ►*n.* A Chinese system of physical exercise designed esp. for self-defense and meditation. [< Mandarin *taì jí (quán),* highest reach (boxing).]

Tai•chung (tī′cho͝ong′, -jo͝ong′) A city of W-central Taiwan SW of Taipei. Pop. 621,566.

tai•ga (tī′gə) ►*n.* The subarctic evergreen forest of N Eurasia just south of the tundra. [Russ. *taĭga.*]

tail (tāl) ►*n.* **1.** The hind part of an animal, esp. when extending beyond the main part of the body. **2.** The bottom, rear, or hindmost part of something. **3a.** The rear of an aircraft. **b.** An assembly of stabilizing planes and control surfaces in this rear portion. **4.** An appendage to the rear or bottom: *the tail of a kite.* **5.** often **tails** *(takes sing. v.)* The reverse side of a coin. **6. tails** A formal evening costume worn by men. ►*adj.* Posterior; hindmost. ►*v. Informal* To follow and keep under surveillance. [< OE *tægel.*] —**tail′less** *adj.*

tail•gate (tāl′gāt′) ►*n.* A hinged board or closure at the rear of a station wagon or other vehicle. ►*v.* **-gat•ed, -gat•ing.** To drive too closely behind (another vehicle). —**tail′gat′er** *n.*

tail•ings (tā′lĭngz) ►*pl.n.* Refuse or dross remaining after ore has been processed.

tail•light (tāl′līt′) ►*n.* A red light mounted on the rear of a vehicle.

tai•lor (tā′lər) ►*n.* One who makes, repairs, and alters garments. ►*v.* **1.** To make (a garment). **2.** To make or adapt for a particular purpose. [< LLat. *tāliāre*, cut.]

tai•lor-made (tā′lər-mād′) ►*adj.* Made or as if made to order.

tail•pipe (tāl′pīp′) ►*n.* The pipe through which exhaust gases from an engine are discharged.

tail•spin (tāl′spĭn′) ►*n.* **1.** The rapid descent of an aircraft in a nose-down spiral spin. **2.** A sudden steep decline or slump.

Tai•nan (tī′nän′) A city of SW Taiwan on the South China Sea. Pop. 609,934.

Taine (tān, tĕn), **Hippolyte Adolphe.** 1828–93. French philosopher and historian.

Tai•no (tī′nō) ►*n., pl.* **-no** or **-nos 1.** A member of an Arawak people of the West Indies who became extinct under Spanish colonization. **2.** The language of this people.

taint (tānt) ►*v.* **1.** To affect with or as if with a disease. **2.** To affect with decay or putrefaction; spoil. See Syns at **contaminate.** ►*n.* **1.** A moral defect considered as a stain or spot. See Syns at **stain. 2.** An infecting touch, influence, or tinge. [< AN *teint*, tinged, and OFr. *ataint*, touched.]

Tai•pei (tī′pā′, -bā′) The capital of Taiwan, in the N part. Pop. 2,327,641.

Tai•wan (tī′wän′). Officially **Republic of China.** Formerly **For•mo•sa** (fôr-mō′sə). A country off SE China comprising the island of **Taiwan** and other smaller islands. Cap. Taipei. Pop. 20,546,500. —**Tai′wan•ese′** (-wä-nēz′, -nēs′) *adj. & n.*

Tai•yu•an (tī′yo͞o-än′, -yüän′) A city of NE China SW of Beijing. Pop. 2,224,580.

Ta•jik (tä-jĭk′, tə-) ►*n., pl.* **-jik** or **-jiks 1.** A member of a people inhabiting Tajikistan and neighboring areas. **2.** Their Iranian language.

Ta•jik•i•stan (tä-jĭk′ĭ-stăn′, -stän′) A region and republic of W-central Asia bordering on Afghanistan and China. Cap. Dushanbe. Pop. 5,993,000.

ta•ka (tä′kə) ►*n.* See table at **currency.** [Bengali *ṭākā* < Skt. *ṭaṅkaḥ*, stamped coin.]

Tak•ak•kaw (tăk′ə-kô′) A waterfall, 503.3 m (1,650 ft), in SE British Columbia, Canada.

take (tāk) ►*v.* **took** (to͝ok), **tak•en** (tā′kən), **tak•ing 1.** To get possession of; capture; seize. **2.** To grasp with the hands. **3.** To carry, convey, or lead to another place. See Usage Note at **bring. 4.** To remove from a place. **5.** To charm; captivate. **6.** To eat, drink, consume, or inhale. **7.** To assume upon oneself; commit oneself to. **8.** *Gram.* To govern: *Intransitive verbs take no direct object.* **9.** To pick out; choose. **10.** To use as a means of conveyance or transportation. **11.** To use as a means of safety: *take shelter.* **12.** To occupy: *take a seat.* **13.** To require: *It takes money to do that.* **14.** To determine through measurement or observation. **15.** To write down: *take notes.* **16.** To make by photography: *take a picture.* **17.** To accept (e.g., something given). **18.** To endure: *take criticism.* **19.** To follow (e.g., a suggestion). **20.** To make or perform: *take a decision.* **21.** To let in; admit. **22.** To interpret or react in a certain manner: *take literally.* **23.** To subtract. **24.** To commit oneself to the study of: *take a course.* **25.** To have the intended effect; work. **26.** To become: *take sick.* —***phrasal verbs:* take after** To follow as an example. **take back** To retract (something stated or written). **take for** To regard as or mistake for: *took him for the boss.* **take in 1.** To include or constitute. **2.** To understand. **3.** To view: *She took in the scene.* **take off 1.** To remove, as clothing. **2.** To rise up in flight, as an airplane. **3.** *Slang* To depart. **take out 1.** To extract; remove. **2.** *Informal* To escort, as a date. **take over** To assume the control or management of. **take to 1.** To become fond of. **2.** To develop as a habit. **take up 1.** To begin again. **2.** To develop an interest in. ►*n.* **1a.** The act or process of taking. **b.** The amount taken, esp. at one time. **2.** The money collected as admission to an event. **3.** The uninterrupted running of a camera or a set of recording equipment, as in filming a movie. —***idioms:* take effect 1.** To become operative, as a law. **2.** To produce the desired reaction. **take place** To happen; occur. [< ON *taka.*] —**tak′er** *n.*

take•off (tāk′ôf′, -ŏf′) ►*n.* **1.** The act of leaving the ground. **2.** *Informal* An imitative caricature or burlesque.

take•out also **take-out** (tāk′out′) ►*adj.* Intended to be eaten off the premises: *takeout pizza.* —**take′-out′** *n.*

take•o•ver also **take-o•ver** (tāk′ō′vər) ►*n.* The act of assuming control.

ta•la (tä′lə) ►*n.* See table at **currency.** [Samoan < E. DOLLAR.]

talc (tălk) ►*n.* A fine-grained mineral used in making talcum powder. [< Pers. *talk.*]

Tal•ca•hua•no (tăl′kə-wä′nō, -hwä′-, täl′kä-) A city of central Chile on the Pacific near Concepción. Pop. 246,853.

tal•cum powder (tăl′kəm) ►*n.* A fine powder made from purified talc, for use on the skin. [< Med.Lat. *talcum*, TALC.]

tale (tāl) ►*n.* **1.** A recital of events or happenings. **2.** A narrative of imaginary events; story. **3.** A deliberate lie. [< OE *talu.*]

tale•bear•er (tāl′bâr′ər) ►*n.* One who spreads malicious gossip. —**tale′bear′ing** *adj. & n.*

tal•ent (tăl′ənt) ►*n.* **1.** A natural or acquired ability; aptitude. **2.** Natural endowment or ability of a superior quality. **3.** A person with such ability. **4.** Any of various ancient units of weight and money. [< Gk. *talanton*, unit of money.] —**tal′ent•ed** *adj.*

tal•is•man (tăl′ĭs-mən, -ĭz-) ►*n.* An object believed to protect or give supernatural powers to its bearer. [< Gk. *telesma*, consecration.] —**tal′is•man′ic** (-măn′ĭk) *adj.*

talk (tôk) ►*v.* **1.** To articulate words. **2a.** To converse by means of spoken language. **b.** To converse about: *talk politics.* **3.** To speak: *talk Arabic.* **4.** To gossip. **5.** To parley or negotiate. **6.** To consult or confer. **7.** To persuade with arguments: *talked them into joining.* —***phrasal verbs:*** **talk back** To reply rudely. **talk down** To address someone with insulting condescension. **talk over** To discuss. ▶*n.* **1.** The act of talking; conversation. **2.** A speech or lecture. **3.** Hearsay, rumor, or speculation. **4.** A subject of conversation. **5.** often **talks** A conference or negotiation. [ME *talken.*] —**talk′er** *n.*

talk•a•tive (tô′kə-tĭv) ▶*adj.* Inclined to talk or converse. —**talk′a•tive•ness** *n.*

talk•ing-to (tô′kĭng-to͞o′) ▶*n., pl.* **-tos** *Informal* A scolding; dressing-down.

talk show ▶*n.* A television or radio show in which people participate in discussions or are interviewed.

tall (tôl) ▶*adj.* **-er, -est 1.** Having greater than ordinary height. **2.** Having a specified height: *a plant three feet tall.* **3.** *Informal* Fanciful or boastful. **4.** Impressively great or difficult: *a tall order to fill.* ▶*adv.* With proud bearing; straight: *stand tall.* [< OE *getæl*, swift.] —**tall′ness** *n.*

Tal•la•has•see (tăl′ə-hăs′ē) The capital of FL, in the NW part. Pop. 124,773.

Tal•ley•rand-Pé•ri•gord (tăl′ē-rănd′pĕr′ĭ-gôr′), **Charles Maurice de.** 1754–1838. French politician and diplomat.

Tal•linn also **Tal•lin** (tăl′ĭn, tä′lĭn). The capital of Estonia, in the NW part on the Gulf of Finland. Pop. 447,672.

tal•low (tăl′ō) ▶*n.* Hard fat obtained from cattle, sheep, or horses and used in candles, soaps, and lubricants. [ME *talow.*] —**tal′low•y** *adj.*

tal•ly (tăl′ē) ▶*n., pl.* **-lies 1.** A reckoning or score. **2.** A stick on which notches are made to keep a count. ▶*v.* **-lied, -ly•ing 1.** To reckon or count. **2.** To correspond or agree. [< Lat. *tālea*, stick.]

tal•ly•ho (tăl′ē-hō′) ▶*interj.* Used to urge hounds on during a fox hunt. [Prob. < OFr. *thialau.*]

Tal•mud (täl′mo͝od, tăl′məd) ▶*n. Judaism* The collection of ancient Rabbinic writings constituting the basis of religious authority in Orthodox Judaism. —**Tal•mu′dic** (-mo͞o′dĭk, -myo͞o′-), **Tal•mu′di•cal** *adj.* —**Tal′mud•ist** *n.*

tal•on (tăl′ən) ▶*n.* The long curved claw esp. of a bird of prey. [< Lat. *tālus*, ankle.]

ta•lus (tā′ləs) ▶*n., pl.* **-li** (-lī). The bone that articulates with the tibia and fibula to form the ankle joint. [Lat. *tālus*, ankle.]

ta•ma•le (tə-mä′lē) ▶*n.* A Mexican dish of fried chopped meat and crushed peppers, wrapped in cornmeal dough and cornhusks and steamed. [< Nahuatl *tamalli.*]

tam•a•rack (tăm′ə-răk′) ▶*n.* An American larch tree. [Prob. of Algonquian orig.]

ta•ma•ri (tə-mä′rē) ▶*n.* Soy sauce made with little or no wheat.

tam•a•rind (tăm′ə-rĭnd′) ▶*n.* **1.** A tropical Asian tree with pods containing an edible acid pulp. **2.** The fruit of this tree. [< Ar. *tamr hindī*, Indian date.]

tam•a•risk (tăm′ə-rĭsk′) ▶*n.* A shrub or small tree with scalelike leaves and white, pink, or red flowers. [< Lat. *tamarīx.*]

tam•bou•rine (tăm′bə-rēn′) ▶*n.* A percussion instrument consisting of a small drumhead with jingling disks fitted into the rim, played by shaking or by striking with the hand. [< OFr. *tambourin*, small drum.]

tame (tām) ▶*adj.* **tam•er, tam•est 1.** Brought from wildness into a domesticated or tractable state. **2.** Gentle; docile. **3.** Insipid; flat. [< OE *tam.*] —**tam′a•ble, tame′a•ble** *adj.* —**tame** *v.* —**tame′ly** *adv.* —**tame′ness** *n.* —**tam′er** *n.*

Tam•er•lane (tăm′ər-lān′). 1336–1405. Mongol conqueror.

Tam•il (tăm′əl, tŭm′-, tä′məl) ▶*n., pl.* **-il** or **-ils 1.** A member of a people of S India and N Sri Lanka. **2.** The Dravidian language of the Tamil. —**Tam′il** *adj.*

Tam•muz (tä′mo͞oz) ▶*n.* A month of the Jewish calendar. See table at **calendar.** [Heb. *Tammūz.*]

tam-o′-shan•ter (tăm′ə-shăn′tər) ▶*n.* A flat-topped, tight-fitting Scottish cap. [After the hero of Burns's poem *"Tam o' Shanter."*]

tamp (tămp) ▶*v.* To pack down tightly by a succession of blows or taps. [Prob. < *tampin*, plug for a gun muzzle.]

Tam•pa (tăm′pə) A city of W-central FL on **Tampa Bay,** an inlet of the Gulf of Mexico. Pop. 280,015.

tam•per (tăm′pər) ▶*v.* **1.** To interfere harmfully; meddle. **2.** To make improper or secret arrangements: *tamper with a jury.* [Prob. < TEMPER.] —**tam′per•er** *n.*

Tam•pe•re (tăm′pə-rā′, täm′-) A city of SW Finland. Pop. 175,504.

Tam•pi•co (tăm-pē′kō, täm-) A city of E-central Mexico near the Gulf of Mexico NNE of Mexico City. Pop. 267,957.

tam•pon (tăm′pŏn′) ▶*n.* A plug of absorbent material inserted into a body cavity or wound. [< OFr., of Gmc. orig.]

tan[1] (tăn) ▶*v.* **tanned, tan•ning 1.** To convert (hide) into leather, as by treating with tannin. **2.** To make brown by exposure to the sun. **3.** *Informal* To thrash; beat. ▶*n.* **1.** A light brown. **2.** The brown color that sun rays impart to the skin. ▶*adj.* **tan•ner, tan•nest 1.** Of the color tan. **2.** Having a suntan. [< Med.Lat. *tannum*, tanbark.]

tan[2] ▶*abbr. Math.* tangent

tan•a•ger (tăn′ĭ-jər) ▶*n.* Any of a family of small New World birds often having brightly colored plumage. [< Tupi *tanagorá.*]

Ta•na•na•rive (tə-năn′ə-rēv′, tä-nä-nä-rēv′) See **Antananarivo.**

tan•bark (tăn′bärk′) ▶*n.* **1.** Tree bark used as a source of tannin. **2.** Shredded bark used to cover a surface such as a circus arena.

Tan•cred (tăng′krĭd). 1078?–1112. Norman Crusader.

tan•dem (tăn′dəm) ▶*n.* **1.** A bicycle built for two riders. **2.** Two or more persons or objects placed one behind the other. ▶*adv.* One behind the other: *rode tandem on the bike.* [Lat., at last.] —**tan′dem** *adj.*

Ta•ney (tô′nē), **Roger Brooke.** 1777–1864. Amer. jurist; the chief justice of the US Supreme Court (1836–64).

tang (tăng) ▶*n.* **1.** A distinctively sharp taste, flavor, or odor. See Syns at **taste. 2.** A projection by which a tool is attached to its handle. [ME *tange*, of Scand. orig.] —**tang′i•ness** *n.* —**tang′y** *adj.*

Tan•gan•yi•ka (tăn′gən-yē′kə, tăng′-) A former country of E-central Africa; joined with

tandem

Zanzibar (1964) to form Tanzania. —**Tan′gan•yi′kan** *adj. & n.*

Tanganyika, Lake. A lake of E-central Africa between Congo (formerly Zaire) and Tanzania.

tan•ge•lo (tăn′jə-lō′) ►*n., pl.* **-los 1.** A hybrid citrus tree derived from grapefruit and tangerine. **2.** The fruit of this tree. [Blend of TANGERINE and *pomelo*, a kind of grapefruit.]

tan•gent (tăn′jənt) ►*adj.* **1.** Making contact at a single point or along a line; touching but not intersecting. **2.** Irrelevant. ►*n.* **1.** A line, curve, or surface touching but not intersecting another line, curve, or surface. **2.** In a right triangle, the ratio of the sine of an acute angle to its cosine. **3.** A sudden digression. [< Lat. *tangēns*, touching.] —**tan′gen•cy** *n.* —**tan•gen′tial** (-jĕshəl) *adj.* —**tan•gen′tial•ly** *adv.*

tan•ger•ine (tăn′jə-rēn′, tăn′jə-rēn′) ►*n.* A mandarin orange with a red-orange skin. [After *Tanger* (Tangier), Morocco.]

tan•gi•ble (tăn′jə-bəl) ►*adj.* **1.** Discernible by the touch; palpable. **2.** Possible to understand or realize. **3.** Real or concrete. ►*n.* **1.** Something palpable or concrete. **2. tangibles** Material assets. [< Lat. *tangere*, touch.] —**tan′gi•bil′i•ty, tan′gi•ble•ness** *n.* —**tan′gi•bly** *adv.*

Tan•gier (tăn-jîr′) also **Tan•giers** (-jîrz′). A city of N Morocco at the W end of the Strait of Gibraltar. Pop. 307,000.

tan•gle (tăng′gəl) ►*v.* **-gled, -gling 1.** To intertwine in a confused mass; snarl. **2.** To be or become entangled. **3.** To snare; entrap. See Syns at **catch. 4.** *Informal* To enter into dispute or conflict: *tangled with the law.* [ME *tangilen*, involve in an embarrassing situation.] —**tan′gle** *n.*

tan•go (tăng′gō) ►*n., pl.* **-gos.** A Latin American ballroom dance in 2/4 or 4/4 time. [Am.Sp.] —**tan′go** *v.*

Tang•shan (tăng′shän′, dăng′-) A city of NE China ESE of Beijing. Pop. 1,484,515.

tank (tăngk) ►*n.* **1.** A large container for liquids or gases. **2.** An enclosed, heavily armored combat vehicle mounted with cannon and guns and moving on caterpillar treads. [< Gujarati (Indic) *tānkh*, cistern, and Port. *tanque*, reservoir.] —**tank′ful′** *n.*

tank•ard (tăng′kərd) ►*n.* A large drinking cup, usu. with a handle and a hinged cover. [ME.]

tank•er (tăng′kər) ►*n.* A ship, plane, or truck built to transport liquids, such as oil, in bulk.

tank top ►*n.* A sleeveless shirt with wide shoulder straps.

tan•ner (tăn′ər) ►*n.* One who tans hides.

tan•ner•y (tăn′ə-rē) ►*n., pl.* **-ies.** An establishment where hides are tanned.

tan•nic acid (tăn′ĭk) ►*n.* A white or yellowish powder derived from certain plants and used in tanning hides and as a medicine.

tan•nin (tăn′ĭn) ►*n.* Tannic acid or another substance having similar uses. [< Med.Lat. *tannum*, tanbark.]

Ta•no•an (tä′nō-ən) ►*n.* An American Indian language family of New Mexico and NE Arizona. —**Ta′no•an** *adj.*

tan•sy (tăn′zē) ►*n., pl.* **-sies.** A plant with buttonlike yellow flower heads and aromatic leaves that are sometimes used medicinally. [< LLat. *tanacētum*, wormwood.]

tan•ta•lize (tăn′tə-līz′) ►*v.* **-lized, -liz•ing.** To excite (another) by exposing something desirable while keeping it out of reach. [< *Tantalus*, Greek mythological figure.] —**tan′ta•li•za′tion** *n.* —**tan′ta•liz′er** *n.* —**tan′ta•liz′ing•ly** *adv.*

tan•ta•lum (tăn′tə-ləm) ►*n. Symbol* **Ta** A very hard, heavy, gray metallic element used to make light-bulb filaments, nuclear reactor parts, and some surgical instruments. At. no. 73. See table at **element.** [< *Tantalus*, Greek mythological figure.]

tan•ta•mount (tăn′tə-mount′) ►*adj.* Equivalent in effect or value. [< AN *tant amunter*, amount to so much.]

tan•tra (tŭn′trə, tăn′-) ►*n.* Any of a comparatively recent body of Hindu or Buddhist religious literature. [Skt. *tantram.*] —**tan′tric** *adj.*

tan•trum (tăn′trəm) ►*n.* A fit of bad temper. [?]

Tan•za•ni•a (tăn′zə-nē′ə) A country of E-central Africa on the Indian Ocean. Official capital Dodoma; de facto capital Dar es Salaam. Pop. 28,846,000. —**Tan•za′ni•an** *adj. & n.*

Tao (dou, tou) ►*n.* **1.** In Taoism, the basic, eternal principle of the universe. **2.** In Confucianism, the right manner of human activity and virtuous conduct. [Chinese (Mandarin) *dào*, way, Tao.]

Tao•ism (dou′ĭz′əm, tou′-) ►*n.* A Chinese philosophy and system of religion based on the teachings of Lao-tzu in the 6th cent. B.C. [< Mandarin *dào*, way.] —**Tao′ist** *n.* —**Tao•is′tic** *adj.*

tap¹ (tăp) ►*v.* **tapped, tap•ping 1.** To strike gently; rap. **2.** To make light clicking sounds. **3.** To select, as for membership in an organization. See Syns at **appoint.** ►*n.* **1a.** A gentle blow. **b.** The sound made by such a blow. **2.** A metal plate attached to the toe or heel of a shoe. [ME *tappen.*]

tap² (tăp) ►*n.* **1.** A faucet; spigot. **2.** Liquor drawn from a spigot. **3.** A tool for cutting an internal screw thread. **4.** A makeshift terminal in an electric circuit. ►*v.* **tapped, tap•ping 1.** To furnish with a spigot or tap. **2.** To pierce in order to draw off liquid. **3.** To draw (liquid) from a vessel or container. **4.** To open outlets from: *tap a water main.* **5a.** To wiretap. **b.** To establish an electric connection in (a power line). **6.** To cut screw threads in. [< OE *tæppa.*]

tap dance ►*n.* A dance in which the rhythm is sounded out by the clicking taps on the heels and toes of a dancer's shoes. —**tap′-dance′** *v.* —**tap dancer** *n.*

tape (tāp) ►*n.* **1.** A narrow strip of strong woven fabric. **2.** A continuous narrow flexible strip of material such as adhesive tape or magnetic tape. **3.** A string stretched across the finish line of a racetrack. **4.** A tape recording. ►*v.*

taped, tap•ing 1. To fasten, secure, or wrap with tape. **2.** To tape-record. [< OE *tæppe*.]

tape deck ►*n.* A tape recorder and player with no amplifier or speaker, used as a component in an audio system.

tape measure ►*n.* A tape marked off in a scale, used for taking measurements.

tape player ►*n.* A self-contained machine for playing tape recordings.

ta•per (tā′pər) ►*n.* **1.** A slender candle or waxed wick. **2.** A gradual decrease in thickness or width of an elongated object. ►*v.* **1.** To make or become gradually narrower or thinner toward one end. **2.** To diminish gradually; slacken off. [< OE *tapor*.] —**ta′per•ing•ly** *adv.*

tape recorder ►*n.* A device for recording and playing back sound on magnetic tape.

tape recording ►*n.* **1a.** A magnetic tape on which sound or images have been recorded. **b.** The material recorded. **2.** The act of recording on this tape. —**tape′-re•cord′** *v.*

tap•es•try (tăp′ĭ-strē) ►*n., pl.* **-tries.** A heavy cloth woven with varicolored designs, usu. hung on walls. [< Gk. *tapēs*, carpet.]

tape•worm (tāp′wûrm′) ►*n.* A long ribbonlike worm that is parasitic in the intestines of vertebrates.

tap•i•o•ca (tăp′ē-ō′kə) ►*n.* A beady starch obtained from the cassava root and used for puddings. [< Tupi *typióca*.]

ta•pir (tā′pər, tə-pîr′) ►*n.* A tropical American or Asian mammal with a heavy body, short legs, and a long fleshy upper lip. [< Tupi *tapiira*.]

tapir
Baird's tapir

tap•room (tăp′ro͞om′, -ro͝om′) ►*n.* A barroom.

tap•root (tăp′ro͞ot′, -ro͝ot′) ►*n.* The main root of a plant, growing straight downward from the stem.

taps (tăps) ►*pl.n.* *(takes sing. or pl. v.)* A military bugle call sounded at night as an order to put out lights and at funerals and memorial services. [Perh. < *taptoo*, TATTOO[1].]

tar[1] (tär) ►*n.* **1.** A dark, oily, viscous material, consisting mainly of hydrocarbons, produced by the destructive distillation of organic substances such as wood, coal, or peat. **2.** A solid residue of tobacco smoke. ►*v.* **tarred, tar•ring.** To coat or surface with tar. [< OE *teru*.]

tar[2] (tär) ►*n.* A sailor. [Poss. < TARPAULIN.]

tar•an•tel•la (tăr′ən-tĕl′ə) ►*n.* **1.** A lively, whirling southern Italian dance. **2.** The music for this dance. [Ital. < TARANTO.]

Ta•ran•to (tä′rän-tō) A city of SE Italy ESE of Naples on the **Gulf of Taranto,** an arm of the Ionian Sea. Pop. 232,200.

ta•ran•tu•la (tə-răn′chə-lə) ►*n., pl.* **-las** or **-lae** (-lē′). Any of various large, hairy, chiefly tropical spiders capable of inflicting a painful bite. [< OItal. *tarantola* < TARANTO.]

Ta•ra•wa (tə-rä′wə, tăr′ə-wä′, tä′rä-) The capital of Kiribati, in the N Gilbert Is. of the W-central Pacific. Pop. 1,956.

tar•dy (tär′dē) ►*adj.* **-di•er, -di•est 1.** Not on time. **2.** Slow; sluggish. [< Lat. *tardus*, slow.] —**tar′di•ly** *adv.* —**tar′di•ness** *n.*

Syns: *tardy, late, overdue* ***Ant:*** *prompt* ***adj.***

tare[1] (târ) ►*n.* Any of several weeds that grow in grain fields. [ME.]

tare[2] (târ) ►*n.* A deduction from gross weight made to allow for the weight of a container. [< Ar. *ṭarḥ*, subtraction.]

tar•get (tär′gĭt) ►*n.* **1a.** An object with a marked surface that is shot at to test accuracy. **b.** Something aimed or fired at. **2.** An object of criticism or attack. **3.** A goal. [< OFr. *targe*, light shield.] —**tar′get** *v.*

tar•iff (tăr′ĭf) ►*n.* **1a.** A list or system of duties imposed on imported or exported goods. **b.** A duty of this kind. **2.** A schedule of prices or fees. [< Ar. *ta'rīf*, notification.]

Tar•king•ton (tär′kĭng′tən), **(Newton) Booth.** 1869–1946. Amer. writer.

tar•mac (tär′măk′) ►*n.* A bituminous road or surface, esp. an airport runway. [Originally a trademark.]

tarn (tärn) ►*n.* A small mountain lake. [ME *tarne*, of Scand. orig.]

tar•nish (tär′nĭsh) ►*v.* **1.** To make or become dull or discolored. **2.** To sully or taint. [< OFr. *ternir*.] —**tar′nish** *n.*

ta•ro (tär′ō, tăr′ō) ►*n., pl.* **-ros.** A tropical Asian plant with broad leaves and a large, starchy, edible tuber. [Of Polynesian orig.]

tar•ot (tăr′ō, tə-rō′) ►*n.* Any of a set of playing cards used in fortunetelling. [< Ital. *tarocco*.]

tarp (tärp) ►*n.* *Informal* A tarpaulin.

tar•pa•per (tär′pā′pər) ►*n.* Heavy paper impregnated with tar, used as a waterproof building material.

tar•pau•lin (tär-pô′lĭn, tär′pə-) ►*n.* Material, such as waterproofed canvas, used to cover and protect things. [?]

tar•pon (tär′pən) ►*n., pl.* **-pon** or **-pons.** A large silvery game fish of Atlantic coastal waters. [?]

tar•ra•gon (tăr′ə-gŏn′, -gən) ►*n.* An aromatic Eurasian herb with leaves used in seasoning. [< Ar. *ṭarḫūn*.]

tar•ry (tăr′ē) ►*v.* **-ried, -ry•ing 1.** To linger or be late. **2.** To wait. **3.** To stay temporarily; sojourn. [ME *tarien*.] —**tar′ri•er** *n.*

tar•sus (tär′səs) ►*n., pl.* **-si** (-sī, -sē). The section of the vertebrate foot between the leg and the metatarsus. [< Gk. *tarsos*, ankle.] —**tar′sal** *adj.*

tart[1] (tärt) ►*adj.* **-er, -est 1.** Having a sharp pungent taste; sour. See Syns at **sour. 2.** Caustic; cutting. [< OE *teart*, severe.] —**tart′ly** *adv.* —**tart′ness** *n.*

tart[2] (tärt) ►*n.* **1.** A pastry shell with shallow sides, no top crust, and any of various fillings. **2.** A prostitute. [< OFr. *tarte*.]

tar•tan (tär′tn) ►*n.* Any of numerous textile patterns of Scottish origin consisting of stripes of varying widths and colors crossed at right angles against a solid background. [Poss. < OFr. *tiretaine*, a kind of fabric.]

tar•tar (tär′tər) ►*n.* **1.** *Dentistry* A hard yellowish deposit on the teeth. **2.** A reddish acid compound deposited on the sides of casks during winemaking. [< Med.Gk. *tartaron*, a chemical.]

Tartar ▸*n.* **1.** also **Ta•tar** (tä′tər) A member of any of the Turkic and Mongolian peoples of central Asia who invaded W Asia and E Europe in the Middle Ages. **2.** often **tartar** A ferocious or violent person.

tartar sauce ▸*n.* Mayonnaise mixed with chopped onion, pickles, and capers and served as a sauce with fish.

Tar•ta•ry (tär′tə-rē) A region of E Europe and N Asia controlled by the Mongols in the 13th and 14th cent.

Tash•kent (tăsh-kĕnt′, täsh-) The capital of Uzbekistan, in the W part W-southwest of Almaty. Pop. 2,094,000.

task (tăsk) ▸*n.* **1.** A piece of assigned work. **2.** A difficult or tedious undertaking. —***idiom:*** **take to task** To reprimand or censure. [< VLat. **taxa*, tax.]

task•bar (tăsk′bär′) ▸*n.* A row of buttons on a computer screen that represent programs that are running.

task force ▸*n.* A temporary grouping of forces for achieving a specific goal.

task•mas•ter (tăsk′măs′tər) ▸*n.* One who imposes heavy work.

Tas•ma•ni•a (tăz-mā′nē-ə, -mān′yə) An island of SE Australia separated from the mainland by Bass Strait. —**Tas•ma′ni•an** *adj. & n.*

Tas•man Sea (tăz′mən) An arm of the S Pacific between SE Australia and W New Zealand.

tas•sel (tăs′əl) ▸*n.* **1.** A bunch of loose threads or cords bound at one end and hanging free at the other, used as an ornament. **2.** Something resembling this, esp. the pollen-bearing inflorescence of a corn plant. ▸*v.* **-seled, -sel•ing** or **-selled, -sel•ling 1.** To fringe or decorate with tassels. **2.** To put forth a tassellike blossom. [ME.]

tassel

taste (tāst) ▸*v.* **tast•ed, tast•ing 1.** To distinguish the flavor of by taking into the mouth. **2.** To eat or drink a small quantity of. **3.** To experience, esp. for the first time. **4.** To have a distinct flavor: *The stew tastes salty.* ▸*n.* **1.** The sense that distinguishes the sweet, sour, salty, and bitter qualities of something placed in the mouth. **2.** The sensation produced by or as if by something in the mouth; flavor. **3.** A small quantity eaten or tasted. **4.** A limited or first experience. **5.** A personal preference. **6.** The faculty of discerning what is aesthetically appropriate: *a room furnished with superb taste.* [< VLat. **tastāre*, touch.] —**tast′a•ble** *adj.* —**tast′er** *n.*

Syns: *taste, flavor, relish, savor, tang* **n.**

taste bud ▸*n.* Any of numerous clusters of cells on the tongue that are primarily responsible for the sense of taste.

taste•ful (tāst′fəl) ▸*adj.* Having, showing, or in keeping with good taste. —**taste′ful•ly** *adv.* —**taste′ful•ness** *n.*

taste•less (tāst′lĭs) ▸*adj.* **1.** Lacking flavor; insipid. **2.** Having or showing poor taste. —**taste′less•ly** *adv.* —**taste′less•ness** *n.*

tast•y (tā′stē) ▸*adj.* **-i•er, -i•est.** Having a pleasing flavor. —**tast′i•ly** *adv.* —**tast′i•ness** *n.*

tat (tăt) ▸*v.* **tat•ted, tat•ting.** To do or make by tatting. [Prob. < TATTING.] —**tat′ter** *n.*

ta•ta•mi (tä-tä′mē, tə-) ▸*n., pl.* **-mi** or **-mis.** Straw matting used as a floor covering esp. in a Japanese house. [J.]

tatami

Ta•tar (tä′tər) ▸*n.* Var. of **Tartar** 1.

Ta•tra Mountains (tä′trə) A range of the Carpathian Mts. in E-central Europe along the Slovakia-Poland border.

tat•ter (tăt′ər) ▸*n.* **1.** A torn and hanging piece of cloth; shred. **2. tatters** Torn and ragged clothing; rags. ▸*v.* To make or become ragged. [ME *tater*, of Scand. orig.]

tat•ter•de•mal•ion (tăt′ər-dĭ-māl′yən, -mā′lē-ən) ▸*n.* A ragamuffin. ▸*adj.* Ragged; tattered. [?]

tat•ting (tăt′ĭng) ▸*n.* **1.** Handmade lace made by looping and knotting a single strand of heavy thread on a small hand shuttle. **2.** The art of making such lace. [?]

tat•tle (tăt′l) ▸*v.* **-tled, -tling 1.** To tell the secrets of another. **2.** To prattle; prate. [ME *tatelen*, stammer.] —**tat′tler** *n.*

tat•tle•tale (tăt′l-tāl′) ▸*n.* One who tells or tattles on others.

tat•too[1] (tă-to͞o′) ▸*n., pl.* **-toos 1.** A call sounded to summon soldiers or sailors to quarters at night. **2.** A rhythmic tapping. [< Du. *taptoe*.] —**tat•too′** *v.*

tat•too[2] (tă-to͞o′) ▸*n., pl.* **-toos 1.** A permanent mark or design made on the skin by a process of pricking and ingraining an indelible pigment. **2.** A similar design made with a temporary dye. ▸*v.* To mark (the skin) with a tattoo. [Of Polynesian orig.] —**tat•too′er** *n.*

tau (tou, tô) ▸*n.* The 19th letter of the Greek alphabet. [Gk.]

taught (tôt) ▸*v.* P.t. and p.part. of **teach.**

taunt (tônt) ▸*v.* To provoke or deride in a jeering manner. ▸*n.* A jeer or gibe. [?] —**taunt′er** *n.* —**taunt′ing•ly** *adv.*

taupe (tōp) ▸*n.* A brownish gray. [< Lat. *talpa*, mole.] —**taupe** *adj.*

Tau•rus (tôr′əs) ▸*n.* **1.** A constellation in the Northern Hemisphere. **2.** The 2nd sign of the zodiac.

Taurus Mountains. A range of S Turkey extending about 563 km (350 mi) parallel to the Mediterranean coast.

taut (tôt) ▸*adj.* **-er, -est 1.** Tight; not slack. See Syns at **tight. 2.** Strained; tense. **3.** Trim; tidy. [ME *tohte*, distended.] —**taut′ly** *adv.* —**taut′ness** *n.*

tau•tol•o•gy (tô-tŏl′ə-jē) ▸*n., pl.* **-gies 1.** Needless repetition of the same sense in different words; redundancy. **2.** *Logic* A statement that includes all logical possibilities and is therefore always true. [< Gk. *tautologos*, redundant.] —**tau′to•log′i•cal** (tôt′l-ŏj′ĭ-kəl), **tau′to•log′ic** *adj.*

tav•ern (tăv′ərn) ▸*n.* **1.** A saloon; bar. **2.** A roadside inn. [< Lat. *taberna.*]

taw•dry (tô′drē) ▸*adj.* **-dri•er, -dri•est 1.** Gaudy and cheap. See Syns at **gaudy. 2.** Shameful; indecent. [Ult. after *Saint Audrey* (died 679).] —**taw′dri•ly** *adv.* —**taw′dri•ness** *n.*

taw•ny (tô′nē) ▸*n.* A light brown to brownish orange. [< AN *taune*, tanned.] —**taw′ni•ness** *n.* —**taw′ny** *adj.*

tax (tăks) ▸*n.* **1.** A contribution for the support of a government required of persons, groups, or businesses within the domain of that government. **2.** An excessive demand; strain. ▸*v.* **1.** To place a tax on (e.g., property). **2.** To exact a tax from. **3.** To make heavy demands upon. **4.** To charge; accuse. [< Med.Lat. *taxāre*, to tax < Lat. *tangere*, touch.] —**tax′a•ble** *adj.* —**tax•a′tion** *n.* —**tax′er** *n.*

tax•i (tăk′sē) ▸*n., pl.* **-is** or **-ies.** A taxicab. ▸*v.* **tax•ied** (tăk′sēd), **tax•i•ing** or **tax•y•ing 1.** To transport or be transported by taxi. **2.** To move slowly on the ground or water before takeoff or after landing.

tax•i•cab (tăk′sē-kăb′) ▸*n.* An automobile that carries passengers for a fare. [< *taxi(meter)* (< Med.Lat. *taxa*, tax) + CAB.]

tax•i•der•my (tăk′sĭ-dûr′mē) ▸*n.* The art or operation of stuffing and mounting animal skins in a lifelike state. [< TAX(O)– + Gk. *derma*, skin.] —**tax′i•der′mist** *n.*

tax•ing (tăk′sĭng) ▸*adj.* Burdensome.

taxo– or **taxi–** or **tax–** ▸*pref.* Order; arrangement: *taxonomy.* [< Gk. *taxis.*]

tax•on•o•my (tăk-sŏn′ə-mē) ▸*n., pl.* **-mies 1.** The classification of organisms in an ordered system that indicates natural relationships. **2.** The science or principles of classification. —**tax′o•nom′ic** (tăk′sə-nŏm′ĭk) *adj.* —**tax′o•nom′i•cal•ly** *adv.* —**tax•on′o•mist** *n.*

tax•pay•er (tăks′pā′ər) ▸*n.* One who pays taxes.

tax shelter ▸*n.* A financial operation that reduces taxes on current earnings.

Tay•lor (tā′lər), **Elizabeth.** b. 1932. British-born Amer. actress.

Taylor, Zachary. 1784–1850. The 12th US President (1849–50).

Tb ▸ The symbol for the element **terbium.**

TB ▸*abbr.* tuberculosis

Tbi•li•si (tə-bə-lē′sē) The capital of Georgia, in the SE part on the Kura R. WNW of Baku. Pop. 1,268,000.

T-bone (tē′bōn′) ▸*n.* A thick steak taken from the small end of the loin and containing a T-shaped bone.

tbs. or **tbsp.** ▸*abbr.* tablespoon

Tc ▸ The symbol for the element **technetium.**

T cell ▸*n.* A principal type of white blood cell that has various roles in the immune system, including recognition of foreign antigens and activation of other immune cells. [*t(hymus-derived) cell.*]

Zachary Taylor
detail of an 1848 portrait

Tchai•kov•sky (chī-kôf′skē), **Peter Ilich.** 1840–93. Russian composer. —**Tchai•kov′sky•an, Tchai•kov′ski•an** *adj.*

TD ▸*abbr.* touchdown

Te ▸ The symbol for the element **tellurium.**

tea (tē) ▸*n.* **1a.** An Asian evergreen shrub with glossy leaves. **b.** The dried processed leaves of this plant, steeped in boiling water to make a beverage. **2.** The beverage thus made. **3.** Any similar drink prepared from the leaves of other plants. **4.** An afternoon reception or social gathering at which tea is served. **5.** *Slang* Marijuana. [< Chin. dial. *te.*]

tea bag ▸*n.* A small porous sack holding enough tea leaves to make an individual serving of tea.

teach (tēch) ▸*v.* **taught** (tôt), **teach•ing 1.** To impart knowledge or skill (to). **2.** To instruct in. **3.** To cause to learn by example or experience. [< OE *tǣcan.*] —**teach′a•bil′i•ty, teach′a•ble•ness** *n.* —**teach′a•ble** *adj.*

teach•er (tē′chər) ▸*n.* One who teaches, esp. one hired to teach.

teach•ing (tē′chĭng) ▸*n.* **1.** The work of a teacher. **2.** A precept or doctrine.

teak (tēk) ▸*n.* **1.** An Asian tree with hard, durable yellowish-brown wood. **2.** The wood of this tree. [< Malayalam *tēkka.*]

tea•ket•tle (tē′kĕt′l) ▸*n.* A covered kettle with a spout and handle, used for boiling water, as for tea.

teal (tēl) ▸*n., pl.* **teal** or **teals 1.** Any of several small wild ducks. **2.** A moderate bluish green. [ME *tele.*] —**teal** *adj.*

team (tēm) ▸*n.* **1.** A group on the same side, as in a game. **2.** A group organized to work together. **3.** Two or more harnessed draft animals. See Usage Note at **collective noun.** ▸*v.* **1.** To harness together to form a team. **2.** To form a team. [< OE *tēam.*]

team•mate (tēm′māt′) ▸*n.* A fellow member of a team.

team•ster (tēm′stər) ▸*n.* **1.** A truck driver. **2.** One who drives a team of draft animals.

team•work (tēm′wûrk′) ▸*n.* Cooperative effort.

tea•pot (tē′pŏt′) ▸*n.* A covered pot with a spout, used for making and serving tea.

tear[1] (târ) ▸*v.* **tore** (tôr, tōr), **torn** (tôrn, tōrn), **tear•ing 1.** To pull apart or into pieces; rend. **2.** To make (an opening) by ripping. **3.** To lacerate. **4.** To separate forcefully; wrench. **5.** To divide or disrupt. **6.** To rush headlong. —***phrasal verb:*** **tear down** To demolish. ►*n.* A rip or rent. —***idiom:*** **tear (one's) hair** To be greatly upset or distressed. [< OE *teran.*]

tear² (tîr) ►*n.* **1.** A drop of the clear salty liquid that lubricates the surface between the eyeball and eyelid. **2. tears** The act of weeping. ►*v.* To fill with tears. [< OE *tēar.*] —**tear′ful** *adj.* —**tear′ful•ly** *adv.* —**tear′i•ly** *adv.* —**tear′i•ness** *n.* —**tear′y** *adj.*

tear•drop (tîr′drŏp′) ►*n.* A single tear.

tear gas (tîr) ►*n.* Any of various agents that irritate the eyes and cause blinding tears.

tear•jerk•er (tîr′jûr′kər) ►*n. Slang* A very sad or sentimental story, drama, or performance.

tea•room (tē′ro͞om′, -ro͝om′) ►*n.* A restaurant serving tea and other refreshments.

tease (tēz) ►*v.* **teased, teas•ing 1.** To annoy; vex. **2.** To make fun of. **3.** To arouse hope, desire, or curiosity without affording satisfaction. **4.** To coax. **5.** To disentangle and dress the fibers of (wool). **6.** To raise the nap of (cloth). **7.** To brush or comb (the hair) toward the scalp for a bouffant effect. [< OE *tǣsan,* comb apart.] —**teas′er** *n.* —**teas′ing•ly** *adv.*

tea•sel (tē′zəl) ►*n.* **1.** A plant with thistlelike flowers surrounded by stiff bristles. **2.** Its bristly flower head, used to raise a nap on fabrics. [< OE *tǣsel.*]

tea•spoon (tē′spo͞on′) ►*n.* **1.** The common small spoon used esp. with tea, coffee, and desserts. **2.** A household cooking measure equal to ⅓ tablespoon (about 5 ml). —**tea′spoon•ful** *n.*

teat (tēt, tĭt) ►*n.* A nipple of the mammary gland. [< OFr. *tete,* of Gmc. orig.]

Te•bal•di (tə-bäl′dē, tē-), **Renata.** b. 1922. Italian-born operatic soprano.

tech (tĕk) *Informal* ►*n.* **1.** A technician. **2.** Technology. **3.** Technical work. ►*adj.* Technical.

tech•ne•ti•um (tĕk-nē′shē-əm, -shəm) ►*n. Symbol* **Tc** A silvery-gray radioactive metal, the first synthetically produced element. At. no. 43. See table at **element.** [< Gk. *tekhnētos,* artificial. See TECHNICAL.]

tech•ni•cal (tĕk′nĭ-kəl) ►*adj.* **1.** Of or derived from technique. **2.** Specialized. **3.** Of the practical, mechanical, or industrial arts: *a technical school.* **4a.** Abstract or theoretical. **b.** Scientific. **5.** Formal rather than practical: *a technical distinction.* **6.** Technological. [< Gk. *tekhnē,* skill.] —**tech′ni•cal•ly** *adv.*

tech•ni•cal•i•ty (tĕk′nĭ-kăl′ĭ-tē) ►*n., pl.* **-ties 1.** The quality or condition of being technical. **2a.** Something meaningful only to a specialist. **b.** A fine point, as of law.

technical sergeant ►*n.* A rank in the US Air Force above staff sergeant.

tech•ni•cian (tĕk-nĭsh′ən) ►*n.* An expert in a technical field or process.

Tech•ni•col•or (tĕk′nĭ-kŭl′ər) ► A trademark for a method of making color movies.

tech•nique (tĕk-nēk′) ►*n.* **1.** The systematic procedure by which a complex or scientific task is accomplished. **2.** also **tech•nic** (tĕk′nĭk) The degree of skill shown in any performance. See Syns at **art¹.** [Fr. < Gk. *tekhnikos,* TECHNICAL.]

tech•noc•ra•cy (tĕk-nŏk′rə-sē) ►*n., pl.* **-cies.** A government or social system controlled by technicians or technical experts. [Gk. *tekhnē,* skill; see TECHNICAL + -CRACY.] —**tech′no•crat** *n.* —**tech′no•crat′ic** *adj.*

tech•nol•o•gy (tĕk-nŏl′ə-jē) ►*n., pl.* **-gies 1.** The application of science, esp. in industry or commerce. **2.** The scientific methods and materials thus used. **3.** High technology. [< Gk. *tekhnē,* skill + -LOGY.] —**tech′no•log′i•cal** (-nə-lŏj′ĭ-kəl) *adj.* —**tech′no•log′i•cal•ly** *adv.* —**tech′nol′o•gist** *n.*

tech•no•pho•bi•a (tĕk′nə-fō′bē-ə) ►*n.* Fear of technology, esp. computers. —**tech′no•phobe′** *n.* —**tech′no•pho′bic** *adj.*

tec•ton•ics (tĕk-tŏn′ĭks) ►*n. (takes sing. v.)* **1.** The geology of the earth's structural features. **2.** The art of large-scale construction. [< Gk. *tektōn,* builder.] —**tec•ton′ic** *adj.*

Te•cum•seh (tĭ-kŭm′sə). 1768–1813. Shawnee leader.

ted•dy bear also **Ted•dy bear** (tĕd′ē) ►*n.* A child's toy bear. [After *Teddy,* nickname of Theodore Roosevelt.]

te•di•ous (tē′dē-əs) ►*adj.* Tiresomely long or dull; boring. [< Lat. *taedium,* TEDIUM.] —**te′di•ous•ly** *adv.* —**te′di•ous•ness** *n.*

te•di•um (tē′dē-əm) ►*n.* Boredom; monotony. [Lat. *taedium* < *taedēre,* to weary.]

tee (tē) ►*n.* **1.** A small peg with a concave top for holding a golf ball for an initial drive. **2.** The area of each golf hole from which the initial drive is made. ►*v.* To place (a golf ball) on a tee. —***phrasal verb:*** **tee off 1.** To drive a golf ball from the tee. **2.** *Slang* To start. [< obsolete Sc. *teaz.*]

teem (tēm) ►*v.* To abound or swarm. [< OE *tīeman,* beget.] —**teem′ing•ly** *adv.*

Syns: *teem, abound, crawl, overflow, swarm* ***v.***

teen (tēn) ►*n.* **1. teens a.** The numbers 13 through 19. **b.** The years of life between ages 13 and 19. **2.** A teenager. ►*adj.* Teenage.

teen•age or **teen-age** (tēn′āj′) also **teen•aged** or **teen-aged** (-ājd′) ►*adj.* Of, for, or involving those aged 13 through 19. —**teen′ag′er** *n.*

tee•ny (tē′nē) also **teen•sy** (tēn′sē) ►*adj.* **-ni•er, -ni•est** also **-si•er, -si•est** *Informal* Tiny. [< TINY.]

tee•pee (tē′pē) ►*n.* Var. of **tepee.**

tee shirt ►*n.* Var. of **T-shirt.**

tee•ter (tē′tər) ►*v.* **1.** To move unsteadily; totter. **2.** To seesaw; vacillate. [ME *titeren.*]

tee•ter-tot•ter (tē′tər-tŏt′ər) ►*n.* See **seesaw** 1.

teeth (tēth) ►*n.* Pl. of **tooth.**

teethe (tē*th*) ►*v.* **teethed, teeth•ing.** To grow or cut one's teeth. [ME *tethen* < *teth,* teeth.]

tee•to•tal•er (tē′tōt′l-ər) ►*n.* One who abstains completely from alcoholic beverages. [< *tee,* pronunciation of 1st letter in *total* + *total (abstinence).*] —**tee•to′tal•ism** *n.*

TEFL ►*abbr.* teaching English as a foreign language

Tef•lon (tĕf′lŏn′) ► A trademark for a nonstick material used to coat cooking utensils.

Te•gu•ci•gal•pa (tē-go͞o′sē-gäl′pä) The capital of Honduras, in the S-central part. Pop. 597,512.

Teh•ran or **Te•he•ran** (tĕ′ə-răn′, -rän′, tē-răn′, -rän′). The capital of Iran, in the N-central part. Pop. 6,750,043.

tek•tite (tĕk′tīt′) ►*n.* A dark glassy rock of possibly meteoric origin. [< Gk. *tēktos,* molten.]

tel. ▸*abbr.* **1.** telegram **2.** telegraph **3.** telephone

Tel A•viv–Ya•fo (tĕl′ä-vēv′-yä′fō) or **Tel A•viv–Jaf•fa** (-jăf′ə, -yä′fə). A city of W-central Israel on the Mediterranean WNW of Jerusalem. Pop. 357,100.

tele– or **tel–** ▸*pref.* **1.** Distance; distant: *telepathy.* **2a.** Telegraph; telephone: *telegram.* **b.** Television: *telecast.* [< Gk. *tēle*, far off.]

tel•e•cast (tĕl′ĭ-kăst′) ▸*v.* To broadcast by television. —**tel′e•cast′** *n.*

tel•e•com•mu•ni•ca•tion (tĕl′ĭ-kə-myo͞o′-nĭ-kā′shən) ▸*n.* often **telecommunications** *(takes sing. v.)* The science and technology of sending messages by electrical or electronic means.

tel•e•com•mute (tĕl′ĭ-kə-myo͞ot′) ▸*v.* **-mut•ed, -mut•ing.** To work at home using a computer connected to the network of one's employer. —**tel′e•com•mut′er** *n.*

tel•e•con•fer•ence (tĕl′ĭ-kŏn′fər-əns, -frəns) ▸*n.* A conference held among people in different locations with telecommunications equipment.

tel•e•gen•ic (tĕl′ə-jĕn′ĭk) ▸*adj.* Presenting an appealing appearance on television. [TELE– + (PHOTO)GENIC.]

tel•e•gram (tĕl′ĭ-grăm′) ▸*n.* A message sent by telegraph.

tel•e•graph (tĕl′ĭ-grăf′) ▸*n.* **1.** A communications system that transmits coded messages by means of unmodulated electric impulses, esp. one in which the transmission and reception stations are connected by wires. **2.** A telegram. ▸*v.* To transmit (a message) by telegraph. —**te•leg′ra•pher** (tə-lĕg′rə-fər), **te•leg′ra•phist** *n.* —**tel′e•graph′ic** *adj.* —**tel′e•graph′i•cal•ly** *adv.* —**te•leg′ra•phy** *n.*

tel•e•ki•ne•sis (tĕl′ĭ-kĭ-nē′sĭs, -kī-) ▸*n.* The movement of objects by scientifically inexplicable means. [TELE– + Gk. *kinēsis*, movement.] —**tel′e•ki•net′ic** (-nĕt′ĭk) *adj.*

tel•e•mar•ket•ing (tĕl′ə-mär′kĭ-tĭng) ▸*n.* The business of marketing goods or services by telephone. —**tel′e•mar′ket•er** *n.*

tel•e•med•i•cine (tĕl′ĭ-mĕd′ĭ-sĭn) ▸*n.* The use of telecommunications to provide health services, as by accessing off-site databases.

te•lem•e•try (tə-lĕm′ĭ-trē) ▸*n.* The automatic measurement and transmission of data from remote sources to receiving stations for recording and analysis. —**tel′e•me′ter** (tĕl′ə-mē′tər) *n.* —**tel′e•met′ric** (tĕl′ə-mĕt′rĭk), **tel′e•met′ri•cal** *adj.*

te•lep•a•thy (tə-lĕp′ə-thē) ▸*n.* Communication through means other than the senses. —**tel′e•path′ic** (tĕl′ə-păth′ĭk) *adj.* —**tel′e•path′i•cal•ly** *adv.* —**te•lep′a•thist** *n.*

tel•e•phone (tĕl′ə-fōn′) ▸*n.* An instrument that converts voice and other sound signals into a form that can be transmitted to remote locations. ▸*v.* **-phoned, -phon•ing.** To speak with (a person) by telephone.

telephone exchange ▸*n.* A central system of switches and other equipment that establishes connections between telephones.

te•leph•o•ny (tə-lĕf′ə-nē) ▸*n.* The transmission of sound between distant stations, esp. by radio or telephone. —**tel′e•phon′ic** (tĕl′ə-fŏn′ĭk) *adj.*

tel•e•pho•to (tĕl′ə-fō′tō) ▸*adj.* Of or relating to a photographic lens or lens system used to produce a large image of a distant object.

tel•e•play (tĕl′ə-plā′) ▸*n.* A play written or adapted for television.

tel•e•scope (tĕl′ĭ-skōp′) ▸*n.* **1.** An arrangement of lenses or mirrors or both that gathers visible light, permitting direct observation or photographic recording of distant objects. **2.** Any of various devices used to detect and observe distant objects by their emission or reflection of invisible radiation. ▸*v.* **-scoped, -scop•ing 1.** To slide inward or outward in overlapping sections, as the cylindrical sections of a small hand telescope do. **2.** To condense. —**tel′e•scop′ic** (-skŏp′ĭk) *adj.*

tel•e•thon (tĕl′ə-thŏn′) ▸*n.* A lengthy television program to raise funds for a charity. [TELE– + (MARA)THON.]

tel•e•type•writ•er (tĕl′ĭ-tīp′rī′tər) ▸*n.* An electromechanical typewriter that either transmits or receives messages coded in electrical signals.

tel•e•vise (tĕl′ə-vīz′) ▸*v.* **-vised, -vis•ing.** To broadcast by television. [< TELEVISION.]

tel•e•vi•sion (tĕl′ə-vĭzh′ən) ▸*n.* **1.** The transmission of visual images, usu. with accompanying sound, as electromagnetic waves. **2.** An electronic apparatus that receives such waves and displays the reconverted images on a screen. **3.** The industry of producing and broadcasting television programs.

tel•ex (tĕl′ĕks′) ▸*n.* **1.** A communications system consisting of teletypewriters connected to a telephonic network. **2.** A message sent or received by telex. [TEL(ETYPEWRITER) + EX(CHANGE).] —**tel′ex′** *v.*

tell (tĕl) ▸*v.* **told** (tōld), **tell•ing 1.** To give an account of; narrate. **2.** To express with words. **3.** To notify; inform. **4.** To give instructions to; direct. **5.** To discover by observation; discern. **6.** To have an effect or impact: *In this game every move tells.* —***phrasal verb:* tell off** *Informal* To rebuke severely; reprimand. [< OE *tellan.*]

tell•er (tĕl′ər) ▸*n.* A bank employee who receives and pays out money.

Teller, Edward. b. 1908. Hungarian-born Amer. physicist.

tell•ing (tĕl′ĭng) ▸*adj.* Having force or effect; striking. —**tell′ing•ly** *adv.*

tell•tale (tĕl′tāl′) ▸*n.* **1.** A tattletale; talebearer. **2.** An indicator; sign.

tel•lu•ri•um (tĕ-lo͝or′ē-əm) ▸*n.* *Symbol* **Te** A brittle, silvery-white metallic element used to alloy stainless steel and lead, in ceramics, and in thermoelectric devices. At. no. 52. See table at **element.** [< Lat. *tellūs*, earth.]

te•mer•i•ty (tə-mĕr′ĭ-tē) ▸*n.* Audacity; nerve. [< Lat. *temere*, rashly.]

temp. ▸*abbr.* **1.** temperature **2.** temporary **3.** *Lat.* tempore (in the time of)

Tem•pe (tĕm′pē′) A city of S-central AZ E of Phoenix. Pop. 141,865.

tem•peh (tĕm′pā′) ▸*n.* A high-protein food made from partially cooked, fermented soybeans. [Indonesian *tempe.*]

tem•per (tĕm′pər) ▸*v.* **1.** To soften or moderate. See Syns at **moderate. 2.** To harden or strengthen (e.g., metal), as by alternate heating and cooling. **3.** To adjust finely; attune. ▸*n.* **1.** A state of mind or emotions; mood. **2.** Calmness; composure. **3a.** A tendency to become angry or irritable. **b.** An outburst of rage. **4.** The degree of hardness of a metal. [< Lat. *temperāre.*]

tem•per•a (tĕm′pər-ə) ►*n.* **1.** A painting medium in which pigment is mixed with water-soluble glutinous materials such as size or egg yolk. **2.** Painting done in this medium. [Ital. < *temperare*, mingle. See TEMPER.]

tem•per•a•ment (tĕm′prə-mənt, tĕm′pər-ə-) ►*n.* **1.** The manner of thinking, behaving, or reacting characteristic of a particular person. **2.** Excessive irritability or sensitiveness. [< Lat. *temperāre*, temper.] —**tem′per•a•men′tal** *adj.* —**tem′per•a•men′tal•ly** *adv.*

tem•per•ance (tĕm′pər-əns, -prəns) ►*n.* **1.** Moderation and self-restraint. **2.** Abstinence from alcoholic liquors.

tem•per•ate (tĕm′pər-ĭt, -prĭt) ►*adj.* **1.** Exercising moderation and self-restraint. **2.** Moderate; restrained. **3.** Not subject to extreme hot or cold weather. —**tem′per•ate•ly** *adv.* —**tem′per•ate•ness** *n.*

Temperate Zone. Either of two latitude zones of the earth, the **North Temperate Zone,** between the Arctic Circle and the tropic of Cancer, or the **South Temperate Zone,** between the Antarctic Circle and the tropic of Capricorn.

tem•per•a•ture (tĕm′pər-ə-cho͝or′, -chər, tĕm′prə-) ►*n.* **1.** The hotness or coldness of a body or environment. **2.** Abnormally high body heat caused by illness; fever. [< Lat. *temperāre*, temper.]

tem•pered (tĕm′pərd) ►*adj.* Having a specified temper or disposition.

tem•pest (tĕm′pĭst) ►*n.* A violent windstorm. [< Lat. *tempestās* < *tempus*, time.]

tem•pes•tu•ous (tĕm-pĕs′cho͞o-əs) ►*adj.* Tumultuous; stormy. —**tem•pes′tu•ous•ly** *adv.* —**tem•pes′tu•ous•ness** *n.*

tem•plate (tĕm′plĭt) ►*n.* A pattern or gauge, such as a thin metal plate, used as a guide in making something accurately. [Prob. < OFr. *temple*, device in a loom.]

tem•ple[1] (tĕm′pəl) ►*n.* **1.** A building dedicated to religious ceremonies or worship. **2.** *Judaism* A synagogue, esp. of a Reform congregation. [< Lat. *templum.*]

tem•ple[2] (tĕm′pəl) ►*n.* **1.** The flat region on either side of the forehead. **2.** The sidepiece of an eyeglass frame. [< Lat. *tempus.*]

tem•po (tĕm′pō) ►*n.*, *pl.* **-pos** or **-pi** (-pē) **1.** The speed at which music is to be played. **2.** A pace. [Ital. < Lat. *tempus*, time.]

tem•po•ral[1] (tĕm′pər-əl, -prəl) ►*adj.* **1.** Of or limited by time. **2.** Worldly; secular. [< Lat. *tempus, tempor-*, time.] —**tem′po•ral•ly** *adv.*

tem•po•ral[2] (tĕm′pər-əl, -prəl) ►*adj.* Of or near the temples of the skull. [< Lat. *tempus, tempor-*, temple.]

temporal bone ►*n.* Either of two bones that form the sides and base of the skull.

tem•po•rar•y (tĕm′pə-rĕr′ē) ►*adj.* Lasting or used for a limited time. ►*n.*, *pl.* **-ies** *Informal* One that works or serves for a limited time. —**tem′po•rar′i•ly** *adv.*

Syns: temporary, acting, interim, provisional ***Ant:*** *permanent* **adj.**

tem•po•rize (tĕm′pə-rīz′) ►*v.* **-rized, -riz•ing 1.** To gain time, as by postponing an action or decision. **2.** To yield to current conditions; compromise. [< Lat. *tempus, tempor-*, time.] —**tem′po•ri•za′tion** *n.*

tempt (tĕmpt) ►*v.* **1.** To try to get (someone) to do wrong, esp. by a promise of reward. **2.** To be attractive to. **3.** To risk provoking: *tempt fate.* **4.** To incline or dispose: *I'm tempted to go.* [< Lat. *temptāre*, try.] —**temp•ta′tion** *n.* —**tempt′er** *n.*

tempt•ress (tĕmp′trĭs) ►*n.* An alluring, bewitching woman. See Usage Note at **-ess.**

tem•pu•ra (tĕm′po͝o-rə, tĕm-po͝or′ə) ►*n.* A Japanese dish of deep-fried batter-dipped vegetables and shrimp or other seafood. [J.]

ten (tĕn) ►*n.* **1.** The cardinal number equal to 9 + 1. **2.** The 10th in a set or sequence. [< OE *tīen.*] —**ten** *adj. & pron.*

ten•a•ble (tĕn′ə-bəl) ►*adj.* Defensible: *a tenable theory.* [< Lat. *tenēre*, hold.] —**ten′a•bil′i•ty, ten′a•ble•ness** *n.* —**ten′a•bly** *adv.*

te•na•cious (tə-nā′shəs) ►*adj.* **1.** Holding firmly, as to a belief; stubborn. **2.** Clinging; adhesive. **3.** Tending to retain; retentive. [< Lat. *tenāx.*] —**te•na′cious•ly** *adv.* —**te•nac′i•ty** (-năs′ĭ-tē), **te•na′cious•ness** *n.*

ten•an•cy (tĕn′ən-sē) ►*n.*, *pl.* **-cies 1.** Possession or occupancy of land or building by title, lease, or rent. **2.** The period of a tenant's occupancy or possession.

ten•ant (tĕn′ənt) ►*n.* **1.** One that pays rent to use or occupy property owned by another. **2.** An occupant. [< Lat. *tenēre*, hold.]

Ten Commandments ►*pl.n. Bible* The ten laws given by God to Moses on Mount Sinai.

tend[1] (tĕnd) ►*v.* **1.** To have a tendency. **2.** To be likely. **3.** To move or extend in a certain direction. [< Lat. *tendere.*]

tend[2] (tĕnd) ►*v.* **1.** To take care of. **2.** To serve at: *tend bar.* **3.** To apply one's attention; attend. [< ME *attenden*, ATTEND.]

Syns: tend, attend, mind, minister, watch **v.**

ten•den•cy (tĕn′dən-sē) ►*n.*, *pl.* **-cies 1.** Prevailing movement; trend. **2.** An inclination to think, act, or behave in a particular way.

ten•den•tious (tĕn-dĕn′shəs) ►*adj.* Promoting a particular point of view; biased. [< Lat. *tendēns*, tending.]

ten•der[1] (tĕn′dər) ►*adj.* **-er, -est 1a.** Delicate; fragile. **b.** Easily chewed. **2.** Young and vulnerable. **3.** Sensitive or sore. **4.** Gentle and loving. **5.** Sentimental; soft. [< Lat. *tener.*] —**ten′der•ly** *adv.* —**ten′der•ness** *n.*

ten•der[2] (tĕn′dər) ►*n.* **1.** A formal offer. **2.** Money: *legal tender.* ►*v.* To offer formally. [< Lat. *tendere*, extend.] —**ten′der•er** *n.*

tend•er[3] (tĕn′dər) ►*n.* **1.** One who tends something. **2.** *Naut.* A vessel attendant on other vessels. **3.** A railroad car attached to the locomotive, carrying fuel and water.

ten•der•foot (tĕn′dər-fo͝ot′) ►*n.*, *pl.* **-foots** or **-feet.** An inexperienced person; novice.

ten•der•heart•ed (tĕn′dər-här′tĭd) ►*adj.* Compassionate. —**ten′der•heart′ed•ly** *adv.* —**ten′der•heart′ed•ness** *n.*

ten•der•ize (tĕn′də-rīz′) ►*v.* **-ized, -iz•ing.** To make (meat) tender. —**ten′der•iz′er** *n.*

ten•der•loin (tĕn′dər-loin′) ►*n.* The tenderest part of a loin of beef or pork.

ten•di•ni•tis also **ten•do•ni•tis** (tĕn′də-nī′tĭs) ►*n.* Inflammation of a tendon. [< NLat. *tendō, tendin-*, TENDON.]

ten•don (tĕn′dən) ►*n.* A band of tough fibrous tissue that connects a muscle with its bony attachment. [< Gk. *tenōn.*]

ten•dril (tĕn′drəl) ►*n.* **1.** A twisting threadlike structure by which a twining plant clings to a support. **2.** Something resembling this. [< OFr.

tendrillon, tender young shoot.]

ten•e•ment (tĕn′ə-mənt) ►*n.* **1.** A building to live in, esp. one rented to tenants. **2.** A rundown, low-rental apartment building whose facilities and upkeep barely meet minimum standards. [< Lat. *tenēre*, hold.]

ten•et (tĕn′ĭt) ►*n.* A doctrine or principle held to be true. See Syns at **doctrine.** [< Lat. *tenēre*, hold.]

ten-gal•lon hat (tĕn′găl′ən) ►*n.* A hat with an exceptionally tall crown and a wide brim.

ten•ge (tĕn-gĕ′) ►*n., pl.* **tenge.** See table at **currency.** [Kazakh and Turkmen.]

Ten•nes•see (tĕn′ĭ-sē′, tĕn′ĭ-sē′) A state of the SE US. Cap. Nashville. Pop. 4,896,641. —**Ten′nes•se′an** *adj. & n.*

Tennessee River. A river of the SE US rising in E TN and flowing about 1,049 km (652 mi) to the Ohio R.

ten•nis (tĕn′ĭs) ►*n.* A game played with rackets and a light ball by two players or two pairs of players on a court divided by a net. [< AN *tenetz*, hold!]

tennis shoe ►*n.* See **sneaker.**

Ten•ny•son (tĕn′ĭ-sən), **Alfred.** 1st Baron Tennyson. 1809–92. British poet. —**Ten′ny•so′ni•an** (-sō′nē-ən) *adj.*

Te•noch•ti•tlán (tĕ-nōch′tē-tlän′) An ancient Aztec capital on the site of present-day Mexico City.

ten•on (tĕn′ən) ►*n.* A projection on a piece of wood shaped for insertion into a mortise to make a joint. [< OFr. < Lat. *tenēre*, hold.]

ten•or (tĕn′ər) ►*n.* **1.** A continuous course. **2.** General sense; drift or purport. **3.** *Mus.* **a.** The highest natural adult male voice. **b.** The range between alto and bass. **c.** A singer, voice, or instrument having this range. [< Lat. < *tenēre*, hold.]

ten•pin (tĕn′pĭn′) ►*n.* **1.** One of the bottle-shaped pins used in bowling. **2. tenpins** *(takes sing. v.)* See **bowling** 1.

tense[1] (tĕns) ►*adj.* **tens•er, tens•est 1.** Tightly stretched; taut. See Syns at **tight. 2.** Feeling mental or nervous tension. **3.** Nerve-racking; suspenseful: *a tense situation.* ►*v.* **tensed, tens•ing.** To make or become tense. [Lat. *tēnsus*, p.part. of *tendere*, stretch.] —**tense′ly** *adv.* —**tense′ness** *n.*

tense[2] (tĕns) ►*n.* Any of the inflected forms of a verb that indicate the time and continuance or completion of the action or state. [< Lat. *tempus*, time.]

ten•sile (tĕn′səl, -sīl′) ►*adj.* **1.** Of or relating to tension. **2.** Capable of being stretched or extended. [< Lat. *tēnsus*, stretched.] —**ten•sil′i•ty** (tĕn-sĭl′ĭ-tē) *n.*

ten•sion (tĕn′shən) ►*n.* **1.** The act of stretching or the condition of being stretched. **2.** A force tending to stretch or elongate something. **3a.** Mental strain. **b.** A strained relationship between people or groups. **c.** Uneasy suspense. **4.** Voltage. [< Lat. *tendere*, *tēns-*, stretch.]

ten•sor (tĕn′sər, -sôr′) ►*n.* A muscle that tenses a body part.

tent (tĕnt) ►*n.* A portable shelter, as of canvas, stretched over a supporting framework of poles with ropes and pegs. [< VLat. **tendita*, stretched.]

ten•ta•cle (tĕn′tə-kəl) ►*n.* An elongated, flexible, unjointed appendage, as of an octopus or squid. [< Lat. *tentāre*, feel.] —**ten•tac′u•lar** (-tăk′yə-lər) *adj.*

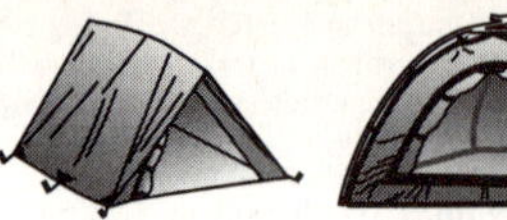

tent
left to right: A-frame and pop models

ten•ta•tive (tĕn′tə-tĭv) ►*adj.* **1.** Not fully worked out or concluded; provisional. **2.** Uncertain; hesitant. [< Lat. *tentāre*, try.] —**ten′ta•tive•ly** *adv.* —**ten′ta•tive•ness** *n.*

ten•ter•hook (tĕn′tər-ho͝ok′) ►*n.* A hooked nail for securing cloth on a drying framework. —***idiom:* on tenterhooks** In a state of suspense or anxiety. [*tenter*, framework for drying + HOOK.]

tenth (tĕnth) ►*n.* **1.** The ordinal number matching the number 10 in a series. **2.** One of ten equal parts. —**tenth** *adv. & adj.*

ten•u•ous (tĕn′yo͞o-əs) ►*adj.* **1.** Long and thin; slender. **2.** Rarefied. **3.** Slight; flimsy. [< Lat. *tenuis*.] —**ten′u•ous•ly** *adv.* —**ten′u•ous•ness, te•nu′i•ty** (tĕ-no͞o′ĭ-tē, -nyo͞o′-) *n.*

ten•ure (tĕn′yər, -yo͝or′) ►*n.* **1a.** The holding of something, as an office or real estate. **b.** A period during which something is held. **2.** The status of holding one's position on a permanent basis. [< Lat. *tenēre*, hold.]

Te•o•ti•hua•cán (tā′ə-tē′wä-kän′) An ancient city of central Mexico; site of the Temple of Quetzalcoatl.

te•pee also **tee•pee** or **ti•pi** (tē′pē) ►*n.* A portable dwelling of certain Native American peoples, consisting of a conical framework of poles covered with skins or bark. [Sioux t^{h}*ípi*, dwelling.]

tep•id (tĕp′ĭd) ►*adj.* Moderately warm; lukewarm. [< Lat. *tepēre*, be lukewarm.] —**te•pid′i•ty, tep′id•ness** *n.* —**tep′id•ly** *adv.*

te•qui•la (tə-kē′lə) ►*n.* An alcoholic liquor distilled from an agave. [After *Tequila*, Mexico.]

tera– ►*pref.* One trillion (10^{12}): *terabyte.* [< Gk. *teras*, monster.]

ter•a•byte (tĕr′ə-bīt′) ►*n.* A unit of computer memory equal to 1,024 gigabytes (2^{40} bytes).

te•rat•o•gen (tə-răt′ə-jən, tĕr′ə-tə-) ►*n.* An agent, such as a drug, that causes malformation of an embryo or fetus. [Gk. *teras*, *terat-*, monster + –GEN.] —**ter′a•to•gen′ic** *adj.*

ter•bi•um (tûr′bē-əm) ►*n. Symbol* **Tb** A soft, silvery-gray rare-earth element, used in x-ray and color television tubes. At. no. 65. See table at **element.** [After *Ytterby*, Sweden.]

ter•cen•ten•a•ry (tûr′sĕn-tĕn′ə-rē, tər-sĕn′tə-nĕr′ē) ►*n., pl.* **-ries.** A 300th anniversary. [Lat. *ter*, thrice + CENTENARY.] —**ter′cen•ten′a•ry** *adj.*

Ter•ence (tĕr′əns). 185?–159? B.C. African-born Roman playwright.

Te•re•sa (tə-rē′sə, -zə, -rā′-), Mother. 1910–97. Albanian-born Indian nun; 1979 Nobel Peace Prize.

Te•resh•ko•va (tə-rĕsh-kō′və), **Valentina Vladmirovna.** b. 1937. Soviet cosmonaut; first woman in space (1963).

ter•i•ya•ki (tĕr′ē-yä′kē) ►*n.* A Japanese dish of grilled or broiled slices of marinated meat or shellfish. [J.]

term (tûrm) ►*n.* **1a.** A limited period of time.

Mother Teresa

b. An assigned period for a person to serve. **c.** A period when a school or court is in session. **2a.** An end or termination. **b.** The end of a normal gestation period: *carried the fetus to term.* **c.** A deadline, as for making a payment. **3a.** A word or phrase having a particular meaning. **b.** **terms** Language of a certain kind: *praised him in glowing terms.* **4.** often **terms** A stipulation or condition: *peace terms.* **5.** **terms** The relationship between persons or groups: *on good terms.* **6.** *Math.* One of the quantities in a fraction, equation, or series. ► *v.* To designate; call. [< Lat. *terminus*, boundary.]

ter•ma•gant (tûr′mə-gənt) ► *n.* A scolding woman; shrew. [ME *Termagaunt*, character in medieval mystery plays.]

ter•mi•nal (tûr′mə-nəl) ► *adj.* **1.** Of or forming a limit, boundary, or end. **2.** Concluding; final. **3.** Of or occurring in a term or each term. **4.** Ending in death; fatal. ► *n.* **1.** A point or part that forms the end. **2.** *Elect.* A position in a circuit at which a connection is normally established or broken. **3.** A railroad or bus station, esp. a terminus. **4.** A device, usu. having a keyboard and video display, through which data can be entered or displayed. [< Lat. *terminus*, boundary.] —**ter′mi•nal•ly** *adv.*

ter•mi•nate (tûr′mə-nāt′) ► *v.* **-nat•ed, -nat•ing.** To bring or come to an end; conclude. —**ter′mi•na•ble** *adj.* —**ter′mi•na′tion** *n.* —**ter′mi•na′tive** *adj.* —**ter′mi•na′tor** *n.*

ter•mi•nol•o•gy (tûr′mə-nŏl′ə-jē) ► *n., pl.* **-gies 1.** The technical terms of a particular field, science, or art; nomenclature. **2.** The study of nomenclature. [< Med.Lat. *terminus*, expression.] —**ter′mi•no•log′i•cal** (-nə-lŏj′ĭ-kəl) *adj.*

ter•mi•nus (tûr′mə-nəs) ► *n., pl.* **-nus•es** or **-ni** (-nī′) **1.** The final point; end. **2.** An end point on a transportation line. [Lat.]

ter•mite (tûr′mīt′) ► *n.* Any of numerous antlike social insects that often feed on wood. [< LLat. *termes*, wood-eating worm.]

term limits ► *pl.n.* A restriction on the number of terms an official may serve.

tern (tûrn) ► *n.* Any of various sea birds resembling gulls but usu. smaller and having a forked tail. [Of Scand. orig.]

ter•na•ry (tûr′nə-rē) ► *adj.* **1.** Composed of three or arranged in threes. **2.** *Math.* **a.** Having the base three. **b.** Involving three variables. [< Lat. *ternī*, three each.]

terp•si•cho•re•an (tûrp′sĭ-kə-rē′ən, -kôr′ē-ən, -kōr′-) ► *adj.* Of dancing. ► *n.* A dancer. [< *Terpsichore*, Greek Muse of dancing.]

terr. ► *abbr.* **1.** terrace **2.** territory

ter•race (tĕr′ĭs) ► *n.* **1.** A porch or balcony. **2.** An open area adjacent to a house serving as an outdoor living space. **3.** A raised bank of earth having vertical or sloping sides and a flat top. **4.** A row of buildings on raised or sloping ground. **5.** A residential street, esp. along the top or slope of a hill. ► *v.* **-raced, -rac•ing.** To form into terraces. [< VLat. **terrācea* < Lat. *terra*, earth.]

ter•ra cot•ta (tĕr′ə kŏt′ə) ► *n.* **1.** A hard ceramic clay used in pottery and construction. **2.** A brownish orange. [Ital.] —**ter′ra-cot′ta** *adj.*

terra fir•ma (fûr′mə) ► *n.* Dry land. [NLat., solid ground.]

ter•rain (tə-rān′) ► *n.* **1.** An area of land; ground. **2.** Topography: *rugged terrain.* [< Lat. *terrēnus*, of the earth.]

ter•ra•pin (tĕr′ə-pĭn) ► *n.* Any of various North American aquatic turtles. [Of Virginia Algonquian orig.]

ter•rar•i•um (tə-râr′ē-əm) ► *n., pl.* **-i•ums** or **-i•a** (-ē-ə). A closed container in which plants and sometimes small animals, such as turtles and lizards, are kept. [Lat. *terra*, earth + –ARIUM.]

ter•res•tri•al (tə-rĕs′trē-əl) ► *adj.* **1.** Of Earth or its inhabitants. **2.** Of or consisting of land. **3.** Living or growing on land. ► *n.* An inhabitant of Earth. [< Lat. *terrestris* < *terra*, earth.]

ter•ri•ble (tĕr′ə-bəl) ► *adj.* **1.** Causing great fear or alarm; dreadful. **2.** Extreme or severe. **3.** Very bad. [< Lat. *terribilis* < *terrēre*, frighten.] —**ter′ri•bly** *adv.*

ter•ri•er (tĕr′ē-ər) ► *n.* Any of several small dogs orig. bred to hunt burrowing animals. [< OFr. *(chien) terrier*, ground (dog) < Lat. *terra.*]

ter•rif•ic (tə-rĭf′ĭk) ► *adj.* **1.** Fine; splendid: *a terrific party.* **2.** Awesome; astounding. **3.** Terrifying. **4.** Terrible; severe. [Lat. *terrificus.*] —**ter•rif′i•cal•ly** *adv.*

ter•ri•fy (tĕr′ə-fī′) ► *v.* **-fied, -fy•ing.** To fill with terror. [Lat. *terrificāre.*]

ter•ri•to•ri•al (tĕr′ĭ-tôr′ē-əl, -tōr′-) ► *adj.* **1.** Of or relating to the geographic area under a given jurisdiction. **2.** Of a particular territory; regional. —**ter′ri•to′ri•al•ly** *adv.*

ter•ri•to•ry (tĕr′ĭ-tôr′ē, -tōr′ē) ► *n., pl.* **-ries 1.** An area of land; region. **2.** The land and waters under the jurisdiction of a government. **3.** often **Territory** A usu. self-governing part of a nation not accorded statehood or provincial status. **4.** An area for which a person is responsible. **5.** A sphere of activity. See Syns at **field.** [< Lat. *territōrium* < *terra*, earth.]

ter•ror (tĕr′ər) ► *n.* **1.** Intense, overpowering fear. **2.** One that instills intense fear. **3.** Violence committed esp. by a group for political purposes. **4.** *Informal* A nuisance; pest. [< Lat. < *terrēre*, frighten.]

ter•ror•ism (tĕr′ə-rĭz′əm) ► *n.* The political use of violence or intimidation. —**ter′ror•ist** *n.* —**ter′ror•is′tic** *adj.*

ter•ror•ize (tĕr′ə-rīz′) ► *v.* **-ized, -iz•ing 1.** To terrify. **2.** To coerce by intimidation or fear. —**ter′ror•i•za′tion** *n.* —**ter′ror•iz′er** *n.*

ter•ry (tĕr′ē) ► *n.* An absorbent pile fabric, usu. of cotton, with uncut loops on both sides. [?]

terse (tûrs) ► *adj.* **ters•er, ters•est.** Brief and to the point; concise. [Lat. *tersus*, p.part. of *tergēre*, cleanse.] —**terse′ly** *adv.* —**terse′ness** *n.*

ter•ti•ar•y (tûr′shē-ĕr′ē) ▸*adj.* **1.** Third in order, degree, or rank. **2. Tertiary** *Geol.* Of or being the 1st period of the Cenozoic Era, including the Pliocene, Miocene, Oligocene, Eocene, and Paleocene epochs. ▸*n.* **Tertiary** The Tertiary Period. [< Lat. *tertius*, third.]

TESL ▸*abbr.* teaching English as a second language

Tes•la (tĕs′lə), **Nikola.** 1856–1943. Serbian-born Amer. engineer and physicist.

tes•sel•late (tĕs′ə-lāt′) ▸*v.* **-lat•ed, -lat•ing.** To form into a mosaic pattern. [< Lat. *tessella*, small cube < Gk. *tessares*, four.] —**tes′sel•la′tion** *n.*

test (tĕst) ▸*n.* **1.** A procedure for critical evaluation of the presence, quality, or truth of something; trial. **2.** A series of questions or problems designed to determine knowledge, intelligence, or ability. **3.** A basis for evaluation or judgment. [< Lat. *testū, testum*, pot.] —**test′er** *n.*

tes•ta•ment (tĕs′tə-mənt) ▸*n.* **1.** Proof; evidence. **2.** A statement of belief. **3.** A legal document providing for the disposition of a person's property after death; will. **4. Testament** Either of the two main divisions of the Christian Bible. [< Lat. *testis*, witness.] —**tes′ta•men′tar•y** (-mĕn′tə-rē, -mĕn′trē) *adj.*

tes•tate (tĕs′tāt′) ▸*adj.* Having made a legally valid will. [< Lat. *testārī*, make a will.]

tes•ta•tor (tĕs′tā′tər, tĕ-stā′tər) ▸*n.* One who has made a legally valid will.

tes•ta•trix (tĕ-stā′trĭks) ▸*n.*, *pl.* **-tri•ces** (-trĭ-sēz′). A woman who has made a legally valid will.

test ban ▸*n.* An agreement between nations to forgo testing of nuclear weapons.

tes•ti•cle (tĕs′tĭ-kəl) ▸*n.* A testis, esp. together with the scrotum. [< Lat. *testiculus*.]

tes•ti•fy (tĕs′tə-fī′) ▸*v.* **-fied, -fy•ing 1.** To make a declaration under oath; submit testimony. **2.** To serve as evidence. See Syns at **indicate. 3.** To declare publicly. [< Lat. *testificārī*.] —**tes′ti•fi′er** *n.*

tes•ti•mo•ni•al (tĕs′tə-mō′nē-əl) ▸*n.* **1.** A statement in support of a particular truth or fact. **2.** A written affirmation of another's character or worth. **3.** A tribute. —**tes′ti•mo′ni•al** *adj.*

tes•ti•mo•ny (tĕs′tə-mō′nē) ▸*n.*, *pl.* **-nies 1a.** A declaration by a witness under oath, as that given before a court. **b.** All such declarations offered in a legal case or hearing. **2.** Supportive evidence; proof. **3.** A public declaration. [< Lat. *testimōnium*.]

tes•tis (tĕs′tĭs) ▸*n.*, *pl.* **-tes** (-tēz). The male reproductive gland. [Lat.]

tes•tos•ter•one (tĕs-tŏs′tə-rōn′) ▸*n.* A steroid hormone responsible for the development of male secondary sex characteristics. [TEST(IS) + STER(OL) + *-one*, suff.]

test tube ▸*n.* A clear cylindrical glass tube used in laboratory experimentation.

tes•ty (tĕs′tē) ▸*adj.* **-ti•er, -ti•est.** Irritable; touchy. [< OFr. *teste*, head.] —**tes′ti•ly** *adv.* —**tes′ti•ness** *n.*

Tet (tĕt) ▸*n.* The lunar New Year as celebrated in Southeast Asia. [Vietnamese *tết*.]

tet•a•nus (tĕt′n-əs) ▸*n.* An often fatal infectious disease marked by spasmodic contraction of voluntary muscles, esp. of the neck and jaw. [< Gk. *tetanos*, rigid.]

tête-à-tête (tāt′ə-tāt′, tĕt′ə-tĕt′) ▸*adv. & adj.* Without the intrusion of a third person. ▸*n.* A private conversation between two persons. [Fr.]

teth•er (tĕ*th*′ər) ▸*n.* **1.** A rope or chain for an animal, allowing it a short radius in which to move about. **2.** The limit of one's resources or endurance. ▸*v.* To fasten with or as if with a tether. [< ON *tjōdhr*.]

Te•ton (tē′tŏn′) ▸*n.*, *pl.* **-ton** or **-tons.** A member of the largest and westernmost of the Sioux peoples.

Teton Range. A range of the Rocky Mts. in NW WY and SE ID.

tetra– or **tetr–** ▸*pref.* Four: *tetrahedron.* [Gk.]

tet•ra•cy•cline (tĕt′rə-sī′klēn′, -klĭn) ▸*n.* A yellow crystalline compound used as an antibiotic. [TETRA– + CYCL(IC) + –INE[2].]

tet•ra•he•dron (tĕt′rə-hē′drən) ▸*n.*, *pl.* **-drons** or **-dra** (-drə). A polyhedron with four faces. —**tet′tra•he′dral** *adj.*

te•tram•e•ter (tĕ-trăm′ĭ-tər) ▸*n.* A line of verse consisting of four metrical feet.

Teu•ton (to͞ot′n, tyo͞ot′n) ▸*n.* **1.** A member of an ancient people, probably of Germanic or Celtic origin, who lived in Jutland until about 100 B.C. **2.** A member of a Germanic-speaking people, esp. a German.

Teu•ton•ic (to͞o-tŏn′ĭk, tyo͞o-) ▸*adj.* **1.** Of or relating to the Teutons. **2.** Of the Germanic languages. ▸*n.* Germanic.

Te•vet (tā′vās, tĕ-vĕt′) ▸*n.* A month of the Jewish calendar. See table at **calendar.** [Heb. *ṭēbēt*.]

Tex•as (tĕk′səs) A state of the S-central US on the Gulf of Mexico. Cap. Austin. Pop. 17,059,805. —**Tex′an** *adj. & n.*

text (tĕkst) ▸*n.* **1.** The wording or words of something written or printed. **2.** The body of a printed work as distinct from a preface, footnote, or appendix. **3.** A Scriptural passage to be read and expounded upon in a sermon. **4.** A subject; topic. **5.** A textbook. [< Lat. *textus* < p.part. of *texere*, weave.] —**tex′tu•al** *adj.*

text•book (tĕkst′bo͝ok′) ▸*n.* A book used for the study of a subject.

tex•tile (tĕks′tīl′, -təl) ▸*n.* **1.** A cloth or fabric, esp. when woven or knitted. **2.** Fiber or yarn for weaving cloth. [< Lat. *textus*, p.part. of *texere*, weave.]

tex•ture (tĕks′chər) ▸*n.* **1.** A structure of interwoven fibers or other elements. **2.** The basic structure or composition of a substance. **3.** The appearance and feel of a surface. [< Lat. *textūra* < *textus*. See TEXT.] —**tex′tur•al** *adj.* —**tex′tured** *adj.*

TGIF ▸*abbr.* thank God it's Friday

Th ▸ The symbol for the element **thorium.**

Th. ▸*abbr.* Thursday

-th[1] ▸*suff.* Var. of **-eth[1].**

-th[2] also **-eth** ▸*suff.* Used to form ordinal numbers: *millionth.* [< OE *-tha*.]

Thack•er•ay (thăk′ə-rē, thăk′rē), **William Makepeace.** 1811–63. British writer.

Thai (tī) ▸*n.*, *pl.* **Thai** or **Thais 1.** A native or inhabitant of Thailand. **2.** The Tai language of Thailand. **3.** Tai. —**Thai** *adj.*

Thai•land (tī′lănd′, -lənd). Formerly **Siam.** A country of SE Asia on the **Gulf of Thailand** (formerly the Gulf of Siam), an arm of the South China Sea. Cap. Bangkok. Pop. 59,396,000.

thal•a•mus (thăl′ə-məs) ►*n., pl.* **-mi** (-mī′). A large mass of gray matter that relays sensory impulses to the cerebral cortex. [< Gk. *thalamos,* inner chamber.] —**tha•lam′ic** (thə-lăm′ĭk) *adj.*

Tha•les (thā′lēz). 624?–546? B.C. Greek philosopher. —**Tha•le′sian** (thā-lē′zhən) *adj.*

tha•lid•o•mide (thə-lĭd′ə-mīd′) ►*n.* A sedative drug found to cause severe birth defects when taken during pregnancy. [*(ph)thal(ic acid)* + *(im)id(e)* + *(i)mide.*]

thal•li•um (thăl′ē-əm) ►*n. Symbol* **Tl** A soft, malleable, highly toxic metallic element used in photocells and infrared detectors. At. no. 81. See table at **element.** [< Lat. *thallus,* green shoot + –IUM.]

Thames (tĕmz) A river of S England flowing about 338 km (210 mi) eastward through London to a wide estuary on the North Sea.

than (*th*ăn, *th*ən) ►*conj.* Used to introduce the second element or clause of an unequal comparison: *She is a better athlete than I.* ►*prep. Informal* In comparison with: *valued no one more than her.* [< OE *thanne.*]

thane (thān) ►*n.* **1.** A freeman granted land by the king in Anglo-Saxon England. **2.** A feudal lord in Scotland. [< OE *thegn.*]

thank (thăngk) ►*v.* **1.** To express gratitude to. **2.** To credit. [< OE *thancian.*]

thank•ful (thăngk′fəl) ►*adj.* Grateful. —**thank′ful•ly** *adv.* —**thank′ful•ness** *n.*

thank•less (thăngk′lĭs) ►*adj.* **1.** Ungrateful. **2.** Not likely to be appreciated: *a thankless job.* —**thank′less•ly** *adv.* —**thank′less•ness** *n.*

thanks (thăngks) ►*pl.n.* Grateful feelings or thoughts; gratitude. ►*interj.* Used to express thanks. —***idiom:*** **thanks to** On account of; because of.

thanks•giv•ing (thăngks-gĭv′ĭng) ►*n.* An act of giving thanks, esp. to God.

Thanksgiving Day ►*n.* The 4th Thursday of Nov., a legal holiday in the US.

Thant (thänt, thănt), **U.** 1909–74. Burmese secretary-general of the United Nations (1961–71).

that (*th*ăt, *th*ət) ►*pron., pl.* **those** (*th*ōz) **1a.** The one designated or implied: *What kind of soup is that?* **b.** The one, thing, or type specified: *The relics found were those of an earlier time.* **2.** Used to introduce a clause, esp. a restrictive clause: *the car that has the flat tire.* **3.** In, on, by, or with which: *She called the day that she arrived.* ►*adj., pl.* **those 1.** Being the one indicated or implied: *that place.* **2.** Being the one further removed or less obvious: *That route is shorter than this one.* ►*adv.* To such an extent: *Is it that difficult?* ►*conj.* **1.** Used to introduce a subordinate clause: *I doubt that you are right.* **2.** Used to introduce an exclamation of desire: *Oh, that I were rich!* [< OE *thæt.*]

Usage: The standard rule is that *that* should be used only to introduce a restrictive (or "defining") relative clause, which serves to identify the entity being talked about. Thus, we say *The house that Jack built has been torn down,* where the clause *that Jack built* tells which house was torn down. Only *which* is to be used with nonrestrictive (or "nondefining") clauses, which give additional information about an entity that has already been identified in the context. Thus, we say *The students in Chemistry 10 have been complaining about the textbook, which* (not *that*) *is hard to follow.* See Usage Note at **this, there.**

thatch (thăch) ►*n.* Plant stalks or foliage used for roofing. ►*v.* To cover with or as if with thatch. [< OE *thæc.*]

Thatch•er (thăch′ər), **Margaret Hilda.** b. 1925. British prime minister (1979–90).

thaw (thô) ►*v.* **1.** To change from a frozen solid to a liquid by gradual warming. **2.** To lose stiffness or numbness by being warmed. **3.** To become warm enough for snow and ice to melt. **4.** To become less reserved. ►*n.* **1.** The process of thawing. **2.** A period during which ice and snow melt. **3.** A relaxation of restraint or tension. [< OE *thawian.*]

THC (tē′āch-sē′) ►*n.* The primary intoxicant in marijuana and hashish. [*t(etra)h(ydro)c(annabinol).*]

the[1] (*th*ē *before a vowel*; *th*ə *before a consonant)* ►*def. art.* **1.** Used before singular or plural nouns and noun phrases that denote particular, specified persons or things: *the shoes I bought.* **2.** Used before a noun or an adjective with generic force: *an animal such as the wolf; the rich.* [< OE.]

the[2] (*th*ē *before a vowel*; *th*ə *before a consonant)* ►*adv.* **1.** Because of that: *thinks the worse of me.* **2.** To that extent; by that much: *the sooner the better.* [< OE *thȳ.*]

the•a•ter or **the•a•tre** (thē′ə-tər) ►*n.* **1.** A building for the presentation of plays, films, or other dramatic performances. **2.** A room with tiers of seats used for lectures or demonstrations. **3.** Dramatic literature or performance. **4.** A setting, as for military operations. [< Gk. *theatron.*]

the•at•ri•cal (thē-ăt′rĭ-kəl) ►*adj.* **1.** Of or suitable for the theater. **2.** Affectedly dramatic. ►*n.* often **theatricals** Stage performances, esp. by amateurs. —**the•at′ri•cal′i•ty** (-kăl′ĭ-tē), **the•at′ri•cal•ness** *n.* —**the•at′ri•cal•ly** *adv.*

the•at•rics (thē-ăt′rĭks) ►*n.* **1.** *(takes sing. v.)* The art of the theater. **2.** *(takes pl. v.)* Theatrical effects or mannerisms.

Thebes (thēbz) **1.** An ancient city of Upper Egypt on the Nile R. in present-day central Egypt. **2.** An ancient city of Greece NW of Athens. —**The′ban** (thē′bən) *adj. & n.*

thee (*th*ē) ►*pron.* The objective case of **thou**[1].

theft (thĕft) ►*n.* The act of stealing; larceny. [< OE *thīefth.*]

their (*th*âr) ►*adj.* The possessive form of **they.** Used as a modifier before a noun: *their house.* [< ON *theira.*]

theirs (*th*ârz) ►*pron. (takes sing. or pl. v.)* The one or ones belonging to them: *The red house is theirs.*

the•ism (thē′ĭz′əm) ►*n.* Belief in the existence of a god or gods. —**the′ist** *n.* —**the•is′tic, the•is′ti•cal** *adj.*

them (*th*ĕm, *th*əm) ►*pron.* The objective case of **they. 1.** Used as the direct or indirect object of a verb. **2.** Used as the object of a preposition. See Usage Note at **I**[1]. [< ON *theim* and OE *thǣm.*]

the•mat•ic (thĭ-măt′ĭk) ►*adj.* Of or being a theme. [Gk. *thematikos.*] —**the•mat′i•cal•ly** *adv.*

theme (thēm) ►*n.* **1.** A topic of discourse or discussion. **2.** The subject of an artistic work.

3. An implicit or recurrent idea; motif. 4. A short written composition. 5. *Mus.* The principal melodic phrase in a composition. [< Gk. *thema.*]

them•selves (*th*ĕm-sĕlvz′, *th*əm-) ▸*pron.* 1. Those ones identical with them. 2. Used reflexively as the direct or indirect object of a verb or as the object of a preposition. 3. Used for emphasis: *We ourselves have heard nothing.*

then (*th*ĕn) ▸*adv.* 1. At that time. 2. Next in time, space, or order. 3. In addition; moreover; besides. 4. In that case: *If it snows, then bring your skis.* 5. As a consequence: *The case, then, is closed.* ▸*n.* That time or moment. ▸*adj.* Being so at that time. [< OE *thenne.*]

thence (*th*ĕns, thĕns) ▸*adv.* 1. From there. 2. From that circumstance or source. 3. *Archaic* Thenceforth. [< OE *thanon.*]

thence•forth (*th*ĕns-fôrth′, -fōrth′, thĕns-) ▸*adv.* From that time forward; thereafter.

thence•for•ward (*th*ĕns-fôr′wərd, thĕns-) also **thence•for•wards** (-wərdz) ▸*adv.* From that time or place onward; thenceforth.

theo– or **the–** ▸*pref.* God: *theocracy.* [< Gk. *theos*, god.]

the•oc•ra•cy (thē-ŏk′rə-sē) ▸*n., pl.* **-cies** 1. A government ruled by or subject to religious authority. 2. A state so governed. **—the′o•crat′** (thē′ə-krăt′) *n.* **—the′o•crat′ic** *adj.* **—the′o•crat′i•cal•ly** *adv.*

The•oc•ri•tus (thē-ŏk′rĭ-təs). 3rd cent. B.C. Greek poet.

The•o•do•ra (thē′ə-dôr′ə, -dōr′-). A.D.508?–548. Byzantine empress (525–548).

The•od•o•ric (thē-ŏd′ər-ĭk). A.D. 454?–526. King of the Ostrogoths (474–526).

The•o•do•sius I (thē′ə-dō′shəs, -shē-əs). A.D. 346?–395. Emperor of Rome (379–395).

the•ol•o•gy (thē-ŏl′ə-jē) ▸*n., pl.* **-gies** 1. The study of the nature of God and religious truth. 2. A system or school of opinions concerning God and religious questions. **—the′o•lo′gi•an** (-ə-lō′jən) *n.* **—the′o•log′i•cal** (-ə-lŏj′ĭ-kəl) *adj.* **—the′o•log′i•cal•ly** *adv.*

the•o•rem (thē′ər-əm, thîr′əm) ▸*n.* 1. An idea that is demonstrably true or is assumed to be so. 2. *Math.* A proposition that has been or is to be proved. [< Gk. *theōrēma.*]

the•o•ret•i•cal (thē′ə-rĕt′ĭ-kəl) also **the•o•ret•ic** (-rĕt′ĭk) ▸*adj.* Of or based on theory. [< Gk. *theōrētikos.*] **—the′o•ret′i•cal•ly** *adv.*

Syns: *theoretical, abstract, academic, hypothetical* **adj.**

the•o•re•ti•cian (thē′ər-ĭ-tĭsh′ən, thîr′ĭ-) ▸*n.* One who formulates, studies, or is expert in the theory of a science or an art.

the•o•rize (thē′ə-rīz′, thîr′īz) ▸*v.* **-rized, -riz•ing.** To formulate theories or a theory. **—the′o•riz′er, the′o•rist** *n.*

the•o•ry (thē′ə-rē, thîr′ē) ▸*n., pl.* **-ries** 1. A set of statements or principles devised to explain a group of facts or phenomena, esp; one that has been repeatedly tested or is widely accepted. 2. The branch of a science or art consisting of its explanatory statements, accepted principles, and methods of analysis, as opposed to practice. 3. Abstract reasoning; speculation. 4. An assumption; conjecture. [< Gk. *theōria.*]

the•os•o•phy (thē-ŏs′ə-fē) ▸*n., pl.* **-phies.** Religious philosophy or speculation about the nature of the soul based on mystical insight into the nature of God. [THEO– + Gk. *sophia*, wisdom.] **—the′o•soph′ic** (-ə-sŏf′ĭk), **the′o•soph′i•cal** *adj.* **—the•os′o•phist** *n.*

ther•a•peu•tic (thĕr′ə-pyōō′tĭk) ▸*adj.* Having healing or curative powers. [< Gk. *therapeuein*, treat medically.] **—ther′a•peu′ti•cal•ly** *adv.*

ther•a•peu•tics (thĕr′ə-pyōō′tĭks) ▸*n. (takes sing. v.)* Medical treatment of disease. **—ther′a•peu′tist** *n.*

ther•a•py (thĕr′ə-pē) ▸*n., pl.* **-pies** 1. Treatment of illness or disability. 2. Psychotherapy. [< Gk. *therapeuein*, treat medically.] **—ther′a•pist** *n.*

there (*th*âr) ▸*adv.* 1. At or in that place. 2. To, into, or toward that place. 3. At that stage, moment, or point. ▸*pron.* Used to introduce a clause or sentence: *There is hope.* ▸*n.* That place or point. [< OE *thǣr.*]

Usage: The demonstrative forms *that there* and *this here* are nonstandard.

there•a•bouts (*th*âr′ə-bouts′) also **there•a•bout** (-bout′) ▸*adv.* 1. Near that place. 2. Approximately.

there•af•ter (*th*âr-ăf′tər) ▸*adv.* From a specified time onward; from then on.

there•at (*th*âr-ăt′) ▸*adv.* 1. At that place; there. 2. At that event; on account of that.

there•by (*th*âr-bī′) ▸*adv.* By that means.

there•fore (*th*âr′fôr′, -fōr′) ▸*adv.* For that reason; consequently.

there•from (*th*âr-frŭm′, -frŏm′) ▸*adv.* From that place, time, or thing.

there•in (*th*âr-ĭn′) ▸*adv.* 1. In that place, time, or thing. 2. In that respect.

there•in•af•ter (*th*âr′ĭn-ăf′tər) ▸*adv.* In a later part.

there•of (*th*âr-ŭv′, -ŏv′) ▸*adv.* 1. Of this, that, or it. 2. From that cause or origin.

there•on (*th*âr-ŏn′, -ôn′) ▸*adv.* On or upon this, that, or it.

The•re•sa or **Te•re•sa** (tə-rē′sə, -zə, -rā′-), Saint. 1515–82. Spanish nun and mystic.

Saint Theresa

there•to (*th*âr-tōō′) ▸*adv.* To that, this, or it.

there•to•fore (*th*âr′tə-fôr′, -fōr′) ▸*adv.* Until that time.

there•un•to (*th*âr′ŭn-tōō′) ▸*adv.* *Archaic* To that, this, or it; thereto.

there•up•on (*th*âr′ə-pŏn′, -pôn′) ▸*adv.* 1. Concerning that matter; upon that. 2. Directly following that. 3. In consequence of that; therefore.

there•with (*th*âr-wĭ*th*′, -wĭth′) ▸*adv.* With that, this, or it.

there•with•al (*th*âr′wĭ*th*-ôl′, -wĭth-) ▸*adv.* With all that, this, or it; besides.

ther•mal (thûr′məl) ▸*adj.* Of, using, producing, or caused by heat. ▸*n.* A rising current of warm air. —**ther′mal•ly** *adv.*

thermo– or **therm–** ▸*pref.* Heat: *thermodynamics.* [< Gk. *thermos*, warm.]

ther•mo•cou•ple (thûr′mə-kŭp′əl) ▸*n.* A device used to measure temperatures, consisting of two dissimilar metals joined at the ends so that an electric current flows when the contacts are at different temperatures.

ther•mo•dy•nam•ics (thûr′mō-dī-năm′ĭks) ▸*n. (takes sing. v.)* Physics that deals with the relationships between heat and other forms of energy. —**ther′mo•dy•nam′ic** *adj.* —**ther′mo•dy•nam′i•cal•ly** *adv.*

ther•mom•e•ter (thər-mŏm′ĭ-tər) ▸*n.* An instrument for measuring temperature. —**ther′mo•met′ric** (thŭr′mō-mĕt′rĭk) *adj.* —**ther•mom′e•try** *n.*

ther•mo•nu•cle•ar (thûr′mō-no͞o′klē-ər, -nyo͞o′-) ▸*adj.* **1.** Of or derived from the fusion of atomic nuclei at high temperatures. **2.** Of atomic weapons based on fusion.

ther•mo•plas•tic (thûr′mə-plăs′tĭk) ▸*adj.* Becoming soft when heated and hard when cooled. ▸*n.* A thermoplastic material.

Ther•mop•y•lae (thər-mŏp′ə-lē) A narrow pass of E-central Greece; site of a Spartan stand against the Persians (480 B.C.).

ther•mos (thûr′məs) ▸*n.* A vacuum bottle. [Orig. a trademark.]

ther•mo•set•ting (thûr′mō-sĕt′ĭng) ▸*adj.* Permanently hardening or solidifying on being heated.

ther•mo•stat (thûr′mə-stăt′) ▸*n.* A device, as in a heating system or an appliance, that senses temperature changes and activates switches controlling the equipment. —**ther′mo•stat′ic** *adj.*

the•sau•rus (thĭ-sôr′əs) ▸*n., pl.* **-sau•ri** (-sôr′ī′) or **-rus•es.** A book of selected words, esp. a dictionary of synonyms and related words. [< Gk. *thēsauros*, treasury.]

these (*th*ēz) ▸*pron. & adj.* Pl. of **this.**

the•sis (thē′sĭs) ▸*n., pl.* **-ses** (-sēz) **1.** A proposition maintained by argument. **2.** A dissertation advancing an original point of view as a result of research. [< Gk.]

thes•pi•an (thĕs′pē-ən) ▸*adj.* Of or relating to drama; dramatic. ▸*n.* An actor or actress. [< THESPIS.]

Thes•pis (thĕs′pĭs). 6th cent. B.C. Greek poet.

Thes•sa•lo•ni•ans (thĕs′ə-lō′nē-ənz) ▸*pl.n. (takes sing. v.)* See table at **Bible.**

Thes•sa•lo•ní•ki (thĕ′sä-lô-nē′kē) or **Sa•lo•ni•ka** (sə-lŏn′ĭ-kə, săl′ə-nē′kə). A city of NE Greece on an inlet of the Aegean Sea. Pop. 406,413.

Thes•sa•ly (thĕs′ə-lē) A region of E-central Greece along the Aegean Sea. —**Thes•sa′lian** (thĕ-sā′lē-ən, -sāl′yən), **Thes′sa•lo′ni•an** *adj. & n.*

the•ta (thā′tə, thē′-) ▸*n.* The 8th letter of the Greek alphabet. [Gk. *thēta.*]

thew (thyo͞o) ▸*n.* often **thews.** Sinew or muscle. [< OE *thēaw*, habit.]

they (*th*ā) ▸*pron.* The ones previously mentioned or implied. [< ON *their.*]

Usage: Use of the third-person plural pronoun *they* to refer to a singular noun or pronoun such as *a person* or *somebody* is common in speech and widespread in many mainstream publications. Nevertheless, many people avoid using *they* in this way in order to adhere to the traditional grammatical rule concerning pronoun agreement. Eighty-two percent of the Usage Panel finds the sentence *The typical student in the program takes about six years to complete their course work* unacceptable. See Usage Note at **I**[1].

they'd (*th*ād) ▸ **1.** They had. **2.** They would.

they'll (*th*āl) ▸ **1.** They will. **2.** They shall.

they're (*th*âr) ▸ They are.

they've (*th*āv) ▸ They have.

thi•a•mine (thī′ə-mĭn, -mēn′) also **thi•a•min** (-mĭn) ▸*n.* A vitamin of the vitamin B complex, found in yeast, meat, and bran and necessary for carbohydrate metabolism. [Gk. *theion*, sulfur + (VIT)AMIN.]

thick (thĭk) ▸*adj.* **-er, -est 1a.** Relatively great in extent from one surface to the opposite; not thin. **b.** Measuring in this dimension: *two inches thick.* **2.** Thickset. **3.** Dense; concentrated. **4.** Having a heavy or viscous consistency. **5.** Having a great number; abounding. **6.** Indistinctly articulated. **7.** Noticeable; conspicuous. **8.** *Informal* Lacking mental agility; stupid. **9.** *Informal* Very friendly; intimate. **10.** *Informal* Excessive. ▸*n.* **1.** The thickest part. **2.** The most intense part: *in the thick of the fighting.* —***idiom:*** **thick and thin** Good and bad times. [< OE *thicce.*] —**thick′ly** *adv.* —**thick′ness** *n.*

thick•en (thĭk′ən) ▸*v.* To make or become thick or thicker. —**thick′en•er** *n.* —**thick′en•ing** *n.*

thick•et (thĭk′ĭt) ▸*n.* A dense growth of shrubs or underbrush. [OE *thiccet.*]

thick•set (thĭk′sĕt′) ▸*adj.* **1.** Having a short wide body; stocky. **2.** Placed closely together.

thick-skinned (thĭk′skĭnd′) ▸*adj.* **1.** Having a thick skin. **2.** Not easily offended.

thief (thēf) ▸*n., pl.* **thieves** (thēvz). One who steals. [< OE *thēof.*]

thieve (thēv) ▸*v.* **thieved, thiev•ing.** To steal. [Perh. < OE *thēofian.*] —**thiev′er•y** *n.*

thigh (thī) ▸*n.* The portion of the leg between the hip and the knee. [< OE *thēoh.*]

thigh•bone (thī′bōn′) ▸*n.* See **femur.**

thim•ble (thĭm′bəl) ▸*n.* A small cup, as of metal or plastic, worn to protect the finger in sewing. [< OE *thūma*, thumb.] —**thim′ble•ful′** *n.*

Thim•phu (thĭm′po͞o′, tĭm′-) The capital of Bhutan, in the W part in the E Himalayas. Pop. 30,340.

thin (thĭn) ▸*adj.* **thin•ner, thin•nest 1a.** Relatively small in extent from one surface to the opposite. **b.** Not great in diameter or cross section; fine. **2.** Lean or slender. **3.** Not dense or concentrated; sparse. **4.** Not rich or heavy in consistency. **5.** Lacking force or substance; flimsy. ▸*v.* **thinned, thin•ning.** To make or become thin or thinner. [< OE *thynne.*] —**thin′ly** *adv.* —**thin′ness** *n.*

thine (*th*īn) ▸*pron. (takes sing. or pl. v.)* Used to indicate the one or ones belonging to thee. ▸*adj.* A possessive form of **thou.** Used instead of *thy* before an initial vowel or *h*: *thine enemy.* [< OE *thīn.*]

thing (thĭng) ▸*n.* **1.** Something that exists; entity. **2a.** A tangible object. **b.** An inanimate object. **3.** A creature. **4a. things** Possessions; belongings. **b.** An article of clothing. **5.** An act, deed, or work. **6.** A thought or notion. **7.** A piece of information. **8.** A matter of concern. **9.** A turn of events. **10. things** The general state of affairs; conditions. **11.** *Slang* A uniquely suitable and satisfying activity: *doing his own thing.* See Syns at **forte**[1]. [< OE *thing.*]

think (thĭngk) ►*v.* **thought** (thôt), **think•ing** **1.** To have or formulate in the mind. **2a.** To ponder. **b.** To reason. **3.** To believe; suppose. **4.** To call to mind; remember. **5.** To visualize; imagine. **6.** To devise or invent: *think up a plan.* **7.** To consider. [< OE *thencan.*] —**think′a•ble** *adj.* —**think′er** *n.*

think tank ►*n.* A research group organized esp. by a government for solving complex problems.

thin•ner (thĭn′ər) ►*n.* A liquid, as turpentine, mixed with paint to reduce viscosity.

thin-skinned (thĭn′skĭnd′) ►*adj.* **1.** Having a thin rind or skin. **2.** Oversensitive.

third (thûrd) ►*n.* **1.** The ordinal number matching the number 3 in a series. **2.** One of three equal parts. **3.** *Mus.* A tone three degrees above or below a given tone in a diatonic scale. **4.** The transmission gear next higher to second in a motor vehicle. [< OE *thridda.*] —**third** *adv. & adj.* —**third′ly** *adv.*

third base ►*n. Baseball* The third base to be reached by a runner. —**third baseman** *n.*

third class ►*n.* **1.** A class of mail including all unsealed printed matter except newspapers and magazines. **2.** Accommodations of the third and usu. lowest order of luxury and price. —**third′-class′** *adv. & adj.*

third-de•gree burn (thûrd′dĭ-grē′) ►*n.* A severe burn in which the skin and underlying tissues are destroyed and sensitive nerve endings are exposed.

third person ►*n.* The form of a verb or pronoun used in referring to a person or thing other than the speaker or the one spoken to.

Third World ►*n.* The developing nations of Africa, Asia, and Latin America.

thirst (thûrst) ►*n.* **1a.** A sensation of dryness in the mouth related to a desire to drink. **b.** The desire to drink. **2.** An insistent desire; craving. ►*v.* **1.** To feel a need to drink. **2.** To yearn. [< OE *thurst.*] —**thirst′i•ly** *adv.* —**thirst′y** *adj.*

thir•teen (thûr-tēn′) ►*n.* **1.** The cardinal number equal to 12 + 1. **2.** The 13th in a set or sequence. [< OE *thrēotīne.*] —**thir•teen′** *adj. & pron.*

thir•teenth (thûr-tēnth′) ►*n.* **1.** The ordinal number matching the number 13 in a series. **2.** One of 13 equal parts. —**thir•teenth′** *adv. & adj.*

thir•ti•eth (thûr′tē-ĭth) ►*n.* **1.** The ordinal number matching the number 30 in a series. **2.** One of 30 equal parts. —**thir′ti•eth** *adv. & adj.*

thir•ty (thûr′tē) ►*n., pl.* **-ties.** The cardinal number equal to 3 × 10. [< OE *thrītig.*] —**thir′ty** *adj. & pron.*

this (*th*ĭs) ►*pron., pl.* **these** (*th*ēz) **1a.** The person or thing present, nearby, or just mentioned. **b.** What is about to be said. **c.** The present event, action, or time. **2.** The nearer or the more immediate one. ►*adj., pl.* **these 1.** Being just mentioned or present. **2.** Being nearer or more immediate. **3.** Being about to be stated or described. ►*adv.* To this extent; so: *never stayed out this late.* [< OE.]

Usage: *This* and *that* are both used as demonstrative pronouns to refer to a thought expressed earlier: *The letter was unopened; that* (or *this*) *in itself casts doubt on the inspector's theory. That* is sometimes prescribed as the better choice in referring to what has gone before. When the referent is yet to be mentioned, only *this* is used: *This* (not *that*) *is what bothers me. We have no time to consider late applications.* See Usage Note at **that, there.**

this•tle (thĭs′əl) ►*n.* Any of numerous weedy plants having prickly leaves and bracts and usu. purplish flowers. [< OE *thistel.*]

this•tle•down (thĭs′əl-doun′) ►*n.* The silky down attached to the seeds of a thistle.

thith•er (thĭ*th*′ər, *th*ĭ*th*′-) ►*adv.* To or toward that place; there. ►*adj.* Being on the more distant side; farther. [< OE *thider.*]

thole pin (thōl) ►*n.* A peg set in pairs in the gunwales of a boat to serve as an oarlock. [< OE *thol.*]

Thom•as (tŏm′əs), Saint. In the Bible, one of the 12 Apostles.

Thomas, Dylan Marlais. 1914–53. Welsh poet.

Thomas à Kem•pis (ə kĕm′pĭs, ä). 1380?–1471. German ecclesiastic and writer.

Thomp•son (tŏmp′sən, tŏm′-), **Benjamin.** Count Rumford. 1753–1814. Amer.-born British physicist.

Thompson, Sir **John Sparrow David.** 1844–94. Canadian prime minister (1892–94).

Thom•son (tŏm′sən), **Virgil Garnett.** 1896–1989. Amer. composer and music critic.

Thor (thôr) ►*n. Myth.* The Norse god of thunder.

tho•rax (thôr′ăks′, thōr′-) ►*n., pl.* **-es** or **tho•ra•ces** (thôr′ə-sēz′, thōr′-) **1.** The part of the vertebrate body between the neck and the diaphragm, partially encased by the ribs; chest. **2.** The middle region of the arthropod body. [< Gk. *thōrax,* breastplate.] —**tho•rac′ic** (thə-răs′ĭk) *adj.*

Tho•reau (thə-rō′, thôr′ō), **Henry David.** 1817–62. Amer. writer. —**Tho•reau′vi•an** *adj.*

tho•ri•um (thôr′ē-əm, thōr′-) ►*n. Symbol* **Th** A radioactive, silvery-white metallic element used in magnesium alloys. At. no. 90. See table at **element.** [< THOR.]

thorn (thôrn) ►*n.* **1a.** A sharp woody spine protruding from a plant stem. **b.** Any of various shrubs, trees, or woody plants bearing such spines. **2.** One that causes pain, irritation, or discomfort. [< OE.] —**thorn′i•ness** *n.* —**thorn′y** *adj.*

thor•ough (thûr′ō, thŭr′ō) ►*adj.* **1.** Complete in all respects. **2.** Painstakingly careful. [< OE *thuruh,* through.] —**thor′ough•ly** *adv.* —**thor′ough•ness** *n.*

thor•ough•bred (thûr′ō-brĕd′, thûr′ə-, thŭr′-) ►*n.* **1.** A purebred or pedigreed animal. **2. Thoroughbred** Any of a breed of horses originating from a cross between Arabian stallions and English mares. ►*adj.* Bred of pure stock; purebred.

thor•ough•fare (thûr′ō-fâr′, thûr′ə-, thŭr′-) ►*n.* A main road or public highway.

thor•ough•go•ing (thûr′ō-gō′ĭng, thûr′ə-, thŭr′-) ►*adj.* **1.** Very thorough; complete. **2.** Absolute; unqualified.

Thorpe (thôrp), **James Francis.** "Jim." 1888–1953. Amer. athlete.

those (*th*ōz) ►*pron. & adj.* Pl. of **that.**

thou (*th*ou) ►*pron.* Used to indicate the one

Jim Thorpe

being addressed, esp. in a religious context. [< OE *thū*.]

though (*thō*) ►*conj.* **1.** Although; while. **2.** Even if. See Usage Note at **although.** ►*adv.* However; nevertheless. [ME, of Scand. orig.]

thought (thôt) ►*v.* P.t. and p.part. of **think.** ►*n.* **1.** The process or power of thinking. **2.** An idea. **3.** A body of ideas. **4.** Consideration; attention. **5.** Intention; expectation. [< OE *gethōht*.]

thought•ful (thôt′fəl) ►*adj.* **1.** Engrossed in thought. **2.** Showing careful thought. **3.** Having or showing regard for others; considerate. —**thought′ful•ly** *adv.* —**thought′ful•ness** *n.*

thought•less (thôt′lĭs) ►*adj.* **1.** Careless; unthinking. **2.** Inconsiderate. —**thought′less•ly** *adv.* —**thought′less•ness** *n.*

thou•sand (thou′zənd) ►*n.* The cardinal number equal to 10 × 100 or 10^3. [< OE *thūsend*.] —**thou′sand** *adj. & pron.*

Thousand Islands. A group of more than 1,800 islands in the St. Lawrence R. at the outlet of Lake Ontario.

Thousand Oaks. A city of S CA W of Los Angeles. Pop. 104,352.

thou•sandth (thou′zəndth, -zənth) ►*n.* **1.** The ordinal number matching the number 1,000 in a series. **2.** One of 1,000 equal parts. —**thou′sandth** *adv. & adj.*

Thrace (thrās) A region and ancient country of the SE Balkan Peninsula N of the Aegean Sea. —**Thra′cian** (thrā′shən) *adj. & n.*

thrall (thrôl) ►*n.* **1.** One held in bondage; slave. **2.** Servitude; bondage. [< ON *thrǣll*.] —**thrall′dom, thral′dom** *n.*

thrash (thrăsh) ►*v.* **1.** To beat with or as if with a whip or flail. See Syns at **beat. 2.** To defeat utterly; vanquish. **3.** To move wildly or violently. [< THRESH.] —**thrash′er** *n.*

thrash•er (thrăsh′ər) ►*n.* Any of various long-tailed New World songbirds. [Perh. < THRUSH.]

thread (thrĕd) ►*n.* **1.** A fine cord made of fibers or filaments twisted together, used in needlework and in weaving cloth. **2.** Something like a thread, as in fineness or length. **3.** A helical or spiral ridge on a screw, nut, or bolt. ►*v.* **1a.** To pass one end of a thread through (e.g., a needle). **b.** To pass a tape or film into or through. **2.** To pass cautiously through. **3.** To machine a thread on (a screw, nut, or bolt). [< OE *thrǣd*.] —**thread′er** *n.* —**thread′y** *adj.*

thread•bare (thrĕd′bâr′) ►*adj.* **1.** Having the nap worn down so that the threads show through. **2.** Shabby; seedy. **3.** Hackneyed.

threat (thrĕt) ►*n.* **1.** An expression of an intention to inflict pain, injury, or evil. **2.** One regarded as a possible danger. [< OE *thrēat*, oppression.]

threat•en (thrĕt′n) ►*v.* **1.** To express a threat against. **2.** To be a source of danger to; menace. **3.** To portend. **4.** To indicate danger or harm. —**threat′en•ing•ly** *adv.*

three (thrē) ►*n.* **1.** The cardinal number equal to 2 + 1. **2.** The 3rd in a set or sequence. **3.** Something having three parts, units, or members. [< OE *thrī*.] —**three** *adj. & pron.*

three-di•men•sion•al (thrē′dĭ-mĕn′shə-nəl, -dī-) ►*adj.* **1.** Of, having, or existing in three dimensions. **2.** Having or appearing to have extension in depth.

three•score (thrē′skôr′, -skōr′) ►*adj.* Sixty. —**three′score′** *n. & pron.*

three•some (thrē′səm) ►*n.* A group of three.

thren•o•dy (thrĕn′ə-dē) ►*n., pl.* **-dies.** A poem or song of lamentation. [Gk. *thrēnos*, lament + *ōidē*, song; see ODE.] —**thren′o•dist** *n.*

thresh (thrĕsh) ►*v.* **1.** To beat (e.g., cereal plants) with a machine or flail to separate the grains or seeds from the straw. **2.** To thrash. [< OE *therscan*.] —**thresh′er** *n.*

thresh•old (thrĕsh′ōld′, -hōld′) ►*n.* **1.** A piece of wood or stone placed beneath a door. **2.** An entrance. **3.** The beginning; outset. **4.** The lowest level or intensity at which a stimulus can be perceived or can produce a given effect. [< OE *therscold*.]

threw (thro͞o) ►*v.* P.t. of **throw.**

thrice (thrīs) ►*adv.* Three times. [Ult. < OE *thrīga*.]

thrift (thrĭft) ►*n.* **1.** Wise economy in managing money and other resources; frugality. **2.** A savings and loan association, credit union, or savings bank. [ME, prosperity.] —**thrift′i•ly** *adv.* —**thrift′i•ness** *n.* —**thrift′y** *adj.*

thrift shop ►*n.* A shop that sells used articles, esp. clothing, as to benefit a charity.

thrill (thrĭl) ►*v.* **1.** To feel or cause to feel a sudden intense sensation. **2.** To enrapture; delight. See Syns at **enrapture. 3.** To quiver; tremble. ►*n.* **1.** A quivering or trembling. **2.** A source or cause of excitement or rapture. [< OE *thȳrlian*, pierce.] —**thrill′er** *n.* —**thrill′ing•ly** *adv.*

thrive (thrīv) ►*v.* **thrived** or **throve** (thrōv), **thrived** or **thriv•en** (thrĭv′ən), **thriv•ing 1.** To make steady progress; prosper. **2.** To flourish. [< ON *thrīfask* < *thrīfa*, seize.] —**thriv′er** *n.*

throat (thrōt) ►*n.* **1.** The anterior portion of the neck. **2.** The portion of the digestive tract that lies between the rear of the mouth and the esophagus. [< OE *throte*.]

throat•y (thrō′tē) ►*adj.* **-i•er, -i•est.** Uttered or sounding as if uttered deep in the throat. —**throat′i•ly** *adv.* —**throat′i•ness** *n.*

throb (thrŏb) ►*v.* **throbbed, throb•bing 1.** To beat rapidly or violently; pound. **2.** To vibrate rhythmically; pulsate. [ME *throbben*.] —**throb** *n.* —**throb′bing•ly** *adv.*

throe (thrō) ►*n.* **1.** A severe pang or spasm of pain. See Syns at **pain. 2. throes** Agonizing struggle or effort. [< OE *thrawu*.]

throm•bo•sis (thrŏm-bō′sĭs) ►*n., pl.* **-ses** (-sēz). The formation or presence of a thrombus.

throm•bus (thrŏm′bəs) ►*n., pl.* **-bi** (-bī). A

blood clot formed in a blood vessel or in a chamber of the heart. [< Gk. *thrombos*, clot.]

throne (thrōn) ►*n.* **1.** A chair occupied by a sovereign or bishop on state or ceremonial occasions. **2.** Sovereign power or rank. [< Gk. *thronos*.]

throng (thrông, thrŏng) ►*n.* A large group of people or things crowded together. See Syns at **crowd.** ►*v.* **1.** To crowd into or around. **2.** To move in a throng. [< OE *gethrang*.]

throt•tle (thrŏt′l) ►*n.* **1.** A valve that regulates the flow of a fluid, such as the valve in an internal-combustion engine that controls the amount of vaporized fuel entering the cylinders. **2.** A lever or pedal controlling such a valve. ►*v.* **-tled, -tling 1.** To regulate the speed of (an engine) with a throttle. **2.** To suppress: *tried to throttle the press.* **3.** To strangle; choke. [< ME *throtelen*, strangle.] —**throt′tler** *n.*

through (thro͞o) ►*prep.* **1.** In one side and out another side of. **2.** In the midst of. **3.** By way of. **4.** By the means or agency of. **5.** Here and there in; around. **6.** From the beginning to the end of. **7.** Done or finished with. ►*adv.* **1.** From one end or side to another end or side. **2.** From beginning to end. **3.** Throughout the whole extent or thickness. **4.** To a conclusion. ►*adj.* **1.** Allowing continuous passage; unobstructed. **2.** Passing or extending from one end, side, or surface to another. **3.** Finished; done. —***idiom:*** **through and through 1.** In every part; throughout. **2.** Completely. [< OE *thurh*.]

through•out (thro͞o-out′) ►*prep.* In, to, through, or during every part of: *throughout the year.* ►*adv.* **1.** Everywhere. **2.** During the entire time or extent.

throve (thrōv) ►*v.* P.t. of **thrive.**

throw (thrō) ►*v.* **threw** (thro͞o), **thrown** (thrōn), **throw•ing 1.** To propel through the air with a swift motion of the hand or arm; fling. **2.** To put with force; hurl. **3.** *Informal* To confuse; perplex. See Syns at **confuse. 4.** To put on or off hastily or carelessly. **5.** To form on a potter's wheel. **6.** To cast: *throw a shadow.* **7.** To arrange or give (e.g., a party). **8.** To activate (a lever or switch). **9.** *Informal* To lose (e.g., a contest) purposely. —***phrasal verbs:*** **throw away** (or **out**) To discard. **throw over** To desert; abandon. **throw up** To vomit. ►*n.* **1.** The act or an instance of throwing. **2.** The distance or height to which something is or can be thrown. **3.** A light coverlet. —***idiom:*** **throw up (one's) hands** To give up in despair. [< OE *thrāwan*.] —**throw′er** *n.*

throw•back (thrō′băk′) ►*n.* A reversion to a former type or ancestral characteristic.

thru (thro͞o) ►*prep., adv., & adj. Informal* Through.

thrum (thrŭm) ►*v.* **thrummed, thrum•ming.** To play (a stringed instrument) idly or monotonously. [Imit.] —**thrum** *n.*

thrush (thrŭsh) ►*n.* Any of various songbirds usu. having brownish upper plumage and a spotted breast. [< OE *thrysce*.]

thrust (thrŭst) ►*v.* **thrust, thrust•ing 1.** To push or drive forcibly. See Syns at **push. 2.** To force into a specified state or condition. **3.** To interject. ►*n.* **1.** A forceful shove. **2a.** A driving force or pressure. **b.** The forward-directed force developed in a jet or rocket engine as a reaction to the rearward ejection of exhaust gases. **3.** A stab. **4.** The essence; point. **5.** Outward or lateral stress in a structure. [< ON *thrȳsta*.]

thru•way also **through•way** (thro͞o′wā′) ►*n.* See **expressway.**

Thu•cyd•i•des (tho͞o-sĭd′ĭ-dēz′). 460?–400? B.C. Greek historian.

thud (thŭd) ►*n.* **1.** A dull sound. **2.** A blow or fall causing such a sound. [Poss. < OE *thyddan*, strike with a weapon.] —**thud** *v.*

thug (thŭg) ►*n.* A cutthroat or ruffian; hoodlum. [Hindi *ṭhag*, perh. < Skt. *sthagaḥ*, a cheat < *sthagayati*, conceals.] —**thug′ger•y** *n.* —**thug′gish** *adj.*

thu•li•um (tho͞o′lē-əm) ►*n. Symbol* **Tm** A bright, silvery rare-earth element, one isotope of which is used in small portable x-ray units. At. no. 69. See table at **element.** [< *Thule*, the northernmost part of the ancient world.]

thumb (thŭm) ►*n.* **1.** The short, thick first digit of the human hand, opposable to the other four digits. **2.** The part of a glove or mitten that covers the thumb. ►*v.* **1.** To scan by turning over pages with the thumb. **2.** To soil or wear by handling. **3.** *Informal* To hitchhike. —***idiom:*** **all thumbs** Clumsy. [< OE *thūma*.]

thumb•nail (thŭm′nāl′) ►*n.* **1.** The nail of the thumb. **2.** *Comp. Sci.* A reduced image of a graphic or a document page. ►*adj.* Brief: *a thumbnail sketch.*

thumb•screw (thŭm′skro͞o′) ►*n.* A screw designed so that it can be turned with the thumb and fingers.

thumb•tack (thŭm′tăk′) ►*n.* A smooth-headed tack that can be pressed into place with the thumb. —**thumb′tack′** *v.*

thump (thŭmp) ►*n.* **1.** A heavy resounding blow. **2.** The muffled sound produced by such a blow. ►*v.* **1.** To beat with or as if with a blunt object so as to produce a muffled sound. **2.** To pound. [Prob. imit.]

thun•der (thŭn′dər) ►*n.* **1.** The booming sound produced by rapidly expanding air along the path of the electrical discharge of lightning. **2.** A sound resembling thunder. ►*v.* **1.** To produce thunder or similar sounds. **2.** To utter loud remarks or threats. [< OE *thunor*.] —**thun′der•ous** *adj.*

Thunder Bay. A city of SW Ontario, Canada, on **Thunder Bay,** an inlet on the NW shore of Lake Superior. Pop. 112,486.

thun•der•bolt (thŭn′dər-bōlt′) ►*n.* A discharge of lightning accompanied by thunder.

thun•der•clap (thŭn′dər-klăp′) ►*n.* A single sharp crash of thunder.

thun•der•cloud (thŭn′dər-kloud′) ►*n.* A large dark cloud that produces thunder and lightning.

thun•der•head (thŭn′dər-hĕd′) ►*n.* The swollen upper portion of a thundercloud.

thun•der•show•er (thŭn′dər-shou′ər) ►*n.* A brief rainstorm accompanied by thunder and lightning.

thun•der•storm (thŭn′dər-stôrm′) ►*n.* An electrical storm with heavy rain.

thun•der•struck (thŭn′dər-strŭk′) ►*adj.* Astonished; stunned.

Thur. ►*abbr.* Thursday

Thur•ber (thûr′bər), **James Grover.** 1894–1961. Amer. writer.

Thurs•day (thûrz′dē, -dā′) ►*n.* The 5th day of

the week. [< OE *thunres dæg*, Thor's day.]

thus (*th*ŭs) ►*adv.* **1.** In this manner. **2.** To a stated degree or extent; so. **3.** Therefore; consequently. [< OE.]

thwack (thwăk) ►*v.* To strike resoundingly with a flat object. [Imit.] —**thwack** *n.*

thwart (thwôrt) ►*v.* To block or hinder; frustrate. ►*n.* A seat across a boat on which a rower may sit. ►*adj.* Transverse. [< ON *thvert*, across.]

thy (*th*ī) ►*adj.* The possessive form of **thou.**

thyme (tīm) ►*n.* An aromatic plant with leaves used as seasoning. [< Gk. *thumon.*]

thy•mine (thī′mēn′) ►*n.* A pyrimidine base that is an essential constituent of DNA. [THYM(US) + -INE².]

thy•mus (thī′məs) ►*n.*, *pl.* **-mus•es.** A small glandular organ, situated behind the top of the breastbone, that plays some part in building resistance to disease but is usu. vestigial after puberty. [< Gk. *thumos.*]

thy•roid (thī′roid′) ►*n.* **1.** The thyroid gland. **2.** A dried powdered preparation of the thyroid gland of certain domestic animals, used in medicine. [Gk. *thureoeidēs.*]

thyroid gland ►*n.* A two-lobed endocrine gland located in front of and on either side of the trachea in humans and producing various hormones.

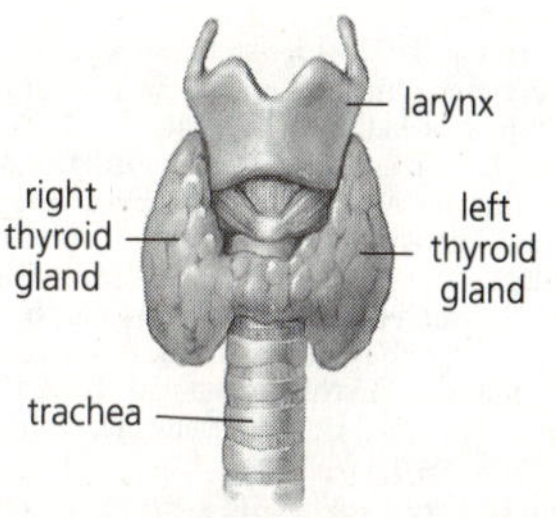

thyroid gland
anterior view

thy•self (*th*ī-sĕlf′) ►*pron. Archaic* Yourself.

ti (tē) ►*n. Mus.* The 7th tone of the diatonic scale. [Alteration of *si.*]

Ti ► The symbol for the element **titanium.**

Tian•jin (tyän′jĭn′) also **Tien•tsin** (tyĕn′tsĭn′). A city of NE China near the Gulf of Bo Hai SE of Beijing. Pop. 5,804,023.

Tian Shan (tyän′ shän′) A mountain range of central Asia extending about 2,414 km (1,500 mi).

ti•ar•a (tē-ăr′ə, -âr′ə, -är′ə) ►*n.* **1.** A bejeweled crownlike ornament worn on the head by women. **2.** The triple crown worn by the pope. [< Gk., turban.]

Ti•ber (tī′bər) A river of central Italy flowing about 406 km (252 mi) through Rome to the Tyrrhenian Sea at Ostia.

Ti•be•ri•us (tī-bîr′ē-əs). 42 B.C.–A.D. 37. Emperor of Rome (A.D. 14–37). —**Ti•be′ri•an** *adj.*

Ti•bet (tə-bĕt′) **1.** A historical region of central Asia between the Himalaya and Kunlun mountains. **2.** See **Xizang.** —**Ti•bet′an** *adj.* & *n.*

Ti•bet•o-Bur•man (tĭ-bĕt′ō-bûr′mən) ►*n.* A branch of the Sino-Tibetan language family that includes Tibetan and Burmese.

tib•i•a (tĭb′ē-ə) ►*n.*, *pl.* **-i•ae** (-ē-ē′) or **-i•as.** The inner and larger of the two bones of the lower leg, extending from the knee to the ankle. [Lat. *tībia*, pipe, shinbone.] —**tib′i•al** *adj.*

tic (tĭk) ►*n.* A spasmodic muscular contraction, usu. of the face or extremities. [Fr.]

tick¹ (tĭk) ►*n.* **1.** A clicking sound made repeatedly by a machine, such as a clock. **2.** A light mark used to check off or call attention to an item. [ME *tek*, light tap.] —**tick** *v.*

tick² (tĭk) ►*n.* Any of numerous bloodsucking parasitic arachnids or louselike insects, many of which transmit diseases. [ME *tik.*]

tick³ (tĭk) ►*n.* **1.** A cloth case for a mattress or pillow. **2.** Ticking. [Prob. ult. < Gk. *thēkē*, receptacle.]

tick•er (tĭk′ər) ►*n.* **1.** A telegraphic instrument that receives news reports and prints them on paper tape. **2.** *Slang* The heart.

ticker tape ►*n.* The paper strip on which a ticker prints.

tick•et (tĭk′ĭt) ►*n.* **1.** A paper slip or card indicating that its holder has paid for admission or a service. **2.** A certificate or license. **3.** An identifying tag; label. **4.** A list of candidates endorsed by a political party; slate. **5.** A summons, esp. for a traffic violation. ►*v.* **1.** To serve with a legal summons. **2.** To tag; label. See Syns at **mark¹.** [< OFr. *estiquet*, notice, label.]

ticket office ►*n.* A location where tickets are sold, esp. for entertainment events or transportation services.

tick•ing (tĭk′ĭng) ►*n.* A strong, tightly woven fabric used to make pillow and mattress coverings.

tick•le (tĭk′əl) ►*v.* **-led, -ling 1.** To touch (the body) lightly so as to cause laughter or twitching movements. **2.** To feel a light tingling on the skin. **3a.** To tease or excite pleasurably. **b.** To please; delight. See Syns at **please.** [ME *tikelen.*] —**tick′le** *n.*

tick•lish (tĭk′lĭsh) ►*adj.* **1.** Sensitive to tickling. **2.** Easily offended or upset. **3.** Requiring tactful handling; delicate. —**tick′lish•ly** *adv.* —**tick′lish•ness** *n.*

tic-tac-toe also **tick-tack-toe** (tĭk′tăk′tō′) ►*n.* A game for two, each trying to make a line of three X's or three O's in a boxlike figure with nine spaces. [Prob. imit.]

tid•al (tīd′l) ►*adj.* Of or affected by tides.

tidal wave ►*n.* **1.** An unusual rise or incursion of water along the seashore. **2.** A tsunami. **3.** An overwhelming manifestation, as of opinion; flood.

tid•bit (tĭd′bĭt′) ►*n.* A choice morsel. [Perh. dial. *tid*, tender + BIT¹.]

tid•dly•winks (tĭd′lē-wĭngks′) ►*pl.n.* *(takes sing. v.)* A game in which players try to snap small disks into a cup by pressing them on the edge with a larger disk. [Poss. dial. *tiddly*, little + WINK.]

tide (tīd) ►*n.* **1a.** The periodic variation in the surface level of the oceans, seas, and other open waters of the earth, caused by gravitational attraction of the moon and sun. **b.** A specific occurrence of such a variation. **c.** The water that moves in such a variation. **2.** An onrush; flow: *a tide of immigration.* See Syns at

flow. 3. A time or season. ▸*v.* **tid•ed, tid•ing.** To drift with the tide. —***phrasal verb:* tide over** To support through a difficult period. [< OE *tīd*, division of time.]

tide•land (tīd′lănd′) ▸*n.* Coastal land submerged during high tide.

tide•wa•ter (tīd′wô′tər, -wŏt′ər) ▸*n.* **1.** Water that inundates land at flood tide. **2.** Water affected by the tides, esp. tidal streams. **3.** Low coastal land drained by tidal streams.

tid•ings (tī′dĭngz) ▸*pl.n.* Information; news. See Syns at **news.** [Perh. < ON *tīdhendi*, events.]

ti•dy (tī′dē) ▸*adj.* **-di•er, -di•est 1.** Orderly and neat. **2.** *Informal* Substantial; considerable. ▸*v.* **-died, -dy•ing.** To put (things) in order. [ME *tidi*, timely.] —**ti′di•ly** *adv.* —**ti′di•ness** *n.*

tie (tī) ▸*v.* **tied, ty•ing** (tī′ĭng) **1.** To fasten or secure with a cord, rope, or strap. **2.** To draw together and knot with strings or laces. **3.** To make (a knot or bow). **4.** To bring or hold together; unite. **5.** To equal (an opponent) in a contest. —***phrasal verbs:* tie in** To coordinate; connect. **tie up 1.** To obstruct. **2.** To keep occupied; engage. **3.** To moor; dock. ▸*n.* **1.** A length, as of cord or string, used for tying. **2.** A necktie. **3.** Something that unites; bond. **4.** An equality, as of votes or scores. **5.** A beam or rod that gives structural support. **6.** A timber laid crosswise to support railway tracks. [< OE *tīgan.*]

tie-dye (tī′dī′) ▸*v.* To dye (fabric) after tying parts of the fabric so that they will not absorb dye, creating a mottled or streaked look. —**tie′-dye′** *n.*

tie-in (tī′ĭn′) ▸*n.* A connection; link.

Tien•tsin (tyĕn′tsĭn′) See **Tianjin.**

Tie•po•lo (tē-ĕp′ə-lō′), **Giovanni Battista.** 1696–1770. Italian painter.

tier (tîr) ▸*n.* One of a series of rows placed one above another. [< OFr. *tire*, row.] —**tier** *v.*

Ti•er•ra del Fue•go (tē-ĕr′ə dĕl fwā′gō) **1.** An archipelago off S South America separated from the mainland by the Strait of Magellan. **2.** The main island of this archipelago.

tie-up (tī′ŭp′) ▸*n.* A temporary stoppage.

tiff (tĭf) ▸*n.* **1.** A fit of irritation. **2.** A petty quarrel. [?] —**tiff** *v.*

ti•ger (tī′gər) ▸*n.* A large carnivorous Asian cat having a tawny coat with black stripes. [< Gk. *tigris.*] —**ti′gress** *n.*

tiger lily ▸*n.* An E Asian plant with large black-spotted reddish-orange flowers.

tight (tīt) ▸*adj.* **-er, -est 1.** Fixed or fastened firmly in place. **2.** Stretched or drawn out fully. **3.** Of such close construction as to be impermeable. **4.** Compact. **5.** Fitting close or too close to the skin; snug. **6.** *Slang* Personally close; intimate. **7.** Constricted. **8.** Stingy. **9.** Difficult: *a tight spot.* **10.** Closely contested. **11.** *Slang* Drunk. ▸*adv.* **-er, -est 1.** Firmly; securely. **2.** Soundly: *sleep tight.* [ME, dense, of Scand. orig.] —**tight′en** *v.* —**tight′ly** *adv.* —**tight′ness** *n.*

Syns: *tight, taut, tense* **adj.**

tight•fist•ed (tīt′fĭs′tĭd) ▸*adj.* Stingy.

tight•lipped also **tight-lipped** (tīt′lĭpt′) ▸*adj.* **1.** Having the lips pressed together. **2.** Loath to speak; close-mouthed.

tight•rope (tīt′rōp′) ▸*n.* A tightly stretched rope on which acrobats perform.

tights (tīts) ▸*pl.n.* A snug stretchable garment covering the body from the waist or neck down.

tight•wad (tīt′wŏd′) ▸*n.* *Slang* A miser.

Ti•gris (tī′grĭs) A river of SW Asia rising in E Turkey and flowing about 1,850 km (1,150 mi) through Iraq to the Euphrates R.

Ti•jua•na (tē′ə-wä′nə, tē-hwä′nä) A city of extreme NW Mexico on the US border S of San Diego. Pop. 429,500.

til•de (tĭl′də) ▸*n.* A diacritical mark (&tide;) placed over the letter *n* in Spanish and over a vowel in Portuguese to indicate nasalization. [Sp. < Lat. *titulus*, superscription.]

tile (tīl) ▸*n.* **1.** A slab, as of baked clay, laid in rows to cover walls, floors, and roofs. **2.** A short length of clay or concrete pipe, used in sewers and drains. **3.** A marked playing piece, as in mahjong. ▸*v.* **tiled, til•ing.** To cover or provide with tiles. [< Lat. *tēgula* < *tegere*, cover.] —**til′er** *n.*

till[1] (tĭl) ▸*v.* To cultivate (land or soil). [< OE *tilian.*] —**till′a•ble** *adj.*

till[2] (tĭl) ▸*prep. & conj.* Until. [< OE *til* < ON.]

till[3] (tĭl) ▸*n.* A drawer or compartment for money, as in a store. [ME *tille.*]

till•age (tĭl′ĭj) ▸*n.* Cultivation of land.

till•er[1] (tĭl′ər) ▸*n.* One that tills land.

til•ler[2] (tĭl′ər) ▸*n.* A lever used to turn a boat's rudder. [< Med.Lat. *tēlārium*, weaver's beam < Lat. *tēla.*]

tilt (tĭlt) ▸*v.* **1.** To slope or cause to slope, as by raising one end; incline. See Syns at **slant. 2.** To thrust (a lance) in a joust. ▸*n.* **1.** A slant; slope. **2.** A joust. **3.** A bias. —***idiom:* at full tilt** *Informal* At full speed. [ME *tilten*, cause to fall.] —**tilt′er** *n.*

tim•ber (tĭm′bər) ▸*n.* **1a.** Trees or wooded land considered as a source of wood. **b.** Wood used as a building material. **2a.** A dressed piece of wood, esp. a structural beam. **b.** A rib in a ship's frame. [< OE, trees for building.] —**tim′bered** *adj.*

tim•ber•line (tĭm′bər-līn′) ▸*n.* The elevation in a mountainous region above which trees do not grow.

timber wolf ▸*n.* See **gray wolf.**

tim•bre (tăm′bər, tĭm′-) ▸*n.* The quality of a sound that distinguishes it from others of the same pitch and volume. [< OFr., drum.]

Tim•buk•tu (tĭm′bŭk-to͞o′, tĭm-bŭk′to͞o) A city of central Mali near the Niger R. NE of Bamako. Pop. 31,925.

time (tīm) ▸*n.* **1a.** A nonspatial continuum in which events occur in apparently irreversible succession. **b.** An interval separating two points on this continuum; duration. **c.** A number, as of years, days, or minutes, representing such an interval. **d.** A similar number representing a specific point on this continuum, reckoned in hours and minutes. **e.** A system by which such intervals are measured or such numbers are reckoned. **2.** often **times** A period; era: *hard times.* **3.** A suitable or opportune moment. **4.** A period designated for a given activity: *harvest time.* **5.** One of several instances. **6.** *Informal* A prison sentence. **7.** The rate of speed of a measured activity: *marching in double time.* **8.** The characteristic beat of musical rhythm. ▸*adj.* **1.** Of or relating to time. **2.** Constructed to operate at a particular moment: *a time release.* **3.** Of or relating to installment buying. ▸*v.* **timed, tim•ing 1.** To set the time for (e.g., an event). **2.** To adjust to keep accurate time. **3.** To adjust the timing of. **4.** To record, set, or maintain the speed, tempo, or duration of. —***idioms:* for the time being** Temporarily. **from time to time** Once in a while. **on time 1.** According to schedule. **2.** By paying in installments. [< OE *tīma.*] —**tim′er** *n.*

time bomb ▸*n.* **1.** A bomb that can be set to detonate at a particular time. **2.** Something that threatens eventual disaster.

time clock ▸*n.* A clock that records the starting and quitting times of employees.

time deposit ▸*n.* A bank deposit that cannot be withdrawn before a specified date.

time-hon•ored (tīm′ŏn′ərd) ▸*adj.* Respected because of age or age-old observance.

time•keep•er (tīm′kē′pər) ▸*n.* One who records time, as in a sports event.

time-lapse (tīm′lăps′) ▸*adj.* Of or being a technique that photographs a slow process at intervals, so that serial projection of the frames gives an accelerated view of the process.

time•less (tīm′lĭs) ▸*adj.* **1.** Eternal. **2.** Unaffected by time; ageless. See Syns at **ageless.** —**time′less•ly** *adv.* —**time′less•ness** *n.*

time•line (tīm′līn′) ▸*n.* **1.** A timetable. **2.** A chronology, esp. a representation of key events in a given time period.

time•ly (tīm′lē) ▸*adj.* **-li•er, -li•est.** Occurring at a suitable or opportune time; well-timed. —**time′li•ness** *n.*

time-out also **time out** (tīm′out′) ▸*n.* A brief cessation of play during a game.

time•piece (tīm′pēs′) ▸*n.* An instrument that measures, registers, or records time.

times (tīmz) ▸*prep. Math.* Multiplied by: *Five times two is ten.*

time-shar•ing (tīm′shâr′ĭng) ▸*n.* **1.** A technique permitting many users simultaneous access to a central computer through remote terminals. **2.** also **time-share** (-shâr′) Joint ownership of vacation property allowing individual use for fixed periods.

times sign ▸*n. Math.* The symbol × used to indicate multiplication.

time•ta•ble (tīm′tā′bəl) ▸*n.* A schedule of the expected times of events, such as arrivals and departures at a railroad station.

time•worn (tīm′wôrn′, -wōrn′) ▸*adj.* **1.** Showing the effects of long use or wear. **2.** Trite.

time zone ▸*n.* Any of the 24 longitudinal divisions of the earth's surface in which a standard time is kept.

tim•id (tĭm′ĭd) ▸*adj.* **-er, -est 1.** Shy. **2.** Fearful and hesitant. [Lat. *timidus.*] —**ti•mid′i•ty, tim′id•ness** *n.* —**tim′id•ly** *adv.*

tim•ing (tī′mĭng) ▸*n.* The regulation of occurrence, pace, or coordination to achieve the most desirable effects.

timing belt ▸*n.* A belt that drives the camshaft in an internal-combustion engine.

Ti•mi•şoa•ra (tē′mē-shwär′ə) A city of W Romania near the Serbian border WNW of Bucharest. Pop. 325,359.

Ti•mor (tē′môr, tē-môr′) An island of SE Indonesia, the easternmost of the Lesser Sundas.

tim•or•ous (tĭm′ər-əs) ▸*adj.* Fearful; timid. [< Lat. *timor,* fear.] —**tim′or•ous•ly** *adv.* —**tim′or•ous•ness** *n.*

Timor Sea. An arm of the Indian Ocean between Timor and Australia.

tim•o•thy (tĭm′ə-thē) ▸*n.* A grass widely cultivated for hay. [Prob. after *Timothy* Hanson, 18th-cent. American farmer.]

Timothy ▸*n.* See table at **Bible.**

Timothy, Saint. 1st cent. A.D. Christian leader and companion of Saint Paul.

tim•pa•ni also **tym•pa•ni** (tĭm′pə-nē) ▸*pl.n.* A set of kettledrums. [Ital. < Gk. *tumpanon,* drum.] —**tim′pa•nist** *n.*

tin (tĭn) ▸*n.* **1.** *Symbol* **Sn** A malleable, silvery metallic element used to coat other metals to prevent corrosion and in alloys such as soft solder, pewter, type metal, and bronze. At. no. 50. See table at **element. 2.** A tin container or box. **3.** *Chiefly Brit.* A can for preserved food. ▸*v.* **tinned, tin•ning 1.** To plate or coat with tin. **2.** *Chiefly Brit.* To pack in tins; can. [< OE.]

tinc•ture (tĭngk′chər) ▸*n.* **1.** A dyeing substance; pigment. **2.** An imparted color; tint. **3.** A trace or vestige. **4.** An alcohol solution of a nonvolatile medicine: *tincture of iodine.* ▸*v.* **-tured, -tur•ing.** To stain or tint with a color. [< Lat. *tingere, tīnct-,* dye.]

tin•der (tĭn′dər) ▸*n.* Readily combustible material used for kindling. [< OE *tynder.*]

tin•der•box (tĭn′dər-bŏks′) ▸*n.* **1.** A box for holding tinder. **2.** A potentially explosive situation.

tine (tīn) ▸*n.* A point or prong, as on a fork. [< OE *tind.*] —**tined** (tīnd) *adj.*

tin•foil also **tin foil** (tĭn′foil′) ▸*n.* A thin pliable sheet of aluminum, tin, or a tin alloy.

tinge (tĭnj) ▸*v.* **tinged** (tĭnjd), **tinge•ing** or **ting•ing 1.** To color slightly; tint. **2.** To affect slightly. [< Lat. *tingere.*] —**tinge** *n.*

tin•gle (tĭng′gəl) ▸*v.* **-gled, -gling.** To have a prickling, stinging sensation, as from cold or excitement. [ME *tinglen.*] —**tin′gle** *n.* —**tin′gler** *n.* —**tin′gly** *adj.*

tin•ker (tĭng′kər) ▸*n.* **1.** A traveling mender of metal household utensils. **2.** A clumsy worker; meddler. ▸*v.* **1.** To work as a tinker. **2.** To make aimless or experimental efforts at repair; fiddle. [ME *tinkere.*]

tin•kle (tĭng′kəl) ▸*v.* **-kled, -kling.** To make or cause to make light metallic sounds, as those of a small bell. [ME *tinklen.*] —**tin′kle** *n.* —**tin′kly** *adj.*

tin•ny (tĭn′ē) ▸*adj.* **-ni•er, -ni•est 1.** Of, containing, or suggesting tin. **2.** Having a thin metallic sound. —**tin′ni•ness** *n.*

tin•sel (tĭn′səl) ▸*n.* **1.** Very thin sheets or strips of a glittering material used as a decoration. **2.** Something showy but basically valueless. [< OFr. *estincelle,* spangle.] —**tin′sel** *adj.*

tin•smith (tĭn′smĭth′) ▸*n.* One who works with light metal, such as tin.

tint (tĭnt) ▸*n.* **1.** A shade of a color, esp. a pale or delicate variation. **2.** A slight coloration. **3.** A trace. **4.** A hair dye. ▸*v.* To give a tint to. [< Lat. *tīnctus,* dyeing.] —**tint′er** *n.*

tin•tin•nab•u•la•tion (tĭn′tĭ-năb′yə-lā′shən) ▸*n.* The ringing or sounding of bells. [< Lat. *tintinnābulum,* small bell.]

Tin•to•ret•to (tĭn′tə-rĕt′ō). 1518–94. Italian painter.

tin•type (tĭn′tīp′) ▸*n.* See **ferrotype.**

ti•ny (tī′nē) ▸*adj.* **-ni•er, -ni•est.** Extremely small; minute. See Syns at **small.** [< ME *tine.*] —**ti′ni•ness** *n.*

tip¹ (tĭp) ▸*n.* **1.** The end of a pointed or projecting object. **2.** A piece meant to be fitted to the end of something. ▸*v.* **tipped, tip•ping 1.** To furnish with a tip. **2.** To cover, decorate, or remove the tip of. [ME.]

tip² (tĭp) ▸*v.* **tipped, tip•ping 1.** To push or knock over; topple. **2.** To tilt. See Syns at **slant. 3.** To raise (one's hat) in greeting. [ME *tipen.*] —**tip** *n.*

tip³ (tĭp) ▸*v.* **tipped, tip•ping.** To strike gently; tap. [< ME *tippe*, a tap.] —**tip** *n.*

tip⁴ (tĭp) ▸*n.* **1.** An extra sum of money given to someone for services rendered; gratuity. **2.** A piece of useful advice or information. [?] —**tip** *v.* —**tip′per** *n.*

ti•pi (tē′pē) ▸*n.* Var. of **tepee.**

tip-off (tĭp′ôf′, -ŏf′) ▸*n. Informal* A piece of inside information; hint or warning.

tip•pet (tĭp′ĭt) ▸*n.* A covering for the shoulders with long ends that hang in front. [ME *tipet.*]

tip•ple (tĭp′əl) ▸*v.* **-pled, -pling.** To drink (alcoholic liquor), esp. habitually. [Perh. < ME *tipeler*, bartender.] —**tip′pler** *n.*

tip•ster (tĭp′stər) ▸*n. Informal* One who sells tips to bettors or speculators.

tip•sy (tĭp′sē) ▸*adj.* **-si•er, -si•est.** Slightly drunk. [< TIP².] —**tip′si•ly** *adv.* —**tip′si•ness** *n.*

tip•toe (tĭp′tō′) ▸*v.* To walk or move quietly or stealthily on one's toes. ▸*adv.* On one's toes. —**tip′toe′** *n.*

tip•top (tĭp′tŏp′) ▸*n.* The highest point; summit. ▸*adj.* Excellent; first-rate.

ti•rade (tī′rād′, tī-rād′) ▸*n.* An angry, often denunciatory speech; diatribe. [< OFr., firing.]

tir•a•mi•su (tîr′ə-mē′so͞o, -mē-so͞o′) ▸*n.* A dessert of cake infused with a liquid such as coffee and layered with a cheese filling. [Ital. *tira mi sù*, pick me up.]

Ti•ra•në also **Ti•ra•na** (tə-rä′nə, tē-). The capital of Albania, in the W-central part. Pop. 244,153.

tire¹ (tīr) ▸*v.* **tired, tir•ing 1.** To make or become weary. **2.** To make or become bored or impatient. [< OE *tyrian.*]

tire² (tīr) ▸*n.* **1.** A covering for a wheel, usu. of hollow rubber filled with compressed air. **2.** A hoop of metal or rubber fitted around a wheel. [ME.]

tired (tīrd) ▸*adj.* **1a.** Fatigued. **b.** Impatient; bored. **2.** Trite: *the same tired rhetoric as always.* —**tired′ly** *adv.* —**tired′ness** *n.*

tire iron ▸*n.* A metal bar with a socket wrench at one end, used for changing tires.

tire•less (tīr′lĭs) ▸*adj.* Not tiring easily; indefatigable. —**tire′less•ly** *adv.*

Syns: *tireless, indefatigable, unflagging, unwearied, weariless* **adj.**

tire•some (tīr′səm) ▸*adj.* Tedious; wearisome. —**tire′some•ly** *adv.* —**tire′some•ness** *n.*

Ti•rol (tə-rōl′, tī-, tī′rōl′) See **Tyrol.**

'tis (tĭz) ▸ It is.

Tish•ri (tĭsh′rē, -rā) ▸*n.* A month of the Jewish calendar. See table at **calendar.** [Heb. *tišrî.*]

tis•sue (tĭsh′o͞o, -yo͞o) ▸*n.* **1.** A fine, very thin fabric, such as gauze. **2.** Thin translucent paper used esp. for packing or wrapping. **3.** A soft absorbent piece of paper used as toilet paper or a handkerchief. **4.** A web; network. **5.** *Biol.* **a.** A group of cells that are similar in form or function. **b.** Cellular matter in general. [< OFr. *tissu*, woven < Lat. *texere*, weave.]

tit¹ (tĭt) ▸*n.* **1.** A titmouse. **2.** Any of various similar small birds. [< TITMOUSE.]

tit² (tĭt) ▸*n.* A teat. [< OE *titt.*]

tit. ▸*abbr.* Title.

Ti•tan (tīt′n) ▸*n.* **1.** *Gk. Myth.* One of a family of giants who were overthrown by the family of Zeus. **2. titan** A person of colossal size, strength, or achievement.

ti•tan•ic (tī-tăn′ĭk) ▸*adj.* Of enormous size or strength; colossal. —**ti•tan′i•cal•ly** *adv.*

ti•ta•ni•um (tī-tā′nē-əm, tĭ-) ▸*n. Symbol* **Ti** A strong, low-density, highly corrosion-resistant, lustrous white metallic element used to alloy metals for low weight, strength, and high-temperature stability. At. no. 22. See table at **element.**

tithe (tīth) ▸*n.* **1.** A tenth part of one's income, contributed esp. to a church. **2.** A tenth part. ▸*v.* **tithed, tith•ing.** To pay a tithe. [< OE *tēotha.*] —**tith′er** *n.*

Ti•tian (tĭsh′ən). 1488?–1576. Italian painter. —**Ti′tian•esque′** *adj.*

Ti•ti•ca•ca (tē′tē-kä′kä), **Lake.** A freshwater lake of South America in the Andes on the Bolivia-Peru border.

tit•il•late (tĭt′l-āt′) ▸*v.* **-lat•ed, -lat•ing.** To excite pleasurably; arouse. [Lat. *tītillāre.*] —**tit′il•lat′ing•ly** *adv.* —**tit′il•la′tion** *n.*

ti•tle (tīt′l) ▸*n.* **1.** An identifying name given to a book, film, or other work. **2.** *Law* **a.** Just cause of possession or control. **b.** The evidence of a right of possession. **c.** The instrument, such as a deed, that constitutes this evidence. **3.** A claim or right. **4a.** A formal appellation, as of rank or office. **b.** Such an appellation used to indicate nobility. **5.** *Sports* A championship. ▸*v.* **-tled, -tling.** To give a title to. [< Lat. *titulus.*]

ti•tled (tīt′ld) ▸*adj.* Having a title, esp. of nobility.

tit•mouse (tĭt′mous′) ▸*n., pl.* **-mice** (-mīs′). A small grayish crested North American bird. [< ME *titmose.*]

Ti•to (tē′tō), Marshal. Josip Broz. 1892–1980. Yugoslavian president (1953–80).

Ti•to•grad (tē′tō-grăd′, -gräd′) See **Podgorica.**

ti•tra•tion (tī-trā′shən) ▸*n.* Determination of the concentration of a solute by measuring the amount of an added reagent needed to complete a reaction. [< OFr. *title*, title.] —**ti′trate′** *v.*

tit•ter (tĭt′ər) ▸*v.* To laugh in a restrained, nervous giggle. [Prob. imit.] —**tit′ter** *n.*

tit•tle (tĭt′l) ▸*n.* The tiniest bit; iota. [< Med. Lat. *titulus*, diacritical mark.]

tit•u•lar (tĭch′ə-lər) ▸*adj.* **1.** Of or constituting a title. **2.** In name only; nominal. [< Lat. *titulus*, title.]

Ti•tus¹ (tī′təs). A.D. 39–81. Emperor of Rome (79–81).

Ti•tus² (tī′təs) ▸*n.* See table at **Bible.**

Titus, Saint. 1st cent. A.D. Christian leader and companion of Saint Paul.

tiz•zy (tĭz′ē) ▸*n., pl.* **-zies** *Slang* A state of nervous confusion; dither. [?]

TKO ▸*abbr.* technical knockout

Tl ▸ The symbol for the element **thallium.**

TLC ▸*abbr.* tender loving care

Tlin•git (tlĭng′gĭt, -kĭt, klĭng′kĭt) ▸*n., pl.* **-git** or **-gits 1.** A member of a Native American people of the coastal and island areas of SE Alaska. **2.** The language of the Tlingit.

Tm ▸ The symbol for the element **thulium.**
TM ▸ *abbr.* trademark
TN ▸ *abbr.* Tennessee
Tnpk. ▸ *abbr.* turnpike
TNT (tē′ĕn-tē′) ▸ *n.* A yellow crystalline compound used as an explosive. [*t(ri)n(itro)t(oluene).*]
to (to͞o; *when unstressed* tə) ▸ *prep.* **1.** In a direction toward. **2.** Reaching as far as. **3.** Toward or reaching a given state. **4.** In contact with; against: *cheek to cheek.* **5.** In front of: *face to face.* **6.** For or of: *the top to the jar.* **7.** Concerning; regarding: *no answer to my letter.* **8.** In a relation with: *parallel to the road.* **9.** As an accompaniment for. **10.** Composing; constituting: *two cups to a pint.* **11.** In accord with: *not to my liking.* **12.** As compared with: *a book superior to his others.* **13a.** Before: *The time is ten to five.* **b.** Up till; until: *worked from nine to five.* **14.** For the purpose of: *went out to lunch.* **15.** Used before a verb to indicate the infinitive: *I'd like to go.* ▸ *adv.* **1.** Into a shut or closed position: *pushed the door to.* **2.** Into a state of consciousness: *The patient came to.* **3.** Into a state of action: *sat down for lunch and fell to.* **4.** *Naut.* Into the wind. [< OE *tō.*]
toad (tōd) ▸ *n.* A froglike, mostly land-dwelling amphibian with rough warty skin. [< OE *tādige.*]
toad•stool (tōd′sto͞ol′) ▸ *n.* An inedible or poisonous mushroom.
toad•y (tō′dē) ▸ *n., pl.* **-ies.** A servile flatterer; sycophant. ▸ *v.* **-ied, -y•ing.** To be a toady to. See Syns at **fawn**[1]. [< TOAD.]
toast[1] (tōst) ▸ *v.* **1.** To heat and brown (e.g., bread). **2.** To warm thoroughly. ▸ *n.* Sliced bread heated and browned. [< Lat. *torrēre, tost-*, parch.]
toast[2] (tōst) ▸ *n.* **1.** The act of raising a glass and drinking in honor of a person or thing. **2.** The person or thing honored in this way. ▸ *v.* To drink to or propose a toast (to). [Poss. < TOAST[1].]
toast•er (tō′stər) ▸ *n.* A mechanical device used to toast bread.
toast•y (tō′stē) ▸ *adj.* **-i•er, -i•est.** Pleasantly warm.
to•bac•co (tə-băk′ō) ▸ *n., pl.* **-cos** or **-coes 1.** A plant native to tropical America, having broad leaves used chiefly for smoking. **2.** The leaves of this plant processed chiefly for use in cigarettes, cigars, snuff, or pipes. **3.** Such products collectively. [Sp. *tabaco.*]
to•bac•co•nist (tə-băk′ə-nĭst) ▸ *n.* A dealer in tobacco and smoking supplies.
To•ba•go (tə-bā′gō) An island of Trinidad and Tobago in the SE West Indies NE of Trinidad.
To•bit (tō′bĭt) ▸ *n.* See table at **Bible.**
to•bog•gan (tə-bŏg′ən) ▸ *n.* A long, narrow, runnerless sled constructed of thin boards curled upward at the front end. ▸ *v.* **1.** To travel on a toboggan. **2.** *Slang* To decline or fall rapidly. [< Micmac *topaghan.*] —**to•bog′gan•er, to•bog′gan•ist** *n.*
toc•ca•ta (tə-kä′tə) ▸ *n. Mus.* A virtuoso, freestyle composition, usu. for the organ, with brilliant runs and scales. [Ital.]
Tocque•ville (tŏk′vĭl), **Alexis Charles Henri Clérel de.** 1805–59. French politician, traveler, and historian.
toc•sin (tŏk′sĭn) ▸ *n.* A warning bell. [< OProv. *tocasenh.*]
to•day (tə-dā′) ▸ *n.* The present day, time, or age. ▸ *adv.* **1.** During or on the present day. **2.** At the present time. [< OE *tō dæge.*]
tod•dle (tŏd′l) ▸ *v.* **-dled, -dling.** To walk with short unsteady steps. [?] —**tod′dler** *n.*
tod•dy (tŏd′ē) ▸ *n., pl.* **-dies.** A hot toddy. [Hindi *tāṛī*, sap of palm.]
to-do (tə-do͞o′) ▸ *n., pl.* **-dos** (-do͞oz′) *Informal* A commotion or stir.
toe (tō) ▸ *n.* **1.** One of the digits of the foot. **2.** The forward part of something worn on the foot. **3.** Something resembling a toe in form, function, or location. ▸ *v.* **toed, toe•ing.** To touch, kick, or reach with the toe. [< OE *tā.*]
toe•a (toi′ə) ▸ *n., pl.* **toea.** See table at **currency.** [Perh. < E. DOLLAR.]
toed (tōd) ▸ *adj.* Having a toe, esp. of a specified number or kind: *an even-toed ungulate.*
TOEFL (tō′fəl) ▸ A trademark for a test of English as a foreign language.
toe•hold (tō′hōld′) ▸ *n.* **1.** A space to support the toe in climbing. **2.** A slight or initial advantage.
toe•nail (tō′nāl′) ▸ *n.* The nail on a toe.
tof•fee (tô′fē, tŏf′ē) ▸ *n.* A chewy candy of brown sugar or molasses and butter. [< TAFFY.]
to•fu (tō′fo͞o) ▸ *n.* A protein-rich food made from an extract of soybeans and used in salads and cooked foods. [< Chin. *dòufŭ.*]
tog (tŏg, tôg) *Informal* ▸ *n.* **togs.** Clothes. ▸ *v.* **togged, tog•ging.** To dress or clothe. [< Lat. *toga*, TOGA.]
to•ga (tō′gə) ▸ *n.* A loose one-piece outer garment worn in public by male citizens in ancient Rome. [Lat.] —**to′gaed** (tō′gəd) *adj.*
to•geth•er (tə-gĕth′ər) ▸ *adv.* **1.** In or into a single group or place. **2.** In or into contact. **3a.** In relationship to one another. **b.** By joint or cooperative effort. **4.** Regarded collectively. **5.** Simultaneously. **6.** In harmony or accord. [< OE *tōgædere.*] —**to•geth′er•ness** *n.*

Usage: *Together with,* like *in addition to,* is often employed following the subject of a sentence or clause to introduce an addition. The addition, however, does not alter the number of the verb, which is governed by the subject: *The king* (singular), *together with two aides, is expected in an hour.* The same is true of *along with, besides,* and *in addition to.*

tog•gle switch (tŏg′əl) ▸ *n.* A switch in which a projecting lever with a spring is used to open or close an electric circuit.
To•gliat•ti also **Tol•yat•ti** (tô-lyät′tē). A city of W Russia on the Volga R. NW of Samara. Pop. 682,256.
To•go (tō′gō′) A country of W Africa on the Gulf of Guinea. Cap. Lomé. Pop. 3,928,000.
To•ho•no O'o•dham (tō-hō′no ō′ə-däm) ▸ *n., pl.* **-dham** or **-dhams.** See **Papago.**
toil[1] (toil) ▸ *v.* **1.** To work strenuously. **2.** To proceed with difficulty. ▸ *n.* Exhausting labor or effort. [< Lat. *tudiculāre*, stir about.] —**toil′er** *n.*
toil[2] (toil) ▸ *n.* often **toils.** Something that entangles: *in the toils of despair.* [< Lat. *tēla*, web.]
toi•let (toi′lĭt) ▸ *n.* **1a.** A disposal fixture for defecation and urination. **b.** A room or booth containing such a fixture. **2.** The act of dressing or grooming oneself. [< OFr. *tellette*, cloth, dim. of *teile*; see TOIL[2].]
toilet paper ▸ *n.* Thin absorbent paper for

cleaning oneself after defecation or urination.
toi•let•ry (toi′lĭ-trē) ▸*n., pl.* **-ries.** An article used in personal grooming or dressing.
toi•lette (twä-lĕt′) ▸*n.* **1.** The process of dressing or grooming oneself; toilet. **2.** A person's dress or style of dress. [Fr. See TOILET.]
toilet water ▸*n.* A scented liquid with a high alcohol content used in bathing or applied as a skin freshener.
to•ken (tō′kən) ▸*n.* **1.** Something serving as an indication or representation; sign. **2.** Something that signifies or evidences authority, validity, or identity. **3.** One that represents a group. **4.** A keepsake. **5.** A piece of stamped metal used as a substitute for currency. ▸*adj.* Done as an indication or a pledge: *a token payment.* [< OE *tācen.*]
to•ken•ism (tō′kə-nĭz′əm) ▸*n.* Symbolic gestures rather than effective action toward a goal.
To•ky•o (tō′kē-ō′, -kyō) The capital of Japan, in E-central Honshu on **Tokyo Bay,** an inlet of the Pacific. Pop. 8,080,286.
to•lar (tō′lär) ▸*n.* See table at **currency.** [Slovene.]
told (tōld) ▸*v.* P.t. and p.part. of **tell.**
To•le•do (tə-lē′dō) **1.** (*also* tō-lĕ′*th*ō) A city of central Spain near the Tagus R. SSW of Madrid. Pop. 57,778. **2.** A city of NW OH on Lake Erie. Pop. 332,943.
tol•er•a•ble (tŏl′ər-ə-bəl) ▸*adj.* **1.** Endurable. **2.** Fairly good; passable. —**tol′er•a•bil′i•ty, tol′er•a•ble•ness** *n.* —**tol′er•a•bly** *adv.*
tol•er•ance (tŏl′ər-əns) ▸*n.* **1.** The capacity for respecting the beliefs or practices of others. **2.** Leeway for variation from a standard. **3.** The capacity to endure hardship or pain. **4.** Resistance, as to a drug. —**tol′er•ant** *adj.* —**tol′er•ant•ly** *adv.*
tol•er•ate (tŏl′ə-rāt′) ▸*v.* **-at•ed, -at•ing 1.** To allow without prohibiting or opposing; permit. **2.** To recognize and respect (the rights, beliefs, or practices of others). **3.** To put up with; endure. [Lat. *tolerāre*, to bear.] —**tol′er•a′tion** *adj.*
Tol•kien (tōl′kēn′, tŏl′-), **J(ohn) R(onald) R(euel).** 1892–1973. British writer.
toll¹ (tōl) ▸*n.* **1.** A fixed tax for a privilege, esp. for passage across a bridge. **2.** A charge for a service, such as a long-distance telephone call. **3.** The amount or extent of loss or destruction, as in a disaster. [< Gk. *telōneion*, tollbooth.]
toll² (tōl) ▸*v.* **1.** To sound (a large bell) slowly at regular intervals. **2.** To announce or summon by tolling. ▸*n.* The sound of a bell being struck. [ME *tollen.*]
toll•booth (tōl′bo͞oth′) ▸*n.* A booth where a toll is collected.
toll•gate (tōl′gāt′) ▸*n.* A gate barring passage until a toll is collected.
Tol•stoy (tōl′stoi, tŏl′-), Count **Leo.** 1828–1910. Russian writer. —**Tol•stoy′an** *adj.*
Tol•tec (tōl′tĕk′, tŏl′-) ▸*n., pl.* **-tec** or **-tecs.** A member of a Nahuatl-speaking people of central and S Mexico whose empire flourished from the 10th to the 12th cent. —**Tol′tec, Tol′tec′an** *adj.*
Tol•yat•ti (tô-lyät′tē) See **Togliatti.**
tom (tŏm) ▸*n.* The male of various animals, esp. a cat or turkey. [< *Tom*, nickname for *Thomas.*]
tom•a•hawk (tŏm′ə-hôk′) ▸*n.* A light ax formerly used as a tool or weapon by certain Native American peoples. See Regional Note at **pone.** [Virginia Algonquian *tamahaac.*] —**tom′a•hawk′** *v.*
to•ma•to (tə-mā′tō, -mä′-) ▸*n., pl.* **-toes 1.** A fleshy, smooth-skinned reddish fruit, eaten as a vegetable. **2.** A plant bearing such fruit. [< Nahuatl *tomatl.*]
tomb (to͞om) ▸*n.* **1.** A place of burial. **2.** A vault or chamber for burial of the dead. [< Gk. *tumbos.*]
tom•boy (tŏm′boi′) ▸*n.* A girl considered boyish or masculine in behavior or manner.
tomb•stone (to͞om′stōn′) ▸*n.* A gravestone.
tom•cat (tŏm′kăt′) ▸*n.* A male cat.
tome (tōm) ▸*n.* A book, esp. a large or scholarly one. [< Gk. *tomos*, section.]
tom•fool•er•y (tŏm-fo͞o′lə-rē) ▸*n., pl.* **-ies 1.** Foolish behavior. **2.** Nonsense.
to•mog•ra•phy (tō-mŏg′rə-fē) ▸*n.* A technique for making detailed x-rays of a predetermined plane section of a solid object. [Gk. *tomos*, section + -GRAPHY.] —**to′mo•gram′** (tō′mə-grăm′) *n.* —**to′mo•graph′** *n.* —**to′mo•graph′ic** *adj.*
to•mor•row (tə-môr′ō, -mŏr′ō) ▸*n.* **1.** The day following today. **2.** The near future. ▸*adv.* On or for the day following today. [< OE *tō morgenne*, in the morning.]
Tomsk (tŏmsk, tômsk) A city of central Russia NE of Novosibirsk. Pop. 497,662.
tom-tom (tŏm′tŏm′) ▸*n.* Any of various small-headed drums that are beaten with the hands. [Hindi *ṭamṭam.*]
-tomy ▸*suff.* Cutting; incision: *lobotomy.* [< Gk. *tomos*, cutting < *temnein*, cut.]
ton (tŭn) ▸*n.* **1a.** A short ton. **b.** A long ton. **c.** A metric ton. See table at **measurement. 2.** *Informal* A very large quantity: *tons of fan mail.* [< OE *tunne*, large cask.]
to•nal•i•ty (tō-năl′ĭ-tē) ▸*n., pl.* **-ties** *Mus.* The arrangement of the tones and chords of a composition in relation to a tonic.
tone (tōn) ▸*n.* **1.** *Mus.* **a.** A sound of distinct pitch, quality, and duration; note. **b.** The largest interval between adjacent notes in the diatonic scale. **2.** The quality of sound. **3.** The pitch of a word or phrase. **4.** Manner of expression: *an angry tone of voice.* **5.** A general quality or atmosphere: *a room with an elegant tone.* **6a.** A color or shade of color. **b.** Quality of color. **7.** *Physiol.* **a.** The tension in resting muscles. **b.** Normal tissue firmness. ▸*v.* **toned, ton•ing 1.** To give a particular tone or inflection to. **2.** *Physiol.* To give tone to. —***phrasal verbs:* tone down** To make less harsh or severe; moderate. **tone up** To make or become brighter or more vigorous. [< Gk. *tonos.*] —**ton′al** *adj.* —**ton′al•ly** *adv.*
tone arm ▸*n.* The arm of a phonograph turntable that holds the cartridge.
ton•er (tō′nər) ▸*n.* One that tones, esp. a powdery ink used dry or suspended in a liquid to produce a photocopy.
Ton•ga (tŏng′gə) A country in the SW Pacific E of Fiji comprising about 150 islands. Cap. Nuku'alofa. Pop. 98,000. —**Ton′gan** *adj. & n.*
tongs (tôngz, tŏngz) ▸*pl.n.* *(takes sing. or pl. v.)* A grasping device consisting of two arms joined at one end by a pivot or hinge. [< OE *tong.*]
tongue (tŭng) ▸*n.* **1.** The fleshy, movable, muscular organ in the mouth that functions in

tasting, chewing, swallowing, and speech. **2.** The tongue of an animal, such as a cow, used as food. **3.** A spoken language. **4.** Quality of utterance: *his sharp tongue.* **5.** Anything resembling a tongue in shape or function. [< OE *tunge.*]

tongue-in-cheek (tŭng′ĭn-chēk′) ▶*adj.* Meant ironically or facetiously.

tongue-tied (tŭng′tīd′) ▶*adj.* Speechless or confused in expression, as from shyness, embarrassment, or astonishment.

tongue twister ▶*n.* **1.** A word or group of words difficult to articulate rapidly. **2.** Something difficult to pronounce.

ton•ic (tŏn′ĭk) ▶*n.* **1.** An invigorating, refreshing, or restorative agent or influence. **2.** *Regional* See **soft drink.** **3.** *Mus.* The first note of a diatonic scale; keynote. ▶*adj.* **1.** Stimulating physical or mental vigor. **2.** *Mus.* Of or based on the tonic or keynote. [< Gk. *tonos,* tone.]

Regional Note: Probably the two most common generic terms for carbonated soft drinks in the United States are *soda,* used in the northeast and the St. Louis area, and *pop,* used from the Midwest westward. In the South all soft drinks are referred to as *cold drinks.* Speakers in and around Boston have a term of their own: *tonic.*

to•night (tə-nīt′) ▶*adv.* On or during the present or coming night. ▶*n.* This night or the night of this day. [< OE *tō niht,* at night. See NIGHT.]

Ton•kin (tŏn′kĭn′, tŏng′-) A historical region of SE Asia on the **Gulf of Tonkin,** an arm of the South China Sea, now forming most of N Vietnam. —**Ton′kin•ese′** (-ēz′, -ēs′) *adj. & n.*

ton•nage (tŭn′ĭj) ▶*n.* **1.** The number of tons of water a ship displaces when afloat. **2.** The capacity of a merchant ship in units of 100 cu. ft. **3.** A charge per ton on cargo. **4.** The total shipping of a country or port, figured in tons. **5.** Weight measured in tons.

ton•sil (tŏn′səl) ▶*n.* A mass of lymphoid tissue, esp. either of two such masses embedded at the back of the mouth. [< Lat. *tōnsillae,* tonsils.] —**ton′sil•lar** *adj.*

ton•sil•lec•to•my (tŏn′sə-lĕk′tə-mē) ▶*n., pl.* **-mies.** Surgical removal of tonsils or a tonsil.

ton•sil•li•tis (tŏn′sə-lī′tĭs) ▶*n.* Inflammation of the tonsils. —**ton′sil•lit′ic** (-lĭt′ĭk) *adj.*

ton•so•ri•al (tŏn-sôr′ē-əl, -sōr-) ▶*adj.* Of barbering or a barber. [< Lat. *tōnsor,* barber.]

ton•sure (tŏn′shər) ▶*n.* **1.** The act of shaving the head, esp. as a preliminary to becoming a priest. **2.** The part of the head so shaved. ▶*v.* **-sured, -sur•ing.** To shave the head of. [< Lat. *tondēre, tōns-,* shear.]

ton•y (tō′nē) ▶*adj.* **-i•er, -i•est** *Informal* Expensive, luxurious, or exclusive.

too (to͞o) ▶*adv.* **1.** In addition; also. **2.** More than enough; excessively: *She worries too much.* **3.** *Informal* Indeed; so: *You will too do it!* [< OE *tō.*]

Usage: *Too* meaning "in addition" or "also" is sometimes used to introduce a sentence: *There has been a cutback in federal subsidies. Too, rates have been increasing.* This usage cannot be called incorrect, but some critics consider it awkward.

took (to͝ok) ▶*v.* P.t. of **take.**

tool (to͞ol) ▶*n.* **1.** A device, such as a saw, used to perform manual or mechanical work. **2.** A machine, such as a lathe, used to cut and shape machine parts. **3.** A means or instrument. **4.** *Comp. Sci.* An application program, esp. one that creates or edits other programs. **5.** A dupe. ▶*v.* **1.** To form, work, or decorate with a tool. **2.** *Slang* To drive or ride in a vehicle. —***phrasal verb:*** **tool up** To furnish tools or machinery for (an industry or factory). [< OE *tōl.*]

tool•bar (to͞ol′bär′) ▶*n.* A row of icons on a computer screen for activating commands or functions.

toot (to͞ot) ▶*v.* To sound a horn or whistle in short blasts. ▶*n.* A blast, as of a horn. [Ult. imit.] —**toot′er** *n.*

tooth (to͞oth) ▶*n., pl.* **teeth** (tēth) **1.** One of a set of hard, bonelike structures rooted in sockets in the jaws, used to bite and chew. **2.** A projecting part resembling a tooth in shape or function, as on a comb. —***idiom:*** **to the teeth** Lacking nothing; completely: *armed to the teeth.* [< OE *tōth.*] —**toothed** *adj.* —**tooth′less** *adj.*

tooth•ache (to͞oth′āk′) ▶*n.* An aching pain in or near a tooth.

tooth•brush (to͞oth′brŭsh′) ▶*n.* A brush for cleaning teeth.

tooth•paste (to͞oth′pāst′) ▶*n.* A paste for cleaning teeth.

tooth•pick (to͞oth′pĭk′) ▶*n.* A small stick for removing food from between the teeth.

tooth•some (to͞oth′səm) ▶*adj.* Delicious; luscious. —**tooth′some•ness** *n.*

top¹ (tŏp) ▶*n.* **1.** The uppermost part, point, surface, or end. **2.** A lid or cap. **3a.** The highest position or rank. **b.** The highest degree or pitch; acme; zenith. ▶*v.* **topped, top•ping 1.** To form, furnish with, or serve as a top. **2.** To reach or go over the top of. **3.** To exceed or surpass. —***idioms:*** **off the top of (one's) head** *Informal* In an impromptu way. **on top of** *Informal* **1.** In control of. **2.** Fully informed about. **3.** In addition to. **4.** Following closely on. [< OE.]

top² (tŏp) ▶*n.* A toy made to spin on the pointed end. [< OE.]

to•paz (tō′păz′) ▶*n.* **1.** A mineral consisting largely of aluminum silicate and valued as a gem. **2.** Any of various yellow gemstones, esp. a yellow variety of sapphire. [< Gk. *topazos.*]

top•coat (tŏp′kōt′) ▶*n.* A lightweight overcoat.

top dog ▶*n.* *Slang* One who has the dominant position or highest authority.

top-drawer (tŏp′drôr′) ▶*adj.* Of the highest importance, rank, or merit.

To•pe•ka (tə-pē′kə) The capital of KS, in the NE part W of Kansas City. Pop. 119,883.

top•er (tō′pər) ▶*n.* A chronic drinker. [< *tope,* drink heavily.]

top•flight (tŏp′flīt′) ▶*adj.* *Informal* First-rate; excellent.

top hat ▶*n.* A man's formal hat with a narrow brim and a tall cylindrical crown.

top-heav•y (tŏp′hĕv′ē) ▶*adj.* Likely to topple because overloaded at the top.

to•pi•ar•y (tō′pē-ĕr′ē) ▶*n., pl.* **-ies 1.** The art of trimming live shrubs or trees into decorative shapes. **2.** A plant so trimmed. [< Gk. *topia,* ornamental gardening.]

top•ic (tŏp′ĭk) ▶*n.* The subject of a speech, essay, thesis, or conversation. [< Gk. *topos,* place.]

top•i•cal (tŏp′ĭ-kəl) ▸*adj.* **1.** Local. **2.** Currently of interest; contemporary. **3.** *Medic.* Of or applied to a localized area of the body. —**top′i•cal′i•ty** (-kăl′ĭ-tē) *n.* —**top′i•cal•ly** *adv.*

top•knot (tŏp′nŏt′) ▸*n.* **1.** A crest or knot of hair or feathers on the crown of the head. **2.** A decorative ribbon or bow worn as a headdress.

top•less (tŏp′lĭs) ▸*adj.* **1.** Having no top. **2.** Not covering the breasts.

top•most (tŏp′mōst′) ▸*adj.* Highest; uppermost.

top-notch or **top•notch** (tŏp′nŏch′) ▸*adj. Informal* First-rate; excellent.

topo– ▸*pref.* Place: *topography.* [< Gk. *topos,* place.]

to•pog•ra•phy (tə-pŏg′rə-fē) ▸*n.* **1.** The physical features of a region. **2.** Detailed description or representation of such features. —**to•pog′ra•pher** *n.* —**top′o•graph′ic** (tŏp′ə-grăf′ĭk), **top′o•graph′i•cal** *adj.* —**top′o•graph′i•cal•ly** *adv.*

top•ping (tŏp′ĭng) ▸*n.* A sauce, frosting, or garnish for food.

top•ple (tŏp′əl) ▸*v.* **-pled, -pling 1.** To push or throw over; overturn. See Syns at **overthrow. 2.** To totter and fall. [< TOP[1].]

tops (tŏps) ▸*adj. Slang* First-rate; excellent.

top•sail (tŏp′səl, -sāl′) ▸*n. Naut.* A square sail set above the lowest sail on the mast of a square-rigged ship.

top-se•cret (tŏp′sē′krĭt) ▸*adj.* Of the highest level of security classification.

top•side (tŏp′sīd′) ▸*adv.* & *adj.* On or to the upper parts of a ship; on deck.

top•soil (tŏp′soil′) ▸*n.* The upper part of soil.

top•sy-tur•vy (tŏp′sē-tûr′vē) ▸*adv.* **1.** Upside-down. **2.** In utter disorder or confusion. ▸*adj.* In a disordered state. [Prob. < TOP[1] + obsolete *terve,* overturn.] —**top′sy-tur′vi•ly** *adv.* —**top′sy-tur′vi•ness** *n.*

toque (tōk) ▸*n.* A woman's small, brimless, close-fitting hat. [Fr.]

tor (tôr) ▸*n.* A rocky peak or hill. [< OE *torr,* prob. of Celt. orig.]

To•rah also **to•rah** (tôr′ə, tōr′ə) ▸*n. Judaism* **1.** The entire body of religious law and learning. **2.** The first five books of the Hebrew Scriptures. See table at **Bible. 3.** The scroll on which these scriptures are written, used in a synagogue during services.

torch (tôrch) ▸*n.* **1a.** A portable light produced by the flame of a burning material wound about the end of a stick. **b.** *Chiefly Brit.* A flashlight. **2.** Something that serves to illuminate or guide. **3.** *Slang* An arsonist. **4.** A portable apparatus that produces a very hot flame by the combustion of gases, used in welding. ▸*v. Slang* To set on fire. [< Lat. *torquēre,* twist.]

tore (tôr, tōr) ▸*v.* P.t. of **tear[1].**

tor•e•a•dor (tôr′ē-ə-dôr′) ▸*n.* A bullfighter. [Sp.]

tor•ment (tôr′mĕnt′) ▸*n.* **1.** Great physical pain or mental anguish. **2.** A source of harassment or pain. ▸*v.* (tôr-mĕnt′, tôr′mĕnt′) **1.** To cause to undergo torment. See Syns at **afflict. 2.** To pester; annoy. [< Lat. *tormentum.*] —**tor•ment′ing•ly** *adv.* —**tor•men′tor, tor•ment′er** *n.*

torn (tôrn, tōrn) ▸*v.* P.part. of **tear[1].**

tor•na•do (tôr-nā′dō) ▸*n., pl.* **-does** or **-dos.** A rotating column of air, usu. accompanied by a funnel-shaped downward extension of a cumulonimbus cloud and moving destructively over a narrow path. [< Sp. *tronada,* thunderstorm.]

To•ron•to (tə-rŏn′tō) The capital of Ontario, Canada, in the S part on Lake Ontario. Pop. 635,395.

tor•pe•do (tôr-pē′dō) ▸*n., pl.* **-does 1.** A cigar-shaped, self-propelled underwater projectile, designed to detonate on contact with or in the vicinity of a target. **2.** Any of various explosive devices. ▸*v.* **-doed, -do•ing.** To attack or destroy with or as if with a torpedo. [Lat. *torpēdō,* electric ray.]

tor•pid (tôr′pĭd) ▸*adj.* **1.** Deprived of the power of motion or feeling. **2.** Dormant; hibernating. **3.** Lethargic; apathetic. [Lat. *torpidus.*] —**tor•pid′i•ty** *n.*

tor•por (tôr′pər) ▸*n.* **1.** A state of inactivity or insensibility. **2.** Lethargy; apathy. [Lat. < *torpēre,* be stiff.] —**tor′po•rif′ic** (-pə-rĭf′ĭk) *adj.*

torque (tôrk) ▸*n.* The tendency of a force to produce rotation about an axis. [< Lat. *torquēre,* twist.] —**torque** *v.*

Tor•rance (tôr′əns, tŏr′-) A city of S CA S of Los Angeles. Pop. 133,107.

tor•rent (tôr′ənt, tŏr′-) ▸*n.* **1.** A turbulent, swift-flowing stream. **2.** A deluge. **3.** An overwhelming outpouring; flood. [< Lat. *torrēre,* burn.] —**tor•ren′tial** (tô-rĕn′shəl, tə-) *adj.*

tor•rid (tôr′ĭd, tŏr′-) ▸*adj.* **-er, -est 1.** Very dry and hot. **2.** Passionate. [Lat. *torridus* < *torrēre,* parch.] —**tor•rid′i•ty, tor′rid•ness** *n.* —**tor′rid•ly** *adv.*

Torrid Zone. The central latitude zone of the earth, between the tropic of Cancer and the tropic of Capricorn.

tor•sion (tôr′shən) ▸*n.* **1.** A twisting or turning. **2.** The stress caused when one end of an object is twisted in one direction and the other end is held motionless. [< Lat. *torquēre, tort-,* twist.] —**tor′sion•al** *adj.*

tor•so (tôr′sō) ▸*n., pl.* **-sos.** The trunk of the human body. [< Lat. *thyrsus,* stalk.]

tort (tôrt) ▸*n. Law* Any wrongful act that does not involve a breach of contract and for which a civil suit can be brought. [< Lat. *torquēre, tort-,* twist.]

torte (tôrt, tôr′tə) ▸*n.* A rich cake made with many eggs, flour, and usu. chopped nuts. [Ger.]

tor•til•la (tôr-tē′yə) ▸*n.* A thin disk of unleavened bread made from cornmeal or wheat flour. [< LLat. *torta,* a kind of bread.]

tor•toise (tôr′tĭs) ▸*n.* Any of various terrestrial turtles. [< Med.Lat. *tortūca.*]

tor•toise•shell (tôr′tĭs-shĕl′) ▸*n.* The translucent brownish outer covering of certain turtles, used to make combs and jewelry.

Tor•to•la (tôr-tō′lə) An island of the British Virgin Is. in the West Indies E of Puerto Rico.

Tor•tu•ga (tôr-to͞o′gə) An island in the West Indies off N Haiti.

tor•tu•ous (tôr′cho͞o-əs) ▸*adj.* **1.** Winding or twisting. **2.** Not straightforward; devious. **3.** Complex. [< Lat. *tortus,* twisted.] —**tor′tu•ous•ly** *adv.* —**tor′tu•ous•ness** *n.*

tor•ture (tôr′chər) ▸*n.* **1.** Infliction of severe pain as a means of punishment or coercion. **2.** Pain or mental anguish. ▸*v.* **-tured, -tur•ing 1.** To subject to torture. **2.** To afflict with great pain or anguish. See Syns at **afflict. 3.** To twist or distort. [< Lat. *torquēre, tort-*, twist.] —**tor′tur•er** *n.* —**tor′tur•ous** *adj.* —**tor′tur•ous•ly** *adv.*

To•ry (tôr′ē, tōr′ē) ►*n., pl.* **-ries 1.** A member of the Conservative Party in Great Britain. **2.** An American who favored the British side during the American Revolution. [< Ir.Gael. *tóraidhe*, robber.] —**To′ry** *adj.* —**To′ry•ism** *n.*

Tos•ca•ni•ni (tŏs′kə-nē′nē), **Arturo.** 1867–1957. Italian conductor.

toss (tôs, tŏs) ►*v.* **1.** To throw lightly. **2.** To throw or be thrown to and fro. **3.** To mix (a salad). **4.** To move or lift (the head) with a sudden motion. **5.** To flip (a coin) to decide something. ***phrasal verb:* toss off** To do effortlessly or casually. ►*n.* **1.** An act of tossing. **2.** An abrupt upward movement, as of the head. [ME *tossen*, poss. of Scand. orig.]

toss•up (tôs′ŭp′, tŏs′-) ►*n. Informal* An even chance or choice.

tot[1] (tŏt) ►*n.* **1.** A small child. **2.** A small amount. [?]

tot[2] (tŏt) ►*v.* **tot•ted, tot•ting.** To total: *totted up the bill.*

to•tal (tōt′l) ►*n.* **1.** An amount obtained by addition; sum. **2.** A whole quantity; entirety. ►*adj.* **1.** Constituting the whole; entire. See Syns at **whole. 2.** Complete; utter. ►*v.* **-taled, -tal•ing** or **-talled, -tal•ling 1.** To determine the sum of. **2.** To amount to. **3.** *Slang* To destroy: *totaled the car.* [< Lat. *tōtus*, whole.] —**to′tal•ly** *adv.*

to•tal•i•tar•i•an (tō-tăl′ĭ-târ′ē-ən) ►*adj.* Of or being a form of government in which the political authority exercises absolute control over all aspects of life and opposition is outlawed. ►*n.* A practitioner or supporter of such a government. [TOTAL + (AUTHOR)ITARIAN.] —**to•tal′i•tar′i•an•ism** *n.*

to•tal•i•ty (tō-tăl′ĭ-tē) ►*n., pl.* **-ties 1.** The quality or state of being total. **2.** An aggregate amount.

tote (tōt) ►*v.* **tot•ed, tot•ing** *Informal* To haul; lug. [Poss. of Bantu orig.]

to•tem (tō′təm) ►*n.* **1.** *Anthro.* **a.** An animal, plant, or natural object serving as a emblem of a clan or family. **b.** A representation of this. **2.** A venerated symbol. [Ojibwa *nindoodem*, my totem.] —**to•tem′ic** (-tĕm′ĭk) *adj.*

totem pole ►*n.* A post carved and painted with a series of family or clan crests, as among certain Native American peoples.

totem pole
Saxman Totem Park, Ketchikan, Alaska

tot•ter (tŏt′ər) ►*v.* **1.** To sway as if about to fall. **2.** To walk unsteadily. [ME *toteren.*] —**tot′ter** *n.* —**tot′ter•y** *adj.*

tou•can (to͞o′kăn′, -kän′) ►*n.* A tropical American bird with brightly colored plumage and a very large bill. [< Tupi *tucano*, bird.]

touch (tŭch) ►*v.* **1.** To cause or permit a part of the body, esp. the hand or fingers, to come in contact with so as to feel. **2.** To be or bring into contact with. **3.** To tap or nudge lightly. **4.** To partake of: *didn't touch her food.* **5.** To disturb or move by handling. **6a.** To adjoin or border. **b.** To come up to; equal. **7.** To treat briefly or allusively: *remarks touching recent events.* **8.** To be pertinent to. **9.** To affect emotionally; move. —***phrasal verbs:* touch down** To land. **touch off 1.** To cause to explode. **2.** To initiate; trigger. **touch up** To improve by making minor changes. ►*n.* **1.** The act or an instance of touching. **2.** The physiological sense by which bodily contact is perceived. **3.** A sensation from a specific contact. **4.** A light push; tap. **5.** A mark or effect left by contact with something. **6.** A small amount; trace. **7.** A characteristic way of doing things. **8.** A facility; knack. **9.** Contact or communication: *Keep in touch.* [< OFr. *touchier.*] —**touch′a•ble** *adj.*

touch-and-go (tŭch′ən-gō′) ►*adj.* Precarious and uncertain in nature or outcome.

touch•down (tŭch′doun′) ►*n.* **1.** *Football* A score of six points, made by moving the ball across the opponent's goal line. **2.** The contact of a landing aircraft or spacecraft with the landing surface.

tou•ché (to͞o-shā′) ►*interj.* Used to acknowledge a hit in fencing or a successful criticism in an argument. [Fr. < p.part. of *toucher*, TOUCH.]

touch•ing (tŭch′ĭng) ►*adj.* Eliciting sympathy or tenderness. —**touch′ing•ly** *adv.*

touch•screen (tŭch′skrēn′) ►*n.* A monitor screen that is responsive to pressure, esp. from a finger or stylus.

touch•stone (tŭch′stōn′) ►*n.* **1.** A hard stone used to test the quality of gold or silver. **2.** A test of authenticity or value; standard. See Syns at **standard.**

touch•y (tŭch′ē) ►*adj.* **-i•er, -i•est 1.** Easily offended or annoyed; oversensitive. **2.** Delicate; difficult: *a touchy situation.* —**touch′i•ly** *adv.* —**touch′i•ness** *n.*

tough (tŭf) ►*adj.* **-er, -est 1.** Strong and resilient. **2.** Hard to cut or chew. **3.** Physically rugged. **4.** Severe; harsh. **5.** Aggressive; pugnacious. **6.** Demanding; difficult. **7.** Strong-minded; resolute. **8.** *Slang* Unfortunate; too bad: *a tough break.* ►*n.* A hoodlum. [< OE *tōh.*] —**tough′ly** *adv.* —**tough′ness** *n.*

tough•en (tŭf′ən) ►*v.* To make or become tough. See Syns at **harden.**

Tou•louse (to͞o-lo͞oz′) A city of S France SE of Bordeaux. Pop. 358,598.

Tou•louse-Lau•trec (to͞o-lo͞oz′lō-trĕk′), **Henri de.** 1864–1901. French artist.

tou•pee (to͞o-pā′) ►*n.* A hairpiece worn to cover a bald spot. [< OFr. *toupe*, tuft.]

tour (to͝or) ►*n.* **1.** A trip with visits to places of interest for business, pleasure, or instruction. **2.** A brief trip to or through a place to see or inspect it. **3.** A journey to fulfill a round of engagements in several places: *a concert tour.* **4.** A period of duty at a single place or job. ►*v.* To make a tour (of). [< Lat. *tornus*, lathe.]

tour de force (to͝or′ də fôrs′, fōrs′) ►*n., pl.*

tours de force (to͝or′). A feat of great virtuosity or strength. [Fr.]

tour•ism (to͝or′ĭz′əm) ►*n.* Tourist travel and accommodation.

tour•ist (to͝or′ĭst) ►*n.* One who travels for pleasure. —**tour′ist•y** *adj.*

tour•ma•line (to͝or′mə-lĭn, -lēn′) ►*n.* A mineral valued, esp. in its green, clear, and blue varieties, as a gemstone. [< Sinhalese *toramalli,* carnelian.]

tour•na•ment (to͝or′nə-mənt, tûr′-) ►*n.* **1.** A contest composed of a series of elimination games or trials. **2.** A medieval jousting or tilting match. [< OFr. *torneier,* TOURNEY.]

tour•ney (to͝or′nē, tûr′-) ►*n., pl.* **-neys.** A tournament. [< VLat. **tornizāre,* turn around.]

tour•ni•quet (to͝or′nĭ-kĭt, tûr′-) ►*n.* A device, usu. a tightly encircling bandage, used to check bleeding in an injured limb. [Fr.]

Tours (to͝or) A city of W-central France on the Loire R. Pop. 129,506.

tou•sle (tou′zəl) ►*v.* **-sled, -sling.** To disarrange or rumple; dishevel. [ME *touselen.*]

Tous•saint L'Ou•ver•ture (to͞o-săɴ′ lo͞o-vĕr-tür′), **François Dominique.** 1743?–1803. Haitian military and political leader.

tout (tout) ►*v.* **1.** To promote or publicize energetically. **2.** To deal in information on racehorses. ►*n.* One who touts. [ME *tuten,* peer at.] —**tout′er** *n.*

tow[1] (tō) ►*v.* To draw or pull behind by a chain or line. See Syns at **pull.** ►*n.* **1.** An act of towing. **2.** Something that tows or is towed. —***idiom:* in tow 1.** Following closely. **2.** Under one's charge. [< OE *togian.*] —**tow′age** *n.* —**tow′er** *n.*

tow[2] (tō) ►*n.* Coarse broken flax or hemp fiber prepared for spinning. [ME.]

to•ward (tôrd, tōrd, tə-wôrd′) ►*prep.* also **to•wards** (tôrdz, tōrdz, tə-wôrdz′) **1.** In the direction of. **2.** In a position facing. **3.** Somewhat before in time. **4.** With regard to. **5.** In partial fulfillment of: *a payment toward the house.* [< OE *tōweard.*]

tow•el (tou′əl) ►*n.* An absorbent cloth or paper used for wiping or drying. ►*v.* **-eled, -el•ing** or **-elled, -el•ling.** To wipe or dry with a towel. [< OFr. *toaille.*]

tow•er (tou′ər) ►*n.* **1.** A tall building or part of a building. **2.** A tall slender structure used for observation, signaling, or pumping. ►*v.* To rise to a conspicuous height. [< Lat. *turris.*]

tow•er•ing (tou′ər-ĭng) ►*adj.* **1.** Of imposing height. **2.** Outstanding; preeminent. **3.** Very great or intense. —**tow′er•ing•ly** *adv.*

tow•head (tō′hĕd′) ►*n.* A person with white-blond hair. —**tow′head′ed** *adj.*

tow•hee (tō′hē, tō-hē′) ►*n.* A North American bird with black, white, and rust-colored plumage in the male. [Imit.]

town (toun) ►*n.* **1.** A population center larger than a village and usu. smaller than a city. **2.** *Informal* A city. **3.** The commercial district of an area. [< OE *tūn,* village.]

town•house or **town house** (toun′hous′) ►*n.* A row house, esp. a fashionable one.

town meeting ►*n.* A legislative assembly of townspeople.

town•ship (toun′shĭp′) ►*n.* **1.** A subdivision of a county in most northeast and Midwest US states. **2.** A public land surveying unit of 36 square miles.

towns•peo•ple (tounz′pē′pəl) ►*pl.n.* The inhabitants or citizens of a town or city.

tow•path (tō′păth′) ►*n.* A path along a canal or river used by animals towing boats.

tox•e•mi•a (tŏk-sē′mē-ə) ►*n.* A condition in which toxins produced by body cells at a local source of infection are contained in the blood. —**tox•e′mic** *adj.*

toxi- or **tox-** ►*pref.* Poison: *toxemia.* [< Lat. *toxicum.*]

tox•ic (tŏk′sĭk) ►*adj.* **1.** Of or caused by a toxin or poison. **2.** Poisonous. ►*n.* A toxic chemical or other substance. —**tox′i•cal•ly** *adv.* —**tox•ic′i•ty** (-sĭs′ĭ-tē) *n.*

tox•i•col•o•gy (tŏk′sĭ-kŏl′ə-jē) ►*n.* The study of poisons and the treatment of poisoning. —**tox′i•co•log′i•cal** (-kə-lŏj′ĭ-kəl), **tox′i•co•log′ic** *adj.* —**tox′i•col′o•gist** *n.*

toxic shock syndrome ►*n.* An acute bacterial infection followed in severe cases by shock, occurring chiefly among women who use vaginal tampons.

tox•in (tŏk′sĭn) ►*n.* A poisonous substance, esp. a protein, produced by living cells or organisms and capable of causing disease when introduced into the body, but also capable of stimulating production of an antitoxin.

toy (toi) ►*n.* **1.** An object for children to play with. **2.** A trifle or bauble. **3.** A very small breed of dog. ►*v.* **1.** To amuse oneself idly. **2.** To treat something casually; flirt: *toyed with the idea.* See Syns at **flirt.** [ME *toye.*]

To•ya•ma (tō-yä′mä) A city of W-central Honshu, Japan, on **Toyama Bay,** an inlet of the Sea of Japan. Pop. 324,073.

Tpk. ►*abbr.* turnpike

TR or **T-R** ►*abbr.* transmit-receive

tr. ►*abbr.* **1.** transitive **2.** translated **3.** transpose **4a.** trust **b.** trustee

trace[1] (trās) ►*n.* **1.** A visible mark or sign of the former presence or passage of some person, thing, or event. **2.** A barely perceivable indication; touch. **3.** A minute amount. ►*v.* **traced, trac•ing 1.** To follow the course or trail of. **2.** To ascertain the successive stages in the development of. **3.** To locate or discover through inquiry. **4.** To draw (a line or figure). **5.** To form (letters) with special care. **6.** To copy by following lines seen through transparent paper. [< Lat. *trahere, tract-,* draw.] —**trace′a•bil′i•ty** *n.* —**trace′a•ble** *adj.* —**trac′er** *n.*

trace[2] (trās) ►*n.* One of two side straps or chains connecting a harnessed draft animal to a vehicle. [< OFr. *trait* < Lat. *trahere, tract-,* haul.]

tracer bullet ►*n.* A bullet that leaves a luminous or smoky trail.

trac•er•y (trā′sə-rē) ►*n., pl.* **-ies.** Ornamental work of interlaced and branching lines.

tra•che•a (trā′kē-ə) ►*n., pl.* **-che•ae** (-kē-ē′) or **-che•as.** A thin-walled tube of cartilaginous and membranous tissue descending from the larynx to the bronchi and carrying air to the lungs; windpipe. [< Gk. *(artēria) trakheia,* rough (artery).] —**tra′che•al** *adj.*

tra•che•ot•o•my (trā′kē-ŏt′ə-mē) ►*n., pl.* **-mies.** The surgical incision into the trachea through the neck.

track (trăk) ►*n.* **1.** A mark, such as a footprint, left in passing. **2.** A path or course; trail. **3a.** A course laid out for running or racing. **b.** Track and field. **4.** A rail or set of parallel rails upon which a train or trolley runs. **5.** A groove, ridge, or rail for a moving device or part. ►*v.* **1.** To follow the tracks of; trail. **2.** To locate by searching diligently: *track down a story.* **3.** To carry on the shoes and deposit: *tracked mud on the rug.* **4.** To observe or monitor, as by radar. —***idioms:* keep track of** To remain informed about. **lose track of** To fail to keep informed about. [< OFr. *trac.*] —**track′a•ble** *adj.* —**track′er** *n.* —**track′less** *adj.*

track and field ►*n.* Athletic events performed on a running track and the adjacent field. —**track′-and-field′** *adj.*

track•ball (trăk′bôl′) ►*n.* A ball mounted in a stationary housing and rotated to control a pointer on a computer screen.

track•ing (trăk′ĭng) ►*n.* The placing of students in a course of study according to ability, achievement, or needs.

tract[1] (trăkt) ►*n.* **1a.** An expanse of land. **b.** A specified area of land. **2.** *Anat.* A system of organs and tissues that together perform a specialized function. [< Lat. *tractus* < p.part. of *trahere*, draw.]

tract[2] (trăkt) ►*n.* A propaganda pamphlet, esp. one put out by a religious or political group. [< Lat. *tractātus*, something discussed.]

trac•ta•ble (trăk′tə-bəl) ►*adj.* **1.** Easily managed or controlled; governable. **2.** Easily worked, as metals; malleable. [< Lat. *tractāre*, manage.] —**trac′ta•bil′i•ty, trac′ta•ble•ness** *n.* —**trac′ta•bly** *adv.*

tract house ►*n.* One of numerous houses of similar or complementary design constructed on a tract of land. —**tract housing** *n.*

trac•tion (trăk′shən) ►*n.* **1.** The act of drawing or pulling or the condition of being drawn or pulled. **2.** Pulling power, as of an engine. **3.** Adhesive friction, as of a wheel on a road. [< Lat. *trahere*, *tract-*, pull.]

trac•tor (trăk′tər) ►*n.* **1.** An automotive vehicle designed for pulling machinery. **2.** A truck having a cab and no body, used for pulling large vehicles. [< Lat. *trahere*, *tract-*, pull.]

trac•tor-trail•er (trăk′tər-trā′lər) ►*n.* A truck consisting of a tractor attached to a semitrailer or trailer, used for transporting loads.

trade (trād) ►*n.* **1.** The business of buying and selling commodities; commerce. **2.** Customers; clientele. **3.** An exchange of one thing for another. **4.** An occupation, esp. one requiring skilled labor; craft. ►*v.* **trad•ed, trad•ing 1.** To engage in buying and selling. **2.** To exchange one thing for another. **3.** To shop regularly at a particular store. [< MLGer., track.] —**trad′er** *n.*

trade-in (trād′ĭn′) ►*n.* Merchandise accepted as partial payment for a new purchase.

trade•mark (trād′märk′) ►*n.* A name, symbol, or other device identifying a product, legally restricted to the use of the owner or manufacturer. ►*v.* **1.** To label (a product) with a trademark. **2.** To register (a name or device) as a trademark.

trade name ►*n.* **1.** A name used to identify a commercial product or service. **2.** The name under which a business firm operates.

trade•off or **trade-off** (trād′ôf′, -ŏf′) ►*n.* An exchange in which something desirable, as a benefit or advantage, is given up for another regarded as more desirable.

trades•man (trādz′mən) ►*n.* **1.** One engaged in retail trade. **2.** A skilled worker.

trade union ►*n.* A labor union. —**trade unionism** *n.* —**trade unionist** *n.*

trade wind (wĭnd) ►*n.* Any of a system of winds occupying most of the tropics, blowing northeasterly in the Northern Hemisphere and southeasterly in the Southern Hemisphere.

trad•ing post (trā′dĭng) ►*n.* A store in a sparsely settled area offering supplies in exchange for local products.

tra•di•tion (trə-dĭsh′ən) ►*n.* **1.** The passing down of a culture from generation to generation, esp. orally. **2a.** A custom handed down. **b.** A set of such customs viewed as a coherent body of precedents influencing the present. See Syns at **heritage.** [< Lat. *trādere*, hand over : TRANS– + *dare*, give.] —**tra•di′tion•al** *adj.* —**tra•di′tion•al•ist** *adj. & n.* —**tra•di′tion•al•ly** *adv.*

tra•duce (trə-dōōs′, -dyōōs′) ►*v.* **-duced, -duc•ing.** To slander; defame. [Lat. *trādūcere.*] —**tra•duce′ment** *n.*

Tra•fal•gar (trə-făl′gər), **Cape.** A cape on the SW coast of Spain NW of the Strait of Gibraltar.

traf•fic (trăf′ĭk) ►*n.* **1.** The commercial exchange of goods; trade. **2a.** The passage of persons, vehicles, or messages through routes of transportation or communication. **b.** The amount, as of vehicles, in transit. **3.** Dealings; communication. ►*v.* **-ficked, -fick•ing.** To carry on trade; deal in. [< OItal. *trafficare*, trade.] —**traf′fick•er** *n.*

traffic circle ►*n.* A circular one-way road at a junction of thoroughfares, facilitating an uninterrupted flow of traffic.

traffic light ►*n.* A road signal for directing vehicular traffic by means of colored lights.

trag•e•dy (trăj′ĭ-dē) ►*n.*, *pl.* **-dies 1.** A drama or literary work in which the main character is brought to ruin or suffers extreme sorrow. **2.** A disastrous event. [< Gk. *tragōidia.*] —**tra•ge′di•an** (trə-jē′dē-ən) *n.* —**tra•ge′di•enne′** (-ĕn′) *n.*

trag•ic (trăj′ĭk) ►*adj.* **1.** Of or having the nature of tragedy. **2.** Writing or performing in tragedy. **3.** Calamitous; disastrous. [< Gk. *tragikos.*] —**trag′i•cal•ly** *adv.*

trag•i•com•e•dy (trăj′ĭ-kŏm′ĭ-dē) ►*n.*, *pl.* **-dies.** A drama combining elements of tragedy and comedy. —**trag′i•com′ic** (-kŏm′ĭk), **trag′i•com′i•cal** *adj.*

trail (trāl) ►*v.* **1.** To drag or allow to drag or stream behind, as along the ground. **2.** To follow the traces or scent of; track. **3.** To lag behind (an opponent). **4.** To extend or grow along the ground or over a surface. **5.** To drift in a thin stream. **6.** To become gradually fainter: *Her voice trailed off.* ►*n.* **1.** Something that hangs loose and long. **2.** Something that follows behind. **3.** A mark or trace left by a moving body. **4.** A marked or beaten path. [ME *trailen.*]

trail bike ►*n.* A small motorcycle designed for off-road riding.

trail•blaz•er (trāl′blā′zər) ►*n.* **1.** One who blazes a trail. **2.** An innovative leader in a field; pioneer. —**trail′blaz′ing** *adj.*

trail•er (trā′lər) ►*n.* **1.** A large transport vehicle hauled by a truck or tractor. **2.** A van drawn by a truck or automobile and used as a dwelling or office.

trailer park ►*n.* An area in which parking space for house trailers is rented.

trail•ing arbutus (trā′lĭng) ►*n.* A low-growing evergreen shrub of E North America.

train (trān) ►*n.* **1.** A series of connected railroad cars. **2.** A long line of moving people, animals, or vehicles. **3.** A part of a gown that trails behind the wearer. **4.** A staff of people following in attendance. **5.** An orderly succession of related events or thoughts. ►*v.* **1.** To coach in or accustom to a mode of behavior or performance. **2.** To make or become proficient with specialized instruction and practice. **3.** To prepare physically, as with a regimen. **4.** To cause (e.g., a plant) to take a desired course or shape. **5.** To focus; aim. See Syns at **aim.** [< OFr. *trainer*, drag.] —**train′a•ble** *adj.* —**train•ee′** *n.* —**train′er** *n.* —**train′ing** *n.*

traipse (trāps) ►*v.* **traipsed, traips•ing.** To walk or tramp about. [Poss. < OFr. *trapasser*, trespass.]

trait (trāt) ►*n.* **1.** A distinguishing feature, as of character. **2.** A genetically determined characteristic or condition. [< Lat. *tractus*, something drawn.]

trai•tor (trā′tər) ►*n.* One who betrays one's country, a cause, or a trust, esp. one who commits treason. [< Lat. *trāditor* < *trādere*, hand over. See TRADITION.] —**trai′tor•ous** *adj.*

Tra•jan (trā′jən). A.D. 53–117. Roman emperor (98–117).

tra•jec•to•ry (trə-jĕk′tə-rē) ►*n.*, *pl.* **-ries.** The path of a projectile or other moving body through space. [< Lat. *trāicere*, *trāiect-*, throw across.]

tram (trăm) ►*n.* **1.** *Chiefly Brit.* A streetcar. **2.** A cable car, esp. one suspended from an overhead cable. **3.** An open wagon run on tracks in a coal mine. [Sc., shaft of a barrow.]

tram•mel (trăm′əl) ►*n.* **1.** A shackle used in teaching horses. **2.** A hindrance or restraint. ►*v.* **-meled, -mel•ing** or **-melled, -mel•ling 1.** To trap or enmesh. See Syns at **hamper**[1]. **2.** To hinder. [< LLat. *trēmaculum*, a kind of net.] —**tram′mel•er** *n.*

tramp (trămp) ►*v.* **1.** To walk with a firm heavy step. **2.** To travel on foot; hike. **3.** To tread down; trample. ►*n.* **1.** The sound of heavy walking or marching. **2.** A walking trip. **3.** One who travels aimlessly about; vagrant. **4.** A prostitute. **5.** A cargo vessel that has no regular schedule but takes on freight whenever it can. [< MLGer. *trampen*.] —**tramp′er** *n.*

tram•ple (trăm′pəl) ►*v.* **-pled, -pling 1.** To beat down with the feet so as to injure or destroy. **2.** To treat harshly or ruthlessly. [ME *tramplen*.] —**tram′ple** *n.*

tram•po•line (trăm′pə-lēn′, -lĭn) ►*n.* A sheet of strong canvas attached with springs to a metal frame and used for gymnastic springing and tumbling. [Ital. *trampolino*.] —**tram′po•lin′er, tram′po•lin′ist** *n.*

trance (trăns) ►*n.* **1.** A hypnotic, cataleptic, or ecstatic state. **2.** Detachment from one's physical surroundings, as in contemplation or daydreaming. **3.** A dazed state. [< Lat. *trānsīre*, go across.]

tran•quil (trăng′kwəl, trăn′-) ►*adj.* Free from agitation; calm. [< Lat. *tranquillus*.] —**tran•quil′li•ty, tran•quil′i•ty** *n.* —**tran′quil•ly** *adv.*

tran•quil•ize also **tran•quil•lize** (trăng′kwə-līz′, trăn′-) ►*v.* **-ized, -iz•ing** also **-lized, -liz•ing 1.** To make or become tranquil. **2.** To sedate. —**tran′quil•i•za′tion** *n.*

tran•quil•iz•er (trăng′kwə-līz′ər, trăn′-) ►*n.* A tranquilizing or depressant drug.

trans. ►*abbr.* **1.** transaction **2.** transitive **3.** translation **4.** transportation **5.** transpose

trans– ►*pref.* **1.** Across; beyond: *transatlantic.* **2.** Change; transfer: *transliterate.* [< Lat. *trāns*, over, across.]

trans•act (trăn-săkt′, -zăkt′) ►*v.* To carry out or conduct (business or affairs). [Lat. *trānsigere*, *trānsāct-* : *trāns-*, over + *agere*, make.] —**trans•ac′tor** *n.*

trans•ac•tion (trăn-săk′shən, -zăk′-) ►*n.* **1.** The act or process of transacting. **2.** Something transacted. —**trans•ac′tion•al** *adj.*

Trans•al•pine Gaul (trăns-ăl′pīn′, trănz-) The part of ancient Gaul NW of the Alps, including modern France and Belgium.

trans•at•lan•tic (trăns′ət-lăn′tĭk, trănz′-) ►*adj.* **1.** On the other side of the Atlantic. **2.** Spanning or crossing the Atlantic.

trans•ax•le (trăns-ăk′səl, trănz-) ►*n.* An automotive part that combines the transmission and the differential, used on vehicles with front-wheel drive. [TRANS(MISSION) + AXLE.]

Trans•cau•ca•sia (trăns′kô-kā′zhə, -zhē-ə, trănz′-) A region of Georgia, Armenia, and Azerbaijan between the Caucasus Mts. and the borders of Turkey and Iran. —**Trans′cau•ca′sian** *adj. & n.*

tran•scend (trăn-sĕnd′) ►*v.* **1.** To go beyond; exceed. **2.** To surpass. **3.** To exist above and independent of. [< Lat. *trānscendere*.] —**tran•scen′dence** *n.* —**tran•scen′dent** *adj.*

tran•scen•den•tal (trăn′sĕn-dĕn′tl) ►*adj.* **1.** Rising above common thought or ideas; exalted; mystical. **2.** *Math.* Of or relating to a real or complex number that is not the root of any polynomial that has positive degree and rational coefficients. —**tran′scen•den′tal•ly** *adv.*

tran•scen•den•tal•ism (trăn′sĕn-dĕn′tl-ĭz′əm) ►*n.* A belief or doctrine asserting the existence of an ideal spiritual reality that transcends the empirical and scientific and is knowable through intuition. —**tran′scen•den′tal•ist** *n.*

trans•con•ti•nen•tal (trăns′kŏn-tə-nĕn′tl) ►*adj.* Spanning or crossing a continent.

tran•scribe (trăn-skrīb′) ►*v.* **-scribed, -scrib•ing 1.** To write or type a copy of. **2.** To write out fully, as from notes. **3.** To adapt or arrange (a musical composition). **4.** To record for broadcast at a later date. [Lat. *trānscrībere*.] —**tran•scrib′er** *n.*

tran•script (trăn′skrĭpt′) ►*n.* Something transcribed; a written or printed copy. [< Lat. *trānscrīptum*.]

tran•scrip•tion (trăn-skrĭp′shən) ►*n.* **1.** The act or process of transcribing. **2.** Something transcribed, esp.: **a.** An adaptation of a musical composition. **b.** A recorded radio or television program.

trans•duc•er (trăns-do͞o′sər, -dyo͞o′-, trănz-) ►*n.* A substance or device, such as a microphone, that converts input energy of one form into output energy of another. [< Lat. *trānsdūcere*, transfer.]

tran•sept (trăn′sĕpt′) ►*n.* Either of the two lateral arms crossing the nave of a cruciform church. [TRANS– + Lat. *saeptum*, partition.]

trans fatty acid (trăns) ►*n.* An unsaturated fatty acid produced by the partial hydrogenation of vegetable oils. [< *trans-*, pref. indicating chemical structure.]

trans•fer (trăns-fûr′, trăns′fər) ►*v.* **-ferred, -fer•ring 1.** To convey, shift, or change from one place, person, or thing to another. **2.** *Law* To make over the possession or legal title of. **3.** To convey (e.g., a design) from one surface to another. **4.** To change from one public conveyance to another. ►*n.* (trăns′fər) **1.** also **trans•fer•al** (trăns-fûr′əl) The conveyance of something from one place or person to another. **2.** One who transfers or is transferred. **3.** A design conveyed by contact from one surface to another. **4.** A ticket entitling a passenger to change from one public conveyance to another. **5.** also **transferal** *Law* A conveyance of title or property from one person to another. [< Lat. *trānsferre* : TRANS– + *ferre*, carry.] —**trans•fer′a•ble, trans•fer′ra•ble** *adj.* —**trans•fer′ence** *n.* —**trans•fer′rer** *n.*

trans•fig•ure (trăns-fĭg′yər) ►*v.* **-ured, -ur•ing 1.** To alter the outward appearance of; transform. See Syns at **convert. 2.** To exalt or glorify. [< Lat. *trānsfigūrāre.*] —**trans•fig′u•ra′tion** *n.*

trans•fix (trăns-fĭks′) ►*v.* **1.** To pierce with or as with a pointed weapon; impale. **2.** To render motionless, as with terror. [Lat. *trānsfīgere, trānsfīx-*.] —**trans•fix′ion** *n.*

trans•form (trăns-fôrm′) ►*v.* **1.** To change markedly in appearance or form. **2.** To change in nature or condition. See Syns at **convert.** [< Lat. *trānsfōrmāre.*] —**trans•form′a•ble** *adj.* —**trans′for•ma′tion** *n.*

trans•form•er (trăns-fôr′mər) ►*n.* A device used to transfer electric energy from one circuit to another.

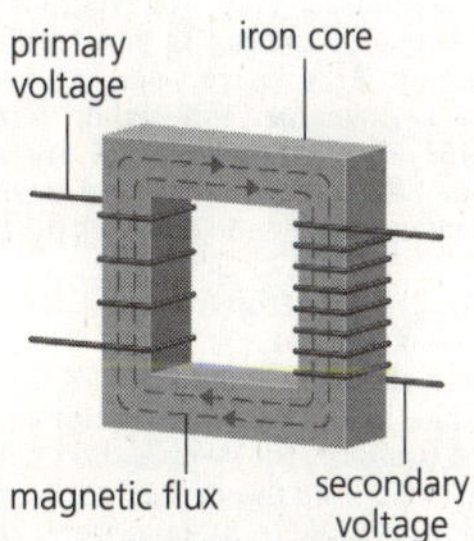

transformer
iron core transformer

trans•fuse (trăns-fyo͞oz′) ►*v.* **-fused, -fus•ing 1.** To transfer (liquid) from one vessel into another. **2.** To permeate; instill. **3.** To administer a transfusion of or to. [< Lat. *trānsfundere, trānsfūs-*, pour out.] —**trans•fus′er** *n.*

trans•fu•sion (trăns-fyo͞o′zhən) ►*n.* **1.** The act or process of transfusing. **2.** The transfer of whole blood or blood products from one individual to another.

trans•gen•dered (trăns-jĕn′dərd, trănz-) ►*adj.* Appearing as or having undergone surgery to become a member of the opposite sex.

trans•gress (trăns-grĕs′, trănz-) ►*v.* **1.** To go beyond or over (a limit). **2.** To act in violation of (a law or commandment). [< Lat. *trānsgredī, trānsgress-*, step across.] —**trans•gres′sion** *n.* —**trans•gres′sor** *n.*

tran•ship (trăn-shĭp′) ►*v.* Var. of **transship.**

tran•si•ent (trăn′zē-ənt, -zhənt, -shənt) ►*adj.* **1.** Passing with time; transitory. **2.** Remaining in a place only a brief time. ►*n.* One that is transient, esp. a person staying a single night at a hotel. [< Lat. *trānsīre*, go over.] —**tran′si•ence, tran′si•en•cy** *n.* —**tran′si•ent•ly** *adv.*

tran•sis•tor (trăn-zĭs′tər, -sĭs′-) ►*n.* **1.** A semiconductor device with at least three terminals, used in a circuit as an amplifier, detector, or switch. **2.** A small portable radio using transistors. [TRANS(FER) + (RES)ISTOR.] —**tran•sis′tor•ize′** *v.*

tran•sit (trăn′sĭt, -zĭt) ►*n.* **1.** The act of passing over, across, or through; passage. **2.** Conveyance of people or goods from one place to another, esp. on a local public transportation system. **3.** A surveying instrument that measures angles. [< Lat. *trānsitus.*]

tran•si•tion (trăn-zĭsh′ən, -sĭsh′-) ►*n.* Passage from one form, state, style, or place to another. —**tran•si′tion•al, tran•si′tion•ar′y** *adj.* —**tran•si′tion•al•ly** *adv.*

tran•si•tive (trăn′sĭ-tĭv, -zĭ-) ►*adj.* Being or using a verb that requires a direct object to complete its meaning. —**tran′si•tive•ly** *adv.* —**tran′si•tive•ness, tran′si•tiv′i•ty** *n.*

tran•si•to•ry (trăn′sĭ-tôr′ē, -tōr′ē, trăn′zĭ-) ►*adj.* Existing only briefly. —**tran′si•to′ri•ly** *adv.* —**tran′si•to′ri•ness** *n.*

trans•late (trăns′lāt′, trănz′-, trăns-lāt′, trănz-) ►*v.* **-lat•ed, -lat•ing 1.** To render in another language. **2.** To put into simpler terms; explain or interpret. **3.** To convey from one form or style to another. **4.** *Phys.* To move from one place to another without rotation. [< Lat. *trānslātus*, p.part. of *trānsferre*, transfer.] —**trans•lat′a•bil′i•ty, trans•lat′a•ble•ness** *n.* —**trans•lat′a•ble** *adj.* —**trans•la′tion** *n.* —**trans′la′tor** *n.*

trans•lit•er•ate (trăns-lĭt′ə-rāt′, trănz-) ►*v.* **-at•ed, -at•ing.** To represent (letters or words) in the corresponding characters of another alphabet. [TRANS– + Lat. *littera*, letter + -ATE[1].] —**trans•lit′er•a′tion** *n.*

trans•lu•cent (trăns-lo͞o′sənt, trănz-) ►*adj.* Transmitting light but diffusing it sufficiently to cause images to be blurred. [< Lat. *trānslūcēre*, shine through.] —**trans•lu′cence, trans•lu′cen•cy** *n.*

trans•mi•grate (trăns-mī′grāt′, trănz-) ►*v.* **-grat•ed, -grat•ing.** To pass into another body after death. Used of the soul. [Lat. *trānsmigrāre.*] —**trans′mi•gra′tion** *n.* —**trans•mi′gra′tor** *n.* —**trans•mi′gra•to′ry** (-grə-tôr′ē, -tōr′ē) *adj.*

trans•mis•sion (trăns-mĭsh′ən, trănz-) ►*n.* **1.** The act or process of transmitting. **2.** Something transmitted. **3.** An automotive assembly of gears that links an engine to a driving axle. **4.** The sending of a signal from a transmitter. —**trans•mis′sive** (-mĭs′ĭv) *adj.*

trans•mit (trăns-mĭt′, trănz-) ►*v.* **-mit•ted, -mit•ting 1.** To send from one person, thing, or place to another. See Syns at **send. 2.** To cause to spread, as an infection. **3.** To impart by heredity. **4.** To send (a signal), as by radio. **5.**

To convey (e.g., force) from one part of a mechanism to another. [< Lat. *trānsmittere*.] —**trans•mis′si•ble, trans•mit′ta•ble** *adj.* —**trans•mit′tal** *n.*

trans•mit•ter (trăns-mĭt′ər, trănz-) ▶*n.* **1.** One that transmits. **2.** Any of various electrical devices used to originate signals, as in radio or telegraphy.

trans•mog•ri•fy (trăns-mŏg′rə-fī′, trănz-) ▶*v.* **-fied** (-fīd′), **-fy•ing.** To change into a different shape or form, esp. one that is fantastic or bizarre. See Syns at **convert.** [?]

trans•mute (trăns-myōōt′, trănz-) ▶*v.* **-mut•ed, -mut•ing 1.** To change from one form, nature, substance, or state into another; transform. See Syns at **convert. 2.** To transfer (an element) into another by nuclear reactions. [< Lat. *trānsmūtāre*.] —**trans•mut′a•bil′i•ty** *n.* —**trans•mut′a•ble** *adj.* —**trans•mut′a•bly** *adv.* —**trans′mu•ta′tion** *n.*

trans•na•tion•al (trăns-năsh′ə-nəl, trănz-) ▶*adj.* **1.** Reaching beyond national boundaries. **2.** Of or involving several nations or nationalities.

trans•o•ce•an•ic (trăns′ō-shē-ăn′ĭk, trănz′-) ▶*adj.* **1.** Situated beyond the ocean. **2.** Spanning or crossing the ocean.

tran•som (trăn′səm) ▶*n.* **1.** A small hinged window above a door. **2.** A horizontal crosspiece over a door or in a window. [Prob. < Lat. *trānstrum*, cross-beam.]

trans•pa•cif•ic (trăns′pə-sĭf′ĭk, trănz′-) ▶*adj.* **1.** Situated on the other side of the Pacific Ocean. **2.** Crossing the Pacific Ocean.

trans•par•ent (trăns-pâr′ənt, -păr′-) ▶*adj.* **1.** Capable of transmitting light so that objects on the other side can be seen clearly. See Syns at **clear. 2.** So fine in texture that it can be seen through; sheer. **3a.** Easily detected; obvious: *transparent lies.* **b.** Free from guile; candid or open. [< Med.Lat. *trānspārēre*, show through.] —**trans•par′en•cy** *n.* —**trans•par′ent•ly** *adv.*

tran•spire (trăn-spīr′) ▶*v.* **-spired, -spir•ing 1.** *Biol.* To give off (vapor containing waste products) through pores or stomata. **2.** To become known. **3.** *Informal* To happen; occur. [< Med.Lat. *trānspīrāre*.] —**tran′spi•ra′tion** (-spə-rā′shən) *n.*

trans•plant (trăns-plănt′) ▶*v.* **1.** To uproot and replant (a growing plant). **2.** To transfer from one place or residence to another. **3.** *Medic.* To transfer (tissue or an organ) from one body or body part to another. —**trans′plant′** *n.* —**trans′plan•ta′tion** *n.*

trans•port (trăns-pôrt′, -pōrt′) ▶*v.* **1.** To carry from one place to another. **2.** To move to strong emotion; enrapture. See Syns at **enrapture. 3.** To send abroad to a penal colony. ▶*n.* (trăns′-pôrt′, -pōrt′) **1.** The act of transporting; conveyance. **2.** Rapture. **3.** A ship or aircraft used to transport troops or military equipment. **4.** A vehicle, as an aircraft, used to transport passengers or freight. [< Lat. *trānsportāre*.] —**trans•port′a•bil′i•ty** *n.* —**trans•port′a•ble** *adj.* —**trans′por•ta′tion** *n.* —**trans•port′er** *n.*

trans•pose (trăns-pōz′) ▶*v.* **-posed, -pos•ing 1.** To reverse or change the order or place of. **2.** *Mus.* To write or perform (a composition) in a key other than the original. [< Lat. *trānspōnere*.] —**trans•pos′er** *n.* —**trans′po•si′tion** (-pə-zĭsh′ən) *n.*

trans•sex•u•al (trăns-sĕk′shōō-əl) ▶*n.* **1.** One whose primary sexual identification is with the opposite sex. **2.** One who has undergone a sex change. —**trans•sex′u•al** *adj.* —**trans•sex′u•al•ism, trans•sex′u•al′i•ty** *n.*

trans•ship (trăns-shĭp′) also **tran•ship** (trăn-shĭp′) ▶*v.* To transfer (cargo) from one conveyance to another for reshipment. —**trans•ship′ment** *n.*

tran•sub•stan•ti•ate (trăn′səb-stăn′shē-āt′) ▶*v.* **-at•ed, -at•ing 1.** To change (one substance) into another; transmute. **2.** *Christianity* To change the substance of (the Eucharistic bread and wine) into the body and blood of Jesus. [Med.Lat. *trānsubstantiāre*.] —**tran′sub•stan′ti•a′tion** *n.*

trans•u•ran•ic (trăns′yōō-răn′ĭk, -rā′nĭk, trănz′-) also **trans•u•ra•ni•um** (-rā′nē-əm) ▶*adj.* Having an atomic number greater than 92. [< TRANS– + URAN(IUM).]

Trans•vaal (trăns-väl′, trănz-) A region of NE South Africa.

trans•ver•sal (trăns-vûr′səl, trănz-) ▶*adj.* Transverse. ▶*n.* *Math.* A line that intersects a system of other lines.

trans•verse (trăns-vûrs′, trănz-, trăns′vûrs′, trănz′-) ▶*adj.* Situated or lying across; crosswise. [< Lat. *trānsvertere*, turn across.] —**trans•verse′** *n.* —**trans•verse′ly** *adv.*

trans•ves•tite (trăns-vĕs′tīt′, trănz-) ▶*n.* A person who dresses and acts in a style or manner of the opposite sex. [TRANS– + Lat. *vestīre*, dress.] —**trans•ves′tism** *n.*

Tran•syl•va•nia (trăn′sĭl-vān′yə, -vā′nē-ə) A historical region of W Romania bounded by the Transylvanian Alps and the Carpathian Mts. —**Tran′syl•va′ni•an** *adj. & n.*

Transylvanian Alps. A range of the S Carpathian Mts. across central Romania.

trap (trăp) ▶*n.* **1.** A device for catching and holding animals. **2.** Any stratagem for betraying, tricking, or exposing an unsuspecting person or group. **3.** A device, such as a U-shaped bend in a drainpipe, for sealing a passage against the escape of foul gases. **4.** A sand trap. **5. traps** *Mus.* Percussion instruments. **6.** *Slang* The human mouth. ▶*v.* **trapped, trap•ping 1.** To catch in or as if in a trap. See Syns at **catch. 2.** To trap furbearing animals. [< OE *træppe*.] —**trap′per** *n.*

trap•door (trăp′dôr′, -dōr′) ▶*n.* A hinged or sliding door in a floor, roof, or ceiling.

tra•peze (tră-pēz′, trə-) ▶*n.* A short horizontal bar suspended from two parallel ropes, used for acrobatics. [< LLat. *trapezium*, TRAPEZOID.]

trap•e•zoid (trăp′ĭ-zoid′) ▶*n.* A quadrilateral with two parallel sides. [< Gk. *trapeza*, table (*tra-*, four + *peza*, foot) + –OID.] —**trap′e•zoi′dal** *adj.*

trap•pings (trăp′ĭngz) ▶*pl.n.* **1.** An ornamental covering for a horse. **2a.** Articles of dress or adornment. **b.** Outward signs; appearance. [< ME *trap*.]

trap•shoot•ing (trăp′shōō′tĭng) ▶*n.* *Sports* Shooting at clay pigeons hurled into the air.

trash (trăsh) ▶*n.* **1.** Discarded material; refuse. **2.** Literary or artistic matter of little merit. **3.** A person or group held in contempt. ▶*v.* *Slang* **1.** To discard. **2.** To wreck or destroy, as by vandalism. [Prob. of Scand. orig.] —**trash′y** *adj.*

trau•ma (trô′mə, trou′-) ▶*n.*, *pl.* **-mas 1.** A serious injury or shock to the body. **2.** An emotional shock that causes lasting psychological damage. [Gk.] —**trau•mat′ic** (-măt′ĭk) *adj.* —**trau′ma•tize′** *v.*

tra•vail (trə-vāl′, trăv′āl′) ►*n.* **1.** Strenuous work; toil. **2.** Tribulation or agony; anguish. **3.** The labor of childbirth. [< LLat. *tripālium,* instrument of torture.] —**tra•vail′** *v.*

trav•el (trăv′əl) ►*v.* **-eled, -el•ing** or **-elled, -el•ling 1.** To go from one place to another; journey. **2.** To be transmitted, as light or sound. **3.** To advance or proceed. **4.** To associate. **5.** To move swiftly. ►*n.* **1.** The act of traveling. **2.** **travels** A series of journeys. [< OFr. *travailler,* to toil.] —**trav′el•er, trav′el•ler** *n.*

trav•e•logue also **trav•e•log** (trăv′ə-lôg′, -lŏg′) ►*n.* A film or illustrated lecture on travel.

tra•verse (trə-vûrs′, trăv′ərs) ►*v.* **-versed, -vers•ing 1.** To travel or pass across, over, or through. **2.** To move to and fro over. **3.** To cross (a slope) diagonally, as in skiing. **4.** To swivel (e.g., a mounted gun) laterally on a pivot. **5.** To extend across. ►*n.* **trav•erse** (trăv′ərs, trə-vûrs′) **1.** The act of traversing. **2.** Something, such as a beam, lying crosswise. ►*adj.* **trav•erse** (trăv′ərs, trə-vûrs′). Transverse. [< OFr. *traverser* < Lat. *trānsversus,* TRANSVERSE.] —**tra•vers′a•ble** *adj.* —**tra•vers′al** *n.* —**tra•vers′er** *n.*

trav•er•tine (trăv′ər-tēn′, -tĭn) ►*n.* A porous calcite deposited from solution in ground or surface waters. [< Lat. *(lapis) tīburtīnus,* (stone) of Tibur (Tivoli), Italy.]

trav•es•ty (trăv′ĭ-stē) ►*n., pl.* **-ties.** A grotesque imitation or likeness. [< Ital. *travestire,* to disguise, parody.] —**trav′es•ty** *v.*

trawl (trôl) ►*n.* A large tapered fishing net that is towed along the sea bottom. ►*v.* To fish with a trawl. [ME *trawelle.*]

trawl•er (trô′lər) ►*n.* A boat equipped for trawling.

tray (trā) ►*n.* A shallow flat receptacle with a raised edge, used for carrying, holding, or displaying articles. [< OE *trēg.*]

treach•er•ous (trĕch′ər-əs) ►*adj.* **1.** Betraying a trust or confidence; traitorous. **2.** Unreliable. **3.** Marked by unforeseen hazards; dangerous or deceptive: *treacherous waters.* —**treach′er•ous•ly** *adv.* —**treach′er•ous•ness** *n.*

treach•er•y (trĕch′ə-rē) ►*n., pl.* **-ies.** Willful betrayal of trust; perfidy. [< OFr. *trichier,* to trick.]

trea•cle (trē′kəl) ►*n.* **1.** Cloying speech or sentiment. **2.** *Chiefly Brit.* Molasses. [< Gk. *thēriakē (antidotos),* (antidote against) wild animals.] —**trea′cly** (-klē) *adj.*

tread (trĕd) ►*v.* **trod** (trŏd), **trod•den** (trŏd′n) or **trod, tread•ing 1.** To walk on, over, or along. **2.** To press beneath the feet; trample. **3.** To walk or dance: *tread a measure.* ►*n.* **1.** The act, manner, or sound of treading. **2.** The horizontal part of a step in a staircase. **3.** The grooved face of a tire. **4.** The part of a shoe sole that touches the ground. [< OE *tredan.*] —**tread′er** *n.*

tread•le (trĕd′l) ►*n.* A pedal operated by the foot to drive a wheel, as in a sewing machine. [< OE *tredel,* step of a stair.] —**tread′le** *v.*

tread•mill (trĕd′mĭl′) ►*n.* **1.** A device operated by walking on an endless belt or on a set of moving steps attached to a wheel. **2.** A monotonous routine.

trea•son (trē′zən) ►*n.* The betrayal of one's country, esp. by aiding an enemy. [< Lat. *trāditiō,* a handing over. See TRADITION.] —**trea′son•a•ble** *adj.* —**trea′son•ous** *adj.*

treas•ure (trĕzh′ər) ►*n.* **1.** Accumulated or stored wealth in the form of money, jewels, or other valuables. **2.** One considered esp. precious or valuable. ►*v.* **-ured, -ur•ing 1.** To value highly. **2.** To store away; hoard. [< Gk. *thēsauros.*] —**treas′ur•a•ble** *adj.*

treas•ur•er (trĕzh′ər-ər) ►*n.* One in charge of funds or revenues, as of a government, corporation, or club.

treas•ure-trove (trĕzh′ər-trōv′) ►*n.* **1.** Treasure found hidden. **2.** A discovery of great value. [AN *tresor trove,* found treasure.]

treas•ur•y (trĕzh′ə-rē) ►*n., pl.* **-ies 1.** A place where treasure is kept. **2.** A place where funds are received, kept, managed, and disbursed. **3.** Such funds or revenues. **4.** **Treasury** A governmental department in charge of the public revenue.

treat (trēt) ►*v.* **1.** To act or behave toward: *treated me fairly.* **2.** To regard and handle in a certain way: *treated the matter as a joke.* **3.** To deal with, handle, or cover. **4.** To provide with food, entertainment, or gifts at one's own expense. **5.** To subject to a process. **6.** To give medical aid to (someone). ►*n.* **1.** Something paid for by someone else. **2.** A special delight or pleasure. [< Lat. *tractāre.*] —**treat′a•ble** *adj.*

Syns: *treat, deal, handle* **v.**

trea•tise (trē′tĭs) ►*n.* A systematic, usu. extensive written discourse on a subject. [< VLat. **tractātīcius,* TRACT[1].]

treat•ment (trēt′mənt) ►*n.* **1.** The act or manner of handling or dealing with someone or something. **2.** The application of remedies to relieve or cure a disease or disorder.

trea•ty (trē′tē) ►*n., pl.* **-ties.** A formal agreement between two or more states. [< Lat. *tractātus,* discussion.]

treb•le (trĕb′əl) ►*adj.* **1.** Triple. **2.** *Mus.* Of or having the highest part, voice, or range. **3.** High-pitched; shrill. ►*n.* **1.** *Mus.* The highest part, voice, instrument, or range. **2.** A high shrill sound or voice. ►*v.* **-led, -ling.** To triple. [< Lat. *triplus.*] —**treb′ly** *adv.*

treble clef ►*n. Mus.* A symbol centered on the second line from the bottom of a staff to indicate G above middle C.

tree (trē) ►*n.* **1.** A perennial woody plant with a main trunk and usu. a distinct crown. **2.** Something resembling a tree: *a clothes tree.* **3.** A diagram showing family lineage. ►*v.* To chase and force up a tree. [< OE *trēow.*] —**tree′less** *adj.*

tree frog ►*n.* A small arboreal frog with long toes terminating in adhesive disks.

tree line ►*n.* **1.** The limit of northern or southern latitude beyond which trees will not grow. **2.** See **timberline.**

tree-of-heav•en (trē′əv-hĕv′ən) ►*n.* A deciduous, rapidly growing tree widely planted as a street tree.

tre•foil (trē′foil′, trĕf′oil′) ►*n.* **1.** A plant, such as a clover, having compound leaves with three leaflets. **2.** An ornament resembling such a leaf. [< Lat. *trifolium.*]

trek (trĕk) ►*v.* **trekked, trek•king.** To make a long difficult journey, esp. through mountains. [Afr., travel by ox wagon < MDu. *trecken,* pull.] —**trek** *n.* —**trek′ker** *n.*

trel•lis (trĕl′ĭs) ► *n.* An open latticework used for training climbing plants. [< Lat. *trilīx*, woven with three threads.] —**trel′lised** *adj.*

trem•a•tode (trĕm′ə-tōd′) ► *n.* Any of numerous parasitic flatworms having external suckers or hooks. [< Gk. *trēmatōdē*, having holes.]

trem•ble (trĕm′bəl) ► *v.* **-bled, -bling 1.** To shake involuntarily, as from excitement, fear, or frailty; quake. **2.** To feel or express fear or anxiety. [< VLat. **tremulāre*.] —**trem′ble** *n.* —**trem′bler** *n.*

tre•men•dous (trĭ-mĕn′dəs) ► *adj.* **1a.** Extremely large; enormous. **b.** *Informal* Marvelous; wonderful. **2.** Capable of making one tremble; awesome or terrible. [< Lat. *tremendus*, terrible.] —**tre•men′dous•ly** *adv.*

trem•o•lo (trĕm′ə-lō′) ► *n., pl.* **-los** *Mus.* A tremulous effect produced either by the rapid repetition of a single tone or by the rapid alternation of two tones. [Ital.]

trem•or (trĕm′ər) ► *n.* **1.** A shaking or vibrating movement, as of the earth. **2.** An involuntary trembling or quivering, as from nervous agitation or disease. [< Lat.]

trem•u•lous (trĕm′yə-ləs) ► *adj.* **1.** Vibrating or quivering; trembling. **2.** Timid; fearful. [< Lat. *tremulus* < *tremere*, tremble.] —**trem′u•lous•ly** *adv.*

trench (trĕnch) ► *n.* **1.** A deep furrow. **2.** A ditch embanked with its own soil and used for concealment and protection in warfare. **3.** A steep-sided valley on the ocean floor. ► *v.* **1.** To cut a trench in. **2.** To fortify with trenches. [< OFr. *trenchier*, cut.]

trench•ant (trĕn′chənt) ► *adj.* **1.** Keen; incisive: *a trenchant argument.* **2.** Caustic; cutting. [< OFr. *trenchier*, cut.] —**trench′an•cy** *n.*

trench coat ► *n.* A belted raincoat with straps on the shoulders and deep pockets.

trench•er (trĕn′chər) ► *n.* A wooden serving board. [< AN *trencher*, cut.]

trench fever ► *n.* An acute infectious disease caused by a microorganism and transmitted by a louse.

trench foot ► *n.* A foot disorder resembling frostbite, often affecting soldiers who must stand in cold flooded trenches.

trench mouth ► *n.* A painful bacterial infection of the mouth and throat.

trend (trĕnd) ► *n.* **1.** A general direction of movement. **2.** A general tendency or inclination. **3.** Current style; vogue: *the latest trend in fashion.* ► *v.* To have a certain direction or tendency. [< OE *trendan*, revolve.]

trend•y (trĕn′dē) ► *adj.* **-i•er, -i•est** *Informal* In accord with the latest fashion. See Syns at **fashionable.** —**trend′i•ly** *adv.* —**trend′i•ness** *n.*

Tren•ton (trĕn′tən) The capital of New Jersey, in the W-central part on the Delaware R. Pop. 88,675.

tre•pan (trĭ-păn′) ► *n.* A trephine. ► *v.* **-panned, -pan•ning.** To trephine. [< Gk. *trupanon*, borer.]

tre•phine (trĭ-fīn′) ► *n.* A surgical saw for cutting out disks of bone, usu. from the skull. ► *v.* **-phined, -phin•ing.** To operate on with a trephine. [< Lat. *trēs fīnēs*, three ends.] —**treph′i•na′tion** (trĕf′ə-nā′shən) *n.*

trep•i•da•tion (trĕp′ĭ-dā′shən) ► *n.* Dread; apprehension. [< Lat. *trepidus*, anxious.]

tres•pass (trĕs′pəs, -păs′) ► *v.* **1.** To commit an offense or sin; transgress or err. **2.** To invade the property or rights of another without consent. **3.** To infringe on the privacy or time of another. [< OFr. *trespasser*.] —**tres′pass** *n.* —**tres′pass•er** *n.*

tress (trĕs) ► *n.* A lock of hair. [< OFr. *tresse*.]

tres•tle (trĕs′əl) ► *n.* **1.** A horizontal bar held up by two pairs of divergent legs and used as a support. **2.** A framework of vertical slanted supports and horizontal crosspieces supporting a bridge. [< Lat. *trānstrum*, beam.]

trey (trā) ► *n., pl.* **treys.** A card or die with three pips. [< Lat. *tria*.]

tri– ► *pref.* **1.** Three: *trisect.* **2a.** Occurring at intervals of three: *trimonthly.* **b.** Occurring three times during: *triweekly.* [< Lat. *trēs* and Gk. *treis*.]

tri•ad (trī′ăd′, -əd) ► *n.* A group of three. [< Gk. *trias*.] —**tri•ad′ic** *adj.*

tri•age (trē-äzh′, trē′äzh′) ► *n.* **1.** A process for sorting injured people into groups based on their need for medical treatment. **2.** A system used to allocate a scarce commodity, esp. in an emergency. [< OFr. *trier*, sort.]

tri•al (trī′əl) ► *n.* **1.** Examination of evidence and applicable law to determine the issue of specified charges or claims. **2.** The act or process of testing or trying. **3.** An effort or attempt. **4.** A test of patience or endurance. **5.** A nuisance; pain. See Syns at **burden**[1]. **6.** A qualifying competition, as in a sport. ► *adj.* **1.** Of a trial. **2.** Provisional; experimental. **3.** Made or done during a test. —***idiom:* on trial** In the process of being tried, as in a court of law. [< AN *trier*, try.]

Syns: *trial, affliction, crucible, ordeal, tribulation* **n.**

tri•an•gle (trī′ăng′gəl) ► *n.* **1a.** The plane figure formed by connecting three points not in a straight line by straight line segments. **b.** Something shaped like a triangle. **2.** A musical percussion instrument formed of a metal bar in the shape of a triangle. —**tri•an′gu•lar** *adj.*

triangle
left to right: right and equilateral models

tri•an•gu•late (trī-ăng′gyə-lāt′) ► *v.* **-lat•ed, -lat•ing.** To measure by using trigonometry. —**tri•ang′gu•la′tion** *n.*

Tri•as•sic (trī-ăs′ĭk) *Geol.* ► *adj.* Of or being the 1st period of the Mesozoic Era, marked by the rise of dinosaurs and the appearance of the earliest mammals. ► *n.* The Triassic Period.

tri•ath•lon (trī-ăth′lən, -lŏn′) ► *n.* An athletic contest consisting of three successive events, usu. long-distance swimming, bicycling, and running. [*tri–* + (DEC)ATHLON.] —**tri•ath′lete** *n.*

tribe (trīb) ► *n.* **1.** A unit of social organization consisting of a number of families, clans, or other groups who share a common ancestry, culture, and typically impermanent leadership. **2.** A group sharing a common distinguishing characteristic. [< Lat. *tribus*, a division of the

Roman people.] —**trib′al** *adj.* —**trib′al•ly** *adv.* —**tribes′man** *n.* —**tribes′wom•an** *n.*

trib•u•la•tion (trĭb′yə-lā′shən) ►*n.* **1.** Great affliction or distress. See Syns at **trial. 2.** An experience that tests one's endurance, patience, or faith. See Syns at **burden[1].** [< Lat. *trībulāre*, oppress.]

tri•bu•nal (trī-byo͞o′nəl, trĭ-) ►*n.* **1.** *Law* A seat or court of justice. **2.** A committee or board appointed to adjudicate in a particular matter. [< Lat. *tribūnus*, tribune.]

trib•une (trĭb′yo͞on′, trĭ-byo͞on′) ►*n.* **1.** An officer of ancient Rome elected by the plebeians to protect their rights. **2.** A protector or champion of the people. [< Lat. *tribūnus*.] —**trib′u•nar′y** (trĭb′yə-nĕr′ē) *adj.*

trib•u•tar•y (trĭb′yə-tĕr′ē) ►*adj.* **1.** Contributory. **2.** Paid in tribute. **3.** Paying tribute. ►*n.*, *pl.* **-ies 1.** A stream that flows into a larger body of water. **2.** One that pays tribute.

trib•ute (trĭb′yo͞ot) ►*n.* **1.** A gift or other acknowledgment of gratitude, respect, or admiration. **2a.** A payment made by one ruler or nation to another in acknowledgment of submission or as the price of protection or security. **b.** A forced payment. [< Lat. *tribuere*, pay.]

trice (trīs) ►*n.* A very short period of time; instant. [< MDu. *trīsen*, hoist.]

tri•cen•ten•ni•al (trī′sĕn-tĕn′ē-əl) ►*adj.* Tercentenary. ►*n.* A tercentenary event or celebration.

tri•ceps (trī′sĕps′) ►*n.*, *pl.* **-ceps•es** (-sĕp′sĭz) also **-ceps.** A large muscle running along the back of the upper arm and serving to extend the forearm. [< Lat., three-headed.]

tri•cer•a•tops (trī-sĕr′ə-tŏps′) ►*n.* A herbivorous dinosaur with three facial horns and a bony plate covering the neck. [NLat. *Tricerātōps*, genus name : TRI– + Gk. *keras*, horn + Gk. *ōps*, face.]

trich•i•no•sis (trĭk′ə-nō′sĭs) ►*n.* A disease caused by eating undercooked pork infested with parasitic worms, causing intestinal disorders, fever, nausea, muscular pain, and edema of the face. [*trichina*, a parasitic worm + –OSIS.]

trick (trĭk) ►*n.* **1.** An act or plan intended to achieve an end by deceptive or fraudulent means. **2.** A mischievous action; prank. **3a.** A peculiar trait; mannerism. **b.** A deceptive or illusive appearance: *a trick of sunlight.* **4a.** A feat requiring special knowledge. **b.** A specialized skill: *the tricks of the trade.* **5.** A feat of magic or legerdemain. **6.** A clever act. **7.** *Games* All the cards played in a single round. ►*v.* To cheat or deceive. ►*adj.* **1.** Involving tricks; tricky. **2.** Weak, defective, or liable to fail: *a trick knee.* —***idiom:*** **not miss a trick** To be extremely alert. [< ONFr. *trikier*, deceive.] —**trick′er** *n.*

trick•er•y (trĭk′ə-rē) ►*n.*, *pl.* **-ies.** The practice or use of tricks; deception.

trick•le (trĭk′əl) ►*v.* **-led, -ling 1.** To flow or fall in drops or in a thin stream. **2.** To proceed slowly or bit by bit. ►*n.* **1.** The act or condition of trickling. **2.** A slow, small, or irregular quantity. [ME *triklen.*]

trick•ster (trĭk′stər) ►*n.* One who plays clever or deceptive tricks.

trick•y (trĭk′ē) ►*adj.* **-i•er, -i•est 1.** Crafty; sly. **2.** Requiring caution or skill. —**trick′i•ly** *adv.* —**trick′i•ness** *n.*

tri•col•or (trī′kŭl′ər) ►*n.* A flag having three colors. ►*adj.* also **tri•col•ored** (-ərd). Having three colors.

tri•corn also **tri•corne** (trī′kôrn′) ►*n.* A hat with the brim turned up on three sides. [< Lat. *tricornis*, three-horned.]

tri•cot (trē′kō) ►*n.* **1.** A fabric knitted so as to resist runs. **2.** A soft ribbed woolen cloth. [Fr. < *tricoter*, knit.]

tri•cy•cle (trī′sĭk′əl, -sĭ-kəl) ►*n.* A three-wheeled vehicle usu. propelled by pedals.

tri•dent (trīd′nt) ►*n.* A long, three-pronged fishing spear or weapon. [< Lat. *tridēns* : TRI– + *dēns*, tooth.]

tried (trīd) ►*v.* P.t. and p.part. of **try.** ►*adj.* Tested and proved to be trustworthy.

tri•en•ni•al (trī-ĕn′ē-əl) ►*adj.* **1.** Occurring every third year. **2.** Lasting three years. ►*n.* A third anniversary. [< Lat. *triennium*, three years.] —**tri•en′ni•al•ly** *adv.*

Tri•este (trē-ĕst′, -ĕs′tē) A city of extreme NE Italy on the **Gulf of Trieste,** an inlet of the Gulf of Venice at the head of the Adriatic Sea. Pop. 229,216.

tri•fle (trī′fəl) ►*n.* **1.** Something of little importance or value. **2.** A small amount. ►*v.* **-fled, -fling 1.** To deal with something as if it were of little significance or value. **2.** To play or toy with something. See Syns at **flirt.** [< OFr. *trufle*, trickery.] —**tri′fler** (trī′flər) *n.*

tri•fling (trī′flĭng) ►*adj.* **1.** Of slight worth or importance. **2.** Frivolous or idle.

tri•fo•cal (trī-fō′kəl, trī′fō′-) ►*adj.* Having three focal lengths. ►*n.* **trifocals.** Eyeglasses having trifocal lenses.

trig (trĭg) ►*adj.* **1.** Smart and trim, as in appearance. **2.** In good condition. [< ON *tryggr*, true.]

trig•ger (trĭg′ər) ►*n.* **1a.** The lever pressed by the finger to discharge a firearm. **b.** A similar device used to release or activate a mechanism. **2.** An event that precipitates other events. [< MDu. *trecker* < *trecken*, pull.] —**trig′ger** *v.*

tri•glyc•er•ide (trī-glĭs′ə-rīd′) ►*n.* A naturally occurring ester of three fatty acids and glycerol that is the chief constituent of fats and oils.

trig•o•nom•e•try (trĭg′ə-nŏm′ĭ-trē) ►*n.* The study of relationships between the sides and the angles of triangles. [Gk. *trigōnon*, triangle + –METRY.] —**trig′o•no•met′ric** (-nə-mĕt′rĭk), **trig′o•no•met′ri•cal** *adj.*

trill (trĭl) ►*n.* **1.** A fluttering or tremulous sound; warble. **2.** *Mus.* The rapid alternation of two tones either a whole or a half tone apart. **3.** *Ling.* **a.** A rapid vibration of one speech organ against another. **b.** A speech sound so pronounced. [Ital. *trillo*.] —**trill** *v.*

tril•lion (trĭl′yən) ►*n.* **1.** The cardinal number equal to 10^{12}. **2.** *Chiefly Brit.* The cardinal number equal to 10^{18}. [Fr.] —**tril′lion** *adj.* —**tril′lionth** *n. & adj.*

tri•lo•bite (trī′lə-bīt′) ►*n.* An extinct three-lobed marine arthropod of the Paleozoic Era. [< Gk. *trilobos*, three-lobed.]

tril•o•gy (trĭl′ə-jē) ►*n.*, *pl.* **-gies.** A group of three related artistic works. [Gk. *trilogia*.]

trim (trĭm) ►*v.* **trimmed, trim•ming 1.** To make neat or tidy by clipping, smoothing, or pruning. **2.** To rid of excess or remove by cutting. **3.** To ornament; decorate. **4.** *Naut.* **a.** To adjust (the sails and yards) so that they receive the wind properly. **b.** To balance (a ship) by shifting its cargo or contents. **5.** To balance (an aircraft) in flight. ►*n.* **1a.** State of order or appearance; condition. **b.** A condition of good health or fitness. **2.** Ornamentation. **3.** Excised or rejected material. **4a.** The readiness of a vessel for sailing. **b.** The balance of a ship. ►*adj.* **trim•mer, trim•mest 1.** In good or neat order. **2.** Having lines of neat and pleasing simplicity. ►*adv.* In a trim manner. [< OE *trymman*, strengthen.] —**trim′ly** *adv.* —**trim′mer** *n.* —**trim′ness** *n.*

tri•mes•ter (trī-mĕs′tər, trī′mĕs′-) ►*n.* **1.** A period of three months. **2.** One of three terms into which an academic year is sometimes divided. [< Lat. *trimēstris*, of three months.]

trim•e•ter (trĭm′ĭ-tər) ►*n.* A line of verse consisting of three metrical feet. —**tri•met′ric** (trī-mĕt′rĭk), **tri•met′ri•cal** *adj.*

trim•ming (trĭm′ĭng) ►*n.* **1.** The act of one that trims. **2.** Something added as decoration. **3. trimmings** Accessories; extras.

trine (trīn) ►*adj.* Threefold; triple. ►*n.* A group of three. [< Lat. *trīnus*.]

Trin•i•dad (trĭn′ĭ-dăd′) An island of Trinidad and Tobago in the Atlantic off NE Venezuela. —**Trin′i•dad′i•an** *adj. & n.*

Trinidad and Tobago. A country of the SE West Indies in the Atlantic off NE Venezuela, comprising the islands of Trinidad and Tobago. Cap. Port of Spain. Pop. 1,257,000.

trin•i•ty (trĭn′ĭ-tē) ►*n., pl.* **-ties 1.** A group of three closely related members. **2. Trinity** In Christian theology, the union of the three divine persons in one God. [< Lat. *trīnitās*.]

trin•ket (trĭng′kĭt) ►*n.* **1.** A small ornament or piece of jewelry. **2.** A trifle. [?]

tri•o (trē′ō) ►*n., pl.* **-os 1.** A group of three. **2.** *Mus.* **a.** A composition for three performers. **b.** The group performing such a composition. [< Ital.]

trip (trĭp) ►*n.* **1.** A going from one place to another; journey. **2.** A stumble or fall. **3.** A maneuver causing someone to stumble or fall. **4.** *Slang* An exciting or hallucinatory experience. **5.** A device for triggering a mechanism. ►*v.* **tripped, trip•ping 1.** To stumble or cause to stumble. **2.** To move nimbly with light rapid steps; skip. **3.** To make or cause to make an error. **4.** To release or be released, as a catch, trigger, or switch. [< OFr. *tripper*, stamp the foot, of Gmc. orig.] —**trip′per** *n.*

tri•par•tite (trī-pär′tīt) ►*adj.* **1.** Composed of or divided into three parts. **2.** Of or executed by three parties: *a tripartite agreement.*

tripe (trīp) ►*n.* **1.** The stomach lining of cattle or other ruminants, used as food. **2.** *Informal* Something of no value; rubbish. [< OFr.]

tri•ple (trĭp′əl) ►*adj.* **1.** Having three parts. **2.** Three times as many or as much. **3.** *Mus.* Having three beats in a measure. ►*n.* **1.** A number or quantity three times as great as another. **2.** A group or set of three; a triad. **3.** *Baseball* A hit that enables the batter to reach third base safely. ►*v.* **-pled, -pling 1.** To make or become three times as great in number or amount. **2.** *Baseball* To make a triple. [< Lat. *triplus*.] —**tri′ply** *adv.*

triple play ►*n.* *Baseball* A play in which three players are put out.

trip•let (trĭp′lĭt) ►*n.* **1.** A group or set of three. **2.** One of three children born at one birth. [TRIPL(E) + (DOUBL)ET.]

tri•plex (trĭp′lĕks′, trī′plĕks′) ►*adj.* Having three parts or divisions: *a triplex cinema.* [Lat.] —**tri′plex′** *n.*

trip•li•cate (trĭp′lĭ-kĭt) ►*n.* One of a set of three identical objects or copies. ►*v.* (-kāt′) **-cat•ed, -cat•ing.** To make three identical copies of. [< Lat. *triplicāre*, to triple.] —**trip′li•ca′tion** *n.*

tri•pod (trī′pŏd′) ►*n.* **1.** A three-legged object, such as a cauldron, stool, or table. **2.** An adjustable three-legged stand, as for supporting a camera or telescope. [< Gk. *tripous*, three-footed : TRI– + *pous*, foot.]

tripod

Trip•o•li (trĭp′ə-lē) **1.** A city of NW Lebanon on the Mediterranean Sea NNE of Beirut. Pop. 198,000. **2.** The capital of Libya, in the NW part on the Mediterranean Sea. Pop. 858,500. —**Tri•pol′i•tan** (trĭ-pŏl′ĭ-tn) *adj. & n.*

trip•tych (trĭp′tĭk) ►*n.* A three-paneled work of art. [< Gk. *triptukhos*, threefold.]

tri•sect (trī′sĕkt′, trī-sĕkt′) ►*v.* To divide into three equal parts. —**tri′sec′tion** *n.*

trite (trīt) ►*adj.* **trit•er, trit•est.** Overused and commonplace; lacking originality. [Lat. *trītus* < p.part. of *terere*, wear out.] —**trite′ly** *adv.* —**trite′ness** *n.*

trit•i•um (trĭt′ē-əm, trĭsh′ē-) ►*n.* A rare radioactive hydrogen isotope with atomic mass 3. [< Gk. *tritos*, third.]

tri•umph (trī′əmf) ►*v.* **1.** To be victorious or successful; win. **2.** To rejoice; exult. ►*n.* **1.** The fact or an instance of being victorious; victory. **2.** Exultation. [< Lat. *triumphāre*.] —**tri•um′phal** *adj.* —**tri•um′phant** *adj.*

tri•um•vir (trī-ŭm′vər) ►*n., pl.* **-virs** or **-vi•ri** (-və-rī′). One of three men sharing civil authority in ancient Rome. [< Lat. : *trium*, of three + *vir*, man.] —**tri•um′vi•ral** *adj.* —**tri•um′vi•rate** (-vər-ĭt) *n.*

triv•et (trĭv′ĭt) ►*n.* **1.** A stand with short feet, used under a hot dish on a table. **2.** A three-legged stand. [< Lat. *tripēs*, three-footed : TRI– + *pēs*, foot.]

triv•i•a (trĭv′ē-ə) ►*pl.n. (takes sing. or pl. v.)* Insignificant or inessential matters. [Lat.]

triv•i•al (trĭv′ē-əl) ►*adj.* **1.** Of little significance or value. **2.** Commonplace. —**triv′i•al′i•ty** (-ăl′ĭ-tē) *n.* —**triv′i•al•ly** *adv.*

triv•i•al•ize (trĭv′ē-ə-līz′) ►*v.* **-ized, -iz•ing.** To reduce to triviality. —**triv′i•al•i•za′tion** *n.*

-trix ►*suff.* A woman who is connected with a specified thing: *testatrix.* [Lat. *-trīx*.]

tro•chee (trō′kē) ►*n.* A metrical foot consisting of a stressed syllable followed by an unstressed syllable, as in *season.* [< Gk. *tro-*

khaios.] —**tro•cha'ic** (-kā'ĭk) *adj.*

trod (trŏd) ►*v.* P.t. and p.part. of **tread.**

trod•den (trŏd'n) ►*v.* P.part. of **tread.**

trog•lo•dyte (trŏg'lə-dīt') ►*n.* **1.** A member of a fabulous or prehistoric race that lived in caves. **2.** A reclusive, reactionary, or brutish person. [< Gk. *Trōglodutai*, cave dwellers.] —**trog'lo•dyt'ic** (-dĭt'ĭk) *adj.*

troi•ka (troi'kə) ►*n.* A Russian carriage drawn by three horses abreast. [Russ. *troĭka.*]

Tro•jan (trō'jən) ►*n.* **1.** A native or inhabitant of ancient Troy. **2.** A person of courageous determination. —**Tro'jan** *adj.*

Trojan War ►*n. Gk. Myth.* The ten-year war waged against Troy by the Greeks, resulting in the destruction of Troy.

troll[1] (trōl) ►*v.* **1.** To fish by trailing a baited line from behind a slowly moving boat. **2a.** To sing in succession the parts of (a round). **b.** To sing heartily. ►*n.* **1.** The act of trolling for fish. **2.** A musical round. [< OFr. *troller*, wander.] —**troll'er** *n.*

troll[2] (trōl) ►*n.* A supernatural creature of Scandinavian folklore, often described as living in caves or under bridges. [< ON.]

trol•ley also **trol•ly** (trŏl'ē) ►*n., pl.* **-leys** also **-lies 1.** A streetcar. **2.** A device that collects electric current and transmits it to the motor of an electric vehicle. **3.** A wheeled carriage or basket suspended from an overhead track. [Poss. < TROLL[1].]

trolley bus ►*n.* A bus that is powered by electricity from an overhead wire.

trolley car ►*n.* A streetcar.

trol•lop (trŏl'əp) ►*n.* **1.** A slovenly woman. **2.** A strumpet. [Perh. < TROLL[1], roll about.]

Trol•lope (trŏl'əp), **Anthony.** 1815–82. British writer.

trom•bone (trŏm-bōn', trəm-, trŏm'bōn') ►*n.* A brass musical instrument with a movable U-shaped slide for producing different pitches. [< Ital. < *tromba*, trumpet.] —**trom•bon'ist** *n.*

tromp (trŏmp) ►*v.* **1.** To tramp. **2.** To trample underfoot. **3.** To trounce. [< TRAMP.]

trompe l'oeil (trômp' loi') ►*n.* A detailed style of painting that gives an illusion of photographic reality. [Fr.]

-tron ►*suff.* Device for manipulating subatomic particles: *betatron.* [Gk., noun suff.]

Trond•heim (trŏn'hām', trôn'-) A city of central Norway on **Trondheim Fjord,** an inlet of the Norwegian Sea. Pop. 140,656.

troop (tro͞op) ►*n.* **1.** A group or company of people, animals, or things. See Syns at **band**[2]. **2a.** A group of soldiers. **b. troops** Military units; soldiers. ►*v.* To move or go as a throng. [< OFr. *trope.*]

troop•er (tro͞o'pər) ►*n.* **1a.** A member of a cavalry unit. **b.** A cavalry horse. **2a.** A mounted police officer. **b.** A state police officer.

trope (trōp) ►*n.* A figure of speech using words in nonliteral ways. [< Gk. *tropos*, a turn.]

tro•phy (trō'fē) ►*n., pl.* **-phies.** A prize or memento received as a symbol of victory. [< Gk. *tropaion.*]

-trophy ►*suff.* Nutrition; growth: *hypertrophy.* [< Gk. *trophē.*]

trop•ic (trŏp'ĭk) ►*n.* **1.** Either of two parallels of latitude, the tropic of Cancer or the tropic of Capricorn, representing the farthest north and south at which the sun can shine directly overhead. **2. tropics** The region of the earth's surface bounded by these latitudes. ►*adj.* Of or concerning the tropics; tropical. [< Gk. *tropē*, a turning.]

-tropic ►*suff.* Changing in a specified way or in response to a specified stimulus: *phototropic.* [< Gk. *tropē*, a turning.]

trop•i•cal (trŏp'ĭ-kəl) ►*adj.* **1.** Of or characteristic of the tropics. **2.** Hot and humid; torrid. —**trop'i•cal•ly** *adv.*

tropical year ►*n.* The time interval between two successive passages of the sun through the vernal equinox; solar year.

tropic of Cancer ►*n.* The parallel of latitude 23°27' north of the equator.

tropic of Capricorn ►*n.* The parallel of latitude 23°27' south of the equator.

tro•pism (trō'pĭz'əm) ►*n.* The turning or bending movement of an organism toward or away from an external stimulus. [< Gk. *tropē*, a turning.]

tro•po•sphere (trō'pə-sfîr', trŏp'ə-) ►*n.* The lowest region of the earth's atmosphere, marked by decreasing temperature with increasing altitude. [Gk. *tropē*, a turning + SPHERE.] —**tro'po•spher'ic** (-sfîr'ĭk, -sfĕr'-) *adj.*

-tropy ►*suff.* The state of turning in a specified way or from a specified stimulus: *phototropy.* [< Gk. *tropos*, changeable.]

trot (trŏt) ►*n.* **1.** The gait of a four-footed animal in which diagonal pairs of legs move forward together. **2.** A gait of a person, faster than a walk; jog. ►*v.* **trot•ted, trot•ting 1.** To go or move at a trot. **2.** To hurry. [< OFr.] —**trot'ter** *n.*

troth (trôth, trŏth, trōth) ►*n.* **1a.** Betrothal. **b.** One's pledged fidelity. **2.** Good faith; fidelity. [< OE *trēowth*, truth.]

Trot•sky or **Trot•ski** (trŏt'skē, trôt'-), **Leon.** 1879–1940. Russian revolutionary theoretician. —**Trot'sky•ite'** *adj. & n.*

trou•ba•dour (tro͞o'bə-dôr', -dōr', -do͝or') ►*n.* **1.** One of a class of 12th and 13th cent. lyric poets in S France, N Italy, and N Spain. **2.** A strolling minstrel. [< OProv. *trobador.*]

trou•ble (trŭb'əl) ►*n.* **1.** A state of distress, affliction, danger, or need. **2.** A source of distress or difficulty. **3.** Inconvenience or bother. **4.** A condition of pain or malfunction. ►*v.* **-bled, -bling 1.** To agitate; stir up. **2.** To afflict with pain or discomfort. **3.** To distress; worry. **4.** To inconvenience; bother. [< Lat. *turbidus*, confused.] —**trou'bler** *n.* —**trou'ble•some** *adj.*

***Syns:** trouble, distress, worry* **v.**

trou•ble•mak•er (trŭb'əl-mā'kər) ►*n.* One who stirs up trouble or strife.

trou•ble•shoot•er (trŭb'əl-sho͞o'tər) ►*n.* One who locates and eliminates sources of trouble.

trough (trôf, trŏf) ►*n.* **1.** A long, narrow, usu. shallow receptacle, esp. for holding water or feed for animals. **2.** A gutter under the eaves of a roof. **3.** A long narrow depression, as between waves. **4.** A low point in a cycle or on a graph. [< OE *trog.*]

trounce (trouns) ►*v.* **trounced, trounc•ing 1.** To thrash; beat. **2.** To defeat decisively. [?]

troupe (tro͞op) ►*n.* A company or group, esp. of touring performers. See Syns at **band**[2]. ►*v.* **trouped, troup•ing.** To tour with a theatrical company. [Fr. TROOP.] —**troup'er** *n.*

trou•sers (trou'zərz) ►*pl.n.* A garment covering the body from the waist to the ankles, divided into sections to fit each leg separately. [< Sc.Gael. *triubhas*.]

trous•seau (tro͞o′sō, tro͞o-sō′) ►*n.*, *pl.* **-seaux** (-sōz, -sōz′) or **-seaus.** The special wardrobe a bride assembles for her marriage. [< OFr.]

trout (trout) ►*n.*, *pl.* **trout** or **trouts.** Any of various edible, chiefly freshwater fishes related to the salmon. [< LLat. *tructa*.]

trove (trōv) ►*n.* A treasure-trove.

trow•el (trou′əl) ►*n.* **1.** A flat-bladed hand tool for leveling, spreading, or shaping substances such as cement. **2.** A small digging tool with a scoop-shaped blade. [< LLat. *truella* < Lat. *trua*, ladle.] —**trow′el** *v.*

troy (troi) ►*adj.* Of or expressed in troy weight. [< *Troyes*, France.]

Troy. An ancient city of NW Asia Minor near the Dardanelles.

troy weight ►*n.* A system of units of weight in which the grain is the same as in the avoirdupois system and the pound contains 12 ounces, 240 pennyweights, or 5,760 grains.

tru•ant (tro͞o′ənt) ►*n.* **1.** One absent without permission, esp. from school. **2.** One who shirks work or duty. [< OFr., beggar.] —**tru′ant** *adj.* —**tru′an•cy** *n.*

truce (tro͞os) ►*n.* A temporary cessation of hostilities by agreement; armistice. [< OE *trēow*, a pledge.]

truck¹ (trŭk) ►*n.* **1.** A heavy motor vehicle for carrying loads. **2.** A two-wheeled barrow for moving heavy objects by hand. **3.** One of the swiveling frames of wheels under each end of a railroad car or trolley car. ►*v.* **1.** To transport by truck. **2.** To drive a truck. [Poss. < TRUCKLE.] —**truck′er** *n.*

truck² (trŭk) ►*v.* **1.** To exchange; barter. **2.** To have dealings or commerce; traffic. ►*n.* **1.** Garden produce raised for the market. **2.** *Informal* Worthless goods; rubbish. **3.** Barter; exchange. **4.** *Informal* Dealings; business. [< ONFr. *troquer*.]

truck•age (trŭk′ĭj) ►*n.* **1.** Transportation of goods by truck. **2.** A charge for this service.

truck•le (trŭk′əl) ►*n.* A small wheel or roller; caster. ►*v.* **-led, -ling.** To be servile or submissive. See Syns at **fawn¹**. [< Lat. *trochlea*, system of pulleys.]

truc•u•lent (trŭk′yə-lənt) ►*adj.* **1.** Disposed to fight; pugnacious. **2.** Savage and cruel; fierce. [Lat. *truculentus*.] —**truc′u•lence** *n.*

Tru•deau (tro͞o-dō′), **Pierre Elliott.** 1919–2000. Canadian prime minister (1968–79 and 1980–84).

trudge (trŭj) ►*v.* **trudged, trudg•ing.** To walk in a laborious, heavy-footed way; plod. [?] —**trudge** *n.* —**trudg′er** *n.*

true (tro͞o) ►*adj.* **tru•er, tru•est 1a.** Consistent with fact or reality; not false or erroneous. **b.** Truthful. **2.** Real; genuine. See Syns at **authentic. 3.** Reliable; accurate. **4.** Faithful; loyal. **5.** Sincerely felt or expressed. **6.** Rightful; legitimate. **7.** Exactly conforming to a rule, standard, or pattern. **8.** Determined with reference to the earth's axis, not the magnetic poles: *true north.* ►*adv.* **1.** Rightly; truthfully. **2.** Unswervingly; exactly. **3.** So as to conform to a type, standard, or pattern. ►*v.* **trued, tru•ing** or **true•ing.** To position (something) so as to make it balanced, level, or square. ►*n.* **1. the true** Truth or reality. **2.** Proper alignment or adjustment: *out of true.* [< OE *trēowe*, trustworthy.] —**true′ness** *n.*

true-blue (tro͞o′blo͞o′) ►*adj.* Loyal or faithful; staunch.

true•love (tro͞o′lŭv′) ►*n.* One's beloved.

truf•fle (trŭf′əl) ►*n.* **1.** An underground fungus valued as a delicacy. **2.** A rich chocolate confection. [< Lat. *tūber*, lump.]

tru•ism (tro͞o′ĭz′əm) ►*n.* A self-evident truth. See Syns at **cliché.** —**tru•is′tic** *adj.*

Tru•ji•llo (tro͞o-hē′yō) A city of NW Peru NW of Lima. Pop. 521,200.

Truk Islands (trŭk, tro͝ok) See **Chuuk Islands.**

tru•ly (tro͞o′lē) ►*adv.* **1.** Sincerely; genuinely. **2.** Truthfully; accurately. **3.** Indeed.

Tru•man (tro͞o′mən), **Harry S.** 1884–1972. The 33rd US President (1945–53).

Harry S. Truman

trump (trŭmp) ►*n.* **1.** often **trumps** A suit in card games that outranks all other suits for the duration of a hand. **2.** A card of such a suit. ►*v.* To play a trump. —***phrasal verb:* trump up** To devise fraudulently. [< TRIUMPH.]

trump•er•y (trŭm′pə-rē) ►*n.*, *pl.* **-ies 1.** Showy but worthless finery. **2.** Nonsense. **3.** Trickery. [< OFr. *tromper*, deceive.]

trum•pet (trŭm′pĭt) ►*n.* **1a.** A soprano brass wind instrument consisting of a long metal tube ending in a flared bell. **b.** Something shaped or sounding like a trumpet. **2.** A resounding call. ►*v.* To sound or proclaim loudly. [< OHGer. *trumpa*, horn.] —**trum′pet•er** *n.*

trun•cate (trŭng′kāt′) ►*v.* **-cat•ed, -cat•ing.** To shorten by or as if by cutting off the end or top. See Syns at **shorten.** [Lat. *truncāre*.] —**trun•ca′tion** *n.*

trun•cheon (trŭn′chən) ►*n.* A short stick carried by police; billy club. [< VLat. **trunciō*, club.] —**trun′cheon** *v.*

trun•dle (trŭn′dl) ►*v.* **-dled, -dling.** To push on wheels or rollers. [< OE *trendel*, circle.]

trundle bed ►*n.* A low bed on casters that can be rolled under another bed for storage.

trunk (trŭngk) ►*n.* **1.** The main woody axis of a tree. **2.** The human body excluding the head and limbs; torso. **3.** A proboscis, esp. the long prehensile proboscis of an elephant. **4.** A main body, apart from tributaries or appendages. **5a.** A covered compartment for luggage and storage, usu. at the rear of an automobile. **b.** A large packing case or box that clasps shut, used as luggage or for storage. **6. trunks** Shorts worn esp. for swimming. [< Lat. *truncus*.]

trunk line ►*n.* A direct line between two telephone switchboards.

truss (trŭs) ►*n.* **1.** A supportive device worn to prevent enlargement of a hernia or the return of a reduced hernia. **2.** A wooden or metal framework designed to support a structure, such as a roof. ►*v.* **1.** To tie up or bind tightly. **2.** To bind the wings or legs of (a fowl) before cooking. **3.** To support or brace with a truss. [< OFr. *trousse*, bundle.]

trust (trŭst) ►*n.* **1.** Firm reliance on the integrity or ability of a person or thing. **2.** Custody; care. See Syns at **care. 3.** Something committed into the care of another; charge. **4a.** The condition and obligation of having confidence placed in one. **b.** One in which confidence is placed. **5.** Reliance on something in the future; hope. **6.** A legal title to property held by one party for the benefit of another. **7.** A combination of firms or corporations for the purpose of reducing competition. ►*v.* **1.** To rely or depend (on); have confidence (in). **2.** To be confident; hope. **3.** To expect with assurance; assume. **4.** To believe. **5.** To entrust. **6.** To grant discretion to confidently. **7.** To extend credit to. —***idiom:* in trust** In the possession or care of a trustee. [ME *truste.*] —**trust'er** *n.*

trus•tee (trŭ-stē') ►*n.* **1.** A person or agent holding legal title to and administering property for a beneficiary. **2.** A member of a board that directs the funds and policy of an institution. —**trus•tee'ship'** *n.*

trust•ful (trŭst'fəl) ►*adj.* Full of trust. —**trust'ful•ly** *adv.* —**trust'ful•ness** *n.*

trust•wor•thy (trŭst'wûr'*th*ē) ►*adj.* Warranting trust; reliable. See Syns at **reliable.** —**trust'wor'thi•ness** *n.*

trust•y (trŭs'tē) ►*adj.* **-i•er, -i•est.** Meriting trust; dependable. See Syns at **reliable.** ►*n., pl.* **-ies.** A trusted person, esp. a convict granted special privileges. —**trust'i•ly** *adv.* —**trust'i•ness** *n.*

truth (tro͞oth) ►*n., pl.* **truths** (tro͞o*th*z, tro͞oths) **1.** Conformity to fact or actuality. **2.** A statement proven to be or accepted as true. **3.** Sincerity; honesty. **4.** Reality; actuality. [< OE *trēowth.*]

Truth, Sojourner. 1797?–1883. Amer. abolitionist and feminist.

Sojourner Truth
photographed c. 1864

truth•ful (tro͞oth'fəl) ►*adj.* **1.** Consistently telling the truth; honest. **2.** Corresponding to reality. —**truth'ful•ly** *adv.* —**truth'ful•ness** *n.*

try (trī) ►*v.* **tried** (trīd), **try•ing 1.** To make an effort (to do something); attempt. **2.** To test in order to determine strength, effect, worth, or desirability. **3a.** To examine or hear (e.g., a case) by judicial process. **b.** To put (a defendant) on trial. **4.** To subject to strain or hardship; tax. **5.** To render (fat). **6.** To smooth, fit, or align accurately. ►*n., pl.* **tries** (trīz). An attempt; effort. [< OFr. *trier*, pick out.]

Usage: The phrase *try and* is commonly used as a substitute for *try to,* as in *Could you try and make less noise?* The usage strikes an inappropriately conversational note in formal writing.

try•ing (trī'ĭng) ►*adj.* Causing strain, hardship, or distress. —**try'ing•ly** *adv.*

try•out (trī'out') ►*n.* A test to ascertain the skills of applicants, as for a sports team.

tryst (trĭst) ►*n.* **1.** An agreement between lovers to meet. **2.** A meeting or meeting place so arranged. [< OFr. *triste*, a waiting place (in hunting).] —**tryst** *v.* —**tryst'er** *n.*

tsar (zär, tsär) ►*n.* Var. of **czar** 1.

tset•se fly (tsĕt'sē, tsē'tsē) ►*n.* A bloodsucking African fly that transmits microorganisms causing diseases such as sleeping sickness. [Of Bantu orig.]

TSgt ►*abbr.* technical sergeant

T-shirt also **tee shirt** (tē'shûrt') ►*n.* A short-sleeved, collarless shirt.

Tsi•nan (jē'nän') See **Jinan.**

Tsing•tao (tsĭng'dou') See **Qingdao.**

Tsi•tsi•har (tsē'tsē'här') See **Qiqihar.**

tsp. ►*abbr.* teaspoon

T-square (tē'skwâr') ►*n.* A T-shaped ruler used for drawing parallel lines.

tsu•na•mi (tso͝o-nä'mē) ►*n., pl.* **-mis.** A very large ocean wave caused by an underwater earthquake or volcanic eruption. [J.]

Tsve•ta•e•va (tsvyĭ-tä'yə-və), **Marina Ivanovna.** 1892–1941. Russian poet.

Tswa•na (tswä'nə, swä'-) ►*n., pl.* **-na** or **-nas 1.** A member of a Bantu people of Botswana and W South Africa. **2.** The Bantu language of the Tswana.

Tu. ►*abbr.* Tuesday

Tu•a•mo•tu Archipelago (to͞o'ə-mō'to͞o) An island group of French Polynesia E of Tahiti.

tub (tŭb) ►*n.* **1.** A round, open, flat-bottomed vessel used for washing, packing, or storing. **2.** A bathtub. [< MDu. or MLGer.]

tu•ba (to͞o'bə, tyo͞o'-) ►*n.* A large, valved, brass wind instrument with a bass pitch. [< Lat., trumpet.]

tu•bal ligation (to͞o'bəl, tyo͞o'-) ►*n.* A method of female sterilization in which the fallopian tubes are surgically tied.

tub•by (tŭb'ē) ►*adj.* **-bi•er, -bi•est.** Short and fat. —**tub'bi•ness** *n.*

tube (to͞ob, tyo͞ob) ►*n.* **1.** A hollow cylinder, esp. one that conveys a fluid or functions as a passage. **2.** A flexible cylindrical container sealed at one end and having a screw cap at the other, for pigments, toothpaste, or other substances. **3a.** An electron tube. **b.** A vacuum tube. **4.** *Chiefly Brit.* A subway. **5.** often **the tube** *Slang* Television. [< Lat. *tubus.*] —**tube'less** *adj.*

tu•ber (to͞o'bər, tyo͞o'-) ►*n.* **1.** A swollen, usu. underground stem, such as the potato, bearing buds from which new plants sprout. **2.** *Biol.* A tubercle. [Lat. *tūber*, lump.] —**tu'ber•ous** *adj.*

tu•ber•cle (to͞o'bər-kəl, tyo͞o'-) ►*n.* **1.** The characteristic lesion of tuberculosis. **2.** *Biol.* A small rounded prominence on the roots of some plants or in the skin or on a bone. [Lat. *tūberculum*, small lump.]

tu•ber•cu•lar (to͞o-bûr′kyə-lər, tyo͞o-) ►*adj.* **1.** Of or covered with tubercles. **2.** Of or affected with tuberculosis.

tu•ber•cu•lin (to͞o-bûr′kyə-lĭn, tyo͞o-) ►*n.* A liquid derived from tubercle bacilli and used in tests for tuberculosis. [Lat. *tūberculum*, tubercle + -IN.]

tu•ber•cu•lo•sis (to͞o-bûr′kyə-lō′sĭs, tyo͞o-) ►*n.* An infectious disease of humans and animals caused by a bacillus and characterized by the formation of tubercles, esp. in the lungs. [Lat. *tūberculum*, tubercle + -OSIS.] —**tu•ber′cu•lous** *adj.*

tube•rose (to͞ob′rōz′, tyo͞ob′-, to͞o′bə-) ►*n.* A tuberous Mexican plant cultivated for its fragrant white flowers. [< feminine of Lat. *tūberōsus*, bearing tubors.]

Tub•man (tŭb′mən), **Harriet.** 1820?–1913. Amer. abolitionist.

Harriet Tubman

tu•bu•lar (to͞o′byə-lər, tyo͞o′-) ►*adj.* Of or having the form of a tube.

tuck (tŭk) ►*v.* **1.** To make one or more folds in. **2.** To turn under the end or edge of in order to secure. **3.** To put in a snug, safe, or concealed place. **4.** To draw in; contract. —***phrasal verb:* tuck in** To make one secure in bed for sleep, esp. by tucking bedclothes into the bed. ►*n.* A flattened pleat or fold, esp. one stitched in place. [ME *tukken.*]

tuck•er (tŭk′ər) ►*v. Informal* To weary; exhaust. [Perh. < TUCK.]

Tuc•son (to͞o′sŏn′) A city of SE AZ SSE of Phoenix. Pop. 405,390.

Tu•cu•mán (to͞o′kə-män′, -ko͞o-) See **San Miguel de Tucumán.**

–tude ►*suff.* Condition, state, or quality: *exactitude.* [< Lat. *-tūdō.*]

Tues. ►*abbr.* Tuesday

Tues•day (to͞oz′dē, -dā′, tyo͞oz′-) ►*n.* The 3rd day of the week. [< OE *Tīwesdæg.*]

tuff (tŭf) ►*n.* A rock composed of compacted volcanic ash. [< OItal. *tufo.*]

tuft (tŭft) ►*n.* A short cluster of strands, as of hair or grass, attached at the base or growing close together. [ME.] —**tuft′ed** *adj.*

tug (tŭg) ►*v.* **tugged, tug•ging 1.** To pull vigorously (at). See Syns at **pull. 2.** To move by pulling with great effort or exertion. **3.** To tow by tugboat. ►*n.* **1.** A strong pull or pulling force. **2.** A tugboat. [< OE *tēon.*]

tug•boat (tŭg′bōt′) ►*n.* A small powerful boat designed for towing or pushing larger vessels.

tug of war ►*n.* **1.** A contest in which two teams tug on opposite ends of a rope, each trying to pull the other across a dividing line. **2.** A struggle for supremacy.

tu•grik (to͞o′grĭk) ►*n.* See table at **currency.** [Mongolian *dughurik.*]

tu•i•tion (to͞o-ĭsh′ən, tyo͞o-) ►*n.* **1.** A fee for instruction, esp. at a school. **2.** Instruction; teaching. [< Lat. *tuērī, tuit-*, protect.] —**tu•i′tion•al, tu•i′tion•ar′y** *adj.*

Tu•la (to͞o′lə) A city of W Russia S of Moscow. Pop. 533,640.

tu•lip (to͞o′lĭp, tyo͞o′-) ►*n.* A bulbous plant widely cultivated for its showy, variously colored flowers. [< Ottoman Turkish *tülbend*, muslin.]

tulip tree ►*n.* A tall tree with tuliplike green and orange flowers.

tulle (to͞ol) ►*n.* A fine starched net of silk, rayon, or nylon, used esp. for veils, tutus, or gowns. [After *Tulle*, France.]

Tul•sa (tŭl′sə) A city of NE OK on the Arkansas R. NE of Oklahoma City. Pop. 367,302.

tum•ble (tŭm′bəl) ►*v.* **-bled, -bling 1.** To perform acrobatic feats, such as somersaults. **2a.** To fall or roll end over end. **b.** To spill or roll out in disorder. **c.** To pitch headlong; fall. **3.** To decline or collapse suddenly. **4.** To cause to fall. **5.** To toss or whirl in a drum or tumbler. [< OE *tumbian*, dance.] —**tum′ble** *n.*

tum•ble•down (tŭm′bəl-doun′) ►*adj.* Dilapidated or rickety.

tum•bler (tŭm′blər) ►*n.* **1.** An acrobat or gymnast. **2.** A drinking glass without a handle or stem. **3.** The part in a lock that releases the bolt when moved by a key. **4.** The drum of a clothes dryer.

tum•ble•weed (tŭm′bəl-wēd′) ►*n.* A densely branched plant that when withered breaks off from the roots and is rolled about by the wind.

tum•brel or **tum•bril** (tŭm′brəl) ►*n.* A two-wheeled cart, esp. one that can be tilted to dump a load. [< OFr. *tomberel.*]

tu•mes•cence (to͞o-mĕs′əns, tyoo-) ►*n.* A swelling or enlarging. [< Lat. *tumēscere*, begin to swell.] —**tu•mes′cent** *adj.*

tu•mid (to͞o′mĭd, tyo͞o′-) ►*adj.* **1.** Swollen; distended. **2.** Overblown; bombastic. [Lat. *tumidus.*] —**tu•mid′i•ty** *n.*

tum•my (tŭm′ē) ►*n., pl.* **-mies** *Informal* The human stomach. [Alteration of STOMACH.]

tu•mor (to͞o′mər, tyo͞o′-) ►*n.* **1.** An abnormal growth of tissue due to uncontrolled, progressive multiplication of cells and serving no physiological function; neoplasm. **2.** A swollen part; swelling. [< Lat.] —**tu′mor•ous** *adj.*

tu•mult (to͞o′mŭlt′, tyo͞o′-) ►*n.* **1.** The din and commotion of a great crowd. **2.** Agitation of the mind or emotions. [< Lat. *tumultus.*] —**tu•mul′tu•ous** (to͞o-mŭl′cho͞o-əs, tyo͞o-) *adj.* —**tu•mul′tu•ous•ness** *n.*

tu•mu•lus (to͞o′myə-ləs, tyo͞o′-) ►*n., pl.* **-li** (-lī′). An ancient grave mound; barrow. [Lat.]

tun (tŭn) ►*n.* A large cask. [< OE *tunne.*]

tu•na (to͞o′nə, tyo͞o′-) ►*n., pl.* **-na** or **-nas 1.** Any of various often large marine food fishes. **2.** also **tuna fish** The canned or processed flesh of tuna. [< Ar. *at-tūn*, TUNNY.]

tun•dra (tŭn′drə) ►*n.* A treeless area of Arctic regions with a permanently frozen subsoil and low-growing vegetation. [Russ.]

tune (to͞on, tyo͞on) ►*n.* **1.** *Mus.* **a.** A melody, esp. a simple one. **b.** A song. **c.** Correct pitch. **d.** Agreement in pitch or key. **2.** Concord or agreement; harmony: *in tune with the times.* **3.** *Electron.* Adjustment of a receiver or circuit for maximum response to a given signal or frequency. ►*v.* **tuned, tun•ing 1.** *Mus.* To put into tune. **2.** To adjust for maximum performance. **3.** *Electron.* To adjust (a receiver) to a desired frequency. [< TONE.] —**tun′a•ble, tune′a•ble** *adj.* —**tune′less** *adj.* —**tune′less•ly** *adv.* —**tune′less•ness** *n.*

tune•ful (to͞on′fəl, tyo͞on′-) ►*adj.* Melodious. —**tune′ful•ly** *adv.* —**tune′ful•ness** *n.*

tun•er (to͞o′nər, tyo͞o′-) ►*n.* **1.** One that tunes. **2.** A device for tuning, esp. an electronic device used to select signals for amplification and conversion to sound.

tune-up (to͞on′ŭp′, tyo͞on′-) ►*n.* An adjustment of a motor or engine to improve working order or efficiency.

tung•sten (tŭng′stən) ►*n.* *Symbol* **W** A hard, brittle, corrosion-resistant gray to white metallic element used in high-temperature structural materials and in electrical elements. At. no. 74. See table at **element.** [Swed.]

Tun•gus•ic (to͝ong-go͞o′zĭk, tŭn-) ►*n.* A subfamily of the Altaic languages of E Siberia and N Manchuria. —**Tun•gus′ic** *adj.*

tu•nic (to͞o′nĭk, tyo͞o′-) ►*n.* **1.** A loose-fitting, knee-length garment worn by the ancient Greeks and Romans. **2a.** A long, plain, close-fitting military jacket. **b.** A long plain blouse. [< Lat. *tunica.*]

tun•ing fork (to͞o′nĭng, tyo͞o′-) ►*n.* A small two-pronged metal device that when struck produces a sound of fixed pitch, used for tuning musical instruments.

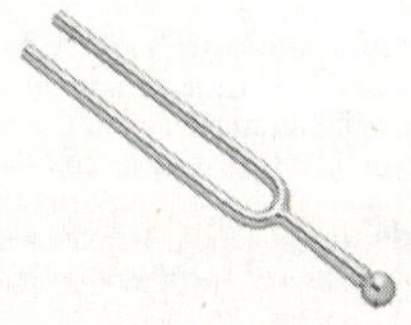

tuning fork

Tu•nis (to͞o′nĭs, tyo͞o′-) The capital of Tunisia, in the N part on the **Gulf of Tunis,** an inlet of the Mediterranean. Pop. 596,654.

Tu•ni•sia (to͞o-nē′zhə, -shə, tyo͞o-) A country of N Africa bordering on the Mediterranean. Cap. Tunis. Pop. 8,733,000. —**Tu•ni′sian** *adj. & n.*

tun•nel (tŭn′əl) ►*n.* An underground or underwater passage. ►*v.* **-neled, -nel•ing** or **-nelled, -nel•ling 1.** To make a tunnel (through or under). **2.** To dig in the form of a tunnel. [< OFr. *tonnelle*, tubular net.]

tunnel vision ►*n.* An extremely narrow outlook; narrow-mindedness.

tun•ny (tŭn′ē) ►*n., pl.* **-ny** or **-nies.** See **tuna** 1. [< Gk. *thunnos.*]

tu•pe•lo (to͞o′pə-lō′, tyo͞o′-) ►*n., pl.* **-los.** A tree of the SE US having soft light wood. [Prob. Creek *'topilwa.*]

Tu•pi (to͞o′pē, to͞o-pē′) ►*n., pl.* **-pi** or **-pis 1.** A member of any of a group of Indian peoples living along the coast of Brazil, in the Amazon River valley, and in Paraguay. **2.** The language of the Tupi. —**Tu′pi•an** *adj.*

tur•ban (tûr′bən) ►*n.* A chiefly Muslim headdress consisting of a long scarf wound around the head. [< Ottoman Turk. *tülbend*, muslin.]

tur•bid (tûr′bĭd) ►*adj.* **1.** Having sediment or foreign particles stirred up or suspended: *turbid water.* **2.** Heavy or dense, as smoke. **3.** In turmoil: *turbid feelings.* [Lat. *turbidus*, disordered.] —**tur′bid•ly** *adv.* —**tur′bid•ness, tur•bid′i•ty** *n.*

tur•bine (tûr′bĭn, -bīn′) ►*n.* A machine in which the kinetic energy of a moving fluid is converted to mechanical power as the fluid turns a series of buckets, paddles, or blades arrayed about the circumference of a wheel or cylinder. [< Lat. *turbō*, spinning top.]

tur•bo•jet (tûr′bō-jĕt′) ►*n.* A jet engine with a turbine-driven compressor.

tur•bo•prop (tûr′bō-prŏp′) ►*n.* A turbojet engine used to drive an external propeller.

tur•bot (tûr′bət) ►*n., pl.* **-bot** or **-bots.** An edible European flatfish. [< OFr. *tourbout.*]

tur•bu•lent (tûr′byə-lənt) ►*adj.* **1.** Violently agitated or disturbed. **2.** Marked by unrest or disturbance. [< Lat. *turbulentus.*] —**tur′bu•lence** *n.* —**tur′bu•lent•ly** *adv.*

tu•reen (to͞o-rēn′, tyo͞o-) ►*n.* A broad, deep, usu. covered dish used esp. for serving soups or stews. [< OFr. *terrin*, earthen < Lat. *terra*, earth.]

turf (tûrf) ►*n.* **1.** Surface earth containing grass and its matted roots; sod. **2.** A piece of cut turf. **3.** A piece of peat burned as fuel. **4.** *Slang* **a.** The range of one's authority or influence. **b.** The area claimed by a gang. **5.** A racetrack for horses. [< OE.]

Tur•ge•nev (to͝or-gān′yəf, -gĕn′-), **Ivan Sergeevich.** 1818–83. Russian writer.

tur•gid (tûr′jĭd) ►*adj.* **1.** Excessively ornate or complex: *turgid prose.* **2.** Swollen or distended, as from fluid. [Lat. *turgidus.*] —**tur•gid′i•ty, tur′gid•ness** *n.*

Tu•rin (to͝or′ĭn, tyo͝or′-) A city of NW Italy on the Po R. Pop. 961,916.

Turk (tûrk) ►*n.* **1.** A native or inhabitant of Turkey. **2.** An Ottoman. **3.** A member of a Turkic-speaking people.

tur•key (tûr′kē) ►*n., pl.* **-keys 1.** A large, widely domesticated North American bird having brownish plumage and a bare wattled head and neck. **2.** *Slang* **a.** A disliked person. **b.** A failure; flop. [< TURKEY.]

Turkey. A country of SW Asia and SE Europe between the Mediterranean and Black seas. Cap. Ankara. Pop. 61,183,000.

turkey vulture ►*n.* A New World vulture with dark plumage and a bare red head and neck.

Turk•ic (tûr′kĭk) ►*n.* A subfamily of the Altaic languages including Turkish. —**Turk′ic** *adj.*

Turk•ish (tûr′kĭsh) ►*adj.* Of Turkey, the Turks, or the Turkish language. ►*n.* The Turkic language of Turkey.

Turkish bath ►*n.* A steam bath followed by a shower and massage.

Turk•men•i•stan (tûrk′mĕn-ĭ-stăn′, -stän′) A region and republic of W-central Asia E of the Caspian Sea. Cap. Ashgabat. Pop. 4,010,000. —**Turk′men** (tûrk′mən) *n. & adj.*

Turks and Cai•cos Islands (tûrks; kā′kəs, kī′kōs) Two island groups of the British West Indies in the Atlantic in the SE Bahamas.

Tur•ku (to͝or′ko͞o′) A city of SW Finland on the

Baltic Sea W of Helsinki. Pop. 160,153.

tur•mer•ic (tûr′mər-ĭk) ►*n.* An Indian plant with yellow flowers and a rootstock that when powdered is used as a condiment and as a yellow dye. [< Med.Lat. *terra merita* : Lat. *terra*, earth + Lat. *merita*, deserved.]

tur•moil (tûr′moil′) ►*n.* Extreme confusion or agitation. [?]

turn (tûrn) ►*v.* **1.** To move or cause to move around an axis or center; rotate or revolve. **2.** To change the position of so as to show the other side. **3.** To shape on a lathe. **4.** To give distinctive form to: *turn a phrase.* **5.** To injure by twisting: *turn an ankle.* **6.** To nauseate; upset. **7a.** To change the direction or course of: *turn the car left.* **b.** To direct or change one's way or course. **8.** To make a course around or about: *turn the corner.* **9.** To set in a specified way or direction. **10.** To antagonize or become antagonistic. **11.** To direct (e.g., the attention or interest) toward or away from something. **12.** To send, drive, or let: *turn the dog loose.* **13.** To have recourse; resort. **14.** To depend on something for success or failure; hinge. **15.** To become: *a lawyer turned novelist.* **16.** To transform or become transformed; change. **17.** To become sour. **18.** To change color. —***phrasal verbs:*** **turn down 1.** To diminish, as the volume of. **2.** To reject. **turn in 1.** To hand in. **2.** To inform on or deliver: *The thief turned himself in.* **3.** *Informal* To go to bed. **turn off 1.** To stop the operation of. **2.** *Slang* To displease or disgust. **turn on 1.** To start the operation of: *Turn on the light.* **2.** *Slang* To please or excite. **turn out 1.** To shut off. **2.** To arrive or assemble. **3.** To produce; make. **4.** To result; end up. **turn over 1.** To think about; consider. **2.** To transfer to another. **turn up 1.** To increase, as the volume of. **2.** To find or be found. **3.** To arrive; appear. ►*n.* **1.** The act of turning; rotation; revolution. **2.** A change of direction: *a left turn.* **3.** A departure or deviation, as in a trend. **4.** A chance or opportunity to do something. **5.** Natural inclination: *a speculative turn of mind.* **6.** A deed or action: *a good turn.* **7.** A short excursion. **8.** A single wind or convolution, as of wire on a spool. **9.** A rendering: *a turn of phrase.* **10.** A momentary shock or scare. —***idioms:*** **by turns** Alternately. **in turn** In the proper order. **out of turn** Not in the proper order. **turn over a new leaf** To change for the better. **turn the tables** To reverse a situation and gain the upper hand. [< Gk. *tornos*, lathe.] —**turn′er** *n.*

turn•a•bout (tûrn′ə-bout′) ►*n.* A shift or reversal in fortune, allegiance, or direction.

turn•a•round (tûrn′ə-round′) ►*n.* A turnabout.

turn•buck•le (tûrn′bŭk′əl) ►*n.* A metal coupling device consisting of an oblong piece internally threaded at both ends into which two pieces of threaded rod are screwed.

turnbuckle

turn•coat (tûrn′kōt′) ►*n.* One who traitorously switches allegiance.

Tur•ner (tûr′nər), **Joseph Mallord William.** 1775–1851. British painter.

Turner, Nat. 1800–31. Amer. slave leader.

turn•ing point (tûr′nĭng) ►*n.* A decisive moment.

tur•nip (tûr′nĭp) ►*n.* **1.** A cultivated plant with a large edible yellow or white root. **2.** The root of this plant. [*tur-*, of unknown orig. + dial. *nepe*, turnip (< Lat. *nāpus*).]

turn•key (tûrn′kē′) ►*n., pl.* **-keys.** A jailer.

turn•off (tûrn′ôf′, -ŏf′) ►*n.* **1.** An exit on a highway. **2.** *Slang* Something distasteful.

turn-on (tûrn′ŏn′, -ôn′) ►*n. Slang* Something that causes pleasure or excitement.

turn•out (tûrn′out′) ►*n.* **1.** The number of people at a gathering; attendance. **2.** An array of equipment. **3.** A widening in a road.

turn•o•ver (tûrn′ō′vər) ►*n.* **1.** The act of turning over; an upset. **2.** An abrupt change; reversal. **3.** A pastry made by covering half of a piece of dough with filling and folding the other half over it. **4a.** The number of times a particular stock of goods is sold and restocked during a given period. **b.** The amount of business transacted during a given period. **5.** The rate of replacement of personnel.

turn•pike (tûrn′pīk′) ►*n.* A toll road, esp. an expressway with tollgates. [ME *turnepike*, spiked barrier.]

turn•stile (tûrn′stīl′) ►*n.* A device for controlling passage from one area to another, usu. consisting of several revolving horizontal arms projecting from a central post.

turn•ta•ble (tûrn′tā′bəl) ►*n.* **1.** The circular rotating platform of a phonograph on which the record is placed. **2.** A circular rotating platform for turning locomotives.

tur•pen•tine (tûr′pən-tīn′) ►*n.* A thin volatile oil, $C_{10}H_{16}$, obtained from certain pine trees and used as a paint thinner, solvent, and medicinally as a liniment. [< Gk. *terebinthos*, a kind of tree.]

tur•pi•tude (tûr′pĭ-to͞od′, -tyo͞od′) ►*n.* Depravity; baseness: *moral turpitude.* [< Lat. *turpis*, shameful.]

tur•quoise (tûr′kwoiz′, -koiz′) ►*n.* **1.** A blue to blue-green mineral of aluminum and copper, prized as a gemstone. **2.** A light bluish green. [< OFr. *turqueis*, Turkish.] —**tur′quoise′** *adj.*

tur•ret (tûr′ĭt, tŭr′-) ►*n.* **1.** A small tower or tower-shaped projection on a building. **2.** A projecting armored structure, usu. rotating horizontally, containing mounted guns and their gunners, as on a warship or tank. [< OFr. *torete* < *tor*, tower.] —**tur′ret•ed** *adj.*

tur•tle[1] (tûr′tl) ►*n.* Any of an order of aquatic or terrestrial reptiles having beaklike jaws and the body enclosed in a bony or leathery shell. [Perh. < OFr. *tortue.*]

tur•tle[2] (tûr′tl) ►*n. Archaic* A turtledove. [< Lat. *turtur.*]

tur•tle•dove (tûr′tl-dŭv′) ►*n.* **1.** An Old World dove with a soft purring call. **2.** See **mourning dove.**

tur•tle•neck (tûr′tl-nĕk′) ►*n.* **1.** A high, close-fitting, turned-down collar. **2.** A garment with such a collar.

Tus•ca•ny (tŭs′kə-nē′) A region of W-central Italy between the N Apennines and the Ligurian and Tyrrhenian seas. —**Tus′can** *adj. & n.*

Tus•ca•ro•ra (tŭs′kə-rôr′ə, -rōr′ə) ▸*n., pl.* **-ra** or **-ras 1.** A member of a Native American people formerly of North Carolina, now in W New York and SE Ontario. **2.** The Iroquoian language of the Tuscarora.

tusk (tŭsk) ▸*n.* A long pointed tooth, as of an elephant, extending outside the mouth. [< OE *tūsc.*] —**tusked** *adj.*

tus•sle (tŭs′əl) ▸*v.* **-sled, -sling.** To struggle roughly; scuffle or wrestle. [ME *tussillen.*] —**tus′sle** *n.*

tus•sock (tŭs′ək) ▸*n.* A clump or tuft, as of grass. [?]

Tut•ankh•a•men (to͞ot′äng-kä′mən). fl. c. 1358 B.C. King of Egypt during the XVIII Dynasty.

tu•te•lage (to͞ot′l-ĭj, tyo͞ot′-) ▸*n.* **1.** The function or role of a guardian; guardianship. **2.** The function or role of a tutor; instruction. **3.** The state of being under a guardian or tutor. [< Lat. *tūtēla.*] —**tu′te•lar′y** (-ĕr′ē) *adj.*

tu•tor (to͞o′tər, tyo͞o′-) ▸*n.* A private instructor, esp. one giving additional or remedial instruction. [< Lat. *tūtor.*] —**tu′tor** *v.* —**tu•to′ri•al** (-tôr′ē-əl, -tōr′-) *adj. & n.*

Tut•si (to͞ot′sē) ▸*n., pl.* **-si** or **-sis.** A member of a Bantu-speaking people of Rwanda and Burundi.

tut•ti-frut•ti (to͞o′tē-fro͞o′tē) ▸*n.* A confection or flavoring that contains a variety of chopped candied fruits. [Ital., all fruits.]

tu•tu (to͞o′to͞o) ▸*n.* A short ballet skirt, usu. having layers of gathered sheer fabric. [Fr.]

Tu•tu (to͞o′to͞o), **Desmond.** b. 1931. South African prelate and antiapartheid leader; 1984 Nobel Peace Prize.

Tu•va•lu (to͞o-vä′lo͞o, to͞o′və-lo͞o′) An island country of the W Pacific N of Fiji. Cap. Fongafale. Pop. 9,000.

tux (tŭks) ▸*n. Informal* A tuxedo.

tux•e•do (tŭk-sē′dō) ▸*n., pl.* **-dos** or **-does.** A man's formal or semiformal suit, usu. black with a tailless jacket and a black bow tie. [After *Tuxedo* Park, New York.]

TV (tē′vē′) ▸*n.* Television.

TVA ▸*abbr.* Tennessee Valley Authority

TV dinner ▸*n.* A frozen precooked meal that needs only to be heated before serving.

Tver′ (tvĕr) A city of W-central Russia on the Volga R. NW of Moscow. Pop. 449,461.

twad•dle (twŏd′l) ▸*n.* Idle talk; nonsense. [Prob. < dial. *twattle.*] —**twad′dle** *v.*

twain (twān) ▸*n., adj., & pron.* Two. [< OE *twēgen.*]

Twain, Mark. See Samuel Langhorne **Clemens.**

twang (twăng) ▸*n.* **1.** A sharp vibrating sound, as of the plucked string of a banjo or guitar. **2.** A strongly nasal tone of voice. [Imit.] —**twang** *v.* —**twang′y** *adj.*

tweak (twēk) ▸*v.* To pinch or twist sharply. [< OE *twiccian.*] —**tweak** *n.*

tweed (twēd) ▸*n.* **1.** A coarse woolen fabric usu. woven of several colors. **2. tweeds** Clothing made of tweed. [< Sc. *tweel,* TWILL.] —**tweed′y** *adj.*

tweet (twēt) ▸*n.* A high chirping sound, as of a young or small bird. [Imit.] —**tweet** *v.*

tweet•er (twē′tər) ▸*n.* A loudspeaker designed to reproduce high-pitched sounds in a high-fidelity audio system.

tweez•ers (twē′zərz) ▸*pl.n. (takes sing. or pl. v.)* Small pincers, usu. of metal, used for plucking or handling small objects. [< obsolete *tweezes.*] —**tweeze** *v.*

twelfth (twĕlfth) ▸*n.* **1.** The ordinal number matching the number 12 in a series. **2.** One of 12 equal parts. —**twelfth** *adv. & adj.*

Twelfth Night ▸*n.* Jan. 5, the eve of Epiphany.

twelve (twĕlv) ▸*n.* **1.** The cardinal number equal to the sum of 11 + 1. **2.** The 12th in a set or sequence. [< OE *twelf.*] —**twelve** *adj. & pron.*

twelve•month (twĕlv′mŭnth′) ▸*n.* A year.

twen•ti•eth (twĕn′tē-ĭth) ▸*n.* **1.** The ordinal number matching the number 20 in a series. **2.** One of 20 equal parts. —**twen′ti•eth** *adv. & adj.*

twen•ty (twĕn′tē) ▸*n., pl.* **-ties.** The cardinal number equal to 2 × 10. [< OE *twēntig.*] —**twen′ty** *adj. & pron.*

twen•ty-twen•ty or **20/20** (twĕn′tē-twĕn′tē) ▸*adj.* Having normal visual acuity.

twerp (twûrp) ▸*n. Slang* An insignificant and contemptible person. [?]

Twi (chwē, chē) ▸*n.* A language of Ghana.

twice (twīs) ▸*adv.* **1.** In two cases or on two occasions; two times. **2.** In doubled degree or amount. [< OE *twiga.*]

twid•dle (twĭd′l) ▸*v.* **-dled, -dling 1.** To turn over or around lightly. **2.** To play with; trifle. —***idiom:* twiddle (one's) thumbs** To do little or nothing; be idle. [Poss. blend of TWIST and FIDDLE.] —**twid′dler** *n.*

twig (twĭg) ▸*n.* A small slender branch. [< OE *twigge.*] —**twig′gy** *adj.*

twi•light (twī′līt′) ▸*n.* **1.** The time of the day when the sun is below the horizon but is casting diffuse light. **2.** The soft indistinct light of this time, esp. after sunset. **3.** A period or condition of decline. [ME.]

twill (twĭl) ▸*n.* A fabric with diagonal parallel ribs. [< OE *twilīc.*]

twin (twĭn) ▸*n.* **1.** One of two offspring born at the same birth. **2.** One of two identical or similar things; counterpart. ▸*adj.* **1.** Born at the same birth. **2.** Being two or one of two identical or like things. **3.** Consisting of two identical or like parts. [< OE *twinn.*]

twin bed ▸*n.* One of a matching pair of single beds.

twine (twīn) ▸*v.* **twined, twin•ing 1.** To twist together; intertwine. **2.** To form by twisting. **3.** To encircle or coil about. **4.** To go in a winding course. ▸*n.* A strong string or cord made of two or more threads twisted together. [< OE *twīn,* double thread.]

twinge (twĭnj) ▸*n.* A sudden sharp physical or emotional pain. See Syns at **pain.** ▸*v.* **twinged, twing•ing.** To feel or cause to feel a sharp pain. [< OE *twengan,* pinch.]

twin•kle (twĭng′kəl) ▸*v.* **-kled, -kling 1.** To shine with slight intermittent gleams. **2.** To be bright or sparkling: *Their eyes twinkled.* **3.** To wink. ▸*n.* **1.** An intermittent gleam of light. **2.** A sparkle of merriment or delight in the eye. **3.** A brief interval; a twinkling. [< OE *twinclian.*] —**twink′ly** *adj.*

twin•kling (twĭng′klĭng) ▸*n.* A brief interval.

twirl (twûrl) ▸*v.* **1.** To rotate or revolve briskly; spin. **2.** To twist or wind (around). [?] —**twirl** *n.* —**twirl′er** *n.*

twist (twĭst) ►*v.* **1.** To entwine (several threads) to produce a single strand. **2.** To wind or coil about something: *twisted the reins around her hand.* **3.** To impart a spiral or coiling shape to. **4a.** To turn or open by turning. **b.** To break by turning: *twist off a small branch.* **5.** To wrench or sprain. **6.** To distort the intended meaning of. **7.** To move in a winding course. **8.** To rotate or revolve. ►*n.* **1.** Something twisted or formed by twisting. **2.** The act of twisting; a spin or twirl. **3.** A sprain or wrench, as of an ankle. **4.** An unexpected turn of events. [ME *twisten.*] —**twist′er** *n.*

twit (twĭt) ►*v.* **twit•ted, twit•ting.** To taunt or tease. ►*n. Slang* An annoying person. [< OE *ætwītan* : *æt*, at + *wītan*, reproach.]

twitch (twĭch) ►*v.* To move or cause to move jerkily or spasmodically. See Syns at **jerk**[1]. ►*n.* **1.** A sudden involuntary muscular movement. **2.** A sudden jerk or tug. [ME *twicchen.*] —**twitch′y** *adj.*

twit•ter (twĭt′ər) ►*v.* To utter a series of light chirping or tremulous sounds. [ME *twiteren.*] —**twit′ter** *n.* —**twit′ter•y** *adj.*

twixt also **′twixt** (twĭkst) ►*prep.* Betwixt.

two (to͞o) ►*n.* **1.** The cardinal number equal to the sum of 1 + 1. **2.** The 2nd in a set or sequence. [< OE *twā.*] —**two** *adj. & pron.*

two-bit (to͞o′bĭt′) ►*adj. Slang* Worth very little; cheap; insignificant.

two bits ►*pl.n.* **1.** *Informal* Twenty-five cents. **2.** *Slang* A petty sum.

two-by-four (to͞o′bī-fôr′, -fōr′) ►*n.* A length of lumber that is 2 inches thick and 4 inches wide or that is trimmed to slightly smaller dimensions.

two-di•men•sion•al (to͞o′dĭ-mĕn′shə-nəl, -dī-) ►*adj.* **1.** Having only two dimensions, esp. length and width. **2.** Lacking depth: *a movie with two-dimensional characters.*

two-faced (to͞o′fāst′) ►*adj.* **1.** Having two faces. **2.** Hypocritical or double-dealing; deceitful. —**two′-fac′ed•ly** (-fā′sĭd-lē, -fāst′lē) *adv.* —**two′-fac′ed•ness** *n.*

two-ply (to͞o′plī′) ►*adj.* Made of two layers, thicknesses, or strands.

two•some (to͞o′səm) ►*n.* Two people together; a couple.

two-step (to͞o′stĕp′) ►*n.* A ballroom dance in 2/4 time with long sliding steps.

two-time (to͞o′tīm′) ►*v. Slang* **1.** To be unfaithful to. **2.** To deceive; double-cross. —**two′-tim′er** *n.*

two-way (to͞o′wā′) ►*adj.* Affording passage or communication in two directions.

TX ►*abbr.* Texas

-ty ►*suff.* Condition; quality: *novelty.* [< Lat. *-tās.*]

ty•coon (tī-ko͞on′) ►*n.* A wealthy and powerful businessperson; magnate. [J. *taikun*, title of a shogun.]

tyke (tīk) ►*n.* **1.** A small child, esp. a boy. **2.** A mongrel or cur. [< ON *tīk*, bitch.]

Ty•ler (tī′lər), **John.** 1790–1862. The 10th US President (1841–45).

tym•pa•ni (tĭm′pə-nē) ►*pl.n.* Var. of **timpani.** —**tym′pa•nist** *n.*

tym•pan•ic membrane (tĭm-păn′ĭk) ►*n.* See **eardrum.**

tym•pa•num (tĭm′pə-nəm) ►*n., pl.* **-na** (-nə) or **-nums 1.** See **middle ear. 2.** See **eardrum.** [< Gk. *tumpanon*, drum.]

John Tyler

Tyn•dale (tĭn′dl), **William.** 1494?–1536. English religious reformer and martyr.

Tyne (tīn) A river, about 129 km (80 mi), of N England flowing to the North Sea.

type (tīp) ►*n.* **1.** A number of people or things sharing common traits; class; category. **2.** One having the features of a group or class: *a type of cactus.* **3.** An example or model; embodiment. **4.** *Print.* **a.** A small block bearing a raised character that leaves a printed impression when inked and pressed on paper. **b.** Such pieces collectively. **c.** Printed or typewritten characters; print. ►*v.* **typed, typ•ing 1.** To typewrite. **2.** To classify according to a particular system. **3.** To typecast. **4.** To represent or typify. [< Gk. *tupos*, impression.]

type•cast (tīp′kăst′) ►*v.* To assign (a performer) repeatedly to the same kind of part.

type•face (tīp′fās′) ►*n. Print.* **1.** The surface of a block of type that makes the impression. **2.** The size or style of type.

type•script (tīp′skrĭpt′) ►*n.* A typewritten copy, as of a book.

type•set (tīp′sĕt′) ►*v.* To set (written material) into type; compose. —**type′set′ter** *n.* —**type′set′ting** *n.*

type•write (tīp′rīt′) ►*v.* To write (something) with a typewriter; type.

type•writ•er (tīp′rī′tər) ►*n.* A machine that prints characters by means of a manually operated keyboard that moves a set of raised types, which strike the paper through an inked ribbon.

ty•phoid (tī′foid′) ►*n.* Typhoid fever. [TYPH(US) + -OID.] —**ty′phoid′** *adj.*

typhoid fever ►*n.* An acute, highly infectious disease caused by a bacillus transmitted by contaminated food or water and marked by high fever, coughing, and red rashes.

ty•phoon (tī-fo͞on′) ►*n.* A tropical cyclone of the W Pacific or Indian Oceans. [Gk. *tuphōn*, whirlwind, Ar. *ṭūfān*, deluge, and Cantonese *taaîfung*, great wind.]

ty•phus (tī′fəs) ►*n.* Any of several infectious diseases caused by microorganisms and marked by severe headache, sustained high fever, delirium, and red rashes. [< Gk. *tuphos*, stupor.] —**ty′phous** (-fəs) *adj.*

typ•i•cal (tĭp′ĭ-kəl) ►*adj.* **1.** Exhibiting the characteristics peculiar to a kind, group, or category; representative. **2.** Conforming to or serving as a type. **3.** Usual; ordinary: *a typical day at the office.* [< Gk. *tupikos.*] —**typ′i•cal•ly** *adv.* —**typ′i•cal•ness, typ′i•cal′i•ty** (-kăl′ĭ-tē) *n.*

typ•i•fy (tĭp′ə-fī′) ►*v.* **-fied** (-fīd′), **-fy•ing 1.**

To serve as a typical example of. **2.** To represent by an image, form, or model; symbolize. —**typ′i•fi′er** *n.*

typ•ist (tī′pĭst) ►*n.* One who operates a typewriter.

ty•po (tī′pō) ►*n., pl.* **-pos** *Informal* A typographical error.

typographical error ►*n.* A mistake in printed copy, esp. one caused by striking an incorrect key on a keyboard.

ty•pog•ra•phy (tī-pŏg′rə-fē) ►*n., pl.* **-phies 1.** The composition of printed material from movable type. **2.** The arrangement and appearance of printed matter. —**ty•pog′ra•pher** *n.* —**ty′po•graph′i•cal** (tī′pə-grăf′ĭ-kəl), **ty′po•graph′ic** *adj.*

ty•ran•ni•cal (tĭ-răn′ĭ-kəl, tī-) also **ty•ran•nic** (-răn′ĭk) ►*adj.* Of or relating to a tyrant or tyranny; despotic. —**ty•ran′ni•cal•ly** *adv.*

tyr•an•nize (tĭr′ə-nīz′) ►*v.* **-nized, -niz•ing 1.** To treat tyrannically; oppress. **2.** To rule as a tyrant. —**tyr′an•niz′er** *n.*

ty•ran•no•saur (tĭ-răn′ə-sôr′, tī-) also **ty•ran•no•saur•us** (tĭ-răn′ə-sôr′əs, tī-) ►*n.* A very large carnivorous dinosaur characterized by small forelimbs and a large head. [Gk. *turannos*, tyrant + *sauros*, lizard.]

tyr•an•nous (tĭr′ə-nəs) ►*adj.* Despotic; tyrannical. —**tyr′an•nous•ly** *adv.*

tyr•an•ny (tĭr′ə-nē) ►*n., pl.* **-nies 1.** A government in which a single ruler is vested with absolute power. **2.** Absolute power, esp. when exercised unjustly or cruelly. **3.** A tyrannical act. **4.** Extreme harshness or severity; rigor. [< Gk. *turannos*, tyrant.]

ty•rant (tī′rənt) ►*n.* **1.** An absolute ruler, esp. an oppressive or cruel one. **2.** A harsh or domineering person. [< Gk. *turannos*.]

tyre (tīr) ►*n. Chiefly Brit.* Var. of **tire**[2].

Tyre. An ancient Phoenician seaport in present-day S Lebanon.

ty•ro (tī′rō) ►*n., pl.* **-ros.** A beginner. [< Lat. *tīrō*, recruit.]

Ty•rol or **Ti•rol** (tə-rōl′, tī-, tī′rōl′). A region of the E Alps in W Austria and N Italy. —**Ty•rol′le•an, Tyr′o•lese′** (tĭr′ə-lēz′, -lēs′, tī′rə-) *adj. & n.*

Tyr•rhe•ni•an Sea (tə-rē′nē-ən) An arm of the Mediterranean between the Italian peninsula and the islands of Corsica, Sardinia, and Sicily.

tzar (zär, tsär) ►*n.* Var. of **czar** 1.

U

u or **U** (yo͞o) ►*n., pl.* **u's** or **U's** also **us** or **Us.** The 21st letter of the English alphabet.

U ► The symbol for the element **uranium.**

UAE ►*abbr.* United Arab Emirates

UAW ►*abbr.* United Automobile Workers

U•ban•gi (yo͞o-băng′gē, o͞o-bäng′-) A river of central Africa flowing about 1,126 km (700 mi) along the NW border of Congo (formerly Zaire) to the Congo R.

u•biq•ui•tous (yo͞o-bĭk′wĭ-təs) ►*adj.* Being or seeming to be everywhere at the same time; omnipresent. [< Lat. *ubīque*, everywhere.] —**u•biq′ui•tous•ly** *adv.* —**u•biq′ui•tous•ness** *n.* —**u•biq′ui•ty** *n.*

U-boat (yo͞o′bōt′) ►*n.* A German submarine. [< Ger. *Unterseeboot* : OHGer. *untar*, under + *See*, sea + *Boot*, boat.]

U-bolt (yo͞o′bōlt′) ►*n.* A U-shaped bolt, fitted with threads and a nut at each end.

U-bolt

uc also **UC** ►*abbr.* uppercase

Uc•cel•lo (o͞o-chĕl′lō), **Paolo.** 1397–1475. Italian painter.

ud•der (ŭd′ər) ►*n.* A baglike organ of female cows, sheep, and goats containing the mammary glands. [< OE *ūder*.]

U•fa (o͞o-fä′) A city of W Russia in the S Ural Mts. Pop. 1,064,000.

UFO (yo͞o′ĕf-ō′) ►*n.* An unidentified flying object.

U•gan•da (yo͞o-găn′də, o͞o-gän′-dä) A country of E-central Africa. Cap. Kampala. Pop. 20,621,000. —**U•gan′dan** *adj. & n.*

ug•ly (ŭg′lē) ►*adj.* **-li•er, -li•est 1.** Displeasing to the eye; unsightly. **2.** Repulsive or offensive; objectionable. **3.** Morally reprehensible; bad. **4.** Threatening or ominous: *ugly black clouds.* **5.** Cross or disagreeable: *an ugly temper.* [< ON *uggligr*, frightful < *uggr*, fear.] —**ug′li•ness** *n.*

Syns: *ugly, hideous, ill-favored, unsightly*
Ant: *beautiful* **adj.**

U•gric (o͞o′grĭk, yo͞o′-) ►*n.* The branch of the Finno-Ugric subfamily of languages that includes Hungarian. —**U′gric** *adj.*

UHF ►*abbr.* ultrahigh frequency

U•jung Pan•dang (o͞o-jo͝ong′ pän-däng′) A city of central Indonesia on SW Sulawesi I. Pop. 709,038.

UK ►*abbr.* United Kingdom

u•kase (yo͞o-kās′, -kāz′, yo͞o′kās′, -kāz′) ►*n.* An authoritative decree; edict. [< Russ. *ukaz*.]

U•kraine (yo͞o-krān′) A republic of E Europe. Cap. Kiev. Pop. 51,910,000.

U•krain•i•an (yo͞o-krā′nē-ən) ►*n.* **1.** A native or inhabitant of Ukraine. **2.** Their Slavic language. —**U•krain′i•an** *adj.*

u•ku•le•le or **u•ke•le•le** (yo͞o′kə-lā′lē, o͞o′kə-) ►*n.* A small four-stringed guitar popu-

ukulele

larized in Hawaii. [Hawaiian *'ukulele.*]

Regional Note: The word *ukulele* is one of a small stock of Polynesian borrowings into American English. Other such words are *aloha* and *luau. Haole* is the Hawaiian word for a white person.

U•laan•baa•tar (o͞o′län-bä′tär′) The capital of Mongolia, in the N-central part. Pop. 515,100.

U•lan-U•de (o͞o-län′o͞o-dĕ′) A city of S-central Russia near Lake Baikal and the Mongolian border. Pop. 363,967.

ul•cer (ŭl′sər) ►*n.* **1.** A lesion of the skin or a mucous membrane accompanied by formation of pus and necrosis of surrounding tissue. **2.** A corrupting condition or influence. [< Lat. *ulcus, ulcer-.*] —**ul′cer•ous** *adj.*

ul•cer•ate (ŭl′sə-rāt′) ►*v.* **-at•ed, -at•ing.** To affect or become affected with an ulcer. —**ul′cer•a′tion** *n.* —**ul′cer•a′tive** (-sə-rā′tĭv, -sər-ə-tĭv) *adj.*

-ule ►*suff.* Small: *ovule.* [Fr. < Lat. *-ulus,* diminutive suff.]

ULF ►*abbr.* ultralow frequency

ul•na (ŭl′nə) ►*n., pl.* **-nas** or **-nae** (-nē). The bone extending from the elbow to the wrist on the side opposite to the thumb. [Lat., elbow.] —**ul′nar** *adj.*

ul•ster (ŭl′stər) ►*n.* A loose, long, often belted overcoat. [< ULSTER.]

Ulster. A historical region of N Ireland.

ult. ►*abbr.* **1.** ultimately **2.** ultimo

ul•te•ri•or (ŭl-tîr′ē-ər) ►*adj.* **1.** Beyond or outside what is evident or admitted: *an ulterior motive.* **2.** Lying beyond or outside of a certain area. [Lat., farther.]

ul•ti•mate (ŭl′tə-mĭt) ►*adj.* **1.** Completing a series, process, or progression. **2.** Fundamental; elemental. **3.** Greatest; extreme. **4.** Farthest; remotest. **5.** Eventual: *hoped for ultimate victory.* ►*n.* **1.** The basic or fundamental fact, element, or principle. **2.** The final point; the conclusion. **3.** The maximum: *the ultimate in sophistication.* [< Lat. *ultimus,* last.] —**ul′ti•mate•ly** *adv.*

ul•ti•ma•tum (ŭl′tə-mā′təm, -mä′-) ►*n., pl.* **-tums** or **-ta** (-tə). A statement of terms that expresses or implies the threat of serious penalties if the terms are not accepted. [< Lat. *ultimātus,* last.]

ul•ti•mo (ŭl′tə-mō′) ►*adv.* In or of the month before the present one. [Lat. *ultimō (mēnse),* in the last (month).]

ul•tra (ŭl′trə) ►*adj.* Going beyond the normal limit; extreme. [< Lat. *ultrā-,* ultra-.]

ultra- ►*pref.* **1.** Beyond: *ultraviolet.* **2.** Extreme; excessive: *ultraconservative.* [< Lat. *ultrā,* beyond.]

ul•tra•con•ser•va•tive (ŭl′trə-kən-sûr′və-tĭv) ►*adj.* Extremely conservative; reactionary.

ul•tra•high frequency (ŭl′trə-hī′) ►*n.* A band of radio frequencies from 300 to 3,000 megahertz.

ul•tra•lib•er•al (ŭl′trə-lĭb′ər-əl, -lĭb′rəl) ►*adj.* Extremely liberal; radical.

ul•tra•ma•rine (ŭl′trə-mə-rēn′) ►*n.* **1.** A blue pigment. **2.** A bright deep blue. ►*adj.* **1.** Of the color ultramarine. **2.** Of or from a place beyond the sea. [< Med.Lat. *ultrāmarīnus,* from beyond the sea : ULTRA– + Lat. *mare,* sea.]

ul•tra•mi•cro•scope (ŭl′trə-mī′krə-skōp′) ►*n.* A microscope with high-intensity illumination used to study very minute objects.

ul•tra•mi•cro•scop•ic (ŭl′trə-mī′krə-skŏp′ĭk) ►*adj.* Too minute to be seen with an ordinary microscope.

ul•tra•mod•ern (ŭl′trə-mŏd′ərn) ►*adj.* Extremely modern in ideas or style. —**ul′tra•mod′ern•ism** *n.* —**ul′tra•mod′ern•ist** *n.*

ul•tra•mon•tane (ŭl′trə-mŏn′tān′, -mŏn-tān′) ►*adj.* **1.** Of or relating to peoples or regions lying beyond the mountains. **2.** Supporting the authority of the pope in ecclesiastical and political matters. [Med.Lat. *ultrāmontānus.*] —**ul′tra•mon′tane′** *n.*

ul•tra•son•ic (ŭl′trə-sŏn′ĭk) ►*adj.* **1.** Relating to acoustic frequencies above the range of human hearing, or above approx. 20,000 hertz. **2.** Of or involving ultrasound.

ul•tra•so•nog•ra•phy (ŭl′trə-sə-nŏg′rə-fē) ►*n.* Diagnostic imaging in which ultrasound is used to visualize an internal body structure or a developing fetus. [ULTRASON(IC) + –GRAPHY.] —**ul′tra•son′o•graph** *n.* —**ul′tra•so•nog′ra•pher** *n.* —**ul′tra•son′o•graph′ic** (-sŏn′ə-grăf′ĭk, -sō′nə-) *adj.*

ul•tra•sound (ŭl′trə-sound′) ►*n.* **1.** Ultrasonic sound. **2.** The use of ultrasonic waves for medical diagnosis or therapy.

ul•tra•vi•o•let (ŭl′trə-vī′ə-lĭt) ►*adj.* Of the range of invisible radiation wavelengths shorter than violet in the visible spectrum and on the border of the x-ray region. ►*n.* Ultraviolet light or the ultraviolet part of the spectrum.

ul•u•late (ŭl′yə-lāt′, yo͞ol′-) ►*v.* **-lat•ed, -lat•ing.** To howl, wail, or lament loudly. [Lat. *ululāre.*] —**ul′u•la′tion** *n.*

U•lys•ses (yo͞o-lĭs′ēz′) ►*n. Myth.* Odysseus.

um•bel (ŭm′bəl) ►*n.* A flat-topped or rounded flower cluster in which the individual flower stalks arise from about the same point. [< Lat. *umbella,* parasol.]

um•ber (ŭm′bər) ►*n.* **1.** A natural brown earth containing ferric and manganese oxides, used as pigment. **2.** Any of the shades of brown produced by umber. ►*adj.* Brownish. [Poss. < UMBRIA.]

um•bil•i•cal (ŭm-bĭl′ĭ-kəl) ►*adj.* Of or located near the navel or umbilical cord. ►*n.* An umbilical cord.

umbilical cord ►*n.* The flexible cordlike structure connecting a fetus at the navel with the placenta and containing blood vessels that transport nourishment to the fetus and remove its wastes.

um•bil•i•cus (ŭm-bĭl′ĭ-kəs, ŭm′bə-lī′kəs) ►*n., pl.* **-ci** (-sī′). See **navel.** [Lat. *umbilīcus.*]

um•bra (ŭm′brə) ►*n., pl.* **-bras** or **-brae** (-brē) **1.** A dark area, esp. the darkest part of a shadow. **2.** The completely dark portion of the shadow cast by one body onto another during an eclipse. [Lat., shadow.] —**um′bral** *adj.*

um•brage (ŭm′brĭj) ►*n.* **1.** Offense; resentment: *took umbrage at their rudeness.* **2.** Shadow or shade. [< Lat. *umbra,* shadow.]

um•brel•la (ŭm-brĕl′ə) ►*n.* **1.** A device for protection from the weather consisting of a collapsible canopy mounted on a central rod. **2.** Something that covers or protects. **3.** Something that encompasses many different elements or groups. [< Lat. *umbella,* parasol.]

Um•bri•a (ŭm′brē-ə) A region of central Italy. —**Um′bri•an** *adj. & n.*

u•mi•ak (o͞o′mē-ăk′) ►*n.* A large open Inuit or

Eskimo boat made of skins stretched on a wooden frame. [Inuit *umiaq*.]

um•laut (o͝om′lout′) ►*n.* **1.** A change in a vowel sound caused by partial assimilation to a sound in the following syllable. **2.** The diacritic mark (¨) placed over a vowel to indicate an umlaut, esp. in German. [Ger.]

um•pire (ŭm′pīr′) ►*n.* **1.** One appointed to rule on plays in various sports, esp. baseball. **2.** One appointed to settle a dispute between other persons or groups. [< OFr. *nonper*, impartial mediator.] —**um′pire′** *v.*

ump•teen (ŭmp′tēn′, ŭm′-) ►*adj. Informal* Large but unspecified in number. [Slang *ump(ty)*, dash in Morse code + *-teen* (in numbers).] —**ump′teenth′** *adj.*

UN ►*abbr.* United Nations

un–[1] ►*pref.* Not: *unhappy.* [< OE.]

un–[2] ►*pref.* **1.** To reverse an action: *unbind.* **2.** To deprive of: *unfrock.* **3.** Used as an intensive: *unloose.* [< OE *ond-*, against.]

un•a•ble (ŭn-ā′bəl) ►*adj.* **1.** Lacking the necessary power, authority, or means. **2.** Incompetent.

un•ac•com•pa•nied (ŭn′ə-kŭm′pə-nēd) ►*adj.* **1.** Going or acting without a companion. **2.** *Mus.* Performed or scored without accompaniment.

un•ac•count•a•ble (ŭn′ə-koun′tə-bəl) ►*adj.* **1.** Impossible to account for; inexplicable. **2.** Not responsible. —**un′ac•count′a•bly** *adv.*

un•ac•cus•tomed (ŭn′ə-kŭs′təmd) ►*adj.* **1.** Not common or usual. **2.** Not habituated: *unaccustomed to a life of stress.*

un•a•dul•ter•at•ed (ŭn′ə-dŭl′tə-rā′tĭd) ►*adj.* **1.** Not mingled or diluted. See Syns at **pure.** **2.** Out-and-out: *the unadulterated truth.*

un•ad•vised (ŭn′əd-vīzd′) ►*adj.* **1.** Not informed. **2.** Rash; imprudent. —**un′ad•vis′ed•ly** (-vī′zĭd-lē) *adv.*

un•af•fect•ed (ŭn′ə-fĕk′tĭd) ►*adj.* **1.** Not changed or affected. **2.** Sincere; genuine. —**un′af•fect′ed•ness** *n.*

un•al•loyed (ŭn′ə-loid′) ►*adj.* **1.** Not in mixture with other metals; pure. **2.** Complete; unqualified. —**un′al•loy′ed•ly** *adv.*

u•nan•i•mous (yo͞o-năn′ə-məs) ►*adj.* **1.** Sharing the same opinions or views. **2.** Based on complete agreement. [< Lat. *ūnanimus*, with one mind.] —**u′na•nim′i•ty** (yo͞o′nə-nĭm′ĭ-tē) *n.* —**u•nan′i•mous•ly** *adv.* —**u•nan′i•mous•ness** *n.*

un•armed (ŭn-ärmd′) ►*adj.* Lacking weapons; defenseless.

un•as•sail•a•ble (ŭn′ə-sā′lə-bəl) ►*adj.* **1.** Impossible to dispute or disprove; undeniable. **2.** Impregnable. —**un′as•sail′a•bil′i•ty** *n.*

un•as•sist•ed (ŭn′ə-sĭs′tĭd) ►*adj.* **1.** Not having assistance; unaided. **2.** *Baseball* Designating a play handled by only one fielder.

un•as•sum•ing (ŭn′ə-so͞o′mĭng) ►*adj.* Not pretentious; modest.

un•at•tached (ŭn′ə-tăcht′) ►*adj.* **1.** Not attached or joined. **2.** Not engaged, married, or involved in a serious relationship.

un•a•vail•ing (ŭn′ə-vā′lĭng) ►*adj.* Not availing; useless. See Syns at **futile.** —**un′a•vail′ing•ly** *adv.*

un•a•void•a•ble (ŭn′ə-voi′də-bəl) ►*adj.* Impossible to avoid; inevitable. See Syns at **certain.** —**un′a•void′a•bil′i•ty** *n.* —**un′a•void′a•bly** *adv.*

un′a•bashed′ *adj.*
un′a•bat′ed *adj.*
un′abridged′ *adj.*
un′ac•cept′ a•bil′i•ty *n.*
un′ac•cept′ a•ble *n.*
un′ac•cept′ a•bly *adv.*
un′ac•com′plished *adj.*
un′ac•count′ a•bil′i•ty *n.*
un′ac•count′a•ble *adj.*
un′ac•count′a•bly *adv.*
un′ac•count′ed *adj.*
un′ac•cred′it•ed *adj.*
un′a•cheiv′a•ble *adj.*
un′ac•knowl′edged *adj.*
un′ac•quaint′ed *adj.*
un′ad•ven′tur•ous *adj.*
un′ad•ver•tised′ *adj.*
un′ad•vis′a•ble *adj.*
un′af•ford′a•ble *n.*
un′a•fraid′ *adj.*
un•aid′ ed *adj.*
un′a•ligned′ *adj.*
un•al′ter•bil′i•ty *adj.*
un•al′ter•a•ble *adj.*
un•al′ter•a•bly *adv.*
un′am•big′u•ous *adj.*
un′am•big′u•ous•ly *adv.*
un•an′a•lize′a•ble *adj.*
un′a•pol′o•get′ic *adj.*
un′ap•peal′ing *adj.*
un′ap•peas′a•ble *adj.*
un•ap′pe•tiz′ing *adj.*
un′ap•pre′ci•at′ed *adj.*
un′ap•proach′a•bil′i•ty *n.*
un′ap•proach′a•ble *adj.*
un′ap•pro′pri•at′ed *adj.*
un′ap•proved′ *adj.*
un•ar′gu•a•ble *adj.*
un•arm′ *v.*
un•asked′ *adj.*
un′as•ser′tive *adj.*
un′as•ser′tive•ness *n.*
un′at•tain′a•bil′i•ty *n.*
un′at•tain′a•ble *adj.*
un′at•test′ed *adj.*
un′at•trac′tive *adj.*
un′at•trib′ut•ed *adj.*
un′a•vail′a•bil′i•ty *n.*
un′a•vail′a•ble *adj.*
un•baked′ *adj.*
un•beat′en *adj.*
un′be•liev′a•ble *adj.*
un′be•liev′ing•ly *adv.*
un•bleached′ *adj.*
un•blem′ished *adj.*
un•blenched′ *adj.*
un•brand′ed *adj.*
un•breath′a•ble *adj.*
un•bridge′a•ble *adj.*
un•bri′dled *adj.*
un•bur′den *v.*
un•caged′ *adj.*
un•ceas′ing *adj.*
un•ceas′ing•ly *adv.*
un•cel′e•brat′ed *adj.*
un•cer′ti•fied′ *adj.*
un•change′a•ble *adj.*
un•change′a•bly *adv.*
un′char•ac•ter•is′tic *adj.*
un•charged′ *adj.*
un•checked′ *adj.*
un•cir′cu•lat′ed *adj.*
un•cir′cum•cised′ *adj.*
un•civ′i•lized′ *adj.*
un•clas′si•fied′ *adj.*
un•clench′ *v.*
un•clut′tered *adj.*
un•coat′ed *adj.*
un•coil′ *v.*
un′col•lect′ed *adj.*
un•com′pen•sat′ed *adj.*
un′com•pet′i•tive *adj.*
un′com•plain′ing *adj.*
un′com•plain′ing•ly *adv.*
un•com′pli•cat′ed *adj.*
un′com•pli•men′ta•ry *adj.*
un′com•pre•hend′ing *adj.*

un•a•ware (ŭn′ə-wâr′) ▸*adj.* Not aware or cognizant. ▸*adv.* Unawares.

Usage: *Unaware,* followed by *of,* is the usual adjectival form modifying a noun or pronoun or following a linking verb: *Unaware of the difficulty, I went ahead. Unawares* is the usual adverbial form: *The rain caught them unawares.*

un•a•wares (ŭn′ə-wârz′) ▸*adv.* **1.** By surprise; unexpectedly. **2.** Without forethought or plan. See Usage Note at **unaware.**

un•bal•anced (ŭn-băl′ənst) ▸*adj.* **1.** Not in balance or not in proper balance. **2.** Mentally deranged. **3.** *Accounting* Not adjusted so that debit and credit correspond.

un•bar (ŭn-bär′) ▸*v.* To open.

un•bear•a•ble (ŭn-bâr′ə-bəl) ▸*adj.* Unendurable; intolerable. —**un•bear′a•bly** *adv.*

un•beat•a•ble (ŭn-bē′tə-bəl) ▸*adj.* Impossible to defeat or surpass.

un•beat•en (ŭn-bēt′n) ▸*adj.* **1.** Never defeated. **2.** Untrodden. **3.** Not beaten or pounded.

un•be•com•ing (ŭn′bĭ-kŭm′ĭng) ▸*adj.* **1.** Not appropriate, attractive, or flattering. **2.** Not proper; indecorous.

un•be•known (ŭn′bĭ-nōn′) ▸*adj.* Occurring or existing without one's knowledge: *a crisis unbeknown to us.* [UN–[1] + obsolete *beknown,* known.]

un•be•lief (ŭn′bĭ-lēf′) ▸*n.* Lack of belief or faith, esp. in religious matters. —**un′be•liev′er** *n.* —**un′be•liev′ing** *adj.*

un•bend (ŭn-bĕnd′) ▸*v.* **1.** To make or become less tense; relax. **2.** To straighten.

un•bend•ing (ŭn-bĕn′dĭng) ▸*adj.* **1.** Not yielding; inflexible. **2.** Aloof and often antisocial. —**un•bend′ing•ly** *adv.*

un•bid•den (ŭn-bĭd′n) also **un•bid** (-bĭd′) ▸*adj.* Not invited, asked, or requested.

un•blink•ing (ŭn-blĭng′kĭng) ▸*adj.* **1.** Without blinking. **2.** Without visible emotion. **3.** Fearless in facing reality. —**un•blink′ing•ly** *adv.*

un•blush•ing (ŭn-blŭsh′ĭng) ▸*adj.* Without shame or embarrassment. —**un•blush′ing•ly** *adv.*

un•bolt (ŭn-bōlt′) ▸*v.* To release the bolts of (a door or gate); unlock.

un•born (ŭn-bôrn′) ▸*adj.* Not yet born.

un•bos•om (ŭn-bo͝oz′əm, -bo͞o′zəm) ▸*v.* **1.** To confide (one's thoughts). **2.** To relieve (oneself) of thoughts or feelings.

un•bound•ed (ŭn-boun′dĭd) ▸*adj.* Having no boundaries or limits.

un•bowed (ŭn-boud′) ▸*adj.* **1.** Not bowed; unbent. **2.** Not subdued.

un•bri•dled (ŭn-brīd′ld) ▸*adj.* **1.** Unrestrained; uncontrolled. **2.** Not fitted with a bridle.

un•bro•ken (ŭn-brō′kən) ▸*adj.* **1.** Not broken; intact. **2.** Uninterrupted; continuous. **3.** Not tamed or broken to harness.

un•bur•den (ŭn-bûr′dn) ▸*v.* To free from a burden or trouble.

un•but•ton (ŭn-bŭt′n) ▸*v.* **1.** To unfasten the buttons (of). **2.** To open or expose as if by unbuttoning.

un•called-for (ŭn-kôld′fôr′) ▸*adj.* **1.** Not required or requested. **2.** Not justified or deserved; unwarranted.

un•can•ny (ŭn-kăn′ē) ▸*adj.* **-ni•er, -ni•est 1.** Peculiarly unsettling; eerie. **2.** So keen and perceptive as to seem preternatural. —**un•can′-**

un′com•pre•hend′ing•ly *adv.*
un•com′pro•mis′ing *adj.*
un•com′pro•mis′ing•ly *adv.*
un′con•ceiv′a•ble *adj.*
un′con•ceiv′a•bly *adv.*
un′con•di′tion•al *adj.*
un′con•di′tion•al•ly *adv.*
un′con•nect′ed *adj.*
un′con•nect′ed•ly *adv.*
un•con′quer•a•ble *adj.*
un•con′quer•a•bly *adv.*
un′con•sol′i•dat′ed *adj.*
un′con•tam′i•nat′ed *adj.*
un′con•test′ed *adj.*
un′con•trol′la•bil′i·ty *n.*
un′con•trol′la•ble *adj.*
un′con•trol′la•bly *adv.*
un′con•trolled′ *adj.*
un′con•tro•ver′sial *adj.*
un′con•tro•ver′sial•ly *adv.*
un′con•vinc′ing *adj.*
un′con•vinc′ing·ly *adv.*
un′cooked′ *adj.*
un′co•op′er•a•tive *adj.*
un′co•op′er•a•tive•ly *adv.*
un′cor•rect′ed *adj.*
un′cor•rob′o•rat′ed *adj.*
un•crit′i•cal *adj.*
un•crowd′ed *adj.*
un•crowned′ *adj.*
un•cul′ti•vat′ed *adj.*
un•curl′ *v.*
un•dam′aged *adj.*
un•dat′ed *adj.*
un′de•bat′a•ble *adj.*
un′de•bat′a•bly *adv.*
un′de•ceiv′a•ble *adj.*
un′de•ceiv′a•bly *adv.*
un′de•ceive′ *v.*
un′de•clared′ *adj.*
un′de•ni′a•ble *adj.*
un′de•ni′a•bly *adv.*
un′de•pend′a•bil′i•ty *n.*
un′de•pend′a•ble *adj.*
un′de•served′ *adj.*
un′de•serv′ed•ly *adv.*
un′de•serv′ing *adj.*
un′de•sired′ *adj.*
un′di•gest′ed *adj.*
un′dig′ni•fied′ *adj.*
un•dip′lo•mat′ic *adj.*
un′dis•turbed′ *adj.*
un•doubt′ed•ly *adv.*
un•doubt′ing *adj.*
un•ed′u•cat′ed *adj.*
un′e•mo′tion•al *adj.*
un′e•mo′tion•al•ly *adv.*
un′em•ploy′a•ble *adj. & n.*
un•err′ing *adj.*
un•err′ing•ly *adv.*
un•fad′ing *adj.*
un•fad′ing•ly *adv.*
un′fa•mil•iar′i•ty *n.*
un•fash′ion•a•ble *adj.*
un•fash′ion•a•bly *adv.*
un•fas′ten *v.*
un•fath′om•a•ble *adj.*
un•fa′vor•a•ble *adj.*
un•fa′vor•a•bly *adv.*
un•fet′ter *v.*
un•fin′ished *adj.*
un•fo′cused *adj.*
un′fore•seen′ *adj.*
un′for•get′ta•bil′i•ty *n.*
un•fund′ed *adj.*
un•fuss′ y *adj.*
un•gen′er•ous *adj.*
un•gen′er•ous•ly *adv.*
un•grate′ful *adj.*
un•grate′ful•ly *adv.*
un•hes′i•tat′ing *adj.*
un•hes′i•tat′ing•ly *adv.*
un•hook′ *v.*
un•hoped′-for′ *adj.*
un•hurt′ *adj.*
un′im•por′tance *n.*
un′im•por′tant *adj.*

ni•ly *adv.* —**un•can′ni•ness** *n.*
un•cer•e•mo•ni•ous (ŭn-sĕr′ə-mō′nē-əs) ▸*adj.* **1.** Without the due formalities; abrupt. **2.** Informal. —**un•cer′e•mo′ni•ous•ly** *adv.*
un•cer•tain (ŭn-sûr′tn) ▸*adj.* **1.** Not known or established; questionable. **2.** Not determined; undecided. **3.** Not having sure knowledge. **4.** Subject to change. —**un•cer′tain•ly** *adv.* —**un•cer′tain•ness** *n.*
un•cer•tain•ty (ŭn-sûr′tn-tē) ▸*n.* **1.** Lack of certainty. **2.** Something uncertain.
un•char•i•ta•ble (ŭn-chăr′ĭ-tə-bəl) ▸*adj.* **1.** Not generous or tolerant. **2.** Unfair or unkind. —**un•char′i•ta•bly** *adv.*
un•chart•ed (ŭn-chär′tĭd) ▸*adj.* Not recorded on a map or plan; unexplored; unknown.
un•chaste (ŭn-chāst′) ▸*adj.* Not chaste or modest. —**un•chaste′ly** *adv.*
un•chris•tian (ŭn-krĭs′chən) ▸*adj.* **1.** Not in accord with the spirit or principles of Christianity. **2.** Not Christian.
un•cial also **Un•cial** (ŭn′shəl, -sē-əl) ▸*adj.* Of a style of writing characterized by somewhat rounded capital letters and found esp. in Greek and Latin manuscripts of the 4th to the 8th cent. A.D. [< Lat. *ūnciālis*, inch-high.] —**un′cial** *n.*
un•civ•il (ŭn-sĭv′əl) ▸*adj.* Discourteous; rude. —**un•civ′il•ly** *adv.*
un•civ•i•lized (ŭn-sĭv′ə-līzd′) ▸*adj.* Not civilized; barbarous.
un•clad (ŭn-klăd′) ▸*adj.* Naked.
un•clasp (ŭn-klăsp′) ▸*v.* **1.** To release or loosen the clasp of. **2.** To release from a grip or embrace.
un•cle (ŭng′kəl) ▸*n.* **1.** The brother of one's mother or father. **2.** The husband of one's aunt. —***idiom:* cry uncle** *Informal* To surrender or submit. [< Lat. *avunculus*, maternal uncle.]
un•clean (ŭn-klēn′) ▸*adj.* **1.** Foul or dirty. **2.** Morally defiled; unchaste. **3.** Ceremonially impure. —**un•clean′ness** *n.*
un•clean•ly (ŭn-klĕn′lē) ▸*adj.* Habitually unclean. —**un•clean′li•ness** *n.*
Uncle Sam (săm) ▸*n.* The government of the US, often personified as a tall thin man with a white beard. [< *US*, abbr. of UNITED STATES.]
Uncle Tom ▸*n.* *Offensive* A Black person regarded as being too deferential to white people. [After *Uncle Tom*, a character in *Uncle Tom's Cabin*, a novel by Harriet Beecher Stowe.]
un•cloak (ŭn-klōk′) ▸*v.* **1.** To remove a cloak or cover from. **2.** To expose; reveal.
un•close (ŭn-klōz′) ▸*v.* To open.
un•clothe (ŭn-klōth′) ▸*v.* To remove the clothing or cover from.
un•coil (ŭn-koil′) ▸*v.* To unwind or become unwound.
un•com•fort•a•ble (ŭn-kŭm′fər-tə-bəl, -kŭmf′tə-, -kŭmf′tər-) ▸*adj.* **1.** Experiencing discomfort; uneasy. **2.** Causing anxiety; disquieting. —**un•com′fort•a•bly** *adv.*
un•com•mit•ted (ŭn′kə-mĭt′ĭd) ▸*adj.* Not pledged to a specific cause or course.
un•com•mon (ŭn-kŏm′ən) ▸*adj.* **1.** Not common; rare. **2.** Wonderful; remarkable. —**un•com′mon•ly** *adv.* —**un•com′mon•ness** *n.*
un•com•mu•ni•ca•tive (ŭn′kə-myōō′nĭ-kā′tĭv, -kə-tĭv) ▸*adj.* Not communicative; reserved. —**un′com•mu′ni•ca′tive•ness** *n.*
un•com•pro•mis•ing (ŭn-kŏm′prə-mī′zĭng) ▸*adj.* Not making concessions; inflexible.
un•con•cern (ŭn′kən-sûrn′) ▸*n.* **1.** Lack of in-

un′in•form′a•tive *adj.*
un′in•form′a•tive•ly *adv.*
un′in•hab′it•a•bil′i•ty *n.*
un′in•hab′it•a•ble *adj.*
un′in•hab′it•ed *adj.*
un′in•hib′it•ed *adj.*
un′in•i′ti•at′ed *adj.*
un′in•spir′ing *adj.*
un′in•spir′ing•ly *adv.*
un′in•struct′ed *adj.*
un′in•struc′tive *adj.*
un′in•sur′a•ble *adj.*
un′in•sured′ *adj.*
un′in•tel′li•gence *n.*
un′in•tel′li•gent *adj.*
un′in•tel′li•gent•ly *adv.*
un′in•tel′li•gi•bil′i•ty *n.*
un′in•tel′li•gi•ble *adj.*
un′in•tel′li•gi•bly *adv.*
un′in•ten′tion•al *adj.*
un′in•ten′tion•al•ly *adv.*
un′in•ter•rupt′ed *adj.*
un′in•vit′ing *adj.*
un′in•vit′ing•ly *adv.*
un•just′ *adj.*
un•jus′ti•fi′a•ble *adj.*
un•jus′ti•fi′a•bly *adv.*
un•just′ly *adv.*
un•kind′ *adj.*
un•kind′ly *adv.*
un•know′a•ble *adj.*
un•know′ing *adj.*
un•known′ *adj.*
un•latch′ *v.*
un•law′ful *adj.*
un•leav′ened *adj.*
un•link′ *v.*
un•man′age•a•bil′i·ty *n.*
un•man′age•a•ble *adj.*
un•man′age•a•bly *adv.*
un•man′ner•ly *adj. & adv.*
un•marked′ *adj.*
un•mar′ried *adj. & n.*
un•meet′ *adj.*
un•mixed′ *adj.*
un′mo•lest′ed *adj.*
un•mo′ti•vat′ed *adj.*
un•muf′fle *v.*
un•my′e•lin•at′ed *adj.*
un•name′a•ble *adj.*
un•named′ *adj.*
un•nec′es•sar′i•ly *adv.*
un•nec′es•sar′y *adj.*
un•no′tice•a•ble *adj.*
un•no′tice•a•bly *adv.*
un′ob•jec′tion•a•ble *adj.*
un′ob•struct′ed *adj.*
un•oc′cu•pied′ *adj.*
un′of•fi′cial *adj.*
un′of•fi′cial•ly *adv.*
un′op•posed′ *adv.*
un′o•rig′i•nal *adv.*
un•or′na•ment′ *v.*
un•or′tho•dox′ *adj.*
un•pack′ *v.*
un•pag′i•nat′ed *adj.*
un′pal•at•a•bil′i•ty *n.*
un•pal′at•a•ble *adj.*
un•pal′at•a•bly *adv.*
un•peo′ple *v.*
un•peo′pled *adj.*
un′per•turbed′ *adj.*
un•pile′ *v.*
un•planned′ *adj.*
un•pleas′ant *adj.*
un•pleas′ant•ly *adv.*
un•pleas′ant•ness *n.*
un•pol′ished *adj.*
un′po•lit′i•cal *adj.*
un•polled′ *adj.*
un•pop′u•lar *adj.*
un′pop•u•lar′i•ty *n.*
un•pop′u•lat′ed *adj.*
un•prac′ticed *adj.*
un•pre•dict′a•bil′i·ty *n.*
un′•pre•dict′a•ble *adj. & n.*

terest; indifference. **2.** Lack of worry or apprehensiveness.

un•con•cerned (ŭn′kən-sûrnd′) ▸*adj.* **1.** Not interested; indifferent. **2.** Not anxious or apprehensive. —**un′con•cern′ed•ly** (-sûr′nĭd-lē) *adv.*

un•con•di•tion•al (ŭn′kən-dĭsh′ə-nəl) ▸*adj.* Without conditions or limitations. —**un′con•di′tion•al•ly** *adv.*

un•con•di•tioned (ŭn′kən-dĭsh′ənd) ▸*adj.* **1.** Unconditional. **2.** *Psychol.* Not resulting from conditioning; unlearned or natural.

un•con•scion•a•ble (ŭn-kŏn′shə-nə-bəl) ▸*adj.* **1.** Not restrained or guided by conscience. **2.** Beyond prudence or reason; excessive. —**un•con′scion•a•bly** *adv.*

un•con•scious (ŭn-kŏn′shəs) ▸*adj.* **1.** Lacking awareness and the capacity for sensory perception. **2.** Temporarily lacking consciousness. **3.** Occurring without conscious awareness: *unconscious resentment.* **4.** Involuntary: *an unconscious mannerism.* ▸*n. Psychol.* The part of the mind that operates without conscious awareness or control. —**un•con′scious•ly** *adv.* —**un•con′scious•ness** *n.*

un•con•sti•tu•tion•al (ŭn′kŏn-stĭ-to͞o′shə-nəl, -tyo͞o′-) ▸*adj.* Not in accord with the constitution of a nation or state. —**un′con•sti•tu′tion•al′i•ty** (-năl′ĭ-tē) *n.* —**un′con•sti•tu′tion•al•ly** *adv.*

un•con•ven•tion•al (ŭn′kən-vĕn′shə-nəl) ▸*adj.* Not adhering to convention; out of the ordinary. —**un′con•ven′tion•al′i•ty** (-năl′ĭ-tē) *n.* —**un′con•ven′tion•al•ly** *adv.*

un•cork (ŭn-kôrk′) ▸*v.* **1.** To draw the cork from. **2.** To free from a constrained state.

un•cou•ple (ŭn-kŭp′əl) ▸*v.* To disconnect.

un•couth (ŭn-ko͞oth′) ▸*adj.* **1.** Crude; unrefined. **2.** Awkward or clumsy. [< OE *uncūth,* unknown, strange.] —**un•couth′ly** *adv.*

un•cov•er (ŭn-kŭv′ər) ▸*v.* **1.** To remove the cover from. **2.** To disclose; reveal. **3.** To remove the hat from (one's head) in respect.

un•cross (ŭn-krôs′, -krŏs′) ▸*v.* To move (e.g., one's legs) from a crossed position.

unc•tion (ŭngk′shən) ▸*n.* **1.** The act of anointing as part of a ceremonial or healing ritual. **2.** An ointment or oil; salve. **3.** Something that serves to soothe; balm. **4.** Affected or exaggerated earnestness. [< Lat. *unguere, ūnct-,* anoint.]

unc•tu•ous (ŭngk′cho͞o-əs) ▸*adj.* **1.** Marked by affected, exaggerated, or insincere earnestness. **2.** Greasy; oily. [< Lat. *ūnctum,* ointment.] —**unc′tu•ous•ly** *adv.* —**unc′tu•ous•ness** *n.*

Syns: *unctuous, fulsome, oily, smarmy* **adj.**

un•cut (ŭn-kŭt′) ▸*adj.* **1.** Not cut. **2.** *Print.* Not slit or trimmed: *uncut pages.* **3.** Not shaped by cutting: *uncut gems.* **4.** Not condensed, abridged, or censored.

un•daunt•ed (ŭn-dôn′tĭd, -dän′-) ▸*adj.* Not discouraged or disheartened; resolutely courageous. —**un•daunt′ed•ly** *adv.* —**un•daunt′ed•ness** *n.*

un•de•cid•ed (ŭn′dĭ-sī′dĭd) ▸*adj.* **1.** Not yet determined or settled. **2.** Not having reached a decision; uncommitted.

un•de•mon•stra•tive (ŭn′dĭ-mŏn′strə-tĭv) ▸*adj.* Not given to expressions of feeling; reserved. —**un′de•mon′stra•tive•ness** *n.*

un•der (ŭn′dər) ▸*prep.* **1.** In a lower position or place than. **2.** Beneath the surface of. **3.** Beneath the guise of: *traveled under a false name.* **4.** Less than; smaller than: *under three years of age.* **5.** Less than the required amount or degree

un′•pre•dict′a•bly *adv.*
un•prej′u•diced *adj.*
un′pre•med′i•tat′ed *adj.*
un′pre•pos•sess′ing *adj.*
un′pre•ten′tious *adj.*
un•priced′ *adj.*
un•prin′ci•pled *adj.*
un′pro•duc′tive *adj.*
un′pro•duc′tive•ly *adv.*
un•prof′it•a•bil′i•ty *n.*
un•prom′is•ing *adj.*
un•prom′is•ing•ly *adv.*
un′pro•pi′tious *adj.*
un′pro•pi′tious•ly *adv.*
un′pro•tect′ed *adj.*
un′pro•voked′ *adv.*
un•quench′a•ble *adj.*
un•quench′a•bly *adv.*
un•ques′tion•a•ble *adj.*
un•ques′tion•a•bly *adv.*
un•read′a•ble *adj.*
un•read′i•ly *adv.*
un•read′i•ness *n.*
un•read′y *adj.*
un′re•al•is′ti•c *adj.*
un′re•al•is′ti•cal•ly *adv.*
un•re′al•ized′ *adj.*
un•rea′son•ing *adj.*
un′re•lent′ing *adj.*
un′re•lent′ing•ly *adv.*
un′re•li′a•bil′ i•ty *n.*
un′re•li′a•ble *adj.*
un′re•li′a•bly *adv.*
un′re•lig′ious *adj.*
un′re•mark′a•ble *adj.*
un′re•mark′a•bly *adv.*
un′re•marked′ *adj.*
un′re•pent′ant *adj.*
un′re•pent′ant•ly *adv.*
un′re•proved′ *adj.*
un′re•quit′ed *adj.*
un′re•quit′ed•ly *adv.*
un′re•spon′sive *adj.*
un′re•spon′sive•ly *adv.*
un′re•spon′sive•ness *n.*
un′re•strained′ *adj.*
un′re•strain′ed•ly *adv.*
un′re•strain′ed•ness *n.*
un′re•straint′ *n.*
un•ripe′ *adj.*
un•ripe′ness *n.*
un•roof′ *v.*
un•safe′ *adj.*
un•said′ *adj.*
un•san′i•tar′y *adj.*
un•sat′is•fac•to′ri•ly *adv.*
un•sat′is•fac′to•ry *adj.*
un•sat′is•fied′ *adj.*
un′sci•en•tif′ic *adj.*
un′sci•en•tif′i•cal•ly *adv.*
un′sub•stan′ti•al′i•ty *n.*
un′suc•cess′ *n.*
un′suc•cess′ful *adj.*
un′suc•cess′ful·ly *adv.*
un•suit′a•bil′i•ty *n.*
un•suit′a•ble *adj.*
un•suit′a•bly *adv.*
un′sus•cep′ti•ble *adj.*
un•swathe′ *v.*
un′sym•met′ri•cal *adj.*
un•throne′ *v.*
un•trou′bled *adj.*
un•twine′ *v.*
un•twist′ *v.*
un•ut′tered *adj.*
un•war′i•ly *adv.*
un•war′y *adj.*
un•wed′ *adj.*
un•wise′ *adj.*
un•work′a•bil′i•ty *n.*
un•work′a•ble *adj.*

of: *under voting age.* **6.** Inferior to in status or rank. **7.** Subject to the authority of: *under a dictatorship.* **8.** Undergoing or receiving the effects of: *under constant care.* **9.** Subject to the obligation of: *under contract.* **10.** Within the group or classification of: *listed under biology.* **11.** In the process of: *under discussion.* **12.** Because of: *under these conditions.* ▸*adv.* **1.** In or into a place below or beneath. **2.** Into a subordinate or inferior condition or position. **3.** So as to be covered or enveloped. **4.** So as to be less than the required amount or degree. ▸*adj.* **1.** Lower. **2.** Subordinate; inferior. **3.** Less than is required or customary. [< OE.]

under– ▸*pref.* **1.** Beneath; below: *underground.* **2.** Inferior; subordinate: *undersecretary.* **3.** Less than normal: *undersized.* [< OE.]

un•der•a•chieve (ŭn′dər-ə-chēv′) ▸*v.* To perform worse or achieve less success than expected. —**un′der•a•chiev′er** *n.*

un•der•age[1] (ŭn′dər-ĭj) ▸*n.* **1.** An amount, as of money, falling short of the listed amount in records of account. **2.** A deficient amount; shortfall.

un•der•age[2] (ŭn′dər-āj′) also **un•der•aged** (-ājd′) ▸*adj.* Below the customary or legal age.

un•der•arm (ŭn′dər-ärm′) ▸*adj.* **1.** Located, placed, or used under the arm. **2.** *Sports* Underhand. ▸*adv.* With an underarm motion or delivery. ▸*n.* The armpit.

un•der•bel•ly (ŭn′dər-bĕl′ē) ▸*n.* **1.** The soft underside of an animal's body. **2.** The vulnerable or weak part.

un•der•bid (ŭn′dər-bĭd′) ▸*v.* **1.** To bid lower than. **2.** *Games* To bid too low. —**un′der•bid′** *n.*

un•der•bite (ŭn′dər-bīt′) ▸*n.* A condition of the teeth in which the lower teeth protrude beyond the upper teeth.

un•der•brush (ŭn′dər-brŭsh′) ▸*n.* Small trees, shrubs, or similar plants growing beneath the taller trees in a forest.

un•der•car•riage (ŭn′dər-kăr′ĭj) ▸*n.* **1.** A supporting framework, as of a motor vehicle. **2.** The landing gear of an aircraft.

un•der•charge (ŭn′dər-chärj′) ▸*v.* To charge (someone) less than is customary or required. —**un′der•charge′** *n.*

un•der•class•man (ŭn′dər-klăs′mən) ▸*n.* A student in the freshman or sophomore class at a secondary school or college.

un•der•clothes (ŭn′dər-klōz′, -klōthz′) ▸*pl.n.* See **underwear.**

un•der•coat (ŭn′dər-kōt′) ▸*n.* **1.** A coat worn beneath another coat. **2.** Short hairs or fur underneath the longer outer hairs of an animal's coat. **3.** also **un•der•coat•ing** (-kō′tĭng) **a.** A coat of sealing material applied before a final coat. **b.** A tarlike substance sprayed on the underside of a vehicle to prevent rusting. —**un′der•coat′** *v.*

un•der•cov•er (ŭn′dər-kŭv′ər) ▸*adj.* Performed or occurring in secret.

un•der•cur•rent (ŭn′dər-kûr′ənt, -kŭr′-) ▸*n.* **1.** A current below another current or a surface. **2.** An underlying tendency or force often contrary to what is superficially evident.

un•der•cut (ŭn′dər-kŭt′) ▸*v.* **1.** To diminish or destroy the effectiveness of; undermine. **2.** To sell at a lower price or work for lower wages than (a competitor). **3.** To make a cut under or below. **4.** *Sports* **a.** To impart backspin to (a ball) by striking downward as well as forward. **b.** To slice (a ball) with an underarm stroke. —**un′der•cut′** *n.*

un•der•de•vel•oped (ŭn′dər-dĭ-vĕl′əpt) ▸*adj.* **1.** Not adequately or normally developed; immature. **2.** Having a low level of economic and technological development. —**un′der•de•vel′op•ment** *n.*

un•der•dog (ŭn′dər-dôg′, -dŏg′) ▸*n.* **1.** One who is expected to lose a contest or struggle. **2.** One who is at a disadvantage.

un•der•done (ŭn′dər-dŭn′) ▸*adj.* Not sufficiently cooked.

un•der•dress (ŭn′dər-drĕs′) ▸*n.* Underwear. ▸*v.* (ŭn′dər-drĕs′) **1.** To dress too informally for the occasion. **2.** To dress without sufficient warmth.

un•der•es•ti•mate (ŭn′dər-ĕs′tə-māt′) ▸*v.* To make too low an estimate of the quantity, degree, or worth of. ▸*n.* (-mĭt). An estimate that is too low. —**un′der•es′ti•ma′tion** *n.*

un•der•ex•pose (ŭn′dər-ĭk-spōz′) ▸*v.* To expose (film) to light for too short a time. —**un′der•ex•po′sure** *n.*

un•der•foot (ŭn′dər-fo͝ot′) ▸*adv.* **1.** Below or under the feet. **2.** In the way.

un•der•gar•ment (ŭn′dər-gär′mənt) ▸*n.* A garment worn under outer garments.

un•der•go (ŭn′dər-gō′) ▸*v.* **1.** To pass through; experience. **2.** To endure; suffer.

un•der•grad•u•ate (ŭn′dər-grăj′o͞o-ĭt) ▸*n.* A college or university student who has not yet received a degree.

un•der•ground (ŭn′dər-ground′) ▸*adj.* **1.** Below the surface of the earth. **2.** Hidden or concealed; clandestine. **3.** Of or relating to avant-garde or experimental films, publications, and art. ▸*n.* **1.** A clandestine, often nationalist, organization working against a government in power. **2.** *Chiefly Brit.* A subway system. **3.** An avant-garde movement. ▸*adv.* (ŭn′dər-ground′) **1.** Below the surface of the earth. **2.** In secret; stealthily.

un•der•growth (ŭn′dər-grōth′) ▸*n.* Low-growing plants, saplings, and shrubs beneath trees in a forest.

un•der•hand (ŭn′dər-hănd′) also **un•der•hand•ed** (ŭn′dər-hăn′dĭd) ▸*adj.* **1.** Done slyly and secretly; sneaky. **2.** *Sports* Executed with the hand brought forward and up from below the level of the shoulder; underarm. —**un′der•hand′** *n.* —**un′der•hand′, un′der•hand′ed** *adv.* —**un′der•hand′ed•ly** *adv.* —**un′der•hand′ed•ness** *n.*

un•der•lie (ŭn′dər-lī′) ▸*v.* **-lay, -lain, -ly•ing** **1.** To be located under or below. **2.** To be the support or basis of; account for.

un•der•line (ŭn′dər-līn′, ŭn′dər-līn′) ▸*v.* **1.** To draw a line under; underscore. **2.** To emphasize. —**un′der•line′** *n.*

un•der•ling (ŭn′dər-lĭng) ▸*n.* A subordinate.

un•der•ly•ing (ŭn′dər-lī′ĭng) ▸*adj.* **1.** Lying under or beneath. **2.** Basic; fundamental. **3.** Present but not obvious; implicit.

un•der•mine (ŭn′dər-mīn′) ▸*v.* **1.** To weaken by wearing away gradually or imperceptibly. **2.** To dig a mine or tunnel beneath.

un•der•most (ŭn′dər-mōst′) ▸*adj.* Lowest in position, rank, or place; bottom. ▸*adv.* Lowest.

un•der•neath (ŭn′dər-nēth′) ▸*adv.* **1.** In or to a place beneath; below. **2.** On the lower face or underside. ▸*prep.* **1.** Under; below; beneath. **2.**

Under the power or control of. ►*adj.* Lower; under. ►*n.* The part or side below or under. [< OE *underneothan* : *under*, UNDER + *neothan*, below.]

un•der•pants (ŭn′dər-pănts′) ►*pl.n.* Briefs or shorts worn as underwear.

un•der•pass (ŭn′dər-păs′) ►*n.* A passage underneath something, esp. a road under another road.

un•der•pin•ning (ŭn′dər-pĭn′ĭng) ►*n.* **1.** A supporting structure or part. **2.** often **underpinnings** *Informal* The legs.

un•der•play (ŭn′dər-plā′, ŭn′dər-plā′) ►*v.* **1.** To act (a role) subtly or with restraint. **2.** To minimize the importance of.

un•der•rate (ŭn′dər-rāt′) ►*v.* To rate too low; underestimate.

un•der•score (ŭn′dər-skôr′, -skōr′) ►*v.* **1.** To underline. **2.** To emphasize; stress. —**un′der•score′** *n.*

un•der•sea (ŭn′dər-sē′) ►*adj. & adv.* Beneath the surface of the sea. —**un′der•seas′** *adv.*

un•der•sec•re•tar•y (ŭn′dər-sĕk′rə-tĕr′ē) ►*n.* An official directly subordinate to a cabinet member. —**un′der•sec′re•tar′i•at** (-târ′ē-ĭt) *n.*

un•der•sell (ŭn′dər-sĕl′) ►*v.* **1.** To sell for a lower price than. **2.** To present in a way that minimizes the value.

un•der•shirt (ŭn′dər-shûrt′) ►*n.* An undergarment worn under a shirt.

un•der•shoot (ŭn′dər-sho͞ot′) ►*v.* **1.** To shoot a projectile short of (a target). **2.** To land an aircraft short of (a landing area).

un•der•shorts (ŭn′dər-shôrts′) ►*pl.n.* Underpants.

un•der•shot (ŭn′dər-shŏt′) ►*adj.* (ŭn′dər-shŏt′) **1.** Driven by water passing from below, as a water wheel. **2.** Having the lower jaw or teeth projecting beyond the upper.

un•der•side (ŭn′dər-sīd′) ►*n.* The side or surface that is underneath.

un•der•signed (ŭn′dər-sīnd′) ►*n., pl.* **-signed.** A signer whose name is at the bottom or end of a document. —**un′der•signed′** *adj.*

un•der•sized (ŭn′dər-sīzd′) also **un•der•size** (-sīz′) ►*adj.* Smaller than normal or sufficient size.

un•der•skirt (ŭn′dər-skûrt′) ►*n.* A skirt worn under another.

un•der•slung (ŭn′dər-slŭng′) ►*adj.* Having springs attached to the axles from below, as on an auto chassis.

un•der•stand (ŭn′dər-stănd′) ►*v.* **-stood** (-sto͝od′), **-stand•ing 1.** To perceive and comprehend the nature and significance of; grasp. **2.** To know thoroughly by close contact or long experience with. **3.** To comprehend the language, sounds, form, or symbols of. **4.** To know and be tolerant or sympathetic toward. **5.** To learn indirectly, as by hearsay. **6.** To conclude; infer. **7.** To accept as an agreed fact: *It is understood that the fee will be 50 dollars.* [< OE *understandan* : UNDER– + *standan*, stand.] —**un′der•stand′a•ble** *adj.* —**un′der•stand′a•bly** *adv.*

un•der•stand•ing (ŭn′dər-stăn′dĭng) ►*n.* **1.** The quality of discernment; comprehension. **2.** The faculty by which one understands; intelligence. **3.** Individual or specified judgment or outlook; opinion. **4.** An agreement between two or more people or groups. **5.** A reconciliation of differences. ►*adj.* Compassionate; sympathetic.

un•der•state (ŭn′dər-stāt′) ►*v.* **1.** To state with less completeness or truth than seems warranted by the facts. **2.** To express with restraint or lack of emphasis, esp. for rhetorical effect. —**un′der•state′ment** *n.*

un•der•stood (ŭn′dər-sto͝od′) ►*adj.* **1.** Agreed on; assumed. **2.** Implicit or implied.

un•der•sto•ry (ŭn′dər-stôr′ē, -stōr′-) ►*n.* An underlying layer of vegetation, esp. beneath a forest's canopy.

un•der•stud•y (ŭn′dər-stŭd′ē) ►*v.* **1.** To study or know (a role) so as to be able to replace a regular performer. **2.** To act as an understudy to. ►*n.* A performer who understudies another.

un•der•take (ŭn′dər-tāk′) ►*v.* **1.** To take upon oneself, as a task. **2.** To pledge or commit (oneself) to.

un•der•tak•er (ŭn′dər-tā′kər) ►*n.* See **funeral director.**

un•der•tak•ing (ŭn′dər-tā′kĭng) ►*n.* **1.** Something undertaken; venture. **2.** A guaranty or promise. **3.** The profession of a funeral director.

un•der-the-count•er (ŭn′dər-*th*ə-koun′tər) ►*adv. & adj.* Transacted or sold illicitly.

un•der•tone (ŭn′dər-tōn′) ►*n.* **1.** An underlying or implied tendency or meaning; undercurrent. **2.** A tone of low pitch or volume. **3.** A pale or subdued color.

un•der•tow (ŭn′dər-tō′) ►*n.* The seaward pull of receding waves after they break on a shore.

un•der•wa•ter (ŭn′dər-wô′tər, -wŏt′ər) ►*adj.* Used, done, or existing beneath the surface of water. —**un′der•wa′ter** *adv.*

un•der•wear (ŭn′dər-wâr′) ►*n.* Clothes worn next to the skin, beneath one's outer clothing.

un•der•weight (ŭn′dər-wāt′) ►*adj.* Weighing less than is normal, healthy, or required.

un•der•world (ŭn′dər-wûrld′) ►*n.* **1.** The part of society organized for and engaged in crime and vice. **2.** *Gk. & Rom. Myth.* The world of the dead; Hades.

un•der•write (ŭn′dər-rīt′) ►*v.* **1.** To assume financial responsibility for. **2.** To sign (an insurance policy) so as to assume liability in case of specified losses. **3.** To agree to buy the unsold part of (stock not yet sold publicly) at a fixed time and price. **4.** To write under, esp. to endorse (a document). —**un′der•writ′er** *n.*

un•de•sir•a•ble (ŭn′dĭ-zīr′ə-bəl) ►*adj.* Not wanted; objectionable. ►*n.* An undesirable person. —**un′de•sir′a•bly** *adv.*

un•dies (ŭn′dēz) ►*pl.n. Informal* Underwear.

un•dis•posed (ŭn′dĭ-spōzd′) ►*adj.* **1.** Not settled, removed, or resolved. **2.** Disinclined; unwilling.

un•do (ŭn-do͞o′) ►*v.* **1.** To reverse or erase; annul. **2.** To untie, disassemble, or loosen. **3.** To open; unwrap. **4a.** To cause the ruin or downfall of; destroy. **b.** To throw into confusion; unsettle.

un•do•ing (ŭn-do͞o′ĭng) ►*n.* **1.** The act of unfastening or loosening. **2a.** The act of bringing to ruin. **b.** A cause or source of ruin. **3.** The act of reversing or annulling something.

un•dress (ŭn-drĕs′) ►*v.* To remove the clothing (of); disrobe. ►*n.* **1.** Informal attire. **2.** Nakedness.

un•due (ŭn-do͞o′, -dyo͞o′) ►*adj.* **1.** Exceeding what is appropriate or normal. **2.** Not just, proper, or legal. **3.** Not yet payable or due.

un•du•lant (ŭn′jə-lənt, ŭn′dyə-, -də-) ▸*adj.* Undulating.

un•du•late (ŭn′jə-lāt′, ŭn′dyə-, -də-) ▸*v.* **-lat•ed, -lat•ing 1.** To move or cause to move in a smooth wavelike motion. **2.** To have a wavelike appearance or form. [< LLat. *undula*, small wave, dim. of Lat. *unda*, wave.]

un•du•la•tion (ŭn′jə-lā′shən, ŭn′dyə-, -də-) ▸*n.* **1.** A wavelike movement. **2.** A wavelike form, outline, or appearance. **3.** One of a series of waves or wavelike segments.

un•du•ly (ŭn-do͞o′lē, -dyo͞o′-) ▸*adv.* Excessively; immoderately: *unduly fearful.*

un•dy•ing (ŭn-dī′ĭng) ▸*adj.* Everlasting.

un•earned (ŭn-ûrnd′) ▸*adj.* **1.** Not gained by work or service. **2.** Not deserved.

un•earth (ŭn-ûrth′) ▸*v.* **1.** To dig up. **2.** To bring to public notice; uncover.

un•earth•ly (ŭn-ûrth′lē) ▸*adj.* **1.** Not of the earth; supernatural. **2.** Unnaturally strange and frightening; eerie.

un•eas•y (ŭn-ē′zē) ▸*adj.* **1.** Lacking ease, comfort, or a sense of security. **2.** Affording no ease or reassurance: *an uneasy calm.* **3.** Awkward or unsure in manner; constrained. —**un•ease′, un•eas′i•ness** *n.* —**un•eas′i•ly** *adv.*

un•em•ployed (ŭn′ĕm-ploid′, -ĭm-) ▸*adj.* **1.** Not having work; jobless. **2.** Not being used; idle. —**un′em•ploy′ment** *n.*

un•e•qual (ŭn-ē′kwəl) ▸*adj.* **1.** Not the same in any measurable aspect. **2.** Asymmetrical. **3.** Irregular; variable. **4.** Not having the required abilities; inadequate. **5.** Not fair. —**un•e′qual•ly** *adv.*

un•e•qualed also **un•e•qualled** (ŭn-ē′kwəld) ▸*adj.* Not matched or paralleled; unrivaled.

un•e•quiv•o•cal (ŭn′ĭ-kwĭv′ə-kəl) ▸*adj.* Open to no doubt or misunderstanding; clear. —**un′e•quiv′o•cal•ly** *adv.*

UNESCO ▸*abbr.* United Nations Educational, Scientific, and Cultural Organization

un•e•ven (ŭn-ē′vən) ▸*adj.* **1.** Not equal, as in size, length, or quality. **2.** Not consistent or uniform. **3.** Not smooth or level. **4.** Not straight or parallel. —**un•e′ven•ly** *adv.* —**un•e′ven•ness** *n.*

un•e•vent•ful (ŭn′ĭ-vĕnt′fəl) ▸*adj.* **1.** Lacking in significant events. **2.** Occurring without disruption. —**un′e•vent′ful•ness** *n.*

un•ex•am•pled (ŭn′ĭg-zăm′pəld) ▸*adj.* Without precedent; unparalleled.

un•ex•cep•tion•a•ble (ŭn′ĭk-sĕp′shə-nə-bəl) ▸*adj.* Beyond any reasonable objection.

Usage: *Unexceptional* and *unexceptionable* are sometimes confused. *Unexceptionable* means "not open to any objection," as in *A judge's ethical standards should be unexceptionable. Unexceptional* generally means "not exceptional, not varying from the usual," as in *Some judges' ethical standards have been unexceptional.*

un•ex•cep•tion•al (ŭn′ĭk-sĕp′shə-nəl) ▸*adj.* **1.** Not varying from a norm; usual. **2.** Not subject to exceptions; absolute. See Usage Note at **unexceptionable.** —**un′ex•cep′tion•al•ly** *adv.*

un•ex•pect•ed (ŭn′ĭk-spĕk′tĭd) ▸*adj.* Coming without warning; unforeseen. —**un′ex•pect′ed•ly** *adv.* —**un′ex•pect′ed•ness** *n.*

un•fail•ing (ŭn-fā′lĭng) ▸*adj.* **1.** Not failing or running out; inexhaustible. **2.** Constant; unflagging. **3.** Infallible. —**un•fail′ing•ly** *adv.*

un•fair (ŭn-fâr′) ▸*adj.* **1.** Not just or evenhanded; biased. **2.** Contrary to laws or conventions, esp. in commerce; unethical. —**un•fair′ly** *adv.* —**un•fair′ness** *n.*

un•faith•ful (ŭn-fāth′fəl) ▸*adj.* **1.** Not faithful; disloyal. **2.** Adulterous. **3.** Not justly representing or reflecting the original; inaccurate. —**un•faith′ful•ly** *adv.* —**un•faith′ful•ness** *n.*

un•fa•mil•iar (ŭn′fə-mĭl′yər) ▸*adj.* **1.** Not within one's knowledge; strange. **2.** Not acquainted; not conversant. —**un′fa•mil•iar′i•ty** (-mĭl-yăr′ĭ-tē, -mĭl′ē-ăr′ĭ-tē) *n.* —**un′fa•mil′iar•ly** *adv.*

un•feel•ing (ŭn-fē′lĭng) ▸*adj.* **1.** Having no sensation; insentient. **2.** Not sympathetic; callous. —**un•feel′ing•ly** *adv.*

un•feigned (ŭn′fānd′) ▸*adj.* Not pretended; genuine.

un•fet•ter (ŭn-fĕt′ər) ▸*v.* To free from restrictions or bonds.

un•fit (ŭn-fĭt′) ▸*adj.* **1.** Inappropriate. **2.** Unqualified. **3.** In poor physical or mental health. ▸*v.* To make unfit; disqualify. —**un•fit′ly** *adv.* —**un•fit′ness** *n.*

un•flag•ging (ŭn-flăg′ĭng) ▸*adj.* Not flagging; untiring. See Syns at **tireless.** —**un•flag′ging•ly** *adv.*

un•flap•pa•ble (ŭn-flăp′ə-bəl) ▸*adj.* Not easily upset; cool. —**un•flap′pa•bil′i•ty** *n.*

un•fledged (ŭn-flĕjd′) ▸*adj.* **1.** Not having the feathers necessary to fly. Used of a young bird. **2.** Inexperienced or immature.

un•flinch•ing (ŭn-flĭn′chĭng) ▸*adj.* Steadfast; resolute. —**un•flinch′ing•ly** *adv.*

un•fold (ŭn-fōld′) ▸*v.* **1.** To open and spread out (something folded). **2.** To remove the coverings from. **3.** To reveal or be revealed gradually.

un•for•get•ta•ble (ŭn′fər-gĕt′ə-bəl) ▸*adj.* Permanently impressed on one's memory; memorable. —**un′for•get′ta•bly** *adv.*

un•formed (ŭn-fôrmd′) ▸*adj.* **1.** Having no definite shape or structure. See Syns at **shapeless. 2.** Immature; undeveloped.

un•for•tu•nate (ŭn-fôr′chə-nĭt) ▸*adj.* **1.** Unlucky. **2.** Causing misfortune; disastrous. **3.** Regrettable; deplorable. ▸*n.* A victim of bad luck. —**un•for′tu•nate•ly** *adv.*

Syns: *unfortunate, hapless, ill-fated, ill-starred, luckless, unlucky* ***Ant:*** *fortunate* ***adj.***

un•found•ed (ŭn-foun′dĭd) ▸*adj.* Not based on fact or sound evidence; groundless. See Syns at **baseless.**

un•fre•quent•ed (ŭn-frē′kwən-tĭd, ŭn′frē-kwĕn′tĭd) ▸*adj.* Receiving few or no visitors.

un•friend•ly (ŭn-frĕnd′lē) ▸*adj.* **1.** Not disposed to friendship. **2.** Unfavorable. —**un•friend′li•ness** *n.*

un•frock (ŭn-frŏk′) ▸*v.* To defrock.

un•furl (ŭn-fûrl′) ▸*v.* To spread or open (something) out.

un•gain•ly (ŭn-gān′lē) ▸*adj.* **-li•er, -li•est 1.** Awkward; clumsy. **2.** Unwieldy. [< UN-[1] + ME *gain*, straight.] —**un•gain′li•ness** *n.*

Un•ga•va Bay (ŭng-gā′və, -gä′-) An inlet of Hudson Strait in NE Quebec, Canada, between N Labrador and **Ungava Peninsula** between Hudson and Ungava bays.

un•god•ly (ŭn-gŏd′lē) ▸*adj.* **1.** Not revering

God; impious. **2.** Sinful; wicked. **3.** Outrageous: *an ungodly hour.* —**un•god′li•ness** *n.*

un•gov•ern•a•ble (ŭn-gŭv′ər-nə-bəl) ▸*adj.* Incapable of being governed or controlled.

un•gra•cious (ŭn-grā′shəs) ▸*adj.* **1.** Lacking courtesy; rude. **2.** Disagreeable. —**un•gra′cious•ly** *adv.* —**un•gra′cious•ness** *n.*

un•guard•ed (ŭn-gär′dĭd) ▸*adj.* **1.** Lacking protection; vulnerable. **2.** Incautious; imprudent.

un•guent (ŭng′gwənt) ▸*n.* A salve; ointment. [< Lat. *unguentum.*]

un•gu•late (ŭng′gyə-lĭt, -lāt′) ▸*adj.* Hoofed. [< Lat. *ungula*, hoof.] —**un′gu•late** *n.*

un•hal•lowed (ŭn-hăl′ōd) ▸*adj.* **1.** Not hallowed or consecrated. **2.** Irreverent; impious.

un•hand (ŭn-hănd′) ▸*v.* To remove one's hand from; let go.

un•hap•py (ŭn-hăp′ē) ▸*adj.* **1.** Not happy; sad. **2.** Not satisfied; discontented. **3.** Unlucky. **4.** Not suitable; inappropriate: *an unhappy choice of words.* —**un•hap′pi•ly** *adv.* —**un•hap′pi•ness** *n.*

un•health•y (ŭn-hĕl′thē) ▸*adj.* **1a.** In ill health; sick. **b.** Symptomatic of ill health. **c.** Conducive to poor health; unwholesome. **2.** Harmful to character; corruptive. —**un′health′i•ly** *adv.* —**un•health′i•ness** *n.*

un•heard (ŭn-hûrd′) ▸*adj.* **1.** Not heard. **2.** Not given a hearing.

un•heard-of (ŭn-hûrd′ŭv′, -ŏv′) ▸*adj.* **1.** Not previously known. **2.** Without precedent.

un•hinge (ŭn-hĭnj′) ▸*v.* **1.** To remove from hinges. **2.** To derange; unbalance.

un•ho•ly (ŭn-hō′lē) ▸*adj.* **1.** Wicked; immoral. **2.** Not hallowed or consecrated. **3.** *Informal* Outrageous. —**un•ho′li•ness** *n.*

un•hook (ŭn-hŏŏk′) ▸*v.* **1.** To remove from a hook. **2.** To unfasten the hooks of.

un•horse (ŭn-hôrs′) ▸*v.* **1.** To cause to fall from a horse. **2.** To overthrow or dislodge.

uni– ▸*pref.* One: *unicycle.* [< Lat. *ūnus*, one.]

u•ni•cam•er•al (yōō′nĭ-kăm′ər-əl) ▸*adj.* Consisting of a single legislative chamber.

UNICEF ▸*abbr.* United Nations Children's Fund (formerly United Nations International Children's Emergency Fund)

u•ni•cel•lu•lar (yōō′nĭ-sĕl′yə-lər) ▸*adj.* Consisting of one cell: *unicellular organisms.*

u•ni•corn (yōō′nĭ-kôrn′) ▸*n.* A fabled creature usu. represented as a horse with a single spiraled horn on its forehead. [< Lat. *ūnicornis*, having one horn.]

u•ni•cy•cle (yōō′nĭ-sī′kəl) ▸*n.* A single-wheeled vehicle usu. propelled by pedals.

un•i•den•ti•fied flying object (ŭn′ī-dĕn′tə-fīd′) ▸*n.* A flying or apparently flying object of an unknown nature, esp. one presumed to be of extraterrestrial origin.

u•ni•form (yōō′nə-fôrm′) ▸*adj.* **1.** Always the same; unvarying. **2.** Being the same as or consonant with another or others. ▸*n.* A distinctive outfit intended to identify those who wear it as members of a specific group. [< Lat. *ūniformis*, of one form.] —**u′ni•for′mi•ty, u′ni•form′ness** *n.* —**u′ni•form′ly** *adv.*

u•ni•fy (yōō′nə-fī′) ▸*v.* **-fied, -fy•ing.** To make into or become a unit; consolidate. [< LLat. *ūnificāre.*] —**u′ni•fi•ca′tion** *n.*

u•ni•lat•er•al (yōō′nə-lăt′ər-əl) ▸*adj.* Of, on, relating to, involving, or affecting only one side. —**u′ni•lat′er•al•ly** *adv.*

uniform
condominiums of identical design

un•im•peach•a•ble (ŭn′ĭm-pē′chə-bəl) ▸*adj.* Beyond doubt, question, or reproach. —**un′im•peach′a•bly** *adv.*

un•in•ter•est•ed (ŭn-ĭn′trĭ-stĭd, -tə-rĕs′tĭd) ▸*adj.* **1.** Without an interest, esp. not having a financial interest. **2.** Not interested; indifferent. See Usage Note at **disinterested.** —**un•in′ter•est•ed•ly** *adv.*

un•ion (yōōn′yən) ▸*n.* **1a.** The act of uniting or the state of being united. **b.** A combination so formed, esp. a confederation of people, parties, or political entities for common interest. **2a.** The state of matrimony; marriage. **b.** Sexual intercourse. **3.** A labor union. **4.** A coupling device for connecting parts, such as pipes or rods. **5.** A design on a flag that signifies the union of two or more sovereignties. **6. Union** The United States of America, esp. during the Civil War. [< LLat. *ūniō* < Lat. *ūnus*, one.]

un•ion•ism (yōōn′yə-nĭz′əm) ▸*n.* **1.** The principle or theory of forming a union. **2.** The principles, theory, or system of a union, esp. a labor union. **3. Unionism** Loyalty to the federal government during the Civil War. —**un′ion•ist** *n.*

un•ion•ize (yōōn′yə-nīz′) ▸*v.* **-ized, -iz•ing.** To organize into or cause to join a labor union. —**un′ion•i•za′tion** *n.* —**un′ion•iz′er** *n.*

union jack ▸*n.* **1.** A flag consisting entirely of a union. **2. Union Jack** The flag of the United Kingdom.

Union of Soviet Socialist Republics. Commonly called **Soviet Union.** A former country of E Europe and N Asia with coastlines on the Baltic and Black seas and the Arctic and Pacific oceans.

union shop ▸*n.* A business or industrial establishment whose employees are required to be or become union members; closed shop.

u•nique (yōō-nēk′) ▸*adj.* **1.** Being the only one of its kind. **2.** Without an equal or equivalent; unparalleled. [< Lat. *ūnicus.*] —**u•nique′ly** *adv.* —**u•nique′ness** *n.*

u•ni•sex (yōō′nĭ-sĕks′) ▸*adj.* Designed for or suitable to both sexes.

u•ni•sex•u•al (yōō′nĭ-sĕk′shōō-əl) ▸*adj.* **1.** Of or for only one sex. **2.** *Bot.* Having either stamens or pistils but not both.

u•ni•son (yōō′nĭ-sən, -zən) ▸*n.* **1a.** Identity of musical pitch. **b.** The combination of parts at the same pitch or in octaves. **2.** A speaking of the same words simultaneously by two or more speakers. **3.** Agreement; concord. —***idiom:* in unison 1.** In complete agreement. **2.** At the same time. [< LLat. *ūnisonus*, with one sound.]

u•nit (yo͞o′nĭt) ▸*n.* **1.** One regarded as a constituent part of a whole. **2a.** A mechanical part or module. **b.** An entire apparatus that performs a specific function. **3.** A precisely specified quantity in terms of which the magnitudes of other quantities of the same kind can be stated. [< UNITY.]

U•ni•tar•i•an (yo͞o′nĭ-târ′ē-ən) ▸*n.* A member of a Christian denomination that rejects the doctrine of the Trinity and emphasizes tolerance in religious belief. —**U′ni•tar′i•an** *adj.* —**U′ni•tar′i•an•ism** *n.*

u•ni•tar•y (yo͞o′nĭ-tĕr′ē) ▸*adj.* **1.** Of or relating to a unit. **2.** Whole. —**u′ni•tar′i•ly** *adv.*

u•nite (yo͞o-nīt′) ▸*v.* **u•nit•ed, u•nit•ing 1.** To bring together so as to form a whole. **2.** To combine (people) in interest, attitude, or action. **3.** To become joined, formed, or combined into a unit. [< Lat. *ūnīre.*]

U•nit•ed Arab Emirates (yo͞o-nī′tĭd) A country of E Arabia, a federation of seven sheikdoms on the Persian Gulf and the Gulf of Oman. Cap. Abu Dhabi. Pop. 1,861,000.

United Kingdom or **United Kingdom of Great Britain and Northern Ireland.** Commonly called **Great Britain.** A country of W Europe comprising England, Scotland, Wales, and Northern Ireland. Cap. London. Pop. 58,091,000.

United Nations. An international organization founded in 1945 to promote peace, security, and development.

United States or **United States of America.** A country of central and NW North America with coastlines on the Atlantic and Pacific. Cap. Washington DC. Pop. 260,651,000.

unit pricing ▸*n.* The pricing of goods on the basis of cost per unit of measure.

u•ni•ty (yo͞o′nĭ-tē) ▸*n., pl.* **-ties 1.** The state or quality of being one; singleness. **2.** The condition of being in accord; harmony. **3.** The combination or arrangement of parts into a whole; unification. **4.** Singleness of purpose or action; continuity. **5.** An ordering of all elements in a work of art or literature so that each contributes to a unified aesthetic effect. **6.** *Math.* The number 1. [< Lat. *ūnitās.*]

univ. ▸*abbr.* **1.** universal **2.** university

u•ni•va•lent (yo͞o′nĭ-vā′lənt) ▸*adj. Chem.* **1.** Having valence 1. **2.** Having only one valence.

u•ni•valve (yo͞o′nĭ-vălv′) ▸*n.* A mollusk having a shell consisting of a single valve or piece. —**u′ni•valve′** *adj.*

u•ni•ver•sal (yo͞o′nə-vûr′səl) ▸*adj.* **1.** Extending to or affecting the entire world; worldwide. **2.** Of, including, or affecting all members of a class or group. See Syns at **general. 3.** Applicable or common to all purposes, conditions, or situations. **4.** Relating to the universe or cosmos. **5.** Knowledgeable about or constituting all or many subjects. **6.** Adapted or adjustable to many sizes or mechanical uses. —**u′ni•ver′sal•ly** *adv.* —**u′ni•ver•sal′i•ty** *n.*

universal donor ▸*n.* A person with group O blood, which is compatible with all other groups in the ABO system.

U•ni•ver•sal•ism (yo͞o′nə-vûr′sə-lĭz′əm) ▸*n.* The theological doctrine that everyone will be saved. —**U′ni•ver′sal•ist** *n. & adj.*

universal joint ▸*n.* A joint or coupling that allows parts of a machine not in line with each other limited freedom of movement in any direction while transmitting rotary motion.

Universal Product Code ▸*n.* A number and bar code that allow a scanner to identify a particular consumer product.

universal time ▸*n.* The mean solar time for the meridian at Greenwich, England, used as a basis for calculating time throughout most of the world.

u•ni•verse (yo͞o′nə-vûrs′) ▸*n.* **1.** All existing things regarded as a whole. **2a.** The earth. **b.** The human race. [< Lat. *ūniversus*, whole.]

u•ni•ver•si•ty (yo͞o′nə-vûr′sĭ-tē) ▸*n., pl.* **-ties.** An institution for higher learning with teaching and research facilities constituting a graduate school, professional schools, and an undergraduate division. [< Med.Lat. *ūniversitās.*]

un•kempt (ŭn-kĕmpt′) ▸*adj.* **1a.** Not combed. **b.** Disorderly or untidy. **2.** Unpolished; rude. [UN–[1] + ME *kembed*, p.part. of *kemben*, comb.]

un•lead•ed (ŭn-lĕd′ĭd) ▸*adj.* Not containing lead: *unleaded gasoline.*

un•learn (ŭn-lûrn′) ▸*v.* To put (something learned) out of the mind; forget.

un•learn•ed (ŭn-lûr′nĭd) ▸*adj.* **1.** Not educated. **2.** (-lûrnd′). Not acquired by training or studying. —**un•learn′ed•ly** *adv.*

un•leash (ŭn-lēsh′) ▸*v.* To release or loose from or as if from a leash.

un•less (ŭn-lĕs′) ▸*conj.* Except on the condition that. [< ME *onlesse.*]

un•let•tered (ŭn-lĕt′ərd) ▸*adj.* Not educated, esp. unable to read and write.

un•like (ŭn-līk′) ▸*adj.* **1.** Not alike; different; dissimilar. **2.** Not equal. ▸*prep.* **1.** Different from; not like. **2.** Not typical of: *It's unlike him not to call.* —**un•like′ness** *n.*

un•like•ly (ŭn-līk′lē) ▸*adj.* **1.** Not likely; improbable. **2.** Likely to fail. —**un•like′li•hood′** *n.* —**un•like′li•ness** *n.*

un•lim•ber (ŭn-lĭm′bər) ▸*v.* To make ready for action.

un•load (ŭn-lōd′) ▸*v.* **1a.** To remove the load or cargo from. **b.** To discharge (cargo or a load). **2a.** To relieve (oneself) of something oppressive; unburden. **b.** To pour forth (one's troubles or feelings). **3a.** To remove the charge from (a firearm). **b.** To discharge (a firearm); fire. **4.** To dispose of, esp. by selling in great quantity. —**un•load′er** *n.*

un•lock (ŭn-lŏk′) ▸*v.* **1a.** To undo (a lock). **b.** To undo the lock of. **2.** To give access to; open. **3.** To provide a key to: *unlock a mystery.*

un•looked-for (ŭn-lo͝okt′fôr′) ▸*adj.* Not expected; unforeseen: *unlooked-for riches.*

un•loose (ŭn-lo͞os′) ▸*v.* **1.** To let loose or unfasten; release. **2.** To relax or ease.

un•luck•y (ŭn-lŭk′ē) ▸*adj.* **1.** Subjected to or marked by misfortune. **2.** Inauspicious. See Syns at **unfortunate. 3.** Disappointing: *an unlucky choice.* —**un•luck′i•ly** *adv.* —**un•luck′i•ness** *n.*

un•make (ŭn-māk′) ▸*v.* **1.** To deprive of position, rank, or authority. **2.** To ruin; destroy. **3.** To alter the nature of.

un•man•nered (ŭn-măn′ərd) ▸*adj.* **1.** Lacking good manners; rude. **2.** Natural and unaffected. —**un•man′nered•ly** *adv.*

un•mask (ŭn-măsk′) ▸*v.* **1.** To remove a mask from. **2.** To disclose the true character of; expose.

un•men•tion•a•ble (ŭn-mĕn′shə-nə-bəl)

▸*adj.* Not fit to be mentioned.

un•mer•ci•ful (ŭn-mûr′sĭ-fəl) ▸*adj.* **1.** Having no mercy; merciless. **2.** Excessive: *unmerciful heat.* —**un•mer′ci•ful•ly** *adv.* —**un•mer′ci•ful•ness** *n.*

un•mis•tak•a•ble (ŭn′mĭ-stā′kə-bəl) ▸*adj.* Obvious; evident. —**un′mis•tak′a•bly** *adv.*

un•mit•i•gat•ed (ŭn-mĭt′ĭ-gā′tĭd) ▸*adj.* **1.** Not diminished or moderated. **2.** Without qualification or exception; absolute.

un•mor•al (ŭn-môr′əl, -mŏr′-) ▸*adj.* Amoral.

un•nat•u•ral (ŭn-năch′ər-əl) ▸*adj.* **1.** In violation of a natural law. **2.** Contrived or constrained; artificial. **3.** In violation of natural feelings or normal or accepted standards. —**un•nat′u•ral•ly** *adv.* —**un•nat′u•ral•ness** *n.*

un•nerve (ŭn-nûrv′) ▸*v.* **1.** To deprive of strength or firmness of purpose. **2.** To make nervous or upset. —**un•nerv′ing•ly** *adv.*

un•num•bered (ŭn-nŭm′bərd) ▸*adj.* **1.** Innumerable; countless. **2.** Not marked with an identifying number.

un•or•gan•ized (ŭn-ôr′gə-nīzd′) ▸*adj.* **1.** Lacking order or unity. **2.** Not unionized.

un•pack (ŭn-păk′) ▸*v.* **1.** To remove the contents of. **2.** To remove (something) from a container.

un•par•al•leled (ŭn-păr′ə-lĕld′) ▸*adj.* Without parallel; unequaled.

un•par•lia•men•ta•ry (ŭn′pär-lə-mĕn′tə-rē, -mĕn′trē) ▸*adj.* Not in accord with parliamentary procedure.

un•peo•ple (ŭn-pē′pəl) ▸*v.* To depopulate (an area).

un•per•son (ŭn′pûr′sən) ▸*n.* A nonperson.

un•plug (ŭn-plŭg′) ▸*v.* **1.** To remove a plug from. **2.** To disconnect (an electric appliance) by removing a plug from an outlet.

un•plugged (ŭn-plŭgd′) ▸*adj.* Relating to music that is not electronically amplified or modified; acoustic. ▸*adv.* Acoustically.

un•plumbed (ŭn-plŭmd′) ▸*adj.* **1.** Not measured or sounded with a plumb. **2.** Not fully examined or explored.

un•prec•e•dent•ed (ŭn-prĕs′ĭ-dĕn′tĭd) ▸*adj.* Having no previous example.

un•pre•pared (ŭn′prĭ-pârd′) ▸*adj.* **1.** Not prepared or ready. **2.** Impromptu. —**un′pre•par′ed•ly** *adv.* —**un′pre•par′ed•ness** *n.*

un•pre•ten•tious (ŭn′prĭ-tĕn′shəs) ▸*adj.* Lacking pretention or affectation; modest. See Syns at **plain.** —**un′pre•ten′tious•ly** *adv.* —**un′pre•ten′tious•ness** *n.*

un•print•a•ble (ŭn-prĭn′tə-bəl) ▸*adj.* Not proper for publication.

un•pro•fes•sion•al (ŭn′prə-fĕsh′ə-nəl) ▸*adj.* **1.** Not conforming to the standards of a profession. **2.** Characteristic of an amateur; inexpert. —**un′pro•fes′sion•al•ly** *adv.*

un•prof•it•a•ble (ŭn-prŏf′ĭ-tə-bəl) ▸*adj.* **1.** Bringing in no profit. **2.** Serving no useful purpose. —**un•prof′it•a•bly** *adv.*

un•qual•i•fied (ŭn-kwŏl′ə-fīd′) ▸*adj.* **1.** Lacking the proper or required qualifications: *unqualified for the job.* **2.** Not modified by conditions or reservations.

un•quote (ŭn-kwōt′) ▸*n.* Used by a speaker to indicate the end of a quotation.

un•rav•el (ŭn-răv′əl) ▸*v.* **1.** To separate (entangled threads). **2.** To separate and clarify the elements of (something mysterious or baffling); solve. See Syns at **solve.**

un•read (ŭn-rĕd′) ▸*adj.* **1.** Not read or studied. **2.** Having read little; unlearned.

un•read•a•ble (ŭn-rē′də-bəl) ▸*adj.* **1.** Illegible. **2.** Not interesting; dull. **3.** Incomprehensible.

un•re•al (ŭn-rē′əl, -rēl′) ▸*adj.* **1.** Not real or substantial. **2.** *Slang* Too good to be true; fantastic. —**un′re•al′i•ty** *n.*

un•rea•son•a•ble (ŭn-rē′zə-nə-bəl) ▸*adj.* **1.** Not governed by reason. **2.** Exceeding reasonable limits. —**un•rea′son•a•ble•ness** *n.* —**un•rea′son•a•bly** *adv.*

Syns: *unreasonable, irrational, excessive*
Ant: *reasonable* **adj.**

un•re•gen•er•ate (ŭn′rĭ-jĕn′ər-ĭt) ▸*adj.* **1.** Not spiritually renewed or reformed; not repentant. **2.** Stubborn.

un•re•lent•ing (ŭn′rĭ-lĕn′tĭng) ▸*adj.* **1.** Relentless; inexorable. **2.** Not diminishing in intensity, pace, or effort.

un•re•mit•ting (ŭn′rĭ-mĭt′ĭng) ▸*adj.* Never slackening; persistent.

un•re•served (ŭn′rĭ-zûrvd′) ▸*adj.* **1.** Not held back for a particular person. **2.** Given without reservation; unqualified. —**un′re•serv′ed•ly** (-zûr′vĭd-lē) *adv.*

un•rest (ŭn-rĕst′, ŭn′rĕst′) ▸*n.* Uneasiness; disquiet: *social unrest.*

un•ri•valed or **un•ri•valled** (ŭn-rī′vəld) ▸*adj.* Unequaled; incomparable.

un•roll (ŭn-rōl′) ▸*v.* **1.** To unwind and open (something rolled up). **2.** To unfold; reveal.

un•ruf•fled (ŭn-rŭf′əld) ▸*adj.* Not agitated; calm.

un•ru•ly (ŭn-ro͞o′lē) ▸*adj.* Difficult or impossible to discipline, control, or rule. [ME *unreuli.*] —**un•ru′li•ness** *n.*

un•sad•dle (ŭn-săd′l) ▸*v.* **1.** To remove a saddle from. **2.** To unhorse.

un•sat•u•rat•ed (ŭn-săch′ə-rā′tĭd) ▸*adj.* **1.** Not saturated. **2.** Of or being a fat, usu. of plant origin, composed predominantly of fatty acids having one or more double bonds in the carbon chain.

un•sa•vor•y (ŭn-sā′və-rē) ▸*adj.* **1.** Distasteful or disagreeable. **2.** Not savory: *an unsavory meal.* **3.** Morally offensive.

un•scathed (ŭn-skā*th*d′) ▸*adj.* Not injured or harmed: *escaped the hurricane unscathed.*

un•schooled (ŭn-sko͞old′) ▸*adj.* **1.** Not educated or instructed. **2.** Not the result of training; natural: *unschooled talents.*

un•scram•ble (ŭn-skrăm′bəl) ▸*v.* **1.** To disentangle; resolve. **2.** To restore (a scrambled message) to intelligible form.

un•screw (ŭn-skro͞o′) ▸*v.* **1.** To take out the screw or screws from. **2.** To loosen, adjust, or remove by rotating.

un•scru•pu•lous (ŭn-skro͞o′pyə-ləs) ▸*adj.* Devoid of scruples; not honorable. —**un•scru′pu•lous•ly** *adv.* —**un•scru′pu•lous•ness** *n.*

un•sea•son•a•ble (ŭn-sē′zə-nə-bəl) ▸*adj.* **1.** Not characteristic of the time of year: *unseasonable weather.* **2.** Poorly timed; inopportune. —**un•sea′son•a•bly** *adv.*

un•seat (ŭn-sēt′) ▸*v.* **1.** To remove from a seat, esp. from a saddle. **2.** To dislodge from a position or office.

un•seem•ly (ŭn-sēm′lē) ▸*adj.* **1.** Not in good taste; grossly improper. **2.** Inappropriate.

un•set•tle (ŭn-sĕt′l) ▸*v.* To make unstable; disturb.
un•set•tled (ŭn-sĕt′ld) ▸*adj.* **1.** Disordered; disturbed. **2.** Likely to change or vary; variable: *unsettled weather.* **3.** Not determined or resolved. **4.** Not paid or adjusted. **5.** Not populated; uninhabited. **6.** Not fixed or established: *an unsettled lifestyle.*
un•sight•ly (ŭn-sīt′lē) ▸*adj.* Unpleasant or offensive to look at; unattractive. See Syns at **ugly.** —**un′sight′li•ness** *n.*
un•skilled (ŭn-skĭld′) ▸*adj.* **1.** Lacking skill or training. **2.** Requiring no training or skill. **3.** Exhibiting a lack of skill; inexpert.
un•so•cia•ble (ŭn-sō′shə-bəl) ▸*adj.* Not disposed to seek the company of others. —**un•so′cia•bil′i•ty** *n.* —**un•so′cia•bly** *adv.*
un•sound (ŭn-sound′) ▸*adj.* **1.** Not dependably strong or solid. **2.** Not physically or mentally healthy. **3.** Not logically valid; fallacious. —**un•sound′ly** *adv.* —**un•sound′ness** *n.*
un•spar•ing (ŭn-spâr′ĭng) ▸*adj.* **1.** Unmerciful; severe. **2.** Not frugal; generous. —**un•spar′ing•ly** *adv.* —**un•spar′ing•ness** *n.*
un•speak•a•ble (ŭn-spē′kə-bəl) ▸*adj.* **1.** Beyond description; inexpressible. **2.** Inexpressibly bad or objectionable. —**un•speak′a•bly** *adv.*

Syns: *unspeakable, indefinable, indescribable, ineffable, inexpressible, unutterable* **adj.**

un•sta•ble (ŭn-stā′bəl) ▸*adj.* **1.** Tending strongly to change: *unstable weather.* **2a.** Fickle. **b.** Lacking control of one's emotions. **3.** Unsteady: *an unstable ladder.* **4a.** Decaying with relatively short lifetime. Used of subatomic particles. **b.** Radioactive. —**un•sta′ble•ness** *n.* —**un•sta′bly** *adv.*
un•stead•y (ŭn-stĕd′ē) ▸*adj.* **1.** Not securely in place; unstable. **2.** Fluctuating; inconstant. **3.** Not even; wavering. —**un•stead′i•ly** *adv.* —**un•stead′i•ness** *n.*
un•stick (ŭn-stĭk′) ▸*v.* To free from being stuck.
un•stop (ŭn-stŏp′) ▸*v.* **1.** To remove a stopper from. **2.** To remove an obstruction from.
un•stressed (ŭn-strĕst′) ▸*adj.* **1.** *Ling.* Not stressed or accented. **2.** Not exposed or subjected to stress.
un•struc•tured (ŭn-strŭk′chərd) ▸*adj.* **1.** Lacking structure. **2.** Not regulated or regimented.
un•strung (ŭn-strŭng′) ▸*adj.* **1.** Having the strings loosened or removed. **2.** Emotionally upset.
un•stud•ied (ŭn-stŭd′ēd) ▸*adj.* **1.** Not contrived; natural. **2.** Not gained by study or instruction.
un•sub•stan•tial (ŭn′səb-stăn′shəl) ▸*adj.* **1.** Lacking material substance; not real. **2.** Flimsy. **3.** Lacking basis in fact.
un•sung (ŭn-sŭng′) ▸*adj.* **1.** Not honored or praised; uncelebrated. **2.** Not sung.
un•tan•gle (ŭn-tăng′gəl) ▸*v.* **1.** To disentangle. See Syns at **extricate.** **2.** To clarify or resolve.
un•taught (ŭn-tôt′) ▸*adj.* **1.** Not instructed. **2.** Not acquired by instruction; natural.
un•thank•ful (ŭn-thăngk′fəl) ▸*adj.* **1.** Ungrateful. **2.** Unwelcome.
un•think•a•ble (ŭn-thĭng′kə-bəl) ▸*adj.* Impossible to imagine; inconceivable.
un•think•ing (ŭn′thĭng′kĭng) ▸*adj.* **1.** Thoughtless or heedless. **2.** Not deliberate; inadvertent. —**un•think′ing•ly** *adv.*
un•tie (ŭn-tī′) ▸*v.* **1.** To undo or loosen (e.g., a knot). **2.** To free from something that binds or restrains.
un•til (ŭn-tĭl′) ▸*prep.* **1.** Up to the time of: *We danced until dawn.* **2.** Before (a specified time): *She can't leave until Friday.* ▸*conj.* **1.** Up to the time that: *We walked until it got dark.* **2.** Before: *You cannot leave until your work is finished.* **3.** To the point or extent that: *I talked until I was hoarse.* [ME.]
un•time•ly (ŭn-tīm′lē) ▸*adj.* **1.** Occurring or done at an inappropriate time; inopportune. **2.** Occurring too soon; premature. —**un•time′li•ness** *n.* —**un•time′ly** *adv.*
un•to (ŭn′to͞o) ▸*prep.* To. [ME.]
un•told (ŭn-tōld′) ▸*adj.* **1.** Not told or revealed. **2.** Beyond description or enumeration.
un•touch•a•ble (ŭn-tŭch′ə-bəl) ▸*adj.* **1.** Not to be touched. **2.** Out of reach; unobtainable. **3.** Beyond criticism, impeachment, or attack. ▸*n.* often **Untouchable** *Hinduism* A member of the class that is considered unclean and defiling by the four Hindu castes.
un•to•ward (ŭn-tôrd′, -tōrd′) ▸*adj.* **1.** Not favorable; unpropitious. **2.** Hard to control; unruly.
un•truth (ŭn-tro͞oth′) ▸*n.* **1.** Something false; a lie. **2.** Lack of truth.
un•tu•tored (ŭn-to͞o′tərd, -tyo͞o′-) ▸*adj.* **1.** Having had no formal education. **2.** Unsophisticated; unrefined.
un•twist (ŭn-twĭst′) ▸*v.* To loosen or separate (something twisted) by turning in the opposite direction; unwind.
un•used (ŭn-yo͞ozd′, ŭn-yo͞ost′) ▸*adj.* **1.** Not in use. **2.** Never having been used. **3.** Not accustomed: *unused to city traffic.*
un•u•su•al (ŭn-yo͞o′zho͞o-əl) ▸*adj.* Not usual or ordinary. —**un•u′su•al•ly** *adv.*
un•ut•ter•a•ble (ŭn-ŭt′ər-ə-bəl) ▸*adj.* **1.** That cannot or must not be uttered or expressed. See Syns at **unspeakable.** **2.** Not capable of being pronounced. —**un•ut′ter•a•bly** *adv.*
un•var•nished (ŭn′vär′nĭsht) ▸*adj.* **1.** Not varnished. **2.** Stated with no effort to soften or disguise; plain.
un•veil (ŭn-vāl′) ▸*v.* **1.** To remove a veil or covering from. **2.** To disclose; reveal.
un•voiced (ŭn-voist′) ▸*adj.* **1.** Not expressed or uttered. **2.** *Ling.* Voiceless.
un•war•rant•ed (ŭn-wôr′ən-tĭd, -wŏr′-) ▸*adj.* Having no justification; groundless. See Syns at **baseless.**
un•wea•ried (ŭn-wîr′ēd) ▸*adj.* **1.** Not tired. **2.** Never wearying. See Syns at **tireless.**
un•well (ŭn-wĕl′) ▸*adj.* In poor health; sick.
un•whole•some (ŭn-hōl′səm) ▸*adj.* **1.** Injurious to health; unhealthy. **2.** Offensive or loathsome. —**un•whole′some•ness** *n.*
un•wield•y (ŭn-wēl′dē) ▸*adj.* Difficult to carry or manage because of bulk or shape.
un•will•ing (ŭn-wĭl′ĭng) ▸*adj.* **1.** Not willing; hesitant. **2.** Done, given, or said reluctantly. —**un•will′ing•ly** *adv.* —**un•will′ing•ness** *n.*
un•wind (ŭn-wīnd′) ▸*v.* **1.** To unroll; uncoil. **2.** To disentangle. **3.** To relax.
un•wit•ting (ŭn-wĭt′ĭng) ▸*adj.* **1.** Not knowing; unaware. **2.** Not intended; unintentional. [ME : UN–[1] + *witting*, knowing (< OE *witan*,

know).] —**un•wit′ting•ly** *adv.*

un•wont•ed (ŭn-wôn′tĭd, -wōn′-, -wŭn′-) ►*adj.* Not habitual or ordinary; unusual.

un•world•ly (ŭn-wûrld′lē) ►*adj.* **1.** Not of this world; spiritual. **2.** Concerned with the spirit or soul. **3.** Not worldly-wise; naive. —**un•world′li•ness** *n.*

un•wor•thy (ŭn-wûr′*th*ē) ►*adj.* **1.** Insufficient in worth; undeserving. **2.** Not suiting or befitting. **3.** Vile; despicable. —**un•wor′thi•ly** *adv.* —**un•wor′thi•ness** *n.*

un•writ•ten (ŭn-rĭt′n) ►*adj.* **1.** Not written or recorded. **2.** Forceful through custom; traditional.

up (ŭp) ►*adv.* **1.** In or to a higher position: *looking up.* **2.** In or to an upright position: *sat up in bed.* **3a.** Above a surface: *coming up for air.* **b.** Above the horizon: *as the sun came up.* **4.** Into consideration: *take up a new topic.* **5.** In or toward a position conventionally regarded as higher, as on a map: *up in Canada.* **6.** To or at a higher price: *stocks going up.* **7.** So as to advance, increase, or improve: *Our spirits went up.* **8.** With or to a greater pitch or volume. **9.** Into a state of excitement or turbulence. **10.** Completely; entirely: *drank it up in a gulp; fastened up the coat.* **11.** Used as an intensifier with certain verbs: *typed up a list.* ►*adj.* **1.** Above a former level; higher: *My grades are up.* **2a.** Out of bed: *was up by seven.* **b.** Standing; erect. **c.** Facing upward. **3.** Raised; lifted: *a switch in the up position.* **4.** Moving or directed upward: *an up elevator.* **5a.** Increasingly excited or agitated; aroused. **b.** *Informal* Cheerful; optimistic. **c.** *Slang* Happily excited; euphoric. **6.** *Informal* Taking place; going on: *wondered what was up back home.* **7.** Being considered; under study: *a contract up for renewal.* **8.** Running as a candidate. **9.** On trial; charged: *up for manslaughter.* ►*prep.* **1.** From a lower to or toward a higher point on: *up the hill.* **2.** Toward or at a point farther along: *up the road.* **3.** Toward the source of: *up the Nile.* ►*n.* **1.** An upward slope; rise. **2.** An upward movement or trend. **3.** *Slang* Excitement or euphoria. ►*v.* **upped, up•ping 1.** To increase: *upped their fees.* **2.** To raise to a higher level. —***idioms:*** **on the up-and-up** Open and honest. **up against** Confronted with; facing. **up to 1.** Occupied with, esp. devising or scheming. **2.** Able to do or deal with. **3.** Dependent on: *It's up to us.* [< OE *up*, upward, and *uppe*, on high.]

up– ►*pref.* **1.** Up; upward: *uphill.* **2.** Upper: *upland.* [< OE *ūp-*, *upp-*.]

up-and-com•ing (ŭp′ən-kŭm′ĭng) ►*adj.* Marked for future success; promising.

U•pan•i•shad (o͞o-pä′nĭ-shäd′) ►*n.* Any of a group of philosophical treatises contributing to the theology of ancient Hinduism, elaborating on the earlier Vedas.

up•beat (ŭp′bēt′) ►*n. Mus.* An unaccented beat occurring before the first beat of a measure. ►*adj. Informal* Optimistic; cheerful.

up•braid (ŭp-brād′) ►*v.* To reprove sharply; reproach. [< OE *ūpbrēdan*.]

up•bring•ing (ŭp′brĭng′ĭng) ►*n.* The rearing and training received during childhood.

UPC ►*abbr.* Universal Product Code

up•com•ing (ŭp′kŭm′ĭng) ►*adj.* Occurring soon; forthcoming.

up•coun•try (ŭp′kŭn′trē) ►*n.* An inland or upland region of a country. —**up′coun′try** *adj. & adv.*

up•date (ŭp-dāt′) ►*v.* To bring up to date. —**up′date′** *n.*

Up•dike (ŭp′dīk′), **John Hoyer.** b. 1932. Amer. writer.

up•draft (ŭp′drăft′) ►*n.* An upward current of air.

up•end (ŭp-ĕnd′) ►*v.* **1.** To stand, set, or turn on one end. **2.** To overturn or overthrow.

up-front or **up•front** (ŭp′frŭnt′) ►*adj. Informal* **1.** Straightforward; frank. **2.** Paid or due in advance: *up-front cash.* —**up′front′** *adv.*

up•grade (ŭp′grād′) ►*v.* **1.** To raise to a higher grade or standard. **2.** *Comp. Sci.* To replace (software or hardware) with a newer or better product. ►*n.* **1.** An upward incline. **2.** *Comp. Sci.* A hardware or software product that is newer or performs better than an earlier version.

up•heav•al (ŭp-hē′vəl) ►*n.* **1.** The process of being heaved upward. **2.** A sudden violent disruption or upset. **3.** *Geol.* A raising of a part of the earth's crust.

up•hill (ŭp′hĭl′) ►*adj.* **1.** Going up a hill or slope. **2.** Difficult; laborious. ►*adv.* (ŭp′hĭl′) **1.** To or toward higher ground; up a slope. **2.** Against adversity; with difficulty.

up•hold (ŭp-hōld′) ►*v.* **1.** To hold aloft. **2.** To prevent from falling; support. **3.** To maintain against opposition. —**up•hold′er** *n.*

up•hol•ster (ŭp-hōl′stər, ə-pōl′-) ►*v.* To supply (furniture) with stuffing, springs, cushions, and covering fabric. [< ME *upholden*, repair.] —**up•hol′ster•er** *n.*

up•hol•ster•y (ŭp-hōl′stə-rē, -strē, ə-pōl′-) ►*n., pl.* **-ies 1.** The materials used in upholstering. **2.** The business of upholstering.

up•keep (ŭp′kēp′) ►*n.* The act or cost of maintaining in proper operation and repair.

up•land (ŭp′lənd, -lănd′) ►*n.* An area of land of high elevation. —**up′land′** *adj.*

up•lift (ŭp-lĭft′) ►*v.* **1.** To raise; elevate. **2.** To raise to a higher social, intellectual, or moral level. **3.** To raise to spiritual or emotional heights; exalt. —**up′lift′** *n.*

up•load (ŭp′lōd′) ►*v.* To transfer (data or programs), usu. from a peripheral computer or device to a central computer.

up•most (ŭp′mōst′) ►*adj.* Uppermost.

up•on (ə-pŏn′, ə-pôn′) ►*prep.* On.

up•per (ŭp′ər) ►*adj.* **1.** Higher in place, position, or rank. **2. Upper** *Geol. & Archaeol.* Being a later division of the period named. ►*n.* **1.** The part of a shoe or boot above the sole. **2.** *Slang* A drug, esp. an amphetamine, used as a stimulant. **3.** An exhilarating experience.

Upper California. See **Alta California.**

up•per•case (ŭp′ər-kās′) ►*adj.* Of or relating to capital letters as distinguished from small letters. —**up′per•case′** *n. & v.*

upper class ►*n.* The highest socioeconomic class in a society. —**up′per-class′** *adj.*

up•per•class•man (ŭp′ər-klăs′mən) ►*n.* A student in the junior or senior class of a secondary school or college.

upper crust ►*n. Informal* The highest social class or group. —**up′per-crust′** *adj.*

up•per•cut (ŭp′ər-kŭt′) ►*n. Sports* A swinging blow directed upward, as in boxing.

upper hand ►*n.* A position of control or advantage.

up•per•most (ŭp′ər-mōst′) ►*adv. & adj.* In the highest position, place, or rank.

Upper Vol•ta (vŏl′tə, vōl′-) See **Burkina Faso.**

up•pi•ty (ŭp′ĭ-tē) ►*adj. Informal* Presumptuous.

up•raise (ŭp-rāz′) ►*v.* To raise or lift up.

up•right (ŭp′rīt′) ►*adj.* **1.** In a vertical position or direction. **2.** Moral; honorable. ►*adv.* Vertically: *walk upright.* ►*n.* Something, such as a goal post, that stands upright. —**up′right′ly** *adv.* —**up′right′ness** *n.*

upright piano ►*n.* A piano having the strings mounted vertically.

up•ris•ing (ŭp′rī′zĭng) ►*n.* A revolt against a constituted government.

up•roar (ŭp′rôr′, -rōr′) ►*n.* A condition of noisy excitement and confusion. [Prob. < MLGer. *uprōr*, upward motion.]

up•roar•i•ous (ŭp-rôr′ē-əs, -rōr′-) ►*adj.* **1.** Causing or accompanied by an uproar. **2.** Hilarious. —**up•roar′i•ous•ly** *adv.* —**up•roar′i•ous•ness** *n.*

up•root (ŭp-ro͞ot′, -ro͝ot′) ►*v.* To remove completely by or as if by pulling up the roots. —**up•root′ed•ness** *n.*

up•scale (ŭp′skāl′) ►*adj.* Intended for or relating to high-income consumers. —**up•scale′** *v.*

up•set (ŭp-sĕt′) ►*v.* **1.** To overturn or cause to overturn; capsize. **2.** To disturb the functioning, order, or course of. **3.** To distress mentally or emotionally. **4.** To overthrow; topple. See Syns at **overthrow.** ►*n.* (ŭp′sĕt′) **1.** The act of upsetting or the condition of being upset. **2.** A disturbance, disorder, or state of agitation. **3.** A game or contest in which the favorite is defeated. ►*adj.* **1.** Overturned; capsized. **2.** Showing symptoms of indigestion. **3.** Emotionally or mentally distressed. [ME *upsetten*, set up.]

up•shot (ŭp′shŏt′) ►*n.* The final result; outcome.

up•side down (ŭp′sīd′) ►*adv.* **1.** With the upper side down. **2.** In great disorder. [< ME *up so doun*, up as if down.] —**up′side-down′** *adj.*

up•si•lon (ŭp′sə-lŏn′, yo͞op′-) ►*n.* The 20th letter of the Greek alphabet. [LGk. *u psilon*, simple u.]

up•stage (ŭp′stāj′) ►*adv.* Toward, at, or on the rear part of a stage. ►*adj.* Of the rear part of a stage. ►*v.* (ŭp-stāj′) **1.** To make (another performer) face away from the audience by assuming a position upstage. **2.** To divert attention or praise from. **3.** To treat haughtily.

up•stairs (ŭp′stârz′) ►*adv.* **1.** Up the stairs. **2.** To or on a higher floor. ►*n.* (ŭp′stârz′) *(takes sing. v.)* The upper part of a building. —**up′-stairs′** *adj.*

up•stand•ing (ŭp-stăn′dĭng, ŭp′stăn′-) ►*adj.* **1.** Standing erect or upright. **2.** Morally upright; honest.

up•start (ŭp′stärt′) ►*n.* A person who attains sudden wealth or importance, esp. one made immodest by the change; parvenu.

up•state (ŭp′stāt′) ►*n.* The northerly section of a US state. —**up′state′** *adv. & adj.*

up•stream (ŭp′strēm′) ►*adv. & adj.* Against the current of a stream.

up•stroke (ŭp′strōk′) ►*n.* An upward stroke.

up•surge (ŭp′sûrj′) ►*n.* A rapid or abrupt rise: *an upsurge in crime.* —**up•surge′** *v.*

up•sweep (ŭp′swēp′) ►*n.* An upward curve or sweep. —**up′sweep′** *v.*

up•swing (ŭp′swĭng′) ►*n.* An upward swing or trend; increase.

up•take (ŭp′tāk′) ►*n.* **1.** A passage for drawing up smoke or air. **2.** Understanding; comprehension: *quick on the uptake.*

up-tem•po also **up•tem•po** (ŭp′tĕm′pō) ►*n., pl.* **-pos.** A fast or lively tempo, as in jazz. —**up′-tem′po** *adj.*

up•tight (ŭp′tīt′) ►*adj. Slang* **1.** Tense; nervous. **2.** Outraged; angry. **3.** Rigidly conventional.

up-to-date (ŭp′tə-dāt′) ►*adj.* Informed of or reflecting the latest information or styles. —**up′-to-date′ness** *n.*

up•town (ŭp′toun′) ►*n.* The upper part of a town or city. ►*adv.* (ŭp′toun′). To, toward, or in the uptown. —**up′town′** *adj.*

up•turn (ŭp′tûrn′, ŭp-tûrn′) ►*v.* **1.** To turn up or over. **2.** To direct upward. ►*n.* (ŭp′tûrn′). An upward movement, curve, or trend, as in business.

up•ward (ŭp′wərd) ►*adv. & adj.* From a lower to a higher place, point, or level. —***idiom:*** **upward (**or **upwards) of** More than; in excess of. —**up′ward•ly** *adv.* —**up′wards** *adv.*

upward mobility ►*n.* Advancement in economic and social standing.

up•wind (ŭp′wĭnd′) ►*adv.* In or toward the direction from which the wind blows. —**up′-wind′** *adj.*

Ur (ûr, o͝or) A city of ancient Sumer in S Mesopotamia on a site in SE Iraq.

u•ra•cil (yo͝or′ə-sĭl) ►*n.* A pyrimidine base that is an essential constituent of RNA. [< UR(EA) + AC(ETIC).]

U•ral-Al•ta•ic (yo͝or′əl-ăl-tā′ĭk) ►*n.* A language group that comprises the Uralic and Altaic families. —**U′ral-Al•ta′ic** *adj.*

U•ral•ic (yo͞o-răl′ĭk) also **U•ra•li•an** (yo͞o-rā′lē-ən) ►*n.* A language family that comprises the Finno-Ugric and Samoyedic subfamilies. —**U•ral′ic** *adj.*

U•ral Mountains (yo͝or′əl) A range of W Russia forming the traditional boundary between Europe and Asia and extending about 2,414 km (1,500 mi) from the Arctic to Kazakhstan.

Ural River. A river of W Russia and W Kazakhstan rising in the S Ural Mts. and flowing about 2,533 km (1,574 mi) to the Caspian Sea.

u•ra•ni•um (yo͞o-rā′nē-əm) ►*n. Symbol* **U** A heavy, radioactive, silvery-white metallic element, used in research, nuclear fuels, and nuclear weapons. At. no. 92. See table at **element.** [< URANUS.]

U•ra•nus (yo͝or′ə-nəs, yo͞o-rā′nəs) ►*n.* **1.** *Gk. Myth.* The earliest supreme god, a personification of the sky. **2.** The 7th planet from the sun, at a distance of approx. 2,869 million km (1,790 million mi) and with a mean diameter of 52,290 km (32,480 mi).

ur•ban (ûr′bən) ►*adj.* Of, relating to, or located in a city. [< Lat. *urbs*, city.]

Urban II. 1042?–99. Pope (1088–99).

ur•bane (ûr-bān′) ►*adj.* **-ban•er, -ban•est.** Polite and refined in manner; suave. [Lat. *urbānus*, URBAN.] —**ur•bane′ly** *adv.*

ur•ban•ite (ûr′bə-nīt′) ►*n.* A city dweller.

ur•ban•i•ty (ûr-băn′ĭ-tē) ►*n.* Refinement and elegance of manner.

ur•ban•ize (ûr′bə-nīz′) ►*v.* **-ized, -iz•ing.** To make urban in nature or character. —**ur′ban•i•za′tion** *n.*
ur•chin (ûr′chĭn) ►*n.* A playful or mischievous youngster; scamp. [< Lat. *ēricius*, hedgehog.]
Ur•du (o͝or′do͞o, ûr′-) ►*n.* An Indic language that is an official language of Pakistan and is also widely used in India.
-ure ►*suff.* **1.** Act; process; condition: *erasure.* **2a.** Function; office: *judicature.* **b.** Body performing a function: *legislature.* [< Lat. *-ūra.*]
u•re•a (yo͞o-rē′ə) ►*n.* A water-soluble compound that is the chief nitrogenous component of the urine in mammals and other organisms. [< Fr. *urée* < *urine*, URINE.]
u•re•mi•a (yo͞o-rē′mē-ə) ►*n.* A toxic condition resulting from kidney disease in which there is retention in the bloodstream of waste products normally excreted in the urine. —**u•re′mic** *adj.*
u•re•ter (yo͞o-rē′tər, yo͝or′ĭ-tər) ►*n.* The long narrow duct that conveys urine from the kidney to the urinary bladder or cloaca. [< Gk. *ourētēr.*]
u•re•thra (yo͞o-rē′thrə) ►*n.*, *pl.* **-thras** or **-thrae** (-thrē). The canal through which urine is discharged and through which semen is discharged in the male. [< Gk. *ourēthra.*] —**u•re′thral** *adj.*
urge (ûrj) ►*v.* **urged, urg•ing 1.** To force or drive forward or onward; impel. **2.** To entreat earnestly and often repeatedly; exhort. **3.** To advocate earnestly; press for. ►*n.* **1.** The act of urging. **2.** An impulse that prompts action or effort. [Lat. *urgēre.*]
ur•gent (ûr′jənt) ►*adj.* **1.** Compelling immediate action; pressing. **2.** Insistent or importunate. —**ur′gen•cy** *n.* —**ur′gent•ly** *adv.*
-urgy ►*suff.* Technique; process: *metallurgy.* [< Gk. *-ourgia* < *ergon*, work.]
u•ric (yo͝or′ĭk) ►*adj.* Relating to, contained in, or obtained from urine.
uric acid ►*n.* A semisolid compound, $C_5H_4N_4O_3$, that is the chief nitrogenous component of the urine in birds, terrestrial reptiles, and insects.
u•ri•nal (yo͝or′ə-nəl) ►*n.* **1.** A place for urinating. **2.** A receptacle for urine.
u•ri•nal•y•sis (yo͝or′ə-năl′ĭ-sĭs) ►*n.* Chemical analysis of urine.
u•ri•nar•y (yo͝or′ə-nĕr′ē) ►*adj.* Of urine or its production, function, or excretion.
urinary bladder ►*n.* A muscular sac in the anterior part of the pelvic cavity in which urine collects before excretion.
u•ri•nate (yo͝or′ə-nāt′) ►*v.* **-nat•ed, -nat•ing.** To excrete urine. —**u′ri•na′tion** *n.*
u•rine (yo͝or′ĭn) ►*n.* The waste product secreted by the kidneys that in mammals is a yellowish, slightly acid fluid discharged through the urethra. [< Lat. *ūrīna.*]
urino– or **urin–** ►*pref.* Urine: *urinalysis.* [< Lat. *ūrīna*, urine.]
URL (yo͞o′är-ĕl′) ►*n.* An Internet address (e.g., *http://www.hmco.com/trade/*), usu. consisting of the access protocol (*http*), the domain name (*www.hmco.com*), and optionally the path to a file (*trade*).
urn (ûrn) ►*n.* **1.** A vase of varying size and shape, usu. having a footed base or pedestal. **2.** A closed metal vessel having a spigot and used for warming or serving tea or coffee. [< Lat. *urna.*]
uro– or **ur–** ►*pref.* **1.** Urine: *uric.* **2.** Urinary tract: *urology.* **3.** Urea: *polyurethane.* [< Gk. *ouron*, urine.]
u•ro•gen•i•tal (yo͝or′ō-jĕn′ĭ-tl) ►*adj.* Of or involving both the urinary and genital structures or functions.
u•rol•o•gy (yo͞o-rŏl′ə-jē) ►*n.* The branch of medicine that deals with the diseases of the urinary tract and urogenital system. —**ur′o•log′ic** (yo͝or′ə-lŏj′ĭk), **ur′o•log′i•cal** *adj.* —**u•rol′o•gist** *n.*
Ur•sa Major (ûr′sə) ►*n.* A constellation containing the seven stars that form the Big Dipper.
Ursa Minor ►*n.* A constellation having the shape of a ladle with Polaris at the tip of its handle.
ur•sine (ûr′sīn′) ►*adj.* Of or characteristic of a bear. [< Lat. *ursus*, bear.]
ur•ti•car•i•a (ûr′tĭ-kâr′ē-ə) ►*n.* See **hives.** [< Lat. *urtica*, nettle.]
U•ru•guay (yo͝or′ə-gwī′, -gwā′) A country of SE South America on the Atlantic and the Río de la Plata. Cap. Montevideo. Pop. 3,167,000. —**U′ru•guay′an** *adj. & n.*
Uruguay River. A river of SE South America rising in S Brazil and flowing about 1,609 km (1,000 mi) to the Río de la Plata.
us (ŭs) ►*pron.* The objective case of **we. 1.** Used as the direct object of a verb: *She saw us.* **2.** Used as the indirect object of a verb: *They offered us free tickets.* **3.** Used as the object of a preposition: *This letter is addressed to us.* **4.** *Informal* Used as a predicate nominative: *It's us.* See Usage Note at **we.** [< OE *ūs.*]
US ►*abbr.* United States
USA ►*abbr.* **1.** United States Army **2.** United States of America
us•a•ble also **use•a•ble** (yo͞o′zə-bəl) ►*adj.* **1.** That can be used: *usable byproducts.* **2.** Fit for use; convenient to use: *a usable reference.* —**us′a•bil′i•ty** *n.* —**us′a•bly** *adv.*
USAF ►*abbr.* United States Air Force
us•age (yo͞o′sĭj, -zĭj) ►*n.* **1.** The act, manner, or amount of using. **2.** A usual, habitual, or accepted practice. **3.** The way in which words or phrases are actually used in a speech community.
USCG ►*abbr.* United States Coast Guard
USDA ►*abbr.* United States Department of Agriculture
use (yo͞oz) ►*v.* **used, us•ing 1.** To put into service; employ. **2.** To avail oneself of; practice. **3.** To conduct oneself toward; treat. **4.** To exploit. **5.** To take habitually, as alcohol or tobacco. **6.** Used in the past tense with *to* to indicate a former state, habitual practice, or custom: *Mail service used to be faster.* —***phrasal verb:* use up** To consume completely. ►*n.* (yo͞os) **1a.** The act of using; employment. **b.** The fact of being used. **2.** The manner of using. **3a.** The privilege of using something. **b.** The ability to use something. **4.** The need or occasion to employ: *have no use for these old clothes.* **5.** The quality of being suitable to an end; usefulness. **6.** A purpose for which something is used. **7.** Accustomed or usual practice. **8.** *Law* **a.** Enjoyment of property, as by occupying or exercising it. **b.** The benefit or profit of lands and tenements held in trust by another. [< Lat. *ūtī*, *ūs-.*] —**us′er** *n.*
used (yo͞ozd) ►*adj.* **1.** Not new; secondhand. **2.** (also yo͞ost). Accustomed; habituated: *We*

still aren't used to such cold winters.

use•ful (yo͞os′fəl) ►*adj.* Having a beneficial use; serviceable. —**use′ful•ly** *adv.* —**use′ful•ness** *n.*

use•less (yo͞os′lĭs) ►*adj.* **1.** Of no beneficial use; futile; ineffective. **2.** Incapable of functioning; ineffectual. See Syns at **futile.** —**use′less•ly** *adv.* —**use′less•ness** *n.*

Use•net or **USE•NET** (yo͞oz′nĕt′) ►*n.* A messaging system that uses a computer network, esp. the Internet, to transfer thematically organized messages.

us•er-friend•ly (yo͞o′zər-frĕnd′lē) ►*adj.* Easy to use or learn to use. —**us′er-friend′li•ness** *n.*

us•er•name (yo͞o′zər-nām′) ►*n.* A sequence of characters used as identification esp. for logging on to a multiuser computer system.

ush•er (ŭsh′ər) ►*n.* **1.** One who escorts people to their seats, as in a theater. **2.** An official doorkeeper, as in a courtroom. **3.** An official who precedes persons of rank in a procession. ►*v.* **1.** To serve as an usher to; escort. **2.** To lead or conduct. See Syns at **guide. 3.** To precede and introduce; inaugurate: *events that ushered in a new era.* [< Lat. *ōstiārius*, doorkeeper.]

USIA ►*abbr.* United States Information Agency

USMC ►*abbr.* United States Marine Corps

USN ►*abbr.* United States Navy

USO ►*abbr.* United Service Organizations

USS ►*abbr.* United States ship

USSR ►*abbr.* Union of Soviet Socialist Republics

usu. ►*abbr.* usually

u•su•al (yo͞o′zho͞o-əl) ►*adj.* **1.** Common; ordinary; normal. **2.** Habitual or customary. [< LLat. *ūsuālis.*] —**u′su•al•ly** *adv.* —**u′su•al•ness** *n.*

u•su•fruct (yo͞o′zə-frŭkt′, -sə-) ►*n. Law* The right to use and enjoy the profits and advantages of something belonging to another as long as the property is not damaged or altered in any way. [< Lat. *ūsusfrūctus.*]

u•su•rer (yo͞o′zhər-ər) ►*n.* One who lends money at interest, esp. at an exorbitant or unlawfully high rate. [< Lat. *ūsūra*, usury.]

u•su•ri•ous (yo͞o-zho͝or′ē-əs) ►*adj.* Relating to, practicing, or being usury. —**u•su′ri•ous•ly** *adv.* —**u•su′ri•ous•ness** *n.*

u•surp (yo͞o-sûrp′, -zûrp′) ►*v.* To seize and hold by force and without legal authority. See Syns at **appropriate.** [< Lat. *ūsūrpāre*, take for one's own use.] —**u′sur•pa′tion** (yo͞o′sər-pā′shən, -zər-) *n.* —**u•surp′er** *n.*

u•su•ry (yo͞o′zhə-rē) ►*n., pl.* **-ries 1.** The practice of lending money and charging the borrower interest, esp. at an exorbitant or illegally high rate. **2.** An excessive or illegally high interest rate. [< Lat. *ūsūra.*]

UT or **Ut.** ►*abbr.* Utah

U•tah (yo͞o′tô′, -tä′) A state of the W US. Cap. Salt Lake City. Pop. 1,727,784. —**U′tahn** *adj. & n.*

Ute (yo͞ot) ►*n., pl.* **Ute** or **Utes 1.** A member of a Native American people of Utah, Colorado, and N New Mexico. **2.** The Uto-Aztecan language of the Ute.

u•ten•sil (yo͞o-tĕn′səl) ►*n.* An instrument or container, esp. one used in a kitchen. [< Lat. *ūtēnsilis*, fit for use.]

u•ter•us (yo͞o′tər-əs) ►*n., pl.* **u•ter•i** (yo͞o′tə-rī′) or **-us•es.** A hollow muscular organ located in the pelvic cavity of female mammals in which the fertilized egg develops. [< Lat.] —**u′ter•ine** (-tər-ĭn, -tə-rīn′) *adj.*

u•tile (yo͞ot′l, yo͞o′tīl′) ►*adj.* Useful. [< Lat. *ūtilis.*]

u•til•i•tar•i•an (yo͞o-tĭl′ĭ-târ′ē-ən) ►*adj.* **1.** Of or in the interests of utility. **2.** Stressing utility over beauty. **3.** Believing in or advocating utilitarianism. ►*n.* One who advocates utilitarianism.

u•til•i•tar•i•an•ism (yo͞o-tĭl′ĭ-târ′ē-ə-nĭz′əm) ►*n.* **1.** The belief that the value of a thing or action is determined by its utility. **2.** The ethical theory that all action should be directed toward achieving the greatest happiness for the greatest number of people.

u•til•i•ty (yo͞o-tĭl′ĭ-tē) ►*n., pl.* **-ties 1.** The quality or condition of being useful; usefulness. **2.** A useful article or device. **3.** An organization, such as a power company, that provides a public service under government regulation. **4.** *Comp. Sci.* A program that performs a specific task related to the management of computer functions, resources, or files. [< Lat. *ūtilis*, useful.]

u•til•ize (yo͞ot′l-īz′) ►*v.* **-ized, -iz•ing.** To put to use. [< Lat. *ūtilis*, useful.] —**u′til•iz′a•ble** *adj.* —**u′til•i•za′tion** *n.* —**u′til•iz′er** *n.*

ut•most (ŭt′mōst′) ►*adj.* **1.** Being or at the most distant limit or point; farthest. **2.** Of the highest or greatest degree, amount, or intensity. [< OE *ūtmest.*] —**ut′most′** *n.*

U•to-Az•tec•an (yo͞o′tō-ăz′tĕk′ən) ►*n.* **1.** A language family of North and Central America that includes Ute, Hopi, Nahuatl, and Shoshone. **2.** A member of a people speaking a Uto-Aztecan language. —**U′to-Az′tec•an** *adj.*

u•to•pi•a (yo͞o-tō′pē-ə) ►*n.* **1.** often **Utopia** An ideally perfect place, esp. in its social, political, and moral aspects. **2.** An impractical, idealistic scheme. [< *Utopia*, a novel by Sir Thomas More.] —**u•to′pi•an** *adj.*

U•trecht (yo͞o′trĕkt′, ü′trĕKHt) A city of central Netherlands SSE of Amsterdam. Pop. 234,139.

U•tril•lo (yo͞o-trĭl′ō), **Maurice.** 1883–1955. French painter.

ut•ter[1] (ŭt′ər) ►*v.* **1.** To send forth with the voice: *uttered a cry.* **2.** To pronounce or speak. [ME *utteren.*] —**ut′ter•a•ble** *adj.*

ut•ter[2] (ŭt′ər) ►*adj.* Complete; absolute; entire: *utter nonsense; utter darkness.* [< OE *ūtera*, outer.]

ut•ter•ance (ŭt′ər-əns) ►*n.* **1a.** The act of uttering; vocal expression. **b.** The power of speaking; speech. **2.** Something uttered or expressed; a statement.

ut•ter•ly (ŭt′ər-lē) ►*adv.* Completely; absolutely; entirely.

ut•ter•most (ŭt′ər-mōst′) ►*adj.* **1.** Utmost. **2.** Outermost. —**ut′ter•most′** *n.*

U-turn (yo͞o′tûrn′) ►*n.* A turn, as by a vehicle, reversing the direction of travel.

UV ►*abbr.* ultraviolet

u•vu•la (yo͞o′vyə-lə) ►*n.* A small, conical, fleshy mass of tissue suspended from the center of the soft palate. [< LLat. *ūvula*, little grape.]

UW ►*abbr.* underwriter

ux•o•ri•ous (ŭk-sôr′ē-əs, -sōr′-, ŭg-zôr′-, -zōr′-) ►*adj.* Excessively submissive or devoted to one's wife. [< Lat. *uxor*, wife.] —**ux•**

o′ri•ous•ly —**ux•o′ri•ous•ness** *n.*

Uz•bek (o͝oz′bĕk′, ŭz′-) ►*n., pl.* **-bek** or **-beks** **1.** A member of a Turkic people inhabiting Uzbekistan and neighboring areas. **2.** The Turkic language of the Uzbeks. [< Uzbek *ŭzbek.*]

Uz•bek•i•stan (o͝oz-bĕk′ĭ-stăn′, -stän′, ŭz-) A republic of W-central Asia. Cap. Tashkent. Pop. 22,349,000.

V

v or **V** (vē) ►*n., pl.* **v's** or **V's** also **vs** or **Vs.** The 22nd letter of the English alphabet.

V[1] ► **1.** The symbol for the element **vanadium.** **2.** *Elect.* The symbol for **potential** 2. **3.** also **v** The symbol for the Roman numeral 5.

V[2] ►*abbr.* **1.** velocity **2.** victory **3.** volt **4.** volume **5.** vowel

v. ►*abbr.* **1.** verb **2.** verse **3.** version **4.** versus **5.** vide **6.** volume (book)

VA ►*abbr.* **1.** Veterans' Administration **2.** or **Va.** Virginia

va•can•cy (vā′kən-sē) ►*n., pl.* **-cies** **1.** The condition of being vacant; emptiness. **2.** An empty space; void. **3.** A position, office, or lodging that is unfilled or unoccupied.

va•cant (vā′kənt) ►*adj.* **1a.** Containing nothing; empty. **b.** Unoccupied. **2a.** Lacking intelligence. **b.** Lacking expression; blank. **3.** Free from activity; idle. [< Lat. *vacāre*, be empty.] —**va′cant•ly** *adv.*

va•cate (vā′kāt′, vā-kāt′) ►*v.* **-cat•ed, -cat•ing** **1.** To make vacant. **2.** *Law* To make void or annul. [Lat. *vacāre*, be empty.]

va•ca•tion (vā-kā′shən, və-) ►*n.* A period of time devoted to rest or relaxation, as from work or study. ►*v.* To take or spend a vacation. —**va•ca′tion•er** *n.*

vac•ci•nate (văk′sə-nāt′) ►*v.* **-nat•ed, -nat•ing.** To inoculate with a vaccine in order to produce immunity to an infectious disease. —**vac′ci•na′tion** *n.*

vac•cine (văk-sēn′, văk′sēn′) ►*n.* A preparation of a weakened or killed pathogen, such as a bacterium or virus, used to vaccinate. [< Lat. *vaccīnus*, of cows.]

vac•il•late (văs′ə-lāt′) ►*v.* **-lat•ed, -lat•ing** **1.** To sway to and fro. **2.** To swing indecisively from one course of action or opinion to another; waver. [Lat. *vacillāre.*] —**vac′il•la′tion** *n.*

va•cu•i•ty (vă-kyo͞o′ĭ-tē, və-) ►*n., pl.* **-ties** **1.** Total absence of matter; emptiness. **2.** An empty space; vacuum. **3.** Emptiness of mind. **4.** Something, esp. a remark, that is vacuous.

vac•u•ole (văk′yo͞o-ōl′) ►*n.* A small, usu. fluid-filled cavity in the cytoplasm of a cell. [Fr. < Lat. *vacuus*, empty.]

vac•u•ous (văk′yo͞o-əs) ►*adj.* **1.** Empty. **2.** Inane; stupid. **3.** Blank; vacant. [< Lat. *vacuus.*] —**vac′u•ous•ness** *n.*

vac•u•um (văk′yo͞o-əm, -yo͞om, -yəm) ►*n., pl.* **-u•ums** or **-u•a** (-yo͞o-ə) **1a.** Absence of matter. **b.** A space relatively empty of matter. **2.** A state or feeling of emptiness; void. ►*v.* To clean with a vacuum cleaner. [Lat. < *vacuus*, empty.]

vacuum bottle ►*n.* A bottle or flask having a vacuum between its inner and outer walls, designed to maintain the desired temperature of the contents.

vacuum cleaner ►*n.* An electrical appliance that cleans surfaces by suction.

vac•u•um-packed (văk′yo͞o-əm-păkt′, -yo͞om-, -yəm-) ►*adj.* Packed in an airtight container.

vacuum tube ►*n.* An electron tube that has an internal vacuum sufficiently high to permit electrons to move with low interaction with any remaining gas molecules.

va•de me•cum (vā′dē mā′kəm) ►*n., pl.* **-cums.** A useful thing that one constantly carries about. [Lat. *vāde mēcum*, go with me.]

Va•duz (vä-do͞ots′, fä-) The capital of Liechtenstein, in the W on the Rhine R. Pop. 4,927.

vag•a•bond (văg′ə-bŏnd′) ►*n.* **1.** A person without a permanent home who moves from place to place; wanderer. **2.** A tramp; vagrant. [< LLat. *vagābundus*, wandering.] —**vag′a•bond′** *adj.* —**vag′a•bond′age** *n.*

va•ga•ry (vā′gə-rē, və-gâr′ē) ►*n., pl.* **-ries** **1.** An erratic or capricious happening. **2.** A whim. [< Lat. *vagārī*, wander.]

va•gi•na (və-jī′nə) ►*n., pl.* **-nas** or **-nae** (-nē). The passage leading from the vulva to the uterus in female mammals. [Lat. *vāgīna*, sheath.] —**vag′i•nal** (văj′ə-nəl) *adj.*

va•grant (vā′grənt) ►*n.* **1.** One who wanders from place to place without a permanent home or livelihood. **2.** One who lives on the streets and constitutes a public nuisance. ►*adj.* **1.** Wandering from place to place; roving. **2.** Moving in a random fashion. [Prob. < OFr. *wacrer*, wander, of Gmc. orig.] —**va′gran•cy** *n.*

vague (vāg) ►*adj.* **vagu•er, vagu•est** **1.** Not clearly expressed or outlined. **2.** Lacking definite shape, form, or character; indistinct. **3.** Indistinctly perceived, understood, or recalled. [< Lat. *vagus.*] —**vague′ly** *adv.* —**vague′ness** *n.*

vain (vān) ►*adj.* **-er, -est** **1.** Not successful; futile. See Syns at **futile.** **2.** Lacking substance or worth; hollow. **3.** Excessively proud of one's appearance or accomplishments; conceited. —***idiom:*** **in vain** **1.** To no avail; without success. **2.** Irreverently or disrespectfully. [< Lat. *vānus*, empty.] —**vain′ly** *adv.*

Syns: *vain, empty, hollow, idle, nugatory, otiose* **adj.**

vain•glo•ry (vān′glôr′ē, -glōr′ē) ►*n., pl.* **-ries** **1.** Excessive pride and vanity. **2.** Vain and ostentatious display. —**vain•glo′ri•ous** *adj.*

Val. ►*abbr.* valley

val•ance (văl′əns, vā′ləns) ►*n.* **1.** An ornamental drapery hung across a top edge, as of a bed. **2.** A decorative frame mounted esp. across the top of a window. [ME.]

vale (vāl) ►*n.* A valley; dale. [< Lat. *vallēs.*]

val•e•dic•tion (văl′ĭ-dĭk′shən) ►*n.* An act or expression of leave-taking. [< Lat. *valedīcere*, say farewell.]

val•e•dic•to•ri•an (văl′ĭ-dĭk-tôr′ē-ən, -tōr′-) ►*n.* The student, usu. with the highest academic rank in a class, who delivers the valedictory at graduation.

val•e•dic•to•ry (văl′ĭ-dĭk′tə-rē) ►*n., pl.* **-ries.** A farewell address, esp. at graduation exercises. —**val′e•dic′to•ry** *adj.*

va•lence (vā′ləns) ►*n. Chem.* **1.** The capacity of an atom or group of atoms to combine in specific proportions with other atoms. **2.** An integer used to represent this capacity. [< Lat. *valēre*, be strong.]

Va•len•ci•a (və-lĕn′shē-ə, -sē-ə) **1.** A region and former kingdom of E Spain on the Mediterranean coast S of Catalonia. **2.** A city of E Spain on the **Gulf of Valencia,** a wide inlet of the Mediterranean Sea. Pop. 749,361. **3.** A city of N Venezuela WSW of Caracas on the W shore of **Lake Valencia.** Pop. 523,000.

-valent ►*suff.* Having a specified valence or valences: *polyvalent.* [< VALENCE.]

val•en•tine (văl′ən-tīn′) ►*n.* **1.** A usu. sentimental card sent to a sweetheart or friend on Saint Valentine's Day. **2.** One's chosen sweetheart on Saint Valentine's Day.

Valentine, Saint. fl. 3rd cent. A.D. Roman Christian martyr.

Val•en•tine's Day or **Val•en•tines Day** (văl′ən-tīnz′) ►*n.* See **Saint Valentine's Day.**

va•le•ri•an (və-lîr′ē-ən) ►*n.* A plant widely cultivated for its small fragrant flowers and for use in medicine as a sedative. [< Med.Lat. *valeriāna*.]

Va•le•ri•an (və-lîr′ē-ən). d. c. A.D. 260. Emperor of Rome (253–260).

val•et (vă-lā′, văl′ā, văl′ĭt) ►*n.* **1.** A man's male servant, who takes care of his clothes and performs other personal services. **2.** An employee, as in a hotel, who performs personal services for guests. [< VLat. **vassellitus*, servant.]

val•e•tu•di•nar•i•an (văl′ĭ-to͞od′n-âr′ē-ən, -tyo͞od′-) ►*n.* A sickly or weak person who is constantly concerned with his or her health. [< Lat. *valētūdō*, health.] —**val′e•tu′di•nar′i•an•ism** *n.*

Val•hal•la (văl-hăl′ə, väl-hä′lə) ►*n. Myth.* In Norse myth, the hall in which Odin received the souls of slain heroes.

val•iant (văl′yənt) ►*adj.* Possessing, showing, or acting with valor; brave. [< Lat. *valēre*, be strong.] —**val′iance** *n.* —**val′iant•ly** *adv.*

val•id (văl′ĭd) ►*adj.* **1.** Founded on evidence or fact; sound: *a valid objection.* **2.** Having legal force; effective: *a valid passport.* [< Lat. *validus*, strong.] —**va•lid′i•ty, val′id•ness** *n.* —**val′id•ly** *adv.*

val•i•date (văl′ĭ-dāt′) ►*v.* **-dat•ed, -dat•ing** **1.** To make legally valid. **2.** To substantiate; verify. —**val′i•da′tion** *n.*

va•lise (və-lēs′) ►*n.* A small piece of hand luggage. [Fr. < Ital. *valigia*.]

Val•i•um (văl′ē-əm) ► A trademark used for the drug diazepam.

Val•kyr•ie (văl-kîr′ē, -kī′rē, văl′kə-rē) ►*n. Myth.* In Norse myth, any of Odin's handmaidens who conducted the souls of the slain to Valhalla.

Val•la•do•lid (văl′ə-də-lĭd′) A city of NW-central Spain NNW of Madrid. Pop. 331,885.

Val•le•jo (və-lā′ō, -hō) A city of W CA on San Pablo Bay N of Oakland. Pop. 109,199.

Val•let•ta (və-lĕt′ə) The capital of Malta, on the NE coast. Pop. 9,149.

val•ley (văl′ē) ►*n., pl.* **-leys** **1.** A long narrow lowland between mountains or hills. **2.** An area drained by a river system. **3.** The area where two slopes of a roof form a drainage channel. [< Lat. *vallēs*.]

Valley Forge. A village of SE PA; site of George Washington's winter headquarters (1777–78).

val•or (văl′ər) ►*n.* Courage and boldness, as in battle; bravery. [< LLat. *valor*.] —**val′or•ous** *adj.*

Val•pa•rai•so (văl′pə-rī′zō) A city of central Chile on the Pacific WNW of Santiago. Pop. 276,756.

val•u•a•ble (văl′yo͞o-ə-bəl, văl′yə-) ►*adj.* **1.** Having high monetary or material value. **2.** Of great importance, use, or service. ►*n.* often **valuables.** A valuable personal possession, such as a piece of jewelry.

val•u•ate (văl′yo͞o-āt′) ►*v.* **-at•ed, -at•ing.** To set a value for; appraise. —**val′u•a′tor** *n.*

val•u•a•tion (văl′yo͞o-ā′shən) ►*n.* **1.** The act of assessing value or price; appraisal. **2.** Assessed value or price.

val•ue (văl′yo͞o) ►*n.* **1.** A fair equivalent or return for something, as goods or services. **2.** Monetary or material worth. **3.** Worth as measured in usefulness or importance; merit. **4.** A principle, standard, or quality considered worthwhile or desirable. **5.** Precise meaning, as of a word. **6.** *Math.* An assigned or calculated numerical quantity. **7.** *Mus.* The relative duration of a tone or rest. **8.** The relative darkness or lightness of a color. **9.** *Ling.* The sound quality of a letter or diphthong. ►*v.* **-ued, -u•ing** **1.** To determine or estimate the value of; appraise. **2.** To regard highly; esteem. **3.** To rate according to relative worth or desirability; evaluate. [< OFr. *valoir*, be worth.] —**val′ue•less** *adj.*

val•ue-add•ed tax (văl′yo͞o-ăd′ĭd) ►*n.* A tax on the estimated market value added to a product or material at each stage of manufacture or distribution.

valve (vălv) ►*n.* **1.** *Anat.* A membranous structure, as in a vein, that prevents the return flow of a fluid. **2a.** A device that regulates the flow of gases or liquids by blocking and opening passageways. **b.** The movable control element of such a device. **c.** A device in a brass wind instrument that permits change in pitch by a rapid varying of the air column in a tube. **3.** A paired or separable structure or part, as of a mollusk shell or seed pod. [< Lat. *valva*, leaf of a door.] —**valved** *adj.*

va•moose (vă-mo͞os′, və-) ►*v.* **-moosed, -moos•ing** *Slang.* To leave hurriedly. [< Sp. *vamos*, let's go.]

vamp[1] (vămp) ►*n.* **1.** The part of a boot or shoe covering the instep and often the toe. **2.** *Mus.* An improvised accompaniment. ►*v.* **1.** To provide with a new vamp. **2.** To patch up. **3.** To improvise. [< OFr. *avanpie*, sock : *avaunt*, before + *pie*, foot (< Lat. *pēs*).] —**vamp′er** *n.*

vamp[2] (vămp) ►*n. Informal* A woman who exploits men esp. by seduction. [< VAMPIRE.] —**vamp** *v.*

vam•pire (văm′pīr′) ►*n.* **1.** A reanimated corpse believed to rise from the grave at night to suck the blood of sleeping people. **2.** A person who preys on others. **3.** Any of various tropical American bats that bite mammals and birds to feed on their blood. [< Ger. *Vampir*, of Slav. orig.]

van¹ (văn) ►*n.* **1.** An enclosed truck or wagon, as for transporting goods or livestock. **2.** A roomy motor vehicle with rear doors and often side panels. **3.** *Chiefly Brit.* A railroad baggage or freight car. [< CARAVAN.]
van² (văn) ►*n.* The vanguard.
va•na•di•um (və-nā′dē-əm) ►*n. Symbol* **V** A bright white, ductile metallic element used in some steels and as a catalyst. At. no. 23. See table at **element.** [< ON *Vanadīs*, a goddess.]
Van Allen belt ►*n.* Either of two zones of highly energetic, charged particles trapped in Earth's magnetic field, surrounding the planet and serving as a source of high-intensity particulate radiation. [After J.A. *Van Allen* (born 1914).]
Van Bu•ren (byo͝or′ən), **Martin.** 1782–1862. The 8th US President (1837–41).

Martin Van Buren
detail of an 1838 portrait

Van•cou•ver (văn-ko͞o′vər) A city of SW British Columbia, Canada, opposite Vancouver Island. Pop. 471,844.
Vancouver, Mount. A peak, 4,873.6 m (15,979 ft), in the St. Elias Mts. of SW Yukon Terr., Canada.
Vancouver Island. An island in the Pacific off SW British Columbia, Canada.
Van•dal (văn′dl) ►*n.* **1. vandal** One who commits vandalism. **2.** A member of a Germanic people that overran Gaul, Spain, and N Africa in the 4th and 5th cent. A.D. and sacked Rome in 455. [Lat. *Vandalus*, of Gmc. orig.]
van•dal•ism (văn′dl-ĭz′əm) ►*n.* Willful or malicious destruction or defacement of public or private property. —**van′dal•ize′** *v.*
Van•der•bilt (văn′dər-bĭlt′), **Cornelius.** 1794–1877. Amer. financier.
Van•dyke (văn-dīk′) ►*n.* A short pointed beard.
Vandyke or **Van Dyck** (văn dīk′), Sir **Anthony.** 1599–1641. Flemish painter.
vane (vān) ►*n.* **1.** A weathervane. **2.** A usu. thin rigid surface radially mounted along an axis that is turned by or used to turn a fluid. **3.** A metal guidance or stabilizing fin attached to the tail of a bomb or other missile. [< OE *fana*, flag.]
van Gogh (văn gō′, gôKH′), **Vincent.** 1853–90. Dutch painter.
van•guard (văn′gärd) ►*n.* **1.** The foremost position in an army or fleet. **2.** The foremost or leading position in a trend or movement. [< OFr. *avaunt garde*.]
va•nil•la (və-nĭl′ə) ►*n.* **1.** A tropical American vine of the orchid family, cultivated for its long narrow seedpods. **2.** The seedpod of this plant. **3.** A flavoring extract prepared from the seedpods of this plant. [Obsolete Sp. *vainilla*, dim. of *vaina*, sheath.]
va•nil•lin (və-nĭl′ĭn, văn′ə-lĭn) ►*n.* A crystalline compound found in vanilla beans and used in perfumes, flavorings, and pharmaceuticals.
van•ish (văn′ĭsh) ►*v.* **1.** To pass out of sight, esp. quickly. See Syns at **disappear. 2.** To pass out of existence. [< Lat. *ēvānēscere*.] —**van′ish•er** *n.*
van•i•ty (văn′ĭ-tē) ►*n., pl.* **-ties 1.** Excessive pride in one's appearance or accomplishments. See Syns at **conceit. 2.** Uselessness; worthlessness. **3a.** Something vain, futile, or worthless. **b.** Something about which one is vain. **4.** A vanity case. **5.** See **dressing table.** [< Lat. *vānus*, empty.]
vanity case ►*n.* **1.** A small handbag or case used for carrying cosmetics or toiletries. **2.** A woman's compact.
vanity plate ►*n.* A license plate for a motor vehicle bearing a combination of letters or numbers selected by the purchaser.
vanity press ►*n.* A publisher that publishes a book at the expense of the author.
van•quish (văng′kwĭsh, văn′-) ►*v.* **1.** To defeat, as in a battle or contest. **2.** To overcome or subdue. [< Lat. *vincere*.] —**van′quish•er** *n.*
van•tage (văn′tĭj) ►*n.* **1.** An advantage in a competition or conflict. **2.** Something, as a strategic position, that provides superiority. **3.** A position affording a comprehensive view or perspective. [< OFr. *avantage*, ADVANTAGE.]
Va•nu•a•tu (vä′no͞o-ä′to͞o). Formerly **New Hebrides.** An island country of the S Pacific E of N Australia. Cap. Vila. Pop. 165,000. —**Va′nu•a′tu•an** *adj. & n.*
Van•zet•ti (văn-zĕt′ē), **Bartolomeo.** 1888–1927. Italian-born Amer. anarchist; executed.
vap•id (văp′ĭd, vā′pĭd) ►*adj.* Lacking liveliness, zest, or interest; flat or dull. [Lat. *vapidus*.] —**va•pid′i•ty, vap′id•ness** *n.*
va•por (vā′pər) ►*n.* **1.** Barely visible or cloudy diffused matter, such as mist, suspended in the air. **2.** The gaseous state of a substance that is liquid or solid under ordinary conditions. **3.** *Archaic* Something insubstantial or fleeting. **4. vapors** *Archaic* Depression or hysteria. ►*v.* **1.** To give off vapor. **2.** To evaporate. [< Lat. *vapor*.]
va•por•ize (vā′pə-rīz′) ►*v.* **-ized, -iz•ing.** To convert or be converted into vapor. —**va′por•i•za′tion** *n.* —**va′por•iz′er** *n.*
vapor lock ►*n.* A pocket of vaporized gasoline in the fuel line of an internal-combustion engine that obstructs the flow of fuel.
va•por•ous (vā′pər-əs) ►*adj.* **1.** Of or resembling vapor. **2a.** Producing vapors; volatile. **b.** Giving off or full of vapors. **3.** Insubstantial, vague, or ethereal. See Syns at **airy.** —**va′por•ous•ness** *n.*
va•pour (vā′pər) ►*n. & v. Chiefly Brit.* Vapor.
va•que•ro (vä-kâr′ō) ►*n., pl.* **-ros** *Regional.* See **cowboy.** [Sp. < *vaca*, cow.]
var. ►*abbr.* **1.** variant **2.** variation **3.** variety
Va•ra•na•si (və-rä′nə-sē) A city of NE-central India on the Ganges R. Pop. 929,270.
Var•gas Llo•sa (vär′gəs yō′sə), **Mario.** b. 1936. Peruvian writer.
var•i•a•ble (vâr′ē-ə-bəl, văr′-) ►*adj.* **1a.** Likely to vary; changeable. **b.** Inconstant; fickle. **2.** *Biol.* Tending to deviate, as from an

established type; aberrant. ►*n.* **1.** Something that is variable. **2.** *Math.* **a.** A quantity capable of assuming any of a set of values. **b.** A symbol representing such a quantity. —**var′i•a•bil′i•ty, var′i•a•ble•ness** *n.* —**var′i•a•bly** *adv.*

var•i•ance (vâr′ē-əns, văr′-) ►*n.* **1a.** Variation; difference. **b.** The degree of such variation. **2.** A difference of opinion; dispute. **3.** *Law* License to engage in an act contrary to a usual rule.

var•i•ant (vâr′ē-ənt, văr′-) ►*adj.* **1.** Exhibiting variation; differing. **2.** Liable to vary; variable. ►*n.* Something exhibiting variation in form from another, as a different spelling of the same word.

var•i•a•tion (vâr′ē-ā′shən, văr′-) ►*n.* **1.** The act, process, or result of varying. **2.** The extent or degree to which something varies. **3.** Something differing from another of the same type. **4.** *Mus.* An altered version of a given theme, diverging from it by melodic ornamentation and by changes in harmony, rhythm, or key.

var•i•col•ored (vâr′ĭ-kŭl′ərd, văr′-) ►*adj.* Having a variety of colors; variegated.

var•i•cose (văr′ĭ-kōs′) ►*adj.* Abnormally swollen or knotted: *varicose veins.* [< Lat. *varix*, swollen vein.] —**var′i•cos′i•ty** *n.*

var•ied (vâr′ēd, văr′-) ►*adj.* **1.** Varying; diverse. **2.** Modified; altered. **3.** Varicolored.

var•i•e•gate (vâr′ē-ĭ-gāt′, vâr′ĭ-gāt′, văr′-) ►*v.* **-gat•ed, -gat•ing 1.** To change the appearance of, esp. by marking with different colors. **2.** To give variety to. [< LLat. *variegāre* : Lat. *varius*, various + *agere*, do.] —**var′i•e•ga′tion** *n.*

va•ri•e•ty (və-rī′ĭ-tē) ►*n.*, *pl.* **-ties 1.** The quality or condition of being various. **2.** A number of different things; assortment. **3.** A group that is distinguished from other groups by a specific characteristic or set of characteristics. **4.** *Biol.* A subdivision of a species consisting of naturally occurring or selectively bred populations or individuals. [< Lat. *varius*, various.] —**va•ri′e•tal** *adj.*

variety show ►*n.* A theatrical entertainment consisting of successive unrelated acts.

variety store ►*n.* A retail store that carries a variety of usu. inexpensive merchandise.

var•i•o•rum (vâr′ē-ôr′əm, -ōr′-, văr′-) ►*n.* An edition of a written work with notes by various scholars and often with various versions of the text. [< Lat. *(ēditiō cum notīs) variōrum*, (edition with the notes) of various persons.]

var•i•ous (vâr′ē-əs, văr′-) ►*adj.* **1a.** Of diverse kinds. **b.** Unlike; different. **2.** Being more than one. **3.** Many-sided; versatile. **4.** Individual; separate. [< Lat. *varius.*] —**var′i•ous•ly** *adv.*

var•let (vär′lĭt) ►*n.* **1.** An attendant or servant. **2.** A rascal; knave. [< OFr.]

var•mint (vär′mĭnt) ►*n.* *Informal* A person or animal considered undesirable or troublesome. [Alteration of VERMIN.]

Var•na (vär′nə) A city of E Bulgaria on the Black Sea NNE of Burgas. Pop. 308,601.

var•nish (vär′nĭsh) ►*n.* **1a.** A paint containing a solvent and a binder, used to coat a surface with a hard, glossy, transparent film. **b.** The smooth coating resulting from the application of this paint. **2.** A deceptively attractive external appearance; gloss. ►*v.* **1.** To cover with varnish. **2.** To gloss: *tried to varnish the truth.* [< OFr. *vernis.*]

var•si•ty (vär′sĭ-tē) ►*n.*, *pl.* **-ties 1.** The principal team representing a university, college, or school, as in sports. **2.** *Chiefly Brit.* A university. [Alteration of UNIVERSITY.]

var•y (vâr′ē, văr′ē) ►*v.* **-ied** (-ēd), **-y•ing 1.** To cause or undergo change; modify or alter. **2.** To give variety to; make diverse. **3.** To be different; deviate. See Syns at **differ.** [< Lat. *variāre.*]

vas (văs) ►*n.*, *pl.* **va•sa** (vā′zə) *Anat.* A vessel or duct. [Lat. *vās*, vessel.]

Va•sa•ri (və-zär′ē, -sär′ē), **Giorgio.** 1511–74. Italian painter, architect, and art historian.

vas•cu•lar (văs′kyə-lər) ►*adj.* Of, characterized by, or containing vessels that carry or circulate fluids, such as blood, lymph, or sap. [< Lat. *vāsculum*, little vessel.]

vas def•er•ens (văs′ dĕf′ər-ənz, -ə-rĕnz′) ►*n.* The duct through which sperm is carried from a testis to the ejaculatory duct. [NLat., duct that carries away.]

vase (vās, vāz, väz) ►*n.* An open container, as of glass, used for holding flowers or for ornamentation. [< Lat. *vās*, vessel.]

va•sec•to•my (və-sĕk′tə-mē) ►*n.*, *pl.* **-mies.** Surgical removal of all or part of the vas deferens, usu. as a means of sterilization.

vaso– or **vas–** ►*pref.* **1.** Blood vessel: *vasoconstriction.* **2.** Vas deferens: *vasectomy.* [< Lat. *vās*, vessel.]

va•so•con•stric•tion (vā′zō-kən-strĭk′shən) ►*n.* Constriction of a blood vessel. —**va′so•con•tric′tor** *n.*

va•so•dil•a•tion (vā′zō-dī-lā′shən, -dĭ-) also **va•so•dil•a•ta•tion** (-dĭl′ə-tā′shən, -dī′lə-) ►*n.* Dilation of a blood vessel. —**va′so•di•la′tor** *n.*

va•so•mo•tor (vā′zō-mō′tər) ►*adj.* Causing or regulating constriction or dilation of blood vessels.

vas•sal (văs′əl) ►*n.* **1.** A person who held land from a feudal lord and received protection in return for homage and allegiance. **2.** A subordinate or dependent. [< VLat. **vassallus*, of Celt. orig.]

vas•sal•age (văs′ə-lĭj) ►*n.* **1.** The condition of being a vassal. **2.** The service, homage, and fealty required of a vassal. **3.** Subordination or subjection; servitude.

vast (văst) ►*adj.* **-er, -est.** Very great in size, amount, intensity, degree, or extent. [Lat. *vāstus.*] —**vast′ly** *adv.* —**vast′ness** *n.*

vat (văt) ►*n.* A large vessel, such as a tub, used to hold or store liquids. [< OE *fæt.*]

VAT ►*abbr.* value-added tax

vat•ic (văt′ĭk) ►*adj.* Of or characteristic of a prophet; oracular. [< Lat. *vātēs*, seer.]

Vat•i•can (văt′ĭ-kən) ►*n.* **1.** The official residence of the pope in Vatican City. **2.** The papal government; papacy.

Vatican City. An independent papal state on the Tiber River within Rome, Italy. Pop. 766.

va•tu (vä′tōō) ►*n.* See table at **currency.** [Indigenous word in Vanuatu.]

vaude•ville (vôd′vĭl′, vōd′-, vô′də-) ►*n.* Stage entertainment offering a variety of short acts such as comedy and song-and-dance routines. [< OFr. *vaudevire*, popular song.] —**vaude•vil′lian** *n.*

vault[1] (vôlt) ►*n.* **1.** An arched structure, usu. of masonry, serving to cover a space. **2.** Something resembling a vault. **3.** A room, such as a storeroom, with arched walls and ceiling, esp. when underground. **4.** A room or compartment for the safekeeping of valuables. **5.** A burial chamber. ▸*v.* To construct, supply, or cover with a vault. [< VLat. **volvitus*, arched.]

vault² (vôlt) ▸*v.* To jump or leap over, esp. with the aid of a support such as the hands or a pole. [< VLat. **volvitāre* < Lat. *volvere*, turn.] —**vault** *n.* —**vault′er** *n.*

vault•ing horse (vôl′tĭng) ▸*n.* A piece of gymnastic equipment with an upholstered body used esp. for vaulting.

vaunt (vônt, vŏnt) ▸*v.* To boast; brag. [< LLat. *vānitāre*.] —**vaunt** *n.*

vb. ▸*abbr.* verb

V-chip (vē′chĭp′) ▸*n.* A computer chip installed in a television to control the display of esp. sexual or violent programs. [V(IEWER) and V(IOLENCE) + CHIP.]

VCR (vē′sē-är′) ▸*n.* An electronic device for recording and playing back video images and sound on a videocassette. [V(IDEO)C(ASSETTE) R(ECORDER).]

VD ▸*abbr.* venereal disease

VDT ▸*abbr.* video display terminal

veal (vēl) ▸*n.* The meat of a calf. [< Lat. *vitellus*.]

Veb•len (vĕb′lən), **Thorstein Bunde.** 1857–1929. Amer. economist.

vec•tor (vĕk′tər) ▸*n.* **1.** *Math.* A quantity completely specified by a magnitude and a direction. **2.** *Pathol.* An organism that carries disease-causing microorganisms from one host to another. [< Lat. *vehere*, *vect-*, carry.]

Ve•da (vā′də, vē′-) ▸*n.* *Hinduism* Any of the oldest Hindu sacred texts, composed in Sanskrit. [Skt. *vedaḥ*, knowledge.] —**Ve′dic** *adj.*

Ve•dan•ta (vĭ-dän′tə, -dăn′-) ▸*n.* *Hinduism* The system of philosophy that further develops the implications in the Upanishads that all reality is a single principle. [Skt. *vedāntaḥ* : *vedaḥ*, VEDA + *antaḥ*, completion.] —**Ve•dan′tic** *adj.*

veep (vēp) ▸*n.* *Slang* A vice president. [Pronunciation of *V.P.*, abbr. of *vice president*.]

veer (vîr) ▸*v.* To turn aside from a course, direction, or purpose. See Syns at **swerve.** [< OFr. *virer*.] —**veer** *n.*

veg (vĕj) ▸*v.* **vegged, veg•ging** *Informal* To engage in relaxing or passive activities. Often used with *out.* [< VEGETATE.]

Vega (vā′gə), **Lope de.** 1562–1635. Spanish playwright.

ve•gan (vē′gən, vĕj′ən) ▸*n.* A vegetarian who eats plant products only. [< VEGETARIAN.]

veg•e•ta•ble (vĕj′tə-bəl, vĕj′ĭ-tə-) ▸*n.* **1a.** A usu. herbaceous plant cultivated for an edible part, such as roots, leaves, or flowers. **b.** The edible part of such a plant. **c.** An organism classified as a plant. **2a.** A dull or passive person. **b.** One who is severely incapacitated, as by coma. [< LLat. *vegetābilis*, enlivening.] —**veg′e•ta•ble** *adj.*

veg•e•tal (vĕj′ĭ-tl) ▸*adj.* **1.** Of or characteristic of plants. **2.** Relating to growth rather than to sexual reproduction; vegetative. [< Lat. *vegetāre*, enliven.]

veg•e•tar•i•an (vĕj′ĭ-târ′ē-ən) ▸*n.* One whose diet consists primarily or wholly of vegetables, grains, and plant products and who eats no meat. —**veg′e•tar′i•an** *adj.* —**veg′e•tar′i•an•ism** *n.*

veg•e•tate (vĕj′ĭ-tāt′) ▸*v.* **-tat•ed, -tat•ing 1.** To grow or sprout as a plant. **2.** To be in a state of physical or mental inactivity or insensibility. [Lat. *vegetāre*, enliven.]

veg•e•ta•tion (vĕj′ĭ-tā′shən) ▸*n.* **1.** The act or process of vegetating. **2.** The plants of an area or region; plant life.

veg•e•ta•tive (vĕj′ĭ-tā′tĭv) ▸*adj.* **1.** Of or characteristic of plants or their growth. **2.** *Biol.* **a.** Of or capable of growth. **b.** Of or functioning in processes such as growth or nutrition rather than sexual reproduction. **c.** Of or relating to asexual reproduction.

ve•he•ment (vē′ə-mənt) ▸*adj.* **1.** Characterized by forcefulness of expression or intensity of emotion; fervid. See Syns at **intense. 2.** Marked by vigor or energy; strong. [< Lat. *vehemēns*.] —**ve′he•mence** *n.* —**ve′he•ment•ly** *adv.*

ve•hi•cle (vē′ĭ-kəl) ▸*n.* **1.** A device or structure for transporting persons or things; conveyance. **2.** A medium through which something is transmitted, expressed, or accomplished. **3.** A substance used as the medium in which active ingredients are applied or administered. [Lat. *vehiculum* < *vehere*, carry.] —**ve•hic′u•lar** (vē-hĭk′yə-lər) *adj.*

veil (vāl) ▸*n.* **1.** A length of often sheer cloth worn by women over the head, shoulders, and often the face. **2.** The life or vows of a nun: *take the veil.* **3.** Something that conceals or obscures: *a veil of secrecy.* ▸*v.* To cover, conceal, or disguise with or as if with a veil. [< Lat. *vēla*.]

vein (vān) ▸*n.* **1.** A vessel through which blood returns to the heart. **2.** One of the branching structures forming the framework of a leaf or an insect's wing. **3.** *Geol.* A long, regularly shaped deposit of an ore; lode. **4.** A long wavy strip of color, as in marble. **5.** A pervading character or quality; strain. See Syns at **streak. 6.** A particular turn of mind: *spoke in a serious vein.* ▸*v.* To mark, form, or decorate with or as if with veins. [< Lat. *vēna*.] —**veined** *adj.*

ve•lar (vē′lər) ▸*adj.* **1.** Of a velum, esp. the soft palate. **2.** *Ling.* Articulated with the back of the tongue touching or near the soft palate.

Ve•láz•quez (və-läs′kĕs), **Diego Rodríguez de Silva y.** 1599–1660. Spanish painter.

Vel•cro (vĕl′krō) ▸ A trademark for a fastening tape used esp. on cloth products.

veldt also **veld** (vĕlt, fĕlt) ▸*n.* Any of the open grazing areas of S Africa. [Afr. *veld*.]

vel•lum (vĕl′əm) ▸*n.* **1.** A fine parchment made from calfskin, lambskin, or kidskin and used in making books. **2.** A paper resembling vellum. [< OFr. *velin*.]

ve•loc•i•ty (və-lŏs′ĭ-tē) ▸*n.*, *pl.* **-ties 1.** Rapidity of motion; speed. **2.** *Phys.* The rate per unit of time at which a body moves in a specified direction. [< Lat. *vēlōx*, fast.]

ve•lour or **ve•lours** (və-lo͝or′) ▸*n.*, *pl.* **-lours** (-lo͝orz′). A closely napped fabric resembling velvet. [< Lat. *villōsus*, hairy.]

ve•lum (vē′ləm) ▸*n.*, *pl.* **-la** (-lə) **1.** A covering or partition of thin membranous tissue. **2.** The soft palate. [Lat., veil.]

vel•vet (vĕl′vĭt) ▸*n.* **1.** A soft fabric having a smooth dense pile and a plain underside. **2.** Something resembling velvet, as in smoothness or softness. **3.** The soft furry covering on the developing antlers of deer. **4.** *Regional* See milk shake. See Regional Note at **milk shake.** [< VLat. **villūtittus.*] —**vel′vet•y** *adj.*

vel•vet•een (vĕl′vĭ-tēn′) ►*n.* A cotton pile fabric resembling velvet. [< VELVET.]

Ven. ►*abbr.* venerable

ve•na ca•va (vē′nə kā′və) ►*n., pl.* **ve•nae ca•vae** (vē′nē kā′vē). Either of two large veins that empty into the right atrium of the heart. [Lat. *vēna*, vein + *cava*, hollow.]

ve•nal (vē′nəl) ►*adj.* Open to, marked by, or susceptible to bribery; corrupt or corruptible. [< Lat. *vēnum*, sale.] —**ve•nal′i•ty** (-năl′ĭ-tē) *n.* —**ve′nal•ly** *adv.*

ve•na•tion (vē-nā′shən, vĕ-) ►*n.* Distribution or arrangement of a system of veins. [< Lat. *vēna*, vein.]

vend (vĕnd) ►*v.* To sell, esp. by peddling. [Lat. *vēndere* : *vēnum*, sale + *dare*, give.]

vend•er or **ven•dor** (vĕn′dər) ►*n.* **1.** One that sells or vends. **2.** A vending machine.

ven•det•ta (vĕn-dĕt′ə) ►*n.* A bitter feud, esp. between two families. [Ital.]

vend•ing machine (vĕn′dĭng) ►*n.* A coin-operated machine that dispenses merchandise.

ve•neer (və-nîr′) ►*n.* **1.** A thin surface layer, as of finely grained wood, glued to a base of inferior material. **2.** A surface show; façade. ►*v.* To overlay with a veneer. [< Ger. *furnieren*, furnish.]

ven•er•a•ble (vĕn′ər-ə-bəl) ►*adj.* **1.** Commanding respect by virtue of age or position. **2.** Worthy of reverence, as by religious association. —**ven′er•a•bil′i•ty** *n.*

ven•er•ate (vĕn′ə-rāt′) ►*v.* To regard with great respect or reverence. [Lat. *venerārī.*] —**ven′er•a′tion** *n.*

ve•ne•re•al (və-nîr′ē-əl) ►*adj.* Of or transmitted by sexual intercourse. [< Lat. *venus*, *vener-*, love.]

venereal disease ►*n.* A contagious disease, such as syphilis or gonorrhea, contracted through sexual intercourse; sexually transmitted disease.

ve•ne•tian blind or **Ve•ne•tian blind** (və-nē′shən) ►*n.* A window blind consisting of thin horizontal adjustable slats that overlap when closed. [< *Venetian*, of Venice.]

Ven•e•zue•la (vĕn′ə-zwā′lə) A country of N South America on the Caribbean Sea. Cap. Caracas. Pop. 21,177,000. —**Ven′e•zue′lan** *adj. & n.*

ven•geance (vĕn′jəns) ►*n.* Infliction of punishment in return for a wrong committed; retribution. [< OFr. *vengier*, AVENGE.]

venge•ful (vĕnj′fəl) ►*adj.* Desiring vengeance; vindictive. —**venge′ful•ly** *adv.* —**venge′ful•ness** *n.*

ve•ni•al (vē′nē-əl, vēn′yəl) ►*adj.* Easily excused or forgiven; pardonable; minor. [< Lat. *venia*, forgiveness.]

Ven•ice (vĕn′ĭs) A city of NE Italy on islets within a lagoon in the **Gulf of Venice,** a wide inlet of the N Adriatic. Pop. 308,717. —**Ve•ne′tian** (və-nē′shən) *n. & adj.*

ve•ni•re (və-nī′rē, -nîr′ē) ►*n.* **1.** A writ summoning prospective jurors. **2.** A panel from which a jury is selected. [< Lat. *venīre*, come.]

ve•ni•re•man (və-nī′rē-mən, -nîr′ē-) ►*n.* A person summoned to jury duty under a venire.

ven•i•son (vĕn′ĭ-sən, -zən) ►*n.* The flesh of a deer used as food. [< Lat. *vēnātiō*, hunting.]

ven•om (vĕn′əm) ►*n.* **1.** A poisonous secretion of an animal, such as a snake or spider, usu. transmitted by a bite or sting. **2.** Malice; spite. [< Lat. *venēnum*, poison.]

ven•om•ous (vĕn′ə-məs) ►*adj.* **1.** Secreting venom: *a venomous snake.* **2.** Full of venom. **3.** Malicious; spiteful.

ve•nous (vē′nəs) ►*adj.* **1.** Of or relating to veins. **2.** Having numerous veins. [< Lat. *vēna*, vein.]

vent[1] (vĕnt) ►*n.* **1.** A means of escape or release; outlet. **2.** An opening permitting escape, as of fumes or a gas. ►*v.* **1.** To give expression to. **2.** To release or discharge through an opening. **3.** To provide with a vent. [< OFr. *vent* and *esvent.*]

vent[2] (vĕnt) ►*n.* A slit in a garment, as in the seam of a pocket. [< OFr. *fente*, slit.]

ven•ti•late (vĕn′tl-āt′) ►*v.* **-lat•ed, -lat•ing 1.** To admit fresh air into to replace stale or noxious air. **2.** To circulate through and freshen. **3.** To provide with a vent, as for airing. **4.** To expose to public discussion or examination. **5.** To aerate or oxygenate (blood). [< Lat. *ventulus*, breeze.] —**ven′ti•la′tion** *n.* —**ven′ti•la′tor** *n.*

ven•tral (vĕn′trəl) ►*adj.* **1.** Of or relating to the abdomen; abdominal. **2.** Of or situated on or close to the anterior aspect of the human body or the lower surface of the body of an animal. [< Lat. *venter*, belly.]

ven•tri•cle (vĕn′trĭ-kəl) ►*n.* A cavity or chamber within a body or an organ, esp.: **a.** Either of the chambers of the heart that contract to pump blood into arteries. **b.** Any of the interconnecting cavities of the brain. [< Lat. *ventriculus.*] —**ven•tric′u•lar** (-trĭk′yə-lər) *adj.*

ven•tril•o•quism (vĕn-trĭl′ə-kwĭz′əm) also **ven•tril•o•quy** (-kwē) ►*n.* The art of projecting one's voice so that it seems to come from another source. [< Lat. *ventriloquus*, speaking from the belly.] —**ven•tril′o•quist** *n.*

Ven•tu•ra (vĕn-to͝or′ə) A city of S CA on the Pacific W of Los Angeles. Pop. 92,575.

ven•ture (vĕn′chər) ►*n.* **1.** An undertaking that is dangerous or of uncertain outcome. **2.** Something, such as money, at hazard in a risky enterprise. ►*v.* **-tured, -tur•ing 1.** To expose to danger or risk. **2.** To brave the dangers of. **3.** To express at the risk of denial, criticism, or censure. **4.** To take a risk; dare. [< ME *aventure*, ADVENTURE.]

ven•ture•some (vĕn′chər-səm) ►*adj.* **1.** Inclined to take risks; daring. See Syns at **adventurous. 2.** Risky; hazardous. —**ven′ture•some•ness** *n.*

ven•tur•ous (vĕn′chər-əs) ►*adj.* Venturesome. —**ven′tur•ous•ness** *n.*

ven•ue (vĕn′yo͞o) ►*n.* **1.** The locality where a crime is committed or a cause of legal action occurs. **2.** The locality from which a jury is called and in which a trial is held. **3.** A place where a gathering is held. [< OFr., a coming < Lat. *venīre*, come.]

Ve•nus (vē′nəs) ►*n.* **1.** *Rom. Myth.* The goddess of love and beauty. **2.** The 2nd planet from the sun, at a mean distance of approx. 108.1 million km (67.2 million mi) and with an average radius of 6,052 km (3,760 mi). —**Ve•nu′sian** (vĭ-no͞o′zhən, -nyo͞o′-) *adj.*

Venus fly•trap (flī′trăp′) ►*n.* An insectivorous plant of the coastal Carolinas, having hinged leaf blades that close and entrap insects.

ver. ▶*abbr.* **1.** verse **2.** version

ve•ra•cious (və-rā′shəs) ▶*adj.* **1.** Honest; truthful. **2.** Accurate; precise. [< Lat. *vērāx.*] —**ve•ra′cious•ness** *n.*

ve•rac•i•ty (və-răs′ĭ-tē) ▶*n., pl.* **-ties 1.** Adherence to the truth; truthfulness. **2.** Conformity to fact or truth; accuracy. **3.** Something that is true. [< Lat. *vērāx*, true.]

Ve•ra•cruz (vĕr′ə-kro͞oz′) A city of E-central Mexico on the Gulf of Mexico E of Puebla. Pop. 284,822.

ve•ran•da or **ve•ran•dah** (və-răn′də) ▶*n.* A usu. roofed porch or balcony extending along the outside of a building. [Hindi *varaṇḍā.*]

verb (vûrb) ▶*n.* The part of speech that expresses existence, action, or occurrence in most languages. [< Lat. *verbum*, word.]

ver•bal (vûr′bəl) ▶*adj.* **1.** Of or associated with words. **2.** Concerned with words only rather than with content or ideas. **3.** Spoken rather than written; oral: *a verbal contract.* **4.** Word for word; literal. **5.** Of or derived from a verb. ▶*n.* A noun or adjective derived from a verb. [< Lat. *verbum*, word.] —**ver′bal•ly** *adv.*

Usage: Because *verbal* can mean both "concerned with words" and "spoken rather than written," care must be given to avoid ambiguity. The phrase *modern technologies for verbal communication* may refer to devices such as radio and the telephone or to devices such as the telegraph and fax machine. In such contexts the word *oral* is available to convey the narrower sense of communication by spoken means.

ver•bal•ize (vûr′bə-līz′) ▶*v.* **-ized, -iz•ing 1.** To express in words. **2.** To convert to use as a verb. **3.** To be verbose. —**ver′bal•i•za′tion** *n.*

ver•ba•tim (vər-bā′tĭm) ▶*adv. & adj.* In the same words; word for word. [< Med.Lat.]

ver•be•na (vər-bē′nə) ▶*n.* Any of various plants cultivated for their showy spikes of variously colored flowers. [Lat. *verbēna*, sacred foliage.]

ver•bi•age (vûr′bē-ĭj, -bĭj) ▶*n.* **1.** An excess of words for the purpose; wordiness. **2.** Wording; diction. [< OFr. *verbier*, chatter.]

ver•bose (vər-bōs′) ▶*adj.* Using more words than is necessary; wordy. See Syns at **wordy.** [< Lat. *verbum*, word.] —**ver•bos′i•ty** (-bŏs′ĭ-tē) *n.*

ver•bo•ten (vər-bōt′n, fĕr-) ▶*adj.* Forbidden; prohibited. [Ger.]

ver•dant (vûr′dnt) ▶*adj.* **1.** Green with vegetation. **2.** Of a green color. [< OFr. *verdoyer*, become green.] —**ver′dan•cy** *n.*

Verde (vûrd), **Cape.** A peninsula of W Senegal projecting into the Atlantic; westernmost point of Africa.

Ver•di (vâr′dē), **Giuseppe.** 1813–1901. Italian composer.

ver•dict (vûr′dĭkt) ▶*n.* **1.** The finding of a jury in a trial. **2.** A judgment; conclusion. [< AN *verdit.*]

ver•di•gris (vûr′dĭ-grēs′, -grĭs′, -grē′) ▶*n.* A green patina formed on copper, brass, and bronze after long exposure to air or seawater. [< OFr. *vert-de-Grice*, green of Greece.]

Ver•dun (vər-dŭn′, vĕr-dœn′) A city of NE France on the Meuse R.; site of a prolonged World War I battle (1916). Pop. 21,516.

ver•dure (vûr′jər) ▶*n.* **1.** The lush greenness of flourishing vegetation. **2.** Green vegetation. [< OFr. < *verd*, green.]

verge[1] (vûrj) ▶*n.* **1.** An edge, rim, or margin. **2.** The point beyond which an action or a condition is likely to begin or occur; brink. **3.** A rod or staff carried as an emblem of authority or office. ▶*v.* **verged, verg•ing.** To border on; approach. [< Lat. *virga*, rod.]

verge[2] (vûrj) ▶*v.* **verged, verg•ing 1.** To slope or incline. **2.** To pass or merge gradually. [Lat. *vergere.*]

verg•er (vûr′jər) ▶*n. Chiefly Brit.* **1.** One who carries a verge, as before a religious dignitary in a procession. **2.** One who takes care of the interior of a church.

Ver•gil (vûr′jəl). See **Virgil.**

ver•i•fy (vĕr′ə-fī′) ▶*v.* **-fied** (-fīd′), **-fy•ing 1.** To prove the truth of; substantiate. **2.** To determine or test the truth or accuracy of; confirm. [< Med. Lat. *vērificāre.*] —**ver′i•fi′a•ble** *adj.* —**ver′i•fi•ca′tion** *n.* —**ver′i•fi′er** *n.*

ver•i•ly (vĕr′ə-lē) ▶*adv.* **1.** In truth; in fact. **2.** Surely; assuredly. [< ME *verrai*, true. See VERY.]

ver•i•si•mil•i•tude (vĕr′ə-sĭ-mĭl′ĭ-to͞od′, -tyo͞od′) ▶*n.* **1.** The quality of appearing to be true or real. **2.** Something that appears to be true or real. [< Lat. *vērīsimilis*, appearing to be true.]

ver•i•ta•ble (vĕr′ĭ-tə-bəl) ▶*adj.* Being truly so called; real or genuine. [< OFr. *verite*, VERITY.] —**ver′i•ta•bly** *adv.*

ver•i•ty (vĕr′ĭ-tē) ▶*n., pl.* **-ties 1.** The quality or condition of being true, factual, or real. **2.** Something, such as a statement or belief, that is true. [< Lat. *vērus*, true.]

Ver•meer (vər-mîr′, -mâr′), **Jan.** 1632–75. Dutch painter.

ver•meil (vûr′məl, -māl′) ▶*n.* **1.** Vermilion. **2.** (vĕr-mā′). Gilded silver, bronze, or copper. [< OFr. *vermeil.*]

ver•mi•cel•li (vûr′mĭ-chĕl′ē, -sĕl′ē) ▶*n.* Pasta in long, very thin strands. [Ital.]

ver•mic•u•lite (vər-mĭk′yə-līt′) ▶*n.* Any of a group of minerals resembling mica and used in heat-expanded form esp. as insulation. [Lat. *vermiculus*, little worm + -ITE[1].]

ver•mi•form (vûr′mə-fôrm′) ▶*adj.* Resembling or shaped like a worm. [< Lat. *vermis*, worm.]

vermiform appendix ▶*n.* A narrow vestigial process projecting from the cecum in the lower right-hand part of the abdomen.

ver•mi•fuge (vûr′mə-fyo͞oj′) ▶*n.* A medicine that expels intestinal worms. [Lat. *vermis*, worm + *fugāre*, drive out.]

ver•mil•ion also **ver•mil•lion** (vər-mĭl′yən) ▶*n.* **1.** A bright red pigment. **2.** A vivid red to reddish orange. [< OFr. *vermeillon* < *vermeil.*] —**ver•mil′ion** *adj.*

ver•min (vûr′mĭn) ▶*n., pl.* **vermin.** Various small animals or insects, such as rats or cockroaches, that are destructive, annoying, or injurious to health. [< Lat. *vermis*, worm.] —**ver′min•ous** *adj.*

Ver•mont (vər-mŏnt′) A state of the NE US bordering on Canada. Cap. Montpelier. Pop. 564,964. —**Ver•mont′er** *n.*

ver•mouth (vər-mo͞oth′) ▶*n.* A sweet or dry wine flavored with aromatic herbs. [< Ger. *Wermut.*]

ver•nac•u•lar (vər-năk′yə-lər) ►*n.* **1.** The standard native language of a country or locality, esp. as distinct from literary language. **2.** A jargon: *the legal vernacular.* [< Lat. *vernāculus*, native.] —**ver•nac′u•lar** *adj.*

ver•nal (vûr′nəl) ►*adj.* Of or occurring in the spring. [Lat. *vērnālis.*] —**ver′nal•ly** *adv.*

Verne (vûrn, vĕrn), **Jules.** 1828–1905. French writer.

Jules Verne

ver•ni•er (vûr′nē-ər) ►*n.* A small scale attached to a main scale, calibrated to indicate fractional parts of the subdivisions of the larger scale. [After Pierre *Vernier* (1580?–1637).]

vernier caliper ►*n.* An L-shaped caliper having a sliding attachment with a vernier.

Ve•ro•na (və-rō′nə) A city of N Italy W of Venice. Pop. 252,689. —**Ve′ro•nese′** (vĕr′ə-nēz′, -nēs′) *adj. & n.*

Ve•ro•ne•se (vĕr′ə-nā′sē, -zē), **Paolo.** 1528–88. Italian painter.

ve•ron•i•ca (və-rŏn′ĭ-kə) ►*n.* Any of various plants that include the speedwells. [NLat.]

Ver•ra•za•no or **Ver•raz•za•no** (vĕr′ə-zä′nō), **Giovanni da.** 1485?–1528? Italian explorer.

Ver•sailles (vər-sī′, vĕr-) A city of N-central France WSW of Paris; site of a palace built by Louis XIV. Pop. 91,494.

ver•sa•tile (vûr′sə-təl, -tīl′) ►*adj.* **1.** Capable of doing many things competently. **2.** Having varied uses or functions. [< Lat. *versāre*, turn.] —**ver′sa•til′i•ty** (-tĭl′ĭ-tē) *n.*

Syns: *versatile, all-around, many-sided, multifaceted, multifarious* **adj.**

verse (vûrs) ►*n.* **1.** Writing arranged according to a metrical pattern; poetry. **2a.** One line of poetry. **b.** A stanza. **3.** A specific type of metrical composition, such as blank verse. **4.** One of the numbered subdivisions of a chapter in the Bible. [< Lat. *vertere*, turn.]

versed (vûrst) ►*adj.* Practiced or skilled; knowledgeable.

ver•si•fy (vûr′sə-fī′) ►*v.* **-fied, -fy•ing 1.** To change from prose into metrical form. **2.** To write verses. —**ver′si•fi•ca′tion** *n.* —**ver′si•fi′er** *n.*

ver•sion (vûr′zhən, -shən) ►*n.* **1.** A description or account from one point of view. **2.** A translation, esp. of the Bible or of a part of it. **3.** A form or variation of an earlier or original type. **4.** An adaptation of a work of art or literature into another medium or style. [< Lat. *vertere, vers-*, turn.]

vers li•bre (vĕr lē′brə) ►*n.* Free verse. [Fr.]

ver•so (vûr′sō) ►*n., pl.* **-sos.** A left-hand page. [NLat. *versō (foliō)*, (with the page) turned.]

ver•sus (vûr′səs, -səz) ►*prep.* **1.** Against: *the plaintiff versus the defendant.* **2.** In contrast with: *death versus dishonor.* [< Lat., turned.]

vert. ►*abbr.* vertical

ver•te•bra (vûr′tə-brə) ►*n., pl.* **-brae** (-brā′, -brē′) or **-bras.** Any of the bones or cartilaginous segments forming the spinal column. [< Lat.] —**ver′te•bral** *adj.*

ver•te•brate (vûr′tə-brĭt, -brāt′) ►*adj.* **1.** Having a backbone or spinal column. **2.** Of the vertebrates. ►*n.* Any of a group of animals, including the fishes, amphibians, reptiles, birds, and mammals, having a segmented spinal column.

ver•tex (vûr′tĕks′) ►*n., pl.* **-ti•ces** (-tĭ-sēz′) or **-tex•es 1.** The highest point; apex or summit. **2a.** The point at which the sides of an angle intersect. **b.** The point on a triangle opposite to and farthest away from its base. **c.** A point on a polyhedron common to three or more sides. [Lat. < *vertere*, turn.]

ver•ti•cal (vûr′tĭ-kəl) ►*adj.* **1.** Being or situated at right angles to the horizon; upright. **2.** Situated at the vertex or highest point; directly overhead. ►*n.* **1.** Something vertical, as a line. **2.** A vertical position. [< Lat. *vertex*, VERTEX.] —**ver′ti•cal•ly** *adv.*

ver•tig•i•nous (vər-tĭj′ə-nəs) ►*adj.* **1.** Turning about an axis. **2.** Affected by vertigo. See Syns at **giddy. 3.** Tending to produce vertigo; dizzying. [< Lat. *vertīgō*, vertigo.]

ver•ti•go (vûr′tĭ-gō′) ►*n., pl.* **-goes** or **-gos.** The sensation of dizziness; giddiness. [< Lat. *vertīgō.*]

ver•vain (vûr′vān′) ►*n.* See **verbena.** [< Lat. *verbēna*, sacred foliage.]

verve (vûrv) ►*n.* **1.** Energy and enthusiasm, as in artistic performance or composition. **2.** Vitality; liveliness. See Syns at **vigor.** [< OFr., fanciful expression.]

ver•y (vĕr′ē) ►*adv.* **1.** In a high degree; extremely: *very happy.* **2.** Truly; absolutely: *the very best advice.* ►*adj.* **-i•er, -i•est 1.** Complete; absolute: *the very end.* **2.** Identical; selfsame: *the very question she asked yesterday.* **3.** Used for emphasis: *the very mountains shook.* **4.** Precise; exact: *the very center of town.* **5.** Mere: *The very thought is frightening.* **6.** Actual: *caught in the very act.* [< OFr. *verai*, true < Lat. *vērus.*]

very high frequency ►*n.* A band of radio frequencies between 30 and 300 megahertz.

very low frequency ►*n.* A band of radio frequencies between 3 and 30 kilohertz.

ves•i•cant (vĕs′ĭ-kənt) ►*n.* A blistering agent, esp. mustard gas. [< Lat. *vēsīca*, blister.] —**ves′i•cant** *adj.*

ves•i•cle (vĕs′ĭ-kəl) ►*n.* **1.** A small bladderlike cell or cavity. **2.** A blister. [< Lat. *vēsīcula.*] —**ve•sic′u•lar** (vĕ-sĭk′yə-lər, və-) *adj.*

Ves•pa•sian (vĕs-pā′zhən, -zhē-ən). A.D. 9–79. Emperor of Rome (69–79).

ves•per (vĕs′pər) ►*n.* **1.** A bell that summons worshipers to vespers. **2.** *Archaic* Evening. [< Lat., evening.]

ves•pers (vĕs′pərz) ►*pl.n. (takes sing. or pl. v.)* A worship service held in the late afternoon or evening. [< Lat. *vespera*, evening.]

ves•per•tine (vĕs′pər-tīn′) ►*adj.* **1.** Of or occurring in the evening. **2.** *Bot.* Opening or blooming in the evening. [< Lat. *vesper*, evening.]

Ves•puc•ci (vĕs-po͞o′chē, -pyo͞o′-), **Amerigo.** 1454–1512. Italian explorer.

ves•sel (vĕs′əl) ►*n.* **1.** A hollow container, as a cup, vase, or pitcher; receptacle. **2.** A ship, large boat, or similar craft. **3.** *Anat.* A duct or other narrow tube that contains or conveys a body fluid. **4.** A person seen as the agent or embodiment, as of a quality. [< Lat. *vāsculum.*]

vest (vĕst) ►*n.* **1.** A sleeveless garment, often having buttons down the front, worn over a shirt or as part of a three-piece suit. **2.** *Chiefly Brit.* An undershirt. ►*v.* **1.** To place in the control of a person or group: *vested his estate in his daughter.* **2.** To invest or endow with power or rights: *vested the council with broad powers.* **3.** To clothe or robe, as in ecclesiastical vestments. [< Lat. *vestis*, garment.]

Ves•ta (vĕs′tə) ►*n. Rom. Myth.* The goddess of the hearth.

ves•tal (vĕs′təl) ►*adj.* Chaste; pure. ►*n.* A woman who is a virgin. [< VESTA.]

vest•ed interest (vĕs′tĭd) ►*n.* **1.** A special interest in protecting or promoting that which is to one's own personal advantage. **2.** A group that has a vested interest.

ves•ti•bule (vĕs′tə-byo͞ol′) ►*n.* **1.** A small entrance hall or lobby. **2.** An enclosed area at the end of a passenger car on a train. **3.** *Anat.* A cavity, chamber, or channel that leads to another cavity. [Lat. *vestibulum.*]

ves•tige (vĕs′tĭj) ►*n.* **1.** A visible trace, evidence, or sign of something that no longer exists or appears. **2.** A remnant. [< Lat. *vestīgium.*]

ves•tig•i•al (vĕ-stĭj′ē-əl, -stĭj′əl) ►*adj.* **1.** Of or constituting a vestige. **2.** *Biol.* Occurring or persisting as a rudimentary or degenerate structure. —**ves•tig′i•al•ly** *adv.*

vest•ment (vĕst′mənt) ►*n.* **1.** A garment, esp. a robe or gown worn as an indication of office. **2.** Any of the ritual robes worn by members of the clergy or assistants at ecclesiastical services or rites. [< Lat. *vestis*, garment.]

vest-pock•et (vĕst′pŏk′ĭt) ►*adj.* Small.

ves•try (vĕs′trē) ►*n., pl.* **-tries 1.** A sacristy. **2.** A meeting room in a church. **3.** A committee elected to administer the temporal affairs of a parish. [< Lat. *vestis*, garment.]

ves•try•man (vĕs′trē-mən) ►*n.* A member of a vestry.

ves•ture (vĕs′chər) ►*n.* **1.** Clothing; apparel. **2.** Something that covers or cloaks. [< *vestīre*, clothe.]

Ve•su•vi•us (vĭ-so͞o′vē-əs), **Mount.** An active volcano, 1,281 m (4,200 ft), of S Italy on the E shore of the Bay of Naples. —**Ve•su′vi•an** *adj.*

vet[1] (vĕt) ►*n. Informal* A veterinarian.

vet[2] (vĕt) ►*n. Informal* A veteran.

vetch (vĕch) ►*n.* A plant having featherlike leaves that end in tendrils and small, variously colored flowers. [< Lat. *vicia.*]

vet•er•an (vĕt′ər-ən, vĕt′rən) ►*n.* **1.** A person of long experience in an activity or capacity. **2.** A person who has served in the armed forces. [Lat. *veterānus* < *vetus*, old.]

Vet•er•ans Day (vĕt′ər-ənz, vĕt′rənz) ►*n.* Nov. 11, observed in the US in honor of veterans of the armed services and in commemoration of the armistice that ended World War I in 1918.

vet•er•i•nar•i•an (vĕt′ər-ə-nâr′ē-ən, vĕt′rə-) ►*n.* A person who practices veterinary medicine.

vet•er•i•nar•y (vĕt′ər-ə-nĕr′ē, vĕt′rə-) ►*adj.* Of the medical or surgical treatment of animals. ►*n., pl.* **-ies.** A veterinarian. [< Lat. *veterīnae*, beasts of burden.]

ve•to (vē′tō) ►*n., pl.* **-toes 1a.** The vested power or constitutional right of a branch of government, esp. of a chief executive, to reject a bill passed by a legislative body and thus prevent or delay its enactment into law. **b.** Exercise of this right. **2.** An authoritative prohibition or rejection of a proposed or intended act. ►*v.* **-toed, -to•ing 1.** To prevent (a legislative bill) from becoming law by exercising the power of veto. **2.** To forbid or prohibit authoritatively. [< Lat. *vetō*, I forbid.]

vex (vĕks) ►*v.* **1.** To annoy; bother. **2.** To cause perplexity in; puzzle. **3.** To debate at length. [< Lat. *vexāre.*]

vex•a•tion (vĕk-sā′shən) ►*n.* **1.** The condition of being vexed; annoyance. **2.** One that vexes. —**vex•a′tious** *adj.*

VF ►*abbr.* **1.** video frequency **2.** visual field

VFW ►*abbr.* Veterans of Foreign Wars

VGA ►*abbr.* video graphics array

VHF ►*abbr.* very high frequency

VHS (vē′āch-ĕs′) ► A trademark for a videotape format.

VI or **V.I.** ►*abbr.* Virgin Islands

vi•a (vī′ə, vē′ə) ►*prep.* By way of. [< Lat. *via*, road.]

vi•a•ble (vī′ə-bəl) ►*adj.* **1.** Capable of living or developing under favorable conditions. **2.** Capable of living outside the uterus. **3.** Feasible; practicable. [< OFr. *vie*, life < Lat. *vīta.*] —**vi′a•bil′i•ty** *n.*

vi•a•duct (vī′ə-dŭkt′) ►*n.* A series of spans or arches used to carry a road or railroad over something, such as a valley or road. [Lat. *via*, road + (AQUE)DUCT.]

viaduct
Tunkhannock Creek Viaduct, Nicholson, Pennsylvania

vi•al (vī′əl) ►*n.* A small container for liquids. [< ME *fiol*, PHIAL.]

vi•and (vī′ənd) ►*n.* **1.** An item of food. **2. viands** Provisions; victuals. [Ult. < *vīvere*, live.]

vi•at•i•cum (vī-ăt′ĭ-kəm, vē-) ►*n., pl.* **-ca** (-kə) or **-cums.** The Eucharist given to a dying person or one in danger of death. [< Lat. *viāticum*, traveling provisions.]

vibes (vībz) ►*pl.n.* **1.** A vibraphone. **2.** *Slang* Vibrations.

vi•brant (vī′brənt) ►*adj.* **1.** Full of vigor or energy. **2.** Produced as a result of vibration; vibrating. —**vi′bran•cy** *n.* —**vi′brant•ly** *adv.*

vi•bra•phone (vī′brə-fōn′) ►*n. Mus.* An instrument similar to a marimba but having metal bars and rotating disks in the resonators to produce a vibrato. [Lat. *vibrāre*, shake + –PHONE.] —**vi′bra•phon′ist** *n.*

vi•brate (vī′brāt′) ► *v.* **-brat•ed, -brat•ing 1.** To move or cause to move back and forth rapidly. **2.** To feel a quiver of emotion. **3.** To shake or tremble. **4.** To produce a sound; resonate. [Lat. *vibrāre.*] —**vi′bra′tor** *n.* —**vi′bra•to′ry** (-brə-tôr′ē, -tōr′ē) *adj.*

vi•bra•tion (vī-brā′shən) ► *n.* **1a.** The act of vibrating. **b.** The condition of being vibrated. **2.** *Phys.* A rapid linear motion of a particle or of an elastic solid about an equilibrium position. **3.** A single complete vibrating motion. **4. vibrations** *Slang* A distinctive emotional aura or atmosphere that is instinctively sensed or experienced.

vi•bra•to (və-brä′tō, vī-) ► *n., pl.* **-tos** *Mus.* A tremulous or pulsating effect produced in an instrumental or vocal tone by slight rapid variations in pitch. [Ital.]

vi•bur•num (vī-bûr′nəm) ► *n.* Any of various shrubs or trees having clusters of small white or pink flowers and berrylike red or black fruit. [Lat. *vīburnum.*]

Vic. ► *abbr.* vicar

vic•ar (vĭk′ər) ► *n.* **1a.** A parish priest in the Church of England. **b.** A cleric in charge of a chapel in the Episcopal Church. **2.** *Rom. Cath. Ch.* A priest who acts for or represents another. [< Lat. *vicārius*, a substitute.]

vic•ar•age (vĭk′ər-ĭj) ► *n.* The residence or benefice of a vicar.

vi•car•i•ous (vī-kâr′ē-əs, -kăr′-, vĭ-) ► *adj.* **1.** Felt or undergone as if one were taking part in the experience or feelings of another. **2.** Endured or done by one person substituting for another. **3.** Acting for another. [< Lat. *vicārius*, substitute.] —**vi•car′i•ous•ly** *adv.* —**vi•car′i•ous•ness** *n.*

vice[1] (vīs) ► *n.* **1a.** Evil; wickedness. **b.** Sexual immorality, esp. prostitution. **2.** A degrading or immoral practice or habit. **3a.** A personal failing; shortcoming. **b.** A defect; flaw. [< Lat. *vitium.*]

vice[2] (vīs) ► *n.* Var. of **vise.**

vi•ce[3] (vī′sē, -sə) ► *prep.* In place of; replacing. ► *adj.* (vīs). Acting as a deputy or substitute for another: *a vice chairman.* [Lat., in place of.]

vice admiral (vīs) ► *n.* A rank, as in the US Navy, above rear admiral and below admiral.

vice president ► *n.* **1.** An officer ranking next below a president, usu. empowered to assume the president's duties under conditions such as absence, illness, or death. **2.** A deputy to a president, esp. in a corporation, in charge of a specific department or location. —**vice-pres′i•den•cy** *n.*

vice•re•gal (vīs-rē′gəl) ► *adj.* Of a viceroy.

vice•roy (vīs′roi′) ► *n.* The governor of a country, province, or colony, ruling as the representative of a sovereign. [Fr.] —**vice′roy′al•ty** *n.*

vi•ce ver•sa (vī′sə vûr′sə, vīs′) ► *adv.* With the order or meaning reversed; conversely. [Lat. *vice versā*, the position being reversed.]

Vi•chy (vĭsh′ē, vē′shē) A city of central France SSE of Paris. Pop. 30,527.

vi•chys•soise (vĭsh′ē-swäz′, vē′shē-) ► *n.* A thick creamy potato soup flavored with leeks or onions, usu. served cold. [Fr. < VICHY.]

vi•cin•i•ty (vĭ-sĭn′ĭ-tē) ► *n., pl.* **-ties 1.** Nearness; proximity. **2.** A nearby or surrounding area; neighborhood. **3.** An approximate degree or amount. [< Lat. *vīcīnus*, neighboring.]

vi•cious (vĭsh′əs) ► *adj.* **1.** Evil; wicked. **2.** Savage and dangerous. **3.** Spiteful; malicious. **4.** Violent; intense. **5.** Marked by a tendency to worsen. [< Lat. *vitium*, evil.] —**vi′cious•ly** *adv.* —**vi′cious•ness** *n.*

vi•cis•si•tude (vĭ-sĭs′ĭ-to͞od′, -tyo͞od′) ► *n.* **1.** The quality of being changeable; mutability. **2.** often **vicissitudes** A sudden or unexpected change or shift. See Syns at **difficulty.** [< Lat. *vicissim*, in turn.]

vic•tim (vĭk′tĭm) ► *n.* **1.** One who is harmed or killed, as by accident or disease. **2.** A living creature offered as a sacrifice during a religious rite. **3.** One who is tricked, swindled, or injured. [Lat. *victima.*]

vic•tim•ize (vĭk′tə-mīz′) ► *v.* **-ized, -iz•ing.** To make a victim of. —**vic′tim•i•za′tion** *n.* —**vic′tim•iz′er** *n.*

vic•tim•less crime (vĭk′tĭm-lĭs) ► *n.* An illegal act having no direct victim.

vic•tor (vĭk′tər) ► *n.* The winner in a fight, battle, contest, or struggle. [< Lat.]

Victor Em•man•u•el I (ĭ-măn′yo͞o-əl). 1759–1824. Sardinian king (1802–21).

Victor Emmanuel II. 1820–78. Italian king (1861–78).

vic•to•ri•a (vĭk-tôr′ē-ə, -tōr′-) ► *n.* A low, four-wheeled carriage for two with a folding top and an elevated driver's seat in front. [After VICTORIA[1].]

Victoria[1]. 1819–1901. Queen of Great Britain and Ireland (1837–1901) and empress of India (1876–1901).

Victoria[2] **1.** The capital of British Columbia, Canada, on SE Vancouver I. Pop. 229,290. **2.** The capital of Hong Kong, China, on the NW coast of Hong Kong I. Pop. 1,183,621. **3.** The capital of Seychelles, on the NE coast of Mahé I. Pop. 23,000.

Victoria, Lake. Also **Victoria Ny•an•za** (nī-ăn′zə, nyän′-). A lake of E-central Africa in Uganda, Kenya, and Tanzania.

Victoria Falls. A waterfall, 108.3 m (355 ft), of S-central Africa in the Zambezi R. between SW Zambia and NW Zimbabwe.

Victoria Island. An island of N-central Northwest Terrs., Canada, in the Arctic Archipelago E of Banks I.

Victoria Land. A region of Antarctica bounded by Ross Sea and Wilkes Land.

Vic•to•ri•an (vĭk-tôr′ē-ən, -tōr′-) ► *adj.* **1.** Of or belonging to the period of the reign of Queen Victoria. **2.** Displaying the moral standards or ideals characteristic of this period. **3.** Being in the highly ornamented, massive style of architecture, decor, and furnishings popular in 19th-cent. England. ► *n.* A person of the Victorian period.

vic•to•ri•ous (vĭk-tôr′ē-əs, -tōr′-) ► *adj.* **1.** Being the winner in a contest or struggle. **2.** Characteristic of or expressing victory. —**vic•to′ri•ous•ly** *adv.* —**vic•to′ri•ous•ness** *n.*

vic•to•ry (vĭk′tə-rē) ► *n., pl.* **-ries 1.** Defeat of an enemy or opponent. **2.** Success in a struggle against difficulties; triumph.

vict•ual (vĭt′l) ► *n.* **1.** Food fit for human consumption. **2. victuals** Food supplies; provisions. ► *v.* **-ualed, -ual•ing** or **-ualled, -ual•**

ling 1. To provide with food. **2.** To lay in food supplies. [< Lat. *vīctus*, nourishment < *vīvere*, live.]

vi•cu•ña also **vi•cu•na** (vī-ko͞on′yə, -ko͞o′nə, -kyo͞o′nə, vĭ-) ►*n.* **1.** A llamalike mammal of the central Andes, having fine silky fleece. **2.** The fleece of the vicuña. [< Quechua *wikuña*.]

vi•de (vī′dē, wē′dā′) ►*v.* See. Used to direct a reader's attention: *vide page 47.* [Lat. *vidē*, sing. imper. of *vidēre*, see.]

vi•del•i•cet (vĭ-dĕl′ĭ-sĕt′, wĭ-dā′lĭ-kĕt′) ►*adv.* That is; namely. Used to introduce examples, lists, or items. [Lat. *vidēlicet*.]

vid•e•o (vĭd′ē-ō′) ►*adj.* **1.** Of or relating to television, esp. televised images. **2.** Of videotape equipment and technology. **3.** *Comp. Sci.* Of the production of images on video displays. ►*n., pl.* **-os 1.** The visual portion of a televised broadcast. **2.** Television. **3.** A videocassette or videotape. **4.** *Comp. Sci.* The appearance of text and graphics on a video display. [Lat. *videō*, I see < *vidēre*, see.]

video camera ►*n.* A portable, hand-held camera that records on videocassettes for playback on a television set.

vid•e•o•cas•sette (vĭd′ē-ō-kə-sĕt′, -kă-) ►*n.* A cassette containing blank or prerecorded videotape.

videocassette recorder ►*n.* A VCR.

vid•e•o•disc also **vid•e•o•disk** (vĭd′ē-ō-dĭsk′) ►*n.* A recording on disk of sounds and images, as of a movie, that can be played back on a television receiver. [Originally a Ger. trademark.]

video display ►*n.* See **display** 2.

video display terminal ►*n.* A computer terminal having a display that uses a cathode-ray tube.

video game ►*n.* An electronic or computerized game played by manipulating images on a video display.

vid•e•o•tape (vĭd′ē-ō-tāp′) ►*n.* A magnetic tape used to record visual images and associated sound for subsequent playback or broadcasting. —**vid′e•o•tape′** *v.*

vie (vī) ►*v.* **vied, vy•ing** (vī′ĭng). To strive for superiority; contend. [< Lat. *invītāre*, invite.]

Vi•en•na (vē-ĕn′ə) The capital of Austria, in the NE part on the Danube R. Pop. 1,560,471. —**Vi′en•nese′** (-ə-nēz′, -nēs′) *adj. & n.*

Vien•tiane (vyĕn-tyän′) The capital of Laos, in the N-central part on the Mekong R. and the Thailand border. Pop. 210,000.

Vi•et•cong (vē-ĕt′kŏng′, -kông′, vyĕt′-) ►*n., pl.* **-cong.** A Vietnamese in or supporting the National Liberation Front of the former South Vietnam. —**Vi•et′cong′** *adj.*

Vi•et•nam (vē-ĕt′näm′, -năm′, vyĕt′-) A country of SE Asia in E Indochina on the South China Sea; divided (1954–1976) into **North Vietnam** and **South Vietnam.** Cap. Hanoi. Pop. 72,510,000.

Vi•et•nam•ese (vē-ĕt′nə-mēz′, vē′ĭt-, vyĕt′-) ►*n., pl.* **-ese 1.** A native or inhabitant of Vietnam. **2.** The language of Vietnam. —**Vi′et•nam•ese′** *adj.*

view (vyo͞o) ►*n.* **1.** An examination or inspection. **2.** An overview. **3.** An opinion; judgment: *my views on politics.* **4.** Field of vision: *disappeared from view.* **5.** A scene or vista. **6.** A picture of a landscape. **7.** A way of showing or seeing something, as from a particular position or angle: *a side view of the house.* **8.** An aim or intention: *laws enacted with a view to ending discrimination.* ►*v.* **1.** To look at; watch. **2a.** To examine or inspect. **b.** To regard; consider. [< Lat. *vidēre*, see.] —**view′er** *n.*

view•find•er (vyo͞o′fīn′dər) ►*n.* A device on a camera that indicates what will appear in the field of view of the lens.

view•point (vyo͞o′point′) ►*n.* A point of view.

vig•il (vĭj′əl) ►*n.* **1.** A watch kept during normal sleeping hours. **2.** The eve of a religious festival as observed by devotional watching. **3.** often **vigils** Ritual devotions observed on the eve of a holy day. [< Lat. *vigilia*.]

vig•i•lance (vĭj′ə-ləns) ►*n.* Alert watchfulness.

vig•i•lant (vĭj′ə-lənt) ►*adj.* On the alert; watchful. —**vig′i•lant•ly** *adv.*

vig•i•lan•te (vĭj′ə-lăn′tē) ►*n.* One, esp. a member of a group of volunteers, who without authority assumes law enforcement powers. [Sp.] —**vig′i•lan′tism, vig′i•lan′te•ism** *n.*

vi•gnette (vĭn-yĕt′) ►*n.* **1.** A decorative design placed at the beginning or end of a book or chapter or along the border of a page. **2.** A picture that shades off into the surrounding color at the edges. **3.** A brief literary or dramatic sketch. [< OFr. *vigne*, vine.]

vig•or (vĭg′ər) ►*n.* **1.** Physical or mental strength or energy. **2.** Strong feeling; enthusiasm or intensity. **3.** Legal effectiveness or validity. [< Lat.]

Syns: *vigor, dash, punch, verve, vim, vitality* ***n.***

vig•or•ous (vĭg′ər-əs) ►*adj.* **1.** Robust; hardy. **2.** Energetic; lively. —**vig′or•ous•ly** *adv.*

vig•our (vĭg′ər) ►*n.* *Chiefly Brit.* Var. of **vigor.**

Vi•king (vī′kĭng) ►*n.* One of a group of seafaring Scandinavian warriors and explorers who plundered the coasts of N and W Europe from the 8th through the 10th cent.

vile (vīl) ►*adj.* **vil•er, vil•est 1.** Loathsome; disgusting. **2.** Unpleasant or objectionable. **3.** Miserably poor; wretched. **4.** Morally low; base. [< Lat. *vīlis*.] —**vile′ly** *adv.* —**vile′ness** *n.*

vil•i•fy (vĭl′ə-fī′) ►*v.* **-fied, -fy•ing.** To speak evil of; defame. [< LLat. *vīlificāre*.] —**vil′i•fi•ca′tion** *n.* —**vil′i•fi′er** *n.*

vil•la (vĭl′ə) ►*n.* **1.** An often large and luxurious country house. **2.** *Chiefly Brit.* A house in a middle-class suburb. [Ital.]

Vil•la (vē′ə), **Francisco.** "Pancho." 1877?–1923. Mexican revolutionary leader.

vil•lage (vĭl′ĭj) ►*n.* **1.** A usu. rural settlement smaller than a town. **2.** An incorporated community smaller in population than a town. **3.** The inhabitants of a village. [< Lat. *vīllāticum*, farmstead.] —**vil′lag•er** *n.*

vil•lain (vĭl′ən) ►*n.* **1.** A wicked or evil person; scoundrel. **2.** (also vĭl′ān′, vĭ-lān′). Var. of **villein.** [< VLat. *vīllānus, serf.]

vil•lain•ous (vĭl′ə-nəs) ►*adj.* **1.** Befitting a villain; wicked. **2.** Unpleasant; vile.

vil•lain•y (vĭl′ə-nē) ►*n., pl.* **-ies 1.** Baseness of mind or character. **2.** Viciousness of conduct or action. **3.** A treacherous or vicious act.

vil•lein also **vil•lain** (vĭl′ən, -ān′, vĭ-lān′) ►*n.* One of a class of feudal serfs who held the legal status of freemen in their dealings with all people except their lord. [ME *vilein*.]

Pancho Villa

Vil•lon (vē-yōN′), **François.** 1431–63? French poet.

Vil•ni•us (vĭl′nē-əs) or **Vil•na** (-nə). The capital of Lithuania, in the SE part ESE of Kaunas. Pop. 581,500.

vim (vĭm) ►*n.* Ebullient vitality and energy. See Syns at **vigor.** [Lat., accusative of *vīs.*]

vin•ai•grette (vĭn′ĭ-grĕt′) ►*n.* **1.** A small decorative bottle or container used for holding an aromatic preparation such as smelling salts. **2.** A dressing made of vinegar or lemon juice and oil. [< OFr. < *vinaigre*, VINEGAR.]

Vin•cent de Paul (vĭn′sənt də pôl), Saint. 1581–1660. French ecclesiastic.

vin•ci•ble (vĭn′sə-bəl) ►*adj.* Capable of being defeated. [< Lat. *vincere*, conquer.]

vin•di•cate (vĭn′dĭ-kāt′) ►*v.* **-cat•ed, -cat•ing 1.** To clear of accusation, blame, suspicion, or doubt with supporting proof. **2.** To substantiate: *vindicate one's claim.* **3.** To justify or prove the worth of, esp. in light of later developments. **4.** To avenge. [< Lat. *vindex*, avenger.] —**vin′di•ca′tion** *n.* —**vin′di•ca′tor** *n.*

vin•dic•tive (vĭn-dĭk′tĭv) ►*adj.* **1.** Disposed to seek revenge; vengeful. **2.** Intended to cause pain or harm; spiteful. [< Lat. *vindicta*, vengeance.] —**vin•dic′tive•ly** *adv.* —**vin•dic′tive•ness** *n.*

vine (vīn) ►*n.* **1a.** A weak-stemmed plant that derives its support from climbing, twining, or creeping along a surface. **b.** The stem of such a plant. **2.** A grapevine. [< Lat. *vīneus*, of wine.]

vin•e•gar (vĭn′ĭ-gər) ►*n.* An impure dilute solution of acetic acid obtained by fermentation and used as a condiment and preservative. [< OFr. *vinaigre* : *vin*, wine + *aigre*, sour (< Lat. *ācer*).]

vin•e•gar•y (vĭn′ĭ-gə-rē, -grē) ►*adj.* **1.** Of or like vinegar; acid. **2.** Unpleasant and irascible.

vine•yard (vĭn′yərd) ►*n.* Ground planted with cultivated grapevines.

vin•i•cul•ture (vĭn′ĭ-kŭl′chər, vī′nĭ-) ►*n.* Viticulture. [Lat. *vīnum*, wine + CULTURE.]

Vin•land (vĭn′lənd) An unidentified coastal region of NE North America visited by Norse voyagers as early as c. 1000.

Vin•son Mas•sif (vĭn′sən mă-sēf′) A peak, 5,142.3 m (16,860 ft), of W Antarctica.

vin•tage (vĭn′tĭj) ►*n.* **1.** The yield of wine or grapes from a vineyard or district during one season. **2.** Wine, usu. of high quality, identified as to year and vineyard or district of origin. **3a.** The harvesting of a grape crop. **b.** The initial stages of winemaking. **4.** A year or period of origin: *a car of 1942 vintage.* ►*adj.* **1.** Of or relating to a vintage. **2.** Of very high quality. **3.** Of the best or most distinctive. [< Lat. *vīndēmia.*]

vint•ner (vĭnt′nər) ►*n.* **1.** A wine merchant. **2.** One who makes wine. [< Lat. *vīnētum*, vineyard.]

vi•nyl (vī′nəl) ►*n.* Any of various typically tough, flexible, shiny plastics, often used for coverings and clothing. [Lat. *vīnum*, wine + -YL.]

vi•ol (vī′əl) ►*n.* Any of a family of stringed instruments, chiefly of the 16th and 17th cent., having a fretted fingerboard, usu. six strings, and played with a bow. [< OProv. *viola.*]

vi•o•la (vē-ō′lə) ►*n.* A stringed instrument of the violin family, slightly larger than a violin, tuned a fifth lower, and having a deeper, more sonorous tone. [< OProv., viola.] —**vi•o′list** *n.*

vi•o•la•ble (vī′ə-lə-bəl) ►*adj.* That can be violated.

vi•o•late (vī′ə-lāt′) ►*v.* **-lat•ed, -lat•ing 1.** To break or disregard (e.g., a law). **2.** To assault (a person) sexually. **3.** To desecrate or defile. **4.** To disturb; interrupt. [< Lat. *violāre* < *vīs*, force.] —**vi′o•la′tive** *adj.* —**vi′o•la′tor** *n.*

vi•o•la•tion (vī′ə-lā′shən) ►*n.* The act or an instance of violating or the condition of being violated.

vi•o•lence (vī′ə-ləns) ►*n.* **1.** Physical force exerted so as to cause damage, abuse, or injury. **2.** An instance of violent action or behavior. **3.** Intensity or severity: *the violence of a hurricane.* **4.** Detriment to meaning, content, or intent: *do violence to a text.* **5.** Vehemence; fervor.

vi•o•lent (vī′ə-lənt) ►*adj.* **1.** Marked by or resulting from great force. **2.** Having or showing great emotional force. **3.** Intense; extreme. See Syns at **intense. 4.** Caused by unexpected force or injury rather than by natural causes: *a violent death.* [< Lat. *violentus* < *vīs*, force.] —**vi′o•lent•ly** *adv.*

vi•o•let (vī′ə-lĭt) ►*n.* **1a.** Any of various low-growing plants having spurred irregular flowers that are characteristically purplish-blue but sometimes yellow or white. **b.** Any of several plants similar to the violet. **2a.** A reddish blue. **b.** The hue of the short-wave end of the visible spectrum. [< Lat. *viola.*]

vi•o•lin (vī′ə-lĭn′) ►*n.* A stringed instrument played with a bow, having four strings tuned at intervals of a fifth, an unfretted fingerboard, and a shallower body than the viol. [Ital. *violino.*] —**vi′o•lin′ist** *n.*

vi•o•lon•cel•lo (vē′ə-lən-chĕl′ō, vī′ə-) ►*n.*, *pl.* **-los.** A cello. [Ital.]

VIP (vē′ī-pē′) ►*n.* *Informal* A very important person.

vi•per (vī′pər) ►*n.* **1.** Any of several venomous Old World snakes having a single pair of long hollow fangs. **2.** A venomous or supposedly venomous snake. **3.** A malicious or treacherous person. [< Lat. *vīpera*, snake < *vīviparus*, VIVIPAROUS.] —**vi′per•ous** *adj.*

vi•ra•go (və-rä′gō, -rā′-, vîr′ə-gō′) ►*n.*, *pl.* **-goes** or **-gos.** A noisy, domineering woman. [Lat. *virāgō* < *vir*, man.]

vi•ral (vī′rəl) ►*adj.* Of or caused by a virus. —**vi′ral•ly** *adv.*

vir•e•o (vîr′ē-ō′) ►*n., pl.* **-os.** Any of various small songbirds having grayish or greenish plumage. [Lat. *vireō*, a kind of bird.]

Vir•gil also **Ver•gil** (vûr′jəl). 70–19 B.C. Roman poet. —**Vir•gil′i•an** (-jĭl′ē-ən) *adj.*

vir•gin (vûr′jĭn) ►*n.* **1.** A person who has not experienced sexual intercourse. **2.** An unmarried woman who has taken religious vows of chastity. **3. Virgin** Mary, the mother of Jesus. ►*adj.* **1.** Of or being a virgin; chaste. **2.** In a pure or natural state. [< Lat. *virgō*, *virgin-*.] —**vir•gin′i•ty** *n.*

vir•gin•al[1] (vûr′jə-nəl) ►*adj.* **1.** Of or befitting a virgin. **2.** Untouched or unsullied; fresh.

vir•gin•al[2] (vûr′jə-nəl) ►*n.* A small legless harpsichord popular in the 16th and 17th cent. [< VIRGIN.]

Vir•gin•ia (vər-jĭn′yə) A state of the E US on Chesapeake Bay and the Atlantic. Cap. Richmond. Pop. 6,216,568. —**Vir•gin′ian** *adj. & n.*

Virginia Beach. An independent city of SE VA on the Atlantic E of Norfolk. Pop. 393,069.

Virginia creeper ►*n.* A North American climbing vine having compound leaves with five leaflets and bluish-black berries.

Virginia reel ►*n.* An American country-dance in which couples perform various steps together to the instructions of a caller.

Virgin Islands 1. A group of islands of the NE West Indies E of Puerto Rico; divided politically into the **British Virgin Islands** to the NE and the Virgin Islands of the United States to the SW. **2.** Officially **Virgin Islands of the United States.** A US territory constituting the SW group of the Virgin Is. Cap. Charlotte Amalie. Pop. 104,000.

Vir•go (vûr′gō) ►*n.* **1.** A constellation in the region of the celestial equator between Leo and Libra. **2.** The 6th sign of the zodiac.

vir•gule (vûr′gyo͞ol) ►*n.* A diagonal mark (/) used esp. to separate alternatives, as in *and/or,* and to represent the word *per,* as in *miles/hour.* [< LLat. *virgula.*]

vir•ile (vîr′əl, -īl′) ►*adj.* **1.** Of or having the characteristics of an adult male. **2.** Having or showing masculine spirit, strength, or power. **3.** Capable of performing sexually as a male; potent. [< Lat. *vir*, man.] —**vi•ril′i•ty** (və-rĭl′ĭ-tē) *n.*

vi•rol•o•gy (vī-rŏl′ə-jē) ►*n.* The study of viruses and viral diseases. —**vi•rol′o•gist** *n.*

vir•tu•al (vûr′cho͞o-əl) ►*adj.* **1.** Existing in essence or effect though not in actual fact or form. **2.** Created, simulated, or carried on by means of a computer or computer network. [< Lat. *virtūs*, excellence. See VIRTUE.] —**vir′tu•al′i•ty** (-ăl′ĭ-tē) *n.*

Usage: The adjectives *virtual* and *digital* and the prefixes *e-* and *cyber-* refer to things carried out chiefly in an electronic medium. *Digital* can be used for most devices or activities that make use of computer technology: *a digital network. Virtual* often refers to things that mimic their physical equivalents: *a virtual tour of a cathedral.* The prefix *e-* is often used in speaking of the Web's commercial applications (*e-commerce*), whereas *cyber-* tends to be used when speaking of computer networks from a broader cultural point of view (*cyberspace*).

vir•tu•al•ly (vûr′cho͞o-ə-lē) ►*adv.* In fact or to all purposes; practically.

virtual reality ►*n.* A computer simulation of a real or imaginary system in real time.

vir•tue (vûr′cho͞o) ►*n.* **1a.** Moral excellence and righteousness; goodness. **b.** An example or kind of moral excellence. **2.** Chastity, esp. in a woman. **3.** A particularly efficacious or beneficial quality; advantage. **4.** Effective force or power. —***idiom:*** **by virtue of** On the basis of. [< Lat. *virtūs* < *vir*, man.]

vir•tu•os•i•ty (vûr′cho͞o-ŏs′ĭ-tē) ►*n., pl.* **-ties.** The technical skill, fluency, or style of a virtuoso.

vir•tu•o•so (vûr′cho͞o-ō′sō, -zō) ►*n., pl.* **-sos** or **-si** (-sē) **1.** A musician with masterly ability, technique, or style. **2.** A person with masterly skill or technique in any field, esp. the arts. [Ital.] —**vir′tu•o′sic** *adj.*

vir•tu•ous (vûr′cho͞o-əs) ►*adj.* **1.** Having or showing virtue, esp. moral excellence. **2.** Chaste; pure. —**vir′tu•ous•ly** *adv.*

vir•u•lent (vîr′yə-lənt, vîr′ə-) ►*adj.* **1.** Extremely infectious, harmful, or poisonous, as a disease or toxin. **2.** Bitterly hostile or antagonistic. [< Lat. *vīrulentus.*] —**vir′u•lence** *n.* —**vir′u•lent•ly** *adv.*

vi•rus (vī′rəs) ►*n.* **1a.** Any of various submicroscopic, often pathogenic parasites that consist essentially of a core of RNA or DNA surrounded by a protein coat and that are typically not considered living organisms. **b.** A disease caused by a virus. **2.** *Comp. Sci.* A self-replicating program that copies itself into other programs on a computer, usu. having negative effects. [Lat. *vīrus*, poison.]

vi•sa (vē′zə) ►*n.* An official authorization appended to a passport, permitting entry into and travel within a particular country or region. [< Lat. *vīsa* < p.part. of *vidēre*, see.]

vis•age (vĭz′ĭj) ►*n.* **1.** The face or facial expression of a person. **2.** Appearance; aspect. [< OFr. < Lat. *vīsus*, appearance < *vidēre*, see.]

vis-à-vis (vē′zə-vē′) ►*prep.* **1.** Compared with. **2.** In relation to. ►*adv.* Face to face. ►*n., pl.* **vis-à-vis** (-vēz′, -vē′). One opposite or corresponding to another; counterpart. [Fr., face to face.]

Vi•sa•yan Islands (vĭ-sī′ən) An island group of the central Philippines in and around the **Visayan Sea** between Luzon and Mindanao. —**Vi•sa′yan** *adj. & n.*

vis•cer•a (vĭs′ər-ə) ►*pl.n.* The internal body organs, esp. those contained within the abdomen and throrax. [< Lat. *vīscus*, *vīscer-*.]

vis•cer•al (vĭs′ər-əl) ►*adj.* **1.** Of, situated in, or affecting the viscera. **2.** Intensely emotional. **3.** Instinctive. —**vis′cer•al•ly** *adv.*

vis•cid (vĭs′ĭd) ►*adj.* Thick and adhesive. Used of a fluid. [LLat. *viscidus.*] —**vis•cid′i•ty** *n.* —**vis′cid•ly** *adv.*

vis•cose (vĭs′kōs′) ►*n.* A thick, golden-brown viscous solution derived from cellulose, used in the manufacture of rayon and cellophane. [VISC(OUS) + -OSE[2].]

vis•cos•i•ty (vĭ-skŏs′ĭ-tē) ►*n., pl.* **-ties.** The condition or property of being viscous.

vis•count (vī′kount′) ►*n.* A nobleman ranking below an earl or count and above a baron. [< Med.Lat. *vicecomes.*]

vis•cous (vĭs′kəs) ►*adj.* **1.** Having relatively high resistance to flow. **2.** Viscid. [< LLat. *vis-*

cum, birdlime.] —**vis′cous•ly** *adv.* —**vis′cous•ness** *n.*

vise also **vice** (vīs) ►*n.* A clamping device, usu. consisting of two jaws closed or opened by a screw or lever, used in carpentry or metalworking to hold a piece in position. [< OFr. *vis,* screw.]

Vish•nu (vĭsh′no͞o) ►*n. Hinduism* A principal Hindu deity, often conceived as a member of the triad including Brahma and Shiva.

vis•i•bil•i•ty (vĭz′ə-bĭl′ĭ-tē) ►*n., pl.* **-ties 1.** The fact, state, or degree of being visible. **2.** The greatest distance under given weather conditions to which it is possible to see without instrumental assistance.

vis•i•ble (vĭz′ə-bəl) ►*adj.* **1.** Capable of being seen. **2.** Manifest; apparent. [< *vidēre, vīs-,* see.] —**vis′i•bly** *adv.*

Vis•i•goth (vĭz′ĭ-gŏth′) ►*n.* A member of the western Goths that invaded the Roman Empire in the 4th cent. A.D. and settled in France and Spain.

vi•sion (vĭzh′ən) ►*n.* **1.** The faculty of sight; eyesight. **2.** Unusual foresight. **3.** A mental image produced by the imagination. **4.** The experience of seeing the supernatural as if with the eyes. **5.** One of extraordinary beauty. [< Lat. *vīsus,* p.part. of *vidēre,* see.]

vi•sion•ar•y (vĭzh′ə-nĕr′ē) ►*adj.* **1.** Marked by vision or foresight. **2.** Having the nature of fantasies or dreams. **3.** Given to impractical or fanciful ideas. **4.** Not practicable; utopian. ►*n., pl.* **-ies 1.** One given to speculative, often impractical ideas. **2.** A seer; prophet. **3.** One having unusual foresight.

vis•it (vĭz′ĭt) ►*v.* **1.** To go or come to see for reasons of business, duty, or pleasure. **2.** To stay with as a guest. **3a.** To afflict or assail. **b.** To inflict punishment on or for; avenge. **4.** *Informal* To converse; chat. ►*n.* **1.** An act or instance of visiting. **2.** A stay as a guest. **3.** The act of visiting in an official capacity: *a doctor's visit.* [< Lat. *vīsitāre* < *vidēre,* see.]

vis•i•tant (vĭz′ĭ-tənt) ►*n.* A visitor; guest.

vis•i•ta•tion (vĭz′ĭ-tā′shən) ►*n.* **1.** A visit, esp. an official inspection or examination. **2.** The right of a divorced or separated parent to visit a child. **3.** A visit of affliction or blessing regarded as being ordained by God. —**vis′i•ta′tion•al** *adj.*

vis•i•tor (vĭz′ĭ-tər) ►*n* One that visits.

vi•sor also **vi•zor** (vī′zər) ►*n.* **1.** A projecting part, as on a cap or the windshield of a car, that protects the eyes from sun, wind, or rain. **2.** The movable front piece of a helmet. [ME *viser* < AN *vis,* VISAGE.]

vis•ta (vĭs′tə) ►*n.* **1.** A distant view, esp. one seen through an opening. **2.** A broad mental view, as of a series of events. [Ital. < *vedere,* see < Lat. *vidēre.*]

VISTA ►*abbr.* Volunteers In Service To America

Vis•tu•la (vĭs′chə-lə, -cho͝o-) A river of Poland, about 1,091 km (678 mi), rising in the W Beskids and flowing to the Gulf of Gdańsk.

vi•su•al (vĭzh′o͞o-əl) ►*adj.* **1.** Of or relating to the sense of sight. **2.** Able to be seen; visible. **3.** Done or executed by sight only. **4.** Of a method of instruction involving sight. [< Lat. *vīsus,* sight. See VISION.] —**vi′su•al•ly** *adv.*

vi•su•al•ize (vĭzh′o͞o-ə-līz′) ►*v.* **-ized, -iz•ing.** To form a mental image or vision of. —**vi′su•al•i•za′tion** *n.* —**vi′su•al•iz′er** *n.*

vi•ta (vī′tə, vē′-) ►*n., pl.* **vi•tae** (vī′tē, vē′tī) **1.** A short biographical or autobiographical account. **2.** A curriculum vitae. [Lat. *vīta,* life. See VITAL.]

vi•tal (vīt′l) ►*adj.* **1.** Of or characteristic of life. **2.** Necessary to the continuation of life. **3.** Full of life; animated. **4.** Of great importance; essential. [< Lat. *vīta,* life.] —**vi′tal•ly** *adv.*

vi•tal•i•ty (vī-tăl′ĭ-tē) ►*n., pl.* **-ties 1.** The capacity to live, grow, or develop. **2.** Vigor; energy. See Syns at **vigor. 3.** The principle or force that distinguishes living from nonliving things.

vi•tal•ize (vīt′l-īz′) ►*v.* **-ized, -iz•ing.** To endow with life, vigor, or energy. —**vi′tal•i•za′tion** *n.* —**vi′tal•iz′er** *n.*

vi•tals (vīt′lz) ►*pl.n.* **1.** The vital body organs. **2.** Essential parts, as of a system.

vital signs ►*pl.n.* The pulse rate, temperature, and respiratory rate of an individual.

vital statistics ►*pl.n.* Statistics concerning births, deaths, marriages, and migrations.

vi•ta•min (vī′tə-mĭn) ►*n.* Any of various organic substances essential in minute amounts for normal growth and activity of the body and obtained naturally from plant and animal foods. [< Lat. *vīta,* life + AMINE.]

vitamin A ►*n.* A vitamin or mixture of vitamins found in fish-liver oils, milk, and some yellow and dark green vegetables, responsible in deficiency for hardening and roughening of the skin and night blindness.

vitamin B ►*n.* **1.** Vitamin B complex. **2.** A member of this complex, esp. thiamine.

vitamin B_1 ►*n.* See **thiamine.**

vitamin B_2 ►*n.* See **riboflavin.**

vitamin B_{12} ►*n.* A complex compound containing cobalt, found esp. in liver and widely used to treat pernicious anemia.

vitamin B complex ►*n.* A group of vitamins including thiamine, riboflavin, niacin, folic acid, biotin, and vitamin B_{12}, occurring chiefly in yeast, liver, eggs, and some vegetables.

vitamin C ►*n.* See **ascorbic acid.**

vitamin D ►*n.* A vitamin that is required for normal growth of teeth and bones and is produced by ultraviolet irradiation of sterols found in milk, fish, and eggs.

vitamin E ►*n.* A vitamin found in plant leaves, wheat germ oil, and milk and used to treat various abnormalities of the muscles, red blood cells, liver, and brain.

vitamin K ►*n.* A vitamin occurring in leafy green vegetables, tomatoes, and egg yolks, that promotes blood clotting and prevents hemorrhaging.

vi•ti•ate (vĭsh′ē-āt′) ►*v.* **-at•ed, -at•ing 1.** To reduce the value or impair the quality of. **2.** To corrupt morally. See Syns at **corrupt. 3.** To invalidate. [< Lat. *vitium,* fault.] —**vi′ti•a′tion** *n.*

vit•i•cul•ture (vĭt′ĭ-kŭl′chər, vī′tĭ-) ►*n.* The cultivation of grapes. [Lat. *vītis,* vine + CULTURE.] —**vit′i•cul′tur•ist** *n.*

Vi•ti Le•vu (vē′tē lĕv′o͞o) The largest of the Fiji Is., in the SW Pacific.

vit•re•ous (vĭt′rē-əs) ►*adj.* **1.** Of or resembling glass; glassy. **2.** Of or relating to the vitreous humor. [< Lat. *vitreus.*]

vitreous humor ►*n.* The clear gelatinous substance that fills the eyeball between the retina and the lens.

vit•ri•fy (vĭt′rə-fī′) ►*v.* **-fied, -fy•ing.** To change or make into glass or a glassy substance, esp. through heat fusion. [< Lat. *vitrum,* glass.] —**vit′ri•fi•ca′tion** *n.*

vit•ri•ol (vĭt′rē-ōl′, -əl) ►*n.* **1a.** See **sulfuric acid. b.** Any of various sulfates of metals. **2.** Bitterly abusive feeling or expression. [< Lat. *vitreolus,* of glass.]

vit•ri•ol•ic (vĭt′rē-ŏl′ĭk) ►*adj.* **1.** Of or derived from vitriol. **2.** Bitterly scathing; caustic.

Vit•syebsk (vēt′syĭpsk) A city of NE Belarus NE of Minsk. Pop. 365,100.

vit•tles (vĭt′əlz) ►*pl.n. Nonstandard* Victuals.

vi•tu•per•ate (vī-to͞o′pə-rāt′, -tyo͞o′-, vĭ-) ►*v.* **-at•ed, -at•ing.** To rail against abusively; berate. [Lat. *vituperāre.*] —**vi•tu′per•a′tion** *n.* —**vi•tu′per•a•tive** *adj.*

vi•va (vē′və, -vä′) ►*interj.* Used to express acclamation, salute, or applause. [Ital., (long) live < Lat. *vīvere,* live.]

vi•va•ce (vē-vä′chā) ►*adv. & adj. Mus.* Lively; briskly. Used as a direction. [Ital. < Lat. *vīvāx,* VIVACIOUS.]

vi•va•cious (vĭ-vā′shəs, vī-) ►*adj.* Full of animation and spirit; lively. [< Lat. *vīvāx* < *vīvere,* live.] —**vi•va′cious•ly** *adv.* —**vi•vac′i•ty** (-văs′ĭ-tē), **vi•va′cious•ness** *n.*

Vi•val•di (vĭ-väl′dē), **Antonio Lucio.** 1675?–1741. Italian composer and violinist.

viv•id (vĭv′ĭd) ►*adj.* **1.** Perceived as bright and distinct; brilliant. **2.** Having intensely bright colors. **3.** Full of the freshness of immediate experience. **4a.** Evoking lifelike mental images. See Syns at **graphic. b.** Active in forming lifelike images: *a vivid imagination.* [Lat. *vīvidus* < *vīvere,* live.] —**viv′id•ly** *adv.* —**viv′id•ness** *n.*

viv•i•fy (vĭv′ə-fī′) ►*v.* **-fied, -fy•ing 1.** To give or bring life to; animate. **2.** To make more lively, intense, or striking; enliven. [< Lat. *vīvus,* alive.]

vi•vip•a•rous (vī-vĭp′ər-əs, vĭ-) ►*adj.* Giving birth to living offspring that develop within the mother's body. [Lat. *vīvus,* alive + -PAROUS.] —**vi′vi•par′i•ty** (vī′və-păr′ĭ-tē, vĭv′ə-) *n.* **vi•vip′a•rous•ly** *adv.*

viv•i•sec•tion (vĭv′ĭ-sĕk′shən) ►*n.* The cutting into or operation upon living animals, esp. for scientific research. [Lat. *vīvus,* alive + (DIS)SECTION.] —**viv′i•sect′** *v.*

vix•en (vĭk′sən) ►*n.* **1.** A female fox. **2.** A quarrelsome, shrewish, or malicious woman. [ME *fixen.*] —**vix′en•ish** *adj.*

viz. ►*abbr. Lat.* videlicet (namely)

viz•ard (vĭz′ərd, -ärd′) ►*n.* A mask. [< VISOR.]

vi•zier (vĭ-zîr′, vĭz′yər) ►*n.* A high officer in a Muslim government, esp. in the Ottoman Empire. [< Ar. *wazīr,* minister.]

vi•zor (vī′zər) ►*n.* Var. of **visor.**

Vla•di•vos•tok (vlăd′ə-və-stŏk′, -vŏs′tŏk′) A city of extreme SE Russia on an arm of the Sea of Japan. Pop. 637,351.

Vla•minck (vlä-măNk′), **Maurice de.** 1876–1958. French artist.

VLF ►*abbr.* very low frequency

VMD ►*abbr. Lat.* Veterinariae Medicinae Doctor (Doctor of Veterinary Medicine)

vo•ca•ble (vō′kə-bəl) ►*n.* A word considered as a sequence of sounds or letters rather than as a unit of meaning. [< Lat. *vocāre,* call.]

vo•cab•u•lar•y (vō-kăb′yə-lĕr′ē) ►*n., pl.* **-ies 1.** All the words of a language. **2.** The sum of words used by a particular person or group. **3.** A list of words and often phrases, usu. arranged alphabetically and defined or translated; lexicon. [< Lat. *vocābulum,* name.]

vo•cal (vō′kəl) ►*adj.* **1.** Of or for the voice. **2.** Uttered or produced by the voice. **3.** Capable of emitting sound or speech. **4.** Full of voices; resounding. **5.** Quick to speak or criticize; outspoken. ►*n.* **1.** A vocal sound. **2.** *Mus.* A singing part: *jazz vocals.* [< Lat. *vōx,* voice.] —**vo′cal•ly** *adv.*

vocal cords ►*pl.n.* A pair of bands or folds of mucous membrane in the larynx that vibrate when pulled together and when air is passed up from the lungs, thereby producing vocal sounds.

vo•cal•ic (vō-kăl′ĭk) ►*adj.* Relating to or having the nature of a vowel.

vo•cal•ist (vō′kə-lĭst) ►*n.* A singer.

vo•cal•ize (vō′kə-līz′) ►*v.* **-ized, -iz•ing 1.** To use the voice, esp. to sing. **2.** To give voice to. **3.** To articulate (a consonant) as a vowel. —**vo′cal•i•za′tion** *n.* —**vo′cal•iz′er** *n.*

vo•ca•tion (vō-kā′shən) ►*n.* **1.** An occupation, esp. one for which a person is particularly suited. **2.** A calling, esp. to a religious career. [< Lat. *vocāre,* call.] —**vo•ca′tion•al** *adj.*

vocational school ►*n.* A school that offers instruction in skilled trades such as mechanics or carpentry.

voc•a•tive (vŏk′ə-tĭv) ►*adj.* Of or being a grammatical case indicating the one being addressed. [< Lat. *vocāre,* call.] —**voc′a•tive** *n.*

vo•cif•er•ate (vō-sĭf′ə-rāt′) ►*v.* **-at•ed, -at•ing.** To cry out loudly and vehemently, esp. in protest. [Lat. *vōciferārī* : *vōx,* voice + *ferre,* carry.]

vo•cif•er•ous (vō-sĭf′ər-əs) ►*adj.* Making an outcry; clamorous. —**vo•cif′er•ous•ly** *adv.* —**vo•cif′er•ous•ness** *n.*

vod•ka (vŏd′kə) ►*n.* A clear alcoholic liquor distilled from a mash of fermented wheat, rye, corn, or potatoes. [Russ. < *voda,* water.]

vogue (vōg) ►*n.* **1.** The prevailing fashion, practice, or style. **2.** Popular acceptance or favor; popularity. [< OFr.] —**vogu′ish** *adj.*

voice (vois) ►*n.* **1a.** Sound produced by the vocal organs of a vertebrate, esp. a human. **b.** The ability to produce such sounds: *lost her voice.* **2.** A specified quality, condition, or pitch of vocal sound. **3.** *Ling.* Expiration of air through vibrating vocal cords, used in the production of vowels and voiced consonants. **4.** A sound resembling vocal utterance: *the voice of the wind.* **5.** *Mus.* **a.** Musical sound produced by vibration of the vocal cords. **b.** A singer: *a choir of 200 voices.* **c.** One of the individual parts or strands in a composition. **6a.** Expression; utterance. **b.** A medium or agency of expression. **c.** The right or opportunity to express a choice or opinion. **7.** *Gram.* A verb form indicating the relation between the subject and the action expressed by the verb. ►*v.* **voiced, voic•ing 1.** To give voice to; utter. **2.** *Ling.* To pronounce with vibration of the vocal cords. **3.** *Mus.* To regulate the tone of (e.g., the pipes of an organ). [< Lat. *vōx.*]

voice box ►*n.* The larynx.

voiced (voist) ►*adj.* **1.** Having a voice or a specified kind of voice: *harsh-voiced.* **2.** *Ling.* Uttered with vibration of the vocal cords, as the consonant *b.*

voice•less (vois′lĭs) ►*adj.* **1.** Having no voice. **2.** *Ling.* Uttered without vibration of the vocal cords, as the consonant *t.* —**voice′less•ly** *adv.* —**voice′less•ness** *n.*

voice mail ►*n.* A computerized system for leaving and receiving telephone messages.

voice-o•ver or **voice•o•ver** (vois′ō′vər) ►*n.* The voice of an unseen narrator in a movie or a television broadcast.

voice•print (vois′prĭnt′) ►*n.* An electronically recorded graphic representation of a person's voice.

void (void) ►*adj.* **1.** Containing no matter; empty. **2.** Not occupied; vacant. **3.** Completely lacking; devoid: *void of understanding.* **4.** Ineffective; useless. **5.** Having no legal force or validity; null. ►*n.* **1.** An empty space; vacuum. **2.** A feeling of emptiness, loneliness, or loss. ►*v.* **1.** To empty. **2.** To excrete (body wastes). **3.** To leave; vacate. **4.** To make void; invalidate. [< Lat. *vacīvus.*] —**void′a•ble** *adj.* —**void′er** *n.*

voile (voil) ►*n.* A sheer fabric of cotton, rayon, silk, or wool used for making lightweight dresses and curtains. [< Lat. *vēlum*, covering.]

vol. ►*abbr.* volume

vol•a•tile (vŏl′ə-tl, -tīl′) ►*adj.* **1.** Evaporating readily at normal temperatures and pressures. **2a.** Tending to vary often. **b.** Inconstant; fickle. **c.** Ephemeral; fleeting. **3.** Tending to violence; explosive. [< Lat. *volāre*, fly.] —**vol′a•til′i•ty** (-tĭl′ĭ-tē) *n.*

vol•a•til•ize (vŏl′ə-tl-īz′) ►*v.* **-ized, -iz•ing** **1.** To become or make volatile. **2.** To evaporate or cause to evaporate.

vol•can•ic (vŏl-kăn′ĭk, vôl-) ►*adj.* **1.** Of or resembling a volcano. **2.** Powerfully explosive: *a volcanic temper.*

vol•ca•nism (vŏl′kə-nĭz′əm) also **vul•ca•nism** (vŭl′-) ►*n.* Volcanic force or activity.

vol•ca•no (vŏl-kā′nō) ►*n.*, *pl.* **-noes** or **-nos** **1.** An opening in the earth's crust through which molten lava, ash, and gases are ejected. **2.** A mountain formed by the materials ejected from a volcano. [< Lat. *Volcānus*, Vulcan.]

Volcano Islands. A group of Japanese islands in the NW Pacific N of the Mariana Is.

vole (vōl) ►*n.* Any of various rodents resembling rats or mice but having a shorter tail. [< obsolete *volemouse.*]

Vol•ga (vŏl′gə) A river of W Russia rising NW of Moscow and flowing about 3,701 km (2,300 mi) to the Caspian Sea.

Vol•go•grad (vŏl′gə-grăd′). Formerly **Stalingrad.** A city of SW Russia on the Volga R. E of Voroshilovgrad. Pop. 996,992.

vo•li•tion (və-lĭsh′ən) ►*n.* **1.** The act of making a conscious choice or decision. **2.** A conscious choice or decision. **3.** The power or faculty of choosing; will. [< Lat. *velle*, *vol-*, wish.] —**vo•li′tion•al** *adj.*

vol•ley (vŏl′ē) ►*n.*, *pl.* **-leys** **1a.** A simultaneous discharge of a number of shots or missiles. **b.** The missiles thus discharged. **2.** A bursting forth of many things together: *a volley of questions.* **3.** *Sports* An act of volleying, esp. in tennis. ►*v.* **1.** To discharge or be discharged in or as if in a volley. **2.** *Sports* To strike (a ball) before it touches the ground. [< Lat. *volāre*, fly.] —**vol′ley•er** *n.*

vol•ley•ball (vŏl′ē-bôl′) ►*n.* **1.** A game played by two teams on a court divided by a high net, in which up to three hits are used to ground the ball on the opposing team's court. **2.** The inflated ball used in this game.

Vó•los (vō′lŏs′) A city of E Greece in Thessaly on the **Gulf of Vólos,** an inlet of the Aegean Sea. Pop. 71,378.

volt (vōlt) ►*n.* The unit of electric potential and electromotive force equal to the difference in potential needed to cause a current of one ampere to flow through a resistance of one ohm. [< Count A. VOLTA.]

Vol•ta (vŏl′tə) A river of W Africa, flowing about 467 km (290 mi) through Ghana to the Gulf of Guinea.

Vol•ta (vōl′tä), Count **Alessandro.** 1745–1827. Italian physicist.

volt•age (vōl′tĭj) ►*n.* Electromotive force or potential difference, usu. expressed in volts.

vol•ta•ic (vŏl-tā′ĭk, vōl-, vôl-) ►*adj.* Of or producing electricity by chemical action; galvanic.

Vol•taire (vōl-târ′, vŏl-). François Marie Arouet. 1694–1778. French philosopher and writer.

volt•me•ter (vōlt′mē′tər) ►*n.* An instrument for measuring potential differences in volts.

vol•u•ble (vŏl′yə-bəl) ►*adj.* Marked by a ready flow of speech; fluent. [< Lat. *volūbilis.*] —**vol′u•bil′i•ty** *n.* —**vol′u•bly** *adv.*

vol•ume (vŏl′yo͞om, -yəm) ►*n.* **1a.** A collection of written or printed sheets bound together; book. **b.** One of the books of a set. **c.** A series of issues of a periodical, usu. covering one calendar year. **2a.** The amount of space occupied by a three-dimensional object or region of space. **b.** The capacity of such a region or of a specified container. **3.** Amount; quantity: *a low volume of business.* **4a.** The amplitude or loudness of a sound. **b.** A control for adjusting loudness. [< Lat. *volūmen*, roll of writing.]

vol•u•met•ric (vŏl′yo͞o-mĕt′rĭk) ►*adj.* Of or relating to measurement by volume. [VOLU(ME) + -METRY + -IC.]

vo•lu•mi•nous (və-lo͞o′mə-nəs) ►*adj.* **1.** Having great volume, fullness, size, or number. **2.** Filling or capable of filling many volumes. **3.** Having many coils; winding. [LLat. *volūminōsus*, having many folds.] —**vo•lu′mi•nous•ly** *adv.* —**vo•lu′mi•nous•ness** *n.*

vol•un•tar•y (vŏl′ən-tĕr′ē) ►*adj.* **1.** Arising from one's own free will. **2.** Acting or done willingly and without constraint or expectation of reward. **3.** Normally controlled by or subject to individual volition. **4.** *Law* Done deliberately; intentional. ►*n.*, *pl.* **-ies.** A piece for solo organ played before, during, or after a religious service. [< Lat. *voluntās*, choice.] —**vol′un•tar′i•ly** (-târ′ə-lē) *adv.*

vol•un•teer (vŏl′ən-tîr′) ►*n.* A person who performs or offers a service of his or her own free will. ►*v.* **1.** To give or offer of one's own accord. **2.** To perform or offer to perform a service of one's own free will.

vol•un•teer•ism (vŏl′ən-tîr′ĭz′əm) ►*n.* Use of or reliance on volunteers.

vo•lup•tu•ar•y (və-lŭp′cho͞o-ĕr′ē) ►*n.*, *pl.* **-ies.** One who is given over to luxury and sensual pleasures. —**vo•lup′tu•ar′y** *adj.*

vo•lup•tu•ous (və-lŭp′cho͞o-əs) ►*adj.* **1.** Of, marked by, or giving sensual pleasure. **2.** Devoted to or indulging in sensual pleasures. **3.** Full and appealing in form. [< Lat. *voluptās*, pleasure.] —**vo•lup′tu•ous•ly** *adv.* —**vo•lup′tu•ous•ness** *n.*

vo•lute (və-lo͞ot′) ►*n.* A spiral, scroll-like formation or decoration. [< Lat. *volūta*.]

vom•it (vŏm′ĭt) ►*v.* **1.** To eject part or all of the contents of the stomach through the mouth. **2.** To eject or discharge in a gush; spew out. ►*n.* Matter ejected from the stomach through the mouth. [< Lat. *vomitāre*.]

voo•doo (vo͞o′do͞o) ►*n.* **1.** A religion practiced chiefly in Caribbean countries, esp. Haiti, in which a supreme God rules a pantheon of local deities, deified ancestors, and saints. **2.** A fetish, spell, or curse holding magic power for adherents of voodoo. **3.** A priest or priestess of voodoo. **4.** Deceptive or delusive nonsense. [Of West African orig.] —**voo′doo•ism** *n.*

vo•ra•cious (vô-rā′shəs, və-) ►*adj.* **1.** Consuming or eager to consume great amounts of food; ravenous. **2.** Exceedingly eager; insatiable. [< Lat. *vorāx*.] —**vo•ra′cious•ly** *adv.* —**vo•rac′i•ty** (-răs′ĭ-tē), **vo•ra′cious•ness** *n.*

Syns: *voracious, gluttonous, rapacious, ravenous* **adj.**

Vo•ro•nezh (və-rô′nĭsh) A city of W Russia on the Don R. SW of Lipetsk. Pop. 898,854.

-vorous ►*suff.* Eating; feeding on: *omnivorous.* [< Lat. *vorāre*, devour.]

vor•tex (vôr′tĕks′) ►*n., pl.* **-es** or **-ti•ces** (-tĭ-sēz′) **1.** A spiral motion of fluid, esp. a whirling mass of water or air; whirlpool or whirlwind. **2.** Something regarded as drawing into its center all that surrounds it. [Lat. < *vertere*, turn.] —**vor′ti•cal** *adj.*

Vosges (vōzh) A mountain range of NE France extending about 193 km (120 mi) parallel to the Rhine R.

vo•ta•ry (vō′tə-rē) ►*n., pl.* **-ries** **1a.** One bound by religious vows. **b.** A devout worshiper. **2.** One who is fervently devoted, as to a leader, activity, or ideal. [< Lat. *vōtum*, vow[1].]

vote (vōt) ►*n.* **1a.** A formal expression of preference for a candidate for office or for a proposed resolution of an issue. **b.** A means by which such a preference is made known, such as a raised hand or a marked ballot. **2.** The number of votes cast in an election or to resolve an issue. **3.** A group of voters: *the rural vote.* **4.** The result of an election. **5.** Suffrage. ►*v.* **vot•ed, vot•ing** **1.** To cast a vote. **2.** To endorse, bring into existence, or make available by vote. **3.** To declare by general consent: *voted the play a success.* [< Lat. *vōtum*, vow[1].] —**vot′er** *n.*

vo•tive (vō′tĭv) ►*adj.* Given or dedicated in fulfillment of a vow. [< Lat. *vōtum*, vow[1].]

vouch (vouch) ►*v.* **1.** To give a personal assurance or guarantee: *I can vouch for his integrity.* **2.** To serve as a guarantee. **3.** To substantiate by supplying evidence. [< AN *voucher*, summon.]

vouch•er (vou′chər) ►*n.* **1.** One that vouches. **2.** A written record, as of an expenditure or transaction. **3.** A certificate representing a credit against future expenditures.

vouch•safe (vouch-sāf′, vouch′sāf′) ►*v.* **-safed, -saf•ing.** To condescend to grant or bestow. [ME *vouchen sauf*, warrant as safe.]

vow[1] (vou) ►*n.* **1.** An earnest promise that binds one to a specified act or mode of behavior. **2.** A declaration or assertion. ►*v.* **1.** To promise solemnly; pledge. See Syns at **promise. 2.** To make a vow. —***idiom:*** **take vows** To enter a religious order. [< Lat. *vōtum* < *vovēre*, to vow.] —**vow′er** *n.*

vow[2] (vou) ►*v.* To declare or assert. [< AVOW.]

vow•el (vou′əl) ►*n.* **1.** A speech sound created by the relatively free passage of breath through the larynx and mouth. **2.** A letter representing a vowel. [< Lat. *vōcālis*, sounding.]

vox pop•u•li (vŏks pŏp′yə-lī′, -lē) ►*n.* Popular opinion. [Lat. *vōx populī*, voice of the people.]

voy•age (voi′ĭj) ►*n.* **1.** A long journey, esp. by sea, to foreign or distant parts. **2.** A journey through outer space. ►*v.* **-aged, -ag•ing.** To make a voyage. [< LLat. *viāticum*, journey.] —**voy′ag•er** *n.*

voy•eur (voi-yûr′) ►*n.* A person who derives sexual gratification from observing the sexual acts of others. [Fr. < OFr. *voir*, see < Lat. *vidēre*.] —**voy•eur′ism** *n.* —**voy′eur•is′tic** *adj.*

VP ►*abbr.* vice president

VS ►*abbr.* veterinary surgeon

vs. ►*abbr.* versus

vss. ►*abbr.* verses

VT also **Vt.** ►*abbr.* Vermont

VTR ►*abbr.* videotape recorder

Vul. ►*abbr.* Vulgate

Vul•can (vŭl′kən) ►*n. Rom. Myth.* The god of fire and metalworking.

vul•ca•nism (vŭl′kə-nĭz′əm) ►*n.* Var. of **volcanism.**

vul•ca•nize (vŭl′kə-nīz′) ►*v.* **-nized, -niz•ing.** To improve the strength, resiliency, and texture of (e.g., rubber) by combining with sulfur or other additives under heat and pressure. —**vul′ca•ni•za′tion** *n.* —**vul′ca•niz′er** *n.*

vulg. ►*abbr.* vulgar

Vulg. ►*abbr.* Vulgate

vul•gar (vŭl′gər) ►*adj.* **1.** Of or associated with the common people. **2.** Of or expressed in language spoken by the common people; vernacular. **3.** Deficient in taste, cultivation, or refinement. **4.** Crudely indecent. [< Lat. *vulgāris* < *vulgus*, common people.] —**vul′gar•ly** *adv.*

vul•gar•i•an (vŭl-gâr′ē-ən) ►*n.* A vulgar person. See Syns at **boor.**

vul•gar•ism (vŭl′gə-rĭz′əm) ►*n.* **1.** Vulgarity. **2a.** A crudely indecent word or phrase; obscenity. **b.** A word, phrase, or manner of expression used chiefly by uneducated people.

vul•gar•i•ty (vŭl-găr′ĭ-tē) ►*n., pl.* **-ties** **1.** The quality or condition of being vulgar. **2.** Something, such as an act or expression, that offends good taste or propriety.

vul•gar•ize (vŭl′gə-rīz′) ►*v.* **-ized, -iz•ing** **1.** To make vulgar; debase. **2.** To popularize. —**vul′gar•i•za′tion** *n.* —**vul′gar•iz′er** *n.*

Vulgar Latin ►*n.* The common speech of the ancient Romans, which is distinguished from standard literary Latin and is the ancestor of the Romance languages.

vul•gate (vŭl′gāt′, -gĭt) ►*n.* **1.** Common speech; vernacular. **2. Vulgate** The Latin edition of the Bible used as the Roman Catholic authorized version. [< LLat. *vulgāta*, popular.]

vul•ner•a•ble (vŭl′nər-ə-bəl) ►*adj.* **1a.** Not protected against harm or injury. **b.** Susceptible to attack; assailable. **c.** Easily affected or hurt, as by criticism. **2.** *Games* In a position to receive greater penalties or bonuses after winning one game of a rubber. [< Lat. *vulnerāre*, to

wound.] —**vul′ner•a•bil′i•ty** *n.* —**vul′ner•a•bly** *adv.*
vul•pine (vŭl′pīn′) ▸*adj.* **1.** Of a fox. **2.** Cunning. [< Lat. *vulpēs*, fox.]
vul•ture (vŭl′chər) ▸*n.* **1.** Any of various large, usu. carrion-eating birds characteristically having dark plumage and a featherless head and neck. **2.** A greedy, opportunistic person. [< Lat. *vultur*.]
vul•va (vŭl′və) ▸*n., pl.* **-vae** (-vē). The external genital organs of the female. [Lat., covering.] —**vul′val, vul′var** *adj.*
vv. ▸*abbr.* verses
v.v. ▸*abbr.* vice versa

W

w[1] or **W** (dŭb′əl-yo͞o, -yo͞o) ▸*n., pl.* **w's** or **W's** also **ws** or **Ws.** The 23rd letter of the English alphabet.
w[2] ▸*abbr.* **1.** weight **2.** width **3.** *Phys.* work
W[1] ▸ The symbol for the element **tungsten.** [< Ger. *Wolfram.* See WOLFRAM.]
W[2] ▸*abbr.* **1.** watt **2.** Wednesday **3.** week **4a.** west **b.** western
w. ▸*abbr.* **1.** wife **2.** also **w/** with
WA ▸*abbr.* Washington
WAAC ▸*abbr.* Women's Army Auxiliary Corps
WAAF ▸*abbr.* Women's Auxiliary Air Force
Wa•bash (wô′băsh′) A river of the E-central US rising in W OH and flowing about 764 km (475 mi) to the Ohio R.
WAC ▸*abbr.* Women's Army Corps
wack•y (wăk′ē) also **whack•y** (hwăk′ē, wăk′ē) ▸*adj.* **-i•er, -i•est** *Slang* **1.** Eccentric. **2.** Crazy; silly. [Prob. < *out of whack.*] —**wack′i•ly** *adv.* —**wack′i•ness** *n.*
Wa•co (wā′kō) A city of E-central TX S of Dallas–Fort Worth. Pop. 103,590.
wad (wŏd) ▸*n.* **1.** A small mass of soft material. **2.** A compressed ball, roll, or lump, as of tobacco. **3.** A plug, as of cloth, used to hold a powder charge in place, as in a muzzleloading gun. **4.** *Informal* A large amount. **5.** *Informal* A large amount of money. ▸*v.* **wad•ded, wad•ding 1.** To compress into a wad. **2.** To pad, pack, line, or plug with wadding. [?]
wad•ding (wŏd′ĭng) ▸*n.* **1.** Wads collectively. **2.** A soft layer of fibrous cotton or wool used for padding. **3.** Material for gun wads.
wad•dle (wŏd′l) ▸*v.* **-dled, -dling.** To walk with short steps that tilt the body from side to side, as a duck does. [< WADE.] —**wad′dle** *n.* —**wad′dler** *n.*
wade (wād) ▸*v.* **wad•ed, wad•ing 1.** To walk in or through a substance, such as water, that impedes movement. **2.** To make one's way arduously. —***phrasal verb:* wade in** (or **into)** To begin or attack resolutely and energetically. [< OE *wadan.*]
wad•er (wā′dər) ▸*n.* **1.** See **wading bird. 2. waders** Waterproof hip boots or trousers.
wa•di (wä′dē) ▸*n., pl.* **-dis** also **-dies 1.** A valley, gully, or streambed in N Africa and SW Asia that remains dry except during the rainy season. **2.** An oasis. [Ar. *wādi.*]
wad•ing bird (wā′dĭng) ▸*n.* A long-legged bird that frequents shallow water.
WAF ▸*abbr.* Women in the Air Force
wa•fer (wā′fər) ▸*n.* **1.** A thin crisp cake, biscuit, or candy. **2.** *Eccles.* A small thin disk of unleavened bread used in the Eucharist. **3.** A small adhesive seal for papers. **4.** *Electron.* A thin semiconductor slice on which an integrated circuit can be formed. [< ONFr. *waufre*, of Gmc. orig.]

waders

waf•fle[1] (wŏf′əl) ▸*n.* A light crisp batter cake baked in a waffle iron. [< MDu. *wāfel.*]
waf•fle[2] (wŏf′əl) ▸*v.* **-fled, -fling** *Informal* To speak or write evasively. [Prob. < obsolete *waff*, yelp.]
waffle iron ▸*n.* An appliance having hinged indented plates that impress a grid pattern into waffle batter as it cooks.
waft (wäft, wăft) ▸*v.* To carry or cause to go gently and smoothly through the air or over water. ▸*n.* **1.** A whiff. **2.** A light breeze. [< *wafter*, convoy ship.]
wag[1] (wăg) ▸*v.* **wagged, wag•ging.** To move or cause to move briskly and repeatedly from side to side, to and fro, or up and down. [ME *waggen.*] —**wag** *n.*
wag[2] (wăg) ▸*n.* A humorous or droll person; wit. [Perh. < WAG[1].] —**wag′ger•y** *n.* —**wag′gish** *adj.* —**wag′gish•ly** *adv.*
wage (wāj) ▸*n.* **1.** Payment for labor or services to a worker. **2. wages** *(takes sing. or pl. v.)* A suitable return or reward. ▸*v.* **waged, wag•ing.** To engage in (e.g., a war or campaign). [< ONFr., of Gmc. orig.]
wa•ger (wā′jər) ▸*n.* Something staked on an uncertain outcome. See Syns at **bet.** ▸*v.* To bet. [< ONFr. *wagier*, pledge.]
wag•gle (wăg′əl) ▸*v.* **-gled, -gling.** To move or wave with short quick motions; wag. [ME *wagelen.*] —**wag′gle** *v.* —**wag′gly** *adj.*
Wag•ner (väg′nər), **Richard.** 1813–83. German composer. —**Wag•ner′i•an** *adj. & n.*
wag•on (wăg′ən) ▸*n.* **1.** A large, four-wheeled vehicle drawn by draft animals or tractor and used esp. for transporting loads. **2a.** A station wagon. **b.** A police patrol wagon. **3.** A child's

low, four-wheeled cart. —***idiom:*** **on the wagon** *Slang* Abstaining from alcohol. [< MDu. *wagen*.]
wagon train ▸*n.* A line or train of wagons traveling cross-country.
wa•hoo (wä-ho͞o′, wä′ho͞o) ▸*n.*, *pl.* **-hoo** or **-hoos.** A tropical marine food and game fish of the mackerel family. [?]
waif (wāf) ▸*n.* **1.** A homeless or forsaken child. **2.** A stray animal. [< AN, stray.]
Wai•ki•ki (wī′kĭ-kē′) A beach and resort district of Oahu I., HI, SE of Honolulu.
wail (wāl) ▸*v.* **1.** To cry loudly and mournfully, as in grief or protest. **2.** To make a mournful, high-pitched sound: *The wind wailed through the trees.* [ME *wailen*, prob. of Scand. orig.] —**wail** *n.* —**wail′er** *n.*
wain (wān) ▸*n.* A large open farm wagon. [< OE *wægn*.]
wain•scot (wān′skət, -skŏt′, -skōt′) ▸*n.* **1.** A facing or paneling, usu. of wood, on the walls of a room. **2.** The lower part of an interior wall when finished in a material different from that of the upper part. [< MDu. *waghenscot*.] —**wain′scot** *v.*
wain•wright (wān′rīt′) ▸*n.* One who builds and repairs wagons.
waist (wāst) ▸*n.* **1.** The part of the human trunk between the bottom of the rib cage and the pelvis. **2a.** The part of a garment that encircles the waist. **b.** A garment that extends from the shoulders to the waistline, as a blouse. **3.** The middle section or part of an object. [ME *wast*.]
waist•band (wāst′bănd′) ▸*n.* A band of material encircling the waist of a garment.
waist•coat (wĕs′kĭt, wāst′kōt′) ▸*n. Chiefly Brit.* A vest.
waist•line (wāst′līn′) ▸*n.* **1a.** The narrowest part of the waist. **b.** The measurement of this part. **2.** The line at which the skirt and bodice of a dress join.
wait (wāt) ▸*v.* **1.** To remain in expectation: *waiting for the bus.* **2.** To be ready for use. **3.** To be in abeyance. **4.** To work as a waiter, waitress, or salesperson. ▸*n.* The act of waiting or the time spent waiting. [< ONFr. *waitier*, watch.]
wait•er (wā′tər) ▸*n.* **1.** One who serves at a table, as in a restaurant. **2.** A tray.
wait•ing room (wā′tĭng) ▸*n.* A room, as in a doctor's office, for the use of people waiting.
wait•ress (wā′trĭs) ▸*n.* A woman who serves at a table. See Usage Note at **-ess.**
waive (wāv) ▸*v.* **waived, waiv•ing 1.** To give up (a claim or right) voluntarily. **2.** To postpone. [< AN *weyver*, abandon.]
waiv•er (wā′vər) ▸*n.* **1.** Intentional relinquishment of a right, claim, or privilege. **2.** The document that waives a right or claim.
wake[1] (wāk) ▸*v.* **woke** (wōk) or **waked** (wākt), **waked** or **wok•en** (wō′kən), **wak•ing 1a.** To become awake: *woke late.* **b.** To stay awake. **c.** To make aware of; alert. **2.** To keep watch or guard, esp. over a corpse. ▸*n.* A watch over a corpse before burial. [< OE *wacan* and *wacian*.]

Regional Note: Northern dialects seem to favor verb forms that change the internal vowel—hence *dove* for the past tense of *dive*, and *woke* for *wake*. Southern dialects tend to prefer forms that add an *-ed*, hence *dived* and *waked*.

wake[2] (wāk) ▸*n.* **1.** The visible track left by something, as a ship, moving through water. **2.** A track or condition left behind; aftermath. [Of Scand. orig.]
wake•ful (wāk′fəl) ▸*adj.* **1a.** Not sleeping. **b.** Without sleep; sleepless. **2.** Watchful; alert. —**wake′ful•ness** *n.*
Wake Island. An island of the W Pacific between HI and Guam.
wak•en (wā′kən) ▸*v.* **1.** To rouse from sleep; awake. **2.** To rouse from an inactive state. [< OE *wæcnan*.] —**wak′en•er** *n.*
Wal•cott (wôl′kŏt′, wŏl′-), **Derek.** b. 1930. West Indian writer; 1992 Nobel.
Wald•heim (wôld′hīm′, vält′-), **Kurt.** b. 1918. Austrian diplomat and politician.
wale (wāl) ▸*n.* **1.** A mark raised on the skin, as by a whip; welt. **2.** A raised ridge in the surface of a fabric such as corduroy. **3.** One of the heavy planks extending along the sides of a wooden ship. ▸*v.* **waled, wal•ing.** To raise wales on (the skin). [< OE *walu*.]
Wales (wālz) A principality of the United Kingdom on the W peninsula of the island of Great Britain. Cap. Cardiff. Pop. 2,790,462.
Wa•le•sa (wä-lĕn′sə, vä-wĕn′sä), **Lech.** b. 1943. Polish leader; 1983 Nobel Peace Prize.
walk (wôk) ▸*v.* **1.** To move or cause to move on foot at a pace slower than a run. **2.** To pass over, on, or through on foot. **3.** To conduct oneself in a particular manner. **4.** *Baseball* To give or be given a base on balls. —***phrasal verbs:*** **walk out** To go on strike. **walk over** *Informal* To treat badly or contemptuously. ▸*n.* **1a.** A manner of walking. **b.** A gait, esp. a slow gait of a horse in which the feet touch the ground one after another. **2.** The act or an instance of walking. **3.** A distance covered in walking. **4.** A sidewalk or other walkway. **5.** *Baseball* A base on balls. [< OE *wealcan*, roll.] —**walk′er** *n.* —**walk′a•ble** *adj.*
walk•a•way (wôk′ə-wā′) ▸*n.* **1.** An easily won contest or victory. **2.** An easy task.
Wal•ker (wô′kər), **Alice.** b. 1944. Amer. writer.

Alice Walker

walk•ie-talk•ie (wô′kē-tô′kē) ▸*n.* A portable sending and receiving radio set.
walk•ing papers (wô′kĭng) ▸*pl.n. Slang* A notice of discharge or dismissal.
walking stick ▸*n.* **1.** A staff used as an aid in walking. **2.** Any of various insects that have the appearance of twigs or sticks.
walk-on (wôk′ŏn′, -ôn′) ▸*n.* A minor, usu. nonspeaking role in a theatrical production.
walk•out (wôk′out′) ▸*n.* **1.** A labor strike. **2.**

The act of leaving or quitting a meeting or organization as a sign of protest.

walk•o•ver (wôk′ō′vər) ►*n.* **1.** A horserace with only one horse entered, won by merely walking the track. **2.** A walkaway.

walk•up also **walk-up** (wôk′ŭp′) ►*n.* **1.** A multistory building with no elevator. **2.** An apartment or office in a walkup.

walk•way (wôk′wā′) ►*n.* A passage for walking.

wall (wôl) ►*n.* **1.** A vertical structure or partition that encloses an area or separates two areas. **2.** A defensive embankment or rampart. **3.** Something resembling a wall in appearance or function: *the stomach wall.* ►*v.* To enclose, surround, or fortify with or as if with a wall. See Syns at **enclose.** [< Lat. *vallum*, palisade.]

wal•la•by (wŏl′ə-bē) ►*n., pl.* **-bies** or **-by.** Any of various Australian marsupials related to the kangaroos but gen. smaller. [Dharuk (Australian) *walaba.*]

Wal•lace, Henry Agard. 1888–1965. Vice President of the US (1941–45).

wall•board (wôl′bôrd′, -bōrd′) ►*n.* See **plasterboard.**

wal•let (wŏl′ĭt) ►*n.* A flat pocket-sized folding case for holding paper money, cards, or photographs. [ME *walet*, knapsack.]

wall•eye (wôl′ī′) ►*n.* **1a.** An eye with a white or opaque cornea. **b.** A disorder in which one eye deviates in orientation from the other. **2.** *pl.* **-eye** or **-eyes** A North American freshwater food and game fish having large staring eyes. —**wall′eyed′** *adj.*

wall•flow•er (wôl′flou′ər) ►*n.* **1.** A cultivated plant with fragrant yellow, orange, or brownish flowers. **2.** One who does not participate in the activity at a social event because of shyness or unpopularity.

Wal•loon (wŏ-lo͞on′) ►*n.* **1.** One of a French-speaking people of Celtic descent inhabiting S and SE Belgium. **2.** Their dialect of French.

wal•lop (wŏl′əp) *Informal* ►*v.* **1.** To beat soundly; thrash. **2.** To strike with a hard blow; impact. **3.** To defeat thoroughly. ►*n.* **1.** A hard blow. **2.** The capacity to create a forceful effect; impact. [< ONFr. **waloper*, gallop.] —**wal′lop•er** *n.*

wal•low (wŏl′ō) ►*v.* **-lowed, -low•ing 1.** To roll around in or as if in mud. **2.** To luxuriate; revel. **3.** To be plentifully supplied: *wallowing in money.* **4.** To move in a clumsy or rolling manner. ►*n.* A muddy pool where animals wallow. [< OE *wealwian.*]

wall•pa•per (wôl′pā′pər) ►*n.* Paper printed with designs or colors and pasted to a wall as a decorative covering. —**wall′pa′per** *v.*

wall-to-wall (wôl′tə-wôl′) ►*adj.* **1.** Completely covering a floor. **2.** *Informal* Present or spreading everywhere.

wal•nut (wôl′nŭt′, -nət) ►*n.* **1a.** Any of several deciduous trees with round sticky fruit that encloses an edible nut. **b.** The nut of a walnut. **2.** The hard, dark brown wood of a walnut. [< OE *wealhhnutu.*]

Wal•pole (wô′pōl′, wŏl′-), **Horace.** 4th Earl of Orford. 1717–97. British writer and historian.

wal•rus (wôl′rəs, wŏl′-) ►*n., pl.* **-rus** or **-rus•es.** A large Arctic marine mammal with two long tusks, tough wrinkled skin, and four flippers. [Du.]

Wal•ton (wôl′tən), **Izaak.** 1593–1683. English writer.

waltz (wôlts, wôls) ►*n.* **1.** A dance in triple time with a strong accent on the first beat. **2.** Music for this dance. ►*v.* **1.** To dance the waltz (with). **2.** *Slang* To move lightly and easily: *waltzed out of the room.* **3.** *Informal* To accomplish a task, chore, or assignment with little effort. [< OHGer. *walzan*, roll.] —**waltz′er** *n.*

Wam•pa•no•ag (wäm′pə-nō′ăg) ►*n., pl.* **-ag** or **-ags 1.** A member of a Native American people of E Rhode Island and SE Massachusetts. **2.** Their Algonquian language.

wam•pum (wŏm′pəm, wôm′-) ►*n.* **1.** Small beads made from polished shells and fashioned into strings or belts, formerly used by certain Native American peoples as currency and jewelry. **2.** *Informal* Money. [Of Massachusett orig.]

wan (wŏn) ►*adj.* **wan•ner, wan•nest 1.** Unnaturally pale; pallid. **2.** Weak or faint. **3.** Sad: *a wan smile.* [< OE *wann*, gloomy, dark.] —**wan′ly** *adv.* —**wan′ness** *n.*

wand (wŏnd) ►*n.* **1.** A slender rod carried as a symbol of office; scepter. **2.** A stick or baton used by a magician, conjurer, or diviner. [< ON *vöndr.*]

wan•der (wŏn′dər) ►*v.* **1.** To move about aimlessly. **2.** To go by an indirect route or at no set pace. **3.** To go astray. **4.** To lose clarity or coherence of thought or expression. [< OE *wandrian.*] —**wan′der•er** *n.* —**wan′der•ing•ly** *adv.*

wan•der•ing Jew (wŏn′dər-ĭng) ►*n.* A trailing plant with usu. variegated foliage, popular as a houseplant.

wan•der•lust (wŏn′dər-lŭst′) ►*n.* A strong or irresistible impulse to travel. [Ger.]

wane (wān) ►*v.* **waned, wan•ing 1.** To decrease gradually in size, amount, intensity, or degree. **2.** To exhibit a decreasing illuminated area from full moon to new moon. **3.** To approach an end: *The old year is waning.* ►*n.* **1.** A gradual decrease or decline. **2.** The period of the moon's waning. [< OE *wanian.*]

wan•gle (wăng′gəl) ►*v.* **-gled, -gling** *Informal* **1.** To make, achieve, or get by contrivance. **2.** To manipulate, esp. fraudulently. [?] —**wang′ler** *n.*

wan•na•be (wŏn′ə-bē′, wôn′-) *Informal* ►*n.* **1.** One who, aspiring to a position, imitates the customs of the one admired. **2.** An imitative product. ►*adj.* Wishing to be; would-be. [< *want to be.*]

want (wŏnt, wônt) ►*v.* **1.** To wish for. See Syns at **desire. 2.** To be without; lack. **3.** To be in need of; require. **4.** To have need. ►*n.* **1.** The condition of lacking something usual or necessary. **2.** Pressing need; destitution. **3.** Something desired. **4.** A defect; fault. [< ON *vanta*, be lacking.]

Usage: When *want* is followed immediately by an infinitive construction, it does not take *for: I want you to go* (not *want for you*). When *want* and the infinitive are separated in the sentence, however, *for* is used: *What I want is for you to go.*

want ad ►*n.* A classified advertisement.

want•ing (wŏn′tĭng, wôn′-) ►*adj.* **1.** Absent; lacking. **2.** Not up to standards or expectations. ►*prep.* **1.** Without. **2.** Minus; less.

wan•ton (wŏn′tən) ►*adj.* **1.** Immoral or unchaste; lewd. **2.** Gratuitously cruel; merciless: *wanton killing.* **3.** Unrestrainedly excessive: *wanton spending.* **4.** Luxuriant; overabundant. **5.** Frolicsome; playful. **6.** Undisciplined. ►*n.* A wanton, esp. immoral person. [ME *wantowen.*] —**wan′ton•ly** *adv.* —**wan′ton•ness** *n.*

wap•i•ti (wŏp′ĭ-tē) ►*n., pl.* **-ti** or **-tis.** A large North American deer having long branching antlers; elk. [Shawnee *waapiti.*]

war (wôr) ►*n.* **1a.** A state or period of armed conflict between nations, states, or parties. **b.** The techniques of war; military science. **2a.** A condition of antagonism or contention. **b.** A determined struggle or attack. ►*v.* **warred, war•ring 1.** To wage war. **2.** To struggle, contend, or fight. [< ONFr. *werre,* of Gmc. orig.]

war•ble (wôr′bəl) ►*v.* **-bled, -bling.** To sing with trills, runs, or other melodic embellishments. ►*n.* The act or sound of warbling. [< ONFr. *werbler,* of Gmc. orig.]

war•bler (wôr′blər) ►*n.* **1.** Any of various small, often yellowish New World songbirds. **2.** Any of various small, often brownish or grayish Old World songbirds.

war chest ►*n.* An accumulation of funds to finance a war effort.

war cry ►*n.* A battle cry.

ward (wôrd) ►*n.* **1.** An administrative division of a city or town, esp. an electoral district. **2.** A division in a hospital: *a maternity ward.* **3.** A division in a prison. **4.** A minor or incompetent person placed under the care or protection of a guardian or a court. **5.** The state of being under guard; custody. **6.** The act of guarding or protecting. **7.** A means of protection. ►*v.* To guard; protect. —***phrasal verb:* ward off** To avert: *ward off disaster.* [< OE *weard,* a watching.]

-ward or **-wards** ►*suff.* Direction toward: *downward; backwards.* [< OE *-weard.*]

war•den (wôrd′n) ►*n.* **1.** The chief administrative official of a prison. **2.** An official charged with the enforcement of certain regulations: *a game warden.* **3.** A churchwarden. [< ONFr. *wardein,* a guard.]

ward•er (wôr′dər) ►*n.* A guard or watcher of a gate or tower. [< ONFr. *warder,* to guard, of Gmc. orig.]

ward heel•er (hē′lər) ►*n.* A worker for the local organization of a political machine.

ward•robe (wôr′drōb′) ►*n.* **1.** A cabinet or closet built to hold clothes. **2.** Garments collectively, esp. all the clothing belonging to one person. **3.** The costumes belonging to a theater. [< ONFr. *warderobe.*]

ward•room (wôrd′ro͞om′, -ro͝om′) ►*n.* The common recreation area and dining room for the commissioned officers on a warship.

ward•ship (wôrd′shĭp′) ►*n.* **1.** The condition of being a ward. **2.** Custody; guardianship.

ware (wâr) ►*n.* **1.** Articles of the same general kind: *hardware; silverware.* **2. wares** Articles of commerce; goods. [< OE *waru.*]

-ware ►*suff.* **1.** Articles of the same general kind, material, or use: *silverware.* **2.** Software: *shareware.* [< WARE. Sense 2 < SOFTWARE.]

ware•house (wâr′hous′) ►*n.* A place in which goods or merchandise are stored. —**ware′house′** (-houz′) *v.*

war•fare (wôr′fâr′) ►*n.* **1.** The act of waging war. **2.** Conflict; strife. [ME.]

war•fa•rin (wôr′fər-ĭn) ►*n.* A white crystalline compound used to kill rodents and medicinally as an anticoagulant. [*W(isconsin) A(lumni) R(esearch) F(oundation)* + *(coum)arin,* a compound.]

war•head (wôr′hĕd′) ►*n.* A section in the forward part of a projectile, such as a guided missile, that contains the explosive charge.

War•hol (wôr′hôl′), **Andy.** 1930?–87. Amer. artist.

war•horse (wôr′hôrs′) ►*n.* **1.** A horse used in combat; charger. **2.** *Informal* One who has been through many struggles.

war•like (wôr′līk′) ►*adj.* **1.** Belligerent; hostile. **2.** Of or relating to war.

war•lock (wôr′lŏk′) ►*n.* A male witch, sorcerer, or wizard. [< OE *wǣrloga,* oath-breaker.]

war•lord (wôr′lôrd′) ►*n.* A military commander exercising civil power in a region, usu. by force of arms.

warm (wôrm) ►*adj.* **-er, -est 1.** Moderately hot. **2.** Preserving or imparting heat: *a warm overcoat.* **3.** Having a sensation of unusually high body heat, as from exercise. **4.** Marked by enthusiasm; ardent: *warm support.* **5.** Excited, animated, or emotional: *a warm debate.* **6.** Recently made; fresh: *a warm trail.* **7.** Close to discovering, guessing, or finding something, as in certain games. **8.** *Informal* Uncomfortable because of danger or annoyance: *Things are warm for the bookies.* ►*v.* **1.** To make or become warm. **2.** To make zealous or ardent; enliven. **3.** To fill with pleasant emotions: *warmed by the sight of home.* **4.** To become ardent, enthusiastic, or animated: *began to warm to the subject.* —***phrasal verb:* warm up** To make or become ready for action, as by exercising or practicing beforehand. [< OE *wearm.*] —**warm′er** *n.* —**warm′ish** *adj.* —**warm′ly** *adv.* —**warm′ness** *n.*

warm-blood•ed (wôrm′blŭd′ĭd) ►*adj.* Maintaining a relatively constant and warm body temperature independent of environmental temperature, as a mammal. —**warm′-blood′ed•ness** *n.*

warm-heart•ed (wôrm′här′tĭd) ►*adj.* Kind; friendly. —**warm′heart′ed•ness** *n.*

war•mon•ger (wôr′mŭng′gər, -mŏng′-) ►*n.* One who advocates or attempts to stir up war. —**war′mon′ger•ing** *n.*

warmth (wôrmth) ►*n.* **1.** The quality or condition of being warm. **2.** Excitement or intensity. [ME.]

warm-up (wôrm′ŭp′) ►*n.* The act, procedure, or period of warming up.

warn (wôrn) ►*v.* **1.** To make aware of present or potential danger; caution. **2.** To admonish as to action or manners. **3.** To notify to go or stay away. **4.** To notify or apprise in advance. [< OE *warnian.*]

warn•ing (wôr′nĭng) ►*n.* **1.** An intimation, threat, or sign of impending danger. **2.** Advice to beware or desist. **3.** Something, such as a signal, that warns. ►*adj.* Acting or serving to warn.

warp (wôrp) ►*v.* **1.** To twist or bend or become twisted or bent out of shape. **2.** To turn or be turned from a proper course; pervert. **3.** To distort. See Syns at **bias. 4.** *Naut.* To move (a vessel) by hauling on a line fastened to an anchor or pier. ►*n.* **1.** The state of being twisted or bent out of shape. **2.** A distortion or twist. **3.**

The threads that run lengthwise in a woven fabric, crossed at right angles to the woof. [< OE *weorpan*, throw away.]

war•path (wôr′păth′, -päth′) ▸*n.* **1.** A course that leads to warfare or battle. **2.** A hostile course or mood.

war•plane (wôr′plān′) ▸*n.* A combat aircraft.

war•rant (wôr′ənt, wŏr′-) ▸*n.* **1.** Authorization or certification; sanction. **2.** Something that assures, attests to, or guarantees; proof. **3.** An order that serves as authorization, esp. a judicial writ authorizing a search, seizure, or arrest. **4.** A certificate of appointment given to a warrant officer. ▸*v.* **1.** To guarantee or attest to the quality, accuracy, or condition of. **2.** To vouch for. **3a.** To guarantee (a product). **b.** To guarantee (a purchaser) indemnification against damage or loss. **4.** To provide adequate grounds for; justify. **5.** To authorize or empower. [< ONFr. *warant*, of Gmc. orig.] —**war′rant•a•bil′i•ty** *n.* —**war′rant•a•ble** *adj.* —**war′ran•tee′** *n.* —**war′ran•ter** *n.*

warrant officer ▸*n.* A military officer intermediate between a noncommissioned and a commissioned rank.

war•ran•ty (wôr′ən-tē, wŏr′-) ▸*n.*, *pl.* **-ties 1.** Official authorization or sanction. **2.** Justification for an act or course of action. **3.** A legally binding guarantee.

war•ren (wôr′ən, wŏr′-) ▸*n.* **1.** An area where small game animals, esp. rabbits, live and breed. **2.** An overcrowded living area. [< ONFr. *warenne*, enclosure.]

Warren. A city of SE MI, a suburb of Detroit. Pop. 144,864.

Warren, Earl. 1891–1974. Amer. jurist; the chief justice of the US Supreme Court (1953–69).

Warren, Robert Penn. 1905–89. Amer. writer and critic.

war•ri•or (wôr′ē-ər, wŏr′-) ▸*n.* One engaged or experienced in battle. [< ONFr. *werreieur.*]

War•saw (wôr′sô′) The capital of Poland, in the E-central part on the Vistula R. Pop. 1,654,491.

war•ship (wôr′shĭp′) ▸*n.* A combat ship.

wart (wôrt) ▸*n.* **1.** A hard rough lump on the skin, caused by a virus. **2.** A similar growth, as on a plant. **3.** A flaw or imperfection. [< OE *wearte.*] —**wart′y** *adj.*

wart hog ▸*n.* A wild African hog having prominent upward-curving tusks and wartlike growths on the face.

war•time (wôr′tīm′) ▸*n.* A time of war.

War•wick (wôr′wĭk) A city of E-central RI on Narragansett Bay. Pop. 85,427.

war•y (wâr′ē) ▸*adj.* **-i•er, -i•est 1.** On guard; watchful. **2.** Prudent; cautious. [< OE *wær.*] —**war′i•ly** *adv.* —**war′i•ness** *n.*

was (wŭz, wŏz; wəz *when unstressed*) ▸*v.* 1st and 3rd pers. sing. p. indic. of **be.**

wa•sa•bi (wä′sə-bē, wə-sä′-) ▸*n.* A pungent green Japanese horseradish, usu. used as a condiment. [Jap.]

Wa•satch Range (wô′săch′) A range of the Rocky Mts. extending about 402 km (250 mi) from SE ID to central UT.

wash (wŏsh, wôsh) ▸*v.* **1.** To cleanse, using water or other liquid, usu. with soap, detergent, or bleach, by immersing, dipping, rubbing, or scrubbing. **2.** To cleanse oneself. **3.** To make moist or wet. **4.** To flow over, against, or past: *waves washed the beach.* **5.** To carry, erode, or destroy by moving water: *Rain washed the topsoil away.* **6.** To rid of corruption; purify. **7.** To separate constituents of (an ore) by immersion in or agitation with water. **8.** *Informal* To hold up under examination: *Your excuse won't wash.* —***phrasal verbs:*** **wash down** To follow the swallowing of (food) with a drink. **wash up 1.** To clean one's hands. **2.** To ruin: *He's washed up as a ballplayer.* ▸*n.* **1.** The act of washing. **2.** A quantity of articles that are to be or have just been washed. **3.** Waste liquid. **4.** A liquid used in washing or coating. **5.** A thin layer of water color or India ink spread on a drawing. **6.** A rush of water. **7.** *Regional* The dry bed of a stream. [< OE *wæscan.*]

Wash. ▸*abbr.* Washington

wash•a•ble (wŏsh′ə-bəl, wôsh′-) ▸*adj.* Capable of being washed without damage.

wash-and-wear (wŏsh′ən-wâr′, wôsh′-) ▸*adj.* Treated so as to require little or no ironing after being washed.

wash•ba•sin (wŏsh′bā′sən, wôsh′-) ▸*n.* A washbowl.

wash•board (wŏsh′bôrd′, -bōrd′, wôsh′-) ▸*n.* A board having a corrugated surface on which clothes can be rubbed during laundering.

wash•bowl (wŏsh′bōl′, wôsh′-) ▸*n.* A basin that can be filled with water for use in washing oneself.

wash•cloth (wŏsh′klôth′, -klŏth′, wôsh′-) ▸*n.* A cloth used for washing oneself.

washed-out (wŏsht′out′, wôsht′-) ▸*adj.* **1.** Lacking color or intensity; faded. **2.** Exhausted.

washed-up (wŏsht′ŭp′, wôsht′-) ▸*adj.* No longer successful or needed; finished.

wash•er (wŏsh′ər, wô′shər) ▸*n.* **1.** One that washes, esp. a machine for washing. **2.** A flat disk, as of metal, placed beneath a nut or at an axle bearing to relieve friction, prevent leakage, or distribute pressure.

wash•ing (wŏsh′ĭng, wô′shĭng) ▸*n.* **1.** Articles washed at one time. **2.** The residue after an ore has been washed.

Wash•ing•ton (wŏsh′ĭng-tən, wô′shĭng-) **1.** A state of the NW US on the Pacific Ocean. Cap. Olympia. Pop. 4,887,941. **2.** The capital of the US, on the Potomac R. between VA and MD and coextensive with the District of Columbia. Pop. 609,909. —**Wash′ing•to′ni•an** (-tō′nē-ən) *adj.* & *n.*

Washington, Booker T(aliaferro). 1856–1915. Amer. educator.

Washington, George. 1732–99. Amer. military leader and 1st US President (1789–97).

Booker T. Washington

George Washington

Washington, Mount. A mountain, 1,917.8 m (6,288 ft), of E NH.
wash•out (wŏsh′out′, wôsh′-) ►*n.* **1.** Erosion of a relatively soft surface, such as a roadbed, by a sudden gush of water. **2.** A total failure or disappointment.
wash•room (wŏsh′ro͝om′, -ro͞om′, wôsh′-) ►*n.* A bathroom, esp. one in a public place.
wash•stand (wŏsh′stănd′, wôsh′-) ►*n.* **1.** A stand designed to hold a basin and pitcher of water for washing. **2.** A stationary bathroom sink.
wash•tub (wŏsh′tŭb′, wôsh′-) ►*n.* A tub used for washing clothes.
wash•y (wŏsh′ē, wô′shē) ►*adj.* **-i•er, -i•est 1.** Watery; diluted. **2.** Lacking strength or intensity: *a washy handshake.*
was•n't (wŭz′ənt, wŏz′-) ► Was not.
wasp (wŏsp, wôsp) ►*n.* Any of various social or solitary insects having a slender body with a constricted abdomen and often inflicting a painful sting. [< OE *wæps.*]
Wasp or **WASP** (wŏsp, wôsp) ►*n.* A white Protestant of Anglo-Saxon ancestry. [*W(hite) A(nglo-)S(axon) P(rotestant).*]
wasp•ish (wŏs′pĭsh) ►*adj.* **1.** Of or suggestive of a wasp. **2.** Easily irritated or annoyed; snappish. —**wasp′ish•ly** *adv.*
wasp waist ►*n.* A very slender or tightly corseted waist. —**wasp′-waist′ed** *adj.*
was•sail (wŏs′əl, wŏ-sāl′) ►*n.* **1a.** A toast given in drinking someone's health. **b.** The drink used in such toasting. **2.** A festivity with much drinking and merriment. ►*v.* To drink to the health of; toast. [< ON *ves heill,* be healthy.] —**was′sail•er** *n.*
Was•ser•mann test (wä′sər-mən) ►*n.* A diagnostic test for syphilis. [After August von *Wassermann* (1866–1925).]
wast (wŏst; wəst *when unstressed*) ►*v. Archaic* 2nd pers. sing. p.t. of **be.**
wast•age (wā′stĭj) ►*n.* **1.** Loss by deterioration or wear. **2.** An amount wasted.
waste (wāst) ►*v.* **wast•ed, wast•ing 1.** To use, consume, or expend thoughtlessly or carelessly. **2.** To lose or cause to lose energy, strength, or vigor: *Disease wasted his body.* **3.** To fail to take advantage of; lose: *waste an opportunity.* **4.** To destroy completely. ►*n.* **1a.** The act or an instance of wasting. **b.** The state of being wasted. **2.** A barren or wild area or expanse. **3.** A useless byproduct. **4.** Garbage; trash. **5.** The undigested residue of food eliminated from the body; excrement. [< Lat. *vāstus,* empty.]
Syns: *waste, consume, dissipate, fritter, squander* ***Ant:*** *save* **v.**
waste•bas•ket (wāst′băs′kĭt) ►*n.* A container for rubbish.
waste•ful (wāst′fəl) ►*adj.* Marked by or inclined to waste. —**waste′ful•ly** *adv.*
waste•land (wāst′lănd′) ►*n.* Land that is desolate, barren, or ravaged.
waste•pa•per (wāst′pā′pər) ►*n.* Discarded paper.
wast•rel (wā′strəl) ►*n.* **1.** One who wastes. **2.** An idler or loafer. [< WASTE.]
watch (wŏch) ►*v.* **1.** To observe carefully or continuously. **2.** To look and wait expectantly or in anticipation: *watch for an opportunity.* **3.** To stay awake deliberately; keep vigil. **4.** To keep a watchful eye on; guard. **5.** To keep up on or informed about: *watch the price of gold.* **6.** To tend (e.g., a flock). See Syns at **tend**[2]. ►*n.* **1.** The act of watching. **2.** A period of close observation. **3.** A person or group of people serving, esp. at night, to guard or protect. **4.** The post or period of duty of a guard or sentinel. **5.** *Naut.* **a.** Any of the periods of time, usually four hours, into which a part of the crew is assigned to duty. **b.** The members of a ship's crew on duty during a specific watch. **6.** A small portable timepiece, esp. one worn on the wrist or carried in the pocket. [< OE *wæccan.*] —**watch′er** *n.*
watch•dog (wŏch′dôg′, -dŏg′) ►*n.* **1.** A dog trained to guard people or property. **2.** One serving as a guardian or protector.
watch•ful (wŏch′fəl) ►*adj.* Closely observant or alert; vigilant. See Syns at **careful.** —**watch′ful•ly** *adv.* —**watch′ful•ness** *n.*
watch•mak•er (wŏch′mā′kər) ►*n.* One who makes or repairs watches.
watch•man (wŏch′mən) ►*n.* A man employed to stand guard or keep watch.
watch•tow•er (wŏch′tou′ər) ►*n.* An observation tower for a guard or lookout.
watch•word (wŏch′wûrd′) ►*n.* **1.** A prearranged reply to a challenge, as from a guard; password. **2.** A rallying cry; slogan.
wa•ter (wô′tər, wŏt′ər) ►*n.* **1.** A clear, colorless, odorless, and tasteless liquid, H_2O, essential for most plant and animal life and the most widely used of all solvents. **2a.** Any of various forms of water, as rain. **b.** often **waters** Naturally occurring mineral water, as at a spa. **3.** A body of water such as a sea, lake, river, or stream. **4.** A body fluid, such as urine, perspiration, or tears. **5.** An aqueous solution of a substance, esp. a gas: *ammonia water.* **6.** A wavy finish or sheen, as of a fabric. **7a.** The transparency and luster of a gem. **b.** A level of excellence: *of the first water.* ►*v.* **1.** To sprinkle, moisten, or supply with water. **2.** To give drinking water to. **3.** To dilute or weaken by or as if by adding water. **4.** To give a sheen to the surface of (silk, linen, or metal). **5.** To produce or discharge fluid, as from the eyes or mouth. [< OE *wæter.*]
wa•ter•bed (wô′tər-bĕd′, wŏt′ər-) ►*n.* A bed whose mattress is a large water-filled plastic bag.
wa•ter•borne (wô′tər-bôrn′, -bōrn′, wŏt′ər-) ►*adj.* Supported or transported by water: *waterborne freight.*
water buffalo ►*n.* A large, often domesticated Asian buffalo with large spreading horns.
Wa•ter•bur•y (wô′tər-bĕr′ē, wŏt′ər-) A city of W-central CT NNW of New Haven. Pop. 108,961.
water cannon ►*n.* A truck-mounted apparatus that fires water at high pressure, used esp. to disperse crowds.
water chestnut ►*n.* **1.** An Asian sedge having an edible corm and cylindrical leaves. **2.** The succulent corm of this plant.
water closet ►*n.* A room or booth containing a toilet and often a washbowl.
wa•ter•col•or (wô′tər-kŭl′ər, wŏt′ər-) ►*n.* **1.** A paint composed of a water-soluble pigment. **2.** A painting that is made with watercolors. —**wa′ter•col′or•ist** *n.*
wa•ter•course (wô′tər-kôrs′, -kōrs′, wŏt′ər-) ►*n.* **1.** A natural or artificial channel through

which water flows. **2.** A stream or river.

wa•ter•craft (wô′tər-krăft′, wŏt′ər-) ▶*n.* A boat or ship.

wa•ter•cress (wô′tər-krĕs′, wŏt′ər-) ▶*n.* A plant growing in freshwater ponds and streams and having pungent edible leaves.

wa•ter•fall (wô′tər-fôl′, wŏt′ər-) ▶*n.* A steep descent of water from a height.

wa•ter•fowl (wô′tər-foul′, wŏt′ər-) ▶*n.* **1.** A water bird, esp. a swimming bird. **2.** Swimming birds, such as ducks and geese, collectively.

wa•ter•front (wô′tər-frŭnt′, wŏt′ər-) ▶*n.* **1.** Land abutting a body of water. **2.** The part of a town or city that abuts water.

water gap ▶*n.* A cleft in a mountain ridge through which water flows.

water hyacinth ▶*n.* A tropical American plant forming dense floating masses in ponds and streams.

wa•ter•ing hole (wô′tər-ĭng, wŏt′ər-) or **water hole** ▶*n.* **1.** A pool where animals come to drink. **2.** *Informal* A place, such as a bar, where drinks are served.

wa•ter•ish (wô′tər-ĭsh, wŏt′ər-) ▶*adj.* Watery.

water lily ▶*n.* Any of various aquatic plants with broad floating leaves and showy, variously colored flowers.

water line ▶*n.* Any of several parallel lines on the hull of a ship that indicate the depth to which the ship sinks under various loads.

wa•ter•logged (wô′tər-lôgd′, -lŏgd′, wŏt′ər-) ▶*adj.* So soaked or saturated with water as to be heavy, sluggish, or unwieldy.

wa•ter•loo (wô′tər-lo͞o′, wŏt′ər-) ▶*n.*, *pl.* **-loos.** A final crushing defeat.

Waterloo. A town of central Belgium near Brussels; site of Napoleon's final defeat (1815).

wa•ter•mark (wô′tər-märk′, wŏt′ər-) ▶*n.* **1.** A mark showing the height to which water has risen. **2.** A translucent design impressed on paper during manufacture and visible when the paper is held to the light. ▶*v.* To mark (paper) with a watermark.

wa•ter•mel•on (wô′tər-mĕl′ən, wŏt′ər-) ▶*n.* **1.** An African vine cultivated for its large edible fruit. **2.** The fruit itself, having a hard green rind and sweet watery reddish flesh.

water moccasin ▶*n.* A venomous snake of lowlands and swampy regions of the S US; cottonmouth.

water ou•zel (o͞o′zəl) ▶*n.* See **dipper** 2. [< OE *ōsle.*]

water pipe ▶*n.* **1.** A pipe that conducts water. **2.** An apparatus for smoking in which the smoke is drawn through a vessel of water.

water polo ▶*n.* A water sport with two teams that try to pass a ball into the other's goal.

wa•ter•pow•er (wô′tər-pou′ər, wŏt′ər-) ▶*n.* The energy produced by running or falling water that is used for driving machinery, esp. for generating electricity.

wa•ter•proof (wô′tər-pro͞of′, wŏt′ər-) ▶*adj.* Impervious to or unaffected by water. ▶*n.* *Chiefly Brit.* A raincoat. —**wa′ter•proof′** *v.*

wa•ter-re•pel•lent (wô′tər-rĭ-pĕl′ənt, wŏt′ər-) ▶*adj.* Resistant to water but not entirely waterproof.

wa•ter-re•sis•tant (wô′tər-rĭ-zĭs′tənt, wŏt′ər-) ▶*adj.* Water-repellent.

wa•ter•shed (wô′tər-shĕd′, wŏt′ər-) ▶*n.* **1.** A ridge of high land dividing two areas drained by different river systems. **2.** The region draining into a body of water. **3.** A turning point. [Poss. translation of Ger. *Wasserscheide* : *Wasser*, water + *Scheide*, divide.]

wa•ter•side (wô′tər-sīd′, wŏt′ər-) ▶*n.* Land bordering a body of water.

water ski ▶*n.* A broad ski used for gliding over water while being towed by a motorboat. —**wa′ter-ski′** *v.* —**wa′ter-ski′er** *n.*

wa•ter•spout (wô′tər-spout′, wŏt′ər-) ▶*n.* **1.** A tornado or lesser whirlwind occurring over water and resulting in a whirling column of air and spray. **2.** A hole or pipe from which water, esp. rainwater, is discharged.

water table ▶*n.* The level below which the ground is saturated with water.

wa•ter•tight (wô′tər-tīt′, wŏt′ər-) ▶*adj.* **1.** So tightly made that water cannot enter or escape. **2.** Unassailable: *a watertight alibi.*

water tower ▶*n.* A standpipe or elevated tank used for storing water.

wa•ter•way (wô′tər-wā′, wŏt′ər-) ▶*n.* A navigable body of water, as a river or canal.

water wheel ▶*n.* A wheel driven by falling or running water, used to power machinery.

water wings ▶*pl.n.* An inflatable device used to support the body of a person learning to swim.

wa•ter•works (wô′tər-wûrks′, wŏt′ər-) ▶*pl.n.* **1.** The water system, including reservoirs, tanks, buildings, pumps, and pipes, of a city or town. **2.** *Informal* Tears.

wa•ter•y (wô′tə-rē, wŏt′ə-) ▶*adj.* **-i•er, -i•est** **1.** Filled with, consisting of, or soaked with water. **2.** Diluted: *watery soup.* **3.** Pale; washed-out. —**wa′ter•i•ness** *n.*

WATS ▶*abbr.* Wide-Area Telecommunications Service

watt (wŏt) ▶*n.* A unit of power equal to one joule per second. [After James WATT.]

Watt, James. 1736–1819. British engineer and inventor.

watt•age (wŏt′ĭj) ▶*n.* **1.** An amount of power, esp. electric power, expressed in watts or kilowatts. **2.** The electric power required by an appliance or device.

Wat•teau (wŏ-tō′, vä-), **Jean Antoine.** 1684–1721. French painter.

wat•tle (wŏt′l) ▶*n.* **1.** A construction of poles intertwined with twigs, reeds, or branches, used for walls, fences, and roofs. **2.** A fleshy, often brightly colored fold of skin hanging from the throat of certain birds. [< OE *watel.*] —**wat′tled** *adj.*

Waugh (wô), **Evelyn (Arthur Saint John).** 1903–66. British writer.

wave (wāv) ▶*v.* **waved, wav•ing 1.** To move or cause to move back and forth or up and down in the air. **2.** To move or swing as in giving a signal. See Syns at **flourish. 3.** To curve or curl, as hair. ▶*n.* **1.** A ridge or swell moving along the surface of a body of water. **2.** An undulating surface movement: *waves of wheat.* **3.** A slight curve or curl, as in the hair. **4.** A movement up and down or back and forth: *a jaunty wave of the hand.* **5.** A surge or rush: *a wave of nausea; a wave of indignation.* **6.** A persistent weather condition: *a heat wave.* **7.** *Phys.* **a.** A disturbance traveling through a medium. **b.** A graphic representation of the variation of such a disturbance with time. [< OE *wafian.*]

wave•band (wāv′bănd′) ►*n.* A range of frequencies, esp. radio frequencies.

wave•form (wāv′fôrm′) ►*n.* The mathematical representation of a wave, esp. a graph obtained by plotting a characteristic of the wave against time.

wave•length (wāv′lĕngkth′, -lĕngth′, -lĕnth′) ►*n.* The distance between one peak or crest of a wave, as of light or sound, and the next corresponding peak or crest.

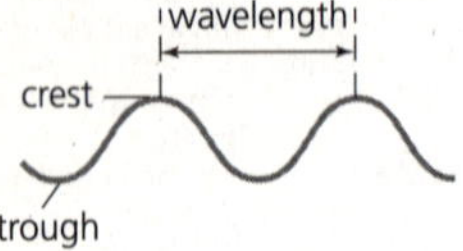

wavelength

wave•let (wāv′lĭt) ►*n.* A small wave; ripple.

wa•ver (wā′vər) ►*v.* **1.** To move or swing back and forth. **2a.** To show or experience irresolution or indecision; vacillate. **b.** To falter or yield: *His resolve began to waver.* **3.** To tremble or quaver, as a voice. **4.** To flicker or glimmer, as light. [ME *waveren.*] —**wa′ver** *n.* —**wa′ver•ing•ly** *adv.*

WAVES ►*abbr.* Women Accepted for Volunteer Emergency Service

wav•y (wā′vē) ►*adj.* **-i•er, -i•est 1.** Abounding or rising in waves: *a wavy sea.* **2.** Marked by or moving in a wavelike form. **3.** Having curls, curves, or undulations: *wavy hair.* —**wav′i•ly** *adv.* —**wav′i•ness** *n.*

wax[1] (wăks) ►*n.* **1a.** Any of various natural, oily or greasy heat-sensitive substances, such as beeswax, consisting of hydrocarbons or fats. **b.** Cerumen. **2.** A preparation containing wax used for polishing. ►*v.* To treat or polish with wax. [< OE *weax.*]

wax[2] (wăks) ►*v.* **1.** To increase gradually in size, amount, intensity, or degree. **2.** To show an increasing illuminated area from new moon to full moon. **3.** To grow or become: *a speaker waxing eloquent.* [< OE *weaxan.*]

wax bean ►*n.* A variety of string bean having yellow pods.

wax•en (wăk′sən) ►*adj.* **1.** Made of wax. **2.** Pale or smooth as wax: *waxen skin.*

wax myrtle ►*n.* An aromatic evergreen shrub of the SE US, having small berrylike fruit with a waxy coating.

wax•wing (wăks′wĭng′) ►*n.* Any of several crested birds having grayish-brown plumage and waxy red tips on the wing feathers.

wax•work (wăks′wûrk′) ►*n.* **1.** A figure made of wax, esp. a life-size wax effigy of a famous person. **2. waxworks** *(takes sing. or pl. v.)* An exhibition of wax figures.

wax•y (wăk′sē) ►*adj.* **-i•er, -i•est 1.** Resembling wax, as in texture. **2.** Full of or covered with wax. —**wax′i•ness** *n.*

way (wā) ►*n.* **1.** A road, route, path, or passage that leads from one place to another. **2.** Space to proceed. **3.** A usual or customary course of action or state of affairs. **4.** Progress or advancement in accomplishing a goal: *worked her way up.* **5.** A course of action: *the easy way out.* **6.** A manner or method of doing: *no way to reach him.* **7.** A habit, characteristic, or tendency: *Things have a way of happening.* **8.** also **ways** (wāz) *(takes sing. v.) Informal* Distance: *The travelers have come a long way.* **9.** A specific direction: *He glanced my way.* **10.** An aspect or feature: *resembles his father in many ways.* **11.** Freedom to do as one wishes: *if I had my way.* **12.** An aptitude or a facility: *has a way with words.* **13.** A condition: *in a bad way financially.* **14.** Vicinity: *out our way.* —***idioms:*** **by the way** Incidentally. **by way of 1.** Through; via. **2.** As a means of: *by way of apology.* **out of the way 1.** In a remote location. **2.** Improper; amiss. **under way** In progress. [< OE *weg.*]

Usage: In American English *ways* is often used as an equivalent of *way* in phrases such as *a long ways to go.* The usage is not incorrect but is regarded as informal.

way•bill (wā′bĭl′) ►*n.* A document giving details and instructions relating to a shipment of goods.

way•far•er (wā′fâr′ər) ►*n.* One who travels, esp. on foot. [ME *weifarere.*] —**way′far′ing** *n. & adj.*

way•lay (wā′lā′) ►*v.* **-laid** (-lād′), **-lay•ing 1.** To lie in wait for and attack from ambush. See Syns at **ambush. 2.** To accost or intercept. —**way′lay′er** *n.*

Wayne (wān), **Anthony.** 1745–96. Amer. Revolutionary general.

-ways ►*suff.* Way, manner, direction, or position: *sideways.* [ME.]

ways and means (wāz) ►*pl.n.* Methods and resources available to accomplish an end, esp. to meet expenses.

way•side (wā′sīd′) ►*n.* The side of a road.

way station ►*n.* A station between principal stations on a route, as of a railroad.

way•ward (wā′wərd) ►*adj.* **1.** Disobedient; willful: *a wayward child.* **2.** Capricious. [< ME *awaiward,* turned away.] —**way′ward•ly** *adv.* —**way′ward•ness** *n.*

WBC ►*abbr.* white blood cell

WbN ►*abbr.* west by north

WbS ►*abbr.* west by south

WC ►*abbr.* water closet

WCTU ►*abbr.* Woman's Christian Temperance Union

we (wē) ►*pron.* **1.** Used to indicate the speaker or writer along with another or others as the subject. **2.** Used instead of *I,* esp. by a sovereign or by a writer. [< OE *wē.*]

Usage: When the pronoun is followed by an appositive noun phrase, the form *us* is frequently encountered where grammatical correctness would require *we,* as in *Us owners* (properly *We owners*) *will have something to say about the contract.* Less frequently, *we* is substituted for *us,* as in *For we students, it's a no-win situation.* Avoid both usages. See Usage Note at **I**[1].

weak (wēk) ►*adj.* **-er, -est 1.** Lacking physical strength, energy, or vigor; feeble. **2.** Likely to fail under pressure, stress, or strain. **3.** Lacking strength of character or will. **4.** Lacking the proper strength or amount of ingredients: *weak coffee.* **5.** Unable to function normally or fully: *a weak heart.* **6.** Lacking aptitude or skill. **7.** Lacking persuasiveness: *a weak argument.* **8.** Lacking power or intensity: *weak light; a weak voice.* **9.** Unstressed or unaccented, as a syllable. [< ON *veikr,* pliant.]

weak•en (wē′kən) ►*v.* To make or become weak or weaker.

weak•fish (wēk′fĭsh′) ►*n.* A marine food and game fish of North American Atlantic waters. [Obsolete Du. *weekvis.*]

weak interaction ►*n.* A fundamental interaction between elementary particles that is responsible for some particle and nuclear decay and for neutrino absorption and emission.

weak-kneed (wēk′nēd′) ►*adj.* Lacking strength of character or purpose.

weak•ling (wēk′lĭng) ►*n.* One of weak constitution or character.

weak•ly (wēk′lē) ►*adj.* **-li•er, -li•est.** Feeble; weak. ►*adv.* In a weak manner.

weak•ness (wēk′nĭs) ►*n.* **1.** The condition or quality of being weak. **2.** A personal defect or failing. **3.** A special fondness or liking: *a weakness for chocolate.*

weal[1] (wēl) ►*n.* Prosperity; well-being. [< OE *wela.*]

weal[2] (wēl) ►*n.* A welt or bump. [< WALE.]

weald (wēld) ►*n. Chiefly Brit.* **1.** A woodland. **2.** An area of open rolling upland. [< OE.]

wealth (wĕlth) ►*n.* **1a.** An abundance of valuable material possessions or resources; riches. **b.** The state of being rich; affluence. **2.** All goods and resources having economic value. [< OE *wela.*]

wealth•y (wĕl′thē) ►*adj.* **-i•er, -i•est.** Having wealth; rich; prosperous. See Syns at **rich.**

wean (wēn) ►*v.* **1.** To accustom (the young of a mammal) to take nourishment other than by suckling. **2.** To rid of a habit or interest: *weaned herself from cigarettes.* **3.** *Informal* To be raised on: *weaned on good literature.* [< OE *wenian.*]

weap•on (wĕp′ən) ►*n.* **1.** An instrument of attack or defense in combat. **2.** A means used to defend against or defeat another. [< OE *wǣpen.*]

weap•on•ry (wĕp′ən-rē) ►*n.* Weapons collectively.

wear (wâr) ►*v.* **wore** (wôr, wōr), **worn** (wôrn, wōrn), **wear•ing 1.** To carry or have on the person: *wear a jacket.* **2.** To have habitually on the person: *wear glasses; wear a beard.* **3.** To display in one's appearance: *wears a smile.* **4.** To bear or maintain in a particular manner: *wears her hair long.* **5a.** To damage, erode, or consume by long or hard use: *shoes worn down at the heels.* **b.** To show the effect of such use: *The tires are starting to wear.* **6.** To produce by constant use or exposure: *wore hollows in the steps.* **7.** To fatigue, weary, or exhaust: *criticism that wore her patience.* **8.** To last under continual or hard use: *a fabric that wears well.* **9.** To pass gradually or tediously: *The hours wore on.* —***phrasal verbs:*** **wear down** To break down or exhaust by relentless pressure or resistance. **wear off** To diminish gradually in effect. **wear out 1.** To make or become unusable through long or heavy use. **2.** To use up or consume gradually. ►*n.* **1.** The act of wearing or the state of being worn; use. **2.** Clothing, esp. of a particular kind or for a particular use: *men's wear; evening wear.* **3.** Gradual impairment or diminution resulting from use or attrition: *The rug is beginning to show wear.* **4.** The ability to withstand use; durability. [< OE *werian.*] —**wear′a•ble** *adj.* —**wear′er** *n.*

wear and tear (târ) ►*n.* Damage or depreciation resulting from ordinary use.

wea•ri•less (wîr′ē-lĭs) ►*adj.* Displaying or feeling no fatigue. See Syns at **tireless.**

wea•ri•some (wîr′ē-səm) ►*adj.* Causing fatigue; tedious. —**wea′ri•some•ly** *adv.* —**wea′ri•some•ness** *n.*

wea•ry (wîr′ē) ►*adj.* **-ri•er, -ri•est 1.** Tired. **2.** Expressive of fatigue: *a weary smile.* **3.** Exhausted of tolerance; impatient: *weary of delays.* ►*v.* **wea•ried** (wîr′ēd), **wea•ry•ing.** To make or become weary. [< OE *wērig.*] —**wea′ri•ly** *adv.* —**wea′ri•ness** *n.*

wea•sel (wē′zəl) ►*n.* **1.** Any of several carnivorous mammals having a long slender body, a long tail, and short legs. **2.** A sneaky or treacherous person. ►*v.* To be evasive; equivocate. [< OE *wesle.*]

weath•er (wĕ*th*′ər) ►*n.* **1.** The state of the atmosphere at a given time and place with respect to temperature, moisture, wind velocity, and barometric pressure. **2.** Bad, rough, or stormy atmospheric conditions. ►*v.* **1.** To expose to or withstand the action of the weather. **2.** To show the effects of exposure to the weather. **3.** To come through safely; survive. [< OE *weder.*] —**weath′ered** *adj.*

weath•er-beat•en (wĕ*th*′ər-bēt′n) ►*adj.* **1.** Worn by exposure to the weather. **2.** Tanned and coarsened from being outdoors: *a weather-beaten face.*

weath•er•board (wĕ*th*′ər-bôrd′, -bōrd′) ►*n.* See **clapboard.**

weath•er-bound (wĕ*th*′ər-bound′) ►*adj.* Delayed, halted, or kept indoors by bad weather.

weath•er•cock (wĕ*th*′ər-kŏk′) ►*n.* **1.** A weathervane, esp. one in the form of a rooster. **2.** One that is fickle.

weath•er•ing (wĕ*th*′ər-ĭng) ►*n.* Any of the chemical or mechanical processes by which rocks exposed to the weather break down.

weath•er•ize (wĕ*th*′ə-rīz′) ►*v.* **-ized, -iz•ing.** To protect against cold weather, as with insulation.

weath•er•man (wĕ*th*′ər-măn) ►*n.* A man who reports and forecasts the weather.

weath•er•proof (wĕ*th*′ər-pro͞of′) ►*adj.* Capable of withstanding exposure to weather without damage. —**weath′er•proof′** *v.*

weather stripping ►*n.* A narrow piece of material installed around doors and windows to protect an interior from external extremes in temperature. —**weath′er-strip′** (wĕ*th*′ər-strĭp′) *v.*

weath•er•vane (wĕ*th*′ər-vān′) ►*n.* A device that pivots on a vertical spindle to indicate wind direction.

weave (wēv) ►*v.* **wove** (wōv), **wo•ven** (wō′vən), **weav•ing 1a.** To make (cloth) by interlacing the threads of the weft and the warp on a loom. **b.** To interlace (e.g., threads) into cloth. **2.** To construct by interlacing or interweaving strips or strands of material: *weave a basket.* **3.** To combine (elements) into a whole. **4.** To interpose (another element) throughout a complex whole: *wove folk tunes into the symphony.* **5.** To spin (a web). **6.** *p.t.* **weaved** To move or progress by winding in and out or from side to side: *weaved through the traffic.* ►*n.* A pattern or method of weaving: *a twill weave.* [< OE *wefan.*] —**weav′er** *n.*

web (wĕb) ►*n.* **1.** A woven fabric, esp. one on a loom or just removed from it. **2.** A latticed or woven structure. **3.** A structure of threadlike filaments spun by spiders. **4.** Something intricately contrived, esp. something that ensnares or entangles: *a web of lies.* **5.** A complex network: *a web of telephone wires.* **6.** A membrane or fold of skin connecting the toes, as of certain amphibians and birds. **7.** The vane of a feather. **8.** often **Web** *Comp. Sci.* The World Wide Web. ▶*v.* **webbed, web•bing 1.** To provide or cover with a web. **2.** To ensnare in or as if in a web. [< OE.] —**webbed** *adj.*

web•bing (wĕb′ĭng) ▶*n.* A strong, narrow, closely woven fabric used esp. for seat belts and harnesses or in upholstery.

web•cast (wĕb′kăst′) ▶*n.* A broadcast of an event over the World Wide Web.

We•ber (vā′bər), Baron **Karl Maria Friedrich Ernst von.** 1786–1826. German composer.

We•ber[1] (vā′bər), **Max.** 1864–1920. German sociologist.

We•ber[2] (wĕb′ər), **Max.** 1881–1961. Russian-born Amer. painter.

web-foot•ed (wĕb′fo͝ot′ĭd) ▶*adj.* Having feet with webbed toes.

web•mas•ter (wĕb′măs′tər) ▶*n.* A person who develops, markets, or maintains websites.

web•page or **Web page** (wĕb′pāj′) ▶*n.* A document on the World Wide Web, often linked to other Web documents.

web•site or **Web site** (wĕb′sīt′) ▶*n.* A set of interconnected webpages, gen. located on the same server, prepared as a collection of information by a person or organization.

Web•ster (wĕb′stər), **Daniel.** 1782–1852. Amer. politician and orator.

Webster, John. 1580?–1625? English playwright.

Webster, Noah. 1758–1843. Amer. lexicographer.

web•worm (wĕb′wûrm′) ▶*n.* Any of various usu. destructive caterpillars that construct webs.

wed (wĕd) ▶*v.* **wed•ded, wed** or **wed•ded, wed•ding 1.** To take as a spouse; marry. **2.** To perform the marriage ceremony for. **3.** To unite closely. [< OE *weddian.*]

Wed. ▶*abbr.* Wednesday

wed•ding (wĕd′ĭng) ▶*n.* **1.** The ceremony or celebration of a marriage. **2.** The anniversary of a marriage. **3.** A close association or union: *a wedding of ideas.*

wedge (wĕj) ▶*n.* **1.** A piece of material, such as metal or wood, tapered for insertion in a narrow crevice and used for splitting, tightening, securing, or levering. **2a.** Something shaped like a wedge: *a wedge of pie.* **b.** *Regional* See **submarine** 2. See Regional Note at **submarine. 3.** Something that intrudes and causes division or disruption. ▶*v.* **wedged, wedg•ing 1.** To split or force apart with or as if with a wedge. **2.** To fix in place with a wedge. **3.** To crowd or squeeze into a limited space. [< OE *wecg.*]

wed•lock (wĕd′lŏk′) ▶*n.* The state of being married; matrimony. [< OE *wedlāc.*]

Wednes•day (wĕnz′dē, -dā′) ▶*n.* The 4th day of the week. [< OE *Wōdnesdæg.*]

wee (wē) ▶*adj.* **we•er, we•est 1.** Very small; tiny. See Syns at **small. 2.** Very early: *the wee hours.* [< OE *wǣge*, weight.]

weed[1] (wēd) ▶*n.* A plant considered undesirable, unattractive, or troublesome, esp. one growing where it is not wanted, as in a garden. ▶*v.* **1.** To clear of weeds. **2.** To eliminate as unsuitable or unwanted: *weed out unqualified applicants.* [< OE *wēod.*] —**weed′er** *n.* —**weed′y** *adj.*

weed[2] (wēd) ▶*n.* **1.** A token of mourning. **2. weeds** The black mourning clothes of a widow. [< OE *wǣd*, garment.]

week (wēk) ▶*n.* **1.** A period of seven days, esp. a period that begins on a Sunday and continues through the next Saturday. **2.** The part of a calendar week devoted to work, school, or business. [< OE *wicu.*]

week•day (wēk′dā′) ▶*n.* Any day of the week except Sunday, or often except Saturday and Sunday.

week•end (wēk′ĕnd′) ▶*n.* The end of the week, esp. the period from Friday evening through Sunday evening. ▶*v.* To spend the weekend.

week•ly (wēk′lē) ▶*adv.* **1.** Once a week. **2.** Every week. **3.** By the week. ▶*adj.* **1.** Occurring, appearing, or done once a week or every week. **2.** Computed by the week. ▶*n., pl.* **-lies.** A publication issued once a week.

week•night (wēk′nīt′) ▶*n.* A night of the week exclusive of Saturday and Sunday.

ween (wēn) ▶*v. Archaic* To think; suppose. [< OE *wēnan.*]

weep (wēp) ▶*v.* **wept** (wĕpt), **weep•ing 1.** To shed (tears) as an expression of emotion, esp. grief; cry. **2.** To ooze or exude (moisture). [< OE *wēpan.*] —**weep′er** *n.* —**weep′y** *adj.*

weep•ing (wē′pĭng) ▶*adj.* **1.** Shedding tears. **2.** Having slender drooping branches.

wee•vil (wē′vəl) ▶*n.* Any of numerous beetles that characteristically have a downward-curving snout and are destructive to nuts, fruits, stems, and roots. [< OE *wifel.*]

weft (wĕft) ▶*n.* **1.** The woof in a woven fabric. **2.** Woven fabric. [< OE *wefta.*]

weigh (wā) ▶*v.* **1.** To determine the weight of by or as if by using a scale or balance. **2.** To consider or balance in the mind; ponder. **3.** *Naut.* To raise (anchor). **4.** To be of a specific weight. **5.** To have consequence or importance: *The decision weighed heavily against us.* See Syns at **count[1]. 6.** To burden or be a burden on; oppress. —***phrasal verb:* weigh in 1.** To be weighed before or after an athletic contest. **2.** *Slang* To contribute to a discussion. [< OE *wegan.*]

weight (wāt) ▶*n.* **1.** A measure of the heaviness of an object. **2a.** The force with which an object is attracted to Earth or another celestial body, equal to the product of the object's mass and the acceleration of gravity. **b.** A unit measure of this force. **c.** A system of such measures. **3.** An object used principally to exert a force by virtue of its gravitational attraction to Earth, esp.: **a.** A solid used as a standard in weighing. **b.** An object used to hold something down. **c.** *Sports* A heavy object, such as a dumbbell, used in weightlifting. **4.** Burden: *the weight of responsibility.* **5.** The greater part; preponderance. **6.** Influence; importance. ▶*v.* **1.** To add heaviness or weight to. **2.** To load down; burden. [< OE *wiht.*]

weight•less (wāt′lĭs) ▶*adj.* **1.** Having little or no weight. **2.** Not experiencing the effects of gravity. —**weight′less•ness** *n.*

weight•lift•ing (wāt′lĭf′tĭng) ▶*n.* The lifting of heavy weights as an exercise or in athletic competition. —**weight lifter** *n.*

weight•y (wā′tē) ►*adj.* **-i•er, -i•est 1.** Heavy. **2.** Burdensome; oppressive. **3.** Of great consequence; momentous: *a weighty matter.* **4.** Having great power or influence: *a weighty argument.* —**weight′i•ly** *adv.* —**weight′i•ness** *n.*

weir (wîr) ►*n.* **1.** A fence placed in a stream to catch fish. **2.** A dam across a river or canal to raise, regulate, or divert the water. [< OE *wer.*]

weird (wîrd) ►*adj.* **-er, -est 1.** Of or suggestive of the supernatural; unearthly. **2.** Of an odd or unusual character; strange. [< OE *wyrd,* fate.] —**weird′ly** *adv.* —**weird′ness** *n.*

weird•o (wîr′dō) ►*n., pl.* **-oes** *Slang* A strange or eccentric person.

wel•come (wĕl′kəm) ►*adj.* **1.** Greeted, received, or accepted with pleasure. **2.** Cordially permitted or invited: *You are welcome to join us.* **3.** Freely granted one's courtesy: *"Thank you." "You're welcome."* ►*v.* **-comed, -com•ing 1.** To greet or entertain cordially or hospitably. **2.** To receive or accept gladly. [< OE *wilcuma,* welcome guest.] —**wel′come** *interj. & n.*

weld (wĕld) ►*v.* **1.** To join (metals) by applying heat and sometimes pressure. **2.** To bring into close association or union. ►*n.* A union or joint produced by welding. [< WELL[1], weld (obs.).] —**weld′er** *n.*

wel•fare (wĕl′fâr′) ►*n.* **1.** Health, happiness, or prosperity; well-being. **2.** Organized efforts, as by an organization, for the betterment of people in need. **3.** Financial or other aid provided, esp. by the government, to people in need. [< OE *wel faran,* fare well.]

welfare state ►*n.* A social system whereby the state assumes primary responsibility for the welfare of its citizens.

well[1] (wĕl) ►*n.* **1.** A deep hole or shaft sunk into the earth to obtain water, oil, gas, or brine. **2.** A container or reservoir for a liquid, such as ink. **3.** A spring or fountain. **4.** An abundant source: *a well of information.* **5.** An open space extending vertically through the floors of a building, as for stairs. **6.** An enclosure in a ship's hold for the pumps. ►*v.* **1.** To rise up. **2.** To pour forth. [< OE *welle.*]

well[2] (wĕl) ►*adv.* **bet•ter** (bĕt′ər), **best** (bĕst) **1.** In a good or proper manner. See Usage Note at **good. 2.** Skillfully: *dances well.* **3.** Satisfactorily: *slept well.* **4.** Successfully: *gets along well with people.* **5.** In a comfortable or affluent manner: *lived well.* **6.** Advantageously: *married well.* **7.** With reason or propriety: *can't very well say no.* **8.** In all likelihood: *You may well need a coat.* **9.** Prudently: *You would do well to obey.* **10.** In a close or familiar manner: *knew them well.* **11.** Favorably: *spoke well of them.* **12.** Thoroughly: *well cooked.* **13.** Perfectly: *I well understand your fears.* **14.** Considerably: *well past noon.* ►*adj.* **better, best 1.** In a satisfactory condition: *All is well.* **2a.** Healthy. **b.** Cured or healed. **3a.** Advisable: *It would be well not to ask.* **b.** Fortunate: *It is well that you stayed.* ►*interj.* **1.** Used to introduce a remark or fill a pause. **2.** Used to express surprise. —***idiom:* as well 1.** In addition. **2.** With equal effect: *I might as well go.* [< OE *wel.*]

we'll (wēl) ► **1.** We will. **2.** We shall.

Wel•land (wĕl′ənd) A city of SE Ontario, Canada, on the **Welland Ship Canal,** 44.4 km (27.6 mi), which connects Lakes Erie and Ontario. Pop. 45,448.

well-ap•point•ed (wĕl′ə-poin′tĭd) ►*adj.* Having a full array of suitable equipment or furnishings.

well-bal•anced (wĕl′băl′ənst) ►*adj.* **1.** Evenly proportioned, balanced, or regulated. **2.** Mentally stable; sensible or sound.

well-be•ing (wĕl′bē′ĭng) ►*n.* The state of being healthy, happy, or prosperous; welfare.

well•born (wĕl′bôrn′) ►*adj.* Of good lineage or stock.

well-bred (wĕl′brĕd′) ►*adj.* Of good upbringing; well-mannered and refined.

well-de•fined (wĕl′dĭ-fīnd′) ►*adj.* Having definite and distinct lines or features.

well-dis•posed (wĕl′dĭ-spōzd′) ►*adj.* Disposed to be kindly, friendly, or receptive.

well-fixed (wĕl′fĭkst′) ►*adj. Informal* Financially secure; well-to-do.

well-found•ed (wĕl′foun′dĭd) ►*adj.* Based on sound judgment, reasoning, or evidence.

well-groomed (wĕl′gro͞omd′) ►*adj.* **1.** Neat and clean in dress and personal appearance. **2.** Carefully tended or cared for.

well-ground•ed (wĕl′groun′dĭd) ►*adj.* **1.** Adequately versed in a subject. **2.** Having a sound basis; well-founded.

well-heeled (wĕl′hēld′) ►*adj.* Wealthy.

Wel•ling•ton (wĕl′ĭng-tən) The capital of New Zealand, on S North I. Pop. 150,100.

Wellington, First Duke of. Arthur Wellesley. "the Iron Duke." 1769–1852. British general and politician.

well-in•ten•tioned (wĕl′ĭn-tĕn′shənd) ►*adj.* Marked by or having good intentions.

well-knit (wĕl′nĭt′) ►*adj.* Strongly knit, esp. strongly and firmly constructed.

well-man•nered (wĕl′măn′ərd) ►*adj.* Polite.

well-mean•ing (wĕl′mē′nĭng) ►*adj.* Well-intentioned.

well•ness (wĕl′nĭs) ►*n.* The condition of good physical and mental health, esp. when maintained by proper diet and exercise.

well-nigh (wĕl′nī′) ►*adv.* Nearly; almost.

well-off (wĕl′ôf′, -ŏf′) ►*adj.* **1.** Well-to-do. **2.** In fortunate circumstances.

well-read (wĕl′rĕd′) ►*adj.* Knowledgeable through having read extensively.

well-round•ed (wĕl′roun′dĭd) ►*adj.* Well-balanced in a range or variety of aspects.

Wells (wĕlz), **H(erbert) G(eorge).** 1866–1946. British writer.

Wells, Ida Bell. 1862–1931. Amer. journalist and reformer.

Ida B. Wells

well-spo•ken (wĕl′spō′kən) ►*adj.* **1.** Chosen or expressed with aptness or propriety. **2.** Courteous in speech.
well•spring (wĕl′sprĭng′) ►*n.* **1.** The source of a stream or spring. **2.** A source; origin.
well-timed (wĕl′tīmd′) ►*adj.* Occurring at an opportune time.
well-to-do (wĕl′tə-do͞o′) ►*adj.* Prosperous; affluent; well-off.
well-turned (wĕl′tûrnd′) ►*adj.* **1.** Shapely: *a well-turned ankle.* **2.** Concisely or aptly expressed: *a well-turned phrase.*
well-wish•er (wĕl′wĭsh′ər) ►*n.* One who extends good wishes to another.
well-worn (wĕl′wôrn′, -wōrn′) ►*adj.* **1.** Showing signs of much wear or use. **2.** Trite.
welsh (wĕlsh, wĕlch) ►*v.* **welshed, welsh•ing** *Informal* **1.** To swindle a person by not paying a debt or wager. **2.** To fail to fulfill an obligation. [?] —**welsh′er** *n.*
Welsh ►*n.* **1.** The people of Wales. **2.** The Celtic language of Wales. —**Welsh** *adj.* —**Welsh′man** *n.* —**Welsh′wom′an** *n.*
Welsh cor•gi (kôr′gē) ►*n.* A dog of a breed originating in Wales, having a long body, short legs, and a foxlike head. [Welsh.]
Welsh rabbit also **Welsh rare•bit** (râr′bĭt) ►*n.* A dish made of melted cheese and sometimes ale, served hot over toast or crackers.
welt (wĕlt) ►*n.* **1.** A usu. leather strip stitched into a shoe between the sole and the upper. **2.** A tape or covered cord sewn into a seam as reinforcement or trimming. **3.** A ridge or bump on the skin caused by a blow or an allergic reaction. ►*v.* **1.** To reinforce or trim with a welt. **2.** To flog. [ME *welte.*]
wel•ter (wĕl′tər) ►*n.* **1.** A confused mass; jumble. **2.** Confusion; turmoil. ►*v.* **1.** To wallow or toss about, as in mud or high seas. **2.** To lie soaked, as in blood. **3.** To roll and surge, as the sea. [< ME *welteren.*]
wel•ter•weight (wĕl′tər-wāt′) ►*n.* A boxer weighing from 136 to 147 lbs., between a lightweight and a middleweight. [< *welter*, boxer.]
Wel•ty (wĕl′tē), **Eudora.** b. 1909. Amer. writer.
wen (wĕn) ►*n.* A harmless cyst containing sebaceous matter. [< OE.]
wench (wĕnch) ►*n.* **1.** A young woman or girl, esp. a peasant girl. **2.** A woman servant. **3.** A wanton woman. [< OE *wencel*, child.]
wend (wĕnd) ►*v.* To proceed on or along (one's way). [< OE *wendan.*]
went (wĕnt) ►*v.* P.t. of **go**[1].
wept (wĕpt) ►*v.* P.t. and p.part. of **weep.**
were (wûr) ►*v.* **1.** 2nd pers. sing. and pl. and 1st and 3rd pers. pl. p.t. of **be. 2.** P. subjunctive of **be.**
we're (wîr) ► We are.
were•n't (wûrnt, wûr′ənt) ► Were not.
were•wolf also **wer•wolf** (wâr′wo͝olf′, wîr′-, wûr′-) ►*n.* In folklore, a person capable of assuming the form of a wolf. [< OE *werewulf* : *wer*, man + *wulf*, wolf.]
wert (wûrt) ►*v. Archaic* 2nd pers. sing. p.t. of **be.**
We•ser (vā′zər) A river, about 483 km (300 mi), of central and NW Germany, flowing to the North Sea.
Wes•ley (wĕs′lē, wĕz′-), **John.** 1703–91. British founder of Methodism (1738).
Wes•sex (wĕs′ĭks) A region and ancient Anglo-Saxon kingdom of S England.
west (wĕst) ►*n.* **1a.** The direction opposite to the earth's axial rotation; the general direction of sunset. **b.** The compass point 270° clockwise from due north. **2.** often **West** The western part of a region or country. **3.** often **West** Europe and the Western Hemisphere. ►*adj.* **1.** To, toward, of, or in the west. **2.** Coming from the west: *a west wind.* ►*adv.* In, from, or toward the west. [< OE.] —**west′ward** *adj. & adv.* —**west′ward•ly** *adj. & adv.* —**west′wards** *adv.*
West, Benjamin. 1738–1820. Amer. painter.
West Bank. A disputed territory of SW Asia between Israel and Jordan W of the Jordan R.; occupied by Israel since 1967.
west•er•ly (wĕs′tər-lē) ►*adj.* **1.** Situated toward the west. **2.** From the west: *westerly winds.* —**west′er•ly** *adv.*
west•ern (wĕs′tərn) ►*adj.* **1.** Of, in, or toward the west. **2.** From the west: *western breezes.* **3.** often **Western** Of or characteristic of western regions or the West. ►*n.* often **Western** A novel, film, or television or radio program having themes or settings characteristic of the American West. [< OE *westerne.*]
west•ern•er also **West•ern•er** (wĕs′tər-nər) ►*n.* A native or inhabitant of the west, esp. the W US.
Western Hemisphere. The half of the earth comprising North America, Central America, and South America.
west•ern•ize (wĕs′tər-nīz′) ►*v.* **-ized, -iz•ing.** To convert to the customs of Western civilization. —**west′ern•i•za′tion** *n.*
Western Sahara also **Spanish Sahara.** A region of NW Africa on the Atlantic coast.
Western Samoa. See **Samoa**[2].
West Germany. A former country (1945–90) of central Europe bordering on the North Sea; reunified with East Germany to form Germany. —**West German** *adj. & n.*
West Indies. An archipelago between SE North America and N South America, separating the Caribbean Sea from the Atlantic and including the Greater Antilles, the Lesser Antilles, and the Bahama Is. —**West Indian** *adj. & n.*
West•pha•lia (wĕst-fāl′yə, -fā′lē-ə) A historical region and former duchy of W-central Germany east of the Rhine R. —**West•pha′lian** *adj. & n.*
West Virginia. A state of the E-central US. Cap. Charleston. Pop. 1,801,625. —**West Virginian** *adj. & n.*
wet (wĕt) ►*adj.* **wet•ter, wet•test 1.** Covered or soaked with a liquid, such as water. **2.** Not yet dry or firm: *wet paint.* **3.** Rainy or foggy. **4.** *Informal* Allowing the sale of alcoholic beverages: *a wet county.* ►*n.* **1.** Moisture. **2.** Rainy weather. ►*v.* **wet** or **wet•ted, wet•ting.** To make or become wet. —***idiom:*** **all wet** *Slang* Entirely mistaken. [< OE *wǣt.*] —**wet′ly** *adv.* —**wet′ness** *n.*
wet blanket ►*n. Informal* One that discourages enjoyment or enthusiasm.
weth•er (wĕth′ər) ►*n.* A castrated ram. [< OE.]
wet•land (wĕt′lănd′) ►*n.* A lowland area, as a marsh, that is saturated with moisture.
wet nurse ►*n.* A woman who suckles another woman's child.

wet•suit also **wet suit** (wĕt′so͞ot′) ►*n.* A tight-fitting permeable suit worn in cold water to retain body heat.

we've (wēv) ► We have.

Wey•den (wīd′n, vīd′n), **Rogier van der.** 1400?–64. Flemish painter.

WH ►*abbr.* watt-hour

whack (hwăk, wăk) ►*v.* To strike with a sharp blow; slap. ►*n.* **1.** A sharp resounding blow. **2.** The sound made by a whack. —***idiom:* out of whack** *Informal* Not functioning correctly. [Prob. imit.]

whack•y (hwăk′ē, wăk′ē) ►*adj. Slang* Var. of **wacky.**

whale[1] (hwāl, wāl) ►*n.* **1.** Any of an order of often very large marine mammals having flippers, a tail with horizontal flukes, and one or two blowholes for breathing. **2.** *Informal* An impressive example: *a whale of a story.* ►*v.* **whaled, whal•ing.** To engage in the hunting of whales. [< OE *hwæl.*]

whale[2] (hwāl, wāl) ►*v.* **whaled, whal•ing.** To strike repeatedly; thrash. [?]

whale•boat (hwāl′bōt′, wāl′-) ►*n.* A long rowboat, pointed at both ends and formerly used in whaling.

whale•bone (hwāl′bōn′, wāl′-) ►*n.* **1.** The elastic horny material forming the fringed plates that hang from the upper jaw of certain whales and strain plankton from the water. **2.** An object made of this material.

whal•er (hwā′lər, wā′-) ►*n.* **1.** One who hunts whales. **2.** A ship used in hunting whales. **3.** A whaleboat.

wham (hwăm, wăm) ►*n.* **1.** A forceful resounding blow. **2.** The sound of such a blow; thud. ►*v.* **whammed, wham•ming.** To strike with resounding impact. [Imit.]

wham•my (hwăm′ē, wăm′ē) ►*n., pl.* **-mies** *Slang* A supernatural spell for causing misfortune; hex. [Perh. < WHAM.]

wharf (hwôrf, wôrf) ►*n., pl.* **wharves** (hwôrvz, wôrvz) or **wharfs.** A landing place or pier where ships may tie up and load or unload. [< OE *hwearf.*]

wharf•age (hwôr′fĭj, wôr′fĭj) ►*n.* **1.** The use of a wharf. **2.** The charges for this usage.

Whar•ton (hwôr′tn, wôr′-), **Edith Newbold Jones.** 1862–1937. Amer. writer.

Edith Wharton

what (hwŏt, hwŭt, wŏt, wŭt; hwət, wət *when unstressed*) ►*pron.* **1a.** Which thing or which particular one of many: *What are you having for dinner?* **b.** Which kind, character, or designation: *What are these objects?* **c.** One of how much value or significance: *What are possessions to a dying man?* **2a.** That which; the thing that: *Listen to what I tell you.* **b.** Whatever thing that: *come what may.* **3.** *Informal* Something: *I'll tell you what.* See Usage Note at **which.** ►*adj.* **1.** Which one or ones: *What train do I take?* **2.** Whatever: *They soon repaired what damage had been done.* **3.** How great: *What a fool!* ►*adv.* How much; how: *What does it matter?* ►*interj.* Used to express surprise or incredulity. [< OE *hwæt.*]

what•ev•er (hwŏt-ĕv′ər, hwŭt-, wŏt-, wŭt-) ►*pron.* **1.** Everything or anything that: *Do whatever you please.* **2.** No matter what: *Whatever happens, we'll meet here tonight.* **3.** *Informal* What: *Whatever does he mean?* ►*adj.* Of any number or kind; any: *Whatever requests you make will be granted.*

Usage: Both *whatever* and *what ever* can be used in sentences such as *Whatever* (or *What ever*) *made her say that?* The same is true of the forms *whoever, whenever, wherever,* and *however* when these expressions are used similarly. In adjectival uses only the one-word form is used: *Take whatever* (not *what ever*) *books you need.*

what•not (hwŏt′nŏt′, hwŭt′-, wŏt′-, wŭt′-) ►*n.* **1.** An unspecified object or article. **2.** A set of open shelves for ornaments.

what•so•ev•er (hwŏt′sō-ĕv′ər, hwŭt′-, wŏt′-, wŭt′-) ►*pron. & adj.* Whatever.

wheat (hwēt, wēt) ►*n.* **1.** A cereal grass widely cultivated for its commercially important edible grain. **2.** The grain of this plant, ground to produce flour. [< OE *hwǣte.*] —**wheat′en** *adj.*

wheat germ ►*n.* The vitamin-rich embryo of the wheat kernel, used as a cereal or food supplement.

Wheat•ley (hwēt′lē, wēt′-), **Phillis.** 1753?–84. African-born Amer. poet.

whee•dle (hwēd′l, wēd′l) ►*v.* **-dled, -dling.** To persuade, attempt to persuade, or obtain by flattery or guile; cajole. [?] —**whee′dler** *n.* —**whee′dling•ly** *adv.*

wheel (hwēl, wēl) ►*n.* **1.** A solid disk or rigid circular ring connected by spokes to a hub, designed to turn around an axle passed through the center. **2.** Something resembling a wheel in appearance or movement. **3.** Something having a wheel as its principal part: *a steering wheel.* **4. wheels** Forces that provide energy, movement, or direction: *the wheels of commerce.* **5.** A revolution or rotation around an axis; turn. **6. wheels** *Slang* A motor vehicle. **7.** *Slang* One with power or influence: *A big wheel at the bank.* ►*v.* **1.** To roll, move, or transport on or as if on wheels. **2.** To turn around or as if around a central axis; revolve or rotate. **3.** To whirl around, changing direction; pivot. [< OE *hwēol.*]

wheel•bar•row (hwēl′băr′ō, wēl′-) ►*n.* A one- or two-wheeled vehicle with handles at the rear, used to carry small loads.

wheel•base (hwēl′bās′, wēl′-) ►*n.* The distance from front to rear axle in a motor vehicle, usu. expressed in inches.

wheel•chair (hwēl′châr′, wēl′-) ►*n.* A chair mounted on large wheels for the use of a sick or disabled person.

wheel•er (hwē′lər, wē′-) ►*n.* **1.** One that wheels. **2.** Something that moves on or is

equipped with wheels: *a three-wheeler.*
wheel•er-deal•er (hwē′lər-dē′lər, wē′-) ►*n. Informal* An aggressive or unscrupulous operator, esp. in business.
wheel•house (hwēl′hous′, wēl′-) ►*n.* See **pilothouse.**
wheel•wright (hwēl′rīt′, wēl′-) ►*n.* One who builds and repairs wheels.
wheeze (hwēz, wēz) ►*v.* **wheezed, wheez•ing.** To breathe with difficulty, producing a hoarse whistling sound. ►*n.* **1.** A wheezing sound. **2.** *Informal* An old joke. [Prob. < ON *hvæsa*, hiss.] —**wheez′er** *n.* —**wheez′i•ly** *adv.* —**wheez′i•ness** *n.* —**wheez′y** *adj.*
whelk (hwĕlk, wĕlk) ►*n.* Any of various large, mostly edible marine snails. [< OE *weoloc.*]
whelm (hwĕlm, wĕlm) ►*v.* **1.** To submerge. **2.** To overwhelm. [ME *whelmen*, overturn.]
whelp (hwĕlp, wĕlp) ►*n.* **1.** A young offspring of an animal, such as a dog or wolf. **2.** An impudent youth. ►*v.* To give birth to whelps. [< OE *hwelp.*]
when (hwĕn, wĕn) ►*adv.* At what time: *When will we leave?* ►*conj.* **1.** At the time that: *in the spring, when the snow melts.* **2.** As soon as: *I'll call you when I get there.* **3.** Whenever: *When the wind blows, all the doors rattle.* **4.** Whereas; although: *playing when she should have been studying.* ►*pron.* What or which time: *Since when are you the expert?* ►*n.* The time or date: *the where and when of the meeting.* [< OE *hwenne.*]
Usage: In informal style *when* is often used after *be* in definitions: *A dilemma is when you don't know which way to turn.* The construction is useful, but it is widely regarded as incorrect or as unsuitable for formal discourse.
whence (hwĕns, wĕns) ►*adv.* **1.** From what place: *Whence came this traveler?* **2.** From what origin or source: *Whence comes this feast?* ►*conj.* By reason of which: *had the same name, whence the error.* [< OE.]
when•ev•er (hwĕn-ĕv′ər, wĕn-) ►*adv.* **1.** At whatever time. **2.** When. See Usage Note at **whatever.** ►*conj.* **1.** At whatever time that. **2.** Every time that: *breaks whenever it rains.*
when•so•ev•er (hwĕn′sō-ĕv′ər, wĕn′-) ►*adv. & conj.* Whenever.
where (hwâr, wâr) ►*adv.* **1.** At or in what place or position: *Where is the telephone?* **2.** From what place or source: *Where did you get this idea?* **3.** To what place or end: *Where is this argument leading?* ►*conj.* **1.** At what or which place: *moved to the city, where jobs are available.* **2a.** In or to a place in which: *Put it where it belongs. Let's go where it's quieter.* **b.** Wherever: *Where there's smoke, there's fire.* ►*n.* **1.** The place or occasion: *the where and when of the performance.* **2.** What place, source, or cause: *Where are you from?* [< OE *hwǣr.*]
Usage: When *where* is used to refer to a point of origin, the preposition *from* is required: *Where did she come from?* When it is used to refer to a point of destination, the preposition *to* is generally superfluous: *Where is she going?* (preferable to *going to*). When it is used to refer to the place at which an event or a situation is located, the use of *at* is widely regarded as regional or colloquial: *Where is the station?* (not *Where is the station at?*).
where•a•bouts (hwâr′ə-bouts′, wâr′-) ►*adv.* About where; in, at, or near what location: *Whereabouts do you live?* ►*n. (takes sing. or pl. v.)* Approximate location: *Her whereabouts are still unknown.*
where•as (hwâr-ăz′, wâr-) ►*conj.* **1.** It being the fact that; inasmuch as. **2.** While at the same time. **3.** While on the contrary.
where•at (hwâr-ăt′, wâr-) ►*conj.* **1.** Toward or at which. **2.** Whereupon.
where•by (hwâr-bī′, wâr-) ►*conj.* In accordance with which; by or through which.
where•fore (hwâr′fôr′, -fōr′, wâr′-) ►*adv.* **1.** For what reason; why. **2.** Therefore. ►*n.* A purpose or cause: *the whys and wherefores of your decision.*
where•in (hwâr-ĭn′, wâr-) ►*adv.* In what way; how: *Wherein have we sinned?* ►*conj.* **1.** In which location; where. **2.** During which.
where•of (hwâr-ŏv′, -ŭv′, wâr-) ►*conj.* **1.** Of what: *I know whereof I speak.* **2.** Of which or when: *ancient lore whereof much is lost.*
where•on (hwâr-ŏn′, -ôn′, wâr-) ►*adv. Archaic* On which or what.
where•so•ev•er (hwâr′sō-ĕv′ər, wâr′-) ►*conj.* Wherever.
where•to (hwâr′to͞o′, wâr′-) ►*adv.* To what place; toward what end. ►*conj.* To which.
where•up•on (hwâr′ə-pŏn′, -pôn′, wâr′-) ►*conj.* **1.** On which. **2.** Following which.
wher•ev•er (hwâr-ĕv′ər, wâr-) ►*adv.* **1.** In or to whatever place: *used red pencil wherever needed.* **2.** Where. See Usage Note at **whatever.** ►*conj.* In or to whichever place or situation: *goes wherever I go.*
where•with (hwâr′wĭth′, -wĭ*th*′, wâr′-) ►*conj.* By means of which.
where•with•al (hwâr′wĭ*th*-ôl′, -wĭth-, wâr′-) ►*n.* The necessary means, esp. financial means.
whet (hwĕt, wĕt) ►*v.* **whet•ted, whet•ting 1.** To sharpen (e.g., a knife); hone. **2.** To make more keen; stimulate. [< OE *hwettan.*]
wheth•er (hwĕ*th*′ər, wĕ*th*′-) ►*conj.* **1.** Used to introduce: **a.** One alternative: *We should find out whether the museum is open.* **b.** Alternative possibilities: *Whether she wins or loses, she can be proud.* **2.** Either: *He passed the test, whether by skill or luck.* [< OE *hwether.*]
whet•stone (hwĕt′stōn′, wĕt′-) ►*n.* A hard, fine-grained stone for honing tools.
whey (hwā, wā) ►*n.* The watery part of milk that separates from the curds, as in the process of making cheese. [< OE *hwæg.*]
which (hwĭch, wĭch) ►*pron.* **1.** What particular one or ones: *Which is your house?* **2.** The one or ones previously mentioned or implied: *my room, which is small and dark; the topic on which she spoke.* **3.** Whichever: *Choose which you like best.* **4.** A thing or circumstance that: *He left early, which was wise.* ►*adj.* **1.** What particular one or ones of a number of things or people: *Which part of town do you mean?* **2.** Any one or any number of; whichever: *Use which door you please.* **3.** Being the one or ones previously mentioned or implied: *It started to rain, at which point we ran.* [< OE *hwilc.*]
Usage: In its use to refer to the contents of sentences and clauses, *which* should be used only when it is preceded by its antecedent. When the antecedent follows, *what* should be used, particularly in formal style: *Still, he has not said he will withdraw, which is more sur-*

prising but *Still, what* (not *which*) *is more surprising, he has not said he will withdraw.* See Usage Note at **that.**

which•ev•er (hwĭch-ĕv′ər, wĭch-) ►*pron.* Whatever one or ones. ►*adj.* Being any one or number: *Take whichever items you please.*

which•so•ev•er (hwĭch′sō-ĕv′ər, wĭch′-) ►*pron. & adj.* Whichever.

whiff (hwĭf, wĭf) ►*n.* **1.** A slight gentle gust of air. **2a.** A brief passing odor carried in the air: *a whiff of perfume.* **b.** A minute trace. **3.** An inhalation, as of air or smoke. ►*v.* **1.** To waft. **2.** To smell or sniff. [Perh. alteration of ME *weffe,* offensive smell.]

whif•fle•tree (hwĭf′əl-trē, wĭf′-) ►*n. Regional* The pivoted horizontal crossbar to which the harness traces of a draft animal are attached. [< *whippletree.*]

Whig (hwĭg, wĭg) ►*n.* **1.** A member of an 18th- and 19th-cent. British political party opposed to the Tories. **2.** A supporter of the war against England during the American Revolution. **3.** A member of a 19th-century American political party formed to oppose the Democratic Party. [Prob. short for *Whiggamore,* one of a body of 17th-cent. Scottish rebels.] —**Whig′ger•y** *n.* —**Whig′gish** *adj.* —**Whig′gism** *n.*

while (hwīl, wīl) ►*n.* **1.** A period of time: *stay for a while.* **2.** The time, effort, or trouble taken in doing something: *It wasn't worth my while.* ►*conj.* **1.** As long as: *fun while it lasted.* **2.** Although: *While I like opera, I'm not a fanatic.* **3.** Whereas: *The soles are leather, while the uppers are canvas.* ►*v.* **whiled, whil•ing.** To spend (time) idly or pleasantly: *while away the hours.* [< OE *hwīl.*]

whi•lom (hwī′ləm, wī′-) ►*adj.* Former: *the whilom editor in chief.* ►*adv. Archaic* At a past time. [< OE *hwīlum,* at times.]

whilst (hwīlst, wīlst) ►*conj. Chiefly Brit.* While. [ME *whilest.*]

whim (hwĭm, wĭm) ►*n.* **1.** A sudden or capricious idea; fancy. **2.** Arbitrary thought or impulse: *governed by whim.* [< *whim-wham,* fanciful object.]

whim•per (hwĭm′pər, wĭm′-) ►*v.* To make soft whining sounds. [Prob. imit.] —**whim′per** *n.* —**whim′per•ing•ly** *adv.*

whim•si•cal (hwĭm′zĭ-kəl, wĭm′-) ►*adj.* **1.** Marked by playful whim or caprice; fanciful. **2.** Erratic in nature or behavior; capricious: *a whimsical personality.* See Syns at **arbitrary.** [< WHIMSY.] —**whim′si•cal′i•ty** (-kăl′ĭ-tē) *n.* —**whim′si•cal•ly** *adv.*

whim•sy also **whim•sey** (hwĭm′zē, wĭm′-) ►*n., pl.* **-sies** also **-seys 1.** An odd or fanciful idea; whim. **2.** A quaint or fanciful quality: *stories full of whimsy.* [Prob. < *whim-wham,* fanciful object.]

whine (hwīn, wīn) ►*v.* **whined, whin•ing 1.** To utter a plaintive, high-pitched sound, as in pain, fear, or supplication. **2.** To complain in a childish fashion. **3.** To make a steady, high-pitched noise: *jet engines whining.* [< OE *hwīnan,* make a whizzing sound.] —**whine** *n.* —**whin′er** *n.* —**whin′y** *adj.*

whin•ny (hwĭn′ē, wĭn′ē) ►*v.* **whin•nied** (hwĭn′ēd, wĭn′-), **whin•ny•ing.** To neigh softly, as a horse. —**whin′ny** *n.*

whip (hwĭp, wĭp) ►*v.* **whipped** or **whipt** (hwĭpt, wĭpt), **whip•ping 1.** To strike with repeated strokes, as with a strap or rod; lash. **2.** To punish by or as if by whipping. **3.** To drive, force, or compel by or as if by whipping. **4.** To beat (e.g., cream or eggs) into a froth or foam. **5.** *Informal* To snatch or remove in a sudden manner: *He whipped off his cap.* **6.** To wrap or bind (e.g., a rope) with twine to prevent unraveling or fraying. **7.** *Informal* To defeat; beat. **8.** To move swiftly or nimbly. **9.** To move like a whip; thrash: *branches whipping in the wind.* —***phrasal verb:* whip up 1.** To arouse; excite: *whip up enthusiasm.* **2.** *Informal* To prepare quickly: *whip up a light lunch.* ►*n.* **1.** A flexible instrument, esp. a rod or thong, used for driving animals or administering punishment. **2.** A whipping or lashing motion or stroke. **3.** A member of a legislative body charged by his or her party with enforcing party discipline and ensuring attendance. **4.** A dessert made of sugar and stiffly beaten egg whites or cream, often with fruit. [ME *wippen.*] —**whip′per** *n.*

whip•cord (hwĭp′kôrd′, wĭp′-) ►*n.* **1.** A worsted fabric with a distinct diagonal rib. **2.** A strong twisted or braided cord sometimes used in making whiplashes. **3.** Catgut.

whip•lash (hwĭp′lăsh′, wĭp′-) ►*n.* **1.** The lash of a whip. **2.** An injury to the cervical spine caused by an abrupt jerking motion of the head, either backward or forward.

whip•per•snap•per (hwĭp′ər-snăp′ər, wĭp′-) ►*n.* An insignificant and pretentious person. [< dial. *snippersnapper.*]

whip•pet (hwĭp′ĭt, wĭp′-) ►*n.* A swift, short-haired dog resembling the greyhound but smaller. [Prob. < WHIP.]

whip•ping boy (hwĭp′ĭng, wĭp′-) ►*n.* A scapegoat.

whip•poor•will (hwĭp′ər-wĭl′, wĭp′-) ►*n.* A brownish insect-eating nocturnal North American bird. [Imit. of its call.]

whip•saw (hwĭp′sô′, wĭp′-) ►*n.* A narrow two-person crosscut saw. ►*v.* **1.** To cut with a whipsaw. **2.** To defeat in two ways at once.

whip•stitch (hwĭp′stĭch′, wĭp′-) ►*v.* To sew with overcast stitches, as in finishing a fabric edge or binding two pieces of fabric together. —**whip′stitch′** *n.*

whipt (hwĭpt, wĭpt) ►*v.* P.t. and p.part. of **whip.**

whir (hwûr, wûr) ►*v.* **whirred, whir•ring.** To move so as to produce an airy vibrating sound. ►*n.* **1.** A whirring sound: *a whir of wings.* **2.** A flurry; bustle. [ME *whirren.*]

whirl (hwûrl, wûrl) ►*v.* **1.** To rotate or cause to rotate rapidly; spin. **2.** To wheel or pivot: *whirled around to face him.* **3.** To have the sensation of spinning; reel. **4.** To move or drive at high speed. ►*n.* **1.** A whirling or spinning motion. **2.** One that whirls or is whirled. **3.** A state of confusion; tumult. **4.** A swift succession or round of events: *the social whirl.* **5.** A state of giddiness or dizziness: *My head is in a whirl.* **6.** *Informal* **a.** A short trip or ride. **b.** A brief or experimental try: *give it a whirl.* [< ON *hvirfla.*] —**whirl′er** *n.*

whirl•i•gig (hwûr′lĭ-gĭg′, wûr′-) ►*n.* **1.** A toy, such as a pinwheel, that whirls. **2.** A merry-go-round. [ME *whirlegigge.*]

whirl•pool (hwûrl′po͞ol′, wûrl′-) ►*n.* **1.** A rapidly rotating current of water; vortex. **2.** A bathtub or pool having submerged jets of warm water.

whirl•wind (hwûrl′wĭnd′, wûrl′-) ►*n.* **1.** A rapidly rotating column of air, such as a tornado, dust devil, or waterspout. **2a.** A tumultuous rush. **b.** A destructive force. ►*adj.* Tumultuous or rapid: *a whirlwind campaign.*

whisk (hwĭsk, wĭsk) ►*v.* **1.** To move or cause to move with quick light sweeping motions. **2.** To whip (eggs or cream). **3.** To move lightly, nimbly, and rapidly. ►*n.* **1.** A quick light sweeping motion. **2.** A whiskbroom. **3.** A kitchen utensil for whipping foodstuffs. [ME *wisken.*]

whisk•broom (hwĭsk′bro͝om′, -bro͞om′, wĭsk′-) ►*n.* A small short-handled broom used esp. to brush clothes.

whisk•er (hwĭs′kər, wĭs′-) ►*n.* **1a. whiskers** The hair on a man's cheeks and chin. **b.** A single hair of a beard or mustache. **2.** One of the long stiff tactile bristles that grow near the mouth of most mammals. **3.** *Informal* A narrow margin: *lost by a whisker.* [ME *wisker* < *wisken*, whisk.] —**whisk′ered, whisk′er•y** *adj.*

whis•key also **-ky** (hwĭs′kē, wĭs′-) ►*n., pl.* **-keys** also **-kies 1.** An alcoholic liquor distilled from grain, such as corn, rye, or barley. **2.** A drink of whiskey. [< Sc.Gael. *uisce beatha*, aqua vitae.]

whis•per (hwĭs′pər, wĭs′-) ►*n.* **1.** Soft speech produced without full voice. **2.** Something uttered very softly. **3.** A rumor or hint: *whispers of scandal.* **4.** A low rustling or sighing sound. ►*v.* **1.** To speak softly. **2.** To tell secretly or privately. **3.** To make a soft rustling sound. [< OE *hwisprian.*] —**whis′per•er** *n.* —**whis′per•y** *adj.*

whist (hwĭst, wĭst) ►*n.* A card game similar to bridge. [< obsolete *whisk.*]

whis•tle (hwĭs′əl, wĭs′-) ►*v.* **1. -tled, -tling** To produce a clear, shrill or musical sound by forcing air through the teeth or pursed lips or by blowing on or through a device. **2.** To make a high-pitched sound when moving swiftly through the air: *The stone whistled past my head.* **3.** To produce by whistling: *whistle a tune.* ►*n.* **1.** A device or instrument for making whistling sounds by means of breath, forced air, or steam. **2.** A sound produced by a whistle or by whistling. —***idiom:* blow the whistle** *Slang* To expose a wrongdoing in the hope of bringing it to a halt. [< OE *hwistlian.*] —**whis′tler** *n.*

Whis•tler (hwĭs′lər, wĭs′-), **James Abbott McNeill.** 1834–1903. Amer. painter.

whistle stop ►*n.* **1.** A town at which a train stops only if signaled. **2.** An appearance of a political candidate in a small town, as on the rear platform of a train.

whit (hwĭt, wĭt) ►*n.* The least bit; iota. [< OE *wiht*, thing.]

white (hwīt, wīt) ►*n.* **1.** The achromatic color of maximum lightness; the color of objects that reflect nearly all light of all visible wavelengths. **2.** The white or whitish part, as of an egg. **3. whites** White trousers or a white outfit. **4.** also **White** A member of a racial group having light skin coloration, esp. one of European origin. ►*adj.* **whit•er, whit•est 1.** Being of the color white. **2.** Light-colored; pale. **3.** also **White** Of or belonging to a racial group having light skin coloration, esp. one of European origin. **4.** Not written on; blank. **5.** Unsullied; pure. **6.** Snowy: *a white Christmas.* **7.** Incandescent. [< OE *hwīt.*] —**whit′en** *v.* —**whit′en•er** *n.* —**white′ness** *n.*

White, Stanford. 1853–1906. Amer. architect.

White, T(erence) H(anbury). 1906–64. British writer.

white ant ►*n.* See **termite.**

white•bait (hwīt′bāt′, wīt′-) ►*n.* The young of various fishes, esp. the herring, considered a delicacy when fried.

white blood cell ►*n.* Any of the whitish nucleated cells in the blood that help protect the body from infection and disease.

white•cap (hwīt′kăp′, wīt′-) ►*n.* A wave with a crest of foam.

white-col•lar (hwīt′kŏl′ər, wīt′-) ►*adj.* Of or relating to workers whose work does not involve manual labor.

white dwarf ►*n.* A whitish star of low luminosity, small size, and very great density.

white elephant ►*n.* **1.** A rare, expensive possession that is a financial burden to maintain. **2.** Something useless or no longer wanted. **3.** A rare whitish form of the Asian elephant.

white feather ►*n.* A sign of cowardice.

white•fish (hwīt′fĭsh′, wīt′-) ►*n.* **1.** Any of various silvery freshwater food fishes. **2.** See **beluga** 2.

white flag ►*n.* A white cloth or flag signaling truce or surrender.

white gold ►*n.* An alloy of gold and nickel, sometimes also containing palladium or zinc, having a pale platinumlike color.

White•hall (hwīt′hôl′, wīt′-) ►*n.* The British civil service. [After *Whitehall*, a street in London, England.]

White•head (hwīt′hĕd′, wīt′-), **Alfred North.** 1861–1947. British mathematician and philosopher.

White•horse (hwīt′hôrs′, wīt′-) The capital of Yukon Terr., Canada, in the S part on the Yukon R. Pop. 14,814.

white-hot (hwīt′hŏt′, wīt′-) *adj.* **1.** So hot as to glow with a bright white light. **2.** Zealous, fervid.

White House ►*n.* **1.** The executive branch of the US government. **2.** The executive mansion of the US President.

white lead (lĕd) ►*n.* A heavy white poisonous compound of lead used in paint pigments.

white lie ►*n.* A trivial, harmless, or well-intentioned untruth.

white matter ►*n.* Whitish nerve tissue, esp. of the brain and spinal cord, consisting chiefly of nerve fibers with myelin sheaths.

White Mountains. A section of the Appalachian Mts. in N NH.

White Nile. A section of the Nile R. in E Africa flowing to Khartoum, where it joins the Blue Nile to form the Nile River proper.

white pine ►*n.* **1.** A timber tree of E North America, having durable, easily worked wood. **2.** The wood of this tree.

white sale ►*n.* A sale of household items, esp. bed sheets, towels, or curtains.

white sauce ►*n.* A sauce made with butter, flour, and milk, cream, or stock.

white slave ►*n.* A woman held unwillingly for prostitution. —**white slavery** *n.*

white•wash (hwīt′wŏsh′, -wôsh′, wīt′-) ►*n.* **1.** A mixture of lime and water, often with whiting, size, or glue added, used to whiten walls and fences. **2.** Concealment or palliation of flaws or failures. ▸*v.* **1.** To paint or coat with whitewash. **2.** To conceal or gloss over (e.g., wrongdoing). See Syns at **palliate.** —**white′wash′er** *n.*

white whale ▸*n.* A small toothed whale usu. of northern waters that is white when mature.

whith•er (hwĭ*th*′ər, wĭ*th*′-) ▸*adv.* To what place, result, or condition. ▸*conj.* **1.** To which specified place or position. **2.** Wherever. [< OE *hwider.*]

whit•ing¹ (hwī′tĭng, wī′-) ▸*n.* A pure white chalk ground and washed for use in paints, ink, and putty. [ME < *whiten*, whiten.]

whit•ing² (hwī′tĭng, wī′-) ▸*n., pl.* **-ing** or **-ings.** A codlike food fish of European Atlantic waters. [< MDu. *wijting.*]

whit•ish (hwī′tĭsh, wī′-) ▸*adj.* Somewhat white.

Whit•man (hwĭt′mən, wĭt′-), **Walt.** 1819–92. Amer. poet.

Whit•ney (hwĭt′nē, wĭt′-), **Eli.** 1765–1825. Amer. inventor of the cotton gin (1793).

Whitney, Mount. A peak, 4,420.7 m (14,494 ft), in the Sierra Nevada of E-central CA.

Whit•sun•day (hwĭt′sən-dē, -dā′, wĭt′-) ▸*n.* See **Pentecost.** [< OE *hwīta sunnandæg*, White Sunday.]

Whit•ti•er (hwĭt′ē-ər, wĭt′-), **John Greenleaf.** 1807–92. Amer. poet.

whit•tle (hwĭt′l, wĭt′l) ▸*v.* **-tled, -tling 1a.** To cut small bits or pare shavings from (a piece of wood). **b.** To fashion in this way. **2.** To reduce gradually: *whittled down my expenses.* [< OE *thwītan.*] —**whit′tler** *n.*

whiz also **whizz** (hwĭz, wĭz) ▸*v.* **whizzed, whiz•zing 1.** To make a whirring or hissing sound, as of an object speeding through air. **2.** To rush past. ▸*n., pl.* **whiz•zes 1.** A whizzing sound. **2.** *Informal* One who has remarkable skill: *a math whiz.* [Imit.]

who (ho͞o) ▸*pron.* **1.** What or which person or persons: *Who left?* **2.** The person or persons that: *The boy who came yesterday has gone.* [< OE *hwā.*]

Usage: The traditional rules that determine the use of *who* and *whom* are relatively simple. *Who* is used for a grammatical subject, where a nominative pronoun such as *I* or *he* would be appropriate, and *whom* is used elsewhere: *I met the man who is taking the job. I met the man whom the committee selected for the job.* • The grammatical rules governing the use of *who* and *whom* apply equally to *whoever* and *whomever.* See Usage Note at **else.**

WHO ▸*abbr.* World Health Organization

whoa (hwō, wō) ▸*interj.* Used as a command to stop, as to a horse.

who'd (ho͞od) ▸ **1.** Who would. **2.** Who had.

who•dun•it (ho͞o-dŭn′ĭt) ▸*n. Informal* A detective story. [< *who done it?.*]

who•ev•er (ho͞o-ĕv′ər) ▸*pron.* **1.** Whatever person or persons: *Whoever comes will be welcomed.* **2.** Who: *Whoever could have dreamed it?* See Usage Notes at **whatever, who.**

whole (hōl) ▸*adj.* **1.** Containing all parts; complete: *whole milk.* **2.** Not divided; in one unit: *a whole loaf.* **3.** Constituting the full amount, extent, or duration: *cried the whole time.* **4.** Not wounded, injured, or impaired. **5.** *Math.* Not fractional; integral. ▸*n.* **1.** All of the component parts or elements of a thing. **2.** A complete entity or system. —***idiom:* on the whole** In general. [< OE *hāl.*] —**whole′ness** *n.*

Syns: *whole, all, entire, total* **adj.**

whole•heart•ed (hōl′här′tĭd) ▸*adj.* Without reservation: *wholehearted approval of the idea.* —**whole′heart′ed•ly** *adv.*

whole note ▸*n.* A musical note having, in common time, the value of four beats.

whole number ▸*n.* **1.** A member of the set of positive integers and zero. **2.** A positive integer. **3.** An integer.

whole•sale (hōl′sāl′) ▸*n.* The sale of goods in large quantities, as for resale by a retailer. ▸*adj.* **1.** Of or engaged in the sale of goods at wholesale. **2.** Made or accomplished extensively and indiscriminately: *wholesale destruction.* ▸*v.* **-saled, -sal•ing.** To sell or be sold at wholesale. —**whole′sale′** *adv.* —**whole′sal′er** *n.*

whole•some (hōl′səm) ▸*adj.* **-som•er, -som•est 1.** Conducive to mental or physical well-being: *a wholesome diet.* **2.** Promoting mental, moral, or social health: *wholesome entertainment.* **3.** Healthy. —**whole′some•ly** *adv.* —**whole′some•ness** *n.*

whole-wheat (hōl′hwēt′, -wēt′) ▸*adj.* Made from the entire grain of wheat, including the bran.

who'll (ho͞ol) ▸ **1.** Who will. **2.** Who shall.

whol•ly (hō′lē, hōl′lē) ▸*adv.* **1.** Completely; entirely. **2.** Exclusively; solely.

whom (ho͞om) ▸*pron.* The objective case of **who.** See Usage Note at **who.**

whom•ev•er (ho͞om-ĕv′ər) ▸*pron.* The objective case of **whoever.** See Usage Note at **who.**

whom•so•ev•er (ho͞om′sō-ĕv′ər) ▸*pron.* The objective case of **whosoever.**

whoop (ho͞op, hwo͞op, wo͞op) ▸*n.* **1.** A loud cry of exultation or excitement. **2.** The paroxysmal gasp typical of whooping cough. ▸*v.* **1.** To utter with a whoop. See Syns at **shout. 2.** To gasp as with whooping cough. **3.** To chase, call, urge on, or drive with a whoop. [< OFr. *hopper*, to whoop.]

whoop•ing cough (ho͞o′pĭng, hwo͞o′-, wo͞o′-) ▸*n.* A highly contagious bacterial disease of the respiratory system, usu. affecting children and marked by spasms of coughing interspersed with deep noisy gasps.

whooping crane ▸*n.* A large, very rare North American crane having black and white plumage and a whooping cry.

whoops (hwo͝ops, wo͝ops, hwo͞ops, wo͞ops) also **woops** (wo͝ops, wo͞ops) ▸*interj.* Used to express apology or mild surprise.

whoosh (hwo͞osh, wo͞osh, hwo͝osh, wo͝osh) ▸*n.* **1.** A soft rushing sound. **2.** A swift movement or flow; rush. [Imit.] —**whoosh** *v.*

whop (hwŏp, wŏp) ▸*v.* **whopped, whop•ping 1.** To strike with a thudding blow. **2.** To defeat soundly; thrash. [ME *whappen.*] —**whop** *n.*

whop•per (hwŏp′ər, wŏp′-) ▸*n. Slang* **1.** Something exceptionally big or remarkable. **2.** A gross lie.

whop•ping (hwŏp′ĭng, wŏp′-) ▸*adj. Slang* Exceptionally large.

whore (hôr, hōr) ▸*n.* A prostitute. [< OE *hōre.*] —**whor′ish** *adj.*

whorl (hwôrl, wôrl, hwûrl, wûrl) ▸*n.* **1.** A form that coils or spirals; curl; swirl. **2.** *Bot.* An arrangement of three or more leaves, petals, or other organs radiating from a single node. [ME *whorle*.]

whorl

who's (ho͞oz) ▸ **1.** Who is. **2.** Who has.

whose (ho͞oz) ▸*adj.* **1.** The possessive form of **who. 2.** The possessive form of **which.** [< OE *hwæs*.]

Usage: *Whose* is acceptable on all levels as a possessive form for both persons and things: *The cabinet, whose decoration was typical of the Regency period, was filled with porcelain.* See Usage Note at **else.**

who•so•ev•er (ho͞o′sō-ĕv′ər) ▸*pron.* Whoever.

W-hr ▸*abbr.* watt-hour

why (hwī, wī) ▸*adv.* For what purpose, reason, or cause: *Why do birds sing?* ▸*conj.* **1.** The reason, cause, or purpose for which: *I know why you left.* **2.** *Informal* For which: *the reason why he's angry.* ▸*n., pl.* **whys.** The cause or reason. ▸*interj.* Used to express mild surprise, indignation, or impatience. [< OE *hwȳ*.]

WI ▸*abbr.* Wisconsin

W.I. ▸*abbr.* West Indies

Wic•ca (wĭk′ə) ▸*n.* A polytheistic Neo-Pagan nature religion whose central deity is a mother goddess. [< OE *wicca*, necromancer.] —**Wic′can** *adj. & n.*

Wich•i•ta (wĭch′ĭ-tô′) A city of S-central KS on the Arkansas R. Pop. 304,011.

wick (wĭk) ▸*n.* A cord or strand of woven fibers, as in a candle, that draws up fuel to the flame by capillary action. [< OE *wēoce*.] —**wick** *v.*

wick•ed (wĭk′ĭd) ▸*adj.* **-er, -est 1.** Evil by nature and in practice. **2.** Playfully mischievous: *a wicked prank.* **3.** Severe and distressing. [< OE *wicca*, sorcerer.] —**wick′ed•ly** *adv.* —**wick′ed•ness** *n.*

wick•er (wĭk′ər) ▸*n.* **1.** A long flexible twig, as of a willow, used in weaving baskets or furniture. **2.** Wickerwork. [ME *wiker*.]

wick•er•work (wĭk′ər-wûrk′) ▸*n.* Woven wicker.

wick•et (wĭk′ĭt) ▸*n.* **1.** A small door or gate, esp. one built into or near a larger one. **2.** A small, often grated window or opening. **3.** In cricket, either of the two sets of three stumps forming the bowler's target. **4.** An arch through which players try to drive their ball in croquet. [< ONFr. *wiket*.]

wick•i•up (wĭk′ē-ŭp′) ▸*n.* A frame hut covered with matting, as of bark or brush, used by certain nomadic Native Americans. [Fox *wiikiyaapi*, wigwam.]

wide (wīd) ▸*adj.* **wid•er, wid•est 1a.** Measured from side to side: *a ribbon two inches wide.* **b.** Extending over a large area from side to side; broad: *a wide road.* **2.** Great in extent or range: *a wide selection.* **3.** Fully open: *look with wide eyes.* **4.** Far from a goal or point: *a shot wide of the mark.* ▸*adv.* **-er, -est 1.** Extensively: *traveled far and wide.* **2.** To the full extent; completely. **3.** So as to miss a target; astray. [< OE *wīd*.] —**wide′ly** *adv.* —**wid′en** *v.* —**wide′ness** *n.*

wide-a•wake (wīd′ə-wāk′) ▸*adj.* **1.** Completely awake. **2.** Alert; watchful.

wide-eyed (wīd′īd′) ▸*adj.* **1.** With the eyes completely open, as in wonder. **2.** Innocent; credulous.

wide•spread (wīd′sprĕd′) ▸*adj.* **1.** Fully opened or extended. **2.** Occurring widely.

wid•geon (wĭj′ən) ▸*n., pl.* **-geon** or **-geons.** A wild freshwater duck having a brownish back and a light head patch. [?]

wid•ow (wĭd′ō) ▸*n.* A woman whose husband has died and who has not remarried. ▸*v.* To make a widow or widower of. [< OE *widuwe*.] —**wid′ow•hood′** *n.*

wid•ow•er (wĭd′ō-ər) ▸*n.* A man whose wife has died and who has not remarried. [ME *widewer*.]

width (wĭdth, wĭtth) ▸*n.* **1.** The state, quality, or fact of being wide. **2.** The measurement of something from side to side.

wield (wēld) ▸*v.* **1.** To handle (e.g., a weapon or tool), esp. capably. **2.** To exercise (e.g., power) effectively. [< OE *wieldan*, rule.]

wie•ner (wē′nər) ▸*n.* A frankfurter. [Ger.]

Wies•ba•den (vēs′bäd′n) A city of W-central Germany on the Rhine R. W of Frankfurt. Pop. 270,873.

Wie•sel (vē′səl), **Elie(zer).** b. 1928. Romanian-born writer and lecturer; 1986 Nobel Peace Prize.

Elie Wiesel

wife (wīf) ▸*n., pl.* **wives** (wīvz). A female spouse. [< OE *wīf*.] —**wife′hood′** *n.* —**wife′ly** *adj.*

wig (wĭg) ▸*n.* A covering of human or synthetic hair worn on the head for personal adornment, as part of a costume, or to conceal baldness. [< PERIWIG.]

wig•gle (wĭg′əl) ▸*v.* **-gled, -gling.** To move or cause to move from side to side with short irregular twisting motions. [ME *wiglen*.] —**wig′gle** *n.* —**wig′gler** *n.* —**wig′gly** *adj.*

Wight (wīt), **Isle of.** An island in the English Channel off S-central England.

wig•wam (wĭg′wŏm′) ▸*n.* A Native American dwelling commonly having an arched or conical framework overlaid with bark, hides, or mats. [Eastern Abenaki *wìkəwαm.*]

Wil•ber•force (wĭl′bər-fôrs′, -fōrs′), **William.** 1759–1833. British politician.

wild (wīld) ►*adj.* **-er, -est 1.** Occurring or living in a natural state; not domesticated or cultivated: *wild geese, wild plants.* **2.** Not inhabited or farmed: *remote, wild country.* **3.** Uncivilized; savage. **4.** Unruly: *wild children.* **5.** Full or suggestive of uncontrolled emotion: *wild with jealousy.* **6.** Extravagant; fantastic: *a wild idea.* **7.** Erratic: *a wild pitch.* **8.** Having a value determined by the cardholder's choice: *deuces wild.* ►*adv.* In a wild manner: *roaming wild.* ►*n.* **1.** A natural or undomesticated state: *plants growing in the wild.* **2.** often **wilds** An uninhabited or uncultivated region. [< OE *wilde.*] —**wild′ly** *adv.* —**wild′ness** *n.*

wild•cat (wīld′kăt′) ►*n.* **1.** Any of various wild felines of small to medium size, as the lynx. **2.** A quick-tempered person. **3.** An oil well drilled in an area not known to be productive. ►*adj.* **1.** Risky or unsound, esp. financially. **2.** Undertaken without official union approval: *a wildcat strike.*

Wilde (wīld), **Oscar (Fingal O'Flahertie Wills).** 1854–1900. Irish-born writer.

wil•de•beest (wĭl′də-bēst′, vĭl′-) ►*n., pl.* **-beests** or **-beest.** See **gnu.** [Obsolete Afr.]

Wil•der (wĭl′dər), **Thornton (Niven).** 1897–1975. Amer. writer.

wil•der•ness (wĭl′dər-nĭs) ►*n.* **1.** An unsettled, uncultivated region left in its natural condition. **2.** A bewildering or threatening vastness. [< OE *wilddēor*, wild beast.]

wild-eyed (wīld′īd′) ►*adj.* Glaring in or as if in anger, terror, madness, or passion.

wild•fire (wīld′fīr′) ►*n.* A raging, rapidly spreading fire.

wild•fowl (wīld′foul′) ►*n.* A wild game bird, such as a duck or quail.

wild-goose chase (wīld′gōōs′) ►*n.* A futile pursuit or search.

wild•life (wīld′līf′) ►*n.* Wild animals and vegetation, esp. in a natural state.

wild rice ►*n.* **1.** A tall aquatic grass of North America, bearing edible grain. **2.** The grain of this plant.

wile (wīl) ►*n.* **1.** A deceitful stratagem or trick. **2.** A disarming or seductive manner, device, or procedure. ►*v.* **wiled, wil•ing 1.** To lure; entice. **2.** To pass (time) agreeably. [< ONFr. *wil*, of Gmc. orig.]

Wil•hel•mi•na (wĭl′ə-mē′nə, vĭl′hĕl-). 1880–1962. Queen of the Netherlands (1890–1948).

Wil•kins (wĭl′kĭnz), **Roy.** 1901–81. Amer. civil rights leader.

will[1] (wĭl) ►*n.* **1.** The mental faculty by which one deliberately chooses a course of action; volition. **2.** Self-control; self-discipline. **3.** A desire, purpose, or determination, esp. of one in authority. **4.** Deliberate intention or wish: *against my will.* **5.** Bearing or attitude toward others; disposition: *full of good will.* **6.** A legal declaration of how a person wishes his or her possessions to be disposed of after death. ►*v.* **willed, will•ing 1.** To decide on; choose. **2.** To yearn for; desire. **3.** To decree, dictate, or order. **4.** To grant in a legal will; bequeath. —***idiom:* at will** Just as or when one wishes. [< OE *willa.*]

will[2] (wĭl) ►*aux.v. P.t.* **would** (wŏŏd) **1.** Used to indicate: **a.** Simple futurity: *They will appear later.* **b.** Likelihood or certainty: *You will regret this.* **c.** Willingness: *Will you help me?* **d.** Requirement or command: *You will report to me now.* **e.** Intention: *I will if I feel like it.* **f.** Customary or habitual action: *They would get together on weekends.* **g.** Probability: *That will be Katie ringing.* **2.** To wish; desire: *Do what you will.* See Usage Note at **shall.** [< OE *willan.*]

Wil•lard (wĭl′ərd), **Emma Hart.** 1787–1870. Amer. educator.

Wil•lem•stad (vĭl′əm-stät′) The capital of the Netherlands Antilles, on the S coast of Curaçao. Pop. 43,547.

will•ful also **wil•ful** (wĭl′fəl) ►*adj.* **1.** Deliberate; voluntary. **2.** Obstinate; stubborn. —**will′ful•ly** *adv.* —**will′ful•ness** *n.*

Wil•liam I[1] (wĭl′yəm). "William the Conqueror." 1027?–87. King of England (1066–87).

William I[2]. Prince of Orange. 1533–84. Dutch governor (1579–84).

William I[3]. 1797–1888. King of Prussia (1861–88); emperor of Germany (1871–88).

William II[1]. 1056?–1100. King of England (1087–1100).

William II[2]. 1859–1941. Emperor of Germany and king of Prussia (1888–1918).

William III. "William of Orange." 1650–1702. King of England, Scotland, and Ireland (1689–1702), Dutch leader (1672–1702), and prince of Orange.

William IV. 1765–1837. King of Great Britain and Ireland (1830–37).

Wil•liams (wĭl′yəmz), **Roger.** 1603?–83. English founder (1662) of Rhode Island.

Williams, Tennessee. 1911–83. Amer. playwright.

Williams, William Carlos. 1883–1963. Amer. poet.

Wil•liams•burg (wĭl′yəmz-bûrg′) A city of SE VA NW of Newport News; site of a restored colonial district. Pop. 11,530.

wil•lies (wĭl′ēz) ►*pl.n. Slang* Feelings of uneasiness; creeps. [?]

will•ing (wĭl′ĭng) ►*adj.* **1.** Disposed or inclined; prepared. **2.** Acting or ready to act gladly. **3.** Done, given, or borne voluntarily. —**will′ing•ly** *adv.* —**will′ing•ness** *n.*

wil•li•waw (wĭl′ē-wô′) ►*n.* A violent gust of cold wind blowing seaward from a mountainous coast. [?]

will-o'-the-wisp (wĭl′ə-*thə*-wĭsp′) ►*n.* **1.** See **ignis fatuus** 1. **2.** A delusive or misleading hope. [< *Will* (nickname for *William*).]

wil•low (wĭl′ō) ►*n.* **1.** Any of various trees or shrubs having usu. narrow leaves and slender flexible twigs. **2.** The wood of a willow. [< OE *welig.*]

wil•low•y (wĭl′ō-ē) ►*adj.* **-i•er, -i•est.** Slender and graceful: *a willowy figure.*

will•pow•er or **will pow•er** (wĭl′pou′ər) ►*n.* The strength of will to carry out one's decisions, wishes, or plans.

wil•ly-nil•ly (wĭl′ē-nĭl′ē) ►*adv. & adj.* **1.** Whether desired or not. **2.** Without order or plan. [< *will ye, nill ye*, be you willing, be you unwilling.]

Wil•ming•ton (wĭl′mĭng-tən) A city of NE DE on the Delaware R. Pop. 71,529.

Wil•son (wĭl′sən), **(James) Harold.** Baron Wilson of Rievaulx. 1916–95. British prime minister (1964–70 and 1974–76).

Wilson, (Thomas) Woodrow. 1856–1924. The 28th US President (1913–21). —**Wil•so′ni•an** (-sō′nē-ən) *adj.*

Woodrow Wilson
detail of a 1921 portrait

wilt[1] (wĭlt) ►*v.* **1.** To lose or cause to lose freshness; droop. **2.** To lose or deprive of energy or vigor; weaken; sap. ►*n.* Any of various plant diseases marked by collapse of terminal shoots, branches, or entire plants. [Poss. < ME *welken.*]

wilt[2] (wĭlt) ►*aux.v. Archaic* 2nd pers. sing. pr.t. of **will**[2].

wi•ly (wī′lē) ►*adj.* **-li•er, -li•est.** Full of wiles; cunning. —**wil′i•ness** *n.*

wim•ble (wĭm′bəl) ►*n.* A hand tool for boring holes. [< AN.] —**wim′ble** *v.*

wimp (wĭmp) ►*n. Slang* A weak, ineffectual person. [Perh. < WHIMPER.] —**wimp′y** *adj.*

wim•ple (wĭm′pəl) ►*n.* A cloth framing the face and drawn into folds beneath the chin, worn by women in medieval times and by certain nuns. [< OE *wimpel.*]

win (wĭn) ►*v.* **won** (wŭn), **win•ning 1.** To achieve victory or finish first in a competition. **2.** To achieve success in an effort. **3.** To receive as a prize or reward. **4.** To obtain or earn. See Syns at **earn. 5.** To succeed in gaining the favor or support of. ►*n.* A victory, esp. in a competition. [< OE *winnan*, strive.] —**win′ner** *n.*

wince (wĭns) ►*v.* **winced, winc•ing.** To shrink or start involuntarily, as in pain or distress; flinch. [ME *wincen*, kick.] —**wince** *n.*

winch (wĭnch) ►*n.* **1.** A stationary hoisting machine having a drum around which is wound a rope or chain attached to the load being lifted. **2.** A crank used to give rotary motion. [< OE *wince*, roller.] —**winch** *v.*

wind[1] (wĭnd) ►*n.* **1.** Moving air, esp. air moving along the ground. **2.** Moving air carrying sound or a scent. **3a.** Respiration: *had the wind knocked out of me.* **b.** Flatulence. **4.** often **winds** *Mus.* **a.** The brass and woodwinds sections of an orchestra. **b.** Wind instruments or their players. **5.** An agent of change or disruption: *the winds of war.* **6.** Empty or boastful talk. ►*v.* **1.** To detect the scent of. **2.** To cause to be out of breath. [< OE *wind.*]

wind[2] (wīnd) ►*v.* **wound** (wound), **wind•ing 1.** To wrap or be wrapped around a center or another object once or repeatedly. **2.** To encircle or be encircled in coils; entwine. **3.** To go along (a twisting course). **4.** To turn (e.g., a crank) in circular motions. **5.** To lift or haul by a windlass or winch. —***phrasal verb:* wind up 1.** To finish; end. **2.** To put in order; settle. **3.** To arrive eventually in a place or situation: *wound up in debt.* ►*n.* A single turn, twist, or curve. [< OE *windan.*] —**wind′er** *n.*

wind[3] (wīnd, wĭnd) ►*v.* **wind•ed** (wīn′dĭd, wĭn′-) or **wound** (wound), **wind•ing,** *Mus.* To sound by blowing (a wind instrument). [< WIND[1].]

wind•bag (wĭnd′băg′) ►*n. Slang* A tiresomely talkative person.

wind•break (wĭnd′brāk′) ►*n.* A hedge, fence, or row of trees serving to lessen or break the force of the wind.

wind•burn (wĭnd′bûrn′) ►*n.* Skin irritation caused by exposure to the wind. —**wind′burned′** *adj.*

wind-chill factor (wĭnd′chĭl′) ►*n.* The temperature of still air that would have the same effect on exposed skin as a given combination of wind speed and air temperature.

wind•fall (wĭnd′fôl′) ►*n.* **1.** A sudden, unexpected piece of good fortune. **2.** A fruit blown down by the wind.

wind•flow•er (wĭnd′flou′ər) ►*n.* See **anemone** 1.

Wind•hoek (vĭnt′ho͝ok′) The capital of Namibia, in the central part. Pop. 88,700.

wind•ing (wīn′dĭng) ►*n.* **1.** Something wound about a center or an object. **2.** A curve or bend, as of a road. ►*adj.* **1.** Twisting or turning; sinuous. **2.** Spiral.

wind•ing-sheet (wīn′dĭng-shēt′) ►*n.* A sheet for wrapping a corpse; shroud.

wind instrument (wĭnd) ►*n. Mus.* **1.** An instrument, such as an oboe or tuba, sounded by a column of air, esp. the breath. **2.** A woodwind, as opposed to a brass instrument.

wind•jam•mer (wĭnd′jăm′ər) ►*n.* A large sailing ship.

wind•lass (wĭnd′ləs) ►*n.* Any of numerous hauling or lifting machines consisting essentially of a horizontal cylinder wound with rope and turned by a crank. [< ON *vindāss.*]

wind•mill (wĭnd′mĭl′) ►*n.* A machine that runs on the energy generated by a wheel of adjustable blades rotated by the wind.

win•dow (wĭn′dō) ►*n.* **1.** An opening constructed in a wall or roof to admit light or air. **2.** A framework enclosing a window. **3.** A windowpane. **4.** An opening that resembles a window. **5.** A temporary period of a specified nature: *a window of opportunity.* **6.** *Comp. Sci.* A rectangular area on a display screen that can be viewed independently of other such areas. [< ON *vindauga.*]

window box ►*n.* A usu. long narrow box for plants, placed on a windowsill or ledge.

win•dow-dress•ing also **win•dow dress•ing** (wĭn′dō-drĕs′ĭng) ►*n.* **1.** Decorative exhibition of retail merchandise in store windows. **2.** A means of improving appearances or creating a falsely favorable impression.

win•dow•pane (wĭn′dō-pān′) ►*n.* A piece of glass in a window.

win•dow-shop (wĭn′dō-shŏp′) ►*v.* To look at merchandise in store windows or showcases without buying. —**win′dow-shop′per** *n.*

win•dow•sill (wĭn′dō-sĭl′) ►*n.* The horizontal ledge at the base of a window opening.

wind•pipe (wĭnd′pīp′) ►*n. Anat.* See **trachea.**

wind•row (wĭnd′rō′) ►*n.* A row, as of leaves

or snow, heaped up by the wind.
wind•shield (wĭnd′shēld′) ►*n.* A framed protective pane of transparent shielding located in front of the occupants of a vehicle.
wind•sock (wĭnd′sŏk′) ►*n.* A tapered, open-ended sleeve pivotally attached to a standard so as to indicate the direction of the wind blowing through it.
Wind•sor (wĭn′zər) A city of SE Ontario, Canada, on the Detroit R. opposite Detroit, MI. Pop. 191,435.
Windsor, Duke of. See **Edward VIII.**
wind•storm (wĭnd′stôrm′) ►*n.* A storm with high winds but little or no rain.
wind•surf•ing (wĭnd′sûrf′ĭng) ►*n.* The sport of sailing while standing on a sailboard. —**wind′surf′** *v.* —**wind′surf′er** *n.*
wind•swept (wĭnd′swĕpt′) ►*adj.* Exposed to or swept by winds.
wind tunnel (wĭnd) ►*n.* A chamber through which air is forced at controlled velocities to study its effect on an object.
wind-up or **wind•up** (wīnd′ŭp′) ►*n.* **1a.** The act of bringing something to an end. **b.** A conclusion; finish. **2.** The movements of a pitcher preparatory to pitching the ball. ►*adj.* Operated by a hand-wound spring.
wind•ward (wĭnd′wərd) ►*adv. & adj.* Toward the wind. —**wind′ward** *n.*
Windward Islands. An island group of the SE West Indies, including the S group of the Lesser Antilles.
wind•y (wĭn′dē) ►*adj.* **-i•er, -i•est 1.** Marked by or abounding in wind. **2.** Exposed to the wind; unsheltered. **3.** Tiresomely talkative. —**wind′i•ly** *adv.* —**wind′i•ness** *n.*
wine (wīn) ►*n.* **1.** The fermented juice of grapes. **2.** The fermented juice of other fruits or plants. ►*v.* **wined, win•ing.** To entertain with wine. [< Lat. *vīnum.*]
wine•glass (wīn′glăs′) ►*n.* A glass, usu. with a stem, from which wine is drunk.
wine•grow•er (wīn′grō′ər) ►*n.* One who owns a vineyard and produces wine.
wine•press (wīn′prĕs′) ►*n.* **1.** A vat in which the juice is pressed from grapes. **2.** A device that presses the juice from grapes.
win•er•y (wī′nə-rē) ►*n., pl.* **-ies.** An establishment at which wine is made.
wine•skin (wīn′skĭn′) ►*n.* A bag, as of goatskin, used for holding and dispensing wine.
wing (wĭng) ►*n.* **1.** One of a pair of movable organs for flying, as of a bird, bat, or insect. **2.** *Informal* A human arm. **3.** An airfoil whose main function is providing lift, esp. either of two such airfoils positioned on each side of the fuselage of an aircraft. **4. wings** The unseen backstage area on either side of a stage. **5.** A structure attached to and connected with a main building. **6.** Either of two groups with opposing views within a larger group; faction. **7a.** Either the left or right flank of an army or a naval fleet. **b.** An air force unit larger than a group but smaller than a division. **8.** *Sports* Either of the forward positions played near the sideline, esp. in hockey. ►*v.* **1.** To move on or as if on wings; fly. **2.** To furnish with wings. **3.** To effect or accomplish by flying. **4.** To wound superficially. —***idioms:*** **on the wing** In flight; flying. **under (one's) wing** Under one's protection. **wing it** *Informal* To improvise; ad-lib. [ME *wenge.*] —**wing′less** *adj.*
wing•ding (wĭng′dĭng′) ►*n. Informal* A lavish or lively party or celebration. [?]
winged (wĭngd, wĭng′ĭd) ►*adj.* **1.** Having wings or winglike appendages. **2.** Soaring with or as if with wings.
wing nut ►*n.* A nut with winglike projections for thumb and forefinger leverage in turning.
wing•span (wĭng′spăn′) ►*n.* Wingspread.
wing•spread (wĭng′sprĕd′) ►*n.* The distance between the tips of the extended wings, as of a bird, insect, or aircraft.
wink (wĭngk) ►*v.* **1.** To close and open one eye deliberately, as to convey a message, signal, or suggestion. **2.** To blink rapidly. **3.** To shine fitfully; twinkle. —***phrasal verb:*** **wink at** To pretend not to notice: *wink at corruption.* ►*n.* **1.** The act of winking. **2.** An instant. **3.** *Informal* A brief period of sleep. [< OE *wincian,* close one's eyes.]
Win•ne•ba•go (wĭn′ə-bā′gō) ►*n., pl.* **-go** or **-gos** or **-goes 1.** A member of a Native American people of Wisconsin, now also in Nebraska. **2.** Their Siouan language.
win•ning (wĭn′ĭng) ►*adj.* **1.** Successful; victorious. **2.** Attractive; charming. ►*n.* **1.** Victory. **2.** often **winnings** Something won, esp. money.
Win•ni•peg (wĭn′ə-pĕg′) The capital of Manitoba, Canada, in the SE part. Pop. 616,790.
Winnipeg, Lake. A lake of S-central Manitoba, Canada.
win•now (wĭn′ō) ►*v.* **1.** To separate the chaff from (grain) by means of a current of air. **2.** To sort into categories, esp. of good and bad. **3.** To separate or get rid of (an undesirable part). [< OE *windwian.*] —**win′now•er** *n.*
win•o (wī′nō) ►*n., pl.* **-os** *Slang* An indigent wine-drinking alcoholic.
win•some (wĭn′səm) ►*adj.* Charming, often in a childlike way. [< OE *wynsum.*] —**win′some•ly** *adv.* —**win′some•ness** *n.*
Win•ston-Sa•lem (wĭn′stən-sā′ləm) A city of N-central NC. Pop. 143,485.
win•ter (wĭn′tər) ►*n.* The usu. coldest season of the year, occurring between autumn and spring. ►*v.* **1.** To spend the winter. **2.** To keep or feed (e.g., livestock) during the winter. [< OE.]
win•ter•green (wĭn′tər-grēn′) ►*n.* **1.** A low-growing evergreen plant of North America, with aromatic leaves and spicy scarlet berries. **2.** An oil or flavoring from this plant.
win•ter•ize (wĭn′tə-rīz′) ►*v.* **-ized, -iz•ing.** To prepare or equip (e.g., an automobile) for winter weather. —**win′ter•i•za′tion** *n.*
win•ter•kill (wĭn′tər-kĭl′) ►*v.* To kill by or die from exposure to cold winter weather. —**win′ter•kill′** *n.*
winter squash ►*n.* Any of several thick-rinded varieties of squash, such as the acorn squash, that can be stored for long periods.
win•ter•time (wĭn′tər-tīm′) ►*n.* The season of winter.
Win•throp (wĭn′thrəp), **John.** 1588–1649. English-born Amer. colonial administrator.
win•try (wĭn′trē) also **win•ter•y** (wĭn′tə-rē) ►*adj.* **-tri•er, -tri•est** also **-ter•i•er, -ter•i•est 1.** Of or like winter; cold. **2.** Suggestive of winter; cheerless: *a wintry smile.*
wipe (wīp) ►*v.* **wiped, wip•ing 1.** To rub, as with a cloth or paper, in order to clean or dry. **2.** To remove, clean, or dry by or as if by rub-

bing. **3.** To rub or pass (e.g., a cloth) over a surface. —***phrasal verb:*** **wipe out 1.** To destroy completely. **2.** *Slang* To murder. [< OE *wīpian.*] —**wipe** *n.* —**wip′er** *n.*

wire (wīr) ▶*n.* **1.** A usu. pliable metallic strand or rod, often electrically insulated, used esp. for structural support or to conduct electricity. **2.** A group of wire strands bundled or twisted together; cable. **3.** An open telephone connection. **4.** *Slang* A hidden microphone, as on a person's body. **5a.** A telegraph service. **b.** A telegram or cablegram. **6.** The finish line of a racetrack. ▶*v.* **wired, wir•ing 1.** To bind, connect, or attach with wires or a wire. **2.** To equip with a system of electrical wires. **3.** *Slang* To install electronic eavesdropping equipment in. **4.** To send by telegraph. **5.** To send a telegram to. [< OE *wīr.*]

wire•haired (wīr′hârd′) ▶*adj.* Having a coat of stiff wiry hair, as certain dogs.

wire•less (wīr′lĭs) ▶*adj.* Having no wire or wires. ▶*n.* **1.** A radiotelegraph or radiotelephone system. **2.** *Chiefly Brit.* Radio.

wire service ▶*n.* A news-gathering organization that distributes syndicated copy electronically to subscribers.

wire•tap (wīr′tăp′) ▶*n.* A concealed listening or recording device connected to a communications circuit. ▶*v.* To monitor (a telephone line) by means of a wiretap.

wir•ing (wīr′ĭng) ▶*n.* A system of electric wires.

wir•y (wīr′ē) ▶*adj.* **-i•er, -i•est 1.** Wirelike, esp. in stiffness; kinky. **2.** Sinewy and lean: *a wiry build.* —**wir′i•ness** *n.*

Wis•con•sin (wĭs-kŏn′sĭn) A state of the N-central US. Cap. Madison. Pop. 4,906,745. —**Wis•con′sin•ite′** *n.*

wis•dom (wĭz′dəm) ▶*n.* **1.** Understanding of what is true, right, or lasting. **2.** Common sense; good judgment. **3.** Scholarly learning. [< OE *wīsdōm.*]

Wisdom of Solomon ▶*n.* See table at **Bible.**

wisdom tooth ▶*n.* One of four rearmost molars on each side of both jaws in humans.

wise[1] (wīz) ▶*adj.* **wis•er, wis•est 1.** Having wisdom; judicious. **2.** Exhibiting common sense; prudent. **3.** Learned; erudite. **4.** Aware; informed: *wise to their tricks.* **5.** *Slang* Rude and disrespectful; impudent. [< OE *wīs.*] —**wise′ly** *adv.*

wise[2] (wīz) ▶*n.* Method or manner of doing; way: *in no wise.* [< OE *wīse.*]

-wise ▶*suff.* Manner, direction, or position: *clockwise.* [< OE *-wīse,* WISE[2].]

Usage: The suffix *–wise* has a long history of use to mean "in the manner or direction of," as in *clockwise.* Since the 1930s, however, the suffix has been widely used in the vaguer sense of "with relation to," as in *Taxwise, it is an unattractive arrangement.* In most writing there is no alternative to paraphrases such as *As far as taxes are concerned, it is an unattractive arrangement.*

wise•a•cre (wīz′ā′kər) ▶*n.* *Slang* A smart aleck. [< MDu. *wijsseggher,* soothsayer < OHGer. *wīssago.*]

wise•crack (wīz′krăk′) ▶*n.* *Slang* A flippant, usu. sardonic remark. —**wise′crack′** *v.*

wish (wĭsh) ▶*n.* **1.** A desire or longing for something. **2.** An expression of a wish. **3.** Something desired or longed for. ▶*v.* **1.** To long for; want: *I wish that you could come.* See Syns at **desire. 2.** To express wishes for; bid: *wished her good night.* **3.** To invoke upon: *I wish them luck.* **4.** To order or entreat: *I wish you to go.* [< OE *wȳscan,* to wish.] —**wish′er** *n.*

wish•bone (wĭsh′bōn′) ▶*n.* The forked bone in front of the breastbone of most birds.

wish•ful (wĭsh′fəl) ▶*adj.* Having or expressing a wish or longing. —**wish′ful•ly** *adv.* —**wish′ful•ness** *n.*

wish•y-wash•y (wĭsh′ē-wŏsh′ē, -wô′shē) ▶*adj.* **-i•er, -i•est** *Informal* Lacking in strength or character; indecisive. [< WASH.]

wisp (wĭsp) ▶*n.* **1.** A small bunch or bundle, as of hair. **2.** One that is thin, frail, or slight. **3.** A faint streak, as of smoke or clouds. [ME.] —**wisp′y** *adj.*

wis•ter•i•a (wĭ-stîr′ē-ə) also **wis•tar•i•a** (wĭ-stâr′-) ▶*n.* A climbing woody vine having racemes of showy purplish or white flowers. [After Caspar *Wistar* (1761–1818).]

wist•ful (wĭst′fəl) ▶*adj.* **1.** Full of wishful yearning. **2.** Pensively sad; melancholy. [< obsolete *wistly,* intently.] —**wist′ful•ly** *adv.* —**wist′ful•ness** *n.*

wit (wĭt) ▶*n.* **1.** Perception and understanding; intelligence. **2a.** often **wits** Keenness and quickness of perception or discernment. **b. wits** Sound mental faculties; sanity. **3a.** The ability to perceive and humorously express the relationship between seemingly incongruous things. **b.** One noted for this ability. —***idiom:*** **at (one's) wits' end** At the limit of one's mental resources; utterly at a loss. [< OE.]

witch (wĭch) ▶*n.* **1a.** A sorceress, esp. in folklore. **b.** A woman believed to practice sorcery. **2.** A follower of Wicca. **3.** A hag. **4.** A spiteful or overbearing woman. **5.** *Informal* A bewitching woman. [< OE *wicce,* witch, and *wicca,* sorcerer.] —**witch′er•y** *n.* —**witch′y** *adj.*

witch•craft (wĭch′krăft′) ▶*n.* Magic; sorcery.

witch doctor ▶*n.* A shamanistic healer.

witch hazel ▶*n.* **1.** A deciduous shrub of E North America having yellow flowers. **2.** An alcoholic solution containing an extract of this plant, used as a mild astringent. [Obsolete *wych,* a kind of elm + HAZEL.]

witch-hunt (wĭch′hŭnt′) ▶*n.* An investigation whose underlying purpose is to identify and harass those with differing views.

witch•ing (wĭch′ĭng) ▶*adj.* **1.** Of or appropriate to witchcraft. **2.** Enchanting.

with (wĭth, wĭth) ▶*prep.* **1.** In the company of: *Did you go with her?* **2.** Next to: *stood with the rabbi.* **3.** Having: *a man with a moustache.* **4.** In a manner characterized by: *performed with skill.* **5.** In the charge or keeping of: *left the cat with the neighbors.* **6.** In the opinion of: *if it's all right with you.* **7.** In support of; on the side of: *I'm with you all the way.* **8.** By the means of: *eat with a fork.* **9.** In spite of. **10.** At the same time as: *gets up with the birds.* **11.** In regard to: *pleased with her decision.* **12.** In comparison or contrast to: *a dress identical with the one I had.* **13.** Having received: *With her permission, he left.* **14.** In opposition to; against: *wrestling with an opponent.* **15.** As a result or consequence of: *sick with the flu.* **16.** So as to be touching or joined to: *linked arms with their partners.* **17.** So as to be free of or separated from: *parted with her husband.* **18.** In the course of: *We grow older with the hours.* **19.** In proportion to: *wines that improve with age.* **20.** As well as: *sing with the best of them.* [< OE.]

with•al (wĭth-ôl′, wĭth-) ▸*adv.* **1.** In addition; besides. **2.** Despite that; nevertheless. **3.** *Archaic* Therewith. [ME.]

with•draw (wĭth-drô′, wĭth-) ▸*v.* **-drew** (-dro͞o′), **-drawn** (-drôn′), **-draw•ing 1.** To take back or away; remove. **2.** To recall or retract. **3.** To move or draw back; retire. **4.** To remove oneself from active participation. [ME *withdrawen.*]

with•draw•al (wĭth-drô′əl, wĭth-) ▸*n.* **1.** The act or process of withdrawing. **2.** Detachment, as from social or emotional involvement. **3a.** Discontinuation of the use of an addictive substance. **b.** The physiological and mental readjustment that accompanies such discontinuation.

with•drawn (wĭth-drôn′, wĭth-) ▸*adj.* **1.** Retiring; shy. **2.** Emotionally unresponsive.

withe (wĭth, wĭth, wīth) ▸*n.* A tough supple twig, esp. of willow, used for binding things together. [< OE *withthe.*]

with•er (wĭth′ər) ▸*v.* **1.** To dry up or shrivel from or as if from loss of moisture. **2.** To lose or cause to lose freshness. **3.** To devastate; stun: *withered them with a glance.* [< ME *widderen.*]

with•ers (wĭth′ərz) ▸*pl.n.* The high part of the back of a horse, located between the shoulder blades. [Prob. < OE *wither-*, against.]

with•hold (wĭth-hōld′, wĭth-) ▸*v.* **-held** (-hĕld′), **-hold•ing 1.** To keep in check; restrain. **2.** To refrain from giving, granting, or permitting. **3.** To deduct (withholding tax) from a salary. [ME *witholden.*]

with•hold•ing tax (wĭth-hōl′dĭng, wĭth-) ▸*n.* A portion of an employee's wages or salary withheld by the employer as partial payment of the employee's income tax.

with•in (wĭth-ĭn′, wĭth-) ▸*adv.* **1.** Inside. **2.** Inside the mind or body; inwardly. **3.** Indoors. ▸*prep.* **1.** Inside. **2.** Inside the limits or extent of. **3.** Inside the fixed limits of: *within one's rights.* **4.** In the scope or sphere of. ▸*n.* An inner position, place, or area: *treachery from within.*

with-it (wĭth′ĭt′, wĭth-) ▸*adj. Slang* Up-to-date.

with•out (wĭth-out′, wĭth-) ▸*adv.* **1.** On the outside. **2.** Outdoors. ▸*prep.* **1a.** Not having; lacking. **b.** Not accompanied by. **2.** At, on, to, or toward the outside or exterior of. [< OE *withūtan.*]

with•stand (wĭth-stănd′, wĭth-) ▸*v.* **-stood** (-sto͝od′), **-stand•ing 1.** To oppose with force or resolution. **2.** To resist successfully. [< OE *withstandan.*]

wit•less (wĭt′lĭs) ▸*adj.* Lacking intelligence or wit; foolish. —**wit′less•ly** *adv.*

wit•ness (wĭt′nĭs) ▸*n.* **1.** One who can give a firsthand account of something seen, heard, or experienced. **2.** Something serving as evidence; sign. **3.** *Law* **a.** One called on to testify in court. **b.** One called on to be present at a transaction to attest to what takes place. **c.** One who signs one's name to a document in attestation of its authenticity. **4.** An attestation; testimony. ▸*v.* **1.** To be present at or have personal knowledge of. **2.** To provide or serve as evidence of. See Syns at **indicate. 3.** To testify to; bear witness. **4.** To be the setting or site of. **5.** To attest to the legality or authenticity of by signing one's name. [< OE *witness* < *wit*, WIT.]

wit•ti•cism (wĭt′ĭ-sĭz′əm) ▸*n.* A witty remark. [WITT(Y) + (CRIT)ICISM.]

wit•ty (wĭt′ē) ▸*adj.* **-ti•er, -ti•est.** Having or showing wit; cleverly humorous. —**wit′ti•ly** *adv.* —**wit′ti•ness** *n.*

Wit•wa•ters•rand (wĭt-wô′tərz-rănd′, -ränd′, -wŏt′ərz-) A region of NE South Africa in S Transvaal.

wives (wīvz) ▸*n.* Pl. of **wife.**

wiz•ard (wĭz′ərd) ▸*n.* **1.** A sorcerer or magician. **2.** A skilled or clever person: *a wizard at math.* [ME *wisard* < *wise*, WISE[1].] —**wiz′ard•ry** *n.*

wiz•ened (wĭz′ənd) ▸*adj.* Withered; shriveled. [< OE *wisnian*, wither.]

wk. ▸*abbr.* week

WL ▸*abbr.* wavelength

WNW ▸*abbr.* west-northwest

WO ▸*abbr.* warrant officer

w/o ▸*abbr.* without

woad (wōd) ▸*n.* **1.** An annual Old World plant with leaves that yield a blue dye. **2.** The dye from this plant. [< OE *wād.*]

wob•ble (wŏb′əl) ▸*v.* **-bled, -bling 1.** To move or rotate with an uneven or rocking motion from side to side. **2.** To tremble or quaver. **3.** To waver or vacillate in one's opinions. [Prob. < LGer. *wabbeln.*] —**wob′ble** *n.* —**wob′bli•ness** *n.* —**wob′bly** *adj.*

Wode•house (wo͝od′hous′), **P(elham) G(renville).** 1881–1975. British writer.

woe (wō) ▸*n.* **1.** Distress or misery, as from grief. **2.** Misfortune; calamity: *economic and political woes.* ▸*interj.* Used to express sorrow or dismay. [< OE *wā*, woe!]

woe•be•gone (wō′bĭ-gôn′, -gŏn′) ▸*adj.* Wretched or pitiful, esp. in appearance.

woe•ful (wō′fəl) ▸*adj.* **1.** Affected by woe; mournful. **2.** Causing woe. **3.** Deplorably bad or wretched: *woeful housing conditions.* —**woe′ful•ly** *adv.* —**woe′ful•ness** *n.*

wok (wŏk) ▸*n.* A metal pan having a convex bottom, used esp. for frying and steaming in Asian cooking. [Cantonese *wŏk.*]

woke (wōk) ▸*v.* P.t. of **wake[1].** See Regional Note at **wake[1].**

wok•en (wō′kən) ▸*v.* P.part. of **wake[1].**

wolf (wo͝olf) ▸*n., pl.* **wolves** (wo͝olvz) **1.** A carnivorous mammal, chiefly of northern regions, related to and resembling the dog. **2.** One regarded as predatory, rapacious, and fierce. **3.** *Slang* A man given to paying unwanted sexual attention to women. ▸*v.* To eat greedily or voraciously. [< OE *wulf.*] —**wolf′ish** *adj.* —**wolf′ish•ly** *adv.*

Wolfe (wo͝olf), **James.** 1727–59. British general in Canada.

Wolfe, Thomas (Clayton). 1900–38. Amer. writer.

wolf•hound (wo͝olf′hound′) ▸*n.* Any of various large dogs orig. trained to hunt wolves.

wolf•ram (wo͝ol′frəm) ▸*n.* See **tungsten.** [Ger.]

Woll•stone•craft (wo͝ol′stən-krăft′, -kräft′), **Mary.** 1759–97. British writer.

Wol•sey (wo͝ol′zē), **Thomas.** 1475?–1530. English prelate and politician.

wol•ver•ine (wo͝ol′və-rēn′) ▸*n.* A solitary, carnivorous mammal of northern forest regions, related to the weasel. [Prob. < WOLF.]

wom•an (wo͝om′ən) ►*n., pl.* **wom•en** (wĭm′ĭn) **1.** An adult female human. **2.** Womankind. **3.** *Informal* A wife, lover, or sweetheart. [< OE *wīfman.*]

wom•an•hood (wo͝om′ən-ho͝od′) ►*n.* **1.** The state of being a woman. **2.** The qualities thought to be appropriate to or representative of women. **3.** Women collectively.

wom•an•ish (wo͝om′ə-nĭsh) ►*adj.* **1.** Characteristic of a woman. **2.** Effeminate.

wom•an•ize (wo͝om′ə-nīz′) ►*v.* **-ized, -iz•ing.** To pursue women lecherously. —**wom′an•iz′er** *n.*

wom•an•kind (wo͝om′ən-kīnd′) ►*n.* Women collectively.

wom•an•ly (wo͝om′ən-lē) ►*adj.* **-li•er, -li•est.** Having qualities usu. attributed to a woman. —**wom′an•li•ness** *n.*

womb (wo͞om) ►*n.* **1.** See **uterus. 2.** A place where something has its earliest development. [< OE *wamb.*]

wom•bat (wŏm′băt′) ►*n.* An Australian marsupial somewhat resembling a small bear. [Indigenous word in Australia.]

wom•en (wĭm′ĭn) ►*n.* Pl. of **woman.**

wom•en•folk (wĭm′ĭn-fōk′) ►*pl.n.* **1.** Women collectively. **2.** The women of a community.

won[1] (wôn) ►*n., pl.* **won.** See table at **currency.** [Korean.]

won[2] (wŭn) ►*v.* P.t. and p.part. of **win.**

won•der (wŭn′dər) ►*n.* **1a.** One that arouses awe, surprise, or admiration; marvel. **b.** The feeling thus aroused. **2.** A feeling of puzzlement or doubt. ►*v.* **1.** To have a feeling of awe or admiration; marvel. **2.** To be filled with curiosity or doubt. **3.** To be inquisitive or in doubt about. [< OE *wundor.*]

Syns: *wonder, marvel, miracle, phenomenon, prodigy, sensation* **n.**

won•der•ful (wŭn′dər-fəl) ►*adj.* **1.** Capable of eliciting wonder; astonishing. **2.** Admirable; excellent. —**won′der•ful•ly** *adv.*

won•der•land (wŭn′dər-lănd′) ►*n.* **1.** A marvelous imaginary realm. **2.** A marvelous real place or scene.

won•der•ment (wŭn′dər-mənt) ►*n.* **1.** Astonishment, awe, or surprise. **2.** A marvel. **3.** Puzzlement or curiosity.

won•drous (wŭn′drəs) ►*adj.* Wonderful. —**won′drous•ly** *adv.*

wonk (wŏngk) ►*n. Slang* **1.** A student who studies excessively. **2.** One who studies an issue or topic thoroughly or excessively. [?]

wont (wônt, wōnt, wŭnt) ►*adj.* **1.** Accustomed or used: *was wont to give generously.* **2.** Likely. ►*n.* Customary practice; habit: *left early, as was her wont.* [ME < *wonen*, to be used to.]

won't (wōnt) ► Will not.

wont•ed (wôn′tĭd, wōn′-, wŭn′-) ►*adj.* Accustomed; usual: *ate with his wonted appetite.*

won ton or **won•ton** (wŏn′tŏn′) ►*n.* A noodle-dough dumpling filled usu. with spiced minced pork or other ground meat. [Cantonese *wān t'ān.*]

woo (wo͞o) ►*v.* **1.** To seek the affection of with intent to romance. **2.** To seek to achieve; try to gain. **3.** To entreat or importune. [< OE *wōgian.*] —**woo′er** *n.*

wood (wo͝od) ►*n.* **1a.** The tough fibrous supporting and water-conducting tissue beneath the bark of trees and shrubs, consisting largely of cellulose and lignin. **b.** This tissue, often cut and dried esp. for building material and fuel. **2.** often **woods** A forest. [< OE *wudu.*]

Wood, Grant. 1892–1942. Amer. artist.

wood alcohol ►*n.* See **methanol.**

wood•bine (wo͝od′bīn′) ►*n.* **1.** Any of various climbing vines, esp. a Mediterranean honeysuckle having yellowish flowers. **2.** See **Virginia creeper.** [< OE *wudubinde.*]

wood•block (wo͝od′blŏk′) ►*n.* See **woodcut.**

wood•chuck (wo͝od′chŭk′) ►*n.* A common North American rodent having a short-legged, heavy-set body and brownish fur. [Prob. of New England Algonquian orig.]

wood•cock (wo͝od′kŏk′) ►*n., pl.* **-cock** or **-cocks.** A game bird having brownish plumage, short legs, and a long bill.

wood•craft (wo͝od′krăft′) ►*n.* **1.** Skill in matters relating to the woods, as hunting or camping. **2.** Skill in working with wood.

wood•cut (wo͝od′kŭt′) ►*n.* **1.** A block of wood with an engraved design for printing. **2.** A print made from a woodcut.

wood•cut•ter (wo͝od′kŭt′ər) ►*n.* One who fells trees and chops wood, as for fuel.

wood duck ►*n.* A brightly colored American duck, the male of which has a large crest.

wood•ed (wo͝od′ĭd) ►*adj.* Covered with trees or woods.

wood•en (wo͝od′n) ►*adj.* **1.** Made of wood. **2.** Without spirit or liveliness. **3.** Clumsy and awkward; ungainly. —**wood′en•ly** *adv.*

Wood•hull (wo͝od′hŭl′), **Victoria Clafin.** 1838–1927. Amer. reformer.

wood•land (wo͝od′lənd, -lănd′) ►*n.* Land covered with trees and shrubs.

wood•peck•er (wo͝od′pĕk′ər) ►*n.* Any of various usu. brightly colored birds that cling to and climb trees and have a chisellike bill for drilling through bark and wood.

wood•pile (wo͝od′pīl′) ►*n.* A pile of wood, esp. for fuel.

wood•ruff (wo͝od′rəf, -rŭf′) ►*n.* A fragrant herb with white flowers. [< OE *wudurofe.*]

wood•shed (wo͝od′shĕd′) ►*n.* A shed in which firewood is stored.

woods•man (wo͝odz′mən) ►*n.* A man who works or lives in the woods or is versed in woodcraft; forester.

woods•y (wo͝od′zē) ►*adj.* **-i•er, -i•st.** Of or suggestive of the woods.

wood•wind (wo͝od′wĭnd′) ►*n. Mus.* Any of a group of wind instruments that includes the bassoon, clarinet, flute, oboe, and saxophone.

wood•work (wo͝od′wûrk′) ►*n.* Something made of wood, esp. wooden interior fittings in a house, as moldings or doors.

wood•y (wo͝od′ē) ►*adj.* **-i•er, -i•est 1.** Forming or consisting of wood: *woody tissue.* **2.** Suggestive of wood. **3.** Wooded.

woof (wo͝of, wo͞of) ►*n.* **1.** The crosswise threads in a woven fabric at right angles to the warp threads. **2.** The texture of a fabric. [< OE *ōwef.*]

woof•er (wo͝of′ər) ►*n.* A loudspeaker designed to reproduce bass frequencies. [< *woof*, dog's bark.]

wool (wo͝ol) ►*n.* **1a.** The dense, soft, often curly hair of sheep and certain other mammals, used as a textile fabric. **b.** A yarn or garment

made of this hair. **2.** A covering or substance suggestive of the texture of true wool. [< OE *wull.*]
wool•en also **wool•len** (wo͝ol′ən) ►*adj.* Made or consisting of wool. ►*n.* often **woolens.** Fabric or clothing made from wool.
Woolf (wo͝olf), **(Adeline) Virginia (Stephen).** 1882–1941. British writer.
wool•gath•er•ing (wo͝ol′găth′ər-ĭng) ►*n.* Indulgence in fanciful daydreams.
wool•ly also **wool•y** (wo͝ol′ē) ►*adj.* **-li•er, -li•est** also **-i•er, -i•est 1a.** Made of or covered with wool. **b.** Resembling wool. **2.** Not sharp or clear: *woolly thinking.* **3.** Lawless and disorderly. ►*n., pl.* **-lies** also **-ies.** A garment made of wool. —**wool′li•ness** *n.*
woolly mammoth ►*n.* A Pleistocene mammoth of cold northern regions.
woom•er•a (wo͝om′ər-ə) ►*n.* A hooked wooden stick used for hurling a spear or dart. [Dharuk (Australian) *wamara.*]
woops (wo͝ops, wo͞ops) ►*interj.* Var. of **whoops.**
wooz•y (wo͞o′zē, wo͝oz′ē) ►*adj.* **-i•er, -i•est 1.** Dazed or confused. **2.** Dizzy or queasy. [?] —**wooz′i•ness** *n.*
Worces•ter (wo͝os′tər) A city of central MA W of Boston. Pop. 169,759.
Worces•ter•shire (wo͝os′tər-shîr, -shər) ►*n.* A piquant sauce of soy, vinegar, and spices.
word (wûrd) ►*n.* **1.** A meaningful sound or combination of sounds, or its representation in writing. **2.** Something said; a remark or comment. **3. words** Discourse or talk; speech. **4. words** *Mus.* Lyrics; text. **5.** An assurance; promise. **6a.** A command or direction. **b.** A verbal signal; password. **7a.** News. See Syns at **news. b.** Rumor. **8. words** An angry argument. **9. Word** The Bible. ►*v.* To express in words. [< OE.] —**word′less** *adj.* —**word′less•ly** *adv.*
word•age (wûr′dĭj) ►*n.* **1.** Words collectively. **2.** The number of words used. **3.** Wording.
word•book (wûrd′bo͝ok′) ►*n.* A lexicon, vocabulary, or dictionary.
word•ing (wûr′dĭng) ►*n.* The way in which something is expressed in words.
word•play (wûrd′plā′) ►*n.* A witty or clever use of words.
word processing ►*n.* The creation, editing, and production of documents and texts by means of computer systems. —**word processor** *n.*
Words•worth (wûrdz′wûrth′), **William.** 1770–1850. British poet.
word•y (wûr′dē) ►*adj.* **-i•er, -i•est.** Using more words than are necessary to convey meaning. —**word′i•ness** *n.*
Syns: *wordy, diffuse, long-winded, prolix, verbose* **adj.**
wore (wôr, wōr) ►*v.* P.t. of **wear.**
work (wûrk) ►*n.* **1.** Physical or mental effort or activity. **2a.** A job; employment: *looking for work.* **b.** A profession or other means of livelihood. **3.** A duty or task. **4a.** The part of a day devoted to an occupation: *met her after work.* **b.** One's place of employment: *I'll call you at work.* **5a.** Something produced as the result of effort. **b.** An act; deed: *charitable works.* **c.** An artistic creation, such as a painting. **d. works** The output of a creative artist. **e. works** Engineering structures. **6. works** *(takes sing. or pl. v.)* A factory or industrial plant: *a steel works.* **7. works** Internal mechanism: *the works of a watch.* **8.** Workmanship: *sloppy work.* **9.** *Phys.* The transfer of energy from one physical system to another. **10. works** *Informal* Everything: *a pizza with the works.* ►*v.* **1.** To exert oneself physically or mentally. **2.** To be employed. **3.** To operate or cause to operate. **4.** To have an effect or influence. **5.** To reach a specified condition through gradual or repeated movement: *The stitches worked loose.* **6.** To proceed laboriously: *worked through the pile of unpaid bills.* **7.** To move in an agitated manner, as with emotion. **8.** To behave in a specified way when processed: *Gold works easily.* **9.** To bring about: *work miracles.* **10.** To shape or forge. **11.** To solve (a problem) by calculation. **12.** To bring to a specified condition by gradual or repeated effort: *worked the nail out of the board.* **13.** *Informal* To arrange or contrive. **14.** To excite or provoke: *worked the mob into a frenzy.* —***phrasal verb:* work out 1.** To solve: *worked out their differences.* **2.** To develop: *work out a plan.* **3.** To prove successful or effective. **4.** To engage in strenuous exercise. —***idiom:* in the works** In preparation; under development. [< OE *weorc.*]
work•a•ble (wûr′kə-bəl) ►*adj.* **1.** Capable of being worked. **2.** Capable of being put into effect; practicable. —**work′a•bil′i•ty** *n.*
work•a•day (wûr′kə-dā′) ►*adj.* **1.** Of or suited for working days. **2.** Mundane; commonplace. [< ME *werkeday*, workday.]
work•a•hol•ic (wûr′kə-hô′lĭk, -hŏl′ĭk) ►*n.* One who has a compulsive and unrelenting need to work. [WORK + (ALCO)HOLIC.]
work•bench (wûrk′bĕnch′) ►*n.* A sturdy table or bench at which manual work is done, as by a machinist or carpenter.
work•book (wûrk′bo͝ok′) ►*n.* **1.** A booklet containing problems and exercises that a student works directly on the pages. **2.** An operating manual, as for an appliance. **3.** A book in which a record of work is kept.
work•day (wûrk′dā′) ►*n.* **1.** A day on which work is usually done. **2.** The part of the day during which one works.
work•er (wûr′kər) ►*n.* **1.** One who works. **2.** One who does manual or industrial labor. **3.** A member of a colony of social insects such as ants or bees, usu. a sterile female, that performs specialized work.
work•fare (wûrk′fâr′) ►*n.* A form of welfare in which aid recipients are required to perform public-service work.
work force ►*n.* **1.** The workers employed in a specific project or activity. **2.** All people working or available to work, as in a nation.
work•horse (wûrk′hôrs′) ►*n.* **1.** A horse used for labor rather than for racing or riding. **2.** *Informal* A person who works tirelessly.
work•house (wûrk′hous′) ►*n.* **1.** A prison in which limited sentences are served at manual labor. **2.** *Chiefly Brit.* A poorhouse.
work•ing (wûr′kĭng) ►*adj.* **1a.** Of, used for, or spent in work. **b.** Functioning. **2.** Sufficient or adequate for using: *a working knowledge of Spanish.* **3.** Serving as a basis for further work: *a working hypothesis.*
work•load (wûrk′lōd′) ►*n.* The amount of work assigned or done in a given time period.
work•man (wûrk′mən) ►*n.* **1.** A man who per-

forms labor for wages. **2.** A craftsman.

work•man•like (wûrk′mən-līk′) ▸*adj.* Befitting a skilled worker; skillfully done.

work•man•ship (wûrk′mən-shĭp′) ▸*n.* **1.** The art of a skilled worker or craftsperson. **2.** The quality of something made.

work•out (wûrk′out′) ▸*n.* **1.** A session of exercise or practice to improve fitness or athletic skill. **2.** A strenuous task.

work•place (wûrk′plās′) ▸*n.* **1.** A place where people are employed. **2.** The work setting in general.

work•shop (wûrk′shŏp′) ▸*n.* **1.** A room, area, or establishment where manual work is done. **2.** An educational seminar in a specified field.

work•space (wûrk′spās′) ▸*n.* An area used or allocated for one's work, as in an office.

work•sta•tion (wûrk′stā′shən) ▸*n.* **1.** An area, as in an office, equipped for one worker, usu. including a computer. **2.** A powerful computer usu. used for processing graphics.

work•ta•ble (wûrk′tā′bəl) ▸*n.* A table designed for a specific activity, as sewing.

work•week (wûrk′wēk′) ▸*n.* The hours or days worked in a week.

world (wûrld) ▸*n.* **1.** The earth. **2.** The universe. **3.** The earth with its inhabitants. **4.** The human race. **5.** The public. **6.** often **World** A specified part of the earth. **7.** A realm or domain. **8.** A sphere of human activity or interest: *the world of sports.* **9.** A particular way of life. **10.** Secular life and its concerns: *a woman of the world.* **11.** A large amount: *did him a world of good.* **12.** A celestial body such as a planet. [< OE *weorold.*]

world•ly (wûrld′lē) ▸*adj.* **-li•er, -li•est 1.** Of or devoted to temporal rather than to religious or spiritual matters. **2.** Sophisticated; cosmopolitan. —**world′li•ness** *n.*

world•ly-wise (wûrld′lē-wīz′) ▸*adj.* Experienced in the ways of the world.

world•wide (wûrld′wīd′) ▸*adj.* Involving or extending throughout the world; universal. —**world′wide′** *adv.*

World Wide Web ▸*n.* The complete set of documents on all Internet servers that use the HTTP protocol, accessible to users via a simple point-and-click system.

worm (wûrm) ▸*n.* **1.** Any of various invertebrates, as an earthworm or tapeworm, having a long, flexible, rounded or flattened body. **2.** Any of various insect larvae having a soft elongated body. **3.** Something that resembles a worm. **4.** An insidiously tormenting or devouring force. **5.** A pitiable or contemptible person. **6. worms** Infestation of the intestines with worms or wormlike parasites. ▸*v.* **1.** To move with or as if with the sinuous crawling motion of a worm. **2.** To elicit by artful or devious means: *wormed a confession out of the suspect.* **3.** To cure of intestinal worms. [< OE *wyrm.*] —**worm′y** *adj.*

worm-eat•en (wûrm′ēt′n) ▸*adj.* **1.** Bored through or gnawed by worms. **2.** Decayed; rotten. **3.** Antiquated; decrepit.

worm gear ▸*n.* **1.** A gear consisting of a spirally threaded shaft and a wheel with teeth that mesh into it. **2.** A worm wheel.

worm•hole (wûrm′hōl′) ▸*n.* **1.** A hole made by a burrowing worm. **2.** *Phys.* A theoretical distortion of space-time in which one location or time is linked with another through a path that is shorter than expected.

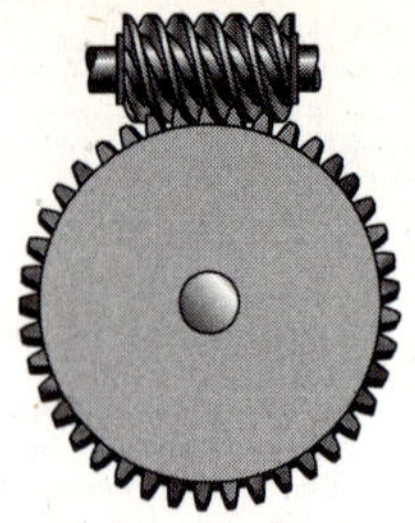

worm gear

worm wheel ▸*n.* The toothed wheel of a worm gear.

worm•wood (wûrm′wo͝od′) ▸*n.* An aromatic herb yielding a bitter extract used in making absinthe. [< OE *wermōd.*]

worn (wôrn, wōrn) ▸*v.* P.part. of **wear.** ▸*adj.* **1.** Affected or impaired by wear or use. **2.** Showing the wearing effects of overwork, care, worry, or suffering.

worn-out (wôrn′out′, wōrn′-) ▸*adj.* **1.** Worn or used until no longer usable. **2.** Thoroughly exhausted; spent.

wor•ri•some (wûr′ē-səm, wŭr′-) ▸*adj.* **1.** Causing worry or anxiety. **2.** Tending to worry.

wor•ry (wûr′ē, wŭr′ē) ▸*v.* **-ried, -ry•ing 1.** To feel uneasy or troubled. See Syns at **brood. 2.** To cause to feel anxious, distressed, or troubled. See Syns at **trouble. 3.** To bother or annoy. **4a.** To pull, bite, or tear at repeatedly. **b.** To touch, move, or handle idly. ▸*n., pl.* **-ries 1.** Mental uneasiness or anxiety. **2.** A source of worry. [< OE *wyrgan,* strangle.] —**wor′ri•er** *n.*

wor•ry•wart (wûr′ē-wôrt′, wŭr′-) ▸*n.* One who worries excessively and needlessly.

worse (wûrs) ▸*adj.* Comp. of **bad, ill.** In a worse manner. ▸*adv.* Comp. of **badly, ill.** [< OE *wyrsa.*]

wors•en (wûr′sən) ▸*v.* To make or become worse.

wor•ship (wûr′shĭp) ▸*n.* **1a.** Reverent love and devotion for a deity or sacred object. **b.** The ceremonies or prayers by which this love is expressed. **2.** Ardent devotion; adoration: *his worship of fame.* **3.** often **Worship** *Chiefly Brit.* Used as a form of address for magistrates and certain other dignitaries: *Your Worship.* ▸*v.* **-shiped, -ship•ing** or **-shipped, -ship•ping 1.** To honor and love as a deity. **2.** To love devotedly. **3.** To participate in religious worship. [< OE *weorthscipe,* worthiness.] —**wor′ship•er** *n.*

wor•ship•ful (wûr′shĭp-fəl) ▸*adj.* **1.** Given to or showing worship. **2.** *Chiefly Brit.* Used as a respectful form of address. —**wor′ship•ful•ly** *adv.*

worst (wûrst) ▸*adj.* Superl. of **bad, ill. 1.** Most inferior, as in quality, condition, health, or effect. **2.** Most severe or unfavorable. ▸*adv.* Superl. of **badly, ill.** In the worst manner or degree. ▸*v.* To gain the advantage over; defeat. ▸*n.* Something that is worst. [< OE *wyrsta.*]

wor•sted (wo͝os′tĭd, wûr′stĭd) ▸*n.* **1.** Firm-textured, compactly twisted woolen yarn made from long-staple fibers. **2.** Fabric made from such yarn. [< ME *worthstede.*]

wort (wûrt, wôrt) ▸*n.* A plant: *liverwort.* [< OE *wyrt.*]

worth (wûrth) ▸*n.* **1.** The quality that renders something desirable, useful, or valuable. **2.** Material or market value. **3.** A quantity of something that may be purchased for a specified sum. **4.** Wealth; riches. ▸*adj.* **1.** Equal in value to something specified. **2.** Deserving of; meriting: *a proposal worth considering.* **3.** Having wealth or riches amounting to. [< OE *weorth.*]

worth•less (wûrth′lĭs) ▸*adj.* **1.** Lacking worth; of no use or value. **2.** Low; despicable. —**worth′less•ness** *n.*

worth•while (wûrth′hwīl′, -wīl′) ▸*adj.* Sufficiently valuable or important to be worth one's time or effort.

wor•thy (wûr′*thē*) ▸*adj.* **-thi•er, -thi•est 1.** Having worth, merit, or value. **2.** Honorable; admirable. **3.** Deserving: *worthy of acclaim.* ▸*n., pl.* **-thies.** An eminent or distinguished person. —**wor′thi•ness** *n.*

would (wo͝od) ▸*aux.v.* P.t. of **will**[2]. **1.** Used after a statement of desire or request: *I wish you would stay.* **2.** Used for politeness: *Would you go with me?* **3.** Used to indicate uncertainty: *It would seem so.* See Usage Note at **if.**

would-be (wo͝od′bē′) ▸*adj.* Desiring or attempting to be: *a would-be actor.*

would•n't (wo͝od′nt) ▸ Would not.

wouldst (wo͝odst) or **would•est** (wo͝od′ĭst) ▸*v. Archaic* 2nd pers. sing. p.t. of **will**[2].

wound[1] (wo͞ond) ▸*n.* **1.** An injury, esp. one in which the skin is torn, pierced, cut, or broken. **2.** An injury to the feelings. ▸*v.* To inflict a wound on. [< OE *wund.*]

wound[2] (wound) ▸*v.* P.t. and p.part. of **wind**[2].

Wound•ed Knee (wo͞on′dĭd) A creek of SW SD, site of a Native American massacre by US troops (1890).

wove (wōv) ▸*v.* P.t. of **weave.**

wo•ven (wō′vən) ▸*v.* P.part. of **weave.**

wow (wou) *Informal* ▸*interj.* Used to express wonder, amazement, or great pleasure. ▸*n.* An outstanding success. ▸*v.* To have a strong and usu. pleasurable effect on.

WPA ▸*abbr.* Work Projects Administration

wpm ▸*abbr.* words per minute

wrack (răk) ▸*n.* **1.** Destruction or ruin. **2.** A remnant of something destroyed. [< OE *wræc,* punishment.]

wraith (rāth) ▸*n.* **1.** An apparition of a living person. **2.** The ghost of a dead person. [?]

Wran•gel Island (răng′gəl) An island of NE Russia in the Arctic Ocean NW of the Bering Strait.

Wran•gell (răng′gəl), **Mount.** A peak, 4,319.7 m (14,163 ft), of the central Wrangell Mts. in S AK.

Wrangell Mountains. A mountain range of S AK extending about 161 km (100 mi) from the Copper R. to the Canadian border.

wran•gle (răng′gəl) ▸*v.* **-gled, -gling 1.** To quarrel noisily or angrily; bicker. **2.** To win or obtain by argument. **3.** To herd (horses or other livestock). ▸*n.* An angry or noisy dispute. [ME *wranglen.*] —**wran′gler** *n.*

wrap (răp) ▸*v.* **wrapped** or **wrapt** (răpt), **wrap•ping 1.** To draw, fold, or wind about in order to cover. **2.** To enclose within a covering; enfold. **3.** To encase and secure (an object), esp. with paper; package. **4.** To clasp, fold, or coil about something. **5.** To envelop or surround, esp. so as to obscure. **6.** To absorb; engross: *wrapped in thought.* —***phrasal verb:*** **wrap up 1.** To finish; conclude. **2.** To summarize; recapitulate. ▸*n.* **1.** An outer garment worn for warmth. **2.** A wrapping or wrapper. **3.** The completion of filming on a movie. —***idiom:*** **under wraps** Secret or concealed. [ME *wrappen.*]

wrap•a•round (răp′ə-round′) ▸*n.* A garment, such as a skirt, that is open to the side and is wrapped around the body.

wrap•per (răp′ər) ▸*n.* **1.** One that wraps. **2.** A material, such as paper, in which something is wrapped. **3.** The tobacco leaf covering a cigar. **4.** A loose robe or negligee.

wrap•ping (răp′ĭng) ▸*n.* The material in which something is wrapped.

wrap-up (răp′ŭp′) ▸*n.* A brief final summary, as of the news.

wrasse (răs) ▸*n.* Any of numerous chiefly tropical, often brightly colored marine fishes. [Cornish *gwragh.*]

wrath (răth) ▸*n.* **1.** Furious, often vindictive anger; rage. **2a.** Punishment or vengeance as a manifestation of anger. **b.** Divine retribution for sin. [< OE *wrǣththu.*] —**wrath′ful** *adj.* —**wrath′ful•ly** *adv.*

wreak (rēk) ▸*v.* **1.** To inflict (e.g., vengeance). **2.** To vent (e.g., anger). [< OE *wrecan.*]

wreath (rēth) ▸*n., pl.* **wreaths** (rē*th*z, rēths) **1.** A ring or circular band, as of flowers or leaves. **2.** A curling or circular form: *a wreath of smoke.* [< OE *writha,* band.]

wreathe (rē*th*) ▸*v.* **wreathed, wreath•ing 1.** To twist or entwine into a wreath. **2.** To coil or spiral. **3.** To encircle with or as if with a wreath. [< WREATH.]

wreck (rĕk) ▸*v.* **1.** To destroy in or as if in a collision. **2.** To dismantle or tear down. **3.** To bring to a state of ruin. See Syns at **blast.** ▸*n.* **1.** The act of wrecking or the state of being wrecked. **2.** A shipwreck. **3a.** The damaged remains, as of a wrecked ship or vehicle. **b.** Debris or cargo cast ashore after a shipwreck. **4.** One in a shattered, broken-down, or worn-out state. [< AN *wrec,* wrecking.]

wreck•age (rĕk′ĭj) ▸*n.* **1.** The act of wrecking or the state of being wrecked. **2.** The debris of something wrecked.

wreck•er (rĕk′ər) ▸*n.* **1.** One that wrecks. **2.** A member of a demolition crew. **3a.** A vehicle or piece of equipment employed in recovering or removing wrecks. **b.** One that salvages wrecked cargo or parts.

wren (rĕn) ▸*n.* Any of various small brownish songbirds having a short, often erect tail. [< OE *wrenna.*]

Wren, Sir **Christopher.** 1632–1723. English architect.

wrench (rĕnch) ▸*n.* **1.** A sudden forcible twist or turn. **2.** An injury produced by twisting or straining. **3.** A sudden surge of emotion. **4.** A tool with fixed or adjustable jaws for gripping, turning, or twisting an object such as a nut. ▸*v.* **1a.** To twist or turn suddenly and forcibly. **b.** To twist and sprain: *wrenched my knee.* **2.** To free by pulling at; yank. See Syns at **jerk**[1]. **3.** To pull at the feelings or emotions of; distress.

4. To distort; pervert. [< OE *wrencan*, twist.]

wrest (rĕst) ▸ *v.* **1.** To obtain by or as if by pulling with violent twisting movements. **2.** To gain or take by force. ▸ *n.* The act of wresting. [< OE *wrǣstan.*] —**wrest′er** *n.*

wres•tle (rĕs′əl) ▸ *v.* **-tled, -tling 1.** To fight by grappling and attempting to throw or immobilize one's opponent. **2.** To contend against in the sport of wrestling. **3.** To struggle to master something: *wrestle with a problem.* [< OE **wrǣstlian.*] —**wres′tle** *n.* —**wres′tler** *n.*

wres•tling (rĕs′lĭng) ▸ *n.* A sport in which two competitors attempt to throw or immobilize each other by grappling.

wretch (rĕch) ▸ *n.* **1.** A miserable, unfortunate, or unhappy person. **2.** A base or despicable person. [< OE *wrecca.*]

wretch•ed (rĕch′ĭd) ▸ *adj.* **-er, -est 1.** Woeful; miserable. **2.** Of a poor or mean character; dismal. **3.** Contemptible; vile. **4.** Of inferior quality. [< ME *wrecche,* WRETCH.] —**wretch′ed•ly** *adv.* —**wretch′ed•ness** *n.*

wri•er (rī′ər) ▸ *adj.* Comp. of **wry.**

wri•est (rī′ĭst) ▸ *adj.* Superl. of **wry.**

wrig•gle (rĭg′əl) ▸ *v.* **-gled, -gling 1.** To turn or twist with sinuous motions; squirm. **2.** To proceed with sinuous motions. **3.** To insinuate or extricate oneself by sly or subtle means. [ME *wrigglen.*] —**wrig′gle** *n.* —**wrig′gly** *adj.*

wrig•gler (rĭg′lər) ▸ *n.* **1.** The larva of a mosquito. **2.** One that wriggles.

Wright (rīt), **Frank Lloyd.** 1869–1959. Amer. architect.

Wright, Orville. 1871–1948. Amer. aviation pioneer; with his brother **Wilbur** (1867–1912) invented the airplane.

Wright, Richard. 1908–60. Amer. writer.

wring (rĭng) ▸ *v.* **wrung** (rŭng), **wring•ing 1.** To twist and squeeze, esp. to extract liquid. **2.** To extract by or as if by twisting or compressing; extort: *wring the truth out of a witness.* **3.** To wrench or twist forcibly or painfully: *wring someone's neck.* **4.** To twist or squeeze (one's hands) in distress. **5.** To anguish or aggrieve. [< OE *wringan.*]

wring•er (rĭng′ər) ▸ *n.* One that wrings, esp. a device in which laundry is pressed between rollers to extract water.

wrin•kle (rĭng′kəl) ▸ *n.* **1.** A small furrow, ridge, or crease on a normally smooth surface, as cloth or the skin. **2.** An ingenious innovation. **3.** A problem or flaw. ▸ *v.* **-kled, -kling 1.** To make a wrinkle or wrinkles in. **2.** To form wrinkles. [Prob. < OE *gewrinclian,* crease.] —**wrin′kly** *adj.*

wrist (rĭst) ▸ *n.* **1.** The joint between the hand and forearm. **2.** The bones of this joint; carpus. [< OE.]

wrist•band (rĭst′bănd′) ▸ *n.* A band, as on a long sleeve, that encircles the wrist.

wrist•watch (rĭst′wŏch′) ▸ *n.* A watch worn on a band that fastens about the wrist.

writ (rĭt) ▸ *n.* **1.** A written order issued by a court, commanding the party to whom it is addressed to perform or cease performing a specified act. **2.** Writings: *holy writ.* [< OE.]

writ•a•ble also **write•a•ble** (rī′tə-bəl) ▸ *adj.* *Comp. Sci.* Capable of recording data: *writable compact disks.*

write (rīt) ▸ *v.* **wrote** (rōt), **writ•ten** (rĭt′n), **writ•ing 1a.** To form (letters, words, or symbols) on a surface with an instrument such as a pen. **b.** To spell. **2.** To form (letters or words) in cursive style. **3.** To compose and set down, esp. in literary or musical form. **4.** To relate or communicate in writing. **5.** To send a letter or note to. **6.** To communicate by letter; correspond. **7.** *Comp. Sci.* To copy (data) to a storage device. —***phrasal verbs:* write in** To cast a vote by inserting (a name not listed on a ballot). **write off 1.** To reduce the book value of. **2.** To cancel from accounts as a loss. [< OE *wrītan.*]

write-in (rīt′ĭn′) ▸ *n.* A vote cast by writing in the name of a candidate not on the ballot.

write-pro•tect (rīt′prə-tĕkt′) ▸ *v.* *Comp. Sci.* To modify (a file or disk) so that its data cannot be edited or erased.

writ•er (rī′tər) ▸ *n.* One who writes, esp. as an occupation.

write-up (rīt′ŭp′) ▸ *n.* A published account, review, or notice.

writhe (rī*th*) ▸ *v.* **writhed, writh•ing.** To twist or squirm, as in pain. [< OE *wrīthan.*]

writ•ing (rī′tĭng) ▸ *n.* **1.** Written form: *Put it in writing.* **2.** Handwriting. **3.** Something written, esp. a literary composition. **4.** The activity, occupation, or style of a writer. **5. Writings** *(takes sing. or pl. v.) Bible* The third of the three divisions of the Hebrew Bible. See table at **Bible.**

Wro•claw (vrôt′släf′) A city of SW Poland on the Oder R. Pop. 643,071.

wrong (rông, rŏng) ▸ *adj.* **1.** Not correct; erroneous. **2a.** Contrary to conscience, morality, law, or custom. **b.** Unfair; unjust. **3.** Not required, intended, or wanted. **4.** Not fitting; inappropriate. **5.** Not in accord with established usage, method, or procedure. **6.** Being the side, as of a garment, that is less finished and not intended to show. ▸ *adv.* **1.** In a wrong manner; erroneously. **2.** Immorally or unjustly. **3.** In an unfavorable way; amiss. See Syns at **amiss.** ▸ *n.* **1.** Something that is wrong. **2.** The condition of being in error or at fault: *in the wrong.* ▸ *v.* **1.** To treat injuriously or dishonorably. **2.** To discredit unjustly; malign. [ME, of Scand. orig.] —**wrong′ly** *adv.*

wrong•do•er (rông′do͞o′ər, rŏng′-) ▸ *n.* One who does wrong. —**wrong′do′ing** *n.*

wrong•ful (rông′fəl, rŏng′-) ▸ *adj.* **1.** Wrong; unjust. **2.** Unlawful: *wrongful death.* —**wrong′ful•ly** *adv.* —**wrong′ful•ness** *n.*

wrong-head•ed (rông′hĕd′ĭd, rŏng′-) ▸ *adj.* Persistently and stubbornly wrong.

wrote (rōt) ▸ *v.* P.t. of **write.**

wroth (rôth) ▸ *adj.* Angry. [< OE *wrāth.*]

wrought (rôt) ▸ *adj.* **1.** Fashioned; created. **2.** Shaped by hammering: *wrought silver.*

wrought iron ▸ *n.* A purified form of iron that is easily shaped, forged, or welded.

wrought-up (rôt′ŭp′) ▸ *adj.* Agitated; excited.

wrung (rŭng) ▸ *v.* P.t. and p.part. of **wring.**

wry (rī) ▸ *adj.* **wri•er** (rī′ər), **wri•est** (rī′ĭst) or **wry•er, wry•est 1.** Dryly humorous. **2.** Temporarily twisted in an expression of distaste or displeasure: *made a wry face.* **3.** Bent to one side; crooked. [< OE *wrīgian,* turn.] —**wry′ly** *adv.* —**wry′ness** *n.*

WSW ▸ *abbr.* west-southwest

wt. ▸ *abbr.* weight

WTO ▸ *abbr.* World Trade Organization

Wu•han (wo͞o′hän′) A city of E China on the Chang Jiang (Yangtze R.). Pop. 3,832,536.

Wup•per•tal (vo͝op′ər-täl′) A city of W-central Germany. Pop. 386,625.

wurst (wûrst, wo͝orst) ▸*n.* Sausage. [Ger.]

WV or **W.Va.** ▸*abbr.* West Virginia

WVS ▸*abbr.* Women's Voluntary Service

WWI ▸*abbr.* World War I

WWII ▸*abbr.* World War II

WWW ▸*abbr.* World Wide Web

WY ▸*abbr.* Wyoming

Wy•an•dot also **Wy•an•dotte** (wī′ən-dŏt′) ▸*n., pl.* **-dot** or **-dots** also **-dotte** or **-dottes 1.** A member of a Native American people of the former Huron confederacy, now in NE Oklahoma. **2.** Their Iroquoian language.

Wy•att or **Wy•at** (wī′ət), Sir **Thomas.** 1503–42. English diplomat.

Wych•er•ley (wĭch′ər-lē), **William.** 1640?–1716. English comic playwright and satirist.

Wyc•liffe, John. 1328?–84. English theologian and religious reformer.

Wy•eth (wī′ĭth), **Andrew.** b. 1917. Amer. painter.

Wy•o•ming (wī-ō′mĭng) A state of the W US. Cap. Cheyenne. Pop. 455,975.

WYSIWYG (wĭz′ē-wĭg′) ▸*adj.* Of or being a word-processing system in which the screen displays text exactly as it will be printed. [*w(hat) y(ou) s(ee) i(s) w(hat) y(ou) g(et).*]

x¹ or **X** (ĕks) ▸*n., pl.* **x's** or **X's** also **xs** or **Xs 1.** The 24th letter of the English alphabet. **2.** A mark inscribed to represent the signature of an illiterate person. **3.** An unknown or unnamed factor, thing, or person. ▸*v.* **x'd, x'ing** or **X'd, X'ing.** To delete or cancel with a series of X's: *x'd out the error.*

x² ▸ The symbol for **abscissa.**

X¹ (ĕks) ▸*n.* A movie rating barring admission to anyone under the age of 17.

X² ▸ **1.** *Elect.* The symbol for **reactance. 2.** also **x** The symbol for the Roman numeral 10.

X³ ▸*abbr.* **1.** Christ (Greek Χριστος, *Khristos*) **2.** Christian **3.** extra

x. ▸*abbr. Bus.* ex

Xan•thus (zăn′thəs) An ancient city of Lycia in present-day SW Turkey.

Xa•vi•er (zā′vē-ər, zăv′ē-), Saint **Francis.** 1506–52. Spanish Jesuit missionary.

x-ax•is (ĕks′ăk′sĭs) ▸*n., pl.* **x-ax•es** (-ăk′sēz) **1.** The horizontal axis of a two-dimensional Cartesian coordinate system. **2.** One of three axes in a three-dimensional Cartesian coordinate system.

X-chro•mo•some (ĕks′krō′mə-sōm′) ▸*n.* The sex chromosome associated with female characteristics, occurring paired in the female and single in the male sex-chromosome pair.

Xe ▸ The symbol for the element **xenon.**

xe•bec (zē′bĕk′) ▸*n.* A small three-masted Mediterranean vessel with both square and triangular sails. [< Ar. dial. *šabbāk.*]

xe•non (zē′nŏn′) ▸*n. Symbol* **Xe** A colorless, odorless, inert gaseous element found in minute quantities in the atmosphere. At. no. 54. See table at **element.** [< Gk. *xenos*, strange.]

Xe•noph•a•nes (zə-nŏf′ə-nēz′). 560?–478? B.C. Greek philosopher.

xen•o•phobe (zĕn′ə-fōb′, zē′nə-) ▸*n.* One unduly fearful or contemptuous of strangers or foreigners. [Gk. *xenos*, foreign + -PHOBE.] **—xen′o•pho′bi•a** *n.* **—xen′o•pho′bic** *adj.*

Xen•o•phon (zĕn′ə-fən, -fŏn′). 430?–355? B.C. Greek soldier and writer.

xer•ic (zĕr′ĭk, zîr′-) ▸*adj.* Of or adapted to an extremely dry habitat. [< Gk. *xēros*, dry.]

xe•rog•ra•phy (zĭ-rŏg′rə-fē) ▸*n.* A dry photographic or photocopying process in which a negative image formed by a resinous powder on an electrically charged plate is transferred to and thermally fixed on a paper or other surface. [Gk. *xēros*, dry + -GRAPHY.] **—xer′o•graph′ic** (zîr′ə-grăf′ĭk) *adj.*

xer•o•phyte (zîr′ə-fīt′) ▸*n.* A plant adapted to living in a dry, arid habitat. [< Gk. *xēros*, dry.] **—xer′o•phyt′ic** (-fĭt′ĭk) *adj.*

Xer•ox (zîr′ŏks) ▸ A trademark for a photocopying process or machine employing xerography.

Xer•xes I (zûrk′sēz). "Xerxes the Great." 519?–465 B.C. King of Persia (486–465).

Xho•sa also **Xo•sa** (kō′sä, -zə) ▸*n., pl.* **-sa** or **-sas 1.** A member of a Bantu people of the E part of Cape Province, South Africa. **2.** The Bantu language of this people.

xi (zī, sī, ksē) ▸*n.* The 14th letter of the Greek alphabet. [Gk. *xei.*]

Xia•men (shyä′mən) also **A•moy** (ä-moi′). A city of E China ENE of Guangzhou. Pop. 639,436.

Xi'an (shē′än′, shyän) also **Si•an** (sē′än′, shē′-). A city of central China SW of Beijing. Pop. 2,872,539.

Xiang Jiang (shyäng′ jyäng′) also **Siang Kiang** (syäng′ kyäng′, shyäng′). A river, about 1,150 km (715 mi), flowing generally northward from SE China.

Xin•gu (shēng-go͞o′) A river of central and N Brazil flowing about 1,979 km (1,230 mi) to the Amazon R.

Xi•zang (shē′dzäng′) or **Ti•bet** (tə-bĕt′). An autonomous region of China in the SW part N and W of the Himalayas. Cap. Lhasa. Pop. 2,196,010.

XL ▸*abbr.* **1.** extra large **2.** extra long

X•mas (krĭs′məs, ĕks′məs) ▸*n.* Christmas. [< *X*, the Greek letter chi, abbr. of *Khristos*, Christ.]

x-ra•di•a•tion (ĕks′rā′dē-ā′shən) ▸*n.* **1.** Treatment with or exposure to x-rays. **2.** Radiation composed of x-rays.

x-ray also **X-ray** (ĕks′rā′) ▸*n.* **1a.** A relatively high-energy photon with a very short wavelength. **b.** A stream of such photons, used in radiography, radiology, radiotherapy, and scientific research. **2.** A photograph taken with x-rays. ▸*v.* **1.** To irradiate with x-rays. **2.** To photograph with x-rays.

Xu•zhou (sho͞o′jō′) also **Sü•chow** (so͞o′chou′, sü′jō′). A city of E China NNW of Nanjing. Pop. 841,000.

xy•lem (zī′ləm) ►*n.* The supporting and water-conducting tissue of vascular plants, consisting primarily of woody tissue. [< Gk. *xulon,* wood.]
xy•loid (zī′loid′) ►*adj.* Of, relating to, or like wood.
xy•lo•phone (zī′lə-fōn′) ►*n.* A percussion instrument consisting of a mounted row of wooden bars graduated in length to sound a chromatic scale, played with two small mallets. —**xy′lo•phon′ist** *n.*

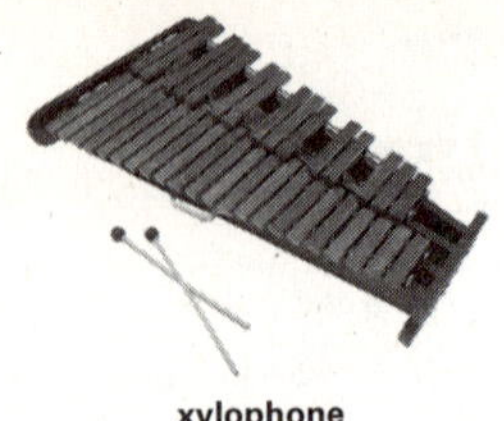
xylophone

Y

y[1] or **Y** (wī) ►*n., pl.* **y's** or **Y's** also **ys** or **Ys.** The 25th letter of the English alphabet.
y[2] ► The symbol for **ordinate.**
Y[1] ► The symbol for the element **yttrium.**
Y[2] ►*abbr.* year
–y[1] or **–ey** ►*suff.* **1.** Characterized by: *rainy.* **2a.** Like: *summery.* **3.** Inclined toward: *sleepy.* [< OE *-ig.*]
–y[2] ►*suff.* **1.** Condition; quality: *jealousy.* **2a.** Activity: *cookery.* **b.** Instance of a specified action: *entreaty.* **3a.** Place for an activity: *cannery.* **b.** Result or product of an activity: *laundry.* **4.** Group: *soldiery.* [< Lat. *-ia.* Sense 2b < Lat. *-ium.*]
–y[3] or **–ie** ►*suff.* **1.** Small one: *doggy.* **2.** Dear one: *sweetie.* **3.** One having to do with or characterized by: *groupie.* [ME *-ie.*]
Y2K (wī′to͞o-kā′) ►*adj.* **1.** Relating to the year 2000. **2.** Relating to the Y2K bug: *Y2K testing.* [Y(EAR) + *2K,* 2000.]
Y2K bug ►*n.* A programming code defect in which a year represented by its last two digits is misinterpreted as being between 1900–99 instead of 2000–99.
yacht (yät) ►*n.* A relatively small sailing or motor-driven vessel, usu. with smart, graceful lines, used for pleasure cruises or racing. [< MLGer. *jachtschip.*] —**yacht** *v.* —**yacht′ing** *n.* —**yachts′man** *n.* —**yachts′wom′an** *n.*
Ya•fo (yä′fō) also **Jaf•fa** (jăf′ə, yä′fə). A former city of W-central Israel on the Mediterranean Sea; part of Tel Aviv–Yafo since 1950.
ya•hoo (yä′ho͞o, yā′-) ►*n., pl.* **-hoos.** A crude or brutish person. See Syns at **boor.** [From the *Yahoos,* characters in *Gulliver's Travels* by Jonathan Swift.]
Yah•weh (yä′wā, -wĕ) also **Yah•veh** (-vā, -vĕ) ►*n.* In the Hebrew Bible, a name of God; Jehovah.
yak[1] (yăk) ►*n.* A shaggy-haired ox of the mountains of central Asia. [Tibetan *gyag.*]
yak[2] (yăk) ►*v.* **yakked, yak•king** *Slang* To talk or chatter persistently. [Imit.] —**yak** *n.*
y'all (yôl) ►*pron. Regional* Var. of **you-all.** See Regional Note at **you-all.**
Yal•ta (yôl′tə) A city of SE Ukraine in the S Crimea on the Black Sea. Pop. 86,000.
Ya•lu Jiang (yä′lo͞o′ jyäng′) A river, about 805 km (500 mi), forming part of the North Korea–China border.
yam (yăm) ►*n.* **1.** The starchy edible root of a tropical vine. **2.** *Regional* See **sweet potato.** See Regional Note at **goober.** [Port. *inhame,* of West African orig.]
yam•mer (yăm′ər) ►*v. Informal* **1.** To complain peevishly; whine. **2.** To jabber; chatter. [ME *yameren,* lament.]
Ya•mous•sou•kro (yä′mo͞o-so͞o′krō) The official capital of Côte d'Ivoire, in the S-central part N of Abidjan.
Ya•mu•na (yŭm′ə-nə) or **Jum•na** (jŭm′nə). A river of N India rising in the Himalayas and flowing about 1,384 km (860 mi) to the Ganges R. at Allahabad.
yang (yăng) ►*n.* The active, male cosmic principle in Chinese dualistic philosophy. [Mandarin *yáng,* sun, light.]
Yan•gon (yäN′gôN′). Formerly **Ran•goon** (răn-go͞on′, răng-). The capital of Myanmar (Burma), in the S part. Pop. 2,458,712.
Yang•tze River (yăng′sē′, -tsē′) See **Chang Jiang.**
yank (yăngk) ►*v.* To pull or extract with or as if with a sudden forceful movement. See Syns at **jerk[1].** ►*n.* A sudden vigorous pull; jerk. [?]
Yank ►*n. Informal* A Yankee.
Yan•kee (yăng′kē) ►*n.* **1.** A native of a northern US state, esp. a New Englander. **2.** A US citizen; American. [?]
Ya•oun•dé (yä-o͞on-dā′) The capital of Cameroon, in the S-central part. Pop. 653,670.
yap (yăp) ►*v.* **yapped, yap•ping 1.** To bark sharply or shrilly; yelp. **2.** *Slang* To talk noisily or stupidly; jabber. ►*n.* **1.** A bark; yelp. **2.** *Slang* Chatter; jabber. **3.** *Slang* The mouth. [Prob. imit.] —**yap′per** *n.*
Ya•qui (yä′kē) ►*n., pl.* **-qui** or **-quis 1.** A member of a Native American people of NW Mexico, now also in S Arizona. **2.** The Uto-Aztecan language of the Yaqui.
yard[1] (yärd) ►*n.* **1.** See table at **measurement. 2.** *Naut.* A long tapering spar slung to a mast to support and spread a sail. [< OE *gerd,* stick.]
yard[2] (yärd) ►*n.* **1.** A tract of ground next to a building. **2.** A tract of ground, often enclosed, used for a specific activity. **3.** An area where railroad trains are made up and cars are switched, stored, and serviced. **4.** An enclosed area for livestock. [< OE *geard.*]
yard•age (yär′dĭj) ►*n.* An amount or length of something measured in yards.
yard•arm (yärd′ärm′) ►*n. Naut.* Either end of a yard of a square sail.
yard•stick (yärd′stĭk′) ►*n.* **1.** A graduated measuring stick one yard in length. **2.** A test or standard used in making a comparison or judgment. See Syns at **standard.**
yar•mul•ke (yär′məl-kə, yä′məl-) ►*n.* A skullcap worn by Jewish men and boys. [Yiddish.]

yarn (yärn) ►*n.* **1.** A continuous strand of twisted threads, as of wool or nylon, used in weaving or knitting. **2.** *Informal* A long, often elaborate story. [< OE *gearn.*]

Ya•ro•slavl (yär′ə-slä′vəl) A city of W-central Russia on the Volga R. NE of Moscow. Pop. 628,302.

yar•row (yăr′ō) ►*n.* Any of several plants having finely dissected foliage and flat, usu. white or yellow flower heads. [< OE *gearwe.*]

yaw (yô) ►*v.* **1.** To swerve off course momentarily or temporarily, as a ship. **2.** To turn about the vertical axis, as a missile. [Perhaps of Scandinavian origin.] —**yaw** *n.*

yawl (yôl) ►*n.* **1.** A two-masted fore-and-aft-rigged sailing vessel with the smaller mast abaft the rudder. **2.** A ship's small boat. [Du. *jol*, poss. < LGer. *jolle.*]

yawn (yôn) ►*v.* **1.** To open the mouth wide with a deep inhalation, as when sleepy or bored. **2.** To open wide; gape. ►*n.* The act of yawning. [< OE *geonian.*] —**yawn′er** *n.*

yaws (yôz) ►*pl.n. (takes sing. or pl. v.)* A highly contagious tropical disease marked by multiple red sores. [< Carib *yaya*, disease.]

y-ax•is (wī′ăk′sĭs) ►*n., pl.* **y-ax•es** (-ăk′sēz) **1.** The vertical axis of a two-dimensional Cartesian coordinate system. **2.** One of three axes in a three-dimensional Cartesian coordinate system.

Yb ► The symbol for the element **ytterbium.**

Y-chro•mo•some (wī′krō′mə-sōm′) ►*n.* The sex chromosome associated with male characteristics, occurring with one X-chromosome in the male sex-chromosome pair.

yd. ►*abbr.* yard (measurement)

ye[1] (*thē*) ►*def. art. Archaic* The. [From the substitution of *y* for þ (th).]

ye[2] (yē) ►*pron. Archaic* You. [< OE *gē.*]

yea (yā) ►*adv.* **1.** Yes; aye. **2.** Indeed; truly. ►*n.* **1.** An affirmative statement or vote. **2.** One who votes affirmatively. [< OE *gēa.*]

yeah (yĕ′ə, yă′ə, yā′ə) ►*adv. Informal* Yes. [< YEA.]

year (yîr) ►*n.* **1a.** The period during which the earth completes one revolution around the sun, equal to 365 days, 5 hours, 49 minutes, and 12 seconds. In the Gregorian calendar, the year begins on January 1 and ends on December 31 and is divided into 12 months, 52 weeks, and 365 days, or 366 days in a leap year. **b.** A corresponding period in other calendars. **2.** A year or part of a year devoted to a special activity: *the academic year.* **3. years** Age, esp. old age. **4. years** A long time. [< OE *gēar.*]

year•book (yîr′bo͝ok′) ►*n.* **1.** A book published every year, containing information about the previous year. **2.** A yearly book published by the graduating class of a school or college.

year•ling (yîr′lĭng) ►*n.* An animal that is one year old or has not completed its second year.

year•long (yîr′lông′, -lŏng′) ►*adj.* Lasting one year.

year•ly (yîr′lē) ►*adj.* Occurring once a year; annual. ►*adv.* Once a year; annually.

yearn (yûrn) ►*v.* **1.** To have a strong or deep desire; long. **2.** To feel deep pity, sympathy, or tenderness. [< OE *geornan.*]

yearn•ing (yûr′nĭng) ►*n.* A deep longing.

year-round (yîr′round′) ►*adj.* Existing, active, or continuous throughout the year.

yeast (yēst) ►*n.* **1.** Any of various unicellular fungi capable of fermenting carbohydrates. **2.** Froth consisting of yeast cells that is present in or added to fruit juices and other substances in the production of alcoholic beverages. **3.** A commercial preparation containing yeast cells and used esp. as a leavening agent. **4.** An agent of ferment or activity. [< OE *gist.*] —**yeast′y** *adj.*

Yeats (yāts), **William Butler.** 1865–1939. Irish writer; 1923 Nobel. —**Yeats′i•an** *adj.*

Ye•ka•te•rin•burg (yĭ-kăt′ər-ən-bûrg′). Formerly (1924–91) **Sverd•lovsk** (sfĕrd-lôfsk′). A city of W-central Russia in the E foothills of the Ural Mts. Pop. 1,350,861.

yell (yĕl) ►*v.* To cry out or utter loudly, as in pain, fright, surprise, or enthusiasm. See Syns at **shout.** [< OE *giellan.*] —**yell** *n.*

yel•low (yĕl′ō) ►*n.* **1a.** Any of a group of colors whose hue is that of ripe lemons. **b.** The hue of the visible spectrum lying between orange and green. **2.** *Regional* The yolk of an egg. ►*adj.* **-er, -est 1.** Of the color yellow. **2.** Having a yellow-brown skin color. **3.** *Slang* Cowardly. **4.** Exploiting, distorting, or exaggerating; sensational: *yellow journalism.* ►*v.* To make or become yellow. [< OE *geolu.*] —**yel′low•ish** *adj.*

yellow card ►*n.* A yellow-colored card shown by a referee, esp. in soccer, to signal a flagrant foul. —**yel′low-card′** *v.*

yellow fever ►*n.* An infectious tropical disease transmitted by mosquitoes and marked by fever, jaundice, and dark-colored vomit resulting from gastrointestinal hemorrhaging.

yellow jack ►*n.* **1.** A yellow flag hoisted on a ship to warn of disease on board. **2.** See **yellow fever.**

yellow jacket ►*n.* A small wasp with yellow and black markings.

Yel•low•knife (yĕl′ō-nīf′) The capital of Northwest Terrs., Canada, on the N shore of Great Slave Lake. Pop. 9,483.

Yellow River. See **Huang He.**

Yellow Sea. An arm of the Pacific between China and the Korean Peninsula.

Yel•low•stone (yĕl′ō-stōn′) A river, about 1,080 km (671 mi), of NW WY and S and E Montana.

yelp (yĕlp) ►*v.* To utter a short sharp bark or cry. [< OE *gielpan*, boast.] —**yelp** *n.*

Yem•en (yĕm′ən, yā′mən) A country of SW Asia at the S tip of the Arabian peninsula; formed when Yemen (or North Yemen) merged with Southern Yemen (1990). Cap. Sana. Pop. 12,672,000. —**Yem′en•ite′, Yem′e•ni** (-ə-nē) *adj. & n.*

yen[1] (yĕn) ►*n.* A yearning or craving. [Cantonese *uên.*] —**yen** *v.*

yen[2] (yĕn) ►*n., pl.* **yen.** See table at **currency.** [J. *en* < Mandarin *yuán*, dollar.]

Ye•ni•sey (yĭ-nĭ-syā′) A river of central Russia flowing about 4,023 km (2,500 mi) to the Kara Sea.

yen•ta (yĕn′tə) ►*n. Slang* A meddlesome or gossipy person, esp. a woman. [Yiddish *yente.*]

yeo•man (yō′mən) ►*n.* **1.** An attendant, servant, or lesser official in a royal or noble household. **2.** A petty officer performing chiefly clerical duties in the US Navy. **3.** A small independent farmer, esp. a member of a former class of small freeholding farmers in England. [ME *yoman.*]

yeo•man•ry (yō′mən-rē) ►*pl.n.* The class of yeomen; small freeholding farmers.

yep (yĕp) ▸*adv. Informal* Yes. [< YES.]
yer•ba ma•té (yâr′bə mä′tā, yûr′bə mä-tā′) ▸*n.* See **maté.** [Am.Sp. : *yerba*, herb + *mate*, maté.]
Ye•re•van also **E•re•van** (yĕ′rĭ-vän′). The capital of Armenia, in the W-central part. Pop. 1,254,000.
yes (yĕs) ▸*adv.* Used to express affirmation, agreement, confirmation, or consent. ▸*n., pl.* **yes•es.** An affirmative response or vote. [< OE *gēse*, so be it!]
ye•shi•va or **ye•shi•vah** (yə-shē′və) ▸*n. Judaism* **1.** A school where students study the Talmud. **2.** An elementary or secondary school with a curriculum that includes religion and culture. [Heb. *yəšîbâ.*]
yes man ▸*n. Informal* One who slavishly agrees with a superior.
yes•ter•day (yĕs′tər-dā′, -dē) ▸*n.* **1.** The day before the present day. **2.** also **yesterdays** Time in the past, esp. the recent past. ▸*adv.* **1.** On the day before the present day. **2.** A short while ago. [< OE *geostran dæg.*]
yes•ter•year (yĕs′tər-yîr′) ▸*n.* **1.** The year before the present year. **2.** Time past.
yet (yĕt) ▸*adv.* **1.** At this time; for the present. **2.** Up to a specified time; thus far. **3.** At a future time; eventually. **4.** Besides; in addition. **5.** Still more; even: *a yet sadder tale.* **6.** Nevertheless: *young yet wise.* ▸*conj.* And despite this; nevertheless. —***idiom:* as yet** Up to the present time. [< OE *gēt.*]

Usage: In formal style *yet* in the sense "up to now" requires that the accompanying verb be in the present perfect, rather than in the simple past: *He hasn't started yet,* not *He didn't start yet.*

ye•ti (yĕt′ē) ▸*n., pl.* **-tis.** See **abominable snowman.** [Alteration of Tibetan *miti.*]
Yev•tu•shen•ko (yĕv′tə-shĕng′kō), **Yevgeny Aleksandrovich.** b. 1933. Soviet poet.
yew (yo͞o) ▸*n.* **1.** A poisonous evergreen tree or shrub having scarlet cup-shaped seeds and flat, dark green needles. **2.** The durable, fine-grained wood of a yew. [< OE *īw.*]
Yid•dish (yĭd′ĭsh) ▸*n.* The language historically of Jews of Central and Eastern Europe, derived principally from medieval German dialects. —**Yid′dish** *adj.*
yield (yēld) ▸*v.* **1a.** To give forth by or as if by a natural process, esp. by cultivation. See Syns at **produce. b.** To furnish or give in return: *an investment that yields high returns.* **2a.** To give over possession of; surrender. **b.** To give up or concede. **3.** To give way to pressure, force, or persuasion: *The door yielded to a gentle push.* **4.** To give place, as to one that is superior. ▸*n.* **1.** An amount yielded, as of a crop. **2.** A profit obtained from an investment; return. [< OE *geldan*, pay.]
yin (yĭn) ▸*n.* The passive, female cosmic principle in Chinese dualistic philosophy. [Mandarin *yīn*, moon, shade.]

yin
yin-yang symbol

yip (yĭp) ▸*n.* A sharp, high-pitched bark; yelp. [Perh. ME *yippe.*] —**yip** *v.*
yip•pee (yĭp′ē) ▸*interj. Informal* Used to express joy or elation.
-yl ▸*suff.* An organic acid radical: *methyl.* [< Gk. *hulē*, wood, matter.]
YMCA ▸*abbr.* Young Men's Christian Association
YMHA ▸*abbr.* Young Men's Hebrew Association
yo•del (yōd′l) ▸*v.* **-deled, -del•ing** or **-delled, -del•ling.** To sing so that the voice fluctuates between the normal chest voice and a falsetto. [Ger. *jodeln.*] —**yo′del** *n.*
yo•ga (yō′gə) ▸*n.* **1.** also **Yoga** A Hindu discipline for training the consciousness to attain perfect spiritual insight and tranquillity. **2.** A system of exercises practiced as part of this discipline. [< Skt. *yogaḥ*, union.]
yo•gi (yō′gē) ▸*n., pl.* **-gis.** One who practices yoga. [< Skt. *yogī* < *yogaḥ*, union. See YOGA.]
yo•gurt also **yo•ghurt** (yō′gərt) ▸*n.* A tart custardlike food prepared from milk curdled by bacteria. [Turk. *yoğurt.*]
yoke (yōk) ▸*n.* **1a.** A crossbar with two U-shaped pieces that encircle the necks of draft animals. **b.** *pl.* **yoke** or **yokes** A pair of draft animals joined by a yoke. **2.** A frame carried across a person's shoulders with equal loads suspended from each end. **3.** A clamp or vise that holds two parts together. **4.** A fitted part of a garment, esp. at the shoulders, to which another piece is attached. **5.** A bond or tie. **6.** Subjugation or bondage. ▸*v.* **yoked, yok•ing 1.** To fit or join with or as if with a yoke. **2.** To join or bind together. [< OE *geoc.*]
yo•kel (yō′kəl) ▸*n.* A rustic; bumpkin. [?]
Yo•ko•ha•ma (yō′kə-hä′mə) A city of SE Honshu, Japan, on the W shore of Tokyo Bay. Pop. 3,288,464.
yolk (yōk) ▸*n.* The yellow portion of an egg of a bird or reptile, serving as nutriment for the developing young. [< OE *geolca.*]
Yom Kip•pur (yôm′ kĭp′ər, kē-po͝or′) ▸*n. Judaism* A holy day observed on the 10th day of Tishri and marked by fasting and prayer for the atonement of sins.
yon (yŏn) ▸*adv. & adj.* Yonder. [< OE *geond.*]
yon•der (yŏn′dər) ▸*adv.* In or at that indicated place. ▸*adj.* Being at an indicated distance, usu. within sight. [< OE *geond.*]
Yon•kers (yŏng′kərz) A city of SE NY N of New York City. Pop. 188,082.
yoo-hoo (yo͞o′ho͞o′) ▸*interj.* Used to call someone at a distance.
yore (yôr, yōr) ▸*n.* Time long past: *days of yore.* [< OE *geāra*, long ago < *gēar*, YEAR.]
York (yôrk) A borough of N England on the Ouse R. ENE of Leeds. Pop. 103,968.
York, Cape 1. The northernmost point of Australia, at the tip of Cape York Peninsula. **2.** A cape of NW Greenland in N Baffin Bay.
York•town (yôrk′toun′) A village of SE VA; site of British surrender in the Revolutionary War (1781).
Yo•ru•ba (yôr′ə-bə, yō-ro͞o-bä′) ▸*n., pl.* **-ba** or **-bas 1.** A member of a West African people living chiefly in SW Nigeria. **2.** The language of the Yoruba. —**Yo′ru•ban** *adj.*

Yo•sem•i•te Valley (yō-sĕm′ĭ-tē) A valley of E-central CA; surrounded by **Yosemite National Park** and including **Yosemite Falls,** 739.6 m (2,425 ft) high.

you (yo͞o) ►*pron.* **1.** The one or ones being addressed: *Is that you?* See Regional Note at **you-all. 2.** One; anyone: *You can't win them all.* [< OE *ēow*.]

you-all (yo͞o′ôl′) also **y'all** (yôl) ►*pron. Regional* You (plural).

Regional Note: The single most famous feature of southern United States dialects is the pronoun *you-all,* probably heard more often in its variant *y'all. You* and *you-all* preserve the singular/plural distinction that English used to have in *thou/you.*

you'd (yo͞od) ► **1.** You had. **2.** You would.

you'll (yo͞ol, yo͝ol; yəl *when unstressed*) ► **1.** You will. **2.** You shall.

young (yŭng) ►*adj.* **-er, -est 1.** Being in an early period of life or development. **2.** Newly begun or formed: *The evening is young.* **3.** Of or suggestive of youth or early life. **4.** Vigorous or fresh; youthful. **5.** Lacking experience; immature. ►*n.* **1.** Young persons collectively: *programs for the young.* **2.** Offspring; brood. [< OE *geong*.] —**young′ish** *adj.*

Young, Andrew Jackson Jr. b. 1932. Amer. diplomat and politician.

Young, Brigham. 1801–77. Amer. Mormon leader.

young•ling (yŭng′lĭng) ►*n.* A young person, animal, or plant.

young•ster (yŭng′stər) ►*n.* A young person.

Youngs•town (yŭngz′toun′) A city of NE OH E of Akron. Pop. 95,732.

your (yo͝or, yôr, yōr; yər *when unstressed*) ►*adj.* The possessive form of **you.** Used as a modifier before a noun: *your boots; your reward.* [< OE *ēower*.]

you're (yo͝or; yər *when unstressed*) ► You are.

yours (yo͝orz, yôrz, yōrz) ►*pron. (takes sing. or pl. v.)* The one or ones belonging to you: *If I can't find my bike, I'll take yours.*

your•self (yo͝or-sĕlf′, yôr-, yōr-, yər-) ►*pron. pl.* **-selves** (-sĕlvz′). That one or those ones identical with you. Used: **a.** Reflexively: *Did you buy yourselves a gift?* **b.** For emphasis: *Do it yourself.*

youth (yo͞oth) ►*n., pl.* **youths** (yo͞oths, yo͞o*thz*) **1.** The condition or quality of being young. **2.** An early period of development or existence, esp. the time of life before adulthood. **3a.** A young person, esp. a young man. **b.** Young people collectively. [< OE *geoguth*.]

youth•ful (yo͞oth′fəl) ►*adj.* **1.** Possessing youth; young. **2.** Characteristic of youth; fresh. **3.** In an early stage; new. —**youth′ful•ly** *adv.* —**youth′ful•ness** *n.*

you've (yo͞ov) ► You have.

yowl (youl) ►*v.* To utter a long, loud, mournful cry; wail. [ME *yowlen*.] —**yowl** *n.*

yo-yo (yō′yō′) ►*n., pl.* **-yos.** A toy consisting of a flattened spool wound with string that is spun down from and reeled up to the hand. [Originally a trademark.]

yr. ►*abbr.* **1.** year **2.** your

yt•ter•bi•um (ĭ-tûr′bē-əm) ►*n. Symbol* **Yb** A soft, bright, silvery rare-earth element used as an x-ray source in some laser materials, and in some special alloys. At. no. 70. See table at **element.** [After *Ytterby*, Sweden.]

yt•tri•um (ĭt′rē-əm) ►*n. Symbol* **Y** A silvery metallic element used to increase the strength of magnesium and aluminum alloys. At. no. 39. See table at **element.** [After *Ytterby*, Sweden.]

yu•an (yo͞o-än′) ►*n., pl.* **-an** or **-ans.** See table at **currency.** [Mandarin *yuán*.]

Yu•ca•tán (yo͞o′kə-tăn′, -tän′) A peninsula mostly in SE Mexico between the Caribbean Sea and the Gulf of Mexico.

yuc•ca (yŭk′ə) ►*n.* Any of a genus of evergreen plants native to North America, having often tall stems and a terminal cluster of white flowers. [Of Taino orig.]

yuck (yŭk) ►*interj. Slang* Used to express rejection or strong disgust. —**yuck′y** *adj.*

Yu•go•sla•vi•a (yo͞o′gō-slä′vē-ə) **1.** A former country of SE Europe (1918–91) on the Balkan Peninsula, comprising the republics of Serbia, Montenegro, Croatia, Slovenia, Macedonia, and Bosnia and Herzegovina. **2.** A country of SE Europe comprising Serbia and Montenegro. Cap. Belgrade. Pop. 10,515,000. —**Yu′go•sla′vi•an** *adj. & n.*

Yuk•on River (yo͞o′kŏn) A river flowing about 3,218 km (2,000 mi) from S Yukon Terr., Canada, through AK to the Bering Sea.

Yukon Territory. A territory of NW Canada E of AK. Cap. Whitehorse. Pop. 23,153.

Yule (yo͞ol) ►*n.* Christmas. [< OE *geōl*.]

yule log ►*n.* A large log traditionally burned in a fireplace at Christmas.

Yule•tide (yo͞ol′tīd′) ►*n.* The Christmas season.

Yu•ma (yo͞o′mə) ► A city of SW AZ on the Colorado R. Pop. 54,923.

yum•my (yŭm′ē) ►*adj.* **-mi•er, -mi•est** *Slang.* Delightful; delicious.

Yu•pik (yo͞o′pĭk) ►*n., pl.* **-pik** or **-piks 1.** A member of a group of Eskimoan peoples of W Alaska and extreme NE Russia. **2.** The languages of the Yupik.

yup•pie (yŭp′ē) ►*n. Informal* A young, affluent, usu. city-dwelling professional. [< *y(oung) u(rban) p(rofessional)*.]

yurt (yûrt) ►*n.* A circular, domed, portable tent used by the nomadic Mongols of central Asia. [Russ. *yurta*.]

yurt

YWCA ►*abbr.* Young Women's Christian Association

YWHA ►*abbr.* Young Women's Hebrew Association

Z

z or **Z** (zē) ▸*n.*, *pl.* **z's** or **Z's** also **zs** or **Zs**. The 26th letter of the English alphabet.

Za•greb (zä′grĕb) The capital of Croatia, in the N part NNW of Belgrade, Yugoslavia. Pop. 867,717.

Za•har•i•as (zə-hăr′ē-əs), **Mildred Ella Didrikson.** "Babe." 1914–56. Amer. athlete.

Babe Didrikson Zaharias

Za•ire (zī′îr, zä-îr′) See **Congo** 1. —**Za•ir′e•an, Za•ir′i•an** *adj. & n.*

Zaire River. See **Congo River.**

Zam•be•zi (zăm-bē′zē) A river, about 2,735 km (1,700 mi), of central and S Africa rising in NW Zambia and flowing to the Mozambique Channel.

Zam•bi•a (zăm′bē-ə) A country of S-central Africa. Cap. Lusaka. Pop. 9,169,000. —**Zam′bi•an** *adj. & n.*

za•ny (zā′nē) ▸*n.*, *pl.* **-nies 1.** A clown; buffoon. **2.** A comical person given to extravagant or outlandish behavior. ▸*adj.* **-ni•er, -ni•est 1.** Ludicrously comical; clownish. **2.** Comical because of incongruity or strangeness; bizarre. [< Ital. dial. *zanni.*] —**za′ni•ly** *adv.* —**za′ni•ness** *n.*

Zan•zi•bar (zăn′zə-bär′) **1.** A region of E Africa, comprising **Zanzibar Island** and several adjacent islands off the NE coast of Tanzania. **2.** A city of Tanzania on the W coast of Zanzibar I. Pop. 133,000.

zap (zăp) ▸*v.* **zapped, zap•ping** *Slang* **1.** To destroy or kill with or as if with a burst of gunfire, flame, or electric current. **2.** To expose to radiation. [Imit.] —**zap′per** *n.*

z-ax•is (zē′ăk′sĭs) ▸*n.*, *pl.* **z-ax•es** (-ăk′sēz). One of three axes in a three-dimensional Cartesian coordinate system.

za•zen (zä′zĕn′) ▸*n.* Meditation as practiced in Zen Buddhism. [J. : *za*, to sit down + *zen*, silent meditation; see Zen.]

zeal (zēl) ▸*n.* Enthusiastic devotion to a cause, ideal, or goal. [< Gk. *zēlos.*]

zeal•ot (zĕl′ət) ▸*n.* One who is zealous, esp. one who is fanatically devoted to a cause. [< Gk. *zēlōtēs.*] —**zeal′ot•ry** *n.*

zeal•ous (zĕl′əs) ▸*adj.* Filled with or motivated by zeal; fervent. —**zeal′ous•ly** *adv.* —**zeal′ous•ness** *n.*

ze•bra (zē′brə) ▸*n.* A swift, wild, horselike African mammal having distinctive overall markings of alternating white and black or brown stripes. [< OPort. *zevro*, wild ass.]

ze•bu (zē′bo͞o, -byo͞o) ▸*n.* A domesticated ox of Asia and E Africa, having a prominent hump and a large dewlap. [Fr. *zébu.*]

Zech•a•ri•ah (zĕk′ə-rī′ə) ▸*n.* **1.** A Hebrew prophet of the 6th cent. B.C. **2.** See table at **Bible.**

zed (zĕd) ▸*n.* *Chiefly Brit.* The letter *z.* [< Gk. *zēta*, zeta.]

Zed•e•ki•ah (zĕd′ĭ-kī′ə). 6th cent. B.C. The last king of Judah (597–586 B.C.).

Zeit•geist (tsīt′gīst′, zīt′-) ▸*n.* The taste and outlook characteristic of a period or generation. [Ger.]

Zen (zĕn) ▸*n.* A school of Buddhism practiced esp. in the Far East asserting that enlightenment can be attained through meditation and self-contemplation rather than through faith and devotion. [J., ult. < Skt. *dhyānam*, meditation.]

Zen Buddhism ▸*n.* Zen.

Zend-A•ves•ta (zĕn′də-vĕs′tə) ▸*n.* The sacred writings of the Zoroastrian religion.

Zeng•er (zĕng′gər, -ər), **John Peter.** 1697–1746. German-born printer in America.

ze•nith (zē′nĭth) ▸*n.* **1.** The point on the celestial sphere that is directly above the observer. **2.** The upper region of the sky. **3.** The highest point above the observer's horizon attained by a celestial body. **4.** The point of culmination; acme. [< Ar. *samt (ar-ra's)*, path (over the head).]

Ze•no of Cit•i•um (zē′nō, sĭt′ē-əm). 335?–263? B.C. Greek Stoic philosopher.

Zeno of E•le•a (ē-lē′ə). 495?–430? B.C. Greek philosopher.

Zeph•a•ni•ah (zĕf′ə-nī′ə) ▸*n.* **1.** A Hebrew prophet of the 7th cent. B.C. **2.** See table at **Bible.**

zeph•yr (zĕf′ər) ▸*n.* **1a.** The west wind. **b.** A gentle breeze. **2.** Any of various soft light fabrics, yarns, or garments. [< Gk. *Zephuros*, god of the west wind.]

zep•pe•lin also **Zep•pe•lin** (zĕp′ə-lĭn) ▸*n.* A rigid airship having a long cylindrical body supported by internal gas cells. [After Count Ferdinand von *Zeppelin* (1838–1917).]

ze•ro (zîr′ō, zē′rō) ▸*n.*, *pl.* **-ros** or **-roes 1.** The numerical symbol 0; cipher. **2.** *Math.* **a.** The identity element for addition. **b.** A cardinal number indicating the absence of any or all units under consideration. **c.** An ordinal number indicating an initial point or origin. **3.** The temperature indicated by the numeral 0 on a thermometer. **4.** *Informal* One having no influence or importance. **5.** The lowest point. ▸*adj.* **1.** Of or being zero. **2a.** Having no measurable or otherwise determinable value. **b.** *Informal* Absent, inoperative, or irrelevant. ▸*v.* **-roed, -ro•ing.** To adjust (an instrument or device) to zero value. —***phrasal verb:* zero in 1.** To aim or concentrate firepower on an exact target location. **2.** To converge intently; close in: *zero in on the cause.* [< Ar. *ṣifr*, cipher.]

zero gravity ▸*n.* The condition of apparent weightlessness occurring when the centrifugal force on a body exactly counterbalances the gravitational attraction on it.

zero hour ▶*n.* The scheduled time for the start of an action, esp. a military operation.

zero population growth ▶*n.* The limiting of population increase to the number needed to replace the existing population.

ze•ro-sum (zîr′ō-sŭm′, zē′rō-) ▶*adj.* Of or being a situation in which a gain on one side necessarily entails an equal loss on another.

zest (zĕst) ▶*n.* **1a.** Flavor or interest; piquancy. **b.** The outermost part of the rind of an orange, lemon, or other citrus fruit, used as flavoring. **2.** Spirited enjoyment; gusto. [Obsolete Fr., citrus peel.] —**zest′ful** *adj.* —**zest′ful•ly** *adv.*
Syns: *zest, gusto, relish* ***n.***

ze•ta (zā′tə, zē′-) ▶*n.* The 6th letter of the Greek alphabet. [Gk. *zēta.*]

Zeus (zo͞os) ▶*n. Gk. Myth.* The principal god of the Greek pantheon, ruler of the heavens and father of other gods and mortal heroes.

Zheng•zhou also **Cheng•chow** (jŭng′jō′). A city of E-central China SSW of Beijing. Pop. 1,752,374.

Zhou En•lai or **Chou En-lai** (jō′ ĕn-lī′). 1898–1976. Chinese revolutionary and politician.

zig•gu•rat (zĭg′ə-răt′) ▶*n.* A temple tower of the ancient Assyrians and Babylonians, having the form of a terraced pyramid. [Assyrian *ziggurratu*, summit.]

ziggurat
c. 2100 B.C. Ziggurat of Ur

zig•zag (zĭg′zăg′) ▶*n.* **1a.** A line or course that proceeds by sharp turns in alternating directions. **b.** One of a series of such sharp turns. **2.** Something, such as a design, marked by zigzags. ▶*adj.* Moving in or having a zigzag. ▶*adv.* In a zigzag manner or pattern. ▶*v.* **-zagged, -zag•ging.** To move in or form a zigzag. [Fr. < Ger. *Zickzack.*]

zilch (zĭlch) ▶*n. Slang* Zero; nothing. [?]

zil•lion (zĭl′yən) ▶*n. Informal* An extremely large indefinite number. [Alteration of *million.*]

Zim•bab•we (zĭm-bäb′wē, -wā). Formerly **Rhodesia.** A country of S Africa. Cap. Harare. Pop. 11,150,000. —**Zim•bab′we•an** *adj. & n.*

zinc (zĭngk) ▶*n. Symbol* **Zn** A bluish-white, lustrous metallic element used to form many alloys, including brass, and in galvanizing iron and other metals. At. no. 30. See table at **element.** ▶*v.* **zinced, zinc•ing** or **zincked, zinck•ing.** To coat or treat with zinc; galvanize. [Ger. *Zink.*]

zinc oxide ▶*n.* An amorphous white or yellowish powder, ZnO, used as a pigment and in pharmaceuticals and cosmetics.

zine or **'zine** (zēn) ▶*n.* **1.** An inexpensive, self-published, underground publication. **2.** An e-zine. [< (MAGA)ZINE.]

zing (zĭng) ▶*n.* **1.** A brief high-pitched humming or buzzing sound. **2.** Liveliness; zip. ▶*v.* **1.** To make a zing. **2.** To move swiftly. **3.** *Informal* To attack verbally. [Imit.] —**zing′y** *adj.*

zing•er (zĭng′ər) ▶*n. Informal* A witty, often caustic remark.

zin•ni•a (zĭn′ē-ə) ▶*n.* A widely cultivated plant with showy, variously colored flower heads. [After J.G. *Zinn* (1727–59).]

Zi•on (zī′ən) also **Si•on** (sī′ən) ▶*n.* **1a.** The historic land of Israel as a symbol of the Jewish people. **b.** The Jewish people; Israel. **2.** A place or religious community regarded as devoted to God. **3.** A utopia.

Zi•on•ism (zī′ə-nĭz′əm) ▶*n.* A Jewish movement that arose in the late 19th cent., orig. seeking to reestablish a Jewish homeland in Palestine and now concerned with the support and development of the state of Israel. —**Zi′on•ist** *adj. & n.*

zip (zĭp) ▶*n.* **1.** A brief, sharp, hissing sound. **2.** Energy; vim. **3.** *Slang* Nothing; nil; zero. ▶*v.* **zipped, zip•ping 1.** To move or act with speed or energy. **2.** To fasten or unfasten with a zipper. [Imit.]

Zip Code ▶ A trademark used for a system designed to expedite the sorting and delivery of mail by assigning a series of numbers to each delivery area in the US.

zip•per (zĭp′ər) ▶*n.* A fastening device consisting of parallel rows of metal, plastic, or nylon teeth on adjacent edges of an opening that are interlocked by a sliding tab. [< ZIP.]

zip•py (zĭp′ē) ▶*adj.* **-pi•er, -pi•est.** Full of energy; lively.

zir•con (zûr′kŏn′) ▶*n.* A brown to colorless mineral, $ZrSiO_4$, that is heated, cut, and polished to form a brilliant blue-white gem. [Ult. < Pers. *āzargūn*, fire color.]

zir•co•ni•um (zûr-kō′nē-əm) ▶*n. Symbol* **Zr** A lustrous, grayish-white, strong, ductile metallic element used chiefly in ceramic and refractory compounds and as an alloying agent. At. no. 40. See table at **element.**

zit (zĭt) ▶*n. Slang* A pimple. [?]

zith•er (zĭth′ər, zĭ*th*′-) ▶*n.* A musical instrument composed of a flat sound box set with strings of graded length, played with the fingertips or a plectrum. [< Gk. *kithara*, ancient musical instrument.] —**zith′er•ist** *n.*

zi•ti (zē′tē) ▶*n.* Pasta in medium-sized, often ridged tubes. [Ital.]

zlo•ty (zlô′tē) ▶*n., pl.* **-ty** or **-tys.** See table at **currency.** [Pol. *złoty* < *złoto*, gold.]

Zn ▶ The symbol for the element **zinc.**

zo•di•ac (zō′dē-ăk′) ▶*n.* **1a.** A band of the celestial sphere extending about 8° to either side of the ecliptic that represents the path of the principal planets, the moon, and the sun. **b.** In astrology, this band divided into 12 equal parts called signs, bearing the name of a constellation for which it was orig. named. **2.** A diagram or figure representing the zodiac. [< Gk. *zōidion*, small figure, zodiacal sign < *zōion*, living thing.] —**zo•di′a•cal** (-dī′ə-kəl) *adj.*

–zoic ▶*suff.* **1.** Relating to a specified manner of animal existence: *protozoic.* **2.** Of a specified geologic era: *Archeozoic.* [< Gk. *zōion*, living being.]

Zo•la (zō′lə, zō-lä′), **Émile.** 1840–1902. French writer and critic.

zom•bie (zŏm′bē) ►*n.* **1.** A voodoo snake god. **2a.** A supernatural power or spell that according to voodoo belief can enter into and reanimate a corpse. **b.** A corpse revived in this way. **3.** One who looks or behaves like an automaton. [< Kimbundu *n-zumbi*, departed spirit.]

zon•al (zō′nəl) ►*adj.* **1.** Relating to a zone. **2.** Divided into zones. —**zon′al•ly** *adv.*

zone (zōn) ►*n.* **1.** An area or region distinguished from adjacent parts by a distinctive feature or characteristic. **2.** Any of the five regions of the surface of the earth that are loosely divided according to prevailing climate and latitude, including the Torrid Zone, the North and South Temperate Zones, and the North and South Frigid Zones. **3.** A section of an area or territory used for a specific purpose: *a residential zone.* ►*v.* **zoned, zon•ing 1.** To divide into zones. **2.** To designate or mark off into zones. [< Gk. *zōnē*, girdle.]

zonk (zôngk, zŏngk) ►*v. Slang* To intoxicate or become intoxicated with drugs or alcohol. [?]

zoo (zo͞o) ►*n., pl.* **zoos 1.** A park or institution in which living animals are kept and exhibited to the public. **2.** *Slang* A place or situation marked by confusion or disorder. [< ZOOLOGICAL GARDEN.]

zoo– or **zo–** ►*pref.* **1.** Animal: *zoology.* **2.** Motile: *zoospore.* [< Gk. *zōion*, living being.]

zo•o•ge•og•ra•phy (zō′ə-jē-ŏg′rə-fē) ►*n.* The biological study of geographic distribution of animals, esp. the causes and effects of such distribution. —**zo′o•ge•og′ra•pher** *n.*

zoological garden ►*n.* See **zoo** 1.

zo•ol•o•gy (zō-ŏl′ə-jē, zo͞o-) ►*n.* **1.** The branch of biology that deals with animals and animal life. **2.** The animal life of a particular area or period. **3.** The characteristics of a particular animal group or category. —**zo′o•log′i•cal** (-ə-lŏj′ĭ-kəl), **zo′o•log′ic** *adj.* —**zo•ol′o•gist** *n.*

zoom (zo͞om) ►*v.* **1.** To make or move with a continuous low-pitched buzzing or humming sound. **2.** To climb suddenly and sharply, as an airplane. **3.** To move about rapidly; swoop. **4.** To simulate movement away from or toward a subject using a zoom lens. [Imit.] —**zoom** *n.*

zoom lens ►*n.* A camera lens whose focal length can be rapidly changed, allowing rapid change in the size of an image.

–zoon ►*suff.* Animal; independently moving organic unit: *spermatozoon.* [< Gk. *zōion*, living being.]

zo•o•plank•ton (zō′ə-plăngk′tən) ►*n.* Plankton that consists of animals.

zo•o•spore (zō′ə-spôr′, -spōr′) ►*n.* A motile, flagellated asexual spore.

Zo•ro•as•ter (zôr′ō-ăs′tər, zōr′-). 6th cent. B.C. Persian prophet who founded Zoroastrianism.

Zo•ro•as•tri•an•ism (zôr′ō-ăs′trē-ə-nĭz′əm) ►*n.* The religious system founded in Persia by Zoroaster, teaching the worship of Ormazd in the context of a universal struggle between the forces of light and of darkness. —**Zo′ro•as′tri•an** *adj. & n.*

zounds (zoundz) ►*interj.* Used to express anger, surprise, or indignation.

zoy•sia (zoi′shə, -sē-ə) ►*n.* Any of several creeping grasses widely cultivated for lawns. [After Karl von *Zois zu Laubach* (1756–1800?).]

Zr ► The symbol for the element **zirconium.**

zuc•chi•ni (zo͞o-kē′nē) ►*n., pl.* **-ni** or **-nis.** A variety of squash having an elongated shape and a smooth, dark-green rind. [Ital. < *zucca*, gourd.]

Zu•lu (zo͞o′lo͞o) ►*n., pl.* **-lu** or **-lus 1.** A member of a people of SE Africa. **2.** The Bantu language of the Zulu. —**Zu′lu** *adj.*

Zu•lu•land (zo͞o′lo͞o-lănd′) A historical region of NE South Africa.

Zu•ni (zo͞o′nē) also **Zu•ñi** (-nyē, -nē) ►*n., pl.* **-ni** or **-nis** also **-ñi** or **-ñis 1.** A member of a Pueblo people of W New Mexico. **2.** The language of the Zuni.

Zu•rich (zo͝or′ĭk) A city of NE Switzerland at the N tip of the **Lake of Zurich.** Pop. 343,981.

zwie•back (swē′băk′, swī′-, zwē′-, zwī′-) ►*n.* A usu. sweetened bread baked first as a loaf and later sliced and toasted. [Ger.]

Zwing•li (zwĭng′lē), **Ulrich.** 1484–1531. Swiss religious reformer. —**Zwing′li•an** *adj. & n.*

zy•de•co (zī′dĭ-kō′) ►*n.* Popular music of S Louisiana played by small groups featuring the guitar, the accordion, and a washboard. [< Louisiana Fr.]

zy•go•sis (zī-gō′sĭs, zĭ-) ►*n., pl.* **-ses** (-sēz). The union of gametes to form a zygote; conjugation.

zy•gote (zī′gōt′) ►*n.* **1.** The cell formed by the union of two gametes, esp. a fertilized ovum before cleavage. **2.** The organism that develops from a zygote. [< Gk. *zugoun*, to yoke.] —**zy•got′ic** (-gŏt′ĭk) *adj.*

zy•mur•gy (zī′mûr′jē) ►*n.* The branch of chemistry that deals with fermentation processes, as in brewing. [Gk. *zumē*, leaven + –URGY.]

PICTURE CREDITS

The editorial and production staff wishes to thank the many individuals, organizations, and agencies that have contributed to the art program of the Dictionary.

Credits on the following pages are arranged alphabetically by boldface entry word. In cases where two or more illustrations complement an entry, the sources follow the order of the illustrations. The following source abbreviations are used throughout the credits: AA - Academy Artworks; AA/ES - Animals Animals/Earth Scenes; AR - Art Resource; CB - Corbis/Bettmann Archive; COR - Corbis; EM - Elizabeth Morales; FPG - FPG International; GC - The Granger Collection, New York; GH - Grant Heilman Photography, Inc.; GP - Globe Photos, Inc.; HAR - H. Armstrong Roberts, Inc.; HM - © School Division, Houghton Mifflin Company; ISI - Index Stock Imagery; LA - Liaison Agency, Inc.; LOC - Library of Congress; PDI - © 2001 PhotoDisc, Inc.; PE - PhotoEdit; PG - Precision Graphics; PI - Positive Images; PR - Photo Researchers, Inc.; SB - Stock, Boston; SS - SuperStock, Inc.; ST - Stone; WWP - AP/Wide World Photos.

abacus HM **Abernathy** COR – Flip Schulke **acanthus** PE – Bill Aron **achene** EM **J. Adams** AR, National Portrait Gallery, Smithsonian Institution **J. Q. Adams** AR, National Portrait Gallery, Smithsonian Institution **adobe** HAR – R. Krubner **adsorb** PG **air-cushion vehicle** PG **Ali** COR – Lynn Goldsmith **amaryllis** HM **ammonite** PDI **amoeba** GH – Runk & Schoenberger **ampoule** SS – Robert Llewellyn **andiron** HM **ankh** HM **anorak** COR – Paul Almasy **Anthony** GC **ao dai** PE – Michael Newman **aoudad** SS **Appomattox** GC **Arafat** GP – James M. Kelly **archer** PE – Tony Freeman **Armstrong** COR **Arthur** GC **asymptote** AA **attitude** HAR – Adamsmith Productions **auger** PDI **avocet** AA/ES – Phyllis Greenberg

bacterium PR – David M. Phillips PR – SPL-CNRI **Baldwin** LOC, Carl Van Vechten Collection **bar graph** AA **baroque** SS **battering ram** GC **Beethoven** LOC **Bell** LOC **berm** PDI **Bernhardt** LOC **bighorn** PR – James Zipp **Black Death** GC **Blair** COR – Peter Turnley **blaze²** SS **blockhouse** ST – James P. Rowan **bok choy** HM **bongo¹** PR – R. Van Nostrand **Bourke-White** CB **bowline** HM **Brady** LOC **Braille** AA **Brant** National Gallery of Canada, Ottawa, Purchased 1951 **bridge¹** AR – Scala **brioche** HM **Brown** COR – The National Archives **Buchanan** SS **bullfrog** PR – Michael P. Gadomski **bundt cake** PDI **Bush** LOC

Cabrini LOC **caliper** PG **candelabrum** HM **caparison** COR – Gianni Dagli Orti **carabiner** HM **caricature** AR – National Portrait Gallery, Smithsonian Institution, Gift of the family of Mr. Charles Dunn **Carson** COR – Underwood & Underwood **Carter** LOC **Cassatt** AR – National Portrait Gallery, Smithsonian Institution **cavalry** GC **cell** Laurel Cook Lhowe **centripetal force** PG **chameleon** AA/ES – Marian Bacon **Chaucer** SS – The Huntington Library, Art Collections, and Botanical Gardens, San Marino, California **Chimera** SS – Archaeological Museum, Florence, Italy and A.K.G., Berlin **Chinese lantern** HM **chopstick** PDI **Churchill** SS – Bridgeman Art Library, London **circle** AA **clean room** ISI – Ed Lallo **Cleveland** SS – Culver Pictures, Inc. **Clinton** Archive Photos – CNP **coat of arms** GC **coliseum** SB – Grant LeDuc **colossus** GC **Columbus** LOC **compass** HM PDI **Confucius** GC **contrail** PDI **convection** PG **Coolidge** SS **cotter pin** AA **cowcatcher** SB – John Elk III **cradleboard** SS **crag** COR – Jon Sparks **crevasse** ISI – David Trask **crosier** SS – Mauro Magliani **cross** AA **cruet** HM **Curie** GC **cyclotron** PG

Dalai Lama GP – Andrea Renault **Dali** COR – Photo B.D.V. **Davis** AR – National Portrait Gallery, Smithsonian Institution **décolletage** SS – The Huntington Library, Art Collections, and Botanical Gardens, San Marino, California **delta wing** COR – NASA **demijohn** HM **dervish** COR – Hans Georg Roth **diagonal** AA **dibble** HM **dish antenna** SB – Bill Gallery **Dix** GC **dodecagon** AA **dodecahedron** AA **doily** HM **domino¹** HM **dormer** SB – Peter Vandermark **Douglass** CB **dreidel** PDI **duffle bag** HM **Dutch door** ISI – Glasheen Graphics

Earhart GC **Easter Island** PDI **eclipse** PG **Eddy** LOC **Edison** GC **Eisenhower** COR **Elizabeth II** GP – © Alpha **endive** HM **equator** Jerry Malone **erosion** COR – Chinch Gryniewicz, Ecoscene **espadrille** HM **ewer** COR – Royal Ontario Museum **extravehicular activity** ISI – Scott Berner

faience COR – Austrian Archives **fault** PG **ferrule** AA **fez** SS **Fillmore** CB **fisheye** PI – Dennis Frates **Fitzgerald** CB **flamenco** PE – Bonnie Kamin **fleur-de-lis** HM **foot** Carlyn Iverson **Ford** GP – James M. Kelly **forelock** PR – Tierbild Okapia **Frank** CB – UPI **French curve** HM **French door** PE – John Neubauer **Fuentes** GP – James M. Kelly

Gandhi LA – Hulton Getty Picture Library **gargoyle** PDI **geisha** SS – Culver Pictures, Inc. **geodesic dome** SS – Mia & Klaus Matthes **Geronimo** COR – Hulton-Deutsch Collection **Gibraltar** ISI –

Rick Strange **Gibson** CB **ginseng** EM **glyph** SB – Michael Dwyer **goggle** PI – Mikki Ansin **gondola** SS AA/ES – Bertram G. Murray **Goya** LOC **Grant** GC **Great Dane** PR – Jacana **guava** COR – Michael Boys **Guevara** LA – Hulton Getty Picture Library **guide dog** AA/ES – Ralph Reinhold

haku HAR – I. Masterson **half note** PG **hand** Carlyn Iverson **Harding** GC **B. Harrison[2]** GC **W. H. Harrison** GC **Hatshepsut** AR – Erich Lessing **Hayes** LOC **hearth** ISI – Kindra Clineff **heel[2]** GH – Alan Pitcairn **henna** SB – John Elk III **hibachi** PDI **hinge** AA **hogan** PR – James Steinberg **Hoover** SS **horn** EM **Horne** GP – Adam Scull **Houston** LOC **Howe** LOC **huarache** HM **hula** COR – Buddy Mays **Hurston** LOC – Carl Van Vechten Collection **hyperbola** AA

Iberian Peninsula PR – SPL-Geospace **icebreaker** COR – Chris Rainier **impacted** PR – SPL **inflorescence** EM **in-line skate** PDI **instrument** HM **Isabella I** GC

jabot SS – The Huntington Library, Art Collections, and Botanical Gardens, San Marino, California **A. Jackson** SS – The Cummer Museum of Art and Gardens, Jacksonville **J. Jackson** SB – Bob Daemmrich **Jefferson** AR – National Portrait Gallery, Smithsonian Institution **jewel box** HM **A. Johnson** GC **L. B. Johnson** Archive Photos **Jordan** COR – Neal Preston **Joseph[2]** AR – National Portrait Gallery, Smithsonian Institution **junk[2]** ST – Vince Streano **kalimba** PDI **Keller** WWP **Kennedy** AR – National Portrait Gallery, Smithsonian Institution **kimono** ISI – Dorian Weber **King, Jr.** COR – Flip Schulke **kookaburra** COR – Clive Druett, Papilio

laboratory GH – Runk & Schoenberger **ladder-back** SS – Christie's Images **LAN** PG **last[3]** PE – Amy Etra **latitude** Jerry Malone **leaf** EM **Lee** COR – The Corcoran Gallery of Art **Lenin** WWP **lever** PG **Liliuokalani** AR – National Portrait Gallery, Smithsonian Institution **Lincoln** CB **lock[1]** HAR – Geopress **lorgnette** HM **louver** SS – Graeme Outerbridge **lute** SB – Peter Vandermark

D. Madison The White House Collection, © White House Historical Association **J. Madison** AR – National Portrait Gallery, Smithsonian Institution **Malcolm X** Black Star – John Launois **manometer** PG **Mao Zedong** LA – Raymond Depardon **Marie Antoinette** SS – Christie's Images **Marshall** SB – Arthur Grace **Mayan** SS – The Newberry Library, Chicago **McKinley** AR – National Portrait Gallery, Smithsonian Institution **Mead** SB – David Austen **megalith** HAR – M. Thonig **mesa** PDI **metamorphosis** EM **minaret** AR **Minoan** COR – Gianni Dagli Orti **mission** GP – Morton Dagawitz **monorail** ST – Robin Smith **Monroe** GC **Morrison** LA – Ulf Andersen **Morse code** AA **Mount Vernon** SS – George Schaub **mule[1]** GH – Grant Heilman **mule[2]** HM **Muñoz Marín** Archive Photo

Napoleon I AR – Giraudon **nautilus** FPG – David Fleetham **neap tide** PG **Nefertiti** SS – Staatliche Museum, Berlin **Neruda** WWP **newel** FPG – Maria Pape PE – Novastock **Nicholas II** GC **Nixon** The Richard Nixon Library and Birthplace **Norgay** COR – Hulton-Deutsch Collection

Oates GP – Andrea Renault **octagon** AA **octahedron** AA **olla** COR – David Muench **oryx** AA/ES – Robert Maier **Osceola** GC **osteoporosis** PR – SPL-Prof. P Motta, Dept. of Anatomy, University "La Sapienza," Rome **overalls** PDI **Owens** Corbis/Bettmann, UPI

pagoda PDI **Pangaea** Jerry Malone **panpipe** PDI **parallelepiped** AA **parallelogram** AA **Parks** AR – National Portrait Gallery, Smithsonian Institution, Gift of the Anheuser-Busch Companies and Artis Lane **Pavlova** CB **Peary** COR – Hulton-Deutsch Collection **personal watercraft** SB – Spencer Grant **petri dish** SS – Charles Orrico **petroglyph** HAR – Wendell Metzen **phoenix** Shahn, Ben. *Phoenix.* (1952). Serigraph, printed in black with watercolor added by hand, composition: 22-3/4 x 21-1/2" (57.9 x 54.7 cm). The Museum of Modern Art, New York. Abby Aldrich Rockefeller Fund. Photograph © 1999 The Museum of Modern Art, New York. © Estate of Ben Shahn/Licensed by VAGA, New York, NY **Picasso** CB **Pierce** GC **piñata** PDI **pitchfork** COR – Dean Conger **platypus** SS **Pocahontas** LOC **Polk** COR – The Corcoran Gallery of Art **pommel horse** FPG – Darryl Zimmerman **pontoon** ISI – J & S Austin **pop art** AR – © 2000 Andy Warhol Foundation and ARS, NY. TM Licensed by Campbell's Soup Co. All Rights Reserved. **porringer** HM **prayer wheel** PDI **prosthesis** PR – Catherine Ursillo **pueblo** SB – Donald Dietz **Pushkin** SS – A.K.G., Berlin **Pythagorean theorem** AA **quatrefoil** COR – Paul Almasy **Quezon y Molina** WWP **quoin** Alan Witschonke

racket[1] HM **Rankin** GC **Rasputin** SS – Culver Pictures, Inc. **Reagan** GC **Red Cloud** COR – Library of Congress **reel[1]** PDI **rest[1]** Tech-Graphics **reverse osmosis** PG **Robinson** Corbis/Bettmann, UPI **E. Roosevelt** The White House Collection, © White House Historical Association **F. D. Roosevelt** GC **T. Roosevelt** GC **rowel** ST – Gary Holscher **ruff** AR – Scala **rune** AR – Werner Forman Archive & Statens Historiska Museet, Stockholm

Sacagawea GC **Saint Bernard** PDI **Sand** LOC **Sanger** Corbis/Bettmann, UPI **sari** COR – Barnabas Bosshart **sarong** SS – Ping Amranand **scoliosis** COR – Lester V. Bergman **Scott** GC **scroll** FPG – Ulf Sjostedt **sea anemone** ST – Norbert Wu **Sequoya** LOC **Seton** GC **sextant** PDI **Shah Jahan** AR – Victoria & Albert Museum, London **M. Shelley** SS – National Portrait Gallery, London **P. Shelley** SS – National Portrait Gallery, London **shoetree** HM **sickle cell anemia** PR – Meckes-Ottawa **Sinai Peninsula** HAR – NASA **Sitting Bull** GC **slipknot** HM **snaffle** HM **snowmobile** GP – Mark E. Gibson **sombrero** PE – Jonathan Nourok **space shuttle** SS – Jack Novak **sphinx** SS – Kurt Scholz **spiral galaxy** COR – NASA **spring tide** PG **spur** PDI COR – Karen Tweedy-Holmes **Stalin** GC **Stanton** *Eminent Women of the Age.* © 1868 by S.M. Betts & Company **stencil** HM **stereoscope** HM **Stone** CB **strainer** HM **stupa** COR – Richard Bickel **Suez Canal** SS **Suleiman I** COR – Ali Meyer **sun** AA **sushi** PDI **swan dive** ST – Bob Torrez

Taft AR – National Portrait Gallery, Smithsonian Institution, Gift of William E. Schevill **tandem** FPG – Arthur Tilley **tapir** AA/ES – Zigmund Lesczcynski **tassel** PDI **tatami** HAR – K. Scholz **Taylor** AR – National Portrait Gallery, Smithsonian Institution **tent** PG **Mother Teresa** GP – Adam Scull **Saint Theresa** AR – Erich Lessing **Thorpe** CB **thyroid gland** Carlyn Iverson **totem pole** GH – Grant Heilman **transformer** PG **triangle** AA **tripod** PDI **Truman** AR – National Portrait Gallery, Smithsonian Institution, Gift of Dean Acheson, Thomas C. Clark, John W. Snyder, Robert A. Lovett, Clinton P. Anderson, Charles F. Brannan, Charles Sawyer, W. Averell Harriman, David K.E. Bruce, Edward H. Foley, Stuart Symington, William McChesney Martin, Clark Clifford, Charles S. Murphy, Ward M. Canaday, and Joseph Stack **Truth** LOC **Tubman** LOC **tuning fork** PDI **turnbuckle** PDI **Tyler** AR – National Portrait Gallery, Smithsonian Institution

U-bolt PDI **ukulele** PDI **uniform** HAR – Linda Burton **Van Buren** AR – National Portrait Gallery, Smithsonian Institution **Verne** GC **viaduct** AA/ES – Michael P. Gadomski **Villa** COR – Hulton-Deutsch Collection

waders ST – David Epperson **Walker** GP – Andrea Renault **B. T. Washington** AR – National Portrait Gallery, Smithsonian Institution **G. Washington** SS – David David Gallery, Philadelphia **wavelength** AA **Wells** GC **Wharton** CB **whorl** EM **Wiesel** COR – Owen Franken **Wilson** PR – Tom McHugh, The National Portrait Gallery, Smithsonian Institution, Transfer from the National Museum of American Art; Gift of the city of New York through the National Art Committee, 1923 **worm gear** AA

xylophone PDI **yin** PG **yurt** PR – Eagy Landau **Zaharias** CB **ziggurat** PR – Georg Gerster

THE SLOW COOKING COLLECTION

THE AUSTRALIAN Women's Weekly

THE SLOW COOKING COLLECTION

CONTENTS

STOVE

COOK IT SLOWLY

Some of the best things in life take time. Casseroles and other slow-cooked meals – such as braises, pot roasts, curries or stews – certainly need time to become hearty, heavenly meals infused with flavour and melt-in-your-mouth tenderness.

They also freeze beautifully, giving you a wonderful comforting meal at the ready. Just reheat and eat.

Slow cooking can be done in an electric slow cooker, on the stove or in the oven. All with the same delicious result.

BEST CUTS FOR SLOW COOKING

Long, slow cooking will tenderise even the toughest cut of meat. Stewing or braising cuts are the best choices. Tough cuts are usually inexpensive, but cutting the meat off the bone yourself can usually save you more money, as you're not paying for the convenience of pre-cut meat, plus it gives you the opportunity to trim off any visible fat.

The best cuts of meat to use are:

* **Beef** topside, oyster, blade, skirt, round, chuck, gravy beef.
* **Veal** osso buco, shanks, shoulder.
* **Lamb** neck chops, boneless shoulder, shanks, boneless forequarter.
* **Pork** forequarter chops, neck, belly, shoulder.
* **Chicken** any pieces on the bone, such as drumsticks, thighs, marylands.

Seafood is generally not suitable for slow cooking as it toughens quickly. However, there are many recipes for sauces that can be slow cooked and the seafood added just before serving. Large octopus will cook and become tender when slow cooked.

BROWN THE MEAT FIRST

As straightforward as most slow cooking recipes are, it is best not to just throw all your ingredients in. Browning the meat first enhances the flavour and gives the meat a beautiful rich colour. Do this in a heated, oiled, large frying pan, in batches, and turning it so that it browns evenly. Be sure to have the pan heated before adding the meat – it's also important to maintain the heat during the browning process; if the pan is not hot enough the meat will stew rather than brown.

THICKENING THE SAUCE

Coating the meat in flour before browning will result in a sauce that is thick enough to make a light coating gravy. If the recipe does not suggest coating the meat, then it is a good idea to thicken the sauce using plain flour or cornflour.

Blending the flour or cornflour with butter or a cold liquid such as water or some of the cooled juices from the pan or slow cooker will help it combine with the cooking juices when stirred in at the end of the cooking time. Simmer, uncovered, for 10 minutes or until sauce thickens.

Another trick to thicken the sauce is to blend some of the cooked vegetables until smooth, and then stir them into the cooking juices.

SLOW COOKERS

Slow cookers are available in a range of shapes and sizes and come with a host of features. We tested the slow-cooker recipes in this cookbook using a 5-litre (20-cup) slow cooker. If you have a smaller or larger cooker you will have to decrease or increase the quantity of food, and almost certainly the liquid content, in the recipes.

The first step when using your slow cooker is to read the manufacturer's instructions, as each cooker will differ depending on its features. It will also outline appropriate safety measures, such as not leaving the appliance unattended at any time.

Some cookers heat from the base and side, while others heat just from the base; some have timers that cut off after the cooking time has expired, while others have timers that will keep the food warm by reducing the temperature until you're ready to eat. It's about finding what works best for you and your slow-cooking needs.

A general rule of thumb is that high heat settings on a slow cooker will cook twice as fast as the lower setting. The longer the meat takes to cook, the more tender and more intense the flavours will be, so if you have the time, set your cooker to a low setting. No matter which setting you use, the food will reach simmering point. Some slow cookers have a warm setting; this is not used for cooking but to maintain the temperature of the food until you're ready to eat.

The high setting comes in handy when you need to add ingredients or to thicken the sauce at the end of the cooking time. Remove the lid and add the ingredients, or the mixture you are using to thicken the sauce, replace the lid and leave it on high for 10–20 minutes.

THE FAT FACTS

When cooking meats over a long period of time, they can often produce a lot of fat, which you will need to remove. The best method is to refrigerate the food first; the fat will set on top of the liquid, and then it can be lifted off and discarded. If you don't have time to refrigerate the food before serving, then there are gadgets available in kitchen/ cookware shops for removing fat: one is a type of 'brush' that sweeps away the fat; the other is a type of jug that separates the fat from the liquid. One of the easiest ways to remove fat is to soak it up using sheets of paper towel, gently placed over the surface of the food.

A NOTE ON DRIED BEANS

Some dried beans need to be cooked before adding to a slow-cooked dish because of a certain chemical they contain. Kidney-shaped beans of all colours and sizes are related to each other and MUST be washed, drained and boiled in fresh water until tender. Add the cooked beans to the slow-cooked dish, just like canned beans. Dried, unsoaked chickpeas and soy beans are fine to use in slow cooking – just rinse them well first; there's no need for overnight soaking before cooking.

FREEZING LEFTOVERS

One of the best things about slow cooking is the ability to cook large amounts of food at once. This allows you to have leftovers that you can freeze for another time. If frozen properly, slow-cooked meals will keep for up to 3 months. There is usually a large quantity of liquid, so transfer the meat and vegetables to appropriate-sized freezer-friendly containers, then pour in enough of the liquid to cover the meat etc. Leave a 2.5cm (1in) space between the food and the lid to allow for expansion, then seal, label and date the container before placing in the freezer.

SLOW COOKER

12

SLOW COOKER

PRESERVES & CONDIMENTS

MIXED BERRY JAM

prep + cook time 4 hours 45 minutes ✻ makes 4 cups

- **1.25kg (2½lb) mixed fresh berries**
- **1kg (2lb) white (granulated) sugar**
- **¼ cup (60ml) lemon juice**

1 Place berries, sugar and juice in a 5-litre (20-cup) slow cooker; stir to coat. Cook, covered, on high for 4 hours.

2 Uncover and adjust setting to 'reduce' (HIGH). Boil, uncovered, stirring occasionally, for 30 minutes or until jam jells when tested (see glossary, page 479).

3 Pour hot jam into hot sterilised jars (see glossary, page 484); seal immediately. Label and date jars when cold. Remove with a clean spoon each time.

Tip *This jam has a softer set than commercial jams.*

BACON JAM

prep + cook time 6 hours 30 minutes * makes 5 cups

- **1kg (2lb) rindless bacon slices, excess fat trimmed, sliced thinly**
- **3 onions (450g), sliced thinly**
- **4 cloves garlic, sliced thinly**
- **⅔ cup (160ml) apple cider vinegar**
- **⅔ cup (150g) firmly packed brown sugar**
- **⅔ cup (160ml) pure maple syrup**
- **1 tablespoon wholegrain mustard**
- **4 sprigs fresh thyme**
- **1 teaspoon instant coffee granules**
- **⅓ cup (80ml) warm water**

1 Heat a large frying pan over medium-high heat. Cook bacon, in batches, until browned lightly. Drain on paper towel.

2 Transfer bacon to a 5-litre (20-cup) slow cooker. Add onion, garlic, vinegar, sugar, maple syrup, mustard, thyme, coffee and the water. Cook, covered, on high for 6 hours. Discard thyme. Skim excess fat. Season with pepper.

3 Process bacon mixture until finely chopped but not pureed. Spoon hot jam into hot sterilised jars (see glossary, page 484); seal immediately. Label and date jars when cold. Remove with a clean spoon each time.

Serving suggestion *Serve on toasted bread with baby spinach leaves, roasted tomatoes and a fried egg.*

CHERRY CHUTNEY

prep + cook time 4 hours 45 minutes * makes 5½ cups

- **1kg (2lb) frozen pitted cherries, thawed**
- **5 medium red apples (750g), peeled, chopped coarsely**
- **2 medium red onions (340g), chopped coarsely**
- **3 cloves garlic, crushed**
- **1 tablespoon finely grated fresh ginger**
- **1 cinnamon stick**
- **2 cardamom pods, bruised**
- **½ cup (110g) caster (superfine) sugar**
- **1 cup (250ml) apple cider vinegar**

1 Combine ingredients in a 5-litre (20-cup) slow cooker. Cook, covered, on high for 4 hours.

2 Discard cinnamon and cardamom. Adjust setting to 'reduce' (HIGH). Boil mixture, uncovered, for 30 minutes or until chutney is thick, stirring occasionally.

3 Spoon hot chutney into hot sterilised jars (see glossary, page 484); seal immediately. Label and date jars when cold. Remove with a clean spoon each time.

Serving suggestion *Spread chutney on crusty bread slices, top with ham and cheese, and grill until cheese melts.*

WECK

PASSATA

prep + cook time 8 hours 30 minutes * makes 6 cups

∗ 1 tablespoon extra virgin olive oil
∗ 2.5kg (5lb) ripe roma (egg) tomatoes, cored
∗ 1½ teaspoons fine salt

1 Place oil in a 5-litre (20-cup) slow cooker. Add tomatoes and sprinkle with salt. Cook, covered, on low for 8 hours; do not stir.

2 Carefully transfer tomatoes, with a slotted spoon, to a sieve. Discard liquid in slow cooker. Blend or process tomatoes, in batches, in a high-powered blender until smooth.

3 Return passata to slow cooker. Adjust setting to 'reduce' (HIGH) and bring to the boil.

4 Pour hot passata into hot sterilised bottles (see glossary, page 484); seal immediately. Label and date bottles when cold.

Tips *If you don't have a high-powered blender, you may need to strain the passata mixture after blending to remove any tomato skins. You can add other flavours to the passata, such as onion, garlic or basil, if you like.*

Serving suggestion
Use passata as a pizza topping, or for stews, soups and as a base for pasta sauces.

Suitable to freeze
at the end of step 2.

PICKLED BEETROOT

prep + cook time 4 hours 20 minutes ✻ makes 5 cups

- **750g (1½lb) trimmed beetroot (beets), peeled, cut into wedges**
- **2 cloves garlic, crushed**
- **2 sprigs fresh thyme, plus extra leaves to serve**
- **2 sprigs fresh rosemary**
- **1 teaspoon mustard seeds**
- **1 teaspoon fennel seeds**
- **1 cup (220g) caster (superfine) sugar**
- **1¼ cups (310ml) white wine vinegar**
- **1¼ cups (310ml) water**

1 Place beetroot, garlic, thyme, rosemary, mustard seeds and fennel seeds in a 5-litre (20-cup) slow cooker. Cook, covered, on high for 4 hours.

2 Just before beetroot is ready, place sugar, vinegar and the water in a small saucepan over medium heat. Cook, stirring, for 2 minutes or until sugar dissolves.

3 Discard thyme and rosemary. Spoon beetroot mixture into hot sterilised jars (see glossary, page 484). Pour enough hot vinegar mixture into jars to cover beetroot; seal immediately. Discard any excess pickling liquid. Label and date jars when cold. Remove with a clean spoon each time. Scatter with extra thyme to serve, if you like.

ORANGE MARMALADE

prep + cook time 3 hours 15 minutes * makes 4 cups

- **1kg (2lb) oranges**
- **1 litre (4 cups) water**
- **1kg (2lb) white (granulated) sugar, approximately**

1 Peel oranges, removing rind and white pith separately. Slice rind thinly and reserve half the pith. Quarter oranges. Slice flesh thinly; reserve any seeds. Tie reserved pith and seeds in muslin.
2 Combine rind, flesh, the muslin bag and the water in a 5-litre (20-cup) slow cooker. Cook, covered, on high for 2 hours. Discard muslin bag.
3 Measure fruit mixture. Allow 1 cup (220g) sugar for each cup of fruit mixture. Return fruit mixture and sugar to slow cooker. Adjust setting to 'reduce' (HIGH) and boil, uncovered, for 40 minutes or until marmalade jells when tested (see glossary, page 479).
4 Pour hot marmalade into hot sterilised jars (see glossary, page 484); seal immediately. Label and date jars when cold. Remove with a clean spoon each time.

Tip *This method of making marmalade will work with most citrus fruits, or a combination of various citrus fruits.*

BREADS

CORN BREAD

prep + cook time 2 hours 30 minutes ✻ serves 10

∗ 1½ cups (225g) self-raising flour
∗ 1 cup (170g) polenta (cornmeal)
∗ 2 teaspoons sea salt
∗ ¼ cup finely chopped fresh flat-leaf parsley
∗ ½ cup (60g) coarsely grated cheddar
∗ 250g (8oz) can corn kernels, drained, rinsed
∗ 250g (8oz) can creamed corn
∗ 2 eggs, beaten lightly
∗ 50g (1½oz) butter, melted
∗ ½ cup (125ml) buttermilk

1 Oil a 5-litre (20-cup) slow cooker. Preheat cooker on high for 30 minutes.
2 Meanwhile, combine flour, polenta, salt, parsley, cheddar and corn kernels in a large bowl. Combine creamed corn, egg, butter and buttermilk in a large jug. Add buttermilk mixture to flour mixture; stir until just combined.
3 Spread mixture into slow cooker insert; smooth top. Cook, covered, on high for 2 hours or until bread sounds hollow when tapped with fingers.
4 Preheat grill (broiler).
5 Carefully turn corn bread, top-side up, onto an oven tray. Cook under grill for 5 minutes or until bread is browned lightly.

Tip *Bread is best made on the day of serving, or reheat, wrapped in foil, in the oven for 15 minutes or until warmed through.*

Serving suggestion *Serve with soups and stews.*

Suitable to freeze *at the end of step 3.*

CHEESY SEED DAMPER

prep + cook time 3 hours 30 minutes * serves 12

- **3 cups (450g) self-raising flour**
- **2 teaspoons sea salt**
- **40g (1½oz) cold butter, chopped**
- **¼ cup (50g) pepitas (pumpkin seed kernels)**
- **¼ cup (35g) sunflower seeds**
- **2 tablespoons linseeds (flaxseeds)**
- **¼ cup (50g) roasted buckwheat**
- **1½ cups (150g) pizza cheese**
- **¾ cup (180ml) buttermilk**
- **½ cup (125ml) water, approximately**

1 Preheat a 5-litre (20-cup) slow cooker on high for 30 minutes.

2 Meanwhile, sift flour and salt into a large bowl; using your fingertips, rub in butter. Stir in seeds, buckwheat and cheese. Stir in buttermilk and enough of the water to make a soft and sticky dough.

3 Turn dough onto a floured surface and knead lightly until smooth. Shape dough into a 16cm (6½in) round on a piece of baking paper. Brush with a little extra buttermilk and sprinkle with a little extra flour. Cut a 1cm (½ in) deep, 10cm (4in) wide cross in top of dough.

4 Lift dough, on baking paper, into slow cooker. Cook, covered, on high for 3 hours or until damper sounds hollow when tapped with fingers.

5 Preheat grill (broiler).

6 Carefully lift damper, on baking paper, from slow cooker; place on an oven tray. Cook under the grill for 5 minutes or until browned lightly.

Tip *Damper is best made on the day of serving, or reheat, wrapped in foil, in the oven for 15 minutes or until warmed through.*

Serving suggestion *Spread with butter and golden syrup, or serve with soups and stews.*

Suitable to freeze *at the end of step 4.*

IRISH SODA RYE BREAD

prep + cook time 3 hours 30 minutes ✻ serves 12

- **2½ cups (375g) white plain (all-purpose) flour**
- **2⅔ cups (330g) rye flour**
- **2 teaspoons sea salt**
- **1 teaspoon bicarbonate of soda (baking soda)**
- **2¾ cups (680ml) buttermilk, approximately**

1 Oil a 5-litre (20-cup) slow cooker. Preheat cooker on high for 30 minutes.
2 Meanwhile, sift flours, salt and bicarbonate of soda into a large bowl. Stir in enough of the buttermilk to make a firm dough.
3 Turn dough onto a floured surface; knead lightly until smooth. Shape dough into a 20cm (8in) round. Brush with a little extra buttermilk and sprinkle with a little extra flour. Cut a 1cm (½in) deep criss-cross pattern in top of dough.
4 Carefully lift dough round and place in slow cooker. Cook, covered, on high for 3 hours or until bread sounds hollow when tapped with your fingers.
5 Preheat grill (broiler).
6 Carefully turn bread, top-side up, onto an oven tray. Cook under the grill for 5 minutes or until browned lightly.

Tip *Bread is best made on the day of serving, or reheat, wrapped in foil, in the oven for 15 minutes or until warmed through.*

Serving suggestion *Spread with butter and orange marmalade (page 23), or serve with soups and stews.*

Suitable to freeze *at the end of step 4.*

TEAR AND SHARE PIZZA SUPREME

prep + cook time 2 hours * serves 6

- **½ cup (135g) drained canned pineapple pieces, chopped coarsely**
- **2 cups (300g) self-raising flour**
- **½ teaspoon bicarbonate of soda (baking soda)**
- **50g (1½oz) cold butter, chopped**
- **¾ cup (180ml) buttermilk, approximately**
- **2 tablespoons pizza sauce with herbs and garlic**
- **2 tablespoons barbecue sauce**
- **½ small red onion (50g), sliced thinly**
- **½ small green capsicum (bell pepper) (75g), sliced thinly**
- **50g (1½oz) sliced pepperoni, chopped coarsely**
- **50g (1½oz) shaved ham, chopped coarsely**
- **50g (1½oz) sliced mushrooms**
- **1½ cups (150g) pizza cheese**

1 Drain pineapple on paper towel.

2 Preheat a 5-litre (20-cup) slow cooker on high for 30 minutes. Line cooker insert with a piece of baking paper.

3 Meanwhile, sift flour and bicarbonate of soda into a large bowl; using your fingertips, rub in butter. Stir in enough of the buttermilk to make a soft, sticky dough.

4 Turn dough onto a floured surface; knead lightly until smooth. Flatten into a 25cm x 30cm (10in x 12in) rectangle. Spread dough with combined sauces, then top with onion, capsicum, pepperoni, ham, mushrooms, drained pineapple and half the cheese.

5 Roll up dough from long side to enclose filling. Cut dough into six scrolls. Place scrolls, just touching, cut-side up, in slow cooker. Scatter with remaining cheese. Cook, covered, on high for 1½ hours or until cooked through.

6 Preheat grill (broiler).

7 Carefully lift scrolls, on baking paper, from slow cooker and place on an oven tray. Cook under grill for 5 minutes or until browned lightly.

Tip *You can use any fillings you like, but be careful not to overstuff the scrolls or they will not cook through.*

Serving suggestion *A leafy green salad.*

SOUPS

SPANISH
OXTAIL AND PEA SOUP

prep + cook time 8 hours 45 minutes * serves 6

- **1.5kg (3lb) oxtails, cut into 5cm (2in) pieces**
- **400g (12½oz) can chickpeas (garbanzo beans), drained, rinsed**
- **400g (12½oz) can diced tomatoes**
- **2 small leeks (400g), white part only, sliced thinly**
- **2 medium carrots (240g), halved, sliced thickly**
- **½ cup (100g) thinly sliced roasted red capsicum (bell pepper)**
- **3 cloves garlic, crushed**
- **2 dried bay leaves**
- **2 teaspoons smoked paprika**
- **1 teaspoon dried chilli flakes**
- **½ cup (125ml) dry sherry**
- **1 litre (4 cups) water**
- **2 cups (500ml) beef stock**
- **250g (8oz) packaged microwave white long grain rice**
- **1 cured chorizo sausage (130g), sliced thinly**
- **⅓ cup fresh flat-leaf parsley leaves**

1 Trim excess fat from oxtail. Combine oxtail, chickpeas, canned tomatoes, leek, carrot, capsicum, garlic, bay leaves, paprika, chilli flakes, sherry, the water and stock in a 5-litre (20-cup) slow cooker. Cook, covered, on low for 8 hours.

2 Heat rice following packet directions.

3 Meanwhile, discard bay leaves from slow cooker. Skim fat from surface. Add rice to cooker and cook, uncovered, on high for 5 minutes or until mixture thickens slightly. Season to taste.

4 Cook chorizo in a heated small frying pan until browned and crisp; drain on paper towel.

5 Divide oxtail among soup bowls, then ladle hot soup into bowls. Top with chorizo and parsley.

Serving suggestion
Warm crusty bread and lemon wedges.

Suitable to freeze
at the end of step 1.

PHO GA

prep + cook time 9 hours * serves 4

- **1.2kg (2½lb) whole chicken**
- **1 large onion (200g), chopped coarsely**
- **5cm (2in) piece fresh ginger, sliced thinly**
- **2 litres (8 cups) water**
- **3 whole star anise**
- **3 green onions (scallions), cut into 5cm (2in) lengths**
- **2 cinnamon sticks**
- **10cm (4in) stalk fresh lemon grass, bruised**
- **1 tablespoon coriander seeds**
- **¼ cup (60ml) fish sauce**
- **¼ cup (60ml) lime juice**
- **2 tablespoons brown sugar**
- **200g (6½oz) rice stick noodles**
- **2 cups (160g) bean sprouts**
- **½ cup small fresh mint leaves**
- **½ cup small fresh coriander (cilantro) leaves**
- **½ cup fresh thai basil leaves**
- **1 fresh long red chilli, seeded, sliced thinly lengthways**
- **1 green onion (scallion), extra, sliced thinly**

1 Place chicken, onion, ginger, the water, star anise, green onion, cinnamon, lemon grass and coriander seeds in a 5-litre (20-cup) slow cooker. Cook, covered, on low for 8 hours.

2 Carefully remove chicken from slow cooker, then shred meat coarsely using two forks; discard skin and bones.

3 Add fish sauce, juice and sugar to stock mixture in slow cooker; stir to combine. Strain cooking liquid through a muslin-lined sieve into a large heatproof bowl; discard solids.

4 Place noodles in a medium heatproof bowl, cover with boiling water and stand for 15 minutes or until tender; drain.

5 Divide noodles and shredded chicken among soup bowls. Ladle hot soup over noodles. Serve topped with sprouts, herbs, chilli and extra green onion.

Serving suggestion *Lime cheeks.*

TOMATO SOUP
WITH BASIL DUMPLINGS

prep + cook time 8 hours 45 minutes * serves 4

∗ 1kg (2lb) over-ripe roma (egg) tomatoes, cored
∗ 400g (12½oz) can whole tomatoes
∗ 3 cloves garlic, peeled
∗ 2 medium onions (300g), quartered
∗ 1 fresh long red chilli, chopped coarsely
∗ 1 stalk celery (150g), trimmed, chopped coarsely
∗ 1 cup (200g) drained roasted red capsicum (bell pepper), chopped coarsely
∗ ¼ cup fresh small basil leaves or micro basil

BASIL DUMPLINGS
∗ 1 cup (150g) self-raising flour
∗ 60g (2oz) cold butter, chopped
∗ 1 egg, beaten lightly
∗ 2 tablespoons basil pesto
∗ 2 tablespoons milk, approximately

1 Place fresh tomatoes, canned tomatoes, garlic, onion, chilli, celery and capsicum in a 5-litre (20-cup) slow cooker. Cook, covered, on low for 7 hours.
2 Cool soup for 10 minutes. Using a stick blender, blend soup until smooth. Season to taste.
3 Make basil dumpling mixture.
4 Carefully drop level tablespoons of the basil dumpling mixture, about 2cm (¾in) apart, on top of soup in slow cooker. Cook, covered, on low for 1 hour or until dumplings are firm to touch and cooked through.
5 Serve soup with dumplings, topped with basil.

BASIL DUMPLINGS Place flour in a medium bowl. Using your fingertips, rub in butter. Stir in egg, pesto and enough of the milk to make a soft, sticky dough.

Serving suggestion
Top with halved mixed baby tomatoes.

Suitable to freeze
at the end of step 2.

POTATO AND CHEDDAR SOUP

prep + cook time 8 hours 30 minutes * serves 4

- **1 stalk celery (150g), trimmed, chopped coarsely**
- **1kg (2lb) potatoes, chopped coarsely**
- **2 medium onions (300g), chopped coarsely**
- **½ small cauliflower (500g), chopped coarsely**
- **3 cloves garlic, sliced thinly**
- **2 cups (500ml) vegetable stock**
- **2 cups (500ml) water**
- **1½ cups (180g) coarsely grated cheddar**
- **⅓ cup (80ml) thickened (heavy) cream**
- **¼ cup fresh micro herbs (optional)**

1 Place celery, potato, onion, cauliflower, garlic, stock and the water in a 5-litre (20-cup) slow cooker. Cook, covered, on low for 8 hours.

2 Add cheddar; stir until cheddar melts. Cool soup for 10 minutes. Using a stick blender, blend soup until smooth. Season to taste.

3 Serve soup drizzled with cream and topped with micro herbs.

Serving suggestion
Garlic bread.

Suitable to freeze
at the end of step 2.

COCONUT PUMPKIN SOUP

prep + cook time 4 hours 30 minutes ✻ serves 4

- **3 cloves garlic, crushed**
- **½ teaspoon dried chilli flakes**
- **1.5kg (3lb) jap pumpkin, chopped coarsely**
- **1 large onion (200g), chopped coarsely**
- **1 cup (250ml) coconut milk**
- **2 cups (500ml) vegetable stock**
- **2 tablespoons roasted unsalted peanuts**
- **1 fresh long red chilli, sliced**
- **¼ cup small fresh coriander (cilantro) leaves**

1 Place garlic, dried chilli, pumpkin, onion, coconut milk and stock in a 5-litre (20-cup) slow cooker. Cook, covered, on high for 4 hours.

2 Cool soup for 10 minutes. Using a stick blender, blend soup until smooth. Season to taste.

3 Serve soup topped with peanuts, fresh chilli and coriander.

Serving suggestion
Thin slices of toasted baguette.

Suitable to freeze
at the end of step 2.

HAM AND CHEESE TORTELLINI BROTH

prep + cook time 5 hours 45 minutes * serves 4

- **3 cloves garlic, crushed**
- **1 medium onion (150g), sliced thinly**
- **400g (12½oz) piece smoked ham**
- **2 tablespoons tomato paste**
- **1 litre (4 cups) chicken stock**
- **3 cups (750ml) water**
- **400g (12½oz) can diced tomatoes**
- **200g (6½oz) frozen green peas**
- **300g (9½oz) ham and cheese tortellini**
- **¼ small white cabbage (300g), shredded finely**
- **⅓ cup (25g) shaved parmesan**

1 Place garlic, onion, ham, tomato paste, stock, the water and canned tomatoes in a 5-litre (20-cup) slow cooker. Cook, covered, on low for 5 hours. Season.

2 Remove ham from slow cooker, then shred meat coarsely using two forks. Return to cooker with peas. Cook, covered, on high for 10 minutes or until peas are tender.

3 Meanwhile, cook tortellini in a large saucepan of boiling salted water until just tender; drain. Divide among bowls.

4 Ladle broth over tortellini. Serve topped with cabbage and parmesan.

Serving suggestion *Crusty olive bread.*

CHICKEN CONGEE

prep + cook time 8 hours 30 minutes * serves 4

∗ 1.2kg (2½lb) whole chicken
∗ 1 medium onion (150g), chopped finely
∗ 50g (1½oz) fresh ginger, sliced thinly
∗ 2 cloves garlic, bruised
∗ 1.5 litres (6 cups) water
∗ 1 cup (200g) white long grain rice
∗ 2 teaspoons peanut oil
∗ 150g (4½oz) fresh shiitake mushrooms, halved if large
∗ 1 dried chinese sausage (lap cheong) (30g), sliced thinly
∗ 2 teaspoons chilli oil
∗ 2 tablespoons fried shallots
∗ 2 green onions (scallions), sliced thinly lengthways

1 Place chicken, onion, ginger, garlic and the water in a 5-litre (20-cup) slow cooker. Cook, covered, on low for 6 hours.

2 Carefully remove chicken from slow cooker, then shred meat coarsely using two forks; discard skin and bones. Strain cooking liquid through a muslin-lined sieve into a large heatproof bowl; discard solids.

3 Return stock mixture to slow cooker with shredded chicken and rice. Cook, covered, on low for 2 hours.

4 Just before serving, heat peanut oil in a medium frying pan over medium-high heat. Cook mushrooms and sausage, stirring, for 5 minutes or until mushrooms are lightly browned and tender.

5 Divide congee among soup bowls. Drizzle with chilli oil. Serve topped with mushroom mixture, shallots and green onion.

HEARTY CORN AND CHICKEN CHOWDER

prep + cook time 8 hours 45 minutes * serves 4

- **1 tablespoon olive oil**
- **1 medium onion (150g), chopped finely**
- **2 rindless bacon slices (130g), cut into 2cm (¾in) pieces**
- **1 stalk celery (150g), trimmed, chopped finely**
- **3 sprigs fresh thyme**
- **2 fresh bay leaves**
- **1.2kg (2½lb) whole chicken**
- **2 trimmed corn cobs (500g)**
- **500g (1lb) potatoes, cut into 2cm (¾in) pieces**
- **1.25 litres (5 cups) chicken stock**
- **1 cup (250ml) milk**
- **2 tablespoons cornflour (cornstarch)**
- **⅓ cup finely chopped fresh chives**

1 Heat oil in a 5-litre (20-cup) slow cooker on 'sear' (HIGH) setting. Cook onion, bacon, celery, thyme and bay leaves, stirring, for 5 minutes or until vegetables soften. Add chicken, corn cobs, potato and stock. Cook, covered, on low for 8 hours.

2 Carefully remove chicken and corn from slow cooker. Shred chicken coarsely using two forks; discard skin and bones. Using a small sharp knife, cut kernels from corn cobs; discard cobs.

3 Stir milk and cornflour in a small bowl until combined. Return chicken and corn to slow cooker with cornflour mixture. Adjust setting to 'reduce' (LOW). Simmer, uncovered, for 10 minutes or until chowder thickens. Season to taste.

4 Serve chowder scattered with fresh chives.

Serving suggestion *Crackers or grilled crusty bread.*

MINESTRONE

prep + cook time 8 hours 30 minutes * serves 4

- **3 cloves garlic, crushed**
- **1 medium onion (150g), chopped finely**
- **1 stalk celery (150g), trimmed, chopped finely**
- **1 medium carrot (120g), chopped finely**
- **2 cups (500ml) vegetable stock**
- **2 tablespoons tomato paste**
- **400g (12½oz) can crushed tomatoes**
- **400g (12½oz) can cannellini beans, drained, rinsed**
- **2 cups (500ml) water, approximately**
- **¾ cup (100g) dried small pasta tubes**
- **150g (4½oz) green beans, trimmed, cut into 3cm (1¼in) lengths**
- **½ cup (60g) frozen green peas**
- **¼ small white cabbage (300g), shredded finely**
- **⅓ cup (25g) finely grated parmesan**
- **½ cup loosely packed fresh flat-leaf parsley leaves**

1 Place garlic, onion, celery, carrot, stock, tomato paste and canned tomatoes in a 5-litre (20-cup) slow cooker. Cook, covered, on low for 6 hours.

2 Add cannellini beans and enough of the water to make a thick soup consistency. Cook, covered, on low for 2 hours. Season to taste.

3 Meanwhile, cook pasta in a large saucepan of boiling salted water until just tender, adding green beans and peas for the last 2 minutes of cooking time; drain.

4 Divide pasta, green beans, peas and cabbage among soup bowls; ladle soup mixture into bowls. Serve topped with parmesan and parsley.

Serving suggestion
Toasted crusty bread.

Suitable to freeze
at the end of step 2.

BEETROOT AND ONION SOUP
WITH MINTY WHIPPED FETTA

prep + cook time 8 hours 30 minutes * serves 6

- **1kg (2lb) baby beetroot (beets)**
- **4 medium parsnips (1kg)**
- **2 large onions (400g)**
- **1 tablespoon olive oil**
- **¼ cup (60ml) balsamic vinegar**
- **2 tablespoons brown sugar**
- **2 cloves garlic, crushed**
- **4 sprigs fresh thyme**
- **1 litre (4 cups) water**

MINTY WHIPPED FETTA

- **180g (5½oz) persian fetta, drained (see tips)**
- **⅓ cup (95g) no-fat Greek-style yoghurt**
- **2 tablespoons finely chopped fresh mint**

1 Trim beetroot, reserving small leaves to serve. Scrub unpeeled beetroot and parsnips; chop coarsely. Thinly slice onions.

2 Heat oil in a 5-litre (20-cup) slow cooker on 'sear' (MEDIUM) setting. Cook onion, stirring, for 15 minutes or until softened and lightly caramelised. Add vinegar and sugar; cook, stirring, for 2 minutes. Add parsnip, beetroot, garlic, thyme and the water; stir to combine. Cook, covered, on low for 8 hours.

3 Cool soup for 10 minutes. Using a stick blender, blend soup until smooth (see tips). Season to taste.

4 Meanwhile, make minty whipped fetta.

5 Serve soup topped with minty whipped fetta and reserved small beetroot leaves.

MINTY WHIPPED FETTA Blend or process fetta and yoghurt until smooth. Stir in mint. Season to taste.

Tips *Reserve some of the marinating oil from the fetta and drizzle over bowls of soup to serve. You may need to add a little extra boiling water if you prefer a thinner soup.*

Serving suggestion *Crusty bread.*

Suitable to freeze *at the end of step 3.*

BEEF AND VEGETABLE SOUP

prep + cook time 9 hours 45 minutes * serves 4

- **1kg (2lb) gravy beef, trimmed, cut into 2.5cm (1in) pieces**
- **1 clove garlic, crushed**
- **1 medium onion (150g), cut into 1cm (½in) pieces**
- **2 stalks celery (300g), trimmed, cut into 1cm (½in) pieces**
- **2 medium carrots (240g), cut into 1cm (½in) pieces**
- **2 medium potatoes (400g), cut into 1cm (½in) pieces**
- **400g (12½oz) can diced tomatoes**
- **1 litre (4 cups) water**
- **2 cups (500ml) beef stock**
- **2 dried bay leaves**
- **1 cup (120g) frozen green peas**
- **⅓ cup coarsely chopped fresh flat-leaf parsley**

1 Combine beef, garlic, onion, celery, carrot, potato, canned tomatoes, the water, stock and bay leaves in a 5-litre (20-cup) slow cooker. Cook, covered, on low for 9 hours.

2 Add peas to slow cooker and cook, covered, for a further 30 minutes. Season to taste.

3 Serve soup topped with parsley.

Serving suggestion
Crusty bread.

Suitable to freeze
at the end of step 2.

4 WAYS WITH TOPPERS

SOUP NUTS AND SEEDS

prep + cook time 10 minutes ✻ makes ¾ cup

Heat 2 tablespoons olive oil in a small non-stick frying pan over medium heat. Add ⅓ cup coarsely chopped natural almonds and ¼ cup pepitas (pumpkin seed kernels); cook, stirring, for 1 minute. Add 1 tablespoon each of coriander seeds and black sesame seeds; cook, stirring, for a further 2 minutes or until lightly toasted. Cool to room temperature.

QUINOA CRISP

prep + cook time 1 hour 30 minutes ✻ makes 2 cups

Preheat oven to 180°C/350°F. Line an oven tray with baking paper. Stir ⅓ cup white quinoa, 2 tablespoons black chia seeds, 2 tablespoons linseeds (flaxseeds), 1 tablespoon extra virgin olive oil and 1 cup water in a small saucepan over medium heat for 12 minutes until mixture is thick and begins to come away from the side of the pan. Add ⅓ cup finely grated parmesan and season; stir for a further 2 minutes. Spread mixture thinly over tray. Cover with a second sheet of baking paper, then roll out to 2mm (⅛in) thick. Bake for 20 minutes, remove top paper, then bake for a further 20 minutes. Carefully turn crisp over and bake for 20 minutes or until golden brown and crisp. Cool, then break into pieces.

ALMOND GREMOLATA

prep + cook time 10 minutes ✻ makes ¾ cup

Coarsely chop ½ cup roasted natural almonds. Heat 30g (1oz) butter in a small saucepan over medium heat; cook, stirring, until beginning to brown, then remove from heat. Add 1 tablespoon finely grated lemon rind and ½ cup chopped fresh flat-leaf parsley.

PARMESAN CRISPS

prep + cook time 20 minutes ✻ makes 12

Preheat oven to 180°C/350°F. Line two oven trays with baking paper. Combine 1 cup finely grated parmesan, 2 teaspoons wholemeal plain (all-purpose) flour, ¼ teaspoon freshly ground black pepper and 1 teaspoon finely chopped fresh rosemary leaves in a small bowl. Place 12 level tablespoons of mixture onto tray, 5cm (2in) apart; flatten to 8cm (3¼in) rounds. Bake for 6 minutes or until pale golden. Working quickly, lift, using a palette knife, and drape over a rolling pin to cool.

SPICY CORN CHOWDER
WITH AVOCADO CREAM

prep + cook time 8 hours 15 minutes * serves 6

- **1 tablespoon extra virgin olive oil**
- **6 trimmed corn cobs (1.5kg), kernels removed**
- **2 medium onions (300g), chopped coarsely**
- **2 cloves garlic, crushed**
- **1 teaspoon ground cumin**
- **1 teaspoon dried oregano**
- **½ teaspoon smoked paprika**
- **1 teaspoon dried chilli flakes (see tip)**
- **1.25 litres (5 cups) vegetable stock or water**
- **300ml pouring cream**
- **½ cup (60g) corn nuts (salted roasted corn kernels)**
- **⅓ cup fresh coriander (cilantro) sprigs**

AVOCADO CREAM

- **1 small avocado (200g), chopped**
- **⅓ cup (80g) sour cream**
- **2 tablespoons lime juice**

1 Heat oil in a 5-litre (20-cup) slow cooker on 'sear' (MEDIUM) setting. Cook corn, onion, garlic, cumin, oregano, paprika and chilli, stirring, for 15 minutes or until softened and lightly caramelised. Add stock and cream. Cook, covered, on low for 7½ hours.

2 Cool soup for 10 minutes. Using a stick blender, blend soup until smooth. Season to taste.

3 Meanwhile, make avocado cream.

4 Serve soup topped with avocado cream, corn nuts and coriander. Season with freshly ground black pepper.

AVOCADO CREAM Blend or process ingredients until smooth. Season to taste.

Tip *You can omit the chilli for those who don't like it spicy.*

Suitable to freeze *at the end of step 2.*

SMOKY CHICKPEA AND TOMATO SOUP

prep + cook time 8 hours 30 minutes * serves 6

- **1.5kg (3lb) tomatoes, quartered (see tip)**
- **1 large onion (200g), chopped coarsely**
- **3 cloves garlic, chopped coarsely**
- **1 stalk celery (150g), trimmed, sliced thickly**
- **3 x 400g (12½oz) cans chickpeas (garbanzo beans), drained, rinsed**
- **1¾ cups (430ml) chicken stock**
- **2 teaspoons smoked paprika**
- **1 tablespoon caster (superfine) sugar**
- **⅓ cup (80g) sour cream**

1 Place tomato, onion, garlic, celery, chickpeas, stock, paprika and sugar in a 5-litre (20-cup) slow cooker. Cook, covered, on low for 8 hours.

2 Using a slotted spoon, transfer 2 cups of the chickpea mixture to a medium bowl; reserve. Stand remaining soup for 10 minutes. Using a stick blender, blend soup until smooth. Stir in reserved chickpea mixture. Season to taste.

3 Serve soup topped with sour cream. Season with freshly ground black pepper.

Tip *Choose the ripest tomatoes you can find.*

Suitable to freeze *at the end of step 2.*

Serving suggestion
Chargrilled bread.

COCK-A-LEEKIE SOUP

prep + cook time 9 hours ✻ serves 6

- **1.2kg (2½lb) whole chicken**
- **2 cloves garlic, sliced thinly**
- **4 medium leeks (1.4kg), white part only, sliced thinly**
- **2 stalks celery (300g), trimmed, sliced thinly**
- **4 sprigs fresh thyme**
- **large pinch cayenne pepper**
- **2.5 litres (10 cups) salt-reduced chicken stock**
- **1 cup (170g) pitted prunes**
- **2 tablespoons coarsely chopped fresh oregano**
- **2 tablespoons coarsely chopped fresh flat-leaf parsley**

1 Place chicken, garlic, leek, celery, thyme, cayenne pepper and 2 litres of the stock in a 5-litre (20-cup) slow cooker. Cook, covered, on low for 8 hours.

2 Carefully remove chicken from slow cooker, then shred meat coarsely using two forks; discard skin and bones.

3 Return shredded chicken to slow cooker with prunes and remaining stock. Cook, covered, on high for 30 minutes or until prunes soften and stock is hot. Discard thyme. Season to taste.

4 Stir oregano and parsley into soup to serve.

Serving suggestion
Damper or soda bread.

Suitable to freeze
at the end of step 3.

CUBAN BLACK BEAN SOUP

prep + cook time 9 hours (+ overnight standing) * serves 6

You will need to soak the beans overnight, so start the recipe the day before.

*** 1½ cups (300g) dried black turtle beans**
*** 1 ham hock (1kg)**
*** 2 tablespoons olive oil**
*** 1 large onion (200g), chopped finely**
*** 1 medium red capsicum (bell pepper) (200g), chopped finely**
*** 3 cloves garlic, crushed**
*** 3 teaspoons ground cumin**
*** 1 teaspoon dried chilli flakes**
*** 400g (12½oz) can crushed tomatoes**
*** 2 litres (8 cups) water**
*** 3 teaspoons dried oregano leaves**
*** 1 teaspoon ground black pepper**
*** 2 tablespoons lime juice**
*** 1 large tomato (220g), chopped finely**
*** ¼ cup coarsely chopped fresh coriander (cilantro)**

1 Place beans in a medium bowl, cover with cold water and stand overnight.
2 Drain and rinse beans, place in a medium saucepan and cover with cold water. Bring to the boil; boil, uncovered, for 15 minutes, then drain.
3 Meanwhile, preheat oven to 220°C/425°F.
4 Roast ham hock on an oven tray for 30 minutes.
5 Heat oil in a large frying pan. Cook onion, capsicum and garlic, stirring, until onion is soft. Add cumin and chilli; cook, stirring, until fragrant.
6 Combine beans, ham hock, onion mixture, canned tomatoes, the water, oregano and pepper in a 5-litre (20-cup) slow cooker. Cook, covered, on low for 8 hours.
7 Remove ham hock from slow cooker. When cool enough to handle, remove meat from bone and shred coarsely; discard skin, fat and bone. Blend or process 2 cups soup mixture until smooth. Return meat to cooker with pureed soup. Stir in juice and fresh tomato. Season to taste.
8 Serve soup topped with coriander.

Serving suggestion
Crusty bread, sour cream or plain yoghurt.

Suitable to freeze
at the end of step 7.

SPICY LENTIL SOUP

prep + cook time 6 hours 15 minutes ✻ serves 4

- **½ cup (100g) dried red lentils**
- **1 litre (4 cups) chicken stock**
- **400g (12½oz) can diced tomatoes**
- **2 dried bay leaves**
- **3 cloves garlic, crushed**
- **⅓ cup (100g) mild indian curry paste**
- **2 small carrots (240g), chopped coarsely**
- **1 stalk celery (150g), trimmed, sliced thinly**
- **2 medium potatoes (400g), chopped coarsely**
- **½ cup (140g) Greek-style yoghurt**
- **½ cup finely chopped fresh coriander (cilantro)**

1 Rinse lentils under cold water until water runs clear; drain.

2 Combine lentils, stock, canned tomatoes, bay leaves, garlic, curry paste, carrot, celery and potato in a 5-litre (20-cup) slow cooker. Cook, covered, on low for 6 hours. Season to taste.

3 Serve soup topped with yoghurt and coriander.

Serving suggestion
Crusty bread.

Suitable to freeze
at the end of step 2.

PUMPKIN SOUP

prep + cook time 6 hours 45 minutes * serves 6

- **30g (1oz) butter**
- **1 tablespoon olive oil**
- **1 large leek (500g), white part only, sliced thinly**
- **1.8kg (3¾lb) butternut pumpkin, chopped coarsely**
- **1 large potato (300g), chopped coarsely**
- **3 cups (750ml) chicken stock**
- **3 cups (750ml) water**
- **½ cup (125ml) pouring cream**
- **1 tablespoon finely chopped fresh chives**

1 Heat butter and oil in a large frying pan. Cook leek, stirring, until soft.

2 Combine leek, pumpkin, potato, stock and the water in a 5-litre (20-cup) slow cooker. Cook, covered, on low for 6 hours.

3 Cool soup for 10 minutes. Blend or process soup, in batches, until smooth. Return soup to slow cooker. Cook, covered, on high for 20 minutes or until hot. Stir in ⅓ cup of the cream. Season to taste.

4 Serve soup drizzled with remaining cream and topped with chives.

Serving suggestion
Toasted sourdough or rye bread.

Suitable to freeze
at the end of step 3 without the cream.

VEGETABLE HARIRA

prep + cook time 8 hours 30 minutes * serves 8

* **2 teaspoons ground cumin**
* **2 teaspoons ground coriander**
* **2 teaspoons sweet smoked paprika**
* **1 teaspoon ground ginger**
* **1 teaspoon ground cinnamon**
* **1 teaspoon dried chilli flakes**
* **¼ teaspoon ground nutmeg**
* **1 large onion (200g), chopped finely**
* **2 medium carrots (240g), chopped finely**
* **4 stalks celery (600g), trimmed, chopped finely**
* **5 medium tomatoes (750g), chopped finely**
* **6 cloves garlic, crushed**
* **2 tablespoons tomato paste**
* **1.5 litres (6 cups) vegetable stock**
* **1 litre (4 cups) water**
* **1 cup (200g) French-style green lentils**
* **400g (12½oz) can chickpeas (garbanzo beans), drained, rinsed**
* **⅓ cup finely chopped fresh flat-leaf parsley**
* **⅓ cup finely chopped fresh coriander (cilantro)**

1 Stir spices in a small frying pan over medium heat for 1 minute or until fragrant.

2 Combine onion, carrot, celery, tomato, garlic, toasted spices, tomato paste, stock, the water and lentils in a 5-litre (20-cup) slow cooker. Cook, covered, on low for 8 hours. Season to taste.

3 Add chickpeas to slow cooker and stir until heated through.

4 Stir in parsley and coriander to serve.

Tip *Harira is a traditional soup that's eaten to break the fast of Ramadan. This is our vegetarian version, but lamb, chicken or beef could be added.*

Serving suggestion *Warmed flat bread and lemon wedges. Drizzle soup with extra virgin olive oil.*

Suitable to freeze *at the end of step 3.*

CHICKEN HOT AND SOUR SOUP

prep + cook time 9 hours * serves 6

*** 1.6kg (3¼lb) whole chicken**
*** 2 medium carrots (240g), chopped coarsely**
*** 2 stalks celery (300g), trimmed, chopped coarsely**
*** 1 large onion (200g), chopped coarsely**
*** 2.5 litres (10 cups) water**
*** 6 fresh kaffir lime leaves, crushed**
*** 2 x 10cm (4in) stalks fresh lemon grass, bruised**
*** 6cm (2½in) piece fresh ginger, grated**
*** 2 fresh long red chillies, sliced thinly**
*** ½ cup (125ml) lime juice**
*** ½ cup (125ml) fish sauce**
*** 3 teaspoons brown sugar**
*** 425g (13½oz) can straw mushrooms, drained, rinsed**
*** 2 baby buk choy (300g), trimmed, chopped coarsely**
*** 200g (6½oz) dried rice vermicelli noodles**
*** ½ cup firmly packed fresh coriander (cilantro) leaves**

1 Remove and discard fat and skin from chicken. Place chicken, carrot, celery, onion and the water in a 5-litre (20-cup) slow cooker. Cook, covered, on low for 8 hours.
2 Carefully remove chicken from slow cooker, then shred meat coarsely using two forks; discard bones. Strain cooking liquid through a muslin-lined sieve or linen tea towel; discard solids.
3 Return strained liquid to slow cooker with lime leaves, lemon grass, ginger, chilli, juice, fish sauce, sugar, mushrooms and shredded chicken. Cook, covered, on high for 30 minutes.
4 Stir in buk choy.
5 Meanwhile, place noodles in a medium heatproof bowl, cover with boiling water and stand for 10 minutes or until softened; drain. Divide noodles among soup bowls. Ladle hot soup over noodles. Serve topped with coriander and fresh sliced chilli, if you like.

Suitable to freeze *at the end of step 3.*

CHICKEN MULLIGATAWNY

prep + cook time 8 hours 30 minutes * serves 4

- **2 medium onions (300g), chopped coarsely**
- **2 cloves garlic, chopped coarsely**
- **2 medium carrots (240g), chopped coarsely**
- **1 stalk celery (150g), trimmed, chopped coarsely**
- **1 fresh long red chilli, chopped coarsely**
- **4cm (1½in) piece fresh ginger, grated**
- **2 chicken marylands (700g)**
- **1 tablespoon mild curry powder**
- **1 teaspoon ground cumin**
- **1 teaspoon garam masala (see tip)**
- **3 cups (750ml) chicken stock**
- **1 cup (250ml) coconut milk**
- **½ cup fresh coriander (cilantro) leaves**

1 Place onion, garlic, carrot, celery, chilli, ginger, chicken, curry powder, cumin, garam masala and stock in a 5-litre (20-cup) slow cooker. Cook, covered, on low for 8 hours.

2 Carefully remove chicken from slow cooker, then shred meat coarsely using two forks; discard skin and bones.

3 Skim fat from surface of vegetable mixture. Blend or process vegetable mixture until smooth. Return shredded chicken to slow cooker with coconut milk and stir to combine.

4 Ladle soup into soup bowls. Scatter with coriander and drizzle with extra coconut milk, if you like.

Tip *Garam masala is a blend of spices, including cloves, cardamom, cinnamon, coriander, fennel and cumin, which are roasted and ground together. Black pepper and chilli can be added for a hotter version.*

Suitable to freeze *at the end of step 3.*

STEWS

TEX-MEX BEEF AND SWEET POTATO STEW

prep + cook time 8 hours 15 minutes * serves 4

- **800g (1½lb) beef chuck steak, cut into 5cm (2in) pieces**
- **1 medium orange sweet potato (400g), unpeeled, cut into 5cm (2in) pieces**
- **1 medium onion (150g), cut into wedges**
- **400g (12½oz) can diced tomatoes**
- **2 teaspoons ground cumin**
- **1 teaspoon dried oregano**
- **2 teaspoons mexican chilli powder**
- **1 fresh long green chilli, chopped finely**
- **3 cloves garlic, crushed**
- **⅔ cup (130g) drained chargrilled capsicum (bell peppers), chopped coarsely**
- **½ cup (125ml) beef stock**
- **⅔ cup fresh coriander (cilantro) leaves**

1 Place beef, sweet potato, onion, canned tomatoes, cumin, oregano, chilli powder, fresh chilli, garlic, capsicum and stock in a 5-litre (20-cup) slow cooker. Cook, covered, on low for 8 hours. Season to taste.

2 Stir in half the coriander. Serve topped with remaining coriander.

Serving suggestion
Grilled corn on the cob, sliced pickled jalapeños, sour cream and lime wedges.

Suitable to freeze
at the end of step 1.

BEEF RENDANG

prep + cook time 8 hours 30 minutes * serves 4

*** ½ cup (40g) desiccated coconut**
*** 10cm (4in) stalk fresh lemon grass, chopped finely**
*** 1 tablespoon finely grated fresh ginger**
*** 4 cloves garlic, quartered**
*** 3 fresh long red chillies, chopped coarsely**
*** 1 medium onion (150g), chopped coarsely**
*** 1½ tablespoons olive oil**
*** 800g (1½lb) beef chuck steak, cut into 5cm (2in) pieces**
*** 2 teaspoons ground coriander**
*** 1 tablespoon grated palm sugar**
*** 1 tablespoon tamarind puree**
*** 1 cinnamon stick**
*** 1 cup (250ml) coconut milk**
*** 2 tablespoons fresh micro herbs (optional)**
*** 1 green onion (scallion), sliced thinly**

1 Process coconut, lemon grass, ginger, garlic, chilli, onions and oil until a smooth paste forms.

2 Heat a 5-litre (20-cup) slow cooker on 'sear' (HIGH) setting. Cook paste, stirring, for 5 minutes or until well toasted and fragrant. Add beef and cook, stirring, for 8 minutes or until browned.

3 Add ground coriander, palm sugar, tamarind, cinnamon and coconut milk to slow cooker; stir to combine. Cook, covered, on low for 8 hours. Season.

4 Serve rendang topped with micro herbs and green onion.

Serving suggestion
Flat bread or steamed rice mixed with red lentils.

Suitable to freeze
at the end of step 3.

TEXAN BRAISED BEEF
WITH POLENTA DUMPLINGS

prep + cook time 8 hours 30 minutes * serves 4

* **¼ cup (35g) plain (all-purpose) flour**
* **2 teaspoons ground cumin**
* **2 teaspoons smoked paprika**
* **2 teaspoons dried oregano**
* **2 tablespoons olive oil**
* **1.2kg (2½lb) beef chuck steak, trimmed, cut into 3cm (1¼in) pieces**
* **2 cured chorizo sausages (340g), sliced thinly**
* **1 large red onion (300g), sliced thinly**
* **3 small (red, yellow and green) capsicums (bell peppers) (450g), chopped coarsely**
* **3 cloves garlic, crushed**
* **¾ cup (180ml) dry red wine**
* **¾ cup (180ml) beef stock**
* **400g (12½oz) can diced tomatoes**
* **1 tablespoon sriracha chilli sauce**
* **⅓ cup fresh coriander (cilantro) leaves**

POLENTA DUMPLINGS

* **¾ cup (110g) self-raising flour**
* **½ cup (85g) polenta (cornmeal)**
* **50g (1½oz) cold butter, chopped**
* **½ cup (50g) pizza cheese**
* **2 tablespoons finely chopped fresh coriander (cilantro)**
* **1 egg, beaten lightly**
* **2 tablespoons milk, approximately**

1 Combine flour, cumin, paprika and oregano in a large bowl; season.

2 Heat oil in a 5-litre (20-cup) slow cooker on 'sear' (HIGH) setting. Coat beef in flour mixture; shake off excess, reserving excess flour. Cook beef, in batches, turning, for 5 minutes or until well browned. Remove from cooker.

3 Cook chorizo in slow cooker, stirring, for 5 minutes or until browned. Remove from cooker.

4 Adjust setting to 'sear' (MEDIUM). Cook onion, capsicum and garlic, stirring, for 5 minutes or until vegetables soften. Sprinkle with reserved excess flour. Cook, stirring, for 3 minutes. Gradually stir in wine, then stock, canned tomatoes and chilli sauce; bring to the boil.

5 Return beef and chorizo to slow cooker. Cook, covered, on low for 7 hours. Season to taste.

6 Make polenta dumpling mixture close to serving.

7 Drop level tablespoons of dumpling mixture, 2cm (¾in) apart, on top of beef mixture. Cook, covered, on high for 30 minutes or until dumplings are firm to touch and cooked through.

8 Serve beef stew and dumplings topped with coriander.

POLENTA DUMPLINGS Place flour and polenta in a medium bowl; using your fingertips, rub in butter. Add cheese and coriander; stir to combine. Stir in egg and enough of the milk to make a soft, sticky dough.

Serving suggestion *Warmed canned black beans and sliced avocado.*

JAMAICAN OXTAIL
WITH BLACK BEANS

prep + cook time 8 hours 45 minutes ✻ serves 6

- **1 tablespoon olive oil**
- **1.6kg (3¼lb) beef oxtail**
- **1 large onion (200g), chopped coarsely**
- **4 cloves garlic, crushed**
- **3 stalks celery (450g), trimmed, chopped coarsely**
- **2 medium carrots (240g), chopped coarsely**
- **1 tablespoon finely grated fresh ginger**
- **2 teaspoons dried chilli flakes**
- **2 teaspoons ground allspice**
- **400g (12½oz) can black-eyed beans, drained, rinsed**
- **400g (12½oz) can diced tomatoes**
- **6 sprigs fresh thyme**
- **2 tablespoons worcestershire sauce**
- **¾ cup (180ml) coconut water**
- **2 tablespoons finely shredded fresh mint leaves**
- **⅓ cup (15g) toasted flaked coconut**

1 Heat oil in a 5-litre (20-cup) slow cooker on 'sear' (HIGH) setting. Cook oxtail, in batches, turning, for 15 minutes or until well browned. Remove from cooker.

2 Carefully drain excess fat from slow cooker, leaving about 2 teaspoons of fat in cooker. Heat cooker on 'sear' (MEDIUM) setting. Cook onion, garlic, celery, carrot and ginger, stirring, for 5 minutes or until vegetables soften. Add chilli and allspice; cook, stirring, for 2 minutes or until fragrant. Return oxtail to cooker with beans, canned tomatoes, thyme, sauce and coconut water; bring to the boil. Cook, covered, on low for 8 hours or until oxtail is very tender.

3 Skim fat from surface of stew. Discard thyme. Season to taste.

4 Serve stew topped with mint and coconut.

Serving suggestion
Steamed or roasted sweet potato, rice or couscous, and lime wedges.

Suitable to freeze
at the end of step 3.

MASSAMAN BEEF CURRY

prep + cook time 8 hours 45 minutes * serves 6

- **2 tablespoons peanut oil**
- **2 large onions (400g), cut into thin wedges**
- **1kg (2lb) gravy beef, chopped coarsely (see tip)**
- **⅔ cup (200g) massaman curry paste**
- **1 cup (250ml) coconut milk**
- **1½ cups (375ml) chicken stock**
- **2 cinnamon sticks**
- **2 dried bay leaves**
- **3 medium potatoes (600g), peeled, chopped coarsely**
- **½ cup (70g) roasted unsalted peanuts**
- **1 tablespoon brown sugar**
- **1 tablespoon fish sauce**
- **⅓ cup fresh coriander (cilantro) leaves**
- **2 tablespoons fried shallots**
- **2 tablespoons roasted unsalted peanuts, extra**

1 Heat half the oil in a 5-litre (20-cup) slow cooker on 'sear' (MEDIUM) setting. Cook onion, stirring, for 10 minutes or until browned lightly. Remove onion from cooker.

2 Heat remaining oil in slow cooker on 'sear' (HIGH) setting. Cook beef, in batches, turning, for 5 minutes or until browned. Add curry paste and cook, stirring, for 1 minute or until fragrant.

3 Return onion to slow cooker with coconut milk, stock, cinnamon, bay leaves, potato and peanuts. Cook, covered, on low for 8 hours.

4 Discard cinnamon sticks. Stir in sugar and fish sauce.

5 Serve curry topped with coriander, fried shallots and extra peanuts.

Tip *Chuck steak is also suitable for this recipe, if you prefer.*

Serving suggestion *Steamed jasmine rice, roti bread and lime wedges.*

BALSAMIC LAMB
WITH POLENTA AND CAVOLO NERO

prep + cook time 6 hours 45 minutes * serves 4

- **¼ cup (35g) plain (all-purpose) flour**
- **½ teaspoon ground cinnamon**
- **pinch chilli powder**
- **2 tablespoons olive oil**
- **1.2kg (2½lb) diced lamb leg**
- **1 large red onion (300g), sliced thickly**
- **1 medium carrot (120g), chopped coarsely**
- **1 stalk celery (150g), trimmed, sliced thickly**
- **3 cloves garlic, crushed**
- **½ cup (125ml) dry red wine**
- **1 cup (250ml) beef stock**
- **¼ cup (60ml) balsamic vinegar**
- **¼ cup (55g) firmly packed brown sugar**
- **¼ cup (70g) tomato paste**
- **2 tablespoons currants**
- **1 dried bay leaf**
- **250g (8oz) cavolo nero (tuscan cabbage), trimmed (see tip)**

CREAMY POLENTA

- **2 cups (500ml) chicken or vegetable stock**
- **2 cups (500ml) milk**
- **1 cup (170g) polenta (cornmeal)**
- **30g (1oz) butter, chopped**
- **½ cup (40g) grated parmesan**

1 Combine flour, cinnamon and chilli in a large bowl; season with sea salt and black pepper.

2 Heat oil in a 5-litre (20-cup) slow cooker on 'sear' (HIGH) setting. Coat lamb in flour; shake off excess, reserving excess flour. Cook lamb, in batches, for 5 minutes, turning, or until well browned. Remove lamb from cooker.

3 Adjust setting to 'sear' (MEDIUM). Cook onion, carrot, celery and garlic, stirring, for 5 minutes or until vegetables soften. Sprinkle with reserved excess flour. Cook, stirring, for 3 minutes. Gradually stir in wine, then stock, vinegar, sugar, tomato paste, currants and bay leaf; bring to the boil.

4 Return lamb to slow cooker. Cook, covered, on low for 6 hours. Discard bay leaf. Season to taste.

5 Just before serving, make creamy polenta.

6 Coarsely chop cavolo nero leaves and add to slow cooker. Cook, covered, on high for 5 minutes or until cavolo nero wilts.

7 Serve creamy polenta topped with lamb and cavolo nero mixture.

CREAMY POLENTA Bring stock and milk to the boil in a large saucepan. Gradually add polenta, whisking until mixture comes to the boil. Reduce heat to low. Cook, stirring, for 5 minutes or until soft and thick. Stir in butter and parmesan. Season to taste. Adjust consistency with a little extra milk, if necessary.

Tip *You will need 1 bunch of cavolo nero for this recipe. You can use kale or silver beet instead of cavolo nero, if you like.*

Suitable to freeze *at the end of step 4.*

MOROCCAN GOAT STEW

prep + cook time 8 hours 30 minutes ✻ serves 4

- **800g (1½lb) boneless goat shoulder, cut into 5cm (2in) pieces (see tips)**
- **1 medium onion (150g), chopped coarsely**
- **3 cloves garlic, crushed**
- **1 tablespoon finely grated fresh ginger**
- **¼ teaspoon saffron threads**
- **¼ teaspoon cayenne pepper**
- **2 teaspoons ground coriander**
- **1 cinnamon stick**
- **½ cup (125ml) chicken stock**
- **400g (12½oz) can chickpeas (garbanzo beans), drained, rinsed**
- **⅔ cup (100g) dried apricots**
- **1 cup (150g) green olives**
- **1 green onion (scallion), sliced thinly lengthways (see tips)**
- **2 tablespoons pine nuts, toasted**

1 Place goat, onion, garlic, ginger, spices, stock and chickpeas in a 5-litre (20-cup) slow cooker. Cook, covered, on low for 8 hours.

2 Stir in apricots and olives. Cook, covered, on high for 15 minutes or until apricots soften. Discard cinnamon. Season to taste.

3 Serve stew topped with green onion and pine nuts.

Tips *You can also make the stew with boneless lamb shoulder. To make green onions curl, place the sliced onions in a small bowl of iced water for 10 minutes, then drain.*

Serving suggestion *Steamed pearl couscous, flat bread or steamed baby potatoes.*

Suitable to freeze *at the end of step 1.*

LAMB AND FENNEL RAGÙ

prep + cook time 8 hours 45 minutes * serves 6

- **¼ cup (35g) plain (all-purpose) flour**
- **2 tablespoons olive oil**
- **1kg (2lb) boneless lamb shoulder, cut into 2.5cm (1in) pieces**
- **1 medium onion (150g), chopped finely**
- **3 cloves garlic, crushed**
- **6 anchovy fillets, chopped finely**
- **½ teaspoon dried chilli flakes**
- **1 teaspoon fennel seeds, crushed lightly**
- **400g (12½oz) can diced tomatoes**
- **⅔ cup (160ml) dry red wine**
- **½ cup (40g) grated parmesan**
- **½ cup fresh basil leaves**

1 Place flour in a large bowl; season.

2 Heat oil in a 5-litre (20-cup) slow cooker on 'sear' (HIGH) setting. Coat lamb in flour and shake off excess. Cook lamb, stirring, for 15 minutes or until well browned.

3 Add onion, garlic, anchovy, chilli, fennel seeds, canned tomatoes and wine; bring to the boil. Cook, covered, on low for 8 hours. Season to taste.

4 Serve ragù topped with parmesan and basil leaves.

Serving suggestion
Pappardelle, mashed potato or crusty bread.

Suitable to freeze
at the end of step 3.

SAUSAGE, LAMB AND BEAN CASSOULET

prep + cook time 8 hours 45 minutes * serves 6

- **2 tablespoons olive oil**
- **3 thick pork sausages (360g)**
- **100g (3oz) piece speck, rind removed, cut into 3cm (1¼in) pieces**
- **900g (1¾lb) boneless lamb shoulder, cut into 3cm (1¼in) pieces**
- **1 large onion (200g), chopped finely**
- **1 bay leaf**
- **5 cloves garlic, chopped finely**
- **2 x 400g (12½oz) cans diced tomatoes**
- **1 cup (250ml) water**
- **2 tablespoons tomato paste**
- **4 x 400g (12½oz) cans white beans, drained, rinsed**
- **2 tablespoons finely chopped fresh flat-leaf parsley**

1 Heat half the oil in a large frying pan over medium-high heat. Cook sausages and speck, turning, until browned. Transfer to a 5-litre (20-cup) slow cooker.

2 Heat same pan over medium-high heat. Cook lamb, in batches, until browned. Transfer to slow cooker. Drain fat from pan.

3 Heat remaining oil in same pan over medium heat. Cook onion and bay leaf, stirring, for 5 minutes or until onion softens. Add garlic and cook, stirring, for 1 minute or until fragrant. Transfer to slow cooker.

4 Add canned tomatoes, the water, tomato paste and beans to slow cooker. Cook, covered, on low for 8 hours.

5 Serve cassoulet topped with parsley.

Tip *There are many French regional variations of cassoulet. For special occasions, add 2 confit duck marylands. Pan-fry them until hot and browned, place on top of hot cassoulet and scatter with chopped parsley.*

Serving suggestion *Lightly toast some fresh breadcrumbs and combine with the chopped parsley; scatter over cassoulet to serve.*

Suitable to freeze *at the end of step 4.*

MULLED WINE PORK
WITH RED WINE CABBAGE

prep + cook time 8 hours 30 minutes * serves 6

*** 3 whole star anise**
*** 2 cinnamon sticks**
*** 2 teaspoons caraway seeds**
*** 6 whole cloves**
*** 2 sprigs fresh rosemary, chopped coarsely**
*** 2 sprigs fresh tarragon, chopped coarsely**
*** 2 cloves garlic, quartered**
*** 2 medium red onions (340g), cut into thick wedges**
*** 1.4kg (2¾lb) piece boneless pork shoulder, rind removed**
*** 1 cup (250ml) dry red wine**
*** 1 cup (250ml) chicken stock**
*** 2 tablespoons worcestershire sauce**
*** 2 tablespoons brown sugar**
*** 2 tablespoons balsamic vinegar**
*** ½ small red cabbage (600g), cut into 6 thick slices**
*** 2 tablespoons fresh tarragon leaves, extra**

SWEET POTATO MASH
*** 2 medium orange sweet potatoes (800g), chopped coarsely**
*** 1 large potato (300g), chopped coarsely**
*** 60g (2oz) butter**

1 Tie spices, herbs and garlic in a muslin bag; secure with kitchen string. Place onion in a 5-litre (20-cup) slow cooker. Top with muslin bag and pork. Pour combined wine, stock, sauce, sugar and vinegar over pork. Cook, covered, on low for 7½ hours. Add cabbage. Cook, covered, on low for a further 30 minutes. Discard muslin bag. Season to taste.
2 Just before serving, make sweet potato mash.
3 Carefully remove pork from slow cooker and break into large chunks.
4 Serve pork with sweet potato mash, and cabbage and onion mixture, drizzled with some of the cooking liquid. Top with extra tarragon.

SWEET POTATO MASH Boil, steam or microwave sweet potato and potato until tender; drain. Mash vegetables with butter in a medium bowl until smooth. Season to taste.

Serving suggestion *Baby spinach and crusty bread to mop up the juices.*

VEAL ROLLS
WITH PROSCIUTTO AND SAGE

prep + cook time 6 hours 30 minutes * serves 4

- **8 slices prosciutto (120g)**
- **8 veal schnitzels (800g)**
- **⅔ cup (130g) drained chargrilled capsicum (bell pepper) strips**
- **8 large fresh sage leaves**
- **1 tablespoon olive oil**
- **1 medium onion (150g), chopped finely**
- **2 cloves garlic, crushed**
- **¼ cup (60ml) dry red wine**
- **400g (12½oz) bottled tomato pasta sauce**

1 Place prosciutto slices on a chopping board; top each slice with a schnitzel. Place capsicum across centre of schnitzels, then top each with a sage leaf. Roll to enclose filling. Secure veal rolls with toothpicks or kitchen string.

2 Heat oil in a 5-litre (20-cup) slow cooker on 'sear' (HIGH) setting. Cook veal rolls, turning, for 10 minutes or until well browned. Add onion, garlic, wine and pasta sauce. Cook, covered, on low for 6 hours. Season to taste.

3 Serve veal rolls with sauce.

Serving suggestion *Soft polenta, pasta, mashed potato or crusty bread. Try topping rolls with gremolata and fried sage leaves.*

PORK VINDALOO

prep + cook time 8 hours 30 minutes * serves 6

- **1.2kg (2½lb) pork scotch fillet (neck)**
- **2 large onions (400g), sliced thinly**
- **5cm (2in) piece fresh ginger, grated finely**
- **2 cloves garlic, grated**
- **400g (12½oz) can diced tomatoes**
- **½ cup (150g) vindaloo curry paste (see tips)**
- **2 tablespoons tomato paste**
- **¾ cup (180ml) beef stock**
- **½ cup fresh coriander (cilantro) leaves**

1 Cut pork into 3cm (1¼in) pieces; discard any visible fat.

2 Place pork, onion, ginger, garlic, canned tomatoes, curry paste, tomato paste and stock in a 5-litre (20-cup) slow cooker. Cook, covered, on low for 8 hours.

3 Serve vindaloo topped with coriander leaves.

Tips *Jars of vindaloo paste are available from most supermarkets. You can also cook the pork in the slow cooker on high for 4 hours. To cook without a slow cooker, simmer curry over low heat, covered, in a heavy-based saucepan for 2 hours or until pork is tender.*

Serving suggestion *Steamed basmati rice and pappadums.*

Suitable to freeze *at the end of step 2.*

SATAY PORK STEW

prep + cook time 4 hours 30 minutes * serves 4

- **700g (1½lb) pork scotch fillet (neck), cut into 5cm (2in) pieces**
- **1 medium red onion (170g), cut into wedges**
- **1 large red capsicum (bell pepper) (350g), sliced thickly**
- **250g (8oz) canned satay sauce**
- **2 tablespoons salt-reduced soy sauce**
- **½ fresh long red chilli, chopped finely**
- **2 tablespoons lime juice**
- **1 green onion (scallion), sliced thinly**
- **¼ cup (35g) coarsely chopped roasted unsalted peanuts**
- **½ fresh long red chilli, extra, sliced thinly**
- **2 tablespoons micro herbs (optional)**

1 Place pork, onion, capsicum, satay sauce, soy sauce and chopped chilli in a 5-litre (20-cup) slow cooker. Cook, covered, on low for 4 hours. Season to taste.

2 Adjust setting to 'reduce' (HIGH). Simmer, uncovered, for 10 minutes or until sauce thickens slightly.

3 Stir in juice and green onion. Serve stew topped with peanuts, extra sliced chilli and micro herbs.

Serving suggestion
Steamed jasmine rice or fried noodles, and cucumber batons.

Suitable to freeze
at the end of step 2.

SWEET AND SOUR PORK

prep + cook time 6 hours 30 minutes * serves 4

- **8 boneless pork spare ribs (1kg)**
- **1 medium red onion (170g), cut into wedges**
- **1 medium red capsicum (bell pepper) (200g), chopped coarsely**
- **2 cloves garlic, crushed**
- **½ teaspoon dried chilli flakes**
- **⅔ cup (160ml) salt-reduced soy sauce**
- **⅔ cup (160ml) salt-reduced tomato sauce**
- **¼ cup (60ml) white wine vinegar**
- **¼ cup (55g) firmly packed brown sugar**
- **½ cup (125ml) apple and pineapple juice (see tips)**
- **2 tablespoons water**
- **1½ tablespoons cornflour (cornstarch)**
- **½ small pineapple (450g), peeled, cored, chopped coarsely**
- **2 teaspoons sesame seeds, toasted**
- **2 green onions (scallions), sliced thinly lengthways (see tips)**

1 Place pork, onion, capsicum, garlic, chilli, sauces, vinegar, sugar and juice in a 5-litre (20-cup) slow cooker. Cook, covered, on low for 6 hours.

2 Combine the water and cornflour in a small bowl until smooth. Stir cornflour mixture and pineapple into slow cooker. Adjust setting to 'reduce' (LOW). Simmer, uncovered, for 10 minutes or until sauce thickens and pineapple is heated through.

3 Serve pork topped with sesame seeds and green onion.

Tips *If apple and pineapple juice is unavailable, just combine apple juice and pineapple juice instead. We placed our green onion strips in a bowl of iced water for about 10 minutes to make them curl.*

Serving suggestion
Steamed jasmine rice and asian greens.

Suitable to freeze
at the end of step 1.

4 WAYS WITH MASH

BASIC POTATO MASH

prep + cook time 30 minutes ✱ serves 4

Place 1kg (2lb) peeled, coarsely chopped potatoes (see tip) in a medium saucepan with enough cold water to barely cover them. Boil, over medium heat, for 15 minutes or until potato is tender; drain. Return potato to pan and mash until smooth (or use a potato ricer or mouli). Add 40g (1½oz) butter and ¾ cup hot milk; fold in gently until mash is smooth. Season to taste. Serve as is or with one of the flavour variations opposite.

Tip *Floury and all-rounder potatoes are best for mash. Try coliban, toolangi delight, king edward or dutch cream.*

MUSTARD AND CHEDDAR MASH

prep + cook time 30 minutes ✻ serves 4

Make Basic Potato Mash (left). When adding the butter and milk, also add 2 tablespoons dijon or wholegrain mustard and 1 cup grated vintage cheddar. Return pan to heat. Stir mash over medium heat until smooth and cheese melts. Season to taste. Serve topped with extra grated vintage cheddar.

OLIVE OIL AND SAGE MASH

prep + cook time 35 minutes ✻ serves 4

Boil 1kg (2lb) potatoes as directed for Basic Potato Mash (left); drain. Wipe pan dry. Heat ⅓ cup olive oil in same pan. Fry 2 thinly sliced cloves garlic and 2 tablespoons sage leaves until crisp. Remove with a slotted spoon. Return potatoes to pan with ½ cup hot milk; mash until smooth. Season to taste. Serve topped with garlic and sage.

KALE MASH

prep + cook time 35 minutes ✻ serves 4

Boil 1kg (2lb) potatoes as directed for Basic Potato Mash (left); drain. Wipe pan dry. Heat ⅓ cup olive oil in pan. Cook 125g (4oz) shredded kale and 1 chopped clove garlic, stirring, over medium heat for 5 minutes until kale wilts. Remove from pan. Return potatoes to pan with 30g (1oz) butter and ¾ cup hot milk; mash until smooth. Stir in kale. Season to taste.

CHICKEN WITH LENTILS, PORT AND PANCETTA

prep + cook time 3 hours 45 minutes ✻ serves 4

- **1 cup (200g) French-style green lentils**
- **2 tablespoons olive oil**
- **8 chicken drumsticks (1.2kg)**
- **2 medium leeks (700g), white part only, sliced thinly**
- **2 medium carrots (240g), halved, sliced thinly**
- **2 stalks celery (300g), trimmed, sliced thickly**
- **100g (3oz) sliced pancetta, chopped coarsely**
- **⅓ cup (95g) tomato paste**
- **2½ cups (625ml) port**
- **1½ cups (375ml) chicken stock**
- **4 sprigs fresh thyme**
- **1 cup (120g) frozen peas, thawed**
- **2 teaspoons fresh thyme leaves, extra**

1 Rinse lentils well; drain.

2 Heat oil in a 5-litre (20-cup) slow cooker on 'sear' (HIGH) setting. Cook chicken, in batches, turning, for 10 minutes or until well browned. Remove from cooker.

3 Adjust setting to 'sear' (MEDIUM). Cook leek, carrot, celery and pancetta, stirring, for 5 minutes or until vegetables soften. Add tomato paste. Cook, stirring, for 3 minutes. Stir in port, stock, thyme and lentils.

4 Return chicken to slow cooker. Cook, covered, on low for 3 hours.

5 Discard thyme. Add peas to slow cooker and stand, covered, for 5 minutes. Season. Serve sprinkled with extra thyme.

Serving suggestion *Creamy polenta, mashed potato or crusty bread to mop up the juices.*

CHICKEN AND SPECK STEW
WITH TARRAGON SCONES

prep + cook time 5 hours * serves 4

- **¼ cup (60ml) olive oil**
- **1kg (2lb) chicken thigh fillets, halved**
- **150g (4½oz) piece speck, chopped finely**
- **2 medium leeks (700g), white part only, sliced**
- **2 cloves garlic, crushed**
- **¼ cup (35g) plain (all-purpose) flour**
- **½ cup (125ml) dry white wine**
- **1½ cups (375ml) chicken stock**
- **⅓ cup (80ml) pouring cream**
- **1 tablespoon wholegrain mustard**
- **½ cup (60g) frozen green peas**

TARRAGON SCONES

- **1 cup (150g) self-raising flour**
- **50g (1½oz) cold butter, chopped**
- **⅓ cup (25g) finely grated parmesan**
- **2 teaspoons finely chopped fresh tarragon**
- **1 egg, beaten lightly**
- **2 tablespoons buttermilk, approximately**

1 Heat 1 tablespoon of the oil in 5-litre (20-cup) slow cooker on 'sear' (HIGH) setting. Cook chicken, in batches, turning, for 5 minutes or until well browned. Remove from cooker.

2 Adjust setting to 'sear' (MEDIUM). Heat remaining oil in slow cooker. Cook speck, leek and garlic, stirring, for 5 minutes or until leek softens. Add flour and cook, stirring, for 3 minutes. Gradually stir in wine, then stock, cream and mustard; bring to the boil.

3 Return chicken to slow cooker. Cook, covered, on low for 4 hours. Season.

4 Make tarragon scone mixture just before serving.

5 Add peas to chicken mixture and stir to combine. Drop level tablespoons of scone mixture, about 2cm (¾in) apart, on top of chicken mixture. Cook, covered, on high for 30 minutes or until scones are firm to touch and cooked through.

6 Serve chicken mixture topped with scones.

TARRAGON SCONES Place flour in a medium bowl; using your fingertips, rub in butter. Stir in parmesan and tarragon, then stir in egg and enough of the buttermilk to make a soft, sticky dough.

Serving suggestion *Top stew with crisp fried shredded leek. Accompany with a leafy green salad.*

CHICKEN, GREEN OLIVE AND PRESERVED LEMON TAGINE

prep + cook time 9 hours * serves 6

- **2 tablespoons olive oil**
- **2 teaspoons ground cinnamon**
- **2 teaspoons ground cumin**
- **2 teaspoons ground coriander**
- **1.8kg (3½lb) whole chicken**
- **1 large onion (200g), sliced thickly**
- **3 cloves garlic, crushed**
- **2 teaspoons finely grated fresh ginger**
- **1 teaspoon dried chilli flakes**
- **½ teaspoon ground turmeric**
- **800g (1½lb) baby potatoes, halved**
- **½ cup (125ml) chicken stock**
- **1 tablespoon honey**
- **1 cup (120g) pitted green olives**
- **1 tablespoon lemon juice**
- **¼ cup fresh flat-leaf parsley leaves**
- **¼ cup fresh coriander (cilantro) leaves**
- **1 tablespoon finely sliced preserved lemon rind (see tip)**

1 Heat half the oil in a 5-litre (20-cup) slow cooker on 'sear' (HIGH) setting. Rub combined cinnamon, cumin and coriander all over chicken. Cook chicken, turning, for 20 minutes or until well browned all over. Remove from cooker.

2 Adjust setting to 'sear' (MEDIUM). Heat remaining oil in slow cooker. Cook onion, garlic, ginger, chilli and turmeric, stirring, for 5 minutes or until onion softens. Add potatoes and cook, stirring, for 5 minutes or until browned. Add stock. Place chicken on top of potatoes and drizzle with honey. Cook, covered, on low for 8 hours.

3 Carefully remove chicken from slow cooker; cover to keep warm. Stir in olives and juice to potato mixture. Season to taste.

4 Cut chicken into pieces. Serve chicken with potatoes and sauce mixture, sprinkled with herbs and rind.

Tip *Preserved lemons are available from delicatessens, specialty food shops and large supermarkets. Use the rind only. Discard the flesh and rinse the rind well under cold water before using.*

Serving suggestion *Steamed couscous and chickpeas.*

BUTTER CHICKEN

prep + cook time 4 hours 45 minutes (+ refrigeration) ✻ serves 6

∗ 12 chicken thigh cutlets (2.4kg), skin removed
∗ 2 tablespoons lemon juice
∗ 1 teaspoon chilli powder
∗ ¾ cup (200g) Greek-style yoghurt
∗ 1 tablespoon finely grated fresh ginger
∗ 2 teaspoons garam masala
∗ 45g (1½oz) butter
∗ 1 tablespoon vegetable oil
∗ 1 medium onion (150g), chopped finely
∗ 4 cloves garlic, crushed
∗ 1 teaspoon ground coriander
∗ 1 teaspoon ground cumin
∗ 1 teaspoon sweet paprika
∗ 2 tablespoons tomato paste
∗ 410g (13oz) can tomato puree
∗ ⅔ cup (160ml) chicken stock
∗ 2 tablespoons honey
∗ 1 cinnamon stick
∗ ⅓ cup (80ml) pouring cream
∗ ½ cup fresh coriander (cilantro) leaves
∗ ⅓ cup (50g) roasted cashews

1 Combine chicken, juice and chilli in a large bowl. Cover and refrigerate for 30 minutes.

2 Stir yoghurt, ginger and half the garam masala into chicken mixture.

3 Heat butter and oil in a 5-litre (20-cup) slow cooker on 'sear' (HIGH) setting. Cook chicken, in batches, turning, for 15 minutes until well browned. Remove from cooker.

4 Add onion and garlic to slow cooker. Cook, stirring, for 5 minutes or until onion softens. Add remaining garam masala, coriander, cumin and paprika; cook, stirring, for 1 minute or until fragrant. Stir in tomato paste, puree, stock, honey and cinnamon. Return chicken to cooker. Cook, covered, on low for 4 hours.

5 Stir in cream. Season to taste.

6 Serve butter chicken topped with coriander leaves and cashews.

Serving suggestion
Steamed basmati rice, warm naan bread and lime wedges.

Suitable to freeze
at the end of step 4.

TURKEY WITH PLUM AND STAR ANISE

prep + cook time 7 hours ✻ serves 4

* **2 turkey drumsticks (1.6kg)**
* **1 tablespoon peanut oil**
* **825g (1¾lb) can whole plums in natural juice**
* **1 medium red onion (170g), sliced thinly**
* **3 small red capsicums (bell peppers) (150g), sliced thinly**
* **4 whole star anise**
* **4 cloves garlic, crushed**
* **1 tablespoon finely grated fresh ginger**
* **1 fresh long red chilli, chopped finely**
* **⅓ cup (80ml) soy sauce**
* **¼ cup (60ml) rice wine vinegar**
* **2 tablespoons grated palm sugar or brown sugar**

1 Remove and discard skin from turkey drumsticks.

2 Heat oil in a 5-litre (20-cup) slow cooker on 'sear' (HIGH) setting. Cook turkey, in batches, turning, for 15 minutes until well browned.

3 Meanwhile, drain plums over a medium bowl; reserve plums and 1 cup juice.

4 Return turkey to slow cooker. Top with onion, capsicum, star anise and drained plums. Combine garlic, ginger, chilli, soy sauce, rice wine, sugar and reserved plum juice in a jug; pour into cooker. Cook, covered, on low for 6 hours.

5 Carefully remove turkey from slow cooker, then shred meat into large chunks; discard bones and star anise. Return shredded turkey to cooker. Season to taste. Serve.

Tip *Depending on the size and shape of your slow cooker, you may need to brown the turkey in a large frying pan in step 2, then transfer to the cooker.*

Serving suggestion *Steamed rice, steamed baby pak choy, fresh coriander (cilantro) sprigs and lime wedges.*

THAI BASIL AND CHILLI CHICKEN WITH CASHEWS

prep + cook time 9 hours * serves 6

- **1.8kg (3½lb) whole chicken**
- **1 medium red onion (170g), sliced thickly**
- **1 medium red capsicum (bell pepper) (200g), sliced thickly**
- **1 medium yellow capsicum (bell pepper) (200g), sliced thickly**
- **2 medium carrots (240g), halved, sliced thickly on the diagonal**
- **4 cloves garlic, quartered**
- **10cm (4in) stalk fresh lemon grass, sliced thinly**
- **4cm (1½in) piece fresh galangal, sliced thinly**
- **3 fresh small red chillies, chopped coarsely**
- **2 tablespoons fish sauce**
- **2 tablespoons grated palm sugar**
- **1 tablespoon vegetable or peanut oil**
- **¾ cup (180ml) chicken stock**
- **2 fresh kaffir lime leaves**
- **2 tablespoons cornflour (cornstarch)**
- **¼ cup (60ml) water**
- **115g (3½oz) baby corn, halved**
- **400g (12½oz) gai lan, trimmed, cut into 5cm (2in) lengths**
- **½ cup (75g) roasted salted cashews**
- **½ cup thai basil leaves**

1 Remove as much skin as possible from the chicken; refrigerate skin until required. Place chicken in a 5-litre (20-cup) slow cooker. Top chicken with onion, capsicums and carrot.

2 Process garlic, lemon grass, galangal, chilli, fish sauce, sugar and oil until smooth. Stir in stock, then pour mixture over chicken in slow cooker. Add lime leaves to cooker. Cook, covered, on low for 8 hours. Skim excess oil from surface.

3 Carefully remove chicken from slow cooker, then break into large chunks; discard bones and lime leaves.

4 Stir cornflour and the water in a small bowl until combined. Add cornflour mixture to slow cooker with corn and gai lan. Adjust setting to 'reduce' (LOW). Simmer, uncovered, for 15 minutes, stirring occasionally, or until sauce thickens. Return chicken to cooker and simmer until heated through. Season to taste.

5 Meanwhile, preheat grill (broiler).

6 Place reserved chicken skin on an oven tray and season. Grill for 15 minutes or until golden and crisp; drain on paper towel. Break crispy skin into pieces.

7 Serve chicken mixture topped with crispy chicken skin, cashews and thai basil.

Serving suggestion *Steamed jasmine rice or roti bread.*

CHICKEN TIKKA MASALA

prep + cook time 4 hours 15 minutes * serves 6

- **1kg (2lb) skinless chicken thigh cutlets**
- **2 x 400g (12½oz) cans diced tomatoes**
- **2 large onions (400g), sliced thinly**
- **⅔ cup (200g) tikka masala curry paste**
- **¼ cup (60ml) pouring cream**
- **1 cup fresh coriander (cilantro) leaves**

1 Combine chicken, canned tomatoes, onion and curry paste in a 5-litre (20-cup) slow cooker. Cook, covered, on high for 4 hours. Season to taste.

2 Stir in cream. Top with coriander to serve.

Serving suggestion
Steamed rice, warmed naan bread and raita (minted yoghurt and cucumber).

Suitable to freeze
at the end of step 1.

MEXICAN BEEF CHILLI MOLE

prep + cook time 8 hours 15 minutes * serves 4

* **1kg (2lb) beef chuck steak, cut into 3cm (1¼in) cubes**
* **2 cups (500ml) beef stock**
* **2 cups (500ml) water**
* **3 chipotle peppers in adobo sauce, chopped finely (see tips)**
* **4 rindless bacon slices (260g), chopped coarsely**
* **1 medium onion (150g), chopped finely**
* **4 cloves garlic, crushed**
* **2 tablespoons tomato paste**
* **400g (12½oz) can black beans, drained, rinsed**
* **410g (13oz) can tomato puree**
* **2 teaspoons ground cumin**
* **2 teaspoons ground coriander**
* **2 teaspoons sweet smoked paprika**
* **¼ teaspoon chilli powder**
* **½ teaspoon ground cinnamon**
* **2 tablespoons finely grated mexican chocolate (see tips)**
* **⅔ cup (80g) grated manchego cheese (see tips)**
* **1 fresh jalapeño chilli, sliced thinly (see tips)**
* **2 green onions (scallions), sliced thinly**

1 Combine beef, stock, the water, chipotle, bacon, onion, garlic, tomato paste, beans, puree and spices in a 5-litre (20-cup) slow cooker. Cook, covered, on low for 8 hours. Season to taste.

2 Stir in chocolate. Season to taste.

3 Serve chilli topped with cheese, jalapeño and green onion.

Tips *Chipotle in adobo sauce and mexican chocolate are available from delicatessens and grocers. If chipotle in adobo sauce is unavailable, use 2–3 tablespoons of hot Mexican-style chilli sauce (adding enough to suit your taste). If mexican chocolate is unavailable, use dark (semi-sweet) chocolate. Manchego is an aged, hard and intensely flavoured Spanish cheese. It is available from delis. Substitute haloumi or fetta if manchego is not available. If fresh jalapeño chillies are unavailable, use slices of bottled pickled jalapeños.*

Serving suggestion
Steamed rice and warmed flat bread.

Suitable to freeze
at the end of step 2.

CHILLI CHICKEN
AND BLACK BEAN STEW

prep + cook time 8 hours 40 minutes * serves 4

* **1 tablespoon olive oil**
* **1 medium onion (150g), chopped finely**
* **1 stalk celery (150g), trimmed, chopped finely**
* **1 large red capsicum (bell pepper) (350g), chopped finely**
* **2 teaspoons mexican chilli powder**
* **1 teaspoon ground coriander**
* **1 teaspoon ground cumin**
* **1 fresh long green chilli, chopped finely**
* **400g (12½oz) can black beans, drained, rinsed**
* **1.2kg (2½lb) whole chicken**
* **2 cups (500ml) water**
* **1½ tablespoons lime juice**
* **⅓ cup coarsely chopped fresh coriander (cilantro)**
* **⅓ cup fresh coriander sprigs**

1 Heat oil in a 5-litre (20-cup) slow cooker on 'sear' (HIGH) setting. Cook onion, celery and capsicum, stirring, for 3 minutes or until vegetables soften. Add chilli powder, coriander, cumin and fresh chilli. Cook, stirring, for 1 minute or until fragrant. Add black beans, chicken and the water. Cook, covered, on low for 8 hours.

2 Carefully remove chicken from slow cooker, then shred meat coarsely using two forks; discard skin and bones.

3 Return shredded chicken to slow cooker with juice; stir to combine. Cook, covered, on high for 15 minutes or until heated through. Stir in chopped coriander. Season to taste.

4 Serve chilli chicken stew topped with coriander sprigs.

Serving suggestion *Steamed rice, grilled tortillas and lime wedges.*

OSSO BUCO
WITH LEMON AND FENNEL SALAD

prep + cook time 8 hours 45 minutes * serves 6

- **¼ cup (35g) plain (all-purpose) flour**
- **2 teaspoons fennel seeds**
- **2 tablespoons olive oil**
- **12 small pieces beef osso buco (1.8kg) (see tips)**
- **1 medium onion (150g), chopped coarsely**
- **1 baby fennel bulb (130g), trimmed, chopped coarsely**
- **2 rindless bacon slices (130g), chopped coarsely**
- **3 cloves garlic, crushed**
- **2 dried bay leaves**
- **pinch saffron threads**
- **½ cup (125ml) dry white wine**
- **1½ cups (375ml) beef stock**
- **1 sprig fresh rosemary**

LEMON & FENNEL SALAD

- **1 baby fennel bulb (130g)**
- **⅓ cup fresh flat-leaf parsley leaves**
- **1 tablespoon finely sliced lemon rind (see tips)**
- **2 teaspoons lemon juice**
- **2 teaspoons olive oil**

1 Combine flour and fennel seeds in a large bowl; season.

2 Heat oil in a 5-litre (20-cup) slow cooker on 'sear' (HIGH) setting. Coat beef in flour mixture; shake off excess, reserving excess flour. Cook beef, in batches, for 5 minutes each side or until well browned. Remove from cooker.

3 Add onion, fennel, bacon, garlic, bay leaves and saffron to slow cooker. Cook, stirring, for 5 minutes or until vegetables soften. Sprinkle with reserved excess flour and cook, stirring, for 3 minutes. Gradually stir in wine and stock; bring to the boil. Add rosemary.

4 Return beef to slow cooker, packing tightly in the cooker. Cook, covered, on low for 8 hours. Discard bay leaves and rosemary. Season to taste.

5 Just before serving, make lemon and fennel salad.

6 Serve osso buco topped with the salad.

LEMON & FENNEL SALAD Trim fennel, reserving fronds. Using a mandoline, V-slicer or sharp knife, shave fennel thinly. Combine fennel with reserved fronds, parsley, rind, juice and oil in a medium bowl. Season to taste.

Tips *Ask the butcher for small pieces (about 3cm/1¼in) of either beef or veal shin (osso buco). Use a zesting tool to make long thin strips of lemon rind. If you don't have one, you can thinly peel the rind from the lemon, avoiding any white pith, then finely slice into long thin strips.*

Serving suggestion *Creamy polenta, mashed potato or crusty bread to mop up the juices.*

Suitable to freeze *at the end of step 4.*

LAMB WITH KALE AND POMEGRANATE

prep + cook time 8 hours 45 minutes * serves 4

*** 1.2kg (2½lb) boneless lamb shoulder, cut into 10cm (4in) chunks**
*** 2 teaspoons ground cumin**
*** 2 teaspoons ground allspice**
*** 2 teaspoons fennel seeds**
*** 1 teaspoon smoked paprika**
*** 1 teaspoon dried chilli flakes**
*** 2 tablespoons olive oil**
*** 1 medium pomegranate (320g)**
*** 1 large onion (200g), sliced thickly**
*** 3 cloves garlic, crushed**
*** 2 teaspoons finely grated fresh ginger**
*** 1 cup (250ml) beef stock**
*** 2 tablespoons pure maple syrup**
*** 1 tablespoon pomegranate molasses**
*** 4 medium kale leaves (140g), trimmed, shredded coarsely**
*** ¼ cup (40g) blanched almonds, roasted, split in half**

1 Combine lamb with spices in a large bowl; season. Heat half the oil in a 5-litre (20-cup) slow cooker on 'sear' (HIGH) setting. Cook lamb, in batches, turning, for 10 minutes or until well browned. Remove from cooker.

2 Meanwhile, cut pomegranate in half. Hold pomegranate, cut-side down, over a sieve placed over a medium bowl and hit the back of the pomegranate with a wooden spoon to release the juice and seeds. Reserve ¼ cup juice and ⅓ cup seeds separately. Refrigerate seeds until required.

3 Adjust setting to 'sear' (MEDIUM). Heat remaining oil in slow cooker. Cook onion, garlic and ginger, stirring, for 5 minutes or until onion softens. Stir in stock, maple syrup, molasses and reserved pomegranate juice. Return lamb to cooker and bring to the boil. Cook, covered, on low for 8 hours.

4 Add kale to slow cooker. Cook, covered, on high for 5 minutes or until kale is wilted. Season to taste.

5 Serve lamb topped with reserved pomegranate seeds and almonds.

Tip *Wear gloves in step 2 when preparing the pomegranate or it will stain your hands. You can use a teaspoon to scrape the seeds out of the cut pomegranate halves, if you prefer.*

Serving suggestion *Steamed pearl couscous, quinoa or rice, and lemon wedges.*

Suitable to freeze *at the end of step 4.*

VEGETARIAN

SPLIT PEA
AND CAPSICUM CURRY

prep + cook time 8 hours 30 minutes * serves 4

*** 1 medium onion (150g), sliced thinly**
*** 500g (1lb) baby potatoes, halved**
*** 1 large carrot (180g), halved, sliced thickly**
*** 1 medium red capsicum (bell pepper) (200g), chopped coarsely**
*** 1 medium yellow capsicum (bell pepper) (200g), chopped coarsely**
*** ⅓ cup (100g) mild indian curry paste**
*** ⅓ cup (85g) yellow split peas**
*** ⅓ cup (85g) green split peas**
*** 8 fresh curry leaves**
*** 2 tablespoons tomato paste**
*** 410g (13oz) can crushed tomatoes**
*** 2 cups (500ml) vegetable stock**
*** 2 cups (500ml) water**
*** 150g (4½oz) sugar snap peas**
*** 1 bunch cavolo nero (tuscan cabbage) (400g), chopped coarsely**
*** ¾ cup (210g) Greek-style yoghurt**
*** ½ cup fresh coriander (cilantro) leaves**

1 Place onion, potato, carrot, capsicums, curry paste, split peas, curry leaves, tomato paste, canned tomatoes, stock and the water in a 5-litre (20-cup) slow cooker. Cook, covered, on low for 8 hours. Season to taste.
2 Stir in sugar snap peas and cavolo nero. Cook, uncovered, on low for 10 minutes or until peas and cavolo nero are tender.
3 Serve curry topped with yoghurt and coriander.

Serving suggestion *Steamed rice and pappadums.*

VEGETABLE STEW
WITH POLENTA DUMPLINGS

prep + cook time 9 hours ✻ serves 4

- **1 medium red onion (170g), cut into wedges**
- **2 medium zucchini (240g), sliced thickly**
- **4 yellow patty pan squash (120g), cut into wedges**
- **1 medium orange sweet potato (400g), chopped coarsely**
- **2 medium carrots (240g), chopped coarsely**
- **1 trimmed corn cob (250g), cut into 6 rounds**
- **1 medium red capsicum (bell pepper) (200g), chopped coarsely**
- **2 flat mushrooms (160g), cut into wedges**
- **3 cloves garlic, crushed**
- **30g (1oz) sachet taco seasoning**
- **2 teaspoons paprika**
- **2 x 400g (12½oz) cans crushed tomatoes**
- **1 cup (250ml) vegetable stock**
- **2 tablespoons fresh flat-leaf parsley leaves**

POLENTA DUMPLINGS

- **1 cup (150g) self-raising flour**
- **2 tablespoons polenta (cornmeal)**
- **60g (2oz) cold butter, chopped**
- **1 egg, beaten lightly**
- **¼ cup (20g) finely grated parmesan**
- **2 tablespoons milk, approximately**

1 Place onion, zucchini, squash, sweet potato, carrot, corn, capsicum, mushroom, garlic, seasoning, paprika, canned tomatoes and stock in a 5-litre (20-cup) slow cooker. Cook, covered, on low for 8 hours.

2 Make polenta dumpling mixture close to serving.

3 Drop level tablespoons of dumpling mixture, about 2cm (¾in) apart, on top of stew. Cook, covered, on low for 30 minutes or until dumplings are firm to touch and cooked through. Serve stew and dumplings topped with parsley.

POLENTA DUMPLINGS Place flour and polenta in a medium bowl; using your fingertips, rub in butter. Stir in egg, parmesan and enough milk to make a soft, sticky dough.

Tip *Add drained, rinsed canned kidney beans or trimmed green beans for the last 10 minutes of cooking time.*

130

SLOW COOKER

VEGETARIAN

BARLEY AND FENNEL RISOTTO

prep + cook time 2 hours 30 minutes * serves 4

*** 1 tablespoon extra virgin olive oil**
*** 20g (¾oz) butter**
*** 1 medium onion (150g), chopped finely**
*** 2 small fennel bulbs (400g), sliced thinly**
*** 2 cloves garlic, crushed**
*** 2 teaspoons fresh thyme leaves**
*** 1 teaspoon fennel seeds, crushed lightly**
*** 1 cup (200g) pearl barley**
*** 2½ cups (625ml) vegetable stock**
*** ½ cup (60g) frozen green peas, thawed**
*** ½ cup (40g) finely grated parmesan**
*** 60g (2oz) snow pea tendrils**
*** 2 teaspoons long strips lemon rind**

1 Heat oil and butter in a 5-litre (20-cup) slow cooker on 'sear' (HIGH) setting. Cook onion, sliced fennel, garlic, thyme and fennel seeds, stirring, for 5 minutes or until vegetables soften. Add barley and cook, stirring, for 2 minutes or until barley is toasted lightly. Add stock. Cook, covered, on low for 2 hours.

2 Add peas and half the parmesan. Season to taste. Stand, covered, for 5 minutes or until peas are heated through.

3 Serve risotto scattered with remaining parmesan, pea tendrils and lemon rind.

Serving suggestion *Grilled bread.*

VEGETARIAN

MUSHROOM STROGANOFF

prep + cook time 3 hours * serves 4

- **¼ cup (60ml) olive oil**
- **12 shallots (300g), halved**
- **200g (6½oz) button mushrooms (see tip)**
- **200g (6½oz) swiss brown mushrooms**
- **375g (12oz) portobello mushrooms, quartered**
- **500g (1lb) cup mushrooms, halved**
- **3 cloves garlic, sliced thinly**
- **2 tablespoons finely chopped fresh thyme**
- **1 tablespoon finely chopped fresh rosemary**
- **2 teaspoons paprika**
- **2 fresh bay leaves**
- **1 cup (250ml) dry white wine**
- **1 tablespoon dijon mustard**
- **1 tablespoon worcestershire sauce**
- **½ cup (120g) crème fraîche**
- **1 tablespoon plain (all-purpose) flour**
- **¼ cup finely chopped fresh chives**

1 Heat 1 tablespoon of the oil in a 5-litre (20-cup) slow cooker on 'sear' (HIGH) setting. Cook shallots and one-third of the mushrooms, stirring, for 5 minutes or until browned. Remove from cooker. Repeat two more times with remaining oil and mushrooms.

2 Return mushroom mixture to slow cooker with garlic, half the thyme, rosemary, paprika, bay leaves and wine. Bring to the boil; boil, uncovered, for 5 minutes or until wine is reduced by half.

3 Add mustard and sauce; stir to combine. Cook, covered, on high for 2 hours. Discard bay leaves.

4 Combine crème fraîche and flour in a small bowl. Stir crème fraîche mixture into mushroom mixture. Adjust setting to 'reduce' (HIGH). Simmer, uncovered, for 10 minutes or until sauce boils and thickens. Season to taste.

5 Serve stroganoff scattered with chives and remaining thyme.

Tip *Use any combination of mushrooms that you prefer.*

Serving suggestion *Buttered wide egg noodles.*

134

SLOW COOKER

VEGETARIAN

INDIAN-STYLE LENTIL STEW

prep + cook time 2 hours 30 minutes * serves 4

- **1 tablespoon olive oil**
- **1 medium onion (150g), chopped finely**
- **3 cloves garlic, crushed**
- **½ teaspoon dried chilli flakes**
- **1 teaspoon ground turmeric**
- **1 tablespoon black mustard seeds**
- **1 cinnamon stick**
- **2 teaspoons ground cumin**
- **1 tablespoon ground coriander**
- **1½ cups (300g) dried green lentils**
- **2½ cups (625ml) vegetable stock**
- **1 cup (250ml) canned coconut cream**
- **150g (4½oz) baby spinach leaves**
- **½ cup (120g) plain yoghurt**
- **2 tablespoons micro herbs (optional)**

1 Heat oil in a 5-litre (20-cup) slow cooker on 'sear' (HIGH) setting. Cook onion and garlic, stirring, for 5 minutes or until softened.

2 Add chilli, turmeric, mustard seeds, cinnamon, cumin and coriander to slow cooker; cook, stirring, for 1 minute or until fragrant.

3 Add lentils, stock and coconut cream; stir to combine. Cook, covered, on low for 2 hours.

4 Discard cinnamon. Stir in spinach. Season to taste. Serve topped with yoghurt and micro herbs.

Serving suggestion *Cauliflower rice or steamed brown rice and grilled roti bread.*

137

SLOW COOKER

VEGETARIAN

BEAN BOURGUIGNON

prep + cook time 4 hours 15 minutes ✻ serves 4

- **600g (1¼lb) swiss brown mushrooms, halved if large**
- **3 x 400g (12½oz) cans butter beans, drained, rinsed**
- **8 shallots (200g), halved**
- **4 cloves garlic, crushed**
- **2 dried bay leaves**
- **6 sprigs fresh thyme**
- **1½ cups (375ml) dry red wine**
- **410g (13oz) can tomato puree**
- **2 teaspoons fresh thyme leaves, extra**

1 Place mushrooms, beans, shallots, garlic, bay leaves, thyme sprigs, wine and puree in a 5-litre (20-cup) slow cooker. Cook, covered, on high for 4 hours.

2 Discard bay leaves and thyme. Season to taste. Serve bourguignon topped with extra thyme.

Serving suggestion *Mashed potato, wilted spinach or toasted crusty bread to mop up the juices.*

138

SLOW COOKER

VEGETARIAN

LENTIL AND CAULIFLOWER STEW WITH CARROT-TOP PESTO

prep + cook time 6 hours * serves 4

- **¾ cup (150g) French-style dried green lentils**
- **400g (12½oz) baby (dutch) carrots with tops**
- **1 tablespoon olive oil**
- **2 medium leeks (700g), white part only, sliced thinly**
- **3 cloves garlic, crushed**
- **2 stalks celery (300g), trimmed, sliced thickly**
- **4 sprigs fresh thyme**
- **2 dried bay leaves**
- **1 cup (250ml) dry white wine**
- **2 cups (500ml) vegetable stock**
- **½ medium cauliflower (750g), cut into medium florets**
- **2 medium kale leaves (70g), stalks removed, shredded coarsely**

CARROT-TOP PESTO

- **1½ cups coarsely chopped reserved carrot tops**
- **1 cup loosely packed fresh mint leaves**
- **2 teaspoons finely grated lemon rind**
- **1 tablespoon lemon juice**
- **1 clove garlic, quartered**
- **½ cup (125ml) extra virgin olive oil**

1 Rinse lentils well; drain.

2 Trim carrots, reserving tops to make pesto.

3 Heat oil in a 5-litre (20-cup) slow cooker on 'sear' (MEDIUM) setting. Cook leek and garlic, stirring, for 10 minutes or until lightly golden. Add carrot, celery, thyme and bay leaves. Cook, stirring, for 5 minutes or until vegetables soften. Add wine and bring to the boil; boil, uncovered, for 1 minute.

4 Add stock, cauliflower and lentils; stir to combine. Cook, covered, on low for 5 hours, stirring occasionally.

5 Discard thyme and bay leaves. Add kale to slow cooker. Cook, covered, on high, for 10 minutes or until kale wilts. Season to taste.

6 Meanwhile, make carrot-top pesto.

7 Serve stew topped with pesto.

CARROT-TOP PESTO Blend or process reserved carrot tops, mint, rind, juice and garlic until finely chopped. With motor operating, add oil in a thin, steady stream; process until smooth. Season to taste.

Serving suggestion *Steamed brown rice or crusty bread to mop up the juices.*

141

SLOW COOKER

VEGETARIAN

STUFFED CAPSICUMS

prep + cook time 3 hours 30 minutes ✻ makes 5

- **2 tablespoons olive oil**
- **1 medium onion (150g), chopped finely**
- **3 cloves garlic, crushed**
- **2 tablespoons tomato paste**
- **1 cup (280g) bottled passata (or see recipe, page 19)**
- **¾ cup (150g) quinoa**
- **1 cup (250ml) chicken stock**
- **400g (12½oz) can brown lentils, drained, rinsed**
- **180g (5½oz) greek fetta, crumbled**
- **⅓ cup (50g) pitted black olives, chopped finely**
- **¼ cup coarsely chopped fresh flat-leaf parsley**
- **¼ cup coarsely chopped fresh basil**
- **5 medium capsicums (1kg) (see tip)**

1 Heat oil in a large frying pan over medium heat. Cook onion and garlic, stirring, for 5 minutes or until onion softens. Add tomato paste, passata, quinoa and stock; bring to the boil. Remove from heat. Stir in lentils, fetta, olives and herbs. Season to taste.

2 Cut tops from each capsicum; reserve tops. Using a small spoon, scoop out the membranes and seeds. Trim bases so that capsicums stand upright. Divide quinoa mixture among capsicums and replace tops.

3 Place stuffed capsicums in a 5-litre (20-cup) slow cooker. Cook, covered, on high for 3 hours.

Tip *Choose capsicums that are taller rather than wider so that they all fit into the slow cooker.*

Serving suggestion *Greek-style yoghurt.*

EGGPLANT PARMIGIANA

prep + cook time 6 hours 45 minutes * serves 4

*** ⅔ cup (160ml) olive oil**
*** 1 medium onion (150g), chopped finely**
*** 2 cloves garlic, crushed**
*** 400g (12½oz) can diced tomatoes**
*** 1 cup (260g) bottled passata (or see recipe, page 19)**
*** ¼ teaspoon dried chilli flakes**
*** 2 medium eggplants (600g), sliced thickly**
*** ¼ cup (35g) plain (all-purpose) flour**
*** ⅔ cup fresh basil leaves, plus extra to serve**
*** 400g (12½oz) bocconcini, torn**
*** ⅔ cup (50g) finely grated parmesan**
*** ½ teaspoon sweet paprika**

1 Heat 1 tablespoon of the oil in a large frying pan over medium heat. Cook onion, stirring, for 5 minutes or until onion softens. Add garlic and cook, stirring, for 1 minute or until fragrant. Stir in canned tomatoes, passata and chilli. Transfer to a medium jug.
2 Toss eggplant in flour to coat; dust off excess. Heat remaining oil in same pan. Cook eggplant, in batches, for 3 minutes each side or until browned. Drain on paper towel.
3 Layer half the eggplant in a 5-litre (20-cup) slow cooker and season. Top with half each of the tomato mixture, basil and bocconcini. Repeat layers one more time. Scatter with parmesan and sprinkle with paprika. Cook, covered, on low for 6 hours.
4 Serve topped with extra basil.

Serving suggestion *Top with toasted coarse breadcrumbs and serve with salad leaves.*

145

SLOW COOKER

VEGETARIAN

QUINOA, BLACK BEAN AND CHIPOTLE CHILLI

prep + cook time 3 hours 30 minutes * serves 4

- **½ cup (100g) tri-colour quinoa**
- **1 tablespoon olive oil**
- **1 medium onion (150g), chopped finely**
- **1 medium red capsicum (bell pepper) (200g), chopped finely**
- **1 medium green capsicum (bell pepper) (200g), chopped finely**
- **3 cloves garlic, crushed**
- **2 teaspoons ground cumin**
- **2 teaspoons dried oregano**
- **½ teaspoon mexican chilli powder**
- **375g (12oz) bottled chipotle thick and chunky salsa**
- **2½ cups (625ml) vegetable stock**
- **2 x 400g (12½oz) cans black beans, drained, rinsed**
- **2 trimmed corn cobs (500g), kernels removed**
- **½ cup fresh coriander (cilantro) sprigs**

1 Rinse quinoa well; drain.
2 Heat oil in a 5-litre (20-cup) slow cooker on 'sear' (HIGH) setting. Cook onion, capsicums and garlic, stirring, for 5 minutes or until vegetables soften. Add cumin, oregano and chilli. Cook, stirring, for 1 minute or until fragrant.
3 Add quinoa, salsa, stock and beans; stir to combine. Cook, covered, on low for 2½ hours.
4 Add corn to slow cooker and cook, covered, on high for 30 minutes or until corn is tender. Season to taste.
5 Serve chilli topped with coriander.

Serving suggestion *Guacamole, corn chips, sour cream and lime cheeks.*

SPINACH AND THREE CHEESE CANNELLONI

prep + cook time 4 hours 45 minutes ✻ serves 6

- **750g (1½lb) frozen spinach, thawed**
- **3½ cups (840g) firm ricotta (see tip)**
- **2 eggs**
- **1 egg yolk**
- **¾ cup (60g) finely grated parmesan**
- **225g (7oz) jar chargrilled eggplant in olive oil, drained, chopped finely**
- **3 cloves garlic, crushed**
- **1 litre (4 cups) bottled passata (or see recipe, page 19)**
- **¾ cup (180ml) pouring cream**
- **¾ cup coarsely chopped fresh basil**
- **400g (12½oz) dried instant cannelloni tubes**
- **1½ cups (180g) pizza cheese**

1 Squeeze excess moisture from spinach. Place spinach, ricotta, eggs, egg yolk, parmesan, eggplant and garlic in a large bowl; stir to combine. Season.

2 Combine passata, cream and basil in a large jug; season.

3 Lightly oil a 5-litre (20-cup) slow cooker. Pour half the passata mixture over the base of the cooker.

4 Spoon or pipe spinach mixture into cannelloni tubes. Arrange cannelloni vertically in slow cooker. Top with remaining passata mixture and sprinkle with pizza cheese. Cook, covered, on low for 4 hours. Stand for 10 minutes before serving.

Tip *Firm ricotta is available from supermarket delis. It is not the same as the soft ricotta found in tubs in the dairy section.*

Serving suggestion *Grated parmesan and extra basil leaves.*

MIXED BEAN, SPINACH AND PANEER ROGAN JOSH

prep + cook time 4 hours 30 minutes * serves 4

∗ ½ cup (150g) rogan josh curry paste
∗ 2 large onions (400g), sliced thinly
∗ 2 teaspoons finely grated fresh ginger
∗ 3 cloves garlic, crushed
∗ 400g (12½oz) can diced tomatoes
∗ 2 x 400g (12½oz) cans four-bean mix, drained, rinsed
∗ 2 dried bay leaves
∗ 2 cups (500ml) vegetable stock
∗ 150g (4½oz) baby spinach leaves
∗ 200g (6½oz) paneer, crumbled
∗ ¼ cup fresh micro herbs (optional)

1 Heat a 5-litre (20-cup) slow cooker on 'sear' (MEDIUM) setting. Cook curry paste, stirring, for 5 minutes or until fragrant. Add onion, ginger, garlic, canned tomatoes, beans, bay leaves and stock; stir to combine. Cook, covered, on low for 4 hours.

2 Stir in spinach and cook, covered, on high for 5 minutes or until spinach wilts. Season to taste.

3 Serve curry topped with paneer and micro herbs.

Serving suggestion
Steamed basmati rice, warmed naan bread, lime wedges and natural yoghurt.

Suitable to freeze
at the end of step 1.

VEGETARIAN

CHEESE, TOMATO
AND OLIVE BREAD PUDDING

prep + cook time 3 hours 30 minutes ✻ serves 6

- **40g (1½oz) butter, softened**
- **6 green onions (scallions), trimmed, sliced thinly**
- **2 cloves garlic, crushed**
- **6 x 1.5cm (¾in) thick slices olive bread (360g)**
- **200g (6½oz) cherry tomatoes**
- **½ cup (80g) pitted black olives, halved**
- **½ cup (40g) finely grated parmesan**
- **100g (3oz) drained persian fetta, crumbled**
- **1 tablespoon coarsely chopped fresh basil**
- **6 eggs**
- **1 cup (250ml) milk**
- **300ml reduced-fat thickened (heavy) cream**
- **¼ teaspoon sweet paprika**

1 Grease a 5-litre (20-cup) slow cooker with a little of the butter.

2 Heat 20g (¾oz) of the butter in a small frying pan. Cook green onion and garlic, stirring, for 5 minutes or until softened.

3 Spread bread with remaining butter; cut each slice in half. Place half the bread in the base of slow cooker. Scatter half the green onion mixture over bread. Layer with half each of the tomatoes, olives, parmesan, fetta and basil. Season to taste. Repeat layers with remaining bread, onion mixture, tomatoes, olives, parmesan, fetta and basil.

4 Whisk eggs, milk and cream together in a large jug; season. Pour egg mixture over bread mixture. Sprinkle with paprika.

5 Cook, covered, on low for 3 hours or until set. Remove insert from slow cooker. Stand for 5 minutes. Serve scattered with basil and extra parmesan, if you like.

Serving suggestion *A green leafy salad.*

153

SLOW COOKER

VEGETARIAN

MOROCCAN-STYLE VEGETABLE STEW WITH HARISSA

prep + cook time 6 hours 30 minutes ✻ serves 4

∗ 1 medium red onion (170g), chopped coarsely
∗ 4 cloves garlic, quartered
∗ 2 teaspoons ground cumin
∗ 2 teaspoons ground coriander
∗ 2 teaspoons sweet paprika
∗ 1 fresh long red chilli, chopped finely
∗ ½ cup coarsely chopped fresh flat-leaf parsley leaves and stalks
∗ 1 cup coarsely chopped fresh coriander (cilantro) leaves and stalks
∗ 2 cups (500ml) vegetable stock
∗ 4 baby eggplants (240g), chopped coarsely
∗ 4 small zucchini (360g), chopped coarsely
∗ 2 small parsnips (240g), chopped coarsely
∗ 2 medium carrots (240g), halved lengthways, then halved crossways
∗ ¼ medium butternut pumpkin (500g), skin on, cut into 8 pieces
∗ 2 medium potatoes (400g), quartered
∗ 2 tablespoons honey
∗ 1 cup (280g) Greek-style yoghurt
∗ 2 tablespoons mild harissa
∗ ⅓ cup loosely packed fresh coriander (cilantro) leaves, extra

1 Blend or process onion, garlic and spices until a smooth paste forms. Combine paste with chilli, herbs and stock in a large jug.

2 Combine vegetables and stock mixture in a 5-litre (20-cup) slow cooker. Cook, covered, on low for 6 hours. Stir in honey. Season to taste.

3 Serve stew topped with yoghurt, harissa and extra coriander.

Serving suggestion *Buttered couscous.*

154

SLOW COOKER

VEGETARIAN

EGGPLANT, OLIVE AND PINE NUT PASTA SAUCE

prep + cook time 6 hours 30 minutes * serves 6

- **3 cloves garlic, chopped finely**
- **2 medium onions (300g), chopped finely**
- **1 fresh long red chilli, chopped finely**
- **1 large eggplant (500g), chopped coarsely**
- **500g (1lb) ripe tomatoes, chopped coarsely**
- **400g (12½oz) can diced tomatoes**
- **½ cup fresh basil leaves**
- **2 tablespoons tomato paste**
- **½ cup (75g) pitted black olives**
- **2 tablespoons pine nuts, toasted**
- **⅓ cup finely shredded fresh basil leaves, extra**

1 Place garlic, onion, chilli, eggplant, fresh and canned tomatoes, basil leaves (reserve a few of the smallest to serve) and tomato paste in a 5-litre (20-cup) slow cooker; stir to combine. Cook, covered, on low for 6 hours. Season to taste.

2 Stir in olives, pine nuts and shredded basil. Scatter reserved small basil leaves over sauce before serving.

Serving suggestion
Short tubular pasta, both casarecce and penne, work well with this pasta sauce.

Suitable to freeze
at the end of step 1.

OVEN

158

OVEN

BREADS

DARK SPICED RYE BREAD

prep + cook time 3 hours 45 minutes * makes 3 loaves

- **4 teaspoons (14g) dried yeast**
- **2 teaspoons caster (superfine) sugar**
- **2 cups (500ml) warm water**
- **½ cup (125ml) extra virgin olive oil**
- **¼ cup (95g) molasses**
- **1 tablespoon caraway seeds**
- **1 teaspoon cumin seeds, toasted**
- **½ cup (75g) sunflower seeds**
- **2 large carrots (360g), peeled, grated coarsely**
- **1 cup (170g) fine cornmeal (maize flour)**
- **3 cups (450g) rye flour**
- **1 cup (300g) plain (all-purpose) flour**
- **⅓ cup (35g) dutch-processed cocoa**
- **1 tablespoon fine salt**
- **½ cup (75g) plain (all-purpose) flour, extra**

1 Whisk yeast, sugar and the water in a large bowl until yeast dissolves. Cover and stand in a warm place for 10 minutes or until mixture is foamy.

2 Stir oil and molasses into yeast mixture, then seeds, carrot, cornmeal and sifted flours, cocoa and salt to form a slightly sticky dough. Turn dough onto a well-floured surface and knead for 10 minutes or until smooth, dusting the surface frequently with the extra flour. Place dough in a large oiled bowl. Cover and stand in a warm place for 1¾ hours or until dough doubles in size.

3 Turn dough onto a floured surface; divide into three portions. Knead each portion until smooth. Shape each portion into a 12cm (4¾in) round. Place on two baking-paper-lined oven trays (place two on one tray and one on a second tray). Cover with clean tea towels and stand in a warm place for 45 minutes or until dough has risen slightly.

4 Preheat oven to 200°C/400°F.

5 Dust loaves with a little more extra flour, then, using a floured small sharp knife, make five or six slashes, in both directions, across each loaf.

6 Bake bread for 40 minutes (swapping trays between shelves halfway through cooking time) or until hollow sounding when tapped. (It is not necessary to swap the trays around in a fan-forced oven as the fan will circulate the heat more evenly.) Transfer loaves to wire racks to cool. Leave for at least 45 minutes before eating.

Serving suggestion
Top with smoked salmon, or eat as a breakfast or sandwich bread.

Suitable to freeze
at the end of step 6.

SEEDED PUMPKIN BREADSTICKS

prep + cook time 4 hours 15 minutes ✻ makes 6 breadsticks

- **900g (1¾lb) butternut pumpkin, halved lengthways, seeds removed**
- **2 teaspoons (7g) dried yeast**
- **1 tablespoon honey**
- **½ cup (125ml) lukewarm water**
- **2 tablespoons vegetable oil**
- **1⅓ cups (200g) wholemeal plain (all-purpose) flour**
- **2 cups (300g) '00' flour, bread flour or plain (all-purpose) flour**
- **½ cup (75g) sunflower seeds**
- **2 tablespoons sesame seeds**
- **1 tablespoon linseeds (flaxseeds)**
- **1 tablespoon sea salt flakes**
- **1 egg, beaten lightly**
- **¼ cup pepitas (pumpkin seed kernels)**
- **1 tablespoon poppy seeds**
- **2 tablespoons sunflower seeds, extra**

1 Preheat oven to 180°C/350°F.

2 Place pumpkin on an oven tray and cover with foil. Bake for 1¼ hours or until very tender. When cool enough to handle, scoop flesh into a medium bowl and mash with a fork; you need 1½ cups mashed pumpkin.

3 Combine yeast, honey and the water in a small bowl; cover with plastic wrap. Stand in a warm place for 10 minutes or until frothy. Stir in oil.

4 Combine sifted flours, sunflower seeds, sesame seeds, linseeds and salt in a large bowl. Add yeast mixture and mashed pumpkin; mix to a soft dough. Knead dough on a floured surface for 10 minutes or until smooth and elastic. (If you have an electric mixer with a dough hook, mix on medium speed for 6 minutes or until smooth and elastic.)

5 Place dough in a large oiled bowl and cover with plastic wrap. Stand in a warm place for 1 hour or until dough doubles in size.

6 Increase oven temperature to 200°C/400°F. Punch down dough with your fist. Knead on a floured surface for 1 minute or until smooth. Roll dough into six 4cm x 30cm (1½in x 12in) lengths and place on a large oiled oven tray (or divide dough into 12 even-sized balls).

7 Cover dough loosely with oiled plastic wrap. Stand in a warm place for 40 minutes or until dough almost doubles in size.

8 Brush dough with egg. Scatter with pepitas, poppy seeds and extra sunflower seeds. Bake for 25 minutes or until golden and bread sounds hollow when tapped. Cool on a wire rack.

Serving suggestion *Split breadsticks lengthways, not cutting all the way through, and stuff with sandwich fillings.*

BUTTERY FRENCH BRIOCHE

prep + cook time 2 hours 30 minutes (+ overnight refrigeration) * makes 1 loaf

You will need to start this recipe the day before. While this bread can be kneaded by hand, it is much easier to incorporate the butter using a bench mixer and dough hook.

*** 4 teaspoons (14g) dried yeast**
*** ⅓ cup (80ml) warm water**
*** ¼ cup (55g) caster (superfine) sugar**
*** 4 cups (600g) plain (all-purpose) flour**
*** 1 teaspoon fine salt**
*** 5 eggs, beaten lightly**
*** 250g (8oz) butter**
*** 1 egg, extra, beaten lightly**
*** 1 tablespoon caster (superfine) sugar, extra**

1 Whisk yeast, the water and 1 tablespoon of the caster sugar in a small bowl until yeast dissolves. Cover and stand in a warm place for 10 minutes or until mixture is frothy.
2 Sift flour, salt and remaining caster sugar into a large bowl, then add yeast mixture and egg; stir until just combined. Turn dough onto a floured surface and knead for 10 minutes or until dough is smooth and elastic.
3 Divide butter into 10 equal portions. Knead each portion of butter into dough, kneading well after each addition, until all the butter is incorporated and dough is smooth and glossy. Place dough in a large bowl. Cover and refrigerate overnight.
4 Preheat oven to 200°C/400°F.
5 Divide dough into three equal portions. Roll each portion into a 45cm (18in) length. Place dough lengths on a large greased oven tray; cross lengths over and under each other into a plait. Cover and stand in a cool place for 1 hour or until dough nearly doubles in size.
6 Brush plait with extra egg and sprinkle with extra sugar. Bake brioche for 10 minutes. Reduce heat to 180°C/350°F and bake for a further 20 minutes or until golden and bread sounds hollow when tapped.

Serving suggestion *Try this for breakfast with soft scrambled eggs and smoked salmon, or with any of our jams or marmalades in* Preserves & Condiments, *pages 12–23.*

CITRUS HAZELNUT BREAD TWIST

prep + cook time 3 hours 45 minutes * serves 8

- **3 teaspoons (10g) dried yeast**
- **1½ tablespoons caster (superfine) sugar**
- **½ cup (125ml) warm milk**
- **2 egg yolks**
- **100g (3oz) butter, melted**
- **¾ cup (180ml) warm water**
- **3 cups (450g) plain (all-purpose) flour**
- **½ teaspoon fine salt**
- **1 cup (140g) roasted skinned hazelnuts**
- **⅓ cup (75g) demerara sugar**
- **1 teaspoon mixed spice**
- **100g (3oz) butter, extra, melted**
- **1 tablespoon finely grated orange rind**
- **1 tablespoon finely grated lemon rind**
- **2 tablespoons demerara sugar, extra**

1 Combine yeast, caster sugar and milk in a large bowl, cover, then stand in a warm place for 10 minutes or until frothy. Add egg yolks, butter, the water, flour and salt; stir until combined. Transfer dough to a lightly floured surface, then knead for 10 minutes or until smooth and elastic. Place dough in a lightly oiled large bowl, cover, then stand in a warm place for 1 hour or until dough doubles in size.
2 Process three-quarters of the hazelnuts for 1 minute or until finely ground. Combine ground nuts in a small bowl with demerara sugar and mixed spice.
3 Preheat oven to 200°C/400°F. Grease a large oven tray.
4 Lightly flour a large piece of baking paper. Roll dough out on paper into a 25cm x 45cm (10in x 18in) rectangle. Lift dough on paper onto tray, cover with plastic wrap, then refrigerate for 1 hour or until firmed slightly (this will assist with shaping the twist).
5 Combine 80g (2½oz) of extra melted butter with the citrus rinds in a small bowl. Brush butter mixture over dough, leaving a 1cm (½in) border. Top with ground hazelnut mixture. Firmly roll dough up from one long side, using the baking paper as a guide. Using a sharp knife, cut the roll in half lengthways. Turn the halves, cut-side out, on the baking paper, then twist together. Form the twisted length into a ring, pressing the two ends together to join.
6 Transfer the ring, carefully lifting it on the baking paper, onto the oven tray. Brush with remaining extra melted butter and sprinkle with extra demerara sugar.
7 Bake for 10 minutes. Reduce oven temperature to 180°C/350°F. Bake for a further 35 minutes or until golden and hollow sounding when tapped. Transfer twist to a wire rack to cool. Top with remaining halved hazelnuts.

Tip *This recipe is best made on the day of serving.*

Serving suggestion *Spread slices of bread with fig jam and top with torn fresh figs.*

FOUR CHEESE PIZZA

prep + cook time 2 hours ✻ serves 4

- **100g (3oz) bocconcini, sliced thinly**
- **½ cup (40g) finely grated parmesan**
- **½ cup (50g) coarsely grated fontina (see tips)**
- **50g (1½oz) gorgonzola, crumbled (see tips)**
- **4 sprigs fresh thyme**

PIZZA DOUGH

- **1½ cups (225g) '00' flour, bread flour or plain (all-purpose) flour**
- **1 teaspoon (4g) dried yeast**
- **1 teaspoon caster (superfine) sugar**
- **1 teaspoon fine table salt**
- **1 tablespoon olive oil**
- **½ cup (125ml) warm water, approximately**

1 Make pizza dough.

2 Preheat oven to 240°C/475°F. Oil a pizza tray or oven tray and place in heated oven.

3 Roll dough into a 35cm (14in) round. Place on tray.

4 Top pizza base with bocconcini, then sprinkle with remaining cheeses.

5 Bake for 15 minutes or until base is browned and crisp. Top with thyme. Serve.

PIZZA DOUGH Combine flour, yeast, sugar and salt in a medium bowl. Make a well in the centre. Stir in oil and enough of the water to mix to a soft dough. Knead dough on a floured surface for 10 minutes or until smooth and elastic. Place dough in a large oiled bowl, cover, then stand in a warm place for 1 hour or until dough doubles in size. Turn dough onto a floured surface and knead until smooth.

Tips *Fontina is an Italian semi-soft cow's milk cheese and can be substituted with gruyère or emmental. Gorgonzola is a blue-veined cheese and can be substituted with other mild blue-veined cheeses. For individual pizzas, divide the dough into four pieces. Roll each piece on a floured surface into 10cm x 20cm (4in x 8in) slipper shapes and bake for 12 minutes.*

Serving suggestion *Scatter with extra fresh thyme leaves and grated parmesan.*

ROASTS & BAKES

LEMON THYME CHICKEN
WITH CAPERBERRY SALSA

prep + cook time 40 minutes (+ standing) ✻ serves 4

∗ 4 chicken breast supremes (1kg) (see tips)
∗ ¼ cup (60ml) olive oil
∗ 2 tablespoons fresh thyme leaves
∗ 1 tablespoon finely grated lemon rind
∗ 1 celeriac (celery root) (750g), peeled
∗ 2 large carrots (360g)
∗ 1 clove garlic, crushed
∗ 2 tablespoons white balsamic vinegar
∗ ½ cup (100g) roasted pepitas (pumpkin seed kernels)
∗ ¾ cup coarsely chopped fresh flat-leaf parsley
∗ 2 tablespoons Greek-style yoghurt
∗ ¼ cup fresh flat-leaf parsley leaves, extra
∗ ¼ cup fresh thyme sprigs, extra

CAPERBERRY SALSA
∗ 1 cup (160g) caperberries
∗ 2 tablespoons olive oil
∗ 2 tablespoons lemon juice
∗ 1½ teaspoons dried pink peppercorns, crushed coarsely

1 Preheat oven to 220°C/425°F. Line an oven tray with baking paper.
2 Combine chicken, 1 tablespoon of the oil, thyme and rind in a large bowl; stand for 10 minutes.
3 Meanwhile, using a vegetable peeler, peel long thin ribbons from the celeriac and carrot (keep the centre core of each vegetable for another use, see tips). Place vegetable ribbons in a large bowl with garlic, vinegar, pepitas, chopped parsley and yoghurt, then season. Stir to combine.
4 Heat remaining oil in a large ovenproof frying pan over medium-high heat. Cook chicken for 3 minutes each side or until browned all over. Transfer to oven and roast for 12 minutes or until cooked through.
5 Meanwhile, make caperberry salsa.
6 Serve chicken with vegetable salad and caperberry salsa, topped with extra herbs and reserved caperberries (from the salsa).

CAPERBERRY SALSA Halve three-quarters of the caperberries, keeping the stems attached; reserve remaining for serving. Combine halved caperberries in a small bowl with oil, juice and peppercorns.

Tips *Chicken breast supreme is a chicken breast with the skin and wing bone attached; ask your butcher to prepare it for you. Alternatively, use chicken breast fillets. You can use the remaining centre core of the celeriac and carrot in a soup.*

LAMB RAGÙ MOUSSAKA

prep + cook time 5 hours 15 minutes ✻ serves 8

- **3 medium eggplants (960g)**
- **cooking-oil spray**
- **80g (2½oz) butter, chopped**
- **½ cup (75g) plain (all-purpose) flour**
- **1 litre (4 cups) milk**
- **1¼ cups (100g) grated parmesan**
- **¾ cup (60g) panko (japanese) breadcrumbs**
- **2 teaspoons finely grated lemon rind**
- **2 teaspoons fresh thyme leaves**

LAMB RAGÙ

- **2kg (4lb) leg of lamb**
- **2 medium onions (300g), chopped**
- **4 cloves garlic, chopped**
- **600g (1¼lb) canned chopped tomatoes**
- **¼ cup (70g) tomato paste**
- **3 bay leaves**
- **½ cup (125ml) red wine**
- **1 teaspoon ground coriander**
- **1 teaspoon ground cumin**
- **2 tablespoons olive oil**

1 Make lamb ragù.

2 Increase oven temperature to 240°C/475°F.

3 Cut eggplants lengthways into medium-thick slices. Spray each side with oil and place on wire racks on oven trays. Roast for 10 minutes or until soft and brown at edges. Remove from oven. Reduce oven to 200°C/400°F.

4 Meanwhile, melt butter in a medium heavy-based saucepan over medium heat. Add flour and stir until mixture bubbles. Gradually pour in milk, whisking continuously until mixture boils and thickens. Add ½ cup (40g) of the parmesan and stir until melted. Remove from heat.

5 Remove lamb from oven bag, then shred meat using two forks; discard bone. Place sauce from oven bag in a large heavy-based saucepan over low heat. Add shredded meat and stir until heated through. Season.

6 Combine breadcrumbs, rind, thyme and remaining parmesan in a medium bowl.

7 Grease a 24cm x 32cm x 6.5cm deep (9½in x 12¾in x 2¾in) (3.5-litre/14-cup) ovenproof dish. Place half the eggplant slices in base of dish. Top with half each of the ragù and white sauce. Repeat layers one more time. Cover white sauce with breadcrumb mixture.

8 Bake for 35 minutes or until golden and heated through.

LAMB RAGÙ Preheat oven to 160°C/325°F. Trim excess fat from lamb, if necessary. Combine onion, garlic, canned tomatoes, tomato paste, bay leaves and wine in a large oven bag. Combine spices in a small bowl. Rub oil then spice mixture over lamb. Place lamb in an oven bag, then place bag on a large oven tray. Seal bag using the tie provided; pierce five or six times near the top of the bag to allow steam to escape during cooking. Roast for 4 hours or until lamb is very tender. Discard bay leaves.

Do ahead *You can make the ragù a day ahead. When cool, shred meat into pieces, then stir into the cooking sauce. Refrigerate until needed. Reheat ragù before continuing from step 6.*

CONFIT DUCK
WITH CANDIED ORANGE

prep + cook time 3 hours 15 minutes (+ refrigeration) * serves 4

- **1 tablespoon fresh thyme leaves**
- **⅓ cup (100g) coarse cooking salt (kosher salt)**
- **2 tablespoons chinese five-spice powder**
- **4 duck marylands (1.2kg)**
- **2 cloves garlic, bruised**
- **2 litres (8 cups) olive oil, approximately**
- **⅓ cup (75g) caster (superfine) sugar**
- **⅓ cup (80ml) water**
- **3 whole cloves**
- **1 medium orange (240g), sliced thinly**
- **120g (4oz) baby rocket (arugula) leaves**
- **⅓ cup (35g) walnut halves, roasted**

DRESSING

- **1 teaspoon dijon mustard**
- **1 tablespoon white wine vinegar**
- **1½ tablespoons olive oil**

1 Combine thyme, salt and five-spice in a small bowl. Place duck in a shallow dish. Rub salt mixture all over duck. Cover and refrigerate for 2 hours.

2 Preheat oven to 130°C/260°F.

3 Wash salt mixture from duck and pat dry with paper towel. Place duck and garlic, tightly packed in a single layer, in a medium ovenproof dish. Pour in enough oil to completely cover duck. Cook duck in the oven for 3 hours or until very tender.

4 Meanwhile, stir sugar, the water and cloves in a large frying pan over medium heat, without boiling, until sugar dissolves. Add orange slices. Bring to the boil, then reduce heat and simmer, uncovered, swirling the pan occasionally, for 1 hour or until liquid is nearly evaporated and oranges are sticky.

5 Make dressing.

6 Carefully remove duck from the oil. Heat 2 tablespoons of the confit cooking oil in a large frying pan over high heat. Cook duck for 2 minutes each side or until golden. Remove from heat.

7 Serve duck with rocket and walnuts drizzled with dressing, accompanied by candied oranges.

DRESSING Place ingredients in a screw-top jar and shake well. Season to taste.

Do ahead *Duck can be cooked up to 4 days ahead; keep covered in oil in the fridge. To reheat duck, remove from oil, place on an oven tray and cook under a preheated grill for 10 minutes or until skin is crisp and heated through.*

SLOW-ROASTED LAMB SHOULDER

prep + cook time 3 hours 45 minutes * serves 4

- **1.3kg (2¾lb) lamb shoulder, shank on**
- **2 tablespoons olive oil**
- **1kg (2lb) potatoes, sliced thickly**
- **2 medium red onions (340g), sliced thickly**
- **4 anchovy fillets, chopped finely**
- **2 garlic bulbs (140g)**
- **1 medium lemon (140g), cut into wedges**
- **3 sprigs fresh rosemary**
- **1 cup (250ml) chicken stock**
- **1 cup (250ml) water or dry white wine**

1 Preheat oven to 180°C/350°F. Season lamb.

2 Heat a flameproof roasting pan over medium-high heat. Add oil, then lamb and cook until lamb is well browned all over. Remove from pan.

3 Layer potato, onion and anchovies in roasting pan; season between layers. Cut garlic bulb in half horizontally and place on vegetables with lemon wedges.

4 Place lamb on top of vegetable mixture. Add rosemary. Pour combined stock and the water over vegetables. Cover pan tightly with two layers of foil. Roast for 1½ hours. Remove foil. Reduce oven to 160°C/325°F and roast for a further 1½ hours or until the meat can be pulled from the bone easily. Transfer lamb to a tray. Cover with foil and rest for 20 minutes. Increase oven to 200°C/400°F.

5 Meanwhile, return vegetable mixture in pan to oven and cook for a further 20 minutes or until browned.

6 Serve lamb with vegetables and lemon.

Serving suggestion *A green salad or greek salad.*

ROAST VEAL RACK
WITH CELERIAC AND POTATO GRATIN

prep + cook time 1 hour 55 minutes * serves 8

*** 2kg (4lb) veal rack (8 cutlets)**
*** 1 cup (250ml) water**
*** ¼ cup (70g) dijon mustard**
*** 2 tablespoons horseradish cream**
*** 2 cloves garlic, crushed**
*** 1½ tablespoons plain (all-purpose) flour**
*** 2 teaspoons dijon mustard, extra**
*** 2 cups (500ml) beef stock**
*** 2 tablespoons finely chopped fresh tarragon**
*** 1 tablespoon coarsely chopped fresh thyme**
*** ¼ cup finely chopped fresh flat-leaf parsley**

CELERIAC & POTATO GRATIN
*** 600ml thickened (heavy) cream**
*** 3 cloves garlic, sliced thinly**
*** 3 teaspoons chopped fresh thyme leaves**
*** 1 medium celeriac (celery root) (750g), trimmed**
*** 3 medium potatoes (600g)**
*** 50g (1½oz) smoked cheddar, grated coarsely**
*** 1 teaspoon fresh thyme, extra**

1 Preheat oven to 180°C/350°F.
2 Make celeriac and potato gratin.
3 Meanwhile, place veal on a wire rack in a flameproof roasting pan. Pour the water into the base of the pan. Combine mustard, horseradish and garlic in a small bowl. Spread mustard mixture over veal and season. Roast veal for last 45 minutes of gratin cooking time or until cooked as desired. Transfer veal to a plate. Cover and rest for 10 minutes.
4 Meanwhile, to make mustard sauce, heat roasting pan over medium-high heat, add flour and cook, whisking, until mixture is smooth and bubbling. Add extra mustard and stock; stir until mixture boils and thickens. Season to taste.
5 Combine herbs and press onto veal. Cut veal into cutlets. Serve veal with gratin and mustard sauce.

CELERIAC & POTATO GRATIN Place cream, garlic and thyme in a medium saucepan over medium heat; bring to a simmer. Remove from heat and stand for 10 minutes. Meanwhile, using a mandoline, V-slicer or sharp knife, thinly slice celeriac and potatoes; combine in a large bowl. Layer celeriac and potato with cream mixture, seasoning with salt and pepper between layers, in a 1.5-litre (6-cup) round ovenproof dish. Scatter with cheese. Cover with foil and bake for 1 hour. Uncover and bake for a further 20 minutes or until tender and golden. Top with extra thyme.

Serving suggestion *Steamed roman or green beans.*

TEA-BRINED ROASTED CHICKEN

prep + cook time 1 hour 45 minutes (+ refrigeration) * serves 4

You will need to start this recipe the day before. One of the challenges of cooking a whole chicken is that the breast meat and leg meat require a different cooking time and temperature from each other, as one is leaner than the other. Brining is the solution to evening out the differences as it adds extra moisture.

*** 1 litre (4 cups) water**
*** ½ cup (30g) russian caravan tea leaves (see tips)**
*** ½ cup (175g) honey**
*** ½ cup (110g) white (granulated) sugar**
*** 2 lemons, 1 sliced, 1 whole**
*** ⅓ cup (40g) sea salt flakes**
*** 1 bunch fresh sage**
*** 1.8kg (3½lb) whole chicken**
*** 1 tablespoon olive oil**

1 Place the water and tea leaves in a saucepan over high heat and bring to the boil. Remove from the heat and stand until cooled. Strain; discard leaves.

2 Stir honey, sugar, sliced lemon and salt flakes through the tea mixture until well combined.

3 Place a large zip-top bag in a large bowl; add half the sage, then the chicken, breast-side down. Carefully pour the tea mixture over the chicken and seal the bag, removing all the air. Refrigerate for 8 hours or overnight, rotating three times.

4 Preheat oven to 180°C/350°F.

5 Remove chicken from brine and pat dry with paper towel; discard brine. Place in a large roasting pan. Place remaining sage and the whole lemon in the chicken cavity, then truss the legs with kitchen string. Drizzle over oil and season with salt and pepper.

6 Roast chicken for 1¼ hours or until the juices run clear when the thickest part of a thigh is pierced. (Cover the parts of the chicken that brown faster with foil.) Rest, covered loosely with foil, for 5 minutes before serving.

Tips *Russian caravan tea is a blend of China black keemun, oolong and lapsang souchong teas. It's not actually from Russia but was transported to Russia from China. It is the lapsang souchong that gives the tea its defining smoky flavour. It is available from select supermarkets and tea shops.*

Serving suggestion *Roasted potatoes and garlic.*

MEATLOAF WITH FIG GLAZE

prep + cook time 1 hour 30 minutes ✻ serves 6

- **2 slices white bread (90g)**
- **½ cup (125ml) milk**
- **1 tablespoon extra virgin olive oil**
- **1 medium carrot (120g), chopped finely**
- **1 trimmed celery stalk (100g), chopped finely**
- **3 shallots (75g), chopped finely**
- **2 cloves garlic, crushed**
- **1kg (2lb) minced (ground) pork and veal (see tips)**
- **1 tablespoon finely chopped fresh oregano**
- **⅓ cup (110g) fig jam**
- **½ cup (115g) glacé ginger**
- **1 tablespoon boiling water**

CARAMELISED SHALLOTS

- **30g (1oz) butter**
- **8 shallots (200g), halved**
- **¼ cup (60ml) dry red wine**
- **6 fresh bay leaves**

1 Preheat oven to 200°C/400°F. Line a large oven tray with baking paper.

2 Place bread and milk in a large bowl; stand for 10 minutes or until milk is absorbed.

3 Meanwhile, heat oil in a large saucepan over medium-high heat. Cook carrot, celery, shallot and garlic for 5 minutes or until soft.

4 Add carrot mixture to bread mixture with pork and veal, and oregano. Season well, then mix well.

5 Shape meatloaf mixture into a 20cm (8in) log in the centre of a 40cm (16in) piece of baking paper. Using the baking paper as a guide, roll to form a 30cm (12in) log. Transfer meatloaf on paper to oven tray.

6 Process jam, ginger and the water until smooth; brush over meatloaf.

7 Bake meatloaf for 45 minutes or until cooked through and browned.

8 Meanwhile, make caramelised shallots.

9 Serve meatloaf topped with shallots.

CARAMELISED SHALLOTS Melt butter in a small ovenproof frying pan over medium heat. Cook shallots, stirring, for 5 minutes or until softened slightly. Add wine and bring to the boil. Transfer pan to the oven. Cook for 15 minutes. Add bay leaves and cook for a further 5 minutes or until shallots are tender and caramelised.

Tips *If you can't find pork and veal mince mixture, then buy 500g (1lb) of each. When making the caramelised shallots, if you don't have an ovenproof frying pan, use a flameproof baking dish instead, or transfer the shallot mixture from the frying pan to an ovenproof dish.*

Serving suggestion *Top meatloaf with bay leaves and serve with mashed potato.*

FIVE-SPICE PORK

prep + cook time 3 hours (+ refrigeration) * serves 12

- **1 large tomato (220g), chopped coarsely**
- **2 tablespoons tomato paste**
- **2 fresh small red chillies, seeded, chopped coarsely**
- **3 teaspoons ground star anise**
- **3 teaspoons ground cinnamon**
- **1 teaspoon ground fennel seeds**
- **¼ teaspoon ground cloves**
- **6 cloves garlic**
- **1 tablespoon finely grated fresh ginger**
- **¼ cup (60ml) soy sauce**
- **1½ tablespoons fish sauce**
- **½ cup (110g) firmly packed brown sugar**
- **2kg (4lb) boneless pork belly, rind removed, fat trimmed**
- **230g (7oz) fresh baby corn**
- **¼ cup (60ml) sesame oil**
- **1 cup (280g) chinese plum sauce**

1 Process tomato, tomato paste, chilli, spices, garlic, ginger, sauces and sugar until mixture forms a paste. Place pork in a glass or ceramic dish, add paste and turn pork to coat. Cover with plastic wrap and refrigerate for 1 hour.

2 Preheat oven to 180°C/350°F.

3 Line a roasting pan with foil, then fit with an oiled wire rack. Remove pork from marinade; reserve marinade. Place pork, fat-side down, on rack in pan. Roast for 30 minutes. Turn pork, brushing with a little reserved marinade. Roast for a further 1 hour, basting every 15 minutes with reserved marinade. Roast for another 30 minutes, without basting, until top is dark brown and crisp. Cool.

4 Combine baby corn and oil in a small bowl, then season to taste; thread onto metal skewers, if you like. Cook on a heated chargrill plate (or barbecue) until corn is lightly charred and just cooked.

5 Serve sliced pork with plum sauce and grilled baby corn. Scatter with thinly sliced green onion, if you like.

Serving suggestion *Serve the pork with bought peking duck pancakes or another flat bread to pile the pork onto.*

4 WAYS WITH ROASTED VEGETABLES

BEETROOT AND WALNUT CRUMBLE

prep + cook time 1 hour ✻ serves 4

Preheat oven to 220°C/425°F. Trim leaves and stalks from 1.5kg (3lb) red beetroot (beets) and 500g (1lb) baby yellow beetroot (beets); wash. Peel red beetroot and cut into six wedges. Keep yellow ones whole. Place all beets on a large piece of foil on an oven tray with 2 bay leaves; drizzle with 1 tablespoon olive oil. Cover with another piece of foil; seal. Roast yellow beets for 30 minutes and red beets for 40 minutes or until tender. Peel yellow beets and halve. Process ½ cup walnuts and ¼ cup fresh flat-leaf parsley until chopped. Toss beetroots with walnut crumble.

ROASTED PARSNIPS WITH SAGE

prep + cook time 1 hour ✻ serves 4

Preheat oven to 200°C/400°F. Cut 1kg (2lb) scrubbed parsnips in half lengthways. Combine parsnips with 2 tablespoons olive oil, ¼ cup firmly packed brown sugar and ½ teaspoon ground nutmeg in a large roasting pan. Season. Roast for 40 minutes. Add ¼ cup fresh sage leaves. Roast for a further 10 minutes or until parsnips are browned and tender, and sage is crisp.

ORANGE AND MAPLE-GLAZED BABY CARROTS

prep + cook time 25 minutes ✻ serves 4

Melt 30g (1oz) butter in a large frying pan over medium heat. Cook 750g (1½lb) trimmed baby (dutch) carrots, turning occasionally, for 8 minutes or until almost tender. Add 2 teaspoons finely grated orange rind, ¼ cup orange juice, 2 tablespoons dry white wine and 2 tablespoons pure maple syrup; bring to the boil. Reduce heat to low. Simmer until liquid is almost evaporated and carrots are tender and caramelised. Serve scattered with ½ cup coarsely chopped roasted hazelnuts and micro herbs, if you like.

ORANGE SWEET POTATO AND CHICKPEAS

prep + cook time 45 minutes ✻ serves 4

Preheat oven to 220°C/425°F. Scrub 1kg (2lb) small orange sweet potatoes. Cut sweet potatoes and 2 medium (340g) red onions lengthways into wedges. Drain a 400g (12½oz) can chickpeas (garbanzo beans); rinse. Place sweet potato, onions, chickpeas and 10 torn sprigs fresh thyme on a baking-paper-lined oven tray. Drizzle with ⅓ cup olive oil; season with salt flakes and freshly ground black pepper. Toss to coat. Roast for 30 minutes or until sweet potato is tender and browned.

187

OVEN

ROASTS & BAKES

CIDER-ROASTED PORK BELLY

prep + cook time 3 hours * serves 4

*** 1.5kg (3lb) piece pork belly, rind on**
*** 2 tablespoons finely chopped fresh rosemary**
*** 1 tablespoon sea salt flakes**
*** 1⅓ cups (330ml) apple cider**
*** 4 medium parsnips (1kg), peeled, cut into quarters**
*** 4 cloves garlic, peeled**
*** 1½ cups (375ml) salt-reduced chicken stock**
*** 2 medium green apples (300g)**
*** 2 x 400g (12½oz) cans brown lentils, drained, rinsed**

1 Preheat oven to 240°C/475°F.

2 Using a sharp knife, score pork rind at 1cm (½in) intervals in a criss-cross pattern. Place pork, rind-side up, in a large roasting pan. Combine rosemary and salt in a small bowl; rub salt mixture over pork. Roast pork, uncovered, for 20 minutes or until rind starts to blister and crackle.

3 Reduce oven to 160°C/325°F. Add cider to pan and roast for 1¼ hours.

4 Add parsnip, garlic and stock to pan. Roast, uncovered, for 45 minutes.

5 Cut unpeeled apples into quarters, add to pan with lentils and roast for a further 30 minutes or until apple is tender. Season to taste.

6 Serve sliced pork with apple mixture.

Tips *To make crisp crackling, the pork rind needs to be really dry: leave the pork rind, uncovered, in the fridge overnight. Cover the pork flesh with plastic wrap to stop it from drying out.*

Serving suggestion *A green salad.*

SLOW-COOKED GREEK LAMB
WITH CHILLI GARLIC BROCCOLINI

prep + cook time 5 hours 30 minutes ✻ serves 4

* **1 medium onion (150g), cut into wedges**
* **4 cloves garlic, unpeeled, bruised**
* **2 bay leaves**
* **3 x 10cm (4in) sprigs fresh rosemary**
* **1.6kg (3¼lb) lamb shoulder on the bone**
* **2 teaspoons extra virgin olive oil**
* **1 teaspoon dried oregano leaves**
* **½ cup (125ml) chicken stock**
* **1 medium lemon (140g), cut into wedges**

CHILLI GARLIC BROCCOLINI

* **½ cup (125ml) water**
* **2 fresh long red chillies, halved lengthways**
* **2 cloves garlic, crushed**
* **20g (¾oz) butter**
* **400g (12½oz) broccolini, trimmed**

1 Preheat oven to 160°C/325°F. Oil the base of a large oven tray. Place onion, garlic, bay leaves and rosemary, then lamb on tray. Rub lamb with oil and scatter with oregano. Season well.

2 Pour stock into base of tray; cover tray tightly with foil. Roast lamb for 5 hours.

3 Increase oven to 200°C/400°F. Remove foil from lamb. Skim fat from the liquid and discard. Spoon pan juices over lamb.

4 Roast lamb, uncovered, for a further 10 minutes or until juices are reduced and lamb is browned.

5 Meanwhile, make chilli garlic broccolini.

6 Drizzle lamb with pan juices and serve with broccolini and lemon wedges.

CHILLI GARLIC BROCCOLINI Bring the water, chilli, garlic and butter to the boil in a large saucepan over medium heat. Season. Add broccolini and cook, covered, for 4 minutes or until broccolini is tender and the water is almost evaporated.

Serving suggestion *Roast potato wedges or mashed potato.*

CREAMY PRAWN AND FISH PIE

prep + cook time 1 hour 30 minutes ✻ serves 8

∗ 1 litre (4 cups) milk
∗ 1 medium leek (350g), white part only, sliced thinly
∗ 1 trimmed celery stalk (100g), sliced thinly
∗ 400g (12½oz) skinless firm white fish fillets, cut into 3cm (1¼in) pieces (see tip)
∗ 400g (12½oz) skinless salmon fillets, cut into 3cm (1¼in) pieces
∗ 80g (2½oz) butter
∗ ½ cup (75g) plain (all-purpose) flour
∗ 1 cup (120g) grated cheddar
∗ 400g (12½oz) uncooked peeled medium prawns (shrimp)
∗ 400g (12½oz) smoked fish (such as trout, haddock or cod), skin removed, flaked
∗ 2 tablespoons finely chopped fresh dill
∗ 2 teaspoons finely grated lemon rind
∗ 1 tablespoon lemon juice
∗ 30g (1oz) butter, extra, chopped finely
∗ 2 sprigs fresh dill, extra

MASH
∗ 1.2kg (2½lb) desiree potatoes
∗ ⅓ cup (80ml) warm milk
∗ 90g (3oz) butter, chopped

1 Place milk, leek and celery in a large saucepan over medium heat; bring to a simmer. Add fish, then simmer over low heat for 10 minutes or until fish is just cooked through. Strain milk mixture into a large bowl; reserve. Transfer fish and vegetables to a medium bowl.
2 Meanwhile, make mash.
3 Preheat oven to 180°C/350°F.
4 Heat butter in cleaned saucepan over medium-high heat. Add flour and cook, stirring, until mixture thickens and bubbles. Gradually add reserved milk; whisk until mixture boils and thickens. Add cheese and stir until smooth. Add cooked fish, prawns, smoked fish, dill, lemon rind and juice; stir to combine. Season. Remove from heat.
5 Transfer fish mixture to a 3-litre (12-cup) ovenproof dish. Top evenly with mash. Using the back of a spoon, swirl mash in a decorative pattern. Dot with extra butter.
6 Bake pie for 45 minutes or until heated through and mash is golden. Serve topped with extra dill.

MASH Boil, steam or microwave potatoes until tender; drain. Mash potato with warmed milk and butter in a large bowl until smooth. Season to taste.

Tip *We used flathead for the firm white fish fillets.*

Do ahead *Pie can be made to the end of step 4 up to 6 hours ahead.*

FALL-APART STICKY LAMB RIBLETS

prep + cook time 4 hours (+ refrigeration) * serves 4

- **4 x 800g (1½lb) lamb riblets (see tip), trimmed, skin off**
- **¼ cup chopped fresh thyme leaves**
- **4 cloves garlic, crushed**
- **1 tablespoon ground cinnamon**
- **1 tablespoon ground cumin**
- **⅔ cup (160ml) whiskey**
- **½ cup (110g) firmly packed brown sugar**
- **2 tablespoons white wine vinegar**
- **2 teaspoons chilli flakes**

1 Place lamb in a glass or ceramic ovenproof dish. Score lamb lightly with a sharp knife.

2 Combine thyme, garlic, spices and whiskey in a medium bowl; rub all over lamb. Cover with plastic wrap and refrigerate for 3 hours.

3 Preheat oven to 160°C/325°F. Line two medium roasting pans with baking paper. Place lamb on wire racks in pans. Cover pans tightly with foil.

4 Roast lamb for 3 hours or until very tender, swapping pans halfway through cooking time. Remove foil and cool slightly.

5 Increase oven to 180°C/350°F. Cut lamb between bones to separate riblets. Rub lamb with combined brown sugar, vinegar and chilli. Return lamb to oven for a further 30 minutes or until caramelised. Season with salt flakes to serve.

tip *Lamb riblets are from the area near the lamb shoulder, above the part that forms a rack of lamb. They are available from the butcher.*

Serving suggestion *Sweet potato wedges and a crisp green salad.*

CHICKEN AND GREEN OLIVE TRAY BAKE

prep + cook time 1 hour 35 minutes ✻ serves 4

- **12 chicken drumsticks (1.8kg) (see tips)**
- **2 tablespoons extra virgin olive oil**
- **½ teaspoon ground white pepper**
- **1 medium lemon (140g)**
- **4 fresh rosemary sprigs**
- **18 baby potatoes (750g)**
- **6 cloves garlic, bruised**
- **2 teaspoons sumac (see tips)**
- **250g (8oz) truss cherry tomatoes**
- **½ cup (75g) green sicilian olives**
- **½ cup (40g) flaked almonds, toasted**
- **½ cup fresh oregano leaves (see tips)**

1 Preheat oven to 180°C/350°F.
2 Place chicken, oil and pepper in a large bowl. Season with salt and toss to combine.
3 Finely grate rind of half the lemon into a small bowl. Peel remaining rind thickly from lemon with a sharp knife so no white pith remains; discard pith. Thinly slice lemon and remove seeds.
4 Line a large deep roasting pan with baking paper. Place lemon slices and rosemary sprigs in pan, then top with potatoes, garlic and chicken. Sprinkle with sumac. Roast for 50 minutes.
5 Add tomatoes and olives to pan. Turn chicken and potatoes; roast for a further 30 minutes or until chicken and potatoes are cooked through.
6 Meanwhile, add almonds to lemon rind and crush lightly. Stir in oregano.
7 Serve chicken and roasted vegetables topped with the almond mixture.

Tips *You could also use 8 chicken thigh cutlets instead of the drumsticks, if you prefer. If you don't have sumac, use sweet paprika instead. Swap oregano for parsley or basil.*

Serving suggestion *Crusty bread and a mixed leaf salad.*

ROAST CHICKEN WITH ALMONDS, SAGE AND SOURDOUGH

prep + cook time 2 hours * serves 4

*** ½ cup (80g) roasted natural almonds, chopped coarsely**
*** 4 fresh sage leaves**
*** 1 teaspoon finely grated lemon rind**
*** 2 cloves garlic, chopped coarsely**
*** ⅓ cup (80ml) extra virgin olive oil**
*** 1.8kg (3½lb) whole chicken**
*** ½ bunch celery (750g), pale inner leaves reserved**
*** 300g (9½oz) sourdough bread**
*** 4 baby parsnips (480g), halved lengthways**
*** 1 bunch (400g) baby heirloom carrots, trimmed leaving 1cm (½in) stalk**
*** 2 cups (500ml) chicken stock**
*** 40g (1½oz) butter, chopped**

ALMOND GREMOLATA
*** ¾ cup (120g) finely chopped roasted natural almonds**
*** 1 clove garlic, crushed**
*** 1 tablespoon finely grated lemon rind**
*** ½ cup finely chopped fresh flat-leaf parsley**

1 Preheat oven to 200°C/400°F. Oil a large roasting dish.

2 Blend or process almonds, sage, rind, garlic and 1½ tablespoons of the oil until a coarse paste forms; season.

3 Pat chicken dry with paper towel. Spread almond mixture evenly over chicken. Place chicken in dish and season.

4 Place celery around chicken. Tear sourdough into 4cm (1½in) pieces. Place bread around chicken and drizzle with remaining oil.

5 Place parsnip, carrot and stock in another large roasting pan, then top with butter. Season. Roast chicken, sourdough and vegetables for 1¼ hours or until chicken is cooked through. Remove dish with chicken from oven. Place sourdough in one bowl and celery in another; cover to keep warm. Turn chicken over so it is breast-side down and cover with foil. Continue to roast parsnip and carrot for a further 20 minutes or until golden and tender.

6 Make almond gremolata.

7 Serve chicken with sourdough and vegetables, topped with almond gremolata.

ALMOND GREMOLATA Combine ingredients in a small bowl.

BEEF AND MUSHROOM PIE

prep + cook time 2 hours 45 minutes * serves 4

- **30g (1oz) butter**
- **900g (1¾lb) beef brisket, cut into 3cm (1¼in) pieces (see tips)**
- **¼ cup (35g) plain (all-purpose) flour**
- **¼ cup (60ml) soy sauce**
- **½ cup (125ml) mirin**
- **½ cup (125ml) sake**
- **1¼ cups (310ml) water**
- **100g (3oz) oyster mushrooms, halved (see tips)**
- **100g (3oz) shiitake mushrooms, quartered (see tips)**
- **1 sheet puff pastry**
- **1 egg**
- **1 egg yolk**
- **½ teaspoon black sesame seeds**
- **½ teaspoon white sesame seeds**

1 Preheat oven to 160°C/325°F.

2 Melt butter in a large dutch oven or other flameproof casserole dish over high heat. Cook beef, in batches, stirring, until browned.

3 Return beef to dish, sprinkle with flour and stir to combine. Gradually stir in soy sauce, mirin, sake and the water until smooth. Cook, covered, in oven for 2 hours or until beef is tender.

4 Increase oven temperature to 200°C/400°F.

5 Add mushrooms to dish and stir to combine. Season. Transfer mixture to a 22cm (9in) pie dish or tin (1-litre/4-cup). Cover dish with pastry. Brush pastry with combined egg and egg yolk. Sprinkle with sesame seeds.

6 Bake pie for 15 minutes or until pastry is browned and filling is heated through.

Tips *You can also use beef chuck steak or gravy beef (boneless shin) instead of the brisket. You can use button, flat or swiss brown mushrooms, if you prefer.*

Do ahead *Filling can be made to the end of step 3 a day ahead and refrigerated. Warm the filling gently before covering with the pastry.*

200

OVEN

ROASTS & BAKES

TWICE-ROASTED DUCK
WITH RHUBARB AND GINGER RELISH

prep + cook time 2 hours (+ cooling) * serves 4

*** 2kg (4lb) whole duck, wings tucked under**
*** 1 large onion (200g), unpeeled, sliced thickly**
*** 6 small floury potatoes (800g), peeled, halved (see tips)**
*** 4 sprigs fresh thyme**

RHUBARB & GINGER RELISH
*** 600g (1¼lb) rhubarb**
*** 20g (¾oz) fresh ginger, julienned**
*** ¾ cup (165g) firmly packed brown sugar**
*** ¼ cup (60ml) red wine vinegar**
*** 10 sprigs fresh thyme**

1 Preheat oven to 200°C/400°F. Pat duck dry inside and out with paper towel. Prick skin all over with a skewer. Season duck all over, inside and out.
2 Place onion in a medium roasting pan; top with duck, breast-side up. Roast for 1 hour, turning halfway through cooking, or until skin is golden brown all over and duck is just cooked through. Remove duck from pan. Reserve ½ cup of the rendered duck fat and the onion slices. Cool duck for 30 minutes. Tip juices out of duck cavity into a small bowl.
3 Meanwhile, boil potatoes in a saucepan of salted water for 15 minutes or until just tender. Drain and return to the pan. Shake pan vigorously to roughen surface of potatoes.
4 Meanwhile, make rhubarb and ginger relish.
5 Place duck on a chopping board. Cut in half lengthways through the breastbone and along both sides of the backbone; discard backbone (see tips).
6 Pour reserved duck fat into a large clean roasting pan; heat in oven for 5 minutes. Add potatoes and spoon hot fat over to coat. Season well. Roast potatoes for 30 minutes, turning occasionally.
7 Transfer duck halves, skin-side up, to pan with potatoes. Turn potatoes. Roast for 20 minutes or until duck skin and potatoes are golden and crisp. Add onion slices and roast for a further 2 minutes or until onion is hot.
8 Cut duck into quarters and serve with potatoes, onion and relish. Scatter with thyme.

RHUBARB & GINGER RELISH Wash rhubarb stalks and cut into 5cm (2in) lengths on the diagonal. Place rhubarb in a small ovenproof dish with remaining ingredients; toss to coat. Stand for 15 minutes. Bake rhubarb mixture on a separate oven shelf to the duck for 10 minutes. Stir gently and bake for a further 8 minutes or until rhubarb is just tender. Remove from oven. Cool without stirring.

Tips *Use a floury potato such as king edward or sebago to get the best crisp roast potatoes. Duck bones and backbone can be used to make stock.*

Serving suggestion *Steamed asparagus, green beans or a crisp green salad.*

RABBIT WITH
FENNEL AND ROSEMARY

prep + cook time 2 hours 30 minutes * serves 4

- **1.5kg (2¾lb) whole rabbit (see tip)**
- **2 tablespoons plain (all-purpose) flour**
- **¼ cup (60ml) olive oil**
- **1 teaspoon fennel seeds**
- **2 medium onions (300g), sliced**
- **2 cloves garlic, sliced thinly**
- **150g (4½oz) speck, cut into batons**
- **¾ cup (180ml) dry white wine**
- **2 tablespoons white wine vinegar**
- **400g (12½oz) can cherry tomatoes**
- **1 tablespoon chopped fresh rosemary leaves**
- **400g (12½oz) cherry truss tomatoes**
- **2 tablespoons chopped fresh flat-leaf parsley**

1 Preheat oven to 180°C/350°F.

2 Cut rabbit into eight pieces; discard belly section of ribcage and backbone. Season flour. Toss rabbit pieces in flour and shake away the excess; reserve remaining flour.

3 Heat 2 tablespoons of the oil in a roasting pan or dutch oven over medium-high heat. Cook rabbit, in batches, for 2 minutes each side or until golden. Remove from pan.

4 Heat remaining oil in same pan over medium-high heat. Cook fennel seeds, onion, garlic and speck, stirring, for 4 minutes or until starting to brown.

5 Add reserved flour and cook, stirring, for 1 minute. Stir in wine and half the vinegar; simmer for 3 minutes or until reduced by half. Add canned tomatoes and rosemary; bring to the boil. Season to taste.

6 Return rabbit to pan and stir gently. Cover tightly with lid or foil. Roast for 1 hour 35 minutes or until tender.

7 Add truss tomatoes and roast, uncovered, for a further 15 minutes or until tomatoes just start to soften.

8 Stir in remaining vinegar. Season to taste. Serve rabbit topped with parsley.

Tip *Ask the butcher to cut the rabbit into pieces, if you like.*

Do ahead *Rabbit can be cooked to the end of step 6 a day ahead and refrigerated. Add the truss tomatoes when reheating.*

Serving suggestion *Soft polenta or mashed potato.*

COFFEE AND CARDAMOM BRISKET

prep + cook time 5 hours 30 minutes (+ overnight refrigeration) * serves 6

You will need to start this recipe the day before.

* **2 teaspoons cumin seeds**
* **2 teaspoons coriander seeds**
* **½ teaspoon cardamom seeds**
* **2 tablespoons ground coffee**
* **2 teaspoons brown sugar**
* **1.5kg (3lb) beef brisket, trimmed**
* **1 cup (250ml) beef stock**
* **1 tablespoon lime juice**
* **½ teaspoon sea salt flakes**
* **1 teaspoon caster (superfine) sugar**
* **1 small red onion (100g), sliced thinly**
* **½ cup (50g) walnuts, roasted, chopped**
* **100g (3oz) persian fetta, crumbled**

1 Place seeds in a small frying pan over medium heat; stir for 1 minute or until fragrant. Using a mortar and pestle or small blender, pound or blend toasted seeds to a powder. Place 1 teaspoon of the spice mix and 1 teaspoon of the coffee in a small bowl; reserve for serving. Add remaining coffee and the brown sugar to the remaining spice mix; season.

2 Rub spice mix over beef in a large bowl. Cover and refrigerate overnight.

3 Preheat oven to 150°C/300°F. Oil a medium roasting pan. Place beef and stock in pan; cover with foil. Roast beef for 5 hours, turning pan halfway through cooking time, or until beef is very tender (beef should be falling apart and easy to shred with two forks).

4 Meanwhile, to make pickled onion, combine juice, salt and caster sugar in a small bowl. Add onion and mix well. Stand for 10 minutes, then drain.

5 Slice then coarsely shred brisket. Serve sprinkled with reserved spice mix, topped with pickled onions, walnuts and fetta.

Tip *The spice rub will look very dark once roasted due to the coffee; however, it will not taste burnt.*

Do ahead *The rub can be made in a large quantity and stored in an airtight container at room temperature for up to 3 months.*

Serving suggestion *Serve with roast pumpkin and a green salad. Leftovers make a delicious sandwich filling with smoky hot or barbecue sauce.*

BEEF RIB ROAST WITH SPICED SALT AND ROASTED ONIONS

prep + cook time 1 hour 50 minutes (+ standing) * serves 8

- **1 tablespoon coriander seeds**
- **1 tablespoon cumin seeds**
- **½ cup (60g) sea salt flakes**
- **¼ teaspoon mixed spice**
- **1 teaspoon freshly ground pepper**
- **3kg (6lb) beef standing rib roast**
- **1 tablespoon olive oil**
- **1 cup (300g) aïoli**

ROASTED ONIONS

- **2 large onions (400g), halved crossways**
- **4 small red onions (400g), quartered**
- **2 bulbs garlic, halved crossways**
- **¼ cup (60ml) olive oil**

1 Preheat oven to 200°C/400°F.

2 Using a mortar and pestle, grind the seeds together until coarsely crushed. Add salt, mixed spice and pepper; mix well. Remove a third of the spiced salt mixture; reserve. Tie beef between ribs with kitchen string. Place beef in a roasting pan, brush with oil and rub with remaining spiced salt mixture.

3 Roast beef for 1½ hours for rare or until cooked as desired (see tip). Rest, covered loosely with foil, for 15 minutes.

4 Meanwhile, make roasted onions.

5 Place reserved spiced salt mixture in a small frying pan; stir over low heat for 1 minute or until fragrant. Cool.

6 Serve beef and onions with aïoli and spiced salt mix, scattered with micro herbs, if you like.

ROASTED ONIONS Place onions and garlic in a roasting pan; drizzle with oil and toss gently. Season. Roast in oven for the last 45 minutes of beef cooking time or until onion is golden and caramelised.

Tip *To test if beef is cooked to your liking, insert a meat thermometer into the centre of the thickest part, not touching any bones. The internal temperature should reach 55°C/130°F for rare, 60°C/140°F for medium-rare, 65°C/150°F for medium and 70°C/158°F for well-done.*

SPANISH-STYLE LEG OF LAMB

prep + cook time 1 hour 45 minutes (+ refrigeration & standing) * serves 10

* **2.2kg (4½lb) easy-carve leg of lamb**
* **1 cured chorizo (170g), chopped**
* **5 cloves garlic, halved**
* **1 tablespoon sweet paprika**
* **1 tablespoon olive oil**
* **½ cup (125ml) dry sherry**
* **2 teaspoons coarsely chopped fresh thyme**

1 Place lamb in a large ovenproof dish. Pierce lamb deeply all over with a sharp knife. Push chorizo and garlic into cuts.

2 Combine paprika, oil and sherry in a small bowl; rub mixture all over lamb. Cover and refrigerate for 3 hours or overnight, turning lamb occasionally in the marinade.

3 Preheat oven to 200°C/400°F.

4 Drain lamb and discard marinade. Place lamb in a large roasting pan. Scatter with thyme. Roast for 1½ hours for medium or until cooked to your liking (see tips). Remove lamb from oven and rest, covered loosely with foil, for 15 minutes before serving.

Tips *The lamb can also be cooked in a covered barbecue, using indirect heat, following the manufacturer's instructions. To test if lamb is cooked to your liking, insert a meat thermometer into the centre of the thickest part, not touching any bones. The internal temperature should reach 60°C/140°F for rare, 60°C–65°C/140°F–150°F for medium-rare, 65°C–70°C/150°F–158°F for medium and 70°C/158°F for medium-well done.*

Serving suggestion *Steamed snow peas and chargrilled lemon halves.*

CASSEROLES

LAMB TAGINE
WITH CHERMOULA

prep + cook time 3 hours 45 minutes ✻ serves 6

*** ¼ cup (60ml) olive oil**
*** 2kg (4lb) boneless lamb shoulder, cut into 5cm (2in) pieces (see tip)**
*** 3 cloves garlic, peeled**
*** 2 dried long red chillies**
*** 800g (1½lb) tomatoes, cored, chopped coarsely**
*** 1 litre (4 cups) chicken stock**
*** 1 cup (250ml) water**
*** ¼ cup (90g) honey**
*** ½ cup (75g) dried apricots, halved**
*** ⅓ cup (55g) natural almonds, toasted, chopped coarsely**
*** ⅓ cup fresh coriander (cilantro) leaves**

CHERMOULA
*** 2 cups chopped fresh coriander (cilantro) leaves, stalks and roots**
*** 2 teaspoons ground cumin**
*** 1 clove garlic, chopped**
*** ½ teaspoon ground turmeric**
*** ¼ cup (60ml) olive oil**
*** 1 tablespoon lemon juice**

1 Preheat oven to 180°C/350°F.
2 Make chermoula.
3 Heat 1 tablespoon of the oil in a dutch oven or other heavy-based casserole dish over high heat. Season lamb with salt and pepper. Cook one-third of the lamb for 5 minutes, turning occasionally, until browned all over. Repeat two more times with remaining oil and lamb.
4 Return lamb to dish with garlic, chillies, tomato, stock, the water, honey and half the chermoula; bring to the boil. Cover and bake in oven for 2 hours. Add apricots and bake, covered, for a further 1 hour or until lamb is tender. Season.
5 Remove lamb and apricots from dish; cover loosely to keep warm. Strain sauce, discarding solids. Return strained sauce to dish. Bring to the boil over high heat. Simmer for 15 minutes or until sauce is reduced and thickened slightly. Return lamb and apricots to dish; heat until warmed through.
6 Serve lamb mixture topped with remaining chermoula, almonds and coriander.

CHERMOULA Process or blend ingredients until smooth. Season to taste.

Tip *You can also make the tagine with beef chuck steak, if you prefer.*

Serving suggestion *Steamed couscous or rice and flat bread.*

Do ahead *Tagine can be made up to 3 days ahead and refrigerated. Chermoula can be made a day ahead; cover surface directly with plastic wrap to seal, then refrigerate.*

neck
12cts
chuck
228 lbs.
13 cts.
brisket
shin
32 lbs
14cts.
GreenBeeKC

RED WINE BEEF STEW
WITH PARMESAN DUMPLINGS

prep + cook time 2 hours 30 minutes * serves 6

- **2 tablespoons olive oil**
- **350g (11oz) piece flat pancetta, cut into 1cm (½in) thick matchsticks**
- **2 medium red onions (340g), cut into thick wedges**
- **1kg (2lb) beef chuck steak, trimmed, cut into 3cm (1¼in) pieces**
- **2 cloves garlic, chopped finely**
- **1 medium carrot (120g), chopped coarsely**
- **2 trimmed celery stalks (200g), sliced thickly**
- **400g (12½oz) can diced tomatoes**
- **2 cups (500ml) dry red wine**
- **2 fresh bay leaves**
- **10g (½oz) finely grated parmesan**

PARMESAN DUMPLINGS

- **1 cup (150g) plain (all-purpose) flour**
- **1 cup (150g) self-raising flour**
- **⅓ cup (10g) finely grated parmesan**
- **125g (4oz) butter, chilled**
- **½ cup (125ml) chilled water, approximately**

1 Preheat oven to 160°C/325°F. Heat oil in a dutch oven or other flameproof casserole dish over medium heat. Add pancetta and onion; cook, stirring, for 2 minutes or until pancetta is golden. Remove pancetta and onion with a slotted spoon.

2 Increase heat to high. Cook beef, in batches, for 3 minutes or until browned all over. Return beef and pancetta mixture to dish. Add garlic, carrot, celery, canned tomatoes, wine and bay leaves; bring to a simmer. Cover and transfer to the oven. Cook for 1½ hours or until beef is almost tender. Season to taste.

3 Meanwhile, make parmesan dumplings.

4 Increase oven to 180°C/350°F. Place dumplings on stew, then scatter with parmesan. Return to oven, uncovered, for 30 minutes or until dumplings are cooked through and browned lightly.

PARMESAN DUMPLINGS Sift flours into a bowl. Stir in parmesan. Coarsely grate butter into bowl; rub in butter with your fingertips. Using a flat-bladed knife, cut enough of the water through flour mixture to just bring it together (see tip). Roll dough into 16 balls.

Tip *Handle dumpling dough as little as possible to keep the texture light and fluffy.*

Do ahead *This recipe can be made to the end of step 2 up to 2 days ahead and refrigerated. Reheat stew, then continue from step 3.*

Suitable to freeze *at the end of step 2.*

LAMB SHANK AND BEAN RAGÙ

prep + cook time 3 hours (+ standing) * serves 4

You will need to start this recipe the day before.

* ½ cup (100g) dried haricot beans
* ½ cup (100g) dried borlotti beans
* 2 tablespoons plain (all-purpose) flour
* 8 french-trimmed lamb shanks (2.4kg) (see tip)
* 2 tablespoons olive oil
* 1 large onion (200g), chopped finely
* 1 medium carrot (120g), chopped finely
* 1 stalk celery (150g), trimmed, chopped coarsely
* 2 cloves garlic, crushed
* 1 fresh long red chilli, chopped finely
* ¼ cup (60ml) balsamic vinegar
* 400g (12½oz) can crushed tomatoes
* 8 anchovies
* 1 cinnamon stick
* 2 sprigs fresh rosemary
* ½ cup (125ml) dry red wine
* 2 cups (500ml) water
* ⅓ cup fresh flat-leaf parsley leaves

1 Place dried beans in a large bowl with enough cold water to cover; stand for 8 hours or overnight.
2 Drain soaked beans and rinse under cold water; drain. Place beans in a medium saucepan with enough water to cover; bring to the boil. Reduce heat and simmer for 15 minutes; drain (beans will not be fully cooked at this stage).
3 Preheat oven to 180°C/350°F.
4 Place flour in a medium bowl; season with salt and pepper. Toss lamb in flour and shake away excess. Heat half the oil in a large dutch oven or other flameproof casserole dish over medium heat. Cook lamb, in batches, turning, until browned all over. Remove from dish and wipe clean, if necessary.
5 Heat remaining oil in dish over medium heat. Cook onion, carrot, celery, garlic and chilli, stirring, for 5 minutes or until onion softens.
6 Return lamb to dish with beans, vinegar, canned tomatoes, anchovies, cinnamon, rosemary, wine and the water; bring to the boil. Cook, covered, in oven for 1 hour, turning shanks halfway through cooking time. Uncover and cook for a further 1 hour or until meat is almost falling off the bone.
7 Just before serving, stir parsley through ragù.

Tip *You can also use 1.2kg (2lb) diced boneless lamb shoulder instead of shanks, if you prefer.*

Serving suggestion *Crusty bread, soft polenta or mashed potato and steamed broccoli.*

CINNAMON AND ORANGE-BRAISED LAMB WITH PUMPKIN

prep + cook time 3 hours 10 minutes ✻ serves 6

*** 1 medium orange (200g)**
*** ¼ cup (60ml) extra virgin olive oil**
*** 2kg (4lb) lamb neck chops (about 20)**
*** ⅓ cup (50g) plain (all-purpose) flour, seasoned**
*** 1 large onion (200g), chopped**
*** 5 cloves garlic, crushed**
*** 2 cinnamon sticks**
*** 2 tablespoons tomato paste**
*** 1.5 litres (6 cups) beef stock**
*** 1.5kg (2¾lb) jap pumpkin, cut into 4cm (1½in) wedges**
*** 150g (4½oz) goat's cheese, crumbled**
*** ⅓ cup (45g) chopped pistachios**
*** 8 sprigs lemon thyme, to serve (optional)**

1 Preheat oven to 150°C/300°F.
2 Using a vegetable peeler, peel six large strips of rind from the orange, avoiding the white pith; reserve the rind. Using a sharp knife, cut all remaining pith from the orange. Cut between membranes, over a bowl to catch any juice, releasing segments.
3 Heat 2 tablespoons of the oil in an 8-litre (16-cup) dutch oven or other heavy-based casserole dish over high heat. Dust lamb in flour to coat; shake away excess. Cook lamb, in batches, for 3 minutes each side or until well browned. Remove from pan.
4 Add onion to pan. Cook over medium heat, stirring occasionally, for 3 minutes or until onion softens. Add garlic, cinnamon, tomato paste and 3 strips of the orange rind. Cook for a further 3 minutes.
5 Return lamb and any resting juices to pan. Cook, stirring to coat, for 2 minutes or until tomato paste has darkened slightly. Add stock and bring to the boil, then cover.
6 Bake lamb for 2½ hours, turning once during cooking, or until lamb is tender.
7 Place pumpkin on a baking-paper-lined oven tray and drizzle with remaining oil; season. Roast pumpkin on a separate oven shelf to the lamb, turning once during cooking, for the last 1½ hours of the lamb cooking time. Skim fat from surface of lamb and discard. Transfer lamb to a bowl and keep warm.
8 Bring sauce to the boil and simmer for 20 minutes or until thickened; season to taste. Return lamb to pan to heat through.
9 Transfer lamb and pumpkin to a serving dish; spoon over sauce. Top with orange segments, goat's cheese, pistachios and remaining orange rind. Scatter with lemon thyme sprigs.

Do ahead *Braised lamb can be made to the end of step 6 a day ahead and refrigerated; skim the fat from the surface before reheating. Roast the pumpkin close to serving.*

BRAISED PORK NECK
AND SHIITAKE MUSHROOMS

prep + cook time 2 hours 30 minutes (+ standing) * serves 4

- **16 dried shiitake mushrooms (30g)**
- **1.5kg (3lb) piece pork neck (scotch fillet roast), fat trimmed**
- **2 tablespoons dark soy sauce**
- **2 tablespoons light soy sauce**
- **5cm (2in) piece fresh ginger, chopped coarsely**
- **2 cloves garlic, chopped**
- **10cm (4in) stalk fresh lemon grass, chopped coarsely**
- **4 kaffir lime leaves**
- **2 tablespoons brown sugar**
- **2 whole star anise**
- **1 litre (4 cups) chicken stock**
- **500g (1lb) fresh rice noodles**
- **1 cup fresh coriander (cilantro) leaves**

1 Place mushrooms in a small bowl, cover with warm water and stand for 30 minutes.

2 Place pork, sauces, ginger, garlic, lemon grass, lime leaves, sugar, star anise, drained mushrooms and stock in a saucepan just large enough to hold the pork. Bring to the boil, then reduce heat to low and simmer, covered, for 2 hours, turning occasionally (as liquid won't cover pork completely).

3 Cook noodles in a large saucepan of simmering water for 2 minutes; drain.

4 Transfer pork to a plate, cover and stand for 5 minutes. Discard star anise.

5 Slice pork. Serve on a bed of noodles, drizzled with some of the cooking liquid, topped with mushrooms and coriander.

Serving suggestion *Steamed asian greens, such as pak choy, choy sum or gai lan.*

BRAISED BEEF
WITH PASTA AND LEMON PANGRATTATO

prep + cook time 4 hours 15 minutes ✻ serves 6

You can serve the braised beef with wide noodles cut from lasagne sheets, as pictured, or any long fresh pasta of your choice or large dried pasta shells.

*** 2 tablespoons olive oil**
*** 1.5kg (3lb) piece beef chuck steak**
*** 2 cups (500ml) beef stock**
*** ¾ cup (180ml) sweet sherry**
*** 1 tablespoon finely chopped preserved lemon rind**
*** 50g (1½oz) butter**
*** 6 cloves garlic, sliced thinly**
*** 400g (12½oz) fresh lasagne pasta sheets, cut into wide lengths**
*** 1 small red onion (100g), halved, sliced thinly**

LEMON PANGRATTATO
*** 4 slices day-old sourdough bread, crusts removed**
*** 25g (¾oz) butter, melted**
*** 2 cloves garlic, sliced**
*** ¼ cup chopped mixed soft herbs (flat-leaf parsley, mint, coriander)**
*** 2 teaspoons finely chopped preserved lemon rind**

1 Preheat oven to 160°C/325°F.
2 Heat oil in a flameproof casserole dish over medium-high heat. Cook beef for 5 minutes or until browned all over. Add stock, sherry, preserved lemon rind, butter and garlic. Transfer to oven and cook, covered, for 3¾ hours or until meat falls apart. Remove beef from dish and, using two forks, pull apart into large pieces.
3 Meanwhile, make lemon pangrattato.
4 Skim fat from surface of cooking liquid in the dish. Place dish on stove over low heat. Cook for 15 minutes or until liquid thickens and reduces by half. Return beef pieces to dish. Season to taste.
5 Cook pasta in a large saucepan of boiling salted water for 2 minutes or until just tender; drain.
6 Add pasta and red onion to beef mixture; toss to mix well. Serve topped with pangrattato.

LEMON PANGRATTATO Tear bread into coarse pieces on an oven tray. Drizzle over butter and scatter with garlic; toss to combine. Bake in the oven for the last 15 minutes of beef cooking time or until golden. Stir in herbs and preserved lemon rind.

Tips *This braised beef would also be great in lasagne or soup, or to fill a pie or tacos.*

SLOW-COOKED OXTAIL IN STOUT

prep + cook time 4 hours (+ standing & refrigeration) * serves 8

You will need to start this recipe the day before.

*** 2 tablespoons olive oil**
*** 3kg (6lb) large pieces oxtail**
*** 1 tablespoon cracked black peppercorns**
*** 2 teaspoons sea salt flakes**
*** 2 tablespoons fresh oregano leaves**
*** 2 tablespoons fresh thyme leaves**
*** 6 cloves garlic, peeled**
*** ¾ cup (165g) firmly packed brown sugar**
*** 2 tablespoons coarsely chopped fresh sage leaves**
*** 3 cups (750ml) stout beer**
*** 50g (1½oz) unsalted butter**
*** 16 pickling onions (580g), peeled (see tip)**
*** 1 cup (170g) pitted prunes**

1 Heat half the oil in a large heavy-based frying pan over medium-high heat. Cook oxtail, in batches, for 14 minutes or until browned all over. Transfer oxtail to a large glass bowl; cool.
2 Blend or process peppercorns, salt, oregano, thyme, garlic and sugar to a paste. If it looks too dry, add 3 teaspoons water.
3 Rub paste all over oxtail. Cover and refrigerate overnight.
4 Preheat oven to 160°C/325°F.
5 Place oxtail, any of the rub, sage and stout in a 6-litre (24-cup) dutch oven or heavy-based flameproof roasting pan; bring to the boil. Cover tightly with lid or foil and bake for 1½ hours.
6 Meanwhile, heat butter and remaining oil in a large heavy-based frying pan over medium heat until foaming. Cook onions, stirring, for 5 minutes or until golden.
7 Add onions and prunes to oxtail mixture. Bake, covered, for a further 1½ hours or until oxtail is falling off the bone.
8 Transfer oxtail and onions to a dish; cover to keep warm. Skim off as much fat as possible from the sauce, then boil over high heat for 2 minutes or until reduced by half. Pour sauce over oxtail and onions. Serve.

Tip *If you don't have a dutch oven or heavy-based flameproof roasting pan, use a regular roasting pan to bake in the oven, then pour the sauce into a saucepan to reduce it on the stove.*

Do ahead *Recipe can be made up to 2 days ahead and refrigerated. Skim the solidified fat from the surface before reheating.*

Suitable to freeze *at the end of step 8.*

12

STAR ANISE, SOY AND BEER-BRAISED BEEF SHIN

prep + cook time 3 hours ✻ serves 4

- **1.2kg (2½lb) boneless beef shin**
- **2 tablespoons olive oil**
- **2 large carrots (360g), chopped coarsely**
- **2 medium onions (300g), chopped coarsely**
- **2 trimmed celery stalks (200g), chopped coarsely**
- **1 clove garlic, crushed**
- **4 whole star anise**
- **1 cup (250ml) port or tawny fortified wine (see tips)**
- **2 cups (500ml) beef stock**
- **1½ cups (375ml) stout beer**
- **¼ cup (60ml) soy sauce**
- **2 teaspoons cornflour (cornstarch)**
- **1 tablespoon water**

1 Preheat oven to 160°C/325°F.

2 Trim excess fat from beef; cut beef into eight large chunks. Season. Heat oil in a 4-litre (16-cup) dutch oven or other flameproof casserole dish over medium-high heat. Cook beef, in batches, for 5 minutes or until browned all over. Remove from dish.

3 Add vegetables, garlic and star anise to dish. Cook, stirring, for 4 minutes or until vegetables start to soften. Add port and bring to the boil. Boil for 3 minutes or until liquid is reduced by half. Return beef to dish with stock. Bring back to the boil, skimming off any scum that rises to the surface. Add stout and soy sauce; bring to the boil. Cover dish with a tight-fitting lid (see tips).

4 Cook beef in oven for 2½ hours or until very tender, stirring halfway through cooking time.

5 Remove beef from dish and cover to keep warm. Strain sauce, discarding solids, and return to dish. Bring sauce to the boil over high heat. Stir cornflour and the water in a small bowl until smooth. Stir into sauce and bring to the boil. Boil sauce for 10 minutes or until reduced and thickened. Return beef to dish; stir until heated through. Season to taste.

Tips *Tawny is the Australian name for fortified wine made in the style of port. If the lid of your casserole dish is not tight-fitting, first cover the dish with foil, then cover with the lid.*

Serving suggestion *Mashed potato and steamed green beans.*

CHICKEN, FENNEL AND ONION BRAISE

prep + cook time 1 hour ✻ serves 4

∗ 4 chicken marylands (1.4kg)
∗ 1 tablespoon olive oil
∗ 2 medium red onions (340g), cut into 8 wedges
∗ 2 baby fennel bulbs (260g), trimmed, quartered
∗ 1 medium lemon (140g), cut into 8 wedges
∗ 1 small bulb garlic, halved crossways
∗ 2 large sprigs fresh rosemary
∗ 1 cup (250ml) chicken stock
∗ 2 teaspoons fennel seeds

1 Preheat oven to 200°C/400°F.

2 Cut three small slashes in the thickest part of each maryland; season. Heat oil in a large flameproof roasting pan over medium-high heat. Cook chicken, turning, for 6 minutes or until browned all over. Add remaining ingredients to pan.

3 Transfer pan to oven and cook for 45 minutes or until chicken is cooked through and vegetables are tender.

4 Serve chicken with vegetables and pan juices.

Serving suggestion *Mashed potato or soft polenta.*

OSSO BUCO
WITH SAFFRON RISOTTO

prep + cook time 2 hours 45 minutes * serves 8

- **1 cup (150g) plain (all-purpose) flour**
- **8 x 3cm (1¼in) thick veal osso buco (2kg)**
- **¼ cup (60ml) olive oil**
- **2 medium onions (300g), chopped finely**
- **2 cloves garlic, crushed**
- **4 medium tomatoes (600g), grated coarsely, skin discarded**
- **2 bay leaves**
- **1 cup (250ml) dry white wine**
- **2 cups (500ml) chicken stock**
- **2 teaspoons finely chopped fresh sage**
- **2 teaspoons finely chopped fresh rosemary**
- **2 teaspoons finely chopped fresh thyme**
- **1 cup (250ml) water**

SAFFRON RISOTTO

- **½ teaspoon saffron threads**
- **¾ cup (180ml) dry white wine**
- **3 cups (750ml) chicken stock**
- **3 cups (750ml) water**
- **90g (3oz) butter**
- **1 large onion (200g), chopped finely**
- **2¼ cups (450g) arborio or carnaroli rice (see tip)**
- **¾ cup (60g) finely grated parmesan**

GREMOLATA

- **2 medium lemons (280g)**
- **½ cup finely chopped fresh flat-leaf parsley**
- **1 clove garlic, crushed**

1 Preheat oven to 170°C/340°F.

2 Place flour in a bowl; season with salt and pepper. Coat osso buco in flour and shake away excess. Heat oil in a large flameproof casserole dish over high heat. Cook osso buco for 2 minutes on each side or until browned. Remove from dish.

3 Cook onion in same dish, stirring, over medium-high heat for 5 minutes or until softened. Add garlic, tomato, bay leaves and wine; bring to the boil. Reduce heat to low and cook for 2 minutes. Add stock, herbs and the water. Return osso buco to dish, stirring to mix well. Bring to the boil. Transfer to oven and cook, covered, turning osso buco halfway through cooking time, for 2 hours or until meat is almost falling off the bone.

4 Thirty minutes before osso buco is cooked, make saffron risotto, then gremolata.

5 Spoon risotto into bowls and top with osso buco. Sprinkle with gremolata to serve.

SAFFRON RISOTTO Combine saffron and wine in a small bowl; stand for 5 minutes. Heat stock and the water in a medium saucepan. Melt half the butter in a large heavy-based saucepan over medium heat. Cook onion for 5 minutes or until softened. Add rice and stir for 1 minute to coat in mixture. Add wine mixture and cook, stirring, for 3 minutes or until liquid almost evaporates. Stir in 1 cup of hot stock mixture; cook, stirring, over low heat until liquid is absorbed. Continue adding stock mixture in 1-cup quantities, stirring until liquid is absorbed after each addition. Cook for 25 minutes in total or until all stock is absorbed and rice is tender. Remove from heat. Stir in parmesan and remaining butter; season.

GREMOLATA Remove rind from lemons with a zester and cut into thin strips (or finely grate). Combine with remaining ingredients in a bowl.

Tip *There are different types of risotto rice and each absorbs liquid differently. Take care with arborio as it is easily overcooked, while carnaroli is more forgiving.*

GINGER-BEER-BRAISED PORK HOCKS

prep + cook time 3 hours 45 minutes ✻ serves 4

- **4 french-trimmed pork hocks, rind removed (4kg)**
- **3 cups (750ml) ginger beer**
- **1 medium onion (150g), sliced thinly**
- **6 cloves garlic, peeled**
- **2 sprigs fresh rosemary**
- **½ cup (170g) ginger marmalade**
- **⅓ cup (120g) honey**
- **1 medium lemon (140g), cut into wedges**
- **fresh rosemary sprigs, extra, to serve**

1 Preheat oven to 160°C/325°F.

2 Place pork in an 8-litre (32-cup) dutch oven or other heavy-based casserole dish. Add ginger beer, onion, garlic, rosemary, ginger marmalade and honey. Roast pork, covered, for 3 hours or until tender, spooning braising liquid over the pork occasionally.

3 Remove pork from dish and cover to keep warm. Skim fat from surface. Place dish with braising liquid over high heat and bring to the boil; boil for 20 minutes or until syrupy. (If the pan or dish you are using is not flameproof, transfer the braising liquid to a medium heavy-based saucepan.)

4 Serve pork with sauce and lemon wedges, topped with extra rosemary sprigs.

Serving suggestion *Mashed potato and a crisp green leaf salad.*

MEXICAN CHICKEN WITH BEANS AND CORN

prep + cook time 2 hours 15 minutes * serves 4

- **1.6kg (3¼lb) whole chicken**
- **1 tablespoon olive oil**
- **1 medium onion (150g), sliced thinly**
- **3 cloves garlic, crushed**
- **1 medium red capsicum (bell pepper) (200g), chopped coarsely**
- **1 medium green capsicum (bell pepper) (200g), chopped coarsely**
- **1 corn cob (250g), trimmed, kernels removed (see tip)**
- **2 tablespoons tomato paste**
- **2 teaspoons ground cumin**
- **2 teaspoons dried oregano**
- **1 teaspoon smoked paprika**
- **1 teaspoon dried chilli flakes**
- **400g (12½oz) can diced tomatoes**
- **2 cups (500ml) chicken stock**
- **2 x 400g (12½oz) cans kidney beans, drained, rinsed**
- **½ cup fresh coriander (cilantro) leaves**
- **8 flour tortillas (400g)**
- **sour cream, to serve**

AVOCADO SALSA

- **1 large avocado (320g), chopped coarsely**
- **1 lebanese cucumber (130g), chopped coarsely**
- **125g (4oz) cherry tomatoes, quartered**
- **1 tablespoon lime juice**
- **1 green onion (scallion), sliced thinly**

1 Pat chicken dry, inside and out, with paper towel. Trim excess fat from chicken.

2 Heat oil in a large saucepan over low heat. Cook onion and garlic, stirring, until onion softens. Add capsicums, corn, tomato paste and spices; cook, stirring, for 2 minutes or until fragrant. Add canned tomatoes and stock to the pan. Add chicken and turn to coat in mixture. Bring to the boil, then reduce heat to low and cook, covered, for 1½ hours.

3 Remove chicken from pan. When cool enough to handle, coarsely shred chicken meat; discard skin and bones.

4 Return meat to pan. Add beans, bring to the boil and cook for 3 minutes or until warmed through. Remove from heat. Season to taste.

5 Meanwhile, make avocado salsa.

6 Top chicken mixture with coriander. Serve with avocado salsa, tortillas and sour cream.

AVOCADO SALSA Combine ingredients in a small bowl; season to taste.

Tip *You can use 250g (8oz) of frozen corn kernels, or a rinsed and drained 400g (12½oz) can of corn kernels instead of fresh, if you prefer.*

Suitable to freeze *at the end of step 4.*

MOROCCAN CHICKEN AND CHICKPEA CASSEROLE

prep + cook time 1 hour ✻ serves 4

*** 1.3kg (2¾lb) chicken thigh fillets**
*** 1 tablespoon moroccan spice mix (see tip)**
*** 2 tablespoons olive oil**
*** 400g (12½oz) can chickpeas (garbanzo beans), drained, rinsed**
*** ½ cup (75g) dried apricots**
*** 1 large onion (200g), sliced thinly**
*** 2 x 400g (12½oz) cans crushed tomatoes**
*** ½ cup (125ml) chicken stock**
*** ¾ cup (150g) tri-coloured quinoa, rinsed**
*** ⅓ cup fresh flat-leaf parsley sprigs**

1 Preheat oven to 200°C/400°F.

2 Place chicken and spice mix in a large bowl; rub to coat.

3 Heat half the oil in a large heavy-based frying pan. Cook chicken, in three batches, for 2 minutes each side or until browned. Transfer chicken to a 4-litre (16-cup) ovenproof dish. Add chickpeas and apricots; stir to combine.

4 Heat remaining oil in same frying pan. Cook onion, stirring, for 10 minutes or until softened. Add canned tomatoes and stock; bring to the boil. Carefully pour tomato mixture over chicken mixture, then cover. Transfer to oven and cook for 15 minutes or until chicken is cooked through. Season to taste.

5 Meanwhile, cook quinoa in a large saucepan of boiling water for 12 minutes or until tender; drain.

6 Top casserole with parsley. Serve with quinoa.

Tip *Moroccan spice mixes often contain a mixture of ground cumin, cinnamon, black pepper, coriander, allspice and cayenne pepper.*

ITALIAN OLIVE AND VEAL CASSEROLE

prep + cook time 2 hours 30 minutes ✻ serves 4

*** 1 tablespoon olive oil**
*** 4 thick pieces veal osso buco (1.2kg)**
*** ¾ cup (90g) pitted green olives, chopped coarsely**
*** 1 medium lemon (140g), quartered**
*** 2 cups (520g) bottled tomato pasta sauce**
*** 2 cups (500ml) water**
*** 4 anchovy fillets, chopped coarsely**
*** ½ cup (120g) firm ricotta cheese**
*** ½ cup (40g) finely grated parmesan**
*** ½ cup coarsely chopped fresh flat-leaf parsley**

1 Preheat oven to 160°C/325°F.

2 Heat oil in a small flameproof roasting pan or dutch oven over medium-high heat. Cook veal, turning, for 6 minutes or until browned all over.

3 Add olives, lemon, sauce and the water to pan; season. Roast, covered, for 2 hours (see tips).

4 Increase oven to 200°C/400°F.

5 Stir anchovy into veal mixture. Top with ricotta and scatter with parmesan. Roast, uncovered, for 15 minutes or until cheese is browned. Top with parsley to serve.

Tips *Place a piece of baking paper, cut to fit inside the pan, onto the surface of the food before it goes into the oven. This will stop the food from browning too much. Cover a roasting pan with foil or a dutch oven with a lid or foil.*

CIDER-BRAISED PORK
WITH PANCETTA LENTILS AND APPLES

prep + cook time 3 hours ✻ serves 4

French-style green lentils are related to the famous French lentils du puy. These green-blue tiny lentils have a hardy nature that allows them to be rapidly cooked without disintegrating.

*** 1.5kg (3lb) pork neck (scotch fillet roast)**
*** ⅓ cup (80ml) olive oil**
*** 1 medium leek (350g), white part only, sliced thinly**
*** 2 teaspoons fennel seeds, crushed lightly**
*** 2 teaspoons coriander seeds, crushed lightly**
*** 2⅔ cups (660ml) apple cider**
*** 100g (3oz) pancetta, chopped finely**
*** 1 small onion (80g), chopped finely**
*** 1 small carrot (70g), chopped finely**
*** 1 stalk celery (150g), trimmed, chopped finely**
*** 1 clove garlic, crushed**
*** ¼ cup (60ml) dry white wine**
*** 1 bay leaf**
*** 2 sprigs fresh thyme**
*** 2 cups (500ml) chicken stock**
*** 1½ cups (375ml) water**
*** 1 cup (200g) dried French-style green lentils, rinsed**
*** 4 medium red apples (600g), quartered**

1 Preheat oven to 160°C/325°F.
2 Trim excess fat from pork. Tie pork with kitchen string at 3cm (1¼in) intervals to form a compact shape.
3 Heat 2 tablespoons of the oil in a large flameproof casserole dish over medium-high heat. Cook pork, turning, for 8 minutes or until browned all over. Remove pork from dish.
4 Add leek to dish. Reduce heat to low and cook, stirring, for 5 minutes or until softened. Add seeds and cook, stirring, for 1 minute or until fragrant. Return pork to dish, add cider and bring to the boil. Transfer to oven. Cook, covered, for 2 hours. Remove lid. Turn pork and cook for a further 30 minutes or until very tender.
5 Meanwhile, to make pancetta lentils, heat 1 tablespoon of the oil in a large frying pan over medium heat. Add pancetta, onion, carrot, celery and garlic. Cook, stirring occasionally, for 7 minutes or until vegetables soften. Increase heat to medium-high. Add wine, bay leaf and thyme. Cook for 1 minute or until most of the cooking liquid evaporates. Add stock, the water and lentils; bring to the boil. Reduce heat and simmer, partially covered, for 20 minutes or until lentils are tender. Discard bay leaf and thyme sprigs. Season to taste.
6 Heat remaining oil in a large frying pan over high heat. Add apple and ¾ cup of the pork braising liquid. Bring to the boil and cook for 5 minutes, turning apples halfway through cooking time, or until they are coloured and heated through and braising liquid is reduced by half. Season to taste.
7 Serve pork with apple, any pan juices and pancetta lentils.

VEGETARIAN

EGGPLANT PARMIGIANA

prep + cook time 1 hour 15 minutes * serves 4

- **⅔ cup (160ml) olive oil**
- **1 medium onion (150g), chopped finely**
- **2 cloves garlic, crushed**
- **400g (12½oz) can diced tomatoes**
- **2 cups (560g) bottled passata (or see recipe, page 19)**
- **¼ teaspoon dried chilli flakes**
- **2 medium eggplants (600g), sliced thickly**
- **¼ cup (35g) plain (all-purpose) flour**
- **⅓ cup fresh basil leaves, plus extra to serve**
- **200g (6½oz) bocconcini, sliced thinly**
- **⅔ cup (50g) finely grated vegetarian parmesan-style cheese**
- **½ teaspoon sweet paprika**

1 Preheat oven to 180°C/350°F.

2 Heat 1 tablespoon of the oil in a large frying pan over medium heat. Cook onion, stirring, for 5 minutes until softened. Add garlic and cook, stirring, until fragrant. Stir in canned tomatoes, passata and chilli; season to taste. Transfer mixture to a medium jug.

3 Toss eggplant in flour to coat; shake off excess. Heat remaining oil in same pan. Cook eggplant, in batches, until browned on both sides; drain on paper towel.

4 Layer half the eggplant in an 18cm x 25cm (7¼in x 10in) ovenproof dish; season. Top with half each of the tomato mixture, basil and bocconcini. Repeat layers one more time, then scatter with parmesan. Sprinkle with paprika.

5 Bake, covered, for 30 minutes. Uncover and bake for a further 15 minutes or until browned and tender. Serve topped with extra basil.

Serving suggestion *A rocket (arugula) salad and crusty bread.*

OVEN

VEGETARIAN

SHALLOT TARTE TATIN

prep + cook time 1 hour 30 minutes (+ standing) * serves 6

*** 1kg (2lb) shallots**
*** 50g (1½oz) butter**
*** 1 tablespoon olive oil**
*** 1 tablespoon light brown sugar**
*** 2 teaspoons finely chopped fresh sage leaves**
*** 2 tablespoons balsamic vinegar**
*** 375g (12oz) roll frozen puff pastry, thawed (see tips)**
*** 150g (4½oz) ashed goat's cheese, sliced**
*** fried sage sprigs, to serve (see tips)**

1 Preheat oven to 160°C/325°F. Place shallots in a medium heatproof bowl with enough boiling water to cover and stand for 4 minutes; drain. Slip off skins. Trim roots, leaving the bases intact. Halve large shallots through the root.
2 Heat butter and oil in a 26cm (10½in) (base measurement) ovenproof frying pan over medium heat. Add shallots, sugar and sage; season. Bring to the boil, add vinegar and stir until combined. Reduce heat and simmer, uncovered, for 10 minutes or until lightly caramelised. Cover pan with lid or foil. Transfer pan to oven and bake for 25 minutes or until shallots are almost tender (there should still be some resistance when a small knife is inserted into the centre). Increase oven to 200°C/400°F.
3 Return pan to stove over medium heat and simmer, uncovered, for 10 minutes or until syrupy. Remove pan from heat and cool for 15 minutes.
4 Meanwhile, unroll pastry and cut into a 28cm (11¼in) round.
5 Place pastry over shallots, pushing down and tucking in edges around inside of pan. Return pan to oven and bake for 25 minutes or until pastry is crisp and golden. Remove from oven and stand for 15 minutes. Invert onto a flat round plate or board. Top with goat's cheese and fried sage. Serve.

Tips *You can use two 24cm (9½in) sheets puff pastry instead of the roll; if you do, cut one sheet in half and press the pieces together on two adjoining sides to make one larger sheet.*

To make fried sage sprigs, heat 20g (¾oz) butter or 1 tablespoon olive oil in a small frying pan. Cook a small handful of fresh sage sprigs until they just change colour. Drain on paper towel.

244

OVEN

VEGETARIAN

KALE AND SILVER BEET SPANAKOPITA

prep + cook time 1 hour 30 minutes ✻ makes 6

- **1.5kg (3lb) silver beet (swiss chard), trimmed (see tips)**
- **350g (11oz) green curly kale (see tips)**
- **400g (12½oz) greek fetta, crumbled**
- **10 green onions (scallions), chopped finely (see tips)**
- **½ cup finely chopped fresh dill**
- **¾ cup finely chopped fresh flat-leaf parsley**
- **2 teaspoons finely grated lemon rind**
- **¼ cup (60ml) lemon juice**
- **3 eggs, beaten lightly**
- **80g (2½oz) butter, melted**
- **2 x 375g (12oz) packets fresh fillo pastry**

1 Preheat oven to 180°C/350°F.

2 Trim 4cm (1½in) off the stalk ends from silver beet and kale; discard. Rinse and drain greens, leaving some water clinging. Tear kale leaves from the centre stem. Cut white stalk from silver beet leaves, cutting into the leaf in a v-shape. Finely chop stems and leaves, keeping them separate.

3 Heat a large saucepan over high heat. Cook stems, stirring occasionally, for 10 minutes or until softened. Drain well. Repeat with chopped leaves. When cool enough to handle, squeeze excess water from greens mixture (this will prevent the pies from becoming soggy).

4 Combine greens, fetta, green onion, herbs, rind, juice and eggs in a large bowl; season with freshly ground black pepper.

5 Butter six 12cm x 17cm (4¾in x 6¾in) (2-cup/500ml) oval oven dishes. Butter half a sheet of fillo pastry, fold in half to make a smaller rectangle, then butter top. Place in dish, allowing pastry to overhang edge. Repeat with two more sheets of pastry, stacking them in the dish; you will now have six layers. Place a sixth of the filling into the tin. Brush half a sheet of fillo with melted butter, fold in half crossways, brush with butter, then fold in half again; trim to fit the top of the pie. Place over filling, then fold in and scrunch the overhanging pastry. Brush top of pie with a little more melted butter. Repeat to make five more pies.

6 Sprinkle a little water over each pie; this will prevent the pastry from burning. Bake for 45 minutes or until golden.

Tips *You will need 1 bunch silver beet and 1 bunch green curly kale for this recipe. Trim the green onions so they are 28cm (11¼in) long; discard the tops.*

Serving suggestion *Snow pea tendrils.*

Suitable to freeze *at the end of step 5. Cook them from frozen, increasing the cooking time slightly, until the pastry is golden and the filling is heated through.*

247

OVEN

VEGETARIAN

PUMPKIN AND CHEESY SMOKED BAKED BEANS

prep + cook time 1 hour ✻ serves 4

- **½ cup (125ml) extra virgin olive oil**
- **1 medium red onion (170g), cut into wedges**
- **350g (11oz) jap pumpkin, chopped (see tips)**
- **3 x 400g (12½oz) cans four-bean mix, drained, rinsed**
- **400g (12½oz) can chickpeas (garbanzo beans), drained, rinsed**
- **⅓ cup (65g) chilli in adobo sauce, chopped finely (see tips)**
- **1 tablespoon honey**
- **2 tablespoons barbecue sauce**
- **1 teaspoon dijon mustard**
- **700g (1½lb) bottled passata (or see recipe, page 19)**
- **¾ cup (90g) coarsely grated cheddar**
- **⅓ cup (40g) coarsely grated smoked cheddar**
- **2 cloves garlic, crushed**
- **4 x 110g (3½oz) ciabatta rolls, halved**

1 Preheat oven to 220°C/425°F.

2 Heat 2 tablespoons of oil in a large ovenproof frying pan over high heat. Cook onion and pumpkin, stirring occasionally, for 4 minutes or until onion softens slightly. Add beans, chickpeas, chilli in adobo sauce, honey, barbecue sauce and mustard. Cook, stirring occasionally, for 3 minutes or until heated through. Stir in passata and bring to the boil. Boil for 3 minutes or until thickened slightly; season to taste.

3 Scatter bean mixture with cheeses. Bake for 20 minutes or until cheese is browned lightly.

4 Meanwhile, combine garlic and remaining oil in a small bowl; season. Brush garlic mixture over cut side of rolls. Place rolls on an oven tray. Bake on a separate shelf to the beans for 6 minutes or until golden.

5 Serve baked beans with torn garlic bread.

Tips *You can use potatoes or an orange sweet potato instead of pumpkin in this recipe, if you prefer. Chipotle chilli in adobo sauce can be found in good grocers and delicatessens.*

ROAST WINTER VEGETABLES
WITH CREAMY POLENTA

prep + cook time 1 hour 30 minutes ✻ serves 8

*** 2 medium kohlrabi (1kg), trimmed, quartered**
*** 2 medium turnips (460g), quartered**
*** 800g (1½lb) small orange sweet potatoes, halved lengthways**
*** 400g (12½oz) baby heirloom carrots, trimmed**
*** 2 bulbs garlic, halved crossways**
*** ¼ cup (60ml) extra virgin olive oil**
*** 2 tablespoons red wine vinegar**
*** 1 cup (220g) pesto (see tip)**
*** 120g (4oz) hard goat's cheese, shaved**
*** ¼ cup fresh flat-leaf parsley leaves**

CREAMY POLENTA
*** 1 litre (4 cups) milk**
*** 1 litre (4 cups) vegetable stock**
*** 2 cups (340g) polenta**
*** 1 cup (80g) finely grated vegetarian parmesan-style cheese**
*** 125g (4oz) mascarpone**

1 Preheat oven to 200°C/400°F. Line two large oven trays with baking paper.

2 Place vegetables and garlic in a large bowl. Drizzle with oil and vinegar, season and toss to coat. Divide vegetables between trays. Roast vegetables for 40 minutes or until garlic is tender. Remove garlic and cover to keep warm. Roast remaining vegetables for a further 30 minutes or until tender and golden.

3 Meanwhile, 20 minutes before vegetables are cooked, make creamy polenta.

4 Pour creamy polenta over a large serving platter, then top with vegetables and pesto. Serve immediately, topped with goat's cheese and parsley.

CREAMY POLENTA Bring the milk and stock to the boil in a large saucepan. Gradually add polenta, whisking constantly, until thickened. Reduce heat to low and simmer, stirring often, for 15 minutes or until smooth. Stir in parmesan and mascarpone; season.

Tip *We used bought walnut and parsley pesto, but you can use your favourite style of pesto, if you prefer.*

251

OVEN

VEGETARIAN

ZUCCHINI, BLACK BEAN AND CORN ENCHILADAS

prep + cook time 1 hour 45 minutes * serves 4

*** 3 large zucchini (450g)**
*** ⅓ cup (80ml) olive oil**
*** 2 trimmed corn cobs (500g)**
*** 8 x 20cm (8in) white corn tortillas**
*** 400g (12½oz) can black beans, drained, rinsed**
*** ½ cup fresh coriander (cilantro) leaves**
*** 100g (3oz) fetta**
*** ¼ cup loosely packed fresh oregano leaves**
*** 1 tablespoon fresh oregano, extra**

ENCHILADA SAUCE
*** 2 x 400g (12½oz) cans crushed tomatoes**
*** 1½ cups (375ml) vegetable stock**
*** 2 tablespoons olive oil**
*** 2 tablespoons coarsely chopped fresh oregano**
*** 2 tablespoons apple cider vinegar**
*** 1 medium onion (150g), chopped coarsely**
*** 1 clove garlic, chopped**
*** 1 tablespoon chopped pickled jalapeños**
*** 1 teaspoon ground cumin**
*** 1 teaspoon caster (superfine) sugar**
*** ¼ teaspoon chilli powder**

1 Preheat oven to 180°C/350°F. Line an oven tray with baking paper. Grease a 25cm x 30cm (10in x 12in) ovenproof dish.

2 Cut zucchini in half lengthways, then cut each half into long thin wedges. Place zucchini on tray and drizzle with half the oil. Roast for 30 minutes or until just tender, then chop coarsely.

3 Meanwhile, make enchilada sauce.

4 Brush corn with 1 tablespoon of the oil. Heat a chargrill pan (or grill or barbecue) over medium-high heat. Cook corn, turning occasionally, for 10 minutes or until golden and tender. Cut kernels from cobs; discard cobs.

5 Reheat chargrill pan over medium-high heat. Cook tortillas for 30 seconds each side or until lightly charred. Transfer to a plate and cover to keep warm.

6 Combine zucchini, beans, coriander, half each of the corn, fetta and oregano, and ½ cup enchilada sauce in a large bowl.

7 Divide zucchini filling evenly among warm tortillas and roll to enclose filling. Place tortillas in dish and brush tops with remaining oil. Spoon remaining enchilada sauce over tortillas, leaving 2cm (¾in) at each end of enchiladas uncovered. Top with remaining fetta and oregano.

8 Bake for 30 minutes or until golden and heated through. Serve topped with remaining corn and extra oregano.

ENCHILADA SAUCE Blend or process ingredients until smooth. Transfer to a medium saucepan and bring to a simmer over medium heat for 20 minutes or until thickened slightly.

252

OVEN

VEGETARIAN

CAULIFLOWER MAC 'N' CHEESE

prep + cook time 1 hour * serves 4

*** 750g (1½lb) cauliflower, trimmed, cut into large florets**
*** 1½ tablespoons extra virgin olive oil**
*** 300g (9½oz) short tubular pasta**
*** 100g (3oz) butter, chopped**
*** ½ cup (75g) plain (all-purpose) flour**
*** 3¼ cups (810ml) hot milk**
*** 2 tablespoons wholegrain mustard**
*** ½ cup (60g) coarsely grated cheddar**
*** ¾ cup (60g) finely grated vegetarian parmesan-style cheese**
*** 2 tablespoons panko (japanese) breadcrumbs**

1 Preheat oven to 240°C/475°F. Grease four 2-cup (500ml) ovenproof dishes.

2 Place cauliflower on a large oven tray, drizzle with oil and season; toss well to combine. Roast for 15 minutes or until almost tender and browned. Reduce oven to 200°C/400°F.

3 Meanwhile, cook pasta in a large saucepan of boiling salted water for 6 minutes (or 2 minutes less than directed on the packet, see tip); drain. Return pasta to pan.

4 Meanwhile, melt butter in a medium saucepan over medium heat. Add flour and cook, stirring, until mixture bubbles and thickens. Gradually whisk in milk until smooth; cook, whisking, until mixture boils and thickens. Remove from heat. Stir in mustard, cheddar and two-thirds of the parmesan until cheeses melt. Add cheese sauce to pasta in pan and toss to combine.

5 Spoon pasta mixture into ovenproof dishes, then press cauliflower pieces into pasta. Scatter over combined breadcrumbs and remaining parmesan.

6 Bake for 20 minutes or until crumbs are golden and mixture is heated through.

Tip *Cooking the pasta in boiling water for 2 minutes less than recommended on the packet directions means that it will still be quite firm and will be perfectly cooked once it has spent time in the oven.*

255

OVEN

VEGETARIAN

CAULIFLOWER 'PIZZA' WITH MOZZARELLA AND ZUCCHINI

prep + cook time 1 hour 25 minutes * serves 4

- **1 small cauliflower (1kg), trimmed, cut into florets**
- **¼ cup (30g) coarsely grated cheddar**
- **1 egg, beaten lightly**
- **¾ cup (60g) coarsely grated vegetarian parmesan-style cheese**
- **½ cup (130g) bottled passata (or see recipe, page 19) (see tips)**
- **2 small zucchini (180g), sliced thinly into ribbons**
- **1 cup fresh basil leaves**
- **1 fresh small red (serrano) chilli, sliced thinly**
- **100g (3oz) mozzarella, torn coarsely**
- **1 tablespoon olive oil**
- **1 tablespoon finely grated lemon rind or strips (see tips)**
- **1 tablespoon lemon juice**

1 Preheat oven to 200°C/400°F. Line two oven trays with baking paper and mark a 22cm (8¾in) round on them; turn paper over.

2 Process cauliflower until finely chopped. Place in a microwave-safe bowl, cover with plastic wrap and microwave on HIGH (100%) for 12 minutes or until tender (alternatively, steam cauliflower, but do not boil it as this will make the crust too soggy); drain. When cool enough to handle, place cauliflower in the centre of a clean tea towel, then gather ends together and squeeze excess moisture from cauliflower.

3 Combine cauliflower, cheddar, egg and ¼ cup of the parmesan in a large bowl; season. Shape cauliflower mixture into marked rounds on trays and smooth the surface. Bake for 25 minutes or until golden.

4 Spread bases with passata. Top each base with a quarter each of the zucchini and basil, then the chilli, mozzarella and remaining parmesan. Bake for 20 minutes or until golden and crisp.

5 Meanwhile, combine oil, rind, juice, and remaining zucchini and basil in a medium bowl; season to taste.

6 Serve pizzas topped with zucchini salad.

Tips *Passata is sieved tomato puree. You could use your favourite pasta sauce instead, if you prefer. If you have one, use a zester to create strips of lemon rind. If you don't have one, peel two long, wide strips of rind from the lemon, avoiding the white pith, then cut them lengthways into thin strips.*

4 WAYS WITH GRAINS

LEMON PISTACHIO COUSCOUS

prep + cook time 15 minutes ⁕ Serves 4

Combine 1 cup couscous, ¾ cup boiling water, 2 teaspoons finely grated lemon rind and ¼ cup lemon juice in a heatproof bowl. Cover and stand for 5 minutes or until liquid is absorbed; fluff with a fork. Meanwhile, stir ½ cup pistachios in a frying pan over medium heat until fragrant; chop coarsely. Heat 2 teaspoons olive oil in same pan, then add 1 crushed clove garlic and 1 finely chopped small red onion. Cook, stirring, until onion softens. Fluff couscous again, then stir through pistachios, onion mixture and ½ cup shredded fresh mint.

PINE NUT AND PARSLEY QUINOA

prep + cook time 20 minutes ⁕ serves 4

Place 1 cup quinoa and 2 cups water in a medium saucepan; bring to the boil. Reduce heat to low. Cook, covered, for 12 minutes or until the water is absorbed and quinoa is tender. Stir in ⅓ cup toasted pine nuts, 2 teaspoons finely grated lemon rind, 2 tablespoons lemon juice and ½ cup finely chopped fresh flat-leaf parsley; season to taste.

BASMATI PILAF

prep + cook time 30 minutes ⁕ serves 4

Melt 20g (¾oz) butter in a medium saucepan. Cook 1 crushed clove garlic, stirring, until fragrant. Add 1 cup brown basmati rice and cook, stirring, for 1 minute. Add 1 cup chicken stock and 1 cup water; bring to the boil. Reduce heat to low and simmer, covered, for 20 minutes or until rice is just tender. Remove from heat. Fluff rice with fork. Stir in ¼ cup coarsely chopped fresh flat-leaf parsley and ¼ cup toasted flaked almonds.

COCONUT RICE

prep + cook time 20 minutes ⁕ serves 4

Place 1½ cups jasmine rice, 270ml canned coconut milk, ⅔ cup (160ml) water and 2 teaspoons finely grated fresh ginger in a medium heavy-based saucepan; season with salt and stir well to combine. Cover pan with a lid and bring to the boil over medium heat. Reduce heat to low and cook for 10 minutes. Turn off heat and stand, covered, for a further 5 minutes before removing lid.

CAULIFLOWER AND LENTIL PARMIGIANA

prep + cook time 1 hour ✻ serves 4

∗ 1kg (2lb) cauliflower, cut into 1.5cm (¾in) slices (see tip)
∗ ½ cup (75g) plain (all-purpose) flour, seasoned
∗ 2 eggs, beaten lightly
∗ 1½ cups (90g) panko (japanese) breadcrumbs
∗ ½ cup (40g) finely grated vegetarian parmesan-style cheese
∗ cooking-oil spray
∗ 250g (8oz) cherry tomatoes, halved
∗ 180g (5½oz) bocconcini, torn
∗ ½ cup fresh basil leaves

LENTIL BOLOGNESE
∗ 2 tablespoons olive oil
∗ 1 large onion (200g), chopped finely
∗ 2 cloves garlic, crushed
∗ 2 tablespoons coarsely chopped fresh basil leaves
∗ 1 teaspoon dried oregano leaves
∗ 400g (12½oz) can diced tomatoes
∗ 400g (12½oz) can tomato puree
∗ 400g (12½oz) can brown lentils, drained, rinsed

1 Preheat oven to 200°C/400°F. Line a large oven tray with baking paper.
2 Toss cauliflower slices in flour and shake away excess. Dip in egg, then in combined breadcrumbs and parmesan to coat; place on oven tray. Coat cauliflower liberally with cooking-oil spray. Bake for 30 minutes or until golden brown.
3 Meanwhile, make lentil bolognese.
4 Place cauliflower in a shallow ovenproof dish. Spoon lentil bolognese over cauliflower. Top with cherry tomatoes and bocconcini; season. Bake for 15 minutes or until bocconcini melts. Top with basil to serve.

LENTIL BOLOGNESE Heat oil in a large saucepan over medium heat. Cook onion, stirring, for 5 minutes or until browned lightly. Stir in garlic, herbs, canned tomatoes and tomato puree; simmer for 5 minutes. Add lentils and simmer, covered, for 4 minutes or until sauce thickens; season.

Tip *Because of the shape of a whole cauliflower, you will get irregular-sized slices.*

261

OVEN

VEGETARIAN

VEGETABLE CASSOULET

prep + cook time 1 hour 50 minutes (+ standing) * serves 4

Cassoulet is a slow-cooked French casserole, traditionally containing meat (typically pork sausages, goose, duck or mutton), pork skin (couennes) and white beans (haricots blancs). This is our vegetarian version, topped with crisp herby bread.

*** 2 teaspoons olive oil**
*** 4 shallots (100g), halved**
*** 3 cloves garlic, sliced thinly**
*** 2 medium carrots (240g), chopped coarsely**
*** 200g (6½oz) swiss brown mushrooms, halved**
*** 1 cup (250ml) dry white wine**
*** 2 medium zucchini (240g), chopped coarsely**
*** 1½ cups (375ml) vegetable stock**
*** 700g (1½lb) bottled passata (or see recipe, page 19)**
*** 1 teaspoon finely chopped fresh thyme leaves**
*** 400g (12½oz) can borlotti beans, drained, rinsed**

BREAD TOPPING
*** 1 tablespoon olive oil**
*** 1 small onion (80g), chopped finely**
*** 1 clove garlic, crushed**
*** 2 teaspoons finely grated lemon rind**
*** 2 teaspoons finely chopped fresh thyme leaves**
*** ½ wholegrain and seed sourdough loaf (220g), torn into 2cm (¾in) pieces**
*** 2 tablespoons coarsely chopped fresh flat-leaf parsley**

1 Preheat oven to 180°C/350°F.

2 Heat oil in a large flameproof casserole dish over medium-high heat. Cook shallots, garlic, carrot and mushrooms, stirring, for 5 minutes or until vegetables are just tender. Add wine and bring to the boil; boil until liquid is reduced by half. Add zucchini, stock, passata, thyme and beans; return to the boil. Remove from heat. Transfer to oven. Cook, covered, for 50 minutes.

3 Meanwhile, make bread topping.

4 Season cassoulet to taste and scatter with bread topping. Return to oven and cook, uncovered, for 10 minutes or until bread topping is browned.

BREAD TOPPING Heat oil in a large frying pan over medium-high heat. Cook onion, stirring, for 5 minutes or until soft. Add garlic, rind, thyme and bread; cook, stirring, for 10 minutes or until bread browns lightly. Stir in parsley.

Serving suggestion *A bitter leaf salad.*

POTATO AND OLIVE-FILLED BANANA CHILLIES

prep + cook time 1 hour 40 minutes * serves 4

*** 40g (1½oz) butter**
*** 2 tablespoons olive oil**
*** 3 cloves garlic, crushed**
*** 2 teaspoons ground cumin**
*** 2 teaspoons dried oregano**
*** 600g (1¼lb) potatoes, cut into 1cm (½in) pieces**
*** 3 large tomatoes (660g), cut into 1cm (½in) pieces**
*** 1 cup (120g) pitted green olives, chopped coarsely**
*** 2 cups (240g) coarsely grated cheddar**
*** 8 red or yellow banana chillies (1.3kg) (see tip)**
*** 50g (1½oz) watercress**
*** ⅓ cup fresh oregano leaves**

TOMATO SAUCE
*** 1 tablespoon olive oil**
*** 1 medium red onion (170g), chopped coarsely**
*** 1 clove garlic, crushed**
*** 1 tablespoon ground cumin**
*** 2 teaspoons dried oregano**
*** 2 x 400g (12½oz) cans diced tomatoes**
*** ½ cup (125ml) water**

1 Preheat oven to 180°C/350°F.
2 Heat butter and oil in a large frying pan over medium-high heat. Cook garlic, cumin, dried oregano and potato, stirring occasionally, for 10 minutes or until potato is browned. Add tomato and olives; cook, stirring, for 10 minutes or until liquid evaporates. Transfer to a large bowl to cool. Stir in cheddar.
3 Meanwhile, using a sharp knife, make a small horizontal cut in each chilli 1cm (½in) below the stem, then make a lengthways slit, starting from the horizontal cut and ending 1cm (½in) from tip, taking care not to cut all the way through. Discard membrane and seeds. Carefully divide filling among chillies.
4 Make tomato sauce.
5 Pour tomato sauce into a small ovenproof dish, then position chillies on sauce. Cover and bake for 40 minutes or until chillies are tender. Serve chillies topped with watercress and fresh oregano.

TOMATO SAUCE Heat oil in a large saucepan over medium-high heat. Cook onion, garlic, cumin and oregano, stirring, for 5 minutes or until onion softens. Add canned tomatoes and the water; bring to the boil. Reduce heat and simmer, uncovered, for 10 minutes.

Tip *Banana chillies are sweet in flavour when ripe and have a lighter flavour than capsicum (bell pepper), with very little heat.*

CHILLI BEAN PIE
WITH CORNBREAD CRUST

prep + cook time 1 hour * serves 6

- **1 tablespoon extra virgin olive oil**
- **1 medium onion (150g), chopped finely**
- **1 medium green capsicum (bell pepper) (200g), chopped finely**
- **2 cloves garlic, crushed**
- **2 teaspoons mexican chilli powder**
- **1 teaspoon ground cumin**
- **2 x 400g (12½oz) cans diced tomatoes**
- **1½ cups (375ml) vegetable stock**
- **4 x 400g (12½oz) cans four-bean mix, drained, rinsed**
- **¼ cup finely chopped fresh coriander (cilantro)**
- **¾ cup (110g) self-raising flour**
- **¾ cup (125g) polenta**
- **90g (3oz) butter, chopped coarsely**
- **1 egg, beaten lightly**
- **⅓ cup (40g) coarsely grated cheddar**
- **125g (4oz) can corn kernels, drained**
- **2 tablespoons milk, approximately**

TOMATO & LIME SALSA

- **400g (12½oz) mixed baby heirloom tomatoes, halved**
- **½ cup fresh coriander (cilantro) leaves**
- **½ small red onion (50g), sliced thinly**
- **2 tablespoons lime juice**

1 Heat oil in a large saucepan over medium-high heat. Cook onion, capsicum and garlic, stirring, for 5 minutes or until onion softens. Add chilli and cumin; cook, stirring, for 1 minute or until fragrant. Add canned tomatoes, stock and beans; bring to the boil. Reduce heat and simmer for 15 minutes or until sauce thickens slightly. Stir in coriander and season to taste.

2 Meanwhile, preheat oven to 200°C/400°F. Place flour and polenta in a medium bowl; rub in butter. Stir in egg, cheddar, half the corn and enough milk to make a soft, sticky dough.

3 Spoon bean mixture into a 2-litre (8-cup) ovenproof dish. Drop tablespoons of corn mixture on top of bean mixture, then top with remaining corn. Bake for 20 minutes or until browned.

4 Meanwhile, make tomato and lime salsa.

5 Serve chilli bean pie with salsa.

TOMATO & LIME SALSA Combine ingredients in a small bowl; season to taste.

OVEN

VEGETARIAN

SWEET POTATO CANNELLONI

prep + cook time 1 hour 45 minutes * serves 6

* **3 medium orange sweet potatoes (1.2kg), unpeeled**
* **500g (1lb) fresh ricotta**
* **1 egg, beaten lightly**
* **2 green onions (scallions), sliced thinly**
* **¼ cup finely chopped fresh flat-leaf parsley**
* **2 tablespoons finely chopped fresh thyme**
* **2 cups (160g) finely grated vegetarian parmesan-style cheese**
* **150g (4½oz) sourdough, crust removed, torn into small pieces**
* **¼ cup (40g) pine nuts**
* **½ teaspoon ground nutmeg**
* **¼ cup (60ml) olive oil**
* **extra fresh flat-leaf parsley and sliced green onion (scallion), to serve**

1 Preheat oven to 200°C/400°F. Place one of the orange sweet potatoes on an oven tray. Bake for 1 hour or until tender. Cool. Reduce temperature to 160°C/325°F.

2 Meanwhile, peel remaining orange sweet potatoes. Using a mandoline, V-slicer or sharp knife, cut sweet potatoes lengthways into 3mm (⅛in) thin slices. Trim slices to 6cm x 12cm (2½in x 4¾in) rectangles; you need 36 rectangles (see tips).

3 Bring a large saucepan of water to the boil; season. Add half the sweet potato slices and boil for 1½ minutes or until softened. Remove from pan with a slotted spoon and place on a tray to cool. Repeat with remaining orange sweet potato slices.

4 When cool enough to handle, remove skin from baked sweet potato. Place sweet potato flesh in a processor with ricotta; process until smooth. Transfer to a large bowl. Stir in egg, green onion, herbs and half the parmesan; season.

5 Grease a 4-litre (16-cup) shallow ovenproof dish (you can also use two 2-litre/8-cup shallow ovenproof dishes). Place 1 heaped tablespoon of filling at the short end of a sweet potato slice; roll to enclose filling. Place, seam-side down, in dish. Repeat with remaining sweet potato slices and filling until dish is filled, in a single layer.

6 Combine sourdough, pine nuts and nutmeg in a medium bowl with remaining parmesan and 2 tablespoons of the oil. Scatter mixture over sweet potato cannelloni.

7 Bake for 15 minutes or until top is golden and crunchy. Serve topped with extra parsley and green onion, drizzled with remaining oil.

Tips *There will be some trimmings from slicing the orange sweet potatoes, which can be chopped and used in soups or for purees and mashes. You could layer the orange sweet potato slices and filling mixture instead of rolling them, if you prefer.*

269

OVEN

VEGETARIAN

POTATO AND MUSHROOM PIE

prep + cook time 2 hours (+ cooling) * serves 6

- **50g (1½oz) butter**
- **1 large onion (200g), chopped finely**
- **2 cloves garlic, crushed**
- **1kg (2lb) mixed mushrooms, sliced (see tips)**
- **½ cup (125ml) dry white wine**
- **1 cup (125g) finely grated gruyère (see tips)**
- **1 cup (80g) finely grated vegetarian parmesan-style cheese**
- **1 tablespoon finely chopped fresh rosemary**
- **1kg (2lb) small desiree potatoes, unpeeled, cut into 5mm (¼in) slices (see tips)**
- **⅓ cup (80ml) milk**
- **300ml thickened (heavy) cream**
- **1 tablespoon fresh rosemary sprigs, extra**

1 Preheat oven to 180°C/350°F. Grease six 2-cup shallow ovenproof dishes.

2 Melt butter in a large saucepan over medium heat. Cook onion and garlic, stirring occasionally, for 5 minutes or until onion is soft but not browned. Add half the mushrooms and cook, stirring occasionally, for 5 minutes. Add remaining mushrooms and cook, stirring occasionally, for 8 minutes or until mushrooms release their juices and most of the liquid evaporates. Stir in wine and bring to the boil, then reduce heat. Simmer until liquid is reduced by half. Remove from heat; season to taste.

3 Combine cheeses and chopped rosemary in a small bowl. Place a layer of potato slices, slightly overlapping, to cover base of dishes, then top with half each of the mushroom and cheese mixtures. Repeat with another layer of potato slices and remaining mushroom mixture. Arrange remaining potato slices, overlapping, around the edge of the dishes. Stir milk and cream together, then pour over potato layers. Refrigerate remaining cheese mixture.

4 Cover dishes loosely with foil. Bake for 45 minutes or until bubbling. Remove foil. Scatter remaining cheese mixture over potato. Bake for a further 30 minutes or until potato is tender and top is golden. Stand for 15 minutes. Serve topped with extra rosemary.

Tips *We used a combination of king brown, swiss brown and button mushrooms, but you can use any combination of mushrooms you prefer. You will need to study cheese labels and do a little research as some cheese is made from animal rennet; however, increasingly, many are also being made with non-animal forms of rennet. Use a mandoline or V-slicer to cut the potatoes into very thin slices.*

SWEETS

TIRAMISU SELF-SAUCING PUDDING

prep + cook time 1 hour * serves 8

- **1 cup (150g) self-raising flour**
- **2 tablespoons dutch-processed cocoa**
- **½ cup (110g) caster (superfine) sugar**
- **½ cup (125ml) milk**
- **1 egg, beaten lightly**
- **2 tablespoons golden syrup**
- **150g (4½oz) butter, melted, cooled**
- **1 cup (220g) firmly packed brown sugar**
- **1 tablespoon instant espresso coffee granules**
- **1 cup (250ml) boiling water**
- **¼ cup (60ml) sweet marsala**
- **½ cup (125ml) thickened (heavy) cream**
- **2 teaspoons dutch-processed cocoa, extra**

MASCARPONE CREAM

- **250g (8oz) mascarpone**
- **¾ cup (180ml) thickened (heavy) cream**
- **2 tablespoons icing (confectioners') sugar**

1 Preheat oven to 180°C/350°F. Grease a 1.5-litre (6-cup) shallow ovenproof dish.

2 Sift flour and cocoa into a large bowl. Stir in caster sugar, milk, egg, syrup and half the butter. Spread mixture into dish.

3 Stir brown sugar, coffee granules and the water in a medium heatproof jug until sugar dissolves. Stir in marsala, cream and remaining butter. Slowly pour coffee mixture, over the back of a spoon, over pudding batter.

4 Bake pudding for 40 minutes or until firm in the centre. Stand for 5 minutes.

5 Meanwhile, make mascarpone cream.

6 Dust pudding with extra cocoa. Serve with mascarpone cream.

MASCARPONE CREAM Beat mascarpone, cream and sifted icing sugar in a small bowl with an electric mixer until soft peaks form.

Tip *This pudding is best made close to serving, as the sauce will thicken and be absorbed if left to stand.*

CHOCOLATE TART
WITH POACHED PEARS

prep + cook time 2 hours (+ refrigeration & freezing) * serves 12

* **125g (4oz) cold butter, chopped**
* **¼ cup (40g) icing (confectioners') sugar**
* **1¼ cups (185g) plain (all-purpose) flour**
* **1 tablespoon dutch-processed cocoa**
* **1 egg yolk**
* **1 tablespoon chilled water**
* **400g (12½oz) dark (semi-sweet) chocolate, chopped**
* **200g (6½oz) butter, chopped coarsely, extra**
* **2 eggs**
* **1 tablespoon plain (all-purpose) flour**

POACHED PEARS

* **½ cup (125ml) lemon juice**
* **½ cup (175g) honey**
* **2 cups (500ml) water**
* **½ cup (110g) caster (superfine) sugar**
* **1 teaspoon vanilla extract**
* **6 pears (1.2kg), peeled, quartered**

HONEYED WALNUTS

* **¾ cup (75g) walnuts**
* **1 tablespoon honey**

1 To make pastry, process butter, icing sugar, flour and cocoa until mixture resembles breadcrumbs. Add egg yolk and the water; process until ingredients come together. Wrap in plastic wrap and refrigerate for 30 minutes.

2 Roll pastry between sheets of baking paper until 5mm (¼in) thick. Freeze for 5 minutes. Lift pastry into an 11cm x 35cm (4½in x 14in) rectangular loose-based fluted tart tin, pressing into sides. Trim edges. Prick base all over with a fork. Freeze for 20 minutes.

3 Meanwhile, preheat oven to 200°C/400°F.

4 Place tin on an oven tray; line with baking paper and fill with dried beans or rice. Bake for 15 minutes, then remove paper and beans. Bake for a further 10 minutes or until browned lightly. Cool on tray.

5 Reduce oven to 180°C/350°F.

6 Stir chocolate and extra butter in a heatproof medium bowl over a saucepan of simmering water until just melted. Remove bowl from pan. Whisk in egg and flour until just combined. Pour mixture into pastry case and smooth surface.

7 Bake tart for 20 minutes or until just set. Cool. Cover and refrigerate for 3 hours or overnight.

8 Meanwhile, make poached pears and honeyed walnuts.

9 Stand tart at room temperature for 30 minutes before serving. Drizzle with the poached pear syrup and top with walnuts. Dust tart with extra cocoa, if you like. Serve with poached pears.

POACHED PEARS Heat juice, honey, the water, sugar and vanilla in a medium saucepan over low heat. Cook, stirring, until sugar dissolves. Bring to the boil over high heat, then reduce heat to low-medium. Add pears and cook for 20 minutes or until just tender. Remove pears from syrup with a slotted spoon. Return syrup to the boil over high heat; boil for 10 minutes or until thickened slightly.

HONEYED WALNUTS Place walnuts on a baking-paper-lined oven tray. Drizzle with honey and toss to coat. Bake at 180°C/350°F for 12 minutes, stirring halfway through cooking time, until golden. Cool.

APPLE CINNAMON CRUNCH CAKE

prep + cook time 2 hours (+ standing) * serves 8

- **8 small red apples (800g) (see tip)**
- **1.5 litres (6 cups) water**
- **2 cups (440g) caster (superfine) sugar**
- **1 cinnamon stick**
- **180g (6oz) butter, softened**
- **2 teaspoons vanilla extract**
- **1 cup (220g) caster (superfine) sugar, extra**
- **3 eggs**
- **1 cup (120g) almond meal**
- **1½ cups (225g) self-raising flour**
- **½ cup (125ml) buttermilk**

CINNAMON CRUNCH TOPPING

- **45g (1½oz) butter**
- **¼ cup (55g) firmly packed brown sugar**
- **¼ cup (35g) plain (all-purpose) flour**
- **1½ teaspoons ground cinnamon**

1 Peel apples, leaving stems intact.

2 Combine the water, sugar and cinnamon in a saucepan large enough to hold apples in a single layer. Stir over high heat, without boiling, until sugar dissolves. Bring to the boil, then add apples. Cover with a round of baking paper and a heatproof plate to keep apples submerged in syrup. Return to the boil. Reduce heat and simmer, covered, for 8 minutes or until apples are tender. Remove apples from pan with a slotted spoon. Cool for 10 minutes.

3 Preheat oven to 160°C/325°F. Insert base of a 26cm (10½in) springform pan upside down in pan to make cake easier to remove. Grease pan and line base with baking paper.

4 Beat butter, vanilla and extra sugar with an electric mixer until light and fluffy. Beat in eggs, one at a time. Stir in almond meal, sifted flour and buttermilk, in two batches. Spread mixture into pan.

5 Place apples, evenly spaced, around outside edge of pan, pushing them down to the base of pan. Bake cake for 30 minutes.

6 Meanwhile, make cinnamon crunch topping.

7 Crumble topping over cake. Bake for a further 45 minutes. Stand cake in pan for 15 minutes.

CINNAMON CRUNCH TOPPING Melt butter in a small saucepan, then stir in remaining ingredients. Refrigerate for 15 minutes.

Tip *We used very small pink lady apples.*

Serving suggestion
Dust cake with icing (confectioners') sugar and serve with pouring or thick cream.

277

OVEN

SWEETS

MAPLE-BAKED WINTER FRUITS

prep + cook time 55 minutes * serves 6

- **1 medium orange (240g)**
- **1 cup (250ml) dry white wine**
- **3 small red apples (390g)**
- **3 corella pears (300g)**
- **30g (1oz) unsalted butter, softened**
- **½ cup (125ml) pure maple syrup**
- **450g (14½oz) rhubarb, trimmed, cut into 12cm (4¾in) lengths**
- **250g (8oz) mascarpone or crème fraîche**

1 Preheat oven to 180°C/350°F.

2 Using a vegetable peeler, peel rind from orange in one long strip, if possible. Squeeze juice from orange. Place rind, juice and wine in a large shallow baking dish.

3 Halve apples crossways and trim the bases slightly to give them a flat surface to sit on. Halve the pears lengthways and trim the rounded skin sides slightly to give them a flat surface to sit on. Place apples and pears in baking dish, trimmed-sides down.

4 Rub softened butter generously over apples and pears, then drizzle with maple syrup. Cover dish with foil and bake for 20 minutes. Add rhubarb and bake, covered, for a further 10 minutes. Remove foil and bake for a further 5 minutes or until all fruit are tender.

5 Combine mascarpone with 2 tablespoons of the cooking liquid from the baked fruit.

6 Serve baked fruit drizzled with cooking liquid, with mascarpone.

Serving suggestion *Almond biscotti or shortbread.*

PEANUT BUTTER CHOCOLATE CAKE

prep + cook time 1 hour 50 minutes ✻ serves 12

- **½ cup (50g) dutch-processed cocoa**
- **½ cup (125ml) boiling water**
- **185g (6oz) butter, softened**
- **1½ cups (330g) caster (superfine) sugar**
- **1 teaspoon vanilla extract**
- **3 eggs**
- **¼ cup (70g) smooth peanut butter**
- **1½ cups (225g) self-raising flour**
- **½ cup (75g) plain (all-purpose) flour**
- **¾ cup (180ml) buttermilk**
- **220g (7oz) peanut-butter-filled milk chocolate (33% cocoa), chopped coarsely**

PEANUT BUTTER GANACHE

- **360g (11½oz) white chocolate, chopped**
- **2 tablespoons smooth peanut butter**
- **½ cup (125ml) pouring cream**

1 Preheat oven to 180°C/350°F. Grease a deep 20cm (8in) square cake pan; line base and sides with baking paper.

2 Stir cocoa and the water in a small heatproof jug until cocoa dissolves. Cool for 10 minutes.

3 Beat butter, sugar and vanilla in a small bowl with an electric mixer until pale and fluffy. Beat in eggs, one at a time, then cocoa mixture and peanut butter until combined (mixture may look curdled at this stage). Beat in sifted dry ingredients and buttermilk, in two batches, until smooth. Spread mixture into pan.

4 Bake cake for 1¼ hours or until a skewer inserted into the centre comes out clean. Stand cake in pan for 5 minutes before turning, top-side up, onto a wire rack to cool.

5 Meanwhile, make peanut butter ganache.

6 Beat cold peanut butter ganache with an electric mixer until pale and fluffy. Spread ganache on top of cooled cake and top with peanut-butter-filled chocolate.

PEANUT BUTTER GANACHE Place chocolate and peanut butter in a medium heatproof bowl. Heat cream in a small saucepan until almost boiling; pour over chocolate mixture, whisking until smooth. Cover and refrigerate for 1 hour, stirring occasionally, until mixture is chilled and thickened.

Do ahead *The cake can be made up to 3 days ahead and stored in an airtight container at room temperature. The peanut butter ganache is best made on the day of serving.*

POACHED QUINCE AND CHESTNUT CAKE

prep + cook time 4 hours * serves 12

- **2 medium quince (700g), peeled, quartered, cored**
- **2 cups (440g) caster (superfine) sugar**
- **½ cup (125ml) sweet marsala**
- **2 cinnamon sticks, halved**
- **1 vanilla bean, split lengthways**
- **1 litre (4 cups) water**
- **1¼ cups (185g) self-raising flour**
- **100g (3oz) almond meal**
- **½ teaspoon baking powder**
- **1 teaspoon mixed spice**
- **250g (8oz) butter, softened**
- **1 cup (220g) firmly packed brown sugar**
- **1 cup (220g) unsweetened chestnut puree**
- **3 eggs**
- **¼ cup (60ml) milk**

CRUMBLE TOPPING

- **⅓ cup (50g) plain (all-purpose) flour**
- **⅓ cup (75g) firmly packed brown sugar**
- **⅔ cup (80g) finely chopped walnuts**
- **75g (2½oz) butter, chopped**

1 Place quince, caster sugar, marsala, cinnamon, vanilla bean and the water in a large saucepan over high heat; bring to the boil. Reduce heat to low and simmer for 2 hours or until quince is tender and syrup reduced. Using a slotted spoon, transfer quince into a medium bowl to cool. Reserve syrup and cinnamon; discard vanilla bean. Cut quince quarters in half.

2 Meanwhile, make crumble topping.

3 Preheat oven to 180°C/350°F. Grease a deep 24cm (9½in) springform pan; line base with baking paper.

4 Push flour, almond meal, baking powder and mixed spice through a fine sieve into a bowl. Beat butter and brown sugar in a large bowl with an electric mixer until pale and fluffy. Add chestnut puree and beat until smooth. Beat in eggs, one at a time, until just combined. Fold in flour mixture and milk until combined. Spread mixture into pan, arrange 12 quince wedges in a circular pattern, then place 4 wedges in the centre. Scatter crumble over top.

5 Bake cake for 1¼ hours or until a skewer inserted into the centre comes out clean. Stand cake in pan for 10 minutes before transferring to a wire rack to cool. Serve warm or cooled, drizzled with reserved syrup and topped with reserved cinnamon sticks.

CRUMBLE TOPPING Combine flour, sugar and walnuts in a small bowl. Rub in butter until mixture forms coarse crumbs.

SPICED PUMPKIN AND HONEY PIES

prep + cook time 1 hour 45 minutes (+ refrigeration & cooling) * makes 6

*** 1½ cups (225g) plain (all-purpose) flour**
*** 125g (4oz) cold butter, chopped**
*** 2 tablespoons icing (confectioners') sugar**
*** 1 egg yolk**
*** 1 tablespoon chilled water**
*** 1 egg yolk, extra**
*** ½ cup (125ml) thick (double) cream**
*** 3 teaspoons honey**
*** ¼ cup (25g) coarsely chopped walnuts**

SPICED PUMPKIN FILLING
*** 1kg (2lb) jap or butternut pumpkin, chopped coarsely**
*** pinch sea salt**
*** ¾ teaspoon ground ginger**
*** ½ teaspoon ground cinnamon**
*** 2 eggs**
*** 2 tablespoons milk**
*** ¼ cup (90g) honey**
*** 2 tablespoons caster (superfine) sugar**

1 To make pastry, process flour, butter and icing sugar until mixture resembles breadcrumbs. Add egg yolk and the water; process until ingredients come together. Divide pastry into six portions, wrap each in plastic wrap and refrigerate for 30 minutes.

2 Meanwhile, make spiced pumpkin filling.

3 Roll pastry between sheets of baking paper until large enough to line six 10cm (4in) round, 3cm (1¼in) deep loose-based tart tins. Lift pastry into tins, pressing into bases and sides. Trim edges. Prick bases all over with a fork. Cover and refrigerate for 20 minutes.

4 Meanwhile, preheat oven to 180°C/350°F.

5 Place tins on an oven tray; line each with baking paper and fill with dried beans or rice. Bake pastry cases for 15 minutes. Remove paper and beans. Bake for a further 10 minutes or until browned lightly. Cool on tray.

6 Spoon pumpkin filling into pastry cases. Brush tops with extra egg yolk. Bake pies for 25 minutes or until set and light golden.

7 Serve pies topped with dollops of cream, drizzled with honey and scattered with walnuts.

SPICED PUMPKIN FILLING Boil, steam or microwave pumpkin until just tender; drain. Process pumpkin, salt, ginger and cinnamon until smooth. Add eggs, milk, honey and sugar; process until smooth. Cool.

Do ahead *The pies can be made a day ahead and refrigerated. Before serving, reheat in a 160°C/325°F oven for 10 minutes or until warm.*

WARM STRAWBERRY AND RHUBARB CRUMBLES

prep + cook time 50 minutes * serves 6

- 500g (1lb) rhubarb
- 250g (8oz) strawberries
- ¼ cup (55g) caster (superfine) sugar
- 2 teaspoons vanilla extract
- 2 eggs
- ¼ cup (55g) caster (superfine) sugar, extra
- 1 tablespoon cornflour (cornstarch)
- 300ml pouring cream
- 1 cup (250ml) milk
- 2 teaspoons vanilla extract, extra

CRUMBLE

- ½ cup (75g) self-raising flour
- ¼ cup (55g) demerara sugar
- 60g (2oz) cold butter, chopped finely
- ½ cup (60g) coarsely chopped pecans

1 Preheat oven to 180°C/350°F.

2 Trim rhubarb and chop into 5cm (2in) pieces. Hull strawberries. Combine rhubarb, strawberries, sugar and vanilla in a shallow baking dish. Bake, uncovered, for 20 minutes or until rhubarb softens.

3 Meanwhile, make crumble.

4 Whisk eggs, extra sugar and cornflour in a medium saucepan over medium heat until combined. Gradually whisk in cream and milk; cook, whisking, until mixture boils and thickens. Remove from heat and stir in extra vanilla.

5 Pour custard into six bowls. Top with rhubarb mixture, then crumble.

CRUMBLE Line an oven tray with baking paper. Combine sifted flour and sugar in a medium bowl; rub in butter until crumbly, then stir in pecans. Spoon mixture in a thin layer onto tray. Bake for 15 minutes or until mixture is browned lightly. Cool for 10 minutes before crumbling mixture coarsely.

PLUM AND HAZELNUT CLAFOUTIS

prep + cook time 1 hour ✻ serves 6

* **500g (1lb) red-fleshed plums**
* **60g (2oz) butter, softened**
* **½ cup (110g) caster (superfine) sugar**
* **4 eggs**
* **½ cup (60g) hazelnut meal**
* **300ml pouring cream**
* **¼ cup (70g) roasted skinless hazelnuts, halved**
* **1½ teaspoons icing (confectioners') sugar**

1 Preheat oven to 180°C/350°F.

2 Cut plums in half; remove and discard stones. Place plums, cut-side up, in a greased 1-litre (4-cup) shallow ovenproof dish.

3 Beat butter and sugar in a large bowl with an electric mixer until light and fluffy. Whisk in eggs, one at a time, then whisk in hazelnut meal and cream until just combined. Pour batter in between plums.

4 Bake clafoutis for 40 minutes or until golden and a knife inserted into the centre comes out clean.

5 Serve clafoutis warm, topped with hazelnuts and dusted with icing sugar.

Serving suggestion *Pouring cream or custard.*

TANGELO TART
WITH CANDIED BLOOD ORANGES

prep + cook time 1 hour 50 minutes (+ refrigeration & standing) * serves 8

*** 1½ cups (225g) plain (all-purpose) flour**
*** 2 tablespoons icing (confectioners') sugar**
*** 125g (4oz) cold butter, chopped**
*** 1 egg yolk**
*** 1 tablespoon chilled water**
*** 1 tablespoon finely grated tangelo rind**
*** ½ cup (125ml) strained freshly squeezed tangelo juice**
*** 5 eggs**
*** ¾ cup (165g) caster (superfine) sugar**
*** 300ml pouring cream**

CANDIED BLOOD ORANGES
*** ½ cup (110g) caster (superfine) sugar**
*** 1½ cups (375ml) water**
*** ½ cup (125ml) strained freshly squeezed blood orange juice**
*** 3 medium blood oranges (480g), cut into 5mm (¼in) slices**
*** ½ cup (180g) honey**

1 To make pastry, process flour, icing sugar and butter until mixture resembles breadcrumbs. Add egg yolk and the water; process until ingredients just come together. Wrap pastry in plastic wrap and refrigerate for 30 minutes.

2 Grease a 23cm (9¼in), 3cm (1¼in) deep round loose-based tart tin. Roll pastry between sheets of baking paper until 3mm (⅛in) thick and large enough to line the tin. Lift pastry into tin and ease into the base and side. Trim edge. Prick base all over with a fork. Cover and refrigerate for 20 minutes.

3 Meanwhile, preheat oven to 190°C/375°F.

4 Place tin on an oven tray; line pastry with baking paper and fill with dried beans or rice. Bake for 10 minutes, then remove paper and beans. Bake for a further 10 minutes or until browned lightly. Cool on tray.

5 Reduce oven to 170°C/325°F.

6 Whisk rind, juice, eggs, caster sugar and cream in a large bowl until combined. Strain mixture into pastry case.

7 Bake tart for 35 minutes or until just set. Cool. Cover and refrigerate for 3 hours or overnight.

8 Make candied blood oranges.

9 Stand tart at room temperature for 30 minutes before serving. Top with half the candied oranges and a little syrup. Serve tart cut into slices with remaining candied oranges and syrup.

CANDIED BLOOD ORANGES Stir sugar, the water and juice in a large frying pan over medium heat until sugar dissolves. Add orange slices and simmer for 20 minutes or until rind is soft. Add honey to pan and simmer for a further 15 minutes or until slices are candied and syrup is thickened.

Do ahead *The tart can be made a day ahead and refrigerated. The candied blood oranges are best made close to serving.*

SPICED SPONGE AND RHUBARB ROULADE

prep + cook time 45 minutes (+ cooling) * serves 10

- **5 eggs, separated**
- **⅔ cup (150g) caster (superfine) sugar**
- **1½ tablespoons hot water**
- **80g (2½oz) white chocolate, grated finely**
- **⅔ cup (100g) self-raising flour**
- **1 teaspoon ground cinnamon**
- **½ teaspoon ground nutmeg**
- **¼ teaspoon ground cloves**
- **¼ teaspoon ground cardamom**
- **¼ cup (55g) caster (superfine) sugar, extra**

ROASTED RHUBARB

- **500g (1lb) rhubarb, trimmed, cut into 5cm (2in) lengths**
- **⅓ cup (75g) firmly packed brown sugar**
- **2 teaspoons finely grated orange rind**
- **1 tablespoon orange juice**
- **2.5cm (1in) piece fresh ginger, grated**

MASCARPONE CREAM

- **½ cup (125ml) thickened (heavy) cream**
- **1 cup (250g) mascarpone**

1 Preheat oven to 200°C/400°F. Grease a 26cm x 32cm (10½in x 12¾in) swiss roll pan; line base with baking paper, extending the paper 5cm (2in) over the long sides.

2 Beat egg yolks and sugar in a medium bowl with an electric mixer for 5 minutes or until very thick. Pour the hot water down the inside of the bowl, add chocolate, then gently fold in combined sifted flour and spices until just combined. Transfer to a medium bowl.

3 Beat egg whites in a medium bowl with an electric mixer until soft peaks form. Fold egg whites into chocolate mixture, in two batches, until just combined. Spread mixture into pan.

4 Bake cake for 12 minutes or until golden and sponge springs back when pressed lightly with a finger.

5 Meanwhile, place a piece of baking paper, cut just larger than the pan, on a work surface; sprinkle evenly with extra sugar. Turn hot sponge onto sugar-covered paper. Peel away lining paper. Trim any crisped edges with a sharp knife. Working quickly, and using paper as a guide, roll sponge up from a long side. Cool for 5 minutes. Unroll sponge, remove paper and reroll. Cover with a clean tea towel. Cool.

6 Meanwhile, make roasted rhubarb and mascarpone cream.

7 Unroll sponge and spread with mascarpone cream, leaving a 2.5cm (1in) border. Top with rhubarb. Reroll sponge to enclose filling. Serve roulade drizzled with rhubarb cooking juices.

ROASTED RHUBARB Combine ingredients in a small shallow baking dish. Roast in oven for 10 minutes, stirring halfway through cooking time, or until rhubarb is tender.

MASCARPONE CREAM Beat cream and mascarpone in a small bowl with an electric mixer until soft peaks form.

Tip *This recipe is best made on the day of serving.*

la Mode à tout prix 1943

RUSTIC APPLE PIE

prep + cook time 1 hour 20 minutes (+ refrigeration) ✻ serves 8

∗ 4 medium red apples (600g)
∗ 1 cup (220g) caster (superfine) sugar
∗ 2 teaspoons finely grated lemon rind
∗ 1 tablespoon lemon juice
∗ 3 cups (750ml) water
∗ 2 cups (300g) plain (all-purpose) flour
∗ 1 tablespoon caster (superfine) sugar, extra
∗ 125g (4oz) cold unsalted butter, chopped
∗ ⅓ cup (80ml) iced water, approximately
∗ 2 tablespoons milk
∗ ¼ cup (55g) demerara sugar
∗ 1 tablespoon flaked natural almonds

1 Peel and core apples; cut into six wedges. Place apple in a medium saucepan with caster sugar, rind, juice and the water; bring to the boil. Reduce heat to low and simmer for 10 minutes or until tender. Using a slotted spoon, transfer apple to a medium bowl. Simmer syrup for 15 minutes or until reduced to ¾ cup. Cool.

2 Meanwhile, process flour, extra sugar and butter until crumbly. Add enough of the iced water until ingredients just come together. Press dough into a ball, wrap in plastic wrap and refrigerate for 30 minutes.

3 Preheat oven to 180°C/350°F.

4 Roll dough between two large sheets of baking paper into a 35cm (14in) round. Remove top layer of paper, then carefully slide dough, on bottom layer of paper, onto a large oven tray.

5 Pile apple into the centre of the dough, leaving a 7cm (2¾in) border. Fold pastry edge up and around apple. Brush milk over pastry and sprinkle with demerara sugar.

6 Bake pie for 40 minutes or until the pastry is golden brown.

7 Just before serving, spoon some of the syrup over the pie and scatter with almonds.

Tip *If you would like to give the pie some colour, scatter some frozen raspberries or blueberries over the apples before wrapping in the pastry.*

Serving suggestion *Cream, ice-cream or custard.*

Do ahead *The pie can be made 6 hours ahead. Reheat 20 minutes before serving.*

MANDARIN POSTRE CHAJÁ

prep + cook time 2 hours 25 minutes ✻ serves 8

- **4 egg whites**
- **1 cup (220g) caster (superfine) sugar**
- **1 teaspoon cornflour (cornstarch)**
- **⅔ cup (150g) caster (superfine) sugar, extra**
- **⅓ cup (80ml) water**
- **6 medium mandarins (1.2kg), peeled, segmented, rind reserved**
- **600ml pouring cream**
- **1 cup (300g) dulce de leche**
- **⅔ cup (95g) roasted peanuts, chopped coarsely**

SPONGE CAKE

- **3 eggs**
- **⅓ cup (75g) caster (superfine) sugar**
- **½ cup (75g) plain (all-purpose) flour**
- **50g (1½oz) butter, melted, cooled**

1 Preheat oven to 180°C/350°F.

2 Make sponge cake.

3 Reduce oven to 100°C/210°F. Grease and line two large oven trays.

4 Beat egg whites in a medium bowl with an electric mixer until soft peaks form. Add sugar, 1 tablespoon at a time, beating continuously until thick and glossy. Beat in cornflour. Spread five 10cm (4in) rounds of mixture 3cm (1¼in) apart on trays (don't worry about making the rounds perfect as the meringues will be broken up).

5 Bake meringues for 2 hours or until dry. Turn off oven and cool meringues in the oven with door closed. Break cooled meringues into rough pieces.

6 Meanwhile, place extra sugar and the water in a medium saucepan over high heat; stir, without boiling, until sugar dissolves. Bring to the boil. Add mandarin segments and reserved mandarin rind; stir well, without damaging mandarin segments. Cook for 5 minutes or until syrup is reduced and segments are plump. Discard rind. Cool mandarin segments in syrup.

7 Beat cream in a medium bowl with an electric mixer until soft peaks form. In a 4-litre (16-cup) glass trifle bowl, layer one-third each of the sponge, cream, meringue, mandarin segments and syrup, dulce de leche and peanuts. Repeat twice more to make three layers.

SPONGE CAKE Grease a 20cm (8in) round cake pan; line base with baking paper. Beat eggs and sugar in medium bowl with an electric mixer for 5 minutes or until light and fluffy. Sift over flour and gently fold in to combine. Drizzle melted butter over the batter and gently fold in to combine. Spoon mixture into pan; smooth the surface. Bake for 20 minutes or until cake is golden and springs back when touched lightly. Cool in pan for 5 minutes before turning onto a wire rack to cool completely. Break cooled cake into chunks.

正田
有機

BARBECUE

SMOKING

PORT-SMOKED BEEF

prep + cook time 1 hour 15 minutes (+ overnight refrigeration & standing) * serves 8

Different smoking wood chips add different flavours to meat, but not in the way you might necessarily expect. The aroma of the wood doesn't actually carry through to the meat; rather, it is the way in which that particular wood burns, which in turn affects the amount of smoke produced and just how smoky the meat will be. You'll find smoking wood chips at hardware or barbecue supply shops.

You will need to start this recipe the day before.

EQUIPMENT
*** 1 cup (125g) smoking wood chips (see note above)**
*** barbecue smoker box**
*** charcoal or gas barbecue**

PORT-SMOKED BEEF
*** 2 tablespoons olive oil**
*** 2 cloves garlic, crushed**
*** ¼ cup (60ml) port or tawny fortified wine (see tip)**
*** 2 tablespoons coarsely chopped fresh oregano**
*** 1.5kg (3lb) piece beef eye fillet, trimmed**
*** 1 cup (250ml) port or tawny fortified wine, extra**

1 Combine oil, garlic, port and oregano in a large bowl. Add beef and turn to coat in marinade. Cover and refrigerate overnight.
2 Meanwhile, combine smoking chips and extra port in a small bowl. Cover and stand overnight.
3 Cook beef, uncovered, on a heated oiled barbecue until just browned all over. Place beef in a lightly oiled deep doubled disposable aluminium roasting tray. Place drained smoking chips in smoker box. Place smoker box alongside beef on the barbecue.
4 Cook beef in a covered barbecue at 180°C/350°F for 45 minutes for medium or until cooked to your liking. Remove beef from barbecue and cover. Rest for 10 minutes before carving.

Tip *Tawny is the Australian name for fortified wine made in the style of port.*

Serving suggestion *Roasted jap pumpkin wedges, aïoli or your favourite relish or chutney. Scatter with micro herbs, if you like.*

Extra
Deli
Pastrami

NEW YORK DELI PASTRAMI

prep + cook time 3 hours 30 minutes (+ refrigeration) * serves 12

Pastrami, the iconic deli meat, starts with corned (salted) beef, which gives the meat its characteristic dense texture that enables thin slicing. Next, the meat is cured with a spice mixture before being smoked at a low temperature to cook and flavour it.

You will need to start this recipe at least 8 hours ahead.

EQUIPMENT

*** 8 x 5cm (2in) pieces apple or pecan smoking wood chips**
*** charcoal barbecue**
*** meat thermometer**

PASTRAMI

*** 1.6kg (3¼lb) piece corned silverside**
*** ¼ cup (20g) coriander seeds**
*** 1 tablespoon yellow mustard seeds**
*** 1 tablespoon fennel seeds**
*** 1 tablespoon black peppercorns**
*** ¼ cup (55g) firmly packed brown sugar**
*** 2 tablespoons sea salt flakes**
*** 1 tablespoon smoked paprika**

1 Trim beef of any fat. Place beef in a large container, cover with cold water and refrigerate for 2 hours to remove excess salt. Drain, then rinse under cold water and pat dry with paper towel. Set aside on a tray.

2 Meanwhile, using a mortar and pestle, pound seeds and peppercorns until coarsely crushed. Add sugar, salt and paprika; stir to combine. Sprinkle spice mix over beef on tray, then turn, pressing spices into meat to coat. Cover and refrigerate for 8 hours or overnight for flavours to develop.

3 Set up a charcoal barbecue for smoking and indirect grilling. Preheat to low heat (110°C/230°F). Add one piece of wood to coals. Place beef on greased barbecue and cook for 3 hours. Increase heat to 140°C/280°F or until the pastrami reaches an internal temperature of 70°C/160°F on a meat thermometer. (Alternatively, insert a skewer and touch it to the inside of your wrist; it should feel warm.)

4 Remove pastrami from the barbecue and cool to room temperature. Once cool, wrap in baking paper and refrigerate in an airtight container for up to 2 weeks, or freeze for up to 3 months.

Serving suggestion *Cut pastrami into paper thin slices and pile high on rye bread with mustard and pickles. For a proper reuben sandwich, toast sandwich with pastrami, sauerkraut, swiss cheese, pickles and thousand island dressing.*

TEXAN-SMOKED PORK RIBS

prep + cook time 2 hours 30 minutes (+ overnight refrigeration) * serves 4

American-style pork ribs are also known as baby back ribs. They are cut from the top of the rib cage, are slightly curved, taper in size and carry more meat on and in between the ribs than spare ribs. Usually the ribs are sold in racks of between 10 and 13 ribs.

You will need to start this recipe the day before.

EQUIPMENT

- **2 cups (225g) hickory smoking wood chips**
- **barbecue smoker box**
- **charcoal or gas barbecue**

RIBS

- **3kg (6lb) American-style pork ribs**
- **2 tablespoons sweet paprika**
- **1 tablespoon ground cumin**
- **1 teaspoon cayenne pepper**
- **1 teaspoon onion powder**
- **1 teaspoon garlic powder**
- **1 tablespoon sea salt flakes**
- **1 tablespoon brown sugar**

BARBECUE SAUCE

- **2 cups (500ml) barbecue sauce**
- **½ cup (125ml) beer**
- **½ cup (125ml) pure maple syrup**
- **¼ cup (60ml) apple cider vinegar**

1 Using a small knife, trim membrane from the back of the ribs. Place ribs on a tray. Combine remaining ingredients in a small bowl. Rub spice mixture over the top of the ribs. Cover and refrigerate overnight.

2 Soak half the wood chips in a small bowl of water for 30 minutes; drain. Combine soaked and remaining dry wood chips in a barbecue smoker box. Place in a preheated medium-hot (180°C/350°F) barbecue; close barbecue lid. Leave for 10 minutes or until chips begin to smoke.

3 Meanwhile, make barbecue sauce.

4 Brush ribs with a little of the sauce. Place ribs on a barbecue rack overhanging the smoker box in the barbecue. (Alternatively, place over a wire rack on the grill side plate for indirect heat.) Cook ribs in covered barbecue for 1¾ hours, brushing with sauce every 15 minutes, or until ribs are tender and darkly glazed.

5 Serve ribs cut into short lengths, with remaining sauce.

BARBECUE SAUCE Bring ingredients to the boil in a medium saucepan over high heat. Reduce heat and simmer for 8 minutes or until liquid is reduced and sauce is thickened slightly.

Serving suggestion *Barbecued corn, coleslaw and wedges of lime.*

SMOKED OCEAN TROUT

prep + cook time 1 hour 45 minutes (+ overnight refrigeration) ✻ serves 8

Smoking a side (fillet) of ocean trout is surprisingly easy. There's a little bit of waiting while the fish is brining, but the active time is very short. While we've specified a charcoal barbecue for its flavour, you can also use a gas barbecue.

You will need to start this recipe the day before.

EQUIPMENT
*** 8 x 5cm (2in) pieces of mesquite or hickory smoking wood chips**
*** charcoal barbecue**

SMOKED OCEAN TROUT
*** 3 litres (12 cups) water**
*** 1 cup (250g) rock salt**
*** ½ cup (110g) firmly packed brown sugar**
*** 2 fresh bay leaves, torn**
*** 2 sprigs fresh dill, bruised**
*** 1 clove garlic, crushed**
*** 1 teaspoon coriander seeds, crushed lightly**
*** 1 teaspoon black peppercorns, crushed lightly**
*** 1.4kg side (fillet) ocean trout, skin on (see tip)**

1 Combine the water, salt and sugar in a large saucepan over medium heat; bring to the boil, stirring to dissolve the sugar and salt. Stand brine until cooled.

2 Transfer brine to a large clean airtight container, large enough to fit the trout snugly. Add bay, dill, garlic, coriander and peppercorns; stir to combine. Add trout and weigh down with a small plate, if necessary, to keep it submerged in brine. Cover and refrigerate for 8 hours.

3 Drain trout, discarding brine. Rinse under cold water and pat dry with paper towel. Place on a wire rack over a tray. Refrigerate overnight or until flesh is dry and sticky.

4 Preheat a charcoal kettle barbecue to 120°C/250°F. Add wood chips to the coals. Place trout, skin-side down, on the grills. Smoke for 1 hour or until cooked through.

5 Remove trout from the barbecue. Cool to room temperature, then keep refrigerated in an airtight container for up to 5 days.

Tip *You can also smoke portions of trout fillet rather than a whole side, if you prefer; however, you will need to reduce the brining and cooking times.*

Serving suggestion *Serve trout with crème fraîche as part of a buffet with salads and baguette. Leftovers can be flaked through salads, pasta or scrambled eggs.*

GARLIC AND ROSEMARY SMOKED LAMB

prep + cook time 1 hour 30 minutes (+ refrigeration) * serves 6

To cook using indirect heat on a gas barbecue, first place the food in a preheated, covered barbecue. Turn the burners off directly under the food, while keeping the side burners on. With a charcoal barbecue, place coals against the sides, leaving the centre rack of the barbecue empty. A disposable aluminium baking dish can be placed here to catch fat drips.

You will need to start this recipe the day before.

EQUIPMENT
- **2 cups (225g) smoking wood chips**
- **barbecue smoker box**
- **charcoal or gas barbecue**

GARLIC & ROSEMARY SMOKED LAMB
- **1kg (2lb) boned rolled lamb loin**
- **4 cloves garlic, halved**
- **2 tablespoons fresh rosemary sprigs**
- **1 teaspoon dried chilli flakes**
- **1 teaspoon sea salt flakes**
- **1 tablespoon olive oil**

1 Pierce lamb in eight places with a sharp knife; push garlic and half the rosemary into cuts. Sprinkle lamb with chilli and salt. Rub all over with oil. Cover and refrigerate for 3 hours or overnight.

2 Meanwhile, soak smoking chips in a large bowl of water for 2 hours.

3 Cook lamb, uncovered, on a heated oiled barbecue until browned all over. Place drained smoking chips in smoker box on barbecue next to lamb. Cook lamb in a covered barbecue, using indirect heat, for 1¼ hours for medium or until cooked to your liking. Remove lamb from barbecue. Scatter with remaining rosemary. Cover loosely with foil and rest for 10 minutes before carving.

Tip *This is a very easy recipe to double or triple to feed a crowd. Alternatively, barbecue one piece to eat on the day and a second to eat over the following few days.*

Serving suggestion *Orange sweet potato mash or wedges and salsa verde.*

FRENCH-STYLE BACON

prep + cook time 3 hours (+ 3 days refrigeration) * makes 2kg

Ventrèche is a French form of bacon from south-western France. There are two styles: one that is cured and rolled (but not smoked) and is the equivalent of Italian pancetta, while the other is smoked and is much like streaky bacon, except rolled. Our recipe is for the second style. If you can, try to find meat from a heritage pig breed.

You will need to cure the pork 3 days ahead.

EQUIPMENT
*** 8 x 5cm (2in) pieces mesquite or apple blend smoking wood chips**
*** charcoal barbecue**
*** meat thermometer**

FRENCH-STYLE BACON
*** ⅓ cup (30g) sea salt flakes**
*** ¼ cup (40g) crushed black peppercorns**
*** 2kg (4lb) piece of female pork belly (see tip)**

1 Combine sea salt and pepper; sprinkle over pork and press to coat. Transfer pork to a large zip-top bag and add any remaining salt mixture. Seal and refrigerate for 3 days to allow pork to cure, turning occasionally to cure evenly.
2 Rinse pork briefly under cold running water and pat dry with paper towel. Roll pork belly to form a cylinder, then tie at 2cm (¾in) intervals with kitchen string to secure. Set pork aside for 30 minutes to come to room temperature.
3 Preheat a charcoal kettle barbecue or off-set barbecue for indirect grilling to 120°C/250°F. Add a piece of wood to the coals, place grill on barbecue, then pork on grill. Cover with lid and smoke for 2½ hours or until cooked through and pork reaches 65°C/149°F on a meat thermometer. (Add more charcoal and wood pieces as you cook, to maintain the barbecue temperature.)
4 Set pork aside to cool. Wrap and refrigerate until required. Bacon will keep, refrigerated, for up to 8 days, or freeze for up to 3 months.

Tip *The meat of female pigs tends to be less 'porky-tasting' than that of uncastrated male pigs. You will need to order it from a good-quality butcher.*

Serving suggestion
Cut thin slices (or small cubes) and fry as you would bacon and eat with fried eggs. Use in quiches, soups, potato salad or in spaghetti carbonara.

MARJORAM AND MALT VINEGAR TOMATOES

prep + cook time 1 hour 30 minutes (+ standing) * makes 500g

Mesquite is a hard wood with a low-moisture content that burns slowly and hot, so it transfers a stronger smoke taste to food than milder fruit woods. You could kill two birds with one stone and also smoke another one of our recipes at the same time as the tomatoes, such as the texan-smoked pork ribs on page 302.

EQUIPMENT

*** 250g (8oz) mesquite smoking wood chips**
*** charcoal or gas barbecue**

MARJORAM & MALT VINEGAR TOMATOES

*** 1.5kg (1½lb) mixed tomatoes (halved if large) (see tip)**
*** 2 tablespoons extra virgin olive oil**
*** 1 tablespoon malt vinegar**
*** 1 clove garlic, sliced finely**
*** ¼ cup fresh marjoram or oregano leaves**

1 Place wood chips in a small bowl, cover with water and leave to soak for 1 hour; drain.

2 Place tomatoes, oil, vinegar, garlic and marjoram in a large bowl; season with salt and pepper. Carefully turn several times to coat the tomatoes in mixture.

3 Preheat a charcoal kettle barbecue or a gas barbecue to low-medium heat. Place the wood chips around the coals or in a smoker box and cover with the barbecue lid. Cook for 5 minutes or until smoke appears.

4 Place a large double sheet of aluminium foil over the grills. Place marinated tomatoes in a single layer on foil. Cook tomatoes, covered, for 1¼ hours or until the tomatoes are softened and smoked.

5 Serve immediately, or transfer to an airtight container and store in the fridge for up to 5 days.

Tip *We used a mix of vine-ripened gourmet tomatoes, cherry tomatoes and kumatoes, but you can use whatever is available.*

Serving suggestion *Pile into baguettes as part of a sandwich filling, or use in salads or pasta dishes. You could also use the tomatoes to make a smoky tomato sauce.*

STOVE

PRESERVES & CONDIMENTS

ROSEMARY AND FENNEL JAM

prep + cook time 1 hour 30 minutes ✻ makes 5 cups

This preserve is best made during autumn and winter months when large fennel bulbs are at their most abundant and cheapest. Baby summer fennel doesn't work quite as well since it is not as moist.

*** 1½ tablespoons extra virgin olive oil**
*** 4 large fennel bulbs (2.2kg), trimmed, sliced thinly (see tip)**
*** 1 medium onion (150g), sliced thinly**
*** 6 cloves garlic, chopped**
*** 2 tablespoons yellow mustard seeds**
*** 2 tablespoons finely chopped fresh rosemary**
*** 2½ cups (550g) firmly packed brown sugar**
*** 2 cups (500ml) malt vinegar**
*** 1½ tablespoons sea salt flakes**
*** freshly ground black pepper**

1 Heat oil in a large saucepan over low-medium heat. Cook fennel, onion, garlic, mustard seeds and rosemary, stirring occasionally, for 40 minutes or until fennel and onion are very soft and browned lightly.

2 Add sugar, vinegar, salt and pepper to taste. Stir over high heat, without boiling, until sugar dissolves. Bring to the boil, then reduce heat and cook, stirring occasionally, for 30 minutes or until thick.

3 Spoon hot jam into hot sterilised jars (see glossary, page 484); seal immediately. Label and date jars when cold. Store in the fridge for up to 6 months. Remove with a clean spoon each time.

Tip *Slice the fennel in a food processor or with a mandoline.*

Serving suggestion *Try this with cheese, grilled meats or sausages, or in burgers and sandwiches.*

INDIAN TOMATO RELISH

prep + cook time 1 hour 30 minutes * makes 6 cups

The relish can be eaten immediately; however, the flavours will improve even further if allowed to stand for 3 days first.

*** 1.5kg (3lb) vine-ripened tomatoes**
*** 90g (3oz) fresh ginger, peeled, chopped coarsely**
*** 8 cloves garlic, chopped coarsely**
*** 2 fresh long green chillies, seeded, chopped coarsely**
*** 1¼ cups (310ml) apple cider vinegar**
*** ½ cup (125ml) olive oil**
*** 3 teaspoons brown mustard seeds**
*** 1 tablespoon ground cumin**
*** 1 tablespoon smoked paprika**
*** 3 teaspoons ground turmeric**
*** 2 teaspoons nigella seeds (see tip)**
*** 1 teaspoon ground chilli powder**
*** 400g (12½oz) can crushed tomatoes**
*** ⅔ cup (150g) firmly packed brown sugar**
*** 2 teaspoons sea salt flakes**

1 Using a small sharp knife, score the base of each tomato with a small cross. Place in a saucepan of boiling water for 1 minute or until the skins start to split. Remove with a slotted spoon to a bowl of iced water. Peel and discard tomato skins. Coarsely chop tomatoes.

2 Process ginger, garlic, chilli and 2 tablespoons of the vinegar to a smooth paste.

3 Heat oil in a large saucepan over medium heat. Cook mustard seeds, stirring, for 20 seconds or until seeds start to pop. Add ginger paste and stir for 2 minutes or until softened. Add cumin, paprika, turmeric, nigella seeds and ground chilli; stir until well combined. Add fresh and canned tomatoes, sugar, salt and remaining vinegar. Simmer, stirring occasionally, for 55 minutes or until mixture is a thick, rich sauce consistency.

4 Spoon hot relish into hot sterilised jars (see glossary, page 484); seal immediately. Label and date jars when cold. Store in a cool, dark place for up to 6 months. Refrigerate after opening and remove with a clean spoon each time.

Tip *Nigella seeds are black with an onion-like taste and are often found scattered on turkish bread with sesame seeds. You will find them in delis and greengrocers that sell spices.*

Serving suggestion
Try this with fried eggs, rice dishes or with barbecued meats.

CARAMELISED ROAST FIG AND TEA JAM

prep + cook time 1 hour 15 minutes ✻ makes 2 cups

Roasting the figs before boiling the jam allows their juices to caramelise and concentrate the fig taste.

*** 5 large figs (400g), stalks removed, quartered lengthways**
*** 2 cups (440g) jam-setting sugar (see tip)**
*** 3 teaspoons loose-leaf earl grey tea**
*** 1 cup (250ml) boiling water**
*** 1 medium granny smith apple (150g), peeled, grated coarsely**

1 Preheat oven to 200°C/400°F. Grease and line an oven tray with baking paper.
2 Place figs on tray; sprinkle with 2 tablespoons of the sugar. Roast for 40 minutes or until tender and juices are caramelised.
3 Meanwhile, combine tea leaves and the boiling water in a medium heatproof jug; steep for 10 minutes, then strain, reserving the liquid.
4 Place roasted figs and apple in a large saucepan over high heat; cook, stirring occasionally, for 5 minutes or until apple is softened. Add ¾ cup of the tea and remaining sugar; stir, without boiling, until sugar dissolves. Bring to the boil; boil, uncovered, without stirring, for 15 minutes or until jam jells when tested (see glossary, page 479). Stir in remaining tea.
5 Pour hot jam into hot sterilised jars (see glossary, page 484); seal immediately. Label and date jars when cold. Store in a cool, dark place for up to 12 months. Refrigerate after opening. Remove with a clean spoon each time.

Tip *Jam-setting sugar is a special blend of sugar containing naturally occurring pectin and citric acid. It is used with fruit that is naturally low in pectin, such as figs. Jam sugar can be found in supermarkets and delis.*

Serving suggestion
Try this spread over french toast for brunch or spooned over frozen yoghurt for a snack.

321

STOVE

PRESERVES & CONDIMENTS

PEACH AND PLUM HOARDER'S JAM

prep time 20 minutes (+ 2 weeks standing) * makes 8 cups

While this is called a jam, it is anything but; really it is a wonderful concoction of boozy fruit and fruit-infused alcohol. It is known by a variety of names: hoarder's jam, rumptoff (rum was originally used) and bachelor jam; however, the common theme of all of them is preserving summer's bounty of fruit.

You will need to start this recipe 2 weeks in advance.

- **1 large just-ripe peach (220g), quartered**
- **4 medium plums, halved**
- **4 medium apricots, halved**
- **2¼ cups (495g) caster (superfine) sugar**
- **3 long strips orange rind**
- **2 vanilla beans, split lengthways**
- **2⅔ cups (660ml) brandy, rum or gin, approximately**

1 Combine fruit and sugar in a large bowl; stand for 1 hour.

2 Transfer fruit mixture to a clean 2-litre (8-cup) wide-mouth jar. Add the rind and vanilla bean. Pour alcohol over the fruit, making sure fruit is immersed (you may need to add a little extra depending on the height and width of the jar).

3 Fill a small zip-top sandwich bag with a little water and place over the fruit to keep them submerged in alcohol. Label and date jar. Set aside in a cool, dark place for at least 2 weeks, and up to 3 months, turning the jar occasionally. Refrigerate after opening. Remove with a clean spoon each time.

Tip *Try making hoarder's jam with blood plums, summer berries, gin and a cinnamon stick.*

Serving suggestion *Use the soaked fruit in trifles, upside-down cakes, crumbles and ice-cream. Use the fruit-infused brandy, rum or gin in punches and cocktails, or to moisten syrup cakes.*

CARROT CAKE CONSERVE

prep + cook time 1 hour 30 minutes * makes 6 cups

- **1kg (2lb) carrots, grated coarsely**
- **2 litres (8 cups) water**
- **⅔ cup (160ml) lemon juice**
- **1 tablespoon ground ginger**
- **1 teaspoon ground cinnamon**
- **½ teaspoon freshly grated nutmeg (see tip)**
- **1 teaspoon vanilla bean paste**
- **1 cup (220g) firmly packed brown sugar**
- **3 cups (660g) caster (superfine) sugar**
- **2 medium green apples (300g), grated coarsely**
- **440g (14oz) can crushed pineapple in natural juice**
- **½ cup (75g) raisins**

1 Place carrot, the water, juice, spices and vanilla in a large saucepan; bring to the boil. Reduce heat and simmer, covered, for 45 minutes or until carrot is soft.

2 Add sugars, apple, pineapple and raisins to the pan. Stir over high heat, without boiling, until sugar dissolves. Bring to the boil; boil for 30 minutes or until thick, stirring occasionally during the last 10 minutes of cooking to prevent the jam sticking.

3 Pour hot jam into hot sterilised jars (see glossary, page 484); seal immediately. Label and date jars when cold. Store in a cool, dark place for up to 6 months. Refrigerate after opening. Remove with a clean spoon each time.

Tip *It is always better to grate nutmeg freshly as it will have the best taste; however, if all you have is ground, that is fine to use too.*

Serving suggestion *Spread over irish soda bread or a walnut or other grainy bread, with ricotta or cream cheese and a dusting of ground cinnamon. You could also serve with warm waffles and vanilla ice-cream as a dessert.*

THE WORLD
KRAFT
BLENDED
PASTEURISED
PACKED

BRAISES

BRAISED
BEEF BRISKET

prep + cook time 2 hours ✻ serves 4

- **1kg (2lb) beef brisket, trimmed**
- **2 tablespoons vegetable oil**
- **1 small onion (80g), sliced thinly**
- **2 cloves garlic, crushed**
- **2cm (¾in) piece fresh ginger, grated**
- **2 tablespoons fish sauce**
- **1 tablespoon dark soy sauce**
- **1 tablespoon light brown sugar**
- **1 teaspoon chinese five-spice powder**
- **2 x 10cm (4in) stalks fresh lemon grass, halved crossways**
- **2 cups (500ml) water**
- **150g (4½oz) snake beans, cut into 5cm (2in) lengths**
- **¾ cup (105g) crushed peanuts**
- **⅓ cup fresh vietnamese mint leaves**

1 Cut beef into 3cm (1¼in) pieces. Heat half the oil in a large saucepan. Cook beef, in batches, until browned. Remove from pan.

2 Heat remaining oil in same pan. Cook onion, garlic and ginger for 5 minutes until onion softens.

3 Return beef to pan with sauces, sugar, five-spice, lemon grass and the water; bring to the boil. Reduce heat and simmer, covered, for 1¼ hours or until beef is tender. Discard the lemon grass. Add beans and ½ cup of the peanuts. Simmer for 15 minutes. Season to taste.

4 Serve beef topped with remaining peanuts and mint leaves.

Suitable to freeze *at the end of step 3.*

LAMB ROGAN JOSH

prep + cook time 2 hours 30 minutes * serves 10

One of the signature recipes of Kashmiri cuisine, rogan josh was originally brought to the Kashmir region by the Moghuls and is now eaten the world over. It is a particular favourite of British curry houses.

*** 1 bunch fresh coriander (cilantro)**
*** 1½ tablespoons vegetable oil**
*** 1.2kg (2½lb) boned lamb shoulder, cut into 5cm (2in) pieces**
*** 2 medium onions (300g), sliced thinly**
*** 4 cloves garlic, crushed**
*** ⅔ cup (200g) rogan josh curry paste**
*** 410g (13oz) can tomato puree**
*** 1 cup (250ml) water**
*** 1kg (2lb) orange sweet potatoes, cut into 2.5cm (1in) pieces**
*** 3 x 400g (12½oz) cans chickpeas (garbanzo beans), drained, rinsed**
*** 150g (4½oz) baby spinach leaves**

1 Finely chop coriander stems and roots; reserve leaves for serving.
2 Heat 1 tablespoon of the oil in a large heavy-based saucepan over high heat. Cook lamb, in batches, for 5 minutes or until browned. Remove from pan.
3 Reduce heat to medium. Cook onion and garlic, stirring, for 4 minutes or until onion softens. Stir in chopped coriander stems and roots. Add curry paste and cook, stirring, for 1 minute or until fragrant. Add lamb, tomato puree and the water; stir to combine. Bring to the boil, then reduce heat and cook, covered, over low heat for 1½ hours.
4 Add sweet potato to pan; cook, covered, for 30 minutes or until lamb and vegetables are tender. Stir in chickpeas and spinach; season to taste. Top with reserved coriander leaves to serve.

Tip *You can also cook this recipe in a 180°C/350°F oven for 2 hours.*

Serving suggestion *Steamed basmati rice and pappadums.*

Suitable to freeze.

BALSAMIC-BRAISED CHICKEN

prep + cook time 1 hour 30 minutes * serves 4

- **3 stalks fresh flat-leaf parsley**
- **3 sprigs fresh thyme**
- **2 dried bay leaves**
- **4 chicken marylands (1.4kg)**
- **1 tablespoon olive oil**
- **1 large carrot (180g), halved crossways, then halved lengthways**
- **1 large onion (200g), cut into thick wedges still attached to root**
- **2 stalks celery (300g), trimmed, cut into thirds**
- **1½ cups (375ml) white balsamic vinegar**
- **¼ cup (60ml) balsamic vinegar**
- **½ cup (125ml) chicken stock, heated**
- **extra sprigs fresh thyme, to serve**

1 Tie parsley, thyme and bay leaves, using kitchen string, into a small bundle.

2 Trim any fat from chicken. Cut two slashes in the thickest part of the thighs. Season.

3 Heat oil in a large flameproof casserole dish over medium heat. Cook chicken, skin-side down, for 8 minutes or until browned. Transfer to a plate.

4 Add carrot, onion and celery to dish; cook, stirring occasionally, for 5 minutes or until starting to brown. Add herb bundle and both vinegars; bring to the boil. Reduce heat to low and simmer for 10 minutes or until reduced by half.

5 Place chicken on top of vegetables. Add hot stock, cover and simmer for 45 minutes or until chicken is just cooked. Stand for 10 minutes. Transfer chicken and vegetables to a serving dish. Return casserole dish to medium heat and bring to the boil, then reduce heat and boil for 5 minutes or until liquid is reduced by a third. Skim fat from surface. Season to taste.

6 Serve chicken and vegetables drizzled with sauce, topped with extra thyme sprigs.

Tip *Use a casserole dish large enough for chicken to fit in a single layer.*

Serving suggestion *Wilted silver beet (swiss chard) or rainbow chard leaves.*

CHICKEN TIKKA
WITH CAULIFLOWER RICE

prep + cook time 1 hour * serves 4

Cauliflower rice is a really great healthy alternative to white rice, if you are watching your carb intake. You just need a food processor to break up the florets into rice-sized pieces.

*** 1 tablespoon peanut oil**
*** 800g (1½lb) chicken thigh fillets, sliced thickly**
*** 1 medium onion (150g), cut into wedges**
*** 1 large red capsicum (bell pepper) (350g), chopped coarsely**
*** 250g (8oz) truss cherry tomatoes**
*** ⅓ cup (100g) tikka curry paste**
*** 2 fresh long green chillies, sliced thinly**
*** 300ml light cooking cream**
*** ¾ cup fresh coriander (cilantro) leaves**

RAITA
*** ¾ cup (200g) Greek-style yoghurt**
*** 1 lebanese cucumber (130g), seeded, chopped finely**
*** 1 tablespoon finely chopped fresh mint leaves**

CAULIFLOWER RICE
*** 1 small cauliflower (1kg), stems chopped finely, florets chopped coarsely**

1 Heat oil in a large deep frying pan over medium-high heat. Cook chicken, in batches, until browned all over. Remove from pan.
2 Add onion, capsicum and tomatoes to same pan, reduce heat to medium and cook, stirring, for 5 minutes or until onion softens. Remove tomatoes from pan and cover to keep warm. Add curry paste and half the chilli to pan; cook, stirring, for 2 minutes or until fragrant. Return chicken to pan with cream and bring to the boil. Reduce heat to low; cook for 10 minutes or until chicken is cooked through. Remove from heat. Return tomatoes to pan and keep warm.
3 Make raita and cauliflower rice.
4 Top chicken tikka with coriander and remaining chilli. Serve with cauliflower rice and raita.

RAITA Combine ingredients in a small bowl; season to taste.

CAULIFLOWER RICE Process cauliflower until finely chopped and resembling rice. Place cauliflower in a large frying pan over medium heat; cook, stirring occasionally, for 10 minutes or until just tender. Season to taste.

HEALTHY BUTTER CHICKEN

prep + cook time 1 hour 5 minutes (+ standing) * serves 4

- **1 cup (150g) raw cashews**
- **6 chicken drumsticks (900g)**
- **600ml buttermilk**
- **2 tablespoons ground turmeric**
- **1 tablespoon ground cumin**
- **1 tablespoon ground cinnamon**
- **1 tablespoon ground coriander**
- **1 tablespoon sweet paprika**
- **¾ teaspoon ground cloves**
- **1 tablespoon olive oil**
- **1 large onion (200g), chopped coarsely**
- **2 tablespoons tomato paste**
- **1 medium orange sweet potato (400g), cut into 2cm (¾in) rounds**
- **1 medium swede (225g), cut into 2cm (¾in) wedges**
- **3 cups (750ml) chicken stock**
- **2 trimmed corn cobs (500g), cut into 2cm (¾in) rounds**
- **60g (2oz) watercress sprigs**
- **extra raw cashews, to serve**

1 Place cashews in a medium bowl, cover with cold water and stand for 30 minutes.

2 Meanwhile, place chicken, buttermilk and spices in a large bowl; stir well to coat chicken completely. Cover and refrigerate for 30 minutes.

3 Drain chicken, reserving marinade. Heat oil in a large heavy-based saucepan over high heat. Cook chicken for 2 minutes on each side or until fragrant.

4 Add onion to pan and cook, stirring, for 2 minutes or until starting to soften. Stir in tomato paste and reserved marinade. Cook for 2 minutes or until mixture comes to a simmer and is fragrant.

5 Add sweet potato, swede and stock to pan; stir to combine. Bring to the boil, reduce heat to low and cook, covered, for 35 minutes or until chicken is falling off the bone and vegetables are tender when a small knife is inserted. Add corn during the last 10 minutes of cooking time.

6 Meanwhile, drain cashews, reserving ½ cup of soaking liquid. Process cashews and reserved liquid until a smooth paste forms (use a high-powered blender, if you have one, as this will achieve a very smooth result).

7 Add cashew paste to pan and stir until well combined to thicken sauce; cook for a further 5 minutes or until sauce thickens and coats the back of a wooden spoon. Season to taste.

8 Serve butter chicken topped with watercress and extra cashews.

Serving suggestion *Steamed basmati rice and warmed naan bread.*

COQ AU VIN

prep + cook time 1 hour 30 minutes * serves 4

Literally meaning 'rooster in wine', this is a quintessential French peasant dish. Braising slowly for hours was a favourite way of transforming tougher, less common meats into a hearty and nourishing meal.

- **750g (1½lb) spring onions**
- **¼ cup (60ml) extra virgin olive oil**
- **4 rindless bacon slices (390g), chopped coarsely**
- **310g (10½oz) button mushrooms**
- **2 cloves garlic, crushed**
- **8 chicken thigh fillets (880g)**
- **¼ cup (35g) plain (all-purpose) flour**
- **2 cups (500ml) dry red wine**
- **1½ cups (375ml) chicken stock**
- **2 tablespoons tomato paste**
- **3 bay leaves**
- **4 sprigs fresh thyme**
- **2 sprigs fresh rosemary**

1 Trim green ends from spring onions, leaving 4cm (1½in) of the stem attached; trim roots. Heat 1 tablespoon of oil in a large heavy-based frying pan. Cook spring onions, stirring, for 5 minutes or until browned all over. Transfer to a large bowl.

2 Add bacon, mushrooms and garlic to pan. Cook, stirring, until bacon is crisp and mushrooms are lightly browned. Transfer to bowl with spring onions.

3 Coat chicken in flour and shake off excess. Heat remaining oil in same pan. Cook chicken, in batches, turning occasionally, for 8 minutes or until browned all over; drain on paper towel.

4 Return chicken, bacon mixture and spring onions to pan. Add wine, stock, tomato paste, bay leaves, thyme and rosemary. Bring to the boil, then reduce heat to low and cook for 35 minutes or until chicken is tender and sauce thickens slightly.

Serving suggestion *Mashed potato or toasted sourdough bread to mop up the juices.*

SRI LANKAN SEAFOOD CURRY

prep + cook time 1 hour 45 minutes * serves 10

- **1.75kg (3½lb) firm white fish fillets**
- **1kg (2lb) uncooked large king prawns (shrimp)**
- **3 fresh long green chillies**
- **2 large onions (600g), chopped coarsely**
- **6 cloves garlic, chopped coarsely**
- **4cm (1½in) piece fresh ginger, chopped coarsely**
- **2 tablespoons olive oil**
- **1 tablespoon ground cumin**
- **3 teaspoons ground turmeric**
- **¼ cup fresh curry leaves**
- **750g (1½lb) ripe tomatoes, chopped**
- **1½ cups (375ml) chicken or fish stock**
- **2 cups (500ml) coconut cream**
- **1 tablespoon fish sauce**
- **1½ teaspoons caster (superfine) sugar**

TOMATO SAMBAL

- **3 medium ripe tomatoes (450g), cut into 1cm (½in) pieces**
- **1 small red onion (100g), chopped finely**
- **1 fresh long green chilli, seeded, chopped finely**
- **2 teaspoons tamarind concentrate**
- **1 teaspoon brown sugar**
- **2 tablespoons fresh coriander (cilantro) leaves**
- **½ cup (25g) coconut flakes, toasted**

COCONUT RICE

- **800ml canned coconut milk**
- **2⅔ cups (680ml) water**
- **4 cups (800g) basmati rice**

1 Cut fish into 6cm (2½in) pieces. Shell and devein prawns, leaving tails intact. Cover and refrigerate seafood separately until required.

2 Remove seeds from half the chillies, then coarsely chop all chillies. Process chilli, onion, garlic and ginger until finely chopped.

3 Heat oil in a large heavy-based saucepan over medium heat. Cook onion mixture, stirring, for 7 minutes or until softened. Reduce heat to low. Add cumin, turmeric and curry leaves; cook, stirring, for 5 minutes. Increase heat to high. Add tomato and stock; bring to the boil. Reduce heat and simmer for 15 minutes. Add coconut cream. Simmer for a further 10 minutes or until vegetables are tender and flavours are developed. Stir in fish sauce and sugar; season.

4 Meanwhile, make tomato sambal and coconut rice.

5 Add fish to curry sauce; simmer for 2 minutes. Add prawns. Simmer for a further 3 minutes or until prawns and fish are just cooked through.

6 Top curry with extra curry leaves, if you like. Serve with tomato sambal and coconut rice.

TOMATO SAMBAL Combine all ingredients except coconut in a medium bowl; season. Cover and refrigerate until required. Just before serving, stir in coconut flakes.

COCONUT RICE Bring coconut milk and the water to the boil in a large saucepan over medium heat. Add rice and return just to the boil, then cover with a tight-fitting lid. Reduce heat to the lowest setting. Cook for 16 minutes or until rice is tender and liquid absorbed. Remove from heat and stand, covered, for 10 minutes. Fluff rice with a fork.

PANANG LAMB CURRY

prep + cook time 2 hours 30 minutes ✻ serves 8

Panang curry is a type of red Thai curry that is thick, salty and sweet, with a nutty peanut flavour. The addition of peanut butter helps to bring out the flavour when using a bought curry paste.

*** 1 tablespoon peanut oil**
*** 1.5kg (3lb) boneless lamb shoulder, cut into 5cm (2in) pieces**
*** ½ cup (150g) panang curry paste**
*** 2½ cups (625ml) coconut cream**
*** 1 cup (250ml) beef or chicken stock, or water**
*** 2 tablespoons fish sauce**
*** ¼ cup (65g) grated palm sugar**
*** 2 tablespoons peanut butter**
*** 4 kaffir lime leaves**
*** 225g (7oz) can sliced bamboo shoots, drained, rinsed**
*** 1 small red capsicum (bell pepper) (150g), sliced thinly**
*** 200g (6½oz) green beans, trimmed**
*** ½ cup fresh coriander (cilantro) leaves**

1 Heat oil in a large flameproof casserole dish over high heat. Cook lamb, in batches, for 5 minutes or until browned. Return all lamb to dish.
2 Add curry paste to same dish; cook, stirring, for 1 minute or until fragrant. Stir in coconut cream, stock, fish sauce, sugar, peanut butter and lime leaves; bring to the boil. Reduce heat to low and cook, covered, for 2 hours or until lamb is tender.
3 Stir in bamboo shoots, capsicum and green beans. Cook, covered, for a further 10 minutes or until vegetables are tender. Season to taste.
4 Serve curry topped with coriander.

Tip *If the curry is too thin at the end of the cooking time, simmer, uncovered, until thickened. If too thick, stir in a little extra coconut cream or stock.*

Serving suggestion *Steamed jasmine rice.*

STUFFED CALAMARI

prep + cook time 1 hour 35 minutes ✻ serves 4

- **500g (1lb) uncooked prawns (shrimp), peeled, deveined, chopped finely**
- **½ cup (40g) quinoa flakes**
- **1 teaspoon finely grated lemon rind**
- **250g (8oz) haloumi, coarsely grated**
- **6 baby calamari (630g), cleaned, tentacles reserved**
- **2 tablespoons extra virgin olive oil, plus extra**
- **1 small onion (80g), chopped finely**
- **1 teaspoon smoked paprika**
- **½ cup (125ml) dry white wine**
- **800g (1½lb) napoletana pasta sauce**
- **1 cup (250ml) chicken stock**
- **½ teaspoon dried chilli flakes**
- **1 teaspoon brown sugar**
- **⅓ cup coarsely chopped fresh flat-leaf parsley, plus extra to serve**

1 To make stuffing, place prawn, quinoa, rind and haloumi in a large bowl; stir to combine well. Finely chop calamari tentacles and stir into prawn mixture. Season with pepper.

2 Divide stuffing mixture among calamari hoods and secure openings with toothpicks.

3 Heat 1 tablespoon of the oil in a large deep frying pan over medium-high heat. Add calamari and cook, turning, for 8 minutes or until golden all over. Transfer to a plate and set aside.

4 Heat the remaining oil in same frying pan. Add onion and cook, stirring, for 3 minutes or until softened. Add paprika and cook, stirring, for 30 seconds. Add wine and simmer for 3 minutes or until almost evaporated. Stir in pasta sauce, stock, chilli and sugar; bring to the boil. Return calamari to pan. Reduce heat to low and cook, stirring, turning calamari occasionally, for 35 minutes or until calamari is tender. Stir in chopped parsley.

5 Remove calamari from sauce and remove toothpicks, then cut into thick slices on the diagonal. Serve stuffed calamari on top of sauce with a drizzle of extra olive oil and scattered with extra chopped parsley.

Serving suggestion *Lemon wedges and crusty bread.*

NAVARIN OF LAMB

prep + cook time 1 hour 50 minutes * serves 4

- **2 tablespoons olive oil**
- **8 lamb noisettes (800g) (see tip)**
- **1 large onion (200g), sliced thickly**
- **2 cloves garlic, crushed**
- **2 tablespoons plain (all-purpose) flour**
- **1 cup (250ml) water**
- **3 cups (750ml) chicken stock**
- **½ cup (125ml) dry red wine**
- **400g (12½oz) can diced tomatoes**
- **¼ cup (70g) tomato paste**
- **2 bay leaves**
- **2 sprigs fresh rosemary**
- **2 stalks celery (300g), trimmed, cut into 5cm (2in) lengths**
- **150g (4½oz) green beans, trimmed, halved**
- **20 baby (dutch) carrots (400g), trimmed**
- **200g (6½oz) mushrooms**
- **1 cup (120g) frozen peas**

1 Heat oil in a large saucepan. Cook lamb, in batches, until browned. Remove from pan.

2 Cook onion and garlic in same pan, stirring, until onion softens. Add flour and cook, stirring, until mixture bubbles and thickens. Gradually add the water, stock and wine; stir until mixture boils and thickens.

3 Return lamb to pan with canned tomatoes, tomato paste, bay leaves and rosemary; bring to the boil. Reduce heat and simmer, covered, for 30 minutes.

4 Add celery, beans, carrots and mushrooms to pan. Simmer, covered, for a further 30 minutes or until vegetables are tender. Add peas and simmer, uncovered, until peas are just tender.

5 Remove and discard toothpicks from lamb. Serve.

Tip *Lamb noisettes are lamb sirloin chops with the bone removed and the 'tail' wrapped around the meaty part of the chop and secured with a toothpick.*

Serving suggestion *Mashed potato.*

Suitable to freeze.

4 WAYS WITH GREEN VEGETABLES

BROCCOLINI AND CRUMBS

prep + cook time 15 minutes ✻ serves 4

Heat ⅓ cup olive oil in a frying pan over medium heat. Stir ¾ cup panko (japanese) breadcrumbs and 1 teaspoon salt flakes for 5 minutes or until golden. Add 4 cloves thinly sliced garlic and stir for 3 minutes or until cooked. Add ¼ cup fresh flat-leaf parsley leaves and 1 teaspoon grated lemon rind. Boil 460g (14½oz) trimmed broccolini for 3 minutes until tender; drain. Toss broccolini with crumb mixture.

BRUSSELS SPROUTS, DUKKAH AND HONEY

prep + cook time 10 minutes ✻ serves 4

Trim ends from 500g (1lb) brussels sprouts and discard. Cut brussels sprouts in half. Place in a bowl with 2 tablespoons each honey and olive oil. Season with salt and pepper. Toss well to combine. Heat a non-stick frying pan over medium heat. Cook sprouts, cut-side down, for 2 minutes or until tender. Turn over and cook for 2 minutes or until browned. Add 2 tablespoons dukkah and toss to combine.

CHARGRILLED ASPARAGUS

prep + cook time 10 minutes ✻ serves 4

Trim 2cm (¾in) from the ends of 480g (15½oz) asparagus. Preheat a chargrill pan. Group asparagus in threes, side-by-side, then thread two toothpicks through each group to hold them together. Brush asparagus with 2 tablespoons each combined kecap manis and olive oil. Chargrill for 2 minutes each side. Serve with baby rocket and lime wedges.

SILVER BEET WITH PINE NUTS

prep + cook time 10 minutes ✻ serves 4

Trim 6cm (2½in) from stem ends of 380g (12oz) silver beet (swiss chard) and discard. Coarsely chop remaining silver beet, keeping leaves and white stems separate. Heat ¼ cup olive oil in a frying pan over medium heat. Cook 1 large thinly sliced red onion, white silver beet stems and ⅓ cup raisins, stirring, for 5 minutes. Add leaves and stir for 8 minutes or until tender. Stir in ½ cup toasted pine nuts.

PORK WITH BEANS AND BEER

prep + cook time 2 hours 40 minutes * serves 8

- **3 cloves garlic, crushed**
- **½ teaspoon freshly ground black pepper**
- **1.8kg (3½lb) pork neck (scotch fillet roast)**
- **1 tablespoon olive oil**
- **3 rindless bacon slices (195g), chopped finely**
- **2 medium onions (300g), sliced thinly**
- **2 teaspoons caraway seeds**
- **1½ cups (375ml) beer**
- **1 cup (200g) dried haricot beans**
- **1½ cups (375ml) chicken stock**
- **¼ small (300g) white cabbage, shredded finely**

1 Rub combined garlic and pepper all over pork. Secure pork with kitchen string at 2cm (¾in) intervals to make an even shape.

2 Heat oil in a large flameproof roasting pan. Cook pork until browned all over, then remove from pan.

3 Cook bacon, onion and seeds in same pan, stirring, until onion is soft and bacon is browned lightly.

4 Return pork to pan with beer, beans and stock. Simmer, covered, for 2 hours or until beans and pork are tender. Remove pork from pan. Add cabbage and cook, stirring, until just wilted.

5 Serve pork with bean mixture.

KOREAN BRAISED BEEF RIBS
WITH KIMCHI AND DAIKON NOODLES

prep + cook time 2 hours 30 minutes ✻ serves 4

Kimchi actually refers to any salted and fermented vegetable in Korean cuisine, but by far the most recognisable of these is baechu kimchi, kimchi made with wombok (chinese cabbage). Koreans are said to eat roughly 18kg of kimchi per person annually.

∗ 1 tablespoon vegetable oil
∗ 1kg (2lb) beef short ribs, cut 6cm (2½in) high
∗ 1 bunch green onions (scallions) (300g)
∗ 1 tablespoon finely chopped fresh ginger
∗ 2 cloves garlic, crushed
∗ 2 tablespoons sesame oil
∗ 2 tablespoons rice wine vinegar
∗ 1 tablespoon soy sauce
∗ 1 tablespoon gochujang (korean red chilli paste)
∗ 1 litre (4 cups) water
∗ 1 cup (100g) kimchi
∗ 1 medium firm pear (230g), grated coarsely
∗ 100g (3oz) fresh shiitake mushrooms
∗ 1 large daikon (800g)
∗ 500g (1lb) baby buk choy, quartered lengthways
∗ 100g (3oz) enoki mushrooms
∗ 1 tablespoon sesame seeds
∗ ½ teaspoon gochugaru (korean red pepper flakes)

1 Heat vegetable oil in a large heavy-based saucepan or flameproof casserole dish over high heat. Season ribs, then cook, turning occasionally, for 8 minutes or until browned all over.
2 Chop the white part of the green onions; reserve green tops for serving and refrigerate. Add chopped green onion, ginger and garlic to pan; cook, stirring, for 30 seconds or until fragrant.
3 Place sesame oil, rice wine, soy sauce and gochujang in a large jug; whisk until combined. Add mixture to pan with the water, kimchi and pear; bring to a simmer. Cook, covered, over low heat, stirring every 30 minutes, for 2 hours or until beef is tender and falls away from the bone. Add shiitake mushrooms to pan for the last 30 minutes of cooking time.
4 Meanwhile, use a julienne peeler, spiraliser, julienne attachment on a mandoline or V-slicer to cut daikon into long thin strips. Cook daikon in a large saucepan of boiling salted water for 3 minutes or until just tender; drain well.
5 Place buk choy and enoki mushrooms on top of braised beef rib mixture. Cook, covered, for a further 2 minutes or until vegetables are just tender.
6 Trim the green tops of the onions and cut into long thin strips. Top ribs with green onion strips, sprinkled with seeds and gochugaru. Serve with daikon noodles.

'OSSO BUCO' SQUID

prep + cook time 1 hour 30 minutes * serves 4

- **2 tablespoons olive oil**
- **1 medium carrot (120g), chopped finely**
- **2 trimmed celery stalks (200g), chopped finely**
- **1 medium onion (150g), chopped finely**
- **2 cloves garlic, chopped finely**
- **1 tablespoon finely chopped fresh rosemary**
- **1 cup (250ml) dry white wine**
- **2 x 400g (12½oz) cans diced tomatoes**
- **2 teaspoons caster (superfine) sugar**
- **800g (1½lb) cleaned squid hoods, sliced into 1cm (½in) thick rings, tentacles reserved**

GREMOLATA BUTTER TOASTS

- **50g (1½oz) butter, softened**
- **1 tablespoon finely chopped fresh flat-leaf parsley**
- **1 tablespoon finely grated lemon rind**
- **1 clove garlic, crushed**
- **8 slices sourdough bread (400g)**

1 Heat oil in a large heavy-based saucepan over medium heat. Add carrot, celery, onion, garlic and rosemary. Cook, stirring, for 10 minutes or until carrot is tender. Add wine and cook for 2 minutes. Add canned tomatoes and sugar; bring to the boil. Add squid, reduce heat to low and cook, covered, for 1 hour or until squid is tender. Season to taste.

2 Make gremolata butter toasts.

3 Scatter squid mixture with remaining lemon rind (from gremolata butter toasts) and fresh parsley leaves, if you like. Serve with gremolata butter toasts.

GREMOLATA BUTTER TOASTS Combine butter, parsley, 2 teaspoons of the lemon rind and garlic in a small bowl; season. Reserve remaining lemon rind for serving. Cook bread on a heated oiled chargrill plate (or pan) for 2 minutes on each side or until char marks appear. Spread with gremolata butter.

Do ahead *This recipe can be made the day before; cover and refrigerate.*

VEAL, MUSHROOMS
AND POTATOES WITH CREAM SAUCE

prep + cook time 1 hour * serves 4

- **60g (2oz) butter**
- **400g (12½oz) veal fillet, sliced thinly**
- **3 shallots (75g), halved**
- **200g (6½oz) swiss brown mushrooms, halved or quartered (see tip)**
- **500g (1lb) kipfler (fingerling) potatoes, cut into 1cm (½in) slices**
- **⅓ cup (80ml) dry white wine**
- **1 cup (250ml) chicken stock**
- **1 tablespoon worcestershire sauce**
- **2 teaspoons dijon mustard**
- **250g (8oz) crème fraîche**
- **¼ cup chopped fresh chives**
- **50g (1½oz) baby spinach leaves**

1 Melt a third of the butter in a large non-stick frying pan over high heat. Cook veal for 1 minute on each side or until browned lightly. Transfer to a plate and cover to keep warm.

2 Heat another third of the butter in same pan. Add shallot and mushroom; cook, stirring, for 5 minutes or until liquid evaporates. Remove from pan.

3 Melt remaining butter in same pan, add potato and cook, stirring, for 10 minutes or until lightly browned and tender. Remove from pan.

4 Add wine to pan and cook, stirring, for 1 minute or until reduced slightly. Add stock, sauce and mustard; bring to the boil. Reduce heat to low-medium and simmer for 3 minutes or until reduced by half. Whisk in crème fraîche and half the chives.

5 Return potato, mushroom mixture and veal to pan to warm through. Add spinach and stir to combine. Serve topped with remaining chives. Season to taste.

Tip *Swiss brown mushrooms have a stronger flavour than button mushrooms, which can be used instead, if you prefer.*

STEWS

PORK, MUSHROOM AND MARSALA STEW

prep + cook time 2 hours 15 minutes ✱ serves 4

- **1kg (2lb) boneless pork shoulder, chopped coarsely (see tips)**
- **¼ cup (35g) plain (all-purpose) flour**
- **2 tablespoons olive oil**
- **4 shallots (100g), sliced thinly**
- **2 cloves garlic, sliced thinly**
- **300g (9½oz) swiss brown mushrooms, halved**
- **1 tablespoon chopped fresh rosemary**
- **1 cup (250ml) marsala (see tips)**
- **1 cup (250ml) chicken stock**
- **1 cup (250ml) water**
- **1 tablespoon tomato paste**
- **½ cup coarsely chopped fresh flat-leaf parsley**

1 Coat pork in flour and shake off excess. Heat oil in a large saucepan or flameproof roasting pan. Cook pork, in batches, until browned all over.

2 Cook shallot, garlic, mushrooms and rosemary in same pan, stirring occasionally, until mushrooms are browned. Add marsala and cook, stirring, for 30 seconds.

3 Return pork to pan with stock, the water and tomato paste; bring to the boil. Reduce heat and simmer, covered, for 1¾ hours, stirring occasionally, or until pork is tender. Season to taste.

4 Serve marsala stew scattered with parsley.

Tips *You can use other cuts of stewing pork for this dish, such as pork neck (scotch), if you prefer. Marsala is an Italian fortified wine. Substitute with madeira, port or dry sherry, if unavailable.*

Suitable to freeze *at the end of step 3.*

CHILLI BEEF
WITH CORNBREAD DUMPLINGS

prep + cook time 1 hour 10 minutes ✻ serves 4

∗ 1 tablespoon olive oil
∗ 1 medium onion (150g), chopped coarsely
∗ 800g (1½lb) minced (ground) beef
∗ 3 cloves garlic, crushed
∗ 2 teaspoons ground cumin
∗ 2 teaspoons smoked paprika
∗ ½ teaspoon cayenne pepper (optional)
∗ 400g (12½oz) can kidney beans, drained, rinsed
∗ 2 x 400g (12½oz) cans diced tomatoes
∗ 1 cup (250ml) beef stock
∗ 1 cup (250ml) water
∗ 1 tablespoon brown sugar

CORNBREAD DUMPLINGS
∗ 1⅓ cups (200g) self-raising flour
∗ ⅓ cup (55g) polenta
∗ ¼ cup (30g) coarsely grated cheddar
∗ ¼ cup (60g) creamed corn
∗ 1 egg, beaten lightly
∗ ½ cup (125ml) milk

1 Heat oil in a large saucepan (see tips). Cook onion, beef, garlic, cumin, paprika and cayenne pepper, stirring, until beef is browned.
2 Add beans to pan with canned tomatoes, stock, the water and sugar; bring to the boil. Reduce heat and simmer for 30 minutes, stirring occasionally. Season to taste.
3 Meanwhile, make cornbread dumpling mixture.
4 Roll level tablespoons of the dumpling mixture into balls (see tips) and place on top of beef mixture in pan. Cook, covered, for 15 minutes or until dumplings are cooked.

CORNBREAD DUMPLINGS Combine sifted flour, polenta and cheddar in a medium bowl, then stir in creamed corn, egg and milk.

Tips *Use a wide saucepan so you have more surface area for the dumplings to cook. Use wet hands when rolling the dumplings to stop them sticking.*

BEEF AND PORCINI MUSHROOM STEW WITH PARMESAN MASH

prep + cook time 2 hours 15 minutes (+ standing) * serves 4

Mushrooms have a moreish savoury taste known as 'umami' and are a good source of vitamins B and D. Here they add a richness to the stew, and the cheesy parmesan mash ensures none of the delicious juices are wasted.

*** 25g (¾oz) dried porcini mushrooms**
*** 1 cup (250ml) beef stock**
*** 2 tablespoons olive oil**
*** 1.5kg (3lb) gravy beef, cut into 5cm (2in) pieces**
*** 1 large onion (200g), chopped coarsely**
*** 2 cloves garlic, crushed**
*** 2 tablespoons tomato paste**
*** 400g (12½oz) can cherry tomatoes**
*** 1 bay leaf**
*** 250g (4oz) button mushrooms, halved**
*** ¼ cup fresh flat-leaf parsley leaves**

PARMESAN MASH
*** 1kg (2lb) floury potatoes (see tips), peeled, cut into large pieces**
*** ¾ cup (180ml) pouring cream**
*** 75g (2½oz) butter, chopped**
*** 1 cup (80g) finely grated parmesan**

1 Place porcini mushrooms and stock in a small bowl; stand for 10 minutes. Drain, reserving stock. Finely chop mushrooms.
2 Heat oil in a large flameproof casserole dish or heavy-based saucepan over medium-high heat. Cook beef, in batches, turning, until browned all over. Remove from dish.
3 Cook onion and garlic in same dish, stirring, for 3 minutes or until softened. Return beef to dish and add tomato paste, canned tomatoes, bay leaf, porcini mushrooms and reserved stock. Bring to the boil, then reduce heat to low and simmer, covered, for 30 minutes. Add button mushrooms and cook, uncovered, for a further 1 hour or until meat is tender. Season to taste.
4 Meanwhile, make parmesan mash.
5 Top stew with parsley and scatter with finely grated parmesan, if you like. Serve with parmesan mash.

PARMESAN MASH Boil potato in a saucepan of salted water for 15 minutes or until tender. Drain and leave for a few minutes to dry. Heat cream and butter in same pan over low-medium heat. Add potato, mashing into milk mixture with a potato masher until smooth. Remove from heat. Stir in parmesan until combined. Season to taste.

Tips *Floury potatoes have a high starch content so tend to fall apart when cooked. They are great for mashing, and for roasting too, as their flesh becomes fluffy and the outside crisp. If you use a potato ricer to mash potatoes, add pressed potatoes to the warm cream, then stir the butter and parmesan in.*

KIPFLER AND SMOKED PORK SAUSAGE GOULASH

prep + cook time 1 hour * serves 4

Originally a stew from Hungary, a goulash is characterised by its spices, particularly smoked paprika, and is known for its heartiness. Here we use pork sausage meat and kipfler potatoes for a fast version, so dinner can be on the table in no time at all.

- **2 tablespoons olive oil**
- **500g (1lb) good-quality pork sausages**
- **2 small red onions (200g), cut into wedges**
- **500g (1lb) small kipfler (fingerling) potatoes, scrubbed, halved lengthways**
- **2 cloves garlic, crushed**
- **2 tablespoons tomato paste**
- **2¼ teaspoons smoked paprika**
- **½ teaspoon fennel seeds**
- **400g (12½oz) can crushed tomatoes**
- **1 cup (250ml) chicken stock**
- **⅓ cup (80g) sour cream**
- **½ cup (55g) coarsely chopped walnuts, toasted**

1 Heat oil in a large heavy-based frying pan over high heat. Squeeze pieces of sausage out of skins into pan and cook, stirring occasionally, for 5 minutes or until golden brown. Remove from pan with a slotted spoon and drain on paper towel.

2 Add onion and potato to same pan; cook, stirring occasionally, for 5 minutes or until onion softens. Return sausage to pan, then add garlic, tomato paste, 2 teaspoons of the paprika and fennel seeds; cook, stirring, for 2 minutes or until fragrant. Add canned tomatoes and stock; bring to the boil. Reduce heat to medium and simmer, covered, for 20 minutes or until potato is tender and sauce reduces slightly. Season.

3 Serve goulash topped with sour cream, walnuts, remaining paprika and baby parsley leaves, if you like.

Do ahead *Goulash can be made to the end of step 2 up to 2 days ahead and refrigerated in an airtight container.*

PORK AND FENNEL RAGÙ
WITH SWEET POTATO GNOCCHI

prep + cook time 2 hours 50 minutes (+ cooling) * serves 6

*** 1.6kg (3¼lb) piece boneless pork shoulder**
*** 2 tablespoons plain (all-purpose) flour**
*** 1 tablespoon extra virgin olive oil**
*** 2 medium leeks (700g), white part only, sliced thinly**
*** 2 trimmed celery stalks (200g), chopped coarsely**
*** 2 medium fennel bulbs (600g), sliced thinly, fronds reserved**
*** 4 cloves garlic, chopped**
*** 1 teaspoon chopped fresh thyme leaves**
*** ¼ teaspoon dried chilli flakes**
*** 2 cups (500ml) chicken stock**
*** 2 cups (500ml) water**
*** 1 cup (120g) green sicilian olives**
*** 1 tablespoon lemon juice**

SWEET POTATO GNOCCHI
*** 1kg (2lb) orange sweet potatoes, unpeeled**
*** 120g (4oz) soft goat's cheese, crumbled (see tips)**
*** 2 egg yolks**
*** 1 cup (150g) plain (all-purpose) flour, approximately**

1 Remove rind and trim fat from pork. Cut pork into six pieces; toss in flour and shake away excess. Heat oil in a flameproof casserole dish over high heat. Cook pork, in batches, for 10 minutes or until browned lightly all over. Remove from dish.
2 Cook leek, celery and sliced fennel in same dish over medium heat, stirring, for 8 minutes or until softened. Add garlic, thyme and chilli; cook, stirring, for 1 minute or until fragrant. Add stock and the water; bring to the boil. Return pork to dish; stir to cover with liquid. Reduce heat to low and cook, covered, stirring occasionally, for 2 hours or until tender.
3 Meanwhile, make sweet potato gnocchi.
4 Remove pork from pan and shred into smaller pieces. Return pork to pan and add olives and juice. Season to taste. Cover and keep warm over low heat.
5 Cook gnocchi, in batches, in a large saucepan of boiling salted water for 2 minutes or until gnocchi float to the surface. Remove gnocchi with a slotted spoon and drain on paper towel.
6 Top gnocchi with ragù. Serve scattered with reserved fennel fronds.

SWEET POTATO GNOCCHI Place whole sweet potatoes in a medium saucepan and cover with cold water. Cover pan with lid and bring to the boil. Reduce heat to low-medium and simmer, partially covered, for 45 minutes or until tender. Drain. Cool slightly, then peel. Mash sweet potato in a large bowl until smooth. Cool to room temperature. Stir in cheese and egg yolks; season. Add enough of the flour to form a soft, slightly sticky dough. Divide dough into six portions. Roll each portion on a floured workbench into a 2cm (¾in) thick log. Using a floured knife, cut logs into 2cm (¾in) lengths. Place gnocchi in a single layer on a large plastic-wrap-lined tray. Cover and refrigerate until required.

Tips *You can use drained persian fetta instead of goat's cheese, if you prefer. Prepare the ragù several hours or a day ahead; refrigerate until cold, then remove any fat from the surface before reheating.*

IRISH STEW
WITH CARROT-TOP SALSA VERDE

prep + cook time 2 hours 45 minutes ✻ serves 4

∗ ⅓ cup (80ml) olive oil
∗ 1kg (2lb) boneless lamb neck, cut into 5cm (2in) pieces
∗ 1 medium onion (150g), chopped
∗ 1 trimmed celery stalk (100g), chopped finely
∗ 3 cloves garlic, crushed
∗ 1.25 litres (5 cups) chicken stock
∗ 400g (12½oz) baby (dutch) carrots with tops, trimmed, tops reserved (see tip)
∗ 1 medium swede (225g), cut into six wedges
∗ ½ cup (70g) roasted hazelnuts, chopped coarsely

CARROT-TOP SALSA VERDE
∗ 1½ cups fresh flat-leaf parsley leaves
∗ 1½ tablespoons fresh lemon thyme leaves
∗ 1 tablespoon capers
∗ 1 small clove garlic, crushed
∗ 1 teaspoon brown sugar
∗ ½ cup (125ml) extra virgin olive oil
∗ 1½ tablespoons white wine vinegar

1 Heat 2 tablespoons of the oil in a large heavy-based saucepan over high heat. Cook lamb, in batches, for 5 minutes, turning occasionally, until browned all over. Remove from pan. (If the base of the pan starts to burn, add 2 tablespoons water and stir to lift meat sticking to the base of the pan.)

2 Reduce heat to medium and add remaining oil to pan. Cook onion, celery and garlic, stirring occasionally, for 10 minutes or until softened. Return lamb to pan, add stock and bring to the boil. Reduce heat to low and cook, covered, for 2 hours or until meat is tender.

3 Meanwhile, wash reserved carrot tops; you need ½ cup firmly packed tops for salsa verde, and some extra to serve. Make carrot-top salsa verde.

4 Increase heat to high and return stew to the boil. Add carrots and swede. Simmer, uncovered, for 15 minutes or until liquid thickens slightly. Season to taste.

5 Serve stew topped with hazelnuts and salsa verde.

CARROT-TOP SALSA VERDE Blend or process ingredients with reserved ½ cup carrot tops (from step 3) until well combined; season to taste. Refrigerate until needed.

Tip *Storing baby carrots with the leaves attached reduces their shelf life dramatically, so cut the tops off as soon as you can. Wrap the tops in damp paper towel, then refrigerate until needed.*

IRISH LAMB
AND BARLEY STEW

prep + cook time 2 hours 5 minutes * serves 6

- **2 tablespoons olive oil**
- **1kg (2lb) diced lamb shoulder**
- **1 large onion (200g), chopped coarsely**
- **2 medium carrots (240g), chopped coarsely**
- **2 stalks celery (300g), trimmed, chopped coarsely**
- **2 cloves garlic, crushed**
- **1 litre (4 cups) chicken stock**
- **2 cups (500ml) water**
- **1 cup (200g) pearl barley**
- **4 sprigs fresh thyme**
- **3 medium potatoes (600g), chopped coarsely**
- **2 cups (160g) finely shredded white cabbage**
- **⅓ cup finely chopped fresh flat-leaf parsley**

1 Heat half the oil in a large saucepan. Cook lamb, in batches, until browned. Remove lamb from pan.

2 Heat remaining oil in same pan. Cook onion, carrot, celery and garlic, stirring, until vegetables soften. Return lamb to pan with stock, the water, barley and thyme; bring to the boil. Reduce heat and simmer, covered, for 1 hour, skimming fat from surface occasionally.

3 Add potato to pan and simmer, uncovered, for 20 minutes or until potato is tender. Add cabbage and simmer, uncovered, until cabbage is just tender. Discard thyme. Season to taste.

4 Serve stew scattered with parsley.

Serving suggestion
Irish soda bread.

Suitable to freeze
at the end of step 2.

SWEET AND SOUR PORK STEW WITH COCONUT RICE

prep + cook time 1 hour ✻ serves 6

∗ 1 tablespoon cornflour (cornstarch)
∗ 1 egg, beaten lightly
∗ 2 tablespoons soy sauce
∗ 1kg (2lb) pork neck (scotch fillet roast), cut into 2cm (¾in) pieces
∗ 2 tablespoons olive oil
∗ 1 medium red onion (170g), chopped coarsely
∗ 30g (1oz) piece fresh ginger, cut into matchsticks
∗ 4 cloves garlic, sliced
∗ 3 fresh long red chillies, sliced thinly
∗ 1 medium red capsicum (bell pepper) (200g), chopped coarsely
∗ 700g (1½lb) pineapple, peeled, core removed, chopped coarsely
∗ 2 medium tomatoes (300g), chopped coarsely
∗ ¾ cup (180ml) rice wine vinegar
∗ 1 cup (250ml) chinese cooking wine (shao hsing)
∗ 2½ tablespoons honey
∗ 3 green onions (scallions), green tops sliced thinly, white part reserved for coconut rice
∗ ½ cup (75g) roasted salted cashews, chopped
∗ 1 lime (65g), cut into wedges

COCONUT RICE
∗ 1 tablespoon olive oil
∗ 2 cups (360g) brown jasmine rice
∗ 400ml can coconut cream
∗ 2½ cups (625ml) water

1 Combine cornflour, egg and soy sauce in a large bowl. Add pork and toss to coat. Season. Heat oil in a large saucepan over high heat. Cook pork, stirring, for 5 minutes or until browned. Using a slotted spoon, transfer pork to a heatproof bowl.

2 Add red onion, ginger, garlic and chilli to pan; cook, stirring, for 4 minutes or until soft. Add capsicum and cook, stirring, for 3 minutes. Add pineapple, tomato, pork and any pork resting juices, rice wine, cooking wine and honey to pan. Reduce heat to low and cook for 20 minutes or until sauce thickens. Season to taste.

3 Meanwhile, make coconut rice.

4 Top coconut rice with pork stew. Scatter with sliced green onion tops and cashews. Serve with lime wedges.

COCONUT RICE Finely chop the reserved white part of the green onion. Heat oil in a medium saucepan over high heat. Cook chopped green onion, stirring, for 2 minutes or until softened. Add rice and cook, stirring, for 1 minute or until coated in oil. Add coconut cream and the water; bring to the boil. Reduce heat to low and cook, stirring occasionally, for 20 minutes or until most of the liquid is absorbed. Remove pan from heat. Stand, covered, for 5 minutes or until rice is tender. Fluff rice with a fork. Season to taste.

PERI PERI COCONUT PORK CURRY

prep + cook time 1 hour * serves 4

- **1 tablespoon olive oil**
- **1kg (2lb) pork fillets, cut 5cm (2in) pieces**
- **1 medium onion (150g), chopped coarsely**
- **¼ cup (60ml) sweet sherry**
- **225g (7oz) packet keralan coconut curry sauce**
- **120g (4oz) peri peri sauce**
- **165ml can coconut milk**
- **1 cup (250ml) water**
- **2 tablespoons tomato paste**
- **200g (6½oz) broccolini, trimmed, halved**
- **⅓ cup (25g) shredded coconut**
- **500g (1lb) basmati microwave rice (see tip)**
- **¼ cup fresh micro mint**
- **1 teaspoon black sesame seeds**

1 Heat oil in a large heavy-based saucepan over high heat. Cook pork, in batches, until browned all over. Return pork to pan.

2 Add onion and sherry to pan. Cook, stirring, for 3 minutes or until onion softens. Add sauces, coconut milk, the water and tomato paste; bring to the boil. Reduce heat and simmer, covered, for 15 minutes. Stir in broccolini and simmer, covered, for 10 minutes or until pork is tender and cooked through. Cut pork into thin slices and return to pan. Season. Cook, uncovered, for a further 5 minutes or until the sauce thickens slightly.

3 Meanwhile, stir coconut in a medium frying pan over low heat for 3 minutes or until golden. Remove coconut from the pan immediately to prevent over-browning.

4 Microwave rice following packet directions. Place rice in a medium bowl with coconut and stir to combine.

5 Top curry with mint and sesame seeds. Serve with coconut rice.

Tip *You can cook your own rice instead of using microwave rice, if you prefer. You will need 1 cup (250g) raw basmati rice to make 500g cooked.*

FRAGRANT VIETNAMESE-STYLE BEEF STEW

prep + cook time 2 hours 50 minutes * serves 4

This is a simple and fresh take on the Vietnamese stew called bò kho, a spicy and warming dish which, in Vietnam, is traditionally eaten for breakfast. Serve stew with steamed basmati rice, over rice noodles, or with a crusty french baguette to soak up all the juices.

*** 1 tablespoon rice bran oil**
*** 1kg (2lb) beef chuck steak, cut into 3cm (1¼in) cubes**
*** 2 medium red onions (340g)**
*** 1 stalk lemon grass, bruised, quartered**
*** 1 teaspoon chinese five-spice powder**
*** 3 whole star anise**
*** 2 whole cloves**
*** ¼ teaspoon cardamom seeds**
*** 5 medium tomatoes (750g), chopped**
*** 1 litre (4 cups) water**
*** ¼ cup (60ml) fish sauce**
*** 2 tablespoons lime juice**
*** 1 teaspoon sea salt flakes**
*** 2 bunches mixed heirloom baby (dutch) carrots (800g), trimmed, peeled**
*** 125g (4oz) baby corn, sliced on the diagonal**
*** 1 cup (80g) bean sprouts**
*** 1 cup fresh thai basil sprigs (see tip)**
*** 1 fresh long red chilli, sliced thinly**
*** 1 lime (65g), cut into wedges**

1 Heat oil in a large heavy-based saucepan or flameproof casserole dish over high heat. Cook beef, in two batches, for 5 minutes or until browned all over. Remove from pan.
2 Chop 1 onion coarsely. Reduce heat to medium. Cook chopped onion, stirring, for 5 minutes or until softened. Add lemon grass and spices; cook, stirring, for 1 minute or until fragrant. Stir in tomato and cook, stirring occasionally, for 4 minutes or until softened.
3 Return beef to pan. Add the water, fish sauce, and season with a little freshly ground black pepper. Bring to the boil, then reduce heat to low and cook, covered, stirring occasionally, for 2 hours or until beef is very tender.
4 Meanwhile, slice remaining onion thinly. Combine sliced onion with juice and salt in a medium glass or ceramic bowl. Stand, covered, for at least 1 hour. Drain before using.
5 Add carrots and corn to beef mixture. Simmer, covered, for 20 minutes or until vegetables are tender. Season to taste.
6 Top stew with bean sprouts, pickled onion, basil and chilli. Serve with lime wedges.

Tip *If you can't find fresh thai basil, use coriander instead.*

Do ahead *Stew can be made a day ahead and refrigerated in an airtight container, or it will freeze for up to 2 months. Make the pickled onion on the day of serving.*

PROVENÇALE BEEF STEW

prep + cook time 1 hour 45 minutes ✻ serves 4

If you wouldn't drink it, don't cook with it: that's the rule of thumb for choosing wine for cooking. Cheap and inferior-quality wines will impart a less pleasant flavour than a great drinking wine.

∗ 2 tablespoons extra virgin olive oil
∗ 1kg (2lb) gravy beef, cut into 2cm (¾in) pieces
∗ 2 rindless bacon slices (130g), chopped coarsely
∗ 1 medium leek (350g), white part only, sliced thinly
∗ 2 medium carrots (240g), diced
∗ 1 stalk celery (150g), trimmed, diced
∗ 2 cloves garlic, crushed
∗ 400g (12½oz) can crushed tomatoes
∗ 1½ cups (375ml) beef stock
∗ 1 cup (250ml) dry red wine
∗ 2 bay leaves
∗ 4 sprigs fresh thyme
∗ 6 sprigs fresh flat-leaf parsley
∗ 2 medium zucchini (240g), sliced
∗ ½ cup (75g) pitted kalamata olives

1 Heat oil in a large heavy-based saucepan over high heat. Cook beef, in batches, for 5 minutes or until browned all over. Remove from pan.
2 Cook bacon, leek, carrot, celery and garlic in same pan, stirring, for 5 minutes or until leek softens.
3 Return beef to pan and add canned tomatoes, stock, wine, bay leaves, thyme and parsley; bring to the boil. Reduce heat to low and cook, covered, for 1 hour, stirring occasionally.
4 Add zucchini and olives. Cook, covered, for 30 minutes or until beef is tender.
5 Remove and discard thyme and parsley before serving.

Serving suggestion *Mashed potato or crusty bread to mop up the sauce.*

4 WAYS WITH POLENTA

SOFT POLENTA

prep + cook time 20 minutes ✻ serves 6

Bring 3 cups milk and 2 cups chicken (or vegetable) stock to the boil in a large saucepan. Gradually add 2 cups polenta, stirring continuously. Reduce heat and simmer, stirring, for 10 minutes or until polenta thickens. Stir in an extra 1 cup milk and ¼ cup finely grated parmesan until cheese melts. Season with sea salt and freshly ground black pepper.

LEMON THYME POLENTA

prep + cook time 20 minutes ✻ serves 6

Bring 3 cups milk and 2 cups chicken (or vegetable) stock to the boil in a large saucepan. Gradually add 2 cups polenta, stirring continuously. Reduce heat and stir in 2 teaspoons lemon thyme leaves. Simmer for 10 minutes or until polenta thickens. Stir in an extra 1 cup milk, 1 teaspoon finely grated lemon rind and ¼ cup finely grated parmesan until cheese melts. Serve topped with extra lemon thyme and finely grated parmesan, if you like.

OLIVE POLENTA

prep + cook time 20 minutes ⁕ serves 6

Bring 3 cups milk and 2 cups chicken (or vegetable) stock to the boil in a large saucepan. Gradually add 2 cups polenta, stirring continuously. Reduce heat and simmer, stirring, for 10 minutes or until polenta thickens. Stir in an extra 1 cup milk, 75g (2½oz) coarsely chopped pitted kalamata olives and ¼ cup finely grated parmesan until cheese melts. Season to taste.

CHEESY PESTO POLENTA

prep + cook time 20 minutes ⁕ serves 6

Bring 3 cups milk and 2 cups chicken (or vegetable) stock to the boil in a large saucepan. Gradually add 2 cups polenta, stirring continuously. Reduce heat and simmer, stirring, for 10 minutes or until polenta thickens. Stir in an extra 1 cup milk, 150g (4½oz) chunky basil dip and ¼ cup finely grated parmesan until cheese melts. Serve topped with extra finely grated parmesan, if you like.

SPANISH CHICKEN, SAFFRON AND TOMATO STEW

prep + cook time 1 hour * serves 4

- **pinch saffron threads**
- **¼ cup (60ml) hot water**
- **4 x 150g (4½oz) skinless chicken thigh cutlets**
- **1 medium red onion (70g), sliced thinly**
- **30g (1oz) piece salami, chopped coarsely**
- **2 cloves garlic, crushed**
- **2 x 400g (12½oz) cans cherry tomatoes**
- **400g (12½oz) can cannellini beans, drained, rinsed**
- **⅓ cup (80g) chargrilled capsicum (bell pepper) strips**
- **350g (11oz) broccolini, trimmed (see tip)**
- **2 tablespoons coarsely chopped fresh flat-leaf parsley**
- **4 x 20g (¾oz) slices ciabatta**

1 Combine saffron and the hot water in a jug.

2 Heat a large deep non-stick frying pan over medium heat. Add chicken and cook, turning, for 6 minutes or until browned all over. Remove from pan.

3 Add onion and salami to pan. Cook, stirring, for 3 minutes or until onion is softened. Add garlic and cook, stirring, for 1 minute or until fragrant.

4 Add canned tomatoes and saffron mixture to pan; bring to the boil. Return chicken to pan. Reduce heat to low and cook, covered, for 25 minutes or until sauce thickens slightly.

5 Add beans and capsicum. Simmer, uncovered, for 5 minutes or until chicken is cooked through.

6 Meanwhile, boil, steam or microwave broccolini until tender; drain.

7 Scatter stew with parsley. Serve with broccolini and torn ciabatta.

Tip *You can swap the broccolini with any steamed green vegetable: asparagus, brussels sprouts, green beans, broccoli, spinach and zucchini are all good choices.*

Suitable to freeze *at the end of step 5.*

AUTUMN CHICKEN FRICASSÉ

prep + cook time 1 hour 15 minutes ✻ serves 4

*** 20g (¾oz) dried porcini mushrooms**
*** 1 cup (250ml) boiling water**
*** 1 tablespoon olive oil**
*** 4 chicken thigh fillets (680g), cut into thirds**
*** 1 large onion (200g), sliced thinly**
*** 2 cloves garlic, crushed**
*** 4 portobello mushrooms (200g), trimmed, sliced thickly**
*** 200g (6½oz) swiss brown mushrooms**
*** ½ cup (125ml) dry white wine (see tip)**
*** 2½ cups (625ml) chicken stock**
*** 400g (12½oz) kipfler (fingerling) potatoes, unpeeled, quartered lengthways**
*** 1 tablespoon fresh thyme leaves**

BUTTERMILK SCONES
*** 2 cups (300g) self-raising flour**
*** ¼ teaspoon bicarbonate of soda (baking soda)**
*** 1 teaspoon sea salt flakes**
*** 60g (2oz) cold butter, chopped coarsely**
*** ¾ cup (180ml) buttermilk**
*** 1 tablespoon fresh thyme leaves**
*** 1 tablespoon finely chopped fresh sage**
*** olive-oil spray**

1 Place porcini mushrooms and the boiling water in a small bowl; stand for 10 minutes. Drain, reserving soaking liquid.

2 Meanwhile, heat oil in a flameproof casserole dish or large heavy-based saucepan over high heat. Add chicken; cook for 3 minutes on each side or until golden brown. Transfer to a plate.

3 Reduce heat to medium. Add onion and cook, stirring, for 5 minutes or until softened. Add garlic, portobello and swiss brown mushrooms, drained porcini and strained reserved soaking liquid. Cook, stirring, for 8 minutes or until mushrooms are softened. Add wine, bring to a simmer and cook for 5 minutes or until reduced slightly.

4 Return chicken to pan. Add stock and potato. Bring to the boil, then reduce heat to low-medium and cook, covered, for 25 minutes. Remove lid and cook for a further 10 minutes or until chicken and potato are tender and sauce reduces slightly.

5 Meanwhile, make buttermilk scones.

6 Scatter chicken fricassé with thyme and fresh sage leaves, if you like; season to taste. Serve with buttermilk scones.

BUTTERMILK SCONES Preheat oven to 180°C/350°F. Grease and line a large oven tray with baking paper. Place flour, bicarbonate of soda and salt in a medium bowl; rub in butter. Stir in buttermilk and herbs to make a soft, sticky dough. Place 12 spoonfuls of dough onto lined tray and spray lightly with oil. Bake for 15 minutes or until light golden and cooked through. Transfer to a wire rack to cool.

Tip *If you prefer, omit the white wine and replace it with extra stock, so you would use 3 cups (750ml) chicken stock in total and add it all at once in step 4.*

FISHERMAN'S STEW
WITH TURMERIC ROUILLE

prep + cook time 1 hour ✻ serves 4

*** 1 tablespoon olive oil**
*** 1 medium onion (150g), sliced thickly**
*** 2 cloves garlic, sliced thinly**
*** 2 baby fennel bulbs (260g), sliced thinly, fronds reserved**
*** 1 fresh long red chilli, sliced thinly**
*** pinch saffron threads (see tips)**
*** 1 bay leaf**
*** 2 cups (500ml) salt-reduced vegetable stock**
*** 2 cups (500ml) water**
*** 400g (12½oz) can cherry tomatoes**
*** 2 blue swimmer crabs (650g), quartered, cleaned**
*** 300g (9½oz) firm white fish fillet, cut into 4cm (1½in) pieces**
*** 8 large uncooked prawns (shrimp) (560g), peeled, deveined, with tails intact**
*** 2 medium calamari (320g), cleaned, sliced, tentacles reserved**

TURMERIC ROUILLE
*** 2 egg yolks**
*** 1 clove garlic, chopped coarsely**
*** 2 teaspoons white balsamic vinegar**
*** 1 teaspoon dijon mustard**
*** ½ teaspoon finely grated fresh turmeric**
*** 1 cup (250ml) extra virgin olive oil**

1 Heat oil in large heavy-based saucepan over medium-high heat. Cook onion, garlic and fennel, stirring, for 5 minutes or until softened. Add chilli, saffron and bay leaf; cook, stirring, for 2 minutes or until fragrant. Add stock, the water and canned tomatoes; bring to the boil. Reduce heat to low and cook, covered, for 30 minutes.

2 Meanwhile, make turmeric rouille.

3 Add crab, fish, prawns and calamari to pan. Cook, covered, for 8 minutes or until seafood is just cooked.

4 Top stew with reserved fennel fronds. Serve with turmeric rouille.

TURMERIC ROUILLE Process yolks, garlic, vinegar, mustard and turmeric in a small food processor until smooth. Gradually add oil in a thin stream until mixture is thick and emulsified. Season to taste.

Tips *Use a tiny pinch of saffron powder instead of saffron threads, if you prefer. You could also use a bought mayonnaise with a little fresh or ground turmeric stirred through it, instead of making the turmeric rouille.*

SEAFOOD STEW

prep + cook time 1 hour * serves 4

Bouillabaisse, by any other name, was created by the fishermen of Marseille from the items of their daily catch that weren't sold to restaurants. The recipe varies, depending on what fish and shellfish are available on the day of cooking.

- **4 cleaned baby squid hoods (480g)**
- **2 baby fennel bulbs (260g)**
- **2 tablespoons lemon juice**
- **1 tablespoon olive oil**
- **2 medium onions (300g), chopped finely**
- **4 cloves garlic, crushed**
- **3 x 5cm (2in) pieces orange rind**
- **1 fresh long red chilli, chopped finely**
- **pinch saffron threads**
- **⅓ cup (80ml) dry white wine**
- **2 x 400g (12½oz) cans diced tomatoes**
- **1 litre (4 cups) fish stock**
- **1kg (2lb) large uncooked king prawns (shrimp), peeled, deveined, with tails intact**
- **200g (6½oz) pipis, scrubbed**
- **250g (8oz) small black mussels, scrubbed, beards removed (see tip)**
- **200g (6½oz) baby octopus, cleaned**
- **2 tablespoons thin strips orange rind, extra**

1 Insert a large knife into a squid hood. Using a small sharp knife, cut 1cm (½in) thick slices on one side of squid. Repeat with remaining hoods.

2 Trim fennel, reserving fronds. Using a mandoline, V-slicer or sharp knife, cut fennel into very thin slices. Place fennel and juice in a small bowl; toss to coat.

3 Heat oil in a large saucepan. Cook onion, stirring, until soft. Add garlic and cook, stirring, for 1 minute.

4 Stir rind, chilli, saffron and wine into onion mixture; cook, stirring, for 2 minutes. Add canned tomatoes and simmer for 10 minutes or until mixture thickens slightly. Add stock and simmer for 20 minutes or until liquid is reduced by about a quarter.

5 Add squid, prawns, pipis, mussels and octopus to pan. Cover and simmer, stirring occasionally, for 5 minutes or until seafood is cooked.

6 Serve stew topped with fennel mixture, reserved fennel fronds and extra rind.

Tip *Not all mussels open up during cooking, even after excessive cooking. You do not have to discard these; just open carefully with a knife and cook a little more.*

FISH AND FENNEL STEW

prep + cook time 1 hour ✻ serves 4

You can add extra seafood to this stew, such as uncooked prawns and mussels, if you like.

∗ ¼ cup (60ml) extra virgin olive oil
∗ 1 medium onion (150g), chopped finely
∗ 2 medium fennel bulbs (600g), sliced thinly, fronds reserved
∗ 2 cloves garlic, crushed
∗ 1 fresh long red chilli, sliced thinly
∗ ½ cup (125ml) dry white wine
∗ 3 cups (750ml) fish stock
∗ 2 x 400g (12½oz) cans diced tomatoes
∗ ¼ teaspoon caster (superfine) sugar
∗ 750g (1½lb) firm white fish fillets, cut into 3cm (1¼in) pieces (see tip)
∗ 2 tablespoons coarsely chopped fresh flat-leaf parsley
∗ 4 slices seeded sourdough bread (280g)
∗ 2 teaspoons finely grated lemon rind
∗ 1 medium lemon (140g), cut into cheeks

1 Heat 1½ tablespoons of the oil in a large saucepan over medium heat. Add onion and fennel; cook, stirring, for 5 minutes or until softened. Add garlic and chilli; cook for 1 minute or until fragrant.

2 Add wine and bring to the boil. Add stock, canned tomatoes and sugar; bring to the boil. Reduce heat to low-medium and cook, covered, for 20 minutes. Season. Add fish and cook, covered, stirring occasionally, for a further 5 minutes or until fish is cooked through. Stir in parsley.

3 Just before serving, heat a chargrill pan (or plate) over medium heat. Brush bread with remaining oil and cook for 1 minute each side or until golden and lightly charred.

4 Top stew with rind and reserved fennel fronds. Serve with grilled sourdough and lemon cheeks.

Tip *We used snapper in this recipe.*

OREGANO LAMB STEW
WITH GNOCCHI

prep + cook time 2 hours 45 minutes * serves 6

*** 2 tablespoons olive oil**
*** 1kg (2lb) boneless lamb shoulder, chopped coarsely**
*** 2 medium onions (300g), sliced thickly**
*** 2 cloves garlic, sliced thinly**
*** 2 teaspoons dried oregano**
*** ½ teaspoon ground cinnamon**
*** 400g (12½oz) can diced tomatoes**
*** 3 cups (750ml) beef stock**
*** 1 tablespoon tomato paste**
*** 2 teaspoons caster (superfine) sugar**
*** 500g (1lb) potato gnocchi (see tip)**
*** ½ cup (40g) finely grated parmesan cheese**
*** ½ cup fresh oregano leaves**

1 Heat oil in a large saucepan. Cook lamb, in batches, until browned. Remove from pan.
2 Meanwhile, cook onion in same pan, stirring, for 5 minutes or until softened. Add garlic, dried oregano and cinnamon; cook, stirring, until fragrant.
3 Return lamb to pan with canned tomatoes, stock, tomato paste and sugar; bring to the boil. Reduce heat and simmer, covered, for 2 hours, stirring occasionally.
4 Uncover and bring to the boil; boil for 10 minutes. Stir in gnocchi and cook, uncovered, for 5 minutes or until gnocchi are tender and sauce thickens. Season to taste.
5 Serve stew topped with parmesan and fresh oregano leaves.

Tip *We used 'fresh' pre-made potato gnocchi, available from the refrigerated section of most supermarkets.*

Serving suggestion *A green salad.*

Suitable to freeze *at the end of step 3.*

SOUPS

SPICED PUMPKIN SOUP
WITH CINNAMON CREAM

prep + cook time 50 minutes * serves 4

- **1 tablespoon olive oil**
- **1 medium onion (150g), chopped coarsely**
- **1 clove garlic, crushed**
- **2 teaspoons ground cumin**
- **½ teaspoon ground coriander**
- **1kg (2lb) butternut pumpkin, chopped coarsely**
- **2 medium potatoes (400g), chopped coarsely**
- **2 cups (500ml) water**
- **1½ cups (375ml) vegetable stock**
- **5cm (2in) strip orange rind**

CINNAMON CREAM

- **⅔ cup (160ml) thickened (heavy) cream**
- **½ teaspoon ground cinnamon**

1 Heat oil in a large saucepan over medium heat. Cook onion and garlic, stirring, for 5 minutes or until onion softens. Add spices and cook, stirring, for 1 minute until fragrant. Add pumpkin, potato, the water, stock and rind; bring to the boil. Reduce heat and simmer, covered, for 20 minutes or until vegetables are tender. Remove pan from heat and cool, uncovered, for 10 minutes.

2 Meanwhile, make cinnamon cream.

3 Blend or process soup, in batches, until smooth. Return soup to same pan and stir over low heat until warmed through. Season to taste.

4 Ladle soup into bowls and serve topped with cinnamon cream.

CINNAMON CREAM Beat ingredients in a small bowl with an electric mixer until soft peaks form.

Tips *To make pumpkin skin easier to remove, place pumpkin in a microwave-safe dish. Microwave on HIGH (100%) for 1 minute. Place on cut side for stability, then cut off the skin.*

Suitable to freeze *at the end of step 3, except omit making the cinnamon cream in step 2.*

393

STOVE

SOUPS

PARSNIP SOUP
WITH KALE CHIPS

prep + cook time 1 hour 20 minutes (+ standing) ✱ serves 8

∗ 2kg (4lb) parsnips, peeled, chopped coarsely
∗ 2 medium onions (300g), chopped coarsely
∗ 1 stalk celery (150g), trimmed
∗ 3 cloves garlic, quartered
∗ 1.5 litres (6 cups) water
∗ 1 litre (4 cups) chicken or vegetable stock
∗ ⅓ cup (80ml) olive oil
∗ 6 cloves garlic, extra, bruised
∗ ½ cup (125ml) pouring cream
∗ 2 tablespoons lemon juice

KALE CHIPS
∗ 200g (6½oz) green kale, washed, dried
∗ 1 clove garlic, crushed
∗ 2 tablespoons extra virgin olive oil
∗ 2 tablespoons dukkah

1 Place parsnip, onion, celery, quartered garlic, the water and stock in a large saucepan; bring to the boil. Reduce heat and simmer, covered, for 1 hour or until tender. Remove pan from heat and cool, uncovered, for 10 minutes.

2 Meanwhile, heat oil and extra garlic in a small saucepan over medium heat. When oil begins to sizzle, remove pan from heat to cool. When cool, discard garlic.

3 Meanwhile, make kale chips.

4 Blend or process soup, in batches, until smooth. Return soup to pan and stir in cream; heat over medium-high heat until hot. Season. Stir in juice.

5 Ladle soup into bowls. Serve drizzled with garlic oil, topped with kale chips.

KALE CHIPS Preheat oven to 220°C/425°F. Tear the leafy part of the kale from stalks, then tear into 3cm (1½in) pieces; discard stalks. Place kale on two large oven trays lined with baking paper. Combine garlic and oil; drizzle half over each tray of kale, then toss well to combine. Spread kale out in a single layer. Bake for 8 minutes, turning kale and swapping trays from top to bottom halfway through cooking time, or until kale is crisp. Season with salt and sprinkle with dukkah.

Suitable to freeze *the soup at the end of step 4.*

POTATO AND SEAFOOD CHOWDER

prep + cook time 1 hour * serves 4

- **1 medium onion (150g), chopped coarsely**
- **2 trimmed celery stalks (200g), chopped coarsely**
- **1 clove garlic, chopped**
- **2 tablespoons extra virgin olive oil**
- **200g (6½oz) speck, rind removed, chopped coarsely**
- **2 tablespoons plain (all-purpose) flour**
- **¼ teaspoon ground nutmeg**
- **3 cups (750ml) hot milk**
- **400g (12½oz) desiree potatoes, cut into 1cm (½in) pieces**
- **2 cups (500ml) fish stock**
- **500g (1lb) pot-ready clams (see tip)**
- **12 large uncooked prawns (shrimps) (840g), peeled, deveined, with tails intact**
- **400g (12½oz) boneless firm white fish, cut into 5cm (2in) pieces**
- **2 whole medium calamari (500g), cleaned, scored, cut into 4cm (1½in) pieces, tentacles reserved**
- **8 scallops, without roe (200g)**
- **⅓ cup (80ml) thickened (heavy) cream**
- **2 tablespoons finely chopped fresh tarragon**
- **¼ cup chopped fresh chives**
- **toasted sourdough bread, to serve**

1 Process onion, celery and garlic until chopped finely.

2 Heat 1 tablespoon of the oil in a large heavy-based saucepan or deep frying pan over medium heat. Add speck and cook for 5 minutes or until starting to crisp. Add onion mixture and cook, stirring, for 5 minutes or until softened but not coloured.

3 Add flour and cook, stirring, for 1 minute. Add nutmeg and milk, stirring to combine well. Add potato and stock; bring to the boil. Reduce heat to low and cook for 5 minutes.

4 Stir in clams and cook, covered, for 4 minutes or until opened. Add prawns, fish and scored calamari pieces; cook for 3 minutes. Add scallops and cook for a further 1 minute. Stir in cream until heated through.

5 Heat remaining oil in a small heavy-based frying pan over high heat. Cook reserved calamari tentacles for 1 minute or until a little crisp.

6 Divide chowder among bowls. Top with calamari tentacles and scatter with fresh herbs. Serve with toasted bread.

Tip *Pot-ready clams have already had sand purged from them and require no preparation. To purge clams yourself, place them in salted water for several hours; allow 1½ tablespoons sea salt to 1 litre (4 cups) cold water. Remove clams from water carefully; do not drain in a colander as you may add the sand back to the clams.*

ROASTED TOMATO SOUP
WITH BROCCOLI PESTO

prep + cook time 1 hour (+ standing) * serves 4

*** 1kg (2lb) vine-ripened tomatoes, quartered**
*** 3 cloves garlic, unpeeled**
*** 3 sprigs fresh thyme**
*** 1 medium onion (150g), chopped**
*** ½ teaspoon sea salt flakes**
*** ¼ cup (60ml) extra virgin olive oil**
*** 3 cups (750ml) vegetable stock**
*** 1 tablespoon pine nuts, toasted**
*** baby basil leaves, to serve**

BROCCOLI PESTO
*** 100g (3oz) broccoli, chopped**
*** 1 clove garlic, crushed**
*** 1½ tablespoons pine nuts, toasted**
*** 1½ tablespoons grated parmesan**
*** 1½ tablespoons coarsely chopped fresh basil leaves**
*** ¼ cup (60ml) olive oil**

1 Preheat oven to 220°C/425°F.

2 Place tomato, garlic, thyme and onion in a baking dish; sprinkle with salt flakes and season with freshly ground black pepper. Drizzle with oil and toss to coat tomatoes. Roast for 30 minutes or until tomatoes are very soft and coloured around the edges.

3 Meanwhile, make broccoli pesto.

4 Transfer roasted tomato mixture to a medium saucepan. Squeeze garlic out of skins and add to tomato mixture. Remove and discard thyme stalks. Add stock to pan and bring to the boil, then remove from heat. Stand for 10 minutes to cool slightly. Blend or process mixture until smooth. Return soup to pan and stir over low heat until hot. Season.

5 Ladle soup into bowls. Top with broccoli pesto, pine nuts, basil and extra fresh tomato, if you like.

BROCCOLI PESTO Add broccoli to a small saucepan of boiling water. Bring to the boil and simmer for 2 minutes. Drain, then refresh in cold water; drain well. Process broccoli with remaining ingredients until combined. Season to taste.

Suitable to freeze *soup and pesto, separately.*

HEARTY CURRIED VEGETABLE AND CHICKPEA SOUP

prep + cook time 1 hour * serves 4

- **1 tablespoon olive oil**
- **2 cloves garlic, crushed**
- **2 teaspoons finely grated fresh ginger**
- **1 large onion (200g), chopped**
- **300g (9½oz) pumpkin, cut into 2cm (¾in) cubes**
- **1 medium potato (200g), cut into 2cm (¾in) cubes**
- **2 medium carrots (240g), chopped coarsely**
- **1 tablespoon curry powder**
- **2 teaspoons cumin seeds, toasted (see tip)**
- **1 litre (4 cups) vegetable stock**
- **200g (6½oz) cauliflower, cut into small florets**
- **400g (12½oz) can chickpeas (garbanzo beans), drained, rinsed**
- **4 pappadams**
- **⅓ cup (95g) Greek-style yoghurt**
- **1 tablespoon baby coriander leaves**

1 Heat oil in a large saucepan over medium heat. Cook garlic, ginger, onion, pumpkin, potato and carrot, stirring, for 5 minutes or until vegetables soften. Add curry powder and half the cumin seeds; cook, stirring, until fragrant.

2 Stir in stock. Bring to the boil, then reduce heat and simmer for 20 minutes or until vegetables are just tender. Stir in cauliflower and chickpeas. Simmer for 15 minutes or until cauliflower is tender. Season to taste.

3 Microwave pappadams on HIGH (100%) for 30 seconds or until puffed.

4 Ladle soup into bowls. Top with yoghurt, coriander and remaining cumin seeds. Serve soup with pappadams.

Tip *To toast cumin seeds, stir seeds in a small frying pan over medium heat for 2 minutes or until fragrant; remove from heat.*

Suitable to freeze *at the end of step 2.*

MINT, BROAD BEAN AND HAM SOUP

prep + cook time 2 hours 30 minutes * serves 4

- **2 teaspoons olive oil**
- **1 large onion (200g), chopped coarsely**
- **2 stalks celery (300g), trimmed, chopped coarsely**
- **1 medium carrot (120g), chopped coarsely**
- **2 cloves garlic, crushed**
- **1kg (2lb) ham hock**
- **2 litres (8 cups) water**
- **3 cups (450g) frozen broad (fava) beans**
- **1 tablespoon lemon juice**
- **⅓ cup finely chopped fresh mint**

1 Heat oil in a large saucepan. Cook onion, celery, carrot and garlic, stirring, until vegetables soften. Add ham hock and the water; bring to the boil. Reduce heat and simmer, covered, for 1½ hours. Uncover and simmer for 30 minutes.

2 Meanwhile, place beans in a medium heatproof bowl, cover with boiling water and stand for 5 minutes; drain. Peel away grey skins.

3 Remove ham hock from soup. When cool enough to handle, remove meat from bone and shred coarsely; discard skin and bone.

4 Add beans to soup and simmer, uncovered, for 5 minutes or until beans are tender. Cool soup for 10 minutes.

5 Using a hand-held blender, blend soup in pan until almost smooth. Return ham meat to soup with juice and stir over low heat until hot. Season to taste.

6 Ladle soup into bowls and serve topped with mint.

Suitable to freeze *at the end of step 5.*

CREAMY CELERIAC SOUP
WITH SCALLOPS

prep + cook time 50 minutes ✻ serves 4

- **50g (1½oz) butter**
- **2 tablespoons extra virgin olive oil**
- **1 medium onion (150g), chopped coarsely**
- **1kg (2lb) celeriac (celery root), peeled, chopped coarsely**
- **1 stalk celery (150g), trimmed, chopped**
- **2 cloves garlic, quartered**
- **1.25 litres (5 cups) salt-reduced vegetable stock**
- **8 scallops without roe (200g) (see tip)**
- **4 rindless bacon slices (250g), halved lengthways**
- **¼ cup (60ml) pouring cream**
- **1 tablespoon lemon juice**
- **1 tablespoon fresh thyme leaves**

1 Heat half the butter and half the oil in a large saucepan over medium heat. Cook onion, celeriac, celery and garlic, stirring occasionally, for 10 minutes or until softened. Stir in stock and bring to the boil. Reduce heat to low and simmer, covered, for 20 minutes or until celeriac is tender. Cool for 10 minutes.

2 Meanwhile, wrap each scallop with a strip of bacon and secure with a toothpick. Cover and refrigerate until required.

3 Blend or process soup, in batches, until smooth. Return soup to pan with cream and stir over medium heat until hot. Season to taste. Cover to keep warm.

4 Melt remaining butter and oil in a large frying pan over high heat. Season scallops, then cook for 2 minutes on one side and 1 minute on the other side, or until scallops are almost cooked through. Transfer to a plate. Remove frying pan from heat and stir in juice.

5 Remove toothpicks from the scallops. Ladle soup into warm bowls. Top with scallops, scatter with thyme and drizzle with the lemon mixture.

Tip *You can use scallops with the roe, if you prefer.*

Suitable to freeze *at the end of step 1.*

MINESTRONE

prep + cook time 4 hours (+ refrigeration) * serves 6

- **1 ham hock (1kg)**
- **1 medium onion (150g), quartered**
- **1 stalk celery (150g), trimmed, chopped coarsely**
- **1 teaspoon black peppercorns**
- **1 bay leaf**
- **4 litres (16 cups) water**
- **1 tablespoon olive oil**
- **1 large carrot (180g), chopped finely**
- **2 stalks celery (200g), extra, trimmed, chopped finely**
- **3 cloves garlic, crushed**
- **¼ cup (70g) tomato paste**
- **2 large tomatoes (440g), chopped finely**
- **1 small leek (200g), white part only, sliced thinly**
- **1 cup (100g) small pasta shells**
- **400g (12½oz) can white beans, drained, rinsed**
- **½ cup coarsely chopped fresh flat-leaf parsley**
- **½ cup coarsely chopped fresh basil**
- **½ cup (40g) shaved parmesan**

1 Preheat oven to 220°C/425°F.

2 Roast ham hock and onion in a medium baking dish for 30 minutes.

3 Place hock and onion in a large saucepan with celery, peppercorns, bay leaf and the water; bring to the boil. Reduce heat and simmer for 2 hours.

4 Remove hock from broth. Strain broth through a fine sieve or colander into a large heatproof bowl; discard solids. Allow broth to cool. Cover and refrigerate until cold.

5 Remove ham from hock and shred coarsely; discard bone, fat and skin.

6 Meanwhile, heat oil in a large saucepan. Cook carrot and extra celery, stirring, for 2 minutes. Add shredded ham, garlic, tomato paste and tomato; cook, stirring, for 2 minutes.

7 Skim fat from surface of broth. Pour broth into a large measuring jug and add enough water to make 2 litres (8 cups). Add broth to pan and bring to the boil. Reduce heat and simmer, covered, for 20 minutes.

8 Add leek, pasta and beans to pan; bring to the boil. Reduce heat and simmer, uncovered, until pasta is tender. Remove from heat and stir in herbs.

9 Ladle soup into bowls and serve topped with parmesan.

Tip *Make the broth up to the end of step 4 a day ahead so that it chills long enough for the fat to solidify on top. Skim away the fat before reheating the broth, then continue with the recipe.*

BROCCOLI AND KALE SOUP
WITH LEMON CRÈME FRAÎCHE

prep + cook time 1 hour ✻ serves 4

- **200g (6½oz) kale leaves, stems removed, chopped coarsely**
- **1½ tablespoons olive oil**
- **1 large onion (200g), chopped finely**
- **3 cloves garlic, chopped finely**
- **1.5 litres (6 cups) vegetable stock**
- **650g (1¼lb) sebago potatoes, chopped (see tips)**
- **450g (14½oz) broccoli, cut into florets, stems sliced thinly**
- **1 cup fresh flat-leaf parsley leaves**
- **1 cup (240g) crème fraîche**
- **1 tablespoon finely grated lemon rind**
- **shredded lemon rind, to serve**

1 Preheat oven to 180°C/350°F.

2 Rub 50g (1½oz) of the kale with 2 teaspoons of the oil. Place on an oven tray and bake for 10 minutes or until crisp.

3 Meanwhile, heat remaining oil in a large saucepan over low heat. Cook onion and garlic, stirring, for 8 minutes or until softened.

4 Add stock and potato; bring to the boil. Reduce heat to low and simmer, covered, for 15 minutes or until potato is very tender.

5 Add broccoli and simmer, covered, for 10 minutes or until vegetables are tender.

6 Stir in remaining kale and parsley; cook for a further 1 minute or until just wilted. Remove soup from heat and stand for 10 minutes to cool slightly. Blend or process mixture until smooth. Return soup to pan and stir over low heat until hot. Season to taste.

7 Combine crème fraîche and grated rind in a small bowl; season.

8 Ladle soup into bowls. Top with crème fraîche mixture, kale chips and shredded rind.

Tips *Sebago is a white-fleshed potato. You can use any white all-purpose non-waxy potato for this recipe. If using a jug blender or food processor to blend soup, stand for 10 minutes to cool slightly before blending (as otherwise the heat build-up can cause the lid to blow off).*

Suitable to freeze *the soup at the end of step 6*

THAI RED CURRY SWEET POTATO SOUP

prep + cook time 1 hour (+ standing) * serves 4

* **1kg (2lb) orange sweet potatoes, peeled, cut into chunks**
* **2 tablespoons vegetable oil**
* **1 large onion (200g), chopped**
* **2 tablespoons thai red curry paste**
* **1 tablespoon grated fresh ginger**
* **2 teaspoons finely chopped trimmed coriander (cilantro) roots**
* **1 litre (4 cups) vegetable stock**
* **1 cup (250ml) water**
* **1 tablespoon fish sauce**
* **1 tablespoon lime juice**
* **2 teaspoons brown sugar**
* **¾ cup (200g) coconut yoghurt**
* **½ cup baby shiso or coriander (cilantro) leaves**
* **1 tablespoon fried shallots**
* **lime cheeks, to serve**

1 Preheat oven to 200°C/400°F. Toss the sweet potato with 1 tablespoon of the oil in a small roasting pan; season. Roast for 20 minutes or until golden and tender.

2 Heat remaining oil in a large saucepan over medium-high heat. Cook onion, stirring, for 5 minutes or until softened. Add curry paste, ginger and coriander roots; cook, stirring, for 1 minute or until fragrant.

3 Add sweet potato, stock and the water to pan; bring to the boil. Reduce heat to low and simmer, covered, for 20 minutes. Remove from heat and stand for 5 minutes. Blend soup using a stick blender until smooth.

4 Add fish sauce, juice, sugar and yoghurt to soup; stir over medium heat until hot. Season to taste.

5 Ladle soup into bowls. Top with shiso leaves and shallots. Serve with lime cheeks.

Tip *You can also use a jug blender to blend soup for a smoother consistency. If using a jug blender, stand soup for 10 minutes to cool slightly before blending (as otherwise the heat build-up can cause the lid to blow off).*

Suitable to freeze *at the end of step 3.*

CHICKEN, CHORIZO AND OKRA GUMBO

prep + cook time 3 hours 15 minutes ✻ serves 8

- **1.5kg (3lb) whole chicken**
- **2 medium carrots (240g), chopped coarsely**
- **2 stalks celery (300g), trimmed, chopped coarsely**
- **1 medium onion (150g), chopped coarsely**
- **12 black peppercorns**
- **1 dried bay leaf**
- **3 litres (12 cups) water**
- **60g (2oz) butter**
- **1 small onion (80g), extra, chopped finely**
- **2 cloves garlic, crushed**
- **1 medium red capsicum (bell pepper) (200g), chopped finely**
- **2 teaspoons dried oregano**
- **1 teaspoon sweet paprika**
- **¼ teaspoon cayenne pepper**
- **¼ teaspoon ground clove**
- **¼ cup (35g) plain (all-purpose) flour**
- **¼ cup (70g) tomato paste**
- **400g (12½oz) can crushed tomatoes**
- **100g (3oz) okra, halved on the diagonal**
- **1 cup (200g) white medium-grain rice**
- **1 cured chorizo sausage (170g), sliced thinly**

1 Place chicken in a large saucepan with carrot, celery, onion, peppercorns, bay leaf and the water; bring to the boil. Reduce heat and simmer, covered, for 1½ hours.

2 Remove chicken from pan. Strain broth through a fine sieve into large heatproof bowl; discard solids. When chicken is cool enough to handle, shred meat coarsely; discard skin and bones.

3 Melt butter in a large saucepan. Cook extra onion and garlic, stirring, until onion softens. Add capsicum, oregano and spices; cook, stirring, until fragrant. Add flour and tomato paste; cook, stirring, for 1 minute. Gradually stir in broth and canned tomatoes; bring to the boil, stirring. Stir in okra and rice. Simmer, uncovered, stirring occasionally, for 15 minutes or until rice is tender.

4 Heat a large oiled frying pan and cook chorizo until browned; drain on paper towel.

5 Add chorizo and shredded chicken to gumbo. Stir over medium heat until hot. Season to taste.

Do ahead *If you want to cook this gumbo a day ahead, the flavours will meld and deepen, making the soup even more delicious. Follow the recipe through to the end of step 2, then cool broth, cover and refrigerate overnight. Refrigerate shredded chicken separately in an airtight container. Continue with the recipe the following day.*

BEETROOT AND GIN SOUP
WITH PUMPERNICKEL CRUMBS

prep + cook time 1 hour (+ standing) * serves 4

*** 50g (1½oz) butter**
*** ¼ cup (60ml) olive oil**
*** 1 large onion (200g), chopped coarsely**
*** 1kg (2lb) beetroot (beets), peeled, grated coarsely**
*** 1 large potato (300g), chopped coarsely**
*** 1 medium fennel bulb (300g), chopped coarsely, fronds reserved**
*** 1 large tomato (220g), chopped coarsely**
*** 1.75 litres (7 cups) vegetable or beef stock**
*** 3 slices pumpernickel bread (195g), torn into coarse crumbs**
*** ½ cup (125ml) gin (see tip)**
*** ⅓ cup (80g) sour cream**
*** ⅓ cup (25g) flaked natural almonds, toasted**

1 Heat butter and 1 tablespoon of the oil in a large saucepan over low-medium heat. Cook onion, stirring occasionally, for 8 minutes or until soft. Add beetroot, potato, fennel and tomato. Cook, stirring occasionally, for 10 minutes or until fennel is golden and caramelised. Stir in stock and bring to the boil. Reduce heat to low and simmer, covered, for 20 minutes or until potato and beetroot are tender. Remove from heat and stand for 10 minutes.

2 Blend or process soup, in batches, until smooth. Return soup to pan and stir over medium heat for 5 minutes or until hot.

3 Meanwhile, heat remaining oil in a medium frying pan over high heat. Cook pumpernickel crumbs, stirring occasionally, for 2 minutes or until crumbs are crisp; drain on paper towel.

4 Stir gin into hot soup; season.

5 Ladle soup into warm bowls. Top with sour cream, pumpernickel crumbs, almonds and reserved fennel fronds.

Tip *If you prefer, you can omit the gin.*

Suitable to freeze *after blending in step 2.*

Serving suggestion
This soup can also be served chilled.

SEAFOOD BISQUE

prep + cook time 2 hours * serves 8

A seafood bisque has a deep luxurious seafood flavour, which comes from cooking both the fish fillets and prawns in their shells to create the richly flavoured stock. The fish is removed and the remaining mixture is then blended (shells and all) to form a smooth, silky soup.

- **1.5kg (3lb) uncooked large king prawns (shrimp)**
- **2 tablespoons olive oil**
- **1 medium onion (150g), chopped coarsely**
- **2 cloves garlic, crushed**
- **1 medium carrot (120g), chopped**
- **1 celery stalk (150g), chopped**
- **6 sprigs fresh thyme**
- **¼ cup fresh flat-leaf parsley leaves**
- **2 tablespoons tomato paste**
- **2 litres (8 cups) water**
- **½ cup (125ml) dry white wine**
- **800g (1½lb) firm white fish fillets, skinned**
- **400g (12½oz) can crushed tomatoes**
- **3 medium potatoes (600g), chopped**
- **½ cup (120g) crème fraîche**
- **⅓ cup (80ml) lemon juice**
- **fresh flat-leaf parsley leaves, extra, to serve**

1 Shell and devein 8 prawns, keeping tails intact. Place shells and heads in a large bowl. Reserve shelled prawns in a small bowl, cover and refrigerate until required.

2 Heat half the oil in a large heavy-based saucepan over high heat. Cook onion, garlic, carrot and celery, stirring, for 5 minutes or until onion begins to soften. Add prawn shells and heads, with remaining unshelled prawns to pan. Cook, stirring, for 5 minutes or until prawns change colour. Stir in thyme, parsley and tomato paste. Add the water and wine; bring to the boil.

3 Reduce heat to low-medium, add fish and simmer for 20 minutes, skimming the surface occasionally with a ladle to remove any scum. Using a slotted spoon, transfer fish to a large bowl and cover until required. Increase heat to medium and add canned tomatoes and potato; season. Cook for 40 minutes or until stock mixture reduces slightly. Cool for 10 minutes.

4 Blend stock mixture, in batches, until smooth. Push blended puree through a fine sieve into a clean medium saucepan over heat and return to the boil.

5 Meanwhile, heat remaining oil in a large frying pan over medium-high heat. Cook reserved prawns for 1 minute on each side or until just cooked through. Flake reserved fish into bite-sized pieces.

6 Stir crème fraîche and juice into soup; season to taste. Ladle soup into bowls. Top with flaked fish, prawns and parsley. Serve with lemon wedges, if you like.

BROWN RICE CONGEE
WITH FRIED GARLIC

prep + cook time 2 hours 25 minutes * serves 6

- **6 cloves garlic**
- **1.75 litres (7 cups) water**
- **2 cups (500ml) chicken or vegetable stock**
- **1½ cups (300g) brown rice**
- **2 tablespoons finely chopped fresh ginger**
- **4 green onions (scallions), sliced thinly**
- **200g (6½oz) chicken breast fillet**
- **½ cup (125ml) vegetable oil**
- **2 tablespoons tamari**
- **½ cup fresh coriander (cilantro) leaves**
- **2 teaspoons toasted sesame seeds**

1 Finely chop 1 garlic clove and thinly slice remaining garlic cloves.

2 Place the water, stock, rice, chopped garlic, ginger and a quarter of the green onion in a large saucepan; bring to the boil. Add chicken and return to the boil. Reduce heat to low and cook, partially covered, for 12 minutes or until chicken is cooked through. Remove chicken from soup and cool for 10 minutes. Shred chicken coarsely.

3 Return soup to the boil. Reduce heat to low and cook, partially covered, for 1½ hours or until rice breaks down and forms a thick porridge consistency.

4 Meanwhile, heat oil in a small saucepan over medium heat. Cook sliced garlic for 1 minute or until golden. Remove garlic with a slotted spoon; drain on paper towel. Reserve garlic-infused oil.

5 Add shredded chicken and tamari to rice mixture; stir over low heat until warmed through. Top congee with fried garlic slices, coriander, sesame seeds and remaining green onion. Serve drizzled with reserved garlic-infused oil.

Tips *Frying garlic tempers the flavour, bringing out a natural sweetness. Just be careful to fry it quickly as overcooking will make it bitter. For a vegetarian version, use vegetable stock and omit the chicken and add some tofu.*

Serving suggestion *Steamed asian greens.*

CREAMY CORN AND CRAB SOUP

prep + cook time 1 hour (+ standing) ✻ serves 4

- **3 cobs corn (1.2kg)**
- **20g (¾oz) butter**
- **2 medium onions (300g), chopped coarsely**
- **1 tablespoon chopped fresh coriander (cilantro) roots (see tip)**
- **1 litre (4 cups) vegetable stock**
- **300ml pouring cream**
- **½ cup (120g) sour cream**
- **140g (4½oz) cooked crab meat**
- **2 tablespoons fresh coriander (cilantro) leaves**
- **1 tablespoon sweet sherry**

1 Remove husks and silks from corn. Cut kernels from cobs; you will need 3 cups.

2 Melt butter in a large saucepan over medium heat. Cook onion, corn and coriander roots, stirring, for 15 minutes or until onion and corn are softened.

3 Add stock and simmer, partially covered, for 20 minutes for flavours to develop and until vegetables are tender. Stand for 10 minutes to cool slightly.

4 Blend or process soup until smooth. Return soup to pan with pouring cream. Stir over low heat until hot; season to taste.

5 Ladle soup into bowls. Top with sour cream, crab meat and coriander. Drizzle with sherry and season with freshly ground black pepper.

Tip *You will need 1 bunch coriander for the coriander roots.*

Suitable to freeze *after blending soup in step 4.*

VEGETARIAN

PINE NUT AND CHICKPEA STEW

prep + cook time 1 hour 30 minutes (+ overnight standing) * serves 4

- **1 cup (200g) dried chickpeas (garbanzo beans)**
- **1 tablespoon extra virgin olive oil**
- **1 medium onion (150g), chopped finely**
- **2 cloves garlic, crushed**
- **1 fresh long red chilli, chopped finely**
- **400g (12½oz) can diced tomatoes**
- **1 cup (280g) bottled passata (or see recipe, page 19)**
- **285g (9oz) bottled piquillo peppers, drained, chopped coarsely**
- **1 cup (250ml) vegetable stock or water**
- **¼ teaspoon saffron threads (see tip)**
- **1½ tablespoons pine nuts, toasted**
- **¼ cup (30g) finely grated vegetarian parmesan-style cheese**
- **¼ cup fresh flat-leaf parsley leaves**

1 Soak chickpeas in cold water overnight; drain.

2 Place drained chickpeas in a large saucepan with plenty of water; bring to a simmer over high heat and simmer for 1 hour or until tender. Drain.

3 Heat oil in a large heavy-based saucepan over medium-high heat. Cook onion, stirring, for 5 minutes or until onion softens. Add garlic and chilli; cook, stirring, for 1 minute or until fragrant.

4 Add canned tomatoes, passata, peppers, stock, saffron and chickpeas; bring to the boil. Reduce heat to low-medium and simmer for 15 minutes or until reduced slightly. Season to taste.

5 Serve stew topped with pine nuts, parmesan and parsley.

Tip *The saffron will give the stew a Spanish flavour; however, it will be just as nice without it, if you don't have any on hand.*

Serving suggestion *Toasted multigrain sourdough bread.*

CHILLI BEANS
WITH CHIMICHURRI

prep + cook time 1 hour * serves 4

*** 1 tablespoon extra virgin olive oil**
*** 1 large onion (200g), chopped finely**
*** 2 teaspoons ground cumin**
*** 2 teaspoons ground coriander**
*** 1 teaspoon mexican chilli powder**
*** 400g (12½oz) can red kidney beans, drained, rinsed**
*** 400g (12½oz) can chickpeas (garbanzo beans), drained, rinsed**
*** ¼ cup chopped chipotle chillies in adobo sauce**
*** 2 x 400g (12½oz) cans diced tomatoes**
*** 1 cup (250ml) water**

CHIMICHURRI
*** ½ small red onion (50g), chopped finely**
*** 1 clove garlic, chopped finely**
*** ½ teaspoon sweet paprika**
*** ½ cup (125ml) olive oil**
*** 1½ tablespoons red wine vinegar**
*** ½ cup finely chopped fresh flat-leaf parsley**
*** 2 tablespoons finely chopped fresh oregano**

1 Heat oil in a large saucepan over medium heat. Cook onion, stirring, for 5 minutes or until onion softens. Add cumin, ground coriander and chilli powder; cook, stirring, for 1 minute or until fragrant.

2 Add beans, chickpeas, chipotle mixture, canned tomatoes and the water; bring to the boil. Reduce heat to low and cook gently for 35 minutes for flavours to develop and until sauce thickens.

3 Meanwhile, make chimichurri.

4 Top chilli beans with chimichurri to serve.

CHIMICHURRI Combine ingredients in a small bowl; season.

Serving suggestion *Serve with sour cream and baked corn tortillas. To make baked corn tortillas, spray corn tortillas with cooking-oil spray and sprinkle with sweet paprika, then bake in a preheated 200°C/400°F oven for 5 minutes or until crisp.*

424

STOVE

VEGETARIAN

CHICKPEA, EGGPLANT AND PUMPKIN CURRY

prep + cook time 1 hour ✻ serves 6

You could use a variety of vegetables instead of the eggplant and pumpkin in this curry, if you like, such as orange sweet potato, carrot, cauliflower or other root vegetables.

*** 2 tablespoons vegetable oil**
*** 1 medium onion (150g), sliced thickly**
*** 1 clove garlic, crushed**
*** 2cm (¾in) piece fresh ginger, grated finely**
*** 2 fresh small red thai (serrano) chillies, chopped finely**
*** 1 teaspoon ground cumin**
*** ½ teaspoon ground turmeric**
*** ¼ teaspoon ground cardamom**
*** ¼ teaspoon ground fennel**
*** 8 baby eggplants (480g), sliced thickly**
*** 1kg (2lb) butternut pumpkin, cut into 1cm (½in) slices**
*** 400g (12½oz) can diced tomatoes**
*** 400ml can coconut cream**
*** 1 cup (250ml) vegetable stock**
*** 1 tablespoon tomato paste**
*** 400g (12½oz) can chickpeas (garbanzo beans), drained, rinsed**
*** ½ cup fresh mint leaves**

1 Heat oil in a large heavy-based saucepan over medium-high heat. Cook onion, garlic, ginger and chilli, stirring, for 8 minutes or until onion softens. Add spices and eggplant; cook, stirring, for 2 minutes.

2 Add pumpkin, canned tomatoes, coconut cream, stock and tomato paste; bring to the boil. Reduce heat to low-medium and cook for 20 minutes. Add chickpeas and simmer for a further 10 minutes or until vegetables are tender. Season to taste.

3 Serve curry topped with mint leaves and fresh sliced long red chilli, if you like.

Serving suggestion *Steamed jasmine rice.*

SRI LANKAN POTATO AND PEA CURRY WITH FRIED EGGS

prep + cook time 1 hour ✻ serves 4

Curry powders are a blend of ground spices used for making Indian and some South-East Asian dishes. They usually consist of dried chilli, cinnamon, coriander, cumin, fennel, cardamom and turmeric.

∗ 4 medium potatoes (800g), chopped coarsely (see tip)
∗ ¼ cup (60g) ghee
∗ 1 medium onion (150g), sliced thinly
∗ 4 cloves garlic, chopped finely
∗ 2½ tablespoons finely chopped fresh ginger
∗ 2 sprigs fresh curry leaves
∗ 1 tablespoon curry powder
∗ 1½ teaspoons brown mustard seeds
∗ ½ teaspoon ground turmeric
∗ 2 fresh long green chillies, sliced thinly
∗ 400g (12½oz) can chickpeas (garbanzo beans), drained, rinsed
∗ 1 cup (120g) frozen peas
∗ ½ cup (125ml) water
∗ ½ teaspoon finely grated lime rind
∗ 1 tablespoon lime juice
∗ 4 eggs
∗ 2 green onions (scallions), sliced thinly
∗ 1 cup fresh coriander (cilantro) leaves

1 Place potatoes in a large saucepan with enough cold water to just cover; bring to the boil. Boil over medium heat for 15 minutes or until tender; drain.

2 Heat 2 tablespoons of the ghee in a large heavy-based frying pan over medium heat. Cook onion, stirring, for 5 minutes or until softened. Add garlic, ginger, curry leaves, curry powder, seeds, turmeric and half the chilli; cook, stirring, for 1 minute or until fragrant.

3 Add potato, chickpeas, peas and the water; bring to the boil. Reduce heat to medium and simmer for 3 minutes or until peas are tender. Stir in rind and juice; season to taste.

4 Heat remaining ghee in a large frying pan over medium-high heat. Cook eggs, in batches, for 2 minutes or until the whites are set and yolks are cooked to your liking.

5 Serve curry topped with fried eggs, green onion, coriander and remaining chilli.

Tip *We used dutch cream potatoes in this recipe.*

428

STOVE

VEGETARIAN

ROOT VEGETABLE TAGINE

prep + cook time 1 hour ✻ serves 4

Ras el hanout is a Moroccan spice blend that can be found at some supermarkets and specialty food stores. Literally translating to 'top of the shop', it can include up to 12 different spices and is used in many savoury dishes, and rubbed on meat or fish.

∗ ¼ cup (60ml) olive oil
∗ 2 small parsnips (240g), quartered lengthways
∗ 2 small carrots (140g), quartered lengthways
∗ 1 small orange sweet potato (250g), quartered lengthways
∗ 1 medium onion (150g), chopped coarsely
∗ 4 cloves garlic, sliced thinly
∗ 1½ tablespoons ras el hanout (see tips)
∗ 2 x 400g (12½oz) cans diced tomatoes
∗ 400g (12½oz) can chickpeas (garbanzo beans), drained, rinsed
∗ 1 cup (170g) pitted prunes
∗ 1½ cups (375ml) vegetable stock
∗ 2 cups (400g) couscous
∗ 2 cups (500ml) boiling water
∗ 1 cup (280g) Greek-style yoghurt
∗ 2 teaspoons harissa paste
∗ 2 tablespoons thinly sliced preserved lemon rind (see tips)
∗ ¼ cup (40g) pomegranate seeds
∗ ½ cup fresh mint leaves

1 Heat oil in a large heavy-based saucepan over medium heat. Cook parsnip, carrot, sweet potato, onion, garlic and ras el hanout, stirring occasionally, for 10 minutes or until tender.
2 Add canned tomatoes, chickpeas, prunes and stock; bring to the boil. Reduce heat to low and simmer, covered, for 40 minutes or until vegetables are tender. Season.
3 Meanwhile, combine couscous and the water in a large heatproof bowl, cover and stand for 5 minutes or until liquid is absorbed. Fluff with a fork.
4 Place yoghurt in a small bowl and swirl through harissa.
5 Top tagine with preserved lemon, pomegranate seeds and mint. Serve with couscous and harissa yoghurt.

Tips *To make your own ras el hanout, combine 1 teaspoon each ground coriander, ground cumin, cinnamon and paprika with ½ teaspoon each ground cardamom, ground ginger and ground turmeric. Preserved lemon is available at delis and some supermarkets. Remove and discard the flesh, rinse the rind well, then slice thinly. You will need about 2 preserved lemon wedges (70g) for this recipe.*

431

STOVE

VEGETARIAN

MUSHROOM RAGÙ
WITH SOFT POLENTA

prep + cook time 1 hour ✻ serves 4

*** 30g (1oz) butter**
*** 500g (1lb) cup mushrooms, sliced thickly**
*** 3 cloves garlic, crushed**
*** ½ cup (125ml) vegetable stock**
*** 150g (4½oz) soft goat's cheese**
*** ¼ cup fresh flat-leaf parsley leaves**

SOFT POLENTA
*** 2 cups (500ml) milk**
*** 2 cups (500ml) vegetable stock**
*** 1¼ cups (210g) coarse polenta (cornmeal)**
*** 40g (1½oz) butter, chopped**
*** ¾ cup (60g) finely grated vegetarian parmesan-style cheese (see tip)**

1 Make soft polenta.

2 Start cooking the mushroom ragù three-quarters of the way through cooking polenta. Heat butter in a large heavy-based frying pan over high heat. Cook mushrooms, stirring occasionally, for 5 minutes or until mushrooms are browned lightly and most of the liquid evaporates. Season. Add garlic and cook, stirring, until fragrant. Stir in stock and bring to the boil. Reduce heat to medium and simmer for 2 minutes or until most of the liquid evaporates. Season to taste. Cover to keep warm.

3 Pour polenta immediately onto a serving board or plate. Using the back of a spoon, make slight indents in polenta. Spoon mushroom ragù over polenta, using a slotted spoon, then drizzle with some of the pan juices. Top with small chunks of goat's cheese and scatter with parsley. Serve immediately.

SOFT POLENTA Bring milk and stock to the boil in a large saucepan. Gradually add polenta, whisking continuously; return to a simmer and whisk for 2 minutes. Reduce heat to low and simmer, whisking occasionally at first, then more frequently as the polenta thickens, for 40 minutes or until thick and no longer grainy. Stir in butter and parmesan. Season to taste.

Tip *Traditionally, parmesan is made with calf rennet. When purchasing, check ingredients to see that the cheese is vegetarian (make sure it doesn't contain calf rennet).*

Serving suggestion *A mixed herb salad.*

STOVE

VEGETARIAN

VEGIE DRAWER DHAL WITH CHEESE BALLS

prep + cook time 1 hour 15 minutes * serves 4

This recipe can be made with any vegetables you have in the fridge, especially those looking a bit sad. Add 'hard' vegetables, such as carrots or potato that require longer cooking, at step 2, and 'soft' vegetables, such as peas, towards the end of step 3.

*** 250g (8oz) cottage cheese**
*** ¾ cup (105g) cornflour (cornstarch)**
*** 2¼ teaspoons garam masala**
*** 3 cloves garlic, crushed**
*** 2 tablespoons vegetable oil**
*** 1 medium onion (150g), chopped finely**
*** 1 bunch fresh coriander (cilantro) (100g) (see tips)**
*** 2 tablespoons grated fresh ginger**
*** 2 fresh long red chillies, chopped finely**
*** 2 cups (240g) coarsely chopped vegetables (such as pumpkin, baby eggplant, cauliflower, peas, spinach)**
*** 1 cup (200g) dried red lentils**
*** 1 litre (4 cups) vegetable stock**
*** 2 cups (400g) basmati rice**
*** 3 cups (750ml) water**
*** vegetable oil, extra, for deep-frying**

1 Combine cottage cheese, ½ cup of the cornflour, ¼ teaspoon of the garam masala and 1 clove garlic in a medium bowl. Season. Refrigerate until required.
2 Heat oil in a large saucepan over medium heat. Cook onion, stirring, for 5 minutes or until softened. Remove leaves from coriander and reserve for serving. Finely chop coriander stalks and roots; add to pan with ginger, 1 chilli, remaining garam masala and garlic, and any 'hard' vegetables that take longer to cook; cook for 2 minutes.
3 Add lentils and stock to pan; bring to the boil. Reduce heat to low and cook, stirring occasionally, for 25 minutes. Add any 'soft' vegetables and cook for a further 5 minutes or until all vegetables are cooked.
4 Meanwhile, place rice and the water in a medium saucepan; bring to the boil. Cover, reduce heat and cook for 15 minutes. Remove pan from heat and stand, covered, for 5 minutes.
5 Fill a large saucepan one-third full with extra oil; heat to 180°C/350°F (or until a cube of bread turns golden in 15 seconds). Using damp hands, roll 2-teaspoon quantities of cheese mixture into balls. Roll balls in remaining cornflour to coat. Deep-fry balls, in batches, for 1 minute or until light golden and crisp; drain on paper towel.
6 Top dhal with cheese balls, remaining chilli and reserved coriander leaves.

Tips *Wash coriander roots well before using. The cheese balls may take on a rustic, slightly 'burst' appearance if left in the oil for too long. This is fine; they will just not look as round.*

Serving suggestion *Steamed basmati rice.*

435

STOVE

VEGETARIAN

SWEET POTATO AND EGGPLANT CURRY WITH CAVOLO NERO

prep + cook time 1 hour * serves 6

Meaning 'black cabbage' in Italian, cavolo nero is more delicate and sweet than its relative curly kale, while possessing many of the same great nutritional qualities. It is rich in protein, fibre, antioxidants, vitamins A, C, and K, and folate.

- **650g (1¼lb) baby eggplants**
- **olive-oil spray**
- **⅓ cup (80ml) olive oil**
- **1 large onion (200g), chopped finely**
- **4cm (1½in) piece fresh ginger, chopped finely**
- **1 fresh small red chilli, chopped finely**
- **2 cloves garlic, crushed**
- **4 cardamom pods, crushed lightly**
- **1 teaspoon garam marsala**
- **1 teaspoon ground cumin**
- **1 teaspoon ground turmeric**
- **800g (1½lb) orange sweet potatoes, cut into 3cm (1¼in) pieces**
- **270ml canned coconut milk**
- **400g (12½oz) can diced tomatoes**
- **1 cup (250ml) vegetable stock**
- **1 tablespoon brown mustard seeds**
- **24 fresh curry leaves**
- **400g (12½oz) cavolo nero (tuscan cabbage), chopped coarsely**
- **2 tablespoons water**

1 Preheat oven to 180°C/350°F. Line two oven trays with baking paper.
2 Quarter eggplants lengthways, place on trays and spray with oil. Bake for 20 minutes or until golden and soft.
3 Heat 2 tablespoons of the oil in a large heavy-based saucepan over medium-high heat. Cook onion, ginger, chilli and garlic for 3 minutes. Reduce heat to low and add cardamom, garam marsala, cumin and turmeric; cook for 2 minutes until fragrant. Increase heat to medium and add sweet potato; stir to coat in spices.
4 Add coconut milk to pan with canned tomatoes and stock; bring to the boil. Reduce heat to low-medium and simmer, covered, for 20 minutes or until sweet potato is tender. Stir in eggplant and return to the boil. Season to taste.
5 Meanwhile, heat remaining oil in a large frying pan over medium-high heat. Cook mustard seeds, stirring, for 1 minute or until seeds pop. Add curry leaves and cook for 1 minute. Stir in cavolo nero and the water; cook, covered, until just wilted. Season to taste.
6 Serve curry with cavolo nero mixture.

Serving suggestion *Steamed basmati rice and Greek-style yoghurt.*

436

STOVE

VEGETARIAN

ALMOST VEGETARIAN MUSHROOM ORECCHIETTE

prep + cook time 1 hour * serves 4

This recipe is great for those times when some want a little meat and others want to abstain from it altogether, since the pancetta can be added or omitted as you please.

*** 30g (1oz) butter**
*** 1 tablespoon olive oil**
*** 1 medium onion (150g), chopped finely**
*** 2 cloves garlic, crushed**
*** 1 cup (250ml) dry white wine**
*** 200g (6½oz) swiss brown mushrooms, sliced**
*** 300ml pouring cream**
*** 200g (6½oz) sliced pancetta (optional)**
*** 500g (1lb) dried orecchiette pasta (see tip)**

GREMOLATA CRUMBS
*** 30g (1oz) butter**
*** 1 ciabatta roll (100g), torn coarsely**
*** 2 cloves garlic, crushed**
*** 2 tablespoons chopped fresh flat-leaf parsley**
*** 2 teaspoons finely grated lemon rind**

1 Heat butter and oil in a medium frying pan. Cook onion and garlic, stirring, for 5 minutes or until onion is soft. Add wine to pan and boil, uncovered, until reduced by half. Stir in mushrooms and cook, stirring occasionally, over medium heat for 5 minutes or until softened. Add cream and stir over medium heat for 2 minutes or until thickened slightly. Season to taste. Cover to keep warm.

2 Meanwhile, if using pancetta, preheat oven to 180°C/350°F. Place pancetta in a single layer on an oven tray lined with baking paper. Bake for 10 minutes or until golden and crisp.

3 Make gremolata crumbs.

4 Cook pasta in a large saucepan of boiling salted water until just tender. Drain, reserving ¼ cup cooking water. Return pasta to pan.

5 Add hot sauce to pasta and toss gently to combine. If mixture is a little thick, add some of the reserved pasta water. Serve pasta topped with crumbled pancetta (if using) and the gremolata crumbs.

GREMOLATA CRUMBS Heat butter in a small saucepan over medium heat; add torn bread and garlic. Cook, stirring, for 2 minutes or until bread is golden brown. Remove from heat and stir in parsley and rind.

Tip *Look for an artisanal brand of orecchiette, as these are more robust (they will also take longer to cook).*

Serving suggestion
A green salad.

VEGETARIAN CHILLI WITH GUACAMOLE

prep + cook time 1 hour ✻ serves 4

Chocolate might seem like an odd choice to add to a savoury dish, but the inclusion of dark chocolate adds body, colour and flavour to this vegetarian chilli. Use a good-quality chocolate, with 70% cocoa solids, so as to not make the chilli too sweet.

∗ 2 stalks celery (300g)
∗ 2 tablespoons olive oil
∗ 1 large onion (200g), chopped coarsely
∗ 1 medium yellow capsicum (bell pepper) (200g), chopped coarsely
∗ 1 large red capsicum (bell pepper) (350g), chopped coarsely
∗ 2 fresh long red chillies, chopped finely
∗ 1 tablespoon smoked paprika
∗ 3 cloves garlic, crushed
∗ 2 teaspoons ground coriander
∗ 2 teaspoons fresh oregano leaves
∗ 2 cups (500ml) vegetable stock
∗ 400g (12½oz) can diced tomatoes
∗ 40g (1½oz) dark chocolate (70% cocoa), grated
∗ 400g (12½oz) can four-bean mix, drained, rinsed
∗ 1 teaspoon caster (superfine) sugar
∗ ¾ cup (90g) finely grated vintage cheddar
∗ 1 packet (156g) blue corn chips (see tip)

GUACAMOLE
∗ 2 medium avocados (500g)
∗ 2 tablespoons lime juice

1 Make guacamole.
2 Wash celery stalks well; remove leafy tips and reserve. Chop celery into 1cm (½in) pieces. Heat oil in a large saucepan over medium heat. Cook celery, onion and capsicums, stirring, for 5 minutes or until softened. Add chilli, paprika, garlic, coriander and oregano; cook, stirring, for 1 minute or until fragrant. Add stock and canned tomatoes; bring to a simmer. Simmer, stirring occasionally, for 10 minutes or until thickened. Add chocolate, beans and sugar; cook, stirring, for 5 minutes or until dark and glossy. Season to taste.
3 Top chilli with cheddar and reserved celery leaves. Serve with guacamole and corn chips.

GUACAMOLE Halve avocados; remove seeds. Place avocado flesh in a medium bowl with juice; season to taste. Mash with a fork until smooth. Cover and refrigerate until required.

Tip *Use yellow corn chips or tortilla chips, if you can't find blue corn chips.*

PASTA WITH NUT PASTE, PEAR AND BORLOTTI BEANS

prep + cook time 55 minutes * serves 4

While this recipe is geared for Autumn, you can swap ingredients for the seasons. In spring, use broad beans instead of borlotti beans, and bitter salad greens instead of radicchio.

*** 600g (1¼lb) fresh borlotti beans, shelled**
*** ½ cup (80g) blanched almonds, roasted**
*** ½ cup (50g) walnuts, roasted**
*** 1 clove garlic, crushed**
*** ¼ cup coarsely chopped fresh flat-leaf parsley**
*** ½ teaspoon freshly ground black pepper**
*** ½ cup (125ml) extra virgin olive oil**
*** 375g (13oz) penne pasta**
*** 2 medium pears (460g), unpeeled, cut into thin wedges**
*** 1 tablespoon olive oil, extra**
*** 1 medium radicchio (200g), leaves separated, torn**
*** 120g (4oz) blue cheese, crumbled**
*** ¼ cup fresh flat-leaf parsley sprigs, extra**

1 Place borlotti beans in a large saucepan of cold water. Bring to the boil; boil for 25 minutes or until tender. Drain.

2 Process nuts, garlic, parsley and pepper until finely chopped. With the motor operating, gradually pour in ¼ cup of the oil until combined. Season with salt.

3 Cook pasta in a large saucepan of boiling salted water for 8 minutes or until almost tender. Drain, reserving ½ cup of the cooking water. Return pasta to pan and cover to keep warm.

4 Meanwhile, season the pear. Heat extra oil in a large frying pan over medium heat. Cook pear for 2 minutes each side or until golden; drain on paper towel. Add beans to same pan, stirring for 2 minutes until heated through.

5 Add nut paste to pasta with enough reserved cooking water for the paste to coat the pasta (do not return the pan to the heat or the nut paste will thicken and make the mixture dry). Add pear, beans and radicchio; toss gently to combine. Season.

6 Serve pasta topped with cheese and parsley sprigs, drizzled with remaining oil.

Tip *For a contrasting texture, top the pasta with a little shaved raw pear.*

STOVE

VEGETARIAN

POTATO GNOCCHI
WITH MUSHROOMS AND THYME

prep + cook time 1 hour (+ refrigeration) * serves 4

Cooking the potatoes whole with the peel on keeps the potatoes dry and fluffy – doing this helps to create lightly textured pillows of gnocchi.

*** 2 tablespoons olive oil**
*** 375g (12oz) assorted mushrooms, sliced thinly (see tip)**
*** 2 teaspoons finely chopped fresh lemon thyme**
*** 2 cloves garlic, crushed**
*** 300ml pouring cream**
*** ⅓ cup (25g) finely grated vegetarian parmesan-style cheese**
*** 2 teaspoons fresh lemon thyme, extra**

POTATO GNOCCHI
*** 500g (1lb) desiree potatoes, unpeeled**
*** 1 egg, beaten lightly**
*** 15g (½oz) butter, melted**
*** 2 tablespoons finely grated vegetarian parmesan-style cheese**
*** 1 cup (150g) plain (all-purpose) flour, approximately**

1 Make potato gnocchi.
2 Heat oil in a large frying pan over high heat. Cook mushrooms and thyme, allowing the mushrooms to brown well before turning, for 5 minutes or until golden. Add garlic and stir for 30 seconds or until softened. Add cream and bring to the boil. Reduce heat and simmer, uncovered, until sauce thickens. Stir in half the parmesan. Season to taste.
3 Meanwhile, cook gnocchi, in batches, in a large saucepan of boiling water until gnocchi float to the surface and are cooked through. Remove from pan with a slotted spoon to a bowl. Cover keep warm.
4 Once all gnocchi are cooked, add to mushroom sauce and stir gently. Serve topped with remaining parmesan and extra thyme sprigs.

POTATO GNOCCHI Boil whole potatoes until tender; drain. When cool enough to handle, peel away skins. Mash potatoes using a ricer or potato masher into a medium bowl. Stir in egg, butter, parmesan and enough flour to make a firm dough. Divide dough into four portions. Roll each portion on a floured surface into 2cm (¾in) thick ropes. Cut each rope into 2cm (¾in) pieces. Place gnocchi in a single layer on a lightly floured tray. Cover and refrigerate for 1 hour.

Tip *Try using a variety of mushrooms, such as flat, cup, button, portobello, oyster and enoki, keeping small mushrooms halved or whole and slicing larger types.*

STOVE

VEGETARIAN

THAI YELLOW CURRY

prep + cook time 1 hour * serves 4

- **1 tablespoon rice bran oil**
- **1 medium red onion (170g), sliced thinly**
- **¼ cup (75g) yellow curry paste**
- **2 cloves garlic, crushed**
- **10cm (4in) stalk fresh lemon grass, bruised**
- **4 kaffir lime leaves, shredded finely**
- **1⅔ cups (410ml) coconut milk**
- **1 cup (250ml) water**
- **750g (1½lb) orange sweet potatoes, unpeeled, scrubbed, chopped coarsely**
- **200g (6½oz) green beans, trimmed**
- **250g (8oz) assorted asian mushrooms (see tips)**
- **1 tablespoon grated palm sugar**
- **1 tablespoon vegetarian oyster sauce**
- **2 tablespoons lime juice**
- **1 fresh long red chilli, seeded, sliced thinly**
- **¼ cup (20g) fried shallots (see tips)**
- **½ cup fresh thai basil leaves**

1 Heat oil in a wok or large heavy-based saucepan over high heat. Add onion and cook, stirring, for 5 minutes or until onion softens. Add curry paste, garlic, lemon grass and lime leaves; cook, stirring, for 1 minute or until fragrant.

2 Add coconut milk, the water and sweet potato; bring to the boil. Reduce heat to medium and simmer for 20 minutes or until sweet potato is just tender. Stir in beans and mushrooms; simmer for a further 5 minutes or until vegetables are tender. Stir in sugar, oyster sauce and juice.

3 Serve curry topped with chilli, fried shallots and thai basil.

Tips *We used a mix of shiitake, oyster and enoki mushrooms in this recipe, but you can use swiss brown or button instead, if you prefer. Fried shallots are available from Asian food stores and some supermarkets.*

447

STOVE

VEGETARIAN

BEETROOT, HALOUMI AND RICE WINTER SALAD

prep + cook time 40 minutes ✻ serves 4

- **1 cup (200g) brown rice**
- **⅓ cup (80ml) extra virgin olive oil**
- **1 small red onion (100g), cut into wedges**
- **1 teaspoon ground cumin**
- **1 teaspoon ground coriander**
- **400g (12½oz) can chickpeas (garbanzo beans), drained, rinsed**
- **500g (1lb) vacuum-packed cooked beetroot (beets), quartered (see tip)**
- **100g (3oz) baby spinach leaves**
- **1 cup fresh mint leaves**
- **½ cup (50g) walnuts, roasted, chopped coarsely**
- **2 tablespoons balsamic glaze**
- **200g (6½oz) haloumi, sliced**

1 Cook rice in a large saucepan of boiling salted water for 25 minutes or until just tender; drain.

2 Meanwhile, heat 1 tablespoon of the oil in a large frying pan over medium heat. Add onion and cook, stirring, for 5 minutes or until tender. Add cumin and coriander; cook, stirring, for 30 seconds or until fragrant. Add chickpeas and beetroot; stir until heated through.

3 Combine rice, spinach, mint and walnuts in a large bowl. Drizzle with combined 1 tablespoon of the balsamic glaze and 2 tablespoons of the remaining oil. Add beetroot and chickpea mixture; season to taste. Mix gently.

4 Heat remaining 1 tablespoon of the oil in a large frying pan over high heat. Cook haloumi for 2 minutes each side or until golden.

5 Serve salad with haloumi, drizzled with remaining balsamic glaze.

Tip *To cook beetroot from scratch, scrub 500g (1lb) medium-sized trimmed beetroot (beets). Add to a saucepan of boiling water, then reduce heat to a simmer and cook for 45 minutes or until a small knife can easily be inserted into one. Drain. Cool for 5 minutes. When cool enough to handle, peel away skins.*

448

STOVE

VEGETARIAN

BROWN RICE AND MUSHROOM BOWL WITH DUKKAH EGGS

prep + cook time 1 hour ✻ serves 4

- **1⅓ cups (265g) brown rice**
- **4 eggs**
- **¼ cup (60ml) extra virgin olive oil**
- **1 small onion (80g), chopped finely**
- **2 cloves garlic, crushed**
- **200g (6½oz) swiss brown mushrooms**
- **4 kale leaves (100g), stems removed, torn coarsely**

DUKKAH

- **½ cup (80g) pine nuts**
- **1 cup (160g) dry-roasted almonds**
- **1 teaspoon sea salt flakes**
- **1 tablespoon black sesame seeds**
- **2 tablespoons coriander seeds**
- **2 tablespoons cumin seeds**
- **2 teaspoons fennel seeds**

1 Make dukkah.

2 Cook rice in a medium saucepan of boiling salted water for 25 minutes or until just tender; drain.

3 Meanwhile, add eggs to a saucepan of water; bring to the boil; boil, uncovered, for 4 minutes for soft-boiled. Drain and rinse eggs under cold water until cool enough to handle, then peel.

4 Heat oil in a large non-stick frying pan over medium heat. Cook onion, stirring, for 5 minutes or until softened. Add garlic and mushrooms. Cook, stirring occasionally, for a further 5 minutes or until mushrooms are browned. Add kale leaves and cook, stirring, for 3 minutes or until wilted. Stir in rice. Season to taste.

5 Roll eggs in dukkah to coat. Divide rice mixture among bowls. Top with halved eggs and remaining dukkah mixture.

DUKKAH Stir pine nuts in a small frying pan over medium heat for 3 minutes or until golden. Place in a food processor with almonds and salt. Place sesame, coriander, cumin and fennel seeds in same pan. Stir over medium heat for 2 minutes or until sesame seeds are golden. Add to the food processor; stand until cooled. Pulse the nuts and seeds until finely chopped. Place in a jar and seal. Store at room temperature.

SWEETS

SLOW-COOKED QUINCE

prep + cook time 4 hours * serves 4

- **½ cup (110g) caster (superfine) sugar**
- **2 tablespoons honey**
- **1 bay leaf**
- **1 whole star anise**
- **3 cups (750ml) water**
- **2 large quinces (800g)**

1 Place sugar, honey, bay leaf, star anise and the water in a large saucepan. Stir over medium heat until sugar dissolves.

2 Peel quinces, halve, then cut each half into quarters; remove cores. Add quince to the syrup and cook over medium heat until syrup comes to a simmer. Cover quince with a piece of baking paper cut to fit the size of the pan. Simmer, covered, over low heat for 3½ hours or until quince is soft and rose-coloured.

3 Serve quince with the poaching liquid.

Do ahead *Cook a double or triple batch of quinces and keep them in their syrup in the fridge, covered, for up to 3 days.*

Serving suggestion *For breakfast, serve with porridge or muesli. For dessert, serve with vanilla ice-cream, thick (double) cream, custard or yoghurt.*

DARK CHOCOLATE PANCAKES WITH MARMALADE

prep + cook time 1 hour ✻ makes 20

* **4 eggs**
* **⅓ cup (75g) caster (superfine) sugar**
* **2 cups (500ml) milk**
* **180g (5½oz) dark (semi-sweet) chocolate, grated finely**
* **60g (2oz) butter, melted**
* **1¾ cups (260g) self-raising flour**
* **½ teaspoon salt**
* **½ cup (50g) dutch-processed cocoa (see tip)**
* **cooking-oil spray**
* **250g (8oz) crème fraîche**
* **⅓ cup (115g) orange or cumquat marmalade**

1 Beat eggs and sugar in a small bowl with an electric mixer for 5 minutes or until thick. Gently stir in milk, chocolate and butter.

2 Sift flour, salt and cocoa into a large bowl. Whisk in egg mixture gradually until batter is smooth.

3 Heat a large heavy-based frying pan over low heat and spray lightly with oil. Pour ¼ cup of the batter into pan; cook until bubbles appear on the surface. Turn pancake and cook for 2 minutes or until cooked through. Remove from pan and cover to keep warm. Repeat with remaining batter, spraying with oil as needed.

4 Serve pancakes topped with crème fraîche and marmalade.

Tip *Dutch-processed cocoa refers to cocoa that has had an alkaline added during a process called 'dutching', which was perfected in Holland, resulting in a richer chocolate taste and colour.*

Serving suggestion *Instead of the crème fraîche and marmalade, you could also serve these pancakes with fresh cream and berries, dusted with a little icing sugar.*

Suitable to freeze *at the end of step 3.*

CROSTOLI CHIPS
WITH VANILLA CUSTARD CREAM

prep + cook time 1 hour (+ standing & refrigeration) ✻ serves 6

- **⅔ cup (100g) plain (all-purpose) flour**
- **⅓ cup (50g) self-raising flour**
- **1½ tablespoons icing (confectioners') sugar**
- **1 teaspoon vanilla extract**
- **2 teaspoons olive oil**
- **1 egg**
- **1 tablespoon marsala, approximately**
- **canola oil, for deep-frying**
- **icing (confectioners') sugar, extra**
- **250g (8oz) strawberries, halved**

VANILLA CUSTARD CREAM

- **2 cups (500ml) milk**
- **⅔ cup (150g) caster (superfine) sugar**
- **4 egg yolks**
- **⅓ cup (50g) plain (all-purpose) flour**
- **⅔ cup (160ml) thickened (heavy) cream**
- **2 teaspoons vanilla extract**

1 Make vanilla custard cream.

2 Place flours and icing sugar in a food processor; process to combine. Add vanilla, oil, egg and enough marsala until ingredients just come together. Knead dough on a floured surface until smooth. Wrap in plastic wrap and stand at room temperature for 30 minutes.

3 Cut dough in half. Working with one piece at a time, lightly flour dough, pressing with the palm of your hand to flatten slightly. Using a pasta machine with rollers at the widest setting, dust the rollers with flour, then feed the dough, one piece at a time, through the pasta machine four times, folding the dough in half each time, until you get an even rectangle. Reduce setting one notch each time, until dough is 1mm thick. Place on a lightly floured work surface. Use a crinkled-edged ravioli cutter to cut dough into 5cm x 12cm (2in x 4¾in) strips. Make two small slits in the centre of each strip.

4 Heat oil in a large saucepan over medium heat to 180°C/350°F. Cook strips, in batches, for 15 seconds each side or until light golden and crisp; drain on paper towel. Cool.

5 Dust crostoli chips with extra sifted icing sugar. Serve with strawberries and custard cream.

VANILLA CUSTARD CREAM Warm milk in a medium saucepan over medium heat until just below boiling. Whisk together sugar, yolks and flour in a small bowl until smooth. Whisk hot milk into egg yolk mixture. Return mixture to same pan and cook, whisking, over low heat for 5 minutes or until mixture boils and thickens. Cover surface of custard directly with plastic wrap and cool for 15 minutes. Refrigerate for 30 minutes or until chilled. Beat cream and vanilla in a small bowl with an electric mixer until soft peaks form, then whisk into custard until smooth.

Tip *Flavour the custard with orange liqueur, grated orange rind or finely chopped chocolate, if you like.*

Do ahead *Crostoli chips can be made a day ahead and stored in an airtight container; dust with icing sugar just before serving. Custard can be made a day ahead and stored, covered, in the fridge.*

SPELT CRÊPES WITH POACHED PEAR AND BLUEBERRIES

prep + cook time 55 minutes (+ standing) * serves 4

*** 2 eggs**
*** 1 cup (250ml) milk**
*** ⅓ cup (50g) plain (all-purpose) spelt flour**
*** ⅓ cup (50g) wholemeal plain (all-purpose) spelt flour**
*** 360g (11½oz) soft ricotta (see tips)**
*** 2 tablespoons pure maple syrup**
*** 1 teaspoon ground cinnamon**
*** 2 teaspoons soft butter**

POACHED PEAR & BLUEBERRIES
*** ½ cup (125ml) dry red wine**
*** ½ cup (125ml) freshly squeezed orange juice**
*** 1 cinnamon stick**
*** 2 tablespoons pure maple syrup**
*** 2 small corella pears (300g), unpeeled (see tips)**
*** 125g (4oz) blueberries**

1 Make poached pear and blueberries.
2 Process eggs, milk and flours until smooth. Transfer to a jug and stand for 20 minutes.
3 Whisk ricotta, maple syrup and cinnamon in a small bowl until smooth.
4 Brush a heated 20cm (8in) crêpe pan with a little of the butter. Pour scant ¼ cup of batter into pan, swirling to coat the base. Cook crêpe for 30 seconds or until browned underneath. Turn crêpe and cook for a further 10 seconds or until browned lightly underneath. Transfer to a plate and cover to keep warm. Repeat with remaining butter and batter to make eight crêpes in total.
5 Spread 2 tablespoons of the ricotta mixture over one-quarter of each crêpe. Fold crêpes into quarters over filling. Serve crêpes with poached fruit, drizzled with the poaching liquid.

POACHED PEAR & BLUEBERRIES Bring wine, juice, cinnamon and maple syrup to the boil in a medium saucepan over medium heat. Meanwhile, quarter and core pears; cut into thin wedges. Add pear to wine mixture and simmer for 10 minutes or until tender. Add blueberries. Remove from heat.

Tips *Buy ricotta fresh from the deli; it should be moist. The cooking time of the pears will depend on their ripeness.*

458

STOVE

SWEETS

CARAMEL GINGER STEAMED PUDDING WITH CUSTARD

prep + cook time 1 hour 50 minutes (+ standing) * serves 8

*** 1 cup (220g) caster (superfine) sugar**
*** ½ cup (125ml) water**
*** ½ cup (110g) crystallised ginger, sliced thinly**
*** ¼ cup (90g) honey**
*** 125g (4oz) butter, softened**
*** 1 teaspoon freshly grated nutmeg**
*** 1 teaspoon ground ginger**
*** 2 eggs**
*** ¾ cup (110g) plain (all-purpose) flour**
*** ¾ cup (110g) self-raising flour**
*** ½ cup (125ml) milk**

CALVADOS CUSTARD
*** 1 vanilla bean, split lengthways**
*** 1½ cups (375ml) milk**
*** 1 cup (250ml) pouring cream**
*** 4 egg yolks**
*** ¼ cup (55g) caster (superfine) sugar**
*** 3 teaspoons cornflour (cornstarch)**
*** 2 tablespoons calvados (apple brandy) (see tip)**

1 Cook half the sugar in a small saucepan over medium-high heat for 3 minutes, swirling pan often, until sugar is deep golden. Remove from heat and carefully pour in the water all at once (mixture will boil). Return to heat and cook for 3 minutes or until caramel has mostly dissolved. Stand for 5 minutes.
2 Grease a 1.5-litre (6-cup) pudding steamer and lid; line base of steamer with baking paper.
3 Sprinkle two-thirds of the crystallised ginger onto the base of steamer and drizzle with honey.
4 Beat butter, remaining sugar and spices in a small bowl with an electric mixer until light and fluffy. Beat in eggs, one at a time. Stir in sifted flours and remaining crystallised ginger, then milk and cooled caramel, in two batches.
5 Pour pudding mixture into steamer. Cover steamer with the lid. Alternatively, place a sheet of baking paper on a sheet of foil; fold a 5cm (2in) pleat longways through the centre. Cover steamer with pleated baking paper and foil, paper-side down (this allows the pudding to expand during steaming); secure with kitchen string. Place steamer in a large saucepan with enough boiling water to come halfway up the side of the steamer. Cover pan with a tight-fitting lid. Boil pudding for 1½ hours, replenishing the water as necessary to maintain its level. Remove steamer from pan and stand for 10 minutes before turning onto a serving plate.
6 Meanwhile, make calvados custard.
7 Serve pudding with custard.

CALVADOS CUSTARD Scrape seeds from vanilla bean into a medium saucepan, then add milk and cream. Cook, stirring, over medium heat until mixture comes to a gentle simmer. Remove from heat. Whisk egg yolks, sugar and cornflour in a medium heatproof bowl until combined. Strain hot milk mixture over egg yolk mixture, whisking constantly. Return mixture to cleaned pan and cook, stirring, over low heat for 2 minutes until custard thickens and coats the back of a wooden spoon. Stir in calvados.

Tip *You can use brandy instead of the calvados.*

Suitable to freeze *at the end of step 5.*

461

STOVE

SWEETS

COCONUT FRITTERS
WITH MANGO, CHILLI AND LIME

prep + cook time 50 minutes * serves 4

- **1 young drinking coconut (1.2kg)**
- **2 medium bananas (400g), mashed**
- **¼ cup (60ml) coconut cream**
- **⅔ cup (100g) plain (all-purpose) flour**
- **1 teaspoon baking powder**
- **¾ cup (60g) shredded coconut**
- **2½ tablespoons coconut nectar or agave syrup**
- **rice bran oil, for deep-frying**
- **2 tablespoons lime juice**
- **1 medium mango (430g), sliced thinly**
- **1½ tablespoons finely grated lime rind**
- **1 fresh long red chilli, seeded, sliced thinly**

1 Insert the tip of a small knife into the soft spot on the base of the coconut, using a twisting action. Place coconut over a glass and drain coconut water (reserve for another use). Wrap coconut in a clean towel; break open with a hammer or by smashing it on the floor. Spoon out the soft coconut flesh; you should have about ½ cup (90g) of the flesh. Thinly slice coconut flesh.

2 Combine fresh coconut, banana, coconut cream, ½ cup of the flour, baking powder, ¼ cup of the shredded coconut and 2 teaspoons of the coconut nectar in a large bowl.

3 Combine remaining flour and shredded coconut in a medium bowl. Roll level tablespoons of coconut mixture into balls, then roll balls in flour mixture.

4 Fill a wok one-third with oil and heat to 160°C/325°F (or until a cube of bread browns in 25–30 seconds). Deep-fry coconut balls, in batches, for 2½ minutes or until golden and cooked through; drain on paper towel.

5 Meanwhile, combine juice and remaining coconut nectar in a small bowl. Stir in mango, rind and chilli.

6 Serve fritters with mango mixture and syrup.

Serving suggestion *Lime wedges for extra tang.*

COCONUT SAGO
WITH GINGER AND PALM SUGAR SYRUP

prep + cook time 40 minutes (+ refrigeration) * serves 6

*** ¾ cup (150g) sago**
*** 400ml can coconut milk**
*** 2¼ cups (560ml) water**
*** ⅓ cup (75g) caster (superfine) sugar**
*** 200g (6½oz) piece of pineapple, peeled, sliced thinly**

GINGER & PALM SUGAR SYRUP
*** 220g (7oz) dark palm sugar, grated finely**
*** ¼ cup (60ml) water**
*** 20g (¾oz) piece ginger, peeled, sliced thinly**

1 Place sago, coconut milk and 1 cup of the water in a medium heavy-based saucepan; soak for 30 minutes.
2 Place pan with sago mixture over medium heat and bring to the boil, stirring. Reduce heat to low. Add remaining water and cook, stirring occasionally, for 10 minutes or until sago is tender. Remove from heat and stir in sugar until dissolved.
3 Spoon sago pudding into six serving glasses. Cover and refrigerate for 2 hours or until chilled.
4 Make ginger and palm sugar syrup.
5 Serve sago topped with pineapple slices, drizzled with sugar syrup.

GINGER & PALM SUGAR SYRUP Stir ingredients in a medium saucepan over low heat until sugar dissolves. Increase heat to high and bring to the boil; boil for 8 minutes or until thickened. Cool.

Do ahead *Sago and syrup can be made a day ahead. Refrigerate sago, and store syrup in an airtight container at room temperature.*

CHOCOLATE-FILLED CROISSANT DOUGHNUTS

prep + cook time 2 hours 15 minutes (+ standing & refrigeration) ✻ makes 16

- **4 teaspoons (14g) dried yeast**
- **1 teaspoon caster (superfine) sugar**
- **1 cup (250ml) lukewarm water**
- **250g (8oz) chilled butter, cut into 2cm (¾in) pieces**
- **3⅓ cups (500g) plain (all-purpose) flour**
- **1 cup (220g) caster (superfine) sugar, extra**
- **¼ teaspoon salt**
- **vegetable oil, for deep-frying**

CHOCOLATE CUSTARD

- **1¼ cups (310ml) milk**
- **3 egg yolks**
- **⅓ cup (75g) caster (superfine) sugar**
- **1½ tablespoons plain (all-purpose) flour**
- **2 tablespoons cocoa powder**

1 Combine yeast, sugar and the water in a small jug. Stand in a warm place for 10 minutes or until frothy.

2 Meanwhile, pulse butter, flour, ⅓ cup (75g) of the extra sugar and salt in a food processor for a few seconds, in short bursts, until butter is the size of small peas.

3 Transfer flour mixture to a large bowl. Add yeast mixture and stir until ingredients almost come together. Using your hands, bring ingredients together to form a dough in the bowl (the butter will still be visible). Cover bowl tightly with plastic wrap and stand in a warm place for 1 hour or until doubled in size.

4 Meanwhile, make chocolate custard.

5 Turn dough onto a floured sheet of baking paper and dust with flour. Top with another sheet of baking paper. Roll out to a 20cm x 40cm (8in x 16in) rectangle. Fold dough into thirds by bringing the bottom third over the middle third, then the top third down to cover the folded dough. Repeat rolling out and folding, then wrap in plastic wrap and freeze for 10 minutes.

6 With a short end of the dough in front of you, repeat step 5 two more times.

7 Roll dough out on a lightly floured surface until 1cm (½in) thick. Using a 7.5cm (3in) round cutter, cut 16 rounds from pastry, rerolling dough, if necessary. Place rounds on baking-paper-lined oven trays. Using a 3cm (1¼in) round cutter, cut holes from centres; place 'holes' on trays. Cover loosely with plastic wrap; stand in a warm place for 1 hour or until doubled in size.

8 Fill a large saucepan or wok one-third full with oil. Heat to 160°C/325°F (or until a cube of bread turns golden in about 25 seconds). Deep-fry dough, in batches, for 2 minutes each side or until golden and cooked through. Drain on paper towel, then dust, one at a time, in remaining extra sugar.

9 Spoon custard into a piping bag fitted with a 5mm (¼in) plain tube. When doughnuts are cool enough to handle, pipe custard through the base of each doughnut at four or five points (to allow custard to be evenly distributed). Serve warm.

CHOCOLATE CUSTARD Bring milk almost to the boil in a small saucepan over medium heat. Meanwhile, whisk egg yolks, sugar, sifted flour and sifted cocoa in a medium bowl until combined. Gradually whisk in hot milk. Return mixture to pan and stir over heat until custard boils and thickens. Strain through a fine sieve into a bowl. Cover surface of custard with plastic wrap and refrigerate until required.

INDIVIDUAL GLUTEN-FREE BOILED PUDDINGS

prep + cook time 2 hours 15 minutes (+ overnight standing) * makes 6

You will need to start this recipe the day before.

- **1kg (2lb) dried mixed fruit**
- **1 large apple (200g), grated coarsely**
- **½ cup (125ml) orange-flavoured liqueur**
- **1 tablespoon finely grated orange rind**
- **2 teaspoons mixed spice**
- **2 teaspoons ground cinnamon**
- **125g (4oz) butter, softened**
- **½ cup (110g) firmly packed dark brown sugar**
- **2 eggs**
- **2 cups (140g) stale gluten-free white breadcrumbs**
- **½ cup (60g) tapioca flour**
- **1 cup (135g) gluten-free plain (all-purpose) flour, plus 1 cup extra**
- **6 x 35cm (14in) squares unbleached calico**

1 Combine mixed fruit, apple, liqueur, rind, mixed spice and cinnamon in a large bowl. Cover with plastic wrap and stand at room temperature overnight.

2 Beat butter and sugar in a small bowl with an electric mixer until pale. Beat in eggs, one at a time. Stir egg mixture into fruit mixture. Add breadcrumbs and combined sifted flours; stir to combine.

3 Fill a boiler three-quarters full of hot water and cover with a tight-fitting lid; bring to the boil. Get ready 1 metre (3ft) of kitchen string, plus extra flour. Wearing thick rubber gloves and using tongs, dip pudding cloths, one at a time, into boiling water; boil for 1 minute, then remove. Squeeze excess water from cloths. Spread hot cloths on bench and rub 2 tablespoons of the extra flour into centre of each cloth to cover an area of 20cm (8in) in diameter, leaving flour a little thicker in centre of cloth where 'skin' on the pudding needs to be thickest. Divide pudding mixture equally among cloths, placing in centre of each cloth. Gather cloths around mixture, avoiding any deep pleats, and pat into round shapes. Tie cloths tightly with string, as close to mixture as possible. Tie loops in string. Lower the three puddings into boiling water. Cover and boil for 2 hours, replenishing with boiling water as necessary to maintain water level.

4 Working with one pudding at a time, lift a pudding from the water using a wooden spoon through the string loop. Do not put pudding on bench; suspend from spoon by placing over the rungs of an upturned stool or wedging the spoon in a drawer. Twist end of cloth around the string to avoid it touching the pudding. Hang pudding for 10 minutes. Repeat with remaining puddings.

5 Place puddings on a board. Cut strings carefully and peel back cloths. Turn puddings onto plate, then carefully peel cloth away completely. Stand for 20 minutes or until skin darkens and puddings becomes firm.

Serving suggestion *Gluten-free custard or ice-cream.*

DAIRY AND GLUTEN-FREE STEAMED CHRISTMAS PUDDING

prep + cook time 7 hours (+ overnight standing) * serves 12

You will need to start this recipe the day before.

- **750g (1½lb) dried mixed fruit**
- **1 large apple (200g), grated coarsely**
- **½ cup (125ml) dry sherry**
- **1 tablespoon finely grated orange rind**
- **2 teaspoons mixed spice**
- **1 teaspoon ground cinnamon**
- **dairy-free spread, for greasing**
- **125g (4oz) dairy-free spread**
- **½ cup (110g) firmly packed brown sugar**
- **2 eggs**
- **2 cups (140g) stale gluten-free breadcrumbs**
- **½ cup (65g) gluten-free plain (all-purpose) flour**
- **½ cup (60g) tapioca flour**

1 Combine mixed fruit, apple, sherry, rind, mixed spice and cinnamon in a large bowl. Cover with plastic wrap and stand at room temperature overnight.

2 Grease a 2-litre (8-cup) pudding basin or steamer with spread. Line base with a small round of baking paper. Place a 30cm x 40cm (12in x 16in) piece of baking paper on a sheet of foil cut to the same size; fold a 5cm (2in) pleat longways through the centre.

3 Beat spread and sugar in a small bowl with an electric mixer until pale. Beat in eggs, one at a time. Stir egg mixture into fruit mixture. Add breadcrumbs and combined sifted flours; stir to combine. Spoon mixture into basin. Top with the pleated baking paper and foil, paper-side down (this allows pudding to expand during steaming); secure with kitchen string (or the lid).

4 Place an inverted saucer in the base of a large saucepan. Place pudding basin on the saucer. Pour enough boiling water into the pan to come halfway up the side of the basin. Cover with a tight-fitting lid. Boil pudding for 6 hours, replenishing with boiling water as necessary to maintain the water level.

5 Remove pudding basin from water. Stand pudding for 10 minutes before turning out.

Do ahead *The pudding can be made a week ahead; cover and store in the fridge. Alternatively, you can freeze the pudding for up to 3 months. To reheat frozen pudding, thaw for 3 days in the fridge, then remove from fridge 12 hours before reheating. Return pudding to pudding basin and steam for 2 hours following instructions in step 4.*

Serving suggestion *Dried figs and a drizzle of golden syrup.*

STOCKS

SLOW-COOKER CHICKEN STOCK

prep + cook time 6 hours 40 minutes (+ cooling & refrigeration) * makes 2.75 litres (11 cups)

Preheat oven to 220°C/450°F. Place 2 chicken carcasses (1kg), cut into pieces, in a roasting pan; roast for 30 minutes. Reserve pan juices. Transfer to a 6-litre (24-cup) slow cooker. Add 1 medium quartered onion, 1 large chopped carrot, 2 chopped celery stalks, 6 sprigs fresh thyme, 2 teaspoons black peppercorns, reserved pan juices and 2.75 litres (11 cups) water. Cook, covered, on low for 6 hours. Strain stock through a fine sieve into a bowl; discard solids. Cool. Cover and refrigerate for 12 hours or overnight. Refrigerate for up to 1 week or freeze for up to 1 month. Bring to the boil before using.

SLOW-COOKER BEEF STOCK

prep + cook time 8 hours 40 minutes (+ cooling & refrigeration) * makes 3 litres (12 cups)

Preheat oven to 220°C/450°F. Place 1kg (2lb) beef bones, cut into 8cm (3¼in) lengths, in a roasting pan; roast for 30 minutes. Transfer to a 6-litre (24-cup) slow cooker. Add 1 medium quartered onion, 1 large chopped carrot, 2 chopped celery stalks, 2 fresh bay leaves, 2 teaspoons black peppercorns and 3 litres (12 cups) water. Cook, covered, on low for 8 hours. Strain stock through a fine sieve into a bowl; discard solids. Cool. Cover and refrigerate for 12 hours or overnight. Refrigerate for up to 1 week or freeze for up to 1 month. Bring to the boil before using.

STOVE-TOP CHICKEN STOCK

prep + cook time 2 hours 15 minutes * makes 3.5 litres (14 cups)

Combine 2kg (4lb) chicken bones, 2 medium chopped onions, 2 chopped trimmed celery stalks, 2 medium chopped carrots, 3 bay leaves, 2 teaspoons black peppercorns and 5 litres (20 cups) water in a large saucepan or stockpot; bring to the boil. Reduce heat and simmer for 2 hours, skimming surface occasionally. Strain stock through a fine sieve into a large heatproof bowl; discard solids. Cool slightly, then refrigerate stock to cool completely. Skim and discard surface fat before using. Refrigerate for up to 1 week or freeze for up to 1 month. Bring to the boil before using.

STOVE-TOP BEEF STOCK

prep + cook time 5 hours 15 minutes * makes 3.5 litres (14 cups)

Preheat oven to 200°C/400°F. Roast 2kg (4lb) meaty beef bones for 1 hour or until browned. Transfer bones to a large saucepan or stockpot. Add 2 chopped medium onions, 2 chopped trimmed celery stalks, 2 medium chopped carrots, 5.5 litres (22 cups) water, 3 bay leaves and 2 teaspoons black peppercorns; bring to the boil. Reduce heat and simmer for 3 hours, skimming surface occasionally. Add an extra 3 litres (12 cups) water and simmer for 1 hour. Strain stock through a fine sieve into a large heatproof bowl; discard solids. Cool slightly, then refrigerate stock to cool completely. Skim and discard surface fat before using. Refrigerate for up to 1 week or freeze for up to 1 month. Bring to the boil before using.

STOVE-TOP VEGETABLE STOCK

prep + cook time 1 hour 45 minutes * makes 3.5 litres (14 cups)

Combine 2 large chopped carrots, 2 large chopped parsnips, 4 medium chopped onions, 10 chopped trimmed celery stalks, 4 bay leaves, 2 teaspoons black peppercorns and 6 litres (24 cups) water in a large saucepan or stockpot; bring to the boil. Reduce heat and simmer for 1½ hours, skimming surface occasionally. Strain stock through a fine sieve into a large heatproof bowl; discard solids. Cool slightly, then refrigerate stock to cool completely. Skim and discard surface fat before using. Refrigerate for up to 1 week or freeze for up to 1 month. Bring to the boil before using.

STOVE-TOP FISH STOCK

prep + cook time 30 minutes * makes 2.5 litres (10 cups)

Combine 1.5kg (3lb) white-fleshed fish bones, 1 medium chopped onion, 2 chopped trimmed celery stalks, 2 bay leaves, 1 teaspoon black peppercorns and 3 litres (12 cups) water in a large saucepan or stockpot; simmer gently, uncovered, for 20 minutes. Strain stock through a fine sieve into a large heatproof bowl; discard solids. Cool slightly, then refrigerate to cool completely. Refrigerate for up to 1 week or freeze for up to 1 month. Bring to the boil before using.

GLOSSARY

ALLSPICE
also known as pimento or jamaican pepper; so-named because it tastes like a combination of nutmeg, cumin, clove and cinnamon. Available whole (a dark-brown berry the size of a pea) or ground.

ALMONDS
blanched brown skins removed.
flaked paper-thin slices.
ground also called almond meal; nuts are powdered to a coarse flour-like texture.
slivered small pieces cut lengthways.

BAKING PAPER
also called parchment paper or baking parchment; a silicone-coated paper that is primarily used for lining baking pans and oven trays so cakes and biscuits don't stick, making removal easy.

BAKING POWDER
a raising agent consisting mainly of two parts cream of tartar to one part bicarbonate of soda (baking soda).

BARLEY
a nutritious grain used in soups and stews. Hulled barley, the least processed, is high in fibre. Pearl barley has had the husk removed, then been steamed and polished so that only the 'pearl' of the original grain remains, much the same as white rice.

BASIL
sweet the most common type of basil; used extensively in Italian dishes and one of the main ingredients in pesto
thai also called horapa; different from holy basil and sweet basil in both look and taste, having smaller leaves and purplish stems. It has a slight aniseed taste and is one of the identifying flavours of Thai food.

BAY LEAVES
aromatic leaves from the bay tree, available fresh or dried; adds a strong, slightly peppery flavour.

BEANS
black-eyed also called black-eyed peas or cow peas. Mild-flavoured and thin-skinned, so they cook faster than most other beans. Often served in the American south with pork and cornbread.
black turtle also known as black or black kidney beans; an earthy-flavoured dried bean completely different from the better-known chinese black beans (which are fermented soy beans).
borlotti also called roman beans or pink beans, can be eaten fresh or dried. Interchangeable with pinto beans due to their similarity in appearance – pale pink or beige with dark red streaks.
broad (fava) also called windsor and horse beans; available dried, fresh, canned and frozen. Fresh should be peeled twice (discarding both the outer long green pod and the beige-green tough inner shell); the frozen beans have had their pods removed but the beige shell still needs removal.
butter cans labelled butter beans are, in fact, cannellini beans. Confusingly butter is also another name for lima beans, sold both dried and canned; a large beige bean having a mealy texture and mild taste.
cannellini small white bean similar in appearance and flavour to haricot, great northern and navy beans, all of which can be substituted for the other.
green also known as french or string beans (although the tough string they once had has generally been bred out of them), this long thin fresh bean is consumed in its entirety once cooked.
haricot the haricot bean family includes navy beans and cannellini. All are mild-flavoured white beans which are interchangeable.
kidney medium-sized red bean, slightly floury in texture, yet sweet in flavour.
snake long (about 40cm/16in), thin, round, fresh green bean; Asian in origin with a taste similar to green beans. Are also known as yard-long beans because of their (pre-metric) length.
soy the most nutritious of all legumes; high in protein, low in carbohydrate, and the source of products such as tofu, soy milk, soy sauce, tamari and miso. Also available dried and canned.
white a generic term we use for canned or dried cannellini, haricot, navy or great northern beans belonging to the same family, phaseolus vulgaris.

BEEF
blade taken from the shoulder; isn't as tender as other cuts of beef, so it needs slow-roasting to achieve best results.
brisket a cheaper cut from the belly; available with or without bones as a joint for slow-roasting, or for stewing and casseroling as cubes or mince.
cheeks the cheek muscle of a cow. It's a very tough and lean cut of meat and is most often used for braising or slow cooking to produce a tender result.
chuck from the neck and shoulder of the cow; tends to be chewy but flavourful and inexpensive. A good cut for stewing or braising.
corned silverside also known as topside roast; sold vacuum-sealed in brine.
gravy beef also known as beef shin or shank, cut from the lower shin.
osso buco literally meaning 'bone with a hole', osso buco is cut from the shin of the hind leg. It is also known as knuckle.
oxtail a flavourful cut originally from the ox but today more likely to be from any beef cattle; requires long, slow cooking so it is perfect for curries and stews.
sausages seasoned and spiced minced (ground) beef mixed with cereal and packed into casings. Also known as snags or bangers.
shank see gravy beef, above.
short ribs cut from the rib section; usually larger, more tender and meatier than pork spare ribs.

BEETROOT (BEETS)
also known as red beets; firm, round root vegetable.

BICARBONATE OF SODA (BAKING SODA)
a raising agent.

BREADCRUMBS
fresh bread, usually white, processed into crumbs.
packaged prepared fine-textured but crunchy white breadcrumbs; good for coating foods that are to be fried.
panko (japanese) breadcrumbs available in two kinds: larger pieces and fine crumbs; have a lighter texture than Western-style ones. Available from Asian food stores and most supermarkets.
stale crumbs made by grating, blending or processing 1- or 2-day old bread.

BROCCOLINI
a cross between broccoli and chinese kale; long asparagus-like stems with a long loose floret, both completely edible. Resembles broccoli but is milder and sweeter in taste.

BUK CHOY
also called bok choy, pak choi, chinese white cabbage or chinese chard; has a fresh, mild mustard taste.

BUTTERMILK
originally the term given to the slightly sour liquid left after butter was churned from cream, today it is made from

no-fat or low-fat milk to which specific bacterial cultures have neen added. Despite its name, it is actually low in fat.

CAPERBERRIES
olive-sized fruit formed after the buds of the caper bush have flowered; usually sold pickled in a vinegar brine with stalks intact.

CAPERS
grey-green buds of a warm climate (usually Mediterranean) shrub, sold either dried and salted or pickled in a vinegar brine. Capers must be rinsed well before using.
baby capers those picked early; very small, fuller-flavoured and more expensive than the full-sized ones.

CARAWAY SEEDS
the small, half-moon-shaped dried seed from a member of the parsley family; adds a sharp anise flavour when used in both sweet and savoury dishes. Used widely in foods such as rye bread, harissa and the classic Hungarian fresh cheese, liptauer.

CARDAMOM
a spice native to India and used extensively in its cuisine; can be purchased in pod, seed or ground form. Has a distinctive aromatic, sweetly rich flavour.

CAVOLO NERO
or tuscan cabbage, a staple in Tuscan country cooking. It has long, narrow, wrinkled leaves and a rich and astringent mild cabbage flavour. It doesn't lose its volume like silver beet or spinach when cooked, but it does need longer cooking.

CELERIAC (CELERY ROOT)
tuberous root with knobbly brown skin, white flesh and a celery-like flavour. Keep peeled celeriac in acidulated water to stop it discolouring. It can be grated and eaten raw in salads; used in soups and stews; boiled and mashed like potatoes; or sliced thinly and deep-fried as chips.

CHEESE
bocconcini from the diminutive of 'boccone', meaning mouthful in Italian; walnut-sized, baby mozzarella; a delicate, semi-soft, white cheese traditionally made from buffalo milk. Sold fresh, it spoils rapidly so will only keep, refrigerated in brine, for 1 or 2 days at the most.
cheddar the most common cow's milk 'tasty' cheese; should be aged, hard and have a pronounced bite.
cottage fresh, white, unripened curd cheese with a grainy consistency and a fat content of 15% to 55%.
fetta Greek in origin; a crumbly textured goat's or sheep's milk cheese, having a sharp, salty taste. Ripened and stored in salted whey; particularly good cubed and tossed into salads.
goat's made from goat's milk; has an earthy, strong taste. Available in soft, crumbly and firm textures, in various shapes and sizes, and sometimes rolled in ash or herbs.
gruyère a hard-rind Swiss cheese with small holes and a nutty, slightly salty flavour. A popular cheese for soufflés.
haloumi a Greek Cypriot cheese with a semi-firm, spongy texture and very salty sweet flavour. Ripened and stored in salted whey; best grilled or fried, it holds its shape well on being heated. Eat while still warm as it becomes tough and rubbery on cooling.
mascarpone an Italian fresh cultured-cream product made in much the same way as yoghurt. Whiteish to creamy yellow in colour, with a buttery-rich, luscious texture. Soft, creamy and spreadable, it is used in Italian desserts and as an accompaniment to fresh fruit.
mozzarella soft, spun-curd cheese originating in southern Italy where it was traditionally made from water-buffalo milk. Now generally made from cow's milk, it is the most popular pizza cheese because of its low melting point and elasticity when heated.
parmesan also called parmigiano; a hard, grainy cow's milk cheese originating in Italy. Reggiano is the best variety.
ricotta a soft, sweet, moist, white cow's milk cheese with a low fat content and a slightly grainy texture. The name roughly translates as 'cooked again' and refers to ricotta's manufacture from a whey that is itself a by-product of other cheese-making.

CHICKEN
breast fillet breast halved, skinned and boned.
drumsticks leg with skin and bone intact.
maryland leg and thigh still connected in a single piece; bones and skin intact.
small chicken also known as spatchcock or poussin; no more than 6 weeks old, weighing a maximum of 500g (1lb). Spatchcock is also a cooking term to describe splitting a small chicken open, flattening out then grilling.
thigh skin and bone intact.
thigh cutlets thigh with skin and centre bone intact; sometimes found skinned with bone intact.
thigh fillets skin and bone removed.

CHILLI
available in many types and sizes. Use rubber gloves when seeding and chopping fresh chillies as they can burn your skin. Removing membranes and seeds lessens the heat level.
ancho mild, dried chillies commonly used in Mexican cooking.
cayenne pepper dried, long, thin-fleshed, extremely hot, ground red chilli.
chipotle (pronounced cheh-pote-lay) the name used for jalapeño chillies once they've been dried and smoked. With a deep, intensely smoky flavour, rather than a searing heat, chipotles are dark brown, almost black, and wrinkled in appearance.
flakes dried, deep-red, dehydrated chilli slices and whole seeds.
green any unripened chilli; also some particular varieties that are ripe when green, such as jalapeño, habanero, poblano or serrano.
jalapeño (pronounced hah-lah-pain-yo) fairly hot, medium-sized, plump, dark green chilli; available pickled, sold canned or bottled, and fresh from greengrocers.
long green any unripened chilli.
long red available both fresh and dried; a generic term used for any moderately hot, thin, long (6cm–8cm/2¼in–3¼in) chilli.
powder can be used as a substitute for fresh chillies (½ teaspoon ground chilli powder to 1 chopped medium fresh chilli).
thai (serrano) also known as 'scuds'; tiny, very hot and bright red in colour.

CHINESE COOKING WINE (SHAO HSING)
also called chinese rice wine; made from fermented rice, wheat, sugar and salt. Found in Asian food shops; if you can't find it, use mirin or sherry.

CHIVES
related to the onion and leek; have a subtle onion flavour. Used more for flavour than as an ingredient.
garlic chives also known as chinese chives; are strongly flavoured, have flat leaves and are eaten as a vegetable, usually in stir-fries.

CHOCOLATE

choc bits also called chocolate chips or chocolate morsels; available in milk, white and dark chocolate. Made of cocoa liquor, cocoa butter, sugar and an emulsifier, they hold their shape in baking and are ideal for decorating.
couverture a term used to describe a fine quality, very rich chocolate high in both cocoa butter and cocoa liquor. This type of chocolate requires tempering when used to coat, but not if used in baking, mousses or fillings.
dark (semi-sweet) also called luxury chocolate; made of a high percentage of cocoa liquor and cocoa butter, and little added sugar. Unless stated otherwise, we use dark chocolate in this book, as it's ideal for use in desserts and cakes.
melts small discs of compounded milk, white or dark chocolate ideal for melting and moulding.
milk most popular eating chocolate, mild and very sweet; similar in make-up to dark with the difference being the addition of milk solids.
white contains no cocoa solids but derives its sweet flavour from cocoa butter. Very sensitive to heat.

CINNAMON

available in pieces (called sticks or quills) and ground into powder; one of the world's most common spices, used as a sweet, fragrant flavouring for both sweet and savoury foods.

CLOVES

dried flower buds of a tropical tree; can be used whole or in ground form. They have a strong scent and taste so should be used sparingly.

COCOA POWDER

also known as unsweetened cocoa; cocoa beans (cacao seeds) that have been fermented, roasted, shelled, ground into powder then cleared of most of the fat content. Unsweetened cocoa is used in hot chocolate drink mixtures; milk powder and sugar are added to the ground product.
dutch cocoa treated with an alkali to neutralise its acids. It has a reddish-brown colour, mild flavour and is easy to dissolve in liquids.

COCONUT

cream obtained commercially from the first pressing of the coconut flesh alone, without the addition of water; the second pressing (less rich) is sold as coconut milk. Available in cans and cartons at most supermarkets.
desiccated concentrated, dried, unsweetened and finely shredded coconut flesh.
flaked dried flaked coconut flesh.
milk not the liquid found inside the fruit (coconut water), but the diluted liquid from the second pressing of the white flesh of a mature coconut (the first pressing produces coconut cream). Available in cans and cartons at most supermarkets.
shredded unsweetened thin strips of dried coconut flesh.

CORIANDER (CILANTRO)

bright-green-leafed herb with a pungent flavour. The leaves, stems and roots of coriander are also used. Wash under cold water, removing any dirt clinging to the roots; scrape the roots with a small flat knife to remove some of the outer fibrous skin. Also available ground or as seeds; these should not be substituted for fresh coriander as the tastes are completely different.

CORNFLOUR (CORNSTARCH)

available made from corn or wheat (wheaten cornflour gives a lighter texture in cakes); used as a thickening agent in cooking.

COUSCOUS

a fine, dehydrated, grain-like cereal product made from semolina; it swells to three or four times its original size when liquid is added. It is eaten like rice with a tagine, as a side dish or salad ingredient.

CRANBERRIES

available dried and frozen; have a rich, astringent flavour and can be used in sweet and savoury dishes. The dried version can usually be substituted for or with other dried fruit.

CREAM

pouring also known as pure or fresh cream. It has no additives and contains a minimum fat content of 35%.
sour a thick, commercially cultured sour cream with a minimum fat content of 35%.
thick (double) a dolloping cream with a minimum fat content of 45%.
thickened (heavy) a whipping cream that contains a thickener. It has a minimum fat content of 35%.

CRÈME FRAÎCHE

a mature, naturally fermented cream (minimum fat content 35%), having a velvety texture and slightly tangy, nutty flavour. Crème fraîche, a French variation of sour cream, can boil without curdling and be used in sweet and savoury dishes.

CUMIN

also known as zeera or comino; resembling caraway in size, cumin is the dried seed of a plant related to the parsley family. Its spicy, almost curry-like flavour is essential to the traditional foods of Mexico, India, North Africa and the Middle East. Available dried as seeds or ground.

CURRY LEAVES

available fresh or dried and have a mild curry flavour; use like bay leaves.

CURRY PASTES

some recipes in this book call for commercially prepared pastes of varying strengths and flavours. Use whichever one you feel best suits your spice-level tolerance.
green hottest of the traditional thai pastes; particularly good in chicken and vegetable curries, and a great addition to stir-fry and noodle dishes.
korma a mix of mostly heat-free spices; forms the base of a mild, slightly nutty-tasting slow-cooked curry.
massaman has a rich, spicy flavour reminiscent of Middle Eastern cooking; favoured by southern Thai cooks for use in hot and sour stew-like curries and satay sauces.
panang based on the curries of Penang, an island off the north-west coast of Malaysia, close to the Thai border. A complex, sweet and milder variation of red curry paste; good with seafood and for adding to soups and salad dressings.
red a popular curry paste; a hot blend of red chilli, garlic, shallot, lemon grass, salt, galangal, shrimp paste, kaffir lime peel, coriander, cumin and paprika. It is milder than the hotter Thai green curry paste.
rogan josh a medium-hot blend that is a specialty of Kashmir in northern India. It contains tomatoes, fenugreek, coriander, paprika and cumin.
tikka in Indian cooking, the word 'masala' loosely translates as paste and the word 'tikka' means a bite-sized piece of meat, poultry or fish, or sometimes a cutlet. Tikka paste is any maker's choice of spices and oils, mixed into a mild paste, frequently coloured

red. Used for marinating or for brushing over meat, seafood or poultry, before or during cooking instead of as an ingredient.
vindaloo a Goan combination of vinegar, tomatoes, pepper and other spices that exemplifies the Portuguese influence on that part of India's coast.
yellow one of the mildest Thai pastes; it is similar in appearance to Indian curries as they both include yellow chilli and fresh turmeric. Good blended with coconut in vegetable, rice and noodle dishes.

CURRY POWDER
a blend of ground spices used for making Indian and some South-East Asian dishes. Consists of dried chilli, cumin, cinnamon, coriander, fennel, mace, fenugreek, cardamom and turmeric. Available mild or hot.

CUSTARD POWDER
instant mixture used to make pouring custard; similar to North American instant pudding mixes.

DATES
fruit of the date palm tree, eaten fresh or dried, on their own or in dishes. About 4cm–6cm (1½in–2¼in) in length, oval and plump, thin-skinned, with a honey-sweet flavour and sticky texture.

DILL
also called dill weed; used fresh or dried, in seed form or ground. Its feathery, frond-like fresh leaves are grassier and more subtle than the dried version or the seeds (which slightly resemble caraway in flavour). Use dill leaves with smoked salmon and sour cream, poached fish or roast chicken; use the seeds with simply cooked vegetables or home-baked dark breads.

DRIED CURRANTS
dried tiny, almost black raisins so named from the grape type native to Corinth, Greece; most often used in jams, jellies and sauces (the best-known of which is the English cumberland sauce). These are not the same as fresh currants, which are the fruit of a plant in the gooseberry family.

DUCK
we use whole ducks in some recipes; available from specialty chicken shops, markets and some supermarkets.
breast fillets boneless whole breasts, with the skin on.
chinese barbecued traditionally, in China, cooked in special ovens; dipped into and brushed during roasting with a sticky sweet coating made from soy sauce, sherry, ginger, five-spice, star anise and hoisin sauce. Available from Asian food shops as well as dedicated Chinese barbecued meat shops.
maryland thigh and drumstick still connected with the skin on.

DUKKAH
an Egyptian specialty spice mixture made up of roasted nuts, seeds and an array of aromatic spices.

EGGPLANT
also known as aubergine. Ranging in size from tiny to very large, and in colour from pale green to deep purple. Can also be purchased chargrilled, packed in oil, in jars.
baby also known as finger or japanese eggplant; very small and slender so can be used without disgorging.
thai also known as makeua prao, golf ball-sized eggplants available in different colours but most commonly green traced in off-white; crisper than the common purple variety, they have bitter seeds that must be removed before using.

FENNEL
also called finocchio or anise; a crunchy green vegetable slightly resembling celery that's eaten raw in salads, fried as an accompaniment, or used as an ingredient in soups and sauces. Also the name given to the dried seeds of the plant which have a stronger licorice flavour.

FENUGREEK
a member of the pea family, the seeds have a bitter taste; the ground seeds are used in Indian curries, powders and pastes.

FIGS
best eaten in peak season, at the height of summer. Vary in skin and flesh colour according to type not ripeness. When ripe, figs should be unblemished and bursting with flesh; nectar beads at the base indicate when a fig is at its best. Figs are also glacéd, dried or canned in sugar syrup; these are usually sold at health-food stores, Middle Eastern food shops or specialty cheese counters.

FIVE-SPICE POWDER (CHINESE FIVE-SPICE)
A fragrant mixture of ground cinnamon, cloves, star anise, sichuan pepper and fennel seeds.

FLOUR
plain (all-purpose) unbleached wheat flour, the best for baking: the gluten content ensures a strong dough for a light result.
rice very fine, almost powdery, gluten-free flour; made from ground white rice. Used in baking, as a thickener, and in some Asian noodles and desserts.
self-raising all-purpose plain or wholemeal flour with baking powder and salt added; make at home in the proportion of 1 cup plain or wholemeal flour to 2 teaspoons baking powder.
wholemeal also known as wholewheat flour; milled with the wheat germ so is higher in fibre and more nutritional than plain flour.

GAI LAN
also known as chinese broccoli, gai larn, kanah, gai lum and chinese kale; appreciated more for its stems than its coarse leaves.

GALANGAL
a rhizome with a hot ginger-citrusy flavour; used similarly to ginger and garlic. Use fresh ginger if unavailable.

GARAM MASALA
a blend of spices including cardamom, cinnamon, cloves, coriander, fennel and cumin, roasted and ground together. Black pepper and chilli can be added for a hotter version.

GHEE
a type of clarified butter where the milk solids are cooked until they are a golden brown, which imparts a nutty flavour and sweet aroma; this fat has a high smoking point so can be heated to a high temperature without burning. Used as a cooking medium in most Indian recipes. Available from many Indian supermarkets. Replace with clarified butter, if you can't find it.

GINGER
fresh also called green or root ginger; the thick gnarled root of a tropical plant.

ground also called powdered ginger; used as a flavouring in baking but cannot be substituted for fresh ginger.

GRAVY POWDER
an instant gravy mix made with browned flour. Plain flour can be used instead for thickening. Available from supermarkets in a variety of flavours.

GREASING/OILING PANS
use butter or margarine (for sweet baking), oil or cooking-oil spray (for savoury baking) to grease baking pans; overgreasing pans can cause food to overbrown. Use paper towel or a pastry brush to spread the oil or butter over the pan. Try covering your hand with a small plastic bag then swiping it into the butter or margarine.

HARISSA
a Moroccan sauce or paste that's made from dried chillies, cumin, garlic, oil and caraway seeds. The paste, available in a tube, is extremely hot and should not be used in large amounts; bottled harissa sauce is milder. Available from Middle Eastern food shops and some supermarkets.

HAZELNUTS
also known as filberts; plump, grape-sized, rich, sweet nuts having a brown skin that is removed by rubbing heated nuts together vigorously in a tea towel.
ground made by grounding hazelnuts to a coarse flour texture for use in baking or as a thickening agent.

HONEY
the variety sold in a squeezable container is not suitable for the recipes in this book.

JAM, JELLING POINT
There are a few visual clues that a jam is almost ready – the mixture will appear thickened with about half of the liquid evaporated. During the end stage it is a good idea to stir the jam gently to ensure it isn't catching on the base of the pan.
A jam is ready when it has reached 'jelling point'. To test it, place two or three small saucers in the freezer at the start of making the jam, then drop a small spoonful onto the chilled saucer. Jam that is pulpy in texture should jell to a spreadable consistency within several minutes. Jam with pieces of fruit suspended in it, such as marmalade, will develop a skin over the top; push the jam with your finger, the skin will wrinkle if the jam is ready.
If the jam is not jelling, return it to the heat and boil it again, this might only take a few minutes. If the jam refuses to set, try adding 2 tablespoons lemon juice. Reboil the jam and test it again.
If this fails, use commercial pectin (available at supermarkets and health-food stores) to set the jam.

KAFFIR LIME
also known as magrood, leech lime or jeruk purut. The wrinkled, bumpy-skinned green fruit of a small citrus tree originally grown in South Africa and South-East Asia.
kaffir lime leaves also known as bai magrood, sold fresh, dried or frozen; looks like two glossy dark green leaves joined end to end, forming a rounded hourglass shape. A strip of fresh lime peel may be substituted for each kaffir lime leaf.

LAMB
chump cut from just above the hind legs to the mid-loin section; can be used as a piece for roasting or cut into chops.
cutlet small, tender rib chop; sometimes sold french-trimmed, with all the fat and gristle at the narrow end of the bone removed.
forequarter chops cut from the shoulder.
leg cut from the hindquarter; can be boned, butterflied, rolled and tied, or diced.
rolled shoulder boneless section of the forequarter, rolled and secured with string or netting.
sausage, merguez small, spicy sausage believed to have originated in Tunisia but eaten in North Africa, France and Spain; traditionally made with lamb and easily recognised because of its chilli-red colour. Can be fried, grilled or roasted; available from many butchers, delis and specialty sausage stores.
shank forequarter leg; sometimes sold as drumsticks or frenched shanks if the gristle and narrow end of the bone are discarded and the remaining meat trimmed.
shoulder large, tasty piece having much connective tissue so is best pot-roasted or braised. Makes the best mince.

LEEK
a member of the onion family, the leek resembles a green onion but is much larger and more subtle in flavour. Tender baby or pencil leeks are essentially young, slender leeks; available early in the season, they can be cooked and eaten whole like asparagus with minimal cooking. Adult leeks are usually trimmed of most of the green tops then chopped or sliced and cooked as an ingredient in stews, casseroles and soups.

LEMON GRASS
also known as takrai, serai or serah. A tall, clumping, lemon-smelling and -tasting, sharp-edged aromatic tropical grass; the white lower part of the stem is used, finely chopped, in many South-East Asian dishes. Can be found in supermarkets, greengrocers and Asian food shops.

LENTILS (RED, BROWN, YELLOW)
dried pulses often identified by and named after their colour. Eaten by cultures all over the world, most famously perhaps in the dhals of India.
French-style a local cousin to the famous (and very expensive) French lentils du puy; green-blue, tiny lentils with a nutty, earthy flavour and a hardy nature that allows them to be rapidly cooked without disintegrating.

LIQUEUR, ORANGE-FLAVOURED
such as curaçao, Grand Marnier or Cointreau.

MACADAMIAS
native to Australia; fairly large, slightly soft, buttery rich nut. Should always be stored in the fridge to prevent their high oil content turning them rancid.

MANGO
tropical fruit originally from India and South-East Asia. With skin colour ranging from green to yellow and deep red; fragrant, deep yellow flesh surrounds a large flat seed. Slicing off the cheeks, cross-hatching them with a knife then turning them inside out shows the sweet, juicy flesh at its best. Mangoes can also be used in curries and salsas, or pureed for ice-cream, smoothies or mousse.

MAPLE-FLAVOURED SYRUP
also called golden or pancake syrup; made from sugar cane. It is not a substitute for pure maple syrup.

MAPLE SYRUP
also called pure maple syrup; distilled from the sap of sugar maple trees found only in Canada and the USA. Maple-flavoured syrup or pancake syrup are not an adequate substitutes for the real thing.

MARJORAM
closely related to and similar in flavour to oregano, but milder and sweeter. Delicious in herb mixtures for omelettes, stuffings, herb scones, and herb and cream cheese sandwiches. As with oregano, many chefs prefer dried marjoram to fresh.

MARSALA
a sweet, fortified Italian wine to which additional alcohol has been added, most commonly in the form of brandy. Produced in the region surrounding the Sicilian city of Marsala and recognisable by its intense amber colour and complex aroma, it is available in a range of styles, from sweet to dry.

MAYONNAISE, WHOLE-EGG
commercial mayonnaise of high quality made with whole eggs and labelled as such; some prepared mayonnaises substitute emulsifiers such as food starch, cellulose gel or other thickeners to mimic the same thick and creamy consistency but never achieve the same rich flavour. Must be refrigerated once opened.

MINT
the most commonly used variety of mint is spearmint; it has pointed, bright-green leaves and a fresh flavour.

MIRIN
a Japanese champagne-coloured cooking wine made of glutinous rice and alcohol. It is used just for cooking and should not be confused with sake. A seasoned sweet mirin, manjo mirin, made of water, rice, corn syrup and alcohol, is used in dipping sauces.

MIXED DRIED FRUIT
a mix of sultanas, raisins, currants, mixed peel and cherries.

MIXED SALAD LEAVES
also called mesclun; a salad mix of young lettuce and other green leaves, including baby spinach leaves, mizuna and curly endive.

MIXED SPICE
a classic spice mixture generally containing caraway, allspice, coriander, cumin, nutmeg and ginger, although cinnamon and other spices can be added. It is used with fruit and in cakes.

MOLASSES
a thick, dark brown syrup, the residue from the refining of sugar; available in light, dark and blackstrap varieties. Its slightly bitter taste is an essential ingredient in American cooking, found in foods such as gingerbread, shoofly pie and boston baked beans.

MOROCCAN SEASONING
available from most Middle Eastern food stores, spice shops and major supermarkets. A blend of turmeric, cinnamon and cumin adds a Moroccan flavour to cooking.

MORTAR AND PESTLE
a cooking tool whose design has remained the same over the centuries: the mortar is a bowl-shaped container and the pestle a rounded, bat-shaped tool. Together, they grind and pulverise spices, herbs and other foods. The pestle is pressed against the mortar and rotated, grinding the ingredient between the two surfaces. Essential for curry pastes and crushing spices.

MUSHROOMS
button small, cultivated white mushrooms with a mild flavour.
dried porcini also known as cèpes; the richest-flavoured mushrooms. Expensive, but because they're so strongly flavoured, only a small amount is required.
enoki cultivated mushrooms also called enokitake; tiny long-stemmed, pale mushrooms that grow and are sold in clusters, and can be used that way or separated by slicing off the base. They have a mild fruity flavour and are slightly crisp in texture.
flat large, flat mushrooms with a rich earthy flavour, ideal for filling and barbecuing. They are sometimes misnamed field mushrooms which are wild mushrooms.
oyster also called abalone; grey-white mushrooms shaped like a fan. Prized for their smooth texture and subtle, oyster-like flavour. Also available in pink.
portobello mature, fully opened swiss browns; large, dark brown mushrooms with full-bodied flavour; ideal for filling or barbecuing.
shiitake when fresh are also known as chinese black, forest or golden oak mushrooms. Large, meaty and, although cultivated, have the earthiness and taste of wild mushrooms. When dried, they are known as donko or dried chinese mushrooms; rehydrate before use.
swiss brown also known as roman or cremini. Light to dark brown mushrooms with full-bodied flavour; suited for use in casseroles or being stuffed and baked.

MUSLIN
inexpensive, undyed, finely woven cotton fabric called for in cooking to strain stocks and sauces; if unavailable, use a clean chux or linen tea towel.

MUSTARD
dijon pale brown, distinctively flavoured, fairly mild-tasting French mustard.
seeds, black also called brown mustard seeds; more pungent than the yellow (or white) seeds used in prepared mustards.
wholegrain also known as seeded. A French-style coarse-grain mustard made from crushed mustard seeds and Dijon-style French mustard.

NOODLES
dried rice also called rice stick noodles. Made from rice flour and water; available flat and wide or very thin (vermicelli). Must be soaked in boiling water to soften.
fresh rice also called ho fun, khao pun, sen yau, pho or kway tiau, depending on the country of manufacture; the most common form of noodle used in Thailand. Can be purchased in strands of various widths or large sheets of about 500g (1lb), which are to be cut into the desired size. Chewy and pure white, they do not need pre-cooking before use.
rice stick also called sen lek, ho fun or kway teow; especially popular South-East Asian dried rice noodles. They come in different widths (thin used in soups, wide in stir-fries), but all should be soaked in hot water to soften. The traditional noodle used in pad thai which, before soaking, measures about 5mm in width.
rice vermicelli also called sen mee, mei fun or bee hoon. Used throughout Asia in spring rolls and cold salads; similar to bean threads, only longer and made with rice flour instead of mung bean starch. Before using, soak the dried noodles in hot water until softened, boil them briefly, then rinse with hot water.

GLOSSARY

NUTMEG
a strong and pungent spice ground from the dried nut of an evergreen tree native to Indonesia. Usually found ground but the flavour is more intense from a whole nut, available from spice shops, so it's best to grate your own.

OIL
cooking spray we use a cholesterol-free cooking spray made from canola oil.
olive made from ripened olives. Extra virgin and virgin are the first and second presses, respectively, of the olives and are therefore considered the best; 'light' refers to taste not fat levels.
peanut pressed from ground peanuts; most commonly used oil in Asian cooking because of its high smoke point (capacity to handle high heat without burning).
sesame roasted, crushed, white sesame seeds; a flavouring rather than a cooking medium.
vegetable oils sourced from plant rather than animal fats.

OKRA
also called bamia or lady fingers. A green, ridged, oblong pod with a furry skin. Native to Africa, this vegetable is used in Indian, Middle Eastern and South American cooking. Can be eaten on its own; as part of a casserole, curry or gumbo; used to thicken stews or gravies.

OLIVES
black have a richer and more mellow flavour than the green ones and are softer in texture. Sold either plain or in a piquant marinade.
green those harvested before fully ripened and are, as a rule, denser and more bitter than the black variety.

ONIONS
baby also called pickling and cocktail onions; are baby brown onions but are larger than shallots. To peel, cover with boiling water and stand for 2 minutes, then drain. The skins will slip off easily.
brown and white interchangeable; white onions have a more pungent flesh.
green (scallions) also called, incorrectly, shallots; an immature onion picked before the bulb has formed, with a long, bright-green edible stalk.
red also known as spanish, red spanish or bermuda onion; a sweet-flavoured, large, purple-red onion.
shallots also called french or golden shallots or eschalots; small and elongated with a brown skin.
spring an onion with a small white bulb and long, narrow green-leafed tops.

ORANGE FLOWER WATER
concentrated flavouring made from orange blossoms.

OREGANO
a herb, also known as wild marjoram; has a woody stalk and clumps of tiny, dark-green leaves. Has a pungent, peppery flavour.

PAPRIKA
ground, dried, sweet red capsicum (bell pepper); there are many grades and types available, including sweet, hot, mild and smoked.

PARSLEY
a versatile herb with a fresh, earthy flavour. There are about 30 varieties of curly parsley; the flat-leaf variety (also called continental or italian parsley) is stronger in flavour and darker in colour.

PARSNIP
their nutty sweetness is especially good when steamed and dressed with a garlic and cream sauce or in a curried parsnip soup, or simply baked. Available all year but the cold develops their sweet/savoury flavour in winter.

PASTA
fettuccine fresh or dried ribbon pasta made from durum wheat, semolina and egg. Also available plain or flavoured.
fresh lasagne sheets thinly rolled wide sheets of plain or flavoured pasta; they do not need par-boiling before being used in cooking.
gnocchi Italian 'dumplings' made of potatoes, semolina or flour; can be cooked in boiling water or baked with sauce.
macaroni tube-shaped pasta available in various sizes; made from semolina and water; does not contain eggs.
pappardelle from the Italian verb pappare, meaning 'to gobble up', pappardelle are broad, flat or frilly, ribbons of pasta. Goes well with red meat sauces (rabbit is a Tuscan favourite), chunky tomato and mushroom sauces as in pappardelle boscaiola, or with cream.
penne Italian for 'pen', this dried pasta resembles a quill and has angled ends and ridges to hold chunky sauces. Penne are also available in a smooth variety.
risoni small rice-shaped pasta; very similar to orzo, another small pasta.
spaghetti long, thin solid strands of pasta.
tagliatelle long, flat strips of wheat pasta, slightly narrower and thinner than fettuccine.

PATTY-PAN SQUASH
also known as crookneck or custard marrow pumpkins; a round, slightly flat summer squash that is yellow to pale-green in colour and has a scalloped edge. Has a firm white flesh and a distinct flavour.

PEANUTS
also called groundnut; not in fact a nut but the pod of a legume. We mainly use raw (unroasted) or unsalted roasted peanuts.

PEAS
green also known as garden peas; must be shelled and their pods never eaten. Peas in the pod will yield just under half their weight of shelled peas. Peas in the pod are available fresh and shelled peas are available frozen.
snow also called mangetout; a variety of garden pea, eaten pod and all (although you may need to string them). Used in stir-fries or eaten raw in salads. Snow pea sprouts are available from supermarkets or greengrocers and are usually eaten raw in salads or sandwiches.
sugar snap also called honey snap peas; fresh small pea that can be eaten, whole, pod and all, similarly to snow peas.

PECANS
native to the US and now grown locally; pecans are golden brown, buttery and rich. Good in savoury as well as sweet dishes; walnuts are a good substitute.

PEPITAS (PUMPKIN SEEDS)
the pale green kernels of dried pumpkin seeds; they can be bought plain or salted.

PEPPERCORNS
black picked when the berry is not quite ripe, then dried until it shrivels and the skin turns dark brown/black. It's the strongest flavoured of the three (white, green and black) – slightly hot with a hint of sweetness.
green soft, unripe berry of the pepper plant, usually sold packed in brine (occasionally found dried, packed in salt). Has a distinctive fresh taste.

pepper medley a mixture of black, white, green and pink peppercorns, coriander seeds and allspice, sold in disposable grinders in supermarkets.
pink a dried berry from a type of rose plant grown in Madagascar, usually sold packed in brine (occasionally found freeze-dried); they possess a distinctive pungently sweet taste.
sichuan also known as szechuan or chinese pepper, native to the Sichuan province of China. A mildly-hot spice that comes from the prickly ash tree. Although not related to the peppercorn family, its small, red-brown aromatic berries look like black peppercorns and have a distinctive peppery-lemon flavour and aroma. They should always be dry-roasted to bring out the flavour.
white less pungent; has been allowed to ripen, after which the skin is removed and the berry is dried. The result is a smaller, smoother-skinned, light-tan berry with a milder flavour.

PINE NUTS
also called pignoli; not a nut but a small, cream-coloured kernel from pine cones. They are best roasted before use to bring out the flavour.

PISTACHIOS
green, delicately flavoured nuts inside hard off-white shells. Available salted or unsalted in their shells; you can also buy them shelled. We use the weight of shelled nuts in our recipes.

POACH
a cooking term to describe gentle simmering of food in liquid (generally water or stock); spices or herbs can be added to impart their flavour.

POLENTA
also known as cornmeal; a ground, flour-like cereal made of dried corn (maize) sold in several different textures. Also the name of the dish made from it.

POMEGRANATE
dark-red, leathery-skinned fresh fruit about the size of an orange filled with hundreds of seeds, each wrapped in an edible lucent-crimson pulp having a unique tangy sweet-sour flavour.

POPPY SEEDS
small, dried, bluish-grey seeds of the poppy plant, with a crunchy texture and a nutty flavour. Can be purchased whole or ground from most supermarkets and delicatessens.

PORK
American-style spare ribs usually sold in long slabs or racks of 10 to 12 ribs, trimmed so little fat remains; slather with barbecue sauce before cooking.
belly fatty cut sold in rashers or in a piece, with or without rind or bone.
cutlets cut from ribs.
ham hock the lower portion of the leg; includes the meat, fat and bone. Most have been cured, smoked or both, but fresh hocks are sometimes available.
hand of pickled pork the 'hand' is a portion of leg and breast. You may need to order this from the butcher in advance.
loin chops or roasting cut from the loin.
neck sometimes called pork scotch fillet; a boneless cut from the foreloin.
pancetta an Italian unsmoked bacon; pork belly cured in salt and spices then rolled into a sausage shape and dried for several weeks. Used, sliced or chopped, as an ingredient rather than eaten on its own.
prosciutto a kind of unsmoked Italian ham; salted, air-cured and aged, it is usually eaten uncooked.
sausage, chorizo of Spanish origin, made from coarsely minced (ground) smoked pork and highly seasoned with garlic, chilli powder and other spices.
sausage, italian pork available as both sweet, which is flavoured with garlic and fennel seeds, and hot, which has chilli added.
scotch fillet sometimes called neck; a boneless cut from the foreloin.
shoulder joint sold with the bone in or out.

POTATOES
baby also called chats; not a separate variety but an early harvest with very thin skin.
coliban round, smooth white skin and flesh; good for baking and mashing.
desiree oval, smooth and pink-skinned, waxy yellow flesh; good in salads, boiled and roasted.
idaho also known as russet burbank; russet in colour, delicious baked.
king edward slightly plump and rosy; great mashed.
lasoda round, red skin with deep eyes, white flesh; good for mashing or roasting.
pink-eye small, off-white skin, deep purple eyes; good steamed and boiled, great baked.
pontiac large, red skin, deep eyes, white flesh; good grated, boiled and baked.
sebago white skin, oval; good fried, mashed and baked.
spunta large, long, yellow flesh, floury; great mashed and fried.

PRESERVED LEMON RIND
a North African specialty; lemons are quartered and preserved in salt and lemon juice or water. To use, remove and discard pulp. Squeeze juice from rind, then rinse well and slice thinly.

QUINCE
yellow-skinned fruit with hard texture and astringent, tart taste; eaten cooked or as a preserve. Long, slow cooking makes the flesh a deep rose pink.
quince paste a thick quince preserve which is sliceable; served on a cheese platter; goes well with cheeses such as brie and camembert. Available from most supermarkets and delicatessens.

RADICCHIO
a red-leafed Italian chicory with a refreshing bitter taste that's eaten raw and grilled. Comes in varieties named after their places of origin, such as round-headed Verona or long-headed Treviso.

RAISINS
dried sweet grapes (traditionally muscatel grapes).

RAITA
a minted yoghurt and cucumber dish served as a cooling accompaniment to fiery curries.

RAS EL HANOUT
a classic spice blend used in Moroccan cooking. The name means 'top of the shop' and is the very best spice blend a spice merchant has to offer. Most versions contain over a dozen spices, including cardamom, nutmeg, mace, cinnamon and ground chilli.

RHUBARB
a plant with long, green-red stalks; becomes sweet and edible when cooked.

RICE
arborio small, round grain rice well-suited to absorb a large amount of liquid; the high level of starch makes it especially suitable for risottos for its classic creaminess.

basmati a white, fragrant long grain rice; the grains fluff up when cooked. Wash several times before cooking.
brown retains the high-fibre, nutritious bran coating that's removed from white rice when hulled. It takes longer to cook than white rice and has a chewier texture. Once cooked, the long grains stay separate, while the short grains are soft and stickier.
jasmine a long grain white rice recognised around the world as having a perfumed aromatic quality; moist in texture, it clings together after cooking. Sometimes substituted for basmati rice.
medium grain previously sold as calrose rice; extremely versatile rice that can be substituted for short or long grain rices if necessary.
wild not a member of the rice family but the seed of an aquatic grass native to the cold regions of North America. Wild rice has a strong nutty taste and can be expensive, so is best combined with brown and white rices in pulaos, stuffings and salads.
wild rice blend a packaged blend of white long grain rice and wild rice. With its dark brown, almost black grains, crunchy, resilient texture and smoky-like flavour, wild rice contrasts nicely with mild-tasting white rice. Perfect with fish, lentils, in pulaos or added to soups.

ROASTING/TOASTING
nuts and dried coconut can be roasted in the oven to restore their fresh flavour and release their aromatic essential oils. Spread them evenly onto an oven tray then roast in a moderate oven for about 5 minutes. Desiccated coconut, pine nuts and sesame seeds roast more evenly if stirred over low heat in a heavy-based frying pan; their natural oils will help turn them golden brown.

ROCKET (ARUGULA)
also called rugula and rucola; peppery green leaf eaten raw in salads or used in cooking. Baby rocket leaves are smaller and less peppery.

ROSEMARY
pungent herb with long, thin pointy leaves; use large and small sprigs, and finely chop leaves.

SAFFRON
stigma of a member of the crocus family, available ground or in strands; imparts a yellow-orange colour to food once infused. The quality can vary greatly; the best is the most expensive spice in the world. Should be stored in the freezer.

SAGE
pungent herb with narrow, grey-green leaves; slightly bitter with a slightly musty mint aroma. Refrigerate fresh sage wrapped in paper towel and sealed in a plastic bag for up to 4 days. Dried sage comes whole, crumbled or ground. It should be stored in a cool, dark place for no more than three months.

SAKE
also known as Japanese cooking rice wine and ryori shu. Made from alcohol (about 14%), rice, salt and corn syrup; often used in marinades for meat and fish. In cooking, it is often used to add body and flavour to various tsuyu (soup stock) and sauces, or to make nimono (simmered dishes) and yakimono (grilled dishes).

SAMBAL OELEK
also called ulek or olek; an Indonesian salty paste made from ground chillies and vinegar.

SAUCES
char siu a Chinese barbecue sauce made from sugar, water, salt, fermented soy bean paste, honey, soy sauce, malt syrup and spices. Found at most supermarkets.
fish also called nam pla or nuoc nam; made from pulverised salted fermented fish, most often anchovies. Has a very pungent smell and strong taste, so use according to your taste level.
hoisin barbecue sauce made from salted fermented soy beans, onions and garlic; used as a marinade or baste, or to accentuate stir-fries and barbecued or roasted foods. Available from Asian food shops and supermarkets.
oyster Asian in origin, this rich, brown sauce is made from oysters and their brine, cooked with salt and soy sauce, and thickened with starches.
soy also known as sieu; made from fermented soy beans. Several variations are available:
dark – deep brown, almost black in colour; rich, with a thicker consistency than other types. Pungent but not particularly salty; good for marinating.
japanese – an all-purpose low-sodium soy sauce made with more wheat content than its Chinese counterparts; fermented in barrels and aged. Possibly the best table soy and the one to choose if you only want one variety.
light – fairly thin in consistency and, while paler than the others, the saltiest tasting; used in dishes in which the natural colour of the ingredients is to be maintained. Not to be confused with salt-reduced or low-sodium soy sauces.
Tabasco brand name of an extremely fiery sauce made from vinegar, thai red chillies and salt.
tamari a thick, dark soy sauce made mainly from soy beans without the wheat used in standard soy sauces.
tomato pasta made from a blend of tomatoes, herbs and spices.
worcestershire this dark-coloured condiment is made from garlic, lime, soy sauce, tamarind, onions, molasses, anchovies, vinegar and seasonings.

SEAFOOD
blue swimmer crab also known as sand crab, blue manna crab, bluey, sand crab or sandy. Substitute with lobster, balmain or moreton bay bugs.
fish fillet, firm white includes bream, flathead, whiting, snapper, dhufish, redfish and ling.
mussels must be tightly closed when bought, indicating they are alive. Before cooking, scrub the shells with a strong brush and remove the 'beards'. Some mussels might not open – you do not have to discard these, just open with a knife and cook a little more if you wish. Varieties include black and green-lip.
ocean trout a farmed fish with pink, soft flesh. From the same family as the atlantic salmon; one can be substituted for the other.
octopus usually tenderised before you buy them; both octopus and squid require either long slow cooking (usually for the large molluscs) or quick cooking over high heat (usually for the small molluscs) – anything in between will make the octopus tough and rubbery.
prawns (shrimp) varieties include, school, king, royal red, sydney harbour, tiger. Can be bought uncooked (green) or cooked, with or without shells.
salmon red-pink firm flesh with few bones; moist delicate flavour.

SEMOLINA
coarsely ground flour milled from durum wheat; the flour used in making gnocchi, pasta and couscous.

SESAME SEEDS
black and white are the most common of this small oval seed; however, there are also red and brown varieties. The seeds are used as an ingredient and

as a condiment. Roast the seeds in a heavy-based frying pan over low heat.

SHERRY
fortified wine consumed as an aperitif or used in cooking. Sherries differ in colour and flavour; sold as fino (light, dry), amontillado (medium sweet, dark) and oloroso (full-bodied, very dark).

SILVER BEET (SWISS CHARD)
also called, incorrectly, spinach; has fleshy stalks and large leaves and can be prepared as for spinach.

SPINACH
also called english spinach and incorrectly, silver beet. Baby spinach leaves are best eaten raw in salads; the larger leaves should be added last to soups, stews and stir-fries, and should be cooked until barely wilted.

SPLIT PEAS
a variety of yellow or green pea grown specifically for drying. When dried, the peas usually split along a natural seam. Whole and split dried peas are available packaged in supermarkets and in bulk in health-food stores.

STAR ANISE
dried star-shaped pod with an astringent aniseed flavour; used to flavour stocks and marinades. Available whole and ground, it is an essential ingredient in five-spice powder.

STERILISING JARS
It's important the jars be as clean as possible; make sure your hands, the preparation area, tea towels and cloths etc are clean, too. The aim is to finish sterilising the jars and lids at the same time the mixture is ready to be bottled. Hot preserves should be bottled into hot, dry clean jars. Jars that aren't sterilised properly can cause deterioration of the preserves during storage.
Here are three methods for sterilising jars. Always start with cleaned washed jars and lids.

1. Put the jars and lids through the hottest cycle of a dishwasher without using any detergent.
2. Lie the jars down in a boiler with the lids, cover them with cold water, then cover the boiler with a lid. Bring the water to the boil over high heat and boil the jars for 20 minutes.
3. Stand the jars upright, without touching each other, on a wooden board on the lowest shelf in the oven. Turn the oven to the lowest possible temperature, close the oven door and leave the jars to heat through for 30 minutes.

Next, remove the jars from the oven or dishwasher with a towel, or from the boiling water with tongs and rubber-gloved hands; the water will evaporate from hot wet jars quite quickly. Stand the jars upright and not touching each other on a wooden board, or a bench covered with a towel to protect and insulate the bench.
Pour hot preserves into hot jars until the jars are filled to the top (in most cases, unless indicated otherwise by the recipe). Secure the lids tightly, hold the jars firmly with a towel or an oven mitt while doing this, then leave the mixture at room temperature to cool before labelling and storing.

SUGAR
brown a soft, finely granulated sugar retaining molasses for its characteristic colour and flavour:
dark brown – a moist, dark brown sugar with a rich, distinctive full flavour from molasses syrup.
light brown – a very soft, finely granulated sugar that retains molasses for its colour and flavour.
caster (superfine) finely granulated table sugar.
demerara small-grained golden-coloured crystal sugar.
icing (confectioners') also known as powdered sugar; pulverised granulated sugar crushed together with a small amount of cornflour (cornstarch).
palm also called nam tan pip, jaggery, jawa or gula melaka; made from the sap of the sugar palm tree. Light brown to black in colour and usually sold in rock-hard cakes; use light brown sugar if unavailable.
pure icing (confectioners') also known as powdered sugar.
raw natural brown granulated sugar.
vanilla available in supermarkets, usually among the spices, or you can make your own by putting a couple of vanilla beans in a jar of caster (superfine) sugar.
white (granulated) coarse, granulated table sugar, also known as crystal sugar.
yellow rock available from Asian supermarkets. It's mainly used in braises and sauces as it gives them a lustre and glaze.

SULTANAS
also called golden raisins; dried seedless white grapes.

SUMAC
a purple-red, astringent spice ground from berries growing on shrubs that flourish wild around the Mediterranean; adds a tart, lemony flavour to dips and dressings and goes well with barbecued meat. Can be found in Middle Eastern food stores.

SWEDE
so-named in England and Australia, the hard, slightly yellow root vegetable that slightly resembles a large dried turnip is called a neep in Scotland and rutabaga in the United States. Because this vegetable thrives in the cold, it has always been popular in Scandinavia, especially in Sweden, hence the name. The swede is a great tasting vegetable with a delicate sweetness and flavour that hints of the freshness of cabbage and turnip.

TAMARIND
the tamarind tree produces clusters of hairy brown pods, each of which is filled with seeds and a viscous pulp, that are dried and pressed into the blocks of tamarind found in Asian food shops. Gives a sweet-sour, slightly astringent taste to marinades, pastes, sauces and dressings.

TAMARIND CONCENTRATE (OR PASTE)
the distillation of tamarind pulp into a condensed compacted paste with a sweet-sour, slightly astringent taste. Thick and purple-black, it requires no soaking. Found in Asian food stores.

TARRAGON
french tarragon, with its subtle aniseed flavour, complements chicken, eggs and veal, and is perfect in a béarnaise sauce. It is also one of the herbs that make up the French fines herbs. Russian and Mexican tarragons are slightly coarser in taste.

THYME
a basic herb of French cuisine widely used in Mediterranean countries to flavour meats and sauces. A member of the mint family, it has tiny grey-green leaves that give off a pungent minty,

light-lemon aroma. Dried thyme comes in both leaf and powder form. Dried thyme should be stored in a cool, dark place for no more than three months. Fresh thyme should be stored in the refrigerator, wrapped in a damp paper towel and placed in a sealed bag for no more than a few days.

TOFU
also known as bean curd, an off-white, custard-like product made from the 'milk' of crushed soy beans; comes fresh as soft or firm. Leftover fresh tofu can be refrigerated in water (which is changed daily) for up to 4 days.
silken tofu refers to the method by which it is made – where it is strained through silk.

TOMATOES
bottled pasta sauce a prepared sauce; a blend of tomatoes, herbs and spices.
canned whole peeled tomatoes in natural juices; available crushed, chopped or diced. Use undrained.
cherry also called tiny tim or tom thumb tomatoes; small and round.
egg also called plum or roma; these are smallish, oval-shaped tomatoes much used in Italian cooking or salads.
paste triple-concentrated tomato puree used to flavour soups, stews and sauces.
puree canned pureed tomatoes.
roma (egg) also called plum; these are smallish, oval-shaped tomatoes much used in Italian cooking or salads.
semi-dried partially dried tomato pieces in olive oil; softer and juicier than sun-dried, these are not a preserve thus do not keep as long as sun-dried.
sun-dried tomato pieces that have been dried with salt; this dehydrates the tomato and concentrates the flavour. We use sun-dried tomatoes packaged in oil, unless stated otherwise.
truss small vine-ripened tomatoes with vine still attached.

TREACLE
thick, dark syrup not unlike molasses; a by-product of the sugar refining process.

TURMERIC
also called kamin; a rhizome related to galangal and ginger. Must be grated or pounded to release its acrid aroma and pungent flavour. Known for the golden colour it imparts, fresh turmeric can be substituted with the more commonly found dried powder, in the proportion of 1 teaspoon ground turmeric for every 20g (¾oz) fresh turmeric. Be aware that fresh turmeric stains your hands and plastic utensils such as chopping boards and spatulas.
ground turmeric fresh turmeric root is dried and ground, resulting in the rich yellow powder that gives many Indian dishes their characteristic yellow colour. It is intensely pungent in taste but not hot.

VANILLA
bean dried, long, thin pod from a tropical golden orchid; the minuscule black seeds inside the bean impart a luscious flavour in baking and desserts. Place a whole bean in a jar of sugar to make vanilla sugar; a bean can be used three or four times.
extract obtained from vanilla beans infused in water; a non-alcoholic version of essence.
paste made from vanilla beans and contains real seeds. Highly concentrated: 1 teaspoon replaces a whole vanilla bean. Found in most supermarkets in the baking section.

VEAL
osso buco also called veal shin, usually cut into 3cm–5cm (1¼in–2in) thick slices and used in the famous Italian slow-cooked casserole of the same name.
rack row of small chops or cutlets.
scaloppine a piece of lean steak hammered with a meat mallet until almost see-through; cook over high heat for as little time as possible.
schnitzel thinly sliced steak.

VIETNAMESE MINT
not a mint at all but a pungent and peppery narrow-leafed member of the buckwheat family. Not confined to Vietnam, it is also known as cambodian mint, pak pai (Thailand), laksa leaf (Indonesia), daun kesom (Singapore) and rau ram in Vietnam. It is a common ingredient in Thai foods, particularly soups, salads and stir-fries.

VINEGAR
balsamic originally from Modena, Italy, there are now many balsamic vinegars on the market ranging in pungency and quality depending on how, and for how long, they have been aged. Made from the juice of Trebbiano grapes; it is a deep rich brown colour with a sweet and sour flavour. Quality can be determined, up to a point, by price; use the most expensive sparingly.
white balsamic a clear and lighter version of balsamic vinegar; it has a fresh, sweet, clean taste.
brown malt made from fermented malt and beech shavings.
cider (apple cider) made from crushed fermented apples.
rice a colourless vinegar made from fermented rice and flavoured with sugar and salt. Sherry can be substituted.
white made from the spirit of cane sugar.
wine made from a blend of either red or white wines.

WALNUTS
a rich, flavourful nut. Should be plump and firm, not shrivelled or soft. Have a high oil content so store in the fridge.

WATERCRESS
one of the cress family, a large group of peppery greens used raw in salads, dips and sandwiches, or cooked in soups. Highly perishable so it must be used as soon as possible after purchase.

WHITE SWEET POTATO
less sweet than orange sweet potato; has an earthy flavour and a purple flesh beneath its white skin and is best baked.

WITLOF
also known as belgian endive; related to and confused with chicory. A versatile vegetable, it tastes as good cooked as it does eaten raw. Grown in darkness like white asparagus to prevent it becoming green; looks somewhat like a tightly furled, cream to very light-green cigar. The leaves can be removed and used to hold a canapé filling; the whole vegetable can be opened up, stuffed then baked or casseroled; and the leaves can be tossed in a salad with other vegetables.

WOMBOK (NAPA CABBAGE)
also called chinese cabbage or peking cabbage; elongated in shape with pale green, crinkly leaves. The most common cabbage in South-East Asia; can be shredded or chopped and eaten raw or braised, steamed or stir-fried.

YOGHURT, GREEK-STYLE
often made from sheep's milk that is strained in a cloth (traditionally muslin) to remove the whey and to give it a thick, smooth, creamy consistency, almost like whipped cream.

UNIVERSAL

CONVERSION CHART

MEASURES

One Australian metric measuring cup holds approximately 250ml; one Australian metric tablespoon holds 20ml; one Australian metric teaspoon holds 5ml. The difference between one country's measuring cups and another's is within a two- or three-teaspoon variance and will not affect your cooking results. North America, New Zealand and the United Kingdom use 15ml tablespoons.

All cup and spoon measurements are level. The most accurate way of measuring dry ingredients is to weigh them. When measuring liquids, use a clear glass or plastic jug with the metric markings.

We use large eggs with an average weight of 60g.

DRY MEASURES

METRIC	IMPERIAL
15g	½ oz
30g	1oz
60g	2oz
90g	3oz
125g	4oz (¼ lb)
155g	5oz
185g	6oz
220g	7oz
250g	8oz (½ lb)
280g	9oz
315g	10oz
345g	11oz
375g	12oz (¾ lb)
410g	13oz
440g	14oz
470g	15oz
500g	16oz (1lb)
750g	24oz (1½ lb)
1kg	32oz (2lb)

LIQUID MEASURES

METRIC	IMPERIAL
30ml	1 fluid oz
60ml	2 fluid oz
100ml	3 fluid oz
125ml	4 fluid oz
150ml	5 fluid oz
190ml	6 fluid oz
250ml	8 fluid oz
300ml	10 fluid oz
500ml	16 fluid oz
600ml	20 fluid oz
1000ml	1¾ pints

LENGTH MEASURES

METRIC	IMPERIAL
3mm	⅛ in
6mm	¼ in
1cm	½ in
2cm	¾ in
2.5cm	1in
5cm	2in
6cm	2½ in
8cm	3in
10cm	4in
13cm	5in
15cm	6in
18cm	7in
20cm	8in
23cm	9in
25cm	10in
28cm	11in
30cm	12in (1ft)

OVEN TEMPERATURES

The oven temperatures in this book are for conventional ovens; if you have a fan-forced oven, decrease the temperature by 10–20 degrees.

	°C (CELSIUS)	°F (FAHRENHEIT)
Very slow	120	250
Slow	150	300
Moderately slow	160	325
Moderate	180	350
Moderately hot	200	400
Hot	220	425
Very hot	240	475

INDEX

A

B

C

D

E

F

G

H

I

J

K

K

L

M

P

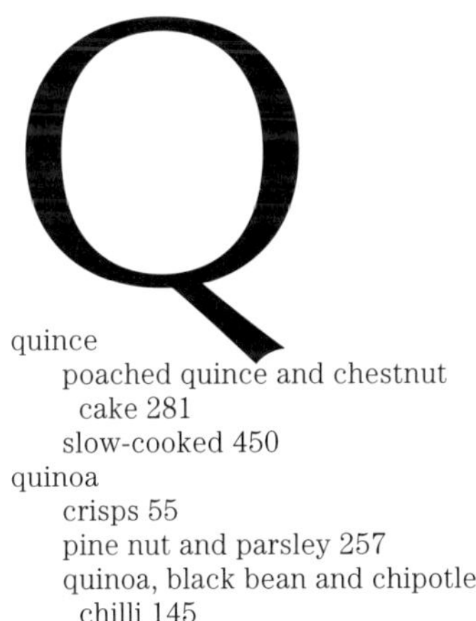

R

S

T

V

Z

First published in 2019 by Bauer Media Books, Australia.
Bauer Media Books is a division of Bauer Media Pty Ltd.

BAUER MEDIA GROUP

Chief executive officer Paul Dykzeul
Chief financial officer Andrew Stedwell

BAUER MEDIA BOOKS

Publisher Sally Eagle
Acting publisher Simone Aquilina
Editorial & food director Sophia Young
Creative director Hannah Blackmore
Managing editor Stephanie Kistner
Food editors Sophia Young, Leanne Kitchen
Designer Bernhard Schmitz
Senior editor Chantal Gibbs
Operations manager David Scotto
Business development manager Meg Kennedy

Cover photography
Photographer James Moffatt
Stylist Bernie Smithies
Photochef Rebecca Lyall

Printed in China by 1010 Printing International

A catalogue record for this book is available from the National Library of Australia.

ISBN: 978-1-92569-544-1 (hardrback)

Published by Bauer Media Books,
a division of Bauer Media Pty Ltd,
54 Park St, Sydney; GPO Box 4088,
Sydney, NSW 2001, Australia
Ph +61 2 8116 9334; Fax +61 2 9126 3702
www.awwcookbooks.com.au

International rights manager Simone Aquilina
saquilina@bauer-media.com.au; ph +61 2 8268 6278

To order books
phone 136 116 (within Australia) or
order online at www.awwcookbooks.com.au

Send recipe enquiries to:
recipeenquiries@bauer-media.com.au